BASEBALL AMERICA'S ULTIMATE

# DRAFT BOOK

COMPILED & EDITED BY ALLAN SIMPSON

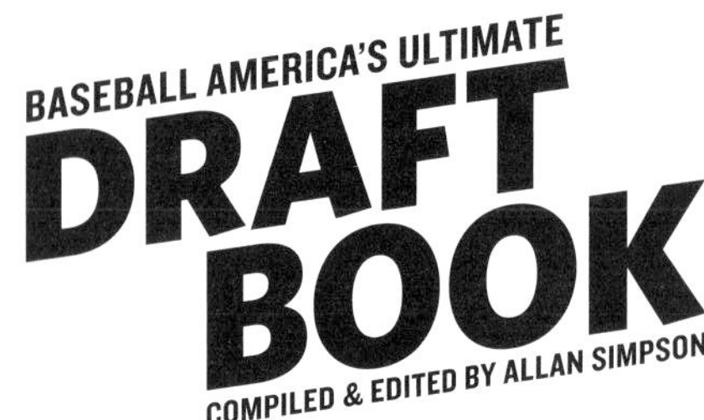


## EDITOR

Allan Simpson


## ACKNOWLEDGEMENTS

Baseball America's Ultimate Draft Book is the most ambitious undertaking ever attempted in capturing the 50-year history of the baseball draft—or any draft, for that matter. It was researched, compiled and edited by the publication's founder and longtime editor, Allan Simpson, who is nationally recognized for his expertise on the baseball draft.

Simpson authored the first edition of the book in 1989, spending the better part of two years poring through clippings and microfilms, talking with scouts and scouting directors, along with some of the more intriguing players and personalities of the first 25 years of the draft era, to accumulate information for that book. Not only has he updated those files with more current information, but he has compiled and edited the most recent 25 years (plus 2016), liberally taking information from Baseball America's extensive coverage of the draft through the years, to provide a comprehensive overview of the full history of the draft. Of particular note is the wealth of signing bonus information that Simpson has painstakingly gathered through the years.

While Simpson has assembled, compiled and written much of the content in the book largely from scratch, he has utilized extensively the draft content that was written eloquently through the years by many of his peers at Baseball America like Jim Callis, John Manuel, Alan Schwarz, Will Lingo, J.J. Cooper, Mike Berardino, Josh Boyd, Jon Scher, Danny Knobler, David Rawnsley and Alan Matthews. Longtime Baseball America correspondents Ken Leiker, Tracy Ringolsby, Peter Gammons, Jayson Stark, Jerry Crasnick and numerous others contributed to the cause to varying degrees. Callis and Leiker, in particular, played an instrumental role in the first draft volume and much of their handiwork then is evident in the current volume. Leiker also lent his assistance in editing the book, while Callis was involved in the proofing process.

Special credit also goes to Lingo, BA's publisher who edited the product and provided plenty of guidance along the way; and also to Sara Hiatt McDaniel, BA's production manager, who oversaw all of the book's production efforts.

Special acknowledgment is also accorded:

- The baseball commissioner's office, especially Roy Krasik, senior director of major league operations, and Chuck Fox, manager, amateur relations.
- The Sporting News, whose extensive coverage of developments leading up to the draft's adoption in 1964 largely enabled us to piece together the story on the evolution of the draft on pages 23-27 as well as various other developments in the early years.


## HOW TO USE THIS BOOK

Statistical information for this book runs through the 2015 season. While we have included the 2016 draft and relevant happenings from the 2016 season (such as Matt Bush reaching the major leagues), most of the information in the book goes through 2015 to avoid partial-season statistics.

In each chapter from 1965-2016, we've included an At A Glance overview—effectively thumbnail sketches to highlight some of the highlights (and lowlights) that helped to define a draft class. Beginning in 2012, we did not include some of the categories because sufficient time had not passed to properly define an appropriate selection.

Most of the categories we included require no explanation; but others do, including the following.

- **SECOND BEST/ON SECOND THOUGHT/SECOND TO NONE/SECOND TIME AROUND:** The best second-round pick in that year's draft.
- **LATE-ROUND FIND:** The best player drafted after the 10th round.
- **NEVER TOO LATE:** The last player drafted who reached the major leagues.
- **OVERLOOKED:** The best player who signed as a nondrafted free agent.
- **MINOR LEAGUE TAKE:** The most significant minor league career by a first-round pick.


**Baseball America®**

MAJORS • MINORS • PROSPECTS • DRAFT • COLLEGE • HIGH SCHOOL

BASEBALL AMERICA • P.O. Box 12877, Durham, NC 27709 • Phone (919) 682-9635

### THE TEAM

**GENERAL MANAGER** Will Lingo *@willingo*

#### EDITORIAL

**EDITOR IN CHIEF** John Manuel *@johnmanuelba*
**MANAGING EDITOR** J.J. Cooper *@jjcoop36*
**ASSOCIATE EDITORS** Matt Eddy *@matteddyba*, Kyle Glaser *@KyleAGlaser*
**NEWS EDITOR** Josh Norris *@jnorris427*
**WEB EDITOR** Vincent Lara-Cinisomo *@vincelara*
**NATIONAL WRITERS** Ben Badler *@benbadler*, Teddy Cahill *@tedcahill*
**ASSISTANT EDITORS** Michael Lananna *@mlananna*, Jim Shonerd *@jimshonerdba*
**EDITORIAL ASSISTANT** Hudson Belinsky *@hudsonbelinsky*
**INTERNS** Will Bryant, Alex Simon

#### PRODUCTION

**DESIGN & PRODUCTION DIRECTOR** Sara Hiatt McDaniel
**MULTIMEDIA MANAGER** Linwood Webb
**PRODUCTION MANAGER** Inna Cazares

#### ADVERTISING

**ADVERTISING DIRECTOR** George Shelton
**DIGITAL SALES MANAGER** Larry Sarzyniak
**MARKETPLACE MANAGER** Kristopher M. Lull
**MARKETING MANAGER** Abbey Langdon

#### BUSINESS

**CUSTOMER SERVICE** Ronnie McCabe, C.J. McPhatter
**ACCOUNTING/OFFICE MANAGER** Hailey Carpenter
**TECHNOLOGY MANAGER** Brent Lewis

#### COLUMNISTS

**JERRY CRASNICK** ESPN
**PETER GAMMONS** MLB Network
**TRACY RINGOLSBY** MLB.com
**JAYSON STARK** ESPN

#### STATISTICAL SERVICE

MAJOR LEAGUE BASEBALL ADVANCED MEDIA

### ACTION / OUTDOOR GROUP

#### MANAGEMENT

**PRODUCTION DIRECTOR** Kasey Kelley
**FINANCE DIRECTOR** Adam Miner

#### SALES & MARKETING

**VP, SALES** Kristen Ude
**SALES ANALYST** Mozelle Martinez
**SALES & MARKETING SPECIALIST** Aaron Santanello

#### DESIGN

**CREATIVE DIRECTOR** Marc Hostetter

#### EVENTS

**EVENTS DIRECTOR** Scott Desidero
**VP/GM, DEW TOUR** Adam Cozens
**OPERATIONS DIRECTOR, DEW TOUR** Anthony Dittman

#### DIGITAL

**DIRECTOR OF ENGINEERING** Jeff Kimmel
**SENIOR PRODUCT MANAGER** Marc Bartell
**DIGITAL CONTENT STRATEGIES MANAGER** Kristopher Heineman

#### FACILITIES

**MANAGER** Randy Ward
**OFFICE COORDINATOR** Ruth Hosea
**IT SUPPORT SPECIALIST** James Rodney

#### MANUFACTURING OPERATIONS

**VP, MANUFACTURING OPERATIONS** Greg Parnell
**ARCHIVIST** Thomas Voehringer

### TEN: THE ENTHUSIAST NETWORK, LLC

**CHAIRMAN** Peter Englehart
**CHIEF EXECUTIVE OFFICER** Scott P. Dickey
**CHIEF FINANCIAL OFFICER** Bill Sutman
**PRESIDENT, AUTOMOTIVE** Scott Bailey
**EVP/GM, SPORTS & ENTERTAINMENT** Norb Garrett
**CHIEF MARKETING OFFICER** Jonathan Anastas
**CHIEF COMMERCIAL OFFICER** Eric Schwab
**CHIEF CREATIVE OFFICER** Alan Alpanian
**EVP, OPERATIONS** Kevin Mullan
**VP, EDITORIAL & ADVERTISING OPERATIONS** Amy Diamond
**SVP/GM, PERFORMANCE AFTERMARKET** Matt Boice
**VP, FINANCIAL PLANNING** Mike Cummings
**SVP, AUTOMOTIVE DIGITAL** Geoff DeFrance
**SVP, AFTERMARKET AUTOMOTIVE CONTENT** David Freiburger
**SVP, IN-MARKET AUTOMOTIVE CONTENT** Ed Loh
**SVP, DIGITAL, SPORTS & ENTERTAINMENT** Greg Morrow
**SVP, DIGITAL ADVERTISING OPERATIONS** Elisabeth Murray
**SVP, MARKETING** Ryan Payne

#### CONSUMER MARKETING, ENTHUSIAST MEDIA SUBSCRIPTION COMPANY, INC.

**SVP, CIRCULATION** Tom Slater
**VP, RETENTION & OPERATIONS FULFILLMENT** Donald T. Robinson III

# After five decades, draft finally comes of age

While most of us who are old enough remember where we were when Bill Mazeroski hit his magical home run in 1960, or when we learned of President Kennedy's assassination in 1963, or saw man's first landing on the moon in 1969, I could tell you where I was on June 8, 1965, when Rick Monday became the first player selected in the inaugural Major League Baseball draft.

I was a high school student in Kelowna, British Columbia, on my lunch hour, when I heard the announcement on my local radio station.

The moment was inconsequential, but it resonated with me over the years and explains why the draft became an integral part of Baseball America's coverage when the publication was launched 16 years later in the garage of my home in Canada.

Others developed a fascination for the NFL and NBA drafts—even the NHL draft, for those of us who were born and raised north of the border. My passion was always the baseball draft.

It was the last of the drafts to be instituted, and while it was conducted in relative anonymity through the years—partly because of the obscurity of the players involved, partly because MLB preferred to keep it that way—the baseball draft has become a meaningful event on the baseball calendar every year in early June.

Though it still gets nowhere near the media coverage the other drafts receive, the baseball draft has surged in popularity in recent years and remains the singular event that Baseball America most identifies with.

After 50 years, it's even fair to say that the baseball draft has come of age, and it's an appropriate time to chronicle a half century of draft history.

Beginning with Monday, who was selected by the Kansas City Athletics with the first pick in the first draft, some 70,000 players have been drafted through the years, and every single name can be found in the pages that follow. The list runs the gamut from Hall of Famers—34, to be exact—to countless late-round picks who never played the game professionally.

Of course, the most insightful way to look at the baseball draft is in hindsight. We did that in 1989 when we published a thorough recap of the first 25 years, and we've outdone ourselves with this volume. Not only have we included many of the same storylines and anecdotes, but we now have access to thousands of signing bonuses that allow us to tell the story through an entirely different prism.

But even as we've seen the average signing bonus for first-rounders climb from $42,516 in 1965, to $176,008 in 1989, to a staggering $2,897,778 in 2016, and the scouting of baseball talent has become much more sophisticated in the process, we still believe the 1968 Los Angeles Dodgers produced the single greatest draft ever, and 1985 remains the richest draft on record.

■ ■ ■

The baseball draft is similar to its football and basketball counterparts in that it is the link that ties together the professional and amateur ranks, and rewards teams most in need of a talent infusion. The obvious difference is that the baseball draft is much more of an inexact science and draws its talent from multiple sources, not just the college ranks. It rarely includes a household name, though Stephen Strasburg and Bryce Harper in 2009 and 2010 were obvious exceptions—as was the signing of Bo Jackson by the Kansas City Royals in 1986.

Ken Griffey Jr. and Mike Piazza meant little to the average baseball fan at the time they were drafted in the late 1980s, but with the advantage of looking at the stellar careers of both players that led to their selection to the Hall of Fame in 2016, the draft status of both players comes more clearly into focus. Griffey, a product of the 1987 draft, is the first No. 1 overall pick ever elected to Cooperstown; Piazza, a 62nd-round afterthought in 1988, is the latest selection ever to be enshrined.

They illustrate the inexact nature of the draft. It was that way in 1965 and remains so 50 years later. The reality is that seven of 10 first-round picks, on average, ever reach the majors, and just 13.9 percent of drafted players overall.

That's why teams need 40 or 50 rounds (or more) to separate the wheat from the chaff, and explains why just 22 draft picks have gone directly to the big leagues since 1965. Mistakes are plentiful, but the uncertainty makes the baseball draft all the more intriguing.

For every Alex Rodriguez or Chipper Jones that has come along, there has been a Matt Bush or Brien Taylor—first-rounders with equally high expectations who never came close to fulfilling them.

The NFL and NHL drafts (seven rounds), and NBA (two rounds) have relatively small, more clearly defined player pools. The baseball draft combines high school seniors, junior college players, college juniors and college seniors. There has never been a requirement to declare for the draft, as occurs in basketball and football; in baseball, everyone's eligible at least twice before they're a college senior.

Despite its inexactness, the draft can shape a team's fortunes for years to come, for better or worse. The Atlanta Braves made 14 straight postseason appearances beginning in the early 1990s, while the Pittsburgh Pirates went 20 straight years with a losing record over relatively the same period—both driven in large measure by their success (or lack thereof) in acquiring talent in the draft.

■ ■ ■

When I launched Baseball America 35 years ago, the baseball draft had little national exposure, yet it was at the forefront of our coverage from the very start, especially after we accurately pegged Mike Moore and Joe Carter as the top two picks in 1981.

As recently as 17 years ago, when Josh Hamilton and Josh Beckett went off the board 1-2, just as we projected, the draft still got little exposure because Major League Baseball refused to promote it, even to the point of withholding the names of every player drafted beyond the first round for a week—and even then refusing to divulge the rounds of the players for four more months. Ostensibly, MLB's approach was aimed at keeping information away from agents and college coaches at a time of significant bonus inflation.

The clandestine efforts by the powers that be to keep the public in the dark—and often the drafted players themselves, in many cases—and forgo an obvious opportunity to market the game only spurred my resolve to expose this inequity. As the then-editor of Baseball America, I was determined to get my hands on the entire draft list (from sources and friends in the industry) and publicize it while the iron was still hot.

We promoted our intentions to do just that in the weeks leading up to the 1998 draft. When MLB got wind of our plans, only at that point did it back off its stance and agree to publish the list immediately, and in its entirety. MLB's rationale was that if BA was going to publish the list anyway, then everyone should have access to it.

In the years since then, MLB has a done a full 180 in its approach to the draft, and now promotes it as one of its special events on the calendar. Traffic on its own website sees a noticeable spike around the draft, and the commissioner's office has even taken an active role in transitioning the draft into a made-for-TV event (if only for the first two rounds), originating from MLB Network's studio in Secaucus, N.J.

While the baseball draft still has a long way to go to become a must-see event for casual baseball fans, all the recent developments to transform the draft into what it has become got me thinking that I might have been onto something all along, that the adoption of the baseball draft in 1965 had historical relevance. I just might have been 50 years ahead of my time.

**ALLAN SIMPSON**
EDITOR

# Draft's constant has been change

It was in a setting of great intrigue and anticipation, as well as an aura of mystery, that 20 major league teams kicked off baseball's first amateur draft on June 8, 1965. Some 200 observers, including club officials and baseball executives from the commissioner's office and the minor leagues, along with members of the media and photographers, gathered for two days at New York's Commodore Hotel to select a total of 826 players.

Unlike the stodgy selection process in later years, which was shrouded in secrecy to prevent enemy forces from pirating privileged scouting information, baseball's first draft was conducted in a carnival-like atmosphere.

"There was tremendous excitement," recalled the late Lou Gorman, then Baltimore's assistant farm director and later Boston's general manager. "We'd all end up at Toots Shor's bar or someplace the night before the draft. There would be all kinds of rumors flying around."

After holing up in hotel rooms for several days planning strategy, club officials emerged for two days of concentrated name-calling that found its light moments, and a few contentious ones.

"There was a lot of cross-chatter in the draft room," said the late Johnny Johnson, who headed up the New York Yankees delegation. "One guy would yell out, 'How the hell could they select that bum!', and then someone else would say, 'Damn it, he was our next guy!' "

RUSS REED

**Reggie Jackson (left) and Rick Monday played together at Arizona State and were the A's first two first-round picks**

Art Stewart, a Chicago-based scout who attended the event with the Yankees delegation and one of the few people from the first gathering still active in the game in his role as a longtime scouting executive with the Kansas City Royals, remembered the first draft as being a little more disorderly.

"It was chaos, absolute chaos," Stewart said. "Clubs didn't know how to prepare for it. The Yankees were no different."

Pittsburgh Pirates general manager Joe Brown, now deceased, recalled how disorganized his team's first draft was.

"We really went into it blind," Brown said. "We all brought trunkfuls of player reports to New York and sat in the hotel room for four or five days. The scouting director put all the reports in the order he had, and then we'd bring up each name and consider it."

Brown said the Pirates went to New York with a list of 450 players they would pick if available.

"That was an inordinate number," he said, when asked back in the 1980s. "We wouldn't have that number now. I don't think too many clubs have failed to improve on their initial method. I really don't think that we were too successful in the early years."

The Pirates ended up selecting 41 players in 1965, including seven who would go on to play in the big leagues. But it was clearly a lesson in trial and error, as it took 18 picks before the Pirates would snag their

**SELECT GROUP**

## Drafted Players Inducted in Hall of Fame

| Draft Year | Player, Pos. | Club (Round) | Induction Year |
|---|---|---|---|
| 1965 | Johnny Bench, c | Reds (2) | 1989 |
| | Nolan Ryan, rhp | Mets (10) | 1999 |
| 1966 | Reggie Jackson, of | Athletics (1) | 1993 |
| | * Tom Seaver, rhp | Braves (Jan. S-1) | 1992 |
| 1967 | Carlton Fisk, c | Red Sox (Jan. R-1) | 2000 |
| 1969 | Bert Blyleven, rhp | Twins (3) | 2011 |
| | Goose Gossage, rhp | White Sox (9) | 2008 |
| 1970 | # Bruce Sutter, rhp | Cubs (NDFA) | 2006 |
| 1971 | Jim Rice, of | Red Sox (1) | 2009 |
| | George Brett, 3b | Royals (2) | 1999 |
| | Mike Schmidt, 3b | Phillies (2) | 1995 |
| 1972 | Dennis Eckersley, rhp | Indians (3) | 2004 |
| | Gary Carter, c | Expos (3) | 2003 |
| 1973 | Robin Yount, ss | Brewers (1) | 1999 |
| | Dave Winfield, of | Padres (1) | 2001 |
| | Eddie Murray, 1b | Orioles (3) | 2003 |
| 1975 | Andre Dawson, of | Expos (11) | 2010 |
| 1976 | Rickey Henderson, of | Athletics (4) | 2009 |
| | Wade Boggs, 3b | Red Sox (7) | 2005 |
| 1977 | Paul Molitor, ss | Brewers (1) | 2004 |
| | Ozzie Smith, ss | Padres (4) | 2002 |
| 1978 | Cal Ripken Jr., ss | Orioles (2) | 2007 |
| | Ryne Sandberg, ss | Phillies (20) | 2005 |
| 1981 | Tony Gwynn, of | Padres (3) | 2007 |
| 1982 | Kirby Puckett, of | Twins (Jan. R-1) | 2001 |
| 1984 | Greg Maddux, rhp | Cubs (2) | 2014 |
| | Tom Glavine, lhp | Braves (2) | 2014 |
| 1985 | Barry Larkin, ss | Reds (1) | 2012 |
| | Randy Johnson, lhp | Expos (2) | 2015 |
| | John Smoltz, rhp | Tigers (22) | 2015 |
| 1987 | Ken Griffey Jr., of | Mariners (1) | 2016 |
| | Craig Biggio, c | Astros (1) | 2015 |
| 1988 | Mike Piazza, c | Dodgers (62) | 2016 |
| 1989 | Frank Thomas, 1b | White Sox (1) | 2014 |

**Contract voided; signed by Mets via lottery.*
*#Undrafted; signed by Cubs as non-drafted free agent.*

## By The Numbers

**70,866** Total number of players drafted, 1965-2016

**17** Most players drafted in one year by one club to reach majors (Mets, 1982)

**495.7** Accumulated WAR (Wins Above Replacement) for the first round of the 1985 draft, easily the best on record

**10.7** Accumulated WAR for the first round of the 1975 draft, easily the lowest on record

**6** Number of first-round picks (June, regular phase) who never played professional baseball

**8** Number of Heisman Trophy winners who have been selected in baseball draft

**9** Most consecutive picks at start of draft to reach majors (Rangers, 1987)

**18** Number of first-round picks the Yankees have lost for signing major league free agents

**100** Number of first-round picks (1965-2009) who failed to advance beyond Class A first future big leaguer.

Despite some chaos, baseball's first draft was accomplished with unexpected precision. Arrangements were made by commissioner Ford Frick and his staff, who began planning the event six months in advance—or as soon as the draft was officially adopted at the 1964 Winter Meetings.

Each club had a table with space for up to eight people. American League clubs were aligned in one row, National League clubs in another. On the first day, the 20 major league organizations drafted 320 players in the first six hours—about one per minute. Another 506 players were drafted over a nine-hour period the following day.

Boston became the first organization to stop drafting. The Red Sox passed after making 20 picks, selecting 13 fewer players than Philadelphia. As an indicator of the different philosophies clubs adopted, the Houston Astros drafted 72 players. Four clubs—Pittsburgh, Milwaukee, Cleveland and Detroit—exchanged scouting reports to give them better coverage of the country.

It was apparent that teams didn't have the draft down to a science. The teams themselves were responsible for determining a player's eligibility, and 13 selections were voided. Several picks were nullified under the American Legion protection rule that prevented teams from drafting Legion players who had not yet turned 17 and had Legion eligibility remaining. One such selection, catcher Robert Yodice, 16, would go on to be the No. 1 choice in a short-lived Legion draft at the end of the summer.

In other cases, an incorrect spelling of a player's name resulted in forfeiture of the pick if the player was subsequently drafted by a second team. Negotiating rights would go to the club which properly identified the player.

While there was general satisfaction with how the first draft was conducted, one obvious flaw was uncovered. It involved the selection of players in the later rounds at the Class A level. Technically, major league teams drafted players for themselves in the first round, and on behalf of their farm teams in succeeding rounds. They were permitted two picks in Triple-A (effectively, rounds 2-3) and four at Double-A (rounds 4-7), for a total of seven picks. Each club had a single affiliate in Triple-A and Double-A, so in each of the first seven rounds, teams had one selection.

In Class A, however, the number of selections an organization could make in each round was determined by the number of farm clubs it had at that level. Some had two, others had as many as five. Additionally, the order of selection in each Class A round did not follow from the order in the first seven rounds; effective with the eighth round, it was based on the previous year's final standings in the eight

## Ten Iconic Draft Moments

Bo Jackson

**1 BO KNOWS BASEBALL.** The Royals scored a major coup for baseball with their bold, calculated move in 1986 to snatch away Bo Jackson, the reigning Heisman Trophy winner and No. 1 overall pick in that year's football draft, from the NFL. With his exceptional power/speed package, Jackson may be the greatest raw talent to play in the draft era, and his impact on the game—even in his brief, injury-riddled career—was substantial.

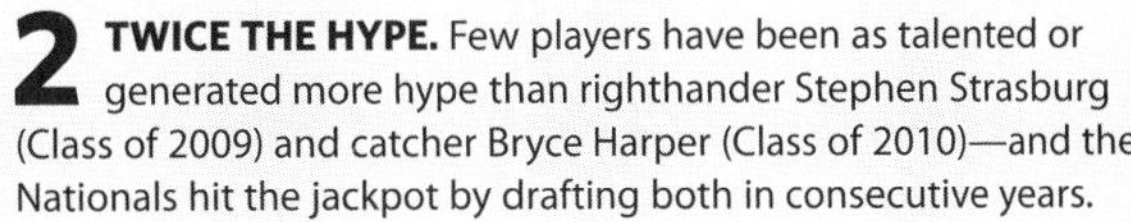

**2 TWICE THE HYPE.** Few players have been as talented or generated more hype than righthander Stephen Strasburg (Class of 2009) and catcher Bryce Harper (Class of 2010)—and the Nationals hit the jackpot by drafting both in consecutive years.

**3 SIGN OF THINGS TO COME.** The Yankees sent shock waves through the industry in 1991, when they signed North Carolina prep lefthander Brien Taylor, the No. 1 overall pick, to a $1.55 million bonus—almost three times the existing record. Taylor's contract triggered an unprecedented wave of bonus escalation that would continue largely unabated over the better part of the next two decades. Taylor's promising career fell apart, and he topped out in Double-A after he injured his shoulder in an offseason fight.

**4 SACRIFICIAL LAMB.** Texas schoolboy lefthander David Clyde fashioned one of the greatest careers in prep baseball annals, making him a near slam-dunk choice as the No. 1 pick in 1973. The Rangers showed no hesitation in drafting him, and the move played right into the hands of owner Bob Short, who saw in Clyde a windfall opportunity to give his ailing franchise a significant shot in the arm. Clyde was promoted directly to the Rangers rotation, and not only won his much-hyped debut, but the sideshow that accompanied it provided Short's transplanted Rangers their first-ever sellout. Short's cash grab, however, came at a significant cost as an emotionally scarred, ill-prepared Clyde went just 18-33 in his big league career.

**5 OPPORTUNISTIC STRIKE.** The Loophole Free-Agent Fiasco of 1996 brought the bonus escalation issue to a head. First-rounders Travis Lee (Twins), John Patterson (Expos), Matt White (Giants) and Bobby Seay (White Sox) all became free agents after challenging a little-enforced rule that required clubs to tender formal contract offers to their draft picks within 15 days of being selected. Expansion teams in Arizona and Tampa Bay saw a windfall opportunity to add frontline talent not otherwise available to them. Between them, the Diamondbacks and Devil Rays signed all four players, shelling out signing bonuses totaling roughly $30 million.

**6 ULTIMATE HUMAN INTEREST STORY.** Jim Abbott was born without a right hand but never let his handicap stand in his way. After a standout college career at Michigan, Abbott was taken by the Angels with the eighth pick in the 1988 draft, then led the U.S. to gold that fall at the Seoul Olympics. Understandably, the atmosphere in Anaheim was at a fever pitch the following spring when Abbott made his pro debut as one of just 22 picks in draft history to play in a major-league game without first appearing in the minors.

**7 LIGHTNING ROD FOR CONTROVERSY.** The baseball draft has had its share of noteworthy holdouts and contentious signings, but few reverberated through the game quite like that of outfielder J.D. Drew. His impact was felt over the course of two drafts (1997 and 1998) and led to a renaming of the event itself.

**8 THE DILEMMA.** Major league teams routinely agonize in selecting one player over another, particularly with the No. 1 pick overall. The 1966 draft serves as a constant reminder of the stakes involved. The Mets came down to California high school catcher Steve Chilcott or Arizona State outfielder Reggie Jackson with the No. 1 pick. They opted for Chilcott.

**9 FINALLY, A WORKABLE SOLUTION.** For the better part of 25 years, the draft served its intended purpose, but in the early 1990s bonuses skyrocketed. From a first-round average of $176,008 in 1989, the norm grew to more than $2 million by 2001 and peaked at $2,653,375 in 2011. Thereafter a new labor agreement ushered in the most-sweeping changes to the draft since the process began, including the establishment of aggregate signing bonus pools, which set limits on the amount that teams could spend on their draft picks, with penalties in the form of fines and forfeited draft picks if a team failed to comply.

**10 AGE OF ENLIGHTENMENT.** The baseball draft may never be confused with the NFL and NBA drafts in terms of popularity, but it has become exponentially more visible—and popular—over the last decade, stemming from Major League Baseball's decision to finally promote the draft as a meaningful event on the baseball calendar.

different Class A leagues in existence at the time. With 60 Class A clubs in all, a maximum of 60 players could be taken in each round.

Conceivably, one organization could reach its quota in each round before another made its first selection, and that's what happened in the case of the Minnesota Twins, who were entitled to five of the first 16 picks. They were able to secure all five players before 11 organizations drew even one player in each Class A round. The San Francisco Giants had to wait until the 39th pick to make their initial selection.

"The present arrangement in the Class A phase of the draft doesn't do what it was intended to do, distribute the talent equally," said St. Louis general manager Bob Howsam, whose club had to wait until the 24th pick in each round. "Certainly the weaker clubs are entitled to draw first, but each organization should have an equal opportunity."

With the exception of an immediate change in the Class A rule and minor changes regarding the eligibility of college players, the draft essentially worked the same way for years to come. Only with a lot less hoopla and fanfare.

## BACK TO THE FUTURE

Fast forward 50 years, and the draft remains Major League Baseball's primary conduit for distributing the young, unrefined talent percolating in the nation's college and high school ranks. For the most part, it has continued to be conducted in the socialist way intended—in a fair and equitable manner, with priority given to teams at the bottom of the standings. In other words, those with the greatest need of a talent infusion to become competitive.

Ken Griffey Jr.

The draft is still held in early June—coincidentally on June 8 in 2015, the same day the 1965 draft began and a true 50th anniversary—so as to strategically slot into a narrow window that allows most of the top amateur prospects eligible for selection to complete their spring schedules, get drafted and sign, all in time to begin their pro careers by the end of June, on the bottom rungs of the minor leagues.

The draft also originates again from New York, though mostly from Major League Baseball headquarters. It is also conducted in relatively the same, systematic manner as the process in 1965 that set the wheels in motion, while even allowing for some of the levity that characterized the first draft.

## 25 LARGEST BONUSES

| | Player, Pos. | Club (Order) | Bonus |
|---|---|---|---|
| 1. | Gerrit Cole, rhp | Pirates '11 (1) | $8,000,000 |
| 2. | * Stephen Strasburg, rhp | Nationals '09 (1) | $7,500,000 |
| | Bubba Starling, of | Royals '11 (5) | $7,500,000 |
| 4. | Kris Bryant, 3b | Cubs '13 (2) | $6,708,400 |
| 5. | Carlos Rodon, lhp | White Sox '14 (3) | $6,582,000 |
| 6. | Jameson Taillon, rhp | Pirates '10 (2) | $6,500,000 |
| | Dansby Swanson, ss | Diamondbacks '15 (1) | $6,500,000 |
| 8. | * Danny Hultzen, lhp | Mariners (2) | $6,350,000 |
| | Mark Appel, rhp | Astros '13 (1) | $6,350,000 |
| 10. | Donavan Tate, of | Padres '09 (3) | $6,250,000 |
| | * Bryce Harper, c | Nationals '10 (1) | $6,250,000 |
| 12. | Buster Posey, c | Giants '08 (5) | $6,200,000 |
| | Nick Senzel, 3b | Reds '16 (2) | $6,200,000 |
| 14. | Tim Beckham, ss | Rays '08 (1) | $6,150,000 |
| 15. | Justin Upton, ss | Diamondbacks '05 (1) | $6,100,000 |
| | Mickey Moniak, of | Phillies '16 (1) | $6,100,000 |
| 17. | Matt Wieters, c | Orioles '07 (5) | $6,000,000 |
| | * Pedro Alvarez, 3b | Pirates '08 (2) | $6,000,000 |
| | Eric Hosmer, 1b | Royals '08 (3) | $6,000,000 |
| | * Dustin Ackley, of | Mariners '09 (2) | $6,000,000 |
| | * Anthony Rendon, ss | Nationals '11 (6) | $6,000,000 |
| | Byron Buxton, of | Twins '12 (2) | $6,000,000 |
| | Tyler Kolek, rhp | Marlins '14 (2) | $6,000,000 |
| 24. | Alex Bregman, ss | Astros '15 (2) | $5,900,000 |
| 25. | * David Price, lhp | Rays '07 (1) | $5,600,000 |

**Signed major league contract.*

Obviously, that's too simplistic to sum up 50 years of draft history. It neglects many of the twists and turns, both the tumultuous and the sublime, that have impacted baseball at all levels over the last half century, many of which have filtered through to the draft, and even played a hand in retooling, if not necessarily reshaping it. But in many respects, the draft now is in relatively the same spot as it was in good, old 1965—even as it went through something of a 360-degree transformation to arrive back where it all started.

The 50th anniversary affair kicked off just down the road from New York, in Secaucus, N.J., at MLB's own state-of-the art television headquarters. The first two rounds were staged in prime time as a made-for-TV extravaganza, and in the spirit of 1965, was replete with its own bells and whistles as some of the stars of draft lore like Reggie Jackson (Class of 1966), Mike Schmidt (Class of 1971), Andre Dawson (Class of 1975) and Ken Griffey Jr. (Class of 1987) were on hand to signify the event's golden anniversary. They were accompanied by a handful of the top prospects in the 2015 draft, plus a couple of token representatives from every club in the game. Naturally, colorful Hall of Famer Tommy Lasorda was there representing the Los Angeles Dodgers, further enlivening the proceedings.

But that's about where any similarity between the 2015 draft and the one staged in 1965 ended.

Though the public announcement of each pick on the first night was made from New Jersey, including the first round by commissioner Rob Manfred, all the decision-making and deliberations by the clubs themselves were handled in the solitude of temporarily assembled draft rooms in major league stadiums around the country, complete with a maze of computers and telephones, and whiteboard lists of the top prospects eligible. Once the first two rounds came and went, the draft was removed from the public spotlight almost entirely. On days two and three, the process shifted back to the commissioner's office, and resumed in its customary rapid-fire, conference-call format, much like it's been done since 1972, when the open format and unwieldy ballroom environment was abandoned in favor of a more efficient, though far more impersonal setting.

In contrast to 20 teams that took part in the inaugural process, 30 clubs participated in 2015—thanks to four waves of major league expansion over the last half-century.

While teams were allowed to draft players at will 50 years earlier and for the next 27 years, they are limited to 40 rounds now.

But just as the order of selection in 1965 was altered by the quirky, convoluted distribution of extra picks based on the number of Class A farm clubs in a team's minor league system, the 2015 rotation was randomly adjusted, too, to provide compensation to teams for major league players lost

## DRAFT AT WAR

The Top 25 players in the draft era, based on Wins Above Replacement, as determined by Baseball Reference (baseball-reference.com):

| | Player, Pos. | Drafted (Round) | WAR | Bonus |
|---|---|---|---|---|
| 1. | Barry Bonds, of | Pirates '85 (1) | 162.5 | $125,000 |
| 2. | Roger Clemens, rhp | Red Sox '83 (1) | 140.3 | $121,000 |
| 3.* | Alex Rodriguez, ss | Mariners '93 (1) | 115.9 | $1,000,000 |
| 4. | Rickey Henderson, of | Athletics '76 (4) | 111.0 | $10,000 |
| 5. | Tom Seaver, rhp | Mets '66 (FA) | 110.5 | $40,000 |
| 6. | Mike Schmidt, 3b | Phillies '71 (2) | 107.0 | $32,500 |
| 7. | Greg Maddux, rhp | Cubs '84 (2) | 106.8 | $75,000 |
| 8. | Randy Johnson, lhp | Expos '85 (2) | 102.1 | $60,000 |
| 9.* | Albert Pujols, 3b | Cardinals '99 (13) | 99.7 | $30,000 |
| 10. | Cal Ripken, ss | Orioles '78 (2) | 95.6 | $20,000 |
| 11. | Bert Blyleven, rhp | Twins '69 (3) | 95.4 | $15,000 |
| 12. | Wade Boggs, 3b | Red Sox '76 (7) | 90.9 | $7,500 |
| 13. | George Brett, 3b | Royals (2) | 88.4 | $25,000 |
| 14. | Chipper Jones, ss | Braves '90 (1) | 85.1 | $275,000 |
| 15. | Ken Griffey Jr., of | Mariners '87 (1) | 83.7 | $160,000 |
| 16. | Mike Mussina, rhp | Orioles '90 (1) | 83.0 | $250,000 |
| 17. | Nolan Ryan, rhp | Mets '65 (10) | 81.8 | $12,000 |
| 18. | Tom Glavine, lhp | Braves '84 (2) | 81.4 | $80,000 |
| 19. | Curt Schilling, rhp | Red Sox '86 (Jan.-S/2) | 79.9 | $15,000 |
| 20. | Jeff Bagwell, 3b | Red Sox '89 (4) | 79.5 | $32,500 |
| 21. | Robin Yount, ss | Brewers '73 (1) | 77.1 | $60,000 |
| 22. | Ozzie Smith, ss | Padres '77 (4) | 76.5 | $5,000 |
| 23. | Paul Molitor, ss | Brewers '77 (1) | 75.5 | $77,500 |
| 24. | Johnny Bench, c | Reds '65 (2) | 75.2 | $6,000 |
| 25. | Lou Whitaker, 2b | Tigers '75 (5) | 74.8 | $11,000 |

**Active player (WAR rating through 2015 season)*

through free agency and priority draft picks they were unable to sign in 2014. There was also special dispensation awarded to small-market clubs in the form of "competitive-balance" picks, providing further proof that the draft remains a pawn in the game's never-ending quest to achieve parity among its constituents.

The lack of parity, or competitive balance in baseball was certainly on everyone's mind back in 1964, when the game was at a crossroads. There were two major issues that threatened the industry: out-of-control signing bonuses to untried amateur prospects, and the dizzying dominance displayed by one club, the all-powerful Yankees.

The solution was to implement a systematic player draft, effective with the 1965 season. It was hoped that a draft would cure all the game's ills by killing two birds with one stone.

Teams had tired of the Yankees dynasty, and the way they had thoroughly dominated the sport practically since the end of World War II. And bonuses were getting so out of hand that they were consistently topping the annual salaries of the game's top stars, and even threatening the financial viability of a number of franchises. The more clubs spent on bonuses to try to remain competitive, the less that was available to prop up a sagging player-development system, which had become fully dependent on major league subsidization for its very survival.

It was baseball's version of Catch-22.

**FIRST OVERALL PICKS**

June, regular phase

| Year | Team | Player, Pos. | School | Bonus |
|---|---|---|---|---|
| 1965 | Athletics | Rick Monday, of | Arizona State | $100,000 |
| 1966 | Mets | Steve Chilcott, c | Antelope Valley HS, Lancaster, Calif. | $75,000 |
| 1967 | Yankees | Ron Blomberg, 1b | Druid Hills HS, Atlanta | $75,000 |
| 1968 | Mets | Tim Foli, ss | Notre Dame HS, Sherman Oaks, Calif. | $74,000 |
| 1969 | Senators | Jeff Burroughs, of | Woodrow Wilson HS, Long Beach, Calif. | $88,000 |
| 1970 | Padres | Mike Ivie, c | Walker HS, Decatur, Ga. | $75,000 |
| 1971 | White Sox | Danny Goodwin, c | Central HS, Peoria, Ill. | Did not sign |
| 1972 | Padres | * Dave Roberts, 3b | Oregon | $70,000 |
| 1973 | Rangers | * David Clyde, lhp | Westchester HS, Houston | $65,000 |
| 1974 | Padres | * Bill Almon, ss | Brown | $90,000 |
| 1975 | Angels | * Danny Goodwin, c | Southern | $150,000 |
| 1976 | Astros | Floyd Bannister, lhp | Arizona State | $100,000 |
| 1977 | White Sox | Harold Baines, of | St. Michaels (Md.) HS | $32,000 |
| 1978 | Braves | * Bob Horner, 3b | Arizona State | $162,000 |
| 1979 | Mariners | Al Chambers, 1b | John Harris HS, Harrisburg, Pa. | $60,000 |
| 1980 | Mets | Darryl Strawberry, of | Crenshaw HS, Los Angeles | $152,500 |
| 1981 | Mariners | Mike Moore, rhp | Oral Roberts | $100,000 |
| 1982 | Cubs | Shawon Dunston, ss | Thomas Jefferson HS, Brooklyn, N.Y. | $135,000 |
| 1983 | Twins | Tim Belcher, rhp | Mount Vernon Nazarene (Ohio) College | Did not sign |
| 1984 | Mets | Shawn Abner, of | Mechanicsburg (Pa.) HS | $150,500 |
| 1985 | Brewers | B.J. Surhoff, c | North Carolina | $150,000 |
| 1986 | Pirates | Jeff King, 3b | Arkansas | $180,000 |
| 1987 | Mariners | Ken Griffey Jr., of | Moeller HS, Cincinnati | $160,000 |
| 1988 | Padres | Andy Benes, rhp | Evansville | $235,000 |
| 1989 | Orioles | * Ben McDonald, rhp | Louisiana State | $350,000 |
| 1990 | Braves | Chipper Jones, ss | The Bolles School, Jacksonville, Fla. | $275,000 |
| 1991 | Yankees | Brien Taylor, lhp | East Carteret HS, Beaufort, N.C. | $1,550,000 |
| 1992 | Astros | Phil Nevin, 3b | Cal State Fullerton | $700,000 |
| 1993 | Mariners | * Alex Rodriguez, ss | Westminster Christian HS, Miami | $1,000,000 |
| 1994 | Mets | Paul Wilson, rhp | Florida State | $1,550,000 |
| 1995 | Angels | Darin Erstad, of | Nebraska | $1,575,000 |
| 1996 | Pirates | Kris Benson, rhp | Clemson | $2,000,000 |
| 1997 | Tigers | Matt Anderson, rhp | Rice | $2,505,000 |
| 1998 | Phillies | * Pat Burrell, 3b | Miami (Fla.) | $3,150,000 |
| 1999 | Devil Rays | Josh Hamilton, of | Athens Drive HS, Raleigh, N.C. | $3,960,000 |
| 2000 | Marlins | Adrian Gonzalez, 1b | Eastlake HS, Chula Vista, Calif. | $3,000,000 |
| 2001 | Twins | Joe Mauer, c | Cretin-Derham Hall, St. Paul, Minn. | $5,150,000 |
| 2002 | Pirates | Bryan Bullington, rhp | Ball State | $4,000,000 |
| 2003 | Devil Rays | * Delmon Young, of | Camarillo (Calif.) HS | $3,700,000 |
| 2004 | Padres | Matt Bush, ss | Mission Bay HS, San Diego | $3,150,000 |
| 2005 | Diamondbacks | Justin Upton, ss | Great Bridge HS, Chesapeake, Va. | $6,100,000 |
| 2006 | Royals | * Luke Hochevar, rhp | None | $3,500,000 |
| 2007 | Rays | * David Price, lhp | Vanderbilt | $5,600,000 |
| 2008 | Rays | Tim Beckham, ss | Griffin (Ga.) HS | $6,150,000 |
| 2009 | Nationals | * Stephen Strasburg, rhp | San Diego State | $7,500,000 |
| 2010 | Nationals | * Bryce Harper, c | JC of Southern Nevada | $6,250,000 |
| 2011 | Pirates | Gerrit Cole, rhp | UCLA | $8,000,000 |
| 2012 | Astros | Carlos Correa, ss | Puerto Rico Baseball Academy, Gurabo, P.R. | $4,800,000 |
| 2013 | Astros | Mark Appel, rhp | Stanford | $6,350,000 |
| 2014 | Astros | Brady Aiken, lhp | Cathedral Catholic HS, San Diego | Did not sign |
| 2015 | Diamondbacks | Dansby Swanson, ss | Vanderbilt | $6,500,000 |
| 2016 | Phillies | Mickey Moniak, of | La Costa Canyon HS, Carlsbad, Calif. | $6,100,000 |

**Signed to major league contract*

familiar turf for the Yankees, with their deep pockets and rich tradition, as they had long been used to buying up the best talent around.

Ron Blomberg, referred to in some quarters as the second coming of Mickey Mantle (who was then on his last wobbly legs in pinstripes), was the player the Yankees chose to pin their hopes on, but he didn't come close to changing the team's fortunes, and the Yankees remained largely a non-factor for the next decade. That enabled other teams to grab a share of the spotlight—and even the once-woeful New York Mets upstaged their crosstown rivals by winning the 1969 World Series.

But the clearest indicator that parity ruled the game occurred over the 10-year period from 1978-87, when 10 different clubs won the World Series. If it was competitive balance the game sought, it got it in spades over that stretch, and for the most part, competitive balance remains a buzzword in today's game.

Also about that time, the minor leagues, which had dipped from 460 clubs at the height of the post-World War II boom to 121 teams in the mid-60s, when the draft was enacted, began a remarkable renaissance. It germinated in places like Nashville, Tenn.; Columbus, Ohio; and Durham, N.C., and interest quickly mushroomed across the minor league landscape. Spurred on by a wave of stadium construction in the 1980s and 1990s, and even a hit movie, "Bull Durham," the minor leagues prospered like never before and soon became largely self-sufficient.

The draft, on its own accord, can't take credit for the parity that took hold in the majors, or the newfound popularity of the minors, or even the solid footing the game overall is on today on almost every front. But it's no coincidence that the greatest era of prosperity the game has known has largely paralleled the 50 years the draft has existed. So it's safe to say that the draft has played a vital role in the game's growth through the years.

"Despite all the changes to the eco-

## DRAFT PARALLELS GAME

The implementation of a draft addressed one of baseball's biggest problems almost overnight, as it led to an immediate and dramatic curtailment of bonus payments.

Outfielder Rick Monday, who enjoys eternal notoriety as the No. 1 pick in the first draft, was awarded a $104,000 contract—$100,000 in the form of a signing bonus, $4,000 under baseball's scholarship program to complete four more semesters of college at Arizona State—by the Kansas City Athletics, the one and only club he could now negotiate with. Monday's bonus was not only less than half the record amount of $205,000 the Los Angeles Angels paid outfielder Rick Reichardt in 1964, when open bidding for talent ruled the day, but it remained the largest bonus paid out in the first 10 years of the draft.

The other issues at the time of the draft's implementation took a little longer to deal with, but it's noteworthy that the Yankees, for all their dominance prior to the draft's inception (nine World Series appearances in 10 years), suddenly became old and decrepit in the very year the draft was implemented. A year later, they tumbled to the bottom of the American League standings. The reward for their incompetence? The first kick at the can in the 1967 draft—

nomics of baseball in the last 50 years, all clubs still view the draft as one of the most important elements in building a competitive team," said Dan Halem, chief legal officer for Major League Baseball. "The draft has been a primary factor in the ability of clubs from smaller markets to field championship-caliber teams."

For all it has done to help level the playing field, individual clubs can still use creativity and ingenuity to make the most of the draft. Throw in a little luck, and the draft era is littered with examples of clubs that just plain outsmarted their competition, and reaped the rewards of success on the playing field.

The Kansas City-based A's laid the foundation for World Series championship teams that came to fruition in Oakland from 1972-74, by getting an early jump in the draft, and the Dodgers' windfall crop of 1968, long hailed as the greatest single-year draft haul in history, propelled the club to a steady stream success in the 1970s, culminating in a World Series title in 1981.

The 1976 draft was the springboard that lifted the Detroit Tigers to a World Series title in 1984, and the 1986 Mets can point to a string of powerful drafts in the early '80s as the biggest contributing factor in their success. In the 1982 draft alone, the Mets drafted a record 17 players, including Dwight Gooden in the first round, who would go on to play in the big leagues.

Of more recent vintage, the St. Louis Cardinals capitalized on astute drafting to produce World Series champions in 2006 and 2011. Same goes for the Giants, who rode the magic arm of 2007 first-rounder Madison Bumgarner to their third World Series conquest in five years in 2014.

Dwight Gooden

On the flip side, the Atlanta Braves were doomed to dark years late in the 1980s, in large part because of their stunning futility in the 1981 draft. The Braves selected 48 players that year, and not a single one played a day in the big leagues—the only time in draft history that a team has whiffed on all its picks. Among 34 players taken in the June, regular phase, only one advanced as high as Triple-A. It didn't help the Braves that they didn't have second- or third-round picks that year, but they also rolled the dice on their top pick, Washington high school outfielder Jay Roberts, a top football recruit who didn't play baseball his senior year in high school while partaking instead in track and field. Not surprisingly, Roberts hit .187 with nine home runs in four minor league seasons, none above Class A.

Ever wonder why the Pirates went on their record-setting 20-year run, from 1993-2012, of never finishing above .500? Point to bad drafting, and a lot of it. In more years than they care to remember, the Pirates either made misguided selections or were victims of their own penny-pinching as an abundance of premium picks never materialized into contributors, and in all too many cases didn't even crack the big leagues. They repeatedly passed over more skilled talent. But then, the Pirates have a long history of squandering draft picks, as eight times from 1965-78 their top selection failed to advance beyond Class A.

Cincinnati's Big Red Machine was a force in the mid-1970s, in large measure because of astute drafting. But six years after winning the second of back-to-back World Series in 1976, a series of dreadful drafts sent it tumbling to the bottom of the National League standings.

More recently, the Astros had the dubious distinction of drafting first overall for an unprecedented three years in a row, after a succession of poor drafts in the early part of the century that resulted in the first three 100-loss seasons in Astros history. By drafting first again in 2014, the Astros tied the Mets and San Diego Padres as teams that have had the No. 1 pick as many five times over the life of the draft. The Pirates, Seattle Mariners and Tampa Bay Rays have selected first four times.

The Red Sox and Cardinals, meanwhile, have not only never picked first, but remain the only two teams that have never had one of the first two selections over the 50-year life of the June regular phase.

## YOUR CHANCES . . .

Based on 61,719 players drafted from 1965-2009 (ignoring 2010-16 because a sizeable number of potential major leaguers drafted in those years are still in the minor leagues, and would skew the results), your chances of reaching the big leagues if you are a drafted player of any kind:

**13.9%**

Obviously, a player drafted in the first round has the greatest chance of reaching the majors, and here are the odds for every other round through the top 10 rounds (June, regular phase only). Predictably, a player's chances decrease with every succeeding round.

First Round **69.4%**
Supplemental First Round **56.7%**
Second Round **47.0%**
Third Round **37.0%**
Fourth Round **31.4%**
Fifth Round **29.8%**
Sixth Round **25.4%**
Seventh Round **23.0%**
Eighth Round **19.2%**
Ninth Round **18.9%**
Tenth Round **18.4%**

### BONUS ESCALATION

For the first 10 to 12 years of the draft, signing bonuses were held in check and the average first-round bonus of $42,516 in 1965 changed only marginally. The Twins even got away with paying Bob Jones, their No. 1 pick in 1966, a bonus of $9,000—the record low for a first-rounder.

The greatest challenge to the game's status quo, however, occurred in 1976 with the advent of major league free agency. With players no longer bound in perpetuity to one club—often the club that drafted and signed them—they were suddenly free to market their services to the highest bidder. The historic ruling not only led to an immediate and exponential increase in major league salaries, but had a profound impact on the finances of the game over the next quarter century, particularly with all the labor strife between players and management that followed.

Free agency didn't have an immediate impact on the draft, though bonus records were set and broken on several occasions shortly after its onset. High-profile first-rounders Bob Horner (Braves) and Kirk Gibson (Tigers) were responsible for the first noteworthy bonus increases in 1978, and lefthander Bill Bordley, a high-profile University of Southern California dropout, and a somewhat obscure prospect drafted by the Yankees in the second round in 1979, Todd Demeter, pushed the mark to the $200,000 barrier and above a year later. But things remained relatively calm for the better part of the next decade.

Storm clouds, however, were beginning to brew all around.

Soon, the trickle-down effect of free agency, with the staggering increases in major league salaries that came in its wake, caught the draft firmly in its clutches and resulted in a similar leap in signing bonuses in the late 1980s.

## TOUGH SIGNS

### Most Times Drafted

**TWO-DRAFT ERA (1965-86)**

| No. | Player, Pos. | First | Last |
|---|---|---|---|
| 7 | *Reid Braden, 1b | 1965 | 1968 |
| | John Bryant, of | 1979 | 1984 |
| | Bill Dobbs, lhp | 1965 | 1970 |
| | *Herb Hofvendahl, of | 1965 | 1969 |
| | Luis Medina, 1b-of | 1981 | 1985 |
| | Pete Varney, c | 1966 | 1971 |

**ONE-DRAFT ERA (1987-2016)**

| No. | Player, Pos. | First | Last |
|---|---|---|---|
| 6 | Mark Hendrickson, lhp | 1992 | 1997 |

**Includes one voided selection*

The Baltimore Orioles had the No. 1 pick in 1989 and engaged in a nasty, contentious negotiation with pitcher Ben McDonald, which lasted all summer. McDonald eventually agreed to a record $824,300, three-year major league contract that provided for a bonus of $350,000 (also a record). Little more than a week later, the Toronto Blue Jays signed John Olerud, a mere third-round pick that year, to an $800,000, three-year deal that included a $575,000 bonus, another record.

By then, the financial state of the game was on such solid footing that spending lavishly on amateurs wasn't seen as a crisis. But in 1991, the industry was rocked to its core by the staggering $1.55 million bonus the Yankees, drafting first overall again, lavished on North Carolina prep pitcher Brien Taylor. The bonus was nearly three times the existing mark set in 1989 by Olerud and tied earlier in 1991 by Mike Kelly, the player drafted right after Taylor.

**STRAIGHT TO THE TOP**

## Draft Picks Who Skipped Minor Leagues

| Year | Team | Player, Pos. | School | Debut Date |
|---|---|---|---|---|
| 1967 | Orioles | Mike Adamson, rhp | Southern California | July 1, 1967 |
| 1970 | Indians | Steve Dunning, rhp | Stanford | June 14, 1970 |
| 1971 | Cubs | Burt Hooton, rhp | Texas | June 17, 1971 |
| | Brewers | Rob Ellis, 3b/of | Michigan State | June 18, 1971 |
| | Senators | Pete Broberg, rhp | Dartmouth | June 20, 1971 |
| 1972 | Padres | Dave Roberts, 3b | Oregon | June 7, 1972 |
| 1973 | Phillies | Dick Ruthven, rhp | Fresno State | April 17, 1973 |
| | Padres | Dave Winfield, of | Minnesota | June 19, 1973 |
| | Rangers | David Clyde, lhp | HS--Houston | June 27, 1973 |
| | Twins | Eddie Bane, lhp | Arizona State | July 4, 1973 |
| 1975 | Athletics | Denny Walling, of | Clemson | Sept. 7, 1975 |
| 1978 | Athletics | Mike Morgan, rhp | HS--Las Vegas, Nev. | June 11, 1978 |
| | Braves | Bob Horner, 3b | Arizona State | June 16, 1978 |
| | Blue Jays | Brian Milner, c | HS--Fort Worth, Texas | June 23, 1978 |
| | Athletics | Tim Conroy, lhp | HS--Monroeville, Pa. | June 23, 1978 |
| 1985 | Expos | * Pete Incaviglia, of | Oklahoma State | April 8, 1986 |
| 1988 | Angels | Jim Abbott, lhp | Michigan | April 8, 1989 |
| 1989 | Blue Jays | John Olerud, 1b | Washington State | Sept. 3, 1989 |
| 1993 | Dodgers | Darren Dreifort, rhp | Wichita State | April 7, 1994 |
| 1995 | Athletics | Ariel Prieto, rhp | None | July 2, 1995 |
| 2000 | Padres | Xavier Nady, 3b | California | Sept. 30, 2000 |
| 2009 | Reds | Mike Leake, rhp | Arizona State | April 11, 2010 |

** Debuted with Rangers*

From that point on, the floodgates opened, and the most contentious two-decade period in draft history ensued as bonuses continued to grow unchecked. In its time-honored tradition of using a heavy hand to try to squelch rising bonus payments, management tried every way imaginable—some legal, some not—to put a drag on the bonus explosion.

But as Pat Gillick, general manager of the 1992-93 World Series champion Blue Jays, put it: "The business is talent, and the draft is the biggest pool of talent. Pennants are won by drafting and signing free agents."

**Louisiana State righthander Ben McDonald was one of the symbols of the bonus escalation that hit the draft**

The very essence of the draft soon came under fire, however, as the industry grappled with measures to get a handle on runaway inflation. The efforts teams made to rein in bonuses paralleled the labor strife at the time, which eventually brought the game to its knees in 1994 with the most damaging strike in history.

With the game squarely back on its feet by 1996, things took a historic turn early that year when Cuban righthander Livan Hernandez, who was not subject to the draft as an international player, signed on the open market for $2.5 million—the largest bonus awarded to an amateur prospect. Later that year, four first-round draft picks were declared free agents when improperly tendered contracts, and pitcher Matt White and first baseman Travis Lee went on to sign exorbitant bonuses of $10.2 million and $10 million, respectively, with the expansion Devil Rays and Arizona Diamondbacks. Those clubs also signed the other two free agents, pitchers John Patterson and Bobby Seay, and tried to justify their investment as a once-in-a lifetime opportunity to give their fledgling franchises a head start.

Those staggering bonuses only strengthened the resolve of high-powered agents like Scott Boras, who engineered White's windfall deal, and masterminded several other record deals. He said the developments of 1996 were conclusive evidence that a draft system artificially stunts bonuses.

"What we've seen happen in the last two years, first internationally and then domestically, has given us a great barometer on the true worth of a select number of quality amateur players," Boras said. "The market has changed, and I know from experience that there are many teams willing to pay optimum dollars for a premium talent."

MLB moved quickly to close the loophole, but fear of additional fallout in 1997 caused teams to take a more cautious approach. In many cases, players were chosen on the basis of signability, not ability. Several first-round picks reached agreement before the draft, an illegal tactic but a common one nonetheless. Others were passed over in the first round because their asking price was deemed too steep.

Still, the record for a player signing with the club that drafted him was broken again in 1997—on two occasions. Pitcher Rick Ankiel, a player who had been in the running to go first overall but slid all the way to the second round (72nd overall), signed for $2.5 million, only to be topped by Matt Anderson, the No. 1 selection. Anderson, another pitcher, signed with the Tigers for $2.505 million after holding out for six months. With all the chaos swirling around them, the Tigers, along with other clubs, were put in the unenviable position of having to defend themselves against paying $10 million bonuses—even as they were spending record amounts.

The second player picked in the 1997 draft, however, had no qualms about challenging the system as it existed. Outfielder J.D. Drew, a Boras client, set the bar in his negotiations with the Philadelphia Phillies based on what the loophole free agents received a year earlier, not the $2 million figure that pitcher Kris Benson received in 1996 as the first overall pick.

Boras engaged in a bitter negotiation with the Phillies, and his client never did sign. Drew subsequently signed on with an independent league club rather than return to college at Florida State for his senior year. Amid concerns that Drew would contest the legality of the draft in the courts because he was no longer an amateur, Major League Baseball moved to make changes aimed at thwarting Drew's efforts—even renaming the process the First-Year Player Draft to remove all references to the word "amateur." Drew was stymied in his efforts to follow through on his threat, was redrafted a year later by the Cardinals with the fifth pick in the first round, and signed somewhat uneventfully.

Even with the restrictive nature of a draft to hold bonuses in check, they still continued to grow at a rapid rate. By 2001, the average bonus for a first-rounder was $2,154,280. By 2008, it was $2,449,785.

In 2009 and 2010, the Washington

Nationals, coming off successive last-place finishes, hit on an unexpected bonanza by having two of the highest-profile players in draft history, pitcher Stephen Strasburg and then-catcher Bryce Harper, fall into their laps in consecutive years, But the Nationals had to open their pocketbooks to sign the pair, and it cost them a record $15 million, including a bonus of $7.5 million, to corral Strasburg, and only slightly less to secure Harper.

That still wasn't the end of all the bonus madness, though, and the documented draft bonus record of $8 million was set in 2011, when the Pirates showered that amount on pitcher Gerrit Cole, the top pick in that year's draft. The average bonus for all first-rounders that year was $2,653,375, also a record.

Finally, enough was enough.

Late in 2011, an accord between ownership and the Players Association put teeth into regulations as they related to bonuses. Per terms of a new Collective Bargaining Agreement that made the draft a focal point for the first time ever, enforceable guidelines were put in place that governed the size of bonus payments, and penalized clubs if they exceeded them. Since then, teams have continued to pay out sizeable bonuses through the early rounds, but more in a spirit of cooperation. Over the last four years, there has been little of the rancor and bitter feelings that characterized the draft through much of its recent history.

With a real tool in hand to control bonuses, and the game on solid footing financially—and even awash in cash—there is as much peace and satisfaction surrounding the draft now as almost any time since its inception. Just another way the draft has come full circle.

### BEST DRAFTS

**1. DODGERS, 1968.** This highly acclaimed draft has stood the test of time as the roll call of established big leaguers included the likes of Garvey, Cey, Buckner, Lopes, Paciorek, Ferguson, Valentine, Alexander.

**2. METS, 1982.** Dwight Gooden headed up a list of 17 future big-leaguers—still a record for one draft.

**3. TIGERS, 1976.** Eight years after they drafted Alan Trammell, Jack Morris, Dan Petry and Steve Kemp, the Tigers romped to victory in the 1984 World Series. Inconceivably, they failed to sign Hall of Famer Ozzie Smith.

**4. RED SOX, 1976.** The Red Sox were overshadowed in the same year by the Tigers, but had a significant haul on their own in securing the likes of Wade Boggs, Bruce Hurst and John Tudor.

**5. ROYALS, 1986.** Landing Bo Jackson in the fourth round rates as the greatest coup in draft history. Tom Gordon was icing on the cake.

Chipper Jones, No. 1 selection in the 1990 draft, could soon join Ken Griffey Jr. as top overall picks in the Hall of Fame

## DRAFT DYNAMICS

Over the 50-year life of the draft, some 70,866 players have been drafted. We've seen 34 Hall of Famers be picked, plus thousands more who earned the distinction of being drafted and never played professionally. Those represent the extremes in what the draft has offered.

To get more of an up-close look at the meat of the issue, to see what has transpired with the huge volume of more mainstream selections, it's worth taking a guided tour through 50-plus years of draft history. Unless otherwise indicated, our focus will be on the conventional June regular phase.

Through the years, we've seen:

■ 1,440 players drafted in the first round. Many, as expected, have gone on to enjoy long and fruitful careers—players like Jackson, the second overall pick in 1966 (behind the long-forgotten Steve Chilcott). Surprisingly, Jackson remained the highest draft selection on record to reach the Hall until 2016, when Griffey became the first player drafted first overall to be enshrined in Cooperstown.

Chipper Jones (Class of 1990), now retired, is surely destined to join Griffey, and there may even be room one day for a disgraced Alex Rodriguez (Class of 1993).

■ Only 69.4 percent of all first-rounders drafted from 1965-2009 reach the promised land (judgment on 2010-16 remains incomplete because of players in those classes still toiling in the minors). That percentage doesn't compare favorably to an almost 100 percent success rate in the football and basketball drafts, where first-rounders move on as a matter of routine to play in the NFL and NBA. Even in the NHL, the success rate for first-rounders is roughly 92 percent.

■ 13.9 percent of all players ever drafted (all phases) reach the big leagues, including Rickey Henderson (Class of 1976), who played more games (3,081) over a 25-year career that any drafted player. That number also accounts for players whose big league careers amounted to a proverbial cup of coffee, including a select crop of draft picks who played just a single game in the majors.

The poster-child for that group is Larry Yount (Robin's brother), a 1968 draft pick who holds an even more unique distinction as the only pitcher in major league history to appear in the record books, yet never face a batter. He was injured during warm-ups in his only outing, had to be removed and never appeared in another contest.

■ An even 100 first-rounders who not only failed to reach the majors, but never moved beyond Class A, including six in 1977. For every unqualified success like Dave Winfield (Class of 1973) or Mike Trout (Class of 2009), there are colossal failures like Kevin Brandt (Class of 1979) and Mark Snyder (Class of 1982). Brandt was released by the Twins out of Rookie ball, little more than a year after being drafted, while the injury-plagued Snyder never won a game in professional baseball.

Meanwhile, six first-rounders through the years didn't even sign to play professionally.

■ Mike Piazza (Class of 1988), a 62nd-round afterthought who not only reached the majors, but enjoyed a long and distinguished career that led to his selection

### WORST DRAFTS

**1. BRAVES, 1981.** First-round pick Jay Roberts was a big mistake, and it never got any better. Only one player reached even Triple-A.

**2. ATHLETICS, 1979-80.** Maverick A's owner Charlie Finley fired all his scouts and the results were predictable. Over the two-year period, the A's signed 21 of 87 picks, no impact players among them.

**3. GIANTS, 1982.** Barry Bonds (the major league career home run leader) and Pete Incaviglia (the collegiate home run leader) were among eight picks in the first 10 rounds who went unsigned.

**4. ROYALS, 2001.** The Royals set back the franchise for years by sticking their necks out on Colt Griffin, the hardest thrower in the draft, and Roscoe Crosby, the best athlete. They never came close to getting a return on their investment.

**5. ASTROS, 2007.** The Astros didn't sign a player in the first four rounds—no small reason why the franchise earned the unique distinction of drafting first overall from 2012-14.

## MAJOR LEAGUE CONTRACTS

Only a handful of drafted players have been signed to major league contracts, which required them to be placed on a team's 40-man roster immediately. The practice was disallowed in 2012. Just the signing bonus of players signed to major league contracts from 1965-85 is noted; the full value of the contract is indicated for players from 1986-2012.

| Year | Player, Pos. | Club (Round) | Bonus | Contract |
|---|---|---|---|---|
| 1967 | **Mike Adamson, rhp** | **Orioles (June S-1)** | **$75,000** | |
| 1970 | **Steve Dunning, rhp** | **Indians (1)** | **$50,000** | |
| 1971 | **Burt Hooton, rhp** | **Cubs (June S-1)** | **$57,500** | |
| | **Rob Ellis, of** | **Brewers (June S-1)** | **$59,250** | |
| | **Pete Broberg, rhp** | **Senators (June S-1)** | **$83,000** | |
| 1972 | Dave Roberts, 3b | Padres (1) | $70,000 | |
| | * Dan Larson, rhp | Cardinals (1) | $40,000 | |
| 1973 | **Dave Winfield, of** | **Padres (1)** | **$50,000** | |
| | * **David Clyde, lhp** | **Rangers (1)** | **$65,000** | |
| | **Eddie Bane, lhp** | **Twins (1)** | **$30,500** | |
| 1974 | Bill Almon, ss | Padres (1) | $90,000 | |
| 1975 | Danny Goodwin, c | Angels (1) | $150,000 | |
| | Chris Knapp, rhp | White Sox (1) | $10,000 | |
| | Rick Cerone, c | Indians (1) | $55,000 | |
| | Jim Gideon, rhp | Rangers (1) | $50,000 | |
| | **Denny Walling, of** | **Athletics (June S-1)** | **$50,000** | |
| | Eddy Putman, c | Cubs (Jan. S-1) | $30,000 | |
| 1977 | Terry Kennedy, c | Cardinals (1) | $50,000 | |
| | * Brian Greer, of | Padres (1) | $60,000 | |
| 1978 | * **Mike Morgan, rhp** | **Athletics (1)** | **$50,000** | |
| | **Bob Horner, 3b** | **Braves (1)** | **$162,000** | |
| | Kirk Gibson, of | Tigers (1) | $150,000 | |
| | * **Brian Milner, c** | **Blue Jays (7)** | **$140,000** | |
| | * **Tim Conroy, lhp** | **Athletics (1)** | **$30,000** | |
| 1979 | Bill Bordley, lhp | Giants (FA) | $200,000 | |
| 1985 | **Pete Incaviglia, of** | **Expos (1)** | **$150,000** | |
| 1986 | Bo Jackson, of | Royals (4) | $100,000 | $1,066,000 |
| 1989 | Ben McDonald, rhp | Orioles (1) | $350,000 | $824,000 |
| | **John Olerud, 1b** | **Blue Jays (3)** | **$575,000** | **$800,000** |
| 1990 | * Todd Van Poppel, rhp | Athletics (1) | $500,000 | $1,200,000 |
| 1992 | Pete Janicki, rhp | Angels (1) | $90,000 | $215,000 |
| 1993 | * Alex Rodriguez, ss | Mariners (1) | $1,000,000 | $1,300,000 |
| 1998 | Pat Burrell, 1b | Phillies (1) | $3,150,000 | $8,000,000 |
| | J.D. Drew, of | Cardinals (1) | $3,000,000 | $7,000,000 |
| | Chad Hutchinson, rhp | Cardinals (2) | $2,300,000 | $3,400,000 |
| 1999 | * Josh Beckett, rhp | Marlins (1) | $3,625,000 | $7,000,000 |
| | Eric Munson, c | Tigers (1) | $3,500,000 | $6,750,000 |
| 2000 | * David Espinosa, ss | Reds (1) | None | $2,950,000 |
| | Dane Sardinha, c | Reds (2) | None | $1,950,000 |
| | **Xavier Nady, 3b** | **Padres (2)** | **$1,100,000** | **$2,850,000** |
| | Jace Brewer, ss | Devil Rays (5) | $450,000 | $1,200,000 |
| 2001 | Mark Prior, rhp | Cubs (1) | $4,000,000 | $10,500,000 |
| | Dewon Brazelton, rhp | Devil Rays (1) | $4,200,000 | $4,800,000 |
| | Mark Teixeira, 3b | Rangers (1) | $4,500,000 | $9,500,000 |
| 2002 | * Adam Loewen, lhp | Orioles (1) | $3,200,000 | $4,020,000 |
| | Jeremy Guthrie, rhp | Indians (1) | $3,000,000 | $4,000,000 |
| | Jeff Baker, 3b | Rockies (4) | $200,000 | $2,000,000 |
| 2003 | * Delmon Young, of | Rays (1) | $3,700,000 | $5,800,000 |
| | Rickie Weeks, 2b | Brewers (1) | $3,600,000 | $4,790,000 |
| 2004 | Justin Verlander, rhp | Tigers (1) | $3,120,000 | $4,500,000 |
| | Philip Humber, rhp | Mets (1) | $3,000,000 | $4,200,000 |
| | Jeff Niemann, rhp | Devil Rays (1) | $3,200,000 | $5,200,000 |
| | Stephen Drew, ss | Diamondbacks (1) | $4,000,000 | $5,500,000 |
| 2005 | Mike Pelfrey, rhp | Mets (1) | $3,550,000 | $5,250,000 |
| | Craig Hansen, rhp | Red Sox (1) | $1,325,000 | $4,000,000 |
| 2006 | Max Scherzer, rhp | Diamondbacks (1) | $3,000,000 | $4,300,000 |
| | Luke Hochevar, rhp | Royals (1) | $3,500,000 | $5,250,000 |
| | Andrew Miller, lhp | Tigers (1) | $3,550,000 | $5,450,000 |
| 2007 | David Price, lhp | Devil Rays (1) | $5,600,000 | $8,500,000 |
| | * Rick Porcello, rhp | Tigers (1) | $3,580,000 | $7,000,000 |
| | Andrew Brackman, rhp | Yankees (1) | $3,350,000 | $4,550,000 |
| | Julio Borbon, of | Rangers (1-S) | $800,000 | $1,300,000 |
| 2008 | Pedro Alvarez, 3b | Pirates (1) | $6,000,000 | $6,335,000 |
| | Brian Matusz, lhp | Orioles (1) | $3,200,000 | $3,472,500 |
| | Yonder Alonzo, 1b | Reds (1) | $2,000,000 | $4,550,000 |
| 2009 | Stephen Strasburg, rhp | Nationals (1) | $7,500,000 | $15,107,104 |
| | Dustin Ackley, of | Mariners (1) | $6,000,000 | $7,500,000 |
| | * Jacob Turner, rhp | Tigers (1) | $4,700,000 | $5,500,000 |
| | Aaron Crow, rhp | Royals (1) | $1,500,000 | $3,000,000 |
| 2010 | Bryce Harper, c | Nationals (1) | $6,250,000 | $9,900,000 |
| | Yasmani Grandal, c | Reds (1) | $2,000,000 | $3,200,000 |
| | Zack Cox, 3b | Cardinals (1) | $2,000,000 | $3,200,000 |
| 2011 | Danny Hultzen, lhp | Mariners (1) | $6,350,000 | $8,500,000 |
| | Trevor Bauer, rhp | Diamondbacks (1) | $3,400,000 | $4,450,000 |
| | * Dylan Bundy, rhp | Orioles (1) | $4,000,000 | $6,250,000 |
| | Anthony Rendon, 3b | Nationals (1) | $6,000,000 | $7,200,000 |
| | Matt Purke, lhp | Nationals (3) | $2,750,000 | $4,150,000 |

** High school selection.*
*Players who began their career in major leagues in bold.*

to the Hall of Fame. Even Piazza, though, doesn't stack up to Clay Condrey (Class of 1996), a 94th-rounder and the latest draft selection ever to have his day in the sun. Condrey was drafted by the Yankees, who selected another future big leaguer, Scott Seabol, in the 88th round of the same draft.

■ Eight Heisman Trophy winners be drafted, along with five players taken No. 1 overall in the NFL draft. Bo Jackson (Class of 1986) fits both descriptions, yet ended up signing with baseball's Royals—a development that arguably ranks as the iconic moment in draft history.

■ 22 players get drafted and move directly to the big leagues, though that phenomenon has occurred only once since 2000. It happened with relative frequency in the 1970s, often as a publicity gimmick, and only Horner in 1978, and possibly Burt Hooton (Class of 1971) and Winfield in 1973, could make convincing cases for legitimately skipping the minor leagues.

Horner stepped right off the Arizona State campus and into a Braves uniform, and went on to win National League rookie-of-the-year honors. That same year, the Blue Jays gave Brian Milner a chance to start his career at the top as an inducement to pass up an opportunity to play college football. Milner, 18, got four hits in two games, before being sent to the minors. He was never heard from again.

David Clyde

A case for starting their careers in the big leagues could be made for some of the high-profile college arms of the draft era like Strasburg, David Price (Class of 2007), Mark Prior (Class of 2001), McDonald (Class of 1989), Gregg Olson (Class of 1988), Greg Swindell (Class of 1986), Roger Clemens (Class of 1983) and Floyd Bannister (Class of 1976), and position players like Mark Teixeira (Class of 2001), Drew (Classes of 1997-98) and Will Clark (Class of 1985).

Similarly, Rodriguez (Class of 1993) and Yount (Class of 1973) are two of the most advanced high school talents of the draft era. Both began their major league careers at 18, and might have held their own by starting on top. In all instances, big league clubs avoided any sense of temptation by easing in the players in the minors leagues.

■ Teenage pitching phenoms like Gooden (Class of 1982), Kerry Wood (Class of 1995) and Jose Fernandez (Class of 2011) mesmerize us with their sheer talent, and all left their mark on the game. David Clyde (Class of 1973) and Taylor (Class of 1991), the only high school pitchers ever selected No. 1 overall prior to 2014, might have made a similar impression, but weren't as fortunate as their promising careers crashed and burned.

And who knows how many other high-profile young arms might have impacted the game in a positive way had they not ended up on the scrap heap by hurting their arms.

For sheer hype in draft history, though, no one can touch Strasburg and Harper, who attracted untold media attention while being drafted first overall by the Nationals in consecutive years.

■ Players like Pete Varney (Class of 1971) and Luis Medina (Class of 1985) reach the majors after being drafted a record-tying seven times each. The elusive Varney was the first overall pick in a draft phase on three different occasions. Bill Dobbs, meanwhile, was also drafted seven times between 1965 and 1970, and never did sign a pro contract.

Obviously, the opportunity to pass through that many drafts occurred in the days (1966-86) when a player could be chosen as often as twice a year, before both phases of the old January draft, along with the secondary phase in June, were folded into a single, solitary phase in 1987.

The modern-day version of a draft dodger is 6-foot-10 Mark Hendrickson, who chose to pursue a career in basketball, first in college at Washington State and then briefly in the NBA. All the while, he continued being selected in the baseball draft, for six straight years from 1992-97, and baseball's persistence finally paid off when he was signed by the Blue Jays just prior to the 1998 draft.

■ Our share of contentious negotiations through the years, involving high-profile prospects like Tim Belcher (Class of 1983), Pete Incaviglia (Class of 1985), McDonald (Class of 1989), Jason Varitek (1993-94) and Drew (1997-98). Incaviglia, who shattered NCAA home run records at Oklahoma State, refused to sign with the Montreal Expos as the eighth overall pick in 1985, and subsequently demanded a trade to a team that was prepared to let him begin his career in the majors. He was dealt to the Texas Rangers, and sure enough the cocky, confident Incaviglia did open the 1986 season with that club.

Shortly thereafter, baseball enacted the "Pete Incaviglia Rule," which essentially forbid teams from trading draft picks until one year after they sign. Incaviglia, at least, went on to sign a contract, unlike famed draft holdout Matt Harrington (Classes of 2000-04).

The draft has seen nothing to quite match the bizarre circumstances surrounding Harrington, who might have been the No. 1 pick in 2000 had his bonus demands not scared off the Florida Marlins, who ended up taking first baseman Adrian Gonzalez as a compromise choice. Despite being drafted four more times after his 2000 draft debacle, Harrington never signed a contract with a big league club, and toiled instead in the obscurity of independent leagues.

Danny Thomas

In stark contrast to some of the draft's more infamous holdouts, Dave Roberts (Class of 1972) started at third base for the Padres one day after being drafted.

■ Players like Tom Seaver (Class of 1966), Bill Bordley (Class of 1979) and Billy Cannon Jr. (Class of 1980), along with the loophole free agents of 1996 involved in the most controversial scenarios in draft history, and their intriguing storylines have stood the test of time.

■ Players struggle to live up to the considerable expectations of being a first-round pick, and often collapse under the weight. Two of the sadder cases in draft history involved 1972 first-rounders, Danny Thomas (Brewers) and John Harbin (Dodgers), who became so distraught with their circumstances surrounding failed careers that they committed suicide.

They are among 22 players drafted in the first round in the first 10 years of the draft who have since passed on. Most died of natural causes, but three died as active players: Thurman Munson (Class of 1968), who perished in a private-plane crash, Tom Maggard (Class of 1968) from complications from an insect bite and Mike Miley (Class of 1974) in a car accident.

■ The fall of former first overall picks like Taylor (Class of 1991) and Matt Bush (2004), who ended up in prison. Bush actually reached the big leagues with the Rangers in 2016, after his imprisonment; Taylor never got there. Darryl Strawberry (Class of 1980) ended up in jail, too, but at least had a long, productive major league career, although it fell short of expectations because of his own drug use. John Wyatt (Class of 1965), John D'Acquisto (Class of 1970), Billy Simpson (Class of 1976), Gooden (Class of 1982) and Kevin Dean (Class of 1985) are other first-round picks through the years who ended up behind bars once their playing careers ended.

Those are just a sampling of the storylines that have made draft history so intriguing and compelling.

## BONUS PROGRESSION RECORD

Here's how the top bonus has evolved through the draft era (for players signing with the team that drafted them):

| Year | Player, Pos. | Club (Round) | Bonus |
|---|---|---|---|
| 1965 | Rick Monday, of | Athletics (1) | $100,000 |
| 1975 | * Danny Goodwin, c | Angels (1) | $150,000 |
| 1978 | * Kirk Gibson, of | Tigers (1) | $150,000 |
| | * Bob Horner, 3b | Braves (1) | $162,000 |
| 1979 | Todd Demeter, 1b | Yankees (2) | $208,000 |
| 1988 | Andy Benes. rhp | Padres (1) | $235,000 |
| 1989 | Tyler Houston, c | Braves (1) | $241,500 |
| | * Ben McDonald, rhp | Orioles (1) | $350,000 |
| | * John Olerud, 1b | Blue Jays (3) | $575,000 |
| 1991 | Mike Kelly, of | Braves (1) | $575,000 |
| | Brien Taylor, lhp | Yankees (1) | $1,550,000 |
| 1994 | Paul Wilson, rhp | Mets (1) | $1,550,000 |
| | Josh Booty, ss | Marlins (1) | $1,600,000 |
| 1996 | Kris Benson, rhp | Pirates (1) | $2,000,000 |
| 1997 | Rick Ankiel, lhp | Cardinals (2) | $2,500,000 |
| | Matt Anderson, rhp | Tigers (1) | $2,505,000 |
| 1998 | * J.D. Drew, of | Cardinals (1) | $3,000,000 |
| | * Pat Burrell, 1b | Phillies (1) | $3,150,000 |
| | Mark Mulder, lhp | Athletics (1) | $3,200,000 |
| | Corey Patterson, of | Cubs (1) | $3,700,000 |
| 1999 | Josh Hamilton, of | Devil Rays (1) | $3,960,000 |
| 2000 | Joe Borchard, of | White Sox (1) | $5,300,000 |
| 2005 | Justin Upton, ss | Diamondbacks (1) | $6,100,000 |
| 2008 | Tim Beckham, ss | Rays (1) | $6,150,000 |
| | Buster Posey, c | Giants (1) | $6,200,000 |
| 2009 | Donavan Tate, of | Padres (1) | $6,250,000 |
| | * Stephen Strasburg, rhp | Nationals (1) | $7,500,000 |
| 2011 | Gerrit Cole, rhp | Pirates (1) | $8,000,000 |

**Signed to major league contract.*

Unlike in football and basketball, where most draft picks are finished products at the time they are selected, and often known quantities, the anonymity of the baseball draft makes almost all players relative unknowns at the time of their selection. Their stories generally only come to light with the benefit of hindsight.

After all, who knew, or really even cared in 1984 that a skinny righthander from Las Vegas, or a young lefthander from Massachusetts with a passion for hockey, would blossom into two of the greatest pitching artists the game has ever known—as teammates, no less. But Greg Maddux and Tom Glavine are now two of the most compelling figures ever drafted.

### AN INEXACT SCIENCE

Much of the draft's charm is preserved in its unpredictable and inexact nature. Who would ever have predicted that Johnny Bench, signed by the Cincinnati Reds for $6,000 as a second-rounder in 1965, would become the first player from the draft era to be elected to the Hall of Fame, or that Seaver would be the first pitcher to reach 300 wins and Nolan Ryan the game's all-time strikeout leader—especially after Seaver was the 193rd pick overall, and Ryan the 295th in the same draft.

To take the crapshoot nature of the inaugural 1965 draft a step further, more players (five) signed that year as nondrafted free agents, including future all-star infielders Don Money and Larry Bowa, were more deserving of being drafted in the first round based on Wins Above Replacement than all but two players actually drafted in the first round (one being Monday).

Those were some of the unlikely, unintended consequences of the first draft, but it's not like the process has become exponentially more sophisticated through the years, transitioning it out of the realm of being an inexact science. Hardly.

The most productive drafts ever actually occurred in the 1980s. The decade from 1981-90 produced the highest yield of future big leaguers overall (14.8 percent), in the first 10 rounds (35.3 percent) and in the first round (73.5 percent). Additionally, the 1986 draft produced more big leaguers overall (246) than any draft in history (until it was recently topped by 2008), and the 1987 draft had the highest percentage of players (42.5 percent) selected in the first 10 rounds who reached the big leagues.

For sheer impact talent, though, no draft in history can touch 1985.

With headliners like Barry Bonds, Barry Larkin, Rafael Palmeiro, Will Clark and B.J. Surhoff, the star-quality talent that came out of the first round of that draft trumps any draft in history—though 2005 or 2008, in time, could give it a run for its money. Led by that quintet, the cumulative WAR of the first round in 1985 is 495.7—easily better than the first round of any draft. The talent didn't stop there, either, as Randy Johnson went in the second round and John Smoltz was a 22nd-round afterthought. Johnson and Smoltz were inducted in the Hall of Fame together in 2015. And that doesn't even begin to address considerable talents like Bobby Witt, one of the best pure arms ever drafted, and Incaviglia, who were the third and eighth picks overall. Bo Jackson, possibly the greatest athlete of the draft era, was also drafted in 1985, though he lasted until the 20th round because of his football obligations at Auburn, and didn't sign for another year.

It's no coincidence that the 1985 draft was heavily weighted toward college talent as most of the top prospects had also factored prominently into the top 10 rounds of the 1982 draft, as unsigned high school players. Bonds, a second-rounder in 1982, failed to sign with the Giants that year over a paltry difference of $5,000.

In terms of the end result, there can be little disputing the 1985 draft's lofty WAR ranking, but that measuring stick doesn't differentiate whether a player signed with the team that drafted him, so the cumulative WAR from Rounds 1-5 in 1982 (845.3) is actually higher than for 1985 (749.0). In addition to Bonds, Larkin and Jackson were both unsigned second-rounders in 1982, which largely accounts for that round producing the highest WAR on record. Additionally, Clark and Johnson were unsigned fourth-rounders that year, which explains why that round has the highest all-time WAR score.

And lest anyone forget, the 1984 draft produced the bulk of that year's U.S. Olympic team, which has been universally praised as the single greatest amateur team ever assembled.

So the relatively short period of just six years, from 1982-87, featured five of the best drafts on record. It also bears noting that the 1981 draft, strong in its own right, has historical significance as that was the year there was a dramatic swing in draft demographics that fueled the string of strong drafts in the '80s.

Seventeen of 26 first-round picks came from the college ranks in 1981, as well as 34 of the first 50—double the previous record. The swing from high school to college talent was felt throughout the 1981 draft as twice as many college players as high school players were selected that year, and a record-low 113 prep players were signed overall. By 1985, the influence of college baseball on the draft had become so pronounced that 11 of the first 12 selections were from the college ranks, and most drafts since have been more skewed toward college talent.

## All In The Family

### THREE-GENERATION ACTS

**Ray, Bob and Bret (from left to right) made the Boones baseball's first three-generation big league family**

**1. BOONES.** Ray Boone played 13 years in the majors, setting the tone for son Bob (Phillies '69), grandsons Bret (Mariners '90) and Aaron (Reds '94), who all played at least 13 years, as well.

**2. BELLS.** Narrowly edged out by the Boones as game's first three-generation family; grandfather Gus played 15 years in majors and spawned son Buddy (Indians '69), grandsons David (Indians '90) and Mike (Rangers '93).

**3. HAIRSTONS.** Sammy Hairston had a brief career in 1951, but sons Johnny (Cubs '65) and Jerry (White Sox '70) followed in his footsteps; Jerry's sons Jerry Jr. (Orioles '97) and Scott (Diamondbacks '01) also had their day in the sun.

**4. COLEMANS.** Three-generations of Colemans included Joe Sr., a big-leaguer from 1942-55; Joe Jr. (Senators '65, first round) and Casey (Cubs '08).

**5. SCHOFIELD/WERTH.** Dick Schofield was a 19-year big leaguer; Dick Jr. (Angels '81, first round) also had a long career. Daughter Kim is the mother of Jayson Werth (Orioles '97, first round).

### FATHER-SON ACTS

**Tom Grieve (right) saw his son, Ben, become a first-round pick in 1994, 18 years after he was a first-rounder**

**1. GRIFFEYS.** Ken Sr. (Reds '69) had solid 19-year career in the majors, but was upstaged by his Hall-of-Fame son Ken Jr. (Mariners '87, first round). They became the first father-son act to play together in the big leagues.

**2. GRIEVES.** Tom (Senators), the sixth pick in '66, and Ben (Athletics), the second pick in '94, were the first father-son first-round picks.

**3. MCRAES.** Hal (Reds '65) was closing out a 19-year career in the majors with the Royals, when the team drafted son Brian in the first round in '85.

**4. GORDONS.** Tom (Royals '86) had a 21-year career in the majors; sons Dee (Dodgers '08) and Nick (Twins '14, first round) also appear destined for lengthy careers.

**5. FIELDERS.** Cecil (Royals '82) led the majors in homers twice, and hit 319 in his career; son Prince (Brewers '02, first round) led in homers once, had 311 homers overall through 2015.

**6. BURROUGHS.** Jeff (Senators) was the first overall pick in 1969 and won an A.L. MVP award five years later; son Sean (Padres '98, first round) fell short of lofty expectations.

**7. MAYBERRYS.** John Sr. (Astros '67) had 255 homers; John Jr. (Mariners '02; Rangers '05) will fall short of that number despite being a two-time first-rounder.

**8. SWISHERS.** Steve (White Sox '73) and Nick (Athletics '02) were both first-rounders and major league all-stars.

**9. DRABEKS.** Kyle (Phillies '06, first round) was expected to upstage his father Doug (White Sox '83), a former Cy Young Award winner and 155-game winner, but fell short.

**10. VAN SLYKES.** Andy (Cardinals '79, first round) played 13 years in the majors; sons Scott (Dodgers) and A.J. (Cardinals) were both selected in '05; Scott reached majors.

### BROTHER ACTS

**1. UPTONS.** Tough to top B.J. (Devil Rays) the No. 2 pick in 2002, and younger brother Justin (Diamondbacks) the No. 1 selection in 2005.

**2. YOUNGS.** Dmitri (Cardinals) was the fourth overall pick in 1991, only to be upstaged 11 years later by Delmon (Devil Rays), the No. 1 selection in 2002.

**3. DREWS.** Unprecedented for one family to produce three first-rounders: J.D. (Phillies '97, Cardinals '98), Tim (Indians '97) and Stephen (Diamondbacks '04).

**4. BRETTS.** John (Braves) and Ken (Red Sox, first round) were drafted in 1966, but they just blazed a trail for Hall of Famer George (Royals '71).

**5. MURRAYS.** Of five brothers to play pro ball, Eddie (Orioles '73) reached the Hall of Fame, Rich (Giants '75) reached the majors.

**6. WEAVERS.** Jeff (Tigers '98) and Jered (Angels '04) were both first-rounders and won 100-plus games in the majors.

**7. BENES.** Andy (Padres) was the top pick in 1988 and paved the way for Alan (Cardinals '93, first round).

**8. LANSFORDS.** Carney's success in the majors as a third-rounder (Angels '75) set the stage for Phil (Indians '78) and Jody (Padres '79), both first-rounders.

**9. CLARKS.** Isaiah (Brewers '84) and Phil (Tigers '85) were first-round picks, but both were upstaged in the majors by older brother Jerald (Padres '85), a 12th-rounder.

**10. WEEKS.** Rickie (Brewers) was the second pick in 2003, while younger brother Jemile (Athletics) was taken nine picks later in 2008.

## MOST-HYPED DRAFT PICKS

BILL MITCHELL

**1. STEPHEN STRASBURG, RHP, NATIONALS '09.** Considered a once-in-a-generation pitcher, both his selection in the draft and debut in Washington a year later drew unprecedented attention.

**2. BRYCE HARPER, C, NATIONALS '10.** The hype began building when he appeared on the cover of Sports Illustrated at 16 and was dubbed "The Chosen One."

**3. BO JACKSON, OF, ROYALS '86.** Most of the hype came from his football accomplishments, but his raw athletic ability transcended baseball like few others.

**4. JIM ABBOTT, LHP, ANGELS '88.** Some 150 media representatives, four Japanese TV crews and 50,000 fans took in the big-league debut of baseball's most-celebrated one-handed pitcher.

**5. DAVID CLYDE, LHP, RANGERS '73.** A Texas schoolboy legend, he proved an immediate artistic and financial success, winning his debut at 18 before the first packed house in the Rangers two-year history.

**6. MARK PRIOR, RHP, CUBS '01.** Described as the greatest pitcher in college baseball history, he instantly became the savior who would lead the Cubs out of a near-100 year wilderness.

**7. ALEX RODRIGUEZ, SS, MARINERS '93.** He arrived in the majors at 18 and is one of the few players in draft history whose accomplishments matched his considerable hype.

**8. BEN MCDONALD, RHP, ORIOLES '89.** He was proclaimed the No. 1 pick in the draft two years before his selection, and the hype only continued to build.

**9. KEN GRIFFEY JR., OF, MARINERS '87.** Not only was he the first son of an active big leaguer to go No. 1, but he eventually played alongside his father in the same outfield.

**10. TODD VAN POPPEL, RHP, ATHLETICS '90.** The Texas prep phenom had the size, stuff and acclaim to become a legend, but never came close to fulfilling expectations.

## FIRST ROUND BONUS PROGRESSION

| Year | Average | Change | Year | Average | Change |
|---|---|---|---|---|---|
| 1965 | $42,516 | | 1991 | $365,596 | +44.5% |
| 1966 | $44,430 | +4.5% | 1992 | $481,893 | +31.9% |
| 1967 | $42,898 | -3.4% | 1993 | $613,037 | +27.2% |
| 1968 | $43,850 | +2.2% | 1994 | $790,357 | +28.9% |
| 1969 | $43,504 | -0.8% | 1995 | $918,019 | +16.1% |
| 1970 | $45,230 | +3.9% | 1996* | $944,404 | +2.9% |
| 1971 | $45,197 | -0.1% | 1997 | $1,325,536 | +40.4% |
| 1972 | $44,952 | -0.5% | 1998 | $1,637,667 | +23.1% |
| 1973 | $48,832 | +8.6% | 1999 | $1,809,767 | +10.5% |
| 1974 | $53,333 | +9.2% | 2000 | $1,872,586 | +3.5% |
| 1975 | $45,661 | -16.8% | 2001 | $2,154,280 | +15.0% |
| 1976 | $49,631 | +9.2% | 2002 | $2,106,793 | -2.2% |
| 1977 | $48,813 | -1.6% | 2003 | $1,765,667 | -16.2% |
| 1978 | $67,892 | +39.1% | 2004 | $1,958,448 | +10.9% |
| 1979 | $68,094 | +0.2 | 2005 | $2,108,000 | +3.0% |
| 1980 | $74,025 | +8.7% | 2006 | $1,933,333 | -4.2% |
| 1981 | $78,573 | +6.1% | 2007 | $2,098,083 | +8.5% |
| 1982 | $82,615 | +5.1% | 2008 | $2,449,785 | +16.8% |
| 1983 | $87,236 | +5.6% | 2009 | $2,434,800 | -1.0% |
| 1984 | $105,392 | +20.8% | 2010 | $2,220,965 | -8.8% |
| 1985 | $118,115 | +12.1% | 2011 | $2,653,375 | +19.5% |
| 1986 | $116,300 | -1.6% | 2012 | $2,475,167 | -6.7% |
| 1987 | $128,480 | +10.5% | 2013 | $2,641.538 | +6.7% |
| 1988 | $142,540 | +10.9% | 2014 | $2,612,109 | -1.1% |
| 1989 | $176,008 | +23.5% | 2015 | $2,774,945 | +6.2% |
| 1990 | $252,577 | +43.5% | 2016 | $2,897,778 | +4.4% |

**Does not include loophole free agents.*

On the contrary, the first round of the draft (June, regular phase) from 1965-80 was heavily populated by high school players, with 296 selections overall, compared to just 78 from the four-year college ranks and one from junior college. In 1971, all 24 players drafted in the first round were from high school. Those numbers are skewed, though, as many of the better college players from that era were subject only to the secondary phase, especially if they were redrafts. The rules that applied to previously drafted players were frequently amended, and eventually almost all college players became the domain of the June regular phase by the mid-70s.

In 1977, more college than high-school players were drafted overall, and that number has never reversed itself.

The draft has been an evolving process from the outset, and just as there was a heavy emphasis on high school talent in the early years before a dramatic shift to college talent in the 1980s, the pendulum swung back toward high school players in later years, especially as bonuses began to rise appreciably and clubs made more of a concerted effort to sign the best prep talent.

After a lull in the 1990s as teams grappled with escalating bonuses and often drafted irrationally, the success rate of players reaching the majors and having impact careers has climbed over the last dozen years—stemming in large measure from a more sophisticated approach teams have taken in the draft. The 2005 and 2008 classes, in particular, look like two of the best ever.

But before we anoint the last 20 years as an age of sophistication, two of the darkest drafts ever, 1999 and 2000, should be fresh in our memory banks. Those were the two most maligned, mismanaged drafts in history, as signing bonuses were so volatile that teams drafted players as much on the basis of signability as ability.

The 1999 draft is the only one on record where fewer than half the players selected in the first round (14 of 30) became big leaguers; 2000 is the only year when more second-rounders (17) made the majors than the first (16). In the two years combined, just 30 of 60 first-rounders reached the majors, while 31 in the second round achieved the feat.

Major League Baseball was in a quandary at the time, as it couldn't legally force its clubs to restrict bonuses at a time of the most rampant inflation in the draft's history. But it did put pressure on them to toe the line more responsibly—or else bear the wrath of the commissioner's office. Given a choice, most teams spent.

Acrimony between clubs and player agents often reached new lows, and the most contentious negotiation in draft history, between the Colorado Rockies and Harrington, played out in 2000.

Big league clubs soon learned the error of their ways and began targeting the best available talent again—even if it came at a cost. The 2004 and 2005 drafts quickly became the most productive ever, with a record-low of just four first-rounders in each of those years failing to reach the big leagues. That feat had occurred only once before, in 1990. The 2008 draft then came along and topped them all, with just three first-rounders failing to reach the majors.

For sheer futility in draft history, we have to go back a few years.

The 1973 draft got off to an auspicious start with the selection of two future Hall of Famers (Winfield and Yount) and a major league all-star (John Stearns) in the first four picks. The fourth player in the group was the star-crossed Clyde, who by all rights should have enjoyed a long and productive career had he not been exploited for financial gain by Rangers owner Bob Short in an obvious cash grab to bail out his struggling team. Overall, that draft produced 139 future big leaguers, the lowest number on record.

Two years later, the 1975 draft established its own marks for futility. The talent that year wasn't necessarily the weakest ever, but the way it was distributed in the first round certainly was. Just 12 of 24 first-rounders played in the big leagues, but that included only one of the first five selections: none other than Danny Goodwin, who owns the rare distinction of becoming the only player selected twice with the first

## LATE-ROUND BOOMS

**1. MIKE PIAZZA, C, DODGERS '88 (62ND ROUND).** Drafted as a favor to Dodgers manager (and godfather) Tommy Lasorda, Piazza became the best offensive catcher in big league history.

**2. JOHN SMOLTZ, RHP, TIGERS '85 (22ND ROUND).** The Tigers managed to talk him out of Michigan State, but regrettably pedaled him to the Braves in a trade-deadline deal.

**3. RYNE SANDBERG, SS, PHILLIES '78 (20TH ROUND).** The Phillies took a chance on the Washington State football recruit, but then unwisely dealt him to the Cubs as a minor leaguer.

**4. KEITH HERNANDEZ, 1B, CARDINALS '71 (42ND ROUND).** Hernandez played sparingly as a prep senior, but the Cardinals took a flier and signed him to a $30,000 bonus.

**5. KENNY LOFTON, OF, ASTROS '88 (17TH ROUND).** A basketball star in college at Arizona, Lofton wisely picked baseball; to the regret of the Astros, he became a star after being traded to Cleveland.

**6. ANDY PETTITTE, LHP, YANKEES '90 (22ND ROUND).** The Yankees signed Pettitte and catcher Jorge Posada (24th round) as draft-and-follows in the same draft; they became a foundation of the team's success over the next two decades.

**7. BRET SABERHAGEN, RHP, ROYALS '82 (19TH ROUND).** He won the first of two Cy Young Awards with the Royals at age 21.

**8. MARK BUEHRLE, LHP, WHITE SOX '98 (38TH ROUND).** With 214 career wins, he was the most successful player drafted in 1998.

**9. OREL HERSHISER, RHP, DODGERS '79 (17TH ROUND).** While Al Chambers was the No. 1 pick in 1979, Hershiser and Don Mattingly (Yankees, 19th round) languished deep into that year's draft.

**10. BUDDY BELL, 3B, INDIANS '69 (16TH ROUND).** He spent 18 years in the majors, was a five-time all-star, six-time Gold Glover.

overall pick in the June regular phase—in 1971, and again in 1975.

With an overall WAR of just 10.7, the first round of the 1975 draft easily ranks as the worst on record (at 61.9, 1970 was next). Just three players, catcher Rick Cerone, outfielder Clint Hurdle and infielder Dale Berra, had careers of at least 10 years. Perhaps most curious, big league teams saw fit to sign more players that year to rare major league contracts (six, including Goodwin) than any draft in history, though all six did eventually reach the big leagues, including four that year.

If there was any sense of salvation, future Hall of Famer Andre Dawson came out of that year's draft, though he was miscast as an 11th-rounder, while one-time career saves leader Lee Smith went in the second round, future American League batting champion Carney Lansford was taken in the third and five-time all-star Lou Whitaker was a fifth-round selection.

### IMPERFECT SYSTEM

With notable exceptions, the rate of drafted players reaching the major leagues has generally risen through the years. Any number of reasons can be offered for the increase, but much of it can be attributed simply to the benefits gained through 50 years of trial and error, and more sophisticated scouting that has evolved through the course of time.

The game has seen significant technical advances, notably in the proliferation of radar guns. Fewer prospects have fallen through the cracks since the introduction of the Major League Scouting Bureau in the mid-70s, with the wider net it casts, and the proliferation of showcase events in recent years has afforded scouts a greater opportunity to see top prospects perform on multiple occasions, while also playing against superior competition. The growing use of analytics has enabled clubs to dissect players in ways previously unimagined.

There have been significant medical advances, none more significant than Tommy John surgery. That practice, first performed on its namesake in 1974, has revived the careers of numerous pitchers who otherwise would have been shelved permanently, as occurred with regularity in the early years of the draft.

Advances in coaching at the college level, and the improvement in college baseball generally, have been instrumental in the draft's evolution, though the introduction of aluminum bats in 1973 presented its own set of challenges.

To be sure, radar guns, Tommy John surgery, the best-selling book "Moneyball" and aluminum bats were not part of the scouting vernacular in 1965.

Projecting the future worth of amateur players was an inexact science in 1965, and despite the changing dynamics and all the modern-day advances the game has seen, the result remains unpredictable.

The best scouts in the game haven't been able to predict the future worth of a typical 18-year-old prospect with any sense of accuracy, even with hundreds of games in the minor leagues to hone and polish his skills. Body type, makeup and devotion to a very unforgiving sport are among the traits that a scout must analyze and assess, yet as in many walks of life, the journey to the big leagues is peppered with challenges, and it often equates to survival of the fittest whether a player makes it or not.

The failure rate of 30 percent among first-rounders alone speaks directly to the degree of difficulty involved in scouting baseball talent. Over the course of 50 years, numerous players with the physical gifts to play in the majors have fallen by the wayside because they lacked the aptitude to get the most out of their natural ability, or the mental strength to stand up to the pressure and grind of baseball.

## FIRST-ROUND BUSTS

**1. KEVIN BRANDT, OF, TWINS '79.** His ill-fated career lasted just 47 games (.155, one homer) before the Twins admitted to the error of their ways and unceremoniously released Brandt.

**2. MARK SNYDER, RHP, INDIANS '82.** Plagued by arm problems from the outset, he never won a game in pro ball. His career totals: 0-5, 7.41 in 11 appearances over three seasons.

**3. BRUCE COMPTON, OF, INDIANS '77.** He never got untracked in four years in the minors, hitting .143 overall with two homers.

**4. JOHNNY JONES, C, SENATORS '67.** Jones lasted just two years in the Senators organization, hitting .150 with one homer.

**5. KEN THOMAS, C, ORIOLES '72.** His 90-game career totals (.148, one home run) said it all.

**6. JAY ROBERTS, OF, BRAVES '81.** He played four seasons in the Braves system, hit .187 with nine homers and struck out 247 times in 226 games.

**7. JACOB SHUMATE, RHP, BRAVES '94.** By walking 436 in 313 innings, it led to a 14-30, 7.07 career record.

**8. WADE TOWNSEND, RHP, ORIOLES '04/DEVIL RAYS '05.** Despite being taken with the eighth overall pick in consecutive drafts, he went 7-21, 5.59 in 64 career appearances.

**9. BILL BENE, RHP, DODGERS '88.** With 489 walks in 444 career innings, Bene never conquered his well-documented control issues, leading to a 15-30, 5.59 career mark.

**10. MATT BUSH, SS, PADRES '04 (1ST OVERALL).** The Padres regretted taking Bush, a local product, before he played his first game as a pro. He ran into numerous off-field issues and never performed to expectations, though he did reach the big leagues with the Rangers in 2016.

With so much projection involved in the scouting of a young player, a scout never knows for sure what he's got.

"You can measure a kid's arm, his swing and his running time to first base, but there's something more important that's only a wild guess," said Harding Peterson in 1975, at the time the Pirates scouting director. "What you draft is usually a kid 18 years old, who's got a girlfriend and who's batted cleanup and hit .600 all his life. Now he's leaving that girl, going to a minor league team where they play a game every day, and playing with a bunch of guys who have also hit .600 all their life. There's no way you can measure how a kid is gonna react to all that."

Those words still ring true today. But it is clear to anyone who has studied draft history and scouting tendencies, that there are patterns to successful drafting. Certain kinds of draft picks, historically, are better risks than others; others offer more potential reward, and it is the risk/reward dynamic that often governs a team's scouting philosophy.

Carlton Fisk

It speaks volumes about the risky nature of drafting high school righthanders, for instance, that not a single player in that demographic has ever been selected No. 1 overall, though a prep righty has gone second on seven occasions, most prominently J.R. Richard in 1969 and Josh Beckett in 1999. No high school righthander drafted anywhere in the first round has been selected to the Hall of Fame, though Rick Sutcliffe (Class of 1973), Gooden (1982), Wood (1995), Roy Halladay (1995), Adam Wainwright (2000) and Zack Greinke (2002) have had noteworthy careers; the recently retired Halladay, in particular, could be destined for Cooperstown. Despite being shut out on first-rounders, the Hall of Fame does include five prep righthanders from the draft era that are enshrined: Ryan (1965, 10th round), Bert Blyleven (1969, third round), Goose Gossage (1970, ninth round), Dennis Eckersley (1972, third round) and Maddux (1982, second round).

## DIFFERENCES IN DRAFT

For all the apparent similarities between the first draft in 1965 and the draft today, there are plenty of differences.

Perhaps most obvious is there were two drafts annually in the beginning, both divided into a regular and secondary phase, compared to just one now. It was out of fear of legal repercussions that the extraneous phases were present in the early years—and the 1966 draft even had five phases with the inclusion of the late-summer draft geared toward American Legion players, though that phase lasted just two years.

The institution of a baseball draft was in the discussion stage for years. It met resistance at almost every step, and even when the procedure was finally ratified in 1964, there was a faction of owners who expressed concern, chiefly on legal grounds, that Congress might view a draft as a restraint on freedom of choice, which conceivably could end up jeopardizing baseball's sacred antitrust status.

To counter some of the lingering legal concerns, the provision was made for two baseball drafts each year (one conducted in June, the other in January), which effectively doubled the opportunity for players to be drafted. Moreover, provisions were put in place for players that went unsigned in one draft to be placed in a special pool, or secondary phase, in the following draft, effectively exposing them to a wider spectrum of teams. From the start, most draft picks were channeled through the June, regular phase, but the other phases provided their share of talent for roughly 20 years before the draft was finally consolidated into a single, all-encompassing phase in 1987.

By then, there were no longer fears of reprisal by Congress over the legality of a draft system. If anything, there was growing concern among big league officials that four draft phases each year, with four separate first rounds, was providing leverage for draft picks in the lower-profile phases, who were equating their worth with increasing frequency to players drafted in comparable slots in the more talent-laden June regular phase. All this at a time when bonuses were starting to climb at a progressive clip.

While both phases of the January draft, and the secondary phase in June were rendered extinct almost 30 years ago, some noteworthy talent came from those drafts.

The January regular phase produced two Hall of Famers: Carlton Fisk (Class of 1967) and Kirby Puckett (Class of 1982), though the success rate overall of players taken in that phase was substantially below the norm. Of 4,622 players selected, only 369 (or 8.0 percent) became big leaguers.

By contrast, the secondary phase of both the January and June drafts didn't produce any Hall of Famers—though Seaver was drafted in the January phase in 1966, before his contract was voided and he subsequently signed with the Mets as a free agent. But those phases produced more than their share of future big leaguers. Among 2,041 players selected in the January secondary phase over a 20-year period, 320 (or 15.7 percent) played in the majors, while 380 (or 20.0 percent) of 1,897 players taken in the June secondary phase hit paydirt.

Through the years, there have been various other changes in draft rules—some adopted to address unintended consequences, others to accommodate evolving changes in the game overall. The often volatile state of signing bonuses also played

## BONUS RECORDS BY ROUND

### ROUNDS 1-50

| | Player, Pos., Club | Year | Bonus |
|---|---|---|---|
| **1** | **Gerrit Cole, rhp, Pirates** | **2011** | **$8,000,000** |
| 1-S | Daz Cameron, of, Astros | 2015 | $4,000,000 |
| 2 | Josh Bell, of, Pirates | 2011 | $5,000,000 |
| 3 | Matt Purke, lhp, Nationals | 2011 | $2,750,000 |
| **4** | **A.J. Cole, rhp, Nationals** | **2010** | **$2,000,000** |
| 5 | Ryan Westmoreland, of, Red Sox | 2008 | $2,000,000 |
| 6 | Jack McGeary, lhp, Nationals | 2007 | $1,800,000 |
| 7 | Brett Hunter, rhp, Athletics | 2008 | $1,100,000 |
| 8 | Colton Cain, lhp, Pirates | 2009 | $1,125,000 |
| 9 | Clay Holmes, rhp, Pirates | 2011 | $1,200,000 |
| 10 | * Luis Cota, rhp, Royals | 2003 | $1,050,000 |
| 11 | Chris Huseby, rhp, Cubs | 2006 | $1,300,000 |
| 12 | Mike Rozier, lhp, Red Sox | 2004 | $1,575,000 |
| **13** | **Jimmy Barthmaier, rhp, Astros** | **2003** | **$750,000** |
| 14 | Dillon Maples, rhp, Cubs | 2011 | $2,500,000 |
| 15 | J.P. Ramirez, of, Nationals | 2008 | $1,000,000 |
| 16 | * Sean Smith, rhp, Indians | 2001 | $1,200,000 |
| 17 | Ryan Hafner, rhp, Pirates | 2010 | $450,000 |
| **18** | **Mark Trumbo, rhp/3b, Angels** | **2004** | **$1,425,000** |
| **19** | *** Ryan Mattheus, rhp, Rockies** | **2003** | **$700,000** |
| 20 | Quinton Miller, rhp, Pirates | 2008 | $900,000 |
| **21** | **Travis Ishikawa, 1b, Giants** | **2002** | **$955,000** |
| 22 | Amir Garrett, lhp, Reds | 2011 | $1,000,000 |
| **23** | **Drake Britton, lhp, Red Sox** | **2007** | **$700,000** |
| 24 | Reggie Pruitt, of, Blue Jays | 2015 | $500,000 |
| 25 | * Nick Pesco, rhp, Indians | 2002 | $465,000 |
| **26** | *** Sean Henn, lhp, Yankees** | **2000** | **$1,701,000** |
| 27 | Garrison Lassiter, ss, Yankees | 2008 | $675,000 |
| **28** | *** Blake Hawksworth, rhp, Cards** | **2001** | **$1,475,000** |
| 29 | Bryan Dobzanski, rhp, Cardinals | 2014 | $700,000 |
| 30 | Rowdy Tellez, 1b, Blue Jays | 2013 | $850,000 |
| **31** | *** Humberto Sanchez, rhp, Tigers** | **2001** | **$1,000,000** |
| **32** | *** Jordan Zimmerman, lhp, Mariners** | **1994** | **$325,000** |
| **33** | *** Kurt Birkins, rhp, Orioles** | **2000** | **$395,000** |
| 34 | Tyler Watson, lhp, Nationals | 2015 | $400,000 |
| 35 | * Cameron Reimers, rhp, Blue Jays | 1998 | $250,000 |
| | Matt Fairel, lhp, Reds | 2008 | $250,000 |
| 36 | * Ryan Miller, lhp, Indians | 2006 | $450,000 |
| 37 | * Drew Miller, rhp, Padres | 2005 | $300,000 |
| **38** | **Jarred Cosart, rhp, Phillies** | **2008** | **$550,000** |
| **39** | **Andy LaRoche, 3b, Dodgers** | **2003** | **$1,000,000** |
| 40 | * Stephen Marek, rhp, Angels | 2004 | $800,000 |
| 41 | Frank Curreri, c, Diamondbacks | 2004 | $200,000 |
| **42** | *** Jesse Chavez, rhp, Rangers** | **2002** | **$225,000** |
| 43 | Ty Washington, ss, Reds | 2011 | $300,000 |
| 44 | * Shane Reedy, rhp, Cardinals | 2001 | $500,000 |
| | Evan DeLuca, lhp, Yankees | 2009 | $500,000 |
| 45 | * Mike Rodriguez, lhp, Dodgers | 2001 | $275,000 |
| 46 | * Mario Mendoza, rhp, Angels | 1998 | $225,000 |
| 47 | * Matt Bruback, rhp, Cubs | 1997 | $685,000 |
| **48** | *** Bobby Wilson, c, Angels** | **2002** | **$153,000** |
| 49 | Jason Smith, rhp, Red Sox | 2003 | $125,000 |
| 50 | Kyle Stroup, rhp, Red Sox | 2008 | $150,000 |

### AFTER 50TH ROUND

| | Player, Pos., Club | Year | Bonus |
|---|---|---|---|
| 69 | * Roger Carter, rhp, Devil Rays | 1996 | $275,000 |

### OTHER PHASES

| | Player, Pos., Club | Year | Bonus |
|---|---|---|---|
| **Jan.-R** | **Roy Smalley, ss, Rangers** | **1974** | **$95,000** |
| **Jan.-S** | **Ricky Wright, lhp, Dodgers** | **1980** | **$115,000** |
| **June-S** | **Mike Adamson, rhp, Orioles** | **1967** | **$85,000** |

*Major leaguers in bold. *Signed as draft-and-follow.*

a hand in dictating change.

When Monday, the top pick in the 1965 draft, and Jackson, the No. 2 selection a year later, both played in college at Arizona State (before eventually becoming teammates with the Kansas City/Oakland A's), they each spent only a single year on the varsity level for the Sun Devils. College freshmen weren't eligible to play varsity sports of any kind at the time, and Major League Baseball's college rule permitted players to be drafted following their sophomore year. Monday was just 19 when he signed with Kansas City.

By contrast, top college talents like Winfield and Goodwin were full-fledged college seniors with four years of varsity experience under their belts when they were drafted and signed—Winfield by the Padres with the fourth overall pick in 1973, Goodwin by the Angels with the No. 1 selection in 1975. By the time Monday and Jackson left school, and Winfield and Goodwin came along, both sets of college rules had been amended. A change in NCAA rules as they pertained to freshmen eligibility enabled Winfield and Goodwin to play on varsity teams as freshmen at the University of Minnesota and Southern University, respectively, and yet neither became eligible for the baseball draft until they were seniors because of their age.

MLB's amended college rule was aimed at protecting colleges by requiring players to stay in school at least a year longer, and while most collegians were draft-eligible as juniors, the rule had an additional provision that players must be age 21 within 45 days of the draft. Goodwin missed the mark as a junior by nearly two months, Winfield by three, and both had little recourse but to wait until they were seniors to be drafted—though Winfield may have stayed anyway as he was an all-Big 10 Conference power forward in basketball on a nationally ranked team.

The same restrictive age clause impacted a number of other college stars in the 1970s. Arizona State shortstop Alan Bannister and Southern California outfielder Steve Kemp, for two, chose to handle their situations differently than Winfield and Goodwin. Bannister, an unsigned first-round pick in the 1969 draft, would have been a slam-dunk first-rounder in 1972 had he been draft-eligible as junior, or even in 1973 if he had returned to college as senior. Kemp was undrafted as a high-school senior, but improved his stock immeasurably in college and would have been an early first-rounder as a junior.

But since both Bannister and Kemp, because they weren't 21, weren't eligible as juniors and didn't want to spend another year in college, their only recourse was to drop out of college during the fall semester in order to become eligible for the lower-profile January draft. Both ended up being taken with the No. 1 overall pick in the regular phase of their respective drafts—Bannister in January 1973, Kemp in January 1976. The college rule was amended once again later in 1976 to permit all college juniors, regardless of age, to become eligible. That rule is still in place today.

The advent of free agency in 1976 also had draft implications, as it was used as a tool to help compensate clubs which had lost meaningful free agents in the previous offseason. Typically, a team that lost a free agent received the first- or second-round selections from the team that signed the player. The Yankees were overly aggressive in their pursuit of free agents from the start, and through the years forfeited as many as 18 first-round selections in the draft. At the opposite end of the free-agent scale, the Expos were routinely hit hard by defections, especially after the 1989 season. With all the extra picks they received as compensation, they had a rare, windfall opportunity in the 1990 draft, selecting 10 players in the first two rounds.

The number of players drafted through the years has varied, depending on the number of rounds—though there was no limit through 1991, and from 1993-97. In 1992, and again from 1998-2011, the draft comprised 50 rounds. Since 2012, it has been 40 rounds. The most players drafted in any year occurred in 1996, when there were 1,740 selections. The 2014 and 2015

## CAREER LEADERS/DRAFTED PLAYERS

(Through 2015)

### GAMES

| Player, Pos., Drafted by | |
|---|---|
| 1. Rickey Henderson, of, Athletics '76 (4) | 3,081 |
| 2. Eddie Murray, 1b, Orioles '73 (3) | 3,026 |
| 3. Cal Ripken Jr., ss, Orioles '78 (2) | 3,001 |
| 4. Barry Bonds, of, Pirates '85 (1) | 2,986 |
| 5. Dave Winfield, of, Padres '73 (1) | 2,973 |

### BATTING AVERAGE

| Player, Pos., Drafted by | |
|---|---|
| 1. Tony Gwynn, of, Padres '81 (3) | .338 |
| 2. Wade Boggs, 3b, Red Sox '76 (7) | .328 |
| 3. Kirby Puckett, of, Twins '82 (Jan.-R/1) | .318 |
| 4. Todd Helton, 1b, Rockies '95 (1) | .316 |
| 5. *Joe Mauer, c, Twins '01 (1) | .313 |

### HITS

| Player, Pos., Drafted by | |
|---|---|
| 1. Derek Jeter, ss, Yankees '92 (1) | 3,465 |
| 2. Paul Molitor, ss, Brewers '77 (1) | 3,319 |
| 3. Eddie Murray, 1b, Orioles '73 (3) | 3,255 |
| 4. Cal Ripken Jr., ss, Orioles '78 (2) | 3,184 |
| 5. George Brett, 3b, Royals '71 (2) | 3,154 |

### HOME RUNS

| Player, Pos., Drafted by | |
|---|---|
| 1. Barry Bonds, of, Pirates '85 (1) | 762 |
| 2. *Alex Rodriguez, ss, Mariners '93 (1) | 687 |
| 3. Ken Griffey Jr., of, Mariners '87 (1) | 630 |
| 4. Jim Thome, ss, Indians '89 (13) | 612 |
| 5. Mark McGwire, 1b, Athletics '84 (1) | 583 |

### RBIS

| Player, Pos., Drafted by | |
|---|---|
| 1. *Alex Rodriguez, ss, Mariners '93 (1) | 2,055 |
| 2. Barry Bonds, of, Pirates '85 (1) | 1,996 |
| 3. Eddie Murray, 1b, Orioles '73 (3) | 1,917 |
| 4. Ken Griffey Jr., of, Mariners '87 (1) | 1,836 |
| 5. Rafael Palmeiro, of, Cubs '85 (1) | 1,835 |

### STOLEN BASES

| Player, Pos., Drafted by | |
|---|---|
| 1. Rickey Henderson, of, Athletics '76 (4) | 1,406 |
| 2. Tim Raines, 2b, Expos '77 (5) | 808 |
| 3. Vince Coleman, of, Cardinals '82 (10) | 752 |
| 4. Willie Wilson, of, Royals '74 (1) | 668 |
| 5. Kenny Lofton, of, Astros '88 (17) | 622 |

### ON-BASE PERCENTAGE

| Player, Pos., Drafted by | |
|---|---|
| 1. Barry Bonds, of, Pirates '85 (1) | .444 |
| 2. *Joey Votto, 1b, Reds '02 (2) | .423 |
| 3. Frank Thomas, 1b, White Sox '89 (1) | .419 |
| 4. Wade Boggs, 3b, Red Sox '76 (7) | .415 |
| 5. Todd Helton, 1b, Rockies '95 (1) | .414 |

### SLUGGING PERCENTAGE

| Player, Pos., Drafted by | |
|---|---|
| 1. Barry Bonds, of, Pirates '85 (1) | .607 |
| 2. Mark McGwire, 1b, Athletics '84 (1) | .588 |
| 3. Manny Ramirez, of, Indians '91 (1) | .585 |
| 4. *Albert Pujols, 3b, Cardinals '99 (13) | .581 |
| 5. Albert Belle, of, Indians '87 (2) | .564 |

George Brett and Nolan Ryan rank among the most successful draft picks in history

### EARNED RUN AVERAGE

| Player, Pos., Drafted by | |
|---|---|
| 1. *Clayton Kershaw, lhp, Dodgers '06 (1) | 2.43 |
| 2. Andy Messersmith, rhp, Angels '66 (June-S/1) | 2.86 |
| 3. Tom Seaver, rhp, Braves '66 (Jan.-S/1) | 2.86 |
| 4. Trevor Hoffman, rhp, Reds '89 (11) | 2.87 |
| 5. John Franco, lhp, Dodgers '81 (5) | 2.89 |

### WINS

| Player, Pos., Drafted by | |
|---|---|
| 1. Greg Maddux, rhp, Cubs '84 (2) | 355 |
| 2. Roger Clemens, rhp, Red Sox '83 (1) | 354 |
| 3. Nolan Ryan, rhp, Mets '65 (10) | 324 |
| 4. Tom Seaver, rhp, Braves '66 (Jan.-S/1) | 311 |
| 5. Tom Glavine, lhp, Braves '84 (2) | 305 |

### INNINGS PITCHED

| Player, Pos., Drafted by | |
|---|---|
| 1. Nolan Ryan, rhp, Mets '65 (10) | 5,386 |
| 2. Greg Maddux, rhp, Cubs '84 (2) | 5,008 |
| 3. Bert Blyleven, rhp, Twins '69 (3) | 4,970 |
| 4. Roger Clemens, rhp, Red Sox '83 (1) | 4,917 |
| 5. Tom Seaver, rhp, Braves '66 (Jan.-S/1) | 4,783 |

### SAVES

| Player, Pos., Drafted by | |
|---|---|
| 1. Trevor Hoffman, rhp, Reds '89 (11) | 601 |
| 2. Lee Smith, rhp, Cubs '75 (2) | 478 |
| 3. John Franco, lhp, Dodgers '81 (5) | 424 |
| 4. Billy Wagner, lhp, Astros '93 (1) | 422 |
| 5. Dennis Eckersley, rhp, Indians '72 (3) | 390 |

### STRIKEOUTS

| Player, Pos., Drafted by | |
|---|---|
| 1. Nolan Ryan, rhp, Mets '65 (10) | 5,386 |
| 2. Randy Johnson, lhp, Expos '85 (2) | 4,875 |
| 3. Roger Clemens, rhp, Red Sox '83 (1) | 4,672 |
| 4. Bert Blyleven, rhp, Twins '69 (3) | 3,701 |
| 5. Tom Seaver, rhp, Braves '66 (Jan.-S/1) | 3,640 |

*Active in 2016.

totals of 1,215 were the smallest since the draft was consolidated from four phases to one in 1987. Prior to that, the fewest number in any year occurred in 1974, when 1,020 players were selected overall, and just 726 in the June, regular phase.

With the consolidation of the draft into a single phase, it provided for a spinoff draft-and-follow rule, whereby unsigned draft picks (mostly junior-college players) remained property of the team that drafted them until a week prior to the following year's draft. Once a player's season was complete, he had the option of signing with the team that drafted him or going back into the draft pool.

On numerous occasions, players subject to the draft-and-follow rule made significant progress while under the control of the team that drafted them, and ended up receiving bonuses that were out of proportion for the rounds they were drafted. First-rounder Adam Loewen (Class of 2002) set the standard for a draft-and-follow with the $3.4 million bonus he received from the Orioles just a week before the 2003 draft, but more significant was the $1.78 million deal 26th-rounder Sean Henn (Class of 2000) signed with the Yankees.

With bonuses continuing to rise, the draft-and-follow process was phased out in 2007, as part of a new Collective Bargaining Agreement. In its place came a signing deadline of Aug. 15, by which time all draft picks must be signed. But with numerous first-rounders and other high-profile selections using the deadline as leverage, often waiting until the 11th hour to sign, and also effectively wasting a summer of minor league development in the process, that rule was later amended in the next CBA to a July 15 deadline.

Numerous other rules were incorporated into the draft process through the years, which helped to define the draft today and its place on the baseball landscape.

It remains to be seen where the draft is headed over the next few years, but it is safe to say that the drafting of more and more familiar names like Strasburg and Harper, and possibly the adoption of a worldwide draft and an even greater effort on the part of MLB to promote the draft as a viable entity, will only lead to more public acceptance. The draft's profile may never approach the NBA and NFL drafts in terms of widespread appeal, but looking back, those sports may be hard pressed to top all the storylines, and all the intriguing twists and turns, that have come from 50 years of history in the baseball draft.

Above all, it can now be written that the draft has done largely what it was intended to do in 1965—level the playing field, and provide some sort of cost containment with signing bonuses—and baseball is a better game because of it.

## THEY WERE DRAFTED?

***STEVE BARTKOWSKI, 1B, ORIOLES '74 (19TH ROUND).** One of the nation's top power-hitting prospects in college at California, Bartkowski focused on football when he became the No. 1 pick in the 1975 NFL draft.

**TOM BRADY, C, EXPOS '95 (18TH ROUND).** A four-time Super Bowl champion quarterback with the New England Patriots, Brady earned attention as a lefthanded-hitting catcher in California before concentrating on football in college at Michigan.

**MARSHALL FAULK, OF, ANGELS '93 (43RD ROUND).** Faulk never played baseball at San Diego State, but was the second pick in the 1994 NFL draft and became a member of the NFL Hall of Fame.

***MIKE GARRETT, OF, DODGERS '70 (35TH ROUND).** Even after winning the 1965 Heisman Trophy for USC and playing five years in the NFL, Garrett had a yearning to play baseball professionally—and nearly did after being drafted by the Dodgers.

**DAN MARINO, RHP, ROYALS '79 (4TH ROUND).** In the 1979 draft, the Royals took two future Hall of Famers—NFL Hall of Famers, that is, in Marino and John Elway (17th round). While Elway played baseball at Stanford and briefly in the Yankees system, Marino never played at Pitt.

**CAZZIE RUSSELL, 1B, ATHLETICS '66 (27TH ROUND).** Three weeks before he was taken by the New York Knicks with the No. 1 pick in the 1966 NBA draft, Russell worked out for a number of clubs and displayed impressive raw power. He never played baseball in four years at Michigan.

**CAREY SCHUELER, LHP, WHITE SOX '93 (43RD ROUND).** The only female ever drafted, Schueler was the daughter of then-White Sox general manager Ron Schueler.

***KENNY STABLER, LHP, YANKEES '66 (10TH ROUND).** Stabler pitched in college at Alabama before playing 15 years in the NFL as a lefthanded-throwing quarterback. He was selected to the NFL Hall of Fame in 2016.

***CHARLIE WARD, SS, YANKEES '94 (18TH ROUND).** Ward, the 1993 Heisman Trophy winner for Florida State, was selected twice in the baseball draft and in the first-round of the 1994 NBA draft, but never in football.

**JAMEIS WINSTON, OF, RANGERS '12 (15TH ROUND).** Winston had early-round potential as both a pitcher and outfielder at Florida State, but focused on football after winning the 2013 Heisman Trophy and becoming the No. 1 pick in the 2015 NFL draft.

*Considers only players that never played baseball professionally.*
**Drafted on multiple occasions.*

## THEY WEREN'T DRAFTED?

**BOBBY BONILLA, OF, PIRATES '81.** The Pirates signed Bonilla for $3,000; little more than a decade later, he was the highest-paid player in the game. Over a 16-year career, he slugged 287 home runs.

**TOM CANDIOTTI, RHP, ROYALS '80.** After going undrafted in 1979 and pitching that summer for an independent minor league team, Candiotti's contract was purchased a year later. From such humble beginnings, he won 151 games over 16 big league seasons as a knuckleballer.

**DANNY DARWIN, RHP, RANGERS '76.** Once Darwin was passed over in the January 1976 draft and had a breakout junior-college season that spring, he was fair game to sign with the highest bidder and accepted a $37,500 offer (first-round money) from the Rangers. In 21 big league seasons, he won 171 games.

**BRIAN DOWNING, C, WHITE SOX '69.** Signed out of a California junior college for $2,000, Downing played 20 years in the majors, hitting 275 home runs.

**TOBY HARRAH, SS, PHILLIES '66.** Harrah accepted a $500 bonus to sign with the Phillies, but never played a game for that club as a four-time all-star in a 17-year big league career.

**KEVIN MITCHELL, 3B, METS '80.** Mitchell signed with the Mets for $2,500, and reached the pinnacle of his 13-year career in 1989 by winning National League MVP honors for the Giants, leading the NL in homers (47) and RBIs (125).

**DON MONEY, 3B, PIRATES '65.** Passed over in the first draft, Money signed with the Pirates two weeks later (for no bonus), only to be dealt to the Phillies in a 4-for-1 trade for Hall of Famer Jim Bunning two years later. Over 16 years, he became a four-time all-star.

**DAN QUISENBERRY, RHP, ROYALS '75.** The sidearming Quisenberry was the game's dominant reliever over a six-year stretch from 1980-85, leading the American League in saves five times.

**BRUCE SUTTER, RHP, CUBS '71.** Though drafted by the Senators` in 1970 (21st round), he was signed by the Cubs as a free agent a year later. He is the only non-drafted player (in the draft era) inducted in the Hall of Fame. In 12 major league seasons, he saved 300 games.

**FRANK WHITE, 2B, ROYALS '70.** The best-known product of the Royals' short-lived Baseball Academy, White spent his entire 18-year major league career in a Royals uniform, winning eight Gold Gloves.

# Reichardt bonus triggered draft

Rick Reichardt had the world in the palm of his hand in the summer of 1964.

He was 21, 6-foot-3, 210 pounds, good-looking and articulate. "The first time I saw him," broadcaster Joe Garagiola would say a couple of years later, "I thought he fell off the cover of a Wheaties box."

Better still, Reichardt could really hit a baseball. Every major league team wanted him, and an escalating bonus war resulted. When Kansas City Athletics owner Charles O. Finley found out Reichardt planned to sign with the Los Angeles Angels, he hopped on his private plane and flew to Madison, Wis., to try and persuade Reichardt to sign with his club.

"At the 11th hour, Finley basically doubled his offer, which put it much, much more than what I signed for," Reichardt said later. "I was too honorable in those days to change my mind. If I could change my mind today, I probably would. The bottom line is the dollar. He flew into my hometown to romance us, but the horse had left the barn."

Reichardt accepted Los Angeles' offer of $205,000 just before a June 24 press conference at the lush Continental Hotel in Hollywood, property of Angels owners Gene Autry and Bob Reynolds. The bonus was the biggest in baseball history.

It came in a year when teams would collectively spend the staggering sum of $7 million to sign unproven amateur talent—more than they spent on salaries for major league players—and was the single biggest development that led to the creation of baseball's amateur draft in 1965.

## BASEBALL FOLLOWS LEAD OF NFL

The concept of a draft was hardly new. The National Football League implemented the procedure in 1936 as a means of distributing talent from the college ranks on an equitable basis; the National Basketball Association followed suit in 1947 and the National Hockey League came on board in 1963. If anything, baseball was a little slow in coming to the table.

For years, Major League Baseball steadfastly resisted the concept of a draft—on moral, legal and competitive grounds.

It was argued that a draft would penalize the industrious teams and be a form of socialism. The powerful Los Angeles Dodgers were opposed to it.

"We were against it for many reasons," general manager Buzzie Bavasi told The Sporting News in 1964. "No. 1, I don't think it will equalize the talent because clubs that were making personnel mistakes under the old system will make them under this one. No. 2, it won't save the money some expect because you still have to pay a boy what he's worth.

"No. 3, it's a form of socialism because the boy can sell his talents in only one place—unlike football which has the NFL, AFL and Canada. No. 4, it penalizes the industrious."

Dodgers' owner Walter O'Malley, in particular, had concerns over the draft's legality. "It boils right down to this," he said. "Is the thing going to leave us open to restraint of trade and/or antitrust litigation? I have grave doubts about its legality and apparently our attorney does, too, because he wouldn't offer us any assurance that we wouldn't wind up in trouble."

Baseball, unlike the other professional sports, had operated under an antitrust exemption since Supreme Court Justice Oliver Wendell Holmes bestowed favorable treatment for baseball in 1922. There was concern that a draft, which would restrict a player's freedom and bargaining power, would jeopardize baseball's special standing.

The game's leaders also feared Congress would take an adverse stance on the premise that a baseball draft would deal primarily with high school players, or minors.

Opponents of a draft, however, were in the minority. Teams like the Dodgers and New York Yankees opposed it not on legal principle, but more for selfish reasons.

"There was some concern whether or not governmental interference would happen, whether some of the players and their representatives would challenge it," said Lee MacPhail, the Baltimore Orioles general manager in 1964 and mastermind of the powerful Yankees teams of the 1950s and early '60s. "But some clubs preferred things go on as they were, if they felt they were getting more than their fair share. They didn't want to change that.

"In the 10 years I was farm director of the Yankees (1949-58), we won nine pennants and won the World Series five years in a row. Kids wanted to sign with the Yankees, the most glamorous team in baseball at the time."

Coming out of Wisconsin, Rick Reichardt signed with the Angels for a $205,000 bonus that shocked the industry

Instead of a draft, baseball enacted its own measures to legislate the payment of bonuses to untried amateur talent by punishing those clubs that spent excessively.

Procuring talent was generally on a first-come, first-served basis. Scouts scoured the country, attended games, got to know players and their families. The teams that were able to sell their organization as the most attractive one or simply had the deepest pockets invariably secured the best talent. Not surprisingly, the system tended to reinforce competitive imbalance.

By 1964, it was apparent the game was in need of systematic change. The very future of baseball was at a crossroads.

The Reichardt contract merely underscored the danger signs lurking all around. Not only were signing bonuses out of control and competitive balance being seriously threatened, but the game's player-development system was rotting at the core.

Wealthy teams like the Yankees were spending more and more to acquire the best amateur talent. The more they spent, the more successful they became. Smaller-market teams were committing financial suicide to keep pace.

## BONUS RUSH STARTED IN 1946

In 1936, the year the NFL instituted

its draft, the Cleveland Indians signed 17-year-old Iowa farmboy Bob Feller to a contract. The price? One dollar.

Players yearned then for the opportunity to play professional baseball, and were happy just for the chance. There was little competition among clubs for a player's services, no matter how talented he was.

By 1942, America's efforts in World War II siphoned off much of the available baseball talent. The supply of players suddenly became limited. Competition drove the Detroit Tigers to sign University of Michigan outfielder Dick Wakefield to an unprecedented bonus of $52,000.

Suddenly, the rush was on.

By the end of World War II, baseball had entered a new era—a golden era. Interest in the game spread like wildfire. Minor league teams sprung up all over and competition for players became fierce. Teams had to offer signing bonuses to top players to remain competitive.

For the next two decades, major league officials wrestled with problems stemming from reckless spending and the competition for new recruits. Various solutions were proposed. None worked. Almost all were revised annually or simply thrown out.

"Traditionally, baseball has had three ways to combat bonuses," said former Houston Astros president Tal Smith, whose involvement in the game at the executive level predated the draft era. "We've had the bonus rule, the first-year player draft and the Rule IV draft. None has been completely effective."

The bonus rule was in effect from 1946-50, and from 1953-57. In its simplest form, it required a club to carry a player on its roster, often with no chance of being farmed to the minor leagues, if the player signed a bonus in excess of a fixed amount, usually from $4,000-$6,000. The first-year draft rule, which was in effect from 1959 until the draft began in 1965, mandated an organization protect its top first-year pro prospects on its 40-man roster, or risk losing them to waivers or the annual Rule V draft.

"The bonus rule was difficult to enforce," Smith said in a 2005 interview. "There were always rumors or suspicions of under-the-table payments to friends or relatives to circumvent the rule. And yet if you adhered to the intent of the rule, it was a detriment to the player's development. It just didn't work.

"The first-year rule was detrimental to a club that scouted and signed a player, then stood to lose him after only one year. But I still think it was the most effective means of curbing bonuses. What we have today is not effective. The draft no longer works in the way it was intended to work—to limit bonuses and level the playing field. It was effective for 20 years, but with all the bonus escalation it's become a detriment to some of the small-market clubs."

### RULE ENCOURAGED CHEATING

At the 1946 Winter Meetings, baseball made its first concerted effort to curtail escalating bonuses by instituting the bonus rule. A bonus player was designated as anyone signed to a contract that exceeded a fixed level ($6,000 for a player signed by a major league team).

The rules that went into effect often required bonus players to be placed on big league rosters before they were ready to play at that level and remain there for two years. They could not be sent to the minors without being placed on irrevocable waivers.

Over the next four years, various amendments to the bonus rule were written to curb teams from spending to excesses. But bonus payments continued to escalate.

In 1947, the Philadelphia Phillies spent $65,000 to sign 18-year-old lefthander Curt Simmons. A year later, the Boston Braves shelled out $75,000 for another young lefty, Johnny Antonelli, who began his career in the big leagues—much to the chagrin of veterans like Johnny Sain, who felt underpaid. They also resented the huge bonuses being paid to teenagers, who ate up roster spots—and had to remain there or be subject to waivers. The Tigers gave the same amount, plus two automobiles, to sign catcher Frank House, 18.

Teams would do a lot of creative things in those days to dodge the bonus rule. Jackie Jensen, hero of the 1949 Rose Bowl, was paid $75,000 by the Pacific Coast League's Oakland Oaks, the largest bonus ever given to a minor league player. The Pittsburgh Pirates wanted to sign Jensen for that amount, as did the Yankees. Oakland had a close working relationship with the Yankees at the time and signed Jensen at their behest. The Oaks let him play in the minor leagues for a year then traded him along with second baseman Billy Martin to the Yankees for $80,000 and four players. Because the Yankees acquired Jensen in a trade, he was not subject to the bonus rule.

In January 1950, the Pirates took bonus payments to a new level when general manager Branch Rickey astounded the industry—much like he had done four years earlier in signing Jackie Robinson for the Brooklyn Dodgers—by signing lefthander Paul Pettit to baseball's first $100,000 bonus. The Pirates got almost no return on the deal as the sore-armed Pettit won only one game in the big leagues.

By then, it had become apparent that the bonus rule was not an effective deterrent in restraining clubs from paying out huge bonuses. After a four-year trial and numerous attempts to abandon it, the bonus rule was repealed at the 1950 Winter Meetings.

With no restrictions in effect, clubs continued their spending frenzy for the next two years.

During the five-year period from 1953-57, proposals were repeatedly introduced to amend or abolish the bonus rule, all amid charges of under-the-table payments to sidestep its restrictive terms. Numerous clubs were penalized for bending the rules.

"We'd pass a bonus rule and by the time we got out of the room, we already figured a way to skin the cat," Tigers general manager Jim Campbell said. "There was no way really to police it. You could hire a kid's uncle as a scout. He might actually be qualified, but it was still questionable."

The Orioles became baseball's biggest spender of the bonus rule era—and its most penalized club. Under new GM/manager Paul Richards, the Orioles spent roughly $700,000 in 1955 on untested players, including Arkansas high school third baseman Brooks Robinson, 18, who went on to play in six big league games that season.

The bonus rule routinely stymied the careers of young players, who often rotted away on major league benches. University of Cincinnati lefthander Sandy Koufax received a $25,000 bonus from the Dodgers in 1955, and had to stay on the big league roster for two years. He pitched in only

## BONUS PROGRESSION RECORD

### Pre-Draft Era

Reliable information on signing bonuses in the pre-draft era is sketchy, with bonuses often intertwined with a player's salary, distorted to circumvent various bonus rules of that era or, in the case of under-the-table payments, going unreported altogether.

There was no systematic method of paying out bonuses in those days, unlike in the draft era when half the signing bonus is generally paid upon approval of the contract and the other half early in the next calendar year. In many cases, some of the top bonuses of the pre-draft period were paid out over several years—such as 10, in the case of Paul Pettit, baseball's first $100,000 bonus baby.

Based on available information, here is the progression of signing-bonus records in the pre-draft era, beginning with Dick Wakefield's $52,000 bonus in 1942—the unofficial start of baseball's bonus era:

| Year | Player, Pos., Club | Bonus |
|---|---|---|
| 1942 | Dick Wakefield, of, Tigers | $52,000 |
| 1946 | Bobby Brown, 3b, Yankees | $56,000 |
| | Tookie Gilbert, 1b, Giants | $60,000 |
| 1947 | Curt Simmons, lhp, Phillies | $65,000 |
| 1948 | Johnny Antonelli, lhp, Braves | $75,000 |
| | Frank House, c, Tigers | $75,000 |
| 1950 | Paul Pettit, lhp, Pirates | $100,000 |
| 1951 | Ted Kazanski, ss, Tigers | $100,000 |
| | Billy Joe Davidson, rhp, Indians | $100,000 |
| 1952 | Marty Keough, of, Red Sox | $100,000 |
| 1957 | John DeMerit, of, Braves | $100,000 |
| | Bob "Hawk" Taylor, c, Braves | $112,000 |
| 1958 | Dave Nicholson, of, Orioles | $120,000 |
| | Denis Menke, ss, Braves | $125,000 |
| 1960 | Danny Murphy, rhp, Cubs | $130,000 |
| | Randy Hundley, c, Giants | $132,000 |
| 1961 | Bob Bailey, ss, Pirates | $175,000 |
| 1964 | Rick Reichardt, of, Angels | $205,000 |

101 innings in 1955 and 1956 and wasn't totally effective for another six years.

Attempts to wipe out the controversial bonus rule, assailed as being counterproductive to player development, were vigorously lobbied at the 1955 and '56 Winter Meetings, but were unsuccessful.

In 1957, the World Series champion Milwaukee Braves handed out the biggest bonus ever, signing catcher Bob "Hawk" Taylor, for $112,000. Finally, at the '57 Winter Meetings, the much-abused bonus rule was abolished. Continued cheating and lack of enforceability led to its repeal.

## FIRST-YEAR RULE ADOPTED

With repeal of the bonus rule, major league clubs went on their greatest spending spree ever in 1958. It was estimated that $6 million in bonuses were paid out.

Baltimore spent a record $120,000 for power-hitting outfielder Dave Nicholson, a high school dropout. Milwaukee topped that record several months later, signing shortstop Denis Menke for $125,000. Ohio State basketball star Frank Howard signed with the Dodgers for $108,000.

In an effort to curb such heavy spending, an unrestricted draft of all first-year players on minor league rosters was passed at the 1958 Winter Meetings. The rule specified that any free agent signed after Dec. 31, 1958, would be subject to the Rule V draft following his first season of Organized Ball if not placed on a 40-man major league roster. Furthermore, the rule required players to be kept on a major league team's 25-man roster the following year if drafted, rather than be sent to the minors for seasoning.

At the 1959 Winter Meetings, a proposal introducing a formal draft of amateur talent was made, but it proved to be five years before its time and was defeated. Meanwhile, bonuses only continued to rise.

In 1960, the Chicago Cubs signed Danny Murphy, 17, to a record $130,000 bonus and immediately placed him in the big leagues. A year later, expansion teams were awarded to Houston, New York, Washington and Los Angeles, causing the scramble for talent to become more furious than ever. Bonus payments reached new levels that threatened baseball's financial well-being. In the first six months of 1961, teams handed out a record $5.23 million in bonuses.

The Boston Red Sox signed local high school star Bob Guindon for $130,000, but that figure was topped in rapid succession by the Pirates, who signed Bob Bailey, an 18-year-old shortstop from Long Beach, Calif., to a $175,000 bonus.

"Maybe we have to be saved from ourselves," Braves general manager John McHale said. "I think it's unfortunate that this is the system. A club like ours must be competitive. To achieve this, we must get

### PRE-DRAFT SPOTLIGHT: RICK REICHARDT

ASSOCIATED PRESS

Rick Reichardt was an unlikely candidate to change the course of baseball history. He played little baseball in high school because the season lasted only 15 games, and went to the University of Wisconsin on a football scholarship.

Freshmen were ineligible for NCAA competition in 1961, so he sat out a year. As a sophomore, he played in the Badgers' 42-37 Rose Bowl loss to Southern California, and the next year, led the Big Ten Conference with 26 pass receptions. Baseball, at first, was just an excuse to get out of spring football practice.

It quickly developed into much more. In 1963, he led the Big Ten with a .429 average in league play, a feat he repeated the next year at .472. His .443 overall average in 1964 set a Badgers record that still stands, and The Sporting News named him college player of the year. On June 24, 1964, he signed with the Los Angeles Angels for a bonus of $205,000—a record figure that led to the implementation of the baseball draft a year later.

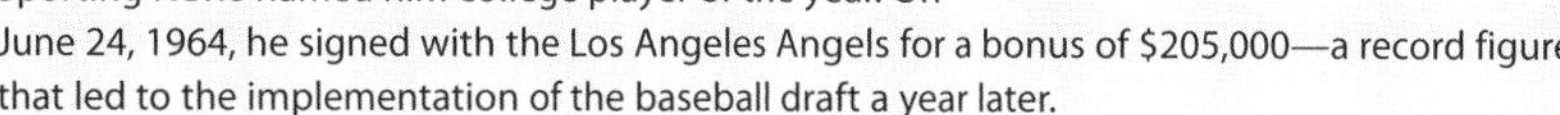

"In 14 years of baseball association, I never have seen a young prospect I personally wanted more for my club," Angels farm director Roland Hemond said shortly after Reichardt signed. "With Mr. (Gene) Autry and Mr. (Bob) Reynolds, we watched him in a doubleheader against Illinois some weeks ago. Rick hit three homers, stole home and was robbed of another homer because the outfielder was able to reach over the fence and snag the ball.

"We sure loved it, even if the price did go up with every hit."

Reichardt decided he wanted to play baseball because it offered more longevity than football. So he and his father laid some ground rules: Rick would not try out, or get involved in an auction, and visited ballparks where he might want to play.

Looking back, Reichardt said he was a little naive.

"I was basically a kid from Wisconsin who hadn't left Wisconsin," he said. "My experience with other major cities and ballparks was nonexistent. Teams like Boston, if I had known the kinds of money they paid a normal player and how Fenway Park would have helped my career, I might have looked at them more seriously."

Reichardt chose the Angels because he liked Autry and Reynolds, and the team was building Anaheim Stadium. The money was a primary consideration, and there were other factors.

"I might have been swayed a bit by the glitz of Hollywood," he said. . . . "The inducement to play in the minor leagues in Hawaii. I wasn't as pragmatic as I should have been, but it turned out still OK."

After 188 minor-league games, mostly in the Pacific Coast League, and two September tours with the Angels, Reichardt arrived in the major leagues to stay in 1966.

"I will be sincerely surprised if Rick isn't the American League's next superstar," said Bill Rigney, his manager. "He comes along at a time when the league needs a Frank Merriwell-type as its leader, and if there was ever a man cut out to lead others, Reichardt is that man.

"What I mean is that Mickey Mantle probably won't play too much longer, and now we've got a player who can dominate the league."

Reichardt seemed on the way to fulfilling those expectations for the first four months of 1966. Then his season crashed to a halt.

The previous winter, he had learned he had congenital kidney blockage, which manifested itself in high blood pressure and severe headaches. After returning from a road trip in late July, he woke up one morning with an unbelievable headache.

"My roommate, Clyde Wright, literally carried me to his car, and took me to a doctor," Reichardt said. "Three days later, I was in Rochester, Minn., having my kidney removed. It was quite traumatic."

Reichardt returned to pinch-hit on the season's final day, finishing with 16 home runs and 44 RBIs in 89 games.

"And that was playing a month with a bone bruise," he said. "I hit three home runs in a series with Washington before we returned to Anaheim. There's no question in my mind I would have hit 30 home runs with about 100 RBIs . . . After that, I didn't have the same resiliency I did before.

"I had some good, decent seasons, but I couldn't sustain it for a long period of time. What kind of test case do you have to compare it to? Not many players play baseball with only one kidney."

In 11 seasons and 997 games, Reichardt hit .261 with 116 homers, though he thinks his kidney problem cut down his production. So does Hemond, still active in the game as a special advisor to the general manager for the Arizona Diamondbacks.

"He was well on his way," Hemond said. "He gave every indication of having an even better career . . . He wasn't quite the same afterward."

ballplayers. If you're not prepared to pay, well, you just stand by and watch somebody else sign 'em.

"No, I don't know how to stop it. We've tried all kinds of ways, including several bonus rules. But nothing has worked. If a draft system similar to that used by football and basketball would hold up under our justice system, then maybe that would be the answer."

From 1958-63, an estimated $45 million was spent on bonuses and first-year player salaries.

"We can't go on like this," an AL official said. "Most of the clubs are mortgaging their future to meet the present competition. If it is illegal to put all the kids in a pool, let's find out why it is illegal. Let's find out from Washington what we can do to make it legal. I think the commissioner should concentrate on nothing else but this for the rest of the summer. We will be bankrupt unless something is done."

By 1962, the minor leagues had shrunk to 18 leagues as three more folded under the financial strain. A year later, two more leagues bit the dust, reducing the number to 16, the lowest total since 1933.

Meanwhile, bonus payments ran the gamut in 1962. The Houston Colt .45s signed 105 free agents for an estimated $900,000. By contrast, the Cubs signed only six, none for more than $8,000.

Sentiment for an amateur draft continued to gain groundswell support, but the chief obstacle remained the fear that Organized Baseball might lose its preferred antitrust status. "Baseball's lawyers tell us this is not the time to try and get into a free-agent draft," St. Louis Cardinals general manager Bing Devine said.

By 1964, continued disenchantment over the first-year rule had the game's top officials looking at other solutions. Though the rule put no ceiling on bonus payments, it penalized those clubs that spent too much money on too many players.

The rule was intended to give the have-not clubs a better chance to compete for free-agent talent, but five years later it had not worked out that way. While it did cut down on bonus spending to a certain extent, the weaker teams could not protect enough young players to rebuild quickly enough. Worse, it retarded the development of some of the game's best prospects.

Among others, the New York Mets were opponents of the rule because they said it curtailed the signing of players, made major leaguers out of boys who should be in the minors and was generally harmful to baseball.

Even the Dodgers, who won the 1963 World Series while carrying two first-year players on their 25-man roster, were disgruntled with the rule.

"Any rule," a Dodgers official said, "that puts the best prospects in a more or less inactive status in the second year of their career is, regardless of its other purposes, a silly rule."

Sandy Koufax saw his development made more difficult by baseball's bonus rule, which kept him in the big leagues

MacPhail, chairman of the committee which drafted the first-year rule, became an outspoken critic.

"It served a purpose in a way, helping reduce the bonus spending which threatened to run us all into bankruptcy," he said, "but it just hasn't quite worked the way we hoped it would. By all rules of common sense, it should have worked.

"The reason I think the rule should be changed is that baseball's primary job is still to give the public the best possible product and you're not doing that when you carry that many kids who can't help you."

While a majority of clubs were opposed to the first-year rule, few were willing to junk it until something better came along.

MacPhail advocated a draft. He felt it offered numerous benefits.

"First, it would enable us to put the best possible product on the field since we wouldn't have to push veterans off our rosters to protect inexperienced kids," he said. "Secondly, costs could be kept within reason. And thirdly, the plan would give every club a chance to get its fair share of the new talent."

## FRAMEWORK FOR DRAFT LAID

On Jan. 15, 1964, at a historic top-level meeting in New York, club owners unanimously authorized commissioner Ford Frick and league presidents Joe Cronin (American) and Warren Giles (National) to formulate a proposal for a free-agent draft. The proposal was to be ready by August.

In the meantime, spending for free agents reached new levels in 1964. Reichardt singlehandedly saw to that, but Finley's A's also spent like no other team that year, signing 80 players to bonuses totaling some $634,000. The A's finished last in the American League in 1964, but Finley was relentless in his pursuit of free agents.

On the heels of another wild spending spree that year, it was expected that the owners would overwhelmingly support Frick's master plan for a free-agent draft when they convened Aug. 10-11 in Chicago to hear the commissioner's proposal. Approval by both leagues was needed.

But proponents of a draft received a jolting setback when only half of the 20 clubs supported Frick's plan, which was similar in scope to the drafts in football and basketball. Even though the Yankees had dominated the American League for years, just two AL clubs supported Frick's draft proposal. Eight of 10 National League clubs supported the plan. The dissenting clubs said their reluctance stemmed from the risk that a draft might be subject to investigation by the House Judiciary Committee. The owners simply could not shake their fear of possible congressional intervention.

As a result, the draft proposal was tabled. Meanwhile, the sentiment was to keep the controversial first-year rule with several modifications.

Prospects for a draft, which appeared doomed less than three months earlier, then took a sudden swing toward becoming reality when major league general managers met in Ligonier, Pa., on Oct. 28, and a show of hands indicated at least 14 teams favored its adoption. The dissenters included the Athletics, Colt .45s, Mets and Washington Senators. The Dodgers were not present, but were known to be strongly against any draft proposal.

Two weeks later, the owners met again in Phoenix and ratified the decision to go forward with a draft, with six teams now opposed to its implementation. The Colt .45s had swung their vote in favor, while the Cardinals and Angels joined the outspoken Dodgers in voicing their objections.

It appeared the proponents would finally see their dreams of a draft become reality. All it needed was formal passage at the Winter Meetings.

"The free-agent draft will help solve our biggest problem: player procurement and development," Indians general manager Gabe Paul said. "It'll help equalize our teams. We have to do something to give the weaker teams greater incentive.

"Football has gone ahead unafraid of legal obstacles and they had more obstacles when they instituted their draft than we do now. They have benefited by our mistakes.

It's about time for us to profit by their experience."

When the 1964 Winter Meetings opened in Houston Nov. 30, there was still doubt whether the plan would pass. Clubs had continued to switch their stance on the issue in informal polls. The influential Yankees were now on the side of those voting against.

When it came to an official vote, the proponents won out. The margin was 13-7 in favor.

Even the Dodgers, the most outspoken against adoption of a draft, were willing to give it a try once they saw the writing on the wall. "We opposed it and we are still opposed to it," O'Malley said, "but we are willing to go along with the rest and give it a try. Our attorneys have assured us the rule isn't legal. But if it isn't, let's find out. Baseball shouldn't run scared."

The draft became official when it was ratified by the National Association. Five negative votes could have blocked it, but at a meeting on Dec. 2, the 16 minor leagues still in existence gave the proposal unanimous endorsement.

## THE WORKING INGREDIENTS

Baseball's new free-agent draft would function in a manner similar to those in the NFL and NBA. All eligible talent would be placed in a common pool, with every team given an equal opportunity to select in turn. When a team selected a player, it would gain exclusive rights to negotiate with him.

Baseball, however, introduced several notable differences.

First, three drafts would be held each year instead of one. A summer meeting would be held in early June, a winter session in mid-January. A third draft, limited to American Legion players not eligible to sign until Sept. 1, would be held in late summer.

The new Rule IV draft would be open to permanent residents of the United States only, with a focus on high school graduates and college players who had attained sophomore standing or age 21.

Where a football team retained permanent negotiating rights to a draftee, a baseball club's rights terminated 15 days before the next draft session. If a player had not signed prior to the 15-day closed period, he went back into a special pool of previously drafted players.

Rule IV draft regulations specified that big league clubs would make their selections in reverse order of the previous year's finish. In 1965, the American League would draft first, with Kansas City having the first selection.

The draft had an immediate impact on signing bonuses. While five players signed bonuses of $100,000 or more in 1964, only No. 1 overall pick Rick Monday signed a contract in six figures in 1965, while the average first-round bonus that year was $42,516.

No one would top Monday's $100,000 bonus for another 10 years, when Danny Goodwin, who was drafted No. 1 overall in both 1971 and 1975, signed for $150,000.

By all accounts, adoption of the draft in 1964 proved to be a blessing for baseball. It was the root that enabled the game to grow and prosper.

"It's an unqualified success," MacPhail said in the late 1980s. "Certainly, it's evened competition. It's given teams that have a difficult time competing for free-agent talent a fair share, or even more than a fair share. Close races in all divisions today goes back to the free agent draft. If you didn't have it today, it would be a disaster."

## DRAFT'S INEXACT NATURE

At best, the baseball draft has remained an inexact science through the years.

"Picking high school and college kids is the most unscientific, inexact of all the evaluations of talent," said Syd Thrift, former Pirates and Orioles general manager. "The reason is these kids are the furthest away from the major leagues.

"Unlike in football and basketball, whose drafts deal with more finished products, the best players drafted in baseball, even the top college players, invariably need to develop and refine their skills for several seasons in the minor leagues."

Over 51 years, only 22 of more than 70,000 players drafted went directly from high school or college to the major leagues. Of that total, five never had to back track to the minor leagues for additional seasoning.

"In football and basketball," Toronto Blue Jays general manager Pat Gillick said, "they're drafting guys after they've spent three or four years in what is the equivalent of our farm system. The caliber of play in college baseball is not equivalent to that of basketball and football.

"It's not a very exacting science. No matter how much testing you try to do, you never really know how a young guy is going to react to a pro situation until he plays in one."

Even a former No. 1 overall draft pick acknowledged how hit-and-miss the baseball draft can be. "The draft is at best a shot in the dark," said Bill Almon, the No. 1 pick in 1974. "That's the reason they draft so many players."

Former Red Sox scout Joe Stephenson may have said it best, when describing how unpredictable the baseball draft can be.

"We belong to the 4-H club," Stephenson said. "You hope you find a prospect. You hope you get him in the draft. You hope you can sign him. And you hope he can play."

## IN FOCUS: PAUL PETTIT

Paul Pettit might have been one of the most overpaid players of the bonus era, but you could never fault him for giving it less than an honest effort. He stuck around professional baseball for an agonizing 11 years. His payoff? One major league victory.

Pettit was baseball's first $100,000 bonus baby. Following graduation from Narbonne High in Harbor City, Calif., he signed 10 annual installments of $10,000 with the Pittsburgh Pirates on Jan. 31, 1950. The 18-year-old lefthander was so determined to justify the investment that all he ended up doing was hurting his arm and ruining his career.

"I tried to do too much too soon," Pettit said. "I read all the predictions and tried to make them come true too soon."

Pettit worked only 94 innings in 1950 at Double-A New Orleans, walking 76 while compiling a 2-7, 5.17 record. He debuted with the Pirates on May 4, 1951, but arm problems limited him to two games. A year later, Pettit earned his only win.

Elbow problems finally forced Pettit to give up pitching in 1954. To his credit, he didn't take the money and run.

The hard-luck bonus baby turned his attention to becoming a first baseman/outfielder and went to the low minors. He eventually worked his way back to Triple-A, but after seven seasons he gave it up. He never returned to the big leagues.

For Pettit, who went on to get his master's degree and became a teacher, it was never supposed to turn out that way.

He was known as the "Wizard of Whiff." As an amateur he pitched six no-hitters, three of them in a row, and struck out 945 batters in 549 innings. In one 12-inning game, he struck out 27 batters.

He was such a sure bet for stardom that Hollywood director Frederick Stephani signed him to a personal services contract while Pettit was still in high school, granting exclusive rights to Pettit's services as a potential actor and athlete. Stephani in turn sold the contract to the Pirates.

There were charges that Stephani had acted as an agent for the Pirates, constituting a violation of baseball's high school rule.

Commissioner Happy Chandler cleared the Pirates after an investigation, but the ruling was unpopular with major league owners and contributed to the downfall of Chandler as commissioner months later.

# 1965

## AT A GLANCE

### This Date In History
**WINTER DRAFT:** None
**SUMMER DRAFT:** June 8-9
**LEGION DRAFT:** Aug. 24

### Best Draft
**KANSAS CITY ATHLETICS.** The A's kicked off baseball's first draft with **RICK MONDAY**, and ended up grabbing nine more future major leaguers. Monday, **SAL BANDO** (6) and **GENE TENACE** (11) all were instrumental in the team's success in the early 1970s, after the move to Oakland.

### Worst Draft
**HOUSTON ASTROS.** The Astros drafted more players (72) and future big leaguers (11) than anyone, but just three of the 30 players they signed reached Houston—and they combined to play in just 26 games.

### First-Round Bust
**KEN PLESHA, C, WHITE SOX.** A 19-year-old catcher from Notre Dame, Plesha never advanced beyond Class A in three pro seasons, while hitting .186 with three homers and also struggling in the field.

### On Second Thought
**JOHNNY BENCH, C, REDS.** Bench signed for $6,000 as a second-round pick, but it was evident early that he was destined for greatness. He became the first drafted player to be enshrined in the Hall of Fame.

### Late-Round Find
**NOLAN RYAN, RHP, METS (10TH ROUND).** Ryan, baseball's all-time strikeout king with 5,714 over a distinguished 27-year career, lasted until the 295th pick—technically the 10th round, though he was the Mets' 12th pick overall. After Ryan fanned 455 in 291 minor league innings, it was obvious that clubs had seriously underestimated his considerable upside.

### Never Too Late
**OTIS THORNTON, C, ASTROS (28TH ROUND).** While technically a 28th-round pick because

# Kansas City gets A for effort in first draft

ASSOCIATED PRESS

Kansas City scout Art Lilly (right), signs Rick Monday, the first pick in the first draft, as his mother Nelda and A's owner Charles Finley look on

Most major league teams didn't know what to expect from baseball's first amateur draft, but the Kansas City Athletics went in prepared. The A's had the initial selection by virtue of finishing last in the American League the previous year.

"We don't want to pat ourselves on the back, but we did study the system," said Hank Peters, then the A's assistant general manager. "I think we organized ourselves well. I remember clubs talked to us about it after the draft, asking how we did it."

The A's used the initial selection, to no one's surprise, on 19-year-old Arizona State outfielder Rick Monday.

"Every now and then a player comes along who's head and shoulders above the crowd," Peters said. "We really didn't have much trouble selecting him. We zeroed in on him pretty early. We had Art Lilly, one of our top scouts at the time, following him. It was a case where we didn't have to argue the merits of three or four players."

At a time when college sophomores were eligible for the draft and freshmen were not eligible to play varsity sports, Monday hit .359 with a school-record 11 homers in his only season at Arizona State. Four days after his selection, with Kansas City owner Charles O. Finley in the stands, Monday led the Sun Devils to their first College World Series championship. He homered as ASU beat Ohio State, 2-1, in the deciding game.

On June 15, Finley flew to Monday's Santa Monica, Calif., home and signed him to a $100,000 bonus contract, an amount that was roughly half what outfielder Rick Reichardt earned from the Los Angeles Angels a year earlier on the open market.

Finley essentially handed over to Monday the equivalent amount he received from the Houston Astros the previous week for the sale of veteran first baseman Jim Gentile.

Led by Monday, Kansas City had an excellent draft, claiming 10 players who would reach the big leagues. The list included third baseman Sal Bando, Monday's Arizona State teammate who was selected MVP of the College World Series. He hit .480 at Omaha, and set then-CWS records for hits (12) and total bases (21). Bando, a sixth-round selection, signed for $25,000.

Combined with some of the fine young talent like Jim (Catfish) Hunter, Lew Krausse, Rollie Fingers, John (Blue Moon) Odom, Jim Nash, Joe Rudi and Skip Lockwood that the A's had been stockpiling over the final two years of the free-agent era, plus a 1966 draft that would net future

## 1965: THE FIRST ROUNDERS

| CLUB: PLAYER, POS., SCHOOL | HOMETOWN | B-T | HT | WT | AGE | BONUS | FIRST YEAR | LAST YEAR | PEAK LEVEL (YEARS) |
|---|---|---|---|---|---|---|---|---|---|
| **1. Athletics: Rick Monday, of, Arizona State** | **Santa Monica, Calif.** | **L-L** | **6-2** | **190** | **19** | **$100,000** | **1965** | **1984** | **Majors (19)** |
| First pick in first draft was college player of year for national champ Sun Devils, went on to hit 241 homers in 19-year big-league career; now a Dodgers announcer. | | | | | | | | | |
| **2. Mets: Les Rohr, lhp, West HS** | **Billings, Mon.** | **L-L** | **6-5** | **200** | **19** | **$50,000** | **1965** | **1970** | **Majors (3)** |
| Born in England, raised in Montana, big lefty was supposed to be centerpiece of talented young Mets pitching crop, but injuries limited him to 24 innings. | | | | | | | | | |
| **3. Senators: Joe Coleman, rhp, Natick HS** | **Natick, Mass.** | **R-R** | **6-3** | **165** | **18** | **$65,000** | **1965** | **1982** | **Majors (15)** |
| As son of Joe, father of Casey, was part of rare three-generation family; reached majors in 1965, won 142 games in career, had long tenure as pitching coach. | | | | | | | | | |
| **4. Astros: Alex Barrett, ss, Atwater HS** | **Winton, Calif.** | **R-R** | **6-0** | **175** | **18** | **$40,000** | **1965** | **1971** | **Class AAA (3)** |
| Holds distinction of being first draft pick not to reach majors; hit .209 overall in seven-year minor league career; later became prominent lawyer in Hawaii. | | | | | | | | | |
| **5. Red Sox: Billy Conigliaro, of, Swampscott HS** | **Swampscott, Mass.** | **R-R** | **6-0** | **175** | **17** | **$62,500** | **1965** | **1973** | **Majors (5)** |
| Brother of Tony, the young star whose career was derailed by a beaning in 1967; brothers played together briefly in Sox outfield, but neither career went as hoped. | | | | | | | | | |
| **6. Cubs: Rick James, rhp, Coffee HS** | **Florence, Ala.** | **R-R** | **6-2** | **200** | **17** | **$40,000** | **1965** | **1970** | **Majors (1)** |
| Not to be confused with musician Rick James of "Super Freak" fame; the pitcher surfaced for three games in majors at 19, spent rest of career in minors. | | | | | | | | | |
| **7. Indians: Ray Fosse, c, Marion HS** | **Marion, Ill.** | **R-R** | **6-3** | **210** | **18** | **$28,000** | **1965** | **1979** | **Majors (12)** |
| Had 12-year big league career (.256 BA, 61 HRs overall), spent last 20 years in A's broadcast booth, but best known for his collision with Pete Rose in '70 ASG. | | | | | | | | | |
| **8. Dodgers: John Wyatt, ss, Bakersfield HS** | **Bakersfield, Calif.** | **L-R** | **6-2** | **200** | **17** | **$40,000** | **1965** | **1970** | **Class A (3)** |
| First-round bust in more ways than one—first for six-year career that peaked in Class A, later for being the ringleader in major drug-smuggling ring. | | | | | | | | | |
| **9. Twins: Eddie Leon, ss, Arizona** | **Tucson, Ariz.** | **R-R** | **5-11** | **165** | **18** | **Unsigned** | **1967** | **1975** | **Majors (8)** |
| Went unsigned as first-rounder out of Arizona in both 1965 and 1966 (June/secondary phase), but went on to play eight seasons in majors, hit .236 overall. | | | | | | | | | |
| **10. Pirates: Wayne Dickerson, of, Ensley HS** | **Birmingham, Ala.** | **L-L** | **6-1** | **178** | **17** | **$25,000** | **1965** | **1969** | **Class A (4)** |
| Three-sport Alabama prep star never advanced past Class A in 5 seasons in Pirates system; hit .262 with 28 homers overall, but career derailed by illness, injury. | | | | | | | | | |
| **11. Angels: # Jim Spencer, 1b, Andover HS** | **Glen Burnie, Md.** | **L-L** | **6-2** | **190** | **18** | **$32,500** | **1965** | **1982** | **Majors (15)** |
| Enjoyed solid 15-year career in majors, hitting 146 homers (second to Rick Monday among 1965 first-rounders), earned two Gold Gloves; died of heart attack at 58. | | | | | | | | | |
| **12. Braves: Dick Grant, 1b/lhp, Watertown HS** | **Watertown, Mass.** | **L-L** | **6-4** | **205** | **18** | **$23,000** | **1965** | **1971** | **Class AA (3)** |
| Began seven-year career in Braves system as a hitter (.252, 49 HR) before switching to mound in 1971; went 7-0 in A ball before being done in by torn rotator cuff. | | | | | | | | | |
| **13. Tigers: Gene Lamont, c, Hiawatha HS** | **Kirkland, Ill.** | **L-R** | **6-1** | **180** | **18** | **$33,000** | **1965** | **1977** | **Majors (5)** |
| Has managed or coached in minors/majors every year since 1978; homered in first big-league AB, but went deep just four times in brief playing career. | | | | | | | | | |
| **14. Giants: Al Gallagher, 3b, Santa Clara** | **Daly City, Calif.** | **R-R** | **6-0** | **180** | **19** | **$40,000** | **1965** | **1980** | **Majors (4)** |
| Nicknamed "Dirty Al" because he refused to wash uniform during 25-game win streak in college; short career as player, but long one as minor league manager. | | | | | | | | | |
| **15. Orioles: Scott McDonald, rhp/1b, Marquette HS** | **Yakima, Wash.** | **R-R** | **6-1** | **195** | **18** | **$30,000** | **1965** | **1970** | **Class AA (1)** |
| Drafted as a pitcher, but hurt his elbow in first start in 1966 and never pitched again; Orioles switched him to first base and he never rose above Double-A. | | | | | | | | | |
| **16. Reds: Bernie Carbo, 3b, Livonia HS** | **Garden City, Mich.** | **L-R** | **5-11** | **170** | **17** | **$30,000** | **1965** | **1980** | **Majors (12)** |
| NL Rookie of the Year in 1970 for Reds (.310, 21 HRs), then hit noted 1975 World Series homer against them; after playing, noted for revelations of heavy drug use. | | | | | | | | | |
| **17. White Sox: # Ken Plesha, c, Notre Dame** | **McCook, Ill.** | **R-R** | **5-11** | **185** | **19** | **$20,000** | **1965** | **1968** | **Class A (4)** |
| Sox could have had Johnny Bench, but went instead for local catching prospect who hit .186 with three homers and never rose above Class A in four seasons. | | | | | | | | | |
| **18. Phillies: Mike Adamson, rhp, Point Loma HS** | **San Diego** | **R-R** | **6-2** | **175** | **17** | **Unsigned** | **1967** | **1971** | **Majors (3)** |
| Phils never came close to matching prep star's reported $100,000 price tag; went to USC and resurfaced as No. 1 pick in secondary phase in '67, debuted in majors. | | | | | | | | | |
| **19. Yankees: Bill Burbach, rhp, Wahlert HS** | **Dickeyville, Wis.** | **R-R** | **6-4** | **205** | **17** | **$35,000** | **1965** | **1972** | **Majors (3)** |
| Flashed promise for Yankees as 1969 rookie, but career unraveled a year later with severe case of flu; he lost his control and never won another game . | | | | | | | | | |
| **20. Cardinals: # Joe DiFabio, rhp, Delta State (Miss.)** | **Cranford, N.J.** | **R-R** | **5-11** | **195** | **21** | **$16,000** | **1965** | **1971** | **Class AAA (3)** |
| Defending World Series champs were reluctant to spend, settled for low-ceiling college arm who went 7-0, 0.95 as junior, 45-34, 3.28 in seven seasons in minors. | | | | | | | | | |

*# Deceased.*

Hall of Famer Reggie Jackson, the A's were in the midst of assembling a list of prospects that would soon be the envy of the game.

For all practical purposes, they were assembling a juggernaut, and it would all culminate in consecutive World Series titles from 1972-74.

### MONDAY GAINS NOTORIETY

As the first pick in the first draft, Monday's place in baseball history was set. Yet he has rarely dwelled on it.

"I don't feel like I've gotten a lot of notoriety from it," he said. "It's more like a flashback. Every June it comes up. The moment for me was that it was an opportunity to get with a club where I had a chance to get to the big leagues quicker than with some other organization."

Though the amount Monday received—$100,000 as a bonus, plus $4,000 under baseball's college-scholarship plan to complete his education at ASU—fell far short of what Reichardt received, Monday says he never regretted that his turn came up just after the rules were changed.

"I couldn't decide whether a draft system was good or bad," he said. "I had a million people giving me advice, but nobody had been through it before. What I did was I gave Charlie a tax-free dollar amount that I was looking for, and basically let him split it up any way he wanted.

"I don't think it would have made much difference in what I got, but I think possibly the draft may result in some of the players not fortunate enough to be drafted in the first round getting less to sign than they would have otherwise."

Bobby Winkles, Monday's coach at Arizona State, remembers that various people suggested to Monday that he should challenge the draft, since it restricted his rights to negotiate with any team. "But Rick wasn't that kind of guy," said Winkles, "and neither was I. He ended up with quite a bit

## AT A GLANCE

of the convoluted way players were drafted in 1965, Thornton was the Astros' 68th selection—and the latest pick that year to reach the majors. After signing for $500, he spent 10 years in the Astros system and surfaced for three games in 1973.

### Overlooked

**DON MONEY, SS, PIRATES.** The draft was hardly an exact science when it was launched in 1965, and 49 players who signed as non-drafted free agents that year reached the big leagues. Money, a Maryland high school product who signed with the Pirates, was the best of the bunch, though he was dealt to Philadelphia while in the minor leagues. The Phillies signed a shortstop of their own in 1965, **LARRY BOWA**, prompting the move of Money to third base. Both players enjoyed 16-year major league careers. Money hit .261 with 176 home runs; Bowa hit .260 with 15 homers.

### International Gem

**WILLIE MONTANEZ, OF, CARDINALS.** Montanez, a Puerto Rican signed for $10,000, had an eventful 14-year major league career. After playing five years in the Cardinals farm system, he was sent to Philadelphia on April 8, 1970, to complete the historic Oct. 7, 1969, trade after Cardinals outfielder Curt Flood refused to report to his new team. Montanez played for nine major league teams, hitting .275 with 139 homers and 820 RBIs.

### Minor League Take

**BERNIE CARBO, 3B, REDS.** No 1965 first-rounder had a standout minor league career, but Carbo hit .274 with 59 homers and 35 stolen bases in 550 games as a springboard to winning National League rookie of the year honors in 1970.

**CONTINUED ON PAGE 30**

## AT A GLANCE

CONTINUED FROM PAGE 29

### One Who Got Away

**TOM SEAVER, RHP, DODGERS (8TH ROUND).** The Dodgers had a future Hall of Famer sitting in their own backyard but made little effort to sign Seaver, a sophomore righthander at USC. He returned to school, remained eligible for the January 1966 draft as a 21-year-old and ended up signing with the Mets—though it wasn't without controversy as Seaver was initially drafted and signed by the Braves, only to have his contract voided.

### He Was Drafted?

**MIKE GARRETT, OF, PIRATES (41ST ROUND).** As the last player drafted by the Pirates, Garrett made a prudent decision to stay in school at USC, and went on to win the Heisman Trophy that fall as a running back for the Trojans. He later went on to play for the American Football League's Kansas City Chiefs, as well as the NFL's San Diego Chargers after the two leagues merged. Garrett's interest in baseball would never subside. The Dodgers drafted him in 1966 and again in 1970, when he was 26 and an established NFL running back.

### Did You Know . . .

**RICK MONDAY** was dropped by the Alaska Goldpanners, when that summer-league power was forced to pare its roster to the 16-player limit for the 1964 National Baseball Congress tournament in Wichita, Kan. With a team of top collegians, including future stars like Seaver and **GRAIG NETTLES**, the Goldpanners finished second in the event.

### They Said It

Mets executive **BING DEVINE** on **LES ROHR**, the second selection overall: "If I ever saw a young pitcher who looked like a 20-game winner, this is it."—*Rohr won two games in his major league career.*

of money."

Finley, an opponent of the draft, was adamant that he made Monday a fair offer. "The fact we signed him for $100,000," said Finley, "showed that Kansas City did not attempt to take advantage of the youngster in the draft."

Finley and Lilly closed the deal during a two-hour conference at Monday's home. "It was more conversation than negotiation," Finley added. "We had a meeting of minds from the start."

Monday was quick to credit Winkles and John McNamara, who both became major league managers, for enabling him to adjust to the pressures inherent with being a top draft pick.

Lilly, the scout who followed Monday throughout his sophomore season at ASU, had no hesitation in calling Monday a superior prospect to Reichardt.

"Every time I see Rick, he impresses me that much more," Lilly said at the time of the draft. "He's the best prospect I've seen in all my years of scouting. I firmly feel that he is a far better prospect now than Reichardt. He appears to have a great deal more talent."

Monday, who came close to accepting a $20,000 offer from the Los Angeles Dodgers out of high school, truly emerged as a top prospect during his sophomore year at ASU.

"He had an outstanding year for us," Winkles said. "He could run, play center field, he had a good arm and he hit with some power. It was kind of obvious from the number of scouts around that he was going to be the No. 1 pick."

For the most part, Monday handled the pressures inherent in being a top draft pick in stride.

"Being a No. 1 pick places a lot of attention and a lot of pressure on an individual," he said. "There was no pressure for me, really. I was fortunate that I got with people immediately who knew what they were doing."

Monday started his pro career at Lewiston, Idaho, of the short-season Class A Northwest League, hitting .271 with 13 homers. He broke in with Kansas City on Sept. 3, 1966 after spending most of that season at Double-A Birmingham.

Once he reached Kansas City, however, Monday said fans had unfair expectations. "A lot of people thought that my being No. 1 in the draft—especially with all the publicity I got—that I would be hitting home runs all over the place," he said. "When I didn't do it, they were down on me. But I was never a home run hitter. Yet in their mind, the No. 1 player, if he's a hitter, should be a home run hitter.

"In college, I never hit many, either. What they signed me for were the other things I do with the bat, plus my running, throwing and defense."

In his 19-year major league career, Monday hit .264 with 241 home runs. He played his first six seasons with the A's, his next five with the Chicago Cubs and finished his career in 1984 with the Dodgers.

### EAGER ANTICIPATION

Baseball's first draft was held over a two-day period at New York's Commodore Hotel. Some 200 front-office officials and scouts from 20 organizations gathered, along with commissioner Ford Frick and his staff. There was also a sizeable delegation of minor league officials, media and photographers.

### How They Should Have Done It

Based on the career WAR (Wins Above Replacement, as calculated by Baseball-Reference.com) numbers achieved by all the players eligible for the 1965 draft, here's how the first round should have unfolded. Numbers in parentheses indicate the round when the player was actually drafted

| | Player, Pos. | Actual Draft | WAR | Bonus |
|---|---|---|---|---|
| 1. | Nolan Ryan, rhp | Mets (10) | 81.8 | $12,000 |
| 2. | Johnny Bench, c | Reds (2) | 75.2 | $6,000 |
| 3. | Graig Nettles, 3b | Twins (4) | 68.0 | $15,000 |
| 4. | Sal Bando, 3b | Athletics (6) | 61.6 | $25,000 |
| 5. | Gene Tenace, ss | Athletics (11) | 46.8 | $1,500 |
| 6. | Amos Otis, of | Red Sox (5) | 42.6 | $8,000 |
| 7. | Don Money, ss | Pirates (NDFA) | 36.3 | None |
| 8. | Rick Monday, of | Athletics (1) | 33.2 | $100,000 |
| 9. | Bob Watson, of | Astros (NDFA) | 28.2 | $3,200 |
| 10. | Hal McRae, ss | Reds (6) | 27.9 | $15,000 |
| 11. | Ken Holtzman, lhp | Cubs (4) | 27.6 | $40,000 |
| 12. | Ron Reed, rhp | Braves (NDFA) | 25.5 | None |
| 13. | Larry Hisle, of | Phillies (2) | 24.9 | $50,000 |
| 14. | Freddie Patek, ss | Pirates (12) | 24.1 | $1,000 |
| 15. | Steve Renko, rhp | Mets (16) | 24.0 | $10,000 |
| 16. | Joe Coleman, rhp | Senators (1) | 23.7 | $65,000 |
| 17. | Stan Bahnsen, rhp | Yankees (4) | 22.9 | $27,000 |
| 18. | Larry Bowa, ss | Phillies (NDFA) | 22.6 | $2,000 |
| 19. | Marty Pattin, rhp | Angels (7) | 20.4 | $17,200 |
| 20. | Jim Bibby, rhp | Mets (NDFA) | 19.5 | None |

| | Top 3 Unsigned Players | | | Year Signed |
|---|---|---|---|---|
| 1. | Tom Seaver, rhp | Dodgers (8) | 111.0 | 1966 |
| 2. | Darrell Evans, 3b | Cubs (10) | 58.5 | 1967 |
| 3. | Andy Messersmith, rhp | Tigers (3) | 40.2 | 1966 |

Predictably, pre-draft speculation centered around who would be the top pick and how the process itself would unfold.

Provisions of the new Rule IV draft specified that major league teams would select their own pick in the first round, then draft on behalf of their minor league affiliates in succeeding rounds. They would also select in reverse order of the previous year's finish through the first three rounds—even though picks in the second and third rounds technically belonged to their Triple-A club. The picks in rounds four through seven were those of their Double-A club, made in reverse order of the record for Double-A teams in 1964.

Beginning with the eighth round, the order of selection changed radically, depending on the number of player-development contracts with Class A clubs that each organization had, and the records of those clubs in the preceding season. A pick was made for every Class A club in each round—making for a total of 60 selections—and it didn't matter whether a big-league team fielded five A-level farm clubs, like the Philadelphia Phillies and Minnesota Twins, or as few as two, as in the case of five clubs. The Phillies, drafting on behalf of their Bakersfield club in the California League, had the initial pick in each round.

The Twins took advantage of that inequality by making five selections in the eighth round and in each succeeding round before the St. Louis Cardinals made even one in the same round. The rule caused plenty of backlash from clubs getting the short end of the stick, and was changed effective with the 1966 draft to equalize the number of selections among clubs in the Class A phase.

The consensus among clubs was that Monday and Montana high school lefthander Les Rohr were the best available talents, and they went 1-2—Monday to Kansas City, Rohr to the New York Mets. Both players were 19, though Monday already had two years of college under his belt.

Beyond Monday and Rohr, clubs took disparate views of the top prospects. Most teams brought follow lists to New York of 300-350 players, and many still had upward of 50 names on their boards when the process ended.

Houston ended up making 72 selections in all, followed by Baltimore with 68. Boston dropped out after selecting just 20 players.

In contrast to Kansas City, which drafted seven future major leaguers with its first 10 picks, Pittsburgh was shut out through 17 rounds—even as it claimed to have landed three of the top seven players on its pre-draft board. But the Pirates made significant headway late in the action by landing several future big leaguers, including righthanders Bob Moose and Gene Garber with their 18th and 20th picks, and shortstop Freddie Patek with their 22nd. The side-arming Garber would go on to pitch in 931 games, fifth-most among pitchers at the time he retired after the 1988 season.

### UNFULFILLED PROMISE RUNS RAMPANT

Of the 20 players drafted in the first round, 13 would go on to reach the major leagues. Yet only Monday and Massachusetts high school righthander Joe Coleman, picked third overall by the Washington Senators, were bona fide first-round selections—at least as measured by WAR (Wins Above Replacement). Several other factors showed what a crapshoot the first draft was. Future Hall of Fame talents like Tom Seaver (Dodgers, 193rd overall) and Nolan Ryan (Mets, 295th overall) weren't even among the first 150 players drafted. Johnny Bench lasted until the second round.

Moreover, 49 domestic players signed as non-drafted free agents in 1965 and went on to play in the big leagues. Five of those players, led by shortstop Don Money, cracked the list of the 20 best players signed in 1965.

Rohr, a promising 6-foot-5 lefthander, showed every indication of justifying his selection after the Mets tabbed him with the second pick overall.

## Fastest To The Majors

| Player, Pos. | Drafted (Round) | Debut |
|---|---|---|
| 1. Ken Holtzman, lhp | Cubs (4) | Sept. 4, 1965 |
| 2. * Joe Coleman, rhp | Senators (1) | Sept. 28, 1965 |
| 3. Clyde Wright, lhp | Angels (6) | June 15, 1966 |
| 4. Ron Keller, rhp | Twins (8) | July 9, 1966 |
| 5. Rick Monday, of | Athletics (1) | Sept. 3, 1966 |
| * Charlie Vaughan, lhp | Braves (4) | Sept. 3, 1966 |
| Sal Bando, 3b | Athletics (6) | Sept. 3, 1966 |

**LAST PLAYER TO RETIRE:** Nolan Ryan, rhp (Sept. 22, 1993)

** High school selection.*

## DRAFT SPOTLIGHT: NOLAN RYAN

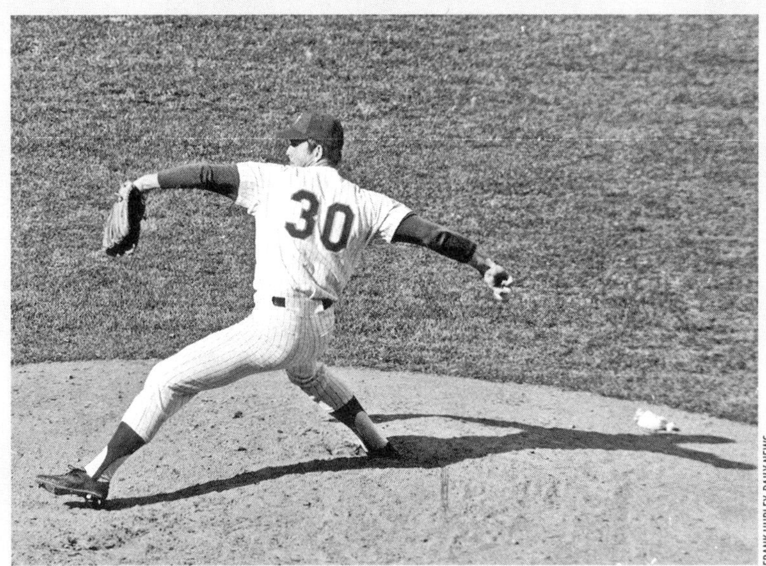


FRANK HURLEY, DAILY NEWS

**Dogged scouting allowed the Mets to grab Nolan Ryan after other teams lost interest in his senior season**

Over his 27-year major league career, Nolan Ryan was the greatest strikeout artist and most unhittable pitcher the game has ever known. His 5,714 strikeouts and nine-inning average of 6.6 hits allowed are records that may never be broken.

So how did Ryan, who had unmistakable talent in high school, go largely unrecognized in the 1965 draft, lasting until the 295th pick overall?

"It's very easy to explain," said Red Murff, the Texas-based scout who signed Ryan for the Mets. "It's the system we have. We know the kids in our territory, but the national crosschecker has the last say. A kid has to be good on the right day to get drafted high, and Nolan had the worst day of his life the day Bing Devine was in to see him pitch."

Murff blamed Ryan's poor showing that day in the spring of his senior year at Alvin (Texas) High on an overzealous high school coach.

"Nolan had been wild in his last start," recalled Murff, "and his coach made him pay the price. The day before Devine came in to see him, he had him throw 30 minutes of hard batting practice. Then he made him run until he puked. He pitched him the next day. Understandably, he looked bad. Nolan had the best arm I'd ever seen, but because of that one game, I couldn't sell him to our organization. Beyond that, it's always been a mystery to me why other organizations never saw in him what I saw."

Murff began tracking Ryan as a sophomore in high school, then really began to take note a year later. "I swear he threw over 100 mph as a junior," Murff said. "There were no radar guns in those days, but he had the best arm I'd ever seen—not just in high school, in my life. And I'd seen (Bob) Feller and (Sandy) Koufax."

Murff or a Mets bird-dog scout watched every game Ryan threw as a senior. A blister on his middle finger—from throwing a complete game almost immediately after reporting from basketball—impaired Ryan's performance early in the season. He lost three times and scouts estimated that his velocity had dipped into the 80s. Some scouts lost interest. Murff never backed off. He knew a good arm when he saw one, and was one of the few scouts who saw Ryan regain his fastball just before the draft. Ryan pitched in 27 of Alvin's 32 games, starting 20 times. He compiled a 19-3 record and struck out 211. Of Murff, Ryan once said: "He seemed to see something in me no one else did."

The Mets had already drafted 11 players when Murff finally convinced the team to select Ryan. Almost immediately, Ryan proved to be something special. At Class A Greenville, Ryan pitched a one-hitter while striking out a South Atlantic League-record 21 batters, highlighting a streak of 25 consecutive scoreless innings to start the 1966 season. "I remember Devine called me right after that," Murff said. "He was ecstatic. He said, 'That Ryan has got to have the best arm I've ever seen.' I kept telling him that the year before."

Ryan finished his first full season by striking out 313 batters in 205 innings, including six in a three-inning, big league stint with the Mets in September. He would go on to strike out 300 hitters in a season six times, including 383 in 1973 after the Mets traded him to the Angels, and 301 in 1989 at age 42. Eleven times he led his league in strikeouts.

Said Murff: "He was able to keep going because he never had arm problems. He's always had the perfect delivery. It starts perfect; it ends perfect. I've still never seen an arm that's close to his."

**WORTH NOTING**

BOSTON RED SOX

**BILLY CONIGLIARO** (Red Sox, 5th overall) was the first drafted player to have an agent. Of his $62,500 bonus, $12,500 was earmarked for his agent.

In addition to the regular June draft, a special draft was held in August for those American Legion players who were not yet 17 as of Jan. 1, 1965, but would be 17 later in the year and had participated in Legion competition that summer. Only 12 players were selected. **ROBERT YODICE**, 16, a catcher from Brooklyn, N.Y., was picked first overall by the Mets and promptly signed for $17,000. He later tore his rotator cuff in a home-plate collision, and never advanced beyond Class A in the Mets system. The only player selected in the short-lived Legion draft to ever reach the big leagues was catcher **EARL WILLIAMS**, selected by the Milwaukee Braves. He went on to slug 138 homers in an eight-year career. A proposal was submitted to major league general managers that October that the Legion draft be abolished and incorporated with the regular June draft. It was rejected, but a year later, when only eight players were selected, the Legion draft was phased out.

Including shortstop **EDDIE LEON** (Twins) and righthander **MIKE ADAMSON** (Phillies), first-rounders who went unsigned, 28 players taken in the first five rounds of the 1965 draft did not agree to terms with the teams that drafted them. That was one short of the record of 29, set in 1979. One of the players who went unsigned was Oklahoma high school lefthander **BILL DOBBS**, a fifth-round pick of

He kicked off his career in style in Double-A, and stymied the Dodgers twice in three starts after reaching the big leagues in short order in September 1967.

But the English-born Rohr, who went 23-0 with a 0.64 ERA as a senior at a Montana high school, was never quite the same after being forced to take the mound for the Mets in an April 15, 1968, game against Houston. He worked the final three innings of a 1-0, 24-inning loss, after pitching batting practice earlier in the day. Rohr's arm swelled up almost immediately and it was later determined he had torn a tendon in his elbow. He made two more abbreviated pitching appearances for the Mets, sandwiched around an extended stay on the disabled list, but he was done after just 24 innings.

By all accounts, a healthy Rohr should have been a centerpiece on a young Mets pitching staff that played a pivotal role in leading the team to an unexpected triumph in the 1969 World Series.

While Rohr would win only two big league games, the Mets gained a measure of redemption with the selection nine rounds later of Ryan, the game's strikeout king with a career total of 5,714.

Joe Coleman

Two of the next three picks after Rohr were Boston high school products, both with intriguing backgrounds.

Coleman's father won 52 major league games from 1942-55, and the younger Coleman, 18, would be in the big leagues himself two months after being drafted. In his two 1965 starts for the Senators, Coleman posted a pair of complete-game victories after compiling a 2-10 record in the minors prior to his callup. He also went 7-19 in Double-A a year later after being returned to the minors for more seasoning.

Boston, with the fifth pick, went for outfielder Billy Conigliaro, brother of budding Red Sox star Tony Conigliaro. Red Sox officials expressed great elation when Billy was still available and wanted the brothers to play in the same outfield.

The story began like a fairy tale, for both brothers. Tony Conigliaro was on his way to winning the 1965 American League home run title, at 20 the youngest player ever to do so. The day Billy was drafted, he was wearing a cap and gown during graduation ceremonies at Swampscott High. Tony, on hand for the occasion, learned that Boston had made Billy the fifth overall pick. Tony interrupted the ceremony to announce the news to the crowd, which gave Billy an ovation.

"I didn't know it was the Red Sox who drafted me until Tony made the announcement from the platform," Billy said. "I was hoping it would be the Sox, but I thought some other major league club would beat them to the punch."

The Red Sox signed Billy two days later for a bonus of $60,000—nearly three times the $22,500 bonus they gave Tony three years earlier.

## Top 25 Bonuses

| | Player, Pos. | Drafted (Round) | Order | Bonus |
|---|---|---|---|---|
| 1. | **Rick Monday, of** | **Athletics (1)** | **1** | **$100,000** |
| 2. | ***Alan Foster, rhp** | **Dodgers (2)** | **28** | **$96,000** |
| 3. | ***Joe Coleman, rhp** | **Senators (1)** | **3** | **$65,000** |
| 4. | ***Billy Conigliaro, of** | **Red Sox (1)** | **5** | **$62,500** |
| 5. | ***Les Rohr, lhp** | **Mets (1)** | **2** | **$50,000** |
| | ***Larry Hisle, of** | **Phillies (2)** | **38** | **$50,000** |
| 7. | *Alex Barrett, ss | Astros (1) | 4 | $40,000 |
| | ***Rick James, rhp** | **Cubs (1)** | **6** | **$40,000** |
| | *John Wyatt, ss | Dodgers (1) | 8 | $40,000 |
| | **Al Gallagher, 3b** | **Giants (1)** | **14** | **$40,000** |
| | *Ken Fila, lhp | Giants (3) | 54 | $40,000 |
| | **Ken Holtzman, lhp** | **Cubs (4)** | **66** | **$40,000** |
| | **Terry Harmon, ss** | **Phillies (5)** | **98** | **$40,000** |
| 14. | ***Bill Burbach, rhp** | **Yankees (1)** | **19** | **$35,000** |
| 15. | ***Gene Lamont, c** | **Tigers (1)** | **13** | **$33,000** |
| 16. | ***Jim Spencer, 1b** | **Angels (1)** | **11** | **$32,500** |
| 17. | *Scott McDonald, rhp | Orioles (1) | 15 | $30,000 |
| | ***Bernie Carbo, 3b** | **Reds (1)** | **16** | **$30,000** |
| | **Keith Lampard, of** | **Astros (2)** | **24** | **$30,000** |
| | *Roger Hayward, rhp | Pirates (2) | 30 | $30,000 |
| | Don Johnson, c | Braves (2) | 32 | $30,000 |
| 22. | ***Ray Fosse, c** | **Indians (1)** | **7** | **$28,000** |
| 23. | **Stan Bahnsen, rhp** | **Yankees (4)** | **79** | **$27,000** |
| 24. | *Ken Poulsen, 3b | Red Sox (3) | 45 | $26,000 |
| | **Rich Robertson, rhp** | **Giants (5)** | **94** | **$26,000** |

*Major leaguers in bold. *High school selection.*

While the Conigliaro brothers teamed up on occasion from 1969-71, it was bittersweet because Tony was never the same after being struck in the face by a pitched ball in 1967. When Tony was unexpectedly traded to the California Angels, Billy came to his brother's defense and was highly critical of the Red Sox for the manner in which they dispatched his brother. Billy's career fizzled a short time later.

Two first-round picks from 1965 went unsigned.

Minnesota, selecting ninth, failed to come to terms with University of Arizona shortstop Eddie Leon. The Twins, who developed a history of not signing their top picks, reportedly offered Leon a signing bonus of just $6,500, and it would be two more years before Leon, who became a three-time All-American at Arizona, would sign a contract. The Twins also didn't sign their second- and third-round picks in 1965.

Philadelphia couldn't reach agreement with its top pick, righthander Mike Adamson, a San Diego high school product who was just 6-6 as a senior. Adamson, who asked for a reported $100,000, enrolled at Southern California rather than sign with the Phillies. He would be drafted with the first overall pick in the secondary phase of the June 1967 draft, and become the first player from the draft era to move directly to the big leagues.

### BENCH, RYAN EXCEL

While Seaver, a sophomore righthander from USC, went unsigned in the 1965 draft and resurfaced in the January 1966 draft, the Hall of Fame careers of both Bench and Ryan took off almost immediately—even as Bench signed with the Cincinnati Reds for just $6,000 and Ryan for $12,000 with the Mets.

## Largest Bonuses By Round

| | Player, Pos. | Club | Bonus |
|---|---|---|---|
| 1. | **Rick Monday, of** | **Athletics** | **$100,000** |
| 2. | ***Alan Foster, rhp** | **Dodgers** | **$96,000** |
| 3. | *Ken Fila, lhp | Giants | $40,000 |
| 4. | **Ken Holtzman, lhp** | **Cubs** | **$40,000** |
| 5. | **Terry Harmon, ss** | **Phillies** | **$40,000** |
| 6. | **Sal Bando, 3b** | **Athletics** | **$25,000** |
| 7. | **Marty Pattin, rhp** | **Angels** | **$17,200** |
| 8. | *Roger Harrington, rhp | Mets | $13,500 |
| 9. | Gary Girouard, rhp | Yankees | $10,000 |
| | *Larry Hall, of | Astros | $10,000 |
| 10. | ***George Lauzerique, rhp** | **Athletics** | **$13,000** |

*Major leaguers in bold. *High school selection.*

Bench, the first player from the draft era to reach the Hall of Fame, was selected by the Reds with the 36th pick overall—the 16th selection in the second round.

"I was totally surprised Cincinnati drafted me," Bench said, "because I hadn't talked to any of their scouts and I hadn't expected anyone to pick me that high."

He did not worry about the small bonus he received from the Reds. He was just determined to get on with his career.

"I know they have plans for me," he said. "It doesn't scare me. I'm looking forward to it. It doesn't matter how much talking is done. It's all up to me. I have to do it myself."

As a standout high school and American Legion player in Binger, Okla., where he was valedictorian of his high school class of 22, Bench excelled in several sports and at several positions, including pitcher. He was 16-0 on the mound in his high school career before suffering his first defeat as a senior, which came on the heels of a bus accident that killed two of his teammates.

It was mostly at the urging of his father Ted, who believed that catching provided the quickest path to the major leagues, that Bench went behind the plate as a pro. A year after signing, he became such a hit in fewer than 100 games for Peninsula of the Class A Carolina League, that a parade escorted him out of town when he was promoted to Triple-A Buffalo. He broke his thumb in his first game there, but returned a year later and earned minor league player of the year honors for his power-hitting exploits and stellar work behind the plate.

By September 1967, Bench was in the big leagues to stay. He was the National League rookie of the year in 1968, and earned the first of two NL MVP awards two years later.

"I never thought everything would come so fast," Bench said. "But my father said catching was the quickest way to the big leagues, because that's what they needed. And I've been planning on being in the majors since the first grade."

Bench spent his entire 17-year career in Cincinnati, establishing standards for defensive excellence while hitting 389 lifetime home runs. He was elected to the Hall of Fame in 1989.

Like Bench, the hard-throwing Ryan had unmistakable talent in high school that largely went unrecognized in the 1965 draft, and resulted

BOB LYNN

**Oklahoma prep standout Johnny Bench lasted until the second round, but became the first drafted player to reach the Hall of Fame**

in his lasting until the 295th pick overall.

But Ryan finished his first full season of professional baseball in 1966 by striking out 313 batters in 205 innings, including six in a three-inning big-league stint in September. Over the next 26 years, he became the greatest strikeout pitcher in major league history. Ryan would go on to strike out 300 hitters in a season on six occasions, including 383 in 1973 in the second season after the Mets traded him to the Angels. Eleven times he led his league in strikeouts.

### CURIOUS DODGERS DRAFT

The Dodgers were one of the more vocal opponents of the draft, mainly because it would put them at a competitive disadvantage. As one of the wealthier teams in the game, the Dodgers would no longer be able to simply outbid other clubs for the services of the best amateur talent.

But they still used their financial muscle in the first draft when they took high school righthander Alan Foster, one of the elite prospects in the draft and a player in their own backyard. Foster's dad, a wealthy Beverly Hills doctor, told numerous scouts before the draft that his son wouldn't sign because he was going to USC.

"Some clubs figured the father might want to scare off other clubs so that one of the Los Angeles clubs would get him," a rival scouting director said.

Sure enough, the Dodgers drafted Foster in the second round and ended up signing him for a bonus of $96,000—second only to the bonus the A's gave Monday as the top pick.

Foster reached the big leagues in 1967 and showed flashes of brilliance in a 10-year career, but never quite lived up to expectations.

The Dodgers made a curious choice with their first selection (eighth overall) by taking John

### WORTH NOTING

the White Sox. He went on to an All-American career at Oklahoma State and through his years in college was drafted a record-tying seven times, but never signed a professional contract. Two other players from the 1965 draft, first baseman **REID BRADEN** (Red Sox, 10th round) and outfielder **HERB HOFVENDAHL** (Mets, 14th round) would also be drafted seven times, but both subsequently signed.

■ The Braves drafted Florida high school shortstop **WAYNE GARRETT** in the sixth round. He joined two older brothers, Adrian and James, who were already in the Braves system. Adrian and Wayne would each go on to play in the big leagues.

■ Of 838 players that were drafted in 1965, 140 would go on to play in the big leagues, representing a success rate of 16.7 percent. Only the 1976 (18.2 percent) and 1986 (17.3 percent) drafts would send a higher proportion of draft picks to the majors before the draft was consolidated into one phase effective with the 1987 draft.

■ For all the attention that **RICK MONDAY** received for being the draft's ultimate No. 1 pick, he actually gained more notoriety for an incident that occurred at Dodger Stadium in 1976, while a member of the Cubs. Two men scrambled on to the field during a Dodgers-Cubs encounter April 25 and began dousing an American flag with lighter fluid. While they fumbled for matches, Monday swooped in and snatched away the flag. He was hailed far and wide as an American hero. "It was a spur-of-the-moment thing," Monday said. "I'm proud to have done what I did, but if anyone else had been in my position, I'm sure they'd have done the same thing. I get kind of angry, actually, when people remember me just for the flag incident. I spent 19 years in the big leagues and made two all-star teams. I had a pretty good career."

## IN FOCUS: KEN HOLTZMAN

Illinois lefthander Ken Holtzman was the first drafted player to reach the major leagues. He debuted with the Chicago Cubs on Sept. 4, 1965.

For Holtzman to remain a big leaguer, however, it required some ingenuity on the part of the Cubs.

A draft of another kind—the military draft—was a foreboding presence at the time. Holtzman managed to sidestep that draft in 1966 and continue to take a regular turn in the Cubs rotation by remaining a student. He transferred to the Chicago branch of the University of Illinois, making him available to the Cubs for all home games, though only weekend games on the road. That arrangement prevailed until June.

While the tactic worked in 1966, with Holtzman going 11-16 as a major league rookie, military service finally caught up with him in 1967. He lost three months of the season, spoiling an otherwise perfect (9-0) campaign.

The military draft impacted numerous other 1965 draft picks. As in Holtzman's case, players had to remain in school (under 2-S student classification) to avoid being drafted, and possibly ending up in Vietnam.

Why did the Cubs go to such lengths to defer Holtzman's military commitment in 1966? Holtzman's potential. "Ken is a better pitcher right now than Sandy Koufax at the same stage," said then-manager Leo Durocher.

Wyatt, a shortstop from nearby Bakersfield. Wyatt was a top college recruit as a quarterback and may have been the best all-around athlete taken in the first round. But few Dodgers scouts were aware of him, and the decision to draft Wyatt was made at the behest of Dodgers general manager Al Campanis, who had scouted Wyatt himself and taken a liking to him.

Wyatt failed to climb above Class A in six seasons in the Dodgers system, and even spent his final season as a pitcher in hopes of salvaging the $40,000 investment the Dodgers made in him.

Wyatt ended up making headlines for all the wrong reasons later in life when he was arrested in 1984 for being the ringleader of a major drug smuggling ring, and served time in jail on charges of tax evasion and conspiracy to defraud the IRS. At the time of his arrest, Wyatt owned a 2,600-acre ranch, a house valued at $8 million and a chain of fitness studios in central California.

With the third of their three picks in the eighth round of the 1965 draft, the Dodgers selected Seaver, then a lightly scouted, and relatively unknown 20-year-old righthander from USC. When Seaver, who had gone 10-2 in his only season for the Trojans, demanded a $70,000 bonus to pass on his junior year at USC, the Dodgers balked and subsequently lost his rights.

As a 21-year-old, Seaver was eligible for the draft's new secondary phase the following January, and his selection by the Atlanta Braves set off a chain of events that became one of the most fascinating chapters in draft history. The upshot of it all, to the Dodgers' regret, was that Seaver ended up signing with the Mets and went on to a Hall of Fame career.

### COLLEGES PLAY SECONDARY ROLE

College World Series champion Arizona State (54-8) became the first NCAA team to win 50 games in a season in 1965, and the Sun Devils, led by Monday, had more draft selections (eight) than any other college. But the overall impact of college baseball was marginal.

Besides Monday, just four other collegians were taken in the first round. Leon, the second player selected, didn't sign, and catcher Ken Plesha (White Sox), who was academically ineligible to play that spring at Notre Dame as a 19-year-old sophomore, and Delta State (Miss.) righthander Joe DiFabio were somewhat surprise selections. Plesha ($20,000) and DiFabio ($16,000) signed for the smallest bonuses given to first-rounders.

Overall, just 43 percent of the players selected were from the college ranks, and some of the top-rated college talent went in later rounds because of questions surrounding their signability.

## Highest Unsigned Picks

**JUNE / REGULAR PHASE ONLY**

| Player, Pos., Team (Round) | College | Re-Drafted |
|---|---|---|
| Eddie Leon, ss, Twins (1) | * Arizona | Cubs '66 (S/1) |
| Mike Adamson, rhp, Phillies (1) | USC | Orioles '67 (S/1) |
| Randy Kohn, c, Mets (2) | Georgia | Dodgers '67 (S/4) |
| Stan Bell, rhp, Senators (2) | Manatee (Fla.) CC | Tigers '66 (Jan.-S/1) |
| John Hetrick, of, Red Sox (2) | Maryland | Tigers '67 (S/1) |
| Del Unser, of, Twins (2) | * Mississippi State | Pirates '66 (Jan.-S/4) |
| Sandy Vance, rhp, Angels (2) | Stanford | White Sox '67 (S/2) |
| Doug Carson, ss, Tigers (2) | Santa Clara | Pirates '67 (S/3) |
| Glen Smith, of, Giants (2) | * Arizona State | Twins '66 (Jan.-S/5) |
| Danny Thompson, ss, Yankees (2) | Oklahoma State | Reds '67 (S/4) |

**TOTAL UNSIGNED PICKS:** Top 5 Rounds (25), Top 10 Rounds (62)

**Returned to same school*

Ohio State sophomore righthander Steve Arlin merited first-round consideration after a dominating performance in the College World Series, while also going 13-2 overall and leading the nation 165 strikeouts in 141 innings. In one of the greatest games ever pitched in Omaha, Arlin went all 15 innings to beat Washington State, 1-0, while allowing three hits and striking out 20.

Arlin, though, was a straight-A student in dentistry at Ohio State, and that caused teams to pass on him in the early rounds. The Detroit Tigers finally took him in the 12th round.

"Even a bonus of $60,000-$80,000 might not entice him to sign," reasoned one scouting executive, "and so a club couldn't sacrifice a top draft pick to take him."

Arlin was equally dominating as a junior in 1966 in leading Ohio State to a national title, and ended up signing with the Phillies for a bonus of $77,500.

Columbia's All-America shortstop Archie Roberts was also a consensus first-round talent, but he slipped because he had already signed to play with the NFL's Cleveland Browns and planned to attend medical school. The Cardinals took him in the 22nd round.

Though he lasted until the fourth round, Illinois All-America lefthander Ken Holtzman was paid like a first-rounder by signing with the Cubs for $40,000. He became the first drafted player to reach the major leagues. After a dominating performance in the lower minors to begin his career, he was in the big leagues to stay by September.

Holtzman won 74 games in six years in Chicago, before being traded to Oakland in 1971—in a straight-up swap for Monday, no less. Obviously, the deal had major draft implications as it involved the first player drafted and the first drafted player to reach the major leagues.

## One Team's Draft: Kansas City Athletics

| Pick. Player, Pos. | Bonus | Pick. Player, Pos. | Bonus | Pick. Player, Pos. | Bonus |
|---|---|---|---|---|---|
| **1. Rick Monday, of** | **$100,000** | 5. * Richard Suggs, ss | $8,000 | 9. Don Lando, of | Did not sign |
| **2. Joe Keough, 1b** | **$24,000** | **6. Sal Bando, 3b** | **$25,000** | **10. * George Lauzerique, rhp** | **$13,000** |
| 3. * Bob Stinson, c | Did not sign | 7. Scott Reid, of | Did not sign | Other* Gene Tenace (20), ss | $1,500 |
| **4. * Pete Koegel, of/1b** | **$25,000** | 8. * Frank Riggins, of | Did not sign | | |

*Major leaguers in bold. *High school selection.*

# 1965 Draft List

**Did not sign. Major leaguers in bold, with first and last years noted. Order of selection indicated in parentheses. For the first five rounds of the June Regular Phase and the first round of all other phases, the peak level of each player is noted. @ Order of selection determined by 1964 won-loss records of Class A minor-league affiliates.*

## BALTIMORE ORIOLES

**June—Regular Phase**

**Major League and Class AAA Selections (15)**

1. Scott McDonald, rhp-1b, Marquette HS, Yakima, Wash.—(AA)
2. Dick Horton, c, Dartmouth University.—(High A)
3. **Frank Tepedino, 1b, Wingate HS, Brooklyn, N.Y.—(1967-71)**

**Class AA Selections (18)**

4. Kenny Purvis, of, Nelson County HS, Lovingston, Va.—(Rookie)
5. *James Taylor, 3b-of, Southern Methodist University.—DNP

DRAFT DROP *Returned to Southern Methodist; re-drafted by Mets, January 1966/secondary phase (1st round)*

6. **Bill Dillman, rhp, Wake Forest University.—(1967-70)**
7. *Frank Chambers, rhp, Mississippi State University.

**Class A Selections @**

**8th Round**

8. Don Roth, of, Spring Arbor (Mich.) College.
9. Dave Halford, ss, Plainfield HS, Hancock, Wis.
10. *Tom Weir, c, Brigham Young University.
11. *Tom Chiles, rhp, Texas A&M University.

**9th Round**

12. *Tom Lawton, rhp, University of Connecticut.
13. *Bob Schaefer, ss, University of Connecticut.

DRAFT DROP *Major league manager (1991, 2005)*

14. *Ronnie Paul, lhp, Texas Christian University.

**10th Round**

15. Quash Thompson, rhp, Jones HS, Orlando, Fla.
16. *Jimmy Carter, ss-3b, Trinity (Texas) University.
17. *Dick Hicks, rhp, Fair Park HS, Shreveport, La.
18. Will Beauchemin, rhp, Holy Spirit HS, Pt. Pleasant, N.J.

**11th Round**

19. *Dave Grangaard, 3b, Camelback HS, Phoenix.
20. Harry Brown, lhp, Baltimore City HS, Baltimore.
21. **Charlie Sands, c, Newport News (Va.) HS.—(1967-75)**

**12th Round**

22. John Rawls, rhp, East Carolina University.
23. ***Lowell Palmer, rhp, Norte Del Rio HS, Sacramento, Calif.—(1969-74)**
24. Brent Vines, rhp, Mound City (Ill.) HS.
25. *Jack McCall, ss, Clemson University.

**13th Round**

26. *Dennis Lamb, 3b, Brigham Young University.
27. *Ron Lanza, of, University of Maine.
28. *Frank Antone, rhp, Lawton HS, Fort Sill, Okla.

**14th Round**

29. Cliff Matthew, c, North Carolina A&T State University.
30. Dave Coleman, c, Northeastern University.
31. *Steve Garman, ss, Caldwell (Idaho) HS.

DRAFT DROP *Brother of Mike Garman, first-round draft pick, Red Sox (1967); major leaguer (1969-78)*

32. *Leroy McDonald, ss, Las Cruces (N.M.) HS.

**15th Round**

33. *Allie Prescott, p, Kingsbury HS, Memphis, Tenn.
34. Robert Jones, ss, Grambling University.
35. *Ray Frank, of, Southern University.

**16th Round**

36. *Mike Burns, of, Mississippi State University.
37. Dan DeVito, 1b, Stamford (Conn.) HS.
38. *Larry Linville, of, Bellingham (Wash.) HS.
39. Stanley Bowen, of-1b, Knox City HS, Novelity, Mo.

**17th Round**

40. Dennis Denning, c-3b, College of St. Thomas (Minn.).
41. *Henry Tenney, ss-of, Vista (Calif.) HS.
42. *Jim Brown, lhp, Englewood (Colo.) HS.

**18th Round**

43. Mike Hebert, lhp, Terrebonne HS, Thibodeaux, La.
44. *Leonard Sheflott, rhp, University of Vermont.
45. Charles Van Camp, 1b, Minot State (N.D.) College.
46. *Dale Ehler, c, University of Oregon.

**19th Round**

47. Bill Grimes, rhp, Northwest Classen HS, Oklahoma City, Okla.
48. *Calvin Fisk, rhp, University of New Hampshire.

DRAFT DROP *Brother of Carlton Fisk, major leaguer (1969-93)*

49. *Greg Riddoch, ss, Colorado State University.

DRAFT DROP *Major league manager (1990-92)*

50. *Jim Wendell, of, La Habra (Calif.) HS.

**20th Round**

51. *Percy Sensabaugh, rhp, Virginia Military Institute.
52. *Bob Malloy, rhp, Shenandoah (Va.) JC.
53. *Charles Drediger, rhp, Bordentown (N.J.) Military Academy.
54. John Stephens, of, Loyola (La.) University.

**21st Round**

55. Rich Thoms, lhp, Austin (Texas) College.
56. *Wayne Britton, of, East Carolina University.

DRAFT DROP *Scouting director, Red Sox (1993-2001)*

57. *Steve Lough, of, Patapsco HS, Baltimore.
58. *Glen Wallace, rhp, Butler HS, Florence, Ala.

**22nd Round**

59. *Steve Andragia, of, Notre Dame HS, Bridgeport, Conn.
60. Gary Carnegie, 3b-of, Connelly HS, Pittsburgh.
61. *Dale Dulaney, rhp, Chicago Teachers College.
62. *Gary Smith, rhp, Alpena (Mich.) CC.

**23rd Round**

63. *John Rockwell, rhp, Santa Ana (Calif.) HS.
64. *Paul Knight, lhp, Avon Lake HS, Lorain, Ohio.
65. *Michael Kenyon, lhp, Ithaca (N.Y.) College.
66. *Roger Hansen, lhp, Muskegon (Mich.) HS.

**24th Round**

67. *Ed Southard, of, University of Arizona.
68. Carl Cmejrek, 1b-of, University of Michigan.
69. *Tom Moeller, 2b, University of Denver.
70. *George Grzegerek, ss, St. Edward's (Texas) University.

**August—American Legion Phase (16)**

No selection.

## BOSTON RED SOX

**June—Regular Phase**

**Major League and Class AAA Selections (5)**

1. **Billy Conigliaro, of, Swampscott (Mass.) HS.—(1969-73)**

DRAFT DROP *Brother of Tony Conigliaro, major leaguer (1964-75)*

2. *John Hetrick, of, Hershey (Pa.) HS.—(AA)

DRAFT DROP *Attended Maryland; re-drafted by Tigers, June 1967/secondary phase (1st round)*

3. **Ken Poulsen, 3b, Birmingham HS, Van Nuys, Calif.—(1967)**

**Class AA Selections (15)**

4. Fred Marden, lhp, Brandeis (Mass.) University.—(High A)
5. **Amos Otis, ss, Williamson HS, Mobile, Ala.—(1967-84)**
6. Jim L. Thomas, lhp, Cal State Sacramento.
7. **Jim Hutto, 3b-rhp, Pensacola (Fla.) HS.—(1970-75)**

**Class A Selections @**

**8th Round**

8. Doug Shores, c, Northeast HS, Greensboro, N.C.
9. *Ron Shotts, 3b, Chaffey HS, Ontario, Calif.
10. Tony Ciarpelli, lhp, Genesee HS, Syracuse, N.Y.

**9th Round**

11. *Dennis Best, of, Gillespie (Ill.) HS.
12. *Manuel Washington, ss, Paragould (Ark.) HS.
13. *Michael Weber, rhp, Greenville HS, Pocahontas, Ill.

**10th Round**

14. Wayne Fuzzard, lhp, McCarthy HS, Fort Pierce, Fla.
15. Bill Farmer, rhp, Choctaw (Okla.) HS.
16. *Reid Braden, 1b, Cerritos (Calif.) JC.

**11th Round**

17. Brian Edgerly, of, Colgate University.
18. **Ray Jarvis, rhp, Hope HS, Providence, R.I.—(1969-70)**
19. John Iannelli, rhp, East Boston (Mass.) HS.

**12th Round**

20. William Barkley, ss, Sam Houston State University.

**August—American Legion Phase (6)**

1. *Mike McCall, ss, Greenville (S.C.) HS.—(High A)

## CALIFORNIA ANGELS

**June—Regular Phase**

**Major League and Class AAA Selections (11)**

1. **Jim Spencer, 1b, Andover HS, Glen Burnie, Md.—(1968-82)**

DRAFT DROP *Grandson of Ben Spencer, major leaguer (1913)*

2. ***Sandy Vance, rhp, Pasadena (Calif.) HS—(1970-71)**

DRAFT DROP *Attended Stanford; re-drafted by White Sox, June 1967/secondary phase (2nd round)*

3. ***Dick Baney, rhp, Anaheim (Calif.) HS.—(1969-74)**

DRAFT DROP *Returned to Anaheim (Calif.) HS; re-drafted by Red Sox, January 1966/secondary phase (1st round)*

**Class AA Selections (7)**

4. John Olerud, c, Washington State University.—(AAA)

DRAFT DROP *Father of John Olerud, major leaguer (1989-2005)*

5. **Joe Henderson, 3b-rhp, Edison HS, Fresno, Calif.—(1974-77)**

DRAFT DROP *Uncle of Dave Henderson, first-round draft pick, Mariners (1977); major leaguer (1981-94)*

6. **Clyde Wright, of-lhp, Carson-Newman (Tenn.) College.—(1966-75)**

DRAFT DROP *Father of Jaret Wright, first-round draft pick, Indians (1994); major leaguer (1997-2007)*

7. **Marty Pattin, rhp, Eastern Illinois University.—(1968-80)**

DRAFT DROP *Baseball coach, Kansas (1982-87)*

**Class A Selections @**

**8th Round**

8. Tom Soderstrom, ss, Lexington (Mass.) HS.
9. *Craig Schell, rhp, Monterey (Calif.) HS.

**9th Round**

10. *Bob Crosby, rhp, Monroe HS, Bronx, N.Y.
11. Gus Gregory, of, University of Illinois.

**10th Round**

12. Gary Wormelduff, rhp, Sunset HS, Hayward, Calif.
13. *Jack Glover, lhp, Banks HS, Birmingham, Ala.

**11th Round**

14. John Enos, ss, Millikan HS, Lakewood, Calif.
15. Sam Gafford, lhp, South HS, Bakersfield, Calif.

**12th Round**

16. **Jarvis Tatum, of, Edison HS, Fresno, Calif.—(1968-70)**
17. Bob Smithson, rhp, Everett (Wash.) CC.

**13th Round**

18. Terry Thompson, 3b-rhp, Newport Harbor HS, Newport Beach, Calif.
19. George Dugan, lhp, Murray State University.

**14th Round**

20. Richard Totten, 2b, Coachella HS, Thermal, Calif.
21. **Doug Griffin, 2b, El Monte HS, La Puente, Calif.—(1970-77)**

**August—American Legion Phase (12)**

No selection.

## CHICAGO CUBS

**June—Regular Phase**

**Major League and Class AAA Selections (6)**

1. **Rick James, rhp, Coffee HS, Florence, Ala.—(1967)**
2. **Ken Rudolph, c, Los Angeles CC.—(1969-77)**
3. Greg Werdick, ss, Crawford HS, San Diego.–(AA)

**Class AA Selections (1)**

4. **Ken Holtzman, lhp, University of Illinois.—(1965-79)**

DRAFT DROP *First drafted player to reach majors (Sept. 4, 1965)*

5. Ronald Webb, of, Hillcrest HS, Springfield, Mo.—(Low A)
6. *Ron Drake, c, Long Beach (Calif.) CC.
7. **Garry Jestadt, ss, Fremont HS, Sunnyvale, Calif.—(1969-72)**

**Class A Selections @**

**8th Round**

8. *Richard Johnson, rhp, Mount San Antonio (Calif.) JC.
9. **Joe Decker, rhp, Petaluma (Calif.) HS.—(1969-79)**
10. Duane Rossman, ss, Washington State University.

**9th Round**

11. ***Tom House, lhp, Nogales HS, La Puente, Calif.—(1971-78)**
12. David Amman, rhp, Cocoa Beach (Fla.) HS.

**10th Round**

13. ***Darrell Evans, 3b, Muir HS, Altadena, Calif.—(1969-89)**
14. *John Thomas, of, Morehouse HS, Bastrop, La.
15. Henry Knittel, rhp, Holy Cross College.

**11th Round**

16. **Johnny Hairston, c, Southern University.—(1969)**

DRAFT DROP *Son of Sam Hairston, major leaguer (1951) • Brother of Jerry Hairston Sr., major leaguer (1973-89) • Uncle of Jerry Hairston Jr., major leaguer (1998-2013) • Uncle of Scott Hairston, major leaguer (2004-14)*

17. Craig Glassco, rhp, Glendora (Calif.) HS.

**12th Round**

18. Bob Rossi, 2b-3b, Loyola (Md.) College.
19. John Burnett, 1b, Skyline HS, Oakland, Calif.
20. **Jim Williams, of, Harry Ells HS, Richmond, Calif.—(1969-70)**

**13th Round**

21. Joseph Doerr, 3b, West Liberty State (W.Va.) College.
22. *Robert Beran, of, Bishop Amat HS, Rosemead, Calif.

**14th Round**

23. *Lamar LaBauve, 1b, Southeastern Louisiana University.
24. Thomas Finnegan, ss, Washington (Pa.) College.
25. Larry Lobb, lhp, Bangor (Pa.) HS.

**15th Round**

26. *Steve Wright, rhp, Andrew Hill HS, San Jose, Calif.
27. Nathaniel Perkins, ss, Benedict (S.C.) College.

**16th Round**

28. John Hermanek, rhp, Bradley University.
29. (void) *John Bacot, of, Alabama A&M University.
30. Ronnie Renner, c, West Virginia University.

DRAFT DROP *Father of Mary Lou Retton, 1984 Olympic gold medalist*

**August—American Legion Phase (5)**

No selection.

## CHICAGO WHITE SOX

**June—Regular Phase**

**Major League and Class AAA Selections (17)**

1. Ken Plesha, c, University of Notre Dame.—(High A)
2. Fred Kovner, of, Old Dominion University.—(AA)
3. Mickey Abarbanel, lhp, Monmouth College.—(AAA)

**Class AA Selections (20)**

4. **Fred Rath, rhp, Baylor University.—(1968-69)**

DRAFT DROP *Father of Fred Rath, major leaguer (1998)*

5. *Bill Dobbs, lhp, Marshall HS, Oklahoma City, Okla.—DNP

DRAFT DROP *Attended Oklahoma State; re-drafted by Braves, June 1967/secondary phase (2nd round)*

6. Emmett Molisee, of, Western HS, Las Vegas, Nev.
7. *Allan Smith, lhp, Manual HS, Peoria, Ill.

**Class A Selections @**

**8th Round**

8. Ron Markowski, of-ss, Central Catholic HS, Pittsburgh.
9. Richard Newhart, ss, San Clemente HS, San Juan Capistrano, Calif.
10. **Ron Lolich, 3b-of, Central Catholic HS, Portland, Ore.—(1971-73)**

DRAFT DROP *Cousin of Mickey Lolich, major leaguer (1963-79)*

**9th Round**

11. John Sluka, 2b, Western Michigan University.
12. Robert Bladek, lhp, Rich East HS, Matteson, Ill.
13. Greg Howell, c, Austin Catholic HS, Detroit.

**10th Round**

14. *Richard Noffke, rhp, Boylan HS, Rockford, Ill.
15. ***John Montague, rhp, Newport HS, Newport News, Va.—(1973-80)**
16. *Richard Slicker, lhp, Edison HS, Tulsa, Okla.

**11th Round**
17. *Clifford Foster, 1b, Sexton HS, Lansing, Mich.
18. *Randy Carroll, 2b, Georgia Tech.
19. *Dave Barton, inf, Ithaca (N.Y.) College.

**12th Round**
20. *Ron Davini, c, Anaheim (Calif.) HS.
**21. Paul Edmondson, rhp, Cal State Northridge.—(1969)**
22. *Dewey Weaver, rhp, Pasco HS, Dade City, Fla.

**13th Round**
23. Tom Cottrell, of-3b, Cal State Northridge.
24. *Bob Hergenrader, lhp, University of Nebraska.
25. *Robert Karlblom, of, Augustana (Ill.) College.

**14th Round**
26. Lawrence Lembo, of-1b, Manhattan College.
27. *Elvatous Peters, of, Southern University.
28. *Jim Hogan, rhp, University of Redlands (Calif.).

**15th Round**
29. Robert Chandler, rhp-of, Wilson HS, Easton, Pa.
30. Jim Ackley, rhp, Hayward (Wis.) HS.
DRAFT DROP *Brother of Fritz Ackley, major leaguer (1963-64)*
**31. Danny Lazar, lhp, Indiana State University.—(1968-69)**

**16th Round**
32. *John Miklos, lhp, Valparaiso University.
33. *Pete Ciganovich, rhp, Bowen HS, Chicago.
34. Paul Lovrich, rhp, Eisenhower HS, Blue Island, Ill.

**17th Round**
35. *Joe Bloom, lhp, Notre Dame HS, North Hollywood, Calif.
36. Leland White, lhp, Hueneme HS, Oxnard, Calif.
37. *Michael White, c, Costa Mesa (Calif.) HS.

**18th Round**
38. *Robert Lawler, lhp, Manatee (Fla.) JC.
39. Tim McLain, rhp, Bremen HS, Chicago.
DRAFT DROP *Brother of Denny McLain, major leaguer (1963-72)*
40. *Joe Holladay, ss, Duncan (Okla.) HS.

**19th Round**
41. Ken Eby, 3b, Purdue University.

**August—American Legion Phase (18)**

No selection.

## CINCINNATI REDS

**June—Regular Phase**

**Major League and Class AAA Selections (16)**
**1. Bernie Carbo, 3b, Livonia HS, Garden City, Mich.—(1969-80)**
**2. Johnny Bench, c, Anadarko HS, Binger, Okla.—(1967-83)**
DRAFT DROP *First drafted player elected to Baseball Hall of Fame, 1989*
3. *John Olagues, rhp, Tulane University.—(AA)
DRAFT DROP *Returned to Tulane; re-drafted by Indians, June 1966/secondary phase (1st round)*

**Class AA Selections (17)**
4. Carl Richardson, ss, Taft HS, Cincinnati.—(AAA)
5. Louis Keller, c, Oconomowoc (Wis.) HS.–(High A)
**6. Hal McRae, ss, Florida A&M University.—(1968-87)**
DRAFT DROP *Father of Brian McRae, first-round draft pick, Royals (1985); major leaguer (1990-99) • Major league manager (1991-2002)*
7. Lester Fulleylove, lhp, Edgewood HS, Atco, N.J.

**Class A Selections @**

**8th Round**
**8. *John Morlan, of-rhp, West HS, Columbus, Ohio—(1973-74)**
9. Tom Murphy, ss, Lufkin (Texas) HS.

**9th Round**
10. Mike Tyler, c, El Camino HS, San Francisco.
11. *Jim Scheschuk, c, University of Texas.
12. *Arthur Boyd, rhp, Escambia HS, Pensacola, Fla.

**10th Round**
13. *Pat Brown, of, Permian HS, Odessa, Texas.
14. Jerry Baker, rhp, Elgin (Ill.) CC.

**11th Round**
15. Joseph Barnes, lhp, Pfeiffer (N.C.) College.
16. Norman Singleton, c, Grandview (Iowa) JC.
17. Tom Ford, of, Fair Park HS, Shreveport, La.

**12th Round**
**18. *Oscar Brown, of, Poly HS, Long Beach, Calif.—(1969-73)**
DRAFT DROP *Brother of Ollie Brown, major leaguer (1965-77)*
19. *Charles Kline, lhp, Western Michigan University.

**13th Round**
20. *Bill Frost, rhp, University of California.
DRAFT DROP *First overall draft pick, June 1966/secondary phase, Giants*
21. George Nichols, rhp, Parker HS, Birmingham, Ala.
22. Alan Baur, c, Christian Brothers HS, Memphis, Tenn.

**14th Round**
23. *Ron Rowell, of, Central HS, Tulsa, Okla.
24. Larry Holly, rhp, Northeast HS, St. Petersburg, Fla.

**15th Round**
25. Glen Flake, rhp, Assumption HS, East St. Louis, Ill.
**26. *Paul Reuschel, rhp, Central HS, Camp Point, Ill.—(1975-79)**
DRAFT DROP *Brother of Rick Reuschel, major leaguer (1972-91)*
27. *Ken Williams, c, East Lansing (Mich.) HS.

**16th Round**
28. Lynn Coleman, of, Potosi (Mo.) HS.
29. Carlton Barnes, ss, East Carolina University.

**17th Round**
30. *Vic Prather, of, Rogers HS, Tulsa, Okla.
31. Harlan Hinds, of, Odessa (Texas) JC.
32. *Larry McWherter, of, El Camino (Calif.) JC.

**August—American Legion Phase (15)**

No selection.

## CLEVELAND INDIANS

**June—Regular Phase**

**Major League and Class AAA Selections (7)**
**1. Ray Fosse, c, Marion (Ill.) HS.—(1967-79)**
2. John Sandknop, ss-2b, Knox County HS, Edina, Mo.—(AA)
3. Ronald Constantino, rhp, Monson (Mass.) HS.—(AAA)

**Class AA Selections (9)**
4. William Perry, of, Palatka (Fla.) HS.—(AA)
5. *Fred Kampf, rhp, Shore Regional HS, Monmouth Beach, N.J.—(AA)
DRAFT DROP *Attended Miami (Fla.); re-drafted by Athletics, June 1967/secondary phase (1st round)*
6. *Phil O'Neil, lhp-1b, St. Peter HS, Worcester, Mass.
7. John Fouse, of-rhp, University of Arizona.

**Class A Selections @**

**8th Round**
8. Ron Arnold, rhp, Northwestern State University.
**9. Vic Albury, 1b-lhp, Key West (Fla.) HS.—(1973-76)**

**9th Round**
**10. *Greg Washburn, rhp, Coal City (Ill.) HS.—(1969)**
11. *Lou Pieserb, lhp, Brother Rice HS, Chicago.

**10th Round**
12. *Ronnie Matney, of, Duncan (Okla.) HS.
13. *Dave Flettrich, ss, Tulane University.

**11th Round**
14. *Frank Favia, c-of, West Leyden HS, Franklin Park, Ill.
15. Harold Joyce, of, Kaimuki HS, Honolulu, Hawaii.

**12th Round**
16. (void) *James Baker, of, McKinley HS, Columbus, Ohio.
17. *James Goodwin, rhp, Southwest HS, Miami.

**13th Round**
18. *Frank Borgia, ss-3b, Central HS, Scranton, Pa.
19. *Fred Kos, 1b, Northeastern University.

**14th Round**
20. James Renfro, rhp, Red Bank HS, Chattanooga, Tenn.
21. *Kenneth Suzawa, lhp, Baldwin HS, Kahului, Hawaii.

**15th Round**
22. *Tom Lundgren, lhp, Forest View HS, Rolling Meadows, Ill.
23. *Charles Bottom, ss, Lincoln (Ill.) JC.

**16th Round**
24. (void) *Tom Schweitzer, lhp, Fairmont State (W.Va.) College.
25. *Howard Arndt, rhp, Republic (Mo.) HS.

**17th Round**
26. *Harold Burke, rhp-of, Parsippany (N.J.) HS.
27. (void) *Ray DeRiggi, lhp-of, Vailsburg HS, Newark, N.J.

**18th Round**
28. *Thomas Lomack, of, Lincoln HS, Tallahassee, Fla.
29. *Dennis Malseed, rhp-3b, St. James HS, Woodlyn, Pa.

**19th Round**
30. *Mark Devitt, c, Dartmouth (Mass.) HS.
31. *Harry McCarthy, of, Huntington (W.Va.) HS.

**20th Round**
32. *Eugene Sidor, c, Nassau (N.Y.) CC.
33. *Frank Spaziani, rhp, Clark (N.J.) Regional HS.

**21st Round**
34. *Larry Hansen, of-3b, Jefferson HS, Portland, Ore.

**August—American Legion Phase (8)**
1. *Dan Ford, of, Hamden (Conn.) HS.—(AA)
2. *Donald Melville, lhp, Saegertown (Pa.) HS.
3. *Joel McMasters, rhp, Bay HS, Lake City, Ark.

## DETROIT TIGERS

**June—Regular Phase**

**Major League and Class AAA Selections (13)**
**1. Gene Lamont, c, Hiawatha HS, Kirkland, Ill.—(1970-75)**
DRAFT DROP *Major league manager (1992-2000)*
2. *Doug Carson, ss, Bishop Armstrong HS, Sacramento, Calif.—(Low A)
DRAFT DROP *Attended Santa Clara; re-drafted by Pirates, June 1967/secondary phase (3rd round)*
**3. *Andy Messersmith, rhp, University of California.—(1968-79)**
DRAFT DROP *Returned to California; re-drafted by Angels, June 1966/secondary phase (1st round)*

**Class AA Selections (11)**
**4. *Bob Reed, rhp, University of Michigan.—(1969-70)**
DRAFT DROP *Returned to Michigan; re-drafted by Tigers, June 1966/secondary phase (2nd round)*
5. Thomas White, 3b, Dorman HS, Spartanburg, S.C.—(Low A)
6. Dennis Grossini, lhp, Lompoc (Calif.) HS.
7. *William Bradley, ss, Palestine (Texas) HS.

**Class A Selections @**

**8th Round**
8. Alex Bike, c, Notre Dame HS, Bridgeport, Conn.
9. James Young, lhp, Cherry Hill HS, Inkster, Mich.
**10. Gary Taylor, rhp, Central Michigan University.—(1969)**

**9th Round**
11. Ronald Kirk, of, Bloomsburg (Pa.) University.
12. *Kris Krebs, ss, Dykes HS, Atlanta.
13. *Dennis Deptula, 2b, University of Michigan.
14. *Vince Bigone, 3b-of, St. Ignatius HS, San Francisco.

**10th Round**
15. Nick Ross, rhp, Divine Child HS, Inkster, Mich.
16. *Kenneth Hall, lhp, Nassau (N.Y.) CC.
17. Shelburn Morton, rhp, Oak Grove HS, Paragould, Ark.

**11th Round**
18. Neil Branch, inf, Thomas Jefferson HS, Elizabeth, N.J.
19. *Thomas Kelly, of, Holy Cross College.
20. Thomas Hamm, of, Georgetown University.
21. Darrell Hollar, inf-of, Lima (Ohio) Senior HS.

**12th Round**
**22. *Rick Austin, lhp, Lakes HS, Tacoma, Wash.—(1970-76)**
**23. *Steve Arlin, rhp, Ohio State University.—(1969-74)**
24. *Arnie Chonko, 1b, Ohio State University.

**13th Round**
25. Robert Felber, inf, CC of Baltimore.
26. *Danny Talbott, 1b-of, University of North Carolina.
DRAFT DROP *17th-round draft pick, San Francisco 49ers/National Football League (1967)*
27. *Joe Hauptman, c, Granite City (Ill.) HS.
**28. *Ray Peters, rhp, Nichols HS, Buffalo, N.Y.—(1970)**

**14th Round**
29. Milton Bender, inf, Northern HS, Detroit.
**30. *Terry Ley, lhp, Madison HS, Portland, Ore.—(1971)**
31. *Neil Pittman, rhp, Parkview HS, Springfield, Mo.

**15th Round**
32. *Ed Staron, of, Western Michigan University.
33. *Martin Brown, rhp, Edison HS, Tulsa, Okla.
34. *Buddy White, rhp, Rutgers University.
35. *Tom Brown, ss, Jupiter (Fla.) HS.

**16th Round**
36. *Steve Kokor, rhp, Alta Loma (Calif.) HS.
**37. Bill Butler, lhp, Herndon (Va.) HS.—(1969-77)**
38. (void) *Robert Yodice, c, Lafayette HS, Brooklyn, N.Y.
DRAFT DROP *First overall draft pick, August 1965/American Legion draft, Mets*

**17th Round**
39. John Huizenga, c, Western Michigan University.
40. *Craig Bozich, of, Aurora Central HS, Denver.
41. Steve Vanderlip, rhp, West Ottawa HS, Holland, Mich.
42. Vic Sorrell, ss, North Carolina State University.
DRAFT DROP *Son of Vic Sorrell, major leaguer (1928-37)*

**18th Round**
43. *Robert Bixler, rhp, Miami (Ohio) University.
44. Ralph Foytack, rhp, Moscow (Pa.) HS.
DRAFT DROP *Nephew of Paul Foytack, major leaguer (1953-64)*

**August—American Legion Phase (14)**

No selection.

## HOUSTON ASTROS

**June—Regular Phase**

**Major League and Class AAA Selections (4)**
1. Alex Barrett, ss, Atwater HS, Winton, Calif.–(AAA)
**2. Keith Lampard, of, University of Oregon.—(1969-70)**
3. Jim Monin, ss, University of Kentucky.—(AA)

**Class AA Selections (16)**
**4. *Pat Jacquez, rhp, Stagg HS, Stockton, Calif.—(1971)**
DRAFT DROP *Attended San Joaquin Delta (Calif.) CC; re-drafted by Cubs, June 1967/secondary phase (3rd round) • Father of Thomas Jacquez, major leaguer (2000)*
5. *Billy Martin, of-inf, Colonial Heights (Va.) HS.—DNP
DRAFT DROP *Attended Randolph-Macon (Va.) College; re-drafted by Senators, June 1967/secondary phase (7th round)*
6. David Fyfe, rhp, Hillsborough HS, Tampa.
7. Ken Chelini, lhp, Galileo HS, San Francisco.
DRAFT DROP *Son of Italo Chelini, major leaguer (1935-37)*

**Class A Selections @**

**8th Round**
8. *Dan Rudanovich, of, University of Missouri.
9. Larry Hall, of, Centreville HS, Church Hill, Md.
**10. Danny Walton, of, Bishop Amat HS, La Puente, Calif.—(1968-80)**

**9th Round**
**11. *Gary Gentry, rhp, Phoenix (Ariz.) JC.—(1969-75)**
12. Carl Ergenzinger, c-3b, Dover (Del.) HS.
13. Jerry Causey, 1b, University of Denver.

**10th Round**
14. Richard Perini, rhp, Fresno State University.
15. *Bill Seinsoth, 1b-lhp, Arcadia (Calif.) HS.
16. *Bill Tsoukalas, lhp, Lincoln HS, Seattle.

**11th Round**
17. *Jim Armstrong, ss, Arizona State University.
**18. *Tom Murphy, rhp, Ohio University.—(1968-79)**
19. *John Hurst, of, Live Oak (Fla.) HS.

**12th Round**
20. *J.B. Jackson, 1b, Roxton HS, Honey Grove, Texas.
21. Dave Anderson, 3b, Western Michigan University.
22. Joseph Vari, 3b-c, William Penn HS, New Castle, Del.

**13th Round**
23. John Francis, c, Bakersfield (Calif.) JC.
24. *Joe Borowy, rhp, Baltimore.
**25. *Buzz Stephen, rhp, Fresno State University.—(1968)**

**14th Round**
26. *Rusty Adkins, 1b, Clemson University.
27. *Michael Willis, lhp, Alameda HS, Denver.
28. *Steve Barrett, of, Artesia (N.M.) HS.

**15th Round**
29. *Gary Hughes, rhp, Monterey HS, Lubbock, Texas.
30. *Paul Suchow, rhp, York HS, Elmhurst, Ill.

31. *Berry Cohen, rhp, Senn HS, Chicago.

**16th Round**

32. *Pascal Renn, rhp, Wake Forest University.
33. Eugene Garritt, of, University of Delaware.
34. *Robert Yingling, ss-2b, St. Joseph's HS, West New York, N.J.

**17th Round**

35. Ralph Barrier, rhp-1b, Hillsdale (Va.) HS.
36. ***Jerry DaVanon, of, San Diego Mesa JC.—(1969-77)**

**DRAFT DROP** *Father of Jeff DaVanon, major leaguer (1999-2004)*

37. Louis McKown, lhp, Wichita Falls (Texas) HS.

**18th Round**

38. Stephen Molberg, 1b, Pampa (Texas) HS.
39. *Paul Alderete, of, Los Angeles Pierce JC.
40. (void) *Doug Parsons, c, Bishop Armstrong HS, Sacramento, Calif.

**19th Round**

41. Wayne Miller, ss, Lambuth (Tenn.) College.
42. Don Sessions, c, University of Colorado.
43. *Gary Butcher, rhp, Los Angeles Harbor JC.

**20th Round**

44. *Arthur Gainous, 1b, Moore HS, Waco, Texas.
45. Edward Earlywine, 2b, University of New Mexico.
46. ***Mel Behney, lhp, Verona (N.J.) HS.—(1970)**

**21st Round**

47. Jack Goings, 3b, Whitehaven HS, Memphis, Tenn.
48. *Patrick Kendig, rhp, South Hunterdon HS, Ringoes, N.J.
49. Harry Mohr, 3b, University of Colorado.

**22nd Round**

50. Robert Grzymala, lhp, St. Mary's HS, East Northport, N.Y.
51. Alfred Pettes, of, Las Cruces (N.M.) HS.
52. *Scotty Long, ss, Auburn University.

**23rd Round**

53. Henry Boykin, 1b-rhp, Phillips (Texas) HS.
54. *Lionel Jones, of, Southern University.
55. Gary Fields, inf, Northeast Louisiana University.

**24th Round**

56. ***Rich Nye, lhp, University of California.—(1966-70)**

**DRAFT DROP** *First player from 1966 draft to reach majors (Sept. 16, 1966)*

57. *Richard Bechtel, ss, Rider College.
58. *Jerry Day, c, Midwest City (Okla.) HS.

**25th Round**

59. *Roy Myers, of, Overton HS, Memphis, Tenn.
60. *Jon Ives, rhp, Berner HS, Massapequa, N.Y.
61. *Jan Adelman, of, University of Mississippi.

**26th Round**

62. ***Billy Harris, ss, Wilmington (N.C.) College.—(1968-69)**
63. John Vignone, of, Susquehanna (Pa.) University.
64. Joe Entiero, c, St. Gabriel HS, Hazelton, Pa.

**27th Round**

65. (void) *Glen Borkhuis, of, Syracuse University.
66. *Mario Gillio, c, Don Bosco Prep HS, East Paterson, N.J.
67. *Dale Fincher, c, Waxahachie (Texas) HS.

**28th Round**

68. **Otis Thornton, c-rhp, Westfield HS, Docena, Ala.—(1973)**
69. *Jerry Borga, 3b-c, Easton (Md.) HS.
70. Ralph Gonzales, c, Atwater (Calif.) HS.

**29th Round**

71. *Richard Licini, 1b-of, Iona Prep HS, Eastchester, N.Y.
72. Reginald Thomas, of, Los Angeles.

**August—American Legion Phase (3)**

No selection.

## KANSAS CITY ATHLETICS

**June—Regular Phase**

**Major League and Class AAA Selections (1)**

1. **Rick Monday, of, Arizona State University.—(1966-84)**

**DRAFT DROP** *First drafted player*

2. **Joe Keough, 1b, Mount San Antonio (Calif.) JC.—(1968-73)**

**DRAFT DROP** *Brother of Marty Keough, major leaguer (1956-66) • Uncle of Matt Keough, major leaguer (1977-86)*

3. ***Bob Stinson, of, Miami Senior HS.—(1969-80)**

**DRAFT DROP** *Attended Miami-Dade CC North; re-drafted by Dodgers, June 1966/secondary phase (1st round)*

**Class AA Selections (19)**

4. **Peter Koegel, of-1b, Seaford (N.Y.) HS.—(1970-72)**
5. Richard Suggs, ss, Hart HS, Saugus, Calif.–(Low A)
6. **Sal Bando, 3b, Arizona State University.—(1966-81)**

**DRAFT DROP** *Brother of Chris Bando, major leaguer (1981-89) • General manager, Brewers (1991-99)*

7. ***Scott Reid, of, Cerritos (Calif.) JC.—(1969-70)**

**DRAFT DROP** *Scouting director, Cubs (1986-87)*

**Class A Selections @**

**8th Round**

8. *Frank Riggins, of, Centralia (Kan.) HS.
9. *Don Lando, of, Ithaca (N.Y.) College.
10. **George Lauzerique, rhp, George Washington HS, New York.—(1967-70)**
11. John Dunn, rhp, Bryant HS, Woodside, N.Y.

**9th Round**

12. Donnie Weeks, rhp, Minor HS, Adamsville, Ala.
13. *Terry L'Ange, rhp, University of Missouri.
14. Craig Gambs, 1b, Richmond (Calif.) HS.
15. **Bobby Brooks, of, Los Angeles Harbor JC.—(1969-73)**

**10th Round**

16. *John Thomas, lhp, Westmont (Calif.) College.
17. Donald Arp, rhp, Berry (Ga.) College.
18. Larry Vlasin, 2b-ss, Madrid (Neb.) HS.
19. *Jerry Burgess, c, North Tonawanda (N.Y.) HS.

**11th Round**

20. **Gene Tenace, ss, Valley HS, Lucasville, Ohio.—(1969-83)**

**DRAFT DROP** *Major league manager (1991)*

21. Jim Buker, rhp, Weymouth (Mass.) HS.
22. Mike Strode, 2b, University of Missouri.
23. *Troy Garey, ss, Bullard HS, Fresno, Calif.

**12th Round**

24. Pete Britton, 3b, University of Virginia.
25. *Brandt Jackson, c, Buena HS, Ventura, Calif.
26. James Blakeney, c, William Carey (Miss.) College.
27. *Stephen Nelson, rhp, Natick HS, Braintree, Mass.

**13th Round**

28. ***Greg Garrett, lhp, Hart HS, Newhall, Calif.—(1970-71)**
29. *Darryl Hester, lhp, Byng HS, Ada, Okla.
30. James Gibney, rhp, Susquehanna (Pa.) University.
31. *Roger Jackson, rhp, North Kansas City (Mo.) HS.

**14th Round**

32. *Jackie Creel, rhp, Phillips HS, Birmingham, Ala.
33. *Pete Middlekauff, 1b, Stanford University.
34. *Bob Biletnikoff, of, University of Miami.
35. *Gary Shephard, of, Duffy HS, Niagara Falls, N.Y.

**15th Round**

36. *Ronald Pietila, ss, Sweetwater Union HS, National City, Calif.
37. *Mike Koritko, ss, Notre Dame HS, Stratford, Conn.
38. *Charles Casey, rhp, University of Florida.
39. David Sellers, rhp, Independence, Mo.

**16th Round**

40. *Jeff Herter, rhp, Kansas City, Mo.
41. John Fleischaur, c-of, Ventura, Calif.
42. Victor Majewski, rhp, Villanova University.
43. Gene Barisano, ss, Ben Franklin HS, Manhattan, N.Y.

**17th Round**

44. *Gary Avery, of, Fremont HS, Los Angeles.
45. James Watts, ss, Howard University.
46. *Ron Gorey, rhp-of, San Clemente (Calif.) HS.
47. *Ronnie Hillman, lhp, Ada (Okla.) HS.

**18th Round**

48. John Budnick, rhp, Bound Brook (N.J.) HS.

**August—American Legion Phase (2)**

1. *Ray DeRiggi, lhp-of, Vailsburg HS, Newark, N.J.—(AA)

## LOS ANGELES DODGERS

**June—Regular Phase**

**Major League and Class AAA Selections (8)**

1. John Wyatt, ss, Bakersfield (Calif.) HS.–(High A)
2. **Alan Foster, rhp, Los Altos HS, Hacienda Heights, Calif.—(1967-76)**
3. Mike Criscione, c, Syracuse University.–(High A)

**Class AA Selections (10)**

4. George Mercado, of, Bishop Dubois HS, New York.—(Low A)
5. John Radosevich, lhp, West Virginia University.—(High A)
6. *Peter Barnes, of, Southern University.
7. *Gary Griffith, rhp, Anadarko (Okla.) HS.

**DRAFT DROP** *Brother of Darrell Griffith, major leaguer (1963-66)*

**Class A Selections @**

**8th Round**

8. James Johnson, of, Las Vegas (Nev.) HS.
9. *Paul Dennenbaum, 1b, Syracuse University.
10. ***Tom Seaver, rhp, University of Southern California.—(1967-86)**

**DRAFT DROP** *Elected to Baseball Hall of Fame, 1992*

**9th Round**

11. Joe Austin, 1b, University of Southern California.
12. *Richard Binder, lhp, Waterloo (Ill.) HS.
13. *Terrance Derringer, rhp, Southwest HS, Miami.

**10th Round**

14. Stephen McGreevy, 1b-of, University of Kansas.
15. **Leon Everitt, rhp, Pemberton HS, Marshall, Texas.—(1969)**
16. (void) *Mike McCall, ss, Greenville (S.C.) HS.

**11th Round**

17. *Johnny Alexander, inf, Whitmire (S.C.) HS.
18. *Rod Austin, of, Santa Clara University.
19. *George Lewark, ss, University of Colorado.

**12th Round**

20. *William Maxwell, rhp, Central HS, Tulsa, Okla.
21. *Daro Quiring, rhp, Stanford University.
22. *Eric Krumlauf, 3b, Shaker Heights (Ohio) HS.

**13th Round**

23. ***Rich Hinton, lhp, Marana (Ariz.) HS.—(1971-79)**
24. Fred Moulder, ss, Oklahoma State University.
25. *Jon Keirns, of, Edmond (Okla.) HS.

**14th Round**

26. Robert Harvey, 3b, Marshall HS, Oklahoma City, Okla.
27. Rhett Thompson, 3b, Del Mar HS, San Jose, Calif.
28. ***Gary Moore, of, University of Texas.–(1970)**

**15th Round**

29. Kyle Carlin, rhp, Sulphur (La.) HS.
30. Dennis Jensen, ss, Jacksonville University.

**August—American Legion Phase (7)**

1. (void) *Barry Snyder, c, Little Rock, Ark.—DNP
2. (void) *Frank Stanek, 1b, Omaha, Neb.

## MILWAUKEE BRAVES

**June—Regular Phase**

**Major League and Class AAA Selections (12)**

1. Dick Grant, 1b-lhp, Watertown (Mass.) HS.–(AA)
2. Don Johnson, c, University of Southern California.—(AAA)
3. Douglas G. King, of, Northeastern HS, Manchester, Pa.—(AA)

**Class AA Selections (4)**

4. **Charlie Vaughan, lhp, Brownsville (Texas) HS.—(1966-69)**
5. William Bates, rhp, Washington (Pa.) College.—(High A)
6. **Wayne Garrett, ss, Sarasota (Fla.) HS.—(1969-78)**

**DRAFT DROP** *Brother of Adrian Garrett, major leaguer (1966-76)*

7. Steve Godfrey, ss, Stonewall, Okla.

**Class A Selections @**

**8th Round**

8. Jeff Albies, 2b, Long Island University.
9. Albert Thompson, of, Narbonne HS, Harbor City, Calif.

**9th Round**

10. Thomas Randecker, rhp, Lock Haven, Pa.
11. Nick Van Lue, 1b, Carson HS, Wilmington, Calif.

**10th Round**

12. *Craig Scoggins, of, Cerritos (Calif.) JC.

**DRAFT DROP** *15th-round draft pick, San Diego Chargers/ National Football League (1967)*

13. Bobby Christensen, ss, Cal State Northridge.

**11th Round**

14. *Earl Lombardo, inf-of, Rider College.
15. Ted Bashore, 1b, UCLA.

**12th Round**

16. *Kenneth Lohnes, c, Mayfair HS, Lakewood, Calif.
17. David Lobb, rhp, Pacelli HS, Austin, Minn.

**13th Round**

18. *John Respondek, rhp, Yorktown, Texas.
19. *Daniel Hootstein, of, Harvard University.

**14th Round**

20. ***John Noriega, rhp, University of Utah.–(1969-70)**
21. ***Ken Tatum, rhp, Mississippi State University.—(1969-74)**

**15th Round**

22. Monte Sharpe, lhp, Auburn University.
23. Douglas Hidden King, of, University of Connecticut.

**16th Round**

24. *George Girard, lhp, Marblehead (Mass.) HS.
25. *Peter Lentine, 1b-lhp, Birmingham HS, Encino, Calif.

**17th Round**

26. Darryl Wilkins, 2b-ss, University of Southern California.
27. *William Ferguson, c, Ray HS, Corpus Christi, Texas.

**18th Round**

28. *Jerry Foglia, rhp, Woodbridge (N.J.) HS.
29. Richard Small, of, Long Island University.

**19th Round**

30. *Steve Wrenn, 1b, Wake Forest University.
31. *William Craig, rhp, Williamson (W.Va.) HS.

**20th Round**

32. *John Reynolds, c, Grosse Pointe (Mich.) HS.
33. ***Bill Zepp, rhp, University of Michigan.—(1969-71)**

**21st Round**

34. *Richard Schaffer, c-3b, Birmingham HS, Encino, Calif.
35. Joe Beck, 1b, Kansas State University.

**22nd Round**

36. *James McFarland, rhp, North Platte, Neb.
37. Daniel Waraksa, 2b-ss, Seton Hall University.

**23rd Round**

38. ***Duffy Dyer, c-of, Arizona State University.—(1968-81)**
39. ***Dan Frisella, rhp, Washington State University.—(1967-76)**

**DRAFT DROP** *Died as active major leaguer (Jan. 1, 1977)*

**24th Round**

40. (void) *Glenn Wallace, rhp, Butler HS, Florence, Ala.

**August—American Legion Phase (11)**

1. **Earl Williams, c-rhp, Montclair (N.J.) HS.—(1970-77)**
2. *William Speaks, 1b, Newark (Ohio) HS.

## MINNESOTA TWINS

**June—Regular Phase**

**Major League and Class AAA Selections (9)**

1. ***Eddie Leon, ss, University of Arizona.—(1968-75)**

**DRAFT DROP** *Returned to Arizona; re-drafted by Cubs, June 1966/secondary phase (1st round)*

2. ***Del Unser, of, Mississippi State University.—(1968-82)**

**DRAFT DROP** *Returned to Mississippi State; re-drafted by Pirates, January 1966/secondary phase (4th round) • Son of Al Unser, major leaguer (1942-45)*

3. *John Dow, of, Bemidji (Minn.) HS.—(High A)

**DRAFT DROP** *No school; re-drafted by Reds, June 1966/ secondary phase (1st round).*

**Class AA Selections (14)**

4. **Graig Nettles, 3b, San Diego State University.—(1967-88)**

**DRAFT DROP** *Brother of Jim Nettles, major leaguer (1970-81)*

5. Neil McPhee, ss, Northeastern University.—(High A)

**DRAFT DROP** *Baseball coach, Northeastern (1986-2014)*

6. Terry Graham, 1b, Carson City (Nev.) HS.
7. Mickey Johnston, c, Drewry Mason HS, Ridgeway, Va.

**Class A Selections @**

**8th Round**

8. **Ron Keller, rhp, Indiana University.—(1966-68)**
9. *William Drummond, rhp, Buena Vista (Iowa) Coll.

10. Johnnie Johnson, c, Americus (Ga.) HS.
11. John Healy, rhp, Lane Tech HS, Chicago.
12. *Tom Burgess, rhp, Phoenix (Ariz.) JC.

9th Round

13. *Jack Palmer, lhp, Cretin HS, St. Paul, Minn.
14. *Kenneth Holt, lhp, Campbell HS, Brookneal, Va.
15. *Paul Coleman, rhp, Cal Poly Pomona.
16. *John Herbst, lhp, University of Southern California.
17. Alan Nordberg, rhp-of, University of Massachusetts.

10th Round

18. *Jim Vopicka, ss, University of Illinois.
19. *Fred Mazurek, of, University of Pittsburgh.

DRAFT DROP *Wide receiver, National Football League (1965-66)*

20. *Ronald Van Dyke, rhp, Hilltop HS, Chula Vista, Calif.
21. Louis Smith, 3b, Cal Poly Pomona.
22. Gary Finch, lhp, Memorial HS, Eau Claire, Wis.

11th Round

23. *Stump Merrill, c, University of Maine.

DRAFT DROP *Major league manager (1990-91)*

24. Joseph Racer, c, Madison HS, Aroda, Va.
25. *Steven Waters, c, Whittier (Calif.) College.
26. Jim Mack, lhp, Cicero (Ill.) HS.
27. *Randy Humphrey, lhp, Carson HS, Torrance, Calif.

12th Round

28. Bill Ferrell, rhp, University of Tennessee.
29. (void) *Steve Kokor, rhp-of, Baseline HS, Alta Loma, Calif.
30. Alvin Hazewinkle, rhp, Eau Claire HS, Columbia, S.C.
31. Paul Mankowski, 2b, Buffalo (N.Y.) HS.
32. Joe Romary, 2b-ss, University of Wisconsin.

13th Round

33. Walter Harrison, rhp, Male HS, Louisville, Ky.
34. Craig MacKay, 2b, University of Utah.
35. *John Tartera, 1b, University of Vermont.
36. *Joseph Braithwaite, 1b, Atlantic City (N.J.) HS.
37. Bill Gray, of, University of Arkansas.

14th Round

**38. *Frank Brosseau, rhp-of, University of Minnesota.—(1969-71)**

39. Bob Purkhiser, rhp, Purdue University.
40. Conrad Bradison, ss, Memorial HS, Eau Claire, Wis.
41. Doug Dobrei, 1b-lhp, Michigan State University.
42. Jim Duffy, of, Westmont (Ill.) HS.

15th Round

43. Jerome Cawley, 3b, University of Minnesota.

**44. Bob Gebhard, rhp, University of Iowa.—(1971-74)**

DRAFT DROP *General manager, Rockies (1991-99); general manager, Diamondbacks (2005)*

45. *Walter Manuel, ss, Lafayette University.
46. Jerry Gleisner, rhp, Cathedral HS, New Ulm, Minn.
47. *Gary Bodak, of-1b, Sayreville (N.J.) HS.

16th Round

48. Luis Lagunas, 2b, Arizona State University.
49. *Rick Manning, 2b, Holy Cross College.
50. Larry Deaton, rhp, Edgewater HS, Orlando, Fla.
51. Aubrey Clore, rhp, Madison (Va.) HS.
52. Bob Rommes, rhp, Mabel (Minn.) HS.

**August—American Legion Phase (10)**

No selection.

## NEW YORK METS

**June—Regular Phase**

**Major League and Class AAA Selections (2)**

**1. Les Rohr, lhp, West HS, Billings, Mon.—(1967-69)**

2. *Randy Kohn, c, Greenville (S.C.) HS.—(High A)

DRAFT DROP *Attended Georgia; re-drafted by Dodgers, June 1967/secondary phase (4th round)*

**3. Joe Moock, ss, Louisiana State University.—(1967)**

**Class AA Selections (6)**

**4. Ken Boswell, 2b, Sam Houston State University.—(1967-77)**

5. *Doug Brittelle, rhp, Massapequa (N.Y.) HS.–DNP

DRAFT DROP *Attended Rutgers; re-drafted by Dodgers, June 1967/secondary phase (16th round) • Drafted by Kentucky Colonels/American Basketball Association (1969)*

6. Harold Roberson, rhp, Central Michigan University.
7. Mike McClure, 3b-ss, Texas A&M University.

**Class A Selections @**

8th Round

8. Roger Harrington, rhp, Fremont HS, Sunnyvale, Calif.
9. Louis Williams, c, Patterson HS, Baltimore.

9th Round

10. *Roger Stevens, of, Pasadena (Calif.) CC.

**11. Jim McAndrew, rhp, University of Iowa.—(1968-74)**

DRAFT DROP *Father of Jamie McAndrew, first-round draft pick, Dodgers (1989); major leaguer (1995-97).*

10th Round

**12. Nolan Ryan, rhp, Alvin (Texas) HS.—(1966-93)**

DRAFT DROP *Elected to Baseball Hall of Fame, 1999 • President, Rangers (2008-13)*

13. Dave Hayes, 2b-of, Balboa HS, San Francisco.

11th Round

14. Gary Burnett, c, East Central (Okla.) JC.
15. Jack Stroud, lhp, University of Missouri.

12th Round

16. *Wayne Drier, of, Billings (Mon.) HS.
17. *John Ferguson, rhp, Union HS, DeSoto, Ga.

13th Round

18. Carl Nicholsen, 2b, Columbia Basin (Wash.) CC.
19. *Kenneth Brownell, lhp, Watsonville (Calif.) HS.

14th Round

20. *Herb Hofvendahl, of, Miramonte HS, Orinda, Calif.
21. Kenneth Williamson, of-1b, Orange (Va.) HS.

15th Round

22. *John Sauerbier, rhp, Chrisman HS, Independence, Mo.
23. (void) *Al Thomas, of, Narbonne HS, Torrance, Calif.

16th Round

**24. Steve Renko, 1b-rhp, University of Kansas.—(1969-83)**

25. Jerry Bark, lhp, University of Maryland.

17th Round

**26. *Jim Hibbs, c, Stanford University.—(1967)**

27. Wayne Burdette, inf, Bowling Green State University.

18th Round

28. Jim Nichols, rhp, University of Arizona.
29. *John Green, rhp-1b, Jones Valley HS, Birmingham, Ala.

19th Round

30. Tom Garrett, ss, Lincoln HS, San Diego.
31. *James Moore, rhp, Homer (La.) HS.

20th Round

32. Frank Pickens, of, Washburn (Kan.) University.
33. *Rudolph Luehs, 1b, Lincoln HS, San Francisco.

21st Round

34. *Michael Carty, of, Downey (Calif.) HS.

**35. Don Shaw, lhp, San Diego State University.—(1967-72)**

22nd Round

36. *Ron Kyner, of, Arvin (Calif.) HS.
37. *Dave Aldrich, rhp, Mount Diablo HS, Concord, Calif.

23rd Round

38. Ray Stadler, c, Arizona State University.
39. *James Lawson, ss, Antioch (Calif.) HS.

24th Round

40. Jim Dix, of, St. Louis University.
41. *Malcolm Petty, rhp, University of Tennessee.

25th Round

42. Andrew Shea, 2b, St. Helena HS, Bronx, N.Y.
43. *Jerry Boehmer, 3b, St. Louis University.

26th Round

**44. Joe Campbell, of, Morehead State University.—(1967)**

45. *Toby Frymire, c, Penn State University.

27th Round

46. Gary Strom, rhp, San Jose State University.

**47. Barry Raziano, rhp-of, East Jefferson HS, Kenner, La.—(1973-74)**

28th Round

48. *Ron Delplanche, 3b, University of Oregon.
49. *Robert Oliver, lhp, University of Texas.

29th Round

50. *Mike Welton, c, Billings (Mon.) HS.
51. Antonio Liberti, c, Adams HS, Ozone Park,N.Y.

30th Round

52. *Alexander MacLean, of, Horton Watkins HS, Ladue, Mo.

**August—American Legion Phase (1)**

1. Robert Yodice, c, Lafayette HS, Brooklyn, N.Y.—(High A)
2. *Ed Johnson, of, New Dorp HS, Staten Island, N.Y.

## NEW YORK YANKEES

**June—Regular Phase**

**Major League and Class AAA Selections (19)**

**1. Bill Burbach, rhp, Wahlert HS, Dickeyville, Wis.—(1969-71)**

**2. *Danny Thompson, ss, Capren (Okla) HS.—(1970-76)**

DRAFT DROP *Attended Oklahoma State; re-drafted by Reds, June 1967/secondary phase (4th round); died as active major leaguer (Dec. 10, 1976)*

3. *Dennis Baldridge, of, University of Oregon.–(AA)

DRAFT DROP *Returned to Oregon; re-drafted by Yankees, June 1966/secondary phase (3rd round)*

**Class AA Selections (8)**

**4. Stan Bahnsen, rhp, University of Nebraska.—(1966-82)**

5. Louis Howell, c, Kentucky Wesleyan College.—(AAA)

DRAFT DROP *Son of Dixie Howell, major leaguer (1940-58)*

6. *John Hurley, rhp, Port Richmond HS, Staten Island, N.Y.

**7. *Darcy Fast, lhp, North Thurston HS, Olympia, Wash.—(1968)**

**Class A Selections @**

8th Round

8. *Scott Lund, rhp, West HS, Davenport, Iowa.
9. Gary Girouard, rhp, University of Nebraska-Omaha.
10. Fred Dawson, of, Henderson State (Ark.) University.

9th Round

11. James Alvey, of-1b, Leitchfield (Ky.) HS.
12. *Donald Alley, c, Adams State (Colo.) College.
13. Robert Hall, 3b, Villanova University.

10th Round

14. Dwain Davidson, 3b, Mountain Home (Ark.) HS.
15. *Steve Mezich, c, Seattle University.
16. Morton Zenor, 1b-of, Lawton (Iowa) HS.

11th Round

**17. Mickey Scott, lhp, Newburg (N.Y.) Free Academy.—(1972-77)**

18. Kerry Compton, lhp, Pittsburg State (Kan.) University.
19. Larry Shawn, rhp, Owensboro (Ky.) HS.

12th Round

20. Richard Ruggles, 2b, University of Kansas.
21. *Clifton Sisco, of, College HS, Bartlesville, Okla.
22. James Bidwell, rhp, Holy Cross College.

13th Round

**23. *Tom Gramly, rhp, San Angelo (Texas) JC.—(1968)**

24. James Eubanks, lhp, Arkansas AM&N University.
25. James Rees, of, University of Southern California.

14th Round

26. *Steve Rudanovich, of, University of Utah.
27. *Harry Wright, of, Cheshire Academy, Great Neck, N.Y.
28. George Blaum, 1b, Bellport (N.Y.) HS.

15th Round

29. Lewis Lawson, 3b, Tech HS, Terre Haute, Ind.
30. Jim Fink, rhp, Richmond (Calif.) HS.
31. T.L. Porter, of, The Citadel.

16th Round

32. *Jeff Burns, c, Plattsburg (N.Y.) HS.
33. Paul Bruinsma, 2b, Sioux Center (Iowa) HS.

**34. Tom Shopay, of, Dean (Mass.) JC.–(1967-77)**

17th Round

35. James N. Smith, rhp, Denmark (S.C.) HS.
36. *Terry Childers, c, Richmond Academy, Augusta, Ga.

DRAFT DROP *Father of Jason Childers, major leaguer (2006) • Father of Matt Childers, major leaguer (2002-05)*

37. *Terry Harrison, rhp, Pendleton (Ore.) HS.

18th Round

38. *Dennis Trame, rhp, Quincy (Ill.) College.
39. *Neil Weber, rhp, Appleton (Wis.) HS.

**40. *Dick Such, rhp, Elon College.—(1970)**

**August—American Legion Phase (20)**

No selection.

## PHILADELPHIA PHILLIES

**June—Regular Phase**

**Major League and Class AAA Selections (18)**

**1. *Mike Adamson, rhp, Point Loma HS, San Diego.—(1967-69)**

DRAFT DROP *Attended Southern California; re-drafted by Orioles, June 1967/secondary phase (1st round, 1st pick); first player from 1967 draft to reach majors (July 1, 1967)*

**2. Larry Hisle, of, Portsmouth (Ohio) HS.—(1968-82)**

**3. Billy Champion, rhp, Shelby (N.C.) HS.—(1969-76)**

**Class AA Selections (5)**

4. John Parker, rhp, Davie County HS, Cooleemee, N.C.—(AAA)

**5. Terry Harmon, ss, Ohio University.—(1967-77)**

**6. *Bob Chlupsa, rhp, Manhattan University.—(1970-71)**

DRAFT DROP *13th-round draft pick, San Diego Rockets/ National Basketball Association (1967)*

7. *Steve Sharp, rhp, Washington HS, Kansas City, Kan.

**Class A Selections @**

8th Round

8. Del Wilber, ss, Purdue University.

DRAFT DROP *Son of Del Wilber, major leaguer (1946-54)*

9. *Orville Hollrah, rhp, University of Missouri.

**10. *Ken Szotkiewicz, 2b, Salesianum HS, Wilmington, Del.—(1970)**

11. Thomas Capowski, ss, Fordham University.
12. *Donald Cook, rhp, Long Island University.

9th Round

**13. *Dick Mills, rhp, Parsons (Iowa) College.—(1970)**

DRAFT DROP *Father of Ryan Mills, first-round draft pick, Twins (1996)*

14. Richard Trolliet, rhp, Wisconsin State Teachers College.
15. Tommy Chapman, lhp, Clemson University.
16. Gordon Knutson, lhp, Glendale, Calif.
17. Gilbert Barnett, 2b, California (Pa.) University.

10th Round

18. *Edward Cott, c, Nichols HS, Buffalo, N.Y.
19. Dan Crothers, of, Jackson (Ohio) HS.
20. Terry Craven, of, Cal State Northridge.
21. *James Cain, 3b, Madison Central HS, Waco, Ky.
22. Charles Brown, of, Brown HS, Atlanta.

11th Round

23. *Jan Fait, of, New Philadelphia (Ohio) HS.
24. Lloyd Ennis, 1b, Wicomico HS, Salisbury, Md.
25. Michael Mathias, rhp, Hunter (N.Y.) College.
26. George Fowlkes, rhp, Cal Poly Pomona.
27. *Len Zandy, rhp-1b, Fordham University.

12th Round

28. *Charles Shreve, rhp, Cathedral Prep HS, Erie, Pa.
29. Don Novick, of, New York University.
30. Terry Ricketts, rhp, Hillsdale (Mich.) HS.
31. Ken Huebner, of, Florida Southern College.
32. *Dale Blazure, of, North Hunterdon HS, Pottersville, N.J.

13th Round

33. Lavis York, 1b, West Georgia College.

DRAFT DROP *Nephew of Rudy York, major leaguer (1934-48)*

**August—American Legion Phase (17)**

1. No selection.
2. Ricky Fuller, c, Hoover HS, Fresno, Calif.

## PITTSBURGH PIRATES

**June—Regular Phase**

**Major League and Class AAA Selections (10)**

1. Wayne Dickerson, of, Ensley HS, Birmingham, Ala.—(High A)
2. Roger Hayward, rhp, Pontiac North HS, Pontiac, Mich.—(AA)
3. Dick Hendrix, rhp, Princeton HS, Cincinnati.—(AAA)

**Class AA Selections (2)**
4. Ed Berube, 3b, Colby (Maine) College.—(Low A)
5. Bob Settle, rhp, Woodrow Wilson HS, Portsmouth, Va.—(AAA)
6. Ronald Young, lhp, Canton South HS, Canton, Ohio.
7. *Steve Schneider, ss, University of Minnesota.

**Class A Selections @**

**8th Round**
8. *Terry Thompson, 1b, Sunset HS, Beaverton, Ore.
9. Larry Killingsworth, rhp, Jordan HS, Long Beach, Calif.
10. *Kerry Dean, rhp, Mansfield (Ohio) HS.

**9th Round**
11. Zelman Jack, of, Pittsburg (Calif.) HS.
12. Douglas Watkins, lhp, Bloomsburg HS, Cheverly, Md.
13. Jack Clark, of, St. Charles (Mo.) HS.

**10th Round**
14. Terry Sparks, rhp, Minford (Ohio) HS.
15. Irvin Melton, rhp, Aulander (N.C.) HS.
16. Paul Giglio, of, Flushing HS, Whitestone, N.Y.

**11th Round**
17. Sammy Angott, inf-rhp, Ohio University.
DRAFT DROP *Son of Sammy Angott, World lightweight boxing champion (1940-44)*
**18. Bob Moose, rhp, Franklin Area HS, Export, Pa.—(1967-76)**
19. *Bob Shannon, of, Natchez, Miss.

**12th Round**
**20. Gene Garber, rhp, Elizabethtown (Pa.) HS.—(1969-88)**
**21. *Jophery Brown, rhp, Grambling University.—(1968)**
**22. Freddie Patek, ss, Seguin, Texas.–(1968-81)**

**13th Round**
23. Sonny Custer, rhp, James Madison HS, Vienna, Va.
24. Preston Bentley, of, Washington (Ohio) HS.
25. Roger Banze, rhp, Francis Hall HS, St. Louis.

**14th Round**
**26. *Tom Dettore, rhp, McMillan HS, Canonsburg, Pa.—(1973-76)**
27. *Alan Putz, 3b, Rockville (Conn.) HS.
28. David Tolley, 3b-c, Grove City (Pa.) College.

**15th Round**
29. *Greg Chlan, p, Westfield (N.J.) HS.
**30. Lou Marone, lhp, San Diego Mesa JC.—(1969-70)**
**31. Jim Nelson, rhp, Burbank HS, Sacramento, Calif.—(1970-71)**

**16th Round**
32. Benny Grove, inf, Frederick (Md.) HS.
33. Robert Roadarmel, rhp, Florida Southern College.
34. *Mike Nickels, lhp, Pulaski HS, Milwaukee.

**17th Round**
35. David Warmbrod, rhp, Jackson, Tenn.
36. Gregory Marotz, rhp, Colgate University.
37. *Glen Borkhuis, rhp, Syracuse University.

**18th Round**
38. Rich Jackson, rhp, Rockhurst (Mo.) College.
39. *Berke Reichenbach, 3b, Ohio University.
40. Dennis Pierce, lhp, Canaseraga HS, Swain, N.Y.

**19th Round**
41. *Mike Garrett, of, University of Southern California.
DRAFT DROP *1965 Heisman Trophy winner; running back, National Football League (1966-73)*

**August—American Legion Phase (9)**

No selection.

## ST. LOUIS CARDINALS

**June—Regular Phase**

**Major League and Class AAA Selections (20)**
1. Joe DiFabio, rhp, Delta State (Miss.) University.—(AAA)
2. Terry Milani, 1b, Lewis (Ill.) University.–(High A)
3. Billy Wolff, of, University of Cincinnati.—(AAA)

**Class AA Selections (13)**
**4. Harry Parker, rhp, Collinsville (Ill.) HS.—(1970-76)**
5. Jerry Pruett, rhp, Lehman HS, Canton, Ohio.—(AA)
6. *Frank Portera, c, Mississippi State University.
7. *Dave Renkiewicz, of, Mount Carmel HS, Wyandotte, Mich.

**Class A Selections @**

**8th Round**
8. Mike Hensley, 3b, Del City (Okla.) HS.
9. Theodore Friel, rhp, Dartmouth College.
10. Fred Van Iten, c, University of Dubuque (Iowa).

**9th Round**
11. Fred Brigham, ss, University of Wyoming.
12. *William Close, rhp, St. Mary's HS, Waltham, Mass.
13. C.A. McGowan, rhp, Memphis State University.

**10th Round**
14. Michael Davis, ss, Galesburg (Ill.) HS.
15. *Ray Henningsen, 2b, Santa Clara University.
16. Louis Fiore, rhp, Glendale (Calif.) HS.

**11th Round**
17. Edward Tivis, 3b, Kansas City, Mo.
18. *Bruce Hinkel, rhp, Marmac Community HS, McGregor, Iowa.
19. *Jay Schloemer, lhp, Lincoln (Ill.) JC.

**12th Round**
20. Jack Singer, of, Princeton University.
21. *Eugene Breinig, rhp, Merced (Calif.) HS.
**22. *Dan McGinn, lhp, University of Notre Dame.—(1968-72)**

**13th Round**
23. *James Townsend, ss, Shasta Union HS, Redding, Calif.
24. *Robert Bender, 1b, Goodlettsville, Tenn.
25. *Mike Kistner, lhp, Jackson (Mo.) HS.

**14th Round**
26. *Robert Carlson, rhp, American International (Mass.) College.
27. Ron Jancek, lhp, Weber State (Utah) College.
**28. Jerry Robertson, rhp, Washburn (Kan.) University.—(1969-70)**

**15th Round**
29. *Duane Freemon, 1b, University of Utah.
30. *Bobby Smith, 3b, Bacone (Okla.) JC.
31. *William Carino, c, Immaculate HS, Revere, Mass.

**16th Round**
32. *John Frye, of-3b, Manatee (Fla.) JC.
33. Joe Gegg, c, St. Louis University.
34. *Mel Workman, rhp, Moweaqua (Ill.) HS.

**17th Round**
35. *Robert Gustafson, of, Rollins (Fla.) College.
36. *William Lierman, rhp, Granite City, Ill.
37. *Ronald Masterson, rhp, Soddy (Tenn.) HS.

**18th Round**
38. Robert Cox, of, Stanford University.
39. *Isaac Barnes, c, North Chattanooga (Tenn.) HS.
**40. *Rich Hacker, ss, New Athens (Ill.) HS.—(1971)**

**19th Round**
41. *Richard Devarney, ss, University of Maine.
**42. *Peter Hamm, rhp, Soquel (Calif.) HS.—(1970-71)**
43. *William Ray, 2b, Lee HS, Brownsboro, Ala.

**20th Round**
44. John Olander, of-c, Cal State Sacramento.
45. Jesse Cleveland, of, Alabama State University.
46. *David Hanbury, 1b, Oswego (N.Y.) HS.

**21st Round**
47. *Jim Gretta, 1b-of, Arizona State University.
48. *Ray Glinsky, rhp, University of Akron.
49. *John Pierce, rhp, Bacone (Okla.) JC.

**22nd Round**
50. *Trenton Jackson, of, University of Illinois.
51. *Archie Roberts, ss-3b, Columbia University.
DRAFT DROP *Quarterback, National Football League (1967)*
52. *Sanford Marks, rhp, Beverly Hills (Calif.) HS.

**23rd Round**
53. Robert Schanze, 3b, Fresno State University.
54. Marlyn Baum, rhp, Luther (Iowa) College.
55. *Tommy Thompson, ss-3b, El Cajon (Calif.) HS.

**24th Round**
**56. John Sipin, ss, Watsonville (Calif.) HS.—(1969)**
57. Ernie DeFilippis, of, Long Island University.
58. *William Monroe, lhp, Napa, Calif.

**25th Round**
59. *Dale Ford, 1b-of, Washington State University.
60. Butch Thompson, c, University of Texas.
61. *Paul DeLoca, rhp, St. Francis (N.Y.) College.

**August—American Legion Phase (19)**
1. No selection.
2. Robert Sankey, ss, Phillipsburg (Pa.) HS.

## SAN FRANCISCO GIANTS

**June—Regular Phase**

**Major League and Class AAA Selections (14)**
**1. Alan Gallagher, 3b, Santa Clara University.—(1970-73)**
2. *Glen Smith, of, Arizona State University.—(AA)
DRAFT DROP *Returned to Arizona State; re-drafted by Twins, January 1966/secondary phase (5th round)*
3. Ken Fila, lhp, Archbishop Ryan HS, Omaha, Neb.—(Low A)

**Class AA Selections (12)**
4. Hal Jeffcoat, rhp-of, Robinson HS, Tampa.—(AAA)
DRAFT DROP *Son of Hal Jeffcoat, major leaguer (1948-59)*
**5. Rich Robertson, rhp, Santa Clara University.—(1966-71)**
6. John Marsden, 3b-of, West Torrance (Calif.) HS.
7. Doug McMillan, rhp, Santa Monica HS, Malibu, Calif.

**Class A Selections @**

**8th Round**
8. David Matthews, rhp, Reading (Pa.) HS.
9. *Richard Hardiman, c, Mortimer Jordan HS, Warrior, Ala.
10. *Dick White, 1b-of, South Torrance HS, Torrance, Calif.

**9th Round**
**11. Chris Arnold, ss, Arcadia (Calif.) HS.—(1971-76)**
12. *Michael Smith, of, Whitehaven HS, Memphis, Tenn.
13. Seth Marty, c, Sierra HS, Whittier, Calif.

**10th Round**
14. Howard Martin, of, Santa Clara University.
15. *Albert Strane, ss, St. Elizabeth HS, East Oakland, Calif.
DRAFT DROP *Twin brother of Alvin Strane, 36th-round draft pick, Giants (1965)*
16. *Jon Baker, rhp, Sunset HS, Portland, Ore.

**11th Round**
17. Jay Reed, of, Washington Union HS, Easton, Calif.
18. *Gary Ford, lhp, Bullis Prep HS, Walnut Creek, Calif.
19. John Guthrie, of-inf, Alhambra HS, Phoenix, Ariz.

**12th Round**
20. Larry Tolliver, rhp, Bakersfield (Calif.) JC.
21. Noel Finley, 2b, Roosevelt HS, Fresno, Calif.
**22. Ron Bryant, lhp, Davis (Calif.) HS.—(1967-75)**

**13th Round**
23. Val Bush, of, Eastern Illinois University.
24. *Alan Diamond, c, University of California.
25. *John Biedenbach, inf-of, Michigan State University.

**14th Round**
26. Joe Pollack, rhp, University of Minnesota.
27. *Mike Perkins, ss, Dorsey HS, Los Angeles.
28. Gene Vidoni, c, Eastern Illinois University.

**15th Round**
29. *James Jordan, 2b, Ouachita Baptist (Ark.) University.
30. *Richard Kwasny, lhp, La Canada (Calif.) HS.
31. Mike Hutson, c, Reedley (Calif.) JC.

**16th Round**
32. Ralph Durgin, rhp, Rancho HS, North Las Vegas, Nev.
33. Al Deravin, of, Sierra HS, Torrance, Calif.
34. Mike Zink, 1b-c, Wilson HS, Tacoma, Wash.

**17th Round**
35. *Richard Roberts, lhp, Southwest HS, St. Louis.
36. *Alvin Strane, 2b, St. Elizabeth HS, East Oakland, Calif.
DRAFT DROP *Twin brother of Albert Strane, 15th-round draft pick, Giants (1965)*
**37. (void) * Mark Schaeffer, lhp, Cleveland HS, Los Angeles.—(1972)**

**18th Round**
38. Joe Madden, rhp, University of Iowa.
39. Ron Grossmiller, inf, Phoenix (Ariz.) JC.
40. Windy Currie, 1b-of, Olympia HS, Columbia, S.C.

**August—American Legion Phase (13)**

No selection.

## WASHINGTON SENATORS

**June—Regular Phase**

**Major League and Class AAA Selections (3)**
**1. Joe Coleman, rhp, Natick (Mass.) HS.—(1965-79)**
DRAFT DROP *Son of Joe Coleman, major leaguer (1942-55) • Father of Casey Coleman, major leaguer (2010-14) • First 1965 high school draft pick to reach majors (Sept. 28, 1965)*
2. *Stan Bell, rhp, Headland HS, College Park, Ga.—(AA)
DRAFT DROP *Attended Manatee (Fla.) JC; re-drafted by Tigers, January 1966/secondary phase (1st round)*
**3. Gene Martin, of, Dougherty HS, Albany, Ga.—(1968)**

**Class AA Selections (3)**
4. *Richard Zank, lhp, Neillsville (Wis.) HS.—(AA)
DRAFT DROP *No school; re-drafted by Indians, January 1966/secondary phase (8th round).*
5. *Arthur Pauls, rhp, St. Rita HS, Chicago.—(High A)
DRAFT DROP *Attended Lewis (Ill.); re-drafted by Giants, June 1967/secondary phase (10th round)*
6. John Taylor, ss, Alleghany HS, Clifton Forge, Va.
7. Fred Jacobs, 2b, Carleton (Minn.) College.

**Class A Selections @**

**8th Round**
8. Eddie Lupton, lhp, University of Notre Dame.
**9. *Garry Hill, rhp, Garinger HS, Charlotte, N.C.—(1969)**

**9th Round**
10. *Dennis McKernan, of, Kutztown (Pa.) University.
11. Richard Hense, of, University of Wisconsin.

**10th Round**
12. *Richard Koslick, ss, Bishop Egan HS, Levittown, Pa.
13. (void) *Gil Torres, of, Morris HS, New York.

**11th Round**
14. John Cashman, rhp, St. Joseph's University.
**15. Tom Ragland, ss, North HS, Detroit.—(1971-73)**

**12th Round**
16. Gary Dameron, ss, Battle Creek (Mich.) HS.
**17. *Dick Tidrow, rhp, Mount Eden (Calif.) HS.—(1972-84)**

**13th Round**
**18. Bill Gogolewski, rhp, Oshkosh (Wis.) HS.—(1970-75)**
19. Richard Drew, c, North HS, Detroit.

**14th Round**
20. *Kenneth Jones, rhp, Forrest HS, Jacksonville, Fla.
21. Ronald Rosenow, ss, Bonduel HS, Shawano, Wis.

**15th Round**
22. *Tom Cook, rhp-c, Sarasota (Fla.) HS.
23. *Richard Jones, rhp, Valparaiso University.

**16th Round**
24. *Larry Price, lhp, Racine HS, Portland, Ohio.
**25. Dick Billings, of, Michigan State University.—(1968-75)**

**August—American Legion Phase (4)**

No selection.

# 1966

## AT A GLANCE

### This Date In History
**WINTER DRAFT:** Jan. 29.
**SUMMER DRAFT:** June 7-8.
**LEGION DRAFT:** Aug. 24.

### Best Draft
**LOS ANGELES DODGERS.** They drafted eight future big leaguers, including **CHARLIE HOUGH** (8), **BILL RUSSELL** (9), **BILLY GRABARKEWITZ** (12) and **TED SIZEMORE** (15), though this group stopped well short of their vaunted 1968 haul.

### Worst Draft
**DETROIT TIGERS.** The Tigers wasted their first two picks in the June regular phase on **RICK KONIK** and **SCOTT FIELDS**, who never ended up playing pro ball, and got fewer than 100 big league games from the players they did sign.

### First-Round Bust
**STEVE CHILCOTT, C, METS.** One of two 1-1 picks over the life of the draft who didn't play a single big league game, Chilcott's promising career was significantly compromised by a string of injuries. Still, he hit .248 overall in just 337 minor league games over seven seasons.

### Second To None
**JOHNNY OATES, C, WHITE SOX.** Oates went unsigned in 1966 as a catcher out of Virginia Tech, but had the most successful career—first as a player, later as a manager—among all second-rounders drafted that year. He died of a brain tumor in 2004.

### Late-Round Find
**TED SIZEMORE, 2B, DODGERS (15TH ROUND).** Sizemore began a 12-year major league career in 1969 by winning National League rookie of the year honors for the Dodgers, dividing his time between second base and shortstop. He would play almost every position on the field over his career, and hit .262 overall. He played for five clubs, enjoying his greatest success in St. Louis.

# Mets make wrong call on Chilcott vs. Jackson

Eleven years after the New York Mets took catcher Steve Chilcott with the first overall pick in the 1966 draft, Reggie Jackson provided a vivid reminder of their Great Mistake.

Playing for the Yankees, Jackson hit the pinnacle of his Hall of Fame career by slamming three home runs in Game Six of the 1977 World Series to power the Yankees to the first of consecutive titles.

The Mets had to wonder what might have been. They had an opportunity to take Jackson in the 1966 draft, but went instead for Chilcott, one of the worst decisions of the draft era.

As Jackson celebrated, Chilcott had been out of professional baseball for five years, never having reached the big leagues. Jackson, picked second by the Kansas City Athletics out of Arizona State, became one of the most colorful and controversial players in baseball history. At the time he retired in 1987, he held records for draft-era players for games (2,820) and home runs (563), while playing on five World Series championship teams—three with the Athletics, the other two with the Yankees.

Chilcott and Jackson were rated even as prospects on the eve of the 1966 draft. They were the top two players on every team's preferred lists. The Mets settled on Chilcott because of a pronounced organizational need for catching. "It was a position pick," acknowledged Joe McDonald, a longtime baseball executive who was in the Mets front office at the time. "We did not feel that we had an adequate catching prospect in the organization."

Chilcott's career was plagued by injuries. Over a seven-year minor league career, he played in only 331 games before getting released by the Yankees, of all teams, in 1972.

The Mets did their homework on Chilcott, 17, a promising lefthanded hitter who hit .500 with 11 homers and 38 RBIs in 25 games in the spring of 1966 at Antelope Valley High in Lancaster, Calif.

They sent venerable Casey Stengel, then the club's vice president of Western scouting, in to see him. Chilcott went 4-for-4, leaving Stengel to say: "One look is enough for me. This boy has all the tools to become a major league hitter."

Several other Mets scouts and front-office officials went in to take a look at Chilcott, including general manager Bing Devine and Bob Scheffing, the club's director of player development.

Stengel's opinion proved decisive in giving the nod to Chilcott, and he was the one who contacted the young catcher to tell him that he had been drafted by the Mets. Chilcott, who passed up offers to play quarterback in college, signed two weeks later to a bonus contract of $75,000.

## 'GEE, WHAT WAS WRONG WITH ME?'

Broken dreams are as common as home runs in baseball, but Chilcott's dream died a little harder than most. When he returned home to Southern California after being released by the Yankees, he was 23—and a failure.

OAKLAND ATHLETICS

The 1966 draft will always be remembered as the one that included future Hall of Famer Reggie Jackson, but unfortunately for the Mets, he was the second pick, after New York took catcher Steve Chilcott

"I became the answer to a great trivia question," he said. Who was the player taken in the 1966 draft, one slot ahead of future Hall of Famer Reggie Jackson? For a quarter century, Chilcott was the only player selected first in the June draft who never played in the big leagues.

Over the years, the Mets were accused of everything from stupidity to racism for selecting Chilcott instead of Jackson. But in 1966, the consensus was that Jackson and Chilcott were on equal footing.

"I went down to the draft that day," said Whitey Herzog, a Mets coach in 1966. "After it was over, I remember Bing Devine going around to the tables and asking the other clubs who they had No. 1. Nine had Chilcott and 10 had Reggie. At that time, you couldn't have gone wrong with either one."

While Stengel, who was retired and living in Glendale, Calif., sided with Chilcott, Dee Fondy, another Mets scout, recommended Jackson.

"One of my comments in our draft meeting was I felt Reggie would be in the major leagues by 1968," said Fondy, who also said he had no qualms with Chilcott: "He did everything you want to see. He had power and a strong, accurate arm. He ran well for his size and position. He had a good feel for playing the game and was such a good competitor. It was all there. Maybe if he hadn't

## 1966: THE FIRST ROUNDERS

| CLUB: PLAYER, POS., SCHOOL | HOMETOWN | B-T | HT. | WT. | AGE | BONUS | FIRST YEAR | LAST YEAR | PEAK LEVEL (YEARS) |
|---|---|---|---|---|---|---|---|---|---|
| **JUNE—REGULAR PHASE** | | | | | | | | | |
| 1. Mets: Steve Chilcott, c, Antelope Valley HS | Lancaster, Calif. | L-R | 5-11 | 185 | 17 | $75,000 | 1966 | 1972 | Class AAA (1) |
| One of classic busts of draft era, though string of injuries were major contributing cause; played in just 337 minor league games (2 above AA), hit .248 with 39 HRs. | | | | | | | | | |
| 2. Athletics: Reggie Jackson, of, Arizona State | Wyncote, Pa. | L-L | 6-0 | 197 | 20 | $80,000 | 1966 | 1987 | Majors (21) |
| In sharp contrast to Chilcott, became Hall of Famer; Mr. October played on five World Series champs, slugged 563 homers, fanned record 2,597 times in career. | | | | | | | | | |
| 3. Astros: # Wayne Twitchell, rhp, Woodrow Wilson HS | Portland, Ore. | R-R | 6-6 | 220 | 18 | $35,000 | 1966 | 1979 | Majors (10) |
| Reached Triple-A in first season, didn't make MLB debut until 1970, after Astros gave up on him; went 48-65, 3.98 in 10-year career, appeared in '73 All-Star Game. | | | | | | | | | |
| 4. Red Sox: # Ken Brett, lhp, El Segundo HS | El Segundo, Calif. | L-L | 6-0 | 175 | 17 | $56,000 | 1966 | 1981 | Majors (14) |
| Everyone but Red Sox saw George's older brother as center fielder in high school; at 19, became youngest pitcher ever in World Series; elbow issues stymied career. | | | | | | | | | |
| 5. Cubs: # Dean Burk, rhp, Highland HS | Highland, Ill. | R-R | 6-5 | 205 | 18 | $35,000 | 1966 | 1972 | Class AAA (2) |
| Spun seven no-hitters in high school, but never achieved goal of pitching in majors after arm problems while going 35-54, 4.12 in seven minor league seasons. | | | | | | | | | |
| 6. Senators: Tom Grieve, of, Pittsfield HS | Pittsfield, Mass. | R-R | 6-2 | 185 | 18 | $35,000 | 1967 | 1979 | Majors (9) |
| One of best athletes ever from western Mass. has had long, varied career in game as player, front-office exec, broadcaster for Rangers; son Ben also a first-rounder. | | | | | | | | | |
| 7. Cardinals: Leron Lee, of, Grant Union HS | Sacramento, Calif. | L-R | 6-1 | 195 | 18 | $24,500 | 1967 | 1976 | Majors (8) |
| Fell short of expectations in eight major league seasons (.250-31-152), but achieved stardom in Japan, along with brother Leon, for record-breaking 11-year career. | | | | | | | | | |
| 8. Angels: Jim DeNeff, ss, Indiana | Holland, Mich. | R-R | 6-2 | 190 | 19 | $50,000 | 1966 | 1971 | Class AAA (2) |
| Viewed as a better prospect than Rick Reichardt by Angels scout who signed both players; hit .231 with 51 homers in six-year minor league career. | | | | | | | | | |
| 9. Phillies: Mike Biko, rhp, W.W. Samuell HS | Dallas | R-R | 6-1 | 185 | 17 | $35,000 | 1966 | 1970 | Class A (3) |
| Pitched Samuell High to only state baseball title ever won by Dallas high school in 1965, but five-year pro career (31-22, 4.23) never advanced beyond Class A. | | | | | | | | | |
| 10. Yankees: Jim Lyttle, of, Florida State | Harrison, Ohio | L-R | 6-0 | 173 | 20 | $43,000 | 1966 | 1976 | Majors (8) |
| Set records in baseball, started for hoops team at Florida State; played eight nondescript seasons in majors, but enjoyed success in seven years in Japan. | | | | | | | | | |
| 11. Braves: Al Santorini, rhp, Union HS | Union, N.J. | R-R | 6-1 | 190 | 18 | $50,000 | 1966 | 1974 | Majors (6) |
| Piled up 50-1 record in schoolboy play and debuted in Double-A; appeared in just one game for Braves before lost to Padres in expansion draft; 17-38 in career. | | | | | | | | | |
| 12. Indians: John Curtis, lhp, Smithtown Central HS | Smithtown, N.Y. | L-L | 6-2 | 180 | 18 | Unsigned | 1968 | 1984 | Majors (15) |
| Went unsigned, spent two years in college at Clemson, resurfaced as first-round pick of Red Sox (June '68/secondary); produced 89-97 record in 15-year career. | | | | | | | | | |
| 13. Reds: Gary Nolan, rhp, Oroville HS | Oroville, Calif. | R-R | 6-3 | 190 | 18 | $40,000 | 1966 | 1977 | Majors (10) |
| Enjoyed one of most-spectacular debuts ever by high school pick; struck out 163 in 114 innings in minors in '66, fanned 208 as National League rookie a year later. | | | | | | | | | |
| 14. Tigers: Rick Konik, 1b, St. Andrews HS | Detroit | L-L | 6-1 | 175 | 18 | Unsigned | Never Played Pro Ball | | |
| Starred in Legion play as two-way player, but one of six first-rounders in draft history who never signed; drafted two more times, then disappeared from radar. | | | | | | | | | |
| 15. Pirates: Richie Hebner, ss, Norwood HS | Norwood, Mass. | L-R | 6-1 | 210 | 19 | $28,000 | 1966 | 1985 | Majors (18) |
| One of best prep hockey players of his day in Massachusetts; Pirates had to counter offer from Boston Bruins to land sweet-swinging future 18-year big leaguer. | | | | | | | | | |
| 16. Orioles: Ted Parks, ss, California | Berkeley, Calif. | R-R | 5-11 | 185 | 19 | $35,000 | 1966 | 1971 | Class AAA (2) |
| Even as first-rounder, upstaged on his college team by three big arms: Bill Frost (No. 1, secondary phase), Andy Messersmith, Rich Nye (first '66 pick to reach majors). | | | | | | | | | |
| 17. Giants: Bob Reynolds, rhp, Ingraham HS | Seattle | R-R | 5-11 | 195 | 19 | $25,000 | 1966 | 1979 | Majors (4) |
| Fastball reached 100 mph in four-year career in majors (14-16, 3.15, 21 SV), but never fully built on dominating debut in minors (10-1, 1.89, 114 IP/183 SO). | | | | | | | | | |
| 18. White Sox: Carlos May, of, A.H. Parker HS | Birmingham, Ala. | B-R | 6-0 | 205 | 18 | $21,000 | 1966 | 1977 | Majors (10) |
| Brother of Lee May hit 18 homers in half-season as rookie in 1969, before losing half his thumb in accident with Marine Reserves; still played 10 seasons in majors. | | | | | | | | | |
| 19. Dodgers: Larry Hutton, rhp, Greenfield Central HS | Greenfield, Ind. | R-R | 6-1 | 185 | 18 | $50,000 | 1966 | 1971 | Class AA (3) |
| Career began with a bang in Rookie ball (9-4, 3.03, 119 IP/142 SO), but never corraled major control issues over balance of six-year career while going 22-28, 4.33. | | | | | | | | | |
| 20. Twins: Bob Jones, 3b, No school | Dawson, Ga. | L-R | 5-10 | 185 | 18 | $9,000 | 1966 | 1969 | Class A (1) |
| Twins set draft record by spending only $9,000 on their first-rounder, and got what they paid for: a player who never advanced beyond Class A in four seasons. | | | | | | | | | |
| **JANUARY—REGULAR PHASE** | | | | | | | | | |
| 1. Athletics: # Don Lohse, rhp, Indiana | Mehlville, Mo. | R-R | 6-4 | 185 | 19 | $17,000 | 1966 | 1970 | Class AA (1) |
| Draft eligible after dropping out of school following freshman year at Indiana; went 15-30, 4.56 in five years in minors; died in jeep accident in 1975. | | | | | | | | | |
| **JANUARY—SECONDARY PHASE** | | | | | | | | | |
| 1. Tigers: Stan Bell, rhp, Manatee (Fla.) JC | College Park, Ga. | R-R | 6-2 | 190 | 18 | Unsigned | 1967 | 1970 | Class AA (3) |
| One of most elusive players in draft's formative years; finally signed in 1967 after passing up three previous offers; went 23-28, 3.80 in four minor league seasons. | | | | | | | | | |
| **JUNE—SECONDARY PHASE** | | | | | | | | | |
| 1. Giants: Bill Frost, rhp, California | Rialto, Calif. | R-R | 6-2 | 195 | 20 | $30,000 | 1966 | 1971 | Class AAA (2) |
| Unsigned Reds 12th-rounder from 1965 developed into top college arm, set NCAA record with 169 Ks in season, but never reached majors in six pro years. | | | | | | | | | |

*# Deceased.*

been injured, he still wouldn't have made the big leagues. But your instincts told you his future was very bright."

Thirteen months after he was drafted, while playing for Winter Haven in the Class A Florida State League, Chilcott was hitting .290 and leading the league in doubles. But as he dove headfirst back to second base on a pickoff play, an infielder landed hard on Chilcott's right shoulder, leaving him with an ache that would not go away. He missed the balance of the 1967 season, and most of the next two.

"They couldn't diagnose what was wrong," Chilcott said. "It felt like there was about four inches of space between by shoulder and my arm."

Chilcott had a series of cortisone shots to deal with the constant pain, and it wasn't until 1970 that his injury was properly diagnosed as a chronic semi-dislocation. Doctors estimated the shoulder had dislocated 15 times since the injury.

## AT A GLANCE

### Never Too Late

**BOBBY RANDALL, 2B, DODGERS (55TH ROUND).** The Dodgers were persistent in their pursuit of Randall. They drafted him out of a Kansas high school and again as a college sophomore at Kansas State two years later, and finally got him in 1969 in the second round of the June secondary phase. Randall never got a chance to play in the big leagues until he was traded to Minnesota, where he played five seasons.

### Overlooked

**TOBY HARRAH, SS, PHILLIES.** Scouts who pursued Harrah as an Ohio high school talent believed he was headed for college, so passed on him in the draft. Phillies scout Tony Lucadello, however, discovered that Harrah was not in college but was working in a factory. He promptly signed him for $500. To Lucadello's regret, the Senators selected Harrah from the Phillies in the Rule 5 draft a year later, and he went on to a productive 18-year career. Harrah hit .264 overall with 195 homers and 918 RBIs.

### International Gem

**JOSE CRUZ, OF, CARDINALS.** One of the greatest players ever signed out of Puerto Rico, Cruz hit .284-165-1,077 with 317 stolen bases in a 19-year big league career—13 of them in Houston after the Cardinals sold his contract to the Astros. The Cardinals, who signed Cruz for $5,000, also signed his younger brothers, Hector (in 1970, for $12,000) and Tommy (in 1969, for $6,000), who also played in the big leagues. Jose Cruz Jr. was the third overall pick in the 1995 draft.

### Minor League Take

**REGGIE JACKSON, OF, ATHLETICS.** He didn't stay long (182 games), but Jackson left a lasting

CONTINUED ON PAGE 42

## AT A GLANCE

CONTINUED FROM PAGE 41

impression in places like Class A Modesto and Double-A Birmingham, for his explosive raw power and all-around tools. As a 19-year-old, his considerable assets also included above-average speed and a powerful right-field throwing arm. In his abbreviated minor league career, he hit .295-40-129 with 21 stolen bases.

### One Who Got Away

**JOHN CURTIS, LHP, INDIANS.** Curtis was the first of two first-rounders in 1966 who didn't sign. He spent two years in college at Clemson, and was drafted in the first round again (June/secondary phase) by the Red Sox two years later. He would go on to win 89 games in a 15-year career.

### He Was Drafted?

**CAZZIE RUSSELL, OF, ATHLETICS (27TH ROUND).** Russell had already been the No. 1 pick in the 1966 NBA draft, but had yet to sign with the New York Knicks when the A's took a flier. Russell never played baseball in college, but worked out with the White Sox prior to the 1966 draft and hit several balls into the seats at Comiskey Park.

### Did You Know . . .

While **STEVE ARLIN**, the Phillies first-round pick in the June secondary phase, left a lasting impression on college baseball in the 1965 and '66 College World Series, his professional impact never approached that of his grandfather, Harold Arlin, who broadcast the first major league game on radio in 1921 for Pittsburgh station KDKA.

### They Said It

Angels scout **NICK KAMZIC**, whose signing of Rick Reichardt in 1964 was a key development that led to the draft, on 1966 first-round pick **JIM DENEFF**: "Deneff has as much potential as Reichardt."—*Deneff never reached the big leagues.*

"After the surgery, I got back about 90 percent of the strength in my arm for throwing," Chilcott said. "But I didn't release the ball as fast anymore. And the big thing, I never was the same hitter again, and that supposedly was my strongest asset.

"I'd been a dead-pull hitter. I felt as if no one could throw a fastball by me. But after the injury, I wasn't able to hit the same way. It affected my concentration and I had a tough time adjusting. I went from a good prospect to an average player, and there are a million average lefthanded-hitting catchers."

Steve Chilcott

Subsequent injuries, including a severely broken right hand and a split kneecap, further dimmed Chilcott's potential. The Mets traded him to the Yankees after the 1971 season. He was released several weeks before the June 1972 draft, having played two games above Double-A.

Over the years, Chilcott had plenty of time to reflect on a career gone awry: "When I see that, I think, Gee, what was wrong with me? I was a kid who had as much desire and dedication to play big league baseball as anybody else. I'd like to know what I could have done differently."

### JACKSON GARNERS HIGHEST BONUS

Jackson, 20, was a sophomore outfielder at Arizona State and a highly regarded defensive back on the football team. He hit .327 in his only season of varsity competition, and set school records for home runs and RBIs. Jackson's 15 homers were second in the nation to Washington State's Dale Ford, who set an NCAA record with 17, while his 65 RBIs were second to Arizona's Eddie Leon, who finished with a college record 75.

It was the second straight year the A's went for an Arizona State product, following Rick Monday. Jackson signed for a bonus of $80,000—$5,000 of which was earmarked for a new car. While it was the largest bonus paid out in 1966, it was $20,000 less than Monday had received. Kansas City's West Coast scout Bob Zuk had zeroed in on Jackson during his sophomore year at Arizona State. The A's also sent farm director Eddie Robinson to watch Jackson play. Both raved about his talent.

"I couldn't believe my eyes," Robinson said. "For the first time, I saw a prospect who rated plus in every category: arm, legs, glove, bat and bat power."

The draft worked out perfectly for the A's, as Jackson was the player they wanted all along. The only debate was where Jackson would begin his pro career. Because Jackson had played only one season of varsity baseball and was less advanced in baseball than he was in football, Zuk wanted Jackson to start at the lowest levels of the minor leagues.

"(A's owner Charles O.) Finley wanted Reggie in Double-A, but (scouting director) Ray Swallow and I fought that tooth and nail," Zuk said. "Reggie, at that time of his career, did not have a lot of confidence. I told Charley, 'If you put him in Double-A, we may never hear of Reggie again.' "

Zuk got his wish. Jackson began his career at Lewiston of the short-season Northwest League. Two weeks later he was promoted to Modesto of the Class A California League, where his massive raw power showed itself. In 68 games at Modesto, Jackson hit .298 with 23 homers and 71 RBIs.

He reached Double-A Birmingham a year later and was there a couple of months before the major league club beckoned. Jackson was called up to Kansas City on June 9, 1967—a year to the day after he signed. He lasted 21 years in the big leagues.

### ECKERT'S FIRST TASK

For the only time in draft history, the 1966 draft featured three phases. In addition to the June draft, which included the likes of Chilcott and Jackson, and the obscure American Legion draft in late August (which was abolished at the 1966 Winter Meetings), a new January phase was introduced.

Fear of legal repercussions was a principal reason for a second draft. Some owners and executives contended that a draft was illegal because it deprived players of the right to bargain on the open market, so they contended that a second draft would demonstrate that players wouldn't be held too long by the organization that drafted them.

The January draft, one of the first official orders of business for new commissioner William "Spike" Eckert, featured a regular phase for recent high school graduates, junior-college players and others who were 21, and a secondary phase for previously drafted players who were eligible again.

## How They Should Have Done It

Based on the career WAR (Wins Above Replacement, as calculated by Baseball-Reference.com) numbers achieved by all the players eligible for the 1966 draft, here's how the first round should have unfolded. Numbers in parentheses indicate the round when the player was actually drafted

| | Player, Pos. | Actual Draft | WAR | Bonus |
|---|---|---|---|---|
| 1. | * Tom Seaver, rhp | Braves (Jan.-S/1) | 111.0 | $51,000 |
| 2. | Reggie Jackson, of | Athletics (1) | 74.0 | $80,000 |
| 3. | Toby Harrah, of | Phillies (NDFA) | 51.2 | $500 |
| 4. | Andy Messersmith, rhp | Angels (June-S/1) | 40.2 | $39,000 |
| 5. | Charlie Hough, rhp | Dodgers (8) | 39.5 | $5,000 |
| 6. | Richie Hebner, 3b | Pirates (1) | 32.9 | $28,000 |
| 7. | Bill Russell, of | Dodgers (9) | 31.0 | $14,000 |
| 8. | Joe Niekro, rhp | Cubs (June-S/3) | 29.9 | $4,000 |
| 9. | Gary Nolan, rhp | Reds (1) | 25.9 | $40,000 |
| 10. | Dave Cash, ss | Pirates (5) | 25.2 | $8,000 |
| 11. | Steve Braun, ss | Twins (10) | 17.6 | $5,000 |
| 12. | Ken Brett, lhp/of | Red Sox (1) | 16.6 | $56,000 |
| | Del Unser, of | Senators (June-S/1) | 16.6 | $10,000 |
| 14. | Cliff Johnson, c | Astros (5) | 16.2 | $10,000 |
| 15. | Ted Sizemore, c | Dodgers (15) | 16.1 | $8,000 |
| 16. | Carlos May, of | White Sox (1) | 10.4 | $21,000 |
| 17. | Mike Jorgensen, 1b | Mets (4) | 9.3 | $10,000 |
| 18. | Clay Kirby, rhp | Cardinals (3) | 7.1 | $8,000 |
| 19. | George Stone, lhp | Braves (5) | 7.0 | $25,500 |
| 20. | Steve Kline, rhp | Yankees (7) | 6.9 | $16,000 |

| | Top 3 Unsigned Players | | | Year Signed |
|---|---|---|---|---|
| 1. | Darrell Evans, 3b | Tigers (June-S/5) | 58.5 | 1967 |
| 2. | Ron Cey, 3b | Mets (19) | 53.3 | 1968 |
| 3. | Steve Garvey, 3b | Twins (3) | 37.6 | 1968 |

**Selection by Braves voided; signed with Mets after special lottery.*

Eckert's leadership was tested immediately in a case involving University of Southern California righthander Tom Seaver, who was drafted by the Atlanta Braves in the first round of the secondary phase. Seaver signed with the Braves a month after the draft for a bonus of $40,000, but Eckert nullified the contract because USC had already begun its 1966 spring schedule. But because Seaver had signed a contract, he was also no longer eligible to play in college, per NCAA regulations.

Eckert set up a special drawing for Seaver's services, and the Mets, Philadelphia Phillies and Cleveland Indians elected to join in the proceedings. The Mets pulled Seaver's name out of a hat.

A total of 197 players were selected in the first January draft, including 95 in the regular phase, which would be the fewest ever. Righthander Don Lohse, who had left Indiana University, was picked first in the regular phase by Kansas City. Manatee (Fla.) Junior College righthander Stan Bell was selected first by Detroit in the secondary phase and went unsigned. Bell also passed up an offer in the 1965 draft as a second-round pick of the Washington Senators, which made him eligible for the secondary phase seven months later.

### HIGH EXPECTATIONS FOR '66 CROP

The June draft, conducted over two days at New York's Roosevelt Hotel—the same site as the inaugural 1965 draft—was also split into two phases. The regular phase saw 833 players claimed, the secondary 104.

Veteran talent sleuth Paul Richards, a former general manager who spent the spring as a super-scout for the Phillies, offered his assessment of the available talent: "Last year, I was wondering whether we could pick up as many as three players. But this year, there is more quality than in any year since World War II. Give me the entire 20 of the first round and, in three years, I guarantee you that team would make trouble for anybody. And I mean anybody."

Just 12 of those first-rounders eventually played in the big leagues, and only Jackson became an unqualified star. Lefthander Ken Brett (Red Sox), righthander Gary Nolan (Reds), third baseman Richie Hebner (Pirates) and outfielder Carlos May (White Sox) did become established big leaguers.

Three first-rounders never advanced beyond Class A, while Michigan high school first baseman Rick Konik didn't sign with the Detroit Tigers and never played professional baseball—even after being drafted two more times.

Richards' assessment of the talent was on the mark, however, when it came to first impressions. Rarely has there been a draft when so many high-

### Fastest To The Majors

| | Player, Pos. | Drafted (Round) | Debut |
|---|---|---|---|
| 1. | Rich Nye, lhp | Cubs (14) | Sept. 16, 1966 |
| 2. | Tom Seaver, rhp | Braves (Jan.-S/1) | April 13, 1967 |
| 3. | * Gary Nolan, rhp | Reds (1) | April 15, 1967 |
| 4. | Joe Niekro, rhp | Cubs (June-S/3) | April 16, 1967 |
| 5. | Reggie Jackson, of | Athletics (1) | June 9, 1967 |

**LAST PLAYER TO RETIRE:** Charlie Hough, rhp (July 26, 1994)

**High school selection.*

### DRAFT SPOTLIGHT: TOM SEAVER

**Tom Seaver was not an overwhelming prospect as an amateur, but he came on strong late in his college career and shot to the majors**

Tom Seaver went into the Baseball Hall of Fame in 1992 with the highest percentage of votes (98.84) of any player on record at the time. It culminated a brilliant 20-year major league career that included 311 wins and three Cy Young Awards.

But there was little in Seaver's amateur background to indicate that he would evolve into one of the game's greatest pitchers.

Seaver began his pro career in a swirl of controversy in 1966, when his rights were awarded to the New York Mets in a special lottery arranged by the commissioner's office. The Atlanta Braves had selected Seaver in the secondary phase of the January draft, with the last pick in the first round, and agreed to terms on a $40,000 bonus on Feb. 24. But because the University of Southern California had already begun its 1966 spring schedule, Seaver was ineligible to sign and commissioner William Eckert nullified the contract. Because Seaver had signed a contract, the NCAA also ruled that he was no longer eligible to play in college. It was a classic Catch-22 scenario.

Seaver's father threatened a lawsuit, and in an unprecedented move, Eckert set up a special drawing for Seaver's services with a condition that the pitcher would be paid a bonus of at least $50,000. The Mets, Philadelphia Phillies and Cleveland Indians elected to participate, and on April 3, 1966, the Mets had the good fortune to pull Seaver's name out of a hat. A day later, they signed him to a contract that provided a bonus of $51,000.

Eckert also fined the Atlanta organization $500 and forbid the Braves from signing Seaver for a period of at least three years.

"I did it for the interest of the boy and the public," Eckert said. "The youngster had previously signed a contract with another club in good faith, only to learn that he had been improperly contacted. It was not his fault the contract was later invalidated."

Seaver made an immediate impression on Mets officials, especially after getting off to a hot start at Triple-A Jacksonville. "He's the best pitching prospect in the minor leagues," proclaimed Jacksonville manager Solly Hemus. "Wonder Boy reminds me of Robin Roberts the way he throws, only he's faster than Roberts. He knows what he's doing and has great poise. If he's not injured, he's going to be one of the big stars of the game."

Seaver went 12-12, 3.13 with 188 strikeouts in 210 innings at Jacksonville in his one and only season in the minors. A year later, he was in the big leagues to stay, and by 1969 steered the Miracle Mets to their improbable World Series triumph, winning 25 games.

But it wasn't always that way for Seaver. As a high school senior in Fresno, Calif., in 1962, a 5-foot-10, 165-pound Seaver was so frail that few colleges showed interest. He spent the next year working in a local packing plant and in the Marines, and when he enrolled at Fresno City College in the fall of 1963 he matured into the team's ace.

Seaver joined the USC rotation in the spring of 1965, and while he went 10-2, 2.47, his raw stuff didn't overwhelm scouts and he wasn't picked until the eighth round of baseball's inaugural draft by the Los Angeles Dodgers. The two sides never came close to a deal, as Seaver's $70,000 asking price was not met by Dodgers scout Tommy Lasorda.

As a 21-year-old junior, Seaver was eligible for the draft's new secondary phase the following January, and almost overnight became a prospect with legitimate raw stuff.

"Some clubs wouldn't give him more than $4,000 because he had a below-average fastball," veteran Southern California scout Al Kubski said. "But he pitched against a team called the Crosby All-Stars just before the draft and was facing active major leaguers. He struck out 12 in five innings. I found out then that, yes, a fastball can be improved after a pitcher becomes older. It's unusual but it can happen, as I saw with Seaver."

## WORTH NOTING

The top players in both college football and college basketball were among those drafted in 1966. **MIKE GARRETT**, the 1965 Heisman Trophy winner who last played baseball briefly as an outfielder for Southern California in the spring of 1965, was selected in the January draft by the Dodgers. While he chose to play for the American Football League's Kansas City Chiefs, he never gave up on his goal to play professional baseball—even after he had established himself as one of the top running backs in the NFL. He was selected by the Dodgers again in 1970.

Michigan's **CAZZIE RUSSELL** starred in basketball for four years at Michigan, leading to his selection by the New York Knicks as the No. 1 pick in the 1966 NBA draft. It wasn't a slam dunk that the 6-foot-5 Russell would simply pursue an NBA career, however, as he played baseball in high school and in summer-league competition while at Michigan, and always maintained that baseball was his preferred sport. Russell, who grew up in Chicago, was invited to work out with the White Sox just prior to the 1966 baseball draft, and launched several balls into the upper deck at old Comiskey Park. Shortly thereafter, he indicated he might consider baseball as a career choice . . . "if baseball made me the right offer." It was not to be, and Russell went on to an all-star career in the NBA over the next 12 years.

**CHARLES CHASE**, a first-round pick of the Twins in the January secondary phase out of a California junior college, became noted as the only draft pick known to have died in action in the Vietnam War. After hitting .269 for the Twins entry in the Rookie-level Gulf Coast League in 1966, Chase entered the service that fall. He spent the following year in training and soon thereafter received his orders to report to Southeast Asia. He was killed by hostile

end players stood out in their professional debuts.

Jackson set an early tone with his impressive power display in the California League, but it was the high school arms that stole the spotlight. Nolan went 7-3, 1.82 and struck out 163 in 104 innings, while walking just 30, in the short-season Northern League. Righthander "Bullet Bob" Reynolds (Giants) went a combined 10-1, 1.89 with 183 strikeouts in 114 innings in the Rookie-level Pioneer and Class A California leagues. Righthander Al Santorini (Braves) more than held his own against stiffer competition in the Double-A Texas League by going 3-2, 1.69 with 49 strikeouts in 48 innings. Righthander Wayne Twitchell (Astros), the third pick overall, reached Triple-A in his debut, while righthander Dean Burk (Cubs) and lefthander Larry Hutton (Dodgers) shared the Pioneer League lead in wins while striking out 249 between them in 229 innings.

One of the draft's great truisms is that first-year success in the minor leagues is not always an accurate barometer of success in the big leagues, and it certainly proved true with the 1966 class.

Not only did the hard-throwing Nolan overwhelm his competition in the lower minors, but he was equally spectacular a year later when the Cincinnati Reds elevated the 18-year-old California product to a spot in their rotation.

Less than a year after receiving a $40,000 bonus out of a small northern California high school, Nolan struck out 15 San Francisco Giants in a game, including future Hall of Famer Willie Mays four times. Though he went 110-70, 3.03 overall in a 10-year big league career, he never again topped the 206 strikeouts he achieved as a rookie.

Reynolds never came close to achieving the success he experienced in his dazzling 1966 debut, in large measure because he never developed another pitch to accompany his blazing fastball, which was routinely clocked in triple digits. He went 14-16, 3.15 with 21 saves in parts of four major league seasons, but spent the bulk of his 14-year career in the minors.

Ken Brett

Nolan wasn't the only teenage pitching prodigy to make his mark in 1967. In the World Series between the St. Louis Cardinals and Boston Red Sox, Ken Brett, barely 19, worked in two games in relief for the Red Sox, making him the youngest pitcher ever to appear in the World Series.

"Nothing ever fazed him. We had no hesitation about putting him on the World Series roster, none at all," recalled Dick Williams, Boston's rookie manager. "He had the guts of a burglar."

Brett had a 15-year major league career but became better known as George Brett's older brother. Ken, as the fourth overall pick in the 1966 draft, actually commanded more attention out of El Segundo (Calif.) High than George would five years later.

The elder Brett went 30-3 as a pitcher in his high school career, but the Red Sox were the only team that wanted him as a pitcher. "The other teams would have drafted him as a center fielder," brother George said. "He might have been a Hall of Famer, he was just such a natural. The ball jumped off his bat. A lot of people said he was the best hitter in the family, and maybe he was."

Shortly after the 1967 World Series, Brett spent six months in the Army Reserve and missed spring training in 1968. He returned to action too quickly after finishing his military duty, and in his first outing that season, in Triple-A, he was left in the game for nine innings. He soon developed elbow trouble that plagued him the rest of his career.

Brett would go on to pitch with 10 different big league teams, including a 1981 season in Kansas City as a teammate of his brother. But with an overall record of 83-85, he never lived up to expectations. "The worst curse in life," Brett would later say, "is unlimited potential."

## Top 25 Bonuses

| Player, Pos. | Drafted (Round) | Order | Bonus |
|---|---|---|---|
| **1. Reggie Jackson, of** | **Athletics (1)** | **2** | **$80,000** |
| **2. Steve Arlin, rhp** | **Phillies (June-S/1)** | **(13)** | **$77,500** |
| 3. * Steve Chilcott, c | Mets (1) | 1 | $75,000 |
| **4. * Ken Brett, lhp/of** | **Red Sox (1)** | **4** | **$56,000** |
| **5. Tom Seaver, rhp** | **# Braves (Jan.-S/1)** | **(20)** | **$51,000** |
| 6. Jim DeNeff, ss | Angels (1) | 8 | $50,000 |
| *** Al Santorini, rhp** | **Braves (1)** | **11** | **$50,000** |
| * Larry Hutton, rhp | Dodgers (1) | 19 | $50,000 |
| **9. Bob Reed, rhp** | **Tigers (June-S/2)** | **(22)** | **$46,000** |
| **10. Jim Lyttle, of** | **Yankees (1)** | **10** | **$43,000** |
| **11. * Gary Nolan, rhp** | **Reds (1)** | **13** | **$40,000** |
| **12. Andy Messersmith, rhp** | **Angels (June-S/1)** | **(12)** | **$39,000** |
| 13. Bob Biletnikoff, of | Yankees (Jan.-S/1) | (17) | $38,000 |
| **14. * Tom Griffin, rhp** | **Astros (Jan.-R/1)** | **(4)** | **$36,500** |
| **15. * Wayne Twitchell, rhp** | **Astros (1)** | **3** | **$35,000** |
| * Dean Burk, rhp | Cubs (1) | 5 | $35,000 |
| *** Tom Grieve, of** | **Senators (1)** | **6** | **$35,000** |
| * Mike Biko, rhp | Phillies (1) | 9 | $35,000 |
| Ted Parks, ss | Orioles (1) | 16 | $35,000 |
| **Oscar Brown, of** | **Braves (June-S/1)** | **(7)** | **$35,000** |
| **21. * Gary Ryerson, lhp** | **Giants (13)** | **257** | **$33,000** |
| Berke Reichenbach, ss | White Sox (June-S/1) | (4) | $33,000 |
| 23. * Fabian Mang, lhp/1b | Braves (2) | 31 | $30,000 |
| * Leo Pinnick, lhp | Twins (2) | 40 | $30,000 |
| **25. * Richie Hebner, 3b** | **Pirates (1)** | **15** | **$28,000** |

*Major leaguers in bold. *High school selection.*
*#Signing voided; signed with Mets after special drawing.*

## ARLIN HEADLINES COLLEGE CROP

Only four college players were picked in the first round of the June regular phase. With the notable exception of Jackson, it wasn't a noteworthy crop, and Indiana third baseman Jim DeNeff (Angels) and California shortstop Ted Parks (Orioles) never reached the majors.

Most of the better college talent, notably Ohio State righthander Steve Arlin, Cal righthander Bill Frost and Arizona shortstop Eddie Leon, had been drafted a year earlier, and so was available in the secondary phase.

Arlin, who led Ohio State to a College World Series title, and Leon, who set an NCAA single-season RBI record, were expected to be in consideration for the first selection overall. But the

Ohio State's Steve Arlin was one of the best college pitchers ever, but his pro career never took off in part because of his passion for . . . dentistry?

Giants were wary that both would be tough signs and settled on Frost, who signed for $30,000.

Frost, who set an NCAA single-season record with 169 strikeouts in 128 innings, went 12-3, 1.12 for the Golden Bears as their staff ace. A year earlier, the 6-foot-3, 195-pound Frost was the No. 3 starter in the Bears rotation behind righthander Andy Messersmith and lefthander Rich Nye, and a 13th-round selection of the Reds.

Messersmith, who also went unsigned in 1965, went in the secondary phase to the Angels with the 12th overall pick, while Nye, undrafted a year earlier, went to the Cubs in the 14th round of the regular phase. Frost never reached the majors after toiling in the minors for six years.

Nye, on the other hand, became the first player from the 1966 draft to reach the majors, marking the second year in a row that distinction was achieved by a lefthander selected by the Cubs. In 1965, the pitcher was Ken Holtzman; Nye found his way to Chicago in September.

Messersmith went on to assemble the best career of the trio, winning 130 games in a 12-year career, and gained even more notoriety for his role in the historic 1975 decision by arbitrator Peter Seitz to strike down baseball's reserve clause and usher in the era of free agency.

Leon was taken by the Cubs with the third pick overall. And just like a year earlier, when he refused to sign with Minnesota as the eighth overall pick, he again did not sign. He finally signed with Cleveland in 1967, as a second-round pick in the June secondary phase, but by then his stock had slipped and he received a bonus of just $10,500.

Arlin was the most publicized—and most expensive—college pitcher in the 1966 draft. A two-time Ohio State All-American, he almost singlehandedly pitched the Buckeyes to the 1966 College World Series title. The 6-foot-3, 190-pound workhorse finished every game the Buckeyes won at Omaha, and went to the mound five times in a six-day stretch. He allowed just two runs in 21 innings, striking out 28, and was the tournament MVP.

Arlin slipped to the 12th round of the 1965 draft because of his bonus demands and turned down a reported $80,000 offer from the Tigers, gambling that a better bonus offer would come along in 1966. Just like in 1965, Arlin's asking price scared off prospective suitors, but the Phillies snagged him with the 13th pick in the secondary phase. His signing bonus of $77,500 was the second-largest in the 1966 draft.

"Without any question," Phillies special-assignment scout Gene Martin said, "he is the most outstanding college pitcher I have seen in years."

Arlin never lived up to his college billing, in part because his true passion was dentistry. His con-

## Largest Bonuses By Round

| | Player, Pos. | Club | Bonus |
|---|---|---|---|
| **1.** | **Reggie Jackson, of** | **Athletics** | **$80,000** |
| 2. | * Fabian Mang, lhp | Braves | $30,000 |
| | * Leo Pinnick, lhp | Twins | $30,000 |
| **3.** | **Jim Magnuson, lhp** | **White Sox** | **$18,000** |
| **4.** | *** Leslie Cain, lhp** | **Tigers** | **$16,000** |
| **5.** | **George Stone, lhp** | **Braves** | **$25,500** |
| **6.** | *** Mike Nagy, rhp** | **Red Sox** | **$24,000** |
| 7. | John Beaton, rhp | Giants | $18,000 |
| 8. | Michael Floyd, of | Angels | $16,000 |
| **9.** | *** Bill Russell, of** | **Dodgers** | **$14,000** |
| 10. | * William Cupp, c | Braves | $10,000 |
| **Jan/R** | *** Tom Griffin, rhp** | **Astros (1)** | **$36,500** |
| Jan/S | Bob Biletnikoff, of | Yankees (1) | $38,000 |
| **Jun/S** | **Steve Arlin, rhp** | **Phillies (1)** | **$77,500** |

*Major leaguers in bold. *High school selection.*

## WORTH NOTING

action on June 11, 1968, at age 21.

■ **REGGIE JACKSON** reached Kansas City on June 9, 1967—a year to the day after he signed with the A's—and lasted 21 years in the big leagues. He was sixth on the all-time list with 563 home runs, while his 2,597 strikeouts were more than anyone who ever played. Jackson's slugging exploits were everything the A's hoped for when they signed him in 1966. He had tied the national collegiate home run record that season, although it was re-broken later in the year. But at the time, Jackson was not just the one-tool power hitter he became late in his major league career. When he enrolled at Arizona State, Jackson was an all-around athlete. He was an All-American running back at Cheltenham High in Wyncote, Pa., attracting 51 scholarship offers for football. Only three schools offered him baseball scholarships, so Jackson went to Arizona State as a defensive back who played baseball on the side. When Jackson was 20, he ran the 100-yard dash in 9.7 seconds. Scouts who saw him expected a five-tool player and frequently compared him to Willie Mays. Reggie responded by telling reporters that "Mays has always been my hero, my idol, my ideal."

■ Mississippi State shared the lead in both January (five) and June (nine) for most players drafted from one college. Hillcrest High of Springfield, Mo., gained special merit in June by having six players drafted—a record for high schools that stood for years.

■ The annual American Legion draft was held in late August, but its fate was sealed when teams selected just eight players in the proceedings. It was in this draft that catcher **PETE VARNEY**, who would go on to be drafted a record seven times before finally signing in 1971 with the White Sox, was first selected.

## IN FOCUS: GARY NOLAN

Less than a year after being drafted in the first round out of a small northern California high school, 18-year-old Cincinnati Reds righthander Gary Nolan struck out 15 San Francisco Giants in a National League game, including future Hall of Famer Willie Mays four times. "Nobody's ever done that to me before," Mays said.

"He's the best-looking pitcher I've seen this spring—and I mean the best," veteran National League umpire Augie Donatelli said of Nolan, just before he opened the 1967 season by striking out the side in the first inning of a 7-3 win over the Houston Astros. Nolan would go on to post a 14-8, 2.58 record while striking out 206 in 227 innings.

But on a cold, blustery day in his first start in spring training in 1968, Nolan walked off the mound in the second inning, after making just two pitches, with a strained shoulder.

Arm problems would plague Nolan throughout his 10-year major league career, all but one with the Reds. Though he would assemble an otherwise impressive 110-70, 3.03 record overall, he never again topped the 206 strikeouts he achieved as a rookie or dominated hitters quite like he did as a precocious teenager.

tract with the Phillies allowed him to enter dental school that fall, and to report late to spring training each year. Arlin never reached Philadelphia and was selected by San Diego in the National League expansion draft in 1968. In six major league seasons, mostly pitching for bad Padres teams, Arlin went 34-67. He led the NL in losses in 1971 and '72. After being traded to Cleveland in 1973, he retired on the first day of spring training the following year to become a full-time dentist.

### MILITARY ACCIDENT SLOWS MAY

May, picked 18th overall by the Chicago White Sox, was well on his way to becoming the American League rookie of the year in 1969, envisioning a career that might rival that of his older brother Lee, then the power-hitting first baseman of the Reds.

But on Aug. 11, 1969, while on maneuvers with his Marine Reserve unit at Camp Pendleton, Calif., May lost the top joint of his right thumb when a mortar shell accidentally fired. The injury cost him the balance of the season and necessitated immediate surgery, along with eventual bone and skin grafting.

"I'll be playing baseball again. I love the game," he said three days after the accident. "I figure I'll have to cut down on my stroke a little bit. And I will have to change my grip to control throws. But I'll play again."

May did return to play 10 years in the big leagues. But his career total of 90 home runs fell far short of expectations after he broke in as a 21-year-old rookie and hit 18 homers in half a season.

Hebner carved out a fine 18-year major league career, hitting .276 with 203 homers, after the Pittsburgh Pirates took him with the 15th pick. As one of the best high school hockey players ever developed in Massachusetts, Hebner also drew interest from the NHL's Boston Bruins, who were prepared to offer him $10,000.

"I'd rather play baseball," was Hebner's response, and he quickly inked a $28,000 bonus offer from the Pirates. He was in Pittsburgh three years later, and his best and most memorable season may have come as a rookie in 1969, when he was hitting over .400 well into May. He finished the year at .301—the highest single-season average of his career.

Throughout his big league career, which ended in 1985, and over most of the time after that when he was a minor league manager and hitting coach, Hebner worked in the offseason as a grave-digger for his family-owned cemetery in Norwood, Mass.

Outfielders Tom Grieve (Senators) and Leron Lee (Cardinals), the sixth and seventh picks in the 1966 draft, were the last two first-rounders to sign as they weighed offers to play college football. Both had modest major league careers but made an impact in other ways.

### Highest Unsigned Picks

**JUNE / REGULAR PHASE ONLY**

| Player, Pos., Team (Round) | College | Re-Drafted |
|---|---|---|
| John Curtis, lhp, Indians (1) | Clemson | Red Sox '68 (S/1) |
| Rick Konik, 1b, Tigers (1) | None | Athletics '67 (Jan.-S/1) |
| C.E. Bryson, of, Cubs (2) | None | Never |
| Pat Skrable, of, Phillies (2) | Bakersfield (Calif.) JC | Phillies '67 (Jan.-S/1) |
| Scott Fields, lhp, Tigers (2) | Ohio | Never |
| Johnny Oates, c, White Sox (2) | * Virginia Tech | Orioles '67 (Jan.-S/1) |
| John D'Auria, rhp, Astros (3) | * Arcadia (Calif.) HS | Tigers '67 (Jan.-S/3) |
| Lou Camilli, 3b, Senators (3) | * Texas A&M | Indians '67 (S/3) |
| Bill Gillean, rhp, Angels (3) | Cerritos (Calif.) JC | Braves '67 (Jan.-S/1) |
| Patrick Amos, ss, Phillies (3) | Texas | Never |

**TOTAL UNSIGNED PICKS:** Top 5 Rounds (27), Top 10 Rounds (71)

**Returned to same school*

Grieve, a three-sport standout and one of the nation's top-rated quarterbacks with a scholarship offer from Michigan, signed with the Senators on Aug. 15, after the team agreed to let him attend college for two years. Two decades and a franchise shift later, Grieve was directing the fortunes of the Texas Rangers as the team's general manager. He later became a broadcaster for the club.

Tom Grieve

Lee had numerous offers to play college football before deciding on a baseball career. Once his time in the U.S. majors ended in 1976, he went on to an 11-year career in Japan. His .320 career batting average is still the highest mark in Japanese baseball history for players with more than 4,000 at-bats. He also set records for foreign players for hits (1,579), home runs (283) and RBIs (912).

Lee's younger brother Leon, a ninth-round draft pick of the Cardinals in 1971 who never reached the big leagues in the U.S., also enjoyed considerable success in Japan, hitting .308 with 268 homers and 884 RBIs in 10 seasons.

Leron Lee was one of four 1966 first-rounders whose careers ended with a tour of duty in Japan. May played there for four years, Reynolds one and outfielder Jimmy Lyttle (Yankees) had a productive seven-year stint.

The notoriety of Grieve and Lee wouldn't end with their own careers, as Grieve's son Ben would become the second overall pick in the 1992 draft, making them the first father-son first-round picks. Lee's nephew Derrek (Leon's son) also became a first-round selection a year later.

### One Team's Draft: Los Angeles Dodgers

| Player, Pos. | Bonus | Player, Pos. | Bonus | Player, Pos. | Bonus |
|---|---|---|---|---|---|
| 1. * Larry Hutton, rhp | $50,000 | 5. * Gordon Allen, of | Did not sign | **9. * Bill Russell, of** | **$14,000** |
| **2. * John Gamble, ss** | **$15,000** | 6. * Dennis James, lhp | $18,000 | 10. * Dennis Thornton, 1b | $6,000 |
| 3. Rich Thompson, 2b | $15,000 | 7. * James Doran, of | Did not sign | **Other Ted Sizemore (15), c** | **$8,000** |
| 4. * Jerry Bagwell, ss | $4,500 | **8. * Charlie Hough, inf/rhp** | **$5,000** | | |

*Major leaguers in bold. *High school selection.*

# 1966 Draft List

**Did not sign. Major leaguers in bold, with first and last years noted. Order of selection indicated in parentheses. For the first five rounds of the June Regular Phase and the first round of all other phases, the peak level of each player is noted.*

## ATLANTA BRAVES

### January—Regular Phase (12)

1. Robert Ritchie, of, Bryant Stratton Business College, Lynnfield, Mass.—(Rookie)
2. Pete Rivera, lhp, Wilson HS, Los Angeles.
3. Jack Crist, ss, Los Angeles Harbor JC.
4. *Jack Patterson, 1b, William Jewell (Mo.) JC.
5. Ray Burner, rhp, Jersey City, N.J.
6. Greg Rineer, ss, Jersey City, N.J.

### January—Secondary Phase (20)

1. **(void) *Tom Seaver, rhp, University of Southern California.—(1967-86)**

DRAFT DROP *Elected to Baseball Hall of Fame, 1992*

2. *Donald Lando, of, Ithaca (N.Y.) College.
3. *Orville Hollrah, rhp, University of Missouri.
4. Darryl Hester, lhp, Byng HS, Ada, Okla.
5. *Pete Middlekauff, 1b-rhp, Stanford University.

### June—Regular Phase (11)

1. **Al Santorini, rhp, Union (N.J.) HS.—(1968-73)**
2. Fabian Mang, lhp-1b, Jesuit HS, New Orleans, La.—(AA)
3. ***Frank Duffy, ss, Stanford University.—(1970-79)**

DRAFT DROP *Returned to Stanford; re-drafted by Reds, June 1967/secondary phase (1st round)*

4. John Laberrique, c, Loyola Marymount University.—(High A)
5. **George Stone, lhp-1b, Louisiana Tech.—(1967-75)**
6. *Reid Braden, 1b, Cerritos (Calif.) JC.
7. *Chuck Koselke, 1b, Western Michigan University.
8. *Jerald Hurt, rhp, University of Missouri.
9. *Sam Narron, c, East Carolina University.

DRAFT DROP *Son of Sam Narron, major leaguer (1935-43) • Cousin of Jerry Narron, major leaguer (1979-87); major league manager (2001-07) • Father of Sam Narron, major leaguer (2004-05)*

10. William Cupp, c-1b, Banning HS, Wilmington, Calif.
11. *Pat Harrison, ss, University of Southern California.

DRAFT DROP *Baseball coach, Pepperdine (1995-96); baseball coach, Mississippi (1997-2000)*

12. Chet Bergalowski, c, Mississippi State University.
13. ***Buddy Harris, rhp, Roxborough (Pa.) HS.—(1970-71)**
14. John Stewart, rhp, University of Southern California.
15. Bob Toney, 3b, Oklahoma State University.
16. *Roger Cain, of, Roosevelt HS, Los Angeles.
17. *Charlie Brown, rhp, Central Connecticut State University.
18. Rudolph Green, c, Douglas HS, Oklahoma City, Okla.
19. *Rod O'Brien, 3b, Lakewood HS, Long Beach, Calif.
20. *Bill Hanley, of, Sacred Heart HS, Waterbury, Conn.
21. John Guest, 1b-of, Parker HS, Greenville, S.C.
22. Kenneth Smith, c, Central HS, Phenix City, Ala.
23. *Walter Peto, 2b, Seton Hall University.
24. *Glenn Lusk, 1b, Mississippi State University.
25. *Dana Halvorson, 1b-of, Rogers HS, Spokane, Wash.
26. Ray Allen, rhp, El Camino (Calif.) JC.
27. *David Wright, c, Anniston (Ala.) HS.
28. Vincent Petrarca, ss, St. Peter's College.
29. *Stanley Rand, 1b-of, Wheatley HS, San Antonio, Texas.
30. *Kenneth Perrin, rhp, Texas A&M University.
31. *Jimmy Gruber, ss, Edgewater HS, Orlando, Fla.
32. *Jimmy Jackson, lhp, Grambling University.
33. ***Gary Ross, rhp, Port Vue-Liberty HS, Port Vue, Pa.—(1968-77)**
34. *Brian Bach, rhp, Kingston (N.Y.) HS.
35. *Larry McGary, c, Hillsborough HS, Tampa.
36. *Brantley Jones, lhp-1b, Kingsbury HS, Memphis, Tenn.
37. Bobby Buckner, 2b, Napa (Calif.) HS.

DRAFT DROP *Brother of Bill Buckner, major leaguer (1969-90)*

38. Jim O'Loughlin, lhp, Chicago.
39. *Peter Riffle, lhp, Adams HS, Adamstown, Pa.
40. Ralph Wells, 3b, Auburn University.
41. Marvin Murphy, 1b, Southeast Lauderdale HS, Meridian, Miss.
42. John Lee, 1b, Webster HS, Minden, La.
43. *Richard Allred, ss, Tulsa, Okla.
44. Leroy Brown, of, Emporia State (Kan.) University.
45. *Ron Romaniello, c, Torrington (Conn.) HS.
46. *Terry Kirkpatrick, c, Mona Shores HS, Muskegon, Mich.
47. **Roe Skidmore, c-1b, Millikin (Ill.) University.—(1970)**
48. *Richard Sauget, c, University of Notre Dame.
49. Stan Evans, c, Bowling Green State University.
50. John Pitrulis, c, St. Procopius (Ill.) College.
51. William Matuez, rhp, Seton Hall University.
52. *Thomas Tidball, ss, Southeast HS, Lincoln, Neb.
53. *Larry Brown, rhp, Wichita (Kan.) HS.
54. *Robert Schnietz, ss, Christian Brothers (Tenn.) College.
55. James Conklin, rhp, Tuxedo (N.Y.) HS.
56. *Ronald Schroeder, 1b-of, Cleo Springs (Okla.) HS.
57. *Patrick Colombo, 3b, Nassau (N.Y.) CC.

### June—Secondary Phase (7)

1. **Oscar Brown, of, University of Southern California.—(1969-73)**

DRAFT DROP *Brother of Ollie Brown, major leaguer (1965-77)*

2. **Gary Neibauer, rhp, University of Nebraska.—(1969-73)**
3. (void) *Reid Braden, 1b, Lakewood (Calif.) JC.
4. *Daniel Hootstein, of, Harvard University.
5. *Frank Portera, c, Mississippi State University.
6. *Dennis Trame, rhp, Quincy (Ill.) College.

### August—American Legion Phase (12)

1. *Guy McTheny, rhp-c, Sarasota (Fla.) HS–(Low A)
2. *Jack Goldberg, 2b, Union, N.J.

## BALTIMORE ORIOLES

### January—Regular Phase (15)

1. (void) *Russell Vitallo, rhp, Berkshire (Mass.) CC.—(Low A)
2. Carlos Evans, c, University of Wisconsin.
3. **Alonzo "Candy" Harris, 3b, Fremont HS, Los Angeles.—(1967)**
4. *Paul Dumais, lhp, Holy Cross College.
5. *Edwin Maras, rhp, South Dakota State University.
6. *Steve Melfa, rhp, Franklin & Marshall (Pa.) College.
7. Bert Jones, c, Buffalo State College.
8. *Dick Wieczezak, ss, Seton Hall University.
9. Doug Ward, rhp, Annapolis (Md.) HS.
10. Dan Prebenda, lhp, Livonia, Mich.
11. *Harry Stelly, lhp, Lafayette, La.
12. Paul Fleshner, ss, Kankakee, Ill.

### January—Secondary Phase (7)

1. ***Gary Gentry, rhp, Phoenix (Ariz.) JC.—(1969-75)**
2. *Stump Merrill, c, University of Maine.

DRAFT DROP *Major league manager (1990-91)*

3. *Steve Wright, rhp, San Jose (Calif.) CC.
4. *Paul Dennenbaum, 1b, Syracuse University.
5. *Larry Linville, of, Mesa (Colo.) College.
6. *Fred Kos, 1b, Northeastern University.
7. Alan Diamond, c, University of California.
8. *Herb Hofvendahl, of, Diablo Valley (Calif.) JC.

### June—Regular Phase (16)

1. Ted Parks, ss, University of California.—(AAA)
2. James Kelly, c, Ensley HS, Birmingham, Ala.—(AA)
3. *Wayne Francinques, ss, Jesuit HS, New Orleans.—(AA)

DRAFT DROP *Attended Tulane; re-drafted by White Sox, June 1969/regular phase (10th round)*

4. Randolph Coon, ss, Dover Plains (N.Y.) HS.—(Short-season A)
5. ***Jan Dukes, lhp, Santa Clara University.—(1969-72)**

DRAFT DROP *Returned to Santa Clara; re-drafted by Senators, January 1967/secondary phase (1st round)*

6. *Stephen Rogers, lhp, Bethlehem Central HS, Delmar, N.Y.
7. Ron Norris, rhp, Hillcrest HS, Springfield, Mo.
8. Louis Coccia, c, Toledo University.
9. **Leon Brown, ss, Grant Union HS, Sacramento, Calif.—(1976)**
10. *Scott Morton, lhp, Iowa State University.
11. **Terry Crowley, 1b-of, Long Island University.—(1969-83)**
12. Dan Kerns, 3b-of, University of Maryland.
13. *Jack Johnson, 3b-of, West Virginia Wesleyan University.
14. *Minton White, 1b-of, University of Texas.
15. Richard Rhine, rhp, Penn State University.
16. *Bill Borelli, 1b, Serra HS, Burlingame, Calif.
17. *Ned Turnbull, lhp, University of Virginia.
18. *Ellsworth Jones, lhp-1b, James Monroe HS, Bronx, N.Y.
19. Henry Medlin, lhp, Robinson (Texas) HS.
20. *Lawrence Pyle, of, Parsippany HS, Tabor, N.J.
21. *Glen Bisbing, 3b, Rider College.
22. *Daniel Beard, rhp, Lakewood (Calif.) HS.
23. Larry Blixt, c, Parsons (Iowa) College.
24. *Jim Skeins, ss, Ranger (Texas) JC.
25. *Preston Nash, ss, City College HS, Baltimore.
26. *Tommy Campbell, of, Jackson State University.
27. Richard Pecore, rhp, St. Joseph's HS, Baltimore.
28. Donald Genussa, 1b, Loyola (La.) University.
29. *Frank Bon Vardo, rhp, University of Maryland.
30. *Bruce Taylor, of, Perth Amboy (N.J.) HS.

DRAFT DROP *First-round draft pick, San Francisco 49ers/ National Football League (1970); defensive back, NFL (1970-77)*

31. *Larry Kleem, lhp, Elder HS, Cincinnati.
32. *Hugh Hamilton, lhp, Lamar HS, Houston.
33. Richard Stevenson, rhp, Parkville HS, Baltimore.
34. *Charles Moore, 1b, Poly HS, Long Beach, Calif.
35. *Fred Fagan, c, San Francisco.
36. *Robert Guerrera, rhp, Crosby HS, Waterbury, Conn.
37. Donald Atkins, lhp, Housatonic Valley HS, Falls Village, Conn.
38. *Larry Piquet, ss, North Eugene (Ore.) HS.
39. Ronnie Shelton, lhp, Johnson City (Ill.) HS.

DRAFT DROP *Writer/director, movie "Bull Durham"*

40. *Billy Ferguson, rhp, Holy Cross HS, New Orleans, La.
41. *Steve Corpuel, 1b, Poly HS, Pacoima, Calif.
42. *Ronald Soucie, lhp, John Baptist HS, Brewer, Maine.
43. Vaughn Kovach, rhp, West Virginia University.
44. *Jim Magnuson, of, JC of San Mateo (Calif.).
45. *Jeff Slipp, of-lhp, Las Vegas, Nev.
46. *Colby Howe, 2b-3b, Menlo-Atherton HS, Menlo Park, Calif.
47. ***Norm Angelini, lhp, JC of San Mateo (Calif.).—(1972-73)**
48. *John Shafer, c, Madison HS, Portland, Ore.
49. Gary Holt, lhp, New Bern (N.C.) HS.

### June—Secondary Phase (8)

1. Buddy White, rhp, Rutgers University.—(High A)
2. *Jim Scheschuk, c, University of Texas.
3. *Greg Riddoch, ss, Colorado State University.

DRAFT DROP *Major league manager (1990-92)*

4. Edward Maras, 1b-rhp, South Dakota State University.
5. *Herb Hofvendahl, of, Diablo Valley (Calif.) JC.

### August—American Legion Phase (15)

No selection.

## BOSTON RED SOX

### January—Regular Phase (3)

1. *Jim Rife, c, Lebanon Valley (Pa.) College.—(Low A)
2. **Mark Schaeffer, lhp, Cleveland HS, Canoga Park, Calif.—(1972)**
3. Donald Fox, rhp, Cooley HS, Detroit.
4. Donnie Peters, rhp, Tusculum (Tenn.) College.

### January—Secondary Phase (9)

1. **Dick Baney, rhp, Anaheim (Calif.) HS.—(1969-74)**
2. Daniel Rudanovich, of, University of Missouri.
3. *Kenneth Hall, lhp, Nassau (N.Y.) CC.
4. ***Jophery Brown, rhp, Grambling University.—(1968)**

### June—Regular Phase (4)

1. **Ken Brett, lhp-of, El Segundo (Calif.) HS.—(1967-81)**

DRAFT DROP *Brother of George Brett, major leaguer (1973-93)*

2. Joseph McCullough, ss, William L. Dickinson HS, Jersey City, N.J.—(AA)
3. Rick Hoban, lhp, West HS, Cleveland.—(AA)
4. ***Skip Jutze, c, Central Connecticut State University.—(1972-77)**

DRAFT DROP *Returned to Central Connecticut State; re-drafted by Tigers, June 1967/secondary phase (3rd round).*

5. Wayne McGhee, c, Fresno State University.—(High A)
6. **Mike Nagy, rhp, St. Helena HS, Bronx, N.Y.—(1969-74)**
7. Danny Smith, ss, Red Lion HS, Windsor, Pa.
8. Roger McComas, lhp, Odessa, Texas.
9. *Ernie Aguirre, c, Bakersfield (Calif.) HS.
10. *Nick DeFlorio, ss, Carey HS, Franklin Square, N.Y.
11. Bill Hathaway, c, Palm Springs (Calif.) HS.
12. Thomas Stephenson, rhp, Anaheim, Calif.
13. Richard Guy, 3b, Jemison (Ala.) HS.
14. Harry Greenfield, of, Husson (Maine) College.
15. Bernard Burns, of, Indiana (Pa.) University.
16. **Ed Phillips, rhp, Colby (Maine) College.—(1970)**
17. Dennis Udy, rhp, University of Utah.
18. William O'Neill, c, Windsor Locks (Conn.) HS.
19. John Frye, of, Michigan State University.
20. Bernard Linn, rhp, Grossmont HS, El Cajon, Calif.
21. *Eugene Collins, rhp, Choctawhatchee HS, Fort Walton Beach, Fla.
22. James Chenevert, of, Redemptorist HS, Baton Rouge, La.
23. *Jack Fulmer, 3b, Arkansas State University.
24. *James Whinery, 3b, Thomas Downey HS, Modesto, Calif.
25. *Steve Egan, c, Pittsburg State (Kan.) University.
26. Richard Goedert, 1b, Mira Costa (Calif.) JC.
27. Otis Griggs, c, Andalusia (Ala.) HS.
28. Louis Inman, 3b, Mississippi College.

### June—Secondary Phase (14)

1. Donald Cook, rhp, Long Island University.—(AAA)
2. Jim Rife, c, Lebanon Valley (Pa.) College.
3. **Dick Mills, rhp, Parsons (Iowa) College.—(1970)**

DRAFT DROP *Father of Ryan Mills, first-round draft pick, Twins (1996)*

4. *George Girard, lhp, Marblehead, Mass.

### August—American Legion Phase (3)

No selection.

## CALIFORNIA ANGELS

### January—Regular Phase (7)

1. *Ron Cherry, c, John Francis Poly HS, Sun Valley, Calif.—DNP
2. **Vern Geishert, rhp, University of Wisconsin.—(1969)**
3. ***Randy Bobb, c, Verdugo Hills HS, Sunland, Calif.—(1968-69)**

### January—Secondary Phase (5)

1. Jim Vopicka, ss, University of Illinois.—(AAA)
2. Paul Alderette, of-c, Los Angeles Pierce JC.
3. *Randy Humphrey, lhp, Los Angeles Harbor JC.
4. *Kenneth Suzawa, lhp, Fresno (Calif.) CC.
5. ***Oscar Brown, of, Compton (Calif.) JC.—(1968-73)**

DRAFT DROP *Brother of Ollie Brown, major leaguer (1965-77)*

### June—Regular Phase (8)

1. Jim DeNeff, ss, Indiana University.—(AAA)
2. David Frost, rhp, Lawton (Okla.) HS.—(AA)
3. *Bill Gillean, rhp, Mayfair HS, Lakewood, Calif.—DNP

DRAFT DROP *Attended Cerritos (Calif.) JC; re-drafted by Braves, January 1967/secondary phase (1st round).*

4. *Jim Suskiewich, lhp, Beaver Falls (Pa.) HS.—(AA)

**DRAFT DROP** *Attended Indiana; re-drafted by Angels, June 1968/secondary phase (4th round).*

5. Buddy Lawhorn, ss, West Haven HS, Memphis, Tenn.—(Low A)
6. John Dickson, c-of, Edison HS, Fresno, Calif.
7. *Robert Smith, rhp, St. John's University.
8. Michael Floyd, of, Fullerton (Calif.) JC.
9. ***Ken Forsch, rhp, Sacramento (Calif.) CC.—(1970-86)**

**DRAFT DROP** *Brother of Bob Forsch, major leaguer (1974-89)*

10. Tim Hewes, c, Bakersfield (Calif.) JC.
11. ***Jim Barr, rhp, Lynwood (Calif.) HS.—(1971-83)**
12. *Larry Bishop, c, Howe HS, Indianapolis, Ind.
13. Anthony Mitchell, rhp, Lincoln HS, San Diego.
14. Paul Devaney, rhp, DeSales HS, Geneva, N.Y.
15. Jack McCall, ss, Clemson University.
16. *Glenn Pickren, rhp, Seminole HS, St. Petersburg, Fla.
17. **Bruce Christensen, ss, Chatsworth HS, Canoga Park, Calif.—(1971)**
18. **Randy Brown, c, Florida State University.—(1969-70)**
19. *Alan Jackson, lhp, St. Clements HS, Somerville, Mass.
20. ***Dave LaRoche, lhp, West Torrance (Calif.) HS.—(1970-83)**

**DRAFT DROP** *Father of Adam LaRoche, major leaguer (2004-15) • Father of Andy LaRoche, major leaguer (2007-13)*

21. *Irl Davis, rhp, Bishop Montgomery HS, Redondo Beach, Calif.
22. (void) *Louis Mellini, rhp, Beverly Hills (Calif.) HS.
23. William Moray, 3b, Santa Monica (Calif.) HS.
24. *Thomas Buchenberger, rhp, St. John's University.
25. *Clarence Smith, rhp, St. Francis (N.Y.) College.
26. *Dan Stolingrosz, 3b, Cleveland HS, Canoga Park, Calif.
27. Richard Well, rhp, Bakersfield (Calif.) HS.
28. Donnie Gaston, c, Ventura (Calif.) JC.
29. Dan Pollard, 1b, Fresno State University.
30. *Forest Hartline, 2b, Pasadena (Calif.) CC.
31. ***Bill Bonham, rhp, Francis Poly HS, Pacoima, Calif.—(1971-80)**
32. Jon Levig, lhp, San Fernando HS, Mission Hills, Calif.
33. Richard Ganulin, 1b, UCLA.
34. *Marvin Madruga, ss, Mount Whitney HS, Visalia, Calif.
35. **Steve Hovley, of, Stanford University.—(1969-73)**

#### June—Secondary Phase (12)

1. **Andy Messersmith, rhp, University of California.—(1968-79)**
2. **Ken Tatum, rhp, Mississippi State University.—(1969-74)**
3. Steve Schneider, ss, University of Minnesota.

#### August—American Legion Phase (7)

1. *Louis Mellini, rhp-3b, Beverly Hills (Calif.) HS—(Low A)

## CHICAGO CUBS

#### January—Regular Phase (6)

1. John Dudek, c, Tuley HS, Chicago.—(AAA)
2. John Killebrew, of, Arizona Western JC.
3. Frank White, c, South Carolina Area Trade School.
4. Billy Johns, 1b, Virginia Tech.

#### January—Secondary Phase (15)

1. No selection.
2. *Sanford Marks, lhp, Los Angeles CC.

#### June—Regular Phase (5)

1. Dean Burk, rhp, Highland (Ill.) HS.—(AAA)
2. *C.E. Bryson, of, Findlay (Ohio) HS.—DNP

**DRAFT DROP** *No school; never re-drafted*

3. Bob Owens, c, Henderson HS, West Chester, Pa.—(High A)
4. Dick Curbow, of, Central HS, Springfield, Mo.—(Low A)

**White Sox first-round pick Carlos May hit 18 home runs in half a season as a rookie in 1969, but a military accident that August cost him part of his right thumb and dented his career**

CHICAGO WHITE SOX

5. Marcus Rhaney, lhp, Middleton HS, Tampa.—(Low A)
6. Ed Bruksch, 3b, University of Minnesota.
7. *Pat O'Brien, lhp, University of Arizona.
8. Jerry Szukala, 1b, University of Illinois.
9. *John Miller, rhp, Academy of the Immaculate Heart of Mary, Coeur D'Alene, Idaho.
10. *Clyde Kuehn, of, Belleville (Ill.) HS.
11. Elby Bushong, c, California Western University.
12. Elvatous Peters, of, Southern University.
13. Bobby Eyer, ss, Loyola HS, Los Angeles.
14. **Rich Nye, lhp, University of California.—(1966-70)**

**DRAFT DROP** *First player from 1966 draft to reach majors (Sept. 16, 1966)*

15. Jeff Rude, of, Southern Oregon University.
16. *Charles Jones, lhp, Central HS, Mobile, Ala.
17. *Ron Del Planche, ss, University of Oregon.
18. *James Silestrini, of, Bullard HS, Fresno, Calif.
19. Rickey Davis, c, Parkview HS, Springfield, Mo.
20. Dale Ford, 1b, Washington State University.
21. Thomas Whelan, c-1b, San Diego State University.
22. *Michael Nichols, lhp, Bakersfield (Calif.) HS.
23. Dana Freudeman, lhp, Central HS, Canton, Ohio.
24. *Steve Hanson, rhp, Saratoga (Calif.) HS.
25. *David Kent, rhp, Hillsborough HS, Tampa.
26. David McKelvey, c-3b, Rider College.
27. Bruce Carmichael, 2b-ss, Santa Clara University.
28. Michael Klahr, ss, Albright (Pa.) College.
29. *Bill Grogan, rhp, Clarkston (Wash.) HS.
30. *Pat Hartigan, rhp, Columbia Basin (Wash.) CC.
31. **Bill Stoneman, rhp, University of Idaho.—(1967-74)**

**DRAFT DROP** *General manager, Angels (1999-2007)*

32. Dale Ehler, c, University of Oregon.
33. Ronald Pearson, of, Phoenix (Ariz.) JC.
34. Earl Lombardo, 2b, Rider College.
35. James Nealey, rhp, Corona (Calif.) HS.
36. Bruce Johnson, of, Wilson HS, Portland, Ore.
37. Fred Rodriguez, 2b, East Carolina University.
38. **Archie Reynolds, rhp, Paris (Texas) JC.—(1968-72)**

#### June—Secondary Phase (3)

1. ***Eddie Leon, ss, University of Arizona.—(1968-75)**

**DRAFT DROP** *First-round pick (9th overall), Twins (1965)*

2. **Jophery Brown, rhp, Grambling University.—(1968)**
3. **Joe Niekro, rhp, West Liberty State (W. Va.) College.—(1967-88)**

**DRAFT DROP** *Brother of Phil Niekro, major leaguer (1964-87) • Father of Lance Niekro, major leaguer (2003-07)*

4. *Ray Henningsen, 2b, Santa Clara University.

#### August—American Legion Phase (6)

No selection.

## CHICAGO WHITE SOX

#### January—Regular Phase (17)

1. *Howard "Buddy" Gordon, 1b-of, University of Southern California.—(AA)
2. James Barton, rhp, University of Akron.
3. Ronald Ellis, rhp-of, Portsmouth, Va.
4. Dean DeBuhr, rhp, Wayne State (Neb.) College.
5. *Al Crawford, 3b, Miami-Dade CC North.
6. *Dick Schryer, of, University of Michigan.
7. *Stephen Moates, rhp, Miami-Dade CC North.

#### January—Secondary Phase (11)

1. *Clifford Foster, 1b-of, Lansing (Mich.) CC.—(AA)
2. Steven Kokor, rhp, Alta Loma (Calif.) JC.
3. Pete Lentine, 1b-lhp, Los Angeles Pierce JC.
4. *Gerald Boehmer, 3b, St. Louis University.
5. *Bill Drummond, rhp, Buena Vista (Iowa) College.
6. *Robert Hergenrader, lhp, University of Nebraska.
7. *Joe Bloom, rhp, Los Angeles Pierce JC.

#### June—Regular Phase (18)

1. **Carlos May, of, Parker HS, Birmingham, Ala.—(1968-77)**

**DRAFT DROP** *Brother of Lee May, major leaguer (1965-82)*

2. ***Johnny Oates, c, Virginia Tech.—(1970-81)**

**DRAFT DROP** *Returned to Virginia Tech; re-drafted by Orioles, January 1967/secondary phase (1st round); major league manager (1991-2001)*

3. **Jim Magnuson, lhp, University of Wisconsin-Oshkosh.—(1970-73)**
4. Karl Simon, of, Central HS, South Bend, Ind.—(High A)
5. **Ken Frailing, lhp, Marion (Wis.) HS.—(1972-76)**
6. Gary Lewis, c, Colton (Calif.) HS.
7. *David Speas, ss, Clairemont HS, San Diego.
8. *Randy Coley, 1b, Providence HS, Lockport, Ill.
9. *Dennis Jones, lhp, Jetmore (Kan.) HS.
10. ***Mike Adams, ss, Loara HS, Anaheim, Calif.—(1972-78)**

**DRAFT DROP** *Son of Bobby Adams, major leaguer (1946-59) • Nephew of Dick Adams, major leaguer (1947)*

11. Bob Mewes, c, Colorado State University.
12. Gary Kirtlan, 1b-of, Clarksburg (Calif.) HS.
13. *John Posen, 3b-of, Morton East HS, Cicero, Ill.
14. *William Hess, lhp, Roncalli HS, Aurora, Ill.
15. ***Mike Thompson, rhp, Ponca City (Okla.) HS.—(1971-75)**
16. **Chuck Brinkman, c, Ohio State University.—(1969-74)**

**DRAFT DROP** *Brother of Eddie Brinkman, major leaguer (1961-75)*

17. *Samuel Watts, ss, Froebel HS, Gary, Ind.
18. *Robert Mitchell, c, Lynwood (Calif.) HS.
19. *Thomas Tutko, inf, Hastings (Neb.) College.
20. *Stephen Vaughn, of-1b, Southeast Missouri State University.
21. Jerry Florence, of, East HS, Wichita, Kan.
22. ***Greg Garrett, lhp, Los Angeles Pierce JC.—(1970-71)**
23. *Andrew Thomas, rhp, Indiana State University.
24. John Marcum, lhp, St. Louis University.
25. *Jim Limke, rhp, Minot State (N.D.) University.
26. *John Zotz, rhp, Danville (Ill.) HS.
27. ***Bobby Fenwick, 2b-ss, University of Minnesota.—(1972-73)**
28. James Daun, rhp-of, Chilton (Wis.) HS.
29. *Marv Galliher, inf, Lincoln HS, San Diego.
30. Melvin McCoy, lhp, Magnolia HS, Stanton, Calif.
31. *Paul Faust, of, University of Minnesota.
32. David Smith, rhp, Schaghticoke (N.Y.) HS.
33. *John Davasko, rhp, St. Louis University.
34. ***Geoff Zahn, lhp, University of Michigan.—(1973-85)**

**DRAFT DROP** *Baseball coach, Michigan (1996-2001)*

35. Thomas Henvey, inf, Lincoln HS, Yonkers, N.Y.
36. *Robert Breitzman, inf, Glenbrook North HS, Northbrook, Ill.
37. **Art Kusnyer, c, Kent State University.—(1970-78)**
38. (void) *Earl Kennedy, inf, Bakersfield (Calif.) JC.
39. *Lawrence Hammer, rhp, Fenger HS, Chicago.
40. *Edmond Curran, rhp, St. Louis University.
41. *Ken Kozil, rhp, Glenbrook North HS, Northbrook, Ill.

#### June—Secondary Phase (4)

1. Berke Reichenbach, inf, Ohio University.-(AAA)
2. *Jim Armstrong, ss, Arizona State University.
3. *Clifford Foster, 1b-of, Lansing (Mich.) CC.
4. Orville Hollrah, rhp, University of Missouri.
5. Gerry Boehmer, 3b, St. Louis University.
6. Frank Chambers, rhp, Mississippi State University.

#### August—American Legion Phase (17)

No selection.

## CINCINNATI REDS

#### January—Regular Phase (14)

No selection.

#### January—Secondary Phase (10)

1. **Dan McGinn, lhp, University of Notre Dame.—(1968-72)**
2. Joseph Braithwaite, 1b, Atlantic City, N.J.
3. *Walter Manuel, ss, Lafayette College.
4. **John Noriega, rhp, University of Utah.—(1969-70)**
5. *Archie Roberts, ss, Holyoke, Mass.

**DRAFT DROP** *Quarterback, National Football League (1967).*

#### June—Regular Phase (13)

1. **Gary Nolan, rhp, Oroville (Calif.) HS.—(1967-77)**

**DRAFT DROP** *First 1966 high school draft pick to reach majors (April 15, 1967)*

2. **Darrell Chaney, ss, Morton HS, Hammond, Ind.—(1969-79)**
3. Mike Oates, rhp, Glenbard West HS, Glen Ellyn, Ill.—(AA)
4. *Tommy Williams, c, Mount Carmel HS, Los Angeles.—(AA)

DRAFT DROP *Attended East Los Angeles JC; re-drafted by Mets, June 1968/secondary phase (2nd round).*
5. *Richard Washburn, rhp, College of St. Thomas (Minn.).—DNP
DRAFT DROP *Never re-drafted*
6. *Steve Steitz, rhp-1b, East Longmeadow (Mass.) HS.
7. David Grawe, rhp, Elder HS, Cincinnati.
8. James Cartlidge, of, Livingston (Ala.) University.
9. *David Reeves, rhp, Americus (Ga.) HS.
10. *Jeffrey Pryor, rhp, Evans HS, Orlando, Fla.
11. *Ricky Schwartz, of, Texas A&M University.
12. *Edward Robbins, rhp, Hillsboro (Ohio) HS.
13. *Thomas Dryja, of-lhp, Riverside HS, Buffalo, N.Y.
14. Donnell Goodwin, ss, Edison HS, Stockton, Calif.
15. *Thomas Henderson, rhp, Northeastern Oklahoma State University.
16. *James Babyak, ss, University of Massachusetts.
17. Claude Passeau, rhp, Mississippi State University.
18. *Larry Housley, 2b-3b, Colton (Calif.) HS.
19. Robert Orange, rhp, Morgan Park HS, Chicago.
**20. *Rick Henninger, rhp, Hastings (Neb.) HS.—(1973)**
21. (void) *David Smith, 3b-ss, Red Lion HS, Windsor, Pa.
22. Isaac Fuggett, of, Douglas HS, Oklahoma City, Okla.
23. *Bob Leatherwood, 2b, University of California.
24. *Timothy White, c, Denton (Texas) HS.
25. *Donald Van Deusen, ss, Concord (W.Va.) College.
26. *Mickey Smith, c, University of Illinois.
27. *Conrad DeNeault, rhp, University of Missouri.

#### June—Secondary Phase (11)

1. *John Dow, of, Bemidji, Minn.—(High A)
**2. *Dick Tidrow, rhp, Chabot (Calif.) JC—(1972-84)**
3. *Stan Bell, rhp, Manatee (Fla.) JC.
DRAFT DROP *First overall draft pick, January 1966/ secondary phase, Giants*
4. *Thomas Kelly, of, Holy Cross College.
5. *Steve Radulovich, 1b, University of Utah.

#### August—American Legion Phase (14)

No selection.

## CLEVELAND INDIANS

#### January—Regular Phase (11)

**1. Ted Ford, of, Richland, N.J.—(1970-73)**
2. Kenneth Showalter, ss, New Martinsville, W.Va.
3. Dave Singerman, rhp, Cuyahoga (Ohio) CC.
**4. Phil Hennigan, rhp, Sam Houston State University.—(1969-73)**
5. Wilma Evans, of, Pittsburgh.
6. *Dave Pratt, lhp, Tennessee Tech.
**7. *Joe Niekro, of-rhp, West Liberty State (W.Va.) College.—(1967-88)**
DRAFT DROP *Brother of Phil Niekro, major leaguer (1964-87) • rather of Lance Niekro, major leaguer (2003-07)*
**8. *Gary Neibauer, rhp, University of Nebraska.—(1969-73)**

#### January—Secondary Phase (3)

1. *Kris Krebs, ss, Manatee (Fla.) JC.—(AAA)
2. J.B. Jackson, of-1b, Kilgore (Texas) JC.
3. *Jackie Kreel, rhp, Gulf Coast (Fla.) JC.
4. *Arnie Chonko, 1b, Ohio State University.
5. Dennis Deptula, 2b, University of Detroit.
6. *Michael Burns, of, Mississippi State University.
7. *Robert Bixler, rhp, Miami (Ohio) University.
8. Richard Zank, lhp, Neilsville, Wis.

#### June—Regular Phase (12)

**1. *John Curtis, lhp, Smithtown Central HS, Smithtown, N.Y.—(1970-84)**
DRAFT DROP *Attended Clemson; re-drafted by Red Sox, June 1968/secondary phase (1st round)*
2. Billy Lynch, lhp-of, Paul Blazer HS, Ashland, Ky.—(Low A)
3. Terry Taylor, of, Soquel HS, Belmont, Calif.—(High A)
4. William Kyle, 1b, University HS, Beverly Hills, Calif.—(High A)
5. Dick Davis, 3b, Pembroke State (N.C.) University.—(High A)
6. Gary Sprague, ss-2b, Florida State University.
7. *Harold Harris, 3b-ss, Hewitt Trussville HS, Birmingham, Ala.
8. Stephen Reid, ss, DeSales HS, Geneva, N.Y.
9. *Daniel McNulty, 2b-ss, Waterloo (N.Y.) HS.
10. Ollie Coffey, c, East Technical HS, Cleveland.
11. Clifford Lee, 2b, Campbell HS, Smyrna, Ga.
12. Jack Sexton, of, Titusville (Fla.) HS.
13. *Billy Ray Palmer, rhp, Rice University.
**14. Russ Nagelson, 1b, Ohio State University.—(1968-70)**
15. James Wingate, rhp, Trinity (Texas) University.
16. Jerry Kremer, ss, University of Maryland.
17. Ronald Hart, ss, Frederick (Md.) HS.
18. *Michael Hastings, of, Ithaca (N.Y.) HS.
19. *Robert Bossom, 1b, Columbia University.
20. Jerry Clark, ss, Rose HS, Greenville, N.C.
21. *Richard Holliday, rhp, Westminster (Pa.) College.
22. *Michael Brannan, of, Broughton HS, Raleigh, N.C.
23. Robert Biscan, rhp, Morton HS, Hammond, Ind.
24. Larry Edwards, rhp, Erskine (S.C.) College.
25. *Mike Carruthers, 1b, Pembroke State (N.C.) University.
26. *Seaton Daly, c, Santa Clara University.
**27. Billy Harris, ss-2b, UNC Wilmington.—(1968-69)**
28. *Ronald Henson, lhp, Rice University.
29. Donald DelMazzio, of, Norwalk, Conn.
30. *John Vance, c, Glasgow (Ky.) HS.
**31. *Jack Lind, 3b, Arizona State University.—(1974-75)**
32. *William Kollman, 3b, Chamberlin HS, Twinsburg, Ohio.
33. *Dale Dunham, rhp, Central HS, Bay City, Mich.
34. *Dick Hall, rhp, Memphis Catholic HS, Memphis, Tenn.

#### June—Secondary Phase (16)

1. John Olagues, rhp, Tulane University.—(High A)
2. Terry Thompson, 1b, Columbia Basin (Wash.) CC.
**3. *Scott Reid, ss-of, Cerritos (Calif.) JC.—(1969-70)**
DRAFT DROP *Scouting director, Cubs (1986-87)*
**4. Tom Gramly, rhp, Texas Christian University.—(1968)**
5. *Stephen Moates, rhp, Miami-Dade CC North.
6. Randy Carroll, 2b, Georgia Tech.
7. *Charlie Watson, rhp, Clemson University.

#### August—American Legion Phase (11)

No selection.

## DETROIT TIGERS

#### January—Regular Phase (13)

1. Tim Marting, ss, Hillsborough (Fla.) JC.—(AAA)
2. (void) *Robert Bellemare, rhp, Post (Conn.) JC.
3. Kenneth Youngblood, c, Little Rock, Ark.
**4. Jon Warden, lhp, Harrisburg, Ohio.–(1968)**

#### January—Secondary Phase (1)

1. *Stan Bell, rhp, Manatee (Fla.) JC.—(AA)
2. *Ray Glinsky, rhp, University of Akron.
3. *Steve Schneider, ss, University of Minnesota.
4. Jerry Foglia, rhp, Woodridge (N.J.) HS.
5. *Glen Borkhuis, rhp, Syracuse University.
**6. *Ken Tatum, rhp, Mississippi State University.—(1969-74)**
7. *Frederick Manning, 2b, Holy Cross College.
8. *Dennis Trame, rhp, Quincy (Ill.) College.
9. *Ed Staron, of, Western Michigan University.

#### June—Regular Phase (14)

1. *Rick Konik, 1b, St. Andrews HS, Detroit.—DNP
DRAFT DROP *No school; re-drafted by Athletics, January 1967/secondary phase (1st round)*
2. *Scott Fields, lhp, Elgin HS, Larue, Ohio.—DNP
DRAFT DROP *Attended Ohio; never re-drafted*
3. Bob Gilhooley, ss, University of Michigan.–(AAA)
**4. Leslie Cain, lhp, El Cerrito (Calif.) HS.—(1968-72)**
5. Eugene Spatz, 3b, Alexander HS, Elmsford, N.Y.—(AAA)
6. Robert Welz, 1b, Harvard University.
7. Hagan Anderson, inf, University of Massachusetts.
8. Mike Irish, c, Grand Ledge (Mich.) HS.
9. Dan Bootcheck, lhp-1b, Michigan City (Ind.) HS.
DRAFT DROP *Father of Chris Bootcheck, first-round draft pick, Angels (2000); major leaguer (2003-06)*
10. Brian Cusino, rhp, Monroe Catholic Central HS, Erie, Mich.
11. *Bob Kloss, rhp-3b, St. Ladislaus HS, Detroit.
12. Chandler Simonds, 1b, University of Michigan.
13. *Vic Pilar, lhp, Thurston HS, Redford Township, Mich.
14. Herbert Doebler, rhp, Utica (Mich.) HS.
15. *Gary Krupinski, c, St. Hedwig HS, Detroit.
16. *Rodney Pryor, lhp, McLeansboro (Ill.) HS.
17. Randy Hooper, of, Pacific HS, San Bernardino, Calif.
18. *John Mayer, lhp, Western Michigan University.
19. Jim Blight, rhp, Michigan State University.
20. *Ron Allen, ss, Scott HS, Toledo, Ohio.
21. Robert Buchanan, rhp, East HS, Buffalo, N.Y.
22. *Richard Schlesinger, lhp, Kansas State University.
23. *Thomas Lomicky, inf, St. Joseph's HS, West New York, N.J.
24. *John Johnson, c, Northwest Classen HS, Oklahoma City, Okla.
25. James Martin, lhp, East Brunswick (N.J.) HS.
26. Nathaniel Dixon, rhp, Tuskegee (Ala.) HS.
27. Vincent Ammerata, ss, Ossining (N.Y.) HS.
28. *Ronald Koehler, lhp, Belleville Township HS, Belleville, Ill.
29. *Harry Gonso, c, Findlay (Ohio) HS.
30. *Ron Timko, rhp, Plains (Pa.) HS.
31. Ron Goulet, of, Flint (Mich.) JC.
32. *Tom Lee, of, Poindexter Legion HS, Springfield, Mo.
33. *Charles Haje, of, Wheaton (Md.) HS.
34. *Mark Kenney, 3b-of, Jamaica HS, Long Island, N.Y.
35. *Frank Sullivan, rhp, Piscataway HS, New Market, N.J.
**36. *Jim Johnson, lhp-of, Western Michigan University.—(1970)**

#### June—Secondary Phase (2)

1. Richard DeVarney, ss, University of Maine.—(High A)
**2. Bob Reed, rhp, University of Michigan.—(1969-70)**
3. Paul Coleman, rhp, Cal Poly Pomona.
4. *George Grzegerek, ss, St. Edward's (Texas) University.
**5. *Darrell Evans, inf, Pasadena (Calif.) CC.—(1969-89)**
6. *Alan Putz, 3b, Cheshire (Conn.) Academy.
7. *Rusty Adkins, 2b-of, Clemson University.
**8. *Bill Zepp, rhp, University of Michigan.—(1969-71)**

#### August—American Legion Phase (13)

No selection.

## HOUSTON ASTROS

#### January—Regional Phase (4)

**1. Tom Griffin, rhp, Grant HS, Sun Valley, Calif.—(1969-82)**
2. Herman Johnson, 1b, Jefferson HS, Los Angeles.
3. Stan Robinson, rhp, Jefferson HS, Los Angeles.
4. *Joe Dawkins, 1b, Fremont HS, Los Angeles.
5. *Oliver Kozloski, c-of, Blinn (Texas) JC.
6. Robert Santee, rhp, Carverdale HS, Houston.
7. *Timothy Ware, ss, Spring Branch HS, Houston.

#### January—Secondary Phase (4)

1. Joel McMasters, rhp-1b, Southern Baptist (Ark.) JC.—(AAA)
2. John Respondek, rhp, Texas A&I University.

#### June—Regular Phase (3)

**1. Wayne Twitchell, rhp, Woodrow Wilson HS, Portland, Ore.—(1970-79)**
2. Butch Crook, lhp, Georgia Tech.—(AA)
3. *John D'Auria, rhp, Arcadia (Calif.) HS.—(Low A)
DRAFT DROP *Returned to Arcadia (Calif.) HS; re-drafted by Tigers, January 1967/secondary phase (3rd round)*
**4. *Elliott Maddox, 3b, Union (N.J.) HS.—(1970-80)**
DRAFT DROP *Attended Michigan; re-drafted by Tigers, June 1968/secondary phase (1st round)*
**5. Cliff Johnson, c, Wheatley HS, San Antonio, Texas.—(1972-86)**
6. Tom Koziol, inf, LaSalle HS, Miami.
7. Rick Lynn, inf, Edwardsville (Ill.) HS.
**8. Fred Stanley, ss, Monte Vista HS, Whittier, Calif.—(1969-82)**
9. Sli Harvey, 1b, Aransas Pass (Texas) HS.
10. *J.D. Hill, of, Edison HS, Stockton, Calif.
DRAFT DROP *First-round draft pick, Buffalo Bills/ National Football League (1971); wide receiver, NFL (1971-77)*
11. *John Caruso, rhp, Franklin K. Lane HS, Ozone Park, N.Y.
12. Robert Dickman, c, Rutgers University.
13. *Douglas Hansen, rhp, Hoover HS, Fresno, Calif.
14. Alan Pauska, 1b-of, Phillipsburg (N.J.) HS.
15. Mike Cole, rhp, Southern Baptist (Ark.) JC.
16. *James Kobi, ss, King's (Pa.) College.
17. *William Green, 3b, Central Missouri State University.
18. *Cyrus Lee, lhp, Jones HS, Little Rock, Ark.
19. William Steinkamp, c, Highland HS, Albuquerque, N.M.
**20. *Ed Goodson, ss, Fries HS, Ivanhoe, Va.—(1970-77)**
21. *Frank Van Devender, rhp, San Diego Mesa JC.
**22. Bob Watkins, rhp, Compton (Calif.) HS.—(1969)**
23. *William Wright, rhp, South Park HS, Beaumont, Texas.
24. *John Fletcher, c, Lee HS, Columbus, Miss.
**25. *Dan Monzon, 2b, Buena Vista (Iowa) College.—(1972-73)**
26. *Bobby Anderson, c, Boulder (Colo.) HS.
DRAFT DROP *First-round draft pick, Denver Broncos/ National Football League (1970); running back, NFL (1970-75)*
27. *Benny Looper, c, Granite (Okla.) HS.
DRAFT DROP *Uncle of Braden Looper, first-round draft pick, Cardinals (1996); major leaguer (1998-2006) • Father of Aaron Looper, major leaguer (2003)*
28. *Jerry Marion, of, University of Wyoming.
29. *Edmund Mantie, rhp, Syracuse University.
30. Robert Cassady, inf, Neshaminy HS, Langhorne, Pa.
31. Boyd Van Patten, of, Springville (Utah) HS.
32. *Steve Evans, rhp, Northville (Mich.) HS.
33. Donald Moore, 3b, Halifax County HS, South Boston, Va.
34. *Jeffrey Bowman, rhp, Downey HS, Modesto, Calif.
35. Patrick Warren, of, Miami (Ohio) University.
36. *Phillip Jones, lhp, Jasper (Texas) HS.
37. Mark Scally, rhp, Curley HS, Miami.
38. Herbert Peterson, c, Rosenwald HS, Panama City, Fla.
39. *Jerome Hall, of, Arlington HS, Fort Worth, Texas.

#### June—Secondary Phase (5)

1. *Larry Linville, of, Mesa (Colo.) College.–(Low A)
2. *Al Crawford, of, Miami-Dade CC North.
3. Paul Dennenbaum, 1b, Syracuse University.
4. *Stephen Lohrer, inf, Nassau (N.Y.) CC.

#### August—American Legion Phase (4)

1. *Gerald Johnson, lhp, Newberg, Ore.

## KANSAS CITY ATHLETICS

#### January—Regular Phase (1)

1. Don Lohse, rhp, Indiana University.—(AA)
2. Bill Geiger, rhp, Keyport (N.J.) HS.
3. James Shotton, rhp, Marion (Ill.) HS.
4. *Jeff Hansen, 1b, Farmingdale (N.Y.) JC.
5. *David Ray, rhp, University of Alabama.
6. *Charlie Watson, rhp, Clemson University.

#### January—Secondary Phase (19)

1. *Ron Drake, c, Long Beach (Calif.) CC.—(AAA)
2. Leonard Zandy, rhp, Fordham University.
3. *Frank Chambers, rhp, Mississippi State University.
4. *Frank Portera, c, Mississippi State University.

#### June—Regular Phase (2)

**1. Reggie Jackson, of, Arizona State University.—(1967-87)**
DRAFT DROP *Elected to Baseball Hall of Fame, 1993*
2. Roger Washington, of, Los Angeles.—(AAA)

3. John Greene, of, Brigham Young University.—(High A)
4. *Billy Cotton, c, McCook (Neb.) HS.—(AAA)

DRAFT DROP *Attended Arizona State; re-drafted by Mets, June 1968/secondary phase (1st round)*

5. **Dave Hamilton, lhp, Edmonds (Wash.) HS.—(1972-80)**
6. ***Warren Bogle, lhp, University of Miami.—(1968)**
7. Clarence Vaughns, 3b, Jordon HS, Los Angeles.
8. Tom Brooks, rhp, St. James HS, Chester, Pa.
9. Frank Fall, rhp, McClatchy HS, Sacramento, Calif.
10. *Nick Radakovic, rhp, University of Michigan.
11. *Tom Binkowski, 1b, Michigan State University.
12. Ed Howell, lhp, Florida State University.
13. *Jack Gehrke, ss, University of Utah.

DRAFT DROP *Wide receiver, National Football League (1968-71)*

14. *Ronald Berta, c, Moravian (Pa.) College.
15. Darrell Baker, rhp, Holbrook (Mass.) HS.
16. John Shearer, lhp, Carlisle (Pa.) HS.
17. Joe Tassone, c, Port Chester (N.Y.) HS.
18. Ed Green, of, University of San Diego.
19. *Robert Rogers, 3b, Salem, Ore.
20. ***Larry Burchart, rhp, Oklahoma State University.—(1969)**
21. Bruce Ocken, rhp, Turlock (Calif.) HS.
22. *Clarence Cleveland, 1b-of, Albany (Ga.) HS.
23. *Michael Lisetski, ss, Rider College.
24. *Allen Ramsey, 3b, Somerville (N.J.) HS.
25. *Rex Hein, rhp, Rockhurst HS, Kansas City, Mo.
26. *Steve Smith, 2b, Poly HS, Long Beach, Calif.
27. *Cazzie Russell, 1b, University of Michigan.

DRAFT DROP *First overall draft pick, National Basketball Association (1966); forward, NBA (1966-78)*

28. *Norbert Beddow, rhp-of, Aurora (Colo.) HS.
29. *John Sellers, inf, Northeast Oklahoma State University.
30. Henry Gunther, of, New London (Conn.) HS.
31. *Eli Lyles, of, City College HS, Baltimore.
32. *Russell Hyder, ss, Boulder (Colo.) HS.
33. Thomas Matakanski, c, Hyde Park, Mass.
34. *Harold Werntz, rhp, Temple University.
35. Charles Lynch, rhp, Sayreville HS, Morgan, N.J.
36. *Tom Binder, rhp, Ganesha HS, Pomona, Calif.

**June—Secondary Phase (20)**

1. Dennis McKernan, 1b-of, Kutztown (Pa.) University.—(Low A)
2. *Charles Kline, lhp, Western Michigan University.
3. Paul Dumais, lhp, Holy Cross College.
4. Don Lando, of, Ithaca (N.Y.) College.

**August—American Legion Phase (1)**

1. ***Pete Varney, c, North Quincy, Mass.—(1973-76)**

DRAFT DROP *First overall draft pick, January 1967/secondary phase, Astros; first overall pick, June 1971/secondary phase (active), White Sox*

2. Bruce Bates, rhp-of, Billings, Mont.

## LOS ANGELES DODGERS

**January—Regular Phase (20)**

1. James Roberts, rhp, University of Alabama.—(AA)
2. Ivey Armstrong, 2b-of, Miami-Dade CC North.
3. Robert Childress, 3b, Methacton HS, Norristown, Pa.
4. Albert Choate, rhp, Sam Houston State University.
5. Jorge Benitez, 1b, Miami-Dade CC North.

**January—Secondary Phase (14)**

1. *John Herbst, lhp, University of Southern California.—(High A)
2. Henry Tenney, of, Vista HS, Valley Center, Calif.
3. **Jim Hibbs, c, Stanford University.—(1967)**
4. *Mike Garrett, of, University of Southern California.

DRAFT DROP *1965 Heisman Trophy winner; running back, National Football League (1966-73)*

**June—Regular Phase (19)**

1. Larry Hutton, rhp, Greenfield (Ind.) HS.—(AA)
2. **John Gamble, ss, Carson City (Nev.) HS.—(1972-73)**
3. Rich Thompson, 2b, Pembroke State (N.C.) University.—(High A)
4. Jerry Bagwell, ss, Wren HS, Liberty, S.C.–(Low A)
5. *Gordon Allen, of, Ludlow (Mass.) HS.—(High A)

DRAFT DROP *Attended Deerfield (Mass.) Academy; re-drafted by Reds, January 1967/secondary phase (2nd round)*

6. Dennis James, lhp, Albany (Ga.) HS.
7. *James Doran, of, Madison Township HS, Parlin, N.J.
8. **Charlie Hough, inf-rhp, Hialeah (Fla.) HS.—(1970-94)**
9. **Bill Russell, of, Pittsburg (Kan.) HS.—(1969-86)**

DRAFT DROP *Major league manager (1996-98)*

10. Dennis Thornton, 1b, Eisenhower HS, Decatur, Ill.
11. *Kenneth Burrow, c, DeAnza HS, Pinole, Calif.
12. **Billy Grabarkewitz, 3b, St. Mary's (Texas) University.—(1969-75)**
13. Romel Canada, of, Chester (Pa.) HS.
14. James Raynor, rhp, East Carolina University.
15. **Ted Sizemore, c, University of Michigan.—(1969-80)**
16. Allen Shiflet, c, McCallum HS, Austin, Texas.
17. Kenneth Raab, rhp, Northview HS, Covina, Calif.
18. *Craig Menzl, 1b, Islip HS, Long Island, N.Y.
19. Leslie Parker, rhp-of, King HS, Tampa.
20. ***Loyd Colson, rhp-inf, Gould (Okla.) HS.—(1970)**
21. John Jiles, of, North Cobb HS, Acworth, Ga.
22. Ronald Sutton, rhp, Tate HS, Molino, Fla.
23. James Frye, rhp, Northern HS, Pontiac, Mich.
24. Bill Ralston, 2b, Cal Poly Pomona.
25. *Bob Perruchon, of, Vallejo (Calif.) JC.
26. *Wayne Danson, c-of, Forrest HS, Jacksonville, Fla.
27. *Lawrence Land, rhp, Bamberg (S.C.) HS.
28. Tom Alger, lhp, Hudson (N.Y.) HS.
29. *Michael Pierce, lhp, Rincon HS, Tucson, Ariz.
30. Steven Howder, of, CC of San Francisco.
31. *Radford Mawhinney, of-1b, Santa Maria (Calif.) HS.
32. James Arkell, of, Claremont (Calif.) College.
33. Ronald Reece, rhp, Campbell HS, Smyrna, Ga.
34. James McCray, of, San Diego State University.
35. *Buzz Nitschke, c, Fresno State University.
36. *Mark Harris, rhp, University of Maryland.
37. Robert Johnson, lhp, Trenton (Mo.) HS.
38. Steven Hockensmith, 1b, Florida Southern College.
39. *Billy Carthel, of-inf, Sul Ross State (Texas) University.
40. **Ray Lamb, rhp, University of Southern California.—(1969-73)**
41. Donald Spain, rhp, Eisenhower HS, Decatur, Ill.
42. Donny Tidwell, rhp, New Diana (Texas) HS.
43. Julio Guerrero, ss, Centralia HS, San Angelo, Texas.
44. *John Shulock, 3b, Vero Beach (Fla.) HS.

DRAFT DROP *Umpire, Major League Baseball (1979-2002)*

45. *Dicky Shaw, ss, Central State (Okla.) University.
46. Jeffrey King, rhp, Mainland HS, Daytona Beach, Fla.
47. Richard LeBlanc, lhp, Forrest HS, Jacksonville, Fla.
48. Lamar Haynes, lhp, Chipola (Fla.) JC.
49. *Jody Gioffoni, rhp, Santa Monica HS, Malibu, Calif.
50. *Kenneth Wiedemann, 2b, West Covina (Calif.) HS.
51. *Mark Johnson, of, University of New Mexico.
52. Walter Pierce, of, William Carey (Miss.) College.
53. *Jack Butorac, rhp, Montebello (Calif.) HS.
54. *David Lindsey, lhp, Fremont HS, Los Angeles.
55. ***Bobby Randall, ss, Gove (Kan.) HS.—(1976-80)**

DRAFT DROP *Baseball coach, Iowa State (1985-95); baseball coach, Kansas (1996-2002)*

56. Frank Staab, rhp, Hays (Kan.) HS.
57. *John Thurston, c-ss, Bishop Molloy HS, Bronx, N.Y.
58. *Adrian Zabala, rhp, University of Florida.
59. *William Scott, ss, Germantown Academy, Philadelphia.
60. *Tom Smith, rhp, Foley (Ala.) HS.
61. Reed Raynor, rhp, Hamilton HS, Robbinsville, N.J.
62. *Robert Chandler, 2b, Rollins (Fla.) College.

**June—Secondary Phase (15)**

1. **Bob Stinson, c-of, Miami-Dade CC North.—(1969-80)**
2. Dick Schryer, of, University of Michigan.
3. James Carter, 3b, Trinity (Texas) University.
4. John Green, rhp, Gulf Coast (Fla.) CC.
5. *John Herbst, lhp, University of Southern California.

CHICAGO WHITE SOX

**The Dodgers found eight future big leaguers in the 1966 draft process, though they waited until the eighth round to select righthander Charlie Hough, a future knuckleball artist**

**August—American Legion Phase (20)**

No selection.

## MINNESOTA TWINS

**January—Regular Phase (19)**

1. Charles Chase, of, JC of San Mateo (Calif.).—(Rookie)

DRAFT DROP *Only drafted player to die in combat action, Vietnam War (June 11, 1968)*

2. *Antone Cardoza, rhp, JC of the Sequoias (Calif.).
3. **Tom Hall, lhp, Riverside, Calif.—(1968-77)**
4. Michael Sheftall, rhp, Jones HS, Houston.
5. *Barry Kubishta, rhp, Gardena (Calif.) HS.
6. Harold Steinback, 3b, Vallejo (Calif.) JC.
7. *Fred Shuey, of, University of Southern California.
8. *Tom Cole, of, Wake Forest University.
9. *Richard Holmes, rhp, Michigan State University.

**January—Secondary Phase (15)**

1. *Bob Crosby, rhp, New York.—(AA)
2. ***Buzz Stephen, rhp, Fresno State University.—(1968)**
3. *Tom Cook, c, Manatee (Fla.) JC.
4. Joseph Borowy, rhp, Baltimore.
5. Glenn Smith, of, Arizona State University.

**June—Regular Phase (20)**

1. Bob Jones, 3b, Dawson, Ga.—(High A)
2. Leo Pinnick, lhp, Billings (Mon.) HS.—(High A)
3. ***Steve Garvey, 3b, Chamberlain HS, Tampa.—(1969-87)**

DRAFT DROP *Attended Michigan State; re-drafted by Dodgers, June 1968/secondary phase (1st round)*

4. *Robert Desjardins, c, La Habra (Calif.) HS.—(Rookie)

DRAFT DROP *Attended Fullerton (Calif.) JC; re-drafted by White Sox, January 1967/secondary phase (2nd round)*

5. *Dayle Campbell, 1b-of, Pepperdine University.—(AA)

DRAFT DROP *Returned to Pepperdine; re-drafted by Orioles, June 1967/secondary phase (4th round)*

6. *Richard Gouin, of, Pomona Catholic HS, Pomona, Calif.
7. Robert Weisenberg, rhp, North HS, Omaha, Neb.
8. Raymond Huett, ss-rhp, Palomar (Calif.) JC.
9. *James Needham, rhp-of, Loomis Prep School, South Windsor, Conn.
10. **Steve Braun, ss-2b, Hopewell Valley HS, Titusville, N.J.—(1971-85)**
11. Mike Holbrook, of, Hoover HS, Fresno, Calif.
12. Ron Chesebro, lhp, Mayfair HS, Lakewood, Calif.
13. Thomas Maurer, lhp, College of St. Thomas (Minn.).
14. *Bruce Wade, rhp, North HS, Torrance, Calif.
15. Claude Fontenot, ss, San Fernando HS, Pacoima, Calif.
16. Joseph Proctor, c, Beekmantown HS, Plattsburgh, N.Y.
17. ***Chuck Scrivener, ss, Poly HS, Baltimore.—(1975-77)**
18. *Mike Sigman, rhp, Kearney HS, San Diego.
19. *Thomas Stack, c, Calvert Hall HS, Baltimore.
20. *Denny Brady, 1b, Purdue University.
21. *Dan Vossler, rhp-1b, Porterville (Calif.) HS.
22. Michael Moran, ss, University HS, Waco, Texas.
23. Ronnie Barr, inf, Phoenix (Ariz.) JC.
24. Mike Colin, rhp, University of Washington.
25. Robert Ziegler, rhp, Iowa State University.
26. Larry Walters, rhp, Santiago HS, Garden Grove, Calif.
27. Larry Jerrel, of, Montana State University.
28. ***Tommy Moore, of-rhp, John Glenn HS, Norwalk, Calif.—(1972-77)**
29. *Steve Suetters, of, Loyola HS, Los Angeles.
30. *Robert Bentley, rhp, University of Notre Dame.
31. Dave Hoffman, of, University of Minnesota.
32. Bob Castiglione, rhp, New York University.
33. Bill Hahn, of, St. Louis University.
34. Ralph Perez, 3b, Washington HS, Los Angeles.
35. *Steven Wood, lhp, Kansas State University.
36. Phil Johnson, rhp, Iowa Teachers College.
37. Richard Barnes, 3b, South Dakota State University.
38. **(void) *Roger Freed, of, Mount San Antonio (Calif.) JC.—(1970-79)**
39. Neil Baskin, 3b, Long Island University.

40. *Bill Farmer, lhp-1b, Seton HS, Endwell, N.Y.
41. *John Clifton, lhp, Chapman (Calif.) College.
42. Henry Dennis, rhp, Chatham (N.Y.) HS.
43. *Robert Vaughn, rhp, Cerritos (Calif.) JC.
44. Richard Erisman, rhp, Lenape HS, Vincentown, N.J.
45. Steve Kadison, 3b, Brown University.
46. Willis Lancaster, c, Franklin HS, New York.
47. *Thomas Staach, rhp, University of Iowa.
48. *Roger Zahn, lhp, New Ulm (Minn.) HS.
49. James Koosa, 1b, Cardinal Newman HS, Columbia, S.C.

**June—Secondary Phase (6)**

1. **Buzz Stephen, rhp, Fresno State University.—(1968)**
2. *Gary Smith, rhp, Alpena (Mich.) CC.
3. Steven Waters, c, Whittier (Calif.) College.
4. Richard Holmes, rhp, Michigan State University.
5. Robert Hergenrader, lhp, University of Nebraska.
6. Pete Middlekauff, 1b, Stanford University.
7. Tommy Cole, of, Wake Forest University.

**August—American Legion Phase (19)**

No selection.

## NEW YORK METS

**January—Regular Phase (2)**

1. Barry Carter, ss, Chambersburg (Pa.) HS.—DNP
2. Robert Sabo, rhp, Ohio University.
3. Mike Griffith, lhp, Fresno State University.
4. *Tim Keely, ss, Chatham (N.J.) HS.
5. *John Cervi, 1b-3b, Erie (N.Y.) CC.

**January—Secondary Phase (18)**

1. *James Taylor, of, Southern Methodist University.—DNP
2. Michael Kenyon, lhp, Ithaca (N.Y.) College.
3. Dewey Weaver, rhp, Pasco HS, Dade City, Fla.
4. *Gary Smith, rhp, Alpena (Mich.) CC.
5. Ron Kyner, of, Arvin (Calif.) HS.
6. ***Scott Reid, 3b-of, Cerritos (Calif.) JC.—(1969-70)**

DRAFT DROP *Scouting director, Cubs (1986-87)*

**June—Regular Phase (1)**

1. Steve Chilcott, c, Antelope Valley HS, Lancaster, Calif.—(AAA)
2. Byron Von Hoff, rhp, Batavia (Ill.) HS.—(High A)

DRAFT DROP *Brother of Bruce Von Hoff, major leaguer (1965-67)*

3. Donald Linehan, lhp, Mount Vernon HS, Lorton, Va.—(High A)
4. **Mike Jorgensen, 1b-of, Francis Lewis HS, Queens, N.Y.—(1968-85)**
5. Richard Dost, rhp, James Madison HS, Vienna, Va.—(High A)
6. Eddie Lindblad, rhp, Piper (Kan.) HS.
7. Wayne Ryan, 2b, Hillcrest HS, Springfield, Mo.
8. Simon Ashbrook, c, Wellsburg (W.Va.) HS.
9. *Gary Matz, ss-3b, Loyola HS, Baltimore.
10. *Russ Vitallo, rhp, Berkshire (Mass.) CC.
11. Nyal Leslie, 3b, University of Arizona.
12. Mike Minster, c, Fairfax HS, Los Angeles.
13. Michael Eppler, of-2b, University of Tulsa.
14. Ed Palat, of, Grainger HS, Kinston, N.C.
15. Dave Rose, c, River Local HS, Hannibal, Ohio.
16. *Charles Lelas, 1b, Springfield (Mass.) College.
17. Richard Summers, c, University of Texas.
18. ***Rod Gaspar, of, Long Beach State University.—(1969-74)**

DRAFT DROP *Father of Cade Gaspar, first-round draft pick, Tigers (1994)*

19. ***Ron Cey, 3b, Mount Tahoma HS, Tacoma, Wash.—(1971-87)**
20. **Ernie McAnally, rhp, Paris (Texas) JC.—(1971-74)**
21. Jim Gravley, 1b, Cal State Los Angeles.
22. William Blucher, 3b, Towson State University.
23. *John Herzing, lhp, Washington (Mo.) University.
24. Frank Lolich, rhp, Brigham Young University.
25. *Terry Parks, lhp, Fremont HS, Sunnyvale, Calif.
26. *Walter Lampmann, of, Manatee (Fla.) JC.
27. Chris Putnam, of, Cal State Los Angeles.
28. Mike Martin, of, Florida State University.

DRAFT DROP *Baseball coach, Florida State (1980-)*

29. *Arnold Nyulassy, 1b, Eastern Kentucky University.
30. Richard Adams, rhp, Chesterfield (S.C.) HS.
31. Willie Richardson, rhp-ss, Burnet (Texas) HS.
32. ***Kurt Bevacqua, 2b, Miami-Dade CC North.—(1971-85)**
33. *Ron Pinsenschaun, of, Eastern Kentucky University.
34. *Jim Beck, c, Durham (N.C.) HS.
35. *Robert Walter, lhp, Santa Clara University.
36. *John Meyer, c, University of Cincinnati.
37. *Neil Rivenburg, of, Southern Oregon University.
38. John Smith, rhp, Irondequoit HS, Rochester, N.Y.
39. *George Sutton, of, Clemson University.
40. Bob Willet, 3b, Ohio University.
41. *Franklin Stover, rhp, William Carey (Miss.) College.
42. *Tom Schweitzer, lhp, Fairmont State (W.Va.) College.
43. Jim Zerilla, rhp-1b, Parsons (Iowa) College.
44. Maury Hopkins, 3b, Florida State University.
45. *John Mispagel, c, Santa Clara University.
46. *Steve Brasher, rhp, University of Arizona.
47. Robert Haines, rhp, Columbia Basin (Wash.) CC.
48. Billy Haynes, rhp, East Rowan County HS, Granite Quarry, N.C.
49. *Hank Marion, ss, Pioneer HS, San Jose, Calif.
50. *Owen Toy, of, University of Nevada.
51. *John Hilts, rhp, University of Wyoming.
52. *Steve Seale, c, Hillcrest HS, Springfield, Mo.

**June—Secondary Phase (9)**

1. **Duffy Dyer, c, Arizona State University.—(1968-81)**
2. Ronnie Paul, lhp, Texas Christian University.
3. **Dan Frisella, rhp, Washington State University.—(1967-76)**

DRAFT DROP *Died as active major leaguer (Jan. 1, 1977)*

4. Steve Wright, rhp, San Jose (Calif.) CC.
5. Roger Stevens, of, University of California.
6. *Rod Austin, of, Santa Clara University.
7. *Tim Keeley, ss, Chatham (N.J.) HS.
8. *Henry Urbanowicz, 1b, Southwest Missouri JC.

**August—American Legion Phase (2)**

1. *Bob Moore, rhp-1b, Klamath Union HS, Klamath Falls, Ore.—DNP

DRAFT DROP *Tight end, National Football League (1971-78)*

## NEW YORK YANKEES

**January—Regular Phase (9)**

1. Thomas Matheson, c, Eagle Rock HS, Los Angeles.—(High A)
2. *Dennis Pearson, rhp, Pasadena (Calif.) CC.
3. Michael Bruckner, rhp, Bakersfield (Calif.) JC.

**January—Secondary Phase (17)**

1. Bob Biletnikoff, of, University of Miami.—(AAA)

DRAFT DROP *17th-round draft pick, New York Jets/ National Football League (1967)*

2. ***Darrell Evans, 3b, Pasadena (Calif.) CC.—(1969-89)**
3. *John Ferguson, rhp, Abraham Baldwin Agricultural (Ga.) JC.
4. *Alan Putz, of, Cheshire Prep School, Rockville, Conn.
5. *Scotty Long, ss, Auburn University.
6. *Paul Coleman, rhp, Cal Poly Pomona.

**June—Regular Phase (10)**

1. **Jim Lyttle, of, Florida State University.—(1969-76)**
2. **Gary Timberlake, lhp, Meade County HS, Brandenburg, Ky.—(1969)**
3. Dave Wolfe, c, Buena Vista (Iowa) College.—(High A)
4. Robert Starr, of, Fullerton (Calif.) HS.—(High A)
5. Carl Black, rhp, Central Missouri State University.—(High A)
6. Alvin Hodges, of, Yanceyville (N.C.) HS.
7. **Steve Kline, rhp, Lake Chelan (Wash.) HS.—(1970-77)**
8. *Michael McFarland, rhp, University of Missouri.
9. *Gary Laney, inf, Clinton (S.C.) HS.
10. *Ken Stabler, lhp, University of Alabama.

DRAFT DROP *Quarterback, National Football League (1970-84)*

11. Roger Dutton, of, Northern Illinois University.
12. Bill Fisher, rhp, Tahlequah HS, Hulbert, Okla.
13. *Ken O'Brien, rhp, Hewlett HS, Woodmere, N.Y.
14. David Ross, c-of, Pittsburg State (Kan.) University.
15. *Rich Donnelly, c, Xavier University.
16. Jerry Matney, lhp, Northside HS, Vernon, Texas.
17. *Richard Buff, inf, Rossville (Ga.) HS.
18. **Joe Pactwa, lhp-of, North Thornton HS, Calumet, Ill.—(1975)**
19. Earl Hash, of, University of Richmond.
20. Jeff Hopkins, of, Wesleyan (Conn.) University.
21. *Julian Karp, rhp, Washington State University.
22. *Marvin Tucker, inf, Truman HS, Independence, Mo.
23. *Clarence Stoner, 1b-of, Penn State University.
24. *Tom Porter, inf, Zephyrhills (Fla.) HS.
25. Robert Dearrah, rhp, Tulane University.
26. Louie Bunch, c, Central HS, Springfield, Mo.
27. *Lamar Davis, 1b, University of Maryland.
28. Dallas Jones, c, Belhaven (Miss.) College.
29. *John Lee, inf-of, Linfield (Ore.) College.
30. *Tim Marks, rhp-of, Manual HS, Peoria, Ill.
31. *Tommie Iseminger, 1b, Hillcrest HS, Springfield, Mo.
32. *Jim Smith, inf, Lewiston (Idaho) HS.
33. *Fred Keimel, lhp, Berkeley Heights (N.J.) HS.
34. *Freddie Dukes, lhp, Central HS, Chattanooga, Tenn.
35. *Robert Robbins, lhp, Gowanda (N.Y.) Senior HS.
36. *Gary Washington, 1b, Mississippi State University.
37. Carl Ingrim, c, Glenville State (W.Va.) College.
38. *Bobby Bryant, lhp, University of South Carolina.

DRAFT DROP *Defensive back, National Football League (1968-80)*

39. Richard Olsen, inf, Iowa State University.
40. *James Price, rhp, Skyline HS, Salt Lake City.
41. Louis Polisano, of, Glassboro State (N.J.) College.
42. David Steen, rhp, Elk Horn, Iowa.
43. *Michael Karkut, lhp, Bayonne (N.J) HS.
44. William Mason, of, American University.
45. *Jim Pope, rhp, Pasco (Wash.) HS.
46. *Robert Parker, c, Duval HS, Lanham, Md.
47. Robert Height, of, Shaw (N.C.) University.
48. *Roy Waye, 1b, Lynn View HS, Kingsport, Tenn.
49. *William Shepherd, rhp, Rogers HS, Spokane, Wash.
50. *Al Simmons, rhp, University of Idaho.
51. *Roger Banks, c, Mars Hill (N.C.) College.
52. *Steven Richman, inf, Columbia University.
53. *Luis Flores, c, Lafayette HS, Brooklyn, N.Y.
54. **Rusty Torres, of, New York Vocational HS, Jamaica, N.Y.—(1971-80)**
55. *Gil Scharringhausen, rhp, Portland State University.
56. Thomas Bongiorno, c, Seton Hall University.
57. Ron Lewis, 1b, Temple University.
58. Ernest Recob, of, Kansas State University.
59. *Kelly Prior, rhp, University of Florida.
60. Tom Bettecher, lhp, Buffalo State College.
61. *Richard Carlson, of, Buffalo State College.
62. *Frank Brennan, rhp, Fairleigh Dickinson University.
63. Matt Galante, inf, St. John's University.

DRAFT DROP *Major league manager (1999)*

**June—Secondary Phase (10)**

1. Walter Manuel, ss, Lafayette University.—(AAA)
2. *Steve Wrenn, 1b, Wake Forest University.
3. Dennis Baldridge, of, University of Oregon.
4. *Terry L'Ange, rhp, University of Missouri.
5. Steven Mezich, c, Seattle University.
6. John Patterson, 1b, William Jewell (Mo.) College.
7. Glen Borkhuis, rhp, Syracuse University.

**August—American Legion Phase (9)**

1. *Gregory Croft, rhp, Glenbrook South HS, Glenview, Ill.—DNP

## PHILADELPHIA PHILLIES

**January—Regular Phase (10)**

1. **John Vukovich, 3b-ss, American River (Calif.) JC.—(1970-81)**

DRAFT DROP *Major league manager (1986-88)*

**January—Secondary Phase (6)**

1. **Lowell Palmer, rhp, American River (Calif.) JC.—(1969-74)**
2. *John Green, rhp, Gulf Coast (Fla.) JC.

**June—Regular Phase (9)**

1. Michael Biko, rhp, W.W. Samuell HS, Dallas.—(High A)
2. *Pat Skrable, of, Bakersfield (Calif.) HS.—(AAA)

DRAFT DROP *Attended Bakersfield (Calif.) JC; re-drafted by Phillies, January 1967/secondary phase (1st round)*

3. *Patrick Amos, ss, Arlington Heights HS, Fort Worth, Texas.—DNP

DRAFT DROP *Attended Texas; never re-drafted*

4. **Ken Reynolds, lhp, New Mexico Highlands University.—(1970-76)**
5. *Charlie West, of, University of Texas-El Paso.—(High A)

DRAFT DROP *Returned to Texas-El Paso; re-drafted by Reds, January 1968/regular phase (1st round); defensive back, National Football League (1968-79)*

6. Michael Beaver, rhp, Worland (Wyo.) HS.
7. *William Camp, rhp, Nathan Hale HS, Tulsa, Okla.
8. Marty Meagher, ss, Rolling Hills (Calif.) HS.
9. *Randy Moseley, lhp, Waxahachie (Texas) HS.
10. David Myers, 1b, Chambersburg (Pa.) HS.
11. Gregg Hansen, c, Wagner College.
12. James Jones, of, Moore HS, Waco, Texas.
13. Smith Holland, rhp, The Citadel.
14. Jack Foreman, rhp, Shelby (Ohio) HS.
15. (void) *Frederick Grooms, rhp-of, Wilson HS, San Francisco.
16. Barry Miller, 2b, Hempfield Area HS, Youngwood, Pa.
17. *Philip MacDonald, of, Crescenta HS, La Crescenta, Calif.
18. *Thomas Schleer, lhp, Wayne (N.J.) HS.
19. *Richard Corsetto, rhp, Gannon (Pa.) University.
20. James McNeil, c, North Plainfield (N.J.) HS.
21. *Ronald Fournier, 1b, Pasadena (Calif.) CC.
22. *James Sanders, rhp, Southside HS, Florence, S.C.
23. *Earl Vickers, of, Fresno State University.
24. Richard Seminoff, rhp, University of Arizona.
25. Ben Farrell, rhp, David Lipscomb (Tenn.) College.
26. *Jodie Beeler, c, W.W. Samuell HS, Dallas.

**June—Secondary Phase (13)**

1. **Steve Arlin, rhp, Ohio State University.—(1969-74)**
2. Stump Merrill, c, University of Maine.

DRAFT DROP *Major league manager (1990-91)*

3. Richard Johnson, rhp, University of Arizona.
4. *Tom Cook, c, Manatee (Fla.) JC.

**August—American Legion Phase (10)**

No selection.

## PITTSBURGH PIRATES

**January—Regular Phase (16)**

1. Kent Smith, of, Sacramento (Calif.) CC.—(Low A)
2. *James Minnette, rhp, Columbia Basin (Wash.) CC.
3. *Willie Somerset, of, Duquesne University.

**January—Secondary Phase (8)**

1. *Fred Mazurek, of, University of Pittsburgh.—DNP

DRAFT DROP *Wide receiver, National Football League (1965-66)*

2. ***Frank Brosseau, of, University of Minnesota.—(1969-71)**
3. Dennis Malseed, rhp, St. James HS, Woodlyn, Pa.
4. ***Del Unser, of-1b, Mississippi State University.—(1968-82)**

DRAFT DROP *Son of Al Unser, major leaguer (1942-45)*

5. *Richard Devarney, ss, University of Maine.
6. ***Dick Mills, rhp, Parsons (Iowa) College.—(1970)**

DRAFT DROP *Father of Ryan Mills, first-round draft pick, Twins (1996)*

7. *Danny Talbott, 1b-of, University of North Carolina.

DRAFT DROP *17th-round draft pick, San Francisco 49ers/ National Football League (1967)*

8. *David Barton, ss, Ithaca (N.Y.) College.

**June—Regular Phase (15)**

1. **Richie Hebner, ss, Norwood (Mass.) HS.—(1968-85)**

**2. Jim Minshall, rhp, Newport Catholic HS, Melbourne, Ky.—(1974-75)**
3. Dick Grimaldi, rhp, Proctor HS, Utica, N.Y.—(Low A)
4. Dave Lambert, of, University of Washington.—(Low A)
**5. Dave Cash, ss, Proctor HS, Utica, N.Y.—(1969-80)**
**6. Gene Clines, 2b-of, Ells HS, Richmond, Calif.—(1970-79)**
**7. Bill Laxton, lhp, Audubon (N.J.) HS.—(1970-77)**
DRAFT DROP *Father of Brett Laxton, major leaguer (1999-2000)*
8. Stanley Baker, c, 71st HS, Fayetteville, N.C.
9. Paul Pierce, of, Pittsfield (Mass.) HS.
10. Robert McKee, lhp, Etna HS, Pittsburgh.
11. Dave Arrington, rhp-of, DeAnza HS, El Sobrante, Calif.
**12. *Ron Schueler, rhp, Hays HS, Catherine, Kan.—(1972-79)**
DRAFT DROP *General manager, White Sox (1991-2000)*
13. Raymond Heller, rhp, Wicomico HS, Salisbury, Md.
14. Robert Sherry, ss, University of Washington.
15. *William Stone, of, Warren Easton HS, New Orleans, La.
16. *James Kovalsky, c, Washington (N.J.) HS.
17. *James Lawrence, c, Deep Creek HS, Chesapeake, Va.
18. Jim Palm, of, Carlmont HS, Belmont, Calif.
19. Michael Fuchs, lhp, Parkersburg (W.Va.) HS.
20. Robert Butkus, lhp, Bowdoin (Maine) College.
21. John Murphy, of, McCloud, Calif.
22. Larry Stout, rhp, Huntington (Ind.) College.
23. Calvin Bailey, rhp, West Virginia State College.
24. Robin Porter, c-of, Virginia Military Institute.
25. Douglas Stanley, of, West Virginia University.
26. *Taylor Toomey, lhp, University of Colorado.
27. *Paul Mann, rhp, Afton HS, St. Louis.
28. Walter Joyner, of-lhp, Western Maryland College.
29. Gerry McCabe, rhp-of, Cripple Creek-Victor HS, Victor, Colo.
30. *Edwin Figueroa, c, George Washington HS, New York.
31. *James Engel, rhp, Bensenville, Ill.
32. *Gary Johnson, inf, University of Idaho.
33. *Michael Horn, rhp, Boone County HS, Florence, Ky.
34. *Rick Jaggars, rhp, Gonzaga University.
35. *James Skovron, rhp, Pentucket Regional HS, West Newbury, Mass.
36. Donald Messinese, lhp, Crossland HS, Washington, Md.
37. Joseph Johnson, rhp, Loyal Sock HS, Williamsport, Pa.
**38. *Rich Hand, rhp, Lincoln HS, Seattle.—(1970-73)**
DRAFT DROP *First overall draft pick, June 1969/secondary phase, Indians*
39. *Ronald Epperson, rhp, Hudson Bay HS, Vancouver, Wash.
40. *Charles Dupuis, of, Evergreen, Wash.
41. *Philip Scarpellino, 1b, University of New Haven.

**June—Secondary Phase (19)**

**1. Frank Brosseau, of, University of Minnesota.—(1969-71)**
2. *Ken Lohnes, c, Cerritos (Calif.) JC.
3. *David Barton, ss, Ithaca (N.Y.) College.
4. *James Minnette, inf, Columbia Basin (Wash.) CC.
5. *Danny Talbott, 1b-of, University of North Carolina.
DRAFT DROP *17th-round draft pick, San Francisco 49ers/National Football League (1967)*

**August—American Legion Phase (16)**

No selection.

## ST. LOUIS CARDINALS

**January—Regular Phase (8)**

1. *Henry Urbanowitz, 1b, Jasper (Mo.) JC.—DNP
2. Jesse DuBose, lhp, Smith HS, Ozark, Ala.
3. James Moore, 2b-ss, El Dorado, Ark.

**January—Secondary Phase (2)**

1. Jon Baker, rhp, Columbia Basin (Wash.) CC.—(High A)
2. *Ken Lohnes, c, Cerritos (Calif.) JC.
3. *William Carino, c, Mount Hermon (Mass.) HS.

**June—Regular Phase (7)**

**1. Leron Lee, 1b-of, Grant Union HS, Sacramento, Calif.—(1969-76)**
DRAFT DROP *Uncle of Derrek Lee, major leaguer (1997-2006)*
2. Danny Barrett, ss, Hillcrest HS, Springfield, Mo.—(Low A)
**3. Clay Kirby, rhp, Washington HS, Arlington, Va.—(1969-76)**
**4. *Bob Spence, 1b, Santa Clara University.—(1969-71)**
DRAFT DROP *Returned to Santa Clara; re-drafted by White Sox, January 1967/secondary phase (1st round)*
5. Don Cooksey, rhp-of, O'Fallon Tech HS, St. Louis.—(Low A)
6. *Ed Bauer, lhp, Columbus HS, Bronx, N.Y.
7. Jerry Bartee, ss, Central HS, Omaha, Neb.
DRAFT DROP *Father of Kimera Bartee, major leaguer (1996-2001)*
8. Charlie Stewart, of, Oklahoma Baptist College.
9. Gary Ford, 3b, Ventura (Calif.) HS.
10. *Cole Shumaker, lhp, Maben (Miss.) HS.
11. Dewayne Wendt, ss, Deshler (Ohio) HS.
12. Joe Atilee, rhp, B.C. Elmore HS, Houston.
13. Terrence Murphy, 2b, Cardinal Mooney HS, Rochester, N.Y.
14. Douglas Lukens, rhp, Washington State University.
15. *Frank Patterson, of, Grambling University.
16. Monte Little, ss, Ayden (N.C.) HS.
17. *Dale Reed, lhp, Glendale HS, Springfield, Mo.
18. *Jerry Paetzhold, lhp, Sparta HS, Ellis Grove, Ill.
19. *Gary Ratliff, of,East Central HS, Tulsa, Okla.
20. Clement Nowakowski, rhp, Washington HS, Chicago.
21. *Michael Noonan, lhp, Foothill (Calif.) JC.
22. *Robert Sharp, rhp, Torrance (Calif.) HS.
23. *Jerry Meadows, rhp, West Virginia University.
24. Lew Wright, rhp, College Park HS, Pleasant Hill, Calif.
25. Dale Hill, 3b-c, Iowa City (Iowa) HS.
**26. *Jim Panther, rhp, Southern Illinois University.—(1971-73)**
27. George Bruns, 2b, Manhattan College.
28. Bob Schaefer, ss, University of Connecticut.
DRAFT DROP *Major league manager (1991, 2005)*
29. Robert Moone, 1b, St. Rita HS, Chicago.
30. *Jerry Sabourin, lhp, Cleveland HS, St. Louis.
31. *Stephen Dean, 1b, Mount Whitney HS, Visalia, Calif.
32. Bill Cheslock, 1b-of, Hofstra University.
33. Eddie Dixon, 3b-rhp, Hiwassee (Tenn.) JC.
34. Fred Covey, rhp, Phillipsburg (Pa.) HS.
35. Earl Nursement, of, University of Nevada.
36. Ken Kurtz, 2b, University of Arizona.
37. *William Flood, of-c, University of Connecticut.
38. (void) *John Manginelli, 3b, Irvington (N.J.) HS.
39. *Phil Trombino, 1b, Iona College.
40. *Mike Pruett, lhp, Ritenour HS, Overland, Mo.
41. Bruce MacLean, rhp, Bowdoin (Maine) College.
42. Buddy Smith, rhp, Chipola (Fla.) JC.
43. Lanny Guyer, 2b, Southern Oregon University.
44. *Jan Biggs, c, Bullard HS, Fresno, Calif.
45. Michael Steele, 1b, San Diego State University.
46. Larry Azevedo, rhp, Hilmar (Calif.) HS.

**June—Secondary Phase (17)**

**1. Jerry DaVanon, 2b, Westmont (Calif.) College.—(1969-77)**
DRAFT DROP *Father of Jeff DaVanon, major leaguer (1999-2007)*
**2. *Bob Chlupsa, rhp-1b, Manhattan University.—(1970-71)**
DRAFT DROP *13th-round draft pick, San Diego Rockets/National Basketball Association (1967)*
3. *Bruce Hinkel, lhp, Upper Iowa University.

**August—American Legion Phase (8)**

No selection.

## SAN FRANCISCO GIANTS

**January—Regular Phase (18)**

1. Gary Bowman, of, Garden City, Mich.—(High A)
2. *Stephen Lohrer, of, Nassau (N.Y.) CC.
**3. *Tony Muser, 1b-lhp, San Diego Mesa JC.—(1969-78)**
DRAFT DROP *Major league manager (1997-2002)*

**January—Secondary Phase (12)**

**1. *Dick Tidrow, rhp, Chabot (Calif.) JC.—(1972-84)**

**June—Regular Phase (17)**

**1. Bob Reynolds, rhp, Ingraham HS, Seattle.—(1969-75)**
2. Joseph Hebert, ss, Baton Rouge (La.) HS.—(Short-season A)
3. James Carroll, rhp, Mississippi State University.—(High A)
**4. *Rich Folkers, lhp, Ellsworth (Iowa) JC.—(1970-77)**
DRAFT DROP *Returned to Ellsworth (Iowa) JC; re-drafted by White Sox, January 1967/secondary phase (3rd round)*
**5. *David Lemonds, of-lhp, Garinger HS, Charlotte, N.C.—(1969-72)**
DRAFT DROP *Attended North Carolina; re-drafted by Cubs, June 1968/secondary phase (1st round; 1st pick)*
6. Keith Wade, of, Muir HS, Pasadena, Calif.
7. John Beaton, rhp, Murray State University.
8. *Steve Barnhill, of, Hinkley HS, Aurora, Colo.
9. *Gerald Christman, lhp, Deshler (Ohio) HS.
10. *Jack Grasing, lhp, Villanova University.
**11. Bernie Williams, of, St. Elizabeth HS, Oakland, Calif.—(1970-74)**
**12. *Mike Sadek, c, University of Minnesota.—(1973-81)**
**13. Gary Ryerson, lhp, Rolling Hills HS, Palos Verdes, Calif.—(1972-73)**
14. *Gary Kollman, ss, University of Wyoming.
15. *Robert Hoey, 3b, Assumption HS, East St. Louis, Ill.
16. Robert DeLong, lhp, Willow Glen HS, San Jose, Calif.
**17. Don Hahn, of, Campbell HS, San Jose, Calif.—(1969-75)**
18. Dale Spier, rhp, Arizona State University.
19. *Clifford Farmer, rhp, Hillcrest HS, Springfield, Mo.
20. *Ted Rohde, of, Sierra HS, Toll House, Calif.
21. *Daniel Blood, 2b, Arcadia (Calif.) HS.
**22. *Frank Baker, ss, University of Southern Mississippi.—(1970-74)**
23. Charles Hopkins, rhp, University of Oregon.
24. *Michael Babler, rhp, St. Elizabeth HS, San Lorenzo, Calif.
25. Marc Michel, of, University of Iowa.
26. Mike Wysocki, rhp, University of Georgia.
27. *Don Kirkland, rhp-inf, Southern Illinois University.
28. *Terry Stofer, of, Key West (Fla.) HS.
29. Roy Johnson, rhp, Canoga Park HS, Woodland Hills, Calif.
30. *Tom Burgess, rhp, Phoenix (Ariz.) JC.
**31. John Harrell, c, West Valley (Calif.) JC.—(1969)**
32. Jerry Anding, rhp, Cal State Northridge.
33. *Phillip Thomas, rhp-inf, Tonganoxie (Kan.) HS.
34. *Ray Strable, rhp, JC of the Sequoias (Calif.).
35. *James Dew, c, Mayville, N.D.
36. Brad Dodge, of, Jordan HS, Long Beach, Calif.
37. Rusty York, of, Phoenix (Ariz.) JC.
38. *Richard Wanless, rhp, Quincy (Mass.) HS.
39. *Mike Ford, c, Lewis (Ill.) University.
40. *Bob Garcia, of, JC of the Sequoias (Calif.).

**June—Secondary Phase (1)**

1. Bill Frost, rhp, University of California.—(AAA)
2. *Kris Krebs, ss, Manatee (Fla.) JC.
**3. *Gary Gentry, rhp, Phoenix (Ariz.) JC.—(1969-75)**
**4. *Tom Murphy, rhp, Ohio University.—(1969-79)**
5. *David Pratt, lhp, Tennessee Tech.

**August—American Legion Phase (18)**

No selection.

## WASHINGTON SENATORS

**January—Regular Phase (5)**

1. Tim Zajeski, rhp, South Holland, Ill.—(AA)
2. Gary Kolumbus, of, Waller HS, Chicago.

**January—Secondary Phase (13)**

**1. *Bob Stinson, of-c, Miami (Fla.) Senior HS.—(1969-80)**
**2. *Bob Reed, rhp, University of Michigan.—(1969-70)**
3. *John Miklos, lhp, Valparaiso University.
4. *Percy Sensabaugh, rhp, Virginia Military Institute.
5. *Terry L'Ange, rhp, University of Missouri.
6. *George Grzegerek, ss, St. Edward's (Texas) University.
7. *John Biedenbach, 3b, Michigan State University.
**8. Dick Such, rhp, Elon College.—(1970)**
9. *Lionel Jones, of, Southern University.

**June—Regular Phase (6)**

**1. Tom Grieve, of-c, Pittsfield (Mass.) HS.—(1970-79)**
DRAFT DROP *Father of Ben Grieve, first-round draft pick, Athletics (1994); major leaguer (1997-2004) • General manager, Rangers (1984-94)*
2. Sonny Bowers, ss, John Marshall HS, Oklahoma City, Okla.—(AA)
**3. *Lou Camilli, 3b, Texas A&M University.—(1969-72)**
DRAFT DROP *Returned to Texas A&M; re-drafted by Indians, June 1967/secondary phase (3rd round)*
4. Wallace Smallwood, rhp, Martinsburg (W.Va.) HS.—(AAA)
5. Gerald Merlet, ss-3b, Beloit (Wis.) HS.—(AA)
6. *Kim Hillstrom, rhp, Central Michigan University.
7. (void) *John Fryer, rhp, Brevard (Fla.) CC.
8. *John Bowman, lhp, Trinity (Texas) University.
9. Robert Miller, 3b, Lewis (Ill.) University.
10. *Larry Herring, lhp, Dillon (S.C.) HS.
11. Wayne Brescher, c, Southeastern Louisiana University.
12. Jack Merlet, 2b, Northern Illinois University.
13. John Michael, ss, Morrow (Ohio) HS.
**14. *Dan Neumeier, rhp, Gresham (Wis.) HS.—(1972)**
15. *Geoff Petrie, rhp, Springfield (Pa.) HS.
DRAFT DROP *First-round draft pick, Portland Trail Blazers/National Basketball Association (1970); guard, NBA (1970-76)*
16. LeRoy Visor, ss, Park HS, Racine, Wis.
17. *Nick Furlong, rhp, Iona Prep School, New Rochelle, N.Y.
18. Duane Kalmer, c, Quincy (Ill.) College.
19. *Edward Cook, ss-of, Bridgewater (Va.) College.
20. *Mickey Yates, of, Texas Christian University.
21. *Charles Miller, rhp, Waynesville (Ohio) HS.
22. *William Kelley, rhp, Archbishop Curley HS, Baltimore.
23. *William Wright, lhp, Montgomery (Md.) JC.
24. *Mike Flanagan, rhp, University of North Carolina.
**25. Gerry Schoen, rhp, Loyola (La.) University.—(1968)**
**26. *Gerry Pirtle, rhp, Nathan Hale HS, Tulsa, Okla.—(1978)**
27. Walter Collins, rhp, Norview HS, Norfolk, Va.
28. Richard Bucholtz, rhp, Burlington (Wis.) HS.
29. *Richard Wicks, lhp, Lake Charles (La.) HS.
30. *Dick Snyder, of, Davidson College.
DRAFT DROP *Forward, National Basketball Association (1966-79)*
31. *Bruce Baudier, rhp, Louisiana State University.
32. Jerry Etheridge, of, Bamberg (S.C.) HS.
33. *Chris Kougias, 1b, Fort Hunt HS, Alexandria, Va.
34. *Dave Cichon, c, Eastern HS, Bristol, Conn.

**June—Secondary Phase (18)**

**1. Del Unser, of-1b, Mississippi State University.—(1968-82)**
DRAFT DROP *Son of Al Unser, major leaguer (1942-45)*
2. John Biedenbach, 3b, Michigan State University.
3. John Miklos, lhp, Valparaiso University.
4. Fred Shuey, of, University of Southern California.

**August—American Legion Phase (5)**

No selection.

# 1967

# Yankees' fall leads to rare No. 1 pick in draft

The fall was sudden and dramatic. The New York Yankees, the most successful and most celebrated team in American sports history, inexplicably found themselves on the bottom looking up just two years after winning nine American League titles in 10 years.

Their consolation prize: the No. 1 pick in the 1967 draft—one of only two times in the draft's history they held that distinction.

The Yankees had little doubt what kind of player they were looking for to restore their tattered image. Trying to elicit memories of Mickey Mantle, who was a year away from retiring but epitomized their glory days of the 1950s and early '60s, the Yankees went after Ron Blomberg, a power hitter with the potential to play center field. It was no coincidence that Blomberg was also Jewish, and the Yankees were quietly hoping that he would appeal to a large Jewish population in New York.

The feelings were definitely mutual, and the thought of playing in front of New York crowds and dealing with the New York media thrilled Blomberg. At 18, he appeared to have everything neatly planned out for him.

"The Yankees have always been my favorite team, and Mantle my favorite player," he said. "I had always dreamed of being a major league ballplayer. I had three goals. I wanted to be a Yankee, to win a batting title, and to have a monument built in honor of me like those in honor of (Babe) Ruth and (Lou) Gehrig.

"I remember becoming a Yankees fan watching Mantle on TV. They were so exciting in those years. They were down, yes, when I was drafted, but that only meant a better opportunity for me."

Blomberg, primarily a pitcher/first baseman at Druid Hills High in Atlanta, hit .472 with five home runs and 45 RBIs as a prep senior. Though he had offers from all over the country to play basketball in college, Blomberg knew at an early age what he wanted to do with his career and quickly agreed with the Yankees on a bonus of $65,000.

"I feel Ronnie is the best pro prospect to come along in several years," said Yankees general manager Lee MacPhail, in announcing Blomberg's signing. "We had six of our scouts watch Ronnie and they unanimously agreed that he was the one we should sign. I figure it will take him about three years to reach the majors."

Blomberg reached New York right on schedule, but he became little more than a platoon player with the Yankees. He became best known as baseball's first designated hitter in 1973—a role that seemed to symbolize the shortcomings that became apparent in his game.

Though the Yankees settled on Blomberg, the team had numerous holes to fill. They had been plagued by problems at shortstop, in particular,

ASSOCIATED PRESS

Ron Blomberg, with his parents and Yankees manager Ralph Houk, looked like a dream pick for the downtrodden Yankees, but he ended up being remembered as the first DH in major league history

since the retirement of Tony Kubek after the 1965 season, and some speculated that they might opt for Terry Hughes, a slick-fielding prep shortstop from South Carolina, to solve their woes at the position. Hughes went one pick later to the Chicago Cubs.

Idaho high school righthander Mike Garman was hailed as the other prospect in a clearly defined pre-draft top three in the June regular phase, and right on cue, he went to the Boston Red Sox.

The best overall talent in the 1967 draft, according to most scouts, however, was University of Southern California righthander Mike Adamson, who was relegated to the lower-profile secondary phase because he had previously been drafted—in 1965, in the first round by Philadelphia. Adamson was claimed by the Baltimore Orioles with the top pick in that phase, and not only signed for the largest bonus ($75,000) in 1967, but earned the distinction of becoming the first drafted player to begin his career in the big leagues.

For all the attention paid to Blomberg and Adamson, and other top prospects in both phases of the June draft, none came close to matching the accomplishments of the lone Hall of Famer to emerge from the Class of 1967: Carlton Fisk, known at the University of New Hampshire primarily for his acumen on the basketball court. Fisk was selected with the fourth pick in the regular phase of the January draft, and signed with the Red Sox for the meager sum of $10,000.

## EARNED ACCLAIM AS FIRST DH

As the No. 1 pick in the draft, Blomberg saw his selection as a one-way track to the Hall of Fame. Others thought so, too.

But Blomberg's career never materialized the way he hoped it would, and the closest he got to the Hall of Fame was the bat that went on display

## AT A GLANCE

### This Date In History

**WINTER DRAFT:** Jan. 28.
**SUMMER DRAFT:** June 6-7.

### Best Draft

**BALTIMORE ORIOLES.** The O's snagged **BOBBY GRICH** and **DON BAYLOR** with their first two picks in the June regular phase, so after signing those two future all-stars it was all right that they got almost no production from their remaining 62 picks in that phase—and nothing out of **MIKE ADAMSON**, the first overall pick in the secondary phase who received the highest bonus in the 1967 draft.

### Worst Draft

**PHILADELPHIA PHILLIES.** The Phillies not only got no mileage out of their top pick in the June regular phase (**PHIL MEYER**) for the third draft in a row, but none of the 24 players they selected in that phase reached the big leagues.

### First-Round Bust

**JOHNNY JONES, C, SENATORS.** If it was a high school catcher the Senators were looking for with the fifth pick, then **TED SIMMONS** was available for the taking. Instead, they went for Jones, a Tennessee prep product who became one of the most over-matched first-rounders in draft history—hardly the career predicted by Senators scout Hillis Layne, who claimed: "He's the best-looking prospect I've seen. If he develops, he has the chance to become a superstar."

### Second To None

**VIDA BLUE, LHP, ATHLETICS.** The A's whiffed on their first-round pick in 1967, **BRIEN BICKERTON**, who didn't reach the majors, but hit paydirt a round later with another lefthander. Blue was a sensation as a 21-year-old, winning both the American League's MVP and Cy Young awards while going 24-8, 1.82 with 301 strikeouts.

CONTINUED ON PAGE 54

## AT A GLANCE

CONTINUED FROM PAGE 53

### Late-Round Find

**DUSTY BAKER, OF, BRAVES (26TH ROUND).** Despite his low standing in the draft, Baker surfaced in the majors at 19 and went on to a 19-year career.

### Never Too Late

**ROGER HAMBRIGHT, RHP, YANKEES (67TH ROUND).** The Yankees landed a pitcher who drove in a run in a major league game that he saved in 1971, his only big league season. That feat wouldn't happen again for the Yankees for 38 years, when Mariano Rivera did it while earning his 500th save. Hambright's career amounted to 18 appearances (and two saves).

### Overlooked

**ANDRE THORNTON, 1B, PHILLIES.** The Phillies made up for a bad draft by signing the power-hitting Thornton, a product of a local high school. Unfortunately they traded him to Cleveland in 1972, before he played a game in his hometown, and he went on to hit 253 homers in the big leagues.

### International Gem

**CESAR CEDENO, OF, ASTROS.** Signed out of the Dominican Republic for $8,000 at 16 and a major leaguer by 19, Cedeno showed power, speed and defensive excellence in center field. He quickly became one of baseball's biggest stars. "At 22," said Astros manager Leo Durocher, "Cesar is as good or better than Willie (Mays) at the same age." Cedeno became the second player in big league history to hit 20 homers and steal 50 bases in a season, and he did it three years in a row (1972-74). He also won five Gold Gloves in a 17-year career.

### Minor League Take

**JOHN MAYBERRY, 1B, ASTROS.** Mayberry debuted in the majors in 1968 at 19, but continued to add to his impressive

## 1967: THE FIRST ROUNDERS

| CLUB: PLAYER, POS., SCHOOL | HOMETOWN | B-T | HT. | WT. | AGE | BONUS | FIRST YEAR | LAST YEAR | PEAK LEVEL (YEARS) |
|---|---|---|---|---|---|---|---|---|---|
| **JUNE—REGULAR PHASE** | | | | | | | | | |
| 1. Yankees: Ron Blomberg, 1b, Druid Hills HS | Atlanta | L-R | 6-1 | 185 | 18 | $65,000 | 1967 | 1978 | Majors (8) |
| Proclaimed great Jewish hope by Yankees, but played in just 461 big league games, batting .293 with 52 homers; became best known as game's first DH. | | | | | | | | | |
| 2. Cubs: Terry Hughes, ss, Dorman HS | Spartanburg, S.C. | R-R | 6-1 | 185 | 18 | $50,000 | 1967 | 1976 | Majors (3) |
| South Carolina prep product was drafted for glovework, raw power potential; hit .209 with solo homer in 54 big league games, spent 10 years in minors. | | | | | | | | | |
| 3. Red Sox: Mike Garman, rhp, Caldwell HS | Caldwell, Idaho | R-R | 6-3 | 200 | 17 | $54,000 | 1967 | 1979 | Majors (9) |
| Highest-ever pick from Idaho; like others in draft's big three, his career fell short of expectations, with 22-25 record, 3.63 ERA, with five clubs over nine years. | | | | | | | | | |
| 4. Mets: Jon Matlack, lhp, Henderson HS | West Chester, Pa. | L-L | 6-3 | 185 | 17 | $55,000 | 1967 | 1983 | Majors (13) |
| Became one of Big Three in Mets rotation in early 1970s, alongside Seaver, Koosman; NL Rookie of the Year in '72, MVP of '74 ASG, won 125 games in 13 years. | | | | | | | | | |
| 5. Senators: Johnny Jones, c, Loretto HS | St. Joseph, Tenn. | L-R | 6-1 | 195 | 17 | $30,000 | 1967 | 1970 | Class A (2) |
| First of four catchers taken in first round; overmatched at plate in four pro seasons, none above Class A; hit just .150 with one homer, 191 strikeouts in 426 ABs. | | | | | | | | | |
| 6. Astros: John Mayberry, 1b, Northwestern HS | Detroit | L-L | 6-3 | 207 | 17 | $40,000 | 1967 | 1982 | Majors (15) |
| Two-time all-state basketball player in Michigan, became two-time AL all-star after being acquired by Royals; hit 255 homers in 15 years; John Jr. also first-rounder. | | | | | | | | | |
| 7. Athletics: # Brien Bickerton, lhp, Santana HS | Santee, Calif. | L-L | 6-2 | 190 | 17 | $15,000 | 1967 | 1975 | Class AAA (1) |
| Went 23-49, 4.58 in eight minor league seasons after A's landed Monday and Jackson in first round of first two drafts; died in horrific head-on car wreck in 2005. | | | | | | | | | |
| 8. Reds: Wayne Simpson, rhp, Centennial HS | Los Angeles | R-R | 6-5 | 205 | 18 | $40,000 | 1967 | 1978 | Majors (6) |
| At 13-1 in 1970 for Reds, was in midst of one of great rookie seasons ever, but his season and career came crashing down when he tore rotator cuff on July 31. | | | | | | | | | |
| 9. Angels: Mike Nunn, c, Ben L. Smith HS | Greensboro, N.C. | L-R | 6-0 | 178 | 18 | $35,000 | 1967 | 1972 | Class AAA (1) |
| Pre-draft scouting reports accurately projected him as solid defender with questionable bat; hit .209 with 14 homers in six minor league seasons. | | | | | | | | | |
| 10. Cardinals: Ted Simmons, c, Southfield HS | Southfield, Mich. | B-R | 6-0 | 185 | 17 | $30,000 | 1967 | 1984 | Majors (21) |
| Overshadowed by Johnny Bench during most of his 21-year career, but with .285 average and 248 homers, was a better overall hitter than the Hall of Famer. | | | | | | | | | |
| 11. Indians: Jack Heidemann, ss, Brenham HS | Brenham, Texas | R-R | 6-0 | 165 | 17 | $22,500 | 1967 | 1979 | Majors (8) |
| Gifted defender became Indians everyday shortstop at 20; hurt shoulder following spring, never saw regular work again, spent bulk of 13-year career in minors. | | | | | | | | | |
| 12. Braves: Andy Finlay, of, Luther Burbank HS | Sacramento, Calif. | R-R | 6-0 | 185 | 17 | $23,000 | 1967 | 1971 | Class AA (2) |
| Career got off to fast start in Braves system but unraveled and led to a trade to expansion Padres; hit .242 with 32 homers in 407 minor league games. | | | | | | | | | |
| 13. White Sox: Dan Haynes, 3b, Headland HS | East Point, Ga. | R-R | 6-2 | 210 | 17 | $20,000 | 1967 | 1974 | Class AAA (3) |
| Prolific power hitter on prep/Legion championship teams, homered 76 times in eight seasons in minors, but career doomed by .243 average after switch to 1B. | | | | | | | | | |
| 14. Phillies: Phil Meyer, lhp, Pius X HS | Downey, Calif. | L-L | 6-1 | 185 | 18 | $65,000 | 1967 | 1972 | Class AAA (1) |
| Flashed impressive raw stuff for young LHP, but unrefined delivery, frequent absences for military duty led to control issues; in six seasons, went 22-24 overall. | | | | | | | | | |
| 15. Tigers: Jim Foor, lhp, McCluer HS | Ferguson, Mo. | L-L | 6-2 | 165 | 17 | $35,000 | 1967 | 1976 | Majors (3) |
| Undistinguished career included 6 innings spread over three major league seasons, 56-47 mark with five organizations in minors; traded twice for first-rounders. | | | | | | | | | |
| 16. Pirates: Joe Grigas, of, Coyle HS | Brockton, Mass. | L-L | 6-0 | 170 | 18 | $12,000 | 1967 | 1970 | Class A (3) |
| Bucs coughed up smallest first-round bonus in 1967, and Massachusetts prep product never advanced above low Class A in 4 minor league seasons. | | | | | | | | | |
| 17. Twins: Steve Brye, 3b/of, St. Elizabeth HS | Oakland, Calif. | R-R | 6-1 | 190 | 18 | $32,000 | 1967 | 1979 | Majors (9) |
| Star of 1966 Legion national champs, also earned all-NorCal honors over three years in HS at three different positions; .258 career average with Minnesota. | | | | | | | | | |
| 18. Giants: Dave Rader, c, South HS | Bakersfield, Calif. | L-R | 5-11 | 165 | 18 | $22,000 | 1967 | 1980 | Majors (10) |
| Fourth catcher tabbed in first round went on to solid 10-year career; second in 1972 NL rookie voting, hit .257 with 30 homers, 245-180 BB-SO ratio for career. | | | | | | | | | |
| 19. Orioles: Bobby Grich, ss, Woodrow Wilson HS | Long Beach, Calif. | R-R | 6-2 | 180 | 18 | $35,000 | 1967 | 1986 | Majors (17) |
| Used player-of-year season at Rochester in 1971 (.336-32-83) as springboard to 17-year career with Orioles/Angels, complete with all-star honors, Gold Gloves. | | | | | | | | | |
| 20. Dodgers: Donnie Denbow, 3b, Southern Methodist | Dallas | R-R | 6-2 | 185 | 21 | $55,000 | 1967 | 1970 | Class A (4) |
| Wide receiver at SMU was only college selection in first two rounds of '67 draft; never hit and quit midway through fourth season in Class A to take job as teacher. | | | | | | | | | |
| **JANUARY—REGULAR PHASE** | | | | | | | | | |
| 1. Cubs: # Alec DiStaso, rhp, Wilson HS | Los Angeles | R-R | 6-2 | 185 | 18 | $8,000 | 1967 | 1970 | Majors (1) |
| Elbow issues compromised career; obvious Tommy John surgery candidate if procedure had existed; pitched in two games for Cubs, later became police officer. | | | | | | | | | |
| **JANUARY—SECONDARY PHASE** | | | | | | | | | |
| 1. Astros: Pete Varney, c, Deerfield Academy | North Quincy, Mass. | R-R | 6-3 | 215 | 17 | Unsigned | 1971 | 1977 | Majors (4) |
| Holds distincton of being No. 1 pick overall in three drafts, also selected record-tying seven times; finally signed in 1971 after football/baseball career at Harvard. | | | | | | | | | |
| **JUNE—SECONDARY PHASE** | | | | | | | | | |
| 1. *Orioles: Mike Adamson, rhp, Southern California | San Diego | B-R | 6-3 | 195 | 19 | $75,000 | 1967 | 1971 | Majors (3) |
| Unsigned first-rounder in 1965 got largest bonus in '67, became first drafted player to begin career in majors, but never won a major league game. | | | | | | | | | |

**Signed to major league contract. # Deceased.*

in Cooperstown after he used it to become baseball's first DH in 1973. It was a dubious honor, a way of telling Blomberg, then in his fourth season with the Yankees, that his days as a major leaguer were numbered.

"He had good tools, and he was ideal for Yankee Stadium because he really pulled the ball, line drives to right field," MacPhail remembered later. "He should have been a great major league player."

Blomberg hit .293 during his eight-year career. Injuries forced him out of the outfield and eventually right out of the lineup when the Yankees also decided he couldn't hit lefthanded pitching.

"Yeah, I'm the answer to a trivia question," he acknowledged. "It's a thrill and an honor to have any spot in the Hall of Fame, but I'd rather have accomplished something like Mickey, Reggie or Hank Aaron. Being the first designated hitter is all right, but I'd trade it in a minute for 20 good major league seasons.

## How They Should Have Done It

Based on the career WAR (Wins Above Replacement, as calculated by Baseball-Reference.com) numbers achieved by all the players eligible for the 1967 draft, here's how the first round should have unfolded. Numbers in parentheses indicate the round when the player was actually drafted

| | Player, Pos. | Actual Draft | WAR | Bonus |
|---|---|---|---|---|
| 1. | Bobby Grich, ss | Orioles (1) | 71.0 | $35,000 |
| 2. | Carlton Fisk, c | Red Sox (Jan.-R/1) | 68.3 | $10,000 |
| 3. | Darrell Evans, 3b | Athletics (June-S/7) | 58.5 | $10,000 |
| 4. | Ted Simmons, c | Cardinals (1) | 50.2 | $30,000 |
| 5. | Vida Blue, lhp | Athletics (2) | 45.5 | $25,000 |
| 6. | Ken Singleton, of | Mets (Jan.-R/1) | 41.8 | $5,000 |
| 7. | Jon Matlack, lhp | Mets (1) | 39.7 | $55,000 |
| 8. | Dusty Baker, of | Braves (26) | 36.9 | $14,000 |
| 9. | Jerry Reuss, lhp | Cardinals (2) | 35.5 | $15,000 |
| 10. | Don Baylor, of | Orioles (2) | 28.3 | $7,500 |
| 11. | Rick Dempsey, c | Twins (15) | 25.4 | $6,000 |
| 12. | John Mayberry, 1b | Astros (1) | 24.8 | $40,000 |
| 13. | Richie Zisk, of | Pirates (3) | 24.7 | $32,000 |
| 14. | Andre Thornton, 1b | Phillies (NDFA) | 24.1 | $10,000 |
| 15. | Dave Goltz, rhp | Twins (5) | 23.2 | $10,000 |
| 16. | Gary Lavelle, lhp | Giants (20) | 19.4 | $500 |
| 17. | Steve Yeager, c | Dodgers (4) | 17.8 | $8,000 |
| 18. | Jim Colborn, rhp | Cubs (NDFA) | 16.0 | $400 |
| 19. | Dave LaRoche, lhp | Angels (Jan.-S/5) | 15.3 | $6,500 |
| 20. | Ralph Garr, 2b | Braves (3) | 14.7 | $30,000 |

| | Top 3 Unsigned Players | | | Year Signed |
|---|---|---|---|---|
| 1. | Steve Rogers, rhp | Yankees (60) | 45.1 | 1971 |
| 2. | Davey Lopes, 2b | Giants (8) | 42.0 | 1968 |
| 3. | Chris Chambliss, 1b | Reds (31) | 27.4 | 1970 |

"Unfortunately, I did not fulfill my potential, because of injuries. You can't look back and think about what would have happened had I only stayed healthy. Even with the injuries, I played in the majors for eight years. I had a good career, but not a great career."

While Blomberg fell short of expectations, Hughes and Garman, who were selected immediately after him, did so to an even greater degree, though Garman carved out a nine-year major league career as a reliever.

Hughes, 18, was No. 1 on the preferential list of the Cubs, who were selecting second, so they were happy they got their man. He was the first player from the June draft to sign, agreeing to a $50,000 bonus.

"Our report on this boy," Cubs vice president John Holland said, "is that he has no faults. He could step onto the field right now and hold his own with the glove. He is a tremendous shortstop."

Hughes, a .615 hitter as a high school senior, would hit only .209 in 54 big league games—just two with the Cubs, and none as a shortstop.

Garman signed with the Red Sox for a bonus of $54,000. He was an unusually attractive commodity because he married at 15 and was the father of a six-week old son. At the time, teams also had to consider ways to keep players from military service, and married players were among those who were exempt.

The careers of Hughes and Garman later became intertwined, with the two players eventually being included in the same trade in 1973.

Before that, however, Red Sox scout Mace Brown had tracked Hughes extensively in 1967, and wanted Boston to acquire his rights in the worst way. For two months, he got his wish.

A year after signing with the Cubs, Hughes spent the first two months of the 1968 season playing for the Red Sox farm club at Greenville of the low Class A Western Carolinas League. He would commute to Greenville every day from his home in nearby Spartanburg, S.C.

The Cubs loaned Hughes to the Boston organization so that he could attend Spartanburg Methodist Junior College while continuing his playing career uninterrupted. That way, he was classified as a student and could avoid the military draft.

Hughes hit .283 in 58 games for Greenville before returning to the Cubs organization when school was out for the summer. At Greenville, he teamed with Garman, briefly giving the Red Sox two of the first three players drafted in 1967.

By picking third, Boston had, to Brown's regret, just missed getting Hughes.

"I wanted to sign Hughes more than any boy I've ever seen," said Brown, who scouted Hughes extensively in high school and watched him play on a daily basis while he was loaned to Greenville. "He's got all the equipment."

Terry Hughes

Hughes ended an undistinguished major league career in 1974 in Boston, of all places, after being traded there a year earlier in a deal with St. Louis that included Garman.

As a member of the Red Sox for parts of four seasons, the first three as a starter, Garman won just two games while posting a 5.26 ERA. He later went on to pitch for four more big league teams, almost exclusively as a reliever, and went 22-27 overall in his career.

A farm boy from Caldwell, Idaho, Garman admitted that he never quite adjusted to life in the fast lane. He also learned, to his regret, that he couldn't bust his fastball by big league hitters like he had in high school.

"It took me months, years to realize that I couldn't throw my fastball by every hitter, that I could not strike out 17 batters a game, that I wasn't the big star I had been in Caldwell," Garman said late in his career. "When that finally came to me I went to bed a lot of nights thinking I'd be released the next day."

As the prototypical big fish in a small pond, Garman was a star in every sport imaginable while in high school. UCLA offered him a full scholarship to play basketball. He also had a chance to be a better quarterback than his brother Steve, who was then the starter at the University of Idaho and subsequently labored as a two-year minor leaguer in the San Francisco Giants system. Baseball? Garman was so overpowering as a pitcher that he averaged well over two strikeouts an inning his senior year.

Garman went on to pitch professionally for 14

### AT A GLANCE

minor league resume over the next three seasons before finally securing regular duty in 1972, after being dealt from the Astros to Royals. Overall, Mayberry hit .301 with 73 homers in 438 games, while also assembling a 260-188 walk-strikeout ratio.

### One Who Got Away

**DAVE KINGMAN, RHP, ANGELS (2ND ROUND).** Kingman became renowned for his prodigious slugging, which included 442 career home runs, but was better known as an amateur as a power pitcher. Had he elected to sign in 1967 with the Angels, who drafted him as a pitcher, he may never have tapped into his massive power potential.

### He Was Drafted?

**ARCHIE MANNING, SS, BRAVES (43RD ROUND).** Manning's fame derived from his own career as a quarterback, along with those of sons Peyton and Eli, but he was also hotly pursued as a shortstop by baseball scouts, beginning in 1967, when he was drafted by the Braves out of Drew (Miss.) High. He was drafted three more times at Ole Miss, but it became apparent that football was his sport when he was taken with the No. 2 pick in the 1971 NFL draft.

### Did You Know . . .

While No. 1 pick **RON BLOMBERG** didn't come close to fulfilling expectations in a seven-year major league career, he was elected to the National Jewish Sports Hall of Fame in 2004.

### They Said It

Cubs general manager **JOHN HOLLAND** on **TERRY HUGHES**, selected second overall: "This boy has no faults. He could step onto the field right now and hold his own with the glove. He is a tremendous shortstop."—*Hughes played in 54 big league games; two with the Cubs, none at shortstop.*

## DRAFT SPOTLIGHT: VIDA BLUE

Vida Blue could have pursued a football career, but a late push by the A's put him on the diamond

Vida Blue had unmistakable talent as a high school quarterback. He might have become the first African-American quarterback to win a Heisman Trophy had he decided to accept a scholarship offer to play football at the University of Houston.

"I didn't care much for baseball when I was 16 or 17," Blue said, "and after my senior year, I was sure my career was in football. But all that changed the following spring in a state playoff game."

That's when Blue threw the last of his seven no-hitters in high school, and recorded all 21 outs via strikeouts. Numerous scouts were on hand to witness the overwhelming performance, including two from the Kansas City Athletics.

"My assistant and I were the only white people among the 4,000 black high school kids," A's scout Tom Ferrick said. "We really stood out."

Shortly thereafter, the A's drafted Blue—though not until the second round. After deliberating almost the entire summer between football and an offer from the A's, Blue finally chose baseball.

"Football was a factor," said Blue, who threw for 3,484 yards and 35 touchdown passes, while also rushing for 1,600 yards in his senior year at DeSoto High in Mansfield, La. "I told the college recruiters that I thought football was my better sport. Houston was probably the most interested in me. They had just begun to implement a run-and-shoot offense which was almost identical to what our high school did."

Fate intervened on the A's behalf and steered Blue to baseball. Blue's father had died during his senior year. As the oldest of six children, it left him as the man of the house, and when the A's agreed on Aug. 28 to enrich their bonus offer to $25,000, Blue signed. All things considered, it was a modest sum in relation to some of the bonuses paid out to the top prospects in 1967, but $10,000 more than the A's gave their first-round pick, Brien Bickerton, who also signed at the last minute.

Blue signed too late to play during the 1967 season, but was an immediate hit in the minor leagues a year later. Despite an 8-11 record at Burlington of the Class A Midwest League, he struck out an eye-popping 231 in 152 innings. He continued to mow down minor league hitters over the better part of the next two years, and by the time he reached the big leagues for good in September 1970, he had struck out 508 in 389 innings.

With a fastball that occasionally reached 100 mph and his ability to pound the strike zone on a regular basis, the best was yet to come.

On Sept. 21, 1970, Blue threw a no-hitter for Oakland against the Minnesota Twins. A year later, at 22, he became the rage of the baseball world as he went 24-8, 1.82 and struck out 301 in 312 innings. His performance was so overpowering that he won both the American League's MVP and Cy Young awards—becoming the youngest player from his league ever to win both.

Blue should have been on top of the world after his spectacular 1971 season, but he was miserable. With a salary of just $16,000, he was easily the most underpaid player in the game, and A's owner Charles O. Finley was in no hurry to reward Blue for his sudden and spectacular accomplishments. The two engaged in a protracted contract dispute that caused Blue to miss the start of the 1972 season as a holdout.

Drained by his long, bitter dispute with Finley, Blue won only six games in 1972 and never again quite equaled his astonishing 1971 season, though he went on to win 209 games and struck out 1,875 over 17 years.

Late in a career that was defined by highs and lows, Blue hit rock bottom after he was convicted for possession of cocaine. He served time in jail and was suspended from the game, though he later came back and pitched three more seasons. His troubles with substance abuse would continue to haunt him after he retired, though, and he was jailed again almost 20 years later.

"Vida should have made it to the Hall of Fame, but he got derailed," said Ferrick, the A's scout who signed Blue. "He ran with party people instead of tending to business and never had the years he should have had."

years, but the game was never quite as easy again as it had been in high school.

### REAL TALENT IN LATER ROUNDS

As it turned out, the careers of Blomberg, Hughes and Garman, not to mention Adamson, never came close to measuring up to the those of some of the players found later in the first round of the regular phase of the 1967 draft—notably Ted Simmons (Cardinals, 10th overall) and Bobby Grich (Orioles, 19th)—but also second-rounders like Vida Blue (Athletics) and Don Baylor (Orioles), and even Dusty Baker (Braves), an overlooked selection in the 26th round.

And that doesn't even begin to address Fisk or Darrell Evans, a California junior-college product who had been drafted four times previously but finally decided to sign with the Kansas City A's after being a lowly seventh-round pick in the June secondary phase. Evans went on to hit 414 home runs in a 21-year big league career. Like Fisk, he signed for the modest sum of $10,000.

Fisk was one of the more unlikely players to evolve into a Hall of Famer.

He was primarily a pitcher in high school in Charlestown, N.H., but his athletic focus then and into an abbreviated college career at the University of New Hampshire was on basketball.

"What I really wanted to be," Fisk once said, "was a power forward for the Boston Celtics."

But at 6-foot-2, Fisk was savvy enough to know that wasn't going to happen, and he often said the smartest thing he did in baseball was become a catcher.

Despite playing in little more than 100 games in high school and American Legion, plus an abbreviated schedule on the freshman team at New Hampshire, Fisk was selected by the Red Sox with the fourth pick in the regular phase of the January 1967 draft. Boston was attracted by his athleticism and his potential as a hitter.

At first, Fisk was suspicious of the move, seeing himself as the token New Englander the Red Sox often took to pacify the team's passionate fan base.

"I really didn't believe they thought I was going to make much of myself," he said.

But Fisk quickly embarked on a career with the Red Sox, and eventually the Chicago White Sox, that would rank among the greatest by a catcher in major league history. At the time he retired in 1993, after 24 years, he was baseball's all-time leader in games caught, with 2,226 (since passed in 2009 by Pudge Rodriguez), and in home runs

### Fastest To The Majors

| | Player, Pos. | Drafted (Round) | Debut |
|---|---|---|---|
| 1. | #Mike Adamson, rhp | Orioles (June-S/1) | July 1, 1967 |
| 2. | Mike Paul, lhp | Indians (20) | May 27, 1968 |
| 3. | Tom Murphy, rhp | Angels (Jan.-S/1) | June 13, 1968 |
| 4. | Darcy Fast, lhp | Cubs (June-S/6) | June 15, 1968 |
| 5. | Gary Ross, rhp | Cubs (Jan.-S/1) | June 28, 1968 |

**FIRST HIGH SCHOOL SELECTIONS:** Jimmy McMath, of (Cubs-2, Sept. 7, 1968); Dusty Baker, of (Braves-26, Sept. 7, 1968)

**LAST PLAYER TO RETIRE:** Carlton Fisk, c (June 22, 1993)

*#Debuted in major leagues.*

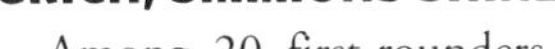

## Top 25 Bonuses

| | Player, Pos. | Drafted (Round) | Order | Bonus |
|---|---|---|---|---|
| 1. | Mike Adamson, rhp | Orioles (June-S/1) | (1) | #$75,000 |
| 2. | * Ron Blomberg, 1b | Yankees (1) | 1 | $65,000 |
| | * Phil Meyer, rhp | Phillies (1) | 14 | $65,000 |
| 4. | * Jon Matlack, lhp | Mets (1) | 4 | $55,000 |
| | Donnie Denbow, 3b | Dodgers (1) | 20 | $55,000 |
| 6. | * Mike Garman, rhp | Red Sox (1) | 3 | $54,000 |
| 7. | * Terry Hughes, ss | Cubs (1) | 2 | $50,000 |
| | * Larry Keener, rhp | Phillies (2) | 34 | $50,000 |
| 9. | * John Mayberry, 1b | Astros (1) | 6 | $40,000 |
| | * Wayne Simpson, rhp | Reds (1) | 8 | $40,000 |
| 11. | * Mike Nunn, c | Angels (1) | 6 | $35,000 |
| | * Jim Foor, lhp | Tigers (1) | 15 | $35,000 |
| | * Bobby Grich, ss | Orioles (1) | 19 | $35,000 |
| 14. | * Bob McLachlin, lhp | Phillies (3) | 54 | $33,000 |
| 15. | * Steve Brye, 3b | Twins (1) | 17 | $32,000 |
| | * Richie Zisk, of | Pirates (3) | 56 | $32,000 |
| 17. | * John Jones, c | Senators (1) | 5 | $30,000 |
| | * Ted Simmons, c | Cardinals (1) | 10 | $30,000 |
| | Ralph Garr, 2b | Braves (3) | 52 | $30,000 |
| | William Rainer, of | Dodgers (3) | 60 | $30,000 |
| | Garry Hill, rhp | Braves (June-S/1) | (8) | $30,000 |
| | Jimmie Jackson, lhp | Cardinals (June-S/1) | (10) | $30,000 |
| 23. | * Jimmy McMath, of | Cubs (2) | 22 | $28,500 |
| | Jim Dunegan, rhp | Cubs (Jan.-R/2) | (21) | $28,500 |
| 25. | John Hetrick, of | Tigers (June-S/1) | (17) | $27,500 |

*Major leaguers in bold. *High school selection. #Major league contract.*

by a catcher, with 351 (later passed in 2004 by Mike Piazza).

He also forever established himself as a New England folk hero when he hit his dramatic home run in Game Six of the 1975 World Series. The enduring image of Fisk jumping and waving the ball fair as he frolicked to first base is still considered by many to be one of baseball's greatest moments.

In contrast to Fisk, Adamson entered the game with considerable fanfare.

In addition to being an unsigned first-round pick in baseball's first draft in 1965, Adamson was the signature talent available in the secondary phase of the 1967 draft after a brief, but dominating college career at USC.

BOSTON RED SOX

**Carlton Fisk**

The Orioles showed little hesitation in taking the 19-year-old righthander with the No. 1 pick, and after he worked out with the team for 10 days before finally signing, they showed even less restraint in starting off Adamson in the big leagues. In the process, he became the first player in the draft era to begin his career without benefit of minor league seasoning.

But Adamson quickly looked overmatched facing big league hitters and the Orioles sent him back to the minor leagues. He made brief appearances with the major league club over the next two years, but never won a game in an aborted big league career.

### GRICH, SIMMONS SHINE

Among 20 first-rounders drafted in the June regular phase, Simmons and Grich enjoyed the best major league careers. Simmons played for 21 years, hitting .285 with 248 homers, while Grich hung around for 17 years, hitting .266 with 224 homers. Grich, in particular, was known for his excellence defensively. Though drafted as a shortstop, Grich set records for the highest fielding average in a season by a second baseman on two occasions.

Had a debilitating injury not intervened, the greatest first-rounder in 1967 might well have been righthander Wayne Simpson, drafted eighth overall by the Cincinnati Reds out of a Los Angeles high school.

Simpson appeared to have it all in the summer of 1967. With a powerful right arm, he could deliver fastballs with such velocity that he drew comparisons to recently retired Hall of Famer Sandy Koufax. He could also throw footballs almost 90 yards downfield.

"I had my pick of schools. USC. UCLA. Name it," Simpson said. "But most of them wanted to switch me to end and I felt I could make it quicker in baseball."

After signing with the Reds for a bonus of $40,000, he was not only in the big leagues by 1970, but a National League all-star that season, as well. Simpson was 14-1 on July 31 that year for the World Series-bound Reds, when everything suddenly unraveled. Years later, he still remembered in graphic detail the pitch to Hall of Famer Billy Williams that proved his undoing.

"I had no pain, no warning," he said. "That's what was so puzzling. One pitch and it popped . . .

"I threw one more pitch and got Williams out. But my arm started shaking and jumping around. It was like taking a knife and sticking it in your shoulder. I've never experienced pain like that before."

Simpson, then 21, had pitched nearly 500 innings in the previous year and a half between the minors, majors and a spectacular season in winter ball, utilizing a pitching motion that put too much strain on his arm. He would never experience major league success again.

Doctors diagnosed a torn rotator cuff in his shoulder, at a time when the term hadn't yet become fashionable and when the injury wasn't even considered treatable. A surgeon told Simpson he needed three to four years of complete rest to rehabilitate the injury.

"I didn't believe it," Simpson said. "I thought he was saying it for effect, to convince me that I had to get complete rest. Three years? Impossible."

Simpson continued to pitch and spent seven more years in the game, bouncing between the majors and minors, and wound up with a final big league record of 36-31, 4.37. In the end, he lost much of the use in his once-envied right arm trying to salvage his fading career.

While giving baseball one more shot in Mexico in 1978, he noticed a cramping sensation in his biceps. He couldn't tie his shoelaces or comb his hair. One day the cramps were especially bad, and a doctor gave him an injection. As Simpson

### WORTH NOTING

■ With the abandonment of the short-lived American Legion draft, which existed in 1965 and 1966 and resulted in just 20 players being picked, all eligible Legion players were incorporated in the June draft in 1967, though they were still prevented from signing until their Legion season was complete. One prominent 1967 draft pick impacted by the revised Legion rule was 17-year-old lefthander **JON MATLACK**, picked fourth overall by the Mets. Matlack, who won 22 straight games and tossed seven no-hitters in a celebrated high school career, didn't sign until Aug. 9. He began his pro career a year later and went on to win 125 games for the Mets and Rangers.

■ Outfielder **JIMMY MCMATH** was an unlikely candidate to become the first high school selection from the 1967 draft to reach the big leagues. Picked in the second round by the Cubs, McMath debuted little more than a year later on Sept. 7, 1968, at age 19, after hitting .388 in 51 games at low Class A Quincy to begin the 1968 season and .263 after a promotion to Double-A. He went 2-for-14 and drove in a pair of runs in six games with the Cubs. But that ended up becoming the extent of McMath's big league career. He was sent back to the minors to begin the 1969 season, and his career would only go backward from there as he had a series of run-ins with managers in the Cubs system, prompting him to quit the game on one occasion.

CONTINUED ON PAGE 58

## WORTH NOTING

CONTINUED FROM PAGE 57

He was also suspended on another, before finally being released in 1971 while in Double-A. "People still say I messed up," said McMath, who died in 2010. "I'll never live that down."

■ If nothing else, **RALPH GARR** could hit. He was a free swinger with a remarkable skill for driving balls to all fields, and won a National League batting title in 1974, at .353, while becoming a career .306 hitter in 13 major league seasons. He also won a Triple-A International League batting title with a .386 average in 1970, and led all NAIA hitters at the college level in 1967 with an improbable .585 average, while playing for Grambling State. That accomplishment led to Garr being drafted in the third round that year by the Braves, but Garr always insisted, especially after achieving success over an extended career in the majors, that he would have gone much higher, possibly as early as the first round if anybody had believed his Grambling batting figures were authentic. "They looked at my college average and thought it was a joke," he said. "They must have thought the pitchers were throwing underhanded. They got me cheaper than I was worth. I had the credentials but I didn't get the big money."

■ For longevity, few teams ever got as much mileage out of their first two June draft picks as Baltimore and St. Louis in 1967. The Cardinals took catcher **TED SIMMONS** with the 10th pick overall and lefthander **JERRY REUSS** with the 30th. Simmons, a .285 hitter with 248 home runs, played 21 major league seasons before hanging 'em up, while Reuss was a 220-game winner over 22 seasons. Not to be outdone, the Orioles selections of shortstop **BOBBY GRICH** (19th overall) hit .266 with 224 homers in 17 seasons, while outfielder **DON BAYLOR** (39th overall) hit .260 with 338 homers over 19 years.

warmed up, his hand went rigid and turned completely white. Within hours, he was on a jet to California to undergo the first of a series of arterial-bypass surgeries in an attempt to restore a normal pulse to his arm. In the process, nerve pathways had to be severed to increase blood flow.

In addition to dangerously high blood pressure, Simpson found out that he had an accumulation of blood clots, similar to those that led to a stroke and prematurely ended the career of Houston Astros star J.R. Richard. Pitching in pain for so many years only exacerbated the problem.

"Baseball is a business, a win-at-all-costs business," Simpson said. "Even if a guy is at 50 percent effectiveness, they'll use him if he can win. But what if it wrecks his arm?"

When asked years later who threw the hardest in all his years behind the plate, Hall of Famer Johnny Bench did not hesitate to name Simpson. "He wore me out," Bench said. "No one threw harder than he did in 1970. I've never seen more explosive stuff."

### PREP SELECTIONS DOMINATE DRAFT

A total of 1,166 selections were made in the June draft in 1967: 975 in the regular phase, and 191 in the secondary phase. That would make it the busiest June draft on record until 1987, when both January phases and the June secondary phase were abolished and consolidated into a single June phase. The Yankees also drafted a then-record 74 players in the regular phase.

The increase in the number of players drafted was attributed to a renewed emphasis on high school talent. A change in baseball's college-eligibility rule, effective with the 1967 draft, restricted the selection of college players in the regular phase to graduates or previously undrafted players who were 21 (within 45 days of the draft's conclusion).

Not only did the high school ranks dominate the draft overall and result in more players from that demographic signing contracts (341) than any draft in history, but the early rounds were skewed like no draft ever as well. Of the 40 players selected in the first two rounds of the regular phase, 39 were prep products—the lone exception being Donnie Denbow, a Southern Methodist University senior picked by the Los Angeles Dodgers with the last pick in the first round.

High school players have been a notably riskier demographic than their college counterparts throughout draft history, and the preponderance of high school picks in 1967 predictably resulted in fewer players reaching the majors from the June regular phase than any draft in history. Just 85 (or 8.7 percent) of the 975 selections made it, as did a record-low 43 (or 21.5 percent) of the 200 players claimed in the first 10 rounds.

### Largest Bonuses By Round

| | Player, Pos. | Club | Bonus |
|---|---|---|---|
| **1.** | ***Ron Blomberg, 1b** | **Yankees** | **$65,000** |
| | *Phil Meyer, lhp | Phillies | $65,000 |
| 2. | *Larry Keener, rhp | Phillies | $50,000 |
| 3. | *Bob McLachlin, lhp | Phillies | $33,000 |
| 4. | *Gary King, ss | Mets | $20,000 |
| 5. | Three tied at | | $10,000 |
| **6.** | ***Dennis Saunders, rhp** | **Tigers** | **$18,000** |
| 7. | *Lynn Adams, ss | Tigers | $15,000 |
| 8. | *John Landry, 1b | Pirates | $10,000 |
| 9. | *Donald Camy, rhp | Athletics | $13,000 |
| 10. | *Daniel Evans, lhp | Astros | $10,000 |
| | ***Charlie Hudson, lhp** | **Mets** | **$10,000** |
| **Jan/R.** | **Jim Dunegan, rhp** | **Cubs (2)** | **$28,500** |
| **Jan/S.** | **Bob Spence, 1b** | **White Sox (1)** | **$27,000** |
| **Jun/S.** | **Mike Adamson, rhp** | **Orioles (1)** | **$75,000** |

*Major leaguers in bold. *High school selection.*

The college-dominated secondary phase, by contrast, produced significantly different results. While previously undrafted college players like Denbow were subject to the more restrictive rules that went into effect in 1967, previously drafted collegians like Adamson, a sophomore, were grandfathered in under the old draft rules. The upshot was the most productive secondary phase on record, as 46 (or 23.7 percent) of a record 194 players drafted in that phase played in the majors.

Previously, baseball's college rule allowed the drafting and signing of all college sophomores, such as Arizona State's Rick Monday and Reggie Jackson—the first collegians drafted in 1965 and 1966, respectively—but that provision was amended at the 1966 Winter Meetings and became effective Jan. 1, 1967. The rule change was designed to benefit the nation's college programs, generally providing them protection from the draft until a player completed his junior year.

College baseball also received another shot in the arm in 1967 as freshmen became eligible to play varsity sports for the first time (though it wasn't until 1972 that the NCAA extended the same privilege to football and basketball). The typical college player would now play three years at the varsity level before being draft eligible. In the past, most of the top college players left as sophomores after playing just a single varsity season.

### TROJANS, DEVILS WIELD INFLUENCE

Arizona State and USC, which began a run of eight consecutive College World Series titles between them in 1967, had the greatest impact on the June draft, with eight selections apiece. USC's Adamson led off the secondary phase, and was followed in quick order by ASU sophomore catcher Randy Bobb—whose big league career was almost

### One Team's Draft: Baltimore Orioles

| | Player, Pos. | Bonus |
|---|---|---|
| **1.** | ***Bobby Grich, ss** | **$35,000** |
| **2.** | ***Don Baylor, of** | **$7,500** |
| 3. | *Greg Arnold, rhp | $11,000 |
| 4. | *Chris Farasopolous, 2b | Did not sign |
| **5.** | ***David Johnson, rhp** | **$6,000** |
| 6. | *Ronny Stewart, of | $3,000 |
| 7. | *Wayne Hoots, of | $3,000 |
| 8. | *Lou Lanehardt, lhp | Did not sign |
| 9. | Fred Kuppers, c | Did not sign |
| 10. | *Robert Blakely, of/1b | Did not sign |
| **Other** | **Mike Adamson (S/1), rhp** | **$75,000** |

*Major leaguers in bold. *High school selection.*

BOB LYNN

Eighth overall pick Wayne Simpson was a National League all-star by 1970, but a shoulder injury late that year cut his career short

as inconsequential as Adamson's, as he garnered just a single hit in 10 at-bats.

The college player of the year, Arizona State junior righthander Gary Gentry, a transfer from Phoenix College, was somewhat overlooked in the draft and lasted until the third round of the secondary phase, when he was finally selected by the Mets. The 6-foot, 180-pound Gentry set an NCAA record that season with 229 strikeouts in 174 innings, while posting a 17-1, 1.14 record.

He capped off his season by going 2-0 with 31 strikeouts in 23 innings at the College World Series, including a 14-inning win over Stanford in the semifinals as the Sun Devils won for the second time in three years, beating Houston 11-2 in the final. Two years later, Gentry would post 13 wins as a rookie for the Mets who won a World Series of a more significant kind. That capped an amazing stretch of success for Gentry, at both the amateur and professional levels.

"I never played on a team that didn't expect to win," said Gentry, "so what happened with the Mets in 1969 was a natural transition for me. I was accustomed to winning. In 1965, in junior college, we won the national championship; in 1966, we got there again, but lost in the final. In '67, at Arizona State, we won the NCAA championship; that same year, I spent the last two months of the season with Williamsport and we won the (Double-A Eastern League) title. In 1968, when I was with Jacksonville, we won the (Triple-A International League) championship there, too. So when I came up to the Mets in '69, I never thought anything except winning."

Arm problems got the best of Gentry, however, limiting his major league career to seven years.

Also in 1967, Colorado State shortstop Greg Riddoch tied the NCAA record of 17 home runs in a season, set a year earlier by Washington State's Dale Ford. Riddoch, who never played but later managed and coached in the big leagues, accomplished the task in just 26 games. Like Gentry, he lasted until the third round of the secondary phase.

## THE EPSTEIN FACTOR

Seldom has an active major leaguer had as profound an effect on the draft as first baseman Mike Epstein did in 1967.

At the time, Epstein, 24, was one of the most noted young players in the game. A 6-foot-4, 230-pound slugger who received a $50,000 bonus from Baltimore following the 1964 Olympics, Epstein piled up some of the best numbers in the minor leagues in 1965 and 1966, narrowly missing back-to-back triple crowns.

Epstein opened the 1967 season with the Orioles, but balked when Baltimore attempted to option him to the minor leagues after a slow start. The Orioles were forced to shop Epstein around, and traded him to Washington little more than a week before the 1967 draft. The Yankees had also expressed a strong interest in Epstein, but were unwilling to part with ace pitcher Mel Stottlemyre to complete the deal. Rebuffed, they made up their minds to go for Blomberg, who like Epstein was Jewish and wielded a big bat.

Epstein's influence didn't stop there. The Senators, set to choose fifth, were primed to take first baseman John Mayberry. But having just dealt for Epstein, they decided against taking another first baseman and instead went for more of a sleeper pick, catcher Johnny Jones, who had hit no homers that spring for a Tennessee high school team that won just one game. Predictably, Jones went on to hit a meager .150 in a four-year pro career that never advanced past Class A.

Mayberry? He was taken by Houston with the next pick and went on to become one of the most prolific home run hitters of his era, hitting 255 in a 15-year big league career. "It was between Jones and Mayberry," Senators general manager George Selkirk said. "We decided to go with the catcher because of the Mike Epstein deal."

Epstein soon fizzled as a power hitter and the Senators would continue to bring up the rear in the American League for years to come, which led to a transfer of the franchise to Texas in the early 1970s.

## Highest Unsigned Picks

**JUNE/REGULAR PHASE ONLY**

| Player, Pos., Team (Round) | College | Re-Drafted |
|---|---|---|
| Danny Graham, ss, Red Sox (2) | UCLA | Never |
| Dave Kingman, rhp, Angels (2) | Harper (Ill.) JC | Orioles '68 (Jan. -S/1) |
| Gary Myers, of, Mets (3) | JC of San Mateo (Calif.) | Red Sox '69 (Jan. S/1) |
| Bruce Harkey, rhp, Angels (3) | None | Mets '68 (Jan.-S/1) |
| Bart Johnson, rhp, Cardinals (3) | Brigham Young | White Sox '68 (S/1) |
| Chris Ward, of, White Sox (3) | Chabot (Calif.) JC | Cubs '68 (S/3) |
| Chris Farasopolous, 2b, Orioles (4) | Brigham Young | Never |
| Dudley Mitchell, of/1b, Red Sox (4) | Colorado | Padres '71 (S/3) |
| Steve Busby, rhp, Giants (4) | USC | Royals '71 (S/2) |
| Ken Caldwell, 3b, Senators (5) | South Carolina | Never |

**TOTAL UNSIGNED PICKS:** Top 5 Rounds (20), Top 10 Rounds (56)

### IN FOCUS: MIKE ADAMSON

The Baltimore Orioles showed little hesitation in taking Mike Adamson with the No. 1 pick in the secondary phase of the June 1967 draft, and even less in starting off the 19-year-old righthander in the big leagues—making him the first player in the draft era to begin his career without minor league seasoning.

O's general manager Harry Dalton said he had no doubt that Adamson was up to the task.

"After watching Mike work, and then watching the guys we already have work, we figured he could help us—now," Dalton said. "This wasn't an inducement to get him to sign. We really figure he can help. If it turns out that Mike's over his head, which is a possibility, then we may have to send him out."

The Orioles initially planned to start Adamson in a game on June 29, but realized he had not started a game in more than a month, and decided to break him in more gently as a reliever. He made his debut July 1. Adamson, who went 8-3, 2.20 while striking out 143 in 101 innings in a dominating sophomore season at Southern California, lasted just three appearances in Baltimore and looked overmatched by big league hitters.

He made brief appearances with the Orioles the next two years, but ended up with a 0-4, 7.46 record in just 25 major league innings overall.

# 1967 Draft List

*Did not sign. Major leaguers in bold, with first and last years noted. Order of selection indicated in parentheses. For the first five rounds of the June Regular Phase and the first round of all other phases, the peak level of each player is noted.*

## ATLANTA BRAVES

### January—Regular Phase (11)

1. *Travis Washington, of, Bacone (Okla.) JC.—DNP
2. Charles Swanson, rhp, Los Angeles Valley JC.
3. William Adelman, 1b, Broward (Fla.) CC.
4. *James O'Leary, rhp-of, Dutchess (N.Y.) CC.
5. John Simmers, rhp, Buena Park, Calif.
6. Mike Gutierrez, 2b, Los Angeles CC.
7. *Phillip Cardwell, inf-of, Manatee (Fla.) JC.
8. *John Brett, 3b-of, El Camino (Calif.) JC.

DRAFT DROP *Brother of George Brett, major leaguer (1973-93) • Brother of Ken Brett, first-round draft pick, Red Sox (1966); major leaguer (1967-81)*

9. *Donald Smith, rhp-1b, CC of Baltimore.
10. *Frank Slaton, 1b-lhp, Antelope Valley (Calif.) JC.
11. *Mark Loper, 3b-of, American River (Calif.) JC.
12. Eric Larson, 3b, Los Angeles Pierce JC.
13. *Rick Senger, c, CC of Baltimore.
14. *C.T. Coe, c, Navarro (Texas) JC.
15. Edward Silverman, lhp, Fairleigh Dickinson University.
16. Alan Goldberg, c, Trenton (Mo.) JC.

### January—Secondary Phase (3)

1. *Bill Gillean, rhp, Cerritos (Calif.) JC.—DNP
2. Stan Bell, rhp, Manatee (Fla.) JC.

DRAFT DROP *First overall draft pick, January 1966/ secondary phase, Tigers*

3. **Ron Schueler, rhp, Fort Hays State (Kan.) College.—(1972-79)**

DRAFT DROP *General manager, White Sox (1991-2000)*

4. ***Chuck Scrivener, ss, CC of Baltimore.—(1975-77)**
5. *Frank Patterson, of, Grambling University.
6. ***Kurt Bevacqua, 2b, Miami-Dade CC North.—(1971-85)**
7. ***Gerry Pirtle, rhp, Bacone (Okla.) JC.—(1978)**
8. *Marvin Tucker, 2b, Independence, Mo.
9. *Jerry Marion, of, University of Wyoming.
10. ***Greg Garrett, lhp, Newhall, Calif.—(1970-71)**

### June—Regular Phase (12)

1. Andy Finlay, of, Luther Burbank HS, Sacramento, Calif.—(AA)
2. Dennis Dalton, rhp, Altavista (Va.) HS.—(AA)
3. **Ralph Garr, 2b, Grambling University.—(1968-80)**
4. **Bob Didier, c, Glen Oaks HS, Baton Rouge, La.—(1969-74)**
5. *Hal Ziegler, 3b, Coatesville (Pa.) Area HS.—DNP

DRAFT DROP *Attended Trinidad State (Colo.) JC; never re-drafted*

6. Ronald Owens, rhp, Lake Hamilton HS, Pearcy, Ark.
7. *Bobby Croswell, ss, Central HS, Jackson, Miss.
8. *Dave Elmendorf, of, Westbury HS, Houston.

DRAFT DROP *Defensive back, National Football League (1971-79)*

9. *Billy Hodge, c, Austin HS, Bryan, Texas.
10. *Edward Rios, of-lhp, Luther Burbank HS, Sacramento, Calif.
11. Terry Hankins, ss, Canoga Park HS, Woodland Hills, Calif.
12. *Buzz Patterson, rhp, Newark Academy, Far Hills, N.J.
13. Bryon Kennedy, c, Page HS, Greensboro, N.C.
14. Richard Wurstner, ss-2b, Turner HS, Buffalo, N.Y.
15. Mark Vanderwater, c, Parsippany (N.J.) HS.
16. Robert Andrews, lhp, San Jose, Calif.
17. Bob Wiswell, lhp, UCLA.
18. *John Wilmouth, 1b, McCluer HS, St. Louis.
19. *Carl Mayfield, c, Kennedy HS, Denver.
20. *Edward Fisher, ss, Campbell University.
21. James Brittan, lhp, Maplewood HS, St. Louis.
22. *Howard Hall, 1b-of, Bogalusa, La.
23. *Gary Moleberg, 3b-1b, Pampa (Texas) HS.
24. John Patterson, 2b-ss, Altamont (Ill.) HS.
25. Mike Testa, of, Morris Hills Regional HS, Parsippany, N.J.
26. **Dusty Baker, of, Del Campo HS, Carmichael, Calif.—(1968-86)**

DRAFT DROP *First 1967 high school draft pick to reach majors (Sept, 7, 1968); major leaguer manager (1993-2013)*

Underrated talent marked the 1967 draft, including longtime player and manager Dusty Baker (right), a 26th-round pick of the Braves

27. *Donald Autry, ss, Blair HS, Pasadena, Calif.
28. Sammy Boatman, of, Murphy HS, Mobile, Ala.
29. *Thomas Urquhart, rhp, Merriam (Kan.) HS.
30. *David Byerly, of, Permian HS, Odessa, Texas.
31. Bob Churchich, 3b, University of Nebraska.
32. Joseph Fanning, c, Central Connecticut University.
33. *Gene Rinaldi, ss, Miami-Dade CC North.
34. George Sahadi, 1b, Lafayette HS, Brooklyn, N.Y.
35. *Michael Magness, rhp, Cedartown (Ga.) HS.
36. *Willie Frazier, ss, Meridian (Miss.) HS.
37. *Derk Hoving, c, Tascosa HS, Amarillo, Texas.
38. *William Wright, rhp, Marysville, Calif.
39. *Craig Lown, rhp, Roncillo HS, Pueblo, Colo.

DRAFT DROP *Son of Turk Lown, major leaguer (1951-62)*

40. *Russell Ross, ss, Fairfax (Va.) HS.
41. Keith Walters, rhp, Saratoga, Calif.
42. *Gerald Burton, of, Ritenour HS, St. Louis.
43. *Archie Manning, ss, Drew (Miss.) HS.

DRAFT DROP *First-round draft pick, New Orleans Saints/ National Football League (1971); quarterback, NFL (1971-84) • Father of Peyton Manning, quarterback, NFL (1998-2015) • Father of Eli Manning, quarterback, NFL (2004-15)*

44. *Alan Bush, lhp, Quincy (Ill.) HS.
45. Allen Jillison, lhp, Southern Regional HS, Manalawki, N.J.
46. *Charles Atkinson, ss, Hillside (N.J.) HS.
47. *Harry Brinson, lhp, Harding HS, Oklahoma City.
48. *Thomas Trailer, of, Lee HS, Montgomery, Ala.

### June—Secondary Phase (8)

1. **Garry Hill, rhp, University of North Carolina.—(1969)**
2. *Bill Dobbs, lhp, Oklahoma State University.
3. **Tom House, lhp, University of Southern California.—(1971-78)**
4. *Harold Harris, 3b, Gulf Coast (Fla.) CC.
5. *Dennis Parks, of, Long Beach (Calif.) CC.
6. *William Craig, rhp, Morehead State University.
7. *Luis Flores, c, Gardner-Webb College.

## BALTIMORE ORIOLES

### January—Regular Phase (20)

1. Brent Nickoloff, 2b-ss, Torrance (Calif.) HS.—(High A)
2. **Lew Beasley, of, Sparta (Va.) HS—(1977)**
3. Herman Grant, rhp, Riverview HS, Boykins, Va.
4. Stanley Martin, ss, Los Angeles Valley JC.
5. *Bill Kirkpatrick, rhp, CC of San Francisco.
6. Tom Kober, rhp, Allentown, Pa.
7. *Thomas Keyser, c, Allegany (Md.) CC.
8. *Michael Jones, ss, Washington HS, San Francisco.
9. *Howard Casey, lhp, Treasure Valley (Ore.) CC.
10. *Joe Arnold, rhp, Miami-Dade CC North.

DRAFT DROP *Baseball coach, Florida (1984-94)*

11. Lawrence Korpisch, 1b, Southeastern Illinois JC.
12. Frank Joyal, c, Fryeburg Academy HS, Burlington, Vt.
13. Tommy Williams, rhp, Thomasville, Ga.

### January—Secondary Phase (10)

1. **Johnny Oates, c, Virginia Tech.—(1970-81)**

DRAFT DROP *Major league manager (1991-2001)*

2. *Steve Steitz, 3b, Worcester Academy, East Longmeadow, Mass.
3. **John Montague, rhp, Old Dominion University.—(1973-80)**
4. *Al Crawford, of, Miami-Dade CC North.
5. *Greg Riddoch, ss, Colorado State University.

DRAFT DROP *Major league manager (1990-92)*

6. *Jimmie Skeins, ss, Ranger (Texas) JC.
7. *Jodie Beeler, c, W.W. Samuell HS, Dallas.
8. Daniel Beard, rhp, Lakewood, Calif.
9. John Hilts, rhp, University of Wyoming.
10. *Michael Noonan, lhp, Foothill (Calif.) JC.
11. Larry Piquet, of, Eugene, Ore.
12. (void) *Herb Hofvendahl, of, St. Mary's (Calif.) College.
13. *William Farmer, lhp, Endwell, N.Y.
14. *Taylor Toomey, lhp, University of Colorado.

### June—Regular Phase (19)

1. **Bobby Grich, ss, Woodrow Wilson HS, Long Beach, Calif.—(1970-86)**
2. **Don Baylor, of, Austin (Texas) HS.—(1970-88)**

DRAFT DROP *Major league manager (1993-2002)*

3. Greg Arnold, rhp, Southern HS, Baltimore.—(AAA)
4. *Chris Farasopolous, 2b, North HS, Torrance, Calif.—DNP

DRAFT DROP *Attended Brigham Young; never re-drafted; defensive back, National Football League (1971-74)*

5. **David Johnson, rhp, Cooper HS, Abilene, Texas.—(1974-78)**
6. Ronny Stewart, of, Balboa HS, San Francisco.
7. Wayne Hoots, of, Hendersonville (N.C.) HS.
8. *Lou Lanehardt, lhp, Patapsco HS, Baltimore.
9. *Fred Kuppers, c, Los Angeles Valley JC.
10. *Robert Blakeley, of-1b, Griffin HS, Springfield, Ill.
11. William Ray, lhp, Belleville (Mich.) HS.
12. Robert Sorrentino, lhp, Notre Dame HS, Bridgeport, Conn.
13. *Michael Wertz, ss, McCallum HS, Austin, Texas.
14. *Dave Schmid, of, Mount St. Joseph HS, Baltimore.
15. *James Reynolds, rhp, Messick HS, Memphis, Tenn.
16. *Dave Kropfelter, c, Mount St. Joseph HS, Baltimore.
17. Mike Duggan, 2b, Bishop Barry HS, St. Petersburg, Fla.
18. Winston Presley, rhp, Jefferson HS, Los Angeles.
19. *Sam Cook, of, San Bernardino (Calif.) HS.
20. ***Doug Rau, lhp, Columbus (Texas) HS.—(1972-81)**
21. *Earl Nance, lhp, George Wythe HS, Richmond, Va.
22. *Terry Wedgewood, ss-3b, Bosse HS, Evansville, Ind.
23. *Billy DeMars, ss, Irondequoit HS, Rochester, N.Y.

DRAFT DROP *Son of Billy DeMars, major leaguer (1948-51)*

24. David Ekelund, 1b, Wilton (Conn.) HS.
25. *Bob Williams, of, Sammamish HS, Kirkland, Wash.
26. *Ronald Hale, rhp, Highland Springs (Va.) HS.
27. *Roy Swanson, rhp, Warren (Pa.) HS.
28. *James Davies, of, Brookston (Ind.) HS.
29. *Larry Mongillo, of, Serra HS, San Mateo, Calif.
30. Dave Harter, lhp, Cardinal Dougherty HS, Buffalo, N.Y.
31. *Dan Ryan, 1b, Columbia Basin (Wash.) CC.
32. *Joe Crocker, c, Goldendale HS, Centerville, Wash.
33. *Richard Wagener, lhp, Andover HS, Linthicum

Heights, Md.
34. *Bill Carroll, of, Cal State Los Angeles.
35. Edward Watts, 3b, Maggie Walker HS, Richmond, Va.
36. *W.J. Blane, 1b, Georgia Tech.
37. Edward Gilkes, of, Northeast HS, St. Petersburg, Fla.
38. *Bill Borelli, 1b, JC of San Mateo (Calif.).
39. *Lee Chilton, rhp, Edison HS, Stockton, Calif.
40. *James Cherwa, rhp, Frank W. Cox HS, Virginia Beach, Va.
41. *Dave Dingman, c, Churchill HS, Eugene, Ore.
42. *Henry Hoxit, rhp, John F. Kennedy HS, Willingboro, N.J.
43. Doug Hatten, lhp, Naches (Wash.) HS.
44. John Gonzales, lhp, Metropolitan State (Colo.) College.
45. *Jim Snyder, of, East Carolina University.
46. *Robert Wilczynski, 1b-of, St. Francis HS, Toledo, Ohio.
47. *Robert Taylor, rhp, Colonial Heights (Va.) HS.
48. Len Pupo, of, Gonzaga University.
49. Charles Sylvester, 2b, St. Petersburg (Fla.) HS.
50. *Hunter Hollar, rhp, Broadway HS, Singers Glen, Va.
51. *Joseph MacDonald, of, Bishop Hendricken HS, Warwick, R.I.
52. *Phil Honeycutt, 3b, Shawnee (Okla.) HS.
53. Alan Kwiatkowski, lhp, Airport (Mich.) CC.
54. *George Ferguson, ss, University of Maine.
55. *Gene Ammann, rhp, Lakeside HS, Decatur, Ga.
56. *Carl Bennett, c, Edison HS, Stockton, Calif.
57. (void) *Jimmy Blackmon, rhp, Rock Hill (S.C.) HS.
58. *Richard Coble, rhp, Jacksonville (Ill.) HS.
59. *Mike Ehlers, c, Centerville (Iowa) JC.
60. James Thomas, inf-of, Colby (Maine) College.
61. *Steve Webber, rhp, Muscatine (Iowa) CC.
DRAFT DROP *Baseball coach, Georgia (1981-96)*
62. *Barry Woodruff, lhp, Woodside (Calif.) HS.
63. *Mike Young, rhp, JC of San Mateo (Calif.).
64. *Tom Skendarian, of, Brown University.

#### June—Secondary Phase (1)

1. **Mike Adamson, rhp, University of Southern California.—(1967-69)**
DRAFT DROP *First-round draft pick (18th overall), Phillies (1965); first player from 1967 draft to reach majors (July 1, 1967)*
2. Gil Scharringhausen, rhp, Portland State University.
3. *Danny Talbott, 3b, University of North Carolina.
DRAFT DROP *17th-round draft pick, San Francisco 49ers/ National Football League (1967)*
4. *Dayle Campbell, of, Pepperdine University.
5. Jerry Meadows, rhp, West Virginia University.
6. *Bill Ferguson, c, Texas Christian University.
7. *Michael McFarland, rhp, University of Missouri.
8. (void) *Gary Smith, rhp, Michigan State University.
9. *Bill Seinsoth, 1b, University of Southern California.
10. *Dan Enger, 1b-of, Birmingham HS, Van Nuys, Calif.
11. *Robert Walter, lhp, Santa Clara University.
12. *Steve Garman, ss-rhp, University of Idaho.
DRAFT DROP *Brother of Mike Garman, major leaguer (1969-78)*

## BOSTON RED SOX

#### January—Regular Phase (4)

1. **Carlton Fisk, c, Charlestown, N.H.—(1969-93)**
DRAFT DROP *Elected to Baseball Hall of Fame, 2000*
2. **Don Newhauser, rhp, Broward (Fla.) CC—(1972-74)**
3. ***Craig Skok, lhp, Broward (Fla.) CC—(1973-79)**

#### January—Secondary Phase (18)

1. *Harold Harris, ss, Hewitt-Trussville HS, Birmingham, Ala.—(Low A)
2. Michael Koritko, of, Housatonic (Conn.) CC.
3. *Bobby Bryant, lhp, University of South Carolina.
DRAFT DROP *Defensive back, National Football League (1968-80)*

4. *Jack Fulmer, 3b, Arkansas State University.
5. ***Geoff Zahn, lhp, University of Michigan.—(1973-85)**
DRAFT DROP *Baseball coach, Michigan (1996-2001)*
6. *Charles Kline, lhp, Michigan State University.
7. ***Bill Zepp, rhp, University of Michigan.—(1969-71)**

#### June—Regular Phase (3)

1. **Mike Garman, rhp, Caldwell (Idaho) HS.—(1969-78)**
DRAFT DROP *Brother of Steve Garman, 12th-round draft pick, Orioles, June 1967/secondary phase*
2. *Danny Graham, ss, Bishop Montgomery HS, Torrance, Calif.—(AA)
DRAFT DROP *Attended UCLA; never re-drafted*
3. Chris Cross, c, Englewood HS, Jacksonville, Fla.—(High A)
4. *Dudley Mitchell, of-1b, Thomas Jefferson HS, Denver.—(High A)
DRAFT DROP *Attended Colorado; re-drafted by Padres, June 1971/secondary phase (3rd round, delayed) • Son of Dale Mitchell, major leaguer (1946-56)*
5. *Michael Witt, of, McLane HS, Fresno, Calif.—(Short-season A)
DRAFT DROP *Attended Fresno (Calif.) CC; re-drafted by Braves, January 1968/secondary phase (3rd round)*
6. Samuel Phillips, rhp, Eastern Hills HS, Fort Worth, Texas.
7. Alan Wolfenbarger, ss, Rutledge (Tenn.) HS.
8. *Steven Salata, c-of, Trinity Pawling Prepartory HS, Oneonta, N.Y.
9. *Cal Meier, ss, Grossmont (Calif.) JC.
10. Mark Kleibl, 3b, Norland HS, Miami.
11. *Ronald Sheppard, 3b, Altus (Okla.) HS.
12. John Newton, ss, Manteca (Calif.) HS.
13. Lawrence Bellm, rhp, Southern Illinois University-Edwardsville.
14. *James Thurston, 3b-ss, Central HS, Little Rock, Ark.
15. James Powers, c, St. Bernard HS, Waterford, Conn.
16. Michael Spellman, lhp, St. Bernard HS, Waterford, Conn.
17. *Michael James, of-ss, McKinney (Texas) HS.
18. *Tommy Harmon, c, Eastern Hills HS, Fort Worth, Texas.
19. Walter Povlick, rhp, East Central HS, Tulsa, Okla.

#### June—Secondary Phase (5)

1. Kris Krebs, ss, Manatee (Fla.) JC.—(AAA)
2. Ray Henningsen, 2b, Santa Clara University.
3. Rod Austin, of, Santa Clara University.
4. John Clifton, lhp, Chapman (Calif.) College.
5. Neil Rivenburg, of, Southern Oregon University.
6. Stephen Eagan, c, Pittsburg State (Kan.) University.

## CALIFORNIA ANGELS

#### January—Regular Phase (10)

1. David McCormick, rhp, El Camino (Calif.) JC.—(AA)
2. Gary Butcher, rhp, Santa Monica (Calif.) CC.
3. Michael Brown, c, Porterville (Calif.) JC.
4. Bruce Davis, inf, Los Angeles Pierce JC.
5. *Wayne Kjorvestad, ss, Mount San Antonio (Calif.) JC.
6. *Kenneth Pfau, rhp, El Camino (Calif.) JC.
7. *Dennis Parks, c-of, Long Beach (Calif.) CC.

#### January—Secondary Phase (6)

1. **Tom Murphy, rhp, Ohio University.—(1968-79)**
2. Ed Bauer, lhp, Gulf Coast (Fla.) CC.
3. *Seaton Daly, c, Santa Clara Univeristy.
4. ***Bill Bonham, rhp, Los Angeles Valley JC.—(1971-80)**
5. **Dave LaRoche, lhp, Torrance, Calif.—(1970-83)**
DRAFT DROP *Father of Adam LaRoche, major leaguer (2004-15) • Father of Andy LaRoche, major leaguer (2007-13)*
6. *Norbert Beddow, of-rhp, Mesa (Colo.) College.
7. *Rod Austin, of, Santa Clara University.
8. *Dan Stoligrosz, 3b, Los Angeles Valley JC.
9. *Marvin Madruga, ss, JC of the Sequoias (Calif.).

10. *Minton White, rhp-of, University of Texas.

#### June—Regular Phase (9)

1. Mike Nunn, c, Ben L. Smith HS, Greensboro, N.C.—(AAA)
2. ***Dave Kingman, rhp, Mount Prospect (Ill.) HS.—(1971-86)**
DRAFT DROP *Attended Harper (Ill.) JC; re-drafted by Orioles, January 1968/secondary phase (1st round); first overall draft pick, June 1970/secondary phase, Giants*
3. *Bruce Harkey, rhp, La Habra (Calif.) HS.—(AA)
DRAFT DROP *No school; re-drafted by Mets, January 1968/secondary phase (1st round)*
4. David Biber, of, Ramona HS, Riverside, Calif.—(Low A)
5. *Stanley Zawacki, of, Weequahic HS, Newark, N.J.—DNP
DRAFT DROP *No school; re-drafted by Braves, January 1968/secondary phase (8th round)*
6. *Rudy Kinard, 2b, Druid Hills HS, Decatur, Ga.
7. Terrance Thompson, rhp, Plant City (Fla.) HS.
8. *Thomas Tikker, c, Los Angeles CC.
9. *Douglas Ross, lhp, Cranford (N.J.) HS.
10. Gerald Lanning, lhp, Brookville (Ind.) HS.
11. Lawrence Rybicki, rhp, Niagara Falls (N.Y.) HS.
12. James Englehardt, lhp, Brigham Young University.
13. Charlie Oakes, 1b-c, Cal State Los Angeles.
14. *Edward Fields, rhp, Sunnyside (Wash.) HS.
15. *Steven Elliott, lhp, Highland HS, Yakima, Wash.
16. John Lyles, ss, Bethel (Tenn.) College.
17. *Steve Moore, of, San Marcos HS, Goleta, Calif.
18. Gregory Smith, lhp, Thousand Oaks (Calif.) HS.
19. *Richard David, 1b, UC Santa Barbara.
20. Robert Foderaro, lhp, Brigham Young University.
21. Craig Baker, rhp, Dayton, Ohio.
22. *Michael Derrington, lhp-1b, Reitz HS, Evansville, Ind.
23. Rich Shibley, ss-2b, Cal State Los Angeles.
24. Dennis Heberlein, 1b, Eisenhower HS, Yakima, Wash.
25. John Jackson, 3b, Southwestern (Calif.) JC.
26. Don Peracchi, 1b, Fresno State University.
27. ***Ed Crosby, 2b, Woodrow Wilson HS, Long Beach, Calif.—(1970-76)**
DRAFT DROP *Father of Bobby Crosby, first-round draft pick, Athletics (2002); major leaguer (2003-07)*
28. Roy Lee, c-1b, Edison HS, Fresno, Calif.
29. *Carl Wright, rhp, Holt HS, Cottondale, Ala.

#### June—Secondary Phase (19)

1. **Greg Washburn, rhp, Lewis (Ill.) University.—(1969)**
2. *Marv Galliher, 2b-of, San Diego Mesa CC.
3. Tim Hewes, c, Bakersfield (Calif.) JC.
4. *Craig Schell, rhp, UC Santa Barbara.
5. *Stephen Dean, 1b-of, JC of the Sequoias (Calif.)
6. ***Brent Strom, lhp, University of Southern California.—(1972-77)**
7. Bob Perruchon, of, Fresno State University.
8. *Mike Babler, rhp, Chabot (Calif.) JC.

## CHICAGO CUBS

#### January—Regular Phase (1)

1. **Alec DiStaso, rhp, Wilson HS, Los Angeles.—(1969)**
2. **Jim Dunegan, rhp, Bacone (Okla.) JC.—(1970)**
3. **Earl Stephenson, lhp, Campbell University—(1971-78)**
4. Edward Howell, c, Olanta, Pa.
5. Theodore Marcopulos, ss, Washington, D.C.

#### January—Secondary Phase (7)

1. **Gary Ross, rhp, Portvue, Pa.—(1968-77)**
2. Jim Armstrong, ss, Arizona State University.
3. *Mike Lisetski, ss, Rider College.
4. **Pat Jacquez, rhp, San Joaquin Delta (Calif.) JC.—(1971)**
DRAFT DROP *Father of Thomas Jacquez, major leaguer (2000)*
5. *David Barton, ss, Ithaca (N.Y.) College.

#### June—Regular Phase (2)

1. **Terry Hughes, ss, Dorman HS, Spartanburg, S.C.—(1970-74)**
2. **Jimmy McMath, of, Druid HS, Tuscaloosa, Ala.—(1968)**
DRAFT DROP *First 1967 high school draft pick to reach majors (Sept. 7, 1968)*
3. Terry Bongiovanni, rhp, O.H. Platt HS, South Meriden, Conn.—(AA)
4. Tom Krawczyk, ss, Central Michigan University.—(AAA)
5. Terrell Jones, c, Parkersburg HS, Washington, W.Va.—(Low A)
6. Bruce Dixon, of, Jones HS, Washington Shores, Fla.
7. *Michael Redling, rhp, Pleasant Hill (Calif.) HS.
8. Allen Robinson, of, Tennessee State University.
9. *Edgar Thomas, 1b, Pioneer HS, Whittier, Calif.
10. Joe Reyda, lhp, Upsala (N.J.) College.
11. John Lung, 3b, UCLA.
12. Charles Pollock, lhp, Farmington HS, Rachel, W.Va.
13. *David Classen, 3b-c, St. Louis (Mo.) HS.
14. Dick Arbogast, rhp, South Harrison HS, West Milford, W.Va.
15. Lloyd Kingfisher, rhp, Bacone (Okla.) JC.
16. *Richard Tekavec, c, Jefferson-Morgan HS, Jefferson, Pa.
17. John Merten, rhp, Rider College.
18. Thomas Brown, rhp, Washington State University.
19. Q.V. Lowe, rhp, Auburn University.
20. ***Gary Lance, rhp, Dentsville HS, Columbia, S.C.—(1977)**
21. *Allen Dukate, rhp, Admiral King HS, Lorain, Ohio.
22. Martin Miller, of, DePaul HS, Chicago.
23. *Bruce Olson, rhp, Montclair (Calif.) HS.
24. John Johnson, of, North Chicago (Ill.) HS.
25. *David Stone, lhp, Kittanning (Pa.) HS.
26. *Leonard Bible, c, Murrah HS, Jackson, Miss.
27. Dennis Rockwell, 1b, Pacific Grove (Calif.) HS.
28. *Larry Sheffield, lhp, Gainesville (Fla.) HS.
29. *Donald Davis, 3b, Randleman (N.C.) HS.
30. Charles Hunt, rhp, Washington HS, Portland, Ore.

#### June—Secondary Phase (2)

1. **Randy Bobb, c, Arizona State University.—(1968-69)**
2. *Doug Hansen, rhp, Fresno (Calif.) CC.
3. *Larry Hanson, 3b, University of Oregon.
4. ***Ken Forsch, rhp, Oregon State University.—(1970-86)**
DRAFT DROP *Brother of Bob Forsch, major leaguer (1974-89)*
5. *Joe Arnold, rhp, Miami-Dade CC North.
DRAFT DROP *Baseball coach, Florida (1984-94)*
6. **Darcy Fast, lhp, Warner Pacific (Ore.) College.—(1968)**
7. Michael Flanagan, lhp, Yakima Valley (Wash.) JC.

## CHICAGO WHITE SOX

#### January—Regular Phase (14)

1. *John Jacobson, c, Bloom (Ill.) JC.—DNP

#### January—Secondary Phase (4)

1. **Bob Spence, 1b-of, Santa Clara University.—(1969-71)**
2. Robert Desjardins, c, Fullerton (Calif.) JC.
3. ***Rich Folkers, lhp, Ellsworth (Iowa) JC.—(1970-77)**
4. Thomas Tutko, of-inf, Hastings (Neb.) College.
5. *Jack Gehrke, ss, University of Utah.
DRAFT DROP *Wide receiver, National Football League (1968-71)*

#### June—Regular Phase (13)

1. Dan Haynes, 3b, Headland HS, East Point, Ga.—(AAA)
2. Stuart Singleton, ss-of, Hudson Bay HS, Vancouver, Wash.—(AA)
3. ***Chris Ward, of, Arrojo HS, San Lorenzo, Calif.—(1972-74)**
DRAFT DROP *Attended Chabot (Calif.) JC; re-drafted by Cubs/June 1968 (3rd round)*
4. Marty Morrison, 1b-3b, Center Township HS, Monaca, Pa.—(Low A)
5. *Mike Slade, rhp, Washington & Lee HS, Arlington, Va.—(AA)
DRAFT DROP *Attended Florida State; re-drafted by Senators, June 1970/secondary phase (7th round)*

6. **Dennis O'Toole, rhp, De la Salle HS, Chicago.—(1969-73)**
DRAFT DROP *Brother of Jim O'Toole, major leaguer (1958-67)*
7. Stephen Krull, rhp, Purdue University.
8. *Norman Kraft, 3b-of, Father Judge HS, Philadelphia.
9. Bill Cooper, rhp, Edison HS, Miami, N.J.
10. *James Rafferty, ss, Groves HS, Birmingham, Mich.
11. *Kurt Aschermann, c, Ossining (N.Y.) HS.
12. *Thomas Wright, of, Santa Ana Valley HS, Santa Ana, Calif.
13. Steven Agerton, 3b-ss, Foothill HS, Bakersfield, Calif.
14. Gerald Hall, c-of, Western HS, Anaheim, Calif.
15. *Joe Bowen, 3b-1b, Robinson HS, Norfolk, Va.
16. *Kent Calderan, ss, Castro Valley (Calif.) HS.
17. George Weimer, rhp, East Aurora HS, Aurora, Ill.
18. *John Amoroso, lhp, Orange (Calif.) HS.
19. Martin Sauble, 1b, North Hagerstown (Md.) HS.
20. Kenneth Valentine, ss, South French Broad HS, Asheville, N.C.
21. *Gary Cook, of, Magnolia HS, Anaheim, Calif.
22. *Craig Perkins, c, Western HS, Rossmore, Calif.
23. *Victor LaDuna, ss, Williamson HS, Mobile, Ala.
24. *Frank Grundler, ss, Thornton Fractional South HS, Lansing, Ill.
25. *Dick Hanselman, lhp, St. John's River (Fla.) CC.
26. Steve Ostrowski, lhp, Lyons-LaGrange HS, Brookfield, Ill.
27. *Ken Ottoson, rhp, Chadron State (Neb.) College.
28. *Leon Filbeck, rhp, Santa Ana Valley HS, Santa Ana, Calif.
29. Steve Humphrey, 1b-of, Fullerton (Calif.) JC.
30. *Charlie Wolfe, lhp, Bethel HS, Colquitt, Ga.
31. ***Jim Norris, of, Seaford (N.Y.) HS.—(1977-80)**
32. *Lee Jacobsen, of, Kearney State (Neb.) College.
33. John Hankammer, rhp, Gibault HS, Waterloo, Ill.
34. Dick Jones, rhp, Miami (Ohio) University.
35. Tim Foy, c, Father Judge HS, Philadelphia.
36. *Thomas Gehrke, 3b-of, St. Joseph HS, Westchester, Ind.
37. Willie Garrison, lhp, Alabama State University.
38. Kenneth Quarles, of, Gardena HS, Los Angeles.
39. (void) *Earl Vickers, of, Fresno State University.
40. *Al Fritz, rhp, Maine West HS, Des Plaines, Ill.
41. Larry Steward, rhp, Wilson HS, Tifton, Ga.
42. *Albert Holland, of, Brevard (Fla.) JC.
43. *Toby Heath, lhp, Santa Ana (Calif.) HS.
44. Richard Ortner, c, San Luis Obispo (Calif.) HS.
45. Bob DeFries, rhp, Brother Rice HS, Oaklawn, Ill.
46. *David Rusco, 2b-ss, San Luis Obispo (Calif.) HS.
47. *Douglas McGrath, rhp, Ossining (N.Y.) HS.
48. *Mike McCarter, c-of, Arcadia Valley HS, Ironton, Mo.
49. *Thomas Fuller, c, Point Loma HS, San Diego.
50. *Lawrence Ulanski, rhp, St. Laurence HS, Chicago.
51. Roger Benko, lhp, Northwestern University.
52. Gary Hoskins, of, Union (Tenn.) University.

**June—Secondary Phase (11)**

1. *Herb Hofvendahl, of, St. Mary's (Calif.) College.—(AA)
2. ***Sandy Vance, rhp, Stanford University.—(1970-71)**
3. *Pat Harrison, 2b, University of Southern California.
DRAFT DROP *Baseball coach, Pepperdine (1995-96); baseball coach, Mississippi (1997-2000)*
4. Charles Kline, lhp, Western Michigan University.
5. *Vince Bigone, of-3b, Santa Clara University.
6. *Dave Renkiewicz, rhp, University of Michigan.
7. *Chuck Koselke, 1b, Western Michigan University.
8. Jim Limke, rhp, Minot State (N.D.) College.
9. Neil Weber, rhp, University of Minnesota.
10. *John Hurley, rhp, University of Michigan.
11. *Richard Licini, 1b, University of Notre Dame.

## CINCINNATI REDS

**January—Regular Phase (7)**

1. Marvin Branscomb, of, Gardena (Calif.) HS.—(AA)
2. *Don Enger, of, Birmingham HS, Van Nuys, Calif.
3. *Bill Sims, c, Oak Hill, Va.
4. Donald Hacker, ss, West Chester (Pa.) University.
5. *David Gunter, rhp, Bacone (Okla.) JC.
6. *Larry Stroman, 2b, San Antonio (Texas) JC.

**January—Secondary Phase (11)**

1. *David Speas, inf, San Diego Mesa JC.—(High A)
2. *Gordon Allen, of, Deerfield Academy, Ludlow, Mass.
3. *Frank Bon Vardo, rhp, University of Maryland.
4. *Gary Ratliff, of, Bacone (Okla.) JC.
5. *Robert Robbins, lhp, Gowanda, N.Y.
6. *John Sellers, ss, Northeastern Oklahoma State University.
7. Edward Curran, rhp, St. Louis CC-Meramec.
8. ***Norm Angelini, lhp, JC of San Mateo (Calif.).—(1972-73)**

**June—Regular Phase (8)**

1. **Wayne Simpson, rhp, Centennial HS, Los Angeles.—(1970-77)**
2. Wayne Holsopple, rhp, Bedford (Ohio) HS.—(High A)
3. Dick Pooschke, ss, Benson HS, Portland, Ore.—(High A)
4. **Fred Kendall, c, Torrance (Calif.) HS.—(1969-80)**
DRAFT DROP *Father of Jason Kendall, first-round draft pick, Pirates (1992); major leaguer (1996-2010)*
5. *Robert Watts, of, Eastern HS, Bristol, Conn.—DNP
DRAFT DROP *No school; never re-drafted*
6. Michael Pstragowski, rhp, Central HS, Manchester, N.H.
7. James Lewis, c, Gardena (Calif.) HS.
8. Steve Cochran, lhp, New Palestine (Ind.) HS.
9. Bob DeGrate, lhp-of, Moore HS, Waco, Texas.
10. Jerry Cole, 1b, Glen Oaks HS, Baton Rouge, La.
11. *Art Ramsey, lhp, St. Albans (W.Va.) HS.
12. *Gordon 'Scooter' Longmire, ss, Tracy (Calif.) HS.
DRAFT DROP *16th-round draft pick, Dallas Cowboys/ National Football League (1972)*
13. *John Hale, c, Huntington (W.Va.) HS.
14. Samuel Greenwood, of, Villanova University.
15. *Patrick Martin, lhp, Palmetto HS, Miami.
16. *Robert Cramer, rhp, New London (Conn.) HS.
17. William Mottershead, rhp, Boca Ciega HS, St. Petersburg, Fla.
18. Kenneth Geiger, rhp, Perkins HS, Sandusky, Ohio.
19. *Paul Walton, rhp, Amesbury (Mass.) HS.
20. *Rick Farizo, rhp, De la Salle HS, New Orleans, La.
21. Keith Pridgen, ss, South Greene HS, Snow Hill, N.C.
22. ***Terry Wilshushen, 3b-rhp, Carson HS, Lakewood, Calif.—(1973)**
23. *Edgar Avila, 1b-lhp, Miami-Dade CC North.
24. James Angelo, 2b, Southern HS, Philadelphia.
25. Sheldon Andrens, of, University of Southern California.
26. *Robert Beck, lhp, East Brunswick (N.J.) HS.
27. ***John Young, 1b, Mount Carmel HS, Los Angeles.—(1971)**
DRAFT DROP *Founder, Reviving Baseball in Innercities (RBI) program*
28. Daniel Hootstein, of, Harvard University.
29. **Dave Tomlin, lhp, West Union (Ohio) HS.—(1972-86)**
30. *John Lynn, 1b, Creston (Iowa) HS.
31. ***Chris Chambliss, 1b, Mira Costa (Calif.) JC.—(1971-88)**
DRAFT DROP *First overall draft pick, January 1970/ regular phase, Indians*
32. *Billy Robertson, 2b, Cisco (Texas) JC.
33. *Reuben Halliburton, rhp, Moore HS, Waco, Texas.
34. *Roger Menaugh, of, John Marshall HS, Oklahoma City, Okla.
35. *Eddie Bravo, 3b, Miami-Dade CC North.
36. Thomas Hooper, 3b, Texas Christian University.
37. *Jerome Thomas, rhp, Hamburg (Iowa) HS.
38. Johnnie Williamson, lhp-1b, Childersburg (Ala.) HS.
39. *Roger Tipton, lhp, Cisco (Texas) JC.
40. *Paul Simon, of, Cardinal O'Hara HS, Havertown, Pa.
41. *Leo Bouvet, rhp, Boys HS, Brooklyn, N.Y.
42. *Robert Zavorskas, ss, Bucknell University.
43. Jerry Flick, rhp, New Miami HS, Hamilton, Ohio.
44. *Joel Green, ss, Memorial HS, Tulsa, Okla.
45. Bob Renninger, lhp, Keystone HS, LaGrange, Ohio.
46. *Alfred Lee, of, Rice Lake (Wis.) HS.
47. *Terry Edwards, of, Memorial HS, Tulsa, Okla.
48. *Ray Nygard, 3b, Superior (Wis.) HS.
49. *Mike Mores, rhp, Holy Cross HS, Norridge, Ill.
50. *Greg Wilcox, lhp, West Bend (Wis.) HS.
51. *William Povia, ss, Hamilton East HS, Trenton, N.J.
52. *Ron Spain, ss, Rayburn HS, Houston.
53. *Donald Sasso, 1b, Sacred Heart HS, Waterbury, Conn.
54. Thomas Peppler, c, Princeton University.
55. Franklin Thompson, lhp, Manatee (Fla.) JC.
56. *Joseph Gavel, 3b-1b, Gulf Coast (Fla.) CC.
57. David Abell, 1b, Ridgway (Ill.) HS.
58. Larry Broeman, lhp, Reitz HS, Evansville, Ind.
59. *Ralph Kirkland, of, Waco (Texas) HS.
60. Kenneth Jones, 2b, Kashmere HS, Houston.
61. *William Barr, 1b, Dover (Okla.) HS.
62. *Timothy Boese, rhp, Lake Forest HS, Lake Bluff, Ill.
63. *Don Churchwell, of, Mark Smith HS, Macon, Ga.
64. *Larry Phillippe, rhp, Fort Myers (Fla.) HS.
65. *Wendell Starrick, ss, Marion (Ill.) HS.
66. *Danny Peelman, 1b-of, North Posey HS, Poseyville, Ind.
67. *Richard Moss, of, Lakeland (Fla.) HS.
68. *Wayne Church, rhp, Gardner-Webb College.
69. *Freddie Steinmark, ss, Wheat Ridge (Colo.) HS.
DRAFT DROP *Subject of hit 2015 movie "My All-American"*
70. *John Fodor, c, University of Southern California.
71. Bill Sluka, of, University of Denver.
72. *Allen Criswell, lhp, Bucknell University.

**June—Secondary Phase (6)**

1. **Frank Duffy, ss, Stanford University.—(1970-79)**
2. Al Crawford, of, Miami-Dade CC North.
3. Greg Riddoch, ss, Colorado State University.
DRAFT DROP *Major league manager (1990-92)*
4. ***Danny Thompson, ss, Oklahoma State University.—(1970-76)**
DRAFT DROP *Died as active major leaguer (Dec. 10, 1976)*
5. *Richard Wanless, rhp, Lakemont Academy HS, Quincy, Mass.
6. *Thomas Kelly, of, Holy Cross College.
7. *Bill Kirkpatrick, rhp, CC of San Francisco.
8. *William Close, rhp, Holy Cross College.
9. *Edward Cott, c, Cornell University.
10. *James O'Leary, rhp, Dutchess (N.Y.) CC.
11. *Roger Jackson, rhp, University of Kansas.
12. **Kurt Bevacqua, 2b, Miami-Dade CC North.—(1971-85)**

## CLEVELAND INDIANS

**January—Regular Phase (12)**

1. Roger Sexton, 3b, Ohio State Universtiy.—(Rookie)
2. John Kasper, 3b, Western Michigan University.
3. David Beber, of, Fort Wayne, Ind.
4. James Underhill, of, Dinwiddie (Va.) HS.
5. James Randall, rhp, Columbia Basin (Wash.) CC.
6. William Hutchens, c, Beckley (W.Va.) College.
7. *Dennis Droege, rhp, Highland (Kan.) CC.
8. *Max Winfield, rhp, Panola (Texas) JC.
9. Leslie Williams, of-inf, West Virginia University.
10. *John Ferguson, rhp, Abraham Baldwin Agricultural (Ga.) JC.
11. Jim Braxton, rhp, University of North Carolina-Wilmington.

**January—Secondary Phase (16)**

1. Ron Allen, 2b-of, Toledo (Ohio) JC.—(AAA)
2. Steve Wrenn, 1b, Wake Forest University.
3. (void) *David Reeves, rhp, South Georgia JC.
4. **Dick Tidrow, rhp, Chabot (Calif.) JC.—(1972-84)**
5. *Luis Flores, c, Gardner-Webb College.
6. Robert Bender, 1b-of, Goodlettsville, Tenn.
7. *John Meyer, c, University of Cincinnati.
8. Billy Ray Palmer, rhp, Rice University.
9. Michael Pierce, lhp, Eastern Arizona JC.
10. Adrian Zabala, rhp, University of Florida.
11. *George Grzegerek, ss, St. Edward's (Texas) University.
12. *Robert Guerrera, rhp, Cheshire Academy, Waterbury, Conn.
13. *Richard Snyder, of, North Canton, Ohio.
14. *Billy Carthel, of-inf, Sul Ross State (Texas) University.
15. Ronald Masterson, rhp, Soddy, Tenn.

**June—Regular Phase (11)**

1. **Jack Heidemann, ss, Brenham (Texas) HS.—(1969-77)**
2. **Mark Ballinger, rhp, Thousand Oaks HS, Newbury Park, Calif.—(1971)**
3. Charles Cichosz, c, Benilde HS, St. Louis Park, Minn.—(Low A)
4. Mac Crossan, rhp, Clark (Wash.) JC.—(AAA)
5. **Ed Farmer, rhp, St. Rita HS, Chicago.—(1971-83)**
6. *William Reuss, of, UC Santa Barbara.
7. Tim Sanders, rhp, Tehachapi (Calif.) HS.
8. Ronald Zuber, rhp, Colorado State University.
9. **Vic Correll, c, Georgia Southern College.—(1972-80)**
10. *Thomas Jenner, ss, Lake Mills (Wis.) HS.
11. *Richard Ogle, rhp, Bozeman (Mon.) HS.
12. Richard Dickinson, 2b, Milford (Conn.) Academy.
13. Ray Cox, c, Auburn University.
14. *Jay Ray Rokey, of, Westwood HS, Mesa, Ariz.
15. *Charles Sprinkle, ss, Arizona Western JC.
16. Larry Gallagher, rhp, Garfield HS, Terre Haute, Ind.
17. Ronald Butterfield, lhp, Murray HS, Salt Lake City.
18. Michael Schroeder, rhp, Waco (Texas) HS.
19. William Kohl, lhp, Gnadenhutten (Ohio) HS.
20. **Mike Paul, lhp, University of Arizona.—(1968-74)**
21. Richard Pack, 1b, Stow (Ohio) HS.
22. *William Gray, 2b, Randleman HS, High Point, N.C.
23. *Ronald Hunt, ss, Miami-Dade CC North.
24. Ed Southard, of, University of Arizona.
25. Kevin Casey, of, Avondale HS, Avondale Estates, Ga.
26. Tom Taylor, ss, Compton (Calif.) CC.
27. *Phillip Still, 2b, DeKalb HS, Decatur, Ga.
28. Jerry McConnell, rhp, Ohio University.
29. *John Hathaway, rhp, Fredonia (N.Y.) HS.
30. Larry McDivitt, rhp, Buckeye HS, Medina, Ohio.
31. *Tim Huntley, of, Creek County HS, Prineville, Ore.
32. Mike Yetter, 3b, Hemet (Calif.) HS.
33. *Thomas Callan, ss, CC of San Francisco.
34. **Jack Brohamer, ss, Huntington Beach (Calif.) HS.—(1972-80)**
35. *Bill Moynier, rhp, Bakersfield (Calif.) JC.
36. *Elwood Walker, rhp, Salt Lake City.
37. Fred Reedy, lhp, Northeast HS, St. Petersburg, Fla.
38. *Joe Staples, c, Texas A&M University.
39. Ladon Green, of, Jordan HS, Columbus, Ga.
40. Bo Rein, ss, Ohio State University.
DRAFT DROP *Seventh-round draft pick, Baltimore Colts/ National Football League (1967); football coach, North Carolina State (1976-79)*
41. *Michael Burns, of, University of Oklahoma.
42. *Brad Lawson, ss, Boardman HS, Youngstown, Ohio.
43. *Charles Paparone, ss, Ellet HS, Akron, Ohio.
44. *Craig Erbland, 1b, Mount Union (Ohio) College.
45. Robert Brooder, rhp, Southern Connecticut State University.
46. *Bill Bright, rhp, Cocoa (Fla.) HS.
47. *Terry Blitz, rhp, McMahon HS, Norwalk, Conn.
48. *John Walker, c, Sacramento (Calif.) CC.
49. John Stephenson, 3b, Ben L. Smith HS, Greensboro, N.C.
50. *Michael Leppa, 3b, Costa Mesa (Calif.) HS.
51. *Gary Zipfel, of-1b, Tinora HS, Defiance, Ohio.
52. *Gilbert Marrujo, c, Coachella Valley HS, Indio, Calif.
53. Bob Dorn, lhp, Cal Poly San Luis Obispo.
54. *Gerald Robert, rhp, Brevard (Fla.) CC.
55. James McMahon, c, Iona College.
56. *William Hendricks, lhp, Brush HS, Cleveland.
57. Kenneth Dean, rhp, Wichita State University.
58. *Alex Duncan, rhp, Poland (Ohio) Seminary.
59. *Ken Burt, rhp, Chaffey (Calif.) JC.
60. *Ron Opatkiewicz, ss, Covina (Calif.) HS.

61. *Dave Phares, c, Hemet (Calif.) HS.
62. *Joseph Bienko, rhp, Dunkirk (N.Y.) HS.

**June—Secondary Phase (15)**

1. Ronald Henson, lhp, Rice University.—(AA)
2. **Eddie Leon, ss, University of Arizona.—(1968-75)**
DRAFT DROP *First-round draft pick (9th overall), Twins (1965)*
3. **Lou Camilli, 3b, Texas A&M University.—(1969-72)**
4. Dennis Brady, 1b, Purdue University.
5. ***Rich Hinton, lhp, University of Arizona.—(1971-79)**
6. Stephen Lohrer, of, Parsons (Iowa) College.
7. *Jim Goodwin, rhp, University of Miami.
8. John Meyer, c, University of Cincinnati.
9. Max Winfield, rhp, Panola (Texas) JC.

## DETROIT TIGERS

**January—Regular Phase (16)**

1. *James Carter, 3b, Golden West (Calif.) JC.—DNP
2. Michael Kotzin, 1b, Fullerton (Calif.) JC.
3. Mike Murray, c, Cypress (Calif.) JC.
4. *Terry Schofield, c, Fullerton (Calif.) JC.

**January—Secondary Phase (2)**

1. **Mike Adams, ss, Fullerton (Calif.) JC.—(1972-78)**
DRAFT DROP *Son of Bobby Adams, major leaguer (1946-59) • Nephew of Dick Adams, major leaguer (1947)*
2. *Danny Talbott, 1b-3b, University of North Carolina.
DRAFT DROP *17th-round draft pick, San Francisco 49ers/National Football League (1967)*
3. John D'Auria, rhp, Arcadia (Calif.) HS.
4. *Ken Lohnes, c, Cerritos (Calif.) JC.
5. Michael Hastings, of, Ithaca (N.Y.) College.
6. *Robert Smith, rhp, St. John's University.
7. *Roger Banks, c, Mars Hill (N.C.) College.

**June—Regular Phase (15)**

1. **Jim Foor, lhp, McCluer HS, Ferguson, Mo.—(1971-73)**
2. Robert Ware, rhp, Hugenot HS, Richmond, Va.—(AAA)
3. James Tanner, of, Robinson HS, Tampa.—(AA)
4. Leslie Tanona, of, University of Michigan.—(AA)
5. **Paul Jata, c, Long Island City (N.Y.) HS.—(1972)**
6. **Dennis Saunders, rhp, Pioneer HS, Whittier, Calif.—(1970)**
7. Lynn Adams, ss, St. Elizabeth HS, Oakland, Calif.
8. James Wosman, c-1b, Augustinian Academy HS, St. Louis.
9. ***Larry Fritz, lhp, Whiting (Ind.) HS—(1975).**
10. *Mike Deniro, 3b, Chaney HS, Campbell, Ohio.
11. Gary McGhee, 2b, East HS, Knoxville, Tenn.
12. *Henry Bunnell, of-lhp, St. Peter's Catholic HS, Scranton, Pa.
13. *Jerry Killian, lhp, St. Matthews HS, Flint, Mich.
14. *Gilbert LaHaine, 1b, Everett HS, Lansing, Mich.
15. **Ike Blessitt, of, Hamtramck (Mich.) HS.—(1972)**
16. *Steve Allen, of, Berkeley (Calif.) HS.
17. *Marvin Gurley, rhp, MacKenzie HS, Detroit.
18. *Richard Szal, rhp, Chaminade HS, Long Island, N.Y.
19. *William Castle, ss, Southeast HS, Oklahoma City, Okla.
20. Doug Swiss, c, Northville (Mich.) HS.
21. ***Danny Fife, rhp, Clarkston (Mich.) HS.—(1973-74)**
22. Jess Rossiter, rhp, Evart (Mich.) HS.
23. *Donald Honne, lhp, Richfield HS, Waco, Texas.
24. Ricky Sayle, of, Memphis State University.
25. Dale Scilley, ss, Washington State University.
26. ***Jim Burton, lhp, Rochester (Mich.) HS.—(1975-77)**
27. *Peter Perpich, rhp, O'Rafferty HS, Lansing, Mich.
28. *Lanny Yost, ss, Clintondale HS, Mount Clemens, Mich.
29. *Jack McCloud, lhp, Kettering HS, Drayton, Mich.
30. *Richard Highduke, ss, Chaminade HS, Long Island, N.Y.
31. *Daniel Carroll, 1b, Grand Island (N.Y.) HS.
32. Carl Schulz, ss, University of Toledo.
33. Pete McKenzie, 2b, Auburn University.
34. Lee Sage, lhp, Ada (Ohio) HS.
35. Darrell Schneller, rhp, Sturgeon (Mo.) HS.
36. **Gary Ignasiak, lhp, St. Mary's HS, Anchorville, Mich.—(1973)**
DRAFT DROP *Brother of Mike Ignasiak, major leaguer (1991-95)*
37. Mike Marshall, ss, Mount Healthy HS, Cincinnati.
38. Marvin Isensee, 1b, Sparta (Wis.) HS.
39. *Richard Miceli, c, Waterford-Kettering HS, Drayton Plains, Mich.
40. *Greg Plant, 2b-ss, Sylvania (Ohio) HS.
41. *Dan Rounds, rhp, Arroyo HS, San Lorenzo, Calif.
42. *Ralph Darin, rhp, River Rouge (Mich.) HS.
43. *Philip Rashead, c, St. Agnes HS, Flint, Mich.
44. William Mullins, of, Paintsville (Ky.) HS.
45. *Thomas Jackson, ss, Citrus (Calif.) JC.
46. Robert Counterman, c, Linden (N.J.) HS.
47. James Sangregario, of, St. Ladislaus HS, Hamtramck, Mich.
48. *Richard Cutler, ss-3b, Bayside HS, Whitestone, N.Y.
49. *Richard Wacheli, rhp, Dieruff HS, Allentown, Pa.
50. *Richard Shirk, 3b-rhp, Cocalico HS, Denver, Pa.
51. *Dan Jackson, inf-rhp, Scott HS, Toldeo, Ohio.

**June—Secondary Phase (17)**

1. John Hetrick, of, University of Maryland.—(AA)
2. ***Geoff Zahn, lhp, University of Michigan.—(1973-85)**
DRAFT DROP *Baseball coach, Michigan (1996-2001)*
3. ***Skip Jutze, c, Central Connecticut State University.—(1972-77)**
4. ***Mel Behney, lhp, Michigan State University.—(1970)**
5. *Tom Lundgren, lhp, University of Missouri.
6. *Tom Binkowski, 1b-of, Michigan State University.
7. Louis Ganious, 1b, Southern University.
8. *John Herzing, lhp, Washington (Mo.) University.
9. *Wayne Danson, of, Gulf Coast (Fla.) CC.
10. *Roy Myers, of, Memphis State University.

## HOUSTON ASTROS

**January—Regular Phase (5)**

1. Jack Van Vleck, rhp, Everett (Wash.) CC.—(High A)
2. *James Kinds, rhp, Kashmere HS, Houston.
3. *John Thomas, c, Barbers Hill HS, Mount Belvieu, Texas.

**January—Secondary Phase (1)**

1. ***Pete Varney, c, Deerfield (Mass.) Academy.—(1973-76)**
DRAFT DROP *First overall draft pick, August 1966/American Legion phase, Athletics; first overall draft pick, June 1971/secondary phase (active), White Sox*
2. Nik Radakovic, rhp, University of Michigan.
3. ***Jim Johnson, lhp, Western Michigan University.—(1970)**
4. *Jerry Meadows, rhp, West Virginia University.
5. *Frank Vandevender, rhp, San Diego Mesa CC.

**June—Regular Phase (6)**

1. **John Mayberry, 1b-of, Northwestern HS, Detroit.—(1968-82)**
DRAFT DROP *Father of John Mayberry, first-round draft pick, Mariners (2002); first-round draft pick, Rangers (2005); major leaguer (2009-15)*
2. **Jay Schlueter, of, Central HS, Phoenix.—(1971)**
3. Craig Hilden, lhp, Bellarmine Prep, Tacoma, Wash.—(High A)
4. Lewis Brown, 3b, Laney (Calif.) JC.—(AA)
5. Douglas Olson, rhp, Bergenfield (N.J.) HS.—(High A)
6. Dale Weatherford, c, William Chrisman HS, Independence, Mo.
7. John Kryczowski, lhp, Hamtramck (Mich.) HS.
8. Gary Long, c, Byng (Okla.) HS.
9. Jeff Morrell, of-3b, Byng (Okla.) HS.
10. Daniel Evans, lhp, Irvington HS, Fremont, Calif.
11. *George Hunt, 1b, Clearwater (Fla.) HS.
12. Gerald Johnson, rhp, Merced (Calif.) HS.
13. *John Ritter, rhp, Kimball HS, Royal Oak, Mich.
14. Steve Grover, lhp, Calvert HS, Prince Frederick, Md.
15. Tom Suchanek, rhp, Greenfield (Mass.) CC.
16. Ken Hovance, of, Toms River (N.J.) HS.
17. Ricky Wilson, 3b, Denison HS, Pottsboro, Texas.
18. Ricky Hartzog, of, Provine HS, Jackson, Miss.
19. *Don Jumper, rhp, Jasper (Texas) HS.
20. Wayne Brechtel, rhp, Johnsonburg (Pa.) HS.
21. *George Shaw, rhp, Panola (Texas) JC.
22. Kenneth McCary, of, Wayne HS, Byars, Okla.
23. *Paul Greer, c, Prestonburg (Ky.) HS.
24. Emmitt Money, rhp, Avon Park (Fla.) HS.
25. Larry Franklin, rhp, Central HS, Springfield, Mo.
26. *Larry Caldwell, of, Mission (Texas) HS.
27. *Michael Cahill, lhp, St. Xavier HS, Cincinnati.
28. *Jerry Proctor, inf, Muir HS, Pasadena, Calif.
29. *James Evans, rhp, Christian Brothers HS, Memphis, Tenn.
30. *Donald Paulsen, of, Lyman HS, Casselberry, Fla.
31. *Pat McKean, lhp, Palo Duro HS, Amarillo, Texas.
32. *Bob Danaher, rhp, Montpelier (Vt.) HS.
33. Shane Hummell, c, Washington Township HS, Blackwood, N.J.
34. *David Buchanan, 3b, Muir HS, Pasadena, Calif.
35. *Robert Warner, rhp, Stroudsburg (Pa.) HS.
36. Steven Ritchie, lhp, Boca Ciega HS, Treasure Island, Fla.
37. *Glen Hassell, lhp, Rusk (Texas) HS.
38. *Carl Hayes, ss, Robstown (Texas) HS.
39. Geoff Price, 2b, Muir HS, Pasadena, Calif.
40. *Louie Gavrell, rhp-of, Tyler (Texas) JC.
41. *John Burger, c, Forest Park HS, Beaumont, Texas.
42. *Bruce Haynes, rhp, Hopkins (Minn.) HS.

**June—Secondary Phase (4)**

1. Kim Hillstrom, rhp, Central Michigan University.—(High A)
2. Gordon Allen, of, Deerfield (Mass.) Academy HS.
3. ***Pete Varney, c, Deerfield (Mass.) Academy HS.—(1973-76)**
DRAFT DROP *First overall draft pick, August 1966/Legion phase, Athletics; first overall draft pick, June 1971/secondary phase (active), White Sox*
4. Mike Flanagan, rhp, University of North Carolina.
5. *Raymond DeRiggi, of-1b, Seton Hall University.
6. *Tom Schweitzer, lhp, Fairmont State (W.Va.) College.
7. ***Jack Lind, ss, Arizona State University.—(1974-75)**
8. *Stephen Hanson, rhp, West Valley (Calif.) JC.

## KANSAS CITY ATHLETICS

**January—Regular Phase (8)**

1. ***Ken Hottman, of, Sacramento (Calif.) CC.—(1971)**
2. *Walter Adey, lhp, Hudson Valley (N.Y.) CC.
3. *George Stephanos, lhp, Arizona Western JC.
4. *Hubert Perkins, of, Iowa State University.

**January—Secondary Phase (12)**

1. *Rick Konik, 1b, Detroit.—DNP
DRAFT DROP *First-round draft pick (14th overall), Tigers (1966)*
2. Roger Cain, of, East Los Angeles JC.
3. *Walter Lampmann, of, Manatee (Fla.) JC.
4. Nick Deflorio, ss, New York Tech.
5. **Jim Panther, rhp, Southern Illinois University.—(1971-73)**
6. Russ Vitallo, rhp, University of Massachusetts.
7. *Rusty Adkins, 2b, Clemson University.
8. *Kelly Prior, rhp, University of Florida.
9. *James Gruber, ss, Seminole (Fla.) CC.
10. *Richard Allred, ss-rhp, Mesa (Ariz.) CC.

**June—Regular Phase (7)**

1. Brien Bickerton, lhp, Santana HS, Santee, Calif.—(AA)
2. **Vida Blue, lhp, DeSoto HS, Mansfield, La.—(1969-86)**
3. Gary Coleman, c, Colonial HS, Orlando, Fla.—(AA)
4. Victor Schamarelli, of, Hillside (N.J.) HS.–(Low A)
5. *Gene Dusan, c, Lakewood (Calif.) HS.—(AAA)
DRAFT DROP *Attended Long Beach (Calif.) CC; re-drafted by Senators, January 1968/secondary phase (1st round)*
6. Carl Ives, rhp, Plantation HS, Fort Lauderdale, Fla.
7. Joe Robinson, ss, Mineola (N.Y.) HS.
8. *Bruce Raible, rhp, Western Hills HS, Cincinnati.
9. Donald Camy, rhp, Alisal HS, Salinas, Calif.
10. Lazaro Mata, c, Miami (Fla.) HS.
11. ***Eric Soderholm, 3b, South Georgia JC.—(1971-80)**
DRAFT DROP *First overall draft pick, June 1968/secondary phase, Twins • Brother of Dale Soderholm, first-round draft pick, Twins (1971)*
12. *Steve Mikulic, ss, Thornridge HS, Dolton, Ill.
13. *Bill Harkins, rhp, Holbrook (Mass.) HS.
14. Bill Aubertin, rhp, Washington HS, Keller, Wash.
15. Ray Elder, 3b, Rubidoux HS, Riverside, Calif.
16. *Rex Kern, 3b, Lancaster (Ohio) HS.
DRAFT DROP *Defensive back, National Football League (1971-74)*
17. Bob Pirnik, c, Woodbridge (N.J.) HS.
18. *Mark Resser, lhp, Skyline HS, Oakland, Calif.
19. Samuel Lovelace, ss-2b, Burbank HS, Sacramento, Calif.
20. *Steve Zimmerman, lhp, Fortune HS, Dearborn, Mich.
21. David Rhodenbaugh, rhp, Fort Lauderdale (Fla.) HS.
22. *John Austin, rhp, Northeast Guilford HS, Greensboro, N.C.
23. Ron Gordon, of, Pasadena (Calif.) CC.
24. Joe Grace, 3b, St. Joseph's University.
25. Sheldon Spicher, ss, Clark (Wash.) JC.
26. Robert Stickels, rhp, University of Nebraska.
27. Clyde Steele, lhp, Bakersfield HS, Costa Mesa, Calif.
28. Clarence Stoner, 1b, Penn State University.
29. *Moody Jackson, of, South Mountain HS, Phoenix.
30. Donald Ruris, 2b, Hofstra University.
31. *Robert Schiffner, lhp, Morris Hills HS, Rockaway, N.J.
32. *Thomas Kaehler, of, Cleveland HS, Reseda, Calif.
33. *Randy Smith, 1b, Lincoln Land (Ill.) JC.
34. Douglas Ross, rhp, Crown Point Central HS, Crown Point, N.Y.
35. Parke Davidson, ss, Texas Christian University.
36. Michael Heinitz, c, Sacramento (Calif.) HS.
37. *Larry Gonsalves, rhp, Fresno State University.
38. Ron Fisher, c, Elizabethtown (Pa.) College.
39. *Allen Simas, rhp, Sacramento (Calif.) CC.
40. *Ernest Fimbres, of, Tucson (Ariz.) HS.
41. David Margolius, c, Lexington (Mass.) HS.
42. *Gregory Hill, of, Los Angeles.
43. **(void) *Reggie Sanders, of, Venice (Calif.) HS.—(1974)**
44. *Ed Assaf, rhp, University of Southern Mississippi.
45. Joe Emanuel, c-1b, North Bend (Neb.) HS.
46. Norb Pena, rhp, Nicholls State University.
47. Garland Godwin, 1b, Alcorn State University.
48. James Burns, of, Lafayette College.
49. *James Veryzer, of, Islip (N.Y.) HS.

**June—Secondary Phase (13)**

1. *Fred Kampf, rhp, University of Miami.–(AA)
2. LaDon Boyd, rhp, Florida State University.
3. *Ronnie Shotts, of, Stanford University.
4. **Warren Bogle, lhp, University of Miami.—(1968)**
5. ***Ray Peters, rhp, Harvard University.—(1970)**
6. Rusty Adkins, 2b, Clemson University.
7. **Darrell Evans, 3b, Pasadena (Calif.) CC.—(1969-89)**
8. Kelly Prior, rhp, University of Florida.
9. Ronald Berta, c, Moravian (Pa.) College.
10. Bob Yingling, 2b-of, University of Miami.

## LOS ANGELES DODGERS

**January—Regular Phase (19)**

1. Travis King, rhp, South Georgia JC.—(AA)
2. James Herbert, lhp, Southern University.

**January—Secondary Phase (17)**

1. ***Larry Burchart, rhp, Oklahoma State University.—(1969)**
2. James Doran, of, Staunton (Va.) Military

Academy.
3. *Jeffrey Bowman, rhp, Modesto (Calif.) JC.
4. Maurice Smith, c-of, University of Illinois.
5. Paul Devaney, rhp, Rochester (N.Y.) Business Institute.
6. *Mike Babler, rhp, Chabot (Calif.) JC.
7. (void) *Eldon Jones, lhp, Trinidad State (Colo.) JC.

**June—Regular Phase (20)**

1. Donnie Denbow, 3b, Southern Methodist University.—(High A)
2. Thomas Harris, ss, Central Gwinnett HS, Lawrenceville, Ga.—(High A)
3. William Rainer, of, Southern Methodist University.—(High A)
4. **Steve Yeager, c, Meadowdale HS, Dayton, Ohio.—(1972-86)**
5. ***Ron Cash, ss, Lakeside HS, Decatur, Ga.—(1973-74)**

DRAFT DROP *Attended Manatee (Fla.) JC; re-drafted by Braves, June 1968/secondary phase (4th round) • Uncle of Kevin Cash, major leaguer (2002-10); major league manager (2015)*

6. *Ken Hansen, rhp, Maryvale HS, Phoenix.
7. *Rusty Bodkin, of, Fort Lauderdale (Fla.) HS.
8. Aubrey Saxon, lhp, Pelzer, S.C.
9. Gary Wedel, 3b, Gardena (Calif.) HS.
10. Carmine Marceno, 1b, Christopher Columbus HS, Bronx, N.Y.
11. Chuck Boggs, c, West Virginia University.
12. Robert Lamber, lhp, New York City Technical JC.
13. Kara Hall, inf, Dos Palos HS, Los Banos, Calif.
14. *James Loll, 1b-rhp, Crespi HS, Reseda, Calif.
15. *Glenn Woodruff, c, Aliceville (Ala.) HS.
16. *John Donovan, rhp, St. Peter's HS, Staten Island, N.Y.
17. *Robert Knight, 2b-ss, King HS, Temple Terrace, Fla.
18. Don Stoulil, 3b, Alemany HS, Sunland, Calif.
19. Abraham Sears, ss-of, Perry (Okla.) HS.
20. Larry King, rhp, Willingham HS, Macon, Ga.
21. *Bruce Matte, rhp, Miami (Ohio) University.

DRAFT DROP *Seventh-round draft pick, Washington Redskins/National Football League (1967)*

22. *Leon Murray, 1b, Fremont HS, Los Angeles.

DRAFT DROP *Brother of Eddie Murray, major leaguer (1977-97) • Brother of Rich Murray, major leaguer (1980-83)*

23. Malcolm Bass, 2b-3b, Gulf Coast (Fla.) CC.
24. Norman Dermody, rhp, Seton Hall University.
25. James Hughes, ss, Okawville (Ill.) HS.
26. *James Norton, c, Alemany HS, San Fernando, Calif.
27. *Michael Rapkin, lhp, Monroe HS, Sepulveda, Calif.
28. *Greg Smith, rhp, Sierra HS, Whittier, Calif.
29. James Flynn, rhp, Roosevelt HS, Fresno, Calif.
30. James Brunnworth, rhp, Edwardsville (Ill.) HS.
31. *Ronald Thompson, rhp-1b, Roosevelt HS, Atlanta.
32. *David Thompson, of, Santa Barbara (Calif.) HS.
33. *John Brannigan, lhp, Cliffside Park HS, Fairview, N.J.
34. *Robert Huellemeier, rhp, Mount DeSales HS, Macon, Ga.
35. *William Wright, c, Carson-Newman (Tenn.) College.
36. Chava Flores, ss, Artesia (N.M.) HS.
37. *Greg Mattinson, of, Grossmont (Calif.) JC.
38. *Charles Kingsbury, 3b, Claremont (Calif.) HS.
39. *Willie Strickland, of, Fremont HS, Los Angeles.
40. *Gene Martin, 3b, Santa Monica (Calif.) HS.
41. Larry Tingle, rhp, Yerington (Nev.) HS.
42. *Douglas Barker, rhp-of, Davis (Calif.) HS.
43. Dennis Murphy, rhp, Southwest HS, Miami.
44. *James O'Brien, of, Sacred Heart HS, San Francisco.
45. *Phillip Cabibi, 2b, Garey HS, Pomona, Calif.
46. *James Southworth, rhp, Los Angeles Valley JC.
47. Gene Willetts, c, Johnson-Wales (Mass.) CC.
48. *William Susa, rhp, Reseda (Calif.) HS.
49. *Steven Napoli, of, Alemany HS, San Fernando, Calif.
50. *John Marino, c, Los Angeles Valley JC.
51. David Conway, of-1b, Los Angeles Valley JC.
52. William Graves, rhp, Westmont (Calif.) College.
53. *Harold Armstrong, ss, Hueneme HS, Oxnard, Calif.
54. *Steven Lee, lhp, Monroe HS, Granada Hills, Calif.
55. *Joe Jacobsen, c, Roosevelt HS, Fresno, Calif.
56. *Michael McPartlin, 3b, Niagara County (N.Y.) CC.
57. *David Dale, rhp, Culver Military Academy, Pittsburgh.
58. *Steven Easton, lhp, Sierra HS, Whittier, Calif.
59. *David Lloyd, of, Jefferson HS, Los Angeles.
60. Patrick Manahan, 3b, Sylmar (Calif.) HS.
61. *Albert Rossi, 2b, St. Francis HS, Pasadena, Calif.
62. *Frank Rucker, lhp, Ensley HS, Birmingham, Ala.
63. **Bruce Ellingsen, lhp, Lakewood (Calif.) HS.—(1974)**
64. *Francis Karmelich, c, Fermin Lasuen HS, San Pedro, Calif.
65. ***Tom Lundstedt, c, Prospect HS, Arlington Heights, Ill.—(1973-75)**
66. *Antonio Latour, lhp, Indian River (Fla.) CC.
67. *Craig Fox, lhp, Ithaca (N.Y.) College.
68. (void) *Bart Bell, 2b, Mesa (Ariz.) CC.
69. *Harold Murray, c, Smith Cotton HS, Sedalia, Mo.
70. *Keith Lieppman, ss, Southwest HS, Kansas City, Mo.

**June—Secondary Phase (14)**

1. *Pat Brown, of, University of Texas.—(AA)
2. *Robert Bosson, 1b, Columbia University.
3. **Larry Burchart, rhp, Oklahoma State University.—(1969)**
4. Randy Kohn, c, University of Georgia.
5. Jim Scheschuk, c, University of Texas.
6. Jackie Creel, rhp, Gulf Coast (Fla.) CC.
7. David Speas, 3b, San Diego Mesa JC.
8. *Walter Adey, lhp, Hudson Valley (N.Y.) CC.
9. *Jon Keirns, of, Central State (Okla.) University.
10. *Lucky Thompson, ss, University of San Diego.
11. *Clarence Cleveland, of-3b, Chipola (Fla.) JC.
12. *Larry Linville, of, Arizona State University.
13. *Pat O'Brien, lhp, University of Arizona.
14. *Bruce Wade, rhp, El Camino (Calif.) JC.
15. *Richard Binder, lhp, University of Illinois.
16. *Doug Brittelle, rhp, Rutgers University.

DRAFT DROP *Drafted by Kentucky Colonels/American Basketball Association (1969)*

17. *Glenn Bisbing, 3b, Rider College.

## MINNESOTA TWINS

**January—Regular Phase (18)**

1. Leonard Weems, of, Ecorse (Mich.) HS.–(High A)
2. *Jack Nelson, rhp, Fullerton (Calif.) JC.
3. *Joe Miller, rhp, Orange Coast (Calif.) JC.
4. Gerald Ruettiman, rhp, St. Paul, Minn.
5. Marv Danielson, 3b, Silver Bay, Minn.

**January—Secondary Phase (14)**

1. Clifford Foster, of-1b, Sexton HS, Lansing, Mich.—(AA)
2. *Rod O'Brien, 3b, Long Beach (Calif.) CC.
3. Edwin Figueroa, c, George Washington HS, New York.
4. Larry Housley, 3b, San Bernardino Valley (Calif.) JC.
5. *Doug Hansen, rhp, Fresno (Calif.) CC.
6. *Scott Morton, lhp, Iowa State University.
7. *Ted Rohde, of, Fresno (Calif.) CC.
8. *John Herbst, lhp, University of Southern California.
9. *Thomas Kelly, of, Holy Cross College.

**June—Regular Phase (17)**

1. **Steve Brye, 3b-of, St. Elizabeth HS, Oakland, Calif.—(1970-78)**
2. Bob Storm, 3b, Adams HS, South Bend, Ind.—(AAA)
3. Tom Norman, 3b, Truman HS, Independence, Mo.—(Rookie)
4. Bill Perkins, c, Montclair (Calif.) HS.—(High A)
5. **Dave Goltz, rhp, Rothsay (Minn.) HS.—(1972-83)**
6. Mark Strader, c, Jefferson HS, Lafayette, Ind.
7. Daniel Mellars, ss, Penn Hills HS, Verona, Pa.
8. Anthony Serenelli, ss-3b, Trenton Cathedral HS, Morrisville, Pa.
9. Steve Simon, rhp, Pius X HS, Lynwood, Calif.
10. Danny Long, c, Calhoun (Tenn.) HS.
11. ***Al Hrabosky, lhp, Savanna HS, Anaheim, Calif.—(1970-82)**
12. Don Brown, rhp, Clarksville (Tenn.) HS.
13. **Steve Luebber, rhp, Joplin (Mo.) HS.—(1971-81)**
14. *Nils Lambert, lhp, Curtis HS, Staten Island, N.Y.
15. **Rick Dempsey, c, Crespi HS, Simi Valley, Calif.—(1969-92)**
16. Dan Humay, ss, University of Illinois.
17. Ray Shoup, of, Ohio State University.
18. *Keith Spicer, of, University of Michigan.
19. Robert Gamache, rhp, West HS, Garden City, Mich.
20. Gary Reierson, of, University of Minnesota.
21. Larry Rathje, of, University of Iowa.
22. *James Enlund, rhp, West Allis Central HS, West Allis, Wis.
23. John Shulock, 3b, Brevard (Fla.) CC.

DRAFT DROP *Umpire, Major League Baseball (1979-2002)*

24. **Jim Obradovich, 2b, Fort Knox (Ky.) HS.—(1978)**
25. Michael Shields, lhp, Waukesha Memorial HS, Waukesha, Wis.
26. Frank Archuleta, of, Hanford (Calif.) HS.
27. Ken Gill, rhp-of, Brevard (Fla.) CC.
28. *Louis Billmeier, rhp, Kuemper HS, Carroll, Iowa.
29. Robert Fitzner, c, University of Denver.
30. *Daniel Adams, 3b-ss, West Allis Central HS, West Allis, Wis.
31. Walter Evanik, of, Kearney (N.J.) HS.
32. Patrick Smith, 2b-ss, Robersonville (N.C.) HS.
33. ***Jake Brown, c, Wheatley HS, Houston.—(1975)**
34. Mike Cichon, rhp, Pomona (Calif.) HS.
35. *William Templeton, rhp, Elmira, N.Y.
36. *Ronald Pritchett, rhp, Ganesha HS, Pomona, Calif.
37. Larry Agrella, ss-3b, Camden HS, San Jose, Calif.
38. *Mel Bannon, ss, St. Francis HS, Pasadena, Calif.
39. William Rahm, rhp, Iowa State University.
40. *Patrick Knutzen, lhp, El Camino (Calif.) JC.
41. Mike Ford, c, Lewis (Ill.) University.
42. *Henry Baker, 3b, Liberty HS, Hinesville, Ga.
43. *Neal Kalberer, lhp, St. Marys Central HS, Bismarck, N.D.
44. *Gary Hohman, c, Steinert HS, Trenton, N.J.
45. *Tim Bodle, rhp, Lancaster (Texas) HS.
46. *Robert Berezowitz, c, Whitewater State (Wis.) College.
47. Lloyd Brunick, rhp, Yankton (S.D.) HS.
48. Vern Gove, of, Randolph (Wis.) HS.
49. Robert Meyer, lhp, Wartburg (Iowa) College.
50. *Michael Vogel, ss, St. Thomas Academy, St. Paul, Minn.
51. *Rick Pope, rhp, El Rancho HS, Pico Rivera, Calif.

**June—Secondary Phase (3)**

1. ***Ken Szotkiewicz, ss, Georgia Southern College.—(1970)**
2. **Dan Monzon, ss, Buena Vista (Iowa) College.—(1972-73)**
3. *David Grangaard, 3b, Arizona State University.
4. Steve Richman, ss, Columbia University.
5. **Mike Sadek, c, University of Minnesota.—(1973-81)**
6. *Michael Noonan, lhp, Foothill (Calif.) JC.
7. Clifford Farmer, rhp, Crowder (Mo.) JC.
8. Jim Townsend, inf-of, Santa Clara University.
9. **Pete Hamm, rhp, Stanford University.—(1970-71)**
10. ***Craig Skok, lhp, Broward (Fla.) CC.—(1973-79)**

## NEW YORK METS

**January—Regular Phase (3)**

1. **Ken Singleton, of, Mount Vernon, N.Y.—(1970-84)**
2. *Dan DeMichele, of-3b, Vermont Academy, Cranston, R.I.
3. Thomas Grubb, rhp, Lexington, N.C.
4. ***Ike Blessitt, of, Hamtramck (Mich.) HS.—(1972)**
5. *Arnie Chonko, 1b, Ohio State University.

**January—Secondary Phase (19)**

1. Tommy Campbell, of, Jackson State University.—(AA)
2. ***Scott Reid, 3b-of, Cerritos (Calif.) JC.—(1969-70)**

DRAFT DROP *Scouting director, Cubs (1986-87)*

3. Richard Carlson, 1b-of, Buffalo State College.
4. *John Mispagel, c, Santa Clara University.
5. ***Bob Chlupsa, rhp, Manhattan College.—(1970-71)**

DRAFT DROP *13th-round draft pick, San Diego Rockets, National Basketball Association (1967)*

6. *Jim Whinery, 3b, Modesto (Calif.) JC.
7. Dennis Trame, rhp, Quincy (Ill.) College.
8. *Terry Stofer, of, Key West, Fla.
9. Charles Haje, of, Montgomery (Md.) JC.
10. **Tommy Moore, of-rhp, Cerritos (Calif.) JC.—(1972-77)**
11. *Ken Stabler, lhp, University of Alabama.

DRAFT DROP *Quarterback, National Football League (1970-84).*

12. *Reid Braden, 1b, Cerritos (Calif.) JC.

**June—Regular Phase (4)**

1. **Jon Matlack, lhp, Henderson HS, West Chester, Pa.—(1971-83)**
2. Dan Carey, lhp, Hastings (Minn.) HS.—(AA)
3. *Gary Myers, of, Hoover HS, Fresno, Calif.—(AA)

DRAFT DROP *Attended JC of San Mateo (Calif.); re-drafted by Red Sox, January 1969/secondary phase (1st round).*

4. Gary King, ss, El Segundo (Calif.) HS.—(High A)
5. Jackie Adams, of, Monrovia (Calif.) HS.—(AA)
6. Russell Seals, rhp, Calhoun (Tenn.) HS.
7. *Barry Sheldon, rhp, Batavia (N.Y.) HS.
8. Mike McCready, rhp, El Segundo (Calif.) HS.
9. Fred Howard, 1b, Hoover HS, Fresno, Calif.
10. **Charlie Hudson, lhp-of, Tupelo (Okla.) HS.—(1972-75)**
11. **Jesse Hudson, lhp, DeSoto HS, Mansfield, La.—(1969)**
12. Tom Horne, lhp, Puyallup (Wash.) HS.
13. *Tim Bograkos, 1b, Central HS, Flint, Mich.
14. *Wendell Franke, ss-rhp, Hooper (Neb.) HS.
15. Charles Landis, of, University of Wisconsin-La Crosse.
16. *John Frilling, of, Covington Catholic HS, Covington, Ky.
17. Forrest Dover, rhp, High Point College.
18. Warren Holmes, of, Norland HS, Miami.
19. *Joseph Tillman, 3b, Murphy HS, Mobile, Ala.
20. *Steve Broege, lhp, Westlake HS, Thornwood, N.Y.
21. *Donald Russell, 3b, Southern HS, Baltimore.
22. Dennis Lingenfelter, rhp, Atwater HS, Winton, Calif.
23. *Michael Lersch, lhp, Hinkley HS, Aurora, Colo.
24. Bob Bryant, c, Chico (Calif.) HS.
25. Peter Cappelli, c, Highland HS, Albuquerque, N.M.
26. *Jerry Perkins, lhp, Wirt HS, Miller, Ind.
27. *Gene Salmon, 1b, Del Rio (Texas) HS.
28. Steve McMillan, 2b, Cerritos (Calif.) JC.
29. Roger Spagnuolo, ss, Sexton HS, Lansing, Mich.
30. *Larry Kiser, lhp, Dobyns-Bennett HS, Kingsport, Tenn.
31. *Mike Pietrantonio, ss, Bordentown (N.J.) Military Academy.
32. *Dan Pastorini, ss, Bellarmine Prep HS, San Jose, Calif.

DRAFT DROP *First-round draft pick, Houston Oilers/National Football League (1971); quarterback, NFL (1971-83)*

33. Del Corral, of, Foothill (Calif.) JC.
34. *William Luftig, ss, Wantagh (N.Y.) HS.
35. *Bill Olsen, lhp, Eureka (Calif.) HS.
36. David Lipp, 2b, Mount Tahoma HS, Tacoma, Wash.
37. John Bachman, c, Edison Tech HS, Rochester, N.Y.
38. **David Schneck, lhp-of, Whitehall (Pa.) HS.—(1972-74)**
39. Mark Crandall, lhp, Washington State University.
40. (void) *Robert Thomas, 1b, Dartmouth College.
41. Joseph Abene, 3b, Hillsborough HS, Tampa.
42. *Ken Henderson, 1b, Long Beach (N.Y.) HS.
43. *Robert Larson, rhp-ss, Alhambra (Calif.) HS.
44. *Melvin McNeil, of, Grambling University.
45. *Mike Swenton, of, Ward HS, Kansas City, Kan.
46. *Frank Alfano, ss, Crawford HS, San Diego.
47. Allen Clements, rhp, University of Texas.
48. *Roy Myers, 3b, Youngstown State University.
49. *James Bergholtz, ss, Hicksville (N.Y.) HS.
50. **Tom Robson, 1b, Utah State University.—(1974-75)**
51. Frank Ujcich, rhp, Wellsburg, W.Va.

52. *George Carter, of, St. Bonaventure University.
DRAFT DROP *13th-round draft pick, Buffalo Bills/ National Football League (1967)*
53. *Harry Saferight, c, Meadowbrook HS, Richmond, Va.
54. Martin Gearhart, of, Xenia (Ohio) HS.
55. Gary Coombs, lhp, Cordova HS, Rancho Cordova, Calif.
56. *William Seyfert, 1b, Newfield HS, Selden, N.Y.
57. Charles Merlo, ss, Morehead State University.
58. *Robert Shearer, of, Newport (Ky.) HS.
59. *Timothy Uraskevich, rhp, SUNY-Buffalo.
60. Richard Shelly, c, Zanesville (Ohio) HS.

**June—Secondary Phase (20)**

1. **Rich Folkers, lhp, Parsons (Iowa) College.—(1970-77)**
2. **Rod Gaspar, of, Long Beach State University.—(1969-74)**
DRAFT DROP *Father of Cade Gaspar, first-round draft pick, Tigers (1994)*
3. **Gary Gentry, rhp, Arizona State University.—(1969-75)**
4. Steve Brasher, rhp, University of Arizona.
5. Ronald Matney, lhp, Sam Houston State University.
6. *Neil Pittman, rhp, University of Missouri.
7. *Jim Brown, lhp, Arizona State University.
8. **Rich Hacker, ss, Southern Illinois University.—(1971)**
9. Buzz Nitschke, c, Fresno State University.
10. *William Maxwell, rhp, Oklahoma State University.
11. *Franklin Riggins, of-lhp, University of Kansas.
12. Sam Narron, c, East Carolina University.
DRAFT DROP *Son of Sam Narron, major leaguer (1935-43) • Cousin of Jerry Narron, major leaguer (1979-87); major league manager, (2001-06) • Father of Sam Narron, major leaguer (2004-05)*
13. Rick Senger, c, CC of Baltimore.
14. *Reid Braden, 1b-of, University of Southern California.

## NEW YORK YANKEES

**January—Regular Phase (2)**

1. *Michael Flanagan, lhp, Yakima Valley (Wash.) JC.—(AA)
2. Charles Burton, rhp, Dallas Baptist College.
3. *Michael Bertrand, c, Columbia Basin (Wash.) CC.
4. *Ken Carmack, rhp, Yakima Valley (Wash.) JC.
5. *Stanley Sass, c-3b, Skagit Valley (Wash.) CC.
6. *Gary Sauer, lhp, Columbia Basin (Wash.) CC.

**January—Secondary Phase (20)**

1. Harry Wright, of, University of Pennsylvania.—(Low A)
2. *Bruce Wade, rhp, El Camino (Calif.) JC.
3. **Terry Ley, lhp, Clark (Wash.) JC.—(1971)**
4. *William Shepherd, rhp, Columbia Basin (Wash.) CC.
5. James Babyak, ss, Westfield State (Mass.) College.
6. *Al Simmons, rhp, University of Idaho.
7. Patrick Hartigan, rhp, Columbia Basin (Wash.) CC.
8. *Wayne Danson, Gulf Coast (Fla.) CC.

**June—Regular Phase (1)**

1. **Ron Blomberg, 1b, Druid Hills HS, Atlanta.—(1969-78)**
DRAFT DROP *First designated hitter, major leagues (1973)*
2. Alfonzo Neal, 3b, Womack HS, Longview, Texas.—(High A)
DRAFT DROP *Son of Charlie Neal, major leaguer (1956-63)*
3. Jimmy Yawn, 2b, University of Mississippi.—(AA)
4. **Larry Gowell, rhp, Edward Little HS, Auburn, Maine.—(1972)**
5. Billy Barlow, c-3b, Kingsbury HS, Memphis, Tenn.—(AA)
6. *Tim Feldhaus, inf, Bonita HS, La Verne, Calif.
7. Philip Ranneberger, of-rhp, Frederick HS, Buckeystown, Md.
8. Stanton Evenhus, rhp, Eastmont HS, Rock Island, Wash.
9. Robert Carson, inf, Federal Way (Wash.) HS.
10. Les Gibbens, lhp, Vallivue HS, Caldwell, Idaho.
11. *Donnie Davis, 3b, Pascagoula (Miss.) HS.
12. Brian Engle, ss, Lewiston (Idaho) HS.
13. *Michael Gomez, rhp, University HS, Spokane, Wash.
14. Daniel Bohannon, ss, Stagg HS, Stockton, Calif.
15. **Jim Deidel, c, Mullen HS, Denver.—(1974)**
16. Craig Fellows, rhp, Fort Hamilton HS, Brooklyn, N.Y.
17. David Gunderman, 2b-ss, Mater Dei HS, Fullerton, Calif.
18. *Richard Cross, ss, Carson HS, Torrance, Calif.
19. *Michael Ball, 3b, Hoover HS, San Diego.
20. Gerald Wickman, lhp, University of Minnesota.
21. *Daniel Bina, rhp, West Salem (Wis.) HS.
22. *Robert Vaught, rhp, Santa Ana (Calif.) JC.
23. Barney Scholl, of, Chapman (Calif.) College.
24. Richard Ordway, rhp, University of Maine.
25. Joseph Gill, of, University of San Francisco.
26. *Ronald Watts, lhp, Wichita West HS, Wichita, Kan.
27. Thomas Porthen, rhp, Foster HS, Riverton Heights, Wash.
28. **Loyd Colson, rhp-inf, Bacone (Okla.) JC.—(1970)**
29. Robert Hefflinger, 1b, Cleveland HS, Portland, Ore.
30. Ken Johnson, rhp, University of Idaho.
31. *Douglas Braun, c, Salinas (Calif.) JC.
32. Willie Elmore, c, Livingston (Ala.) University.
33. *Tommy Monroe, c, Shades Valley HS, Birmingham, Ala.
34. *Michael Baier, ss, Calvert Hall HS, Baltimore.
35. *David Gonzalez, ss, St. Augustine HS, San Diego.
36. *Jerry McCollough, of-1b, La Puente (Calif.) HS.
37. Walter Peto, ss, Seton Hall University.
38. Joseph Hindelang, rhp, Temple University.
39. *James Corcoran, ss, Gonzaga Prep HS, Spokane, Wash.
40. *Jerre Algeo, inf, Central HS, Springfield, Mo.
41. *John Wiley, rhp, Lincoln HS, Portland, Ore.
42. Nelson Straley, c, Bishop Montgomery HS, Hawthorne, Calif.
43. ***Mike Reinbach, of, Granite Hills HS, El Cajon, Calif.—(1974)**
44. *Dana Ryan, 2b, Arkansas State University.
45. ***Sam Ewing, 1b-of, Overton HS, Nashville, Tenn.—(1973-78)**
46. Gerry Vanaman, 2b, Chapman (Calif.) College.
47. *Dennis Gideon, lhp, Chaffey (Calif.) JC.
48. Jerry Schultz, 2b-3b, University of North Dakota.
49. *Walter Failor, rhp-1b, Aberdeen (Wash.) HS.
50. Denis Murray, lhp, Cal Poly Pomona.
51. Jeffery Mason, ss, Deerfield (Ill.) HS.
52. Dale Braumberger, rhp, Cal Poly Pomona.
53. *Atheophilus Jermany, rhp, Roosevelt HS, Portland, Ore.
54. *Randy Nelson, 3b, Magnolia HS, Anaheim, Calif.
55. *Randy Vataha, ss, Rancho Alamitos HS, Garden Grove, Calif.
DRAFT DROP *Wide receiver, National Football League (1971-77)*
56. Andrew Bottin, of-1b, Meadowdale HS, Edmonds, Wash.
57. Donald Keeler, 1b, Snohomish (Wash.) HS.
58. Craig Keister, lhp, Marysville (Wash.) HS.
59. *Gerald Bosch, of, CC of San Francisco.
60. ***Steve Rogers, rhp, Glendale HS, Springfield, Mo.—(1973-85)**
61. Michael Fowler, lhp, Columbia HS, Richland, Wash.
62. *Steve Wiencek, ss, Claremont (Calif.) HS.
63. Paul Branca, c, Brentwood (N.Y.) HS.
64. *John Pavlik, of, Springfield (Ore.) HS.
65. *Charles Zecco, lhp, Burlington HS, Edgewater Park, N.J.
66. *Frank Whigham, ss, Seminole HS, Sanford, Fla.
67. **Roger Hambright, rhp, Columbia River HS, Vancouver, Wash.—(1971)**
68. *Wayne Stephens, ss, Charter Oaks HS, Covina, Calif.
69. *Michael Hunt, rhp, Kennewick (Wash.) HS.
70. *Kelly Godfrey, rhp-of, South Hills HS, Covina, Calif.
71. *Larry McClenny, rhp, Shadle Park HS, Spokane, Wash.
72. *Michael Bubalo, of-1b, Lincoln HS, Portland, Ore.
73. *Robert Scott, c, Rossville (Ga.) HS.
74. Thomas Gill, ss, St. Francis (N.Y.) College.
75. *Greg Wellman, lhp, Forest Hills HS, West Palm Beach, Fla.
76. David Walsh, ss, Enterprise HS, Redding, Calif.
77. Donald Van Deusen, ss, Concord (W.Va.) College.

**June—Secondary Phase (9)**

1. Charles Lelas, 1b-of, Springfield (Mass.) College.—(High A)
2. **Frank Baker, ss, University of Southern Mississippi.—(1970-74)**
3. *Ron Davini, c, Arizona State University.
4. Gary Washington, 1b, Mississippi State University.
5. Bruce Baudier, rhp, Louisiana State University.
6. William Shepherd, rhp, Columbia Basin (Wash.) CC.
7. **Gerry Pirtle, rhp, Bacone (Okla.) JC.—(1978)**
8. ***Norm Angelini, lhp, JC of San Mateo (Calif.).—(1972-73)**
9. (void) *Rich Donnelly, c, Xavier University.
10. *Harold Werntz, rhp, Temple University.
11. *Steve Sharp, rhp, University of Missouri.
12. Al Simmons, rhp, University of Idaho.

## PHILADELPHIA PHILLIES

**January—Regular Phase (13)**

1. Michael Coble, rhp, Long Beach (Calif.) CC.—(AA)
2. **Buck Martinez, c, Sacramento (Calif.) CC.—(1969-86)**
DRAFT DROP *Major league manager (2001-02)*

**January—Secondary Phase (15)**

1. Pat Skrable, of, Bakersfield (Calif.) JC.—(AAA)
2. Ernest Aguirre, inf, Bakersfield (Calif.) JC.
3. ***Darrell Evans, 3b-rhp, Pasadena (Calif.) CC.—(1969-89)**
4. *Stephen Smith, 3b, Poly HS, Long Beach, Calif.
5. *Richard Corsetto, rhp-of, Harford (Md.) CC.

**June—Regular Phase (14)**

1. Phil Meyer, lhp, Pius X HS, Downey, Calif.—(AAA)
2. Larry Keener, rhp, Wheeler HS, Marietta, Ga.—(Low A)
3. Bob McLachlin, lhp, Tenafly (N.J.) HS.—(High A)
4. Nicholas Graybeal, c, Tennessee HS, Bristol, Tenn.—(Short-season A)
5. *Red Daniels, of, Las Cruces (N.M.) HS.—(AA)
DRAFT DROP *Attended New Mexico; re-drafted by Dodgers, June 1970/secondary phase (3rd round)*
6. *Terry Mathias, ss, Clear Creek HS, League City, Texas.
7. Bruce Hotchkiss, of, Ellsworth (Iowa) JC.
8. Robert Stevens, lhp, St. Viator HS, Mount Prospect, Ill.
9. *Michael Schomaker, of-c, Stanford University.
10. Terry Howarth, 1b, Westchester (Calif.) HS.
11. Donald Thomson, rhp, Newell (Iowa) HS.
12. Frank Odum, c, Jesup HS, Odum, Ga.
13. Dennis Davies, c, Murray (Utah) HS.
14. *Eugene Stack, rhp, Harding HS, Oklahoma City, Okla.
15. Jose Sanchez, rhp, Coachella Valley HS, Indio, Calif.
16. Jeff Beattie, rhp, Warwick (N.Y.) HS.
17. Henry Jacquez, of, Amos Alonzo Stagg HS, Stockton, Calif.
18. Robert Kenny, rhp, Parsons (Iowa) College.
19. Joseph Anderson, of, Rahway HS, Winfield Park, N.J.
20. *John Maczuga, of, Franklin (N.J.) HS.
21. *Milton Jackson, rhp, University of Tulsa.
22. *Don Keenan, c, Pensacola (Fla.) HS.
23. Kenneth Bangsberg, lhp, San Diego Mesa CC.
24. Anthony Giresi, lhp, Fair Lawn (N.J.) HS.

**June—Secondary Phase (18)**

1. *Doug Sandstedt, lhp, Benson HS, Omaha, Neb.—(High A)
2. **Scott Reid, of, Arizona State University.—(1969-70)**
DRAFT DROP *Scouting director, Cubs (1986-87)*
3. Bob Leatherwood, 2b, University of California.
4. *Tom Cook, c, Manatee (Fla.) JC.
5. *Steve Smith, ss-3b, Long Beach (Calif.) CC.
6. Jim Magnuson, of, University of California.

## PITTSBURGH PIRATES

**January—Regular Phase (15)**

1. *Ronald Ritter, rhp, Shelby HS, Shelbyville, Ky.—DNP
2. *Joe Staton, 1b-of, Seattle (Wash.) CC.
3. *Edward Lemmon, rhp-inf, Robert Morris (Ill.) College.
4. *Dick Wieczezak, 3b, Seton Hall University.
5. David Etter, 1b, Chambersburg (Pa.) Area HS.
6. Bobby Herring, rhp, Gainesville (Ga.) JC.

**January—Secondary Phase (13)**

1. *Kris Krebs, ss, Manatee (Fla.) JC.—(AAA)
2. James Minette, inf, Columbia Basin (Wash.) CC.
3. *Frank Brennan, rhp, Fairleigh Dickinson University.
4. *Richard Wanless, rhp, North Quincy (Mass.) HS.
5. *Bill Tsoukalas, lhp, Everett (Wash.) CC.
6. *Cliff Farmer, rhp, Hillcrest HS, Springfield, Mo.

**June—Regular Phase (16)**

1. Joe Grigas, of, Coyle HS, Brockton, Mass.—(Low A)
2. Alvin Sells, rhp, Sullivan HS, Kingsport, Tenn.—(AA)
3. **Richie Zisk, of, Parsippany (N.J.) HS.—(1971-83)**
4. Mike Roberts, 3b, Mount Eden HS, Hayward, Calif.—(Rookie)
5. Bill McBrayer, ss, Williamson (W.Va.) HS.—(High A)
6. Harry Tobergte, rhp, Badin HS, Hamilton, Ohio.
7. Dennis Vaughn, c, Los Gatos (Calif.) HS.
8. John Landry, 1b, Istrouma HS, Baton Rouge, La.
9. Ted Taylor, 3b-of, Florida A&M University.
10. Darrell Brown, ss-3b, East Bank HS, Handley, W.Va.
11. William Spikes, of, Central Memorial HS, Bogalusa, La.
DRAFT DROP *Brother of Charlie Spikes, first-round draft pick, Yankees (1969); major leaguer (1972-80)*
12. Garry Helms, ss, Clemson University.
13. Meredith Cox, rhp, Centennial HS, Compton, Calif.
14. Tom Saunches, c, DuQuoin (Ill.) HS.
15. Tyrone Hines, ss, Mount Pleasant HS, Schenectady, N.Y.
16. Charles Malitz, of-1b, Texas A&M University.
17. Howard Deacon, c, Wayland (Mass.) HS.
18. Paul Strauch, rhp, Danvers (Mass.) HS.
19. *Jack Burns, of-rhp, George Washington HS, Denver.
20. Paul Keany, 3b, University of Maine.
21. James Iglehart, of, Castlemont HS, Oakland, Calif.
22. *Michael Derrig, lhp, Lincoln-Way HS, Makena, Ill.
23. *George Arnott, 2b, Santa Cruz (Calif.) HS.
24. *James Topping, lhp, Maine Central Institute, Lewiston, Maine.
25. *Dave Rose, rhp, San Carlos (Calif.) HS.
26. *Lee Lamb, rhp, Bremen HS, Midlothian, Ill.
27. *Donald Schroeder, rhp, Long HS, Longview, Wash.
28. *Donald Barnes, rhp, Marietta (Ohio) HS.
29. Lewis Green, ss, Healdsburg (Calif.) HS.
30. J.T. Ingram, rhp, Dos Palos (Calif.) HS.
31. Terry Gardner, rhp, McNary HS, Salem, Ore.
32. *Lyle Wilber, rhp, Goldendale (Wash.) HS.
33. *Don Anderson, rhp, Pennington Prep HS, Westfield, N.J.
34. *Jerry Vitatoe, 3b-of, St. Joseph's HS, Oakland, Calif.
35. Perry Dunn, ss-3b, Blanchard HS, Augusta, Ga.
36. *Tommy Grayson, inf, Guilford (N.C.) College.
37. **Lorenzo Lanier, of, John Adams HS, Cleveland.—(1971)**
38. *Bob Auriegemma, rhp, South City HS, San Francisco.
39. Daryl French, rhp, Bainbridge HS, Winslow, Wash.

40. *Danny Brown, 2b, Benton HS, St. Joseph, Mo.
41. *William Hager, lhp, West Allegheny HS, Imperial, Pa.
42. *Edward Perry, of-1b, Bethlehem Central HS, Delmar, N.Y.

**June—Secondary Phase (12)**

**1. *John Morlan, of, Ohio University.—(1973-74)**
2. *Mike Lisetski, ss, Rider College.
3. Doug Carson, c, Santa Clara University.
4. Frank Brennan, rhp, Fairleigh Dickinson University.
5. Tom Buchenberger, rhp, St. John's University.
6. *Taylor Toomey, lhp, University of Colorado.
**7. *Rick Austin, lhp, Washington State University.—(1970-76)**
8. *Edward Mantie, rhp, Syracuse University.
**9. *Tom Dettore, rhp, Juniata (Pa.) College.—(1973-76)**

## ST. LOUIS CARDINALS

**January—Regular Phase (9)**

1. Fred Grooms, rhp, Wilson HS, San Francisco.—(High A)
2. *Doug Sandstedt, lhp, Benson HS, Omaha, Neb.
3. *Ronald Lemery, c, Jefferson (Mo.) HS.
4. *Jackie Creel, rhp, Gulf Coast (Fla.) CC.

**January—Secondary Phase (9)**

1. *Jim Scheschuk, c, University of Texas.—(Short-season A)
2. *Stephen Dean, 1b, JC of the Sequoias (Calif.).
3. *Clarence Cleveland, rhp, Chipola (Fla.) JC.
4. *Tom Cook, c, Manatee (Fla.) JC.
5. Bruce Hinkel, lhp, Marquette, Iowa.

**June—Regular Phase (10)**

**1. Ted Simmons, c-of, Southfield (Mich.) HS.—(1968-88)**
DRAFT DROP *General manager, Pirates (1992-93)*
**2. Jerry Reuss, lhp, Ritenour HS, Overland, Mo.—(1969-90)**
**3. *Bart Johnson, rhp, Torrance (Calif.) HS.—(1969-77)**
DRAFT DROP *Attended Brigham Young; re-drafted by White Sox, June 1968/secondary phase (1st round)*
4. Ron McCollum, c, Shaker HS, Latham, N.Y.—(Low A)
5. *Matt Sterling, rhp, Thomas Jefferson HS, Denver.
DRAFT DROP *Attended Wyoming; never re-drafted*
6. *Paul Womble, ss, Wyandotte HS, Kansas City, Kan.
7. John Polovina, rhp, St. Francis HS, Altadena, Calif.
8. Larry Koch, rhp, Nassau (N.Y.) CC.
9. *James Braxton, 1b-of, Connellsville (Pa.) HS.
**10. *Lenny Randle, ss, Centennial HS, Compton, Calif.—(1971-82)**
11. Alfred Buchta, rhp, New York University.
12. Jeffrey Ice, rhp, Treadwell HS, Memphis, Tenn.
13. *Raymond Wood, of-1b, Central HS, Omaha, Neb.
14. *William Kelly, rhp-1b, Reading (Mass.) HS.
15. David Polcari, of, Medford (Mass.) HS.
16. Mel Pettigrew, of, Hanford Union HS, Hanford, Calif.
17. John Carroll, rhp, Fordham University.
18. Ronnie Roberts, lhp, Hay Long HS, Mount Pleasant, Tenn.
19. *Richard Wilson, rhp, Milliken HS, Long Beach, Calif.
20. *Thomas Dunn, 1b, Arroyo HS, San Lorenzo, Calif.
21. Stanley Dyson, 3b-of, Santa Fe HS, Santa Fe Springs, Calif.
22. John Howard, 1b-lhp, Assumption HS, East St. Louis, Ill.
23. Glenn Marshall, 1b, Los Angeles (Calif.) HS.
24. Bob Richardson, rhp, Weymouth (Mass.) HS.
25. Freddie Jamison, rhp, Carver HS, Memphis, Tenn.
26. Thomas Kuczynski, lhp-of, Braintree (Mass.) HS.
27. Paul Kacera, 3b, Granite City (Ill.) HS.
28. Bob Bonalewicz, c, Parsons (Iowa) College.
29. James Scieres, c, Arkansas State University.
30. *Wesley Rutledge, rhp, Troy State University.
31. *Randolph Siebert, rhp, Glendale (Calif.) HS.
32. *Richard McHale, lhp, Villa Park (Calif.) HS.
**33. *Pat Osburn, lhp-1b, Clearwater (Fla.) HS.—(1974-75)**
34. *Joel Hall, c, Waukegan (Ill.) HS.
35. *Orlando Ortega, of, Cypress (Calif.) JC.
36. Freddie Smith, c, Jefferson HS, Los Angeles.
37. *Mark Driscoll, 2b, Arlington (Mass.) HS.
38. Benny Haynie, rhp, Northeast Mississippi JC.
39. *Richard Householder, ss-of, Fontana (Calif.) HS.
40. Richard Rix, of, University Lake HS, Hartland, Wis.
41. *Malcolm Beard, ss, Dartmouth College.
42. *Robert Olszewski, of, St. Anthony HS, Long Beach, Calif.

**June—Secondary Phase (10)**

1. Jimmie Jackson, lhp, Grambling University.—(AA)
2. *Charlie West, of, University of Texas-El Paso.
DRAFT DROP *Defensive back, National Football League (1968-79)*
3. Phil Trombino, 1b, Iona College.
4. *Stephen Steitz, lhp-of, Worchester (Mass.) Academy.
**5. Bob Chlupsa, rhp, Manhattan University.—(1970-71)**
DRAFT DROP *13th-round draft pick, San Diego Rockets/ National Basketball Association (1967)*
6. Jerry Sabourin, lhp, St. Louis.
7. *William Holt, lhp, Lynchburg (Va.) College.
8. *Phil O'Neil, of, Holy Cross College.

## SAN FRANCISCO GIANTS

**January—Regular Phase (17)**

**1. *Von Joshua, of, Chabot (Calif.) JC.—(1969-80)**
**2. *Brent Strom, lhp, San Diego (Calif.) CC.—(1972-77)**
3. Fred Fegen, c, University of San Francisco.
4. *William Price, of, Fremont HS, Los Angeles.

**January—Secondary Phase (5)**

1. *Marv Galliher, inf, San Diego Mesa JC.—(AAA)
2. *John Dow, of, Bemidji, Minn.
3. *Ray Strable, rhp, JC of the Sequoias (Calif.).
4. *Bobby Garcia, of-rhp, JC of the Sequoias (Calif.).
5. *Daniel Blood, 2b, Citrus (Calif.) JC.
6. (void) *Jim Magnuson, c-of, JC of San Mateo (Calif.).
7. *Michael Pruett, lhp, Overland, Mo.

**June—Regular Phase (18)**

**1. Dave Rader, c, South Bakersfield (Calif.) HS.—(1971-80)**
2. Michael Roby, 1b, East Waterloo (Iowa) HS.—(Short-season A)
**3. Don Carrithers, rhp, Lyndale HS, Lynwood, Calif.—(1970-77)**
**4. *Steve Busby, rhp, Fullerton (Calif.) HS.—(1972-80)**
DRAFT DROP *Attended Southern California; re-drafted by Royals, June 1971/secondary phase, delayed (2nd round)*
5. *Marty Pfenninger, ss, Hunterdon Central HS, Flemington, N.J.—(Rookie)
DRAFT DROP *Attended Temple; re-drafted by Orioles, June 1970 (36th round)*
6. Mike Welker, lhp, Pleasant Valley HS, Chico, Calif.
7. *Larry Price, of, Coachella Valley HS, Coachella, Calif.
**8. *Davey Lopes, of, Washburn (Kan.) University.—(1972-87)**
DRAFT DROP *Major league manager (2000-02)*
9. *James Gasbarro, inf, Catholic Memorial HS, Hyde Park, Mass.
10. *Robert Tate, ss, Bacone (Okla.) HS.
**11. Jim Willoughby, rhp, Gustine (Calif.) HS.—(1971-78)**
12. Osvaldo Bosch, of, Haaren HS, New York.
13. Rosendo Cedeno, 1b-of, DeWitt Clinton HS, Bronx, N.Y.
14. Gene Cook, 2b, Redondo Beach (Calif.) HS.
15. *Pat Westley, ss, North HS, Phoenix.
16. Anthony Ketelsleger, rhp, Rio Hondo (Calif.) JC.
17. *Gary Houston, lhp, James Lick HS, San Jose, Calif.
18. Freddie Glass, rhp, University of Alabama.
19. Larry Iten, c, Calexico (Calif.) HS.
**20. Gary Lavelle, lhp, Liberty HS, Bethlehem, Pa.—(1974-87)**
21. Van Fixico, 2b, Bacone (Okla.) JC.
22. Garry Pinnow, of-1b, University of Wisconsin.
23. *Dan Guerrero, c, El Rancho HS, Pico Rivera, Calif.
24. *Glen Davis, 2b, North HS, Phoenix.
25. *John Floyd, 1b, Gordo (Ala.) HS.
26. *Bobby Wade, c, University of Mississippi.
27. *Martin Downen, rhp, Brigham Young University.
28. *Gregory Yarbrough, lhp, Shaw (Miss.) HS.
**29. *Rick Sawyer, rhp, Bakersfield (Calif.) JC.—(1974-77)**
30. *Donald Elam, rhp, San Francisco State University.
31. Michael Newsom, inf-rhp, Western HS, Las Vegas, Nev.
32. *Robert Huddelston, of, Catalina HS, Tucson, Ariz.
33. David Voss, 1b, Wilson HS, Tacoma, Wash.
34. Jeff Campbell, rhp, Livingston (Ala.) University.
35. *Wayne Mitchell, of, Richmond Union HS, Richmond, Calif.
36. Leonard Cargill, rhp, Fresno (Calif.) CC.
37. *Vache Bahadurian, 1b, Forest Hills (N.Y.) HS.
38. Robert Kenney, rhp, Rutgers University.
39. *Donald Weber, lhp, Highland Park HS, St. Paul, Minn.
40. *John Terista, ss, Ithaca (N.Y.) College.
41. *Bob Graczyk, rhp, Proviso West HS, Bellwood, Ill.
42. Douglas Theriault, lhp, Puyallup (Wash.) HS.
43. *Michael Miller, 1b, West Chester (Pa.) HS.
44. *Mickey Cureton, of, Centennial HS, Compton, Calif.
45. *Dave Gillette, c-of, Alhambra HS, Phoenix.
46. Marty Coil, 1b, San Francisco State University.
47. *Lynn Sparks, lhp, Cal State Chico.
48. *Gary Shade, 2b, Reynoldsburg (Ohio) HS.
49. Joe Wischnowski, rhp, Illinois State University.

**June—Secondary Phase (16)**

**1. Bobby Fenwick, ss, University of Minnesota.—(1972-73)**
**2. *Ken Hottman, of, Sacramento (Calif.) CC.—(1971)**
**3. Jim Johnson, lhp-of, Western Michigan University.—(1970)**
4. Earl Vickers, of, Fresno State University.
5. *Tom Brown, ss, University of Miami.
6. *Mike Willis, lhp, University of Colorado.
7. Jack Fulmer, 3b, Arkansas State University.
**8. *Chuck Scrivener, ss, CC of Baltimore.—(1975-77)**
9. *Jerald Hurt, rhp, University of Missouri.
10. *Arthur Pauls, rhp, Lewis (Ill.) University.

## WASHINGTON SENATORS

**January—Regular Phase (6)**

1. Robert Stach, 1b, Southern HS, West River, Md.—(AA)

**January—Secondary Phase (8)**

**1. Jan Dukes, lhp, Santa Clara University.—(1969-72)**
2. *Gary Washington, 1b, Mississippi State University.
3. *Ray Henningsen, 2b, Santa Clara University.
4. *Michael Weber, lhp, Southern Illinois University-Edwardsville.
5. *Sam Narron, c, East Carolina University.
DRAFT DROP *Son of Sam Narron, major leaguer (1935-43) • Cousin of Jerry Narron, major leaguer (1979-87); major league manager, Texas Rangers (2001-06) • Father of Sam Narron, major leaguer (2004-05)*
6. *Lamar Davis, 1b, University of Maryland.
7. *Charlie Watson, lhp, Clemson University.
8. (void) *Terry L'Ange, rhp, University of Missouri.

**June—Regular Phase (5)**

1. Johnny Jones, c, Loretto HS, St. Joseph, Tenn.—(High A)
2. Dexter Baker, lhp-of, St. Catherine's HS, Racine, Wis.—(High A)
**3. Mike Thompson, rhp, Ponca City (Okla.) HS.—(1971-75)**
4. *Ken Caldwell, 3b, Mecklenburg HS, Huntersville, N.C.—(AA)
DRAFT DROP *Attended South Carolina; never re-drafted*
**5. Ike Brookens, rhp, Chambersburg HS, Fayetteville, Pa.—(1975)**
DRAFT DROP *Cousin of Tom Brookens, major leaguer (1979-90)*
6. Michael Schooff, lhp, Woodbridge (Va.) HS.
7. Melvin Lowe, of, Lakewood (N.J.) HS.
8. *Thomas Elgin, lhp, North Hagerstown (Md.) HS.
9. *Chris Cammack, 3b, Fayetteville (N.C.) HS.
10. Robert Koehler, rhp, Rider College.
**11. Rich Stelmaczek, c, Mendel Catholic HS, Chicago.—(1971-74)**
12. *Rick Eisenacher, rhp, Albert Einstein HS, Wheaton, Md.
13. Wayne Stack, ss, St. John's University.
**14. *Ray Bare, rhp, Southwest HS, Miami.—(1972-77)**
15. *Joseph Frye, rhp, Fairmont (N.C.) HS.
16. *Bruce Kinder, ss, Broward (Fla.) CC.
17. Robert George, lhp, Brooklyn Park HS, Baltimore.
18. Gordon Steinbach, of, Ripon (Wis.) College.
19. *Richard Astor, 3b, New Brunswick HS, Milltown, N.J.
20. Dale Gambill, 2b-rhp, Clearwater (Fla.) HS.
21. Gary Carter, rhp, Brunswick (Md.) HS.
22. Jeffrey Drexler, rhp, Oshkosh (Wis.) HS.
23. Roger Sheridan, of, Quincy (Ill.) College.
24. Thomas Worthington, 3b, Fairmont East HS, Kettering, Ohio.
25. *Ralph Owens, ss, Falls Church (Va.) HS.
26. *Lyle Edwards, of, Western Carolina University.
27. Richard Bechtel, ss-2b, Rider College.
28. *Howard Williams, 3b, Garfield HS, Terre Haute, Ind.
29. Robert Corwin, c, Little Miami HS, Morrow, Ohio.
30. *Donald Burkhalter, rhp, Pensacola (Fla.) HS.
31. Dale Hillard, c-of, Clinton-Massie HS, Clarksville, Ohio.
32. Dick Baldwin, of, Bradley University.
33. *Edwin Mossman, 3b, William Chrisman HS, Independence, Mo.
34. George Hubal, rhp, Trenton Catholic HS, Trenton, N.J.
35. Delbert Marcus, c, Elkton (Md.) HS.
**36. Bobby Jones, 1b, Elkton (Md.) HS.—(1974-86)**
37. *Frank Fillman, lhp, DuVal HS, Lanham, Md.
38. Lawrence Mischik, lhp, Rider College.
39. *William Metcalf, lhp, Ripon (Wis.) College.
40. *William Wood, rhp, Warren County HS, Front Royal, Va.
41. Terry Brecher, ss, Western Illinois University.
**42. John Wockenfuss, 3b-rhp, Dickinson HS, Wilmington, Del.—(1974-85)**

**June—Secondary Phase (7)**

1. Gary Ratliff, of, Bacone (Okla.) JC.—(AAA)
2. Larry Herring, lhp, Baptist (S.C.) College.
**3. *Paul Reuschel, rhp, Western Illinois University.—(1975-79)**
DRAFT DROP *Brother of Rick Reuschel, major leaguer (1972-91)*
4. *Edward Cook, of, Bridgewater (Va.) College.
5. *Rick Konik, 1b, Detroit.
DRAFT DROP *First-round draft pick (14th overall), Tigers (1966)*
6. *Richard Hicks, rhp, Louisiana State University.
7. *Billy Martin, of, Randolph-Macon (Va.) University.
8. *Don Kirkland, rhp, Southern Illinois University.

# 1968

# Dodgers' class stands as best in draft annals

Bill Buckner, Tom Paciorek and Steve Garvey (from left to right) were among the 15 major leaguers Dodgers scouts found in the 1968 drafts

Baseball's draft was still in its infancy in 1968, a mere toddler of three. Al Campanis, then scouting director for the Los Angeles Dodgers, didn't know quite yet how to treat it, so he went to someone who did.

The National Football League had staged a draft for 32 years, and Campanis figured he could learn something there. He called on San Diego Chargers coach Sid Gillman, who handed him off to Al LoCasale, then in charge of San Diego's draft.

"He actually showed me how to draft," Campanis said of LoCasale, who later became the right-hand man of Los Angeles Raiders owner Al Davis. "He explained the difference between drafting the best athlete and going for need. He showed us how to rank players on a scale of 100 based on fundamental skills. He took a neophyte and taught me how to approach a draft and I think this helped us."

To their checklist of available players, Campanis and his staff added extra weight for intangibles, including mental toughness and the desire to win.

"We told our scouts to look for the cream," Campanis said. "We didn't just want a major league prospect. We wanted a Dodgers prospect. They learned to look out for the very best."

The Dodgers' approach bore fruit quickly. Out of the 1968 draft came such names as Garvey and Cey, Lopes and Buckner, Valentine and Paciorek, Zahn and Alexander. In all, the Dodgers selected a then-record 15 players (12 in June, three in January) who would play in the big leagues. It was no ordinary bunch, either, as they mined the nucleus of Dodgers championship teams for years to come in this draft.

No team in the draft's history may ever have extracted more talent from one crop.

Three of the players, first baseman Steve Garvey, second baseman Davey Lopes and third baseman Roy Cey, would eventually combine with shortstop Bill Russell—a product of the Dodgers' 1966 draft, another significant haul—to spend almost nine

## AT A GLANCE

### This Date In History

**WINTER DRAFT:** Jan. 27
**SUMMER DRAFT:** June 6-7

### Best Draft

**LOS ANGELES DODGERS.** With a 15-player haul that included the likes of Garvey, Cey, Lopes, Buckner, Ferguson, Valentine, Paciorek and Alexander, the Dodgers had a draft for the ages.

### Worst Draft

**OAKLAND ATHLETICS.** The A's got off on the wrong foot in the June regular phase when they failed to sign their first two picks, and four of their first six. They also didn't sign a future big leaguer in the first 25 rounds. This draft signaled the beginning of a downturn for the A's farm system.

### First-Round Bust

**MARTY COTT, C, ASTROS.** Cott, the third player drafted in the June regular phase, had a two-game cameo in Triple-A in his first pro season. It never got any better, and his career fell apart in Class A in 1970, at age 19.

### On Second Thought

**CHARLIE DUDISH, SS/OF, GIANTS.** Dudish was taken in the second round by the Giants, but would have gone early in the first had he not been such a prized football recruit. His career as a quarterback at Georgia Tech quickly fizzled amid injuries and suspensions. Dudish tried baseball after being drafted again in 1971 by the Padres, and then again with the Braves in 1973, but neither was successful.

### Late-Round Finds

**KEN FORSCH, RHP, ASTROS (18TH ROUND)/ BOB FORSCH, RHP/3B, CARDINALS (26TH ROUND).** The Forsch brothers each had 16-year major league careers, and between them won 282 games. They are also the

CONTINUED ON PAGE 68

## AT A GLANCE

CONTINUED FROM PAGE 67

only brother combo to throw no-hitters. Ken, drafted out of Oregon State, went 114-113 from 1970-86, while Bob went 168-136 from 1974-89 after signing out of a Sacramento high school.

### Never Too Late

**BOBBY SHELDON, SS, DODGERS (52ND ROUND).** A California high school product, Sheldon went to Loyola Marymount rather than signing with the Dodgers. He still became the latest 1969 draft to reach the majors as he was drafted by the Brewers in 1972 (22nd round) and spent parts of three seasons with that club.

### Overlooked

**ENOS CABELL, 1B, ORIOLES.** One of six 1968 free agents who reached the big leagues, the Los Angeles Harbor JC product signed with the Orioles for $2,500 but got his career break in 1974 when traded to Houston. He hit .281 with 45 homers and 191 stolen bases over the next eight seasons, playing mostly at third base. He spent 15 years in the majors.

### International Gem

**MANNY TRILLO, 2B, PHILLIES.** Signed by Philadelphia for $500 in 1968, the Venezuelan never played for the Phillies until 1979. He was selected from the Phillies by the A's in the 1969 minor league Rule 5 draft, and later traded to the Cubs. From there, he was traded again to the Phillies. Over a 17-year career, mostly as a second baseman, Trillo hit .263 with 61 homers.

### Minor League Take

**GREG LUZINSKI, OF, PHILLIES.** Dodgers first-rounder **BOBBY VALENTINE** won two MVP awards in three seasons on his ascent to the big leagues, but Luzinski, drafted six picks later, made a steadier step-by-step progression and posted louder

## 1968: THE FIRST ROUNDERS

| CLUB: PLAYER, POS., SCHOOL | HOMETOWN | B-T | HT. | WT. | AGE | BONUS | FIRST YEAR | LAST YEAR | PEAK LEVEL (YEARS) |
|---|---|---|---|---|---|---|---|---|---|
| **JUNE—REGULAR PHASE** | | | | | | | | | |
| 1. Mets: Tim Foli, ss, Notre Dame HS | Canoga Park, Calif. | R-R | 5-11 | 185 | 17 | $74,000 | 1968 | 1985 | Majors (16) |
| Journeyman shortstop spent 16 years in majors; dependable in field, hit just .251, with 25 home runs; driven player best-known for his fiery, combative personality. | | | | | | | | | |
| 2. Athletics: Pete Broberg, rhp, Palm Beach HS | Palm Beach, Fla. | R-R | 6-3 | 195 | 18 | Unsigned | 1971 | 1978 | Majors (8) |
| A's made futile attempt to sign Florida prep star set on Ivy League education; resurfaced in 1971 as No. 1 pick in June secondary phase, went straight to majors. | | | | | | | | | |
| 3. Astros: Marty Cott, c, Hutchinson Tech HS | Buffalo | L-R | 6-3 | 185 | 17 | $47,000 | 1968 | 1970 | Class AAA (1) |
| Astros looked for long-term solution behind plate, but he struggled offensively (.231), in field (38 errors, 23 passed balls), lasted just three seasons in minors. | | | | | | | | | |
| 4. Yankees: # Thurman Munson, c, Kent State | Canton, Ohio | R-R | 5-11 | 185 | 19 | $45,000 | 1968 | 1979 | Majors (11) |
| Heart and soul of Yankees, first team captain since Gehrig; won rookie, MVP awards, led team to consecutive World Series titles before untimely death in plane crash. | | | | | | | | | |
| 5. Dodgers: Bobby Valentine, of, Rippowam HS | Stamford, Conn. | R-R | 5-10 | 185 | 18 | $65,000 | 1968 | 1979 | Majors (10) |
| Proclaimed as next great Dodgers star, but never developed; career came crashing down with Angels when he badly hurt leg in collision with outfield fence. | | | | | | | | | |
| 6. Indians: Michael Weaver, ss, Paxon HS | Jacksonville, Fla. | L-R | 6-1 | 180 | 18 | $32,000 | 1968 | 1973 | Class AA (2) |
| Indians cut losses, released him out of spring training in 1974 after he hit nine homers, had just 123 RBIs in five seasons; played just 20 games above Class A. | | | | | | | | | |
| 7. Braves: # Curtis Moore, of, Denison HS | Denison, Texas | L-R | 6-1 | 180 | 18 | $12,500 | 1968 | 1974 | Class AAA (1) |
| Languished for seven years in Braves system, hit .263 overall with 54 HR; spent five seasons in Mexico, finally hit stride in 1976 (28 homers, drew 129 walks). | | | | | | | | | |
| 8. Senators: Donnie Castle, lhp/of, Coldwater HS | Coldwater, Miss. | L-L | 6-1 | 190 | 18 | $35,000 | 1969 | 1978 | Majors (1) |
| Pitched Memphis Legion squad to national title in 1968 prior to signing; spent almost all of 10-year career in minors as hitter (.232 overall, 115 homers). | | | | | | | | | |
| 9. Pirates: Dick Sharon, of, Sequoia HS | Redwood City, Calif. | R-R | 6-2 | 185 | 18 | $25,000 | 1968 | 1976 | Majors (3) |
| Began nine-year career in Pittsburgh system, but contract allowed him to demand trade if he didn't crack deep Pirates OF; sent to Tigers, played three years in bigs. | | | | | | | | | |
| 10. Orioles: Junior Kennedy, ss, Arvin HS | Arvin, Calif. | R-R | 6-0 | 180 | 17 | $38,500 | 1968 | 1983 | Majors (7) |
| Given name is Junior; spent 10 years in minors and didn't reach majors until traded to Reds; utility infielder for bulk of seven-year career, hitting .248 in 447 games. | | | | | | | | | |
| 11. Phillies: Greg Luzinski, 1b, Notre Dame HS | Prospect Heights, Ill. | R-R | 6-1 | 200 | 17 | $50,000 | 1968 | 1984 | Majors (15) |
| "The Bull" breezed through minors (113 HRs in four years), became dominant force at plate in early years with Phillies, hit .309-39-130 in best season in 1976. | | | | | | | | | |
| 12. Angels: Lloyd Allen, rhp, Selma HS | Selma, Calif. | R-R | 6-1 | 180 | 18 | $75,000 | 1968 | 1979 | Majors (7) |
| Signed largest bonus in '68 draft, threw as hard as anyone in class; had success early on as closer, but arm problems led to 8-25, 4.69 record, shortened his career. | | | | | | | | | |
| 13. Reds: Tim Grant, rhp, Riverview HS | Boykins, Va. | L-R | 6-0 | 185 | 18 | $20,000 | 1968 | 1971 | Class A (3) |
| Reds hit jackpot with first-rounders from 1965-67, but '68 pick never surfaced above Class A; went 23-20, 3.79 on mound, became primarily a hitter at end. | | | | | | | | | |
| 14. White Sox: Rich McKinney, ss, Ohio | Troy, Ohio | R-R | 6-0 | 185 | 21 | $35,000 | 1968 | 1977 | Majors (7) |
| College All-American in 1968 (.391-7-24), preceded Hall of Famer Mike Schmidt as Ohio shortstop; success harder to come by in majors, hit .225 in utility role. | | | | | | | | | |
| 15. Cubs: Ralph Rickey, of, Oklahoma | Oklahoma City | B-R | 6-4 | 200 | 21 | $28,500 | 1968 | 1973 | Class AAA (4) |
| Former Sooners kicker spent six years in Cubs system, last four in Triple-A; began career as power-hitting prospect (.242-40-153), finished on mound (17-22, 4.15). | | | | | | | | | |
| 16. Twins: Alex Rowell, of, Luther (Iowa) College | North Chicago, Ill. | R-R | 6-1 | 195 | 21 | $12,000 | 1968 | 1970 | Class AA (2) |
| All-conference all four years in baseball/basketball at small Iowa college, but athletic success never translated to minors; hit .271 and played just three years. | | | | | | | | | |
| 17. Giants: Gary Matthews, of, San Fernando HS | Pacoima, Calif. | R-R | 6-2 | 185 | 17 | $30,000 | 1968 | 1987 | Majors (16) |
| "Sarge" enjoyed productive 16-year career with five clubs, hit .281-234-978, stole 183 bags, drew 940 walks; Gary Jr. also had success in 12-year career. | | | | | | | | | |
| 18. Tigers: Murray Robinson, of, Thomas Dale HS | Chester, Va. | L-R | 6-1 | 190 | 18 | $15,000 | 1968 | 1975 | Class AAA (3) |
| "Smokey" would have been a sure hit in Detroit, but his eight-year career, spent entirely in Tigers system, peaked in Triple-A; hit .251 with 86 homers. | | | | | | | | | |
| 19. Cardinals: # James "Butch" Hairston, of, Roth HS | Dayton, Ohio | L-R | 6-0 | 175 | 17 | $20,000 | 1968 | 1972 | Class A (5) |
| Spent five years (281 games) in Cardinals system, none above Class A (career totals: .264-7-90, 21 SB); later went on to earn two Master's degrees at Ohio State. | | | | | | | | | |
| 20. Red Sox: # Tom Maggard, of/c, John Glenn HS | Norwalk, Calif. | R-R | 6-6 | 215 | 18 | $40,000 | 1968 | 1973 | Class AAA (1) |
| Six-foot-6 catcher hit .233 with 47 homers in six years in Red Sox system; set to back up Carlton Fisk in 1974, but died in September 1973 after insect bite. | | | | | | | | | |
| **JANUARY—REGULAR PHASE** | | | | | | | | | |
| 1. Athletics: George Hendrick, of, Fremont HS | Los Angeles | R-R | 6-3 | 195 | 18 | $20,000 | 1968 | 1988 | Majors (18) |
| Never played high school ball, became immediate hit in pros by leading Midwest League in batting; went on to hit .278 with 267 HRs, 1,111 RBIs in 18-year career. | | | | | | | | | |
| **JANUARY—SECONDARY PHASE** | | | | | | | | | |
| 1. Twins: Eric Soderholm, ss, South Georgia JC | Miami | R-R | 6-0 | 190 | 19 | $23,500 | 1968 | 1980 | Majors (9) |
| Nine-year career in majors (.264 BA, 102 HRs), highlighted by comeback season with Chisox in 1977 (.280, 25 HRs) after being sidelined by knee injury. | | | | | | | | | |
| **JUNE—SECONDARY PHASE** | | | | | | | | | |
| 1. Cubs: Dave Lemonds, lhp, North Carolina | Charlotte | L-L | 6-2 | 170 | 19 | $50,000 | 1968 | 1974 | Majors (2) |
| Led Charlotte team coached by his dad to Legion World Series title in 1965, followed by successful college career at UNC; went 4-8, 2.99 in two big league seasons. | | | | | | | | | |

*# Deceased.*

seasons together, culminating with a victory in the 1981 World Series. That is the longest run of any infield quartet in history, and broke the record that had belonged to the fabled Cubs' crew of Tinker to Evers to Chance.

"It's a record that can't be broken," Garvey said years later. "You can't keep one guy for eight years, never mind four."

The 1968 draft was not regarded as a particularly strong one overall. Just 11 of 20 first-round picks from the June regular phase reached the majors, a record low. The college crop, in particular, was thin, and it took more than a year for the first member of the Class of 1968 to surface in the big leagues.

It's just that one team got more than its share of talent. The Dodgers drafted more players in 1968 than anyone, some 101 in all, but they didn't get first kick at the can as they drafted fifth overall in the June regular phase and 13th in the secondary

## How They Should Have Done It

Based on the career WAR (Wins Above Replacement, as calculated by Baseball-Reference.com) numbers achieved by all the players eligible for the 1968 draft, here's how the first round should have unfolded. Numbers in parentheses indicate the round when the player was actually drafted

| | Player, Pos. | Actual Draft | WAR | Bonus |
|---|---|---|---|---|
| 1. | Ron Cey, 3b | Dodgers (June-S/3) | 53.3 | $21,000 |
| 2. | Thurman Munson, c | Yankees (1) | 45.9 | $45,000 |
| 3. | George Foster, of | Giants (Jan.-R/3) | 44.0 | $2,000 |
| 4. | Davey Lopes, 2b | Dodgers (Jan.-S/2) | 42.0 | $10,000 |
| 5. | Steve Garvey, 3b | Dodgers (June-S/1) | 37.6 | $39,000 |
| 6. | Garry Maddox, of | Giants (Jan.-R/2) | 36.7 | $1,500 |
| 7. | Cecil Cooper, 1b | Red Sox (6) | 35.8 | $5,000 |
| 8. | Doyle Alexander, rhp | Dodgers (9) | 35.5 | $5,000 |
| 9. | Bob Forsch, rhp | Cardinals (26) | 35.1 | $8,000 |
| 10. | Gary Matthews, of | Giants (1) | 30.2 | $30,000 |
| 11. | George Hendrick, of | Athletics (Jan.-R/1) | 28.9 | $20,000 |
| 12. | Ken Forsch, rhp | Astros (18) | 26.4 | $10,000 |
| 13. | Ben Oglivie, of | Red Sox (11) | 26.3 | $20,000 |
| 14. | Greg Luzinski, 1b | Phillies (1) | 26.1 | $50,000 |
| 15. | Al Bumbry, of | Orioles (11) | 24.5 | None |
| 16. | Paul Splittorff, lhp | Royals (25) | 23.5 | $1,500 |
| 17. | Oscar Gamble, of | Cubs (16) | 23.0 | $1,000 |
| 18. | Bill Lee, lhp | Red Sox (22) | 22.2 | $4,000 |
| 19. | Eric Soderholm, ss | Twins (Jan.-S/1) | 21.5 | $23,500 |
| 20. | Joe Ferguson, of | Dodgers (8) | 20.9 | $8,000 |

| | Top 3 Unsigned Players | | | Year Signed |
|---|---|---|---|---|
| 1. | Burt Hooton, rhp | Mets (5) | 35.9 | 1971 |
| 2. | Mickey Rivers, of | White Sox (Jan-R/1) | 32.3 | 1969 |
| 3. | Jim Barr, rhp | Phillies (June-S/3) | 19.2 | 1970 |

phase. And they didn't even sign eight of the first 16 players they drafted in the regular phase.

For the second time in three years, the New York Mets led off the proceedings, and again went for a California high school player—in this case, shortstop Tim Foli. He would play 16 years in the big leagues, though he never amounted to much more than a journeyman infielder.

Foli, whose older brother Ernie signed a six-figure contract with the Los Angeles Angels in 1962 but never reached the big leagues, was selected out of Notre Dame High in Canoga Park, Calif. The Mets signed him to a $74,000 bonus, roughly the same figure they paid catcher Steve Chilcott two years earlier.

The Oakland Athletics and Houston Astros whiffed with the next two selections, as the A's didn't sign Florida prep righthander Pete Broberg with the second pick, and New York high school catcher Marty Cott, chosen third by the Astros, never came close to reaching the big leagues.

But the draft came alive with the next two selections. Future all-star catcher Thurman Munson went to the New York Yankees with the fourth pick, and the Dodgers began their historic run by selecting "can't-miss" prospect Bobby Valentine.

### DODGERS SCORE EARLY, OFTEN

For the Dodgers to pull off the greatest talent haul in draft history required more than progressive thinking. It also took a shift in philosophy, a relatively high draft position and a lot of luck.

To that point in their 10 years in Los Angeles, the Dodgers were best known for pitching. They were determined to complement that with a revamped offense.

"In our meeting before the 1968 draft, I remember telling (owner) Peter (O'Malley), who wasn't very involved at the time, that we were going for bats," Campanis said. "At the time, we couldn't get a hit. If you're hungry, you eat. So when we had the choices, we went for a Garvey and Cey, a Buckner and Valentine. Every time we had a tough choice to make, we went for the better hitter."

One of those difficult decisions came with the fifth overall pick. Campanis narrowed his club's choices to Valentine, a multi-sport high school star from Stamford, Conn., and Bill Buckner, a hitting machine from Napa, Calif.

"We ended up getting both," Campanis said. "We went for Valentine first because he was the better athlete with better speed, even though Buckner was the better hitter."

With Valentine and Buckner, who went on to accumulate 2,715 hits in a 22-year major league career and won a National League batting title in 1980, the Dodgers then added outfielder Tom Paciorek in the fifth round, catcher Joe Ferguson in the eighth and righthander Doyle Alexander in the ninth. With two of their first three picks in the secondary phase, the Dodgers landed Garvey and Cey, a pair of hard-hitting third basemen from the collegiate ranks. Lopes was a product of the January draft.

Most of that talent assembled that summer on a power-packed Ogden team that cruised to a Rookie-level Pioneer League title.

"Without a doubt, it was the best Rookie league team I'd ever seen," said manager Tommy Lasorda, who would go on to major league greatness himself. "Find me another Rookie club that had three eventual big league stars in the starting lineup."

Two years later, at Spokane of the Triple-A Pacific Coast League, things hadn't changed much.

Valentine led the PCL in batting at .340, while collecting 211 hits (69 for extra bases). Buckner was third at .335, Paciorek seventh at .326. Garvey took a .319 average with him when called up by the Dodgers at midseason. With arguably the greatest minor league team in the draft era, Spokane won the PCL's Northern Division title by 26 games, then crushed a veteran Hawaii team 4-0 for the league championship.

Fred Nelson, a second baseman drafted that year from Arizona State and later a prominent scout, credited the success of that draft not just to the scouting department, but to the team's player-development staff. He was quick to point out that Lopes (and Russell) were outfielders when they signed, while Garvey was a third baseman.

"What the Dodgers were able to do was recognize talent, while also recognizing what the organization could do to make them better," Nelson said. "They put together an infield that only had one guy (Cey) at the position he was playing when he signed, and it played together longer than any in history. It wasn't by accident."

The Dodgers made 71 selections in the regular phase of the June draft, 17 more than any other club.

"I think we had nine farm clubs at the time," said Bill Schweppe, then an assistant to farm direc-

**AT A GLANCE**

numbers overall in four years (.299-113-377).

### One Who Got Away

**PETE BROBERG, RHP, ATHLETICS.** A total of 108 players were selected in the first five rounds of the June regular phase in 1968, and 28 went unsigned—the highest ratio in draft history. The college defections started early with Broberg, the second pick overall. He sought a reported $150,000 bonus but chose to attend Dartmouth instead.

### He Was Drafted?

**KENNY STABLER, LHP, ASTROS (2ND ROUND, JANUARY/REGULAR PHASE).** The Astros took the University of Alabama quarterback three days after he was picked in the second round of the NFL draft by the Oakland Raiders. Stabler, a lefthander who pitched briefly early in his career for the Crimson Tide, went on to the Pro Football Hall of Fame after a 15-year career in the NFL.

### Did You Know . . .

A three-sport star at Texas-El Paso, **CHARLIE WEST** was the Reds' first-round pick in the January secondary phase and was also drafted by the NFL's Minnesota Vikings (second round). After receiving a $27,500 bonus (the largest paid by the Reds that year), West played in just 19 games for Class A Tampa, hitting .183 in 60 at-bats, before deciding he'd had enough with baseball. He went on to spend 12 years in the NFL as a defensive back.

### They Said It

**NELSON BURBRINK**, Mets scouting director on **TIM FOLI**, the first overall pick: "Foli has good power, good hands, a good arm . . . I wasn't the only one to see him. Bob Scheffing (who became Mets GM in 1970) scouted him, too. Each time Scheffing saw him, he hit a home run."—*Foli hit just 25 homers in a 16-year career, none with the Mets.*

## DRAFT SPOTLIGHT: THURMAN MUNSON

Thuman Munson appeared to be on a Hall of Fame career trajectory when he died in a plane crash in 1979 at age 32

Thurman Munson was the first college player drafted in 1968. He was the best talent to emerge from his class and became the heart and soul of New York Yankees teams that captured back-to-back World Series titles in 1977-78. His place in the Hall of Fame seemed assured, but for the plane crash that snuffed out his life in the prime of his career.

As a high school graduate in 1965, Munson wasn't drafted—or even scouted. That was because he never caught at Lehman High in Canton, Ohio, until his senior year, and even then only sparingly.

"That year, we had a pitcher who threw so hard that no one else could catch him," Munson said. "I volunteered to catch him although I had never caught before. I caught him five or six times and that was all my high school catching. Look, I just loved baseball so much that I would play anywhere. I didn't care."

Munson was primarily a shortstop. He was pursued by multiple colleges for his football skills, but just three offered him a scholarship to play baseball. Yet he committed to that sport and made huge strides in college at Kent State while transitioning to catcher.

Still, he had something to prove in the summer of 1967, following his sophomore year, when he agreed to play in the Cape Cod League. Munson showed his skills behind the plate and led the Cape with a .420 batting average. Scouts praised him for his defensive prowess, especially his quick release. He picked a man off base in nine straight games,

"That's where scouts really saw me," Munson said. "I really had some kind of year there."

Veteran scout Harry Hesse had alerted the Yankees, and they had scout Gene Woodling, an ex-big leaguer, follow his every move as a junior at Kent State. Munson responded by hitting a career-best .413 with three homers and 30 RBIs in 25 games.

The Yankees jumped on Munson with the fourth pick overall, though there was debate until the night before the draft whether to take Munson or Illinois prep slugger Greg Luzinski. Yankees manager Ralph Houk swung the vote to Munson by expressing his preference for the player who would help the team the soonest. Naturally, that was Munson.

"He was our first choice all the way," said Yankees farm director Johnny Johnson. "He can play in a high classification right now."

Munson signed for a $45,000 bonus, broke in at Double-A Binghamton and hit .301. He would have won the Eastern League batting title if he had enough plate appearances to qualify. After missing most of the 1969 season while on military duty, Munson was in the big leagues to stay by September, after playing fewer than 100 games in the minors.

He was the American League's Rookie of the Year in 1970, and soon became the centerpiece of a Yankees team that would make consecutive World Series appearances from 1976-78. On Aug. 2, 1979, at 32, Munson died in the crash of his private plane.

Over his 11-year career with the Yankees, he hit .292 with 113 home runs. He was a seven-time all-star, a three-time Gold Glover and the AL. MVP in 1976. Munson remains part of Yankee lore. In the clubhouse at old Yankee Stadium, his corner locker was left with only an empty chair, a mirror, and above, a small plate with his retired No. 15.

"That locker symbolizes Thurman and is there for memory," said former teammate Bobby Murcer, who spoke at the funeral. "Thurman is there and always will be."

On the surface, Munson was gruff and temperamental. He assailed writers trying to interview him, accusing them of misrepresenting his views. He rarely smiled. He avoided signing autographs or displaying emotion. To those who knew him best, though, Munson was a tough competitor who often played hurt. He was the consummate family man, a model parent who was generous with his time and money. At every opportunity, he flew home to Canton to spend time with his wife and three children. He was at home, flying his private plane that fateful day when he crashed attempting a landing.

"In a real tough situation, it was not Reggie (Jackson) you feared most, it was Thurman," said Steve Stone, a college teammate. "Thurman would always find a way to get the runner home. Whether it was with the arm or the bat, he found a way to beat you.

"This was a guy who absolutely detested losing. He always gave everything he had and for that he was appreciated by teammates and even opponents."

tor Fresco Thompson and later Thompson's successor. "The draft was in its infancy and we didn't have much experience. The thought was that you didn't know how well you would do signing these players, so you better draft as many as you can.

"I view that draft as a nine-plus, reserving a 10 for somebody who might come along and do a better job. But that won't be easy. It's hard to conceive of any organization being that good or that fortunate."

### METS FOLLY: TAKING FOLI

The decision by the Mets to go for Foli, 17, with the No. 1 pick was a last-minute one.

"We didn't decide until after midnight and we had to make a late call to the coast to check on Foli's availability and his physical condition," said Nelson Burbrink, the Mets' director of player development. "We had been undecided between Foli and Lloyd Allen, a righthanded pitcher, but the fact that we might need a little hitting made the difference and we took Foli."

Foli played 16 seasons in the majors, but just two years with the Mets.

Meanwhile, Allen, the other player the Mets gave final consideration to before settling on Foli, earned the largest bonus ($75,000) of any player in the 1968 draft. One of the hardest throwers in the class, Allen was taken by the California Angels with the 12th pick, and rose quickly to the big leagues, making his first appearance in 1969 at age 19. Two years later, he settled in as the Angels' closer and had 15 saves, but just as quickly lost that role and his career never took off, though arm problems were a contributing factor. In seven major league seasons, he went 8-25, 4.69 overall.

Had he indicated more of a willingness to sign, Broberg may have been the top selection. However, it was well known to scouts that Broberg was committed to an Ivy League education at Dartmouth. Broberg's father Gus, a prominent attorney in Palm Beach, Fla., was a three-time All-American basketball player at Dartmouth from 1939-41 and determined that his son would get a similar education.

A's owner Charles O. Finley decided Broberg was worth the gamble, and his newly relocated Oakland club selected Broberg with the second overall pick. Despite negotiations that went into six figures, Broberg stuck to his conviction and rejected all offers.

The 6-foot-3 righthander dominated his competition at Dartmouth for three years and signed with the Washington Senators in 1971 as the No. 1 pick in the June secondary phase. He made his

### Fastest To The Majors

| | Player, Pos. | Drafted (Round) | Debut |
|---|---|---|---|
| 1. | Bill Lee, lhp | Red Sox (22) | June 25, 1969 |
| 2. | Dave Lemonds, lhp | Cubs (June-S/1) | June 30, 1969 |
| 3. | Thurman Munson, c | Yankees (1) | Aug. 8, 1969 |
| 4. | *Oscar Gamble, of | Cubs (16) | Aug. 27, 1969 |
| 5. | Steve Garvey, 3b | Dodgers (June-S/1) | Sept. 1, 1969 |

**LAST PLAYER TO RETIRE:** Bill Buckner, of (May 30, 1990)

** High school selection.*

## Top 25 Bonuses

| Player, Pos. | Drafted (Round) | Order | Bonus |
|---|---|---|---|
| 1. * **Lloyd Allen, rhp** | **Angels (1)** | **12** | **$75,000** |
| 2. * **Tim Foli, ss** | **Mets (1)** | **1** | **$74,000** |
| 3. * **Bobby Valentine, ss** | **Dodgers (1)** | **5** | **$65,000** |
| 4. **John Curtis, lhp** | **Red Sox (June-S/1)** | **(10)** | **$60,000** |
| 5. * **Greg Luzinski, 1b** | **Phillies (1)** | **11** | **$50,000** |
| **Dave Lemonds, lhp** | **Cubs (June-S/1)** | **(1)** | **$50,000** |
| 7. * Marty Cott, c | Astros (1) | 3 | $47,000 |
| 8. **Thurman Munson, c** | **Yankees (1)** | **4** | **$45,000** |
| * **Bill Buckner, of** | **Dodgers (2)** | **25** | **$45,000** |
| * Jeff Wang, of | Phillies (2) | 31 | $45,000 |
| 11. * Tom Maggard, of | Red Sox (1) | 20 | $40,000 |
| 12. **Steve Garvey, 3b** | **Dodgers (June-S/1)** | **(13)** | **$39,000** |
| 13. * **Junior Kennedy, ss** | **Orioles (1)** | **10** | **$38,500** |
| 14. * **Donnie Castle, lhp/1b** | **Senators (1)** | **8** | **$35,000** |
| **Rich McKinney, ss** | **White Sox (1)** | **14** | **$35,000** |
| * **Rich Chiles, of** | **Astros (2)** | **23** | **$35,000** |
| George Kazmarek, of | Mets (Jan.-R/1) | (2) | $35,000 |
| **Ed Goodson, ss** | **Giants (June-S/1)** | **(3)** | **$35,000** |
| 19. * Michael Weaver, of | Indians (1) | 6 | $32,000 |
| 20. * Donald Dickerson, 1b | Mets (2) | 21 | $31,000 |
| 21. * **Gary Matthews, of** | **Giants (1)** | **17** | **$30,000** |
| * Ken Johnson, ss | Yankees (2) | 24 | $30,000 |
| * **Bill Greif, rhp** | **Astros (3)** | **43** | **$30,000** |
| * Steven Kogut, c | Yankees (4) | 64 | $30,000 |
| * Dan Covert, 1b | Indians (4) | 66 | $30,000 |
| **Bart Johnson, rhp** | **White Sox (June-S/1)** | **(2)** | **$30,000** |
| Robert Elliot, rhp | Yankees (Jan.-R/1) | (3) | $30,000 |

*Major leaguers in bold. *High school selection.*

debut in the big leagues without the benefit of minor league seasoning.

Houston had an opportunity to go for Munson, an established college catcher, with the third pick overall, but the Astros cast their lot with Cott, an unproven high school receiver.

"We think that Cott is just a shade away from being a major league catcher right now," said Tal Smith, the Astros' director of player personnel. "He's that fine a receiver."

Except for a two-game stint in Triple-A in his first pro season, Cott never advanced beyond Class A in three seasons before quitting in 1971, at age 20. He was placed on the restricted list before being released by the Astros in 1972. In 199 minor league games, Cott hit just .231 with 14 homers and struggled even more behind the plate, committing 38 errors.

Curiously, the Astros tested both of their first two selections, Cott and outfielder Rich Chiles, at the Triple-A level in their first pro seasons—even though both players were high school picks. Chiles, a future big leaguer, hit .446 in 32 games at Covington of the Rookie-level Appalachian League, and held his own at Triple-A Oklahoma City by hitting .262 in 43 games.

### YANKEES SCORE BIG WITH MUNSON

Munson, the first of four college players drafted in the first round of the June regular phase, went to the Yankees with the fourth pick. He proved to be the best first-round selection in 1968 as he went on to an all-star career over 12 seasons in New York, before he was killed in a plane crash in 1979.

Munson's untimely death underscored the tragedy that afflicted the 1968 draft, with three first-round picks who died while active players.

Catcher Tom Maggard, picked 20th overall in the regular phase by the Boston Red Sox, had an adverse and ultimately fatal reaction to an insect bite while at Triple-A Pawtucket in 1973. Shortstop Danny Thompson, Minnesota's first pick in the secondary phase, died of leukemia in 1976, ending a seven-year major league career.

The circumstances surrounding Maggard's death were somewhat of a mystery at the time, but what was known is that Maggard was bitten by some type of bug midway through the International League season. His right forearm swelled up considerably, but it soon healed and Maggard seemed to have recovered.

He then developed back pains that were attributed to the physical demands of catching. X-rays revealed nothing, but eventually Maggard was unable to catch any longer. Blood tests were never taken.

The Red Sox decided to send Maggard home early to be examined by local doctors, but while driving west from Pawtucket, he could get no farther than a relative's home in Maryland before the pain became too much.

BOSTON RED SOX

Tom Maggard

Maggard's wife, accompanying him on the trip, called his mother, who took a plane to meet him. By then, Maggard was so weak that he could not dress himself, and his mother and wife put him on a plane for California. He arrived home Sept. 7, and two days later was dead, the cause attributed to a staph infection that started in his arm and spread to his vital organs.

Thompson, who had been an all-American shortstop at Oklahoma State prior to being drafted, was about to embark on his fourth season with the Minnesota Twins in 1973, when a preseason physical taken the day before his 26th birthday revealed that he had leukemia. He went on to play four more seasons, his last after being traded by the Twins to the Texas Rangers, and died less than 10 weeks after the 1976 season concluded.

### VALENTINE, DUDISH IN HEAVY DEMAND

Foli and Broberg created headlines by becoming the first two selections in the regular phase of the 1968 draft, but the most noted high school players were a pair of electrifying two-sport stars: Valentine and Charlie Dudish.

Dudish, a record-setting quarterback from Georgia and the son of former NFL running back Andy Dudish, was the most hotly recruited prep football player in years. He had offers from more than 200 colleges, but didn't make a commitment until he determined first where he stood in the baseball draft.

Valentine, a running back, was the only football player in Connecticut prep history to be named all-state for three years. Like Dudish, he had scholarship offers from upward of 200 colleges, includ-

### WORTH NOTING

Before signing with the Senators as their first-round pick (eighth overall), lefthander **DONNIE CASTLE** posted a 17-1 record and was named the American Legion player of the year after pitching Memphis Post 1 to victory in the 1968 American Legion World Series. As a senior that spring at Coldwater (Miss.) High, Castle pitched back-to-back no-hitters and struck out 20 of 21 batters in a game. For all of Castle's mound success as an amateur, he was a standout two-way player and the Senators elected to make him a hitter almost exclusively in the pro ranks. He reached the big leagues in that role with the Rangers in 1973, but success with the bat was fleeting as his career in the majors lasted only four games. He made nine pitching appearances in the minors, going 0-1, 8.18.

**MICKEY MCCARTY,** drafted in the 26th round by the Indians in 1968 out of Texas Christian, became the first of only three athletes ever to be selected in three different professional sports drafts. The 6-foot-7, 240-pound McCarty was all-Southwest Conference in baseball (as a lefthanded pitcher) and basketball in 1967 and 1968, and hadn't played football since high school, yet chose to pursue a career in the NFL after being drafted in the fourth round in 1968 by the Kansas City Chiefs. He was also selected by the NBA's Dallas Chaparrals in the 14th round. McCarty played only briefly for the Chiefs, as mostly a tight end and kick returner. Later in life, he twice survived heart trans-

CONTINUED ON PAGE 72

## WORTH NOTING

CONTINUED FROM PAGE 71

plant surgery, before dying of cancer in 2010 at 63.

■ As impressive as the Dodgers' celebrated 1968 draft class was, it could easily have taken on iconic status had righthander **SANDY VANCE**, selected in the second round of the June secondary phase, not encountered career-ending arm problems early in his career with the Dodgers, and first baseman **BILL SEINSOTH**, picked in the seventh round of the same phase, not elected to delay his signing with the Dodgers for another year, before dying in a 1969 car accident. Vance went 32-3 in a three-year career with Stanford, and was 15-3 with 158 strikeouts in 131 innings in his first season in the Dodgers system, while Seinsoth, a two-time All-American, was selected the Most Outstanding Player in the 1968 College World Series for champion USC.

■ Righthander **BART JOHNSON** did not enjoy as much success as others drafted in the June secondary phase, but was the most athletic player selected. The tall, lanky Johnson not only threw exceptionally hard, but was named the California basketball player of the year as a prep senior in 1967, when he rebuffed a third-round offer from the Cardinals in favor of playing basketball at Brigham Young. He averaged 28 points a game for the freshman team. Johnson did not play baseball while at BYU, however, so he was eligible for the 1968 draft. The White Sox were so enamored of his potential as a pitcher that they drafted him with the second pick overall and gave him a $30,000 signing bonus to give up a basketball career that had obvious NBA potential. After a dominant season in 1969 at Class A Appleton, where he went 16-4, 2.17 with 200 strikeouts in 170 innings, Johnson was promoted to the majors. At 19, he was one of the most impressive natural talents ever to don a White Sox uniform and showed flashes of

ing Southern California, which came calling with an offer that would make him a logical successor at tailback to the departing O.J. Simpson.

Both players were in demand by major league teams as well, with the Dodgers jumping on Valentine with the fifth pick. Dudish, a power-hitting shortstop/outfielder, had the talent to be considered in that range, after hitting .647 and posting a 0.50 ERA as a senior at Avondale High, but tumbled out of the first round because teams couldn't get a handle on how sincere he was about playing baseball. He eventually went to the San Francisco Giants in the second round.

Sure enough, Dudish ended up choosing football, with Georgia Tech as his college of choice. His decision was announced on national TV, after the Giants made a last, desperate push to sign him, reportedly offering a bonus of $100,000.

"We didn't know where we were going to go—football or baseball," said Dudish's father. "In the end, we turned down a substantial baseball offer."

Bobby Valentine

Dudish never came close to fulfilling expectations at Georgia Tech as his career was wracked by injuries and suspensions related to missing classes. He was dismissed from the team for a final time near the end of his sophomore year.

With his football career in shambles, Dudish tried to resurrect his athletic career by returning to baseball. He was drafted by the Padres with the 12th pick overall in the June 1971 secondary phase, and signed for $10,000. But he struggled in all phases after being away from the game for three years, and went 2-for-28 in a short stay at Lodi of the Class A California League. He was released after little more than a month.

He subsequently hooked on with the Atlanta Braves in 1973, and hit .280 with a homer in 107 at-bats at Greenwood of the Class A South Atlantic League, but a wrist injury from his football days had robbed him of his power. He never played baseball again.

Dudish also fell victim to drug and alcohol abuse, and they were a major contributing factor in his once-promising career ending up in ruin. "It was a nightmare," Dudish said, reflecting on his career and the burden of expectations. "By all rights, I should be dead."

Valentine dealt with his own unrealistic expectations when he signed with the Dodgers as their top draft pick, especially after he went on to win minor league MVP honors twice in three years.

"He's one of the most exciting kids I've ever seen come into the game . . . He's just a baby, but he's going to be the next leader of the Dodgers," said Lasorda, who managed Valentine throughout his minor league career before going on to his highly successful tenure with the big league club.

Of all the members of the vaunted Class of 1968, Valentine was the one chosen first. He was

### Largest Bonuses By Round

| | Player Pos. | Club | Bonus |
|---|---|---|---|
| 1. | ***Lloyd Allen, rhp** | **Angels** | **$75,000** |
| 2. | ***Bill Buckner, 1b** | **Dodgers** | **$45,000** |
| | *Jeff Wang, of | Phillies | $45,000 |
| 3. | ***Bill Greif, rhp** | **Astros** | **$30,000** |
| 4. | *Steven Kogut, c | Yankees | $30,000 |
| | *Dan Covert, 1b | Indians | $30,000 |
| 5. | *Kerry Horn, of | Giants | $18,500 |
| 6. | Adrian Kent, of | Yankees | $8,000 |
| 7. | **Tom Bradley, rhp** | **Angels** | **$13,000** |
| 8. | **Jim Howarth, of** | **Giants** | **$12,000** |
| 9. | ***Larry Doby Johnson, c** | **Indians** | **$10,000** |
| | Greg Schubert, of | Athletics | $10,000 |
| 10. | **Harvey Shank, rhp** | **Angels** | **$5,000** |
| Jan/R. | George Kazmarek, of | Mets (1) | $35,000 |
| Jan/S. | Steven Salata, c | Cubs (1) | $27,000 |
| Jun/S. | **John Curtis, lhp** | **Red Sox (1)** | **$60,000** |

*Major leaguers in bold. *High school selection.*

the one most expected to shine.

Valentine had everything in high school. A three-sport star at Rippowam High in Stamford, he was proclaimed as the best prep athlete ever to come from Connecticut. He was the student body president, the lead in his school's senior play.

As a first-round pick in baseball, he had all the tools. He could run, he could hit, he could throw. He did everything with a smooth, effortless grace that said he was born to play ball.

The Dodgers' original plan was to build their infield around Valentine, but bad timing and misfortune would stalk the "can't-miss" prospect.

After tearing up the PCL for Spokane in 1970, Valentine, 20, was ready for the big leagues. But it was evident almost from the start that he never quite fit in with the Dodgers. The team had difficulty determining whether he was a shortstop or an outfielder, or even a second baseman. Or whether he had the maturity to play in the big leagues.

The outspoken Valentine ruffled feathers in Los Angeles in two seasons, playing mostly in a utility role. Finally, in November 1972, the Dodgers sent Valentine to the Angels in a blockbuster deal involving Frank Robinson and Andy Messersmith—just as his mentor, Lasorda, was being named the Dodgers' third-base coach.

"My biggest misfortune," Valentine said later, "would be getting to the big leagues as soon as I did."

Then on May 17, 1973, taking a rare turn in the outfield, Valentine raced back on a long fly ball by Oakland's Dick Green and attempted a leaping catch against the center-field wall. The ball hit the top of the eight-foot fence and bounced over. Valentine's spikes ripped through the canvas covering and caught in the chain-link fence behind it. He fell to the ground writhing in pain, the broken bones in his right leg protruding through the skin five inches above the ankle.

Valentine's leg was in a cast for five months. Complications set in. The leg had not been set properly and when his bones healed, his ankle tilted backward some 17 degrees.

"They said that they'd have to re-break my leg and then it would be 18 months more," said

Valentine, who declined to have a second operation for fear that it would end his career.

Valentine would never be the same. He attempted a comeback the following spring with the Angels, hitting .261 in 117 games, but the speed that made him one of the game's most electrifying young players was gone. From that point, Valentine was little more than a utility player, bouncing back and forth between the majors and minors. It became a struggle, both physically and emotionally, for the once-gifted athlete.

"Coming back and seeing my leg was bent, was going to be ugly and I wasn't going to be able to run well, that was really hard," said Valentine, who would later make his mark on the game by managing three big league teams. "I knew that from then on, when I hit the ball and ran, the spectators and the managers and the scouts weren't going to say, God, what an exciting ballplayer!"

### SLIM PICKINGS IN COLLEGE RANKS

Southern California won the 1968 College World Series, beating Southern Illinois 4-3 in the final. The Trojans had more players drafted (eight) than any other college, but flaky lefthander Bill Lee, a 12-game winner for the Trojans, was the only player of note. Despite lasting until the 22nd round, Lee became the first player from the 1968 draft to reach the big leagues.

Munson (Kent State), a first-round selection in the regular phase, and Garvey (Michigan State) and Cey (Washington State) proved to be considerable talents, but the overall quality of the college crop in the 1968 draft was weak.

That stemmed from the ramifications of a change in baseball's college rule, effective with the 1967 draft, which allowed the selection of college sophomores in that draft (and again in 1968) if they had been drafted previously, but prohibited other college players from being picked until they were juniors. Effectively, many top collegians who otherwise might have been a central part of the 1968 talent pool were skimmed off a year earlier.

Munson was the first college player selected in the regular phase, and really the only one from the early rounds who left his mark on the game.

North Carolina lefthander Dave Lemonds was the first player selected in the secondary phase. He was named the College Player of the Year by The Sporting News, even though he won just six games that spring for the Tar Heels. Overall, he went 6-1, 1.49 with 96 strikeouts in 72 innings. Lemonds landed in the big leagues little more than a year after signing with the Chicago Cubs for $50,000, but won just four games, none with the Cubs.

Lefthander John Curtis (10th overall), who chose a two-year college career at Clemson after going unsigned as a first-round pick of the Cleveland Indians in 1966, and Garvey (13th overall), an unsigned third-rounder that year who went on to a successful career in both baseball and football at Michigan State, were also selected in the first round of the secondary phase.

### BORN TO BE A DODGER

As much as anyone, Garvey became a centerpiece of the successful Dodgers teams of the 1970s and early '80s, hitting .301 with 211 homers and 992 RBIs in his 14 years with the club. He won the National League MVP award in 1974, was a 10-time all-star and went on to set an NL record for consecutive games played (1,207). He also won four Gold Gloves at first base after breaking in as a third baseman. His shortcomings at the hot corner early in his career, stemming from a steady stream of throwing errors, were well known, though his arm was never the same after he separated his shoulder while playing football in college.

Cey, the player who eventually replaced Garvey at third for the Dodgers, had as productive a major league career as anyone from 1968. He played 17 years in the big leagues, the first 12 with the Dodgers, and slammed 316 homers while driving in 1,139 runs. But Garvey was the player born to be a Dodger. Growing up in Tampa, his father, a Greyhound bus driver, transported the Dodgers when they came to the Tampa area to play spring games. And young Steve would routinely take a couple of days off from school to travel along and even serve as the team's batboy.

When the Dodgers didn't draft him in 1966 out of Tampa's Chamberlain High, he chose to attend Michigan State. As a sophomore, he was a starter at cornerback on the football team, and an All-American at third base on the baseball team. When the Dodgers did draft him, after he hit .376 with nine homers for the Spartans, he left no doubt where his allegiance lay.

"I sincerely believe there is such a thing as a Dodger," he said. "I don't think there is such a thing as a Padre or a Brave or a Met. I sincerely think I was born to be a Dodger."

The Dodgers also drafted Paciorek, a two-time All-America defensive back at Houston who was selected by the Miami Dolphins in the 1968 NFL draft. Paciorek hit .364 with six home runs as a senior at Houston, and opted for baseball over football. He played 18 years in the big leagues.

### NOT ALL IS LOST FOR A'S

The Kansas City Athletics from 1965-67 made as much headway in the draft as any big league club. They tabbed talented players like outfielders Rick Monday and Reggie Jackson, and lefthander Vida Blue in consecutive years, among a number of other future big leaguers.

## One Team's Draft: Los Angeles Dodgers

| Player, Pos. | Bonus | Player, Pos. | Bonus | Player, Pos. | Bonus |
|---|---|---|---|---|---|
| **1. *Bobby Valentine, of** | **$65,000** | **5. Tom Paciorek, of** | **$20,000** | **9. *Doyle Alexander, rhp** | **$4,000** |
| **2. *Bill Buckner, 1b** | **$45,000** | 6. *Bob Auger, 1b | Did not sign | 10. *Rich Anderson, rhp | Did not sign |
| 3. Sonny Johnson, of | $12,500 | 7. *Joseph Barkauskas, c | Did not sign | **Other Steve Garvey (S/1), 3b** | **$39,000** |
| **4. *Mike Pazik, lhp** | **Did not sign** | **8. Joe Ferguson, of** | **$8,000** | | |

*Major leaguers in bold. *High school selection.*

### WORTH NOTING

brilliance over the next few seasons, especially in 1971, when he went 12-10, 2.93 and saved 14 games. But the outspoken Johnson's career was wracked by injuries and controversy, and overall he went only 43-51, 3.94 while being used as both a starter and reliever. Johnson never did play basketball again, though he talked openly about a possible career in the NBA. "He was the best basketball player I ever faced," said Paul Westphal, a former USC All-American and then a rising star with the NBA's Boston Celtics. Johnson later became a longtime scout for the White Sox.

■ The Yankees selected a familiar name in the secondary phase of the January draft. They took Columbia Basin (Wash.) Junior College righthander **WILLIAM SHEPHERD**, a fifth-rounder, for the fourth draft in a row and again were unsuccessful in signing him.

■ The Twins released **ALEX ROWELL**, their first-round pick, on July 7, 1970, after he did not report that year. All along, the Twins had thought Rowell's absence was because he was enlisted in the military.

■ The January draft saw a then-record 290 selections made—128 in the regular phase, 162 in the secondary phase—including three by the poorly prepared Cubs that were voided. Their first selection in the regular phase, pitcher **DAVE BALDWIN**, had been signed the previous November by Detroit; the two other picks violated the college rule. "It's truly puzzling," said Vedie Himsl, the Cubs' assistant director of player procurement and development. "Baldwin's name wasn't among the ineligibles so we assumed he was available. Oddly enough, the Tigers selectors sat at the table next to ours and said nothing when we made our first call." The National Association, which administered draft selections, later advised the Cubs of the mix-up.

## IN FOCUS: TIM FOLI

The New York Mets selected Tim Foli with the No. 1 pick in the 1968 draft because of the California high school shortstop's offensive potential.

"We had been undecided between Foli and Lloyd Allen, a righthanded pitcher," said Nelson Burbrink, Mets director of player development. "The fact that we might need a little hitting in the organization made the difference and we took Foli.

"He has good power, good hands, a good arm, but only average speed. He reminds me of Jim Fregosi, except Fregosi can run a little better."

The light-hitting shortstop never homered in the 102 major league games he played for the Mets. Foli played for eight big-league teams, hitting .251 with 25 homers overall.

The high-strung Foli was known for his fiery personality and explosive temper. Shortly after a clubhouse altercation in 1972 with coach Joe Pignatano, the Mets packaged Foli to Montreal in a 3-for-1 deal that brought outfielder Rusty Staub to New York.

Foli was driven by an intense desire to both win and excel, and grew increasingly frustrated when he failed to meet his lofty expectations. He often lashed out, and frequently got into confrontations with opposing players, umpires and even teammates.

The transplanted Oakland A's in 1968 took an immediate and significant step back by failing to sign either of their first two picks in the June regular phase—Broberg and outfielder John Shelley, who opted to play football at Oklahoma—and failing to draft anyone of substance.

Over the next dozen years, the A's would allow numerous other premium draft picks to go unsigned, though the erosion of the team's player-development program was masked by the success at the big league level, highlighted by the consecutive World Series titles from 1972-74.

The A's at least scored in the January draft in 1968 with the selection of outfielder George Hendrick with the No. 1 pick in the regular phase.

Hendrick, who went on to an 18-year big league career, had recently graduated from Fremont High in Los Angeles, making him draft-eligible. But he didn't play baseball in high school, stemming from a dispute with a coach while a freshman; he was spotted by the A's playing on weekends with a Pittsburgh Pirates-sponsored semi-pro team.

"We think Hendrick has the potential of Rick Monday and Reggie Jackson," said Ray Swallow, head of the A's scouting operation.

Hendrick's pro career started with a bang. He won the Class A Midwest League batting title in his first season—one of only a handful of players in draft history to win a full-season batting title in the same year he was drafted.

With the selection of Garry Maddox in the second round and George Foster one round later in the January regular phase, the Giants appeared to be drafting their outfield of the future in 1968—especially after landing Gary Matthews with their first-round pick in June. The Giants, however, failed to realize the talent in their midst, as all enjoyed their best years in the majors after leaving the Giants, either in trades or via free agency.

Gary Matthews

Foster hit four of his 348 career homers in a Giants uniform before being sent to Cincinnati in 1971 in a deal for shortstop Frank Duffy and pitcher Vern Geishert.

Maddox, a .285 career hitter and an eight-time Gold Glove winner as one of the game's best defensive center fielders, played three of his 15 seasons in San Francisco. He went to Philadelphia in 1975 in a deal for first baseman Willie Montanez.

Matthews was signed as a free agent by Atlanta following the 1976 season after five years with the Giants. In all, he played 16 seasons, hitting .281 with 234 homers.

### EXPANSION PANIC

With expansion of the major leagues in 1969 from 20 to 24 teams, Major League Baseball made provision for the four new clubs to participate in the 1968 draft in order to begin building a talent base. The new teams took part in the June proceedings only, and were not permitted to start selecting until the end of the fourth round of both the regular and secondary phases.

Because the American League had committed to expanding to Kansas City and Seattle in October 1967, the Royals and Pilots were much better prepared than their National League counterparts. Expansion franchises weren't awarded to Montreal and San Diego until May 27—little more than a week before the 1968 draft.

Both Kansas City and Seattle had already established farm teams in the short-season New York-Penn League to send their players to. The Expos and Padres had no time to make such arrangements, yet were still allowed to participate in the draft—with the stipulation that they begin negotiations with their picks within 15 days of their selection, or the players would become free agents.

The Expos selections were made by Gerry Snyder, the leader in Montreal's bid to land an expansion team and the No. 3 man in the Montreal municipal government. Because the team hadn't had time to hire a single front office official, Snyder worked from scouting reports other teams were willing to share with him. Montreal selected 15 players, but signed only six, all to 1969 contracts. None would play in the big leagues.

Unsigned righthander Mike Swain, the Expos' top pick (fourth round), later said the Expos didn't contact him for six weeks after the draft, and then offered him $500 to sign. He rejected that offer and was never drafted again. The Expos even drafted a Canadian, outfielder Richard Trembecki, who was better known at the University of Denver for his hockey skills. The selection was later voided because Canadians weren't subject to selection.

San Diego signed five of the 19 players it drafted. One, catcher Ronnie McGarity, was placed with St. Louis' club in the Rookie-level Gulf Coast League, while the other four signed 1969 contracts. The Padres' selections were made by Eddie Leishman, longtime general manager of San Diego's franchise in the Pacific Coast League.

Kansas City was the best prepared of the expansion teams. The Royals had already invested in an extensive scouting operation and got off to a running start by signing 26 players, including lefthander Paul Splittorff, a 25th-round pick who would go on to win 166 major league games.

The Pilots signed 13 players, including future Twins manager Tom Kelly.

## Highest Unsigned Picks

**JUNE/REGULAR PHASE ONLY**

| Player, Pos., Team (Round) | College | Re-Drafted |
|---|---|---|
| Pete Broberg, rhp, Athletics (1) | Dartmouth | Senators '71 (S/1) |
| John Shelley, of, Athletics (2) | Oklahoma | Never |
| Gordon Carter, of, Angels (2) | USC | Giants '71 (S/2) |
| John Langerhans, 1b, Twins (2) | Texas | Brewers '71 (S/3) |
| Charlie Dudish, ss/of, Giants (2) | Georgia Tech | Padres '71 (S/1) |
| Bernie Boehmer, c, Mets (3) | St. Louis CC-Meramec | Indians '70 (Jan.-S/3) |
| Richard Trapp, ss, Yankees (3) | * Florida | Royals '69 (Jan.-S/12) |
| James Sams, rhp, Pirates (3) | Miami (Ohio) | Indians '71 (S/2) |
| John Harbin, ss, Angels (3) | Newberry (S.C.) | Dodgers '72 (1) |
| Rich Lenard, rhp, Reds (3) | Indiana | Never |

**TOTAL UNSIGNED PICKS:** Top 5 Rounds (28), Top 10 Rounds (67)

**Returned to same school*

# 1968 Draft List

**Did not sign. Major leaguers in bold, with first and last years noted. Order of selection indicated in parentheses. For the first five rounds of the June Regular Phase and the first round of all other phases, the peak level of each player is noted.*

## ATLANTA BRAVES

**January—Regular Phase (8)**

**1. Jim Breazeale, c, Houston.—(1969-78)**
2. *Arnold Murillo, 1b, Canoga Park (Calif.) HS.
3. Michael McCammon, rhp, Indian River (Fla.) CC.
4. *Daniel Ketcherside, rhp, St. Louis CC-Meramec.
5. *Robert Fendlor, lhp, Miami-Dade CC North.
6. *James Lancaster, 1b, Odessa, Texas.
7. *Robert Hooper, of, Sardis (Texas) HS.

**January—Secondary Phase (20)**

1. *Gary Ross, lhp, Arizona Western JC.—(AA)
2. *David Byerly, of, Odessa (Texas) JC.
3. *Mike Witt, of, Fresno (Calif.) CC.
4. *Richard Wilson, rhp, Long Beach (Calif.) CC.
5. *Richard Cross, inf, Los Angeles CC.
6. *Mike Rapkin, lhp, Los Angeles Valley JC.
7. *Derk Hoving, c, Amarillo, Texas.
8. *Stan Zawacki, of, Newark, N.J.

**June—Regular Phase (7)**

1. Curtis Moore, of, Denison (Texas) HS.—(AAA)
2. Danny Landis, rhp, Franklin Heights HS, Columbus, Ohio.—(Low A)
**3. Clint Compton, ihp, Robert E. Lee HS, Montgomery, Ala.—(1972)**
**4. Mike McQueen, lhp, Spring Branch HS, Houston.—(1969-74)**
5. Roger Reid, ss, Weber State (Utah) College.—(High A)
6. John Burns, c, Eastern Illinois University.
7. Lee Grotelueschen, ss, Southeast HS, Lincoln, Neb.
8. *Cecil Johnson, 3b, Dorsey HS, Los Angeles.
9. *James Shebesta, lhp, Paschal HS, Fort Worth, Texas.
**10. *Mike Beard, lhp, Central HS, Little Rock, Ark.—(1974-77)**
**11. John Fuller, 1b, Lynwood (Calif.) HS.—(1974)**
12. Johnny Brown, 3b, North Jefferson HS, Warrior, Ala.
13. *Sylvan Rothschild, ss, Coronado HS, El Paso, Texas.
14. *David Thornton, of, Grant HS, Sacramento, Calif.
15. Grady Little, c, Garinger HS, Charlotte, N.C.
DRAFT DROP *Major league manager (2002-07) • Brother of Bryan Little, major leaguer (1982-86)*
16. *Richard Perry, lhp, William Chrisman HS, Independence, Mo.
17. Calvin Kelley, ss-2b, Richmond Union HS, Richmond, Calif.
18. Charles Townson, ss-2b, Waxahachie (Texas) HS.
19. Robin Ostebo, lhp, Johnson HS, St. Paul, Minn.
20. *Danny Heck, ss, Leuzinger HS, Hawthorne, Calif.
21. *Mose Adolph, of, Manual Arts HS, Los Angeles.
22. Richard Sandate, lhp, West Oso HS, Corpus Christi, Texas.
23. Ron Taylor, rhp, Bonneville (Utah) College.
24. William McEntire, lhp, Alpine (Texas) HS.
25. *John Conover, rhp, Santa Ana (Calif.) HS.
26. Terry Muck, 2b, Bethel (Minn.) College.
27. *Gary Robson, rhp, John Burroughs HS, Los Angeles.
28. *Richard Law, lhp, Owensboro, Ky.
29. *Frank Saenz, rhp, Los Angeles (Calif.) HS.
30. Harold Burke, rhp-of, Villanova University.
**31. *Rudy Arroyo, lhp, Mountain View (Calif.) HS.—(1971)**
32. *Kenneth Hess, rhp, Dixie HS, New Lebanon, Ohio.
33. *Dale Burch, rhp, De la Salle HS, New Orleans, La.
34. *David Kaster, rhp, South HS, Omaha, Neb.
35. Rowland Houston, of-inf, Poly HS, Long Beach, Calif.
36. *Glen Gilmore, rhp, Burke HS, Omaha, Neb.
37. *Johnny Glover, lhp, Appling HS, Macon, Ga.

**June—Secondary Phase (7)**

1. *Larry Pyle, of, University of Miami.—(AA)
2. *Gary Ross, lhp, Arizona Western JC.
3. Jim Sanders, rhp, University of North Carolina-Wilmington.
**4. *Ron Cash, ss, Manatee (Fla.) JC.–(1973-74)**
DRAFT DROP *Uncle of Kevin Cash, major leaguer (2002-10); major league manager (2015)*
5. Richard Wilson, rhp, Long Beach (Calif.) CC.
6. *Bob Bridges, lhp, Arizona Western JC.

## BALTIMORE ORIOLES

**January—Regular Phase (9)**

**1. Tom Walker, rhp, Brevard (Fla.) CC.—(1972-77)**
DRAFT DROP *Father of Neil Walker, first-round draft pick, Pirates (2004); major leaguer (2009-15)*
2. *Edward Northrup, rhp, George Mason University.
3. *Tom Hannibal, lhp, Clark (Wash.) JC.
4. *Leonard Scott, rhp, Baltimore (Md.) HS.
5. John Gage, c-1b, Wheeling (W.Va.) College.
6. *William Campbell, lhp, Warrenton, Va.
7. *Larry Lorenz, of-1b, Santa Clara (Calif.) HS.
8. *Michael Houck, lhp, Hudson Valley (N.Y.) CC.

**January—Secondary Phase (9)**

**1. *Dave Kingman, rhp-of, Harper (Ill.) JC—(1971-86)**
DRAFT DROP *First overall draft pick, June 1970/secondary phase, Giants*
**2. *Ron Cash, ss, Manatee (Fla.) CC.—(1973-74)**
DRAFT DROP *Uncle of Kevin Cash, major leaguer (2002-10); major league manager (2015)*
3. *Leon Murray, 1b, Los Angeles CC.
DRAFT DROP *Brother of Eddie Murray, major leaguer (1977-97) • Brother of Rich Murray, major leaguer (1980-83)*
4. *Joe Arnold, rhp, Miami-Dade CC North.
DRAFT DROP *Baseball coach, Florida (1984-94)*
5. *George Ferguson, 3b, University of Maine.
6. *Joe Crocker, c, Spokane (Wash.) CC.
7. *William Close, rhp, Holy Cross College.
8. *Carl Bennett, c, San Joaquin Delta (Calif.) JC.
9. *Michael Ehlers, c, Centerville (Iowa) JC.
10. *James O'Brien, of-c, San Francisco.

**June—Regular Phase (10)**

**1. Junior Kennedy, ss, Arvin (Calif.) HS.—(1974-83)**
DRAFT DROP *Brother of Jim Kennedy, major leaguer (1970)*
2. Michael Herson, rhp, University of Maryland.—(AAA)
3. Conrad Herrman, rhp, Sterling HS, Somerdale, N.J.—(High A)
**4. Jesse Jefferson, rhp, Carver HS, Midlothian, Va.—(1973-81)**
**5. Ron Dunn, 2b, Hoover HS, Fresno, Calif.—(1974-75)**
6. Richard Wurkits, c, Hoover HS, Fresno, Calif.
7. Danny Hart, ss, Troup County HS, LaGrange, Ga.
8. *Gerald Tassa, lhp, Washington & Lee HS, Arlington, Va.
9. Larry Jones, rhp, Oak Park HS, Kansas City, Mo.
10. *Lloyd Lightfoot, ss, North Carolina A&T State University.
**11. Al Bumbry, of, Virginia State University.—(1972-85)**
12. Dexter Tielke, rhp, West Columbia (Texas) HS.
**13. *Bill Fahey, c, Redford Union HS, Redford, Mich.—(1971-83)**
DRAFT DROP *First overall draft pick, January 1970/secondary phase, Senators • Father of Brandon Fahey, major leaguer (2006-08)*
14. *Donald Henderson, lhp, Tucker (Ga.) HS.
15. Robert Roth, lhp, Bowen HS, Chicago.
16. *Johnny Spriggs, 1b, Luling (Texas) HS.
17. Walter Hamm, of, University of South Dakota.
18. George Manz, rhp, University of Maryland.
19. *Larry Tipton, ss-2b, Robstown (Texas) HS.
20. Leonard Finch, 3b, Napa (Calif.) HS.
**21. Rich Coggins, of, Garey HS, Pomona, Calif.—(1972-76)**
22. Robert Bosley, lhp, Essex (Md.) CC.
23. *Larry Schutzius, of, Hinkley HS, Aurora, Colo.
24. *Ken Wamble, ss, South Houston (Texas) HS.
25. *Fred Williams, rhp, Sollers Point HS, Baltimore.
26. Wayne Zaskoda, ss, El Campo (Texas) HS.
27. Harold Warden, of, R.L. Turner HS, Carrolton, Texas.
28. John Blanchard, c, Colorado State University.
29. *James Kechura, inf-of, James Monroe HS, Bronx, N.Y.
30. *Roger Mayer, c-1b, Englewood (Colo.) HS.
**31. *Bill Bonham, rhp, Los Angeles Valley JC.—(1971-80)**
32. Rickey Gray, ss, Mumford HS, Detroit.
**33. *Bill Stein, 2b, Brevard (Fla.) CC.–(1972-85)**
34. *John Stephens, of-rhp, Gulf Coast (Fla.) CC.
35. Norman Seidel, rhp, Kenwood HS, Baltimore.
36. Jerrold Szostak, rhp, Quigley South HS, Chicago.
37. Pennington Hebron, ss, Hanover, Md.
38. Charles Lacy, inf, Odessa (Texas) JC.
39. *James Latouralle, ss, East Longmeadow (Mass.) HS.
40. *Robert Bower, 1b-3b, Ypsilanti (Mich.) HS.
41. Joseph Bartlett, of, University of New Hampshire.
42. *Ronald Bennett, lhp, Wayne County HS, Jesup, Ga.
43. Eddie Williams, lhp, University of Oklahoma.
44. *Stan Gatto, lhp, Suffolk (N.Y.) CC.
45. Lonnie Teasley, lhp, Lincoln HS, Taylor, S.C.
46. Grady Pierce, rhp, Griffin (Ga.) HS.
47. *Paul McGlain, lhp, Lincoln HS, San Francisco.
48. *Glenn Wallace, rhp, Mississippi State University.
49. *Tom Boland, rhp, South Georgia JC.
50. *Al Cleveland, rhp, Chipola (Fla.) JC.

**June—Secondary Phase (4)**

1. Derk Hoving, c, Amarillo (Texas) JC.—(AA)
2. *Charles Jones, lhp, Grambling University.
3. Eldon Jones, lhp, University of Southern Colorado.
4. William Kelley, rhp, University of Virginia.
5. Michael Houck, lhp, Hudson Valley (N.Y.) CC.
6. *Steven Rogers, of-lhp, University of Massachusetts.
7. *William Hunt, ss, Louisiana State University.

## BOSTON RED SOX

**January—Regular Phase (19)**

1. Walter Ransom, ss, South Gate (Calif.) HS.—(High A)
2. *Thomas Combs, of, American River (Calif.) JC.
3. Ronald Falls, rhp, Grossmont (Calif.) JC.
4. Mickey Whitson, rhp, Gulf Coast (Fla.) CC.

**January—Secondary Phase (15)**

1. Doug Sandstedt, lhp, Omaha (Neb.) HS.—(High A)
2. *Wendell Franke, inf, Mesa (Ariz.) CC.
3. *John Walker, c, Sacramento (Calif.) CC.
4. Thomas Skendarian, of, Brown University.
5. *Gerald Burton, of, St. Louis CC-Meramec.
6. *Larry Gonsalves, rhp, Fresno State University.
7. *Pat Brown, of, University of Texas.

**June—Regular Phase (20)**

1. Tom Maggard, of-c, John Glenn HS, Norwalk, Calif.—(AAA)
2. Curtis Suchan, ss-of, Jesuit HS, Tampa.—(AA)
**3. Lynn McGlothen, rhp, Grambling HS, Simsboro, La.—(1972-82)**
4. Allen Collins, c, Glendora (Calif.) HS.—(High A)
5. Manny Crespo, ss, Miami Senior HS.—(AAA)
**6. Cecil Cooper, 1b, Brenham (Texas) HS.—(1971-87)**
DRAFT DROP *Major league manager (2007-09)*
7. Hal Kurtzman, ss, University HS, Beverly Hills, Calif.
8. Roy Handel, c, Columbus (Ga.) HS.
9. Ed Baird, rhp, University of Connecticut.
10. *Michael O'Banion, c, Dos Palos (Calif.) HS.
**11. Ben Oglivie, 1b-of, Roosevelt HS, Bronx, N.Y.—(1971-86)**
12. Robert Overmiller, 3b-1b, Red Lion HS, Sexton, Pa.
13. Frank Mannerino, of, Oak Lawn (Ill.) Community HS.
14. Terry Williams, rhp, Davenport (Iowa) West HS.
15. *Thomas King, lhp, Acton-Boxborough HS, West Acton, Mass.
16. Bill Brown, 1b, Fresno State University.
17. Michael Collins, lhp, West Covina (Calif.) HS.
18. Lonnie Keeter, 3b, David Douglas HS, Portland, Ore.
19. *Curtis Jordan, of, Middle Georgia JC.
20. Jeff Grate, ss, Harvard University.
21. Frank Addonizo, c, St. John's University.
**22. Bill Lee, lhp, University of Southern California.—(1969-82)**
DRAFT DROP *First player from 1968 draft to reach majors (June 25, 1969)*
23. Stan Moss, inf, University of Alabama.
24. *Doug Miller, c-of, Klamath Union HS, Klamath Falls, Ore.
25. *Robert Hoepfinger, of, Timon HS, Buffalo, N.Y.
26. William Croken, c, Malden (Mass.) HS.
27. Roger Ward, lhp, Chaminade HS, Fort Lauderdale, Fla.
28. *Felix Skalski, 3b, Kalamazoo Valley (Mich.) JC.
29. Thomas Walsh, rhp, Tilton-Northfield HS, Tilton, N.H.
30. Blaine Young, lhp, Bishop Stang HS, Fairhaven, Mass.
31. Michael Neal, lhp, Shasta (Calif.) JC.
32. Michael Harvison, inf, Polytechnical HS, Fort Worth, Texas.
33. Richard Perry, c-1b, St. Johnsville (N.Y.) HS.
34. George Reebe, of, Natick (Mass.) HS.
35. Jeff Guenther, rhp, Katella HS, Anaheim, Calif.
36. *Michael Comuso, rhp, Lawrence Central HS, Lawrence, Mass.

**June—Secondary Phase (10)**

**1. John Curtis, lhp, Clemson University.—(1970-84)**
DRAFT DROP *First-round draft pick (12th overall), Indians (1966)*
2. *Ronald Soucie, lhp, Husson (Maine) College.
3. Richard Wicks, lhp, McNeese State University.
4. Alan Truskowski, lhp, St. Clair County (Mich.) CC.
5. *Nicholas Furlong, rhp, University of Notre Dame.

## CALIFORNIA ANGELS

**January—Regular Phase (11)**

1. *Robert Johnson, rhp, Los Angeles Pierce JC.—(Short-season A)
2. Jim Cesario, 3b, Torrance (Calif.) HS.
3. *James Stern, lhp, South Georgia JC.
4. *David Landress, 2b, Los Angeles Pierce JC.
5. *James Eichmeier, lhp, Arizona Western JC.
6. *Richard Leavitt, of, Cerritos (Calif.) JC.
7. *Thomas Tanner, of, Cerritos (Calif.) JC.
8. *Rusty Swisher, rhp, Los Angeles Pierce JC.

**January—Secondary Phase (13)**

1. Dayle Campbell, 1b, Pepperdine University.—(AA)
2. Pat Knutzen, lhp, El Camino (Calif.) JC.
**3. *Paul Reuschel, rhp, Western Illinois University.—(1975-79)**
DRAFT DROP *Brother of Rick Reuschel, major leaguer (1972-91)*
4. David Thompson, of, Santa Barbara (Calif.) CC.
5. *Ronald Pritchett, rhp, Mount San Antonio (Calif.) JC.
6. *William Susa, rhp, Los Angeles Pierce JC.
7. *Lee Chilton, of, San Joaquin Delta (Calif.) JC.
8. *Jim Pope, rhp, Columbia Basin (Wash.) CC.

**June—Regular Phase (12)**

**1. Lloyd Allen, rhp, Selma (Calif.) HS.—(1969-75)**
2. *Gordon Carter, of, Sunny Hills HS, Fullerton, Calif.—(High A)
DRAFT DROP *Attended Southern California, re-drafted by Giants, June 1971/secondary phase, delayed (2nd round) • Brother of Gary Carter, major leaguer (1974-1992)*
3. *John Harbin, ss, Berea HS, Greenville, S.C.—(Short-season A)
DRAFT DROP *Attended Newberry (S.C.) College; re-drafted by Dodgers, 1972 (1st round)*
4. Rick Hansen, rhp, McLane HS, Fresno, Calif.–(AA)
5. *Dennis Wallin, c, Rio Americano HS, Sacramento, Calif.—DNP
DRAFT DROP *Attended American River (Calif.) JC; re-drafted by Yankees, January 1969/secondary phase (2nd round)*
6. Gregory Dehn, c, Anoka (Minn.) HS.
**7. Tom Bradley, rhp, University of Maryland.—(1969-75)**
DRAFT DROP *Baseball coach, Jacksonville (1979-90); baseball coach, Maryland (1991-2000)*

8. Randy Niles, ss, Santa Monica (Calif.) JC.
9. Toy McCord, ss, University of South Carolina.
**10. Harvey Shank, rhp, Stanford University.—(1970)**
11. Jose Quinones, of, Staten Island (N.Y.) CC.
12. Brian Nelson, lhp, Cal State Los Angeles.
**13. *Rick Auerbach, ss, Taft HS, Woodland Hills, Calif.—(1971-81)**
14. Damon Howell, ss, Edison HS, Fresno, Calif.
15. *Robert Hubbard, rhp, Spencerport (N.Y.) HS.
16. James Malloney, rhp, Sacred Heart Academy, Cumberland, R.I.
17. *William Jenkins, 2b, Orange Coast (Calif.) JC.
18. Frank Russo, lhp, Everett (Mass.) HS.
19. Jerry Carr, rhp, Bolsa Grande HS, Garden Grove, Calif.
20. Constantine Cirasuolo, of, Whitesboro (N.Y.) HS.
21. *Gary Addeo, 1b-of, Pius X HS, Downey, Calif.
22. *Gene Tate, ss, Turlock (Calif.) HS.
23. *Richard Mahlmann, lhp, Hanford (Calif.) HS.
24. *Van Winters, rhp, McLane HS, Fresno, Calif.
25. Stephen Romero, rhp, Simi Valley (Calif.) HS.
26. Daniel Loomer, ss, Golden State (Calif.) JC.
27. *Rodney Sooter, rhp, Holy Savior Menard HS, Alexandria, La.
28. John Schroeder, rhp, UC Santa Barbara.
29. *Lionel Schoebridge, 1b-c, Lyndhurst (N.J.) HS.
30. *Bobby Wheeler, 1b, Sunny Hills HS, Fullerton, Calif.
31. Jerry Feldman, 1b, Cal State Los Angeles.
32. Craig Hansen, 1b, University of Denver.
33. Ronald St. Clair, rhp, Bakersfield (Calif.) JC.
34. *Glenn Spicer, rhp, Grant HS, North Hollywood, Calif.
35. *Thomas Utman, ss, Menlo (Calif.) JC.
36. Matt Moschetti, 3b, Cal State Fullerton.
37. *Dennis Gallagher, ss, East Nicholas (Calif.) HS.
38. Greg Henard, ss-3b, Tulare (Calif.) HS.
39. *Verdell Adams, of, Jefferson HS, Portland, Ore.

#### June—Secondary Phase (14)

1. Larry Hanson, ss, University of Oregon.—(AAA)
2. Michael Schomaker, c, Stanford University.
3. Martin Pavlik, lhp, Wilson (Ill.) JC.
4. Jim Suskiewich, lhp, Indiana University.
5. *Michael Babler, rhp, Chabot (Calif.) JC.
6. Michael Lersch, lhp, Mesa (Ariz.) CC.
7. *Charles Kurkjian, 3b, Fresno (Calif.) CC.
8. *Craig Schell, rhp, UC Santa Barbara.

## CHICAGO CUBS

#### January—Regular Phase (16)

1. (void) *Dave Baldwin, lhp, Manatee (Fla.) JC.—(High A)
2. *Darryl Thomas, lhp, Long Beach (Calif.) CC.
3. *Steve Simonian, rhp, Fresno (Calif.) CC.
4. *Jake Molina, ss, San Diego CC.
5. Curtis Barto, ss, Montgomery, Pa.
6. *Robert Petretta, of, San Diego CC.
7. (void) *N.D. Bingham, rhp, Texas Christian University.
8. *Patrick Roark, of, San Diego Mesa JC.
9. (void) *Thomas Palmer, rhp, University of Delaware.

#### January—Secondary Phase (10)

1. Steven Salata, c, Oneonta (N.Y.) HS.—(Low A)
2. *Dennis Parks, of, University of Southern California.
3. Mike Lisetski, ss, Rider College.
4. *Bill Grogan, rhp, Yakima (Wash.) Valley JC.
5. Tim Feldhaus, ss, Mount San Antonio (Calif.) JC.
6. *Thomas Kaehler, of, Los Angeles Valley JC.
7. Dennis Gideon, lhp, Chaffey (Calif.) JC.

#### June—Regular Phase (15)

1. Ralph Rickey, of, University of Oklahoma.—(AAA)
**2. Matt Alexander, 3b, Grambling University.—(1973-81)**
3. *Jeff Pederson, of, Fermin Lasuen HS, San Pedro, Calif.—DNP
DRAFT DROP *Attended Southern California; never re-drafted*
4. Michael Roe, rhp, East Providence HS, Riverside, R.I.—(AA)
5. (void) *Eldridge Blake, of, St. Thomas, Virgin Islands.—DNP
DRAFT DROP *Attended University of Virgin Islands; never re-drafted*
6. Randolph Richardson, c, Pfeiffer (N.C.) College.
7. *Thomas McDermott, ss, Northwest HS, St. Louis.
8. Joe Biercevicz, rhp, Shelton HS, Huntington, Conn.
9. Ron Jones, lhp, Covina HS, West Covina, Calif.
10. *Don Henrichs, rhp, Enumclaw (Wash.) HS.
11. *Nicholas Eichelberger, ss, Trinity Prep, Allentown, Pa.
12. *Scott Taylor, rhp, Mansfield (Pa.) University.
13. Richard Barnes, lhp, Lane Tech HS, Chicago.
14. *Kim West, rhp, St. Albans (W.Va.) HS.
15. *Wayne Anderson, 1b, Lakes HS, Tacoma, Wash.
**16. Oscar Gamble, of, George Washington Carver HS, Montgomery, Ala.—(1969-85)**
DRAFT DROP *First 1968 high school draft pick to reach majors (Aug. 27, 1969)*
17. *Robert Johnston, lhp, Fike HS, Wilson, N.C.
18. *Tim Gurp, of, Phoenix (Ariz.) JC.
19. Phil Brown, rhp, Manteca (Calif.) HS.
20. Bob Micheletti, c, University of Minnesota.
21. Paul Zahn, rhp, Parsons (Iowa) College.
22. Michael Nye, of, Ribault HS, Jacksonville, Fla.
23. *James Mottine, rhp, Red Bank (N.J.) HS.
24. Denny Taylor, lhp, West Virginia University.
25. James Bryan, of, Guilford (N.C.) College.
26. *Herbert Sikes, 3b, Leon HS, Tallahassee, Fla.
27. Jimmie Walters, ss, Georgia Southern College.
28. Terry Childers, c, Georgia Southern College.
DRAFT DROP *Father of Matt Childers, major leaguer (2002-05) • Father of Jason Childers, major leaguer (2006)*
29. Paul Starman, rhp, University of Iowa.
30. *Bill Dorothy, 2b, Bacone (Okla.) JC.
31. *Ken Wastradowski, lhp, Centralia (Wash.) HS.
32. *Mike Hetman, c, Hudson Valley (N.Y.) CC.

#### June—Secondary Phase (1)

**1. Dave Lemonds, lhp, University of North Carolina.—(1969-72)**
2. Robert Breitzman, 2b, Illinois State University.
**3. Chris Ward, of, Chabot (Calif.) JC.–(1972-74)**
**4. Paul Reuschel, rhp, Western Illinois University.—(1975-79)**
DRAFT DROP *Brother of Rick Reuschel, major leaguer (1972-91)*
5. Allen Simas, of, Sacramento (Calif.) CC.
6. *Gary Houston, lhp, San Jose (Calif.) CC.
7. Tom Binkowski, 1b, Michigan State University.

## CHICAGO WHITE SOX

#### January—Regular Phase (13)

**1. *Mickey Rivers, of, Miami-Dade CC North.—(1970-84)**
2. *Martin Pavlik, lhp, Wilson (Ill.) JC.

#### January—Secondary Phase (19)

**1. *Chris Ward, of, Chabot (Calif.) JC.—(1972-74)**
2. *Bill Dobbs, lhp, Oklahoma State University.
3. *Dick Hanselman, lhp, St. John's River (Fla.) CC.
4. Joe Bowen, 3b-1b, Norfolk (Va.) HS.
5. *Jerre Algeo, 2b, Poteau (Mo.) JC.
6. *Don Lamb, rhp, Thornton (Ill.) CC.

#### June—Regular Phase (14)

**1. Rich McKinney, ss-3b, Ohio University.—(1970-77)**
**2. Hugh Yancy, ss, Sarasota (Fla.) HS.—(1972-76)**
**3. Lamar Johnson, c, Wenonah HS, Birmingham, Ala.—(1974-82)**
4. Dennis Deck, lhp, Magnolia HS, Anaheim, Calif.—(AAA)
5. *Tom Wittum, 3b, Round Lake (Ill.) HS.—DNP
DRAFT DROP *Attended Northern Illinois; never re-drafted; punter, National Football League (1973-77)*
6. Robert Giesler, lhp, LaPorte (Ind.) HS.
7. *Collis James, c, Mobile County Training School, Prichard, Ala.
8. Leonard Massaro, rhp, Richmond (Calif.) HS.
9. *William Menk, lhp, Lincoln HS, Philadelphia.
10. Lawrence Jackson, of-1b, Wenonah HS, Birmingham, Ala.
11. *James Kiley, ss, Reading (Mass.) HS.
12. Jim Redmon, ss, Western Michigan University.
13. *Garrett Berry, c, Sunny Hills HS, Fullerton, Calif.
**14. Rich Moloney, rhp, Brookline (Mass.) HS.—(1970)**
15. Richard Propson, lhp, Stockbridge (Wis.) HS.
**16. Stan Perzanowski, rhp, Morton HS, Hammond, Ind.—(1971-78)**
17. *Thomas Heinrich, of, Hayward (Wis.) HS.
18. William Hansen, 1b, Long Island University.
19. *Bobby Lail, lhp, Crest HS, Shelby, N.C.
20. Kenny Brooks, rhp, Wilkes Central HS, Wilkesboro, N.C.
21. Rod Pommes, of-3b, Santa Clara University.
22. *Robert Kleinholz, 1b-lhp, Loara HS, Anaheim, Calif.
23. John Fiene, c, Westside HS, Omaha, Neb.
24. Larry Bashford, 3b, Anaheim (Calif.) HS.
25. Dana Ryan, 2b, Arkansas State University.
26. Stephen Spanich, rhp, Quincy (Ill.) College.
27. *Mark Jones, 1b, Crowder (Mo.) JC.
28. *Bruce Finkbeiner, inf-of, Colorado State University.
29. *Dale Reed, lhp, Crowder (Mo.) JC.
30. Charles Auchmutey, rhp, Avondale HS, Avondale Estates, Ga.
31. Nathander Pettaway, 1b, St. Elmore HS, Theodore, Ala.

#### June—Secondary Phase (2)

**1. Bart Johnson, rhp, Torrance, Calif.—(1969-77)**
**2. Ken Hottman, of, Sacramento (Calif.) CC.—(1971)**
**3. Dan Neumeier, rhp, University of Wisconsin-Oshkosh.—(1972)**
4. *Dave Renkiewicz, rhp, University of Michigan.
5. *Michael Nichols, 1b-lhp, Biola (Calif.) University.
6. Larry Linville, of, Arizona State University.
7. *Franklin Riggins, of, University of Kansas.

## CINCINNATI REDS

#### January—Regular Phase (14)

1. *Donald Shrum, rhp, Houston (Texas) HS.—(Rookie)
2. *Freddie Howard, 1b-of, Paris (Texas) JC.
3. William Morton, c, Pittsburgh (Pa.) HS.
4. Charles Beck, rhp, Lincoln HS, Summit, Mo.
5. *David Ward, rhp, Eastern Oklahoma State JC.
6. Jerry Turk, rhp, Fort Valley State (Ga.) College.
7. Charles Higgins, rhp, Jefferson State (Ala.) JC.
8. *William Davis, c, Midway (Pa.) HS.

#### January—Secondary Phase (16)

1. Charlie West, of, University of Texas-El Paso.—(High A)
DRAFT DROP *Defensive back, National Football League (1968-79)*
**2. *Chris Chambliss, 1b, Mira Costa (Calif.) JC.—(1971-88)**
DRAFT DROP *First overall draft pick, January 1970/ regular phase, Indians*
3. *Michael Wertz, ss, Wharton County (Texas) JC.
4. Michael James, 2b, Dallas Baptist University.
5. Michael Willis, lhp, University of Colorado.
6. *Edward Stack, rhp, Cameron (Okla.) University.
7. *Donald Jumper, rhp, Jasper, Texas.
8. Glenn Bisbing, c, Rider College.

#### June—Regular Phase (13)

1. Tim Grant, rhp, Riverview HS, Boykins, Va.—(High A)
**2. Milt Wilcox, rhp, Crooked Oak HS, Oklahoma City, Okla.—(1970-86)**
3. *Rich Lenard, rhp, LaPorte (Ind.) HS.—DNP
DRAFT DROP *Attended Indiana; never re-drafted*
4. Edward May, lhp, McLain HS, North Tulsa, Okla.—(High A)
5. Edward Upstone, rhp, Walter Lutheran HS, Lyons, Ill.—(High A)
6. Albert Faix, lhp, Pennsylvania Ridge HS, Sellersville, Pa.
7. Phillip Freeman, of-1b, Wasson HS, Colorado Springs, Colo.
8. William Hoelzer, of, Clinton (Mich.) HS.
9. Carl Williamson, rhp, El Rancho HS, Pico Rivera, Calif.
10. Edward Street, lhp, Horace Scott HS, Modena, Pa.
11. Henry Kopps, of, Brazosport HS, Lake Jackson, Texas.
12. Thomas Dittmar, of-1b, Belleville (Texas) HS.
13. Vincent Coleman, 1b-3b, St. Joseph HS, Jackson, Miss.
14. Robert Flint, rhp, Provine HS, Jackson, Miss.
15. Doug Dreier, rhp, Red Bluff (Calif.) HS.
16. Robert Welsh, ss, Cathedral HS, Trenton, N.J.
17. *Don Sweetland, c, William S. Hart HS, Saugus, Calif.
18. Jeffrey Brelsford, c, Mainland HS, Daytona Beach, Fla.
19. Theodore Bryand, 2b, South French HS, Asheville, N.C.
20. *Wade Kleckley, rhp, Brookland-Cayce HS, Lexington, S.C.
21. Benjamin Williams, c-of, Grambling University.
22. Gregory Siereveld, inf, Taft HS, Hamilton, Ohio.
23. Keith West, of, Gustine (Calif.) HS.
24. *Jonathan Tate, rhp, Tompkins HS, Savannah, Ga.
**25. *Mike Willis, lhp, Hillsboro HS, Nashville, Tenn.—(1977-81)**
26. *Russell Davis, lhp, Capitol Hill HS, Oklahoma City, Okla.
27. *Craig White, of, Fairfax (Va.) HS.
28. *John Mindell, rhp, Okarche (Okla.) HS.
29. *James Kelley, 2b, Arlington (Texas) HS.
30. *Kenneth Burke, rhp, William Bryant HS, Moultrie, Ga.
31. *Gregory Faux, rhp, Provo (Utah) HS.
32. Larry Feltner, rhp, High Point HS, College Park, Md.
33. *Ronald Fisher, rhp, Olympus HS, Salt Lake City.
34. *Gerald Daugherty, c, Cy-Fair HS, Houston.
35. *Michael O'Connor, lhp, Anderson HS, Cincinnati.
36. *Michael Carter, ss-3b, John Tyler HS, Tyler, Texas.
37. *Glen Olsen, rhp, Wilson HS, Sinking Springs, Pa.
38. *Bobby Thompson, rhp, Edmond (Okla.) HS.
39. Gregg Slape, of, Sul Ross State (Texas) University.
40. *Stephen Boron, rhp, George Washington HS, Philadelphia.
41. *Kent Estep, rhp, Grandfield (Okla.) HS.
42. Bobby Lemley, inf, Marshall University.
43. *James Mertens, 1b, Fairmont State (W.Va.) College.
44. *Patrick Korsnick, of, Wheeling Central HS, Wheeling, W.Va.

#### June—Secondary Phase (5)

**1. Mel Behney, lhp, Michigan State University.—(1970)**
2. (void) *Jeff Pryor, rhp, Florida Southern College.
3. *Darryl Thomas, lhp, Long Beach (Calif.) CC.
4. *Donald Schroeder, rhp, Grays Harbor (Wash.) JC.
5. *Freddie Howard, 1b-lhp, Paris (Texas) JC.
6. *David Reeves, rhp, University of Georgia.
7. (void) *Wayne Church, rhp, East Tennessee State University.

## CLEVELAND INDIANS

#### January—Regular Phase (5)

1. *Lambert Ford, of, Vineland (N.J.) HS.—(AA)
2. *Rick Dierker, rhp, Woodland Hills (Calif.) HS.
DRAFT DROP *Brother of Larry Dierker, major leaguer (1964-77); major league manager (1997-2001)*
3. Bruce Killion, rhp, North Charleston, S.C.
4. *Donald Barnum, rhp, Chabot (Calif.) JC.
5. Allan Boyd, c, Baltimore (Md.) HS.
6. *Clarence Smith, rhp, St. Francis (N.Y.) College.
7. *Jeff Fuller, 2b, Canoga Park (Calif.) HS.
8. Tom Penders, of, University of Connecticut.
DRAFT DROP *Basketball coach, Texas (1988-98); basketball coach, Houston (2004-10)*

#### January—Secondary Phase (5)

**1. *Ray Bare, rhp, Miami-Dade CC North.—(1972-77)**
2. Harold Harris, 3b-ss, Gulf Coast (Fla.) CC.
**3. Rick Sawyer, rhp, Bakersfield (Calif.) JC.—(1974-77)**
4. *Leon Filbeck, rhp, Santa Ana (Calif.) JC.
5. Wayne Danson, of, Gulf Coast (Fla.) CC.
6. Edwin Staples, c, Texas A&M University.
7. Robert Cramer, rhp, Mitchell (Conn.) JC.
8. *Taylor Toomey, lhp, University of Colorado.
9. *William Moynier, rhp, Bakersfield (Calif.) JC.

10. *Roy Waye, 1b, Kingsport, Tenn.
11. *Roger Jackson, rhp, University of Kansas.
12. *Larry Phillippe, rhp, Edison (Fla.) CC.

### June—Regular Phase (6)

1. Michael Weaver, ss-of, Paxon HS, Jacksonville, Fla.—(AA)
2. Mike Parks, 3b, Lakewood (Calif.) HS.—(High A)
3. **Bob Kaiser, lhp, Weber HS, Ogden, Utah.—(1971)**
4. Danay Covert, 1b, Stephen F. Austin HS, Austin, Texas.—(AAA)
5. Larry Shaw, of-1b, Matawan (N.J.) HS.—(High A)
6. John Howell, lhp, Robert E. Lee HS, Midland, Texas.
7. Richard Napolitano, rhp, St. John's University.
8. Ken Stauffer, c, Margaretta HS, Castalia, Ohio.
9. **Larry Doby Johnson, c, East Tech HS, Cleveland.—(1972-78)**
10. *Ken Conlin, 2b, East Valley HS, Yakima, Wash.
11. **Vince Colbert, rhp, East Carolina University.—(1970-72)**
12. **Chuck Machemehl, rhp, Texas Christian University.—(1971)**
13. Cecil Bankhorn, ss, David Lipscomb (Tenn.) College.
14. *Dana Baltzer, ss, Hoover HS, San Diego.
15. Mike Carruthers, 1b, Pembroke State (N.C.) University.
16. ***Steve Stone, rhp, Kent State University.—(1971-81)**
17. Robert Shaps, of, Shaker Heights (Ohio) HS.
18. **John Lowenstein, ss, UC Riverside.—(1970-85)**
19. Jimmy Hobgood, lhp, Pensacola (Fla.) HS.
20. *George Gibson, ss, Tate HS, Cantonment, Fla.
21. Donald Hayward, rhp, Pontiac Northern HS, Pontiac, Mich.
22. *Robert Shearer, ss, Indian River (Fla.) CC.
23. Gary Lear, c, Columbia, Mo.
24. *Douglas Bozeman, 2b, Fremont HS, Los Angeles.
25. *Mickey McCarty, lhp, Texas Christian University.

DRAFT DROP *One of three athletes drafted in three sports; fourth-round draft pick, Kansas City Chiefs/National Football League (1969); tight end, NFL (1969); 15th-round draft pick, Chicago Bulls/National Basketball Association (1968); 14th-round draft pick, Dallas Chaparrals/American Basketball Association (1968)*

26. *Stephen Fahsbender, lhp, North Bakersfield (Calif.) HS.
27. *Frank Hagen, of, Napa (Calif.) HS.
28. Richard Schwartz, lhp, St. John's University.
29. ***Doug Bird, rhp, Pomona (Calif.) HS.—(1973-83)**
30. Walter Hallberg, 3b, Pascagoula (Miss.) HS.
31. *Robert Eriksen, rhp, Bullard HS, Fresno, Calif.
32. Jerry Stitt, of, University of Arizona.

DRAFT DROP *Baseball coach, Arizona (1997-2001)*

33. ***Dave Augustine, c, Miami-Dade CC South.—(1973-74)**
34. Michael Selland, 3b, DeAnza HS, El Sobrante, Calif.
35. Robert Love, rhp, Baldwin-Wallace (Ohio) College.
36. *Tim Mackin, rhp, Hudson Bay HS, Vancouver, Wash.
37. *James Gailey, of, Lake Wales (Fla.) HS.
38. James Bogard, c, Mohawk HS, Sycamore, Ohio.
39. *Franco Garcia, inf-of, Westfield (Mass.) HS.
40. *Alan White, rhp-ss, Buckeye Central HS, New Washington, Ohio.
41. *William Becker, of, Bowling Green State University.
42. *Harold Smith, ss, Elwood City (Pa.) HS.
43. *Mickey Knight, rhp, Michigan State University.
44. *Dan Miller, rhp, Sandusky (Ohio) HS.
45. *Bruce Cannon, 3b, Oberlin (Ohio) HS.
46. *Walter Sharrock, rhp, Jupiter (Fla.) HS.
47. *Gary Harover, of-1b, Pendleton (Ore.) HS.
48. *Wayne Milan, rhp, Stranahan HS, Fort Lauderdale, Fla.

### June—Secondary Phase (6)

1. **Rick Austin, lhp, Washington State University.—(1970-76)**
2. *Pat Brown, of, University of Texas.
3. *Dale Dunham, rhp, Central Michigan University.
4. ***John Morlan, rhp, Ohio University.—(1973-74)**
5. Leon Filbeck, rhp, Santa Ana (Calif.) JC.
6. ***Ray Bare, rhp, Miami-Dade CC North.—(1972-77)**
7. *Ron Davini, c, Arizona State University.
8. *William Moynier, rhp, Bakersfield (Calif.) HS.
9. Larry Price, of, JC of the Desert (Calif.).

## DETROIT TIGERS

### January—Regular Phase (17)

1. *James Carter, 3b, Golden West (Calif.) JC.—DNP
2. (void) *Thomas Jackson, ss, Citrus (Calif.) JC.
3. *Richard Garner, c, Santa Rosa (Calif.) JC.
4. *James Poole, c, Detroit (Mich.) HS.
5. *Nicholas Parilla, rhp, Staunton (Va.) Military Academy.
6. George Moore, of, Detroit (Mich.) HS.
7. **Bill Slayback, rhp, Glendale (Calif.) JC.—(1972-74)**
8. Arthur Clifford, rhp, Quincy, Mass.
9. Rodger Beckman, ss, Muskegon (Mich.) CC.

### January—Secondary Phase (3)

1. **Ken Szotkiewicz, ss, Georgia Southern College.—(1970)**
2. **Chuck Scrivener, ss, CC of Baltimore.—(1975-77)**
3. Tommy Grayson, 2b, Guilford (N.C.) College.
4. ***Bob O'Brien, lhp, University of Arizona.—(1971)**
5. *Steve Smith, 3b, Long Beach (Calif.) CC.
6. Jerry Killian, lhp, Flint (Mich.) JC.
7. *Harry Saferight, c, Manatee (Fla.) JC.
8. ***Terry Wilshusen, rhp, Torrance, Calif.—(1973)**
9. Vache Bahadurian, 1b, New York CC.
10. *William Carroll, of, Alhambra, Calif.

### June—Regular Phase (18)

1. Murray "Smokey" Robinson, of, Thomas Dale HS, Chester, Va.—(AAA)
2. **Bob Molinaro, of, Essex Catholic HS, Newark, N.J.—(1975-83)**
3. Ray Blosse, rhp, High Point College.—(AAA)
4. Thomas Casteller, rhp, John F. Kennedy HS, Taylor, Mich.—(High A)
5. *Thomas Miller, of, Reading (Pa.) HS.—DNP

DRAFT DROP *Did not sign, never re-drafted*

6. Frank Fisher, rhp, Wayne (Mich.) HS.
7. Daryl Busen, rhp, Fordson HS, Dearborn, Mich.
8. ***Ross Grimsley, lhp, Frayser HS, Memphis, Tenn.—(1971-82)**

DRAFT DROP *Son of Ross Grimsley, major leaguer (1951)*

9. *John Hyde, lhp, Loyola Academy, Chicago.
10. **Marvin Lane, of, Pershing HS, Detroit.—(1971-76)**
11. Mark Grove, of, Anchor Bay HS, New Baltimore, Mich.
12. *Terry Rutledge, 3b-of, McLain HS, Tulsa, Okla.
13. Howard Johnson, ss, Milton (Wis.) College.
14. Robert Cole, 1b, West Portsmouth (Ohio) HS.
15. *Rex Campbell, c, Beaver Local HS, East Liverpool, Ohio.
16. Spencer Horn, ss, Fort Cobb (Okla.) HS.
17. Robert LaFrance, c, Natick (Mass.) HS.
18. **Bob Strampe, rhp, Janesville (Wis.) HS.—(1972)**
19. *Matthew Rockwood, of, Grand Rapids (Mich.) JC.
20. *Barry Perteler, rhp, Swartz Creek HS, Gaines, Mich.
21. Anthony Amendola, rhp, Aviation Tech HS, New York.
22. *Michael Crim, rhp, Hickman HS, Columbia, Mo.
23. **Don Leshnock, lhp, Youngstown State University.—(1972)**
24. Bill Puryear, rhp, Highland Park (Mich.) HS.
25. Edward Laborio, rhp, Cranston (R.I.) HS.
26. John Bevil, lhp, Baylor University.
27. Donald Murphy, c, St. Mary's HS, Sacramento, Calif.
28. *John Zbercot, c, South Lake HS, St. Clair Shores, Mich.
29. Lary Lohse, lhp, Seaman (Ohio) HS.
30. *Terry Greene, inf, Republic (Mo.) HS.
31. Richard Foulk, lhp, South Torrance (Calif.) HS.
32. Wayne Hamilton, inf, Airport HS, New Boston, Mich.
33. Stephen Cushmore, lhp, Princeton University.
34. *Keith Kasparovitch, lhp, Punahou HS, Honolulu, Hawaii.
35. *John Cabral, lhp, Kaimuki HS, Honolulu, Hawaii.
36. *Dennis Primeau, inf, Northville HS, Novi, Mich.
37. Mark Pratt, rhp, Monroe (Mich.) HS.
38. *Michael Longstreth, ss, Harding HS, Oklahoma City, Okla.
39. Thomas Breving, of, Xavier University.
40. Arthur Grassing, rhp, Bourne HS, Flushing, N.Y.
41. *Alfred LiVecchi, rhp, Lane HS, Queens Village, N.Y.
42. *Shawn Howitt, 1b, Central HS, Battle Creek, Mich.
43. *Robert Hileman, rhp, Staunton (Va.) Military Academy.
44. Joseph Pellechi, inf, Fordham University.
45. Joseph Martin, rhp, Shippensburg (Pa.) HS.

### June—Secondary Phase (20)

1. **Elliott Maddox, 3b-of, University of Michigan.—(1970-80)**
2. *John Hurley, rhp, University of Michigan.
3. *Ronald Wayne, lhp, Laney (Calif.) JC.
4. Steve Smith, 3b, Long Beach (Calif.) CC.
5. *Barry Sheldon, rhp, Genesee (N.Y.) CC.

## HOUSTON ASTROS

### January—Regular Phase (4)

1. **Glenn Adams, of, Springfield (Mass.) College.—(1975-82)**
2. *Ken Stabler, lhp, University of Alabama.

DRAFT DROP *Quarterback, National Football League (1970-84)*

### January—Secondary Phase (12)

1. Michael McFarland, rhp, University of Missouri.—(AA)
2. ***Sandy Vance, rhp, Stanford University.—(1970-71)**
3. *Bob Williams, of, Yakima Valley (Wash.) JC.
4. *Ronald Shepard, 3b-of, Altus, Okla.

### June—Regular Phase (3)

1. Marty Cott, c, Hutchinson Technical HS, Buffalo, N.Y.—(AAA)
2. **Rich Chiles, of, Winters (Calif.) HS.—(1971-78)**
3. **Bill Greif, rhp, Reagan HS, Austin, Texas.—(1971-76)**
4. Larry Mansfield, 1b, University of Tennessee.—(AA)
5. **Larry Yount, rhp, Taft HS, Woodland Hills, Calif.—(1971)**

DRAFT DROP *Brother of Robin Yount, first-round draft pick, Brewers (1973); major leaguer (1974-1993)*

6. John Grant, lhp, Westchester HS, Los Angeles.
7. *Greg Pavlick, rhp-3b, Thomas A. Edison HS, Alexandria, Va.
8. Raylan Hoellwarth, c, Lodi (Calif.) HS.
9. Andrew Williams, inf, Jesuit HS, New Orleans, La.
10. Carlos Alfonso, inf, Naples (Fla.) HS.
11. Kenneth Barnes, rhp, Skyline HS, Idaho Falls, Idaho.
12. *Henry Yeargan, ss, Wayne County HS, Jesup, Ga.
13. Lester Roos, ss, Temple University.
14. *Wendall Clowers, lhp, City HS, Chattanooga, Tenn.
15. Clinton Burr, rhp, Cocoa HS, Rockledge, Fla.
16. *Curtis Boans, of, Dunedin HS, Clearwater, Fla.
17. *Dave Snow, 3b, Bellflower (Calif.) HS.

DRAFT DROP *Baseball coach, Loyola Marymount (1985-88); baseball coach, Long Beach State (1989-2001)*

18. **Ken Forsch, rhp, Oregon State University.—(1970-86)**

DRAFT DROP *Brother of Bob Forsch, 26th-round draft pick, Cardinals (1968); major leaguer (1974-89)*

19. Rodney Clabo, of, Temple University.
20. James Baasse, ss, Hammond-Morton HS, Hammond, Ind.
21. Edward Ontiveros, rhp, Bakersfield (Calif.) HS.
22. *Don Hager, c, Sherman HS, Seth, W.Va.
23. *John Euller, rhp, Milford Mill HS, Baltimore.
24. *Darrell Jones, rhp, Comanche (Okla.) HS.
25. John Canty, lhp, University of Massachusetts.
26. Steven Miller, lhp, Dowling HS, Des Moines, Iowa.
27. Harmon Bove, c, Burlington (Vt.) HS.
28. John Fox, c-of, Lansdowne HS, Baltimore.
29. David Doyle, ss, Lynwood (Calif.) HS.
30. *Clifford Powers, inf, South Broward HS, Dania, Fla.
31. *Steven Griffith, rhp, Pacifica HS, Garden Grove, Calif.
32. *Phil Corddry, lhp, University of Maryland.
33. Alan Peters, rhp, Verbum Dei HS, Los Angeles.
34. *Ronald Garlin, of, McArthur HS, Hollywood, Fla.
35. *Gary Klass, ss, Reitz Memorial HS, Evansville, Ind.
36. *James Fallers, lhp-of, Mount Pleasant HS, Wilmington, Del.

### June—Secondary Phase (15)

1. **Buddy Harris, rhp, University of Miami.—(1970-71)**
2. David Grangaard, 3b, Arizona State University.
3. Joe Arnold, rhp, Arizona State University.

DRAFT DROP *Baseball coach, Florida (1984-94)*

4. Richard Hicks, rhp, Louisiana State University.
5. Lambert Ford, of, Vineland HS, Richland, N.J.

## KANSAS CITY ROYALS

### June—Regular Phase (24)

1-3. No selections.

4. Kenneth O'Donnell, ss, Neptune (N.J.) HS.–(AA)
5. John Nelson, of, Duarte (Calif.) HS.—(High A)
6. *Mark Tanner, 1b-rhp, Neshannock HS, New Castle, Pa.

DRAFT DROP *Son of Chuck Tanner, major leaguer (1955-72); major league manager (1970-88) • Brother of Bruce Tanner, major leaguer (1985)*

7. **Lance Clemons, lhp-of, West Chester (Pa.) University.—(1971-74)**
8. *Clark Ullom, lhp, Shawnee Mission South HS, Shawnee Mission, Kan.
9. **Monty Montgomery, rhp, Pfeiffer (N.C.) College.—(1971-72)**
10. Robert Lawson, rhp, Cox HS, Virginia Beach, Va.
11. *Robert Nelson, rhp, Roosevelt HS, Seattle.
12. Cornelius Drew, of, Dendron (Va.) HS.
13. Jim Hannah, c, Washington State University.
14. Thomas Crichton, 2b, Santa Cruz (Calif.) HS.
15. Michael Ginn, c, Bakersfield (Calif.) HS.
16. ***Dane Iorg, ss, Arcata (Calif.) HS.—(1977-86)**

DRAFT DROP *Brother of Garth Iorg, major leaguer (1978-87)*

17. Paul Walker, rhp, Colorado School of Mines.
18. *Mark Fuller, lhp, Chatham (La.) HS.
19. *Vincent Shawver, rhp, Shawnee Mission North HS, Shawnee Mission, Kan.
20. *Joe Pupo, rhp, Gonzaga HS, Spokane, Wash.
21. *Ronnie Botica, rhp, Shreveport, La.
22. *Mike Proffit, lhp, Ensley HS, Birmingham, Ala.
23. Jackson Chandler, rhp, Prince Edward Academy, Farmville, Va.
24. Greg With, 3b, University of New Mexico.
25. **Paul Splittorff, lhp, Morningside (Iowa) College.—(1970-84)**
26. *Patrick Smith, ss, Bellarmine Prep, Tacoma, Wash.
27. *Jerry Merchant, ss, San Bernardino (Calif.) HS.
28. Bruce Pomeroy, c, James Madison HS, Vienna, Va.
29. Richard Long, rhp, Kansas State University.
30. *Thomas Cason, of, South Georgia JC.
31. *Gary Rainbow, rhp, North Syracuse (N.Y.) HS.
32. Thomas Moore, rhp, Rider College.
33. Roland Panepinto, ss-2b, Fort Union (Va.) Military HS.
34. *James Walker, rhp, San Bernardino (Calif.) HS.
35. *Tim Steele, 1b-of, Downey (Calif.) HS.
36. *James Masters, rhp, Jesuit HS, Carmichael, Calif.
37. *Steve Noreiga, rhp-of, Jesuit HS, Tampa.
38. *Stephan Metro, inf-of, Arvada West HS, Golden, Colo.
39. *John Medlin, of, College of William & Mary.
40. Donald Hacker, ss, West Chester (Pa.) University.
41. *Steve Patchin, c, Joplin (Mo.) HS.
42. Norman Taylor, rhp, Greene Central HS, Snow Hill, N.C.

43. *Kurt Lohrke, ss, Jesuit HS, Carmichael, Calif.
44. *David Edson, ss, Terra Linda HS, San Rafael, Calif.
45. Walter Tobler, of, Wilson HS, Portsmouth, Va.
46. Greg Chlan, rhp, Rider College.
47. John Marshall, ss, University of Arkansas.
48. Terry Schofield, c, San Diego State University.
49. *Michael McDonald, c-1b, Vermont Academy HS, Rutland, Vt.
50. Wayne Flanagan, 3b, Loudon Valley HS, Leesburg, Va.
51. *Whitey Reid, lhp, T.C. Williams HS, Alexandria, Va.
52. *Pete Gigonovich, of, Butler University.
53. Larry Largent, rhp, Kansas State University.

**June—Secondary Phase (22)**

1-3. No selections.
4. Rex Hein, rhp, University of Missouri.
5. *Gary Hohman, c, Bordentown (N.J.) Military Academy.
6. *Jack Gehrke, ss-2b, University of Utah.
DRAFT DROP *Wide receiver, National Football League (1968-71)*
7. *Thomas Lundgren, lhp, University of Missouri.
8. *William Maxwell, rhp, Oklahoma State University.
9. *John Walker, c, Sacramento (Calif.) CC.

## LOS ANGELES DODGERS

**January—Regular Phase (6)**

1. Larry Hall, 1b-of, Broward (Fla.) CC.—(High A)
2. *Bonnie Smith, c-3b, Los Angeles (Calif.) HS.
3. *Craig Brown, 1b, Chipola (Fla.) JC.
4. Ted Rohde, of, Fresno (Calif.) CC.
5. *Ronnie Hilton, 2b, Gulf Coast (Fla.) CC.
6. *Tommy Graham, of, Harbor City (Calif.) HS.
7. *Lynn Morrison, of, Long Beach (Calif.) CC.
8. Gordon Crook, of, Arizona State University.
9. Bruce Price, lhp, Chaffey (Calif.) JC.
10. Donald Pierce, 1b, San Francisco (Calif.) HS.

**January—Secondary Phase (6)**

1. Marv Galliher, inf, San Diego Mesa JC.—(AAA)
2. **Davey Lopes, of, Washburn (Kan.) University.—(1972-87)**
DRAFT DROP *Major league manager (2000-02)*
3. *Steve Moore, of, Santa Barbara (Calif.) CC.
4. Randy Smith, of, Lincoln Land (Ill.) JC.
5. **Geoff Zahn, lhp, University of Michigan.—(1973-85)**
DRAFT DROP *Baseball coach, Michigan (1995-2001)*
6. *David Grangaard, 3b, Arizona State University.
7. Greg Wellman, lhp, Palm Beach (Fla.) JC.
8. *James Loll, inf, Los Angeles Pierce JC.
9. *Thomas Jackson, ss, Citrus (Calif.) JC.
10. ***Ed Crosby, 2b, Long Beach (Calif.) CC.—(1970-76)**
DRAFT DROP *Father of Bobby Crosby, first-round draft pick, Athletics (2001); major leaguer (2003-2010)*
11. *John Marino, c, Los Angeles Valley JC.
12. *Gregory Smith, rhp, Rio Hondo (Calif.) JC.
13. *William Templeton, rhp, Elmira, N.Y.

**June—Regular Phase (5)**

1. **Bobby Valentine, of, Rippowam HS, Stamford, Conn.—(1969-79)**
DRAFT DROP *Major league manager (1985-2012)*
2. **Bill Buckner, 1b, Napa HS, Vallejo, Calif.—(1969-90)**
3. Sonny Johnson, of, South Carolina State College.—(AA)
4. ***Mike Pazik, lhp, Lynn English HS, Lynn, Mass.—(1975-77)**
DRAFT DROP *Attended Holy Cross; re-drafted by Yankees, June 1971/secondary phase, delayed (1st round)*
5. **Tom Paciorek, of-1b, University of Houston.—(1970-87)**
DRAFT DROP *Ninth-round draft pick, Miami Dolphins/ National Football League (1968) • Brother of Jim Paciorek, major leaguer (1987) • Brother of John Paciorek, major leaguer (1963)*
6. *Bob Auger, 1b, Putnam (Conn.) HS.
7. *Joseph Barkauskas, c, Piscataway (N.J.) HS.
8. **Joe Ferguson, of, University of the Pacific.—(1970-83)**
9. **Doyle Alexander, rhp, Woodlawn HS, Birmingham, Ala.—(1971-89)**
10. *Rich Anderson, rhp, Trumbull (Conn.) HS.
11. Robert S. Baxter, c, Lower Dauphin HS, Hummelstown, Pa.
12. *Charles Land, of, Midwest City (Okla.) HS.
13. *Tom Pratt, lhp, Righetti HS, Santa Maria, Calif.
14. Frederick Willard, 3b-1b, San Francisco, Calif.
15. *Jeff Port, 3b, Birmingham HS, Encino, Calif.
16. *Artie Brown, rhp, New York University.
17. **Bob Gallagher, of, Stanford University.—(1972-75)**
18. Fred Nelson, 2b, Arizona State University.
19. *Jeff Stout, ss, LaPuente (Calif.) HS.
20. Ted Gilje, lhp, College Park HS, Pleasant Hill, Calif.
21. James Rich, of, Centennial HS, Compton, Calif.
22. Brooks Anderson, of-1b, Cardinal McCloskey HS, Albany, N.Y.
23. Danny Copeland, of-c, West Newton (Pa.) HS.
24. *Milton Guggia, 2b, Santa Maria (Calif.) HS.
25. Tom Sowinski, rhp, St. John's University.
26. *Robert Baxter, of, Southampton (N.Y.) HS.
27. *Albert Strane, ss, Santa Clara University.
DRAFT DROP *Twin brother of Alvin Strane, 28th-round draft pick, Dodgers (1968)*
28. *Alvin Strane, 2b, Santa Clara University.
DRAFT DROP *Twin brother of Albert Strane, 29th-round draft pick, Dodgers (1968)*
29. *Bob Wissler, of-2b, Cal Poly Pomona.
30. (void) *Roy Nelson, lhp, Vigor HS, Mobile, Ala.
31. *Richard Breese, rhp, Port Chester (N.Y.) HS.
32. *Dennis Major, 1b, Laney (Calif.) JC.
33. Michael St. John, rhp, West Valley (Calif.) JC.
34. *Alan Blair, ss-of, Leeds HS, Odenville, Ala.
35. William Estey, ss, University of New Hampshire.
36. Roger Wallace, rhp-of, Englewood HS, Jacksonville, Fla.
37. Danny Nichols, 3b, Kansas State University.
38. *James Curnow, c, Morristown HS, Morris Plains, N.J.
39. *Thomas Joyce, ss, Solano (Calif.) CC.
40. *Jim Mueller, of, Arkansas State University.
41. *Samuel Pasquatonio, c, Franklin (Mass.) HS.
42. Richard Dorsch, rhp, Valparaiso University.
43. *Peter Brown, rhp, Hayward (Calif.) HS.
44. *John Rushing, lhp, Tuscaloosa HS, Northport, Ala.
45. Kenneth Van Bell, rhp, Richmond Hill (N.Y.) HS.
46. *Gary Whittemore, lhp, University of New Mexico.
47. *Gary Weese, rhp, Midwest City (Okla.) HS.
48. *John Fargnoci, 1b, Bryant HS, Astoria, N.Y.
49. Edgar Ott, lhp, Rutgers University.
50. *Kenneth Pfau, rhp, El Camino (Calif.) JC.
51. Robert Woodruff, of, Port Chester (N.Y.) HS.
52. ***Bob Sheldon, ss, Montebello (Calif.) HS.—(1974-77)**
53. *Charles Elwis, lhp, Marshall HS, Los Angeles.
54. *Beau Robinson, 1b, Central HS, Springfield, Mo.
55. *Tod Rush, lhp, Montebello (Calif.) HS.
56. *Anthony Embessi, rhp, Bristol (Pa.) HS.
57. *Steven Angelo, inf, Montebello HS, Pico Rivera, Calif.
58. *Douglas Blake, of, Hackettstown (N.J.) HS.
59. *Jeff Paquette, c-of, Lincoln HS, San Francisco.
60. *Gary Welch, of-c, San Rafael (Calif.) HS.
61. Merritt Barnes, ss, University of San Francisco.
62. *Chester Teklinski, rhp, Tarentum (Pa.) HS.
63. Lee Driggers, of, Colonial HS, Orlando, Fla.
64. *Jeffrey Burns, c, Rollins (Fla.) College.
65. Charles Cochrane, ss, Lincoln HS, San Francisco.
66. William Homik, c, University of Southern California.
67. Charles Calver, rhp, Cal Poly Pomona.
68. Peter Scarpati, rhp, St. Francis (N.Y.) College.
69. Stephen Krines, 3b, Villanova University.
70. John DeBrino, rhp, Bishop Gibbons HS, Schenectady, N.Y.
71. *Carl Amendola, c, Plainedge HS, Massapequa, N.Y.

**June—Secondary Phase (13)**

1. **Steve Garvey, 3b, Michigan State University.—(1969-87)**
2. **Sandy Vance, rhp, Stanford University.—(1970-71)**
3. **Ron Cey, 3b, Washington State University.—(1971-87)**
4. *Bruce Kinder, ss, Florida Southern College.
5. *Bill Seinsoth, 1b, University of Southern California.
6. *Ellsworth Jones, lhp, New York University.
7. ***Bobby Randall, ss, Kansas State University.—(1976-80)**
DRAFT DROP *Baseball coach, Iowa State (1985-95); baseball coach, Kansas (1996-2002)*

## MINNESOTA TWINS

**January—Regular Phase (15)**

1. *David Hoot, of, Houston (Texas) HS.—DNP
2. *Bob Bridges, lhp, Arizona Western JC.
3. Allen Fenchel, of, Laney (Calif.) JC.
4. *Larry Klein, lhp, Venice (Calif.) HS.
5. Danny Humphries, rhp, Pico Rivera, Calif.
6. *Louis Rodriguez, 1b, New York (N.Y.) HS.

**January—Secondary Phase (1)**

1. **Eric Soderholm, ss, South Georgia JC.—(1971-80)**
DRAFT DROP *Brother of Dale Soderholm, first-round draft pick, Twins (1971)*
2. *Bill Borelli, 1b, JC of San Mateo (Calif.).
3. *Joe Jacobsen, c, Fresno (Calif.) CC.
4. *Eugene Rinaldi, ss, Miami-Dade CC North.
5. *Barry Sheldon, rhp, Batavia, N.Y.
6. *Edgardo Avila, 1b, Miami-Dade CC North.
7. *Robert Huddleston, of, Arizona Western JC.

**June—Regular Phase (16)**

1. Alex Rowell, of, Luther (Iowa) College.—(AA)
2. *John Langerhans, 1b, South San Antonio (Texas) HS.—(AA)
DRAFT DROP *Attended Texas; re-drafted by Brewers, June 1971/secondary phase, delayed (3rd round) • Father of Ryan Langerhans, major leaguer (2002-13)*
3. Michael Cavanaugh, ss, Birmingham HS, Van Nuys, Calif.—(High A)
4. **Jim Nettles, of, San Diego State University.—(1970-81)**
DRAFT DROP *Brother of Graig Nettles, major leaguer (1967-88)*
5. *Harvey Winn, 2b, Loara HS, Anaheim, Calif.—DNP
DRAFT DROP *Attended Oregon; never re-drafted*
6. Avery Morris, of, Franklin County HS, Estill Springs, Tenn.
DRAFT DROP *Father of Bryan Morris, first-round draft pick, Dodgers (2006); major leaguer (2012-15)*
7. *John Roatche, c, Hatboro (Pa.) HS.
8. *Timothy Evans, ss, Littleton (Colo.) HS.
9. Mike Brooks, ss, West Covina (Calif.) HS.
10. *Gary Bradshaw, rhp, Lake Worth (Fla.) HS.
11. Ron Oglesby, rhp, Ramona HS, Riverside, Calif.
12. *Mike Morrison, lhp-of, La Vista HS, Brea, Calif.
13. *Frank Cordaro, rhp, Teaneck (N.J.) HS.
14. *Paul Commando, c, Christopher Columbus HS, Bronx, N.Y.
15. *Frank Tokash, rhp, Westfield (N.J.) HS.
16. *Thomas Fast, rhp, Brighton (Colo.) HS.
17. Gary Majdoch, lhp, University of Wisconsin-Eau Claire.
18. **Jerry Terrell, 2b, Mankato State (Minn.) University.—(1973-80)**
19. Samuel Faria, of, Hingham (Mass.) HS.
20. *Michael Pivec, of, Calvert Hall HS, Baltimore.
21. Russ Rolandson, ss-2b, University of Minnesota.
22. James Hansen, c, University of Wisconsin-Stevens Point.
23. Mark Hartig, rhp, Mullen HS, Denver.
24. Buryl Hemerick, rhp, Costa Mesa HS, Huntington Beach, Calif.
25. Gregory Wendorf, lhp, University of Wisconsin-Stevens Point.
26. *Thomas Lolos, c, Parsons (Iowa) College.
27. *John Kiefer, ss, Princess Anne HS, Virginia Beach, Va.
28. Thomas Bryan, c, Seminole HS, Sanford, Fla.
29. Phil Edwards, 2b, East Mecklenburg HS, Charlotte, N.C.
30. *Daniel Patrovich, lhp, Valdosta State (Ga.) College.
31. Lee Ware, of, Glassboro State (N.J.) College.
32. *Nick Nicosia, of, University of Florida.
33. David Skog, lhp, St. Louis Park HS, Minneapolis.
34. Kenneth Meek, ss, Montclair State (N.J.) College.

**June—Secondary Phase (18)**

1. **Danny Thompson, ss, Oklahoma State University.—(1970-76)**
DRAFT DROP *Died as active major leaguer (Dec. 12, 1976)*
2. Gary Matz, 3b-of, Boston College.
3. *William Camp, rhp, Oklahoma State University.
4. *Bill Dobbs, lhp, Oklahoma State University.
5. *Jerry Paetzhold, lhp, Southern Illinois University-Edwardsville.

## MONTREAL EXPOS

**June—Regular Phase (21)**

1-3. No selections.
4. *Mikel Swain, rhp, Ohio State University.—(Low A)
DRAFT DROP *Did not sign, never re-drafted*
5. *Frank Ward, rhp, Southern Tech (Ga.) Institute.—(High A)
DRAFT DROP *Returned to Southern Tech; re-drafted by Red Sox, June 1969/secondary phase (1st round)*
6. Roger Nelson, c, Lincoln (Neb.) HS.
7. *Kevin Bryant, ss, Winter Haven (Fla.) HS.
8. *William Kendall, 3b, University of Minnesota.
9. Ross Hoffman, 1b, UCLA.
10. *Carlton Exum, rhp, Maynard Evans HS, Orlando, Fla.
11. Dave Hartman, lhp, Iowa State University.
12. *John Palmer, lhp, St. Paul, Minn.
13. Larry Woltz, 3b-of, DeKalb (Ga.) JC.
14. Joseph Marecki, ss, Miami-Dade CC North.
15. (void) *Richard Trembecki, of, University of Denver.
16. Richard Turner, rhp, Eau Gallie HS, Melbourne, Fla.
17. *William Seagraves, rhp-1b, Edgewater HS, Orlando, Fla.
18. *Michael Fulford, 3b, Miami-Dade CC South.

**June—Secondary Phase (23)**

No selection.

## NEW YORK METS

**January—Regular Phase (2)**

1. George Kazmarek, of-1b, Baltimore Institute.—(AAA)
2. *Larry Sozzi, inf-c, CC of San Francisco.

**January—Secondary Phase (4)**

1. Bruce Harkey, rhp, La Habra (Calif.) HS.–(High A)
2. Michael Derrig, lhp, Joliet (Ill.) JC.
3. *Fred Kampf, rhp, University of Miami.
4. *Bill Bright, rhp-of, Brevard (Fla.) CC.
5. *Michael Lersch, lhp, Mesa (Ariz.) CC.
6. Bruce Matte, rhp, Miami (Ohio) University.
DRAFT DROP *Seventh-round draft pick, Washington Redskins/National Football League (1967)*
7. *Reid Braden, 1b, University of Southern California.
8. *Tim Uraskevich, rhp, SUNY-Buffalo.
9. *Bob Danaher, rhp, Miami-Dade CC North.
10. *Moody Jackson, of, Phoenix (Ariz.) JC.
11. *Charles Kingsbury, inf-of, San Diego CC.

**June—Regular Phase (1)**

1. **Tim Foli, ss, Notre Dame HS, Canoga Park, Calif.—(1970-85)**
2. Donald Dickerson, 1b, Ensley HS, Birmingham, Ala.—(AA)
DRAFT DROP *Brother of Wayne Dickerson, first-round draft pick, Pirates (1965)*
3. *Bernie Boehmer, c, St. Dominic HS, O'Fallon, Ill.—(AAA)
DRAFT DROP *Attended St. Louis CC-Meramec; re-drafted by Indians, January 1970/secondary phase (3rd round)*
4. Alan Dodson, rhp, Sweetwater HS, National City, Calif.—(AA)
5. ***Burt Hooton, rhp, King HS, Corpus Christi, Texas.—(1971-85)**
DRAFT DROP *Attended Texas; re-drafted by Cubs, June 1971/secondary phase, delayed (1st round); first player from 1971 draft to reach majors (June 17, 1971)*
6. *Robert Masteller, lhp, Midwest City (Okla.) HS.
7. **Charlie Williams, rhp, Parsons (Iowa) College.—(1971-78)**

8. Marvin Leonard, lhp, DeWitt Clinton HS, Bronx, N.Y.
**9. *Jack Pierce, of, San Jose (Calif.) HS.—(1973-75)**
**10. Hank Webb, rhp, Copaigue (N.Y.) HS.—(1972-77)**
**11. Don Rose, rhp, Stanford University.—(1971-74)**
12. James Ziegler, of, Colorado State University.
13. *Stuart Pugh, lhp-of, Mascoutah (Ill.) HS.
**14. John Milner, of, South Fulton HS, East Point, Ga.—(1971-82)**
15. *Kenneth Dempsey, of, Ensley HS, Birmingham, Ala.
16. John Gurganus, rhp, Westwood HS, Palestine, Texas.
17. Leonard Carroll, c, Bergen Catholic HS, Oradell, N.J.
18. *Harley House, rhp, Piedmont Hills HS, San Jose, Calif.
19. *John Penn, 1b, Ferrum (Va.) JC.
20. Scott Goodwin, rhp, Reseda (Calif.) HS.
21. *John Severs, of, West Mecklenburg HS, Charlotte, N.C.
22. *Steve Turigliatto, c, Long Beach (Calif.) CC.
23. *Wayne Young, c, Sleepy Hollow HS, Tarrytown, N.Y.
24. *Daniel Misko, lhp, Tuscaloosa (Ala.) HS.
25. *Paul Patterson, rhp, Canton (N.Y.) HS.
26. Terry DeWald, 2b, University of Arizona.
27. Glenn Stitzel, 2b, Millersville (Pa.) University.
28. Daniel Murphy, rhp, Technical HS, Springfield, Mass.
29. *Charles Covey, 3b, Pasadena (Calif.) CC.
30. *Frank Szoke, ss, Whitehall HS, Cementon, Pa.
31. *Gary Morgan, 1b, Austin (Minn.) HS.
32. *Greg Archer, lhp-1b, Corcoran (Calif.) HS.
33. *Frederick Donaldson, ss, Loudon County HS, Leesburg, Va.
34. Edward Young, 3b, Johnson HS, Savannah, Ga.
35. *Harold Wilkerson, c, Fike HS, Wilson, N.C.
36. *Michael Bettega, lhp, Menlo (Calif.) JC.
37. Eugene Zawatski, lhp, Boston University.
38. Charlie Carr, of, University of North Carolina.
39. *Joe Kilby, of, Lincoln HS, Tacoma, Wash.
40. David Colon, rhp, Reicher HS, Waco, Texas.
41. James Malone, rhp, Union (Utah) HS.
42. Gary Hill, of, Sacramento (Calif.) CC.
43. *William Todd, lhp, Ritenour HS, St. Louis.
44. *Richard Seymour, c, St. Mary's HS, Ogdensburg, N.Y.

### June—Secondary Phase (11)

1. *Billy Cotton, c, Arizona State University.—(AAA)
2. Tommy Williams, c, East Los Angeles JC.
**3. *Ray Peters, rhp, Harvard University.—(1970)**
4. *John Whitehurst, c, Albemarle (N.C.) JC.
**5. *Rich Hand, rhp, University of Puget Sound.—(1970-73)**
DRAFT DROP *First overall draft pick, June 1969/secondary phase, Indians; first player from 1969 draft to reach majors (April 9, 1970)*
6. *Mickey Wertz, ss, Wharton County (Texas) JC.
7. *Mike Sigman, rhp, Santa Clara University.
**8. *Mickey Rivers, of, Miami-Dade CC North.—(1970-84)**
9. *Vince Bigone, of, Santa Clara University.

## NEW YORK YANKEES

### January—Regular Phase (3)

1. Robert Elliot, rhp, Massapequa, N.Y.—(AA)
2. *Robert Singer, of-lhp, Los Angeles CC.
3. Harry McCandless, rhp, Kansas City, Mo.
4. *Ron Wayne, lhp, Laney (Calif.) JC.
**5. *John Andrews, of-lhp, Pasadena (Calif.) CC.—(1973)**
6. *Ken Carmack, rhp, Yakima Valley (Wash.) JC.
7. *Raleigh Rhodes, p, De Anza (Calif.) JC.
8. *Melvin Oden, rhp-c, Wenatchee Valley (Wash.) CC.
9. Douglas Duncan, rhp, Spokane (Wash.) CC.
10. John Manginelli, 3b, Irvington, N.Y.

### January—Secondary Phase (7)

1. Billy Olsen, lhp, JC of the Redwoods (Calif.).–(AA)
2. Douglas Hansen, rhp, Fresno (Calif.) CC.
3. *Thomas Tikker, c, Los Angeles CC.

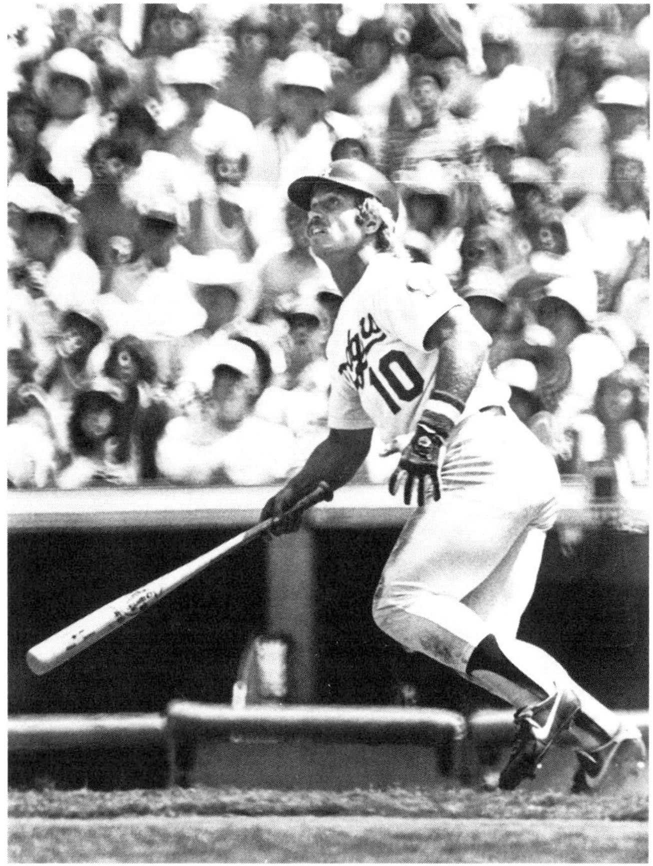


**Ron Cey was one of the less heralded members of the Dodgers' fabled Class of '68, but he had as productive a major league career as anyone, hitting 316 homers in 17 seasons**

4. Bruce Olson, rhp, Chaffey (Calif.) JC.
5. *William Shepherd, rhp, Spokane (Wash.) CC.
6. *Gary Houston, lhp, San Jose (Calif.) CC.

### June—Regular Phase (4)

1. Thurman Munson, c, Kent State University.—(1969-79)
DRAFT DROP *Died as active major leaguer (Aug. 2, 1979)*
2. Kenneth Johnson, ss, Redwood HS, Larkspur, Calif.—(AA)
3. *Richard Trapp, ss, University of Florida.—DNP
DRAFT DROP *Returned to Florida; re-drafted by Royals, January 1969/secondary phase (12th round); wide receiver, National Football League (1968-69)*
4. Steven Kogut, c, Upland (Calif.) HS.—(High A)
**5. George Zeber, ss, Loara HS, Anaheim, Calif.—(1977-78)**
6. Dave Kent, of, Parsons (Iowa) College.
**7. Wayne Nordhagen, of, Treasure Valley (Ore.) CC.—(1976-83)**
8. Patrick Denning, c, Schurz HS, Chicago.
9. *Howard Casey, lhp, Treasure Valley (Ore.) CC.
10. Alonzo Ramirez, rhp, El Campo (Texas) HS.
11. *Steve Hanzlik, rhp, Douglas HS, Portland, Ore.
**12. *Duane Kuiper, ss, Racine East HS, Sturtevant, Wis.—(1974-85)**
13. *Rickie Clements, lhp, Sadler HS, Whitesboro, Texas.
14. Robert McDaniel, of, University of Missouri.
15. *Pat Sonneman, 3b-of, Mount Tahoma HS, Tacoma, Wash.
16. *Ronnie Saunders, 1b-c, Burt HS, Clarksville, Tenn.
17. Lee Choate, 1b, Central HS, Chattanooga, Tenn.
18. Patrick Cluney, 1b, Trinity (Texas) University.
19. *Jeff Carpenter, ss, Owensboro Catholic HS, Owensboro, Ky.
20. *Mike Siani, ss, New Dorp HS, Staten Island, N.Y.
DRAFT DROP *First-round draft pick, Oakland Raiders/National Football League (1972); wide receiver, NFL (1972-80)*
21. *Vernon Gilmore, of, Willamette (Ore.) University.
22. *Terry Pollreisz, of, University of Portland.
DRAFT DROP *Baseball coach, Portland (1987-97)*
23. Ken Lange, rhp, Glassboro State (N.J.) College.
24. *Jim Hefflinger, lhp, Cleveland HS, Portland, Ore.
25. David Reid, lhp, Sessar (Ill.) HS.
26. Richard Monroe, c, Colton (Calif.) HS.
27. Richard Koslick, 3b-ss, Tennessee Tech.
28. Julius Bender, 3b, Ellsworth (Iowa) JC.
29. *Gerald Keigley, 3b, St. Joseph HS, Greenville, Miss.
30. John Pogonelski, rhp, Hamden (Conn.) HS.
31. Timothy O'Connell, of-1b, Xavier University.
32. Daniel Schirrips, rhp, Lafayette HS, Brooklyn, N.Y.
33. *Jeff Geach, ss, Del Campo HS, Carmichael, Calif.
34. *Eddie Pyatt, rhp, Glendale HS, Springfield, Mo.
35. *Daniel Velander, rhp, Franklin HS, Portland, Ore.
36. *John Mills, rhp, Wenatchee (Wash.) HS.
37. Douglas D'Addario, of, Kensington HS, Buffalo, N.Y.
38. *Rick Schoener, of-1b, Marinette (Wis.) HS.
39. *Jim Huff, rhp-of, Del Valle HS, Walnut Creek, Calif.
40. *Bill Jones, rhp, El Cerrito (Calif.) HS.
41. *William McDermott, 1b, Moorpark (Calif.) HS.
42. Michael Miller, of, Kaupan HS, Wichita, Kan.
43. *Bruce Zimmerman, rhp, Ukiah (Calif.) HS.

### June—Secondary Phase (8)

1. Ray DeRiggi, lhp, Seton Hall University.—(AA)
2. George Ferguson, ss-3b, University of Maine.
3. *Sammy Fletcher, c, Mississippi State University.
4. *Bill Ferguson, c, Texas Christian University.
5. *Thomas Hannibal, lhp, Clark (Wash.) JC.
6. *Jerre Algeo, 2b, Poteau (Okla.) JC.
7. Richard Buff, 3b, University of Georgia.

## OAKLAND ATHLETICS

### January—Regular Phase (1)

**1. George Hendrick, of, Fremont HS, Los Angeles.—(1971-88)**
**2. Reggie Sanders, of, Venice (Calif.) HS.—(1974)**
3. *Michael Prieto, of, JC of San Mateo (Calif.).
4. *Paul Williams, c, Mitchell (Conn.) JC.
5. *William Coppola, rhp, Hudson Valley (N.Y.) CC.
6. John Luman, rhp-of, Vermont Technical JC.
7. *Jack Gehrke, ss, University of Utah.
DRAFT DROP *Wide receiver, National Football League (1968-71)*

### January—Secondary Phase (17)

1. Gene Dusan, c, Long Beach (Calif.) CC.—(AAA)
**2. *Ray Peters, rhp, Harvard University.—(1970)**
3. *Glenn Woodruff, c, Marion (Ala.) Military Institute.
4. *Michael Magness, rhp, Manatee (Fla.) JC.
5. *Mark Reeser, lhp, Laney (Calif.) JC.
6. Charles Sprinkle, ss, Arizona Western JC.
7. *Gerald Hurt, rhp, University of Missouri.
8. *Edward Cook, of, Bridgewater (Va.) College.
9. *Tom Binkowski, of, Michigan State University.
10. *Gary Hohman, c, Bordentown Military Institute, Trenton, N.J.
11. *Allen Simas, rhp, Sacramento (Calif.) CC.

### June—Regular Phase (2)

**1. *Pete Broberg, rhp, Palm Beach (Fla.) HS.—(1971-78)**
DRAFT DROP *Attended Dartmouth; re-drafted by Senators, June 1971/secondary phase (1st round, 1st pick)*
2. *John Shelley, of, Casady HS, Oklahoma City, Okla.—DNP
DRAFT DROP *Attended Oklahoma; never re-drafted; 17th-round draft pick, Buffalo Bills/National Football League (1972)*
3. Charles Chaney, c-3b, Los Angeles.—(AA)
4. *Steven Tingle, ss, Pleasure Ridge Park HS, Louisville, Ky.—DNP
DRAFT DROP *Attended Kentucky; never re-drafted*
5. William Lucas, 3b, Westfield (Mass.) HS.—(Low A)
**6. *Rich Troedson, lhp, Camden HS, San Jose, Calif.—(1973-74)**
7. Buddy Copeland, rhp, University of Georgia.
8. Edward Bacak, rhp, Carroll HS, Corpus Christi, Texas.
9. Greg Schubert, of, Washington State University.
10. Patrick Tatum, rhp, Roger Ludlowe HS, Fairfield, Conn.
11. *Bob Koeppel, lhp-of, Limestone HS, Bartonville, Ill.
DRAFT DROP *First overall draft pick, January 1972/secondary phase, Twins*
12. *Gene Stohs, lhp, Grand Island (Neb.) HS.
13. Phillip Murnahan, rhp, Ironton (Ohio) HS.
14. *Charles Walker, of, Lakeside HS, Atlanta.
15. Steve Mastin, rhp, Florida State University.
16. *Steve Wilmet, lhp, St. Norbert HS, West DePere, Wis.
17. Stephen Cooley, of-1b, University of North Dakota.
18. Mike Peden, c, Auburn University.
19. William Ingram, rhp, Idaho State University.
20. Augusta Massingill, ss, Englewood HS, Jacksonville, Fla.
21. Alan Hefferon, rhp, Brown University.
22. *Mark Arnold, rhp, William Chrisman HS, Independence, Mo.
23. Mason Elvrom, c-of, Clover Park HS, Tacoma, Wash.
24. Robert Gibble, rhp, Bloomsburg (Pa.) University.
25. *Mark Tschopp, rhp, Jefferson HS, Cedar Rapids, Iowa.
**26. John Strohmayer, rhp, University of the Pacific.—(1970-74)**
27. *Jim Jachym, lhp, Westfield (Mass.) HS.
28. *John Renhow, of, North Dakota State University.
29. *Ernie Henrickson, rhp-of, Snohomish (Wash.) HS.
30. *Jerry Devins, rhp-of, Owensboro Catholic HS, Owensboro, Ky.
31. *Douglas Smith, ss-2b, Buena Vista (Iowa) College.

### June—Secondary Phase (12)

1. Tom Cook, c, Florida State University.—(AAA)
2. Tommy Smith, rhp, Auburn University.
3. *Herb Hofvendahl, of, St. Mary's (Calif.) College.
4. Fred Kampf, rhp, University of Miami.

## PHILADELPHIA PHILLIES

**January—Regular Phase (12)**

1. Stephen Cates, lhp, Sunland (Calif.) HS.—(AAA)
2. *Edward Kelly, rhp, Dayton, Ohio.
3. James Alviso, rhp, Livermore, Calif.
4. *Lawrence Hardin, 2b, Polk (Fla.) CC.
5. *Carl London, of, Coatesville, Pa.
6. *Charles Kurkjian, 3b, Fresno (Calif.) CC.

**January—Secondary Phase (8)**

1. *Pat Harrison, 2b, University of Southern California.—(AAA)
DRAFT DROP *Baseball coach, Pepperdine (1995-96); baseball coach, Mississippi (1997-2000)*
2. David Rusco, ss, Cuesta (Calif.) JC.
3. Louis Lanehardt, lhp, Baltimore.
4. *Donald Burkhalter, ss-rhp, Gulf Coast (Fla.) CC.
5. *Michael Schomaker, of-c, Stanford University.

**June—Regular Phase (11)**

**1. Greg Luzinski, 1b, Notre Dame HS, Prospect Heights, Ill.—(1970-84)**
DRAFT DROP *Father of Ryan Luzinski, first-round draft pick, Dodgers (1992)*
2. Jeff Wang, of, South Torrance (Calif.) HS.—(High A)
3. William Lash, rhp-of, Windsor Locks (Conn.) HS.—(Low A)
**4. *Buddy Schultz, lhp, Shaw HS, East Cleveland, Ohio.—(1975-79)**
DRAFT DROP *Attended Miami (Ohio); re-drafted by Cubs, 1972 (6th round)*
5. Allen Bowers, of, Mount Vernon HS, Fort Belvoir, Va.—(High A)
6. Willie Jones, of, Southern HS, Philadelphia.
7. Brian Hansen, c, SUNY-Buffalo.
8. Edward Goldstone, inf, Yale University.
9. *Phillip Harvey, rhp, Washington HS, Kansas City, Kan.
10. Wilbur Cole, of, Southside HS, Florence, S.C.
11. William Geitz, lhp, West Deptford (N.J.) HS.
12. Roger Noble, lhp, Trotwood (Ohio) HS.
13. John Lee, rhp, Great Falls, Mon.
14. Jerry Coker, ss, Manning (S.C.) HS.
15. Robert Cunningham, rhp, Middle Tennessee State University.
16. *Harry Rogers, of, Curwensville HS, Grampian, Pa.
17. Rick Lang, of, Santa Clara HS, Oxnard, Calif.
18. Robert Keister, rhp, Sayreville (N.J.) HS.
19. Daniel Brigham, ss, Berlin (N.H.) HS.
20. Robert Maltsberger, c, Shoreline HS, Seattle.
21. Phil Locanto, 2b, Western Michigan University.
22. *Robert Coultas, of, Alhambra HS, Martinez, Calif.
23. Ronald Carnutt, of, Camden HS, San Jose, Calif.
24. *Charlie Janes, rhp, Kingston (N.Y.) HS.
25. *Larry Robertson, lhp, Lower Dauphin HS, Hummelstown, Pa.
26. *Ronald Collier, rhp, Mansfield (Pa.) University.
27. *Larry Tarver, c, Arvin (Calif.) HS.
28. *Michael Brown, inf, Wilmington (Del.) HS.
29. *John Malone, 3b, Maine-Endwell HS, Endwell, N.Y.
30. Charles Pesce, c, University of Delaware.

**June—Secondary Phase (9)**

1. *Pat Harrison, 2b, University of Southern California.—(AAA)
DRAFT DROP *Baseball coach, Pepperdine (1995-96); baseball coach, Mississippi (1997-2000)*
2. *Edgardo Avila, lhp, Miami-Dade CC North.
**3. *Jim Barr, rhp, University of Southern California.—(1971-83)**
4. Tom Schleer, lhp, Kentucky Wesleyan College.
5. Reid Braden, 1b-3b, University of Southern California.

## PITTSBURGH PIRATES

**January—Regular Phase (10)**

1. *Sam Viney, 1b-rhp, San Joaquin Delta (Calif.) JC.—(Short-season A)
2. *Kevin Crain, rhp, Cabrillo (Calif.) JC.
3. Mark McLeod, c-3b, California (Md.) HS.
4. Steve Lewis, rhp, Bakersfield (Calif.) HS.
5. Thomas Davis, of, San Jose (Calif.) CC.
6. Robert Johnson, lhp, Salem (W.Va.) College.
7. *Peter Poldiak, rhp, Gulf Coast (Fla.) CC.

**January—Secondary Phase (18)**

1. *Robert Taylor, rhp, Richard Bland (Va.) JC.–DNP
2. *Jim Snyder, of, East Carolina University.
**3. Tom Dettore, rhp-c, Juniata (Pa.) College.—(1973-76)**
4. *Edward Mantie, rhp, Syracuse University.
5. *Jerry Vitatoe, 3b-of, Oakland (Calif.) HS.
6. *Donald Schroeder, rhp, Grays Harbor (Wash.) JC.

**June—Regular Phase (9)**

**1. Dick Sharon, of, Sequoia HS, Redwood City, Calif.—(1973-75)**
2. Brad Gratz, lhp, George Schafer HS, Southgate, Mich.—(AA)
3. *James Sams, rhp, Cuyahoga Falls (Ohio) HS.—(High A)
DRAFT DROP *Attended Miami (Ohio); re-drafted by Indians, June 1971/secondary phase, delayed (2nd round)*
4. Mike Marine, rhp, Warren HS, Downey, Calif.—(Low A)
**5. *Wayne Garland, rhp, Cohn HS, Nashville, Tenn.—(1973-81)**
DRAFT DROP *Attended Gulf Coast (Fla.) CC; re-drafted by Cardinals, January 1969/secondary phase (1st round, 1st pick)*
6. *Peter Halfman, of, Jesuit HS, Sacramento, Calif.
7. *David Van Volkenburg, lhp, Cathedral Prep, Erie, Pa.
8. Michael Cooper, rhp, Kokomo (Ind.) HS.
9. Frank Barlew, 3b, Montour HS, Pittsburgh.
10. *Ray Borowicz, ss, Huntington (N.Y.) HS.
**11. Milt May, ss, St. Petersburg (Fla.) HS.—(1970-84)**
DRAFT DROP *Son of Pinky May, major leaguer (1939-43)*
12. Thomas Fratto, of, Cambridge Latin HS, Cambridge, Mass.
13. *David Entrekin, c, Coatesville (Pa.) Area HS.
**14. Bruce Kison, rhp, Pasco (Wash.) HS.—(1971-85)**
15. Rudolph Brooks, 1b, Berkeley (Calif.) HS.
16. *Richard Hurt, rhp, Lihon HS, Nashville, Tenn.
17. Charles Hines, 3b, Florida State University.
**18. *Paul Mitchell, rhp, Worcester (Mass.) Academy.—(1975-80)**
19. *Mike Groves, of, Seminole HS, Largo, Fla.
20. Steve McFarland, inf, Sammamish HS, Bellevue, Wash.
21. *Joe Urbanovitch, c, Villanova University.
22. Thomas Whalan, 2b-ss, Lowell (Mass.) HS.
23. *Dennis Franklin, rhp, Gonzalez Tate HS, Cantonment, Fla.
24. Randy Beringer, ss, Tigard (Ore.) HS.
25. Gary Conboy, rhp, Genesee (N.Y.) CC.
26. *Keith Scruggs, rhp, Alleghany City HS, Iron Gate, Va.
27. *Marvin Tucker, of, Central Missouri State University.
28. *Anthony Giordano, c, Most Holy Trinity HS, Brooklyn, N.Y.
29. *Stanley Grout, rhp, Perry (Iowa) Senior HS.
30. Larry Barefoot, rhp, Hallsboro HS, Whiteville, N.C.
31. Scott Roswald, of, San Juan HS, Citrus Heights, Calif.
32. Robert Hessler, rhp, Hampton (Va.) HS.
33. Stephen Bentley, rhp, Stoneham (Mass.) HS.
34. *Paul Marcek, rhp, Archbishop Rummel HS, Omaha, Neb.
35. *Roger Wright, c, Northeast Lauderdale HS, Meridian, Miss.
36. Thomas Rambeau, lhp, York (Pa.) College.
37. *Michael Price, ss-of, Technical HS, Oakland, Calif.
38. Barry Houser, lhp, West Chester (Pa.) University.

**June—Secondary Phase (19)**

1. Edward Northrop, rhp, Alexandria, Va.—(Short-season A)
2. James Skovron, rhp, West Newbury, Mass.
3. *Alan Putz, 1b, Springfield (Mass.) College.
4. *Wayne Harlan, inf, Yakima Valley (Wash.) JC.

## ST. LOUIS CARDINALS

**January—Regular Phase (20)**

1. Michael Maselbas, rhp, American International (Mass.) University.—(High A)
2. *Frank Buchan, of, Marshalltown (Iowa) CC.
3. *Jim Pettee, 2b-of, Manatee (Fla.) JC.
4. *Elmer Dize, rhp, Mount Olive (N.C.) JC.

**January—Secondary Phase (14)**

**1. *Ken Hottman, of, Sacramento (Calif.) CC.—(1971)**
2. *Michael Babler, rhp, Chabot (Calif.) JC.
**3. *Rick Austin, lhp, Washington State University.—(1970-76)**
**4. Skip Jutze, c, Central Connecticut State University.—(1972-77)**
5. *Douglas Braun, c, Vallejo (Calif.) JC.
6. Rusty Bodkin, of, Broward (Fla.) CC.

**June—Regular Phase (19)**

1. James "Buth" Hairston, of, Roth HS, Dayton, Ohio.—(High A)
2. Wade Boyett, rhp-ss, Davidson HS, Mobile, Ala.—(High A)
3. *Mark Kitchell, of, Mamaroneck (N.Y.) HS.—DNP
DRAFT DROP *No school; re-drafted by Mets, June 1969/secondary phase (2nd round)*
4. Dick McVay, rhp-of, Norway (Iowa.) HS.—(AAA)
5. David Sagaser, lhp, Taft (Calif.) HS.—(High A)
6. Jackie Stripling, rhp-ss, Holdenville (Okla.) HS.
**7. Tom Heintzelman, 2b, Parsons (Iowa) College.—(1973-78)**
DRAFT DROP *Son of Ken Heintzelman, major leaguer (1937-52)*
8. Ted Hemenway, rhp, Mehlville (Mo.) HS.
9. Lawrence Hebert, 3b, Sacramento (Calif.) CC.
10. Donald Picard, lhp, Lyndon State (Vt.) College.
11. Bill Caudell, c, Manchester HS, Richmond, Va.
12. *William Wall, rhp, Skaneateles (N.Y.) HS.
13. *Michael Larkin, rhp, Plantation (Fla.) HS.
14. Don Kirkland, ss, Southern Illinois University.
15. *Paul Arendt, 3b-ss, Thomas Jefferson HS, Denver.
16. *Mike Douglas, 1b, Dominguez HS, Paramount, Calif.
17. George Greer, of, University of Connecticut.
DRAFT DROP *Baseball coach, Wake Forest (1988-2004)*
18. *Darrell Downey, ss-c, Ventura (Calif.) HS.
19. Ben Farley, lhp-1b, Cleveland HS, St. Louis.
20. Guy Gaumont, of, Loyola HS, Los Angeles.
21. David Hansen, rhp, Ygnacio Valley HS, Concord, Calif.
22. Ernest Vierra, c-of, Sacramento (Calif.) CC.
**23. *Craig Swan, rhp, Millikan HS, Long Beach, Calif.—(1973-84)**
24. *Gary Howard, c, Yuba City (Calif.) HS.
25. Gerald Bryant, lhp, Amherst (Va.) County HS.
**26. Bob Forsch, 3b-rhp, Hiram Johnson HS, Sacramento, Calif.—(1974-89)**
DRAFT DROP *Brother of Ken Forsch, 18th-round draft pick, Astros (1968); major leaguer (1970-86)*
27. *Mark Lopinot, rhp, St. Louis CC-Meramec.
28. *James Martin, c, Jones Valley HS, Birmingham, Ala.
29. *John Davsko, rhp, St. Louis University.
30. *Nicholas Stipanovich, rhp, Boston University.
31. Glenn Essman, c, Riverview HS, St. Louis.
32. *Albert Johnson, of, Los Angeles (Calif.) HS.
**33. Tim Plodinec, rhp, University of Arizona.—(1972)**
34. Steven Frohman, of, Long Island University.
35. Daniel Ford, rhp-of, Quinnipiac (Conn.) College.

AP WIRE PHOTO

**Tim Foli, the No. 1 overall selection in 1968, autographs a ball for his mother immediately after signing with the Mets for a $74,000 bonus**

36. Chet Jackson, of, Kirkwood (Mo.) HS.
37. George Newman, ss, Hartnell (Calif.) CC.
**38. *Ed Halicki, rhp, Kearny (N.J.) HS.—(1974-80)**
39. Gerald Aanonsen, ss, Wittenberg (Wis.) HS.
40. *John Hathaway, c, Lewiston (Idaho) HS.
41. *Eric Maitland, inf, Gettysburg (Pa.) HS.
42. *Wayne Johnson, lhp, Brewer HS, Fort Worth, Texas.
43. *Ronnie Diggle, ss-2b, Dominguez HS, Paramount, Calif.
44. Scott Sulprizio, 1b, Diablo Valley (Calif.) JC.
45. *Michael Dickens, ss, Central Catholic HS, Melbourne, Fla.
46. *Stephen Brassey, inf, San Leandro (Calif.) HS.

**June—Secondary Phase (17)**

1. Steve Evans, rhp, University of Michigan.—(AA)
2. Benny Looper, c, Southwestern Oklahoma State University.

DRAFT DROP *Father of Aaron Looper, major leaguer (2003) • Uncle of Braden Looper, first-round draft pick, Cardinals (1996); major leaguer (1998-2007)*

3. Dennis Parks, of, Long Beach State University.
4. *Brian Bach, rhp, University of Connecticut.
5. David Cichon, c-rhp, Amherst (Mass.) College.
6. Mike Ehlers, c, Ellsworth (Iowa) JC.
7. *Ron Pritchett, rhp, Mount San Antonio (Calif.) JC.

## SAN DIEGO PADRES

**June—Regular Phase (23)**

1-3. No selections.
4. *Luciano Hernandez, rhp, Solano Beach (Calif.) HS.—(Rookie)

DRAFT DROP *No school; re-drafted by Padres, January 1969/secondary phase (5th round)*

5. John Preston, rhp, Sweetwater HS, Chula Vista, Calif.—(High A)
6. *Bob McRoberts, of, Crawford HS, El Cajon, Calif.
**7. David Robinson, of, San Diego State University.—(1970-71)**

DRAFT DROP *Brother of Bruce Robinson, first-round draft pick, Athletics (1975); major leaguer (1978-80)*

8. *Alan Hansen, rhp, La Mesa (Calif.) HS.
9. *Dale Davis, lhp, Kearny HS, San Diego.
10. *Andy Hancock, c, Furman University.
11. *Matthew Rosiek, rhp, Indian River (Fla.) CC.
**12. *David Moates, of, Manatee (Fla.) JC.—(1974-76)**
13. *Robert Thompson, inf, Clairemont HS, San Diego.
**14. *Jim Crawford, lhp, Tucson (Ariz.) HS.—(1973-78)**
15. Ronnie McGarity, c-rhp, North Cobb HS, Kennesaw, Ga.
16. *Nacho Bracamontes, lhp, Sweetwater HS, Chula Vista, Calif.
17. *Ted Tomasovich, of, Georgia Tech.
18. Ron Drake, c, University of Southern California.
19. *Earl Altschuler, 3b, Crawford HS, San Diego.

**June—Secondary Phase (21)**

1-3. No selections.
**4. *Rich Hinton, lhp, University of Arizona.—(1971-79)**
**5. Bob O'Brien, lhp-1b, University of Arizona.—(1971)**
6. *Richard Gouin, of, California Western University.

## SAN FRANCISCO GIANTS

**January—Regular Phase (18)**

1. Steve Sibley, lhp, El Camino (Calif.) JC.–(High A)
**2. Garry Maddox, of, San Pedro (Calif.) HS.—(1972-86)**
**3. George Foster, of, El Camino (Calif.) JC.—(1969-86)**
4. *Alan Truskowski, lhp, Wallace (Ala.) JC.
5. *Wayne Harlan, 3b, Yakima Valley (Wash.) JC.
6. *Jim Bianchi, ss, Boise (Idaho) JC.
7. *Lawrence Haynes, of, Baton Rouge, La.

**January—Secondary Phase (2)**

1. Steve Garman, rhp-ss, University of Idaho.—(Short-season A)

DRAFT DROP *Brother of Mike Garman, first-round draft pick, Red Sox (1967); major leaguer (1969-78)*

2. *Tim Huntley, of, Spokane (Wash.) CC.
3. Don Paulsen, of, Altamonte Springs, Fla.
4. *Pat Westley, ss, Phoenix (Ariz.) JC.
5. *Tom Schweitzer, lhp, Fairmont State (W.Va.) College.
6. Edgar Thomas, 1b-lhp, Whittier, Calif.
7. *John Frilling, of, Indian River (Fla.) CC.
8. *Ed Assaf, rhp, University of Southern Mississippi.
9. *Martin Pfenninger, ss, Temple University.

**June—Regular Phase (17)**

**1. Gary Matthews, of, San Fernando HS, Pacoima, Calif.—(1972-87)**

DRAFT DROP *Father of Gary Matthews Jr., major leaguer (1999-2010)*

2. *Charlie Dudish, ss-of, Avondale HS, Avondale Estates, Ga.—(High A)

DRAFT DROP *Attended Georgia Tech; re-drafted by Padres, June 1971/secondary phase, delayed (1st round) • Son of Andy Dudish, running back/ National Football League (1946-47)*

3. Alan Cowgill, rhp, Bradley University.—(High A)
4. *Ken Rutkowski, of-rhp, SUNY-Buffalo.—DNP

DRAFT DROP *Returned to SUNY-Buffalo; re-drafted by Red Sox, January 1969/secondary phase (2nd round)*

5. Kerry Horn, of-3b, Fairfield (Ala.) HS.—(Low A)
6. Thomas Impliazzo, c, Eagle Rock (Calif.) HS.
7. Jake Jacobson, c, Hamline (Minn.) University.
**8. Jim Howarth, of, Mississippi State University.—(1971-74)**
9. *Richard McKinley, rhp, Pittsburg (Calif.) HS.
10. Keith Haney, c, California State (Pa.) Teachers College.
11. *Tommie Nichols, ss, University of Mississippi.
12. *Jose Basterrechea, rhp, Flushing (N.Y.) HS.
13. Gary Schafer, ss, Mount Rubidoux HS, Riverside, Calif.
14. Todd Martin, ss, Del Mar HS, San Jose, Calif.
15. *William Fitzgerald, c, Tulane University.
16. Ken Cornell, 3b-of, Roosevelt HS, Wyandotte, Mich.
17. *Michael Ward, 2b, Marion, S.C.
18. *James LaRusso, 3b, Monmouth (N.J.) College.
19. *Robert Horton, c, Dean Attendance Center, Leland, Miss.
20. *Pat Bekeza, of-inf, University of Southern Colorado.
21. *Doug Balne, lhp, New Caanan (Conn.) HS.
22. *Cary Livingston, of, West Jefferson HS, Gretna, La.
23. *Pat Cech, rhp, Maryvale HS, Phoenix, Ariz.
24. John Petrock, ss, Somerville (N.J.) HS.
25. *Robert McLeod, rhp, Georgetown (Ky.) College.
26. *Joseph Campanario, rhp-of, St. Elizabeth HS, Oakland, Calif.
27. *Mike Balogh, rhp, O'Hara HS, Buffalo, N.Y.
28. *Michael Koski, 2b, Las Plumas HS, Oroville, Calif.
29. *Kent Corley, 2b, Sandy Springs HS, Atlanta.
30. *Ralph Dick, of, Mesa (Ariz.) CC.
31. Hugh Woolridge, of, John Harris HS, Harrisburg, Pa.
32. *Steve Holdren, of, Mountain Home (Idaho) HS.
33. George Bochow, 1b-of, New York University.
**34. *Rob Ellis, 3b-of, Ottawa Hills HS, Grand Rapids, Mich.—(1971-75)**
35. *Allen Weendone, rhp, Hicks Memorial HS, Selma, Ala.
36. Tommy Hanegan, ss, Ocala, Fla.
37. Tommy Palmertree, lhp, Burbank HS, Sacramento, Calif.

**June—Secondary Phase (3)**

**1. Ed Goodson, ss, East Tennessee State University.—(1970-77)**
2. *Harry Saferight, c, Manatee (Fla.) JC.
3. *Patrick Roark, of, San Diego Mesa JC.
4. Edmund Mantie, rhp, Syracuse University.
5. (void) *Tom Schweitzer, lhp, Fairmont State (W.Va.) College.
6. *Gerald Christman, lhp, University of Michigan.
7. Dick Hanselman, lhp, St. John's River (Fla.) CC.

## SEATTLE PILOTS

**June—Regular Phase (22)**

1-3. No selections.
4. Marty West, c, Rock Hill (S.C.) HS.—(Short-season A).
5. *Greg Brosterhous, ss-rhp, Klamath Falls (Ore.) HS.—-DNP

DRAFT DROP *Attended Oregon; never re-drafted*

6. *Roger McSwain, of, Crest HS, Shelby, N.C.
**7. Bill Parsons, rhp, Riverside (Calif.) CC.—(1971-74)**
**8. Tom Kelly, of, St. Mary's HS, South Amboy, N.J.—(1975)**

DRAFT DROP *Major league manager (1986-2001)*

9. Milton Jordan, 3b, Lanier HS, Macon, Ga.
10. Larry Pickett, rhp, Chaffey HS, Ontario, Calif.
11. Frankie Kimball, c, Trinity (Texas) University.
12. *Mike Baldwin, lhp, Sacramento (Calif.) CC.
13. *Ronnie Slingerman, 3b, James Madison HS, Vienna, Va.
14. *Willie Laughridge, rhp, Rock Hill (S.C.) HS.
15. *Phillip Basler, 1b, Truman HS, Independence, Mo.
16. *Roger Sizoo, c, Citrus (Calif.) JC.
17. *Mike Staffieri, ss, Sunny Hills HS, Fullerton, Calif.
18. *Jim Silvey, 2b, Ritenour HS, St. Louis.
**19. Wilbur Howard, of, Holbrook HS, Lowell, N.C.—(1973-78)**
20. *Henry Talbot, of, Boise, Idaho.
21. Gary Upton, c, Bradley University.
22. Wayne Sullivan, rhp, Belmont Abbey (N.C.) College.
23. *Dario Pini, ss-3b, Sequoia HS, Redwood City, Calif.
24. Nelson Gibson, rhp, Clemson University.
25. *Larry Angell, rhp, Shoreline HS, Seattle.
26. *Ronald Kelam, of, Southwest HS, St. Louis.
27. *Mitch Laird, rhp, Woodward (Okla.) HS.
28. *Perry Allen, rhp, Sulphur (Okla.) HS.
29. *Steve Downs, 3b, Taft HS, Chicago.
30. *Barry Herron, c, Kansas State University.
31. Wayne Vincent, lhp, Florida State University.
32. Larry Nero, rhp, Los Angeles.

**June—Secondary Phase (24)**

1-3. No selections.
4. David Etter, of-1b, Shippensburg (Pa.) University.

## WASHINGTON SENATORS

**January—Regular Phase (7)**

1. Jimmy Blackmon, rhp, Rock Hill (S.C.) HS.—(AA)
2. *John Whitehurst, c, Albemarle (N.C.) JC.
3. *Richard Myers, c, Manasquan, N.J.
4. DeWayne Chambers, of, Florida Memorial College.

**January—Secondary Phase (11)**

**1. *Danny Thompson, ss, Oklahoma State University.—(1970-76)**

DRAFT DROP *Died as active major leaguer (Dec. 10, 1976)*

2. *Kent Calderan, ss, Chabot (Calif.) JC.
3. William Holt, lhp, Lynchburg (Va.) College.
4. David Schmid, lhp, Catonsville (Md.) CC.
5. *Donald Keenan, c-of, Gulf Coast (Fla.) CC.
6. Chuck Koselke, 1b, Western Michigan University.
7. (void) *Bruce Kinder, ss, Florida Southern College.
8. *Robert Knight, ss, South Georgia JC.

**June—Regular Phase (8)**

**1. Donnie Castle, lhp-1b, Coldwater (Miss.) HS.—(1973)**
**2. Jimmy Mason, ss, Murphy HS, Mobile, Ala.—(1971-79)**
3. Rickey Rogers, ss, New Carlisle (Ohio) HS.—(AA)
4. *Alan Schwartz, rhp, Douglas MacArthur HS, Wantagh, N.Y.—DNP

DRAFT DROP *Attended Duke; re-drafted by Reds, June 1971/secondary phase, delayed (3rd round)*

**5. Jeff Terpko, rhp, Sayre (Pa.) HS.—(1974-77)**
**6. *Mike Cubbage, ss-3b, Lane HS, Charlottesville, Va.—(1974-81)**

DRAFT DROP *Major league manager (1991)*

7. *Harold Richmond, rhp, Travis HS, Austin, Texas.
8. Gene Wiley, rhp, Threadgill HS, Greenwood, Miss.
9. *Bruce Clarke, rhp-of, West HS, Pawtucket, R.I.
**10. Larry Biittner, lhp-1b, Buena Vista (Iowa) College.—(1970-83)**
**11. *Chris Speier, ss, Alameda (Calif.) HS.—(1971-89)**

DRAFT DROP *Father of Justin Speier, major leaguer (1998-2007)*

12. *Rick Oliver, of-3b, Patapsco HS, Baltimore.
13. *Robert Eldridge, rhp, Robert Morris (Ill.) JC.
14. *Sherwood Hahn, of, Virginia Tech.
15. Jeff Janek, lhp, Harold Richards HS, Oak Lawn, Ill.
16. Darrel Hetzler, 1b, Central HS, Xenia, Ohio.
17. Roy Adams, of-c, Roth HS, Dayton, Ohio.
18. Robert Shutts, rhp, Northwestern University.
19. Bill Davidson, rhp, King HS, Tampa.
20. Jeffrey Vollweiler, rhp, American University.
21. *Berry McQueen, rhp, Garrett HS, Charleston, S.C.
22. *Alan Lobb, lhp, Bangor (Pa.) HS.
23. *Jerry Tagge, inf-c, West HS, Green Bay, Wis.

DRAFT DROP *First-round draft pick, Green Bay Packers/ National Football League (1972); quarterback, NFL (1972-74)*

**24. *Jim Cox, ss, Bloomington (Ill.) HS.—(1973-76)**
25. Pat Kuehner, 1b, University of Southern California.
26. Richard Guarnera, ss, Baltimore University.
27. Gary Sargent, lhp, Indiana University.
28. *Harold Graff, c, Illinois Wesleyan University.
29. *Barnes Yelvington, rhp, Lee Woodward HS, Black Creek, N.C.
30. Albert Richards, ss, University of Maryland.
31. *Kenneth McGregor, ss, Gulf Coast (Fla.) CC.

**June—Secondary Phase (16)**

**1. Rick Henninger, rhp, University of Missouri.—(1973)**
2. *Glen Pickren, rhp, University of Florida.
3. *Don Burkhalter, rhp, Gulf Coast (Fla.) CC.
4. *Paul Williams, c, Mitchell (Conn.) JC.
5. *Ed Cott, c, Cornell University.
6. *Bill Bright, of-rhp, Brevard (Fla.) CC.

# 1969

## AT A GLANCE

### This Date In History
**WINTER DRAFT:** Feb. 1
**SUMMER DRAFT:** June 5-6

### Best Draft
**CINCINNATI REDS. DON GULLETT** (1), **RAWLY EASTWICK** (3) and **KEN GRIFFEY** (29) were all key pieces for the Big Red Machine's World Series championship teams in 1975-76. Gullett reached the big leagues to open the 1970 season. Remarkably, it would be another 13 seasons before the next Reds first-rounder (Nick Esasky, a 1978 pick who debuted in 1983) appeared in Cincinnati.

### Worst Draft
**PITTSBURGH PIRATES. ED RATLEFF** (6), a first-rounder in the 1973 NBA draft who went on to play five seasons for the Houston Rockets, became the best-known player the Bucs drafted in 1969. None of the players they signed that year played in more than 17 big league games.

### First-Round Bust
**TED NICHOLSON, 3B, WHITE SOX.** The Sox gambled on the untested Nicholson with the third pick, gave him a bonus of $15,000, and went bust as the Mississippi high school product played in just 152 minor league games. Nicholson did lose two full years (1971-72) while serving in Vietnam. He was released early in the 1973 season.

### Second To None
**LARRY GURA, LHP, CUBS.** Though he won an NCAA-record 19 games for College World Series champion Arizona State, Gura lasted until the second round (36th pick overall). He went on to win 126 games over 15 big league seasons.

### Late-Round Find
**KEN GRIFFEY, OF, REDS (29TH ROUND).** Despite being an afterthought in the 1969 draft, Griffey went on to hit .296—12 points

# Early promise fades for Burroughs, Richard

AP PHOTOS

Ted Williams called Jeff Burroughs the best 18-year-old hitter he had ever seen, but his major league career leveled off after a fast start

California high school outfielder Jeff Burroughs was acknowledged as the best hitting prospect in the 1969 draft, and few disputed that Louisiana prep righthander James Rodney Richard was the elite pitching prospect. Appropriately, they went off the board 1-2 in the June regular phase, with the Washington Senators snapping up Burroughs, and the Houston Astros tabbing the 6-foot-8 Richard.

By age 24, Burroughs had won the American League MVP award and become one of baseball's premier power hitters. In 1978-79, Richard posted consecutive 300-strikeout seasons while establishing himself as the premier power arm in the game.

The future was bright for both. Or so it seemed.

Burroughs never again matched his high-water mark of 1974, when he hit .301 with 118 RBIs for the Texas Rangers, while Richard's promising career took a tragic turn in 1980, when he was felled by a life-threatening stroke, at age 30, and never pitched another big league game.

Burroughs was so highly regarded a hitter out of Woodrow Wilson High in Long Beach, Calif., that no less an authority than Ted Williams called him "the best 18-year-old hitter I've ever seen."

Williams was manager of the Senators at the time, and instrumental in the club's selection of Burroughs as the No. 1 pick.

"He doesn't have an outstanding arm or outstanding speed, but he has an outstanding bat," said the Hall of Famer. "He has everything it takes to be one of the finest righthanded hitters in the game in three or four years."

Burroughs signed with the Senators for a bonus of $88,000—the largest handed out in 1969.

Jack Sheehan, Washington's chief scout, echoed Williams' sentiments by saying Burroughs "has the best power of any 18-year-old I've ever seen."

"He was the best all-around hitter available," Senators farm director Hal Keller agreed.

Most clubs agreed with the Senators that he was the most attractive player available.

Burroughs impressed Williams and other Senators officials with a batting-practice onslaught of home runs prior to the draft at Anaheim Stadium, home of the California Angels.

## 1969: THE FIRST ROUNDERS

| CLUB: PLAYER, POS., SCHOOL | HOMETOWN | B-T | HT. | WT. | AGE | BONUS | FIRST YEAR | LAST YEAR | PEAK LEVEL (YEARS) |
|---|---|---|---|---|---|---|---|---|---|
| **JUNE—REGULAR PHASE** | | | | | | | | | |
| **1. Senators: Jeff Burroughs, of, Woodrow Wilson HS** | **Long Beach, Calif.** | **R-R** | **6-1** | **200** | **18** | **$88,000** | **1969** | **1985** | **Majors (16)** |
| Made MLB debut at 19, won AL MVP (.301-25-118 in 1974) at 23, but 16-year career disappointed after that (.261, 240 HRs); son Sean also a first-rounder. | | | | | | | | | |
| **2. Astros: J.R. Richard, rhp, Lincoln HS** | **Ruston, La.** | **R-R** | **6-8** | **225** | **19** | **$39,000** | **1969** | **1983** | **Majors (10)** |
| Big, dominant pitcher looked like sure Hall of Famer (107-71, 3.15, pair of 300 SO seasons) before he was felled by stroke in 1980; never pitched in majors again. | | | | | | | | | |
| **3. White Sox: Ted Nicholson, 3b, Oak Park HS** | **Laurel, Miss.** | **R-R** | **6-5** | **200** | **20** | **$15,000** | **1969** | **1973** | **Class A (2)** |
| Sox got what they paid for; he lost all of 1971-72 seasons to military duty, never advanced above A-ball, hit .252 with 12 homers in parts of three years. | | | | | | | | | |
| **4. Mets: Randy Sterling, rhp, Key West HS** | **Key West, Fla.** | **L-R** | **6-4** | **193** | **18** | **$52,500** | **1969** | **1975** | **Majors (1)** |
| Pitching was on the minds of Amazin' Mets in '69, but he spent most of seven-year career in Triple-A, went 60-56, 3.40; surfaced for three games with Mets in '74. | | | | | | | | | |
| **5. Angels: Alan Bannister, ss, John F. Kennedy HS** | **Buena Park, Calif.** | **R-R** | **6-0** | **175** | **17** | **Unsigned** | **1973** | **1985** | **Majors (12)** |
| Rejected Angels offer, became college star at Arizona State; drafted No. 1 overall in 1973 (January/regular phase), but never starred in majors as expected. | | | | | | | | | |
| **6. Phillies: Mike Anderson, 1b, Timmonsville HS** | **Timmonsville, S.C.** | **R-R** | **6-3** | **187** | **17** | **$51,000** | **1969** | **1981** | **Majors (9)** |
| Enjoyed almost identical minor league career as Greg Luzinski, Phils' first-rounder a year earlier, but never matched him in nine years in majors (.246-28-134). | | | | | | | | | |
| **7. Twins: Paul Ray Powell, of, Arizona State** | **Eloy, Ariz.** | **R-R** | **6-0** | **190** | **20** | **$45,000** | **1969** | **1975** | **Majors (3)** |
| College player of year in '69 (.360-11-73) led Sun Devils to national title, but MLB career fizzled (.167-1-2 in 30 games); later became a catcher, Triple-A lifer. | | | | | | | | | |
| **8. Dodgers: Terry McDermott, c, St. Agnes HS** | **West Hempstead, N.Y.** | **R-R** | **6-4** | **205** | **18** | **$50,000** | **1969** | **1976** | **Majors (1)** |
| Played nine games for Dodgers in 1972, but moved to first base and spent bulk of career at Triple-A Albuquerque; later became sportscaster in that city. | | | | | | | | | |
| **9. Athletics: Don Stanhouse, rhp/3b, DuQuoin HS** | **DuQuoin, Ill.** | **R-R** | **6-2** | **185** | **18** | **$33,000** | **1969** | **1983** | **Majors (10)** |
| Began career as 3B, but A's saw more upside on mound; spent 10 years in majors as reliever, went 38-54, 3.84 with 64 SV; played for four Hall of Fame managers. | | | | | | | | | |
| **10. Pirates: Bob May, rhp, Merritt Island HS** | **Merritt Island, Fla.** | **R-R** | **6-0** | **175** | **17** | **$15,000** | **1969** | **1970** | **Class A (1)** |
| Florida prep product pitched two years in minors for Pirates, went 5-7, 3.97 in 20 appearances; 1971-73 seasons lost to military duty, never resumed pro career. | | | | | | | | | |
| **11. Yankees: Charlie Spikes, 3b/of, Central Memorial HS** | **Bogalusa, La.** | **R-R** | **6-2** | **195** | **18** | **$30,000** | **1969** | **1980** | **Majors (9)** |
| Rising prospect when Yankees dealt him to Cleveland for 3B Graig Nettles; hit 23 homers as rookie, but never clicked under demanding manager Frank Robinson. | | | | | | | | | |
| **12. Braves: Gene Holbert, c, Palmyra HS** | **Campbelltown, Pa.** | **B-R** | **6-1** | **210** | **17** | **$10,000** | **1969** | **1972** | **Class AA (1)** |
| Switch-hitting catcher signed with Braves for smallest bonus in first round, had unproductive four-year career (.228-7-104); was on restricted list in 1973-74. | | | | | | | | | |
| **13. Red Sox: Noel Jenke, of, Minnesota** | **Owatonna, Minn.** | **L-L** | **6-1** | **215** | **22** | **$85,000** | **1969** | **1971** | **Class AAA (2)** |
| Red Sox thought they scored a coup in signing three-sport college star; started career in AAA, never hit to expectations before quitting in 1971 to pursue NFL career. | | | | | | | | | |
| **14. Reds: Don Gullett, lhp, McKell HS** | **Lynn, Ky.** | **R-L** | **6-0** | **190** | **18** | **$25,000** | **1969** | **1978** | **Majors (9)** |
| Cracked Reds Opening Day roster at 19, became force as starter/reliever; played on four straight World Series champs (1975-78); career cut short by torn rotator cuff. | | | | | | | | | |
| **15. Indians: Alvin McGrew, of, A.H. Parker HS** | **Fairfield, Ala.** | **R-R** | **6-2** | **175** | **17** | **$40,000** | **1969** | **1976** | **Class AAA (3)** |
| Three-sport high school standout chose offer from Indians over chance to play football/basketball in college; played eight years in minors, .hit .269-46-237, 68 SB. | | | | | | | | | |
| **16. Cubs: Roger Metzger, ss, St. Edward's (Texas)** | **San Antonio** | **L-R** | **6-0** | **165** | **21** | **$26,000** | **1969** | **1980** | **Majors (11)** |
| Light-hitting, Gold-Glove SS played just two games with Cubs before trade to Astros; career ended when he lost tips off four fingers in industrial accident. | | | | | | | | | |
| **17. Orioles: Don Hood, lhp, Southside HS** | **Florence, S.C.** | **L-L** | **6-2** | **175** | **19** | **$17,500** | **1969** | **1983** | **Majors (10)** |
| Played on four straight state championship teams in high school; pitched for five teams over 10 years in majors, mostly as reliever, went 34-35, 3.79 with 6 SV. | | | | | | | | | |
| **18. Giants: Mike Phillips, ss, MacArthur HS** | **Irving, Texas** | **L-R** | **6-0** | **170** | **18** | **$30,000** | **1969** | **1983** | **Majors (11)** |
| Prep shortstop hung on for 11 years in majors in utility role; played for five teams, hit .240-11-45 overall; later became VP of corporate/group sales for Royals. | | | | | | | | | |
| **19. Tigers: Lenny Baxley, 1b, Enterprise HS** | **Redding, Calif.** | **L-L** | **6-2** | **185** | **18** | **$20,000** | **1969** | **1973** | **Class A (3)** |
| Once hit five homers in Little League game, excelled in three sports in high school; raw power never developed in five seasons in minors, none above Class A. | | | | | | | | | |
| **20. Cardinals: # Charles Minott, lhp/1b, Royal Oak HS** | **Covina, Calif.** | **L-L** | **6-4** | **200** | **17** | **$38,000** | **1969** | **1971** | **Class A (1)** |
| Spent first year in minors as pitcher (2-5, 4.31), second as hitter in A-ball (.304-5-32); diagnosed with Hodgkin's Disease in spring training 1972, died at 27. | | | | | | | | | |
| **21. Pilots: Gorman Thomas, ss, James Island HS** | **Charleston, S.C.** | **R-R** | **6-2** | **190** | **18** | **$50,000** | **1969** | **1986** | **Majors (13)** |
| Only first-round pick in Pilots history achieved folk-hero status in Milwaukee for long-ball/strikeout feats; hit 164 HR in minors, 268 in 13 years in majors. | | | | | | | | | |
| **22. Expos: Balor Moore, lhp, Deer Park HS** | **Deer Park, Texas** | **L-L** | **6-3** | **185** | **18** | **$24,800** | **1969** | **1981** | **Majors (8)** |
| Went 9-1, 0.41 in first pro season and was in majors 11 months after being drafted; went 28-48, 4.52 in eight seasons, hampered by shoulder/knee injuries. | | | | | | | | | |
| **23. Royals: Johnny Simmons, ss, Childersburg HS** | **Childersburg, Ala.** | **R-R** | **5-11** | **165** | **18** | **Unsigned** | **Never Played Pro Ball** | | |
| No. 4 on Royals follow list, hit .519 and excelled as SS/RHP in high school, but chose to play football at Auburn; never drafted in baseball again. | | | | | | | | | |
| **24. Padres: Randy Elliott, 1b, Camarillo HS** | **Camarillo, Calif.** | **R-R** | **6-2** | **190** | **18** | **$20,000** | **1969** | **1980** | **Majors (4)** |
| Streaky hitter played parts of four seasons in majors from 1972-80, career derailed by 1972 shoulder injury; hit .215 in majors, .297-78-411 in 703 games in minors. | | | | | | | | | |
| **JANUARY—REGULAR PHASE** | | | | | | | | | |
| **1. Astros: Derrel Thomas, ss, Dorsey HS** | **Los Angeles** | **B-R** | **6-0** | **160** | **18** | **$16,000** | **1969** | **1985** | **Majors (15)** |
| Eligible for January draft as December HS grad; went on to 15-year career in majors for eight teams as utility player; later spent time in jail on cocaine charges. | | | | | | | | | |
| **JANUARY—SECONDARY PHASE** | | | | | | | | | |
| **1. Cardinals: Wayne Garland, rhp, Gulf Coast (Fla.) CC** | **Nashville, Tenn.** | **R-R** | **6-0** | **195** | **18** | **Unsigned** | **1969** | **1981** | **Majors (9)** |
| Didn't sign in January, but did with Orioles in June; capitalized on 20-7 season with O's in 1976, signed historic 10-year deal in first wave of MLB free agency. | | | | | | | | | |
| **JUNE—SECONDARY PHASE** | | | | | | | | | |
| **1. Indians: Rich Hand, rhp, Puget Sound (Wash.)** | **Bellevue, Wash.** | **R-R** | **6-1** | **185** | **20** | **$17,000** | **1969** | **1974** | **Majors (4)** |
| First player from 1969 draft class to reach majors; overuse in 1970 led to elbow injuries early, shoulder issues later; went 24-37 in four major league seasons. | | | | | | | | | |

*# Deceased.*

## AT A GLANCE

higher than his more-celebrated son—in a 19-year major league career.

### Never Too Late

**AL COWENS, OF, ROYALS (75TH ROUND).** The expansion Royals needed all the players they could find to fill out rosters for six farm clubs, and made 118 selections in the 1969 draft—including a then-record 90 in the June regular phase. They stumbled upon Cowens, the latest pick that year to reach the majors, and saw him enjoy a 13-year big league career.

### Overlooked

**BRIAN DOWNING, C/OF, WHITE SOX.** Downing was cut from high school and junior college teams, but got signed out of a tryout camp at a time when major league teams were scrambling to find players to replace those lost to military duty at the height of the Vietnam War. He became the most productive free-agent signing of the draft era. In 20 seasons (13 with the Angels), he hit .267, and proved to be a player ahead of his time as he hit 275 homers and drew 1,197 walks in a then-unconventional role as a leadoff hitter.

### International Gem

**JOAQUIN ANDUJAR, RHP, REDS.** Signed out of the Dominican Republic at 17 for $2,500, Andujar never found his groove with the Reds in six minor league seasons before being dealt to the Astros. He went on to win 127 big league games over the next 13 seasons, including 20 with the Cardinals in 1984.

### Minor League Take

**GORMAN THOMAS, OF, PILOTS.** Stormin' Gorman had a noteworthy major league career as the only first-round pick in Seattle Pilots history. He slammed 268 homers in 1,435 games over 13 seasons, while also striking out

**CONTINUED ON PAGE 84**

## AT A GLANCE

CONTINUED FROM PAGE 83

1,339 times. His all-or-nothing approach also characterized his minor league career. In 709 games, Thomas went deep 164 times (including 51 homers in 1974 at Triple-A Sacramento), while striking out 827 times.

### One Who Got Away

**JOHNNY SIMMONS, SS, ROYALS.** Angels first-rounder **ALAN BANNISTER** didn't sign as the fifth overall pick in 1969, but he resurfaced as the No. 1 pick in the 1973 draft (January/regular phase) after three outstanding college seasons at Arizona State. Simmons, the other first-rounder in 1969 to go unsigned, was lost for good when he chose a college football career at Auburn.

### He Was Drafted?

**JOHNNY RODGERS, SS, DODGERS (38TH ROUND).** Rodgers was drafted out of an Omaha high school, but never played baseball in college at Nebraska, where he won the Heisman Trophy in 1972.

### Did You Know . . .

**ELI BORUNDA,** San Diego's second-round pick, quit the Padres in 1970 after going 0-9 at Triple-A Salt Lake City to join the Jehovah's Witness ministry. Over the next three years, two more Padres players—ex-big league catcher Ron Slocum and 1971 second-rounder Willie Boynton—left baseball at the height of their careers to join the religious organization.

### They Said It

**REGGIE JACKSON**, on Arizona State baseball/football standout **PAUL RAY POWELL,** a former teammate drafted in the first round by the Twins: "He's a cinch future major league star . . . a much superior outfielder to what I was at Arizona State."—*Powell hit one homer in his short big league career, 562 fewer than Jackson.*

"Working out with Ted Williams was quite an experience," said Burroughs, who hit .569 as a high school senior. "I've always been a Williams fan. You could say he's been my idol. I was a little boy when he was playing."

Burroughs would play briefly for Williams in Washington, but enjoyed his greatest success as a member of the Rangers, after the Senators franchise moved to Arlington, Texas, following the 1971 season. The obvious peak came with his 1974 MVP award.

Richard, meanwhile, was so overpowering at Lincoln High in Ruston, La., that he didn't allow an earned run in his senior year, while going 11-0. For his career, he was 28-0 with four perfect games.

The Astros initially identified the tall, gangly Richard, along with a pair of athletic outfielders from small hamlets in the South—Charlie Spikes of Bogalusa, La., and Alvin McGrew of Fairfield, Ala.—as the players they would seriously consider with the No. 2 pick overall.

"But after we saw J.R., there was no doubt in our minds," said Tal Smith, the Astros' director of player personnel. "The raw ability was just awesome. It was more of a gamble with J.R. than we thought it would have been with McGrew or Spikes, but the potential was so much greater. Our scouts felt that Richard had a Bob Gibson fastball. He was the top pitching prospect in the country."

### BURROUGHS, OTHERS MOVE QUICKLY

From the moment he signed with Washington, Burroughs was on the fast track to the big leagues. It was against Williams' better judgment that Burroughs was called up in his first full pro season, but owner Bob Short was notoriously impatient. He would later exploit two more No. 1 overall picks—Pete Broberg (1971) and David Clyde (1973)—by starting their professional careers in the big leagues, so he pushed for Burroughs, 19, to be called up on July 20, 1970, little more than a year after he signed with the Senators, for an ill-fated two-week stint.

Burroughs had already been challenged that season, by beginning the 1970 season with the Senators' Triple-A farm club at Denver, curiously at the request of Bears general manager Jim Burris, who felt the power-hitting outfielder was capable of making the leap from Rookie ball. Despite a 1-for-24 start, Burroughs was beginning to gain the measure of Triple-A pitching when Short called. Burroughs struggled in his debut for the Senators, getting two singles in six games, and it would be another year before he returned to the big leagues again.

"We realize it was a bad mistake to call Burroughs up last year," Senators vice president Joe Burke said after Burroughs was called up for good.

Among other things, Burroughs struggled adapting to the hitting philosophy preached by Williams, one of the game's all-time great batsmen.

"Williams was a dead pull hitter, and he thought everyone should be," Burroughs said. "He used to say, 'You make history off the inside pitch.' And he considered pitchers to be the stupidest people in the world.

"He was very helpful to everybody. The problem was we just couldn't do it as well, because we weren't Ted Williams. He would get frustrated and say we had this God-given ability. He couldn't understand that we just weren't as good."

While Burroughs struggled with his premature promotion to the Senators, two other teenagers in the Class of 1969, both pitchers, made seamless transitions to the big leagues and were entrenched by the time he broke in.

Lefthander Don Gullett, Cincinnati's first-round pick (14th overall), opened the 1970 season in the Reds bullpen, and went on to post a 5-2, 2.42 record in 44 appearances as a rookie for the National League champions.

Minnesota's Bert Blyleven, a third-round pick, moved into the Twins rotation two months after his 19th birthday, and went on to assemble a 10-9, 3.18 record in 25 starts, while walking 47 and striking 135 in 164 innings.

Both pitchers went on to successful big league careers, with Blyleven becoming the only player drafted and signed in 1969 who became a Hall of Famer—though he wasn't elected until 2011, in his 14th year of eligibility. Blyleven, who was born in the Netherlands and reared in Canada before moving with his family to California, was advanced for his age, mainly because of his tantalizing curve—a pitch that was self-taught.

Gullett's career, while successful, was shortened because of a torn rotator cuff in his pitching shoulder. In nine years, working as both a starter

## How They Should Have Done It

Based on the career WAR (Wins Above Replacement, as calculated by Baseball-Reference.com) numbers achieved by all the players eligible for the 1969 draft, here's how the first round should have unfolded. Numbers in parentheses indicate the round when the player was actually drafted

| | Player, Pos. | Actual Draft | WAR | Bonus |
|---|---|---|---|---|
| 1. | Bert Blyleven, rhp | Twins (3) | 95.4 | $15,000 |
| 2. | Dwight Evans, of | Red Sox (5) | 66.7 | $10,500 |
| 3. | Buddy Bell, 2b | Indians (16) | 65.9 | None |
| 4. | Brian Downing, c | White Sox (NDFA) | 51.4 | $2,000 |
| 5. | Ken Griffey, of | Reds (29) | 34.5 | None |
| 6. | Mickey Rivers, of | Braves (June-S/2) | 32.3 | $2,000 |
| 7. | Bob Boone, 3b | Phillies (6) | 27.4 | $18,000 |
| 8. | Bill North, of | Cubs (12) | 26.7 | $12,000 |
| 9. | Kent Tekulve, rhp | Pirates (NDFA) | 26.3 | None |
| 10. | J.R. Richard, rhp | Astros (1) | 22.3 | $39,000 |
| 11. | Larry Gura, lhp | Cubs (2) | 21.7 | $30,000 |
| 12. | Dan Driessen, 3b | Reds (NDFA) | 20.4 | None |
| 13. | Lee Lacy, 3b | Dodgers (Jan.-R/2) | 20.1 | $15,000 |
| 14. | Gorman Thomas, ss | Pilots (1) | 19.8 | $50,000 |
| 15. | Don Gullett, lhp | Reds (1) | 18.5 | $25,000 |
| 16. | Jeff Burroughs, of | Senators (1) | 17.7 | $88,000 |
| 17. | Steve Stone, rhp | Giants (Jan.-S/4) | 17.6 | $10,000 |
| 18. | Jim Slaton, rhp | Pilots (15) | 17.5 | $5,000 |
| 19. | Rick Miller, of | Red Sox (2) | 15.6 | $25,000 |
| 20. | Al Cowens, ss | Royals (75) | 15.2 | $4,500 |
| 21. | Mike Easler, 3b | Astros (14) | 12.9 | None |
| 22. | Alan Ashby, c | Indians (3) | 11.1 | $15,000 |
| 23. | Jim Essian, c | Phillies (NDFA) | 10.9 | $7,000 |
| 24. | Al Hrabosky, lhp | Cardinals (Jan.-R/1) | 10.6 | $20,000 |
| **Top 3 Unsigned Players** | | | | **Year Signed** |
| 1. | Dave Winfield, rhp | Orioles (40) | 64.0 | 1973 |
| 2. | Doug DeCinces, 3b | Padres (18) | 41.6 | 1970 |
| 3. | Jim Sundberg, c | Athletics (6) | 40.3 | 1973 |

and reliever, the hard-throwing southpaw posted a 109-50 record, and had the distinction of pitching on four straight World Series champions—with Cincinnati's Big Red Machine in 1975-76, with the New York Yankees from 1977-78 after signing with that club as a free agent—before his career ended at 27 due to persistent shoulder problems.

Gullett made 11 appearances at short-season Class A Sioux Falls in 1969, after being drafted, before making the Reds staff out of spring training a year later—the same career path successfully traveled three years earlier by Reds 18-year-old pitching sensation Gary Nolan. Gullett had enjoyed a spectacular, multi-sport career at Kentucky's McKell High, and had dozens of offers to play both football and basketball in college before the Reds lured him to baseball with a $25,000 signing bonus. In his signature games as a high school senior, Gullett scored all 72 points—11 via touchdown, six on extra-points—in a 72-0 win in football, tallied 47 points in basketball and struck out 20 of 21 in baseball while spinning a perfect game.

Without the shoulder problems that prematurely ended his career, Gullett may have joined Blyleven in the Hall of Fame.

"You never know what may have happened," Gullett said years later, after returning to the game as a pitching coach. "There's always a chance of injury. It was just unfortunate in my career. If I had stayed healthy, there is the chance I could have been very successful."

### PREP TALENT IN LATE ROUNDS

There was more of a high school flavor to the 1969 draft than any in history, with 63.5 percent of all selections in June coming from that demographic. The total of 723 high school selections was more than three times the number in 1985.

Of 24 players drafted in the first round, 21 were from the prep ranks—and that didn't even include a number of mid- to late-round selections who enjoyed productive big league careers, and in hindsight would have been slam-dunk first-rounders. Among them were the likes of outfielder Dwight Evans (Red Sox, fifth round), third baseman Buddy Bell (Indians, 16th round) and outfielder Ken Griffey (Reds, 29th round)—to say nothing of outfielder Al Cowens, a lowly 75th-round selection of the Kansas City Royals.

In contrast to those players, and even the success enjoyed by Burroughs, Richard and Gullett, short-lived as it may have been, the first round of the June regular phase as a whole never measured up to expectations.

Four selections failed to even advance beyond

## Fastest To The Majors

| | Player, Pos. | Drafted (Round) | Debut |
|---|---|---|---|
| 1. | Rich Hand, rhp | Indians (June-S/1) | April 9, 1970 |
| 2. | * Don Gullett, lhp | Reds (1) | April 10, 1970 |
| 3. | Larry Gura, lhp | Cubs (2) | April 30, 1970 |
| 4. | * Balor Moore, lhp | Expos (1) | May 21, 1970 |
| 5. | * Bert Blyleven, rhp | Twins (3) | June 5, 1970 |

**LAST PLAYER TO RETIRE:** Bert Blyleven, rhp (Oct. 4, 1992)

**High school selection.*

## DRAFT SPOTLIGHT: J.R. RICHARD

GLUF PHOTO

**J.R. Richard was one of the most dominant righthanders ever when he was struck down by a stroke in 1980, never returning to the big leagues**

J.R. Richard was so dominating a pitcher at Lincoln High in Ruston, La., that as a senior, he didn't allow an earned run. His athletic ability extended well beyond his pitching skills, however, and the Houston Astros, who selected him with the second pick in the 1969 draft, had plenty of competition for his services.

There was concern that the towering Richard would accept a basketball scholarship from Southern, one of many colleges to pursue him for his hoops skills. Richard, 19, was also the quarterback of his high school team for four years. For added measure, he homered four times and drove in 10 runs in one game as a senior in a lopsided 48-0 victory, while also spinning a no-hitter.

Tal Smith, the Astros' director of player personnel, wasn't the only high-level scouting official who saw Richard in the spring of 1969 and left impressed. "I went over to work him out one time, and got a little ol' kid to catch him," recalled Mel Didier, then scouting director for the Montreal Expos. "Every time he'd catch one of J.R.'s pitches, it would knock him back about a foot, it seemed. It was unbelievable the arm that guy had."

Overpowering as he was, Richard didn't know some of the basics of pitching. "When he went to Covington (Va.) for Rookie ball," Smith said, "he didn't know how to throw from a stretch. He hadn't needed that in high school; that's how dominating he'd been."

Richard signed with the Astros for a bonus of $39,000. On Sept. 15, 1971, he made his first major league start, striking out 15 San Francisco Giants. By 1976, he won 20 games. In 1978, he became the first righthander in National League history to strike out more than 300 batters in a season (303), and he followed that with a 313-strikeout season.

In 1980, Richard was the most dominant righthander in the game. He had a 10-4, 1.89 record in the first half and started the All-Star Game for the National League. He pitched two scoreless innings in Dodger Stadium, with his fastball clocked at 100 mph.

Then in a flash, it was over.

On July 30, 1980, Richard collapsed in the Astrodome during a workout. A blood clot in his right shoulder had moved into the carotid artery in his neck, the main supplier of blood to the brain. He suffered a massive stroke.

"I should have died right then," Richard said. "Anyone else would have been dead."

Multiple surgeries restored the circulation in his shoulder, but his coordination and reflexes never fully returned. Richard did not play in 1981. His comeback attempts in 1982 and 1983 were unsuccessful, though he did pitch a combined 117 innings in the Astros farm system. "I had to learn to do things all over again," Richard said.

In 1984, the Astros released Richard. Soon thereafter, he was destitute. In 1993, Richard was found living under a bridge a few miles from the Astrodome.

When the game—and almost his life—was taken from him, Richard had a 107-71, 3.15 record in the big leagues. He struck out 1,493 in 1,606 innings.

In hindsight, there had been warning signs. Richard frequently had talked about his arm feeling fatigued that season. After he pulled himself out of his first start after the All-Star Game, the Astros placed him on the disabled list. Doctors determined that he had a blood clot on his right side but said he was in no danger and could return to baseball.

Richard later sued the team and its doctors, eventually settling out of court for a reported $1 million. It was small consolation for a pitcher who might have become one of the best in baseball history.

"I'm bitter in a lot of ways," he said. "What has happened could have been prevented. It should have been prevented. My entire life was shattered. I didn't reach my prime. It was all taken from me when I was coming along. Who knows how much better I would have gotten or what kind of records I would have put up?"

## WORTH NOTING

■ Though no one realized it at the time, the 1969 draft produced several players who became centerpieces of some of the more prominent family acts in the draft era. Chief among them were **BOB BOONE** (Phillies, sixth round) and **BUDDY BELL** (Indians, 16th round), both of whom enjoyed long and productive major league careers, following in the footsteps of their fathers, and paving the way for their sons. Boone's father Ray played in the majors, and the Boones made baseball history in 1992, when Bob's son Bret also reached the majors, making the Boones the game's first three-generation family. Not to be outdone, the Bell family gained the same distinction in 1995, when David Bell, Buddy's son, reached the majors, to join his father and Buddy's father, Gus Bell, in select company. By 2015, the feat had been achieved four times, with the Coleman and Hairston families joining the Boones and Bells.

■ **JEFF BURROUGHS**, the top overall pick in the 1969 draft, earned his own historical footnote when son Sean became a first-rounder in 1998. **KEN GRIFFEY**, while only a 29th-rounder when he was drafted in 1969, was responsible for producing the first overall pick in the 1986 draft, Ken Griffey Jr.

■ Bell closed out an 18-year major league career in 1989 with numbers that were remarkably similar to his father, Gus, who toiled in the big leagues for 15 seasons. Buddy hit .280; his dad .281.

### Top 25 Bonuses

| Player, Pos. | Drafted (Round) | Order | Bonus |
|---|---|---|---|
| **1. *Jeff Burroughs, of** | **Senators (1)** | **1** | **$88,000** |
| 2. Noel Jenke, of | Red Sox (1) | 13 | $85,000 |
| **3. *Randy Sterling, rhp** | **Mets (1)** | **4** | **$52,500** |
| **4. *Mike Anderson, 1b** | **Phillies (1)** | **6** | **$51,000** |
| **5. *Terry McDermott, c** | **Dodgers (1)** | **8** | **$50,000** |
| ***Gorman Thomas, ss** | **Pilots (1)** | **21** | **$50,000** |
| *John Brown, rhp | Senators (2) | 25 | $50,000 |
| **8. Paul Ray Powell, of** | **Twins (1)** | **7** | **$45,000** |
| 9. *Alvin McGrew, of | Indians (1) | 15 | $40,000 |
| **10. *J.R. Richard, rhp** | **Astros (1)** | **2** | **$39,000** |
| 11. *Charles Minott, lhp/of | Cardinals (1) | 20 | $38,000 |
| *James Winters, of | Orioles (4) | 89 | $38,000 |
| 13. Michael Kimbrell, 2b | Dodgers (Jan.-R/1) | (5) | $35,000 |
| **14. *Don Stanhouse, rhp/3b** | **Athletics (1)** | **9** | **$33,000** |
| 15. *Dave Chorley, of | Angels (2) | 29 | $32,500 |
| **16. *Charlie Spikes, 3b/of** | **Yankees (1)** | **11** | **$30,000** |
| ***Mike Phillips, ss** | **Giants (1)** | **18** | **$30,000** |
| **Larry Gura, lhp** | **Cubs (2)** | **40** | **$30,000** |
| **19. Wayne Garland, rhp** | **Orioles (June-S/1)** | **(5)** | **$28,000** |
| **20. *Stan Papi, ss** | **Astros (2)** | **26** | **$27,000** |
| **21. Roger Metzger, ss** | **Cubs (1)** | **16** | **$26,000** |
| ***Joe Nolan, c** | **Mets (2)** | **28** | **$26,000** |
| Gary Myers, of | Red Sox (Jan.-S/1) | (4) | $26,000 |
| 24. Several tied at | | | $25,000 |

*Major leaguers in bold. *High school selection.*

Class A, though the careers of third baseman Ted Nicholson, drafted third overall by the Chicago White Sox, and righthander Bob May (Pirates, 11th), were affected by military duty.

The St. Louis Cardinals got just two years of minor league service—one as a pitcher, one as a hitter—from their top pick, lefthander Charles Minott (20th overall). He was diagnosed with Hodgkin's Disease in spring training of 1972 and died five years later.

Ken Griffey

Two first-round picks, shortstops Alan Bannister (Angels, 5th) and Johnny Simmons (Royals, 23rd), didn't sign at all. Bannister enjoyed a spectacular college career at Arizona State before becoming the first overall pick in the January 1973 draft (regular phase), while Simmons chose a football career at Auburn and was never heard from again on the diamond.

But no first-rounder in the 1969 crop failed quite as spectacularly as Nicholson, a 20-year-old Mississippi high school product. Not only had he missed a year of school because of a childhood illness, making him the oldest high school product ever drafted in the first round, but his selection also raised eyebrows because his high school in Laurel, Miss., didn't even field a baseball team.

Most other clubs did not hold Nicholson in the same regard as the White Sox, and the crosstown Cubs had him rated as no better than the 70th best player available in their predraft rankings.

Nicholson was spotted by White Sox scouts Walt Widmayer and Sam Hairston while playing for the semi-pro Laurel Black Cats. A year earlier, Widmayer and Hairston had discovered outfielder Carlos May, an Alabama high school product who became a successful first-round pick for the Sox. They hoped to catch lightning in a bottle again by tapping the 6-foot-5 Nicholson with the third pick overall.

"He's got more power than May," White Sox farm director Glen Miller said at the time, justifying his club's decision.

Nicholson, who was signed to a bonus of just $15,000 (equaling the smallest bonus paid out in the first round in 1969), proved a major disappointment. He played in just 152 games over a five-year stretch in the White Sox system, hitting only five homers, though he lost two full years (1971-72) while serving the war effort in Vietnam. Nicholson was released early in the 1973 season after it had become apparent that his skills had significantly eroded while being away from the game for an extended period.

Of the three college selections in the first round, the most disappointing by far was Minnesota senior outfielder Noel Jenke, drafted 13th overall by the Red Sox. He began his career in Triple-A, but was laboring at Double-A Pawtucket in 1971, hitting .238 with three homers and 17 RBIs in 52 games, when he retired from the game to pursue a career in the National Football League.

Jenke's biggest problem, it seemed, was choosing which sport he wanted to pursue at the professional level. He had his pick of three after starring for three years in hockey and football for the Gophers, while also batting .400 with 12 home runs as a right fielder in 1969, in his only varsity baseball season. Basically, he was Dave Winfield before Dave Winfield.

The Minnesota Vikings claimed Jenke in the 1969 NFL draft, and though he was never drafted in hockey, the Chicago Blackhawks held his negotiation rights and made a concerted effort to sign him after his stellar hockey career with the Gophers. (As a side note, Jenke is generally credited with being the first U.S. college player to use a curved stick.)

The Red Sox were the last team to come calling for Jenke's services, but made the biggest statement by signing him to an $85,000 bonus offer—the second largest handed out in 1969.

Jenke wasn't just a talented all-around athlete; his aggressive attitude caught the eye of coaches and scouts.

"Jenke is the meanest competitor we've had here since I've been the coach," Gophers baseball coach Dick Siebert said. "Off the field, you can't meet a nicer boy. But once the game starts, look out. I never saw any more determination in an athlete."

The Red Sox were also impressed by Jenke's tenacity and talent, and sent six different scouts to check him out in the spring of 1969.

"I was one of them myself," Boston scouting director Neil Mahoney said. "We all came away feeling that the boy has the potential to be an outstanding player."

But the potential didn't translate into results—not on the baseball field, at least. Jenke, who subsequently played linebacker for four years in the

NFL, showed little raw power as a pro, hitting only five homers in parts of three seasons.

"He was a major disappointment. His hitting was his biggest problem," said Ed Kenney, then the Red Sox farm director. "He was a leader in football when he played in college, and we thought it would carry over in baseball. But it didn't."

## POWELL, GURA SPARK ARIZONA STATE

Arizona State dominated the collegiate ranks in 1969. Not only did the Sun Devils win the College World Series for the third time in five years, but their impact on the draft was significant.

The Sun Devils had more players drafted (eight) than any other college—and their take included both the first college position player drafted, outfielder Paul Ray Powell, and first college pitcher, lefthander Larry Gura. Powell was claimed by the Twins with the seventh pick overall, while Gura lasted deep into the second round before being claimed by the Cubs with the 36th pick overall.

Gura was fresh from tossing a 10-1, six-hit victory over Tulsa in the CWS championship game, which enabled the Joliet, Ill., product to set a collegiate record for wins in a season with 19, breaking the record of 18 set by Southern California's Bruce Gardner in 1960. Gura finished with a 19-2, 1.01 record, along with 195 strikeouts in 169 innings.

Powell was named the collegiate player of the year after hitting .364 with 11 home runs and 74 RBIs, while setting NCAA season records for hits (89) and total bases (162). He was proclaimed, in some quarters, a better overall prospect than former ASU star Reggie Jackson, the second overall pick in the 1966 draft and a rising major league star at the time of Powell's selection.

None other than Jackson himself tabbed Powell a can't-miss prospect.

"He's a much superior outfielder to what I was at Arizona State," Jackson said. "He's a football player who has a lot of courage, and can run and throw. Within two years, he will be a star in the majors."

Like Jackson, Powell enrolled at ASU to play football, and he became a defensive co-captain as an underclassman. The baseball careers of both in college were supposed to be mere afterthoughts—and evolved only after Sun Devils football coach Frank Kush reluctantly gave both permission to skip spring football to play baseball.

### Largest Bonuses By Round

| | Player, Pos. | Club | Bonus |
|---|---|---|---|
| 1. | ***Jeff Burroughs, of** | **Senators** | **$88,000** |
| 2. | *John Brown, rhp | Senators | $50,000 |
| 3. | Several tied at | | $15,000 |
| 4. | *James Winters, of | Orioles | $38,000 |
| 5. | ***David Criscione, c** | **Senators** | **$25,000** |
| 6. | **Bob Boone, 3b** | **Phillies** | **$18,000** |
| 7. | *Stan Templeton, of | Cardinals | $12,000 |
| 8. | John Dolinsek, of | Astros | $15,000 |
| 9. | Donzell McDonald, of | Pirates | $8,000 |
| 10. | *Ron Mitchell, of | Dodgers | $13,600 |
| Jan/R. | Michael Kimbrell, 2b | Dodgers (1) | $35,000 |
| Jan/S. | Gary Myers, of | Red Sox (1) | $26,000 |
| **Jun/S.** | **Wayne Garland, rhp** | **Orioles (1)** | **$28,000** |

*Major leaguers in bold. *High school selection.*

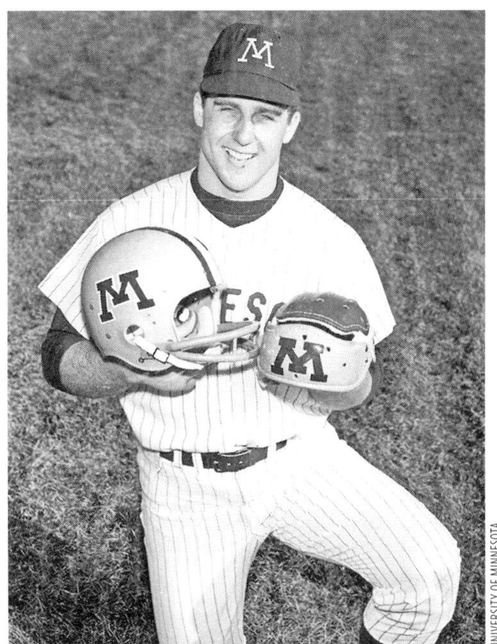
UNIVERSITY OF MINNESOTA

**Noel Jenke seemed to have all the attributes to be a baseball (or hockey) star, but he ultimately found more success as an NFL player**

Bobby Winkles, the ASU baseball coach who soon left the Sun Devils to manage the Angels, coached the pair and said: "At the same stage, I'd say Powell is a better outfielder than Jackson was in college. Powell is not a free swinger like Jackson, but he is more consistent. Both are equally fast but Jackson has the better arm."

The Twins signed Powell to a $45,000 bonus and were so impressed that they immediately began talking of him as another Harmon Killebrew.

"I'm not Harmon Killebrew," Powell said emphatically. "I consider myself more of a line-drive hitter than a long-ball, home run man."

Powell never came close to living up to his lofty expectations. He garnered only 30 at-bats in his brief big league career, and hit his only career homer in a Twins uniform in 1971, the same year Killebrew clubbed his 500th.

With the notable exception of the two high-powered programs at Southern California and Arizona State, college baseball's influence on the draft had yet to manifest in the late 1960s, and two of the elite talents in the college game in 1969, Stanford third baseman Bob Boone and USC first baseman Bill Seinsoth, both seniors, were largely overlooked. Boone went to the Philadelphia Phillies in the sixth round, while Seinsoth, who had been drafted four times previously, was taken by the Los Angeles Dodgers with their first pick in the secondary phase.

Until then, neither player had shown much inclination for pro ball and had spent the previous three summers playing alongside one another in Fairbanks, Alaska, for the Alaska Goldpanners.

Boone got an $18,000 signing bonus from the Phillies, and went on to a 19-year major league career as a catcher after being converted from third base. With his father Ray, and sons Bret and Aaron, he became a part of the first three-generation family in the majors in 1992, and gained further recognition by catching more games in the

### WORTH NOTING

In homers, Gus edged his son, 206-201. The elder Bell enjoyed his greatest success as a member of the Reds, and Buddy, a product of Cincinnati's Moeller High, was disappointed that the Reds not only didn't draft him in 1969, but also showed little interest. "It was an initial shock," said Bell, who ended up being selected in the 16th round by Ohio's other major league team, Cleveland.

■ **DAVE WINFIELD**, who became a first-round pick in 1973 out of the University of Minnesota and a member of baseball's Hall of Fame 28 years after that, was drafted by Baltimore in 1969—in the 40th round, as a pitcher out of a Minnesota high school. A scouting report by Twins area scout Cobby Saatzer, written in scouting vernacular common in that era, didn't paint a rosy picture for Winfield's future: "A colored boy with some real good power. Will have to play first base or outfield because of his running speed, which is 4.2 (down the line). Has pretty good hands. Has to make more contact to be a prospect. Has trouble with the low pitches."

■ No college pitcher was drafted in the first round of the June regular phase in 1969, but that was hardly a reflection on a lack of quality arms in the college game. It's just that the top talent was not in the 1969 draft. Had he been eligible, Texas freshman righthander **BURT HOOTON** almost certainly would have been a premium pick. Hooton shut out eventual champion Arizona State, 4-0, in the first round of the College World Series to push his mark on the season to 12-0, 0.88. In 102 innings, he struck out 136 while allowing just 47 hits. Hooton, an unsigned fifth-round pick of the Mets out of a Texas high school in 1968, would go on to dominate college hitters for two more years at Texas on his way to becoming the second overall selection in the secondary phase of the June 1971 draft.

## IN FOCUS: BERT BLYLEVEN

Bert Blyleven didn't play baseball until well into his childhood years. He quickly made up for lost time.

Born Rik Aalbert Blyleven in Zeist, Holland, in 1951, Blyleven moved with his family to Canada at age 2 and lived in Saskatoon, Saskatchewan until he was 6. The family then moved to Southern California, and it wasn't until his father took him to see Sandy Koufax pitch for the Dodgers in the early 1960s that he became interested in baseball.

He thrived at Santiago High in Garden Grove, where he developed his trademark curve, and the Dodgers were ready to draft him in the first round in 1969. But in one of his final outings as a senior, he got shelled. "There were 32 scouts in the stands at the start," Blyleven recalled. "Thirty-one of them must have left by the third inning." One who stayed was Twins scout Jesse Flores, and the Twins drafted him in the third round. He quickly signed for $15,000.

Blyleven soon filled out his 6-foot-3 frame, added velocity to his fastball and overwhelmed hitters in the low minors. At 19, he became the youngest pitcher in the majors when he was called up on June 2, 1970. He got the win that day and nine more that season, and was well on his way to a career total of 287 wins over 22 years that propelled him into the Hall of Fame.

big leagues than anyone at the time he retired.

The 6-foot-4, 200-pound Seinsoth, the 1968 College World Series MVP, signed for $25,000 with the Dodgers after hitting .368 with 14 homers and 52 RBIs as a senior for the Trojans. By almost all accounts, he was destined to become a top slugger in the big leagues.

But Seinsoth died in a car accident in September 1969, immediately after completing his first season in the Dodgers organization. He hit 10 homers in a half-season at high Class A Santa Barbara.

"I've always felt, had the accident not occurred, we might not have had Steve Garvey playing first base for the Dodgers all those years," USC coach Rod Dedeaux said. "Bill Seinsoth was an outstanding major league prospect. He had big league power, an outstanding throwing arm as a former pitcher, the agility as a former basketball player, and soft hands to be a good defensive first baseman. Bill had a great attitude, he had the intelligence. He had a can't-miss label. All he lacked was running speed."

Seinsoth was killed when his Volkswagen was lifted off the road by a gust of wind in the California desert. The car flipped over, and Seinsoth was tossed out.

"With seat belts, it might have been different," Dedeaux said. "He was one of my favorites."

### KUHN IN COMMAND

The June segment of the 1969 draft was the first conducted under the leadership of Bowie Kuhn. He took over as commissioner for the deposed William Eckert, who resigned under fire the previous December. Eckert's last official duty was to oversee the two January draft phases.

Between the January and June drafts that year, a total of 1,478 players were selected—a record that stood until 1989, when the draft was consolidated into a single June phase. Much of the increase was attributed to four new expansion clubs joining the major league fold in 1969.

The Kansas City Royals, who were stocking six new farm clubs in 1969, selected a draft record 98 players in June, including 90 in the regular phase. The Montreal Expos followed by selecting 78 (75 in the regular phase).

To their chagrin, the Royals were unable to sign Simmons, their first-round selection. He was a .517 hitter at Childersburg (Ala.) High who went on to play football at Auburn, where he teamed up with 1970 Heisman Trophy winner Pat Sullivan. Simmons would never play pro ball, becoming one of just six first-round picks never to do so.

The Royals, however, landed the equivalent of a first-rounder in the 75th round, when they lucked into Cowens, who played 13 years in the majors and was runner-up in AL MVP voting in 1977.

### Highest Unsigned Picks

**JUNE/REGULAR PHASE ONLY**

| Player, Pos., Team (Round) | College | Re-Drafted |
|---|---|---|
| Alan Bannister, ss, Angels (1) | Arizona State | Phillies '73 (Jan.-R/1) |
| Johnny Simmons, ss/rhp, Royals (1) | Auburn | Never |
| Peter Helt, lhp, Yankees (2) | Michigan | Never |
| Jim Kocoloski, ss, Expos (2) | Michigan | Never |
| Richard Soriano, of, White Sox (3) | Miami-Dade CC | Angels '70 (S/1) |
| John La Rose, lhp, Yankees (3) | * Cumberland (R.I.) HS | Red Sox '70 (S/1) |
| Bo Kleiber, ss, Mets (4) | Ohio | Mets '71 (29) |
| Bob Anderson, rhp, White Sox (5) | N.C. State | Never |
| John Doherty, of, Pirates (5) | None | Angels '70 (Jan.-S/1) |
| Michael Elwood, rhp, Indians (5) | Michigan | Angels '72 (5) |

**TOTAL UNSIGNED PICKS:** Top 5 Rounds (11), Top 10 Rounds (56)

**Returned to same school*

The first-round picks of the Expos (lefthander Balor Moore), Seattle Pilots (outfielder Gorman Thomas) and San Diego Padres (Randy Elliott) all reached the majors, with Thomas achieving the most success, slugging 268 home runs over a 13-year career.

Thomas achieved the distinction of being the only first-round pick (June, regular phase) in the history of the Pilots, when the ill-fated franchise moved from Seattle to Milwaukee and became the Brewers. More notably, Thomas twice led the American League in home runs. He also became the franchise's career homer leader, in three separate stints with the Seattle/Milwaukee organization.

Unlike expansion cousins Kansas City and San Diego, which shared a Double-A farm club at Elmira, N.Y., in 1969, neither Montreal nor Seattle had Double-A affiliations that year. That cost both teams in the draft as the Expos and Pilots were prevented from making third-round selections in both phases of the January and June drafts.

Al Cowens

From a technical standpoint, major league teams made picks in the third round on behalf of their Double-A affiliates. But with no Double-A clubs, the Expos and Pilots were forced to pass in the third round, a penalty that angered Seattle general manager Marvin Milkes.

"It was wrong and it was unfair," Milkes said. "Here they won't let us pick from Double-A because we don't have a Double-A team. But last year, they let San Diego and Montreal pick at the Class A level when neither had an A-team."

### One Team's Draft: Boston Red Sox

| Player, Pos. | Bonus | Player, Pos. | Bonus | Player, Pos. | Bonus |
|---|---|---|---|---|---|
| 1. Noel Jenke, of | $85,000 | **5. *Dwight Evans, of** | **$10,500** | 9. *Robert Kerr, rhp | $10,000 |
| **2. Rick Miller, of** | **$25,000** | 6. Michael Cummings, ss | $8,000 | 10. *William Hernandez, of | Did not sign |
| **3. Buddy Hunter, 2b/3b** | **$15,000** | **7. *Steve Barr, lhp** | **$8,000** | **Other* Dave Coleman (18), 3b** | **$10,000** |
| **4. *Jim Wright, rhp** | **$5,000** | 8. *Eric Brown, c | Did not sign | | |

*Major leaguers in bold. *High school selection.*

# 1969 Draft List

**Did not sign. Major leaguers in bold, with first and last years noted. Order of selection indicated in parentheses. For the first five rounds of the June Regular Phase and the first round of all other phases, the peak level of each player is noted.*

## ATLANTA BRAVES

### January—Regular Phase (11)

1. *Robert Beach, rhp, Cabrillo (Calif.) JC.—DNP
2. Michael Magness, rhp, Manatee (Fla.) JC.
3. *William Clark, rhp, San Francisco State University.
4. *Billy Rhoden, rhp, Palm Beach (Fla.) JC.

DRAFT DROP *Brother of Rick Rhoden, first-round draft pick, Dodgers (1971); major leaguer (1974-89)*

5. *Steven Hembree, ss, Navarro (Texas) JC.
6. *Curtis Dockery, rhp, Houston.
7. *David Allen, lhp, Westark (Ark.) CC.
8. *John Haarmeyer, rhp, Blinn (Texas) JC.
9. *Charles Lecroy, 3b, Gardner-Webb (N.C.) JC.

### January—Secondary Phase (15)

1. *Harry Saferight, c, Manatee (Fla.) JC.—(AAA)
2. Jeffrey Geach, 2b, American River (Calif.) JC.
3. ***Jack Pierce, 1b, San Jose (Calif.) CC.—(1973-75)**
4. *Peter Halfman, of, American River (Calif.) JC.
5. *William Fitzgerald, c, Tulane University.
6. *Bobby Lail, lhp, Gardner-Webb (N.C.) JC.
7. *Roger McSwain, of, Gardner-Webb (N.C.) JC.

### June—Regular Phase (12)

1. Gene Holbert, c, Palmyra HS, Campbelltown, Pa.—(AA)
2. **Leo Foster, ss, Holmes HS, Covington, Ky.—(1971-77)**
3. **Larvell Blanks, ss, San Felipe HS, Del Rio, Texas.—(1972-80)**
4. Russell Dillon, lhp, Novato (Calif.) HS.—(AAA)
5. Howard Duckworth, c, Boerne (Texas) HS.—(Rookie)
6. **Jimmy Freeman, lhp, Nathan Hale HS, Tulsa, Okla.—(1972-73)**
7. Mike Walseth, 1b, University of Minnesota.
8. *Michael Rusk, rhp, Gunn HS, Los Altos, Calif.
9. *James Gardner, rhp, Martinsville, Va.
10. *Steven Gardner, 3b, Weber State (Utah) College.
11. *Alan Rome, rhp, Warren Easton HS, New Orleans.
12. Gary Hagen, rhp, Alton (Ill.) HS.
13. Tom Heierle, c, Santiago HS, Garden Grove, Calif.
14. *Walt Sumner, of, Florida State University.

DRAFT DROP *Defensive back, National Football League (1969-74)*

15. *Leroy Thomas, c-1b, Sam Houston HS, San Antonio, Texas.
16. Charles Westerhouse, rhp, Duquoin (Ill.) HS.
17. *John Nickerson, c, Pittsburg (Texas) HS.
18. *Gil Untemeyer, 3b, Andrew Jackson HS, Jacksonville, Fla.
19. Marc Mengo, 1b-3b, Blackford HS, San Jose, Calif.
20. **Bucky Guth, ss, West Virginia University.—(1972)**
21. David Gourieux, rhp, Murray State University.
22. *George Horton, c-of, Upsala (Pa.) College.
23. *John Yeglinski, of, Sheepshead Bay HS, Brooklyn, N.Y.
24. *John Librandi, of, Ribault HS, Jacksonville, Fla.
25. *Ray Coley, c, Valparaiso University.
26. James Nageleisen, of, Covington, Ky.
27. *Ronald Middleton, rhp, Lake Land (Ill.) JC.
28. *Cecil Walley, lhp, Fruitdale HS, Vinegar Bend, Ala.
29. Stan Babieracki, lhp, St. John's University.
30. Richard Dahlgren, 1b, Indiana (Pa.) University.
31. Richard Atkinson, 2b-3b, Greenville (Ill.) College.
32. *James Toms, rhp, Lawton (Okla.) HS.
33. *Michael LaMacchia, of, Antonian HS, San Antonio, Texas.
34. *Al Ryan, ss, De la Salle HS, New Orleans, La.
35. *Robert Roemer, c-3b, Thornridge HS, South Holland, Ill.

### June—Secondary Phase (16)

1. *Gary Robson, rhp, Los Angeles CC.—(AAA)
2. **Mickey Rivers, of, Miami-Dade CC North.—(1970-84)**
3. *Bert Yeargan, ss, Brewton Parker (Ga.) JC.
4. *Sigmund Gancasz, c, Queensborough (N.Y.) CC.

## BALTIMORE ORIOLES

### January—Regular Phase (18)

1. *Rick Dierker, rhp, Los Angeles Pierce JC.—(AA)

DRAFT DROP *Brother of Larry Dierker, major leaguer (1964-77); major league manager (1997-2001)*

2. *Rudi Strickland, lhp, Indian River (Fla.) CC.
3. Robert Fields, rhp, Allegany (Md.) CC.
4. *Ken Caudle, c-3b, East Los Angeles JC.
5. *Victor Sutherland, lhp, Brevard (Fla.) CC.
6. *Carl Bennett, c, San Joaquin Delta (Calif.) JC.
7. *Michael Morris, rhp, CC of San Francisco.
8. *Roger Carmine, lhp, JC of San Mateo (Calif.).
9. James Edgar, rhp, Solano (Calif.) CC.
10. Joseph Walsh, rhp, University of Maine.

### January—Secondary Phase (18)

1. *Richard Wanless, rhp, Quincy, Mass.—(Low A)
2. *Phillip Corddry, lhp, University of Maryland.
3. John Austin, rhp, Greensboro, N.C.
4. *Peter Perpich, rhp, Lansing (Mich.) CC.
5. *Bruce Cannon, 3b, Oberlin, Ohio.
6. Terry Pollreisz, inf-of, University of Portland.

DRAFT DROP *Baseball coach, Portland (1987-97)*

7. *Stephen Boland, rhp, South Georgia JC.
8. *Michael Babler, rhp, Chabot (Calif.) JC.
9. *Michael Balogh, rhp, Niagara University.
10. *Glen Pickren, rhp, University of Florida.
11. *Stan Gatto, lhp, Selden, N.Y.

### June—Regular Phase (17)

1. **Don Hood, lhp, Southside HS, Florence, S.C.—(1973-83)**
2. James Stafford, 1b, San Pedro (Calif.) HS.—(High A)
3. Terry Clapp, ss, Southeast Guilford HS, Liberty, N.C.—(AAA)
4. James Winters, of-1b, St. Francis HS, Mountain View, Calif.—(High A)
5. Mark Weems, rhp, La Puente HS, Azusa, Calif.—(AAA)
6. **David Skaggs, c, North Torrance HS, Lawndale, Calif.—(1977-80)**
7. William O'Connor, 2b, Mount Miguel HS, Lemon Grove, Calif.
8. Greg Simendinger, rhp, Brandywine (Del.) JC.
9. Frank Coleman, rhp-3b, Clearwater (Fla.) HS.
10. Walter Harrison, c-of, King George (Va.) HS.
11. *Ralph Radtke, c, Waukegan East HS, Waukegan, Ill.
12. *Rich Fillings, lhp, Catonsville (Md.) HS.
13. *Gary Szakacs, 1b-of, Mira Loma HS, Sacramento, Calif.
14. Jeffrey Bonardel, rhp, Whippany Park HS, Whippany, N.J.
15. *Charles Clanton, of, Bradshaw HS, Florence, Ala.
16. *Kent Murdock, ss, Clearfield (Utah) HS.
17. Daniel Yaccarino, rhp, Port Richmond HS, Staten Island, N.Y.
18. *John Tatem, rhp, Pocomoke HS, Pocomoke City, Md.
19. Marvin Hines, of, North Lenoir HS, LaGrange, N.C.
20. ***Dick Ruthven, of-rhp, Irvington HS, Fremont, Calif.—(1973-86)**

DRAFT DROP *First-round draft pick (8th overall), Twins (1972); first overall draft pick, January 1973/secondary phase, Phillies; first player from 1973 draft to reach majors (April 17, 1973)*

21. Oscar Delbusto, c, Jackson HS, Miami.
22. Gregory Hansen, rhp, University of Utah.
23. Brian Swasey, 2b, Portland, Maine.
24. *John Saunders, c, Campolindo HS, Lafayette, Calif.
25. *Greg Parrish, lhp, Glendale (Ariz.) CC.
26. ***Mike Barlow, rhp, Syracuse University.—(1975-81)**
27. Ray Patterson, of, Dominguez HS, Compton, Calif.
28. *Walter Wolfe, lhp, Lawrenceville (Ill.) HS.
29. *Willie Jones, 1b, Bowen HS, Chicago.
30. *Jay Anderson, c, Chico (Calif.) HS.
31. *Fred Yilling, c, Mississippi State University.
32. *Michael Jones, lhp, Hazel Park (Mich.) HS.
33. Thomas Souza, ss, Alhambra HS, Martinez, Calif.
34. *Douglas Cash, ss, DeKalb (Ga.) JC.
35. *Michael Thompson, of, Phillips (Okla.) University.
36. *Robert Wilson, ss, Mountain Lakes (N.J.) HS.
37. *John Shaw, 2b, University of Mississippi.
38. Donald Finch, ss, Gloucester (N.J.) HS.
39. *Michael Timms, 3b, Airline HS, Bossier City, La.
40. ***Dave Winfield, rhp-of, Central HS, St. Paul, Minn.—(1973-95)**

DRAFT DROP *Elected to Baseball Hall of Fame, 2001; one of three athletes drafted in three professional sports; first-round draft pick (4th overall), Padres (1973); 17th-round draft pick, Minnesota Vikings/National Football League (1973); fifth-round draft pick, Atlanta Hawks/National Basketball Association (1973); sixth-round draft pick, Utah Stars/American Basketball Association (1973); first college selection, 1973 draft, to reach majors (June 19, 1973)*

41. *Kenneth Bauer, 3b, North Bergen (N.J.) HS.
42. *James Pikula, of-c, Fernandina Beach (Fla.) HS.
43. *Robert Boddie, rhp, Woodlawn HS, Shreveport, La.
44. *Richard Stevens, rhp, Berkeley HS, Oakland, Calif.
45. Michael Beitey, rhp-of, Vancouver (Wash.) HS.
46. *Donald Sever, 2b, St. Francis HS, Redwood City, Calif.
47. *Charles Stone, c, East Los Angeles JC.
48. *Michael Chitwood, rhp, South Mountain HS, Phoenix.
49. William Wooten, c, Logan HS, Stallings, W.Va.
50. (void) *Richard Brown, of, Sunnyvale, Calif.

### June—Secondary Phase (5)

1. **Wayne Garland, rhp, Gulf Coast (Fla.) CC.—(1973-81)**

DRAFT DROP *First overall draft pick, January 1969/secondary phase, Cardinals*

2. *Gary Bradshaw, rhp, Miami-Dade CC North.
3. *David Kropfelder, c, CC of Baltimore.
4. Steven Turigliatto, c, University of Southern California.
5. *Michael Pivec, of, CC of Baltimore.

## BOSTON RED SOX

### January—Regular Phase (14)

1. Bill Norton, 1b, Merrimack (Mass.) College.—(High A)
2. Richard Licini, 1b, University of Notre Dame.
3. ***Johnny Grubb, of, Manatee (Fla.) JC.—(1972-87)**
4. *William Hamilton, c, Broward (Fla.) CC.

### January—Secondary Phase (4)

1. Gary Myers, of, JC of San Mateo (Calif.).—(AA)
2. *Ken Rutkowski, c-rhp, SUNY-Buffalo.
3. John Zbercot, c, St. Clair Shores (Mich.) JC.
4. *Ronald Garlin, of, Miramar Isles (Fla.) HS.
5. *Wayne Milan, rhp, Broward (Fla.) CC.
6. *John Stephens, of, Gulf Coast (Fla.) CC.
7. Gerald Daughtry, c, Blinn (Texas) JC.

### June—Regular Phase (13)

1. Noel Jenke, of, University of Minnesota.—(AAA)

DRAFT DROP *Linebacker, National Football League (1971-74)*

2. **Rick Miller, of, Michigan State University.—(1971-85)**
3. **Buddy Hunter, 2b-3b, Pershing (Neb.) College.—(1971-75)**
4. **Jim Wright, rhp, Coopersville (Mich.) HS.—(1978-79)**
5. **Dwight Evans, 3b-of, Chatsworth HS, Northridge, Calif.—(1972-91)**
6. Michael Cummings, ss, Grambling University.
7. **Steve Barr, lhp, Carson HS, Torrance, Calif.—(1974-76)**
8. *Eric Brown, c, Morristown East HS, Morristown, Tenn.
9. Robert Kerr, rhp, Arvada HS, Denver.
10. *William Hernandez, of-c, George Washington HS, New York.
11. Clark Adkins, of, Ray HS, Corpus Christi, Texas.
12. *Lindsay Graham, rhp, Dulaney HS, Timonium, Md.
13. *Vaughan Sykes, rhp, Mebane, N.C.
14. *Greg McCollum, 1b, Meadowdale HS, Lynwood, Wash.
15. David Klastava, rhp-inf, Scotch Plains (N.J.) HS.
16. *James Torres, of, Arlington Heights HS, Fort Worth, Texas.
17. Donald Small, 1b-rhp, Southwestern HS, DeLeon Springs, Fla.
18. **Dave Coleman, 3b, Stebbins HS, Dayton, Ohio.—(1977)**
19. *Perry Renfro, lhp, Butler HS, Huntsville, Ala.
20. *Larry Smith, of, Tennessee Tech.
21. Thomas Kramer, c, Dieruff HS, Allentown, Pa.
22. Fernando Santiago, 1b, Monroe HS, Bronx, N.Y.
23. *Scott Sholbe, ss, Grand Junction (Colo.) HS.
24. *Donald Rhoden, ss, Franklin County HS, Winchester, Tenn.
25. James Bryant, rhp, Columbia State (Tenn.) CC.

### June—Secondary Phase (9)

1. Frank Ward, rhp, Southern Tech (Ga.) JC.—(High A)
2. Phillip Corddry, lhp, University of Maryland.
3. John Fletcher, c, Mississippi State University.
4. *David Allen, lhp, Westark (Ark.) CC.

## CALIFORNIA ANGELS

### January—Regular Phase (4)

1. *Randall Bayer, 1b, Mesa (Ariz.) CC.—(High A)
2. *Robert Singer, of, Los Angeles CC.
3. Terry Logan, 1b, Panola (Texas) JC.
4. *William Thomas, 3b, Menlo (Calif.) JC.
5. ***John Andrews, of-lhp, Pasadena (Calif.) CC.—(1973)**
6. *Gary McEwen, lhp, Torrance, Calif.
7. *Robert Wolf, rhp, Cerritos (Calif.) JC.
8. *Ray Leavitt, of, Cerritos (Calif.) JC.
9. *Thor Skogan, of, Sierra (Calif.) JC.
10. *Donald Pfister, c, Pasadena (Calif.) CC.
11. *Dwight Johnson, of, De Anza (Calif.) JC.
12. *Kent Calderan, ss, Chabot (Calif.) JC.
13. *Bruce Rosenthal, c-3b, Pasadena (Calif.) CC.
14. Terry Tulley, rhp, Chaffey (Calif.) JC.

### January—Secondary Phase (14)

1. *Sherwood Hahn, rhp-of, Virginia Tech.—DNP
2. *Franklin Riggins, of, University of Kansas.
3. Charles Elwis, lhp, Los Angeles CC.
4. *Ronnie Diggle, of, Cerritos (Calif.) JC.
5. *Pat Sonneman, 3b, Columbia Basin (Wash.) CC.
6. *David Edson, ss, Menlo (Calif.) JC.
7. *Lawrence Schutzius, of, Mesa (Ariz.) JC.
8. *Kenneth Pfau, rhp, Torrance, Calif.
9. *Dale Davis, lhp, San Diego CC.
10. *William Kendall, 3b, University of Minnesota.

### June—Regular Phase (5)

1. ***Alan Bannister, ss, Kennedy HS, Buena Park, Calif.—(1974-85)**

DRAFT DROP *Attended Arizona State; re-drafted by Phillies, January 1973/regular phase (1st round, 1st pick)*

2. David Chorley, of, Millikan HS, Long Beach, Calif.—(AAA)
3. Sam Ashford, ss, Western HS, Ensley, Ala.—(AAA)
4. **Rudy Meoli, ss, Royal Oak HS, Covina, Calif.—(1971-79)**
5. James Erautt, rhp, Helix HS, Lemon Grove, Calif.—(High A)
6. Rich Bailey, of, Millikan HS, Long Beach, Calif.
7. Michael Martorella, 1b, Monterey Peninsula (Calif.) JC.
8. *Murphy Eppinette, rhp, Chalmette HS, Arabi, La.
9. John Schroeder, ss, Magnolia HS, Anaheim, Calif.
10. *David Bishop, lhp, Mountain Lakes (N.J.) HS.
11. ***Jim Wohlford, 2b, Mount Whitney HS, Visalia, Calif.—(1972-86)**
12. Rick Young, lhp, Larkin HS, Streamwood, Ill.
13. Larry Hunt, of, Arcadia HS, Temple City, Calif.
14. Eric Shiffer, 3b, Lakewood (Calif.) HS.
15. David Marikos, c, El Segundo (Calif.) HS.
16. *Steve Dix, of, Normandy HS, St. Louis.
17. *David Babcock, c, Springfield HS, Battle Creek, Mich.
18. Thomas Benedict, lhp, Chaffey (Calif.) JC.
19. *Anthony Piraino, c, Lakewood (Calif.) HS.
20. *Thomas Lundgren, lhp, University of Missouri.
21. *Noel Sweeney, c, Katella HS, Anaheim, Calif.
22. Louis Pasierb, lhp, Bradley University.
23. Joseph Muto, ss, San Juan HS, Carmichael, Calif.
24. *Jeffrey Wingert, c-of, Chaffey HS, Ontario, Calif.

**25. Andy Hassler, lhp, Palo Verde HS, Phoenix.—(1971-85)**
26. *Bruce Patras, ss, Hogan HS, Vallejo, Calif.
27. *Bob Beyn, rhp, Taft (Calif.) HS.
28. Don Neugebauer, 1b, Cal State Fullerton.
DRAFT DROP *Father of Nick Neugebauer, major leaguer (2001-02)*
29. Anthony Spano, of, Chapman (Calif.) College.
30. *Gregory Sikora, of, Lincoln HS, San Francisco.
31. James Langrill, lhp, Saddleback (Calif.) CC.
32. *Gary Wann, rhp, Orange (Calif.) HS.
33. *Paul Husband, of, Wingfield HS, Jackson, Miss.
34. Jared Holve, 1b-lhp, Clovis (Calif.) HS.
35. Stephen Rosen, of, El Rancho HS, Pico Rivera, Calif.
36. *Richard Cox, lhp, Cal State Fullerton.
37. Phil Rose, c, University of Houston.
38. *Joseph Mecca, of-rhp, Dunmore (Pa.) HS.

### June—Secondary Phase (23)

1. *Robert Beach, rhp, Cabrillo (Calif.) JC.—DNP
2. Bruce Heinbechner, lhp, Los Angeles Pierce JC.
3. Charles Jones, lhp, Grambling University.

## CHICAGO CUBS

### January—Regular Phase (15)

1. *Edgar Pate, lhp, Gardena (Calif.) HS.—(AA)
2. *Donald Highstreet, rhp, Cerritos (Calif.) JC.
3. *Edward Spell, rhp, Louisburg (N.C.) JC.
4. Robert Woods, 2b, Atlantic (N.J.) CC.
5. *Fred Mims, of, Spoon River (Ill.) JC.
6. Dennis King, c, Claremont-Mudd (Calif.) College.

### January—Secondary Phase (11)

1. Joe Urbanovich, c, Villanova University.—(Low A)
2. *Gary Ross, lhp, Arizona Western JC.
3. *Dana Baltzer, ss, San Diego.
4. Nacho Bracomontes, lhp, Chula Vista, Calif.

### June—Regular Phase (16)

**1. Roger Metzger, ss, St. Edward's (Texas) University.—(1970-80)**
**2. Larry Gura, lhp, Arizona State University.—(1970-85)**
3. Gary James, lhp, Channel Islands HS, Oxnard, Calif.—(Low A)
4. James Davis, 1b, McKinley HS, Canton, Ohio.—(Low A)
5. Dan Corder, rhp, El Cajon (Calif.) HS.—(AAA)
6. *Kevin Kooyman, c, St. Mary's HS, Lodi, Calif.
7. James Brunette, 3b, Lewis (Ill.) University.
8. Robert White, of, Fort Cherry HS, Hickory, Pa.
9. *Ed McLarty, 1b, University of Mississippi.
**10. Jim Todd, rhp, Millersville (Pa.) University.—(1974-79)**
11. *Robert Crain, ss, Muir HS, Altadena, Calif.
**12. Bill North, of, Central Washington University.—(1971-81)**
13. *Curtis Zimmerman, 1b, De la Salle HS, New Orleans, La.
14. *Dan Hansen, ss, Western HS, Anaheim, Calif.
15. Steve Eckert, rhp, Moline (Ill.) HS.
16. *Jay Smith, rhp, Boca Ciega HS, Treasure Island, Fla.
17. Arthur Ganious, 1b, Southern University.
18. Thomas Hulderman, of, Monongah HS, Carolina, W.Va.
19. *Steve Kemnitzer, of, Klamath Falls (Ore.) HS.
20. Rufus Holton, of, St. John's River (Fla.) CC.
21. Gary Canepa, rhp, Lodi (Calif.) HS.
**22. *Dave Oliver, 2b, Franklin HS, Stockton, Calif.—(1977)**
23. Horace Porter, 2b, Pfeiffer (N.C.) College.
24. James Johnson, 3b, Cal State Chico.
25. Ralph Pipes, rhp, Fresno (Calif.) HS.
26. *Carlos Suarez, lhp, Miami Beach (Fla.) HS.
27. *Randy Benson, lhp, East Rowan HS, Granite Quarry, N.C.
DRAFT DROP *Son of Vern Benson, major leaguer (1943-53); major league manager (1977)*
28. *Andy Nelson, rhp, Everett (Wash.) HS.
29. Richard Bennett, rhp, East Meadow HS, Long Island, N.Y.
30. Michael Derr, ss, Mansfield (Pa.) University.
31. *Gary Ghidinelli, c, Santa Cruz (Calif.) HS.
32. *Carl Shumaker, of, Seminole (Fla.) CC.
**33. Pat Bourque, of, Holy Cross College.—(1971-74)**
34. William Mansfield, rhp, Jacksonville University.
35. Phil Reser, of, University of Idaho.
36. *Tom Rosa, ss, Coral Park HS, Miami.
37. *Dick Gold, 2b, Florida State University.
38. Arthur Oordt, 1b, Westmar (Iowa) College.

### June—Secondary Phase (24)

1. Gary Ross, lhp, Arizona Western JC.—(AA)
2. *Richard Wanless, rhp, Quincy, Mass.
3. John Meyer, lhp, Ocean County (N.J.) JC.

## CHICAGO WHITE SOX

### January—Regular Phase (6)

1. Richard Motsinger, ss-3b, Wingate (N.C.) JC.—(Short-season A)
2. *Russell Almquist, lhp, Los Angeles Pierce JC.
3. Robert Ebersole, c-1b, Hagerstown (Md.) JC.
4. *Larry Sisk, of, Gardner-Webb (N.C.) JC.
5. *Kirk Berger, rhp, York (Pa.) College.
6. *Gerald Kelly, 3b, Gulf Coast (Fla.) JC.

### January—Secondary Phase (20)

1. Ron Davini, c-of, Arizona State University.—(AAA)
**2. *Pat Osburn, lhp, Manatee (Fla.) JC.—(1974-75)**
3. *Gary Bradshaw, rhp, Miami-Dade CC North.
4. Louis Billmeier, rhp, University of Nebraska-Omaha.
5. *Ronald Kelam, of, St. Louis.
6. *Douglas Smith, inf, Buena Vista (Iowa) College.

### June—Regular Phase (3)

1. Ted Nicholson, 3b, Oak Park HS, Laurel, Miss.—(Low A)
2. Michael Atkinson, rhp, Carol City HS, Miami.—(AA)
3. *Richard Soriano, of, Hialeah HS, Miami.—DNP
DRAFT DROP *Attended Miami-Dade CC North; re-drafted by Angels, June 1970/secondary phase (1st round)*
4. Bill Clark, 3b, Southern Illinois University.—(AA)
5. *Bob Anderson, rhp, Joliet (Ill.) West HS.—DNP
DRAFT DROP *Attended North Carolina State; never re-drafted*
6. *Doug Wessel, rhp, Webster Groves (Mo.) HS.
**7. Bruce Kimm, c, Norway (Iowa) HS.—(1976-80)**
DRAFT DROP *Major league manager (2002)*
8. Anthony Rodriguez, ss, St. Philip HS, Chicago.
9. *Ruben Garcia, lhp, Brownfield (Texas) HS.
10. Wayne Francinques, ss, Tulane University.
11. Duane Shaffer, rhp, Garden Grove (Calif.) HS.
DRAFT DROP *Scouting director, White Sox (1991-2000)*
12. Steven Tiemeier, lhp, Indian Hills (Iowa) CC.
13. *Wayne Pitcock, of-1b, Arkansas State University.
14. Thomas Fuller, c, San Diego CC.
15. *William Berger, 2b, Coronado HS, Scottsdale, Ariz.
16. *Thomas Cain, rhp, Wartburg (Iowa) College.
17. *David Breshers, 2b, University of Iowa.
18. Jim MacDonnell, lhp, University of Wyoming.
**19. Glenn Redmon, 3b, University of Michigan.—(1974)**
20. Barry O'Sullivan, 1b, Southern Illinois University.
21. *Patrick Sullivan, 1b, Verona (N.J.) HS.
22. *Timm Moore, of, Ellsworth (Iowa) JC.
23. Charlie Cromer, rhp, Appalachian State University.
24. *Alan Lindsay, lhp, Cherryville (N.C.) HS.
25. Mark Marquess, 1b, Stanford University.
DRAFT DROP *Baseball coach, Stanford (1977-2015)*
26. Cleothus Jackson, lhp, Jackson State University.
27. Dan Rourke, ss, Upper Iowa University.
28. *Timothy Peden, c, Kermit (Texas) HS.
29. Gregg Boehning, lhp, Jefferson HS, Lafayette, Ind.
30. Lewis Braddy, ss, Stillman (Ala.) College.
31. Kenneth Samuels, rhp, Stillman (Ala.) Colllege.
32. Gary Isakson, of-rhp, Elmwood Park (Ill.) HS.
33. *James Pratt, of, Chatard HS, Indianapolis.
34. Allen Rajanen, c, Superior (Wis.) HS.
35. Fred Norton, of, Connellsville (Pa.) HS.
36. *Louis Lodigiani, of, South San Francisco HS.

### June—Secondary Phase (17)

1. Mike Baldwin, lhp, Sacramento (Calif.) CC.—(AAA)
2. *William Thomas, 3b, Menlo (Calif.) JC.
**3. Rich Hinton, lhp, University of Arizona.—(1971-79)**
4. Jim Mueller, of, Arkansas State University.

## CINCINNATI REDS

### January—Regular Phase (13)

1. John Jackson, rhp, Mount San Antonio (Calif.) JC.—(AAA)
2. *Buford Wood, rhp, Bacone (Okla.) JC.
3. *Richard Burch, of-3b, Blinn (Texas) JC.
4. *Orman Warren, rhp, East Los Angeles JC.
5. *Benton Ragland, 3b, Ranger (Texas) JC.
6. Tim White, c, University of Arizona.
7. Gene Sarazen, 1b-of, North Texas State University.
8. *Michael Campbell, rhp, Hill (Texas) JC.

### January—Secondary Phase (17)

**1. Ross Grimsley, lhp, Jackson State (Tenn.) CC.—(1971-82)**
DRAFT DROP *Son of Ross Grimsley, major leaguer (1951)*
2. Ted Tomasovich, 1b, Georgia Tech.
3. *Perry Allen, rhp, Murray State (Okla.) JC.
4. *Daniel Misko, lhp, Gulf Coast (Fla.) JC.
5. *Nicholas Furlong, rhp, University of Notre Dame.
6. *James Mertens, 1b, Fairmont State (W.Va.) College.

### June—Regular Phase (14)

**1. Don Gullett, lhp, McKell HS, Lynn, Ky.—(1970-78)**
DRAFT DROP *First 1969 high school draft pick to reach majors (April 10, 1970)*
2. Kent Burdick, of, Parker HS, Janesville, Wis.—(AA)
**3. Rawly Eastwick, rhp, Haddonfield (N.J.) HS.—(1974-81)**
4. Mike Ruddell, ss-rhp, Lakewood (Calif.) HS.—(AAA)
5. Clarence Cooper, lhp-1b, Frederick (Md.) HS.—(AA)
6. Barry Powell, ss, Pleasanton (Texas) HS.
7. Ronald Steele, of, Wichita Heights HS, Wichita, Kan.
8. Robert Gallagher, of, Pennsville (N.J.) HS.
9. *Emery Mitchell, c, Encina HS, Sacramento, Calif.
10. Phillip Babcock, rhp, Fort Ann HS, Comstock, N.Y.
11. Steven Miller, rhp, Marshall University.
**12. Nardi Contreras, rhp, Tampa (Fla.) Catholic HS.—(1980)**
13. Tim Bolton, lhp, Minor HS, Birmingham, Ala.
14. *Ray Guy, rhp, Thomson (Ga.) HS.
DRAFT DROP *Punter, National Football League (1973-86)*
15. Robert Dreher, c, Springdale (Pa.) HS.
**16. *Mike Cosgrove, lhp, Bourgade HS, Phoenix.—(1972-76)**
17. Richard Homan, rhp, Springfield (Mass.) Tech HS.
18. *Ronald Procter, c, Frederick (Md.) HS.
19. Kerry Hardiman, rhp, St. Bernard Parish (La.) CC.
**20. *Tommy Spencer, of, Gallie Academy HS, Gallipolis, Ohio.—(1978)**
21. *Larry O'Brien, 1b, Lakewood HS, Long Beach, Calif.
22. *Jackie Brown, ss-of, Starmount-Boonville HS, Jonesville, N.C.
23. *Roger Gregg, c, Southwestern (Calif.) JC.
24. *Robert McConnaugh, ss, West Liberty State (W.Va.) College.
25. *Michael Couzzi, inf-of, Trenton State (N.J.) College.
**26. *Mac Scarce, lhp, Manatee (Fla.) JC.—(1972-78)**
27. DeWayne Kerr, of-rhp, Corsicana (Texas) HS.
28. *Randall Fowler, c, Eunice (N.M.) HS.
**29. Ken Griffey, of, Donora (Pa.) HS.—(1973-91)**
DRAFT DROP *Father of Ken Griffey Jr., first overall draft pick, Mariners (1987); major leaguer (1989-2010)*
30. *Stephen Klinger, lhp, Bloomsburg (Pa.) University.
31. Ronald Swaim, lhp, Sparkman HS, Madison, Ala.
32. *Ronald Hayes, rhp, Monahans (Texas) HS.
33. Robert Young, ss, Rutgers University.
34. *Melvin Robinson, lhp, Tarboro (N.C.) HS.
35. *Michael Clancy, c, Bishop Kelley HS, Tulsa, Okla.
36. Rowe Miller, c, O.D. Wyatt HS, Fort Worth, Texas.

### June—Secondary Phase (14)

**1. *Johnny Grubb, of, Manatee (Fla.) JC.—(1972-87)**
2. Bill Ferguson, c, Texas Christian University.
3. Richard Burch, of, Blinn (Texas) JC.
4. Carl Bennett, c, San Joaquin Delta (Calif.) JC.
5. *James Mertens, 1b, Fairmont State (W.Va.) College.

## CLEVELAND INDIANS

### January—Regular Phase (16)

1. *Steve Wahl, 2b-ss, Los Angeles.—DNP
2. *Allen Hardin, ss, Polk (Fla.) CC.
3. *Rocky Jackson, 2b, Yakima Valley (Wash.) JC.
4. *David Chaffee, lhp-1b, Newman Prep, Melrose, Mass.
5. *Barry Parker, c, Southern Tech (Ga.) JC.
6. Donald Gray, inf, CC of Baltimore.
7. *William Hall, of-lhp, San Joaquin Delta (Calif.) JC.
8. *Christopher Scott, 2b, Cleveland.
9. *Steven Wood, lhp, Kansas State University.
10. *John Meyer, lhp, Ocean County (N.J.) JC.
11. *Peter Poldiak, rhp, Gulf Coast (Fla.) CC.
12. *Stanley Charzewski, c, College of Staten Island (N.Y.).

### January—Secondary Phase (6)

1. *Frank Ward, rhp, Southern Tech (Ga.) JC.—(High A)
2. *Bill Jenkins, ss, Orange Coast (Calif.) JC.
3. *Freddie Howard, of-1b, Paris (Texas) JC.
**4. *Rich Hinton, lhp, University of Arizona.—(1971-79)**
5. *Craig Schell, rhp, UC Santa Barbara.
6. *Alex Duncan, rhp, Cuyahoga (Ohio) CC.
7. *Ken Conlin, ss, Columbia Basin (Wash.) CC.
8. *Barry Herron, c, Kansas State University.
9. *William Hunt, ss, Louisiana State University.
10. *Larry Tipton, ss-2b, Blinn (Texas) JC.
11. *Johnny Rushing, lhp, John C. Calhoun (Ala.) CC.
12. *Mitchell Laird, rhp, Oklahoma Military Academy.

### June—Regular Phase (15)

1. Alvin McGrew, of, A.H. Parker HS, Fairfield, Ala.—(AAA)
2. Victor Ambrose, 2b, University of Albuquerque.—(AA)
**3. Alan Ashby, c, San Pedro (Calif.) HS.—(1973-89)**
4. Richard Derrickson, rhp, Lafayette HS, Lexington, Ky.—(AA)
5. *Michael Elwood, rhp, West Bloomfield HS, Orchard Lake, Mich.—(High A)
DRAFT DROP *Attended Michigan; re-drafted by Angels, 1972 (5th round)*
6. Michael Pompili, rhp, University of Toledo.
7. Jerry Bond, of, Southern Illinois University.
**8. Rob Belloir, ss, Mercer University.—(1975-78)**
9. *William Duffy, lhp, Kimball HS, Dallas.
10. Michael Young, 2b, Timmonsville (S.C.) HS.
11. Thomas Sullivan, rhp, Dover (Del.) HS.
12. *Robert Perkins, lhp, Lake Wales (Fla.) HS.
13. Rick Magnante, 3b, UC Santa Barbara.
14. Richard Ray, of, Prosser (Wash.) HS.
15. *Stanley Hamlin, rhp, Taft (Calif.) HS.
**16. Buddy Bell, 2b, Moeller HS, Cincinnati.—(1972-89)**
DRAFT DROP *Major league manager, (1996-2007) • Son of Gus Bell, major leaguer (1950-64) • Father of David Bell, major leaguer (1995-2006) • Father of Mike Bell, major leaguer (2000)*
17. Gary Gloede, of, Parker HS, Janesville, Wis.
18. Daniel Maluzhinsky, rhp, Lamphere HS, Madison Heights, Mich.
19. Carl Wiggins, of, Latta HS, Sellers, S.C.
20. *Robert Verbeck, c, Ward HS, Kansas City, Kan.
21. Roger Williams, 3b-ss, Raytown (Mo.) HS.
22. Gary Ruby, lhp, Arizona State University.
23. Mike Easom, 3b, Florida State University.

24. Nicholas Hockett, lhp, Northeast HS, St. Petersburg, Fla.
25. Ernest McMahan, rhp, Garrett HS, Charleston Heights, S.C.
26. John Wheeler, rhp, Tampa.
27. Jerry Haggard, 2b, Texas Tech.
28. *Dennis Smith, 1b, Bowling Green HS, Weston, Ohio.
**29. *Ken Kravec, lhp, Midpark HS, Middleburg Heights, Ohio.—(1975-82)**
30. Vincent Pope, of, Glenville HS, Cleveland.
31. Mike Bradley, c, Norte Vista HS, Riverside, Calif.
32. Bill Tsoukalas, lhp, Seattle University.
33. Denny Thomas, lhp, Perkins HS, Sandusky, Ohio.
34. Harry Fry, rhp, Harding HS, Marion, Ohio.
35. *Rex Carrow, 2b, East Lansing (Mich.) HS.
36. Tommie Bozich, ss, Northeast HS, St. Petersburg, Fla.
37. James Koch, c, St. Mary's (Texas) University.
38. Ray Johnson, of-1b, Mount San Antonio (Calif.) JC.
39. *James Smith, of, Montebello HS, Monterey Park, Calif.
40. William Dew, of, University of North Carolina-Wilmington.
41. Perry Yearwood, rhp, Randolph-Macon (Va.) College.
42. James Sanders, 3b, Ledford HS, Thomasville, N.C.
43. *Donald Wallace, 1b-of, San Bernardino Valley (Calif.) JC.

### June—Secondary Phase (1)

**1. Rich Hand, rhp, University of Puget Sound.—(1970-73)**

DRAFT DROP *First player from 1969 draft to reach majors (April 9, 1970)*

2. *Robert Eldridge, rhp, Southern Illinois University.
3. Stephen Boland, rhp, South Georgia JC.
4. *Bill Dobbs, lhp, Oklahoma State University.
5. *William Camp, rhp, Oklahoma State University.

## DETROIT TIGERS

### January—Regular Phase (20)

1. *Ralph Edwards, c-of, Miami-Dade CC North.—DNP
2. Michael Belcik, c, University of Toledo.
3. *Michael Chaney, of, Chabot (Calif.) JC.
4. *William Knight, c, Port Huron (Mich.) JC.
5. Jack Nelson, rhp, Fullerton (Calif.) JC.
6. Joe McIlvaine, rhp, St. Charles Seminary, Narberth, Pa.

DRAFT DROP *Scouting director, Mets (1981-85) • General manager, Padres (1990-93); general manager, Mets (1993-97)*

### January—Secondary Phase (16)

**1. *John Young, 1b, Fullerton (Calif.) JC.—(1971)**

DRAFT DROP *Founder, Reviving Baseball in Innercities (RBI) program*

2. Bruce Finkbeiner, of, University of Colorado.
3. *Peter Brown, rhp, Chabot (Calif.) JC.
4. Nils Lambert, lhp, College of Staten Island (N.Y.).
5. *Edwin Mossman, 3b, Central Missouri State University.

### June—Regular Phase (19)

1. Lenny Baxley, 1b, Enterprise HS, Redding, Calif.—(High A)
2. Harry Kendrick, c, Michigan State University.—(AAA)
**3. Bill Gilbreth, lhp, Abilene Christian (Texas) University.—(1971-74)**
4. James Newhook, of, St. Helena HS, Whitestone, N.Y.—(High A)
5. Owen Hether, ss, Norwood (Mich.) College.—(High A)
**6. Lerrin LaGrow, rhp, Arizona State University.—(1970-80)**
7. *Daniel Bielski, rhp, Michigan State University.
8. Jim Smith, rhp, University of Connecticut.
9. Mark Giegler, ss, Milford (Mich.) HS.
10. Robert Service, ss, Central HS, Ilion, N.Y.
11. *Wayne Miller, lhp, Newark (Calif.) HS.
12. Michael Fremuth, rhp, Princeton University.
13. *Kris Silverthorn, of, Thomas Jefferson HS, Dallas.
14. *Brad Van Pelt, rhp, Owosso (Mich.) HS.

DRAFT DROP *Linebacker, National Football League (1973-86)*

15. *Eugene LaFave, rhp, St. Francis DeSales HS, Detroit.
16. Dave DuBois, lhp, Elsie HS, Ovid, Mich.
17. *Bruce Vida, rhp, Ecorse (Mich.) HS.
18. Richard Schroellucke, ss, Algonac (Mich.) HS.
19. Richard Krumm, rhp, Eastern Michigan University.
20. *Daniel Gibson, rhp, Hazelwood (Mo.) HS.
21. *Gary Gentle, c, Belleville (Mich.) HS.
22. *Frank Crachiolo, c, St. Ambrose HS, Detroit.
**23. *Doug Konieczny, rhp, St. Ladislaus HS, Detroit.—(1973-77)**
24. Mike Jacobs, of, Ohio Northern University.
25. *Timothy Dean, inf-rhp, Mansfield (Ohio) HS.
26. *John Scotto, of-rhp, Holy Cross HS, Queens Village, N.Y.
27. *Daniel Ruth, 1b, University of Colorado.
28. *John Womack, c, Ecorse (Mich.) HS.
29. Stephen Knowlton, lhp, Genesee (Mich.) HS.
30. *Anthony Aquila, rhp, Woodbridge HS, Avenel, N.J.
31. Dan McGraw, 2b, Cass Tech HS, Detroit.
32. *Robert Dillow, c, Loyola HS, Bayside, N.Y.
33. *Robert Moug, 3b, Redford HS, Detroit.
34. *Edward Plomer, c, Redford HS, Detroit.

### June—Secondary Phase (21)

1. *Bill Bright, of, Brevard (Fla.) CC.—(AAA)
2. *George Pugh, lhp, Mesa (Ariz.) CC.
3. *Stephen Steitz, 3b-of, Springfield (Mass.) College.

## HOUSTON ASTROS

### January—Regular Phase (1)

**1. Derrel Thomas, ss, Dorsey HS, Los Angeles.—(1971-85)**
**2. *Craig Caskey, lhp, Yakima Valley (Wash.) JC.—(1973)**
3. *Charles Benjamin, c, St. Petersburg (Fla.) JC.

### January—Secondary Phase (3)

1. Bob McRoberts, of, Grossmont (Calif.) JC.—(Short-season A)
2. Gary Howard, of, Yuba (Calif.) CC.
3. Herman Jordan, of, Middle Georgia JC.
4. *Bill Bright, inf-of, Brevard (Fla.) CC.

### June—Regular Phase (2)

**1. J.R. Richard, rhp, Lincoln HS, Ruston, La.—(1971-80)**
**2. Stan Papi, ss, Bullard HS, Fresno, Calif.—(1974-81)**
3. Harlan Keller, c, Taft (Calif.) HS.—(Short-season A)
4. Larry Elenes, rhp, Western HS, Buena Park, Calif.—(AAA)
5. Robert Fernley, ss, Torrance (Calif.) HS.—(Short-season A)
6. *Willard Ester, rhp, Carver HS, Houston.
7. Bruce Thomas, rhp, Queen Anne HS, Centerville, Md.
8. John Dolinsek, of, Arizona State University.
9. Anthony Sturtevant, of, McGill Institute HS, Mobile, Ala.
10. Leroy Martin, rhp, Alisal HS, Salinas, Calif.
11. *Thomas White, lhp, Amherst (Mass.) HS.
12. *Charles Bates, ss-3b, Dominguez HS, Compton, Calif.

DRAFT DROP *First-round draft pick (19th overall), Tigers (1973)*

13. Mark Keller, lhp, Woodrow Wilson HS, Long Beach, Calif.
**14. Mike Easler, 3b, Benedictine HS, Cleveland.—(1973-87)**
15. Jerome Hutchinson, rhp, Raines HS, Jacksonville, Fla.
16. *Vernon Davis, rhp, Tucson (Ariz.) HS.
17. *Jack Rhine, c, Riviera Beach (Fla.) HS.
18. Henry Moore, lhp, Centennial HS, Los Angeles.
19. *Mike Nelson, 1b, Eisenhower HS, Yakima, Wash.
20. (void) *Albert Hughes, ss, Beckley, W.Va.
21. *Cecil Norris, of, South Park HS, Beaumont, Texas.
22. *James Hooks, ss, Jones (Okla.) HS.
23. Kyle Shook, rhp, Beaumont (Texas) HS.
24. Charles Taylor, rhp, Eastern Kentucky University.
25. Thom Lehman, lhp, University of Miami.
26. Alan Schmidt, 2b, University of Dayton.
27. Adolph Carter, ss, Courter Tech, Cincinnati.
28. *Arnold Alaniz, inf, Kingsville (Texas) HS.
29. *Gary Bullion, rhp, Weslaco (Texas) HS.

### June—Secondary Phase (22)

1. Matthew Rosiek, rhp, Indian River (Fla.) CC.—(AAA)

## KANSAS CITY ROYALS

### January—Regular Phase (22)

1. Ronald Opatkiewicz, ss, Mount San Antonio (Calif.) JC.—(Low A)
2. *Dennis Nicholson, rhp, JC of the Sequoias (Calif.).
3. *Steve Lee, lhp, Los Angeles Valley JC.
4. *Edward Hopkins, 1b, Kansas State University.
5. *Larry Prieto, 2b, Fresno (Calif.) CC.
6. Steve Moore, of, Santa Barbara (Calif.) CC.
7. *Reginald Carney, 1b, Fork Union (Va.) Military Academy.
8. *John Jackson, of, Pasadena (Calif.) CC.

### January—Secondary Phase (24)

1. *Darrell Downey, c, Ventura (Calif.) JC.—DNP
2. *Charles Kurkjian, 3b, Fresno (Calif.) CC.
3. Lloyd Lightfoot, ss, North Carolina A&T State University.
4. Van Winters, rhp, Fresno (Calif.) CC.
5. *Dennis Gallagher, ss, Yuba (Calif.) CC.
6. Dave Thornton, of, American River (Calif.) JC.
7. Paul Walton, rhp, Amesbury, Mass.
9. *Steve Griffith, rhp, Golden West (Calif.) JC.
10. James Kleckley, rhp, Columbia (S.C.) HS.
11. Tom Pratt, lhp, Hancock (Calif.) JC.
12. *Richard Trapp, ss, University of Florida.

DRAFT DROP *Wide receiver, National Football League (1968-69)*

### June—Regular Phase (23)

1. *Johnny Simmons, ss-rhp, Childersburg (Ala.) HS.—DNP

DRAFT DROP *Attended Auburn; never re-drafted*

2. Dale Phillips, ss, Fresno (Calif.) HS.—(AA)
3. A.C. Mosley, 1b, Mobile (Ala.) County Training HS.—(Rookie)
**4. Al Autry, rhp, Grace Davis HS, Modesto, Calif.—(1976)**
**5. Keith Marshall, of, Loara HS, Anaheim, Calif.—(1973)**
6. Edward Siracusa, of, Los Gatos (Calif.) HS.
7. *Jerry Manto, c, Poly HS, Long Beach, Calif.
8. Tom Lugo, ss, Sweetwater Union HS, National City, Calif.
9. *Stephen Bryant, lhp, Andalusia (Ala.) HS.
10. James Smith, c, Centennial HS, Compton, Calif.
11. Thomas Luck, lhp, Spotsylvania HS, Bumpass, Va.
**12. *Eric Raich, rhp, Dominguez HS, South Gate, Calif.—(1975-76)**

DRAFT DROP *First overall draft pick, January 1972/ regular phase, Indians*

13. James Buzzard, ss, Glynn Academy, Brunswick, Ga.
14. Michael McGrath, lhp, Pershing (Neb.) College.
15. *David Sasser, 1b, Groves HS, Garden City, Ga.
**16. Jim York, rhp, UCLA.—(1970-76)**
17. *Murry Parish, rhp, Carroll HS, Corpus Christi, Texas.
18. *David Bewley, rhp, Sarasota (Fla.) HS.
19. James Pappas, c, John F. Kennedy HS, Bethpage, N.Y.
20. Ron Clark, rhp, Santa Fe HS, Norwalk, Calif.
21. Toby Heath, 1b, Santa Ana (Calif.) JC.
22. Louis Cruz, rhp, Southern State (Ohio) CC.
23. *Robert Maneely, rhp, St. Joseph HS, Deptford, N.J.
24. John Stankey, of, Westmont (Calif.) College.
25. Hugh Waln, of, Fauquier HS, Warrenton, Va.
26. *John Jones, lhp, Russell (Ky.) HS.
27. Art Demery, rhp, Wasco Union HS, Wasco, Calif.
28. Randy Hammon, rhp, Serra HS, Gardena, Calif.
29. Greg Kinder, rhp, La Habra (Calif.) HS.
30. Victor Price, of, Langley HS, McLean, Va.
31. Michael Prieto, of, JC of San Mateo (Calif.).
32. Gary Sanserino, ss, UCLA.
33. *Kenneth Comer, ss, Minnetonka HS, Excelsior, Minn.
34. Nathaniel Riggin, ss, Highland Springs (Va.) HS.
35. *Lou Berthelson, c, Simi (Calif.) HS.
36. *Dan Knight, c, Darlington Prep, Lyndale, Ga.
37. Edward McFarland, 2b, Bowdoin (Maine) College.
38. *George Chavez, rhp, Delano (Calif.) HS.
39. *George Wheeler, rhp, Sidney Lanier HS, Montgomery, Ala.
40. Timothy Pickering, 3b, Camarillo (Calif.) HS.
41. Lloyd Gladden, rhp, Cal State Los Angeles.
42. Mike Witt, of, Fresno (Calif.) CC.
43. *Wesley Jermyn, ss, Baptist HS, Los Angeles.
44. Guy Hansen, rhp, UCLA.
45. *John Varga, ss-2b, Queen Anne HS, Seattle.
46. *Mike Fitzsimmons, of, Monterey Union HS, Del Ray Oaks, Calif.
**47. Frank Ortenzio, of, San Joaquin Memorial HS, Fresno, Calif.—(1973)**
48. *Joseph Borchard, of, Moorpark (Calif.) JC.

DRAFT DROP *Father of Joe Borchard, first-round draft pick, White Sox (2000); major leaguer (2002-07)*

49. Charles Burt, rhp, Southwest Missouri State University.
50. Larry Newton, ss, Roxboro HS, Hurdle Mills, N.C.
51. Gerald Metivier, 3b, Cal State Los Angeles.
52. Steven Lizak, 2b, St. John's University.
53. Dean Owens, 3b, West Torrance (Calif.) HS.
54. *Gene Kerr, rhp, Montebello (Calif.) HS.
55. Mike Ballantine, rhp, Anaheim (Calif.) HS.
56. Michael Patrick, rhp, Rancho Alamitos HS, Garden Grove, Calif.
57. *John Helfrick, 3b, Hoover HS, San Diego.
58. *Glen Berberet, 1b, Long Beach (Calif.) CC.
59. Frank Wright, 1b, Cal State Los Angeles.
60. *Ray Brown, rhp, Long Beach (Calif.) CC.
61. *Charles Dickinson, ss, Hattiesburg (Miss.) HS.
62. *Robert McKeel, rhp, Harding (Ark.) University.
63. *Robert Spohr, rhp, Hilltop HS, Chula Vista, Calif.
64. *David Hazelip, rhp, Trezevant HS, Memphis, Tenn.
65. *James Lasher, rhp, John F. Kennedy HS, Utica, N.Y.
66. *Robert Lopresti, rhp, Birmingham HS, Encino, Calif.
67. Kim Giffoni, rhp, Santa Monica HS, Malibu, Calif.
68. *Rick Richardson, 1b, Churchland HS, Chesapeake, Va.
69. *Robert Williams, rhp, Pius X HS, Downey, Calif.
70. *David Brunell, rhp, Bell (Calif.) HS.
71. *Larry Klein, lhp, Santa Monica (Calif.) JC.
72. *Steve Bisceglia, rhp, Bullard HS, Fresno, Calif.
73. *Donald Shaw, 3b, Pacific Palisades (Calif.) HS.
74. *Richard Auckland, 1b, West Chester (Pa.) University.
**75. Al Cowens, ss, Centennial HS, Los Angeles.—(1974-86)**
76. *John Behrens, 2b, San Joaquin Memorial HS, Fresno, Calif.
77. *Robert Proechel, c, Franklin Academy, Malone, N.Y.
78. *Bill Akers, c, Burlington (Colo.) HS.
79. *Gary Mack, 2b, Western HS, Los Alamitos, Calif.
80. Donald Weir, rhp, University of Nevada-Reno.
81. Mark Stoner, ss, Burroughs HS, Ridgecrest, Calif.
82. William Olin, 2b, Pasadena (Calif.) CC.
83. *Gary Rausch, lhp, Girard HS, Lake City, Pa.
84. *Richard Haderer, rhp, Mills HS, Burlingame, Calif.
85. Steven Nielsen, lhp, Cal Poly Pomona.
86. Brian Smith, rhp, North Torrance (Calif.) HS.
87. *Mike Seberger, rhp, Bellflower (Calif.) HS.
88. *Gregory Hopkins, of, Darlington Prep HS, Lyndale, Ga.
89. *Roy Petersen, of-1b, Somerville (Mass.) HS.
90. *James Beal, 2b, Westchester HS, Los Angeles.

### June—Secondary Phase (15)

1. Michael Nichols, lhp, Biola (Calif.) University.—(Low A)
2. Stanley Grout, rhp, Perry, Iowa.
**3. Doug Bird, rhp, Mount San Antonio (Calif.) JC.—(1973-83)**
4. Thomas Joyce, ss-2b, San Francisco State University.
5. Jeff Stout, 3b-ss, Mount San Antonio (Calif.) JC.
6. *Gary Addeo, rhp, Cerritos (Calif.) JC.

7. *Stephen Griffith, rhp, Golden West (Calif.) JC.
8. *Larry Diel, ss, Cerritos (Calif.) JC.

## LOS ANGELES DODGERS

**January—Regular Phase (5)**

1. Michael Kimbrell, 2b, Birmingham, Ala.–(High A)
**2. Lee Lacy, 3b, Laney (Calif.) JC.—(1972-87)**
3. *Carl Salyers, rhp, Southwestern Christian (Texas) JC.
**4. Bob O'Brien, lhp, Fresno (Calif.) CC.—(1971)**
5. *Dean Voegerl, lhp, Trinidad State (Colo.) JC.
6. *Dave Maas, 2b, Fullerton (Calif.) JC.

**January—Secondary Phase (9)**

1. Pat Harrison, ss, University of Southern California.—(AAA)
DRAFT DROP *Baseball coach, Pepperdine (1995-96); baseball coach, Mississippi (1997-2000)*
2. *William Camp, rhp, Oklahoma State University.
3. *George Pugh, lhp, Mesa (Ariz.) CC.
4. *Bill Ferguson, 1b-c, Texas Christian University.
5. *Alan Putz, 1b, Springfield (Mass.) College.

**June—Regular Phase (8)**

**1. Terry McDermott, c, St. Agnes HS, West Hempstead, N.Y.—(1972)**
2. Elvin Ervin, lhp, Putnam City HS, Bethany, Okla.—(High A)
3. Albert Dawson, rhp, Lyndhurst (N.J.) HS.–(AAA)
4. Bob Long, of, Texas A&M University.—(AA)
DRAFT DROP *17th-round draft pick, Chicago Bears/ National Football League (1972)*
5. Mark Meschuk, rhp, St. Bernard HS, El Segundo, Calif.—(High A)
**6. Stan Wall, lhp, Raytown (Mo.) South HS.—(1975-77)**
7. Jim Cardasis, of, New York University.
8. Kenneth Bruno, ss, Cliffside Park HS, Palisades Park, N.J.
9. Larry President, lhp, Temple (Texas) HS.
10. Ron Mitchell, of, Agua Fria HS, Avondale, Ariz.
11. John Hughes, 1b, Parkwood HS, Joplin, Mo.
12. Stanley Russell, rhp-1b, Villa Park HS, Anaheim, Calif.
13. *Ronald Dolan, 2b, Seton Hall University.
14. Arthur Pauls, rhp, Lewis (Ill.) University.
**15. *Roy Staiger, ss, Bacone (Okla.) JC.—(1975-79)**
16. *Jimmy Page, rhp, Hardesty (Okla.) HS.
17. *Edgar Bellamy, ss-2b, Fort Cobb (Okla.) HS.
18. *Mark Pastrovich, lhp, Mascoutah (Ill.) HS.
19. *Anthony Blakley, ss, Sullivan West HS, Kingsport, Tenn.
20. *Donald Sweetland, c, Saddleback (Calif.) CC.
21. Joseph Szewezyk, 1b-of, New York University.
**22. Royle Stillman, of, North Torrance HS, Torrance, Calif.—(1975-77)**
23. Manuel Washington, of, Mississippi State University.
24. David Allen, lhp, California Western College.
25. *William Owen, 3b, Millington (Tenn.) HS.
**26. *Jim Fuller, of, San Diego CC.—(1973-77)**
27. *Johnny Hatcher, rhp, Andrews (Texas) HS.
28. *Harry Chapman, rhp, Sarasota (Fla.) HS.
29. *George Horman, c-3b, Crawford HS, San Diego.
30. *Nick Devirgilis, of, Sarasota (Fla.) HS.
31. *Jeff Hogan, ss, Florida State University.
32. *Raymond Ippolito, ss, New York University.
33. *Robert Cox, rhp, Southeast HS, Wichita, Kan.
34. Vince D'Amico, 1b, University of Albuquerque.
35. Jerry Arnold, lhp, Woodward (Okla.) HS.
36. *William Wyles, lhp, New Mexico Military Institute.
37. *Gary Granville, of, El Camino (Calif.) JC.
38. *Johnny Rodgers, inf-of, Tech HS, Omaha, Neb.
DRAFT DROP *Heisman Trophy winner (1972); first-round draft pick, San Diego Chargers/National Football League (1973); wide receiver, NFL (1977-78)*
39. *Gary Erskine, of-lhp, Anderson (Ind.) HS.
DRAFT DROP *Son of Carl Erskine, major leaguer (1948-59)*
40. Dennis Haren, of, Bishop Montgomery HS, Torrance, Calif.
41. *Rod Boone, c, Crawford HS, San Diego.
DRAFT DROP *Son of Ray Boone, major leaguer (1948-60) • Brother of Bob Boone, sixth-round draft pick, Phillies (1969); major leaguer (1972-90); major league manager (1995-2003)*
42. Robert Sicilia, of, Rogers HS, Spokane, Wash.
43. Robert Payne, of, UC Riverside.

**June—Secondary Phase (8)**

1. Bill Seinsoth, 1b, University of Southern California.—(High A)
**2. Bobby Randall, ss, Kansas State University.—(1976-80)**
DRAFT DROP *Baseball coach, Iowa State (1984-94); baseball coach, Kansas (1995-2001)*
3. Steven Wilmet, lhp, St. Norbert (Wis.) College.
4. Randall Bayer, of-1b, Mesa (Ariz.) CC.

## MINNESOTA TWINS

**January—Regular Phase (8)**

1. Gary Willburn, c, Gardena (Calif.) HS.—(Low A)
2. Jimmy Smith, 1b, Van Nuys (Calif.) HS.
3. *Chuck Erickson, of, Northridge (Calif.) HS.
4. Mark Scoville, ss, Riverside (Calif.) CC.
5. *John Gaylord, lhp, Chaffey (Calif.) JC.
6. Kelly Godfrey, of, Mount San Antonio (Calif.) JC.
7. Ralph Zuniga, rhp, Chaffey (Calif.) JC.
8. *Barry Woodruff, lhp, JC of San Mateo (Calif.)
9. Ray Strable, rhp, Fresno State University.
10. Ron Shotts, of-3b, Stanford University.
11. *Leroy McDonald, ss, Grand Canyon College.

**January—Secondary Phase (10)**

1. John Hurley, rhp, University of Michigan.—(AA)
2. Tommy Nichols, ss, University of Mississippi.
3. *Richard Perry, rhp, Independence (Mo.) HS.
4. *Gary Addeo, rhp, Paramount (Calif.) HS.
5. Bob Wissler, ss, Cal Poly Pomona.
6. Ronald Pritchett, rhp, Mount San Antonio (Calif.) JC.
7. Roger Mayer, c, University of Colorado.
8. *Mike Douglas, 1b, Cerritos (Calif.) JC.
9. *Jim Mueller, of, Arkansas State University.
10. *Richard Gouin, of, California Western College.
11. *Robert Shearer, ss-2b, Indian River (Fla.) CC.

**June—Regular Phase (7)**

**1. Paul Ray Powell, of, Arizona State University.—(1971-75)**
2. Ron McDonald, 3b, South Hills HS, Covina, Calif.—(AA)
**3. Bert Blyleven, rhp, Santiago HS, Garden Grove, Calif.—(1970-92)**
4. Ronald Adams, lhp, Thomas Jefferson HS, Carter Lake, Iowa.—(Short-season A)
5. Byron Emick, of, Grand Ledge (Mich.) HS.—(Rookie)
6. Richard Osentowski, of, Kearney State (Neb.) College.
7. Greg Jaycox, rhp-1b, Channel Islands HS, Oxnard, Calif.
**8. *Rick Burleson, ss, Warren HS, South Gate, Calif.—(1974-87)**
9. John Braun, rhp, Marion (Wis.) HS.
10. *Gary Atwell, of, Kennedy HS, Buena Park, Calif.
11. Thomas Schmidt, rhp, Central HS, La Crosse, Wis.
12. *Gregory Bero, c, Serra HS, Gardena, Calif.
13. Bill Barnes, lhp, South Hills HS, Covina, Calif.
14. Mike Dion, c, St. Paul HS, Santa Fe Springs, Calif.
15. Reynold Lyczak, 3b-ss, Burlington HS, Burlington Township, N.J.
16. Dan Vossler, rhp, UC Riverside.
17. James Koering, rhp, University of Iowa.
18. *Rand Rasmussen, ss, Millikan HS, Long Beach, Calif.
19. Ted Remington, rhp, Parsons (Iowa) College.
20. *Gregory Zail, rhp, St. Paul HS, Santa Fe Springs, Calif.
21. Kenneth Knight, of, Victoria HS, Telferner, Texas.
22. Joseph Bochy, c, Jefferson HS, Falls Church, Va.
23. William Giffin, rhp, Eastern Michigan University.
24. Greg Gustafson, c, Bellingham (Wash.) HS.
25. *Jerry Johnson, lhp, Oregon State University.
26. *Brent Estee, lhp, Pershing (Neb.) College.
27. Thomas Thompson, 3b, Fairfax (Va.) HS.
28. *Michael Evans, lhp, Woodbridge (Va.) HS.
29. Robert Love, 3b, Hixon HS, Chattanooga, Tenn.
30. (void) *Daniel Boettcher, rhp, Radnor HS, Rosemont, Pa.
31. Arthur Gordon, rhp, Washington HS, Cairo, Ga.
32. Richard Judkins, rhp, Goffstown (N.H.) HS.
**33. Jim Hughes, rhp, St. Bernard HS, Los Angeles.—(1974-77)**
34. James Michael, rhp, Loras (Iowa) College.
35. David Schmidt, ss, Fresno State University.
36. Wayne Parks, rhp, St. Cloud State (Minn.) University.
37. Charles Wheeler, ss, Buena Vista (Ga.) HS.
38. (void) *Wilson Raines, rhp, Johnson HS, Laurinburg, N.C.
39. Steve Hardin, rhp, Pisgah HS, Canton, N.C.
40. David Nieman, of, Augustana (S.D.) College.
41. Jeff Snowdon, lhp, Thomas Jefferson HS, Denver.
42. Keith Sonnichen, of-rhp, Carthage (Wis.) College.
43. *Craig Barnes, lhp, South Hills HS, Covina, Calif.
44. Neal Emerson, lhp, Coon Rapids (Minn.) HS.
45. Lee Palas, lhp, Elvader HS, St. Olaf, Iowa.
46. *Michael Dlugach, c, Overton HS, Memphis, Tenn.
47. *James Skogstad, rhp, Metropolitan State (Colo.) College.
48. *Jim Otto, ss, North Hennepin (Minn.) CC.

**June—Secondary Phase (3)**

1. Ralph Dick, of, Arizona State University.–(High A)
2. Leroy McDonald, ss, Grand Canyon College.
3. *Peter Halfman, of, American River (Calif.) JC.
4. Patrick Bekeza, of, University of Southern Colorado.
5. *George Swanson, of-1b, Miami-Dade CC North.
**6. *Ron Cash, 3b-ss, Manatee (Fla.) JC.—(1973-74)**
DRAFT DROP *Uncle of Kevin Cash, major leaguer (2002-10); major league manager (2015)*

## MONTREAL EXPOS

**January—Regular Phase (21)**

1. *Larry Diel, ss, Cerritos (Calif.) JC.—DNP
2. *Robert Flynn, of-2b, Miami-Dade CC North.
3. No selection.
4. *William Greener, of, Hill (Texas) JC.
5. Keith LeFevre, rhp, Marrero, La.
6. *Mike Henderson, rhp, Mount San Antonio (Calif.) JC.
7. Steve Wagner, 1b-of, Mount San Antonio (Calif.) JC.
8. *Norman Boles, c, Springfield, Mo.
9. *Charles Ramshaw, ss, University of Southern California.

**January—Secondary Phase (23)**

1. *Gene Salmon, 1b, University of Texas.–(Rookie)
2. *Alan Hansen, rhp, Grossmont (Calif.) JC.
3. No selection.
4. *Roger Sizoo, c, Citrus (Calif.) JC.
5. *Jeff Stout, 3b, Mount San Antonio (Calif.) JC.
6. Steve Angelo, rhp-3b, Rio Hondo (Calif.) JC.

**June—Regular Phase (22)**

**1. Balor Moore, lhp, Deer Park (Texas) HS.—(1970-80)**
2. *Jim Kocoloski, ss, Shady Side Academy, Monroeville, Pa.—DNP
DRAFT DROP *Attended Michigan; never re-drafted*
3. No selection.
4. John Reid, ss, Colgate University.—(AA)
5. Elisco Pompa, of, Mission (Texas) HS.—(AAA)
6. *Harry Conlan, of, West Haven (Conn.) HS.
7. *Todd Brentlinger, rhp, Los Altos (Calif.) HS.
8. *Bill Sanford, c, Los Altos (Calif.) HS.
9. *Timothy Coffin, rhp, Palos Verdes HS, Rolling Hills, Calif.
10. *Robert Mollenhauer, 2b, St. Mary HS, Elizabeth, N.J.
11. Lincoln Clark, ss, Northwestern HS, Detroit.
12. *Richard Brown, of-1b, DeAnza (Calif.) JC.
13. Stephen Keller, rhp, Loyola Marymount University.
14. Robert Schleider, rhp, A&M Consolidated HS, College Station, Texas.
15. Glenn Vickery, rhp, Ben C. Rain HS, Mobile, Ala.
16. James Sparkman, of-rhp, University of Houston.
17. *Brad Graff, ss, Appleton (Wis.) HS.
18. John Reen, c, Seminole (Fla.) CC.
19. Randolph Brunner, 1b-rhp, Westminster HS, Atlanta.
20. *Jack Garrett, rhp, Eastern Hills HS, Fort Worth, Texas.
21. *David Fressa, rhp, Clawson (Mich.) HS.
22. Gerard Castaldo, c-ss, Bayonne (N.J.) HS.
23. Brian Abraham, lhp, Biloxi (Miss.) HS.
24. *Thomas Mims, of, Drew (Miss.) HS.
25. Donald Klinger, 2b, Rider College.
26. Pat Russell, rhp, Nazareth HS, Brooklyn, N.Y.
27. *Joseph Flannery, of-rhp, South Plainfield (N.J.) HS.
28. *James Ellison, lhp, Peterson HS, Santa Clara, Calif.
29. James Rispoli, of, University of New Haven.
30. Mike Popevec, c, San Jose State University.
31. *James Hatfield, rhp, Hydro (Okla.) HS.
32. *Mike Kedulich, c, Workman HS, La Puente, Calif.
33. *Albert Nocciolo, c, William S. Hart HS, Saugus, Calif.
34. *Steve Gulloti, ss-3b, Sierra HS, Whittier, Calif.
35. Boris Kopylow, rhp, Sierra HS, Whittier, Calif.
36. Jerry McClain, rhp, Santa Clara University.
37. *Paul Meaut, lhp, Notre Dame HS, Biloxi, Miss.
38. *Daniel Cook, 3b, Southwest Missouri State University.
**39. Terry Humphrey, c-1b, Los Angeles CC.—(1971-79)**
40. Ed Fisher, rhp, Valdosta State (Ga.) College.
41. *Henry Holmes, 1b, Forest Hill HS, West Palm Beach, Fla.
42. *Martin Henderson, 1b, Nassau (N.Y.) CC.
43. Robert Williams, rhp, St. Louis CC-Meramec.
44. *Gerard Mosley, 2b, Kirkwood (Mo.) HS.
45. *Bill Borelli, of-1b, Santa Clara University.
46. Terry Tuck, of, San Antonio, Texas.
47. Jack Robinson, of, Cincinnati.
48. *Lee Pelekoudas, rhp, Homestead HS, Sunnyvale, Calif.
49. Dave LaPointe, ss, University of Vermont.
50. *Steve Fanning, 3b, Southampton (N.Y.) HS.
51. *Lawrence Bock, ss, Riviera Beach (Fla.) HS.
52. *Lloyd DeFoor, c, Calhoun (Ga.) HS.
53. *Arnold Braden, lhp, Orange Park (Fla.) HS.
54. *Steve Whitaker, rhp, Brevard (Fla.) JC.
55. Gary Wilhelm, 2b-of, Cherry Hill HS, Inkster, Mich.
56. *Timothy Williams, of, Courter Tech HS, Cincinnati.
57. *Larry Calufetti, c, Harrisburg (Ill.) HS.
58. *Dennis Holmberg, inf, Baker HS, Columbus, Ga.
59. *Benny Howard, rhp, Ben C. Rains HS, Mobile, Ala.
60. Sam Kershaw, 1b, Levittown, Pa.
61. *Frank Serrano, rhp-of, Clifton HS, Bronx, N.Y.
62. *Jeffrey Peoples, of-rhp, Montgomery Bell Academy, Nashville, Tenn.
63. *Steve Loiselle, c, Channel Islands HS, Oxnard, Calif.
64. *Eugene McElwain, lhp, Manhattan Prep, Bronx, N.Y.
65. *Arthur Simon, ss, Hialeah (Fla.) HS.
66. *Patrick Moore, c, Mira Costa HS, Manhattan Beach, Calif.
67. *Francis Slayer, 3b, Ferndale (Wash.) HS.
68. *Thomas Peavey, rhp, Ingraham HS, Seattle.
69. *John Spelaliere, ss, Erasmus Hall HS, Brooklyn, N.Y.
70. *Frank Zawatski, c, Bound Brook (N.J.) HS.
**71. Tony Scott, of, Withrow HS, Cincinnati.—(1973-84)**
72. John Gentile, c, CC of Baltimore.
73. *Linwood Forte, ss, Munford HS, Detroit.
74. Rick Down, of, Southgate (Mich.) HS.
75. *Butch Stinson, lhp, Cohn HS, Nashville, Tenn.
76. *Lavery Hiegel, c, St. Francis HS, Palo Alto, Calif.

**June—Secondary Phase (10)**

1. *Mike Weathers, 2b, Cerritos (Calif.) JC.—(AAA)
DRAFT DROP *Baseball coach, Long Beach State (2002-10)*
2. *Ronnie Diggle, c-of, Cerritos (Calif.) JC.
3. No selection.
4. James LaRusso, 2b, Monmouth College.

## NEW YORK METS

**January—Regular Phase (3)**

1. *Bruce Heinbechner, lhp, Pacoima (Calif.) HS.—(AAA)

2. Ken Esposito, lhp, Nassau (N.Y.) CC.
3. *Doug Brittelle, rhp, Rutgers University.
DRAFT DROP *Draft pick, Kentucky Colonels/American Basketball Association (1969)*
4. *Dave Carey, rhp, Hastings, Minn.

**January—Secondary Phase (13)**

1. *Billy Cotton, c, Arizona State University.—(AAA)
2. Jerry Perkins, lhp, Indiana University.
3. *Greg Archer, 1b, JC of the Sequoias (Calif.).
4. *Joe Kilby, of, Big Bend (Wash.) CC.
5. *Vince Bigone, of-3b, Santa Clara University.
6. *Mike Sigman, rhp, Santa Clara University.
7. Bob McLeod, rhp, Georgetown (Ky.) College

**June—Regular Phase (4)**

**1. Randy Sterling, rhp, Key West (Fla.) HS.—(1974)**
**2. Joe Nolan, c, Southwest HS, St. Louis.—(1972-85)**
3. Garnett Davis, c-of, East HS, Columbus, Ohio.—(High A)
4. *Bo Kleiber, ss, Vandalia-Butler HS, Vandalia, Ohio.—DNP
DRAFT DROP *Attended Ohio; re-drafted by Mets, 1971 (29th round)*
5. Michael Kowalski, rhp, Stratford (Conn.) HS.—(Short-season A)
6. Cecil Reynolds, rhp, New Hanover HS, Wilmington, N.C.
7. Joseph Murray, rhp, St. Bernard HS, New London, Conn.
8. *Kenneth Ossola, 3b, St. Louis University.
9. *Vernon Temple, c, Beaumont (Texas) HS.
10. *Clifford Ker, rhp, Granada Hills (Calif.) HS.
11. John Tregilgus, ss, Lawton (Okla.) HS.
12. *Ludwig Benedetti, ss, Sheepshead Bay HS, Brooklyn, N.Y.
13. Gary Betts, 1b, Easton (Pa.) HS.
14. *Paul Caffrey, of-rhp, Seton Hall Prep, South Orange, N.J.
15. *Thomas Ball, rhp, Orange-Stark HS, Orange, Texas.
16. *Kevin Tennant, c, Molloy HS, Queens, N.Y.
17. *Elroy Othold, rhp, St. Paul HS, Shiner, Texas.
18. Gerald Davis, ss, Parker HS, Janesville, Wis.
19. Victor Worry, lhp, Pfeiffer (N.C.) College.
20. *Scotty Kurtz, lhp, Northwest Missouri State University.
**21. Lute Barnes, 2b, Oregon State University.—(1972-73)**
22. John Main, rhp, Lyons (N.Y.) HS.
23. *Douglas Farrell, rhp-of, Mooney HS, Rochester, N.Y.
24. *Bruce Swanson, rhp, Rio Americano HS, Sacramento, Calif.
**25. *Vic Harris, ss, Los Angeles Valley JC.—(1972-80)**
26. *Richard Kelly, c, Brighton (Colo.) HS.
**27. Buzz Capra, rhp, Illinois State University.—(1971-77)**
28. Von Opolous, lhp, West HS, Salt Lake City.
29. George Leckrone, rhp-ss, Dover (Pa.) HS.
30. *Robert Steinberg, 1b-of, University of Scranton (Pa.).
**31. George Theodore, 1b-of, University of Utah.—(1973-74)**
32. *Harold Hess, of, Seaford HS, Wantagh, N.Y.
33. Greg Allen, c, Pembroke State (N.C.) University.
34. *Robert Murphy, 1b-c, University of Tulsa.
35. Edmond Robinson, lhp, Webber HS, Eastover, S.C.
36. *Joseph Panele, lhp, LaSalle HS, Niagara Falls, N.Y.
37. Thomas Kilgore, 3b, University of Utah.
38. *Randall Shipp, rhp-c, South Sevier HS, Joseph, Utah.
39. *Dave Nelson, rhp, Viewmont HS, Bountiful, Utah.
40. *Larry Burke, ss, Marietta (Ohio) HS.
41. *John Monick, lhp-of, Wyoming Prep School, Kingston, Pa.
42. Ed LaBorde, c, Bethany (Pa.) College.
43. *Bruce Clouser, of, St. Joseph's University.
44. *James Newman, lhp, Big Springs (Texas) HS.
45. *Donald McLeod, rhp, Niagara-Wheatfield HS, Niagara Falls, N.Y.
46. *Ronald Drews, rhp, Old Dominion University.
DRAFT DROP *Son of Karl Drews, major leaguer (1946-54) • Father of Matt Drews, first-round draft pick, Yankees (1993)*
47. *Steve Jasinski, rhp, Chicopee Comprehensive HS, Chicopee, Mass.
48. *Craig Menzi, of, Adelphi (N.Y.) University.
49. *Jerry Goode, lhp, Marist HS, Bayonne, N.J.
50. *Robert Cary, ss, Greenwood (S.C.) HS.
51. *Charles Prorok, rhp, Newman HS, Cheektowaga, N.Y.
52. *Jack MacKay, ss, Valley Stream HS, Franklin Square, N.Y.

**June—Secondary Phase (12)**

1. Billy Cotton, c, Arizona State University.—(AAA)
2. Mark Kitchell, of, Larchmont, N.Y.
**3. Larry Fritz, 1b, Arizona State University.—(1975)**
4. Richard Breese, rhp, University of Albuquerque.
5. *Michael Balogh, rhp, Niagara County (N.Y.) CC.
6. Nicholas Furlong, rhp, University of Notre Dame.
**7. *John Andrews, lhp, Pasadena (Calif.) CC.—(1973)**

## NEW YORK YANKEES

**January—Regular Phase (12)**

1. *Gregory Marshall, of, Laney (Calif.) JC.—(Low A)
2. *Gary Marks, lhp, Golden West (Calif.) JC.
3. Reinaldo Ramos, of, Chicago.
4. John Schlesinger, ss-3b, JC of the Redwoods (Calif.).
5. *Michael Warwick, c, Contra Costa (Calif.) JC.
6. *Toni Breckel, rhp, Centralia (Wash.) JC.

**January—Secondary Phase (2)**

1. Larry Pyle, of, University of Miami.—(AA)
2. *Dennis Wallin, c, American River (Calif.) JC.
3. *Rickie Clements, lhp, Grayson County (Texas) JC.
4. Donald Schroeder, rhp, Grays Harbor (Wash.) JC.
**5. *Jim Barr, rhp, University of Southern California.—(1971-83)**
6. *Gary Robson, rhp, Los Angeles CC.
7. *James LaRusso, 3b-2b, Monmouth College.
8. *Ken Wastradowski, lhp, Centralia (Wash.) JC.

**June—Regular Phase (11)**

**1. Charlie Spikes, 3b-of, Central Memorial HS, Bogalusa, La.—(1972-80)**
2. *Peter Helt, lhp, Morristown (N.J.) HS.—DNP
DRAFT DROP *Attended Michigan; never re-drafted*
**3. *John LaRose, lhp, Cumberland (R.I.) HS.—(1978)**
DRAFT DROP *Returned to Cumberland (R.I.) HS; re-drafted by Red Sox, June 1970/secondary phase (1st round)*
4. Fred Frazier, 2b, Hoover HS, Fresno, Calif.–(AAA)
5. Clemont Sanders, of, Marshall HS, Chicago.—(AAA)
6. Marion Prince, ss-rhp, Walker HS, Atlanta.
7. Jorge Maduro, c, University of Miami.
8. *Todd Sprecher, c, South Eugene (Ore.) HS.
9. David Kilgore, 1b, Beloit Memorial HS, Beloit, Wis.
**10. Ken Crosby, rhp, Brigham Young University.—(1975-76)**
11. Paul Jenious, rhp, Booker T. Washington HS, Memphis, Tenn.
12. *Eric Long, rhp, Stagg HS, Stockton, Calif.
13. Thomas O'Connor, of, South Hills Catholic HS, Pittsburgh.
14. John Colunio, ss, Ashland (Ohio) College.
**15. *John Tamargo, c, Tampa Catholic HS, Tampa.—(1976-80)**
16. *Robert Finley, rhp, Darlington (Wis.) HS.
17. Francis Combs, c, North Carolina State University.
18. Leroy Gardner, of, Bacone (Okla.) JC.
19. Alan Tetrault, of-1b, Technical HS, Springfield, Mass.
20. *Keith Harding, of, Lewiston (Idaho) HS.
21. *John McLean, rhp, Overton HS, Nashville, Tenn.
22. *Steve Greenough, lhp, South Eugene (Ore.) HS.
23. Ricky Kriz, of, University of Northern Iowa.
24. Pat Brown, of, University of Texas.
**25. *Larry Hardy, rhp, University of Texas.—(1974-76)**
26. *Henry Garcia, ss, Grant HS, Sacramento, Calif.
27. *James Gorton, rhp, Chaminade HS, Rosedale, N.Y.
28. Terry Vargason, lhp, Borah HS, Boise, Idaho.
29. Paul Swanson, rhp, Milford (Conn.) HS.
30. *Duane Donahoo, inf-of, Christian Brothers HS, Memphis, Tenn.
31. Donald Palmer, 1b, David Douglas HS, Portland, Ore.
32. Paul Baretta, ss, Southern Connecticut State University.
33. *Michael Venable, rhp-of, Blanchet HS, Seattle.
34. Greg Buys, 1b-c, Kennett (Mo.) HS.
35. Oliver Lyons, of, Pilgrim HS, Warwick, R.I.
36. *Christopher Boyle, ss, East HS, Wichita, Kan.
37. Danny Dalonzo, rhp, Lincoln HS, Stockton, Calif.
38. *Steve Connolly, 1b, Central Catholic HS, Norwalk, Conn.
39. *Brian Cogan, lhp, Saratoga Springs, N.Y.
40. *Tom Farrias, rhp, New Bedford (Mass.) HS.
41. *James Linnin, c, Port Chester (N.Y.) HS.
42. *Jack McDonald, rhp, Pullman (Wash.) HS.
43. *Gregory Branum, 3b-of, LaCrosse HS, Hooper, Wash.
44. *Joel DeTray, rhp, Clarkston (Wash.) HS.
45. Christopher Barker, rhp, McNary HS, Salem, Ore.
46. *Dean Mick, ss-3b, Foster HS, Seattle.
47. *Kenneth O'Brien, rhp, Villanova University.
48. Kenneth Bennett, 1b, West HS, Wichita, Kan.
49. Arthur Cooper, 1b, Rodeo (Calif.) HS.
50. *Prentice McGray, of, Edison HS, Stockton, Calif.

**June—Secondary Phase (13)**

1. *Joe Kilby, of, Big Bend (Wash.) CC.—DNP
2. Ronald Collier, rhp, Mansfield (Pa.) University.
3. *Daniel Velander, rhp, Portland, Ore.
4. *Wayne Adkison, 2b, Yakima Valley (Wash.) JC.
5. Beau Robinson, of-1b, Bacone (Okla.) JC.

## OAKLAND ATHLETICS

**January—Regular Phase (10)**

1. Marshall Crossan, rhp, San Jose (Calif.) CC.—(AA)
2. *Daniel Pritchett, of, El Camino (Calif.) JC.
3. *Reggie Tredaway, 3b, Sul Ross State (Texas) University.
4. *Doug McCoy, rhp, Miami-Dade CC South.

**January—Secondary Phase (12)**

1. Darryl Thomas, lhp, Long Beach (Calif.) CC.—(Short-season A)
2. *Steve Wilmet, lhp, St. Norbert (Wis.) College.
3. *Pat Bekeza, of-inf, University of Southern Colorado.
4. *Jerre Algeo, 2b, Poteau (Mo.) JC.
5. *Gary Houston, lhp, San Jose (Calif.) CC.

**June—Regular Phase (9)**

**1. Don Stanhouse, rhp-ss, DuQuoin (Ill.) HS.—(1972-82)**
**2. Tommy Sandt, ss, Pacifica HS, Garden Grove, Calif.—(1975-76)**
**3. Steve Lawson, lhp, San Lorenzo HS, San Leandro, Calif.—(1972)**
4. Bob Williams, c, Washington State University.—(AA)
5. Joseph Williamson, 1b, Bartlett Yancey HS, Yanceyville, N.C.—(Short-season A)
**6. *Jim Sundberg, c, Galesburg (Ill.) HS.—(1974-89)**
7. *Dave Wiggins, of, McLane HS, North Fresno, Calif.
**8. Glenn Abbott, rhp, North Little Rock (Ark.) HS.—(1973-84)**
9. *Michael Hanson, rhp, Walla Walla (Wash.) HS.
10. *Ivan Dempsey, c, Science Hill HS, Johnson City, Tenn.
11. *Michael Logelin, 2b, Loyola Marymount University.
12. *John Adeimy, ss, Forest Hill HS, West Palm Beach, Fla.
**13. *John Stearns, c, Thomas Jefferson HS, Denver.—(1974-84)**
DRAFT DROP *First-round draft pick (2nd overall), Phillies (1973); 17th-round draft pick, Buffalo Bills/National Football League (1973)*
14. Samuel LeClair, of, Bridegewater-Raynham Regional HS, Bridgewater, Mass.
15. Billy Swope, rhp, Forest Park HS, Beaumont, Texas.
16. *John Lenahan, rhp, Salesianum HS, Wilmington, Del.
17. Dick Meier, of, Central HS, Davenport, Iowa.
18. James Capehart, of, Bertie HS, Windsor, N.C.
**19. Charlie Chant, ss, Narbonne HS, Harbor City, Calif.—(1975-76)**
20. *Chris Vella, lhp, Notre Dame HS, Van Nuys, Calif.
21. Wilson Rainer, rhp, Johnson HS, Laurinburg, N.C.
22. *Andrew Bielanskie, c, Savanna HS, Anaheim, Calif.
23. David Cavazza, rhp, Milford (Mass.) HS.
24. *Michael McKinney, rhp, St. James HS, Chester, Pa.
25. Joseph Lasorsa, rhp, Boston University.
26. Michael Foyer, c, Sierra (Calif.) JC.
27. *Clare Leifer, of, University of Washington.
28. Ronnie Wynne, ss, Williamston (N.C.) HS.
29. Dennis Myers, 1b, American River (Calif.) JC.
30. *Brian Applegate, ss, El Cajon (Calif.) HS.
31. Alan Castro, c, Cabrillo (Calif.) JC.
32. *Terry Mayer, 1b-3b, La Sierra HS, Carmichael, Calif.
33. William Linehan, lhp, Peabody (Mass.) HS.
34. Jack Knutson, rhp, Hudson Bay HS, Vancouver, Wash.

**June—Secondary Phase (7)**

1. William Fitzgerald, c, Tulane University.—(AA)
2. *Dennis Wallin, c, American River (Calif.) JC.
3. Russell Almquist, lhp, Los Angeles Pierce JC.
4. *Larry Prieto, 2b, Fresno (Calif.) CC.

## PHILADELPHIA PHILLIES

**January—Regular Phase (7)**

**1. *Terry Enyart, lhp, Chipola (Fla.) JC.—(1974)**
2. Dennis Weiner, 1b, Philadelphia.
3. *John Clear, 1b-of, Wilmington, Calif.
4. Richard Kelly, 2b, St. Joseph's University.

**January—Secondary Phase (7)**

1. Douglas Barker, rhp, Sacramento (Calif.) CC.—(High A)
2. Frank Hagen, inf, Napa Valley (Calif.) JC.
3. *Michael Wertz, ss, Dallas Baptist University.
4. *Lawrence Tarver, c, Bakersfield (Calif.) JC.
5. *Robert Coultas, rhp, Diablo Valley (Calif.) JC.
6. *Kevin Bryant, inf, Valencia (Fla.) CC.

**June—Regular Phase (6)**

**1. Mike Anderson, 1b, Timmonsville (S.C.) HS.—(1971-79)**
DRAFT DROP *Brother of Kent Anderson, major leaguer (1989-90)*
**2. Mike Rogodzinski, of, Southern Illinois University.—(1973-75)**
3. Bobby Wiltshire, rhp, Coahoma County HS, Clarksdale, Miss.—(High A)
**4. Mike Wallace, lhp, James Madison HS, Vienna, Va.—(1973-77)**
5. Robert Malcolm, rhp, Tennessee Tech.—(High A)
**6. Bob Boone, 3b, Stanford University.—(1972-90)**
DRAFT DROP *Major league manager (1995-2003) • Son of Ray Boone, major leaguer (1948-60) • Brother of Rod Boone, 41st-round draft pick, Dodgers (1969) • Father of Bret Boone, major leaguer (1992-2005) • Father of Aaron Boone, major leaguer (1997-2006)*
7. Craig Scramuzzo, rhp, St. Philip HS, Chicago.
8. *Allan Matson, of, St. John's University.
9. Dennis Iverson, rhp, Winona State (Minn.) University.
10. Dan Benoit, c, Western Michigan University.
11. *Roger Pattillo, ss, Ouachita Baptist (Ark.) University.
12. Joseph Emer, 2b, St. Norbert (Wis.) College.
13. Richard Giallella, of, Rider College.
14. *Patrick Rusco, 1b, San Luis Obispo (Calif.) HS.
15. *Richard Magner, c, Xavier HS, Middletown, Conn.
**16. Ron Diorio, rhp, University of New Haven.—(1973-74)**
17. Willie Sledge, of, Basic HS, Henderson, Nev.
18. Ken Ward, rhp-of, Seton Hall University.
19. Lloyd Hutchinson, of-inf, University of Colorado.

DRAFT DROP *Father of Chad Hutchinson, first-round draft pick, Braves (1995); major leaguer (2001)*
20. Michael Whalin, lhp, Hughes HS, Cincinnati.
21. Thomas Coplin, lhp, Laton (Calif.) HS.
22. Charles Paglierani, of, American International University.
23. Phillip Morgan, 3b, Ohio State University.
24. *David Merchant, ss, Harding HS, Marion, Ohio.
25. Chuck Kniffin, lhp, Nassau (N.Y.) CC.
26. Donald Kinzel, 2b, San Jose State University.
27. Fred Ruben, 3b, Delaware State College.
28. (void) *Ellsworth Jones, lhp, New York University.
29. *Daryl Arenstein, 1b, Rolling Hills (Calif.) HS.
30. Larry Coffin, ss, Oakton HS, Vienna, Va.
31. James Dietz, c, Moravian (Pa.) College.

**June—Secondary Phase (6)**

1. Allen Joyce, ss, Scranton, Pa.—(Rookie)
2. *Cal Meier, ss, University of Southern California.
3. ***Rudy Arroyo, lhp, Foothill (Calif.) JC.—(1971)**
4. *Ellsworth Jones, lhp, New York University.

## PITTSBURGH PIRATES

**January—Regular Phase (9)**

1. Arthur Meza, c, Stockton (Calif.) HS.—(Low A)
2. Mack McKay, ss, New Orleans.
3. *William Woodruff, rhp, Georgia State University.
4. *William Shepherd, rhp, Spokane (Wash.) CC.
5. *Bruce Irvin, c-rhp, St. Petersburg (Fla.) JC.
6. Thomas Fitzgerald, ss, Rahway (N.J.) HS.
7. Paul Giroux, inf, Ithaca (N.Y.) College.
8. *Billy Updegraff, c, Hagerstown (Md.) JC.
9. *George Swanson, of, Miami-Dade CC North.
10. *Allen Joyce, ss, North Scranton, Pa.
11. *Sigmund Gancasz, c, Queensborough (N.Y.) CC.

**January—Secondary Phase (5)**

1. **John Morlan, of-rhp, Ohio University.—(1973-74)**
2. *Matthew Rosiek, rhp, Indian River (Fla.) CC.
3. *Wayne Harlan, inf, Yakima Valley (Wash.) JC.
4. *Gerald Bryant, lhp, Lynchburg (Va.) College.
5. *John Mills, rhp, Wenatchee Valley (Wash.) CC.

**June—Regular Phase (10)**

1. Bob May, rhp, Merritt Island (Fla.) HS.—(Short-season A)
2. Jim Johnson, of, Brandywine HS, Niles, Mich.—(Low A)
3. **Fred Cambria, rhp, St. Leo (Fla.) College.—(1970)**
4. **Jim McKee, rhp, Otterbein (Ohio) College.—(1972-73)**
5. ***John Doherty, of, Reading (Mass.) HS.—(1974-75)**

DRAFT DROP *No school; re-drafted by Angels, January 1970/secondary phase (1st round)*

6. *Ed Ratleff, rhp, East HS, Columbus, Ohio.

DRAFT DROP *First-round draft pick, Houston Rockets/ National Basketball Association (1973); forward, NBA (1973-78)*

7. Michael Semp, of, Macomb (Mich.) CC.
8. Donzell McDonald, of, Poly HS, Long Beach, Calif.

DRAFT DROP *Father of Donzell McDonald, major leaguer (2001-02) • Father of Darnell McDonald, first-round draft pick, Orioles (1997), major leaguer (2004-13)*

9. John Griggs, ss, Central HS, Phenix City, Ala.
10. *William Robinson, of-rhp, North Carolina A&T State University.
11. *James Horton, lhp, Ypsilanti (Mich.) HS.
12. *Dennis Odom, ss, Kearny HS, San Diego.
13. Gary Meyer, rhp, Merritt Island (Fla.) HS.
14. *Ronald Van Saders, c, Woodridge HS, Moonachie, N.J.
15. *Walter Biercevicz, lhp-of, Norwalk State Tech (Conn.) JC.
16. David Lee, rhp, Wettermark HS, Boyce, La.
17. (void) *Donald Boettger, rhp-1b, Radnor-Delaware County HS, Radnor, Pa.
18. *Frank Shimerola, lhp, Bishop Ryan HS, Omaha, Neb.
19. *Jack Baker, 1b-lhp, Maury HS, Norfolk, Va.
20. *Joe Munoz, of-ss, Miller HS, Corpus Christi, Texas.
21. Peter Hughes, ss, Southbridge (Mass.) HS.
22. Daniel Quinn, rhp, Buffalo State College.
23. *Robert Polinsky, rhp, Panther Valley HS, Lansford, Pa.
24. Jim Clark, ss, Catholic HS, Owensboro, Ky.
25. Scott Dwyer, 2b-3b, Burbank HS, Sacramento, Calif.
26. George Stanley, rhp, Bridgewater HS, Raynham, Mass.
27. *Michael Kowalski, rhp, Cocoa (Fla.) HS.
28. *Dennis Chambliss, rhp, Sidney Lanier HS, Macon, Ga.
29. *Stafford Branch, rhp, Scotia (N.Y.) Senior HS.
30. Brian Blaney, rhp, Methuen (Mass.) HS.
31. Douglas Storum, c, Brevard (Fla.) CC.
32. ***Doug Ault, of-lhp, Panola (Texas) JC.—(1976-80)**
33. *Michael Smollen, c, Lake Worth (Fla.) HS.
34. *Eugene Sackett, c, McClatchy HS, Sacramento, Calif.
35. *Dave Pyles, inf, East HS, East Bremerton, Wash.
36. *David Krull, inf-of, University of Iowa.
37. Michael Snipes, ss, Martin County HS, Stuart, Fla.
38. *Larry Green, 3b, Dean (Mass.) JC.
39. *Joseph Levulis, lhp, Frontier Central HS, Blasdell, N.Y.
40. *David Kegris, c, John Harris HS, Harrisburg, Pa.
41. William Maher, lhp, Johnstown (Pa.) HS.
42. *Leonard Jankiewicz, 1b, Lancaster (N.Y.) HS.
43. Dennis Slagle, rhp, Bethlehem-Center HS, Richeyville, Pa.
44. *Gary Gaiser, rhp, West Seneca (N.Y.) HS.
45. *Victor Sharek, 3b-rhp, Lincoln HS, Wampum, Pa.
46. *John Waffle, ss, Cardinal Mooney HS, Rochester, N.Y.
47. *Edward Spoth, 1b-ss, DeSales Catholic HS, East Amherst, N.Y.
48. Joseph Secor, rhp-of, Elkton (Md.) HS.

**June—Secondary Phase (4)**

1. Rudi Strickland, lhp, Indian River (Fla.) CC.—(Low A)
2. ***Glenn Borgmann, c, Miami-Dade CC North.—(1972-80)**
3. ***Jim Barr, rhp, University of Southern California.—(1971-83)**
4. *Gerald Bryant, lhp, Amherst County HS, Madison Heights, Va.
5. Ken Wastradowski, lhp, Centralia (Wash.) JC.
6. *William Jenkins, ss, Orange Coast (Calif.) JC.

## ST. LOUIS CARDINALS

**January—Regular Phase (19)**

1. **Al Hrabosky, lhp, Fullerton (Calif.) JC.—(1970-82)**
2. **Ed Crosby, 2b, Long Beach (Calif.) CC.—(1970-76)**

DRAFT DROP *Father of Bobby Crosby, first-round draft pick, Athletics (2001); major leaguer (2003-06)*

3. *David Jakubs, 3b-ss, University of Cincinnati.
4. *John Phillips, rhp, Moorpark (Calif.) JC.
5. Jack Butorac, rhp, Cal State Los Angeles.
6. *Glenwood Arbuckle, lhp, Trenton (Mo.) JC.

**January—Secondary Phase (1)**

1. ***Wayne Garland, rhp, Gulf Coast (Fla.) CC.—(1973-81)**
2. *Artie Brown, rhp, New York University.
3. **Ray Bare, rhp, Miami-Dade CC North.—(1972-77)**
4. Robert Auger, 1b-rhp, Putnam, Conn.
5. Nicholas Stipanovich, rhp, Boston University.
6. Herb Hofvendahl, of, St. Mary's (Calif.) College.
7. *Brian Bach, rhp, University of Connecticut.

**June—Regular Phase (20)**

1. Charles Minott, lhp-of, Royal Oak HS, Covina, Calif.—(High A)
2. John Nixon, ss, New Hanover HS, Wilmington, N.C.—(High A)

DRAFT DROP *Father of Trot Nixon, first-round draft pick, Red Sox (1993); major leaguer (1996-2008)*

3. **Mick Kelleher, ss, University of Puget Sound.—(1972-82)**
4. **Bill Stein, ss, Southern Illinois University.—(1972-85)**
5. John Heenan, of, Lincoln HS, San Jose, Calif.—(High A)
6. Greg Millikan, lhp, Occidental (Calif.) College.
7. Stanley Templeton, of, Weatherford (Okla.) HS.
8. Russ Caldarella, of-ss, Millikan HS, Long Beach, Calif.
9. ***Bucky Dent, 3b, Hialeah (Fla.) HS.—(1973-84)**

DRAFT DROP *Major league manager (1989-90)*

10. Barry Poris, 1b-lhp, CC of New York.
11. ***Bill Madlock, 3b, Eisenhower HS, Decatur, Ill.—(1973-87)**
12. Gary Collins, 1b, Southern Illinois University-Edwardsville.
13. Paul Sheehan, rhp, Burlington (Mass.) HS.
14. *Michael Timmel, rhp, Terra Linda HS, San Rafael, Calif.
15. *George Coval, c, Philipsburg (Pa.) HS.
16. Gary Barakat, 2b, Cliffside Park HS, Palisades, N.J.
17. *Andres Frank, of, Castro Valley (Colo.) HS.
18. *Alex West, c, Fairfax HS, Los Angeles.
19. Henry Daugherty, 3b, University of South Alabama.
20. *Roger Schmuck, of-1b, Mesa (Ariz.) CC.
21. *Joe Krsnich, of-inf, Kapaun Memorial HS, Wichita, Kan.
22. *Maurice Robert, of-rhp, Richfield HS, Waco, Texas.
23. Jim Ciotti, rhp, Salem (Ohio) HS.
24. Tony Partin, rhp, North Hampton HS, Cape Charles, Va.
25. Ray Colin, of, Long Beach (Calif.) CC.
26. Ronald Dyson, c-3b, Technical HS, Oakland, Calif.
27. *Robert Munson, rhp, Choate Prep, Wallingford, Conn.
28. John Kitchen, rhp, University of Massachusetts.
29. *Joaquin Saiz, of, Fort Lee (N.J.) HS.
30. Brad Plant, lhp, Mound (Minn.) HS.
31. **Ken Reitz, ss, Jefferson HS, Daly City, Calif.—(1972-82)**
32. *Robert Dance, c, Colonial Heights (Va.) HS.
33. John Sawatski, c, Hall HS, Little Rock, Ark.

DRAFT DROP *Son of Carl Sawatski, major leaguer (1948-63)*

34. Tim McEnderfer, c, Cornell University.
35. *William Hall, lhp, San Joaquin Delta (Calif.) JC.
36. Lonnie Croslow, ss, Modesto (Calif.) JC.
37. (void) *Michael Mantorella, 1b, Monterey Peninsula (Calif.) JC.
38. *John Herzing, lhp, Washington (Pa.) University.
39. Robert Fulewider, 2b, California Lutheran University.
40. John St. George, 2b-ss, Whittier (Calif.) College.

**June—Secondary Phase (18)**

1. Gary Marks, of, Golden West (Calif.) JC.—(AA)
2. Alan Putz, of, Springfield (Mass.) College.
3. *Gary Houston, lhp, San Jose (Calif.) CC.
4. (void) *John Jackson, 3b-of, University of California.
5. Kent Calderan, ss, Chabot (Calif.) JC.

## SAN DIEGO PADRES

**January—Regular Phase (23)**

1. Don Keenan, c, Gulf Coast (Fla.) CC.—(High A)
2. *Willie Buchanon, of-inf, Mira Costa (Calif.) JC.

DRAFT DROP *First-round draft pick, Green Bay Packers/ National Football League (1973); defensive back, NFL (1972-82)*

3. *Gary Dunkelberger, rhp, Orange Coast (Calif.) JC.
4. *Eric Swanson, rhp, San Diego CC.
5. *David Dowdy, c, Lower Columbia (Wash.) JC.
6. Thomas O'Day, ss, Fort Lauderdale, Fla.
7. John Baca, c, Los Angeles.
8. *Ronnie Helton, rhp, Gulf Coast (Fla.) CC.
9. Charles Taylor, rhp, Vallejo, Calif.

**January—Secondary Phase (21)**

1. Jose Basterrechea, rhp, Flushing, N.Y.—(Rookie)
2. ***Ron Cash, ss, Manatee (Fla.) JC.–(1973-74)**
3. ***Rudy Arroyo, lhp, Foothill (Calif.) JC.—(1971)**
4. Kenneth McGregor, ss, Gulf Coast (Fla.) CC.
5. *Luciano Hernandez, rhp, Del Mar, Calif.
6. *Beau Robinson, 1b-of, Muskogee (Okla.) JC.
7. *Andy Hancock, c, Furman University.

**June—Regular Phase (24)**

1. **Randy Elliott, 1b, Camarillo (Calif.) HS.—(1972-80)**
2. Eli Borunda, rhp, Thomas Jefferson HS, San Antonio, Texas.—(AAA)
3. Joe DiSarcina, ss, University of Massachusetts.—(High A)

DRAFT DROP *Uncle of Gary DiSarcina, major leaguer (1989-2000)*

4. Eddie Rundle, of, Lamar University.—(Rookie)
5. Gil Vidrio, ss, Sweetwater HS, National City, Calif.—(High A)
6. Richard Longhurst, of, Pocatello (Idaho) HS.
7. *Stephen Peck, rhp, DeAnza HS, Richmond, Calif.
8. *William Berkes, 3b-c, Robinson HS, Tampa.
9. Aubrey Anderson, rhp, Escambia HS, Pensacola, Fla.
10. *John Dean, 2b, Calhoun (Ga.) HS.
11. Grant Steer, of, University of San Francisco.
12. *Dennis Loewe, rhp, Pershing (Neb.) College.
13. Guy Eargle, of, University of South Carolina.
14. Danny Young, rhp, Lodi HS, Stockton, Calif.
15. Wayne Zurburg, c, Broward (Fla.) CC.
16. Gregory Sinclair, rhp, University of San Francisco.
17. *James Kirkland, of, Savannah (Ga.) HS.
18. ***Doug DeCinces, 3b, Los Angeles Pierce JC.—(1973-87)**
19. *David Fussell, c, University of Chattanooga.
20. *Richard Horn, of, Avondale HS, Decatur, Ga.
21. David Kostival, 3b, Athens HS, Chauncey, Ohio.
22. Brian Brown, of-c, James Monroe HS, Bronx, N.Y.
23. *John Blue, lhp, Tempe (Ariz.) HS.
24. Michael Anders, of, Gonzaga University.
25. Marvin Sherzer, rhp, University of South Florida.
26. *Rick Simmons, rhp, Rogers HS, Spokane, Wash.
27. Rich Zinniger, lhp, Brigham Young University.
28. *Gregory Prickett, of, Middle Georgia JC.
29. *Kenneth Robinson, rhp-of, Oakland (Calif.) HS.
30. *Michael Dishman, 3b, Washington HS, Portland, Ore.
31. Lawrence Whiteside, rhp, Dixie Hollins HS, St. Petersburg, Fla.
32. *Earl Austin, 3b, Dos Palos (Calif.) HS.
33. *Michael Wells, ss-of, Normal (Ill.) Community HS.

**June—Secondary Phase (20)**

1. David Jakubs, 3b, University of Cincinnati.—(High A)
2. *Willie Buchanon, of, Mira Costa (Calif.) JC.

DRAFT DROP *First-round draft pick, Green Bay Packers/ National Football League (1973); defensive back, NFL (1972-82)*

3. *Freddie Howard, of-1b, Paris (Texas) JC.

## SAN FRANCISCO GIANTS

**January—Regular Phase (17)**

1. *Daniel Bondon, of-inf, San Pedro (Calif.) HS.—DNP
2. *James Stedman, rhp, Mesa (Ariz.) CC.
3. *Joseph Jacobsen, c-1b, Fresno (Calif.) CC.
4. *Robert Garcia, of-rhp, JC of the Sequoias (Calif.).
5. *Scott Wolfe, 2b, JC of the Sequoias (Calif.).
6. ***Glenn Borgmann, c-1b, Miami-Dade CC North.—(1972-80)**
7. *Larry Dierks, lhp, JC of the Sequoias (Calif.).
8. *Randall Shroll, rhp, JC of Southern Idaho.

**January—Secondary Phase (19)**

1. *Thomas Frye, of-rhp, Fairmont, N.C.—DNP
2. *Howard Casey, lhp, Umpqua (Ore.) CC.
3. *Pat Cech, rhp, Glendale (Ariz.) CC.
4. **Steve Stone, rhp, Kent State University.—(1971-81)**
5. Edgardo Avila, lhp-of, Miami-Dade CC North.

**June—Regular Phase (18)**

1. **Mike Phillips, ss, MacArthur HS, Irving, Texas.—(1973-83)**
2. Jack Woolsey, of, Kansas State University.—(AA)
3. **Horace Speed, of, Banning HS, Compton, Calif.—(1975-79)**
4. Randy Mohler, ss, Taylor (Ind.) University.—(AA)
5. Raymond Lombardo, c, Crespi HS, Encino, Calif.—(High A)

**6. Steve Ontiveros, 3b, Bakersfield (Calif.) HS.—(1973-80)**
**7. Gary Thomasson, of, Oceanside (Calif.) HS.—(1972-80)**
8. Guy Homoly, of, Illinois State University.
9. *Peter Franklin, of-ss, Morristown (N.J.) Prep HS.
10. Mike Fisher, of-inf, El Centro (Calif.) HS.
**11. Skip Pitlock, lhp, Southern Illinois University.—(1970-75)**
12. John Sielicki, lhp, Hartford (Conn.) Public HS.
13. Rich Miller, 3b, Ithaca (N.Y.) College.
14. *John Conners, of, Gardena (Calif.) HS.
**15. *Derek Bryant, of, Henry Clay HS, Lexington, Ky.—(1979)**
16. Mike Murphy, 1b, Ohio University.
17. Randy Kapano, of, Citrus (Calif.) JC.
18. Mike O'Brien, rhp, Phoenix (Ariz.) JC.
19. Rick Carden, lhp, Hawthorne (Calif.) HS.
20. *David Marshall, 1b, Solano (Calif.) CC.
21. Rick Gallagher, 1b, Cal Poly Pomona.
22. *Manuel Zepeda, 1b, El Monte (Calif.) HS.
23. *Eubulus Marsh, of, Solano (Calif.) CC.
24. *Larry Ike, rhp, Ottawa Hills HS, Grand Rapids, Mich.
25. Michael Powers, c, Henderson State (Ark.) University.
26. *William Lazzerini, lhp, Notre Dame HS, Sherman Oaks, Calif.
27. Jim Hoggarth, c, Oglethorpe (Ga.) University.
28. *Donald Crew, of, Alabama Christian College.
29. Edgar Ward, of, Arlington (Texas) HS.
30. Edward Hart, c, Westmont HS, San Jose, Calif.
31. *Jeffrey Hershkowitz, rhp, Springfield Gardens HS, Jamaica, N.Y.
32. *Michael McCormick, rhp, Boise (Idaho) HS.
33. *Allen Thomas, rhp, Rochester (Mich.) HS.
34. *Jerry Vitatoe, 1b-3b, Laney (Calif.) JC.
35. *Jim Chapados, 1b, Chehalis (Wash.) HS.
36. Joseph Sadelfeld, lhp, Ohio State University.
37. Cephus Mayo, 2b-3b, Treasure Valley (Ore.) CC.
38. *Jeffrey Bouton, rhp, Nutley (N.J.) HS.
39. Mark Brewster, of, Northern Arizona University.
40. *Richard Binder, lhp, University of Illinois.

### June—Secondary Phase (2)

**1. Jake Brown, c, Southern University.—(1975)**
2. *Daniel Ragland, 3b, Ranger (Texas) JC.
3. *Dave Carey, rhp, Hastings, Minn.
4. *Rick Dierker, rhp, Los Angeles Pierce JC.
DRAFT DROP *Brother of Larry Dierker, major leaguer (1964-77); major league manager (1997-2001)*

## SEATTLE PILOTS

### January—Regular Phase (24)

1. *Mike Weathers, 2b, Cerritos (Calif.) JC.—(AAA)
DRAFT DROP *Baseball coach, Long Beach State (2002-10)*
**2. Jerry Bell, rhp, Southwestern (Tenn.) College.—(1971-74)**
3. No selection.
4. *Lloyd Breshers, rhp, Centerville (Iowa) JC.
5. Jeffrey Lemon, rhp, Long Beach, Calif.
6. *Randall Brown, of, Sacramento (Calif.) CC.

### January—Secondary Phase (22)

**1. Ray Peters, rhp, Harvard University.—(1970)**
2. *Henry Yeargan, ss, Brewton Parker (Ga.) JC.
3. No selection.
4. *Bill Dobbs, lhp, Oklahoma State University.
5. *Bonnie Smith, 1b, Los Angeles.
6. *Bruce Kinder, ss, Florida Southern College.
**7. Rick Auerbach, ss, Los Angeles Pierce JC.—(1971-81)**
**8. *Doug Bird, rhp, Mount San Antonio (Calif.) JC.—(1973-83)**
**9. *Duane Kuiper, ss, Indian Hills (Iowa) CC.—(1974-85)**
10. *Michael Longstreth, ss, Eastern Oklahoma A&M JC.
11. David Renkiewicz, rhp, University of Michigan.
12. *Nick Nicosia, of, University of Florida.

### June—Regular Phase (21)

**1. Gorman Thomas, ss-rhp, James Island HS, Charleston, S.C.—(1973-86)**
2. Steve Beasley, 1b, Jesup (Ga.) HS.—(Low A)
3. No selection.
4. Stephen Harvey, rhp, Ingraham HS, Seattle.—(AA)
**5. Gary Martz, of-rhp, West Valley HS, Spokane, Wash.—(1975)**
6. *Larry Hollyfield, of, Compton (Calif.) HS.
DRAFT DROP *Seventh-round draft pick, Portland Trail Blazers/National Basketball Association (1973)*
7. Charles Loseth, rhp, Estancia HS, Costa Mesa, Calif.
8. *Kenneth Braun, ss, DuPont Manual HS, Louisville, Ky.
9. *John Vance, c-1b, Western Kentucky University.
10. *Gary King, ss, Clay HS, South Bend, Ind.
11. *James Kinsley, rhp, Herricks HS, New Hyde Park, N.Y.
12. Earl Gilbert, rhp-of, Pascagoula (Miss.) HS.
13. *Dwane Doel, of, Plantation HS, Fort Lauderdale, Fla.
14. Robert Green, 3b, Boston College.
**15. Jim Slaton, rhp, Antelope Valley (Calif.) JC.—(1971-86)**
16. *Jeffrey Ryser, ss, Bellaire HS, Houston.
**17. Bobby Coluccio, of-inf, Centralia (Wash.) HS.—(1973-78)**
18. *Jerry Lewis, 1b, Palm Springs (Calif.) HS.
19. John Terranova, lhp, McKean HS, Wilmington, Del.
20. Charles Williams, of, Locke HS, Los Angeles.
**21. Bob Hansen, 1b-of, University of Massachusetts.—(1974-76)**
22. *James Juniel, of, Richmond (Calif.) HS.
23. *Richard Jones, lhp, Davidson HS, Mobile, Ala.
24. Billy Turner, rhp, East HS, Des Moines, Iowa.
25. *Marc Rhea, ss, Sehome HS, Bellingham, Wash.
26. Rudolph Toth, 1b, Northampton (Pa.) HS.
27. *Steve Cain, rhp, North Kansas City (Mo.) HS.
28. *Michael Lynch, lhp, Norman (Okla.) HS.
29. John Pankow, lhp, University of Washington.
30. *James Greggerson, lhp, Ysleta HS, El Paso, Texas.
31. *Bruce Maxwell, c, Madison HS, Portland, Ore.
32. Virgil Smith, of, Sacramento (Calif.) HS.
33. Norman Hill, 2b, Mobile County Training School, Magazine, Ala.
34. *Gene Moser, of, Edmonds (Wash.) HS.
35. *Jack Wilson, of, Sarasota (Fla.) HS.
36. Johnny Martin, 3b, Union (Tenn.) University.
37. John Conzatti, rhp, Centralia (Wash.) HS.
38. *Zack Rogers, 1b-lhp, Butler (Ala.) HS.
39. *William Fuller, lhp, Great Neck South HS, Great Neck, N.Y.
40. *Ricky Patrylo, rhp, Manville (N.J.) HS.
41. *Herbert Williams, c, Sacramento (Calif.) HS.
42. James Spencer, 1b-3b, Falls Church (Va.) HS.
43. Bobby Cook, inf, Latta (S.C.) HS.
44. Stan Walton, lhp-of, Spartanburg (S.C.) HS.
45. *John Petronaci, rhp, Montclair (N.J.) HS.
46. *Michael Weaver, 2b, Maplewood HS, Richmond Heights, Mo.
47. Albert Strane, of, Santa Clara University.

### June—Secondary Phase (11)

**1. *Pat Osburn, lhp, Manatee (Fla.) JC.—(1974-75)**
2. Edgar Pate, lhp, Los Angeles CC.
3. No selection.
4. *Ernie Henrickson, rhp-of, Everett, Wash.
5. Donald Schmonsky, rhp, Jamestown (N.Y.) CC.

## WASHINGTON SENATORS

### January—Regular Phase (2)

**1. Joe Lovitto, c, San Pedro (Calif.) HS—(1972-75)**
2. *Lyn Martin, ss, St. Johns River (Fla.) JC.
3. *Tim Martin, 2b, St. Johns River (Fla.) JC.
4. *Daniel Baker, c-of, Montgomery (Md.) JC.
5. *Rick Cassata, 3b, Syracuse University.
DRAFT DROP *Quarterback, Canadian Football League (1968-76)*
6. *Donald Schmonsky, rhp, Jamestown (N.Y.) CC.
7. *Jon Roth, lhp, Niagara County (N.Y.) CC.
8. James Bottoms, of, Seabrook, Md.
9. *Brian Moore, 1b, Waterloo, Iowa.
10. *Michael Pich, c, Salisbury, Md.

### January—Secondary Phase (8)

**1. *Mickey Rivers, of, Miami-Dade CC North.—(1970-84)**
2. *Gerald Tassa, lhp-of, Wingate (N.C.) JC.
3. Fred Williams, rhp, Baltimore.
4. *Bill Seinsoth, 1b, University of Southern California.
5. *Scott Taylor, rhp, Mansfield (Pa.) University.
6. *Ronald Collier, rhp, Mansfield (Pa.) University.
7. *Michael Pivec, of, Baltimore.

### June—Regular Phase (1)

**1. Jeff Burroughs, of, Woodrow Wilson HS, Long Beach, Calif.—(1970-85)**
DRAFT DROP *Father of Sean Burroughs, first-round draft pick, Padres (1998); major leaguer (2002-05)*
2. John Brown, rhp, Bishop Denis J. O'Connell HS, Arlington, Va.—(AA)
3. *Jim Officer, lhp, Madison HS, Portland, Ore.—(AA)
DRAFT DROP *Attended Oregon; re-drafted by Angels, June 1971/secondary phase (1st round)*
**4. Pete Mackanin, 3b-ss, Brother Rice Catholic HS, Chicago.—(1973-81)**
DRAFT DROP *Major league manager (2005, 2007, 2015)*
**5. David Criscione, c, Dunkirk (N.Y.) HS.—(1977)**
6. *Geoffrey Brandt, of-rhp, El Camino HS, Carmichael, Calif.
7. Melvin Williams, of, Pembroke State (N.C.) University.
8. *Eric Florence, c, Waynesville (Ohio) HS.
9. Ricky Rowe, ss, Georgetown (S.C.) HS.
10. *Claude Renfro, rhp-1b, Red Bank HS, Chattanooga, Tenn.
11. Eugene Lightford, of, Boys HS, Brooklyn, N.Y.
12. Vernon Saatzer, lhp, St. Thomas Military HS, St. Paul, Minn.
13. *James Sullivan, lhp, LaJunta (Colo.) HS.
14. *Darrell Darrow, ss, Jordan HS, Long Beach, Calif.
15. Donald Shields, rhp, Northwestern State University.
16. *Randall Goede, lhp, Valparaiso University.
17. *David Cooper, rhp, Wallace HS, Gary, Ind.
18. Michael Pettit, rhp, St. Catherines Catholic HS, Racine, Wis.
19. Gordon Broseker, of-rhp, Northern HS, Baltimore.
20. *Daniel Tracy, rhp, Muskogee (Okla.) HS.
21. Farley Banks, ss-c, Gwynn Park HS, Aquasco, Md.
22. *Steven Hegens, rhp, Spingarn HS, Washington, D.C.
23. *Charles Krause, lhp, Palo Alto (Calif.) HS.
24. Jack Crable, of, Moeller HS, Cincinnati.
25. *Norman Jones, ss, Haddonfield (N.J.) HS.
26. *Gabriel Padilla, rhp, Johnston HS, Austin, Texas.
27. *Kristian Sorensen, rhp, Santa Cruz (Calif.) HS.
28. James Herzog, 2b, St. Catherines Catholic HS, Racine, Wis.
29. *John Hickey, c, Belmont Abbey (N.C.) College.
30. Jerry Ginter, rhp, Falls HS, International Falls, Minn.
**31. *Chuck Seelbach, rhp, Dartmouth University.—(1971-74)**
32. William Brykczynski, rhp, Thornridge HS, Dolton, Ill.
33. *Joseph Cork, ss, Manhattan Prep HS, Bronx, N.Y.
34. *Paul Burton, lhp, Archbishop Kennedy HS, Conshohocken, Pa.
**35. *Tippy Martinez, of-lhp, LaJunta (Colo.) HS.—(1974-88)**
36. Roger Gifford, c-of, Lewis (Ill.) University.
37. James Cleary, of, Mitchellville, Md.
38. Robert Ormond, lhp, Princeton (N.C.) HS.
39. Edward Layman, rhp, Belmont Abbey (N.C.) College.
40. *Robert Guinan, 2b, Manhattan Prep HS, New York.
41. *Daniel Wolfe, rhp, Cardinal Mindszenty HS, Dunkirk, N.Y.
42. *Jim Callison, of, Wake Forest University.
**43. Steve Foucault, 3b-rhp, South Georgia College.—(1973-78)**
44. Edward Hose, rhp-of, Williamsport (Md.) HS.
45. *Randy Kersten, 2b, Central HS, Naperville, Ill.
46. *Harry Martell, 3b-rhp, Archbishop Curley HS, Baltimore.
47. *William Eckler, of, SUNY-Fredonia.
48. *Loren Marz, of, Cassadaga Central HS, Sinclairville, N.Y.

### June—Secondary Phase (19)

1. *Sherwood Hahn, rhp-1b, Virginia Tech.—DNP
**2. *Pete Varney, c, Harvard University.—(1973-76)**
DRAFT DROP *First overall draft pick, June 1966/American Legion phase, Athletics; first overall draft pick, January 1968/secondary phase, Astros; first overall draft pick, June 1971/secondary phase, active, White Sox*
3. *Bruce Irvin, c, St. Petersburg (Fla.) JC.
**4. Dave Moates, of, Florida State University.—(1974-76)**
5. *Douglas Smith, 2b, Buena Vista (Iowa) College.

# 1970

## AT A GLANCE

### This Date In History
**WINTER DRAFT:** Jan. 17
**SUMMER DRAFT:** June 4-5

### Best Draft
**CHICAGO WHITE SOX. GOOSE GOSSAGE** (9) landed in the Hall of Fame, while sidekick **TERRY FORSTER** (2) had a lengthy major league career. **LEE RICHARD** (1) didn't pan out, but another shortstop, **BUCKY DENT** (top pick in June/secondary phase), did.

### Worst Draft
**NEW YORK METS.** The defending World Series champions failed to capitalize on their newfound glory. They didn't sign their top two picks in the June regular phase, and had only one future big leaguer, reserve outfield **BRUCE BOISCLAIR** (20), of 41 picks overall in that phase.

### First-Round Bust
**GARY POLCZYNSKI, SS, REDS.** Between Don Gullett (1969 draft/1970 debut) and Nick Esasky (1978/1983), the Reds didn't bring a first-round talent to the majors for 13 years—a key reason why the wheels fell off the Big Red Machine. Polczynski contributed by hitting .193 over a four-year minor league career.

### Second Best
**TERRY FORSTER, LHP, WHITE SOX.** Forster outpitched Gossage for the first five years of their careers and saved 69 games from 1972-74 as the primary closer for the Sox, though Gossage grabbed the reins from that point on, finishing with 124 wins and 310 saves. Forster chalked up 54 wins and 127 saves over 16 years.

### Late-Round Find
**DAVE PARKER, OF, PIRATES (14TH ROUND).** Parker passed on college football after a knee injury as a Cincinnati high school senior, and he welcomed the chance to play baseball—even after falling to the 14th round and

# Ivie's fragile makeup undoes Padres career

The San Diego Padres were so proud to showcase Mike Ivie, the No. 1 pick in the 1970 draft, that they immediately brought the 17-year-old catcher and his parents to San Diego to introduce him to the local press and let him work out with the major league team.

Ivie, a 6-foot-2, 200-pound Georgia high school product, went behind the plate to catch batting practice before a Padres game. His first few throws back to the pitcher were crisp and precise, but his next one innocuously nicked the edge of the L-screen, protecting the pitcher.

"That, Rook, is why they're sending you to Tri-Cities, because you can't throw the ball straight back to the pitcher," jawed veteran Chris Cannizzaro, the regular Padres catcher.

Little did anyone know, but it was the beginning of the end for the talented youngster.

A few days later, the wide-eyed Ivie made his pro debut at Tri-Cities of the short-season Class A Northwest League and knew almost immediately that something wasn't right, especially after one of his throws back to the pitcher sailed into center field, allowing the winning run to score. Ivie had taken Cannizzaro's off-the-cuff remark personally and developed a mental block.

"He was afraid to throw the ball back to the pitcher," recalled Ivie's father Bill, who had been his coach in Connie Mack League ball in Decatur, Ga. "Mike always had a strong, accurate arm in high school, but it became a psychological thing with him."

Ivie, who received a $75,000 signing bonus from the Padres, soon became so tormented over the travails of catching that he simply refused to go behind the plate. On two occasions, he bolted the organization—partly out of humiliation and frustration, partly out of fear of failure.

His promise behind the plate never blossomed as he developed a loathing for the position—which he was so well equipped to play that no less an authority than Johnny Bench once remarked, "He has the softest hands, the best catcher's hands I've ever seen."

Ivie overcame the tribulations he endured early in his young career to reach San Diego for good in 1975, when he was almost exclusively a first baseman, and went on to play with three other clubs in a tumultuous major league career that almost mercifully ended in 1983. But not before he spent two terms on the disabled list with a malady listed as mental exhaustion.

In the end, Ivie ended up catching in just nine games in the big leagues.

"People ask me if we made a mistake on Ivie," said Bob Fontaine Sr., San Diego's scouting director in 1970. "It wouldn't have made any difference who had the first pick. Ivie was going to be the first player taken. He could have caught at the major

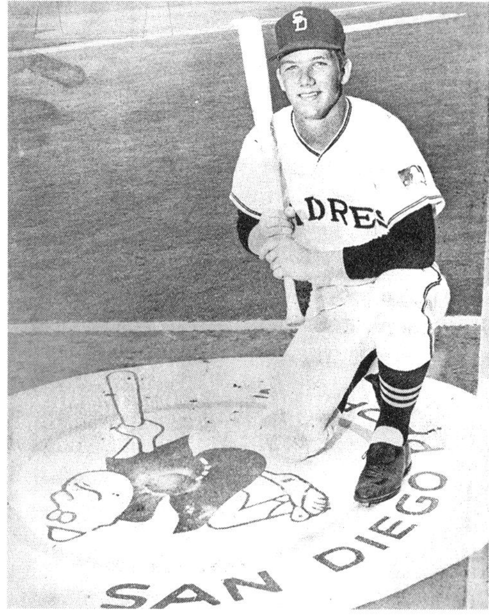

Scouts still rave about Mike Ivie's natural ability behind the plate, but an offhand remark before his pro career started seemed to start him on a downhill spiral that sabotaged his major league potential

league level the day we signed him. He was the best kid catcher I ever had seen and I haven't seen anyone better since. He had great hands, balance, the throwing arm and he had an instinct and feel for the game."

## CATCHERS DOMINATE FIRST ROUND

Led by Ivie, the focus in the 1970 draft was on catchers like no other draft in history. Three of the first four selections in the June regular phase were high school catchers, and a record six backstops went in the first round.

San Diego earned the right to draft Ivie via a coin flip. The Padres and Montreal Expos, their 1969 National League expansion cousins, finished their first seasons with identical 52-110 records. By coming out on the wrong end, the Expos slipped to No. 3 in the pecking order, as the No. 2 spot was reserved for the American League club (Cleveland Indians) with the poorest won-loss mark in 1969.

The Expos also ended up taking a catcher, North Carolina prep talent Barry Foote. Foote had a solid, if unspectacular 10-year career in the majors, hitting .230 overall with 57 homers for four different clubs.

But neither the Padres nor Expos claimed the catcher who went on to enjoy the best career: Darrell Porter, who went to the Milwaukee Brewers with the fourth pick. Porter, known for his outstanding defensive skills and the ability to hit for power from the left side, played in the big leagues from 1971-87, hitting .247 with 188 home runs. He reached Milwaukee at 19 and played six

## 1970: THE FIRST ROUNDERS

| CLUB: PLAYER, POS., SCHOOL | HOMETOWN | B-T | HT. | WT. | AGE | BONUS | FIRST YEAR | LAST YEAR | PEAK LEVEL (YEARS) |
|---|---|---|---|---|---|---|---|---|---|
| **JUNE—REGULAR PHASE** | | | | | | | | | |
| 1. Padres: Mike Ivie, c, Walker HS | Decatur, Ga. | R-R | 6-2 | 198 | 17 | $75,000 | 1970 | 1983 | Majors (11) |
| All the tools to be an elite catcher with soft hands/raw power, but consumed by fear of failure; hit .269 with 81 HRs in 11 years, fell far short of expectations. | | | | | | | | | |
| 2. Indians: Steve Dunning, rhp, Stanford | San Diego | R-R | 6-2 | 205 | 21 | $50,000 | 1970 | 1978 | Majors (7) |
| Became second player of draft era to debut in majors, but never fulfilled college expectations (13-2, 1.83, 108 IP/144 SO); went just 23-41, 4.56 for five clubs. | | | | | | | | | |
| 3. Expos: Barry Foote, c, Smithfield-Selma HS | Smithfield, N.C. | R-R | 6-3 | 205 | 18 | $44,000 | 1970 | 1982 | Majors (10) |
| Second of three premium catchers drafted had pedestrian 10-year career in majors (.230, 57 HRs), before long tenure as coach; son Derek became sixth-rounder. | | | | | | | | | |
| 4. Brewers: # Darrell Porter, c, Southeast HS | Oklahoma City | L-R | 6-0 | 193 | 18 | $70,000 | 1970 | 1987 | Majors (17) |
| Debuted at 19, enjoyed flashes in long career (.291-20-112 for Royals in '79; World Series MVP for Cards in 1982); cocaine affected career, killed him in 2002. | | | | | | | | | |
| 5. Phillies: Mike Martin, lhp, Olympia HS | Columbia, S.C. | L-L | 6-1 | 185 | 18 | $29,000 | 1970 | 1978 | Class AAA (2) |
| Brother Jerry went undrafted, played 11 years in majors; Mike's career stymied by elbow issues, and he tried hitting for two years before returning to mound. | | | | | | | | | |
| 6. White Sox: Lee Richard, ss, Southern | Port Arthur, Texas | R-R | 6-0 | 160 | 21 | $46,500 | 1970 | 1978 | Majors (5) |
| Nicknamed "Bee Bee" in high school because he was a hard-throwing pitcher; great speed but struggled at plate (.209-2-29) in abbreviated big league career. | | | | | | | | | |
| 7. Astros: Randy Scarbery, rhp, Roosevelt HS | Fresno, Calif. | R-R | 6-1 | 180 | 17 | Unsigned | 1973 | 1980 | Majors (2) |
| First two-time first-round pick in June regular phase; drafted by A's in 1973 after successful career at USC, spent two unproductive years in majors (3-10, 4.50). | | | | | | | | | |
| 8. Royals: Rex Goodson, c/of, Pine Tree HS | Longview, Texas | R-R | 5-11 | 190 | 18 | $40,000 | 1970 | 1973 | Class AA (1) |
| Catcher in HS, but Royals immediately moved Texas football recruit to OF to take advantage of superior athleticism; spent four years in minors, hit .274-17-121. | | | | | | | | | |
| 9. Dodgers: Jim Haller, rhp, Creighton Prep | Omaha, Neb. | R-R | 6-5 | 205 | 18 | $42,000 | 1970 | 1975 | Class AAA (2) |
| Lanky righthander with questionable mechanics, predictably hurt arm toward end of six-year career in minors; never advanced past Triple-A, went 18-18, 3.65. | | | | | | | | | |
| 10. Angels: Paul Dade, 3b/of, Nathan Hale HS | Seattle | R-R | 5-11 | 175 | 18 | $20,000 | 1970 | 1982 | Majors (6) |
| Had 13-year career and won batting title in Triple-A; spent parts of six seasons in majors (.270-10-107), but never flashed enough power to earn regular work. | | | | | | | | | |
| 11. Cardinals: Jim Browning, rhp, Emma Sansom HS | Gadsden, Ala. | R-R | 6-0 | 180 | 18 | $25,000 | 1970 | 1975 | Class AA (2) |
| Went 2-0, 0.56 in three games in Cards system before getting shipped to Phillies to complete 1969 trade when Curt Flood failed to report; went 26-23 in minors. | | | | | | | | | |
| 12. Yankees: # Dave Cheadle, lhp, Asheville HS | Asheville, N.C. | L-L | 6-2 | 180 | 19 | $57,500 | 1970 | 1978 | Majors (1) |
| Had dominant prep career (56 IP/119 SO as a senior), spent eight years in minors, made two relief appearances with Braves, fanned Pete Rose for only strikeout. | | | | | | | | | |
| 13. Pirates: John Bedard, rhp, Springfield Tech HS | Springfield, Mass. | R-R | 6-2 | 195 | 17 | $38,000 | 1970 | 1974 | Class A (4) |
| Spent five seasons in Pirates system, never advanced beyond Class A; used first as pitcher (15-28, 5.60), later as catcher (.202-0-15); brother also played for Bucs. | | | | | | | | | |
| 14. Senators: Chip Maxwell, 3b/ss, Zane Trace HS | Kingston, Ohio | L-R | 6-1 | 195 | 17 | $32,500 | 1970 | 1974 | Class AAA (1) |
| Had plenty of promise as prep senior (11-0 as pitcher, .642 BA as SS), but five-year career in minors fell short of expectations; hit .242 with 13 HRs. | | | | | | | | | |
| 15. Reds: Gary Polczynski, ss, Nathan Hale HS | West Allis, Wis. | R-R | 6-0 | 169 | 18 | $25,000 | 1970 | 1973 | Class AAA (1) |
| Ended Reds' early run of success in draft by hitting .193 with nine HRs, committing 93 errors as 2B in four seasons in minors; later became coach at his alma mater. | | | | | | | | | |
| 16. Red Sox: Jimmie Hacker, ss, Temple HS | Temple, Texas | L-R | 5-11 | 170 | 18 | Unsigned | 1974 | 1975 | Class AA (2) |
| Chose Texas A&M rather than signing with Red Sox; drafted by Braves in 1974 (5th round), and his pro career lasted just two years (.251-2-59 overall). | | | | | | | | | |
| 17. Giants: John D'Acquisto, rhp, St. Augustine HS | San Diego | R-R | 6-2 | 205 | 18 | $27,500 | 1970 | 1983 | Majors (10) |
| Spent 10 years in majors (57-58, 4.42) with fastball comparable to Nolan Ryan's; retired after elbow surgery in 1983; later jailed on fraud/money-laundering charges. | | | | | | | | | |
| 18. Athletics: Dan Ford, of, Fremont HS | Los Angeles | R-R | 6-2 | 185 | 18 | $29,500 | 1971 | 1985 | Majors (11) |
| "Disco Dan" spent four years buried in A's system before getting his break with trade to Twins; spent nine of 11 years in MLB as regular, hit .270 with 121 HRs. | | | | | | | | | |
| 19. Cubs: Gene Hiser, of, Maryland | Baltimore | L-L | 5-10 | 175 | 21 | $35,000 | 1970 | 1976 | Majors (5) |
| Hit .338 with 11 HRs, 44 RBIs (both school records) as Maryland All-American; debuted in Triple-A but never got untracked in five years in majors (.202-1-18). | | | | | | | | | |
| 20. Tigers: Terry Mappin, c, Durrett HS | Louisville, Ky. | L-R | 6-0 | 200 | 18 | $45,000 | 1970 | 1973 | Class AA (1) |
| Received largest bonus given out by Tigers at time to draft pick after hitting .473 with 10 HRs as HS senior; four-year career peaked in Double-A, hit .245-21-110. | | | | | | | | | |
| 21. Braves: Ron Broaddus, rhp, Brazosport HS | Freeport, Texas | R-R | 6-4 | 190 | 17 | $15,000 | 1971 | 1974 | Class A (4) |
| Went 33-1 in HS, spurned Texas A&M offer; injured knee after signing and required surgery and extensive rehab; went 4-15, 5.24, career peaked in A-ball. | | | | | | | | | |
| 22. Twins: Bob Gorinski, ss, Mount Pleasant HS | Calumet, Pa. | R-R | 6-3 | 215 | 18 | $60,000 | 1970 | 1979 | Majors (1) |
| Led team coached by dad to state title as prep SR; one of most-feared sluggers in minors (163 HRs in 9 years), but hit just .195-3-22 in 1977, in lone crack at majors. | | | | | | | | | |
| 23. Mets: George Ambrow, ss, Poly HS | Long Beach, Calif. | R-R | 6-0 | 190 | 18 | Unsigned | Never Played Pro Ball | | |
| Told Mets not to draft him because of his commitment to USC, which he fulfilled; all-conference as a freshman, but then his career was cut down by knee injuries. | | | | | | | | | |
| 24. Orioles: James West, c, Vashon HS | St. Louis | B-R | 6-3 | 190 | 17 | $15,000 | 1970 | 1973 | Class A (1) |
| Yet another first-round prep catcher, struggled behind plate in pros (52 G, 20 errors, 20 passed balls), spent most of failed career as 1B/OF in O's/Expos low minors. | | | | | | | | | |
| **JANUARY—REGULAR PHASE** | | | | | | | | | |
| 1. Indians: Chris Chambliss, 1b, UCLA | Aiea, Hawaii | L-R | 6-1 | 200 | 21 | $25,000 | 1970 | 1988 | Majors (17) |
| Dropped out of UCLA and won Triple-A batting title right out of the gate; hit .279, 185 HRs over 18 years in majors, delivered legendary homer in '76 ALCS for Yanks. | | | | | | | | | |
| **JANUARY—SECONDARY PHASE** | | | | | | | | | |
| 1. Senators: Bill Fahey, c, St. Clair County (Mich.) CC | Detroit | L-R | 6-0 | 195 | 20 | $31,500 | 1970 | 1983 | Majors (11) |
| Carved out 11-year career in majors as backup catcher, hit .241 with 7 HRs in 383 games; later became coach; son Brandon spent three years with Orioles as infielder. | | | | | | | | | |
| **JUNE—SECONDARY PHASE** | | | | | | | | | |
| 1. Giants: Dave Kingman, rhp/of, Southern California | Mount Prospect, Ill. | R-R | 6-6 | 210 | 21 | $80,000 | 1970 | 1987 | Majors (16) |
| Prodigious all-or-nothing slugger known for long home runs, high strikeouts; played 16 years in majors, went deep 442 times, struck out 1,816 times. | | | | | | | | | |

*# Deceased.*

## AT A GLANCE

signing for a $6,000 bonus with the Pirates. He went on to a 19-year career in the majors, winning two National League batting titles, while hitting .290 overall with 334 homers.

### Never Too Late

**MIKE BACSIK, RHP, ORIOLES (55TH ROUND).** Bacsik was the latest player drafted in 1970 to reach the majors, though he didn't sign for another three years as a nondrafted free agent with the Rangers. He spent five years in the majors from 1975-80, posting an 8-6, 4.43 record. His son Mike, a 1996 draft pick of the Indians, also had a five-year career, from 2001-07.

### Overlooked

**FRANK WHITE, 2B, ROYALS.** White was the first and best graduate of the Royals short-lived Baseball Academy, a novel concept of Royals owner Ewing Kauffman in the early 1970s to attract the best athletes and mold them into baseball players. He played 18 season with the Royals, hit .255 with 160 homers, played in five All-Star Games and won eight Gold Glove Awards.

### International Gem

**SIXTO LEZCANO, OF, BREWERS.** Signed out of Puerto Rico at age 16 for $5,000, Lezcano spent the first seven seasons of a 12-year major league career with the Brewers. He became the only player to hit two Opening Day grand slams, in 1978 and 1980, and won a Gold Glove while with the Brewers. Over his career, he hit .271 with 148 home runs.

### Minor League Take

**BOB GORINSKI, OF, TWINS.** The 6-foot-3, 215-pound Gorinski showed more raw power in the minors than any 1970 first-rounder, leading his league in home runs on four occasions and hitting 163 homers in nine seasons. He topped

CONTINUED ON PAGE 98

## AT A GLANCE

CONTINUED FROM PAGE 97

the Triple-A Pacific Coast League with 28 in 1976, a year before making his debut with the Twins, but his big league career lasted only 54 games. He hit just .195 with three homers.

### Ones Who Got Away

**RANDY SCARBERY, RHP, ASTROS (1ST ROUND); GEORGE AMBROW, SS, METS (1ST ROUND).** Southern California landed one of the greatest recruiting crops in NCAA history in 1970. In Scarbery and Ambrow, they secured a pair of unsigned first-rounders, though their biggest catch may have been outfielder **FRED LYNN**, an unsigned third round-pick of the Yankees.

### He Was Drafted?

**JAMES STREET, RHP, INDIANS (31ST ROUND).** Street was the quarterback who went 20-0 as a starter and led Texas to a national football title in 1969, and the father of major league all-star pitcher and Texas All-American Huston Street. Street carved out his own career as a standout pitcher with the Longhorns, going 29-8 over three seasons and earning All-America honors twice. He died of a heart attack in 2013.

### Did You Know . . .

Dodgers first-rounder **JIM HALLER** had elbow surgery on Sept. 25, 1974, by orthopedic surgeon Dr. Frank Jobe. That same day, Jobe performed his historic ulnar collateral ligament surgery on another Dodgers pitcher, Tommy John.

### They Said It

Padres president **BUZZIE BAVASI** on No. 1 draft pick **MIKE IVIE**: "In my 40 years in the game, I would have to say Ivie is the biggest disappointment I've had. He could have been one of the greatest catchers of all time. If a scout could tell what was inside the young man, the scout would be worth a million dollars a year. But you never know."

years with the Brewers, but achieved his greatest success after being traded, first to Kansas City and then to St. Louis. At the height of his career, Porter was a three-time all-star with the Royals from 1978-80. He also earned MVP honors in both the National League Championship Series and World Series in 1982 for the champion Cardinals.

Like Ivie, Porter was plagued by his own personal demons. He was one of the first American professional athletes to publicly admit he had a problem with substance abuse. His admission came shortly after Porter enjoyed his best season, in 1979, when he batted .291 for the Royals, hit 20 homers, drove in 112 runs and led the American League with 119 walks.

Porter admitted that offseason to being deep into chemical dependency throughout most of his career—dating back to his early days with the Brewers. During spring training, he acknowledged that he had an addiction problem, and subsequently enrolled in an Arizona substance-abuse clinic. He spent six weeks in rehab before rejoining the Royals, but a reformed Porter was not the same player, and his discontent sharpened when he failed to regain his 1979 form. By midseason of 1982, he became a frequent target of fan abuse in St. Louis, and his production—save for his brief respite in postseason play that year—continued to deteriorate over three more years with the Cardinals.

Darrell Porter

"I'd been fairly successful the whole time I was doing drugs," Porter observed later. "When I stopped doing them, I just struggled."

In 1984, Porter wrote a revealing autobiography, in which he detailed his life in baseball and his struggles with substance abuse. It offered a harrowing portrait of a man driven to the edge.

"I didn't even drink in high school," he wrote. "But when I got into baseball, I was suddenly batting .204 and I found that four or five beers tasted terrific. I began using alcohol, which is a drug, and uppers and downers and cocaine, and I smoked a lot of marijuana cigarettes. It started as a social thing, but after a while being high became the reality. Soon, baseball was the only thing left.

"I guess I was schizoid. Baseball was one world and partying was another."

Porter returned to Kansas City once he retired, and despite all indications of turning his life around, he died in 2002 in what an autopsy described as "the toxic effects of cocaine."

### IVIE IN CLASS OF HIS OWN

While Porter and Foote were seen as legitimate major league prospects and went on to lengthy careers, they were definitely considered consolation prizes after Ivie, the big catch in 1970.

Ivie actually had a poor senior season at Decatur's Walker High by batting .258 and hitting only one homer—a sharp drop from his junior year, when he hit .550 with 21 homers—but scouts were so hypnotized by his stellar work behind the plate that they didn't seem to notice.

There was no indication then that he would develop a phobia over such a routine act as returning the ball back to the pitcher, but Cannizzaro's innocent comment hit Ivie like an avalanche. He couldn't shake the perceived slight from the back of his mind, and soon dreaded all notions of catching—something that had come easily and naturally to him almost his entire life. He saw it as his first professional failure.

Ivie caught on a regular basis the better part of his first two seasons in the Padres system, hitting a combined .288 with 18 homers and 87 RBIs. And while he also committed 34 errors—many on errant throws—there were no overt indications of the anguish he was going through, and the Padres had no misgivings over promoting him to the big leagues in September 1971. He more than held his own in six games, hitting .471 while playing flawlessly behind the plate.

But the following spring in big league camp, Ivie would walk away from baseball for the first time. He double-pumped and triple-pumped before returning the ball to the pitcher so frequently during spring training that Padres manager Preston Gomez finally lost patience. "Throw the ball! Throw the ball!" Gomez screamed.

That night, Ivie went home to Georgia. He did not return until six weeks later, and only after

## How They Should Have Done It

Based on the career WAR (Wins Above Replacement, as calculated by Baseball-Reference.com) numbers achieved by all the players eligible for the 1970 draft, here's how the first round should have unfolded. Numbers in parentheses indicate the round when the player was actually drafted

| | Player, Pos. | Actual Draft | WAR | Bonus |
|---|---|---|---|---|
| 1. | Rick Reuschel, rhp | Cubs (3) | 70.0 | $11,000 |
| 2. | Goose Gossage, rhp | White Sox (9) | 42.0 | $8,000 |
| 3. | Doug DeCinces, 3b | Orioles (Jan.-S/3) | 41.6 | $5,000 |
| 4. | Darrell Porter, c | Brewers (1) | 40.8 | $70,000 |
| 5. | Dave Parker, of | Pirates (14) | 40.0 | $6,000 |
| 6. | Bill Madlock, ss/3b | Senators (Jan.-S/5) | 38.0 | $1,000 |
| 7. | Frank White, 2b | Royals (NDFA) | 34.7 | None |
| 8. | John Denny, rhp | Cardinals (29) | 32.4 | $500 |
| 9. | Jim Barr, rhp | Giants (June-S/3) | 31.1 | $10,000 |
| 10. | Chris Speier, ss | Giants (Jan.-S/2) | 30.5 | $10,000 |
| 11. | Chris Chambliss, 1b | Indians (Jan.-R/1) | 27.4 | $25,000 |
| 12. | Rick Burleson, ss | Red Sox (Jan.-S/5) | 22.7 | $26,000 |
| 13. | Bake McBride, of | Cardinals (37) | 22.6 | $2,500 |
| 14. | Terry Forster, lhp | White Sox (2) | 20.7 | $17,500 |
| 15. | Doc Medich, rhp | Yankees (30) | 19.8 | $5,000 |
| 16. | Bill Bonham, rhp | Cubs (NDFA) | 18.6 | $2,000 |
| 17. | Bucky Dent, ss | White Sox (June-S/1) | 17.4 | $12,000 |
| 18. | Dave Kingman, rhp/of | Giants (June-S/1) | 17.3 | $80,000 |
| 19. | Rick Waits, lhp | Senators (5) | 14.7 | $12,000 |
| 20. | Bill Campbell, rhp | Twins (NDFA) | 13.1 | $1,000 |
| | Ray Knight, 3b | Reds (10) | 13.1 | None |
| 22. | Greg Gross, of | Astros (4) | 12.8 | $14,000 |
| 23. | Dan Ford, of | Athletics (1) | 11.8 | $29,500 |
| 24. | Lenny Randle, 2b | Senators (June-S/1) | 11.5 | $20,000 |

| Top 3 Unsigned Players | | | | Year Signed |
|---|---|---|---|---|
| 1. | Fred Lynn, of | Yankees (3) | 49.9 | 1973 |
| 2. | Phil Garner, 2b | Expos (8) | 29.7 | 1971 |
| 3. | Roy Smalley, ss | Expos (35) | 27.8 | 1974 |

the organization agreed to let him play first base at Double-A Alexandria. Ivie had a fine 1972 season (.291 with 24 home runs) and was invited to join the Padres in September—as a catcher. He declined.

Bill Ivie later remembered finding a notepad in his son's room, after Mike had left for spring training in 1972. On the pad was an outline of a baseball diamond with a straight line drawn from the catcher to the pitcher. Underneath, Mike had written, "I can do it, I can do it, I can do it."

Ivie quit again in 1973, just before the Hawaii Islanders, San Diego's Triple-A affiliate, were to start a 26-game road trip in June. Ivie also dreaded air travel, and he said the thought of that much time in an airplane was more than he could bear. He sat out the rest of the season and was coaxed into returning in 1974 and saw some brief, late-season action in San Diego.

In 1975, Ivie finally made the Padres for good. He would catch in only three games in the next three years before being traded to San Francisco before the 1978 season. He caught his last game on July 5, 1976, in Chicago.

"He stepped back there and played like he'd never been away," Fontaine said. "The Cubs won the game when a guy stole second and went to third because Ivie's throw went into center field. The second baseman didn't cover, but Mike still blamed himself. He said, 'Never again.' "

Ivie's career then took him to Houston and Detroit, before it all came to an end in 1983. He hit .269 with 81 homers and 411 RBIs over 11 seasons, but his legacy is one of the biggest disappointments of the draft era.

As the first overall pick in the 1970 draft, Ivie was the center of attention. He admitted that he tried to play up to everyone's expectations—both in high school and professional baseball. When he didn't, it proved to be his downfall.

"I was the No. 1 draft choice," he said. "I set certain standards for the No. 1 choice and I didn't think I was living up to them. As a No. 1 draft choice, I thought I was supposed to be perfect—hit a home run every time up and throw out everybody who tried to steal. I wasn't doing that so I thought I was failing."

"In my 40 years in the game, I would have to say Ivie is the biggest disappointment I've had," said Buzzie Bavasi, the Padres general manager in the early 70s. "He could have been one of the greatest catchers of all time. That's why I say if a scout could tell what was inside the young man, the scout would be worth a million dollars a year. But you never know."

## Fastest To The Majors

| | Player, Pos. | Drafted (Round) | Debut |
|---|---|---|---|
| 1. | # Steve Dunning, rhp | Indians (1) | June 14, 1970 |
| 2. | Chris Speier, ss | Giants (Jan.-S/1) | April 7, 1971 |
| | Lee Richard, ss | White Sox (1) | April 7, 1971 |
| 4. | * Terry Forster, lhp | White Sox (2) | April 11, 1971 |
| 5. | Chris Chambliss, 1b | Indians (Jan.-R/1) | May 28, 1971 |

**LAST PLAYER TO RETIRE:** Goose Gossage, rhp (Aug. 8, 1994)

*#Debuted in major leagues. *High school selection.*

## DRAFT SPOTLIGHT: DAVE KINGMAN

CREDIT CREDIT

Dave Kingman was a standout two-way player at Southern California

Mike Ivie was the No. 1 pick in the 1970 draft, but had he been eligible, University of Southern California slugger Dave Kingman would have given Ivie a run for his money.

As it was, the San Francisco Giants were happy to get Kingman with the top pick in the secondary phase, and signed him for $80,000—$5,000 more than Ivie received.

Because the towering Kingman had been drafted twice and wasn't eligible for the regular phase of the draft, it has been lost in history somewhat what kind of a prospect he was coming out of USC—as both a hitter and pitcher.

Kingman became one of the most prodigious sluggers in major league history, hitting 442 homers in 16 seasons. But he was known primarily as a pitcher when he arrived at USC in 1969 after a year at an Illinois junior college, and went 11-4, 1.38 as a sophomore. He may have lacked command, but scouts were intrigued with his long, powerful frame and superior velocity.

"He was absolutely a major league prospect as a pitcher," said Rod Dedeaux, Kingman's coach at USC. "He had an outstanding curveball and a wicked slider. His fastball was in the 90s and he loved to pitch."

The 6-foot-6, 210-pound Kingman also belted four home runs and drove in 16 runs for the Trojans in 1969—in 32 at-bats. That summer, he played several games in the outfield for the Alaska Goldpanners, while also doubling as one of the team's top pitchers, and hit seven more homers, including some tape-measure shots.

Soon thereafter, the Big Switch was on. It had become so apparent to Dedeaux that Kingman's bat should be in the lineup on an everyday basis that he converted Kingman to a full-time outfielder—over Kingman's objections. Kingman responded by hitting .417 with 12 doubles, eight homers and 25 RBIs in 25 games—not including six extra-base hits in three exhibition games against the Los Angeles Dodgers early in the spring—but missed half the season after breaking his arm and tearing knee ligaments in a collision with another player. Kingman didn't pitch an inning in 1970 for the Trojans, who were on their way to the first of five consecutive College World Series championships.

Scouts were quick to hail him as the best power-hitting prospect in the 1970 draft, and Kingman was even being compared by some to Babe Ruth for his two-way exploits.

Upon signing with the Giants, Kingman hit 15 homers in 60 games for Double-A Amarillo in his first extended test as a hitter, then belted another 26 in 105 games for Triple-A Phoenix in 1971. From that point on, Kingman was in the big leagues.

"He's one of the strongest men I've ever seen," said Phoenix general manager Rosy Ryan. "He has a chance of becoming one of the game's greatest sluggers."

Ryan was a former roommate of Ruth's during a brief big league stint with the New York Yankees, and in 1924 became the first National League pitcher to hit a home run in World Series competition.

Dedeaux, who coached for 42 years at USC, rated Kingman the best power hitter who ever played for him. "He had outstanding power," Dedeaux said. "Nobody who played here had as much, and we've had some other good ones in Mark McGwire and Dave Hostetler. Reggie Jackson once asked me if I had ever seen anybody with as much power in college as him and I told him Kingman had.

"The thing we have to be thankful for was that there was no designated hitter rule at the time, so everybody had to hit. Dave showed he had the power to hit the ball a long way. He certainly was not a polished hitter, but showed he could hit it a long way."

## WORTH NOTING

■ College World Series champion Southern California had more players drafted in June than any four-year college, but the five Trojans selections marked the fewest number ever for the school with the most picks in a single draft. A greater focus was placed on the junior-college ranks in 1970, and Florida's Miami-Dade North Community College had the most players drafted in both January (12) and June (six). The 12 January selections were a record that would last until Sacramento (Calif.) City College had 13 players drafted in 1983.

■ The June 1970 draft was conducted while Curt Flood's $3 million lawsuit against Major League Baseball, challenging the game's reserve clause, was still making its way through the court system. Had Flood, the former Cardinals outfielder who was traded against his will following the 1969 season and sat out 1970, won his suit, it likely would have rendered all future drafts illegal. Flood lost his case, thus preserving baseball's anti-trust exemption and the ability of baseball (and other sports) to control the way players enter the sport.

■ The Dodgers raised eyebrows by taking a stab at running back **MIKE GARRETT** of the Super Bowl champion Kansas City Chiefs. Garrett, the 1965 Heisman Trophy winner who was also drafted by the Dodgers in 1966, was in the final year of a five-year pact with the Chiefs. "I intend to play baseball and will negotiate with the Los Angeles Dodgers," said the 26-year-old Garrett, who had maintained throughout his career that he wanted to give baseball a try once his football contract ran out. Garrett had played baseball in college while at USC, but negotiations with the Dodgers never materialized. He remained with the Chiefs.

■ The Pirates drafted the most players in both January (37) and June (65). None of the 28 players the Pirates

## PADRES CONSIDERED LOCAL PRODUCT

Peter Bavasi, San Diego's director of minor league operations, said the Padres narrowed their choice for the No. 1 pick in the June regular phase down to Ivie and Stanford pitcher Steve Dunning.

"Dunning is a hometown boy from San Diego and we took that into consideration," Bavasi said. "But we decided that for the long run, Ivie would suit our needs best."

Had he been eligible for the June regular phase, University of Southern California slugging outfielder Dave Kingman almost certainly would have been in the discussion as well. But because he had previously been drafted, the 6-foot-6 Kingman was eligible only for the secondary phase, and the San Francisco Giants were happy to snap him up with the top pick. They signed him for an $80,000 bonus, the largest figure in that year's draft.

Dunning went to Cleveland with the second pick, and the Indians were so enthralled that they elected to elevate the hard-throwing righthander to the big leagues 10 days after his selection.

Veteran Indians scout Loyd Christopher called Dunning the best prospect he'd ever signed. "Steve Dunning throws as fast as anybody on the Indians staff except (Sam) McDowell," Christopher said. "And he'll match Sam every once in a while."

CLEVELAND INDIANS

Steve Dunning

As Stanford's ace in the spring of 1970, Dunning electrified scouts by beating No. 1 and eventual College World Series champion USC twice within a seven-day period, 2-1 and 7-2, striking out 17 batters in the first game and 15 in the second. Earlier in the season, he struck out 19 and allowed only a bloop single against Air Force, but lost 2-1 on three ninth-inning errors. Overall, Dunning went 13-2, 1.83, striking out 144 in 108 innings. He was named the college player of the year by The Sporting News.

Dunning went from the Stanford Indians (as they were known then) to the Cleveland Indians in a single jump, moving immediately into the rotation. His arrival in Cleveland was greeted with more fanfare than any pitcher since 1936, when 18-year-old Bob Feller broke in.

Dunning's first start on June 14 attracted a crowd of 25,380 to Cleveland's Municipal Stadium—a significant gathering in 1970. Dunning struck out the first hitter he faced (Tommy Harper), hurled five effective innings and was the winning pitcher in a 9-2 victory over Milwaukee.

"I admitted thinking to myself," he said later, "this isn't so tough. I guess I figured it always would be the way it was that day."

Dunning's best game in the majors came on Opening Day the following year. He threw a one-hitter against Washington, which prompted Senators manager Ted Williams to say that Dunning would be "some kind of pitcher one day."

But that was about as good as it would get for Dunning. Like Ivie, his promising career fell short of expectations. Dunning went 12-23 with Cleveland over his first year and a half and eventually was sent to the minor leagues. By the time he retired in 1979, at age 30, he'd been with eight major league organizations and posted a 23-41 record over seven seasons.

The Indians were convinced when they signed Dunning to a $50,000 bonus that he was ready for the big leagues. He was originally ticketed to open in Triple-A, but Indians manager Alvin Dark got a chance to see Dunning work out and pushed for him to be re-signed to a major league contract. He made his big league debut despite not having pitched in a game in more than a month.

"It wasn't my idea," Dunning said. "That's the way the Indians wanted it."

When later asked if he had experienced too much too soon, Dunning didn't find fault with the Indians.

"No, I don't think I was mishandled," he said in 1973. "I'll never know whether starting out at the top helped me or hindered me. I could have pitched in the minors all three years I've been in pro ball and I still wouldn't know as much as I do now.

"If I had been in the minors all along, I'd probably still be trying to throw my fastball past everybody. I know I can't do that."

Dunning claimed he never lost anything off the fastball that warranted his being the second player selected in the 1970 draft, and blamed his failure on lack of consistency and a quality breaking ball.

"I threw in the high 90s, though they didn't have those sophisticated radar guns they have now," he said. "Back then, it was Sam McDowell and me. They said I was the second-hardest

### Top 25 Bonuses

| | Player, Pos. | Drafted (Round) | Order | Bonus |
|---|---|---|---|---|
| **1.** | **Dave Kingman, rhp/of** | **Giants (June-S/1)** | **(1)** | **$80,000** |
| **2.** | ***Mike Ivie, c** | **Padres (1)** | **1** | **$75,000** |
| **3.** | ***Darrell Porter, c** | **Brewers (1)** | **4** | **$70,000** |
| **4.** | ***Bob Gorinski, ss** | **Twins (1)** | **22** | **$60,000** |
| **5.** | ***Dave Cheadle, lhp** | **Yankees (1)** | **12** | **$57,500** |
| **6.** | ***Greg Terlecky, rhp** | **Cardinals (5)** | **107** | **$55,000** |
| **7.** | **Steve Dunning, rhp** | **Indians (1)** | **2** | **$50,000** |
| **8.** | **Lee Richard, ss** | **White Sox (1)** | **6** | **$46,500** |
| 9. | *Terry Mappin, c | Tigers (1) | 20 | $45,000 |
| **10.** | ***Barry Foote, c** | **Expos (1)** | **3** | **$44,000** |
| 11. | *Jim Haller, rhp | Dodgers (1) | 9 | $42,000 |
| 12. | *Rex Goodson, c/of | Royals (1) | 8 | $40,000 |
| | *Richard Earle, rhp | Yankees (2) | 36 | $40,000 |
| | *Fred Wegner, of | Red Sox (2) | 40 | $40,000 |
| 15. | *John Bedard, rhp | Pirates (1) | 13 | $38,000 |
| 16. | *David Lawson, rhp | Yankees (4) | 84 | $37,000 |
| **17.** | **Gene Hiser, of** | **Cubs (1)** | **19** | **$35,000** |
| 18. | *Chip Maxwell, 3b | Senators (1) | 14 | $32,500 |
| **19.** | ***Chip Lang, rhp** | **Expos (2)** | **27** | **$32,000** |
| **20.** | **Bill Fahey, c** | **Senators (Jan.-S/1)** | **(1)** | **$31,500** |
| **21.** | ***Paul Dade, 3b/of** | **Angels (1)** | **10** | **$30,000** |
| | *Price Thomas, of | Brewers (3) | 52 | $30,000 |
| **23.** | ***Dan Ford, of** | **Athletics (1)** | **18** | **$29,500** |
| 24. | *Mike Martin, lhp | Phillies (1) | 5 | $29,000 |
| 25. | *Charles Ross, lhp | Red Sox (4) | 86 | $28,000 |
| | *Dewey Forry, of | Dodgers (5) | 105 | $28,000 |

*Major leaguers in bold. *High school selection.*

## Largest Bonuses By Round

| | Player, Pos. | Club | Bonus |
|---|---|---|---|
| 1. | ***Mike Ivie, c** | **Padres** | **$75,000** |
| 2. | *Richard Earle, rhp | Yankees | $40,000 |
| | *Fred Wegner, of | Red Sox | $40,000 |
| 3. | *Price Thomas, of | Brewers | $30,000 |
| 4. | *David Lawson, rhp | Yankees | $37,000 |
| 5. | ***Greg Terlecky, rhp** | **Cardinals** | **$55,000** |
| 6. | ***David Downs, rhp** | **Phillies** | **$23,500** |
| 7. | *Dan Field, c | Phillies | $10,000 |
| | ***Don DeMola, rhp** | **Yankees** | **$10,000** |
| 8. | Frank Rossi, 1b | Yankees | $15,000 |
| 9. | ***Phil Mankowski, 3b** | **Tigers** | **$10,000** |
| | ***Joe Gilbert, lhp** | **Expos** | **$10,000** |
| 10. | *Rob Andrews, of | Orioles | $12,000 |
| Jan/R. | *John Klitsner, 1b | Red Sox (1) | $23,000 |
| **Jan/S.** | **Bill Fahey, c** | **Senators (1)** | **$31,500** |
| **Jun/S.** | **Dave Kingman, rhp/of** | **Giants (1)** | **$80,000** |

*Major leaguers in bold. *High school selection.*

thrower in the league. My career was limited because I never had an effective breaking pitch. And to be successful as a starter, you need something in addition to a fastball. I was a one-pitch pitcher most of my career."

Cleveland also had the No. 1 pick that year in the January regular phase, and went for UCLA first baseman Chris Chambliss. He had a highly productive junior season in 1969 for the Bruins, leading the powerful Pacific-8 Conference with 15 home runs, but wasn't eligible for the draft in June because he wouldn't be 21 until December. His only recourse to become eligible for the January 1970 draft was to drop out of school the previous fall.

Chris Chambliss

Chambliss made a name for himself that summer when he teamed with Dunning to lead the semi-pro Anchorage Glacier Pilots, in their first year of existence, to the National Baseball Congress championship. Chambliss was named MVP of the Wichita-based NBC tournament, and oddly, after signing with the Indians for a bonus of $25,000, made his pro debut right back in Wichita in 1970, and won the Triple-A American Association batting title that season with a .342 average.

Chambliss would go on to a productive career in the big leagues, hitting .279 with 185 homers, but enjoy his greatest success with the Yankees and later the Atlanta Braves.

### USC WINS FIRST OF FIVE TITLES

Kingman became the top pick in the secondary phase in June, even as he missed half the 1970 season with a broken arm and torn knee ligaments, sustained in an outfield collision with another USC player. He was relatively new to his role as an everyday player after being primarily a pitcher prior to his junior season with the Trojans, but Kingman hit .417 with eight homers in 25 games, and that was enough for the Giants to jump on him with the No. 1 pick in the secondary phase.

Even as Kingman didn't pitch an inning for USC in 1970, the Trojans went on to win the first of five consecutive College World Series titles. They got maximum mileage out of lefthander Brent Strom (13-1, 2.26), who was selected third overall in the secondary phase in June by the New York Mets, and righthander Jim Barr (14-2), who like Kingman was also drafted by the Giants.

Barr made a pair of prolonged relief appearances at the CWS for the victorious Trojans, beating Texas, 8-7, in 14 innings and Florida State, 2-1, in 15 innings in the championship game. In all, he worked 16 innings in the two contests.

MVP honors at Omaha, though, went to Florida State ace Gene Ammann, who allowed two runs in 18 innings. Ammann, drafted in the third round (secondary phase) by Milwaukee, went 15-0, 0.66, striking out 150 in 137 innings. His college success never translated into an appearance in the big leagues.

USC went a long way toward sustaining its superiority at the college level by landing a pair of unsigned first-round picks from the 1970 draft in righthander Randy Scarbery (Astros) and shortstop George Ambrow (Mets). The Trojans added to their recruiting haul by nabbing outfielder Fred Lynn, picked in the third round by the Yankees. Unlike Scarbery and Lynn, who both became prominent picks in the 1973 draft after three college seasons at USC, Ambrow's career never materialized, and he never even played the game professionally.

The unfulfilled careers of Ivie (because of performance) and Ambrow (because of injury) set the tone for the first round of the 1970 draft—one of the weakest in draft history. Only Porter had a career worthy of being taken in the first round, though outfielder Dan Ford (Athletics), who was selected with the 18th pick, had a representative career. A third first-rounder, in addition to Scarbery and Ambrow, also went unsigned as the Red Sox failed to sway shortstop Jimmie Hacker, the 16th pick overall, from attending Texas A&M.

Only four pitchers taken in the first round went on to work in the majors, and they all had losing records while going a combined 60-103. The biggest winner of the bunch was righthander John

## One Team's Draft: Chicago White Sox

| | Player, Pos. | Round |
|---|---|---|
| 1. | **Lee "Bee Bee" Richard, ss** | **$46,500** |
| 2. | ***Terry Forster, lhp** | **$17,500** |
| 3. | ***Jerry Hairston, of** | **$10,000** |
| 4. | *Harold McClain, lhp | $14,000 |
| 5. | *Dale Lydecker, of | Did not sign |
| 6. | **Jim Geddes, rhp** | **$13,000** |
| 7. | *Dennis Weidman, of | $5,000 |
| 8. | Steve Foran, lhp | Did not sign |
| 9. | ***Rich "Goose" Gossage, rhp** | **$8,000** |
| 10. | *Lyn Hamilton, c | Did not sign |
| **Other** | ***Bucky Dent (S/1), ss** | **$12,000** |

*Major leaguers in bold. *High school selection.*

## WORTH NOTING

selected in the January regular phase would play in the big leagues, however, and only two of their 102 picks overall saw service in Pittsburgh.

■ Despite selecting a record 357 players overall in the January draft, held again at the Americana Hotel in New York, major league owners decided that all January drafts in the future would be conducted via a conference call originating from the commissioner's office. The status quo would hold for June, but within three years that phase would also be staged by a conference-call arrangement.

■ The player's name was never made public, but one of the selections in the January draft in 1970 was of a player who had died in a car accident a week before the draft. The selection was voided.

■ A team other than a major league club participated in the baseball draft for the first time in 1970. The Bend Rainbows, a member of the short-season Class A Northwest League, were entitled to make selections on behalf of the Hawaii Islanders of the Triple-A Pacific Coast League, because the Rainbows had a partial working agreement with the Islanders. "Hawaii is going to develop its own farm system, and Bend is the first team in the system," explained Northwest League president John Carbray, who made the selections on Bend's behalf. "Hawaii is projecting five years ahead when it hopes to get a major league franchise." Bend picked three players in January and seven in June, but was not permitted to select until the fourth round (technically, the Class A round) of any phase. Independent minor league clubs had the right to select amateur players from the outset of the draft in 1965, but the practice happened only on rare occasions through the years before being banned altogether nearly 40 years later.

**IN FOCUS: GEORGE AMBROW**

Southern California won the first of five consecutive College World Series titles in 1970, then capitalized on their success by securing a pair of unsigned first-round picks from the 1970 draft in righthander Randy Scarbery (Astros) and shortstop George Ambrow (Mets). While Scarbery became a first-round pick again three years later, Ambrow never played the game professionally.

Fresh out of a Long Beach, Calif., high school, Ambrow hit .314 with three homers, 12 doubles and five triples as the shortstop for USC's 1971 national championship team.

"He had everything," USC coach Rod Dedeaux said. "He had great speed, could field the ball, could hit and had an outstanding arm."

Then, his knees went. Ambrow had operations on both knees following the 1971 season and never played again. Though he was drafted again with a token 18th-round pick in 1974 by the California Angels, Ambrow became one of six first-round draft picks to never play a professional baseball game.

"I think he had five knee operations all together," Dedeaux said. "They came to find out later it was probably a genetic thing, but the injuries were probably brought on by athletics. It was really disappointing, especially for a kid like him. He had such great desire and was such a great prospect, but he just had a defect in his knees."

D'Acquisto (Giants), who went 34-51, 4.56 in 10 seasons for eight different teams, despite being one of the hardest throwers in the big leagues in the 1970s. His blazing fastball was often included in the same class as Hall of Famer Nolan Ryan's.

D'Acquisto hung it up in 1983 after undergoing arm surgery, but he was back in the news a decade later when he served time in jail for his part in a fraud and money-laundering scheme.

For the most part, the best talent in the 1970 draft wasn't apparent or fully appreciated at the time. Two future Hall of Famers came from the class—both mid- to late-round, high school righthanders who would make their mark as relief pitchers.

Rich "Goose" Gossage was selected by the Chicago White Sox in the ninth round, and signed for a bonus of just $8,000. Bruce Sutter went in the 21st round to the Washington Senators, who made little effort to sign him. Sutter enrolled in college at Old Dominion, but soon dropped out and signed in 1971 as a nondrafted free agent with the Chicago Cubs for $500.

In the early 1970s, it was uncommon for major league teams to cast young, hard throwers in the role of a closer. That position was generally earmarked for veteran pitchers on the decline. All that changed in 1972 with the emergence in Chicago of two young relief artists. White Sox manager Chuck Tanner gambled that Terry Forster, the club's second-round pick in 1970, and Gossage, both 20, could hold up his bullpen as his team chased Oakland for the American League West title.

They did. The White Sox won 87 games as Forster, a lefthander, posted a 6-5, 2.25 record with 29 saves (second in the league), while Gossage went 7-1, 4.28 in a set-up role.

"They were the best young relief pitching tandem I've ever seen in baseball," said veteran front-office executive Roland Hemond, then Chicago's farm director.

Not only were Forster and Gossage both 1970 draft picks, but they enjoyed remarkably similar careers. They both jumped to the big leagues from Class A ball—Forster at 19, Gossage at 20—and became starters for the only times in their careers with the White Sox in 1976, after which they were packaged in a trade for outfielder Richie Zisk and went to the Pirates.

Both were also granted free agency following the 1977 season. Within a day of each other, they went their separate ways—Gossage to the Yankees, Forster to the Dodgers—only to hook up against one another in the 1978 World Series.

In 16 major league seasons, Forster pitched in 614 games. Gossage appeared in 1,002 contests in 22 years, and separated himself later in his career with his dominance in a long relief role, which resulted in 124 wins and 310 saves, and led to his selection to the Hall of Fame.

The Pirates struggled to make sense of the 1970 draft, as they selected 37 players in January and not a future big leaguer among them. They also didn't sign a future big leaguer in the June regular phase through 13 rounds. Yet they still benefited from two of the best players in that year's draft, outfielder Dave Parker and third baseman Bill Madlock, who went on to win six National League batting championships between them.

Parker, a physically imposing Cincinnati high school product, lasted until the 14th round because of concerns over a knee injury he sustained while playing football in his senior year. The Pirates took a chance and signed him for $6,000, and were almost immediately rewarded when the 6-foot-5 Parker quickly blossomed into one of the game's top prospects and won back-to-back batting crowns with a .338 average in 1977 and .334 mark in 1978.

Though he didn't sign with the Pirates originally, Madlock was a product of the 1970 draft as he was taken with a fifth-round pick in the January regular phase by the Senators out of an Iowa junior college. Prior to being acquired by Pittsburgh in 1979 in a midseason, six-player deal with the Giants, Madlock had already won two NL batting titles. He subsequently won two more in a Pirates uniform—at .341 in 1981 and .323 in 1983.

Goose Gossage symbolized some of the unappreciated talent in the 1970 draft class, as a ninth-round pick who reached the Hall of Fame

## Highest Unsigned Picks

**JUNE/REGULAR PHASE ONLY**

| Player, Pos., Team (Round) | College | Re-Drafted |
|---|---|---|
| Randy Scarbery, rhp, Astros (1) | USC | Athletics '73 (1) |
| Jimmie Hacker, 3b, Red Sox (1) | Texas A&M | Braves '74 (5) |
| George Ambrow, ss, Mets (1) | USC | Angels '74 (Jan.-S/18) |
| Ken Pape, ss, Brewers (2) | Texas | Rangers '73 (5) |
| Roger Choate, c, Phillies (2) | South Carolina | Never |
| Dale Holland, 2b, Athletics (2) | Mississippi State | Never |
| Mike Ibarguen, rhp, Tigers (2) | San Jacinto (Texas) JC | Jan. '71 (Jan.-S/1) |
| Gary Nevinger, rhp, Mets (2) | Georgia | Mets '73 (3) |
| Fred Lynn, of, Yankees (3) | USC | Red Sox '73 (2) |
| Steve Baumiller, rhp, Senators (3) | Florida Southern | Indians '73 (16) |

**TOTAL UNSIGNED PICKS:** Top 5 Rounds (23), Top 10 Rounds (53)

# 1970 Draft List

**Did not sign. Major leaguers in bold, with first and last years noted. Order of selection indicated in parentheses. For the first five rounds of the June Regular Phase and the first round of all other phases, the peak level of each player is noted.*

## ATLANTA BRAVES

### January—Regular Phase (22)

1. *Curran Percival, rhp, San Diego Mesa JC.—(AAA)
2. **Jack Pierce, 1b, San Jose (Calif.) CC.—(1973-75)**
3. *William Collins, rhp, Manatee (Fla.) JC.
4. *Willie Harper, rhp, Douglasville, Ga.
5. Ray McGhee, 2b, Jersey City, N.J.
6. *Pat Cech, rhp, Glendale (Ariz.) CC.

### January—Secondary Phase (20)

1. *Dennis Loewe, rhp, Pershing (Neb.) College.—(Short-season A)
2. *Ronald Dolan, of-3b, Seton Hall University.
3. *Steve Steitz, 3b, Springfield (Mass.) University.
4. Sigmund Gancasz, c, Queensborough (N.Y.) CC.
5. *Ken Wamble, 3b, Lamar University.

### June—Regular Phase (21)

1. Ron Broaddus, rhp, Brazosport HS, Freeport, Texas.—(High A)
2. **Adrian Devine, rhp, Ball HS, Galveston, Texas.—(1973-80)**
3. **Rod Gilbreath, ss-rhp, R.H. Watkins HS, Laurel, Miss.—(1972-78)**
4. **Rowland Office, of, McClatchy HS, Sacramento, Calif.—(1972-83)**
5. *James Summers, rhp, Memorial HS, Tulsa, Okla.—DNP

DRAFT DROP *No school; never re-drafted*

6. *William Lawrence, rhp, Ramsey HS, Birmingham, Ala.
7. Michael Knox, rhp, West Waterloo (Iowa) HS.
8. *Andy Johnson, ss, Athens (Ga.) HS.

DRAFT DROP *Running back, National Football League (1974-81)*

9. David Bogacki, lhp, New Jersey HS, Woodbury, N.J.
10. *Jerry Simmons, lhp, Webster HS, Tulsa, Okla.
11. *William Griffith, 1b, Wade Hampton HS, Greenville, S.C.
12. *Gary Knuckles, 3b, Richmond (Calif.) HS.
13. Lendon Brookins, 3b, Texas Southern University.
14. *Merle Jordan, lhp-of, Roseville (Calif.) HS.
15. Wallace Jones, rhp, University of Tampa.
16. *Gary Cavallo, rhp, Seton Hall University.
17. *Ronald Robinson, ss-rhp, St. Augustine HS, New Orleans, La.
18. Perry Chapple, rhp, E.B. Erwin HS, Center Point, Ala.
19. Thomas Watson, rhp-of, Deering HS, Portland, Maine.
20. *Ray Huard, inf, Princeton University.
21. Scotty Selph, c, Robert E. Lee HS, Montgomery, Ala.
22. *George Howay, lhp, Imbay (Mich.) HS.
23. *Gaylin Papst, ss-of, Danville (Ill.) HS.
24. Wilson Stallworth, rhp, North Carolina A&T University.
25. Terry Smythe, rhp, North Torrance (Calif.) HS.
26. *Gary Ellefson, rhp-inf, Dell Rapids (S.D.) HS.
27. Glenn Landesberg, lhp, University of Bridgeport (Conn.).
28. *Lyman Willis, rhp, North Hampton HS, Eastville, Va.
29. *Michael Morrison, ss, Sam Houston HS, San Antonio, Texas.
30. *Mike Dorn, lhp, Corinth (Miss.) HS.

### June—Secondary Phase (13)

1. *Billy Hodge, c, Texas A&M University.—(AAA)
2. *Robert Jones, of, Amherst (Mass.) College.
3. ***Johnny Grubb, of, Florida State University.—(1972-87)**
4. *Keith Lieppman, 3b, University of Kansas.

## BALTIMORE ORIOLES

### January—Regular Phase (23)

1. William Seltzer, c, Hagerstown (Md.) JC.—(High A)
2. Nathaniel Turner, 3b, Southside HS, Effingham, S.C.
3. Terrence Jones, of, Lower Columbia (Wash.) JC.
4. *Gerald Tassa, lhp, Wingate (N.C.) College.
5. *Gerard Fell, of-1b, CC of Baltimore.
6. *William Cameron, of, Gulf Coast (Fla.) CC.
7. *William Pierce, lhp, Glassboro (N.J.) HS.
8. *John Stenglein, of-1b, Miami-Dade CC North.
9. Lynn Murdock, of, Tarrant County (Texas) JC.
10. *Bruce Mierkowicz, 1b, St. Clair County (Mich.) CC.
11. Ronald Kavanaugh, lhp, Panhandle State (Okla.) University.
12. Michael Pittruzello, of, Central Connecticut State University.

### January—Secondary Phase (17)

1. **Mike Reinbach, of, UCLA.—(1974)**
2. **Jim Fuller, 1b, San Diego Mesa JC.—(1973-77)**
3. **Doug DeCinces, 3b, Los Angeles Pierce JC.—(1973-87)**
4. *Mike Cuozzi, 2b-of, Trenton State (N.J.) College.
5. Robert McConnaughy, ss, West Liberty State (W.Va.) College.
6. James Juniel, of, Contra Costa (Calif.) JC.
7. (void) *Jay Smith, rhp, Treasure Island, Fla.
8. (void) *Dan Pritchett, of, El Camino (Calif.) JC.
9. Gerald Bryant, lhp, Madison Heights, Va.

### June—Regular Phase (24)

1. James West, c, Vashon HS, St. Louis.—(High A)
2. Michael Satterlee, c, Roosevelt HS, Portland, Ore.—(AA)
3. Edward Blake, rhp, Assumption HS, East St. Louis, Ill.—(AA)

DRAFT DROP *Son of Ed Blake, major leaguer (1951-57)*

4. Dan Beerbower, 3b, Taft (Calif.) HS.—(AA)
5. Edward House, lhp, Parker HS, Birmingham, Ala.—(High A)
6. ***Ron Hodges, c, Appalachian State University.—(1973-84)**
7. Don Hickey, c-ss, High Point College.
8. Anthony Leopaldi, of, Bloomfield (N.J.) HS.
9. **Tim Nordbrook, ss, Loyola (Md.) College.—(1974-79)**
10. **Rob Andrews, of, South Torrance (Calif.) HS.—(1975-79)**
11. Sylvester Caudle, of, Dorsey HS, Los Angeles.
12. **Herb Hutson, rhp, Georgia Southern College.—(1974)**
13. George Underwood, rhp, Logan (W.Va.) HS.
14. Olen Bartley, ss, Artesia HS, Lakewood, Calif.
15. Randy Lee, lhp, Laurel (Del.) HS.
16. *Robert Loughery, rhp, Northeast HS, Pasadena, Md.
17. *Jacky Akin, 1b, Panola (Texas) JC.
18. Michael Ivancin, lhp, Bishop Barry HS, St. Petersburg, Fla.
19. *Huntington Batjer, lhp, Central HS, San Angelo, Texas.
20. *Casey Ortez, of, Stagg HS, Stockton, Calif.
21. *Oren Myers, 1b, R.H. Watkins HS, Laurel, Miss.
22. *Steven Prestridge, rhp, Central HS, Jackson, Miss.
23. Hugh Platt, c, La Puente (Calif.) HS.
24. *Floyd Hartley, 2b, CC of Baltimore.
25. *Ronald Hancock, of, Cocoa (Fla.) HS.
26. *George Boggan, lhp, Calloway HS, Jackson, Miss.
27. James Blackwood, 2b, Pfeiffer (N.C.) College.
28. *Tom Seybold, lhp, University of Florida.
29. ***Bobby Myrick, lhp, Blair HS, Hattiesburg, Miss.—(1976-78)**
30. *John Jeter, of, Spingarn HS, Washington, D.C.
31. *Gary Boyajian, rhp, River Dell HS, River Edge, N.J.
32. *Reginald Leonard, of, Princeton HS, Cincinnati.
33. *Gary Brown, rhp, Elon College.
34. Douglas Felderman, c, North Torrance HS, Torrance, Calif.
35. Ross Miller, rhp, University of Wyoming.
36. Martin Pfenninger, ss, Temple University.
37. *Darrell Devitt, rhp, Billings, Mon.
38. Rich May, 1b, SUNY-Buffalo.
39. Peter Miller, ss, Grand Rapids (Mich.) JC.
40. *Dan Parma, of, Kennedy HS, Buena Park, Calif.
41. *Randolph Delerio, c, Dos Palos (Calif.) HS.
42. *Michael Ginocchio, rhp, Santa Monica HS, Los Angeles.
43. *John Marzulla, rhp-1b, Belmar HS, Spring Lake, N.J.
44. *Preston Douglas, of, Pembroke State (N.C.) University.
45. *Al Ryan, 2b, Gulf Coast (Fla.) CC.

DRAFT DROP *Son of Connie Ryan, major leaguer (1942-54)*

46. *Robert Cobb, rhp, Fresno (Calif.) CC.
47. *Guy Robinette, 3b, Jefferson HS, Roanoke, Va.
48. James Fields, of, Georgia Southern College.
49. *Ricardo Urbano, lhp, Los Gatos (Calif.) HS.
50. *Daniel Ferguson, c, Sahuaro HS, Tucson, Ariz.
51. *Thomas Melson, ss, Lakewood (Colo.) HS.
52. *Michael Buchelman, ss, Wilcox HS, Santa Clara, Calif.
53. *David Ellis, of, New London (Conn.) HS.
54. *Michael Rzepiennik, rhp, Dundalk HS, Baltimore.
55. ***Mike Bacsik, rhp, Bishop Dunne HS, Dallas.—(1975-80)**

DRAFT DROP *Father of Mike Bacsik, major leaguer (2001-05)*

56. Greg Montgomery, c, Lincoln HS, Denver.
57. Donald Belluomini, lhp, JC of San Mateo (Calif.).

### June—Secondary Phase (24)

1. Claude Renfro, rhp-1b, Gulf Coast (Fla.) CC.—(AA)
2. William Wood, c, Los Angeles Valley JC.
3. *Michael Cuozzi, 2b-of, Trenton State (N.J.) College.
4. *Rich Fillings, lhp, Indian River (Fla.) CC.
5. *John Librandi, of, Manatee (Fla.) JC.
6. *Rick Eisenacher, rhp, Auburn University.
7. Gene Salmon, 1b, University of Texas.
8. *Gerard Fell, 1b-c, CC of Baltimore.
9. *Kevin Bryant, 2b, Valencia (Fla.) CC.
10. *Phil Still, 3b, Mississippi State University.

## BOSTON RED SOX

### January—Regular Phase (15)

1. John Klitsner, 1b, Birmingham HS, Encino, Calif.—(AA)
2. Wayne Milam, rhp, Broward (Fla.) CC.
3. Steve Miller, c, University of Virginia.
4. *Larry Patton, of-lhp, Columbia State (Tenn.) CC.
5. *James Paul, rhp, Henry Ford (Mich.) CC.
6. Shawn Harris, rhp, Johnson & Wales (R.I.) JC.
7. James Jackson, rhp, Fullerton (Calif.) JC.

### January—Secondary Phase (5)

1. **Rick Burleson, ss, Warren HS, South Gate, Calif.—(1974-87)**
2. *Robert Perkins, lhp, Manatee (Fla.) JC.
3. Harry Chapman, rhp, Sarasota (Fla.) HS.
4. *Edgar Bellamy, 2b, Fort Cobb (Okla.) HS.
5. *Donald Rhoton, ss, Columbia State (Tenn.) CC.

### June—Regular Phase (16)

1. *Jimmie Hacker, 3b, Temple (Texas) HS.—(AA)

DRAFT DROP *Attended Texas A&M; re-drafted by Braves, 1974 (5th round)*

2. Fred Wegner, of, Fresno (Calif.) HS.—(High A)
3. *John Schmidt, 3b-rhp, Lutheran HS, Denver.—DNP

DRAFT DROP *Attended Colorado; never re-drafted*

4. Chuck Ross, lhp, Woodrow Wilson HS, Long Beach, Calif.—(AAA)
5. Donald Dudley, rhp, St. Joseph Central HS, St. Joseph, Mo.—(High A)
6. Tom Jones, rhp, Carson-Newman (Tenn.) College.
7. Jerry Spencer, rhp, East Central (Miss.) JC.
8. Keith Durant, of-rhp, Rippowam HS, Stamford, Conn.
9. Kenneth Watkins, rhp, Southwest Missouri State University.
10. Michael Mooney, c, Cardinal Dougherty HS, Buffalo, N.Y.
11. Ramsey Koschak, of, Central HS, San Angelo, Texas.
12. *John Binks, lhp, Forest Park HS, Beaumont, Texas.
13. **Tim Blackwell, 3b-c, Crawford HS, San Diego.—(1974-83)**
14. Leo Veleas, of, University of New Haven.
15. Peter Peckham, lhp, Mount Pleasant HS, Providence, R.I.
16. Anthony McLin, of, Stillman (Ala.) College.
17. William Kouns, rhp, William Carey (Miss.) College.
18. Jack Wick, ss, San Pedro (Calif.) HS.
19. *Bruce Kombrinck, p, Gulf Coast (Fla.) CC.
20. Robert Caballero, of, Loyola (La.) University.
21. *Kenneth Kollmyer, rhp, Hoover HS, San Diego.
22. Karl King, rhp-of, Ansonia (Conn.) HS.
23. Chad Nielsen, 1b, Ogden (Utah) HS.
24. *Jerry DeWitt, rhp-of, El Dorado HS, Orange, Calif.
25. Dave Barton, 1b, Costa Mesa HS, Santa Ana, Calif.
26. Dick Nichols, 2b, Florida State University.
27. (void) *George Maldonado, of, University of Nevada-Reno.
28. *James Duckhorn, of, Reedley (Calif.) JC.
29. John Sinclair, of, Husson (Maine) College.
30. *Frank Johnstone, p, Alvin (Texas) HS.

### June—Secondary Phase (14)

1. **John LaRose, lhp, Cumberland (R.I.) HS.—(1978)**
2. *Dave Elmendorf, of, Texas A&M University.

DRAFT DROP *Defensive back, National Football League (1971-79)*

3. Larry O'Brien, 1b-of, Long Beach (Calif.) CC.
4. Alan Jackson, lhp, Northeastern University.
5. *Charles Bates, 3b-ss, Los Angeles CC.

DRAFT DROP *First-round draft pick (19th overall), Tigers (1973).*

## CALIFORNIA ANGELS

### January—Regular Phase (9)

1. *Paul Sands, rhp, Lakewood (Calif.) HS.—(AA)
2. **Morris Nettles, of, Venice (Calif.) HS.—(1974-75)**
3. (void) *Jim Chapman, ss, Columbia Basin (Wash.) CC.
4. *Thomas Williams, of, Solano (Calif.) CC.
5. Albert Borchetta, lhp, Greenwich, Conn.
6. *Alan Gomez, ss, Foothill (Calif.) JC.
7. *Jerry Reasonover, 2b, Gulf Coast (Fla.) CC.
8. John Clear, 1b-of, Los Angeles Harbor JC.

### January—Secondary Phase (7)

1. **John Doherty, of, Reading, Mass.—(1974-75)**
2. *Gary Granville, of, El Camino (Calif.) JC.
3. *Robert Beyn, rhp, Taft (Calif.) JC.
4. *Sherwood Hahn, 1b-of, Virginia Tech.
5. Thomas Lundgren, lhp, University of Missouri.
6. *Walt Sumner, of, Florida State University.

DRAFT DROP *Defensive back, National Football League (1969-74)*

7. Darrell Darrow, 2b, Long Beach (Calif.) CC.

### June—Regular Phase (10)

1. **Paul Dade, 3b-of, Nathan Hale HS, Seattle.—(1975-80)**
2. **Dan Briggs, lhp-1b, Sonoma (Calif.) HS.—(1975-82)**
3. Gary Talley, lhp, South Garland (Texas) HS.—(High A)
4. *David Freeborn, ss, Shafter HS, Buttonwillow, Calif.—(High A)

DRAFT DROP *No school; re-drafted by Dodgers, January 1971/secondary phase (2nd round)*

5. **John Balaz, of, San Diego CC.—(1974-75)**
6. Michael Browne, rhp, Sterling HS, Houston.
7. **Dick Lange, rhp, Central Michigan University.—(1972-75)**
8. **Doug Howard, 1b, Brigham Young University.—(1972-76)**
9. *Brad Duncan, rhp, El Camino HS, Sacramento, Calif.
10. *Allen Baker, c, Erwin HS, Birmingham, Ala.
11. *Gene Delyon, 3b, Los Altos (Calif.) HS.
12. Ronald Marquez, of-ss, Lakewood (Calif.) HS.
13. William Rothan, rhp, Western Hills HS, Cincinnati.
14. Richard Case, rhp, Park Ridge (N.J.) HS.
15. ***Steve Stroughter, of, Redwood HS, Visalia, Calif.—(1982)**
16. Antonio Barbosa, lhp, University of Texas-Pan American.
17. *John C. Bush, rhp, San Gabriel (Calif.) HS.

**18. *Michael Edwards, ss, Jefferson HS, Los Angeles.—(317)**
DRAFT DROP *Twin brother of Marshall Edwards, major leaguer (1977-80) • Brother of Dave Edwards, major leaguer (1978-82)*
19. *Mark Robinson, rhp, Key West (Fla.) HS.
20. Brian Woodward, rhp, Woodland (Wash.) HS.
21. Robert Groth, of, Fresno State University.
22. *Walt Kaczmarek, rhp, Santa Clara (Calif.) HS.
23. *John S. Bush, of, Central HS, Miami.
**24. Sid Monge, lhp, Brawley (Calif.) HS.—(1975-84)**
25. *Dennis Nadeau, ss, Alvirne HS, Hudson, N.H.
26. *Ray Hall, ss-2b, Roosevelt HS, Fresno, Calif.
27. *Richard Hennes, of, Huntington Park (Calif.) HS.
28. Laron Matlock, of, Ventura (Calif.) JC.
29. Willie Goldwire, c, John F. Kennedy HS, Riviera Beach, Fla.
30. *Everett Turner, of, San Lorenzo (Calif.) HS.
31. *Patrick Daniels, lhp, University of Idaho.
**32. *Mike Krukow, c-rhp, San Gabriel (Calif.) HS.—(1976-89)**
33. *Walt Sweeney, lhp, Petaluma (Calif.) HS.
34. Bob Johnson, rhp, Cal State Northridge.
35. *Dana Dismukes, rhp, Foothill (Calif.) JC.
36. (void) *Richard Adkins, rhp, MacArthur HS, Pasadena, Texas.
37. *Dennis Palla, of, Shafter HS, Buttonwillow, Calif.
38. *Doug Colvard, of, Lincoln HS, Stockton, Calif.
39. *Gene Moreau, of, Edison HS, Fresno, Calif.

**June—Secondary Phase (22)**

1. *Richard Soriano, of, Miami-Dade CC North.—DNP
2. *Pat Cech, rhp, Glendale (Ariz.) CC.
3. *Ken Harris, of, Pasadena (Calif.) CC.
**4. *Mike Potter, of, Mount San Antonio (Calif.) JC.—(1976-77)**
5. *Todd Sprecher, c, Yakima Valley (Wash.) JC.
6. *Rick Dierker, rhp, Los Angeles Pierce JC.
DRAFT DROP *Brother of Larry Dierker, major leaguer (1964-77); major league manager (1997-2001)*

## CHICAGO CUBS

**January—Regular Phase (20)**

**1. Pete LaCock, 1b, Taft HS, Woodland Hills, Calif.—(1972-80)**
DRAFT DROP *Son of Peter Marshall (Hollywood actor)*
2. *Greg Gaffey, 1b, Lincoln Land (Ill.) JC.
3. *Ronald Hardin, of, Polk (Fla.) CC.
4. Walter Hirsch, of, Ocean County (N.J.) JC.
5. *Ronald Kendall, ss, Forest Hill HS, West Palm Beach, Fla.

**January—Secondary Phase (22)**

1. James Clouser, of, St. Joseph's University.—(Low A)
2. Dennis Odom, ss, San Diego CC.
3. Robert Maneely, rhp, St. Joseph's HS, Deptford, N.J.
4. *Larry Green, c, Doane (Neb.) College.
**5. *Chuck Seelbach, rhp, Dartmouth University.—(1971-74)**
6. *Ellsworth Jones, lhp, New York University.
7. *Angelo Mecca, of, Keystone (Pa.) JC.
8. *Jack Wilson, of, Sarasota (Fla.) HS.

**June—Regular Phase (19)**

**1. Gene Hiser, of, University of Maryland.—(1971-75)**
2. Dyain Frazier, lhp, Elmore HS, Houston.—(AA)
**3. Rick Reuschel, rhp, Western Illinois University.—(1972-91)**
DRAFT DROP *Brother of Paul Reuschel, major leaguer (1975-79)*
4. *Tim Doerr, ss, Granite Hills HS, El Cajon, Calif.—(AA)
DRAFT DROP *Attended UCLA; re-drafted by Reds, 1974 (18th round)*
5. Tom Badcock, lhp, Springfield (Mass.) College.—(AAA)
6. William Butts, of, Fowler (Calif.) HS.
7. Thomas O'Brien, of, Hoover HS, Fresno, Calif.
8. Calvin White, 1b, Maggie (Calif.) HS.
9. Jimmy Kelly, lhp, Brazosport HS, Freeport, Texas.
10. *Jeff Oscarson, ss, Saguaro HS, Scottsdale, Ariz.
**11. *Jackson Todd, rhp, Will Rogers HS, Tulsa, Okla.—(1977-81)**
12. *Mike Sylvester, rhp, Moeller HS, Cincinnati.
13. Bill Huisman, 2b, Kansas State University.
14. Nicholas McKenzie, c, Moses Lake (Wash.) HS.
15. Robert Watson, of, Western Illinois University.
16. Craig Schwerman, rhp, Western Illinois University.
17. *Benny Castillo, 2b, Coral Park HS, Miami.
**18. *Jeff Schneider, lhp, Alleman HS, Rock Island, Ill.—(1981)**
19. Michael Fink, ss, Middlesex (N.J.) HS.
20. Donald Schuldies, of, Granite Hills HS, El Cajon, Calif.
21. Gary Guenther, inf, Modesto (Calif.) JC.
22. *James Riddell, rhp, Hillsborough HS, Tampa.
23. *Mitch Fahland, c, Libby (Mon.) HS.
24. *Gregg Schnurr, of, Troy HS, Fullerton, Calif.
25. *Kevin McNichol, inf, James Monroe HS, Bronx, N.Y.
26. *James Walton, rhp, Allegany HS, Cumberland, Md.
27. Clinton Henderson, of-rhp, Bethune HS, Shreveport, La.
28. *Dean Boger, lhp, Falls Church (Va.) HS.
29. Mark Thomas, rhp, MacMurray (Ill.) College.
30. Michael Weiss, rhp, Quincy (Ill.) HS.
31. *Glenn Bryant, rhp, Aldine HS, Houston.
32. *Robert Vandersluis, rhp, Northwest Nazarene (Idaho) College.
33. Jim Bianchi, ss, Boise State University.
34. Robert Schell, ss, Clay HS, South Bend, Ind.
35. Glenn Stinson, of, MacMurray (Ill.) College.
36. Bruce Hildebrandt, rhp, Pace (N.Y.) University.
37. *David Landers, of, St. Joseph's University.
38. *Cecil Evans, lhp, Carlsbad (N.M.) HS.
39. *Thomas Amanti, rhp, New London (Conn.) HS.
40. Gary McKenna, rhp, Providence College.
41. *Bill Capps, 2b, Arlington (Texas) HS.
42. Gary Hogan, rhp, Broward (Fla.) CC.
43. Charles Benjamin, 1b, St. Petersburg (Fla.) JC.
44. Lawrence Pratt, c, South Broward HS, Hollywood, Fla.
45. *Thomas Stafford, of, Robert E. Lee HS, Jacksonville, Fla.
46. Thomas McBean, of, Husson (Maine) College.
47. Michael Clampitt, ss, Hobbs (N.M.) HS.

**June—Secondary Phase (17)**

**1. Tom Lundstedt, c, University of Michigan—(1973-75)**
2. Steve Steitz, 3b, Springfield (Mass.) College.
3. Kurt Ascherman, c, Springfield (Mass.) College.

White Sox second-rounder Terry Forster saved 69 games from 1972-74 as the team's closer

## CHICAGO WHITE SOX

**January—Regular Phase (5)**

**1. *Duane Kuiper, ss, Indian Hills (Iowa) CC.—(1974-85)**
2. *Archibald Cameron, rhp, Miami-Dade CC North.
3. Barry Curlee, of, East Rowan HS, Granite Quarry, N.C.
4. Dan McDonough, c, Indian Hills (Iowa) CC.
5. *Joel Sexton, rhp, Indian Hills (Iowa) CC.
6. James Rice, c, Fullerton (Calif.) JC.
7. *Michael Misler, lhp, Miami-Dade CC North.
8. *Daniel Hinzman, lhp, Indian Hills (Iowa) CC.
9. Larry Shoup, of, Cypress (Calif.) JC.
10. *Bruce Meredith, lhp, Ellsworth (Iowa) JC.

**January—Secondary Phase (21)**

1. *Rick Dierker, rhp, Los Angeles Pierce JC.—(AA)
DRAFT DROP *Brother of Larry Dierker, major leaguer (1964-77); major league manager (1997-2001)*
2. Emery Mitchell, c, American River (Calif.) JC.
3. *Gary Mack, 2b, Cypress (Calif.) JC.
**4. *John Tamargo, c, Miami-Dade CC North.—(1976-80)**

**June—Regular Phase (6)**

**1. Lee Richard, ss, Southern University.—(1971-76)**
**2. Terry Forster, lhp, Santana HS, Santee, Calif.—(1971-86)**
DRAFT DROP *First 1970 high school draft pick to reach majors (April 11, 1971)*
**3. Jerry Hairston, of, Gardendale HS, Birmingham, Ala.—(1973-89)**
DRAFT DROP *Son of Sam Hairston, major leaguer (1951) • Brother of John Hairston, major leaguer (1969) • Father of Jerry Hairston, major leaguer (1998-2013) • Father of Scott Hairston, major leaguer (2004-14)*
4. Harold McClain, lhp, Beaver Falls (Pa.) HS.—(AAA)
5. *Dale Lydecker, of, Nyack (N.Y.) HS.—(Short-season A)
DRAFT DROP *Attended North Carolina; never re-drafted*
**6. Jim Geddes, rhp, Ohio State University.—(1972-73)**
7. Dennis Weidman, of, Lampeter-Strasburg HS, South Lancaster, Pa.
8. *Steve Foran, lhp, University of Denver.
**9. Rich Gossage, rhp, Wasson HS, Colorado Springs, Colo.—(1972-94)**
DRAFT DROP *Elected to Baseball Hall of Fame, 2008*
10. *Lyn Hamilton, c, Headland HS, East Point, Ga.
11. *Mike Hefftner, lhp, Erie (Colo.) HS.
12. Mike Drewett, 3b, Pine Bluff (Ark.) HS.
13. Steven Houck, of, Oklahoma State University.
14. *Gary Wagner, rhp, Maine East HS, Niles, Ill.
15. *Jimmy Collins, rhp, Southern University.
16. Dennis Smith, of, Neshaminy HS, Levittown, Pa.
17. Richard Lucke, of, University of Notre Dame.
18. *Arnold Costell, lhp, MacArthur HS, South Wantagh, N.Y.
19. Gregory Mathey, rhp-of, Thornton HS, Harvey, Ill.
**20. Bruce Miller, ss, Indiana University.—(1973-76)**
21. Gene Duhe, rhp, Nicholls State University.
22. *Jay Parker, c, Clay HS, South Bend, Ind.
23. *Joseph Lang, c-3b, Cardinal Dougherty HS, Buffalo, N.Y.
24. Allan Paganucci, rhp, University of San Francisco.
25. Cliff Hayes, of-inf, Jackson State University.
26. Michael Reynolds, c, Catawba (N.C.) College.
27. *Stephen Hazan, lhp, Mission Viejo (Calif.) HS.
28. Rusty Bourg, rhp, Arkansas State University.
29. Richard DeMay, rhp, Elgin (Ill.) HS.
30. *Bruce Mitchell, inf, Little Rock Central HS, Little Rock, Ark.
31. *Stephen Sroba, of, Neshaminy HS, Trevose, Pa.
32. Frank Buchan, of, Upper Iowa University.

**June—Secondary Phase (6)**

**1. Bucky Dent, 3b, Miami-Dade CC North.—(1973-84)**
2. *Henry Baker, 3b, Southern University.
3. *Archie Manning, ss, University of Mississippi.
DRAFT DROP *First-round draft pick, New Orleans Saints/National Football League (1971); quarterback, NFL (1971-84) • Father of Peyton Manning, quarterback, NFL (1998-2015) • Father of Eli Manning, quarterback, NFL (2004-15)*

## CINCINNATI REDS

**January—Regular Phase (16)**

1. *Dale Harrington, rhp, Odessa (Texas.) JC.—(High A)
**2. Joel Youngblood, c-ss, Stephen F. Austin HS, Houston.—(1976-89)**
3. Frank Martin, lhp, San Joaquin Delta (Calif.) JC.
4. *Larry Wondercheck, lhp, Long Beach (Calif.) CC.
5. *Charles Haymes, c-2b, Chicago.
6. *Larry Hammer, rhp, New Mexico Highlands University.
7. *Stephen Thompson, lhp, Jackson, Tenn.
8. *Mark Fouse, rhp, Connors State (Okla.) JC.

**January—Secondary Phase (18)**

1. William Wall, rhp, Auburn (N.Y.) JC.—(High A)
2. James Kirkland, of, South Georgia JC.
3. *Anthony Blakley, ss-2b, Brewton Parker (Ga.) JC.
4. *Johnny Spriggs, of, Angelo State (Texas) University.
5. Stephen Klinger, lhp, Bloomsburg (Pa.) University.
6. *Norman Jones, inf, Atlantic (N.J.) CC.

**June—Regular Phase (15)**

1. Gary Polczynski, ss, Nathan Hale HS, West Allis, Wis.—(AAA)
2. Rex Jackson, rhp, Rubidoux HS, Riverside, Calif.—(High A)
3. Barry Ulsh, 1b, Middletown (Pa.) Area HS.—(High A)

4. Bill Pinkham, c, Jeffersonville (Ind.) HS.—(High A)
5. *Huey Rice, rhp, Leon HS, Tallahassee, Fla.—DNP

DRAFT DROP *No school; never re-drafted*

**6. Tom Carroll, rhp, North Allegheny HS, Pittsburgh.—(1974-75)**
7. *Eugene Quirk, of, Wahconah Regional HS, Dalton, Mass.
**8. Will McEnaney, lhp, Springfield North HS, Springfield, Ohio.—(1974-79)**
9. *Greg Sinatro, ss-3b, LaSalle Academy, Hartford, Conn.

DRAFT DROP *Brother of Matt Sinatro, major leaguer (1981-92)*

**10. Ray Knight, rhp-3b, Dougherty HS, Albany, Ga.—(1974-88)**

DRAFT DROP *Major league manager (1996-97, 2003)*

11. Ira Damren, 1b, East Carteret HS, Beaufort, N.C.
12. William Smith, c, Hope Mills (N.C.) HS.
13. Christopher Jones, of, Azusa Pacific (Calif.) University.
14. Eddie Hill, rhp, University of North Carolina.
15. Pat McGehee, of, Oceanside (Calif.) HS.
16. *Doug Kotar, of, Canon-McMillan HS, Muse, Pa.

DRAFT DROP *Running back, National Football League (1974-81)*

17. Jesse Helton, ss, East Texas Baptist University.
18. David Hagadorn, rhp, Mansfield (Pa.) University.
**19. Pat Zachry, rhp, Richfield HS, Waco, Texas.—(1976-85)**
20. *Don Golden, of, Valdosta (Ga.) HS.
21. *Don Kreke, rhp, Mater Dei HS, Bartelso, Ill.
**22. *Rick Williams, rhp, Merced HS, El Nido, Calif.—(1978-79)**

DRAFT DROP *Son of Dick Williams, major leaguer (1951-64); major league manager (1967-88)*

23. Rick DeFelice, c, University of Cincinnati.
24. *John Maier, rhp, Laurel Valley HS, New Florence, Pa.
25. Lawrence Basey, of, Martinsburg (W.Va.) HS.
26. Stan Norman, of, Fairfield University.
27. Eric Boyd, 1b-c, CC of Baltimore.
28. Jim Mavroleon, rhp, West Virginia University.
29. Richard Blackstone, of, Fairmont State (W.Va.) College.
30. *Victor Mantoni, 3b, Hopedale (Mass.) HS.
31. *Jack Risdon, lhp, Edmond (Okla.) HS.
32. *Burke Suter, rhp, Towson (Md.) Senior HS.
33. *Robert Steinberg, 1b, University of Scranton (Pa.).
34. *Lawrence Gustafson, c-3b, Oakcrest HS, Mays Landing, N.J.
35. *David Moharter, lhp, Bloomsburg (Pa.) University.
36. *Stephen Carrigan, ss, Archbishop Curley HS, Baltimore.
37. *Mark Hoffman, lhp, Titusville (Fla.) HS.
38. *Gary Richter, 2b, Pleasanton (Texas) HS.
39. *Stephen Parker, of, Mainland HS, Northfield, N.J.
40. *Jeffrey Bradford, rhp, Dundalk HS, Baltimore.
41. *John Wiggins, rhp, Plant City (Fla.) HS.
42. Thomas Collins, rhp, New York University.
43. *Larry Cole, ss, Weber State (Utah) College.
44. Ronald Williamson, of-inf, Hallsboro (N.C.) HS.
45. *Michael Racobaldo, rhp, Woodrow Wilson HS, Camden, N.J.
46. *Charles Cundari, lhp, Westlake HS, Hawthorne, N.Y.
47. *Richard Ryan, rhp, Iowa Central CC.

### June—Secondary Phase (9)

**1. Pat Osburn, lhp, Florida State University.—(1974-75)**
**2. *Jim Norris, of, University of Maryland.—(1977-80)**
**3. *Duane Kuiper, ss, Indian Hills (Iowa) CC.—(1974-85)**
4. *Mike Dickens, 3b, Catawba (N.C.) College.

## CLEVELAND INDIANS

### January—Regular Phase (1)

**1. Chris Chambliss, 1b, UCLA.—(1971-88)**
2. *Brian Lieckfelt, rhp, St. Clair County (Mich.) CC.
3. Dennis Queen, lhp, St. Clair County (Mich.) CC.
4. John Detter, rhp, Nickerson (Kan.) HS.
5. Michael Burger, 3b, Brewton Parker (Ga.) JC.
6. *William Smith, lhp, Mount San Antonio (Calif.) JC.
7. James Valenty, 3b-of, St. Petersburg (Fla.) JC.

### January—Secondary Phase (15)

1. Gary King, ss, South Bend, Ind.—(Low A)
2. William Hernandez, c, College of Staten Island (N.Y.).
3. *Bernie Boehmer, c, St. Louis CC-Meramec.
4. William Hendricks, lhp, Miami (Ohio) University.
5. Carlos Suarez, lhp, Miami-Dade CC North.
6. *Randall Goede, lhp, Valparaiso University.

### June—Regular Phase (2)

**1. Steve Dunning, rhp, Stanford University.—(1970-77)**

DRAFT DROP *First player from 1970 draft to reach majors (June 14, 1970)*

2. Bill Flowers, of, Courter Tech HS, Cincinnati.—(AAA)
3. Harry Shaughnessy, of, Western Michigan University.—(Class AA)
4. Jeff Baker, rhp, Charter Oak HS, Glendora, Calif.—(Rookie)
**5. Tommy Smith, of, North Carolina State University.—(1973-77)**
6. Ron Salyers, lhp, Admiral King HS, Lorain, Ohio.
**7. *Jim Kremmel, lhp, University of New Mexico.—(1973-74)**
8. *Paul Miles, of, Paulding (Ohio) HS.

DRAFT DROP *Eighth-round draft pick, Baltimore Colts/ National Football League (1974)*

9. Gary Tucker, 1b, Leto HS, Tampa.
**10. Dennis Kinney, lhp, Bedford HS, Temperance, Mich.—(1978-82)**
11. *David Hasbach, rhp, Palatine (Ill.) HS.

DRAFT DROP *First overall draft pick, January 1974/ secondary phase, Royals*

12. James Beyersdorf, rhp, Freeland HS, Saginaw, Mich.
13. *Richard Katz, 3b, Platt HS, Meriden, Conn.
14. Dan Stoligrosz, 3b, University of Southern California.
15. Randy Peterson, c, Warren HS, Downey, Calif.
16. Thomas Burkert, lhp, Eastern Michigan University.
17. *Byron Florence, of, Roosevelt HS, East Chicago, Ind.
18. *Mike Kavanaugh, ss-c, Patterson HS, Baltimore.
19. Dave Jacome, ss, University of Arizona.
20. Dave Ruhe, of-1b, St. Joseph's (Ind.) College.
21. *Craig Paterniti, rhp, Falconer (N.Y.) HS.
22. Dean Schneider, 1b, Capital (Ohio) University.
23. Thomas Kelley, rhp, Aurora (Colo.) HS.
24. *Steven Schultz, lhp, Rancho HS, Las Vegas, Nev.
**25. *Sam Bowen, of-rhp, Glynn Academy HS, Brunswick, Ga.—(1977-80)**
**26. Jeff Newman, c-1b, Texas Christian University.—(1976-84)**
27. Michael Green, 3b, East HS, Atlanta.
28. *Mel Cuckovich, 3b-ss, Hiram Johnson HS, Sacramento, Calif.
29. *Ward Glazebrook, 1b, Coalinga (Calif.) HS.
30. *James Robertson, c, Bay HS, Bay Village, Ohio.
31. *James Street, rhp, University of Texas.

DRAFT DROP *Father of Huston Street, first-round draft pick, Athletics (2004); major leaguer (2005-15)*

32. *Robert Brough, lhp, Woodmore HS, Woodville, Ohio.
33. *John Pilewski, rhp, Bowsher HS, Toledo, Ohio.
34. Jack Darnell, rhp, Monterey HS, Lubbock, Texas.
35. Donald Kennedy, lhp, Hiram (Ohio) College.

### June—Secondary Phase (4)

1. *Mike Swenton, of, University of Oklahoma.—(AA)
2. *Curran Percival, rhp, San Diego Mesa JC.
3. Robert Eldridge, rhp, Southern Illinois University.
**4. *Doug Ault, of-lhp, Panola (Texas) JC.—(1976-80)**

## DETROIT TIGERS

### January—Regular Phase (19)

1. *Timothy Steele, 1b, Cerritos (Calif.) JC.—(AA)
2. Douglas Brittelle, rhp, Rutgers University.

DRAFT DROP *Draft pick, Kentucky Colonels/American Basketball Association (1969)*

**3. *Mike Potter, of, Mount San Antonio (Calif.) JC.—(1976-77)**
4. *Raymond Kennett, rhp, Connors State (Okla.) JC.
5. *John Orr, of, Finney HS, Detroit.
6. *Michael Strickland, of, Northwestern HS, Detroit.

### January—Secondary Phase (23)

1. *Steven Cash, ss, DeKalb (Ga.) JC.—(Rookie)
2. Jeff Hogan, 3b, Florida State University.
3. Michael Pivec, of, CC of Baltimore.
4. *Rand Rasmussen, ss, Long Beach (Calif.) CC.
5. *Richard Auckland, 1b-of, West Chester (Pa.) University.

### June—Regular Phase (20)

1. Terry Mappin, c, Durrett HS, Louisville, Ky.—(AA)
2. *Mike Ibarguen, rhp, Sam Rayburn HS, Pasadena, Texas.—(AA)

DRAFT DROP *Attended San Jacinto (Texas) JC; re-drafted by Cardinals, January 1971/secondary phase (1st round).*

3. *James Chamberlain, lhp, Ben L. Smith HS, Greensboro, N.C.—(AA)

DRAFT DROP *Attended North Carolina; never re-drafted*

4. Daniel Grant, c, Westchester HS, Los Angeles.—(High A)
5. Tom Lantz, rhp, Akron East HS, Akron, Ohio.—(AA)
6. Alan Locasio, c, St. Francis (N.Y.) College.
7. *Paul Spivey, of, Robert E. Lee HS, Montgomery, Ala.
**8. John Knox, 2b, Bowling Green State University.—(1972-75)**
**9. Phil Mankowski, 3b, Bishop Turner HS, Cheektowaga, N.Y.—(1976-82)**
**10. Fernando Arroyo, rhp, Burbank HS, Sacramento, Calif.—(1975-86)**
11. *William Smith, ss, Manzano HS, Albuquerque, N.M.
12. *Gary Hampton, of, Fresno (Calif.) HS.
13. James Bebout, of, Morgan HS, Stockport, Ohio.
14. David Baye, rhp, Southern Connecticut State University.
15. Ted Brazell, of, St. Louis CC-Meramec.
16. *Glenn Knight, rhp, Allen Park (Mich.) HS.
17. Albert Kaminski, ss, University of Minnesota.
18. *Charles Coe, ss, St. Louis CC-Meramec.
19. *Curt Grote, ss, Hoyleton (Ill.) HS.
20. David Deluca, rhp, Syracuse University.
**21. Fred Holdsworth, rhp, Northville (Mich.) HS.—(1972-80)**
22. Kenneth Forfar, rhp, Kearny (N.J.) HS.
23. *Dennis Hindman, rhp, Brethren (Mich.) HS.
24. Carl Cavanaugh, rhp, University of Tampa.
25. Richard Fairbanks, of, Brigham Young University.
26. *Dean Jones, lhp, Virginia HS, Bristol, Va.
27. Carmine Perotta, rhp, Florida Southern College.
28. *Thomas DeBeche, rhp, St. Agnes Cathedral HS, Massapequa Park, N.Y.
29. Steven Strack, ss, Niagara Falls (N.Y.) Senior HS.
30. Randy Brady, of, Zeeland HS, Holland, Mich.
31. Fred Bruntrager, lhp, SUNY-Cortland.
32. *Tim Pierce, rhp, Kenmore East HS, Tonawanda, N.Y.
33. William Crowley, 3b, Holy Cross College.
34. Jonathan Gold, of, Monmouth College.

### June—Secondary Phase (12)

**1. Chuck Seelbach, rhp, Dartmouth College.—(1971-74)**
2. James Bergholz, ss, Kings (Pa.) College.
3. *Jerry Reasonover, ss, Gulf Coast (Fla.) CC.
4. *William Collins, rhp, Manatee (Fla.) JC.

## HOUSTON ASTROS

### January—Regular Phase (8)

1. *William Wood, c, Los Angeles Valley JC.—(AAA)
2. *Kent Froede, of, Southwestern (Calif.) JC.
3. *Kenneth Doria, 3b, Gulf Coast (Fla.) CC.
4. *Mason Bean, c, South Georgia JC.
5. (void) Larry Carino, 2b, Ridgewood, N.J.

### January—Secondary Phase (14)

1. *Robert Masteller, lhp, Grayson County (Texas) JC.—(Rookie)
**2. Mike Cosgrove, lhp, Phoenix (Ariz.) JC.—(1972-76)**
3. Steven Gardner, 3b, Weber State (Utah) College.
4. Jerry Lewis, 1b, JC of the Desert (Calif.).

### June—Regular Phase (7)

**1. *Randy Scarbery, rhp, Roosevelt HS, Fresno, Calif.—(1979-80)**

DRAFT DROP *Attended Southern California; re-drafted by Athletics, 1973 (1st round)*

2. Alton Williams, ss, Webb HS, Oxford, N.C.—(High A)
3. Don Stratton, rhp, Los Altos (Calif.) HS.—(AAA)
**4. Greg Gross, of, Red Land HS, Etters, Pa.—(1973-89)**
5. Ronald DeJean, rhp, Aurora Central HS, Aurora, Colo.—(AA)
6. Richard Busby, ss, Bessemer (Ala.) HS.
7. John McLaren, c, Westbury HS, Houston.

DRAFT DROP *Major league manager (2007)*

8. Rick Sanderlin, of, Mission Bay HS, San Diego.
9. Tom Wise, inf, Madison HS, Portland, Ore.
10. Gordon Crane, rhp, Birmingham HS, Van Nuys, Calif.
11. Lennard Davis, of, Mainland HS, Daytona Beach, Fla.
12. *Lonnie Kruger, rhp, Silver Lake (Kan.) HS.

DRAFT DROP *Basketball coach, Atlanta Hawks/National Basketball Association (2000-03); basketball coach, Nevada-Las Vegas (2004-11); basketball coach, Oklahoma (2011-2015)*

13. Alan Horne, rhp, Dougherty HS, Albany, Ga.

DRAFT DROP *Father of Alan Horne, first-round draft pick, Angels (2001)*

14. William Gardner, rhp, DeLand (Fla.) HS.
**15. *Joe Wallis, of, McCluer HS, Florissant, Mo.—(1975-79)**
16. *Lawrence Kinn, lhp, New Riegel (Ohio) HS.
17. *Joseph Chelli, rhp, Linden (Calif.) HS.
18. *Richard Marcet, rhp, McGill HS, Mobile, Ala.
19. Brad McRoberts, rhp, Santana HS, El Cajon, Calif.
20. David Wing, ss, Will Rogers HS, Tulsa, Okla.
21. Anthony Lang, of, Central HS, Mobile, Ala.
22. James Provenzeno, lhp, University of Arizona.
23. *Thomas Walsh, lhp, St. Maria Goretti HS, Hagerstown, Md.
24. *Brad Omlid, 2b, Cleveland HS, Seattle.
25. James Streleski, lhp, Puyallup (Wash.) HS.

### June—Secondary Phase (11)

1. Don Russell, 3b, Clemson University.—(AAA)
2. *Jim Burnes, rhp, Glendale (Ariz.) CC.
3. *Stan Butkus, rhp, Miami-Dade CC North.

## KANSAS CITY ROYALS

### January—Regular Phase (7)

1. *Jack Peres, rhp, Los Angeles Harbor JC.—DNP
2. James Webb, lhp, Western Kentucky University.
**3. Greg Minton, rhp, San Diego Mesa JC.—(1975-90)**
4. *Wayne Currin, of, Louisburg (N.C.) JC.
5. John Joseph, of, Chabot (Calif.)) JC.
6. *Larry McDaniel, c, Bacone (Okla.) JC.
7. *Rick Halsey, 3b, San Diego Mesa JC.
8. *Joe Meyers, ss, James Monroe HS, Mission Hills, Calif.
9. Gary Hubbs, c, Cal Poly Pomona.
10. *Steven Shaw, of, Prince George's (Md.) CC.

### January—Secondary Phase (13)

1. *Ronnie Diggle, of, Cerritos (Calif.) JC.—(AAA)
2. *Cal Meier, ss, University of Southern California.
**3. Jim Wohlford, ss, JC of the Sequoias (Calif.).—(1972-86)**
4. *Gary Wann, rhp, Fullerton (Calif.) JC.
5. *Dean Mick, ss, Yakima Valley (Wash.) JC.

### June—Regular Phase (8)

1. Rex Goodson, c, Pine Tree HS, Longview, Texas.—(AA)
2. John Johnson, ss, Little Rock Central HS, Little Rock, Ark.—(AAA)
3. David Allen, lhp, Haverford Township HS, Havertown, Pa.—(Low A)
**4. Tom Poquette, of, Memorial HS, Eau Claire, Wis.—(1973-82)**
5. *Arthur Grzeskowiak, 1b, Sterling Morton East HS, Cicero, Ill.—DNP

DRAFT DROP *Attended Miami (Ohio); never re-drafted*
6. Paul Pelz, rhp, Neff HS, La Mirada, Calif.
7. Rich Lashmet, ss, Chatsworth HS, Canoga Park, Calif.
8. Bruce Griggs, rhp, Thornridge HS, Thornton, Ill.
9. Mack Payne, rhp, Arkansas A&M University.
10. Noel Paulson, 2b, Golden West (Calif.) JC.
11. Stanley Jackson, 1b, Thornton HS, Harvey, Ill.
12. *Ed Bowman, 3b, Santa Barbara (Calif.) HS.
13. *James Ferguson, of, John F. Kennedy HS, Richmond, Calif.
14. Brad Rooker, lhp, North Torrance (Calif.) HS.
15. John Hurst, 2b, Shrewsbury (Mass.) HS.
16. Robert McDonald, c, Chambersburg (Pa.) HS.
17. *Alvin Harper, ss, Webster HS, Minden, La.
18. *Allan Houston, rhp, Woburn (Mass.) HS.
19. Darrell Gambero, rhp, Fresno State University.
20. Lonne Reed, of, Fremont HS, Los Angeles.
21. *Marv Chamberlain, c, Mark Morris HS, Longview, Wash.
22. *Jack Winchester, 3b, Inglewood (Calif.) HS.
23. *Rick Bloomer, of, Oak Park HS, Kansas City, Mo.
24. *Steve Taylor, lhp, Pasadena (Calif.) CC.
25. Gerald Clark, c, Wahama HS, New Haven, W.Va.
26. Chris Crews, ss, Westside HS, Omaha, Neb.
27. *Rudy Sgontz, c, Loara HS, Anaheim, Calif.
28. Scott McManis, rhp, Sunset HS, Portland, Ore.
29. *Donald Jones, lhp, Arcadia (Calif.) HS.
30. *John Rowley, lhp, Buffalo (Okla.) HS.
31. *Steve Lee, lhp, Cal State Northridge.
32. James Feiler, lhp, Unionville HS, West Chester, Pa.
33. Gary Schlagenhauf, of, UC Davis.
34. Don Campbell, lhp, Western Montana College.
35. *John Stefanski, ss, New London (Conn.) HS.
36. Peter Dunn, c, Stetson University.
37. (void) *James Streleski, lhp, Puyallup (Wash.) HS.
38. *Joseph Lewandowski, of, Plainedge HS, North Massapequa, N.Y.

**June—Secondary Phase (2)**

1. Tommy Harmon, c, University of Texas.—(AAA)
2. Cal Meier, ss, University of Southern California.
3. John Gaylord, c, Chaffey (Calif.) JC.
4. Gary Houston, lhp, San Jose State University.
5. *Timothy Steele, 1b, Cerritos (Calif.) JC.
6. *Bruce Mierkowicz, 1b, St. Clair County (Mich.) CC.
7. Jack Burns, rhp, Denver.

## LOS ANGELES DODGERS

**January—Regular Phase (10)**

1. *Jim Burnes, rhp, Glendale (Ariz.) CC.—DNP
2. *Edward Womboldt, c, Indian Hills (Iowa) CC.
3. *David Holmes, c, Glendale (Ariz.) CC.
4. Ralph Davis, rhp, Alice (Texas) HS.
5. *Kenneth Harris, 1b, Pasadena (Calif.) CC.

**January—Secondary Phase (10)**

**1. *John LaRose, lhp, Cumberland, R.I.—(1978)**
2. *Kevin Kooyman, c, Grossmont (Calif.) JC.
3. Bruce Raible, rhp, Cincinnati.
**4. *Mike Barlow, rhp, Syracuse University.—(1975-81)**

**June—Regular Phase (9)**

1. Jim Haller, rhp, Creighton Prep HS, Omaha, Neb.—(AAA)
2. Randy Fairbanks, lhp, Satellite (Fla.) HS.—(AA)
**3. Lance Rautzhan, lhp, Blue Mountain HS, Pottsville, Pa.—(1977-79)**
4. Ricky Nitz, rhp, Hoover HS, Glendale, Calif.—(AAA)
5. Dewey Forry, of, Terra Linda HS, San Rafael, Calif.—(AAA)
6. *James Vaeth, rhp, Seaford (N.Y.) HS.
7. Thomas Jenkins, of, University of Tulsa.
8. *Rex Peters, 1b, Midland Park (N.J.) HS.
9. John Snider, 3b-of, Fairfield Union HS, Pleasantville, Ohio.
10. Wayne Ristig, 2b, Chapman (Calif.) College.
11. *Creighton Tevlin, of, Canoga Park (Calif.) HS.
12. *Patrick Paulson, lhp, East Haven (Conn.) HS.
13. Norm Brown, of, University of California.
14. Thomas Corder, ss, San Jose State University.
15. *John Cosmos, 1b-lhp, Sacred Heart HS, San Francisco.
16. Mike Plunkett, rhp, Emporia State (Kan.) University.
**17. *Mike Vail, ss, Archbishop Mitty HS, San Jose, Calif.—(1975-84)**
18. *Larry Tolbert, rhp, East Central HS, Tulsa, Okla.
19. Paul Barnes, of, Middle Georgia JC.
20. Phil Keller, rhp, Stanford University.
21. Albert Taylor, rhp, Kearny HS, San Diego.
22. Wayne Burney, 1b, Northeast Louisiana University.
23. Les Rogers, 3b, University of Tulsa.
24. *Francisco Suarez, ss, Hialeah (Fla.) HS.
25. *Dennis Abel, of, San Francisco State University.
26. Thomas Gleason, lhp, Cleveland HS, Reseda, Calif.
27. *John Wade, c, Pasadena (Calif.) HS.

DRAFT DROP *Son of Ben Wade, major leaguer (1948-55)*
28. Ron Hall, lhp, University of Oklahoma.
29. Steve Wilson, rhp, South Georgia JC.
30. *James Ivey, lhp, East Point, Ga.
31. *Bruce Collins, rhp, South San Francisco (Calif.) HS.
32. *Thaddeus Rowe, inf, Brookland-Cayce HS, West Columbia, S.C.
**33. Greg Shanahan, rhp, Humboldt State (Calif.) University.—(1973-74)**
34. *Chris Kinsel, c, St. Augustine HS, Bonita, Calif.
35. *Mike Garrett, of, Marina del Rey, Calif.

DRAFT DROP *1965 Heisman Trophy winner; running back, National Football League (1966-73)*
36. *Mark Andresen, of, Garden Grove (Calif.) HS.
37. *Michael Sanders, 3b, Daniel HS, Clemson, S.C.
38. *Maury Damkroger, c, Northeast HS, Lincoln, Neb.

DRAFT DROP *Running back, National Football League (1974-75)*
39. Vandon Mattison, lhp, Kennedy HS, Sacramento, Calif.
40. *Scott Waltemate, rhp, Steeleville (Ill.) HS.

**June—Secondary Phase (7)**

**1. Doug Rau, lhp, Texas A&M University.—(1972-81)**
2. *George Pugh, lhp, Mesa (Colo.) College.
3. Joe Daniels, of, University of New Mexico.
4. Ken O'Brien, rhp, Villanova University.
5. *Paul Womble, 3b, University of Kansas.

## MILWAUKEE BREWERS/ SEATTLE PILOTS

**January—Regular Phase (3)**

1. George Bacher, of, Quincy (Mass.) JC.—DNP
2. *James Timmons, c, Arizona Western JC.
3. Guy McTheny, of-c, University of Florida.
4. *William Bell, ss, Jefferson State (Ala.) JC.
5. *Dennis Clark, c, Chaffey (Calif.) JC.
6. *Gary Malcom, of, Elkhart (Ind.) HS.

**January—Secondary Phase (19)**

1. Gary Bradshaw, rhp, Miami-Dade CC North.—(High A)
2. *Charles Bates, 3b, Cerritos (Calif.) JC.

DRAFT DROP *First-round draft pick (19th overall), Tigers (1973)*
3. *Robert Crain, ss, Pasadena (Calif.) CC.
4. *Earl Austin, 3b, Dos Palos, Calif.
5. Dennis Holmberg, 3b, Brewton Parker (Ga.) JC.
6. *Bruce Irvin, c, St. Petersburg (Fla.) JC.
7. David Kropfelder, c, CC of Baltimore.
8. *Gilbert Untermeyer, 3b, St. John's River (Fla.) CC.

**June—Regular Phase (4)**

**1. Darrell Porter, c, Southeast HS, Oklahoma City, Okla.—(1971-87)**
**2. *Ken Pape, ss, MacArthur HS, San Antonio, Texas.—(1976)**

DRAFT DROP *Attended Texas; re-drafted by Rangers, 1973 (5th round)*
3. Price Thomas, of, Shaw HS, Mobile, Ala.—(AA)
4. Jerry O'Neill, lhp, St. Agnes HS, Baldwin Park, N.Y.—(AAA)
5. Carl Austerman, rhp, Glendale (Ariz.) HS.—(AAA)
**6. Bill Travers, lhp, Norwood (Mass.) HS.—(1974-83)**
7. Duane Espy, 2b, Santa Monica (Calif.) HS.
8. Marion Jackson, of, Jackson HS, Miami.
9. *John Nunnenkamp, rhp, Freeport (N.Y.) HS.
10. Ken Collins, rhp, Clackamas (Ore.) CC.
11. *Steve Behlen, lhp, Clovis (Calif.) HS.
12. Darryl Steen, rhp, Jefferson HS, Los Angeles.
13. *Richard Baker, lhp, Terry Parker HS, Jacksonville, Fla.
14. Charles Capello, lhp, Long Island University.
15. *Charles Manley, of, Springfield (Mass.) Tech HS.
16. Brian Muir, of, David Douglas HS, Portland, Ore.
17. *Pat Marble, rhp, Yucca Valley (Calif.) HS.
18. *William Varner, lhp, Roberts HS, Decorah, Iowa.
19. *Andrew Kemp, rhp, Pasadena (Calif.) HS.
20. *Frank Dziadul, 3b, Seminole (Fla.) HS.
21. *John McMillan, rhp, Parkton HS, North Red Springs, N.C.
22. Michael Seufer, of, Franklin Heights HS, Columbus, Ohio.
23. Dennis Yard, rhp, Northridge, Calif.
24. *Donald Cooke, lhp, Monsignor Pace HS, Opa Locka, Fla.
25. Paul Lang, rhp, SUNY-Buffalo.
26. *Victor Zaremba, of-p, Colorado Springs (Colo.) HS.
27. *Rex Landis, c, Franklin Heights HS, Columbus, Ohio.
28. Thomas Steadman, ss, Archbishop Carroll HS, Washington, D.C.
29. Ronald Harred, c, Southwestern Oklahoma State University.

**June—Secondary Phase (8)**

1. Whitey Adams, 3b, University of Mississippi.—(AAA)
2. *Earl Nance, lhp, Auburn University.
3. Gene Ammann, rhp, Florida State University.
**4. *John Tamargo, c, Miami-Dade CC North.—(1976-80)**

## MINNESOTA TWINS

**January—Regular Phase (21)**

1. *Sayle Brown, rhp, Glendale (Calif.) JC.—DNP
2. *Stanley Butkus, rhp, Miami-Dade CC North.
3. *Daniel Hensley, rhp, JC of the Sequoias (Calif.).
4. *Perry Yawn, of, University of Alabama.
5. Tom Wayne, 2b, Miami Shores, Fla.
6. *James Curtis, c, Newhall (Calif.) JC.

**January—Secondary Phase (11)**

1. *George Pugh, lhp, Mesa (Ariz.) CC.—DNP
2. Thomas Cain, rhp, Wartburg (Iowa) College.
3. Mark Pastrovich, lhp, Three Rivers (Mo.) CC.
4. Frank Tokash, rhp, Fairleigh Dickinson University.
**5. (void) *Glenn Borgmann, c, Miami-Dade CC North.—(1972-80)**
**6. *Jim Barr, rhp, University of Southern California.—(1971-83)**
7. Mel Bannon, ss, Santa Clara University.

**June—Regular Phase (22)**

**1. Bob Gorinski, ss, Mount Pleasant HS, Calumet, Pa.—(1977)**
**2. Mark Wiley, rhp, La Mesa, Calif.—(1975-78)**
3. John Hasbrouck, c, Albany (Minn.) HS.—(AA)
4. Peter Meyers, lhp, James Monroe HS, Sepulveda, Calif.—(High A)
5. *Ron Herring, rhp, Greenville (Ala.) HS.—(High A)

DRAFT DROP *Attended Chipola (Fla.) JC; re-drafted by Tigers, January 1971/secondary phase (3rd round)*
6. Randy Beach, ss, North Torrance (Calif.) HS.
7. *Mike Hughes, p, Lynwood (Calif.) HS.
8. *Dennis Allar, rhp-c, Minnetonka HS, Excelsior, Minn.
9. Gregory Goularte, of-c, Gavilan (Calif.) JC.
10. Samuel Hess, c, Turner Ashby HS, Dayton, Va.
11. Dave Saylor, c, Granada Hills (Calif.) HS.
12. Michael Wagner, rhp, Robertsdale (Ala.) HS.
13. *Manny Estrada, ss, Bishop Amat HS, Covina, Calif.
**14. *Steve Staggs, inf, Cerritos (Calif.) JC.—(1977-78)**
15. Harold Allen, lhp, Highland Springs HS, Richmond, Va.
16. Frank Schuster, lhp, East Aurora (Ill.) HS.
17. Frank Ciaramella, 3b, St. John's University.
18. *Sylvester Washington, 1b-of, Locke HS, Los Angeles.
19. Paul Haugen, rhp, Granada Hills (Calif.) HS.
20. Robert Gause, rhp, Cal State Fullerton.
21. Edmund Savold, rhp, St. Francis (N.Y.) College.
22. *Robert Kelly, lhp, Greeley Central HS, Greeley, Colo.
23. *Daniel Koontz, ss, Hoover HS, Fresno, Calif.
24. John Geitner, of, Sturgeon Bay (Wis.) HS.
25. Derry Deguire, ss, Los Angeles Harbor JC.
26. William Letsom, lhp, Tremper HS, Kenosha, Wis.
27. Nicholas Metz, c, Denmark HS, Maribel, Wis.
28. *Kevin Hunt, of, Doane (Neb.) College.

DRAFT DROP *Offensive tackle, National Football League (1972-78)*
29. George Dixon, lhp, Springfield (Mass.) College.
30. Bruce Wachutka, rhp, St. Louis Park (Minn.) HS.
31. Harold Brown, of-1b, Holdenville (Okla.) HS.
32. Barry Roderick, ss, Amherst (Mass.) College.
33. *Gregg Klee, lhp, Port Richmond HS, Staten Island, N.Y.
34. *Brad Van Mierlo, lhp, Royal Oak HS, Covina, Calif.
35. *Chris Charnish, of, University of Wisconsin-Platteville.
36. Phillip Flodin, c, University of Minnesota.
37. *Dennis Cline, ss, Conrad HS, Wilmington, Del.
38. *Lindsay Hoyer, c, Edina (Minn.) HS.
39. Dan Blood, 2b, Cal Poly Pomona.
40. *William Finck, rhp, Tennyson HS, Hayward, Calif.
41. Michael Ladd, c, Deering HS, Portland, Maine.
42. Terry Cupples, rhp, Wayne State (Neb.) University.
43. *Barry Traynor, rhp, Gahr HS, Norwalk, Calif.
44. Joe Hanzlik, lhp, Edison HS, Minneapolis.
45. Ronald Davison, ss-rhp, Springfield (Minn.) HS.
46. *Lawrence Siedow, of, Shakopee (Minn.) HS.

**June—Secondary Phase (18)**

1. Dan Guerrero, c, Occidental (Calif.) College.—(High A)
2. Dennis Loewe, rhp, Pershing (Neb.) College.
3. *Tom Rosa, ss, Miami-Dade CC South.
4. *Stan Hamlin, rhp, Bakersfield (Calif.) JC.

## MONTREAL EXPOS

**January—Regular Phase (4)**

1. Frank Hale, c, Mount San Antonio (Calif.) JC.—(AA)
2. *Craig Park, rhp, Venice (Calif.) HS.
3. *John Wilhoit, rhp, DeKalb (Ga.) JC.
4. *Gary Crawford, rhp, Lamar (Colo.) CC.
5. *Dirk Dunbar, 1b, Southeastern (Iowa) CC.
6. *Neal Mersch, rhp, Arizona Western JC.

**January—Secondary Phase (8)**

1. *Larry O'Brien, 1b-of, Long Beach (Calif.) CC.—(Low A)
2. Clifford Ker, rhp, Los Angeles Valley JC.
3. *Arthur Simon, ss, Miami-Dade CC North.
4. *George Horton, c, Upsala (N.J.) College.
5. *Ken O'Brien, rhp, Villanova University.
6. *James Curnow, c, Morristown, N.J.
7. David Krull, of, University of Iowa.
8. *Carlton Exum, rhp, Orlando, Fla.

**June—Regular Phase (3)**

**1. Barry Foote, c, Selma HS, Smithfield, N.C.—(1973-82)**
**2. Chip Lang, rhp, North Hills HS, Pittsburgh.—(1975-76)**

DRAFT DROP *Uncle of Neil Walker, first-round draft pick, Pirates (2004); major leaguer (2009-15)*
3. Randy Viefhaus, 1b, Lafayette HS, Ellisville, Miss.—(AAA)
4. James Horsch, rhp, Bellaire HS, Houston.—(AA)
**5. Pat Scanlon, 3b, Richfield (Minn.) HS.—(1974-77)**
6. Ray Mullinax, 3b, Will Rogers HS, Tulsa, Okla.
7. Cannon Smith, 1b, C.L. Walker HS, Atlanta.
**8. *Phil Garner, 2b, University of Tennessee.—(1973-88)**

DRAFT DROP *Major league manager (1992-2007)*
**9. Joe Gilbert, lhp, Newton HS, Jasper, Texas.—(1972-73)**
10. Mike Liebeck, of, Long Beach (Calif.) CC.

11. *Richard Carter, rhp, North Arlington (N.J.) HS.
12. Wallace Wright, ss-rhp, Mickens HS, Dade City, Fla.
13. *Jeff Hooper, lhp, Granada Hills (Calif.) HS.
**14. Jerry White, of, Washington HS, San Francisco.—(1974-86)**
15. *James Healy, ss, Parsippany HS, Lake Hiawatha, N.J.
16. *Theodore Schelmay, c, Bayonne (N.J.) HS.
17. James Sloan, ss, William Penn Charter HS, Philadelphia.
**18. Dale Murray, rhp, Blinn (Texas) JC.—(1974-85)**
19. Ray Valenzuela, of, Bassett HS, LaPuente, Calif.
20. *Daniel Tripp, lhp, West Ottawa HS, Holland, Mich.
21. Michael McCord, rhp, Westport HS, Louisville, Ky.
22. *Bernard Kirschner, of-ss, Yorkton HS, Arlington, Va.
23. *John Stansik, rhp, St. Alphonsus HS, Dearborn, Mich.
24. Lee Collins, c, Mountain Lakes (N.J.) HS.
25. Craig Van Bogelen, rhp, Arlington HS, Poughkeepsie, N.Y.
26. *Embry Pendarvis, ss, Northeast HS, Oklahoma City, Okla.
27. Robert Patin, rhp, St. Joseph HS, Jackson, Miss.
28. Charlie Jackson, 3b-rhp, Crockett (Texas) HS.
29. *Alex Pastore, of-3b, Hightstown (N.J.) HS.
30. *Gene Allen, ss, Biloxi (Miss.) HS.
31. *William Berryhill, c, Bartlesville (Okla.) HS.
32. (void) *Anthony Buckley, rhp-of, Ridley Township HS, Swarthmore, Pa.
33. *Stephen Marino, c, Winthrop (Mass.) HS.
34. *John McLish, of, John Marshall HS, Edmond, Okla.

DRAFT DROP *Son of Cal McLish, major leaguer (1944-64).*

**35. *Roy Smalley, ss, Westchester HS, Los Angeles.—(1975-87)**

DRAFT DROP *First overall draft pick, January 1974/regular phase, Rangers • Son of Roy Smalley, major leaguer (1948-58) • Nephew of Gene Mauch, major leaguer (1944-57); major league manager (1960-87)*

36. *Wade Fatheree, 1b, Rockdale (Texas) HS.
37. *Max Goldstein, 1b, Turlock (Calif.) HS.
38. *Horace Holmes, lhp, McComb-Gibson HS, Summit, Miss.

### June—Secondary Phase (5)

**1. *Sam Ewing, of, University of Tennessee.—(1973-78)**
2. *Jim Corcoran, ss-2b, University of California.
3. Dale Harrington, rhp, Odessa (Texas) JC.
4. Douglas Balne, lhp, New Canaan, Conn.

## NEW YORK METS

### January—Regular Phase (24)

1. Richard Avalos, of, San Fernando HS, Pacoima, Calif.—(High A)
2. David Chew, of-3b, Contra Costa (Calif.) JC.
3. *Clarence Bass, of, Southwood (N.C.) College.
4. *John Fargnoli, c, Brevard (Fla.) CC.
5. *Ronald Burns, rhp, North Greenville (S.C.) JC.
6. Marvin Tucker, of-2b, University of Southern Colorado.
7. *James Gailey, c, Manatee (Fla.) JC.

### January—Secondary Phase (24)

**1. Roy Staiger, ss, Bacone (Okla.) JC.—(1975-79)**
2. *Larry Prieto, 2b, Fresno (Calif.) CC.
3. *Gary Breshears, 2b, University of Iowa.
4. *Craig Menzl, 1b, Adelphi University.

### June—Regular Phase (23)

1. *George Ambrow, ss, Poly HS, Long Beach, Calif.—DNP

DRAFT DROP *Attended Southern California; re-drafted by Angels, January 1974/secondary phase (18th round)*

2. *Gary Nevinger, rhp, Vandalia (Ill.) HS.—(High A)

DRAFT DROP *Attended Georgia; re-drafted by Mets, 1973 (3rd round)*

3. Michael Graham, of, Pershing (Neb.) College.—(High A)
4. Ronnie Collins, ss, Pembroke State (N.C.) University.—(High A)
5. *George Schneider, lhp, Cold Spring Harbor HS, Lloyd Harbor, N.Y.—DNP

DRAFT DROP *Attended Furman; never re-drafted*

6. Steven Warden, rhp-3b, Sullivan East HS, Bluff City, Tenn.
7. Rex Phelps, rhp, Copper Basin HS, Farner, Tenn.
8. Randy Pugh, rhp, Calistoga (Calif.) HS.
9. Thomas Hallums, 1b, South Carolina State College.
10. *James Pittman, rhp, Messick HS, Memphis, Tenn.
11. David Barb, rhp, Elkins (W.Va.) HS.
12. Bryan Hartman, rhp, Trinity (Texas) University.
13. *Jesse Carter, c, Central HS, Murfreesboro, Tenn.
14. *William Bishop, 1b, James Monroe HS, Bronx, N.Y.
15. Robert Bartlett, rhp, Arkansas Tech University.
16. Roman Schmidt, c, Riverview HS, Sarasota, Fla.
17. Thomas Sheppard, rhp, Cal State Los Angeles.
18. *Steven Carp, rhp-inf, Canarsie HS, Brooklyn, N.Y.
19. *Russell Cauley, lhp, Hooks HS, Leary, Texas.
**20. Bruce Boisclair, of, Killingly HS, Danielson, Conn.—(1974-79)**
21. *Lawrence Neal, of, Laney (Calif.) JC.
22. Richard Wustefeld, rhp, Wantagh (N.Y.) HS.
23. Edward Grady, of, Nichols (Ga.) HS.
24. Allan Rommes, rhp, Caledonia (Minn.) HS.
25. Carroll Talbert, 3b, Boonsboro (Md.) HS.
26. *Robert Sherman, rhp, Seminole (Fla.) CC.
27. Richard Williams, rhp, Chariho HS, Carolina, R.I.
28. *Nicholas Welshmeyer, rhp, Bishop O'Dowd HS, Castro Valley, Calif.
29. Terry Deremer, ss, Fairmont State (W.Va.) College.
30. *Dennis Zimmerman, of, Albright (Pa.) College.
31. Jeff Anderson, of, Jackson State University.
32. Timothy DeCaminada, 1b, University of Portland.
33. Daryl Tollinche, of, William Allen HS, Allentown, Pa.
34. *John Lonchar, c, Euclid (Ohio) HS.
35. *Steve Bossi, of, Contra Costa (Calif.) JC.
36. *Michael McGuire, of, Amherst HS, Snyder, N.Y.
37. *Dave Williams, rhp, Coshocton (Ohio) HS.
38. *Ron Lyons, of, Mason County (Ky.) HS.
39. *John Mullins, rhp, Paul Blazer HS, Ashland, Ky.
40. Larry Potash, lhp, Gannon (Pa.) University.
41. *Michael Basinger, 3b-1b, Los Banos (Calif.) HS.

### June—Secondary Phase (3)

**1. Brent Strom, lhp, University of Southern California.—(1972-77)**
2. *Andrew Bielanski, c, Fullerton (Calif.) JC.
3. Ken Wamble, 2b, Odessa (Texas) JC.
4. *Stephen Cash, ss, Dekalb (Ga.) JC.

## NEW YORK YANKEES

### January—Regular Phase (11)

1. Ron Hinckley, rhp, St. John's River (Fla.) CC.—(Rookie)
2. John Mercado, 1b-3b, Ranger (Texas) JC.
3. *John Gaylord, lhp, Chaffey (Calif.) JC.
4. *Lawrence Knight, rhp, Ranger (Texas) JC.
5. *Robert Coultas, rhp, Diablo Valley (Calif.) JC.
6. *James Henley, lhp, Eagle Rock HS, Los Angeles.
7. (void) *Gary Leach, rhp, Yakima Valley (Wash.) JC.
8. Jim Hefflinger, rhp, Mount Hood (Ore.) CC.

### January—Secondary Phase (3)

1. Wayne Pitcock, 1b, Arkansas State University.—(High A)
2. *Todd Sprecher, c, Yakima Valley (Wash.) JC.
3. David Hazelip, rhp, Columbia State (Tenn.) CC.
4. Joel DeTray, rhp, Columbia Basin (Wash.) CC.
5. Dan Velander, rhp, Lower Columbia (Wash.) CC.
6. *Jack McDonald, rhp, Spokane (Wash.) CC.
7. Eugene Moser, of, Bellevue (Wash.) CC.

### June—Regular Phase (12)

**1. Dave Cheadle, lhp, Asheville (N.C.) HS.—(1973)**
2. Richard Earle, rhp, Highland Park (N.J.) HS.—(AAA)
**3. *Fred Lynn, of, El Monte (Calif.) HS.—(1974-90)**

DRAFT DROP *Attended Southern California; re-drafted by Red Sox, 1973 (2nd round)*

4. David Lawson, rhp, Germantown Academy, Flourtown, Pa.—(AA)
5. Ned Jayjack, c, Normandy HS, Parma, Ohio.—(High A)
6. Doug Stodgel, ss, Cal State Los Angeles.
**7. Don DeMola, rhp, Commack South HS, Commack, N.Y.—(1974-75)**
8. Frank Rossi, 1b, Montclair State (N.J.) College.
9. Tom Robbins, of, Belhaven (Miss.) College.
10. Julio Hernandez, ss, Miami (Fla.) Senior HS.
11. (void) *Kevin Rusnak, of, Ohio State University.
12. Wes Vandenburg, of, Hastings (Mich.) HS.
13. Thomas Hannibal, lhp, University of Portland.
14. *Mike McNeilly, rhp-ss, Lower Columbia (Wash.) CC.
15. Richard Bianchi, c, St. Anthony HS, Trenton, N.J.
16. *Duane Wirth, rhp, St. Mary's HS, Mesa, Ariz.
17. Dick Clark, c, Anderson (Mo.) HS.
18. Robert Behar, rhp, James Monroe HS, New York.
19. Bill Sheets, lhp, Eastern Oregon State College.
20. John Shaw, 2b, University of Mississippi.
21. George Beattie, ss, South Portland (Maine) HS.
22. Carlos Rodriguez, ss, Brandeis HS, New York.
23. Irving Homs, c-of, Lehman (N.Y.) College.
24. Clark Babbitt, rhp, Western Washington University.
25. *Tom Martell, lhp, Taft HS, Lincoln City, Ore.
26. Clyde Armstrong, lhp, Capitol Hill HS, Oklahoma City, Okla.
27. William Kolstad, lhp, Reynolds HS, Troutdale, Ore.
28. *Randy Fink, lhp, Columbia River HS, Vancouver, Wash.
29. *Willie Morales, c, Tucson (Ariz.) HS.
**30. Doc Medich, rhp, University of Pittsburgh.—(1972-82)**
31. *Byron Burns, rhp, Kelso (Wash.) HS.
32. *Oscar James, of, Owensboro (Ky.) HS.
33. *Jim Cody, rhp, Big Bend (Wash.) CC.
34. Robin Hippi, rhp, Central Washington University.
35. *Richard Ralston, rhp, Spokane (Wash.) CC.
36. *Joe Krsnich, inf-of, Wichita (Kan.) HS.

DRAFT DROP *Son of Rocky Krsnich, major leaguer (1949-53)*

37. *Kyle Johnson, 2b, Helena (Mon.) HS.
38. Tom Couples, rhp, Seattle University.

DRAFT DROP *Brother of Fred Couples (PGA golfer)*

39. Robert Nielsen, of, University of Minnesota.
40. John Bakis, 3b, Norwich (Vt.) University.
41. *Jerry Schuster, lhp, West HS, Billings, Mon.
42. *Dave Michael, lhp-of, Pendleton (Ore.) HS.
43. *Randy Brummitt, lhp, McNary HS, Salem, Ore.
44. *John Wade, lhp, West Seattle HS.
45. *Keith Metheny, rhp, Kentridge HS, Kent, Wash.

DRAFT DROP *Son of Bud Metheny, major leaguer (1943-46)*

46. *Charles Gardinier, ss, Oregon College of Education.

### June—Secondary Phase (16)

1. Greg Gaffey, 1b, Lincoln (Mo.) University.—(Rookie)
2. Jerry Johnson, lhp, Oregon State University.

## OAKLAND ATHLETICS

### January—Regular Phase (17)

1. Phil LaGore, rhp, Monroe HS, Panorama City, Calif.—(Low A)
2. *Marv Owen, of, Fullerton (Calif.) JC.

DRAFT DROP *Wide receiver, National Football League (1973-74)*

3. (void) *Jack Brushert, of, Chapman (Calif.) College.
**4. *Mitchell Page, of, Compton (Calif.) CC.—(1977-84)**
5. Michael Morrison, lhp, Fullerton (Calif.) JC.
**6. (void) *Mark Wiley, rhp, Cal Poly Pomona.—(1975-78)**
7. *Carl Jones, 2b, Los Angeles CC.
8. (void) *John Vaught, rhp, Chapman (Calif.) College.
9. John Phillips, rhp, Thousand Oaks HS, Newbury Park, Calif.
10. *Lois Ridley, c-3b, Santa Monica (Calif.) JC.
11. *Jerry McCullough, of-1b, Mount San Antonio (Calif.) JC.
12. *Darrell Cox, rhp, Locke HS, Compton, Calif.
13. (void) *Allan Wise, of, Chapman (Calif.) College.

### January—Secondary Phase (9)

**1. Vic Harris, ss, Los Angeles Valley JC.—(1972-80)**
2. *Robert Eldridge, rhp, Southern Illinois University.
3. *John Librandi, of, Manatee (Fla.) JC.
4. *Mike Seberger, rhp, Cerritos (Calif.) JC.
5. Mike Logelin, 2b, Loyola Marymount University.

### June—Regular Phase (18)

**1. Dan Ford, of, Fremont HS, Los Angeles.—(1975-85)**
2. *Dale Holland, 2b, Riverview HS, Sarasota, Fla.—DNP

DRAFT DROP *Attended Mississippi State; never re-drafted*

3. David Murphy, 3b-ss, Ceres (Calif.) HS.—(Short-season A)
4. Dale Sanner, of, Rubidoux HS, Riverside, Calif.—(AAA)
5. *David Wooley, c, Bellaire (Texas) HS.—(High A)

DRAFT DROP *Attended Sam Houston State; never re-drafted*

6. *Darroll Phillips, rhp-of, Lincoln HS, Stockton, Calif.
7. Steve Cole, rhp, Carson HS, Torrance, Calif.
8. Bill Van Bommel, rhp, Menasha (Wis.) HS.
9. *Mark Hamilton, 1b, Ruston (La.) HS.
10. Mike Kowalik, rhp, Kennedy HS, Sacramento, Calif.
11. Alan Griffin, rhp, Mira Costa HS, Hermosa Beach, Calif.
12. *Paul Bagnasco, 3b, Cabrillo (Calif.) JC.
13. *Daryl Fuchs, c, Evansville (Wis.) HS.
14. Steve Tomasetti, c-of, North Quincy (Mass.) HS.
15. *Frank Baumgardner, rhp, Carol City HS, Opa Locka, Fla.
16. *Ron Corbett, rhp, Suffolk (Mass.) University.
17. David Smith, c, St. James HS, Brookhaven, Pa.
18. *Michael McManus, 1b-of, Mount San Antonio (Calif.) JC.
19. *Jack Brushert, of, Chapman (Calif.) College.
20. *Jim Golden, lhp, University of Portland.
21. Ron Brenner, rhp, Morningside (Iowa) College.
22. *Russ Schroeder, ss, Sam Rayburn HS, Pasadena, Texas.
23. Eldon Jones, lhp, University of Southern Colorado.
24. *Doug Cornett, c, Madison Central HS, Richmond, Ky.
25. *Mike Gerakos, 3b, Fullerton (Calif.) JC.

### June—Secondary Phase (20)

1. Bernie Boehmer, c, St. Louis CC-Meramec.—(AA)
2. *Ronnie Diggle, of, Cerritos (Calif.) JC.
3. Dennis Primeau, ss, St. Clair County (Mich.) CC.
4. *James Gailey, of, Manatee (Fla.) JC.

## PHILADELPHIA PHILLIES

### January—Regular Phase (6)

1. Russ Klobas, of, Laney (Calif.) JC.—(AA)
2. James Goodwin, rhp, Georgia Southern College.
3. George Hodge, 3b, Sacramento (Calif.) CC.
4. Ken Fuller, rhp, Chabot (Calif.) JC.

### January—Secondary Phase (16)

1. Allan Matson, of, St. John's University.—(High A)
2. *Claude Renfro, rhp-1b, Gulf Coast (Fla.) CC.
3. *William Menk, lhp, Philadelphia.
4. *Gary Szakacs, 1b, American River (Calif.) JC.

### June—Regular Phase (5)

1. Mike Martin, lhp, Olympia HS, Columbia, S.C.—(AAA)

DRAFT DROP *Brother of Jerry Martin, major leaguer (1974-84)*

2. *Roger Choate, c, Alleghany HS, Sparta, N.C.—DNP

DRAFT DROP *Attended South Carolina; never re-drafted*

3. David Selinsky, lhp, Klamath Falls (Ore.) HS.—(Low A)
4. Ken Fowler, rhp, Red Springs (N.C.) HS.—(Rookie)
5. Bruce Butler, 1b-of, Elk Grove HS, Sacramento, Calif.—(High A)
**6. David Downs, rhp, Viewmont HS,**

ASSOCIATED PRESS

**Dave Parker was better known as a football prospect coming out of high school in Cincinnati, and lasted until the 14th round, where the Pirates grabbed him and saw him quickly blossom**

**Bountiful, Utah.—(1972)**
DRAFT DROP *Brother of Kelly Downs, major leaguer (1986-93)*
7. Dan Field, c, St. Joseph HS, West Chester, Pa.
**8. Fred Andrews, ss, Lincoln Heights (Ohio) HS.—(1976-77)**
9. Lawrence Utz, rhp, Cypress Lake HS, Cape Coral, Fla.
10. David Yates, 2b, University of Delaware.
**11. Craig Robinson, ss, Wake Forest University.—(1972-77)**
12. Fred Thomason, lhp, Ball State University.
13. *Robert Worthington, 2b, Calvert Hall HS, Timonium, Md.
14. John Dusenbury, c, Asheville (N.C.) HS.
15. *William Emerson, rhp, Haddonfield (N.J.) HS.
16. Robert Wilson, rhp-of, JC of the Redwoods (Calif.).
17. *James Dennor, of-1b, Northern Illinois University.
18. Rick Fusari, of-rhp, Central Connecticut State University.
19. *Eric Wharton, of, Delaware State College.
20. *Scott Ferguson, 3b, Wauwatosa (Wis.) HS.
21. William McGonigle, inf, Santa Clara University.
**22. Erskine Thomason, rhp, Erskine (S.C.) College.—(1974)**
23. *Stanley Sweitham, ss, Polytechnic HS, Baltimore.
24. Chris Bradford, rhp, Diablo Valley (Calif.) JC.
25. *Jeff Kalish, 3b, New York University.
26. (void) *Tom Jones, rhp, Carson-Newman (Tenn.) College.
27. Mark Brown, rhp, University of Delaware.
**28. Bob Beall, of-1b, Oregon State University.—(1975-80)**
29. Malcolm Smoot, c, Ohio University.
30. Kevin Rusnak, of, Ohio State University.

### June—Secondary Phase (19)

1. Thomas Urquardt, rhp, Phillips (Okla.) University.—(Short-season A)
2. Philip Jones, ss, Spokane (Wash.) CC.
3. Robert Masteller, lhp, Grayson County (Texas) JC.
4. Gary Szakacs, 1b, American River (Calif.) JC.
5. *Chris Cammack, 3b, North Carolina State University.

## PITTSBURGH PIRATES

### January—Regular Phase (14)

1. *Alan Jackson, lhp, Northeastern University.—(AA)
2. *Ronald Erion, 3b-1b, San Joaquin Delta (Calif.) JC.
3. *Steven Darden, rhp, South Georgia JC.
4. *Clinton Olson, rhp, Big Bend (Wash.) CC.
5. *Charlie Roberts, rhp, Bellevue (Wash.) CC.
6. *Richard Counts, ss, St. Petersburg (Fla.) JC.
7. *James Heard, ss, Dalton (Ga.) JC.
8. *Steven Hunter, c, Yakima Valley (Wash.) JC.
9. *Peter Castle, rhp, Niagara County (N.Y.) CC.
10. *Stephen Dorsch, lhp, Concordia (N.Y.) College.
11. Ken Fulton, c, Duquesne University.
12. *Robbie Harms, c, Lakeland (Ill.) CC.
13. *Ted Cooper, 2b, Morgan State University.
14. Joseph Say, c-of, Kenmore East HS, Sterling Heights, Mich.
15. *David Sosnoskie, c-3b, Shamokin Area (Pa.) HS.
16. (void) *Kirk Berger, rhp-of, York (Pa.) College.
17. *Robert Deremer, of, Allegany HS, Cumberland, Md.
18. *Robert Brown, rhp, Connellsville Area HS, South Connellsville, Pa.
19. *Mark Mooney, rhp, Catonsville (Md.) CC.
20. *Terry Derfler, c, Pine Grove (Pa.) HS.
21. Stephen Bosley, rhp, Catonsville (Md.) CC.
22. *Barry Barns, rhp-of, West Perry HS, Blain, Pa.
23. *Anthony Joseph, lhp, Lincoln HS, Ellwood City, Pa.
24. *Carl Woolford, lhp-1b, Anne Arundel (Md.) CC.
25. *William Beauchamp, 1b-lhp, Overlea HS, Baltimore.
26. *Edward Griffin, rhp, Montgomery (Md.) JC.
27. *Bruce James, of-1b, Woodlawn HS, Baltimore.
28. *Kyle Roher, c, Wesley (Del.) College.

### January—Secondary Phase (4)

1. *Richard Soriano, of, Miami-Dade CC North.—DNP
2. (void) *Richard Wanless, rhp, Quincy, Mass.
3. John Vance, c, Western Kentucky University.
4. Henry Hyde Jr., lhp, Loyola (Ill.) University.
5. Frank Shimerdla, lhp, Bishop Ryan HS, Omaha, Neb.
6. *Gary Gaiser, rhp, SUNY-Buffalo.
7. *David Pyles, ss-2b, Olympic (Wash.) JC.
8. *Joe Munoz, of-ss, Miller HS, Corpus Christi, Texas.
9. *Alan Lindsay, lhp, Gaston (N.C.) Tech.

### June—Regular Phase (13)

1. John Bedard, rhp-c, Springfield (Mass.) Tech HS.—(Low A)
2. Kenneth Waiss, rhp, DePew (N.Y.) HS.—(Low A)
3. Scott Johnson, rhp, Millersburg Military Institute, Florence, Ky.—(High A)
4. Eddie Sherlin, of-2b, Gallatin (Tenn.) Senior HS.—(AA)
5. Chester Gunter, rhp, Edison HS, Fresno, Calif.—(AA)
6. Gary Gandy, of, Westbury HS, Houston.
7. Brad Albertson, ss, Cascade HS, Everett, Wash.
8. *John Simontacchi, c, Fremont HS, Sunnyvale, Calif.
9. Richard Stuart, c, Central Kitsap HS, Bremerton, Wash.
10. Rich Standart, ss, St. Mary's HS, Stockton, Calif.
**11. *John Caneira, rhp, Naugatuck (Conn.) HS.—(1977-78)**
12. Jim Sanderson, 1b, Charter Oaks HS, Covina, Calif.
13. Richard DeMaria, 1b, Springfield (Mass.) Tech HS.
**14. Dave Parker, of, Courter Tech HS, Cincinnati.—(1973-91)**
15. Gary Kelley, of, McClatchy HS, Sacramento, Calif.
16. Theodia Johnson, 3b-of, Allen Carver HS, Cincinnati.
17. Robert Stewart, ss, Westwood (N.J.) HS.
18. Gary Abram, rhp, Union HS, Tulsa, Okla.
19. Richard Swinchock, lhp, Bethlehem-Center HS, Clarksville, Pa.
20. Charles Arrendale, rhp, Marian (Ind.) College.
21. Ed Robbins, rhp, Ohio University.
22. *Ken St. Pierre, c, Danvers (Mass.) HS.
**23. Ed Ott, 3b-c, Muncy (Pa.) HS.—(1974-81)**
24. Kenneth Stollmeyer, of, Charter Oak HS, Glendora, Calif.
25. *Ron Hooks, of, Far Rockaway (N.Y.) HS.
26. *Greg Van Gaver, rhp, O'Dea HS, Seattle.
27. *Charles Ringer, ss, Dearborn Heights, Mich.
28. *Bennie Allison, 3b-1b, Ursuline HS, Youngstown, Ohio.
29. Richard Berry, ss, Washtenaw (Mich.) CC.
30. *Calvin Jones, 3b-ss, Edison HS, Philadelphia.
31. Pat Cassaday, of-rhp, Miles (Iowa) Community HS.
32. Terry Bowman, 1b, Pensacola (Fla.) HS.
33. *David Keigan, rhp, Braintree (Mass.) HS.
34. *Paul Kurpiel, of, Chaminade HS, Dayton, Ohio.
35. *John Keough, rhp, Rockland (Mass.) HS.
36. *Greg Bish, rhp, Northeastern Oklahoma JC.
37. *Carlos Hughes, lhp, Aurora (N.C.) HS.
38. *Stan Rosenbrock, ss, Brighton (Colo.) HS.
39. *Robert Clites, rhp, Mapletown HS, Bobtown, Pa.
40. *Mark Whiting, 3b-of, Grand Junction (Colo.) HS.
41. *Stephen Jarrard, 2b, Bellaire HS, Houston.
42. *Michael Wood, of, Brookhaven HS, Columbus, Ohio.
43. Arthur Rousseau, rhp, Washtenaw (Mich.) CC.
44. Carl Hewlett, rhp, Marshall University.
45. Steve Evert, of, Washington State University.
46. Richard Stephenson, of-1b, Idaho State University.
47. John Sullivan, c, Washington State University.
48. *Michael Rollins, 1b-c, Beaver Falls (Pa.) HS.
49. *Ray Parr, lhp, Shorecrest HS, Seattle.
50. *David Mroczkowski, ss, Bridgeport (Ohio) HS.
51. *Edwin McGraw, rhp, Downingtown (Pa.) HS.
52. *Jeff Silfies, 1b, Northampton County Area (Pa.) CC.
53. *James Caviglia, c, Santa Clara University.
54. *Dave Chambers, rhp, University of Puget Sound.
55. *Stew Casterline, c-rhp, Mansfield (Pa.) University.
56. *John Bowling, lhp, LaRue County HS, Hodgensville, Ky.
57. *Jerry Gomez, lhp, Bishop Ryan HS, Omaha, Neb.
58. *Dennis Peters, rhp, Turner HS, Beloit, Wis.
59. *Ray Baye, rhp, Northampton (Mass.) HS.
60. Anthony Buckley, rhp-of, Ridley Township HS, Swarthmore, Pa.

### June—Secondary Phase (15)

1. Richard Astor, of-3b, Edinboro (Pa.) University.—(Short-season A)
2. Clinton Olson, rhp, Big Bend (Wash.) CC.
3. *Peter Castle, rhp, Monroe (N.Y.) CC.
4. *James Heard, ss, Dalton (Ga.) JC.
5. *Steve Hunter, c, Yakima Valley (Wash.) JC.

## ST. LOUIS CARDINALS

### January—Regular Phase (12)

1. Donald Reed, rhp, Wilson HS, Easton, Pa.—(High A)
2. David Fitzmaurice, 1b, St. John's University.
**3. Mike Tyson, ss, Indian River (Fla.) CC.—(1972-81)**
4. Pascal Johnson, 1b-of, Eastern Oklahoma State JC.
5. *Edwin Steverson, of, San Diego Mesa JC.
6. Greg Garver, of, Chaffey (Calif.) JC.
7. *Van Winters, rhp, Fresno (Calif.) CC.
8. *Luis Jiminez, ss, Chaffey (Calif.) JC.
9. *Darrell Cederlind, 3b, Chaffey (Calif.) JC.

### January—Secondary Phase (6)

**1. *Bucky Dent, 3b, Miami-Dade North CC.—(1973-84)**
DRAFT DROP *Major league manager (1989-90)*
2. *Bill Dobbs, lhp, Oklahoma State University.
3. *Rich Fillings, lhp, Indian River (Fla.) CC.
**4. Rudy Arroyo, lhp, Foothill (Calif.) JC.—(1971)**
5. Staff Branch, rhp, Hudson Valley (N.Y.) CC.
6. *Wayne Miller, lhp, Ohlone (Calif.) JC.
7. *George Chavez, rhp, Delano (Calif.) HS.
8. Richard Brown, of, Cal Poly San Luis Obispo.
9. *Peter Halfman, of, American River (Calif.) JC.

### June—Regular Phase (11)

1. Jim Browning, rhp-ss, Emma Sansom HS, Gadsden, Ala.—(AA)
2. Ron Kinner, c-of, Dunbar HS, Lubbock, Texas.—(AA)
3. Eddie Wheeler, ss, Sarasota (Fla.) HS.—(AAA)
4. Mark Covert, rhp, Boulder (Colo.) HS.—(AA)
**5. Greg Terlecky, rhp, West Covina (Calif.) HS.—(1975)**
6. Robin Sievers, 3b, Hazelwood HS, St. Louis.
DRAFT DROP *Son of Roy Sievers, major leaguer (1949-65)*
**7. Don Durham, rhp-of, Western Kentucky University.—(1972-73)**
**8. *Bob Allietta, c, Lawrence HS, Falmouth, Mass.—(1975)**
9. Fred Warner, rhp, Lake Forest (Ill.) College.
**10. Marc Hill, c, Elsberry (Mo.) HS.—(1973-86)**
11. *Paul Dyer, lhp, St. Ignatius College Prep HS, San Francisco.
12. John Hund, ss-2b, Wilson HS, Long Beach, Calif.
13. *Thomas Kennedy, ss, Northport (N.Y.) HS.
14. Ray Cingle, 1b, Bald Eagle HS, Clarence, Pa.
15. Dennis Duhan, rhp, Orange-Stark HS, Orange, Texas.
16. *Zane Grubbs, lhp, Brenham (Texas) HS.
17. *Michael Ford, 3b, Elk City HS, Woodward, Okla.
18. *Bruce Madden, ss, Danvers (Mass.) HS.
19. Ricky Shepard, lhp, Gorham (Ill.) HS.
20. Mark Hale, 1b, Blinn (Texas) JC.
21. *Richard Wilson, lhp-of, Pendleton (S.C.) HS.
22. Virgil Erickson, c, Wartburg (Iowa) College.
23. *Stan Kerby, rhp-of, Meridian HS, Mound City, Ill.
24. *Farrell Vincent, rhp, Christian Brothers HS, Memphis, Tenn.
25. Ken Faria, 1b, Mission HS, San Jose, Calif.
26. *Dennis Bean, lhp, Newport Harbor HS, Costa Mesa, Calif.
27. *Ed Orizzi, c, Shrewsbury (Mass.) HS.
28. *Eugene Reinke, 1b, Mesa (Ariz.) CC.
**29. John Denny, rhp, Prescott (Ariz.) HS.—(1974-86)**
30. *Roy Meisner, of, West Valley (Calif.) JC.
31. John Davis, rhp, Russellville (Ark.) HS.
32. *Wilmer Aaron, ss, Manual Arts HS, Los Angeles.
33. Mark Gasperino, 1b, Pasadena (Calif.) CC.
34. Willie Farrow, lhp-of, Fremont HS, Los Angeles.
35. *Clif Holland, lhp, San Carlos (Calif.) HS.
36. *Clint Myers, 3b, Lakewood (Calif.) HS.
DRAFT DROP *Father of Corey Myers, first-round draft pick, Diamondbacks (1999)*
**37. Bake McBride, lhp-of, Westminster (Mo.) College.—(1973-83)**
38. *Robert Jurgensen, rhp, Lakeland Regional HS, Ringwood, N.J.
39. Thomas Kimak, rhp, Pequannock (N.J.) HS.
40. Stephen Yetsko, 3b, Lakeland Regional HS, Skyline Lake, N.J.
41. Danny Reynolds, c, Hollywood (Fla.) HS.

### June—Secondary Phase (23)

1. *Paul Sands, rhp, Bacone (Okla.) JC.—(AA)
2. Bill Bright, of, Louisiana State University.
3. *David Breshears, 2b, University of Iowa.
4. *Craig Barnes, 1b, Mount San Antonio (Calif.) JC.
5. *Craig Menzl, lhp, Adelphi (N.Y.) College.

## SAN DIEGO PADRES

### January—Regular Phase (2)

**1. John Scott, ss, Centennial HS, Los Angeles.—(1974-77)**

2. Mike Chapman, of, San Diego Mesa JC.
3. *Barry Parker, c-1b, Southern Tech (Ga.) Institute.
4. *Kevin Bryant, ss, Valencia (Fla.) CC.
5. *Larry Sweat, lhp-of, Grossmont (Calif.) JC.

**January—Secondary Phase (12)**

1. Dan Bielski, rhp, Michigan State University.—(AAA)
**2. *Doug Ault, of, Panola (Texas) JC.—(1976-80)**
3. *Robert Beach, rhp, Cabrillo (Calif.) JC.
4. Henry Yeargan, ss, Brewton Parker (Ga.) JC.
5. Roger Gregg, c, Southwestern (Calif.) JC.

**June—Regular Phase (1)**

**1. Mike Ivie, c, Walker HS, Decatur, Ga.—(1971-83)**
**2. Dan Spillner, rhp, Federal Way (Wash.) HS.—(1974-85)**
3. Fred Seibly, rhp, Granada Hills (Calif.) HS.—(High A)
**4. Steve Simpson, rhp, Washburn (Kan.) University.—(1972)**
5. Ulysees Wilson, ss, Florida A&M University.—(AAA)
**6. Bob Davis, rhp-ss, Locust Grove (Okla.) HS.—(1973-81)**
7. Richard Arendell, 3b, Mayfair HS, Bellflower, Calif.
8. Wayne Rettig, lhp, Davenport Central HS, Davenport, Iowa.
9. Robert Gibson, rhp, McLain HS, Tulsa, Okla.
10. Ed Evilsizor, 3b-of, Kearny HS, San Diego.
11. *Marvin Webb, 2b, John F. Kennedy HS, San Pablo, Calif.
12. Ronald Olson, rhp, Clayton Valley HS, Concord, Calif.
**13. *Steve Dillard, ss, Saltillo (Miss.) HS.—(1975-82)**
14. Nick Perlozza, 1b, High Point College.
15. John Krawiecki, rhp, University of New Haven.
16. Doug Hunt, of, San Diego State University.
17. *Ron Scott, of, Eastern Oregon State College.
**18. Ralph Garcia, rhp, University of Nevada-Las Vegas.—(1972-74)**
19. William Morrell, lhp, Ferris State (Mich.) College.
20. *Thomas Hurn, of-1b, Central HS, Cedar Rapids, Iowa.
21. *Terry Farmer, rhp, Jordan HS, Columbus, Ga.
22. *Roger Keilig, c, San Carlos HS, Redwood City, Calif.
**23. Larry Hardy, rhp, University of Texas.—(1974-76)**
24. Michael Smith, of, Pacific (Ore.) University.
25. Dick Brown, lhp, University of Oklahoma.

**June—Secondary Phase (21)**

1. Bob Graczyk, rhp, Illinois State University.—(AA)
2. *Steve Easton, lhp, Brigham Young University.
3. *William Bell, ss, Jefferson State (Ala.) JC.

## SAN FRANCISCO GIANTS

**January—Regular Phase (18)**

**1. Randy Moffitt, rhp, Long Beach State University.—(1972-83)**
DRAFT DROP *Brother of Billie Jean King (Hall of Fame tennis player)*
2. Charles Erickson, of, Los Angeles Pierce JC.
3. *Bruce Frankum, rhp, Valencia (Fla.) CC.
4. Steve Faria, c-1b, Ohlone (Calif.) JC.
5. *Mike Hansen, rhp, San Diego CC.
6. Terry Nelson, inf-of, Antelope Valley (Calif.) JC.
7. *Russ Atterbery, c, JC of the Siskiyous (Calif.).
8. *Dennis Primeau, ss, St. Clair County (Mich.) CC.
9. *Arthur Carpenter, lhp, Lower Columbia (Wash.) JC.
10. *James Whaley, 3b-of, St. Clair County (Mich.) CC.
11. *Charles Berg, of, Bakersfield (Calif.) JC.
12. *Lamar Crook, of, JC of the Sequoias (Calif.).
13. *Bruce Courtmanch, rhp, Bellevue (Wash.) CC.
14. Gary Williams, rhp, Shoreline (Wash.) CC.
15. *Philip Jones, inf, Spokane (Wash.) CC.
16. *Steven Schrader, inf, El Camino (Calif.) JC.
17. Robert Ulrich, rhp, Fresno State University.

**January—Secondary Phase (2)**

**1. Chris Speier, ss, Laney (Calif.) JC.—(1971-89)**
DRAFT DROP *Father of Justin Speier, major leaguer (1998-2007)*
2. *Stan Hamlin, rhp, Bakersfield (Calif.) JC.
3. Andrew Nelson, rhp, Everett (Wash.) CC.
4. *Brian Applegate, ss, San Diego Mesa JC.
5. *Craig Barnes, 1b-lhp, Mount San Antonio (Calif.) JC.
6. Clare Leifer, 2b, Marysville, Wash.
7. *Ernie Henrickson, rhp, Washington State University.
8. *John Behrens, inf, Fresno (Calif.) CC.

**June—Regular Phase (17)**

**1. John D'Acquisto, rhp, St. Augustine HS, San Diego.—(1973-82)**
**2. Butch Metzger, rhp, Kennedy HS, Sacramento, Calif.—(1974-78)**
3. Kyle Hypes, lhp-of, Santana HS, Lakeside, Calif.—(AAA)
4. *Mark Lucich, 1b, Eureka (Calif.) HS.—(AA)
DRAFT DROP *Attended Stanford; never re-drafted*
**5. *Jim Otten, rhp, Mesa (Ariz.) CC.—(1974-81)**
DRAFT DROP *Returned to Mesa (Ariz.) CC; re-drafted by Red Sox, January 1971/secondary phase (1st round)*
6. *Mark Hance, 1b, South Bakersfield (Calif.) HS.
7. Michael Haynes, of, San Diego (Calif.) HS.
8. *Bill Taylor, inf, San Dieguito HS, Encinitas, Calif.
9. Bill Bates, rhp, Eisenhower HS, Rialto, Calif.
10. John Parslow, rhp, Fermin Lasuen HS, San Pedro, Calif.
11. John Ogden, rhp, Far Rockaway HS, Broad Channel, N.Y.
12. Eugene Alim, inf, Imperial Beach (Calif.) HS.
13. *Stan Mann, ss, Southwest HS, St. Louis.
14. *Jim Hogan, of, Golden West (Calif.) JC.
DRAFT DROP *First overall draft pick, January 1971/secondary phase, Bend Rainbows (Northwest League)*
15. *Robert Miller, of, Grant Union HS, Sacramento, Calif.
16. *Vern Wilkins, 1b, Mesa (Ariz.) CC.
17. Thomas Smith, ss, Lincoln HS, San Diego.
18. *Ray Cocco, 2b, Sequoia HS, Redwood City, Calif.
19. Glenn Milani, 1b, Mendel Catholic HS, Chicago.
20. *Bill Sero, ss, Garfield Heights (Ohio) HS.
21. Steven Tener, rhp, Stagg HS, Stockton, Calif.
22. *Michael Hall, rhp, Mesa (Colo.) College.
23. Rick Schroeder, 2b, University of Wisconsin-Oshkosh.
24. *Mark Crane, ss, Flint Central HS, Flint, Mich.
**25. Doug Capilla, lhp, Westmont HS, Campbell, Calif.—(1976-81)**
26. *John Fuzak, 3b, Alma (Mich.) College.
**27. *Warren Brusstar, rhp, Napa (Calif.) HS.—(1977-85)**
28. *Tom Hofer, c, Mountain Home (Idaho) HS.
29. Dale Dunham, rhp, Central Michigan University.
30. Steve Franceschi, rhp, University of the Pacific.
31. Jim Vaughn, rhp, Seton HS, Chandler, Ariz.
32. *Paul Djakanow, 3b-1b, Chadsey HS, Detroit.
33. *Ernest Moen, ss, Golden West (Calif.) JC.
34. *Eric Geister, rhp, East Detroit (Mich.) HS.
35. *Ben Heise, ss, Vacaville (Calif.) HS.
DRAFT DROP *Brother of Bob Heise, major leaguer (1967-77)*
36. *Mike Henley, lhp, Vacaville (Calif.) HS.
37. *David Whitney, lhp, Astoria (Ore.) HS.
38. *Steve Borsczwski, c, Seton Hall University.
39. *Samuel Shea, rhp, Winona State (Minn.) University.
40. Kenneth Danielson, of-1b, Wagner College.

**June—Secondary Phase (1)**

**1. Dave Kingman, rhp-of, University of Southern California.—(1971-86)**
**2. *Pete Varney, 1b, Harvard University.—(1973-76)**
DRAFT DROP *First overall draft pick, June 1966/American Legion phase, Athletics; first overall draft pick, January 1968/secondary phase, Astros; first overall draft pick, June 1971/secondary phase (active), White Sox*
**3. Jim Barr, rhp, University of Southern California.—(1971-83)**

## WASHINGTON SENATORS

**January—Regular Phase (13)**

1. (void) *Julian Hines, rhp, Tryon, N.C.—DNP
2. *Guy Freeland, rhp, Mount San Antonio (Calif.) JC.
**3. *Mardie Cornejo, rhp, Miami (Ohio) JC.—(1978)**
DRAFT DROP *Father of Nate Cornejo, first-round draft pick, Tigers (1998); major leaguer (2001-04).*
4. David Wisniewski, ss, SUNY Tech JC-Alfred.
5. (void) *Don Thomas, rhp, Olar HS, Denmark, S.C.

**January—Secondary Phase (1)**

**1. Bill Fahey, c, St. Clair County (Mich.) CC.—(1971-83)**
DRAFT DROP *Father of Brandon Fahey, major leaguer (2006-08)*
2. *Bill Borelli, 1b, Santa Clara University.
3. *David Carey, rhp, University of Minnesota.
4. *Ray Coley, c, Valparaiso University.
**5. Bill Madlock, ss-3b, Southeastern (Iowa) CC.—(1973-87)**
6. *Arnold Braden, lhp, Orange Park, Fla.
7. *James Kiley, ss, University of Massachusetts.
8. *Walt Biercevicz, of-lhp, Norwalk (Conn.) CC.
9. *Tom Rosa, ss, Miami-Dade CC South.

**June—Regular Phase (14)**

1. Charles "Chip" Maxwell, 3b-ss, Zane Trace HS, Kingston, Ohio.—(AAA)
2. Art DeFilippis, lhp-of, Stamford Catholic HS, Stamford, Conn.—(AAA)
3. *Steve Baumiller, rhp, Forest Hill HS, West Palm Beach, Fla.—(Rookie)
DRAFT DROP *Attended Florida Southern; re-drafted by Indians, 1973 (16th round)*
4. Gary Jackson, lhp, Hicksville (N.Y.) HS.–(Low A)
**5. Rick Waits, lhp, Therrell HS, Atlanta.—(1973-85)**
6. *Richard Baker, rhp, Holy Cross HS, Lynchburg, Va.
7. Rick Kemp, lhp, Kankakee (Ill.) CC.
8. *Paul Stombaugh, of, High Point HS, College Park, Md.
9. David Daniels, ss, Union (N.J.) HS.
10. *Harvey Willis, ss, George Washington HS, Danville, Va.
11. Tim French, lhp, South Charleston (W.Va.) HS.
12. *Edgar DeFore, rhp, Lanier HS, Macon, Ga.
13. Edward Szado, lhp, Providence College.
**14. *Joe Simpson, of, Norman (Okla.) HS.—(1975-83)**
15. *Mike Kirchoff, of, Miami-Dade CC South.
16. Francis Obermeier, 3b, St. Louis University.
17. Steve Greenberg, 1b, Yale University.
DRAFT DROP *Son of Hank Greenberg, major leaguer (1930-47)*
18. *Rick Colzie, rhp-ss, Miami-Dade CC South.
**19. *Jerry Remy, 2b, Somerset (Mass.) HS.—(1975-84)**
20. Larry Brooks, rhp, David Douglas HS, Portland, Ore.
**21. *Bruce Sutter, rhp, Donegal HS, Mount Joy, Pa.—(1976-88)**
DRAFT DROP *Elected to Baseball Hall of Fame, 2006*
22. *Les Kozlowski, lhp, Quigley Prep HS, Chicago.
23. *Dave Cosgrove, rhp, University of Minnesota.
24. James Redmon, rhp-of, Washburn (Kan.) University.
25. *William Robbins, rhp, Calhoun (Ga.) HS.
26. *Greg Baldwin, of, Dykes HS, Atlanta.
27. *George McCollum, lhp, Edgewater HS, Orlando, Fla.
28. Bobby Billings, of, Appalachian State University.
29. *Fred Gianiny, lhp, Wheaton (Md.) HS.
30. *Brad Fulk, 2b, South Hagerstown HS, Hagerstown, Md.
31. Sam Miller, rhp, Appalachian State University.
32. *Tim Sherrill, 1b, Miami-Dade CC South.
33. *John O'Connor, c, Hammond HS, Alexandria, Va.
34. Sylvester Swindler, of, University of Southwestern Louisiana.
35. *Danny Evans, rhp, Miami-Dade CC South.
36. Ken Rhyne, c, Pfeiffer (N.C.) College.
37. *Gordon Slade, of, Davidson College.
38. *Robert Boschulte, 2b, University of Wisconsin.
39. *Todd Brenizer, lhp, Greenville (Tenn.) HS.
40. Bruce Sydnor, c, Robert E. Peary HS, Rockville, Md.
41. John Bennett, rhp, Coral Park HS, Miami.
42. *Anthony Giordano, c-of, Miami-Dade CC North.
43. Mark Munoz, c, Carol City HS, Miami.
44. *Roger Mammen, of, Hartsburg-Emden HS, Emden, Ill.
45. *Brian Lovett, rhp, Coral Park HS, Miami.
46. *Robert Woodland, rhp, Suitland (Md.) HS.
47. Johnny Gasque, rhp-ss, Latta HS, Dillon, S.C.

**June—Secondary Phase (10)**

**1. Lenny Randle, inf, Arizona State University.—(1971-82)**
**2. *Mardie Cornejo, rhp, Wellington, Kan.—(1978)**
DRAFT DROP *Father of Nate Cornejo, first-round draft pick, Tigers (1998); major leaguer (2001-04).*
3. Francis Karmelich, c, UC Riverside.
4. Archie Cameron, rhp, Miami-Dade CC North.
5. Dennis Auckland, 1b, West Chester (Pa.) University.
6. *Larry Prieto, 2b, Fresno (Calif.) CC.
7. Mike Slade, rhp, Arlington, Va.
8. *Shawn Harris, rhp, Johnson & Wales (R.I.) JC.

## BEND RAINBOWS (CLASS A NORTHWEST LEAGUE)

**January—Regular Phase (1)**

1-3. No selections.
4. *Ken Suzawa, lhp, Baldwin HS, Kahului, Hawaii.

**January—Secondary Phase (1)**

1-3. No selections.
4. *Jeff Wingert, c, Chaffey (Calif.) JC.
5. *Gary Addeo, rhp, Cerritos (Calif.) JC.

**June—Regular Phase (1)**

1-3. No selections.
4. *Tom Boyd, lhp, Wilcox HS, Santa Clara, Calif.—(AAA)
DRAFT DROP *Attended West Valley (Calif.) JC; re-drafted by Phillies, January, 1970/secondary phase (1st round)*
5. *Charles Chatham, lhp, Ramona HS, Riverside, Calif.—DNP
DRAFT DROP *No school; never re-drafted*
6. Tom Trebelhorn, c-3b, Portland State University.
DRAFT DROP *Major league manager (1986-94)*
7. Jim Van Wyck, ss, University of Oregon.
8. Phil Bushman, of, University of Oregon.
9. Allan Wise, of, Chapman (Calif.) College.
10. *Gary Roma, 3b-of, Chaffey (Calif.) JC.

**June—Secondary Phase (1)**

No selection.

# 1971

## AT A GLANCE

### This Date In History
**WINTER DRAFT:** Jan. 13
**SUMMER DRAFT:** June 8-9

### Best Draft
**KANSAS CITY ROYALS.** The Royals targeted **ROY BRANCH** (1) and **GEORGE BRETT** (2) with their first pick, and gambled by taking Branch first that Brett would still be available the second time around. He was, and the Royals added **MARK LITTELL** (12), **STEVE BUSBY** (June/secondary phase) and **JOHN WATHAN** (January/regular phase).

### Worst Draft
**CHICAGO WHITE SOX.** The Sox drafted catcher **DANNY GOODWIN** with the No. 1 pick, and didn't sign him and seven of their selections in the first 10 rounds—including three additional future big leaguers.

### First-Round Bust
**WILLIAM "SUGAR BEAR" DANIELS, RHP, ATHLETICS.** Daniels was invited to big league spring training in 1972 by A's owner Charlie Finley, who personally nicknamed him "Sugar Bear." He made such a favorable impression with his superior raw stuff that he nearly cracked the Opening Day roster, but Daniels' career never took off after he was assigned to Class A to begin the '72 season.

### On Second Thought
**GEORGE BRETT, SS, ROYALS; MIKE SCHMIDT, SS, PHILLIES.** In one of the great coincidences in draft history, the two Hall of Famers were drafted with back-to-back picks in the second round. Both were drafted as shortstops and began their careers at that position, but soon moved to their more natural positions and became arguably the two greatest third basemen in baseball history.

### Late-Round Find / Never Too Late
**KEITH HERNANDEZ, 1B, CARDINALS (42ND ROUND).** Not only was Hernandez,

# Teams find big talent, just not in first round

The regular phase of the June 1971 draft got off on the wrong foot when the Chicago White Sox selected catcher Danny Goodwin with the No. 1 overall pick but were unable to sign the 17-year-old Illinois high school product.

Three picks later, the Montreal Expos took Condredge Holloway, a shortstop from the Alabama prep ranks, who also chose not to sign.

By the time the top half of the first round was complete, the talent selected was so thin that journeyman infielder Tom Veryzer, a lifetime .241 hitter selected 11th by the Detroit Tigers, would become the most productive big leaguer drafted.

But things got better. Considerably better.

Future Hall of Famer Jim Rice and Frank Tanana, who would win 240 games in the majors, were among those selected later in the first round.

George Brett and Mike Schmidt, two of the greatest third basemen in baseball history and both first-ballot Hall of Famers, were called in the second round—with back-to-back picks.

Future Cy Young Award winner Ron Guidry was taken a round later.

Keith Hernandez, one of the best first basemen of his generation, wasn't tabbed until the 42nd round. Bruce Sutter? The future Hall of Famer wasn't drafted at all.

There have been few drafts over 50 years when the talent, especially the elite-level talent, was so grossly misread as this one.

It may be no coincidence that the 1971 draft—the June regular phase, at least—was the last one in which the entire first round was higher-risk, high school selections. It wasn't until the White Sox led off the second round by drafting Ohio State outfielder Bill Sharp that a college player was taken.

That no college player went in the first round was not an indictment of the 1971 college crop. To the contrary. It's just that almost all the high-profile candidates, like pitchers Pete Broberg (Dartmouth) and Burt Hooton (Texas), and outfielder Rob Ellis (Michigan State), weren't eligible for the regular phase because they had already been drafted—Broberg with the second pick overall in 1968. That trio likely would have gone 1-2-3 under more inclusive rules, just like they went off the board in the lower-profile secondary phase.

In the end, the best college talent to emerge from the 1971 draft, regardless of phase, was Schmidt, a previously undrafted high school senior and two-time All-American at Ohio University. He lasted until the 30th pick of the regular phase, when he was finally tabbed by the Philadelphia Phillies. Brett, unquestionably the best high school selection in 1971, went one pick earlier, to the Kansas City Royals.

On any numbers of counts, the outstanding careers of Brett and Schmidt have been linked ever since.

Teams found little success in the first round of the 1971 draft, but in the second round and other phases, Hall of Famers like George Brett, the Royals' second-round pick, were waiting to be plucked

## ROYALS, PHILS LUCK OUT

Brett and Schmidt were prime targets of the Royals and Phillies, and both clubs gave serious consideration to taking them in the first round. But both elected to roll the dice, hoping that Brett and Schmidt would still be available the second time around. To their good fortune, they were.

Both the Royals and Phillies cast their lot with high school pitchers in the first round, choosing two players named Roy: Roy Branch in the case of the Royals, Roy Thomas in the case of the Phillies. Both reached the big leagues, but neither came close to the success enjoyed by Brett and Schmidt.

In 21 years with the Royals, Brett posted a significantly higher batting average than Schmidt, .305 to .267, but Schmidt had a leg up with the power numbers he accumulated over 18 years. Schmidt hit 548 homers, while Brett had 305. In RBIs, they were practically a dead heat as Brett's total of 1,596 topped Schmidt by one.

Both spent their entire careers with the same club, and may have reached the pinnacle of their success in the same year, 1980. Brett, who flirted with .400 much of the season before settling at .390, was the American League MVP. Schmidt (.286-48-121) earned the same honor in the National League, and was MVP of the World Series, won by the Phillies over the Royals in six games.

Brett and Schmidt both began their careers in the minors, somewhat inauspiciously, as short-

## 1971: THE FIRST ROUNDERS

| CLUB: PLAYER, POS., SCHOOL | HOMETOWN | B-T | HT. | WT. | AGE | BONUS | FIRST YEAR | LAST YEAR | PEAK LEVEL (YEARS) |
|---|---|---|---|---|---|---|---|---|---|
| **JUNE—REGULAR PHASE** | | | | | | | | | |
| 1. White Sox: Danny Goodwin, c, Central HS | Peoria, Ill. | L-R | 6-1 | 195 | 17 | Unsigned | 1975 | 1985 | Majors (7) |
| Draft's only two-time No. 1 selection hit .495-9-27 as prep senior; never came close to signing amid rumors he was looking for rich $100,000 bonus to skip college. | | | | | | | | | |
| 2. Padres: Jay Franklin, rhp, James Madison HS | Vienna, Va. | R-R | 6-2 | 185 | 18 | $65,000 | 1971 | 1977 | Majors (1) |
| Elevated to majors from Rookie ball in first season, worked 6 IP for Padres; hurt arm the next spring and sat out 1972, never returned as career/life fell apart. | | | | | | | | | |
| 3. Brewers: Tom Bianco, ss, Sewanhaka HS | Elmont, N.Y. | B-R | 5-11 | 185 | 18 | $50,000 | 1971 | 1979 | Majors (1) |
| First of three picks from Long Island in top 11 in this draft; got brief shot in majors in 1975 (.176-0-0 in 34 AB), sandwiched between nine years in minors. | | | | | | | | | |
| 4. Expos: Condredge Holloway, ss, Robert E. Lee HS | Huntsville, Ala. | R-R | 6-0 | 175 | 17 | Unsigned | Never Played Pro Ball | | |
| Expos always maintained their $75,000 offer was trumped by "outside forces" to steer two-sport star to college; first black QB in SEC history, later played in CFL. | | | | | | | | | |
| 5. Royals: Roy Branch, rhp, Beaumont HS | St. Louis | R-R | 5-11 | 180 | 17 | $50,000 | 1971 | 1980 | Majors (1) |
| Compared to Bob Gibson while growing up in St. Louis, but never fully recovered after injuring his arm the day before '71 draft; later served time in Mexican jail. | | | | | | | | | |
| 6. Phillies: Roy Thomas, rhp, Lompoc HS | Lompoc, Calif. | R-R | 6-5 | 195 | 17 | $65,000 | 1971 | 1990 | Majors (8) |
| Well-traveled player spent most of 20-year career in minors, posting 116-91, 3.55 record; won 20 games, including 14 with Mariners, in parts of eight MLB seasons. | | | | | | | | | |
| 7. Senators: Roger Quiroga, rhp, Ball HS | Galveston, Texas | R-R | 6-1 | 180 | 18 | $50,000 | 1972 | 1975 | Class A (3) |
| Traded to Phillies in Curt Flood deal before playing for Senators; limited to three seasons by arm injury (went 24-21, 4.08); later became mayor of Galveston. | | | | | | | | | |
| 8. Cardinals: Ed Kurpiel, 1b/lhp, Archbishop Molloy HS | Hollis, N.Y. | L-L | 6-3 | 210 | 17 | $83,750 | 1971 | 1978 | Class AAA (5) |
| Signed largest bonus in draft on strength of massive raw power; went deep 100 times in seven-year career, including five in Triple-A, but never played in majors. | | | | | | | | | |
| 9. Indians: David Sloan, rhp, Santa Clara HS | Santa Clara, Calif. | R-R | 6-1 | 175 | 19 | $40,000 | 1971 | 1976 | Class AA (1) |
| Still talked about as biggest arm ever to come from his hometown; reached Double-A in debut, but career derailed by injury and went 11-24, 5.03 overall in minors. | | | | | | | | | |
| 10. Braves: # Taylor Duncan, ss, Grant Union HS | Sacramento, Calif. | R-R | 5-10 | 165 | 18 | $25,000 | 1971 | 1980 | Majors (2) |
| Broke his ankle in first pro season and never fully recovered; reached MLB briefly in 1977-78, but spent bulk of career in minors (.283-74-469); died of stroke at 50. | | | | | | | | | |
| 11. Tigers: # Tom Veryzer, ss, Islip HS | Islip, N.Y. | R-R | 6-2 | 175 | 18 | $23,000 | 1971 | 1984 | Majors (12) |
| Hit .225-4-20 in pro debut, but earned MVP honors in Appy League because of magic glove; played 12 years in majors with four clubs, hit .241 with 14 HRs. | | | | | | | | | |
| 12. Astros: Neil Rasmussen, ss, Arcadia HS | Arcadia, Calif. | R-R | 6-2 | 185 | 18 | $40,000 | 1971 | 1978 | Class AA (3) |
| Hit .223 with 5 HRs in three years in Astros system, released after he refused move to mound; played five more years in minors after getting picked up by Brewers. | | | | | | | | | |
| 13. Angels: Frank Tanana, lhp, Catholic Central HS | Detroit | L-L | 6-2 | 180 | 17 | $50,000 | 1971 | 1993 | Majors (21) |
| Hard-throwing, dominant lefty looked destined for Cooperstown before hurting shoulder; forced to become a finesse pitcher, he still earned 240 wins in 21 years. | | | | | | | | | |
| 14. Mets: Rich Puig, 2b, Hillsborough HS | Tampa | L-R | 5-11 | 165 | 18 | $40,000 | 1971 | 1976 | Majors (1) |
| Drafted for his glove, he struggled in the field much of his career (67 errors in one two-year stretch), while hitting .234 overall; went hitless in 10 at-bats in majors. | | | | | | | | | |
| 15. Red Sox: Jim Rice, of, T.L. Hanna HS | Anderson, S.C. | R-R | 6-1 | 200 | 18 | $30,000 | 1971 | 1989 | Majors (16) |
| One of the best hitters of his generation; hit .298 with 382 homers in 16 years with Red Sox, highlighted by MVP season in '78; elected to Hall of Fame on final try. | | | | | | | | | |
| 16. Cubs: Jeff Wehmeier, rhp, Brebeuf Jesuit HS | Indianapolis | R-R | 6-4 | 185 | 18 | $44,000 | 1971 | 1973 | Class A (2) |
| Son of Herm Wehmeier, 14-year big leaguer; Jeff's career never materialized as he went 9-15, 5.08 in three seasons; released in '73, the same year his father died. | | | | | | | | | |
| 17. Athletics: Wlliam Daniels, rhp, MacKenzie HS | Detroit | R-R | 6-4 | 195 | 17 | $25,000 | 1972 | 1975 | Class A (4) |
| Nicknamed "Sugar Bear" by A's owner Charlie Finley, also described as righthanded Vida Blue; nearly cracked A's roster in 1972, never came close to majors again. | | | | | | | | | |
| 18. Giants: Frank Riccelli, lhp, Christian Brothers HS | Syracuse, N.Y. | L-L | 6-2 | 185 | 18 | $29,000 | 1971 | 1982 | Majors (3) |
| Hailed as most dominant arm ever to come out of Syracuse prep ranks, had one-hit/20-SO game as senior; went 3-3, 4.39 overall in brief major league time. | | | | | | | | | |
| 19. Yankees: Terry Whitfield, of, Palo Verde HS | Blythe, Calif. | L-R | 6-2 | 190 | 18 | $35,000 | 1971 | 1988 | Majors (10) |
| Known for his bat, had success in minors (.286-85-453) and showed flashes in majors (.281-33-179), but found greatest success in Japan (85 HRs in three years). | | | | | | | | | |
| 20. Dodgers: Rick Rhoden, rhp, Atlantic HS | Boynton Beach, Fla. | R-R | 6-3 | 195 | 18 | $45,000 | 1971 | 1989 | Majors (16) |
| Overcame osteomyelityis as child to win 151 games in majors, earn all-star/Silver Slugger honors, later became biggest money winner on celebrity golf tour. | | | | | | | | | |
| 21. Twins: Dale Soderholm, ss, Coral Park HS | Miami | R-R | 6-3 | 165 | 18 | $31,000 | 1971 | 1978 | Class AAA (5) |
| Younger brother of big leaguer Eric, also drafted by Twins; spent all but one season of eight-year minor league career in Twins system, hit .233-47-260 overall. | | | | | | | | | |
| 22. Pirates: Craig Reynolds, ss, John H. Reagan HS | Houston | L-R | 6-0 | 170 | 18 | $30,000 | 1971 | 1989 | Majors (15) |
| Drafted by Bucs, but spent bulk of career with hometown Astros, hit .256; later became pastor of Houston church; son Kyle was sixth-rounder in 2008. | | | | | | | | | |
| 23. Orioles: # Randy Stein, rhp, Ganesha HS | Pomona, Calif. | R-R | 6-4 | 200 | 18 | $20,000 | 1971 | 1983 | Majors (4) |
| Spent 13 years in pros, including parts of four in majors (5-6, 5.72); later became prominent insurance salesman, died in 2011 due to early onset of Alzheimer's. | | | | | | | | | |
| 24. Reds: # Mike Miley, ss, East Jefferson HS | New Orleans | B-R | 6-1 | 180 | 18 | Unsigned | 1974 | 1976 | Majors (2) |
| Like Holloway, passed on first-round offer to become QB in Southeastern Conference; drafted in first round again in 1974, died in car crash in 1977. | | | | | | | | | |
| **JANUARY—REGULAR PHASE** | | | | | | | | | |
| 1. Padres: Dave Hilton, 3b, Southwest Texas JC | Pearland, Texas | R-R | 6-1 | 185 | 20 | $10,000 | 1971 | 1981 | Majors (4) |
| Spent freshman year at Rice, headed to juco after big summer in Jayhawk League to become draft-eligible; went on to play four years in majors, hit .213-6-33. | | | | | | | | | |
| **JANUARY—SECONDARY PHASE** | | | | | | | | | |
| 1. Bend (A): James Hogan, of, Golden West (Calif.) JC | Westminster, Calif. | L-L | 6-0 | 170 | 20 | $10,000 | 1971 | 1974 | Class AAA (1) |
| Rare No. 1 pick by independent club; set Golden West records for homers, steals; traded to Angels in '72, played four years in minors (.249-21-152, 40 SB). | | | | | | | | | |
| **JUNE—SECONDARY PHASE (DELAYED)** | | | | | | | | | |
| 1. *Senators: Pete Broberg, rhp, Dartmouth | Palm Beach, Fla. | R-R | 6-3 | 195 | 21 | $83,000 | 1971 | 1978 | Majors (8) |
| Unsigned as No. 2 pick in 1968, became dominant arm in college, made pro debut in Senators rotation; struggled with command in big leagues, went 41-71. | | | | | | | | | |
| **JUNE—SECONDARY PHASE (ACTIVE)** | | | | | | | | | |
| 1. White Sox: Pete Varney, c/1b, Harvard | North Quincy, Mass. | R-R | 6-3 | 235 | 22 | $12,500 | 1971 | 1977 | Majors (4) |
| Finally signed after being drafted a record-tying seventh time following baseball/football career at Harvard; played in 69 games in majors, hit .247 with five homers. | | | | | | | | | |

**Signed to major league contract. # Deceased.*

## AT A GLANCE

who went on to hit .296 over a 17-year major league career, overlooked in the 1972 draft, but he was also the lowest pick that year to reach the majors. Hernandez was at least paid like a future star from the start as his $30,000 signing bonus was higher than the bonuses received by several first-rounders.

### Overlooked

**BRUCE SUTTER, RHP, CUBS.** Sutter was an unsigned 21st-round pick in the 1970 draft, but still qualifies as the only player from the draft era to be elected to the Hall of Fame after signing as a nondrafted free agent. The Cubs took a chance on the Old Dominion University drop-out by signing him for $500 three months after the 1972 draft's conclusion.

### International Gem

**TONY ARMAS, OF, PIRATES.** The Pirates get credit for signing Armas for $5,000 on Jan. 18, 1971, but the Venezuelan outfielder played only four games in Pittsburgh before being packaged to Oakland in a nine-player deal during spring training in 1977. Over the next 13 seasons, all in the American League, Armas went on to slug 251 homers, twice leading the league in that category.

### Minor League Take

**ROY THOMAS, RHP, PHILLIES.** Thomas, the sixth player drafted in 1971, went on to win 20 games in the majors over parts of eight seasons, but holds the unwanted distinction of winning more minor league games (116, from 1971-90) than any first-round pitcher in draft history.

### One Who Got Away

**CONDREDGE HOLLOWAY, SS, EXPOS.** In Danny Goodwin (first) and Holloway (fourth), two of the first four picks in the 1971 draft went

CONTINUED ON PAGE 112

## AT A GLANCE

CONTINUED FROM PAGE 111

unsigned—making it the most futile draft on record in terms of premium talent getting away. Unlike Goodwin, who signed four years later after being drafted No. 1 overall again, Holloway was lost for good when he rejected an offer from the Expos in order to play football at Tennessee. After college, he went on to play 13 years in the Canadian Football League.

### He Was Drafted?

**JOE THEISMANN, SS, TWINS (39TH ROUND).** Although Theismann never played baseball at Notre Dame, he was drafted by the Twins in 1971 with their 39th and last pick. Theismann, who excelled in baseball at a New Jersey high school, rejected both the Twins nominal offer and a fourth-round opportunity in that year's NFL draft to play three seasons in the Canadian Football League. He returned to the U.S. in 1974 to play 12 seasons in the NFL and was the winning quarterback for the Washington Redskins in Super Bowl 17.

### Did You Know . . .

A's second rounder **RON WILLIAMSON** became the subject of the first non-fiction book by best-selling author John Grisham, *The Innocent Man: Murder and Injustice in a Small Town,* which documents Williamson's wrongful conviction and his subsequent exoneration of his death sentence in a 1988 case that involved the rape and murder of an Oklahoma woman.

### They Said It

Milwaukee Brewers general manager **FRANK LANE** on **ROB ELLIS**, who began his career in the big leagues: "He's all baseball. If he can't play in the big leagues right now, I don't know who can. He has a chance to be a real star."—*Ellis hit .198 in an abbreviated big league career that lasted 36 games.*

stops. And they encountered their share of early struggles at the plate, before turning a corner and establishing themselves as two of the best offensive players of their generation.

Unlike Brett, Schmidt wasn't drafted out of high school—in part because he had two knee operations from playing football.

"I was your basic late bloomer," Schmidt said. "I was about the fourth or fifth best baseball player in school—a .250 hitter, and if you don't hit .400 in high school, nobody knows you're alive. I was always the kid with potential, but the only time I was a real star was in Little League. After that, I just seemed to be missing something."

Mike Schmidt

After graduating from Fairview High in Dayton, Ohio, Schmidt walked on in two sports at Ohio. He made the freshman basketball team, but was forced to quit that sport because his knees wouldn't hold up. They never bothered him playing baseball, though, and he went on to play four years of shortstop. He led the Bobcats to a berth in the 1970 College World Series, but wasn't drafted as a junior because he wasn't 21. But he finally earned a full scholarship by returning for his senior year.

Schmidt had a rough start to his professional career. He was called up to the Phillies late in 1972, and finished that season hitting .206 with one home run in 13 games. The next year, Schmidt hit just .196 with 136 strikeouts in his first full season, playing 132 games.

But in 1974, Schmidt arrived. He made the first of his 12 all-star teams that year and led all major leaguers in home runs (36). He duplicated that feat over the next two seasons, and won eight home run titles in all. He won the first of nine consecutive Gold Glove Awards in 1976, and the first of three NL MVP awards in 1980.

Brett, meanwhile, was no sure thing himself coming out of El Segundo (Calif.) High. The youngest of four brothers who played professionally, George demonstrated the least athletic prowess of the bunch initially, and it was the second-oldest Brett brother, Ken, who was 33-3 as a pitcher and hit .484 in high school, who was ticketed for stardom. He preceded George by five years and was the fourth overall pick in the 1966 draft.

"He was the best thing ever to come out of my hometown," Brett said. "He was better than anyone in everything in high school—baseball, football, you name it. Hey, he pitched for the Red Sox in the World Series when he was 19."

At 5-foot-1 and 105 pounds, George was nearly cut from the JV team as a freshman at El Segundo High. His highest batting average in high school was .351, and he lacked his brother's intense approach to the game.

"George was very well known, being from Southern California, but he wasn't a great tools guy," said then-Royals assistant scouting director Herk Robinson. "He was a heart, brain and guts type of player who could hit."

## How They Should Have Done It

Based on the career WAR (Wins Above Replacement, as calculated by Baseball-Reference.com) numbers achieved by all the players eligible for the 1971 draft, here's how the first round should have unfolded. Numbers in parentheses indicate the round when the player was actually drafted

| | Player, Pos. | Actual Draft | WAR | Bonus |
|---|---|---|---|---|
| 1. | Mike Schmidt, ss | Phillies (2) | 107.0 | $32,500 |
| 2. | George Brett, ss | Royals (2) | 88.4 | $25,000 |
| 3. | Keith Hernandez, 1b | Cardinals (42) | 60.1 | $30,000 |
| 4. | Frank Tanana, lhp | Angels (1) | 57.9 | $50,000 |
| 5. | Ron Guidry, lhp | Yankees (3) | 48.1 | $11,000 |
| 6. | Jim Rice, of | Red Sox (1) | 47.2 | $30,000 |
| 7. | Steve Rogers, rhp | Expos (June-S/1) | 45.1 | $27,500 |
| 8. | Rick Rhoden, rhp | Dodgers (1) | 35.9 | $45,000 |
| | Burt Hooton, rhp | Cubs (June-S/1) | 35.9 | $57,500 |
| 10. | Phil Garner, 2b | Athletics (Jan.-S/1) | 29.7 | $15,000 |
| 11. | Bruce Sutter, rhp | Cubs (NDFA) | 24.6 | $500 |
| 12. | Jerry Mumphrey, of | Cardinals (4) | 22.4 | $6,000 |
| 13. | Mike Caldwell, lhp | Padres (12) | 18.7 | $1,500 |
| 14. | Johnny Grubb, of | Padres (Jan.-S/1) | 16.6 | $5,000 |
| 15. | Steve Busby, rhp | Royals (June-S/2) | 16.3 | $18,500 |
| 16. | Dennis Lamp, rhp | Cubs (3) | 15.4 | $10,000 |
| 17. | Larry Herndon, of | Cardinals (3) | 15.1 | $12,000 |
| 18. | Jerry Remy, 2b | Angels (Jan.-S/8) | 14.4 | |
| 19. | Larry Andersen, rhp | Indians (7) | 14.2 | $10,000 |
| 20. | Art Howe, 3b | Pirates (NDFA) | 13.9 | None |
| 21. | Craig Reynolds, ss | Pirates (1) | 13.1 | $30,000 |
| 22. | Charlie Moore, c | Brewers (5) | 10.3 | $15,000 |
| 23. | Rob Wilfong, 2b | Twins (13) | 7.8 | $10,000 |
| 24. | Terry Whitfield, of | Yankees (1) | 5.9 | $35,000 |

| | Top 3 Unsigned Players | | | Year Signed |
|---|---|---|---|---|
| 1. | Roy Smalley, ss | Red Sox (Jan.-S/4) | 27.8 | 1974 |
| 2. | Mike Flanagan, lhp | Astros (16) | 26.3 | 1973 |
| 3. | Warren Cromartie, of | White Sox (7) | 16.2 | 1973 |

The Royals considered Brett for their first-round pick (fifth overall), but they decided to go with Branch, a St. Louis high school product who they believed had the potential to become another Bob Gibson, even amid reports that he had injured his elbow working out for the hometown Cardinals the day before the draft.

After signing for a bonus of $25,000—less than half the $56,000 bonus his brother had received from the Boston Red Sox five years earlier—Brett began his professional career at Billings in the Rookie-level Pioneer League at shortstop, his high school position. He had trouble going to his right defensively and soon shifted to third base.

In his first three minor league seasons, Brett never topped .300 or hit more than 10 home runs. He also struggled with the Royals when called up in 1974, with the swing he had always patterned after Red Sox Hall of Famer Carl Yastrzemski.

Later in 1974, Brett fell under the influence of noted hitting guru Charlie Lau, who transformed his approach. He taught him patience at the plate, to go to the opposite field and to concentrate on hitting the ball where it was pitched. From that point on, Brett became a hitting machine. He went on to collect 3,154 hits, the most ever by a third baseman. He also became one of only four players in major league history to accumulate 3,000 hits, 300 home runs and a career .300 average.

## SENATORS TAB BROBERG

Not only were Broberg, Hooton and Ellis the first three picks in the secondary phase of the 1971 draft, but all started their professional careers in the major leagues—becoming just three of 22 players in draft history to be so recognized.

None had careers that stood up to some of the best high school talent taken in the regular phase, and only Hooton had any long-term staying power.

The Washington Senators had the No. 1 pick in the secondary phase. By that time their owner, politician Bob Short, had soured on the Washington market. His Senators were in desperate straits financially and a year removed from becoming the Texas Rangers. Short had installed himself as his team's general manager, and was not averse to putting his own interests ahead of the team's long-term outlook. Short had been expected to go after Ellis with the No. 1 pick, but went instead for Broberg because he felt he had the best chance to give his club an immediate boost. Farm director Hal Keller supported the decision.

"He has a real good fastball," Keller said. "He's had some problems with control but he can make it in any league as long as he throws strikes with his fastball. He's as fine a pitcher as I've seen in a long, long time."

Broberg had been a hot commodity since turning down the Oakland A's as the second pick overall in the 1968 draft. He was still in demand three years later, despite an unimpressive 5-5 record his junior year in college at Dartmouth. His 1.43 ERA and 127 strikeouts in 82 innings were a truer indication of his potential.

Broberg's father, a judge in West Palm Beach, Fla., played an instrumental role in negotiations with the Senators, just as he did with the A's three years earlier when Oakland owner Charles O. Finley offered a reported $175,000 to sway his son away from an Ivy League education.

"I was too young to sign then," Broberg said. "I wasn't ready for pro ball. I would probably have been eaten alive. I don't regret passing up the bonus. When I was drafted in 1968, Mr. Finley had nothing to offer but a lot of money. It's unrealistic to think someone would give me that much now. It's a different market for players now."

The Senators signed Broberg to a bonus of $83,000, but the overall value of the deal exceeded $100,000, a club record, when a major league salary and other incentives were factored in.

Broberg, 21, signed in part because he wanted an opportunity to start his career in the big leagues. He got his wish, and made his debut 12 days after

### Fastest To The Majors

| | Player, Pos. | Drafted (Round) | Debut |
|---|---|---|---|
| 1. | # Burt Hooton, rhp | Cubs (June-S/1) | June 17, 1971 |
| 2. | # Rob Ellis, of | Brewers (June-S/1) | June 18, 1971 |
| 3. | # Pete Broberg, rhp | Senators (June-S/1) | June 20, 1971 |
| 4. | * Jay Franklin, rhp | Padres (1) | Sept. 4, 1971 |
| | Mike Caldwell, lhp | Padres (12) | Sept. 4, 1971 |

**LAST PLAYER TO RETIRE:** Larry Andersen, rhp (July 31, 1994)

*#Debuted in major leagues. *High school selection.*

## DRAFT SPOTLIGHT: BURT HOOTON

Burt Hooton holds a unique place in baseball history as one of the only pitchers to find sustained major league success using a knuckle-curve

Burt Hooton was a three-time All-American at Texas and one of the most dominant college pitchers of the draft era. He wrapped up a prolific career with the Longhorns in 1971 by going 11-2, 1.11, with a national-best 153 strikeouts in 97 innings, which fattened his career totals to 35-3, 1.14 with 386 strikeouts in 291 innings.

Few players ever burst onto the draft stage with more impressive credentials, and the Chicago Cubs showed no hesitation in taking Hooton with the second pick in the June secondary phase, or bringing him immediately to the big leagues to begin his professional career.

Hooton debuted with the Cubs on June 17, days after signing for a bonus of $57,500. He gave up three runs in three innings, though he hadn't pitched in a game in three weeks. He was shipped out to Triple-A Tacoma shortly thereafter, but if ever there was a pitcher equipped to pitch in the big leagues right out of college, Hooton was it.

His great equalizer was his trademark pitch, a baffling knuckle-curve. He unleashed that weapon on unsuspecting PCL hitters, striking out 135 in 102 innings, while posting a 1.68 ERA. In one outing, he tied a 66-year old PCL record by striking out 19. Hooton was back up with the Cubs in September. As a precocious 21-year-old, he beat the New York Mets twice—the first time on a three-hit, 15-strikeout effort, the second on a two-hit shutout.

Never has a player showed such domination in the major leagues in the same year he was drafted, and to their obvious regret, the Mets had drafted Hooton out of high school three years earlier, but didn't sign him.

Hooton didn't gain his early notoriety for his spectacular pitching as much as for his knuckle-curve. The pitch quickly became the rage of baseball, as no one else in the big leagues threw it, a delectable part-curve, part-knuckleball with a sharp downward bite.

"That ball breaks like its falling off a table," Cubs manager Leo Durocher raved. "Without a doubt, it's the sharpest curve I've seen since the one thrown by Tommy Bridges."

Hooton pitched a no-hitter the following April against Philadelphia, but soon too much advice and too much tinkering from too many pitching coaches left him confused. It took the edge off his meal ticket, and he never again displayed for the Cubs the remarkable dominance he did to start his career. He was basically a two-pitch pitcher in college, and early in his days as a pro, but scouts and coaches wanted to see a greater assortment. They didn't think he'd last as a starter with just two pitches.

Tommy Lasorda, who saw Hooton at his best in the PCL in 1971 while managing at Spokane, was stunned to see him three years later while a coach with the Los Angeles Dodgers. "He was the finest-looking pitcher I'd ever seen come directly out of college," Lasorda said. "Three years later, when I saw him pitching for the Cubs, I couldn't believe he was the same player. He was overweight, he looked unsure of himself, and he looked unhappy."

By the time he was traded to Los Angeles prior to the 1975 season, at Lasorda's urging, Hooton's career record stood at 34-44. With the Dodgers, he soon found a sympathetic pitching coach in Red Adams. Through Adams' tutelage, he got straightened around and would go on to win 117 more big league games—mostly by emphasizing his killer knuckle-curve, a pitch be began throwing at age 14 in Pony League.

"I tried to throw a regular knuckleball," Hooton said. "I couldn't throw it the regular way and the knuckle-curve is what I came up with. I fold my thumb underneath the ball and grip the seams on top with the knuckles of my first two fingers. Unlike a regular knuckler, which doesn't revolve at all, the knuckle-curve does have a little spin to it."

## WORTH NOTING

■ Among those drafted in 1971 were three renowned, future NFL quarterbacks: **JOE THEISMANN**, **ARCHIE MANNING** and **STEVE BARTKOWSKI**. Only Theismann never played baseball in college. At the time he was drafted by the Twins, Theismann had already signed to play with the Canadian Football League's Toronto Argonauts. Manning, drafted twice in 1971, was in the midst of contract negotiations with the NFL's New Orleans Saints when drafted in June by the White Sox. Bartkowski was drafted out of high school in 1971 by the Royals and went on to set University of California home run records, but cast his lot with the NFL when the Atlanta Falcons made him the No. 1 pick overall in 1975.

■ For the first time, the January draft was conducted by telephone from commissioner Bowie Kuhn's office. The total cost: $4,000. "For the average West Coast club, the draft used to cost about $2,000," said Johnny Johnson, chief administrator to Kuhn. "That included travel, hotel bills and entertainment for local area scouts. They saved all that expense."

■ A total of 938 players were selected in the three phases of the June draft. That continued a downward spiral from the 1,139 players that were drafted two years earlier, and 1,032 in 1970. The spiral would bottom out in 1974, with 725 selections.

■ On the same day the June draft began, Bruce Gardner, one of the greatest college pitchers of the pre-draft era, was found dead near the pitcher's mound at USC, his alma mater. He died of a self-inflicted gunshot wound to his left temple. Clutched in his right hand was his USC degree and a plaque that proclaimed him an All-American in 1960, the year he wrapped up his historic college career with an overall 40-5 record. Gardner played three seasons in the Dodgers organization, winning 31

**Pitching for last-place teams wore on righthander Pete Broberg, the first pick in a star-studded June secondary phase out of Dartmouth**

he was drafted, on Father's Day. He shut out the Red Sox for six innings and left in the seventh with the shutout still intact, though Boston rallied to win 4-3.

Broberg, who retired at 29, never quite lived up to his press clippings. He never had a winning season in eight years in the big leagues, bowing out with a 41-71 record. But he never had much of a chance.

"I just got tired of playing for last-place teams," he said. "I played on some horrible teams that did not have a good attitude or a good record."

Hooton was more heralded than Broberg over the course of his college career at Texas, and even more was expected of him in the short term. The Chicago Cubs took him with the second pick overall in the secondary phase.

The Cubs immediately brought Hooton to the big leagues for one start against St. Louis, on June 17, but he hadn't pitched in a game in three weeks and gave up three runs in three innings. He was then shipped out to Tacoma of the Triple-A Pacific Coast League after one outing.

Ellis, the third player taken in the secondary phase, stepped right off the Michigan State campus and into a Milwaukee Brewers uniform. As a college junior, Ellis hit .407 with a school-record 14 homers, and his performance left little doubt in the minds of Brewers personnel that he was ready to be a big leaguer.

"We're delighted to have him," Brewers general manager Frank Lane said. "He's all baseball. If he can't play in the big leagues right now, I don't know who can. He has a chance to be a real star."

Expectations were high when the Brewers traded away veteran first baseman Mike Hegan to clear a spot for Ellis, and Ellis singled off Oakland's Catfish Hunter in his first big league at-bat. Ellis, though, hit .198 in 36 games his first season with the Brewers. It would be three more years before another big league opportunity came his way. By then, the promise had faded.

## VARNEY FINALLY SIGNS

The 1971 draft marked the last time that college players who were drafted out of high school would be subject to automatic selection in the June secondary phase. In the future, all college players not drafted in the previous 13 months would be included in the regular phase.

As a transitional step, the 1971 June secondary phase was split into two segments: an active phase, for players drafted as recently as January, and a delayed phase, for players drafted prior to 1971. As 1968 draft picks, players like Broberg, Hooton and Ellis were eligible for the delayed phase.

The White Sox had first selection in the active phase and went for Harvard's two-time All-America catcher Pete Varney, who was drafted a record-tying seventh time. With his college eligibility finally exhausted, Varney signed with Chicago.

Varney went on to play seven years of professional baseball and spent parts of four seasons in the big leagues, hitting .247 in 69 games with the White Sox and Braves.

The White Sox gained the rights to Varney in the secondary phase by luck of the draw, but earned the No. 1 pick in the June regular phase by having the poorest record (56-106) in the American League in 1970. White Sox player personnel director Roland Hemond ended any suspense by announcing two days before the draft that Goodwin would be his team's choice. Goodwin, who hit .494 with nine home runs and 27 RBIs in 28 games as a senior for Peoria Central High, was generally regarded as the top player available, though was heavily scouted by just three teams.

"We've been getting questions from all sides about the choice and rather than dodge them, we decided to make the announcement," Hemond

### Top 25 Bonuses

| | Player, Pos. | Drafted (Round) | Order | Bonus |
|---|---|---|---|---|
| 1. | * Ed Kurpiel, 1b | Cardinals (1) | 8 | $83,750 |
| **2.** | **Pete Broberg, rhp** | **Senators (June-S/1)** | **(1)** | **#$83,000** |
| **3.** | *** Jay Franklin, rhp** | **Padres (1)** | **2** | **$65,000** |
| | *** Roy Thomas, rhp** | **Phillies (1)** | **6** | **$65,000** |
| **5.** | **Rob Ellis, 3b** | **Brewers (June-S/1)** | **(3)** | **#$59,250** |
| **6.** | **Burt Hooton, rhp** | **Cubs (June-S/1)** | **(2)** | **#$57,500** |
| **7.** | *** Tom Bianco, 3b** | **Brewers (1)** | **3** | **$50,000** |
| | *** Roy Branch, rhp** | **Royals (1)** | **5** | **$50,000** |
| | * Roger Quiroga, rhp | Senators (1) | 7 | $50,000 |
| | *** Frank Tanana, lhp** | **Angels (1)** | **13** | **$50,000** |
| **11.** | *** Rick Rhoden, rhp** | **Dodgers (1)** | **20** | **$45,000** |
| 12. | * Jeff Wehmeier, rhp | Cubs (1) | 16 | $44,000 |
| 13. | * David Sloan, rhp | Indians (1) | 9 | $40,000 |
| | * Neil Rasmussen, ss | Astros (1) | 12 | $40,000 |
| | *** Rich Puig, 2b** | **Mets (1)** | **14** | **$40,000** |
| | *** Jim Burton, lhp** | **Red Sox (June-S/1)** | **(5)** | **$40,000** |
| **17.** | *** Paul Seibert, lhp** | **Astros (3)** | **60** | **$36,500** |
| 18. | * James Vosk, rhp | Red Sox (3) | 63 | $36,000 |
| **19.** | *** Terry Whitfield, of** | **Yankees (1)** | **19** | **$35,000** |
| | **Mike Pazik, lhp** | **Yankees (June-S/1)** | **(13)** | **$35,000** |
| **21.** | **Mike Schmidt, ss** | **Phillies (2)** | **30** | **$32,500** |
| 22. | * Dale Soderholm, ss | Twins (1) | 21 | $31,000 |
| **23.** | *** Jim Rice, of** | **Red Sox (1)** | **15** | **$30,000** |
| | *** Craig Reynolds, ss** | **Pirates (1)** | **22** | **$30,000** |
| | Mike Ibarguen, rhp | Cardinals (Jan.-S/1) | (16) | $30,000 |
| | **Keith Hernandez, 1b** | **Cardinals (42)** | **785** | **$30,000** |

*Major leaguers in bold. *High school selection. #Major league contract.*

## Largest Bonuses By Round

| | Player, Pos. | Club | Bonus |
|---|---|---|---|
| 1.* | Ed Kurpiel, 1b | Cardinals | $83,750 |
| **2.** | **Mike Schmidt, ss** | **Phillies** | **$32,500** |
| **3.*** | **Paul Seibert, lhp** | **Astros** | **$36,500** |
| 4. | Four tied at | | $20,000 |
| 5.* | Charles Gibbon, lhp | Angels | $26,000 |
| 6.* | Jeff Kalil, of | Angels | $16,000 |
| 7. | Greg Marshall, of | Royals | $15,000 |
| 8. | Jerry Devine, of | Brewers | $10,000 |
| 9.* | Freddie Tate, of | Brewers | $15,000 |
| 10.* | Kevin Carr, rhp/of | Yankees | $12,000 |
| Jan/R. | James Cates, 1b | Tigers (1) | $20,000 |
| Jan/S. | Mike Ibarguen, rhp | Cardinals (1) | $30,000 |
| **Jun/S(A)** | **Pete Broberg, rhp** | **Senators (1)** | **$83,000** |
| Jun/S(D) | David Kaster, rhp | Astros (1) | $16,000 |

*Major leaguers in bold. *High school selection.*

said. "After all the hours we've spent in making this decision, we'd look pretty stupid if we hadn't made up our minds by at least 48 hours before the draft."

But it may have backfired on the White Sox. They committed to Goodwin, a 6-foot-1, 195-pound lefthanded hitter with 3.9-second speed to first, before ever determining his contractual demands. From their initial meeting, the White Sox knew that Goodwin would be a tough sign.

"He's way out of line with his money demands, so we had to back off for the time being," Sox vice president Stu Holcomb said of their early negotiations. "He wants more than $100,000 and he wants it now, not spread over a number of years."

The White Sox were pressed financially at the time and never closed the gap on Goodwin, and failed to sign 20 of their 34 June picks. Goodwin, one of three first overall picks in the June regular phase not to sign, opted for Southern University, where he played for four years before being drafted first overall again in 1975 by the California Angels. For all the hype he generated in two different drafts, Goodwin's career never lived up to it.

### COMPETITION FROM SEC FOOTBALL

Two other first-round picks from 1971 went unsigned. Holloway and Mike Miley, both high school shortstops, decided instead to play quarterback in the football-rich Southeastern Conference.

The Expos, picking fourth, failed to sign Holloway despite making him a substantial bonus offer. Officially, Holloway needed his mother's consent (under Alabama law) to sign with the Expos because he was only 17, and didn't get it. The popular rumor of the day, however, was that the Expos never matched what University of Tennessee boosters provided Holloway in the way of inducements for him to quarterback their football team.

The Expos offered Holloway an $80,000 bonus as well as a big league contract and a September promotion, and the promise that slick-fielding shortstop Bobby Wine would be his personal infield instructor at the major league level. Team president John McHale also told his mother, "I will personally tuck him into bed every night."

All those benefits, however, couldn't close the deal. Holloway played baseball four years for the

**Unsigned first-rounder Condredge Holloway went on to a standout football/baseball career at Tennessee, but he never played pro ball**

Volunteers, winning All-America honors in 1975 when he led the Southeastern Conference in hitting at .396. Holloway had become the first regular black quarterback in SEC history, and in three seasons rolled up 4,068 yards of total offense, more than any Volunteer before him.

Holloway's future was in Canada—but not in Montreal, in the Canadian Football League. The Atlanta Braves drafted him again in the 10th round after his senior year, but he opted again to stay with football and never played pro baseball. The NFL's New England Patriots drafted Holloway in the 12th round in 1975, but wanted to convert him to a defensive back, so Holloway signed with the CFL's Ottawa Rough Riders, who promised him that he could remain a quarterback. In 13 seasons in the CFL with three teams, he passed for 25,193 yards and ran for another 3,167. In 1982, when he passed for 4,661 yards and 31 touchdowns for the Toronto Argonauts, he won the Schenley Award as the league's outstanding player.

Miley, meanwhile, turned down the Cincinnati Reds as the last pick in the first round in favor of a football career at Louisiana State. He quarterbacked the Tigers for three years and signed with the Angels in 1974, again as a first-round pick. He was killed in a car accident early in his major league career.

### TROUBLED CAREERS FOR TWO PITCHERS

The talent at the top took another pronounced hit when the first two pitchers drafted, Jay Franklin (Padres, second overall) and Branch (Royals, fifth), failed to win a game between them in the big leagues while making a combined five appearances.

Both players never came close to achieving their ceiling because of arm injuries. Later, they fell on hard times personally.

Franklin, signed to a $65,000 bonus by the

### WORTH NOTING

games, but broke his ankle in spring training in 1964, and was on the disabled list that season before being released.

■ The short-season Northwest League's Bend Rainbows, the only club without a major league affiliation in 1971, elected to take part in the draft for the second year in a row and made the first selection in the January secondary phase. They went for Golden West Junior College outfielder **JIM HOGAN**, and signed him for a bonus of $10,000. It would be the last time that a minor league club would take part in the draft until Boise, also of the Northwest League, selected two players in 1989.

■ Springfield (Mass.) College righthander **WILLIE BOYNTON** became a second-round pick of the Padres in 1971 after leading the NCAA ranks with 15.7 strikeouts/nine innings. A year later, he posted a 12-5, 2.90 record at Double-A Alexandria, but walked away from baseball and joined the Jehovah's Witness religious organization. It was the second time in three drafts that the Padres had lost a second-rounder to the sect.

■ As the first-round pick of the Cardinals (eighth overall), first baseman **ED KURPIEL** received the highest bonus in the 1971 draft, $83,750. While he never played in a big league game in a nine-year professional career, Kurpiel was on the bench, in a Cardinals uniform for the first time, on the night of Sept. 10, 1974, when Lou Brock stole bases 104 and 105 to break Maury Wills' single-season stolen-base record of 104.

■ Southern California (53-13) won the second of five consecutive College World Series championships in 1971, beating Southern Illinois 7-2 in the final. A youthful USC squad had just six players drafted, with their best prospect being righthander **STEVE BUSBY** (11-2), a second-round

CONTINUED ON PAGE 116

**WORTH NOTING**

CONTINUED FROM PAGE 115

pick of the Royals in the secondary (delayed) phase who signed for a bonus of $18,500. Busby went on to win 56 games in three years with the Royals before a rotator-cuff injury short-circuited his career.
In the first round of the same phase, the Royals went for Arizona State All-American first baseman **ROGER SCHMUCK**, who hit .432, batted safely that season in an NCAA-record 45 straight games, and set collegiate records for most hits (98) and RBIs (80). Schmuck signed for $17,000, but hit just .211 with 14 home runs in three minor league seasons. Other top collegians taken in the first round of the June secondary phase were Tulsa righthander **STEVE ROGERS** (Expos) and Michigan lefthander **JIM BURTON** (Red Sox), selected fourth and fifth overall. Rogers pitched his team into the College World Series and went on to win 158 games over 13 years in the majors, all with the Expos. Burton had a record-setting career with the Wolverines, but is best remembered for being the loser in Game Seven of the 1975 World Series, when he came on in the ninth inning of 3-3 game between the Reds and Red Sox, and surrendered the decisive run in a Reds 4-3 win.

■ The focus in the June secondary phase was on top college talent, but one of the more noteworthy selections was outfielder **CHARLES DUDISH**, who went 10th overall to the Padres. Three years earlier, Dudish, a quarterback, was one of the hottest recruits in college football history, but also a second-round pick of the Giants. He chose to play football at Georgia Tech, but his college career never materialized because of injuries and suspensions. He decided to give baseball one last, belated shot, signing with the Padres for $10,000, but failed miserably in a brief trial in the Class A California League and was released after little more than a month.

Padres, reached the big leagues at age 18, little more than two months after he was drafted. His promotion came on the heels of a dominating season at Tri-Cities of the short-season Northwest League that included a 17-strikeout game and no-hitter in his final start. It culminated a whirlwind rise from high school, where Franklin went 13-1 his senior year and led Vienna's James Madison High to the Virginia state 3-A title by striking out 42 in two playoff games.

Franklin made three abbreviated September appearances for the Padres, and off that showing was expected to earn a starting job as a teenager in 1972 with the Padres. He never got the chance.

Franklin attended a camp for Padres prospects prior to spring training, and cut loose a 90-plus mph fastball before his arm was ready. His right elbow immediately swelled up.

"It scared me to death," Franklin said. "I could feel it. I knew something terrible had happened. I walked right off the mound. They said they could see my elbow crinkle from the sidelines as soon as I threw the pitch. They sent me to some doctors, and the doctors told me to take a year off."

Franklin followed orders and never pitched an inning that season, and never pitched in the big leagues again. He hung on and pitched in the minor leagues until 1977, but was never the same.

Branch was rated the No. 1 prospect in the 1971 draft by the Royals, who acknowledged being stunned that he was still available with the fifth choice overall. He had a 7-0, 0.59 record his senior year at Beaumont High in St. Louis. After one game that spring, a scout called his office to file a report on Branch, and was asked if he was a good fielder. "I don't know," the scout replied. "He struck out every batter." Almost every scouting report indicated Branch had the potential to develop in the manner of another righthander in town: Gibson the Cardinals great.

"I was completely overwhelmed by him in high school," Royals scouting director Lou Gorman said. "He's a carbon copy of Gibson in his poise, motion, follow-through and the way he wears his uniform. He even walks off the mound like Gibson. A lot of kids that age can throw hard, but this kid's fastball just exploded and he had complete command of his curveball.

"I thought he would be an outstanding pitcher in the big leagues. Not average. Outstanding. I couldn't wait to get the reports from Rookie league. I thought he would strike out 14 to 15 a game, just completely overwhelm the Rookie league at 17."

The Royals followed through on their intent to draft Branch, even though there were indications that Branch had hurt his arm working out for the Cardinals a day before the draft, and had walked off the mound holding his elbow.

"We called the Cardinals and George Silvey, their scouting director, told us, 'No, as far as they saw, Branch was all right,' " Tom Ferrick, a Royals scouting consultant, said. "Now we were really mixed up. We went 'round the table and the vote was split. If Branch isn't OK, Brett would be a heck of a No. 1, but we decided to take a chance on Branch. I thought if he was healthy he might be the outstanding righthander in the league for years to come. He was the best pitching prospect I had ever seen."

To the Royals' regret, the concerns about Branch's arm proved accurate.

His early reports were less than overwhelming and he subsequently needed elbow surgery to remove bone chips after just three games for Rookie-level Kingsport. The following year was largely lost to rehabilitation, and the third to a serious hernia condition. Branch drifted from team to team in the organization, never pitching above Double-A. He tried the patience of frustrated managers and coaches in the Royals system.

Gorman never lost faith in Branch, and within a year of being named general manager of the expansion Seattle Mariners in 1977, he traded for Branch. After a poor start in Triple-A, Branch was sent to Nuevo Laredo of the Mexican League, where he spent two summers rekindling interest in his arm.

Branch made two starts for Seattle in the final month of the 1979 season, but failed to make an impression by going 0-1, 8.18 in 11 innings. He was released, and the following spring failed to make San Francisco's Triple-A club.

TOM DIPACE
Roy Branch

Branch drifted south of the border again in 1981 and 1982. One day in May 1982, the Nuevo Laredo team bus, bound for Mexico City, was stopped and searched by federal agents. Guns and marijuana were found, and three American pitchers, including Branch, were detained. He was imprisoned immediately and wasn't released for some six months. Baseball turned the other way while he was incarcerated, and what hope was left for Branch had evaporated in a Mexican jail cell.

Franklin's career also ended after his own series of injuries and surgeries to his elbow and shoulder reduced him to a sidearmer with a well below average fastball. The Padres sent him home, and his once-promising career was over at age 23.

"I was too young and inexperienced," said

## One Team's Draft: Kansas City Royals

| Player, Pos. | Bonus | Player, Pos. | Bonus | Player, Pos. | Bonus |
|---|---|---|---|---|---|
| **1. *Roy Branch, rhp** | **$50,000** | 5. *David Masser, of | $13,000 | 9. *James Ross, rhp | $8,000 |
| **2. *George Brett, ss** | **$25,000** | 6. *George Feeley, of | $8,000 | **10. *Jerry Maddox, ss** | **Did not sign** |
| 3. *Charles Smith, of | $20,000 | 7. Greg Marshall, of | $15,000 | **Other Steve Busby (S/2), rhp** | **$18,500** |
| **4. *Joe Zdeb, 3b** | **$20,000** | 8. Gary Dunkleberger, rhp | $3,500 | | |

*Major leaguers in bold. *High school selection.*

## Highest Unsigned Picks

**JUNE/REGULAR PHASE ONLY**

| Player, Pos., Team (Round) | College | Re-Drafted |
|---|---|---|
| Danny Goodwin, c, White Sox (1) | Southern | Angels '75 (1) |
| Condredge Holloway, ss, Expos (1) | Tennessee | Braves '75 (10) |
| Mike Miley, ss, Reds (1) | Louisiana State | Angels '74 (1) |
| Jim Umbarger, lhp, Indians (2) | Arizona State | Indians '74 (16) |
| Paul Zobeck, lhp, White Sox (3) | Yavapai (Ariz.) JC | Angels '73 (Jan.-R/4) |
| Eddy Putman, c, Senators (3) | USC | Cubs '75 (Jan.-S/1) |
| Dennis Lewallyn, rhp, Braves (3) | Chipola (Fla.) JC | Dodgers '72 (Jan.S/1) |
| Ken Huizenga, of, Athletics (3) | USC | Red Sox '75 (Jan.-R/1) |
| Steve Hergenrader, c, White Sox (4) | Fresno (Calif.) CC | Expos '72 (Jan.-S/2) |
| Greg Cochran, rhp, Phillies (4) | Arizona State | Athletics '75 (2) |

**TOTAL UNSIGNED PICKS:** Top 5 Rounds (18), Top 10 Rounds (52)

Franklin, reflecting on his major league debut at 18. "It was a mental struggle. But I go back and there's lots of things I would have done differently if I had been more mature. I just wasn't mature enough to be pitching in the major leagues. I had the fastball, but as far as intermingling with the rest of the players, it was tough. They were all older than me and had more experience."

Franklin's life crumbled once his baseball career ended. He encountered mental-health issues following a divorce and the suicide of his father, and was lucky to be alive after he jumped from a fourth-story window in a Virginia courthouse during a court-sanctioned mental health assessment in 1991. He was eventually diagnosed as a paranoid schizophrenic with fixed delusions.

Jay Franklin

"For the last 10 years, I've been pretty much depressed all the time," Franklin admitted in a 2012 interview. "I get paranoid. I think everybody knows my business, which my business is not too good in the last 15 years. I have some things that I wish I had never done."

While Franklin and Branch at least pitched in the big leagues, three other high school arms drafted in the first round in 1971 didn't even get out of Class A before the bottom fell out on their careers.

One such pick, Oakland's William Daniels, received a $25,000 bonus and spent the remainder of the 1971 season traveling with the major league team. He became a daily companion of Finley, the maverick A's owner, who bestowed the nickname of "Sugar Bear" on Daniels.

Though Daniels never pitched an inning for the A's in 1971, he was extended an invitation to major league camp the following spring, and so impressed the A's coaching staff with his long, lanky frame and impressive raw stuff that he nearly cracked the club's Opening Day roster. He was one of the last three players cut.

That would be as close as Daniels would ever get to the big leagues again. He was sent to Class A to officially begin his career and never progressed from there. On two occasions over the next three years, he was banished to co-op clubs before finally being released in 1974. The Tigers gave the Michigan high school product a second chance but cut Daniels midway through the 1975 season. In 57 career appearances, Daniels went 14-17, 5.47; in 268 innings, he walked 258 while striking out 234.

### RICE, TANANA STAND OUT

If the first round of the 1971 draft experienced its share of disappointments, there were three players, in particular—Rice, Tanana and righthander Rick Rhoden—who enjoyed long and distinguished careers.

Rice, a South Carolina product picked 15th overall by the Red Sox, became one of the top hitters of his generation and went on to hit .298 with 382 home runs over 16 years, all with the Red Sox. Unlike Brett and Schmidt, though, he had to wait to get into Cooperstown, winning election on his 15th and final try on the ballot.

The Angels appeared to have a Hall of Famer of their own in Tanana, who at 24 had already led the American League in ERA (2.54 in 1977) and strikeouts (269 in 1975), and had set an AL record for lefthanders by striking out 17 in a game. However, Tanana injured a tendon in his left arm in 1977 and was never the same pitcher again.

A classic power pitcher capable of blowing his fastball by hitters prior to the injury, Tanana had to learn how to pitch with a finesse-oriented approach. His career eventually took him back to Detroit, where he had been a baseball and basketball star at Central Catholic High. Overall, Tanana won 240 games in a 21-year career.

Rhoden, drafted 20th overall by the Dodgers, pitched 16 years in the majors, winning 151 games. His career accomplishments are all the more noteworthy as Rhoden was stricken with osteomyelitis as a child, an affliction that damaged his right knee so severely that his left leg had to be shortened so it wouldn't significantly outgrow his right leg. He injured his knee landing on a pair of rusty scissors as an 8-year-old and was required to wear a brace for three years.

"It doesn't bother me at all now," Rhoden said in the midst of his long, successful big-league career. "I can do anything now but run."

Hernandez, who went on to become a .300-hitting, all-star first baseman in the big leagues, signed a bonus contract in 1971 befitting his impending stardom. At $30,000, his bonus was more in line with a typical first-rounder, not a player who had lasted all the way to the 42nd round, the 783rd player draft overall.

The most-decorated athlete ever produced at Capuchino High in Millbrae, Calif., Hernandez, 17, starred in baseball, basketball and football, but scared scouts off by not playing his senior year of high school after a disagreement with his coach. He resurrected his career during summer-league play, in the Mid-Peninsula Joe DiMaggio League, hitting more than .500 while also being one of the league's top pitchers. The Cardinals signed him with a significantly-revised bonus offer just before he was scheduled to enroll at the University of California.

### IN FOCUS: PETE VARNEY

In an era when some American youngsters were trying to figure out ways to avoid being drafted into military service in Vietnam, Harvard catcher Pete Varney became a draft dodger of a different sort.

"I have no regrets whatsoever about not signing earlier," said Varney, who was drafted seven times before finally signing with the White Sox in 1971. "Harvard was a very good process for me to go through. It taught me a great deal about myself and my education has been a good insurance policy for me."

Varney was 17 in 1966 when he graduated from high school in North Quincy, Mass. His age made him ineligible for the June draft that year, but two months later he was drafted for the first time by the Athletics in the since-abandoned American Legion draft. He did not sign, and delayed his entrance into Harvard for a year by attending a Massachusetts prep school.

The Astros drafted Varney out of Deerfield Academy in both January and June 1967, but the highly touted catcher decided he couldn't pass up an Ivy League education—or a chance to play both baseball and football.

"Had it been anywhere else that had accepted me, I probably would have signed to play baseball then," said Varney.

# 1971 Draft List

**Did not sign. Major leaguers in bold, with first and last years noted. Order of selection indicated in parentheses. For the first five rounds of the June Regular Phase and the first round of all other phases, the peak level of each player is noted.*

## ATLANTA BRAVES

### January—Regular Phase (9)

1. *Joe Turnbull, of-1b, Seminole (Fla.) CC.—(Low A)

### January—Secondary Phase (20)

**1. *Pete Varney, c-1b, Harvard University.—(1973-76)**

DRAFT DROP *First overall draft pick, June 1966/American Legion phase, Athletics; first overall draft pick, January 1968/secondary phase, Astros • First overall draft pick, June 1971/secondary phase (active), White Sox*

2. *John Adeimy, ss, Miami-Dade CC South.
3. *Jerry Gomez, lhp, Omaha, Neb.
4. Jimmy Collins, rhp, Southern University.

### June—Regular Phase (10)

**1. Taylor Duncan, ss, Grant Union HS, Sacramento, Calif.—(1977-78)**
**2. Jamie Easterly, lhp, Crockett (Texas) HS.—(1974-87)**
**3. *Dennis Lewallyn, rhp, Escambia HS, Pensacola, Fla.—(1975-82)**

DRAFT DROP *Attended Chipola (Fla.) JC; re-drafted by Dodgers, January 1972/secondary phase (1st round)*

4. Pat McKean, lhp, Texas Tech.—(AAA)
5. Rob Pitre, rhp, Rosemead (Calif.) HS.—(High A)
6. *Brian Stone, of, El Camino HS, Sacramento, Calif.
7. Larry Smith, lhp, Arroyo HS, El Monte, Calif.
8. *Jerry Willeford, of-c, Sam Houston HS, Houston.
**9. *Mike Stanton, rhp, Santa Fe HS, Lakeland, Calif.—(1975-85)**
10. *Mike Dempsey, rhp, Grimsley HS, Greensboro, N.C.
**11. Junior Moore, 3b, John F. Kennedy HS, Richmond, Calif.—(1976-80)**
12. *James Foxwell, ss, Bridgewater-Raritan East HS, Martinsville, N.J.
13. *Larry Silveira, c, San Luis Obispo (Calif.) HS.
14. *George Gilbreath, rhp, North Greenville (S.C.) JC.
15. Larry Hendrickson, rhp, Santa Rosa (Calif.) JC.
16. Calvin Smith, ss, Harper HS, Atlanta.
**17. Biff Pocoroba, c, Canoga Park (Calif.) HS.—(1975-84)**
18. *William Daves, c, Guthrie (Okla.) HS.
19. *Peter Dann, rhp, Metuchen (N.J.) HS.
20. *Rod Spence, 3b, St. Augustine HS, San Diego.

DRAFT DROP *Brother of Bob Spence, major leaguer (1969-71)*

21. William Lorillard, lhp, Robert E. Lee HS, San Antonio, Texas.
22. *Scott McHenry, rhp, Bridgewater-Raritan East HS, Somerville, N.J.
23. *Larry Liedy, ss, Staten Island (N.Y.) CC.
24. *Rick Dively, of, Saguaro HS, Scottsdale, Ariz.
25. Roger Williams, of, Texas Christian University.

### June—Secondary Phase/Delayed (18)

**1. Mike Beard, lhp, University of Texas.–(1974-77)**

### June—Secondary Phase/Active (10)

**1. *Ron Hodges, c, Appalachian State University.—(1973-84)**

## BALTIMORE ORIOLES

### January—Regular Phase (24)

1. Edward Jordan, c, Los Angeles Pierce JC.–(AAA)
2. Richard David, 1b, Honululu, Hawaii.
3. Allan Wyatt, of-1b, Los Angeles Pierce JC.
4. *Jimmie Martin, of, Glendale (Calif.) JC.
5. *Mike Pulaski, of, Indian River (Fla.) CC.
6. Dennis Silvey, 1b, Mount Hood (Ore.) CC.
7. Harry Bilyeu, c, Glendale (Calif.) JC.
8. Curt Daniels, 2b, Oregon State University.
9. *Perry Kozlowski, rhp, Santa Rosa (Calif.) JC.
10. *Larry Hartman, rhp, JC of San Mateo (Calif.).
11. *Robert Brassea, ss, Canada (Calif.) JC.

### January—Secondary Phase (19)

1. Wilmer Aaron, ss, Los Angeles Valley JC.—(AA)
2. John Euler, rhp, University of North Carolina.
3. *Richard Baker, rhp, Lynchburg, Va.
4. *Robert Sherman, rhp, Seminole (Fla.) CC.
5. *Darrell Devitt, rhp, Mesa (Ariz.) CC.
6. Tom Seybold, lhp, University of Florida.
7. *John O'Connor, c, Alexandria, Va.
8. *Chris Cammack, 3b, North Carolina State University.
9. *Randy Delerio, c, Dos Palos (Calif.) HS.

### June—Regular Phase (23)

**1. Randy Stein, rhp, Ganesha HS, Pomona, Calif.—(1978-82)**
2. Doug Patterson, rhp, Stark HS, Orange, Texas.—(AA)

DRAFT DROP *Father of John Patterson, first-round draft pick, Expos (1996); major leaguer (2002-07)*

**3. Kiko Garcia, ss, Ygnacio Valley HS, Walnut Creek, Calif.—(1976-85)**
4. Myrl Smith, lhp, Franklin Senior HS, Reisterstown, Md.—(AAA)
5. Mark Pettit, ss, Bishop Montgomery HS, Lomita, Calif.—(High A)

DRAFT DROP *Son of Paul Pettit, baseball's first $100,000 bonus baby; major leaguer (1951-53)*

6. Tim Hoyles, rhp, Princeton HS, Cincinnati.
**7. *Hank Small, of, Dykes HS, Atlanta.–(1978)**
8. *Anthony Davis, of, San Fernando HS, Pacoima, Calif.

DRAFT DROP *Running back, National Football League (1977-79)*

9. Peter Quinlan, of, North Reading (Mass.) HS.
10. Russell Parker, of-rhp, Southside HS, Effingham, S.C.
11. *Stephen Johnson, ss, Barboursville HS, Huntington, W.Va.
12. *Michael Arrington, rhp, Bethel HS, Hampton, Va.
13. Horace Richardson, lhp-of, College of William & Mary.
14. *Larry Meekins, rhp, Franklin HS, Owings Mills, Md.
15. *William Bollman, c, Westbury HS, Houston.
16. *Roger McSwain, of, Gardner-Webb College.
17. Billy Hamilton, lhp, Dumas (Texas) HS.
18. *Dan Marple, of, Hueneme HS, Oxnard, Calif.
19. *Otis Zagorski, of, Havelock (N.C.) HS.
20. Kim Hall, ss, Maryland State College.
21. Carey Shea, c, Georgia Southern College.
22. Frank Bowling, of-3b, Cleveland HS, Reseda, Calif.
23. Charles Heil, 1b, Serra HS, Hawthorne, Calif.
24. Paul Kreins, 1b, College Park HS, Pleasant Hills, Calif.
25. *Leo Szarek, lhp, Whitehouse HS, Somerville, N.J.
26. *Donald Rogers, c, Louisburg (N.C.) JC.
27. *James Thompson, rhp, Lake Havasu (Ariz.) HS.
28. *John Paull, c, Laurel Highlands HS, Lemont Furnace, Pa.
29. *David Christiansen, lhp, Grant HS, Sherman Oaks, Calif.
30. *Dennis Watson, rhp, Van Nuys HS, Arleta, Calif.
31. *John Kelly, 3b-of, Crenshaw HS, Los Angeles.
32. *Robert Keller, rhp, Xenia (Ohio) HS.
33. *Thomas Foster, ss, Aloha (Ore.) HS.
34. *Tyrus Neely, ss, Macomb (Mich.) CC.
35. *Brian Jones, c, Edmondson HS, Baltimore.
36. *Steve Cannady, c, Bellarmine Prep, Campbell, Calif.
37. *Frank Kunnen, c, Clearwater Catholic HS, Clearwater, Fla.
38. *Ken Bruchanski, rhp, St. Clement HS, Centerline, Mich.
39. *Rocky Manuel, ss, Portage Northern HS, Portage, Mich.
40. *Richard Cahill, lhp, Tigard (Ore.) HS.
41. *Chandler Myers, rhp, Narbonne HS, Harbor City, Calif.
42. *Timothy Fox, rhp, Gulf Coast (Fla.) CC.

### June—Secondary Phase/Delayed (7)

**1. Paul Mitchell, rhp, Old Dominion University.—(1975-80)**
2. *Bob Koeppel, lhp-of, Bradley University.

DRAFT DROP *First overall draft pick, January 1972/secondary phase, Twins*

3. Joe Pupo, rhp, Santa Clara University.

### June—Secondary Phase/Active (9)

1. Robert Sekel, rhp, Niagara County (N.Y.) CC.—(AAA)
2. *Rod Walker, rhp, Mississippi Gulf Coast JC.
3. *Robert Loughery, rhp, Anne Arundel (Md.) CC.
4. *Rick Colzie, rhp-ss, Miami-Dade CC South.

## BOSTON RED SOX

### January—Regular Phase (16)

1. *Howard Echols, 3b, Columbia State (Tenn.) CC.—(Low A)
2. *Craig Kimball, c, San Francisco.
3. Dwayne Mayberry, of, San Francisco.
**4. *Eric Rasmussen, rhp, Indian Hills (Iowa) CC.—(1975-83)**
5. Michael Averill, of, Fullerton (Calif.) JC.
6. *Elliott Jones, rhp, Vanderbilt University.
7. Dale Bjerke, rhp, St. Clair County (Mich.) CC.

### January—Secondary Phase (21)

**1. *Jim Otten, rhp, Mesa (Ariz.) CC.–(1974-81)**
2. Steve Foran, lhp, University of Denver.
**3. *John Tamargo, c, Miami-Dade CC North.—(1976-80)**
**4. *Roy Smalley, ss, Los Angeles.—(1975-87)**

DRAFT DROP *First overall draft pick, January 1974/regular phase, Rangers • Son of Roy Smalley, major leaguer (1948-58) • Nephew of Gene Mauch, major leaguer (1944-57); major league manager (1960-87)*

5. *Steve Boryczewski, c, Seton Hall University.

### June—Regular Phase (15)

**1. Jim Rice, of, T.L. Hanna HS, Anderson, S.C.—(1974-89)**

DRAFT DROP *Elected to Baseball Hall of Fame, 2009*

2. Milt Jefferson, 3b, Manual Arts HS, Los Angeles.—(AA)
3. Jim Vosk, rhp, Middletown HS, Red Bank, N.J.—(AAA)
4. Tom Pokorski, lhp, Northview HS, Covina, Calif.—(High A)
5. Tom Cassell, ss, Mansfield (Pa.) University.–(AA)
6. Terry Stokes, ss, University of Pittsburgh.
7. Paul Flanagan, of, Columbus HS, Dorchester, Mass.
8. James Snypes, of, University of South Alabama.
**9. Bill 'Bugs' Moran, rhp, Louisburg (N.C.) JC.—(1974)**
10. Michael Sherwood, ss, Bella Vista HS, Fair Oaks, Calif.
11. Paul Smith, c-of, South HS, Framingham, Mass.
12. David Sauve, 2b, University of Maryland.
13. Clyde Zimmerman, ss, Southern Columbia HS, Catawissa, Pa.
14. James Barrineau, rhp, South Boston (Mass.) HS.
15. Thomas Cason, of, Jacksonville State University.
16. Chester Lucas, of, Citronelle (Ala.) HS.
17. *Richard Wehner, lhp, St. Clement HS, Detroit.
18. Stephen Chapman, lhp, University of Minnesota.
19. Kelly Jones, rhp, Boise (Idaho) HS.
20. Kenneth Nicar, c, Sam Houston HS, Houston.
21. *Jerry Stamps, c, Jess Lanier HS, Bessemer, Ala.
22. John Seymour, c-3b, St. Lawrence (N.Y.) Univ.
23. Ken Inglis, lhp, Montclair State (N.J.) College.
24. *Richard Seid, c, Oak Park (Mich.) HS.
**25. Mark Bomback, rhp, Durfee HS, Fall River, Mass.—(1978-82)**
**26. Jack Baker, 1b, Auburn University.—(1976-77)**
27. *Ronnie Goodman, c-of, Port Jefferson HS, Mount Sinai, N.Y.
28. *Steve Kooshkalis, rhp, Peabody (Mass.) HS.

### June—Secondary Phase/Delayed (5)

**1. Jim Burton, lhp, University of Michigan.—(1975-77)**
2. Keith Scruggs, rhp, Lynchburg (Va.) College.
3. Kurt Lohrke, ss, Santa Clara University.

DRAFT DROP *Son of Jack "Lucky" Lohrke, major leaguer (1947-53)*

**4. *Duane Kuiper, ss, Southern Illinois University.—(1974-85)**
5. Mike Hansen, rhp, Arizona State University.
6. *Steve Prestridge, rhp, Delta State (Miss.) University.
7. Bill Todd, lhp, University of Missouri.

### June—Secondary Phase/Active (7)

1. *Lynn McKinney, rhp, Rio Hondo (Calif.) JC.–(AAA)
2. Earl Nance, lhp, Auburn University.
3. Henry Baker, 3b, Southern University.

## CALIFORNIA ANGELS

### January—Regular Phase (14)

1. Earl Austin, 3b, West Hills (Calif.) JC.—(Rookie)
2. Larry Dierks, lhp, University of Arizona.
3. *Darold Nogle, of, Rio Hondo (Calif.) JC.
4. *Alan Cox, rhp, Fullerton (Calif.) JC.
5. *Dan Everts, rhp, Rio Hondo (Calif.) JC.
6. *William Weyl, lhp-1b, Santa Rosa (Calif.) JC.

### January—Secondary Phase (7)

**1. Bob Allietta, c, Falmouth, Mass.—(1975)**
2. *Michael McManus, 1b-of, Mount San Antonio (Calif.) JC.
3. *Robert Loughery, rhp, Pasadena, Md.
**4. *Michael Edwards, ss, Los Angeles.—(1977-80)**

DRAFT DROP *Twin brother of Marshall Edwards, major leaguer (1981-83) • Brother of Dave Edwards, 7th-round draft pick, Twins (1971); major leaguer (1978-82)*

5. *Craig Barnes, 1b, Mount San Antonio (Calif.) JC.
6. *John Wade, c, Seattle.
7. *Mitch Fahland, c, Libby, Mon.
**8. Jerry Remy, 2b, Roger Williams (R.I.) College.—(1975-84)**

### June—Regular Phase (13)

**1. Frank Tanana, lhp, Catholic Central HS, Detroit.—(1973-93)**
**2. Ron Jackson, 3b, Wenonah HS, Birmingham, Ala.—(1975-84)**
**3. Billy Smith, ss, John Jay HS, San Antonio, Texas.—(1975-81)**
4. David Christiansen, c, Inglewood (Calif.) HS.—(AAA)
5. Charles Gibbon, lhp, Leuzinger-Lawndale HS, Hawthorne, Calif.—(AA)
6. Jeff Kalil, of, Isaac Elston HS, Michigan City, Ind.
7. Frankie George, of, St. Augustine HS, San Diego.
8. Steve Miller, rhp-of, Atwater HS, Winton, Calif.
9. David Evans, rhp, Sparta (N.C.) HS.
10. Thomas Whiteley, rhp, Temple City (Calif.) HS.
11. Ed Romager, rhp, Erwin HS, Birmimgham, Ala.
12. *Steve Trella, rhp, Servite HS, Anaheim, Calif.
13. Mark Block, c, Bellarmine Prep HS, Los Gatos, Calif.
14. Jim Uruburu, lhp, Cal Poly Pomona.
15. *David Barnes, 2b-ss, East Valley HS, Yakima, Wash.
16. Mike Wade, rhp, Cave Springs HS, Roanoke, Va.
17. Melvin Aaron, of, University of California.
18. *Michael Martinez, rhp, Montebello (Calif.) HS.
19. Steve Wiencek, 2b, Cal Poly Pomona.
20. Peter Levin, lhp, UCLA.
21. *Steve Kelley, rhp, Cupertino (Calif.) HS.
22. *Steve Ross, of, UC Santa Barbara.
23. Tom Smith, 1b-of, Ohio University.
24. *Michael Payne, rhp, Mississippi Delta JC.
25. *Michael Gleason, of, Gonzaga Prep HS, Spokane, Wash.
26. *Mike Gatlin, ss, Chaffey HS, Ontario, Calif.

DRAFT DROP *First overall draft pick, June 1974/secondary phase, Reds*

27. Randy Wilson, 1b, Sylmar (Calif.) HS.
28. Ken Barker, rhp, Claremont (Calif.) HS.
29. *Michael Daley, 1b, Marion (Wis.) HS.
30. Oscar Fisher, of, Southern University.
31. *Edward Gale, lhp, Peoria Central HS, Peoria, Ill.
32. *Joe Cipriano, rhp, Delsea Regional HS, Franklinville, N.J.
33. *Dennis O'Connor, c, Soquel HS, Santa Cruz, Calif.
34. Frank Kenyon, lhp, Bonita HS, San Dimas, Calif.
35. *Joe Groetsch, rhp-ss, North Catholic HS, Pittsburgh.
36. *Jesse Mendoza, of-c, Bishop Amat HS, La Puente, Calif.
37. Thomas Floyd, rhp, Baptist Christian (La.) College.
38. *John Palmer, lhp, Corona Del Mar HS, Newport Beach, Calif.
39. *Ron Wrigley, rhp, St. Augustine HS, San Diego.
40. *Frank Welch, rhp, Walterboro (S.C.) HS.

41. *Alan Brumfield, inf-c, George Washington HS, Danville, Va.
42. *David Judnick, rhp, Novato (Calif.) HS.
43. *Ed Piecynski, rhp, Pittston (Pa.) HS.
44. *Carl Peternell, c, Miraleste HS, Rolling Hills, Calif.
45. *Ray Bolton, rhp, Moorpark (Calif.) JC.

**June—Secondary Phase/Delayed (11)**

1. Jack Donovan, rhp, Seton Hall University.–(AAA)
2. Ron Botica, rhp, Louisiana Tech.
3. *Steve Fahsbender, lhp, Claremont-Mudd (Calif.) College.

**June—Secondary Phase/Active (3)**

1. Jim Officer, lhp, University of Oregon.—(AA)
2. Darroll Phillips, rhp-of, Laney (Calif.) JC.
3. *Gary Hampton, 2b-of, Fresno (Calif.) CC.
4. *Tom Martell, lhp, Linn-Benton (Ore.) CC.

## CHICAGO CUBS

**January—Regular Phase (15)**

1. *Perry Danforth, ss, Indian Hills (Iowa) CC.—(AA)
2. *Richard Koch, lhp, Indian Hills (Iowa) CC.
3. *James Kick, rhp, St. Louis CC-Meramec.

**January—Secondary Phase (22)**

1. Gary Brown, rhp, Elon College.—(Low A)
2. ***Steve Stroughter, of, JC of the Sequoias (Calif.)—(1982)**
3. *William Bishop, 1b, Bronx, N.Y.

**June—Regular Phase (16)**

1. Jeff Wehmeier, rhp, Brebeuf HS, Indianapolis.—(Low A)

DRAFT DROP *Son of Herm Wehmeier, major leaguer (1945-58)*

2. Steven Haug, c, Wood River (Ill.) HS.—(AAA)
3. **Dennis Lamp, rhp, St. John Bosco HS, Los Alamitos, Calif.—(1977-92)**
4. Max Stewart, of, Hilltop HS, Chula Vista, Calif.—(Low A)
5. **Rob Sperring, 3b-ss, University of the Pacific.—(1974-77)**
6. Johnny Jenkins, ss, Riverview HS, Sarasota, Fla.
7. **Jim Tyrone, of, Pan American University.—(1972-77)**

DRAFT DROP *Brother of Wayne Tyrone, major leaguer (1976)*

8. *William Stark, c, Chaffey HS, Ontario, Calif.
9. *David Bartholomew, 1b, Kearny HS, San Diego.
10. *Randy Davidson, 2b, Robert E. Lee HS, Huntsville, Ala.
11. *Curtis Wright, rhp, Edison HS, Fresno, Calif.
12. ***Dave Bergman, 1b, Maine South HS, Park Ridge, Ill.—(1975-92)**
13. Danny Humble, of, Central Greene HS, Waynesburg, Pa.
14. *Gary Hunt, rhp, Ravenswood (W.Va.) HS.
15. *William Smith, of, Hoggard HS, Wilmington, N.C.
16. John Anderson, lhp, John Brown (Ark.) University.
17. *Dwight Ausbon, ss, Locke HS, Los Angeles.
18. Robert Kleen, 3b, Central HS, St. Louis.
19. *Terry Teale, c, McClatchy HS, Sacramento, Calif.
20. Michael Gutierrez, ss, Merced (Calif.) HS.
21. Walt Barnes, 2b, Gunn HS, Palo Alto, Calif.
22. *Mike Denevi, ss, Los Gatos (Calif.) HS.
23. *Guy Hollingsworth, lhp, South Natchez (Miss.) HS.
24. Terry Thompson, rhp, Pillow Academy, Greenwood, Miss.
25. Cameron Jury, rhp, William Jewell (Mo.) College.

**June—Secondary Phase/Delayed (2)**

1. **Burt Hooton, rhp, University of Texas.—(1971-85)**

DRAFT DROP *First player from 1971 draft to reach majors (June 17, 1971)*

2. Joel Green, ss, University of Miami.

**June—Secondary Phase/Active (18)**

1. ***Jim Otten, rhp, Mesa (Ariz.) CC.–(1974-81)**

## CHICAGO WHITE SOX

**January—Regular Phase (2)**

1. *Larry O'Brien, rhp, Indian Hills (Iowa) CC.—(High A)
2. *Gary Conley, of, Miami-Dade CC North.
3. *Joe Wolf, c-1b, University of Northern Iowa.

**January—Secondary Phase (5)**

1. **Sam Ewing, of-1b, University of Tennessee.—(1973-78)**
2. Paul Sands, rhp, Bacone (Okla.) JC.
3. *Earl Nance, lhp, Auburn University.
4. *James Hamilton, c, East Point, Ga.

**June—Regular Phase (1)**

1. ***Danny Goodwin, c, Peoria Central HS, Peoria, Ill.—(1975-82)**

DRAFT DROP *Attended Southern; re-drafted by Angels, 1975 (1st round, 1st pick)*

2. **Bill Sharp, of, Ohio State University.—(1973-76)**
3. *Paul Zobeck, lhp, Central HS, Pueblo, Colo.—DNP

DRAFT DROP *Attended Yavapai (Ariz.) CC; re-drafted by Angels, January 1973/regular phase (4th round)*

4. *Steve Hergenrader, c, McLane HS, Fresno, Calif.—(High A)

DRAFT DROP *Attended Fresno (Calif.) CC; re-drafted by Expos, January 1972/secondary (2nd round)*

5. Eddie Holly, rhp, Unaka HS, Elizabethton, Tenn.—(Low A)
6. ***Jack Kucek, rhp, Newton Falls (Ohio) HS.—(1974-80)**
7. ***Warren Cromartie, of, Jackson HS, Miami.—(1974-91)**
8. ***Barry Bonnell, 2b, Milford (Ohio) HS.—(1977-86)**

DRAFT DROP *First overall draft pick, January 1975/ secondary phase, Phillies*

9. Kurt Best, rhp, Austin (Minn.) HS.
10. *Robert Willis, of, Monroe HS, Pacoima, Calif.
11. David Leisman, rhp, Michigan State University.
12. *Ricardo Fuentes, ss, Miami (Fla.) Senior HS.
13. *Jay Kuhnie, rhp, Eastern Michigan University.
14. *Benny McGrumby, ss-of, Centennial HS, Los Angeles.
15. Don Bolte, lhp, Canoga Park (Calif.) HS.
16. *Randy Braxton, 2b, Clairemont HS, San Diego.
17. **Jeff Holly, lhp, Aviation HS, Redondo Beach, Calif.—(1977-79)**
18. Rey Santiago, 1b, Washington HS, East Chicago, Ind.
19. *Frank Klancer, rhp, Barberton (Ohio) HS.
20. *Mike Curran, 3b, Jefferson HS, Cedar Rapids, Iowa.
21. *Douglas Blue, lhp, Gering (Neb.) HS.
22. *William Choat, lhp, Huffman HS, Birmingham, Ala.
23. Jack Friess, of, University of Wisconsin-Oshkosh.
24. Michael McConnell, c, Whiting (Ind.) HS.
25. James Davis, lhp, Woodrow Wilson HS, Camden, N.J.
26. *Robert Bianco, ss, Norton East HS, Cicero, Ill.

**June—Secondary Phase/Delayed (23)**

1. Craig Lown, rhp, University of Southern Colorado.—(Low A)

DRAFT DROP *Son of Turk Lown, major leaguer (1951-64)*

2. *Ralph Darin, rhp, Central Michigan University.

**June—Secondary Phase/Active (1)**

1. **Pete Varney, c-1b, Harvard University.—(1973-76)**

DRAFT DROP *First overall draft pick, June 1966/American Legion phase, Athletics; first overall draft pick, January 1968/secondary phase, Astros*

2. *William Taylor, inf, Mira Costa (Calif.) JC.
3. *Archie Manning, ss, University of Mississippi.

DRAFT DROP *First-round draft pick, New Orleans Saints/ National Football League (1971); quarterback, NFL (1971-84) • Father of Peyton Manning, quarterback, NFL (1998-2015) • Father of Eli Manning, quarterback, NFL (2004-15)*

4. *Frank Baumgardner, rhp, Miami-Dade CC North.

## CINCINNATI REDS

**January—Regular Phase (23)**

1. Eddie Tobin, of, Baptist Christian (La.) College.—(High A)
2. Joe Munoz, of-1b, Bacone (Okla.) JC.
3. Brian Williams, of-1b, Cynthiana, Ky.
4. *Mike Pfitzer, rhp, Mesa (Ariz.) CC.
5. *Charles Haymes, of-inf, Chicago.
6. *Tom Rima, of, Indian Hills (Iowa) CC.
7. *Dan Hinzman, lhp, Indian Hills (Iowa) CC.

**January—Secondary Phase (12)**

1. *Gaylin Pabst, ss-of, Danville Area (Ill.) CC.—DNP
2. *Chris Charnish, of, University of Wisconsin-Platteville.
3. *Billy Hodge, c, Texas A&M University.
4. Richard Soriano, of, Miami-Dade CC North.
5. *Gary Ellefson, rhp, Dell Rapids (S.D.) HS.

**June—Regular Phase (24)**

1. ***Mike Miley, ss, East Jefferson HS, New Orleans.—(1975-76)**

DRAFT DROP *First-round draft pick (10th overall), Angels (1974); died as active major leaguer (Jan. 6, 1977)*

2. David Covert, 1b, Meridian (Miss.) HS.—(AA)
3. Richard Coleman, of, Lane Tech HS, Chicago.—(Rookie)
4. Ernie Pupo, rhp, Gonzaga Prep, Spokane, Wash.—(Short-season A)
5. **Don Werner, c, East HS, Appleton, Wis.—(1975-82)**
6. Paul Howland, lhp, McClain HS, Greenfield, Ohio.
7. **Dave Revering, 1b, Bella Vista HS, Fair Oaks, Calif.—(1978-82)**
8. *Pat Williams, rhp, Camden HS, San Jose, Calif.
9. Gary Myers, rhp, Flat River HS, Esther, Mo.
10. Frank Ford, 1b-of, North HS, Minneapolis.
11. *Scott Torosian, rhp, Hoover HS, Fresno, Calif.
12. Allen Knight, c, Bossier City (La.) HS.
13. Jerry Bowles, rhp, Southeastern Louisiana Univ.
14. *Randy Johnston, c-3b, Wichita West HS, Wichita, Kan.
15. *Doug Horton, rhp, Virginia Tech.
16. *Dennis Simon, rhp, Monongahela Valley Catholic HS, Findleyville, Pa.
17. *Edward Burzo, of, Levittown (N.Y.) Division HS.
18. Michael Heintz, lhp, Lower Moreland HS, Huntington Valley, Pa.
19. John Hale, c, West Virginia University.
20. Andres Delgado, rhp, George Washington HS, New York.
21. Mike Marchovecchio, of-3b, Roncalli HS, Pueblo, Colo.
22. *Carl Person, of, Miami-Dade CC South.
23. ***Dave Collins, 1b-of, Stevens HS, Rapid City, S.D.—(1975-90)**
24. *Pat Tormey, ss, St. Augustine HS, La Mesa, Calif.
25. Robert Edmond, 2b, Fort Valley State (Ga.) College.
26. *Gary Mashburn, rhp, Fulton HS, Knoxville, Tenn.
27. Larry Cole, of, Salem (Va.) College.
28. *Lorenzo Ladaga, c, Hialeah (Fla.) HS.
29. *Robin Ogle, 1b, Tallawanda HS, Oxford, Ohio.

DRAFT DROP *Grandson of Walter Alston, major leaguer (1936); major league manager (1954-76)*

30. *Craig Kliebl, rhp, Norland HS, Miami Beach, Fla.
31. *Melvin Barkham, ss, Gulfport (Miss.) HS.

**June—Secondary Phase/Delayed (6)**

1. Stan Borowicz, ss, Ithaca (N.Y.) College.—(AAA)
2. Ken Hansen, rhp, Arizona State University.
3. *Alan Schwartz, rhp, Duke University.

**June—Secondary Phase/Active (20)**

1. Darrell Devitt, rhp, Mesa (Ariz.) CC.—(AA)
2. *Tom Rima, of, Indian Hills (Iowa) CC.

## CLEVELAND INDIANS

**January—Regular Phase (10)**

1. *William Malacrida, of-c, Valencia (Fla.) CC.–DNP
2. *Bill Dancy, ss, Seminole (Fla.) CC.

**January—Secondary Phase (23)**

1. *Steve Behlen, lhp, Fresno (Calif.) CC.—DNP
2. *Dan Tripp, lhp, Holland, Mich.
3. *Gary Cavallo, rhp, Seton Hall University.
4. *Mark Robison, rhp, Key West, Fla.
5. **Jim Norris, of, University of Maryland.—(1977-80)**

**June—Regular Phase (9)**

1. David Sloan, rhp, Santa Clara (Calif.) HS.–(AA)
2. ***Jim Umbarger, lhp, Grant HS, Van Nuys, Calif.—(1975-78)**

DRAFT DROP *Attended Arizona State; re-drafted by Indians, 1974 (16th round)*

3. **Wayne Cage, lhp-1b, Ruston HS, Choudrant, La.—(1978-79)**
4. Donnie Howse, 3b, Central HS, Murfreesboro, Tenn.—(High A)
5. *John Novak, lhp, Padua HS, Middleburg Heights, Ohio.—(High A)

DRAFT DROP *Attended Ohio; re-drafted by Expos, 1974 (9th round)*

6. Jamie Traber, of, McLane HS, Fresno, Calif.
7. **Larry Andersen, rhp, Interlake HS, Bellevue, Wash.—(1975-94)**
8. Delmas Culp, c, West HS, Columbus, Ohio.
9. Larry Marshall, of, San Fernando (Calif.) HS.
10. Terry Wedgewood, 3b, Purdue University.
11. *Stephen Clancy, c, Bacone (Okla.) JC.
12. Jimmy Johnson, c-inf, Rosamond (Calif.) HS.
13. Donald Cordonnier, 1b, Russia (Ohio) HS.
14. *Mark Rogers, of, Rancho Alamitos HS, Garden Grove, Calif.
15. Jimmy Denny, of, Columbus (Ga.) HS.
16. Richard Kavanaugh, rhp, Troy (Miss.) HS.
17. *Ken Harbin, 2b, Parker HS, Greenville, S.C.
18. Thomas Roberts, 1b, University of Toledo.
19. Anthony Manning, of, Shaker Heights (Ohio) HS.
20. Brian Sullivan, rhp, Western Michigan University.
21. Ron Ellis, ss, Ohio State University.
22. Richard Langdon, lhp, Southern Illinois University.
23. *Jeffrey Roser, rhp, Okaloosa-Walton (Fla.) JC.
24. (void) Lawrence Longa, 1b-of, Central Catholic HS, Cleveland.
25. *Donald Reece, 3b-rhp, Cordova HS, Rancho Cordova, Calif.
26. *Lamar Jones, rhp, Roswell (Ga.) HS.
27. ***Mike Eden, 3b, Southern Illinois University.—(1976-78)**

**June—Secondary Phase/Delayed (17)**

1. ***Jim Cox, ss, University of Iowa.—(1973-76)**
2. James Sams, rhp, Miami (Ohio) University.
3. Steve Mikulic, ss, University of Arizona.

**June—Secondary Phase/Active (21)**

1. *Keith Metheny, rhp, Green River (Wash.) CC.—(Short-season A)

## DETROIT TIGERS

**January—Regular Phase (12)**

1. Kim Cates, 1b, Fullerton (Calif.) JC.—(High A)
2. George Hart, c, Brookdale (N.J.) CC.
3. Gary Bond, rhp, Los Angeles CC.
4. Fred Strine, rhp, Ohio State University.

**January—Secondary Phase (11)**

1. Gary Rausch, lhp, Lake City, Pa.—DNP
2. *Don Kreke, rhp, Belleville Area (Ill.) CC.
3. *Ron Herring, rhp, Chipola (Fla.) JC.
4. *Ray Huard, ss, Princeton University.
5. *Rick Eisenacher, rhp, Auburn University.

**June—Regular Phase (11)**

1. **Tom Veryzer, ss, Islip (N.Y.) HS.—(1973-84)**
2. **Dennis DeBarr, lhp, Kennedy HS, Fremont, Calif.—(1977)**
3. Ben Hunt, ss, Bel Air HS, El Paso, Texas.–(Rookie)
4. Ramon Gimenez, c, New York City Technical JC.—(AA)
5. Billy Michael, of, Stonewall Jackson HS, Charleston, W.Va.—(AA)
6. Jeff Natchez, of, Southwestern HS, Flint, Mich.
7. **Gene Pentz, rhp, Johnstown (Pa.) HS.—(1975-78)**
8. *David Bowden, ss, Kathleen HS, Lakeland, Fla.
9. Don Leslie, rhp, Jefferson HS, Lafayette, Ind.
10. *Frank Catalano, of, East Meadow (N.Y.) HS.
11. Robert Nemcek, rhp, Central HS, Little Falls, N.Y.
12. Lawrence Bracco, rhp, Deer Lakes HS, Creighton, Pa.
13. **Gary Christenson, lhp, Memorial HS, New Hyde Park, N.Y.—(1979-80)**
14. *Mitch Lukevics, rhp, Liberty HS, Bethlehem, Pa.
15. *Vince Buszko, rhp, South River (N.J.) HS.
16. *Marvin Otto, c, Starpoint HS, Lockport, N.Y.

17. *Dennis McLain, lhp, Southeastern HS, Detroit.
18. Maurice Horton, ss, East St. Louis (Ill.) HS.
19. Robert Shortell, rhp, St. John's University.
20. *Curtis Bishop, lhp, Roswell (N.M.) HS.
21. *John Gutowski, rhp, Piscataway (N.J.) HS.
22. *Michael Johnson, lhp, Robinson (Ill.) HS.
23. Robert Flanders, of, Brown University.
24. Glenn Faulk, lhp, Rosemead HS, El Monte, Calif.
25. Scott Thompson, 3b, Memorial HS, Manchester, N.H.
26. Jim Eschen, inf, Wake Forest University.
27. Andy Kanoza, ss, Central Michigan University.
28. Stewart Sims, 3b, Snyder (Texas) HS.
29. Richard Miceli, rhp, Western New Mexico University.
30. Roberto Perez, 3b, Miami (Fla.) Senior HS.
31. Michael Corbett, of, Liverpool (N.Y.) HS.
32. *Paul Bock, lhp, Mishawaka (Ind.) HS.
33. *Edmund Besch, rhp, Orchard Park (N.Y.) HS.
34. Greg Gromek, ss, Florida State University.
35. *Robert Brown, rhp, Brother Rice HS, Birmingham, Mich.
36. Mark Palmer, rhp, La Quinta HS, Westminster, Calif.
37. *Kent Marsh, ss, Caledonia (Mich.) HS.

**June—Secondary Phase/Delayed (21)**

1. Charles Coe, ss, Kansas State University.—(Short-season A)
2. **Danny Fife, rhp, University of Michigan.—(1973-74)**
3. **Ron Cash, ss, Florida State University.—(1973-74)**

DRAFT DROP *Uncle of Kevin Cash, major leaguer (2002-10); major league manager (2015)*

**June—Secondary Phase/Active (11)**

1. Arnold Costell, lhp, Nassau (N.Y.) CC.—(Low A)

## HOUSTON ASTROS

**January—Regular Phase (11)**

1. Blake Green, rhp, Bakersfield (Calif.) JC.—(AAA)
2. *Richard Bubash, rhp, Boyce (Pa.) CC.

**January—Secondary Phase (4)**

1. **Doug Konieczny, rhp, St. Clair County (Mich.) CC.—(1973-77)**
2. *Alan Horne, rhp, Albany, Ga.

DRAFT DROP *Father of Alan Horne, first-round draft pick, Indians (2001)*

3. *Rick Colzie, inf-rhp, Miami-Dade CC South.
4. *William Taylor, inf, Mira Costa (Calif.) JC.

**June—Regular Phase (12)**

1. Neil Rasmussen, ss, Arcadia (Calif.) HS.—(AA)
2. **Art Gardner, lhp-of, South Leake HS, Walnut Grove, Miss.—(1975-78)**
3. **Paul Siebert, lhp, Edina (Minn.) HS.—(1974-78)**

DRAFT DROP *Son of Dick Siebert, major leaguer (1932-45)*

4. David Warburton, rhp, Nathan Hale HS, Tulsa, Okla.—(Rookie)
5. *Jim Donker, rhp, Arcadia HS, Phoenix.—DNP

DRAFT DROP *No school; never re-drafted*

6. Marc Cochran, c, Hayfield HS, Alexandria, Va.
7. William McLaurine, lhp, Laverne (Okla.) HS.
8. *Joe Yocum, rhp, Bullard HS, Fresno, Calif.
9. Michael Hart, c, Westmont HS, San Jose, Calif.
10. Gary Smith, lhp, Concord HS, Gilman, Vt.
11. John Kimbley, of, Dumas (Texas) HS.
12. *Mike Patrick, lhp, St. Joseph's HS, Wickliffe, Ohio.
13. *Michael Galloway, lhp, W.A. Berry HS, Birmingham, Ala.
14. *William Sutton, lhp, Laverne (Okla.) HS.
15. ***Mike Flanagan, lhp, Memorial HS, Manchester, N.H.—(1975-92)**

DRAFT DROP *General manager, Orioles (2003-07)*

16. John Cook, ss, Mount Everett HS, Sheffield, Mass.
17. Gil Stafford, c, Maryvale HS, Phoenix.

DRAFT DROP *Baseball coach, Grand Canyon (1981-2000)*

18. *James Baker, ss, Camden County HS, Waverly, Ga.
19. James Todd, rhp, Connersville (Ind.) HS.

**June—Secondary Phase/Delayed (8)**

1. ***Rich Troedson, lhp, Santa Clara University.—(1973-74)**
2. Robert Blakley, of-1b, Southern Illinois University.
3. *Ray Guy, rhp, University of Southern Mississippi.

DRAFT DROP *First-round draft pick, Oakland Raiders/ National Football League (1973); punter, NFL (1973-86)*

**June—Secondary Phase/Active (4)**

1. David Kaster, rhp, University of Nebraska-Omaha.—(Rookie)

## KANSAS CITY ROYALS

**January—Regular Phase (4)**

1. **John Wathan, c, University of San Diego.—(1976-85)**

DRAFT DROP *Major league manager (1987-92) • Father of Dusty Wathan, major leaguer (2002)*

2. *Michael Bauer, rhp, University of Wisconsin.
3. *Billy Simmons, 1b-of, Westark (Ark.) CC.

**January—Secondary Phase (15)**

1. ***Ron Hodges, c, Appalachian State University.—(1973-84)**
2. *Archie Manning, ss, University of Mississippi.

DRAFT DROP *First-round draft pick, New Orleans Saints/ National Football League (1971); quarterback, NFL (1971-84) • Father of Peyton Manning, quarterback, NFL (1998-2015) • Father of Eli Manning, quarterback, NFL (2004-15)*

3. *Gary Roma, 3b-of, Chaffey (Calif.) JC.

**June—Regular Phase (5)**

1. **Roy Branch, rhp, Beaumont HS, St. Louis.—(1979)**
2. **George Brett, ss, El Segundo (Calif.) HS.—(1973-93)**

DRAFT DROP *Elected to Baseball Hall of Fame, 1999 • Brother of Ken Brett, first-round draft pick, Red Sox (1966); major leaguer (1967-81)*

3. Charles Smith, of, Sherwood HS, Olney, Md.—(AAA)
4. **Joe Zdeb, 3b, Maine South HS, Park Ridge, Ill.—(1977-79)**
5. David Masser, of, Pueblo County HS, Pueblo, Colo.—(Rookie)
6. George Feeley, of, West HS, Rockford, Ill.
7. Greg Marshall, of, San Jose State University.
8. Gary Dunkleberger, rhp, Chapman (Calif.) College.
9. James Ross, rhp, Sam Houston HS, Houston.
10. ***Jerry Maddox, ss, Neff HS, La Mirada, Calif.—(1978)**
11. *Michael McGee, ss, Gerstmeyer HS, Terre Haute, Ind.
12. **Mark Littell, rhp, Gideon (Mo.) HS.—(1973-82)**
13. *Samuel Howell, rhp, Cardinal Newman HS, West Palm Beach, Fla.
14. Craig Perkins, c, University of Southern California.
15. Gerald Mifsud, of, Edinboro (Pa.) University.
16. *Tim Ryan, lhp, San Joaquin Memorial HS, Fresno, Calif.
17. Tim Howard, lhp, Wahama HS, New Haven, W.Va.
18. Charles Butler, rhp, Saddleback HS, Santa Ana, Calif.
19. ***Mike Dupree, of, Roosevelt HS, Fresno, Calif.—(1976)**
20. Ricky Romans, lhp, Jeffersonville (Ind.) HS.
21. *David Cargo, 1b, Concord (Calif.) HS.
22. ***Larry Demery, rhp, Locke HS, Los Angeles.—(1974-77)**
23. Kent Agler, rhp, Cal Poly San Luis Obispo.
24. Joe Carbone, 2b, Ohio University.
25. Steve Hudson, rhp, Mayfair HS, Lakewood, Calif.
26. Randy Johnson, rhp, Aviation HS, Manhattan Beach, Calif.
27. *Mike Walsh, rhp, Neff HS, La Mirada, Calif.
28. *Steven Ingram, rhp, Maryvale HS, Phoenix.
29. *Tom Apa, c, Jesuit HS, Portland, Ore.
30. *James Housley, of, Taft HS, Tarzana, Calif.
31. *Steven Jones, 1b, Garden Grove (Calif.) HS.
32. *Ron Hill, 2b, David Douglas HS, Portland, Ore.
33. *Steve Bartkowski, 1b, Buchser HS, Santa Clara, Calif.

DRAFT DROP *First overall draft pick, Atlanta Falcons/ National Football League (1975); quarterback, NFL (1975-86)*

34. *Charles Cleveland, rhp, Bibb HS, Centerville, Ala.

**June—Secondary Phase/Delayed (15)**

1. Roger Schmuck, of-1b, Arizona State University.—(High A)
2. **Steve Busby, rhp, University of Southern California.—(1972-80)**
3. Mark Arnold, rhp, Kansas State University.

**June—Secondary Phase/Active (13)**

1. *Gary Anglin, lhp, Ventura (Calif.) JC.—DNP
2. **Steve Staggs, inf, Cerritos (Calif.) JC.—(1977-78)**

## LOS ANGELES DODGERS

**January—Regular Phase (19)**

1. Steven Olsen, lhp, American River (Calif.) JC.—(Rookie)
2. Don Standley, rhp, Fullerton (Calif.) JC.
3. *Paul Few, rhp, Chipola (Fla.) JC.

**January—Secondary Phase (14)**

1. Jim Corcoran, ss, University of California.—(AA)
2. David Freeborn, ss, Buttonwillow (Calif.) HS.
3. *Francisco Suarez, ss, Miami-Dade CC North.

**June—Regular Phase (20)**

1. **Rick Rhoden, rhp, Atlantic HS, Boynton Beach, Fla.—(1974-89)**
2. Greg Reinecker, rhp, Edgewood HS, La Puente, Calif.—(High A)
3. Ricky Green, rhp, Chino (Calif.) HS.—(AA)
4. *Michael Frazier, c, Elmore HS, Houston.—(Rookie)

DRAFT DROP *Attended Texas A&M; re-drafted by Indians, 1974 (8th round)*

5. **Rex Hudson, rhp, Nathan Hale HS, Tulsa, Okla.—(1974)**
6. Chris Mayo, lhp, Hillsdale HS, San Mateo, Calif.
7. *Chuck Redmon, ss, Moore (Okla.) HS.
8. *Terry Stupy, c, Los Alamitos (Calif.) HS.
9. Thad Philyaw, of, Gunn HS, Palo Alto, Calif.
10. Thomas Urban, rhp, Mount Miguel HS, La Mesa, Calif.
11. Stan Watkins, lhp, Pacifica HS, Garden Grove, Calif.
12. *Terry Senn, 2b, University of San Francisco.
13. *Chris Sans, 1b, Texas A&M University.
14. **John Hale, of-3b, Wasco (Calif.) HS.—(1974-79)**
15. Leon Wood, 2b-ss, Polk (Fla.) CC.
16. *Al Arthur, rhp, Lake Oswego (Ore.) HS.
17. James Conn, ss, Vanderbilt University.
18. *Pat McNally, 1b, Redlands (Calif.) HS.
19. *Robert Austin, rhp, Cleveland HS, Northridge, Calif.
20. Hiawatha Roberson, of, Canada (Calif.) JC.
21. ***Larry Wolfe, ss-rhp, Cordova HS, Rancho Cordova, Calif.—(1977-80)**
22. Curtis Hires, c, Thomas Jefferson HS, Brooklyn, N.Y.
23. Ed Carroll, lhp, El Segundo HS, Hawthorne, Calif.
24. *William Hattis, rhp, New Trier East HS, Glencoe, Ill.
25. Mike Harrelson, of-2b, University of Georgia.
26. Dana Hendershott, lhp, University of San Francisco.
27. Bobby Johnson, of-c, Southern University.
28. *John Coon, rhp-of, Las Vegas (Nev.) HS.
29. **Kevin Pasley, c, Chaminade HS, Bethpage, N.Y.—(1974-78)**
30. Doug Radestock, lhp, Santana HS, San Diego.
31. ***Kim Andrew, ss, Monroe HS, Sepulveda, Calif.—(1975)**
32. *Steve Rhodin, 1b, Ypsilanti (Mich.) HS.
33. Michael Vinci, 3b-ss, Lakeland HS, Peekskill, N.Y.
34. *Ted Schultz, ss, Escondido (Calif.) HS.
35. ***Tom Hume, rhp, Northeast HS, St. Petersburg, Fla.—(1977-87)**
36. *Willis Gallop, rhp, Santa Fe HS, Alachua, Fla.
37. Michael Thomas, of, Kirkman HS, Chattanooga, Tenn.
38. *Mike Sudduth, lhp, Holtville (Calif.) HS.
39. *Keath Chauncey, of, Polk (Fla.) CC.
40. *Sam Ceci, c, University of Southern California.
41. Randy Hoppe, c, Santa Rosa (Calif.) JC.
42. Michael Collins, lhp, Long Beach State University.
43. *Richard Rogers, 3b, McLain HS, Tulsa, Okla.
44. *Ron Wrona, ss, Bishop Kelley HS, Tulsa, Okla.

DRAFT DROP *Brother of Rick Wrona, major leaguer (1988-94)*

45. *Eddie Ford, ss, Great Neck (N.Y.) South HS.

DRAFT DROP *First-round draft pick (20th overall), Red Sox (1974) • Son of Whitey Ford, major leaguer (1950-67)*

46. *Joe Camp, 1b, North Florida JC.
47. *Mike Trifiolis, 1b, West Orange (N.J.) HS.
48. *Don Stackpole, c, Elsinore (Calif.) HS.

**June—Secondary Phase/Delayed (20)**

1. Steve Patchin, c, University of Missouri.–(AAA)
2. Tim Evans, ss, University of Colorado.
3. Pat Paulson, lhp, University of New Haven.
4. Roy Petersen, of-1b, University of Southern Colorado.
5. *Mike Siani, ss, Villanova University.

DRAFT DROP *First-round draft pick, Oakland Raiders/ National Football League (1972); wide receiver, NFL (1972-80)*

**June—Secondary Phase/Active (14)**

1. *Mike Pfitzer, rhp, Mesa (Ariz.) CC.—(High A)
2. Roger Keilig, c, Canada (Calif.) JC.

## MILWAUKEE BREWERS

**January—Regular Phase (6)**

1. ***Don Collins, lhp, South Georgia JC.—(1977-80)**
2. *Douglas David, rhp, Providence College.
3. No selection.
4. *Dean Mick, 3b, Yakima Valley (Wash.) JC.

**January—Secondary Phase (17)**

1. Rick Oliver, of-3b, CC of Baltimore.—(AAA)
2. *Mark Hance, 1b, Bakersfield (Calif.) JC.
3. *Tom Rosa, ss, Miami-Dade CC North.
4. *John LiBrandi, of, Manatee (Fla.) JC.
5. John Bush, of, Miami.

**June—Regular Phase (3)**

1. **Tommy Bianco, ss, Sewanhaka HS, Elmont, N.Y.—(1975)**
2. **Larry Anderson, rhp, El Rancho HS, Pico Rivera, Calif.—(1974-77)**
3. No selection.
4. Robert Dunn, of, Kennett Square (Pa.) HS.—(Low A)
5. **Charlie Moore, c-3b, Minor HS, Birmingham, Ala.—(1973-87)**
6. Edwin Kurtz, rhp, Duncan Fletcher HS, Atlantic Beach, Fla.
7. ***Dan Boitano, rhp, Hoover HS, Fresno, Calif.—(1978-82)**
8. Jerry Devins, of, University of South Alabama.
9. Freddie Tate, of, Minor HS, Birmingham, Ala.
10. **Tom Hausman, rhp, La Verne (Calif.) HS.—(1975-82)**
11. **Kevin Kobel, lhp, St. Francis HS, Colden, N.Y.—(1973-80)**
12. *Jim McCutchin, rhp, Levelland (Texas) HS.
13. *Stephen Tinsley, 1b-of, Roxanna (Ill.) HS.
14. Paul Minton, lhp, Northeastern University.
15. *Mike Merritt, rhp, New Hanover HS, Wilmington, N.C.
16. Scott Mork, ss, Eastern Hills HS, Fort Worth, Texas.
17. *Robert Tyler, lhp, Ribault HS, Jacksonville, Fla.
18. *Donald Fisher, lhp, Pennridge HS, Perkasie, Pa.
19. *Robert Steif, rhp, Wausau (Wis.) HS.
20. *Steve Kendall, rhp, McKean HS, Wilmington, Del.
21. *Duane Bickel, rhp, Orchard View HS, Muskegon, Mich.
22. *Michael Schrader, ss, Sam Houston HS, Houston.
23. *Walter Pierson, lhp, Delaware Valley HS, Milford, N.J.
24. *Larry Riddle, rhp, Banks HS, Birmingham, Ala.

**June—Secondary Phase/Delayed (3)**

1. **Rob Ellis, 3b-of, Michigan State University.—(1971-75)**

2. Scott Larson, rhp-ss, Occidental (Calif.) College.
DRAFT DROP *Brother of Dan Larson, first-round draft pick, Cardinals (1972); major leaguer (1976-82)*
3. *John Langerhans, 1b, University of Texas.
DRAFT DROP *Father of Ryan Langerhans, major leaguer (2002-07)*

**June—Secondary Phase/Active (23)**

1. Gary Cavallo, rhp, Seton Hall University.—(AAA)

## MINNESOTA TWINS

**January—Regular Phase (22)**

1. *Jerry Mayberry, rhp, San Jose, Calif.—DNP
2. *Gary Anglin, lhp, Ventura (Calif.) JC.
3. *Rulon Herren, of, Cabrillo (Calif.) JC.
4. William Osborne, rhp, Lynchburg (Va.) College.
5. *Cary Wifler, rhp, Denver.

**January—Secondary Phase (13)**

1. Jeffrey Hooper, lhp, Los Angeles Valley JC.—(High A)
2. *Stephen Hazan, lhp, Mission Viejo, Calif.
3. *Stephen Easton, lhp, Brigham Young University.
4. *Richard Hunt, of, Doane (Neb.) College.

**June—Regular Phase (21)**

1. Dale Soderholm, ss, Coral Park HS, Miami.–(AAA)
DRAFT DROP *Brother of Eric Soderholm, first overall draft pick, January 1968/secondary phase; major leaguer (1971-80)*
2. Michael Uremovich, c, Waukegan (Ill.) HS.—(High A)
3. Scott Marchael, lhp, Woodrow Wilson HS, Long Beach, Calif.—(Low A)
4. Robert Gallagher, of, Mount Miguel HS, Spring Valley, Calif.—(High A)
5. Steve Marquardt, rhp, Poly Tech HS, North Hollywood, Calif.—(Low A)
6. William Kissell, ss, Royal Oak HS, Covina, Calif.
7. **Dave Edwards, c, Jefferson HS, Los Angeles.—(1978-82)**
DRAFT DROP *Brother of Marshall Edwards, major leaguer (1981-83) • Brother of Michael Edwards, fourth-round draft pick, Angels (January 1971/secondary phase); major leaguer (1977-80)*
8. Marty Hulse, rhp, Santiago HS, Garden Grove, Calif.
9. *Claude Westmoreland, of, Washington Union HS, Fresno, Calif.
10. *Rick Bethke, lhp, Bellflower (Calif.) HS.
11. Stephen Blood, rhp, Woodsville (N.H.) HS.
12. Mark Burris, 3b, Wood River (Ill.) HS.
13. **Rob Wilfong, 2b, Northview HS, Covina, Calif.—(1977-87)**
14. Thomas Finch, c, Fairfield University.
15. Greg Rogers, ss, Northview HS, Covina, Calif.
16. Jerry Lundin, ss, Iowa State University.
17. *Phil Convertino, of, Bishop Amat HS, Arcadia, Calif.
18. Edward Goldbaum, of, John H. Francis Poly HS, North Hollywood, Calif.
19. (void) *James Patterson, rhp, Ithaca (N.Y.) College.
20. *Randy Young, rhp, West Torrance (Calif.) HS.
21. *Terry Nance, rhp, Monterey Peninsula (Calif.) JC.
22. Mark Connor, rhp, Manhattan College.
23. *Thomas Mace, inf-of, CC of Baltimore.
24. Stuart Friedman, c, Lynchburg HS, River Edge, N.J.
25. James Bachtell, 2b-ss, Randolph-Macon (Va.) College.
26. Reginald Rowe, rhp, University of Tulsa.
27. Jack Maloof, of, University of La Verne (Calif.).
28. Lon Galli, lhp, University of Wisconsin.
29. Bruce Skoglund, c-of, Central HS, Duluth, Minn.
30. Louis Anemone, 2b, St. Francis (N.Y.) College.
31. *Steve Shimek, ss, Little Falls HS, Fort Ripley, Minn.
32. *Robert Mayhew, lhp, Arcadia (Calif.) HS.
33. *Rex Hendricks, lhp, Littleton (Colo.) HS.
34. Randy Atchison, ss, Kerkhoven (Minn.) HS.
35. *Thomas Carpenter, rhp-ss, Craig HS, Janesville, Wis.
36. ***Chuck Baker, ss, Orange HS, Garden Grove, Calif.—(1978-81)**
37. Dan Solters, rhp, Cal Poly Pomona.
38. John Katrosh, 1b-of, Trenton State (N.J.) College.
39. *Joe Theismann, ss, University of Notre Dame.
DRAFT DROP *Quarterback, National Football League (1974-85)*

**June—Secondary Phase/Delayed (9)**

1. **Glenn Borgmann, c-1b, University of South Alabama.—(1972-80)**
2. *John Roatche, c, Florida State University.
3. Ken Dempsey, of, Auburn University.
4. Ken Braun, ss, Western Kentucky University.
5. Richard Mahlmann, lhp, Fresno State University.
6. Mike Ball, 3b, University of Southern California.
7. Clark Ullom, lhp-of, University of Kansas.

**June—Secondary Phase/Active (15)**

1. *Randy Delerio, c, West Hills (Calif.) JC.—(Short-season A)
2. *Dan Everts, rhp, Rio Hondo (Calif.) JC.
3. Jeff Kalish, 3b, New York University.
4. Francisco Suarez, 3b, Miami-Dade CC North.
5. *Rick Eisenacher, rhp, Auburn University.
6. *Ray Hall, ss-2b, Fresno (Calif.) CC.

## MONTREAL EXPOS

**January—Regular Phase (3)**

1. John Scalia, rhp, Brentwood, N.Y.—(AA)
2. *Chris Hall, of, Bacone (Okla.) JC.
3. *Harvey Smith, ss, Cincinnati.
4. *Terry Ray, rhp, Blinn (Texas) JC.
5. *Ward Lyons, 3b, Mount San Antonio (Calif.) JC.
6. *Dale Fell, lhp, Palm Beach (Fla.) JC.
7. *Ron Mahood, of, Houston Baptist University.

**January—Secondary Phase (6)**

1. Harry Conlan, of, West Haven, Conn.—(Short-season A)
2. Richard Baker, lhp, Jacksonville, Fla.
3. *Vern Wilkins, 1b, Mesa (Ariz.) CC.
4. *Gary Hampton, c, Fresno, Calif.
5. Michael Lynch, lhp, Grayson County (Texas) JC.
6. *Duane Wirth, rhp, Mesa, Ariz.
7. *John Wiggins, rhp, Plant City, Fla.
8. *Mike Cuozzi, inf-of, Trenton State (N.J.) College.
9. *Williams Collins, rhp, Manatee (Fla.) JC.

**June—Regular Phase (4)**

1. *Condredge Holloway, ss, Robert E. Lee HS, Huntsville, Ala.—DNP
DRAFT DROP *Attended Tennessee; re-drafted by Braves, 1975 (10th round); 12th-round draft pick, New England Patriots/National Football League (1975); quarterback, Canadian Football League (1975-87)*
2. **Dan Warthen, lhp, Omaha North HS, Omaha, Neb.—(1975-78)**
3. Glen Tackitt, lhp, S.H. Rider HS, Wichita Falls, Texas.—(High A)
4. David Carey, rhp, U.S. Military Academy.—(High A)
5. Otto Kemper, 2b, Brenham (Texas) HS.—(High A)
6. **Larry Lintz, ss-2b, San Jose State University.—(1973-78)**
7. *Dan Marrelli, 2b, West HS, Salt Lake City.
8. Walter Rothe, of-1b, University of Texas.
9. Steven Ayers, lhp, Walker HS, Decatur, Ga.
10. Sam Viney, of-3b, UC Davis.
11. *Ken Daughty, of-inf, Lamar (Colo.) CC.
12. *Wayne Pinkerton, ss, Humphreys Academy, Hollandale, Miss.
13. *Steve Cline, rhp, Hagerstown (Md.) JC.
14. *John Andrews, ss, Lincoln (Ill.) HS.
15. *Wes Moore, rhp, Western Hills HS, Cincinnati.
16. *Dale Brock, of, St. Augustine HS, New Orleans.
DRAFT DROP *Cousin of Lou Brock, major leaguer (1961-79)*
17. *Mike Moran, ss, Biloxi (Miss.) HS.
18. *John Van Brunt, c, Crawford (N.J.) HS.
19. *Eugene Martin, 2b, Covington Catholic HS, Covington, Ky.
20. *Jeffrey Washington, of, Ypsilanti (Mich.) HS.
21. *Ken Ward, ss, Calhoun HS, Merrick, N.Y.
22. Steve Tucker, rhp, Warren HS, Downey, Calif.
23. ***Gary Alexander, c, Los Angeles Harbor JC.—(1975-81)**
24. *Michael Grover, of, El Cajon (Calif.) HS.
25. *Tom Cusick, ss-2b, MacArthur HS, San Antonio, Texas.
26. David Drumright, rhp, Kansas HS, Ottawa, Kan.
27. *Ralph Petrillo, 3b-of, Newburgh (N.Y.) HS.
28. *J.P. Pierson, of, Washington HS, Phoenix.
29. Ed Riley, ss, Neshaminy HS, Levittown, Pa.
30. *Robert Lucy, 1b, Lee (Mass.) HS.
31. *Tom Joyce, lhp, Clawson (Mich.) HS.
32. ***Al Woods, 1b, St. Elizabeth HS, Oakland, Calif.—(1977-86)**
33. Leonard Bonk, ss-2b, Catholic Central HS, Monroe, Mich.
34. *Thomas Jones, of-rhp, Douglas HS, Oklahoma City, Okla.
35. *Samuel Guarino, c, Stamford Catholic HS, Stamford, Conn.
36. *Ernest Bessette, ss, Naugatuck (Conn.) HS.
37. Brian Finnerty, c-1b, Pace (N.Y.) University.
38. Rich Sanfillipo, ss, Montclair State (N.J.) College.

**June—Secondary Phase/Delayed (4)**

1. **Steve Rogers, rhp, University of Tulsa.—(1973-85)**
2. Bobby Croswell, ss, Mississippi State University.
3. ***Sam Bowen, of-rhp, Brunswick (Ga.) JC.—(1977-80)**

**June—Secondary Phase/Active (8)**

1. *Ron Herring, rhp, Chipola (Fla.) JC.—(High A)
2. *Larry O'Brien, rhp, Indian Hills (Iowa) CC.

## NEW YORK METS

**January—Regular Phase (13)**

1. *Dan Pettyjohn, c, Yavapai (Ariz.) JC.—DNP
2. Joel Elderkin, 3b, Chabot (Calif.) JC.
3. *Keith Buckingham, rhp, Lincoln Land (Ill.) JC.
4. *Steve Janosik, rhp, Wenatchee Valley (Wash.) CC.
5. **Francisco Estrada, rhp, Cuesta (Calif.) JC.—(1971)**
6. Victor Rose, lhp, Connors State (Okla.) JC.

**January—Secondary Phase (10)**

1. James Evans, rhp, Memphis, Tenn.—(High A)
2. Rich Wagener, lhp, West Virginia University.
3. ***Mardie Cornejo, rhp, Wellington, Kan.—(1978)**
DRAFT DROP *Father of Nate Cornejo, first-round draft pick, Tigers (1998); major leaguer (2001-05)*
4. *Steve Bossi, of, Contra Costa (Calif.) JC.
5. Paul Womble, 3b, University of Kansas.

**June—Regular Phase (14)**

1. **Rich Puig, 2b, Hillsborough HS, Tampa.—(1974)**
2. Jimmy Kidder, 2b, Jay HS, San Antonio, Texas.–(AAA)
3. John Busco, ss, Mount St. Michael HS, Bronx, N.Y.—(AAA)
4. Earnest Page, of, Carver HS, Birmingham, Ala.—(Short-season A)
5. *Terry Grantham, rhp, McClenaghan HS, Florence, S.C.—DNP
DRAFT DROP *No school; never re-drafted*
6. Isaac Small, of, Deland HS, DeLeon Springs, Fla.
7. Clarence Burgy, rhp, Bellaire (Ohio) HS.
8. Carlos Sagredo, of, Taft HS, Bronx, N.Y.
9. **Rick Baldwin, of-rhp, Downey HS, Modesto, Calif.—(1975-77)**
10. Ernie DiStasi, c, Ansonia (Conn.) HS.
11. (void) *Ralph Darin, rhp, Central Michigan University.
12. Tommy Scott, 1b, Herbert Hoover HS, Elkview, W.Va.
13. *Michael Bahnick, rhp, Rider College.
14. *Michael Aldridge, of, East Carolina University.
15. *Ray Forgie, rhp, Coronado HS, Scottsdale, Ariz.
16. *Bob Hampton, of, Leigh HS, San Jose, Calif.
17. *Ron Beaurivage, 1b, Memorial HS, Manchester, N.H.
18. *Pat McMahon, lhp, Bishop Kenny HS, Jacksonville, Fla.
19. *Steve Marlow, 1b, Skyline HS, Salt Lake City.
20. Michael Anderson, lhp, Hollywood Hills HS, West Hollywood, Fla.
21. *Aaron Randall, 1b, Vigor HS, Whistler, Ala.
22. *Robert Frisby, lhp, McCluer HS, Ferguson, Mo.
23. **Mark DeJohn, 3b, Wilson HS, Middletown, Conn.—(1982)**
24. *William Roche, rhp, Jackson HS, Jacksonville, Fla.
25. *Roger Danson, ss, Wolfson HS, Jacksonville, Fla.
26. Richard Holman, rhp, Milton (Wis.) College.
27. Gil Hodges Jr., 1b, Long Island University-C.W. Post.
DRAFT DROP *Son of Gil Hodges, major leaguer (1943-63); major league manager (1963-71)*
28. *Paul Kreke, rhp, Mater Dei HS, New Baden, Ill.
29. Tony Maya, rhp, Ajo (Ariz.) HS.
30. Scott Stevens, lhp, Lakewood (Calif.) HS.
31. Steve Pierce, lhp, Gainesville (Ga.) JC.
32. Don Pooschke, of, Benson HS, Portland, Ore.
33. *Glen Canfield, c, Glendale (Calif.) JC.
34. *David Levet, of, Bountiful (Utah) HS.
35. William Leeper, c, Fernandina HS, Fernandina Beach, Fla.

**June—Secondary Phase/Delayed (24)**

1. *Richard Anderson, rhp, University of New Haven.—(AAA)
2. Greg Pavlick, rhp-3b, University of North Carolina.
3. Paul Bagnasco, 3b, Santa Clara University.
4. John Severs, of, Clemson University.
5. *Alan Lobb, lhp, Elizabethtown (Pa.) College.

**June—Secondary Phase/Active (12)**

1. Edgar DeFore, rhp, Macon, Ga.—(Rookie)
2. ***Don Collins, lhp, South Georgia JC.—(1977-80)**
3. Michael McManus, rhp, Mount San Antonio (Calif.) JC.
4. *Dan Pettyjohn, c, Yavapai (Ariz.) JC.
5. Joel Elderkin, 3b, Chabot (Calif.) JC.

## NEW YORK YANKEES

**January—Regular Phase (20)**

1. *Steve Bissett, 2b-ss, JC of San Mateo (Calif.)—(High A)
2. *Roscoe Goehring, rhp, Diablo Valley (Calif.) JC.
3. Jim Alexander, rhp, Yakima Valley (Wash.) JC.

**January—Secondary Phase (25)**

1. *Dave Elmendorf, of, Texas A&M University.—DNP
DRAFT DROP *Defensive back, National Football League (1971-79)*
2. *Roger Keilig, c, Redwood City, Calif.
3. Russ Cauley, lhp, Leary, Texas.
4. *Tom Martell, lhp, Lincoln City, Ore.
5. Jim Golden, lhp, University of Portland.
6. *Michael Venable, rhp-of, Bellevue (Wash.) CC.
7. *Byron Burns, rhp, Kelso, Wash.
8. *Keith Metheny, rhp Kent, Wash.
9. *Dennis Cline, ss, Wilmington, Del.

**June—Regular Phase (19)**

1. **Terry Whitfield, of, Palo Verde HS, Blythe, Calif.—(1974-86)**
2. Stephen Lindsey, 3b, McLane HS, Fresno, Calif.—(AA)
3. **Ron Guidry, lhp, University of Southwestern Louisiana.—(1975-88)**
4. John Williams, of, Tulare Union HS, Tulare, Calif.—(High A)
5. **Larry Murray, of, Phillips HS, Chicago.—(1974-79)**
6. Larry Walker, c, Ramona (Calif.) HS.
7. Robert Arnold, rhp, West Snyder HS, McClure, Pa.
8. Joe Blake, rhp, Simpson (Iowa) College.
9. Phil Still, 3b, Mississippi State University.
10. Kevin Carr, rhp-of, Colgan HS, Pittsburg, Kan.
11. Tony Sevy, lhp, Hillcrest HS, Springfield, Mo.
12. *Steven Gullotti, ss, Rio Hondo (Calif.) JC.
13. ***Mike Paxton, rhp, Oakhaven HS, Memphis, Tenn.—(1977-80)**
14. James Dodson, lhp, Washburn HS, Topeka, Kan.
15. *Mickey Beard, rhp, French HS, Beaumont, Texas.
16. Larry Raschke, rhp, Gonzaga University.
17. Joel Hall, c, Northwestern University.
18. Jeffrey Davis, 1b, Harwich HS, West Harwich, Mass.
19. *Stephen Burks, lhp, Cabot (Ark.) HS.
20. *Joe Eberhard, ss, Memorial HS, Joplin, Mo.
21. *Michael Berger, rhp, Tacoma (Wash.) HS.

22. Roger Johanson, rhp, Eastmont HS, East Wenatchee, Wash.
23. *Gerald Collins, lhp, Warren HS, Downey, Calif.
24. *Michael Guischer, rhp, Mount Hood (Ore.) CC.
25. *Ken Swygard, lhp, Portland, Ore.
26. *Brad Trickey, ss, Jefferson HS, Cedar Rapids, Iowa.
27. Bill Stearns, c, University of Wyoming.
DRAFT DROP *Brother of John Stearns, first-round draft pick, Phillies (1973); major leaguer (1974-84)*
28. *Gary Owens, inf, College of the Ozarks (Mo.).
29. Roger Adams, 2b, University of Tulsa.
30. Jerry Anderson, rhp, McGuire (N.J.) AFB.
31. *Vince Doherty, rhp, Linfield (Ore.) College.
32. *Greg Branum, 3b-of, Spokane Falls (Wash.) CC.

**June—Secondary Phase/Delayed (13)**

1. **Mike Pazik, lhp, Holy Cross College.—(1975-77)**
2. Robert Schiffner, lhp, Princeton University.
3. Phil Honeycutt, 3b, University of Tulsa.

**June—Secondary Phase/Active (17)**

1. David Bishop, lhp, West Chester (Pa.) University.—(High A)
2. *Steve Hunter, c, Yakima Valley (Wash.) JC.
3. *Greg Van Gaver, rhp, Bellevue (Wash.) CC.
4. *Byron Burns, rhp, Lower Columbia (Wash.) JC.
5. Steve Janosik, rhp, Wenatchee Valley (Wash.) CC.

## OAKLAND ATHLETICS

**January—Regular Phase (18)**

1. *Lynn McKinney, rhp, Rio Hondo (Calif.) JC.–(AAA)
2. Lynn Minner, 1b, Louisville, Ky.
3. *Roger Whitley, rhp, Foothill (Calif.) JC.
4. *Dan Fitzgerald, c, Solvang, Calif.
5. ***Rich Dauer, ss, San Bernardino Valley (Calif.) JC.—(1976-85)**
DRAFT DROP *First-round draft pick (24th overall), Orioles (1974)*
6. *Duane Roberts, 1b-of, Ventura (Calif.) JC.

**January—Secondary Phase (3)**

1. **Phil Garner, 3b, University of Tennessee.—(1973-88)**
DRAFT DROP *Major league manager (1992-2007)*
2. Keith Lieppman, 3b, University of Kansas.
3. ***Steve Staggs, 2b, Cerritos (Calif.) JC.—(1977-78)**
4. *John Cosmos, lhp, San Francisco.
5. *Terry Farmer, rhp, Columbus, Ga.
6. *Charles Bates, 3b-ss, Compton (Calif.) CC.
DRAFT DROP *First-round draft pick (19th overall), Tigers (1973)*
7. *Doug Cornett, c, Richmond, Ky.
8. Rudy Sgontz, c, Anaheim, Calif.
9. Ron Corbett, rhp, Suffolk (Mass.) University.
10. *Stan Hamlin, rhp, Bakersfield (Calif.) JC.
11. *Dan Parma, of, Buena Park, Calif.

**June—Regular Phase (17)**

1. William "Sugar Bear" Daniels, rhp, MacKenzie HS, Detroit.—(High A)
2. Ron Williamson, of-c, Asher (Okla.) HS.–(High A)
3. *Ken Huizenga, of, Glendora (Calif.) HS.—(AAA)
DRAFT DROP *Attended Southern California; re-drafted by Red Sox, January 1975/regular phase (1st round)*
4. Stan Bockewitz, lhp, Pana (Ill.) HS.—(AAA)
5. Kirk Thomas, rhp, Kennewick (Wash.) HS.—(High A)
6. Ron Lollis, c, Gonzaga Prep HS, Spokane, Wash.
7. Charles Gipson, 1b, Santa Ana (Calif.) HS.
DRAFT DROP *Father of Charles Gipson, major leaguer (1998-2005)*
8. Kirk Allison, of, El Segundo (Calif.) HS.
9. *John Beckman, lhp, Springfield (Ill.) HS.
10. Ray Leavitt, ss, Charter Oak HS, Glendora, Calif.
11. *Tim Hamilton, 2b, Edmonds (Wash.) HS.
12. Nicholas Parrilla, rhp, Parsons (Iowa) College.
13. James George, rhp, University of Southern California.
14. Ron Roller, of, Bellevue (Wash.) CC.
15. Richard Keller, of, Nashville (Ill.) HS.
16. Billy Matthews, c-3b, Kirkland Tech HS, Chattanooga, Tenn.
17. *Jeff Reinke, lhp, Pasadena (Calif.) HS.
18. *Jeff DeBell, rhp-ss, Sammamish HS, Bellevue, Wash.
19. *Michael Kee, of, Palo Verde HS, Tucson, Ariz.
20. *Greg Sanossian, rhp, St. Anthony HS, Long Beach, Calif.
21. *Greg Kessler, of-inf, Laguna Beach (Calif.) HS.
22. *Stephen Chipp, rhp, Santa Clara University.
23. Ronald Wilson, rhp-1b, Charter Oak HS, Glendora, Calif.
24. Robert Wolf, rhp, Chapman (Calif.) College.
25. *Ben Heise, ss, Yavapai (Ariz.) JC.
DRAFT DROP *Brother of Bob Heise, major leaguer (1967-77)*
26. *Richard Harris, ss, Westwood HS, Mesa, Ariz.
27. *Ricky Holoubek, ss, Wilson HS, Los Angeles.

**June—Secondary Phase/Delayed (19)**

1. Mike Weathers, 2b, Chapman (Calif.) College.—(AAA)
DRAFT DROP *Baseball coach, Long Beach State (2002-10)*
2. *Mike McNeilly, rhp-ss, Gonzaga University.
3. *James Horton, lhp, Eastern Michigan University.

**June—Secondary Phase/Active (19)**

1. Steve Easton, lhp, Brigham Young University.—(AA)
2. Ron Corbett, rhp, Suffolk (Mass.) University.
3. *Charles Bates, 3b, Los Angeles CC.
DRAFT DROP *First-round draft pick (19th overall), Tigers (1973)*

## PHILADELPHIA PHILLIES

**January—Regular Phase (5)**

No selection.

**January—Secondary Phase (18)**

1. Thomas Boyd, lhp, West Valley (Calif.) JC.–(AAA)
2. *David Bishop, lhp, West Chester (Pa.) University.
3. *Henry Baker, 3b, Southern University.
4. *Gary Boyajian, rhp, River Edge, N.J.
5. *George McCollum, lhp, Orlando, Fla.

**June—Regular Phase (6)**

1. **Roy Thomas, rhp, Lompoc (Calif.) HS.—(1977-87)**
2. **Mike Schmidt, ss, Ohio University.—(1972-89)**
DRAFT DROP *Elected to Baseball Hall of Fame, 1995*
3. Gary Kinard, rhp, North Charleston (S.C.) HS.—(Short-season A)
4. *Greg Cochran, rhp, Lowell HS, Whittier, Calif.—(AAA)
DRAFT DROP *Attended Arizona State; re-drafted by Athletics, 1975 (2nd round)*
5. Robert Ray, rhp-of, Alleghany County HS, Iron Gate, Va.—(Rookie)
6. Jan Barber, rhp, James Lick HS, San Jose, Calif.
7. Larry Dombkowski, of, Elston HS, Michigan City, Ind.
8. **Mac Scarce, lhp, Florida State University.—(1972-78)**
9. Alan McLaughlin, 2b, Eastern Michigan University.
10. *Mike Girazian, rhp, Selma HS, Kingsburg, Calif.
11. William Letsch, lhp, St. Catherine HS, Racine, Wis.
12. *Robert Barr, lhp, Van Horn HS, Independence, Mo.
13. Alfonso Rodriguez, rhp-of, Miami (Fla.) Senior HS.
14. Pat Lowrey, lhp, JC of Lake County (Ill.).
15. Roger Skalisky, rhp, Wenatchee (Wash.) HS.
16. *Mike Hannah, 1b, Ohio University.
17. Ken Kurtz, lhp, Lincoln HS, Stockton, Calif.
18. Gary Poteet, rhp, Hiwassee (Tenn.) JC.
19. John Boyd, c, L.D. Bell HS, Hurst, Texas.
20. Jay Thornton, 3b, Boone HS, Orlando, Fla.
21. Terry Periman, lhp, University of Missouri.
22. *Billy Olsen, rhp, Mineral Area (Mo.) JC.
23. *Greg Ferguson, rhp, Arlington Heights HS, Fort Worth, Texas.
24. Dan Greenhalgh, rhp, Folsom (Calif.) HS.
25. Mickey White, c, Rutgers University.
DRAFT DROP *Scouting director, Indians (1991-93); scouting director, Pirates (1999-2001)*
26. Mike Walsh, rhp, Broward (Fla.) CC.
27. Terry Ford, ss, Middle Georgia JC.
28. Billy Anderson, ss, University of South Carolina.
29. Jerome Johnson, rhp, Ben Eielson HS, Fairbanks, Alaska.
30. Randy Smith, rhp, Wahama HS, New Haven, W.Va.
31. *Mark Gehrig, 1b, Diablo Valley (Calif.) JC.
32. *Dan Hebel, rhp-1b, Lima (Ohio) HS.
33. *Charles Franklin, 3b, Santa Clara University.
34. *Doug Dickmann, c, St. Mary's HS, St. Louis.
35. Harry Saferight, c, Richmond, Va.
36. David Croft, rhp, Monte Vista HS, Danville, Calif.
37. *Edmond Peres, of-3b, Fort Myers (Fla.) HS.
38. Thomas Higgins, 2b, Wilkes (Pa.) College.
39. *David Quay, rhp, Penn Highlands HS, Lewistown, Pa.

**June—Secondary Phase/Delayed (22)**

1. **Dane Iorg, ss, Brigham Young University.—(1977-86)**
DRAFT DROP *Brother of Garth Iorg, major leaguer (1978-87)*
2. James Greggerson, lhp, University of Texas-El Paso.
3. Larry Kiser, lhp, University of North Carolina.

**June—Secondary Phase/Active (16)**

1. Don Kreke, rhp, Belleville Area (Ill.) CC.–(High A)
2. Steve Bissett, 2b-ss, JC of San Mateo (Calif.).
3. *Tom Rosa, ss, Miami-Dade CC South.

## PITTSBURGH PIRATES

**January—Regular Phase (21)**

1. *Alejandro Lopez, 2b, New Brunswick, N.J.—DNP
2. Randy Richards, rhp, University of Akron.
3. *Ron Harrison, rhp, American River (Calif.) JC.
4. *Michael Meseberg, of, Yakima Valley (Wash.) JC.
5. *Robert Sekel, rhp, Niagara University.
6. Anthony Blakley, ss, Brewton Parker (Ga.) JC.
7. *Dan DeBattista, 3b, Allegheny (Pa.) JC.
8. *Davis May, rhp, Gulf Coast (Fla.) CC.

**January—Secondary Phase (2)**

1. Robert Jones, of, Amherst (Mass.) College.–(AA)
2. *Robert Miller, of, Sacramento, Calif.
3. *Jim Cody, rhp, Big Bend (Wash.) CC.
4. *James Healy, ss, Lake Hiawatha, N.J.
5. *John Wade, lhp, Seattle.
6. *Rich Ralston, rhp, Spokane (Wash.) CC.
7. *Tim Pierce, rhp, Tonawanda, N.Y.
8. David Landers, of, St. Joseph's University.
9. *Steve Hunter, c, Yakima Valley (Wash.) JC.
10. Ronald Robinson, ss-rhp, New Orleans.
11. *Ray Hall, ss-2b, Fresno (Calif.) CC.
12. *Greg Van Gaver, rhp, Bellevue (Wash.) CC.
13. *Carlos Hughes, lhp, Aurora, N.C.

**June—Regular Phase (22)**

1. **Craig Reynolds, ss, John H. Reagan HS, Houston.—(1975-89)**
2. **Doug Bair, rhp, Bowling Green State University.—(1976-90)**
3. Ron Knaub, 1b, Anaheim (Calif.) HS.—(High A)
4. Mike Scaglione, rhp, Mindszenty HS, Dunkirk, N.Y.—(Rookie)
5. *Steve Gerlecz, 3b, Sedalia (Mo.) HS.—(High A)
DRAFT DROP *Attended State Fair (Mo.) CC; re-drafted by Pirates, January 1973/regular phase (10th round)*
6. Ray Lilley, rhp, Tarboro (N.C.) HS.
7. George Whileyman, rhp, Sam Houston State University.
8. *Ronald Bell, rhp, Sunny Hills HS, Fullerton, Calif.
9. Rodney Davis, rhp, Whetstone HS, Columbus, Ohio.
10. *James McKinney, ss, Ensley HS, Birmingham, Ala.
11. Thomas Prazych, rhp, Central HS, Scranton, Pa.
12. Elliott Jones, rhp, Vanderbilt University.
13. Oscar Johnson, lhp, Dos Palos (Calif.) HS.
14. *Richard Prior, of, Trinity-Pawling Prep, Peabody, Mass.
15. Luther Anderson, of, Jefferson HS, Los Angeles.
16. Paul Bostic, c, Carson-Newman (Tenn.) College.
17. Bruce Westbrook, rhp, Southeast HS, Bradenton, Fla.
18. Richard Bedard, inf, Amherst (Mass.) College.
19. Terry Collins, ss, Eastern Michigan University.
DRAFT DROP *Major league manager (1994-2015)*
20. John Darnell, lhp-1b, R.L. Osborne HS, Marietta, Ga.
21. Allen Dukate, rhp, Miami (Ohio) University.
22. *Bob Lesslie, rhp, St. Louis CC-Meramec.
DRAFT DROP *First overall draft pick, June 1972/secondary phase, Dodgers*
23. *Edward Smith, ss-3b, Washington State University.
24. Danny Waelchli, rhp, Kutztown (Pa.) University.
25. *David Naberezny, ss, Oliver HS, Pittsburgh.
26. John Herrscher, rhp, Central Catholic HS, Kingston, Pa.
27. Charles Flint, rhp, Danvers (Mass.) HS.
28. *Herman Maston, 2b, Wasco (Calif.) HS.
29. Richard Thomas, rhp, North Hills HS, Pittsburgh.
30. John Caruso, ss-2b, Regis (Colo.) College.
31. Joe Nagy, of, Keystone (Pa.) JC.

**June—Secondary Phase/Delayed (14)**

1. Tom Thomas, 3b, Washington State University.—(AAA)
2. *Douglas Farrell, rhp-of, Niagara University.
3. Gary Shade, 2b, Ohio University.

**June—Secondary Phase/Active (24)**

No selection.

## ST. LOUIS CARDINALS

**January—Regular Phase (7)**

1. *Rand Rasmussen, ss, Long Beach (Calif.) CC.—DNP
2. *Tom Zimmerman, rhp, University of Nebraska.
3. Mark Cresse, c, Golden West (Calif.) JC.
4. *Tommy Zimmer, 2b-c, Manatee (Fla.) JC.
DRAFT DROP *Son of Don Zimmer, major leaguer (1954-65); major league manager (1972-99)*
5. *Gary Matthews, lhp, Columbia State (Tenn.) CC.
6. *John Behrens, ss-1b, Fresno (Calif.) CC.
7. Bob Kennedy Jr., rhp, Mesa (Ariz.) CC.
DRAFT DROP *Son of Bob Kennedy, major leaguer (1939-57); major league manager (1963-68) • Brother of Terry Kennedy, first-round draft pick, Cardinals (1977); major leaguer (1978-91)*
8. *Edward Hora, lhp, Brigham Young University.
9. *John Alesci, ss, Miami-Dade CC.
10. *Jeff Neal, lhp, Fresno (Calif.) CC.
11. ***Rick Langford, of-rhp, Manatee (Fla.) JC.—(1976-86)**
12. *Rodney Walker, rhp, Pascagoula, Miss.
13. *Mike Sinovich, 1b, St. Louis CC-Florissant Valley.

**January—Secondary Phase (16)**

1. Mike Ibarguen, rhp, San Jacinto (Texas) JC.–(AA)
2. *Al Ryan, 2b, Gulf Coast (Fla.) CC.
DRAFT DROP *Son of Connie Ryan, major leaguer (1942-54); major league manager (1975-77)*
3. Mark Andresen, of, Garden Grove, Calif.
4. **Mike Vail, ss, DeAnza (Calif.) JC.—(1975-84)**
5. *William Finck, rhp, Hayward, Calif.
6. **Mike Potter, of, Mount San Antonio (Calif.) JC.—(1976-77)**
7. Robert Cobb, rhp, Fresno (Calif.) CC.
8. *Marvin Webb, 2b, San Pablo, Calif.

**June—Regular Phase (8)**

1. Ed Kurpiel, 1b-of, Archbishop Molloy HS, Hollis, N.Y.—(AAA)
2. Gary Christophel, lhp, Mount Healthy HS, Cincinnati.—(High A)
3. **Larry Herndon, of, Douglas HS, Memphis, Tenn.—(1974-88)**
4. **Jerry Mumphrey, ss-of, Chapel Hill HS, Tyler, Texas.—(1974-88)**
5. *Steven Copeland, lhp, St. Patrick's HS, Vallejo, Calif.—DNP
DRAFT DROP *No school; never re-drafted*
6. Charles Blakely, c, Northeast Missouri State University.
7. Gary Trumbauer, lhp, Thousand Oaks (Calif.) HS.
8. *Steven Greene, 2b, Fremont HS, Los Angeles.
9. Leon Lee, 3b, Grant HS, Sacramento, Calif.
DRAFT DROP *Brother of Leron Lee, major leaguer (1969-76) • Father of Derrek Lee, first-round draft pick, Padres (1993); major leaguer (1997-2011)*
10. Greg LaMendola, rhp, Western HS, Buena Park, Calif.
11. **Jim Dwyer, of, Southern Illinois University.—(1973-90)**
12. John Grijalva, 3b-c, Pasadena HS, Sierra Madre,

Calif.
13. *Mark Wogan, rhp, Saguaro HS, Scottsdale, Ariz.
14. Fred Zwiefel, inf, University of Missouri-St. Louis.
15. Shelby Hill, rhp, West HS, Morristown, Tenn.
16. Gary Raco, inf, Reedley (Calif.) JC.
17. *John Park, rhp, Nathan Hale HS, Tulsa, Okla.
18. *William Poe, rhp, Waterford HS, Pontiac, Mich.
19. *Donald Redoglia, ss, Pasadena (Calif.) HS.
20. *Arthur Adams, lhp, Wellesley (Mass.) HS.
21. Monte Bolinger, 1b, Lompoc (Calif.) HS.
22. Marty DeMerritt, rhp, South San Francisco (Calif.) HS.
23. Charles Voskovitch, lhp, South HS, Commack, N.Y.
24. James Walthour, 3b, St. Louis CC-Meramec.
25. Jethro Mills, lhp-of, Newton (Mass.) HS.
26. Mark Penbarthy, c, Los Angeles Baptist College.
27. *James Hinkleman, rhp, Bowen HS, Lansing, Ill.
28. *Mark Mazzucco, rhp, Raritan HS, Hazlet, N.J.
29. *Rickey Ritschel, rhp, Rogers HS, Tulsa, Okla.
30. *Alan Gifford, rhp-inf, Wayne Hills HS, Wayne, N.J.
31. *Steve Walsh, lhp, University HS, St. Louis.
32. *William Lankford, of, Mark Twain HS, New London, Mo.
33. *Roger Walton, rhp, Hannibal (Mo.) HS.
34. Mark Mueller, 3b-ss, St. Louis CC-Florissant Valley.
DRAFT DROP *Son of Don Mueller, major leaguer (1948-59)*
**35. *Sam Hinds, rhp-ss, International School, Hague, Holland.—(1977)**
36. James Linehan, rhp, Peabody (Mass.) HS.
37. *Milton Holt, lhp, Phillips Andover Prep, Andover, Mass.
38. *William Drescher, c, Clarkston HS, Congers, N.Y.
39. *Forrest Meek, rhp, Roosevelt HS, Fresno, Calif.
40. *James Fiack, c, UC Davis.
41. *Lee Daney, rhp, U.S. Military Academy.
**42. Keith Hernandez, 1b, Capuchino HS, Millbrae, Calif.—(1974-90)**
43. *Don Hairston, rhp, Channel Islands HS, Oxnard, Calif.
44. *Michael Laurent, rhp, Valley HS, Albuquerque, N.M.
45. William Kelly, rhp, Harvard University.

**June—Secondary Phase/Delayed (16)**
1. Rick Pope, rhp, UCLA.—(AA)
2. Jim Silvey, 2b, University of Tulsa.
3. Steve Broege, lhp, Iona College.
4. *Jim Jachym, lhp, University of Connecticut.

**June—Secondary Phase/Active (2)**
1. Mike Swenton, of, University of Oklahoma.–(AA)
**2. *Roy Smalley, ss, Los Angeles CC.–(1975-87)**
DRAFT DROP *First overall draft pick, January 1974/ regular phase, Rangers • Son of Roy Smalley, major leaguer (1948-58) • Nephew of Gene Mach, major leaguer (1944-57); major league manager (1960-87)*
3. Tommy Zimmer, c-2b, Manatee (Fla.) JC.
DRAFT DROP *Son of Don Zimmer, major leaguer (1954-65); major league manager (1972-99)*

## SAN DIEGO PADRES

**January—Regular Phase (1)**
**1. Dave Hilton, 3b, Southwest Texas JC.—(1972-75)**
2. Anthony Glassman, of, University of Rochester.
3. No selection.
4. *William Sims, 1b, San Joaquin Delta (Calif.) JC.
5. *Wendell Stephens, rhp, East Los Angeles JC.

**January—Secondary Phase (24)**
**1. Johnny Grubb, of, Florida State University.—(1972-87)**
2. Robert Johnston, lhp, Atlanta Christian College.
3. Marc Rhea, ss, Mesa (Ariz.) CC.
4. *Ricardo Urbano, lhp, Los Gatos, Calif.

**June—Regular Phase (2)**
**1. Jay Franklin, rhp, James Madison HS, Vienna, Va.—(1971)**
DRAFT DROP *First 1971 high school draft pick to reach majors (Sept. 4, 1971)*
2. Willie Boynton, rhp, Springfield (Mass.) College.—(AA)
3. No selection.
4. Craig Settles, ss-3b, Point Loma HS, San Diego.—(AA)
**5. Dave Freisleben, rhp, Sam Rayburn HS, Pasadena, Texas.—(1974-79)**
6. Don Elliott, ss, Norway (Iowa) HS.
**7. Frank Snook, rhp, Grand Canyon College.—(1973)**
**8. Joe Goddard, c, Marshall University.—(1972)**
9. *Johnny Green, c, Grant HS, Sacramento, Calif.
10. Melvin Lord, 1b, Fresno (Calif.) HS.
**11. *Bill Almon, ss, Veterans Memorial HS, Warwick, R.I.—(1974-88)**
DRAFT DROP *First overall draft pick, Padres (1974)*
**12. Mike Caldwell, lhp, North Carolina State University.—(1971-84)**
13. *Fred Mims, of, University of Iowa.
14. Robert Hill, 1b-rhp, Bowling Green State University.
15. *Greg Richards, rhp, Palos Verdes HS, Palos Verdes Estates, Calif.
16. Robert Marshall, of, Davidson HS, Mobile, Ala.
17. Duane Larson, 2b, Santa Clara University.
18. Gary Myron, rhp, University of San Diego.
19. *Jeff Spagnola, of, El Modena HS, Orange, Calif.
20. Anthony Ponticelli, rhp, Johnston (R.I.) HS.

**June—Secondary Phase/Delayed (12)**
1. Charlie Dudish, ss-of, Georgia Tech.—(High A)
DRAFT DROP *Son of Andy Dudish, running back/National Football League (1946-48)*
2. *Ricky Rucker, lhp, University of Alabama.
3. *Dudley Mitchell, of-1b, University of Colorado.
DRAFT DROP *Son of Dale Mitchell, major leaguer (1946-56)*

**June—Secondary Phase/Active (22)**
1. Billy Hodge, c, Texas A&M University.—(AAA)

## SAN FRANCISCO GIANTS

**January—Regular Phase (17)**
1. *Robert Makoski, 1b, St. Clair County (Mich.) CC.—(Low A)
2. Richard Thompson, lhp, Cypress (Calif.) JC.
3. *Joseph Remcisz, ss, St. Clair County (Mich.) CC.
4. *David Harness, 1b-of, El Camino (Calif.) JC.
5. Matt Werderber, rhp, Lower Columbia (Wash.) JC.
6. *David Bryant, ss, Mount Hood (Ore.) CC.
7. George Maldonado, of, University of Nevada.
8. *Chris Tust, of, Lower Columbia (Wash.) JC.
9. *Michael Ferney, rhp, Yavapai (Ariz.) JC.
10. *Robert Burton, rhp-of, JC of the Sequoias (Calif.).
11. *James Cannon, rhp, JC of the Sequoias (Calif.).

**January—Secondary Phase (8)**
1. *Mike Swenton, of, University of Oklahoma.–(AA)
2. *Rudy Kinard, 2b, University of Tennessee.
3. *Tim Sherrill, 1b, Miami-Dade CC South.
4. Stephen Lee, lhp, Cal State Northridge.
5. *Paul Djakonow, 3b, Detroit.
**6. *Warren Brusstar, rhp, Napa, Calif.—(1977-85)**
7. Robert Vandersluis, rhp, Northwest Nazarene (Idaho) College.
8. *David Whitney, lhp, Astoria, Ore.

**June—Regular Phase (18)**
**1. Frank Riccelli, lhp, Christian Brothers HS, Syracuse, N.Y.—(1976-79)**
2. Tony Pepper, 1b-of, Grant HS, Sacramento, Calif.—(AAA)
**3. Willie Prall, lhp, Upsala (N.J.) College.—(1975)**
**4. *Rick Anderson, rhp, Southern California Christian HS, Inglewood, Calif.—(1979-80)**
DRAFT DROP *Attended Los Angeles Valley JC; re-drafted by Yankees, January 1972/secondary phase (1st round)*
**5. Skip James, 1b-of, University of Kansas.—(1977-78)**
6. *Ed Gilliam, of, Locke HS, Los Angeles.
7. Scott Wolfe, 2b, Fresno State University.
8. Al Smith, of, Adrian (Mich.) College.
9. David Walski, 3b, UC Santa Barbara.
**10. *Craig Caskey, lhp, University of Puget Sound.—(1973)**
11. *Charles Bordes, ss, University of Southwestern Louisiana.
**12. *Terry Cornutt, rhp, Linn-Benton (Ore.) CC.—(1977-78)**
13. *Gerard Thomas, lhp, West Scranton (Pa.) HS.
14. *Greg Lyon, lhp, Sayreville HS, Parlin, N.J.
15. *Rick Duncan, c, Central HS, Chattanooga, Tenn.
16. *Brian Masella, of-1b, Peddie HS, Bordentown, N.J.
17. *Michael Rankin, c, Bartlett HS, Memphis, Tenn.
18. *Pedro Santiago, of, James Monroe HS, Bronx, N.Y.
19. *Mark Servais, 2b, St. Mary's (Minn.) College.
20. Jay Dillard, rhp, Branham HS, San Jose, Calif.
21. Phil Beall, ss, Baylor University.
22. *Steve Miller, rhp, Miramonte HS, Orinda, Calif.
23. Frank Reyes, rhp, Allan Hancock (Calif.) JC.
24. *Terry Brown, lhp, University of Miami.
25. *David Chapman, rhp, Newark (Del.) HS.
26. *James Snoots, 3b, Johnson HS, Thurmond, Md.
27. Bruce Wright, of, University of Richmond.
28. *Francis Sansosti, rhp-1b, Curley HS, Baltimore.
29. *Connie Smith, ss-rhp, East Texas Baptist University.
30. *Robert Schaeffer, c, El Segundo (Calif.) HS.
31. David Fuqua, rhp, Bend (Ore.) HS.
**32. Greg Thayer, rhp, St. Cloud State (Minn.) University.—(1978)**
33. *James Howard, of, North Central HS, Indianapolis.
34. *William Wesley, rhp, Moeller HS, Cincinnati.
35. *Tim Kampa, rhp, Lewiston (Idaho) HS.
**36. *Juan Eichelberger, rhp, Balboa HS, San Francisco.—(1978-88)**
37. *Craig Clark, 2b-ss, Foothill (Calif.) JC.
38. *Roy Hadden, rhp, Mountain View (Calif.) HS.
39. *Kenny Roberts, rhp, Lawndale (Calif.) HS.
40. *John Chapman, rhp, Fort Myers (Fla.) HS.
41. *Donald Cooke, lhp, Miami-Dade CC North.
42. Harold Ingle, ss, Campbell University.
43. *Seldon Morton, 1b-lhp, Jefferson HS, Daly City, Calif.
44. *John Fennell, rhp, Minico HS, Rupert, Idaho.

**June—Secondary Phase/Delayed (10)**
1. *Paul Patterson, rhp, Ithaca (N.Y.) College.–(AAA)
2. Gordon Carter, of, University of Southern California.
DRAFT DROP *Brother of Gary Carter, major leaguer (1974-92)*
3. Bill Adkison, 3b-of, Central Washington University.

**June—Secondary Phase/Active (6)**
**1. Steve Stroughter, of, JC of the Sequoias (Calif.).—(1982)**
2. *Terry Farmer, rhp, Chipola (Fla.) JC.

## WASHINGTON SENATORS

**January—Regular Phase (8)**
1. Steven Raines, rhp, University of Tennessee.—(High A)
2. *Mike Coronado, ss, San Diego CC.
3. *Raleigh Riddle, 2b-ss, Miami-Dade CC North.
4. *Kenneth Benson, lhp, West Valley (Calif.) JC.
5. *Terry Dreamer, rhp, Pershing (Neb.) College.
6. *Greg Ojeda, ss, West Valley (Calif.) JC.
7. *Peter Catalanotte, 1b, Phoenix (Ariz.) JC.

**January—Secondary Phase (9)**
**1. Jim Kremmel, lhp, University of New Mexico.—(1973-74)**
2. *Curran Percival, rhp, San Diego Mesa JC.
3. *Frank Baumgardner, rhp, Opa Locka, Fla.
4. *Jeff Kalish, 3b, New York University.
5. David Moharter, lhp, Bloomsburg (Pa.) University.

**June—Regular Phase (7)**
1. Roger Quiroga, rhp, Ball HS, Galveston, Texas.—(High A)
2. Bill Amason, rhp, Lake Worth (Fla.) HS.—(Low A)
**3. *Eddy Putman, c, Northview HS, Covina, Calif.—(1976-79)**
DRAFT DROP *Attended Southern California; re-drafted by Cubs, January 1975/secondary phase (1st round)*
4. David Harper, rhp, Boone HS, Orlando, Fla.—(AAA)
5. *Joe Burgess, lhp, Davenport (Okla.) HS.—DNP
DRAFT DROP *Attended Eastern Oklahoma State JC; re-drafted by Red Sox, January 1972/secondary phase (2nd round)*
**6. Greg Pryor, 2b, Florida Southern College.—(1976-86)**
7. *Leslie Clark, ss, Prince Edward County HS, Farmville, Va.
8. *Michael Agosto, of, Clairemont HS, San Diego.
9. James Penner, rhp, McLane HS, Fresno, Calif.
10. Alberto Zamora, rhp, Miami (Fla.) Senior HS.
11. *Louie Lamoure, ss, Bullard HS, Fresno, Calif.
12. Steven Eckinger, 3b, Central Missouri State University.
13. *Gary Kelson, rhp, Miami Beach (Fla.) HS.
14. *Rick Tomlin, lhp, George Wythe HS, Richmond, Va.
15. *William Carleton, lhp, Miami-Dade CC South.
16. Robert Spinner, of, Emporia State (Kan.) University.
17. *Tom Stoddard, c, Lake Worth (Fla.) HS.
18. *Mark Rott, c-of, Ynagcio Valley HS, Concord, Calif.
19. *Marcelino Huerta, 3b, H.B. Plant HS, Tampa.
20. Robert Frye, rhp, Ashbrook HS, Gastonia, N.C.
21. *John Herman, of, Overton HS, Nashville, Tenn.
22. Gary Boyce, of, Michigan State University.
23. *Walt Rzepiennik, rhp, CC of Baltimore.
24. Ken Flowers, lhp, Littlefield HS, Lumberton, N.C.
25. *James Van Der Beek, rhp, Lafayette College.
26. Richard Revta, c, Lehigh University.
**27. *Stan Thomas, rhp, University of New Haven.—(1974-77)**
28. Larry Mohme, 3b, Highland HS, New Douglas, Ill.
29. *Frank Weisse, of, Lafayette College.
30. *Jesse Campbell, c, Jackson HS, Miami.
31. *Dan Domski, lhp, Rockford West HS, Rockford, Ill.
32. Bruce Cease, 1b, Miami-Dade CC South.
33. *Selven Watts, of, Colonial Beach (Va.) HS.
34. Royce Hayes, of, Western Carolina University.
35. *Lawrence Rettenmund, 2b, Michigan State University.

**June—Secondary Phase/Delayed (1)**
**1. Pete Broberg, rhp, Dartmouth College.—(1971-78)**
DRAFT DROP *First-round draft pick (2nd overall), Athletics (1968)*
**2. Mike Cubbage, ss-3b, University of Virginia.—(1974-81)**
DRAFT DROP *Major league manager (1991)*
3. Henry Bunnell, of-rhp, George Washington University.
4. *Joe Barkauskas, c, Lafayette College.

**June—Secondary Phase Active (5)**
1. Vern Wilkins, 1b, Mesa (Ariz.) CC.—(AAA)
2. *Steve Behlen, lhp, Fresno (Calif.) CC.

## BEND RAINBOWS (CLASS A NORTHWEST LEAGUE)

**January—Regular Phase (1)**
1-3. No selections.
4. *Wayne Kiefer, Golden West (Calif.) JC.
5. *Dean Lyman, Fullerton (Calif.) JC.

**January—Secondary Phase (1)**
1. Jim Hogan, of, Golden West (Calif.) JC.—(AAA)

**June—Regular Phase (1)**
1-3. No selections.
4. Bill Bolden, rhp, Santa Ana Valley HS, Santa Ana, Calif.—(High A)
5. Mike Lacheur, c, Bonita HS, La Verne, Calif.—(Short-season A)
6. Fred Morgan, 1b-c, Pomona (Calif.) HS.
7. *Greg Clark, inf, Fullerton (Calif.) JC.
8. *Bill Hobbs, of, Fullerton (Calif.) JC.
9. *Norm Kepner, c, Fullerton (Calif.) JC.
10. Thomas Turner, 3b, Fullerton (Calif.) JC.

**June—Secondary Phase/Delayed (1)**
No selection.

**June—Secondary Phase/Active (1)**
No selection.

# 1972

## AT A GLANCE

### This Date In History

**WINTER DRAFT:** Jan. 12
**SUMMER DRAFT:** June 6-7

### Best Draft

**TEXAS RANGERS.** In his first year in a new market, Rangers owner Bob Short didn't have a No. 1 overall pick to exploit for short-term gain as he did on three occasions (Jeff Burroughs/1969, Pete Broberg/1971, David Clyde/1973), allowing the Rangers to identify a draft-high 13 future big leaguers, including **ROY HOWELL** (1) and **MIKE HARGROVE** (25)—though seven went unsigned.

### Worst Draft

**CINCINNATI REDS.** In an all-too-familiar script in the 1970s, the Reds botched their first-round pick (**LARRY PAYNE**) and didn't produce a big leaguer among players they drafted in June. The club's foundation was beginning to show cracks because of its ineptitude in the draft, and crumbled a decade later.

### First-Round Bust

**KEN THOMAS, C, ORIOLES.** It didn't take the O's long to realize they had made a big mistake in drafting Thomas, as they released him after just 90 minor league games—all but seven in Rookie ball. His career totals: .148, one home run, 27 errors, 32 passed balls.

### On Second Thought

**JOHN CANDELARIA, LHP, PIRATES.** Five second-rounders in 1972 enjoyed better careers than all but two first-rounders. Candelaria was the most successful of the bunch, winning 177 games in a 19-year career.

### Late-Round Find

**MIKE HARGROVE, 1B, RANGERS (25TH ROUND).** A product of obscure Northwestern Oklahoma State, Hargrove became a Rangers regular by 1974 and went on to a productive 12-year career in the majors, posting a .396

# Tragedy underscores mediocre talent crop

No. 1 overall pick Dave Roberts began his career in the majors with the Padres, but he spent most of it in a utility role, with a .239 career average

The 1972 draft began with high expectations when the San Diego Padres selected University of Oregon infielder Dave Roberts with the No. 1 pick in the June regular phase, and started him at third base in a game against the Pittsburgh Pirates a day later. No drafted player ever began his big league career more quickly.

Padres scouting director Bob Fontaine offered high praise for Roberts: "He is the most-advanced prospect we've ever picked up in the draft."

Cleveland Indians minor league director Paul O'Dea expressed similar enthusiasm over his club's selection of New York high school infielder Rick Manning with the second pick overall.

"Manning is the best-looking kid we've seen in many years," O'Dea said. "He's got a great swing and could come fast. He has the batting potential to hit 30 home runs a year in the big leagues."

Those hopeful statements ran counter to the prevailing wisdom that the 1972 draft was substandard in both depth and impact talent. And while the class did ultimately produce two Hall of Famers, Gary Carter and Dennis Eckersley—California high school products taken three picks apart in the third round—the first round did end up being one of the worst in draft history.

Leading the way, neither Roberts nor Manning ever quite lived up to their press clippings.

After a strong start, Roberts never again played consistently like a No. 1 pick. A mysterious back ailment sidelined him to start the 1974 season and he never got untracked, hitting .167 in 113 games. His career began a downhill slide from that point. Manning's power never manifested as predicted. Over 13 major league seasons, he homered just 56 times while hitting .257.

They set a tone for the entire first round as only two players who signed, lefthander Scott McGregor (Yankees, 14th overall), and shortstop Chet Lemon (Athletics, 22nd) enjoyed careers that warranted their lofty draft status. Neither played a single game in the majors with the team that drafted them, however.

The high-end talent that came from the second round trumped that in the first, and four players signed as nondrafted free agents outstripped the first-rounders. And that says nothing of players like Carter and Eckersley, who slipped mysteriously to the third round.

Not only did the first round end up becoming one of the most underachieving lots in draft history, but it was further scarred by two of the most tragic developments in the 50-year history of the draft: the suicide deaths of Danny Thomas (Brewers, sixth) and John Harbin (Dodgers, 17th).

Moreover, Lyman Bostock, who overcame being a lowly 26th-round draft pick of the Minnesota Twins to become one of the stars of the 1972 class, died at the height of his career when he was the unintended victim of a drive-by shooting in 1978.

Indeed, no other draft in history has been so scarred by tragedy.

## 1972: THE FIRST ROUNDERS

| CLUB: PLAYER, POS., SCHOOL | HOMETOWN | B-T | HT. | WT. | AGE | BONUS | FIRST YEAR | LAST YEAR | PEAK LEVEL (YEARS) |
|---|---|---|---|---|---|---|---|---|---|
| **JUNE—REGULAR PHASE** | | | | | | | | | |
| 1. *Padres: Dave Roberts, 3b, Oregon | Corvallis, Ore. | R-R | 6-3 | 215 | 21 | $70,000 | 1972 | 1982 | Majors (10) |
| Debuted with Padres a day after signing, looked ready to blossom after hitting .286 with 21 HRs in 1973, but hit skids a year later, became backup catcher. | | | | | | | | | |
| 2. Indians: Rick Manning, ss, LaSalle HS | Niagara Falls, N.Y. | L-R | 6-0 | 175 | 17 | $57,500 | 1972 | 1987 | Majors (13) |
| Never became power threat Indians envisioned, but developed into solid big leaguer, Gold-Glove outfielder in 13-year career; hit .257 overall, went deep 56 times. | | | | | | | | | |
| 3. Phillies: Larry Christenson, rhp, Marysville HS | Marysville, Wash. | R-R | 6-4 | 215 | 18 | $50,000 | 1972 | 1983 | Majors (11) |
| Dominated as prep senior (0.28 ERA, 72 IP/143 SO), made Phillies Opening Day roster a year later, went on to win 83 games before career doomed by elbow issues. | | | | | | | | | |
| 4. Rangers: Roy Howell, 3b, Lompoc HS | Lompoc, Calif. | L-R | 6-1 | 190 | 18 | $40,000 | 1972 | 1985 | Majors (11) |
| First pick for first-year Rangers started career in Double-A, made it to Texas by 1974; hit .261 with 80 HRs in 12 years, also saw time with Blue Jays, Brewers. | | | | | | | | | |
| 5. Expos: Bobby Goodman, c, Bishop Byrne HS | Memphis | R-R | 6-2 | 195 | 18 | $60,000 | 1972 | 1977 | Class AAA (1) |
| Goodman, not third-rounder Gary Carter, was supposed to be Expos' catcher of future; career ravaged by injuries, and he hit .240 with 36 HRs in six years. | | | | | | | | | |
| 6. Brewers: # Danny Thomas, 1b/of, Southern Illinois | East Carondelet, Ill. | R-R | 6-2 | 190 | 21 | $50,000 | 1972 | 1979 | Majors (2) |
| Most tragic career of draft era? After his promising career fizzled, he was overcome by depression, bizarre behavior and committed suicide in Alabama jail cell. | | | | | | | | | |
| 7. Reds: Larry Payne, rhp, Huntsville HS | Bedias, Texas | R-R | 6-0 | 180 | 18 | $50,000 | 1972 | 1978 | Class AAA (4) |
| Reds missed mark again on top draft pick and struck out on every selection in June phase; Payne went 49-43, 3.54 in seven seasons in minors, all in Reds system. | | | | | | | | | |
| 8. Twins: Dick Ruthven, rhp, Fresno State | Fremont, Calif. | R-R | 6-2 | 185 | 21 | Unsigned | 1973 | 1986 | Majors (14) |
| Prep outfielder made huge strides as pitcher in college, fanned 153 in 111 IP as junior; rejected Twins offer, redrafted in January 1973 and pitched 14 MLB seasons. | | | | | | | | | |
| 9. Astros: Steve Englishbey, of, South Houston HS | Houston | L-L | 6-1 | 193 | 17 | $25,000 | 1972 | 1978 | Class AAA (1) |
| Astros steered hometown boy away from career as QB at Houston, but he didn't pan out; hit .225 with 58 HRs in six years and was released after smashing locker. | | | | | | | | | |
| 10. Angels: Dave Chalk, 3b, Texas | Dallas | R-R | 5-10 | 175 | 21 | $31,000 | 1972 | 1981 | Majors (9) |
| Three-time Texas All-American set school career mark with .362 BA, signed after senior year; spent nine years with Angels, three other clubs, hit .252-15-243. | | | | | | | | | |
| 11. Braves: Preston Hanna, rhp, Escambia HS | Pensacola, Fla. | R-R | 6-1 | 180 | 17 | $40,000 | 1972 | 1983 | Majors (8) |
| Went 13-0, 0.31, pitched perfect game as prep senior, but found going much tougher in minors (43-47, 4.24), majors (17-25, 4.61) as he struggled to throw strikes. | | | | | | | | | |
| 12. White Sox: Mike Ondina, of, Cordova HS | Rancho Cordova, Calif. | L-R | 6-2 | 190 | 18 | $52,000 | 1972 | 1979 | Class AAA (2) |
| Along with Jerry Manuel (No. 20), became first set of prep teammates to be picked in first round; spent all eight years of career in minors, hit .254 with 57 homers. | | | | | | | | | |
| 13. Mets: Richard Bengston, c, Richwoods HS | Peoria, Ill. | R-R | 6-3 | 195 | 18 | $22,000 | 1972 | 1976 | Class AA (1) |
| Three-sport star in high school, began five-year pro career with Mets as catcher, ended it as first baseman with Expos; reached Double-A, hit .254-34-214 overall. | | | | | | | | | |
| 14. Yankees: Scott McGregor, lhp, El Segundo HS | El Segundo, Calif. | L-L | 6-0 | 180 | 18 | $72,500 | 1972 | 1988 | Majors (13) |
| Prep teammate of George Brett set state record with 51 wins in stellar HS career; signed by Yankees, but earned all 138 wins in majors while with Orioles. | | | | | | | | | |
| 15. Cubs: Brian Vernoy, lhp, La Quinta HS | Westminster, Calif. | L-L | 6-3 | 180 | 18 | $26,000 | 1972 | 1975 | Class A (3) |
| Went 7-3, 1.15, spun two no-hitters as prep senior, but uneventful pro career ended after three years when released by Cubs with 15-19, 3.70 career record. | | | | | | | | | |
| 16. Red Sox: # Joel Bishop, ss, McClatchy HS | Sacramento, Calif. | R-R | 6-2 | 180 | 18 | $45,000 | 1972 | 1973 | Class A (1) |
| All-star QB in high school quit football as senior to focus on baseball; quit baseball midway through second pro season, citing mistrust of Red Sox coaches. | | | | | | | | | |
| 17. Dodgers: # John Harbin, ss, Newberry (S.C.) College | Greenville, S.C. | R-R | 6-1 | 195 | 21 | $30,000 | 1972 | 1972 | Class A (1) |
| Lasted only one year in pros after knees, already damaged from football, were injured in spring camp in 1973; distraught at end of career, later committed suicide. | | | | | | | | | |
| 18. Royals: Jamie Quirk, ss, St. Paul HS | Whittier, Calif. | B-R | 6-3 | 180 | 17 | $78,000 | 1972 | 1992 | Majors (18) |
| Took largest bonus of 1972 to sign Notre Dame QB recruit; became super utilityman in 18-year MLB career, never got more than 300 ABs in a season. | | | | | | | | | |
| 19. Giants: Rob Dressler, rhp, Madison HS | Portland, Ore. | R-R | 6-3 | 175 | 18 | $30,000 | 1972 | 1980 | Majors (5) |
| Went 7-4, 0.38 with 72 IP/122 SO as prep SR, played on four straight state champs; success tougher to come by in majors, went 11-23, 4.17 with three clubs. | | | | | | | | | |
| 20. Tigers: Jerry Manuel, ss, Cordova HS | Rancho Cordova, Calif. | R-R | 5-11 | 165 | 18 | $48,000 | 1972 | 1986 | Majors (5) |
| Best athlete in rich Sacramento prep ranks turned down UCLA grid offer; played 1,281 games in minors, then played (five years), managed (nine years) in majors. | | | | | | | | | |
| 21. *Cardinals: Dan Larson, rhp, Alhambra HS | Alhambra, Calif. | R-R | 6-1 | 180 | 17 | $53,500 | 1972 | 1984 | Majors (7) |
| Went 112-81, 4.07 in 12 years in minors, also played seven seasons in majors, went 10-25, 4.40 with 3 clubs, earned World Series ring with 1980 Phillies. | | | | | | | | | |
| 22. Athletics: Chet Lemon, ss, Fremont HS | Los Angeles | R-R | 5-11 | 175 | 17 | $20,000 | 1972 | 1990 | Majors (16) |
| Had productive 16-year career as major league OF with White Sox, Tigers, hit .273-215-884 overall; later developed Chet Lemon's Juice, youth baseball juggernaut. | | | | | | | | | |
| 23. Pirates: Dwayne Peltier, ss, Servite HS | Anaheim, Calif. | R-R | 6-1 | 180 | 17 | $50,500 | 1973 | 1976 | Class AA (1) |
| Leveraged big bonus with late signing, showed early promise as power-hitting 3B, but career fizzled; later became successful financial adviser. | | | | | | | | | |
| 24. Orioles: Ken Thomas, c, Clear Fork HS | Bellville, Ohio | R-R | 5-11 | 180 | 18 | $15,000 | 1972 | 1973 | Class A (1) |
| O's bombed twice in three years by taking prep catcher with top pick; Thomas hit .148-1-25, had 27 errors/32 passed balls in 85 games behind plate. | | | | | | | | | |
| **JANUARY—REGULAR PHASE** | | | | | | | | | |
| 1. Indians: Eric Raich, rhp, Southern California | South Gate, Calif. | R-R | 6-4 | 225 | 20 | $22,500 | 1972 | 1978 | Majors (2) |
| Dropped out of USC to become eligible for January draft, top pick in lean crop; pitched two years for Indians in 1975-76, went 7-8, 5.85; also 33-63 in minors. | | | | | | | | | |
| **JANUARY—SECONDARY PHASE** | | | | | | | | | |
| 1. Twins: Bob Koeppel, lhp/of, Bradley | Peoria, Ill. | L-L | 6-0 | 200 | 21 | N/A | 1972 | 1973 | Class AA (1) |
| Didn't sign with Orioles in 1971 despite hitting .484 for Bradley, leading nation in RBIs/game; Southern League all-star (.274-9-71) in second and final pro season. | | | | | | | | | |
| **JUNE—SECONDARY PHASE** | | | | | | | | | |
| 1. Dodgers: Bob Lesslie, rhp, Kansas State | St. Louis | R-R | 6-3 | 215 | 21 | $12,000 | 1972 | 1977 | Class AAA (2) |
| All-Big Eight Conference performer at Kansas State went 56-56 in six-year career in minors; later became CEO of prominent life-insurance company. | | | | | | | | | |

**Signed to major league contract. # Deceased.*

## AT A GLANCE

on-base average while hitting .290 with 80 homers. He drew 965 walks vs. 550 strikeouts. Had he not been gunned down in 1978, at the prime of his career, **LYMAN BOSTOCK**, drafted by the Twins in the 26th round, would have been a deserving candidate.

### Never Too Late

**GIL KUBSKI, OF, PIRATES (40TH ROUND).** The 40th and last pick of the Pirates in 1972, Kubski didn't sign until 1975, when he was drafted by the Angels, who employed his father Al as a scout at the time. The younger Kubski reached the Angels briefly in 1980. Like Al, who scouted for more than 40 years, Gil also became best-known for his contributions as a scout.

### Overlooked

**JOHN MONTEFUSCO, RHP, GIANTS.** Montefusco, **LARRY PARRISH**, **CLAUDELL WASHINGTON** and **GARY WARD** were among the players signed as nondrafted free agents in 1972. The edge goes to Montefusco, signed by the Giants out of a New Jersey junior college. He posted a 90-83, 3.54 record in 13 major league seasons, won National League rookie of the year honors in 1975 and was an all-star a year later when he won a career-high 16 games.

### International Gem

**JORGE ORTA, 2B, WHITE SOX.** Orta, 21, was a veteran of five professional seasons in his native Mexico when his contract was purchased prior to the 1972 season. He started at shortstop for the White Sox, was sent to the minors for more seasoning, but returned later that year and went on to play 16 years in the majors, hitting .278 with 130 homers overall.

### Minor League Take

**JERRY MANUEL, SS, TIGERS.** Of all the first-rounders in 1972,

CONTINUED ON PAGE 126

## AT A GLANCE

CONTINUED FROM PAGE 125

no one persevered in the minor leagues longer than Manuel, who toiled for 17 seasons. In 1,281 games, he hit .255 with 43 homers; he also spent parts of five seasons in the majors. It helped to prepare Manuel for two managerial stints in the majors.

### One Who Got Away

**DICK RUTHVEN, RHP, TWINS.** Ruthven, one of six first-round picks the Twins didn't sign through the years, elected not to return to Fresno State for his senior year. He sat out that fall, became the first pick in the secondary phase of the January draft in 1973, and stepped immediately into a Phillies uniform.

### He Was Drafted?

**RAY GUY, RHP, BRAVES (17TH ROUND).** The only punter to become a first-round NFL draft pick and a member of the Pro Football Hall of Fame, Guy was selected on three occasions in the baseball draft. As a pitcher at Southern Mississippi, he struck out 266 in 221 innings, while authoring a 16-strikeout game and no-hitter.

### Did You Know . . .

**DAVE LOGAN,** a 19th-round pick of the Reds in 1972 out of a Colorado high school, is one of just three athletes (with Mickey McCarty and Dave Winfield) to be drafted in three different sports. He was picked in 1976 by the NBA's Kansas City Kings (ninth round) and NFL's Cleveland Browns (third round). Logan played nine seasons in the NFL, and became a prominent radio personality and high school football coach in Denver.

### They Said It

Cleveland farm director **PAUL O'DEA** on **RICK MANNING**, the second overall pick: "He has the batting potential to hit 30 or more home runs a year in the big leagues."—*Manning hit 56 in a 13-year career.*

## ROBERTS, MANNING SET TONE

The 6-foot-3, 215-pound Roberts was the first college player selected first overall since the inaugural draft in 1965, when the Kansas City Athletics took Arizona State outfielder Rick Monday.

Roberts matriculated at Oregon, near his hometown of Corvallis, Ore., when he wasn't drafted out of high school and couldn't interest Arizona State or any Sun Belt school in his baseball skills. As a freshman he was better known for his basketball skills, and didn't even play varsity baseball. But he began to attract the attention of scouts when he was the starting shortstop for the runner-up U.S. entry at the 1970 World Cup in Colombia, as well as for the Alaska Goldpanners, the nation's ranking summer-league baseball power, in 1970 and 1971.

He opened the pivotal 1972 college season at third base for Oregon, though he soon moved back to shortstop. He hit .410 and set school records for homers (12) and RBIs (47). In 144 at-bats, he struck out once.

As the draft neared, some thought the Padres would use the No. 1 pick on third baseman Dave Chalk of Texas, but he ended up going to the California Angels with the 10th selection overall.

The Padres took Roberts and signed him within a matter of hours to a major league contract that provided a $70,000 bonus.

"We just drafted the player we felt was the best in the country," said Peter Bavasi, the Padres farm director. "It just so happens that we need help at third base, but it was only a coincidence that Roberts plays third."

One night later, Roberts was at third base for the Padres. He held his own over the balance of the 1972 season, and a year later showed he belonged by hitting .286 with 21 home runs, 18 in the second half. He was touted as one of the game's rising power hitters. But then the bottom fell out. He struggled out of the gate in 1974, and soon was on a shuttle between San Diego and the Padres' Triple-A farm club in Hawaii. With each demotion, the hope he would regain his stroke diminished. He even became a catcher in hopes of preserving his fading career.

Rick Manning

While Roberts became an accomplished defender behind the plate and eventually played every position except pitcher during his 10-year career, his relationship with the Padres became rocky. He never felt like he got a fair shake in San Diego, particularly from Padres president Buzzie Bavasi.

"When you're in an organization a long time," Roberts said, "people in the organization, coaches, managers, the front office . . . they all made me feel I wasn't appreciated. They look at you and see the negative things you do instead of the things you do well."

It all ended for Roberts in 1982, in Philadelphia as a backup catcher. His career average: .239.

After the Padres went for Roberts, the Indians sought to address a pressing need for power.

"We have our strategy mapped out," Indians general manager Phil Seghi said a day before the draft. "We're going for the game-winner, the one-swing guy who wins games. We are going for power. We're not concerned about high batting averages."

The Indians were convinced they found their man in Manning, a .614 hitter at La Salle High in Niagara Falls, N.Y., who didn't strike out a single time his senior year. While Manning, who was signed for a bonus of $57,500, proved to be an exceptional defensive center fielder in a career split between Cleveland and Milwaukee, he was hardly the power hitter Indians officials envisioned.

Manning was not only upstaged by the Indians' third-round pick, Eckersley, but by three less heralded ball players with New York birthrights: lefthander John Candelaria (Pirates, second round), righthander Dennis Leonard (Royals, second round) and second baseman Willie Randolph (Pirates, seventh round).

Candelaria won 177 games in a 19-year career, Leonard won 144 times over 12 seasons, and Randolph hit .276, stole 271 bases and was a standout defender over 18 seasons.

Had the enigmatic, 6-foot-7 Candelaria shown a greater inclination to play baseball as a teenager, he almost certainly would have played his way into the first round in the 1972 draft and possibly become the best player in the entire class.

## How They Should Have Done It

Based on the career WAR (Wins Above Replacement, as calculated by Baseball-Reference.com) numbers achieved by all the players eligible for the 1972 draft, here's how the first round should have unfolded. Numbers in parentheses indicate the round when the player was actually drafted

| | Player, Pos. | Actual Draft | WAR | Bonus |
|---|---|---|---|---|
| 1. | Gary Carter, c | Expos (3) | 69.8 | $35,000 |
| 2. | Willie Randolph, ss | Pirates (7) | 65.6 | $9,000 |
| 3. | Dennis Eckersley, rhp | Indians (3) | 63.0 | $25,000 |
| 4. | Chet Lemon, ss | Athletics (1) | 55.3 | $20,000 |
| 5. | John Candelaria, lhp | Pirates (2) | 42.4 | $38,000 |
| 6. | Mike Hargrove, 1b | Rangers (25) | 30.2 | $2,000 |
| 7. | Dennis Leonard, rhp | Royals (2) | 26.3 | $16,000 |
| 8. | Bob Knepper, lhp | Giants (2) | 22.1 | $20,000 |
| 9. | Scott McGregor, lhp | Yankees (1) | 20.4 | $72,500 |
| 10. | John Montefusco, rhp | Giants (NDFA) | 20.0 | None |
| 11. | Claudell Washington, of | Athletics (NDFA) | 19.4 | $3,000 |
| 12. | Bruce Bochte, 1b/of | Angels (2) | 19.2 | $15,000 |
| 13. | Ernie Whitt, c | Red Sox (15) | 18.5 | $3,500 |
| 14. | Randy Jones, lhp | Padres (5) | 18.1 | $3,000 |
| 15. | Gary Ward, of | Twins (NDFA) | 17.6 | $1,000 |
| 16. | Ellis Valentine, of | Expos (2) | 16.9 | $20,000 |
| 17. | Ray Burris, rhp | Cubs (17) | 16.4 | $4,000 |
| 18. | Dave Collins, 1b | Angels (June-S/1) | 16.0 | $12,000 |
| 19. | Larry Parrish, 3b | Expos (NDFA) | 15.5 | $12,000 |
| 20. | Don Aase, rhp | Red Sox (6) | 15.3 | $10,000 |
| 21. | Lyman Bostock, of | Twins (26) | 13.1 | $4,000 |
| 22. | Vern Ruhle, rhp | Tigers (17) | 12.9 | $4,000 |
| 23. | Craig Swan, rhp | Mets (3) | 12.7 | $15,000 |
| 24. | Leon Roberts, of | Tigers (10) | 12.1 | $5,000 |

| | Top 3 Unsigned Players | | | Year Signed |
|---|---|---|---|---|
| 1. | Jim Sundberg, c | Rangers (8) | 40.3 | 1973 |
| 2. | Roy Smalley, ss | Red Sox (Jan.-S/5) | 27.8 | 1974 |
| 3. | Jason Thompson, lhp/1b | Dodgers (15) | 24.9 | 1975 |

Born in New York of Puerto Rican parents, Candelaria's passion growing up was for basketball, and he excelled at hoops. He scored 1,318 points in his last three seasons at LaSalle Academy in Lower Manhattan.

Candelaria didn't even play baseball as a junior or senior because his high school dropped the sport. Pirates scout Dutch Deutsch, however, remembered Candelaria's baseball ability and encouraged the Pirates to take a second-round flier on him. "I put in the back of my mind that when he grew up, we might find him again," Deutsch said.

Candelaria scoffed at Deutsch's initial offer of a $15,000 bonus, and went to Puerto Rico to play amateur basketball. He was invited to try out for the Puerto Rican national team for the 1972 Olympics. The Pirates continued to pursue Candelaria, but even the intervention of Pirates great Roberto Clemente, a Puerto Rican icon, couldn't sway him.

Later that summer, Pirates super-scout Howie Haak, who was a folk hero in the Caribbean with his scouting exploits, took the task of getting Candelaria signed. He was authorized to go as high as $40,000 and finally got him to agree to a bonus of $38,000. Haak found Candelaria early one morning in a small hamlet in rural Puerto Rico. Candelaria had been out the night before celebrating another basketball victory, and quickly signed.

Candelaria began a rapid rise through the Pirates system. By the time he reached Pittsburgh in 1975, his minor league record was 28-11. Two years after that, he won 20 games for the Pirates.

### CLASS TOUCHED BY TRAGEDY

Roberts was the first college player drafted in 1972, Thomas the second. He was taken by the Milwaukee Brewers with the sixth pick overall out of Southern Illinois University. Harbin went later in the first round to the Los Angeles Dodgers out of South Carolina's tiny Newberry College.

Thomas was a ballplayer with a seemingly brilliant future, but never seemed fulfilled even as he achieved his goal of playing in the big leagues. Before long, he went through a radical behavioral change and quickly played his way out of the major leagues. His life continued to spiral, and in 1980 committed suicide in a Mobile, Ala., jail cell.

Harbin, a third-round draft pick in 1968, passed up an opportunity to sign with the Angels for the chance to play both baseball and football at Newberry. "I wanted to go to school," he said, "and I also wanted to play football. I guess I really had football on my mind then. But mainly I wanted to get my four years of education."

### Fastest To The Majors

| | Player, Pos. | Drafted (Round) | Debut |
|---|---|---|---|
| 1. | # Dave Roberts, 3b | Padres (1) | June 7, 1972 |
| 2. | Jim Crawford, lhp | Astros (14) | April 6, 1973 |
| 3. | Ray Burris, rhp | Cubs (17) | April 8, 1973 |
| 4. | * Larry Christenson, rhp | Phillies (1) | April 13, 1973 |
| 5. | Dave Lemanczyk, rhp | Tigers (16) | April 15, 1973 |

**LAST PLAYER TO RETIRE:** Dennis Eckersley, rhp (Sept. 26, 1998)

*#Debuted in major leagues. *High school selection.*

## DRAFT SPOTLIGHT: DANNY THOMAS

Danny Thomas showed great natural ability, but he struggled to cope with daily life

Danny Thomas was the sixth overall pick in the 1972 draft. Drafted by the Milwaukee Brewers, he had a seemingly brilliant future as a power-hitting outfielder.

"He had a lot going for him as a prospect," said Tony Siegle, assistant scouting and farm director for the Brewers. "Everyone thought he would be a good hitter with power. He had a fine throwing arm, was an above-average outfielder and had above-average speed."

The Brewers signed Thomas for a bonus of $50,000. For three years, the investment looked solid, but in 1975 he slugged an umpire in the Double-A Eastern League and was suspended for the remainder of the season. A year later, however, he won a triple crown in a return to the league, batting .325 with 29 home runs and 83 RBIs, which earned Thomas a late-season promotion to the big leagues. The Brewers made him their left fielder, and in 32 games he hit .276 with four homers.

Instead of satisfaction after his breakthrough 1976 season, though, Thomas felt pressure to live up to expectations, and emptiness from having already reached his goals.

"Danny told me after he got to the big leagues it wasn't quite what he thought it was going to be," said Ricky Patterson, Thomas' best friend since childhood. "He said, 'I'm playing with the best, but there are guys in Triple-A and Double-A who are just as good.'

"When he reached his goal to play in the big leagues, he didn't have any other goals. Nothing could have measured up to what he had built the big leagues up to be in his mind. He kept looking and looking for more, and it drove him crazy."

After that, Thomas showed a radical change in behavior.

The first warning sign came when Thomas went to Venezuela for winter ball after the 1976 season. He attempted suicide by downing at least 75 muscle-relaxing pills. The Brewers arranged for Thomas' return to Milwaukee and placed him under psychiatric care. Thomas embraced the Worldwide Church of God, which his mother had followed during his youth. When he reported for spring training in 1977, he told the Brewers his religion prohibited him from playing from sundown Friday until sundown Saturday. Brewers manager Alex Grammas began calling him "The Sundown Kid," and the nickname stuck.

Thomas made the Brewers roster and flourished early in the 1977 season, batting cleanup five days a week. But as his average fell below .300 and the Brewers saw things which indicated religion hadn't changed his lifestyle, their tolerance diminished. He was dispatched to Triple-A Spokane. He had just turned 26 and would never take another swing in the major leagues.

"He was as happy as a lark when he heard he was being sent down," Siegle said. "Our general manager said, 'Did we send him to Spokane or on a trip to the Caribbean?'"

By August, Thomas was batting .237 at Spokane and sinking into a deep depression. The Brewers demoted him to Double-A, but Thomas refused to report and sat out the rest of the season. Milwaukee invited him to minor league spring training in 1978, but when Thomas said he would report only to major league camp, the Brewers released him.

Thomas and his wife and two children were living in poverty in a shack without plumbing or electricity on the outskirts of Spokane, when the Boise Buckskins, an independent entry in the short-season Northwest League, offered him a contract for the 1978 season, promising him time off from sundown Friday until sundown Saturday.

Thomas played little more than half the Buckskins' games, and yet won the NWL batting title at .358, while hitting 11 homers. He moved to the Inter-American League in 1979, but the league folded midway through its first season. His career was over. Thomas took his pregnant wife and two children to Illinois, where he grew up, before moving in February 1980 to his childhood home of Prichard, Ala., just outside Mobile.

"As the season came around, and he realized he would never play again, that bothered him," Judy Thomas said. "Everything he did would just go wrong. Little things. Big things."

His best friend saw a man in dire straits. Patterson tried to talk Judy into committing her husband, but she refused. Thomas got psychiatric care for a month as an outpatient at the University of South Alabama Medical Center. Two months after he stopped going for treatment, he was arrested for sexually assaulting his children's 12-year-old babysitter.

Thomas died in a Mobile jail cell on June 12, 1980. He hanged himself using his clothing. He was 29. The sun finally had set on the tormented life of The Sundown Kid.

**WORTH NOTING**

■ The University of Southern California won a third consecutive College World Series in 1972, but not a single Trojans player was selected in the June draft. **ERIC RAICH**, the first player selected in the regular phase of the January draft, undoubtedly would have been picked had he not chosen to drop out of school the previous fall. The Trojans (50-13) featured a sophomore-dominated lineup that included the likes of pitcher Randy Scarbery (13-2) and outfielder Fred Lynn (.326, national-best 14 homers), who would be top draft picks in 1973. It was another sophomore, unheralded Russ McQueen, who led the Trojans to the national title. He won three games and saved another at the College World Series, where the Trojans came out of the loser's bracket to subdue powerful Arizona State. The supposedly invincible Sun Devils (64-6) won more games than any college team in history to that point, had a 1.76 team ERA and 24 shutouts and featured three pitchers—Eddie Bane (who would be the Twins' first-round pick in 1973), **CRAIG SWAN** (Mets, third round) and **JIM CRAWFORD** (Astros, 14th round)—who would all be in the big leagues by 1973.

■ Arizona State had more players drafted (eight) than any college in 1972, but the team's unquestioned star, junior shortstop Alan Bannister, wasn't among them. Bannister was ineligible because he didn't reach his 21st birthday within the required 45 days of the draft. He turned 21 on Sept. 3, and six days later withdrew from school in order to become eligible for the January 1973 draft. He was the first player selected in the regular phase. While it didn't benefit Bannister, there was a twist in the draft rules in 1972 that impacted previously drafted college players. In the past, all such players would have been channeled through the secondary phase in January or June, but for the first time, they became eligible for the

Harbin played football for two years at Newberry before he was sidelined with a knee injury. A shortstop on the diamond, he hit .408 with six homers as a junior and almost certainly would have signed then, but he wasn't yet 21 and therefore ineligible for the 1971 draft under the rules at the time. As a senior, he hit .340 with five homers.

"I've been coaching for 31 years," said Horace Turbeville, Harbin's coach at Newberry and later the baseball coach at Winthrop College, "and he had the best arm I saw in college—ever. He had good power, he could run, he was going to be outstanding. There was no question in my mind he would have gone to the big leagues."

The Dodgers made the 6-foot-1, 190-pounder their first-round pick and planned to move him to the outfield. "He was a good-looking athlete," recalled Lamar North, the Dodgers scout who signed Harbin. "He was an all-around player. He could run, throw and hit."

Harbin went on to hit .313 with three home runs and 55 RBIs, along with 62 walks, in an impressive debut with the Dodgers, while playing mostly at short-season Spokane.

But Harbin's career with the Dodgers was amazingly short-lived. He tore up his knee, already surgically repaired from football, in his first spring training and never answered the bell for the 1973 season. Additional surgery didn't correct the damage. His career was over.

By playing in only a half-season in 1972 after signing with the Dodgers, it marked the shortest professional career ever for a first-round draft pick.

"He was a great prospect," said Larry Corrigan, a teammate of Harbin's who would go on to a long career in the game as a scout. "He was the No. 1 draft choice of the Dodgers, but his knees were all blown out from football. He had all the talent in the world, but football ruined his baseball career."

Harbin's life after baseball took a pronounced downward turn. He returned to South Carolina to coach and teach in high school, but continued frustration over his lost opportunity caused his personal life to collapse. He split up with his wife, quit his job and suffered from severe depression.

In 1983, Harbin took his life.

"They called it a chemical mental imbalance," Turbeville said. "He was very depressed over the turn of events in his life."

Bostock was a third prominent member of the 1972 draft whose life—and promising career—ended tragically.

A late-round selection of the Twins after leading Cal State Northridge to the second of consecutive NCAA Division II national championships, Bostock quickly established himself as one of the steals of the draft era. His .311 career average, over four seasons, was the best in his draft class.

Bostock, 27, had just signed a lucrative contract with the Angels after the 1977 season. With the Angels in Chicago for a weekend series in September 1978, Bostock was visiting friends in nearby Gary, Ind., when he was gunned down, a victim of mistaken identity.

## Top 25 Bonuses

| | Player, Pos. | Drafted (Round) | Order | Bonus |
|---|---|---|---|---|
| 1. | ***Jamie Quirk, ss** | **Royals (1)** | **18** | **$78,000** |
| 2. | ***Scott McGregor, lhp** | **Yankees (1)** | **14** | **$72,500** |
| 3. | **Dave Roberts, 3b** | **Padres (1)** | **1** | **#$70,000** |
| 4. | *Bobby Goodman, c | Expos (1) | 5 | $60,000 |
| 5. | ***Dan Larson, rhp** | **Yankees (1)** | **21** | **#$58,500** |
| 6. | ***Rick Manning, ss** | **Indians (1)** | **2** | **$57,500** |
| 7. | *Mike Ondina, of | White Sox (1) | 12 | $52,000 |
| 8. | *Dwayne Peltier, ss | Pirates (1) | 23 | $50,500 |
| 9. | ***Larry Christenson, rhp** | **Phillies (1)** | **3** | **$50,000** |
| | **Danny Thomas, 1b/of** | **Brewers (1)** | **6** | **$50,000** |
| | *Larry Payne, rhp | Reds (1) | 7 | $50,000 |
| 12. | ***Jerry Manuel, ss** | **Tigers (1)** | **20** | **$48,000** |
| 13. | *Joel Bishop, ss | Red Sox (1) | 16 | $45,000 |
| 14. | ***Roy Howell, 3b** | **Rangers (1)** | **4** | **$40,000** |
| | ***Preston Hanna, rhp** | **Braves (1)** | **11** | **$40,000** |
| | ***Tom Underwood, lhp** | **Phillies (2)** | **29** | **$40,000** |
| 17. | ***John Candelaria, lhp** | **Pirates (2)** | **47** | **$38,000** |
| 18. | Bob Grossman, rhp | Indians (2) | 26 | $35,000 |
| | ***Gary Carter, c** | **Expos (3)** | **53** | **$35,000** |
| 20. | **Dave Chalk, 3b** | **Angels (1)** | **10** | **$31,000** |
| | **Tito Landrum, of** | **Cardinals (NDFA)** | | **$31,000** |
| 22. | John Harbin, ss | Dodgers (1) | 17 | $30,000 |
| | ***Rob Dressler, rhp** | **Giants (1)** | **19** | **$30,000** |
| | *Michael Allen, rhp | Padres (2) | 27 | $30,000 |
| 25. | *Cleo Smith, 1b | Dodgers (2) | 41 | $27,500 |

*Major leaguers in bold. *High school selection. #Major league contract.*

### THE CALIFORNIA FACTOR

The redeeming feature of the 1972 draft was the emphasis on players from California, the nation's top talent-producing state. Eleven of 24 first-rounders were products of the Golden State, as were nine second-rounders.

Third baseman Roy Howell was the first Californian picked, fourth overall to the Texas Rangers, and signed for $40,000. Lemon, who signed with Oakland for $20,000, was the most successful, with a 16-year career in the majors.

The 1972 draft marked the first time that two players from the same high school became first-round picks. The Chicago White Sox chose outfielder Mike Ondina from Cordova High near Sacramento with the 12th pick overall, while the Detroit Tigers went for his teammate, shortstop Jerry Manuel, with the 20th pick. Ondina signed for $52,000; the more athletic, well-rounded Manuel received $48,000 by leveraging a football scholarship offer from UCLA.

Though Ondina never reached the big leagues, Manuel did, along with two other Cordova players: Nyls Nyman and Randy Lerch. Nyman was a 16th-round pick of the White Sox in 1972; Lerch was an eighth-rounder in 1973.

Another Sacramento area product, shortstop Joel Bishop, was selected with the 16th overall pick by the Boston Red Sox. Bishop was an all-state quarterback in his junior year at McClatchy High, but gave up football to concentrate on baseball.

"They'll have to tear the uniform off him," said longtime Sacramento-based scout Ron King.

After signing for a bonus of $45,000, Bishop's professional career fizzled after 120 games. He simply quit in the midst of the 1973 season at Winter Haven of the Class A Florida State League, claiming he was tired of the mistrust and mistreatment from the coaching staff.

"Joel had the physical skills, but he walked away

disillusioned," said Bernie Church, his coach at McClatchy High. "His heart wasn't into it. He lost his desire and drive."

No player in the 1972 draft received a bonus of $100,000, but two Southern California prep products received the largest figures: Jamie Quirk, who received $78,000 from the Kansas City Royals as the 18th pick overall, and McGregor, who got $72,500 from the Yankees as the 14th pick.

Quirk was one of the nation's top quarterback recruits, with offers from the nation's top college programs, and had committed to Notre Dame.

"All I wanted to do was get a scholarship so I could go to college," Quirk said. "I really wasn't thinking baseball. The scouts would come out, but I guess they figured I liked football best. I liked football during football season, baseball during baseball season.

"It really surprised me when I heard I was a first-round draft choice. Boy, that was something. It had been pretty hectic until I settled on Notre Dame. Then came the baseball draft and I had to make another decision."

Most clubs passed on the 6-foot-4, 190-pound Quirk early because of his football commitment, so he was there for the Royals.

"He has all the tools you'd look for in a major league shortstop," said Lou Gorman, Kansas City's scouting director. "Baseball cannot afford to keep losing this kind of boy to football. Baseball has to uphold its prestige by signing this sort of boy."

Quirk went on to play 18 years in the big leagues, but had to improvise all along the way to prolong his career. He learned to become a versatile player, and actually caught in 525 games compared to just 22 at shortstop.

McGregor was one of the most decorated high school players of his era. A teammate of George Brett at powerful El Segundo High, McGregor won a state record 51 games and was a two-time California Interscholastic Federation sectional player of the year.

Though he didn't have overpowering stuff, McGregor was a control specialist with an outstanding pickoff move, and was far enough along when he signed with the Yankees that they started him off with their Class A Fort Lauderdale club in Florida State League. He languished in that organization until 1976, before being packaged to Baltimore in a 10-player deal.

McGregor spent all 13 years of his major league career in an Orioles uniform, winning 138 games.

## Largest Bonuses By Round

| | Player, Pos. | Club | Bonus |
|---|---|---|---|
| 1. | ***Jamie Quirk, ss** | **Royals** | **$78,000** |
| 2. | ***Tom Underwood, lhp** | **Phillies** | **$40,000** |
| 3. | ***Gary Carter, c** | **Expos** | **$35,000** |
| 4. | Four tied at | | $15,000 |
| 5. | *Mitch Bobinger, lhp | Dodgers | $21,000 |
| 6. | **Bill Nahorodny, c** | **Phillies** | **$25,000** |
| 7. | *Quency Hill, lhp | Phillies | $18,000 |
| 8. | Three tied at | | $8,000 |
| 9. | ***Craig Cacek, of** | **Mets** | **$16,000** |
| 10. | *Charles Hammond, of | Braves | $12,500 |
| Jan/R. | James Owen, rhp | Rangers (1) | $25,000 |
| Jan/S. | Three tied at | | $20,000 |
| Jun/S. | Bob Lesslie, rhp | Dodgers (1) | $12,000 |
| | **Dave Collins, of** | **Angels (1)** | **$12,000** |

*Major leaguers in bold. *High school selection.*

**Third-round pick Dennis Eckersley established himself as a starter with the Indians, then built his Hall of Fame credentials as a closer**

### ECKERSLEY, CARTER WORTH THE WAIT

Carter and Eckersley may have been part of one of the most successful California draft crops of all time, but they were fringe components as the 21st and 22nd players taken from the state. But it was evident early on that both were special talents.

The Expos spent their first-round pick in 1972 on Memphis prep catcher Bobby Goodman, but they also took Carter two rounds later with the intent of making him a catcher—even though he caught sparingly in high school.

Barry Foote, drafted by the Expos with the third overall pick in 1971, was entrenched as the starting catcher when Carter arrived. The Expos put Carter in right field, but he still managed to see action in 66 games behind the plate in 1975 as Foote's understudy. It wasn't until 1977, after an injury-plagued 1976 season, that Carter took over as Montreal's No. 1 catcher. Over the next several years, Carter, nicknamed "The Kid" for his youthful exuberance, honed his Hall of Fame skills with both the Expos and Mets, leading the latter to a World Series title in 1986. By the time he wrapped up his career in 1992 as an 11-time all-star and three-time Gold Glove winner, he was a .262 career hitter with 324 homers and 1,225 RBIs.

Carter was elected to the Hall of Fame in 2003; less than a decade later, on Feb. 16, 2012, he was dead of a brain tumor. "Gary was a champion," said longtime Expos pitcher Steve Rogers, who played alongside Carter in Montreal. "He was a gamer in every sense of the word—on the field and in life. He made everyone else around him better, and he made me a better pitcher."

The Indians also struck gold in the third round

### WORTH NOTING

regular phase, provided they had not been drafted in the previous 13 months.

■ The A's won the 1972 World Series but had another in a string of unproductive drafts that would doom the franchise in the coming years. After selecting future big leaguer **CHET LEMON** in the first round, the A's didn't sign their next four picks and seven of their first 11.

■ Just 849 players were drafted in June, the lowest total since the first draft in 1965. The January draft also suffered from attrition as the 267 players selected were the fewest since 1966. There was talk of abandoning the January process because first-rounders in January were beginning to equate themselves with first-rounders in the June regular phase. But the ongoing fear of legal action kept the January draft alive for another 15 years. The January draft gave players an opportunity to be drafted a second time each year, and in baseball's view did not unduly restrict their access to employment.

■ Two of the most celebrated high school players to go unsigned in 1972 were a pair of University of Texas recruits: lefthander **RICH WORTHAM**, who slipped to the White Sox in the fifth round, and righthander **JIM GIDEON**, the Tigers' selection in the third round. Wortham posted 50 wins (then an NCAA record) in a four-year career with the Longhorns, while Gideon won 19 games in 1974 (tying an NCAA record) and went 17-0 for Texas' national championship team in 1975.

■ First baseman **RANDY BASS**, the Twins seventh-round pick, never distinguished himself playing for five teams over six big league seasons, but had a memorable career in the minors and in Japan, earning him iconic status in the nation. Bass won back-to-back Central League triple crowns in 1985-86, and established a Japanese record for foreign players by bashing 54 homers in 1985.

## IN FOCUS: GARY CARTER

Gary Carter was an excellent all-around athlete at Sunny Hills High in Fullerton, Calif., and captained the baseball, basketball and football teams. An All-America quarterback, he received more than 100 college offers before committing to play football at UCLA. But he tore ligaments in his right knee as a senior, and that convinced him that baseball might be his best option.

He had been an outfielder to that point in his career. When he was drafted in the third round by the Expos and signed for a bonus of $35,000, he learned that the Expos wanted him as a catcher.

"The scouts thought I could do it," he said. "They thought I had the athletic ability and the leadership qualities. But at first, I was the worst catcher you'd ever seen. It was very frustrating and discouraging."

Carter spent his first three seasons in the minors learning the intricacies of catching, and soon moved past injury-plagued Bobby Goodman, the Expos' first-round pick in 1972, on the team's depth chart. He was still somewhat of a novice behind the plate when he joined the Expos full-time in 1975 and spent most of that season in right field, but was already proclaimed the team's catcher of the future. He took over the role a year later and fashioned a Hall of Fame career at the position.

by selecting Eckersley, who also was a high school quarterback at Fremont's Washington High in the Bay Area. He gave up football as a senior to focus all his efforts on baseball.

A staunch San Francisco Giants fan growing up, Eckersley had his sights set there.

"When I was drafted, and the Cleveland scout (Loyd Christopher) called to tell me, I thought to myself, 'Oh, no, not the Indians,' " he said. "I was really hoping the Giants would pick me because I felt I had a better chance to get to the big leagues sooner with them. But as it turned out, it was a break because the Indians needed pitching, too."

Three days after graduating from high school, the 17-year-old Eckersley reported to Reno of the Class A California League. He spun a shutout in his first outing. After going 17-13 at Reno in his first two seasons, Eckersley emerged in 1974, when he went 14-3 in the Double-A Texas League, and led that league with 163 strikeouts in 167 innings.

A year later, Eckersley made the Indians staff as a reliever. After 10 straight scoreless appearances, spanning 14 innings, he moved into the rotation and defeated the defending World Series champion A's in consecutive starts to push his record to 3-0, 0.28. From there he went on to become the American League rookie pitcher of the year.

Though he had significant success as a starter early on in his 24-major league career, Eckersley earned his greatest acclaim as a dominant closer after being traded to Oakland in 1987. From 1988-92, he saved 220 games—a major league record over a five-year span. He finished his career with 390 saves, along with 171 wins, and was enshrined in Cooperstown in 2004, in his first year of eligibility.

### MORE FAILURES THAN SUCCESSES

While the class of 1972 was one of the weakest in draft history, it had its moments as Roberts debuted in the big leagues, and Fresno State righthander Dick Ruthven, the eighth overall pick, did the same—although not until 1973, after he went unsigned by the Twins and was re-drafted by the Phillies the following January.

Ruthven debuted in the Philadelphia rotation alongside Larry Christenson, the Phillies' first-round selection (third overall) in 1972, whose only pro experience was a half year in Rookie ball. Christenson was 19, less than a year removed from high school in Marysville, Wash., when he broke in with the Phillies. He beat the Mets 7-1 in his big league debut and later won 19 games for a division championship team in 1977. But arm problems ended his 11-year career in 1983.

More than anything, the first round of the 1972 draft was known for its unfulfilled promise, and tragedy. Another first-rounder, Goodman, narrowly escaped death himself as a result of a strange on-field incident. Montreal, selecting fifth overall, took the player generally regarded as the best catching prospect in the draft.

"Had we drafted No. 1," Expos player-development director Mel Didier said, "we would have still selected him as our No. 1 pick."

Goodman signed with the Expos for a bonus of $60,000, the largest in club history. But he never reached the big leagues in an injury-riddled career.

His career started on its downhill cycle on July 10, 1973, at Class A West Palm Beach. He hit a double-play grounder, but the shortstop's relay throw to first base was wide and struck Goodman in the head. He fell to the ground, unconscious.

The errant throw left him with a concussion, but when Goodman hit the ground, he also separated his throwing shoulder. After an operation on his shoulder he stopped breathing. The staff at Halifax General Hospital in Daytona Beach, Fla., had to revive him.

"I just vaguely remember the hospital," he said. "I remember waking up there and my first thought was that the bus driver got into an accident and had killed us all."

The rash of injuries continued. In 1974, Goodman tore up his right knee swinging a bat in spring training; struggled with impaired vision stemming from the incident the year before; was in a car wreck and hurt his back; and accidentally stabbed himself in the chest when the ice pick he was using to fix his mitt slipped. Then he broke his hand in instructional league that October.

"He was so injury-prone," Fanning said. "His whole career was filled with trauma."

The injuries thwarted Goodman's chances of playing in the big leagues, and he retired at age 24—but not before suing the Expos over the treatment of his initial injuries in 1973. The two sides settled out of court.

## Highest Unsigned Picks

**JUNE/REGULAR PHASE ONLY**

| Player, Pos., Team (Round) | College | Re-Drafted |
|---|---|---|
| Dick Ruthven, rhp, Twins (1) | None | Phillies '73 (Jan.-S/1) |
| Randy Wallace, 3b, Reds (2) | Tennessee | Cubs '75 (3) |
| Clay Westlake, c/1b, Twins (2) | Arizona State | Expos '76 (15) |
| Garrett Strong, of, Athletics (2) | Arizona State | Giants '75 (4) |
| Gene Stohs, of, White Sox (3) | * Nebraska | Indians '73 (Jan.-S/2) |
| Paul Adams, c, Royals (3) | Virginia Tech | Rangers '76 (27) |
| Mike Kirkland, 3b, Giants (3) | Arkansas | Never |
| Jim Gideon, rhp, Tigers (3) | Texas | Rangers '75 (1) |
| Jim Willis, 1b, Athletics (3) | Oregon | Astros '75 (Jan.-S/1) |
| John Poloni, lhp, Pirates (3) | Arizona State | Rangers '75 (6) |

**TOTAL UNSIGNED PICKS:** Top 5 Rounds (26), Top 10 Rounds (61)

**Returned to same school*

## One Team's Draft: Texas Rangers

| Player, Pos. | Bonus | Player, Pos. | Bonus | Player, Pos. | Bonus |
|---|---|---|---|---|---|
| **1. * Roy Howell, 3b** | **$40,000** | **5. Rich Wortham, lhp** | **Did not sign** | 9. * Steve Correll, rhp | Did not sign |
| **2. Ron Pruitt, c/of** | **$16,500** | 6. * Mel Barrow, ss | $6,500 | 10. Wayne Popiolek, rhp | Did not sign |
| 3. * Jeff Scott, rhp/c | $15,000 | 7. * Mark Ackerman, rhp | Did not sign | **Other Mike Hargrove (25), 1b** | **$2,000** |
| **4. * Brian Doyle, ss** | **$13,000** | **8. * Jim Sundberg, c** | **Did not sign** | | |

*Major leaguers in bold. *High school selection.*

# 1972 Draft List

**Did not sign. Major leaguers in bold, with first and last years noted. Order of selection indicated in parentheses. For the first five rounds of the June Regular Phase and the first round of all other phases, the peak level of each player is noted.*

## ATLANTA BRAVES

### January—Regular Phase (12)

1. *Ray Humphries, rhp, San Bernardino Valley (Calif.) JC.—(High A)
2. *Laconia Graham, rhp, Ranger (Texas) JC.
3. Kenneth Miller, rhp, Bellevue (Wash.) CC.
4. *Barry Rawls, of-rhp, Bronx (N.Y.) CC.
5. *David Fillipone, c, Seton Hall University.

### January—Secondary Phase (10)

1. *Mike McNeilly, rhp-ss, Gonzaga University.—(Rookie)
2. ***Sam Bowen, of-rhp, Brunswick (Ga.) JC.—(1977-80).**
3. *Jeff DeBell, rhp-ss, Bellevue (Wash.) CC.

### June—Regular Phase (11)

1. **Preston Hanna, rhp, Escambia HS, Pensacola, Fla.—(1975-82)**
2. George Lusic, rhp, San Pedro (Calif.) HS.—(AAA)
3. Bobby Jack, 1b, University of Oklahoma.—(High A)
4. *Mickey Lashley, rhp, College HS, Bartlesville, Okla.—(AA)

DRAFT DROP *Attended Oklahoma; re-drafted by White Sox, 1975 (8th round); baseball coach, Texas-San Antonio (1996-2000)*

5. *Denny Martindale, 2b-rhp, North HS, Torrance, Calif.—DNP

DRAFT DROP *Attended Southern California; re-drafted by Royals, June 1975/secondary phase (3rd round)*

6. *Stephen Cook, 3b, North Miami (Fla.) HS.
7. Gary Scavone, rhp, Meyers HS, Wilkes-Barre, Pa.
8. ***Ken Phelps, 1b, Ingraham HS, Seattle.—(1980-90)**
9. Bobby Buford, rhp, New Hope (Ala.) HS.
10. Charles Hammond, of, Lee's Summit (Mo.) HS.
11. *Jan Ehemann, lhp, Glen Este HS, Batavia, Ohio.
12. Ken Alfred, lhp, Nicholls State University.
13. George Tydings, rhp, West Palm Beach, Fla.
14. *Anton Rosentritt, c, St. Edward's (Texas) University.
15. *Dwayne Wilson, 2b, Shamrock HS, Decatur, Ga.
16. *Greg McCollum, 1b, University of Puget Sound.
17. *Ray Guy, rhp, University of Southern Mississippi.

DRAFT DROP *First-round draft pick, Oakland Raiders/ National Football League (1973); punter, NFL (1973-86)*

18. Conrad Pressley, of, Roberson HS, Asheville, N.C.
19. *James Yaeger, lhp, Northwest Classen HS, Oklahoma City, Okla.
20. Pat Herring, rhp, Raytown (Mo.) HS.
21. *Charles Leonard, rhp, East HS, Memphis, Tenn.
22. Mike Fitzgerald, 1b, University of Tennessee-Chattanooga.
23. Ken Zarski, rhp, Wake Forest University.
24. *Steve Renner, rhp, Wooddale HS, Memphis, Tenn.
25. John Travis, rhp, West Georgia College.
26. *Timothy Fox, rhp, Gulf Coast (Fla.) CC.

### June—Secondary Phase (11)

1. Mike Bahnick, rhp, Rider College.—(Rookie)
2. **Don Collins, lhp, South Georgia JC.—(1977-80)**
3. *Jim Gattis, 3b, Los Angeles Valley JC.

## BALTIMORE ORIOLES

### January—Regular Phase (23)

1. Cass Safrit, ss, Pfeiffer (N.C.) College.—(AA)
2. Larry Green, rhp, Tyler (Texas) JC.
3. *Martin Bladen, c, Southwood (N.C.) JC.
4. *Jim Gattis, 3b, Los Angeles Valley JC.
5. Ricardo Urbano, lhp, Los Gatos, Calif.
6. *Carroll Palmer, lhp, Treasure Valley (Ore.) CC.
7. *Jeff McKay, rhp, Treasure Valley (Ore.) CC.
8. Jack Winchester, 3b, El Camino (Calif.) JC.
9. *Mickey Hall, rhp, Santa Monica (Calif.) JC.
10. William Siebler, 1b-c, Antelope Valley (Calif.) JC.
11. Dan Tippit, rhp, Antelope Valley (Calif.) JC.
12. *Terry Bernard, rhp, Los Angeles Valley JC.
13. *Don Hurst, of, Phoenix (Ariz.) JC.

### January—Secondary Phase (11)

1. Leslie Clark, ss, Prince Edward HS, Farmville, Va.—(Short-season A)
2. *Rick Tomlin, lhp, Manatee (Fla.) JC.
3. *Ricky Holoubek, ss, Pasadena (Calif.) CC.
4. *Walt Rzepiennik, rhp, CC of Baltimore.
5. *David Barnes, 2b-ss, Bellevue (Wash.) CC.
6. *David Christiansen, lhp, Los Angeles Valley JC.
7. *Richard Cahill, lhp, Mount Hood (Ore.) CC.
8. *Thomas Foster, ss, Treasure Valley (Ore.) CC.
9. *Dennis Watson, rhp, Los Angeles Valley JC.
10. *Frank Kunnen, c, Miami-Dade CC North.

### June—Regular Phase (24)

1. Ken Thomas, c, Clear Fork HS, Bellville, Ohio.—(High A)
2. John O'Rear, ss, Tarrant (Ala.) HS.—(AAA)
3. Randy Benson, lhp, Pfeiffer (N.C.) College.—(AAA)

DRAFT DROP *Son of Vern Benson, major leaguer (1943-53); major league manager (1977)*

4. Blake Doyle, 2b, Caverna HS, Cave City, Ky.—(AAA)

DRAFT DROP *Brother of Denny Doyle, major leaguer (1970-77) • Twin brother of Brian Doyle, fourth-round draft pick, Rangers (1972); major leaguer (1978-81)*

5. Gary Robson, rhp, UCLA.—(AAA)
6. Rodney Lee, of, Highlands HS, North Highlands, Calif.
7. Nathaniel Clayton, of, Atlanta Baptist College.
8. *Joseph Miller, of, Brandywine HS, Wilmington, Del.
9. John Adam, rhp, Gardena (Calif.) HS.
10. *Don Henley, of, Ewing HS, Trenton, N.J.
11. **Bobby Brown, of-3b, Northampton HS, Eastville, Va.—(1979-85)**
12. Greg Patterson, lhp, Royal HS, Simi Valley, Calif.
13. Henry Holmes, lhp, Belmont Abbey (N.C.) College.
14. ***Rick Honeycutt, lhp, Lakeview HS, Fort Oglethorpe, Ga.—(1977-97)**
15. *James Joiner, c, Deland (Fla.) HS.
16. *Jeff Grantz, ss, Bel Air (Md.) HS.
17. David Garcia, rhp, Royal HS, Thousand Oaks, Calif.
18. ***Nate Snell, rhp, Roberts HS, Vance, S.C.—(1984-87)**
19. John Tatem, rhp, Virginia Tech.
20. **Mike Willis, lhp, Vanderbilt University.—(1977-81)**
21. *Ken Califano, lhp-of, Essex (Md.) CC.
22. **Willie Royster, c, Spingarn HS, Washington, D.C.—(1981)**
23. *Donald Broom, of, Buna (Texas) HS.
24. *Larry Pike, lhp, St. Petersburg (Fla.) JC.
25. *Winiam Sempsrott, rhp, Danville (Ill.) HS.
26. Dale Vineyard, ss, Mehlville HS, St. Louis.
27. *John Riehs, lhp, LaGrange (Texas) HS.
28. ***John Flinn, rhp, Monroe HS, Sepulveda, Calif.—(1978-82)**
29. Jim Buckner, of, Yavapai (Ariz.) JC.

DRAFT DROP *Brother of Bill Buckner, major leaguer (1969-90)*

30. *Lee Heath, of, Taylor HS, Barberville, Fla.
31. Howard McPike, rhp, Bowling Green (Mo.) HS.
32. *Kevin Gilmartin, ss, Alemany HS, Sepulveda, Calif.
33. Michael Kroll, c, Tampa (Fla.) Catholic HS.
34. *Don Lyons, 1b, Riordan HS, San Francisco.
35. Clarence Laubach, of-1b, Central Columbia HS, Mifflinville, Pa.
36. *John Kennedy, ss, Arvin (Calif.) HS.
37. *Tony Milledge, 3b, Manatee HS, Palmetto, Fla.

DRAFT DROP *Father of Lastings Milledge, first-round draft pick, Mets (2003); major leaguer (2006-11)*

38. William Fraser, of, Thurston HS, Detroit.
39. *Robert Wood, 2b, St. Petersburg (Fla.) JC.
40. *Rick Peterson, lhp, Mount Lebanon (Pa.) HS.
41. *Rufus Cook, 1b, Silsbee (Texas) HS.
42. *Scott Margolin, c, Gardena (Calif.) HS.
43. *Stan Shoaf, rhp, St. Petersburg (Fla.) HS.
44. *Eugene Cunningham, 1b, James Monroe HS, Fredericksburg, Va.

### June—Secondary Phase (22)

1. *Mel Washington, c-of, Los Angeles Valley JC.—(High A)
2. *Steve Cline, rhp, Hagerstown (Md.) JC.
3. *Richard Cahill, lhp, Mount Hood (Ore.) CC.
4. *Chris Wibberley, rhp, El Camino (Calif.) JC.
5. *Thomas Forster, ss, Treasure Valley (Ore.) CC.
6. *David Christiansen, lhp, Los Angeles Valley JC.
7. *Keath Chauncey, of, Polk (Fla.) CC.

## BOSTON RED SOX

### January—Regular Phase (15)

1. *Clif Holland, lhp, Canada (Calif.) JC.—(Low A)
2. *Jimmie Williams, rhp, Indian Hills (Iowa) CC.
3. Harold Stutte, rhp, Contra Costa (Calif.) JC.
4. John Webb, 2b, Seminole (Fla.) CC.

### January—Secondary Phase (3)

1. Ken Daughty, of, Lamar (Colo.) CC.—(Short-season A)
2. *Joe Burgess, lhp, Eastern Oklahoma State JC.
3. *Larry Meekins, rhp, Louisburg (N.C.) JC.
4. *Ralph Darin, rhp, Central Michigan University.
5. ***Roy Smalley, ss, Los Angeles CC.—(1975-87)**

DRAFT DROP *First overall draft pick, January 1974/ regular phase, Rangers • Son of Roy Smalley, major leaguer (1948-58) • Nephew of Gene Mauch, major leaguer (1944-57); major league manager (1960-87)*

### June—Regular Phase (16)

1. Joel Bishop, ss, McClatchy HS, Sacramento, Calif.—(High A)
2. **Steve Dillard, ss, University of Mississippi.—(1975-82)**
3. Randy Markley, of, Lynwood HS, Long Beach, Calif.—(High A)
4. Ronnie Sims, rhp, Dorman HS, Una, S.C.—(High A)
5. Bill Fewox, rhp, Truman HS, Kansas City, Mo.—(High A)
6. **Don Aase, rhp, Savanna HS, Anaheim, Calif.—(1977-90)**
7. Steven Samuelson, rhp, College of St. Thomas (Minn.).
8. Mark Jones, 2b, Arlington Heights HS, Fort Worth, Texas.
9. Ludwig Benedetti, ss, Long Island University.
10. **Andy Merchant, c, Auburn University.—(1975-76)**
11. Steve Tarbell, c, Upland (Calif.) HS.
12. ***Donnie Moore, of, Monterey HS, Lubbock, Texas.—(1975-88)**
13. *Joseph Spaulding, of, Connors State (Okla.) JC.
14. *Bill Bohne, ss, Blinn (Texas) JC.
15. **Ernie Whitt, c, Macomb (Mich.) CC.—(1976-91)**
16. *Ray Boneschans, rhp, Oak Ridge HS, Orlando, Fla.
17. Al Ryan, 2b, University of South Alabama.

DRAFT DROP *Son of Connie Ryan, major leaguer (1942-54); major league manager (1975-77)*

18. Robert Leonard, 3b, Panola (Texas) JC.
19. Herb Loveless, rhp, Ionia (Mich.) HS.
20. *David Chapman, inf, Compton (Calif.) HS.
21. *Richard Marshall, rhp, South Park HS, Beaumont, Texas.
22. Barry Sbragia, rhp, Washington State University.

### June—Secondary Phase (20)

1. Brad Hanson, ss, Valencia (Fla.) CC.—(High A)

## CALIFORNIA ANGELS

### January—Regular Phase (9)

1. **Tom Donohue, of, Nassau (N.Y.) CC.—(1979-80)**
2. Tim Burns, rhp, Austin Peay State University.
3. *Paul Levar, rhp, Spokane Falls (Wash.) CC.
4. *Robert Perkins, rhp, St. Clair County (Mich.) CC.
5. *Michael Lee, rhp, Miami-Dade CC North.
6. *Craig White, of, Clemson University.
7. *Darrell Dickens, rhp, Contra Costa (Calif.) JC.

### January—Secondary Phase (23)

1. ***Craig Caskey, lhp, University of Puget Sound.—(1973)**
2. *Jeff Spagnola, of, Santa Ana (Calif.) JC.
3. *Mike Bahnick, rhp, Rider College.
4. *Jerry Stamps, c, Gulf Coast (Fla.) CC.
5. *Jim Jachym, lhp, University of Connecticut.
6. *Larry Liedy, ss, Staten Island (N.Y.) CC.
7. *Michael Roche, rhp, Seminole (Fla.) CC.

### June—Regular Phase (10)

1. **Dave Chalk, 3b, University of Texas.—(1973-81)**
2. **Bruce Bochte, 1b-of, Santa Clara University.—(1974-86)**
3. Alan Dopfel, rhp, Massachusetts Institute of Technology.—(AAA)
4. **Dave Machemer, ss, Central Michigan University.—(1978-79)**
5. Michael Elwood, rhp, University of Michigan.—(High A)
6. *George Milke, rhp, Marion HS, San Diego.
7. *Donald Houston, c, Murphy HS, Los Angeles.
8. George Lugosan, ss, Washington HS, Chicago.
9. Anthony Gilcrease, c, Patrick Henry HS, San Diego.
10. Dennis Barry, 1b-of, Ball State University.
11. Kevin Thiel, lhp, Marion (Wis.) HS.
12. ***Bill Paschall, rhp, Kempsville HS, Virginia Beach, Va.—(1978-81)**
13. *Brad Van Pelt, rhp, Michigan State University.

DRAFT DROP *Linebacker, National Football League (1973-86)*

14. John Stoffel, lhp, University of Wisconsin.
15. Richard Laubert, 3b, Palos Verdes HS, Palos Verdes Estates, Calif.
16. *Dan Lahoue, 1b, Henry Ford (Mich.) CC.
17. Jeff Brock, rhp, California Lutheran University.
18. *James Kopatz, c, Lanphier HS, Springfield, Ill.
19. *Theis Meyer, rhp, Bakersfield (Calif.) HS.
20. Jude Tassone, 2b, University of San Francisco.
21. *Michael Perkins, 1b-of, Cohn HS, Nashville, Tenn.
22. *James Hallowell, 1b-of, Buena HS, Ventura, Calif.
23. *Brian Smith, c, Calhoun HS, Merrick, N.Y.
24. *Mark Barr, rhp, Golden West (Calif.) JC.

DRAFT DROP *Brother of Jim Barr, major leaguer (1971-83)*

25. *Patrick Pridy, ss, Excelsior HS, Norwalk, Calif.
26. William McCorkle, 1b-c, Azusa Pacific (Calif.) University.

### June—Secondary Phase (6)

1. **Dave Collins, 1b-of, Mesa (Ariz.) CC.—(1975-90)**
2. ***Sam Bowen, 2b, Brunswick (Ga.) JC.—(1977-80)**

## CHICAGO CUBS

### January—Regular Phase (16)

1. *Rex Peters, 1b, Lafayette College.—DNP
2. Dana Corey, of, University of Maine.
3. Tom Myette, 2b-of, Nassau (N.Y.) CC.
4. *Mark Miller, 2b, Ranger (Texas) JC.

### January—Secondary Phase (20)

1. *Greg Van Gaver, rhp, Bellevue (Wash.) CC.—(Rookie)
2. Johnny Green, c, Central Arizona JC.
3. *John Langerhans, 1b, University of Texas.

DRAFT DROP *Father of Ryan Langerhans, major leaguer (2002-13)*

4. *Mark Rogers, of, Golden West (Calif.) JC.

### June—Regular Phase (15)

1. Brian Vernoy, lhp, La Quinta HS, Westminster, Calif.—(High A)
2. Clifford Hall, of, Tamalpais HS, Marin City, Calif.—(AA)
3. **Mike Gordon, c, Brockton (Mass.) HS.—(1977-78)**
4. *Blair Stouffer, 3b-ss, Alamo Heights HS, San Antonio, Texas.—(AAA)

DRAFT DROP *Attended Texas; re-drafted by Rangers, 1975 (5th round)*

5. *Tommy West, of-1b, Gainesville (Ga.) HS.—DNP

DRAFT DROP *Attended Tennessee; never re-drafted; football coach, Clemson (1993-99); football coach, Memphis (2001-09)*

6. **Buddy Schultz, lhp, Miami (Ohio) University.—(1975-79)**
7. Stanley Buky, ss, Avondale HS, Avondale Estates, Ga.

8. Bill Droege, of, Kansas State University.
9. Craig Cerratani, 1b-of, Melrose (Mass.) HS.
10. Doug Carvalho, of, Durfee HS, Fall River, Mass.
11. Peter Dresser, lhp, University of New Hampshire.
12. John Repetto, rhp, Arlington (Mass.) HS.
13. Robert Ott, rhp, Quincy (Ill.) College.
14. Mark Monaghan, c, Middle Township HS, Highlands, N.J.
15. Gary Young, lhp, Texas Wesleyan College.
16. Fred Kreiger, rhp, Allegany HS, Cresaptown, Md.
**17. Ray Burris, rhp, Southwestern Oklahoma State University.—(1973-87)**
18. Randy Gettman, of, Adams State (Colo.) College.
19. James Conroy, lhp, Penn State University.
**20. Wayne Tyrone, 2b, Pan American University.—(1976)**
DRAFT DROP *Brother of Jim Tyrone, major leaguer (1972-77)*
21. Mark Tanner, 1b-rhp, Penn State University.
DRAFT DROP *Son of Chuck Tanner, major leaguer (1955-72); major league manager (1970-88) • Brother of Bruce Tanner, major leaguer (1985)*
22. *James Skripko, rhp, North Hunterdon Regional HS, Hampton, N.J.
23. Robert McCowan, ss, McMinn County HS, Athens, Tenn.
24. *Harry Martell, rhp, University of Maryland.
25. Theodore Echols, 1b, Fairmont State (W.Va.) College.
**26. *Mike Ramsey, ss, Roswell (Ga.) HS.—(1978-85)**
27. Joe Patterson, of, College of Idaho.

#### June—Secondary Phase (15)

1. *Bob Brescher, rhp, Miami-Dade CC South.—DNP
2. *Paul Levar, rhp, Spokane Falls (Wash.) CC.

## CHICAGO WHITE SOX

#### January—Regular Phase (11)

1. Murphy Eppinette, rhp, Northeast Louisiana University.—(Low A)
2. *Bob Brescher, rhp, Miami-Dade CC South.
3. Postell Johnson, of, Miami-Dade CC North.
4. *Dennis Aderholt, rhp, Mitchell (N.C.) CC.
5. *Don Boyer, 1b-of, Miami-Dade CC South.

#### January—Secondary Phase (7)

1. Paul Patterson, rhp, Ithaca (N.Y.) College.—AAA)
2. *Jay Kuhnie, rhp, Eastern Michigan University.
3. Roger McSwain, of, Gardner-Webb College.
4. *Frank Baumgardner, rhp, Miami-Dade CC North.

#### June—Regular Phase (12)

1. Mike Ondina, of, Cordova HS, Rancho Cordova, Calif.—(AAA)
2. Cleo Kilpatrick, of, Washington HS, Tulsa, Okla.—(AAA)
3. *Gene Stohs, lhp-of, University of Nebraska.—DNP
DRAFT DROP *Returned to Nebraska; re-drafted by Indians, January 1973/secondary phase (2nd round).*
**4. *Bruce Robinson, c, La Jolla (Calif.) HS.—(1978-80)**
DRAFT DROP *Attended Stanford; re-drafted by Athletics, 1975 (1st round) • Brother of Dave Robinson, major leaguer (1970-71)*
5. Tom King, lhp, La Porte HS, Hamlet, Ind.—(Low A)
**6. George Enright, c, Hialeah (Fla.) HS.—(1976)**
7. Eric Thomas, ss, West End HS, Birmingham, Ala.
**8. *Mike Overy, rhp, Olivet Nazarene (Ill.) College.—(1976)**
9. John Shermer, rhp, Appalachian State University.
10. Glenn Bryant, rhp, San Jacinto (Texas) JC.
11. David Sandoval, rhp, Norte Vista HS, Riverside, Calif.
12. *Gary Parks, lhp, Noblesville (Ind.) HS.
13. Eddie Echols, 3b, Jacksonville State University.
14. Joseph Pomykala, of, Lewis (Ill.) University.
15. *Wayne Horkey, c, Spalding HS, Granville, Iowa.
**16. Nyls Nyman, of, Cordova HS, Rancho Cordova, Calif.—(1974-77)**
DRAFT DROP *Brother of Chris Nyman, major leaguer (1982-83)*
17. Tate Easton, lhp, Birmingham-Southern College.
18. *Mike Umfleet, ss, Lafayette HS, Ballwin, Mo.
19. *Rick Dominik, rhp, St. Louis Park (Minn.) HS.
20. Ron Slingerman, 3b-rhp, High Point College.
21. Gary Whaley, 3b-1b, Birmingham-Southern College.
22. *Alan Wasik, c, Lewis (Ill.) University.
23. *Douglas May, of-1b, West HS, Greeley, Colo.
**24. *Jim Lentine, of, Sierra HS, Whittier, Calif.—(1978-80)**

#### June—Secondary Phase (16)

1. *Clif Holland, of-lhp, Canada (Calif.) JC.—(Low A)

## CINCINNATI REDS

#### January—Regular Phase (8)

1. Greg Sinatro, ss-3b, Miami-Dade CC South.–(AAA)
DRAFT DROP *Brother of Matt Sinatro, major leaguer (1981-92)*
2. Tommy Mutz, c, Cochise County (Ariz.) CC.
3. *Bert Francks, rhp, CC of Morris (N.J.).
4. *Farrell Vincent, rhp, Southwest Texas JC.
5. *Keith Overbeck, rhp, Dana (Neb.) College.
6. *Lewis Reasonover, ss, Gulf Coast (Fla.) CC.
7. *Gary Erskine, of-lhp, University of Texas.
DRAFT DROP *Son of Carl Erskine, major leaguer (1948-59)*
8. Perry Renfroe, lhp, Jacksonville State University.

#### January—Secondary Phase (16)

**1. Tom Hume, rhp, Manatee (Fla.) JC.—(1977-87)**
2. Larry O'Brien, rhp, Indian Hills (Iowa) CC.
3. *Ron Herring, rhp, Chipola (Fla.) JC.

#### June—Regular Phase (7)

1. Larry Payne, rhp, Huntsville HS, Bedias, Texas.—(AAA)
2. *Randy Wallace, 3b-of, Englewood HS, Jacksonville, Fla.—DNP
DRAFT DROP *Attended Tennessee; re-drafted by Cubs, 1975 (3rd round)*
3. David Embree, 2b, Bishop Gallagher HS, Harper Woods, Mich.—(Rookie)
4. Keith Joseph, lhp, Skyline HS, Salt Lake City.—(Short-season A)
5. *Bernie Hittner, rhp, Bishop Amat HS, West Covina, Calif.—DNP
DRAFT DROP *Attended Stanford; never re-drafted*
6. Mike Staffieri, ss, Brigham Young University.
7. David Moore, rhp, Lafayette HS, Lexington, Ky.
8. Robert Cummings, 3b, West HS, Phoenix, Ariz.
9. *James Petersen, lhp, Waupun (Wis.) Senior HS.
10. Michael Westerman, ss, Freeport (Pa.) HS.
11. Wallace Lester, rhp, Carlsbad (N.M.) HS.
12. Keith Halgerson, rhp, Lincoln HS, Sioux Falls, S.D.
13. Kelly Phipps, lhp, Yuma (Ariz.) HS.
14. Pat Sylvester, 3b-2b, JC of the Desert (Calif.).
15. Ben Castillo, rhp, Iolani HS, Kailua, Hawaii.
16. *Matt Polinski, c, Evanston (Ill.) Senior HS.
17. Donald Lewis, of-3b, Claremont-Mudd (Calif.) College.
18. *Lonnie Salyers, rhp, University of Texas-Arlington.
19. *Mark Kilmurray, ss, University of New Haven.
20. John Savute, 2b-3b, Wichita Heights HS, Wichita, Kan.
**21. *Dan Dumoulin, rhp, Kokomo (Ind.) HS.—(1977-78)**
22. *Marty O'Malley, c, Winner (S.D.) HS.
**23. *Ron Hassey, ss, Tucson (Ariz.) HS.—(1978-91)**
24. *Dennis Miscik, 1b, Mount Pleasant HS, Calumet, Pa.
25. Ron Van Saders, c, William Paterson (N.J.) College.
26. Andre Rabouin, c, University of Texas-Pan American.
27. *Jay Toubl, rhp, Milton (Wis.) College.
28. *Johnny Williams, of, Talladega (Ala.) HS.
29. *Steve Nichols, lhp, Jacksonville University.
30. *Dave Logan, ss-rhp, Wheat Ridge (Colo.) HS.
DRAFT DROP *One of three athletes drafted in three professional sports; ninth-round draft pick, Kansas City Kings/National Basketball Association (1976); third-round draft pick, Cleveland Browns/National Football League (1976); wide receiver, National Football League (1976-84)*
31. William Davis, rhp, Central HS, Knoxville, Tenn.

#### June—Secondary Phase (9)

No selection.

## CLEVELAND INDIANS

#### January—Regular Phase (1)

**1. Eric Raich, rhp, University of Southern California.—(1975-76)**
2. Anthony Giammaresis, ss, Broward (Fla.) CC.
3. Clyde Fink, of, East Rowan HS, Salisbury, N.C.
4. *Michael Smith, rhp, DeAnza (Calif.) JC.
5. *Charles Petrillo, 2b, St. Clair County (Mich.) CC.
6. *John Keough, p, Miami-Dade CC North.
7. *Michael Johnson, rhp, Bacone (Okla.) JC.

#### January—Secondary Phase (21)

**1. Duane Kuiper, ss, Southern Illinois University.—(1974-85)**
**2. *Don Collins, lhp, South Georgia JC.—(1977-80)**
3. *William Taylor, inf, Mira Costa (Calif.) JC.
4. *Mike Hannah, 1b, Ohio University.
5. Edward Burzo, of, Nassau (N.Y.) CC.
6. *Alan Lobb, lhp, Elizabethtown (Pa.) College.
7. *Ben Heise, ss, Yavapai (Ariz.) JC.
DRAFT DROP *Brother of Bob Heise, major leaguer (1967-77)*

#### June—Regular Phase (2)

**1. Rick Manning, ss, LaSalle HS, Niagara Falls, N.Y.—(1975-87)**
2. Bob Grossman, rhp, University of Maryland.—(AAA)
**3. Dennis Eckersley, rhp, Washington Union HS, Fremont, Calif.—(1975-98)**
DRAFT DROP *Elected to Baseball Hall of Fame, 2004*
4. *John Sciarra, ss, Bishop Amat HS, Alhambra, Calif.—DNP
DRAFT DROP *Attended UCLA; re-drafted by Orioles, 1974 (7th round); quarterback/defensive back, National Football League (1978-83)*
5. *Jeff Feramisco, of, Fresno (Calif.) HS.—(High A)
DRAFT DROP *Attended Fresno CC; re-drafted by Angels, January 1973/secondary phase (1st round)*
6. Rex Bynum, of, University of Alabama.
7. Kris Yoder, c, Savanna HS, Buena Park, Calif.
8. Robert Hickey, ss, High Point College.
**9. *Mike Armstrong, rhp, North Shore HS, Sea Cliff, N.Y.—(1980-87)**
**10. *Pete Redfern, rhp, Sylmar (Calif.) HS.—(1976-82)**
DRAFT DROP *First overall draft pick, January 1976/secondary phase, Twins; first player from 1976 draft to reach majors (May 15, 1976)*
11. Ken Kirchner, lhp, Richmond Heights (Ohio) HS.
12. Dick Combs, c, Lakeland (Fla.) HS.
13. *James Eden, rhp, Solon (Ohio) HS.
14. *Dan Shaw, rhp, Stanford University.
15. Larry Unser, 2b-of, Marian (Ind.) College.
16. *George Gospodinoff, lhp, Norte Vista HS, Riverside, Calif.
17. *Manuel Alfonsin, inf-of, Miami Springs HS, Hialeah, Fla.
18. *Thomas Lyons, rhp, Notre Dame HS, Biloxi, Miss.
19. *Kent Juday, inf, Clay HS, South Bend, Ind.
20. *David Mandell, lhp, Maumee (Ohio) HS.
21. Brian Dingess, lhp, Garden Grove (Calif.) HS.
22. Dan Van Auken, rhp, St. Petersburg (Fla.) JC.
23. Ed Arsenault, rhp-1b, Robinson HS, Tampa.
24. *Phillip Francis, rhp, Solon (Ohio) HS.
25. *Greg Redding, rhp, Hillsborough HS, Tampa.
26. *Michael Melvin, ss, Deep Creek HS, Chesapeake, Fla.
**27. *Dan O'Brien, rhp, Bishop Berry HS, St. Petersburg, Fla.—(1978-79)**
28. *James Shade, rhp, Reynoldsburg (Ohio) HS.
29. Steve Rametta, inf, Gladstone HS, Covina, Calif.
30. *Ken Bolek, of, University HS, Chardon, Ohio.
31. *Ken Grolle, rhp, Los Altos (Calif.) HS.
32. *Robert Rossi, rhp, Corning (N.Y.) West HS.
33. *Bob Purkey Jr., rhp, Bethel Park (Pa.) HS.
DRAFT DROP *Son of Bob Purkey, major leaguer (1954-66)*
34. *Steve Meisner, inf-of, Fontana HS, Alta Loma, Calif.
35. *Dennis Smith, 1b, Miami (Ohio) University.
**36. *Rick Langford, of-rhp, Manatee (Fla.) JC.—(1976-86)**
37. Robert Meyer, 3b, Aurora, Ind.

#### June—Secondary Phase (2)

**1. *Rich Dauer, ss-2b, San Bernardino Valley (Calif.) JC.—(1976-85)**
DRAFT DROP *First-round draft pick (24th overall), Orioles (1974)*
2. John Langerhans, 1b, University of Texas.
DRAFT DROP *Father of Ryan Langerhans, major leaguer (2002-13)*
3. Michael Smith, rhp, De Anza (Calif.) JC.
4. *Rick Bethke, lhp, Cerritos (Calif.) JC.
5. Charles Hendrix, rhp, Grossmont (Calif.) JC.

## DETROIT TIGERS

#### January—Regular Phase (19)

1. Alfred Callis, lhp, Fullerton (Calif.) JC.—(High A)
**2. Dan Gonzales, of, Fullerton (Calif.) JC.—(1979-80)**
3. Brian Sheekey, rhp, Union County (N.J.) JC.
4. *Ronald Horgett, c, DeKalb (Ga.) JC.
5. Daniel Kaupla, rhp, Fullerton (Calif.) JC.
**6. Art James, of, Macomb (Mich.) CC.—(1975)**
7. *Carl Benson, of, Lamar (Colo.) CC.
8. John Davies, rhp, University of Toledo.
9. *David Lloyd, rhp, Macomb (Mich.) CC.

#### January—Secondary Phase (19)

1. *Curtis Bishop, lhp, Bacone (Okla.) JC.—DNP
2. *Mitch Lukevics, rhp, Bethlehem, Pa.
3. *John Van Brunt, c, Mesa (Ariz.) CC.
4. Frank Weisse, of, Lafayette College.

#### June—Regular Phase (20)

**1. Jerry Manuel, ss, Cordova HS, Rancho Cordova, Calif.—(1975-82)**
DRAFT DROP *Major league manager (1998-2010)*
2. John Valle, 3b, Holy Cross HS, New York.—(AAA)
DRAFT DROP *Brother of Dave Valle, major leaguer (1984-96)*
**3. *Jim Gideon, rhp, Bellaire HS, Houston.—(1975)**
DRAFT DROP *Attended Texas; re-drafted by Rangers, 1975 (1st round)*
**4. Dan Meyer, 2b, Santa Ana (Calif.) JC.—(1974-85)**
5. James Murray, lhp, St. Mary's Prep HS, Orchard Lake Village, Mich.—(Low A).
6. *Jeffrey Potter, lhp, Lincoln HS, Elwood City, Pa.
7. Roy Haney, c, Byng HS, Ada, Okla.
8. Nat Calamis, ss, St. John's University.
9. Gary Stollar, c, Westmoor HS, Daly City, Calif.
**10. Leon Roberts, of, University of Michigan.—(1974-84)**
11. *Allan Striano, of, C.W. Post University.
12. Stephen Litras, ss, Floral Park (N.Y.) HS.
13. John Larkin, lhp, Syracuse University.
14. *Gary Kennedy, of, Dacula (Ga.) HS.
15. Douglas Ratford, of, St. John's University.
**16. Dave Lemanczyk, rhp, Hartwick (N.Y.) College.—(1973-80)**
**17. Vern Ruhle, rhp, Olivet (Mich.) College.—(1974-86)**
18. *Philip Vaden, rhp, Western HS, Detroit.
**19. Mark Wagner, ss, Harbor HS, Ashtabula, Ohio.—(1976-84)**
20. John Petrolla, 3b, Cardinal Mooney HS, Poland, Ohio.
21. Fred Winner, lhp, Lycoming (Pa.) College.
22. *Steve Bartolin, lhp, Youngstown State University.
23. Greg Kuhl, rhp, Jefferson Davis HS, Montgomery, Ala.
24. Allen Szaroleta, rhp, St. Joseph's HS, Perth Amboy, N.J.
25. *Paul Cormier, rhp, University of New Hampshire.
26. Dennis Ray, of, Garden City (Mich.) East HS.
**27. George Cappuzzello, lhp, Ursuline Catholic HS, Girard, Ohio.—(1981-82)**
28. *Lloyd Sprockett, ss, Warren Reserve HS, Warren, Ohio.
29. *Bruce Fitzma, rhp, Central Christian HS, Grand Rapids, Mich.
30. *Charles Morrison, lhp, Parkview HS, Springfield, Mo.
31. Richard McDonagh, lhp, Walt Whitman HS, Huntington Station, N.Y.
32. John Yalden, rhp, St. John's University.

33. *Rick Wolff, 2b, Harvard University.

**June—Secondary Phase (12)**

1. Michael McGuire, of, Cornell University.—(High A)

## HOUSTON ASTROS

**January—Regular Phase (10)**

1. *William Meyer, ss, Indian River (Fla.) CC.—(AA)
2. *Howard Ashlock, lhp, Palm Beach (Fla.) JC.
3. *David Meites, lhp, Bowling Green State University.

**January—Secondary Phase (14)**

1. *Rick Bethke, lhp, Cerritos (Calif.) JC.—(AAA)

**June—Regular Phase (9)**

1. Steve Englishbey, of, South Houston (Texas) HS.—(AAA)
2. Stan Floyd, c, George Wythe HS, Richmond, Va.—(High A)
3. Lonnie Newland, ss, Hobbs (N.M.) HS.—(Rookie)
4. David Brooks, rhp, Merced (Calif.) HS.—(Rookie)
5. Kenny Reed, 2b, Arizona State University.—(AAA)
6. Donnie Sims, of, Dorman HS, Spartanburg, S.C.
7. *Michael Odum, of, Tucson (Ariz.) HS.
8. *Wayne Williams, ss, Abilene (Texas) HS.
9. *Wymon Winton, c, Cotaco HS, Somerville, Ala.
10. David Ralstin, of, Homestead HS, Palo Alto, Calif.
11. *Pete Padgett, rhp, Del Valle HS, Walnut Creek, Calif.
12. ***Roy Lee Jackson, rhp, Opelika (Ala.) HS.—(1977-86)**
13. *Kevin Stephenson, rhp, Lyman HS, North Orlando, Fla.
14. **Jim Crawford, lhp, Arizona State University.—(1973-78)**
15. *Richard Koenig, of, Cardinal Newman HS, West Palm Beach, Fla.
16. Michael Markl, 2b, University of Texas.
17. Paul Dillard, ss, Douglas HS, Oklahoma City, Okla.
18. *Alexander Taylor, rhp, Blair HS, Hattiesburg, Miss.
19. *John Revere, of, Patterson Co-op HS, Dayton, Ohio.
20. *Ted Yoak, rhp-inf, Hamilton Community HS, Dorr, Mich.
21. Tom Changnon, lhp, Stanford University.
22. John Calzia, rhp, University of La Verne (Calif.).
23. Dennis Nagel, rhp, University of Cincinnati.
24. Ben Ochoa, rhp, University of La Verne (Calif.).
25. *Gary Addeo, rhp, Cal State Los Angeles.
26. *Robert Diliberto, rhp-of, Mansfield University.

**June—Secondary Phase (7)**

1. *Bob Gerdes, rhp, Miami-Dade CC South.—(High A)
2. *Lawrence Lee, c, Martinez, Calif.

## KANSAS CITY ROYALS

**January—Regular Phase (17)**

1. Kenzie Davis, of, Chaffey (Calif.) JC.—(AA)
2. *Ron McDonald, rhp, Louisburg (N.C.) JC.
3. Jerry Gomez, lhp, Yavapai (Ariz.) JC.

**January—Secondary Phase (9)**

1. ***Dave Collins, 1b-of, Mesa (Ariz.) CC.—(1975-90)**
2. ***Mike Stanton, rhp, Miami-Dade CC South.—(1975-85)**
3. *Byron Burns, rhp, Lower Columbia (Wash.) JC.
4. *Michael Walsh, rhp, Cerritos (Calif.) JC.
5. ***Mike Dupree, of, Fresno (Calif.) CC.—(1976)**
6. ***Jerry Maddox, ss, Cerritos (Calif.) JC.—(1978)**
7. *Steven Jones, 1b, Garden Grove, Calif.

**June—Regular Phase (18)**

1. **Jamie Quirk, ss, St. Paul HS, Whittier, Calif.—(1975-92)**
2. **Dennis Leonard, rhp, Iona College.—(1974-86)**
3. *Paul Adams, c, Castlewood HS, Dante, Va.—DNP

Twins 26th-rounder Lyman Bostock was a draft steal, but his life was cut short when he was fatally wounded as an innocent bystander in a 1978 drive-by shooting in Gary, Ind.

DRAFT DROP *Attended Virginia Tech; re-drafted by Rangers, 1976 (27th round)*

4. *Doug Wessel, rhp, Vanderbilt University.—(AA)

DRAFT DROP *Returned to Vanderbilt; re-drafted by Orioles, June 1973/secondary phase (1st round)*

5. Karl Jacobsen, c, Valley Central HS, Montgomery, N.Y.—(Low A)
6. John Rockwell, 2b, Lane (Tenn.) College.
7. Dale Stevener, of, Francis Howell HS, New Melle, Mo.
8. Stan Butkus, rhp, University of South Alabama.
9. Shaun Howitt, of, Michigan State University.
10. Kevin Bova, of, Long Branch (N.J.) HS.
11. **Rodney Scott, 3b, Arlington HS, Indianapolis.—(1975-82)**
12. *Scott Gardner, rhp, Riverview HS, Sarasota, Fla.
13. *Mike Bartell, ss, Encinal HS, Alameda, Calif.

DRAFT DROP *Grandson of Dick Bartell, major leaguer (1927-46)*

14. Jeff Grossick, lhp, Menominee (Mich.) HS.
15. Joseph McNamara, rhp, Bethlehem Central HS, Delmar, N.Y.
16. **George Throop, rhp, Long Beach State University.—(1975-79)**
17. *Pat Curran, of, Golden West (Calif.) JC.
18. Craig Bowser, rhp, University of La Verne (Calif.).
19. David Bradford, ss, Murray State University.
20. Juan Quesada, 3b-1b, DeWitt Clinton HS, New York.
21. *John Keisler, rhp, Long Beach State University.
22. Reginald Knapper, rhp, Chartiers Houston HS, Houston, Pa.
23. *Robert Glass, 3b, Lakeland (Fla.) HS.
24. *Doug Duncan, c, Hillcrest HS, Dallas.
25. Roman Bailey, rhp, Union (Tenn.) University.
26. Dennis Gallagher, of, Chapman College.
27. *Thomas Davis, rhp, Loara HS, Anaheim, Calif.
28. Mark Brown, c, Gloucester (Mass.) HS.
29. Doug Buchanan, c, Eastern (Pa.) College.
30. Don Spare, ss, Chapman (Calif.) College.
31. *Greg Fairbanks, rhp, Satellite Beach (Fla.) HS.
32. Bernard Hunting, 3b-ss, Rockford (Mich.) HS.
33. *James Auringer, ss-rhp, Corcoran HS, Syracuse, N.Y.
34. Mike Roberts, c, University of North Carolina.

DRAFT DROP *Baseball coach, North Carolina (1978-98)• Father of Brian Roberts, first-round draft pick, Orioles (1999); major leaguer (2001-14)*

35. Rod Boone, of, Stanford University.

DRAFT DROP *Son of Ray Boone, major leaguer (1948-60) • Brother of Bob Boone, major leaguer (1972-90); major league manager (1995-2003)*

36. John Urzi, 2b-ss, San Jose State University.
37. Eric Littell, c, Gideon (Mo.) HS.

DRAFT DROP *Brother of Mark Littell, major leaguer (1973-82)*

**June—Secondary Phase (8)**

1. *Mike Payne, rhp, Delta State (Miss.) University.—DNP
2. ***Jerry Maddox, ss, Cerritos (Calif.) JC.–(1978)**

## LOS ANGELES DODGERS

**January—Regular Phase (18)**

1. John Adams, rhp, Phoenix, Ariz.—(Low A)
2. *Tim Hosler, of-3b, South Georgia JC.
3. *Allen Polofsky, lhp, Miami-Dade CC South.

**January—Secondary Phase (8)**

1. **Dennis Lewallyn, rhp, Chipola (Fla.) JC.—(1975-82)**
2. James Vanderbeek, rhp, Lafayette College.
3. *Francis Sansosti, rhp-1b, Essex (Md.) CC.
4. *Mike Siani, ss, Villanova University.

DRAFT DROP *First-round draft pick, Oakland Raiders/ National Football League (1972); wide receiver, NFL (1972-80)*

5. Chris Sans, 1b, Texas A&M University.

**June—Regular Phase (17)**

1. John Harbin, ss, Newberry (S.C.) College.—(Short-season A)
2. Cleo Smith, 1b-of, Harry Ells HS, Richmond, Calif.—(AAA)
3. **Bobby Detherage, rhp-of, Hillcrest HS, Springfield, Mo.—(1980)**
4. Larry Corrigan, c-rhp, Iowa State University.—(AAA)

DRAFT DROP *Baseball coach, Iowa State (1981-84); scouting director, Twins (1992-93)*

5. Mitch Bobinger, lhp, Chico (Calif.) HS.—(AAA)
6. Al Torregano, c, University of Southwestern Louisiana.
7. *James Fleming, ss, St. Peter's HS, New Brunswick, N.J.
8. Stephen Plut, of, St. Francis HS, San Carlos, Calif.
9. Robert Stewart, rhp, Magnolia HS, Anaheim, Calif.
10. William Kooyman, 3b, St. Mary's (Calif.) College.
11. Terry Zorger, 3b, Huntington (Ind.) College.
12. Jere Nolan, of, University of California.
13. *Henry Boguszewski, rhp, Glen Cove (N.Y.) HS.
14. Michael Rushde, of, Fontana (Calif.) HS.
15. ***Jason Thompson, lhp-1b, Apple Valley (Calif.) HS.—(1976-86)**
16. *Doug Schaefer, rhp, Lindberg HS, Afton, Mo.
17. **Glenn Burke, of, Merritt (Calif.) JC.—(1976-79)**
18. Richard Magner, c, Rollins College.
19. Leonard Wouters, rhp, Hampton Bays (N.Y.) HS.
20. ***John Littlefield, rhp, Azusa (Calif.) HS.—(1980-81)**
21. *John Freedman, 3b, Claremont (Calif.) HS.
22. *Richard Jacobs, lhp, University of Oklahoma.
23. *Dale Forchetti, ss, Neshaminy HS, Levittown, Pa.
24. *Don Redoglia, ss-2b, Pasadena (Calif.) CC.
25. *Kenneth Smith, of, Jefferson HS, Daly City, Calif.
26. *Buff White, lhp, Folsom HS, Orangevale, Calif.
27. *David Rothermel, 3b, Hillcrest HS, Springfield, Mo.
28. Steven O'Brien, rhp, Maryvale HS, Phoenix.
29. *Samuel Roberts, 1b, Tennessee HS, Bristol, Tenn.
30. Brian Felda, of, University of Wisconsin-Oshkosh.
31. Michael Parnow, 2b, JC of Marin (Calif.).
32. James Fiack, c, UC Davis.
33. Charles Walker, of, Atlanta Baptist College.
34. *Jeff Chandler, lhp, Davis (Calif.) HS.
35. ***Craig Minetto, lhp, Amos Alonzo Stagg HS, Stockton, Calif.—(1978-81)**
36. *David Baker, c, Pacific HS, San Leandro, Calif.
37. *Tom Haley, c, Binger (Okla.) HS.
38. ***Bob Shirley, lhp, Putnam City HS, Oklahoma City, Okla.—(1977-87)**
39. *Tim Lewis, lhp-1b, Germantown Academy, Norristown, Pa.

**June—Secondary Phase (1)**

1. Bob Lesslie, rhp, Kansas State University.–(AAA)
2. Michael Rzepiennik, rhp, CC of Baltimore.
3. *Robin Ogle, 1b, Miami-Dade CC South.

DRAFT DROP *Grandson of Walter Alston, major leaguer (1936); major league manager (1954-76)*

## MILWAUKEE BREWERS

**January—Regular Phase (5)**

1. Robert Alexander, rhp, St. Clair County (Mich.) CC.—(AA)
2. Vincent Roberto, of, University of Miami.

**January—Secondary Phase (17)**

1. ***Terry Cornutt, rhp, Linn-Benton (Ore.) CC.—(1977-78)**
2. Tim Hamilton, 2b, Mesa (Ariz.) CC.
3. *Fred Mims, of, University of Iowa.

**June—Regular Phase (6)**

1. **Danny Thomas, 1b-of, Southern Illinois University.—(1976-77)**
2. Jerry Mantlo, c, Arizona State University.—(AAA)
3. Roger Alexander, rhp, Norman (Okla.) HS.—(AAA)

4. *Ronald Pearce, rhp, Gordon HS, Douglasville, Ga.—DNP

DRAFT DROP *Attended Georgia Tech; never re-drafted*

5. Rick Richardson, 1b-of, North Carolina State University.—(AA)
6. Thomas Diedel, lhp, Mullen HS, Denver.
7. Kent Jackson, of, Arizona State University.
8. James Blaine, rhp, Midwest City HS, Oklahoma City, Okla.
9. *Henry McGowan, 3b-of, Grandfield (Okla.) HS.
10. Victor Sanchez, ss, Pentucket HS, West Newbury, Mass.
11. David Simplot, rhp-c, Sehome HS, Bellingham, Wash.
12. Sam Killingsworth, c, Cleveland (Miss.) HS.
13. *Kip Coughlan, 3b, Highland Springs (Va.) HS.
14. William Davidson, rhp, Chaffey HS, Ontario, Calif.
15. **Roger Miller, rhp, Uniontown HS, Mill Run, Pa.—(1974)**
16. *Thomas Sohns, ss-2b, Dunmore (Pa.) HS.
17. Mark Young, lhp, Roswell (N.M.) HS.
18. Wayne Politelli, 3b, Pilgrim HS, Warwick, R.I.
19. Mike Duncan, rhp, Arvin HS, Lamont, Calif.
20. *Greg Marshall, rhp, Northmont HS, Englewood, Ohio.
21. William Collins, c, George Washington University.
22. **Bob Sheldon, ss, Loyola Marymount University.—(1974-77)**
23. *Carl Sapp, rhp, Dominguez HS, Compton, Calif.
24. **Greg Erardi, rhp, Liverpool (N.Y.) HS.—(1977)**
25. Charles Solano, rhp, Wayne State (Neb.) College.
26. Al Widmar, rhp, University of Tulsa.

DRAFT DROP *Son of Al Widmar, major leaguer (1947-52)*

27. *Robert Jantz, of, Shattuck (Okla.) HS.
28. *Fred Nachbar, c, Rockhurst HS, Shawnee, Kan.

**June—Secondary Phase (10)**

1. Roger Danson, ss, Seminole (Fla.) CC.—(AA)

## MINNESOTA TWINS

**January—Regular Phase (7)**

1. Lew Lerner, rhp, San Fernando Valley State (Calif.) College.—(AAA)
2. *William Bishop, 1b, Yavapai (Ariz.) JC.
3. John Pangle, rhp, Parsons (Iowa) College.
4. Tom Mitterholzer, of, San Fernando Valley State (Calif.) College.

**January—Secondary Phase (1)**

1. *Bob Koeppel, lhp-of, Bradley University.—(AA)
2. Joseph Yocum, rhp, Fresno (Calif.) CC.
3. ***Warren Cromartie, of, Miami-Dade CC North.—(1974-91)**

**June—Regular Phase (8)**

1. ***Dick Ruthven, rhp, Fresno State University.—(1973-86)**

DRAFT DROP *No school; re-drafted by Phillies, January 1973/secondary phase (1st round, 1st pick); first player from 1973 draft to reach majors (April 17, 1973)*

2. *Clay Westlake, c-1b, Loara HS, Anaheim, Calif.—(High A)

DRAFT DROP *Attended Arizona State; re-drafted by Expos, 1976 (15th round)*

3. **Willie Norwood, of, University of La Verne (Calif.).—(1977-80)**
4. William Daniels, rhp, Montebello (Calif.) HS.—(High A)
5. Tommy Franklin, c, T.C. Roberson HS, Arden, N.C.—(Low A)
6. **Doug Clarey, ss, Homestead (Calif.) HS.—(1976)**
7. **Randy Bass, 1b, Lawton (Okla.) HS.—(1977-82)**
8. *William Cowens, ss, Centennial HS, Compton, Calif.

DRAFT DROP *Brother of Al Cowens, major leaguer (1974-86)*

9. *Michael Baier, ss-2b, University of Maryland.
10. ***Dave Stegman, of, Lompoc (Calif.) HS.—(1978-84)**
11. Kevin Cooney, rhp, Montclair State (N.J.) College.
12. *William Stiegemeier, rhp, University of Kansas.
13. ***Pete Falcone, lhp, Lafayette HS, Brooklyn, N.Y.—(1975-84)**
14. Dan Kelly, c-ss, Unionville HS, Chester, Pa.
15. *Mike Nelson, of, Stanford University.
16. Thomas Boettcher, 3b, Madison, Wis.
17. *Steve Wilkins, of, The Dalles (Ore.) HS.
18. *Kenneth Wright, of, Centennial HS, Compton, Calif.
19. Mike Gerakos, 3b, UCLA.
20. *Lindsay Hoyer, c, University of Minnesota.
21. *James Saunders, 3b, Prince Edward HS, Crewe, Va.
22. *Gary Sargent, inf, Bemidji (Minn.) HS.

DRAFT DROP *Second-round draft pick, Los Angeles Kings/ National Hockey League (1974); defenseman, NHL (1975-83)*

23. *John Brooks, of, Northwestern University.
24. Lee Sturtevant, rhp, Laconia (N.H.) HS.
25. *Kevin Hanzlik, c, Edison HS, Minneapolis.
26. **Lyman Bostock, of, Cal State Northridge.—(1975-78)**

DRAFT DROP *Died as active major leaguer (Sept. 23, 1978)*

27. *Michael Thissen, rhp, Columbus HS, Waterloo, Iowa.
28. David Morrison, of-rhp, Mission Bay HS, San Diego.
29. *Richard Metzger, ss, Hoover HS, Fresno, Calif.
30. Michael Coronado, ss, Cal State Los Angeles.
31. *Carlos Moreno, lhp, Lennox HS, Inglewood, Calif.
32. William O'Connor, rhp, Kingsborough (N.Y.) CC.
33. David Anna, rhp, Jefferson HS, Edgewater, Colo.
34. Gary Martin, lhp, Alpaugh (Calif.) HS.
35. *Terry Ryan, lhp, Parker HS, Janesville, Wis.

DRAFT DROP *Scouting director, Twins (1986-92); general manager, Twins (1994-2007, 2011-15)*

36. *Michael Hickman, rhp, Tustin (Calif.) HS.

**June—Secondary Phase (18)**

1. *John Eichholtz, rhp, Fresno (Calif.) CC.–(High A)
2. **Al Woods, 1b, Laney (Calif.) JC.—(1977-86)**

## MONTREAL EXPOS

**January—Regular Phase (6)**

1. Wayne Piper, rhp, Creighton University.—(High A)
2. Carl Baker, of, La Puente (Calif.) HS.
3. *Rhinehart Dallas, of, Baltimore.
4. *James Hamilton, c, Middle Georgia JC.
5. ***Michael Edwards, ss, Los Angeles CC.—(1977-80)**

DRAFT DROP *Brother of Dave Edwards, major leaguer (1978-82) • Twin brother of Marshall Edwards, major leaguer (1981-83)*

6. *Richard Davidson, c, Columbia State (Tenn.) CC.

**January—Secondary Phase (2)**

1. **Jim Cox, ss, University of Iowa.—(1973-76)**
2. *Steve Hergenrader, c, Fresno (Calif.) CC.
3. *William Daves, c, Motlow State (Tenn.) CC.
4. *Steve Cline, rhp, Hagerstown (Md.) JC.
5. *Edward Gale, lhp, Palm Beach (Fla.) JC.

**June—Regular Phase (5)**

1. Bobby Goodman, c, Bishop Byrne HS, Memphis, Tenn.—(AAA)
2. **Ellis Valentine, c-of, Crenshaw HS, Los Angeles.—(1975-85)**
3. **Gary Carter, c, Sunny Hills HS, Fullerton, Calif.—(1974-92)**

DRAFT DROP *Elected to Baseball Hall of Fame, 2003*

4. Roger DeLazzer, of, Lake Park HS, Itasca, Ill.—(High A)
5. **Dennis Blair, rhp, Eisenhower HS, Rialto, Calif.—(1974-80)**
6. *Terrence Mackey, rhp, MacArthur HS, San Antonio, Texas.
7. *Thomas Wise, lhp-of, Bayonne (N.J.) HS.
8. Luis Jonas, of, Erasmus Hall HS, Brooklyn, N.Y.
9. Gary Bryant, rhp, Madison HS, San Diego.
10. *David Bedrosian, 2b, McLane HS, Fresno, Calif.
11. **J. Michael Hart, 1b-of, Kalamazoo Valley (Mich.) CC.—(1980)**
12. *Rickey Ferguson, rhp, Haskell (Okla.) HS.
13. Michael Criss, rhp, Los Altos HS, Reseda, Calif.
14. *Kevin Morel, ss, Oxen Hill (Md.) HS.
15. Larry Lein, c, Green River (Wash.) CC.
16. ***Rick Matula, rhp, Wharton (Texas) HS.—(1979-81)**
17. ***Mark Mercer, lhp, West HS, Minneapolis.—(1981)**
18. ***Keith Drumright, 2b, Hillcrest HS, Springfield, Mo.—(1978-81)**
19. *Don Flanagan, c-rhp, Stephen F. Austin HS, Houston.
20. Kevin Young, of, Portage (Pa.) HS.
21. *Scott Mackey, lhp, Marengo (Ill.) HS.
22. *Michael Amatulli, 3b-of, Wayne Hills Regional HS, Wayne, N.J.
23. Mario Hewitt, 3b-of, St. John's University.
24. *Kevin Carney, c, Burlington (Vt.) HS.
25. *Randy Johnson, rhp, Brooklyn Center (Minn.) HS.
26. *Glen Smith, ss-3b, Bordentown (N.J.) Regional HS.
27. *Mike Williamson, rhp, Hillsdale HS, San Mateo, Calif.
28. *Dennis Connally, c, Redondo Beach (Calif.) HS.
29. *Lawrence Groover, lhp, Temple (Texas) JC.
30. *Vollon Dixon, of, Morningside HS, Inglewood, Calif.

**June—Secondary Phase (13)**

1. **Craig Caskey, lhp, University of Puget Sound.—(1973)**
2. *Laconia Graham, rhp, Ranger (Texas) JC.

## NEW YORK METS

**January—Regular Phase (14)**

1. Ronnie Diggle, of, UCLA.—(AAA)
2. John Lenahan, rhp, Villanova University.
3. John Blue, lhp, Tempe, Ariz.
4. *Steven Kennedy, rhp, San Jacinto (Texas) JC.
5. **Randy Tate, rhp, John C. Calhoun (Ala.) CC.—(1975)**
6. *Robert Youse, rhp, Glendale (Ariz.) CC.

**January—Secondary Phase (24)**

1. Michael Agosto, of, San Diego Mesa JC.—(AA)
2. **Ron Hodges, c, Appalachian State University.—(1973-84)**
3. *Roger Danson, ss, Seminole (Fla.) CC.
4. Ernest Bessette, ss, Post (Conn.) JC.
5. Terry Senn, 2b, University of San Francisco.

**June—Regular Phase (13)**

1. Richard Bengston, c, Richwoods HS, Peoria, Ill.—(AA)
2. Craig Skoglund, of, Clairemont HS, San Diego.—(Low A)
3. **Craig Swan, rhp, Arizona State University.—(1973-84)**
4. ***Andy Replogle, rhp, Snider HS, Fort Wayne, Ind.—(1978-79)**

DRAFT DROP *Attended Kansas State; re-drafted by Cardinals, 1975 (9th round)*

5. ***Randy McGilberry, rhp, Satsuma HS, Saraland, Ala.—(1977-78)**

DRAFT DROP *Attended Louisiana Tech; re-drafted by Royals, 1975 (14th round)*

6. **Brock Pemberton, 1b, Marina HS, Huntington Beach, Calif.—(1974-75)**
7. *Jeff Kleinbaum, 1b-of, Martin Van Buren HS, Bayside, N.Y.
8. *Larry Ike, rhp, Michigan State University.
9. **Craig Cacek, of, Monroe HS, Sepulveda, Calif.—(1977)**
10. Gary Perritt, lhp, Hanford (Calif.) HS.
11. *Bob Polinsky, rhp, Delaware Valley (Pa.) College.
12. Ken Perry, ss, Abbeyville (La.) HS.
13. Dennis Solari, rhp, Irvington HS, Fremont, Calif.
14. Jeffrey Grose, lhp, Colonia HS, Iselin, N.J.
15. *David Wiggins, of, San Diego State University.
16. Glenn Harper, of, San Pedro (Calif.) HS.
17. George Marshall, lhp, Northwest Cabarrus HS, Concord, N.C.
18. *Timothy Huff, rhp, West Forsyth HS, Winston-Salem, N.C.
19. *Clyde Lineberry, of, Parry McCluer HS, Buena Vista, Va.
20. *Duke Ribar, rhp, Steubenville (Ohio) HS.
21. Gregory Dobson, of-lhp, Bethune-Cookman College.
22. Robert Cheesman, of, Ledyard (Conn.) HS.
23. *Eric Magee, rhp, Haddonfield (N.J.) HS.
24. ***Craig Mitchell, rhp, Shadle Park HS, Spokane, Wash.—(1975-77)**

DRAFT DROP *First overall draft pick, June 1973/second-ary phase, Athletics*

25. *Greg Vogel, inf, Northampton HS, Cherryville, Pa.
26. *Tom Swenson, rhp, Rio Linda (Calif.) HS.
27. *Bruce Caldwell, rhp, DeKalb (Ga.) JC.
28. John Trevisan, c, Elizabethtown (Pa.) College.
29. *Bo Kleiber, ss, Ohio University.
30. *Randy Owens, rhp, Bamberg (S.C.) HS.
31. Gregory Hill, c, Santa Monica (Calif.) JC.
32. Augie Garbatini, rhp, University of Connecticut.
33. *Ray Davis, rhp, Southeast Bulloch HS, Brooklet, Ga.
34. *Michael Hasley, lhp, Oakdale (Calif.) HS.
35. *Chuck Rogers, rhp, Findlay (Ohio) HS.
36. Michael Henderson, rhp, Azusa Pacific University.
37. John Slosar, 1b-of, University of Connecticut.
38. *William Robinson, of, Delaware State College.
39. *Charles Steffen, lhp-1b, Jefferson HS, Rochester, N.Y.
40. *Paul Stombaugh, of, Clemson University.
41. *Alex Pastore, of, Miami-Dade CC North.
42. *Bryan Jones, ss, Haddonfield (N.J.) HS.
43. *Dan Forsythe, rhp, St. Paul (Minn.) North HS.
44. Tim Juran, lhp, Valparaiso University.
45. Kirk Berger, of, Millersville (Pa.) HS.

**June—Secondary Phase (3)**

1. Mike McNeilly, rhp, Gonzaga University.—(Rookie)

## NEW YORK YANKEES

**January—Regular Phase (13)**

1. *Joe Krsnich, 3b-of, Wichita State University.—(AA)
2. *Mike Lester, 3b, Bellevue (Wash.) CC.
3. Fred Luzzi, 2b, Sacramento (Calif.) CC.
4. *Lawrence Lee, c, Broward (Fla.) CC.
5. *Richard Green, 3b, Mesa (Ariz.) CC.

**January—Secondary Phase (5)**

1. **Rick Anderson, rhp, Los Angeles Valley JC.—(1979-80)**
2. Steven Greene, 2b, Los Angeles Valley JC.
3. *John Herman, of, Motlow State (Tenn.) CC.
4. ***Larry Wolfe, ss-rhp, Sacramento (Calif.) CC.—(1977-80)**
5. *Pat Williams, rhp, West Valley (Calif.) JC.

**June—Regular Phase (14)**

1. **Scott McGregor, lhp, El Segundo (Calif.) HS.—(1976-88)**
2. **Ken Clay, rhp, E.C. Glass HS, Lynchburg, Va.—(1977-81)**
3. Dennis Irwin, c, Hanford (Calif.) HS.—(AAA)
4. **Mickey Klutts, ss, El Rancho HS, Pico Rivera, Calif.—(1976-83)**
5. **Darryl Jones, ss, Westminster (Pa.) College.—(1979)**

DRAFT DROP *Brother of Lynn Jones, major leaguer (1979-86)*

6. Ed Ricks, rhp, Grambling University.
7. Earl Howell, c, Blair HS, Hattiesburg, Miss.
8. John Yeglinski, of, Long Island University.
9. Donald White, of-3b, Grambling HS, Simsboro, La.
10. Gaylord Browne, ss, John Brown (Ark.) University.
11. *Michael Rusk, rhp, San Jose State University.
12. Terry Quinn, c, University of Nevada-Reno.
13. Alfred Alwurm, lhp, Glendale (Calif.) HS.
14. *Doug Slocum, rhp, Mesa (Ariz.) CC.
15. Daniel Elko, of, Woodrow Wilson HS, Levittown, Pa.
16. Jim Lawler, rhp, Buena Vista (Iowa) College.

DRAFT DROP *Baseball coach, Gonzaga (1978-79); baseball coach, Texas-El Paso (1980-84); baseball coach, Arkansas-Little Rock (2006-08)*

17. *Michael Milligan, c, East Jefferson HS, Metairie, La.
18. *Paul Burnett, 1b-rhp, Temple HS, Vicksburg, Miss.
19. Bob Artemenko, rhp, Northwestern University.
20. *Bradley Davis, rhp, Milwaukie (Ore.) HS.
21. **Bob Kammeyer, rhp, Stanford University.—(1978-79)**

22. *Larry Hart, 1b, Darien (Conn.) HS.
23. Scott Rahl, 1b, University of New Haven.
24. Linwood Fisher, 1b, Newburgh (N.Y.) Free Academy.
25. Raymond Ventura, ss, Seekonk (Mass.) HS.
26. *Len Glowzenski, rhp, Mater Dei HS, New Monmouth, N.J.
27. Robert Wilson, of, William Paterson (N.J.) College.
28. Ronald Spann, 1b, Western Connecticut State University.
29. *Paul Caffrey, of, Seton Hall University.
30. Paul Lancaster, c, Ouachita Baptist (Ark.) University.
31. *Bill Simpson, ss, Cleveland HS, Portland, Ore.
32. *John Varga, 2b-ss, Seattle University.
33. Tim Wanner, 3b, University of Denver.

**June—Secondary Phase (14)**

1. Joe Barkauskas, c, Lafayette College.—(AA)
2. *Greg Van Gaver, rhp, Bellevue (Wash.) CC.
3. Brian Stone, of, Sacramento, Calif.

## OAKLAND ATHLETICS

**January—Regular Phase (21)**

1. *Charles Hendrix, rhp, Grossmont (Calif.) JC.—(Rookie)
2. *Sylvester Washington, of-1b, Los Angeles CC.
3. *Marv Thompson, ss-of, Rio Hondo (Calif.) JC.
4. Joe Lindsey, c-of, Compton, Calif.
5. *Don Lewis, of, Claremont-Mudd (Calif.) College.
6. *Robert Franks, rhp, Glendale (Calif.) JC.
7. *Chris Wibberly, rhp, El Camino (Calif.) JC.
8. David Love, rhp, San Bernardino Valley (Calif.) JC.
9. ***Rich Dauer, ss-2b, San Bernardino Valley (Calif.) JC.—(1976-85)**

DRAFT DROP *First-round draft pick (24th overall), Orioles (1974)*

10. **Bob Lacey, lhp, Central Arizona JC.—(1977-84)**
11. *Greg Motter, rhp, Imperial Valley (Calif.) JC.

**January—Secondary Phase (13)**

1. *Steve Trella, rhp, Fullerton (Calif.) JC.—(AA)
2. *Bill Hobbs, of, Fullerton (Calif.) JC.
3. *Gary Anglin, lhp, Ventura (Calif.) JC.
4. *Steven Ingram, rhp, Glendale (Ariz.) CC.

**June—Regular Phase (22)**

1. **Chet Lemon, ss, Fremont HS, Los Angeles.—(1975-90)**
2. *Garrett Strong, of, Fontana (Calif.) HS.

DRAFT DROP *Attended Arizona State; re-drafted by Giants, 1975 (4th round)*

3. *Jim Willis, 1b, The Dalles (Ore.) HS.

DRAFT DROP *Attended Oregon; re-drafted by Astros, January 1975/secondary phase (1st round)*

4. *Ken McKinney, 3b, Hazel Green (Ala.) HS.

DRAFT DROP *Attended Columbia State (Tenn.) JC; re-drafted by Angels, January 1973/secondary phase (6th round)*

5. *R.J. Harrison, c, Millikan HS, Long Beach, Calif.

DRAFT DROP *Attended Arizona State; re-drafted by Cardinals, 1975 (23rd round); scouting director, Rays (2006-15)*

6. Tim Indie, rhp, Camarillo (Calif.) HS.
7. Clarence Harrell, rhp, Montevallo HS, Wilton, Ala.
8. Jack Bastable, 3b-c, University of Missouri.
9. ***Dennis Littlejohn, c, North Torrance (Calif.) HS.—(1978-80)**
10. *Richard Olson, c, Washington HS, Fresno, Calif.
11. *Don Saulnier, lhp, Waltham (Mass.) HS.
12. **Chris Batton, rhp, St. Bernard's HS, Los Angeles.—(1976)**
13. *David Gronlund, 3b, Norte Vista HS, Riverside, Calif.
14. Ricky Tronerud, rhp-of, Hoover HS, San Diego.
15. ***Bobby Pate, 3b-of, Compton HS, Gardena, Calif.—(1980-81)**
16. Randy Taylor, rhp, Antelope Valley HS, Lancaster, Calif.
17. John Brownlee, rhp, South Wichita (Kan.) HS.
18. *Jim Rollins, rhp, Glendale (Calif.) HS.
19. *Chester Franklin, ss, Channel Islands HS, Oxnard, Calif.
20. *Bob Mosco, ss, Ganesha HS, Pomona, Calif.
21. *James Chellis, c, Bishop Hartley HS, Columbus, Ohio.
22. *David Hamilton, of, Locke HS, Los Angeles.
23. Ken Templeton, of, Santa Ana (Calif.) Valley HS.
24. *Ray Anderson, 2b-ss, Bonita HS, Claremont, Calif.
25. *Cliff Goodknight, rhp, Venice (Calif.) HS.
26. *Dennis Sherow, of, Compton (Calif.) HS.
27. *Mark Davison, rhp-of, Kennedy HS, Buena Park, Calif.
28. Thomas Tessar, rhp-c, Central Missouri State University.
29. Charles Barnes, of, Dominguez HS, Compton, Calif.
30. Dennis Root, lhp, Cal Poly Pomona.
31. Albert Curtis, ss, Sir Francis Drake HS, Mill Valley, Calif.
32. *Ronald Ward, inf, El Cerrito HS, Richmond, Calif.

**June—Secondary Phase (24)**

1. *J.P. Pierson, of, Glendale (Ariz.) CC.—(Low A)

The Pirates worked long and hard to sway second-round pick John Candelaria from playing basketball, and their diligence paid off as he won 177 games in a 19-year major league career

## PHILADELPHIA PHILLIES

**January—Regular Phase (4)**

1. Ricky Knepper, 3b, Boonsboro, Md.—(Rookie)
2. Ernest Gonzalez, of, Polk (Fla.) CC.
3. *Brad Hanson, ss, Valencia (Fla.) CC.
4. *Tom Gallo, rhp-of, Ulster (N.Y.) CC.
5. *Michael Jacobsen, 2b, Fresno (Calif.) CC.
6. *Michael Lucide, of, Diablo Valley (Calif.) JC.

**January—Secondary Phase (22)**

1. Mark Rott, c-of, Diablo Valley (Calif.) JC.—(Short-season A)
2. *Keath Chauncey, of, Polk (Fla.) CC.
3. Randy Delerio, c, West Hills (Calif.) JC.
4. *Mike Girazian, rhp, Fresno (Calif.) CC.
5. Charles Franklin, 3b, Encino, Calif.

**June—Regular Phase (3)**

1. **Larry Christenson, rhp, Marysville (Wash.) HS.—(1973-83)**

DRAFT DROP *First 1972 high school draft pick to reach majors (April 13, 1973)*

2. **Tom Underwood, lhp, Kokomo (Ind.) HS.—(1974-84)**

DRAFT DROP *Brother of Pat Underwood, first-round draft pick, Tigers (1976); major leaguer (1979-83)*

3. Rickey White, 2b, Fresno (Calif.) HS.—(Rookie)
4. John Guarnaccia, of, Downers Grove (Ill.) HS.—(AA)
5. Elliott Morton, c, Peachtree HS, Atlanta.—(Rookie)
6. **Bill Nahorodny, c, St. Clair County (Mich.) CC.—(1976-84)**
7. Quency Hill, lhp, Bryan Adams HS, Dallas.
8. ***Wayne Krenchicki, ss, Ewing HS, Ewing Township, N.J.—(1979-86)**
9. Kevin Bryant, 3b, Florida Southern College.
10. Ronald DeFeo, 3b, University of Bridgeport (Conn.).
11. Eddie Grime, lhp, Archbold (Ohio) HS.
12. *Randy Davidson, 2b, Columbia State (Tenn.) CC.
13. *Kerry Getter, rhp, University of Pennsylvania.
14. Jeff Wilson, c-of, McLane HS, Fresno, Calif.
15. William Dennis, lhp-of, Havre De Grace (Md.) HS.
16. James Meerpohl, rhp, Bowling Green State University.
17. Billy Beverly, lhp, Georgiana (Ala.) HS.
18. Walt Stolzenthaler, of, Staten Island (N.Y.) CC.
19. Rex Carrow, 2b, Michigan State University.
20. *David Lockett, rhp, Cleburne (Texas) HS.
21. Matthew Allison, of, Morris Knolls HS, Denville, N.J.
22. Dennis Lee, of, Cleburne (Texas) HS.
23. Pat McCoy, rhp, University of Northern Colorado.
24. *William Zisk, rhp-of, Roseville (Calif.) HS.
25. *Raymond Kennett, rhp, University of Tulsa.

**June—Secondary Phase (17)**

1. ***Dan Boitano, rhp, Fresno (Calif.) CC.—(1978-82)**
2. *Richard Davidson, c, Columbia State (Tenn.) CC.

## PITTSBURGH PIRATES

**January—Regular Phase (24)**

1. *Dennis Bolden, rhp, Chipola (Fla.) JC.—(Low A)
2. David Gaynor, 1b, New Mexico Highlands University.
3. *Joel Misler, rhp, Miami-Dade CC North.
4. Jerry Goode, rhp, Bayonne, N.J.
5. ***Jim Morrison, 3b, South Georgia JC.—(1977-88)**
6. *Ken Donaldson, c, Bellevue (Wash.) CC.
7. Alan Drechsler, lhp, Monroe (N.Y.) CC.
8. *Michael Kirkpatrick, rhp, Bucks County (Pa.) CC.
9. *Joe Blandford, of, Charles County (Md.) CC.
10. *Michael McGuire, of, Cornell University.
11. *Tom Holliday, c, Yavapai (Ariz.) JC.

DRAFT DROP *Father of Matt Holliday, major leaguer (2004-15); baseball coach, Oklahoma State (1997-2003)*

**January—Secondary Phase (4)**

1. Rick Anderson, rhp, University of New Haven.—(AAA)
2. Gerard Thomas, lhp, Scranton, Pa.
3. *Doug Farrell, rhp-of, Niagara University.
4. *Don Fisher, lhp, Polk (Fla.) CC.
5. Keith Matheny, rhp, Green River (Wash.) CC.
6. John Paull, c, Lemont Furnace, Pa.
7. **Larry Demery, rhp, Los Angeles CC.—(1974-77)**

**June—Regular Phase (23)**

1. Dwayne Peltier, ss, Servite HS, Anaheim, Calif.—(AA)
2. **John Candelaria, lhp, LaSalle Academy, Brooklyn, N.Y.—(1975-93)**
3. ***John Poloni, lhp, Lutheran West HS, Allen Park, Mich.—(1977)**

DRAFT DROP *Attended Arizona State; re-drafted by Rangers, 1975 (6th round)*

4. **Tim Jones, rhp, Ponderosa HS, El Dorado Hills, Calif.—(1977)**
5. *Gary Anderson, rhp, Thornridge HS, South Holland, Ill.—DNP

DRAFT DROP *No school; never re-drafted*

6. **Ken Macha, 1b-3b, University of Pittsburgh.—(1974-81)**

DRAFT DROP *Major league manager (2003-10)*

7. **Willie Randolph, ss-c, Tilden HS, Brooklyn, N.Y.—(1975-92)**

DRAFT DROP *Major league manager (2005-08)*

8. Michael Redden, rhp, Brother Rice HS, Chicago.
9. Robert Mazur, of, Charleroi (Pa.) HS.
10. *Scott Gunderson, rhp, Marysville HS, Stanwood, Wash.
11. *Michael Cones, ss, San Jacinto (Texas) JC.
12. *Craig Allegrezza, rhp, Milford (Mass.) HS.
13. Kim West, rhp, West Virginia University.
14. Mike Skinner, of-3b, Potomac State (W.Va.) JC.
15. Michael Gipaya, lhp, St. Louis HS, Honolulu.
16. William Estes, lhp, Rockford, Ill.
17. Ray Castaldi, of, St. James HS, Parkside, Pa.
18. Tim Flaherty, rhp, Rockville (Conn.) HS.
19. Wayne Eckert, 3b, Goose Creek HS, Hanahan, S.C.
20. Robert Rudi, rhp, South Philadelphia (Pa.) HS.
21. Alan Albert, lhp, Clear Springs (Md.) HS.
22. *John Hoffman, rhp, Snohomish HS, Lake Stevens, Wash.
23. Michael Busby, ss, Bessemer (Ala.) HS.
24. Charles Janes, rhp, Dartmouth College.
25. Michael Gonzalez, rhp, Kelly HS, Chicago.
26. Paul Burton, lhp, Villanova University.
27. Joel Sexton, rhp, Louisiana State University.
28. **Butch Alberts, 3b, University of Cincinnati.—(1978)**
29. *Richard Hudson, rhp, Century (Fla.) HS.
30. Larry Snowden, lhp-of, Monroe County HS, Monroeville, Ala.
31. *Evan Edge, c, Gadsden (Ala.) HS.
32. *Brian Bochow, ss, Duke University.
33. *Stan Boskovich, lhp, Albert Gallatin HS, Masontown, Pa.
34. *Mike Gannon, c, Central Washington University.
35. Michael Burgess, rhp, Robert E. Lee HS, Baytown, Texas.
36. *Doug Zimmerman, c, Slippery Rock (Pa.) University.
37. Luther Wrenn, of, Seymour (Ind.) HS.
38. *Doug Zavodny, of, McKinley HS, Buffalo, N.Y.
39. *Jerome Yankrick, lhp-1b, Greater Latrobe HS, Hostetter, Pa.
40. ***Gil Kubski, 3b, Granada Hills (Calif.) HS.—(1980)**

**June—Secondary Phase (23)**

1. ***Jim Morrison, 3b, South Georgia JC.—(1977-88)**

2. Dennis Simon, rhp, Finleyville, Pa.
3. *Donald Fisher, lhp, Polk (Fla.) CC.

## ST. LOUIS CARDINALS

### January—Regular Phase (22)

1. *Bob Gerdes, rhp, Miami-Dade CC South.—(High A)
2. *John Eichholtz, rhp, Fresno (Calif.) CC.
3. *Mark Klein, rhp, Broward (Fla.) CC.
4. *Charles Ellis, of, Los Angeles Valley JC.
5. *Richard Chapman, rhp-1b, St. Petersburg (Fla.) JC.
6. *Malvin Washington, c-of, Los Angeles Valley JC.
7. ***Keith Smith, of, Manatee (Fla.) JC.—(1977-80)**
8. Collier Black, rhp, Middle Georgia JC.

### January—Secondary Phase (18)

1. ***Dan Boitano, rhp, Fresno (Calif.) CC.—(1978-82)**
2. Scott Torosian, rhp, Fresno (Calif.) CC.
3. *Ricardo Fuentes, ss, Miami-Dade CC North.
4. William Poe, rhp, Pontiac, Mich.

### June—Regular Phase (21)

1. **Dan Larson, rhp, Alhambra (Calif.) HS.—(1976-82)**
2. Gary Blackwell, ss, Ben C. Rains HS, Mobile, Ala.—(AAA)
3. John Crider, of, Carlsbad (N.M.) HS.—(High A)
4. Dave Bialas, c, Bellaire (Texas) HS.—(AAA)
5. Rick Hetherington, ss, Fresno (Calif.) HS.—(Low A)
6. Tommy Washington, ss, Snyder (Texas) HS.
7. Ray Scott, lhp, Hardaway HS, Columbus, Ga.
8. Fred McGaha, of-inf, Louisiana Tech University.
9. **Mike Proly, rhp, St. John's University.—(1976-83)**
10. Dan Radison, 3b-c, Southern Illinois University.
11. Lawrence Aubel, rhp, University of South Alabama.
12. Rick Simmons, rhp, University of Idaho.
13. *Chris Lynch, rhp, Columbus HS, Miami.
14. Michael Camuso, rhp, University of Lowell (Mass.).
15. Mike Proffitt, lhp, Mississippi State University.
16. *Harold Harsh, of, Blairsville (Pa.) HS.
17. Gary Hernandez, 1b-of, University of California.

**DRAFT DROP** *Brother of Keith Hernandez, major leaguer (1974-90)*

18. *Steve King, c, Hoggard HS, Wilmington, N.C.
19. *Danny Starr, c-rhp, White Station HS, Memphis, Tenn.
20. James Gorton, rhp, Manhattan College.
21. John Jacobs, of, Metropolis (Ill.) Community HS.
22. *Michael Hill, rhp, Puxico (Miss.) HS.
23. *Michael Murphy, rhp, Hoover HS, Fresno, Calif.
24. Burt Nordstrom, rhp, Humboldt State (Calif.) University.
25. James Romanosky, rhp, Columbia University.
26. *Ted Milton, of, Mississippi State University.
27. *Phil Willingham, 2b, Satsuma HS, Saraland, Ala.
28. William Bird, inf, Edgewood HS, West Covina, Calif.
29. Stan Allison, ss, Central HS, Little Rock, Ark.
30. *James Martinez, c, Cosumnes River (Calif.) JC.
31. Blake Zimmerman, c, Weber State (Utah) College.
32. Philip McCollough, rhp, Harriman (Tenn.) HS.
33. *Greg Wolk, rhp, Crystal City (Mo.) HS.
34. Patrick Hamman, rhp, Canoga Park (Calif.) HS.
35. Joseph Kubeck, rhp, Springfield (Mass.) College.
36. Johnny Glenn, of-2b, University of Arizona.
37. *Robert Matzenbacher, of, Marissa (Ill.) HS.
38. *Charles Mitchell, of, Barstow (Calif.) CC.
39. *Steve Allietta, ss-2b, Lawrence HS, Falmouth, Mass.
40. Bruce Henderson, 1b, Long Island University.
41. *Joseph Rezzuti, of, Northeastern University.

### June—Secondary Phase (21)

1. *Ray Humphries, rhp, San Bernardino Valley (Calif.) JC.—(High A)

## SAN DIEGO PADRES

### January—Regular Phase (2)

1. Cliff Butcher, rhp, University of Tulsa.—(AA)
2. Mike Heftner, lhp, University of Southern Colorado.
3. *Clarence Poitier, 3b-2b, Miami-Dade South CC.

### January—Secondary Phase (6)

1. **Rich Troedson, lhp, Santa Clara University.—(1973-74)**
2. Mark Servais, 2b, St. Mary's (Minn.) University.

### June—Regular Phase (1)

1. **Dave Roberts, 3b, University of Oregon.—(1972-82)**

**DRAFT DROP** *First player from 1972 draft to reach majors (June 7, 1972)*

2. Mike Allen, rhp, Marple-Newtown HS, Newtown Square, Pa.—(AAA)
3. Gary Walls, ss, Birmingham (Ala.) HS.—(AA)
4. Charles Brown, of, South Leake HS, Walnut Grove, Miss.—(Short-season A)
5. **Randy Jones, lhp, Chapman (Calif.) College.—(1973-82)**
6. Bill Hall, 2b, University of Virginia.
7. Edward Arkema, rhp, J. Sterling Morton East HS, Cicero, Ill.
8. Don Leege, c, Furman University.
9. ***Dave Heaverlo, rhp, Central Washington University.—(1975-81)**

**DRAFT DROP** *Father of Jeff Heaverlo, first-round draft pick, Mariners (1999)*

10. **Jerry Turner, of, Venice HS, Culver City, Calif.—(1974-83)**
11. *Stephen Conley, rhp, Deering HS, Portland, Maine.
12. **Rusty Gerhardt, lhp, Clemson University.—(1974)**
13. *Dennis Whitehead, c, University of South Alabama.
14. *Guy Todd, rhp, Richfield HS, Waco, Texas.
15. Thomas Armstrong, 2b, University of Denver.
16. William Dorsey, rhp, Fitch HS, Mystic, Conn.
17. Craig Bromann, rhp, University of Denver.
18. Gary Phillips, 3b-of, Helix HS, Lemon Grove, Calif.
19. *Marv Owen, of, San Diego State University.

**DRAFT DROP** *Wide receiver, National Football League (1973-74)*

### June—Secondary Phase (5)

1. ***Warren Cromartie, of, Miami-Dade CC North.—(1974-91)**

## SAN FRANCISCO GIANTS

### January—Regular Phase (20)

1. Ken Kollmeyer, lhp, San Diego CC.—(High A)
2. **Reggie Walton, 1b, Compton (Calif.) JC.—(1980-82)**
3. *Mike LaBare, of, Bakersfield (Calif.) JC.
4. *Craig Cornwell, rhp, Pasadena (Calif.) CC.
5. James Emery, lhp, JC of San Mateo (Calif.).
6. *Harold Sinclair, 3b, Bee County (Texas) JC.
7. Barry Moss, of, Los Angeles Pierce JC.
8. *Kevin Darke, p, Chaffey (Calif.) JC.
9. *Lou Irwin, p, JC of the Sequoias (Calif.).
10. *Mark Hance, 1b, Bakersfield (Calif.) JC.
11. *Michael Turk, 1b, Vallejo (Calif.) JC.
12. *Michael Supernak, p, Miami-Dade CC North.
13. *Jeff Bartelt, p, Treasure Valley (Ore.) CC.
14. *Greg Brinkley, of, Treasure Valley (Ore.) CC.
15. Henry Jones, inf, Lower Columbia (Wash.) JC.

### January—Secondary Phase (12)

1. Kenny Roberts, rhp, El Camino (Calif.) JC.—(High A)
2. **Gary Alexander, c, Los Angeles Harbor JC.—(1975-81)**
3. *Joe Barkauskas, c, Lafayette College.
4. *Terry Farmer, rhp, Chipola (Fla.) JC.
5. *J.P. Pierson, of, Glendale (Ariz.) CC.
6. Seldon Morton, 1b-lhp, Skyline (Calif.) JC.
7. *Lamar Jones, rhp, DeKalb (Ga.) JC.

### June—Regular Phase (19)

1. **Rob Dressler, rhp, Madison HS, Portland, Ore.—(1975-80)**
2. **Bob Knepper, lhp, Calistoga (Calif.) HS.—(1976-90)**
3. *Mike Kirkland, 3b, Pasadena (Texas) HS.—DNP

**DRAFT DROP** *Attended Arkansas; never re-drafted; quarterback, National Football League (1976-78)*

4. Jerry Scarcella, rhp, Walt Whitman HS, Huntington Station, N.Y.—(High A)
5. Joe Meade, ss, Chandler (Ariz.) HS.—(Low A)
6. *James Crosta, ss, Union (N.J.) HS.
7. ***Brian Asselstine, of, Allan Hancock (Calif.) JC.—(1976-81)**
8. William Adams, c, Rider College.
9. R.J. Englert, of, Texas A&M University.
10. *John Racanelli, lhp, Terra Nova HS, Pacifica, Calif.
11. Tim Bull, 1b-of, St. Louis CC-Meramec.
12. Tim Day, c, San Jose State University.
13. ***Orlando Gonzalez, 1b, Miami-Dade CC South.—(1976-80)**
14. ***Lenn Sakata, 2b, Treasure Valley (Ore.) CC.—(1977-87)**
15. Steve Greenough, lhp, University of Oregon.
16. John Harrison, of, Los Angeles Pierce JC.
17. *Isaac Giminez, ss, Bronx (N.Y.) CC.
18. Thomas O'Donnell, lhp, Arroyo HS, El Monte, Calif.
19. *Paul Parker, p, Montclair State (N.J.) College.
20. *John Lacey, 1b, Bergenfield (N.J.) HS.
21. *Mike Gillespie, p, Iowa State University.
22. Charles Polk, of, Narbonne HS, Harbor City, Calif.
23. Roger Rasmussen, rhp, Monrovia HS, Newport Beach, Calif.
24. **Ed Halicki, rhp, Monmouth College.—(1974-80)**
25. *Robert Alonzo, inf, Carl Hayden HS, Phoenix, Ariz.
26. *Doug Cushman, p, Lee HS, Springfield, Va.
27. *Roberto Ayala, 3b, Chandler (Ariz.) HS.
28. *Michael Younce, ss, Millington (Tenn.) HS.
29. William Binder, c, Princeton University.
30. *Thomas Boutin, of, Melvindale (Mich.) HS.
31. Harlan Highfill, rhp, Central HS, Little Rock, Ark.
32. *Jackie Johnson, ss, Salem (N.J.) CC.
33. Wendell Stephens, rhp, Los Angeles CC.
34. Rick Glazebrook, 1b, Arizona State University.
35. Gene Lanthorn, rhp, Oregon College of Education.
36. Ken Conlin, ss, Eastern Washington University.
37. *Ray Mallott, of, Findlay (Ohio) College.
38. *Bill Przygocki, rhp, Central HS, Bay City, Mich.
39. *Rick Burley, lhp, San Jacinto (Texas) JC.
40. *Peter Cervantes, c-3b, Abraham Lincoln HS, Los Angeles.
41. *Reland McFadden, 1b, Evander Child HS, Bronx, N.Y.
42. *Stan Jakubowski, rhp, Union (N.J.) HS.
43. *Rogelio Dominguez, of-c, Miami (Fla.) Senior HS.
44. Greg Brust, 3b, Arizona State University.
45. Mike Rupcich, c, Arizona State University.
46. Carl Wesley, of, East Texas Baptist University.

### June—Secondary Phase (19)

1. Lewis Reasonover, ss, Gulf Coast (Fla.) CC.—(Rookie)
2. Jeff McKay, rhp, Treasure Valley (Ore.) CC.
3. *Sylvester Washington, of-1b, Los Angeles CC.
4. **Terry Cornutt, rhp, Linn-Benton (Ore.) CC.—(1977-78)**
5. *Craig Cornwell, rhp, Pasadena (Calif.) CC.

## TEXAS RANGERS

### January—Regular Phase (3)

1. James Owen, rhp, San Jose (Calif.) CC.—(AA)
2. Vincent Ujdur, c, Diablo Valley (Calif.) JC.
3. *Bob Tompkins, p, Mesa (Ariz.) CC.
4. *James Lacey, inf-rhp, Cabrillo (Calif.) JC.

### January—Secondary Phase (15)

1. Charles Bordes, ss, University of Southwestern Louisiana.—(AAA)
2. *R.B. Bell, rhp, Fullerton (Calif.) JC.
3. *Michael Rankin, c, Columbia State (Tenn.) CC.
4. *Ray Forgie, rhp, Mesa (Ariz.) CC.
5. *Robin Ogle, 1b, Miami-Dade CC South.

**DRAFT DROP** *Grandson of Walter Alston, major leaguer (1936); major league manager (1954-76)*

### June—Regular Phase (4)

1. **Roy Howell, 3b, Lompoc (Calif.) HS.—(1974-84)**
2. **Ron Pruitt, c-of, Michigan State University.—(1975-83)**
3. Jeff Scott, rhp-c, Kankakee-Eastridge HS, St. Anne, Ill.—(AA)

**DRAFT DROP** *Scouting director, Indians (1987-88); scouting director, Tigers (1994-96)*

4. **Brian Doyle, ss, Caverna HS, Cave City, Ky.—(1978-81)**

**DRAFT DROP** *Brother of Denny Doyle, major leaguer (1970-77) • Twin brother of Blake Doyle, fourth-round draft pick, Orioles (1972)*

5. ***Rich Wortham, lhp, Odessa (Texas) HS.—(1978-83)**

**DRAFT DROP** *Attended Texas; re-drafted by Mets, 1975 (14th round)*

6. Mel Barrow, ss, Harlan HS, Chicago.
7. *Mark Ackerman, rhp, Sunny Hills HS, Fullerton, Calif.
8. ***Jim Sundberg, c, University of Iowa.—(1974-89)**
9. *Steve Correll, rhp, Blue Island HS, New Ringgold, Pa.
10. Wayne Popiolek, rhp, Reavis HS, Chicago.
11. ***Bo McLaughlin, rhp, Amelia (Ohio) HS.—(1976-80)**

**DRAFT DROP** *First-round draft pick (14th overall), Astros (1975)*

12. *Robert Allinder, of, Truman HS, Independence, Mo.
13. ***George Frazier, rhp, Hillcrest HS, Springfield, Mo.—(1978-87)**
14. ***Gil Rondon, rhp, DeWitt Clinton HS, New York.—(1976-79)**
15. *Perry Pryor, rhp, Evans HS, Orlando, Fla.
16. Charles Fowke, ss, Manatee (Fla.) JC.
17. *Donnelly Douglas, lhp, Amherst (Mass.) College.
18. *Sam Leonard, rhp, St. Michael's HS, Royal Oak, Mich.
19. **Bobby Thompson, ss, Harding HS, Charlotte, N.C.—(1978)**
20. *Dennis Thornbury, lhp, Palomar (Calif.) JC.
21. Mark Mullen, c, Amelia (Ohio) HS.
22. ***Garry Hancock, of, Brandon HS, Seffner, Fla.—(1978-84)**
23. James Pascarella, 2b, University of New Haven.
24. *Wesley Goodale, rhp, Forest Hills HS, West Palm Beach, Fla.
25. **Mike Hargrove, 1b, Northwestern Oklahoma State University.—(1974-85)**

**DRAFT DROP** *Major league manager (1991-2007)*

26. *Tom Farias, rhp, American International (Mass.) College.
27. Stephen Cartier, of, Jupiter (Fla.) HS.
28. *Michael Collodi, of-c, Colorado School of Mines.
29. *Brian Herosian, lhp-1b, University of Connecticut.
30. James Raynor, rhp, Rollins (Fla.) College.
31. *Larry Sisk, of, Gardner-Webb College.
32. Lawrence Chapman, ss-rhp, Fort Pierce Central HS, Fort Pierce, Fla.
33. *Joseph Setticase, of, Miami (Fla.) Senior HS.
34. *James Brittain, c, Escambia HS, Pensacola, Fla.
35. *Edward Mock, rhp, Escambia HS, Pensacola, Fla.
36. Kevin Murtha, 1b, St. Mary's (Calif.) College.
37. *Samuel Thomas, rhp, Chamberlain HS, Tampa.
38. *Barry Redmond, ss, Brandon HS, Seffner, Fla.
39. Joseph LaRocca, 1b, University of Notre Dame.
40. Nelson King, rhp-of, Colorado School of Mines.
41. Bill Skeens, of-rhp, Indian Hills HS, Oakland, N.J.
42. *Jack Rhine, c, Florida Southern College.
43. *John Butler, of, Miami-Dade CC South.
44. *Richard Mallman, rhp, Prospect HS, Saratoga, Calif.

### June—Secondary Phase (4)

1. *R.B. Bell, rhp, Fullerton (Calif.) JC.—(AAA)
2. ***Mike Stanton, rhp, Miami-Dade CC South.—(1975-85)**
3. *Ron Herring, rhp, Chipola (Fla.) JC.
4. **Keith Smith, of, Manatee (Fla.) JC.—(1977-80)**
5. *Terry Farmer, rhp, Chipola (Fla.) JC.
6. *William Meyer, ss, Indian River (Fla.) CC.
7. *Mike Siani, ss, Villanova University.

**DRAFT DROP** *First-round draft pick, Oakland Raiders/National Football League (1972); wide receiver, NFL (1972-80)*

1973

# Clyde jumps to majors, at expense of career

David Clyde was 18. A Texan. Baseball's No. 1 draft pick. The most gifted young pitcher to come along in years.

To Texas Rangers owner Bob Short, he was like a gift from heaven.

Three weeks after Clyde completed what may have been the greatest high school pitching career ever, Short showcased his prized lefthander against the Minnesota Twins. With bands, amusement shows and grass-skirted Polynesian dancers as a backdrop, along with a battalion of reporters, Clyde's June 27 debut was a smashing success, both artistically and financially. He walked the first two hitters in the first inning, then struck out the side. He pitched five innings, allowing only one hit. He flashed his 95 mph fastball. He won.

Most important to Short, at least, Clyde's debut marked the first sellout since the struggling Rangers franchise moved to suburban Dallas from Washington, D.C., after the 1971 season. He had the crowd abuzz with excitement. For the first time, he had Texans talking baseball, not the Dallas Cowboys.

"We needed something like this to stay in business," Short said after Clyde wowed a sellout crowd of 35,698. "You don't want to read too much into one five-inning performance, but we think David is the kind of player the people of this area can identify with. He's young, he's a Texan, and a winner. Isn't it ironic that it took an 18-year-old high school pitching star to pack the house, even when the debut of major league baseball two years ago wouldn't do it?"

No debut in draft history attracted more attention than Clyde's. He was a folk hero in Texas as a teenager.

The young lefthander was prominently featured in Sports Illustrated prior to becoming the only high school pitcher in the first 25 years of the draft to be the No. 1 pick. He signed the largest contract paid an 18-year-old to that point in the draft's evolution—some $125,000, according to Short, although the actual bonus was only $65,000.

Clyde enjoyed a spectacular career at Houston's Westchester High. In his senior year, he went 18-0. He struck out a then-high school record 328 batters in 148 innings. He tossed 14 shutouts. He allowed three earned runs (0.18 ERA). He finished with a streak of 55 consecutive scoreless innings. He pitched shutouts in all five Texas 5-A playoff games, allowing no hits three times, one hit in the other two contests. For his career, Clyde was 53-13, 0.65, including a 7-7 record as a prep freshman. He struck out a still-standing national record 843 batters in 475 innings.

Whitey Herzog, manager of the Rangers in 1973, was among those sent out to scout Clyde.

"At 18," Herzog said, "he was as good as any kid I ever saw, including Nolan Ryan, Gary Gentry,

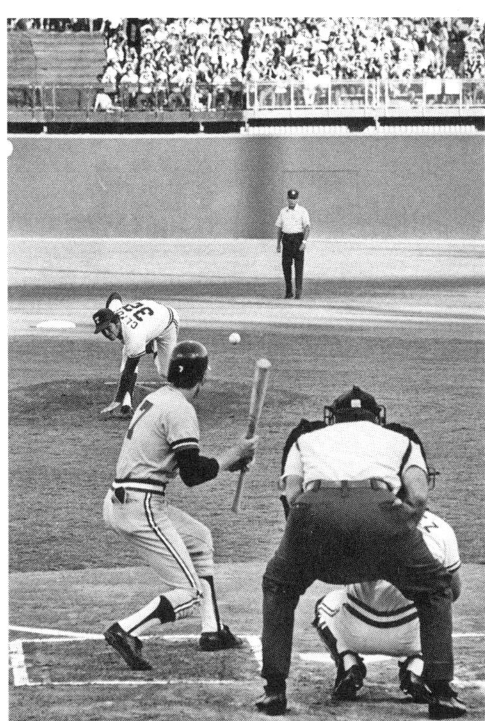

FORT WORTH STAR TELEGRAM

**David Clyde generated excitement for the Rangers when he went straight to the big leagues and won his debut before a packed house**

Jon Matlack and Tug McGraw. He had a good fastball, a great curveball, a great delivery, poise and control. Boy, that kid had an arm on him in high school. Some of those kids went up to the plate shaking when he was pitching."

Others routinely called him the next coming of Sandy Koufax, and after signing his contract Clyde stated that his goal was to "become the greatest pitcher ever." Clyde wore No. 32, made famous by Koufax, who retired seven years earlier.

Legendary Pirates scout Howie Haak saw Clyde, and said he was the real thing. "His curve is outstanding," Haak said. "His fastball is better than a great many pitchers in the major leagues today. In fact, it is my opinion that this boy could pitch in the major leagues right now."

Such accolades further hyped his debut.

"The pressure on the kid was tremendous," Herzog said. "We held up the game for 30 minutes to let the crowd in."

Herzog's idea was to let Clyde pitch a few games in the big leagues, then send him to the minors. But Clyde would attract another 33,010 fans to his second start, and Short resisted. Without his prized young pitcher on the mound, the Rangers drew a paltry 6,000 a contest. Clyde remained with the Rangers over the balance of the 1973 season, and though he won his first start in impressive fashion, he finished the campaign with a 4-8, 5.03 record.

"It was the worst thing for him, mentally and

## AT A GLANCE

### This Date In History
**WINTER DRAFT:** Jan. 10
**SUMMER DRAFT:** June 5-6

### Best Draft
**BALTIMORE ORIOLES.** The O's drafted future big leaguers in all four phases, and scored their biggest coup by tabbing a pair of stalwarts in the June regular phase: Hall of Famer **EDDIE MURRAY** in the third round and lefthander **MIKE FLANAGAN**, who won 141 games for the franchise, in the seventh.

### Worst Draft
**CINCINNATI REDS.** Several Cincinnati drafts in the 1970s played a key role in the demise of the Big Red Machine, and this may have been the worst of all. Starting with underachieving outfielder **BRAD KESSLER** in the first round, the Reds didn't sign one player in 1973 who became a big leaguer. Only one, 33rd-rounder **RICK COLZIE**, advanced as far as Triple-A.

### First-Round Bust
**BILLY TAYLOR, OF, ANGELS.** The seventh pick overall, Taylor deliberated most of the summer between playing football at Georgia and signing a $40,000 bonus contract with the Angels. He signed and won a Rookie-level Pioneer League batting title in his first pro season (1974), but never advanced beyond low Class A.

### On Second Thought
**FRED LYNN, OF, RED SOX.** Two years after being passed over in the first round of the 1973 draft, Lynn was well on his way to winning Rookie-of-the-Year and MVP honors for the American League champion Red Sox.

### Late-Round Find
**JACK CLARK, RHP/OF, GIANTS (13TH ROUND).** One of the most feared power hitters of his era, Clark lasted until the middle rounds of the 1973

CONTINUED ON PAGE 138

## AT A GLANCE

CONTINUED FROM PAGE 137

draft. The reason? Most clubs saw Clark as a pitcher after he posted an 11-3, 1.25 record with 99 strikeouts in 95 innings as a high school senior in Covina, Calif. The Giants quickly saw that Clark was an everyday player. He became a .300 hitter at every stop in the system and hit 340 homers with 1,180 RBIs in an 18-year big league career.

### Never Too Late

**BRYN SMITH, RHP, CARDINALS (49TH ROUND).** Smith didn't sign with the Cardinals, but agreed to terms with the Orioles a year later as a nondrafted free agent before going on to win 108 games in a 13-year big league career.

### Overlooked

**RON LEFLORE, OF, TIGERS.** Leflore's story is one of the more amazing in baseball history. He had never played organized baseball until he was serving time for armed robbery in Michigan State Prison. Word of his talent filtered out, and the Tigers scouted him and signed him to a contract in July 1973 that allowed him to meet the conditions for parole. His rags-to-riches story became the subject of a 1978 made-for-TV movie, and he hit .288 and stole 455 bases in nine major league seasons, including 97 in 1980.

### International Gem

**DENNIS MARTINEZ, RHP, ORIOLES.** Martinez, the first Nicaraguan player ever to reach the big leagues, won 245 games (the most ever by a Latin American pitcher) over a 23-year career. The Orioles signed him for $3,000.

### Minor League Take

**JERRY TABB, 1B, CUBS.** Tabb's career never panned out as expected (.226, six homers in 74 games), but he was a star in college at Tulsa, winning College World Series MVP honors as a freshman and All-

## 1973: THE FIRST ROUNDERS

| CLUB: PLAYER, POS., SCHOOL | HOMETOWN | B-T | HT. | WT. | AGE | BONUS | FIRST YEAR | LAST YEAR | PEAK LEVEL (YEARS) |
|---|---|---|---|---|---|---|---|---|---|
| **JUNE—REGULAR PHASE** | | | | | | | | | |
| 1. *Rangers: David Clyde, lhp, Westchester HS | Houston | L-L | 6-1 | 180 | 18 | $65,000 | 1973 | 1981 | Majors (5) |
| Texas schoolboy hero debuted in majors at 18, attracted first sellout crowd in Rangers history; exposed to too much too soon, and his promising career unraveled. | | | | | | | | | |
| 2. Phillies: John Stearns, c, Colorado | Denver | R-R | 6-0 | 195 | 21 | $53,000 | 1973 | 1985 | Majors (11) |
| Two-sport star weighed NFL option from Buffalo Bills, went with baseball after leading nation in homers; appeared in 4 all-star games, set record for SBs by catcher. | | | | | | | | | |
| 3. Brewers: Robin Yount, ss, Taft HS | Woodland Hills, Calif. | R-R | 6-0 | 165 | 17 | $60,000 | 1973 | 1993 | Majors (20) |
| Half season in NY-P League was all it took to launch Hall of Fame careeer; debuted for Brewers at 18, went on to win 2 MVP awards and collect 3,142 hits. | | | | | | | | | |
| 4. *Padres: Dave Winfield, rhp/of, Minnesota | St. Paul, Minn. | R-R | 6-6 | 195 | 21 | $65,000 | 1973 | 1995 | Majors (22) |
| One of the best athletes of draft era launched career in San Diego, never spent a day in minors; 3,110 hits, 465 homers, 7 Gold Gloves led him to Hall of Fame. | | | | | | | | | |
| 5. Indians: Glenn Tufts, 1b, Raynham HS | Bridgewater, Mass. | R-R | 6-3 | 200 | 18 | $40,000 | 1973 | 1977 | Class AA (2) |
| Prep slugger's career never got untracked after horrific car accident left him with badly damaged leg; released in 1977 after hitting .240 with just 20 homers. | | | | | | | | | |
| 6. Giants: Johnnie LeMaster, ss, Paintsville HS | Paintsville, Ky. | R-R | 6-3 | 165 | 17 | $38,000 | 1973 | 1987 | Majors (12) |
| Set MLB record with inside-the-park homer in first AB, but hit just .222 with 22 homers in 12-year career and became the focus of Giants fans' frustration. | | | | | | | | | |
| 7. Angels: Billy Taylor, of, Windsor Forest HS | Savannah, Ga. | L-R | 5-11 | 190 | 18 | $50,000 | 1973 | 1976 | Class A (3) |
| All-state QB weighed Georgia offer before signing with Angels; won Pioneer League batting title (.344) in pro debut, but hit .222 in 3 years in low Class A after that. | | | | | | | | | |
| 8. Expos: Gary Roenicke, ss, Edgewood HS | West Covina, Calif. | R-R | 6-3 | 195 | 18 | $65,000 | 1973 | 1988 | Majors (12) |
| Slugged 25 homers for O's in first season (1979), but never became a star in 12-year career; brother Ron managed and played in majors, son Josh also reached MLB. | | | | | | | | | |
| 9. Royals: Lew Olsen, rhp, San Ramon Valley HS | Alamo, Calif. | R-R | 6-5 | 220 | 18 | $64,000 | 1973 | 1979 | Class AAA (2) |
| Chose Royals over baseball/football offer from Stanford, but languished in minors for 7 seasons; developed sore arm in Rookie ball and never recovered his velocity. | | | | | | | | | |
| 10. Braves: Pat Rockett, ss, Robert E. Lee HS | San Antonio, Texas | R-R | 5-10 | 165 | 18 | $40,000 | 1973 | 1980 | Majors (3) |
| San Antonio prep star had offer to be WR at Texas, chose career with Braves; started parts of 3 seasons at SS, but plagued by anemic bat (.214 BA, 1 HR in 411 AB). | | | | | | | | | |
| 11. *Twins: Eddie Bane, lhp, Arizona State | Westminster, Calif. | R-L | 5-9 | 160 | 21 | $30,500 | 1973 | 1980 | Majors (3) |
| Crafty lefty had standout career at ASU, going 41-4 and setting NCAA strikeout records, but ended up making his mark on the game as a shrewd judge of talent. | | | | | | | | | |
| 12. Cardinals: Joe Edelen, 3b/rhp, Gracemont HS | Gracemont, Okla. | R-R | 6-0 | 175 | 17 | $58,000 | 1973 | 1983 | Majors (2) |
| Two-way prep standout started career as an everyday player, but anemic bat (.232, 18 HRs) led to the mound and got him a brief major league opportunity. | | | | | | | | | |
| 13. Yankees: Doug Heinold, rhp, Stroman HS | Victoria, Texas | R-R | 6-3 | 175 | 19 | $65,000 | 1973 | 1978 | Class AAA (4) |
| Won 13 games, posted 0.37 ERA as prep senior, and went 45-40, 2.83 in six minor league seasons, but an arm injury in Triple-A derailed his career. | | | | | | | | | |
| 14. Mets: Lee Mazzilli, of, Abraham Lincoln HS | Brooklyn, N.Y. | B-R | 6-1 | 175 | 18 | $50,000 | 1974 | 1989 | Majors (14) |
| Local product was a youth speed-skating champion and played with flair; went on to a 14-year major league career; later managed Orioles, became an actor. | | | | | | | | | |
| 15. Orioles: Mike Parrott, rhp, Camarillo HS | Camarillo, Calif. | R-R | 6-4 | 200 | 18 | $20,000 | 1973 | 1986 | Majors (5) |
| Upstaged by Orioles picks Eddie Murray, Mike Flanagan, but spent 5 years in majors; won 14 games for Seattle in 1979, only to lose 16 in a row a year later. | | | | | | | | | |
| 16. Cubs: Jerry Tabb, 1b, Tulsa | Altus, Okla. | L-R | 6-2 | 190 | 21 | $37,000 | 1973 | 1978 | Majors (3) |
| MVP of '71 College World Series as a freshman, but his college and minor league success at the plate never translated to majors; hit .226 with 6 HRs in 74 games. | | | | | | | | | |
| 17. Red Sox: Ted Cox, c, Midwest City HS | Midwest City, Okla. | R-R | 6-3 | 190 | 18 | $35,000 | 1973 | 1981 | Majors (5) |
| He was named minors' top player in 1977 in Triple-A and set MLB record with hits in first six ABs for Red Sox, but ended his career with a .245 batting average. | | | | | | | | | |
| 18. Dodgers: Ted Farr, c, Shadle Park HS | Spokane, Wash. | R-R | 6-0 | 187 | 18 | $48,000 | 1973 | 1977 | Class AAA (1) |
| Sore shoulder dogged him from the start; had surgery in second pro season and never bounced back; hit .235 with 39 HRs in five years in Dodgers system. | | | | | | | | | |
| 19. Tigers: Charles Bates, 1b, Cal State Los Angeles | Los Angeles | B-R | 6-0 | 210 | 21 | $25,000 | 1973 | 1976 | Class AA (3) |
| Drafted 5 times previously based on his potential with the bat, juco standout signed after first NCAA Division I season; hit .259 in 4 seasons in minors. | | | | | | | | | |
| 20. Astros: Calvin Portley, ss, Longview HS | Longview, Texas | R-R | 5-10 | 165 | 18 | $24,000 | 1973 | 1978 | Class AA (4) |
| Top prep RB recruit took the money from home-state Astros, but never got above Double-A in 6 minor league seasons; hit .228 overall, went deep just once. | | | | | | | | | |
| 21. White Sox: Steve Swisher, c, Ohio | Parkersburg, W.Va. | R-R | 6-2 | 200 | 21 | $40,000 | 1973 | 1983 | Majors (9) |
| Traded to Cubs after just six months; selected to 1976 NL all-star team and gained notoriety as father of Nick, also a first-rounder and MLB all-star. | | | | | | | | | |
| 22. Reds: Brad Kessler, of, Claremont HS | Claremont, Calif. | R-R | 6-1 | 200 | 17 | $35,000 | 1973 | 1976 | Class AA (1) |
| Prep football/baseball star hit .609 as a junior, .429 as senior, but never came close to fulfilling Reds' expectations, hitting .235 in four minor league seasons. | | | | | | | | | |
| 23. Athletics: Randy Scarbery, rhp, Southern California | Fresno, Calif. | R-R | 6-1 | 180 | 20 | $32,500 | 1973 | 1980 | Majors (2) |
| Two-time first-rounder played on 3 championship teams at USC, but found success tougher to come by in pro ranks; assembled 3-10 mark in major leagues. | | | | | | | | | |
| 24. Pirates: Steve Nicosia, c, North Miami Beach HS | North Miami Beach, Fla. | R-R | 5-11 | 195 | 17 | $38,000 | 1973 | 1985 | Majors (8) |
| Steadily climbed through the ranks to achieve an 8-year big league career mostly as a backup catcher, including on Pittsburgh's 1979 World Series champs. | | | | | | | | | |
| **JANUARY—REGULAR PHASE** | | | | | | | | | |
| 1. Phillies: Alan Bannister, ss, Arizona State | Buena Park, Calif. | R-R | 5-11 | 175 | 21 | $85,000 | 1973 | 1985 | Majors (12) |
| After record-setting junior season at ASU, withdrew in fall to become draft-eligible in January; got largest 1973 bonus, but his 12-year career disappointed a bit. | | | | | | | | | |
| **JANUARY—SECONDARY PHASE** | | | | | | | | | |
| 1. Phillies: Dick Ruthven, rhp, Fresno State | Fremont, Calif. | R-R | 6-3 | 190 | 21 | $62,500 | 1973 | 1986 | Majors (14) |
| Phils owned No. 1 pick in both January drafts, opted for Ruthven after he didn't sign with Twins as first-rounder previous June; debuted in majors in April. | | | | | | | | | |
| **JUNE—SECONDARY PHASE** | | | | | | | | | |
| 1. A's: Craig Mitchell, rhp, Spokane Falls (Wash.) CC | Spokane, Wash. | R-R | 6-3 | 190 | 19 | $10,000 | 1973 | 1979 | Majors (3) |
| Drafted previously by Yankees and Mets, went to World Series champ A's in talent-diluted June secondary phase; reached majors briefly, went 0-2, 7.82. | | | | | | | | | |

**Signed to major league contract.*

## How They Should Have Done It

Based on the career WAR (Wins Above Replacement, as calculated by Baseball-Reference.com) numbers achieved by all the players eligible for the 1973 draft, here's how the first round should have unfolded. Numbers in parentheses indicate the round when the player was actually drafted

| | Player, Pos. | Actual Draft | WAR | Bonus |
|---|---|---|---|---|
| 1. | Robin Yount, ss | Brewers (1) | 77.1 | $60,000 |
| 2. | Eddie Murray, 1b | Orioles (3) | 68.2 | $25,500 |
| 3. | Dave Winfield, of | Padres (1) | 64.0 | $65,000 |
| 4. | Jack Clark, rhp/of | Giants (13) | 52.9 | $10,000 |
| 5. | Fred Lynn, of | Red Sox (2) | 49.9 | $40,000 |
| 6. | Jim Sundberg, c | Rangers (Jan.-S/1) | 40.3 | $10,000 |
| 7. | Dwayne Murphy, of | Athletics (15) | 33.0 | $6,000 |
| 8. | Mike Flanagan, lhp | Orioles (7) | 26.3 | $5,000 |
| 9. | Mike Krukow, rhp | Cubs (8) | 24.1 | $9,000 |
| 10. | Ruppert Jones, of | Royals (3) | 22.5 | $21,000 |
| 11. | John Stearns, c | Phillies (1) | 19.5 | $53,000 |
| 12. | Dick Ruthven, rhp | Phillies (Jan.-S/1) | 18.6 | $62,500 |
| 13. | Ron LeFlore, of | Tigers (NDFA) | 17.8 | $2,500 |
| 14. | Warren Cromartie, of | Expos (June-S/1) | 16.2 | $20,000 |
| 15. | Gary Roenicke, ss | Expos (1) | 15.5 | $65,000 |
| 16. | Lee Mazzilli, of | Mets (1) | 15.4 | $50,000 |
| 17. | Wayne Gross, 1b | Athletics (9) | 15.0 | $7,000 |
| 18. | Mike Heath, c | Yankees (2) | 13.4 | $30,000 |
| 19. | Len Barker, rhp | Rangers (3) | 12.7 | $16,000 |
| 20. | LaMarr Hoyt, rhp | Yankees (5) | 12.4 | $15,000 |
| 21. | Rick Langford, rhp | Pirates (NDFA) | 11.0 | None |
| 22. | Bob McClure, lhp | Royals (June-S/3) | 10.8 | $5,000 |
| 23. | Joe Sambito, lhp | Astros (17) | 9.0 | $2,500 |
| 24. | Pete Falcone, lhp | Giants (June-S/1) | 8.9 | $6,000 |

| Top 3 Unsigned Players | | | | Year Signed |
|---|---|---|---|---|
| 1. | Floyd Bannister, lhp | Athletics (3) | 26.9 | 1976 |
| 2. | Bob Stanley, rhp | Dodgers (9) | 24.3 | 1974 |
| 3. | Jeff Reardon, rhp | Expos (23) | 19.2 | 1977 |

physically," Herzog said. "He ran with the veterans at night. He didn't have a chance to learn the game and how to conduct himself.

"I warned them they might lose a great pitcher. He was a good kid and a tough competitor, but he was into something he couldn't handle."

### WINFIELD, BANE START ON TOP

Clyde wasn't the only high-profile pick from the 1973 draft to debut in the big leagues.

Days after outfielder Dave Winfield, picked fourth overall by the San Diego Padres, was named MVP of the College World Series for a Minnesota team that didn't even reach the championship game, the Padres thrust him into their starting lineup on June 19. The Twins did the same July 4 with their first-round pick, Arizona State lefthander Eddie Bane (11th overall), who like Clyde attracted a sellout crowd to his debut.

A fourth player, Philadelphia Phillies righthander Dick Ruthven, also debuted in the big leagues. But Ruthven, the top pick in the January secondary phase, at least had the benefit of an entire spring training before making his first big league appearance on April 17.

The 6-foot-6 Winfield remains one of the greatest athletes ever drafted.

As a basketball player, Winfield was a starting forward on Minnesota's nationally ranked hoops squad. Following his senior year, he was drafted by the National Basketball Association's Atlanta

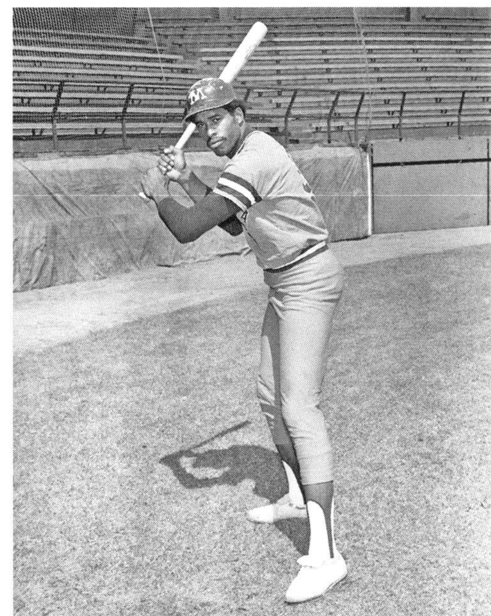

Few athletes in history can match Dave Winfield, who was a two-way star at Minnesota and was drafted in three professional sports

Hawks and the American Basketball Association's Utah Stars. The National Football League's Minnesota Vikings also recognized Winfield's potential. They drafted him in 1973 as a prospective tight end, even though he never played a down in college.

Baseball? Winfield was no ordinary talent there, either. Prior to signing with the Padres as an outfielder, Winfield was better known for his pitching exploits. In fact, it wasn't until the previous summer, while playing for the National Baseball Congress champion Alaska Goldpanners, that Winfield started playing with any regularity in the outfield—and then only because another player unexpectedly signed a pro contract. Scouts said Winfield's talent was so exceptional that he would have been a first-round pick at any position.

"We want him as an everyday player," Padres player personnel director Bob Fontaine said. "With his ability to run and hit and throw, we think he would be more of an asset in the lineup every day."

"I really think that I could do either," Winfield said. "But they think of me as an outfielder, so that's what I'll be."

Though drafted by the Padres to play a position, the hard-throwing Winfield left his mark as a pitcher. His final performance was one of the most remarkable in college baseball history.

The scene: the semifinals of the 1973 College World Series. Against a University of Southern California team that would go on to win its fourth title in a row and included such future big leaguers as Fred Lynn, Roy Smalley, Rich Dauer and Steve Kemp, Winfield was working on a one-hit shutout with 15 strikeouts through eight innings. He led 7-0, but tired in the ninth and was lifted. Incredibly, USC rallied to score eight runs in the inning, and won 8-7. Earlier in the series, Winfield beat Oklahoma 1-0, striking out 14. For the year, he was 9-1 with 109 strikeouts in 82 innings. He never pitched again.

Following the CWS, Winfield signed with San

## AT A GLANCE

America honors as a junior. In the minors, he also had better credentials than any first-rounder in 1973, hitting .295 overall with 98 homers and 391 RBIs, though it never translated into major league success.

### One Who Got Away

**FLOYD BANNISTER, LHP, ATHLETICS (3RD ROUND).** The A's took a stab at drafting Bannister out of Seattle's Kennedy High, where he went 16-0, 0.00 as a senior. He did not sign and went on to have a spectacular college career at Arizona State that led to his being the top pick in the 1976 draft.

### He Was Drafted?

**BRAD VAN PELT, RHP, CARDINALS (JANUARY/SECONDARY, 1ST ROUND); PIRATES (JUNE/SECONDARY, 5TH ROUND).** Numerous big league teams tried to lure Van Pelt, a standout pitching prospect in high school and at Michigan State, but he was steadfast in his desire to play football and went on to become a five-time all-pro linebacker in a 14-year NFL career.

### Did You Know . . .

**LEE MAZZILLI,** selected first overall by the Mets in 1973 out of a local high school, was an eight-time national youth speed-skating champion. He also established a Class A California League record by stealing seven bases in one game.

### They Said It

**WHITEY HERZOG,** on the way the Rangers mishandled No. 1 pick **DAVID CLYDE** by sending him straight to the big leagues: "It was the worst thing for him, physically and mentally. He ran with the veterans at night . . . He didn't have a chance to learn the game and how to conduct himself. I warned them they might lose a great pitcher. He was a good kid and a tough competitor, but he was into something he couldn't handle."

## DRAFT SPOTLIGHT: ROBIN YOUNT

Robin Yount jumped to the major leagues at age 18 and didn't slow down until he reached the Hall of Fame

Robin Yount was 18, less than a year out of high school, when Milwaukee Brewers manager Del Crandall spotted him for the first time.

"The talent was obvious," Crandall said. "It was the fourth or fifth day of spring training, and I said to him, 'You want some ground balls?' He said yes. Well, you know how rough some of those Arizona infields are. He made this one look as smooth as glass by the way he was scooping up all those balls. I hit him 20 or 25, then walked over to (Brewers director of baseball operations) Jim Wilson and said to him, 'Is there any possible reason why an 18-year-old kid can't open up as our shortstop?' Wilson said, 'I don't see why not.'"

The rest was history. Yount, who hit .285 in 64 games at Newark of the short-season New York-Penn League in his pro debut, opened the 1974 season in Milwaukee—the youngest player in the big leagues, playing a position that might have been the most demanding in the game. He was still five months shy of his 19th birthday.

The quiet but confident Yount survived four hitless games to begin his career, but held his own at the plate and in the field over the balance of the 1974 season, and went on to spend the next 19 years as a regular with the Brewers. He played the first 12 at shortstop, and the final eight as an outfielder when his powerful throwing arm began going lame.

A .285 hitter overall, Yount achieved his 3,000th career hit in 1992, becoming the third-youngest player in major league history to achieve the feat. He went on to collect 3,142, won two American League MVP awards, in 1982 and 1989, and still holds Brewers career records in most offensive categories. He was selected to the Hall of Fame in 1999, in his first year of eligibility.

To Yount, age was never a factor when he broke in with the Brewers. "I don't think about my age," he said during his rookie season. "I can't worry about how old I am. There are too many other things for me to think about."

Yount hit .455 with three homers as a high school senior in Woodland Hills, Calif., and fanned 17 in nine innings of relief duty on his way to being named the Los Angeles city player of the year and the third pick in the draft. He was signed by Brewers scouting director Jim Baumer, who five years earlier signed Robin's older brother Larry for the Houston Astros. "We had quite a go of it before he signed," remembered Baumer. "They wanted more money than we were willing to give."

Yount finally agreed to a $60,000 bonus on June 27, becoming one of the last first-rounders to sign, and passing on a college career at Arizona State. Less than a year later, when Yount was already Milwaukee's starting shortstop, he quipped to Baumer, "See? I told you I should have been given more money."

Diego for a package deal worth roughly $100,000, including a bonus of $65,000. He remains one of only three athletes over the 50-year life of the baseball draft to be chosen in three different professional drafts. The other two—Mickey McCarty and Dave Logan—both elected to play in the NFL.

"I decided on baseball because I think I'm better at that and because I think I can get more money doing it than anything else," Winfield said, foreshadowing the enormous 10-year contract he signed with the New York Yankees as a free agent after the 1979 season. "I never reached my full potential in basketball. I know I can play the game. A lot of people wonder if I could have made it in basketball."

Fontaine was quick to recognize Winfield's unique talent. "There's no limit," he said. "He can become as great as he wants to be. Physically, there's nothing he can't do in this game."

Winfield began his career in San Diego and never spent a day in the minor leagues. He went on to play 22 seasons in the majors, compiling a .283 batting average with 3,110 hits and 465 home runs, while also stealing 223 bases. He also won seven Gold Gloves for his defensive excellence.

Oddly, Twins scouting director George Brophy said his club had no interest in drafting Winfield, a hometown boy with enormous local appeal, but that became academic as Winfield was gone when the Twins made their initial selection. They went for Bane, a crafty southpaw who went 15-1 as a junior at Arizona State in 1973, and a remarkable 41-4 in three years. He also established NCAA single-season (192) and career (505) strikeout records.

Bane pitched the only perfect game in ASU history against Cal State Northridge on March 2, striking out 19 in the process. In a spring exhibition game, he beat the California Angels, 3-2, striking out nine.

"That game took him out of the realm of being just another good college pitcher," Sun Devils coach Jim Brock said.

Twins officials became convinced that Bane, the college player of the year, could help the major league club immediately after watching him shut down Winfield's Minnesota team, 3-0 with 12 strikeouts, in his only start at the College World Series. "He showed me in Omaha that he has command and poise," Brophy said.

A day after Clyde, the high school sensation and No. 1 pick, made his debut in front of a packed house in Texas, tight-fisted Twins owner Calvin Griffith declared that Bane would begin his career under similar pomp and circumstance. A packed house Griffith got, but he made Bane a sacrificial lamb in the process.

### Fastest To The Majors

| | Player, Pos. | Drafted (Round) | Debut |
|---|---|---|---|
| 1. | # Dick Ruthven, rhp | Phillies (Jan.-S/1) | April 17, 1973 |
| 2. | # Dave Winfield, of | Padres (1) | June 19, 1973 |
| 3. | *# David Clyde, lhp | Rangers (1) | June 27, 1973 |
| 4. | # Eddie Bane, lhp | Twins (1) | July 4, 1973 |
| 5. | Jim Sundberg, c | Rangers (Jan.-S/1) | April 4, 1974 |

**LAST PLAYER TO RETIRE:** Eddie Murray, 1b (Sept. 20, 1997)

*#Debuted in major leagues. *High school selection.*

## Top 25 Bonuses

| Player, Pos. | Drafted (Round) | Order | Bonus |
|---|---|---|---|
| **1. Alan Bannister, ss** | **Phillies (Jan.-R/1)** | **(1)** | **$85,000** |
| **2. * David Clyde, lhp** | **Rangers (1)** | **1** | **#$65,000** |
| **Dave Winfield, of/rhp** | **Padres (1)** | **4** | **#$65,000** |
| *** Gary Roenicke, ss** | **Expos (1)** | **8** | **$65,000** |
| * Doug Heinold, rhp | Yankees (1) | 13 | $65,000 |
| 6. * Lew Olsen, lhp | Royals (1) | 9 | $64,000 |
| **7. Dick Ruthven, rhp** | **Phillies (Jan.-S/1)** | **(1)** | **$62,500** |
| **8. * Robin Yount, ss** | **Brewers (1)** | **3** | **$60,000** |
| **9. * Joe Edelen, 3b/rhp** | **Cardinals (1)** | **12** | **$58,000** |
| **10. John Stearns, c** | **Phillies (1)** | **2** | **$53,000** |
| 11. * Billy Taylor, of | Angels (1) | 7 | $50,000 |
| *** Lee Mazzilli, of** | **Mets (1)** | **14** | **$50,000** |
| 13. * Ted Farr, c | Dodgers (1) | 18 | $48,000 |
| 14. * Glenn Tufts, 1b | Indians (1) | 5 | $40,000 |
| *** Pat Rockett, ss** | **Braves (1)** | **10** | **$40,000** |
| **Steve Swisher, c** | **White Sox (1)** | **21** | **$40,000** |
| **Fred Lynn, of** | **Red Sox (2)** | **41** | **$40,000** |
| * Mike Paciorek, of | Dodgers (2) | 42 | $40,000 |
| **19. * Johnnie LeMaster, ss** | **Giants (1)** | **6** | **$38,000** |
| *** Steve Nicosia, c** | **Pirates (1)** | **24** | **$38,000** |
| **21. Jerry Tabb, 1b** | **Cubs (1)** | **16** | **$37,000** |
| **22. * Ted Cox, ss** | **Red Sox (1)** | **17** | **$35,000** |
| * Brad Kessler, of | Reds (1) | 22 | $35,000 |
| 24. * John Hughes, c | Phillies (4) | 74 | $32,500 |
| **25. Eddie Bane, lhp** | **Twins (1)** | **11** | **#$30,500** |

*Major leaguers in bold. *High school selection. #Major league contract.*

Bane, 21, made his professional debut July 4 in front of the largest regular-season crowd in Twins history: 45,890. The game was delayed 15 minutes to allow the throng of fans to reach their seats.

He dazzled Kansas City with his curve, control and craftiness, stopping the Royals on three hits over seven innings. He left leading 2-1 in a game the Twins eventually lost, 5-4.

"They figured they might as well see what I had right off the bat," Bane said. "We got caught up in a whirlwind."

Thereafter, it was all downhill for Bane. The crafty little lefty didn't win a game in 1973, going 0-5, 4.92 in 23 appearances, including six starts. With the exception of a couple of brief return engagements to Minnesota in 1975 and 1976, when he won a combined seven games, he spent the rest of his career in the minor leagues.

"I'd like to think I was ready for the big leagues right out of college," Bane said later, "but I wasn't. Maybe if I had gone to the minor leagues for one year, it would have been different."

But Bane also felt the Twins gave up on him after that first season. "That one year was enough for Minnesota," he said. "After that, they started looking for somebody else. They formed an opinion on what I did that first year. That really isn't fair, but it happens a lot in baseball. Once you get a bad rap, it stays with you."

In the end, Bane's size proved to be his undoing.

"All my life," the 5-foot-9, 165-pound Bane said, "people told me I was too small. I was too small for high school football, too small for high school baseball, too small for the colleges, too small for the big leagues."

Bane may have been small in stature but he overcame his lack of physical presence, especially in college, by resorting to and relying on the finer points of pitching—some legal, some not. He had uncanny control of all his pitches and baseball intelligence that went well beyond his years. He employed every trick in the book to deceive hitters, and admitted deploying a spitball, at times.

"I was cutting the ball, scuffing the ball, throwing spitballs in college," Bane said. "You were just trying to get any edge you could on the hitters. I used Firm-Grip, pine tar, that type of stuff to make the breaking pitch break better."

But Bane said there was a big difference between pitching to college hitters and veteran, savvy big leaguers. He didn't exactly overwhelm Triple-A hitters, either, with his limited arsenal.

Eddie Bane

"I had an excellent curve in college and everybody knew it," he said. "It got to the point where hitters would see it coming and start swinging. I got a lot of strikeouts that way. They didn't even have to be strikes a lot of times. Up there the hitters are a little more disciplined. They didn't swing at it as much. And everybody knows I'm not going to throw the ball by anybody."

Bane was left defenseless when the trademark curve that made him so effective in the amateur ranks deserted him as a professional.

"I had been in pro ball about a year," he said, "when the curve just disappeared. Suddenly, it wasn't there anymore. I somehow lost it. I didn't hurt my arm. I remember a guy watching me pitch and asking me when I hurt my arm. I didn't."

The trick pitches that Bane mastered at ASU helped him survive when his bread-and-butter pitch went astray, but he soon drifted through the minors, and eventually went to Mexico to pitch before he hung it up in 1981.

Bane later went on to become one of the most respected judges of pitching talent in the game as a scout, and had a noteworthy stint as scouting director of the Los Angeles Angels.

Despite the attention Winfield and Bane earned as two of 22 players in draft history to debut in the big leagues, however, everything paled in comparison to the intrigue surrounding Clyde, who scouts agreed was head and shoulders above the rest of the talent in the regular phase of the June draft.

"You have Clyde far above everybody else, and then there's a big drop off down to whatever comes after him," said Lou Fitzgerald, Southwest area scout for the Phillies, who had the second pick. "We'd love to have him, but we don't see any way Texas can pass him by. Everybody I've talked to said he is by far the best talent available."

### STAR QUALITY IN FIRST ROUND

The top four picks in the June regular phase reached the big leagues faster than any quartet in draft history. The third pick overall, shortstop Robin Yount, was 18, with a half-season of minor league experience under his belt, when he opened

### WORTH NOTING

■ The Cardinals used the 12th pick in the 1973 draft to pick **JOE EDELEN**, who still holds the distinction of being part of the greatest combined strikeout game in prep baseball annals. While a junior in October 1971 at Gracemont (Okla.) High, Edelen hooked up with Asher High's Billy Brimm in the Oklahoma Class B fall state championship game. The contest went 17 innings and Asher won 1-0 to capture the second of five straight state titles, but the game was noteworthy because both Brimm (37) and Edelen (35) went the distance and combined to strike out 72 batters. Edelen allowed just three hits and walked two.

■ Southern California won its fourth consecutive College World Series championship in 1973, beating Arizona State in the championship game, 4-3, for the second year in a row. But it was a highly charged early-season encounter between the two powers—or, more specifically, between **EDDIE BANE**, ASU's record-breaking lefthander, and **FRED LYNN**, the talented Trojans center fielder—that helped shape the 1973 draft. The matchup attracted a throng of scouts from around the country, and Bane upstaged Lynn by fanning him four times. It cemented Bane's standing as a first-rounder and probably knocked down Lynn to the second round. "As cocky as I was then, I was pretty sure I was better than Fred Lynn," Bane said later. "Here's Fred Lynn, one of the greats, drafted in the second round, basically because I ate him up. Here I am in the first round. That shouldn't have happened. But it did."

■ The Trojans featured righthander **RANDY SCARBERY** (15-2, 1.83), who became the first player of the draft era to be selected in the first round of the June regular phase on two different occasions. In 1970, Scarbery was drafted by the Astros out of a Fresno, Calif.,

CONTINUED ON PAGE 142

## WORTH NOTING

CONTINUED FROM PAGE 141

high school, but rejected a reported $65,000 offer. Three NCAA championships and 31 wins later, Scarbery was again drafted in the first round by the Athletics. This time, the offer was substantially less: $32,500. Scarbery pitched with Oakland's Triple-A club for five seasons without ever seeing the big leagues. He finally reached his goal in 1979, with the White Sox. By then his spirit and his skills had eroded. He went 3-10 in his two seasons with the White Sox. Scarbery expressed no regrets about his decision as a prep senior to turn down the Astros big offer and postpone his pro debut. "I always felt I did the right thing in going to school," he said near the end of his brief big league career. "I might have become discouraged playing a year or two in Class A. I'm happy with my decision. But you can't help thinking about the huge salaries Fred Lynn, Roy Smalley and Dave Kingman, guys I played with in college, are getting now."

■ Ranger (Texas) won the 1973 Junior College World Series, almost entirely on the strength of righthander **DONNIE MOORE**, who set tournament records for wins, innings and strikeouts. Not only did Moore win all of Ranger's games, but no pitcher has ever duplicated his record of four wins since. Moore had been the third overall pick in the secondary phase of the January draft in 1973, and the Cubs made sure he wouldn't re-enter the June draft by signing him to a $25,000 bonus after the tournament. Moore carved out a solid big league career as a closer, but became one of the tragic figures of the 1973 draft when in 1986, as a member of the Angels, he gave up one of the most memorable home runs in baseball history—a shot by Boston's Dave Henderson that propelled the Red Sox into the World Series. Overcome by grief from that incident, he killed himself less than three years later.

the 1974 season at shortstop for the Milwaukee Brewers. John Stearns, a power-hitting catcher from the University of Colorado selected second by Philadelphia, was up with the Phillies later in the 1974 season.

Like Winfield, Stearns was an acknowledged two-sport star in college. Not only did he lead the NCAA ranks with 15 homers and a .819 slugging average in 1973, while batting .413, but he also was an all-Big Eight Conference safety who was drafted by the NFL's Buffalo Bills earlier in the year.

Stearns wasn't sure whether he wanted to pursue a career in baseball or football. He thought his chances of making it were better in football, but the Phillies made up his mind for him, steering him to baseball with a $53,000 signing bonus. A year later, he was in the big leagues.

"Baseball is a much harder game to play," he said. "Hitting is the hardest thing I've ever had to do athletically. Before I heard I went second in the draft, I really thought it would be easier to make an NFL club."

John Stearns

Stearns wasn't selected until the 17th round of the NFL draft by the Bills, but that wasn't indicative of his ability.

"I heard that I went low in the football draft because most of the teams knew I'd go high in the baseball draft," he said. "As a matter of fact, (Buffalo) coach (Lou) Saban called me during the NFL draft to ask about my plans to play football or baseball.

"I was very surprised to be chosen second in the baseball draft. I was pretty sure I'd go in the first round, but to be chosen second, well, I wasn't prepared for that."

Stearns went on to play a single game with the Phillies, on Sept. 22, 1974, before being swapped to the New York Mets in a six-player deal that brought pitcher Tug McGraw to Philadelphia following that season.

He was a four-time all-star with the Mets, and in 1978 set a modern National League record for stolen bases by a catcher with 25. But in 1982, he severely injured a tendon in his throwing arm. An arduous two-year rehabilitation period failed to restore the snap in his arm, and his career was effectively over after the injury. In 810 games in the majors, he hit .260 with 46 homers.

Stearns and Winfield also shared the plight of being college seniors who were ineligible for the draft in 1972 as juniors, because they were not 21. It would be another three years before that rule was amended, making all college juniors eligible for selection.

### TALENT THINS OUT QUICKLY

The star power at the top of the 1973 draft was as significant as any draft in history, and it remains the only one with two Hall of Famers (Yount and Winfield) among the initial four selections.

### Largest Bonuses By Round

| | Player, Pos. | Club | Bonus |
|---|---|---|---|
| **1.** | *** David Clyde, lhp** | **Rangers** | **$65,000** |
| 2. | * Ron Selak, rhp | Cardinals | $42,500 |
| **3.** | *** Eddie Murray, lhp** | **Orioles** | **$25,500** |
| 4. | * John Hughes, c | Phillies | $32,500 |
| **5.** | *** Dave Geisel, lhp** | **Cubs** | **$24,500** |
| **6.** | *** Mike Dimmel, of** | **Dodgers** | **$17,000** |
| 7. | * Steve Grimes, 3b | Giants | $25,000 |
| **8.** | *** Randy Lerch, lhp** | **Phillies** | **$20,000** |
| 9. | * Thomas Frizzi, of | Pirates | $10,000 |
| 10. | * James Barrett, lhp | White Sox | $15,000 |
| **Jan/R.** | **Alan Bannister, ss** | **Phillies (1)** | **$85,000** |
| **Jan/S.** | **Dick Ruthven, rhp** | **Phillies (1)** | **$62,500** |
| **Jun/S.** | **Warren Cromartie, 1b/of** | **Expos (1)** | **$20,000** |

*Major leaguers in bold. *High school selection.*

Yet the 1973 draft overall was considered one of the leanest ever. The talent thinned out noticeably after the first four selections, and only 110 players from both June phases reached the big leagues, a record low. Of that number, 36 went unsigned.

There was growing concern among baseball officials at the time that the talent overall was beginning to dry up, as only 785 players were selected. That total would bottom out a year later.

In stark contrast to Yount and Winfield, two of the next three selections, first baseman Glenn Tufts (Indians, fifth overall) and outfielder Billy Taylor (Angels, seventh), never came close to reaching the big leagues, though in the case of Tufts it stemmed from a horrific car accident five months after he was drafted by Cleveland.

Tufts was returning to his Bridgewater, Mass., home on a rainy night when his car skidded on slick pavement, sideswiped a parked car and smashed into a telephone pole.

"I knew I was hurt," said Tufts, who was able to free himself from his car. "I felt the pain in my ankle and hip. I just hoped it wasn't serious."

Tufts sustained a broken pelvis, broken ribs, damaged kidneys and a broken left leg. All were serious injuries, but he was expected to recover with normal rehabilitation. Yet Tufts remained in the hospital until January, had to walk with crutches, then a cane. By spring training, he was back in uniform with the Indians.

It didn't seem possible that his promising career was over. But it essentially was.

From the start of spring training, it was obvious that Tufts was still injured. He hobbled badly, the pain was evident and intense. X-rays were taken but showed no reason for his continued discomfort.

After beginning the 1974 season on the disabled list, Tufts finally found the reason for his piercing pain in another x-ray. A sliver of bone was wedged inside his foot, just below the left ankle. It had been hidden in previous pictures.

"The doctors told us it would require breaking two joints to get to the trouble," Indians farm director Bob Quinn said. "They told us the risk was too great. The leg might be damaged further. They didn't want to try it."

Tufts was advised of the reluctance of surgeons to operate. But he was unwavering.

"I thought I might not play again if I had the operation," he said, "but I knew I wouldn't play again if I didn't have it."

In June, a year after he was drafted, Tufts had surgery. Three pins were put into his foot. He was on crutches for six months, by which time his leg atrophied so much it became thinner than his forearm. Finally the pins were removed and he began another round of rehabilitation. The pain diminished. Again Tufts reported to spring training—20 months since he last played. But the recovery was slow and he had lost his conditioning.

"He hobbled so badly," Quinn said, "we wouldn't let him run."

Tufts started the 1975 season on the inactive roster at Class A San Jose and eventually was activated in a DH role. Slowly, he began to get his stroke back. Toward the end of the season, he began playing first base again. He hit .270 in 102 games, with nine homers.

After the season, Tufts had another operation to fuse bones in his ankle, which was designed to increase his mobility. It was an operation that should have been done to begin with.

Glenn Tufts

Tufts continued to work hard to return himself to the form he displayed at Bridgewater-Raynham High, where he hit more than .500 three years in a row and was a feared young slugger. He was the first three-time, all-state baseball player in Massachusetts since Tony Conigliaro, one of the greatest players in New England prep history.

But Tufts' efforts to rehabilitate his career were all in vain. Over the next two seasons, he failed miserably in two promotions to Double-A, hitting .115 and .163. By 1977, at age 22, his career was finished. He returned home, embittered over his failure to realize his boyhood dream.

A schoolboy hero, Tufts eventually became the baseball coach at Bridgewater State College. He later became an instructor, minor league manager and longtime scout in the Northeast for the San Francisco Giants. He had plenty of time to reflect on a major league career that never was.

"Just to play in the big leagues . . . one game," said Tufts, who received a $40,000 bonus to sign with the Indians. "I knew I had the ability, but I didn't get a chance. A lot of first-rounders don't make it, but they went as far as their ability took them. For me, it just wasn't meant to be. That's the only way you can think about it, or else it will drive you crazy."

Injuries also played a key role in the fortunes of a second player chosen in the top 10 picks in 1973, righthander Lew Olsen, who was selected ninth overall by the Royals. In Olsen's case, he believes his baseball career ended the day it started.

After signing out of San Ramon High in Alamo, Calif., Olsen immediately reported to the Royals' Rookie-league Billings club in the Pioneer League.

"I threw BP the first day I got to Billings, and I think that's when it all started," Olsen said. "I was a young kid. I had been a first-round pick, then I joined the club and I felt like I still had to go out and impress people. It was wrong. Boy, was it wrong. A few days later, I couldn't even push a door with my right arm."

Olsen, who accepted a $64,000 bonus from the Royals to pass up a scholarship offer to play both football and baseball at Stanford, made just three brief appearances in Billings, working 10 innings.

The 6-foot-4, 220-pound righthander soon began making steady progress in the Royals system, reaching Triple-A in 1976, but rarely displayed the 90-plus mph velocity that he was known for in high school. Instead, he developed a reputation as a short-armer who relied more on finesse than raw power to get hitters out.

Olsen believes he became that type of pitcher because of the pain he endured throughout his seven-year career, though Royals officials said it was probably due to his mechanics.

He finally had arm surgery in April 1978, causing him to miss that season. A year later, when the Royals sent him back to the Rookie-level Gulf Coast League, back where it all started for him six years earlier, he knew his career was over. In 106 minor league appearances, Olsen went 33-35, 3.26. He struck out just 270 in 594 innings.

In the end, though, the biggest disappointment of all in the 1973 draft might have been Clyde.

"His first six starts, he pitched very well," Herzog said. "But after that it was all downhill. After a couple of homers were hit off him, he lost confidence and couldn't get his curve over. The hitters just laid back for his fastball.

"I felt sorry for him. I told his mother I'd take care of him, but I got fired."

Billy Martin replaced Herzog as manager of the Rangers in 1974. Clyde started fast, winning his first three games, but things would never again be the same for the young lefthander. He lost nine games in a row and the confidence of Martin, who engaged in a power struggle with the Texas front office. He demanded that Clyde be sent to the minor leagues, to no avail. Caught in the middle, a bewildered Clyde went 31 days without so much as even warming up on the sidelines.

"Billy didn't want me there and the front office

## One Team's Draft: Baltimore Orioles

| Player, Pos. | Bonus | Player, Pos. | Bonus | Player, Pos. | Bonus |
|---|---|---|---|---|---|
| **1. *Mike Parrott, rhp** | **$20,000** | 5. *Michael Hile, lhp | $17,000 | 9. *David Obal, c | $6,000 |
| 2. *Jerry Guinn, rhp | $25,000 | 6. Ricky Ryser, rhp | $5,000 | 10. *Steven Ramsey, ss | Did not sign |
| **3. *Eddie Murray, 1b** | **$25,500** | **7. Mike Flanagan, lhp** | **$5,000** | **Other John Flinn (Jan.-S/2), rhp** | **$5,000** |
| 4. *Don Whiting, of | $15,000 | 8. Ed Bowman, 3b/c | Did not sign | | |

*Major leaguers in bold. *High school selection.*

### WORTH NOTING

■ The team Moore beat in the final, Gulf Coast (Fla.) JC, was absent its best pitcher, **BOB PURKEY JR.**, son of the longtime big league pitcher. Purkey, a second-round pick of the Dodgers in the secondary phase of the January 1973 draft, collapsed while swimming prior to the opening of the tournament, remained in a coma and subsequently died of an undiagnosed heart ailment.

■ For only the second time in the draft's early history, every first-round pick in the June regular phase signed—even Cal State Los Angeles first baseman **CHARLES BATES**, who had been drafted five times previously. Bates, the 19th overall pick, was signed primarily for his bat, but went on to hit .259 with 22 homers in four minor league seasons, while never advancing beyond Double-A.

■ The Red Sox' selection in the first round of the January/regular phase was voided by the commissioner's office when it was revealed that third baseman **LLOYD THOMPSON** was attending the University of New Mexico. Players from four-year colleges were not eligible for the January phase. Boston officials believed Thompson was still enrolled at Blinn (Texas) Junior College.

■ A change in draft rules in 1973 provided that players who had been selected at least 13 months previously would become eligible for selection in the regular phase of the June draft. In the past, re-drafted players like Stearns and Winfield would have been relegated to the secondary phase. With that change, a record-low 38 players were selected in the secondary phase.

■ In the last year wood bats were used in the college ranks, Arizona State set an NCAA record for team batting average (.333), while USC established a season mark for homers. ASU had more players drafted than any other college (seven) in June.

**IN FOCUS: EDDIE MURRAY**

Eddie Murray was one of the last great players to emerge from a golden era of baseball in inner-city Los Angeles. From roughly 1955-1980, the playgrounds teemed with players bent on following in the footsteps of Jackie Robinson, Willie Mays and Hank Aaron.

Even against the backdrop of increasing racial tension—symbolized by the Watts riots of 1965—and economic strife, baseball offered a way out for the likes of Reggie Smith, Bobby Tolan, Willie Crawford and Bob Watson, among the many African-Americans who reached the pinnacle of the game. One school alone, Fremont High, produced 18 future big leaguers in that period.

No one from that era of baseball in Los Angeles impacted the game quite like Murray, and all four of his brothers also went on to professional careers. Ozzie Smith was a teammate of Murray's at Locke High in 1973, and became no less a star, though he took a more circuitous route to the Hall of Fame as he was passed over in the 1973 draft.

Though Murray wasn't selected until the third round, he was in the big leagues by 1977, when he was American League rookie of the year, and went on to hit .287 with 504 home runs and 1,917 RBIs in an esteemed 21-year career.

did, and I paid the price," Clyde said later. "I didn't pitch for 31 days and nothing was explained to me. I was afraid to ask what I could do about it. It was just one of those political things."

He was eventually sent out, but by then the dream was tarnished. Clyde's out pitch, his curve, was long gone by that time, never to return on a consistent basis. Over the years, Clyde battled arm injuries, broken marriages, a drinking problem—and ultimately, the spectre of unfulfilled potential. By 1981, he was finished.

Clyde, who went 18-33 as a major leaguer, never expressed resentment for the way he was handled. But he often wondered how things might have been had he been allowed to develop his craft in the minor leagues from the start.

"Things would have been different," he said. "I'm not the first kid who got used, and I won't be the last. But I don't regret anything. I had my opportunity. I can say I was there."

As disappointing as Clyde's career, as well as those of numerous other first-rounders, turned out, the baseball draft has a way of leveling the field with the unexpected success of players selected in later rounds. There was no better example of that in the 1973 draft than first baseman Eddie Murray, a future Hall of Famer who wasn't selected until the third round by the Baltimore Orioles.

### PHILLIES PICK FIRST TWICE

The Phillies earned the right to pick first in the regular phase of the January draft because of their lowly 59-97 record in the strike-shortened 1972 season, and lucked out in also obtaining the top selection in the secondary phase, where the order was established randomly.

It appeared to be a significant coup at the time for the downtrodden Phillies as it enabled them to scoop up the two players who would have been slam-dunk first-round picks in June had they elected to return to college for their senior years. Both dropped out during the fall, making them eligible in January.

In the regular phase, the Phillies went for shortstop Alan Bannister, Arizona State's two-time All-American. Like Stearns and Winfield, Bannister was not draft-eligible in 1972 after his junior year at ASU, because he wasn't 21 at the time. Bannister signed for $85,000, the largest bonus awarded in 1973. In all probability, he would have been one of the top two or three picks in June had he elected to play his senior year of college.

Bannister, an unsigned first-round pick of the Angels in 1969 out of a California high school, deliberated long and hard whether to drop out of college, but finally decided it was the prudent thing to do to get his blossoming baseball career rolling at the professional level.

"I had done as much as I could in college and figured it was time to give pro baseball a try," Bannister said in announcing his decision, Sept. 14, 1972. "I just felt that the money and the bonus of spring training next year has to make it worth my while. Besides, I couldn't get myself up for another spring of Northern Colorado, Wisconsin and Texas-El Paso."

"It's not your everyday situation," ASU coach Jim Brock said. "Almost every scout I've talked to regards him as the top prospect in the nation."

In 1972 at Arizona State, Bannister established NCAA records for hits (101), RBIs (90) and total bases (177) while hitting .380 and stealing 28 bases. A year earlier, he set a college record with 13 triples.

By many accounts, he was the best prospect to come out of the college ranks to that point in the draft era—or at least since ASU slugger Reggie Jackson in 1966—among baseball officials surveyed.

The Phillies had every expectation that Bannister would be a star at the big league level.

"He can field, he can run, he can throw, he can steal bases," said Merrill Combs, the Phillies' southern California scout who had tracked Bannister for years. "He's a shortstop with all the tools it takes to play shortstop. He's also a good enough athlete to adjust to any position they decide he can play to help them the most—third, second, center field. He's just an outstanding prospect."

Because veteran Larry Bowa was entrenched as the Phillies shortstop, Bannister played in only 50 games in Philadelphia. A career .270 hitter, he lasted 12 years in the big leagues—never quite fulfilling all the expectations that were heaped on him in 1973.

In the secondary phase, the Phillies landed Ruthven, who was Minnesota's first-round pick (eighth overall) the previous June as a junior, but went unsigned and chose not to return to Fresno State, where in 1972 he was 10-3 with 153 strikeouts in 111 innings.

With Bannister and Ruthven on board, along with the selection of Stearns in June, Philadelphia appeared to have gained a windfall opportunity to reverse years of losing at the big league level. The Phillies did in fact become one of the elite teams in the game over most of the remainder of the decade—though not because of the contributions of Bannister, Ruthven or Stearns.

Ruthven gave the Phillies pitching staff an immediate lift, opening the 1973 season with the big league club, but went 17-24 in two-plus years in Philadelphia before being traded to Atlanta. Bannister spent all of the 1973 season in Triple-A, and never became a fixture with the Phillies, while Stearns played all of one game in Philadelphia before being traded to the Mets.

## Highest Unsigned Picks

**JUNE/REGULAR PHASE ONLY**

| Player, Pos., Team (Round) | College | Re-Drafted |
|---|---|---|
| Bruce Tonascia, of/c, Angels (2) | USC | Angels '76 (34) |
| Jim Gaudet, c, Braves (3) | Tulane | Royals '76 (6) |
| Steve Day, ss, Padres (3) | Texas | Giants '76 (36) |
| Floyd Bannister, lhp, Athletics (3) | Arizona State | Astros '76 (1/1) |
| Lynn Garrett, ss, Rangers (4) | Arizona | Indians '77 (11) |
| Tom Kinkelaar, rhp, Mets (4) | Miami (Ohio) | Not drafted |
| Bobby Mitchell, of, Giants (5) | USC | Dodgers '77 (7) |
| Mike Colbern, c, Royals (5) | Arizona State | White Sox '76 (2) |
| Tom Steinmetz, ss, Dodgers (5) | Iowa | Expos '76 (23) |
| Andrew Mason, 3b, Rangers (6) | Oregon State | Rangers '75 (Jan.-S/3) |

**TOTAL UNSIGNED PICKS:** Top 5 Rounds (9), Top 10 Rounds (51)

**Did not sign. Major leaguers in bold, with first and last years noted. Order of selection indicated in parentheses. For the first five rounds of the June Regular Phase and the first round of all other phases, the peak level of each player is noted.*

# 1973 Draft List

## ATLANTA BRAVES

### January—Regular Phase (9)

1. *Mike Kirkpatrick, rhp, Bucks County (Pa.) CC.—(High A)
2. *Mike Vernier, 3b, Aquinas (Mich.) College.
3. *Robert Kraft, 1b, Bellevue (Wash.) CC.
4. Mike Trifilois, 1b, Lafayette College.

### January—Secondary Phase (15)

1. **Brian Asselstine, of, Hancock (Calif.) JC.—(1976-81)**
2. ***Pete Falcone, lhp, Kingsborough (N.Y.) CC.—(1975-84)**
3. John Lacey, 1b, Bergen (N.J.) CC.

### June—Regular Phase (10)

1. **Pat Rockett, ss, Robert E. Lee HS, San Antonio, Texas.—(1976-78)**
2. Steve Stone, c, Doherty HS, Worcester, Mass.—(AA)
3. ***Jim Gaudet, c, Jesuit HS, New Orleans.—(1978-79)**

DRAFT DROP *Attended Tulane; re-drafted by Royals, 1976 (6th round)*

4. Bill Downing, ss, University of San Francisco.—(AA)
5. Paul Wagner, ss, Dickinson (Pa.) College.—(Rookie)
6. Jimmy Arline, of, Wilby HS, Waterbury, Conn.
7. *Alvin Jones, of, Seguin (Texas) HS.
8. *Randy Quintrell, lhp, Newton County HS, Covington, Ga.
9. Greg Kastner, rhp, Missouri Western State College.
10. Roger Cador, of, Southern University.

DRAFT DROP *Baseball coach, Southern University (1985-2015)*

11. *Mark Knose, rhp, Harrison (Ohio) HS.
12. *Gary Atwell, of, Arizona State University.
13. *Charles Phillips, lhp, La Quinta HS, Garden Grove, Calif.
14. George Ban, c, Kennedy HS, Sacramento, Calif.
15. *Adam Smith, rhp, Southland Academy, Americus, Ga.
16. **Terry Harper, rhp-of, Douglas County HS, Douglasville, Ga.—(1980-87)**
17. *Steve Barlow, lhp, Morehouse (Ga.) College.
18. *David Whitehurst, of-rhp, Walker HS, Decatur, Ga.
19. **Larry Bradford, lhp, Clark HS, Chicago.—(1977-81)**
20. *Rick Hays, rhp, Charter Oak HS, Glendora, Calif.
21. *Craig Hillard, of, Salisbury (N.C.) HS.
22. *Steve Barrett, 2b, Murray State University.
23. Michael Yates, rhp, Fairfield University.
24. Bobby Malone, c, Sullivan East HS, Piney Flats, Tenn.
25. Leland Byrd, ss, Gainesville (Ga.) HS.
26. William King, rhp, Southwest DeKalb HS, Decatur, Ga.
27. John McLean, rhp, Vanderbilt University.
28. *Mark Hamilton, 1b, North Springs HS, Sandy Springs, Ga.
29. *Jim Busby, lhp-of, Leesburg HS, Yalaha, Fla.

DRAFT DROP *Son of Jim Busby, major leaguer (1950-62)*

30. Anthony Taylor, of, Clark Atlanta College.

### June—Secondary Phase (14)

No selection.

## BALTIMORE ORIOLES

### January—Regular Phase (16)

1. Cleve Reed, of, Southeastern Oklahoma State University.—(Rookie)
2. *Richard Cuoco, 2b, Los Angeles Valley JC.

DRAFT DROP *Scouting director, Angels (1978-80)*

3. *Martin Fleming, rhp, Cypress (Calif.) JC.
4. *Jeff Budrick, p, Los Angeles Valley JC.
5. *Rickey Holoubek, ss, Pasadena (Calif.) CC.
6. ***Mark Lee, rhp, El Camino (Calif.) JC.—(1978-81)**
7. *Michael Manns, p, El Camino (Calif.) JC.
8. *Tom Kotchman, c, Chipola (Fla.) JC.

DRAFT DROP *Father of Casey Kotchman, first-round draft pick, Angels (2001); major leaguer (2004-13)*

9. *Alton Caesar, 3b-of, Sierra (Calif.) JC.

### January—Secondary Phase (16)

1. Alfred Aulwurm, lhp, Glendale (Calif.) JC.—Rookie)
2. **John Flinn, rhp, Los Angeles Valley JC.—(1978-82)**
3. **Gil Rondon, rhp, New York.—(1976-79)**
4. *James Joiner, c, Seminole (Fla.) CC.
5. *Richard Cahill, lhp, Mount Hood (Ore.) CC.
6. *Rufus Cook, 1b, Panola (Texas) JC.
7. *Don Lyons, 1b, San Francisco CC.
8. *Scott Margolin, c, East Los Angeles JC.

### June—Regular Phase (15)

1. **Mike Parrott, rhp, Camarillo (Calif.) HS.—(1977-81)**
2. Jerry Guinn, rhp, Maud (Okla.) HS.—(Rookie)
3. **Eddie Murray, c-1b, Locke HS, Los Angeles.—(1977-97)**

DRAFT DROP *Elected to Baseball Hall of Fame, 2003 • Brother of Rich Murray, major leaguer (1980-83)*

4. Don Whiting, of, Lincoln HS, San Diego.—(AAA)
5. Michael Hile, lhp, Venice HS, Los Angeles.—(AA)
6. Ricky Ryser, rhp, Texas Wesleyan College.
7. **Mike Flanagan, lhp, University of Massachusetts.—(1975-92)**

DRAFT DROP *General manager, Orioles (2003-08)*

8. *Ed Bowman, 3b-c, University of Southern California.
9. David Obal, c, St. John College HS, Silver Spring, Md.
10. *Steven Ramsey, ss, Westchester HS, Houston.
11. *Mike Hilderbrandt, c, Woodland (Calif.) HS.
12. *Kenny Alderman, ss, Radford (Va.) HS.
13. *Errect Ridley, of, Venice (Calif.) HS.
14. *Greg Davis, of, Oral Roberts University.
15. Russ Peach, lhp, Murray State University.
16. Robert George, rhp, Poly HS, Arleta, Calif.
17. ***Jerry Garvin, lhp, Merced (Calif.) HS.—(1977-82)**
18. Martin Parrill, 3b, Findlay (Ohio) College.
19. Dennis McMillan, rhp, Hermitage HS, Richmond, Va.
20. *Brett Terrill, 1b, Bowie (Md.) HS.
21. Michael Perez, rhp, Armijo HS, Fairfield, Calif.
22. David Highmark, lhp, Dartmouth College.
23. *Dan Beitey, rhp, Clark (Wash.) JC.
24. Vernon Snyder, of, Northern HS, Grantsville, Md.
25. *Timothy Smith, 3b, Bishop Montgomery HS, Hermosa Beach, Calif.
26. *Robert Ehrig, c, Los Angeles Valley JC.
27. *Robert Davis, lhp, Albemarle (N.C.) JC.
28. ***Chuck Porter, rhp, Perry Hall (Md.) HS.—(1981-85)**

### June—Secondary Phase (7)

1. Doug Wessel, rhp, Vanderbilt University.—(AA)
2. Richard Cuoco, 2b, Los Angeles Valley JC.

DRAFT DROP *Scouting director, Angels (1978-80)*

3. *James Dimeo, rhp, Essex (Md.) CC.
4. ***Bobby Pate, 3b-of, Mesa (Ariz.) CC.—(1980-81)**

## BOSTON RED SOX

### January—Regular Phase (18)

1. (void) *Lloyd Thompson, 3b, Blinn (Texas) JC.—(High A)
2. *William Daves, c, Motlow State (Tenn.) CC.
3. *Brian McCune, p, Clark (Wash.) JC.
4. *Larry Howser, ss-2b, Manatee (Fla.) JC.

DRAFT DROP *Brother of Dick Howser, major leaguer (1961-68); major league manager (1978-86)*

5. *Ted Updike, 1b, San Diego Mesa JC.

### January—Secondary Phase (22)

1. *Mike Payne, rhp, Delta State (Miss.) University.—DNP
2. ***Bobby Pate, 3b-of, San Diego Mesa JC.—(1980-81)**
3. *Michael Hill, p, Three Rivers (Mo.) CC.
4. *Kevin Stephenson, rhp, Seminole (Fla.) CC.
5. Greg McCollum, 1b, University of Puget Sound.
6. Mark Kilmurray, ss, University of New Haven.
7. Tom Farias, rhp, American International (Mass.) College.
8. *Glen Smith, ss-3b, Bordentown, N.J.

### June—Regular Phase (17)

1. **Ted Cox, ss, Midwest City (Okla.) HS.—(1977-81)**
2. **Fred Lynn, of, University of Southern California.—(1974-90)**
3. Charles Meyers, 2b, Oklahoma State University.—(AA)
4. Curran Percival, rhp, Chapman (Calif.) College.—(AAA)
5. **Rick Jones, lhp, Forrest HS, Jacksonville, Fla.—(1976-78)**
6. Glenn Bannister, c, University of Oklahoma.
7. *William St. Claire, lhp, Springfield (Mass.) Technical HS.
8. **Butch Hobson, 3b, University of Alabama.—(1975-82)**

DRAFT DROP *Major league manager (1992-94)*

9. Rick Berg, of, Apple Valley HS, Hesperia, Calif.
10. Roswell Brayton, rhp, Harvard University.
11. *Chris DiLorenzo, rhp, West Rome (Ga.) HS.
12. Barrett Jackson, of-1b, Piscataway HS, Plainfield, N.J.
13. Jack Medick, c, University of Nebraska.
14. James Lease, rhp, William Carey (Miss.) College.
15. *Carmen Coppol, rhp, Claymont (Del.) HS.
16. Lanny Phillips, 3b-of, University of Oklahoma.
17. James Bodinski, c, North Attleboro (Mass.) HS.
18. *Mike Cunico, ss, Pueblo (Colo.) Central HS.
19. Michael Bennett, of, Western Illinois University.
20. Collin Youtz, lhp, Lebanon (Pa.) HS.
21. Greg Eastin, lhp, Ridge HS, Basking Ridge, N.J.
22. Larry Morello, of, Lafayette HS, Brooklyn, N.Y.

### June—Secondary Phase (5)

No selection.

## CALIFORNIA ANGELS

### January—Regular Phase (8)

1. Randy Smith, lhp, Three Rivers (Mo.) CC.—(AA)
2. *Marvin Townsend, ss, Albemarle (N.C.) JC.
3. *Pat Perrino, 3b-c, Henry Ford (Mich.) CC.
4. *Paul Zobeck, lhp, Yavapai (Ariz.) JC.
5. *Larry Eubanks, of, Glendale (Ariz.) CC.
6. Gary Beese, c, Lewis (Ill.) University.
7. *Len Patterson, c, Laney (Calif.) JC.
8. *Tim Hurley, 3b-of, Spokane (Wash.) CC.
9. *Art Bordley, lhp, El Camino (Calif.) JC.

DRAFT DROP *Brother of Bill Bordley, first-round draft pick, Brewers (1976); major leaguer (1980)*

10. *Larry Hutton, of, Long Beach (Calif.) CC.
11. *Clark Maynard, 1b, Greenfield (Mass.) CC.

### January—Secondary Phase (4)

1. *Jeff Feramisco, of, Fresno (Calif.) CC.—(High A)
2. **Mike Overy, rhp, Olivet (Mich.) College.—(1976)**
3. Malvin Washington, c-of, Los Angeles Valley JC.
4. *Kevin Carney, c, Burlington, Vt.
5. *Ron Ward, inf, Contra Costa (Calif.) JC.
6. *Kenny McKinney, 3b, Columbia State (Tenn.) CC.
7. *Ken Nelson, of, Stanford University.
8. *James Yaeger, lhp, Connors State (Okla.) JC.
9. *Mike Mulligan, c, Chipola (Fla.) JC.
10. *Ted Milton, of, Mississippi State University.
11. *Tom Rezzuti, of, Northeastern University.

### June—Regular Phase (7)

1. Billy Taylor, of, Windsor Forest HS, Savannah, Ga.—(Low A)
2. *Bruce Tonascia, of-c, Napa (Calif.) HS.—(Low A)

DRAFT DROP *Attended Southern California; re-drafted by Angels, June 1976/regular phase (34th round)*

3. **Pat Kelly, c, Santa Maria (Calif.) HS.–(1980)**

DRAFT DROP *Father of Casey Kelly, first-round draft pick, Red Sox (2008); major leaguer (2012-15)*

4. Doug Slettvet, rhp, Lakewood (Calif.) HS.—(AA)
5. Robert Johnson, of, Lakewood (Calif.) HS.—(Rookie)
6. Steve Brisbin, c, Lakewood (Calif.) HS.
7. *Carl Gardner, 3b, Miami-Dade CC North.
8. ***Steven Burke, rhp, Tokay HS, Lodi, Calif.—(1977-78)**
9. *Lee Overton, c, Sacramento (Calif.) HS.
10. Clinton Sander, of, Nathan Hale HS, Seattle.
11. Lawrence Rush, 1b, Venice HS, Culver City, Calif.
12. ***Brian Kingman, rhp, Santa Monica (Calif.) JC.—(1979-83)**
13. Glenn Prichard, rhp, Verdugo HS, Tujunga, Calif.
14. Bob Makoski, 1b, Ohio University.
15. ***Dan Boone, lhp, Cerritos (Calif.) JC.—(1981-90)**
16. *Bob DiPietro, lhp, Stanford University.
17. Roger Smith, ss, Florida State University.
18. *Mitchell Delmonico, ss, Napa (Calif.) HS.
19. Rhoderick Wallace, of, South San Francisco HS.
20. *Brian Rhode, lhp, East HS, Wichita, Kan.
21. ***Jim Dorsey, rhp, Cleveland HS, Los Angeles.—(1980-85)**
22. ***Ray Smith, c-1b, Abraham Lincoln HS, San Diego.—(1981-83)**
23. Bill Berger, 2b, Arizona State University.
24. *Tim Brill, c, Olney (Pa.) HS.
25. Keith McVicker, ss, Leigh HS, San Jose, Calif.
26. Dean Jelmini, of, Loyola Marymount University.
27. *Willie McIntyre, of, Hueneme HS, Oxnard, Calif.
28. Robert Verbeck, c, Missouri Western State College.
29. *David Farley, rhp, Yucaipa (Calif.) HS.
30. *Zackary Butler, c, Robert E. Lee HS, Huntsville, Ala.
31. *Wilson Plunkett, of, University of Southern Mississippi.

### June—Secondary Phase (21)

1. *David Bedrosian, 2b, Fresno (Calif.) CC.—(High A)
2. *Kevin Morel, ss, Indian River (Fla.) CC.
3. *Martin Fleming, rhp, Cypress (Calif.) JC.
4. *Dennis Sherow, of, Compton (Calif.) CC.

## CHICAGO CUBS

### January—Regular Phase (15)

1. *Wayne Benson, of, Ranger (Texas) JC.—(AAA)
2. *Charles Pfab, inf, Middle Georgia JC.
3. Travis Roberts, rhp, South Georgia JC.

### January—Secondary Phase (3)

1. **Donnie Moore, rhp-of, Ranger (Texas) JC.—(1975-88)**
2. Lawrence Groover, lhp, Temple (Texas) JC.
3. *Paul Levar, rhp, Spokane Falls (Wash.) CC.

### June—Regular Phase (16)

1. **Jerry Tabb, 1b, University of Tulsa.—(1976-78)**
2. Darrell Turner, rhp, Ocoee (Fla.) HS.—(AAA)
3. Earle Chew, of, Temple University.—(AA)
4. Billy Burleson, rhp-1b, Pine Bluff (Ark.) HS.—(High A)
5. **Dave Geisel, lhp-1b, Tonawanda (N.Y.) HS.—(1978-85)**
6. **Joe Wallis, of, Southern Illinois University.—(1975-79)**
7. August Juricic, 2b, Joliet (Ill.) Central HS.
8. **Mike Krukow, rhp, Cal Poly San Luis Obispo.—(1976-89)**
9. Greg Collins, c, Vanderbilt University.
10. *Emeel Salem, ss, Mountain Brook (Ala.) HS.
11. Byron Wilkerson, rhp, Harrison HS, Evansville, Ind.
12. Stephen Pearsall, of, Assumption (Mass.) College.
13. Byron Loomans, ss, Central (Iowa) College.
14. Steve Haglund, Cleveland HS, Reseda, Calif.
15. Richard Meek, of, Ponderosa HS, Shingle Springs, Calif.
16. Kevin Markert, c, Albany (Ga.) HS.
17. Richard Ware, lhp, Southern Illinois University.
18. *George Sullivan, rhp, Hueytown (Ala.) HS.
19. Vernon Temple, rhp, Rice University.
20. *John Barnfield, lhp, Niles North HS, Glenview, Ill.
21. Stephen Clancy, c, University of Texas.
22. Mack Parker, 1b, South Leake HS, Walnut Grove, Miss.
23. *Ralph Chafin, of, Northeast HS, Macon, Ga.
24. *Robert Lehtola, ss, Rio Americano HS, Sacramento, Calif.
25. *Michael Giobbi, rhp, Deering HS, Portland, Maine.

26. Richard Poythress, ss, South Georgia JC.
27. Ken Kral, of, Southern Illinois University.
28. Robbie Hatfield, ss, Mount Pleasant (Texas) JC.
29. *Marvin Wooten, 1b, Rocky Mount (N.C.) HS.
30. *Rocky Thompson, c, Thomas Jefferson HS, San Antonio, Texas.
31. *Vincent Hillyer, lhp, Thayer Academy, Weymouth, Mass.

**June—Secondary Phase (10)**

1. *Ken McKinney, 3b, Yavapai (Ariz.) JC.—(Short-season A)

## CHICAGO WHITE SOX

**January—Regular Phase (22)**

1. Barnes Yelverton, rhp, UNC Wilmington.—(Low A)
2. Mickey Hickerson, 2b, University of North Carolina.
3. Kenny Bagwell, 2b, Clemson University.

**January—Secondary Phase (24)**

1. *Stephen Cook, 3b, Miami-Dade CC North.—(High A)

**June—Regular Phase (21)**

**1. Steve Swisher, c, Ohio University.—(1974-82)**
DRAFT DROP *Father of Nick Swisher, first-round draft pick, Athletics (2002); major leaguer (2004-15)*
**2. Jim Otten, rhp, Arizona State University.—(1974-81)**
**3. Ken Kravec, lhp, Ashland (Ohio) College.—(1975-82)**
4. Bill Kautzer, rhp, Nekoosa (Wis.) HS.—(Low A)
5. Curt Minges, 3b, Concord (Calif.) HS.—(Low A)
6. Robert Palmer, c, Corona del Mar HS, Newport Beach, Calif.
7. *Philip Nerone, 3b, Baldwin HS, Pittsburgh.
8. Manny Estrada, ss-3b, Cal State Los Angeles.
9. *Julio Alonso, lhp, Power Memorial HS, Bronx, N.Y.
10. James Barrett, of, Hillcrest HS, Springfield, Mo.
11. Douglas Fortune, of-1b, University of New Haven.
12. William Lehman, rhp, Edison HS, Edison Township, N.J.
13. Robert Klein, rhp, Memorial HS, Beloit, Wis.
14. *Michael Cross, ss-2b, Oklahoma State University.
15. Bobby Tucker, of, University of Tennessee.
16. *Monte Kruse, lhp, George-Little Rock (Iowa) HS.
17. *William Tucker, lhp, Bloom HS, Chicago Heights, Ill.
**18. Mike Squires, of-1b, Western Michigan University.—(1975-85)**
19. *Andrew Gallo, rhp, Magnolia HS, Anaheim, Calif.
20. Jeff Sovern, 3b-c, Central Michigan University.
**21. *Chris Nyman, ss, Cordova HS, Rancho Cordova, Calif.—(1982-83)**
DRAFT DROP *Brother of Nyls Nyman, major leaguer (1974-77)*
22. Michael Wolf, ss, Hart HS, Saugus, Calif.
23. Nick Medrano, of, Cal State Dominguez Hills.
24. *Nicholas Bandow, of, Jacobs HS, Stevens Point, Wis.
25. *Don Davis, 3b, Portage Northern HS, Portage, Mich.
26. *Sal Rende, lhp, Eisenhower HS, Blue Island, Ill.
27. *Greg Klette, rhp, Washburn HS, Minneapolis.
28. Barry Smith, rhp, Cummings HS, Burlington, N.C.
29. Roy Coulter, lhp, Cregier HS, Chicago.
30. David Vanderloop, ss, Kaukauna (Wis.) HS.
31. Don Bridges, rhp, Hoggard HS, Wilmington, N.C.
32. *Glen Bright, rhp, Western Carolina University.
33. Michael Dlugach, c, Memphis State University.
34. *Randy Davidson, 2b, Columbia State (Tenn.) CC.
35. Donald Miller, rhp, Thornwood HS, South Holland, Ill.
36. *Terry Hough, rhp, Glendale HS, Springfield, Mo.
37. Phil Mullen, lhp, Methodist (N.C.) College.
38. Tony Johnson, of, Vallejo (Calif.) HS.
39. *Phil Klimas, 3b, Hubbard HS, Chicago.
40. *Tom Mee, ss-rhp, Prior Lake (Minn.) HS.

**June—Secondary Phase (11)**

1. Mark Jackson, c, Long Beach (Calif.) CC.—(Low A)

## CINCINNATI REDS

**January—Regular Phase (21)**

**1. *Gary Lucas, lhp, Riverside (Calif.) CC.—(1980-87)**
2. Jon Ellefson, rhp, University of North Dakota.
3. *John Higgins, of-p, Indian Hills (Iowa) CC.
4. *Steven Hargest, p, Suffolk County (N.Y.) CC.
5. *Terry Willis, p, Lake Sumter (Fla.) CC.

**January—Secondary Phase (9)**

1. Jeff Chandler, lhp, Sacramento (Calif.) CC.—(AA)
2. *Paul Parker, p, Montclair State (N.J.) College.
3. *Ray Guy, rhp, University of Southern Mississippi.
DRAFT DROP *First-round draft pick, Oakland Raiders/ National Football League (1973); punter, NFL (1973-86)*

**June—Regular Phase (22)**

1. Brad Kessler, of, Claremont (Calif.) HS.—(AA)
2. Richard Jensen, lhp, Tooele (Utah) HS.—(AA)
3. Wallace Williams, c, Merritt Island (Fla.) HS.—(High A)
4. Pat Garvey, rhp, Ashtabula (Ohio) HS.—(High A)
5. Marlon Styles, c, Aiken HS, Cincinnati.—(High A)
6. *Reed Schielke, lhp, Boulder (Colo.) HS.
7. James Kulina, lhp, Lower Dauphin HS, Hummelstown, Pa.
8. *Stephan Jackson, 2b, Wesleyan Academy, Chatom, Pa.
9. George Meier, c, Mercy HS, University City, Mo.
10. Joseph Nichols, rhp, Central Catholic HS, Pittsburgh.
11. *Richard Barrett, rhp, Goochland (Va.) HS.
**12. *Jay Howell, rhp, Fairview HS, Boulder, Colo.—(1980-94)**
13. Richard Kuhn, lhp, Swissvale HS, Pittsburgh.
14. *Jeff Lang, lhp, McNicholas HS, Cincinnati.
15. *Alfred Henkel, lhp, Churchland HS, Portsmouth, Va.
16. Donald Hawkins, c, Buffalo Gap HS, Churchville, Va.
17. *Robert Ferber, of, Sahuaro HS, Tucson, Ariz.
18. Curtis Runyon, of-inf, Temple (Texas) JC.
19. James McNeil, rhp, Bacone (Okla.) JC.
20. Ronald Reagan, of, Southeastern Oklahoma State University.
21. *Joseph Waugh, of-1b, Barboursville HS, Huntington, W.Va.
22. John Underwood, rhp, Royal Oak HS, Covina, Calif.
23. *Jeff Scheumack, rhp, Spring Woods HS, Houston.
24. *Phil Bittle, 1b-of, Douglas (Ariz.) HS.
25. *Paul Downey, lhp, Columbia State (Tenn.) CC.
26. *Michael Knight, of, Mainland HS, Holly Hills, Fla.
27. Sammy Heasley, lhp, Lamar (Colo.) CC.
28. Pierre Lyons, rhp, Riverdale HS, Murfreesboro, Tenn.
29. Jerry Rodgers, of, Gonzaga University.
30. George Knowles, rhp, Rider College.
31. *Chester Czaplicki, rhp, Rider College.
32. *Mark Unsoeld, c, Charter Oak HS, Glendora, Calif.
33. Rick Colzie, of, Florida State University.
34. *William Martin, rhp, Shaw HS, Mobile, Ala.

**June—Secondary Phase (22)**

**1. *Gary Lucas, lhp, Riverside (Calif.) CC.—(1980-87)**

## CLEVELAND INDIANS

**January—Regular Phase (6)**

1. Jim McCutchin, rhp, University of Texas.—(AAA)
2. *Jerry Devine, of, Rose State (Okla.) JC.
3. *Donnie Sasser, inf-c, Middle Georgia JC.
4. *William Tiedemann, inf, Yavapai (Ariz.) JC.
5. *Paul Faulk, of, Seminole (Fla.) CC.
6. *Danny Howell, c, Brunswick (Ga.) JC.
7. *James Postel, p, Orange Coast (Calif.) JC.

**January—Secondary Phase (12)**

1. *Don Saulnier, lhp, Massachusetts Bay CC.—(High A)
2. *Gene Stohs, lhp-of, University of Nebraska.
3. *Manuel Alfonsin, inf-of, Miami-Dade CC North.
4. Clyde Lineberry, of, Southwood (Va.) JC.
5. *Dennis Whitehead, c, University of South Alabama.

**June—Regular Phase (5)**

1. Glenn Tufts, 1b, Raynham HS, Bridgewater, Mass.—(AA)
**2. Tommy McMillan, ss, Jacksonville University.—(1977)**
**3. Dave Oliver, 2b, Cal Poly San Luis Obispo.—(1977)**
4. Tom McGough, rhp, Greater Johnstown (Pa.) HS.—(AAA)
5. Vassie Gardner, of, Dorsey HS, Los Angeles.—(AAA)
6. Norman Werd, lhp, Indiana University.
7. Rock Weeks, c, Western HS, Buena Park, Calif.
8. Mike Moran, ss, Gulf Coast (Fla.) CC.
9. *Gary Ezell, ss-rhp, Elgin (Okla.) HS.
10. *Les Hemby, c, Blinn (Texas) JC.
11. Don Flanagan, rhp, San Jacinto (Texas) JC.
12. Joseph Bodine, lhp, Emma Sansom HS, Gadsden, Ala.
13. Tim Holden, lhp, Cleveland State University.
14. John Conover, rhp, Humboldt State (Calif.) University.
15. Joseph Cork, ss, Fordham University.
16. Steve Baumiller, rhp, Florida Southern College.
17. *Stephen Lee, rhp, Hattiesburg (Miss.) HS.
18. *Tom Hinrichs, 3b, Yuba City (Calif.) HS.
19. *Dan Walker, rhp, Malone (Ohio) College.
20. Robert Daub, c, Hicksville (N.Y.) HS.
21. *Donald Carr, rhp-of, Lufkin (Texas) HS.
22. *Cliff Mays, rhp, Central Catholic HS, Portland, Ore.
23. *Danny Miller, rhp-inf, Los Angeles Pierce JC.
24. Curtis Zimmerman, 1b, Tulane University.
25. *Billy Sorrell, rhp, Andrew HS, High Point, N.C.
26. *Mark Wezet, rhp, Evansville (Ind.) Memorial HS.
27. *Danny Rollin, of, Petal (Miss.) HS.
28. *Steve Scott, rhp, East Ridge HS, St. Anne, Ill.
29. *James Boulter, lhp, King Philip Regional HS, Norfolk, Mass.
30. *Richard Chappell, 3b, Griffith (Ind.) HS.
31. *Edward Wright, 2b, Churchland HS, Portsmouth, Va.
32. Stephen Proniewych, 1b, Idaho State University.
33. *Robert Wilmot, rhp, Clintondale HS, Mount Clemons, Mich.
34. *Bradford Hoch, ss-3b, North Florida JC.
35. *Ron Harrington, c, Petal (Miss.) HS.
36. *Gary Smith, of, Deering HS, Portland, Maine.
37. *Vincent Degrouttola, rhp, Archbishop Rummel HS, Metairie, La.
38. *Frank Toups, inf, Brother Martin HS, New Orleans.
39. *Danny White, inf, Arizona State University.
DRAFT DROP *Quarterback, National Football League (1976-87)*
40. *Douglas Dye, of, College of Wooster (Ohio).
41. Wilburt Avery, ss, Baldwin-Wallace (Ohio) College.
42. *Michael Rachuba, lhp, Start HS, Toledo, Ohio.

**June—Secondary Phase (15)**

1. *Alex Pastore, of, University of South Alabama.—(High A)

## DETROIT TIGERS

**January—Regular Phase (20)**

1. Steve Trella, rhp, Fullerton (Calif.) JC.—(AA)
2. *Dino Hloros, p, St. Clair County (Mich.) CC.
3. Lary Graves, rhp, Washtenaw (Mich.) JC.
4. *Francis Sansosti, rhp, Essex (Md.) CC.

**January—Secondary Phase (8)**

1. Larry Ike, rhp, Michigan State University.—(AA)
2. *Gary Kennedy, of, Brewton-Parker (Ga.) JC.
3. *Phil Vaden, rhp, Detroit.

**June—Regular Phase (19)**

1. Charles Bates, 3b, Cal State Los Angeles.—(AA)
2. Kevin Slattery, ss, Oceanside (N.Y.) HS.–(Low A)
**3. Bob Adams, 3b, UCLA.—(1977)**
4. Robert Trudo, of, Brookfield HS, Masury, Ohio.—(Rookie)
5. Michael Elders, rhp, Clay HS, Oregon, Ohio.—(AA)
6. Greg Shippy, c, Garrett HS, Auburn, Ind.
7. *Robert Stadnika, rhp, Eisenhower HS, Saginaw, Mich.
8. Elliott Moore, lhp, Michigan State University.
9. Joseph Simbolick, c, Seymour (Conn.) HS.
10. *Joe Carroll, rhp, Rogers HS, Tulsa, Okla.
11. *Ken Gregory, of, North Plainfield (N.J.) HS.
12. Michael Ray, rhp, Cairo (Ga.) HS.
**13. *Charlie Puleo, rhp, Bloomfield (N.J.) HS.—(1981-89)**
14. Ronald Jones, of, Highland Park (Mich.) HS.
15. Tom Butler, ss, Texas Christian University.
16. Curtis Morgan, 1b, Western HS, Detroit.
17. Thomas Walko, of, Cardinal Mooney HS, Poland, Ohio.
18. *Michael St. Louis, lhp, Ithaca (N.Y.) College.
19. Anthony Jonas, of, Long Island University.
20. Charles Moore, c, Northeast HS, Macon, Ga.
21. William Madden, rhp, St. Joseph's HS, Pittsfield, Mass.
22. Mike Hughes, lhp, Lamar University.
23. Roy Marks, rhp, Parsons (Iowa) College.
24. Jeff Bouton, rhp, Monmouth College.
DRAFT DROP *Brother of Jim Bouton, major leaguer (1962-78)*
25. *Richard Flynn, rhp, Keyport HS, Union Beach, N.J.
26. *Richard Sherkel, c, Penn State University.
27. *Frederick Petersen, rhp, Commack (N.Y.) South HS.
28. Fred Swanson, of, Pine River HS, Tustin, Mich.

**June—Secondary Phase (23)**

No selection.

## HOUSTON ASTROS

**January—Regular Phase (19)**

1. *Robert Nickeson, ss, West Valley (Calif.) JC.—(AA)

**January—Secondary Phase (5)**

**1. Mike Stanton, rhp, Miami-Dade CC South.—(1975-85)**
2. Donald Broom, of, McNeese State University.

**June—Regular Phase (20)**

1. Calvin Portley, ss, Longview (Texas) HS.—(AA)
2. Scott Gregory, rhp, Palos Verdes HS, Palos Verdes Estates, Calif.—(High A)
3. David Aloi, rhp, Edgewood HS, West Covina, Calif.—(AAA)
4. Michael Jones, of, Fremont HS, Inglewood, Calif.—(High A)
**5. Mike Mendoza, rhp, McClintock HS, Tempe, Ariz.—(1979)**
6. *Stephen Williams, rhp, Milton (Fla.) HS.
7. Eric Brown, c, Tennessee Tech.
**8. *Ken Landreaux, of, Dominguez HS, Compton, Calif.—(1977-87)**
DRAFT DROP *First-round draft pick (6th overall), Angels (1976)*
9. Michael Holland, 1b, Charter Oak HS, Covina, Calif.
10. Steven Oberweather, ss, Lee's Summit (Mo.) HS.
11. Ron Roznovsky, rhp, University of Texas.
12. Nathan Stewart, of, Le Tourneau (Texas) College.
13. *Kelly Cordes, lhp, Prescott (Ariz.) HS.
**14. *Bobby Clark, ss, Perris (Calif.) HS.—(1979-85)**
15. *Steve Woitock, 2b, Dana (Neb.) College.
16. *Richard Nesloney, rhp, Tuloso-Midway HS, Corpus Christi, Texas.
**17. Joe Sambito, lhp, Adelphi (N.Y.) University.—(1976-87)**
**18. *Mike Davey, lhp, Gonzaga University.—(1977-78)**
19. *Jerry Halstead, 1b, St. Petersburg (Fla.) JC.

**June—Secondary Phase (20)**

No selection.

## KANSAS CITY ROYALS

**January—Regular Phase (10)**

1. *Marty French, rhp, Grossmont (Calif.) JC.—(AA)
2. Karel deLeeuw, of, Glendale (Ariz.) CC.

**January—Secondary Phase (20)**

1. J.P. Pierson, of, Glendale (Ariz.) CC.—(Low A)
2. Bradley Davis, rhp, Mount Hood (Ore.) CC.

**June—Regular Phase (9)**

1. Lew Olsen, rhp, San Ramon HS, Alamo, Calif.—(AAA)
2. Brian Trifiolis, c, West Orange (N.J.) HS.—(Low A)
3. **Ruppert Jones, of, Berkeley (Calif.) HS.—(1976-87)**

DRAFT DROP *First player selected, Major League Baseball expansion draft, Mariners (Nov. 5, 1976)*

4. Ronnie Sutler, ss, Buckingham HS, Dillwyn, Va.—(Rookie)
5. ***Mike Colbern, c, Hawthorne (Calif.) HS.—(1978-79)**

DRAFT DROP *Attended Arizona State; re-drafted by White Sox, 1976 (2nd round)*

6. Bob Kellison, of, San Diego State University.
7. Danny Link, rhp, North Davidson HS, Lexington, N.C.
8. Bob Falcon, lhp, Texas A&M University.
9. *Ron Miles, lhp, Marion (S.C.) HS.
10. Jim Peterson, rhp, St. Mary's HS, Gaylord, Mich.
11. Willie Clark, rhp, Jackson State University.
12. Chris Evers, rhp, Wayzata (Minn.) HS.
13. ***Sandy Wihtol, rhp, Homestead HS, Sunnyvale, Calif.—(1979-82)**
14. *John Yandle, lhp, Lake Oswego (Ore.) HS.
15. Jeff White, of, Wakefield HS, Arlington, Va.
16. Ruben Garcia, lhp, Texas Tech.
17. *Tom Ricks, ss, Valencia HS, Placentia, Calif.
18. Gary Williams, lhp, Fenger HS, Chicago.
19. Richard Rich, rhp, Loara HS, Anaheim, Calif.
20. *Xavier Dixson, of, St. Mary's (Calif.) College.
21. Greg Kuhnke, of, Nekoosa (Wis.) HS.
22. *Charles Stevens, of, Princeton (N.C.) HS.
23. *Robert MacHale, ss, Villa Park HS, Orange, Calif.
24. Clyde Athman, c, Healy HS, Pierz, Minn.
25. *Dan Burns, c, St. Bernard HS, Hawthorne, Calif.
26. ***Chuck Baker, ss, Santa Ana (Calif.) JC.—(1978-81)**
27. *Manny Chavez, 2b, Whittier (Calif.) HS.
28. *Robert Bechtelheimer, rhp, Herndon HS, Fairfax, Va.
29. Dwight Favors, 1b, Manual Arts HS, Los Angeles.
30. Alex Gorgie, rhp, Rancho Alamitos HS, Garden Grove, Calif.
31. *Robert Sellers, 1b, W.T. Woodson HS, Annandale, Va.
32. Dwayne Taggart, of, Los Angeles Southwest CC.
33. Brian Slagle, rhp, Huntington Beach (Calif.) HS.
34. Marvell McKinney, inf, East HS, Memphis, Tenn.
35. Darrell Parker, of, Woodside HS, Palo Alto, Calif.
36. *Mark Gesquiere, rhp, Aviation HS, Manhattan Beach, Calif.
37. David Bewley, rhp, University of LaVerne (Calif.).
38. *Bob Goodyear, lhp, Lutheran HS, Inglewood, Calif.
39. Jim Lemon, 2b, Creighton University.

DRAFT DROP *Son of Jim Lemon, major leaguer (1950-63)*

40. *Mike Ongarato, of, Rolling Hills HS, Palos Verdes, Calif.
41. *Robert Price, ss, Eastern Wayne HS, Goldsboro, N.C.
42. Elvin Lowe, 2b, Parkview HS, Little Rock, Ark.
43. Ellis Clayton, ss, Springfield (Ore.) HS.
44. Kenneth Wright, lhp, Kailua (Hawaii) HS.
45. *Dale Cline, rhp, Bridgeton (N.J.) HS.
46. Steven Barnes, rhp, Willamette HS, Eugene, Ore.
47. *Mike Gatlin, 3b, Chaffey (Calif.) JC.

DRAFT DROP *First overall draft pick, June 1974/secondary phase, Reds*

48. William Heigel, c, San Jose State University.
49. Jimmy Kelley, c, University of Texas-Arlington.
50. Michael Larkin, rhp, University of Wyoming.
51. *Dave Klungreseter, lhp, Cal State Fullerton.
52. *Robert Allen, 3b, University of Arizona.

**June—Secondary Phase (19)**

1. *Clif Holland, lhp, University of Southern California.—(Low A)
2. Paul Caffrey, of, Seton Hall University.
3. **Bob McClure, lhp, JC of San Mateo (Calif.).—(1975-93)**
4. ***Rob Picciolo, inf, Santa Monica (Calif.) JC.—(1977-85)**

## LOS ANGELES DODGERS

**January—Regular Phase (17)**

1. Wesley Moore, rhp, Yavapai (Ariz.) JC.—(Low A)
2. *Michael Boyd, of, Chipola (Fla.) JC.
3. ***Bob McClure, lhp, JC of San Mateo (Calif.).—(1975-93)**
4. *Jeff Moore, 1b-3b, Middle Georgia JC.
5. *Jeff Hill, of, Phoenix (Ariz.) JC.
6. *Terry Nance, rhp, Monterey Peninsula (Calif.) JC.

**January—Secondary Phase (17)**

1. Guy Todd, rhp, Blinn (Texas) JC.—(AA)
2. *Bob Purkey Jr., rhp, Gulf Coast (Fla.) CC.

DRAFT DROP *Son of Bob Purkey, major leaguer (1954-66)*

3. ***Craig Minetto, lhp, San Joaquin Delta (Calif.) JC.—(1978-81)**

**June—Regular Phase (18)**

1. Ted Farr, c, Shadle Park HS, Spokane, Wash.—(AAA)
2. Mike Paciorek, ss, St. Mary's HS, Detroit.—(Low A)

DRAFT DROP *Brother of John Paciorek, major leaguer (1963) • Brother of Tom Paciorek, major leaguer (1970-87) • Brother of Jim Paciorek, major leaguer (1987)*

3. **Joe Simpson, of, University of Oklahoma.—(1975-83)**
4. Mark Hance, 3b, Fresno State University.—(AA)
5. *Tom Steinmetz, ss, Canevin Catholic HS, Carnegie, Pa.—(Low Class A)

DRAFT DROP *Attended Iowa; re-drafted by Expos, 1976 (23rd round)*

6. **Mike Dimmel, of, Logansport (Ind.) HS.—(1977-79)**
7. David Richards, c, Proviso East HS, Forest Park, Ill.
8. Brad Drysdale, rhp, Brawley (Calif.) Union HS.
9. ***Bob Stanley, rhp, Kearny (N.J.) HS.—(1977-89)**
10. *Mark Wilson, of-3b, Ashland (Ore.) HS.
11. Charles Barrett, rhp, Rancho HS, North Las Vegas, Nev.

DRAFT DROP *Brother of Marty Barrett, first overall draft pick, June 1979/secondary phase; major leaguer (1982-91) • Brother of Tommy Barrett, major leaguer (1988-92)*

12. William Collins, rhp, University of South Alabama.
13. Daniel Smith, rhp, Covina HS, West Covina, Calif.
14. James Mitchell, ss, Cardinal Mooney HS, Rochester, N.Y.
15. *Kelly Snider, 1b, Hillcrest HS, Springfield, Mo.
16. Edward Davis, 3b-of, West Jefferson HS, Marrero, La.
17. Robert Arceneaux, c, Manual Arts HS, Los Angeles.
18. ***Tom Dixon, rhp-3b, Boone HS, Orlando, Fla.—(1977-83)**
19. *Charles James, of, Manual Arts HS, Los Angeles.
20. *Marty Kunkler, lhp, Lindbergh HS, St. Louis.
21. Russell Holland, rhp, Parksley (Va.) HS.

**June—Secondary Phase (16)**

1. William Meyer, ss, University of Michigan.—(AA)

## MILWAUKEE BREWERS

**January—Regular Phase (4)**

1. Michael Robinson, of, Shoreline (Wash.) CC.—(Low A)
2. *James Diventi, rhp, Essex (Md.) CC.

**January—Secondary Phase (6)**

1. *Scott Gunderson, rhp, Bellevue (Wash.) CC.—DNP

**June—Regular Phase (3)**

1. **Robin Yount, ss, Taft HS, Woodland Hills, Calif.—(1974-93)**

DRAFT DROP *Elected to Baseball Hall of Fame, 1999 • Brother of Larry Yount, major leaguer (1971)*

2. Joe Slaymaker, lhp, Newport HS, Bellevue, Wash.—(Low A)
3. Garry Conn, rhp, Bentley HS, Flint, Mich.—(AA)
4. Mark Plunkett, rhp, Edmonds (Wash.) HS.—(Low A)
5. Michael Gilbert, 2b, Hartsville (S.C.) HS.–(Low A)
6. John Buffamoyer, c, Berea HS, Greenville, S.C.
7. *Carey Scarborough, ss-2b, Bishopville (S.C.) HS.
8. Jerry Costain, 1b-of, Toms River South HS, Toms River, N.J.
9. Jeffrey Barker, rhp, Claremont (Calif.) HS.
10. Charles Moore, c, Western Branch HS, Chesapeake, Va.
11. Terry Ervin, of, Wilson HS, Los Angeles.
12. Jack Chilton, lhp, Maryvale HS, Phoenix, Ariz.
13. James Bendick, of, Shenendehowa HS, Ballston Lake, N.Y.
14. Paul Ausman, lhp, Regis HS, Eau Claire, Wis.
15. *Terry Unruh, rhp, Enid (Okla.) HS.
16. Terry Frawley, lhp, Bodley HS, Fulton, N.Y.
17. Perry Danforth, ss-2b, University of New Mexico.
18. Raymond Rudolph, ss-c, Tottenville (N.Y.) HS.
19. Richard Baker, lhp, Monte Vista HS, La Mesa, Calif.
20. William Smith, ss, Dominican HS, Milwaukee.
21. *Mike Schisler, rhp, Georgia Tech.

**June—Secondary Phase (13)**

1. *Scott Gunderson, rhp, Bellevue (Wash.) CC.—DNP

## MINNESOTA TWINS

**January—Regular Phase (12)**

1. Joe Honce, of, West Virginia University.—(High A)
2. *Dan Argee, of, Cosumnes River (Calif.) JC.
3. *Scott Wilson, 3b, Golden West (Calif.) JC.
4. Arthur Castillo, of, Fullerton (Calif.) JC.
5. William Brock, lhp, Manatee (Fla.) JC.
6. *David Morris, of, Citrus (Calif.) JC.

**January—Secondary Phase (18)**

1. *Dennis Sherow, of, Compton (Calif.) CC.—(AAA)
2. *R.B. Bell, rhp, Fullerton (Calif.) JC.
3. ***Jerry Maddox, 3b, Cerritos (Calif.) JC.—(1978)**

**June—Regular Phase (11)**

1. **Eddie Bane, lhp, Arizona State University.—(1973-76)**

DRAFT DROP *Scouting director, Angels (2004-10)*

2. Eddie McMahon, ss, University of Massachusetts.—(High A)
3. Russ Noah, of, Loyola Marymount University.—(AA)
4. Michael Beck, ss, Oakton HS, Vienna, Va.—(Low A)
5. Richard Tintor, c, Hibbing (Minn.) HS.—(Low A)
6. ***Darrell Jackson, lhp, Locke HS, Los Angeles.—(1978-82)**
7. **Luis Gomez, ss, UCLA.—(1974-81)**
8. *Sam Donabedian, of, McLane HS, Fresno, Calif.
9. **Larry Wolfe, ss, Sacramento (Calif.) CC.—(1977-80)**
10. ***Ken Schrom, rhp, Grangeville (Idaho) HS.—(1980-87)**
11. ***Jerry Reed, rhp, Enka HS, Asheville, N.C.—(1981-90)**
12. Archie Amerson, ss, Morse HS, San Diego.
13. *James Worth, rhp, Edgewood HS, West Covina, Calif.
14. *Rob Klebba, 3b, La Crescenta (Calif.) HS.
15. Mike Seberger, rhp, Cal Poly Pomona.
16. Michael Dodd, c, Golden West (Calif.) JC.
17. *Gary Bishop, 1b, Poly Institute, Baltimore.
18. ***Ricky Peters, ss, Dominguez HS, Compton, Calif.—(1979-86)**
19. *Dan Grimm, rhp, Fresno State University.
20. *Richard Douglass, rhp-1b, San Clemente (Calif.) HS.
21. Michael Messman, rhp, Marshall HS, Portland, Ore.
22. *Frank Meyers, lhp, De La Salle HS, Minneapolis.
23. Dave Garcia, rhp, Stevens Institute of Technology (N.Y.).
24. Robert Daniels, 2b, Long Island University.
25. Brad Duncan, rhp, Fresno State University.
26. Paul Franco, rhp, Cal State Los Angeles.
27. **(void) *Gary Woods, of, Santa Barbara (Calif.) CC.—(1976-85)**
28. *Robbie Henderson, ss, Clairemont HS, San Diego.

DRAFT DROP *Brother of Ken Henderson, major leaguer (1965-80)*

29. Jerry Matejka, lhp, Breckenridge (Minn.) HS.
30. *Bill Sanford, c, Washington State University.

**June—Secondary Phase (9)**

1. *Wayne Williams, ss, Ranger (Texas) JC.—(High A)
2. *Bob Nickeson, ss, West Valley (Calif.) JC.
3. *Michael Buckingham, rhp, Gulf Coast (Fla.) CC.
4. *Marty French, rhp, Grossmont (Calif.) JC.

## MONTREAL EXPOS

**January—Regular Phase (7)**

1. Tom Ford, lhp, Eastern Michigan University.—(High A)
2. Mark Cunningham, ss, Diablo Valley (Calif.) JC.
3. *Hubert Hewitt, inf, Merritt (Calif.) JC.
4. Steve Melton, 3b, John Brown (Ark.) University.
5. Jack Spence, lhp, Alamogordo, N.M.
6. *Dan Henry, ss-of, San Bernardino Valley (Calif.) JC.
7. *Jay Seccombe, ss, Chabot (Calif.) JC.
8. *Thomas Slater, c, Mesa (Ariz.) CC.
9. *Kenneth Snyder, p, Chabot (Calif.) JC.
10. *Greg Ballard, rhp, Garey HS, Pomona, Calif.

DRAFT DROP *First-round draft pick, Washington Bullets/National Basketball Association (1977); forward, NBA (1977-89)*

11. *Stephen Gooding, 1b, Catonsville (Md.) CC.
12. *Lee Sneath, p, Foothill (Calif.) JC.
13. Jimmie Williams, rhp, Indian Hills (Iowa) CC.
14. *Robert Willis, p, Valencia (Fla.) CC.

**January—Secondary Phase (21)**

1. *David Bedrosian, 2b, Fresno (Calif.) CC.—(High A)
2. ***Dan Boitano, rhp, Fresno (Calif.) CC.—(1978-82)**
3. Bill Bohne, ss, Blinn (Texas) JC.
4. David Gronlund, 3b, Riverside (Calif.) CC.

**June—Regular Phase (8)**

1. **Gary Roenicke, ss, Edgewood HS, West Covina, Calif.—(1976-88)**

DRAFT DROP *Brother of Ron Roenicke, major leaguer (1981-88); major league manager (2011-15) • Father of Josh Roenicke, major leaguer (2008-13)*

2. Ed Creech, ss, Mercer University.—(AAA)

DRAFT DROP *Scouting director, Expos (1994-97); scouting director, Cardinals (1998); scouting director, Pirates (2001-07)*

3. Rickey Hughes, 1b-of, Gaston HS, Gadsden, Ala.—(High A)
4. Daniel Smith, of-3b, Westchester HS, Los Angeles.—(High A)
5. Bruce Shannon, 3b, Jacksonville University.—(AA)
6. *Pat Kelleher, rhp, Servite HS, Los Alamitos, Calif.
7. *Dennis Doss, rhp, Memorial HS, Joplin, Mo.
8. Michael Marvelle, of, Quincy (Mass.) HS.
9. David Heffner, of, Gardner-Webb College.
10. *Mark Carpenter, lhp, Los Alamitos (Calif.) HS.
11. *Earl Thornton, lhp, Holtville HS, Deatsville, Ala.
12. Greg Biagini, 1b-of, Iowa State University.
13. *Greg Chandler, c, Everett (Wash.) HS.
14. *Eugene Frey, of, Redwood HS, Corte Madero, Calif.
15. *Greg Ballard, rhp, Pomona, Calif.

DRAFT DROP *First-round draft pick, Washington Bullets/National Basketball Association (1977); forward, NBA (1977-89)*

16. *David Koza, lhp-of, Torrington, Wyo.
17. *Terry Kieffer, lhp, Indian Hills (Iowa) CC.
18. *Bill Harris, lhp, St. Francis HS, Mountain View, Calif.
19. *Mike Henderson, ss, Lincoln HS, Stockton, Calif.
20. *Jerry Keller, c-1b, Seaholm HS, Birmingham, Mich.
21. Larry Brown, rhp, Morningside HS, Inglewood, Calif.
22. Matt Dinkle, rhp, Nicholls State University.

**23. *Jeff Reardon, rhp, Wahconah HS, Dalton, Mass.—(1979-94)**
24. Elgin Battles, rhp, Waianae (Hawaii) HS.
**25. Tim Ireland, 2b, Chabot (Calif.) JC.—(1981-82)**
26. *Scott Moffitt, 3b, Cottonwood HS, Salt Lake City.
27. *Robin Robinson, of, Centennial HS, Los Angeles.
28. Paul Joyce, rhp, Louisiana State University.
29. *Bruce Freeberg, rhp, Edgewood HS, West Covina, Calif.
30. *David Steck, rhp, Patrick Henry HS, San Diego.
31. *Steve Viefhaus, ss, Ellisville, Mo.

**June—Secondary Phase (6)**

**1. Warren Cromartie, of, Miami-Dade CC North.—(1974-91)**

## NEW YORK METS

**January—Regular Phase (13)**

1. Jimmie Johnson, rhp, University of Arkansas-Little Rock.—(High A)
2. *Melvin Anderson, of-1b, Los Angeles CC.
3. *Andrew Jackson, ss, Yakima Valley (Wash.) JC.
4. *Thomas Guess, 1b, Hillsborough (Fla.) CC.
5. *Mark Kramer, of, Yakima Valley (Wash.) JC.
6. *Eudaldo Oliveros, ss, Miami-Dade CC North.

**January—Secondary Phase (11)**

1. *Doug Wessel, rhp, Vanderbilt University.—(AA)
2. *Bob Gerdes, rhp, Miami-Dade CC South.
3. *Chris Lynch, rhp, Miami-Dade CC South.
4. *Michael Hasley, lhp, Modesto (Calif.) JC.
5. *Charles Steffen, lhp-1b, Monroe (N.Y.) CC.

**June—Regular Phase (14)**

**1. Lee Mazzilli, of, Lincoln HS, Brooklyn, N.Y.—(1976-89)**
DRAFT DROP *Major league manager (2004-05)*
**2. Jackson Todd, rhp, University of Oklahoma.—(1977-81)**
3. Gary Nevinger, rhp, University of Georgia.—(High A)
4. *Tom Kinkelaar, rhp, Mundelein (Ill.) HS.—DNP
DRAFT DROP *Attended Miami (Ohio); never re-drafted*
5. Johnny Williams, of, T.R. Robinson HS, Tampa.—(Rookie)
6. Rich Miller, of, West Chester (Pa.) University.
7. Michael Papa, of, Lafayette HS, Brooklyn, N.Y.
8. *Tom Baxter, rhp, Bayonne (N.J.) HS.
9. John Courtney, rhp, Corrigan (Texas) HS.
10. *John Brass, rhp, West HS, Bakersfield, Calif.
11. Gary Blaylock, 1b, Union (Tenn.) University.
12. David Lozano, ss, San Joaquin Delta (Calif.) JC.
13. James Matthews, ss, Luling (Texas) HS.
14. Gary Albert, rhp, Eastern Lebanon County HS, Myerstown, Pa.
15. *Ronald Reynolds, ss, Central HS, Savanna, Tenn.
16. Dennis Jackson, 1b, Tottenville HS, Staten Island, N.Y.
17. Chris Ryba, rhp, SUNY-Stony Brook.
18. Ron King, rhp, Redmond (Wash.) HS.
19. *Ronnie Hildreth, rhp, Vigor HS, Prichard, Ala.
20. Richard Harris, of, Arizona State University.
**21. Mardie Cornejo, rhp, University of Tulsa.—(1978)**
DRAFT DROP *Father of Nate Cornejo, major leaguer (2001-05)*
22. *Garnett Houghton, rhp, Ohlone (Calif.) JC.
23. Robert Salinger, c, St. Leo (Fla.) College.
24. Randy Trapp, of, Eastern Illinois University.
25. Brian Canfield, 3b, Lafayette College.
26. *Harry Tabler, c, Elder HS, Cincinnati.
DRAFT DROP *Brother of Pat Tabler, first-round draft pick, Yankees (1976); major leaguer (1981-92)*
27. *Colin Leisher, ss, Summit (N.J.) HS.
28. Larry Calufetti, c, Southern Illinois University.
29. Paul Dyer, lhp, University of California.
30. Alan Osmundson, c, Tottenville HS, Staten Island, N.Y.
31. *Matt Gondak, of, Redwood HS, Larkspur, Calif.
32. *Charles Fore, rhp, Flomaton (Ala.) HS.
**33. *Warren Brusstar, rhp, Fresno State University.—(1977-85)**
34. Kevin Meistickle, rhp, Thiel (Pa.) College.
35. Ed Wallace, ss, Southern Tech (Ga.) Institute.
36. Michael Neumann, rhp, Kennedy HS, Chicago.

**June—Secondary Phase (24)**

No selection.

## NEW YORK YANKEES

**January—Regular Phase (14)**

1. *Greg Kane, c, Yavapai (Ariz.) JC.—(High A)
2. Steve Hergenrader, c-of, Fresno (Calif.) CC.
3. *Dean Engler, rhp, Clark (Wash.) JC.
4. *David Jost, inf, Foothill (Calif.) JC.
5. *Joe Eberhard, ss, Crowder (Mo.) JC.
6. *Michael Lester, 3b, Bellevue (Wash.) CC.

**January—Secondary Phase (14)**

1. Bob Polinsky, rhp, University of Delaware.—(AAA)
2. *Wayne Horkey, c, Granville, Iowa.
**3. *Craig Mitchell, rhp, Spokane Falls (Wash.) CC.—(1975-77)**
DRAFT DROP *First overall draft pick, June 1973/secondary phase, Athletics*
4. *Brian Herosian, lhp-1b, University of Connecticut.

**June—Regular Phase (13)**

1. Doug Heinold, rhp, Stroman HS, Victoria, Texas.—(AAA)
**2. Mike Heath, ss, Hillsborough HS, Tampa.—(1978-91)**
3. Howard Shoff, rhp, William Penn HS, York, Pa.—(Short-season A)
**4. Kerry Dineen, of, University of San Diego.—(1975-78)**
**5. LaMarr Hoyt, rhp, Keenan HS, Columbia, S.C.—(1979-86)**
6. Sheldon Gill, c, Jordan HS, Long Beach, Calif.
7. Steve Coulson, 3b-of, Murray State University.
**8. Garth Iorg, ss, Arcata (Calif.) HS.—(1978-87)**
DRAFT DROP *Brother of Dane Iorg, major leaguer (1977-86) • Father of Eli Iorg, first-round draft pick, Astros (2005)*
9. *Craig Harvey, rhp-c, Laverne (Okla.) HS.
10. Jack Shupe, 1b, Wayne State (Nebraska) University.
11. *Barry Barritt, c, Thomas Jefferson HS, Council Bluffs, Iowa.
12. Craig White, of-1b, Clemson University.
13. Jim Sullivan, lhp, Colorado State University.
14. *Don Lenhof, rhp, Erlanger (Ky.) HS.
15. Lee Boettchner, rhp, Winona State (Minn.) University.
16. Tim Grice, 3b-c, University of Minnesota.
17. *James Roach, rhp, West Bakersfield (Calif.) HS.
18. *Ron Pederson, lhp, Rock Valley (Iowa) Community HS.
19. Bob Majczan, rhp, Villanova University.
20. *David Hasbach, rhp, Miami (Ohio) University.
DRAFT DROP *First overall draft pick, January 1974/secondary phase, Royals*
21. Gary Blevins, rhp, Princeton University.
22. Donald Moore, c-3b, Green Hills (Ohio) Community HS.
23. *Mark Erickson, 1b, Clark (Wash.) JC.
24. *James Hill, of, Belleville HS, Millstadt, Ill.
25. *Collin Morrison, lhp, Livermore (Calif.) HS.
26. Richard Melts, c-rhp, Yonkers (N.Y.) HS.
27. Robert Wasilak, c, Kearny (N.J.) HS.
28. *Jack Patchin, c, Crowder (Mo.) JC.

**June—Secondary Phase (3)**

1. Wayne Benson, of, Ranger (Texas) JC.—(AAA)
2. Dean Engler, rhp, Clark (Wash.) JC.
3. *Kevin Nelson, lhp, JC of Southern Idaho.
4. *Greg Kane, c, Yavapai (Ariz.) CC.

## OAKLAND ATHLETICS

**January—Regular Phase (24)**

**1. Mike Norris, rhp, CC of San Francisco.—(1975-90)**
2. *John Morris, rhp, Cypress (Calif.) JC.
3. *Clark Beam, rhp-2b, Mitchell (N.C.) CC.
4. *Steven Williams, rhp, Golden West (Calif.) JC.
5. *Gordon Blakeley, of, Golden West (Calif.) JC.

**January—Secondary Phase (10)**

**1. *Warren Cromartie, of, Miami-Dade CC North.—(1974-91)**
2. Carl Sapp, rhp, Compton, Calif.
3. *John Freedman, 3b, Citrus (Calif.) JC.

**June—Regular Phase (23)**

**1. Randy Scarbery, rhp, University of Southern California.—(1979-80)**
DRAFT DROP *First-round draft pick (7th overall), Astros (1970) • Brother of Rickey Scarbery, 44th-round draft pick, Cardinals (1973)*
2. James Tuttle, rhp-of, Roger Bacon HS, Cincinnati.—(High A)
**3. *Floyd Bannister, lhp, Kennedy HS, Seattle, Wash.—(1977-92)**
DRAFT DROP *Attended Arizona State; re-drafted by Astros, 1976 (1st round, 1st pick)*
4. Ransom Voelkel, lhp, DeKalb HS, Auburn, Ind.—(Short-season A)
5. Steve Staniland, rhp, Santa Clara University.—(AA)
6. Mack Harrison, ss-2b, Watkins HS, Laurel, Miss.
**7. Matt Keough, 3b-rhp, Corona Del Mar (Calif.) HS.—(1977-86)**
DRAFT DROP *Son of Marty Keough, major leaguer (1956-66) • Nephew of Joe Keough, major leaguer (1968-73)*
**8. Derek Bryant, of, University of Kentucky.—(1979)**
**9. Wayne Gross, 1b, Cal Poly Pomona.—(1976-86)**
10. *Scott Freebairn, c, Detroit Country Day HS, Royal Oak, Mich.
11. Richard Zoss, lhp, East Detroit HS, Warren, Mich.
12. *Danny Hall, 2b, Federal-Hocking HS, Coolville, Ohio.
DRAFT DROP *Baseball coach, Kent State (1988-93); baseball coach, Georgia Tech (1994-2015)*
13. David Moore, rhp, Marshall HS, West Sacramento, Calif.
14. *Stan Skidgel, rhp, Oakmont HS, Roseville, Calif.
**15. Dwayne Murphy, of, Antelope Valley HS, Lancaster, Calif.—(1978-89)**
16. *Monty Hannah, of, Eastmoor Academy HS, Columbus, Ohio.
17. Gary Rump, c, Lahser HS, Bloomfield Hills, Mich.
18. James Biehl, rhp-of, Garden Grove (Calif.) HS.
19. Marty Stajduhar, 3b, University of La Verne (Calif.).
20. Scott Gilchrist, c, Granada Hills HS, Northridge, Calif.
21. Bill Hobbs, of-1b, UCLA.
22. William Zedalis, rhp, Eisenhower HS, Rialto, Calif.
**23. *Jeff Rineer, lhp, Penn Manor HS, Pequea, Pa.—(1979)**
24. *William Dwyer, ss, Arlington (Mass.) HS.
25. William Undegaff, c, High Point College.
26. *James Dobens, rhp-ss, Bishop Guertin HS, Nashua, N.H.
27. Robert Mollenhauer, 2b, Lafayette College.
28. Gary Williams, rhp, Los Alamitos HS, Cypress, Calif.
29. *John Boggan, rhp, Manhattan Academy, Jackson, Miss.
30. David Sparks, ss, Ohio University.
31. Rick Ingalls, of-2b, Cal State Los Angeles.

**June—Secondary Phase (1)**

**1. Craig Mitchell, rhp, Spokane Falls (Wash.) CC.—(1975-77)**
2. *Don Lyons, 1b, San Francisco CC.

## PHILADELPHIA PHILLIES

**January—Regular Phase (1)**

**1. Alan Bannister, ss, Arizona State University.—(1974-85)**
DRAFT DROP *First-round draft pick (5th overall), Angels (1969).*
2. Greg Gold, rhp, Diablo Valley (Calif.) JC.
3. Andrew Russo, c, LeMoyne College.
4. *Errol Moore, of, Sacramento (Calif.) CC.
5. *Rick Talley, p, San Jacinto (Texas) JC.
6. *Joe Griffin, c, Polk (Fla.) CC.
**7. Rick Bosetti, 2b, Shasta (Calif.) JC.—(1976-82).**
8. Dennis Perry, rhp, Ranger (Texas) JC.
9. *Gene Litle, rhp, West Valley (Calif.) JC.

**January—Secondary Phase (1)**

**1. Dick Ruthven, rhp, Fresno State University.—(1973-86)**
DRAFT DROP *First-round draft pick (8th overall), Twins (1972) • First player from 1973 draft to reach majors (April 17, 1973)*
2. *Don Fisher, lhp, Polk (Fla.) CC.
3. *Paul Caffrey, of, Seton Hall University.
4. William Zisk, rhp-of, Roseville, Calif.

**June—Regular Phase (2)**

**1. John Stearns, c, University of Colorado.—(1974-84)**
DRAFT DROP *17th-round draft pick, Buffalo Bills/National Football League (1973)*
**2. Todd Cruz, ss, Western HS, Detroit.—(1978-84)**
3. Ronald Jackson, 3b, Central HS, St. Joseph, Mo.—(Low A)
4. John Hughes, c, Nathan Hale HS, Tulsa, Okla.—(AA)
**5. Jim Wright, rhp, Benton HS, St. Joseph, Mo.—(1981-82)**
**6. Manny Seoane, rhp, Tampa (Fla.) Catholic HS.—(1977-78)**
7. *Steve Kesses, of, North Haven (Conn.) HS.
**8. Randy Lerch, lhp, Cordova HS, Rancho Cordova, Calif.—(1975-86)**
9. Dan Fitzgerald, of, University of New Mexico.
10. Lawrence Hicks, of, University of Texas-Arlington.
11. *Jeff Malinoff, 1b, UC Irvine.
12. *Glen Halvorson, of, Edmonds (Wash.) HS.
13. Mark Crane, ss, University of Michigan.
14. Darrell Flowers, lhp, Cairo (Ill.) HS.
15. *Bruce Hodges, rhp, Sarasota (Fla.) HS.
16. Stephen Thornton, lhp, Pearl HS, Nashville, Tenn.
17. Oliver Bell, lhp, Encino HS, Sacramento, Calif.
18. Mark Ammons, 1b-of, Bowling Green State University.
19. Mark Klein, rhp, Broward (Fla.) CC.
20. *Ken Bourque, lhp, Fermi HS, Enfield, Conn.
21. *James Cullen, rhp, Farmingdale (N.Y.) HS.
22. Joseph O'Brien, rhp, University of Tennessee.

**June—Secondary Phase (12)**

**1. Dan Boitano, rhp, Fresno (Calif.) CC.—(1978-82)**

## PITTSBURGH PIRATES

**January—Regular Phase (23)**

1. Paul Nelson, of, Sacramento (Calif.) CC.—(High A)
2. *Michael Buckingham, rhp, Gulf Coast (Fla.) CC.
3. *Ray Parr, lhp, Bellevue (Wash.) CC.
4. *Larry Prewitt, rhp, Sierra (Calif.) JC.
5. *David Quay, rhp, Tennessee Tech.
6. *Paul Risso, p, JC of San Mateo (Calif.).
7. *Harold Flewelling, p, Shippensburg, Pa.
8. John Hall, rhp-2b, Mineral Area (Mo.) JC.
9. *Ron Sciarro, p, University of Kentucky.
10. Steve Gerlecz, of, State Fair (Mo.) CC.
11. *William Muoio, p, Monroe (N.Y.) CC.
12. *Dale Przybysz, rhp, Erie (N.Y.) CC.
13. *Frank Jarosiewicz, rhp-3b, Staunton (Va.) Military Academy.

**January—Secondary Phase (19)**

1. Richard Olson, c, Fresno (Calif.) CC.—(High A)
2. *Sam Leonard, rhp, Yavapai (Ariz.) JC.
3. *Harry Martell, 3b-rhp, University of Maryland.
4. *John Hoffman, rhp, Lamar (Colo.) CC.
5. *Richard Hudson, rhp, Chipola (Fla.) JC.
6. *Mike Collodi, of-c, Colorado School of Mines.

**June—Regular Phase (24)**

**1. Steve Nicosia, c, North Miami Beach (Fla.) HS.—(1978-85)**
2. Doug Nelson, lhp, Manatee (Fla.) JC.—(AAA)
**3. Mitchell Page, of, Cal Poly Pomona.—(1977-84)**
4. Randy Sealy, rhp, Brazoswood HS, Clute, Texas.—(AAA)
5. Randy Brandt, lhp-1b, Frazier HS, Newell, Pa.—(AA)
6. Dennis Davis, rhp, Martin County HS, Stuart, Fla.
7. Henry Welty, c, Whitesboro (N.Y.) HS.

8. Robert Hall, ss, Concord HS, Wilmington, Del.
9. Thomas Frizzi, of, Mira Loma HS, Sacramento, Calif.
10. Ken Barnes, ss, Gulf Coast (Fla.) CC.
11. Larry Kinn, lhp, Eastern Michigan University.
12. Nicholas Bredy, of, Hiram Johnson HS, Sacramento, Calif.
13. Randy Hopkins, lhp, Livingston (Ala.) University.
14. Wesley Edwards, ss, Berea HS, Greenville, S.C.
15. *Richard Rhodes, lhp, Vanderbilt University.
16. Joe Turnbull, of, High Point College.
17. Vincent Frye, lhp-of, Monessen (Pa.) HS.
18. Joseph Corrado, rhp-of, Deer Lakes HS, Gibsonia, Pa.
19. Joseph Neal, lhp, St. Joseph's University.
20. Dennis Blomberg, rhp, Hibbing (Minn.) HS.
21. Stephen Dorsch, lhp, Concordia (N.Y.) College.
22. Robert Cecil, of, High Point College.
23. Michael Kavanagh, rhp, Villanova University.
24. *David Chappell, of-1b, West Allegheny HS, Imperial, Pa.
25. Joseph Piscotty, of, SUNY-Buffalo.
26. Stanley Schroer, lhp, Louisiana State University.
27. *Michael Williams, lhp, Brazoswood HS, Clute, Texas.
28. *Lawrence Jones, rhp, Seminole (Fla.) HS.
29. *Paul Anthony, lhp, Lancaster (N.Y.) HS.
30. *Tom Kettinger, of, University of Michigan.
31. *Craig Cordt, rhp, Marshalltown (Iowa) HS.

#### June—Secondary Phase (2)

1. **Mark Mercer, lhp, Hill (Texas) JC.—(1981)**
2. Charles Steffen, lhp-1b, Monroe (N.Y.) CC.
3. *William Sempsrott, rhp, Danville, Ill.
4. *Marvin Townsend, ss, Albemarle (N.C.) CC.
5. *Brad Van Pelt, rhp, Michigan State University.

DRAFT DROP *Linebacker, National Football League (1973-86)*

## ST. LOUIS CARDINALS

#### January—Regular Phase (11)

1. Larry Storti, 2b, Long Beach (Calif.) CC.–(High A)
2. *Don Hogestyn, of, Broward (Fla.) CC.
3. *Mark Jackson, c, Long Beach (Calif.) CC.
4. *Chris Loafman, rhp, DeAnza (Calif.) JC.
5. *Richard Smith, lhp, Miami-Dade CC North.
6. *Lynn Merrell, p, Bakersfield (Calif.) JC.
7. *Dean Cummings, p, Ohlone (Calif.) JC.
8. *John Smith, p, Ohlone (Calif.) JC.
9. *Roger Parker, p, Pascagoula, Miss.
10. *Bill Beno, lhp, Manatee (Fla.) JC.

#### January—Secondary Phase (7)

1. *Brad Van Pelt, rhp, Michigan State University.—DNP

DRAFT DROP *Linebacker, National Football League (1973-86)*

2. Kip Coughlan, 3b, Richmond, Va.
3. Tony Milledge, 3b, Manatee (Fla.) JC.

DRAFT DROP *Father of Lastings Milledge, first-round draft pick, Mets (2003); major leaguer (2006-11)*

4. *Paul Cormier, rhp, University of New Hampshire.

#### June—Regular Phase (12)

1. **Joe Edelen, 3b-rhp, Gracemont (Okla.) HS.—(1981-82)**
2. Ron Selak, rhp, El Cerrito (Calif.) HS.—(AAA)
3. Paul Husband, of, University of Mississippi.—(AA)
4. Clint Myers, 3b, Arizona State University.–(AAA)

DRAFT DROP *Father of Corey Myers, first-round draft pick, Diamondbacks (1999)*

5. **Randy Wiles, lhp, Louisiana State University.—(1977)**
6. **John Tamargo, c, Georgia Southern College.—(1976-80)**
7. *Richard Hand, c, Union (N.J.) HS.
8. *James Bradford, lhp, Pine Bluff (Ark.) HS.
9. *Steve Whitehead, ss, Ramona HS, Riverside, Calif.
10. Steve Pasternak, rhp, University of Missouri.
11. David Martin, 1b-of, Kennedy-King (Ill.) JC.
12. *Thomas Cook, 1b, Lenoir City (Tenn.) HS.
13. John Stosz, of, Amherst (Mass.) Regional HS.
14. *Jim Peterson, rhp, Sonora HS, Fullerton, Calif.
15. Donald Boyd, of, Meridian (Miss.) HS.
16. *Gene Laguna, 3b, Union (N.J.) HS.
17. Ronald Aront, ss, Union (N.J.) HS.
18. Frank Nuzzo, 3b, Everett (Mass.) HS.
19. Jimmy Wise, rhp, University of Iowa.
20. Ricky Steen, ss, Big Spring (Texas) HS.
21. David Sandlin, lhp-of, UNC Wilmington.
22. Michael Ford, 3b-c, University of Oklahoma.
23. Dennis Starr, c, University of Mississippi.
24. James Beal, of, University of LaVerne (Calif.).
25. *Dick Jauron, ss, Yale University.

DRAFT DROP *Defensive back, National Football League (1973-80); head coach, Chicago Bears/NFL (1999-2003); head coach, Buffalo Bills/NFL (2006-09)*

26. *Don Walker, 1b-of, Centralia (Ill.) HS.
27. *Dana Pearson, lhp, Cobden (Ill.) HS.
28. *Carmen Caldwell, 1b-of, Jay HS, San Antonio, Texas.
29. Robert Corcoran, rhp, Yale University.
30. *Don Cardoza, of, JC of the Sequoias (Calif.).
31. *Dana McManus, rhp, Palomar (Calif.) CC.
32. **Eric Rasmussen, rhp, Louisiana State University.—(1975-83)**
33. Keith Cochran, 2b, University of Arkansas.
34. Ernie Rosseau, of, University of South Alabama.
35. *Gerald Ako, rhp, Aiea HS, Honolulu.
36. Kris Sorenson, rhp, San Jose State University.
37. Jeff Peeples, rhp, Vanderbilt University.
38. Gary Walker, rhp, University of Nebraska-Omaha.
39. George Chisolm, 1b, Callaway HS, Jackson, Miss.
40. Steve Sherrill, c, University of the Pacific.
41. *Tim Hotop, rhp, Mexico (Mo.) HS.
42. ***Gil Patterson, of-rhp, Norland HS, North Miami Beach, Fla.—(1977)**
43. *James Burress, rhp, Valley HS, Las Vegas, Nev.
44. *Rickey Scarbery, rhp, Roosevelt HS, Fresno, Calif.

DRAFT DROP *Brother of Randy Scarbery, first-round draft pick, Athletics (1973); major leaguer (1979-80)*

45. Thurman Smith, of, University of Arkansas.
46. *Russell Hamilton, of-rhp, Reedley (Calif.) JC.
47. Tommy Neal, of, University of Arkansas.
48. Stephen Ballard, 1b, University of Arkansas.
49. ***Bryn Smith, rhp, Santa Maria (Calif.) HS.—(1981-93)**
50. Richard Shaw, 3b, Tuskegee (Ala.) Institute.
51. *John Dominianni, 3b, Upsala (N.J.) College.
52. Bert Francks, rhp, CC of Morris (N.J.).

#### June—Secondary Phase (8)

1. William Daves, c, Motlow State (Tenn.) CC.—(AAA)

## SAN DIEGO PADRES

#### January—Regular Phase (3)

1. **Dave Wehrmeister, rhp, Northeast Missouri State University.—(1976-85)**
2. *Phil Williams, c, Saddleback (Calif.) CC.
3. *Mike Parkinson, ss, Mount San Antonio (Calif.) JC.
4. **Mike Dupree, rhp-of, Fresno (Calif.) CC.—(1976)**

#### January—Secondary Phase (13)

1. Dan Shaw, rhp, Stanford University.—(AA)
2. *Wayne Williams, ss, Ranger (Texas) JC.

#### June—Regular Phase (4)

1. **Dave Winfield, rhp-of, University of Minnesota.—(1973-95)**

DRAFT DROP *Elected to Baseball Hall of Fame, 2001 • One of three athletes drafted in three professional sports; fifth-round draft pick, Atlanta Hawks/National Basketball Association (1973); sixth-round draft pick, Utah Stars/American Basketball Association (1973); 17th-round draft pick, Minnesota Vikings/National Football League (1973)*

2. **Mike Champion, ss, Foothill HS, Santa Ana, Calif.—(1976-78)**
3. *Steve Day, ss, Lufkin (Texas) HS.—(Short-season A)

DRAFT DROP *Attended Texas; re-drafted by Giants, 1976 (36th round)*

4. Jerry Stone, c, Loyola Marymount University.—(AAA)
5. Nathaniel Harmon, rhp, Taft HS, Cincinnati.—(Short-season A)
6. *Steven Hogan, of-inf, Grant HS, Sacramento, Calif.
7. *Butch Stinson, lhp-of, David Lipscomb College.
8. Jay Smith, rhp, Florida Southern College.
9. John McAllen, lhp, Cal State Los Angeles.
10. Peter Cusick, c, Monmouth College.
11. Dwight Adams, c, Los Angeles (Calif.) HS.
12. Dale Torcato, 3b, Woodland (Calif.) HS.

DRAFT DROP *Father of Tony Torcato, first-round draft pick, Giants (1998); major leaguer (2002-05)*

13. **Joe McIntosh, rhp, Washington State University.—(1974-75)**
14. Bob Polock, 2b, University of Illinois.
15. Gregory Zail, rhp, UCLA.
16. *Samuel Nicholson, rhp, University of Texas.
17. *Glen Johnson, c-of, Stanford University.
18. *Tim Pettorini, of, Bowling Green State University.
19. *Gregory Kruciak, lhp, St. Gerard HS, San Antonio, Texas.
20. *Ray Crawford, ss-of, Santa Ana (Calif.) HS.
21. Scott Brown, 1b, UC Santa Barbara.

#### June—Secondary Phase (18)

No selection.

## SAN FRANCISCO GIANTS

#### January—Regular Phase (5)

1. John Andrews, ss, Lincoln Land (Ill.) JC.—(AA)
2. ***Rob Picciolo, ss, Santa Monica (Calif.) JC.—(1977-85)**
3. *Bill Malpass, ss-2b, West Valley (Calif.) JC.
4. James Davidson, rhp-of, Linn-Benton (Ore.) CC.
5. *William Kolarik, p, Los Angeles Valley JC.
6. *Kevin Nelson, lhp, JC of Southern Idaho.
7. *Mark Weldon, inf, Green River (Wash.) CC.
8. *Thomas Park, p, Bellevue (Wash.) CC.
9. *Stephen Corn, p-1b, Spokane Falls (Wash.) CC.
10. *Doug Johnson, p, Scottsdale (Ariz.) CC.

#### January—Secondary Phase (23)

1. **Dave Heaverlo, rhp, Central Washington University.—(1975-81)**

DRAFT DROP *Father of Jeff Heaverlo, first-round draft pick, Mariners (1999)*

2. *Steve Wilkins, of, Treasure Valley (Ore.) CC.
3. Dennis Smith, 1b, Miami (Ohio) University.
4. *Robert Alonzo, inf, Phoenix (Ariz.) CC.
5. *Bill Przygocki, rhp, St. Clair County (Mich.) CC.
6. *Craig Cornwell, rhp, Pasadena (Calif.) CC.
7. *Peter Cervantes, c-3b, Los Angeles CC.

#### June—Regular Phase (6)

1. **Johnnie LeMaster, ss, Paintsville (Ky.) HS.—(1975-87)**
2. Ernest Young, c, Denby HS, Detroit.—(AA)
3. **Jeff Little, lhp, Woodmore HS, Woodville, Ohio.—(1980-82)**
4. Terry Coomer, rhp, Noblesville (Ind.) HS.—(Rookie)
5. ***Bobby Mitchell, of, Chatsworth (Calif.) HS.—(1980-83)**

DRAFT DROP *Attended Southern California; re-drafted by Dodgers, 1977 (7th round)*

6. **Tommy Toms, rhp, East Carolina University.—(1975-77)**
7. Steve Grimes, 3b, Point Loma HS, San Diego.
8. Tony Cabrera, 3b, Hialeah (Fla.) HS.
9. *Bobby McClellan, c, Emma Sansom HS, Gadsden, Ala.
10. **Eddie Plank, rhp, University of Nevada-Reno.—(1978-79)**
11. *Tommy Jarmon, of, Edison HS, Stockton, Calif.
12. Gerald Anderson, of, Edgewood HS, West Covina, Calif.
13. **Jack Clark, rhp-of, Gladstone HS, Covina, Calif.—(1975-92)**
14. *Karl Gordon, ss, Montclair State (N.J.) College.
15. *Robert Simons, c, Logansport (Ind.) HS.
16. Arturo Marin, 2b, Pasadena (Calif.) CC.
17. Stephen Williams, lhp, Swanton (Ohio) HS.
18. *Jeffrey Ross, lhp, Ellwood P. Cubberley HS, Palo Alto, Calif.
19. Frank Zawatski, c, Lehigh University.
20. Carroll Palmer, lhp, Treasure Valley (Ore.) CC.
21. ***Dan Graham, 3b, Mesa (Ariz.) CC.—(1979-81)**
22. *James Schak, rhp, Newark (N.J.) College of Engineering.
23. *Kevin Tennant, c, Seton Hall University.
24. *James Bertram, rhp, La Jolla (Calif.) HS.
25. *Darnell Waters, inf, Fremont HS, Oakland, Calif.
26. Robert Sparks, of, Castlemont HS, Oakland, Calif.
27. *George Hahn, c, Campbell (Calif.) HS.

DRAFT DROP *Brother of Don Hahn, major leaguer (1969-75)*

28. Lee Cook, lhp, Treasure Valley (Ore.) CC.
29. *Stewart Bringhurst, rhp-c, Crestmoor HS, San Bruno, Calif.
30. *Gavin Long, rhp, Westmoor HS, Pacifica, Calif.

#### June—Secondary Phase (4)

1. **Pete Falcone, lhp, Kingsborough (N.Y.) CC.—(1975-84)**

## TEXAS RANGERS

#### January—Regular Phase (2)

1. Brad Fulk, 2b, Air Force Academy.—(AA)
2. ***Jeff Schneider, lhp, Iowa State University.—(1981)**
3. *Zane Grubbs, lhp, University of Texas.

#### January—Secondary Phase (2)

1. **Jim Sundberg, c, University of Iowa.—(1974-89)**
2. *Rick Bethke, lhp, Cerritos (Calif.) JC.
3. *Kevin Morel, ss, Indian River (Fla.) CC.
4. *Donnelly Douglas, lhp, Amherst (Mass.) College.
5. *Ray Boneschans, rhp, Valencia (Fla.) CC.
6. *Richard Mallman, rhp, West Valley (Calif.) JC.
7. *William Robinson, of, University of Delaware.

#### June—Regular Phase (1)

1. **David Clyde, lhp, Westchester HS, Houston.—(1973-79)**

DRAFT DROP *First 1973 high school draft pick to reach majors (June 27, 1973)*

2. Rich Shubert, lhp, Bryant HS, Astoria, N.Y.—(AA)
3. **Len Barker, rhp, Neshaminy HS, Trevose, Pa.—(1976-87)**
4. *Lynn Garrett, ss, Berkeley (Calif.) HS.—(AAA)

DRAFT DROP *Attended Arizona; re-drafted by Indians, 1977 (11th round)*

5. **Ken Pape, ss, University of Texas.—(1976)**
6. *Andrew Mason, 3b, Charter Oak HS, Covina, Calif.
7. Drew Nickerson, rhp, Reseda (Calif.) HS.
8. *Wayne Steele, lhp, Hoover HS, San Diego.
9. Don Thomas, 3b, University of California.
10. Steven Strickland, lhp, Fort Myers (Fla.) HS.
11. John Weber, ss-of, LaSalle HS, Niagara Falls, N.Y.
12. Ray Rainboldt, rhp, Cleveland (Okla.) HS.
13. *Eugene Norman, rhp, San Gorgonio HS, Highland, Calif.
14. *Gerald Erb, rhp, Wahconah Regional HS, Dalton, Mass.
15. Gary Wright, of-1b, Albert Einstein HS, Kensington, Md.
16. *Mark Peters, rhp, Morton HS, Hammond, Ind.
17. Gary Hubka, 3b, Memorial HS, Beloit, Wis.
18. *Walt Kaczmarek, rhp, Santa Clara University.
19. *Roland Keys, ss, Morristown (N.J.) HS.
20. *Mike Merritt, rhp, University of North Carolina.
21. Walter Gawaluch, ss, Texas Wesleyan College.
22. Greg Keen, rhp, Miami-Dade CC South.
23. Jonathan Astroth, of, Southern Methodist University.
24. *Barry Mollencupp, c, Harlem HS, Loves Park, Ill.
25. Gene Delyon, 3b, Santa Clara University.
26. Lindsey Graham, rhp, Clemson University.
27. *Nicholas Peterson, lhp, Stanford University.
28. ***Billy Sample, 3b, Andrew Lewis HS, Salem, Va.—(1978-86)**
29. Rudy Jaramillo, of, University of Texas.
30. **Dan Duran, 1b, Foothill (Calif.) JC.—(1981)**
31. Don Bodenhamer, 3b, Texas Christian University.
32. (void) *Mark Hance, 3b, Fresno State University.
33. Michael Mehaffie, rhp-of, Kimball HS, Dallas.
34. *Frederic Wade, 3b, Columbus HS, Miami.
35. *Steve Polan, ss, El Camino HS, Sacramento, Calif.
36. *Gary Wiencek, c, Citrus (Calif.) JC.

#### June—Secondary Phase (17)

1. *Jeff Feramisco, of, Fresno (Calif.) CC.—(High A)

# 1974

## AT A GLANCE

### This Date In History
**WINTER DRAFT:** Jan. 9
**SUMMER DRAFT:** June 5-6

### Best Draft
**CALIFORNIA ANGELS.** Seven of the first eight, and nine of the first 12 players the Angels drafted played in the majors, an unprecedented success rate in the first 15 years of the draft.

### Worst Draft
**OAKLAND ATHLETICS.** Despite winning three consecutive World Series titles from 1972-74, the A's never built on it in the draft. They failed to sign their first three picks in 1974, and six of their top 10.

### First-Round Bust
**RON SOREY, 3B, EXPOS.** The only first-rounder not to reach at least Double-A, Sorey played five seasons in the Expos and Blue Jays systems, hitting a combined .239 with 22 homers.

### Second Time Around
**BUTCH WYNEGAR, C, TWINS.** Wynegar set the bar high with the success he enjoyed in his first two seasons in the minors (.323 with 27 home runs in 199 games), and by becoming the youngest player, at 20, to play in the All-Star Game. But his first two years with the Twins proved to be his best, and his 13-year career in the majors fell short of expectations.

### Late-Round Find
**JIM GANTNER, 2B, BREWERS (12TH ROUND).** With apologies to one-season wonder Mark Fidrych, a 10th-round pick of the Tigers who electrified the baseball world as a rookie in 1976 with his zany mound antics and 19-win season, the steady Gantner had the more productive career. In 17 seasons in the majors, all with the Brewers, he hit .274. He also fielded the ball at a .985 clip, and was a double-play partner of Hall of Famer Robin Yount for a number of years before Yount moved to center field in 1985.

# Scarce talent prompts aggressive signings

The 1974 draft was significant as a low point in the 50-year evolution of the process because teams selected fewer players in June that year (726) than in any draft in history, with 689 taken in the regular phase and 37 in the secondary phase. Those numbers pointed to a more far-reaching problem that major league teams were beginning to come to grips with.

"The apparent reduction in the quality of talent available at the free-agent level has to raise serious questions as to the quality of our product at the major league level 10 or 15 years from today," said a concerned Lou Gorman, vice president of player development for the Kansas City Royals. "If this alarming trend continues, I shudder to think what we will be marketing as Major League Baseball in the future.

"We must do everything humanly and financially possible to revitalize, rejuvenate and redirect the high school baseball programs in this country."

Baseball, to its credit, recognized the issue, and did its part in the 1974 draft to address it by luring athletes away from other sports—specifically football—like no draft before.

The most noteworthy two-sport athlete targeted was Louisiana State's Mike Miley, a star shortstop on the baseball team and the starting quarterback on the football squad.

Three years earlier, Miley had passed up a first-round offer from the Cincinnati Reds to play football at LSU, but now it was baseball's chance to turn the tables and grab the upper hand in the Miley sweepstakes.

With the 10th pick overall in the first round, the California Angels went after Miley, who the previous January led LSU to victory over Penn State in the Orange Bowl. It took a $90,000 package, including a $75,000 signing bonus, for the Angels to persuade Miley, one of the top signal callers in the college game, to give up his senior year of football.

"It was the toughest decision I ever had to make," Miley said. "I had to decide whether my future was in football or baseball."

There was speculation that Miley might take advantage of a new NCAA policy that enabled athletes to be professionals in one sport while maintaining their amateur standing in another. But the Southeastern Conference's interpretation of the rule was more stringent, and when push came to shove, baseball scored a coup by winning Miley's services outright.

Unfortunately, Miley was killed in a car accident three years later.

No player from the 1974 draft class went on to become a Hall of Famer, but the Atlanta Braves' Dale Murphy was probably the closest. He was picked fifth overall that year, as a catcher out of an Oregon high school, though it wasn't until he moved permanently to the outfield in 1980 that his career took off.

BROWN UNIVERSITY

Brown shortstop Bill Almon was the Padres' target with the No. 1 pick in 1974, after they took a flier on him three years earlier out of high school, but he never became an impact player in the big leagues

He became a two-time National League MVP and in the 1980s, only Mike Schmidt (313) hit more home runs than Murphy's 308. Only Eddie Murray (996) surpassed Murphy's 929 RBIs.

## MIXED SIGNALS IN FIRST ROUND

While fewer players (983) were drafted overall in 1974—counting both phases in January and June—than in any year since the inaugural draft in 1965, when there was only one phase, major league clubs began to figure out the intricacies of baseball's primary talent procurement process with a greater sense of precision. On many counts, the 1974 draft was the most successful to date.

A higher percentage of draft picks overall (16.4 percent) reached the majors, as did players taken in both the first 10 rounds of the June regular phase (32.1 percent) and the first round (75 percent, or 18 of 24).

Of the seven most successful players in that year's draft, as measured by WAR (Wins Above Replacement), six were first-rounders, while the seventh was former University of Southern California shortstop Roy Smalley Jr., the top pick in the January regular phase who also commanded

## 1974: THE FIRST ROUNDERS

| CLUB: PLAYER, POS., SCHOOL | HOMETOWN | B-T | HT. | WT. | AGE | BONUS | FIRST YEAR | LAST YEAR | PEAK LEVEL (YEARS) |
|---|---|---|---|---|---|---|---|---|---|
| **JUNE—REGULAR PHASE** | | | | | | | | | |
| 1. *Padres: Bill Almon, ss, Brown | Warwick, R.I. | R-R | 6-3 | 170 | 21 | $90,000 | 1974 | 1988 | Majors (15) |
| Tall, rangy Ivy Leaguer played 15 years in majors with eight clubs, hit .254 with 36 homers; had all-star season with White Sox in 1981, but mostly utility role. | | | | | | | | | |
| 2. Rangers: Tommy Boggs, rhp, Lanier HS | Austin, Texas | R-R | 6-2 | 201 | 18 | $87,500 | 1974 | 1985 | Majors (9) |
| Texas recruit started, ended major league career with Rangers, achieved greatest success with Braves; went 20-44, 4.22 overall, hung it up in 1986 with arm issues. | | | | | | | | | |
| 3. Phillies: Lonnie Smith, of, Centennial HS | Compton, Calif. | R-R | 5-9 | 177 | 18 | $55,000 | 1974 | 1994 | Majors (17) |
| Talented but flawed player hit .288 with 98 homers, 370 steals in majors, was starter on five World Series teams; career tainted by his part in 1980s drug scandal. | | | | | | | | | |
| 4. Indians: Tom Brennan, rhp, Lewis (Ill.) | Oak Lawn, Ill. | R-R | 6-1 | 180 | 21 | $45,000 | 1974 | 1986 | Majors (5) |
| One-man team in leading Lewis to '74 NAIA World Series title (12-1, 1.17, 86 IP/144 SO); finally broke into majors at 28, went 9-10, 4.40 as reliever. | | | | | | | | | |
| 5. Braves: Dale Murphy, c, Woodrow Wilson HS | Portland, Ore. | R-R | 6-4 | 195 | 18 | $43,750 | 1974 | 1993 | Majors (18) |
| Hit .462-5-28 in 16 games as prep SR; played catcher, then first base in early stages of 18-year career, but became one of game's best when moved to OF in 1980. | | | | | | | | | |
| 6. Brewers: Butch Edge, rhp, El Camino HS | Sacramento, Calif. | R-R | 6-3 | 195 | 17 | $47,500 | 1974 | 1983 | Majors (1) |
| Lost to Toronto in 1976 expansion draft; went 3-4, 5.23 for Jays in only MLB season in 1979, then spent balance of career in minors, where he went 33-44, 3.95. | | | | | | | | | |
| 7. Cubs: Scot Thompson, of, Knoch HS | Renfrew, Pa. | L-L | 6-2 | 160 | 18 | $40,000 | 1974 | 1985 | Majors (8) |
| His high school didn't field a team, so scouts judged him in workouts, Legion ball; went hitless in first 39 pro at-bats, but rebounded to hit .262 in 620 MLB games. | | | | | | | | | |
| 8. White Sox: Larry Monroe, rhp, Forest View HS | Mount Prospect, Ill. | R-R | 6-4 | 200 | 17 | $58,000 | 1974 | 1979 | Majors (1) |
| Longtime Sox scouting exec got his pro start in organization; reached majors in 1976, but developed shoulder problems after five appearances in only season. | | | | | | | | | |
| 9. Expos: Ron Sorey, 3b, Stebbins HS | Dayton, Ohio | R-R | 6-1 | 200 | 19 | $43,000 | 1974 | 1978 | Class A (3) |
| Expos sorry they wasted pick on Wisconsin quarterback recruit; never progressed beyond Class A for Expos, Blue Jays, hit .239-22-135 with 84 steals. | | | | | | | | | |
| 10. Angels: # Mike Miley, ss, Louisiana State | Metairie, La. | B-R | 6-1 | 180 | 21 | $75,000 | 1974 | 1976 | Majors (2) |
| Rejected Reds first-round offer in 1971 to play QB at LSU; promising MLB career had just started when he died in a single-car wreck in January 1977. | | | | | | | | | |
| 11. Pirates: # Rod Scurry, lhp, Proctor Hug HS | Sparks, Nev. | L-L | 6-2 | 180 | 18 | $35,000 | 1974 | 1988 | Majors (8) |
| Central figure in early 1980s drug scandal that rocked Pirates; went 19-32, 3.24 in eight major league seasons, died in 1992 of cocaine-induced heart attack. | | | | | | | | | |
| 12. Yankees: Dennis Sherrill, ss, South Miami HS | Miami | R-R | 6-0 | 165 | 18 | $55,000 | 1974 | 1980 | Majors (2) |
| Disappointment on several fronts when Yanks passed on ex-batboy Eddie Ford, Whitey's son, and went for Miami prep shortstop; played just five games in majors. | | | | | | | | | |
| 13. Cardinals: Garry Templeton, ss, Santa Ana Valley HS | Santa Ana Valley, Calif. | R-R | 5-11 | 170 | 18 | $37,500 | 1974 | 1991 | Majors (16) |
| Career soared in St. Louis after six major league seasons (.305-25-281), but pace slipped when he became disgruntled, traded to Padres for Ozzie Smith. | | | | | | | | | |
| 14. Twins: Ted Shipley, ss, Vanderbilt | Chattanooga, Tenn. | R-R | 6-1 | 170 | 21 | $35,000 | 1974 | 1976 | Class AA (2) |
| Best college career of three SEC shortstops taken in first round, but never got untracked in three seasons in minors (.238-6-87); later became Vermont college coach. | | | | | | | | | |
| 15. Astros: Kevin Drake, of, Cabrillo HS | Lompoc, Calif. | R-R | 6-3 | 200 | 18 | $71,125 | 1974 | 1977 | Class AAA (1) |
| Astros paid significant bonus to pry two-sport standout away from UCLA football career; never distinguished himself in four seasons in minors (.228-11-98, 50 SBs). | | | | | | | | | |
| 16. Tigers: Lance Parrish, 3b, Walnut HS | Diamond Bar, Calif. | R-R | 6-4 | 215 | 17 | $60,000 | 1974 | 1975 | Majors (19) |
| Spent senior high school season at hot corner, but Tigers quickly re-established him as everyday catcher, leading to a 19-year career at position, 324 homers. | | | | | | | | | |
| 17. Mets: Cliff Speck, rhp, Beaverton HS | Beaverton, Ore. | R-R | 6-3 | 190 | 17 | $30,000 | 1974 | 1988 | Majors (1) |
| Released by Mets after four seasons because of injuries, control issues, but perservered, finally reached majors in 1986 at age 29, with fifth organization. | | | | | | | | | |
| 18. Royals: Willie Wilson, of, Summit HS | Summit, N.J. | R-R | 6-3 | 195 | 18 | $90,000 | 1974 | 1994 | Majors (19) |
| Three-sport prep star had 200 college football offers; bonus expectations scared off numerous clubs, but Royals rewarded by taking run at speedy leadoff hitter. | | | | | | | | | |
| 19. Giants: Terry Lee, 2b, San Luis Obispo HS | San Luis Obispo, Calif. | L-R | 6-1 | 175 | 18 | $25,000 | 1974 | 1981 | Class AAA (2) |
| Son of Tom Lee, celebrated multi-sport athlete/coach at Cal Poly, brother of current Poly baseball coach Larry Lee; career peaked in Triple-A in 1981 (.271-47-293). | | | | | | | | | |
| 20. Red Sox: Eddie Ford, ss, South Carolina | Great Neck, N.Y. | B-R | 6-1 | 165 | 20 | $50,000 | 1974 | 1977 | Class AAA (1) |
| Grew up among Yankee royalty as Whitey's son, played in college for Bobby Richardson; drafted by rivals, struggled in four seasons at plate (.236-11-98), in field. | | | | | | | | | |
| 21. Dodgers: Rick Sutcliffe, rhp, Van Horn HS | Kansas City, Mo. | L-R | 6-5 | 205 | 17 | $50,000 | 1974 | 1994 | Majors (18) |
| Easily most successful pitcher taken in first round; won 171 games in 18 MLB seasons, was NL Rookie of Year in '79, led AL in ERA in '82, won Cy Young in '84. | | | | | | | | | |
| 22. Athletics: Jerry Johnson, c/rhp, McCallum HS | Austin, Texas | R-R | 6-2 | 185 | 18 | Unsigned | 1975 | 1985 | Class AAA (4) |
| Unsigned, re-drafted following January by Cardinals; spent first four seasons of 11-year career in minors as catcher (.200-4-49), last seven on mound (51-68, 3.75). | | | | | | | | | |
| 23. Reds: Steve Reed, rhp, Fort Wayne HS | Fort Wayne, Ind. | R-R | 6-1 | 185 | 18 | $25,000 | 1974 | 1980 | Class AAA (1) |
| Showed early promise by going 19-11, 2.37 in first two seasons, but hurt arm, released in 1977; signed on with Brewers as reliever, pitched three more years. | | | | | | | | | |
| 24. Orioles: Rich Dauer, ss/3b, Southern California | Colton, Calif. | R-R | 6-0 | 175 | 21 | $20,000 | 1974 | 1985 | Majors (10) |
| Hit .387-15-92, set NCAA record for hits in leading USC to fifth straight national title in 1974; became better known with O's as dependable defender at 2B. | | | | | | | | | |
| **JANUARY—REGULAR PHASE** | | | | | | | | | |
| 1. Rangers: Roy Smalley, ss, Southern California | Los Angeles | B-R | 6-1 | 185 | 21 | $95,000 | 1974 | 1987 | Majors (13) |
| Great pedigree as son of big leaguer, nephew of Gene Mauch, two-year starter on national champion; played 13 years in majors, hit .257 with 163 HRs, solid in field. | | | | | | | | | |
| **JANUARY—SECONDARY PHASE** | | | | | | | | | |
| 1. Royals: David Hasbach, rhp, Miami (Ohio) | Palatine, Ill. | R-R | 6-3 | 205 | 22 | $7,500 | 1975 | 1979 | Class AAA (3) |
| Royals gambled top pick on injury-plagued pitcher, who missed '74 college season with elbow surgery; reached Triple-A in first season, but never went further. | | | | | | | | | |
| **JUNE—SECONDARY PHASE** | | | | | | | | | |
| 1. Reds: Mike Gatlin, 3b, Arizona | Ontario, Calif. | R-R | 6-1 | 190 | 21 | Unsigned | 1975 | 1979 | Class AAA (3) |
| Passed up Reds offer, slipped to fifth round next January when re-drafted by Twins; signed after leading Arizona in homers, RBIs; played five years in minors. | | | | | | | | | |

**Signed to major league contract. # Deceased.*

## AT A GLANCE

### Never Too Late

**RANDY JOHNSON, 3B, ORIOLES (39TH ROUND).** This one, while also from California, didn't sign with the Orioles, was re-drafted by the Mets in 1978 out of San Jose State and went on to play three years in the majors, from 1982-84, with the Braves. He went on to a long career as a scout and minor league instructor.

### Overlooked

**TOMMY HERR, 2B, CARDINALS.** The best of 24 players signed as non-drafted free agents in 1974 who eventually found their way to the big leagues, Herr signed for $10,000 and played 13 seasons in the majors, most prominently with the Cardinals. In 1985, he led that club to a World Series berth by driving in 110 runs, while hitting .302.

### International Gem

**ALFREDO EDMEAD, OF, PIRATES.** No international player who signed in 1974 went on to a notable big league career. But stardom was predicted for Edmead, a 17-year-old from the Dominican Republic who died on Aug. 22, 1974, after colliding with a teammate at Class A Salem while both were chasing a pop fly in a Carolina League game. He hit .314 with 61 stolen bases in his only minor league season.

### Minor League Take

**LONNIE SMITH, OF, PHILLIES.** Smith, the third player drafted in 1974, was champing at the bit to join a power-packed Phillies lineup in the late 1970s. But with no openings, he was forced to play four full seasons at Triple-A Oklahoma City from 1976-79, during which time he hit .307, scored 393 runs and stole 171 bases. He finally earned his shot at the big leagues with the World Series champion Phillies in 1980, and went on to hit .288 over a 17-year big league career.

CONTINUED ON PAGE 152

## AT A GLANCE

CONTINUED FROM PAGE 151

### One Who Got Away

**PAUL MOLITOR, SS, CARDINALS (28TH ROUND).** The only Hall of Famer connected to the 1974 draft, Molitor didn't sign out of high school with the Cardinals. Three years later, he was snapped up by the Brewers with the third pick overall and went on to a 21-year major league career.

### He Was Drafted?

**STEVE BARTKOWSKI, 1B, ORIOLES (19TH ROUND).** The last of four future NFL players drafted by the Orioles in 1974, Bartkowski came the closest to pursuing a baseball career. He was pegged by numerous clubs as a potential first-rounder but had a disappointing junior season and tumbled in the draft. That fall, he became the top passing quarterback in the nation, and his potential baseball career was history when he became the No. 1 pick in the NFL draft the following spring.

### Did You Know . . .

Every pitcher drafted in the first round in 1974 had a losing record in the minor leagues, with one exception: **TOM BRENNAN,** who began his pro career in Triple-A, yet took more than seven years to crack the majors. Brennan went 91-84 in the minors, while the combined record of the other eight first-round arms was 396-486.

### They Said It

**ROY SMALLEY JR.,** on being drafted first overall in January by Texas: "The two people in baseball I most respect are my father and uncle (Gene Mauch). They both told me there's not a better manager in the game than Billy Martin."—*Martin was fired less than two months after Smalley reached the big leagues with the Rangers; over a 13-year career, he played for 15 different managers, including his uncle Gene.*

the largest bonus ($95,000) that year.

In no other draft to date did the elite-level talent come off the board with such precision—even as there was no obvious talent like a future Hall of Famer to choose from (save for Paul Molitor, a late-round selection in 1974, who didn't sign and was re-drafted in 1977).

But if 1974 was the most successful draft at least on one score, it came at a cost as three first-rounders were at the center of well-documented drug scandals that rocked the game in the early 1980s.

Lonnie Smith (Phillies, third) and Rod Scurry (Pirates, 11th) were central figures in the infamous Pittsburgh drug trials of 1985. Smith was granted immunity from prosecution in exchange for his testimony, but was one of seven players suspended for a year by new commissioner Peter Ueberroth. The suspension was later commuted in exchange for fines, submission to drug testing and public service. Scurry testified, but was not punished for his involvement with drugs.

Willie Wilson (Royals, 18th) was implicated along with several Kansas City teammates in 1983. He pleaded guilty to misdemeanor drug charges for attempting to purchase cocaine, and served 81 days in jail. Wilson was also suspended for the 1984 season by commissioner Bowie Kuhn, though the suspension was later reduced on appeal.

Smith and Wilson both managed to pick up the pieces from their drug involvement and went on to resume long and otherwise successful careers in the majors. Scurry wasn't as fortunate, as continued heavy drug use cost him his life. Four years after he retired in 1988, he died of a cocaine-induced heart attack.

Smith's road to success was a roller-coaster ride. Never known for defensive excellence, Smith once led Triple-A American Association outfielders in errors four years in a row (1976-79) while playing for Oklahoma City, but also hit .307 and scored 393 runs over the same span.

Lonnie Smith

After finally cracking the Phillies roster in 1980, he played a contributing role as the team won the World Series. Two years later, after being traded by Philadelphia to St. Louis, he was runner-up in the National League MVP voting to Murphy, as the Cardinals won the World Series. In all, Smith was a starter for five teams through the years that played in the World Series.

But Smith also became heavily involved with drugs, spent time in the minor leagues and was released. Down but not out, Smith came charging back to win NL comeback player of the year honors with Atlanta in 1989.

### PADRES FIND JOY IN ALMON

Miley and Smalley were the highest-profile and best-known shortstops in the 1974 draft class, but both players were upstaged in that year's draft by a lesser-known college shortstop in Brown University's Bill Almon. The San Diego Padres plucked the Ivy Leaguer with the No. 1 selection in the June regular phase.

The Padres had a longstanding interest in the tall, rangy Almon, as they also drafted him in 1971 out of high school in Warwick, R.I. Three years later, the Padres' patience paid off and they finally got their man.

"I'm really pleased to be with San Diego," Almon said at the time of his signing. "I like the organization and the people I've dealt with. I couldn't be happier if I had been drafted by any other club."

As a high school talent, Almon had scouts from every major league team hot on his trail. The Milwaukee Brewers, for one, were prepared to draft him in the first round.

Prior to the 1971 draft, however, Almon wrote to every major league club, thanking them for their interest and explaining that he had decided to go to college. Brown University, not exactly a baseball factory, won the Almon sweepstakes.

The Padres took a chance anyway, drafting Almon in the 10th round, and though he turned them down, his name was tucked away in their futures file.

"I knew I wasn't going to sign then, and the Padres knew it too," Almon said. "But they weren't drafting too many people then, and they thought it was worth the risk. Frankly, I didn't think I was

## How They Should Have Done It

Based on the career WAR (Wins Above Replacement, as calculated by Baseball-Reference.com) numbers achieved by all the players eligible for the 1974 draft, here's how the first round should have unfolded. Numbers in parentheses indicate the round when the player was actually drafted

| | Player, Pos. | Actual Draft | WAR | Bonus |
|---|---|---|---|---|
| 1. | Dale Murphy, c | Braves (1) | 46.3 | $43,750 |
| 2. | Willie Wilson, of | Royals (1) | 45.3 | $90,000 |
| 3. | Lance Parrish, 3b | Tigers (1) | 39.3 | $60,000 |
| 4. | Lonnie Smith, of | Phillies (1) | 38.4 | $55,000 |
| 5. | Rick Sutcliffe, rhp | Dodgers (1) | 34.3 | $40,000 |
| 6. | Roy Smalley, ss | Rangers (Jan.-R/1) | 27.8 | $95,000 |
| 7. | Garry Templeton, ss | Cardinals (1) | 27.7 | $37,500 |
| 8. | Butch Wynegar, c | Twins (2) | 26.4 | $25,000 |
| 9. | Bob Stanley, rhp | Red Sox (Jan.-S/1) | 24.3 | $4,000 |
| 10. | Tommy Herr, 2b | Phillies (NDFA) | 23.3 | $10,000 |
| 11. | Jim Gantner, 2b | Brewers (12) | 22.4 | $3,000 |
| 12. | Ed Whitson, rhp | Pirates (6) | 21.8 | $5,000 |
| 13. | Jim Clancy, rhp | Rangers (4) | 21.3 | $7,500 |
| 14. | Shane Rawley, lhp | Expos (June-S/2) | 21.1 | $5,000 |
| 15. | Moose Haas, rhp | Brewers (2) | 17.6 | $22,500 |
| | Bryn Smith, rhp | Orioles (NDFA) | 17.6 | $1,000 |
| 17. | Rance Mulliniks, ss | Angels (3) | 17.2 | $25,000 |
| 18. | Julio Cruz, 2b | Angels (NDFA) | 16.9 | Unavailable |
| 19. | Pete Vuckovich, rhp | White Sox (3) | 16.5 | $16,000 |
| 20. | Rich Dauer, ss/3b | Orioles (1) | 14.4 | $20,000 |
| 21. | Rick Camp, rhp | Braves (7) | 12.3 | $5,000 |
| 22. | Jim Morrison, 3b | Phillies (5) | 12.1 | $12,500 |
| 23. | Steve Henderson, of | Reds (5) | 11.5 | $2,500 |
| | Bill Caudill, rhp | Cardinals (8) | 11.5 | $10,000 |
| | Mark Fidrych, rhp | Tigers (10) | 11.5 | None |

| | Top 3 Unsigned Players | | | Year Signed |
|---|---|---|---|---|
| 1. | Paul Molitor, ss | Cardinals (28) | 75.5 | 1977 |
| 2. | Bob Welch, rhp | Cubs (14) | 44.2 | 1977 |
| 3. | Scott Sanderson, rhp | Royals (11) | 28.1 | 1977 |

mature enough, either mentally or physically, for professional baseball at that time."

With the first pick in 1974, the Padres did not hesitate to go back after the Brown shortstop, who hit .362 as a junior with a school-record 10 home runs and 31 RBIs. He was signed to a major league contract that included a $90,000 bonus.

Almon expressed a desire to start his career in the big leagues, just like Padres first-round picks Dave Roberts (1972) and Dave Winfield (1973) before him, but he acquiesced to the Padres' wishes for him begin his career in the minors—though with the promise of a September callup.

After working out with the big league club for five days, Almon was sent to Triple-A Hawaii. But he sat on the bench there, in large measure because the Islanders owned many of their own players at the time and had a say in who would play. Almon hit just .222 in 14 games before being sent to Alexandria of the Double-A Texas League, where he hit .186 in 25 contests. Despite his struggles at the plate, he still earned a September shot with the Padres under provisions of the major league contract he signed. In his first 16 big league games, he hit .316.

Almon finally took over as San Diego's regular shortstop in 1977, but was moved to second base a year later to accommodate a slick-fielding rookie, Ozzie Smith. Almon soon fell out of favor with Padres management, and never clicked in trials with the Montreal Expos and New York Mets over the next two years. He briefly resurrected his fading career with the Chicago White Sox in 1981, his best season.

Over a 15-year career in the majors, while playing for eight different teams, Almon never hit with much authority, batting .254 with 36 homers.

"When I first signed, I gave professional baseball too much credit," said Almon, reflecting on his career. "I didn't take the approach that I had to do something right in the first place to be where I was. That was a major mistake. I finally just decided to play my game and took the approach that I would be successful if I did what I did best."

If it was a familiar face that the Padres went for in selecting Almon with the top pick, the Texas Rangers used a familiar script in making the second pick.

A year after securing Texas schoolboy David Clyde with the No. 1 pick, the Rangers went for another hard-throwing Texan, Austin righthander Tommy Boggs. The Rangers, however, were much more patient with Boggs than they were with Clyde, and resisted any temptation of promoting

## Fastest To The Majors

| | Player, Pos. | Drafted (Round) | Debut |
|---|---|---|---|
| 1. | Jack Kucek, rhp | White Sox (2) | Aug. 8, 1974 |
| 2. | Bill Almon, ss | Padres (1) | Sept. 2, 1974 |
| 3. | Jim Umbarger, lhp | Rangers (16) | April 8, 1975 |
| 4. | Roy Smalley, ss | Rangers (Jan.-R/1) | April 30, 1975 |
| 5. | Mike Miley, ss | Angels (1) | July 6, 1975 |

**FIRST HIGH SCHOOL SELECTION:** Butch Wynegar, c (Twins/2, April 9, 1976).

**LAST PLAYER TO RETIRE:** Lance Parrish, c (Sept. 23, 1995).

## DRAFT SPOTLIGHT: DALE MURPHY

As great as Dale Murphy's career ended up, Braves officials can't help but wonder what might have been had he stayed a catcher

No player from the 1974 draft class went on to the Hall of Fame, but Dale Murphy, a two-time National League MVP, was probably the closest. The Braves picked him fifth overall that year, as a catcher out of an Oregon high school, though it wasn't until he moved to the outfield in 1980 that his career took off.

Murphy was the first bona fide prospect to come along in Atlanta since the Braves moved from Milwaukee almost a decade earlier. He was the crown jewel of the farm system and expected to be the game's next great catcher. There was eager anticipation among Braves officials when Murphy arrived in 1977.

"Oh my, yes, he was a catcher!" raved Braves scouting director Paul Snyder, recalling Murphy's formative years. "As a scout, you're always looking for that kind of arm strength and hitting ability from a catcher. He had a chance to be a great one."

The Braves had groomed Murphy carefully in the minor leagues when they put him behind the plate in a spring game in 1977 against the Yankees, who repeatedly took advantage of the inexperienced 20-year-old. Twice they pulled off successful delayed steals when Murphy double-pumped, then refused to throw the ball through to second base. Later, he threw the ball down the left-field line on an steal of third. After the game, Braves manager Dave Bristol so berated Murphy that it forever undermined his confidence. Even though Murphy developed into one of the game's top all-around outfielders, Bristol's treatment of him remained a sore point to longtime Braves officials.

"Nobody ever should have talked to Dale like that," said Snyder, his anger obvious.

His confidence shaken, Murphy returned to the minor leagues in 1977. While he hit .305 with 22 homers at Triple-A Richmond, he wasn't the catcher he had been. When he opened the 1978 season in the Atlanta lineup, it was at first base. The Braves continued trying to restore Murphy's confidence behind the plate, however, and he continued to catch sporadically, working 21 games in 1978 and 27 more in 1979. Finally, they gave up.

In 1980, the Braves got veteran Chris Chambliss to play first and manager Bobby Cox moved Murphy to the outfield. It proved to be an astute move as Murphy quickly began to fulfill his true potential. He won the first of consecutive National League MVP awards in 1982 and also began a streak of five consecutive Gold Glove Awards.

When Murphy was a senior at Woodrow Wilson High in Portland, Ore., in 1974, scouts were a fixture at his games. Often 20 or more would be on hand to get a firsthand look at the gangly 6-foot-5 catcher with a throwing arm that was second to none. "Defensively, he had the best high school arm I've seen," said Jack Dunn, his high school and American Legion coach, and later the baseball coach at Portland State.

Dunn knew Murphy well. His son and Murphy had been friends since both were young. Dunn had coached him in seventh-grade basketball, and every summer in Legion ball, including 1973 when Murphy led a Portland entry to the American Legion World Series.

The Braves, who were in a scouting combine in 1974 with the Yankees, Angels and Chicago Cubs, assigned crosschecker Bill Wight to follow Murphy, who hit .462 with five homers and 28 RBIs in 16 games his senior year. Almost every report the Braves had on Murphy indicated he would be a defensive specialist. Any offense would be a bonus.

"We had nine reports on Murphy, but Bill Wight was the only scout who said Dale had plus power potential," said Snyder, then an assistant to Braves scouting director Bill Lucas. "As with most big kids, Murphy had a long swing and the chance for error is greater. But Bill was an ex-pitcher who studied hitters carefully, and he determined that his contact ratio would be great enough that he wouldn't be a liability with the bat."

Murphy's offensive prowess proved to be more than just an added bonus.

Murphy also became one of baseball's greatest ambassadors. He was honored with a number of the game's most prestigious off-field awards during his 18-year major league career. "I've never seen a No. 1 draft pick who was so humble," Snyder said. "Over the years, I always had a tough time deciding whether he was a better ballplayer or a better person. In every regard, he's a tremendous human being."

## WORTH NOTING

In a year when the designated-hitter rule and aluminum bats were introduced to the college game, there were fewer college players selected (300) overall than in any June draft ever. It wasn't that the college game didn't have its share of noteworthy accomplishments, or standout performers, in 1974. In fact, the University of Southern California completed the most dominant run in college history by winning its fifth consecutive College World Series title. The Trojans beat Miami, which was making its first trip to Omaha at the beginning of its rise to prominence as a college baseball power, in the final, 7-3. With the unexpected departure of **ROY SMALLEY** to the pro ranks as the top pick in the January 1973 draft, USCs top player was senior third baseman **RICH DAUER**, who would go on to be Baltimore's first-round pick, 24th overall. He set NCAA records for hits (108), total bases (181) and RBIs (92), while hitting .387 with 15 homers for the Trojans. Primarily a third baseman in college, Dauer went on to set records for defensive excellence as a second baseman in a 10-year career with the Orioles.

Santa Clara third baseman **GENE DELYON** established an NCAA single-season home run record with 19, while Miami first baseman **ORLANDO GONZALEZ** stole a record 62 bases. Neither was a prominent factor in the draft, however, as Delyon was drafted ninth overall by the Padres in the June secondary phase, while Gonzalez, the NCAA player of the year, was an 18th-round afterthought of the Indians. The year's biggest winner, Texas sophomore righthander Jim Gideon (19-2), was not eligible for the draft. His 19 wins tied a record set by Arizona State's Larry Gura in 1969.

Drafted in the first round by the Mets in 1974, pitcher **CLIFF SPECK** persevered for 12 years in the minor leagues before finally making the

Boggs straight to the big leagues.

"Boggs isn't as refined as Clyde," said Rangers president Bobby Brown, who took an active role in the signing and later became American League president. "It's not every kid who can step into the major leagues right away. But Boggs may throw harder than Clyde."

Tommy Boggs

Boggs, who had committed to Texas to play both baseball and football, agreed with the Rangers on an $87,500 bonus prior to the draft. It took him two more years to reach the big leagues, but he went only 1-7, 3.49 as a 20-year-old rookie with the Rangers. A year later he was dealt to the Braves in a four-team trade.

He was plagued by arm problems over much of the next seven years, and his career ended in 1986 when he didn't answer the bell after undergoing rotator-cuff surgery. He retired with a 20-44 career record.

### CONCERTED EFFORT TO LURE ATHLETES

When the Reds drafted Miley with the 24th and last first-round pick in 1971, he declined their $65,000 bonus offer. Three years later, when the Angels drafted him with the 10th pick, he decided he couldn't resist their overtures.

"It was a real good contract opportunity for me," said Miley, the second player ever to be a first-rounder in the regular phase of separate June drafts. "This was the time. It is something I would have been foolish to turn down."

Many baseball observers felt Miley might be a tough sign, given his previous decision and the fact he was an emerging star at LSU. But his love of baseball helped him make up his mind.

"I have baseball in my heart and have more confidence on the baseball diamond than I do on the football field," he said.

Though Miley hit only .184 in 14 games with California in 1976, he still was considered the team's shortstop of the future.

But on Jan. 6, 1977, he was killed when his sports car slammed into a culvert in Baton Rouge, La., and overturned. He was 23.

The Royals targeted another top football talent with the 18th pick overall, and spent $90,000—the largest bonus in club history—in order to land Wilson, a New Jersey high school standout. His signing didn't create the same stir in Kansas City that Bo Jackson's would 12 years later, but it did mark a historic development in Royals history.

Wilson was a two-time high school All-American running back at Summit (N.J.) High who ran for a combined 3,693 yards as a junior and senior, scored 401 points over his career, and ran 11 of 24 interceptions back for touchdowns. He was pursued by more than 200 colleges before settling on the University of Maryland.

Wilson went on to become a prototypical artificial-turf player. His speed made him an outstanding defensive center fielder. He also led the American League in triples five times, while his 83 percent stolen-base success rate was one of the best in major league history.

Baseball's renewed motivation to go head-to-head with football, and other sports, to win back some of the better athletes it had been losing didn't stop with Miley and Wilson.

The Houston Astros enticed their first-round selection, Kevin Drake, one of the top running backs in Southern California, to give up a football career at UCLA by allowing him to start out in Triple-A—though that ended up being the highest level he reached. The UCLA football program also came up short by losing a prized linebacker recruit, Lance Parrish, Detroit's first pick.

Not only did the Angels score a coup for baseball by landing Miley in the first round, but they were also successful in attracting high school basketball sensation Mark Wulfemeyer, the leading prep scorer in Southern California history, in the ninth round. It cost the Angels a bonus of $42,500—more than several first-rounders received—even though Wulfemeyer went on to play basketball concurrently at USC, under the NCAA's new two-sport rule, while apprenticing in the Angels system. Ultimately, Wulfemeyer never fulfilled his potential in either sport.

The Baltimore Orioles gave it the old college try, too, but weren't so fortunate in their pursuit of several top two-sport athletes. They drafted four players in the first 20 rounds who later played in the National Football League, including their sixth-round pick, Georgia quarterback Andy Johnson, who had already been drafted and signed by the New England Patriots. UCLA quarterback John Sciarra, who didn't play baseball in college, and USC running back Anthony Davis, a member

### Top 25 Bonuses

| | Player, Pos. | Drafted (Round) | Order | Bonus |
|---|---|---|---|---|
| 1. | **Roy Smalley, ss** | **Rangers (Jan.-R/1)** | **(1)** | **$95,000** |
| 2. | **Bill Almon, ss** | **Padres (1)** | **1** | **#$90,000** |
| | ***Willie Wilson, of** | **Royals (1)** | **18** | **$90,000** |
| 4. | ***Tommy Boggs, rhp** | **Rangers (1)** | **2** | **$87,500** |
| 5. | **Mike Miley, ss** | **Angels (1)** | **10** | **$75,000** |
| 6. | *Kevin Drake, of | Astros (1) | 15 | $71,125 |
| 7. | ***Lance Parrish, 3b** | **Tigers (1)** | **16** | **$60,000** |
| 8. | ***Larry Monroe, rhp** | **White Sox (1)** | **8** | **$58,000** |
| 9. | ***Lonnie Smith, of** | **Phillies (1)** | **3** | **$55,000** |
| | ***Dennis Sherrill, ss** | **Yankees (1)** | **12** | **$55,000** |
| 11. | Eddie Ford, ss | Red Sox (1) | 20 | $50,000 |
| | ***Rick Sutcliffe, rhp** | **Dodgers (1)** | **21** | **$50,000** |
| 13. | ***Butch Edge, rhp** | **Brewers (1)** | **6** | **$47,500** |
| 14. | **Tom Brennan, rhp** | **Indians (1)** | **4** | **$45,000** |
| 15. | ***Dale Murphy, c** | **Braves (1)** | **5** | **$43,750** |
| 16. | *Ron Sorey, 3b | Expos (1) | 9 | $43,000 |
| 17. | *Mark Wulfemeyer, rhp | Angels (9) | 202 | $42,500 |
| 18. | *Mike Martinson, c | Angels (2) | 34 | $40,000 |
| | ***Steve Shirley, lhp** | **Dodgers (2)** | **45** | **$40,000** |
| 20. | ***Garry Templeton, ss** | **Cardinals (1)** | **13** | **$37,500** |
| 21. | ***Rod Scurry, lhp** | **Pirates (1)** | **11** | **$35,000** |
| | Ted Shipley, ss | Twins (1) | 14 | $35,000 |
| | ***Jeff Byrd, rhp** | **Rangers (2)** | **26** | **$35,000** |
| | *Michael Brown, rhp | Orioles (3) | 72 | $35,000 |
| 25. | ***Cliff Speck, rhp** | **Mets (1)** | **17** | **$25,000** |

*Major leaguers in bold. *High school selection. #Major league contract.*

## Largest Bonuses By Round

| | Player, Pos. | Club | Bonus |
|---|---|---|---|
| **1.** | ***Willie Wilson, of** | **Royals** | **$90,000** |
| **2.** | ***Steve Shirley, lhp** | **Dodgers** | **$40,000** |
| | *Mike Martinson, c | Angels | $40,000 |
| 3. | *Michael Brown, rhp | Orioles | $35,000 |
| **4.** | ***Thad Bosley, of** | **Angels** | **$22,000** |
| 5. | *James Mills, 1b | Mets | $16,000 |
| **6.** | ***Jerry Narron, c** | **Yankees** | **$13,000** |
| **7.** | **Sam Bowen, of** | **Red Sox** | **$12,000** |
| **8.** | ***Mark Clear, rhp** | **Phillies** | **$16,000** |
| 9. | *Mark Wulfemeyer, rhp | Angels | $42,500 |
| 10. | Rick Ollar, of | Dodgers | $14,000 |
| **Jan/R.** | **Roy Smalley, ss** | **Rangers (1)** | **$95,000** |
| Jan/S. | Butch Stinson, lhp | White Sox (1) | $9,000 |
| **Jun/S.** | **Sandy Wihtol, rhp** | **Indians (2)** | **$17,000** |

*Major leaguers in bold. *High school selection.*

of the Trojans perennial NCAA championship baseball team, were also selected by the Orioles.

But the most noteworthy two-sport athlete the Orioles drafted in 1974 was University of California first baseman Steve Bartkowski, who was also one of the nation's top quarterbacks. In 1973, as a sophomore, Bartkowski set a school single-season home run record by going deep 12 times. With some of the best raw power in the collegiate ranks, the 6-foot-5 Bartkowski was expected to be one of the top picks in the 1974 baseball draft. But when his home run production tapered off that spring to five, scouts lost interest. So did Bartkowski, insulted that he tumbled all the way to the 19th round. He never played baseball again.

That fall, Bartkowski had a breakthrough senior season in football when he became the top-rated passer in the nation, which led to his becoming the No. 1 pick in the NFL draft a year later. Even after he became an established quarterback in the NFL with the Atlanta Falcons, though, Bartkowski professed that baseball was his favorite sport, that he would have pursued a career in that sport under more favorable circumstances.

"Football was a tool, nothing more," he said. "I played football to get into shape for baseball, never an end unto itself. A lot of scouts came around every year, but they all wanted me to start too far down the line. If I'd been offered a Double-A contract, I'd be playing professional baseball.

"The scouts sometimes accused me of playing football just so I could play one against the other when I got around to signing a contract. Honestly, that never crossed my mind. I was always a baseball player first and I always figured that baseball is where I'd stay."

Baseball also continued its pursuit of Brad Van Pelt, once a top pitching prospect at Michigan State. Even though Van Pelt had a year under his belt with the NFL's New York Giants and later became an all-pro linebacker, he was drafted in January by the St. Louis Cardinals, the fifth time he had been selected in the baseball draft.

### SMALLEY EASY CHOICE

In the January draft, it was a foregone conclusion that Smalley, who contributed to NCAA championships at USC in 1972-73, would be the No. 1 pick in the regular phase. It was the fifth time that Smalley, who played at a junior college as a freshman before enrolling at USC, had been drafted.

"He's got a helluva lot of talent," said Rangers owner Bob Short. "Everybody in the organization . . . me, (manager Billy) Martin, (general manager Dan) O'Brien and (farm director Hal) Keller wanted him. He cost a lot, but we didn't think we could afford not to do it."

Smalley likely would have signed in 1973, when he was a junior, but because he didn't turn 21 within 45 days of that year's draft, he wasn't eligible. Like numerous other high-profile USC players in the 1970s who faced the same dilemma, he was forced to leave school in the fall following his junior season in order to make himself eligible for the January draft.

Roy Smalley

But it was more than a big price tag and his own intuition that told Smalley the timing was right for him to sign.

As the son of 10-year major league shortstop Roy Smalley Sr., and the nephew of one of the game's sharpest managerial minds, Gene Mauch, Smalley relied on their judgment. Both his father and uncle agreed the opportunity was right.

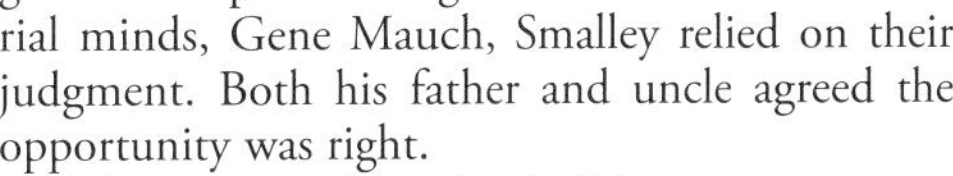

"The two people in baseball I most respect are my father and my uncle," he said. "They both told me there's not a better manager in the game than Billy Martin. So I'm excited about the chance to play for him."

The only question was whether the Rangers would start Smalley out in the big leagues, as they had developed a reputation for doing in recent years. But with the circus surrounding 1973 top draft pick David Clyde still fresh in their minds, the Rangers resisted temptation and elected to send Smalley to Double-A to begin his career.

"A lot of people think Smalley can play major league ball right now," Short said. "It will all depend on how he looks in spring training. Our reports say he has the talent to play in the big leagues and that he is highly motivated."

After spending the entire 1974 season in the minors, Smalley made his big league debut early in 1975, just two months before Martin was fired. Smalley went on to play 13 seasons as a big league shortstop, hitting .257 with 163 homers.

Led by Smalley in January, and Almon and Miley in June, shortstops were in demand in the 1974 draft. Three were plucked in the first round out of the Southeastern Conference: Miley, South Carolina's Eddie Ford (Red Sox) and Vanderbilt's Ted Shipley (Twins). Neither Ford nor Shipley reached the big leagues

It was highly anticipated that Ford, son of Yankees Hall of Famer Whitey Ford, would be selected by the Yankees with the 12th pick overall, especially since his dad was the team's pitching coach at the time and Ford's coach at

### WORTH NOTING

majors with the Braves in 1986. By then, Speck was with his fifth organization. Only two other first-round picks in draft history, Alan Cockrell in 1984 and Alan Zinter in 1989, took longer paths to become a big leaguer.

■ The only college pitcher drafted in the first round in the 1974 June regular phase was Lewis (Ill.) University senior righthander **TOM BRENNAN**, who won three games at the 1974 NAIA World Series to finish the season with a 12-1, 1.17 record and 144 strikeouts in 86 innings. For his career, Brennan, a three-time NAIA All-American, was 44-6. Brennan, drafted fourth overall by the Indians, started his pro career in Triple-A, but it took seven more seasons for him to reach the big leagues, and he would go on to win only nine games at the major league level, working as a reliever.

■ Despite a down season on the field, Arizona State (39-24) tied USC for the most players drafted (six) from a four-year school in June. Miami-Dade North Community College led the way with 12 selections in January, and another seven in June. Arizona State's losses to the draft were compounded when Sun Devils recruits **LONNIE SMITH** (Phillies), **DALE MURPHY** (Braves) and Speck all went in the first round and signed immediately.

■ Arizona State second baseman **BUMP WILLS**, son of Maury, was a projected first-round pick, but his draft hopes, and chances of a lucrative bonus, were dashed when he broke his ankle in a sliding drill, ending his season. Wills lasted until the 12th round and elected not to sign with the Padres. Wills came back to be a first-round pick (sixth overall) of the Rangers in the January secondary phase of the 1975 draft. He was in the big leagues by 1977, though his big league career was over by 1982.

## IN FOCUS: WILLIE WILSON

Most major league clubs thought Willie Wilson's college football commitment was so strong that it made him unsignable. The Royals gladly snapped him up with the 18th overall pick and signed him, though it cost them $40,000 more than they were initially prepared to pay.

"I guess I turned a lot of people off because I was undecided," Wilson said. "I'd rather play baseball than football because football is a game where you can get hurt. The Royals understood that."

Wilson hit .436 his final year in high school and stole 28 straight bases. He also spent most of the season as a catcher because his team didn't have anyone else to play the position.

Al Diez, the Royals scout who kept the closest watch on Wilson, said he was the best athlete he had ever seen. He clocked Wilson circling the bases in 14.4 seconds.

"Al did a really good job of getting close to him and finding out his heart lay with baseball and knowing what his signability was," Royals scouting director Art Stewart said. "Coming up through the minor leagues, everybody was of the attitude he wasn't a switch-hitter. But we started him early and because he is such a great athlete, he was able to make the transition. It certainly paid off because of his great, great speed."

South Carolina was former Yankees great Bobby Richardson. Eddie Ford himself grew up around Yankee Stadium. He knew the facility and the organization like the back of his hand.

But the Yankees went for another shortstop, Dennis Sherrill, a Florida high school product. They hoped Ford would be available when their turn came up again in the second round.

He never lasted that long as the Boston Red Sox, picking eight slots after the Yankees in the first round, stepped up and took the 20-year-old Ford.

"I thought the Yanks would draft me," Ford said. "My father told me the Yankees would draft me in the second round. But I was hoping I would go in the first round. This is really a big thrill."

Whitey Ford's reaction when he found out that his son would not be a Yankee: "Oh boy. I think he would have liked to go to the Yankees. Seeing that the Yankees selected a shortstop, I'm sure he's disappointed. I would have liked him to come with us, too."

The younger Ford, who was encouraged by his father to become a shortstop and Mickey Mantle to become a switch-hitter, was more philosophical.

BOSTON RED SOX

Eddie Ford

"I guess I kinda hoped I'd go with the Yankees," he said. "I mean, after you've grown up with the pinstripes and all that, it means something to you. On the other hand, it's probably best that I go somewhere else where I won't always be Whitey's kid, Eddie Ford Jr."

Boston didn't select Ford to undercut the Yankees.

"We were looking for a real good shortstop," Red Sox farm director Ed Kenney said, "and our reports say he's just that. Outstanding with the glove, good arm, good speed."

At South Carolina, where Ford played under Richardson, a former teammate of his father, Ford hit an ordinary .290 with four homers and 25 RBIs in 56 games his junior year.

His lack of hitting prowess would eventually doom him. In four seasons in the Red Sox system, Ford never hit higher than .251 or more than five homers in a season. He retired following the 1977 season to pursue a career as a lawyer.

Sherrill played briefly in the big leagues with the Yankees—two games in 1978, three in 1980. He actually quit the game along the journey to New York, in 1977, when he went home to Miami, disillusioned with baseball. Sherrill admitted he had a tough time adjusting from high school to the pros. Baseball had been fun in high school, drudgery in the pros.

"I didn't know if I wanted to be a pro ballplayer or an average working man," he said. "Now that I've been through both—the eight-hour work thing and baseball—I see there's a lot of money to be made in baseball."

Of all the shortstops taken in the first round of the 1974 draft, Garry Templeton, selected by the St. Louis Cardinals with the 13th pick, had the best shot at stardom.

A natural righthanded hitter, he learned to switch hit in his first pro season in the Rookie-level Gulf Coast League, and vaulted through the Cardinals system, landing in St. Louis in August of 1976. A year later, he batted .322, and banged out 200 hits with a National League-leading 18 triples.

That kind of production became the norm for Templeton early in his career, and through his first six season with the Cardinals, Templeton had a .305 career average, along with 25 homers, 69 triples and 281 RBIs.

While he had established himself as one of the best young players in the game with his play, Templeton also had become one of the more controversial players in the game with his often indifferent style, veiled threats to quit the game and general boorish actions.

A series of obscene gestures, directed at Cardinals fans who had grown tired of his act, were the final straw, and he was traded to San Diego for the slick-fielding, light-hitting Smith, who thrived in St. Louis and quickly emerged as a Hall of Fame player as a Cardinal. Templeton's career, by contrast, was never the same after he went to San Diego, though he played well enough to remain a starter for another decade.

## Highest Unsigned Picks

**JUNE/REGULAR PHASE ONLY**

| Player, Pos., Team (Round) | College | Re-Drafted |
|---|---|---|
| Jerry Johnson, c, Athletics (1) | Temple (Texas) JC | Cardinals '75 (Jan.-S/1) |
| Kenny Kolkhorst, c/1b, Giants (2) | Baylor | Never |
| Jim Loftin, lhp, Athletics (2) | South Alabama | Orioles '78 (14) |
| Tom Van Der Meersche, rhp, Brewers (3) | Arizona State | Indians '78 (28) |
| John Henderson, c, Cubs (3) | Georgia | Cubs '75 (S/1) |
| Dave Tobik, rhp, Expos (3) | *Ohio | Tigers '75 (Jan.-S/1) |
| LaMart Harris, of, Pirates (3) | Ranger (Texas) JC | Pirates '75 (S/1) |
| Everett Murray, of, Royals (3) | Kentucky | Orioles '75 (S/1) |
| David Wendt, lhp, Athletics (3) | Oklahoma | Never |
| Brandt Humphry, 3b, Padres (4) | Arizona State | Angels '77 (9) |

**TOTAL UNSIGNED PICKS:** Top 5 Rounds (16), Top 10 Rounds (56)

**Returned to same school*

## One Team's Draft: California Angels

| Player, Pos. | Bonus |
|---|---|
| **1. Mike Miley, ss** | **$75,000** |
| 2. *Mike Martinson, c | $40,000 |
| **3. *Rance Mulliniks, ss** | **$25,000** |
| **4. *Thad Bosley, of** | **$22,000** |
| **5. *Stan Cliburn, c** | **$12,000** |
| **6. Gary Wheelock, rhp** | **$8,000** |
| **7. *Ralph Botting, lhp** | **$11,000** |
| **8. *Floyd Chiffer, rhp** | **Did not sign** |
| 9. *Mark Wulfemeyer, rhp | $42,500 |
| **10. *Greg A. Harris, rhp** | **Did not sign** |
| **Other John Caneira (S/1), rhp** | **$9,500** |

*Major leaguers in bold. *High school selection.*

# 1974 Draft List

**Did not sign. Major leaguers in bold, with first and last years noted. Order of selection indicated in parentheses. For the first five rounds of the June Regular Phase and the first round of all other phases, the peak level of each player is noted.*

## ATLANTA BRAVES

**January—Regular Phase (6)**

1. **Larry McWilliams, lhp, Paris (Texas) JC.—(1978-90)**
2. *Tim Graven, lhp, Columbia State (Tenn.) CC.
3. *John Anderson, ss, South Georgia JC.
4. Tom Westlake, 2b, Sacramento (Calif.) CC.
5. *Steven Watson, 1b-of, Spokane Falls (Wash.) CC.
6. *John Schott, rhp, Blinn (Texas) JC.
7. Patrick Hobbs, lhp, Miami-Dade CC North.

**January—Secondary Phase (8)**

1. *Mike Williams, lhp, Temple (Texas) JC.—(AAA)
2. **Mike Davey, lhp, Gonzaga University.—(1977-78)**
3. *Mike Schisler, rhp, Georgia Tech.

**June—Regular Phase (5)**

1. **Dale Murphy, c, Woodrow Wilson HS, Portland, Ore.—(1976-93)**
2. **Joey McLaughlin, rhp, McLain HS, Tulsa, Okla.—(1977-84)**
3. Robert Long, of, Redwood Larkspur HS, Corte Madera, Calif.—(High A)
4. Donald Fletcher, ss, Blount HS, Mobile, Ala.—(Low A)
5. Jimmie Hacker, 3b, Texas A&M University.–(AA)

DRAFT DROP *First-round draft pick (16th overall), Red Sox (1970)*

6. Steven Van Kerns, rhp, San Jacinto (Texas) JC.
7. **Rick Camp, rhp, West Georgia College.—(1976-85)**
8. Steve Oliva, of, Kennedy HS, Granada Hills, Calif.
9. Eric Cervantes, of, Hiram Johnson HS, Sacramento, Calif.
10. **Mickey Mahler, lhp, Trinity (Texas) University.—(1977-86)**

DRAFT DROP *Brother of Rick Mahler, major leaguer (1979-91)*

11. *Tim Costello, lhp, Central-Hower HS, Akron, Ohio.
12. Daniel Newell, 2b, Green River (Wash.) CC.
13. *David Reed, 1b-lhp, Corner HS, Dora, Ala.
14. *Marshall Justice, rhp, South Georgia JC.
15. *Joe McClain, rhp-1b, Happy Valley HS, Johnson City, Tenn.
16. Glen Smith, 2b, David Lipscomb College.
17. *William Taylor, rhp, Ridgeview HS, Atlanta.

**June—Secondary Phase (11)**

1. *Scott McGlamory, rhp, Gulf Coast (Fla.) CC.—DNP

## BALTIMORE ORIOLES

**January—Regular Phase (21)**

1. *Lee Brownell, c, Allan Hancock (Calif.) JC.—DNP
2. Ed Pebley, 3b, Allan Hancock (Calif.) JC.
3. *Sherwin Rogers, 2b, Adrian (Mich.) College.
4. *Alex Torres, ss, JC of the Sequoias (Calif.).
5. *Billy DeYo, lhp, East Los Angeles JC.
6. *Donald Gardner, lhp, Allan Hancock (Calif.) JC.
7. *Edward Montes, of, Bellflower, Calif.
8. *Alton Caesar, ss, Sierra (Calif.) JC.
9. ***Mark Lee, rhp, El Camino (Calif.) JC.—(1978-81)**
10. *John Edwards, c, Carmichael, Calif.
11. *Walt Mason, of, Central Arizona JC.
12. *James Lugo, rhp, Mount San Jacinto (Calif.) JC.
13. *Richard Martinez, of, Mira Costa (Calif.) JC.
14. *Wilburt Ellis, rhp, East Los Angeles JC.
15. *Terry Gray, rhp, Merced (Calif.) JC.

**January—Secondary Phase (3)**

1. Brad Drysdale, rhp, Arizona Western JC.—(Rookie)
2. *Robbie Henderson, ss, San Diego Mesa JC.

DRAFT DROP *Brother of Ken Henderson, major leaguer (1965-80)*

3. *Steve Hogan, of, Central Arizona JC.
4. *Edward Wright, 2b, Albemarle (N.C.) JC.

**June—Regular Phase (24)**

1. **Rich Dauer, ss-3b, University of Southern California.—(1976-85)**
2. Craig Ryan, 1b-of, Cal State Northridge.—(AAA)
3. Michael Brown, rhp, Crescenta Valley HS, La Crescenta, Calif.—(High A)
4. **Mike Darr, rhp, Norco (Calif.) HS.—(1977)**

DRAFT DROP *Father of Mike Darr, major leaguer (1999-2001)*

5. **Randy Miller, rhp, UC San Diego.—(1977-78)**
6. *Andy Johnson, ss, University of Georgia.

DRAFT DROP *Running back, National Football League (1974-81)*

7. *John Sciarra, ss, UCLA.

DRAFT DROP *Quarterback/defensive back, National Football League (1978-83)*

8. Joseph Villa, c, Cantwell HS, Pico Rivera, Calif.
9. *Kenny Washington, 1b-of, Morningside HS, Los Angeles.
10. James Bryan, of, Merced (Calif.) JC.
11. Richard Rickman, ss, Ragsdale HS, Greensboro, N.C.
12. *Dean Phillips, rhp, Paschal HS, Fort Worth, Texas.
13. John Gordy, rhp, James Bennett HS, Salisbury, Md.
14. James Evans, of, Booker T. Washington HS, Norfolk, Va.
15. *Anthony Davis, of, University of Southern California.

DRAFT DROP *Running back, National Football League (1977-79)*

16. Jay Cline, c, Campbell University.
17. Robert Volk, rhp, Lambuth (Tenn.) College.
18. *Marvin Saunders, of, Deep Creek HS, Chesapeake, Va.
19. *Steve Bartkowski, 1b, University of California.

DRAFT DROP *First overall draft pick, Atlanta Falcons/ National Football League (1975); quarterback, NFL (1975-86)*

20. Bernard Bumbrey, of, Stafford HS, Hartwood, Va.
21. *Alan Willett, rhp, Patchogue-Medford HS, Patchogue, N.Y.
22. (void) *Marvin Townsend, ss, Campbell University.
23. *Richard Hudson, rhp, Chipola (Fla.) JC.
24. Creighton Tevlin, of, University of Southern California.
25. Dan Marple, of, Cal Poly San Luis Obispo.
26. *Michael Croswell, ss, Manhattan HS, Jackson, Miss.
27. *Mark Naehring, 1b, LaSalle HS, Cincinnati.

DRAFT DROP *Brother of Tim Naehring, major leaguer (1990-97)*

28. Tom Kibbee, rhp, Mendocino (Calif.) CC.
29. *Bob Hamilton, of, Suitland HS, District Heights, Md.
30. Ricky Ford, inf, Texas Wesleyan College.
31. *Bernard Menapace, c, Broad Run HS, Sterling Park, Va.
32. Rich Katz, 3b, Jacksonville University.
33. *Vernon Crockett, 2b, Huguenot HS, Richmond, Va.
34. *Scott Winston, lhp, Windsor Forest HS, Savannah, Ga.
35. Rich Reichle, 3b, University of Miami.
36. Gus Quiros, rhp, Los Angeles, Calif.
37. *Mark Trapani, rhp, Poly HS, North Hollywood, Calif.
38. William Bird, rhp, Oklahoma State University.
39. Gary Brandenburg, c, Oklahoma State University.
40. ***Randy Johnson, 3b, San Diego Mesa JC.—(1982-84)**
41. Ron DeGrande, of, Stagg HS, Stockton, Calif.

**June—Secondary Phase (14)**

1. Charles James, of, Los Angeles Valley JC.—(High A)
2. Jeff Feramisco, of, Fresno (Calif.) CC.
3. *Robbie Henderson, ss, San Diego Mesa JC.

DRAFT DROP *Brother of Ken Henderson, major leaguer (1965-80)*

4. **Tom Chism, of, Brandywine (Del.) JC.—(1979)**
5. *Alex Torres, ss, JC of the Sequoias (Calif.).

## BOSTON RED SOX

**January—Regular Phase (19)**

1. **Chuck Rainey, rhp, San Diego Mesa JC.—(1978-84)**
2. Ralph Russo, 1b, Quinnipiac College.
3. *Stephen Kolenda, 2b, Stetson University.
4. *James Wargo, ss, Gulf Coast (Fla.) CC.
5. *Brad Liedtke, of-rhp, Fullerton (Calif.) JC.

**January—Secondary Phase (7)**

1. **Bob Stanley, rhp, Kearny (N.J.) HS.—(1977-89)**
2. **Steve Burke, rhp, Merritt (Calif.) JC.—(1977-78)**
3. Greg Kane, c, Yavapai (Ariz.) JC.

**June—Regular Phase (20)**

1. Eddie Ford, ss, University of South Carolina.—(AAA)

DRAFT DROP *Son of Whitey Ford, major leaguer (1950-67)*

2. Jimmy Shankle, c, Monterey HS, Lubbock, Texas.—(AA)
3. Ronny Patrick, lhp, Castlewood (Va.) HS.—(Low A)
4. Charles Reilly, 2b, Adelphi (N.Y.) University.—(AA)
5. *Craig Brooks, of, Richmond (Calif.) HS.—(AAA)

DRAFT DROP *No school; never re-drafted*

6. Robert Klass, rhp, Southern Illinois University.
7. **Sam Bowen, 2b, Valdosta State (Ga.) College.—(1977-80)**
8. Paul McClure, 1b-of, University of Wyoming.
9. **Joel Finch, rhp, Washington HS, South Bend, Ind.—(1979)**
10. *Lee Roy Russell, rhp, Bibb County HS, Brent, Ala.
11. Charles Pinkney, of, Kingsborough (N.Y.) CC.
12. John Tagliarino, rhp, Tampa (Fla.) Catholic HS.
13. *Michael Wholey, rhp, Lakes HS, Tacoma, Wash.
14. Mark Barr, rhp, University of Southern California.

DRAFT DROP *Brother of Jim Barr, major leaguer (1971-83)*

15. Burke Suter, rhp, High Point College.
16. *Jeff Hardy, ss, Gulf Coast (Fla.) CC.
17. *Jackie Snell, lhp, George C. Wallace (Ala.) CC.
18. Jerome Register, of, Valdosta State (Ga.) College.

**June—Secondary Phase (20)**

1. Towny Townsend, ss, Campbell University.—(High A)
2. David Koza, lhp, Eastern Oklahoma State JC.

## CALIFORNIA ANGELS

**January—Regular Phase (9)**

1. *Larry Howser, ss, Manatee (Fla.) JC.—DNP

DRAFT DROP *Brother of Dick Howser, major leaguer (1961-68); major league manager (1978-86)*

2. Pat Cristelli, rhp, University of Puget Sound.
3. *Owen Prather, lhp, Cypress (Calif.) JC.
4. ***Steve Hammond, of, Gulf Coast (Fla.) CC.—(1982)**

DRAFT DROP *Brother of Chris Hammond, major leaguer (1990-2006)*

5. *Edward Nuss, rhp, Valencia (Fla.) CC.
6. Frank Panick, rhp, UCLA.
7. *William Sundquist, 1b, JC of the Redwoods (Calif.).
8. *James Davis, rhp, Long Beach (Calif.) CC.
9. *Scott McGlamory, rhp, Gulf Coast (Fla.) CC.
10. David Drevnak, of, Gulf Coast (Fla.) CC.
11. *Mike Holt, rhp, JC of the Canyons (Calif.).
12. *Gary Wilburn, c, Riverside (Calif.) CC.
13. *Keith Ulrich, lhp, El Camino (Calif.) JC.
14. Juan Delgado, 1b, San Bernardino Valley (Calif.) JC.
15. *Steve Fenoglio, of, Long Beach (Calif.) CC.
16. *Leon Smith, lhp, Hartnell (Calif.) CC.
17. *William Felt, c, American River (Calif.) JC.
18. *George Ambrow, ss-rhp, University of Southern California.

DRAFT DROP *First-round draft pick (23rd overall), Mets (1970)*

**January—Secondary Phase (23)**

1. *David Bedrosian, 2b, Fresno (Calif.) CC.—(High A)
2. *Charles James, of, Los Angeles Valley JC.
3. *Steve Barrett, 2b, Murray State University.
4. Danny Miller, rhp, Los Angeles Pierce JC.
5. ***Dan Boone, lhp, Cerritos (Calif.) JC.—(1981-90)**

**June—Regular Phase (10)**

1. **Mike Miley, ss, Louisiana State University.—(1975-76)**

DRAFT DROP *First-round draft pick (24th overall), Reds (1971); died as active major leaguer (Jan. 6, 1977)*

2. Marty Martinson, c, Lakewood (Calif.) HS.—(AAA)
3. **Rance Mulliniks, ss, Monache HS, Woodville, Calif.—(1977-92)**
4. **Thad Bosley, of, Oceanside (Calif.) HS.—(1977-90)**
5. **Stan Cliburn, c, Forrest Hill HS, Jackson, Miss.—(1980)**

DRAFT DROP *Twin brother of Stew Cliburn, 16th-round draft pick, Giants (1974); major leaguer (1984-88)*

6. **Gary Wheelock, rhp, UC Irvine.—(1976-80)**
7. **Ralph Botting, lhp, Burbank (Calif.) HS.—(1979-80)**
8. ***Floyd Chiffer, rhp, Lakewood (Calif.) HS.—(1982-84)**
9. Mark Wulfemeyer, rhp-of, Troy HS, Fullerton, Calif.
10. ***Greg A. Harris, rhp, Los Alamitos (Calif.) HS.—(1981-95)**
11. Bryant Fahrow, ss, Kankakee (Ill.) CC.
12. **John Verhoeven, rhp, University of La Verne (Calif.).—(1976-81)**
13. *Curtis Anderson, ss, Deerfield (Ill.) HS.
14. Russ McQueen, rhp, University of Southern California.
15. *David Anderson, rhp, Gresham HS, Portland, Ore.
16. William Case, rhp, Antelope Valley (Calif.) JC.
17. *Jackie Smith, lhp, Manatee (Fla.) JC.
18. Donald Johnson, lhp, Palomar (Calif.) JC.
19. *Steve Vaughn, of, Palisades HS, Pacific Palisades, Calif.
20. Kenneth Wright, of, Compton (Calif.) CC.
21. Lamar Wright, lhp, Shorter (Ga.) College.
22. *Carl Spikes, of, Bogalusa (La.) HS.

DRAFT DROP *Brother of Charlie Spikes, first-round draft pick, Yankees (1969); major leaguer (1972-80)*

23. *Barry Acquistapace, rhp, Dos Pueblos HS, Goleta, Calif.
24. *Daniel Owen, rhp, Miami-Dade CC North.
25. Arthur Lorick, of, Florida Air Academy, Melbourne, Fla.
26. *Erol Akchurin, 3b, Burlingame (Calif.) HS.
27. *Paul Kolesnikow, of, Burlingame (Calif.) HS.
28. *Joseph Ducey, c, Foothill HS, Santa Ana, Calif.
29. *Paul Stefan, rhp, Drake University.
30. *Dennis Hawkins, of, Chaffey (Calif.) JC.
31. *Randall Bonner, c, Wheeler HS, Marietta, Ga.
32. John Picone, c, UC Santa Barbara.
33. *James Billuris, of-inf, Del Mar HS, San Jose, Calif.
34. *Tim Cashman, ss, Santa Barbara (Calif.) CC.
35. *Larry Marsh, ss, South Hills HS, Covina, Calif.
36. Gregory Kulesza, rhp, Royal Oak (Mich.) HS.
37. *Gary Wiencek, c, Citrus (Calif.) JC.

**June—Secondary Phase (2)**

1. **John Caneira, rhp, Eastern Connecticut State University.—(1977-78)**
2. Jeff Malinoff, 1b, UC Irvine.

## CHICAGO CUBS

**January—Regular Phase (8)**

1. Eric Grandy, 1b-of, Essex (Md.) CC.—(AA)

**January—Secondary Phase (16)**

1. Karl Gordon, ss, Montclair State (N.J.) College.—(AA)

**June—Regular Phase (7)**

1. **Scot Thompson, of, Knoch HS, Renfrew, Pa.—(1978-85)**
2. **Mike Sember, ss, University of Tulsa.—(1977-78)**
3. *John Henderson, c, Mount DeSales HS, Macon, Ga.—(Low A)

DRAFT DROP *Attended Georgia; re-drafted by Cubs, June 1975/secondary phase (1st round)*

**4. George Riley, lhp, South Philadelphia HS.—(1979-86)**
5. Kevin Drury, ss, Glynn Academy, Brunswick, Ga.—(AAA)
6. David Wood, rhp, Washington HS, South Bend, Ind.
7. *Craig McGinnis, lhp, Powers HS, Flint, Mich.
8. Thomas Deskins, 2b, Paintsville (Ky.) HS.
9. Jeffrey Collins, rhp, Ironton (Ohio) HS.
10. Ken Christensen, rhp-c, Wisconsin Lutheran HS, Cudahy, Wis.
11. *David Hall, of, New Trier HS, Winnetka, Ill.
12. Harvey Selnik, ss, Hart HS, Saugus, Calif.
13. Jack Uhey, rhp, Hart HS, Newhall, Calif.
**14. *Bob Welch, rhp, Hazel Park HS, Ferndale, Mich.—(1978-94)**
DRAFT DROP *First-round draft pick (20th overall), Dodgers (1977)*
15. Steve Hamrick, lhp, Cornell University.
16. Gary Howard, of, Williamson HS, Mobile, Ala.
17. Ronald Hill, c, Delano (Calif.) HS.
18. *Jeff Rowlands, c, Howland HS, Warren, Ohio.
19. Marion Massee, ss, Fitzgerald (Ga.) HS.
20. *Michael Tucker, rhp, Great Falls (Mon.) HS.
21. *Joe Budiselish, c, Linden HS, Stockton, Calif.
22. *Greg Stitzinger, 2b, Mesa (Ariz.) CC.
23. Aaron Randall, 1b, Grambling University.
24. *William Miles, rhp, East HS, Nashville, Tenn.
25. *John Harris, of, Jackson HS, Miami.

**June—Secondary Phase (17)**

No selection.

## CHICAGO WHITE SOX

**January—Regular Phase (7)**

**1. Kevin Bell, 3b, Mount San Antonio (Calif.) JC.—(1976-82)**
2. *Richard Swanson, rhp, Triton (Ill.) JC.
3. Jay Attardi, lhp, Miami-Dade CC North.
4. *Ed Devalasco, rhp, Miami-Dade CC North.
5. Cas Sledzik, c, Mayfair (Ill.) JC.

**January—Secondary Phase (9)**

1. Butch Stinson, lhp-of, Vanderbilt University.—(AAA)
2. *Carl Gardner, 3b, Miami-Dade CC North.
3. *Garnett Houghton, rhp, Ohlone (Calif.) JC.

**June—Regular Phase (8)**

**1. Larry Monroe, rhp, Forest View HS, Mount Prospect, Ill.—(1976)**
**2. Jack Kucek, rhp, Miami (Ohio) University.—(1974-80)**
DRAFT DROP *First player from 1974 draft to reach majors (Aug. 8, 1974)*
**3. Pete Vuckovich, rhp, Clarion (Pa.) University.—(1975-86)**
4. Harris Price, c, Shaler Township HS, Glenshaw, Pa.—(Low A)
5. Ray Katts, of, Southside HS, Sardis, Ala.—(Short-season A)
6. Tommy Toman, of, Gateway HS, Monroeville, Pa.
7. Tony Komadina, lhp, Arizona State University.
8. Donn Seidholz, 3b, Indiana University.
**9. *Jim Farr, rhp, Athens (Pa.) HS.—(1982)**
10. Dennis Sandoval, rhp, Servite HS, Placentia, Calif.
11. Michael Smith, c-rhp, Carver HS, Birmingham, Ala.
12. Paul Bock, lhp, Western Michigan University.
13. Phil Trucks, c, Carol City HS, Opa-Locka, Fla.
14. Edward Olszta, c-of, Providence HS, New Lenox, Ill.
15. *Lawrence Berkery, 1b-lhp, Riverview HS, Sarasota, Fla.
16. *Bill Swiacki, rhp, Choate Prep School, Sturbridge, Mass.
DRAFT DROP *Ninth-round draft pick, New York Giants/ National Football League (1978)*
17. Scott Richartz, ss, Chino (Calif.) HS.
**18. Dave Frost, rhp, Stanford University.—(1977-82)**
19. *James Roach, rhp, Lincoln-Way HS, Mokena, Ill.
20. Ted Loehr, rhp, Stetson University.
21. Marland Easley, c-of, Santa Ana (Calif.) Valley HS.
22. *Joseph Nahay, lhp, Garden Grove HS, Pacifica, Calif.
23. *Albert Paglione, rhp, St. Anthony HS, Trenton, N.J.

**June—Secondary Phase (18)**

1. Phil Nerone, 3b, Miami-Dade CC North.—(Low A)
2. *Michael St. Louis, lhp, Ithaca (N.Y.) College.

## CINCINNATI REDS

**January—Regular Phase (24)**

**1. Mike Armstrong, rhp, University of Miami.—(1980-87)**
2. *Dennie Gentry, rhp, Rose State (Okla.) JC.
3. *Bruce Ryals, of, Florida JC.
4. *Scott Miller, of, St. Petersburg (Fla.) JC.
5. *Alan Kunick, of, Bismarck (N.D.) JC.
6. *Ronnie Corder, ss-3b, Highland (Kan.) CC.
7. *Kevin Gallinari, rhp, Nassau (N.Y.) CC.
8. *Tom Kotchman, 3b, Chipola (Fla.) JC.
DRAFT DROP *Father of Casey Kotchman, first-round draft pick, Angels (2001); major leaguer (2004-13)*

**January—Secondary Phase (22)**

1. James Diventi, rhp, Essex (Md.) CC.—(Low A)
2. *Richard Barrett, rhp, Manatee (Fla.) JC.

**June—Regular Phase (23)**

1. Steve Reed, rhp, Fort Wayne (Ind.) HS.—(AAA)
**2. Mike Grace, 3b, Waterford Mott HS, Pontiac, Mich.—(1978)**
**3. Mike LaCoss, rhp, Mount Whitney HS, Visalia, Calif.—(1978-91)**
4. Jim Reeves, of, University of Texas.—(High A)
**5. Steve Henderson, ss-3b, Prairie View A&M University.—(1977-88)**
6. Mark Pearson, rhp, Alton (Ill.) HS.
7. Bradley Bush, c, Paris (Texas) HS.
8. *Jeff Hansen, of, El Camino HS, Sacramento, Calif.
**9. Ron Oester, ss, Withrow HS, Cincinnati.—(1978-90)**
**10. Lynn Jones, of, Thiel (Pa.) College.—(1979-86)**
DRAFT DROP *Brother of Darryl Jones, major leaguer (1979-86)*
11. Jerry Christensen, rhp, Manzano HS, Albuquerque, N.M.
12. Charles Renneau, rhp, Granite Hills HS, El Cajon, Calif.
13. Paul Marshall, of, Sheridan (Wyo.) HS.
14. Robert Constantine, 3b, Lyman HS, Altamonte Springs, Fla.
**15. Dan Norman, 1b-of, Barstow (Calif.) CC.—(1977-82)**
16. *Kevin Waldrop, rhp, Herrin (Ill.) HS.
17. Randy Walraven, lhp, Alvarado (Texas) HS.
18. Tim Doerr, 3b-1b, UCLA.
19. Brice Kinnamon, c, Cambridge (Md.) HS.
20. William Baggett, of, Rose Sterling HS, Houston.
21. Charles Neal, rhp-1b, Smiley HS, Houston.
22. *John Barron, rhp, Cameron (Texas) HS.
23. Dean Graumann, 2b-ss, University of Tulsa.
24. Tim Dull, rhp, Johnstown (Pa.) Vocational Tech HS.
25. *Scott Burk, ss-rhp, Cherry Creek HS, Englewood, Colo.
DRAFT DROP *Defensive back, National Football League (1979)*
26. John Fuller, c, University of Florida.
27. *George McLean, rhp, New Albany (Ind.) HS.
28. Jim Turner, ss, University of Georgia.
29. *James Russell, 1b-3b, Helix HS, La Mesa, Calif.
30. Stephen Hughes, rhp, Cal State Los Angeles.
31. *David Pugh, ss-of, Highland Park HS, St. Paul, Minn.
32. *Keith Lloyd, lhp, Waltrip HS, Houston.
33. *Timothy Rappe, of-2b, University of Wisconsin.
34. *John Crane, rhp, Martin County HS, Stuart, Fla.
35. *Julian Rodriguez, 3b, Twin Lake HS, West Palm Beach, Fla.
**36. *Andy McGaffigan, rhp, Twin Lake HS, West Palm Beach, Fla.—(1981-91)**

**June—Secondary Phase (1)**

1. *Mike Gatlin, 3b, University of Arizona.—(AAA)

## CLEVELAND INDIANS

**January—Regular Phase (3)**

1. *Stephen Cook, of-3b, Miami-Dade CC North.—(High A)
2. *Francis Legath, ss, St. Petersburg (Fla.) JC.
3. *Steven Gorthy, c, Fresno (Calif.) CC.
4. *Jamie Baby, lhp, Cuyahoga (Ohio) CC.
**5. *Paul Moskau, 3b-rhp, Arizona State University.—(1977-83)**
6. Robert Fulgham, lhp-of, Holmes (Miss.) JC.
7. *Joe Griffin, c, Polk (Fla.) CC.
8. *Glen Lamas, c, Southeastern Louisiana University.
9. Michael Dolf, 2b-ss, JC of the Redwoods (Calif.).
**10. *Garry Hancock, of, Hillsborough (Fla.) CC.—(1978-84)**
11. *Robert Glass, 3b, Manatee (Fla.) JC.
12. *Mark Clemons, ss-2b, Itawamba (Miss.) JC.
13. *John Webster, ss-2b, Panola (Texas) JC.

**January—Secondary Phase (19)**

1. *Mike Merritt, rhp, University of North Carolina.—(Short-season A)
2. *Gary Ezell, ss-rhp, Connors State (Okla.) JC.
3. *Brad Van Pelt, rhp, Michigan State University.
DRAFT DROP *Linebacker, National Football League (1973-86)*

**June—Regular Phase (4)**

**1. Tom Brennan, rhp, Lewis (Ill.) University.—(1981-85)**
2. Rickey Howerton, c, Taft HS, Canoga Park, Calif.—(AA)
3. John Arnold, lhp, Effingham (Ill.) HS.—(AA)
4. *Stanley Mann, ss, Southern Illinois University.—(AA)
DRAFT DROP *Returned to Southern Illinois; re-drafted by Mets, January 1975/secondary phase (1st round)*
5. *Earl Bass, rhp, University of South Carolina.—(AAA)
DRAFT DROP *Returned to South Carolina; re-drafted by Cardinals, June 1975/secondary phase (1st round)*
6. *Karl Schroeder, lhp, John Marshall HS, Oklahoma City, Okla.
7. Steven Hanson, rhp, Andover HS, North Linthicum, Md.
8. *Mike Frazier, c, Texas A&M University.
9. *Ward Wilson, c, Dunedin (Fla.) HS.
10. Ben Heise, ss, University of Arizona.
DRAFT DROP *Brother of Bob Heise, major leaguer (1967-77)*
11. *David Gallino, ss, El Sobrante (Calif.) HS.
12. *Steven Van Deren, c, JC of the Redwoods (Calif.).
13. Thomas Sowles, of, Albion (Mich.) College.
14. Steven Widner, lhp, Gibbs HS, Corryton, Tenn.
15. Stanley Maffey, of, Treasure Valley (Ore.) CC.
16. *David Adeimy, c, Forest Hill HS, West Palm Beach, Fla.
17. Steven Huusfeldt, rhp, Lowell HS, Whittier, Calif.
**18. Orlando Gonzalez, 1b, University of Miami.—(1976-80)**
19. Hurley Mitchell, rhp, Coeburn (Va.) HS.
20. *Jerry Stamps, c-1b, University of South Alabama.
21. Michael Jones, rhp, Colonial HS, Orlando, Fla.
22. *James McBride, rhp, Blair HS, Hattiesburg, Miss.
23. *Kevin Kopp, c, Sylmar (Calif.) HS.
24. Carlos Brooks, c, University of North Carolina.
25. Timothy Fox, rhp, University of Oklahoma.

**June—Secondary Phase (12)**

1. *Ron Montgomery, of, East Los Angeles JC.—DNP
**2. Sandy Wihtol, rhp, DeAnza (Calif.) JC.—(1979-82)**
3. *Danny White, inf, Arizona State University.
DRAFT DROP *Quarterback, National Football League (1976-88)*

## DETROIT TIGERS

**January—Regular Phase (15)**

1. *Randy Nall, of, Citrus (Calif.) JC.—(Rookie)
2. *William Crawford, lhp, Gulf Coast (Fla.) CC.
3. *David Delenick, 1b, St. Clair, Pa.

**January—Secondary Phase (17)**

**1. *Bobby Pate, 3b-of, Mesa (Ariz.) JC.—(1980-81)**

**June—Regular Phase (16)**

**1. Lance Parrish, c-3b, Walnut HS, Diamond Bar, Calif.—(1977-95)**
DRAFT DROP *Father of David Parrish, first-round draft pick, Yankees (2000)*
2. James Taylor, lhp, Franklin County HS, Decherd, Tenn.—(High A)
3. Steve Viefhaus, ss-rhp, St. Louis CC-Meramec.—(AAA)
4. Mel Jackson, ss, LeMoyne-Owen (Tenn.) College.—(AA)
5. Ronald Martinez, of, Buena HS, Ventura, Calif.—(AA)
6. *William Poland, lhp, Crescenta Valley HS, Glendale, Calif.
7. David Balbierz, rhp, Hilbert (N.Y.) JC.
**8. *Dan Morogiello, lhp, Milford Academy, Brooklyn, N.Y.—(1983)**
9. *Jake Battle, c, Western HS, Detroit.
**10. Mark Fidrych, rhp, Worcester Academy HS, Northborough, Mass.—(1976-80)**
11. Stephen Gamby, rhp, Carey (Ohio) HS.
12. William Coury, c, Durfee HS, Fall River, Mass.
13. Brian Kelly, ss, Churchill HS, Livonia, Mich.
14. *Richard Spanton, lhp, Chatard HS, Indianapolis.
**15. *Greg Keatley, c, Miami-Dade CC North.—(1981)**
16. Steven Harris, lhp, Connally HS, West, Texas.
17. Greg Kline, of, Northeastern HS, Mount Wolf, Pa.
18. *John Stocker, 3b, Custer HS, Milwaukee.
**19. Bob Sykes, lhp, Miami-Dade CC North.—(1977-81)**
20. Calvin Jones, ss, Delaware State College.
21. *John Crabtree, lhp, John Marshall HS, Indianapolis, Ind.
22. Clifford Irwin, rhp, University of California.
23. *Terry O'Hearn, of, Catholic Central HS, Grand Rapids, Mich.
24. Robert LaLonde, rhp, Mohawk Valley (N.Y.) CC.
25. John Johnson, rhp, University of South Carolina.
26. Patrick Murphy, lhp, Pepperdine University.
27. Richard Fulton, rhp, Gardner-Webb College.
28. Edward Carroll, of, Raritan HS, Hazlet, N.J.
29. *David Hollifield, of, Kenwood HS, Baltimore.

**June—Secondary Phase (6)**

**1. *Rob Picciolo, ss, Pepperdine University.—(1977-85)**

## HOUSTON ASTROS

**January—Regular Phase (16)**

**1. J.J. Cannon, of, Pensacola (Fla.) JC.—(1977-80)**
2. *Robert Starks, lhp, Canada (Calif.) JC.

**January—Secondary Phase (24)**

1. *Danny White, inf, Arizona State University.—DNP
DRAFT DROP *Quarterback, National Football League (1976-88)*

**June—Regular Phase (15)**

1. Kevin Drake, of, Cabrillo HS, Lompoc, Calif.—(AAA)
2. Jeff Smith, ss, Hoggard HS, Wilmington, N.C.—(AA)
**3. Alan Knicely, rhp, Turner Ashby HS, Bridgewater, Va.—(1979-86)**
4. Fay Thompson, 1b, Vallejo (Calif.) HS.—(AA)
5. David Buckley, lhp, Bellevue (Wash.) CC.—(High A)
6. Ken LaHonta, of, Serra HS, Millbrae, Calif.
**7. *Don Kainer, rhp, Milby HS, Houston.—(1980)**
8. Richard Haynes, 2b-ss, Clemson University.
9. Tom Twellman, 3b, Southern Illinois University-Edwardsville.
10. Greg Jurgenson, lhp, Oregon State University.
11. *Gaylon Austin, lhp, Klein HS, Spring, Texas.
12. Larry Matula, rhp, Temple (Texas) JC.
**13. *Anthony Johnson, of, Northside HS, Memphis, Tenn.—(1981-82)**

**14. *Mickey Hatcher, of, Mesa (Ariz.) HS.—(1979-90)**
15. Tom Rima, of, University of New Orleans.
16. Michael Hasley, lhp, Modesto (Calif.) JC.

**June—Secondary Phase (3)**

**1. *Gil Patterson, of-rhp, Miami-Dade CC South.—(1977)**
**2. *Chuck Baker, ss, Loyola Marymount University.—(1978-81)**

## KANSAS CITY ROYALS

**January—Regular Phase (17)**

**1. Mark Souza, lhp, JC of San Mateo (Calif.).—(1980)**
2. Hal Thomasson, 3b-ss, Laney (Calif.) JC.
3. *Phil Doktor, ss, Citrus (Calif.) JC.
4. *Mike Scott, lhp, Central Arizona JC.
5. *Dale King, rhp, Miami-Dade CC South.
**6. Bobby Castillo, rhp, Los Angeles Valley JC.—(1977-85)**
7. *Rowland George, rhp, Atlantic Cape (N.J.) CC.
8. *Wayne Carmichael, lhp, Atlantic Cape (N.J.) CC.
9. Craig Husband, lhp, University of Oregon.

**January—Secondary Phase (1)**

1. David Hasbach, rhp, Miami (Ohio) University.—(AAA)
2. Xavier Dixson, of, St. Mary's (Calif.) College.
3. Dan Walker, rhp, Malone (Ohio) College.
4. *Steve Woitock, 2b, Dana (Neb.) College.

**June—Regular Phase (18)**

**1. Willie Wilson, of, Summit (N.J.) HS.—(1976-94)**
2. Bobby Edmondson, c, Lakeview HS, Fort Oglethorpe, Ga.—(Low A)
3. *Everett Murray, of, North College Hill HS, Cincinnati.—(Rookie)

DRAFT DROP *Attended Kentucky; re-drafted by Orioles, June 1975/secondary phase (1st round)*

4. Pat Curran, of, Chapman (Calif.) College.—(High A)
5. Thomas Laseter, of, San Jacinto (Texas) JC.—(AA)
**6. *Craig Eaton, rhp, Miami-Dade CC North.—(1979)**
7. Kevin Lahey, rhp, Newburgh (N.Y.) Free Academy.
8. Ed Sempsrott, lhp, Danville (Ill.) HS.
9. *Russ Francis, rhp, University of Oregon.

DRAFT DROP *First-round draft pick, New England Patriots/National Football League (1975); tight end, NFL (1975-87)*

10. *Jeff Campbell, lhp, Unicoi HS, Erwin, Tenn.
**11. *Scott Sanderson, rhp, North HS, Glenbrook, Ill.—(1978-96)**
12. Keith Bridges, of, UC Irvine.
13. *Charles McLean, 3b, Richmond Senior HS, Rockingham, N.C.
14. Ray Humphries, rhp, UC Irvine.
15. *Lawrence Pekarcik, rhp, Damien HS, Pomona, Calif.
16. *Bobby Gabriesheski, of, Raleigh-Egypt HS, Memphis, Tenn.
17. *Gregg Foster, rhp, Marina HS, Huntington Beach, Calif.
18. *David McIntyre, c, Polk Central HS, Tryon, N.C.
19. *Jeff Hemm, c, Nathan Hale HS, Tulsa, Okla.
20. Jerry Peterson, rhp, Ocoee (Fla.) HS.
21. Gary Wright, lhp, Miami (Ohio) University.
22. William Wilson, lhp, Montclair (N.J.) HS.
23. *Thomas Perkins, rhp, Cal State Los Angeles.
24. *Tim O'Neill, rhp, North Torrance (Calif.) HS.
25. John Affinto, of, Linton HS, Schenectady, N.Y.
26. *Mike Parker, 3b, Start HS, Toledo, Ohio.
27. *Douglas Warrick, 3b, Louisburg (N.C.) JC.
**28. *Sammy Stewart, rhp, Montreat-Anderson (N.C.) JC.—(1978-87)**
29. Stewart Colton, lhp, University of Nevada-Reno.
30. Craig Lloyd, 1b, Southern Utah State College.
31. Dale Hrovat, rhp, Arizona State University.
32. Huey Fleming, of, Leon Godchaux HS, Reserve, La.
33. *Michael McLellan, rhp, Kennedy HS, Denver.
34. *Larry Goldetsky, ss, St. Louis Park (Minn.) HS.
35. *Danny Gans, 3b, Torrance (Calif.) HS.

**June—Secondary Phase (8)**

1. Mike Williams, lhp, Temple (Texas) JC.—(AAA)
2. Randy Nall, of, Citrus (Calif.) JC.

## LOS ANGELES DODGERS

**January—Regular Phase (22)**

1. Claude Westmoreland, of, University of California.—(AAA)
2. *Dale Forchetti, ss, University of Southern Mississippi.
3. *Henry Boguszewski, rhp, Nassau (N.Y.) CC.
**4. *Shane Rawley, lhp, Indian Hills (Iowa) CC.—(1978-89)**

**January—Secondary Phase (6)**

1. Don Cardoza, of, JC of the Sequoias (Calif.).—(AAA)
**2. *Jim Dorsey, rhp, Los Angeles Valley JC.—(1980-85)**

**June—Regular Phase (21)**

**1. Rick Sutcliffe, rhp, Van Horn HS, Kansas City, Mo.—(1976-94)**
**2. Steve Shirley, lhp, Terra Nova HS, Pacifica, Calif.—(1982)**
3. Freddie Tisdale, ss, Centennial HS, Los Angeles.—(AAA)
4. Jim Riggleman, 2b-3b, Frostburg State (Md.) College.—(AAA)

DRAFT DROP *Major league manager (1992-2011)*

5. Alvin Harper, ss, Southern University.—(Low A)
6. James Del Vecchio, 2b, Andrew Ward HS, Fairfield, Conn.
7. *Chris Gandy, of, Christian Brothers HS, Sacramento, Calif.
8. Randy Rogers, ss, Texas HS, Texarkana, Texas.
9. Joseph Keller, rhp, Clover Park HS, Tacoma, Wash.
10. Rick Ollar, of, Oklahoma State University.
11. *Scott Anderson, rhp, Lake Oswego (Ore.) HS.
12. *Dwayne Wright, c, Berkeley (Calif.) HS.
13. *Les Pearsey, ss, Brethren HS, Los Angeles.
14. *Jackie Schuman, 2b, Putnam City (Okla.) HS.
15. Richard Oliveri, 3b, Bishop Fallon HS, Buffalo, N.Y.
16. Billy Wilson, rhp, Emporia State (Kan.) University.
17. Michael Laurent, rhp, University of New Mexico.
18. *Ray Murillo, rhp, Agua Fria HS, Avondale, Ariz.
19. *Brian Heublein, lhp, University of Southern California.
20. *Chris Lynch, rhp, Miami-Dade CC North.
21. *Ron Wrobel, lhp, Quigley HS, Chicago.
22. Doug Slocum, rhp, Arizona State University.

**June—Secondary Phase (5)**

1. Robert Glass, 3b, Manatee (Fla.) JC.—(AA)

## MILWAUKEE BREWERS

**January—Regular Phase (5)**

**1. *John Caneira, rhp, Eastern Connecticut State University.—(1977-78)**
**2. *Tom Chism, of, Brandywine (Del.) JC.—(1979)**

**January—Secondary Phase (21)**

1. *Robert Nickeson, ss, West Valley (Calif.) JC.—(AA)

**June—Regular Phase (6)**

**1. Butch Edge, rhp, El Camino HS, Sacramento, Calif.—(1979)**
**2. Moose Haas, rhp, Franklin HS, Owings Mills, Md.—(1976-87)**
3. *Tom Van Der Meersche, rhp, Everett (Wash.) HS.—(Low A)

DRAFT DROP *Attended Arizona State; re-drafted by Indians, 1978 (28th round)*

**4. Barry Cort, rhp, King HS, Tampa.—(1977)**
**5. Gary Beare, rhp, Long Beach State University.—(1976-77)**
6. *Mike Denevi, ss, Santa Clara University.
**7. Steve Bowling, of, University of Tulsa.—(1976-77)**
8. David Sylvia, rhp, Lakewood HS, Long Beach, Calif.
9. *William Taylor, of, St. Augustine HS, San Diego.
10. Cap Pohlman, lhp, Central Michigan University.
11. *Paul Bain, rhp, South Torrance (Calif.) HS.
**12. Jim Gantner, ss, University of Wisconsin-Oshkosh.—(1976-92)**
13. Tom Farina, ss, Pulaski HS, Milwaukee.
14. *Dan Morgan, rhp, Superior (Wis.) HS.
**15. Jerry Augustine, lhp, University of Wisconsin-La Crosse.—(1975-84)**

DRAFT DROP *Baseball coach, Wisconsin-Milwaukee (1995-2006)*

16. *David Pencille, rhp, Amos Alonso Stagg HS, Stockton, Calif.

**June—Secondary Phase (10)**

1. Carey Scarborough, ss-2b, Clemson University.—(Low A)

## MINNESOTA TWINS

**January—Regular Phase (13)**

1. Mark Lockwood, lhp, Fullerton (Calif.) JC.—(High A)
2. *William Nelson, lhp, Miami-Dade CC North.
3. *Doug Thomson, rhp, Rio Hondo (Calif.) JC.
4. *Brian Pulliam, of, Fullerton (Calif.) JC.
5. *John Batton, rhp, Los Angeles Pierce JC.
6. *Neal Patton, rhp, Southwestern (Calif.) JC.
7. *Frank Terriogo, ss, St. Peter's College.
8. *Sam Floyd, ss, Canada (Calif.) JC.
9. Donald Cross, rhp, Fremont, Calif.
10. Wayne Caughey, ss, St. Cloud State (Minn.) University.

**January—Secondary Phase (11)**

**1. Jerry Garvin, lhp, Merced (Calif.) JC.—(1977-82)**
2. *Richard Douglass, rhp-1b, Saddleback (Calif.) CC.
3. *Kevin Morel, ss, Indian River (Fla.) CC.

**June—Regular Phase (14)**

1. Ted Shipley, ss, Vanderbilt University.—(AA)
**2. Butch Wynegar, c, Red Lion HS, York, Pa.—(1976-88)**

DRAFT DROP *First 1974 high school draft pick to reach majors (April 9, 1976)*

3. Dean Olson, lhp, Nogales HS, La Puente, Calif.—(High A)
4. *Michael Lambert, lhp, Culver City (Calif.) HS.—DNP

DRAFT DROP *Attended Southern California; never re-drafted*

5. John Maier, rhp, Penn State University.—(AA)
6. *Curt Etchandy, ss, Santiago HS, Garden Grove, Calif.
7. John Lonchar, c, University of Michigan.
8. *Howard McCann, ss, Oswego (N.Y.) HS.

DRAFT DROP *Father of Brian McCann, major leaguer (2005-14)*

9. Steve Flores, of, La Habra (Calif.) HS.
10. *Steve Kruzelock, c, Venice HS, Mar Vista, Calif.
11. *Tom Costello, p, Newberg HS, Dundee, Ore.
12. *John Helfrick, 3b, San Diego State University.
13. *Dartt Wagner, of, Buchser HS, Santa Clara, Calif.
**14. Bud Bulling, c, Cal State Los Angeles.—(1977-83)**
15. William Bitter, c, Fresno (Calif.) HS.
16. Randy Lee, lhp, Bell Gardens (Calif.) HS.
17. Robb Mayhew, lhp, University of La Verne (Calif.).
18. Theodore Groff, lhp, Lampeter-Strasburg HS, Willow, Pa.
19. Frank Quintero, rhp, Buena Park (Calif.) HS.
20. *Brett Houser, rhp, Millikan HS, Long Beach, Calif.
21. *Ronnie Mears, ss, Pinole (Calif.) HS.
22. *David Enos, ss, Troy HS, Yorba Linda, Calif.
23. Mike Angione, rhp, Iona College.
24. James Volkmar, c, Ithaca (N.Y.) College.
25. *Bill Foley, c, Bowie (Md.) HS.
26. Jesus Lopez, 3b-2b, Eastside HS, Newark, N.J.
27. *Gary Armstrong, ss, El Capitan HS, Lakeside, Calif.
28. *David Pearce, lhp, Kearns HS, Salt Lake City.
29. *Fred Westfall, rhp, Madison HS, San Diego.
30. Charles Alonso, 1b, University of La Verne (Calif.).
31. Mike Heinen, rhp, Cal Poly Pomona.
32. *Bill Hughes, ss, Notre Dame HS, North Hollywood, Calif.
33. Douglas Gildenzoph, rhp, Nekoosa (Wis.) HS.
34. John Torreano, lhp, Albany HS, Berkeley, Calif.
35. *Larry Randel, ss, Magnolia HS, Anaheim, Calif.
**36. *Eric Show, rhp, Ramona HS, Riverside, Calif.—(1981-91)**
37. *Tom Jahnke, of, Richfield HS, Minneapolis.
38. Tom Channel, rhp, Washington HS, Portland, Ore.
39. *Benjamin Chrin, rhp, Whitehall (Pa.) HS.
40. Kent Mariska, of, Jefferson HS, Bloomington, Minn.
41. *Robert Blake, lhp, Cretin HS, St. Paul, Minn.

**June—Secondary Phase (24)**

1. *Gary Bishop, 1b, Indian River (Fla.) CC.—(Rookie)

## MONTREAL EXPOS

**January—Regular Phase (10)**

**1. Joe Kerrigan, rhp, Temple University.—(1976-80)**

DRAFT DROP *Major league manager (2001)*

**2. *Ned Yost, c, Chabot (Calif.) JC.—(1980-85)**

DRAFT DROP *Major league manager (2003-15)*

3. *Bill Przygocki, rhp, St. Clair County (Mich.) CC.
4. *Kent Taylor, ss, East Los Angeles JC.
**5. *Randy Niemann, lhp, JC of the Redwoods (Calif.).—(1979-87)**
6. *John Bass, 3b, Laney (Calif.) JC.
7. Mike Uebbing, rhp, Grossmont (Calif.) JC.
8. Ronald Edwards, rhp, Detroit.
9. *Gary Gronowski, rhp, Valencia (Fla.) CC.
10. Kenneth Snyder, rhp, Chabot (Calif.) JC.
11. William Wood, of, South Georgia JC.
12. *David Oliver, of, Grossmont (Calif.) JC.
13. *Doug Heinz, rhp, San Joaquin Delta (Calif.) JC.
14. *Kevin Kearney, 1b, Laney (Calif.) JC.

**January—Secondary Phase (10)**

1. *Michael St. Louis, rhp, Ithaca (N.Y.) College.—DNP
2. *Steve Williams, lhp, St. Clair County (Mich.) CC.
3. *Dan Grimm, rhp, Fresno State University.
4. *David Koza, lhp-of, Eastern Oklahoma State JC.

**June—Regular Phase (9)**

1. Ron Sorey, 3b, Stebbins HS, Dayton, Ohio.—(High A)
**2. Jerry Fry, ss, Springfield (Ill.) HS.—(1978).**
**3. *Dave Tobik, rhp, Ohio University.—(1978-85)**

DRAFT DROP *Attended Ohio University; re-drafted by Tigers, January 1975/secondary phase (1st round)*

4. Godfrey Evans, ss, Morningside HS, Compton, Calif.—(AA)
5. Randy Fierbaugh, rhp, Ashland (Ohio) College.—(AAA)
6. David Frederickson, rhp, Santa Barbara (Calif.) CC.
**7. Bobby Ramos, c, Jackson HS, Miami.—(1978-84)**
8. Marv Chamberlain, 1b-3b, Washington State University.
9. John Novak, lhp, Ohio University.
**10. *Bob Bonner, 3b, King HS, Corpus Christi, Texas.—(1980-83)**
11. *Tim Richards, c, Westminster (Calif.) HS.
12. Robert Woodland, of, Howard University.
13. Dave Whiteaker, c, Gonzaga University.
14. Bob Bohr, rhp, Central Dauphin HS, Harrisburg, Pa.
15. Joe Meir, rhp, Hillsboro (Ore.) HS.
16. Michael Curran, 3b, Iowa State University.
17. Joe Gonzalez, of-1b, Blinn (Texas) JC.
18. *Robert Dinges, of-1b, Gunn HS, Palo Alto, Calif.
**19. *Hubie Brooks, ss, Dominguez HS, Compton, Calif.—(1980-94)**

DRAFT DROP *First-round draft pick (3rd overall), Mets (1978)*

20. Bill Welsh, ss, St. Anthony's HS, Trenton, N.J.
21. *Stanley Butler, ss, Poly HS, Long Beach, Calif.
22. *Gregg Bemis, lhp, University of Puget Sound.
23. *Lawrence Kalmus, rhp, Gonzalez (Texas) HS.
24. Gary Horstmann, rhp, Blinn (Texas) JC.
25. *Randall Esker, rhp, Valmeyer (Ill.) HS.

26. *Robert Weis, c, Eastmont HS, East Wenatchee, Wash.
27. *Larry Kowalishen, rhp, Chabot (Calif.) JC.
28. Rodney Hampton, 1b-of, Henry Ford (Mich.) CC.
29. *David Thieneman, rhp, Chalmette HS, Meraux, La.
30. *Steve Wilkins, of, Treasure Valley (Ore.) CC.
31. *Gerry Greene, c, Essex (Vt.) HS.
32. *Ronald Irwin, rhp, Northern HS, Pontiac, Mich.
33. *Cleveland Porter, rhp, Ganesha HS, Pomona, Calif.
34. *Richard Casillas, c, San Bernardino (Calif.) HS.
35. *Ted Smith, p-of, San Leandro (Calif.) HS.
36. *Randy Toogood, c, Kailua (Hawaii) HS.
37. *John Riffle, rhp-of, Palisades (Calif.) HS.
38. *Ronald Goodman, lhp, Santa Barbara (Calif.) HS.
39. *Waldo Winborn, of, Buena HS, Sierra Vista, Ariz.

**June—Secondary Phase (13)**

1. Jamie Baby, lhp, Cuyahoga (Ohio) CC.—(High A)
2. **Shane Rawley, lhp, Indian Hills (Iowa) CC.—(1978-89)**

## NEW YORK METS

**January—Regular Phase (18)**

1. *Robert Carroll, rhp, East Los Angeles JC.—(High A)
2. Stan Hough, of, McLennan (Texas) JC.
3. *James Eble, lhp, Roane State (Tenn.) CC.
4. Edward Hicks, ss, Brewton Parker (Ga.) JC.
5. *Antonio Castro, of, Southwestern (Calif.) JC.
6. *Richie Howard, 3b, Middle Georgia JC.
7. Gerald Tenge, rhp, Scottsdale (Ariz.) CC.
8. Randy Peterson, c, Green River (Wash.) CC.

**January—Secondary Phase (20)**

1. *Chuck Fore, rhp, Faulkner State (Ala.) JC.—(AAA)
2. *Colin Leisher, ss, Valencia (Fla.) CC.

**June—Regular Phase (17)**

1. **Cliff Speck, rhp, Beaverton (Ore.) HS.—(1986)**
2. **Dwight Bernard, rhp, Belmont (Tenn.) College.—(1978-82)**
3. Keith Bodie, of, South Shore HS, Brooklyn, N.Y.—(AA)
4. **John Pacella, rhp, Connetquot HS, Oakdale, N.Y.—(1977-86)**
5. James Mills, 1b, Baker (La.) HS.—(Low A)
6. Darrell Lakey, rhp, Redwood HS, Visalia, Calif.
7. Don Driskill, rhp, Jordan HS, Long Beach, Calif.
8. Ed Cipot, of, Highland HS, Highland Park, N.J.
9. Steve Garrison, of, St. Augustine HS, San Diego.
10. *Brian Cherevko, rhp, Buchser HS, Santa Clara, Calif.
11. *John McBride, ss, University of Utah.
12. ***Pat Putnam, 1b, Miami-Dade CC North.—(1977-84)**
13. Stephen Lott, of, Jefferson HS, Tampa.
14. Randy Frankum, rhp, Wharton (Texas) HS.
15. *Ray Cardinalli, of, Monterey (Calif.) HS.
16. William Gifford, ss, Whitehaven HS, Memphis, Tenn.
17. David Richardson, rhp, Alhambra HS, Martinez, Calif.
18. ***Steve Baker, rhp, Monte Vista HS, La Mesa, Calif.—(1978-83)**
19. *Joe Grajewski, rhp, Central Catholic HS, Steubenville, Ohio.
20. **Bobby Myrick, lhp, Mississippi State University.—(1976-78)**
21. Lowell Jacobsen, rhp, Grand View (Iowa) College.
22. Bruce Gustafson, c, University of Minnesota.
23. William Beno, of, Manatee (Fla.) JC.
24. William Daly, 3b, University of Richmond.
25. David Butler, rhp, Cal State Stanislaus.
26. *Michael O'Connor, lhp, Christ the King HS, Glendale, N.Y.
27. *Ralph Jiminez, c, Stevenson HS, Bronx, N.Y.
28. Wayne Bauers, of, Sonoma State (Calif.) University.
29. Robert Leonard, rhp, Salinas (Calif.) HS.
30. Greg Boos, rhp, Wayne State (Neb.) University.
31. ***Gene Krug, 1b, Lamar (Colo.) CC.—(1981)**
32. *Tim Glines, c, Central Catholic HS, Modesto, Calif.
33. Gene Felts, of, Valdosta State (Ga.) College.
34. *Stewart Bringhurst, c, JC of San Mateo (Calif.).
35. *Gene Litle, rhp, University of California.
36. *Steve Marlowe, 1b, University of Utah.
37. *Jim Lysgaard, rhp, JC of San Mateo (Calif.).
38. *Scott Lankford, rhp, Downey HS, Modesto, Calif.

**June—Secondary Phase (7)**

1. **Ned Yost, c, Chabot (Calif.) JC.—(1980-85)**
DRAFT DROP *Major league manager (2003-15)*
2. Antonio Castro, of, Southwestern (Calif.) JC.

## NEW YORK YANKEES

**January—Regular Phase (11)**

1. ***Ken Phelps, of, Mesa (Ariz.) CC.—(1980-90)**
2. *Ron Montgomery, of, East Los Angeles JC.
3. *Jason Tanneberg, lhp, Bellevue (Wash.) CC.

**January—Secondary Phase (5)**

1. *Gene Delyon, 3b, Santa Clara University.—(AA)
2. *Scott Gunderson, rhp, Bellevue (Wash.) CC.
3. Leon Plunkett, of, University of Southern Mississippi.

**June—Regular Phase (12)**

1. **Dennis Sherrill, ss, South Miami (Fla.) HS.—(1978-80)**
2. **Dave Bergman, 1b-of, Illinois State University.—(1975-92)**
3. Jose Alvarez, ss, St. Patrick HS, Elizabeth, N.J.—(AA)
4. Terry Bevington, c, Santa Monica (Calif.) HS.—(AAA)
DRAFT DROP *Major league manager (1995-97).*
5. David Carter, of, Glassboro State (N.J.) College.—(Short-season A)
6. **Jerry Narron, c, Goldsboro (N.C.) HS.—(1979-87)**
DRAFT DROP *Major league manager (2001-07) • Nephew of Sam Narron, major leaguer (1935-43)*
7. *Jeff Jens, rhp, Kennedy HS, Granada Hills, Calif.
8. Richard Fleshman, rhp, American University.
9. Scott Norris, of, University of Arizona.
10. Joe Kwasny, rhp, Kellam HS, Virginia Beach, Va.
11. Edward Orick, lhp, Reading HS, Cincinnati.
12. *Billy Severns, of, University of Oklahoma.
13. Robert Gagg, rhp-ss, Butler HS, Bloomingdale, N.J.
14. Pat Peterson, ss, Southern Illinois University-Edwardsville.
15. Charles Jones, rhp, Walpole (Mass.) HS.
16. *Orville Rhuems, rhp, Colgan HS, Pittsburg, Kan.
17. Sam Mishmash, rhp, Colgan HS, Pittsburg, Kan.
18. Sabah Mendez, rhp, Julia Richmond HS, New York.
19. **Dennis Werth, c-1b, Southern Illinois University-Edwardsville.—(1979-82)**
DRAFT DROP *Stepfather of Jayson Werth, major leaguer (2002-15)*
20. Kevin McNichol, ss, New York University.
21. Gary McMurtry, lhp, Metcalf (Ky.) College.
22. Greg Diehl, rhp, University of Delaware.
23. *Robert Giapponi, of, Mark T. Sheehan HS, Wallingford, Conn.

**June—Secondary Phase (22)**

No selection.

## OAKLAND ATHLETICS

**January—Regular Phase (23)**

1. *Steven Williams, rhp, Golden West (Calif.) JC.—DNP
2. *Kevin LanFranco, lhp, Santa Ana (Calif.) JC.
3. Eddie White, rhp, Riverside (Calif.) CC.
4. *Michael Tennant, rhp, Neosho County (Kan.) JC.
5. *Ronald Smith, 2b, Los Angeles CC.
6. *Robert McKelvey, of-1b, Cerritos (Calif.) JC.
7. *Rodney Brown, 2b, Golden West (Calif.) JC.
8. *Clark Beam, of, Mitchell (N.C.) CC.
9. Richard Peregud, rhp, Saddleback (Calif.) CC.

**January—Secondary Phase (15)**

1. *David Steck, rhp, San Diego Mesa JC.—(AA)
2. *Wayne Steele, lhp, San Diego State University.
3. *Errect Ridley, of, Santa Monica (Calif.) JC.

**June—Regular Phase (22)**

1. *Jerry Johnson, c, McCallum HS, Austin, Texas.—(AAA)
DRAFT DROP *Attended Temple (Texas) JC; re-drafted by Cardinals, January 1975/secondary phase (1st round)*
2. *Jim Loftin, lhp, Ben C. Rains HS, Mobile, Ala.—(Rookie)
DRAFT DROP *Attended South Alabama; re-drafted by Orioles, 1978 (14th round)*
3. *David Wendt, lhp, Shawnee Mission North HS, Merriam, Kan.—DNP
DRAFT DROP *Attended Oklahoma; never re-drafted*
4. Dennis Haines, c, University of Arizona.—(AAA)
5. Don Walker, ss-rhp, Pecos (Texas) HS.—(Short-season A)
6. Don Petrie, rhp, Pembroke Country Day HS, Overland Park, Kan.
7. ***Ron Roenicke, 1b, Edgewood HS, West Covina, Calif.—(1981-88)**
DRAFT DROP *Major league manager (2011-15) • Brother of Gary Roenicke, major leaguer (1976-88)*
8. James Oldham, rhp, Fox HS, Arnold, Mo.
9. *Tom Ruegger, of, Hawthorne (Calif.) HS.
10. *Jerry Ennis, ss, South HS, Bakersfield, Calif.
11. James Moldenhauer, c, University of Minnesota.
12. **Darrell Woodard, ss, Bell HS, Los Angeles.—(1978)**
13. *Michael Wirwas, ss, Inglewood (Calif.) HS.
14. *Richard Brewster, 2b, San Bernardino (Calif.) HS.
15. Nolan Ramirez, ss, Whittier (Calif.) College.
16. Robert Argenti, ss, Lafayette College.
17. Ronald Beaurivage, 1b, University of Massachusetts.
18. Michael Rodriguez, c, Grand Island (N.Y.) HS.
19. **Rick Lysander, rhp, Cal State Los Angeles.—(1980-85)**
20. *Larry Buckle, rhp, Woodrow Wilson HS, Long Beach, Calif.
21. Chris Wibberley, rhp, Loyola Marymount University.
22. *Anthony Williams, of, Santa Monica (Calif.) HS.
23. Robert Salas, rhp, Nogales HS, La Puente, Calif.
24. *Leonard Johnson, of, El Camino (Calif.) JC.
25. *Larry Rosin, rhp, Niles North HS, Skokie, Ill.

**June—Secondary Phase (16)**

1. *Phil Doktor, ss, Citrus (Calif.) JC.—(Rookie)

## PHILADELPHIA PHILLIES

**January—Regular Phase (4)**

1. Neal Cooper, rhp, Texas Wesleyan College.—(AA)
2. Robert Keller, rhp, Austin Peay State University.
3. Donald Ballenger, lhp, Merced (Calif.) JC.
4. *Fernando Tarin, rhp, Mount San Antonio (Calif.) JC.
5. Eudaldo Oliveros, 2b, Miami-Dade CC North.
6. Jerry Houston, rhp, San Jose (Calif.) CC.
7. Ken Berger, of, Valencia (Fla.) CC.
8. *Ron Estes, rhp, JC of Southern Idaho.
9. *Steve Wyatt, lhp, Mesa (Ariz.) CC.
10. *Michael Rector, rhp, San Diego CC.
11. *Harold Adams, of, Bellevue (Wash.) CC.
12. *Dennis Luquet, 2b, Diablo Valley (Calif.) JC.

**January—Secondary Phase (14)**

1. Wayne Williams, ss, Ranger (Texas) JC.—(High A)
2. *Jeff Malinoff, 1b, UC Irvine.
3. ***Dan Graham, 3b, Mesa (Ariz.) CC.—(1979-81)**
4. **Warren Brusstar, rhp, Fresno State University.—(1977-85)**
5. *Walt Kaczmarek, rhp, Santa Clara University.

**June—Regular Phase (3)**

1. **Lonnie Smith, of, Centennial HS, Compton, Calif.—(1978-94)**
2. **Kevin Saucier, lhp, Escambia HS, Warrington, Fla.—(1978-82)**
3. Frank Ciammachilli, rhp, Oceanside (Calif.) HS.—(AA)
4. **Don McCormack, c, Omak (Wash.) HS.—(1980-81)**
5. **Jim Morrison, 3b, Georgia Southern College.—(1977-88)**
6. Keefe Perkins, c, East HS, Denver.
7. *David Tyler, 3b, Lane HS, Charlottesville, Va.
8. **Mark Clear, rhp, Northview HS, Covina, Calif.—(1979-90)**
9. Doyle Sheets, rhp, Grace (Ind.) College.
10. Tim Ryan, lhp, Santa Clara University.
11. John Gibson, lhp, Georgia Southern College.
12. *David Caldwell, of, Northwest Cabarrus HS, Kannapolis, N.C.
13. Todd Brenizer, lhp, Furman University.
14. Larry Wertz, lhp, Las Lomas HS, Walnut Creek, Calif.
15. Doug Harrison, rhp, Adams HS, Rochester, Mich.
16. *Freddie Van Bever, 3b, Brevard (Fla.) CC.
17. John Gambrell, of, University of South Carolina.
18. Vincent Monti, lhp, Lafayette HS, Brooklyn, N.Y.
19. Larry Silveira, c, Cal Poly San Luis Obispo.
20. *Jeffrey Brown, of, U.S. Air Force Academy.
21. Joseph DiBenedetto, lhp, James Madison HS, Brooklyn, N.Y.
22. Jerome Reedy, ss, UC Davis.
23. John Hill, of, Bridgeport (Conn.) HS.
24. Dave Smith, ss, Union HS, Tulare, Calif.
25. *Mike Morrissey, rhp, Schenectady, N.Y.
26. ***Derek Botelho, ss, Boca Raton (Fla.) HS.—(1982-85)**
27. *David Stevens, of, Jesuit HS, Citrus Heights, Calif.
28. *Randy Owens, rhp, Spartanburg Methodist (S.C.) JC.
29. Alan Franklin, 2b, Catawba (N.C.) College.
30. *Steve Kaia, rhp, Bullard HS, Fresno, Calif.
31. Nicolas Ysursa, ss, Idaho State University.
32. *William Heberle, 2b, Encina HS, Sacramento, Calif.

**June—Secondary Phase (19)**

1. ***Ken Phelps, of, Mesa (Ariz.) CC.—(1980-90)**

## PITTSBURGH PIRATES

**January—Regular Phase (12)**

1. *Dan Bishop, rhp, Green River (Wash.) CC.—DNP
2. Dennis Bolden, rhp, University of South Alabama.
3. **Fred Breining, rhp, JC of San Mateo (Calif.).—(1980-84)**
4. *John Pilato, of, Monroe (N.Y.) CC.
5. *Robert Harold, rhp, Monroe (N.Y.) CC.
6. *James Del Re, lhp, Monroe (N.Y.) CC.
7. *Rick Peterson, lhp, Gulf Coast (Fla.) CC.
8. *Edward Todd, of, Marion (Ala.) Military Institute.
9. *Stephen Tanner, lhp, Gulf Coast (Fla.) CC.
10. *Randy Law, ss, Monroe (N.Y.) CC.
11. *John Hoffman, rhp, Lamar (Colo.) CC.
12. *Sam Leonard, rhp, Yavapai (Ariz.) JC.

**January—Secondary Phase (2)**

1. Bob DiPietro, lhp, Stanford University.—DNP
2. *Glen Halvorson, of, Bellevue (Wash.) CC.
3. *Richard Sherkel, c, Penn State University.
4. *William Martin, rhp, Chipola (Fla.) JC.

**June—Regular Phase (11)**

1. **Rod Scurry, lhp, Proctor Hug HS, Sparks, Nev.—(1980-88)**
2. **Gary Hargis, ss, Cabrillo HS, Lompoc, Calif.—(1979)**
3. *LaMart Harris, of, Abilene (Texas) HS.—(AA)
DRAFT DROP *Attended Ranger (Texas) JC; re-drafted by Pirates, June 1975/secondary phase (1st round)*
4. Ray Price, rhp, University of Washington.—(AAA)
5. Roger Wick, c, Hermiston (Ore.) HS.—(High A)
6. **Ed Whitson, rhp, Unicoi County HS, Erwin, Tenn.—(1977-91)**
7. **Mike Edwards, inf, UCLA.—(1977-80)**
DRAFT DROP *Twin brother of Marshall Edwards, major leaguer (1981-83) • Brother of Dave Edwards, major leaguer (1978-82)*
8. Joseph Isaac, rhp, East Laurens HS, Dublin, Ga.
9. Phil Scaffidi, ss, St. Joseph's HS, Buffalo, N.Y.
10. **Bryan Clark, lhp, Madera (Calif.) HS.—(1981-90)**
11. Marion Higgins, c, Minor HS, Birmingham, Ala.

12. *Victor Holmes, rhp, Shoreline HS, Seattle.
13. *Wayne Anderson, lhp, Crenshaw HS, Los Angeles.
14. *Richard Murray, 3b, O'Fallon (Ill.) HS.
15. Claude Smith, rhp, Mercer University.
16. *Bob McIlwain, of, Bainbridge Island (Wash.) HS.
17. *Michael McLeod, rhp, Middle Georgia JC.
18. James Leverenz, rhp, Indianapolis.
19. *Jonathon Walton, 1b-of, Buffalo State College.
20. John Bowling, lhp, University of Kentucky.
21. *Timothy Size, rhp, Spring Hill (Ala.) College.
22. Alfred Rein, of, Martin County HS, Stuart, Fla.
23. Mitchell Nowicki, c, Illinois State University.
24. Walter Cieply, rhp, Monessen (Pa.) HS.
25. *Albert Kissner, rhp, Hamden (Conn.) HS.
26. Ronald Barlow, ss, Shenandoah (Pa.) HS.
27. *William Yarbrough, inf, Sebring (Fla.) HS.
28. *Robert Turner, rhp, Fruitland (Idaho) HS.
29. *Bruce Hunter, ss, Yakima Valley (Wash.) JC.
30. Gregory Yoken, of, Poudre HS, Fort Collins, Colo.
**31. *Rick Sweet, c, Gonzaga University.—(1976-83)**
32. Greg Ferguson, rhp, Oklahoma State University.
33. *Tim Burman, lhp, University of Cincinnati.
34. *Charles Ledbetter, rhp, Clearwater (Fla.) HS.
DRAFT DROP *Brother of Jeff Ledbetter, first-round draft pick, Red Sox (1982)*
35. Frederick Neeland, rhp, Cherryfield (Maine) HS.
36. Tim Hogle, lhp, Moon HS, Coraopolis, Pa.
37. *Jim Stoekel, inf, Harvard University.

### June—Secondary Phase (21)

1. *Alton Caesar, ss, Sierra (Calif.) JC.—DNP
2. *William Cranford, lhp, Gulf Coast (Fla.) CC.

## ST. LOUIS CARDINALS

### January—Regular Phase (14)

**1. John Urrea, rhp, Rio Hondo (Calif.) JC.—(1977-81)**
2. *Bill Simpson, ss, Long Beach (Calif.) CC.
3. Michael Stone, c, Watertown, Conn.
DRAFT DROP *Baseball coach, Massachusetts (1988-2015)*
4. *Gerald Hynko, c, South Georgia JC.
5. Calvin Barr, c-of, Broward (Fla.) CC.
6. *James Weil, rhp, Grand View (Iowa) College.
7. Bill Lobdell, rhp, Broome (N.Y.) CC.
8. James McGuffin, c, Pasadena (Calif.) CC.
9. *Logan Clark, lhp, Mount San Antonio (Calif.) JC.
10. *Michael Antone, of, Chabot (Calif.) JC.

### January—Secondary Phase (18)

1. Alex Pastore, of, University of South Alabama.—(High A)
2. Ed Bowman, 3b-of, University of Southern California.
3. *Clif Holland, lhp, University of Southern California.

### June—Regular Phase (13)

**1. Garry Templeton, ss, Santa Ana (Calif.) Valley HS.—(1976-91)**
2. Bobby Hrapmann ss, Northwestern State University.—(AA)
3. Gregory Herman, lhp, Lakewood (Calif.) HS.—(High A)
4. Ken Grassano, rhp, Springfield Gardens HS, Rosedale, N.Y.—(Low A)
5. Claude Crockett, of, Southern Illinois University.—(High A)
6. *David Perez, ss, Hillsdale HS, San Mateo, Calif.
7. *Jack Lawson, rhp, Scottsdale (Ariz.) HS.
**8. Bill Caudill, rhp, Aviation HS, Redondo Beach, Calif.—(1979-87)**
9. *Michael Cameron, rhp, Council Rock HS, Ivyland, Pa.
10. *Stephen Makwinski, rhp, Sayreville-Warrenton Memorial HS, South Amboy, N.J.
11. Harold Witt, ss-3b, Stebbins HS, Dayton, Ohio.
12. *Charles Maynard, rhp, South San Francisco HS.
13. Dale Carr, 1b-of, Birmingham HS, Encino, Calif.
14. Hugh Mendenhall, of, Cottonwood HS, Salt Lake City.
15. Stan Meek, lhp, University of Oklahoma.
DRAFT DROP *Baseball coach, Oklahoma (1990); scouting director, Marlins (2002-15)*
16. *Randy Rodgers, 1b, North Riverside (Calif.) HS.
17. Michael Murphy, rhp-of, St. Louis CC-Meramec.
18. *James Buggy, lhp, Power Memorial HS, Ozone Park, N.Y.
19. William Cowens, ss, Compton (Calif.) JC.
20. *Peter Rankowitz, rhp, Tolman HS, Pawtucket, R.I.
21. Lonnie Kruger, rhp, Kansas State University.
DRAFT DROP *Coach, Atlanta Hawks/National Basketball Association (2000-03); basketball coach, Texas-Pan American (1979-82); basketball coach, Kansas State (1986-90); basketball coach, Florida (1990-96); basketball coach, Illinois (1996-2000); basketball coach, Nevada-Las Vegas (2004-11); basketball coach, Oklahoma (2011-15)*
**22. *Neil Fiala, 2b, St. John Vianney HS, St. Louis.—(1981)**
**23. *Dave Baker, ss, Granada Hills HS, Northridge, Calif.—(1982)**
DRAFT DROP *Brother of Doug Baker, major leaguer (1984-90)*
24. Len Strelitz, rhp, Temple City (Calif.) HS.
DRAFT DROP *Scouting director, Rangers (1996)*
25. Scott Hohensinner, lhp, Puyallup (Wash.) HS.
26. *Pat Wathall, rhp, Loara HS, Anaheim, Calif.
27. *Glenn Comoletti, lhp, Braintree (Mass.) HS.
**28. *Paul Molitor, ss, Cretin HS, St. Paul, Minn.—(1978-98)**
DRAFT DROP *First-round draft pick (3rd overall), Brewers (1977); elected to Baseball Hall of Fame, 2004; major league manager (2015)*
29. Thomas Valdes, lhp, Baldwin HS, Maui, Hawaii.
30. *Phil Marty, ss, El Camino HS, San Francisco.
31. David Boyer, 3b, Hermann (Mo.) HS.

### June—Secondary Phase (23)

1. Terry Kieffer, lhp, Louisiana State University.—(Rookie)

## SAN DIEGO PADRES

### January—Regular Phase (2)

**1. Tucker Ashford, 3b-ss, Shelby State (Tenn.) CC.—(1976-84)**
2. *Witt Beckman, of, University of Miami.
DRAFT DROP *16th-round draft pick, Chicago Bears/National Football League (1975)*
3. Rodney Jett, lhp, Cypress (Calif.) JC.
4. *Bobby Hottinger, c, Butte (Calif.) JC.
5. *Richard Boss, of, JC of San Mateo (Calif.).

### January—Secondary Phase (4)

**1. *Gil Patterson, of-rhp, Miami-Dade CC South.—(1977)**
2. *Ray Crawford, ss-of, Santa Ana, Calif.

### June—Regular Phase (1)

**1. Bill Almon, ss, Brown University.—(1974-88)**
2. Donnie Alfano, 1b-lhp, Mount Whitney HS, Visalia, Calif.—(AAA)
3. Roger Coe, lhp, University of Toledo.—(AA)
4. *Brandt Humphry, rhp-3b, North Torrance (Calif.) HS.—(AA)
DRAFT DROP *Attended Arizona State; re-drafted by Angels, 1977 (9th round)*
**5. *Lenn Sakata, 2b, Gonzaga University.—(1977-87)**
DRAFT DROP *Returned to Gonzaga; re-drafted by Brewers, January 1975/secondary phase (1st round)*
6. Galen McSpadden, lhp, Southeast Missouri State University.
**7. Jim Wilhelm, 1b-of, Santa Clara University.—(1978-79)**
8. Stuart McCoy, of, Bullard HS, Fresno, Calif.
9. Robert Taylor, ss, Nicholls State University.
10. Lin Hamilton, c, Clemson University.
11. Carl Mayberry, 1b, Floresville (Texas) HS.
**12. *Bump Wills, 2b, Arizona State University.—(1977-82)**
DRAFT DROP *Son of Maury Wills, major leaguer (1959-72)*
13. Ron Gill, rhp, UC Riverside.
14. Rodney Leisle, 2b, Bullard HS, Fresno, Calif.
15. Rod Bovee, lhp, University of the Pacific.
16. Bill Delormier, rhp, San Diego State University.
17. *Steven Roak, rhp, San Pedro (Calif.) HS.
18. Byron Burns, rhp, Gonzaga University.
19. Mark Carroll, rhp, San Jose State University.
20. *James Wilson, rhp-of, Compton (Calif.) HS.

### June—Secondary Phase (9)

1. Gene Delyon, 3b, Santa Clara University.—(AA)
2. Stephen Barrett, 2b, Murray State University.

## SAN FRANCISCO GIANTS

### January—Regular Phase (20)

1. Daniel Smith, lhp-1b, Los Angeles Valley JC.—(Low A)
2. *Arthur Spann, of, Alcorn State University.
3. *Larry Nevarez, rhp, Ventura (Calif.) JC.
4. *Tyrone Osborne, rhp-1b, Berkeley, Calif.
5. *Mark Miggins, 1b, Miami-Dade South CC.
6. *Steven Turner, p, Treasure Valley (Ore.) CC.
7. *Dale Yraguen, rhp, Treasure Valley (Ore.) CC.

### January—Secondary Phase (12)

1. *Clifford Mays, rhp, Clark (Wash.) JC.—DNP
2. *Les Hemby, c, Blinn (Texas) JC.
3. Gary Atwell, of, Arizona State University.
4. Dan Beitey, rhp, Clark (Wash.) JC.
5. Mark Erickson, 1b, Clark (Wash.) JC.

### June—Regular Phase (19)

1. Terry Lee, 2b, San Luis Obispo (Calif.) HS.—(AAA)
2. *Kenny Kolkhorst, c-1b, Waltrip HS, Houston.—DNP
DRAFT DROP *Attended Baylor; never re-drafted*
**3. Alan Wirth, rhp, St. Mary's HS, Mesa, Ariz.—(1978-80)**
4. *Rob Lory, lhp, Buena HS, Ventura, Calif.—DNP
DRAFT DROP *Attended Southern California; never re-drafted*
5. John Proud, ss, San Luis Obispo (Calif.) HS.—(Rookie)
6. Steve Cline, rhp, Clemson University.
7. *Chris Raper, 3b, Austin (Texas) HS.
**8. *Denny Walling, of, Brookdale (N.J.) CC.—(1975-92)**
DRAFT DROP *First overall draft pick, June 1975/secondary phase, Athletics*
9. Michael Kenney, of, University of Albany.
**10. Guy Sularz, of-rhp, North Hollywood (Calif.) HS.—(1980-83)**
11. Steve LaFerrara, c, Molloy HS, Bayside, N.Y.
12. Michael Wilbins, 1b, Southern Illinois University.
13. James Ray, of, Ashland (Ohio) College.
14. Steve Ryan, 1b-rhp, Widener (Pa.) University.
**15. John Henry Johnson, lhp, Sonoma (Calif.) HS.—(1978-87)**
**16. *Stew Cliburn, rhp-ss, Forrest Hills HS, Jackson, Miss.—(1984-88)**
DRAFT DROP *Twin brother of Stan Cliburn, fifth-round draft pick, Angels (1974); major leaguer (1980)*
17. Joe Zagarino, of-1b, Cal Poly San Luis Obispo.
18. *Mike Tulacz, lhp, Wappingers Falls HS, Poughkeepsie, N.Y.
19. Monroe Greenfield, rhp, Gonzaga University.
20. *David Morgan, rhp, Mehlville HS, St. Louis.
21. *Randy Brandt, rhp, Minnesota Lake (Minn.) HS.
**22. *Dave Rozema, rhp, Central HS, Grand Rapids, Mich.—(1977-86)**
23. *Denis Froehlich, ss, Creighton University.
**24. Jeff Yurak, c, Citrus (Calif.) JC.—(1978)**
25. Joseph Small, ss, University of New Haven.
26. *John Shoemaker, ss, Waverly (Ohio) HS.
27. Mike Cash, 2b, Georgia Southern College.
DRAFT DROP *Brother of Ron Cash, major leaguer (1973-74) • Father of Kevin Cash, major leaguer (2002-10); major league manager (2015)*

### June—Secondary Phase (15)

No selection.

## TEXAS RANGERS

### January—Regular Phase (1)

**1. Roy Smalley, ss, University of Southern California.—(1975-87)**
DRAFT DROP *Son of Roy Smalley Sr., major leaguer (1948-58) • Nephew of Gene Mauch, major leaguer (1944-57); major league manager (1960-87)*
2. Glenn Purvis, of, Mesa (Ariz.) CC.
**3. Johnny Sutton, rhp, Plano (Texas) JC.—(1977-78)**
4. *Tim Pagnozzi, ss, Mesa (Ariz.) CC.

### January—Secondary Phase (13)

1. *Jeff Feramisco, of, Fresno (Calif.) CC.—(High A)
2. Rick Hays, rhp, Mount San Antonio (Calif.) JC.
3. Glen Bright, rhp, Western Carolina University.
4. *Gary Bishop, 1b, Indian River (Fla.) CC.

### June—Regular Phase (2)

**1. Tommy Boggs, rhp, Lanier HS, Austin, Texas.—(1976-85)**
**2. Jeff Byrd, rhp, El Capitan HS, Lakeside, Calif.—(1977)**
3. Joseph Russell, c, Miami Lakes HS, Hialeah, Fla.—(AAA)
**4. Jim Clancy, rhp, St. Rita HS, Chicago.—(1977-91)**
5. Ron Norman, lhp, Pembroke State (N.C.) University.—(AAA)
6. David McCarthy, lhp, Bourgade HS, Phoenix.
7. William Patten, lhp, Northrop HS, Fort Wayne, Ind.
8. Ward Smith, lhp, Mira Loma HS, Sacramento, Calif.
9. Eddie Holman, lhp, Louisiana Tech.
10. *Ronald Smith, ss, Elkhart (Ind.) Memorial HS.
11. *Ken O'Brien, ss, Widener (Pa.) University.
12. Danny Tidwell, rhp, Atlantic HS, Delray, Fla.
**13. Rick Lisi, 3b, Pittsfield (Mass.) HS.—(1981)**
14. James Crall, c, Northrop HS, Fort Wayne, Ind.
15. Keath Chauncey, of, Georgia Southern College.
**16. Jim Umbarger, lhp, Arizona State University.—(1975-78)**
17. *Mike Massa, 2b, LaSalle HS, Cincinnati.
**18. Gary Gray, 3b, Southeastern Oklahoma State University.—(1977-82)**
19. Terry Pyka, of, University of Texas.
20. Richard Getter, rhp, Texas Wesleyan College.
21. *Dale Brock, of, Southern University.
DRAFT DROP *Cousin of Lou Brock, major leaguer (1961-79)*
22. *Charles Faubion, rhp, Alhambra HS, Glendale, Ariz.
23. *Wade Leitch, rhp, Sahuaro HS, Tucson, Ariz.
24. *Derrick Jackson, of, Wheaton (Ill.) Central HS.
**25. *Tim Stoddard, rhp, North Carolina State University.—(1975-89)**
26. Darrel Frolin, rhp, Phillips (Okla.) University.
27. *Steven Murray, rhp, Hoover HS, Fresno, Calif.
28. Dave Braden, lhp, Franklin, Ohio.
**29. Bobby Cuellar, rhp, University of Texas.—(1977)**
**30. *Al Holland, lhp, North Carolina A&T State University.—(1977-87)**
31. Robert Worthington, 2b, High Point College.
32. *Johnny Brown, ss, Hartsville (S.C.) HS.
33. *Keith Snider, 1b-ss, New Castle HS, Newport, Va.
34. *Larry Shelton, c, Tunstall HS, Dry Fork, Va.
35. Thomas Smith, ss, Walter Johnson HS, Bethesda, Md.
36. *John Bell, c, Brookville HS, Lynchburg, Va.

### June—Secondary Phase (4)

**1. *Garry Hancock, of, Hillsborough (Fla.) JC.—(1978-84)**
2. Robert Carroll, rhp, East Los Angeles JC.

# 1975

**AT A GLANCE**

### This Date In History

**WINTER DRAFT:** Jan. 9
**SUMMER DRAFT:** June 3-4

### Best Draft

**CALIFORNIA ANGELS.** Though top pick **DANNY GOODWIN** didn't pan out, the Angels drafted 15 future big leaguers—tying the mark (to that point) of the Dodgers and their celebrated 1968 draft class. The most productive picks were **WILLIE AIKENS**, selected with the second overall pick in the January regular phase, and **CARNEY LANSFORD** (3).

### Worst Draft

**MILWAUKEE BREWERS.** The Brewers landed 11-year big leaguer **LENN SAKATA** in January, but drew a blank in June, signing no one who reached the majors.

### First-Round Bust

**ART MILES, SS, EXPOS.** With a .229 average, 10 homers and 119 errors in 284 games, none above Class A, Miles was already struggling. Then his career ended abruptly in August 1977 when his West Palm Beach Expos were celebrating a Florida State League championship and he dove into a shallow pool and broke his neck, leaving him partially paralyzed.

### On Second Thought

**LEE SMITH, RHP, CUBS.** One of the dominant closers in big league history, Smith held the record for career saves (478) for 13 years, before he was surpassed by Trevor Hoffman in 2006. His performance over 18 years easily trumped that of anyone taken in the first round of the June regular phase.

### Late-Round Find

**ANDRE DAWSON, OF, EXPOS (11TH ROUND).** Dawson, righthander **DAVE STEWART** (Dodgers, 16th round) and second baseman **GLENN HUBBARD** (Braves, 20th round) all were overlooked in a maligned 1975 draft. But few players in draft history were ever so misread as

# Goodwin personifies historically weak crop

The contradictions were evident in the 1975 draft—considered, by almost any standard, the weakest draft on record.

Southern University catcher Danny Goodwin set the tone when he was taken by the California Angels with the No. 1 pick, just as he had been in 1971 by the Chicago White Sox out of a Peoria, Ill., high school. He also set high expectations by signing for a bonus of $150,000, some $50,000 more than the existing draft record, established in 1965 by Rick Monday.

And yet Goodwin, for all the hype he generated in two separate drafts, four years apart, ended up becoming one of the biggest flops of the draft era.

The first round of the June regular phase was so miscast that only one player among the first five selected (Goodwin) reached the big leagues. The balance of the first round didn't play out much better as the 24 selections yielded a cumulative WAR (Wins Above Replacement) score of 10.7—easily the poorest recorded for any first round in draft history.

Furthermore, four players signed in 1975 as nondrafted free agents—pitchers Al Holland, Rick Mahler and Dan Quisenberry, and third baseman Ken Oberkbell—went on to have more productive big league careers than all but one first-rounder, catcher Rick Cerone.

Despite being the worst first round in draft annals, a record four first-rounders were signed to major league contracts, all of whom subsequently made their major league debuts later in the 1975 season. Historically, only a privileged few were ever signed to major league deals, and generally they were players considered near slam-dunks to reach the big leagues.

One such player receiving a major league deal was Texas All-American righthander Jim Gideon (17th overall), who signed for $50,000 and made one appearance late in the 1975 season for the home-state Rangers—and never pitched another inning in the big leagues.

Another was former Central Michigan righthander Chris Knapp (11th overall), who received a bonus of just $10,000 from the White Sox, one of the smallest bonuses ever given a first-rounder.

Goodwin and Cerone were also accorded major league deals, though only Cerone, who signed with the Cleveland Indians for $55,000, had a meaningful big league career.

The curious splurge in awarding major league contracts in an otherwise forgettable 1975 draft didn't stop there as another catcher, Eddy Putman (Cubs), the third pick in the January secondary phase, and outfielder Denny Walling (Athletics), the first pick in the June secondary phase, were awarded similar deals. Putman went on to appear in just 43 big league games.

**Checking the AP wire, Danny Goodwin sees that he is the No. 1 pick in the draft for the second time in four years; like most 1975 first-rounders, Goodwin turned out to be a disappointment**

Not all was lost in the 1975 draft, though, as righthander Lee Smith, the game's all-time saves leader when he retired, went in the second round; third baseman Carney Lansford, a future American League batting champion, went in the third; and second baseman Lou Whitaker, part of one of the best double-play tandems in the game's history, went in the fifth.

But the ultimate contradiction in the Class of 1975 may have occurred in the 11th round, where an obscure outfielder from Florida A&M University, Andre Dawson, was drafted and later signed for a bonus of $2,000. He was the only future major leaguer the Montreal Expos signed that year, but became an overnight sensation in the minor leagues and emerged to become the only Hall of Famer the 1975 draft produced.

The appearance of a familiar face like Goodwin at the top of the draft board, plus the arrival of a record-tying six draft picks in the major leagues by September, provided plenty of hope that the 1975 draft would be historic. It was, but for the wrong reasons.

Goodwin's career, so promising when he was drafted, began to unravel almost from the time it started. He never caught a single game in the big

## 1975: THE FIRST ROUNDERS

| CLUB: PLAYER, POS., SCHOOL | HOMETOWN | B-T | HT. | WT. | AGE | BONUS | FIRST YEAR | LAST YEAR | PEAK LEVEL (YEARS) |
|---|---|---|---|---|---|---|---|---|---|
| **JUNE—REGULAR PHASE** | | | | | | | | | |
| 1. *Angels: Danny Goodwin, c, Southern | Peoria, Ill. | L-R | 6-1 | 195 | 21 | $150,000 | 1975 | 1986 | Majors (7) |
| Drafted first overall twice (four years apart), but injured arm after signing with Angels, never caught a game in big leagues; hit .236-13-81 in seven MLB seasons. | | | | | | | | | |
| 2. Padres: Mike Lentz, lhp, Juanita HS | Kirkland, Wash. | R-L | 6-0 | 185 | 18 | $58,000 | 1975 | 1978 | Class AA (2) |
| Went 14-2, 0.47 with 199 SO in dominating prep SR season, but never came close to fulfilling expectations in injury-plagued pro career; 17-22, 4.99 in three years. | | | | | | | | | |
| 3. Tigers: Les Filkins, of, George Washington HS | Chicago | L-L | 5-11 | 185 | 18 | $45,000 | 1975 | 1982 | Class AAA (3) |
| All-state running back spent eight years in Tigers system, but never quite showed enough production to get over big league hump, hit .255 with 60 HRs, 374 RBIs. | | | | | | | | | |
| 4. Cubs: Brian Rosinski, of, Evanston HS | Evanston, Ill. | L-R | 6-0 | 205 | 18 | $46,000 | 1975 | 1981 | Class AAA (2) |
| Similar profile as fellow Illinois product Filkins; hit .283-46-311 in seven seasons; injured leg on day he was supposed to be promoted, never got second chance. | | | | | | | | | |
| 5. Brewers: Rich O'Keefe, lhp, Yorktown Heights HS | Yorktown Heights, N.Y. | L-L | 6-6 | 210 | 17 | $52,000 | 1975 | 1984 | Class AAA (3) |
| Signed with Brewers, spent bulk of career with Reds, released in 1982 with sore arm; had surgery to remove bone chips in elbow, took final shot with Mets. | | | | | | | | | |
| 6. Mets: Butch Benton, c, Godby HS | Tallahassee, Fla. | R-R | 6-1 | 190 | 17 | $30,000 | 1975 | 1991 | Majors (4) |
| Spent nine years in Triple-A with five organizations, hit .270-64-447 overall in minors; also got four brief looks in majors, first in '78 with Mets, hit .162 in 51 games. | | | | | | | | | |
| 7. *Indians: Rick Cerone, c, Seton Hall | Newark, N.J. | R-R | 5-11 | 190 | 21 | $55,000 | 1975 | 1992 | Majors (18) |
| First 1975 pick to reach majors, last first-rounder to retire; hit .245 with 59 HRs in 18 seasons, highlighted by '80 with Yankees (.277-14-85) as Munson replacement. | | | | | | | | | |
| 8. Giants: Ted Barnicle, lhp, Jacksonville State | Sudbury, Mass. | L-L | 5-11 | 170 | 21 | $30,000 | 1975 | 1982 | Class AAA (1) |
| Averaged 18 SO/9 IP at D-II school with 97 mph FB, but didn't overpower minor league hitters in eight seasons; went 35-46, 4.73, before sore elbow ended career. | | | | | | | | | |
| 9. Royals: Clint Hurdle, of, Merritt Island HS | Merritt Island, Fla. | L-R | 6-3 | 195 | 17 | $50,000 | 1975 | 1987 | Majors (10) |
| Billed as "This Year's Phenom" on 1978 Sports Illustrated cover, but didn't meet expectations as player; found much more success as manager with Rockies, Pirates. | | | | | | | | | |
| 10. Expos: Art Miles, ss, Crockett HS | Austin, Texas | L-R | 6-2 | 175 | 18 | $56,000 | 1975 | 1977 | Class A (2) |
| Batted .229 with 10 homers, 119 errors in 284 games over three seasons in minors, then broke his neck in diving accident in 1977 after team won league title. | | | | | | | | | |
| 11. *White Sox: Chris Knapp, rhp, Central Michigan | St. Joseph, Mich. | R-R | 6-5 | 200 | 21 | $10,000 | 1975 | 1983 | Majors (6) |
| Used impressive pro debut in low Class A (6-6, 1.97, 87 IP/99 SO) as springboard to September appearance in Chicago; spent six years in majors, went 36-32, 4.99. | | | | | | | | | |
| 12. Phillies: Sammye Welborn, rhp, Wichita Falls HS | Wichita Falls, Texas | L-R | 6-4 | 195 | 18 | $57,000 | 1975 | 1983 | Class AAA (3) |
| Had three no-hitters, 1.11 ERA in high school, but eight-year pro career peaked in Triple-A, went 47-45, 5.05 overall; wife in synchonized swimming hall of fame. | | | | | | | | | |
| 13. Twins: Rick Sofield, ss, Morristown HS | Morristown, N.J. | L-R | 6-1 | 195 | 18 | $40,000 | 1975 | 1982 | Majors (3) |
| All-state QB/shortstop chose Twins over college at Michigan, spent three years in majors (.243-9-66), went on to long coaching career in college, minors, majors. | | | | | | | | | |
| 14. Astros: Bo McLaughlin, rhp, David Lipscomb | Amelia, Ohio | R-R | 6-5 | 185 | 21 | $40,000 | 1975 | 1985 | Majors (6) |
| Still holds school record for wins (16), single-game strikeouts (19) at Lipscomb, went 10-20, 4.49 in six years in majors, remains active as pitching coach for Rockies. | | | | | | | | | |
| 15. Red Sox: Otis Foster, 1b, High Point | High Point, N.C. | R-R | 6-0 | 210 | 21 | $50,000 | 1975 | 1980 | Class AAA (2) |
| Set NAIA season records for homers (30), RBIs (79) with explosive raw power, but one-dimensional player whose pro career topped out in Triple-A (.271-61-361). | | | | | | | | | |
| 16. Cardinals: David Johnson, lhp, Gaylord HS | Gaylord, Mich. | R-L | 6-1 | 175 | 18 | $30,000 | 1975 | 1981 | Class AA (3) |
| Northern Michigan product earned all-state honors in baseball, basketball, football, but met his match in minors; went 42-34, 3.55 overall in seven seasons. | | | | | | | | | |
| 17. *Rangers: Jim Gideon, rhp, Texas | Houston | R-R | 6-3 | 190 | 21 | $50,000 | 1975 | 1982 | Majors (1) |
| Celebrated college pitcher went 36-2 in final two seasons with Longhorns, but pro career fizzled; made one start in majors, went 17-27, 6.09 in minor leagues. | | | | | | | | | |
| 18. Braves: Donald Young, c, Dos Pueblos HS | Goleta, Calif. | R-R | 6-3 | 190 | 18 | $40,000 | 1975 | 1977 | Class A (2) |
| Underwhelming minor league career ended in A-ball in 1977 (.199-3-40); later graduated from Harvard biz school, became CEO of energy technology company. | | | | | | | | | |
| 19. Yankees: Jim McDonald, 1b, Verbum Dei HS | Los Angeles | L-L | 6-2 | 190 | 17 | $31,500 | 1975 | 1982 | Class AAA (2) |
| Yanks banked on his raw power developing into weapon to attack right-field porch in Yankee Stadium, but just flashed glimpses in minors; hit .259 with 44 homers. | | | | | | | | | |
| 20. Pirates: Dale Berra, ss, Montclair HS | Montclair, N.J. | R-R | 6-0 | 180 | 18 | $50,000 | 1975 | 1988 | Majors (11) |
| Yogi's son excelled in baseball, football, hockey in high school, made MLB debut at 20; modest 11-year career (.236-49-278) overshadowed by role in drug scandal. | | | | | | | | | |
| 21. Athletics: Bruce Robinson, c, Stanford | La Jolla, Calif. | L-R | 6-1 | 185 | 21 | $28,750 | 1975 | 1984 | Majors (3) |
| Set Stanford season record with 13 homers, but lefthanded power never played in big leagues (.228-0-10); career ended when he hurt shoulder in car wreck. | | | | | | | | | |
| 22. Reds: Tony Moretto, of, Harrison HS | Evansville, Ind. | L-R | 6-2 | 170 | 18 | $25,000 | 1975 | 1978 | Class AA (2) |
| Reds were enamored with sweet lefthanded swing, raw power, strong arm, but he never progressed beyond Double-A in four seasons, hit .234-7-70 overall. | | | | | | | | | |
| 23. Orioles: Dave Ford, rhp, Lincoln West HS | Cleveland | R-R | 6-4 | 190 | 18 | $32,000 | 1975 | 1985 | Majors (4) |
| Went 10-1, 0.46 with 5 BB/124 SO ratio in high school, began big league career with 15 scoreless IP; but career (5-6, 4.02) plagued by shoulder/elbow issues. | | | | | | | | | |
| 24. Dodgers: Mark Bradley, ss, Elizabethtown HS | Elizabethtown, Ky. | R-R | 6-0 | 178 | 18 | $40,000 | 1975 | 1984 | Majors (3) |
| Perennial Dodgers prospect beat bushes for eight years, hit .287-83-259 with 240 SBs, only payoff was 9 ABs in majors; later got brief shot with Mets (.204-3-5). | | | | | | | | | |
| **JANUARY—REGULAR PHASE** | | | | | | | | | |
| 1. Padres: Gene Richards, of, South Carolina State | Blair, S.C. | L-L | 6-0 | 175 | 21 | $20,000 | 1975 | 1984 | Majors (8) |
| He and college teammate Willie Aikens went 1-2; mostly a pitcher in college, had monster pro debut (.381, 148 R, 85 steals), reached San Diego by 1977. | | | | | | | | | |
| **JANUARY—SECONDARY PHASE** | | | | | | | | | |
| 1. Phillies: Barry Bonnell, of, Ohio State | Milford, Ohio | R-R | 6-3 | 190 | 21 | $25,000 | 1975 | 1986 | Majors (10) |
| Left school, led U.S. to gold at World Baseball Cup in fall of 1974, won South Atlantic League batting title in pro debut, but traded by Phillies to Braves at midseason. | | | | | | | | | |
| **JUNE—SECONDARY PHASE** | | | | | | | | | |
| 1. *Athletics: Denny Walling, 1b/of, Clemson | Farmingdale, N.J. | L-R | 6-0 | 180 | 21 | $50,000 | 1975 | 1992 | Majors (18) |
| Hit .421-13-60 for Clemson, debuted in majors same year; during 18-year big league career became one of game's best pinch-hitters; had lifetime .271 BA, 49 HRs. | | | | | | | | | |

**Signed to major league contract.*

## AT A GLANCE

Dawson. He was an immediate hit in pro ball, on the way to a 21-year, Hall of Fame career.

### Never Too Late

**DUANE WALKER, OF, GIANTS (34TH ROUND).** One of the last dozen players drafted in 1975, Walker didn't sign with the Giants out of a Texas high school, but did with the Reds (22nd round) a year later out of junior college. He persevered in the Reds system for seven years and went on to play six years in the big leagues, hitting .229 with 24 homers.

### Overlooked

**DAN QUISENBERRY, RHP, ROYALS.** Quisenberry was a marginal prospect, at best, when he signed with the Royals as a nondrafted free agent out of California's La Verne College. His career took off five years later when he mastered a submarine delivery, and he went on to lead the American League in saves five times. Quisenberry relied on pinpoint control, deception and guile to carve out a 12-year career.

### International Gem

**TONY PENA, C, PIRATES.** Pena, a product of the Pirates' rich pipeline to the Dominican Republic, played 18 years in the majors, hitting .260 with 107 home runs, while also winning four Gold Gloves. Had his career not been derailed by a severe beaning in 1984, Puerto Rican shortstop **DICKIE THON** might have upstaged Pena. Thon signed with the Angels for $20,000, while Pena was awarded a $4,000 bonus by the Pirates.

### Minor League Take

**DANNY GOODWIN, C, ANGELS.** While he essentially became a flop in a seven-year big league career after an arm injury rendered him ineffective as a catcher, the lefthanded-hitting Goodwin

CONTINUED ON PAGE 164

## AT A GLANCE

CONTINUED FROM PAGE 163

showed his offensive potential in an extended stay in the minors, hitting .313 with 129 home runs over 860 games.

### One Who Got Away

**BOB HORNER, SS, ATHLETICS (15TH ROUND).** By signing only eight of 25 selections, the A's had little to show for the June regular phase. Had they signed Horner, who went on to a huge college career at Arizona State on his way to becoming the No. 1 pick in the 1978 draft, he could have singlehandedly transformed their draft.

### He Was Drafted?

**DANNY WHITE, SS, INDIANS (JANUARY/SECONDARY, 5TH ROUND).** Though he enjoyed a record-setting career as a quarterback at Arizona State, and played 13 seasons in the NFL with the Dallas Cowboys, White was more in demand as a baseball prospect early in his career at ASU. He was picked four times in the baseball draft, including in 1975 after he had begun his pro career in the World Football League, where he played for two years before joining the Cowboys.

### Did You Know . . .

**TIM STODDARD,** drafted by the White Sox in January (secondary phase, 2nd round), is the only athlete to play for an NCAA basketball champion and World Series champion. The 6-foot-7 Stoddard was a starting forward on North Carolina State's 1974 hoops team, and a reliever for the 1983 Orioles.

### They Said It

Angels scouting director **WALTER SHANNON** on catcher **DANNY GOODWIN,** the No. 1 pick in June: "He was a legitimate No. 1 pick. He could hit, he had a good arm. There was no question he was the player we were going to pick."—*Goodwin hit .236 in 252 big league games, none as a catcher.*

leagues, and played in parts of seven seasons while hitting just .236.

In the end, Goodwin's unfulfilled career was no less a disappointment than those of most other first-rounders in 1975.

Arm problems short-circuited the promising careers of pitchers Mike Lentz (Padres, second overall), the top high school arm, and Gideon, the highest-profile college arm.

But arm injuries also took a toll on rising major leaguers like Knapp and Bo McLaughlin (Astros, 14th), and struck down a handful of others before they reached the big leagues. A serious shoulder injury, stemming from a car accident, sidelined Oakland's No. 1 pick, catcher Bruce Robinson.

Art Miles? In one of the most bizarre injuries ever to hit a first-round pick, Montreal's top selection (10th overall) dove into shallow water in 1977, while in the midst of celebrating a Class A Florida State League championship with teammates. Miles broke his neck in the incident, and remained partially paralyzed.

But mostly, the first round of the 1975 draft was dogged by unfulfilled potential.

### LENTZ EMBARASSED BY FAILURE

If Goodwin ranks as one of the draft's biggest busts, he at least spent parts of seven seasons in the big leagues. Lentz, the player picked immediately after Goodwin, never even reached Triple-A.

As a senior in 1975 at Juanita High in Kirkland, Wash., the lefthanded Lentz went 14-2, 0.47 with 199 strikeouts in 104 innings, and just 22 walks. What's more, he was such an accomplished, all-around talent that he led his prep conference in hitting, at .461, for a second straight season.

"We felt Lentz was an excellent choice," San Diego Padres player personnel director Bob Fontaine said. "He's built along the lines of Don Gullett. He's an all-around athlete."

It didn't take long for the bubble to burst for Lentz, who received a $70,000 package deal from the Padres, including a $58,000 signing bonus. Plagued by injuries, a losing record and an acknowledged lazy attitude, Lentz lasted three seasons in the pro ranks.

Mike Lentz

His career got off on the wrong foot when he dislocated his shoulder at short-season Class A Walla Walla, and then missed the 1976 season with knee surgery. Over the next two seasons, at Double-A Amarillo in 1977 and high Class A Reno in 1978, Lentz went a combined 12-19, 5.54. His career was going nowhere fast and he admitted at the time to feeling burdened by the high expectations of being an early first-round pick.

"I tried real hard those first two years because of the No. 1 thing," he said. "I wanted to show everyone I was a No. 1 pick. It wore off. Then I became lackadaisical."

### How They Should Have Done It

Based on the career WAR (Wins Above Replacement, as calculated by Baseball-Reference.com) numbers achieved by all the players eligible for the 1975 draft, here's how the first round should have unfolded. Numbers in parentheses indicate the round when the player was actually drafted

| | Player, Pos. | Actual Draft | WAR | Bonus |
|---|---|---|---|---|
| 1. | Lou Whitaker, 2b | Tigers (5) | 74.8 | $11,000 |
| 2. | Andre Dawson, of | Expos (11) | 64.4 | $2,000 |
| 3. | Carney Lansford, 3b | Angels (3) | 40.2 | $37,500 |
| 4. | Lee Smith, rhp | Cubs (2) | 29.6 | $28,000 |
| 5. | Dave Stewart, rhp | Dodgers (16) | 26.8 | $11,500 |
| 6. | Dan Quisenberry, rhp | Royals (NDFA) | 25.4 | None |
| 7. | Jason Thompson, lhp/1b | Tigers (4) | 24.8 | $14,000 |
| 8. | Ken Oberkfell, 3b | Cardinals (NDFA) | 22.3 | $8,000 |
| 9. | Rick Mahler, rhp | Braves (NDFA) | 20.3 | None |
| 10. | Glenn Hubbard, 2b | Braves (20) | 19.2 | $1,500 |
| 11. | Gene Richards, of | Padres (Jan.-R/1) | 18.6 | $20,000 |
| 12. | Don Robinson, rhp | Pirates (3) | 18.0 | $24,000 |
| 13. | Bump Wills, 2b | Rangers (Jan.-S/1) | 16.4 | $30,000 |
| 14. | Dave Rozema, rhp | Tigers (Jan.-S/4) | 15.9 | $2,500 |
| 15. | Jim Beattie, rhp | Yankees (4) | 15.4 | $25,000 |
| 16. | Willie Upshaw, of | Yankees (5) | 13.0 | $4,000 |
| 17. | Denny Walling, 1b/of | Athletics (June-S/1) | 12.2 | $50,000 |
| 18. | Al Holland, lhp | Pirates (NDFA) | 12.1 | $9,000 |
| 19. | Tom Brookens, 3b | Tigers (Jan.-R/1) | 11.6 | $12,000 |
| 20. | Rick Cerone, c | Indians (1) | 8.2 | $55,000 |
| 21. | Willie Aikens, 1b | Royals (Jan.-R/1) | 8.0 | $19,000 |
| 22. | Paul Hartzell, rhp | Angels (10) | 6.0 | $4,000 |
| 23. | Dale Berra, ss | Pirates (1) | 5.4 | $50,000 |
| 24. | Tim Stoddard, rhp | White Sox (Jan.-S/2) | 4.8 | None |

| | Top 3 Unsigned Players | | | Year Signed |
|---|---|---|---|---|
| 1. | John Tudor, lhp | Mets (21) | 34.6 | 1976 |
| 2. | Mike Boddicker, rhp | Expos (8) | 31.8 | 1978 |
| 3. | Bob Horner, ss | Athletics (15) | 21.7 | 1978 |

Things got so bad one night in Reno that Lentz, then 30 pounds overweight, was the starting pitcher in an ugly 27-17 loss to Visalia. After that game, a frustrated, disillusioned Lentz had to be talked out of quitting.

"I have been embarrassed," he said. "I've already hit the low point. I can only go up. I'll give it as long as it takes to make the major leagues."

That chance never came. The Padres released Lentz prior to the 1979 season.

Gideon's career with the Rangers began with similar promise. He became the third pitcher in a row from the Lone Star State that the Rangers chose with their first-round pick. But like Lentz, and the two Rangers pitchers before him, David Clyde and Tommy Boggs, Gideon flamed out long before achieving big league success.

A two-time All-American at Texas, Gideon had a 40-6 record in college. As a sophomore, he tied the NCAA record (since broken) of 19 wins; as a junior, he went 17-0, 1.60 and led the Longhorns to their first College World Series title in 25 years. His 17 wins without a loss are still an NCAA record.

"He was as much of a sure thing to pitch in the big leagues as anyone," Texas coach Cliff Gustafson said.

Rangers farm director Hal Keller confirmed as much, saying: "In my opinion, he may be better than some major league fourth starters right now, and he figures to get better. Our scouting reports on him were exceptionally good. He has a good running fastball, tight rotation on his curve and the makings of a good slider. He has good control and a fine knowledge of pitching."

Gideon initially reported to Rookie-level Sarasota for 10 days before finishing out the 1975 minor league season in Triple-A. On Sept. 14, he made a start for the also-ran Rangers, allowing four earned runs in five-plus innings.

There was no way of knowing it then, but that was the extent of Gideon's big league career.

Jim Gideon

A year later, he joined Boggs and Clyde on a star-studded but under-achieving pitching staff at Triple-A Sacramento, but midway through the 1976 season was traded to the Twins in a deal that brought future Hall of Famer Bert Blyleven to the Rangers. Gideon was assigned to the Twins' Triple-A affiliate in Tacoma, and that's where a chronic nerve injury that would short-circuit his career began to act up. He finished that season with a 5-9, 5.49 record, along with an unsightly 120 walks and just 69 strikeouts in 146 innings.

When Gideon struggled again early in the 1977 season, back at Tacoma (2-3, 9.80 with 43 walks in 45 innings), he requested a demotion to Class A to try and work through his troubles. But after two more games of being hit hard and struggling to find the strike zone, he had the first of two surgeries to repair the nerve behind his right shoulder blade that by then had caused the muscles in his shoulder to deteriorate.

After 18 months in rehabilitation, Gideon tried pitching again, but had only moderate success and was released by the Twins in mid-1979. After his second shoulder surgery, Gideon attempted an unsuccessful comeback in 1982 with the Rangers.

### HURDLE HOLDS HOPE

The careers of Goodwin and Lentz never took hold, and neither did those of the two players drafted right after them: outfielders Les Filkins and Brian Rosinski, both Illinois prep products.

The Detroit Tigers took Filkins, a .450 hitter from Chicago's George Washington High, with the third overall pick, while the Chicago Cubs followed by selecting Rosinski, a .517 hitter from

### Fastest To The Majors

| | Player, Pos. | Drafted (Round) | Debut |
|---|---|---|---|
| 1. | Rick Cerone, c | Indians (1) | Aug. 17, 1975 |
| 2. | Danny Goodwin, c | Angels (1) | Sept. 3, 1975 |
| 3. | Chris Knapp, rhp | White Sox (1) | Sept. 4, 1975 |
| 4. | Tim Stoddard, rhp | White Sox (Jan.-S/2) | Sept. 7, 1975 |
| 5. | # Denny Walling, of | Athletics (June-S/1) | Sept. 7, 1975 |

**FIRST HIGH SCHOOL SELECTION:** Dale Berra, ss (Pirates/1, Aug. 22, 1977)
**LAST PLAYER TO RETIRE:** Lee Smith, rhp (July 2, 1997)

*#Debuted in major leagues.*

## DRAFT SPOTLIGHT: DANNY GOODWIN

Danny Goodwin made draft history as the No. 1 pick in two different drafts: in 1971, by the Chicago White Sox as a high school selection from Peoria, Ill., and in 1975, by the California Angels as a college product from Southern University.

The Angels envisioned a franchise cornerstone catcher when they took Danny Goodwin No. 1 overall, but he never lived up to the billing

As an elite catcher with power potential who had stood up to scouting scrutiny, Goodwin appeared destined for stardom. The Angels envisioned a player they would build their franchise around.

But it never came to pass, and Goodwin's promising career curiously unraveled before it ever started.

After signing with the Angels for a draft-record $150,000 bonus, Goodwin was sent to their Double-A affiliate in El Paso. Veteran catching instructor Vern Hoscheit was assigned to get him ready for the big leagues as quickly as possible. On one occasion, Hoscheit thought Goodwin was malingering, and demanded he throw hard for a full 20 minutes.

"I hadn't been playing for almost two months," Goodwin said. "Still the Angels wanted me to go through all kinds of drills right away. They wanted me to throw every day before games. I should have taken it slow. It was probably my fault as much as anybody's, but I was young and I wanted to play. I ended up hurting my arm. But it was just a sore arm. There was no operation, no damage or anything like that. The following year, I got it together again, but by then they had given up on me as a catcher."

The Angels never saw the raw arm strength Goodwin had showcased in college. "He was consistently inaccurate with his throws," Angels scouting director Walter Shannon said. "You could see there was something wrong. Other teams could see it, too, and they began to run on him. He was just not able to throw anymore. He always could hit, and for a catcher he could run OK. But he was just an ordinary catcher once he couldn't throw."

The 6-foot-1, 195-pound Goodwin excelled in all areas of his game in four years at Southern. With a powerful lefthanded stroke, he hit .394 with 20 home runs and 166 RBIs in 169 games, and was equally valued for his skills behind the plate.

"He was a legitimate No. 1 pick," Shannon said. "He could hit and he always had a good arm in high school and college. There was no question he was the player we were going to sign. We determined early on that we were going to take him."

When Goodwin retired from baseball after the 1986 season—his final year spent in Japan—he had never been a catcher in a major league game, not even for one pitch. He played in the majors in parts of seven of his 11 seasons as a pro, but in 252 games (150 as a designated hitter) his batting average was just .236; he also had only 13 home runs.

Goodwin always was a tease, though, because he hit well in the minors throughout his career: .313 with 129 homers and 637 RBIs in 860 games. The Angels were especially intrigued in 1978, when they called him up for a third time. His .360 average for El Paso was the best in the Texas League, and he had drilled 26 homers. He was still catching on occasion, but seeing more time at first base. His days as a catcher clearly were numbered, as Texas League baserunners were successful on all 26 stolen-base attempts against him.

The Angels, though, weren't overly enthralled with him at first base, either. "He never had the agility to play that position," Shannon said. "His lack of agility and slowness afoot showed up more than ever at first base."

Following the 1978 season, the Angels traded Goodwin to the Minnesota Twins.

"It's always remained a mystery to me why he threw so well in high school and college, then couldn't throw in the pros," Shannon said. "Looking back, I guess we made a mistake, but I was sure that he was going to be a major league catcher for a long time."

## WORTH NOTING

■ The June draft was conducted for the first time in 1975 by conference call, originating from the commissioner's office. The January draft had been handled that way since 1972. Baseball went to the conference call instead of an actual draft meeting to save money, and didn't shift to the television-friendly public announcement of picks until 2007.

■ The Major League Scouting Bureau, a service to provide scouting information to all major league clubs and share the cost, was established on Sept. 1, 1974, and made its presence felt for the first time in the 1975 draft. Membership was optional in the early years of the bureau, and 17 of 24 clubs coughed up $115,000 apiece to join in the first year. It was baseball's second attempt at a centralized scouting service, and succeeded the short-lived Central Scouting Bureau, which had been founded in 1968. Most teams viewed a central-scouting concept as an opportunity to cut costs, and as a result numerous scouts were lopped from the payroll of several clubs. "It's senseless," said Expos general manager Jim Fanning, one of the bureau's founding fathers, "to have 20 scouts sitting in the stands looking at one prospect." At the top of the bureau's list of preferred prospects for the 1975 draft were four college players who were drafted in the first round: **DANNY GOODWIN** (Southern), **RICK CERONE** (Seton Hall) and **BRUCE ROBINSON** (Stanford), all catchers, and righthander **JIM GIDEON** (Texas). Cerone, a .410 hitter who set school records for homers (15) and RBIs (64), was Cleveland's first selection (seventh overall). Robinson, a defensive stalwart, set Stanford's single-season home run record with 13.

■ The first amendment in eight years to baseball's college rule was passed in 1975, though it didn't go into effect until the following year.

neighboring Evanston High. The careers of both players bogged down in Triple-A, and they never reached the big leagues.

One early hope to salvage the 1975 draft was outfielder Clint Hurdle, a three-sport star at a Florida high school who turned down a scholarship opportunity to become a quarterback at Miami in order to sign with the Kansas City Royals with the ninth pick overall. In 1967, in his third season in the Royals system, Hurdle hit .328 with 19 home runs at Triple-A Omaha, which earned him a nine-game, season-ending audition in Kansas City.

The next spring, the precocious Hurdle, 20, graced the cover of Sports Illustrated, He was billed "The Next Phenom."

From that moment on, Hurdle was supposed to be on a fast track to the Hall of Fame. But he never came close to fulfilling those unrealistic expectations—and the premature exposure he received as a wide-eyed rookie became an albatross. Other than the 1980 season when the Royals reached the World Series and Hurdle contributed a .294 average, along with 10 homers and 60 RBIs, he never came close to living up to the expectations others had for him. He perceived himself and his career as a failure because he didn't. Over parts of 10 seasons, he appeared in 515 games and hit .259.

"I was ready for the ball," Hurdle says of his spring of 1978. "The sensationalism? I don't think I was ready for that."

Clint Hurdle

Another first-rounder burdened by early expectations was third baseman Dale Berra, son of Hall of Famer Yogi Berra, who was managing the New York Mets in 1975. Dale was drafted by the division rival Pittsburgh Pirates.

"I'm very happy he was drafted by the Pirates, even though they are in our division," Yogi said. "Dale was happy, too."

Because the Mets and Pirates were both in the National League East, the Berras were under specific instructions from commissioner Bowie Kuhn to avoid discussion of Dale's negotiations with the Pirates. It became a moot point two months later when the elder Berra was fired by the Mets.

Dale was the third of Yogi's sons to play professional sports. Larry was a catcher in the Mets system before injuries forced his retirement. Tim was a wide receiver in 1974 for the National Football League's Baltimore Colts.

The youngest Berra was the best athlete of the bunch, and warranted being taken in the first round after hitting .520 with 10 homers and 20 stolen bases as a senior at Montclair (N.J.) High. He accepted a $50,000 bonus from the Pirates over offers to play football and hockey in college.

Berra, the first high school player from the 1975 draft to reach the majors, played 11 seasons in the big leagues, and even got a chance to play briefly for his father in 1985, when he left Pittsburgh as a free agent and signed with the New York Yankees. The elder Berra managed the Yankees at the time, but was fired 16 games into the season, and Dale's stay in New York was short-lived as well.

His .236 career average and 49 homers paled in comparison to his father's Hall of Fame credentials, and Berra's career ended on more of an ominous note as he was implicated as a central figure in the drug culture that infiltrated the Pirates clubhouse in the early 1980s.

### Top 25 Bonuses

| | Player, Pos. | Drafted (Round) | Order | Bonus |
|---|---|---|---|---|
| 1. | **Danny Goodwin, c** | **Angels (1)** | **1** | **#$150,000** |
| 2. | ***Myron White, of** | **Dodgers (2)** | **48** | **$60,000** |
| 3. | *Mike Lentz, lhp | Padres (1) | 2 | $58,000 |
| 4. | *Sammye Welborn, rhp | Phillies (1) | 12 | $57,000 |
| 5. | *Art Miles, ss | Expos (1) | 10 | $56,000 |
| 6. | **Rick Cerone, c** | **Indians (1)** | **7** | **#$55,000** |
| 7. | ***Rick O'Keefe, lhp** | **Brewers (1)** | **5** | **$52,000** |
| 8. | ***Clint Hurdle, of** | **Royals (1)** | **9** | **$50,000** |
| | **Jim Gideon, rhp** | **Rangers (1)** | **17** | **#$50,000** |
| | **Denny Walling, of** | **Athletics (June-S/1)** | **(1)** | **#$50,000** |
| | Otis Foster, 1b | Red Sox (1) | 15 | $50,000 |
| | ***Dale Berra, ss** | **Pirates (1)** | **20** | **$50,000** |
| 13. | *Brian Rosinski, of | Cubs (1) | 4 | $46,000 |
| 14. | *Les Filkins, of | Tigers (1) | 3 | $45,000 |
| 15. | *John Murphy, lhp | Tigers (2) | 27 | $42,500 |
| | ***Frank Pastore, rhp** | **Reds (2)** | **46** | **$42,500** |
| 17. | *Joe Jones, c | Phillies (2) | 36 | $40,000 |
| | ***Rick Sofield, of** | **Twins (1)** | **13** | **$40,000** |
| | **Bo McLaughlin, rhp** | **Astros (1)** | **14** | **$40,000** |
| | *Don Young, c | Braves (1) | 18 | $40,000 |
| | ***Mark Bradley, of** | **Dodgers (1)** | **24** | **$40,000** |
| 22. | ***Carney Lansford, ss** | **Angels (3)** | **49** | **$37,500** |
| 23. | ***Jim Anderson, ss** | **Angels (2)** | **25** | **$32,750** |
| 24. | *Harold Drake, ss | Padres (2) | 26 | $32,500 |
| 25. | **Dave Ford, rhp** | **Orioles (1)** | **23** | **$32,000** |

*Major leaguers in bold. *High school selection. #Major league contract.*

### SILVER LINING IN DRAFT

The 1975 draft was maligned because of a highly unproductive first round, but it was not totally devoid of talent.

Making up for pulling the wrong card on Rosinski, the Cubs nailed their second-round selection by snatching up an ace reliever in Smith. The Angels compensated for Goodwin's futility by tabbing the hot-hitting Lansford two rounds later. The Tigers more than made up for their mistake in drafting Filkins in the first round by landing first baseman Jason Thompson in the fourth round and Whitaker in the fifth.

The Expos lost out on Miles, but hit paydirt in the 11th round by tabbing Dawson, who provided the best evidence of all how twisted, misguided and mistake-filled the 1975 draft turned out.

Dawson became a true five-tool player by hitting 438 home runs, stealing 314 bases and winning eight Gold Gloves in a 21-year career. That put him in select company in baseball history as only Willie Mays and Barry Bonds reached the same 400-home run/300-stolen base/eight Gold Glove threshold. Dawson's accomplishments were achieved while he endured 12 knee surgeries over the course of his career.

"If Andre didn't have bad knees, he would

## Largest Bonuses By Round

| | Player, Pos. | Club | Bonus |
|---|---|---|---|
| **1.** | **Danny Goodwin, c** | **Angels** | **$150,000** |
| **2.** | *** Myron White, of** | **Dodgers** | **$60,000** |
| **3.** | *** Carney Lansford, 3b** | **Angels** | **$37,500** |
| 4. | Three tied at | | $25,000 |
| 5. | * Bob Grant, c | Mets | $25,000 |
| 6. | Dave Baker, c | Phillies | $21,000 |
| **7.** | **Keith Moreland, 3b** | **Phillies** | **$15,000** |
| | * Richard Montejano, rhp | Cardinals | $15,000 |
| 8. | * Greg Bradford, lhp | Phillies | $25,000 |
| **9.** | *** John Flannery, ss** | **Angels** | **$30,000** |
| 10. | * Charles Martin, of | Dodgers | $16,000 |
| **Jan/R.** | **Gene Richards, of** | **Padres (1)** | **$20,000** |
| **Jan/S.** | **Bump Wills, 2b** | **Rangers (1)** | **$30,000** |
| | **Eddy Putman, c** | **Cubs (1)** | **$30,000** |
| **Jun/S.** | **Denny Walling, of** | **Athletics (1)** | **$50,000** |

*Major leaguers in bold. *High school selection.*

have finished with 600 home runs and 500 stolen bases," said former teammate Shawon Dunston.

In many regards, the first rounds of both January drafts and the June secondary phase were more productive than the mainstream June regular phase—both in terms of the No. 1 pick and the next few selections.

Gene Richards

In the January regular phase, the Padres took South Carolina State outfielder Gene Richards with the first pick, and the Angels followed suit by selecting a player from the same school, first baseman Willie Aikens. Only one other time in draft history (Southern California, January 1976/secondary phase) did one college produce the first two picks in a single draft. Richards and Aikens became eligible when South Carolina State abruptly dropped its baseball program in the fall of 1974.

Both players had caught the attention of scouts in the collegiate Valley League the previous summer, with Richards hitting .336 and stealing 32 bases, while Aikens led the league with 17 home runs.

Richards, 21, launched his career with one of the most spectacular seasons by a first-year pro in the draft era. He won the California League batting title with a .381 average, and also led the high Class A league with 148 runs and 85 stolen bases. Two years later, he set a major league record for rookies by stealing 56 bases.

Aikens' first two pro seasons were no less spectacular. He led the Class A Midwest League in 1975 with 91 RBIs, and a year later topped the Double-A Texas League with 117, while slamming 30 home runs.

Though Richards and Aikens proved to be two of the best young hitters to come along in years, neither, strangely enough, was known primarily for his hitting feats at South Carolina State. Richards' specialty was actually pitching. He went 7-2 as a junior and initially had hopes that the Padres would let him pursue that role professionally.

"In school, hitting was always secondary to me," Richards said. "I just wanted to concentrate on throwing strikes. I liked it out there. I figured I could be successful that way."

The lumbering Aikens, a 6-foot-3, 242-pound defensive end, was better known for his hitting on the football field.

"I was a college football player when I signed with the Angels," Aikens said. "I had to work hard to drop 20 pounds by the end of spring training."

If there was a period of adjustment for either, no one seemed to notice.

The Padres stuck Richards in the outfield and told him to learn the position. By 1977, he was one of the most productive hitters and basestealers in the big leagues.

Both Richards, a career .290 hitter with 247 stolen bases, and Aikens, a .271 hitter with 110 home runs, went on to play eight seasons in the big leagues, but both also started to unravel while in their prime.

Because he focused so much on pitching growing up, Richards never learned how to play the outfield with precision. Even with his blazing speed, he couldn't overcome his numerous mistakes with the glove. When he stopped hitting .300, his career was over.

Aikens' problems were more acute. After being traded to Kansas City in 1980, he became heavily involved in cocaine use and was soon banished from the big leagues. He eventually drifted to Mexico, where he became the most prodigious home run hitter to play there since the legendary Hector Espino. He broke Mexican League records for batting (.454) and RBIs (154) in 1986, but was essentially blackballed from the game at that point and never earned another chance to play in the majors. He subsequently spent 14 years in prison on drug-related charges.

In the January secondary phase, outfielder Barry Bonnell was the first pick, and he, too, won a full-season Class A batting title in his first season, leading the Western Carolinas League with a .324 average. Oddly, he won the title while playing for two different teams.

Bonnell, who dropped out of Ohio State after his junior year to become eligible for the January draft, was selected by the Philadelphia Phillies

## One Team's Draft: New York Yankees

| Player, Pos. | Bonus | Player, Pos. | Bonus | Player, Pos. | Bonus |
|---|---|---|---|---|---|
| 1. * Jim McDonald, 1b | $31,500 | **5. * Willie Upshaw, 1b** | **$4,000** | 9. Len Glowzenski, rhp | Did not sign |
| 2. * Benny Lloyd, of | $25,000 | 6. * Leon Laurent, rhp | $7,500 | 10. * Larry Brown, rhp | Did not sign |
| 3. Nate Chapman, of | $6,500 | **7. Mike Fischlin, ss** | **$10,000** | **Other Gil Patterson (S/1), rhp** | **$19,000** |
| **4. Jim Beattie, rhp** | **$25,000** | 8. * Alex Kager, rhp | Did not sign | | |

*Major leaguers in bold. *High school selection.*

### WORTH NOTING

Provisions were made for all college players, no matter what their age, to be subject to selection following their junior season. Previously, a player had to have attained his 21st birthday no later than 45 days after the June draft to be eligible in the same year. The rule change wasn't enacted soon enough to affect Goodwin, the No. 1 pick who was not eligible to sign in 1974 after his junior year in college because he was still 20. It also didn't happen in time to prevent three prominent University of Southern California juniors—pitcher Pete Redfern, catcher Dennis Littlejohn and outfielder Steve Kemp—from dropping out of school in the fall of 1975 in order to become eligible for the January draft in 1976. None was eligible for any of the 1975 drafts under the existing rules. Kemp (who hit .435 with 13 home runs for the Trojans in 1975) was the first player selected in the regular phase in January 1976; Redfern and Littlejohn went 1-2 in the secondary phase.

■ One of the top two-sport athletes drafted in 1975 was outfielder **MYRON WHITE**, a prominent UCLA football recruit who rushed for an Orange County record 4,164 yards over three years at Santa Ana Valley (Calif.) High. White, a second-round pick of the Dodgers, signed for a bonus of $60,000, but got just four at-bats in a brief career with the Dodgers in 1978. In seven minor league seasons, White hit .261 with 64 homers.

■ The Reds' second-round pick was righthander **FRANK PASTORE**, whose bonus of $42,500 (the second-largest in club history at the time) was an incentive to pass up a scholarship offer to Stanford. Pastore went on to post a 48-58, 4.29 record in eight major league seasons, and later became known as the host of one of the nation's most popular Christian talk shows. He died in 2012 after a collision involving his motorcycle on a Los Angeles freeway.

**IN FOCUS: ANDRE DAWSON**

Andre Dawson had his first knee surgery while playing high school football in Miami. After that he concentrated on baseball in college at Florida A&M, but went relatively unnoticed until Montreal Expos coaching aide Billy Adair saw him, and got word to scouting director Mel Didier that he might want to take a look.

Didier saw him as much more than a skinny center fielder known for his defense, the reputation Dawson had at the time. "This young man has as quick a bat as Hank Aaron," Didier wrote in his report. "Dawson has a bat like that, and he can run and he can throw. He's going to be an outstanding player."

Still, Dawson lasted until the 11th round of the 1975 draft. Belying his obscure status, Dawson's talent was obvious from the start. He hit .330 and led the Rookie-level Pioneer League with 13 homers. He could run, hit, throw and play defense like few others in the 1975 draft, and made a rapid rise through the Expos organization. In 186 minor league games before reaching Montreal late in the 1976 season, Dawson hit .343 with 41 homers.

"He was a natural," Angels scouting director Walter Shannon said. "But he was from a small school and very few scouts saw him play. I'm sure if we had to do it all over again, he'd have been the No. 1 pick. But that's hindsight."

and started his career in the WCL with their Spartanburg affiliate. But 23 games into the 1975 season, Bonnell was part of a five-player trade with the Atlanta Braves, who simply shifted him to their WCL club in nearby Greenville. Bonnell later played 10 big league seasons.

In the June secondary phase, the top selection was hard-hitting Clemson outfielder Denny Walling, who became one of the half-dozen 1975 draft picks to debut in the majors in September.

After initially being offered $10,000 by the A's to sign, he finally reached agreement on a $50,000 bonus on Sept. 5 and debuted in the majors two days later—one of only 22 draft picks ever to skip the minors before playing in the big leagues. He played 18 years altogether, and became one of the top pinch-hitters in big league history.

## TREND TOWARD COLLEGE TALENT

Despite the failings of numerous high-profile college stars drafted in 1975, the year signaled a turning point in the impact college baseball would have on the draft going forward.

A record-low total of 188 high school players were signed out of the 1975 draft, as big league clubs were becoming increasingly concerned with the return on higher-risk high school talent, historically the game's primary source of talent. Their focus began shifting to the less-risky talent the college ranks were providing.

A record eight college players were selected in the first round of the June regular phase—though that stemmed as much from rules changes in recent years that made an increasing number of previously drafted players eligible for the regular phase as it did from a change in philosophical approach. By 1977, more college players would be drafted than high school players for the first time, a trend that never reversed itself.

Coincidentally, a new team was crowned the College World Series champion in 1975. Texas won, beating South Carolina 5-1 in the final. The Longhorns (56-6) also had more players drafted (eight) than any college.

Gideon was the only Texas player selected in the first round, but his lefthander sidekick Rich Wortham (15-1, 1.95) would undoubtedly have been a top-round pick, as well, had it not been for a serious accident in the fall of 1974. Wortham was riding atop an equipment lift when it suddenly plunged 20 feet, throwing him to the ground. His left leg was placed in a cast after surgery that removed part of a muscle that was sliced in the accident.

Wortham came back to pitch effectively for Texas and dispatched South Carolina in the CWS championship game. But he lost some of the zip off his fastball after the accident, and major league clubs treated him as damaged goods by ignoring him in the early rounds of the draft. The Mets finally took him in the 14th round.

Unimpressed with their bonus offer, Wortham returned to Texas for his senior year in 1976 and went on to set an NCAA record for career wins (50), breaking the mark of Arizona State's Craig Swan, who won 47 from 1969-72.

Texas' victory in the College World Series ended an eight-year period of almost total domination by college baseball's acclaimed Big Two: Southern California and Arizona State. It was a sign that college baseball, which introduced popular regional tournament play in 1975, was coming of age.

Aluminum bats, adopted for the 1974 season, were beginning to make college baseball a more wide-open offensive game, and a rash of home run records fell in 1975.

The NCAA single-season mark was broken for the second time in two years by Arizona State third baseman Jerry Maddox, who hit 20, while also leading the nation in hits (92), total bases (184) and RBIs (89). As a team, the Sun Devils hit a record 76. South Carolina first baseman Hank Small had 19 on the season, giving him 48 for his career, another record.

The Braves drafted the two sluggers—Small (fourth round) and Maddox (eighth round)—and while both reached the major leagues, they combined to play in just eight games and neither went deep even once. In 1978, Small's career home run mark would be obliterated by Arizona State's Bob Horner, another Braves draft pick—but in 1975, Horner was an unsigned Oakland A's selection.

At the NAIA level, High Point College's Otis Foster took power hitting to a new dimension by establishing a new single-season record with 30 home runs, while batting .478, driving in 75 runs and striking out just 12 times in 48 games. That performance impressed the Boston Red Sox, who drafted Foster in the first round.

Mace Brown, who scouted the Carolinas for the Red Sox in the 1970s, said Foster was the best hitter he'd scouted in 29 years—better even than future Hall of Famer Jim Rice, a South Carolina high school product Brown signed in 1971. "I haven't ever seen a hitter like him," Brown said of Foster. "He hits the ball hard, all over the park."

Foster, however, never hit more than 16 homers in a minor league season, and failed to reach the big leagues.

With the widespread implementation of livelier aluminum bats and the greater sweet spot they provided, scouts faced a new challenge in ascertaining which amateur hitters had genuine major league power. Foster's failure provided concrete evidence that the power didn't always translate.

### Highest Unsigned Picks

**JUNE/REGULAR PHASE ONLY**

| Player, Pos., Team (Round) | College | Re-Drafted |
|---|---|---|
| Rod Boxberger, rhp, Mets (2) | USC | Astros '78 (1) |
| Pat Gillie, rhp, Royals (2) | Arizona State | Brewers '79 (21) |
| Bob Grandas, ss, Tigers (3) | Central Michigan | Athletics '78 (3) |
| Randy Wallace, of, Cubs (3) | *Tennessee | Astros '76 (Jan.-S/2) |
| Kem Wright, rhp, Rangers (3) | Texas | Rangers '78 (24) |
| John Wells, of, White Sox (4) | USC | Never |
| Mike Wright, c, Athletics (4) | Vanderbilt | Tigers '78 (9) |
| Gene Ransom, 2b, Angels (5) | California | Twins '78 (19) |
| Tom Willette, lhp, Padres (5) | N.C. State | Royals '78 (20) |
| Bob Hely, ss, Brewers (5) | Wake Forest | Never |

**TOTAL UNSIGNED PICKS:** Top 5 Rounds (14), Top 10 Rounds (60)

**Returned to same school.*

# 1975 Draft List

**Did not sign. Major leaguers in bold, with first and last years noted. Order of selection indicated in parentheses. For the first five rounds of the June Regular Phase and the first round of all other phases, the peak level of each player is noted.*

## ATLANTA BRAVES

**January—Regular Phase (17)**

1. *Ernie Mauritson, rhp, Chabot (Calif.) JC.—DNP
2. Gary Cavaletto, of, Allan Hancock (Calif.) JC.
3. William Bowman, of, Allan Hancock (Calif.) JC.
4. Dennis Shambaugh, rhp, Mechanicsburg, Pa.

**January—Secondary Phase (21)**

1. *Keith Lloyd, p, Blinn (Texas) JC.—DNP
2. William Cranford, lhp, Gulf Coast (Fla.) CC.

**June—Regular Phase (18)**

1. Donald Young, c, Dos Pueblos HS, Goleta, Calif.—(Low A)
2. **Larry Whisenton, of, Central HS, St. Louis.—(1977-82)**
3. **Gary Cooper, of, Grove HS, Garden City, Calif.—(1980)**
4. **Hank Small, of, University of South Carolina.—(1978)**
5. ***Bob Skube, of, Simi Valley (Calif.) HS.—(1982-83)**

DRAFT DROP *Attended Southern California; re-drafted by Cardinals, June 1978/regular phase (18th round)*

6. James Doherty, ss, Ithaca (N.Y.) College.
7. *John Semarod, of, Monsignor Farrell HS, Staten Island, N.Y.
8. **Jerry Maddox, ss, Arizona State University.—(1978)**
9. Mike Reynolds, of, Blinn (Texas) JC.
10. *Condredge Holloway, ss, University of Tennessee.

DRAFT DROP *First-round draft pick (4th overall), Expos (1971) • 12th-round draft pick, New England Patriots/National Football League (1975) • Quarterback, Canadian Football League (1975-87)*

11. Ricky Carriger, rhp, Elizabethton (Tenn.) HS.
12. **Duane Theiss, rhp, Marietta (Ohio) College.—(1977-78)**
13. Kevin Connolly, c, Rider College.
14. Mike Park, rhp, University of Mississippi.
15. *Donald Eagan, 3b, Glacier HS, Burien, Wash.
16. Dean Marietta, rhp, St. Bonaventure HS, Ventura, Calif.
17. *William Pye, lhp, Avondale HS, Avondale Estates, Ga.
18. William Stewart, 3b, Verbum Dei HS, Compton, Calif.
19. James Shanks, rhp, Harlem (Ga.) HS.
20. **Glenn Hubbard, 2b, Ben Lomond HS, Ogden, Utah.—(1978-89)**
21. *Gary Skow, of, Yavapai (Ariz.) JC.
22. ***Nate Snell, rhp, Tennessee State University.—(1984-87)**
23. *Michael Wooten, 2b, West HS, Knoxville, Tenn.

**June—Secondary Phase (16)**

1. David Stevens, of, American River (Calif.) JC.—(AA)
3. *David Stevens, of, American River (Calif.) JC.
4. *Stan Skidgel, rhp, Cal Poly San Luis Obispo.
5. *Mark Trapani, rhp, Los Angeles Pierce JC.

## BALTIMORE ORIOLES

**January—Regular Phase (24)**

1. Ricky Mayo, rhp, Merced (Calif.) JC.—(AAA)
2. *Donald Kuhnoff, ss, Los Angeles Valley JC.
3. *Greg Broomis, rhp, Los Angeles Valley JC.
4. *Doug Stokke, ss, Long Beach (Calif.) CC.
5. *Scott Hefner, p, Central Arizona JC.
6. *Stephen Maehl, p, Foothill (Calif.) JC.
7. *Michael Kelly, 1b-of, Allan Hancock (Calif.) JC.
8. *Russell Mitchell, p, San Diego Mesa JC.
9. *Tim Feickert, of, Antelope Valley (Calif.) JC.
10. *Julio Acosta, of, Miami-Dade CC North.
11. Mike Pagnozzi, lhp, Tucson, Ariz.

DRAFT DROP *Brother of Tom Pagnozzi, major leaguer (1987-98)*

12. *Paul Mize, 2b, Sierra (Calif.) JC.
13. *Scott Frazier, 3b, Sacramento (Calif.) CC.
14. *James Rogers, p, JC of Southern Idaho.
15. *Joseph Romero, c-3b, Yavapai (Ariz.) JC.
16. *Edward Ribera, p, Yavapai (Ariz.) JC.

**January—Secondary Phase (16)**

1. Mark Gesquiere, rhp, El Camino (Calif.) JC.—(Rookie)
2. *Paul Bain, rhp, El Camino (Calif.) JC.

**June—Regular Phase (23)**

1. **Dave Ford, rhp, Lincoln West HS, Cleveland.—(1978-81)**
2. John Dyer, lhp, McLain HS, Tulsa, Okla.—(Low A)
3. **Steve Lake, c, Lennox (Calif.) HS.—(1983-93)**
4. Samuel Gierhan, rhp, Lakewood (Calif.) HS.—(Low A)
5. Vern Thomas, of, Harlem HS, Thompson, Ga.—(AAA)
6. **Darryl Cias, c, Kennedy HS, Granada Hills, Calif.—(1983)**
7. George Mitchell, ss, Laudon HS, Chevy Chase, Md.
8. *Robert Theoudele, rhp, John F. Kennedy HS, Richmond, Calif.
9. Darwin Luna, rhp, St. Louis HS, Pearl City, Hawaii.
10. Vincent White, of, John F. Kennedy HS, Sacramento, Calif.
11. Mike Ornest, 3b, Beverly Hills (Calif.) HS.

DRAFT DROP *Son of Harry Ornest, owner, St. Louis Blues/ National Hockey League (1983-86)*

12. *Jim Skaalen, 1b-3b, San Diego State University.
13. Greg Ward, rhp, University of South Carolina.
14. *Thomas Vitale, lhp, Belle Vernon, Pa.
15. *Jarrell Wilkerson, lhp, Smithfield (Va.) HS.
16. *Chris Nurse, ss, Bel Air HS, Fallston, Md.
17. Richard McCarthy, ss, University of New Orleans.
18. *Porter Wyatt, rhp, Inglewood HS, Compton, Calif.
19. *Alfred Blank, c, Morrisville (Pa.) HS.
20. ***Mark Esser, lhp, Ketcham HS, Poughkeepsie, N.Y.—(1979)**
21. *Randy Kwist, 1b, Springfield (Mass.) Tech HS.
22. *Bob Knezevich, rhp, Thomas Jefferson HS, Council Bluffs, Iowa.
23. Jack Neimeyer, rhp, Long Beach, Calif.
24. *Bruce Hardy, c-1b, Arizona State University.
25. Randy Vanderhook, c-3b, Bellflower, Calif.
26. Randy Checkos, rhp, Buena Park (Calif.) HS
27. *Charles Moore, rhp, Bayside HS, Virginia Beach, Va.
28. Charles Fletcher, rhp, Manhattan Beach, Calif.
29. *David Hogg, c, Jeannette (Pa.) HS.
30. ***Chris Smith, c, Bishop Montgomery HS, Hermosa Beach, Calif.—(1981-83)**
31. Doug Thiel, 1b-2b, Merced (Calif.) JC.
32. Edwin Lashley, of, Wicomico HS, Salisbury, Md.
33. *Robert Ehrig, c, University of Hawaii.
34. *Ben Hines, ss, Mesa (Ariz.) CC.
35. Robert Walker, rhp, North Central (Ill.) College.

**June—Secondary Phase (5)**

1. Everett Murray, of, University of Kentucky.—(Rookie)
2. Donald Kuhnoff, ss, Los Angeles Valley JC.
3. **Jeff Rineer, lhp, Franklin & Marshall (Pa.) College.—(1979)**
4. *Erik Hendricks, rhp, Chabot (Calif.) JC.

## BOSTON RED SOX

**January—Regular Phase (16)**

1. Walter Bigos, rhp, Cerritos (Calif.) JC.—(AA)
2. *Tim Vranich, ss, St. Petersburg (Fla.) JC.
3. Edward Nuss, rhp, Valencia (Fla.) CC.
4. *James McKenzie, rhp, Solano (Calif.) CC.
5. *David Isaacson, p, JC of the Redwoods (Calif.).

**January—Secondary Phase (14)**

1. Ken Huizenga, of, University of Southern California.—(AAA)
2. *Jerry Ennis, ss, Bakersfield (Calif.) JC.
3. *Chris Gandy, of, Sacramento (Calif.) CC.
4. *Jerry Stamps, c-1b, University of South Alabama.
5. *Mike Morrissey, rhp, Schenectady, N.Y.

**June—Regular Phase (15)**

1. Otis Foster, 1b, High Point College.—(AAA)
2. **Dave Schmidt, c, Mission Viejo (Calif.) HS.—(1981)**
3. **Ed Jurak, ss, San Pedro (Calif.) HS.—(1982-89)**
4. Michael Moore, rhp, Oak Park HS, Kansas City, Mo.—(High A)
5. Larry Hyman, 3b, Irwin County HS, Mystic, Ga.—(High A)
6. Mike Howard, rhp, South Portland (Maine) HS.
7. ***Larry Littleton, of, University of Georgia.—(1981)**
8. Bob Hampton, of, Stanford University.
9. ***Dave Stegman, of, University of Arizona.—(1978-84)**
10. **Dave Stapleton, 2b, University of South Alabama.—(1980-86)**
11. Gary Purcell, of, University of New Orleans.
12. Carlton Steele, of, Westfield State (Mass.) College.
13. Breen Newcomer, lhp, University of Oklahoma.
14. Phillip Welch, rhp, Providence College.
15. Richard Waller, rhp, Montclair State (N.J.) College.
16. David Schoppee, rhp, Deering HS, Portland, Maine.
17. Richard McAlister, c, Louisiana Tech.
18. Happy Vincent, 3b, Palm Springs (Calif.) HS.
19. Thomas Streightiff, of, Juniata (Pa.) College.
20. *Larry Ennis, of, Fairleigh Dickinson University.
21. Timothy Clemmons, of, Southeastern HS, Chillicothe, Ohio.
22. **Mike O'Berry, c, University of South Alabama.—(1979-85)**
23. **Mike Paxton, rhp, Memphis State University.—(1977-80)**
24. *Peter Khoury, of, Durfee HS, Fall River, Mass.

**June—Secondary Phase (11)**

1. Ron Evans, 3b, North Carolina State University.—(AAA)

## CALIFORNIA ANGELS

**January—Regular Phase (2)**

1. **Willie Aikens, 1b, South Carolina State College.—(1977-85)**
2. **Jim Dorsey, rhp, Los Angeles Valley JC.—(1980-85)**
3. Gary Hinshaw, ss, Modesto (Calif.) JC.
4. *Jim Raska, p, CC of Baltimore.
5. ***Bob Walk, rhp, JC of the Canyons (Calif.).—(1980-93)**
6. *James Roach, rhp, Bakersfield (Calif.) JC.
7. *Bob Meadows, p, Seminole (Fla.) CC.
8. *Andy Schardt, 1b, Fullerton (Calif.) JC.
9. *Rodger Bills, p, Idaho Falls, Idaho.
10. Carl Meche, rhp, Northwestern State University.
11. *Hal Jeffrey, p, JC of the Canyons (Calif.).
12. *Mark Miller, p, Central Arizona JC.
13. *David Rhinehart, of, Riverside (Calif.) HS.

**January—Secondary Phase (12)**

1. **Gil Kubski, 3b, Cal State Northridge.—(1980)**
2. Richard Brewster, 2b, San Bernardino Valley (Calif.) JC.
3. Terry Stupy, c, UC Irvine.
4. ***Derek Botelho, ss-rhp, Miami-Dade CC South.—(1982-85)**
5. **Bobby Clark, ss, Riverside (Calif.) CC.—(1979-85)**
6. *Paul Kolesnikow, of, JC of San Mateo (Calif.).
7. *William McIntyre, of, Cal State Northridge.
8. *Albert Paglione, rhp, Valencia (Fla.) CC.

**June—Regular Phase (1)**

1. **Danny Goodwin, c, Southern University.—(1975-82)**

DRAFT DROP *First overall draft pick, June 1971/regular phase, White Sox*

2. **Jim Anderson, ss, Kennedy HS, Granada Hills, Calif.—(1978-84)**
3. **Carney Lansford, ss, Wilcox HS, Santa Clara, Calif.—(1978-92)**

DRAFT DROP *Brother of Phil Lansford, first-round draft pick, Indians (1978) • Brother of Jody Lansford, first-round draft pick, Padres (1979); major leaguer (1982-83)*

4. **Floyd Rayford, c, Manual Arts HS, Los Angeles.—(1980-87)**
5. *Gene Ransom, 2b, Berkeley (Calif.) HS.—DNP

DRAFT DROP *Attended California; re-drafted by Twins, June 1978/regular phase (19th round) • Ninth-round draft pick, Golden State Warriors/National Basketball Association (1979) • Brother of Horace Ransom, 15th-round draft pick, Athletics (1981)*

6. Steve Kelley, rhp, Santa Clara University.
7. *Marvin Cobb, 2b, University of Southern California.

DRAFT DROP *Defensive back, National Football League (1975-77)*

8. Jimmy Brown, rhp, Bogalusa (La.) HS.
9. **John Flannery, ss, Lakewood (Calif.) HS.—(1977)**
10. **Paul Hartzell, rhp, Lehigh University.—(1976-84)**
11. *Steve King, c, University of South Carolina
12. Mike Merritt, rhp, University of North Carolina.
13. Robert Boyd, rhp, Brooklyn Park HS, Baltimore.
14. *Columbus Duncan, of, McDonogh HS, Baltimore.
15. David Hollifield, lhp, Seminole (Fla.) CC.
16. Wayne Williams, of, King George (Va.) HS.
17. Gary Boyle, rhp, Torrance (Calif.) HS.
18. Jerry Quigley, rhp, Lewis (Ill.) University.
19. **Steve Eddy, rhp, United Township HS, Moline, Ill.—(1979)**
20. Robert LaFave, of, Carmen HS, Flint, Mich.
21. *Kim Mason, rhp, Arizona Western JC.
22. ***Ron Musselman, rhp, Louisburg (N.C.) JC.—(1982-85)**
23. *Jim Capoferi, c, Lakeview HS, St. Clair Shores, Mich.
24. *Clarence Syers, rhp, Sylmar (Calif.) HS.
25. *James Morphis, rhp, Harry Ells HS, Richmond, Calif.
26. *Jim Watkins, of, Pike HS, Indianapolis.

DRAFT DROP *First overall draft pick, June 1978/secondary phase, Red Sox*

27. *Jim Schwanke, ss, Yavapai (Ariz.) JC.
28. *Brian Sweet, rhp, Highland HS, Salt Lake City.

**June—Secondary Phase (21)**

1. ***Garry Hancock, of, University of South Carolina.—(1978-84)**
2. *Randy Rogers, 1b, UC Riverside.

## CHICAGO CUBS

**January—Regular Phase (3)**

1. Wayne Doland, rhp, Fairleigh Dickinson University.—(High A)
2. William Mullins, 1b, St. Petersburg (Fla.) JC.
3. *Jeffrey Robinson, ss, Blinn (Texas) JC.

**January—Secondary Phase (3)**

1. **Eddy Putman, c, University of Southern California.—(1976-79)**
2. Michael Perkins, 1b-of, Belmont (Tenn.) College.
3. Michael Cameron, rhp, Ivyland, Pa.

**June—Regular Phase (4)**

1. Brian Rosinski, of, Evanston (Ill.) HS.—(AAA)
2. **Lee Smith, rhp, Castor HS, Jamestown, La.—(1980-97)**
3. *Randy Wallace, of, University of Tennessee.—DNP

DRAFT DROP *Returned to Tennessee; re-drafted by Astros, January 1976/secondary phase (2nd round)*

4. Charles Peoples, c, Columbia HS, Richland, Wash.—(High A)
5. Michael Taylor, rhp, Scotlandville HS, Baton Rouge, La.—(High A)
6. Willis Stewart, 3b, Sam Houston State University.
7. *Bill Hainline, ss, Rogers HS, Spokane, Wash.
8. Chuck Rogers, rhp, University of Michigan.
9. *Ron Kainer, rhp, Sam Houston State University.
10. *Morris Wilmer, of, Louisiana College.
11. Mike Umfleet, ss, University of Oklahoma.
12. Jeffrey Lucchesi, lhp, JC of Marin (Calif.).
13. Michael Moore, rhp, Tennessee Tech.
14. Mike Anderson, of, University of Texas.
15. *Richard Alexander, of, Myers Park HS, Matthews, N.C.

16. *Scott Green, rhp, Kennedy HS, Granada Hills, Calif.
17. Dwight Bryant, of, Decatur (Ga.) HS.
18. *Sam Marsi, rhp, Tomales HS, Port Reyes Station, Calif.
19. James Weber, lhp, University of New Mexico.
20. William Von Ahnen, lhp, Kingsborough (N.Y.) CC.
21. Ricky Brockway, inf, University of Texas-Pan American.
22. *Del Leutbecher, 1b, Katella HS, Anaheim, Calif.
23. *Steve Winfield, rhp, San Augustine (Texas) HS.
24. *Chris Hartig, rhp, Mullen HS, Lakewood, Colo.
25. *Tim Huff, rhp, Gardner-Webb College.
26. Joe Hernandez, of, University of Texas-Pan American.
27. *Steve Bush, ss, University of Kentucky.
28. James Travis, ss, Whitworth (Wash.) College.
29. *Randy Hackney, 1b, University of Michigan.

**June—Secondary Phase (4)**

1. *John Henderson, c, University of Georgia.—DNP
2. Charles Ledbetter, rhp, Valencia (Fla.) CC.

DRAFT DROP *Brother of Jeff Ledbetter, first-round draft pick, Red Sox (1982)*

## CHICAGO WHITE SOX

**January—Regular Phase (12)**

1. *James Dyer, ss, Arizona Western JC.—(AA)
2. *John MacAuley, 2b, Golden West (Calif.) JC.
3. *Monte Bothwell, of, Cypress (Calif.) JC.
4. Robert Madden, rhp, Golden West (Calif.) JC.
5. Marshall Harper, of, Brevard (Fla.) CC.
6. Kent Hunziker, rhp, Golden West (Calif.) JC.
7. Gary Eagle, 2b, Miami-Dade CC North.
8. ***Bruce Bochy, c, Brevard (Fla.) CC.—(1978-87)**

DRAFT DROP *Major league manager (1995-2015) • Father of Brett Bochy, major leaguer (2014-15)*

9. Michael Farrell, rhp, Miami-Dade CC North.
10. (void) *Willie Lee, of, Southwestern Oklahoma State University.

**January—Secondary Phase (20)**

1. *Scott Anderson, rhp, Mesa (Ariz.) CC.—(AA)
2. **Tim Stoddard, rhp, North Carolina State University.—(1975-89)**

DRAFT DROP *Only athlete to win NCAA basketball championship (North Carolina State/1974) and World Series championship (Orioles/1983)*

3. Curtis Etchandy, ss, Golden West (Calif.) JC.
4. Bobby McClellan, c, Gadsden State (Ala.) JC.
5. *Mike Tulacz, lhp, Miami-Dade CC North.
6. *Danny Gans, 3b, Mount San Antonio (Calif.) JC.
7. *Michael Wirwas, ss, Mesa (Ariz.) CC.

**June—Regular Phase (11)**

1. **Chris Knapp, rhp, Central Michigan University.—(1975-80)**
2. Mitch Lukevics, rhp, Penn State University.—(AAA)
3. Thomas Bright, of, Alta Loma (Calif.) HS.—(Low A)
4. *John Wells, of, Hoover HS, San Diego.—(High A)

DRAFT DROP *Attended Southern California; re-drafted by Mets, June 1978/regular phase (19th round)*

5. Phil Bauer, ss, Joliet Central HS, Joliet, Ill.—(AA)
6. *Robert Cochran, lhp, Royal Oak HS, Covina, Calif.
7. Edward Yesenchak, c, Canon-McMillan HS, Canonsburg, Pa.
8. *Mickey Lashley, rhp, University of Oklahoma.

DRAFT DROP *Baseball coach, Texas-San Antonio (1997-2000)*

9. Randy Seltzer, lhp, Parkland HS, Wescosville, Pa.
10. Leo Elter, ss, Shaler HS, Pittsburgh.
11. *Don Hanna, rhp, Yavapai (Ariz.) JC.
12. Ted Schultz, ss, University of San Diego.
13. *David Daniels, of, Edgewood HS, West Covina, Calif.
14. *Mike Dempsey, rhp, North Carolina State University.
15. Peter Maropis, ss, Allegheny (Pa.) College.
16. ***Dan O'Brien, rhp, Florida State University.—(1978-79)**
17. **Marv Foley, c, University of Kentucky.—(1978-84)**
18. *Jeff Simons, lhp, Brevard (Fla.) CC.
19. Jim Handley, rhp, Auburn University.
20. *Clark Langdon, 3b, Lamar (Colo.) CC.
21. ***Harry Chappas, ss, Nova HS, Fort Lauderdale, Fla.—(1978-80)**
22. *Ronald Russell, 3b-of, Christian Brothers HS, Memphis, Tenn.
23. *Roger Mayo, rhp, Jacksonville State University.
24. *Stephen Walsh, lhp, St. Louis University.
25. *Greg Johnson, rhp, Santiago HS, Santa Ana, Calif.
26. *James Green, rhp, Maplesville (Ala.) HS.
27. Tom Joyce, lhp, University of Michigan.
28. Wayne Gottleber, rhp, St. Clair County (Mich.) CC.
29. *Michael Ryan, lhp, Bellaire HS, Houston.
30. *Mark Reese, of, Atherton HS, Louisville, Ky.

DRAFT DROP *Son of Pee Wee Reese, major leaguer (1940-58)*

31. *Brian Zapalac, lhp, Sealy (Texas) HS.

**June—Secondary Phase (9)**

1. *Mike Tulacz, lhp, Miami-Dade CC North.—(High A)
2. Jim Crosta, ss, University of Miami.
3. *Thomas Baxter, rhp, Miami-Dade CC South.

## CINCINNATI REDS

**January—Regular Phase (21)**

1. *James Slaughter, c, Pasadena (Calif.) CC.—DNP
2. *Teddy Asbill, p, Bunch, Okla.
3. Bernard Plent, rhp, Arizona State University.
4. *Mark Clark, of, Antelope Valley (Calif.) JC.

**January—Secondary Phase (5)**

1. Lawrence Pekarcik, rhp, Mount San Antonio (Calif.) JC.—(High A)
2. Mark Unsoeld, c, Mount San Antonio (Calif.) JC.
3. *Tom Baxter, rhp, University of Miami.

**June—Regular Phase (22)**

1. Tony Moretto, of, Harrison HS, Evansville, Ind.—(AA)
2. **Frank Pastore, rhp, Damien HS, Upland, Calif.—(1979-86)**
3. **Paul Moskau, rhp, Azusa Pacific (Calif.) University.—(1977-83)**
4. **Scott Brown, rhp, DeQuincy (La.) HS.—(1981)**
5. Mark Miller, c, El Capitan HS, Lakeside, Calif.—(AAA)
6. Sal Ferrara, rhp, Tampa (Fla.) Catholic HS.
7. Frederick Warren, rhp, Sam Houston State University.
8. *Ed Skribiski, ss, Frontier Regional HS, Sunderland, Mass.
9. Randy Davidson, 2b, Florida State University.
10. ***Don Welchel, rhp, Lake Highland HS, Dallas.—(1982-83)**
11. Marti Wolever, of, St. Albert HS, Council Bluffs, Iowa.

DRAFT DROP *Scouting director, Phillies (1992-2014)*

12. Mark Hopper, ss, Florida Southern College.
13. Lawrence Groves, ss, Encinal HS, Alameda, Calif.
14. Tony Grana, rhp, Gorman HS, Las Vegas, Nev.
15. *Jim McArdle, 3b, Brevard (Fla.) CC.
16. Evan Edge, c, Jacksonville State University.
17. Kelly Jensen, rhp, Utah Technical JC.
18. *Michael Bretz, rhp, Eastern Hills HS, Fort Worth, Texas.
19. Reggie Waller, of, San Diego CC.

DRAFT DROP *Brother of Tye Waller, major leaguer (1980-87) • Scouting director, Padres (1992-93)*

20. *Mark Copeland, rhp, Eastern Hills HS, Fort Worth, Texas.
21. John Huntington, lhp-of, Rancho HS, Las Vegas, Nev.
22. Charles Moore, rhp, Paxon HS, Jacksonville, Fla.
23. Gary Richter, 2b, Grayson County (Texas) JC.
24. *Steve Muccio, ss, DeWitt Clinton HS, Bronx, N.Y.
25. Robert Adams, rhp, East Bay HS, Ruskin, Fla.
26. *Stanley Cannon, of-1b, Woodham HS, Pensacola, Fla.
27. ***Bill Paschall, rhp, University of North Carolina.—(1978-81)**

**June—Secondary Phase (14)**

1. *Scott Burk, ss-rhp, Oklahoma State University.—(AA)

DRAFT DROP *Defensive back, National Football League (1979)*

## CLEVELAND INDIANS

**January—Regular Phase (8)**

1. Michael Vaughn, rhp, West Valley (Calif.) JC.—(High A)
2. *John Hills, lhp, Moorpark (Calif.) JC.
3. Stephen Klein, rhp, Queens (N.Y.) College.
4. *Alfonso Williams, 3b-c, Lawson State (Ala.) CC.
5. *Gary Talbert, c-of, Faulkner State (Ala.) JC.
6. Patrick Washko, 1b-of, Cleveland State University.

**January—Secondary Phase (8)**

1. Craig Harvey, rhp-c, La Verne, Okla.—(AA)
2. Ralph Jiminez, c, Bronx (N.Y.) CC.
3. *Steven Van Deren, c, JC of the Redwoods (Calif.).
4. *Michael Massa, 2b, Miami-Dade CC South.
5. *Danny White, inf, Arizona State University.

DRAFT DROP *Quarterback, National Football League (1976-88).*

6. *David Adeimy, c, Miami-Dade CC North.

**June—Regular Phase (7)**

1. **Rick Cerone, c, Seton Hall University.—(1975-92)**

DRAFT DROP *First player from 1975 draft to reach majors (Aug. 17, 1975)*

2. Daniel Skiba, rhp, South Houston (Texas) HS.—(AA)
3. Bill Hiss, ss, Queens (N.Y.) College.—(AA)
4. Larkin Bullard, rhp, Robert E. Lee HS, Springfield, Va.—(High A)
5. ***Mike Macha, 3b, Rice University.—(1975-80)**

DRAFT DROP *Returned to Rice; re-drafted by Braves, January 1976/secondary phase (1st round)*

6. Jeff Tomski, c, St. Thomas More HS, Milwaukee.
7. *Casey Lindsey, lhp, Billings (Mon.) HS.
8. Larry Harmon, ss, Clover Hill HS, Midlothian, Va.
9. *Jerry Schmidt, rhp, Lewis-Clark State (Idaho) College.
10. **Dave Schuler, lhp, University of New Haven.—(1979-85)**
11. *Marvin Hammock, ss, Carol City HS, Opa Locka, Fla.
12. *William Wilborn, of, McClatchy HS, Sacramento, Calif.
13. *David Erickson, rhp, Escambia HS, Pensacola, Fla.
14. *Roderick Ingram, of, Linfield (Ore.) College.
15. Gary Melson, rhp, Middle Tennessee State University.
16. ***Leo Sutherland, of, Santiago HS, Garden Grove, Calif.—(1980-81)**
17. Angelo LoGrande, 1b, Sehome HS, Bellingham, Wash.
18. Thomas Amenita, rhp, Rider College.
19. *Dennis Firenza, of, Elk Grove HS, Sacramento, Calif.
20. Earl Jordan, of, Virginia Wesleyan College.
21. *Jerome Miller, of, Leland HS, Elizabeth, Miss.
22. *Ronald Rippee, c, Alhambra HS, Martinez, Calif.
23. *Michael Hrnyak, ss, Euclid (Ohio) HS.
24. Richard Ezell, ss, Virginia Wesleyan College.
25. *Ricky Connell, rhp, Indian Hills (Iowa) CC.
26. Barry Glabman, ss, Homewood, Ill.

**June—Secondary Phase (13)**

1. John Brown, of, South Georgia JC.—(AA)
2. *Jackie Snell, lhp, George C. Wallace (Ala.) CC.

## DETROIT TIGERS

**January—Regular Phase (4)**

1. **Tom Brookens, ss, Mansfield (Pa.) University.—(1979-90)**

DRAFT DROP *Twin brother of Tim Brookens, first-round draft pick, January 1975/regular phase, Rangers*

2. *Eric Mustad, rhp, Citrus (Calif.) JC.
3. *Mike Parkinson, ss, Mount San Antonio (Calif.) JC.
4. Alfred DiPietro, c, San Jose (Calif.) CC.
5. Frank Harris, rhp, Fullerton (Calif.) JC.
6. John Romero, ss, Santa Monica (Calif.) CC.
7. *Brian Rusca, rhp, West Valley (Calif.) JC.
8. *Christopher O'Brien, p, Central Arizona JC.
9. *Pat Callahan, c, Broward (Fla.) CC.

**January—Secondary Phase (2)**

1. **Dave Tobik, rhp, Ohio University.—(1978-85)**
2. Thomas Perkins, rhp, Cal State Los Angeles.
3. *Dean Phillips, rhp, Panola (Texas) JC.
4. **Dave Rozema, rhp, Grand Rapids (Mich.) JC.—(1977-86)**

**June—Regular Phase (3)**

1. Les Filkins, of, George Washington HS, Chicago.—(AAA)
2. John Murphy, lhp, St. Francis Prep HS, Brooklyn, N.Y.—(AAA)
3. *Bob Grandas, ss, Central HS, Flint, Mich.—(AAA)

DRAFT DROP *Attended Central Michigan; re-drafted by Athletics, June 1978/regular phase (3rd round)*

4. **Jason Thompson, lhp-1b, Cal State Northridge.—(1976-86)**
5. **Lou Whitaker, 3b, Martinsville (Va.) HS.—(1977-95)**
6. Jeff Reinke, lhp, University of Southern California.
7. Dana McManus, rhp, Chapman (Calif.) College.
8. *Steve Powers, rhp, University of Arizona.
9. *Andy Lopez, ss, UCLA.

DRAFT DROP *Baseball coach, Pepperdine (1989-94); baseball coach, Florida (1995-2001); baseball coach, Arizona (2002-15)*

10. Vicente Diaz, c, Jackson HS, Miami.
11. Paul Vavruska, rhp, St. John's River (Fla.) CC.
12. *Chuck Black, ss, Shawnee HS, Lima, Ohio.
13. *John Racanelli, rhp, University of Southern California.
14. *Steve Morrison, 2b, Farmington-Harrison HS, Farmington, Mich.
15. Don Thomas, rhp, North Baltimore (Ohio) HS.
16. *Karl Boesch, rhp, Clackamas (Ore.) CC.
17. Mike Bartell, ss, Santa Clara University.

DRAFT DROP *Grandson of Dick Bartell, major leaguer (1927-46)*

18. *John Phipps, c, Central HS, Flint, Mich.
19. ***Bruce Berenyi, rhp, Glen Oaks (Mich.) CC.—(1980-86)**
20. *Derek Carrier, ss, Science Hill HS, Johnson City, Tenn.
21. Venoy Garrison, c, UCLA.
22. David Bowden, ss, University of Florida.
23. Julio Alonso, lhp, Lamar University.
24. Wynn Sherman, c-of, Cal Poly Pomona.
25. *Scott McLeod, rhp, Riverview (Mich.) HS.
26. Dexter Redd, of, Hoover HS, San Diego.

**June—Secondary Phase (17)**

1. Phil Doktor, ss, University of Southern California.—(Rookie)
2. *Mike Parkinson, ss, Mount San Antonio (Calif.) JC.
3. *Brian Rusca, rhp, West Valley (Calif.) JC.

## HOUSTON ASTROS

**January—Regular Phase (13)**

1. ***Darrell Brown, ss, East Los Angeles JC.—(1981-84)**
2. John Goetz, c, Rollins (Fla.) College.
3. *Michael Hopkins, p, Shelby State (Tenn.) CC.

**January—Secondary Phase (7)**

1. Jim Willis, 1b, University of Oregon.—(AA)
2. *Steven Murray, rhp, Fresno (Calif.) CC.
3. *James Crosta, ss, Miami-Dade CC South.

**June—Regular Phase (14)**

1. **Bo McLaughlin, rhp, David Lipscomb (Tenn.) College.—(1976-82)**
2. Ed Andersen, rhp, Redwood HS, Greenbrae, Calif.—(High A)
3. Bobby Hallgren, of, Charles F. Adams HS, Clarkston, Wash.—(High A)
4. Jack Cloherty, rhp, St. Patrick's HS, Watertown, Mass.—(High A)
5. **Joe Pittman, 3b, Southern University.—(1981-84)**
6. Michael Lally, of, Peoria (Ariz.) HS.
7. *Arnold McCrary, of, Muir HS, Altadena, Calif.

8. *Frank Aranco, rhp, Union (N.J.) HS.
9. *Jimmy Hickman, of-3b, Loris (S.C.) HS.
10. Scott Makela, 3b, Rochester (N.Y.) Institute of Technology.
11. Gerald Taylor, 1b, Huston-Tillotson (Texas) College.
12. *Lance Gore, lhp, Katella HS, Anaheim, Calif.
13. Donald Pisker, of, Rider College.
14. Michael Tyler, c, St. John's University.
15. Richard Miller, lhp, University of Arkansas.
16. *Phillip Pundt, rhp, Mount St. Joseph HS, Baltimore.
17. Brian Woltman, 3b, Clawson (Mich.) HS.
18. Robert Blank, rhp, University of Arkansas.
19. *Daniel Newell, rhp, Cardington-Lincoln HS, Cardington, Ohio.
20. *Greg Vogel, inf, Penn State University.
21. Robert Wood, 2b, Birmingham-Southern College.
22. Al Osofsky, of, St. John's University.
**23. *Kim Seaman, lhp, Live Oak Academy HS, Moss Point, Miss.—(1979-80)**
24. *Mark Champagne, rhp, Port Neches HS, Groves, Texas.

**June—Secondary Phase (24)**

**1. Bruce Bochy, c, Brevard (Fla.) CC.—(1978-87)**
DRAFT DROP *Major league manager (1995-2015)*
2. *Gerald Green, rhp, Lower Columbia (Wash.) JC.

## KANSAS CITY ROYALS

**January—Regular Phase (10)**

1. Steven Manley, p, Kingsborough (N.Y.) CC.—DNP
2. Frank Mastrangelo, c, Shippensburg (Pa.) University.
3. *Scott Borie, p, Golden West (Calif.) JC.
4. *Timothy Hayes, ss, Cypress (Calif.) JC.
5. *Steven Brooks, p, Huntington Beach, Calif.

**January—Secondary Phase (24)**

1. *Tim Richards, c, Golden West (Calif.) JC.—DNP
2. *Jake Battle, c, Miami-Dade CC North.
3. *Larry Randel, ss, Fullerton (Calif.) JC.

**June—Regular Phase (9)**

**1. Clint Hurdle, of, Merritt Island (Fla.) HS.—(1977-87)**
DRAFT DROP *Major league manager (2002-15)*
2. *Pat Gillie, rhp, Alhambra HS, Phoenix—DNP
DRAFT DROP *Attended Arizona State; re-drafted by Brewers, June 1979/regular phase (21st round)*
3. Bryan Jones, ss, University of Iowa.—(High A)
4. David Winters, rhp, Alfred Bonnabel HS, Kenner, La.—(Short-season A)
**5. Rich Gale, rhp, University of New Hampshire.—(1978-84)**
6. Jack Hudson, c, South Charleston (W.Va.) HS.
7. Kevin Gillen, of, Niles West HS, Skokie, Ill.
8. *James Murphy, c, Port Clinton (Ohio) HS.
9. Steve Lacy, ss, Louisiana Tech.
10. Ron Smith, rhp, Wilcox HS, Santa Clara, Calif.
**11. Danny Garcia, of, Baruch (N.Y.) College.—(1981)**
12. Joe Rothwell, c, Oak Hills HS, Cincinnati.
13. David Burroughs, c, Ketchum (Okla.) HS.
**14. Randy McGilberry, rhp, Louisiana Tech.—(1977-78)**
15. Henry Greene, lhp, McCracken HS, Bluffton, S.C.
16. *Frank Shellenback, c, Barrington HS, Barrington Hills, Ill.
17. Kent Cvejdlik, rhp, Thomas Jefferson HS, Carter Lake, Iowa.
18. *Larry Brown, c, Niceville (Fla.) HS.
19. John Hart, rhp, Mercer University.
20. *Ronnie Ferrell, 3b, Northern HS, Durham, N.C.
21. John Sebastian, rhp, Columbus (Ga.) HS.
**22. *Ron Hassey, 3b, University of Arizona.—(1978-91)**
23. Greg Schuller, c, Independence, Mo.
24. *Gordon Blakeley, 3b, Chapman (Calif.) College.
25. *Mike Hankins, 3b, South Raytown (Mo.) HS.

**June—Secondary Phase (19)**

1. Mike Denevi, ss, Santa Clara University.—(AAA)
2. *William Yarbrough, 3b, Manatee (Fla.) JC.

3. (void) *Denny Martindale, 2b-rhp, University of Southern California.

## LOS ANGELES DODGERS

**January—Regular Phase (23)**

1. Donald Washington, of, Laney (Calif.) JC.—(High A)
2. *Dale Emmer, of, Santa Monica (Calif.) JC.
3. *Gavin Long, rhp, JC of San Mateo (Calif.).
4. *Patrick Buckner, c, Sacramento (Calif.) CC.
5. *Steven Watson, p, Midland (Texas) JC.
6. Mike Tennant, rhp, Crowder (Mo.) JC.
7. Ron Weirum, 2b, Santa Barbara (Calif.) CC.
8. *Terry Watkins, rhp, Sacramento (Calif.) CC.

**January—Secondary Phase (23)**

**1. *Gil Patterson, of-rhp, Miami-Dade South CC.—(1977)**
2. *William Yarbrough, 3b, Manatee (Fla.) JC.
3. *Earl Bass, rhp, University of South Carolina.

**June—Regular Phase (24)**

**1. Mark Bradley, ss, Elizabethtown (Ky.) HS.—(1981-83)**
**2. Myron White, of, Santa Ana (Calif.) Valley HS.—(1978)**
3. Rodney Scheller, rhp, Greeley (Colo.) West HS.—(High A)
4. James Evans, lhp, East Technical HS, Cleveland.—(High A)
5. Marvin Garrison, of, Verbum Dei HS, Compton, Calif.—(AAA)
6. Robert Adams, ss-2b, Fairview HS, Camden, Ark.
7. Kenneth Townsend, rhp, Sonora (Calif.) HS.
8. Jacky Parish, c, University of Oklahoma.
9. *Arthur Toal, ss, Tottenville HS, Staten Island, N.Y.
10. Charles Martin, of, Wheaton (Ill.) North HS.
11. Michael Lake, lhp, Hueneme (Calif.) HS.
12. *Robert Healey, rhp, Roosevelt HS, St. Louis.
13. Robert Lowman, rhp, Mamaroneck HS, Larchmont, N.Y.
14. *Samuel Roberts, 1b, Carson-Newman (Tenn.) College.
15. Robert Stoffle, rhp, Kennedy HS, Sacramento, Calif.
**16. Dave Stewart, rhp, St. Elizabeth HS, Oakland, Calif.—(1978-95)**
DRAFT DROP *General manager, Diamondbacks (2014-15)*
**17. Brad Gulden, c, Chaska HS, Carver, Minn.—(1978-86)**
**18. *Mike Walters, rhp, Alta Loma (Calif.) HS.—(1983-84)**
19. *Robert Dove, rhp, Tustin (Calif.) HS.
20. *William Seney, rhp, Apple Valley (Calif.) HS.
21. *Stephen Youngman, 1b, North Brunswick (N.J.) HS.
22. *Paul Jacobs, of-3b, Kennedy HS, Sacramento, Calif.
23. *Paul Touchstone, rhp, Galveston (Texas) JC.
24. *Robert Newman, rhp, Mount Hood (Ore.) CC.
25. *Kris Kaminska, rhp, Peoria (Ariz.) HS.
26. *Jay Nelson, rhp, Chaska HS, Carver, Minn.
27. *Mitch Dean, rhp, Concord (Calif.) HS.
28. Arthur Fischetti, 2b-3b, Lafayette College.
29. *Michael Otto, rhp, Kennedy HS, Sacramento, Calif.
30. *Paul Lanier, c-3b, Moultrie (Ga.) HS.
31. *Rudy Rufer, ss, Valley Stream HS, Malverne, N.Y.
32. *James Black, ss, Camden (Ark.) HS.
33. *Alan Clark, rhp, Hiawatha HS, Kirkland, Ill.

**June—Secondary Phase (18)**

No selection.

## MILWAUKEE BREWERS

**January—Regular Phase (6)**

1. *Gerald Green, rhp, Lower Columbia (Wash.) JC.—DNP
2. *James Parker, p, Yakima Valley (Wash.) JC.

**January—Secondary Phase (10)**

**1. Lenn Sakata, 2b, Gonzaga University.—(1977-87)**
2. *Mike Denevi, ss, Santa Clara University.

**June—Regular Phase (5)**

1. Rick O'Keefe, lhp, Yorktown Heights (N.Y.) HS.—(AAA)
2. Chuck Ross, c, Tates Creek HS, Lexington, Ky.—(AA)
DRAFT DROP *Father of Robbie Ross, major leaguer (2012-15)*
3. Alvin Edge, rhp, Crawford HS, San Diego.—(AA)
4. Gregory Anderson, of, North HS, Riverside, Calif.—(Low A)
5. *Bob Hely, ss, Fort Lauderdale (Fla.) HS.—DNP
DRAFT DROP *Attended Wake Forest; never re-drafted*
6. *Brian Hayes, lhp, Savanna HS, Buena Park, Calif.
7. John Hannon, rhp, Jacksonville University.
8. *Greg Jemison, of, Seton Hall University.
9. Talmadge Tanks, 1b, George Washington Carver HS, Martinsville, Va.
10. Richard Ford, lhp, Lynn (Mass.) Technical College.
11. Elliott Franklin, ss, Ranger (Texas) JC.
12. Bradley Meagher, lhp, Adirondack Central HS, Forestport, N.Y.
13. Stephen Ruling, rhp, University of South Florida.
14. Gary LaRocque, 2b, University of Hartford.
DRAFT DROP *Scouting director, Mets (1998-2003)*
15. John Morris, rhp, Cal State Los Angeles.
16. *Frank Miloszewski, lhp, Beaver Falls (Pa.) HS.
17. *Jeff Kenaga, of, Lutheran West HS, Dearborn Heights, Mich.
18. Raymond Hall, ss, California State Chico.
**19. *Bob Stoddard, rhp, Live Oak HS, Morgan Hill, Calif.—(1981-87)**
20. David Marino, ss, Carthage (Wis.) College.
21. William Dick, lhp, Cleveland Heights (Ohio) HS.
22. *Jason Passmore, of, Colonial HS, Orlando, Fla.

**June—Secondary Phase (15)**

1. Billy Severns, of, University of Oklahoma.—(AAA)
2. *Jeff Hardy, ss, Gulf Coast (Fla.) CC.

## MINNESOTA TWINS

**January—Regular Phase (14)**

**1. (void) *Vic Bernal, rhp, Cal Poly Pomona.—(1977)**
2. *Donald Albares, 2b, George C. Wallace (Ala.) CC.
**3. *Randy Niemann, lhp, JC of the Redwoods (Calif.).—(1979-87)**
4. *Steve Ross, of, San Jose (Calif.) CC.
5. *Steve Lund, p, Mount Hood (Ore.) CC.
**6. *Vance McHenry, ss, Butte (Calif.) JC.—(1981-82)**
7. *Robert Milostan, of-1b, Itaska, Ill.

**January—Secondary Phase (22)**

1. Mark Wilson, of-3b, Linn-Benton (Ore.) CC.—(Low A)
2. Rick Duncan, c, Vanderbilt University.
3. *Dale Brock, of, Southern University.
DRAFT DROP *Cousin of Lou Brock, major leaguer (1961-79)*
4. *Anthony Davis, of, University of Southern California.
DRAFT DROP *Running back, National Football League (1977-78)*
5. Mike Gatlin, 3b, University of Arizona.
DRAFT DROP *First overall draft pick, June 1974/secondary phase, Reds*

**June—Regular Phase (13)**

**1. Rick Sofield, ss, Morristown (N.J.) HS.—(1979-81)**
2. Stephen Parrott, rhp, Camarillo (Calif.) HS.—(AA)
DRAFT DROP *Brother of Mike Parrott, major leaguer (1977-81)*
3. Steve Douglas, 3b, T.C. Williams HS, Alexandria, Va.—(AAA)
4. Greg Field, rhp, Lake Worth HS, West Palm Beach, Fla.—(AAA)
**5. Dan Graham, c, University of La Verne (Calif.).—(1979-81)**
6. *Bruce Humphrey, 1b, Nathan Hale HS, Tulsa, Okla.
7. Donald Yarborough, c, Lake Worth HS, Fort Pierce, Fla.

8. *Larry Reynolds, 2b, Corvallis (Ore.) HS.
DRAFT DROP *Brother of Don Reynolds, major leaguer (1978-79) • Brother of Harold Reynolds, major leaguer (1983-94)*
9. Mike Bacon, 3b, La Sierra HS, Riverside, Calif.
10. Robert Franz, of, Kennedy HS, Granada Hills, Calif.
11. *Joseph Smith, of, Hogan HS, Vallejo, Calif.
12. Doc Estes, of, Cal State Fullerton.
13. Dennis Mantick, 2b, Western Illinois University.
14. *Peter Brown, lhp, Glens Falls, N.Y.
15. Ronald Jones, rhp, Missouri Western State College.
**16. *Paul Mirabella, lhp, Montclair State (N.J.) College.—(1978-90)**
17. Joseph Kordosky, ss, University of Minnesota.
18. Gregg Gaughran, c, Kennedy HS, Bloomington, Minn.
19. *Gary Bowers, rhp, Anaheim (Calif.) HS.
20. Steve Wagner, rhp, Hazen HS, Renton, Wash.
**21. *Marty Castillo, 3b, Savanna HS, Anaheim, Calif.—(1981-85)**
22. *Wilbert Haslip, 2b, Santa Ana Valley HS, Santa Ana, Calif.
23. Gary Grunsky, lhp, Delano (Calif.) HS.
24. Davis May, rhp, Auburn University.
25. *Gilbert Ramirez, c, Savanna HS, Buena Park, Calif.
26. *Mark Grier, c, Severna Park (Md.) HS.
27. Charles Carvis, rhp, Wilcox HS, Santa Clara, Calif.
28. *George Rath, lhp, Bella Vista HS, Orangevale, Calif.
29. *Steven Rice, rhp, San Joaquin Delta (Calif.) JC.
30. *Mike Arlotta, lhp, Norland HS, Miami.
31. *Walter Podgurski, 2b, Union (N.J.) HS.
32. *Gary Spies, c, Anne Arundel (Md.) CC.
**33. *Steve Christmas, 3b, Colonial HS, Orlando, Fla.—(1983-86)**
34. *Roger Dirkes, ss, Washington State University.
35. Dan Petrowitz, lhp, Edison HS, Minneapolis.
36. Gregg Bemis, lhp, University of Puget Sound.
37. Al Arthur, rhp, Stanford University.

**June—Secondary Phase (3)**

**1. Hosken Powell, of, Chipola (Fla.) JC.—(1978-83)**
2. *Scott Anderson, rhp, Mesa (Ariz.) CC.
3. *Dirk Blankenship, rhp, Blinn (Texas) JC.

## MONTREAL EXPOS

**January—Regular Phase (9)**

1. *John Brown, of, South Georgia JC.—(AA)
2. *Ken Lelek, rhp, Monroe (N.Y.) CC.
3. Randy Eickenhorst, 3b, Gulf Coast (Fla.) CC.
4. *Kevin LaFranco, lhp, Santa Ana (Calif.) JC.
5. *Peter Peltz, ss, Brookdale (N.J.) CC.
6. *Jack Hudson, c, Golden West (Calif.) JC.
7. *Dirk Blankenship, rhp, Blinn (Texas) JC.
8. Larry Horn, rhp-3b, Blinn (Texas) JC.

**January—Secondary Phase (13)**

1. Mark Knose, rhp, University of Toledo.—(High A)
2. *Jeff Hardy, ss, Gulf Coast (Fla.) CC.
3. Larry Goldetsky, ss, Indian Hills (Iowa) CC.
4. *Brian Cherevko, rhp, West Valley (Calif.) JC.
5. *Ronald Goodman, lhp, Santa Barbara (Calif.) CC.

**June—Regular Phase (10)**

1. Art Miles, ss, Crockett HS, Austin, Texas.—(High A)
2. Dale McMullen, of, St. Pius HS, Houston.—(AA)
3. Mitch Cipolla, c, Martin Van Buren HS, Bellerose, N.Y.—(High A)
4. Andrew Dyes, of, Fresno State University.–(AAA)
5. Dale Halvorson, rhp, U.S. Naval Academy.—(Rookie)
6. Ronald Staggs, 1b, East Carolina University.
7. *Rodney Feight, rhp, Everett (Pa.) HS.
**8. *Mike Boddicker, rhp, Norway (Iowa) HS.—(1980-93)**
9. Walter Johnson, c, Anderson HS, Austin, Texas.
10. Jeff Gingrich, rhp, San Jose State University.
**11. Andre Dawson, of, Florida A&M University.—(1976-96)**
DRAFT DROP *Elected to Baseball Hall of Fame, 2010*

12. Bob Weatherford, rhp, MacArthur HS, Decatur, Ill.
13. Mark Ewell, rhp, University of Iowa.
14. *Alphonso Eiland, ss, Inglewood (Calif.) HS.
15. *Craig Smith, lhp, Fort Vancouver (Wash.) HS.
16. *Chick Valley, lhp, San Diego CC.
17. Lloyd Thompson, ss-2b, University of New Mexico.
18. *John Marquardt, of, Alamogordo (N.M.) HS.
19. *Robert Powell, rhp, Bloomington (Calif.) HS.
20. Michael Cooper, c, El Camino (Calif.) JC.
**21. *Rickey Keeton, rhp, Western Hills HS, Cincinnati.—(1980-81)**
22. Tim Stuthard, rhp, Henderson State (Ark.) University.
23. *Ronald Keyes, rhp, R.H. Watkins HS, Laurel, Miss.
24. *Bill Evers, c, Eckerd (Fla.) College.
25. Ray Crowley, 1b, Lewis (Ill.) University.
26. *Michael Krill, lhp, Irvington (N.J.) HS.
27. *Tom Teuchert, rhp, Chaparral HS, Scottsdale, Ariz.
28. *Tom McLish, rhp, Edmond (Okla.) HS.
DRAFT DROP *Son of Cal McLish, major leaguer (1944-64)*
29. *Manuel Mayer, 3b, Irvington (N.J.) HS.
30. *Mark Hredzak, of, Keystone Oaks HS, Pittsburgh.

**June—Secondary Phase (12)**

1. *Del Bender, of, Miami-Dade CC South.—(High A)
2. *Mark Liber, lhp, Mesa (Ariz.) CC.
3. *Frank Williams, c, Louisburg (N.C.) JC.

## NEW YORK METS

**January—Regular Phase (5)**

**1. *Dave Hudgens, 1b, Oroville, Calif.—(1983)**
2. *Fritz Lagergren, 2b, Seminole (Fla.) CC.
3. Rick Sander, rhp, San Bernardino Valley (Calif.) JC.
**4. Marshall Brant, 1b, Santa Rosa (Calif.) JC.—(1980-83)**
5. *Robert Simmons, p, Broward (Fla.) CC.
**6. *Karl Pagel, 1b, Glendale (Ariz.) CC.—(1978-83)**
DRAFT DROP *Brother of Mike Pagel, quarterback, National Football League (1982-93)*

**January—Secondary Phase (9)**

1. Stanley Mann, ss, Southern Illinois University.—(AA)
**2. *Gene Krug, 1b, Lamar (Colo.) CC.—(1981)**
3. *Jackie Smith, lhp, Manatee (Fla.) JC.
**4. *Greg A. Harris, rhp, Long Beach (Calif.) CC.—(1981-95)**
5. John McBride, ss, University of Utah.
6. Gene Litle, rhp, University of California.
7. *Steve Marlowe, 1b, University of Utah.
8. *Stewart Bringhurst, c, JC of San Mateo (Calif.).
9. *Michael Wholey, rhp, Green River (Wash.) CC.

**June—Regular Phase (6)**

**1. Butch Benton, c, Godby HS, Tallahassee, Fla.—(1978-85)**
2. *Rod Boxberger, rhp, Foothill HS, Santa Ana, Calif.—(AA)
DRAFT DROP *Attended Southern California; re-drafted by Astros, June 1978/regular phase (1st round) • Father of Brad Boxberger, major leaguer (2012-15)*
3. George Milke, rhp, University of Southern California.—(AA)
4. Larry Prewitt, rhp, University of the Pacific.—(AAA)
5. Bob Grant, c, Westchester HS, Los Angeles.—(High A)
6. George Bradbury, 2b, Pinole Valley HS, Pinole, Calif.
7. Randy Brown, rhp, Seminole HS, Sanford, Fla.
8. *Steve Houlberg, ss, Southwest HS, Miami.
9. *Frank McCann, ss, University of Delaware.
10. *Chuck McMichael, lhp, Hoover HS, Glendale, Calif.
DRAFT DROP *Scouting director, Rangers (1997-2000)*
11. *Guy Jones, rhp, Shasta HS, Redding, Calif.
12. Gene Bardot, rhp, Southwestern (Calif.) JC.
13. *Richter Armer, of, Fremont HS, Sunnyvale, Calif.
**14. *Rich Wortham, lhp, University of Texas.—(1978-83)**
**15. *Charlie Lea, rhp-1b, Kingsbury HS, Memphis.—(1980-88)**
16. Paul Cacciatore, rhp, Waltham (Mass.) HS.
17. Russell Clark, rhp, Mississippi Gulf Coast JC.
18. *James Noonan, ss, Cordova HS, Rancho Cordova, Calif.
19. *David Pfeiffer, rhp, Green City HS, Winigan, Mo.
20. Gilbert Joseph, rhp, Brownsville HS, Hiller, Pa.
**21. *John Tudor, lhp, Georgia Southern College.—(1979-90)**
22. *John Tillema, rhp, Cupertino (Calif.) HS.
23. *Bob Bonnette, ss, Wellington Academy HS, Neeses, S.C.
24. Jeff Carter, 3b-of, Memphis State University.
25. James Howard, of, Stetson University.
26. Tony Wylie, of, Salinas (Calif.) HS.
27. Kevan Aman, of, Kamiakan HS, Kennewick, Wash.

**June—Secondary Phase (20)**

1. Ward Wilson, c, Valencia (Fla.) CC.—(AA)
2. James Dyer, ss, Arizona Western JC.

## NEW YORK YANKEES

**January—Regular Phase (20)**

1. *Pat McGehee, p, Carson (Calif.) HS.—DNP

**January—Secondary Phase (18)**

1. *Larry Buckle, rhp, Long Beach (Calif.) CC.—(AA)
2. *Ward Wilson, c, Valencia (Fla.) CC.

**June—Regular Phase (19)**

1. Jim McDonald, 1b, Verbum Dei HS, Los Angeles.—(AAA)
2. Benny Lloyd, of, Manual Arts HS, Los Angeles.—(Short-season A)
3. Nate Chapman, of, Jarvis Christian (Texas) College.—(AAA)
**4. Jim Beattie, rhp, Dartmouth College.—(1978-86)**
DRAFT DROP *General manager, Expos (1995-2001); co-general manager, Orioles (2003-05)*
**5. Willie Upshaw, 1b, Blanco (Texas) HS.—(1978-88)**
6. Leonce Laurent, rhp, Lutcher HS, Gramercy, La.
**7. Mike Fischlin, ss, Cosumnes River (Calif.) JC.—(1977-87)**
8. *Alex Kager, rhp, Permian HS, Odessa, Texas.
9. *Len Glowzenski, rhp, Seton Hall University.
10. *Larry Brown, rhp, Norwood (Mass.) HS.
11. *Kent Nicar, rhp, Morgan City (La.) HS.
12. *James Kopatz, c, University of Illinois.
13. *John Hoscheidt, of, Southern Illinois University.
**14. *Danny Boone, lhp, Cal State Fullerton.—(1981-90)**
15. *Greg Sanossian, 1b, St. John's University.
16. Robert Cahall, rhp, Atlantic (N.J.) CC.
17. *Henry Campbell, ss, Yazoo City (Miss.) HS.
18. Robert Smith, of, Philadelphia College of Textiles.

**June—Secondary Phase (7)**

**1. Gil Patterson, of-rhp, Miami-Dade CC South.—(1977)**
**2. Randy Niemann, lhp, JC of the Redwoods (Calif.).—(1979-87)**

## OAKLAND ATHLETICS

**January—Regular Phase (22)**

1. *Del Bender, of, Miami-Dade CC South.—(High A)
2. Gary Medeiros, c, Chabot (Calif.) JC.
3. *Erik Hendricks, rhp, Chabot (Calif.) JC.
4. *Ray Dimick, thp, Los Angeles Pierce JC.

**January—Secondary Phase (4)**

**1. Rob Picciolo, ss, Pepperdine University.—(1977-85)**
2. *Pat Kelleher, rhp, Fullerton (Calif.) JC.
3. *Brian Heublein, lhp, University of Southern California.
4. David Gallino, ss, Contra Costa (Calif.) JC.

**June—Regular Phase (21)**

**1. Bruce Robinson, c, Stanford University.—(1978-80)**
DRAFT DROP *Brother of Dave Robinson, major leaguer (1970-71)*
2. Greg Cochran, rhp, Arizona State University.—(AAA)
3. Randy Green, rhp, Ketchum (Okla.) HS.—(AAA)
4. *Mike Wright, c, Father Ryan HS, Nashville, Tenn.—(High A)
DRAFT DROP *Attended Vanderbilt; re-drafted by Tigers, June 1978/regular phase (9th round)*
5. *Robert Heuck, lhp, John Marshall HS, San Antonio, Texas.—DNP
DRAFT DROP *Attended Texas; re-drafted by Rangers, June 1978/regular phase (18th round)*
6. *Steven Splitt, of, Clairemont HS, San Diego.
7. Steven Malito, of, Central Valley HS, Spokane, Wash.
8. Guy Murphy, rhp, Meridian (Miss.) HS.
9. *Jeffrey Marson, lhp, Logan HS, La Crosse, Wis.
**10. *Tom Wieghaus, c, Rich East HS, Park Forest, Ill.—(1981-84)**
11. *Thomas Underhill, rhp, Central HS, Bristol, Wis.
12. *Mark Paradise, lhp, Marblehead (Mass.) HS.
13. Kenneth Hunter, c, Muir HS, Altadena, Calif.
14. *Robert Harris, rhp, Montgomery Bell Academy HS, Nashville, Tenn.
**15. *Bob Horner, ss, Apollo HS, Glendale, Ariz.—(1978-88)**
DRAFT DROP *First overall draft pick, June 1978/regular phase, Braves*
16. *Steve Benson, ss, Culver City (Calif.) HS.
17. *Kenneth Robinson, of, Ypsilanti (Mich.) HS.
18. *Albert Dunn, c, South San Francisco (Calif.) HS.
19. *George Mahan, rhp, Michigan State University.
20. *George Robins, of, Manual Arts HS, Los Angeles.
21. Howard Robinson, 3b-ss, Dorsey HS, Los Angeles.
22. *Michael Hilliard, 3b, Lincoln HS, San Diego.
23. John Hagman, rhp, St. Olaf (Minn.) College.
**24. *Mike Chris, 1b, Venice HS, Los Angeles.—(1979-83)**
25. *Robert Hardaway, c-of, Inglewood (Calif.) HS.

**June—Secondary Phase (1)**

**1. Denny Walling, of, Clemson University.—(1975-92)**
2. Monte Bothwell, of, Cypress (Calif.) JC.

## PHILADELPHIA PHILLIES

**January—Regular Phase (11)**

1. *Richard Nesloney, rhp, Ranger (Texas) JC.—(High A)
2. Joseph Daniels, ss, Murray Wright HS, Detroit.
3. David Roper, ss, Spartanburg Methodist (S.C.) JC.
4. *Chris Carstensen, of, Moorpark (Calif.) JC.
5. *Michael Benfield, rhp, Spartanburg Methodist (S.C.) JC.
6. *Mark Liber, lhp, Mesa (Ariz.) CC.
7. Cubb Stokes, 1b, University of Tennessee.
**8. *Jack Lazorko, 3b-rhp, Miami-Dade CC South.—(1984-88)**

**January—Secondary Phase (1)**

**1. Barry Bonnell, of, Ohio State University.—(1977-86)**
2. Ken O'Brien, ss, Widener (Pa.) University.
3. Dennis Hawkins, of, Chaffey (Calif.) JC.
4. Steve Kruzelock, c, Santa Monica (Calif.) JC.

**June—Regular Phase (12)**

1. Sammye Welborn, rhp, Wichita Falls (Texas) HS.—(AAA)
2. Joe Jones, c, Columbus (Ga.) HS.—(AA)
3. Ray LaPointe, rhp, Baptist (S.C.) College.—(Low A)
**4. Dickie Noles, rhp, Harding HS, Charlotte, N.C.—(1979-90)**
5. Norberto Roman, c, Manhattan Vocational HS, New York.—(Low A)
6. Dave Baker, c, Stanford University.
**7. Keith Moreland, 3b, University of Texas.—(1978-89)**
8. Greg Bradford, lhp, Legrand (Calif.) HS.
**9. *Dave Van Gorder, c, Chandler (Ariz.) HS.—(1982-87)**
10. *DeVallon Harper, rhp, Alhambra HS, Martinez, Calif.
**11. *Rick Leach, of, Southwestern HS, Flint, Mich.—(1981-90)**
DRAFT DROP *First-round draft pick (13th overall), Tigers (1979); fifth-round draft pick, Denver Broncos/ National Football League (1979)*
12. Mark Rogers, of, Azusa Pacific (Calif.) Univ.
13. *Greg Norris, rhp, Whiteville HS, Brunswick, N.C.
14. Martin Robinson, rhp, Penn HS, Osceola, Ind.
15. Raymond Schmidt, ss, Bishop McNamara HS, Kankakee, Ill.
16. *Jeffrey Brisson, of, Iowa Western CC.
17. James Smoak, of, Baptist College of Florida.
18. James Nickerson, rhp, Pittsburgh (Pa.) HS.
**19. *Dave Rucker, lhp, Eisenhower HS, Rialto, Calif.—(1981-88)**
20. *Kenny Young, of, Amityville (N.Y.) HS.
21. Gregory Stone, rhp, University of South Alabama.
22. *Richard Lipp, of, Grant Island (N.Y.) HS.
**23. *Allan Ramirez, rhp, Victoria (Texas) HS.—(1983)**
24. *Marc Thomas, c-of, San Luis Obispo (Calif.) HS.
25. Don Fowler, rhp, Dana Hills HS, Dana Point, Calif.
26. Jeffrey Johnson, ss, Christian Brothers HS, Quincy, Ill.
27. James Lasak, rhp, Black Hawk (Ill.) JC.
28. Louis Reyes, c-3b, Hillsborough (Fla.) CC.
**29. *Roger Slagle, rhp, University of Kansas.—(1979)**

**June—Secondary Phase (8)**

1. Joe Berriatua, 1b-of, JC of San Mateo (Calif.).—(Short-season A)
2. Tim Pagnozzi, ss, Mesa (Ariz.) CC.
DRAFT DROP *Brother of Tom Pagnozzi, major leaguer (1987-98)*

## PITTSBURGH PIRATES

**January—Regular Phase (19)**

**1. *Hosken Powell, of, Chipola (Fla.) JC.—(1978-83)**
2. Ray Negron, ss, New York Tech.
3. *John Tolan, ss, Big Bend (Wash.) CC.
4. *Frank Williams, c, Louisburg (N.C.) JC.
5. Richard Ferrell, p, Morris Harvey (W.Va.) College.
**6. *Mark Corey, 1b, Central Arizona JC.—(1979-81)**
7. *Russell Aldrich, c, Chipola (Fla.) JC.
8. *Daniel Bishop, rhp, Green River (Wash.) CC.
9. James Keough, p, Ricks (Idaho) JC.
10. *Francis Spetter, c, Three Rivers (Mo.) CC.

**January—Secondary Phase (15)**

1. *Charles Ledbetter, rhp, Valencia (Fla.) CC.—(AA)
DRAFT DROP *Brother of Jeff Ledbetter, first-round draft pick, Red Sox (1982)*
2. *Mike Frazier, c, Texas A&M University.
3. *Gary Smith, of, Valencia (Fla.) CC.
4. Timothy Burman, lhp, University of Cincinnati.

**June—Regular Phase (20)**

**1. Dale Berra, ss, Montclair (N.J.) HS.—(1977-87)**
DRAFT DROP *Son of Yogi Berra, major leaguer (1946-65), major league manager (1964-85) • First 1975 high school draft pick to reach majors (Aug. 22, 1977)*
2. Jeff Pinkus, rhp, Hingham (Mass.) HS.—(Low A)
**3. Don Robinson, rhp, Ceredo-Kenova HS, Kenova, W.Va.—(1978-92)**
4. Larry Olson, c, Katella HS, Anaheim, Calif.—(Low A)
5. Jerry McDonald, of, Banks HS, Birmingham, Ala.—(AAA)
6. *Rob Simond, lhp, Barrington (Ill.) HS.
7. Heyward Edrington, c, McCrorey-Liston HS, Blair, S.C.
8. Jim Busby, of, Florida State University.
DRAFT DROP *Son of Jim Busby, major leaguer (1950-62)*
9. James Johnston, rhp, Shorter (Ga.) College.
10. Steven Fleming, of, Sale HS, Chester, Va.
11. *Greg Stahl, ss, Rolling Hills HS, Rancho Palos Verdes, Calif.
**12. *Ernie Camacho, rhp, Hartnell (Calif.) CC.—(1980-90)**

13. *Ronnie Pearce, rhp, Lake Brantley HS, Altamonte Springs, Fla.
14. David Joyner, 3b, Dalton (Ga.) HS.
15. *David Aronow, rhp, William H. Taft HS, Canoga Park, Calif.
16. Mark Tapia, rhp, University of South Alabama.
17. *Charles Dorgan, lhp, Meadowdale HS, Lynwood, Wash.
18. *Paul Smith, 1b, Clearwater (Fla.) HS.
19. *Frank Lucarelli, rhp, Newport HS, Bellevue, Wash.
20. Mark Saber, ss-3b, University of Georgia.
21. Joe Daniel, c, Mercer University.
22. Robert Semerano, rhp, Orange County (N.Y.) CC.
23. James Burkett, rhp, Mortimer Jordan HS, Morris, Ala.
24. Vaughn Robbins, 1b, Shorter (Ga.) College.
25. *Paul Tasker, c-3b, Dunedin HS, Clearwater, Fla.
26. Harry Summers, c, Shorter (Ga.) College.
27. *Craig Thorpe, rhp, Miami.
28. Jeffrey Woods, ss, West Branch HS, Beloit, Ohio.
29. *Richard Holloway, rhp, Mount Lebanon HS, Pittsburgh.
30. *William Krampe, rhp, Shaler HS, Pittsburgh.
31. *Robert Sims, ss, Lafayette-Jefferson HS, Lafayette, Ind.
32. *Larry McIver, of, Power Memorial HS, New York.
33. *Michael Munns, rhp, Caldwell, Idaho.
34. *John Pennington, ss, Bell (Calif.) HS.

#### June—Secondary Phase (6)

1. *LaMart Harris, of, Ranger (Texas) JC.—(AA)
2. *Ernie Mauritson, rhp, Chabot (Calif.) JC.
3. *Steve Wilkins, of, Oregon State University.

## ST. LOUIS CARDINALS

#### January—Regular Phase (15)

1. Terry Gray, rhp, Merced (Calif.) JC.—(High A)
2. *Ray Gault, rhp, Manatee (Fla.) JC.
3. *Randall Hagerty, 1b, San Diego Mesa JC.
4. *Peter Tereschuk, rhp, Long Beach (Calif.) CC.
5. *Richard Lacey, ss, Anderson (S.C.) JC.

#### January—Secondary Phase (11)

1. Jerry Johnson, c, Temple (Texas) JC.—(AAA)
DRAFT DROP *First-round draft pick (22nd overall), Athletics (1974)*
2. Chuck Redmon, ss, University of Oklahoma.
3. *Erol Akchurin, 3b, JC of San Mateo (Calif.).
4. Brett Houser, rhp, Long Beach (Calif.) CC.
5. *Scott Lankford, rhp, Modesto (Calif.) JC.
6. *Jackie Snell, lhp, George C. Wallace (Ala.) CC.
7. *Tim Glines, c, JC of the Sequoias (Calif.).

#### June—Regular Phase (16)

1. David Johnson, lhp, Gaylord (Mich.) HS.—(AA)
2. **Kelly Paris, ss, Taft HS, Woodland Hills, Calif.—(1982-88)**
DRAFT DROP *Brother of Bret Paris, 24th-round draft pick, Giants (1975)*
3. **Mike Ramsey, ss, Appalachian State University.—(1978-85)**
4. James Propst, rhp, West HS, Columbus, Ohio.—(Low A)
5. Steve Shartzer, of, Southern Illinois University.—(High A)
6. *Dale Eiler, c, Clairemont HS, San Diego.
7. Ralph Costanzo, 3b, Capuchino HS, Millbrae, Calif.
8. Richard Montejano, rhp, Imperial (Calif.) HS.
9. **Andy Replogle, rhp, Kansas State University.—(1978-79)**
10. *Mark Nipp, rhp, Aptos (Calif.) HS.
11. *Scott Stranski, rhp, Mount Vernon (Ill.) HS.
12. **Jim Lentine, of, University of La Verne (Calif.).—(1978-80)**
13. **Alan Olmsted, lhp, Hazelwood East HS, St. Louis.—(1980)**
14. Robert Frantz, lhp, Clarion (Pa.) University.
15. *Steve Romine, of, Wheeler HS, Marietta, Ga.
16. Karl Rieger, lhp, Sam Houston State University.
17. *Randy Rhodes, 2b, Canada (Calif.) JC.
18. David Oliver, rhp, Belleville East HS, Fairview Heights, Ill.
19. *Robert Stephens, ss, Fayetteville (Ark.) HS.
20. *Kell Schmidt, lhp, San Leandro (Calif.) HS.
21. Theis Meyer, rhp, University of Southern California.
22. *Randy Evans, rhp, Catalina HS, Tucson, Ariz.
23. R.J. Harrison, c, Arizona State University.
DRAFT DROP *Scouting director, Rays (2006-15))*
24. Nick Leyva, ss, University of La Verne (Calif.).
DRAFT DROP *Major league manager (1989-91)*
25. Anthony Dennard, rhp, Chipola (Fla.) JC.
26. *Anthony Tornincasa, c-of, Hillsdale HS, San Mateo, Calif.
27. *Michael Finch, lhp, El Capitan HS, Lakeside, Calif.
28. Jeff Borges, ss, San Leandro (Calif.) HS.
29. *Michael Bungarz, lhp, Moreau HS, Hayward, Calif.
30. David Lundsford, 1b, Monte Vista HS, San Diego.
31. George Shuford, of, Kailua (Hawaii) HS.

#### June—Secondary Phase (2)

1. Earl Bass, rhp, University of South Carolina.—(AAA)
2. ***Karl Pagel, 1b, Glendale (Ariz.) CC.—(1978-83)**
DRAFT DROP *Brother of Mike Pagel, quarterback, National Football League (1982-93)*

## SAN DIEGO PADRES

#### January—Regular Phase (1)

1. **Gene Richards, of, South Carolina State College.—(1977-84)**
2. *John Savage, p, West Valley (Calif.) JC.
3. *Regindo Wilkerson, p, St. John's River (Fla.) CC.
4. *Michael Swingle, p, Lincoln Land (Ill.) JC.

#### January—Secondary Phase (19)

1. **Juan Eichelberger, rhp, University of California.—(1978-88)**
2. **Chuck Baker, ss, Loyola Marymount University.—(1978-81)**
3. **Rick Sweet, c, Gonzaga University.—(1978-83)**
4. ***Al Holland, lhp, North Carolina A&T University.—(1977-87)**

#### June—Regular Phase (2)

1. Mike Lentz, lhp, Juanita HS, Kirkland, Wash.—(AA)
2. Harold Drake, ss, Bonita HS, La Verne, Calif.—(AA)
3. **Tony Castillo, c, James Lick HS, San Jose, Calif.—(1978)**
4. Tim Derryberry, of, Chino (Calif.) HS.—(AAA)
5. *Tom Willette, lhp, Plymouth Salem HS, Canton, Mich.—DNP
DRAFT DROP *Attended North Carolina State; re-drafted by Royals, 1978 (20th round)*
6. **Vic Bernal, rhp, Cal Poly Pomona.—(1977)**
7. William Joseph, lhp, Kearny HS, San Diego.
8. Walter Segrest, c, Vallejo (Calif.) HS.
9. Bobby Mitchell, ss-of, University of Richmond.
10. Carl Maglio, inf, Edgewood HS, Madison, Wis.
11. *Ron Driver, lhp, Sam Rayburn HS, Pasadena, Texas.
12. Joe Hicks, of, San Pedro (Calif.) HS.
DRAFT DROP *Father of Aaron Hicks, first-round draft pick, Twins (2008); major leaguer (2013-15)*
13. *Brian Savidge, of, San Mateo (Calif.) HS.
14. Gene Menees, 3b, Vanderbilt University.
15. *Samuel Albert, ss, Toulminville HS, Mobile, Ala.
16. Guy Hollingsworth, lhp, Louisiana State University.
17. Alan Brumfield, ss, High Point College.
18. **Don Reynolds, of, University of Oregon.—(1978-79)**
DRAFT DROP *Brother of Harold Reynolds, major leaguer (1983-94) • Brother of Larry Reynolds, 8th-round draft pick, Twins (1975)*
19. *Michael Coppess, rhp, Chino (Calif.) HS.
20. Kurt Wittmeyer, ss, San Diego State University.
21. Greg Wilkes, rhp, San Diego State University.
22. *Dave Crutcher, rhp, Woodland (Calif.) HS.
23. *James Ridenour, rhp, Vincennes (Ind.) University JC.
24. *James Harris, rhp, Bossier HS, Bossier City, La.
25. Marty French, rhp, San Diego State University.

#### June—Secondary Phase (22)

1. *Larry Buckle, rhp, Long Beach (Calif.) CC.—(AA)

## SAN FRANCISCO GIANTS

#### January—Regular Phase (7)

1. Gene Schmidt, rhp, El Camino (Calif.) JC.—(AAA)
2. Rick Steen, rhp, Ventura (Calif.) JC.
3. *Frank Marini, of, Mount San Antonio (Calif.) JC.
4. ***Dave Hostetler, 1b, Citrus (Calif.) JC.—(1981-88)**
5. *John Guarino, of-1b, Pepperdine University.
6. Alan Ayres, of, Citrus (Calif.) JC.
7. Dennis Lee, 2b, Mount San Antonio (Calif.) JC.
8. Pat Ryan, inf-c, Pasadena (Calif.) CC.
9. *Butch Rowe, ss, West Valley (Calif.) JC.
10. *Joe Berriatua, 1b-of, JC of San Mateo (Calif.).
11. Luis Pereiro, inf, Tampa.
12. *Tom Pagnozzi, ss, Mesa (Ariz.) CC.
13. *John Braas, p, Bakersfield (Calif.) JC.
14. Steve Watson, rhp-of, Spokane Falls (Wash.) CC.
15. *Robert Dahlquist, p-1b, Everett (Wash.) CC.
16. *Mace Magruder, p-of, Bellevue (Wash.) CC.

#### January—Secondary Phase (17)

1. David Anderson, rhp, Arizona Western JC.—(Low A)
2. *Jeffrey Ross, lhp, Fresno State University.
3. *Billy Severns, of, University of Oklahoma.

#### June—Regular Phase (8)

1. Ted Barnicle, lhp, Jacksonville State University.—(AAA)
2. Rick Bradley, c, University of Texas.—(AAA)
3. **Jose Barrios, 1b, South Miami HS.—(1982)**
4. Garrett Strong, of, Arizona State University.—(AA)
5. ***Bob Shirley, lhp, University of Oklahoma.—(1977-87)**
DRAFT DROP *Returned to Oklahoma; re-drafted by Padres, January 1976/secondary phase (1st round)*
6. **Rich Murray, 1b, Locke HS, Los Angeles.—(1980-83)**
DRAFT DROP *Brother of Eddie Murray, major leaguer (1977-97)*
7. George Davis, of, Scottsdale (Ariz.) HS.
8. *Greg Fisher, 3b, Pleasant Hill HS, Concord, Calif.
9. Tom Bhagwatt, of, University of Hawaii.
10. *Dan Massari, 1b, Oklahoma State University.
11. Ted Schoenhaus, of, Seton Hall University.
12. **Greg Johnston, of, Citrus (Calif.) JC.—(1979-91)**
13. Steve Osborne, of, San Francisco CC.
14. Mark Woodbrey, 2b, Amherst (Mass.) College.
15. Doug Schaefer, rhp, University of Oklahoma.
16. *Charles Wyatt, rhp, Foothill (Calif.) JC.
17. Bryan Boyne, ss, Rice University.
18. *James English, 2b, Hazelwood Central HS, St. Louis.
19. *Dan Hartwig, rhp, Quartz Hill HS, Lancaster, Calif.
20. Mark Daugherty, 3b, Hoggard HS, Wilmington, N.C.
21. Howard Mitchell, 2b, Southern Illinois University.
22. **Mike Rowland, rhp, Millikin (Ill.) University.—(1980-81)**
23. Martin Flores, lhp, University of Texas.
24. Bret Paris, ss, Los Angeles Pierce JC.
DRAFT DROP *Brother of Kelly Paris, second-round draft pick, Cardinals (1975); major leaguer (1982-88)*
25. *John Holcomb, of, Carroll HS, Corpus Christi, Texas.
26. *Javier Fierro, 3b, Mount San Antonio (Calif.) JC.
27. *William Eve, 1b, North Miami Beach HS, Opalocka, Fla.
28. Tim Peterson, rhp, Bellevue (Wash.) CC.
29. ***Ron Roenicke, of-1b, Mount San Antonio (Calif.) JC.—(1981-88)**
DRAFT DROP *Brother of Gary Roenicke, major leaguer (1976-88) • Major league manager (2011-15)*
30. *Mark Clifford, rhp, Harrison County HS, Cynthiana, Ky.
31. *Cyrus Smith, of, Callaway HS, Jackson, Miss.
32. Steven Sherman, lhp, Patrick Henry HS, San Diego.
33. ***Tye Waller, 3b, Hoover HS, San Diego.—(1980-87)**
34. ***Duane Walker, lhp-of, Deer Park HS, Pasadena, Texas.—(1982-88)**
35. *Mike Zouras, 3b, El Camino (Calif.) JC.
36. *Kevin Kopp, c, Los Angeles Pierce JC.
37. *Robert Cramer, rhp, R.A. Long HS, Longview, Wash.

#### June—Secondary Phase (10)

1. ***Darrell Brown, ss, East Los Angeles JC.—(1981-84)**
2. *Ray Gault, rhp, Manatee (Fla.) JC.

## TEXAS RANGERS

#### January—Regular Phase (18)

1. Tim Brookens, of, Shenandoah (Va.) College.—(AA)
DRAFT DROP *Twin brother of Tom Brookens, first-round draft pick, January 1975/regular phase, Tigers*
2. *Ron Evans, 3b, Greensboro, N.C.
3. *Greg Fairbanks, rhp, Brevard (Fla.) CC.
4. *Michael MacDonald, p, Columbia State (Tenn.) CC.

#### January—Secondary Phase (6)

1. **Bump Wills, 2b, Arizona State University.—(1977-82)**
DRAFT DROP *Son of Maury Wills, major leaguer (1959-72); major league manager (1980-81)*
2. ***Anthony Johnson, of, Shelby State (Tenn.) CC.—(1981-82)**
3. (void) *Andrew Mason, 3b, Oregon State University.

#### June—Regular Phase (17)

1. **Jim Gideon, rhp, University of Texas.—(1975)**
2. **Eddie Miller, of, Ells HS, Richmond, Calif.—(1977-84)**
3. *Kem Wright, rhp, Paris (Texas) HS.—(AA)
DRAFT DROP *Attended Texas; re-drafted by Rangers, June 1978/regular phase (24th round)*
4. Victor Mabee, ss, Sunnyvale (Calif.) HS.—(AA)
5. Blair Stouffer, 3b-ss, University of Texas.—(AAA)
6. **John Poloni, lhp, Arizona State University.—(1977)**
7. David Rivera, of, King City HS, Greenfield, Calif.
8. *John Shouse, 1b, Chamberlain HS, Tampa.
9. Randall Reynolds, c, York (Pa.) College.
10. *Richard Comeau, rhp, Leominster (Mass.) HS.
11. *Hal Hutchens, rhp, New Hanover HS, Wilmington, N.C.
12. Richard Couch, lhp, Berkeley HS, Oakland, Calif.
13. Wayne Pinkerton, inf, Mississippi State University.
14. John Takacs, ss-2b, West Haven (Conn.) HS.
15. *Glenn Ballard, c, Satellite Beach HS, Indian Harbor Beach, Fla.
16. Mike Bucci, of, West Chester University.
17. Joseph Stewart, of, Burbank HS, Sacramento, Calif.
18. *Dennis Doyle, c, St. Peter's HS, Worcester, Mass.
19. *Michael Smith, rhp, Norwood (Ohio) HS.
20. *Peter Alfano, rhp, Ensley HS, Birmingham, Ala.
21. Harold Kelly, rhp, Plant City (Fla.) HS.
22. Pat Moock, rhp, Louisiana State University.
23. **Larue Washington, ss, Cal State Dominguez Hills.—(1978-79)**
24. *Mark Brisker, of, Colerain HS, Cincinnati.
25. David Chapman, 1b, UCLA.
26. *David Lockett, rhp, Texas A&M University.
27. James Thomas, c, Texas Wesleyan College.
28. William Stone, ss, Toronto (Ohio) HS.
29. Lawrence Burgess, lhp, American Christian HS, Fort Worth, Texas.
30. *Tommy Crain, 1b, Texas Christian University.
31. *Mickey Reichenbach, 1b, University of Texas.
32. *Bruce Poole, lhp, University of South Alabama.
33. (void) *George Tebbetts, 3b, Bradenton HS, Anna Maria, Fla.
DRAFT DROP *Son of Birdie Tebbetts, major leaguer (1936-52); major league manager (1954-1966)*

#### June—Secondary Phase (23)

1. **Pat Putnam, 1b, University of South Alabama.—(1977-84)**

# 1976

## AT A GLANCE

### This Date In History

**WINTER DRAFT:** Jan. 7
**SUMMER DRAFT:** June 8-10

### Best Draft

**DETROIT TIGERS.** The Tigers didn't sign **OZZIE SMITH** (7) but laid the foundation for their 1984 World Series championship team by drafting **ALAN TRAMMELL** (2), **DAN PETRY** (4) and **JACK MORRIS** (5). They also got significant early production from **STEVE KEMP**, the top pick in January (regular phase), before trading him.

### Worst Draft

**SAN FRANCISCO GIANTS.** With the exception of 26th-rounder **JEFF STEMBER**, who pitched in one big league game, the Giants didn't sign a single pick in June who became a big leaguer.

### First-Round Bust

**BILLY SIMPSON, OF, RANGERS.** Several clubs thought Simpson was the best position prospect in the 1976 draft, but he had one of the worst careers of any first-rounder ever. In 189 minor league games, none above Class A, he hit .177 with no home runs while being released by three different clubs. Later, Simpson was convicted for his part in a cocaine-smuggling ring, and spent a number of years in jail.

### Second Time Around

**ALAN TRAMMELL, SS, TIGERS.** Trammell more than made up for Tigers first-rounder **PAT UNDERWOOD** by teaming with Lou Whitaker (Class of 1975) to become one of the best double-play combinations in the game's history. In 20 years with the Tigers, Trammell hit .285 with 185 home runs.

### Late-Round Find

**RICK HONEYCUTT, LHP, PIRATES (17TH ROUND).** Known in recent years as the pitching coach for the Dodgers, Honeycutt had a 21-year career in the majors as a starter and reliever. In

# Draft features lefties, Arizona State talent

Floyd Bannister's selection by the Houston Astros with the No. 1 pick in the 1976 draft was as much of a foregone conclusion as any top selection in draft annals.

A hard-throwing lefthander out of Arizona State, Bannister dominated the nation's collegiate ranks unlike anyone before him, and few after. He led NCAA pitchers in strikeouts two years in a row, fanning 217 in 157 innings as a sophomore in 1975 and 213 more in an NCAA-record 186 innings a year later. He tied the collegiate record for wins (19) in 1976, while posting a 1.45 ERA and completing an NCAA record 17 games. He was college baseball's top player.

From the Astros' perspective, Bannister's selection was overshadowed a bit as it occurred on the same day that the local Rockets chose John Lucas with the No. 1 pick in the NBA draft. But it established a definitive tone for a 1976 process that was uniquely deep in two commodities: lefthanded pitching and Arizona State talent.

Led by Bannister, four of the first five picks in the June regular phase (and five of the first eight) were lefthanders; his selection also highlighted a record 13 Sun Devils throughout.

While Houston's selection of Bannister with the No. 1 pick was established well in advance of the 1976 draft, the Detroit Tigers didn't determine until the 11th hour which of two lefthanders they would take as a consolation prize: Pat Underwood, an Indiana high school product, or Bob Owchinko, a local boy from Eastern Michigan University. They settled on Underwood.

Owchinko went to the San Diego Padres with the fifth pick overall, but not before the Milwaukee Brewers jumped on another southpaw, Bill Bordley, a California high school product with the fourth pick. Illinois prep lefthander Steve Trout, son of Hall of Famer Dizzy Trout, went eighth to the Chicago White Sox.

All the lefthanders eventually played in the big leagues, with varying degrees of success. None had a winning record.

Arizona State's unprecedented impact on the draft began with Bannister and followed in quick order with the selection of outfielder Ken Landreaux by the California Angels with the sixth pick overall. Landreaux was no less a star on Arizona State's 1976 juggernaut than Bannister, as he hit .406 with 15 homers, and set NCAA season records for runs (96), hits (119), total bases (201) and RBIs (93).

With their 13 picks, the Sun Devils became the first college team ever to reach double figures in a single draft, and they had more than twice as many selections as their closest pursuers (Arizona and Oklahoma, with six apiece). Perhaps most telling, 26 of 27 members of that power-packed ASU squad were eventually drafted, and a record 13 reached the big leagues—among them Bob Horner, at the time a freshman shortstop and later the No. 1 pick in the 1978 draft.

Lefthanders and Arizona State products got all the early hype in the 1976 draft, but in the fourth round the Athletics found Rickey Henderson, who became the greatest leadoff hitter of all time

Though the 1976 Sun Devils (65-10) were hailed as one of the greatest college teams ever assembled, and set NCAA records for wins and home runs (87), they failed to reach the championship game of that year's College World Series. Within a week of the draft, the No. 1 Sun Devils were vanquished by upstart Eastern Michigan and archrival and eventual champion Arizona.

In a classic showdown in Omaha featuring the two best lefthanders in the college game, EMU's Owchinko outdueled Bannister, 2-1. The Tigers had set their sights on Owchinko, a local product considered the next best thing to Bannister, but didn't think they could meet his terms.

"The Tigers called me before the draft, but they weren't talking enough money," said Owchinko, who went 14-3, 1.95 as a junior at Eastern Michigan and 29-9, 2.15 over three seasons. "They wouldn't give me a few certain things I wanted."

The Tigers went for the next-best lefthander on their board, Underwood, the younger brother of Philadelphia Phillies lefthander Tom Underwood, a second-round pick four years earlier.

"He's the type of youngster who won't let you cross the plate," said Bill Lajoie, Detroit's director

## 1976: THE FIRST ROUNDERS

| CLUB: PLAYER, POS., SCHOOL | HOMETOWN | B-T | HT. | WT. | AGE | BONUS | FIRST YEAR | LAST YEAR | PEAK LEVEL (YEARS) |
|---|---|---|---|---|---|---|---|---|---|
| **JUNE—REGULAR PHASE** | | | | | | | | | |
| 1. Astros: Floyd Bannister, lhp, Arizona State | Seattle | L-L | 6-1 | 185 | 20 | $100,000 | 1976 | 1992 | Majors (15) |
| Slam-dunk No. 1 choice after brilliant college career, combined 36-6, 1.55 (343 IP/430 SO) as SO/JR; had his moments in 15 years in majors, went just 134-143. | | | | | | | | | |
| 2. Tigers: Pat Underwood, lhp, Kokomo HS | Kokomo, Ind. | L-L | 6-0 | 175 | 19 | $70,000 | 1976 | 1984 | Majors (4) |
| Record-setting career in Indiana prep ranks, but got bogged down in minors in Triple-A; went 13-18, 4.43 in four years in majors, outpitched by older brother Tom. | | | | | | | | | |
| 3. Braves: Ken Smith, 3b, East HS | Youngstown, Ohio | L-R | 6-2 | 190 | 18 | $50,000 | 1976 | 1986 | Majors (3) |
| Hit .500-plus in three high school seasons, flashed raw power, but bat never played in 10 years in Braves system; hit .259-74-426 overall, got brief MLB look. | | | | | | | | | |
| 4. Brewers: Bill Bordley, lhp, Bishop Montgomery HS | Rolling Hills Estates, Calif. | R-L | 6-3 | 185 | 18 | Unsigned | 1979 | 1982 | Majors (1) |
| One of first controversial draft figures; rebuffed Brewers offer, had storied college career, manipulated '79 draft, done in by arm issues; now MLB security chief. | | | | | | | | | |
| 5. Padres: Bob Owchinko, lhp, Eastern Michigan | Detroit | L-L | 6-2 | 190 | 21 | $42,500 | 1976 | 1986 | Majors (10) |
| Star of 1976 College World Series became first pick from June draft to reach majors; couldn't sustain his early promise, went 37-60, 4.28 over 10 years. | | | | | | | | | |
| 6. Angels: Ken Landreaux, of, Arizona State | Compton, Calif. | L-R | 5-11 | 170 | 21 | $82,000 | 1976 | 1989 | Majors (11) |
| Set numerous college records as ASU junior, became minors' top player in 1977 (.357-27-116 in AA/AAA), had 31-game hit streak in majors, played 11 years overall. | | | | | | | | | |
| 7. Cubs: Herm Segelke, rhp, El Camino HS | South San Francisco | R-R | 6-5 | 215 | 18 | $52,500 | 1976 | 1984 | Majors (1) |
| Two-time national punt/pass/kick winner as youngster, dominant senior-league pitcher later in life; went 63-61, 5.29 in minors, worked just 4 IP in majors. | | | | | | | | | |
| 8. White Sox: Steve Trout, lhp, Thornwood HS | South Holland, Ill. | L-L | 6-4 | 195 | 18 | $32,000 | 1976 | 1990 | Majors (12) |
| Son of Dizzy Trout, winner of 170 games in majors, later worked in front office for Sox; same team drafted Steve, who broke in at 20, went 88-92, 4.18 in 12 seasons. | | | | | | | | | |
| 9. Expos: Bob James, rhp, Verdugo Hills HS | Sunland, Calif. | R-R | 6-3 | 220 | 17 | $35,000 | 1976 | 1987 | Majors (8) |
| Starter for six years in Expos system, used as reliever in eight-year major league career; compiled 73 SV for three clubs, including 32 SV for White Sox in 1982. | | | | | | | | | |
| 10. Twins: Jamie Allen, 3b/rhp, Davis HS | Yakima, Wash. | R-R | 5-11 | 195 | 18 | Unsigned | 1979 | 1985 | Majors (1) |
| Led Yakima to Legion title in 1975, Arizona State to CWS championship in 1977; drafted by Mariners in 1979, played only one MLB season in injury-prone career. | | | | | | | | | |
| 11. Giants: Mark Kuecker, ss, Brenham HS | Brenham, Texas | R-R | 5-10 | 152 | 18 | $52,500 | 1976 | 1979 | Class AAA (1) |
| Led HS team to consecutive Texas 3-A titles as power-hitting SS; hit .244 with 12 HRs in climb through Giants system, never answered bell for 1980 season. | | | | | | | | | |
| 12. Rangers: Billy Simpson, of, Lakewood HS | Lakewood, Calif. | B-R | 6-2 | 180 | 18 | $52,500 | 1976 | 1978 | Class A (2) |
| Stood out on nation's best HS team, but disastrous pro career; hit .177-0-51 in three seasons, released by three clubs; later served long prison term on drug charges. | | | | | | | | | |
| 13. Mets: Tom Thurberg, of/rhp, South Weymouth HS | South Weymouth, Mass. | R-R | 6-1 | 185 | 18 | $30,000 | 1978 | 1985 | Class AAA (4) |
| Began career as OF, but didn't hit (.217-14-74 in two seasons), moved to mound; went 36-33, 4.29 over last eight years in minors in Mets/Cardinals systems. | | | | | | | | | |
| 14. Indians: Tim Glass, c, South HS | Springfield, Ohio | R-R | 6-2 | 215 | 18 | $42,500 | 1976 | 1985 | Class AA (5) |
| Caught Indians' attention with loud .459-12-36 season as prep SR; played 10 years in organization, hit .245-131-440 overall, never surfaced above Double-A. | | | | | | | | | |
| 15. Cardinals: Leon Durham, 1b, Woodward HS | Cincinnati | L-L | 6-1 | 200 | 18 | $37,000 | 1976 | 1995 | Majors (10) |
| Had 16 HRs, 11 wins as HS SR; career took off when traded to Cubs for Bruce Sutter, hit .277-147-530 in MLB; extended his career playing in Mexico, indy leagues. | | | | | | | | | |
| 16. Yankees: Pat Tabler, of, McNicholas HS | Cincinnati | R-R | 6-3 | 185 | 18 | $27,500 | 1976 | 1992 | Majors (12) |
| Passed up basketball scholarship to Virginia Tech, quickly became best prospect in Yankees system, but played for five other teams in 12-year big league career. | | | | | | | | | |
| 17. Phillies: Jeff Kraus, ss, Colerain HS | Cincinnati | R-R | 6-1 | 175 | 17 | $60,000 | 1977 | 1981 | Class AA (3) |
| Played 583 games in Phillies organization, never cracked loaded big league roster; released after compiling his best minor league season (.302-2-65) in 1980. | | | | | | | | | |
| 18. Royals: Ben Grzybek, rhp, Hialeah HS | Hialeah, Fla. | L-R | 6-5 | 200 | 18 | $40,000 | 1976 | 1980 | Class AA (4) |
| Hard-throwing RHP showed early promise with Royals, but got bogged down with control issues in Double-A; went 28-41, 3.41 overall, all in Royals system. | | | | | | | | | |
| 19. Dodgers: Mike Scioscia, c, Springfield HS | Morton, Pa. | L-R | 6-2 | 200 | 17 | $44,500 | 1976 | 1994 | Majors (13) |
| Enjoyed long career as big league player, manager; spent 13 years with Dodgers as two-time all-star, hit .259-68-446; hooked on as Angels skipper in 2000. | | | | | | | | | |
| 20. Orioles: Dallas Williams, of, Abraham Lincoln HS | Brooklyn, N.Y. | L-L | 5-11 | 170 | 18 | $34,000 | 1976 | 1987 | Majors (2) |
| Won two Triple-A batting titles in 1980s, hit .285-83-591 with 221 SBs in 1,469 games in minors; earned token 38 ABs in MLB; later coached in majors/minors. | | | | | | | | | |
| 21. Pirates: Jim Parke, rhp, Henry Ford II HS | Sterling Heights, Mich. | R-R | 6-4 | 215 | 18 | $47,500 | 1976 | 1980 | Class A (3) |
| Overcame death of both parents in plane crash while in high school; arm problems curtailed pro career, went 14-15, 4.41 in four seasons, never escaped A-ball. | | | | | | | | | |
| 22. Red Sox: Bruce Hurst, lhp, Dixie HS | St. George, Utah | L-L | 6-4 | 185 | 18 | $42,500 | 1976 | 1994 | Majors (15) |
| Bannister got more acclaim, but Utah prep lefty quiety had impressive run in minors (49-31, 3.08), outpitched No. 1 overall pick in majors (145-113, 3.92). | | | | | | | | | |
| 23. Reds: Mark King, rhp, Owensboro HS | Owensboro, Ky. | R-R | 6-1 | 185 | 18 | $25,000 | 1976 | 1978 | Class A (2) |
| Reds string of poor-performing first-rounders in 1970s persisted; led HS to Kentucky state title as senior, but lasted just three years in pro ball, went 7-24, 5.63. | | | | | | | | | |
| 24. Athletics: Mike Sullivan, rhp, Garfield HS | Woodbridge, Va. | R-R | 5-11 | 173 | 17 | Unsigned | 1979 | 1982 | Class AA (1) |
| Unsigned first-rounder went 10-0, 1.98 for Clemson in 1979, re-drafted by Reds in top round that year, never advanced beyond Double-A in four years in minors. | | | | | | | | | |
| **JANUARY—REGULAR PHASE** | | | | | | | | | |
| 1. Tigers: Steve Kemp, of, Southern California | Arcadia, Calif. | L-L | 6-0 | 195 | 21 | $50,000 | 1976 | 1988 | Majors (11) |
| One of best hitters in USC history blitzed through minors, had success with Tigers; struck in eye shortly after inking rich free-agent deal with Yankees, career declined. | | | | | | | | | |
| **JANUARY—SECONDARY PHASE** | | | | | | | | | |
| 1. Twins: Pete Redfern, rhp, Southern California | Sylmar, Calif. | R-R | 6-2 | 185 | 21 | $30,000 | 1976 | 1982 | Majors (7) |
| Left USC and reached majors after four minor league starts, went 42-48 in seven seasons; nearly died in 1983 Newport Beach diving accident left him paralyzed. | | | | | | | | | |
| **JUNE—SECONDARY PHASE** | | | | | | | | | |
| 1. Braves: Gerald Price, 2b, Diablo Valley (Calif.) JC | Oakland, Calif. | L-R | 5-10 | 160 | 19 | Unsigned | Never Played Pro Ball | | |
| Passed on Braves offer, teamed with Willie McGee to lead Diablo Valley to state juco title in 1977, also played for USC's College World Series champs in 1978. | | | | | | | | | |

## AT A GLANCE

797 career games, he won 109 games and saved 38 others, but didn't pitch a single game for the Pirates, the team that took him out of Tennessee.

### Never Too Late

**PAT SHERIDAN, OF, REDS (36TH ROUND).** The Reds had a curious draft in 1976 as only three of the first 30 picks they made in the June regular phase reached the majors, but four of their last eight did. The last was Sheridan, who didn't sign and was drafted three years later in the third round by the Royals out of Eastern Michigan. He played nine years in the majors.

### Overlooked

**DANNY DARWIN, RHP, RANGERS.** Darwin and fellow righthanders **GREG A. HARRIS** and **STEVE FARR** all had successful careers after being signed in 1976 as nondrafted free agents. Darwin had a dominant spring season for Grayson County (Texas) Community College and might have surged into the first round in June, but ended up signing with the Rangers for $37,500 prior to the draft. He pitched for 21 years with eight different big league clubs and won 171 games.

### International Gem

**PASCUAL PEREZ, RHP, PIRATES.** Perez was a product of the Pirates' pipeline to the Dominican Republic, and signed in January 1976 for $2,000. He had his greatest success over an 11-year career in the majors with the Braves, winning 29 games in 1983-84.

### Minor League Take

**BRUCE HURST, LHP, RED SOX.** As a Utah high school product, Hurst didn't earn anywhere near the acclaim of fellow lefthander Floyd Bannister when the two were first-rounders in 1976. But Hurst learned his craft well in the minors while assembling a 49-31, 3.08

CONTINUED ON PAGE 176

## AT A GLANCE

CONTINUED FROM PAGE 175

record, and went on to outpitch Bannister in the majors, posting a 145-113 mark over 15 years.

### One Who Got Away

**BILL BORDLEY, LHP, BREWERS.** Bordley decided not to sign with the Brewers as the fourth overall pick in 1976 and ended up in college at USC. Three years later, he became one of the most controversial figures in draft history by trying to manipulate the process to direct him to a West Coast team.

### He Was Drafted?

**JIMMIE GILES, 1B-OF, DODGERS (12TH ROUND).** The Dodgers scored an apparent coup by signing the 6-foot-3, 240-pound Giles for just $6,500. But the Alcorn State product was so overmatched in his pro debut, going 4-for-51 with no RBIs and 29 strikeouts, that he quit the game, returned to college to resume his football career and became a third-round pick of the Houston Oilers. Giles went on to play 13 years in the NFL, four as an all-pro tight end.

### Did You Know . . .

**PAT UNDERWOOD,** the second overall pick in the 1976 draft, won his major league debut for the Tigers on May 31, 1979, by outdueling his older brother Tom, then with the Blue Jays,1-0. It didn't get much better than that as he won just 12 more games in his career.

### They Said It

**BILL BORDLEY,** reflecting on his failed career as a pitcher and second career with the Secret Service that ultimately led to his being selected as Major League Baseball's security chief: "Nothing I would have loved more than to be a 20-game winner and win a World Series. It didn't work out. But in the grand scheme of things, I saw the United States while playing ball and saw the World with the Secret Service."

of player development. "He's bigger than his brother and throws harder. We think he can reach the major leagues in two years, just as his brother did."

Underwood didn't make his debut with the Tigers until 1982, and it was no ordinary debut as he hooked up with none other than his brother, then with the Toronto Blue Jays. Younger brother prevailed, 1-0, but Tom Underwood got the last laugh as went on to win 86 games over 11 seasons, while Pat won 13 games in a four-year career.

With Bannister holding out much of the summer before signing with the Astros, Owchinko was the first player from the June draft to reach the big leagues. He was promoted by the Padres in September. While Owchinko pitched a number of dominating games early on, he won just 37 games in a career that fell short of expectations.

The fourth member of the star-studded crop of lefthanders was Bordley, and he may have had the most eventful career of all. He ultimately didn't sign with the Brewers after becoming bogged down in contract negotiations, and opted instead for a college career at Southern California.

Bordley went 26-2 in his first two years at USC and dominated in much the same way Bannister did in his final two seasons for Arizona State. But he became one of the most controversial figures in draft history when he left school a year early and attempted to manipulate the 1979 draft for his own benefit. It took a special ruling by the commissioner's office to resolve his bizarre case.

### CAN'T WIN FOR LOSING

Few pitchers in college history were able to match Bannister's credentials, but Underwood assembled a similar resume at the high school level in Indiana, while surpassing most of the accomplishments of his brother Tom four years earlier at Kokomo High. The younger Underwood still holds Indiana career prep marks for shutouts (22) and strikeouts (637), all the while posting a 0.58 ERA and six no-hitters, including four as a senior.

After signing with the Tigers for a bonus of $70,000, Underwood got off to a quick start and in his first full season he reached Triple-A Evansville, back home in Indiana. But he got bogged down there, spending all or parts of five seasons in Evansville from 1977-83, while mixing in some big league time in Detroit, mostly as a reliever. In 113 games with the Tigers, Underwood went 13-28, 4.43. His career ended early in the 1984 season, when he had ligament damage in his pitching elbow and was released.

Before Bordley secured his place in draft history in 1979, when he disrupted the January phase with his efforts to essentially guarantee a West Coast-based club would draft him, the 6-foot-3, 200-pound lefthander created controversy of a different kind in 1976 when he elected not to sign with the Brewers.

There was much speculation on the size of the bonus the Brewers offered Bordley, a standout pitcher at California's Bishop Montgomery High, who struck out 162 in 85 innings as a senior, posted a 0.72 ERA and even hit .455 as the team's first baseman on days he didn't pitch.

The amount was reportedly $60,000 initially,

## How They Should Have Done It

Based on the career WAR (Wins Above Replacement, as calculated by Baseball-Reference.com) numbers achieved by all the players eligible for the 1976 draft, here's how the first round should have unfolded. Numbers in parentheses indicate the round when the player was actually drafted

| | Player, Pos. | Actual Draft | WAR | Bonus |
|---|---|---|---|---|
| 1. | Rickey Henderson, of | Athletics (4) | 111.0 | $10,000 |
| 2. | Wade Boggs, ss | Red Sox (7) | 90.9 | $7,500 |
| 3. | Alan Trammell, ss | Tigers (2) | 70.3 | $35,000 |
| 4. | Jack Morris, rhp | Tigers (5) | 44.1 | $12,500 |
| 5. | Danny Darwin, rhp | Rangers (NDFA) | 40.5 | $37,500 |
| 6. | Bruce Hurst, lhp | Red Sox (1) | 34.8 | $42,500 |
| 7. | John Tudor, lhp | Red Sox (Jan.-S/3) | 34.6 | $5,000 |
| 8. | Floyd Bannister, lhp | Astros (1) | 26.9 | $100,000 |
| 9. | Mike Scioscia, c | Dodgers (1) | 25.9 | $44,500 |
| 10. | Mike Scott, rhp | Mets (2) | 22.8 | $24,500 |
| 11. | Rick Honeycutt, 1b/lhp | Pirates (17) | 22.3 | $2,000 |
| 12. | Greg A. Harris, rhp | Mets (NDFA) | 20.4 | $20,000 |
| 13. | Steve Kemp, of | Tigers (Jan.-R/1) | 19.5 | $50,000 |
| 14. | Steve Farr, rhp | Pirates (NDFA) | 18.4 | None |
| 15. | Dan Petry, rhp | Tigers (5) | 17.4 | $18,000 |
| 16. | Leon Durham, 1b | Cardinals (1) | 16.1 | $37,000 |
| 17. | Jody Davis, c | Mets (Jan.-R/3) | 15.8 | $4,000 |
| 18. | Jay Howell, rhp | Reds (31) | 15.4 | $2,000 |
| 19. | John Castino, 3b | Twins (3) | 15.0 | $22,500 |
| 20. | Ron Hassey, c | Indians (18) | 14.7 | $1,000 |
| 21. | Steve Trout, lhp | White Sox (1) | 13.5 | $32,000 |
| 22. | Lary Sorensen, rhp | Brewers (8) | 13.2 | $8,000 |
| 23. | Eddie Milner, of | Reds (21) | 12.8 | $2,500 |
| | Bob Brenly, c | Giants (NDFA) | 12.8 | None |
| **Top 3 Unsigned Players** | | | | **Year Signed** |
| 1. | Ozzie Smith, ss | Tigers (7) | 76.5 | 1977 |
| 2. | Willie McGee, of | White Sox (7) | 34.1 | 1977 |
| 3. | Jeff Reardon, rhp | Expos (23) | 19.2 | 1977 |

and later $75,000, but once he turned down the latter amount, Bordley says he was forced to listen to a revised final offer of just $52,000.

"When they went down to that, it really made me question their motives and honesty," Bordley said. "I talked to them at the end and told them I would have been ready to sign for $85,000, and they acted like they would pay it, but I had made a commitment to school.

"Fortunately, I came from a family where money isn't a do-or-die chance. My folks told me not to let money influence my decision too much."

Bordley said he wasn't sure he was ready to sign professionally out of high school anyway.

"To be honest, I think I needed a couple years of experience," he said. "In high school, my fastball was about all I had and all I really needed. I needed more work on my offspeed stuff and setting up hitters. I couldn't control my curve, so I never used it in a pressure situation."

After going 14-0 as a freshman at USC and becoming the only starting pitcher in school history to go through a season unbeaten, Bordley quickly transformed himself into a more complete pitcher. By 1978, he was acknowledged as the best amateur pitcher in the country.

Besides Bordley, two other first-round picks in the 1976 draft went unsigned.

Third baseman Jamie Allen, a .523 hitter at Davis High in Yakima, Wash., and a key member of Yakima's 1975 American Legion national championship team, was selected 10th overall by the Minnesota Twins. Allen indicated to every team that contacted him prior to the draft that he planned to attend college at Arizona State, but the Twins drafted him anyway. He rebuffed their $50,000 offer.

Oakland also failed to reach agreement with Virginia prep righthander Mike Sullivan, the final pick in the first round. The downtrodden A's, reeling from the fallout of dismantling their championship teams from 1971-75, also neglected to sign their second-round pick and five of their first 10. Sullivan went to college at Clemson and three years later was picked in the first round again, by Cincinnati. He never played in the big leagues.

### HENDERSON, BOGGS GRAB SPOTLIGHT

For all the hype over Bannister and Bordley in 1976, and the development of other first-round picks like Bruce Hurst (Red Sox) and Mike Scioscia (Dodgers) into legitimate big leaguers, the best high school talents drafted that year were two future Hall of Famers: Rickey Henderson, a fourth-round pick by Oakland, and Wade Boggs, a seventh-round selection by the Boston Red Sox.

Henderson, a product of local Oakland Tech, signed with the A's for a bonus of $10,000 after seriously considering an offer from the University of Arizona as a running back. Boggs passed on a scholarship offer from South Carolina to become a kicker by signing with the Red Sox for $7,500.

In high school, Henderson was much more accomplished in football than baseball, and twice piled up 1,000 yards in rushing. He was often compared to O.J. Simpson, a fellow Bay Area product, because of his raw speed and explosive running ability. He also hit .435 with 30 stolen bases as a senior, and had it not been for his mother's urging to pursue baseball, Henderson almost certainly would have ended up playing football.

"She was afraid that I might get hurt in football," he said. "I listened to her."

More than anything else in high school, Henderson worked diligently on his basestealing skills, and he largely had the art mastered by his early days in the minors. In his first full season in the A's system, at Class A Modesto in 1977, he stole 95 bases. Five years later, he set the American League standard by stealing 130 bases for the A's.

Over the course of a 25-year career, Henderson became the most accomplished leadoff hitter in the game's history. He set major league records for runs scored (2,295) and stolen bases (1,406), while also hitting .279 with 297 home runs, 1,115 RBIs,

### Fastest To The Majors

| | Player, Pos. | Drafted (Round) | Debut |
|---|---|---|---|
| 1. | Pete Redfern, rhp | Twins (Jan.-S/1) | May 15, 1976 |
| 2. | Bob Owchinko, lhp | Padres (1) | Sept. 25, 1976 |
| 3. | Steve Kemp, of | Tigers (Jan.-R/1) | April 7, 1977 |
| 4. | Bob Shirley, lhp | Padres (Jan.-S/1) | April 10, 1977 |
| | Floyd Bannister, lhp | Astros (1) | April 10, 1977 |

**FIRST HIGH SCHOOL SELECTION:** Alan Trammell, ss (Tigers/2, Sept. 9, 1977)

**LAST PLAYER TO RETIRE:** Rickey Henderson, of (Sept. 19, 2003)

### DRAFT SPOTLIGHT: FLOYD BANNISTER

**Floyd Bannister was one of the most celebrated college pitchers ever, and while he had a long major league career it fell short of expectations**

If ever there was a draft pick who seemed destined to begin his professional career in the big leagues, it was Floyd Bannister, the most dominant college pitcher of his era.

When the Astros selected the talented Arizona State lefthander with the No. 1 pick, however, both parties immediately dashed speculation that he would begin his career on top—as became common practice among elite draft picks in the 1970s.

"I've talked to Houston about starting out in the majors and I don't want to," Bannister said. "I want to go to the minor leagues first and prove myself there. It will give me a chance to get accustomed to professional baseball and not move up too quickly. I've seen too many cases of people starting out in the big leagues and having it hurt them. I'd like to start off low and build my confidence."

The Astros were in full agreement, which worked out well as the two sides struggled to come to a signing agreement. For Bannister, it was the second time in three years he reached a stalemate in draft negotiations. In 1973, after going 16-0, 0.00 for Seattle's Kennedy High, he was taken in the third round by Oakland, but A's owner Charles Finley was in a cost-cutting mode and didn't make Bannister a serious offer. His recourse then was to fulfill his scholarship offer at ASU. This time, Bannister knew all along what his intentions were.

"There was never any doubt I would sign with Houston," he said. "I knew I wasn't going back to school. I just wanted some time to relax and think about the whole situation."

On July 23, the two parties finally reached an accord on a bonus of $100,000.

It was the Astros' intention from the outset to start out Bannister on the bottom rung of their organization, at Covington of the Rookie-level Appalachian League, and he did begin his indoctrination there. Bannister had few qualms over his initial assignment, as he was mindful of the circus-like atmosphere that Eddie Bane, another standout lefthander from ASU, experienced to his detriment just three years earlier when he was drafted in the first round by the Minnesota Twins and made his debut in the majors. Bane never won a game that season, and his career quickly spiraled downward.

Despite a two-month layoff, Bannister overwhelmed the substandard competition he faced in the Appy League; in 13 innings, he allowed three scratch hits, while walking two and striking out 27. That dominating performance left a lasting impression on Covington manager Julio Linares.

"I think he's got to be the best young pitcher I've ever seen," Linares said. "With the stuff he's got, he could pitch in the majors right now."

Bannister made seven minor league appearances over the balance of the 1976 season, including a start in Triple-A in his final outing. A year later, he cracked Houston's Opening Day roster, and was in the big leagues to stay.

But things were never quite as easy again for Bannister. Though he pitched in all or parts of 15 big league seasons, often flashed overwhelming stuff and even led the American League in strikeouts in 1982 while pitching for his hometown Seattle Mariners, Bannister never lived up to his billing. He even developed a reputation for rarely pitching well in pressure-packed games and posted just a 134-143 record overall.

When Bannister had reconstructive shoulder surgery in 1988 and found no takers for his services, he went to Japan for a season, though eventually returned to pitch two more seasons in the U.S. before retiring in 1992.

## WORTH NOTING

■ Among a total of 1,071 players selected in the four phases of the draft in 1976, 195 went on to play in the major leagues. That represented a success rate of 18.2 percent—the best mark of the draft era.

■ Arizona State lefthander **FLOYD BANNISTER** and outfielder **KEN LANDREAUX**, and Eastern Michigan lefthander **BOB OWCHINKO** were the only college players selected in the first round of the June regular phase. However, 65 more college players were drafted overall than the previous year, and 1976 was the last year in the draft's evolution that more high school players were drafted than college players. The change in baseball's college rule that made all juniors automatically eligible for selection, regardless of age, took effect with the June 1976 draft and facilitated much of the increase. Previously only juniors were eligible for selection, provided they had achieved their 21st birthday within 45 days of the draft.

■ Predictably, the Major League Scouting Bureau rated Bannister and fellow lefthander **PAT UNDERWOOD**, who would go on to be the top two picks in the June regular phase, as Nos. 1-2 on its master list of top prospects for the 1976 draft. On the traditional 20-to-80 scouting scale, Bannister received an overall future potential score of 69.3, Underwood 67.6. Oddly, the third-highest grade turned in was for Texas high school righthander, **SCOTT GARDNER** (64.0), who wasn't drafted until the third round.

■ Righthander **RAY GAULT**, a first-round pick (eighth overall) of the Indians in the June secondary phase out of Manatee (Fla.) Junior College, had one of the most dubious careers of any pitcher in the draft era. In four minor league seasons, including one in Triple-A, the hard-throwing Gault went 7-20, 10.01 with 329

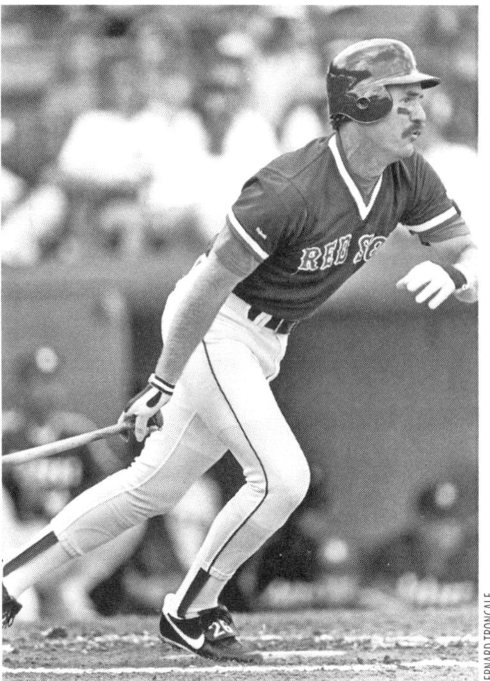


BERNARD TRONCALE

**Wade Boggs lasted until the seventh round because of modest overall tools, but the Red Sox recognized his superior bat skills**

3,055 hits and a .401 on-base average.

Like Henderson, Boggs excelled in baseball and football at Tampa's H.B. Plant High, but everything Boggs did was geared toward a career in baseball. On the advice of his parents, he gave up his role as the team's starting quarterback as a senior, for fear he might get hurt, though he continued to excel as both a left-footed punter and kicker.

With a grade of 40 on the traditional 20-80 scouting scale, Boggs was all but written off as a prospect by the Major League Scouting Bureau and other clubs because he lacked obvious power and speed. But his innate ability to hit to all fields, advanced approach to hitting and uncanny plate discipline appealed to the Red Sox.

Boggs' career got off to an ordinary start as he hit just .263 at Elmira of the short-season New York-Penn League that summer, but that would be the one and only time that the sweet-swinging Boggs hit less than .300 over the first 16 years of his career—six in the minors, 10 in the majors.

He won a batting title in Triple-A in 1981, in his final year in the minors, and went on to win five more in his first seven seasons with the Red Sox. Over 18 major league seasons, including 11 with the Red Sox, he hit .328 overall and set an AL-record with seven consecutive 200-hit seasons.

### SOUTHERN CAL CONNECTION

The January 1976 draft had unusually strong talent, thanks to three premium Southern California dropouts. Righthander Pete Redfern (Twins) and catcher Dennis Littlejohn (Giants) were the first two picks in the regular phase, while outfielder Steve Kemp (Tigers) was the No. 1 selection in the secondary phase. All three left college the previous fall to become eligible.

Though all were juniors in 1975, none were 21 within the required 45 days of that year's draft. A change in baseball's college rule passed in 1975 and made all juniors draft eligible, regardless of age, but the rule wasn't set to go into effect until the June draft in 1976, so it was too late to benefit the USC trio.

Redfern and Littlejohn were both drafted prior to attending USC, but the unheralded Kemp was a walk-on. He enrolled in 1972 as a skinny 155-pound outfielder with few defensive skills, a below-average arm and little speed. He played rarely as a freshman.

By the time Kemp completed his junior season, though, he had set USC's single-season record by hitting .435 (31 points better than the existing mark), while contributing 13 homers and 67 RBIs.

Longtime USC coach Rod Dedeaux called Kemp the best natural hitter he ever had, while others were comparing him to the best all-around players to ever wear Trojan colors.

"I know a lot of people are comparing me with Fred Lynn now because we were both from USC," Kemp said. "But I don't mind. If anything, it's an honor. I guess being the first draft choice and being compared with Lynn put pressure on me, but I think I play better under pressure."

Lynn never hit better than .326 in any of his three years at USC, and yet was the American League MVP and rookie of the year in 1975, just two years after he left school.

With Kemp's prowess at the plate and the dramatic improvement he'd shown in all phases of his game, the Tigers showed no hesitation in selecting him with the first pick in the January draft. They rewarded him with a $50,000 bonus.

In his first season in the Tigers system, Kemp hit .386 in a 52-game trial at Triple-A Evansville, and would have played in the big leagues that year had he not torn ligaments in his ankle in the final week

### Top 25 Bonuses

| | Player, Pos. | Drafted (Round) | Order | Bonus |
|---|---|---|---|---|
| **1.** | **Floyd Bannister, lhp** | **Astros (1)** | **1** | **$100,000** |
| **2.** | **Ken Landreaux, of** | **Angels (1)** | **6** | **$85,000** |
| **3.** | *** Pat Underwood, lhp** | **Tigers (1)** | **2** | **$70,000** |
| 4. | * Jeff Kraus, ss | Phillies (1) | 17 | $60,000 |
| **5.** | *** Herm Segelke, rhp** | **Cubs (1)** | **7** | **$52,500** |
| | * Mark Kuecker, ss | Giants (1) | 11 | $52,500 |
| | * Billy Simpson, of | Rangers (1) | 12 | $52,500 |
| **8.** | *** Ken Smith, 3b** | **Braves (1)** | **3** | **$50,000** |
| | **Steve Kemp, of** | **Tigers (Jan.-R/1)** | **(1)** | **$50,000** |
| 10. | * Jim Parke, rhp | Pirates (1) | 21 | $47,500 |
| **11.** | *** Mike Scioscia, c** | **Dodgers (1)** | **19** | **$44,500** |
| **12.** | **Bob Owchinko, lhp** | **Padres (1)** | **5** | **$42,500** |
| | * Tim Glass, c | Indians (1) | 14 | $42,500 |
| | *** Bruce Hurst, lhp** | **Red Sox (1)** | **22** | **$42,500** |
| 15. | * Ben Grzybek, rhp | Royals (1) | 18 | $40,000 |
| 16. | * Steve Finch, rhp | Rangers (2) | 36 | $38,000 |
| **17.** | **Danny Darwin, rhp** | **Rangers (NDFA)** | | **$37,500** |
| **18.** | *** Leon Durham, 1b** | **Cardinals (1)** | **15** | **$37,000** |
| **19.** | *** Bob James, rhp** | **Expos (1)** | **9** | **$35,000** |
| | *** Alan Trammell, ss** | **Tigers (2)** | **26** | **$35,000** |
| | * Don Ruzek, ss | Dodgers (2) | 43 | $35,000 |
| **22.** | *** Dallas Williams, of** | **Orioles (1)** | **20** | **$34,000** |
| **23.** | *** Steve Trout, lhp** | **White Sox (1)** | **8** | **$32,000** |
| 24. | * Melvin Manning, ss | Brewers (2) | 28 | $31,000 |
| 25. | Five tied at | | | $30,000 |

*Major leaguers in bold. *High school selection.*

## Largest Bonuses By Round

| | Player, Pos. | Club | Bonus |
|---|---|---|---|
| 1. | **Floyd Bannister, lhp** | **Astros** | **$100,000** |
| 2. | * Steve Finch, rhp | Rangers | $38,000 |
| 3. | * Craig Hendrickson, ss | Angels | $30,000 |
| 4. | * Randy Curtis, ss | Phillies | $22,500 |
| 5. | **Greg Keatley, c** | **Cubs** | **$17,000** |
| 6. | *** Ozzie Virgil, c** | **Phillies** | **$18,000** |
| 7. | Kelly Snider, 1b | Dodgers | $17,000 |
| 8. | * Bobby Clark, lhp | Cubs | $20,000 |
| 9. | **Gary Allenson, c** | **Red Sox** | **$8,000** |
| 10. | Duane Gustavson, c | Cubs | $18,000 |
| Jan/R | **Steve Kemp, of** | **Tigers (1)** | **$50,000** |
| Jan/S | **Pete Redfern, rhp** | **Twins (1)** | **$30,000** |
| Jun/S | **Dave Stegman, of** | **Tigers (1)** | **$18,000** |

*Major leaguers in bold. *High school selection.*

of the American Association season.

Kemp hit .318 with 26 homers and 105 RBIs in 1979, his best season with the Tigers, and went on to play 10 big league seasons. But after signing a lucrative deal as a free agent with the New York Yankees in 1983, his career effectively ended that season when he was hit in the head by a batting-practice drive that knocked him unconscious. It left him with blurred vision, and he was never the same.

"I lost vision in my left eye, and that made it a lot more difficult," Kemp said. "I lost depth perception, and it hampered my ability to do the things I did well."

Pete Redfern

Redfern's life turned even more dramatically. After receiving a $30,000 bonus from the Twins, it took Redfern just four appearances in the minors before he made his big league debut. He threw five hitless innings in his first start, and went 8-8, 3.51 as a rookie. He spent seven seasons with the Twins, while posting a career mark of 42-48, 4.54.

He spent the 1983 season in Triple-A in the Dodgers organization, hoping to keep his fading career alive, but it all ended on an October day that year when Redfern went swimming in the Pacific Ocean, off the Southern California coast. He dove into shallow water and broke his neck. Had it not been for the quick actions of a nearby friend, Redfern would have drowned; as it was, the accident left him paralyzed and confined to a wheelchair.

Littlejohn saw action in parts of three major league seasons with the San Francisco Giants, but hit just .203 in 78 games.

Interestingly, the top pick in the June secondary phase in 1976, second baseman Gerald Price, also had ties to USC. He was drafted by the Atlanta Braves while a freshman at California's Diablo Valley Junior College, but didn't sign and returned to that school for his sophomore season. He then transferred to USC for two years, and despite helping to lead the Trojans to a College World Series title as a junior in 1978, he was never drafted during his tenure there and didn't play pro ball.

Another player with significant California ties who escaped detection altogether in the June draft was Greg Harris, a Long Beach City College product and UCLA recruit. Though he went undrafted, Harris almost singlehandedly pitched the Alaska Goldpanners to their fourth National Baseball Congress championship in five years in 1976 by beating the rival Anchorage Glacier Pilots 2-0 in 10 innings in the final.

Harris, who won four games in the tournament to push his record on the summer to 15-3, 2.12, had been drafted three times (twice by the Mets), but because he was passed over in June he was free to sign with any team after the NBC tournament and accepted a $20,000 offer from the Mets. Harris pitched 15 years in the majors and gained his greatest fame in 1995 by pitching to two batters lefthanded, effectively becoming the first switch-pitcher in baseball's modern era.

While Bannister, Owchinko and Landreaux were the only college players selected in the first round of the June regular phase, 65 more college players were drafted overall than the previous year, and 1976 was the last year in the draft's evolution that more high school players were drafted than college players. The change in baseball's college rule that made all juniors eligible for selection drove much of the increase.

### DOMINANT PREP TEAM

If Arizona State was the nation's dominant college team of 1976, then California's Lakewood High was undeniably the best high school team in the land. Four Lancer players were selected in that year's draft, including outfielder Billy Simpson (Rangers), who went in the first round, and shortstop/righthander Don Ruzek (Dodgers), who went in the second. From that California Interscholastic Federation Southern section 4-A championship team, 15 players went on to play professional baseball.

Pitcher/outfielder Stan Williams Jr., an unsigned 11th-round pick of the St. Louis Cardinals, was the star of the Lakewood High powerhouse, though he never played pro ball. He went on to a college career at USC but was plagued by arm problems.

Scouts focused most of their attention on the

## One Team's Draft: Detroit Tigers

| Player, Pos. | Bonus | Player, Pos. | Bonus | Player, Pos. | Bonus |
|---|---|---|---|---|---|
| **1. * Pat Underwood, lhp** | **$70,000** | **5. Jack Morris, rhp** | **$12,500** | 9. * Charles Farmer, c | Did not sign |
| **2. * Alan Trammell, ss** | **$35,000** | 6. * Lawrence Douglas, ss | $2,500 | 10. Michael Burns, rhp | $2,000 |
| 3. * Scott Johnson, c | $25,000 | **7. Ozzie Smith, ss** | **Did not sign** | **Other Steve Kemp (Jan.-R/1), of** | **$50,000** |
| **4. * Dan Petry, rhp** | **$18,000** | **8. Glenn Gulliver, ss** | **Unavailable** | | |

*Major leaguers in bold. *High school selection.*

## WORTH NOTING

walks and just 146 strikeouts in 179 innings. His 1978 season, spent playing for the Bakersfield Outlaws, an independent team in the Class A California League, was an especially rough one as he went 2-10, 10.75 and walked 156 in 72 innings. He led the league with 33 wild pitches and 20 hit batters, and set a league record by serving up six wild pitches in one inning. Gault had been drafted on three other occasions before signing with the Indians.

■ Cincinnati was acknowledged as one of the nation's hotbeds of amateur talent in the 1970s, and the city had a run of three straight picks in the first round in 1976 with the selection of Woodward High first baseman **LEON DURHAM** (Cardinals, 15th overall pick), McNicholas High outfielder **PAT TABLER** (Yankees, 16th) and Colerain High shortstop **JEFF KRAUS** (Phillies, 17th). Additionally, catcher **TIM GLASS** (Indians, 14th) was from nearby Springfield. Durham and Tabler went on to combine for more than 2,000 games in the major leagues, while Kraus and Glass both peaked at Double-A.

■ Major leaguer Andy Messersmith successfully challenged the legality of baseball's reserve clause in 1975, which ushered in the era of free agency a year later. Free to sign with the team of his choice, Messersmith signed a three-year, $1 million deal with the Braves prior to the 1976 season. The landmark Messersmith ruling would eventually have significant implications on the draft. As major leaguers were permitted to play out their options and sign as free agents with other clubs, their former clubs would be awarded draft picks as compensation. The connection of draft picks to major league players created a linkage to player value in the eyes of the Players Association (and arbitrators), thus giving the union a voice in changes to the draft in subsequent years.

## IN FOCUS: BOB OWCHINKO

Bob Owchinko's promising career began with a flourish, only to fizzle out.

On July 16, 1977, little more than a year after the San Diego Padres drafted Owchinko with the fifth pick overall out of Eastern Michigan University, he pitched the best game of his career, coming within five outs of a perfect game against the National League champion Los Angeles Dodgers—and lost, 1-0.

The rookie lefthander went 9-12 that season, but was so impressive that he was saluted as the league's top first-year pitcher. Padres manager Roger Craig hailed him as the best pitching prospect ever drafted by San Diego and predicted the 22-year-old Owchinko would win 20 games the following season.

It never happened, as no matter how well he pitched, he never seemed to win. Owchinko pitched four seasons in San Diego, and went a combined 27-48. He went on to work in parts of six more seasons in the big leagues, but never was able to craft his raw talent into meaningful results. "You see his arm and you keep expecting him to develop into a consistent winner," a scout said when Owchinko was fighting to salvage a career gone awry. "But it should have happened by now if it's going to happen. A lot of clubs wrote him off as a kid who just never learned how to win."

6-foot-2, 175-pound Simpson, who appeared to fit all the physical requirements of a first-rounder with his speed, range and arm strength. He signed with the Texas Rangers for a bonus of $52,500.

"Billy was really a good player," said John Herbold, Simpson's high school coach and later the coach at Cal State Los Angeles. "But one thing about him was he was a little bit older when he graduated. He was 19."

Simpson hit .326 as a senior for Lakewood High, and that modest average proved to be a tipoff on the colossal failings he would endure in pro ball. The Rangers released him within two years after he had hit .151 with no homers in 139 professional games, almost all at the Rookie level. He later signed with the New York Mets, but hit .185 in 50 more games in that organization and was released again. The Padres gave him a third chance, but he didn't make it out of spring training. At 21, Simpson was through, and broke as he misspent all his bonus money.

"He was a bad sign," admitted Joe Klein, the Rangers assistant farm director at the time and Simpson's first manager in pro ball. "He never showed anything. I don't remember one positive thing that he did or one thing he picked up.

"It never was an effort situation. He gave it the best shot he had."

Klein said he believed the Rangers might have been victimized by the club's move to join the Major League Scouting Bureau in 1975. The organization pared its scouting staff to just five or six area scouts as a result, and Klein speculated that the Rangers may have relied too extensively on the bureau's report in evaluating Simpson.

In December 1986, Simpson's name surfaced again—for all the wrong reasons. Then 29, he pleaded guilty to charges related to his involvement in a multimillion-dollar international drug-smuggling ring. One count of conspiracy and two counts of using the telephone to facilitate the commission of a federal crime bought him a 10-year prison sentence.

"Being a No. 1 draft choice, he had farther to fall," Herbold said. "Bill had a lot of tools, but he was at the top of the Empire State Building, and that's a long way down."

### HOME RUN EXPLOSION

Several of Bannister's teammates from Arizona State's 1976 club also had their moments in the big leagues, particularly Horner and Landreaux.

Landreaux's career started slowly as he hit just .220 in Double-A in his first season. But a year later, he was the minor league player of the year when he hit .357 overall with 27 homers and 116 RBIs between Double-A El Paso and Triple-A Salt Lake City. Over an 11-year major league career, he was best remembered for his 31-game hitting streak with the Twins in 1980.

While the Sun Devils won five College World Series championships in a 16-year period from 1965-81, and the 1976 club could do no better than finish third, that team has always been held in high esteem by those close to the ASU program.

"Most of the fans pay more attention to that team than I do," late ASU coach Jim Brock once said, "but as far as people who went on to do well in professional baseball, it was our best."

### Highest Unsigned Picks

**JUNE/REGULAR PHASE ONLY**

| Player, Pos., Team (Round) | College | Re-Drafted |
|---|---|---|
| Bill Bordley, lhp, Brewers (1) | USC | Reds '79 (Jan.-S/1) |
| Jamie Allen, 3b/rhp, Twins (1) | Arizona State | Mariners '79 (2) |
| Mike Sullivan, rhp, Athletics (1) | Clemson | Reds '79 (1) |
| Tom Hawk, rhp, Giants (2) | Arizona State | Astros '80 (5) |
| Tim Brandenburg, lhp, Royals (2) | Kentucky | Never |
| Jerry Don Gleaton, lhp, Orioles (2) | Texas | Rangers '79 (1) |
| Brian Duffy, lhp, Athletics (2) | California | Indians '79 (43) |
| Scott Gardner, rhp, Brewers (3) | Oklahoma | Orioles '79 (28) |
| Mike Madden, lhp, Pirates (3) | No. Colorado | Never |
| James Stehle, lhp, White Sox (4) | * Wilkes (Pa.) | Padres '77 (5) |

**TOTAL UNSIGNED PICKS:** Top 5 Rounds (19), Top 10 Rounds (58)

**Returned to same school.*

Despite losing seven straight games to Arizona State, Arizona (56-17) won the 1976 College World Series. The Wildcats beat ASU for the only time all year in the semifinals in Omaha, eliminating the Sun Devils, then beat Eastern Michigan, 7-1, in the final.

Arizona outfielder Dave Stegman, who hit .430 and set an NCAA record with 30 doubles, was his team's most prominent draft pick, the second player selected in the June secondary phase. Righthander/DH Steve Powers, the Series' most outstanding player, went to the Pirates in the same phase with the 18th selection.

Eastern Michigan got to the championship game behind the twin first-round arms of Owchinko, the fifth pick in 1976, and sophomore righthander Bob Welch (10-3, 1.82), a 1977 selection.

For the third year in a row in 1976, the NCAA single-season home run record fell. In fact, three players broke the old mark of 20, set in 1975 by Arizona State's Jerry Maddox. None of the three record-setters was a factor in the draft.

Wyoming outfielder Bill Ewing set the new standard with 23 homers, but wasn't taken until the fourth round by the Angels. Louisville's Jim LaFountain, who had four homers and 14 RBIs in one game and ended up with 22 long balls on the season, wasn't even drafted. Florida State catcher Terry Kennedy had 21, but as a sophomore wasn't eligible for selection. He became a first-round pick in 1977.

Texas lefthander Rich Wortham also put himself in the NCAA record book in 1976 after posting a 14-2, 1.70 record for the Longhorns. His 14 victories enabled him to finish his career with 50, eclipsing the old mark of 47, set by Arizona State's Craig Swan from 1969-72. Wortham, an elite prospect coming out of high school before hurting himself in a farming accident, wasn't selected until the second round of the January secondary phase. He signed with the Chicago White Sox for $17,500.

Wortham pitched in 83 games for the White Sox through the 1980 season, then was plagued by wildness that ended his career. Over his final three years, all in the minor leagues, Wortham worked 186 innings and walked 206. He went 2-11, 9.40 in his last two seasons.

# 1976 Draft List

**Did not sign. Major leaguers in bold, with first and last years noted. Order of selection indicated in parentheses. For the first five rounds of the June Regular Phase and the first round of all other phases, the peak level of each player is noted.*

## ATLANTA BRAVES

### January—Regular Phase (4)

1. William Free, rhp, Tuskegee (Ala.) Institute.—(AA)
2. *Carl Pankratz, rhp, Temple (Texas) JC.
3. *Larry Wright, lhp, DeKalb (Ga.) JC.

### January—Secondary Phase (10)

1. **Mike Macha, 3b, Rice University.—(1979-80)**
2. ***Dave Stegman, of, University of Arizona.—(1978-84)**
3. ***Bob Stoddard, rhp, Gavilan (Calif.) JC.—(1971-87)**
4. *Condredge Holloway, ss, University of Tennessee.

**DRAFT DROP** *First-round draft pick (4th overall), Expos (1971) • 12th-round draft pick, New England Patriots/National Football League (1975); quarterback, Canadian Football League (1975-87)*

### June—Regular Phase (3)

1. **Ken Smith, 3b, Youngstown East HS, Youngstown, Ohio.—(1981-83)**
2. Dom Chiti, lhp, Raleigh-Egypt HS, Memphis, Tenn.—(AA)

**DRAFT DROP** *Son of Harry Chiti, major leaguer (1950-62)*

3. **Dan Morogiello, lhp, Seton Hall University.—(1983)**
4. Gordon Guzenski, rhp, Benedictine (Kan.) College.—(Low A)
5. **Bruce Benedict, c, University of Nebraska-Omaha.—(1978-89)**
6. **Jim Wessinger, ss, LeMoyne College.—(1979)**
7. *Glynn Tschirhart, ss, St. Mary's (Texas) University.
8. *Tony Jordan, rhp, Rolling Hills HS, Rancho Palos Verdes, Calif.
9. Clayton Elliott, ss, Liberty University.
10. Jerry Keller, c-1b, Eastern Michigan University.
11. James Bagley, of, San Jacinto (Texas) JC.
12. ***Ricky Peters, ss, Arizona State University.—(1979-86)**
13. David Long, of, Loyola Marymount University.
14. **Rick Matula, rhp, Sam Houston State University.—(1979-81)**
15. *David Duff, c, Menchville HS, Newport News, Va.
16. William Tucker, lhp, Eastern Illinois University.
17. Jeffrey Culbreth, rhp, Sylvan HS, Atlanta.
18. ***Ricky Jones, ss-rhp, Towers HS, Decatur, Ga.—(1986)**
19. *Eugene Wisniewski, ss, Holy Ghost Prep HS, Philadelphia.
20. Wyatt Tonkin, rhp, University of Washington.
21. Isaac Seoane, c, Dade HS, Miami.
22. Aaron Hudson, 3b, West Montgomery HS, Mount Gilead, N.C.
23. Bob Brasher, of, Louisiana Tech.
24. *Robert McGraw, 1b, Huffman HS, Birmingham, Ala.
25. Eldgre Huddleston, of, Southwest Missouri State University.
26. *Richard Volz, ss, Antonian HS, San Antonio, Texas.
27. *Clay Stolte, rhp, Highlands HS, San Antonio, Texas.
28. *Rick Montoni, of, University of Miami.

### June—Secondary Phase (1)

1. *Gerald Price, 2b, Diablo Valley (Calif.) JC.—DNP
2. ***Ron Roenicke, of-1b, Mount San Antonio (Calif.) JC.—(1981-88)**

**DRAFT DROP** *Brother of Gary Roenicke, major leaguer (1976-88) • Major league manager (2011-15)*

3. ***John Butcher, rhp, Yavapai (Ariz.) JC.—(1980-86)**

## BALTIMORE ORIOLES

### January—Regular Phase (19)

1. *Raphael Hampton, of, Jackson (Mich.) CC.—(AAA)
2. **Mark Corey, of, Central Arizona JC.—(1979-81)**
3. *Craig Robinson, c-1b, Chipola (Fla.) JC.
4. Howard Ashlock, lhp-1b, Cal Poly Pomona.
5. *Michael Moore, rhp, Cleveland State (Tenn.) CC.
6. Michael Long, rhp, Central Arizona JC.
7. Paul Burgess, rhp, Lancaster, Calif.
8. Pat Espinosa, rhp, UCLA.

### January—Secondary Phase (7)

1. **Wayne Krenchicki, ss, University of Miami.—(1979-86)**
2. *Erik Hendricks, rhp, Chabot (Calif.) JC.
3. *William Yarbrough, 3b, Manatee (Fla.) JC.
4. *Stephen Vaughan, of, University of Arizona.
5. Jim Skaalen, 1b-3b, San Diego State University.
6. Randy Johnson, 3b, San Diego State University.
7. *Paul Tasker, c-3b, Edison (Fla.) CC.

### June—Regular Phase (20)

1. **Dallas Williams, of, Abraham Lincoln HS, Brooklyn, N.Y.—(1981-83)**
2. ***Jerry Don Gleaton, lhp, Brownwood (Texas) HS.—(1979-92)**

**DRAFT DROP** *Attended Texas; re-drafted by Rangers, June 1979/regular phase (1st round); first player from 1979 draft to reach majors (July 11, 1979)*

3. Andrew Davis, 2b, Southeastern Louisiana University.—(High A)
4. Michael Lindal, lhp, Libertyville (Ill.) HS.—(High A)
5. Kevin Jondle, rhp, St. John Bosco HS, Long Beach, Calif.—DNP
6. **Jim Smith, ss, Long Beach State University.—(1982)**
7. *Ronald Adkins, ss, Grambling State University.
8. Kevin Kennedy, c, San Diego State University.

**DRAFT DROP** *Major league manager (1993-96)*

9. Pete Torrez, lhp, Dallas Baptist University.
10. Michael Ithier, 1b, Washington HS, Milwaukee.
11. Robert Welch, rhp, Copiague HS, Lindenhurst, N.J.
12. *John Isley, 1b-of, Hoggard HS, Wilmington, N.C.
13. *Darrell Guillory, rhp, LaGrange HS, Lake Charles, La.
14. Steven Fedoris, rhp, Allderdice HS, Pittsburgh.
15. Evon Martinson, c, Point Loma Nazarene (Calif.) College.
16. Craig Allegrezza, rhp, University of Massachusetts.
17. Anthony Zentgraf, 3b, University of Virginia.
18. *Mark Poehlman, of, Loyola HS, Baltimore.
19. *Don Carfino, ss, St. John Bosco HS, Bellflower, Calif.
20. *Daniel Prior, rhp, Gulf Coast (Fla.) CC.
21. Ed Blankmeyer, 2b, Seton Hall University.

**DRAFT DROP** *Baseball coach, St. John's (1996-2015)*

22. *Fred Benham, c, Abramson HS, New Orleans, La.

### June—Secondary Phase (16)

No selection.

## BOSTON RED SOX

MICHAEL PONZINI

**Other pitchers received more hype, but Red Sox first-rounder Bruce Hurst outperformed them**

### January—Regular Phase (21)

1. *Nate Puryear, rhp, Stillman (Ala.) College.—(AAA)
2. **Dennis Burtt, rhp, Santa Ana (Calif.) JC.—(1985-86)**
3. Steven Schneck, rhp, Kalamazoo Valley (Mich.) CC.
4. *Gary Hoyle, c, Broward (Fla.) CC.
5. *Roscoe Alburtis, 1b, Blinn (Texas) JC.
6. *Jeffrey Spahr, rhp, Gulf Coast (Fla.) CC.
7. **(void) *Terry Leach, rhp, Auburn University.—(1981-93)**
8. *Russell Cain, c, George C. Wallace (Ala.) CC.

### January—Secondary Phase (9)

1. David Tyler, 3b, Vanderbilt University.—(AA)
2. *Greg Jemison, of, Seton Hall University.
3. **John Tudor, lhp, Georgia Southern College.—(1979-90)**
4. Bruce Poole, lhp, University of South Alabama.

### June—Regular Phase (22)

1. **Bruce Hurst, lhp, Dixie HS, St. George, Utah.—(1980-94)**
2. **Glenn Hoffman, ss, Savanna HS, Anaheim, Calif.—(1980-89)**

**DRAFT DROP** *Brother of Trevor Hoffman, major leaguer (1993-2010) • Major league manager (1998)*

3. Mark Twogood, of, Loara HS, Anaheim, Calif.—(Short-season A)
4. *Larry Jones, rhp, Florida State University.—(AAA)

**DRAFT DROP** *Returned to Florida State; re-drafted by Orioles, June 1977/regular phase (5th round)*

5. **Mike Smithson, rhp, University of Tennessee.—(1982-89)**
6. *Ron Kovach, lhp, Grand Junction (Colo.) HS.
7. **Wade Boggs, ss, Plant HS, Tampa.—(1982-99)**

**DRAFT DROP** *Elected to Baseball Hall of Fame, 2005*

8. Ronnie Harrington, c, William Carey (Miss.) College.
9. **Gary Allenson, c, Arizona State University.—(1979-85)**
10. Danny Parks, rhp, Memphis State University.
11. David Denton, 2b, University of Nevada-Las Vegas.
12. **Reid Nichols, 2b, Ocala Forest HS, Ocala, Fla.—(1980-87)**
13. John Edwards, c, University of La Verne (Calif.).
14. *Larry Edwards, lhp, Bishop Walsh HS, LaVale, Md.
15. *Dan Swanson, lhp, Aragon HS, San Mateo, Calif.
16. Bancroft Ormsby, ss, University of Arkansas.
17. Jack Sauer, rhp, Northwestern Business (Ohio) JC.
18. Glenn Fisher, ss, Mansfield (Pa.) University.
19. John Kidd, 3b, SUNY-Buffalo.
20. Mike Ongarato, of, Cal Poly San Luis Obispo.
21. *Frederick Opper, 1b, Mount St. Michaels HS, Mount Vernon, N.Y.
22. **Chico Walker, 2b, Tilden Tech HS, Chicago.—(1980-93)**
23. *Peter Reilly, c, Trinity HS, Manchester, N.H.
24. Jerry King, rhp, San Diego (Calif.) HS.
25. Randy Lamprecht, c, Rice University.
26. John Faccinto, 3b, Bishop Gorman HS, Las Vegas, Nev.

### June—Secondary Phase (22)

1. Steve Miller, rhp, Lower Columbia (Wash.) JC.—(High A)

## CALIFORNIA ANGELS

### January—Regular Phase (5)

1. Steve Tebbetts, of, Florida State University.—(Low A)
2. Stephen Lettric, rhp, San Jose (Calif.) CC.
3. Kenneth Gooch, ss, Yuba (Calif.) CC.
4. **Mark Brouhard, c, Los Angeles Pierce JC.—(1980-85)**
5. **Keith Comstock, lhp, Canada (Calif.) JC.—(1984-91)**
6. *Howard Herl, rhp, Essex (Md.) CC.
7. *Dan Gausepohl, c-of, Long Beach (Calif.) CC.
8. *Joel Crisler, rhp, South Georgia JC.
9. *Jim Christiansen, 3b-of, Fullerton (Calif.) JC.
10. *Michael Shipley, lhp, Barstow (Calif.) CC.
11. Donny Jones, c, Barstow (Calif.) CC.
12. *Marty Serrano, ss, San Jose (Calif.) CC.
13. ***Ron Johnson, 1b, Fullerton (Calif.) JC.—(1982-84)**
14. *Charles Cassell, rhp, Barstow (Calif.) CC.
15. *Steven Balla, rhp, Gavilan (Calif.) JC.
16. *Lawrence Cole, rhp, Butte (Calif.) JC.

### January—Secondary Phase (15)

1. Greg Johnson, rhp, Santa Ana (Calif.) JC.—(High A)
2. ***Mike Chris, 1b-lhp, Los Angeles Pierce JC.—(1979-83)**
3. *Steve King, c, University of South Carolina.
4. ***Ernie Camacho, rhp, Hartnell (Calif.) CC.—(1980-90)**
5. *Greg Stahl, ss, Los Angeles Harbor JC.

### June—Regular Phase (6)

1. **Ken Landreaux, of, Arizona State University.—(1977-87)**
2. **Bob Ferris, rhp, University of Maryland.—(1979-80)**
3. Craig Hendrickson, ss, W.T. Woodson HS, Annandale, Va.—(High A)
4. Bill Ewing, of, University of Wyoming.—(AAA)
5. *Mickey Palmer, of-lhp, West Covina (Calif.) HS.—(High A)

**DRAFT DROP** *Attended Cal State Fullerton; re-drafted by Royals, June 1979/regular phase (5th round)*

6. Steve Whitehead, ss, UC Irvine.

7. **Chuck Porter, rhp, Clemson University.—(1981-85)**
8. Bob Slater, 2b, Cal State Northridge.
9. *Joseph Powell, 1b, Overlea HS, Baltimore.
10. David Moore, 2b, Sahuaro HS, Tucson, Ariz.
11. *Rick Schwenn, rhp, Cal Poly Pomona.
12. **Mike Bishop, 3b, Righetti HS, Santa Maria, Calif.—(1983)**
13. *Joe Carroll, rhp, University of Tulsa.
14. *Jeff Gilbert, of, Cal State Northridge.
15. Don Lyons, 1b, Gonzaga University.
16. William Douglas, c, Sylmar (Calif.) HS.
17. **Ken Schrom, rhp, University of Idaho.—(1980-87)**
18. ***Larry Owen, c, Bowling Green State University.—(1981-88)**
19. *Peter Chapin, rhp, Troy HS, Fullerton, Calif.
20. Scott Moffitt, 3b, University of Utah.
21. *Jon Hansen, of, Santa Barbara (Calif.) HS.
22. *Stan Edmonds, of, Needles (Calif.) HS.
23. Jeffrey Wolf, rhp, Dixie (Utah) JC.
24. *William Sylvester, rhp, Rancho Alamitos HS, Garden Grove, Calif.
25. *Robert Luitwieler, lhp, La Habra (Calif.) HS
26. David DaCosta, 3b, Santana-Santee HS, San Diego.
27. *Tommy Montgomery, lhp, Robert E. Lee HS, Thomaston, Ga.
28. ***Jeff Calhoun, lhp, Parklane Academy HS, McComb, Miss.—(1984-88)**
29. **John Harris, 1b, Lubbock Christian (Texas) College.—(1979-81)**
30. *Keith Vranesh, 3b, Arlington HS, Riverside, Calif.
31. *Bruce Ferguson, rhp, University of Arizona.
32. *Dave Garcia, ss, El Cajon (Calif.) HS.

DRAFT DROP *Son of Dave Garcia, major league manager (1977-82)*

33. *Monte Pries, rhp, Corona del Mar HS, Newport Beach, Calif.
34. *Bruce Tonascia, of-c, University of Southern California.

#### June—Secondary Phase (10)

1. John Racanelli, rhp, University of Southern California.—(AAA)
2. **Danny Boone, lhp, Cal State Fullerton.—(1981-90)**
3. *William Eve, 1b, Miami-Dade CC North.
4. *Michael Shipley, lhp, Barstow (Calif.) CC.
5. Joel Crisler, rhp, South Georgia JC.
6. *Joe Ward, of, Manatee (Fla.) JC.
7. *Charles Cassell, rhp, Barstow (Calif.) CC.

## CHICAGO CUBS

#### January—Regular Phase (8)

1. John Faley, rhp, Camden County (N.J.) CC.—(High A)
2. Bryan Johnson, c, Bellevue (Wash.) CC.
3. **Ron Davis, rhp, Blinn (Texas) JC.—(1978-88)**

DRAFT DROP *Father of Ike Davis, first-round draft pick (2008), major leaguer (2010-15)*

4. Ray Dimick, rhp, Los Angeles Pierce JC.

#### January—Secondary Phase (24)

1. Peter Brown, lhp, Glens Falls, N.Y.—(Rookie)
2. *Steven Winfield, rhp, Panola (Texas) JC.

#### June—Regular Phase (7)

1. **Herm Segelke, rhp, El Camino HS, South San Francisco.—(1982)**
2. Buddy Lowe, rhp, Sarasota (Fla.) HS.—(High A)
3. **Kurt Seibert, ss, Clemson University.—(1979)**
4. **Keith Drumright, 2b, University of Oklahoma.—(1978-81)**
5. **Greg Keatley, c, University of South Carolina.—(1981)**
6. Dan England, rhp, High Point College.
7. ***Odie Davis, ss, Prairie View A&M University.—(1980)**
8. Bobby Clark, lhp, Pleasant Hill HS, Concord, Calif.
9. *Frank D'Antico, rhp, Upsala (N.J.) College.
10. Duane Gustavson, c, University of Wisconsin.
11. *Donald Fusari, lhp, Eastern Connecticut State University.
12. Gordon Hodgson, 3b, Terra Linda HS, San Rafael, Calif.
13. LaVerne Jark, 2b, Northern State (S.D.) College.
14. **Steven Davis, ss, Stanford University.—(1979)**
15. Edwin Mohr, of, Rib Lake (Wis.) HS.
16. *James Funderberk, lhp, Bell HS, Huntington Park, Calif.
17. *Edward Szymanski, lhp, Salesianum HS, Wilmington, Del.
18. Denzil Palmer, ss, Cal State Los Angeles.
19. Joseph Thompson, 1b, Knoch HS, Renfrew, Pa.
20. Richard Herendeen, lhp, Chardon (Ohio) HS.
21. Daniel Brown, lhp, New Haven (Ind.) HS.
22. Douglas McCracken, of, Sunset HS, Portland, Ore.
23. Jared Martin, of, St. Mary's (Calif.) College.
24. *Felix Oroz, lhp, Manogue HS, Reno, Nev.
25. *Brian Snitker, c, University of New Orleans.
26. Tony Messer, 3b, Virginia HS, Bristol, Va.
27. Melvin Godard, 1b, Williamston (N.C.) HS.
28. Richard McClure, rhp, Los Medanos (Calif.) JC.
29. Raymond Powell, lhp, Etowah HS, Attalla, Ala.
30. Bert Newman, 2b, Southern Illinois University.

#### June—Secondary Phase (21)

1. **Karl Pagel, 1b, University of Texas.—(1978-83)**

DRAFT DROP *Brother of Mike Pagel, quarterback, National Football League (1982-93)*

2. John Reiter, rhp, St. Louis CC-Meramec.
3. *Mark Post, lhp, Keystone (Pa.) JC.
4. *Ken Lelek, rhp, Monroe (N.Y.) CC.
5. *Gary Skow, of, Yavapai (Ariz.) JC.
6. Bill Evers, c, Eckerd (Fla.) College.

## CHICAGO WHITE SOX

#### January—Regular Phase (7)

1. *Jesse Baez, c, Cerritos (Calif.) JC.—(AA)
2. *John Reiter, rhp, St. Louis CC-Meramec.
3. *Mike Estes, rhp, Manatee (Fla.) JC.
4. *Robert Kocol, of, Brevard (Fla.) CC.
5. ***Andy McGaffigan, rhp, Palm Beach (Fla.) JC.—(1981-91)**
6. **Fred Howard, rhp, Miami-Dade CC South.—(1979)**

#### January—Secondary Phase (3)

1. **Leo Sutherland, of, Golden West (Calif.) JC.—(1980-81)**
2. **Rich Wortham, lhp, University of Texas.—(1978-83)**
3. *Dennis Sandoval, rhp, Fullerton (Calif.) CC.
4. *Mike Tulacz, lhp, Miami-Dade CC North.
5. *Michael Otto, rhp, Sacramento (Calif.) CC.
6. **Harry Chappas, ss, Miami-Dade CC North.—(1978-80)**
7. ***Mark Esser, lhp, Miami-Dade CC North.—(1979)**
8. *John Racanelli, rhp, University of Southern California.
9. *Robert Healey, rhp, St. Louis CC-Meramec.
10. *Karl Schroeder, lhp, University of Oklahoma.

#### June—Regular Phase (8)

1. **Steve Trout, lhp, Thornwood HS, South Holland, Ill.—(1978-89)**

DRAFT DROP *Son of Dizzy Trout, major leaguer (1939-57)*

2. **Mike Colbern, c, Arizona State University.—(1978-79)**
3. A.J. Hill, ss, Hollywood HS, Los Angeles.—(AAA)
4. *James Stehle, lhp, Wilkes (Pa.) College.—(AA)

DRAFT DROP *Returned to Wilkes College; re-drafted by Padres, June 1977/regular phase (5th round)*

5. *Jerry Stovall, rhp, Hoover HS, Fresno, Calif.—(AA)

DRAFT DROP *Attended Fresno (Calif.) CC; re-drafted by Blue Jays, January 1977/secondary phase (1st round)*

BERNARD TRONCALE

Tigers second-rounder Alan Trammell was the first 1976 high school pick to reach the majors

6. Clay Hicks, rhp, Edmond (Okla.) HS.
7. ***Willie McGee, of, Harry Ells HS, Richmond, Calif.—(1982-99)**
8. **Lorenzo Gray, ss, Lynwood (Calif.) HS.—(1982-83)**
9. Ken Hamman, ss, University of Detroit.
10. Jim Gabella, 2b, Deerfield Beach (Fla.) HS.
11. Rick Thoren, lhp, University of Northern Colorado.
12. *Jeff Wick, lhp, Verdugo Hills HS, Tujunga, Calif.
13. ***Pat Keedy, 1b, Gardendale HS, Birmingham, Ala.—(1985-89)**
14. *Stephen Collins, rhp, CC of San Francisco.
15. Paul Soth, rhp, Marini HS, Westminster, Calif.
16. John Martin, rhp, Big Bend (Ore.) CC.
17. *Mark Blumenschein, lhp, Tecumseh HS, New Carlisle, Ohio.
18. William Parmenter, ss, San Marin HS, Novato, Calif.
19. Keith Rokosz, cf, Troy HS, Fullerton, Calif.
20. Andy Pasillas, c, Cal State Fullerton.
21. ***Ed Olwine, lhp, Greenville (Ohio) HS.—(1986-88)**
22. *John Thetford, rhp, Bartlett HS, Memphis, Tenn.
23. *Glen Watson, of, Maine West HS, Des Plaines, Ill.
24. *Paul Stefan, rhp, Louisiana State University.
25. David Greenaway, 2b, Sterling HS, Magnolia, N.J.
26. *Eugene Zurowski, of, Martin (Tenn.) JC.

#### June—Secondary Phase (14)

1. ***Hubie Brooks, ss, Mesa (Ariz.) CC.—(1980-94)**

DRAFT DROP *First-round draft pick (3rd overall), Mets (1978)*

2. *Greg Stahl, ss, Los Angeles Harbor JC.
3. *Robert Kocol, of, Brevard (Fla.) CC.

## CINCINNATI REDS

#### January—Regular Phase (24)

1. *Roderick Patterson, rhp, Santa Monica (Calif.) JC.—(High A)
2. *Dwayne Mikemann, rhp, Rose State (Okla.) JC.
3. Thomas McClendon, ss, George Wallace (Ala.) CC.
4. *Gary Hill, lhp, Indian Hills (Iowa) CC.
5. Glenn Bonnell, ss, Milford (Ohio) HS.
6. Alfred Nichols, of, Bakersfield (Calif.) JC.
7. *David Froelich, rhp, Indian Hills (Iowa) CC.
8. *Jerry Veale, lhp, Jefferson State (Ala.) JC.

#### January—Secondary Phase (22)

1. **Duane Walker, lhp-of, San Jacinto (Texas) JC.—(1982-88)**
2. Clarence Syers, rhp, JC of the Canyons (Calif.).

#### June—Regular Phase (23)

1. Mark King, rhp, Owensboro (Ky.) Senior HS.—(High A)
2. **Paul Householder, of, North Haven (Conn.) HS.—(1980-87)**
3. Gregory Meyer, lhp, John F. Kennedy HS, Ballwin, Mo.—(AA)
4. *Mark Bingham, ss-1b, Hastings on the Hudson HS, Hastings, N.Y.—DNP

DRAFT DROP *Attended Harvard; never re-drafted*

5. Mark Breitenbach, rhp, Shaler HS, Glenshaw, Pa.—(Low A)
6. *Steve Renfroe, of, Berkmar HS, Lilburn, Ga.
7. **Bill Dawley, rhp, Griswold HS, Lisbon, Conn.—(1983-89)**
8. Michael Kopsky, 3b, Christian Brothers HS, St. Louis.
9. *Pete Rowe, c, Oregon State University.
10. Ronnie Stryker, rhp, Tate HS, Pensacola, Fla.
11. Alfred Welch, of, Seminole (Fla.) HS.
12. *Derek Tatsuno, lhp, Aiea (Hawaii) HS.
13. Bob Mayer, lhp, Florida State University.
14. Thomas Norko, c, Shelton (Conn.) HS.
15. Paul Herring, of, University of Mary Hardin-Baylor (Texas).
16. *Gary Pickert, lhp, Emporia State (Kan.) University.
17. Thomas Dimino, ss, Monroe (N.Y.) CC.
18. Randy Brinkley, lhp, Blanchester (Ohio) HS.
19. *Michael Barrett, rhp, Forest Park HS, Beaumont, Texas.
20. Kevin Jensen, of, Southern Utah State College.
21. **Eddie Milner, of, Central State (Ohio)**

University.—(1980-88)
22. *Paul Homrig, of, San Pedro (Calif.) HS.
23. Butch Harris, of-3b, Wingate (N.C.) College.
24. John Gosse, rhp, Lower Columbia (Wash.) JC.
25. Thomas Sohns, ss, University of Scranton (Pa.).
26. *Abner Johnson, rhp, Creighton University.
27. *James Jones, of, Milby HS, Houston.
28. Donald Carr, of, Texas Wesleyan College.
29. Robert Harold, rhp, University of Illinois.
30. *Douglas Smith, rhp, Southwestern Oklahoma State University.
**31. Jay Howell, rhp, University of Colorado.—(1980-94)**
32. *Dom Antonini, c, Glassboro State (N.J.) College.
**33. *Tim Laudner, c, Park Center HS, Minneapolis.—(1981-89)**
34. David Goodman, c, Coral Park HS, Miami.
**35. *Scotti Madison, ss, Tate HS, Pensacola, Fla.—(1985-89)**
**36. *Pat Sheridan, of, Wayne Memorial HS, Wayne, Mich.—(1981-91)**
37. *Greg Johnson, inf, Taft HS, Hamilton, Ohio.
38. *James Snyder, 1b, Stevenson HS, Livonia, Mich.

**June—Secondary Phase (3)**

**1. Bruce Berenyi, rhp, Northeast Missouri State University.—(1980-86)**
2. Rickey Lear, rhp, Valencia (Fla.) CC.
3. *Jeff Hardy, ss, Florida State University.
4. *Dwayne Mikemann, rhp, Rose State (Okla.) JC.

## CLEVELAND INDIANS

**January—Regular Phase (13)**

1. Julian Rodriguez, rhp, Palm Beach (Fla.) JC.—(High A)
2. *Jaime Lopez, 1b, Yavapai (Ariz.) JC.
3. *Reginald Pearman, 1b, Davidsonville, Md.
4. *Cleo DeWitt, c-of, South Florida JC.
5. *Steven Turco, ss, Broward (Fla.) CC.
6. *Kenneth Jarahek, of, Pensacola (Fla.) JC.
7. *Victor Herold, 1b, Broward (Fla.) CC.
8. *Jeffrey Muehling, lhp, Lincoln Land (Ill.) JC.
9. *Douglas Hogan, rhp, Indian Hills (Iowa) CC.
10. *Jerry Valentine, 3b, Westark (Ark.) CC.
11. *James Johnson, inf, Monroe (N.Y.) CC.

**January—Secondary Phase (17)**

**1. Garry Hancock, of, University of South Carolina.—(1978-84)**
2. George Mahan, rhp, Michigan State University.
3. *Thomas Eagan, 2b, Burien, Wash.
4. Dan Massari, 1b, University of Oklahoma.
5. *Bill Evers, c, Eckerd (Fla.) College.

**June—Regular Phase (14)**

1. Tim Glass, c, Springfield South HS, Springfield, Ohio.—(AA)
2. Sam Spence, rhp, Brandon HS, Mango, Fla.—(AA)
3. Craig Adams, of, Boone HS, Orlando, Fla.—(AA)
4. *Robert Scott, of, Gunn HS, Palo Alto, Calif.—DNP

DRAFT DROP *Attended Santa Clara; never re-drafted*

5. David Fowlkes, c, Decatur (Ga.) HS.—(Low A)
**6. *Bill Scherrer, lhp, Bishop O'Hara HS, Tonawanda, N.Y.—(1982-88)**

DRAFT DROP *First overall draft pick, January 1977/secondary phase, Reds*

7. *Gary Hardie, ss, Georgia Military Academy, Milledgeville, Ga.
8. *Steven Nielsen, rhp, Penn State University.
9. John Teising, lhp, St. Bernard Parish (La.) CC.
10. *Dennis Doss, rhp, American Christian (Mo.) College.
11. William Mitchell, lhp, East Texas Baptist University.
**12. *Joe Beckwith, rhp, Auburn University.—(1979-86)**
13. Kevin Jeansenne, of, University of Southwestern Louisiana.
14. John Buszka, of, SUNY-Buffalo.
15. Duane Wilson, 1b, University of Georgia.
16. Terry Tyson, ss, University of Toledo.
17. *Matthew Schaper, ss-of, Texas City (Texas) HS.
**18. Ron Hassey, c, University of Arizona.—(1978-91)**
19. Troy Wilder, lhp, Oak Harbor (Wash.) HS.
20. *Robert Johnson, ss, Binger (Okla.) HS.
21. Kenneth Preseren, ss, Baldwin-Wallace (Ohio) College.
22. *Randy Puckett, ss, Dinuba (Calif.) HS.
23. *Todd Heimer, lhp, Seton Hall University.
24. *Jim Haggerty, lhp, Grand Junction (Colo.) HS.
25. *Jack Lopez, ss, Sandalwood HS, Jacksonville, Fla.
26. Tony Toups, 2b-of, Louisiana State University.
27. *Joseph Keohane, rhp, Burlington (Mass.) HS.
28. *Gary Hinson, ss, Hillsborough (Fla.) JC.
29. *Morgan Lester, lhp, Sterling HS, Houston.
30. Michael Rowe, 1b, Palm Beach (Fla.) JC.
31. *Charles Gwynn, of, Poly HS, Long Beach, Calif.

DRAFT DROP *Brother of Tony Gwynn, major leaguer (1982-2001) • Brother of Chris Gwynn, major leaguer (1987-96)*

32. *Thomas Cook, lhp, Hamilton-Wenham HS, Hamilton, Mass.
33. *Michael Lynes, lhp, Rolling Hills HS, Rancho Palos Verdes, Calif.
34. *Timothy Newston, c, Pendleton (Ore.) HS.
35. Reggie Smith, rhp-3b, Judson (Ill.) College.

**June—Secondary Phase (8)**

1. Ray Gault, rhp, Manatee (Fla.) JC.—(AAA)
2. Nate Puryear, rhp, Stillman (Ala.) College.
3. *Victor Jacobsen, 3b, Big Bend (Wash.) CC.
4. *Bill Springman, 2b, Cerritos (Calif.) JC.
5. Paul Tasker, c-3b, Edison (Fla.) CC.
**6. *Dave Hostetler, 1b, Citrus (Calif.) JC.—(1981-88)**

## DETROIT TIGERS

**January—Regular Phase (1)**

**1. Steve Kemp, of, University of Southern California.—(1977-88)**
2. *Gerald Price, 2b, Diablo Valley (Calif.) JC.

DRAFT DROP *First overall draft pick, June 1976/secondary phase, Braves*

3. *Mike Yackee, rhp, Citrus (Calif.) JC.
4. *Larry Randel, ss, Fullerton (Calif.) JC.
5. *Brian McCaslin, rhp, Yavapai (Ariz.) JC.
6. Garry Grafton, rhp, Slippery Rock (Pa.) University.
7. Albert Wilson, of, Concordia (Mich.) College.

**January—Secondary Phase (23)**

1. *Ray Gault, rhp, Manatee (Fla.) JC.—(AAA)
**2. *Mike Walters, rhp, Chaffey (Calif.) JC.—(1983-84)**
**3. *Ron Roenicke, of-1b, Mount San Antonio (Calif.) JC.—(1981-88)**

DRAFT DROP *Brother of Gary Roenicke, major leaguer (1976-88) • Major league manager (2011-15)*

4. *Ben Hines, ss, Cypress (Calif.) JC.

**June—Regular Phase (2)**

**1. Pat Underwood, lhp, Kokomo (Ind.) HS.—(1979-83)**

DRAFT DROP *Brother of Tom Underwood, major leaguer (1974-84)*

**2. Alan Trammell, ss, Kearny HS, San Diego.—(1977-96)**

DRAFT DROP *First 1976 high school draft pick to reach majors (Sept. 9, 1977) • Major league manager (2003-05)*

3. Scott Johnson, c, Bonita HS, La Verne, Calif.—(High A)
**4. Dan Petry, rhp, El Dorado HS, Placentia, Calif.—(1979-91)**
**5. Jack Morris, rhp, Brigham Young University.—(1977-94)**
6. Lawrence Douglas, ss, Salem (N.H.) HS.
**7. *Ozzie Smith, ss, Cal Poly San Luis Obispo.—(1978-96)**

DRAFT DROP *Elected to Baseball Hall of Fame, 2001*

**8. Glenn Gulliver, ss, Eastern Michigan University.—(1982-83)**
9. *Charles Farmer, c, Hernando County HS, Brooksville, Fla.
10. Michael Burns, rhp, Alma (Mich.) College.
11. Robert Castleberry, of, Norte Del Rio HS, Sacramento, Calif.
12. Gary Wiencek, c, University of Southern California.
13. John Ward, lhp, Westmont (Calif.) College.
**14. *Rod Booker, ss, Pasadena (Calif.) HS.—(1987-91)**
15. John Northrup, of, Central Michigan University.
**16. Roger Weaver, rhp, SUNY-Oneonta.–(1980)**
17. Herbert Krul, c, University of Toledo.
18. John Sauer, rhp, St. John Vianney Seminary HS, Falls Church, Va.
19. Gordon Blakely, 3b, Chapman (Calif.) College.
20. Larry Corr, rhp, Belmont College.
21. *Robert Jenkins, of, Fairfax HS, Los Angeles.
22. *Ken Castles, lhp, Santa Theresa (Calif.) HS.
**23. Kip Young, rhp, Bowling Green State University.—(1978-79)**
24. Ken Bolek, of, University of Arizona.
25. Scott Bradley, lhp, Lincoln Park (Mich.) HS.
26. *Thomas Schultz, of, Union HS, Grand Rapids, Mich.
27. Gabriel Hernandez, lhp, Flushing HS, Bayside, N.Y.
28. *Brian Francisco, 2b, UC Riverside.
29. *Tracy Harris, rhp, Washington State University.

**June—Secondary Phase (2)**

**1. Dave Stegman, of, University of Arizona.—(1978-84)**
2. Stephen Vaughan, of, Los Angeles Valley JC.
3. Larry Randel, ss, Fullerton (Calif.) JC.

## HOUSTON ASTROS

**January—Regular Phase (2)**

**1. Gary Wilson, rhp, Southern Arkansas University.—(1979)**
2. *Thomas Offerman, lhp, Nassau (N.Y.) CC.
3. *Mark Post, lhp, Keystone (Pa.) JC.

**January—Secondary Phase (18)**

1. *Rodney Feight, rhp, Indian River (Fla.) CC.—DNP
2. *Randy Wallace, 3b-of, University of Tennessee.

**June—Regular Phase (1)**

**1. Floyd Bannister, lhp, Arizona State University.—(1977-92)**
2. Phil Klimas, 3b, St. Xavier (Ill.) College.—(AA)
**3. Reggie Baldwin, c, Grambling State University.—(1978-79)**
**4. Jim Pankovits, 3b, University of South Carolina.—(1984-90)**
5. *Joe Isaacs, rhp, Asher HS, Ada, Okla.—(AA)

DRAFT DROP *Attended Eastern Oklahoma State JC; re-drafted by Twins, January 1978/secondary phase (1st round, 1st pick).*

6. Douglas Jackson, rhp, Madison HS, Houston.
**7. Tom Wiedenbauer, of, Sahuaro HS, Tucson, Ariz.—(1979)**
**8. Dave Smith, rhp, San Diego State University.—(1980-92)**
9. George Ploucher, lhp, Middle Tennessee State University.
10. Jerry Williford, c, University of Houston.
**11. Gary Rajsich, 1b-of, Arizona State University.—(1982-85)**

DRAFT DROP *Scouting director, Orioles (2012-15)*

12. *Ronnie Estes, rhp, Boise State University.
13. Charles Gardner, ss, John Brown (Ark.) University.
14. Randolph Lamb, ss, Ouachita Baptist (Ark.) University.
15. *Ronald Lee, ss, Sharpstown HS, Houston.
16. *Jimmy Johnson, of, Sam Rayburn HS, Pasadena, Texas.
**17. Bert Roberge, rhp, University of Maine.—(1979-86)**
18. *Steven Lerner, lhp, Miami-Dade CC New World Center.
19. *Mike Villegas, rhp, East HS, Phoenix.
20. Jeff Ellison, of, San Diego State University.
21. Randy Rouse, c, John Brown (Ark.) University.
22. Dennis Miscik, lhp, Indiana (Pa.) University.
23. Thomas McCann, 1b, Washington Township HS, Turnersville, N.J.
24. *Douglas Welenc, rhp, Greenfield (Mass.) HS.
25. *Steven Mueller, c, Hondo (Texas) HS.

**June—Secondary Phase (7)**

1. *Robert Healey, rhp, St. Louis CC-Meramec.—(High A)
**2. *Ron Musselman, rhp, Clemson University.—(1982-85)**

## KANSAS CITY ROYALS

**January—Regular Phase (17)**

1. Stephen Beene, c, University of Central Arkansas.—(High A)
2. *Matt Mullins, ss-rhp, Los Angeles Harbor JC.
3. *Charles Maynard, rhp, JC of San Mateo (Calif.).

**January—Secondary Phase (5)**

**1. *Hubie Brooks, ss, Mesa (Ariz.) CC.—(1980-94)**

DRAFT DROP *First-round draft pick (3rd overall), Mets (1978)*

2. *Ron Wrobel, lhp, Yavapai (Ariz.) JC.
**3. Bill Paschall, rhp, University of North Carolina.—(1978-81)**
4. Ron Kainer, rhp, Houston.
5. *Alphonso Eiland, ss, Los Angeles Harbor JC.
6. *George Robins, of-rhp, Santa Monica (Calif.) JC.

**June—Regular Phase (18)**

1. Ben Grzybek, rhp, Hialeah (Fla.) HS.—(AA)
2. *Tim Brandenburg, lhp, Elizabethtown (Ky.) HS.—DNP

DRAFT DROP *Attended Kentucky; never re-drafted*

3. Rich Dubee, rhp, Bridgewater-Raynham HS, Bridgewater, Mass.—(AAA)
4. Thomas Close, c, Canton HS, Plymouth, Mich.—(Rookie)
5. Brad Simmons, lhp, Glendale HS, Springfield, Mo.—(High A)
**6. Jim Gaudet, c, Tulane University.—(1978-79)**
7. Darrell Vosejpka, 3b, Montgomery HS, Lonsdale, Minn.
8. Tim Riley, 3b, University of Nevada-Reno.
9. Timmy Gowen, lhp, Niles (Mich.) HS.
10. Philip Pulido, rhp, Tampa Catholic HS, Tampa.
11. Juan Rodriguez, of, Paterson (N.J.) HS.
12. John Krattli, 3b, University of Kansas.
13. *Theodore French, of, Waterloo (N.Y.) HS.
14. Raymond Prince, rhp, Altus (Okla.) HS.
**15. Ken Phelps, of, Arizona State University.—(1980-90)**
16. Paul Stevens, 2b, Lewis (Ill.) University.

DRAFT DROP *Baseball coach, Northwestern (1988-2015)*

17. Bob Lizarraga, rhp, UCLA.
18. Ed Cowan, rhp, UCLA.
19. *Clyde Simmons, ss, Western HS, Detroit.
20. Victor Mendez, ss, Yonkers (N.Y.) HS.
21. *Galen Cisco, 3b, St. Mary's HS, St. Mary, Ohio.

DRAFT DROP *Son of Galen Cisco, major leaguer (1961-69).*

22. *Gary Guisness, 3b-c, Corona del Mar (Calif.) HS.

**June—Secondary Phase (4)**

1. Frank McCann, ss, University of Delaware.—(AAA)
2. William Yarbrough, 3b, Manatee (Fla.) JC.
3. Marty Serrano, ss, San Jose (Calif.) CC.
4. *Javier Fierro, 3b, Cal State Los Angeles.

## LOS ANGELES DODGERS

**January—Regular Phase (20)**

1. *Michael Wetklow, of, Sacramento (Calif.) CC.—DNP
**2. Dave Patterson, rhp, Cerritos (Calif.) JC.—(1979)**
3. Paul Bain, rhp, El Camino (Calif.) JC.
**4. *Mookie Wilson, of, Spartanburg Methodist (S.C.) JC.—(1980-91)**

DRAFT DROP *Stepfather of Preston Wilson, first-round draft pick (1992); major leaguer (1998-2007)*

5. *Timothy DeWald, rhp, Cypress (Calif.) JC.
6. *Robert Weis, rhp, Sacramento (Calif.) CC.
7. *Mark Garber, rhp, Antelope Valley (Calif.) JC.
8. *Richard Barnhart, rhp, Green River (Wash.) CC.
9. *Rickey Lear, rhp, Valencia (Fla.) CC.
10. *Robert Benda, ss-2b, Palm Beach (Fla.) JC.
11. *Charles Young, rhp-3b, Los Angeles Pierce JC.

**January—Secondary Phase (12)**

1. Jack Lawson, rhp, Phoenix (Ariz.) JC.—(Short-season A)

2. Charles Dorgan, lhp, Green River (Wash.) CC.
3. *Larry Buckle, rhp, Long Beach (Calif.) CC.

**June—Regular Phase (19)**

**1. Mike Scioscia, c, Springfield HS, Morton, Pa.—(1980-92)**
DRAFT DROP *Major league manager (2000-15)*
2. Don Ruzek, ss, Lakewood (Calif.) HS.—(AA)
**3. Max Venable, of, Cordova HS, Rancho Cordova, Calif.—(1979-91)**
DRAFT DROP *Father of Will Venable, major leaguer (2008-15)*
4. Marty Kunkler, lhp, University of Oklahoma.–(AA)
**5. Ted Power, rhp, Kansas State University.—(1981-93)**
**6. Mike Howard, of-3b, Sacramento (Calif.) HS.—(1981-83)**
7. Kelly Snider, 1b, University of Oklahoma.
8. Robert Kownacki, ss, Fairfield University.
9. Charles Phillips, lhp, University of Southern California.
DRAFT DROP *Defensive back, National Football League (1975-79)*
10. Bill Swoope, c, Norfolk Catholic HS, Norfolk, Va.
11. William Martin, rhp, William Carey (Miss.) College.
12. Jimmy Giles, of, Alcorn State University.
DRAFT DROP *Tight end, National Football League (1977-89)*
13. Jim Peterson, rhp, Arizona State University.
14. *Doug Elliott, 2b, Fullerton (Calif.) HS.
**15. Keith MacWhorter, rhp, Bryant (R.I.) College.—(1980)**
**16. Jack Perconte, 2b, Murray State University.—(1980-86)**
17. Miguel Rodriguez, rhp, Adlai Stephenson HS, Bronx, N.Y.
18. Timothy Jones, c-of, Wooster (Ohio) HS.
19. Eric Schmidt, lhp, Mission Viejo (Calif.) HS.
20. Dan Henry, 3b, Loyola Marymount University.
21. Jeff Albert, rhp, C.W. Post (N.Y.) College.
22. Robert Amico, 1b-of, SUNY-Buffalo.
23. *Richard Martini, of, UC Davis.
24. Mickey Lashley, rhp, University of Oklahoma.
DRAFT DROP *Baseball coach, Texas-San Antonio (1997-2000)*
25. *Jose Martinez, ss, South San Francisco HS.
26. George Kaage, 1b, Kankakee (Ill.) CC.
27. Mark Kryka, rhp, Antigo (Wis.) HS.
28. *Steven Silagi, rhp, El Rancho HS, Pico Rivera, Calif.
29. *Mickey Martin, c, U.S. Grant HS, Oklahoma City, Okla.
30. Douglas Foster, of, Compton (Calif.) HS.
31. *John Holland, rhp, South Florence (S.C.) HS.
32. *Stephen Nelson, rhp, Wilson HS, Tacoma, Wash.
33. *Jeff Hunter, 3b, Millard HS, Omaha, Neb.
34. *Mark Wychopen, c, South Houston HS.
**35. *Scott Fletcher, ss, Wadsworth (Ohio) HS.—(1981-95)**
36. *Bruce Scheidegger, rhp, Chadwick (Ill.) HS.
37. Donald Brodell, of, University of Arkansas-Little Rock.
38. *James Riedel, rhp, SUNY-Buffalo.
39. *Gerald Snow, rhp, Madras (Ore.) HS.

**June—Secondary Phase (11)**

1. *Joe Ferri, of, Pasadena (Calif.) CC.—DNP
**2. *Mike Walters, rhp, Chaffey (Calif.) JC.—(1983-84)**

## MILWAUKEE BREWERS

**January—Regular Phase (3)**

1. David Globig, of, University of Minnesota.—(Low A)
2. *Victor Jacobsen, 3b, Big Bend (Wash.) CC.
3. *William LaRosa, rhp, Cuyahoga (Ohio) CC.

**January—Secondary Phase (19)**

1. Jason Passmore, of, Orlando, Fla.—(Low A)
2. Jon Dempsey, rhp, North Carolina State University.

**June—Regular Phase (4)**

**1. *Bill Bordley, lhp, Bishop Montgomery HS, Rolling Hills, Calif.—(1980)**
DRAFT DROP *Attended Southern California; re-drafted by Reds, January 1979/secondary phase (1st round)*

Dodgers first-rounder Mike Scioscia has spent 40 years in the game as a catcher and manager

2. Melvin Manning, ss, Hopewell (Va.) HS.—(AA)
3. *Scott Gardner, rhp, Monterey HS, Lubbock, Texas.—(AA)
DRAFT DROP *Attended Oklahoma; re-drafted by Orioles, June 1979/regular phase (28th round)*
4. Terry Shoebridge, c, Lyndhurst (N.J.) HS.–(AAA)
5. John Roesch, lhp, El Capitan HS, El Cajon, Calif.—(Low A)
6. Andrew Pascarella, 2b, University of Wisconsin.
7. Ronald Jacobs, c, University of Texas.
**8. Lary Sorensen, rhp, University of Michigan.—(1977-88)**
**9. George Frazier, rhp, University of Oklahoma.—(1978-87)**
10. *Steven Guengerich, of, Homestead HS, Cupertino, Calif.
11. Larry Montgomery, rhp, Sharpstown HS, Houston.
12. Garry Pyka, 2b, University of Texas.
**13. Gary Holle, 1b, Siena College.—(1979)**
14. James Quinn, rhp, New Caney HS, Porter, Texas.
15. Jeffrey Harryman, lhp, North HS, Riverside, Calif.
16. Richard Thurman, rhp, Springfield (Mich.) HS.
17. *Tim Peerenboom, 1b, Kimberly HS, Combined Locks, Wis.
18. Eric Restin, ss, St. John's University.
19. Gary Donovan, ss, Portland State University.
20. Chester Nelson, c, Nicholls HS, New Orleans.
21. *George Hill, c, Virginia Tech.
22. Garry Fritch, rhp, University of Wisconsin-Superior.
23. *William Henley, of, Arcadia HS, Temple City, Calif.

**June—Secondary Phase (6)**

**1. *Darrell Brown, ss, Cal State Los Angeles.—(1981-84)**
2. Thomas Offerman, lhp, Nassau (N.Y.) CC.

## MINNESOTA TWINS

**January—Regular Phase (9)**

**1. Bob Veselic, rhp, Mount San Antonio (Calif.) JC.—(1980-81)**
2. *Jim Leicht, rhp, Fullerton (Calif.) JC.
3. John Breaux, rhp, Mount San Antonio (Calif.) JC.
4. John Altman, rhp, Linn-Benton (Ore.) CC.
5. Eugene Montgomery, of, JC of San Mateo (Calif.).
**6. *Joe Charboneau, of, West Valley (Calif.) JC.—(1980-82)**
**7. Kevin Stanfield, lhp, San Bernardino Valley (Calif.) JC.—(1979)**
8. *Lloyd Ard, rhp, Chipola (Fla.) JC.

**January—Secondary Phase (1)**

**1. Pete Redfern, rhp, University of Southern California.—(1976-82)**
DRAFT DROP *First player from 1976 draft to reach majors (May 15, 1976).*
2. Steve Benson, ss, Arizona Western JC.
3. *Mike Arlotta, lhp, Miami-Dade CC North.
4. *Gary Bowers, rhp, Fullerton (Calif.) JC.
5. *Robert Dinges, of-1b, Foothill (Calif.) JC.
6. *Robert Knezerich, rhp, Council Bluffs, Iowa.

**June—Regular Phase (10)**

**1. *Jamie Allen, 3b-rhp, Davis HS, Yakima, Wash.—(1983)**
DRAFT DROP *Attended Arizona State; re-drafted by Mariners, June 1979/regular phase (2nd round)*
**2. Terry Felton, rhp, Baker (La.) HS.—(1979-82)**
**3. John Castino, 3b, Rollins (Fla.) College.—(1979-84)**
4. Warren Allen, ss, Richmond County HS, Hamlet, N.C.—(Low A)
5. *Tony Cameron, lhp, Pepperdine University.—(High A)
DRAFT DROP *Returned to Pepperdine; re-drafted by Mariners, June 1977/regular phase (6th round)*
6. Bill Harris, lhp, Santa Clara University.
7. Paul Cantanese, of, Cupertino HS, Sunnyvale, Calif.
8. Michael Gustave, of, Harford (Md.) CC.
9. *Greg Sporrer, ss, Troy-Fullerton HS, Yorba Linda, Calif.
10. *John Violette, c, St. Bernard HS, Playa Del Rey, Calif.
11. Steve Christian, ss, Piedmont Hills HS, San Jose, Calif.
12. *Ronald Moore, lhp, Troy HS, Yorba Linda, Calif.
13. *Glenn Wendt, ss, Temple (Texas) JC.
14. *Randy Ingle, ss-2b, East Rutherford HS, Forest City, N.C.
15. Steven Hypes, rhp, Milligan (Tenn.) College.
**16. Mark Funderburk, of, Louisburg (N.C.) JC.—(1981-85)**
17. Mark Tomasiak, rhp, Lafayette HS, Chesterfield, Mo.
18. *Joseph Sekora, rhp, Newton Falls (Ohio) HS.
19. John Jones, lhp, Baldwin HS, Milledgeville, Ga.
20. *Tim Byelland, ss, Millikan HS, Long Beach, Calif.
21. Bruce MacPherson, rhp, Cal Poly Pomona.
22. Tom McWilliams, lhp, Morningside (Iowa) College.
23. Wally McMakin, rhp, Louisiana State University.
24. *Preston Banks, 3b, Manual Arts HS, Los Angeles.
25. Donald Tryon, ss, Orange Coast (Calif.) JC.
26. *Jim Brooks, ss, El Rancho HS, Pico Rivera, Calif.
27. Gary Dobbs, lhp, Warren HS, Downey, Calif.
28. Daniel Spain, of, Orange Coast (Calif.) JC.
29. Eric Barstad, lhp, Salinas (Calif.) HS.
30. Bret Williams, rhp, Yucaipa (Calif.) HS.
31. *Michael Davis, ss, Rio Hondo (Calif.) JC.
32. *Joe Scherger, of, Billings (Mon.) HS.

**June—Secondary Phase (24)**

1. Greg Vogel, 2b, Penn State University.—(Low A)
2. *David Froelich, rhp, Indian Hills (Iowa) CC.

## MONTREAL EXPOS

**January—Regular Phase (10)**

1. *Steve Miller, rhp, Lower Columbia (Wash.) JC.—(High A)
2. *Scott Winston, lhp, Chipola (Fla.) JC.
3. Doug Simunic, c, St. Clair County (Mich.) CC.
4. *Michael Mann, p, St. Clair County (Mich.) CC.
**5. *Gary Weiss, 2b, Blinn (Texas) JC.–(1980-81)**
6. *Matthew Gaglione, of, Chipola (Fla.) JC.
7. *Ronnie Mears, 2b-ss, Contra Costa (Calif.) JC.
8. *Robert Volk, c, Cerritos (Calif.) JC.
9. *John Thiele, c, Pasadena (Calif.) CC.
10. Robert Watkins, rhp, Grossmont (Calif.) JC.
11. *Kevin Minter, rhp, Moorpark (Calif.) JC.

**January—Secondary Phase (4)**

1. LaMart Harris, of, Ranger (Texas) JC.—(AA)
2. Stephen Walsh, lhp, St. Louis University.
3. Kurt Boesch, rhp, Clackamas (Ore.) CC.
4. Daniel Newell, rhp, Ohio Dominican College.

**June—Regular Phase (9)**

**1. Bob James, rhp, Verdugo Hills HS, Sunland, Calif.—(1978-87)**
2. Dennis Sherow, rhp, Cal Poly Pomona.—(AAA)
**3. Dan Schatzeder, lhp-of, University of Denver.—(1977-91)**
**4. Bobby Pate, of, Arizona State University.—(1980-81)**
5. Carlton Roberts, lhp, Cabrillo HS, Lompoc, Calif.—(High A)
6. *Anthony Zahradnick, lhp, Arkport (N.Y.) HS.
7. Johnnie Walker, ss, Sacramento (Calif.) HS.
8. John Scoras, c, Montclair State (N.J.) College.
**9. Jack O'Connor, lhp, Yucca Valley (Calif.) HS.—(1981-87)**
10. Michael Tremba, 3b, Connellsville HS, Champion, Pa.
11. Michael Brooks, rhp, Jackson State University.
**12. *Nick Capra, 2b, Lincoln HS, Denver, Colo.—(1982-91)**
13. *Ed Irvine, of, Jordan HS, Long Beach, Calif.
14. Michael Sullivan, rhp, Elder HS, Cincinnati.
15. Clay Westlake, c-1b, Arizona State University.
16. *John Evans, 1b, St. Bernard HS, Los Angeles.
17. *Ray Bozich, of, St. Petersburg (Fla.) JC.
18. *James Gibson, lhp, Texas A&M University.
19. *Tom Chamberlain, rhp, Oregon State University.
20. *Andrew Walker, c, East St. Louis HS.
**21. David Palmer, rhp, Glen Falls (N.Y.) HS.—(1978-89)**

**June—Secondary Phase (17)**

1. Don Hanna, rhp, Arizona State University.–(AA)
2. *Jim Leicht, rhp, Fullerton (Calif.) JC.

## NEW YORK METS

**January—Regular Phase (14)**

1. *Dean Moranda, lhp, Fresno (Calif.) CC.—(High A)
2. ***Mickey Hatcher, of, Mesa (Ariz.) CC.—(1979-90)**
3. **Jody Davis, 1b-c, Middle Georgia JC.—(1981-90)**
4. *Edward Baker, c-3b, DeKalb (Ga.) JC.
5. *Kendall Driggers, rhp, Florida JC.
6. *Alvin Moore, of, South Georgia JC.
7. ***Greg A. Harris, rhp, Long Beach (Calif.) CC.—(1981-95)**
8. Fred Westfall, rhp, San Diego Mesa JC.
9. Theodore O'Neil, rhp, Rollins (Fla.) College.
10. Gary Corrado, lhp, Luzerne County (Pa.) CC.

**January—Secondary Phase (16)**

1. Steven Kesses, of, Duke University.—(High A)
2. *Greg Fisher, 3b, Diablo Valley (Calif.) JC.
3. *Michael Coppess, rhp, Chaffey (Calif.) JC.
4. **Kim Seaman, lhp, Mississippi Gulf Coast JC.—(1979-80)**

**June—Regular Phase (13)**

1. Tom Thurberg, of-rhp, South Weymouth (Mass.) HS.—(AAA)
2. **Mike Scott, rhp, Pepperdine University.—(1979-91)**
3. Curtis Baker, 3b, Fullerton (Calif.) HS.—(Low A)
4. Robert Pappageorgas, ss, Pacific Grove HS, Pebble Beach, Calif.—(Low A)
5. David Riehl, lhp, Deer Park (Texas) HS.—DNP
6. *Scott Brantley, of, Forest HS, Ocala, Fla.

**DRAFT DROP** *Linebacker, National Football League (1980-89)*

7. *Brian Hurse, rhp, Englewood HS, Jacksonville, Fla.
8. ***Barry Evans, ss-3b, West Georgia JC.—(1978-82)**
9. Curtis Fisher, 1b, Georgia Southern College.
10. Elmer Cardwell, 3b, Normandy HS, St. Louis.
11. **Neil Allen, rhp, Ward HS, Kansas City, Kan.—(1979-89)**
12. Robert Grote, rhp, Wright State University.
13. Donald Pearson, rhp, Delphi (Ind.) HS.
14. *Charles Clarke, of, Nicholls HS, New Orleans, La.
15. Charles Warren, of-3b, Brunswick (Ga.) JC.
16. David Owen, lhp, Lynchburg (Va.) College.
17. **Dave Von Ohlen, lhp, Flushing HS, College Point, N.Y.—(1983-87)**
18. *Willie Harmon, inf, Kosciusko (Miss.) HS.
19. *Anthony Guralas, ss-1b, Redwood HS, Larkspur, Calif.
20. *Billy Lott, c, Wayne County HS, Jesup, Ga.
21. *Martin Chargin, inf, Monte Vista HS, San Jose, Calif.
22. Robert Bryant, of, Methodist (N.C.) College.
23. *Marty Kain, rhp, La Quinta HS, Westminster, Calif.
24. *Rob Kauffman, inf, Nathan Hale HS, Tulsa, Okla.
25. Michael Mitchell, lhp, West Muskingum HS, Zanesville, Ohio.
26. *Michael Matlock, rhp-3b, Laytonville (Calif.) HS.
27. James Murphy, 3b-ss, Wittenberg (Ohio) University.
28. Tonus Thomas, of, Franklin, Ill.
29. *Mike Mitskavich, rhp, Central Catholic HS, DuBois, Pa.
30. Keith Shermeyer, inf, Dover (Pa.) HS.
31. Carman Coppol, Elizabethtown (Pa.) College.
32. *Terry Sutcliffe, rhp, Van Horn HS, Kansas City, Mo.

**DRAFT DROP** *Brother of Rick Sutcliffe, major leaguer (1976-94)*

**June—Secondary Phase (9)**

1. Richter Armer, of, DeAnza (Calif.) JC.—(Low A)
2. *Dennis Sandoval, rhp, Fullerton (Calif.) JC.
3. *Michael Coppess, rhp, Chaffey (Calif.) JC.

## NEW YORK YANKEES

**January—Regular Phase (15)**

1. ***John Fulgham, rhp, Yavapai (Ariz.) JC.—(1979-80)**
2. *Theodore Smith, of, Chabot (Calif.) JC.
3. Darnell Waters, ss, Chabot (Calif.) JC.
4. *Jay Elmore, rhp, Longview (Mo.) CC.

**January—Secondary Phase (11)**

1. *William Wilborn, of, Cosumnes River (Calif.) JC.—(High A)

**DRAFT DROP** *Brother of Ted Wilborn, fourth-round draft pick, Yankees, June 1976/regular phase*

2. *Frank McCann, ss, University of Delaware.

**June—Regular Phase (16)**

1. **Pat Tabler, of, McNicholas HS, Cincinnati.—(1981-92)**

**DRAFT DROP** *Brother of Harry Tabler, 21st-round draft pick, Yankees, June 1976/regular phase*

2. Calvin Riggar, lhp, Lennox (Calif.) HS.—(AA)
3. Johnny Crawford, of, Fremont HS, Los Angeles.—(High A)
4. **Ted Wilborn, of, McClatchy HS, Sacramento, Calif.—(1979-80)**

**DRAFT DROP** *Brother of William Wilborn, first-round draft pick, Yankees, January 1976/secondary phase*

5. *Bill Knudson, rhp, University HS, Spokane, Wash.—DNP

**DRAFT DROP** *Attended Gonzaga; never re-drafted*

6. *Dwight Harris, of, Blair HS, Pasadena, Calif.
7. Fred Atkins, rhp, Technical HS, Oakland, Calif.
8. Tim Lewis, lhp, University of South Carolina.
9. *Gordon Hahn, 2b, Santa Clara University.

**DRAFT DROP** *Brother of Don Hahn, major leaguer (1969-75)*

10. Mark Thiel, c, University of Missouri.
11. *Warren Hollier, rhp, Muir HS, Altadena, Calif.
12. *Pat Callahan, c, University of Miami.
13. Garry Smith, of, University of South Florida.
14. *Randy Whistler, c, Lakewood HS, Long Beach, Calif.
15. *Daniel Teel, c, Ridgefield Park (N.J.) HS.
16. Donald Fisk, rhp, University of Nevada-Reno.
17. *Frank Wren, of, Northeast HS, St. Petersburg, Fla.

**DRAFT DROP** *General manager, Orioles (1998-99); general manager, Braves (2007-14)*

18. Mark Softy, rhp, Princeton University.
19. *Paul Semall, rhp, Ohio State University.
20. *Joe Portale, c, St. Edward HS, North Olmsted, Ohio.
21. *Harry Tabler, c, Ohio State University.

**DRAFT DROP** *Brother of Pat Tabler, first-round draft pick, Yankees, June 1976/regular phase*

22. *Richard Clowson, lhp, Ohio State University.
23. Peter Eshelman, lhp, Williams (Mass.) College.
24. ***Chris Welsh, lhp, University of South Florida.—(1981-86)**
25. Don Hogestyn, 2b, University of South Florida.

**June—Secondary Phase (20)**

1. **Roger Slagle, rhp, University of Kansas.—(1979)**
2. *Michael Estes, rhp, Manatee (Fla.) JC.

## OAKLAND ATHLETICS

**January—Regular Phase (23)**

1. *Colin Danielsen, rhp, Pasadena (Calif.) CC.—DNP
2. Christian Jensen, 2b, Trenton State (N.J.) College.
3. Bart Braun, rhp, Solano (Calif.) CC.
4. *Robert Bohnet, 3b, Solano (Calif.) CC.
5. *Joe Ferri, of, Pasadena (Calif.) CC.
6. *Greg Fite, rhp, Laney (Calif.) JC.

**January—Secondary Phase (13)**

1. Tom Baxter, rhp, Hudson County (N.J.) JC.—(High A)
2. Donald Henley, of, Mercer County (N.J.) CC.
3. *Stephen Muccio, ss, Valencia (Fla.) CC.

**June—Regular Phase (24)**

1. *Mike Sullivan, rhp, Garfield HS, Woodbridge, Va.—(AA)

**DRAFT DROP** *Attended Clemson; re-drafted by Reds, June 1979/regular phase (1st round)*

2. *Brian Duffy, lhp-1b, Serra HS, Foster City, Calif.—(High A)

**DRAFT DROP** *Attended California; re-drafted by Indians, June 1979/regular phase (43rd round)*

3. Allan Minker, 1b, Glasgow HS, Newark, Del.—(AA)
4. **Rickey Henderson, of, Technical HS, Oakland, Calif.—(1979-2003)**

**DRAFT DROP** *Elected to Baseball Hall of Fame, 2009*

5. Dave Hornacek, of, Beaver Falls (Pa.) HS.—(Short-season A)
6. *Jeff Walsh, rhp, Archbishop Mitty HS, Santa Clara, Calif.
7. *Jerry Joyce, of, Monterey HS, Seaside, Calif.
8. Vernon Armstead, of, Jefferson HS, Los Angeles.
9. Dom Scala, 3b, St. John's University.
10. *Stan Levi, of, Locke HS, Los Angeles.
11. **Bobby Moore, rhp, John F. Kennedy HS, Sepulveda, Calif.—(1985)**
12. Jim Bennett, of-1b, Edison Street HS, Stockton, Calif.
13. Bryan Meyl, rhp, SUNY-Brockport.
14. Timothy Spaulding, rhp, Montrose (Mich.) HS.
15. *Dale Crummie, c, Locke HS, Los Angeles.
16. Donald Schubert, rhp, Fox Chapel HS, Sharpsburg, Pa.
17. *Mike Myerchin, lhp, Mira Costa HS, Manhattan Beach, Calif.
18. Thomas Wright, c, Belmont College.
19. Kenny McKinney, 2b, Memphis State University.
20. John Kniss, 2b, San Joaquin Delta (Calif.) JC.
21. *Eric Prevost, lhp, San Fernando (Calif.) HS.
22. *Tom Beyers, 1b, Harbor HS, Santa Cruz, Calif.
23. *Jarvis Redwine, of, Inglewood (Calif.) HS.

**DRAFT DROP** *Running back, National Football League (1981-83)*

24. Richard Dziemiela, 3b-ss, Elmhurst (Ill.) College.
25. Michael Nipert, c, Hazen HS, Renton, Wash.
26. *Kevin Darst, 2b, Vallejo (Calif.) HS.
27. Michael Billington, 2b, Forest Park (Mo.) JC.
28. Ron McNeely, of, Memphis State University.
29. *Charles Love, of, Banning HS, Long Beach, Calif.
30. *Philip Tyson, lhp, Centennial HS, Compton, Calif.
31. *John Hanley, c, Grant HS, Van Nuys, Calif.
32. *Elijah Risper, of, Crenshaw HS, Los Angeles.
33. *Michael Hunter, lhp, Vintage HS, Napa, Calif.
34. Brian Bullas, of-2b, University of San Diego.

**June—Secondary Phase (18)**

1. **Ernie Camacho, rhp, Hartnell (Calif.) CC.—(1980-90)**
2. Theodore Smith, of, Chabot (Calif.) JC.
3. ***Bob Stoddard, rhp, Gavilan (Calif.) JC.—(1981-87)**
4. Clyde Patterson, rhp, Santa Monica (Calif.) JC.
5. ***Mike Chris, 1b, Los Angeles Pierce JC.—(1979-83)**

## PHILADELPHIA PHILLIES

**January—Regular Phase (18)**

1. ***Jack Lazorko, rhp, Miami-Dade CC South.—(1984-88)**
2. **Derek Botelho, rhp, Miami-Dade CC South.—(1982-85)**
3. Ricky Burdette, lhp, Chipola (Fla.) JC.
4. *Robert Casanova, 2b, Grossmont (Calif.) JC.
5. **Bob Walk, rhp, JC of the Canyons (Calif.).—(1980-93)**
6. *Tony Dorsey, of-2b, Ranger (Texas) JC.
7. *Michael Glenn, lhp, Ranger (Texas) JC.
8. *Thomas Popovich, 2b-ss, Battle Creek, Mich.
9. *Frank Horak, rhp, Pasadena (Calif.) CC.
10. *Mark Taylor, rhp, St. John's River (Fla.) CC.
11. Erik Nelson, of, Diablo Valley (Calif.) JC.
12. ***Jeff Lahti, rhp, Treasure Valley (Ore.) CC.—(1982-86)**

**January—Secondary Phase (20)**

1. Glenn Ballard, c, Valencia (Fla.) CC.—(AA)
2. *Steve Powers, rhp, University of Arizona.
3. Harvin Hammock, ss, Miami-Dade CC North.

**June—Regular Phase (17)**

1. Jeff Kraus, ss, Colerain HS, Cincinnati.—(AA)
2. Eddie Williams, c, Northwestern HS, Detroit.—(Short-season A)
3. Richard Whaley, lhp, Jacksonville (N.C.) HS.—(Low A)
4. Randy Curtis, ss, Pine Bluff (Ark.) HS.—(Short-season A)
5. **Len Matuszek, of, University of Toledo.—(1981-87)**
6. **Ozzie Virgil, c, Moon Valley HS, Glendale, Ariz.—(1980-90)**

**DRAFT DROP** *Son of Ozzie Virgil, major leaguer (1956-69)*

7. Wallace Nunn, rhp, Holland Hall HS, Tulsa, Okla.
8. Michael Kruzelock, rhp, Venice HS, Mar Vista, Calif.
9. *Duane Evans, 1b, Yuma (Ariz.) HS.
10. William Buchan, 3b, South Weymouth (Mass.) HS.
11. Randy Black, of, Guilford (N.C.) College.
12. Lee Wilson, rhp, Seaside (Ore.) HS.
13. Henry Mack, rhp, George Rogers Clark HS, Winchester, Ky.
14. Brian Watts, rhp, Caseville (Mich.) HS.
15. Brent Adams, rhp, Sonora HS, Jamestown, Calif.
16. Charles Davis, rhp, Richmond County HS, Rockingham, N.C.
17. *Eugene Norman, rhp, UC Irvine.
18. Frank Lucy, c, Arizona State University.
19. Elijah Bonaparte, of, Kennedy HS, Paterson, N.J.
20. *Steven Safranski, of, Putman HS, Mark, Ill.
21. Louis Packer, of, Marshall University.
22. Stephen Hagen, lhp, Elk Grove (Calif.) HS.
23. Thomas Brunswick, ss, Coldwater (Ohio) HS.
24. *George Bertstrom, c, Faulkner State (Ala.) JC.
25. Shawn Kuhn, rhp, Morro Bay HS, Baywood Park, Calif.
26. *John Lohse, 3b, Hamilton City HS, Glenn, Calif.
27. *Stephen Brown, rhp, Morris Harvey HS, Charleston, W.Va.
28. *Keith Walker, lhp, Arlington (Texas) HS.

**June—Secondary Phase (13)**

1. ***Jack Lazorko, rhp-3b, Miami-Dade CC South.—(1984-88)**
2. **Joe Charboneau, of, West Valley (Calif.) JC.—(1980-82)**
3. **Bob Walk, rhp, JC of the Canyons (Calif.).—(1980-93)**
4. *Gary Bowers, rhp, Fullerton (Calif.) JC.

## PITTSBURGH PIRATES

**January—Regular Phase (22)**

1. Michael Imhoff, of, Polk (Fla.) CC.—(Rookie)
2. *Joe Ward, of, Manatee (Fla.) JC.
3. *Ken Lelek, rhp, Monroe (N.Y.) CC.
4. *Hillary Nelson, lhp, Chipola (Fla.) JC.
5. *Chris Keyes, c, Big Bend (Wash.) CC.
6. (void) *John Duda, rhp, Yakima Valley (Wash.) JC.

**January—Secondary Phase (6)**

1. **Larry Littleton, of, University of Georgia.—(1981)**
2. *Jerry Schmidt, rhp, Lewis-Clark State (Idaho) College.
3. *Tim Huff, rhp, Gardner-Webb College.
4. *Phillip Pundt, rhp, Miami-Dade CC North.
5. *Richard Hand, c, Brown University.
6. *Gerald Green, rhp, Lower Columbia (Wash.) JC.
7. *Albert Kissner, rhp, University of New Haven.

**June—Regular Phase (21)**

1. Jim Parke, rhp, Henry Ford II HS, Sterling Heights, Mich.—(High A)
2. **Dorian Boyland, of, University of Wisconsin-Oshkosh.—(1978-81)**
3. ***Mike Madden, lhp, Palmer HS, Colorado Springs, Colo.—(1983-86)**

**DRAFT DROP** *Attended Northern Colorado; never re-drafted*

4. George Goodrich, of, Lincoln HS, Wisconsin Rapids, Wis.—(Low A)
5. James Smith, rhp, University HS, Waco, Texas.—(AAA)
6. Charles Rouse, 2b, Fulton HS, Knoxville, Tenn.
7. ***Don Crow, c, Davis HS, Yakima, Wash.—(1982)**
8. Robert Rock, rhp, Mount Vernon HS, Alexandria, Va.
9. Brian Schwerman, rhp, Libertyville (Ill.) HS.
10. *Don Davisson, of, Rock Hill HS, Kitts Hill, Ohio.
11. Pat Shackelford, rhp, Buchholz HS, Gainesville, Fla.
12. Allen Leech, ss, West Chester (Pa.) University.
13. James Rogers, rhp, Cleveland State (Tenn.) CC.
14. Bob Stadnika, rhp, Central Michigan University.

15. Jeff Greenhalgh, 1b, Valdosta State (Ga.) College.
16. Marvin Evans, 1b, Seminole (Fla.) CC.
**17. Rick Honeycutt, 1b-lhp, University of Tennessee.—(1977-97)**
18. *David Banes, ss, Buchholz HS, Gainesville, Fla.
19. Dick Walterhouse, 2b, University of Michigan.
20. *Jeff Mincey, c, Liberty University.
21. Eric Peterson, lhp, Jacksonville University.
22. George Renfroe, c, Lompoc (Calif.) HS.
23. Terry Burkholder, 2b, West Chester (Pa.) University.
**24. Bob Long, rhp-of, Shorter (Ga.) College.—(1981-85)**
25. Lenny Spicer, of, Walton-Verona HS, Verona, Ky.
26. Gary Fulton, of, Murphy HS, Atlanta.
27. *Ray Dahlman, c-1b, Cabrillo HS, Lompoc, Calif.
28. Richie Howard, 3b, Auburn University.
29. Thomas Burke, of-inf, Northwestern University.
30. *Wade Manning, of, Ohio State University.
31. Laurence Kienzle, lhp, Clarion (Pa.) University.
32. Gene Gentile, of, Allderdice HS, Pittsburgh.
33. Mark Howard, rhp, University of South Alabama.
34. *Scott Kuvinka, 3b-c, Hopewell HS, Aliquippa, Pa.
35. *Ledell Lowe, 1b, University of South Alabama.
36. Richard Baker, c, University of Scranton (Pa.).

**June—Secondary Phase (19)**

1. Steve Powers, rhp, University of Arizona.—(High A)
2. *Mike Zouras, 3b, Long Beach State University.
3. *Thomas Eagan, 3b, Green River (Wash.) CC.

## ST. LOUIS CARDINALS

**January—Regular Phase (16)**

1. Fulvio Bertolotti, c, Merced (Calif.) JC.—(AA)
**2. *John Butcher, rhp, Yavapai (Ariz.) JC.—(1980-86)**
3. *James Harskamp, inf, Merced (Calif.) JC.
4. William Schopp, rhp, Moorpark (Calif.) JC.
5. *John Zalopany, rhp, Grossmont (Calif.) JC.
6. *Randy Toogood, c, Glendale (Ariz.) CC.
7. Roger Nolan, of-1b, North Hills HS, Pittsburgh.
8. *David Mobley, ss, Chipola (Fla.) JC.
9. Ronald Swanson, of, Contra Costa (Calif.) JC.
10. *Mark Hoffman, lhp, Harvard University.

**January—Secondary Phase (14)**

1. *Michael Bungarz, lhp, Chabot (Calif.) JC.—(High A)
2. *Gary Skow, 1b, Yavapai (Ariz.) JC.
**3. Dan O'Brien, rhp, Florida State University.—(1978-79)**
4. *James Kopatz, c, University of Illinois.

**June—Regular Phase (15)**

**1. Leon Durham, 1b-lhp, Woodward HS, Cincinnati.—(1980-89)**
2. Walt Pierce, 3b, Wilcox HS, Santa Clara, Calif.—(AA)
3. Jere Schuler, lhp, Lampeter-Strasburg HS, Lancaster, Pa.—(Low A)
4. Randy Thomas, ss, Lynchburg (Va.) College.—(AAA)
5. Paul Keck, of, San Mateo (Calif.) HS.—(Rookie)
6. *Larry Kuhn, rhp, North Torrance (Calif.) HS.
7. *Bryan Hardy, lhp, Bingham HS, West Jordan, Calif.
8. Denny Martindale, 2b-rhp, Cal Poly San Luis Obispo.
9. Daniel Winslow, c, Buena HS, Sierra Vista, Ariz.
10. Billy Meza, rhp, San Gabriel HS, San Marino, Calif.
11. *Stan Williams Jr., of, Lakewood (Calif.) HS.

DRAFT DROP *Son of Stan Williams, major leaguer (1958-72)*

**12. Gene Roof, ss, St. Mary HS, Paducah, Ky.—(1981-83)**

DRAFT DROP *Brother of Phil Roof, major leaguer (1961-77)*

13. *David Harrigan, ss, Altus (Okla.) HS.
14. John Fedorko, rhp, Bethel (Conn.) HS.
15. *Billy Minor, of-rhp, New Chaney (Texas) HS.
16. Jeff Toothman, 1b-of, Edgewood HS, West Covina, Calif.
17. Frank Marsalan, c, Greensburg Catholic HS, Apollo, Pa.
18. *Keith Gradwohl, rhp, Yakima Valley (Wash.) JC.
19. Kenneth Given, of, Morris Harvey (Ga.) College.
20. Bill Simpson, 3b, University of Arizona.
21. Ray Williams, rhp, Thousand Oaks (Calif.) HS.
**22. Ray Searage, lhp, West Liberty State (W.Va.) College.—(1981-90)**
23. *Greg Moyer, rhp, La Mirada (Calif.) HS.
24. Mike Calise, 3b, Mesa (Ariz.) CC.
25. *Tony Hudson, rhp, San Bernardino (Calif.) HS.
26. Terry Jacob, rhp, Arizona State University.
27. *Steve Schefsky, rhp, Hillsdale HS, San Mateo, Calif.
28. Mark Bumstead, inf, Cal State Northridge.
29. Frank Hunsaker, c, Southern Illinois University.
**30. John Littlefield, rhp, Azusa Pacific (Calif.) University.—(1980-81)**
31. *Russell McDonald, rhp, Monte Vista HS, San Jose, Calif.
32. *Garry Lewis, of-rhp, Dixon (Mo.) HS.
33. *Larry Navilhon, rhp, Crestmoor HS, San Bruno, Calif.
34. David Benoit, ss, Assumption (Mass.) College.

**June—Secondary Phase (15)**

**1. John Fulgham, rhp, Yavapai (Ariz.) JC.—(1979-80)**
**2. *Charlie Lea, rhp, Shelby State (Tenn.) CC.—(1980-88)**
3. *Steven Winfield, rhp, Panola (Texas) JC.

## SAN DIEGO PADRES

**January—Regular Phase (6)**

1. Randal Miller, c, University of New Orleans.—(AA)
2. *Bill Springman, 2b, Cerritos (Calif.) JC.
3. *Stephen Conner, c, Volunteer State (Tenn.) CC.
4. *Milton Smith, 3b, Southwestern (Calif.) JC.

**January—Secondary Phase (8)**

**1. Bob Shirley, lhp, University of Oklahoma.—(1977-87)**
**2. *Dan Boone, lhp, Cal State Fullerton.—(1981-90)**
3. *Stanley Cannon, of-1b, Pensacola (Fla.) JC.
**4. *Roger Slagle, rhp, University of Kansas.—(1979)**

**June—Regular Phase (5)**

**1. Bob Owchinko, lhp, Eastern Michigan University.—(1976-86)**
**2. Steve Mura, rhp, Tulane University.—(1978-85)**
3. Tod Olson, ss, Atwater (Calif.) HS.—(High A)
4. Paul O'Neill, 3b, Texas Wesleyan College.—(AAA)
**5. Jim Beswick, of, East Allegheny HS, North Versailles, Pa.—(1978)**
6. Mark Spatz, ss, Wilson HS, Hacienda Heights, Calif.
7. Daniel Keen, lhp, Coral Park HS, Miami.
8. *Pat Blamey, rhp, Buchser HS, Santa Clara, Calif.
**9. Craig Stimac, c, University of Denver.—(1980-81)**
10. *Mark Daly, lhp, Florida Southern College.
**11. Tom Tellmann, rhp, Grand Canyon College.—(1979-85)**
12. Ronnie Barnett, of, University of Texas-Arlington.
**13. Mark Lee, rhp, Pepperdine University.—(1978-81)**
14. Earl Battey Jr., 3b, UCLA.

DRAFT DROP *Son of Earl Battey, major leaguer (1955-67)*

**15. Broderick Perkins, 1b, St. Mary's (Calif.) College.—(1978-84)**
16. *Tim Muser, ss, Clairemont HS, San Diego.
17. William Hallstrom, ss, Grand Canyon HS, Scottsdale, Ariz.
18. *Steve Glaum, rhp, UC Riverside.
**19. Gary Lucas, lhp, Chapman College.—(1980-87)**
20. Mike Bullock, rhp, St. Mary's (Calif.) College.
21. Dane Ilertson, 1b, Point Loma Nazarene (Calif.) College.
22. *Larry Kowalishen, rhp, University of California.
23. Bobby Dupree, rhp, Grambling State University.
24. Steve Smith, ss, Pepperdine University.
25. *Johnny Jones, of, Lampasas (Calif.) HS.
26. *Robert Denton, of, La Jolla (Calif.) HS.

**June—Secondary Phase (5)**

1. William Wilborn, of, Cosumnes River (Calif.) JC.—(High A)

DRAFT DROP *Brother of Ted Wilborn, fourth-round draft pick, Yankees, June 1976/regular phase*

2. Jerry Schmidt, rhp, Lewis-Clark State (Idaho) College.

## SAN FRANCISCO GIANTS

**January—Regular Phase (12)**

1. Lozando Washington, of, Los Angeles Harbor JC.—(Low A)
2. John Harper, lhp, Los Angeles Pierce JC.
3. Jeff Shourds, of, Garden Grove, Calif.
**4. *Dave Hostetler, 1b, Citrus (Calif.) JC.—(1981-88)**
5. *Jim Wilson, 3b, Cerritos (Calif.) JC.
6. Stephen McKown, rhp, Hutchinson (Kan.) CC.
7. *Steve Huff, rhp, Phoenix (Ariz.) JC.
8. *Eric Mustad, rhp, Citrus (Calif.) JC.
9. *Robert Ruth, rhp, Centralia (Wash.) JC.
10. *Robert Turner, rhp, Treasure Valley (Ore.) CC.

**January—Secondary Phase (2)**

**1. Dennis Littlejohn, c, University of Southern California.—(1978-80)**
2. *Roderick Ingram, of-c, Linfield (Ore.) College.
3. *Daniel Hartwig, rhp, Antelope Valley (Calif.) JC.
4. *Richard Holloway, rhp, Gulf Coast (Fla.) CC.
5. William Krampe, rhp, Pittsburgh.
6. *William Eve, 1b, Miami-Dade CC North.
7. *Robert Cramer, rhp, Columbia Basin (Wash.) CC.
8. *Greg Vogel, 2b, Penn State University.

**June—Regular Phase (11)**

1. Mark Kuecker, ss, Brenham (Texas) HS.—(AAA)
2. *Tom Hawk, rhp, Fairmont West HS, Kettering, Ohio.—(High A)

DRAFT DROP *Attended Arizona State; re-drafted by Astros, June 1980/regular phase (5th round)*

3. John Sylvester, of, University of Tampa.—(High A)
4. *Kevin Rostenkowski, lhp, Perry Meridian HS, Indianapolis.—DNP

DRAFT DROP *Attended Miami (Ohio); never re-drafted*

5. Jeffrey O'Donnell, c, North Hollywood (Calif.) HS.—(Rookie)
6. *John Fenwick, ss, Anoka (Minn.) HS.
7. Richard Farrell, c, St. Xavier (Ill.) College.
8. *Dean Gottler, c, Tates Creek HS, Lexington, Ky.
**9. *Renie Martin, rhp, University of Richmond.—(1979-84)**
10. *Jerome Ahlert, ss, Aiken HS, Cincinnati.
11. Danny Held, of, JC of the Desert (Calif.).
12. Mike Wardlow, of, Southern California Christian College.
13. *Raymond Mass, rhp, Bellevue (Wash.) CC.
14. Bill Tullish, of, North Florida University.
15. Steve Stumpff, 1b, University of Iowa.
16. Ray Cosio, rhp, Miami Senior HS.
17. *Frank Ferroni, lhp, Redwood HS, Mill Valley, Calif.

DRAFT DROP *First overall draft pick, June 1977/secondary phase, Twins*

18. Mike Rex, ss, Linfield (Ore.) College.
19. David Schwartz, of, Shaker Heights (Ohio) HS.
20. *Johnny Hamilton, p, Navajo HS, Altus, Okla.
21. *Robert Pettit, inf, Chandler (Ariz.) HS.
22. *Jeff Ahearn, lhp, St. Genevieve HS, Reseda, Calif.
**23. *Mike Couchee, rhp, Los Gatos (Calif.) HS.—(1983)**
24. Glenn Walker, of, Victor Valley (Calif.) CC.
25. Wayne Pechek, of, University of Oklahoma.
**26. Jeff Stember, rhp, Westfield (N.J.) HS.—(1980)**
27. *David Meyer, 2b, Mira Costa (Calif.) JC.
**28. *Steve Macko, 3b, Baylor University.—(1979-80)**
29. *George Hawkins, of, Shorter (Ga.) College.
30. *Michael Stover, rhp, JC of Southern Idaho.
31. Mike Glinatsis, rhp, Youngstown State University.
32. *Robert Jester, rhp, Trenton State (N.J.) College.
33. *Samuel Dittoe, rhp, Sheridan HS, Somerset, Ohio.
34. *Mike Bates, rhp, Apollo HS, Phoenix.
35. *Robert Everling, rhp, Marion (Ind.) HS.
36. *Steve Day, ss, University of Texas.
37. *Leslie Ream, 2b, Ohio University.
38. James Pryor, c, Cal Poly Pomona.
39. Thomas Boutin, of, Eastern Michigan University.
40. *Sammy Bickham, rhp, Plano HS, Richardson, Texas.

**June—Secondary Phase (23)**

1. *Jim Wilson, 3b, Cerritos (Calif.) JC.—(AAA)
2. Dan Hartwig, rhp, Antelope Valley (Calif.) JC.
3. *Robert Ruth, rhp, Centralia (Wash.) JC.

## TEXAS RANGERS

**January—Regular Phase (11)**

1. *Jerome Hojnacki, 1b, Northwestern University.—DNP
2. *Paul Givens, lhp, San Jose (Calif.) CC.
3. John Phenix, of, Reno, Nevada.

**January—Secondary Phase (21)**

**1. Paul Mirabella, lhp, Montclair State (N.J.) College.—(1978-90)**
2. *Richard Comeau, rhp, Manatee (Fla.) JC.
3. Len Glowzenski, rhp, Seton Hall University.
4. *Jim Watkins, of, Valencia (Fla.) CC.

DRAFT DROP *First overall draft pick, January 1978/secondary phase, Braves*

**June—Regular Phase (12)**

1. Billy Simpson, of, Lakewood (Calif.) HS.—(High A)
2. Steve Finch, rhp, Cordova HS, Rancho Cordova, Calif.—(AAA)
**3. Mike Griffin, rhp, Woodland (Calif.) HS.—(1979-89)**
**4. Brian Allard, rhp, Henry Senachwine HS, Henry, Ill.—(1979-81)**
5. *Paul Rudiman, rhp, Duval HS, Lanham, Md.—(Low A)

DRAFT DROP *No school; re-drafted by Pirates, January 1977/secondary phase (1st round)*

6. David Peterson, c, Wilson HS, Portland, Ore.
7. Ted Davis, rhp, Fairmont Heights HS, Cheverly, Maine.
8. Kerry Keenan, rhp, Slippery Rock (Pa.) University.
9. Alphonso Lewis, of-c, Pensacola (Fla.) HS.
**10. Billy Sample, 3b-of, James Madison University.—(1978-86)**
11. Peter Zilonis, ss, Rindge Tech HS, Cambridge, Mass.
**12. *Andre Robertson, ss, West Orange (Texas) HS.—(1981-85)**
13. *Michael Guman, lhp, Bethlehem Catholic HS, Bethlehem, Pa.
14. James Capowski, ss, Roosevelt HS, Yonkers, N.Y.
15. *Greg Eason, lhp, Escambia HS, Pensacola, Fla.
**16. *Brian Snyder, lhp, Chantilly (Va.) HS.—(1985-89)**

DRAFT DROP *Father of Brandon Snyder, first-round draft pick, Orioles (2005); major leaguer (2010-13)*

17. Glenn Williams, of, San Jose State University.
18. *Richard Hereth, c, Colerain HS, Cincinnati.
19. Mike Jaccar, 3b, Southern Methodist University.
20. Doug Duncan, c, University of Texas.
21. Mike Williamson, rhp, Stanford University.
22. Wayne Wilkerson, 3b-of, American University.
23. *Gordon Hawkins, rhp, Surrattsville HS, Clinton, Md.
24. *Monte McAbee, of, Medford (Ore.) HS.
25. *Vincent Merolla, rhp, James Madison HS, Brooklyn, N.Y.
26. (void) *Timothy Bjelland, ss, Millikan HS, Long Beach, Calif.
27. *Paul Adams, 1b, Virginia Tech.
28. *Tim Knight, of, Daytona Mainland HS, Holly Hill, Fla.

**June—Secondary Phase (12)**

1. Greg Jemison, of, Seton Hall University.—(AA)

# 1977

# Maverick Veeck pulls surprise with Baines

The Chicago White Sox had the No. 1 selection in the 1977 draft, and pitcher Bill Gullickson was supposed to be their guy. He was a hometown boy, a hard-throwing righthander from Joliet, Ill. He was rated No. 1 in the country by the Major League Scouting Bureau.

But White Sox owner Bill Veeck wasn't known as one of the game's most colorful, unpredictable and shrewdest characters for nothing. It surprised few that he had something up his sleeve.

Sure enough, Veeck crossed up everyone by going for a player, first baseman Harold Baines, that he began scouting personally when Baines wasn't even a teenager.

"Our choice was universal," Veeck said. "We scouted him as thoroughly as we scouted anybody, even Gullickson and others. Whenever our scouts looked at Baines, the first line in the report was, 'He has one of the greatest natural swings we've ever seen.' He's an all-around athlete.

"I saw him play in Little League, and he impressed me even then. I've been watching him for six years."

Prior to buying the White Sox franchise in 1976, Veeck lived in Easton, on Maryland's Eastern Shore. Less than 10 miles away, in St. Michaels, lived Baines, who began making a name for himself in the area as a 12-year-old. Intrigued, Veeck often went over to watch him play.

By the time Baines was a senior at St. Michaels High, he hit .532 and was rated the fifth-best player in the country by the Scouting Bureau. Though he hit only two homers in 14 games that spring, most scouts agreed he was the best hitting prospect in the 1977 draft.

"Baines hits a baseball farther than any high schooler I've ever seen except Dave Nicholson, and, of course, a gorilla couldn't hit a ball as far as Nicholson did," White Sox super-scout Paul Richards said. "He reminds me a bit of (former Cubs star) Billy Williams."

Veeck was so determined to take Baines that he and White Sox executive Roland Hemond went to St. Michaels the night before the draft and signed him personally. They weren't taking any chance that the organization might fall victim again to the same public-relations snafu that occurred six years earlier, when the White Sox took catcher Danny Goodwin with the top pick and failed to sign him.

At a time when several White Sox regulars were unsigned and looking to free agency, the cash-strapped Veeck engineered a deal for Baines that included a signing bonus of $32,500—easily the lowest bonus ever paid a No. 1 pick, and the lowest paid to a player in the top half of the first round in 1977.

Many in the industry speculated that the White Sox simply settled for the best player they could afford to sign, and even Gullickson expressed surprise that he wasn't snapped up with the No. 1 pick.

STAR-DEMOCRAT

**Industry observers regarded Harold Baines as a budget pick for the White Sox, but owner Bill Veeck had personally scouted Baines since he was 12, and his major league career lived up to the No. 1 selection**

"I never even heard of Baines," said Gullickson, who was picked second by the Montreal Expos. "I was surprised, because everybody kept saying the White Sox would take me or (Terry) Kennedy. And I kept hearing, 'they need pitching,' 'they need pitching.' I guess they didn't."

For weeks, scouts had singled out Gullickson as the top prospect in the nation. He was clocked at 96 mph and went unbeaten his senior year at Joliet Catholic High, compiling a 12-0, 0.48 record with 188 strikeouts in 87 innings.

"I sort of thought the White Sox would draft me, or maybe Milwaukee," he said. "I was surprised to hear from Montreal. They never talked to me until the morning of the draft."

Gullickson received a $75,000 bonus from the Expos—more than double the amount Baines got. And Gullickson himself was trumped one pick later by the $77,500 bonus the Brewers gave University of Minnesota shortstop Paul Molitor.

Kennedy, a catcher at Florida State and the other player the White Sox gave serious consideration to before settling on Baines, went to the St. Louis Cardinals with the sixth pick. He signed a major league contract that included a $50,000 bonus.

## AT A GLANCE

### This Date In History
**WINTER DRAFT:** Jan. 11
**SUMMER DRAFT:** June 7-9

### Best Draft
**MONTREAL EXPOS.** In the first five rounds, the Expos chose **BILL GULLICKSON** (1), who won 162 games in a 14-year career; **SCOTT SANDERSON** (3), who won 163 over 19 years; and **TIM RAINES** (5), whose 23-year career included a .294 average, 1,571 runs scored and 888 stolen bases.

### Worst Draft
**BALTIMORE ORIOLES.** The only mileage the Orioles got out of the June phases were five hitless at-bats from **DRUNGO HAZEWOOD** (1) and 15 innings from righthander **MARK SMITH** (15).

### First-Round Bust
**BRUCE COMPTON, OF, INDIANS.** A record six first-rounders didn't advance beyond even Class A, but none failed quite so dramatically as Compton (11th overall). He played four seasons in the minors, one with the Indians and three in the Cubs organization, and hit just .143 overall with two homers in 124 games.

### Second To None
**MOOKIE WILSON, OF, METS.** The Mets got solid production from their top two picks in the 1977 draft, Wilson and second baseman **WALLY BACKMAN** (1)—especially during the team's run to a 1986 World Series title. Wilson hit .289 that season, and .274 with 281 stolen bases during 10 seasons with the Mets. Backman batted a team-high .320 in 1986, while hitting .283 with 103 stolen bases over nine seasons with the club.

### Late-Round Find
**CHILI DAVIS, OF, GIANTS (11TH ROUND).** Davis, the first Jamaican-born player to reach the majors, enjoyed a better career

CONTINUED ON PAGE 188

## AT A GLANCE

CONTINUED FROM PAGE 187

than anyone drafted beyond the 10th round in 1986, hitting at a .274 clip with 350 homers and 1,372 RBIs. He later became a successful hitting coach.

### Never Too Late

**TOM NIEDENFUER, RHP, DODGERS (36TH ROUND).** The Dodgers didn't sign Niedenfuer out of Washington's Redmond High as a 1977 draft pick, but managed to get their man three years later out of Washington State, signing him as a non-drafted free agent, and coughing up a signing bonus of $25,000. He went on to pitch 10 years as a reliever in the majors, winning 36 games and saving 97 others.

### Overlooked

**JEFF REARDON, RHP, METS.** Reardon was drafted by the Expos out of a Massachusetts high school in 1973, didn't sign and then was passed over in the 1977 draft after four years at the University of Massachusetts. He signed with the Mets as a non-drafted free agent, and ended up with the Expos in a 1981 trade. Reardon saved 367 games over 16 major league seasons, including a club-record 152 in his six years in an Expos uniform.

### International Gem

**JUNIOR ORTIZ, C, PIRATES.** Ortiz was the best of an unusually weak lot of international signings in 1977. He spent 13 years in the big leagues as a backup catcher, hitting .256 overall.

### Minor League Take

**PAUL MOLITOR, SS, BREWERS.** Molitor spent less time in the minors than any first-rounder in 1977—just 67 games in low Class A—but his post-draft performance ranks among the best-ever among first-rounders. He hit .355 with nine home runs, stole 14 bases in 16 attempts and posted a 47-22 walk-strikeout ratio. A year

## 1977: THE FIRST ROUNDERS

| CLUB: PLAYER, POS., SCHOOL | HOMETOWN | B-T | HT. | WT. | AGE | BONUS | FIRST YEAR | LAST YEAR | PEAK LEVEL (YEARS) |
|---|---|---|---|---|---|---|---|---|---|
| **JUNE—REGULAR PHASE** | | | | | | | | | |
| 1. White Sox: Harold Baines, 1b/of, St. Michaels HS | St. Michaels, Md. | L-L | 6-2 | 175 | 18 | $32,000 | 1977 | 2001 | Majors (22) |
| Personally scouted for years by White Sox owner Bill Veeck, sweet-swinging Maryland product played 22 years in majors, hit .289, added 384 homers, 1,628 RBIs. | | | | | | | | | |
| 2. Expos: Bill Gullickson, rhp, Joliet Catholic HS | Orland Park, Ill. | R-R | 6-3 | 200 | 18 | $75,000 | 1977 | 1983 | Majors (14) |
| No. 1-ranked prospect by scouting bureau broke into majors with Expos at 20, set rookie record with 18 SO game, won 162 games over 14 years with six clubs. | | | | | | | | | |
| 3. Brewers: Paul Molitor, ss, Minnesota | St. Paul, Minn. | R-R | 6-0 | 185 | 20 | $77,500 | 1977 | 1998 | Majors (21) |
| Minnesota All-American needed just 64 games in low Class A to launch Hall of Fame career; hit .306 with 234 homers, 504 steals, played multiple positions. | | | | | | | | | |
| 4. Braves: Tim Cole, lhp, Saugerties HS | Saugerties, N.Y. | L-L | 6-0 | 185 | 18 | $52,500 | 1977 | 1986 | Class AAA (1) |
| Three-sport prep star always intrigued scouts with big fastball, but career doomed by control issues; went 48-64, 5.55 in 10 years in minors, walked 706 in 883 IP. | | | | | | | | | |
| 5. Tigers: Kevin Richards, rhp, Roosevelt HS | Wyandotte, Mich. | R-R | 6-2 | 175 | 19 | $43,500 | 1977 | 1982 | Class AA (3) |
| Tigers believed they drafted carbon copy of zany RHP (and 1976 sensation) Mark Fidrych, but Michigan product was a mirage; went 22-22, 4.42 in minors. | | | | | | | | | |
| 6. *Cardinals: Terry Kennedy, c, Florida State | Mesa, Ariz. | L-R | 6-3 | 220 | 21 | $50,000 | 1977 | 1991 | Majors (14) |
| Son of Cubs GM/longtime MLB OF Bob Kennedy; hit .264 with 113 HRs for four clubs in 14 years in majors, best season with Padres in 1982 (.295-21-97). | | | | | | | | | |
| 7. Angels: Richard Dotson, rhp, Anderson HS | Cincinnati | R-R | 6-1 | 182 | 18 | $60,000 | 1977 | 1990 | Majors (12) |
| Dealt to White Sox for Brian Downing before making big league appearance for Angels; won 111 games in 12 seasons, highlighted by breakout 22-7 mark in 1983. | | | | | | | | | |
| 8. *Padres: Brian Greer, of, Sonora HS | Brea, Calif. | R-R | 6-3 | 210 | 18 | $60,000 | 1977 | 1983 | Majors (2) |
| Signed big league deal as incentive to forgo UCLA football, became first 1977 draft to reach majors but got just 4 ABs over two trials; strikeout-prone in minors. | | | | | | | | | |
| 9. Rangers: David Hibner, ss, Howell HS | Howell, Mich. | R-R | 5-10 | 180 | 18 | $49,500 | 1977 | 1982 | Class A (5) |
| Prep shortstop with speed, raw power fell short of expectations in six seasons in minors, none above Class A; error prone, played way off shortstop, hit just .193. | | | | | | | | | |
| 10. Giants: Craig Landis, ss, Vintage HS | Napa, Calif. | R-R | 6-2 | 200 | 18 | $50,000 | 1977 | 1982 | Class AAA (3) |
| Prominent UCLA QB recruit followed career path of dad, former Gold Glover Jim Landis, but career stalled in Triple-A; eventually became successful agent. | | | | | | | | | |
| 11. Indians: Bruce Compton, of, Norman HS | Norman, Okla. | R-R | 6-2 | 185 | 18 | $32,000 | 1977 | 1980 | Class A (1) |
| Passed up Texas Tech football offer to sign with Indians, lasted only half-season before trade to Cubs; posted woeful numbers: .143-2-34 in four seasons. | | | | | | | | | |
| 12. Cubs: Randy Martz, rhp, South Carolina | Elizabethville, Pa. | L-R | 6-4 | 210 | 21 | $50,000 | 1977 | 1985 | Majors (4) |
| Backup QB for two years at South Carolina who took up pitching as junior, went 14-0; won 11 games for Cubs in 1982, but never won another game in majors. | | | | | | | | | |
| 13. Red Sox: Andrew Madden, rhp, New Hartford HS | New Hartford, N.Y. | R-R | 6-7 | 225 | 17 | $42,500 | 1977 | 1979 | Class A (2) |
| Big RHP fanned 175, played alongside Andy Van Slyke as high school SR; disastrous three-year career in minors, though injuries contributed to 2-11, 4.00 record. | | | | | | | | | |
| 14. Astros: # Ricky Adams, ss, Montclair HS | Montclair, Calif. | R-R | 6-1 | 175 | 18 | $50,000 | 1977 | 1987 | Majors (3) |
| Released by Astros after three years in minors (.248-1-67, 41 SB, 57 errors/123 G at SS); subsequently signed with Angels, spent parts of three seasons in majors. | | | | | | | | | |
| 15. Twins: Paul Croft, of, Morristown HS | Morristown, N.J. | R-R | 6-0 | 175 | 17 | $40,000 | 1977 | 1983 | Class AA (1) |
| Miami football recruit fell out of favor with Twins, spent five years in A-ball before being dealt to Braves; seven-year tally in minors: .262-84-284, 147 SB. | | | | | | | | | |
| 16. Mets: Wally Backman, ss, Aloha HS | Beaverton, Ore. | B-R | 5-10 | 160 | 17 | $35,000 | 1977 | 1983 | Majors (14) |
| Scrappy competitor hit .320, provided top-of-lineup spark for 1986 champion Mets; potential big league managerial shot derailed by legal, financial issues. | | | | | | | | | |
| 17. Athletics: Craig Harris, rhp, Buena HS | Sierra Vista, Ariz. | R-R | 6-5 | 185 | 18 | $35,000 | 1977 | 1983 | Class AA (1) |
| Unlikely first-rounder after he quit his primary sport, basketball, as prep SR; mediocre in minors (18-35, 5.19); wheelchair-bound for 10 years with bone disease. | | | | | | | | | |
| 18. Pirates: Tony Nicely, of, Meadowdale HS | Dayton, Ohio | R-R | 6-0 | 180 | 17 | $45,000 | 1977 | 1980 | Class A (3) |
| First of two Dayton-area first-rounders; had solid first season (.273-3-24) before shoulder injury doomed career; hit .240 overall with four home runs. | | | | | | | | | |
| 19. Orioles: # Drungo Hazewood, of, Sacramento HS | Sacramento, Calif. | R-R | 6-3 | 205 | 17 | $50,000 | 1977 | 1983 | Majors (1) |
| All-around athlete who chose Orioles over chance to play running back at USC; struggled to crack O's roster, got just 5 ABs in majors, hit .240-97-352 in minors. | | | | | | | | | |
| 20. Dodgers: # Bob Welch, rhp, Eastern Michigan | Ferndale, Mich. | R-R | 6-4 | 190 | 20 | $20,000 | 1977 | 1994 | Majors (17) |
| Overcame alcoholism early in career to win 27 games in 1990, 211 over 17-year career divided between Dodgers/A's; died from broken neck in 2014 fall. | | | | | | | | | |
| 21. Royals: Mike Jones, lhp, Sutherland HS | Pittsford, N.Y. | L-L | 6-6 | 215 | 17 | $40,000 | 1977 | 1990 | Majors (4) |
| Went 6-3, 3.21 in 1981 in what looked like long career as Royals starter; broke his neck in wreck that winter, had to reinvent himself, won just five more games. | | | | | | | | | |
| 22. Phillies: Scott Munninghoff, rhp, Purcell Marian HS | Cincinnati | R-R | 6-0 | 175 | 18 | $40,000 | 1977 | 1982 | Majors (1) |
| Won 31 games between high A and Double-A in 1978-79, but career leveled off, made four brief appearances in majors in 1980, hit 3B in only big league AB. | | | | | | | | | |
| 23. Yankees: Steve Taylor, rhp, Delaware | Newark, Del. | R-R | 6-4 | 200 | 21 | $40,000 | 1977 | 1981 | Class AAA (3) |
| With twin brother Jeff (later a longtime scout) as batterymate, went 12-1, 1.59 (102 IP/114 SO) as college SR; topped out in Triple-A after injuring his arm. | | | | | | | | | |
| 24. Reds: Tad Venger, 3b, Hart HS | Newhall, Calif. | L-R | 6-2 | 175 | 18 | $40,000 | 1977 | 1981 | Class A (3) |
| Reds whiffed on eighth straight first-rounder, who failed to advance past Class A; made 33 errors in 37 games in first pro season, hit .258 with 18 homers overall. | | | | | | | | | |
| 25. Blue Jays: Tom Goffena, ss, Sidney HS | Sidney, Ohio | R-R | 6-0 | 160 | 17 | $36,000 | 1977 | 1979 | Class A (2) |
| First pick in Jays history had speed, arm strength, but injured his back lifting weights; missed 1978 season, played in only 145 games as pro, hit .238-0-51. | | | | | | | | | |
| 26. Mariners: # Dave Henderson, of, Dos Palos HS | Dos Palos, Calif. | R-R | 6-2 | 210 | 18 | $58,000 | 1977 | 1994 | Majors (14) |
| Fresno State two-sport recruit hit .315-16-63 in short-season ball and never looked back; hit famous 1986 ALCS homer off Donnie Moore in 14-year MLB career. | | | | | | | | | |
| **JANUARY—REGULAR PHASE** | | | | | | | | | |
| 1. Expos: Kalvin Adams, c, Central Arizona JC | Corpus Christi, Texas | R-R | 6-2 | 190 | 18 | Unsigned | 1977 | 1980 | Class A (3) |
| Expos didn't get their man in January, but did in June after he hit .415-7-77 in juco play; power prospect spent three seasons in minors, seven in Mexico. | | | | | | | | | |
| **JANUARY—SECONDARY PHASE** | | | | | | | | | |
| 1. Reds: Bill Scherrer, lhp, Nevada-Las Vegas | Franklinville, N.Y. | L-L | 6-4 | 180 | 18 | $12,500 | 1977 | 1989 | Majors (7) |
| Spurned Indians as sixth-rounder in 1976, then left UNLV to become eligible in January; pitched in 312 games in minors, 228 in majors (8-10, 4.08). | | | | | | | | | |
| **JUNE—SECONDARY PHASE** | | | | | | | | | |
| 1. Twins: Frank Ferroni, lhp, Central Arizona JC | Mill Valley, Calif. | L-L | 5-11 | 175 | 19 | Unsigned | 1981 | 1981 | Class A (1) |
| Teammate of Kalvin Adams (No. 1 pick in January) rejected Twins offer, wasn't drafted again for four more years (Orioles, January 1981) as career got sidetracked. | | | | | | | | | |

**Signed to major league contract. # Deceased.*

## How They Should Have Done It

Based on the career WAR (Wins Above Replacement, as calculated by Baseball-Reference.com) numbers achieved by all the players eligible for the 1977 draft, here's how the first round should have unfolded. Numbers in parentheses indicate the round when the player was actually drafted

| | Player, Pos. | Actual Draft | WAR | Bonus |
|---|---|---|---|---|
| 1. | Ozzie Smith, ss | Padres (4) | 76.5 | $5,000 |
| 2. | Paul Molitor, ss | Brewers (1) | 75.5 | $77,500 |
| 3. | Tim Raines, ss | Expos (5) | 69.1 | $6,000 |
| 4. | Bob Welch, rhp | Dodgers (1) | 44.2 | $20,000 |
| 5. | Jesse Barfield, of | Blue Jays (9) | 39.4 | $7,500 |
| 6. | Harold Baines, 1b/of | White Sox (1) | 38.6 | $32,000 |
| 7. | Chili Davis, of | Giants (11) | 38.2 | $12,000 |
| 8. | Willie McGee, of | Yankees (Jan.-S/1) | 34.1 | $7,500 |
| 9. | Scott Sanderson, rhp | Expos (3) | 28.1 | $18,500 |
| 10. | Dave Henderson, of | Mariners (1) | 27.5 | $58,000 |
| 11. | Bill Gullickson, rhp | Expos (1) | 23.6 | $75,000 |
| 12. | Mookie Wilson, of | Mets (2) | 22.2 | $28,000 |
| 13. | Dave Righetti, lhp | Rangers (June-R/1) | 21.8 | $1,000 |
| 14. | Terry Kennedy, c | Cardinals (1) | 21.6 | $50,000 |
| 15. | Jeff Reardon, rhp | Mets (NDFA) | 19.3 | None |
| 16. | Richard Dotson, rhp | Angels (1) | 15.4 | $60,000 |
| 17. | Kevin Bass, of | Brewers (2) | 14.8 | $44,000 |
| 18. | Mike Davis, of | Athletics (3) | 14.5 | $15,000 |
| 19. | Mitch Webster, of | Dodgers (23) | 14.4 | $10,000 |
| 20. | Wally Backman, ss | Mets (1) | 13.1 | $35,000 |
| 21. | Brian Harper, c | Angels (4) | 12.3 | $26,000 |
| 22. | Jim Gott, rhp | Cardinals (4) | 10.8 | $10,000 |
| 23. | Terry Leach, rhp | Braves (NDFA) | 10.2 | None |
| 24. | Joe Price, lhp | Reds (4) | 8.3 | $10,000 |
| 25. | Roger Erickson, rhp | Twins (3) | 8.1 | $18,500 |
| 26. | Dave LaPoint, lhp | Brewers (10) | 7.2 | $5,000 |

| | Top 3 Unsigned Players | | | Year Signed |
|---|---|---|---|---|
| 1. | Tony Phillips, ss | Mariners (16) | 50.8 | 1978 |
| 2. | Jesse Orosco, lhp | Cardinals (Jan.-R/7) | 23.9 | 1978 |
| 3. | Bud Black, lhp | Giants (Jan.-R/3) | 21.1 | 1979 |

### DOUBTS ABOUT BAINES, OTHERS

For three years, the White Sox carefully nurtured Baines before unleashing him on the American League. He quickly matured into one of the game's top young hitters, and eventually the leading home run hitter in White Sox history.

If there were reservations about Baines initially, similar concerns existed for Gullickson, Molitor and Kennedy.

Gullickson's issues weren't performance-related as he reached the big leagues briefly at age 20. A year later, he went 10-5, 3.00 for the Expos after being called up in May from Triple-A, and was the top rookie pitcher in the National League.

Gullickson saw his career complicated by diabetes, however. Doctors had diagnosed the disease in March after he lost 20 pounds and was unduly tired from spring-training workouts.

"They said it came on a couple of months before I found out," Gullickson said. "I was scared when I first found out. I didn't know how it would affect my baseball career. When most people first think about being diabetic, they think of a real frail person, one not able to participate in sports. I was no different. Then I thought about Ron Santo, Catfish Hunter and Bobby Clarke. If they did it, so could I."

That September, in a stunning display of power pitching in a game against the Chicago Cubs,

Terry Kennedy's father Bob was the Cubs' GM, but he never got the chance to draft his son when the Cardinals made him the No. 6 pick

Gullickson made the baseball world take notice when he struck out 18—a record for a rookie (later broken by Kerry Wood in 1998) and just one shy of the major league single-game mark.

The illness didn't seem to slow Gullickson during his rookie season, but he was never again quite the same power pitcher he was that night in September 1980. Like Baines, though, he had a commendable major league career. Over 14 seasons, he won 162 games while pitching for five different teams.

The reservations scouts had about Molitor and Kennedy had more to do with the subpar seasons both experienced as college juniors after their breakout sophomore campaigns.

Molitor put himself on the radar for the 1977 draft by hitting .376 with 10 homers for Minnesota in 1976, but pressed a year later with all the attention he received from scouts and slipped to .326 with five homers—even as he led the Gophers to a College World Series berth and set numerous school offensive records.

His selection with the third pick was still a noteworthy achievement, as he was offered only $4,000 by the Cardinals in 1974 as a lowly 28th-round pick out of high school—as a pitcher. He nearly accepted the offer because he didn't have a college scholarship offer at the time, but Minnesota coach Dick Seibert came through a short time later and had the foresight to convert Molitor into a full-time infielder as a Gophers freshman.

The 6-foot-4, 220-pound Kennedy was lightly recruited out of high school as well, but his father Bob was well connected in the industry as a long-time player and executive. Through his friendship with Florida State coach Woody Woodward, he arranged for his son to attend FSU.

While he played sparingly for the Seminoles as a freshman, the younger Kennedy took off a year later, he launched a 21-year career in the majors that led to the Hall of Fame.

**AT A GLANCE**

### One Who Got Away

**TERRY FRANCONA, 1B, CUBS (2ND ROUND).** Francona hit .545 as a sophomore and .769 as a junior at New Brighton (Pa.) High, and likely would have been a first-round pick in the 1977 draft had he not separated his shoulder as a senior. He became a first-rounder three years later after a star-studded college career at Arizona.

### He Was Drafted?

**DANNY AINGE, SS, BLUE JAYS (15TH ROUND).** The expansion Blue Jays took a flier on Ainge, believing they had little chance to sign the three-sport, high school All-American. But they struck a deal that enabled Ainge to juggle baseball and basketball at Brigham Young. When he was drafted by the NBA's Boston Celtics in 1981, Ainge opted for the NBA and went on to a lengthy career as a player and executive. He and Mark Hendrickson are the only players in baseball's draft era to play Major League Baseball and in the NBA.

### Did You Know . . .

From 1974-77, the California Angels drafted more players who played in the big leagues than any other club: 52 future major leaguers, including 12 in 1977. The payoff was American League division championship teams in 1979 and 1982.

### They Said It

**DANNY AINGE,** days before he was drafted by the NBA's Boston Celtics in 1981: "There's no question in my mind, and never will be, that baseball is a better game than basketball. I have a commitment to play baseball, and I plan to honor that commitment."—*Soon after the draft, Ainge reneged on his three-year contract with the Blue Jays to pursue an NBA career.*

## DRAFT SPOTLIGHT: DANNY AINGE

Danny Ainge was the rare athlete with legitimate ability to play at the highest level in both baseball and basketball

Danny Ainge had just signed a three-year contract with the Toronto Blue Jays in 1980, and appeared sincere in his desire to make baseball his career.

"I've had about 15 NBA teams contact me to see what my plans are," Ainge said on the eve of the 1981 NBA draft. "I told them not to waste their draft choices because I have a commitment to baseball. My contract with the Blue Jays does not allow me to play pro basketball. But I guess somebody's going to draft me anyway."

Using the second of two second-round draft picks, the Boston Celtics went for the two-time Brigham Young All-American. Under normal circumstances, the 6-foot-5 Ainge, who averaged 24 points as a senior at BYU, might have been the third pick in the NBA draft, after DePaul's Mark Aguirre and Indiana's Isiah Thomas. But his was not a normal situation. For four years, Ainge played basketball at BYU and baseball in the Toronto organization. He was the Jays' starting third baseman at the time of his selection by the Celtics.

To deter NBA clubs from trying to woo Ainge, the Blue Jays signed him to a contract that provided for a $50,000 salary the first year, $75,000 the second and $100,000 the third. He also accepted a $300,000 bonus for agreeing not to play professional basketball.

Boston gambled on Ainge, but Celtics president Red Auerbach admitted he talked with him several times before the draft. "We think we have a shot at him," Auerbach said.

Ainge reaffirmed his desire to play baseball after being drafted by the Celtics. But he left the door open. "Had any other team but Boston drafted me, there would be zero chance of me playing basketball," he said. "There is no question that Boston has the style and the mystique that appeals to me. But I still want to play baseball."

On June 12, just three days after the NBA draft, Ainge announced he had decided to play basketball. The ensuing tug-of-war over Ainge turned into a legal battle. Ultimately, the courts ruled in favor of the Celtics, enabling him to play basketball.

Ainge played 15 seasons in the NBA, including eight in Boston, and won NBA titles in 1984 and '86. He coached the Phoenix Suns for four seasons after retiring as a player, and became the Celtics general manager in 2003, building the 2008 NBA champions.

Competition for Ainge's services first began at North Eugene High. He was the only Oregon high school athlete ever named all-state in baseball, basketball and football, and he accomplished the feat twice. As in basketball, Ainge would have been a first-round pick in baseball in 1977 had he focused on the sport. The Jays took him in the 15th round.

"We took a flier," Jays GM Pat Gillick said. "If you're faint-hearted, you better not run an expansion club. You've got to gamble, be it in trades or drafts."

Ainge signed for a bonus of $32,500, with the stipulation that he would be allowed to play basketball at BYU and would never be assigned to a classification lower than Triple-A. "I plan on playing college basketball and pro baseball, year by year," he said. "I really don't know what's going to happen when I choose between them."

Ainge reported to Triple-A Syracuse in late April 1978. With no spring training and no minor league experience, he broke in with three hits in his first game and a home run the following day. He struggled the remainder of the season, hitting .229.

A year later, Ainge earned his first playing time with the Blue Jays, batting .237 in 87 games as a rookie second baseman. In 1980, Ainge again rode the Syracuse-Toronto-BYU shuttle, displaying much more skill and success on the basketball court.

By 1981, Ainge was ready to devote his attention to baseball. Or so it seemed. But a .186 average and the Celtics changed that. His legacy in Toronto: 211 games and a .220 average.

later when he moved behind the plate and his raw power began to emerge. He finished the year with 21 homers and 64 RBIs.

Kennedy got off to a slow start in his draft year because of a wrist injury and dipped to just eight homers. But the Cardinals showed no hesitation taking him with the sixth pick.

Bob Kennedy had recently been named general manager of the Cubs, and indicated he would take a shot at drafting him, if available, but he was gone when the Cubs picked 12th. Terry seemed to be an ideal fit for the Cardinals, and he was familiar with the organization because his dad had worked there as the club's farm director and assistant general manager, and he often worked out at Busch Stadium while in high school.

"He has major league power right now," said Cardinals scout Harry Walker, who aggressively pursued Kennedy. "He handles himself well behind the plate and has a strong arm."

Kennedy became the first of six consecutive Cardinals picks in the June regular phase to reach the big leagues, tying a draft record. He went on to play 14 seasons in the big leagues and remained in the game as a longtime minor league manager.

### MOLITOR, SMITH REACH HALL

Molitor, who evolved into a frontline shortstop after three years in college, went to Milwaukee with the third pick despite the formidable presence on that club of Robin Yount, who at 21 was already entrenched at the position. Yount himself had been taken by the Brewers with the third overall pick four years earlier.

By drafting Molitor, the Brewers were hedging their bets in case Yount became a free agent in a couple of years. There were also rumblings that he might move to center field one day or even abandon his baseball career altogether and join the professional golf tour.

After a half-season at low Class A Burlington to begin his career, Molitor had no pretensions about cracking the Milwaukee roster a year later—though Yount had done just that in 1974, when he made the leap from A-ball to the Brewers' starting shortstop job. But Molitor had an impressive training camp and was eager to join the big league club to begin the 1978 season, even if it meant moving to another position.

As it turned out, he became the Opening Day shortstop and remained there for a month when Yount couldn't answer the bell because of a sore foot. When Yount returned, the versatile Molitor never lost his place in the lineup and simply shifted across the bag to second base. He spent the bulk of

### Fastest To The Majors

| | Player, Pos. | Drafted (Round) | Debut |
|---|---|---|---|
| 1. | * Brian Greer, of | Padres (1) | Sept. 13, 1977 |
| 2. | Roger Erickson, rhp | Twins (3) | April 6, 1978 |
| 3. | Paul Molitor, ss | Brewers (1) | April 7, 1978 |
| | Ozzie Smith, ss | Padres (4) | April 7, 1978 |
| 5. | Darrell Jackson, lhp | Twins (9) | June 16, 1978 |

**LAST PLAYER TO RETIRE:** Tim Raines, of (Sept. 29, 2002)

**High school selection.*

## Top 25 Bonuses

| | Player, Pos. | Drafted (Round) | Order | Bonus |
|---|---|---|---|---|
| 1. | **Paul Molitor, ss** | **Brewers (1)** | **3** | **$77,500** |
| 2. | ***Bill Gullickson, rhp** | **Expos (1)** | **2** | **$75,000** |
| 3. | ***Richard Dotson, rhp** | **Angels (1)** | **7** | **$60,000** |
| | ***Brian Greer, of** | **Padres (1)** | **8** | **#$60,000** |
| 5. | ***Dave Henderson, of** | **Mariners (1)** | **26** | **$58,000** |
| 6. | Tim Cole, lhp | Braves (1) | 4 | $52,500 |
| 7. | **Terry Kennedy, c** | **Cardinals (1)** | **6** | **#$50,000** |
| | *Craig Landis, ss | Giants (1) | 10 | $50,000 |
| | **Randy Martz, rhp** | **Cubs (1)** | **12** | **$50,000** |
| | ***Ricky Adams, ss** | **Astros (1)** | **14** | **$50,000** |
| | ***Drungo Hazewood, of** | **Orioles (1)** | **19** | **$50,000** |
| 12. | *David Hibner, ss | Rangers (1) | 9 | $49,500 |
| 13. | *Anthony Nicely, of | Pirates (1) | 18 | $45,000 |
| 14. | ***Kevin Bass, of** | **Brewers (2)** | **29** | **$44,000** |
| 15. | *Kevin Richards, rhp | Tigers (1) | 5 | $43,500 |
| 16. | *Andrew Madden, rhp | Red Sox (1) | 13 | $42,500 |
| 17. | *Tad Venger, 3b | Reds (1) | 24 | $40,000 |
| | ***Mike Jones, lhp** | **Royals (1)** | **21** | **$40,000** |
| | *Paul Croft, of | Twins (1) | 15 | $40,000 |
| | Steve Taylor, rhp | Yankees (1) | 23 | $40,000 |
| | ***Scott Munninghoff, rhp** | **Phillies (1)** | **22** | **$40,000** |
| 22. | *Tom Goffena, ss | Blue Jays (1) | 25 | $36,000 |
| 23. | ***Wally Backman, ss** | **Mets (1)** | **16** | **$35,000** |
| | *Craig Harris, rhp | Athletics (1) | 17 | $35,000 |
| | *Gary Johnson, rhp | Angels (2) | 33 | $35,000 |

*Major leaguers in bold. *High school selection. #Major league contract.*

UNIVERSITY OF MINNESOTA

**Paul Molitor was a lightly recruited pitcher when he ended up at Minnesota, where his conversion to position player paid dividends**

his rookie season at that position while inheriting a permanent role as the Brewers leadoff hitter.

Over the course of a 15-year career with the Brewers, Molitor played every position except pitcher and catcher, though he spent a significant amount of time in a DH role because of the assortment of injuries he sustained. He hit .303 overall with 160 home runs and 412 stolen bases.

Yount spent his entire Hall of Fame career in Milwaukee, but Molitor moved on following the 1992 season, seeking more money than the small-market Brewers were willing to pay. Molitor landed in Toronto for three years and finished his career back home in Minnesota, playing for the Twins.

When he retired in 1998, Molitor was one of four players in big league history to have a lifetime .300 batting average and at least 3,000 hits and 500 stolen bases. He was also the only one of the four to have at least 200 home runs.

Molitor was elected to the Hall of Fame in 2004, and later became the third active Hall of Famer to manage a major league team when he took over the reins of the Twins in 2015.

The only other player from the Class of 1977 to reach Cooperstown was also a college shortstop: slick-fielding Ozzie Smith, an underrated fourth-round pick of the San Diego Padres out of Cal Poly who signed for just $5,000.

Like Molitor, who had Yount above him in the pecking order at shortstop in the Brewers system, Smith had the challenge of unseating incumbent Bill Almon, the first overall pick in the 1974 draft. But Smith followed the same career path as Molitor and leaped straight to the big leagues out of Class A. Not only did he claim the Padres' starting shortstop job to open the 1978 season, but he quickly won over manager Roger Craig on the basis of his wizardry in the field.

"Smith is the best young infielder I've ever seen," Craig said after the acrobatic Smith made a number of spectacular plays in the field as a rookie. "Very soon, he's going to be one of the best shortstops in baseball, if not the best."

Somehow scouts had never seen Smith in such a favorable light. They were always reluctant to deem him worthy of a premium pick—let alone draft him at all early in his career—because of his slight 5-foot-10 frame. Most thought he'd never hit enough in the majors to justify the investment.

After signing with the Padres in 1977 and spending his first pro season at Walla Walla of the short-season Northwest League, Smith slid into the shortstop job a year later. He hit .258 and stole 40 bases for the Padres as a rookie, but was deemed expendable when he hit .231 overall with a single homer in four seasons with that club.

Traded to St. Louis for another, more well-rounded shortstop, Garry Templeton, after the 1981 season, the Wizard of Oz found a home in St. Louis. He became a catalyst on both sides of the ball in leading the Cardinals to a World Series title in his first season, and hit at a .272 clip over the next 15 years, even chipping in with 27 home runs.

But it was his spectacular defense at shortstop that set him apart from any player in his era, and from 1980-92 he won 13 consecutive Gold Gloves. As one of the most dynamic shortstops ever to play the game, he earned his due in Cooperstown as a first-ballot Hall of Famer.

Beyond Molitor and Smith, shortstops were a popular commodity in the 1977 draft, though only one other first-rounder, Wally Backman, an Oregon high school product selected 16th overall by the New York Mets, left his mark in the majors.

A second Oregon prep shortstop, Danny Ainge, was a considerable talent and almost certainly would have gone in the first round as well, had be not also excelled in football and especially basketball. With

### WORTH NOTING

New expansion teams in Toronto and Seattle made their way onto the major league scene in 1977, but a favorable draft position was not part of the $10 million expansion price. The Blue Jays and Mariners both began selecting talent in January, in the Nos. 25 and 26 positions, and the same order held in June. The Mariners had considerably more success with their top pick in the June regular phase, outfielder **DAVE HENDERSON**, than the Blue Jays did with theirs, shortstop **TOM GOFFENA**. Henderson played 14 years in the major leagues, while Goffena's career flamed out after just three seasons in the minors, none above Class A.

Arizona State (57-12) won the 1977 College World Series, beating South Carolina 2-1 in the final. The Sun Devils won on a seventh-inning home run by catcher **CHRIS BANDO**, the younger brother of former ASU star Sal Bando and an unsigned 22nd-round pick of the Brewers in the 1977 draft. Bando was one of a draft-high nine players selected by the Sun Devils, but the real star of that squad was sophomore second baseman Bob Horner, who led the nation with 22 homers, 87 RBIs, 102 hits and 191 total bases. Horner would become the nation's No. 1 draft pick a year later when he set a Division I record with 25 homers.

Eckerd (Fla.) College first baseman Steve Balboni set NCAA Division II records with 26 homers and 77 RBIs while leading that school to a national title. Balboni hit five homers in the D-II World Series, but like Horner was not eligible for the 1977 draft.

**MIKE JONES**, a promising lefthander drafted by the Royals with their first-round pick in 1977, went 6-3, 3.20 as a rookie for the Royals in 1981, but his career—and life—were nearly snuffed

CONTINUED ON PAGE 192

## WORTH NOTING

CONTINUED FROM PAGE 191

out by a grinding car crash following that season near his Pittsford, N.Y., home. Jones sat out the 1982 season while rehabbing his injuries, but continued to pitch for eight more years, almost entirely in the minor leagues. His left arm, badly injured in the accident, was never the same and Jones, who had come up as a power pitcher, had to reinvent himself as a finesse specialist. Over his minor league career, he went 90-74, 3.58.

■ The Rangers had the wisdom to select fireballing lefthander **DAVE RIGHETTI** with their first pick in the January regular phase, and they also drafted his brother **STEVE** in the same phase. But even after Righetti demonstrated a preview of things to come by striking out 20 in a game at Double-A Tulsa, the Rangers made the mistake of shipping him to the Yankees in a 10-player deal little more than a year later. He quickly became one of the game's top relievers in New York, and his 46 saves in 1986 were a then-major league record. Righetti ended up pitching 16 years in the big leagues for five different teams (none of them the Rangers), piling up 82 wins and 252 saves along with a 3.46 ERA in 1,404 career innings.

■ The Giants selected California prep shortstop **CRAIG LANDIS**, the son of former big leaguer Jim Landis, with their top pick in the 1977 draft (10th overall). Once a top quarterback recruit, Landis decided to turn his attention back to football when his baseball career peaked in Triple-A. At 23, he enrolled at Stanford, where he played as a defensive back. By then, his football skills had eroded and he never rose above backup duty with the Cardinal. His Stanford degree came in handy, though. While Landis never made his mark in baseball as a player, he did in later years as a prominent player agent, with Angels star out-

so many options, he was determined to be too great a risk to warrant going in an early round, but the Toronto Blue Jays took a 15th-round flier on him and succeeded in signing him—though they had to allow him to juggle an All-America basketball career at Brigham Young, while also playing baseball with the Jays. They ultimately lost him to the NBA's Boston Celtics.

Tim Raines

The Expos took Florida prep shortstop Tim Raines in the fifth round and had the foresight to move him almost immediately to second base, and eventually to left field, to allow the offensive side of his game to flourish. That it did as Raines became one of the game's most-electrifying leadoff hitters in the game over a 23-year career in the majors. He hit .294 overall, scored 1,571 runs and stole 808 bases, and even contributed 170 home runs.

### COLLEGES PLAY INCREASING ROLE

Molitor and Kennedy were the prime college targets in the June regular phase, but only three other players in that demographic—pitchers Randy Martz (Cubs, 12th overall), Bob Welch (Dodgers, 20th) and Steve Taylor (Yankees, 23rd)—were selected in the first round.

Martz was somewhat of a surprise selection as he didn't even play baseball at South Carolina until his junior year, and yet fashioned a perfect 14-0 mark in leading the Gamecocks all the way to the championship game of the College World Series. Martz had been a third-string quarterback on the football team for three seasons before deciding to give baseball a whirl.

Welch himself led Eastern Michigan to a spot in the national title game a year earlier on the strength of a 10-3, 1.82 record, along with 111 strikeouts in 94 innings. Based on that performance, along with a mid-90s fastball, Welch had expectations of becoming the first college pitcher taken in the 1977 draft, but he missed most of his junior season with an elbow injury and didn't win a game. Nonetheless, he attracted droves of scouts to watch him in bullpen sessions that spring, and the Los Angeles Dodgers showed no hesitation taking him late in the first round.

They were rewarded almost immediately as Welch went 7-4, 2.02 as a rookie in 1978, and gained national fame in that year's World Series by striking out Reggie Jackson with two men on base in the top of the ninth inning of Game Two to preserve a Dodgers win.

Over his career, Welch won 211 games, was part of five World Series teams and became the last major league pitcher to win as many as 25 games. He went 27-6 for the Oakland A's in 1990.

Though just five collegians went in the first round, that number belied the growing influence of the college game on the draft, and 1977 marked the first time in the June regular phase that more

### Largest Bonuses By Round

| | Player, Pos. | Club | Bonus |
|---|---|---|---|
| **1.** | **Paul Molitor, ss** | **Brewers** | **$77,500** |
| **2.** | *** Kevin Bass, of** | **Brewers** | **$44,000** |
| 3. | * Jeff Conner, lhp | Angels | $27,500 |
| 4. | * Kyle Koke, ss | Mariners | $28,000 |
| 5. | Four tied at | | $20,000 |
| 6. | Scott Burk, 3b | Red Sox | $20,000 |
| 7. | * Michael Moore, 1b | Mariners | $16,000 |
| **8.** | *** Brad Havens, lhp** | **Angels** | **$27,000** |
| 9. | Brandt Humphry, 3b | Angels | $17,000 |
| 10. | * Michael Beecroft, rhp | Tigers | $11,000 |
| **Jan/R.** | **Daryl Sconiers, 1b** | **Angels (3)** | **$23,000** |
| Jan/S. | Robert Healey, rhp | Angels (1) | $18,000 |
| **Jun/S.** | **Ron Roenicke, of** | **Dodgers (1)** | **$19,500** |

*Major leaguers in bold. *High school selection.*

collegians (438) were drafted than high school players (392).

That ratio would never reverse itself and, in fact, the trend toward college talent would widen greatly over the years as clubs placed more emphasis on older, more proven college players.

If the game was looking for evidence to justify switching away from untested high school talent, the 1977 draft provided it.

Among the 19 prep players selected in the first round, the unlikely total of six never even advanced beyond Class A—a draft record for futility. The 1978 draft also saw five more first-rounders flame out at the same level.

None of the 1977 first-rounders failed quite so miserably as Cleveland's top selection, outfielder Bruce Compton (11th overall), or Boston's initial pick, righthander Andrew Madden (13th overall). The 6-foot-7 Madden went just 2-11 in three minor league seasons, though arm problems compromised his career. Compton simply fizzled, hitting a feeble .144 over four seasons.

"He was not a good draft," Indians farm director Bob Quinn later admitted. "We made a mistake."

The Texas Rangers took shortstop David Hibner with the ninth pick overall. He lasted six seasons in the minors, including four at Asheville of the Class A South Atlantic League, but hit only .194 overall and was sent packing.

The Pittsburgh Pirates thought they had a potential star in outfielder Tony Nicely (18th overall), until he made an off-balance throw one day early in his career and tore up his shoulder, elbow and wrist—all on the same play. Nicely played in only 95 games, hitting .240.

"He was one of the most physically impressive players the Pirates ever drafted," Pittsburgh farm director Branch Rickey III said. "He had phenomenal muscle strength, but the connective tissue in his shoulder was so elastic, it just snapped. He could never throw again."

The two other first-rounders who failed to advance beyond Class A were shortstop Tom Goffena (Blue Jays, 25th overall), who played only three seasons because of a disabling back injury, and third baseman Tad Venger (Reds, 24th overall), who hit .258 over five seasons but never demonstrated the power the Reds were looking for.

### THE FOOTBALL FACTOR

Outfielder Brian Greer was yet another 1977 first-rounder whose career fell considerably short of expectations. But Greer at least gained the distinction of reaching the big leagues—if only briefly.

Chosen eighth overall by San Diego, the 6-foot-3, 210-pound Greer was a top-rated linebacker and utilized his scholarship offer from UCLA as a bargaining chip in negotiations to extract a three-year, $100,000 major league deal, including the promise of a September promotion to the big leagues. The Padres had no misgivings about extending Greer a rare major league contract.

"He has the chance to become a complete ballplayer," Padres director of player personnel Bob Fontaine said. "He possesses the necessary tools. He is a good runner and thrower, and has a very strong throwing arm. Plus, he's got good size and power."

Greer, who hit .460 as a senior at Sonora High in Brea, Calif., was assigned initially to Walla Walla, where he tied a Northwest League record by drilling three home runs in one game. Nineteen of his 32 hits also went for extra-bases, but more telling were his .188 batting average and league-leading 87 strikeouts in 170 at-bats. Ready or not, the 18-year-old Greer was in San Diego that September and became the first player from the 1977 draft to play in a major league game. In his one at-bat for the Padres in an 18-4 drubbing at the hands of the Dodgers, he struck out. Two years later, he received four more token plate appearances.

Brian Greer

That was the extent of Greer's major league career, but it wasn't the only instance where he played at a level he wasn't equipped to handle.

In training camp in 1978, Greer so impressed the Padres with his massive raw power that they sent him to Amarillo of the Double-A Texas League—and left him there for three years, to sink or swim. He sank.

"I was just lost," Greer said of his tenure in Amarillo. "I didn't know what was going on. I was a lost child in a man's game."

Glenn Ezell, who managed Greer at Amarillo, concurred. "They sent an 18-year-old kid just a year out of high school and shot him into Double-A. They made a mistake, no doubt about it," he said. "It's just like they say, success breeds success and, I guess, failure breeds failure. That's what happened to Brian."

Greer never recovered from the way the Padres mishandled him early in his career. Though he hit a career-high 31 homers in a 1982 season split between Double-A and Triple-A, he also struck out 202 times. On five occasions in his first six years in the minors, he topped his league in strikeouts.

After being banished to Class A in 1983, it was all over for Greer. In seven minor league seasons, he hit just .210 while striking out 997 times in 2,437 at bats.

Ten years after he retired, Greer, then a strapping 250 pounds, showcased his raw power by winning the inaugural National Home Run Derby for men's softball players. His daughter Lauren also excelled at softball, and led Washington to the NCAA softball title in 2009. While at Washington, she met and later married Jake Locker, then the Huskies quarterback and later a first-round pick in the NFL draft.

UCLA lost out to pro ball on a second prized football recruit when shortstop Craig Landis was plucked with the 10th overall pick by the San Francisco Giants. Landis was a talented option quarterback who Bruins coach Terry Donahue felt confident would start as a freshman, but Landis also came from significant baseball lineage, as his father Jim played 11 seasons in the big leagues.

Forced to make a decision between signing with the Giants or playing football at UCLA, Landis chose to follow in his father's footsteps.

"I was a quarterback and I could have gone just about any place I wanted," he said. "But I got drafted by the Giants and decided to play baseball. It was a difficult decision. They didn't offer me as much money as a lot of the No. 1 picks were getting.

"But I felt it was the quickest way to get into professional sports. Football is a rough sport and your career can end so quickly. Most guys who have the choice pick baseball over football."

Landis found success all the way up the ladder in the Giants chain, never hitting less than the .282 figure he compiled at Triple-A Phoenix in 1980. But it wasn't good enough to suit the Giants, who traded him to the Atlanta Braves organization. He played three more seasons in the Braves system and when it became apparent that a big league promotion wasn't imminent, he hung it up.

"I was optimistic at the time that it would work," Landis said. "I hoped to put in a couple of years in the minor leagues and then go to the big leagues. I guess other people expected that of me too, because of my dad."

Greer and Landis both chose careers in baseball over the opportunity to play football at UCLA, and two more 1977 first-rounders passed up a shot to play football for California colleges.

### One Team's Draft: Milwaukee Brewers

| Pick. Player, Pos. | Bonus | Pick. Player, Pos. | Bonus | Pick. Player, Pos. | Bonus |
|---|---|---|---|---|---|
| **1. Paul Molitor, ss** | **$77,500** | 5. * Michael Breslin, rhp | Did not sign | 9. Chris Carstensen, of | $2,000 |
| **2. * Kevin Bass, of** | **$44,000** | 6. Bill Foley, c | $15,000 | **10. * Dave LaPoint, lhp** | **$5,000** |
| 3. * Stan Davis, 1b | $25,000 | 7. * Alan Page, 1b | Did not sign | Other Ron Driver (June-S/1), lhp | $15,000 |
| 4. * Jerry Jenkins, rhp | $15,000 | 8. Steve Day, ss | $5,000 | | |

*Major leaguers in bold. *High school selection.*

#### WORTH NOTING

fielder Mike Trout among his more prominent clients.

■ White Sox owner Bill Veeck was a promotional genius, but the drafting of **HAROLD BAINES**, a player he discovered, wasn't considered just another of his publicity gimmicks. Others in the Chicago organization believed Baines was the real deal, and worthy of being taken with the No. 1 overall pick in the 1977 draft. "Baines is just an average runner, thrower and fielder, but his bat will take care of everything. He's the fellow we wanted. We weren't saving money," White Sox super-scout Paul Richards said. Three days after signing with the White Sox, Baines drove an hour from his home on the Maryland Eastern Shore to Baltimore to join the White Sox for a weekend series against the Orioles. He took batting practice with the big leaguers, but was so in awe of his surroundings that he didn't hit a single ball out of the infield in three turns in the batting cage. Every White Sox player witnessed the unimpressive display, but Veeck quickly wrote it off as nerves getting the best of a young player. Baines got untracked over the next three years in the White Sox farm system, and developed into the leading home run hitter in White Sox history. By the time Baines' 22-year career was over in 2001, Veeck got the last laugh as his protégé retired with a .289 average, 384 homers and 1,628 RBIs.

■ Two players who were unsigned first-round picks in the 1976 draft had standout seasons as college freshmen. Bill Bordley, who was picked fourth overall by the Brewers, went 14-0 for Southern California, while Twins pick Jamie Allen (who went 10th overall) was a key player for Arizona State, going 5-2 as a pitcher and batting .356. Another freshman, Hawaii lefthander Derek Tatsuno, led the nation with 146 strikeouts in 116 innings.

## IN FOCUS: OZZIE SMITH

At Locke High in suburban Los Angeles, Smith played alongside future big leaguers Eddie Murray, Gary Alexander and Darrell Jackson. Those players were all drafted out of high school, but Smith was passed over in the 1973 draft. "I'm sure size had a lot to do with it," Smith said. "I was maybe 130, 135 pounds at the time."

Smith went to college at Cal Poly, and though he didn't start immediately, his unusually advanced actions in the field didn't go unnoticed.

"The first time I saw him, as a freshman, fielding balls with the other players, I noticed he had this instinct for the ball," said Berdy Harr, his college coach. "Right away I knew he was something special. I never taught Ozzie anything about playing defense. He already knew what that was all about. He had a sense of timing, a rhythm I'd never seen before."

Harr may not have taught Smith any of the finer points of defense, but he did encourage him to become a switch-hitter.

A year later, Smith was drafted for the first time, in the seventh round, but the Detroit Tigers offered him only $5,000. Smith was looking for twice that amount and when he didn't get it he returned to Cal Poly for his senior year. He signed in 1977 with the San Diego Padres as a fourth-rounder—for $5,000.

The Baltimore Orioles won the battle for outfielder Drungo Hazewood (19th overall), a running back who had signed to play at the University of Southern California. The expansion Seattle Mariners pried away outfielder Dave Henderson (26th overall), an outstanding tight end prospect, from Fresno State.

Although Greer and Hazewood (five at-bats in 1980) reached the big leagues, only Henderson had any degree of measurable success in baseball among the four high-profile California football recruits.

Henderson played six seasons in Seattle, but attained his place in baseball history after leaving the Mariners for the Boston Red Sox in a 1986 trade. In October that year, Henderson hit his historic two-out, two-run homer in the American League Championship Series off California Angels reliever Donnie Moore to rally the Red Sox from the brink of elimination to an eventual berth in the World Series. Henderson also played a key role for two more World Series teams in Oakland, in 1988-89.

Dave Henderson

Hazewood died of cancer in 2013. Henderson died of a heart attack in 2015.

### BRAVES, BLUE JAYS GO TO COURT

The Braves were a sad-sack franchise in the mid-1970s, losing 94 games in 1975, and 92 more in 1976, the year that maverick Southern businessman Ted Turner bought the team. His motivation was to make the Braves the focal point for his fledgling cable television super-station, but he needed to reverse the club's fortunes on the field to make the Braves a viable product.

To Turner's good fortune, free agency infiltrated the game the same year he took over the Braves, and he was bent on capitalizing on the process to provide his struggling club the quick fix he believed it needed.

Celebrated righthander Andy Messersmith, whose contractual issues with the Dodgers in 1975 were integral in triggering free agency, had already come on board for the 1976 season, and Turner's primary target for 1977 was former Giants all-star outfielder Gary Matthews. He orchestrated the signing of Matthews to a multi-year deal on Nov. 17, 1976, but was almost immediately accused by baseball commissioner Bowie Kuhn of tampering in his courtship of Matthews.

As punishment for illegally contacting Matthews before the 1976 season was even over, Turner was suspended for a year, the Braves were fined $10,000 and penalized with the loss of two premium draft picks: the club's first-round choices in the regular phase in 1977, in both January and June.

The Braves forfeited their January pick, but challenged Kuhn's ruling in the courts to retain their June selection (fourth overall), and were successful. With the reinstatement of the fourth pick, the Braves went for lefthander Tim Cole, who spent 10 years in the minors and never reached the big leagues.

The courts would also get involved in another case involving a noteworthy 1977 draft pick, the Blue Jays' Ainge. That didn't occur for another four years, when the multi-sport star was in the middle of a tug-of-war over his services between the Blue Jays and the Boston Celtics.

Ainge had just signed a new three-year contract with the Blue Jays in 1980, but the Celtics drafted him anyway in 1981, following his senior season at BYU when he won the Wooden Award as college basketball's player of the year. Three days later Ainge announced he had decided to play basketball.

The Blue Jays sued for breach of contract, and eventually both the Celtics and Blue Jays filed lawsuits in U.S. federal court against each other.

The Celtics sought a temporary restraining order to keep the Blue Jays from interrupting contract talks between Ainge and the NBA team. Their suit contended that "Ainge's contract as it purports to prevent Ainge from playing basketball is plainly invalid and unenforceable, and cannot lawfully be invoked to prevent Ainge from playing professional basketball."

The Blue Jays countersued, seeking an injunction that would prevent the Celtics from conducting further negotiations with Ainge and from signing him until 1983, when his Blue Jays contract expired. It also asked that the NBA be prevented from approving any contract Ainge might sign with an NBA team.

Ultimately, the courts ruled in favor of the Celtics, enabling him to play basketball. But the Celtics had to settle with Toronto for an amount in excess of $500,000.

Ainge had first-round talent in baseball had he decided to focus on the sport, but the arrangement that allowed him to juggle careers as a pro baseball and college basketball player worked for four years, until the Celtics threw a wrench into Toronto's best-laid plans.

It would be hard to argue that Ainge didn't make the right call, after a 15-year NBA playing career that led into coaching and then a long tenure as the Celtics' general manager.

## Highest Unsigned Picks

**JUNE/REGULAR PHASE ONLY**

| Player, Pos., Team (Round) | College | Re-Drafted |
|---|---|---|
| Ricky Wright, lhp, Cardinals (2) | Texas | Dodgers '80 (Jan.-S/1) |
| Terry Francona, 1b, Cubs (2) | Arizona | Expos '80 (1) |
| Keith Creel, rhp, Athletics (2) | Texas | Royals '80 (S/1) |
| Jeff White, c, Yankees (2) | Morehead State | Never |
| Dave Hodgins, c, Blue Jays (2) | USC | Never |
| Rick Foley, rhp, Padres (3) | *Santa Clara | Angels '78 (5) |
| Jerry Vasquez, rhp, Rangers (3) | *Arizona State | Mariners '78 (18) |
| Bret Baynham, lhp, Indians (3) | South Carolina | Never |
| Scott Sullivan, of, Red Sox (3) | Santa Clara | Never |
| Steve McQueen, ss, Mets (3) | Gulf Coast (Fla.) CC | Twins '78 (Jan.-S/5) |

**TOTAL UNSIGNED PICKS:** Top 5 Rounds (23), Top 10 Rounds (52)

**Returned to same school.*

# 1977 Draft List

**Did not sign. Major leaguers in bold, with first and last years noted. Order of selection indicated in parentheses. For the first five rounds of the June Regular Phase and the first round of all other phases, the peak level of each player is noted.*

## ATLANTA BRAVES

### January—Regular Phase (3)

1. (Selection forfeited as penalty for tampering with Gary Matthews prior to 1976 major league re-entry draft)
2. Romel Beck, ss, East Los Angeles JC.
3. *Mark Garber, rhp, Antelope Valley (Calif.) JC.
4. *Walter Parmenter, of, Middle Georgia JC.

### January—Secondary Phase (14)

1. *Gerald Price, 2b, Diablo Valley (Calif.) JC.—DNP

**DRAFT DROP** *First overall draft pick, June 1976/secondary phase, Braves*

### June—Regular Phase (4)

1. Tim Cole, lhp, Saugerties (N.Y.) HS.—(AA)
2. **Tony Brizzolara, rhp, University of Texas.—(1979-84)**
3. **Bob Porter, of, Napa (Calif.) HS.—(1981-82)**
4. *Allen Wesolowski, rhp, La Porte (Ind.) HS.—(Short-season A)

**DRAFT DROP** *Attended Eastern Michigan; re-drafted by Brewers, June 1978/secondary phase (1st round)*

5. Richard Wieters, rhp, The Citadel.—(AA)

**DRAFT DROP** *Father of Matt Wieters, first-round draft pick, Orioles (2007); major leaguer (2009-15)*

6. **Albert Hall, ss, Jones Valley HS, Birmingham, Ala.—(1981-89)**
7. George Ramos, of, Seton Hall University.
8. *Reggie King, c, Morgan Park HS, Chicago.
9. *Phil Deriso, lhp, Westover HS, Albany, Ga.
10. Jeffrey Matthews, ss-2b, Mankato State (Minn.) University.
11. *Greg Cypret, ss, University of Missouri.
12. Tom Mee, of, University of Minnesota.
13. *Cody Whitt, rhp, North Springs HS, Atlanta.
14. *Daniel Hejl, c, L.B. Johnson HS, Austin, Texas.
15. Terry Abbott, rhp, Jacksonville State University.
16. Daniel Ballard, rhp, St. Francis (N.Y.) College.
17. **Larry Owen, c, Bowling Green State University.—(1981-88)**
18. Daniel Lucia, rhp, JC of Marin (Calif.).
19. *Quinton Lloyd, of, L.B. Johnson HS, Austin, Texas.
20. ***Mike Brown, rhp, Marshall HS, Vienna, Va.—(1982-87)**
21. *Charlie Locke, rhp, Corrigan (Texas) HS.
22. Darryl Logan, 3b, Asheville (N.C.) HS.
23. Brady Baldwin, c, University of Cincinnati.
24. *Tod Carter, rhp, Washington & Lee HS, Arlington, Va.
25. Thomas LaGrave, rhp, American University.
26. *Daniel England, of, North Eugene (Ore.) HS

### June—Secondary Phase (23)

1. *Mark Martin, c, San Jacinto (Texas) JC.—(Low A)
2. *Billy Bowen, of, Grayson County (Texas) JC.

## BALTIMORE ORIOLES

### January—Regular Phase (20)

1. **John Shelby, ss, Columbia State (Tenn.) CC.—(1981-91)**
2. Tom Rowe, rhp, Rockland (N.Y.) CC.
3. Gerald Coleman, of, Baltimore.
4. *Frederick Lund, rhp, Sacramento (Calif.) CC.
5. *Mike Otto, of, Sacramento (Calif.) CC.
6. Terrence Swinton, ss, CC of Philadelphia.
7. Thomas McWilliams, c, Oakland (Mich.) CC.
8. *Michael Smoot, 3b-c, DeKalb (Ga.) JC.

### January—Secondary Phase (23)

1. Joseph Powell, 1b-3b, Valencia (Fla.) CC.—(High A)
2. *Gary Bozich, 2b, St. Petersburg (Fla.) JC.

### June—Regular Phase (19)

1. **Drungo Hazewood, of, Sacramento (Calif.) HS.—(1980)**
2. Dan Logan, 1b, West Georgia College.—(AAA)
3. Richard Moore, c, South Dorchester HS, Cambridge, Md.—(High A)
4. David Caldwell, of, Clemson University.—(AA)
5. Larry Jones, rhp, Florida State University.—(AAA)
6. Will George, lhp, Pennsauken (N.J.) HS.
7. Mark Van Bever, 2b, University of South Carolina.
8. John Denman, of, American University.
9. **Mark Smith, rhp, American University.—(1983)**
10. Russ Brett, 3b, Santa Clara University.
11. Michael Sherman, c, Goldsboro (N.C.) HS.
12. Steven Polan, 3b, University of La Verne (Calif.).
13. William Marrero, of, Hauppauge HS, Smithtown, N.Y.
14. David Lankster, ss, Middle Tennessee State University.
15. ***Mike Martin, 3b-c, Milwaukie HS, Troutdale, Ore.—(1986)**
16. *Mark Bolton, rhp, Longview (Texas) HS.
17. Tom Eaton, 2b, Tulsa University.
18. Michael Lacasse, 2b, James Madison University.
19. Steve Lesser, rhp, Alderson-Broaddus (W.Va.) College.
20. David Emala, 3b, Johns Hopkins (Md.) University.
21. Robert Whitfield, ss, Alderson-Broaddus (W.Va.) College.
22. *Lorenzo Bundy, ss, Essex HS, Tappahannock, Va.
23. ***Chris Jones, of, Grossmont (Calif.) JC.—(1985-86)**

### June—Secondary Phase (9)

1. Steve Lerner, lhp, University of Miami.—(High A)
2. *Earl Robinson, of, Gulf Coast (Fla.) CC.

## BOSTON RED SOX

### January—Regular Phase (14)

1. *Marcus Bell, rhp, Cleveland State (Tenn.) CC.—DNP
2. *Carl Pankratz, rhp, Temple (Texas) JC.
3. John Morgan, 3b, University of Massachusetts-Lowell.
4. *Rodney Feight, rhp, Indian River (Fla.) CC.
5. Stephen Annarummo, of, Rhode Island College.
6. *Ron Koenigsfeld, ss, Indian Hills (Iowa) CC.

### January—Secondary Phase (17)

1. Jim Wilson, 3b, Cerritos (Calif.) JC.—(AAA)

### June—Regular Phase (13)

1. Andrew Madden, rhp, New Hartford (N.Y.) HS.—(High A)
2. **Bobby Sprowl, lhp, University of Alabama.—(1978-81)**
3. *Scott Sullivan, of, Cupertino HS, Los Gatos, Calif.—DNP

**DRAFT DROP** *Attended Santa Clara; never re-drafted*

4. Erwin Bryant, ss, Columbia State (Tenn.) CC.—(AA)
5. Mark Baum, rhp, Northland HS, Columbus, Ohio.—(AA)
6. Scott Burk, 3b, Oklahoma State University.

**DRAFT DROP** *Defensive back, National Football League (1979)*

7. Richard Parr, of, Greenville (Ill.) College.
8. **Roger LaFrancois, c, University of Oklahoma.—(1982)**
9. Leonard Thompson, c, DeKalb (Ga.) JC.
10. **Steve Shields, rhp, Hokes Bluff HS, Gadsden, Ala.—(1985-89)**
11. *Bill Swiacki, rhp, Amherst (Mass.) College.

**DRAFT DROP** *Ninth-round draft pick, New York Giants/National Football League (1978)*

12. Frank Gill, 2b, Fairfield University.
13. Rick Colbert, c, Joliet Catholic HS, Joliet, Ill.
14. Barry Butera, ss-3b, Tulane University.
15. Al Hulbert, rhp, Westboro (Mass.) HS.
16. Mark Saunders, rhp, Allderdice HS, Pittsburgh.
17. ***Gary Redus, ss-of, Athens State (Ala.) College.—(1982-94)**
18. *Bruce Alexander, rhp, Kokomo (Ind.) HS.
19. Rosaire Viens, rhp, Sacred Heart University.
20. *Ell Roberson, of, Robert E. Lee HS, Baytown, Texas.
21. Russ Laribee, of, University of Connecticut.
22. ***Gerry Davis, 3b, Ewing HS, Trenton, N.J.—(1983-85)**
23. Rick Nesloney, rhp, Lamar University.
24. Mark Kaeterle, ss, Vocational HS, New Bedford, Mass.
25. **Pete Ladd, rhp, University of Massachusetts.—(1979-86)**
26. **Lee Graham, of, Lake Weir HS, Belleview, Fla.—(1983)**

### June—Secondary Phase (7)

1. Steve Collins, rhp, Fresno State University.—(High A)
2. Ronald Lee, ss, Blinn (Texas) JC.

## CALIFORNIA ANGELS

### January—Regular Phase (8)

1. **Alan Wiggins, 2b-of, Pasadena (Calif.) CC.—(1981-87)**
2. Guy Jones, rhp, JC of the Sequoias (Calif.).
3. **Daryl Sconiers, 1b, Orange Coast (Calif.) JC.—(1981-85)**
4. *Steve England, c, Mineral Area (Mo.) JC.
5. *Brian Winship, inf, Yuba (Calif.) CC.
6. *John Hartnell, lhp, El Camino (Calif.) JC.
7. *Barry Acquistapace, rhp, Santa Barbara (Calif.) CC.
8. ***Marty Castillo, 3b, Santa Ana (Calif.) JC.—(1981-85)**
9. *Ron Cooper, rhp, Orange Coast (Calif.) JC.
10. *David Bertulli, 3b, Valencia (Fla.) CC.
11. ***Marty Barrett, 2b, Mesa (Ariz.) CC.—(1982-91)**

**DRAFT DROP** *First overall draft pick, June 1979/secondary phase, Red Sox • Brother of Tommy Barrett, major leaguer (1988-92)*

### January—Secondary Phase (8)

1. Robert Healey, rhp, St. Louis CC-Meramec.—(High A)
2. *Monte Pries, rhp, Orange Coast (Calif.) JC.

### June—Regular Phase (7)

1. **Richard Dotson, rhp, Anderson HS, Cincinnati.—(1979-90)**
2. Gary Johnson, rhp, Deep Creek HS, Chesapeake, Va.—(High A)
3. Jeff Conner, lhp, Trevor Browne HS, Phoenix.—(AAA)
4. **Brian Harper, c, San Pedro HS, Rolling Hills, Calif.—(1979-95)**
5. **Ricky Steirer, rhp, University of Maryland-Baltimore County.—(1982-84)**
6. *Brian Hayes, lhp, University of Southern California.
7. Doug Thomson, rhp, University of La Verne (Calif.).
8. **Brad Havens, lhp, Kimball HS, Royal Oak, Mich.—(1981-89)**
9. Brandt Humphry, 3b, Arizona State University.
10. *Kevin Dukes, lhp, Sahuaro HS, Tucson, Ariz.
11. Michael Heaton, rhp, Butte (Calif.) JC.
12. George Tucker, lhp, Narbonne HS, Culver City, Calif.
13. *John Garcia, rhp, Carl Hayden HS, Phoenix.
14. ***Brian Denman, 1b-rhp, University of Minnesota.—(1982)**
15. *Mark Reeves, c, Spokane Falls (Wash.) CC.
16. Melvin Quarles, of, UC Riverside.
17. *Joseph Plummer, of, St. Anthony's HS, Long Beach, Calif.
18. Steve Trumbauer, c, California Lutheran University.
19. Filiberto Gonzalez, lhp, Sierra (Calif.) JC.
20. *Neal Herrick, rhp, Arundel HS, Jessup, Md.
21. Monte Mendenhall, rhp, University of Nevada-Las Vegas.
22. *Reggie West, of, Santa Ana Valley HS, Santa Ana, Calif.
23. Jesse Plummer, of, Salisbury State (Md.) College.
24. Jim Vallone, lhp, University of La Verne (Calif.).
25. Joey Blyleven, rhp, Santiago HS, Garden Grove, Calif.

**DRAFT DROP** *Brother of Bert Blyleven, major leaguer (1970-92)*

26. *Kim Nelson, 3b, Brigham Young University.
27. Art Miller, lhp, Northwestern Missouri State University.
28. *Les Pearsey, ss, University of Arizona.
29. *John Flares, rhp, Glendale (Ariz.) CC.
30. *Brett Baumann, lhp, Colton (Calif.) HS.
31. ***Dave Meier, ss, Bullard HS, Fresno, Calif.—(1984-88)**
32. ***LaSchelle Tarver, of, Madera (Calif.) HS.—(1986)**
33. *Jim Watkins, of, Valencia (Fla.) CC.

**DRAFT DROP** *First overall draft pick, June 1978/secondary phase, Braves*

### June—Secondary Phase (20)

1. **Mike Walters, rhp, Chaffey (Calif.) JC.—(1983-84)**
2. Michael Stover, rhp, Brigham Young University.
3. *Lyle Brackenridge, ss, Pasadena (Calif.) CC.

## CHICAGO CUBS

### January—Regular Phase (11)

1. *Blane McDonald, c, South Florida JC.—(High A)
2. Lawrence Panella, of, SUNY-New Paltz.
3. Charles Tewell, lhp, Chelmsford, Mass.
4. **Jim Tracy, of, Fairfield, Ohio.—(1980-81)**

**DRAFT DROP** *Major league manager (2001-12)*

5. James Messmer, 3b, Point Park (Pa.) College.
6. *Vincent Noldon, of, Porterville (Calif.) JC.
7. *Tim Mueller, rhp, JC of Southern Idaho.
8. *Randall Carter, ss, Arizona Western JC.

### January—Secondary Phase (11)

1. Jeff Hardy, ss, Florida State University.—(High A)
2. Billy Joe Minor, rhp, Angelina (Texas) JC.

### June—Regular Phase (12)

1. **Randy Martz, rhp, University of South Carolina.—(1980-83)**
2. ***Terry Francona, 1b, New Brighton (Pa.) HS.—(1981-90)**

**DRAFT DROP** *Attended Arizona; re-drafted by Expos, 1980 (1st round, 22nd overall) • Son of Tito Francona, major leaguer (1956-70) • Major league manager (1997-2015)*

3. Randy Clark, rhp, Point Loma HS, San Diego.—(AA)
4. **Dan Rohn, 2b, Central Michigan University.—(1983-86)**
5. **Steve Macko, ss, Baylor University.—(1979-80)**
6. Mike Turgeon, ss, Eastern Connecticut State University.
7. Carl Spikes, of, Southern University.
8. Thomas Spino, lhp, Maine East HS, Niles, Ill.
9. Michael Shepston, c, Phoenix (Ariz.) JC.
10. John Hartin, 1b-of, Missouri Baptist College.
11. Kenneth Veenema, 2b, Cornell University.
12. Michael Wright, lhp, Pattonville HS, Bridgeton, Mo.
13. Joseph Stethers, lhp, Coastal Carolina College.
14. Javier Fierro, 3b, Cal State Los Angeles.
15. Todd Winderfeldt, of, James Madison University.
16. Mark Obal, ss, Northeastern Illinois University.
17. *Dave Weatherman, rhp, West Torrance (Calif.) HS.
18. Joey Cole, rhp, Halifax HS, Vernon Hills, Va.
19. Bill Ross, rhp, Borah HS, Boise, Idaho.
20. *Stephen Maral, c, Marina HS, San Leandro, Calif.
21. *Carl Carlson, 1b-of, Cahokia (Ill.) HS.
22. *Luis Rojas, of, Kennedy HS, New York.
23. *Jay Schwamberger, lhp, Independence HS, Charlotte, N.C.
24. *James Robinson, of, Lake Washington HS, Kirkland, Wash.
25. Paul Brownlee, ss, Fairmont State (W.Va.) University.
26. Eric Robertson, of, Stillman (Ala.) College.
27. Vincent Valentini, rhp, Fairleigh Dickinson University.
28. *Wendell Henderson, c, Leon Godchaux HS, Mount Airy, La.
29. **Gene Krug, 1b, University of Oklahoma.—(1981)**
30. Rick DeLoach, 3b, Stephenville (Texas) HS.
31. John Bargfeldt, rhp-of, Anderson (Ind.) University.
32. *Anthony Veith, 1b, Brainerd, Minn.
33. *Jackie Snell, lhp, Tulane University.
34. William Morgan, of, Alief Hastings HS, Houston.
35. *Jon Putnam, rhp, King HS, Tampa.

36. Philip Rossi, ss, Millersville (Pa.) University.
37. Wilfred Puentes, of, Monmouth College.

**June—Secondary Phase (8)**

1. *David Sullivan, c, Yavapai (Ariz.) JC.—(High A)
2. Jerome Ahlert, ss, Cincinnati.
3. *Marcus Bell, rhp, Cleveland State (Tenn.) CC.

## CHICAGO WHITE SOX

**January—Regular Phase (2)**

1. *Simon Glenn, of, Blinn (Texas) JC.—DNP
2. *Handsome Roundtree, rhp, Orange Coast (Calif.) JC.
3. Jeff Vuksan, c, Miami-Dade CC South.
4. *Pat Rubino, c, JC of the Canyons (Calif.).
5. *Michael Selwood, 3b-c, Golden West (Calif.) JC.
6. (void) *Phillip Francis, rhp, Kent State University.
7. *Martin McDermott, ss-2b, Palm Beach (Fla.) JC.
8. **Mark Esser, lhp, Miami-Dade CC North.—(1979)**
9. Alex Suarez, c-of, Los Angeles Pierce JC.
10. *Pete Teixeira, rhp, Miami-Dade CC South.

DRAFT DROP *Uncle of Mark Teixeira, major leaguer (2003-15)*

11. *Rodolfo Arias, c, Miami-Dade CC South.
12. *Michael Powell, rhp, Manatee (Fla.) JC.
13. Joseph Netzler, rhp, Wautoma, Wis.
14. *Ted May, of, Cleveland State (Tenn.) CC.

**January—Secondary Phase (19)**

1. *Gary Bowers, rhp, Fullerton (Calif.) JC.—(High A)
2. John Hanley, c, Los Angeles Pierce JC.
3. *Robert Kocol, of, Brevard (Fla.) CC.
4. ***Charlie Lea, rhp, Shelby State (Tenn.) CC.—(1980-88)**

**June—Regular Phase (1)**

1. **Harold Baines, 1b-of, St. Michaels HS, Easton, Md.—(1980-2001)**
2. **Rich Barnes, lhp, Lake Worth (Fla.) HS.—(1982-83)**
3. Mark Naehring, 1b, Miami (Ohio) University.—(AAA)

DRAFT DROP *Brother of Tim Naehring, major leaguer (1990-97)*

4. *Dan Hanggie, ss-3b, Brea Olinda HS, Brea, Calif.—(AA)

DRAFT DROP *Attended Cal State Fullerton; re-drafted by Yankees, 1980 (7th round)*

5. *Paul Fox, rhp, San Mateo (Calif.) HS.—(Rookie)

DRAFT DROP *Attended Canada (Calif.) JC; re-drafted by Tigers, June 1979/secondary phase (1st round)*

6. **Rod Allen, of, Santa Monica (Calif.) HS.—(1983-88)**
7. *Perry Swanson, rhp, Rancho HS, Las Vegas, Nev.
8. Ron Woods, rhp, UC Santa Barbara.
9. *Fred Williams, lhp, Fremont HS, Sunnyvale, Calif.
10. Steve Tipa, of, University of New Haven.
11. **Rusty Kuntz, of, Cal State Stanislaus.—(1979-85)**
12. *Dennis Mark, of, West Valley (Calif.) JC.
13. *James Tjader, 2b, Iowa Western CC.
14. Rick Montoni, of, University of Miami.
15. Mike Johnson, of, Cal State Dominguez Hills.
16. *Bob Volk, 3b, Oral Roberts University.
17. ***Terry Bogener, of, University of Oklahoma.—(1982)**
18. Jackie Smith, lhp, Florida State University.
19. **Dewey Robinson, rhp, Southern Illinois University.—(1979-81)**
20. **Ross Baumgarten, lhp, University of Florida.—(1978-82)**
21. Ed Bahns, 1b, Florida Southern College.
22. *Alvin Ruben, 1b, Robert E. Lee HS, Baytown, Texas.
23. David Pencille, rhp, Cal Poly San Luis Obispo.
24. *Orlando Quiroga, rhp, Pima (Ariz.) CC.
25. *Rick Keeler, c, DeSoto (Texas) HS.
26. *Steven Mobley, rhp, DeSoto (Texas) HS.

**June—Secondary Phase (3)**

1. ***Hubie Brooks, of, Arizona State University.—(1980-94)**

DRAFT DROP *First-round draft pick (3rd overall), Mets (1978)*

2. David Daniels, of, West Covina, Calif.
3. *Greg Moyer, of, Cerritos (Calif.) JC.

## CINCINNATI REDS

**January—Regular Phase (23)**

1. Gregg Lorenz, lhp, Indian Hills (Iowa) CC.—(Low A)
2. *Jack Holmes, lhp, Temple (Texas) JC.
3. *David Hanna, rhp, Phoenix (Ariz.) JC.
4. Kevin Knuth, of, Monroe (N.Y.) CC.
5. Walter Paluch, of, Triton (Ill.) JC.
6. *Mike Schultz, rhp, Yakima Valley (Wash.) JC.
7. *Robert Potts, of, Yakima Valley (Wash.) JC.
8. *Ronnie Driver, lhp, San Jacinto (Texas) JC.
9. *Kevin Williams, of, Edmonds (Wash.) CC.
10. *Norman Walker, of, San Jacinto (Texas) JC.
11. *Michael Gouch, rhp, Kingsborough (N.Y.) CC.
12. ***Bob Dernier, of, Longview (Mo.) CC.—(1980-89)**

**January—Secondary Phase (1)**

1. **Bill Scherrer, lhp, University of Nevada-Las Vegas.—(1982-88)**

**June—Regular Phase (24)**

1. Tad Venger, 3b, Hart HS, Newhall, Calif.—(High A)
2. Ray Corbett, c, Samuel Clemens HS, Schertz, Texas.—(AAA)
3. Kevin Mulholland, lhp, Don Bosco Tech HS, Paterson, N.J.—(High A)
4. **Joe Price, lhp, University of Oklahoma.—(1980-90)**
5. Jack Hudson, c, Chapman (Calif.) College.—(AAA)
6. *Kevin Shannon, c, Sharpstown HS, Houston.
7. **Tom Foley, ss, Palmetto HS, Miami.—(1983-95)**
8. **Tony Walker, ss, San Marcos HS, Martindale, Texas.—(1986)**
9. Bill Kuchar, of, Manden HS, Hamden, Conn.
10. Joel Willett, rhp, Aloha (Ore.) HS.
11. Ricky Arnold, rhp, Ceres HS, Modesto, Calif.
12. John Halasz, of, Climax Scott HS, Scotts, Mich.
13. Larry Jackson, rhp, Rockledge (Fla.) HS.
14. Chris Wells, rhp, Bellport (N.Y.) HS.
15. Rick Lombardo, lhp, Florida Southern College.
16. Roger Glynn, lhp, Iowa Western CC.
17. Kelly Becker, lhp, Scottsbluff (Neb.) HS.
18. *Greg Korbe, of, Kansas State University.
19. *Donald Minnick, lhp, Liberty HS, Bedford, Va.
20. Robert Umdenstock, rhp, Lincoln HS, Des Moines, Iowa.
21. Michael Norman, rhp, University of California.
22. Greg Hughes, rhp, Sharpstown HS, Houston.
23. Larry Jensen, rhp, Mankato State (Minn.) University.
24. Wayne Pizer, of, Tigard HS, Tualatin, Ore.
25. Jeff Mihlbachler, rhp, St. Anthony HS, Effingham, Ill.
26. Theophilus Stokes, inf, Guilford (N.C.) College.
27. *Dan Flattery, rhp, St. Edmond HS, Vincent, Iowa.
28. *Mark Abrusley, rhp, Oakdale (La.) HS.
29. *Carlos Matamoras, 2b, South Miami HS.
30. *Dennis Trompeter, rhp, Northwestern University.
31. Robert Morrison, 2b, St. Olaf (Minn.) College.
32. *Dave Perez, ss-2b, Stanford University.
33. *Jeff Morrison, lhp, Atlantic Delray HS, Delray Beach, Fla.
34. *Jeffrey Ayers, rhp, Lake Washington HS, Kirkland, Wash.
35. *Olice King, lhp-1b, Bowen HS, Chicago.

**June—Secondary Phase (15)**

1. Robert Potts, of, Yakima Valley (Wash.) JC.—(Short-season A)
2. *Blane McDonald, c, South Florida JC.

## CLEVELAND INDIANS

**January—Regular Phase (11)**

1. Michael Elliott, lhp, West Hills (Calif.) JC.—(High A)
2. *Earl Robinson, of, Gulf Coast (Fla.) CC.
3. Bobby McCormick, of, Porterville (Calif.) JC.
4. Norm Churchill, lhp, Hillsborough (Fla.) CC.
5. Robert Costa, of, Lakeland (Ohio) CC.
6. Kendall Driggers, rhp, Florida JC.
7. *Chino Cadahia, 1b-c, Miami-Dade CC New World Center.
8. Donald Hubbard, 1b-3b, Seminole (Okla.) JC.
9. *Steven Robbins, 2b-3b, South Georgia JC.
10. Ernest Gibson, ss-of, South Georgia JC.

**January—Secondary Phase (6)**

1. *Frank Ferroni, lhp, Central Arizona JC.—(High A)

DRAFT DROP *First overall draft pick, June 1977/secondary phase, Twins*

2. *Tim Knight, of, Valencia (Fla.) CC.
3. *Pete Alfano, rhp, Jefferson State (Ala.) JC.
4. *James Harris, rhp, Mississippi State University.
5. *Thomas Underhill, rhp, University of Wisconsin.
6. *Jack Lopez, ss, Gulf Coast (Fla.) CC.

**June—Regular Phase (11)**

1. Bruce Compton, of, Norman (Okla.) HS.—(Low A)
2. Sam Davis, of, Jacksonville State University.—(Low A)
3. *Bret Baynham, lhp, Columbus HS, Miami.—DNP

DRAFT DROP *Attended South Carolina; never re-drafted*

4. *Michael Sanford, rhp, Childersburg (Ala.) HS.—DNP

DRAFT DROP *Attended DeKalb South (Ga.) CC; re-drafted by Rangers, June 1979/secondary phase (first round)*

5. ***Tim Lollar, lhp, University of Arkansas.—(1980-86)**

DRAFT DROP *Returned to Arkansas; re-drafted by Yankees, 1978 (4th round)*

6. **Eric Wilkins, rhp, Washington State University.—(1979)**
7. John Dubeau, lhp, Dos Palos HS, Firebaugh, Calif.
8. Scott Dwyer, rhp, Eau Gallie HS, Melbourne, Fla.
9. Stephen McMurray, c, Polk (Fla.) CC.
10. Albert Rausch, ss, Jacksonville University.
11. Lynn Garrett, of, University of Arizona.
12. Glenn Wendt, ss, University of Arizona.
13. Ricky Borchers, lhp, Southeastern Oklahoma State University.
14. **Kevin Rhomberg, 3b, College of St. Francis (Ill.).—(1982-84)**
15. **Jerry Dybzinski, ss, Cleveland State University.—(1980-85)**
16. Brent Hurley, of, Cuyahoga (Ohio) CC.
17. Ben Curry, 1b, Florida State University.
18. Kenneth Rogers, rhp, Faulkner State (Ala.) JC.
19. James Neely, rhp, Iowa Western CC.
20. Greg Johnson, rhp, Cal State Fullerton.
21. Tim Brill, c, St. Joseph's University.
22. *William Musser, rhp, Yorktown HS, Arlington, Va.
23. *David Jaffe, lhp, Keppel HS, Monterey Park, Calif.
24. Reggie Walker, 2b, Tuskegee (Ala.) Institute.
25. *Mitchell Denson, lhp, Tyler (Texas) JC.
26. *William Klank, rhp, Ewing HS, Trenton, N.J.
27. *James Souder, rhp, Bourgade HS, Phoenix, Ariz.
28. Sal Rende, 1b, St. Xavier (Ill.) College.

**June—Secondary Phase (16)**

1. John Shouse, 1b, University of South Florida.—(Short-season A)
2. Steven Robbins, 2b-3b, South Georgia JC.

## DETROIT TIGERS

**January—Regular Phase (6)**

1. Raphael Hampton, of, Jackson (Mich.) CC.—(AAA)
2. *David Witty, rhp, Yavapai (Ariz.) JC.
3. *John Tillema, rhp, DeAnza (Calif.) JC.
4. *Michael Rostas, rhp, Central Arizona JC.
5. *Roy Naas, rhp, Citrus (Calif.) JC.
6. Allan Bauman, lhp, Lakeland (Ohio) CC.
7. Larry Marsh, ss, Mount San Antonio (Calif.) JC.
8. ***Bill Laskey, rhp, Monroe County (Mich.) CC.—(1982-88)**
9. *Michael Murphy, rhp, Macomb (Mich.) CC.
10. Michael Bateman, ss, Riverside (Calif.) CC.

**January—Secondary Phase (10)**

1. **Mike Chris, 1b, West Los Angeles JC.—(1979-83)**
2. *Duane Evans, 1b, Yavapai (Ariz.) JC.
3. Larry Kowalishen, rhp, University of California.

**June—Regular Phase (5)**

1. Kevin Richards, rhp, Roosevelt HS, Wyandotte, Mich.—(AA)
2. Jeff Jackowiak, rhp, St. Joseph HS, South Bend, Ind.—(AA)
3. **Darrell Brown, of, Cal State Los Angeles.—(1981-84)**
4. *Mark McKinney, of, Tennessee HS, Bristol, Tenn.—DNP

DRAFT DROP *Attended North Carolina; never re-drafted*

5. Donald Taylor, 3b, Fair Park HS, Shreveport, La.—(Rookie)
6. Dave Steffen, rhp, Flat Rock (Mich.) HS.
7. **Ricky Peters, of, Arizona State University.—(1979-86)**
8. Kurt Hall, c, Cape Elizabeth (Maine) HS.
9. John Upshaw, c, Emporia State (Kan.) University.
10. Michael Beecroft, rhp, Kennedy HS, Sacramento, Calif.
11. *Bobby Supel, 3b, East Carolina University.
12. Gary Armstrong, ss, San Diego State University.
13. Clifton Wilder, of, Menchville HS, Newport News, Va.
14. **Bruce Robbins, lhp, Blackford HS, Dunkirk, Ind.—(1979-80)**

DRAFT DROP *Brother of Leroy Robbins, 11th-round draft pick, Athletics (1977)*

15. Dale Reis, lhp, UC Riverside.
16. *Willie Hardwick, rhp, Berkeley (Calif.) HS.
17. John Flynn, rhp, Kings Park (N.Y.) HS.
18. ***Willie Lozado, ss, Thomas Jefferson HS, Brooklyn, N.Y.—(1984)**
19. Joe Janton, rhp, UC Santa Barbara.
20. Ted Dasen, 3b, Eastern Michigan University.
21. Gary Champagne, of, Northwood (Texas) Institute.
22. Chuck Irving, rhp, Wake Forest University.
23. Bert Geiger, rhp, Palmetto HS, Miami.
24. *Kevin Balogh, rhp, University of Toledo.
25. *William Crews, of, Memorial HS, Wayne, Mich.
26. *Rod Hodde, 1b, Burton (Texas) HS.
27. *Theodore Geer, c, Park Ridge (N.J.) HS.
28. Ronnie Reasonover, of, Troy State University.
29. Juan Gomez, c, Union HS, Union City, N.J.

**June—Secondary Phase (24)**

1. ***Bill Laskey, rhp, Monroe (N.Y.) CC.—(1982-88)**
2. *David Witty, rhp, Yavapai (Ariz.) JC.
3. *Peter Padgett, rhp, University of Nevada-Reno.

## HOUSTON ASTROS

**January—Regular Phase (13)**

1. *Victor Walters, rhp, Miami-Dade CC South.—(Low A)
2. Don Harkness, ss, Lynn, Mass.
3. *Stephen McLaughlin, rhp, Cleveland State (Tenn.) CC.

**January—Secondary Phase (5)**

1. ***John Butcher, rhp, Yavapai (Ariz.) JC.—(1980-86)**
2. *Mark Grier, c, Anne Arundel (Md.) CC.

**June—Regular Phase (14)**

1. **Ricky Adams, ss, Montclair (Calif.) HS.—(1982-85)**
2. Stan Leland, rhp, Wabash (Ind.) HS.—(AAA)
3. Kevin Houston, lhp, Liberty (Mo.) HS.—(AA)
4. *Terry Byrum, ss, Madison HS, Houston.—(High A)

DRAFT DROP *Attended Houston; re-drafted by Mets, 1979 (35th round)*

5. **Scott Loucks, of, Southeastern Oklahoma State University.—(1980-85)**
6. Jim MacDonald, rhp, Woodsville (N.H.) HS.
7. *Steven Holman, rhp, Old Main HS, North Little Rock, Ark.
8. George Gross, 3b, University of Delaware.
9. Paul Cooper, of, Jackson State University.
10. *Wayne Guinn, rhp, Druid Hills HS, Decatur, Ga.
11. Fred Morris, lhp, LaSalle University.
12. Eddie Curry, lhp, Jackson State University.
13. Joseph Miller, of, Widener (Pa.) University.
14. **Billy Smith, rhp, Sam Houston State University.—(1981)**
15. *Stephen Martin, rhp, Palo Verde HS, Tucson, Ariz.

16. Charles White, rhp, DeKalb (Texas) HS.
17. *Don Robinson, rhp, Mississippi State University.
18. Steven Sitek, rhp, Hot Springs (Ark.) HS.

**June—Secondary Phase (19)**

1. *Victor Walters, rhp, Miami-Dade CC South.—(Low A)

## KANSAS CITY ROYALS

**January—Regular Phase (22)**

1. Cliff Roberts, of, Brevard (Fla.) CC.—(High A)
2. *Jeff Musser, of, Ferrum (Va.) College.
3. Robert Engelmeyer, lhp, Baltimore.
4. *Brad Coxon, ss, Central Arizona JC.

**January—Secondary Phase (25)**

1. *James Funderburk, lhp, Orange Coast (Calif.) JC.—DNP
2. Mark Daly, lhp, Florida Southern College.

**June—Regular Phase (21)**

1. **Mike Jones, lhp, Sutherland HS, Pittsford, N.Y.—(1980-85)**
2. Mike Morley, lhp, Eisenhower HS, Saginaw, Mich.—(AAA)
3. *Russ Davis, rhp, Meridian (Miss.) HS.—(High A)

DRAFT DROP *Attended Mississippi; re-drafted by Royals, 1980 (6th round)*

4. William Miller, rhp, Madison HS, Portland, Ore.—(High A)
5. Phil Westendorf, 1b, Washington State University.—(AA)
6. *Donald Oliver, rhp, Victoria (Texas) HS.
7. **Kelly Heath, ss, Louisburg (N.C.) JC.—(1982)**
8. Gerald Ako, rhp, University of Hawaii.
9. ***Bobby Bonner, ss, Texas A&M University.—(1980-83)**
10. Bret Mitchell, 3b, Clay HS, South Bend, Ind.
11. ***Bill Earley, lhp, Miami (Ohio) University.—(1986)**
12. Kevin Staley, rhp, Louisburg (N.C.) JC.
13. Elwaine Hardike, rhp, Glenbard East HS, Lombard, Ill.
14. Mickey Reichenbach, rhp, University of Texas.
15. Geoffrey Nash, of, Arthur Hill HS, Saginaw, Mich.
16. Rick McGlone, c, Florida State University.
17. Dennis Webb, of, Northwest Missouri State University.
18. Culpepper Smith, c, Leesburg (Fla.) HS.
19. **Renie Martin, rhp, University of Richmond.—(1979-84)**
20. Daniel Wieser, ss, Southeast Missouri State University.
21. *Ronn Dixon, lhp, Glen Oaks HS, Baton Rouge, La.
22. *Stephen Smith, of, Trenton Central HS, Trenton, N.J.
23. *Ken Martinson, c, West HS, Billings, Mon.
24. *Daniel Graham, c, Raytown (Mo.) South HS.

**June—Secondary Phase (22)**

1. *Michael Bates, rhp, Phoenix (Ariz.) JC.—DNP

## LOS ANGELES DODGERS

**January—Regular Phase (19)**

1. *Tim Gloyd, ss, Sacramento (Calif.) CC.—(High A)
2. Jessie Daniels, 2b, Louisburg (N.C.) JC.
3. Rocky Cordova, rhp, Sacramento (Calif.) CC.
4. *Daniel Forer, lhp, Iowa Western CC.
5. Larry Wright, rhp, DeKalb (Ga.) JC.
6. *Ronald Grout, 1b, Wingate (N.C.) College.
7. *Randall May, rhp, Yakima Valley (Wash.) JC.

**January—Secondary Phase (16)**

1. *Mark Martin, c, San Jacinto (Texas) JC.—(Low A)

**June—Regular Phase (20)**

1. **Bob Welch, rhp, Eastern Michigan University.—(1978-94)**
2. **Joe Beckwith, rhp, Auburn University.—(1979-86)**
3. Doug Harrison, rhp, Central Michigan University.—(AAA)
4. John Bush, ss, Ogden (Utah) HS.—(Short-season A)

Dodgers first-round pick Bob Welch overcame early struggles to pitch 17 years in the majors

5. **Mickey Hatcher, of, University of Oklahoma.—(1979-90)**
6. Mark Elliott, 1b, Silver Lake (Kan.) HS.
7. **Bobby Mitchell, of, University of Southern California.—(1980-83)**
8. James Nobles, lhp, Kentucky Wesleyan College.
9. Henry Noble, ss, McIntosh Academy, Darien, Ga.
10. Danny Coulon, rhp, JC of the Sequoias (Calif.).
11. Jack Littrell, rhp, Oldham County HS, Crestwood, Ky.
12. Ken Likewise, lhp, Chaparral HS, Scottsdale, Ariz.
13. *Dennis Delany, c, UCLA.
14. Jerry Bass, rhp, Georgia Tech.
15. Joe Purpura, lhp, West Leyden HS, Melrose Park, Ill.
16. Jesse Baez, c, Cerritos (Calif.) JC.
17. *Ed Reilly, rhp, Fanwood HS, Scotch Plains, N.J.
18. *Sam Favata, 2b, Edgewood HS, Baldwin Park, Calif.
19. *Richard Ross, of, Santa Teresa HS, San Jose, Calif.
20. *Steven Green, rhp, Pepperell HS, Rome, Ga.
21. *Mike Ledna, ss, Buffalo Grove (Ill.) HS.
22. Bobby Brown, of, John Brown (Ark.) University.
23. **Mitch Webster, of, Larned (Kan.) HS.—(1983-95)**
24. *Victor Woods, of, El Cerrito HS, Richmond, Calif.
25. Mike Zouras, 3b, Long Beach State University.
26. Michael Holt, rhp, East Forsyth HS, Kernersville, N.C.
27. *Mark Jakway, of, Hemet (Calif.) HS.
28. Douglas Hogan, rhp, Mineral Area (Mo.) JC.
29. *Melvin Freemen, 3b, Easley (S.C.) HS.
30. *Anthony Bolla, c, Crestmoor HS, San Bruno, Calif.
31. *Scott Hadley, rhp, Central HS, Hinsdale, Ill.
32. *Ronald Kiene, rhp, Stuyvesant HS, Brooklyn, N.Y.
33. *Jeffrey Jordan, rhp, Orangeville (Ill.) HS.
34. *Ken Duckett, of, Reynolds HS, Winston-Salem, N.C.
35. John Shoemaker, ss, Miami (Ohio) University.
36. ***Tom Niedenfuer, rhp, Redmond (Wash.) HS.—(1981-90)**
37. *Todd Roddy, inf, Bellevue (Neb.) HS.

**June—Secondary Phase (17)**

1. **Ron Roenicke, of, UCLA.—(1981-88)**

DRAFT DROP *Brother of Gary Roenicke, first-round draft pick, Expos (1983); major leaguer (1976-88) • Major league manager (2011-15)*

2. *Rick Kranitz, rhp, Yavapai (Ariz.) JC.
3. *Kevin Williams, of-1b, Edmonds (Wash.) CC.

## MILWAUKEE BREWERS

**January—Regular Phase (4)**

1. Daryl Bailey, rhp, Monroe (N.Y.) CC.—(AA)
2. Dale LaBar, 3b, New Castle, Del.
3. *Stephen Ibarguen, rhp, Panola (Texas) JC.
4. Richard Nicholson, rhp, St. Petersburg, Fla.

**January—Secondary Phase (4)**

1. Steve Splitt, of, UCLA.—(AA)
2. Larry Edwards, lhp, Allegany (Md.) CC.
3. *Steven Winfield, rhp, Panola (Texas) JC.

**June—Regular Phase (3)**

1. **Paul Molitor, ss, University of Minnesota.—(1978-98)**

DRAFT DROP *Elected to Baseball Hall of Fame, 2004 • Major league manager (2015)*

2. **Kevin Bass, of, Menlo HS, Menlo Park, Calif.—(1982-95)**
3. Stan Davis, 1b, Halifax HS, Nathalie, Va.—(AAA)
4. Jerry Jenkins, rhp, Royal HS, Simi Valley, Calif.—(AA)
5. *Michael Breslin, rhp, Bellaire HS, Houston.—DNP

DRAFT DROP *Attended Houston; never re-drafted*

6. Bill Foley, c, Clemson University.
7. *Alan Page, 1b, Menlo HS, Redwood City, Calif.
8. Steve Day, ss, University of Texas.
9. Chris Carstensen, of, Cal State Los Angeles.
10. **Dave LaPoint, lhp, Glens Falls (N.Y.) HS.—(1980-91)**
11. Mike Henderson, ss, Arizona State University.
12. Steve Manderfield, lhp, Kimball HS, Royal Oak, Mich.
13. John Skorochocki, ss, Trenton (N.J.) HS.
14. Joe Bob Mitchell, of, Prairie View A&M University.
15. Richard Bross, lhp, Tonawanda (N.Y.) HS.
16. *Larry Groves, rhp-of, Shawnee Mission West HS, Overland Park, Kan.
17. Tim Jordan, of, Edward Little HS, Auburn, Maine.
18. ***Dave Hudgens, 1b, Arizona State University.—(1983)**
19. *Ron Pisel, rhp, Southeastern Illinois JC.
20. Brian Fisher, ss, Tonawanda (N.Y.) HS.
21. *Charles Beverly, rhp, Kelly HS, Wise, Va.
22. ***Chris Bando, c, Arizona State University.—(1981-89)**

DRAFT DROP *Brother of Sal Bando, major leaguer (1966-81)*

23. *Larry Reasonover, 3b, Gulf Coast (Fla.) CC.

**June—Secondary Phase (14)**

1. Ron Driver, lhp, San Jacinto (Texas) JC.—(AA)
2. *Curt Reade, rhp, Hancock (Calif.) JC.

## MINNESOTA TWINS

**January—Regular Phase (16)**

1. Lance Hallberg, ss, San Bernardino Valley (Calif.) JC.—(AA)
2. *Craig Kornfeld, ss, Miami-Dade CC North.
3. Stan Cannon, of, Pensacola (Fla.) JC.
4. Dean Moranda, lhp, Fresno (Calif.) CC.
5. Tim Savage, c, San Bernardino Valley (Calif.) JC.
6. *Russell Fowler, 2b, San Diego Mesa (Calif.) JC.
7. ***Brad Lesley, rhp, Merced (Calif.) JC.—(1982-85)**
8. *Everett Rey, c, San Joaquin Delta (Calif.) JC.
9. *Richard Holloway, rhp, Gulf Coast (Fla.) CC.
10. *Casey Hagan, lhp, Los Angeles Harbor JC.
11. Mark Clapham, rhp, North Carolina State University.
12. *Manuel Adams, of-c, Fresno (Calif.) CC.
13. *Dale Adair, inf, Mount San Antonio (Calif.) JC.
14. *David Free, rhp, San Diego Mesa (Calif.) JC.
15. *Russ Penfold, lhp, Cypress (Calif.) JC.
16. ***Brad Mills, 3b-1b, JC of the Sequoias (Calif.).—(1980-83)**

DRAFT DROP *Father of Beau Mills, first-round draft pick, Indians (2007) • Major league manager (2010-12)*

**January—Secondary Phase (21)**

1. ***Mike Walters, rhp, Chaffey (Calif.) JC.—(1983-84)**
2. *Greg Stahl, ss, Los Angeles Harbor JC.
3. *Greg Moyer, of, Cerritos (Calif.) JC.
4. *Tom Costello, rhp, Oregon State University.

**June—Regular Phase (15)**

1. Paul Croft, of, Morristown (N.J.) HS.—(High A)
2. Bart Nieuwenhuis, lhp, Tombstone HS, Huachuca City, Ariz.—(Rookie)
3. **Roger Erickson, rhp, University of New Orleans.—(1978-83)**
4. Kevin McWhirter, of, San Diego State University.—(AA)
5. ***Rich Bordi, rhp, El Camino HS, San Francisco.—(1980-88)**

DRAFT DROP *Attended Fresno State; re-drafted by Athletics, 1980 (3rd round); first player from 1980 draft to reach majors (July 16, 1980)*

6. Steve Herz, c, Cal State Fullerton.
7. *Tom Jagiela, c, University of Minnesota.
8. *Eddie Rodriguez, ss-2b, Miami Senior HS.
9. **Darrell Jackson, lhp, Arizona State University.—(1978-82)**
10. George Slembecker, ss, Overlea HS, Baltimore.
11. *Mark Mauer, c, Harding HS, St. Paul, Minn.
12. Jose Rodriguez, ss, Flushing HS, Corona, N.Y.
13. Steve McManaman, of, University of Nebraska.
14. Gary Hall, c, Columbus (Ga.) College.
15. Gary Adair, of, Cal State Los Angeles.
16. Michael O'Connor, lhp, St. John's University.
17. Rick Cyburt, ss, Rider College.
18. **Scott Ullger, ss, St. John's University.—(1983)**
19. Ken Angulo, lhp-of, Edgewood HS, West Covina, Calif.
20. Rubio Malone, lhp, Compton (Calif.) HS.
21. *Tony Torres, rhp, Lemoore (Calif.) HS.
22. *Jim David, ss, Bishop Diego HS, Santa Barbara, Calif.
23. *Curt Burkhead, rhp, Crawford HS, San Diego.
24. Eugene Robinson, rhp, University of New Orleans.
25. Timothy Loberg, of-inf, University of Minnesota.
26. Joseph Bennett, 2b, University of New Orleans.
27. Abner Johnson, rhp, Creighton University.
28. Charles Aldridge, rhp, Las Vegas (Nev.) HS.
29. Joseph Tarver, ss, Arvin (Calif.) HS.
30. *Dominic Perry, 2b, Gahr HS, Lakewood, Calif.
31. *Robert Crissman, ss, Gahr HS, Cerritos, Calif.
32. *David Montanari, 2b, Santa Monica (Calif.) HS.

33. *Floyd Brennecke, ss, Azusa Pacific (Calif.) University.
34. Dwight Lewis, rhp, Cal State Fullerton.
35. Gary Bishop, 1b-of, University of Maryland.
36. Jeff Brueggemann, rhp, Stetson University.
37. *Glenn Cupstid, of, Windsor Forest HS, Savannah, Ga.
38. *David Fowke, 2b, Brandon (Fla.) HS.

**June—Secondary Phase (1)**

1. *Frank Ferroni, lhp, Central Arizona JC.—(High A)
2. Gary Bozich, 2b, St. Petersburg (Fla.) JC.

## MONTREAL EXPOS

**January—Regular Phase (1)**

1. *Kalvin Adams, c-3b, Central Arizona JC.—(High A)
2. Bobby Sagers, 3b-of, University of Cincinnati.
3. *Christian Loeffler, c, Wharton County (Texas) JC.
4. *Clifford Mackey, lhp, Linn-Benton (Ore.) CC.
5. *Michael Hobbs, of, Southeastern (N.C.) CC.
6. *William Eady, rhp, Temple (Texas) JC.
7. ***Dan Firova, c, Beeville (Texas) JC.—(1981-88)**
8. Richard Heidorn, ss, Ohio State University.
9. *David Waddell, rhp, Trinidad State (Colo.) JC.
10. *Michael Mann, rhp, St. Clair County (Mich.) CC.
11. Gregory Cox, rhp, Cincinnati.
12. *Gregory Charzanowski, ss, St. Clair County (Mich.) CC.

**January—Secondary Phase (22)**

1. *Allen Pye, lhp, DeKalb (Ga.) JC.—(Short-season A)

**June—Regular Phase (2)**

1. **Bill Gullickson, rhp, Joliet Catholic HS, Orland Park, Ill.—(1979-94)**
2. Greg Staffon, rhp, Hawthorne (Calif.) HS.—(High A)
3. **Scott Sanderson, rhp, Vanderbilt University.—(1978-96)**
4. Scott Anderson, rhp, Oregon State University.—(AA)
5. **Tim Raines, ss, Seminole HS, Sanford, Fla.—(1979-2002)**

DRAFT DROP *Father of Tim Raines Jr., major leaguer (2001-04)*

6. *Chris Day, lhp, Sharpstown HS, Houston.
7. David Hall, of, Rollins College.
8. Bruce McAlister, ss, Rollins College.
9. Thomas Haggerty, 1b, Maryvale HS, Phoenix.
10. *Ronald Brower, 1b, Appalachian State University.
11. Wayne Simmons, ss-2b, R.L. Osborne HS, Marietta, Ga.
12. Jeff Roberts, c, Newark Catholic HS, Newark, Ohio.
13. Randy Trumbull, rhp, Taft HS, Hamilton, Ohio.
14. Stanley Treadway, 1b, Jacksonville State University.
15. Daniel Morgan, rhp, University of Minnesota.
16. Mark Steenken, c, Northern Kentucky University.
17. Steve King, lhp, Middletown (Ohio) JC.
18. John Willis, rhp, Kecoughtan HS, Hampton, Va.
19. *Rob Pietroburgo, lhp, University of Missouri.
20. Harvey Kuenn Jr., 1b, Central HS, Milwaukee.

DRAFT DROP *Son of Harvey Kuenn, major leaguer (1952-66)*

21. Tommy Joe Shimp, rhp, Rose State (Okla.) JC.
22. Walter Coppol, lhp, Claymont (Del.) HS.
23. Tom Steinmetz, 2b, University of Iowa.
24. *Michael Kelly, of, Cordova HS, Rancho Cordova, Calif.
25. Richard Phillips, of-1b, Kentucky State University.
26. **Anthony Johnson, of, LeMoyne-Owen (Tenn.) College.—(1981-82)**
27. Dave Hensil, c-1b, University of Illinois.
28. Jeff Wilson, rhp, University of Cincinnati.
29. *Michael Ruelas, rhp, Alvin (Texas) HS.

**June—Secondary Phase (10)**

1. Kalvin Adams, of-3b, Central Arizona JC.—(High A)

Expos first-rounder Bill Gullickson overcame diabetes to pitch 14 years in the big leagues

## NEW YORK METS

**January—Regular Phase (15)**

1. *David Sullivan, c, Yavapai (Ariz.) JC.—(High A)
2. Robert Rossen, of, St. Petersburg (Fla.) JC.
3. *Donald Hess, c, Lamar (Colo.) CC.
4. *David Vickers, rhp, Lamar (Colo.) CC.
5. *John Hessler, rhp, Crowder (Mo.) JC.
6. *William Wrightson, 1b, DeAnza (Calif.) JC.
7. *Randall Cashore, rhp, Butte (Calif.) JC.

**January—Secondary Phase (3)**

1. *Ronald Lee, ss, Blinn (Texas) JC.—(High A)
2. *Brian Hurse, rhp, Florida JC.
3. *Michael Matlock, rhp-3b, Concordia (Ala.) JC.
4. *Anthony Guralas, ss-1b, Cuesta (Calif.) JC.

**June—Regular Phase (16)**

1. **Wally Backman, ss, Aloha HS, Beaverton, Ore.—(1980-93)**
2. **Mookie Wilson, of, University of South Carolina.—(1980-91)**

DRAFT DROP *Stepfather of Preston Wilson, major leaguer (1998-2007)*

3. *Steve McQueen, ss, Fernandina Beach (Fla.) HS.—(High A)

DRAFT DROP *Attended Gulf Coast (Fla.) CC; re-drafted by Twins, January 1978/secondary phase (5th round)*

4. Ray Lewis, c, Southern University.—(Low A)
5. **Fred Martinez, rhp, Cal State Los Angeles.—(1980-81)**
6. **Brent Gaff, rhp, Churubusco (Ind.) HS.—(1982-84)**
7. William Chamberlain, of, Woodrow Wilson HS, Long Beach, Calif.
8. Jeff Franklin, rhp, South Carroll HS, Mount Airy, Md.
9. Randy Bozeman, rhp, Thomasville Central HS, Thomasville, Ga.
10. August Garrett, of, Locust Valley (N.Y.) HS.
11. *Jean Donalaya, rhp, El Camino HS, San Francisco.
12. Stephen Golden, rhp, Paulding County HS, Rockmart, Ga.
13. Robert Healy, ss, Cal State Hayward.
14. Bert Kizer, 1b, Georgia Tech.
15. Michael Supczenski, of, Wilkes (Pa.) College.
16. *Michael Foster, lhp, Atwater (Calif.) HS.
17. Ron MacDonald, 2b, University of Kansas.
18. Scott Allen, rhp, Mercer University.
19. ***Craig Chamberlain, rhp, Long Beach (Calif.) CC.—(1979-80)**
20. James Olinger, rhp, St. Edward's HS, Elgin, Ill.
21. *Dan Gausepohl, of, Long Beach (Calif.) CC.
22. William Nafziger, c, Woodland (Calif.) HS.
23. Michael Lowry, rhp, Madera (Calif.) HS.
24. *Jack Lambeth, lhp, Hillcrest HS, Springfield, Mo.
25. *Chris Wilmes, 3b, St. Dominic HS, O'Fallon, Mo.
26. Doug Mizzi, lhp, Hicksville (N.Y.) HS.
27. Henri Jones, of, Iowa State University.
28. *Mike McCain, ss, Edmonds (Wash.) HS.
29. Greg Charleston, ss, Florida JC.
30. Duane Howard, rhp-of, Wichita, Kan.
31. Michael Brown, of, Southern Illinois University-Edwardsville.
32. *Sean Mays, ss, Dublin (Calif.) HS.
33. *Brad Jordison, lhp, Hillcrest HS, Sandy, Utah.
34. *Richard Finn, lhp, Northeast HS, St. Petersburg, Fla.
35. *Mark Raust, 1b, Campbell (Calif.) HS.

**June—Secondary Phase (25)**

1. Allen Pye, lhp, DeKalb (Ga.) JC.–(Short-season)
2. ***Bud Black, lhp, Lower Columbia (Wash.) JC.—(1981-95)**

DRAFT DROP *Major league manager (2007-15)*

## NEW YORK YANKEES

**January—Regular Phase (24)**

1. *Robert Moncur, of, Utah Technical JC.—DNP
2. Eddie Mickelsen, ss, Snow (Utah) JC.
3. *Peter Padgett, rhp, University of Nevada-Reno.
4. *James Harper, rhp, Los Medanos (Calif.) JC.
5. Jeffrey Thornton, of, Scottsdale (Ariz.) CC.

**January—Secondary Phase (15)**

1. **Willie McGee, of, Diablo Valley (Calif.) JC.—(1982-99)**

**June—Regular Phase (23)**

1. Steve Taylor, rhp, University of Delaware.—(AAA)
2. *Jeff White, c, Bryan Station HS, Lexington, Ky.—DNP

DRAFT DROP *Attended Morehead State; never re-drafted*

3. **Joe Lefebvre, of, Eckerd (Fla.) College.—(1980-86)**
4. **Roger Holt, ss, University of Florida.—(1980)**
5. Buck Showalter, of, Mississippi State University.—(AAA)

DRAFT DROP *Major league manager (1992-2015)*

6. *Michael Ickowski, rhp, John F. Kennedy HS, Cheektowaga, N.Y.
7. *Erik Hendricks, rhp, Chapman (Calif.) College.
8. Pat Callahan, c, University of Miami.
9. Jamie Werly, rhp, Harvard University.
10. ***Chuck Hensley, lhp, Tulare Union HS, Tulare, Calif.—(1986)**
11. Daniel Moroff, 3b, Valencia (Fla.) CC.
12. Paul Semall, rhp, Ohio State University.
13. *Andy Marston, of-rhp, Dunedin (Fla.) HS.
14. Rex Farrior, c, Jesuit HS, Tampa.
15. Rowland Keys, 2b, Rollins (Fla.) College.
16. *Gerald Weller, 1b-of, Michigan State University.
17. Kenny Baker, of, Wake Forest University.
18. Kevin Murphy, 1b-of, Bates (Maine) College.
19. Mike McLeod, rhp, Florida State University.
20. Dan Schmitz, 2b, Eastern Michigan University.

DRAFT DROP *Baseball coach, Bowling Green (1991-2015)*

21. **Chris Welsh, lhp, University of South Florida.—(1981-86)**
22. *Keith Schrimsher, rhp, Florida JC.
23. Tom Bonfield, 1b, St. Leo (Fla.) College.
24. **(void) *Juan Bonilla, 2b, Florida State University.—(1981-87)**
25. Ron Hess, ss, University of Iowa.
26. Gene Laguna, 3b, Seton Hall University.
27. Stan Saleski, rhp, Eckerd (Fla.) College.

**June—Secondary Phase (11)**

1. Byron Ballard, rhp, Miami-Dade CC North.—(AA)
2. ***Jack Lazorko, rhp, Mississippi State University.—(1984-88)**

## OAKLAND ATHLETICS

**January—Regular Phase (18)**

1. Dennis Wyszynski, rhp, Mercer County (N.J.) CC.—(AA)
2. Pat Dempsey, c, Columbia State (Tenn.) CC.

DRAFT DROP *Brother of Rick Dempsey, major leaguer (1969-92)*

3. *Doug Hunt, rhp, Taft (Calif.) JC.
4. *Bill Haley, rhp, Solano (Calif.) CC.
5. (void) *Larry Adams, rhp, University of Southern California.
6. *Robert Bradford, rhp, Yavapai (Ariz.) JC.
7. *James Evans, lhp, Santa Monica (Calif.) JC.
8. *Michael Boyd, of, Los Angeles Pierce JC.
9. *Ricky Allen, of, Southwestern (Calif.) JC.

**January—Secondary Phase (2)**

1. ***Hubie Brooks, ss-of, Mesa (Ariz.) CC.—(1980-94)**

DRAFT DROP *First-round draft pick (3rd overall), Mets (1978)*

2. Thomas Eagan, 3b, Green River (Wash.) CC.
3. *Kevin Darst, 2b, Solano (Calif.) CC.
4. *Preston Banks, 3b, Southwestern (Calif.) JC.

**June—Regular Phase (17)**

1. Craig Harris, rhp, Buena HS, Sierra Vista, Ariz.—(AA)
2. ***Keith Creel, rhp, Duncanville (Texas) HS.—(1982-87)**

DRAFT DROP *Attended Texas; re-drafted by Royals, June 1980/secondary phase (1st round)*

3. **Mike Davis, of, Hoover HS, San Diego.—(1980-89)**

DRAFT DROP *Brother of Mark Davis, major leaguer (1991)*

4. Dana Berry, 1b, Morgantown (W. Va.) HS.—(AA)
5. *Willie Davis, of, Jefferson HS, Portland, Ore.—DNP

DRAFT DROP *Attended Canada (Calif.) JC; re-drafted by Braves, January 1979/secondary phase (1st round)*

6. **Dave Beard, rhp, Sequoyah HS, Chamblee, Ga.—(1980-84)**
7. Scott Inbach, lhp, Chaparral HS, Las Vegas, Nev.
8. *Bill Repass, c, T.C. Roberson HS, Arden, N.C.
9. *Jay Erdahl, of, Lincoln HS, Seattle.
10. Robert Markham, 1b, Porterville (Calif.) JC.

11. Leroy Robbins, of, University of Kentucky.
DRAFT DROP *Brother of Bruce Robbins, 14th-round draft pick, Tigers (1977); major leaguer (1979-80)*
12. Ted Nowakowski, c, SUNY-Farmingdale.
**13. Jeff Jones, rhp, Bowling Green State University.—(1980-84)**
14. Paul Mize, ss, University of Hawaii.
15. *Maury Ornest, 1b, Beverly Hills (Calif.) HS.
DRAFT DROP *Son of Harry Ornest, owner, St. Louis Blues/ National Hockey League (1983-86)*
16. *Michael Munns, rhp, JC of Southern Idaho.
17. *David Curran, rhp, Pepperdine University.
18. *David Malloy, lhp, Heightstown HS, East Windsor, N.J.
19. *Kerry Sabo, rhp, West Geauga HS, Chesterland, Ohio.
20. *Edward Long, rhp, Fairfax HS, Los Angeles.
21. Dan Donovan, c, Morris Harvey (Ga.) College.
22. *Steve Shields, ss-rhp, Ranger (Texas) JC.
23. Rob Klebba, 2b, Pepperdine University.
24. *Michael Campbell, 3b, North Mesquite (Texas) HS.
**25. Shooty Babitt, inf, Berkeley (Calif.) HS.—(1981)**
26. *Harold Washington, of, Manual Arts HS, Los Angeles.
27. *Rondal Rollin, of, Carson (Calif.) HS.
28. *Ron Nickerson, 3b, Jordan HS, Los Angeles.
29. *Harry Brown, rhp, San Bernardino (Calif.) HS.
30. *David McClain, ss-3b, JC of the Canyons (Calif.).
31. *Mendez Davis, of, Centennial HS, Los Angeles.
32. *Gary Aguirre, ss, Foothill HS, Bakersfield, Calif.
33. *Michael Davis, ss-of, Compton, Calif.
34. Mike Yesenchak, lhp, Canon McMillan HS, Canonsburg, Pa.
35. *Stephen Dicarlo, rhp, Revere (Mass.) HS.
36. *Tom Riley, ss, Blanchet HS, Seattle.
37. *Joe Madrigal, rhp, Ganesha HS, Pomona, Calif.

#### June—Secondary Phase (5)

1. *Richard Holloway, rhp, Gulf Coast (Fla.) CC.–(AA)
2. Jack Holmes, lhp, Temple (Texas) JC.
3. *Dave Morgan, 3b, Fresno (Calif.) CC.
4. *Michael Mann, rhp, St. Clair County (Mich.) CC.
5. Frederick Lund, rhp, Sacramento (Calif.) CC.
6. *Rob Dondero, rhp, Mesa (Ariz.) CC.

## PHILADELPHIA PHILLIES

#### January—Regular Phase (21)

1. *Michael Childs, c, Ranger (Texas) JC.—(Low A)
2. *Byron Ballard, rhp, Miami-Dade CC North.
3. *Doug Laufer, rhp, Paris (Texas) JC.
4. Armando Abreu, lhp, Newark, N.J.
5. *Keith Bonine, rhp, Mesa (Ariz.) CC.
6. Gary Mitchell, rhp, Holyoke (Mass.) CC.
7. *Ernest Lee, of-ss, Ranger (Texas) JC
8. *Scott Job, rhp, JC of Southern Idaho.
9. *John Freed, rhp, Miami-Dade CC South.
10. *Eric Snider, rhp-c, Diablo Valley (Calif.) JC.
11. *David Labrum, rhp, JC of Southern Idaho.

#### January—Secondary Phase (9)

1. John Lohse, 3b, Butte (Calif.) JC.—(High A)
2. *Ray Mass, rhp, Bellevue (Wash.) CC.
3. *Tony Dorsey, of-2b, Fort Worth, Texas.

#### June—Regular Phase (22)

**1. Scott Munninghoff, rhp, Purcell HS, Cincinnati.—(1980)**
2. Earl Neal, 1b, San Bernardino (Calif.) HS.—(AA)
3. Andres Romero, of-1b, Miami HS.—(High A)
**4. George Vukovich, of, Southern Illinois University.—(1980-85)**
5. Keith Washington, of, Atlantic HS, Boynton Beach, Fla.—(AA)
6. John Quijada, ss, Trevor Browne HS, Phoenix.
7. Robert Volkerding, of, Central HS, Cape Girardeau, Mo.
8. Gregory Moore, rhp, East Bakersfield (Calif.) HS.
9. Ronald Smith, ss, Furman University.
10. *Lawrence Davila, rhp, Key West (Fla.) HS.
11. Michael Pace, of, University of Oklahoma.
12. John Daynor, 1b-of, Bradley University.
13. Steve Swain, of, Redondo HS, Redondo Beach, Calif.
14. Collin Sullivan, of, Christian Brothers HS, Sacramento, Calif.
15. *Martin Little, rhp, Ashe Central HS, West Jefferson, N.C.
16. Ernest Gause, lhp, Kingstree HS, Georgetown, S.C.
17. *Roger Godwin, rhp, Fernandina Beach (Fla.) HS.
18. Tom Lombarski, ss, Livingston (N.J.) HS.
19. *Gregory DeHart, rhp, North Hollywood (Calif.) HS.
**20. Greg Walker, c, Coffee HS, Douglas, Ga.—(1982-90)**
21. Anthony Capps, c, Jacksonville (N.C.) HS.
**22. Jerry Reed, rhp, Western Carolina University.—(1981-90)**
23. Dennis Becker, rhp, St. Louis University.
24. *Tim Geddes, rhp, Quartz Hill (Calif.) HS.
25. Wally Goff, lhp, William Penn HS, Bear, Del.
26. Steve Curry, inf, Scottsdale (Ariz.) JC.
27. Jose Castro, ss, Jackson HS, Miami.
**28. *Jim Adduci, of, Brother Rice HS, Oak Lawn, Ill.—(1983-89)**
29. Stuart Miller, c, Portola (Calif.) HS.
30. Ed Cuervo, c-2b, Angelina (Texas) JC.
31. *Kerry Nash, rhp, Miami-Dade CC South.
32. *Randy Wroten, of, Novi HS, Northville, Mich.
33. Chris Bouchee, of, Des Plaines, Ill.

#### June—Secondary Phase (6)

1. Chino Cadahia, 1b-c, Miami-Dade CC New World Center.—(AAA)

## PITTSBURGH PIRATES

#### January—Regular Phase (17)

1. Tom Fiesthumel, lhp, Utica, N.Y.—(Short-season A)
2. Randy Cooney, lhp, Austin, Pa.
3. *Joe Kubit, of, Valencia (Fla.) CC.
4. *Mark Endriss, 2b, Central Arizona JC.
5. Robert Ferguson, lhp, Point Park (Pa.) College.
6. *Joel Pyfrom, rhp, Miami-Dade CC South.

#### January—Secondary Phase (18)

1. Paul Rudiman, rhp, Lanham, Md.—(High A)
2. *David Banes, ss, Manatee (Fla.) JC.
3. *Timothy Newtson, c, Mesa (Ariz.) CC.

#### June—Regular Phase (18)

1. Anthony Nicely, of, Meadowdale HS, Dayton, Ohio.—(High A)
2. Mike Pill, rhp, Edgewood HS, West Covina, Calif.—(Low A)
3. Lance Dodd, rhp, Atholton HS, Laurel, Md.—(High A)
**4. Stew Cliburn, rhp, Delta State (Miss.) University.—(1984-88)**
DRAFT DROP *Twin brother of Stan Cliburn, major leaguer (1980)*
5. Jim Poff, of, Workman HS, Covina, Calif.—(High A)
6. *Randy Smith, rhp, Childersburg (Ala.) HS.
7. Charles Powell, lhp, Fullerton (Calif.) HS.
8. Paul Moore, of, Fort Chiswell HS, Max Meadows, Va.
9. Michael Shoaf, lhp, Carson City (Nev.) HS.
10. Phillip Cyburt, lhp, Brea Olinda HS, Brea, Calif.
**11. Rich Lancellotti, of, Glassboro State (N.J.) College.—(1982-90)**
**12. *Wayne Tolleson, ss, Western Carolina University.—(1981-90)**
13. *Mike Davis, 2b, Parker HS, Janesville, Wis.
14. Gerald Busby, rhp, Chaparral HS, Las Vegas, Nev.
15. Ben Wiltbank, rhp, CC of Baltimore.
16. *Mark Beuclear, rhp, Dickinson (Texas) HS.
17. *Mark Gray, 2b-ss, Gallatin HS, Warsaw, Ky.
**18. *Dennis Rasmussen, lhp, Bear Creek HS, Lakewood, Colo.—(1983-95)**
DRAFT DROP *First-round draft pick (17th overall), Angels (1980)*
19. Wendell Hibbett, of, University of Texas.
20. Casey Clark, ss, University of San Diego.
21. *Rusty Shelton, rhp-c, Gretna HS, Hunt, Va.
22. *Lawrence Dotson, of, San Bernardino (Calif.) HS.
23. Jessie Jones, c, Jackson State University.
24. *Ronald Thurston, c, Woodrow Wilson HS, Long Beach, Calif.
25. *Fulton Walker, of, Martinsburg (W. Va.) HS.
DRAFT DROP *Defensive back, National Football League (1981-86)*
26. *Mark Haley, c, Cabrillo HS, Lompoc, Calif.
27. *Kurt Kingsolver, c, Long Beach (Calif.) CC.
28. *Marvin Fowler, rhp, Madison HS, San Diego.
29. *Paul Doty, rhp, Santana HS, Santee, Calif.
30. Chick Valley, 1b-lhp, San Diego State University.
31. Edward Baker, 2b, DeKalb (Ga.) CC.
32. *Michael Ferguson, rhp, Northview HS, Covina, Calif.
33. *Robert Wicks, rhp, Amador HS, Pleasanton, Calif.
34. *William Metil, 3b, Northgate HS, Bellevue, Pa.
35. Timothy Ganch, 1b, Point Park (Pa.) College.
36. George Hill, of, Virginia Tech.
37. Steven Hawes, c, Tennessee Wesleyan College.
38. *Rick Witt, 3b, Spokane (Wash.) CC.

#### June—Secondary Phase (2)

1. *Bill Springman, 2b, Oral Roberts University.—(AA)
2. Michael Selwood, 3b-c, Golden West (Calif.) JC.
3. *Michael Childs, c, Ranger (Texas) JC.
4. Casey Hagan, lhp, Los Angeles Harbor JC.

## ST. LOUIS CARDINALS

#### January—Regular Phase (5)

1. *Curt Reade, rhp, Allan Hancock (Calif.) JC.—(High A)
2. *Rob Dondero, rhp, Mesa (Ariz.) CC.
3. *Rick Kranitz, rhp, Yavapai (Ariz.) JC.
**4. Tye Waller, 3b, San Diego CC.—(1980-87)**
5. (void) *Randy Wiens, rhp, Merced (Calif.) JC.
6. *Randy Evans, rhp, Central Arizona JC.
**7. *Jesse Orosco, lhp, Santa Barbara (Calif.) CC.—(1979-2003)**
8. *Greg Dees, c, San Bernardino (Calif.) JC.
9. *James Harskamp, ss, Merced (Calif.) JC.
10. *Terry Mixon, 2b, DeKalb South (Ga.) CC.

#### January—Secondary Phase (7)

1. Randy Puckett, ss, Reedley (Calif.) JC.—(Rookie)
2. *Larry Navilhon, rhp, JC of San Mateo (Calif.).
3. *James Snyder, of-1b, St. Clair County (Mich.) CC.

#### June—Regular Phase (6)

**1. Terry Kennedy, c, Florida State University.—(1978-91)**
DRAFT DROP *Son of Bob Kennedy, major leaguer (1939-57); major league manager (1963-68)*
**2. *Ricky Wright, lhp, Paris (Texas) HS.—(1982-86)**
DRAFT DROP *Attended Texas; re-drafted by Dodgers, January 1980/secondary phase (1st round)*
**3. Joe DeSa, 1b, Damien HS, Honolulu, Hawaii.—(1980-85)**
**4. Jim Gott, of-rhp, San Marino (Calif.) HS.—(1982-95)**
**5. Andy Rincon, rhp, St. Paul HS, Pico Rivera, Calif.—(1980-82)**
**6. Jeff Doyle, ss, Oregon State University.—(1983)**
7. Donald Moore, rhp, El Camino Real HS, Woodland Hills, Calif.
8. Leroy Grossini, ss, Santa Barbara (Calif.) CC.
9. Randy Howell, of, Furman University.
10. *Tom Heckman, rhp, Helias HS, Jefferson City, Mo.
11. Tom Chamberlain, rhp, Oregon State University.
12. *Stan Younger, of, Santa Monica (Calif.) HS.
13. *Don Tracey, rhp, Yonkers (N.Y.) HS.
14. Tom Vasche, rhp, Corvallis (Ore.) HS.
15. Kelly Miller, ss, Elon College.
16. Jim Reeves, of, Southern Illinois University.
17. Richard Murray, 3b, Southern Illinois University.
18. *Paul Grame, rhp, Los Altos (Calif.) HS.
19. Mark David, of, University of Houston.
20. *Kernan Ronan, rhp, Brophy Prep HS, Phoenix.
21. Brooks Whitehead, lhp, Westmont (Calif.) College.
22. Rick Cheshire, c, Middle Tennessee State University.
**23. *Floyd Chiffer, rhp, UCLA.—(1982-84)**
24. *Charles Montgomery, rhp, Chipola (Fla.) JC.
25. Barry Cheesman, c, Galesburg (Ill.) HS.
26. Darnell Barnett, of, Cal State Los Angeles.
27. Richard Hay, rhp, Lower Dauphin HS, Middletown, Pa.
28. Dennis Morton, lhp, Helix HS, Lemon Grove, Calif.
29. *John Cherney, rhp, Los Angeles Pierce JC.
**30. *Mike Jeffcoat, lhp, Pine Bluff (Ark.) HS.—(1983-94)**
31. Dennis Cirbo, c, University of Colorado.
**32. Neal Fiala, ss, Southern Illinois University.—(1981)**
33. *Otis Metz, of, New Rochelle (N.Y.) HS.
34. *Kenneth Erickson, rhp, Glendora (Calif.) HS.
35. Jimmy Hickman, of, Newberry (S.C.) College.
36. Vaughn Yadao, lhp, William McKinley HS, Honolulu, Hawaii.
37. *Steve Lane, lhp, Vanderbilt University.
38. Joe Baciotti, of, West Chester (Pa.) University.
39. *Richard Stewart, lhp, Fillmore (Calif.) HS.
40. William Thomas, rhp, Kecoughtan HS, Hampton, Va.
41. Jerry Poston, 1b-of, University of South Alabama.
42. *Deron Thomas, inf, McCluer HS, Ferguson, Mo.
DRAFT DROP *Son of Lee Thomas, major leaguer (1961-68)*

#### June—Secondary Phase (12)

1. *Simon Glenn, of, Blinn (Texas) JC.—DNP
2. *Greg Pastors, ss, Yavapai (Ariz.) JC.
3. Michael Rostas, rhp, Central Arizona JC.
4. Randall Bonner, c, Marietta, Ga.

## SAN DIEGO PADRES

#### January—Regular Phase (7)

1. Kevin Chapman, rhp, Mount San Antonio (Calif.) JC.—(Short-season A)
2. James Haight, lhp, Wilmington (Del.) College.
3. *Michael Bungarz, lhp, Chabot (Calif.) JC.
4. *Mark Boggs, rhp, Cleveland State (Tenn.) CC.

#### January—Secondary Phase (20)

1. *Frank Araneo, rhp, Valencia (Fla.) CC.—DNP

#### June—Regular Phase (8)

**1. Brian Greer, of, Sonora HS, Brea, Calif.—(1977-79)**
DRAFT DROP *First player from 1977 draft to reach majors (Sept. 13, 1977)*
**2. Barry Evans, ss, West Georgia College.—(1978-82)**
3. *Rick Foley, rhp, Santa Clara University.—(AAA)
DRAFT DROP *Returned to Santa Clara; re-drafted by Angels, 1978 (5th round)*
**4. Ozzie Smith, ss, Cal Poly San Luis Obispo.—(1978-96)**
DRAFT DROP *Elected to Baseball Hall of Fame, 2002*
5. James Stehle, lhp, Wilkes (Pa.) College.—(AA)
6. *Nick Harsh, rhp, Mater Dei HS, Santa Ana, Calif.
7. Michael Vint, rhp, Granite Hills HS, El Cajon, Calif.
8. Troy Dixon, rhp, Leuzinger HS, Hawthorne, Calif.
9. Bob Blakley, of, Southwest Missouri State University.
**10. Ron Tingley, of, Ramona HS, Riverside, Calif.—(1982-95)**
11. John Yandle, lhp, Stanford University.
12. George Hahn, c, Santa Clara University.
DRAFT DROP *Brother of Don Hahn, major leaguer (1969-75)*
13. John Alvarez, 3b, Cal State Fullerton.
14. Joe Carroll, rhp, University of Tulsa.
15. Eric Mustad, rhp, Cal State Fullerton.
16. Frank Hardy, 1b, Long Beach State University.
17. Eric Clark, of, Hoover HS, San Diego.
18. Curtis Reed, ss, Joliet (Ill.) West HS.
DRAFT DROP *Brother of Jeff Reed, first-round draft pick, Twins (1980); major leaguer (1984-2000)*
19. John Almon, of, Rhode Island College.
DRAFT DROP *Brother of Bill Almon, first overall draft pick, Padres (1974); major leaguer (1974-88)*
20. Gary Pickert, lhp, Emporia State (Kan.) University.
21. Larry Bowie, c, Jacksonville State University.
22. Gary Ashby, 1b, Texas Tech
**23. *Gary Weiss, 2b, University of Houston.—(1980-81)**
24. Glynn Tschirhart, ss-2b, St. Mary's (Texas) University.
25. Bob Sherwood, rhp, Washington State University.
26. William Wesserman, lhp, Glassboro State (N.J.) University.
27. *Harley Woody, lhp, Lookout Valley HS, Tiftonia, Tenn.

28. *Rob Hertel, 2b, University of Southern California.
DRAFT DROP *Quarterback, National Football League (1978-80) • Brother of Rich Hertel, fifth-round draft pick, 1977 (Blue Jays)*

**June—Secondary Phase (21)**

No selection.

## SAN FRANCISCO GIANTS

**January—Regular Phase (9)**

1. Gareth Ledbetter, c, Santa Ana (Calif.) JC.—(High A)
2. *Lyle Brackenridge, ss, Pasadena (Calif.) CC.
3. ***Bud Black, lhp, Lower Columbia (Wash.) JC.—(1981-95)**
DRAFT DROP *Major league manager (2007-15)*
4. *Randy Meyer, rhp, Mount Hood (Ore.) CC.
5. *Jeff Evans, inf, Golden West (Calif.) JC.
6. *Dennis Gonsalves, rhp, El Camino (Calif.) JC.
7. ***Jeff Lahti, rhp, Treasure Valley (Ore.) CC.—(1982-86)**
8. ***Jay Pettibone, rhp, Fullerton (Calif.) JC.—(1983)**
9. Bart Bass, rhp, San Diego.
10. *Dave Morgan, 3b, Fresno (Calif.) CC.

**January—Secondary Phase (24)**

1. *Mike Bates, rhp, Phoenix (Ariz.) JC.—DNP
2. *Jeff Ahern, lhp, Arizona Western JC.
3. *Stephen Youngman, 1b, Trenton State (N.J.) College.

**June—Regular Phase (10)**

1. Craig Landis, ss, Vintage HS, Napa, Calif.–(AAA)
DRAFT DROP *Son of Jim Landis, major leaguer (1957-67)*
2. **Phil Huffman, rhp, Brazoswood HS, Lake Jackson, Texas.—(1979-85)**
3. Mike Fox, ss, Fontana (Calif.) HS.—(High A)
4. Darnell Baker, of-c, Bishop Gibbon HS, Schenectady, N.Y.—(Low A)
5. *Jon Reelhorn, rhp, Edison HS, Stockton, Calif.—(AAA)
DRAFT DROP *Attended Fresno State; re-drafted by Phillies, 1980 (4th round)*
6. Scott Budner, lhp, Eastern Connecticut State University.
7. George Torassa, c, St. Ignatius HS, San Francisco.
8. Lou Marietta, rhp, St. Bonaventure HS, Ventura, Calif.
9. Glenn Goya, 1b, Colorado State University.
10. *Larry Fobbs, inf, University of Southern California.
11. **Chili Davis, of, Dorsey HS, Los Angeles.—(1981-99)**
12. **Bob Tufts, lhp, Princeton University.—(1981-83)**
13. *Ron Batter, c, JC of San Mateo (Calif.).
14. **Bob Kearney, c, University of Texas.—(1979-87)**
15. ***Jim Farr, rhp, Penn State University.—(1982)**
16. Jeff Stadler, rhp, Mission Bay HS, Pacific Beach, Calif.
17. *Daryl Adams, rhp, Willows (Calif.) HS.
18. *Norm Christensen, rhp, Clairemont HS, San Diego.
19. (void) *Joe Ward, of, University of Florida.
20. ***Ricky Horton, lhp, F.D. Roosevelt HS, Hyde Park, N.Y.—(1984-90)**
21. *James Keyte, lhp, Verdugo Hills HS, Tujunga, Calif.
22. *Albert Ward, rhp, Escambia HS, Pensacola, Fla.
23. *Steve Espinoza, ss, Los Altos HS, Mountainview, Calif.
24. *Joe Lentsch, c, Creighton University.
25. *Weston Mitchell, ss, Campbell (Calif.) HS.
26. *Dan Sijer, lhp, Shoreline (Wash.) CC.
27. *Rodney Hudson, c, Portland State University.

**June—Secondary Phase (4)**

1. John Fenwick, ss, Anoka, Minn.—(High A)
2. ***Dave Hostetler, 1b, University of Southern California.—(1981-88)**

## SEATTLE MARINERS

**January—Regular Phase (25)**

1. Paul Givens, lhp, Fresno (Calif.) CC.—(High A)

The Padres found Ozzie Smith in the fourth round but traded him to the Cardinals in 1981

2. Mark Schuster, 1b, Central Arizona JC.
3. Jeff Cary, rhp, Pensacola (Fla.) JC.
4. *Dan Townsend, of, Yavapai (Ariz.) JC.
5. Alphonso Eiland, of-ss, Palomar (Calif.) JC.
6. *Don Keener, 3b, Chipola (Fla.) JC.
7. *Glen Moon, of, Santa Monica (Calif.) JC.
8. *Porter Wyatt, of, Palomar (Calif.) JC.
9. *Michael Tice, of, DeKalb South (Ga.) CC.
10. James Hall, 2b-ss, Los Angeles.

**January—Secondary Phase (26)**

1. *Dom Antonini, c, Glassboro State (N.J.) University.—DNP
2. John Evans, 1b, Los Angeles Harbor JC.

**June—Regular Phase (26)**

1. **Dave Henderson, of, Dos Palos (Calif.) HS.—(1981-94)**
2. Henry Bender, c, Wilson HS, Tacoma, Wash.—(Short-season A)
3. **Bud Anderson, rhp, Rutgers University.—(1982-83)**
4. Kyle Koke, ss, South Grand Prairie (Texas) HS.—(AA)
5. **Ron Musselman, rhp, Clemson University.—(1982-85)**
6. Tony Cameron, lhp, Pepperdine University.
7. Michael Moore, 1b, Davis HS, Yakima, Wash.
8. Rodney Hobbs, of, Renton HS, Seattle.
9. Tracy Harris, rhp, Washington State University.
10. *John Haley, of, Anacortes (Wash.) HS.
11. ***Bill Latham, lhp, Huffman HS, Birmingham, Ala.—(1985-86)**
12. **Karl Best, rhp, Kent Meridian HS, Kent, Wash.—(1983-88)**
13. Mark Oestreich, of, Florida International University.
14. Tim Hallgren, rhp, Charles F. Adams HS, Clarkston, Wash.
DRAFT DROP *Scouting director, Dodgers (2007-10)*
15. Greg Biercevicz, rhp, University of Connecticut.
16. ***Tony Phillips, ss, Roswell (Ga.) HS.—(1982-99)**
17. Barry Knight, lhp, Hillsborough (Fla.) CC.
18. Lloyd Ard, rhp, Florida International University.
19. Al Weston, of, Michigan State University.
20. Gary McDonnell, 2b, Nicholls State University.
21. Larry Patterson, 3b, Gonzaga University.
22. Calvin King, ss, Southern University-New Orleans.
23. *Rick Ramos, rhp, Lewis (Ill.) University.
24. *Thomas Bloemke, rhp, University of Missouri.
25. *Jack Hills, lhp, Cal State Los Angeles.
26. Scott Miller, of, University of South Florida.
27. *Del Curtis, of, Central Arizona JC.
28. *Larry Eiler, lhp, Arizona State University.
29. *Rick Santarone, c, Cherry Hill (N.J.) HS.
30. Tom Fitzgerald, rhp, Florida International University.
31. *Juan Corey, c, Central HS, Miami.
32. *John Jordan, c, Mount St. Joseph HS, Glen Burnie, Md.

**June—Secondary Phase (26)**

1. Rodolfo Arias, c, Miami-Dade CC South.—(High A)

## TEXAS RANGERS

**January—Regular Phase (10)**

1. **Dave Righetti, lhp, San Jose (Calif.) CC.—(1979-95)**
DRAFT DROP *Brother of Steve Righetti, sixth-round draft pick, January 1977/regular phase (Rangers)*
2. *Phil Cordova, c, Colby (Kan.) CC.
3. *Billy Bowen, of, Grayson County (Texas) JC.
4. *Greg Pastors, ss, Yavapai (Ariz.) JC.
5. Ronald Johnson, 1b, Central Arizona JC.
6. Steve Righetti, 3b, San Jose (Calif.) CC.
DRAFT DROP *Brother of Dave Righetti, first-round draft pick, January 1977/regular phase (Rangers)*
7. *Frankie Meason, 1b, Paris (Texas) JC.

**January—Secondary Phase (12)**

1. Arnold McCrary, of, Los Angeles CC.—(AA)
2. Dennis Doyle, c, Assumption (Mass.) College.
3. *Robert Johnson, rhp, Southwestern Oklahoma State University.

**June—Regular Phase (9)**

1. David Hibner, ss, Howell (Mich.) HS.—(High A)
2. Linvel Mosby, rhp, Pecos (Texas) HS.—(Low A)
3. *Jerry Vasquez, rhp, Arizona State University.—(AA)
DRAFT DROP *Returned to Arizona State; re-drafted by Mariners, 1978 (18th round)*
4. **George Wright, of, Capitol Hill HS, Oklahoma City, Okla.—(1982-86)**
5. Mike Jirschele, ss, Clintonville (Wis.) HS.—(AAA)
6. Patrick Nelson, rhp, Carol City HS, Cooper City, Fla.
7. **Odie Davis, ss, Prairie View A&M University.—(1980)**
8. *Joseph Knight, rhp, Texas HS, Texarkana, Texas.
9. **Bobby Johnson, c, Kimball HS, Dallas.—(1981-83)**
10. Chuck Lamson, lhp, Gloucester County (N.J.) JC.
11. Steven Nielsen, rhp, Penn State University.
12. Ronald Carney, of, Texas Wesleyan College.
13. **Don Kainer, rhp, University of Texas.—(1980)**
14. Glenn Hollands, lhp, Santa Clara University.
15. *James Sutton, rhp, Colton (Calif.) HS.
16. William LaRosa, rhp, Dallas Baptist University.
17. *Ken Jones, rhp, Lennox (Calif.) HS.
18. *Richard Martini, of, UC Davis.
19. James Barbe, 3b, James Madison University.
20. Joseph Carroll, of, Lehigh University.
21. *Terry Mixon, ss, Georgia Southern College.
22. **Ed Lynch, rhp, University of South Carolina.—(1980-87)**
DRAFT DROP *General manager, Cubs (1994-2000)*
23. *John White, rhp, Millikan HS, Long Beach, Calif.
24. *Thad Reece, ss, Porterville (Calif.) HS.
25. Marty Scott, 3b, Dallas Baptist University.
26. *Dewey Porter, c, Munford HS, Detroit.
27. *Douglas Myers, 3b, Indian Lake HS, Huntsville, Ohio.
28. *Jeff Taylor, c, University of Delaware.

**June—Secondary Phase (18)**

1. **John Butcher, rhp, Yavapai (Ariz.) JC.—(1980-86)**
2. *Steve Winfield, rhp, Panola (Texas) JC.

## TORONTO BLUE JAYS

**January—Regular Phase (26)**

1. *Bradford Ross, of, Blinn (Texas) JC.—DNP
2. *Tom Penney, c, Blinn (Texas) JC.
3. Jay Robertson, rhp, Sacramento (Calif.) CC.
DRAFT DROP *Scouting director, Indians (1994-96)*
4. *Michael Wright, rhp, Fresno (Calif.) CC.

**January—Secondary Phase (13)**

1. *Jerry Stovall, rhp, Fresno (Calif.) CC.—(AA)
2. *Michael Barrett, rhp, San Jacinto (Texas) JC.

**June—Regular Phase (25)**

1. Tom Goffena, ss, Sidney (Ohio) HS.—(High A)
2. *Dave Hodgins, c, Buchser HS, Santa Clara, Calif.—DNP
DRAFT DROP *Attended Southern California; never re-drafted*
3. *Jim Teahan, rhp, Esperanza HS, Yorba Linda, Calif.—(AA)
DRAFT DROP *Attended Utah; re-drafted by Athletics, 1980 (18th round)*
4. Daryl Hill, 2b, Peterson HS, Sunnyvale, Calif.—(High A)
5. Rich Hertel, 3b, University of Southern California.—(High A)
DRAFT DROP *Brother of Rob Hertel, 28th-round draft pick, 1977, Padres; quarterback, National Football League (1978-80)*
6. David Rohm, rhp, Fresno State University.
7. Scott Gregory, rhp, University of Southern California.
8. Jack Hollis, rhp, University of New Mexico.
9. **Jesse Barfield, of, Central HS, Joliet, Ill.—(1981-92)**
DRAFT DROP *Father of Josh Barfield, major leaguer (2006-09)*
10. *Mark Armstrong, rhp, Chesterton (Ind.) HS.
11. Pete Rowe, c, Oregon State University.
12. Dwayne Wright, c, St. Mary's (Calif.) College.
13. Rocket Wheeler, 2b, University of Houston.
14. *Randy Brown, rhp, MacArthur HS, Houston.
15. **Danny Ainge, ss, North Eugene (Ore.) HS.—(1979-81)**
DRAFT DROP *Guard, National Basketball Association (1981-95); coach, Phoenix Suns/NBA (1996-99); president/basketball operations, Boston Celtics/NBA (2003-15)*
16. *Steve Leppert, c, Avon Worth HS, Pittsburgh.
DRAFT DROP *Son of Don Leppert, major leaguer (1955)*

**June—Secondary Phase (13)**

1. *Tom Penney, c, Blinn (Texas) JC.—DNP

# Braves go with Horner, but most covet Gibson

Arizona State had two of the top three picks in the 1978 draft, as Bob Horner (left) went to the Braves at No. 1, and Hubie Brooks went to the Mets

Bob Horner had just established NCAA season and career home run records. He went deep in his first professional game as a member of the Atlanta Braves on his way to becoming the National League Rookie of the Year.

But if the Braves had their way, Horner would not have been the No. 1 pick in the 1978 draft. Michigan State's Kirk Gibson was the player the Braves really wanted.

"Gibson stands out. The rest are a box entry," Braves scouting director Paul Snyder said on the eve of the draft. "If I had to compare him with anybody, he's like Mickey Mantle. You don't see that combination of speed and power very often."

Atlanta reluctantly passed on Gibson, and so did the next 10 teams before the Detroit Tigers snapped him up.

Gibson, an outstanding wide receiver and likely first-round pick in the 1979 National Football League draft, scared off the Braves and everyone else because of his football ambitions. He had a year remaining in college, and there were serious doubts that he'd give it up at any cost.

"I definitely want to play my senior year of football," Gibson said. "I'm not going to leave Michigan State. Being an athlete and a student here have been the best experience of my life, and I want it to last as long as possible."

The Tigers worked out Gibson at Tiger Stadium two weeks before the draft and watched him hit several balls into the upper deck. They also had a frank discussion with him over his willingness to play baseball and believed that if he were to sign with anyone, it would be his home-state team.

Atlanta led off the proceedings with Horner, and once the next 10 clubs skipped over Gibson, the Tigers took him with the 12th pick. Within a week, they had worked out a major league deal that allowed Gibson to return to Michigan State for his senior year of football and made him the highest-paid player of the draft era, with a signing bonus of $150,000, with the full value of his contract closer to $185,000.

Just two days later, on June 14, Horner set a new bonus standard by agreeing with the Braves on a $162,000 bonus as part of a major league contract that provided him an additional $21,000 in salary.

Horner was in the Braves lineup three days after that, and in his third at-bat homered against Pittsburgh's Bert Blyleven, setting off a wild celebration among the 18,572 Braves fans who had cheered his every move.

"There hasn't been this much feeling in the crowd since the day Henry (Aaron) hit 715," Snyder said. "It's a shame that we had to lose (9-4), because this is the biggest day I've ever experienced. When you work seven days a week for three months toward something like this, this reward is hard to describe."

Between their bonuses, the euphoria over Horner's debut and the national intrigue generated by Gibson's status as a two-sport star, Horner and Gibson became two of the most celebrated

## AT A GLANCE

### This Date In History
**WINTER DRAFT:** Jan. 10
**SUMMER DRAFT:** June 6-8

### Best Draft
**ATLANTA BRAVES.** The Braves got immediate production by drafting **BOB HORNER** and didn't stop there as they landed future Cy Young Award winner **STEVE BEDROSIAN** (3) and 13-year big leaguer **GERALD PERRY** (11).

### Worst Draft
**BOSTON RED SOX.** In the first year of draft-pick compensation, the Red Sox lost their top three picks in the June regular phase for signing free agents. They also didn't sign **MARTY BARRETT**, their top pick in the secondary phase (though they did get him a year later). All that left them with was one measly big league game from **JOHN LICKERT** (13).

### First-Round Bust
**NICK HERNANDEZ, C, BREWERS.** Hernandez was one of five first-round picks in 1978 who didn't reach Double-A. He was the first one drafted (eighth overall), first one released (July 10, 1981) and had the least productive career. In 238 games over four seasons, Hernandez hit .217; in 192 games behind the plate, he committed 48 errors and had 58 passed balls.

### Second To None
**CAL RIPKEN JR., RHP-SS, ORIOLES.** Ripken became a slam-dunk Hall of Famer with the Orioles, but there was plenty of debate when he was drafted whether he was picked as a favor to his father Cal Sr., and better suited to become a pitcher or third baseman.

### Late-Round Find
**RYNE SANDBERG, SS, PHILLIES (20TH ROUND).** Until Mike Piazza, Sandberg ranked as the lowest-round draft pick to reach the Hall of Fame. He slipped far beyond where his talent

CONTINUED ON PAGE 202

## AT A GLANCE

CONTINUED FROM PAGE 201

warranted because most clubs believed he was headed to Washington State to play football.

### Never Too Late

**CURT WARDLE, LHP, CARDINALS (45TH ROUND).** Wardle passed up an offer to sign out of high school. Three years later, he was chosen in the third round out of UC Riverside. He pitched in only two major league seasons, in 1984-85, and went a combined 8-9, 6.13.

### Overlooked

**BOB OJEDA, LHP, RED SOX.** The Red Sox made up for the loss of their top three picks by signing a pair of free-agent pitchers from the junior-college ranks prior to the draft: Ojeda, a soft-tossing lefthander from California's College of the Sequoias, and hard-throwing **STEVE CRAWFORD**, a righthander from Oklahoma's Rogers State. Expectations were higher for Crawford because of the $38,000 signing bonus he received, compared to just $500 given Ojeda. But Ojeda had the better career of the two, going 110-98, 3.65 over 15 seasons.

### International Gem

**JULIO FRANCO, 2B, PHILLIES.** Franco, a Dominican Republic product, had one of the most interesting careers in baseball history. He hit better than .300 in all five seasons he played in the minors for the Phillies; by the time he finally retired in 2009 at age 49, as the oldest active player in the game for four years running, he had played 23 years in the majors, while also seeing time in Japan, Korea and Mexico.

### Minor League Take

**MATT WINTERS, OF, YANKEES.** Winters hit 190 homers in 12 seasons in the minors (eighth-most all-time among first-rounders), plus another 160 in five

## 1978: THE FIRST ROUNDERS

| CLUB: PLAYER, POS., SCHOOL | HOMETOWN | B-T | HT. | WT. | AGE | BONUS | FIRST YEAR | LAST YEAR | PEAK LEVEL (YEARS) |
|---|---|---|---|---|---|---|---|---|---|
| **JUNE—REGULAR PHASE** | | | | | | | | | |
| 1. *Braves: Bob Horner, 3b, Arizona State | Glendale, Ariz. | R-R | 6-1 | 190 | 20 | $162,000 | 1978 | 1988 | Majors (10) |
| NCAA season/career home run leader stepped right into Braves lineup, hit 23 homers, became NL's top rookie; remainder of career rocked by controversy, injuries. | | | | | | | | | |
| 2. Blue Jays: Lloyd Moseby, 1b, Oakland HS | Oakland, Calif. | L-R | 6-3 | 190 | 18 | $55,000 | 1978 | 1991 | Majors (12) |
| Prep basketball all-American learned to play OF in first pro season, became part of dynamic Jays trio with Bell/Barfield; 169 HRs, 280 SBs in 12 MLB seasons. | | | | | | | | | |
| 3. Mets: Hubie Brooks, ss, Arizona State | Tempe, Ariz. | R-R | 6-0 | 180 | 21 | $50,000 | 1978 | 1994 | Majors (15) |
| Juco transfer spent two years at ASU, hit .396; drafted five times before signing with Mets; career took off when traded to Expos; hit .269-149-824 for five clubs. | | | | | | | | | |
| 4. *Athletics: Mike Morgan, rhp, Valley HS | Las Vegas, Nev. | R-R | 6-3 | 195 | 18 | $50,000 | 1978 | 2002 | Majors (22) |
| A's owner Charlie Finley's sacrificial lamb when began career in majors at 18; recovered from ordeal to pitch 22 years for then-record 12 clubs, won 141 games. | | | | | | | | | |
| 5. Padres: Andy Hawkins, rhp, Midway HS | Waco, Texas | R-R | 6-5 | 205 | 18 | $62,500 | 1978 | 1992 | Majors (10) |
| Superior athlete, prodigious punter in HS; went 84-91, 4.22 in big leagues, only pitcher to win World Series game for Padres, lost 4-0 no-hitter for Yankees. | | | | | | | | | |
| 6. Mariners: Tito Nanni, of/1b, Chestnut Hill Academy | Philadelphia | L-L | 6-4 | 205 | 18 | $101,000 | 1979 | 1985 | Class AAA (3) |
| Four-sport prep standout, top QB recruit held out all summer before signing deal with Mariners that got one club official fired; career peaked in Triple-A, hit. 253. | | | | | | | | | |
| 7. Giants: Bob Cummings, c, Brother Rice HS | Chicago | R-R | 6-2 | 180 | 17 | $50,000 | 1978 | 1986 | Class AAA (1) |
| Never advanced beyond Double-A in seven seasons in Giants system; signed by Mariners, played four more years, hit .258-54-309 overall; later became scout. | | | | | | | | | |
| 8. Brewers: Nick Hernandez, c, Hialeah HS | Hialeah, Fla. | R-R | 6-4 | 195 | 18 | $50,000 | 1978 | 1981 | Class A (3) |
| Chose pro ball over college football, but hit .217-9-65, committed 48 errors in 192 games behind plate, released in 1981; nephew of MLB ump Angel Hernandez. | | | | | | | | | |
| 9. Expos: Glen Franklin, ss, Chipola JC | St. Louis | L-R | 5-10 | 175 | 20 | $50,000 | 1978 | 1984 | Class AAA (2) |
| First juco player drafted in first round; hit .289-40-285, stole 129 bases in seven seasons with three organizations; struggled in field (81 errors in 179 games as SS). | | | | | | | | | |
| 10. Indians: Phil Lansford, ss, Wilcox HS | Santa Clara, Calif. | R-R | 6-3 | 195 | 18 | $68,000 | 1978 | 1981 | Class A (3) |
| Highest-drafted of three Lansford brothers, but achieved least as career peaked in Class A; hit .246-16-135 as 1B/3B, dealt to Blue Jays after first season. | | | | | | | | | |
| 11. Astros: Rod Boxberger, rhp, Southern California | Santa Ana, Calif. | R-R | 6-3 | 185 | 20 | $77,500 | 1978 | 1983 | Class AA (6) |
| College World Series outstanding player for champion USC; had losing record all six years in minors, went 30-55, 4.67 overall; son Brad became big league reliever. | | | | | | | | | |
| 12. *Tigers: Kirk Gibson, of, Michigan State | Waterford, Mich. | L-L | 6-2 | 212 | 21 | $150,000 | 1978 | 1995 | Majors (17) |
| Premium football talent played just one year of baseball in college; Tigers scored coup landing local product, hit .268 in MLB with 255 HRs; also managed in majors. | | | | | | | | | |
| 13. Cubs: Bill Hayes, c, Indiana State | North Platte, Neb. | R-R | 6-1 | 190 | 20 | $62,000 | 1978 | 1987 | Majors (2) |
| His Nebraska HS didn't field baseball team; became top prospect in college, hit .317-13-48 as JR; played five games in majors, has spent 38 years in coaching role. | | | | | | | | | |
| 14. Angels: Tom Brunansky, of, West Covina HS | West Covina, Calif. | R-R | 6-4 | 210 | 17 | $92,500 | 1978 | 1994 | Majors (14) |
| Chose Angels over Stanford football offer, was organization's top prospect when dealt to Twins in 1982; played 14 seasons with six clubs in majors, hit 271 HRs. | | | | | | | | | |
| 15. Cardinals: Bob Hicks, 1b, Gonzalez Tate HS | Pensacola, Fla. | R-R | 6-3 | 190 | 17 | $40,000 | 1978 | 1984 | Class AA (1) |
| Pursued pro career as hitter, batted .237-53-22 over five years in Class A for Cardinals; traded to Rangers in 1983 and tried pitching, but went only 2-3, 7.62. | | | | | | | | | |
| 16. Twins: Lenny Faedo, ss, Jefferson HS | Tampa | R-R | 6-0 | 170 | 18 | $50,000 | 1978 | 1986 | Majors (5) |
| Slick-fielding SS was product of Jefferson High baseball factory that produced numerous prominent big leaguers; spent five years with Twins, hit .252-5-52. | | | | | | | | | |
| 17. Reds: Nick Esasky, ss, Carol City HS | Carol City, Fla, | R-R | 6-3 | 190 | 18 | $40,000 | 1978 | 1992 | Majors (8) |
| Power bat primed for stardom after hitting .277-30-108 for Red Sox in 1989; signed with Braves as free agent but developed vertigo, played just nine more games. | | | | | | | | | |
| 18. Yankees: Rex Hudler, ss, Bullard HS | Fresno, Calif. | R-R | 6-1 | 175 | 17 | $100,000 | 1978 | 1998 | Majors (13) |
| High-energy player passed up football offer from Notre Dame to sign; got buried in deep system, but emerged to play 13 seasons in majors with sis clubs. | | | | | | | | | |
| 19. Pirates: Brad Garnett, 1b, DeSoto HS | DeSoto, Texas | L-L | 6-4 | 205 | 17 | $60,000 | 1979 | 1982 | Class A (4) |
| First of two Pirates first-rounders, neither advanced beyond Class A; career undone by injuries, well-documented alcohol abuse; hit only .210 with 40 homers. | | | | | | | | | |
| 20. Athletics: Tim Conroy, lhp, Gateway HS | Monroeville, Pa. | L-L | 6-0 | 178 | 18 | $30,000 | 1978 | 1989 | Majors (7) |
| Dominant western Pennsylvania prep arm followed same direct path to majors as fellow A's prospect Mike Morgan; 18-32, 4.69 record over seven seasons. | | | | | | | | | |
| 21. Pirates: Jerry Aubin, of, Dougherty HS | Albany, Ga. | R-R | 6-2 | 195 | 17 | $50,000 | 1978 | 1983 | Class A (3) |
| Left Pirates in 1979 after tearing up shoulder, played football at South Carolina before another devastating injury, failed in one final shot at baseball. | | | | | | | | | |
| 22. Orioles: Bob Boyce, 3b, Deer Park HS | Cincinnati | R-R | 6-1 | 175 | 18 | $30,000 | 1978 | 1982 | Class A (3) |
| Played alongside second-rounder Cal Ripken, won Appy League batting title in first season; career doomed by injuries, two elbow surgeries, released in 1982. | | | | | | | | | |
| 23. Phillies: Rip Rollins, 1b/rhp, Alleghany HS | Sparta, N.C. | R-R | 6-2 | 200 | 18 | $50,000 | 1978 | 1984 | Class AA (2) |
| Two-way talent chose Phils over South Carolina QB offer; arm problems led to 16-14, 5.12 record, subsequently became outfielder (.207-13-55). | | | | | | | | | |
| 24. Yankees: Matt Winters, of, Williamsville HS | Williamsville, N.Y. | L-R | 6-3 | 195 | 18 | $40,000 | 1978 | 1989 | Majors (1) |
| Cup of coffee with Royals in 11th pro season, but enjoyed success in minors (.275-190-835, 147 BBs in 1982, 122 RBIs in 1987), also slugged 160 homers in Japan. | | | | | | | | | |
| 25. Royals: Buddy Biancalana, ss, Redwood HS | Greenbrae, Calif. | B-R | 5-11 | 150 | 18 | $53,333 | 1978 | 1988 | Majors (6) |
| Slick fielder gained fame for standout performance in 1985 World Series, good-natured ribbing from David Letterman for offensive skills; career .234 hitter. | | | | | | | | | |
| 26. Yankees: Brian Ryder, rhp, Shrewsbury HS | Shrewsbury, Mass. | R-R | 6-5 | 200 | 18 | $50,000 | 1978 | 1983 | Class AAA (3) |
| With 43-19 record, became can't miss prospect while in Triple-A with Yankees in 1981, but miss he did after being traded that year to Reds for Ken Griffey Sr. | | | | | | | | | |
| **JANUARY—REGULAR PHASE** | | | | | | | | | |
| 1. Blue Jays: Mike Lebo, c, Connecticut | Middletown, Pa. | L-R | 6-4 | 215 | 19 | $43,750 | 1978 | 1982 | Class A (5) |
| Unanimous choice among MLB clubs as best prospect in lean January crop; offense-first catcher hit .241 with 44 homers in five seasons, none above Class A. | | | | | | | | | |
| **JANUARY—SECONDARY PHASE** | | | | | | | | | |
| 1. Twins: Joe Isaacs, rhp, Eastern Oklahoma State JC | Ada, Okla. | L-R | 6-4 | 200 | 20 | $15,000 | 1978 | 1979 | Class AA (1) |
| Unsigned fifth-rounder out of Oklahoma high school in 1976; lasted only two years in Twins system, went 10-15, 4.58, peaked in Double-A. | | | | | | | | | |
| **JUNE—SECONDARY PHASE** | | | | | | | | | |
| 1. Braves: Jim Watkins, c, Florida | Indianapolis | L-R | 6-0 | 175 | 20 | Unsigned | 1979 | 1980 | Class AA (1) |
| Drafted for fourth time, still didn't sign; .375 average was second-best in Florida history; re-drafted by Red Sox in 1979, played three years of pro ball. | | | | | | | | | |

**Signed to major league contract.*

## How They Should Have Done It

Based on the career WAR (Wins Above Replacement, as calculated by Baseball-Reference.com) numbers achieved by all the players eligible for the 1978 draft, here's how the first round should have unfolded. Numbers in parentheses indicate the round when the player was actually drafted

| | Player, Pos. | Actual Draft | WAR | Bonus |
|---|---|---|---|---|
| 1. | Cal Ripken Jr., 3b | Orioles (2) | 95.6 | $20,000 |
| 2. | Ryne Sandberg, ss | Phillies (20) | 67.6 | $25,500 |
| 3. | Dave Stieb, of/rhp | Blue Jays (5) | 57.2 | $28,000 |
| 4. | Tony Phillips, ss | Expos (Jan.-S/1) | 50.8 | $5,000 |
| 5. | Kirk Gibson, of | Tigers (1) | 38.2 | $150,000 |
| | Kent Hrbek, 1b | Twins (17) | 38.2 | $30,000 |
| 7. | Charlie Leibrandt, lhp | Reds (9) | 33.8 | $2,000 |
| 8. | Mike Boddicker, rhp | Orioles (6) | 31.8 | $12,500 |
| 9. | Lloyd Moseby, 1b | Blue Jays (1) | 27.6 | $55,000 |
| 10. | Mike Morgan, rhp | Athletics (1) | 26.6 | $50,000 |
| 11. | Steve Sax, 2b | Dodgers (9) | 25.3 | $15,000 |
| 12. | Bob Ojeda, lhp | Red Sox (NDFA) | 24.5 | $500 |
| 13. | Jesse Orosco, lhp | Twins (Jan.-R/2) | 23.9 | $6,000 |
| 14. | Mike Witt, rhp | Angels (4) | 22.0 | $30,000 |
| 15. | Doug Jones, rhp | Brewers (Jan.-R/3) | 21.8 | $4,000 |
| 16. | Bob Horner, 3b | Braves (1) | 21.7 | $162,000 |
| | Tom Brunansky, of | Angels (1) | 21.7 | $92,500 |
| 18. | Britt Burns, lhp | White Sox (3) | 18.1 | $20,000 |
| 19. | Gary Redus, 2b | Reds (15) | 16.2 | $3,000 |
| 20. | Eric Show, rhp | Padres (18) | 15.9 | $1,000 |
| 21. | Steve Bedrosian, rhp | Braves (3) | 14.9 | $18,000 |
| 22. | Rob Deer, of | Giants (4) | 13.7 | $10,000 |
| 23. | Hubie Brooks, ss | Mets (1) | 12.6 | $50,000 |
| 24. | Vance Law, 2b | Pirates (39) | 10.7 | None |
| 25. | Andy McGaffigan, rhp | Yankees (6) | 10.5 | $6,500 |
| 26. | Dave Valle, c | Mariners (2) | 10.1 | $28,000 |

| Top 3 Unsigned Players | | | | Year Signed |
|---|---|---|---|---|
| 1. | Mark Langston, lhp | Cubs (15) | 50.7 | 1981 |
| 2. | Frank Viola, lhp | Royals (16) | 47.4 | 1981 |
| 3. | Gary Gaetti, 3b | White Sox (June-S/3) | 41.8 | 1979 |

players of the draft era. But their major league careers, while noteworthy, were not the most successful among the cast of players drafted in 1978. They were easily trumped by a handful of others, the most obvious being future Hall of Famer Cal Ripken Jr.

### HORNER A SUBSTITUTE CHOICE

While the Braves were disappointed to pass on Gibson, they were happy to settle for Horner, who hit .412 with 25 homers and 100 RBIs that season for College World Series runner-up Arizona State. He was the No. 1-rated player by the Major League Scouting Bureau, and the winner of the inaugural Golden Spikes Award—college baseball's equivalent of the Heisman Trophy.

"Horner is ranked right close to Gibson in home run power, and on average he's probably a better hitter than Gibson," Snyder said.

Horner, a career .386 hitter who set an NCAA record with 56 homers, played all four infield positions at Arizona State. He was a second baseman most of the 1978 season, but switched to his natural position of third base in early May because of an arm injury to Jamie Allen.

"Seven of our people saw him play second, and four saw him play third," Snyder said. "We were greatly relieved when they moved him. The only doubt we had about him was whether he could make the move to third base."

The Braves had no intention of taking Horner directly to the big leagues when they began negotiations with Horner and his agent, Bucky Woy. But Horner persuaded Braves general manager Bill Lucas to give him a shot.

"I told Mr. Lucas there were no doubts in my mind I could play," Horner said. "I think I'm ready to go. Otherwise, I wouldn't have tried to talk him into it. I came here with the thought of staying and I have confidence I can do well."

Horner proved he belonged by hitting .266 with 23 homers over the balance of the 1978 season. Less than two months later, all the goodwill from Horner's success dissipated when Horner and Woy became entangled in a war of words with Braves officials over Horner's salary for 1979 and the interpretation of the major league contract he had signed.

Woy threatened to seek free-agent status for his client after the Braves offered Horner a $75,000 contract for the coming season. Woy argued that Horner's 1978 salary was $183,000—not $21,000, as the Braves claimed—and under terms of baseball's Basic Agreement he could not be cut more than 20 percent.

The Braves sent Horner a revised offer of $146,400 by the Dec. 20 contract deadline, but stipulated that amount was payable only if it was upheld in arbitration. Marvin Miller, director of the Major League Players Association, jumped in and said the Braves' offer did not constitute a firm offer. Woy then threatened that Horner would sit out the 1979 season if the Braves didn't meet his salary demand of $350,000.

Braves owner Ted Turner said Horner was not worth $300,000 a year, "and the only way he'll get that figure is if he can make that cute blonde hair curl without going to a hairdresser to get a permanent."

Woy and Horner filed a grievance against the Braves on Jan. 25, 1979, asking that Horner be declared a free agent. Horner became a spring-training holdout before finally reporting March 26. He started the 1979 season back at third base for the Braves, but an ankle injury on Opening Day sent him to the sidelines for 33 games.

Finally on June 4, a day before the 1979 draft, an arbitrator, Kansas State law professor Raymond Goetz, granted Horner a pay raise to a figure estimated at $130,000, but refused to grant him free agency. Horner claimed victory, though he said he was disappointed he did not gain his free agency.

"We're terribly disappointed," Woy said. "The remedy is short of what we were expecting. It obviously didn't make us happy. The arbitrator upheld our position that a signing bonus is part of the salary. We were right, but he didn't grant the free agency, which is a big disappointment."

Horner went on to play nine seasons with the Braves, but his career was ravaged by a string of injuries that cost him almost any chance to maximize his considerable offensive skills. He hit 217 home runs, including a record-tying four in one game in 1986.

He became a free agent a year later, but when

## AT A GLANCE

seasons in Japan, but went deep just twice in his only exposure in the majors, in 1989. Winters got buried in a deep Yankees farm system at the prime of his career in the early 1980s.

### One Who Got Away

**TIM WALLACH, 1B, ANGELS (8TH ROUND).** The Angels had Wallach, from right in their own back yard at Cal State Fullerton, firmly in their grasp but could not sign him. A year later, Wallach was taken by the Expos with the 10th pick overall, and went on to a productive 17-year career.

### He Was Drafted?

**BUCK BELUE, OF, WHITE SOX (2ND ROUND).** Belue played baseball four years in college and three more in the Expos system, but is best remembered as the quarterback for Georgia's 1980 national championship football team. The real star of that team was running back Herschel Walker, who narrowly missed winning the Heisman Trophy as a freshman.

### Did You Know . . .

While winning consecutive World Series in 1977-78, the Yankees also had the luxury of drafting three times in the first round in 1978 thanks to the loss of Ron Blomberg and Mike Torrez in the first year that teams were compensated with draft picks for losing free agents. In subsequent years, the tables turned as the Yankees routinely forfeited first-round picks because of their forays into free agency.

### They Said It

All-America wide receiver **KIRK GIBSON**, on playing baseball in college for the first time as a junior: "I didn't think I was going to be the least bit interested. But I enjoyed playing baseball more than I ever imagined. It was unbelievable."—*Gibson enjoyed it so much that he became a first-round pick in 1978, and quickly put football in his past.*

## DRAFT SPOTLIGHT: KIRK GIBSON

As one of the nation's top college-football talents, Gibson had a passion for football. He made it no secret that he played baseball as a youngster only because his father kept encouraging him to. He didn't play baseball at all in his first two years at Michigan State, and did so his junior year only at the prompting of Spartans football coach Darryl Rogers.

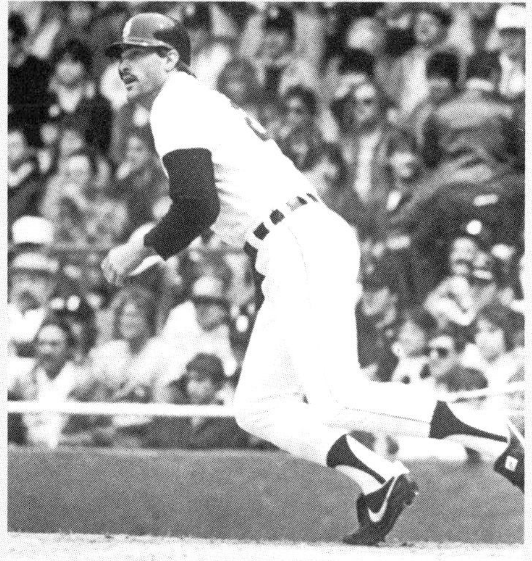

**Kirk Gibson played baseball as a way to get more leverage in the NFL draft, but he ended up making his career on the diamond**

"My whole idea was to get more money from football," Gibson said. "Darryl called me in and said, 'Play baseball. It'll give you more bargaining power.' I didn't think I was going to be the least bit interested. But I enjoyed playing baseball so much more than I ever imagined. It was unbelievable."

Gibson drew attention from scouts on Michigan State's spring trip to Texas, and the Major League Scouting Bureau graded both his speed and power at 80 on the 20-to-80 scouting scale. Bill Lajoie, the Tigers' director of player procurement, did a double-take when he saw that report. He had scouted Gibson in high school and recalled a player badly in need of playing experience. "His only redeeming quality," Lajoie remembered, "was his raw speed."

Gibson hit .390 for the Spartans and showed a rare combination of speed and strength, stealing 21 bases in 22 attempts while bashing a school-record 16 home runs.

"I would never have anticipated that he could have made that much progress in one year," said his father Bob, "but I always thought he had a lot of ability as a baseball player."

Few people outside the baseball world took Gibson's baseball exploits seriously, and Gibson even downplayed his own baseball skills, though some clubs felt it was a deliberate attempt to scare off every team except the Tigers. By mid-April, Lajoie had seen everything in Gibson he needed to see, but the Tigers masked their interest and were conspicuously absent from Michigan State's late-season games.

"What work I did on him, I did early," Lajoie said, "What more did I have to do, see him hit another one 450 feet? The only question was whether we would be able to get him. If you saw him play football, there was a question of whether you should mess with him."

Lajoie orchestrated a secret workout at Tiger Stadium on the eve of the draft. Gibson hit ball after ball into the upper deck, and Lajoie used the opportunity to pin down Gibson and his intentions: "I asked him, 'So Kirk, are you going to be a football player or a baseball player?' He tells me, 'I will play baseball, but only for the Detroit Tigers.' "

Gibson didn't reveal to anyone else before the draft that he would consider signing a baseball contract, even one that allowed him to continue playing football. Because of the personal relationship they established with him, the Tigers felt they had the best chance of landing Gibson. They kept their fingers crossed that he would still be available when it came their turn to select. To their good fortune, he was.

Gibson signed a contract in which he agreed not to pursue a pro football career. He did, however, return to Michigan State for his senior year and set Spartans career records for pass receptions (112), yardage (2,347) and touchdown receptions (24). He was selected in the 1979 NFL draft by the St. Louis Cardinals.

Gibson said he never considered trying to play both sports professionally, as Bo Jackson did later. Only when he struggled in his first full pro year at Triple-A Evansville, did Gibson even talk of resurrecting his football career. It became a moot point by the end of that summer as the Tigers called up Gibson, and even though he hit just .237 in 12 games, he soon forgot about football. By 1984, he had helped the Tigers win a World Series, and from 1984-86 he averaged 28 homers and 31 stolen bases a season.

In 1988, Gibson signed with the Los Angeles Dodgers as a free agent and won the National League MVP award. He became a key figure in another World Series celebration, in a single at-bat in the Dodgers 4-1 series victory over Oakland. Plagued by knee injuries, Gibson came off the bench in the bottom of the ninth inning of Game One and ripped a dramatic two-run homer for a 5-4 victory, a storyline lifted right out of *The Natural*.

he found no takers for his services—which players later discovered was because major league owners had colluded illegally to drive down salaries—he headed for Japan. He returned to spend the 1988 season with the St. Louis Cardinals, but played in just 60 games after injuring his left shoulder. His career ended when he couldn't answer the bell for the 1989 season.

### FINLEY OUTDOES HIMSELF

Four players selected in the 1978 draft began their careers in the big leagues. Horner proved he was ready for the challenge, but none of the other three, all high school selections, lasted more than three games before they were dispatched for much-needed seasoning.

Two of those players, pitchers Mike Morgan and Tim Conroy, were first-round draft picks of the Oakland Athletics. The fourth, catcher Brian Milner, was a seventh-round selection of the Toronto Blue Jays but the recipient of a staggering $140,000 bonus—the third-largest in the 1978 draft behind only Horner and Gibson.

For A's owner Charles O. Finley, starting Morgan and Conroy, both 18, in the majors was his way of immediately recouping his investment in the two players. Morgan, a righthander from Nevada, received a bonus of $50,000; Conroy, a lefthander from Pennsylvania, received $30,000.

Finley was threatening to move the A's out of Oakland because of poor attendance, and an influx of fans was more important to him than the long-range development of a couple of kids.

Finley sent Morgan, the fourth pick overall, to the wolves first.

"I think there's a danger of him getting his head knocked off," Finley said. "But after talking with the kid, I realized there was no possibility of him losing his confidence. He impressed me very much with his cocky confidence. He has a lot of poise."

Morgan debuted against the Baltimore Orioles on June 11, attracting a crowd of 23,123 to Oakland's Alameda County Coliseum, and writers from as far away as New York, Chicago and Boston. Morgan held his own by scattering 10 hits in a complete game, losing 3-0 and recording zero strikeouts. Morgan, who went 7-1, 0.68 and struck out 111 in 72 innings as a senior at Valley High in Las Vegas, said he never asked for the chance to join the A's immediately.

"(Finley) told me if I'm winning and looking good, I'll stay," Morgan said. "If it turns out I need experience, I'll go to the minors."

Morgan was tagged with three losses before he

### Fastest To The Majors

| Player, Pos. | Drafted (Round) | Debut |
|---|---|---|
| 1.*# Mike Morgan, rhp | Athletics (1) | June 11, 1978 |
| 2. # Bob Horner, 3b | Braves (1) | June 16, 1978 |
| 3.*# Brian Milner, c | Blue Jays (7) | June 23, 1983 |
| *#Tim Conroy, lhp | Athletics (1) | June 23, 1978 |
| 5. * Britt Burns, lhp | White Sox (3) | Aug. 5, 1978 |

**LAST PLAYER TO RETIRE:** Jesse Orozco, lhp (Sept. 27, 2003).

*#Debuted in major leagues. *High school draft choice.*

## Top 25 Bonuses

| | Player, Pos. | Drafted (Round) | Order | Bonus |
|---|---|---|---|---|
| 1. | **Bob Horner, 3b** | **Braves (1)** | **1** | **#$162,000** |
| 2. | **Kirk Gibson, of** | **Tigers (1)** | **12** | **#$150,000** |
| 3. | ***Brian Milner, c** | **Blue Jays (7)** | **158** | **#$140,000** |
| 4. | *Tito Nanni, of/1b | Mariners (1) | 6 | $101,000 |
| 5. | ***Rex Hudler, ss** | **Yankees (1)** | **18** | **$100,000** |
| 6. | ***Tom Brunansky, of** | **Angels (1)** | **14** | **$92,500** |
| 7. | Rod Boxberger, rhp | Astros (1) | 11 | $77,500 |
| 8. | *Phil Lansford, ss | Indians (1) | 10 | $68,000 |
| 9. | **Bill Hayes, c** | **Cubs (1)** | **13** | **$62,000** |
| 10. | *Brad Garnett, of | Pirates (1) | 19 | $60,000 |
| 11. | ***Lloyd Moseby, 1b** | **Blue Jays (1)** | **2** | **$55,000** |
| 12. | ***Buddy Biancalana, ss** | **Royals (1)** | **13** | **$53,333** |
| 13. | **Jim Maler, 1b** | **Mariners (Jan.-R/1) (5)** | | **$52,200** |
| 14. | **Hubie Brooks, ss** | **Mets (1)** | **3** | **$50,000** |
| | ***Mike Morgan, rhp** | **Athletics (1)** | **4** | **#$50,000** |
| | *Bob Cummings, c | Giants (1) | 7 | $50,000 |
| | *Nick Hernandez, c | Brewers (1) | 8 | $50,000 |
| | Glen Franklin, ss | Expos (1) | 9 | $50,000 |
| | ***Lenny Faedo, ss** | **Twins (1)** | **16** | **$50,000** |
| | *Jerry Aubin, of | Pirates (1) | 21 | $50,000 |
| | *Rip Rollins, 1b/rhp | Phillies (1) | 23 | $50,000 |
| | *Brian Ryder, rhp | Yankees (1) | 26 | $50,000 |
| | ***Darryl Motley, of** | **Royals (2)** | **51** | **$50,000** |
| 24. | Steve Michael, of | Expos (3) | 61 | $45,000 |
| 25. | Mike Lebo, c | Blue Jays (Jan.-R/1) | (1) | $43,750 |

*Major leaguers in bold. *High school selection. #Major league contract.*

was finally sent to Triple-A Vancouver.

"I got a lot of recognition for that, but it crushed my development," said Morgan, who returned to Oakland in 1979 and went on to spend 22 years in the majors with 12 clubs.

When Morgan was sent out, he was replaced by Conroy, who made two starts, walked nine and allowed four earned runs in five innings. He, too, was sent packing. But unlike Morgan, it would be another four years before a bewildered Conroy would return to the big leagues.

The 1978 draft marked the last time that a high school player would step immediately out of the draft and into a big league uniform.

### RIPKEN, SANDBERG UPSTAGE TOP PICKS

With their first pick in the 1978 draft, the Orioles selected a record-setting, high school third baseman. The player took professional baseball by storm by winning MVP honors in the Rookie-level Appalachian League.

That would seem to be a natural way for Cal Ripken Jr. to begin his career, considering all he would accomplish, but it actually describes Bob Boyce, the Orioles' top selection that year out of Deer Park High in Cincinnati, where he hit .550 and .525 in his final two years of high school, and knocked in 66 runs as a senior.

Boyce outplayed Ripken at Bluefield by hitting .319 with a league-high 19 doubles, playing alongside him in the field while hitting one spot ahead of him in the batting order. Unfortunately, that would be as good as it got for Boyce, whose promising career was destroyed by injuries.

The Orioles took Ripken with the third of three selections they had in the second round, and he thrived as O's officials wondered whether he was better suited to become a pitcher or infielder. Some wondered if he was a legitimate prospect at all, or whether he was drafted as a favor to his father, longtime Orioles minor league manager Cal Ripken Sr.

As a prep senior, Ripken, 17, pitched his Aberdeen High team to the Maryland Class A championship by tossing a two-hitter and striking out 17 to stretch his record on the season to 7-2, 0.70 with 100 strikeouts in 60 innings. He also hit .492, but a majority of scouts who saw Ripken that spring went on days he was scheduled to pitch, and saw more upside on the mound—even as his best pitch was a sinking fastball that most often was clocked in the 80s. As an everyday player, scouts questioned his hitting and running ability.

"Everyone said if they drafted me, it would be as a pitcher," Ripken said. "I didn't know how to feel about that. It was nice to know that there was strong interest in me, but I thought I had enough talent to be a regular player. It might have turned out different if any other team had taken me. I would have probably gone ahead and been a pitcher."

After considerable internal debate, and input from Ripken's father, the Orioles decided to break in the young Ripken as a shortstop. He got off to an inauspicious start. He committed 33 errors in 62 games for Bluefield and failed to go deep even once while hitting behind Boyce in the batting order. He had eight home runs to show for his first 693 professional at-bats.

As Ripken began to grow into his 6-foot-5 frame and his power manifested, the Orioles made the decision to move him to third base in his first full pro season. He played that position all the way up the ladder in the Orioles farm system, though the debate continued whether he was a better fit at third base or shortstop. He reached the majors in 1981 as a third baseman, and appeared to have the ideal profile to remain there.

But Orioles manager Earl Weaver, who liked Ripken as a position player when he was drafted, went against the grain again and decided to

**Believe it or not, many in the Orioles organization doubted whether Cal Ripken Jr. could be an everyday player, much less a shortstop**

### WORTH NOTING

■ The White Sox had little to show for the 22 picks they made in the two June phases of the 1978 draft, signing only eight players. They forfeited their first-round pick for signing free agent Ron Blomberg, and the lone selection who amounted to anything was lefthander **BRITT BURNS**, who went 20-1 with 292 strikeouts in 139 innings while allowing only run over his final two years at Huffman High in Birmingham, Ala. Burns reached the big leagues two months after being drafted, and by age 26 had won 70 games in the majors, including a personal-best 18 in 1985. But a congenital hip disorder forced him to retire prematurely. He attempted a comeback in 1990, but then quit for good after making four minor league appearances.

■ **GARY REDUS**, a 15th-round pick of the Reds, put together one of the most spectacular first seasons of any player in the draft era. Playing for Billings of the Rookie-level Pioneer League, Redus launched his career by hitting .462 with 17 home runs and 42 stolen bases. He led the league in batting, runs (100), hits (117), total bases (199) and steals. He used his big season as a springboard to a 13-year big-league career. "I don't think it made people think of me as a can't-miss prospect," Redus said. "The season was only 68 games long, and it was more like a college season than a pro season. It would be different if someone did that for a 140-game season. If someone did that, I'd say it was pretty incredible."

■ Lefthander **JESSE OROSCO**, who established a major league record for most games pitched in a career (1,252, all but four as a reliever) in a 24-year career from 1979-2003, was a product of the 1978 draft—as an overlooked second-round pick in the January regular phase by the Twins out of Santa Barbara (Calif.) City College,

CONTINUED ON PAGE 206

## WORTH NOTING

CONTINUED FROM PAGE 205

where he was 10-2 in 1977. Though drafted by the Twins, Orosco never pitched a game for that club until his final season. He was traded by the Twins to the Mets in 1979 before making an appearance.

■ The Major League Scouting Bureau report on Tigers first-round pick **KIRK GIBSON**, written on May 19, 1978 by bureau scout Jim Martz: "Best prospect I have ever seen. Outstanding physical specimen. Has the tools and makeup to be an offensive superstar and put people in the seats. Awesome power, excellent runner. Ball jumps off a short swing and quick bat. Highly competitive and confident in his abilities. Has hit several 500-foot-plus home runs this spring. Highly doubtful sign as player is adamant about playing senior year of college football. BASEBALL NEEDS THIS PLAYER."

■ The 1978 draft had special significance because it was the first one where compensation was awarded to teams that lost players through free agency. A complicated and short-lived re-entry draft was the mechanism that provided an orderly process for free agents to sign with other clubs; it was one of the major revisions in the game's reserve clause brought about by the far-reaching Messersmith Decision of 1976. Players with six years of major league service were eligible to gain their freedom by playing out their options, but were eligible to be signed only by the clubs that drafted them. Teams that signed free agents were now obligated to compensate the player's former club with a draft pick. No such compensation was required for the first wave of free agents a year earlier. Distinction was made in the quality of free agents lost. If a player's negotiating rights were claimed by fewer than two teams in the re-entry draft, then no compensation was required. A total of 11 free agents changed clubs

move Ripken back to shortstop once and for all, during his first full season in the majors in 1982. He remained there all the way through the 1997 season, a year before his record streak of playing in 2,632 consecutive games finally ended.

In a 21-year career with the Orioles, Ripken hit .276 with 431 home runs and 1,695 RBIs. He also collected 3,184 hits and was a 19-time all-star, two-time MVP and two-time Gold Glove winner.

Ryne Sandberg was the other 1978 draft pick to earn election to the Hall of Fame. Unlike Ripken, he was an established shortstop as a Washington high school senior and remained there coming up in the Philadelphia Phillies organization. But with Larry Bowa entrenched at shortstop and Mike Schmidt at third base when he was on the cusp of breaking into the major league lineup, the Phillies decided to shift Sandberg to second base.

Before that plan went into action, Sandberg was traded to the Chicago Cubs as a throw-in in a deal involving Bowa, and Bowa's continued presence assured that Sandberg wouldn't play shortstop in the majors. He settled in at second base for the Cubs over a 16-year career and established his Hall of Fame credentials by hitting .285 with 282 homers and 1,061 RBIs. He also stole 344 bases, was a nine-time Gold Glove winner and the National League MVP in 1984.

Sandberg was an afterthought in the 1978 draft, lasting until the 20th round, though it was because most teams considered him unsignable because of his commitment to play football at Washington State. But that didn't deter the Phillies.

"Back then, Philadelphia was one of those organizations that liked to get hard-to-sign players and work on them," said Moose Johnson, a Phillies crosschecker at the time. "Ryne was one of those. What helped us was the Major League Scouting Bureau had him as being worth just $4,000, and unsignable at that value. That kept a lot of scouts from traveling to the Northwest to see him."

Ryne Sandberg

Phillies area scout Bill Harper, however, had developed a close relationship with Sandberg, and when the 20th round came around, he pushed hard for the Phillies to take a chance on Sandberg, a three-sport star in baseball, football and basketball at Spokane's North Central High.

After three days of deliberations, Sandberg accepted the Phillies' $50,000 offer that included a signing bonus of $25,000, plus other incentives.

Scouting also played a vital role in the discovery of another successful player in the Class of 1978, first baseman Kent Hrbek, a 17th-round afterthought who enjoyed a long and productive career with the Minnesota Twins, his hometown team.

Typical of high school players in the colder climate of the upper Midwest, Hrbek went largely unnoticed at Bloomington's Kennedy High. But a concession worker at old Metropolitan Stadium, home of the Twins, tipped off scout Angelo Giuliani that he ought to check out the team's big, power-hitting first baseman. Giuliani did, and was so taken with what he saw that he described Hrbek as "the best prospect from Minnesota I've seen in my 30 years of scouting."

### Largest Bonuses By Round

| | Player, Pos. | Club | Bonus |
|---|---|---|---|
| **1.** | **Bob Horner, 3b** | **Braves** | **$162,000** |
| **2.** | *** Darryl Motley, of** | **Royals** | **$50,000** |
| 3. | Steve Michael, of | Expos | $45,000 |
| **4.** | *** Mike Witt, rhp** | **Angels** | **$30,000** |
| 5. | * Darren Burroughs, lhp | Phillies | $30,000 |
| 6. | Pete Dempsey, ss | Phillies | $27,500 |
| **7.** | *** Brian Milner, c** | **Blue Jays** | **$140,000** |
| 8. | Bill Swiacki, rhp | Dodgers | $18,000 |
| 9. | Mike Wright, of | Tigers | $15,000 |
| | *** Steve Sax, ss** | **Dodgers** | **$15,000** |
| 10. | Rodney Kemp, of | Dodgers | $12,000 |
| **Jan/R.** | **Jim Maler, 1b** | **Mariners (1)** | **$52,200** |
| Jan/S. | Rusty McDonald, rhp | Dodgers (1) | $18,000 |
| **Jun/S.** | **Craig Chamberlain, rhp** | **Royals (1)** | **$18,000** |

*Major leaguers in bold. *High school selection.*

Giuliani was convinced he had a steal in Hrbek, but he was also certain that no other team knew about his hidden gem, so the Twins didn't feel any urgency to draft Hrbek in an early round.

"He was a 17th-rounder who would have been a first-rounder if anyone else would have known about him," Giuliani said.

The Twins treated Hrbek like a 17th-rounder with their initial contract offer of $5,000. He rejected it, and appeared headed for the University of Minnesota when the Twins didn't raise the ante. But in a late-summer American Legion game, with Twins owner Calvin Griffith and farm director George Brophy both on hand at the insistence of Giuliani, Hrbek seized the moment by launching one of the tape-measure home runs he would soon become known for. Suitably impressed, Griffith authorized a $30,000 bonus to sign Hrbek—a figure more in line with what a first-rounder might expect, not a 17th-round afterthought.

Over a 14-year big league career, all with the Twins, Hrbek hit .287 with 340 homers, and played a major role in transforming a perennial sub-.500 team into a two-time World Series champion.

Astute scouting also played a critical role in the scouting and signing of the best pitcher to emerge from the 1978 draft.

Dave Stieb was an All-America outfielder in his first season at Southern Illinois, after transferring there from a California junior college. Most scouts saw Stieb as an everyday player, and a report from a Blue Jays area scout indicated that Stieb could run, throw, defend and hit with power, and said he should be crosschecked as a potential early-round pick on the basis of those tools.

But even with a .394 average and 12 home runs on his resume, Stieb did little to impress veteran Blue Jays scouts Bobby Mattick and Al LaMacchia, who saw him in an early May game against Eastern Illinois. They had all but written him off as a prospect when Stieb was pressed into service as a pitcher late in the game.

Though Mattick and LaMacchia were there to look at Stieb as an outfielder, his appearance on the mound grabbed their attention. "Stieb knocked our eyeballs out," Mattick said. "He was absolutely overpowering. We didn't like him as a hitter, but he sure as hell opened our eyes when he started pitching. We decided to draft him."

Dave Stieb

Stieb pitched in 17 innings for the Salukis that spring, but the Blue Jays stepped up and drafted him in the fifth round on the basis of his lively right arm. Then they took on the tall order of convincing Stieb to become a full-time pitcher. He still saw himself as an everyday player and continued to play center field most of the time as a first-year pro.

He didn't become a full-time pitcher until 1979, and after going 10-2 at two levels in the Jays system Stieb quickly found himself in the big leagues, the first year of an outstanding 15-year career on the mound for the Blue Jays. On the strength of his dominant fastball and slider, he won 175 games.

## MARINERS MIRED IN CONTROVERSY

The Blue Jays made waves in the 1978 draft by spending the exorbitant sum of $140,000 on Milner, a seventh-round pick whose career never materialized because of injuries. The Seattle Mariners, the Jays' 1977 American League expansion cousins, attempted to keep pace by lavishing their own six-figure bonus on outfielder Tito Nanni, the sixth overall pick.

Nanni didn't reach his potential, either, after a failed seven-year career in the minors. But the repercussions over Nanni's signing were immediate and far-reaching.

The Mariners had initially targeted Gibson with their first-round pick, and club officials claim they had been given word that Gibson would sign with them. But a financially strapped ownership group that included entertainer Danny Kaye vetoed the move. The Mariners went to Plan B, and drafted a player they determined was the next best thing to Gibson: the 6-foot-4, 210-pound Nanni, a football/baseball star from Philadelphia. He bore a striking physical resemblance to Gibson, and also could run and hit with power.

The Mariners found out the hard way that Nanni's price tag was in Gibson's range. After relentlessly pursuing him all summer, they finally talked Nanni out of his football commitment to the University of North Carolina on Aug. 22 by agreeing to a bonus of $101,000.

"Tito is the kind of player we have to sign to put together a solid minor league organization," said Mel Didier, the club's director of player development and scouting. "He can drive the ball out of sight and he runs the 40 in 4.7 seconds—outstanding speed for a big fella."

But the signing cost Didier his job, as he had exceeded budget authority by some $50,000 to collar Nanni. Officially, Kip Horsburgh, the Mariners executive director, said he fired Didier because of events stemming from Didier authorizing a "clearly improper contract." Didier's firing created discord throughout the organization.

"We had to sign Nanni," general manager Lou Gorman said in support of Didier. "He can play. We had to sign him."

Didier believed he was improperly fired by the Mariners, and took his case to arbitration. AL president Lee MacPhail was the arbitrator and ruled in favor of the Mariners.

For all the anguish the Mariners went through in signing Nanni, he never reached the big leagues. He hit just .253, and despite his big, athletic frame, hit 66 home runs in 2,775 at-bats.

## FIRST-ROUND FAILURES

In 1977, a record six first-round picks failed to ascend beyond Class A. The attrition rate was slightly better a year later, but five more players bit the dust before reaching Double-A.

The Pittsburgh Pirates failed miserably with both their first-round selections: Texas high school first baseman Brad Garnett (19th overall), who had a well-chronicled battle with alcohol abuse and hit just .210 in five seasons; and Georgia prep outfielder Jerry Aubin (21st overall), who had immediate misgivings about passing up a football scholarship to the University of South Carolina and quit less than a year after signing.

The group of underachievers also included Boyce (22nd overall), the Orioles' top selection whose career was ruined by a steady dose of injuries; catcher Nick Hernandez (eighth overall), a career .217 hitter who was cut loose midway through his fourth season in the Brewers system; and shortstop Phil Lansford (10th overall), who was supposed to be the best of all the Lansford brothers (Carney, an American League batting champion; Joey, a first-rounder in 1980), but lasted only one season in the Cleveland Indians system before being traded away.

The career of Philadelphia's Rip Rollins (23rd overall) also appeared doomed from the start as he was released in 1981 after two seasons as a

### One Team's Draft: Toronto Blue Jays

| Player, Pos. | Bonus | Player, Pos. | Bonus | Player, Pos. | Bonus |
|---|---|---|---|---|---|
| **1. *Lloyd Moseby, 1b** | **$55,000** | **5. Dave Stieb, of/rhp** | **$28,000** | 9. *Tom Stauffer, lhp | Did not sign |
| 2. *Tim Thompson, 1b | $34,500 | 6. *Mike Cuellar, rhp | $13,500 | 10. Alan Montgomery, 3b | $10,000 |
| 3. *Mike Cullen, rhp | $30,000 | **7. *Brian Milner, c** | **$140,000** | Other Mike Lebo (Jan.-R/1), c | $43,750 |
| 4. *Mike Coyne, of | $27,500 | 8. *Brad Burger, rhp | $4,000 | | |

*Major leaguers in bold. *High school selection.*

## WORTH NOTING

following the 1977 season that triggered compensation. The Orioles, who lost pitchers Dick Drago (Red Sox) and Ross Grimsley (Expos), and third baseman Elliot Maddox (Mets) to free agency, gained three compensation picks, all in the second round. The Yankees lost pitcher Mike Torrez and outfielder Ron Blomberg, and were compensated with the first-round picks of the Red Sox and White Sox, respectively. That proved to be one for the books because in coming years, the Yankees became so aggressive in their pursuit of other teams' free agents that they rarely were participants in the first round of the amateur draft. The Yankees got little direct benefit from their three first-rounders as only shortstop **REX HUDLER**, an outstanding high school quarterback who committed to play football at Notre before accepting a $100,000 bonus from the Yankees, ever played in New York. He played in just 29 games with the Yankees over a 13-year career in the majors. Pitcher **BRIAN RYDER** peaked in Triple-A, while outfielder **MATT WINTERS** labored for 11 years in the minors, mostly with the Yankees, before finally getting a chance with the Royals in 1989.

■ Arizona State had two of the first three selections in the draft. Two picks after **BOB HORNER** went to the Braves, shortstop **HUBIE BROOKS** was chosen by the Mets. Catcher **CHRIS BANDO** also went in the second round to the Indians. The Sun Devils had eight players drafted in all, second only to Southern California. Brooks hit .432 and set a Division-I record with 126 hits. Bando, a .415 hitter, led the nation with 30 doubles and 102 RBIs. Following the 1978 season, Arizona State and fellow Western Athletic Conference power Arizona joined the Pacific-8 Conference, creating the Pac-10, and giving the newly aligned Southern Division college baseball's first super conference.

## IN FOCUS: BRIAN MILNER

The Toronto Blue Jays were so determined to sign Brian Milner and build their two-year-old franchise around him that in addition to giving him a $140,000 signing bonus, they promised him he could start his career in the majors.

"I was involved in signing Darrell Porter when I was with the Brewers, and Gary Carter when I was with the Expos," Blue Jays scout Bobby Mattick said, "and I think Brian has more raw ability than either of them."

Milner, a Texas prep product, wasn't picked until the seventh round because teams were convinced he would attend Arizona State on a football/baseball scholarship.

In his big league trial, he started two games for the Jays, getting four hits. In the second game, Milner had three hits, including a triple, as the Jays crushed the powerful Orioles 24-10.

"They wanted me to get a taste of the major leagues," he said. "It really shocked me to be there, but I knew I would be optioned later."

The next day, the Blue Jays farmed out Milner to their Rookie-level Medicine Hat farm club. He was never heard from again.

Milner's promising career was destroyed by injuries. After hitting .239 with 12 homers in 362 games over five years in the minors, Milner was released by the Blue Jays in spring training 1983.

sore-armed pitcher, and another as an outfielder when his arm issues prevented him from pitching any longer. After sitting out most of two years, a rejuvenated Rollins was given a second shot with the Phillies, in Double-A, but went just 7-11, 6.02 over two years in an unsuccessful comeback.

With Garnett and Aubin their latest casualties, the Pirates experienced more than their share of disappointments in the draft's first 15 years with their varied assortment of first-rounders. The unlikely total of eight didn't advance beyond Class A, and their string of poor drafts was a contributing factor in things coming to a head in the three-year period from 1984-86, when the Pirates finished last in the National League East each season.

No draft contributed to the demise more than 1978, when they had two first-round picks and missed badly on both. They threw away a $60,000 bonus on Garnett, another $50,000 on Aubin.

Garnett's issues had mostly to do with alcoholism. He had a succession of injuries over a five-year career, which he attributed to his drinking problems.

"I can blame all my physical problems on alcohol, because going out and being hung over in 90- and 100-degree temperatures is not the thing to do to your body," Garnett said after undergoing alcohol rehabilitation in 1981. "It's easy to start drinking, especially when you're younger. For me, I think it was a combination of being away from home, missing my parents and my girlfriend. In high school, I drank, but not as much as I did when I got into pro ball."

Garnett never hit higher than .231, never advanced past Class A and was out of baseball after 1982. He also found out he owed the federal government $14,000 in back taxes on his bonus because his mother, who was separated from his father, spent most of the money without telling him.

In Aubin's case, he couldn't make up his mind whether he liked baseball or football better, and it proved his undoing.

After an uneventful first year with the Pirates' Rookie-level farm club, Aubin was promoted to Class A Salem. In the first month of the 1979 season, Aubin injured his shoulder on a throw home from right field on a rain-slicked field. He missed the rest of that season, and a doctor told him the injury was so severe that he might not be able to throw again.

When the Pirates appeared to act indifferently towards the injury, Aubin questioned whether he wanted to play baseball any longer and sought out the same South Carolina football coaches who had recruited him two years earlier, when he was a star quarterback at Dougherty High in Albany, Ga. He asked them if it wasn't too late to resume his football career, and he got an encouraging thumbs up to join the Gamecocks squad that fall.

Aubin spent two seasons at South Carolina as a non-scholarship backup, but never played quarterback as his shoulder injury, even after surgery, robbed him of arm strength. He also endured two more football-related surgeries. No longer healthy enough to play football, Aubin contacted the Pirates, asking for a second chance.

He returned to the Pirates for the 1982 season after nearly three years away from the game, but his story ended much like Garnett's. He never hit higher than .238, never advanced past Class A and was out of baseball after a brief trial with the Yankees in 1983.

## Highest Unsigned Picks

**JUNE/REGULAR PHASE ONLY**

| Player, Pos., Team (Round) | College | Re-Drafted |
|---|---|---|
| Steve Raine, rhp, Giants (2) | Arizona State | Royals '80 (Jan.-S/1) |
| Buck Belue, of, White Sox (2) | Georgia | Expos '82 (6) |
| Fran Mullins, ss, Tigers (3) | * Santa Clara | White Sox '79 (3) |
| Mike Moore, rhp, Cardinals (3) | Oral Roberts | Mariners '81 (1) |
| Dave Leeper, of, Twins (3) | USC | Royals '81 (1) |
| Larry Reynolds, of, Padres (4) | * Stanford | Rangers '79 (4) |
| Glenn Gallagher, lhp, Dodgers (4) | Clemson | Blue Jays '81 (3) |
| Dave Seiler, lhp, Cubs (4) | Texas | Phillies '81 (8) |
| Mike Rubel, c, White Sox (4) | CS Fullerton | Astros '81 (6) |
| Mitch Zwolensky, rhp, Rangers (4) | Eastern Michigan | Rangers '81 (11) |

**TOTAL UNSIGNED PICKS:** Top 5 Rounds (14), Top 10 Rounds (53)

**Returned to same school.*

### COLLEGES GET TOP TALENT

The 1978 draft witnessed its share of colossal failures in the first round at the high school level, but it was not an indictment of the high school crop as a whole.

With college baseball becoming a viable option for an increasing number of players, many of the better prospects like Mike Moore, Kevin McReynolds, Mark Langston and Frank Viola, to name four, were paid only passing interest. Three years later, those players became the cornerstone of a draft whose emphasis in the early rounds swung dramatically to college talent for the first time in draft history. Moore, an unsigned third-round pick of the Cardinals in 1978, became the first overall selection in 1981.

More and more colleges were beginning to place greater emphasis on baseball by 1978, enabling the college game to take on an ever-broadening role in the development of future major league talent. But for one last season, Southern California and Arizona State, the two dominant college programs over most of the 1960s and 1970s, still commanded the spotlight. The Trojans beat the Sun Devils, 10-3, in the championship game of the College World Series.

In the first 14 years of the draft, the Trojans and Sun Devils combined to win 10 national titles; over the next 37 years, the former powers combined to win just twice.

Longtime USC coach Rod Dedeaux called his 1978 club his best ever. Twelve members of that team were drafted, including righthander Rod Boxberger (12-1), the College World Series MVP who was drafted in the first round by the Houston Astros. Dedeaux was so impressed with his club that he predicted 10 members would play in the big leagues. Eight did, but Boxberger was not one of them. His unfulfilled career began and ended in Double-A.

# 1978 Draft List

*Did not sign. Major leaguers in bold, with first and last years noted. Order of selection indicated in parentheses. For the first five rounds of the June Regular Phase and the first round of all other phases, the peak level of each player is noted.

## ATLANTA BRAVES

**January—Regular Phase (2)**

1. *Joe Housey, rhp, Miami-Dade CC North.—(AA)
2. Ronald Rudd, 3b, Sacramento (Calif.) CC.
3. James Rogers, rhp, Murray State (Okla.) JC.
4. *Jack McMahon, rhp, Cypress (Calif.) JC.

DRAFT DROP *Son of Don McMahon, major leaguer (1957-74)*

5. *Howard Scott, rhp, DeKalb (Ga.) JC.

**January—Secondary Phase (4)**

1. Mark Martin, c, San Jacinto (Texas) JC.–(Low A)
2. *Stephen Maral, c, Chabot (Calif.) JC.

**June—Regular Phase (1)**

1. **Bob Horner, 3b, Arizona State University.—(1978-88)**
2. **Matt Sinatro, c, Conrad HS, West Hartford, Conn.—(1981-92)**
3. **Steve Bedrosian, rhp, University of New Haven.—(1981-95)**

DRAFT DROP *Father of Cam Bedrosian, first-round draft pick Angels (2010); major leaguer (2014-15)*

4. **Rick Behenna, rhp, Southridge HS, Cutler Ridge, Fla.—(1983-85)**
5. Michael Miller, ss, University of Louisville.—(AAA)
6. Ken Scanlon, ss, Granada Hills HS, Northridge, Calif.
7. *Doyle Wilson, ss, Shorter (Ga.) College.
8. **Jose Alvarez, rhp, University of Southwestern Louisiana.—(1981-89)**
9. *Gary Friedrich, lhp, Donald E. Gavit HS, Hammond, Ind.
10. Jimmy Matthews, 3b, Georgia Southern College.
11. **Gerald Perry, of, McCracken HS, Hilton Head, S.C.—(1983-95)**
12. Bobby Supel, 3b, East Carolina University.
13. *Robert Elsea, lhp, Cleveland State (Tenn.) CC.
14. Lance Gore, lhp, Cal State Fullerton.
15. William Aldridge, rhp, University of Tennessee.
16. Daniel Lopez, of, University of Houston.
17. James Van Deventer, of, Catholic University.
18. *Charles Shearer, rhp, Weber HS, Chicago.
19. *James Harris, lhp, Thomas Jefferson HS, Brooklyn, N.Y.
20. Kevin Balogh, rhp, Toledo, Ohio.
21. Gil Ryan, rhp, Blinn (Texas) JC.
22. *Larry Brown, rhp, Harvard University.
23. Michael Smith, rhp, Massachusetts Bay CC.
24. *Hubert Taylor, rhp, Georgia Southwestern College.
25. Mark Roush, rhp, University of Cincinnati.
26. *Lawrence Dugger, rhp, Eastwood HS, El Paso, Texas.
27. Brad Campbell, rhp, West Georgia College.

DRAFT DROP *Father of Brett Campbell, major leaguer (2006)*

28. *Paul Robinson, 3b, Bishop Nolan HS, Fort Worth, Texas.

DRAFT DROP *Son of Eddie Robinson, major leaguer (1942-57)*

29. *Kerry Cox, of, Tarrant HS, Birmingham, Ala.

**June—Secondary Phase (1)**

1. *Jim Watkins, c, University of Florida.—(AA)
2. Blane McDonald, c, Florida State University.
3. *Jimmy Boring, rhp, DeKalb South (Ga.) CC.

## BALTIMORE ORIOLES

**January—Regular Phase (21)**

1. *Kenny Kurtz, lhp, Seminole (Fla.) CC.—(High A)
2. Daniel Keck, of, Central Arizona JC.
3. *David Jensen, lhp, Edmonds (Wash.) CC.
4. Stanley Hendrickson, of-1b, CC of Philadelphia.
5. George Paul, rhp, Manatee (Fla.) JC.
6. *Curt Kowalski, rhp, Seminole (Fla.) CC.
7. *Ted Dixon, rhp, Angelina (Texas) JC.
8. *John Wood, 3b, Abraham Baldwin Agricultural (Ga.) JC.
9. Charles Proviano, ss, Pittsburgh.
10. *Robert Pigford, rhp, CC of Philadelphia.

**January—Secondary Phase (3)**

1. Eddie Rodriguez, ss, Miami-Dade CC South.—(AA)
2. Mark Bolton, rhp, Longview, Texas.
3. *Lawrence Davila, rhp, Key West, Fla.

**June—Regular Phase (22)**

1. Bob Boyce, 3b, Deer Park HS, Cincinnati.—(High A)
2. **Larry Sheets, of, Lee HS, Staunton, Va.** (Choice from Mets as compensation for free agent Elliott Maddox)**—(1984-93)**
2. Edwin Hook, rhp, Point Loma HS, San Diego (Choice from Expos as compensation for free agent Ross Grimsley).—(AA)
2. **Cal Ripken Jr., 3b, Aberdeen (Md.) HS.—(1981-2001)**

DRAFT DROP *Elected to Baseball Hall of Fame, 2007 • Son of Cal Ripken Sr., major league manager (1985-88) • Brother of Bill Ripken, major leaguer (1987-98)*

2. Cecil Whitehead, c, Valdosta State (Ga.) College (Choice from Red Sox as compensation for free agent Dick Drago).—(High A)
3. **Bobby Bonner, ss, Texas A&M University.—(1980-83)**
4. Tim Norris, rhp, Archbishop Curley HS, Baltimore.—(AA)
5. *Tony Herron, lhp, Sanger (Calif.) HS.—(AAA)

DRAFT DROP *Attended Fresno State; re-drafted by Athletics, 1981 (10th round)*

6. **Mike Boddicker, rhp, University of Iowa.—(1980-93)**
7. **Don Welchel, rhp, Sam Houston State University.—(1982-83)**
8. *Scott Collins, ss, Plymouth-Canton HS, Canton, Ohio.
9. Kurt Fabrizio, 1b, Edmonds (Wash.) CC.
10. Brooks Carey, lhp, Florida State University.
11. *Robin Dreizler, c, Redondo Beach (Calif.) HS.
12. Charles Salagan, lhp, St. Clair County (Mich.) CC.
13. William Purdy, rhp, Niagara University.
14. Jim Loftin, lhp, University of South Alabama.
15. *John Mortillaro, lhp, Smithtown East HS, Nesconset, N.Y.
16. Michael Byars, ss, Canyon HS, Orange, Calif.
17. James Delmonico, of, West Hempstead, N.Y.
18. Marion Thackston, lhp, Huntington (W.Va.) HS.
19. *William Butler, ss, Rossville (Ga.) HS.

**June—Secondary Phase (22)**

1. Juan Corey, c, Miami-Dade CC North.—(High A)

RUSS REED

A's first-rounder Mike Morgan was the first player from the '78 draft to reach the majors

## BOSTON RED SOX

**January—Regular Phase (23)**

1. *Bruce Kastelic, ss, Ranger (Texas) JC.—(AA)
2. ***Matt Young, lhp, Pasadena (Calif.) CC.—(1983-93)**
3. *Milton Ondracek, rhp, San Jacinto (Texas) JC.
4. Dan Weppner, lhp, Palm Beach (Fla.) JC.
5. *Howard Brodsky, c, North Miami Beach (Fla.) HS.
6. *James Funderburk, lhp, Orange Coast (Calif.) JC.

**January—Secondary Phase (13)**

1. **Brian Denman, 1b-rhp, Richfield, Minn.—(1982)**
2. Mark Paradise, lhp, Marblehead, Mass.

**June—Regular Phase (24)**

1. (Choice to Yankees as compensation for free agent Mike Torrez).
2. (Choice to Orioles as compensation for free agent Dick Drago).
3. (Choice to White Sox as compensation for free agent Jack Brohamer).
4. Edward Connors, 3b, North Bergen (N.J.) HS.—(High A)
5. Del Bender, of-1b, Mississippi State University.—(High A)
6. Steve Schaefer, rhp, Alhambra (Calif.) HS.
7. Ken Hagemann, 1b, Tottenville HS, Staten Island, N.Y.
8. Kenny Young, of, University of New Haven.
9. Russ Quetti, ss, University of Maine.
10. Donald Hayford, rhp, Lakeland (Fla.) HS.
11. Craig Vandersteen, lhp, Grand Ledge (Mich.) HS.
12. James Fabiano, ss, Westwood, Maine.
13. **John Lickert, c, Langley HS, Pittsburgh.—(1981)**
14. Lloyd Bessard, of, Abbeville (La.) HS.
15. Robert Parker, of, William Carey (Miss.) College.
16. *Mark Mitchell, rhp, North Hills HS, Pittsburgh.
17. *Steve Reish, rhp, Union City (Ind.) HS.
18. Gary Givens, rhp, Georgia Southern College.
19. Harold Nataupsky, c, Marblehead (Mass.) HS.
20. Keith Pecka, lhp, Kankakee (Ill.) CC.

**June—Secondary Phase (20)**

1. ***Marty Barrett, 2b, Mesa (Ariz.) CC.—(1982-91)**

DRAFT DROP *First overall draft pick, June 1979/secondary phase, Red Sox • Brother of Tommy Barrett, major leaguer (1988-92)*

## CALIFORNIA ANGELS

**January—Regular Phase (13)**

1. *Rick Evans, lhp, El Camino (Calif.) JC.—DNP
2. *Steven Norman, of, Barstow (Calif.) CC.
3. Anthony Dailey, of, Valencia (Fla.) CC.
4. Mark Nocciolo, c, JC of the Canyons (Calif.).
5. *Jeff Hanslovan, lhp, Linn-Benton (Ore.) CC.
6. *Mark Seeger, of, Mesa (Ariz.) CC.
7. *Trent Smith, rhp, Seminole (Fla.) CC.
8. *Arthur Maebe, rhp, Mission (Calif.) JC.
9. *Billy Blizzard, rhp, Barstow (Calif.) CC.
10. *Dave Yobs, 1b, Los Angeles Valley JC.

**January—Secondary Phase (25)**

1. *Simon Glenn, of, Blinn (Texas) JC.—DNP
2. *Stephen Martin, rhp, Pima (Ariz.) CC.

**June—Regular Phase (14)**

1. **Tom Brunansky, of, West Covina (Calif.) HS.—(1981-94)**
2. (Choice to Padres as compensation for free agent Merv Rettenmund).
3. **Dave Engle, 3b, University of Southern California.—(1981-89)**
4. **Mike Witt, rhp, Servite HS, Buena Park, Calif.—(1981-93)**
5. Rick Foley, rhp, Santa Clara University.—(AAA)
6. Gary Clevenger, 3b, Buena HS, Ventura, Calif.
7. Bill Springman, 2b, Oral Roberts University.
8. ***Tim Wallach, 1b, Cal State Fullerton.—(1980-96)**

DRAFT DROP *First-round draft pick (10th overall), Expos (1979)*

9. Preston Freeman, ss, Chandler (Ariz.) HS.
10. *Terry Marshall, lhp, Riverside Christian HS, Mira Loma, Calif.
11. Perry Morrison, rhp, Phoenix (Ariz.) JC.
12. ***Jeff Schattinger, rhp, University of Southern California.—(1981)**
13. *Peter Otero, c, Yavapai (Ariz.) JC.
14. **Dan Whitmer, c, Cal State Fullerton.—(1980-81)**
15. Richard Rommel, rhp, Cal State Fullerton.
16. ***John Christensen, of, Troy HS, Fullerton, Calif.—(1984-88)**
17. *Brian Owens, rhp, Mesa (Ariz.) HS.
18. *Walter Hagerty, c, Altus (Okla.) HS.
19. John Soderman, rhp, Santa Ana, Calif.
20. *Steve Muccio, of, University of New Mexico.
21. *Howard Dashefsky, c, El Camino Real HS, Canoga Park, Calif.
22. *Thomas Saatzer, c, West Brady HS, St. Paul, Minn.

**June—Secondary Phase (6)**

1. *Paul Homrig, 1b, San Pedro, Calif.—DNP
2. *Karl Jastrow, lhp, West Los Angeles JC.

## CHICAGO CUBS

**January—Regular Phase (14)**

1. Joe Hicks, 3b, Florida State University.—(AAA)
2. Craig Kornfeld, ss, Miami-Dade CC North.
3. *Richard Aspenleiter, rhp, Grossmont (Calif.) JC.
4. *Matt Stilwell, of, Linn-Benton (Ore.) CC.
5. *John Kossick, lhp, Houston CC.
6. *Kevin Shuster, c, Pasadena (Calif.) CC.
7. *Todd Wilson, lhp, Mount San Antonio (Calif.) JC.

**January—Secondary Phase (22)**

1. *Michael Campbell, 3b, Panola (Texas) JC.—DNP
2. Andrew Walker, c, East St. Louis, Ill.

**June—Regular Phase (13)**

1. **Bill Hayes, c, Indiana State University.—(1980-81)**
2. **Mel Hall, of, Port Byron HS, Cayuga, N.Y.—(1981-96)**
3. Bubba Kizer, ss, University of Georgia.—(Low A)
4. *Dave Seiler, lhp, Manzano HS, Albuquerque, N.M.—(AA)

DRAFT DROP *Attended Texas; re-drafted by Phillies, 1981 (8th round)*

5. ***Jon Perlman, rhp, Baylor University.—(1985-88)**

DRAFT DROP *Returned to Baylor; re-drafted by Cubs, 1979 (1st round)*

6. Robert Triplett, c, Phillips HS, Chicago.
7. Mark Parker, rhp, Huntington (Ind.) College.
8. *Dave Klipstein, ss, Marshall HS, Milwaukee.
9. *Jeff Groth, of, Bowling Green State University.

DRAFT DROP *Wide receiver, National Football League (1979-85)*

10. John Stockstill, ss, Hurley HS, Crane, Mo.
11. *Mark Lohuis, rhp, Fresno State University.
12. Glenn Swaggerty, rhp, Carter HS, Knoxville, Tenn.
13. *Dave Govea, 1b-of, Poly HS, Arleta, Calif.
14. **Mark Gilbert, of, Florida State University.—(1985)**
15. ***Mark Langston, lhp, Buchser HS, Santa Clara, Calif.—(1984-99)**
16. James Mitchell, ss, James Madison University.
17. *Scott Stranski, rhp, Northwestern University.
18. *Matt Elser, 1b-lhp, Poly HS, Arleta, Calif.
19. Joe McClain, rhp, Milligan (Tenn.) College.
20. Mark Vaji, lhp, Marshall HS, Cleveland.
21. *Chris Adomanis, rhp, Bowie (Md.) HS.
22. *Darrel White, of, Southwest HS, St. Louis.
23. *Joe Beason, rhp, Taylor HS, Kokomo, Ind.
24. Mike Godley, of, Jackson State University.
25. *Richard Raphael, rhp, San Jose State University.
26. Tim Carroll, of, University of Nebraska.
27. Kevin Kirby, rhp, Santa Clara University.
28. Eric Gorman, lhp, West Morris HS, Chester, N.J.
29. Mike Weakman, 3b, Meridian HS, Sanford, Mich.
30. **Mike Diaz, 1b, Terra Nova HS, Pacifica, Calif.—(1983-88)**
31. *Wayne Stone, of, Oral Roberts University.

**June—Secondary Phase (14)**

1. *Jim McManus, rhp, Triton (Ill.) JC.—(Short-season A)
2. *Jeff Stottlemyre, rhp, Yakima Valley (Wash.) JC.

DRAFT DROP *Brother of Mel Stottlemyre, major leaguer (1964-74)*

3. (void) *Greg Moyer, of, Cerritos (Calif.) JC.

## CHICAGO WHITE SOX

**January—Regular Phase (17)**

1. *Mark Christy, rhp, Miami-Dade CC North.—(High A)
2. *John Wolfer, rhp, Miami-Dade CC North.
3. *Jeffrey Orville, rhp, Santa Ana (Calif.) JC.
4. *Duane Dewey, c-1b, Miami-Dade CC North.
5. *Don Brownell, rhp, Seminole (Fla.) CC.
6. *Russ Fowler, inf, San Diego Mesa JC.
7. *Ken Hallin, rhp, Southwestern (Calif.) JC.

**January—Secondary Phase (7)**

1. Vic Walters, rhp, Miami-Dade CC South.–(Low A)
2. *Randy Brown, rhp, San Jacinto (Texas) JC.

**June—Regular Phase (18)**

1. (Choice to Yankees as compensation for free agent Ron Blomberg)
2. David White, 3b, Valdosta (Ga.) HS (Choice from Padres as compensation for free agent Oscar Gamble).—(Low A)
2. *Buck Belue, of, Valdosta (Ga.) HS.—(AA)

DRAFT DROP *Attended Georgia; re-drafted by Expos, 1982 (6th round)*

3. **Britt Burns, lhp, Huffman HS, Birmingham, Ala.—(1978-85)**
3. Mike Maitland, lhp, Monsignor Pace HS, Miami (Choice from Red Sox as compensation for free agent Jack Brohamer).—(AAA)
4. *Mike Rubel, c, Banning (Calif.) HS.—(AAA)

DRAFT DROP *Attended Cal State Fullerton; re-drafted by Astros, 1981 (6th round)*

5. Dennis Keating, of, Marin Catholic HS, San Rafael, Calif.—(AA)
6. *Dom Fucci, 1b-of, Auburn University.
7. *Michael Schoeller, c-1b, Florida Southern College.
8. Ivan Mesa, ss, Miami Springs HS, Hialeah, Fla.
9. *Preston Williams, 1b, Indiana State University.
10. *Brian Stemberger, ss, Eastern Michigan University.
11. Ramon Murillo, rhp, University of Arizona.
12. Mark Platel, rhp, Veghany HS, Del Mor, N.Y.
13. *Rick Witt, ss-3b, Spokane Falls (Wash.) CC.
14. ***Bobby Meacham, ss, Mater Dei HS, Westminster, Calif.—(1983-88)**

DRAFT DROP *First-round draft pick (8th overall), Cardinals (1981)*

15. *Andrew Dawson, ss, Waxahachie (Texas) HS.
16. *William Stroope, 1b, Waxahachie (Texas) HS.
17. *Larry Doby, of, Duke University.

DRAFT DROP *Son of Larry Doby, major leaguer (1947-59)*

18. Thomas Kokas, of-2b, Northwestern University.

**June—Secondary Phase (18)**

1. *Mark Christy, rhp, Miami-Dade CC North.—(High A)
2. *Duane Dewey, c, Miami-Dade CC North.
3. ***Gary Gaetti, 3b, Lake Land (Ill.) CC.—(1981-2000)**

## CINCINNATI REDS

**January—Regular Phase (18)**

1. ***Brad Lesley, rhp, Merced (Calif.) JC.—(1982-85)**
2. Larry Buckel, rhp, Long Beach (Calif.) CC.
3. **Paul Gibson, lhp, Center Moriches (N.Y.) HS.—(1988-96)**
4. *Larry Mikesell, lhp, Brevard (Fla.) CC.
5. Dan Sarrett, c, Valencia (Fla.) CC.
6. *Tim Muench, rhp, Seminole (Fla.) CC.
7. *Kevin Wiebold, rhp, McLennan (Texas) CC.
8. *Robert Day, 3b-ss, North Idaho JC.
9. *James McManus, rhp, Triton (Ill.) JC.
10. *Jeff Fiechtner, rhp, Des Moines Area (Iowa) CC.

**January—Secondary Phase (16)**

1. Wayne Guinn, rhp, DeKalb (Ga.) JC.—(Low A)
2. *Jeff Ayers, rhp, Bellevue (Wash.) CC.

**June—Regular Phase (17)**

1. **Nick Esasky, ss, Carol City (Fla.) HS.—(1983-90)**
2. **Dave Van Gorder, c, University of Southern California.—(1982-87)**
3. Eski Viltz, of, Notre Dame HS, North Hollywood, Calif.—(AA)
4. Mike Kripner, c, Texas Lutheran College.—(AA)
5. **Jeff Lahti, rhp, Portland State University.—(1982-86)**
6. *Ray Townsend, 2b, UCLA.
7. *Tim Greene, lhp, River North Academy, Macon, Ga.
8. Chuck McKinney, rhp, Baden HS, Hamilton, Ohio.
9. **Charlie Leibrandt, lhp, Miami (Ohio) University.—(1979-93)**
10. Chris Stropolo, of, John Curtis HS, Metairie, La.
11. *John Warren, c-of, Wayne County HS, Jesup, Ga.
12. Mike Sullivan, c, Northwest Regional HS, Colebrook, Conn.
13. Byron Jackson, rhp, Rider HS, Wichita Falls, Texas.
14. *Jim Thomas, ss, Southeast HS, Wichita, Kan.
15. **Gary Redus, ss, Athens State (Ala.) College.—(1982-94)**
16. **Skeeter Barnes, 2b, University of Cincinnati.—(1983-94)**
17. **Tom Lawless, ss-2b, Penn State University.—(1982-90)**

DRAFT DROP *Major league manager (2014)*

18. *Mitch Dean, rhp, Arizona State University.
19. *David Anderson, rhp, Western HS, Las Vegas, Nev.
20. Jim Taylor, c, Harding HS, Charlotte, N.C.
21. ***Otis Nixon, ss, Louisburg (N.C.) JC.—(1983-99)**

DRAFT DROP *Brother of Donell Nixon, major leaguer (1987-90)*

22. *John Cook, of, Washington State University.
23. *Kevin Maroney, of, Oakwood HS, Dayton, Ohio.
24. Rick Jendra, ss-2b, Florida International University.
25. Lee Hover, of, University of Oklahoma.
26. *Monte DeRatt, rhp, University of North Carolina.
27. James Mugele, inf, High Point College.
28. *Bill Bakewell, p, University of Arkansas.
29. Alex Neely, rhp, Phillips (Okla.) University.
30. *Joe Stefani, rhp, Dowling HS, Des Moines, Iowa.
31. *Ronald Walling, lhp, Westmont HS, Johnstown, Pa.
32. Cary Hornaman, of, Northern State (S.D.) College.
33. *Stan Johnson, c, Wake Forest University.
34. Charles Engel, rhp, St. Cloud State (Minn.) University.
35. *Kurt Moody, lhp, Hoover HS, Des Moines, Iowa.
36. John LoCasio, lhp, St. Francis DeSales HS, Toledo, Ohio.
37. *Patrick Chester, ss, South Dorchester HS, Cambridge, Md.

**June—Secondary Phase (9)**

1. **Brad Lesley, rhp, Merced (Calif.) JC.—(1982-85)**
2. ***Ralph Citarella, rhp, Brevard (Fla.) CC.—(1983-87)**
3. *Kevin Niewulis, lhp, Louisburg (N.C.) JC.
4. *Gary Kempton, c, Triton (Ill.) JC.

## CLEVELAND INDIANS

**January—Regular Phase (9)**

1. Thomas Anderson, 1b, South Florida JC.—(AA)
2. Robert Conley, ss, Enterprise State (Ala.) JC.
3. Lloyd Turner, ss, Middle Georgia JC.
4. Robin Fuson, rhp, Valencia (Fla.) CC.
5. Keith Hendry, rhp, South Florida JC.
6. *Robert Payne, of, St. John's River (Fla.) CC.
7. Ralph Henriguez, c, Indian River (Fla.) CC.
8. Russell Cain, c, George C. Wallace (Ala.) CC.
9. *James Gardner, c, Miami-Dade CC North.
10. *Joseph Kelihar, 1b-of, St. Petersburg (Fla.) JC.

**January—Secondary Phase (17)**

1. *Mike Bates, rhp, Phoenix (Ariz.) JC.—DNP
2. *Kernan Ronan, rhp, Glendale (Ariz.) CC.

**June—Regular Phase (10)**

1. Phil Lansford, ss, Wilcox HS, Santa Clara, Calif.—(High A)

DRAFT DROP *Brother of Carney Lansford, major leaguer (1978-92) • Brother of Jody Lansford, first-round draft pick, Padres (1979); major leaguer (1982-83)*

2. **Chris Bando, c, Arizona State University.—(1981-89)**

DRAFT DROP *Brother of Sal Bando, major leaguer (1966-81)*

3. Michael Taylor, of, Columbia State (Tenn.) CC.—(AAA)
4. Dane Anthony, rhp, James Buchanan HS, St. Thomas, Pa.—(AA)
5. John Asbell, rhp, Southwest HS, Macon, Ga.—(Low A)
6. Tom Owens, rhp, University of Michigan.
7. ***Mike Young, of, Hayward (Calif.) HS.—(1982-89)**
8. *Eric Porter, c, Waseca (Mich.) HS.
9. Peter Peltz, 3b, Clemson University.
10. Kenneth Henderson, 2b, Worthington, Ohio.
11. Gordon Glaser, rhp, Louisiana College.
12. *Casey Lindsey, lhp, Arizona State University.
13. Robert Hussey, rhp, St. Xavier (Ill.) College.
14. *Mark Meleski, ss, J.R. Tucker HS, Richmond, Va.
15. Gerald Stutzriem, lhp, Rich Central HS, Country Club Hills, Ill.
16. Richard Barnhart, rhp, University of Puget Sound (Wash.).
17. Jerald Hammermeister, 3b, Ellensburg (Wash.) HS.
18. *Howard Lukehardt, lhp, Norwin HS, Huntingdon, Pa.
19. *James McBride, rhp, Jackson State University.
20. *Bob Bonnette, inf, Clemson University.
21. Robert Pfeffer, rhp, Glassboro State (N.J.) College.
22. *Phillip Preliezo, lhp, Christopher Columbus HS, Miami.
23. Chris Barker, of, St. Catherine HS, Racine, Wis.
24. Louis Ganci, rhp, New York Tech.
25. Reid Cassidy, rhp, Colby (Maine) College.
26. Randy Rambis, rhp, San Jose State University.
27. Kenneth Gilmore, 2b-3b, Troy State University.
28. Tom Van Der Meersche, rhp, Arizona State University.
29. *Blaine Smith, rhp, University of North Carolina.
30. *Tim Behler, lhp, University of La Verne (Calif.).
31. *Warner Crumb, rhp, Northhampton HS, Cheriton, Va.
32. *Jay Waid, c, Hewitt HS, Trussville, Ala.
33. *Mike Brecht, lhp, Hazel Park (Mich.) HS.
34. *Ronald Kollmann, rhp, Nampa (Idaho) HS.
35. *Scott August, lhp, Potomac HS, Oxen Hill, Md.
36. Richard Hille, rhp, St. John's University.
37. *George White, rhp, Ballard HS, Seattle.
38. *John Shrewsberry, rhp, Palm Beach (Fla.) JC.
39. Lawrence Beck, lhp, Occidental (Calif.) College.
40. Ron Wrobel, lhp, Grand Canyon College.
41. (void) *Michael Culbert, rhp, Bonanza HS, Las Vegas, Nev.
42. George Ravanis, rhp, Boston College.
43. *Michael Mowrey, rhp, San Gabriel (Calif.) HS.
44. David Warnecke, rhp, McKendree (Ill.) College.
45. *Michael Yackee, rhp, Cal State Los Angeles.
46. *David Spamer, rhp, East Allegheny HS, North Versailles, Pa.
47. *Ron Reeves, rhp, Monterey HS, Lubbock, Texas.
48. *Delbert Stacey, rhp, Rutland (Vt.) HS.

**June—Secondary Phase (13)**

1. *David Grier, rhp, Valencia (Fla.) CC.—(AA)
2. *Doug Wabeke, ss, Grand Rapids (Mich.) JC.
3. *Rick Evans, lhp, El Camino (Calif.) JC.

## DETROIT TIGERS

**January—Regular Phase (11)**

1. **Chris Codiroli, rhp, San Jose (Calif.) CC.—(1982-90)**

DRAFT DROP *Brother of Mike Codiroli, ninth-round draft pick, Athletics (1978)*

2. Kevin Fitzhugh, rhp, Orange Coast (Calif.) JC.
3. *John Cardinali, ss, DeAnza (Calif.) JC.
4. *Steve Conroy, lhp, Citrus (Calif.) JC.
5. *Rich DeVincenzo, lhp, Miami-Dade CC North.
6. *Donald Pierce, lhp, Chaffey (Calif.) JC.
7. Dan O'Connor, c, Central Florida JC.

**January—Secondary Phase (26)**

1. William Klank, rhp, Mercer County (N.J.) CC.—(High A)
2. *Rick Santarone, c, Gulf Coast (Fla.) CC.

**June—Regular Phase (12)**

1. **Kirk Gibson, of, Michigan State University.—(1979-95)**

DRAFT DROP *Seventh-round draft pick, St. Louis Cardinals/National Football League (1979) • Major league manager (2010-14)*

2. Craig Johnson, of, UCLA.—(AA)
3. ***Fran Mullins, ss, Santa Clara University.—(1980-86)**

DRAFT DROP *Returned to Santa Clara; re-drafted by White Sox, 1979 (3rd round)*

4. **Jerry Ujdur, rhp, University of Minnesota.—(1980-84)**
5. **Marty Castillo, 3b, Chapman (Calif.) College.—(1981-85)**
6. *Kevin Martin, ss, Falconer Central HS, Jamestown, N.Y.
7. **Bruce Fields, of, Everett HS, Lansing, Mich.—(1986-89)**
8. Ted Hutson, c, Miami East HS, Fletcher, Ohio.
9. Mike Wright, of, Vanderbilt University.
10. James Simerly, rhp, Chapman (Calif.) College.
11. Art Toal, 2b-ss, University of Oklahoma.
12. Jack Smith, rhp, Glen Oaks (Mich.) CC.
13. David Cassetto, rhp, Western Michigan University.
14. ***Mike Mason, of-lhp, Normandale (Minn.) CC.—(1982-88)**
15. Marvin Saunders, rhp, University of South Alabama.
16. **Dave Rucker, lhp, University of La Verne (Calif.).—(1981-88)**
17. Todd Ervin, 2b, Stanford University.

18. *Mark Jacob, rhp, De La Salle HS, Detroit.
19. *Edwin Schneider, lhp, Indian River (Fla.) CC.
20. John Crawford, c, Delta State (Miss.) University.
21. Michael Untisz, rhp, Fairleigh Dickinson University.
22. Bob Benda, ss, Florida State University.
23. *Gary Baker, 3b, Hazel Park (Mich.) HS.
24. *Tom Grinstead, lhp, Edgewood HS, West Covina, Calif.
25. John Kelley, of, Simon Kenton HS, Independence, Ky.
26. James Wilfong, of, University of La Verne (Calif.).
DRAFT DROP *Brother of Rob Wilfong, major leaguer (1977-87)*
**27. John Martin, lhp, Eastern Michigan University.—(1980-83)**
28. *Holden Smith, of, University of California.
29. Judson Thigpen, rhp, Delta State (Miss.) University.
30. Michael Polvi, rhp, University of Detroit.
31. Ben Bonk, rhp, Central Michigan University.
32. Buddy Slemp, of, Oral Roberts University.

**June—Secondary Phase (12)**

1. *Peter Chapin, rhp, Fullerton (Calif.) JC.—(AA)

## HOUSTON ASTROS

**January—Regular Phase (12)**

1. Greg Smith, of, Canada (Calif.) JC.—(Rookie)
**2. Pat Perry, lhp, Lincoln Land (Ill.) CC.—(1985-90)**
3. *Joe Collins, rhp, Hillsborough (Fla.) CC.

**January—Secondary Phase (14)**

1. *James Tjader, 2b, Iowa Western CC.—(AA)

**June—Regular Phase (11)**

1. Rod Boxberger, rhp, University of Southern California.—(AA)
DRAFT DROP *Father of Brad Boxberger, major leaguer (2012-15)*
**2. Danny Heep, of-lhp, St. Mary's (Texas) University.—(1979-91)**
DRAFT DROP *Baseball coach, Incarnate Word, Texas (1998-2015)*
3. John Hessler, rhp, University of Tulsa.—(AA)
**4. Ron Meridith, lhp, Oral Roberts University.—(1984-87)**
5. Doug Stokke, ss, University of Southern California.—(AAA)
6. *Bob Palmer, c, Chapman (Calif.) College.
7. Greg Cypret, ss, University of Missouri.
8. Larry Ashley, 2b-of, Oakland (Calif.) HS.
9. *Brad Carlson, 3b, Boone HS, Orlando, Fla.
10. *Frank Castro, c, Miami Springs HS, Hialeah, Fla.
DRAFT DROP *First-round draft pick (26th overall), Padres (1981)*
**11. Jack Lazorko, 3b-rhp, Mississippi State University.—(1984-88)**
**12. Tim Tolman, of, University of Southern California.—(1981-87)**
13. *Mike Browning, 1b-rhp, Southridge HS, Miami.
14. Arvis Harper, of, University of Arkansas.
15. Thad Troedson, rhp, San Diego State University.
DRAFT DROP *Brother of Rich Troedson, major leaguer (1973-74)*
16. *Michael Buggs, of, Castlemont HS, Oakland, Calif.
17. *Charles Hutchingson, rhp, West Memphis (Ark.) HS.

**June—Secondary Phase (5)**

**1. *Scott Fletcher, ss, Valencia (Fla.) CC.—(1981-95)**

## KANSAS CITY ROYALS

**January—Regular Phase (26)**

1. *Lee Cline, rhp, JC of Southern Idaho.—DNP
2. *Eugene Picchena, 3b, Edmonds (Wash.) CC.
3. Keith Vranesh, of, Saddleback (Calif.) CC.
4. *Doug Wabeke, ss, Grand Rapids (Mich.) JC.
5. Francis Mouse, ss, Allegany (Md.) CC.
6. Larry Onesi, rhp, Russellton, Pa.
7. *Tom Chevolek, lhp, East Los Angeles JC.
8. John Melody, lhp, Irvington, N.J.
9. *Randy Cornelius, rhp, McKinleyville, Calif.

BILL SETLIFF

Twins hometown hero Kent Hrbek lasted until the 17th round because few knew about him

10. *Michael Koch, c, Scottsdale (Ariz.) CC.

**January—Secondary Phase (5)**

1. Earl Robinson, of, Gulf Coast (Fla.) CC.—DNP
2. Mike Haley, of, Central Arizona JC.
3. *Tony Zahradnick, lhp, Valencia (Fla.) CC.

**June—Regular Phase (25)**

**1. Buddy Biancalana, ss, Redwood HS, Greenbrae, Calif.—(1982-87)**
**2. Darryl Motley, of, Grant HS, Portland, Ore.—(1981-87)**
**3. Mark Ryal, of-lhp, Dewar (Okla.) HS.—(1982-90)**
4. David Mangrum, rhp, Bells (Texas) HS.—(Rookie)
5. David Hogg, c, Northwestern University.—(AAA)
6. Jesse Lucious, of, Rich East HS, Park Forest, Ill.
7. *Tim Rodgers, rhp, Bixby HS, Broken Arrow, Okla.
**8. Jeff Cornell, rhp, University of Missouri.—(1984)**
9. Erik Hendricks, rhp, Chapman (Calif.) College.
10. *Harold Bright, of, Mumford HS, Detroit.
11. Ulises Infante, 3b, St. Patrick's HS, Elizabeth, N.J.
12. Robert Ganger, rhp, Pepperdine University.
13. James Davidson, of, Alma (Mich.) College.
14. Ira Turner, 1b, Bethune-Cookman College.
**15. *Don Heinkel, rhp, Horlick HS, Racine, Wis.—(1988-89)**
**16. *Frank Viola, lhp, East Meadow (N.Y.) HS.—(1982-96)**
17. James Canfield, lhp, Wayne Memorial HS, Wayne, Mich.
18. *Bob Fiala, 3b, Oklahoma City University.
19. *Bradley Kast, lhp, Reading (Mich.) HS.
20. *Tom Willette, lhp, North Carolina State University.
21. Steven Porter, of, Upsala (N.J.) College.
22. Anthony Washington, of, Southeastern Oklahoma State University.
23. Jim McCoy, rhp, University of Texas-Arlington.
**24. Ron Johnson, 1b, Fresno State University.—(1982-84)**
25. Chris Czarka, rhp, Central Michigan University.
26. *Buddy Bailey, c, Lynchburg (Va.) College.
27. *Mark Terrill, rhp, Gilroy (Calif.) HS.
28. *John Seneca, rhp, Seton Hall University.
29. *Charles Curry, 1b, Southern Illinois University.
30. Craig Pippin, rhp, University of Florida.
31. *Gregg Baker, rhp, Marcos de Niza HS, Tampa.

**June—Secondary Phase (2)**

**1. Craig Chamberlain, rhp, University of Arizona.—(1979-80)**
**2. Bill Laskey, rhp, Kent State University.—(1982-88)**
3. Jeff Hanslovan, lhp, Linn-Benton (Ore.) CC.

## LOS ANGELES DODGERS

**January—Regular Phase (22)**

**1. Brian Holton, rhp, Louisburg (N.C.) JC.—(1985-90)**
2. Greg Schultz, ss, Sacramento (Calif.) CC.
3. *Brad Patterson, rhp, Umpqua (Ore.) CC.
4. Matt Reeves, lhp, Sacramento (Calif.) CC.
**5. *Bryan Little, ss, Louisburg (N.C.) JC.—(1982-86)**
DRAFT DROP *Brother of Grady Little, major league manager (2002-07)*
6. *Jimmy Boring, rhp, DeKalb South (Ga.) CC.
7. *Larry Pittman, 1b, Abraham Baldwin Agricultural (Ga.) JC.
8. *Anthony Murdaugh, rhp, University of South Carolina.
9. *Peter Zorich, rhp, Lower Columbia (Wash.) JC.

**January—Secondary Phase (8)**

1. Rusty McDonald, rhp, DeAnza (Calif.) JC.–(AAA)
2. *Dan Sijer, lhp, Shoreline (Wash.) CC.
3. Stephen Smith, rhp-of, Gulf Coast (Fla.) CC.

**June—Regular Phase (21)**

1. (Choice to Pirates as compensation for free agent Terry Forster).
2. Clay Smith, ss, Northwest HS, Oklahoma City, Okla.—(High A)
3. Augie Ruiz, lhp, University of Miami.—(AAA)
4. *Glenn Gallagher, lhp, Peekskill (N.Y.) HS.—(AA)
DRAFT DROP *Attended Clemson; re-drafted by Blue Jays, 1981 (3rd round)*
5. John Robbins, of, Lockhart HS, Union, S.C.—(High A)
**6. Mike Marshall, 1b-rhp, Buffalo Grove (Ill.) HS.—(1981-91)**
7. Mark Nipp, rhp, University of Oklahoma.
8. Bill Swiacki, rhp, Amherst (Mass.) College.
DRAFT DROP *Ninth-round draft pick, New York Giants/ National Football League (1978)*
**9. Steve Sax, ss, Marshall HS, West Sacramento, Calif.—(1981-94)**
DRAFT DROP *Brother of Dave Sax, major leaguer (1982-87)*
10. Rodney Kemp, of, San Jose State University.
11. John Malkin, c, Cardinal Spellman HS, Bronx, N.Y.
12. Francis Wilczewski, rhp, Independence HS, San Jose, Calif.
13. Melvin Meadows, of, White Oak HS, Maysville, N.C.
14. Jeff Kopjo, of-1b, Lyons Township HS, Brookfield, Ill.
15. Stephen Maples, c, Skyline HS, Dallas.
16. Brian Hayes, lhp, University of Southern California.
17. Joe Pocoroba, ss, Crespi HS, Woodland Hills, Calif.
DRAFT DROP *Brother of Biff Pocoroba, major leaguer (1975-84)*
**18. *Eric Bullock, of, South Gate HS, Los Angeles.—(1985-92)**
**19. Gary Weiss, ss, University of Houston.—(1980-81)**
20. *Chris Iwasaki, of, Reedley (Calif.) JC.
21. Dave LaPointe, rhp, Monadnock Regional HS, Troy, N.H.
22. Tom Banducci, rhp, William Floyd HS, Mastic, N.Y.
23. Chris Gandy, 1b, UC Riverside.
24. Warren Reed, lhp, Comfort, Texas.
25. *William Murray, ss, Tamalpais HS, Mill Valley, Calif.
26. *David Albrecht, lhp, Appleton (Wis.) East HS.
27. *James Taylor, c, University of South Carolina.
28. Robert White, lhp, Lake Mills (Wis.) HS.
29. Joe Herbert, of-c, Columbia (Tenn.) HS.
30. *Kevin Patten, of, Miami (Ohio) University.
31. Kent Johnson, rhp, Northside HS, Muncie, Ind.
32. *Dan Forer, lhp, Iowa Western CC.
33. *Michael Vienne, rhp, St. Mary's HS, Natchitoches, La.
34. *Mark Pirruccello, c, Servite HS, Anaheim, Calif.

**June—Secondary Phase (7)**

**1. Dann Bilardello, c, Cabrillo (Calif.) JC.—(1983-92)**
2. *Keith Schrimsher, rhp, University of South Florida.

## MILWAUKEE BREWERS

**January—Regular Phase (7)**

1. Weldon Swift, rhp, University of Maryland-Baltimore County.—(AA)
**2. Doug Loman, of, Bakersfield (Calif.) JC.—(1984-85)**
**3. Doug Jones, rhp, Central Arizona JC.—(1982-2000)**
4. *Larry May, rhp, Central Arizona JC.
5. *Roland Atkins, c, Calhoun (Ala.) CC.
6. Porter Wyatt, ss, Palomar (Calif.) JC.
7. *Robert Duncan, lhp, Blinn (Texas) JC.
8. *Greg Robles, 1b, San Jose (Calif.) CC.
9. *Kyle Farenthold, lhp, Blinn (Texas) JC.
10. Jerry Lewis, of, Central Arizona JC.
11. Eddie Brunson, of, Miami-Dade CC North.
12. *Charles Dinkins, lhp, Miami-Dade CC New World Center.

**January—Secondary Phase (19)**

1. Greg DeHart, rhp, Los Angeles Valley JC.—(High A)
2. *Maury Ornest, 1b, Central Arizona JC.
DRAFT DROP *Son of Harry Ornest, owner, St. Louis Blues/ National Hockey League (1983-86)*
3. *Jerry Joyce, of, West Valley (Calif.) JC.

**June—Regular Phase (8)**

1. Nick Hernandez, c, Hialeah (Fla.) HS.—(High A)
2. (Choice to Mariners as compensation for free agent Ray Fosse)
**3. Rickey Keeton, rhp, Southern Illinois University.—(1980-81)**

4. Rich Olsen, rhp, University of Hawaii.—(AAA)
5. Tim Cook, rhp, Newberry (S.C.) College.—(AAA)
6. Steven Gibson, rhp, Kennedy HS, Granada Hills, Calif.
7. Franklin Thomas, 2b, University of Maryland.
8. Vince Pone, 3b, El Camino Real HS, Woodland Hills, Calif.
9. Dan Gilmartin, ss, Monroe HS, Sepulveda, Calif.
10. Lance Ediger, of, Dallas (Ore.) HS.
11. Columbus Duncan, 1b, University of Virginia.
12. *Jerry DeSimone, ss, Southern Illinois University.
13. Steven Norwood, rhp, University of Virginia.
14. *Tom McLish, rhp, Edmond, Okla.
DRAFT DROP *Son of Cal McLish, major leaguer (1944-64)*
15. *Steve Watson, rhp, East Bay HS, Gibsonton, Fla.
**16. *Tim Teufel, ss, St. Petersburg (Fla.) JC.—(1983-93)**
17. Mark Lepson, rhp, Lansdowne HS, Arbutus, Md.
18. Dean Hall, 1b, University of Hawaii.
**19. *Kevin McReynolds, of, Sylvan HS, North Little Rock, Ark.—(1983-94)**
DRAFT DROP *First-round draft pick (6th overall), Padres (1981)*
20. *Mark Clabough, rhp, Lakewood (Calif.) HS.
21. *Randy Guerra, inf, University of Miami.
22. *Chuckie Canady, c, White Oak HS, Maysville, N.C.
23. *Alan Mayles, rhp, Turner Ashby HS, Harrisonburg, Va.
24. Randy Boyce, lhp, Cal State Dominguez Hills.
25. Humberto Acosta, of, University of Miami.
26. Pat Seegers, of, University of Wisconsin.
27. *Mark Bonner, of, Long Beach (Calif.) CC.
28. James Manship, rhp, University of Arizona.
**29. *Rob Murphy, lhp, Christopher Columbus HS, Miami.—(1985-95)**
30. *Buster Moore, c, Molalla HS, Beaver Creek, Ore.
31. *Steve Krueger, lhp, Garden City (Kan.) CC.
32. *Kevin McKenna, rhp, Lakewood (Calif.) HS.
33. *Michael Woods, ss, Southern University.

**June—Secondary Phase (4)**

1. Allen Wesolowski, rhp, La Porte, Ind.—(Short-season A)
2. James Robinson, of, Edmonds (Wash.) CC.
3. *Robert Smith, of, Orange Coast (Calif.) JC.
4. *James Johnson, ss, Edmonds (Wash.) CC.
5. James Padula, c, Chaffey (Calif.) JC.
6. Daniel Maxson, rhp, DeKalb (Ga.) JC.
7. *Steven Maral, c, Chabot (Calif.) JC.

## MINNESOTA TWINS

**January—Regular Phase (15)**

**1. *Ralph Citarella, rhp, Brevard (Fla.) CC.—(1983-87)**
**2. Jesse Orosco, lhp, Santa Barbara (Calif.) CC.—(1979-2003)**
3. Butch Rowe, ss, San Jose, Calif.
4. *Timothy Madera, of, JC of Marin (Calif.).
5. Steven Green, rhp, Modesto (Calif.) JC.
6. *Richard Austin, c, Cerritos (Calif.) JC.
7. *David Dodson, rhp, San Joaquin Delta (Calif.) JC.
8. *Larry Navilhon, rhp, JC of San Mateo (Calif.).
9. Ronnie Mears, ss-2b, San Pablo, Calif.
10. Art Piccolotti, of, Skyline (Calif.) JC.
11. *Tom Paul, of, Treasure Valley (Ore.) CC.
12. *Gary Forillo, ss, Citrus (Calif.) JC.
13. John Minarcin, rhp, Oneonta, N.Y.

**January—Secondary Phase (1)**

1. Joe Isaacs, rhp, Eastern Oklahoma State JC.–(AA)
**2. *Mike Couchee, rhp, San Jose (Calif.) CC.—(1983)**
**3. *Willie Lozado, ss, Miami-Dade CC New World Center.—(1984)**
4. Harold Washington, of-rhp, Southwestern (Calif.) JC.
5. *Steve McQueen, ss, Gulf Coast (Fla.) CC.

**June—Regular Phase (16)**

**1. Lenny Faedo, ss, Jefferson HS, Tampa.—(1980-84)**
2. Mike Riley, rhp, Agawam (Mass.) HS.—(AA)
**3. *Dave Leeper, lhp-of, Villa Park (Calif.) HS.—(1984-85)**
DRAFT DROP *Attended Southern California; re-drafted by Royals, 1981 (1st round)*
4. Wade Adamson, rhp, South Dakota State University.—(AA)
5. Frank Vilorio, ss, Cal State Fullerton.—(AA)
6. *Nattie George, of, Overfelt HS, San Jose, Calif.
7. Mark Maher, c, Tulane University.
8. Les Pearsey, 2b, University of Arizona.
**9. *Tony Fossas, lhp, University of South Florida.—(1988-99)**
10. *Tom Morris, lhp, Brigham Young University.
DRAFT DROP *Brother of Jack Morris, major leaguer (1977-94)*
11. Don Smith, c, Istrouma HS, Baton Rouge, La.
**12. *Scott Bradley, c, West Essex HS, Essex Fells, N.J.—(1984-92)**
DRAFT DROP *Baseball coach, Princeton (1998-2015)*
13. Ron Grout, 1b, Wingate (N.C.) College.
14. *Craig Shumock, 3b, Chestnut Hill Academy, Willow Grove, Pa.
15. Robert Jones, lhp, Archbishop Curley HS, Baltimore.
16. Michael Williams, c, Wingate (N.C.) College.
**17. Kent Hrbek, 1b, Kennedy HS, Bloomington, Minn.—(1981-94)**
18. Alex Dovalis, 3b, Long Beach (Calif.) CC.
19. *Gene Ransom, ss, University of California.
DRAFT DROP *Brother of Jeff Ransom, fifth-round draft pick, Giants (1978); major leaguer (1981-83) • Ninth-round draft pick, Golden State Warriors/ National Basketball Association (1979)*
20. Kevin Sevcik, rhp, St. Olaf (Minn.) College.
21. *Tom Lounibos, inf, University of San Francisco.
22. Chris Geason, lhp, Augsburg (Minn.) College.
23. *William Guinn, rhp, Beaverton (Ore.) HS.
24. *Edward Castro, rhp, University of Maryland.
25. Robert Holden, c, Glassboro State (N.J.) College.
26. Rufus Thompson, of, Cal Poly Pomona.
27. *Al Mejia, c, Fullerton (Calif.) JC.
28. *Randy Ramirez, rhp, Katella HS, Anaheim, Calif.
29. *Steven Houlberg, ss, University of Alabama.
30. *Randy Filkins, of, West Hills (Calif.) JC.
31. Robert Waldusky, of, University of La Verne (Calif.).
32. *Ron Dearth, 3b, Lakewood (Calif.) HS.
33. *Paul Mancuso, lhp, Shaw HS, Gretna, La.

**June—Secondary Phase (25)**

1. *Bruce Kastelic, ss, Ranger (Texas) JC.—(AA)

## MONTREAL EXPOS

**January—Regular Phase (10)**

1. Gary Hartsock, rhp, Muscatine (Iowa) CC.—(High A)
2. *Charles Barclift, 1b, Louisburg (N.C.) JC.
3. *John Maxom, rhp, DeKalb South (Ga.) CC.
4. *Ken Kellogg, of, Blinn (Texas) JC.
5. *Louis Stawarz, 1b, Manatee (Fla.) JC.
6. *Brian Benedict, c, Palm Beach (Fla.) JC.
7. Renardo Richardson, 3b, Cincinnati.
8. Mark South, rhp, Wright State University.
9. *John Damon, ss, Sacramento (Calif.) CC.
10. Paul Josephson, rhp, Shrewsbury, Conn.

**January—Secondary Phase (10)**

**1. Tony Phillips, ss-2b, New Mexico Military Institute.—(1982-99)**
2. *Larry Reasonover, 3b, Hillsborough (Fla.) CC.
3. Gary Aguirre, ss, Bakersfield, Calif.
4. *Michael Kelly, of, Cosumnes River (Calif.) JC.

**June—Regular Phase (9)**

1. Glen Franklin, ss, Chipola (Fla.) JC.—(AAA)
2. (Choice to Orioles as compensation for free agent Ross Grimsley)
3. Steve Michael, of, Arizona State University.—(AAA)
**4. Dave Hostetler, 1b, University of Southern California.—(1981-88)**
5. Steve Morrison, 3b, University of South Alabama.—(AA)
**6. *Bill Mooneyham, rhp, Atwater HS, Winton, Calif.—(1986)**
7. *Cat Whitfield, of-1b, Middle Georgia JC.
8. David Perez, ss-2b, Stanford University.
**9. Charlie Lea, rhp, Memphis State University.—(1980-88)**
**10. Tom Wieghaus, c, Illinois State University.—(1981-84)**
11. *Dave Clements, ss, East Bay HS, Riverview, Fla.
12. Ronnie Pearce, rhp, Stetson University.
**13. *Jim Deshaies, lhp, Massena (N.Y.) HS.—(1984-95)**
14. Grayling Tobias, of, University of Missouri-St. Louis.
15. Jeff Taylor, lhp, Garfield HS, Garrettsville, Ohio.
16. Jerry George, c, Louisiana College.
17. Rick Ramos, rhp, Lewis (Ill.) University.
**18. Razor Shines, c, St. Augustine (N.C.) College.—(1983-87)**
19. Kevin Mendon, rhp, Emporia State (Kan.) University.
**20. Pat Rooney, of, Eastern Illinois University.—(1981)**
21. *Chris Cawthon, inf, Avondale HS, Avondale Estates, Ga.
22. Steve Lovins, rhp, Northern Kentucky University.

**June—Secondary Phase (24)**

No selection.

## NEW YORK METS

**January—Regular Phase (4)**

1. *Gerry Miller, 1b, Des Moines Area (Iowa) CC.—(Low A)
2. Michael Cannon, of, Middlesex (Conn.) CC.
**3. *Marty Barrett, 2b, Mesa (Ariz.) CC.—(1982-91)**
DRAFT DROP *First overall draft pick, June 1979/secondary phase, Red Sox • Brother of Tommy Barrett, major leaguer (1988-92)*
4. *Ron Graves, rhp, Modesto (Calif.) JC.
**5. *Ricky Jones, 3b-rhp, Chipola (Fla.) JC.—(1986)**
6. *Louis D'Amore, rhp, CC of Morris (N.J.).
7. *Floyd Gow, lhp, Butte (Calif.) JC.
**8. Jamie Nelson, c, Orange Coast (Calif.) JC.—(1983)**
9. *Al Hammack, rhp, Bellevue (Wash.) CC.
10. *Robert Randolph, rhp, Butte (Calif.) JC.

**January—Secondary Phase (24)**

1. *Michael Foster, lhp, Merced (Calif.) JC.—(Low A)
2. *Jack Lambeth, lhp, Westark (Ark.) CC.

**June—Regular Phase (3)**

**1. Hubie Brooks, of, Arizona State University.—(1980-94)**
2. (Choice to Orioles as compensation for free agent Elliott Maddox)
**3. Brian Giles, 2b, Kearny HS, San Diego.—(1981-90)**
4. Don Troyan, 1b, St. John's University.—(High A)
5. Jeff Gossett, ss, Eastern Illinois University.—(High A)
**6. Mike Fitzgerald, c, Lakewood (Calif.) HS.—(1983-92)**
7. *Henry Janssen, c, Scotch Plains (N.J.) HS.
8. James Cooperider, lhp, Central Valley HS, Redding, Calif.
9. Glen Johnson, rhp, Lewis-Clark State (Idaho) College.
10. Richard Lane, c, San Jose State University.
**11. Randy Johnson, ss, San Jose State University.—(1982-84)**
12. *Reggie Whittemore, of, David Lipscomb College.
13. *Jeff Sunderlage, lhp, Elgin (Ill.) HS.
14. Darryl Denby, of, Lincoln HS, San Diego.
15. John Elder, 3b, Frostburg State (Md.) College.
16. James Beck, 1b, Temple University.
17. Randy Pitts, rhp, University of Redlands (Calif.).
18. Michael Tancredi, rhp, Mansfield (Pa.) University.
19. *John Wells, of, University of Southern California.
20. Steve Till, c, Cal State Fullerton.
21. Michael Viggiano, ss, Bricktown (N.J.) HS.
**22. *Mark Davis, lhp, Granada Hills HS, Livermore, Calif.—(1980-97)**
DRAFT DROP *First overall draft pick, January 1979/ secondary phase, Phillies*
23. *Richard Eckleberry, rhp, Flathead HS, Kalispell, Mont.
**24. Rick Anderson, rhp, University of Washington.—(1986-88)**
25. *Clint Harvey, rhp, Coastal Carolina College.
26. Greg Korbe, of, Kansas State University.
**27. *Al Lachowicz, rhp, Canevin Catholic HS, McKees Rock, Pa.—(1983)**
DRAFT DROP *First-round draft pick (24th overall), Rangers (1981)*
28. Gary Hilton, rhp, Canyon HS, Anaheim, Calif.
29. Ronald Walker, 1b, Benedictine (Kan.) College.
30. David Smith, of, Siena College.
31. Marc Siciliano, c, Iona College.

**June—Secondary Phase (3)**

1. *James Tjader, 3b, Iowa Western CC.—(AA)

## NEW YORK YANKEES

**January—Regular Phase (25)**

1. Mark Harris, ss, University of Maryland.—(AA)
DRAFT DROP *Son of Gail Harris, major leaguer (1955-60)*
2. John Franks, rhp, Seminole (Fla.) CC.
3. *Kevin Niewulis, lhp, Louisburg (N.C.) JC.
**4. *Rusty McNealy, of, JC of Southern Idaho.—(1983)**
5. *Dean Foes, lhp, Central Arizona JC.

**January—Secondary Phase (11)**

1. David Garcia, 2b, Grossmont (Calif.) JC.—(High A)
DRAFT DROP *Son of Dave Garcia, major league manager (1977-82)*
2. *James Robinson, of, Edmonds (Wash.) CC.
3. *David Fowke, 2b, Manatee (Fla.) JC.

**June—Regular Phase (26)**

**1. Rex Hudler, ss, Bullard HS, Fresno, Calif.** (Choice from White Sox as compensation for free agent Ron Blomberg)**—(1984-98)**
**1. Matt Winters, of, Williamsville (N.Y.) HS** (Choice from Red Sox as compensation for free agent Mike Torrez)**—(1989)**
1. Brian Ryder, rhp, Shrewsbury (Mass.) HS.—(AAA)
**2. Steve Balboni, 1b, Eckerd (Fla.) College.—(1981-93)**
3. Mark Johnston, of, University of South Alabama.—(AA)
**4. Tim Lollar, lhp-1b, University of Arkansas.—(1980-86)**
5. Pete Khoury, of, Eckerd (Fla.) College.—(High A)
**6. Andy McGaffigan, rhp, Florida Southern College.—(1981-91)**
7. Kevin Hemphill, 3b, Catawba (N.C.) College.
8. Dan Plante, c, Crespi HS, Woodland Hills, Calif.
9. Jeff Taylor, c, University of Delaware.
DRAFT DROP *Brother of Steve Taylor, first-round draft pick, Yankees (1977)*
10. Dan Ledduke, rhp, Florida International University.
11. Mark Moore, lhp, University of South Florida.
12. *Randy Kwist, 3b, Eckerd (Fla.) College.
13. Claude Sammons, 1b-of, Gonzaga University.
**14. *Andy Beene, rhp, Baylor University.—(1983-84)**
15. *Dan Peterson, rhp, Great Falls (Mon.) HS.
**16. Brian Dayett, 3b, St. Leo (Fla.) College.—(1983-87)**
**17. Don Cooper, rhp, New York Tech.—(1981-85)**
DRAFT DROP *Major league manager (2011)*
18. Rich Carlucci, rhp, University of Iowa.
19. Karl Steffen, lhp, Ithaca (N.Y.) College.
20. *Eric Snider, rhp, Washington State University.
21. *Jerome Burgess, c, Atlantic HS, Delray Beach, Fla.
22. *Jeff Ledbetter, 1b, Largo (Fla.) HS.
DRAFT DROP *First-round draft pick (26th overall), Red Sox (1982)*
**23. *Howard Johnson, rhp-3b, Clearwater (Fla.) HS.—(1982-95)**

**June—Secondary Phase (15)**

1. *Joe Housey, rhp, Miami-Dade CC North.—(AA)

## OAKLAND ATHLETICS

**January—Regular Phase (3)**

1. *David Grier, rhp, Valencia (Fla.) CC.—(AA)
2. *Kendall Greene, rhp, Santa Barbara (Calif.) CC.
3. *Thomas McGivney, c, Alvin (Texas) CC.
4. *Karl Jastrow, lhp, West Los Angeles JC.
5. *Jerry Lane, inf, West Los Angeles JC.
6. *James Padula, c, Chaffey (Calif.) JC.

7. *James Johnson, ss, Edmonds (Wash.) CC.
8. *Robert Parr, of, West Los Angeles JC.
9. *Kevin Darst, inf, Solano (Calif.) CC.
**10. *Larry White, rhp, Los Angeles Pierce JC.—(1983-84)**
11. *John Davis, rhp, Solano (Calif.) CC.

**January—Secondary Phase (21)**

**1. *Scott Fletcher, ss, Valencia (Fla.) CC.—(1981-95)**
2. *Mark Beuclear, rhp, San Jacinto (Texas) JC.
3. *Edward Long, rhp, Santa Monica (Calif.) JC.
4. *Joe Madrigal, rhp, Mount San Antonio (Calif.) JC.

**June—Regular Phase (4)**

**1. Mike Morgan, rhp, Valley HS, Las Vegas, Nev.—(1978-2002)**
DRAFT DROP *First player from 1978 draft to reach majors (June 11, 1978)*
**1. Tim Conroy, lhp, Gateway HS, Monroeville, Pa.** (Choice from Rangers as compensation for free agent Mike Jorgensen)**—(1978-87)**
**2. Keith Atherton, rhp, Mathews (Va.) HS.—(1983-89)**
3. Bob Grandas, of, Central Michigan University.—(AAA)
**4. Mike Woodard, 2b, Proviso East HS, Maywood, Ill.—(1985-88)**
**5. Scott Meyer, c, Western Michigan University.—(1978)**
**6. Kelvin Moore, 1b, Jackson State University.—(1981-83)**
7. Chuck Dougherty, lhp, Steubenville (Ohio) HS.
8. *Robert Adams, c, Sherrill Central HS, Sherrill, N.Y.
9. *Mike Codiroli, of, Stanford University.
DRAFT DROP *Brother of Chris Codiroli, major leaguer (1982-90)*
10. Stephen Marlowe, rhp, St. Petersburg Christian HS, Pinellas Park, Fla.
11. Jay Greb, ss, Eagle Point (Ore.) HS.
12. Ron Jensen, lhp, Coronado HS, Scottsdale, Ariz.
13. Bret Cleland, rhp, Corning (Calif.) HS.
14. Omar Minaya, of, Newton HS, Elmhurst, N.Y.
DRAFT DROP *General manager, Expos (2002-04); general manager, Mets (2005-10)*
**15. *Jim Scranton, ss, Palomar (Calif.) JC.—(1984-85)**
16. *Daniel Casey, lhp, Edison (N.J.) HS.
17. Donald Morris, of, University of Oklahoma.
18. Fred DeVito, 3b, Pace (N.Y.) University.
19. *Charles Hollowell, lhp, Plant HS, Tampa.
20. *Tim Byron, rhp, Our Lady of the Valley HS, Florham Park, N.J.
21. *Wymon Smith, rhp, JC of Southern Idaho.
22. *John Lunden, rhp, JC of Southern Idaho.
23. *Casey Schaefer, rhp, North Salem (Ore.) HS.
24. *Bud Yanus, rhp, Eastern Michigan University.
25. *Gregg Mayer, of-rhp, Brick Township HS, Lakewood, N.J.
26. *Stephen Bricker, rhp, Watkins Memorial HS, Etna, Ohio.
27. *Jeffrey Way, c, University HS, Spokane, Wash.
28. *ChuckHernandez, lhp, Tampa Catholic HS, Tampa.
29. *Greg Key, ss, Citrus HS, Inverness, Fla.
30. *Brian Harrison, rhp, Stanford University.
31. Steven Oliver, lhp, Cecil (Md.) CC.
**32. *Greg Booker, 1b-ss, Cummings HS, Burlington, N.C.—(1983-90)**
33. Ralph Jean, rhp, Dover (Del.) HS.
34. *John Moller, lhp, Brookdale (N.J.) CC.
35. *George Cecchetti, 1b, Tokay HS, Stockton, Calif.

**June—Secondary Phase (26)**

1. Michael Kennedy, ss, Linn-Benton (Ore.) CC.—(High A)

## PHILADELPHIA PHILLIES

**January—Regular Phase (24)**

1. Don Woodward, rhp, Central Arizona JC.—(Low A)
2. *Steven Russell, rhp, Muskogee (Okla.) HS.
3. *James Green, of, Panola (Texas) JC.
4. Angelo Ross, of, Pasadena (Calif.) CC.
5. *Gary Venner, c, Ranger (Texas) JC.
6. Juan Parker, of, Truman (Ill.) JC.
7. *Jeffrey Musser, of, Ferrum (Va.) College.

**January—Secondary Phase (20)**

1. Daryl Adams, rhp, Butte (Calif.) JC.—(High A)
2. *Kevin Williams, of, Edmonds (Wash.) CC.

**June—Regular Phase (23)**

1. Rip Rollins, rhp-1b, Alleghany HS, Sparta, N.C.—(AA)
2. Anthony McGill, of, Jones HS, Houston.—(Low A)
3. Dean Martinez, rhp, Pueblo East HS, Pueblo, Colo.—(High A)
**4. Ed Hearn, c, Fort Pierce Central HS, Fort Pierce, Fla.—(1986-88)**
5. Darren Burroughs, lhp, Vinita HS, Langley, Okla.—(AAA)
6. Pete Dempsey, ss, Temple University.
7. Paul Kiess, 1b, Granada Hills HS, Northridge, Calif.
8. Mike Henson, c, San Mateo HS, Foster City, Calif.
9. Dan Prior, rhp, James Madison University.
10. Marty Shoemaker, rhp, Checotah (Okla.) HS.
**11. *Dwight Taylor, of, Fremont HS, Los Angeles.—(1986)**
12. Michael Culbert, rhp, Bonanza HS, Las Vegas, Nev.
13. Bruce Humphrey, 1b, University of Tulsa.
14. Robert Angius, lhp-1b, Lassen HS, Susanville, Calif.
15. Charles Marshall, rhp, Floyd County HS, Willis, Va.
16. *Ron Rendleman, rhp, Bloomington (Calif.) HS.
17. *Michael Kreymborg, rhp, Kelley HS, Tulsa, Okla.
18. Randy Greer, of, Southern California College.
19. Jeff Ulrich, c, Fresno (Calif.) CC.
**20. Ryne Sandberg, ss, North Central HS, Spokane, Wash.—(1981-97)**
DRAFT DROP *Elected to Baseball Hall of Fame, 2005; major league manager (2013-15)*
21. Alvin White, of, University of Northern Colorado.
22. Thomas Popovich, 3b, University of Toledo.
23. John Palmieri, lhp, Pilgrim HS, Warwick, R.I.
**24. *Rick Leach, 1b-of, University of Michigan.—(1981-90)**
DRAFT DROP *First-round draft pick (13th overall), Tigers (1979) • Fifth-round draft pick, Denver Broncos/ National Football League (1979)*
25. Phil Teston, rhp, Land O'Lakes (Fla.) HS.
26. *Michael Vojtesak, rhp, Joliet Central HS, Joliet, Ill.
27. John DeVincenzo, rhp, University of Tampa.
28. Derek Williams, c, Willingboro (N.J.) HS.
29. Steve Harvey, of, Benjamin Franklin HS, Philadelphia.
30. *Sammy Bickham, lhp, Southern Methodist University.

**June—Secondary Phase (21)**

1. *Kendall Greene, rhp, Santa Barbara (Calif.) CC.—DNP
2. *Ken Eriksen, rhp, Citrus (Calif.) JC.

## PITTSBURGH PIRATES

**January—Regular Phase (20)**

1. *Pete Chapin, rhp, Fullerton (Calif.) JC.—(AA)
2. Brent Hillenga, 1b, San Diego Mesa JC.
3. *Mel Locke, rhp, Pasadena (Calif.) CC.
4. *Bill Waag, ss, Lower Columbia (Wash.) JC.
5. *Robert Smith, of, Orange Coast (Calif.) JC.
6. Michael Leveton, 1b, Cromwell, Conn.
7. *Courtney Wyrick, rhp, West Los Angeles JC.
8. *John Garcia, p, Chattahoochee Valley (Ala.) CC.
9. *Joe Nemeth, 1b, Orange Coast (Calif.) CC.

**January—Secondary Phase (12)**

1. *Kurt Kingsolver, c, Long Beach (Calif.) CC.—(AAA)
2. *Lawrence Dotson, of, Orange Coast (Calif.) CC.
3. *Marvin Fowler, rhp, San Diego Mesa JC.
4. *Rob Dondero, rhp, Mesa (Ariz.) CC.

**June—Regular Phase (19)**

1. Brad Garnett, 1b, DeSoto (Texas) HS.—(High A)
1. Jerry Aubin, of, Dougherty HS, Albany, Ga. (Choice from Dodgers as compensation for free agent Terry Forster).—(High A)
2. Brad Palmer, lhp, Escondido (Calif.) HS.—(Low A)
3. Pat Rubino, c, San Diego State University.—(Low A)
4. Thomas Siebert, rhp, Coeur d'Alene (Idaho) HS.—(Low A)
5. Robert Davis, rhp, University of Utah.—(High A)
6. *Don McCarthy, p, Del City (Okla.) HS.
7. *Scott Roberts, rhp, Roosevelt HS, Seattle.
8. Donald Cline, rhp, Piqua, Ohio.
9. Frank Milozewski, rhp, Indiana University.
10. *David Rosenhahn, rhp-ss, West Seneca (N.Y.) HS.
11. Tim Florey, rhp, Brooklyn Park HS, Baltimore.
12. Dennis Jones, of, Kearny HS, Spring Valley, Calif.
13. *Barry Brown, lhp, Lake Worth HS, Fort Worth, Texas.
14. Wesley Hair, 3b-2b, Albany State (Ga.) College.
15. *John Young, c, Henry Ford II HS, Sterling Heights, Mich.
16. Stanton Brown, of, Davidson College.
17. Mike Nedelisky, rhp, Lewis-Clark State (Idaho) College.
**18. John Stuper, rhp, Point Park (Pa.) College.—(1982-85)**
DRAFT DROP *Baseball coach, Yale (1993-2015)*
19. *Jeff Vlha, inf, Fullerton (Calif.) HS.
20. Todd Denby, inf, Fluvanna HS, Scottsville, Va.
**21. Dave Dravecky, lhp, Youngstown State University.—(1982-89)**
22. Thaddeus Reed, of, Glass HS, Lynchburg, Va.
23. *Arbrey Lucas, rhp, Chaparral HS, North Las Vegas, Nev.
24. *David McDonald, lhp, Allegheny (Pa.) CC.
25. *Vince Pellegrini, rhp, Father Judge HS, Philadelphia.
26. John Huey, rhp, Mannington (W.Va.) HS.
**27. Jeff Zaske, rhp, Meadowdale HS, Lynwood, Wash.—(1984)**
28. *David Pascho, rhp, Juanita HS, Kirkland, Wash.
29. *Michael O'Boyle, rhp, Northport HS, Long Island, N.Y.
30. *Mark Johnson, rhp, Kearns (Utah) HS.
31. Dean Rick, lhp, Wilson HS, Sinking Spring, Pa.
32. James Fiori, c, Carlynton HS, Carnegie, Pa.
33. *John West, ss, Granite Falls HS, Marysville, Wash.
34. *Kevin Johnson, rhp, CC of Baltimore.
35. *Geoff Meadows, rhp, Southmoreland HS, Everson, Pa.
36. *Tim Ronan, rhp, University of San Diego.
37. *Albert Brehm, rhp, Foothills HS, Santa Ana, Calif.
38. *Mike Bretz, rhp, Florida State University.
**39. Vance Law, ss, Brigham Young University.—(1980-91)**
DRAFT DROP *Son of Vernon Law, major leaguer (1950-67) • Baseball coach, Brigham Young (2000-12)*
40. *Fenton Lebon, p-of, Lincoln Academy, Newcastle, Maine.

**June—Secondary Phase (23)**

1. Bill Waag, ss, Lower Columbia (Wash.) JC.—(AA)
2. *Tim Muench, rhp, Seminole (Fla.) CC.

## ST. LOUIS CARDINALS

**January—Regular Phase (16)**

1. *Michael Gentry, rhp, Chipola (Fla.) JC.—DNP
2. *Don Sutherland, rhp, Barstow (Calif.) CC.
3. Daniel Pierce, rhp, El Camino (Calif.) JC.
**4. *Gary Gaetti, 3b, Lake Land (Ill.) CC.—(1981-2000)**
5. *Edward Lindsey, lhp, Broward (Fla.) CC.
6. *Gary Kempton, c, Triton (Ill.) JC.
7. *Kevin Coughlon, of, Moorpark (Calif.) JC.
8. *Robert Weirum, 2b, Santa Barbara (Calif.) CC.
9. *Matthew Vejar, 3b, Merced (Calif.) JC.
10. *Kenneth Corzel, rhp, Santa Monica (Calif.) JC.
11. *Kevin Waller, of, San Diego CC.

**January—Secondary Phase (18)**

1. *James David, ss, Santa Barbara (Calif.) CC.—DNP
2. *Ken Eriksen, rhp, Citrus (Calif.) JC.
**3. *Dave Meier, ss, Fresno (Calif.) CC.—(1984-88)**

**June—Regular Phase (15)**

1. Bob Hicks, 1b, Tate HS, Pensacola, Fla.—(AA)
2. David Kable, 1b, West HS, Columbus, Ohio.—(AAA)
**3. *Mike Moore, rhp, Eakly HS, Carnegie, Okla.—(1982-95)**
DRAFT DROP *Attended Oral Roberts; re-drafted by Mariners, 1981 (1st round, 1st overall); first player from 1981 draft to reach majors (April 11, 1982)*
**4. George Bjorkman, c, Oral Roberts University.—(1983)**
5. *Glenn Jones, of, Frankfort (Ky.) HS.—(AAA)
DRAFT DROP *Attended Morehead State; re-drafted by Giants, 1981 (14th round)*
6. Tim Mueller, c, Arroyo HS, San Lorenzo, Calif.
7. Dennis Gadowski, rhp, Central Catholic HS, Cleveland.
8. *Richard Budweg, lhp, Bloomsburg (Pa.) University.
9. *Marty Wilkerson, ss, Corona (Calif.) HS.
10. *Marshall Cook, lhp, Dallas Baptist University.
11. *Jeff Sollars, lhp, Wellington (Ill.) HS.
12. Dennis Delany, c, UCLA.
13. Roosevelt Lett, 3b, Garey HS, Pomona, Calif.
14. Martin Little, rhp, West Jefferson, N.C.
15. *Mike Toothman, of, Edgewood HS, West Covina, Calif.
16. Mike Carpenter, of, UCLA.
17. *Mark Smith, rhp, David Lipscomb HS, Franklin, Tenn.
**18. *Bob Skube, of, University of Southern California.—(1982-83)**
19. *Ken Malone, of, Prairie View A&M University.
20. Jeff Young, of, Trenton (N.J.) HS.
21. John Perlongo, 1b, Ridgefield Park (N.J.) HS.
22. Ray Rivas, 2b, Santa Clara University.
23. *John Carter, 1b-of, Bloomfield (N.J.) HS.
24. Robert Russell, rhp, Paducah (Ky.) CC.
25. *Tom Sauer, rhp, St. Louis CC-Meramec.
26. *Les Kakazu, 3b, Waipahu (Hawaii) HS.
27. Everette Smith, 2b, Furman University.
28. *Gerald Klauser, c, Whitesboro (N.Y.) HS.
29. *Tim Gloyd, ss-2b, Pepperdine University.
30. *Steven Southerland, rhp, De Smet Jesuit HS, Chesterfield, Mo.
31. *Armand Villa, rhp, Sunnyslope HS, Phoenix.
32. James Dieters, 3b, Oakland (Mich.) University.
33. Scott Arigoni, lhp, Cape Cod (Mass.) CC.
34. Paul Wysocki, rhp, Sacred Heart University.
35. Thomas Wertz, rhp, Brighton (Mass.) HS.
36. *Randy Ratcliff, 1b, William Carey (Miss.) College.
37. Reginald Ward, of, Beaumont HS, St. Louis.
38. *Pat Patterson, ss, Miami-Dade CC North.
39. *Frank Horak, rhp, Loyola Marymount University.
40. John Harshbarger, rhp, University of Illinois.
41. Kerry Burchett, rhp, East Tennessee State University.
42. David Picconi, lhp, University of Northern Colorado.
43. *Kevin Pyatte, lhp, Portland, Texas.
44. Peter Beattie, of, Wilson HS, Hacienda Heights, Calif.
**45. *Curt Wardle, lhp, Norco (Calif.) HS.—(1984-85)**
46. Thomas Chandler, of, Bryan (Texas) HS.

**June—Secondary Phase (19)**

1. Jeff Orville, rhp, Santa Ana (Calif.) JC.—(Rookie)
2. *Curt Reade, rhp, Fresno State University.
3. *Don Pierce, lhp, Chaffey (Calif.) JC.
**4. *Ed Vande Berg, lhp, San Bernardino Valley (Calif.) JC.—(1982-88)**

## SAN DIEGO PADRES

**January—Regular Phase (6)**

1. Donald Johnson, lhp, Eastern Michigan University.—(AA)
2. *Jeff Stottlemyre, lhp, Yakima Valley (Wash.) JC.
DRAFT DROP *Brother of Mel Stottlemyre, major leaguer (1964-74)*
**3. *Ed Vande Berg, lhp, San Bernardino Valley (Calif.) JC.—(1982-88)**
4. *James Tunnell, rhp, San Joaquin Delta (Calif.) JC.

**January—Secondary Phase (6)**

**1. Mike Martin, c, Mount Hood (Ore.) CC.—(1986)**
2. Willie Hardwick, rhp, Laney (Calif.) JC.

3. *Reggie West, of, Santa Ana (Calif.) JC.
4. *Robert Wicks, rhp, Chabot (Calif.) JC.

**June—Regular Phase (5)**

1. **Andy Hawkins, rhp, Midway HS, Waco, Texas.—(1982-91)**
2. (Choice to White Sox as compensation for free agent Oscar Gamble)
2. **Doug Gwosdz, c, Madison HS, Houston** (Choice from Angels as compensation for free agent Merv Rettenmund)**—(1981-84)**
3. **George Stablein, rhp, Cal State Dominguez Hills.—(1980)**
4. *Larry Reynolds, of, Stanford University.—(AA)

DRAFT DROP *Returned to Stanford; re-drafted by Rangers, 1979 (4th round) • Brother of Don Reynolds, major leaguer (1978-79) • Brother of Harold Reynolds, major leaguer (1983-94)*

5. **Floyd Chiffer, rhp, UCLA.—(1982-84)**
6. **Tim Flannery, 2b, Chapman (Calif.) College.—(1979-89)**
7. **Steve Fireovid, rhp, Miami (Ohio) University.—(1981-92)**
8. Mike Parker, of, University of Michigan.
9. Tim Hamm, rhp, Soquel HS, Santa Cruz, Calif.
10. Mobil Cox, ss, UCLA.
11. Jack Hills, lhp, Cal State Dominguez Hills.
12. Brad Shames, c, UC Santa Barbara.
13. Greg Patton, rhp, Lower Dauphin HS, Elizabethtown, Pa.
14. Al Richmond, of, St. Mary's (Calif.) College.
15. *Ken Harris, 3b-ss, El Cerrito HS, Berkeley, Calif.
16. Curt Cannedy, 1b, St. Mary's (Calif.) College.
17. Bob Volk, 3b, Oral Roberts University.
18. **Eric Show, rhp, UC Riverside.—(1981-91)**
19. Anthony McGrue, of, Morse HS, San Diego.
20. Syd Church, lhp, University of the Pacific.
21. *Ken McLemore, inf, Morse HS, San Diego.

DRAFT DROP *Brother of Mark McLemore, major leaguer (1986-2004)*

22. *Gregg Sporrer, inf, Cal State Fullerton.
23. *Aaron Cain, 2b-of, University of New Mexico.
24. ***Mark Thurmond, lhp, Texas A&M University.—(1983-90)**
25. ***Paul Noce, ss, Sequoia HS, Redwood City, Calif.—(1987-90)**
26. ***Randy Kramer, rhp, Oak Grove HS, San Jose, Calif.—(1988-92)**

**June—Secondary Phase (11)**

1. Greg Pastors, ss, Oklahoma State University.—(AAA)
2. *Rob Hertel, inf, University of Southern California.

DRAFT DROP *Quarterback, National Football League (1978-79)*

## SAN FRANCISCO GIANTS

**January—Regular Phase (8)**

1. *Greg Byrd, 1b, Columbia State (Tenn.) CC.—DNP
2. Ned Raines, 2b, Seminole (Fla.) CC.

DRAFT DROP *Brother of Tim Raines, major leaguer (1979-2002)*

3. Paul Plinski, inf, Los Angeles Valley JC.
4. *James Evans, lhp, West Los Angeles JC.
5. *Eugene Hernandez, rhp, San Joaquin Delta (Calif.) JC.
6. *Michael Ott, of, Yavapai (Ariz.) JC.
7. *Michael Kennedy, ss, Linn-Benton (Ore.) CC.
8. *Joe Olivas, rhp-inf, San Joaquin Delta (Calif.) JC.
9. Bruce Oliver, 3b-of, San Diego CC.

**January—Secondary Phase (2)**

1. Ron Pisel, rhp, Southeastern Illinois JC.—(AAA)
2. Greg Moyer, of, Cerritos (Calif.) JC.
3. *Norm Christensen, rhp, San Diego CC.

**June—Regular Phase (7)**

1. Bob Cummings, c, Brother Rice HS, Chicago.—(AAA)
2. *Steve Raine, rhp, North Salinas (Calif.) HS.–(AA)

DRAFT DROP *Attended Arizona State; re-drafted by Royals, January 1980/secondary phase (1st round)*

3. David Wiggins, lhp-of, Seminole HS, Sanford, Fla.—(AAA)
4. **Rob Deer, of, Canyon HS, Anaheim, Calif.—(1984-96)**
5. **Jeff Ransom, c, Berkeley (Calif.) HS.—(1981-83)**

DRAFT DROP *Brother of Gene Ransom, 19th-round draft pick, Twins (1978)*

6. *Ken Hall, p, McNicholas HS, Cincinnati.
7. Kelly Anderson, rhp, Ygnacio Valley HS, Concord, Calif.
8. ***Alvin Davis, 3b-of, North HS, Riverside, Calif.—(1984-92)**
9. Chris Barbone, of, Azusa Pacific (Calif.) University.
10. *Dwayne Jackson, of, Locke HS, Los Angeles.
11. **John Rabb, c, Washington HS, Los Angeles.—(1982-88)**
12. *Charles Everett, rhp, Crowley (Texas) HS.
13. Dale Baldwin, 2b, Boise State (Idaho) University.
14. *Greg Norris, rhp, University of North Carolina.
15. Jeff Ahlert, c, Aiken HS, Cincinnati.
16. Ricky Kittrell, lhp, Vanderbilt University.
17. *Steve Roberts, 3b, University of Kentucky.
18. *Bob Taylor, rhp, Thomas Jefferson HS, Port Arthur, Texas.
19. Richard Doss, inf, Eastern Illinois University.
20. *Babe Laufenberg, rhp, Crespi HS, Canoga Park, Calif.

DRAFT DROP *Quarterback, National Football League (1983-89)*

21. **Mark Calvert, rhp, University of Tulsa.—(1983-84)**
22. Darius Copley, of, Lubbock Christian (Texas) College.
23. *Doug Hoppock, rhp-of, Southeast HS, Wichita, Kan.
24. *Kem Wright, rhp, University of Texas.
25. Keith Brooks, of, Martinsburg (W.Va.) HS.
26. *Burl Coker, lhp, Baylor University.
27. Leotis Butler, of, Georgia Southwestern College.
28. *Kevin Clinton, of-rhp, Southeast HS, Wichita, Kan.

DRAFT DROP *Son of Lou Clinton, major leaguer (1960-67)*

29. *Randy Meyer, of, Mount Hood (Ore.) CC.
30. Richard Casillas, c, Oregon College of Education.
31. *Ted Notos, lhp, Grant HS, Portland, Ore.
32. *Mark Brewer, rhp, Coronado HS, Tempe, Ariz.
33. *John Milholland, 2b, Louisa (Va.) HS.

**June—Secondary Phase (17)**

1. Kevin Darst, inf, Solano (Calif.) CC.—(High A)
2. *Greg Byrd, inf, Columbia State (Tenn.) CC.

## SEATTLE MARINERS

**January—Regular Phase (5)**

1. **Jim Maler, 1b, Miami-Dade CC South.—(1981-83)**
2. Anthony Jordan, rhp, Monterey Peninsula (Calif.) JC.
3. ***Dann Bilardello, c, Cabrillo (Calif.) JC.—(1983-92)**
4. *Kirk Komstadius, 3b, Yakima Valley (Wash.) JC.
5. *Kevin Miller, 1b, Cerritos (Calif.) JC.
6. Teddy Adkins, rhp, Palm Beach (Fla.) JC.

**January—Secondary Phase (9)**

1. Richard Alexander, of, Matthews, N.C.–(High A)
2. *Juan Corey, c, Miami-Dade CC North.
3. Carlos Matamoras, 2b, Miami-Dade CC North.

**June—Regular Phase (6)**

1. Tito Nanni, of-1b, Chestnut Hill Academy, Philadelphia.—(AAA)
2. **Dave Valle, c, Holy Cross HS, Bayside, N.Y.—(1984-96)**
2. Rich Naumann, lhp, Bay Village (Ohio) HS (Choice from Brewers as compensation for free agent Ray Fosse).—(High A)
3. Rob Simond, lhp, Southern Illinois University.—(AA)
4. Ron McGee, rhp, Lincoln HS, San Jose, Calif.—(AAA)
5. Werner Lajszky, c, Mater Christi HS, Astoria, N.Y.—(High A)
6. Doug Smith, rhp, University of Oklahoma.
7. **John Hobbs, lhp, Lynchburg (Va.) College.—(1981)**
8. Lazoro Santin, lhp, Rochester Adams HS, Rochester Hills, Mich.
9. Richard Graser, lhp-of, Fort Vancouver HS, Vancouver, Wash.
10. **Bob Stoddard, rhp, Fresno State University.—(1981-87)**
11. **Vance McHenry, ss, University of Nevada-Las Vegas.—(1981-82)**
12. Terry Mixon, ss, Georgia Southern College.
13. *Bill Kampen, rhp, Archbishop Rummel HS, Metairie, La.
14. Rob Pietroburgo, lhp, University of Missouri.
15. Harry Mauch, of, Southern Oregon State.
16. David Nowland, ss, University of Tulsa.
17. Michael Guerra, 3b-of, University of Nevada-Las Vegas.
18. *Jerry Vasquez, rhp, Arizona State University.
19. *Calvin Horhn, of, Des Moines Area (Iowa) CC.
20. Rod Hudson, c, Portland State University.
21. **Dave Edler, 3b, Washington State University.—(1980-83)**
22. Chris Flammang, 1b-of, Sierra HS, Tollhouse, Calif.

**June—Secondary Phase (8)**

1. *Gerald Miller, 1b-of, Des Moines Area (Iowa) CC.—(Low A)
2. *Scott Benedict, c, Palm Beach (Fla.) JC.

## TEXAS RANGERS

**January—Regular Phase (19)**

1. Michael Vickers, lhp, Hill (Texas) JC.—(AA)
2. *Mark Knowles, lhp, Central Arizona JC.
3. *Anthony Stevens, of, Seminole (Fla.) CC.
4. *Richard Derechailo, c, Brookdale (N.J.) CC.
5. *Edward Bailey, c, Paris (Texas) JC.

**January—Secondary Phase (23)**

1. Michael Childs, c, Ranger (Texas) JC.—(Low A)
2. Greg Eason, lhp, Pensacola, Fla.

**June—Regular Phase (20)**

1. (Choice to Athletics as compensation for free agent Mike Jorgensen)
2. Amos Lewis, 3b, Astronaut HS, Mims, Fla.–(AA)
3. David Crutcher, rhp, University of Arizona.–(AAA)
4. *Mitch Zwolensky, rhp, Owosso (Mich.) HS.—(AAA)

DRAFT DROP *Attended Eastern Michigan; re-drafted by Rangers, 1981 (11th round)*

5. *Eric Shellenback, of, Barrington HS, Barrington Hills, Ill.—DNP

DRAFT DROP *Attended Northwestern; never re-drafted*

6. **Terry Bogener, of, University of Oklahoma.—(1982)**
7. Jerry Neufang, c, Hayfield HS, Lorton, Va.
8. **Wayne Tolleson, ss, Western Carolina University.—(1981-90)**
9. Tracy Cowger, of-c, Loyola Marymount University.
10. ***Allan Ramirez, rhp, Rice University.—(1983)**
11. **Chris Smith, of-3b, University of Southern California.—(1981-83)**
12. *Rick Misuraca, 3b, Del City (Okla.) HS.
13. Albert Ortiz, of, Baruch (N.Y.) College.
14. ***Charlie O'Brien, c, Bishop Kelley HS, Tulsa, Okla.—(1985-2000)**
15. *Eddie Greene, lhp, Edward H. White HS, Jacksonville, Fla.
16. Daniel Dixon, of, University of Nebraska.
17. *Brian Piper, rhp, Buena HS, Sierra Vista, Ariz.
18. Ron Gooch, 2b, Southeastern Oklahoma State University.
19. *Howie Shapiro, inf, University of Miami.
20. Keith Shellings, lhp, Southern University.
21. Charles Kwolek, lhp, Providence College.
22. Andrew Tam, rhp, Texas Wesleyan College.
23. *Donald Atkins, ss, Parkview HS, Little Rock, Ark.
24. Stanley Reese, 1b, George Mason University.
25. Cameron Killebrew, of, Brigham Young University.

DRAFT DROP *Son of Harmon Killebrew, major leaguer (1954-75)*

26. David Miller, of, George Mason University.
27. Jeff Zitek, ss, Illinois State University.
28. Wesley Williams, rhp, New Mexico Highlands University.
29. **Jim Farr, rhp, Penn State University.—(1982)**
30. **Gene Nelson, rhp, Pasco County HS, Dade City, Fla.—(1981-93)**
31. Steve Paine, of-c, Dallas Baptist University.
32. *Thomas Blackmon, rhp, South Florence (S.C.) HS.
33. Cecil De Fla Strawn, c, Southern Methodist University.
34. *James Strum, rhp, St. Mark's HS, Wilmington, Del.
35. Keith Walsh, rhp, John F. Kennedy HS, Suffolk, Va.
36. *Harry Oakley, c, Rogers HS, Newport, R.I.
37. David Chapman, 3b, University of Michigan.
38. John Zisk, of, Delaware Valley (Pa.) College.

DRAFT DROP *Brother of Richie Zisk, major leaguer (1971-83)*

39. ***Tim Hulett, ss, Lanphier HS, Springfield, Ill.—(1983-95)**
40. *Jeff Scott, 3b, Port Clinton (Ohio) HS.
41. Alvin Williams, 3b, Jackson State University.
42. *Moses Kyles, ss, Buchanan (Mich.) HS.

**June—Secondary Phase (10)**

1. **Mike Richardt, 3b, Fresno (Calif.) CC.—(1980-84)**
2. Thomas McGivney, c, Alvin (Texas) CC.
3. *David Jensen, lhp, Edmonds (Wash.) CC.

## TORONTO BLUE JAYS

**January—Regular Phase (1)**

1. Mike Lebo, c, University of South Carolina.—(High A)
2. ***Mike Richardt, ss, Fresno (Calif.) CC.—(1980-84)**
3. **Geno Petralli, c, Sacramento (Calif.) CC.—(1982-93)**
4. Michael Kelly, of, Santa Barbara, Calif.

DRAFT DROP *Brother of Pat Kelly, major leaguer (1991-99)*

**January—Secondary Phase (15)**

1. *Rob Hertel, 2b-3b, University of Southern California.—DNP

DRAFT DROP *Quarterback, National Football League (1978-79)*

**June—Regular Phase (2)**

1. **Lloyd Moseby, of-1b, Oakland (Calif.) HS.—(1980-91)**
2. Tim Thompson, 1b, Winter Park (Fla.) HS.—(AAA)
3. Mike Cullen, rhp, Columbus (Wis.) HS.—(AA)
4. Mike Coyne, of, McNicholas HS, Cincinnati.—(Low A)
5. **Dave Stieb, of, Southern Illinois University.—(1979-98)**
6. Mike Cuellar, rhp, Madison HS, Houston.

DRAFT DROP *Son of Mike Cuellar, major leaguer (1959-77)*

7. **Brian Milner, c, Southwest HS, Fort Worth, Texas.—(1978)**
8. Brad Burger, rhp, North Boone HS, Roscoe, Ill.
9. *Tom Stauffer, lhp, Monsignor Bonner HS, Drexel Hill, Pa.
10. Allen Montgomery, 3b, Houston.
11. **Dave Baker, 3b, UCLA.—(1982)**

DRAFT DROP *Brother of Doug Baker, major leaguer (1984-90)*

12. Vincent Williams, of, Sam Houston HS, Houston.
13. Thomas O'Dowd, rhp, Lumen Christi HS, Jackson, Mich.
14. Mark Stoeber, rhp, Northern Kentucky University.
15. *Rob Irwin, lhp, Stanford University.
16. Ronald Harper, of, El Cerrito HS, Richmond, Calif.
17. Richard Palmer, c, West Covina (Calif.) HS.
18. *Robert Heuck, lhp, University of Texas.
19. Terry Watkins, rhp, St. Mary's (Calif.) College.
20. Bill Lajoie, 3b, St. Clair County (Mich.) CC.
21. *Mondel Williams, of, McClatchy HS, Sacramento, Calif.
22. *Russ Dickerson, inf, Harrisonburg (Va.) HS.
23. *John Moses, lhp, Bellaire HS, Houston.
24. *Michael Cunningham, rhp, Highlands HS, Sacramento, Calif.
25. *Jimmie Ranson, 1b, San Diego State University.

**June—Secondary Phase (16)**

1. *Simon Glenn, of, Blinn (Texas) JC.—DNP

# 1979

# Moribund first round belies intriguing class

It's well documented in baseball history that the first round almost always sets the tone for any draft because it usually includes the best prospects and the most intriguing storylines. But that characterization hardly applied to 1979; the high-end talent selected that year was some of the most mundane and unremarkable on record.

Even as a then-record 19 first-rounders went on to play in the major leagues, the crop was fraught with underachievers, even imposters. With one or two exceptions, it was an uninspiring lot.

It included one of the most unproductive first overall picks ever in Al Chambers, and unequivocally the worst first-round pick of them all in Kevin Brandt. It included one of the most hyped failed prospects in the draft era in Brad Komminsk, and one of the most controversial players in the game's history in drug-stained Steve Howe.

It also included a draft-record four selections who went unsigned.

Yet for all the negativity that surrounded the 26 players chosen in the first round in 1979, that year's draft as a whole was one of the most fascinating ever. It's just that almost all the truly noteworthy players and most fascinating accomplishments involved players in the less noticed corners of the draft.

- Bill Bordley, who attempted to manipulate the draft like almost no player before him? He was a product of the normally tranquil January draft.
- Todd Demeter, who set a draft record with his stunning $208,000 bonus, and yet never came close to providing a return on his investment? A second-rounder.
- Derek Tatsuno, who compiled possibly both the greatest season and career resume of any college pitcher ever, but was thwarted in his efforts to capitalize on his exploits by playing in Japan? Another second-rounder.
- Orel Hershiser, the most successful player in the 1979 draft class and one of the best big-game pitchers of the draft era? A 17th-rounder.
- John Elway, who led a wave of the greatest quarterback prospects ever to come along at one time, and might have been the top pick in the 1979 draft if his sole focus was baseball? An 18th-rounder.
- Don Mattingly, undeniably the best pure hitter in the 1979 class? A 19th-rounder.

Fascinating names all, but not a first-rounder in the bunch. And it's safe to say that no player actually drafted in the first round in 1979 had credentials to match the career-defining exploits of those half-dozen players.

### BORDLEY CALLS HIS SHOT

The typically quiet, low-profile January draft took on an interesting twist in 1979 that required the intervention of commissioner Bowie Kuhn.

Orel Hershiser was one of the best big-game pitchers of his era and clearly the most successful player from the 1979 draft, but he lasted until the Dodgers took him in the 17th round

The circumstances surrounded Bordley, a star lefthander who went 26-2 in two seasons at the University of Southern California. He dropped out of school following his sophomore year to become eligible for the January draft, and was considered far and away the top commodity in the secondary phase—if not the best pitching prospect in the amateur ranks, Tatsuno notwithstanding.

He was the winning pitcher in the national championship game for USC in 1978, and longtime Trojans coach Rod Dedeaux said he was the best pitcher he'd ever had.

Bordley, an unsigned first-round pick of the Milwaukee Brewers in 1976, made it clear to every club that desired his services that he wanted to pitch for a West Coast club, ostensibly because of family obligations. His father Art had recently suffered a heart attack and undergone surgery, and his older brother Art Jr., a former minor leaguer, had been badly hurt in a motorcycle accident.

To Bordley's misfortune, Philadelphia, Toronto and Cincinnati had the first three picks in the draft, so his best bet to land with a West Coast club was the California Angels with the fourth pick.

According to Bordley, Angels general manager Buzzie Bavasi had assured him his club would not only accommodate him, making it possible for Bordley to live at home, but also agreed to a $200,000 signing bonus and an immediate job in the big leagues. The trick was to get the teams drafting ahead of the Angels to comply with his wishes.

## AT A GLANCE

### This Date In History
**WINTER DRAFT:** Jan. 9
**SUMMER DRAFT:** June 5-7

### Best Draft
**LOS ANGELES DODGERS.**
**STEVE HOWE** (1) and **GREG BROCK** (13) had lengthy big league careers, but the selection of **OREL HERSHISER** (17) put this draft over the top.

### Worst Draft
**OAKLAND ATHLETICS.**
In one of the most inept drafts ever, the A's failed to sign five of their first six picks in the June regular phase, 13 of their top 16 and 36 of 48 picks overall. Seven picks eventually played in the big leagues, but the lone player the A's signed was **BERT BRADLEY** (36), who worked six innings in Oakland in 1983.

### First-Round Bust
**KEVIN BRANDT, OF, TWINS.**
Brandt ranks as the greatest first-round flop of the draft era. The Twins released him after a year in the organizaion and he played in just 47 games as a pro, all in the Rookie-level Appalachian League, batting .155 with one homer and nine RBIs.

### Second Time Around
**RANDY BUSH, OF, TWINS.**
The Twins bombed with Brandt, but made good a round later by selecting Bush, a serviceable outfielder who hit .251 over a dozen years with the club and was a key contributor on World Series champions in 1987 and 1991.

### Late-Round Find
**OREL HERSHISER, RHP, DODGERS (17TH ROUND).**
Hershiser earned the most Wins Above Replacement of any player drafted in 1979, edging 19th-rounder **DON MATTINGLY** (Yankees) and 23rd-rounder **BRETT BUTLER** (Braves).

### Never Too Late
**MIKE SHARPERSON, SS, PIRATES (41ST ROUND); HERM WINNINGHAM, OF,**

CONTINUED ON PAGE 216

## AT A GLANCE

CONTINUED FROM PAGE 215

**PIRATES (39TH ROUND).** The two latest picks in 1979 to reach the big leagues were unsigned Pirates selections. Sharperson and Winningham had known each other since age 7, grew up down the street from each other in Orangeburg, S.C., were drafted from the same high school and attended the same junior college (Georgia's DeKalb South CC). They both became first-round picks in the secondary phase in 1981. Sharperson played eight seasons in the big leagues; Winningham played in nine.

### Overlooked

**DAN GLADDEN, OF, GIANTS.** A classic over-achiever, Gladden was never drafted out of high school, junior college or at Fresno State. The Giants signed him for no bonus after the 1979 draft, after he begged their Class A Fresno affiliate for a tryout. Gladden worked his way through the Giants system, hitting .300 every step of the way, before getting his first shot in the big leagues late in the 1983 season. A year later, he hit .351 with 31 stolen bases as a rookie; in an 11-year career in the majors, Gladden hit .270-74-446 and stole 222 bases.

### International Gem

**TONY FERNANDEZ, SS, BLUE JAYS. FERNANDO VALENZUELA** made more of a splash when he debuted in spectacular fashion with the Dodgers in 1980, and **JOSE OQUENDO**, a Puerto Rican signed at 16 by the Mets for $12,000, was acknowledged as the big catch on the international front. But Fernandez, a Dominican signed by the Blue Jays for just $3,000, had the best career among all foreign players signed in 1979. In 17 seasons, 12 in Toronto, Fernandez hit .288-94-844, stole 246 bases and fielded the ball at a steady .980 clip.

## 1979: THE FIRST ROUNDERS

| CLUB: PLAYER, POS., SCHOOL | HOMETOWN | B-T | HT. | WT. | AGE | BONUS | FIRST YEAR | LAST YEAR | PEAK LEVEL (YEARS) |
|---|---|---|---|---|---|---|---|---|---|
| **JUNE—REGULAR PHASE** | | | | | | | | | |
| 1. Mariners: Al Chambers, 1b, John Harris HS | Harrisburg, Pa. | L-L | 6-4 | 210 | 18 | $60,000 | 1979 | 1988 | Majors (3) |
| Frame, power potenial drew comparisons to Willie Stargell coming out of high school; played only 57 games in majors, didn't hit (.208-1-11) or adapt to OF. | | | | | | | | | |
| 2. Mets: Tim Leary, rhp, UCLA | Santa Monica, Calif. | R-R | 6-3 | 195 | 20 | $100,000 | 1980 | 1994 | Majors (13) |
| Went 12-3, 2.72 as UCLA junior; spring sensation in 1981, but hurt elbow in season-opener; came back to have long career, though stuff was never the same. | | | | | | | | | |
| 3. Blue Jays: Jay Schroeder, c, Palisades HS | Pacific Palisades, Calif. | R-R | 6-3 | 195 | 17 | $135,000 | 1980 | 1983 | Class A (3) |
| Jays gambled big bonus on two-sport star, but eventually lost him to NFL career after he struggled to hit (.213-36-166) or adapt to outfield in low minors. | | | | | | | | | |
| 4. Braves: Brad Komminsk, of, Shawnee HS | Lima, Ohio | R-R | 6-3 | 187 | 18 | $70,000 | 1979 | 1997 | Majors (8) |
| Billed as the next Dale Murphy when he breezed through minors, debuted in Atlanta in 1983; fell far short (.218, 23 HRs) in eight major league seasons. | | | | | | | | | |
| 5. Athletics: Juan Bustabad, ss, Miami Lakes HS | Hialeah, Fla. | B-R | 5-9 | 145 | 17 | Unsigned | 1980 | 1989 | Class AAA (5) |
| Cuban-born player rejected A's $25,000 offer, became top pick in January '80 draft; didn't hit (.247) in nine seasons in minors, became longtime manager/coach. | | | | | | | | | |
| 6. Cardinals: Andy Van Slyke, of, New Hartford HS | New Hartford, N.Y. | L-R | 6-2 | 190 | 18 | $42,500 | 1980 | 1995 | Majors (13) |
| Preferred basketball to baseball in HS, but became accomplished hitter and Gold Glove OF (.274-164-792, 245 SB) in 13 MLB seasons; son Scott plays for Dodgers. | | | | | | | | | |
| 7. Indians: Jon Bohnet, lhp, Hogan HS | Vallejo, Calif. | B-L | 6-0 | 180 | 18 | $77,500 | 1979 | 1984 | Majors (1) |
| On fast track with 8-1, 0.52 record as prep SR, 6-3, 1.98 mark as first-year pro, reached Cleveland by 1982, but struggled in brief duty with Indians, never returned. | | | | | | | | | |
| 8. Astros: John Mizerock, c, Punxsutawney HS | Punxsutawney, Pa. | L-R | 6-0 | 180 | 18 | $65,000 | 1979 | 1990 | Majors (4) |
| Excelled in baseball, five other sports as star prep athlete; slowed by weak bat in minors, majors (.188-2-24), became longtime manager/coach in minors. | | | | | | | | | |
| 9. White Sox: Steve Buechele, ss, Servite HS | Fullerton, Calif. | R-R | 6-2 | 185 | 18 | Unsigned | 1982 | 1995 | Majors (11) |
| Passed up White Sox offer, became John Elway's roommate at Stanford; drafted by Rangers (1982, fifth round), went on to play 11 years in majors (.245-137-547). | | | | | | | | | |
| 10. Expos: Tim Wallach, 1b/3b, Cal State Fullerton | Tustin, Calif. | R-R | 6-3 | 195 | 21 | $77,500 | 1979 | 1996 | Majors (17) |
| Passed up Angels eighth-round offer as junior, returned to Fullerton, hit .394-23-102, won Golden Spikes Award, led Titans to College World Series title. | | | | | | | | | |
| 11. Twins: Kevin Brandt, of, Nekoosa HS | Nekoosa, Wis. | R-R | 6-0 | 180 | 17 | $25,000 | 1979 | 1980 | Rookie (2) |
| Hit .557-10-31 as prep senior, impressed Twins with power display in workout, but brief pro career was dismal failure; hit .155-1-9 in 47 Rookie-league games. | | | | | | | | | |
| 12. Cubs: Jon Perlman, rhp, Baylor | Carthage, Texas | R-R | 6-3 | 180 | 22 | $50,000 | 1979 | 1988 | Majors (3) |
| Went from walk-on at Baylor to set school record for career wins; Cubs fifth-rounder in 1978 became team's top pick a year later, went 1-2, 6.35 in brief MLB career. | | | | | | | | | |
| 13. Tigers: Rick Leach, of, Michigan | Flint, Mich. | L-L | 6-1 | 180 | 22 | $125,000 | 1979 | 1990 | Majors (10) |
| Second straight year Tigers took state football star with top pick; short on power/speed, long on hitting skills, intangibles, hit .268-18-183 in 10 MLB seasons. | | | | | | | | | |
| 14. Padres: Joe Lansford, 1b, Wilcox HS | San Jose, Calif. | R-R | 6-5 | 220 | 18 | $100,000 | 1979 | 1987 | Majors (2) |
| Indians took brother in first round in 1978; explosive raw power in big frame, hit 138 HRs in minors, just one in majors as path to San Diego blocked by Steve Garvey. | | | | | | | | | |
| 15. Giants: Scott Garrelts, rhp, Buckley-Loda HS | Buckley, Ill. | R-R | 6-4 | 200 | 17 | $50,000 | 1979 | 1995 | Majors (10) |
| Put himself on map with 22 SO game as prep junior; spent 10 years in majors, best season in 1989 (14-5, 2.28), when he led NL in ERA, Giants to World Series. | | | | | | | | | |
| 16. Dodgers: # Steve Howe, lhp, Michigan | Clarkston, Mich. | L-L | 6-1 | 180 | 21 | $75,000 | 1979 | 1996 | Majors (12) |
| Went 7-2, 1.78 and became Michigan's career wins leader; mercurial 12-year MLB career because of frequent substance-abuse issues, went 47-41, 3.03 with 91 SV. | | | | | | | | | |
| 17. Rangers: Jerry Don Gleaton, lhp, Texas | Brownwood, Texas | L-L | 6-3 | 190 | 21 | $53,000 | 1979 | 1993 | Majors (12) |
| Second-round pick out of high school, became first to reach majors in 1979 after 13-1, 1.95 record (111 IP/121 SO) at Texas; went 15-23, 4.25 in 12 seasons. | | | | | | | | | |
| 18. Giants: Rick Luecken, rhp, Spring-Woods HS | Houston | R-R | 6-6 | 218 | 17 | Unsigned | 1983 | 1991 | Majors (2) |
| Career trended down after he passed on Giants offer; won 24 games in four years at Texas A&M, slipped to 28th round in 1983 draft, went 3-5, 5.10 in 78 MLB IP. | | | | | | | | | |
| 19. White Sox: Rick Seilheimer, c, Brenham HS | Brenham, Texas | L-R | 5-11 | 185 | 18 | $50,000 | 1979 | 1986 | Majors (1) |
| Second Sox pick in first round became initial prep selection in 1979 draft to reach majors; debuted at 19, hit .212-1-3 in 21 games, never returned. | | | | | | | | | |
| 20. Reds: Dan Lamar, c, Bellaire HS | Houston | R-R | 6-1 | 195 | 18 | $40,000 | 1979 | 1985 | Class AA (1) |
| Noted by Reds fans as the compensation pick for losing Pete Rose to Phillies; buried in Class A for five years, briefly reached Double-A, hit .276-45-221 overall. | | | | | | | | | |
| 21. Royals: Atlee Hammaker, lhp, East Tennessee State | Alexandria, Va. | L-L | 6-2 | 193 | 21 | $65,000 | 1979 | 1995 | Majors (12) |
| Attended college on hoops scholarship, emerged as baseball talent; became NL all-star/ERA leader in 1983; father-in-law of Indians catcher Yan Gomes. | | | | | | | | | |
| 22. Reds: Mike Sullivan, rhp, Clemson | Woodbridge, Va. | R-R | 6-0 | 170 | 20 | $40,000 | 1979 | 1982 | Class AA (1) |
| First-round pick of A's in 1976 re-emerged as top pick after 10-1, 1.96 junior season at Clemson; pro career peaked in Double-A, won 15 games in minors. | | | | | | | | | |
| 23. Tigers: Chris Baker, of, Livonia Franklin HS | Dearborn Heights, Mich. | R-R | 6-3 | 190 | 18 | $54,000 | 1979 | 1982 | Class A (2) |
| Tigers stayed close to home again with second first-round pick; speed was his best tool, but stole just six bases in four seasons in low minors, hit .247-20-132. | | | | | | | | | |
| 24. Padres: Bob Geren, c, Clairemont HS | San Diego | R-R | 6-2 | 195 | 17 | $52,000 | 1979 | 1992 | Majors (5) |
| Padres stayed close to home in taking San Diego HS player of year; finally reached majors with Yankees in 10th pro season, hit .233-22-76, became A's manager. | | | | | | | | | |
| 25. Dodgers: Steve Perry, rhp, Michigan | Ann Arbor, Mich. | R-R | 6-5 | 215 | 22 | $67,500 | 1979 | 1984 | Class AAA (2) |
| Unprecedented third first-rounder from one college; son of Michigan's sports information director reached Triple-A with Dodgers, went 28-40 in six years. | | | | | | | | | |
| 26. Athletics: Mike Stenhouse, of, Harvard | Cranston, R.I. | L-R | 6-1 | 185 | 21 | Unsigned | 1980 | 1987 | Majors (5) |
| Second unsigned A's pick in first round, offered only $12,000; hit .396-1-30 after .475 freshman year, 10 HRs as sophomore; hit .190-9-40 in five MLB seasons. | | | | | | | | | |
| **JANUARY—REGULAR PHASE** | | | | | | | | | |
| 1. Mets: Neal Heaton, lhp, Sachem HS | Holtsville, N.Y. | L-L | 6-0 | 185 | 18 | Unsigned | 1981 | 1996 | Majors (12) |
| Local product, December HS grad, chose Miami over Mets' $35K offer; went 42-7, 2.03 at Miami, drafted by Indians in 1981, went 80-96 in major league career. | | | | | | | | | |
| **JANUARY—SECONDARY PHASE** | | | | | | | | | |
| 1. Phillies: Mark Davis, lhp, Chabot (Calif.) JC | Livermore, Calif. | L-L | 6-3 | 175 | 18 | $30,000 | 1979 | 1997 | Majors (15) |
| Phils passed on Bill Bordley, big name in draft, for juco lefty who spent 15 years in majors, won NL Cy Young with Padres (4-3, 1.85, 44 SV) in breakout 1989 season. | | | | | | | | | |
| **JUNE—SECONDARY PHASE** | | | | | | | | | |
| 1. Red Sox: Marty Barrett, ss, Arizona State | Las Vegas, Nev. | R-R | 5-10 | 175 | 20 | $28,000 | 1979 | 1991 | Majors (10) |
| Scored winning run for Triple-A Pawtucket in famed 33-inning game in 1981; played 10 seasons in majors (.278-18-314, 57 SB), was ALCS MVP in 1986. | | | | | | | | | |

*# Deceased.*

## How They Should Have Done It

Based on the career WAR (Wins Above Replacement, as calculated by Baseball-Reference.com) numbers achieved by all the players eligible for the 1979 draft, here's how the first round should have unfolded. Numbers in parentheses indicate the round when the player was actually drafted

| | Player, Pos. | Actual Draft | WAR | Bonus |
|---|---|---|---|---|
| 1. | Orel Hershiser, rhp | Dodgers (17) | 56.8 | $10,000 |
| 2. | Brett Butler, of | Braves (23) | 49.5 | $1,000 |
| 3. | Don Mattingly, 1b | Yankees (19) | 42.2 | $22,500 |
| 4. | Gary Gaetti, 3b | Twins (June-S/1) | 41.8 | $3,500 |
| 5. | Andy Van Slyke, of | Cardinals (1) | 41.3 | $42,500 |
| 6. | Tim Wallach, 1b/3b | Expos (1) | 38.3 | $77,500 |
| 7. | Bill Doran, 2b | Astros (6) | 32.7 | $13,000 |
| 8. | Scott Fletcher, ss | Cubs (June-S/1) | 32.0 | $20,000 |
| 9. | Von Hayes, 1b/3b | Indians (7) | 29.6 | $21,000 |
| 10. | Greg Gagne, ss | Yankees (5) | 26.3 | $21,500 |
| 11. | Johnny Ray, 2b | Astros (12) | 24.0 | $1,000 |
| 12. | Howard Johnson, 3b | Tigers (Jan.-S/1) | 22.1 | $12,000 |
| 13. | Gary Pettis, of | Angels (Jan.-R/6) | 22.0 | $5,000 |
| 14. | Bud Black, lhp | Mariners (17) | 21.1 | $1,000 |
| 15. | Mark Eichhorn, rhp | Blue Jays (Jan.-R/2) | 19.6 | $10,000 |
| 16. | Pete O'Brien, 1b | Rangers (15) | 19.2 | $2,000 |
| 17. | Milt Thompson, of | Braves (Jan.-R/2) | 18.7 | $10,000 |
| 18. | Storm Davis, rhp | Orioles (7) | 17.4 | $25,000 |
| 19. | Otis Nixon, 3b/of | Yankees (June-S/1) | 16.6 | $25,000 |
| 20. | Dan Gladden, of | Giants (NDFA) | 15.3 | None |
| 21. | Jose DeLeon, rhp | Pirates (3) | 15.2 | $10,000 |
| | Jeff Russell, rhp | Reds (5) | 15.2 | $20,000 |
| 23. | Brook Jacoby, 3b | Braves (Jan.-R/7) | 14.9 | $5,000 |
| 24. | Tim Leary, rhp | Mets (1) | 12.2 | $100,000 |
| 25. | Steve Howe, lhp | Dodgers (1) | 10.7 | $25,000 |
| 26. | Scott Garrelts, rhp | Giants (1) | 10.0 | $50,000 |

| | Top 3 Unsigned Players | | | Year Signed |
|---|---|---|---|---|
| 1. | Kevin Gross, rhp | Orioles (32) | 28.0 | 1981 |
| 2. | Tom Henke, rhp | Mariners (20) | 23.5 | 1980 |
| 3. | Glenn Davis, 1b | Orioles (31) | 19.5 | 1981 |

All three clubs indicated they would accommodate Bordley—or so he thought. The Phillies and Blue Jays obliged, but the Reds, picking right before the Angels, had a last-minute change of heart and drafted Bordley. When a club official called Bordley to tell him the Reds had drafted him, he hung up on him.

"Today is my 21st birthday and it's the saddest day of my life," said Bordley, expressing his dismay over the change in developments that didn't work in his favor.

For their part, the Reds defended their decision to draft Bordley.

"We talked to him, and we knew he preferred to stay on the West Coast." said Joe Bowen, the Reds vice president in charge of scouting. "But in baseball, you don't get to pick the teams; the teams pick you. He was the best player available, so we took him."

Bordley stuck to his guns and refused to sign with the Reds.

Once their chance to snag Bordley fell through, the Angels explored other options to obtain the prized lefthander and even suggested a trade. But that would require the Reds to sign Bordley first because draft rules prohibited the trading of draft picks. The two clubs moved far enough along on a trade proposal that the Reds agreed to give up Bordley, and in exchange would receive Dickie Thon, a promising young shortstop in the Angels system, plus $75,000. That proposal was vetoed by Major League Baseball's executive council.

That's when a sympathetic Kuhn entered the fray.

After conducting an eight-day investigation that concluded Feb. 13, he voided the Reds' selection of Bordley. Furthermore, he determined that the Angels were guilty of tampering because they had persuaded Bordley to not sign with Cincinnati. Kuhn fined the Angels $15,000 and granted the Reds three of their future draft choices as compensation.

As part of his ruling, Kuhn asked Bordley to submit five teams (besides the Angels) that he would be amenable to signing with, and a special lottery was set up with Kansas City, Los Angeles, Milwaukee, San Francisco and Seattle vying for his negotiating rights. The Giants had luck of the draw, gaining his rights on Feb. 24.

Almost immediately they came to terms with the Bordley on a three-year major league deal that included a $200,000 bonus—the largest paid to any amateur in the draft era to that point.

Unfortunately, Bordley's career with the Giants never worked out because he was derailed by elbow problems within a year, and won just two games in his short-lived big league career.

Under normal circumstances, the Phillies would have drafted Bordley with the No. 1 pick in the January secondary phase. Instead, they settled for another lefthander from California, Mark Davis.

"There were several reasons we didn't draft Bordley," said Phillies farm director Dallas Green. "The obvious one was the bonus he was asking for. It was totally out of line, as far as I was concerned. We also had no June draft pick because we had signed Pete Rose (as a free agent). So I felt I could not jeopardize the entire organization by drafting someone who might be difficult to sign. We felt we had to have a guy we could sign and one who might in a few years produce just as well as Bordley might."

Davis enjoyed considerably more success over a 15-year career and won the National League's Cy Young Award in 1989, as a member of the San Diego Padres.

Neal Heaton, another lefthander, was the first pick in the regular phase in January. A Holtsville, N.Y., product, he was taken by the Mets. Heaton had led his New York-based team to the Connie Mack World Series title the previous summer and was eligible for the January draft because he finished high school in December.

With a narrow window to sign between the draft and his scheduled enrolment date at the University of Miami, Heaton turned down the Mets $38,000 offer. Over the next three years, Heaton won 42 games for the Hurricanes and became an attractive pick again when next eligible for the draft in 1981.

### CHAMBERS LEADS OFF JUNE PHASE

The Seattle Mariners had the first selection in the regular phase of the June draft and narrowed their choice to Chambers and Komminsk. They went for Chambers, a power-hitting first baseman from Pennsylvania, because they believed he might

## AT A GLANCE

### Minor League Take

**TIM WALLACH, 1B, EXPOS.** Wallach led Cal State Fullerton to its first College World Series title in 1979 by hitting 22 homers and driving in an NCAA record-tying 102 runs. He continued his torrid hitting at Double-A Memphis and Triple-A Denver in the Expos system over the next year and a half with a combined 55 homers and 186 RBIs in 219 games, and was in Montreal to stay by 1981.

### One Who Got Away

**DEREK TATSUNO, LHP, PADRES (2ND ROUND).** Despite a 20-1 record and NCAA-record 234 strikeouts in the final season of a spectacular three-year college career at Hawaii, Tatsuno lasted until the second round of the 1979 draft thanks to his desire to pitch professionally in Japan. After trying unsuccessfully for three years to do that, Tatsuno signed with the Brewers in 1982. He never came close to matching his college success.

### He Was Drafted?

**DAN MARINO, RHP, ROYALS (4TH ROUND).** In the same draft that the Royals took Marino, a top prep pitching prospect in Pennsylvania, they took a 17th-round flier on **JOHN ELWAY**. Marino never played baseball again while joining Elway in becoming a college football star and later a record-breaking quarterback in the NFL.

### Did You Know . . .

More first-round picks went unsigned (four) in 1979 (June/regular phase) than any draft in history.

### They Said It

Seattle Mariners scout **BOB HARRISON**, who signed top draft pick **AL CHAMBERS**: "There's no doubt he's going to have 70 power (on the 20-80 scouting scale). And that means 35 to 40 home runs a year, maybe more in our place."—*Chambers homered just twice in his big league career.*

## DRAFT SPOTLIGHT: BILL BORDLEY

Bill Bordley won just two games in his major league career, and made more of a mark on the game as Major League Baseball's vice president of security and facility management.

Those are hardly the kind of credentials that would point to Bordley as one of the most controversial figures of the draft era. But in 1979, as the best-known and most-coveted amateur player in the game, Bordley attempted to manipulate the draft by declaring he would play only for a team near his West Coast home. It eventually worked for him, though not before it became messy and required the intervention of the commissioner's office.

**Bill Bordley was one of the first pitchers to have Tommy John surgery, but it did not work for him and his career fizzled**

The end result was that Bordley signed with the San Francisco Giants for $200,000, the largest bonus paid since the inception of the draft. It was a deal that met the interests of both parties as Bordley, a star lefthander in two years at the University of Southern California, got paid handsomely to pitch close to home, while the Giants suddenly and almost inadvertently had one of the best arms around dumped in their lap.

"He's one of those kids who was brought up to be a ballplayer," said Bing Devine, a longtime executive employed by the Giants at the time. "Unless something happens to his arm, he'll be a good one."

The last time a drafted player had gone through a scenario similar to Bordley's occurred in 1966, when another USC player, Tom Seaver, had a contract he signed with the Atlanta Braves nullified by the commissioner's office. The New York Mets won a special three-team drawing for his services, much like the Giants did with Bordley, and none other than Devine was the Mets' general manager at the time.

Bordley began his career in 1979 with Triple-A Phoenix in the Giants system, posting an 8-11, 4.56 record. He opened the 1980 season back in Phoenix, but was promoted to the Giants in June and won his first two big league starts, both against the Reds, the team that had drafted Bordley in 1979, only for commissioner Bowie Kuhn to override the selection. Seaver, naturally, was the losing pitcher in his first win.

But unbeknownst to anyone, Bordley's arm was beginning unravel by that time and those would be his only victories in the major leagues. His 2-3, 4.65 record for the 1980 Giants turned out to be the extent of his major league career.

Bordley said he felt twinges of pain in his left elbow in his final season at USC, and the pain persisted into his pro career and intensified greatly in 1980. Following that season, Bordley underwent surgery to repair ligaments in his left elbow, but the procedure failed. The following spring, Dr. Frank Jobe rebuilt the elbow using a tendon from Bordley's leg. At the time, Jobe had performed similar surgery on six other pitchers, but only Tommy John had survived to pitch again professionally.

After being forced to sit out the 1981 season, Bordley launched his comeback with Class A Fresno in 1982. But with a fastball that was a shell of the 95 mph offering that launched his career, Bordley posted an uninspiring 5-5, 4.71 record. He was released by the Giants following the season.

Bordley went to spring training with the Braves in 1983 and didn't make the team, and then attempted to salvage his career by pitching in Mexico. But after walking 11 and striking out just one in two starts, he knew he was finished.

It wouldn't be the end of Bordley's career in baseball, however.

After returning to USC and obtaining a degree in business, Bordley took a job with the Secret Service in the agency's investigative division. After working behind the scenes with two U.S. Presidents, he was hired in 2011 to oversee security and facility management for Major League Baseball.

become another Willie Stargell, or even Dave Parker. Chambers was also an all-state defensive end with a college commitment to Arizona State.

That was supposed to be a bargaining chip in his negotiations with the Mariners, but Chambers surprisingly agreed to the club's initial offer of $60,000 a day before the draft. For the Mariners, it represented a nice change of pace from the previous year, when protracted negotiations and a huge bonus for first-round pick Tito Nanni cost player-development director Mel Didier his job.

"I enjoy hitting a baseball much more than getting hit in football," said Chambers of his decision to sign so quickly.

While the Mariners were convinced Chambers was most deserving of being drafted No. 1, none of the teams selecting immediately behind Seattle shared the same sentiment. UCLA righthander Tim Leary, California prep catcher Jay Schroeder and Komminsk, a prep outfielder from Ohio, were generally regarded as the top three prospects—and went off the board in that order with the next three picks.

The Mariners took Chambers primarily because of his raw power potential.

"He has the best bat I've seen for a high school player since Jeff Burroughs," said Seattle farm director Hal Keller, who signed Burroughs for the Washington Senators 10 years earlier. "He has a very short, quick stroke and tremendous power. At this point at age 18, he is just learning the game.

"I just felt you didn't get a chance for a bat like this very often. You could project him as the type of guy who can put people in the seats. He has awesome power."

As a senior at John Harris High in Harrisburg, Pa., playing on a field with no fences, Chambers hit .484 with seven doubles, four triples, four home runs and 28 RBIs in 22 games.

Though Chambers hit .292 in parts of seven seasons in the Mariners farm system, he hit only 73 homers. He was extended four separate trials in Seattle, from 1983-85, that amounted to just 57 games and 120 at-bats, and hit only two home runs while batting .208.

On March 25, 1986, just as the Mariners were breaking camp, they released Chambers.

By drafting Chambers with the first pick in the first round and Arizona State third baseman Jamie Allen with the top pick in the second round, the Mariners thought they had pulled off a coup. Allen, a Yakima, Wash., product and an unsigned first-round pick in 1976, had been mentioned as a possible first overall pick prior to the 1979 season

## Fastest To The Majors

| | Player, Pos. | Drafted | Debut |
|---|---|---|---|
| 1. | Jerry Don Gleaton, lhp | Rangers (1) | July 11, 1979 |
| 2. | Steve Howe, lhp | Dodgers (1) | April 11, 1980 |
| 3. | Brad Mills, 3b | Expos (17) | June 8, 1980 |
| 4. | Mike Kinnunen, lhp | Twins (10) | June 12, 1980 |
| 5. | Bill Bordley, lhp | Reds (Jan.-S/1) | June 30, 1980 |

**FIRST HIGH SCHOOL SELECTION:** Ricky Seilheimer, c (White Sox/1, July 5, 1980)

**LAST PLAYER TO RETIRE:** Mike Maddux, rhp (July 4, 2000)

before being plagued by a recurrence of shoulder woes that impacted his draft year at ASU.

As one of the nation's top collegiate players as a sophomore, Allen hit .347 with 15 homers, but he slumped to .257 with five homers in 35 games as a junior. Shortly after the draft, he had two pins removed from his injured right shoulder. By signing Allen for $57,500, the Mariners were hopeful he would quickly return to the productive offensive player he had been and solidify third base for them.

Allen's shoulder never fully responded. He spent just a single season playing third base for the Mariners, in 1983, and hit .223 with four homers in 86 games.

### THE FOOTBALL FACTOR

Schroeder, a two-sport star from Pacific Palisades, Calif., was chosen third overall by the Toronto Blue Jays, but his commitment to play football at UCLA, as one of the nation's premier quarterback recruits, raised serious doubts whether the Blue Jays would ever sign him. He deliberated most of the summer before finally agreeing to a deal that included a $135,000 bonus and would allow him to play college football while pursuing baseball on the side.

That arrangement persisted for two years before Schroeder, struggling to get ahead in baseball, decided to give up football and concentrate solely on baseball. But Schroeder was never able to become a consistent hitter in a four-year career in the Jays system, batting .213 with 36 home runs in 417 games while striking out 477 times. He never rose above Class A.

Realizing his baseball career was going nowhere, Schroeder let NFL teams know that he was available to pursue a career in pro football—if a team was inclined to draft him, considering he started only one game at quarterback for UCLA. The Washington Redskins took him in the third round of the 1984 NFL draft.

### Top 25 Bonuses

| | Player, Pos. | Drafted (Round) | Order | Bonus |
|---|---|---|---|---|
| 1. | * Todd Demeter, 1b | Yankees (2) | 51 | $208,000 |
| **2.** | **Bill Bordley, lhp** | **† Reds (Jan.-S/1)** | **(3)** | **#$200,000** |
| 3. | * Jay Schroeder, c | Blue Jays (1) | 3 | $135,000 |
| **4.** | **Rick Leach, of** | **Tigers (1)** | **13** | **$125,000** |
| **5.** | **Tim Leary, rhp** | **Mets (1)** | **2** | **$100,000** |
| | *** Joe Lansford, 1b** | **Padres (1)** | **14** | **$100,000** |
| **7.** | *** Ron Shepherd, of** | **Blue Jays (2)** | **29** | **$85,000** |
| **8.** | *** Jon Bohnet, lhp** | **Indians (1)** | **7** | **$77,500** |
| | **Tim Wallach, 3b** | **Expos (1)** | **10** | **$77,500** |
| **10.** | *** Brad Komminsk, of** | **Braves (1)** | **4** | **$70,000** |
| 11. | Steve Perry, rhp | Dodgers (1) | 25 | $67,500 |
| **12.** | *** John Mizerock, c** | **Astros (1)** | **8** | **$65,000** |
| | **Atlee Hammacker, lhp** | **Royals (1)** | **21** | **$65,000** |
| 14. | * Kyle Money, rhp | Phillies (2) | 46 | $64,000 |
| **15.** | *** Al Chambers, 1b/of** | **Mariners (1)** | **1** | **$60,000** |
| **16.** | **Jamie Allen, 3b** | **Mariners (2)** | **29** | **$57,500** |
| 17. | * Chris Baker, of | Tigers (1) | 23 | $54,000 |
| **18.** | **Jerry Don Gleaton, lhp** | **Rangers (1)** | **17** | **$53,000** |
| **19.** | *** Bob Geren, c** | **Padres (1)** | **24** | **$52,000** |
| **20.** | **Jon Perlman, rhp** | **Cubs (1)** | **12** | **$50,000** |
| | *** Rick Seilheimer, c** | **White Sox (1)** | **19** | **$50,000** |
| | *** Scott Garrelts, rhp** | **Giants (1)** | **15** | **$50,000** |
| **23.** | *** Roy Smith, rhp** | **Phillies (3)** | **72** | **$47,500** |
| **24.** | **Marc Sullivan, c** | **Red Sox (2)** | **52** | **$45,000** |
| **25.** | *** Andy Van Slyke, of** | **Cardinals (1)** | **6** | **$42,500** |

*Major leaguers in bold. *High school selection. #Major league contract. †Selection voided; signed with Giants after special lottery.*

ASSOCIATED PRESS

**Seattle went for high school power hitter Al Chambers with the No. 1 overall pick, but he never got more than a big league cup of coffee**

With his failed baseball career in the past, Schroeder earned a backup job with the Redskins, but was thrust into action when starter Joe Theismann suffered the most infamous broken leg in football history in a late-season game against the New York Giants. Schroeder finished the year as the starter and the next year passed for more than 4,000 yards en route to a spot in the Pro Bowl. In 1987, he was instrumental in leading the Redskins to a Super Bowl title. Schroeder went on to play 10 years in the NFL, passing for more than 20,000 yards and 100 touchdowns.

More teams than just the Blue Jays considered Schroeder the top prospect in the 1979 draft. As a catcher, he was big, strong and agile, and had an exceptional throwing arm.

But in most of his four years in the Blue Jays system, Schroeder caught little. When he was not off quarterbacking the UCLA football team, he frittered away his talents in the outfield, with the exception of a disastrous half-season experiment at third base.

With Schroeder a prime exhibit, the 1979 draft featured possibly the greatest collection of dual-sport athletes to ever emerge in one high school class. Many, like Schroeder, were prominent parts of both that year's college football signing crop and the prep baseball draft class.

The 1983 NFL draft provided context for the strength of the class. Considered a landmark draft for quarterbacks, future Pro Football Hall of Fame performers like Elway and Dan Marino were among six QBs drafted in the first round. Running back Curt Warner also was a first-round pick in that draft. All three were heavily recruited

### WORTH NOTING

■ **DEREK TATSUNO**, the University of Hawaii's stellar junior lefthander, compiled arguably the best season ever by a college pitcher. He set still-standing NCAA single-season records for wins (20, in 22 starts) and strikeouts (234), and by leading the NCAA in strikeouts for a third straight year, established a career mark with 541. Tatsuno was coveted by big league teams and drew more than 18,000 fans to see his final start for the Rainbows. But the 5-foot-10, 175-pound lefthander wasn't drafted until the Padres took him with the 40th pick overall. "They found out I may go to Japan," Tatsuno said. "That kind of scared them off. That's why I was drafted in the second round." Tatsuno announced he was spurning a six-figure bonus offer from the Padres to sign with a team in Japan's industrial league, a farm club of the powerful Seibu Lions. Tatsuno wanted to pitch for Seibu, but an agreement between the major leagues of Japan and the U.S. restricted the signing of one another's players, so he was forbidden from doing so. His hope was that no team in the U.S. would draft him again, which would free him to pitch for the Lions. But American teams continued to draft Tatsuno, effectively barring him. "It was a helpless feeling," he said. "As a U.S. citizen, there was nothing I could do to get around it. The only legal way to beat it would have been to give up my citizenship. I didn't think that was a good idea." Finally in 1982, he signed with the Brewers as their first pick in January. He received a bonus of $15,000. With the magic in his left arm all but gone, Tatsuno went 7-2. 6.42 for Double-A El Paso in 1982. He rebounded to go 10-6, 3.24 after being demoted to Class A Stockton in 1983, but the Brewers released him.

■ The 1979 draft set a record for futility when four first-round selections from the June regular phase went

CONTINUED ON PAGE 220

## WORTH NOTING

CONTINUED FROM PAGE 219

unsigned. That included three high school picks, and marked the last time that a team lost a first-round choice to a college baseball scholarship until the Brewers failed to sign righthander Alex Fernandez in 1988. The Giants and White Sox each had two first-round picks; the White Sox lost out to Stanford on shortstop **STEVE BUECHELE** (ninth overall), their first pick, while the Giants failed to sign righthander **RICK LUECKEN** (18th overall), the second of their two first-rounders, who opted to attend Texas A&M. The sad-sack Athletics outdid themselves. In a year when they drew less than 307,000 fans and were in such desperate financial straits that they fired all their scouts, the A's had a pair of first-round selections and came up short on signing both. Florida prep shortstop **JUAN BUSTABAD** (fifth overall) and Harvard outfielder **MIKE STENHOUSE** (26th overall), refused offers from frugal A's owner Charles O. Finley. Bustabad, who was offered $25,000, elected to enroll at Miami-Dade North Community College that fall. Stenhouse, offered $12,000, chose not to return to Harvard, and sat out the fall in order to remain eligible for the January draft. Both players, along with unsigned second-rounder **TOM DODD**, became premium picks in an unusually talent-filled January 1980 draft. The A's signed none of nine picks in the January draft, and three of their first 16 picks in the June regular phase.

■ Cal State Fullerton (60-14), led by college player of the year **TIM WALLACH** (.392-23-102), won its first College World Series title in 1979. Arizona State led all colleges with nine draft picks in the June regular phase—even as the Sun Devils had the poorest record (32-31) in their modern history and finished dead last in the newly expanded Southern Division of the Pacific-10 Conference.

■ The University of Michigan established a draft first when

prep football players in 1979—and were picked in that year's baseball draft.

Interestingly, the Kansas City Royals selected both Elway (18th round) and Marino (fourth round). As blue-chip quarterback recruits, neither expressed more than a passing interest in playing professional baseball out of high school and both went on to distinguished footballs careers, both in college and the NFL.

Had he been considered more signable, Elway almost certainly would have been an early first-round pick in the 1979 baseball draft. According to scouts, he was at least on par as a baseball prospect with Schoeder.

Though Elway, the most celebrated two-sport athlete in the 1979 draft, didn't sign at the time, he was drafted in the second round by the New York Yankees after his sophomore year at Stanford in 1981. He was signed to a $75,000 bonus and played six weeks of minor league baseball in the Yankees system in 1982.

Though he had little intention of pursuing a baseball career beyond his brief dalliance that summer, Elway used the threat of a continuing career for leverage in the next year's NFL draft, when he refused to sign with the Baltimore Colts as the first selection and insisted on being traded to a West Coast team. Elway got his wish, going to Denver and leading the Broncos to five Super Bowl appearances.

In all, the 1979 baseball draft produced at least 13 picks who went on to enjoy outstanding college football careers—including 11 who subsequently were drafted by NFL teams or played in the NFL. Of the 13, only three played in the big leagues.

Rick Leach, the University of Michigan quarterback who finished third in the 1978 Heisman Trophy balloting, opted for a baseball career after he was drafted in the first round by the Detroit Tigers—but only after being picked in the fifth round of the NFL draft by the Denver Broncos two months earlier, and also receiving a significant offer to play in Canada with the Montreal Alouettes.

### KOMMINSK'S CAREER FALLS SHORT

Beyond Chambers, few of the other high-end prospects in the 1979 draft like Leary, Schroeder and Komminsk materialized into bona fide major league players, either. But none proved quite as big a disappointment as Komminsk—considering all the hype he generated almost from the day he was drafted by the Braves with the fourth pick overall.

"Komminsk is the only player who's come along since I've been here who has graded 8 (on the 2-to-8 scouting scale) in both power and running," raved Braves scouting director Paul Snyder. "He has amazing tools everywhere but in his arm."

Komminsk hit .481 with two homers and 20 RBIs in 17 games as a high school senior, and all signs pointed to his becoming the best player the Braves organization had raised since Hank Aaron nearly 30 years earlier. But he was cursed by the high expectations the Braves, and no less an authority than Aaron himself set for him. Aaron labeled him a "can't-miss major leaguer."

### Largest Bonuses By Round

| | Player, Pos. | Club | Bonus |
|---|---|---|---|
| 1. | * Jay Schroeder, c | Blue Jays | $135,000 |
| 2. | * Todd Demeter, 1b | Yankees | $208,000 |
| **3.** | *** Roy Smith, rhp** | **Phillies** | **$47,500** |
| 4. | Three tied at | | $25,000 |
| 5. | Terry Sutcliffe, rhp | Dodgers | $25,000 |
| 6. | * Trent Purcell, of | Phillies | $25,000 |
| **7.** | *** Storm Davis, rhp** | **Orioles** | **$25,000** |
| | Ed Irvine, of | Brewers | $25,000 |
| 8. | * Jeff Nate, ss | Phillies | $16,000 |
| **9.** | **Pete Filson, lhp** | **Yankees** | **$16,000** |
| **10.** | **Dave Owen, ss** | **Cubs** | **$14,000** |
| Jan/R. | John Stevenson, ss | Padres (1) | $26,000 |
| **Jan/S.** | **Mark Davis, lhp** | **Phillies (1)** | **$30,000** |
| **Jun/S.** | **Marty Barrett, 2b** | **Red Sox (1)** | **$28,000** |

*Major leaguers in bold. *High school selection.*

"He will do things Dale Murphy hasn't dreamed of," baseball's reigning home run king boasted after Komminsk toyed with Triple-A pitching in 1983, hitting .334 with 24 homers and 103 RBIs. It was his second near-triple crown performance in the minor leagues in three years.

But if ever there was a ballplayer who seemed set up for a fall, it was Komminsk. For reasons that were never fully understood, the gifted Komminsk suddenly lost his ability to hit once he hit the big time. He was nowhere near the player Aaron and other Braves officials thought he would be.

In Atlanta, the effects of Komminsk's demise were felt long after he left.

"I don't think there's any question Brad set the franchise back," Atlanta general manager Bobby Cox said. "He didn't do some things he should have. We thought he'd be a better player than (Bob) Horner or Murphy."

Komminsk played parts of eight years in the majors with seven different organizations, and hit just .238. He actually established more of a legacy in the minors, hitting .278 with 230 home runs over 16 seasons before serving as a manager for a number of years after retiring as a player.

Brad Komminsk

Expectations also burdened Leary, a hard-throwing righthander from UCLA who was drafted second overall by the Mets. After a dominating spring-training performance in 1981, he was labeled for stardom before he'd ever toed a big league rubber, and even touted as the second coming of Hall of Famer Tom Seaver. The Big Apple was practically his for the taking.

After just one minor league season, Leary earned a spot in the Mets rotation to open the 1981 season. He made his highly anticipated major league debut in 46-degree weather, pitched to seven hitters and blew out his arm.

He was never the same power pitcher again, although he came back to win 78 games in the majors.

## BRANDT'S CAREER A DISASTER

For sheer futility, no first-round pick in 1979—or in draft history, for that matter—matched Minnesota's Brandt, a career .154 hitter. He was such a bust that he drew his release little more than a year after signing with the Twins, without even moving beyond Rookie ball.

Brandt was drafted out of a small Wisconsin high school, where as a senior he hit .557 with 10 home runs and had 19 stolen bases in 18 games. He sold the Twins on drafting him with their first pick solely off his one-day power display at a tryout in Wisconsin Rapids three days before the draft. For two hours, Brandt gave a command performance for Twins scout Ellis Clary, knocking ball after ball out of the park.

"There ain't no more (Harmon) Killebrews," said Clary, "but when we worked Brandt out the other day we had to quit early. He knocked all the baseballs out of the park. I think we got a good prospect."

No other teams projected Brandt so high, and Brandt certainly did not prove to be a legitimate first-round pick. He received less than $25,000 from the Twins to sign—easily the smallest bonus in the first round—and was unceremoniously released after playing in just two games in 1980. His release, on July 6, 1980, marked the earliest date that a team gave up on a first-round pick.

"He was a mistake," admitted Twins assistant farm director Jim Rantz, who succeeded Brophy. "Some kids can go backward on you, and he did. We clearly made a bad choice."

In contrast to Brandt, no player taken in the first round achieved success as early, or as easily as Howe, one of two pitchers the Los Angeles Dodgers drafted from the University of Michigan.

At 27-8, Howe was the winningest pitcher in Wolverines history, and he seemed like a particularly astute pick when he opened the 1980 season in the big leagues and went on to become the National League rookie of the year. In 1981, he saved the final game of the World Series for the Dodgers; a year later, he was an all-star. Almost overnight Howe had become one of the best young lefthanders in the game.

Following the 1982 season, however, Howe's story as one of the more flawed figures of the draft era began to unfold. News came out that he was a cocaine addict, and had been for a period of years—even while in college at Michigan

Howe's major league career, which had looked so promising, was suddenly in serious jeopardy.

Over the next six years, Howe was suspended on numerous occasions for being in violation of baseball's after-care program. The final straw appeared to come in January 1988 when Howe disappeared during a three-day mini-camp while with the Texas Rangers. He did not pitch at all in 1988 or 1989, and it appeared Howe's checkered career was over.

But in early 1990, at age 32, Howe got clearance to resume his drug-tarnished career one more time when commissioner Fay Vincent granted him permission to sign a minor league contract. Like a cat with nine lives he capitalized on the opportunity to pitch in the big leagues for the Yankees, off and on, until 1996. He even survived becoming the second player in major league history to be banned for life because of substance abuse in 1991, upon his seventh and final drug suspension, though he was spared that punishment when the Major League Players Association fought to have his case overturned in the courts on appeal, and succeeded.

While Howe's career off the field was marked by adversity and derailed by repeated struggles with cocaine and alcohol abuse, he was successful on the field over 12 major league seasons. He went 47-41, 3.03 with 91 saves, while pitching for four different clubs, though mostly for the Dodgers and Yankees.

But Howe's life of living dangerously ended in 2006, when he was killed in a single-car accident. He was 48. A toxicology report indicated he had methamphetamine in his system.

## LATE ROUNDERS ENJOY SUCCESS

The first round of the 1979 draft had more than its share of players who didn't realize their potential, or really even come close in many cases, but not all was doom and gloom.

With the sixth pick overall, the Cardinals took New York high school outfielder Andy Van Slyke, who went on to play 13 seasons in the majors. He hit .274 with 164 homers for four clubs, while also winning five Gold Gloves.

The Montreal Expos also made an astute selection with the 10th pick overall.

They took Cal State Fullerton senior first baseman Tim Wallach, who led the Titans to their first College World Series championship by hitting .392 with 23 homers and an NCAA-record tying 102 RBIs. He also won the Golden Spikes Award as the nation's top amateur player.

Wallach homered in his first professional at-bat for Double-A Memphis and went on to hit .327 with 18 home runs in one of the most auspicious debuts of the draft era. He never stopped hitting on his way to Montreal. He went on to hit .257 with 250 homers and 1,125 RBIs in a 17-year major league career. Even more impressive, he adapted from a college first baseman to a three-time Gold Glove winner across the diamond at third base.

No future Hall of Famers came from the 1979 draft class, but Hershiser and Mattingly became

### One Team's Draft: Seattle Mariners

| Player, Pos. | Bonus | Player, Pos. | Bonus | Player, Pos. | Bonus |
|---|---|---|---|---|---|
| **1. *Al Chambers, 1b** | **$60,000** | 5. *Mark Cahill, rhp | $12,500 | 9. Bob Randolph, rhp | $7,500 |
| **2. Jamie Allen, 3b** | **$57,500** | 6. *Kevin King, of | $15,500 | 10. *Chris Henry, c | $7,500 |
| 3. Rick Adair, lhp | $25,000 | **7. Brian Snyder, lhp** | **$10,000** | **Other Bud Black (17), lhp** | **$1,000** |
| **4. *Jim Presley, ss** | **$25,000** | 8. *Scott Stranski, rhp | $7,500 | | |

*Major leaguers in bold. *High school selection.*

### WORTH NOTING

outfielder **RICK LEACH**, and pitchers **STEVE HOWE** and **STEVE PERRY** were all drafted in the first round. Howe (7-2, 1.78) and Perry (4-5, 3.14) were drafted by the Dodgers, while Leach (.315-5-12), the Wolverines quarterback, was picked up by the Tigers. Only four other times in draft history did a school produce three first-rounders in the same draft. It also occurred with Fresno State in 1989, Rice in 2004, Miami in 2008 and Vanderbilt in 2015.

■ The Reds had nine picks in the first two rounds of the June regular and secondary phases—their own four, two as compensation for losing major leaguers Pete Rose and Mike Lum to free agency, and three more from the Angels for tampering charges related to the drafting of **BILL BORDLEY** in January.

■ **DARRELL MILLER**, California's ninth-round draft in 1979, became the first member of a gifted athletic family to showcase his talents on the national stage when he spent the first of five seasons with the Angels in 1984. He was later upstaged by siblings Cheryl and Reggie. Cheryl has been called the greatest women's basketball player ever, while Reggie became a No. 1 draft pick and high-scoring guard with the National Basketball Association's Indiana Pacers.

■ **GLENN DAVIS** and **STORM DAVIS** grew up in the same Jacksonville, Fla., household and were drafted by the Orioles in 1979. But they were not one of the great brother acts of the draft era. In fact, the Davis boys were not even related. Glenn came from a broken home, and it was just coincidence that Glenn's high school baseball coach (Storm's father) had the same last name and asked him to move in with his family. Storm signed in 1979 and was in the Orioles rotation by age 21, while Glenn, after two college seasons, went on to become the greatest home run hitter in Astros history.

## IN FOCUS: TODD DEMETER

Todd Demeter, a highly regarded Oklahoma prep first baseman, was one of the premier prospects in the 1979 class. He had every intention of attending college at Oklahoma before the Yankees offered him a signing bonus of $208,000, which not only set a draft record but also topped the longstanding record $205,000 bonus the Angels paid Rick Reichardt in 1964, which triggered the draft's implementation.

The Yankees had forfeited their first-round pick by signing lefthander Tommy John so boldly went for Demeter, son of former big leaguer Don Demeter, with their second-round selection (51st overall). Demeter's bonus demands scared teams off from drafting him to that point.

"It's a very, very worthwhile bonus," said Jack Butterfield, the Yankees vice president for player development and scouting. "We were delighted that we were able to sign him. He was among our top four on the total draft list. We knew he wanted to go to Oklahoma and we took a chance."

Demeter's career did not come close to expectations. In five seasons, including a brief appearance in Double-A in 1983, he hit .233 with 61 homers and 267 RBIs. He played two seasons in Class A in the Cardinals system to close out his career. He died in 1995 of Hodgkin's disease.

two of the greatest late-round finds in draft history, and arguably the two most successful players in the class.

Overlooked as a 17th-rounder because scouts thought he was too frail and didn't throw hard enough, Hershiser put together the greatest streak of shutout pitching in baseball history by tossing 59 consecutive scoreless innings in 1988. As a reward for that feat, Hershiser became baseball's first $3 million player.

That was quite an accomplishment for a pitcher who didn't crack the varsity roster his first two years at New Jersey's Cherry Hill East High, and was a non-factor as a junior. It was only as a senior that Hershiser's body developed to the point where he was a major contributor, setting school career records for winning percentage, strikeouts and ERA.

On the basis of that performance, Hershiser earned a scholarship to Bowling Green State. But the odds were again stacked against him as he barely played as a freshman and was academically ineligible as a sophomore. He got bigger and stronger that summer, though, and added 5 mph of velocity to his fastball to go 6-2, 2.26 and earn all-Mid-American Conference honors in his draft year.

The Dodgers signed Hershiser for $10,000, and he began his pro career with the same low expectations he had encountered in both high school and college. The initial scouting report on him didn't paint a particularly bright picture, indicating he had poor control, a below-average fastball and threw his curve with improper mechanics. Moreover, it said he rattled easily and had questionable makeup.

Don Mattingly

Hershiser began to address those shortcomings in earnest early in his minor league career with the Dodgers, spent mostly as a reliever, and slowly but surely worked his way up the Dodgers chain. He reached the majors on Sept. 1, 1983, but it wasn't until midway through the 1984 season, when he was elevated to a starting role, that his career began to flourish.

Mattingly was picked two rounds later than Hershiser, but was always considered the better prospect of the two.

As a senior at Reitz Memorial High in Evansville, Ind., Mattingly hit .552. Over four years as a starter, he hit .462 and drove in 140 runs, which tied the national high school record.

Mattingly also played quarterback and defensive back on the football team, guard on the basketball team and pitcher, in addition to first base, on the baseball team. He was talented enough to receive major college offers in each sport, and committed to play basketball at Indiana State.

As good as Mattingly appeared to be at baseball, he had his share of detractors. He was knocked for his lack of both power and speed.

"He didn't show the two tools that were in vogue then," said Jax Robertson, a Yankees scout who followed Mattingly closely for three years. "He didn't show a lot of power, and he didn't pull the ball that much. But when he hit the ball, he hit it squarely, and with authority."

In four years in the Yankees organization, the last in Triple-A, Mattingly hit .349, .358, .314 and .315, though never slugged more than 10 home runs in any season. Because of his status as a 19th-round pick and the lingering concerns over his lack of power and speed, he rarely was accorded the same treatment as Demeter, the team's top draft pick in 1979 who had signed a record contract and was also a first baseman. Mattingly routinely played second fiddle to Demeter in the Yankees system, and that included being consigned to the outfield much of his time in the minors.

Mattingly was an instant hit in New York, however. He won an American League batting crown in his first full season in 1984, edging out teammate Dave Winfield, .343 to .340, while also drilling 23 homers. With his new-found power stroke, the Yankees showed no hesitation in rightfully restoring Mattingly to his natural position at first base. In 1985, he set career highs in homers (35) and RBIs (145), and won the American League MVP award. He also won the first of nine Gold Glove Awards that season.

Though the mighty Yankees were relegated to also-ran status in his heyday years with the team, Mattingly became the face of the franchise in the 1980s with his impressive hitting exploits. He almost certainly would have warranted serious Hall of Fame consideration had his career not been slowed, and derailed entirely after 14 seasons by a disabling back injury. For his career, he hit .307 with 222 home runs, and it's safe to say that Mattingly provided the Yankees the kind of production they expected from Demeter, whose career fizzled out in Double-A.

Not only did the careers of Hershiser and Mattingly surpass those of every player chosen before them in 1979, but a similar case could also be made for outfielder Brett Butler. A lowly 23rd-round selection of the Braves, Butler played 17 seasons in the majors for five different clubs and starred in a leadoff role by hitting .290 with 1,359 runs scored and 558 stolen bases.

## Highest Unsigned Picks

**JUNE/REGULAR PHASE ONLY**

| Player, Pos., Team (Round) | College | Re-Drafted |
|---|---|---|
| Juan Bustabad, ss, Athletics (1) | Miami-Dade CC North | Red Sox '80 (Jan.-S/1) |
| Steve Buechele, ss, White Sox (1) | Stanford | Rangers '82 (5) |
| Rick Luecken, rhp, Giants (1) | Texas A&M | Reds '82 (12) |
| Mike Stenhouse, of, Athletics (1) | Harvard (d/o) | Expos '80 (Jan.-S/1) |
| Tom Dodd, of, Athletics (2) | Oregon (d/o) | Yankees '80 (Jan.-S/1) |
| Scott Glanz, rhp, White Sox (2) | Arkansas | Angels '82 (13) |
| Derek Tatsuno, lhp, Padres (2) | Hawaii | Mets '80 (S/3) |
| Rick Wysocki, lhp, Reds (2) | Southern Illinois | Never |
| #Craig Jones, rhp, Mets (3) | * Army | Braves '80 (4) |
| Ron Romanick, rhp, Blue Jays (3) | Arizona State | Padres '80 (S/1) |

**TOTAL UNSIGNED PICKS:** Top 5 Rounds (29), Top 10 Rounds (62)

*#Selection voided. *Returned to same school.*

# 1979 Draft List

**Did not sign. Major leaguers in bold, with first and last years noted. Order of selection indicated in parentheses. For the first five rounds of the June Regular Phase and the first round of all other phases, the peak level of each player is noted.*

## ATLANTA BRAVES

### January—Regular Phase (3)

1. *Kelly Faulk, rhp, Wharton County (Texas) JC.—(AAA)
2. **Milt Thompson, of, Gaithersburg, Md.—(1984-96)**
3. Rick Coatney, rhp, Westark (Ark.) CC.
4. *Edward Lambeth, lhp, Westark (Ark.) CC.
5. *Randy Porter, lhp, Linn-Benton (Ore.) CC.
6. (void) *Benji de la Rosa, of, Murray State (Okla.) JC.
7. **Brook Jacoby, of, Ventura (Calif.) JC.—(1981-92)**

### January—Secondary Phase (20)

1. *Willie Davis, of, Canada (Calif.) JC.—DNP

### June—Regular Phase (4)

1. **Brad Komminsk, of-1b, Shawnee HS, Lima, Ohio.—(1983-91)**
2. (Choice to Reds as compensation for free agent Mike Lum)
3. Daniel Church, rhp, San Marin HS, Novato, Calif.—(Low A)
4. Ken Ames, rhp, St. Helens HS, Warren, Ore.—(Low A)
5. Bob Luzon, 2b, Westlake HS, Thornwood, N.Y.—(AA)
6. **Mike Payne, rhp, Williston (Fla.) HS.–(1984)**
7. Roy North, rhp, Rider College.
8. David Coghill, lhp, Clackamas (Ore.) CC.
9. **Paul Runge, ss, Jacksonville University.—(1981-88)**
10. *Keith Belcik, c, Clay HS, Oregon, Ohio.
11. Gary Reiter, lhp, Bowling Green State University.
12. Glenn Bockhorn, 2b, Texas Lutheran College.
13. Steve Stieb, c, Southern Illinois University.

DRAFT DROP *Brother of Dave Stieb, major leaguer (1979-98)*

14. Randy Ingle, ss, Appalachian State University.
15. Bret Ferguson, lhp, North Baltimore (Ohio) HS.
16. Buddy Bailey, c, Lynchburg (Va.) College.
17. *Nick O'Connor, rhp, Reading HS, Cincinnati.
18. Harold Williams, 1b, Virginia Tech.
19. Pete Teixeira, rhp, University of Florida.

DRAFT DROP *Uncle of Mark Teixeira, major leaguer (2003-15)*

20. Randy Whistler, c, Arizona State University.
21. Billy Bowen, of, Southeastern Oklahoma State University.
22. Greg Norris, rhp, University of North Carolina.
23. **Brett Butler, of, Southeastern Oklahoma State University.—(1981-97)**
24. *John Shannon, rhp, University of Houston.
25. Robert Kennedy, rhp, Cochise County (Ariz.) CC
26. Chuck Black, 2b, Bowling Green State University.
27. Mike Garcia, 2b, Cal State Fullerton.
28. Tommy Thompson, c, University of Oklahoma.
29. *Eric Call, rhp, Miami-Dade CC South.
30. Arcilio Castaigne, rhp, Texas Wesleyan College.
31. Greg Dikos, 3b, Ball State University.
32. DeWayne Kitts, lhp, Lynchburg (Va.) College.
33. *Jeff Groth, of, Bowling Green State University.

DRAFT DROP *Wide receiver, National Football League (1979-85)*

34. Kevin Patten, of, Miami (Ohio) University.
35. Arthur Neal, of Morehouse (Ga.) College.
36. *Philip Bowie, of, Greenwood (S.C.) HS.
37. Tim Fuller, rhp, Berkmar HS, Norcross, Ga.
38. Russell Kerdolff, rhp, Northern Kentucky University.
39. *Scott Matthews, of, Melbourne (Fla.) HS.

### June—Secondary Phase (24)

No selection.

## BALTIMORE ORIOLES

### January—Regular Phase (20)

1. *Darren Dilks, lhp, Chaffey (Calif.) JC.—(AAA)

DRAFT DROP *First-round draft pick (18th overall), Expos (1981)*

2. Steve Espinoza, ss, Foothill (Calif.) JC.
3. Randy Miller, 2b, Florida JC.
4. *Bill Bond, 1b-rhp, St. Petersburg (Fla.) JC.
5. Gregg Burtt, of, Quinsigamond (Mass.) CC.
6. *Craig Cunard, lhp, Iowa Western CC.
7. *Antonio Barquin, of, Miami-Dade CC South.
8. *Kevin Usher, rhp, Bayport (N.Y.) HS.

### January—Secondary Phase (23)

1. Andy Marston, of-rhp, St. Petersburg (Fla.) JC.—(High A)

### June—Regular Phase (19)

1. (Choice to White Sox as compensation for free agent Steve Stone).
2. Tim Maples, rhp, Pinecrest HS, Southern Pines, N.C.—(AA)
3. ***Bob Melvin, c, Menlo-Atherton HS, Menlo Park, Calif.—(1985-94)**

DRAFT DROP *Attended California; re-drafted by Tigers, January 1981/secondary phase (1st round); major league manager (2003-15)*

4. Greg Dees, 3b, Auburndale (Fla.) HS.—(AA)
5. **Allan Ramirez, rhp, Rice University.—(1983)**
6. Julian Gonzalez, lhp, Tampa Catholic HS, Tampa.
7. **Storm Davis, rhp, University Christian HS, Jacksonville, Fla.—(1982-94)**

DRAFT DROP *Stepbrother of Glenn Davis, 31st-round draft pick, Orioles (1979); major leaguer (1984-93)*

8. Robert Palmer, c, Chapman (Calif.) College.
9. *Jeff Hunter, 3b, University of Nebraska.
10. ***Rod Booker, ss, University of California.—(1987-91)**
11. Mark Jurena, of, University of Louisville.
12. Kenneth Jordan, rhp, William Campbell HS, Brookneal, Va.
13. Terry Schriner, of, Harrisburg (Pa.) HS.
14. David Schuman, of, Seton Hall University.
15. Freddie Smith, rhp, Pasco HS, Dade City, Fla.
16. *Bill Hainline, ss, Gonzaga University.
17. Angelo Blake, 2b, Sacramento (Calif.) CC.
18. Larry Woodhall, lhp, Mankato State (Minn.) University.
19. Lonnie Ivie, c, Blinn (Texas) JC.
20. *Thomas Harrell, ss, Columbus (Ga.) College.
21. Bruss Bowman, 1b, Walt Whitman HS, Bethesda, Md.
22. Manuel Martinez, c, Southmost Texas JC.
23. *Greg Schuler, of, Robinson HS, Fairfax, Va.
24. Gary Zedonak, rhp, Mansfield (Pa.) University.
25. David Pfeiffer, rhp, Northwest Missouri State University.
26. **Bill Swaggerty, rhp, Stetson University.—(1983-86)**
27. *Chris Newman, 1b, Churchill HS, Eugene, Ore.
28. *Scott Gardner, rhp, University of Oklahoma.
29. *Cecil Morris, of, Loyola HS, Los Angeles.
30. John DeLeon, 1b, University City HS, Philadelphia.
31. ***Glenn Davis, 1b-rhp, University Christian HS, Jacksonville, Fla.—(1984-93)**

DRAFT DROP *Stepbrother of Storm Davis, 7th-round draft pick, Orioles (1979); major leaguer (1982-94)*

32. ***Kevin Gross, rhp, Fillmore (Calif.) HS.—(1983-97)**
33. *Rodney Mason, rhp, High Point HS, Beltsville, Md.
34. Charles Williams, ss, Apopka HS, Plymouth, Fla.
35. *Charles Tomaselli, lhp, Clearwater (Fla.) HS.
36. *Jack Leonard, inf, J.R. Tucker HS, Richmond, Va.

### June—Secondary Phase (7)

1. *Joe Housey, rhp, Miami-Dade CC North.—(AA)
2. Fred Conradi, lhp, Centralia (Wash.) JC.

## BOSTON RED SOX

### January—Regular Phase (25)

1. Kevin Kane, rhp, Cuesta (Calif.) JC.—(AAA)
2. *Michael Dolinar, 3b, Bakersfield (Calif.) JC.
3. *Harley Woody, lhp, Columbia State (Tenn.) CC.
4. *Michael Burton, rhp, University of Alabama.
5. *Kenneth Cox, 1b, Columbia State (Tenn.) CC.
6. Lee Pruitt, of-c, Westark (Ark.) CC.
7. Scott Gering, rhp-of, St. John's River (Fla.) CC.
8. Timothy Wadsworth, c-1b, Pensacola, Fla.

### January—Secondary Phase (25)

No selection.

### June—Regular Phase (26)

1. (Choice to Athletics as compensation for free agent Steve Renko)
2. **Marc Sullivan, c, University of Florida.—(1982-87)**

DRAFT DROP *Son of Haywood Sullivan, major leaguer (1955-63); major league manager (1965); part-owner, Red Sox (1981-86)*

3. John Ackley, c, Mahopac HS, Carmel, N.Y.—(AAA)

DRAFT DROP *Father of Dustin Ackley, first-round draft pick, Mariners (2009), major leaguer (2011-15)*

4. *Gib Seibert, of, Sahuaro HS, Tucson, Ariz.—(AAA)

DRAFT DROP *Attended Arizona State; re-drafted by Phillies, 1982 (4th round)*

5. Jim Watkins, of, University of Florida.—(AA)

DRAFT DROP *First overall draft pick, June 1978/second-ary phase, Braves*

6. *Rick Thompson, ss, Glen Oaks HS, Canton, Ohio.
7. **Tom McCarthy, rhp, Carver HS, Plymouth, Mass.—(1985-89)**
8. *Steven True, lhp, Marlow (Okla.) HS.
9. Chuck Sandberg, 1b, University of Florida.
10. Jerry Miklosi, ss, Western Michigan University.
11. ***Tommy Dunbar, of, Middle Georgia JC.—(1983-85)**
12. *Ronnie Perry, ss, Holy Cross College.

DRAFT DROP *Third-round draft pick, Boston Celtics/ National Basketball Association (1980)*

13. *Glen Kuhn, rhp, Sauquoit (N.Y.) HS.
14. *Mickey Meister, rhp, Redwood HS, San Rafael, Calif.
15. Reggie Whittemore, of, David Lipscomb College.
16. *Mark Sewald, rhp, Bishop Montgomery HS, Carson, Calif.
17. *John Leonard, rhp, Connellsville HS, Dawson, Pa.
18. Eddie Lee, of, University of South Alabama.
19. Bob Birrell, lhp, Brandeis (Mass.) University.
20. Jay Fredlund, rhp, Lafayette College.
21. David Holt, c, Fresno State University.
22. Glenn Eddins, 3b, David Lipscomb College.

### June—Secondary Phase (1)

1. **Marty Barrett, 2b, Arizona State University.—(1982-91)**

DRAFT DROP *Brother of Tommy Barrett, major leaguer (1988-92)*

2. Jeems Teller, of, Sacramento (Calif.) CC.

## CALIFORNIA ANGELS

### January—Regular Phase (16)

1. *Dennis Ivy, of-1b, San Joaquin Delta (Calif.) JC.—DNP
2. *Bill Worden, c, Mission (Calif.) JC.
3. ***Al Newman, ss, Chaffey (Calif.) JC.—(1985-92)**
4. Edward Lindsey, lhp, Broward (Fla.) CC.
5. *Don Freeman, ss, West Los Angeles JC.
6. **Gary Pettis, of, Laney (Calif.) JC.–(1982-92)**
7. *Russ Stephans, c, Los Angeles Valley JC.
8. *Stanford Hill, lhp, McLennan (Texas) CC.
9. Robert Klein, rhp, JC of the Canyons (Calif.).
10. Peter Nebrich, 1b, Broward (Fla.) CC.

### January—Secondary Phase (4)

1. ***Otis Nixon, 3b, Louisburg (N.C.) JC.—(1983-99)**

DRAFT DROP *Brother of Donell Nixon, major leaguer (1987-90)*

2. *Ken Eriksen, rhp, Citrus (Calif.) JC.
3. ***Curt Wardle, lhp, San Bernardino Valley (Calif.) JC.—(1984-85)**
4. *Brian Owens, rhp, Mesa (Ariz.) CC.

### June—Regular Phase (15)

1. (Choice to Giants as compensation for free agent Jim Barr)
2. (Choice to Reds as penalty for tampering with amateur free agent Bill Bordley)
3. Mickey Saatzer, rhp, Eisenhower HS, Hopkins, Minn.—(High A)
4. *Eric Barry, lhp, Mount Whitney HS, Visalia, Calif.—(AA)

DRAFT DROP *Attended Cal State Fullerton; re-drafted by Athletics, 1982 (20th round)*

5. **Pat Keedy, 2b, Auburn University.—(1985-89)**
6. Jackie Skaggs, rhp, William Carey (Miss.) College.
7. *Steve Renfroe, of, Auburn University.

DRAFT DROP *Baseball coach, Auburn (2000-03)*

8. Warren Hollier, rhp, Oral Roberts University.
9. **Darrell Miller, c, Cal Poly Pomona.—(1984-88)**

DRAFT DROP *Brother of Reggie Miller, guard/National Basketball Association (1987-2005) • Brother of Cheryl Miller, inductee, Basketball Hall of Fame (1995)*

10. *Bob Gunnarsson, lhp, Lake Havasu (Ariz.) HS.
11. Greg Hanson, c, Southern California College.
12. *Danny Smith, lhp, Southern HS, Cutler Ridge, Fla.
13. Marion Hunter, ss, Kearny HS, San Diego.
14. Jim Celedonia, c, William Carey (Miss.) College.
15. *Don Carfino, ss, University of Southern California.
16. Mark Pangborn, rhp, Rio Hondo (Calif.) JC.
17. *Galdenio Noda, ss, Bell (Calif.) HS.
18. *Andrew Pavlovic, rhp, Yavapai (Ariz.) JC.
19. *Mingo Nunez, ss, Wagner College.
20. Brian Buckley, rhp, UC Davis.
21. *Maurice Christian, of, Texas Southern University.
22. David Duran, rhp, Cal State Los Angeles.
23. Eli Aldrige, of, Prairie View A&M University.
24. Tim Collins, of, Loyola Marymount University.
25. *Paul Wirkus, of, San Diego State University.
26. Jay Kibbe, rhp, Louisiana Tech.
27. *Rod Martin, of, Eisenhower HS, San Bernardino, Calif.
28. *Mike Rizzo, ss-2b, Holy Cross HS, Chicago.

DRAFT DROP *Scouting director, Diamondbacks (2000-06); general manager, Nationals (2009-15)*

29. Frank Pennachio, 3b, University of Southern California.

### June—Secondary Phase (19)

1. (Choice to Reds as penalty for tampering with amateur free agent Bill Bordley)
2. (Choice to Reds as penalty for tampering with Bordley)
3. ***Bill Lindsey, 3b, Broward (Fla.) CC.—(1987)**

## CHICAGO CUBS

### January—Regular Phase (11)

1. Mark Wilkins, rhp, Eastern Michigan University.—(Low A)
2. *David Means, of, Winchester, Ky.
3. *Steve Podraza, c, Brookdale (N.J.) CC.
4. Terry Austin, of, Ranger (Texas) JC.
5. *Michael Maack, lhp, Miami-Dade CC South.
6. *Michael O'Malley, lhp, Triton (Ill.) JC.
7. *Todd Wilson, lhp, Mount San Antonio (Calif.) JC.

### January—Secondary Phase (9)

1. *Mark Christy, rhp, Miami-Dade CC North.—(High A)

### June—Regular Phase (12)

1. **Jon Perlman, rhp, Baylor University.—(1985-88)**
2. Shane Allen, ss, Palm Bay HS, Melbourne, Fla.—(Low A)
3. ***Chuck Crim, rhp, Thousand Oaks (Calif.) HS.—(1987-94)**

DRAFT DROP *Attended Hawaii; re-drafted by Brewers, 1982 (17th round)*

4. Stan Kyles, rhp, Wendell Phillips HS, Chicago.—(AAA)
5. *Steve Gehrke, rhp, Murray (Utah) HS.—(Rookie)

DRAFT DROP *Attended Nebraska; re-drafted by Dodgers, 1982 (12th round)*

6. Michael Buckley, ss, Lakewood (Calif.) HS.
7. Randy LaVigne, of, University of Connecticut.
8. *Tim Thompson, rhp, Jordan HS, Long Beach, Calif.
9. Thomas Morris, lhp, Brigham Young University.

DRAFT DROP *Brother of Jack Morris, major leaguer (1977-94)*

10. **Dave Owen, ss, University of Texas-Arlington.—(1983-88)**

DRAFT DROP *Brother of Spike Owen, first-round draft pick, Mariners (1982); major leaguer (1983-95)*

**11. Ray Soff, rhp, Central Michigan University.—(1986-87)**
12. James Lockett, of, University of Missouri.
13. Joe Fiori, 2b, Point Park (Pa.) College.
14. Jack Upton, 1b-3b, Colorado State University.
15. Kirk Ortega, c, St. Francis (N.Y.) College.
**16. Tom Grant, of, University of New Haven.—(1983)**
17. Brian Hardy, lhp, Brigham Young University.
18. Mark Schiewe, rhp, Buckley Loda HS, Buckley, Ill.
19. Craig Weissmann, rhp, Clairemont HS, San Diego.
**20. *Bryan Oelkers, lhp, Pattonville HS, Overland, Mo.—(1983-86)**
DRAFT DROP *First-round draft pick (4th overall), Twins (1982); first player from 1982 draft to reach majors (April 9, 1983)*
21. Tim Millner, rhp, Illinois State University.
22. Robert Blyth, rhp, Brigham Young University.
**23. *Mark Huismann, rhp, Colorado State University.—(1987)**
24. Sidney Smith, of, Patrick Henry HS, San Diego.
25. Michael Kelley, of, Mississippi State University.
26. Anthony Biafore, ss, Monmouth College.
27. *Joseph Carter, rhp, Helix HS, El Cajon, Calif.
28. Dennis Mork, of, UC Riverside.
**29. *Steve Ziem, rhp, Banning (Calif.) HS.—(1987)**
30. Glenn Millhauser, of, University of Northern Colorado.
31. *Doug Huffman, lhp, North Carolina State University.
32. Michael Thompson, lhp, Fairleigh Dickinson University.
33. *Dave Fabela, c, Aquinas HS, San Bernardino, Calif.
34. *Dave McClure, c, Kapaun Mount Carmel HS, Wichita, Kan.
35. Richard Renwick, rhp, Babson (Mass.) College.
36. Phillip Belmonte, ss, Azusa Pacific (Calif.) University.
37. Howie Shapiro, 2b, University of Miami
38. *Wes Clements, of-1b, University of Arizona.
39. William Trapani, lhp, Bellevue (Neb.) College.

#### June—Secondary Phase (6)

**1. Scott Fletcher, ss, Georgia Southern College.—(1981-95)**
2. Anthony Veith, 1b, University of Minnesota.
3. *John Moller, lhp, Seton Hall University.
4. *John Millholland, ss, Louisburg (N.C.) JC.
5. James McManus, rhp, University of Nebraska.
6. Pedro Bazan, c, Central Arizona JC.

## CHICAGO WHITE SOX

#### January—Regular Phase (10)

1. *Bruce Cooper, rhp, Broward (Fla.) CC.—DNP
2. *Randy Riccardi, c, Miami-Dade CC North.
**3. Randy Johnson, 1b-of, Miami-Dade CC South.—(1980-82)**
4. *Tim Kammeyer, rhp, Southwestern (Calif.) JC.
5. Felix Agapay, 1b-of, University of Illinois.
6. *Allen Black, rhp, West Los Angeles JC.
7. *Robert Brown, ss, Pasadena (Calif.) CC.
8. *Jim David, ss, JC of the Canyons (Calif.).
9. *Richard Kryzsiak, of, Chaffey (Calif.) JC.
10. *Craig Nelson, rhp, Glendale (Ariz.) CC.

#### January—Secondary Phase (17)

1. Gary Friedrich, lhp, Wabash Valley (Ill.) JC.—(Low A)
2. *Paul Doty, rhp, Grossmont (Calif.) JC.

#### June—Regular Phase (9)

**1. *Steve Buechele, ss, Servite HS, Fullerton, Calif.—(1985-95)**
DRAFT DROP *Attended Stanford; re-drafted by Rangers, 1982 (5th round)*
**1. Rick Seilheimer, c, Brenham (Texas) HS** (Choice from Orioles as compensation for free agent Steve Stone)**—(1980)**
DRAFT DROP *First 1979 high school draft pick to reach majors (July 5, 1980)*
2. *Scott Glanz, rhp, Edison HS, Tulsa, Okla.–(Low A)
DRAFT DROP *Attended Arkansas; re-drafted by Angels, 1982 (13th round)*
**3. Fran Mullins, ss, Santa Clara University.—(1980-86)**
4. *Richard Frazier, c, S.R. Butler HS, Huntsville, Ala.—DNP
DRAFT DROP *No school; never re-drafted*
5. Dom Fucci, 1b, Auburn University.—(AAA)
6. Chuck Johnson, rhp, University of Iowa.
7. Mitch Olson, of, Los Alamitos (Calif.) HS.
8. William Mills, rhp, Marathon (Fla.) HS.
9. *Scott Meier, c, Tokay HS, Lodi, Calif.
**10. *Jimmy Key, lhp, Butler HS, Huntsville, Ala.—(1984-98)**
11. Ted Ronshauser, c, San Marin HS, Novato, Calif.
12. Randy Evans, rhp, Oklahoma State University.
13. *Jon Soderberg, rhp, Essex Junction (Vt.) HS.
14. Tom Keating, rhp, University HS, San Diego.
15. *Wayne Fugett, rhp, Valdosta (Ga.) HS.
16. *Darryl Wilks, of, Glenwood HS, Fort Mitchell, Ala.
17. Jim English, 2b-1b, University of Missouri.
18. Mark Jackman, lhp, Birmingham-Southern College.
19. Dennis Vasquez, rhp, University of La Verne (Calif.).
20. Keith Brown, of-1b, University of Southern California.
21. Larry Hall, ss, University of Florida.
22. *Chris Johnston, 3b, Corona del Mar HS, Newport Beach, Calif.
23. *Tom Dieters, ss, Rochester (Mich.) HS.
24. *Reggie Fischer, rhp, Mount Carmel HS, Bellmont, Ill.
25. *Len Kasper, 1b, Proviso West HS, Bellwood, Ill.
26. Keefe Davis, rhp, Los Angeles (Calif.) HS.
27. Dan Williams, 1b, Stetson University.
28. *Kevin Kristan, rhp, Carmel HS, Mundelein, Ill.
29. Albert Likely, 1b, Davison HS, Mobile, Ala.
30. Ron Naclerio, of, St. John's University.
31. *Ray Thoma, 2b, Marist HS, Oak Lawn, Ill.
32. Paul Mainieri, 2b, University of New Orleans.
DRAFT DROP *Baseball coach, Notre Dame (1995-2006); baseball coach, Louisiana State (2007-15)*
33. *Randy Abel, c, Sealy (Texas) HS.
34. Larry Doby, of, Duke University.
DRAFT DROP *Son of Larry Doby, major leaguer (1947-59); major league manager (1978)*

#### June—Secondary Phase (5)

**1. Bob Fallon, lhp, Miami-Dade CC North.—(1984-85)**
2. *Bruce Cooper, rhp, Broward (Fla.) CC.
**3. *Tim Teufel, 2b, Clemson University.—(1983-93)**

## CINCINNATI REDS

#### January—Regular Phase (21)

1. Kevin Waller, of-3b, San Diego CC.—(High A)
2. *Robert Elliott, rhp, Gulf Coast (Fla.) CC.
3. *Kevin Lindsley, rhp, Linn-Benton (Ore.) CC.
4. Larry Raskin, c-1b, Coastal Carolina College.
5. *Dale Chatham, lhp, Gulf Coast (Fla.) CC.
6. Tim Stamper, rhp, Spokane Falls (Wash.) CC.
7. *Richard Rizzo, of-inf, Suffolk County (N.Y.) CC.
8. *Tim Henry, lhp, Paris (Texas) JC.

#### January—Secondary Phase (3)

**1. Bill Bordley, lhp, El Camino (Calif.) JC.—(1980)**
DRAFT DROP *First-round draft pick (fourth overall), Brewers (1976)*
2. *Gary Kempton, c, Triton (Ill.) JC.

#### June—Regular Phase (22)

1. Dan Lamar, c, Bellaire HS, Houston (Choice from Phillies as compensation for free agent Pete Rose).—(AA)
1. Mike Sullivan, rhp, Clemson University.–(High A)
DRAFT DROP *First-round draft pick (24th overall), Athletics (1976)*
**2. Keefe Cato, rhp, Fairfield University** (Choice from Braves as compensation for free agent Mike Lum)**—(1983-84)**
**2. Bob Buchanan, lhp, Riverview HS, Sarasota, Fla.** (Choice from Angels as penalty for tampering with Bill Bordley)**—(1985-89)**
2. *Rick Wysocki, lhp, Lakewood (N.J.) HS.—DNP
DRAFT DROP *Attended Southern Illinois; never re-drafted*
3. *Scott Lindquist, rhp, Kingsburg (Calif.) HS.—DNP
DRAFT DROP *Attended Northern Arizona; never re-drafted; 12th-round draft pick, Los Angeles Raiders/ National Football League (1983)*
4. *Michael Tolbert, rhp, Phillips HS, Chicago.–DNP
DRAFT DROP *Attended Triton (Ill.) JC; re-drafted by Padres, June 1980/secondary phase (3rd round)*
**5. Jeff Russell, rhp, Wyoming HS, Cincinnati.—(1983-96)**
6. Ron Little, of, Asheboro (N.C.) HS.
7. Bob Lapple, c, Davidson College.
8. *Bill Crone, 2b, West Chester (Pa.) University.
9. *Augie Schmidt, ss, Bradford HS, Kenosha, Wis.
DRAFT DROP *First-round draft pick (2nd overall), Blue Jays (2002)*
10. Tony Masone, of, Clemson University.
11. Keith Schrimsher, rhp, Univ. of South Florida.
**12. *Tom Edens, of-rhp, Fruitland (Idaho) HS.—(1987-95)**
**13. *Randy Gomez, c, University of Utah.—(1984).**
14. Rick Myles, lhp, Jackson (Mich.) CC.
15. *Eric Jordan, c, Chaparral HS, North Las Vegas, Nev.
16. Greg Bangert, lhp, Lewis-Clark State (Idaho) College.
17. *Cary Palmer, rhp, Mesa (Ariz.) CC.
18. Rusty Jones, of, University of Texas-Arlington.
19. Kevin Flannery, rhp, Central Michigan University.
**20. Jeff Jones, of, University of Iowa.—(1983)**
21. Kevin Hinds, 2b, Jackson State University.
22. Steven Daniels, rhp, Texas Wesleyan College.
23. Perry Estep, of, West Virginia State College.
24. Nick Fiorillo, lhp, University of Texas-El Paso.
**25. Kurt Kepshire, rhp, University of New Haven.—(1984-86)**
26. Mark Miller, of, UCLA.
27. *Dave Eldredge, c, Punahou HS, Honolulu, Hawaii.
28. Newton Box, lhp, Phillips (Okla.) University.
29. *Robert Slavens, lhp, Westbury HS, Houston.
30. Mike Dowless, rhp, John T. Hoggard HS, Wilmington, N.C.
31. *James Vegara, of, John F. Kennedy HS, Old Bethpage, N.Y.
32. *Kyle Rutledge, 2b, University of New Mexico.
33. *James Melson, rhp, Morgan County HS, Hartselle, Ala.
34. Bill Boddy, c, Start HS, Toledo, Ohio.
35. Rodney Johnson, 3b, Temple University.
**36. *Mike Maddux, rhp, Rancho HS, Las Vegas, Nev.—(1986-2000)**
DRAFT DROP *Brother of Greg Maddux, major leaguer (1986-2008)*
37. Jeff Ayers, rhp, Bellevue (Wash.) CC.
38. Rob Hoover, rhp, University of New Mexico.
39. *Sonny James, of, Fulton (Mo.) HS.
40. *Randy Reed, c, Tennessee Wesleyan College.
41. *Mike Adkins, c, Caldwell (Idaho) HS.
42. *Daniel Klosicki, rhp, Spokane Falls (Wash.) CC.
43. *Mike Fischer, c, Riverview HS, Sarasota, Fla.

#### June—Secondary Phase (16)

1. *Larry Mikesell, lhp, Brevard (Fla.) CC.—(Low A)
1. *Mark Pederson, rhp, Yakima Valley (Wash.) CC (Choice from Angels as penalty for tampering with amateur free agent Bill Bordley).—DNP
2. *Robert Elliott, rhp, Gulf Coast (Fla.) CC (Choice from Angels as penalty for tampering with amateur free agent Bill Bordley).

## CLEVELAND INDIANS

#### January—Regular Phase (8)

1. Francis Regan, rhp, Valencia (Fla.) CC.–(High A)
2. *Jeff Thompson, of, Miami-Dade CC North.
3. *Rod McDonald, rhp, Cuyahoga (Ohio) CC.
4. Roberto Alvarez, 3b-2b, Miami-Dade CC North.
5. *Luis Duarte, c-1b, Miami-Dade CC North.
6. *Joseph Cazares, ss, Imperial Valley (Calif.) JC.
7. *Dave Oliva, of, Los Angeles Valley JC.
8. John Napolitano, rhp, Cohoes, N.Y.
9. *Mike Reddish, c, Indian River (Fla.) CC.
10. Alex Christenson, rhp, Merced (Calif.) JC.
11. *James Winters, 3b, Cuyahoga (Ohio) CC.
12. *Mark Lacy, 1b, St. Petersburg (Fla.) JC.
13. *Larry Pittman, 1b, Abraham Baldwin (Ga.) JC.
14. Tommy Martinez, rhp-of, Hialeah, Fla.
15. Jack Lopez, ss, Miami-Dade CC North.

#### January—Secondary Phase (13)

1. Brad Carlson, of, Edison (Fla.) CC.—(Low A)
2. *Michael Sanford, rhp, DeKalb South (Ga.) CC.

#### June—Regular Phase (7)

**1. Jon Bohnet, lhp, Hogan HS, Vallejo, Calif.—(1982)**
2. Chris Rehbaum, of, St. Joseph's Collegiate HS, Buffalo, N.Y.—(Low A)
3. *Eric Hardgrave, 1b, Bullard HS, Fresno, Calif.—(AA)
DRAFT DROP *Attended Stanford; re-drafted by Padres, 1983 (6th round)*
4. John Hoban, rhp, Cal State Dominguez Hills.—(High A)
5. *Ed Brennan, ss, Sweet Home (Ore.) HS.—(Rookie)
DRAFT DROP *Attended Arizona State; re-drafted by Rangers, 1982 (25th round)*
6. *Dave Landrith, c, Homestead HS, Sunnyvale, Calif.
**7. Von Hayes, 3b, St. Mary's (Calif.) College.—(1981-92)**
8. *Charles Melito, 1b, Tulane University.
9. Ricky Baker, of, San Francisco State University.
10. *Len Bradley, rhp, Clemson University.
11. *Brian Butera, of, Tulane University.
12. Ron Leach, lhp, Fresno State University.
13. Frank Osmulski, c, Summit (N.J.) HS.
14. Jerry Larison, rhp, Lafayette HS, Lexington, Ky.
15. Jack Nuismer, rhp, Vanderbilt University.
16. *Mike Hocutt, 3b, Rogers HS, Michigan City, Ind.
17. Thomas Clancy, rhp, Wilmot HS, Twin Lakes, Wis.
DRAFT DROP *Brother of Jim Clancy, major leaguer (1977-91)*
18. Lawrence Locascio, c, St. Xavier (Ill.) College.
19. George Cecchetti, of, San Joaquin Delta (Calif.) JC.
20. *Larry Smith, ss, Ilion (N.Y.) HS.
21. Leonard Jones, rhp, University of Nevada-Las Vegas.
22. *Ricky Edwards, rhp, Santa Clara University.
23. *Robbie Cobb, ss, Garfield HS, Hamilton, Ohio.
24. *Gary Whisler, 3b, Klamath Union HS, Klamath Falls, Ore.
25. Larry Hrynko, rhp, St. Xavier (Ill.) College.
26. *Chris Sigourney, lhp, Larkin HS, Elgin, Ill.
27. Ralph Hodge, 1b, San Francisco State University.
28. *Thomas Gilchrist, rhp, Newport HS, Bellevue, Wash.
29. Todd Richard, lhp, DeSales HS, Walla Walla, Wash.
30. *Allen Peel, c, Davis (Calif.) HS.
**31. Larry White, rhp, San Francisco State University.—(1983-84)**
32. Michael Jakubowicz, rhp, Clarke HS, Hammond, Ind.
33. *Robert Heath, rhp, Maine East HS, Niles, Ill.
34. *Jeff Walsh, rhp, Santa Clara University.
35. *Joseph Krisik, lhp, Badger HS, Genoa City, Wis.
36. *Stan Osiecki, rhp, Ansonia (Conn.) HS.
37. George Merry, lhp, Ipswich (Mass.) HS.
38. Donald Nicolet, of-3b, Fort Steilacoom (Wash.) CC.
39. *Gerald Drobnick, ss, Euclid (Ohio) HS.
40. Matt Maki, lhp, San Jose State University.
41. *Gary Joseph, rhp-ss, New Iberia (La.) HS.
42. Brian Meier, 3b, San Joaquin Delta (Calif.) JC.
43. *Brian Duffy, lhp, University of California.
44. Bruce Chaney, ss, Washington State University.

#### June—Secondary Phase (25)

1. Weston Mitchell, ss, San Jose (Calif.) CC.—(AA)
2. Stephen Roche, rhp, Sacramento (Calif.) CC.
3. *John Damon, ss, Sacramento (Calif.) CC.
4. Victor Woods, of, Laney (Calif.) JC.
5. *James Glenn, of, Texas A&M University.
6. Bob Ferris, c-inf, Mesa (Ariz.) CC.

## DETROIT TIGERS

#### January—Regular Phase (14)

1. Michael Camp, rhp, Eastern Oklahoma State JC.—(High A)
2. *Dave Kirby, of, Citrus (Calif.) JC.
3. *Brian Stehling, rhp, San Jacinto (Texas) JC.
4. Gary Zelmanski, 1b, St. Clair County (Mich.) CC.

5. *Mike Querrey, 1b, Citrus (Calif.) JC.
6. *Ricky Gamez, ss-2b, Central Arizona JC.
7. *John Collier, rhp, St. Clair County (Mich.) CC.

#### January—Secondary Phase (12)

1. **Howard Johnson, 3b, St. Petersburg (Fla.) JC.—(1982-95)**
2. *Pat Blamey, rhp, San Jose (Calif.) CC.
3. Ell Roberson, of, Baytown, Texas.

#### June—Regular Phase (13)

1. **Rick Leach, of, University of Michigan.—(1981-90)**

DRAFT DROP *Fifth-round draft pick, Denver Broncos/ National Football League (1979)*

1. Chris Baker, of, Livonia Franklin HS, Dearborn Heights, Mich. (Choice from Brewers as compensation for free agent Jim Slaton).—(Low A)
2. Keith Fisher, c, Apopka (Fla.) HS.—(High A)
3. Randy Harvey, of, Poly HS, Riverside, Calif.—(AA)
4. Luis Sanchez, rhp, Monsignor Pace HS, Miami.—(High A)
5. Jon Driver, c, Shelby County HS, Shelbyville, Ky.—(Rookie)
6. David Arnold, ss, La Habra HS, Los Angeles.
7. Charlie Nail, rhp, McClure Academy, Jackson, Miss.
8. Vern Followell, ss, UCLA.
9. Michael Schoeller, 1b, Florida Southern College.
10. *Winston Ficklin, 2b-3b, El Cerrito HS, Richmond, Calif.
11. Anthony Barraco, c, De la Salle HS, Pittsburg, Calif.
12. **Mike Warren, rhp, Fullerton HS, Garden Grove, Calif.—(1983-85)**
13. *Mitch Seoane, 2b, Tampa Catholic HS, Tampa.

DRAFT DROP *Brother of Manny Seoane, major leaguer (1977-78)*

14. Gordon Chretien, rhp, Eastern Michigan University.
15. Jeff Kenaga, of, Western Michigan University.
16. Ron Lindberg, ss, Pace (N.Y.) University.
17. John Lackey, rhp, Florida Southern College.
18. *Steve Hendrix, lhp, Center Line (Mich.) HS.
19. Steve Dunn, lhp, Southwest Missouri State University.
20. *Greg Funk, ss, Serra HS, San Bruno, Calif.
21. Michael Krill, lhp, Irvington, N.J.
22. Ken Baldwin, 2b, Rice University.
23. *Audie Cole, of, Eastern Michigan University.
24. John Wells, of, University of Southern California.
25. William Hardy, of, Alabama State University.
26. *Michael Ward, 1b, Alma (Mich.) HS.
27. Robert Bresnen, lhp, Miami (Ohio) University.
28. Scott Vaughn, rhp, Allen Park (Mich.) HS.
29. *Terry Schalk, rhp, Lakeshore HS, St. Clair Shore, Mich.
30. Randy Nelson, rhp, Cal Poly Pomona.
31. Scott Bollens, rhp, UCLA.
32. Wilson Tucker, of, Belmont College.
33. Mark McKnight, 2b, Pfeiffer (N.C.) College.

#### June—Secondary Phase (17)

1. Paul Fox, rhp, Canada (Calif.) JC.—(Rookie)
2. James Good, of, JC of Southern Idaho.

## HOUSTON ASTROS

#### January—Regular Phase (7)

1. ***Jeff Dedmon, rhp, West Los Angeles JC.—(1983-88)**
2. Mike Penate, rhp, Miami-Dade CC New World Center.
3. *Jeff Etsell, lhp, Palm Beach (Fla.) JC.
4. *Gil Robison, rhp, Centralia (Wash.) JC.

#### January—Secondary Phase (5)

1. *Edwin Schneider, lhp, Indian River (Fla.) CC.—(Low A)
2. *Richard Eckleberry, rhp, JC of Southern Idaho.

#### June—Regular Phase (8)

1. **John Mizerock, c, Punxsutawney (Pa.) HS.—(1983-89)**

DRAFT DROP *Major league manager (2002)*

2. **Ty Gainey, of, Cheraw (S.C.) HS.—(1985-87)**
3. Cliff Wherry, ss, UC Riverside.—(AAA)
4. **Larry Ray, of, Kentucky Wesleyan College.—(1982)**
5. Mark Strucher, 1b-c, Georgia Southern College.—(AAA)
6. **Bill Doran, 2b, Miami (Ohio) University.—(1982-93)**
7. **Mark Ross, rhp, Texas A&M University.—(1982-90)**
8. William Ray, rhp, Oklahoma City University.
9. ***Mark Dempsey, rhp, Ohio State University.—(1982)**
10. Marc Thomas, of, Brigham Young University.
11. Greg Peterson, rhp, Brigham Young University.
12. **Johnny Ray, 2b, University of Arkansas.—(1981-90)**
13. Doug Welenc, rhp, University of Massachusetts.
14. Larry Brown, rhp, Harvard University.
15. Eddie Bonine, rhp, Grand Canyon College.
16. Blaine Smith, rhp, University of North Carolina.
17. Val Primante, c, University of Nebraska.
18. Steve Quealey, rhp, Washington State University.
19. Andrew Rice, lhp, Murray State University.
20. *Orlando Fernandez, 3b-of, Miami Lakes HS, Hialeah, Fla.
21. Mark Lohuis, rhp, Fresno State University.
22. *William Ratterman, lhp, Purcell HS, Cincinnati.
23. Mark Campbell, c, Florida International University.
24. Michael Finch, lhp, San Diego State University.
25. **Chris Jones, of, San Diego State University.—(1985-86)**
26. *Dana Ynostroza, c, Serramonte HS, Daly City, Calif.

#### June—Secondary Phase (20)

1. ***Lemmie Miller, of, Santa Barbara (Calif.) CC.—(1984)**

## KANSAS CITY ROYALS

#### January—Regular Phase (22)

1. **Mike Brewer, rhp, Foothill (Calif.) JC.—(1986)**

DRAFT DROP *Brother of Tony Brewer, major leaguer (1984)*

2. *Tim Cates, rhp, DeKalb South (Ga.) CC.
3. *Alex Christy, 1b, Westerville (Ohio) HS.
4. Roger Patoka, c, University of Wisconsin-Stevens Point.
5. *Curt Thrasher, lhp, Oxnard (Calif.) JC.
6. ***Mike Bielecki, rhp, Valencia (Fla.) CC.—(1984-97)**

#### January—Secondary Phase (21)

1. **Jeff Schattinger, rhp, University of Southern California.—(1981)**
2. *David Anderson, rhp, Arizona Western JC.

#### June—Regular Phase (21)

1. **Atlee Hammaker, lhp, East Tennessee State University.—(1981-95)**
2. John Skinner, rhp, North Carolina State University.—(AA)
3. **Pat Sheridan, of, Eastern Michigan University.—(1981-91)**
4. *Dan Marino, rhp, Central Catholic HS, Pittsburgh.—DNP

DRAFT DROP *Attended Pittsburgh; never re-drafted; first-round draft pick, Miami Dolphins/National Football League (1983); quarterback, NFL (1983-99)*

5. Mickey Palmer, of, Cal State Fullerton.—(High A)
6. Kenneth Pour, rhp, New Athens (Ill.) HS.
7. ***Craig Lefferts, lhp, University of Arizona.—(1983-94)**
8. *Doran Perdue, 2b, Murray State University.
9. Rob Townley, of, Long Beach State University.
10. ***Billy Moore, of, Covina HS, West Covina, Calif.—(1986)**
11. Otis Irvin, ss, Phillips HS, Chicago.
12. Ron Krauss, lhp, Seminole (Fla.) HS.
13. Ron Batter, c, University of Miami.
14. *Osbe Hoskins, 3b, Creston HS, Grand Rapids, Mich.
15. Walt Vanderbush, rhp, College of Wooster (Ohio).
16. Johnny Barnette, of, Spartanburg Methodist (S.C.) JC.
17. *David Sullivan, c, Oklahoma State University.
18. *John Elway, of, Granada Hills HS, Northridge, Calif.

DRAFT DROP *First-round draft pick, Baltimore Colts/ National Football League (1983); quarterback, NFL (1983-98)*

19. Daniel St. Clair, rhp, University of Kansas.
20. Jim Atkinson, 3b, University of North Carolina.
21. Lawrence Grahek, of, University of Minnesota.
22. Dave Luethy, ss, University of Oklahoma.
23. Larry Williams, rhp, Central Michigan University.
24. Vin Yuhas, rhp, Manalapan HS, Englishtown, N.J.
25. **Jeff Twitty, lhp, University of South Carolina.—(1980)**
26. Daniel Fischer, rhp, University of Nevada-Las Vegas.
27. *Craig Herberholz, rhp, Catholic Central HS, Farmington Hills, Mich.
28. *Bryan Nabors, rhp, South Shores HS, Chicago.
29. *Andrew Basten, rhp, Ashwaubenon HS, Green Bay, Wis.
30. *Mark Wakai, c, Cumberland HS, Seabrook, N.J.
31. Craig Patterson, 2b, Florida State University.
32. Ken Kurtz, lhp, Mississippi State University.
33. *James Jones, rhp, Redwood HS, Kentfield, Calif.
34. Al Garray, c, University of Connecticut.
35. *Reggie West, of, Santa Ana (Calif.) JC.
36. Leon Vickers, of, University of Kansas.
37. *Greg Housner, c, Bridgeport HS, Saginaw, Mich.

#### June—Secondary Phase (21)

1. Duane Dewey, c-1b, Louisiana State University.—(AAA)
2. *David McDonald, lhp, Allegheny (Pa.) CC.
3. *David LaBounty, rhp, Yakima Valley (Wash.) JC.
4. *Gil Robison, rhp, Centralia (Wash.) JC.

Dodgers first-rounder Steve Howe mixed on-field success with major off-field struggles

## LOS ANGELES DODGERS

#### January—Regular Phase (23)

1. Robert Silicani, 3b-ss, JC of San Mateo (Calif.).—(Rookie)
2. *Jeems Teller, of, Sacramento (Calif.) CC.
3. *Kyle Dunning, rhp, Linn-Benton (Ore.) CC.
4. *Joseph Siers, rhp, Palm Beach (Fla.) JC.
5. *Phillip Smith, lhp, DeKalb South (Ga.) CC.
6. *Eric Stack, rhp, Lane (Ore.) CC.
7. *James Gleissner, c, Mount San Jacinto (Calif.) JC.

#### January—Secondary Phase (16)

1. Rick Misuraca, 3b, Rose State (Okla.) JC.—(Rookie)
2. *John Millholland, ss, Louisburg (N.C.) JC.
3. *Richard Ross, of, San Jose (Calif.) CC.
4. *Tommy Blackmon, rhp, Spartanburg Methodist (S.C.) JC.

#### June—Regular Phase (24)

1. **Steve Howe, lhp, University of Michigan** (Choice from Pirates as compensation for free agent Lee Lacy)**—(1980-96)**
1. (Choice to Padres as compensation for free agent Derrel Thomas)
1. Steve Perry, rhp, University of Michigan (Choice from Yankees as compensation for free agent Tommy John)—(AAA)
2. David Lanning, 3b, University of Georgia.—(AA)
3. **Don Crow, c, Washington State University.—(1982)**
4. Leo Mann, ss, University of Missouri.—(High A)
5. Terry Sutcliffe, rhp, University of Kansas.—(High A)

DRAFT DROP *Brother of Rick Sutcliffe, first-round draft pick, Dodgers (1974); major leaguer (1976-94)*

6. Dale Holman, of, Louisiana Tech.
7. Tim Gloyd, ss-2b, Pepperdine University.
8. *Jeff Dietrich, lhp, Serramonte HS, Daly City, Calif.
9. Felix Oroz, lhp, University of Wyoming.
10. John Houston, c-3b, John F. Kennedy HS, Sacramento, Calif.
11. Mark Sheehy, 2b, UC Riverside.
12. *Kerwin Danley, of-1b, Dorsey HS, Los Angeles.

DRAFT DROP *Umpire, Major League Baseball (1998-2015)*

13. **Greg Brock, 1b, University of Wyoming.—(1982-91)**
14. Frank Bryant, rhp, North Carolina State University.
15. Tom Beyers, of, Cal Poly San Luis Obispo.
16. Ken Bullock, lhp, University of San Francisco.
17. **Orel Hershiser, rhp, Bowling Green State University.—(1983-2000)**
18. Keith Mohler, of, University of South Alabama.
19. Wayne Kellam, rhp, Indian River HS, Chesapeake, Va.
20. Bill Sobbe, c, Northwest Missouri State University.
21. Clint Wickenscheimer, rhp, Ball State University.
22. Glenn Terry, lhp, Kimball HS, Dallas.
23. David Daniel, rhp, Antelope Valley HS, Hesperia, Calif.

**24. Morris Madden, lhp, Spartanburg Methodist (S.C.) JC.—(1987-89)**
25. *Leonard Collins, ss-of, Hiram Johnson HS, Sacramento, Calif.
26. *Brian Dillard, of, Bloom Township HS, Chicago Heights, Ill.
27. *Harry Kazanjian, c-of, Washington HS, San Francisco.
28. *Kevin Roddy, inf, Bellevue West HS, Bellevue, Neb.
29. *P.J. Schranz, ss, Bloom Township HS, Chicago Heights, Ill.
30. *Ted Salcido, of, Wilson HS, Los Angeles.
31. *James Garcia, rhp, Bell HS, Huntington Park, Calif.
32. *George Page, of, Kennedy HS, Pacoima, Calif.

### June—Secondary Phase (18)

1. Al Mejia, c, Oral Roberts University.—(High A)
2. *Thomas McLaughlin, rhp, Los Angeles CC.
3. *Kyle Dunning, rhp, Linn-Benton (Ore.) CC.
4. *Bill Worden, c, Mission (Calif.) JC.

## MILWAUKEE BREWERS

### January—Regular Phase (24)

1. David Thomas, rhp, Lafayette, Ind.—(High A)
**2. *Jeff Heathcock, rhp, Golden West (Calif.) JC.—(1983-88)**
DRAFT DROP *First overall draft pick, June 1980/secondary phase, Astros*
3. *Larry Robinson, rhp, Compton (Calif.) CC.
4. Benjie Biggus, rhp, Frederick (Md.) CC.
5. *Weston Mitchell, 2b, San Jose (Calif.) CC.
6. Jesse Vasquez, rhp, Los Angeles Harbor JC.
7. *Pedro Bazan, c, Central Arizona JC.
8. *Ricky Daniels, ss, Los Angeles CC.
9. *Jim Woodward, ss, Rio Hondo (Calif.) JC.
10. Brian Meadows, rhp, Yavapai (Ariz.) JC.
11. *Jeff Ronk, 3b, JC of the Canyons (Calif.).
12. *Scott Olshane, rhp, Los Angeles Valley JC.
13. *Tilmon Crownover, rhp, Central Arizona JC.
14. *Daniel Anctile, rhp, Los Angeles Valley JC.
15. *Daryl Pitts, of, Los Angeles CC.
16. *Tim Sinovich, 1b, Cental Arizona JC.
17. Rick Odekirk, lhp, University of Southern California.
18. Scott Job, of, JC of Southern Idaho.
19. *Pedro Perez, inf, Miami-Dade CC New World Center.

### January—Secondary Phase (8)

1. Tony Torres, rhp, JC of the Sequoias (Calif.).—(AA)
2. Ronald Walling, lhp, Johnstown, Pa.
3. Todd Freeman, 3b, Spartanburg Methodist (S.C.) JC.
4. *Ron Thurston, c, Santa Ana (Calif.) JC.
5. *Rick Evans, lhp, El Camino (Calif.) JC.
6. *Karl Watson, rhp, Manatee (Fla.) JC.

### June—Regular Phase (23)

1. (Choice to Tigers as compensation for free agent Jim Slaton)
2. Mark Higgins, of, Central Valley HS, Veradale, Wash.—(Low A)
3. Jon Hansen, of, University of Hawaii.—(AA)
4. Rick Kranitz, rhp, Oklahoma State University.—(AAA)
**5. Andy Beene, rhp, Baylor University.—(1983-84)**
6. Karl McKay, rhp-of, Lafayette HS, Ballwin, Mo.
7. Ed Irvine, of, Arizona State University.
**8. Bill Schroeder, c, Clemson University.—(1983-90)**
9. David Morris, rhp, West Linn (Ore.) HS.
10. Ron Koenigsfeld, ss, Florida International University.
**11. *Paul Zuvella, 2b, Stanford University.—(1982-91)**
12. *Tom Mallon, lhp, W.T. Woodson HS, Fairfax, Va.
**13. Bob Skube, of, University of Southern California.—(1982-83)**
14. *Scott Smith, rhp, Polytechnic HS, Baltimore.
15. *Bruce Hines, 2b, University of La Verne (Calif.).
16. Kurt Kingsolver, c, Cal State Fullerton.
17. Ray Alonzo, of, Grand Canyon College.
18. *Chris Glass, 2b, Hagerstown (Md.) CC.

Tim Wallach was the Expos' first-round pick and spent 16 years in the major leagues

19. Joe Tkac, lhp, Tulane University.
**20. *Don Slaught, c-1b, UCLA.—(1982-97)**
21. *Pat Gillie, rhp, Arizona State University.
22. Kevin McCoy, rhp, Baltimore.
23. *Keith Mucha, 3b, Kennedy HS, Granada Hills, Calif.
24. Frank Galloway, rhp, The Citadel.
25. *James Koontz, rhp, Clarion (Pa.) University.
26. Curt Downs, ss, Los Angeles.
27. *Mike Fulmer, lhp, Antelope Valley HS, Lancaster, Calif.
28. *Danny Marshall, lhp, Cheraw HS, Patrick, S.C.
**29. *Dan Firova, c, Pan American University.—(1981-88)**
30. *Randy Poitevint, 3b, Reseda HS, Sunland, Calif.
31. *Jorge Reyes, lhp, Southwest Senior HS, Miami.
32. *Darren Swanson, rhp, Kent Meridian HS, Kent, Wash.
33. *Eugene Hering, of, Brookdale (N.J.) CC.
34. *Andrew Speck, rhp, Beaverton HS, Aloha, Ore.

### June—Secondary Phase (26)

1. David Grier, rhp, Virginia Tech.—(AA)
2. Randy Meyer, of, UC Santa Barbara.
3. *Chris Cawthon, 1b, DeKalb (Ga.) JC.
4. *Willie Davis, of, Canada (Calif.) JC.
5. *Harold Brown, rhp, Chipola (Fla.) JC.

## MINNESOTA TWINS

### January—Regular Phase (12)

1. *Joe McCarthy, of, Seminole (Fla.) CC.—DNP
2. Scott Stoltenberg, ss-of, Sacramento (Calif.) CC.
3. *Tracy Turner, lhp, El Camino (Calif.) JC.
4. *John Damon, 2b, Sacramento (Calif.) CC.
**5. Eddie Hodge, lhp, Cerritos (Calif.) JC.—(1984)**
6. Alan Jensen, c, South Florida JC.
7. *Bruce Amador, 2b, Modesto (Calif.) JC.
8. *Nelson Page, p, Utah Technical JC.
9. *Trent Smith, rhp, Seminole (Fla.) CC.
10. *Ken Rolfe, ss, Lower Columbia (Wash.) JC.
11. *David Wilson, rhp, Anderson (S.C.) JC.
12. Thomas Paul, of, Treasure Valley (Ore.) CC.
13. *Richard King, p, Solano (Calif.) CC.
14. Rick Kyzer, 3b, South Florida JC.
15. *Lou Sottile, 3b, Seminole (Fla.) CC.
16. Larry May, rhp, Central Arizona JC.

### January—Secondary Phase (19)

1. *Joe Plummer, rhp, Long Beach (Calif.) CC.—(Short-season A)
**2. *Mike Mason, lhp, Normandale (Minn.) CC.—(1982-88)**
3. *Jeff Vlha, 2b, Fullerton (Calif.) JC.
4. *Randy Ramirez, rhp, Fullerton (Calif.) JC.

### June—Regular Phase (11)

1. Kevin Brandt, of, Nekoosa (Wis.) HS.—(Rookie)
**2. Randy Bush, of, University of New Orleans.—(1982-93)**
**3. Tim Laudner, c, University of Missouri.—(1981-89)**
4. Sam Arrington, rhp, Taft (Calif.) HS.—(AA)
5. Bob Konopa, lhp, Bedford (Ohio) HS.—(AA)
6. Rich Shefte, ss, University of Nebraska-Omaha.
7. *David Stokes, 3b, Tulane University.
8. Ron Wilkinson, ss, Chapman (Calif.) College.
9. Paul Voigt, rhp, University of Virginia.
**10. Mike Kinnunen, lhp, Washington State University.—(1980-87)**
11. Bruce Stocker, of, Pima (Ariz.) CC.
12. Rick Beswick, 2b, Lewis & Clark (Ill.) CC.
13. *Todd Taylor, rhp, Upland (Calif.) HS.
**14. *Andre David, of, Cal State Fullerton.—(1984-86)**
15. Manny Colletti, ss, University of New Orleans.
16. Ken Francingues, rhp, Tulane University.
17. Wayne Palica, rhp, Huntington Beach (Calif.) HS.
DRAFT DROP *Son of Erv Palica, major leaguer (1945-56)*
18. Kevin Miller, of, Cerritos (Calif.) JC.
19. Boyce Orosco, rhp, Monache HS, Porterville, Calif.
20. Jack Gurholt, lhp, University of Wisconsin.
21. *Bill Piwnica, ss, Minnetonka (Minn.) HS.
22. Richard Austin, c, Cerritos (Calif.) JC.
23. Tim Fagely, lhp, Winona State (Minn.) University.
24. Bob Mulligan, lhp, John Jay (N.Y.) College.
25. Brandon Rosenberg, of, Glassboro State (N.J.) College.
26. *Randy Newman, lhp, Cypress (Calif.) JC.
27. Bill Lampey, rhp, University of New Orleans.
28. Alfredo Agras, of-c, Miami Springs HS, Hialeah, Fla.
29. *Edward Odin, of, Pacifica HS, Cypress, Calif.
30. *Tom Colburn, c, University of California.
**31. *Tom Nieto, c, Cerritos (Calif.) JC.—(1984-90)**
32. *David Zitkus, lhp, JC of Lake County (Ill.).
33. Derek Bulcock, ss, San Jose State University.
34. *John Lastinger, of, Valdosta (Ga.) HS.

### June—Secondary Phase (11)

**1. Gary Gaetti, 3b, Northwest Missouri State University.—(1981-2000)**
**2. *Randy O'Neal, rhp, Palm Beach (Fla.) JC.—(1984-90)**

## MONTREAL EXPOS

### January—Regular Phase (9)

1. Stephen Roeder, ss, Columbia State (Tenn.) CC.—(High A)
**2. *Jim Weaver, of-1b, Manatee (Fla.) JC.—(1985-89)**
3. *Derrell Baker, 2b, Middle Georgia JC.
**4. *Randy O'Neal, rhp, Palm Beach (Fla.) JC.—(1984-90)**
5. *Chris Campbell, 3b, Panola (Texas) JC.
6. *Rory Brown, lhp, Broward (Fla.) CC.
7. *Steve Mastro, 3b-of, Macomb (Mich.) CC.
8. *Mike Withrow, rhp, Blinn (Texas) JC.
9. *Tracy Cohron, lhp, Middle Georgia JC.
10. *Richard Vitato, inf, Merced (Calif.) JC.
11. *John Baker, rhp, Manatee (Fla.) JC.
12. Blake Byrket, rhp, Muscatine (Iowa) CC.
13. Jim Atkinson, of, Western Kentucky University.
14. *Ric Wilson, c, Mesa (Ariz.) CC.
DRAFT DROP *Scouting director, Angels (2010-15)*
15. George Keen, c, Wittenberg (Ohio) University.

### January—Secondary Phase (14)

1. *Chris Cawthon, 1b, DeKalb (Ga.) JC.—DNP
2. Cat Whitfield, 1b, Middle Georgia JC.
3. (void) Lawrence Dummer, rhp, Arizona Western JC.

### June—Regular Phase (10)

**1. Tim Wallach, 1b, Cal State Fullerton.—(1980-96)**
2. Mike Kwiecinski, ss, Shawnee HS, Warren, Mich. (Choice from Cardinals as compensation for free agent Darold Knowles).—(High A)
2. (Choice to Athletics as compensation for free agent Elias Sosa)
3. (Choice to Pirates as compensation for free agent Duffy Dyer)
**4. *John Russell, c, Norman (Okla.) HS.—(1984-93)**
DRAFT DROP *Attended Oklahoma; re-drafted by Phillies, 1982 (1st round); major league manager (2008-10)*
5. Jim Auten, of, UCLA.—(AA)
**6. Wallace Johnson, 2b, Indiana State University.—(1981-90)**
**7. Mike Gates, 2b, Pepperdine University.—(1981-82)**
8. Bill St. John, lhp, Aiken HS, Cincinnati.
9. Larry Boger, rhp-ss, Del Campo HS, Carmichael, Calif.
10. *Thor Edgel, rhp, Garden Grove (Calif.) HS.
11. Joe Abone, rhp, LeMoyne College.
12. Ronnie Caldwell, rhp-of, McNeese State University.
13. Kirk Forbes, 2b, Tennessee State University.
14. *John Palica, 1b-of, Torrance HS, Lomita, Calif.
15. *Guy Burgess, lhp, Atlantic HS, Delray Beach, Calif.
16. Bobby Ruiz, lhp, Dupont HS, Hermitage, Tenn.
**17. Brad Mills, 3b, University of Arizona.—(1980-83)**
DRAFT DROP *Father of Beau Mills, first-round draft pick, Indians (2007) • Major league manager (2010-12)*
18. *Shayne Hammond, lhp, West Columbus HS, Cerro Gordo, N.C.
19. *Jeff McDonald, rhp, Monta Vista HS, Saratoga, Calif.
20. Chuck Fick, c, Pepperdine University.
DRAFT DROP *Brother of Robert Fick, major leaguer (1998-2007)*
21. Keith White, lhp, Jackson State (Tenn.) CC.
22. *Thomas Scheer, rhp, Burbank HS, Sacramento, Calif.
23. David Flowers, lhp, Methodist (N.C.) College.
24. *David Flores, rhp, Carroll HS, Corpus Christi,

Texas.
25. Bud Yanus, rhp, Eastern Michigan University.
26. David Bradshaw, lhp, Jac-Cen-Del HS, Osgood, Ind.
27. Tommy Montgomery, lhp, Columbus (Ga.) College.
28. *George Foussianes, ss, University of Michigan.
29. Bill Sattler, rhp, Youngstown State University.
**30. *Billy Hatcher, of-rhp, Williams (Ariz.) HS.—(1984-95)**
31. *John McKeon, 2b, Hugh M. Cummings HS, Burlington, N.C.
DRAFT DROP *Son of Jack McKeon, major league manager (1973-2011)*

**June—Secondary Phase (10)**

1. *Mark Christy, rhp, Miami-Dade CC North.—(High A)
2. *Ed Schiavo, rhp, Boyertown, Pa.

## NEW YORK METS

**January—Regular Phase (1)**

**1. *Neal Heaton, lhp, Sachem HS, Holtsville, N.Y.—(1982-93)**
2. Mark Welch, lhp, Indiana Central University.
3. Marques Cooper, of, Three Rivers (Mo.) CC.
4. *Thomas McLaughlin, rhp, Los Angeles CC.
5. *Michael Befort, rhp, Allen County (Kan.) CC.
6. Ron Souza, ss, Butte (Calif.) JC.
7. Ron Graves, rhp, Modesto (Calif.) JC.
8. David Michael, rhp, Dodge City (Kan.) CC.
9. John Semprini, rhp, Des Moines Area (Iowa) CC.
**10. Rusty Tillman, of, Florida JC.—(1982-88)**
11. *Jesse Anderson, rhp, San Diego CC.
12. *Mike Sodders, 3b, Orange Coast (Calif.) JC.
DRAFT DROP *First-round draft pick (11th overall), Twins (1981)*

**January—Secondary Phase (11)**

1. John Violette, c, El Segundo, Calif.—(AAA)
2. Jeff Sunderlage, lhp, Des Moines Area (Iowa) CC.

**June—Regular Phase (2)**

**1. Tim Leary, rhp, UCLA.—(1981-94)**
**2. Jeff Bettendorf, rhp, Lompoc (Calif.) HS.—(1984)**
3. *Craig Jones, rhp, U.S. Military Academy.—(AAA)
DRAFT DROP *Selection voided; returned to U.S. Military Academy; re-drafted by Braves, 1980 (5th round)*
4. David Howard, of, Wichita State University.—(AA)
5. Gary Hardie, ss, Georgia Tech.—(High A)
**6. Ron Gardenhire, 2b, University of Texas.—(1981-85)**
DRAFT DROP *Major league manager (2002-14)*
7. Mike Hennessy, of, Bogota (N.J.) HS.
8. David Buttles, rhp, Kearny HS, San Diego.
9. Lee Shockley, rhp, Parkside HS, Salisbury, Md.
10. *Brooks Wallace, ss, Texas Tech.
11. Bryan Dunbar, c, JC of Marin (Calif.).
12. *Larry Hernandez, of, Jones HS, Orlando, Fla.
13. Doug Elliott, 2b, San Diego State University.
14. *Brick Toifel, c, Davidson HS, Mobile, Ala.
**15. *Walt Terrell, rhp, Morehead State University.—(1982-92)**
16. Bill Hill, of, Brookdale (N.J.) CC.
17. *Todd Davidson, of, North Allegheny HS, Wexford, Pa.
18. *John Bryant, of, El Toro (Calif.) HS.
19. Mike Anicich, 1b, Arizona State University.
**20. *John Leister, rhp, Russell HS, Great Falls, Mon.—(1987-90)**
DRAFT DROP *Drafted by Michigan Panthers/United States Football League (1983)*
21. Ted Damiter, rhp, Shippensburg (Pa.) University.
22. *Joe Scherger, of, University of Nebraska.
23. *Joseph Healy, rhp, Judge HS, Philadelphia.
24. Richard Greenfield, ss, LaSalle University.
25. Scott LaVielle, c, Olympic (Wash.) JC.
26. *Jim Phillips, rhp, Shawnee HS, Shawnee Mission, Kan.
**27. David W. Smith, rhp, Lamar University.—(1984-85)**
28. *Darryl Stephens, 1b, Butte (Calif.) JC.
**29. *Clay Christiansen, rhp, University of Kansas.—(1984)**
30. William Rittweger, 2b, Seton Hall University.

The Mets took Tim Leary in the first round, and he carved out a significant big league career

31. Paul Niggebrugge, of, Temple University.
32. Thomas Miller, lhp, Modesto (Calif.) JC.
33. Michael Privette, rhp, Millikan HS, Long Beach, Calif.
34. *Dan Sprick, of, St. Louis University.
35. *Terry Byrum, ss, University of Houston.
36. David Duff, c, University of Virginia.

**June—Secondary Phase (22)**

**1. *Bill Mooneyham, rhp, Merced (Calif.) JC.—(1986)**
2. Joe Plummer, rhp, Long Beach (Calif.) CC.
3. *Sheldon Andrews, rhp, Lower Columbia (Wash.) JC.

## NEW YORK YANKEES

**January—Regular Phase (26)**

1. James Campbell, rhp, Orange Coast (Calif.) JC.—(Low A)
2. Glenn Swires, 3b, Mount San Antonio (Calif.) JC.
3. Jeff Vanderplas, lhp, Camden County (N.J.) JC.
4. *Gary Higgins, rhp, Columbia State (Tenn.) CC.
5. *Otis Reuban, lhp, Black Hawk (Ill.) JC.
6. George Zimmerer, 2b, San Jose (Calif.) CC.
7. *Ed Schiavo, rhp, Boyertown (Pa.) HS.
8. Rich Santarone, c, Camden County (N.J.) JC.

**January—Secondary Phase (26)**

1. Chuck Hernandez, lhp, Hillsborough (Fla.) CC.—(AA)
2. Alan Mayles, rhp, Louisburg (N.C.) JC.
3. *Dan Peterson, rhp, North Idaho JC.
4. *Jerome Burgess, 1b, Palm Beach (Fla.) JC.
5. *Charles Beverly, rhp, University of North Carolina.

**June—Regular Phase (25)**

1. (Choice to Dodgers as compensation for free agent Tommy John)
2. Todd Demeter, 1b, U.S. Grant HS, Oklahoma City, Okla.—(AA)
DRAFT DROP *Son of Don Demeter, major leaguer (1956-67)*
**3. Freddie Toliver, rhp, San Gorgonio HS, San Bernardino, Calif.—(1984-93)**
4. *Ted Perkins, 1b, El Cerrito HS, Richmond, Calif.—DNP
DRAFT DROP *No school; re-drafted by Indians, June 1981/secondary phase (2nd round)*
**5. Greg Gagne, ss, Somerset (Mass.) HS.—(1983-97)**
**6. Stefan Wever, rhp, UC Santa Barbara.—(1982)**
7. Mike Echstenkamper, of, Ohio University.
8. Huey Gayden, of, Jackson State University.
**9. Pete Filson, lhp, Temple University.—(1982-90)**
10. Richard Budweg, lhp, Bloomsburg (Pa.) University.
11. George Demaria, rhp, El Segundo (Calif.) HS.
12. Michael Free, rhp, Chapman (Calif.) College.
13. David Buffamoyer, c, Clemson University.
14. Randy Guerra, 1b, University of Miami.
**15. Keith Smith, ss, Canyon HS, Canyon Country, Calif.—(1984-85)**
16. Chris Lein, rhp, Florida International University.
17. Rob Teegarden, of, University of Florida.
18. *Mike Dotterer, of, Edison HS, Huntington Beach, Calif.
DRAFT DROP *Son of Dutch Dotterer, major leaguer (1957-61) • Eighth-round draft pick, Los Angeles Raiders/National Football League (1983)*
**19. Don Mattingly, 1b, Reitz Memorial HS, Evansville, Ind.—(1982-95)**
DRAFT DROP *Major league manager (2011-15)*
20. *Sean Everton, of, Santa Clara University.
21. Derwin McNealy, of, Crenshaw HS, Carson, Calif.
22. *Cedric Mack, of, Brazosport HS, Freeport, Texas.
23. Brian Murphy, lhp, Eastern Connecticut State University.
24. Gregg Sporrer, ss, University of La Verne (Calif.).
25. Jeff Rudolph, c-3b, University of Central Florida.
26. Frank Ricci, rhp, Rollins (Fla.) College.
27. Kevin Irot, rhp, Cal Poly San Luis Obispo.
28. John Seneca, rhp, Seton Hall University.
29. *Rusty Piggott, ss, Rollins (Fla.) College.
30. Greg Copeland, rhp, Shaw HS, Cleveland.

**June—Secondary Phase (3)**

**1. Otis Nixon, 3b, Louisburg (N.J.) JC.—(1983-99)**
DRAFT DROP *Brother of Donell Nixon, major leaguer (1987-90)*
2. Scott Benedict, c, University of Georgia.
3. Mark Ochal, rhp, Brookdale (N.J.) CC.

## OAKLAND ATHLETICS

**January—Regular Phase (6)**

**1. *Lemmie Miller, of, Santa Barbara (Calif.) CC.—(1984)**
**2. *Bob Fallon, lhp, Miami-Dade CC North.—(1984-85)**
3. *David Granger, rhp, Santa Barbara (Calif.) CC.
4. *Harold Brown, rhp, Chipola (Fla.) JC.
5. *Fred Conradi, lhp, Centralia (Wash.) JC.
6. *Kirk Komstadius, 3b, Yakima Valley (Wash.) JC.
7. *Al Romero, of, JC of Southern Idaho.

**January—Secondary Phase (10)**

1. *Paul Homrig, 1b, Los Angeles Harbor JC.—DNP
2. *Stephen Maral, c, Chabot (Calif.) JC.

**June—Regular Phase (5)**

1. *Juan Bustabad, ss, Miami Lakes HS, Hialeah, Fla.—(AAA)
DRAFT DROP *Attended Miami-Dade CC North; re-drafted by Red Sox, January 1980/secondary phase (1st round, 1st pick)*
**1. *Mike Stenhouse, of, Harvard University** (Choice from Red Sox as compensation for free agent Steve Renko)**—(1982-86)**
DRAFT DROP *No school; re-drafted by Expos, January 1980/secondary phase (1st round) • Son of Dave Stenhouse, major leaguer (1962-64)*
**2. *Tom Dodd, of, University of Oregon.–(1986)**
DRAFT DROP *No school; re-drafted by Yankees, January 1980/secondary phase (1st round)*
2. Mark Ferguson, rhp, West Muskingum HS, Zanesville, Ohio (Choice from Expos as compensation for free agent Elias Sosa).—(AA)
3. *Ricky McMullen, 2b, William Carey (Miss.) College.—(AAA)
DRAFT DROP *No school; re-drafted by Padres, January 1980/secondary phase (1st round)*
4. *Tom Caulfield, lhp, St. Mary's HS, Jersey City, N.J.—(High A)
DRAFT DROP *Attended Southern Illinois; never re-drafted*
**5. *Ronn Reynolds, c, University of Arkansas.—(1982-90)**
DRAFT DROP *Returned to Arkansas; re-drafted by Mets, 1980 (5th round)*
6. Oscar Burnett, of-3b, Moravia Central HS, Moravia, N.Y.
7. *Robert Ruffus, rhp, Monmouth College.
8. *Jeff Blankenship, rhp, El Dorado HS, Placentia, Calif.
9. *Mark Calvert, rhp, Thomas Stone HS, Waldorf, Md.
10. Paul Spillane, c, Colby (Maine) College.
11. *Craig Roberson, ss, Highland Springs (Va.) HS.
12. *Joe Jacowiak, rhp, St. Joseph's HS, South Bend, Ind.
13. *Jim Stefanski, c, Long Island University.
14. *Mike McCandless, rhp, San Jose (Calif.) CC.
15. Keith Call, rhp, Hammond (Ind.) Tech HS.
16. Paul Stockley, ss, American International (Mass.) College.
17. *Manuel Costa, 3b, Gavilan (Calif.) JC.
18. *Kevin Olson, rhp, Marina HS, Huntington Beach, Calif.
19. *Mike O'Hara, rhp, Covina HS, West Covina, Calif.
20. Robert Wood, rhp, Northeast Louisiana University.
21. Steven Roberts, 3b, University of Kentucky.
22. *Scott Jefferson, of, Berkeley (Calif.) HS.
23. *Jordan Berge, ss, Pueblo East HS, Pueblo, Colo.
24. *Hank Landers, of, Somerville (Mass.) HS.
25. *Ron Sylvia, rhp, Cal State Los Angeles.
26. Ken Corzel, rhp, Long Beach State University.
**27. Bert Bradley, rhp, Brigham Young University.—(1983)**
28. Ed Retzer, rhp, SUNY-Buffalo.
29. Joe Williams, 1b, University of South Florida.
30. *Brian Guinn, ss, Berkeley HS, Richmond, Calif.
31. *Greg Hazel, ss, San Jose (Calif.) CC.
32. *Arthur Sullivan, of, Colby (Maine) College.
33. *Ken Babcock, lhp, Centenary College.
34. John Pignotti, c, Claremont-Mudd (Calif.) College.

**June—Secondary Phase (9)**

1. *Edwin Schneider, lhp, Indian River (Fla.) CC.—(Low A)
2. *Scott Patterson, rhp, Mesa (Ariz.) CC.
**3. *Jeff Dedmon, rhp, West Los Angeles JC.—(1983-88)**

## PHILADELPHIA PHILLIES

**January—Regular Phase (19)**

1. Dean Baugh, of-inf, Butte (Calif.) JC.—DNP
2. *Robert Fischer, rhp, Panola (Texas) JC.
3. Jon Lindsey, ss, Seminole (Okla.) JC.
4. *Grant Priess, c, Blinn (Texas) JC.
5. *Ken Schubert, rhp, St. Clair County (Mich.) CC.
6. *Benny Smith, lhp, Ranger (Texas) JC.
7. *Robert Culley, 3b, Panola (Texas) JC.
8. *Nathan Frierson, rhp, Ranger (Texas) JC.
9. *Don Young, of, Paris (Texas) JC.
10. *Steve D'Ercole, ss, Seminole (Fla.) CC.
11. *Donald Wilson, rhp, Salem (N.J.) CC.
12. *Richard Yraguen, ss, JC of Southern Idaho.

**January—Secondary Phase (1)**

**1. Mark Davis, lhp, Chabot (Calif.) JC.—(1980-97)**
2. *Luis Rojas, of, New York.
3. *Kem Wright, rhp, Paris (Texas) JC.
4. *Ron Rendelman, rhp, San Bernardino Valley

(Calif.) JC.

**June—Regular Phase (20)**

1. (Choice to Reds as compensation for free agent Pete Rose)
2. Kyle Money, rhp, W.W. Samuell HS, Dallas.—(AAA)
3. **Roy Smith, rhp, Mount Vernon (N.Y.) HS.—(1984-91)**
4. **Jay Baller, rhp, Canby (Ore.) HS.–(1982-92)**
5. Herbert Bennett, rhp, Riverdale HS, Fort Myers, Fla.—(Short-season A)
6. Trent Purcell, of, Trotwood (Ohio) HS.
7. Ken Ellenberg, 3b, Carl Albert HS, Midwest City, Okla.
8. Jeff Nate, ss, Dowagiac (Mich.) HS.
9. Matthew Dorin, rhp, Miraleste HS, Rolling Hills, Calif.
10. Rusty Hamric, 2b, Hardin-Simmons (Texas) University.
11. DeWayne Hutchinson, rhp, Yoncalla (Ore.) HS.
12. David Harrigan, c, University of Oklahoma.
13. *Jeff Ahern, lhp, Arizona State University.
14. Adam Conti, rhp, Chicopee (Mass.) HS.
15. Willie Darkis, of, Eastern Oklahoma State JC.
16. Steve Dunnegan, rhp, Kerman (Calif.) HS.
17. Roger Redmond, rhp, Bishop Kelley HS, Tulsa, Okla.
18. Michael Hanson, 3b, Woodway HS, Edmonds, Wash.
19. Robert Barnett, rhp, Oregon (Ill.) HS.
20. Michael Lynes, lhp, UC Riverside.
21. *Mike Knox, ss, Carlisle (Pa.) HS.
22. *Randy Foyt, 3b, Beyer HS, Modesto, Calif.
23. Andrew Owings, ss, Klamath Falls (Ore.) HS.
24. *Tim Reynolds, rhp, Skyline HS, Dallas.
25. David Mitchell, rhp, Leesburg HS, Fruitland Park, Fla.
26. **Kelly Downs, rhp, Viewmont HS, Bountiful, Utah.—(1986-93)**

DRAFT DROP *Brother of Dave Downs, major leaguer (1972)*

27. Russell Gums, rhp, Rio Linda (Calif.) HS.
28. *Brian Henderson, c, South Albany (Ore.) HS.
29. ***Nelson Santovenia, 3b, Southridge HS, Miami.—(1987-93)**
30. Brad Lenaburg, rhp, Southwestern Oklahoma State University.
31. *Keith Robinson, 1b, Julian HS, Chicago.
32. *Curt Warner, of, Pineville HS, Wyoming, W.Va.

DRAFT DROP *First-round draft pick, Seattle Seahawks/ National Football League (1983); running back, NFL (1983-90)*

33. *Deron Gustafson, 2b, Crockett HS, Austin, Texas.

**June—Secondary Phase (4)**

1. Kelly Faulk, rhp, Wharton County (Texas) JC.—(AAA)
2. *Mike Withrow, rhp, Blinn (Texas) JC.

DRAFT DROP *Father of Chris Withrow, first-round draft pick, Dodgers (2007)*

3. *Russ Stephans, c, Los Angeles Valley JC.
4. Ken Martinson, c, Billings, Mont.

## PITTSBURGH PIRATES

**January—Regular Phase (15)**

1. William Nice, lhp, JC of Southern Idaho.—(Low A)
2. *Chris Goodchild, rhp, Santa Monica (Calif.) JC.
3. *Carl Taylor, rhp, Camden County (N.J.) JC.
4. ***Rick Ownbey, rhp, Santa Ana (Calif.) JC.—(1982-86)**
5. *Todd Dinsmore, of, Treasure Valley (Ore.) CC.
6. *Sheldon Andrews, rhp, Lower Columbia (Wash.) JC.
7. *Warren DeLisle, ss, Bellevue (Wash.) CC.
8. *Chris Fazendine, rhp, Yakima Valley (Wash.) JC.
9. *Mark Ochal, rhp, Brookdale (N.J.) CC.

**January—Secondary Phase (18)**

1. *David McDonald, lhp, Allegheny (Pa.) CC.—DNP

**June—Regular Phase (16)**

1. (Choice to Dodgers as compensation for free agent Lee Lacy)
2. Scott Fiepke, lhp, Elizabethtown (Ky.) HS.—(AA)
3. **Jose DeLeon, rhp, Perth Amboy, N.J.** (Choice from Expos as compensation for free agent Duffy Dyer)**—(1983-95)**
3. Scott Kuvinka, 3b, Ohio University.—(High A)
4. **Chris Green, lhp, Dorsey HS, Los Angeles.—(1984)**
5. Conner McGehee, of, Douglas Freeman HS, Richmond, Va.—(AA)
6. *Craig Fitzpatrick, rhp, Fatima HS, Koeltztown, Mo.
7. *John Alvarez, 3b, Helix HS, Lemon Grove, Calif.
8. Andrew Snaith, 2b, Choctawatchee HS, Fort Walton Beach, Fla.
9. Art Ray, rhp, Northern Illinois University.
10. Ken Ford, c, Albany State (Ga.) College.
11. Michael Johnson, rhp, Osseo (Minn.) HS.
12. Terry Salazar, 1b, University of Texas.
13. Wilmot Reedy, 2b, Thomas Jefferson HS, Brooklyn, N.Y.
14. Jim Felt, of, DeKalb (Ga.) JC.
15. Thomas Olszak, of, University of Pennsylvania.
16. **Ron Wotus, ss, Bacon Academy HS, Colchester, Conn.—(1983-84)**
17. *Darryl Stephens, of, Gonzaga Prep HS, Spokane, Wash.
18. *Philip Fritz, ss, Henrico HS, Richmond, Va.
19. *Otis Grant, inf-c, Carver HS, Atlanta.
20. Tim Wheeler, 3b, Dupont HS, Charleston, W.Va.
21. Larry Nicholson, lhp, Ohio University.
22. Mike Quade, of, University of New Orleans.

DRAFT DROP *Major league manager (2010-11)*

23. *Ron Evans, ss, New Hartford (N.Y.) HS.
24. *Kevin Babb, rhp, Taft HS, Rose Lodge, Ore.
25. *Joey Farrill, rhp, Mosley HS, Panama City, Fla.
26. *Jeff Metz, rhp, Connellsville (Pa.) HS.
27. *John Tutt, ss-of, East Rome (Ga.) HS.
28. *Lance Mason, c, Meadowbrook HS, Richmond, Va.
29. *Thomas Bart, rhp-of, Burrell HS, Lower Burrell, Pa.
30. *Greg Tutt, ss-of, East Rome (Ga.) HS.
31. *Roger Lorenzen, of, Oregon College of Education.
32. *Craig Steensen, c, The Hotchkiss School, Newark, Del.
33. *David Blume, 1b, Lewis-Clark State (Idaho) College.
34. Robert Gulaskey, 3b-1b, Elizabeth Forward HS, Elizabeth, Pa.
35. Lawrence Styles, rhp, Penn State University.
36. *Paul Bard, c, Tufts (Mass.) University.

DRAFT DROP *Father of Daniel Bard, first-round draft pick, Red Sox (2006); major leaguer (2009-13) • Father of Luke Bard, first-round draft pick, Twins (2012)*

37. **Joel Skinner, c, Mission Bay HS, San Diego.—(1983-91)**

DRAFT DROP *Son of Bob Skinner, major leaguer (1954-66), major league manager (1968-77) • Major leaguer manager (2002)*

38. *John Peoples, rhp, Dickinson HS, Wilmington, Del.
39. ***Herm Winningham, of, Wilkinson HS, Orangeburg, S.C.—(1984-92)**
40. *Robert Seames, rhp, Telstar HS, Bethel, Maine.
41. ***Mike Sharperson, ss, Wilkinson HS, Orangeburg, S.C.—(1987-95)**
42. Gordon Maki, rhp, Poly HS, Baltimore.
43. *Michael Giedlin, rhp, Alfred Almond HS, Alfred, N.Y.
44. *Paul Cox, lhp, Springbrook HS, Silver Spring, Md.

**June—Secondary Phase (8)**

1. **Mike Bielecki, rhp, Valencia (Fla.) CC.—(1984-97)**
2. *Nattie George, of, San Jose (Calif.) CC.
3. *Rick Witt, 3b, Gonzaga University.

## ST. LOUIS CARDINALS

**January—Regular Phase (5)**

1. *Bob Ferris, 1b, Mesa (Ariz.) CC.—(AAA)
2. Keith Spreckles, ss, Islip, N.Y.
3. *Mike Evans, lhp, Merced (Calif.) JC.
4. *Ronald Sloy, 1b, Mount Hood (Ore.) CC.
5. *Mark Pedersen, rhp, Yakima Valley (Wash.) JC.
6. ***Bill Lindsey, 3b, Broward (Fla.) CC.—(1987)**
7. *Gary Fradella, 1b, Glendale (Calif.) JC.
8. *John Mathews, rhp, Rio Hondo (Calif.) JC.
9. *Kevin Coughlon, of, Oxnard (Calif.) JC.
10. *Sam Cordero, rhp, Eastern Arizona JC.
11. *Thomas Kurant, rhp, Miami-Dade CC North.
12. ***Greg Bargar, rhp, El Camino (Calif.) JC.—(1983-86)**
13. John Rincon, of, Rio Hondo (Calif.) JC.
14. *Steve Heslop, lhp, San Bernardino Valley (Calif.) JC.

**January—Secondary Phase (7)**

1. ***Bill Mooneyham, rhp, Merced (Calif.) JC.—(1986)**
2. *David Jensen, lhp, Edmonds (Wash.) CC.

**Cardinals first-rounder Andy Van Slyke found his most big league success with the Pirates**

**June—Regular Phase (6)**

1. **Andy Van Slyke, of, New Hartford (N.Y.) HS.—(1983-95)**

DRAFT DROP *Father of Scott Van Slyke, major leaguer (2012-15)*

2. (Choice to Expos as compensation for free agent Darold Knowles)
3. ***Ed Vosberg, lhp, Salpointe HS, Tucson, Ariz.—(1986-2002)**

DRAFT DROP *Attended Arizona; re-drafted by Blue Jays, 1982 (11th round)*

4. John Del Monte, of, St. Joseph's University.—(AA)
5. *Mark Roberts, lhp, Myers Park HS, Charlotte, N.C.—(Short-season A)

DRAFT DROP *Attended DeKalb (Ga.) JC; re-drafted by Indians, January 1980/secondary phase (1st round)*

6. Robert Brooks, rhp, Ithaca (N.Y.) College.
7. Bill Fink, of, Greenfield (Ind.) HS.
8. Earl Weaver, rhp, Kutztown (Pa.) University.
9. Mike Kopala, c, Hackensack HS, Rochelle Park, N.J.
10. Jack Ayer, ss, Cal Poly San Luis Obispo.
11. **Tom Dozier, rhp, Richmond (Calif.) HS.—(1986)**
12. Jeff Taylor, lhp, Righetti HS, Santa Maria, Calif.
13. Jeff Warburton, lhp, Granger HS, Salt Lake City.
14. *Tracy Hamilton, ss, Tattnall Square HS, Macon, Ga.
15. Tim Fish, lhp, Whittier Christian HS, Rowland Heights, Calif.
16. ***Steve Stanicek, 1b, Rich East HS, Park Forest, Ill.—(1987-89)**

DRAFT DROP *First-round draft pick (11th overall), Giants (1982) • Brother of Pete Stanicek, major leaguer (1987-88)*

17. *Tony Hudson, rhp, Cal State Fullerton.
18. **Mark Salas, c, Nogales HS, La Puente, Calif.—(1984-91)**
19. *Greg Howe, of, Eisenhower HS, Rochester, Mich.
20. *Doug Latrenta, of, St. John's University.
21. *Lloyd Martin, lhp, Los Altos HS, Hacienda Heights, Calif.
22. *John Krol, 3b, Bishop McGuiness HS, Winston-Salem, N.C.
23. **Terry Clark, rhp, Mount San Antonio (Calif.) JC.—(1988-97)**
24. *Jeff Keeler, rhp, Miami-Dade CC South.
25. Phil Baskerville, of, Elon College.
26. Stan McCauley, 3b, Troy State University.
27. *Kevin House, of, Southern Illinois University.

DRAFT DROP *Wide receiver, National Football League (1980-87)*

**June—Secondary Phase (12)**

1. **Ralph Citarella, rhp, Florida Southern College.—(1983-87)**
2. ***Mike Mason, lhp, Normandale (Minn.) CC.—(1982-88)**

## SAN DIEGO PADRES

**January—Regular Phase (13)**

1. John Stevenson, ss, Los Angeles Valley JC.—(AA)
2. *Carlos Moreno, rhp, Miami-Dade CC New World Center.
3. *Victor Woods, of, Laney (Calif.) JC.
4. Greg Tarnow, c-3b, Rolling Prairie, Ind.
5. ***Larry See, 3b, Cerritos (Calif.) JC.—(1986-88)**

**January—Secondary Phase (22)**

1. *Mondel Williams, of, Sacramento (Calif.) CC.—DNP

**June—Regular Phase (14)**

1. **Joe Lansford, 1b, Wilcox HS, San Jose, Calif.—(1982-83)**

DRAFT DROP *Brother of Carney Lansford, major leaguer (1978-92) • Brother of Phil Lansford, first-round draft pick, Indians (1978)*

1. **Bob Geren, c, Clairemont HS, San Diego** (Choice from Dodgers as compensation for free agent Derrel Thomas)**—(1988-93)**

DRAFT DROP *Major league manager (2007-11)*

2. *Derek Tatsuno, lhp, University of Hawaii.—(AAA)

DRAFT DROP *No school; re-drafted by Mets, June 1980/secondary phase (3rd round)*
3. Steve Johnson, of, Rich East HS, Park Forest, Ill.—(AA)
**4. Mark Parent, c, Anderson HS, Cottonwood, Calif.—(1986-98)**
**5. Mark Thurmond, lhp, Texas A&M University.—(1983-90)**
**6. *Harold Reynolds, ss, Corvallis (Ore.) HS.—(1983-94)**
DRAFT DROP *Brother of Don Reynolds, major leaguer (1978-79) • Brother of Larry Reynolds, fourth-round draft pick, Rangers (1979)*
7. Michael Barba, rhp, Coastal Carolina University.
**8. James Steels, of, Santa Maria (Calif.) HS.—(1987-89)**
9. Corky Wyrick, rhp, Cal Poly San Luis Obispo.
10. Dan Gausepohl, of, UCLA.
11. Jerry DeSimone, ss, Southern Illinois University.
12. *Larry Navilhon, rhp, Cal State Fullerton.
13. Aaron Cain, 2b-of, University of New Mexico.
14. Dave Froelick, rhp, University of New Orleans.
15. *Paul Bradley, c, La Sierra HS, Riverside, Calif.
16. Dave Wilson, rhp, Bethel HS, Hampton, Va.
17. Dan Sijer, lhp, University of Washington.
18. Doug Lulay, of, Oregon College of Education.
19. Alfredo Rodriguez, ss, University of Miami.
20. Dan Danielson, rhp, Long Beach State University.
21. Francisco Gonzalez, 2b-ss, Valdosta State (Ga.) College.
22. Thomas Brokop, rhp, Thornton (Ill.) CC.
23. Rodney Peterson, rhp, Black Hawk (Ill.) JC.
24. *Ronnie Scheer, of, Kentucky HS, Paducah, Ky.
25. *Mark Hoffman, lhp, Mount Eden HS, Hayward, Calif.
26. *Richard Scott, 2b, Gunn HS, Palo Alto, Calif.
27. *Donald Canedo, ss, Hoover HS, San Diego.

**June—Secondary Phase (14)**

**1. *Jeff Heathcock, rhp, Golden West (Calif.) JC.—(1983-88)**
DRAFT DROP *First overall draft pick, June 1980/secondary phase, Astros*

## SAN FRANCISCO GIANTS

**January—Regular Phase (17)**

1. Kevin Johnson, of, Los Angeles CC.—(Low A)
2. Matthew Dunn, c, Brookdale (N.J.) CC.
3. *Mario Ramirez, p, Los Angeles CC.
4. *David LaBounty, rhp, Yakima Valley (Wash.) JC.
5. *Albert Hammack, rhp, Bellevue (Wash.) CC.
6. Ralph Guarante, of, Paterson, N.J.
7. Ronald Perodin, of, Los Angeles CC.
8. *Kurtis Kemp, c, Linn-Benton (Ore.) CC.
9. Arthur Maebe, rhp, JC of the Desert (Calif.).
10. Jerry Lane, c-inf, Santa Monica (Calif.) JC.
11. *Eugene Hernandez, rhp, San Joaquin Delta (Calif.) JC.
12. *Jack Glaze, lhp, Lane (Ore.) CC.

**January—Secondary Phase (24)**

1. *Jeff Stottlemyre, rhp, Yakima Valley (Wash.) JC.—(AA)
DRAFT DROP *Brother of Mel Stottlemyre, major leaguer (1964-74)*

**June—Regular Phase (17)**

**1. Scott Garrelts, rhp, Buckley-Loda HS, Buckley, Ill.** (Choice from Angels as compensation for free agent Jim Barr)**—(1982-91)**
**1. *Rick Luecken, rhp, Spring Woods HS, Houston.—(1989-90)**
DRAFT DROP *Attended Texas A&M; re-drafted by Reds, 1982 (12th round)*
**2. Chris Brown, 3b, Crenshaw HS, Los Angeles.—(1984-89)**
3. David Wilhelmi, rhp, Joliet Catholic HS, Joliet, Ill.—(AA)
**4. Randy Kutcher, ss, Palmdale (Calif.) HS.—(1986-90)**
5. *Louis Burmester, rhp, Herricks HS, Williston Park, N.Y.—DNP
DRAFT DROP *Attended Nassau (N.Y.) CC; re-drafted by Mariners, January 1981/secondary phase (2nd round)*
6. James Dunn, 2b-rhp, Portland State University.
7. Darryl McNealy, 1b, Crenshaw HS, Carson, Calif.
8. Greg Baker, of, Indiana State University.
9. Charles Curry, 1b, Southern Illinois University.
**10. *Scotti Madison, c, Vanderbilt University.—(1985-91)**
**11. Frank Williams, rhp, Lewis-Clark State (Idaho) College.—(1984-89)**
12. Cordie Dillard, 2b, Crenshaw HS, Los Angeles.
13. *David Cardwell, ss, East Tennessee State University.
14. *Lance Junker, of, Mission (Calif.) JC.
15. *Scott Blanke, of, Cypress (Calif.) JC.
**16. Tom O'Malley, 2b, Montoursville (Pa.) HS.—(1982-90)**
17. *Steve Murphy, rhp, Grant HS, North Hollywood, Calif.
18. Michael Woods, ss, Southern University.
19. John Wojcik, of, SUNY-Buffalo.
20. *Paul Ash, of, Delaware State University.
21. *John Ross, 3b, William Paterson (N.J.) College.
22. *Mark Dacko, rhp, James Madison University.
23. *Jim Wilson, c, Franklin HS, Livonia, Mich.
24. David Thornton, rhp, St. Joseph's University.
25. *James Kelly, rhp, Westwood HS, Fort Pierce, Fla.
26. *Bill Zempolich, rhp, Roosevelt HS, Lanham, Md.
27. Jerald Felt, rhp, Mesa (Colo.) College.
28. John Ziccardi, 1b-of, Florida Institute of Technology.
29. Don Jamerson, of, Cal State Hayward.
30. Joe Lorenz, 3b, Lewis (Ill.) University.
31. *Tim Thiessen, ss-3b, Roosevelt HS, Fresno, Calif.
32. Buster Turner, c, Texas A&M University.
33. *David Del Rio, of, Ponderosa HS, Lotus, Calif.
34. *Russell Cleland, c-rhp, El Dorado HS, Placerville, Calif.

**June—Secondary Phase (2)**

1. Chris Goodchild, rhp, Santa Monica (Calif.) JC.—(High A)

## SEATTLE MARINERS

**January—Regular Phase (2)**

1. Michael Hood, c, Washington Academy, Greenville, Miss.—(High A)
2. Don Minnick, lhp, Bedford, Va.
**3. *Carlos Diaz, lhp, Allan Hancock (Calif.) JC.—(1982-86)**
4. *Steve Lawrence, lhp, Yavapai (Ariz.) JC.

**January—Secondary Phase (15)**

1. *Joe Housey, rhp, Miami-Dade CC North.—(AA)

**June—Regular Phase (1)**

**1. Al Chambers, of-1b, John Harris HS, Harrisburg, Pa.—(1983-85)**
**2. Jamie Allen, 3b, Arizona State University.—(1983)**
DRAFT DROP *First-round draft pick (10th overall), Twins (1976)*
3. Rick Adair, lhp, Western Carolina University.—(AAA)
**4. Jim Presley, ss, Escambia HS, Pensacola, Fla.—(1984-91)**
5. Mark Cahill, rhp, East HS, Cranston, R.I.—(AA)
6. Kevin King, of, Chief Sealth HS, Seattle.
**7. Brian Snyder, lhp, Clemson University.—(1985-89)**
DRAFT DROP *Father of Brandon Snyder, first-round draft pick, Orioles (2005); major leaguer (2010-13)*
8. Scott Stranski, rhp, Northwestern University.
9. Bob Randolph, rhp, Arizona State University.
10. Chris Henry, c, North Central HS, Spokane, Wash.
11. Mark Batten, rhp, University of Miami.
12. Mike Codiroli, of, Stanford University.
DRAFT DROP *Brother of Chris Codiroli, major leaguer (1982-90)*
**13. Mike L. Hart, of, University of Wisconsin.—(1984-87)**
14. Joe Georger, rhp, University of Kentucky.
15. *Brian McDonough, rhp, Tottenville HS, Staten Island, N.Y.
16. Charles Colby, ss, Westmont (Calif.) College.
**17. Bud Black, lhp, San Diego State University.—(1981-95)**
DRAFT DROP *Major league manager (2007-15)*
18. *Fred Belak, rhp, Cardinal Spellman HS, Bronx, N.Y.
19. William Gaffney, ss, Adelphi (N.Y.) University.
**20. *Tom Henke, rhp, East Central (Mo.) JC.—(1982-95)**
21. Brian Harrison, rhp, Stanford University.
22. John Cook, of, Washington State University.
23. *David Axenfeld, lhp, Fayetteville-Manilius HS, Manilius, N.Y.
24. Roy Clark, 2b, University of North Carolina.
DRAFT DROP *Scouting director, Braves (2000-09)*
25. Kevin Steger, rhp, New Mexico State University.
26. Jed Murray, rhp, Southern Utah State College.
27. Dale Eiler, c, Arizona State University.
28. Bill Martin, rhp, Quinnipiac College.
29. Chris Hunger, rhp-ss, Edgewood HS, Berlin, N.J.
30. Mark Chelette, 3b-ss, University of Texas.
31. *Daniel McFadden, lhp, Kingstree (S.C.) HS.
32. *Mike Rantz, ss, Moundsview Heights HS, St. Paul, Minn.
33. *Edward Kolo, c, St. Mark's Seminary, Auburn, N.Y.
34. *Jack Thompson, of, Washington State University.
DRAFT DROP *First-round draft pick, Cincinnati Bengals/National Football League (1979); quarterback, NFL (1979-84).*

**June—Secondary Phase (15)**

**1. Carlos Diaz, lhp, Allan Hancock (Calif.) JC.—(1982-86)**
2. Jeff Stottlemyre, rhp, Yakima Valley (Wash.) JC.
DRAFT DROP *Brother of Mel Stottlemyre, major leaguer (1964-74)*

## TEXAS RANGERS

**January—Regular Phase (18)**

1. *Clay Weisinger, rhp, Angelina (Texas) JC.—DNP
2. Keith Showell, of, Prince George's (Md.) CC.
3. *Larry Mikesell, lhp, Brevard (Fla.) CC.
4. *Michael Young, rhp, Trinidad State (Colo.) JC.
5. David Orzel, lhp, Macomb (Mich.) CC.
6. *James Good, of, JC of Southern Idaho.
7. *Lee Cline, rhp, JC of Southern Idaho.
8. *Perry Kilgo, rhp, McLennan (Texas) CC.
9. *Michael Williams, c, Hill (Texas) JC.
10. *Oscar Cardenas, ss, Hill (Texas) JC.
11. *Randy Jones, of, Wenatchee Valley (Wash.) CC.

**January—Secondary Phase (6)**

1. *Arbrey Lucas, rhp, Arizona Western JC.—(AA)
2. Jerry Vasquez, rhp, Arizona State University.
3. Doyle Wilson, ss, Rome, Ga.

**June—Regular Phase (17)**

**1. Jerry Don Gleaton, lhp, University of Texas.—(1979-92)**
DRAFT DROP *First player from 1979 draft to reach majors (July 11, 1979)*
**2. Donnie Scott, c, Tampa Catholic HS, Tampa.—(1983-91)**
**3. Nick Capra, 2b, University of Oklahoma.—(1982-91)**
4. Larry Reynolds, ss, Stanford University.—(AA)
DRAFT DROP *Brother of Don Reynolds, major leaguer (1978-79) • Brother of Harold Reynolds, major leaguer (1983-94); sixth-round draft pick, Padres (1979)*
5. Mark Gammage, rhp, Osborn HS, Detroit.—(Low A)
6. Shelton McMath, of, Texas A&M University.
7. Larry D'Onofrio, c, College of St. Francis (Ill.).
8. Michael Roberts, rhp, Baylor University.
9. *Jeff Johnson, rhp, Muir HS, Pasadena, Calif.
10. William Goodman, 2b, George Washington University.
11. Mel Gilliam, lhp, Florida A&M University.
**12. Tony Fossas, lhp, University of South Florida.—(1988-99)**
13. Bobby Ball, of, Cal State Dominguez Hills.
14. Mike Behudian, 2b-of, Fairfield University.
**15. Pete O'Brien, 1b, University of Nebraska.—(1982-93)**
16. James Hager, rhp, Newberry (S.C.) College.
17. *Steve Brigante, 2b, Lubbock Christian (Texas) College.
18. *Joe Kucharski, rhp, Surrattsville HS, Clinton, Md.
DRAFT DROP *First-round draft pick (24th overall), Orioles (1982)*
19. *Larry Hamilton, of, Morehead State University.
20. *James Hawkins, c, Herndon HS, Reston, Va.
21. *Homer Moncrief, rhp, Jackson State University.
22. *Steven Davis, of, Middle Georgia JC.
23. James Schaefer, of, Southwest Missouri State University.
24. *Andy Ortiz, lhp, Roselle Catholic HS, Roselle, N.J.
25. Elwood Zebley, c, Towson State University.
**26. Dave Schmidt, rhp, UCLA.—(1981-92)**
27. Stanley Baker, ss, Dallas Baptist University.
28. Jorge Gomez, ss, Macomb (Mich.) CC.
29. Charles Stafford, of, Dallas Baptist University.
**30. Jay Pettibone, rhp, Chapman (Calif.) College.—(1983)**
31. *Daryl Frazier, rhp, Midwestern State (Texas) University.
32. Gordon Ricossa, lhp, Southern Methodist University.
33. *Joe Dellasega, 1b, Colgan HS, Pittsburg, Kan.
**34. Ray Fontenot, lhp, McNeese State University.—(1983-86)**
35. Rodger Bastien, ss, Michigan State University.
36. *Mitch Ashmore, c, Centenary College.
37. *Thomas Smith, rhp, University of Minnesota.
38. Stephen Romey, 1b-3b, Kent State University.

**June—Secondary Phase (23)**

1. *Michael Sanford, rhp, DeKalb South (Ga.) CC.—DNP
2. *Joe McCarthy, of, Seminole (Fla.) CC.
3. *Jerome Burgess, 1b, Delray Beach, Fla.

## TORONTO BLUE JAYS

**January—Regular Phase (4)**

1. *Scott Patterson, rhp, Valencia (Fla.) CC.—DNP
**2. Mark Eichhorn, ss-rhp, Cabrillo (Calif.) JC.—(1982-96)**
3. *Stephen Roache, rhp, Sacramento (Calif.) CC.
4. *Craig Charron, ss, Merced (Calif.) JC.
**5. *Jeff Moronko, 3b, San Jacinto (Texas) JC.—(1984-87)**
6. *Randy Brown, rhp, San Jacinto (Texas) JC.

**January—Secondary Phase (2)**

1. *Nattie George, of, San Jose (Calif.) CC.—(Low A)

**June—Regular Phase (3)**

1. Jay Schroeder, c, Palisades HS, Pacific Palisades, Calif.—(High A)
DRAFT DROP *Quarterback, National Football League (1985-94)*
**2. Ron Shepherd, of, Kilgore (Texas) HS.—(1984-86)**
**3. *Ron Romanick, rhp, Newport HS, Bellevue, Wash.—(1984-86)**
DRAFT DROP *Attended Arizona State; re-drafted by Padres, June 1980/secondary phase (1st round)*
**4. Andre Robertson, 2b, University of Texas.—(1981-85)**
5. Keith Walker, lhp-of, University of Texas.–(AAA)
6. Robert Tackitt, rhp, Mount Diablo HS, Concord, Calif.
7. John Seiber, rhp, Sweet Home (Ore.) HS.
8. Mark Liber, lhp, Pepperdine University.
9. Mark Holton, rhp, Elizabeth Forward HS, Buena Vista, Pa.
10. *Matt Ford, rhp, Bossier City (La.) HS.
11. Randy Ford, lhp, Western Michigan University.
12. Vern Ramie, 1b, University of Hawaii.
13. Brian Stemberger, 3b, Eastern Michigan University.
14. Paul White, of, North Carolina State University.
15. *Tim Cassell, rhp, El Cerrito HS, Pinole, Calif.
16. *Jack McMahon, rhp, Cal State Dominguez Hills.
DRAFT DROP *Son of Don McMahon, major leaguer (1957-74)*
**17. *Jeff M. Robinson, rhp, Troy HS, Yorba Linda, Calif.—(1987-92)**
18. Jeff Vail, 1b-rhp, St. Xavier (Ill.) College.
19. Phillip Turner, 1b, Mott (Mich.) CC.
20. Lee Wetenkamp, 3b, University of Wisconsin.

**June—Secondary Phase (13)**

1. Kem Wright, rhp, University of Texas.—(AA)
2. *Darren Dilks, lhp, Chaffey (Calif.) JC.
DRAFT DROP *First-round draft pick (18th overall), Expos (1981)*

# 1980

## AT A GLANCE

### This Date In History
**WINTER DRAFT:** Jan. 11
**SUMMER DRAFT:** June 3-5

### Best Draft
**CINCINNATI REDS.** The demise of the Big Red Machine came about largely because of a succession of first-round failures and unproductive drafts in the 1970s, but the Reds turned the page to the 1980s by selecting **RON ROBINSON** (1), **DANNY TARTABULL** (3), **ERIC DAVIS** (8) and **SCOTT TERRY** (12).

### Worst Draft
**TORONTO BLUE JAYS.** The Jays had winning seasons in the majors every year from 1983-93, despite being blanked in the 1980 draft. Among 34 players they selected in January and June, they didn't sign a single future big leaguer. **GARRY HARRIS**, the second overall pick in the June regular phase, didn't even advance beyond Double-A.

### First-Round Bust
**LEBO POWELL, C, PHILLIES.** Powell evoked a wide range of opinion among Phillies scouts on his worth as a prospect before he was drafted, and gave his detractors plenty of ammunition in a career that fell far short of expectations. He hit .231 with 18 homers in three seasons in the system, while committing 37 errors and 44 passed balls. But he was sent packing because of off-field indiscretions, including involvement with drugs.

### Second Best
**TIM TEUFEL, 2B, TWINS.** Teufel became a second-rounder after setting Cape Cod League records for home run (16) and RBIs (52) in the summer of 1979, and hitting .396-10-63 as a Clemson All-American in 1980; he became a big leaguer on the strength of a .323-27-100 season in the Triple-A International League in 1983. In 11 seasons in the majors, Teufel hit .254-86-379 playing for three teams.

# Mets begin revival by hitting on Strawberry

It was 1980. The New York Mets had hit the skids.

For three straight years, the Mets finished dead last in the National League East. Three years later, they would complete an unenviable streak of five last-place finishes in seven years.

But a reawakening began in 1980, in the midst of all their misery, when the Mets began drafting a succession of top players who formed the cornerstone of what would become baseball's model franchise, a budding dynasty. The 1986 World Series triumph was testament to their rising fortune.

Beginning with the June 1980 draft, the Mets drafted 69 players over the next six years who reached the big leagues, including a record 17 in 1982. No team came close to matching that total during the period. Not in quality, not in quantity.

It all began with the first pick in 1980 when the Mets, in their first year under new ownership, went for a strapping high school outfielder from Los Angeles. Darryl Strawberry's talent was obvious from the start.

"He's the best prospect I've seen in the last 30 years," veteran Philadelphia Phillies scout Hugh Alexander said.

By taking Strawberry with the top pick and signing him to a $152,500 bonus, the Mets gained the distinction of drafting the only player in draft history who was picked first, received the largest bonus and posted the highest WAR (Wins Above Replacement) rating in his draft class.

Strawberry was also the first high school player in the 1980 draft to reach the majors, and his arrival in New York in 1983 was not only met with great fanfare but marked a dramatic turnaround in the Mets' fortunes—especially with other talented players like Dwight Gooden in the pipeline.

From 1983-90, the 6-foot-6 Strawberry was one of the most electrifying players in the game. He was a feared slugger, known for his intimidating presence in the batter's box, his long, looping swing and prodigious home runs. In his eight seasons with the Mets, he drilled a club-record 252 homers, drove in 733 runs and stole 191 bases. In 1987, his best season, he went deep 39 times while stealing 36 bases.

But Strawberry's time also featured controversy and turbulence, and his 17-year career ultimately fell far short of the Hall of Fame trajectory once projected for him.

The Mets had two other first-round picks in the 1980 draft, and four of the first 28 selections. It was a golden opportunity to begin catching up to their competition, though the careers of outfielder Billy Beane (23rd overall) and catcher John Gibbons (24th) never panned out as hoped. Beane and Gibbons gained more notoriety in the game once they retired.

Beane became the general manager of the

ASSOCIATED PRESS

Crenshaw High's Darryl Strawberry headed up an exceptional group of players in Southern California in the 1980 draft and was the No. 1 overall pick by the Mets, leading that franchise's resurgence

Oakland A's and the focal point of a best-selling book and movie, Moneyball, which chronicled his club's use of analytics. Gibbons went on to serve two stints as manager of the Toronto Blue Jays.

Oddly, in a five-pick stretch late in the first round, Beane, Gibbons and two other future big league managers, Rich Renteria (Pirates, 20th) and Terry Francona (Expos, 22nd), were selected. John Farrell (A's, ninth round), Lloyd McClendon (Mets, eighth round), Dave Miley (Reds, second round) and Bryan Price (Twins, 21st round) were picked in later rounds, making it the greatest collection of future managers in one draft. During the 2014 season, six 1980 draft picks were piloting big league clubs.

The Mets had reason to exult by selecting a draft-high 10 players who would play in the big leagues, as well as signing a future National League MVP in Kevin Mitchell, an overlooked California high school player, as a free agent. But the crosstown Yankees had cause for despair.

The Yankees had the worst draft in their history. Among 54 selections in January and June, only three players were signed who reached the big leagues—each of whom played just a single year. They forfeited their first two picks in June for signing free agents Rudy May and Bob Watson, and didn't sign four of their next six picks, including Louisiana prep star Billy Cannon. His selection,

## 1980: THE FIRST ROUNDERS

| CLUB: PLAYER, POS., SCHOOL | HOMETOWN | B-T | HT. | WT. | AGE | BONUS | FIRST YEAR | LAST YEAR | PEAK LEVEL (YEARS) |
|---|---|---|---|---|---|---|---|---|---|
| **JUNE—REGULAR PHASE** | | | | | | | | | |
| **1. Mets: Darryl Strawberry, of, Crenshaw HS** | **Los Angeles** | **L-L** | **6-6** | **180** | **18** | **$152,500** | **1980** | **1999** | **Majors (17)** |
| Consensus No. 1 pick became one of most feared sluggers in game, with 335 HRs, 1,000 RBIs, yet also known for drug addiction that short-circuited his stardom. | | | | | | | | | |
| **2. Blue Jays: Garry Harris, ss, Herbert Hoover HS** | **San Diego** | **R-R** | **5-9** | **165** | **17** | **$58,000** | **1980** | **1983** | **Class AA (1)** |
| Athletic SS with power/speed had difficult time adapting to pace of pro game; hit .244-32-177 and played his way off short with 62 errors in 74 games. | | | | | | | | | |
| **3. Braves: Ken Dayley, lhp, Portland** | **The Dalles, Ore.** | **L-L** | **6-0** | **180** | **21** | **$90,500** | **1980** | **1993** | **Majors (11)** |
| Went 8-2, 1.58, led NCAA in strikeout ratio (85 IP/138 SO) as college junior; went 33-45, 3.64 with 39 SV as starter/reliever in unremarkable major league career. | | | | | | | | | |
| **4. Athletics: Mike King, lhp, Morningside (Iowa) College** | **Sioux City, Iowa** | **L-L** | **6-1** | **180** | **21** | **$35,000** | **1980** | **1984** | **Class AAA (2)** |
| Spectacular Division II college success (seven no-hitters, 0.48 ERA; 174 IP/49 H/304 SO in career), did not translate; struggled to throw strikes in pros, blew out arm. | | | | | | | | | |
| **5. Padres: Jeff Pyburn, of, Georgia** | **Athens, Ga.** | **R-R** | **6-2** | **205** | **22** | **$103,500** | **1980** | **1982** | **Class AAA (1)** |
| Ex-Georgia QB had breakout year with school record 15 HRs, 66 RBIs; chose baseball over NFL, hit .295-12-136 in three seasons in minors and didn't show power. | | | | | | | | | |
| **6. Mariners: Darnell Coles, ss, Dwight D. Eisenhower HS** | **Rialto, Calif.** | **R-R** | **6-1** | **180** | **18** | **$82,500** | **1980** | **1992** | **Majors (14)** |
| UCLA wide receiver recruit hit .513 as prep SR, might have been No. 1 pick if didn't hurt knee; played 14 years in majors, hit .245-75-368, twice hit 3 HRs in game. | | | | | | | | | |
| **7. Giants: Jessie Reid, 1b, Lynwood HS** | **Lynwood, Calif.** | **L-L** | **6-0** | **202** | **18** | **$75,000** | **1980** | **1989** | **Majors (2)** |
| Career .500-plus bat in HS, hit Pioneer League-best .366 in MVP season as first-year-pro, .268-111-614 in 10 years in minors, just 10 ABs in major leagues. | | | | | | | | | |
| **8. White Sox: Cecil Espy, of, Point Loma HS** | **San Diego** | **B-R** | **6-3** | **185** | **17** | **$65,000** | **1980** | **1994** | **Majors (8)** |
| Left mark on majors with speed, defense, switch-hitting ability; hit .244-7-108 with 103 SBs playing for four teams; stole 358 bags in long career in minors. | | | | | | | | | |
| **9. Dodgers: Ross Jones, ss, Miami** | **Hialeah, Fla.** | **R-R** | **6-2** | **185** | **20** | **$61,000** | **1980** | **1988** | **Majors (3)** |
| Led Hialeah to Legion title in 1978, won Cape Cod batting title (.413) in 1979, hit .329-4-51 as Miami junior in 1980, spent three years in majors (none in L.A.). | | | | | | | | | |
| **10. Indians: Kelly Gruber, ss, Westlake HS** | **Austin, Texas** | **R-R** | **6-0** | **175** | **18** | **$80,000** | **1980** | **1997** | **Majors (10)** |
| Multi-sport high school star signed to play football at Texas; career took off after Toronto made him Rule 5 pick; hit .259-117-445 before back injury ended career. | | | | | | | | | |
| **11. Cubs: Don Schulze, rhp, Lake Park HS** | **Roselle, Ill.** | **R-R** | **6-3** | **205** | **17** | **$62,500** | **1980** | **1993** | **Majors (6)** |
| Grew up Cubs fan, debuted in Chicago at 20; went 15-25, 5.47 overall for five teams; sued Famous Chicken for $2 million after separating his shoulder in collision. | | | | | | | | | |
| **12. Twins: Jeff Reed, c, Joliet West HS** | **Joliet, Ill.** | **L-R** | **6-1** | **183** | **18** | **$60,000** | **1980** | **2001** | **Majors (17)** |
| Solid defender spent 17 seasons in majors with six clubs, mostly as backup, hit .250-61-323; began at Rookie-level Elizabethton, where he has coached since 2002. | | | | | | | | | |
| **13. Phillies: Lebo Powell, c, Pine Forest HS** | **Pensacola, Fla.** | **R-R** | **5-11** | **215** | **18** | **$55,000** | **1980** | **1982** | **Class A (2)** |
| Had size, power, arm strength to be big league catcher, but hampered by off-field issues, cut loose after three seasons; hit .231-18-87, struggled defensively. | | | | | | | | | |
| **14. Rangers: Tim Maki, rhp, Carroll HS** | **Huntertown, Ind.** | **R-R** | **6-2** | **210** | **18** | **$50,000** | **1980** | **1984** | **Class A (4)** |
| Former catcher became pitcher in HS, spun consecutive no-hitters; struggled to throw strikes in five seasons in minors, went 9-26, 5.42 overall (302 IP/203 BB). | | | | | | | | | |
| **15. Cardinals: Don Collins, rhp, Ferguson HS** | **Newport News, Va.** | **R-R** | **6-2** | **190** | **17** | **$50,000** | **1980** | **1983** | **Class A (4)** |
| Left unprotected after three years in Cards system because of elbow issues, taken by Brewers in Rule 5 draft; 1983 elbow surgery ended career, went 28-20, 3.71. | | | | | | | | | |
| **16. Royals: # Frank Wills, rhp, Tulane** | **New Orleans** | **R-R** | **6-2** | **200** | **21** | **$75,000** | **1980** | **1991** | **Majors (9)** |
| Punter, All-American pitcher at Tulane (5-3, 2.81, 64 IP/75 SO); hard thrower plagued by wildness early in career, went 22-26, 5.08 in nine years in majors. | | | | | | | | | |
| **17. Angels: Dennis Rasmussen, lhp, Creighton** | **Lakewood, Colo.** | **L-L** | **6-6** | **200** | **21** | **$57,500** | **1980** | **1995** | **Majors (12)** |
| Also played basketball at Creighton; overcame suspect mechanics that got him traded twice before winning his first game in majors, to post 91-77, 4.15 record. | | | | | | | | | |
| **18. Tigers: Glenn Wilson, 3b, Sam Houston State** | **Channelview, Texas** | **R-R** | **6-1** | **195** | **21** | **$62,500** | **1980** | **1993** | **Majors (10)** |
| Hit .439-11-58 as college JR, began pro career as 3B, became strong-armed OF; traded by Tigers for Willie Hernandez (AL MVP) prior to '84 season. | | | | | | | | | |
| **19. Reds: Ron Robinson, rhp/ss, Woodlake HS** | **Woodlake, Calif.** | **R-R** | **6-4** | **200** | **18** | **$92,500** | **1980** | **1992** | **Majors (9)** |
| Spun national record three perfect games as prep SR, came within out of another with Reds in 1988; plagued by elbow problems in majors; went 48-39, 3.63. | | | | | | | | | |
| **20. Pirates: Rich Renteria, ss, South Gate HS** | **South Gate, Calif.** | **R-R** | **5-9** | **180** | **18** | **$40,000** | **1980** | **1994** | **Majors (5)** |
| Batted .331 to lead Carolina League in 1982, .442 to lead Mexican League in 1991; hit .237-4-41 with three clubs in five seasons; stint as Cubs manager in 2014. | | | | | | | | | |
| **21. Braves: Jim Acker, rhp, Texas** | **Freer, Texas** | **R-R** | **6-2** | **215** | **21** | **$65,000** | **1980** | **1993** | **Majors (10)** |
| Rode Atlanta-to-Toronto shuttle most of 10-year career in majors, with two stints in each organization; posted overall 33-49, 3.97 record with 30 saves. | | | | | | | | | |
| **22. Expos: Terry Francona, of, Arizona** | **New Brighton, Pa.** | **L-L** | **6-2** | **190** | **21** | **$80,000** | **1980** | **1990** | **Majors (10)** |
| Son of Tito, 15-year big leaguer; decorated college career at Arizona, managerial career with three teams in majors; playing career compromised by knee injuries. | | | | | | | | | |
| **23. Mets: Billy Beane, of, Mount Carmel HS** | **Rancho Bernardo, Calif.** | **R-R** | **6-3** | **185** | **18** | **$125,000** | **1980** | **1989** | **Majors (6)** |
| Promising playing career never came together; hit just .219-3-29 in six big league seasons; blossomed as front-office exec with A's, became face of Moneyball. | | | | | | | | | |
| **24. Mets: John Gibbons, c, MacArthur HS** | **San Antonio** | **R-R** | **5-11** | **190** | **17** | **$55,000** | **1980** | **1990** | **Majors (2)** |
| Played 18 games in majors with Mets, had lengthy career as minor league catcher (.253-89-454 over 11 years), before becoming big league coach/manager. | | | | | | | | | |
| **25. Brewers: Dion James, of, McClatchy HS** | **Sacramento, Calif.** | **L-L** | **6-1** | **170** | **17** | **$50,000** | **1980** | **1996** | **Majors (11)** |
| Hit .300-plus all way up line before debuting with Brewers in 1983; played 11 years in majors with four clubs on strength of bat, speed, defense, hit .288-32-266. | | | | | | | | | |
| **26. Orioles: # Jeff Williams, of, Princeton HS** | **Cincinnati** | **L-L** | **6-1** | **175** | **17** | **$32,500** | **1980** | **1989** | **Class AAA (1)** |
| Hit .346 in Appy League in first season, but no higher than .268 over next seven seasons in minors with five organizations; died in motorcycle accident in 2006. | | | | | | | | | |
| **JANUARY—REGULAR PHASE** | | | | | | | | | |
| **1. Blue Jays: Colin McLaughlin, rhp, Connecticut** | **Woodbury, Conn.** | **R-R** | **6-5** | **210** | **20** | **$50,000** | **1980** | **1989** | **Class AAA (8)** |
| Dropped out of UConn after going 12-2, 2.30 as freshman, leading team to CWS; pitched nine years in minors with Blue Jays, went 50-56, 4.54 with 30 SV. | | | | | | | | | |
| **JANUARY—SECONDARY PHASE** | | | | | | | | | |
| **1. Red Sox: Juan Bustabad, ss, Miami-Dade CC North** | **Hialeah, Fla.** | **B-R** | **5-11** | **150** | **19** | **$50,000** | **1980** | **1989** | **Class AAA (4)** |
| Rejected A's $25,000 offer as fifth pick in 1979 draft, earned double from Red Sox; hit .247 with 6 HRs in nine seasons in minors, became longtime manager/coach. | | | | | | | | | |
| **JUNE—SECONDARY PHASE** | | | | | | | | | |
| **1. Astros: Jeff Heathcock, rhp, Oral Roberts** | **Westminster, Calif.** | **R-R** | **6-4** | **190** | **20** | **$42,000** | **1980** | **1990** | **Majors (4)** |
| Went 10-4, 2.43 for ORU in dominant 1-2 pitching punch with Mike Moore (top pick in '81 draft); made 56 appearances for Astros from 1983-88, went 9-9, 3.76. | | | | | | | | | |

*# Deceased.*

## AT A GLANCE

### Late-Round Find

**DARREN DAULTON, C, PHILLIES (25TH ROUND).** The Phillies made a costly error by taking the underachieving Powell with their first pick, but more than made up for it 24 picks later by selecting Daulton. The Kansas high school product went on to play 14 years in the majors with the Phils; in his best season in 1982, he hit .270 with 27 homers and a National League-leading 109 RBIs.

### Never Too Late

**JEFF ROBINSON, RHP, PADRES (40TH ROUND).** The 6-foot-6 Robinson wasn't ready to sign as a 40th-round pick out of a California high school in 1980, but was more than ready as a third-round selection of the Tigers three years later out of Azusa Pacific University. He pitched six seasons in the majors, winning 47 games.

### Overlooked

**TOM CANDIOTTI, RHP, ROYALS.** Candiotti won 151 games over 17 seasons in the big leagues, utilizing mostly a knuckleball, but his story is more about the drive and determination it took for him to even get there. He rewrote the St. Mary's (Calif.) record book, but hurt his arm and wasn't drafted as a fifth-year senior in 1979. Candiotti hooked on with the independent Victoria Mussels of the short-season Northwest League and pitched well enough for his contract to be purchased in 1980 by the Royals. The Brewers claimed him in the Rule 5 draft, and he reached the majors with them in 1983.

### International Gem

**JOSE RIJO, RHP, YANKEES.** Rijo signed out of the Dominican Republic at age 16 for $3,000. He went 2-8, 4.76 in his one big league season in New York before spending the balance of a 14-year career with the A's and Reds. Overall, he com-

CONTINUED ON PAGE 232

## AT A GLANCE

CONTINUED FROM PAGE 231

piled a 116-91, 3.24 record, though he lost five years to an arm injury at the height of his career.

### Minor League Take

**JESSIE REID, OF, GIANTS.** Reid got just 10 major league at-bats in a 14-year professional career, including the first nine in the Giants organizations and the last four in Japan and Mexico. During his extended tour in the minors, Reid had more homers (111) and RBIs (614) than any 1980 first-rounder.

### One Who Got Away

**BILLY CANNON, SS, YANKEES (3RD ROUND).** Cannon never played professional baseball after the commissioner's office ruled that the Yankees and Cannon family conspired to mislead other clubs about Cannon's signing intentions. His rights went to the Indians, who could not sign him.

### He Was Drafted?

**RONNIE PERRY, SS, WHITE SOX (3RD ROUND).** Perry was a record-setting guard in basketball in high school and at Holy Cross, and an outstanding shortstop. He was drafted in the third round of both the NBA and baseball drafts in 1980, and played two seasons at Double-A in the White Sox system after he failed to crack the Boston Celtics roster.

### Did You Know . . .

The Blue Jays didn't draft a single big leaguer in either June phase of the draft, but five first-round picks signed by other clubs in 1980 eventually played in Toronto.

### They Said It

San Diego's Hoover High coach **BOB WARNER** on shortstop **GARRY HARRIS**, the second overall pick in the 1980 draft: "I'll bet my wife and children that he'll make it to Toronto."—*Harris never did, peaking in Double-A.*

with their top pick (third round), generated complaints from several clubs that they were duped into believing Cannon was unsignable.

Commissioner Bowie Kuhn ruled that the Yankees had conspired with Cannon and his family to persuade other teams to pass on him. He voided the pick and held a special lottery for Cannon's services, where every team but the Yankees could bid on Cannon's rights. At the cost of a third-round pick in the 1981 draft, the Cleveland Indians acquired Cannon's rights, but were unable to sign him.

Cannon's selection by the Yankees was one of the most controversial in draft history, and while it didn't work out, it also did not dissuade Steinbrenner and his club from gambling premium picks on high-risk football players in future drafts.

In 1981, the Yankees went for Stanford quarterback John Elway. After a three-month courtship, he agreed to play six weeks in the Yankees farm system in 1982 but abandoned baseball when he was picked first overall in the 1983 NFL draft.

Alabama prep running back Bo Jackson was targeted by the Yankees in 1982, but he resisted their overtures and chose to play football at Auburn. He won the 1985 Heisman Trophy and became the No. 1 pick in the 1986 NFL draft, before unexpectedly signing with the Kansas City Royals.

### CALIFORNIA DREAMIN'

The 1980 draft featured a preponderance of high school players from Southern California. Five of the first eight picks were from the region, and it was noteworthy that all were African-Americans at a time when more black players were in the big leagues than at any point in the game's history. That number peaked in 1981, when 18.7 percent of all major leaguers were African-American.

With the No. 1 choice, the Mets narrowed their decision to four Southern California products, and ultimately to two: Crenshaw High's Strawberry and Darnell Coles, a prep All-America wide receiver from Eisenhower High in Rialto who had signed to play football at UCLA.

Darnell Coles

Strawberry led Crenshaw to the L.A. city basketball championship as a senior, so was late reporting for baseball. But in 14 games that spring, he hit .400 with six homers and stole eight bases. He also went 1-1 with three saves in limited action as a pitcher. Coles hit .513. The Mets settled on Strawberry, in part because Coles injured his knee the previous fall playing football and required surgery. He went five picks later to the Seattle Mariners.

"He is just a pure hitter with major league power," said Mets area scout Roger Jongewaard, who threw his support behind Strawberry. "He has good instincts for his age, runs like a deer and his arm is better than adequate."

Strawberry held out for five weeks, baiting the Mets with a combined baseball/basketball offer from Oklahoma State.

## How They Should Have Done It

Based on the career WAR (Wins Above Replacement, as calculated by Baseball-Reference.com) numbers achieved by all the players eligible for the 1980 draft, here's how the first round should have unfolded. Numbers in parentheses indicate the round when the player was actually drafted

| | Player, Pos. | Actual Draft | WAR | Bonus |
|---|---|---|---|---|
| 1. | Darryl Strawberry, of | Mets (1) | 42.0 | $152,500 |
| 2. | Tom Candiotti, rhp | Royals (NDFA) | 41.5 | None |
| 3. | Eric Davis, ss | Reds (8) | 35.9 | $18,000 |
| 4. | Kevin Mitchell, of | Mets (NDFA) | 29.0 | $2,500 |
| 5. | Tom Henke, rhp | Rangers (June-S/4) | 23.5 | $5,000 |
| 6. | Danny Tartabull, ss | Reds (3) | 23.1 | $30,000 |
| 7. | Darren Daulton, c | Phillies (25) | 22.8 | $10,000 |
| 8. | Don Slaught, c | Royals (7) | 19.4 | $8,000 |
| 9. | Mark Portugal, rhp | Twins (NDFA) | 18.1 | None |
| 10. | Oil Can Boyd, rhp | Red Sox (16) | 17.7 | $8,000 |
| 11. | Kelly Gruber, ss | Indians (1) | 16.5 | $80,000 |
| 12. | Harold Reynolds, 2b | Mariners (June-S/1) | 15.8 | $30,000 |
| 13. | Tim Teufel, 2b | Twins (2) | 15.3 | $15,000 |
| 14. | Jim Eisenreich, of | Twins (16) | 13.4 | $2,000 |
| 15. | Glenn Wilson, 3b | Tigers (1) | 12.9 | $62,500 |
| 16. | Tim Burke, rhp | Pirates (2) | 12.4 | $35,000 |
| 17. | Dennis Rasmussen, lhp | Angels (1) | 11.4 | $57,500 |
| 18. | Randy Ready, 3b | Brewers (6) | 10.9 | $11,000 |
| 19. | Walt Terrell, rhp | Rangers (33) | 10.8 | $3,000 |
| 20. | Tom Niedenfuer, rhp | Dodgers (NDFA) | 10.6 | $25,000 |
| 21. | Craig Lefferts, lhp | Cubs (9) | 9.3 | $7,500 |
| 22. | Joe Hesketh, lhp | Expos (2) | 8.7 | $35,000 |
| 23. | Ron Robinson, rhp | Reds (1) | 8.2 | $92,500 |
| 24. | Matt Young, lhp | Mariners (2) | 7.6 | $35,000 |
| 25. | Ed Vande Berg, lhp | Mariners (13) | 7.0 | $1,000 |
| 26. | Tim Hulett, 2b | White Sox (Jan.-S/3) | 6.7 | $52,500 |

| Top 3 Unsigned Players | | | | Year Signed |
|---|---|---|---|---|
| 1. | Doug Drabek, rhp | Indians (4) | 29.8 | 1983 |
| 2. | Terry Steinbach, 3b | Indians (16) | 24.3 | 1983 |
| 3. | Rick Aguilera, rhp | Cardinals (37) | 22.4 | 1983 |

The Blue Jays had the second pick, and every one of their top-level talent sleuths, including general manager Pat Gillick, fingered Garry Harris as the best available talent.

"He was the pick of the country as far as I was concerned," said Jays crosschecker Bob Zuk. "I saw him play four games this season, and I think he should have been the first pick. He is a very good-looking prospect, a shortstop who hits for average and will steal some bases."

Harris hit .426 with two homers and was successful on all 16 stolen-base attempts for San Diego's Hoover High, Ted Williams' alma mater, but never came close to fulfilling his potential with the Blue Jays. In his first 76 games as a pro, Harris committed 62 errors at shortstop and soon shifted to second base. His career peaked in Double-A, where he hit .224 with five stolen bases in 1983, his final season.

In addition to Strawberry, Harris and Coles, first baseman Jessie Reid (Giants, seventh overall) and outfielder Cecil Espy (White Sox, eighth) were the other Southern Californians who went in the top eight selections. Both reached the majors briefly, but spent the bulk of their careers in the minors.

Four more California high school products, including Beane, went in the back half of the first round. Beane was in the running to go No. 1, but scared off the Mets and other clubs because of a college commitment to Stanford. The $125,000 signing bonus he received from the Mets was second only to Strawberry's.

"There are more blue-chippers in this draft than we've had for the past few years," Seattle farm director Hal Keller said on the eve of the draft. "There are more good pitchers overall than I've seen in quite a while."

That view proved to be a little optimistic as the 1980 draft fell short of expectations overall, and few of the top pitching prospects panned out.

Nineteen of 26 first-rounders played in the big leagues, just like in 1979, and once again much of the best talent came from the most unlikely of sources. Three of the most productive players signed in 1980 were nondrafted free agents—righthanders Tom Candiotti and Mark Portugal, along with Mitchell—and they had more productive careers than every first-rounder but Strawberry.

Mitchell, a high school dropout, signed with the Mets for a bonus of $2,500 on Nov. 16, 1980. He had been a gang member and survived multiple gunshot wounds as a teenager in San Diego, but found baseball as an outlet. He went on to become a two-time all-star and the 1989 National League MVP while playing for the San Francisco Giants, but was known for his unpredictable and sometimes volatile behavior off the field as well as his brilliance on it. Over a 13-year career in the majors from 1983-98, Mitchell played for eight clubs, batting .284 with 234 homers overall.

One of the overlooked players was Eric Davis, a close childhood friend of Strawberry's who also excelled in baseball and basketball at rival Fremont High. Even as Southern California was teeming with scouts in 1980, Davis didn't attract anywhere near the attention Strawberry received, and he slipped through to the eighth round, where he was selected by the Cincinnati Reds. To Reds scout Larry Barton Jr., who signed Davis for $18,000, the apparent snub was a case of exposure.

"The school he came from, Fremont, was basically down in the ghetto," Barton said. "There wasn't so many white people who would go in there. There wasn't so many scouts."

Davis, then a skinny shortstop with a pronounced hitch in his swing, was worked out by only four major league organizations: the Reds, Dodgers, Angels and Brewers. Almost everyone believed his focus was basketball, not baseball. To Chief Bender, the Reds farm director who watched Davis hit .219 as an error-prone shortstop in his

## Fastest To The Majors

| | Player, Pos. | Drafted (Round) | Debut |
|---|---|---|---|
| 1. | Rich Bordi, lhp | Athletics (3) | July 16, 1980 |
| 2. | Terry Francona, of | Expos (1) | Aug. 19, 1981 |
| 3. | Dan Firova, c | Mariners (Jan.-S/2) | Sept. 1, 1981 |
| 4. | Tom Gorman, lhp | Expos (4) | Sept. 2, 1981 |
| 5. | Jim Eisenreich, of | Twins (16) | April 6, 1982 |

**FIRST HIGH SCHOOL SELECTION:** Darryl Strawberry, of (Mets/1, May 6, 1983)

**LAST PLAYER TO RETIRE:** Eric Davis, of (Oct. 7, 2001)

## DRAFT SPOTLIGHT: BILLY CANNON

Baseball was making a concerted attempt in the late 1970s and early 1980s to beat other sports in their pursuit of multi-sport athletes.

MLB quashed Billy Cannon's predraft arrangement with the Yankees, the Indians failed to sign him, and he never played professional baseball

But the Yankees, emboldened by their success in attracting major league free agents to New York, tried to pull a fast one on the other clubs in 1980 with their solicitation of Billy Cannon Jr., son of the 1959 Heisman Trophy winner. As a player with an intriguing two-sport background, Cannon was the kind of player Yankees owner George Steinbrenner coveted.

But by forfeiting their picks in the first two rounds in that year's draft, the Yankees were obvious longshots in the Cannon sweepstakes. Almost every other club viewed him as a first-round talent, so he was sure to be gone by the time the Yankees made their first selection.

Shortly before the draft, however, Cannon's father advised all clubs that his son intended to go to college and indicated only an offer in excess of $250,000 would make him change his mind. Teams passed on Cannon through the first two rounds.

But the Yankees, who paid out a draft record $208,000 bonus to Todd Demeter a year earlier, weren't scared off. They went for Cannon, 18, and he was set to accept a huge bonus contract from Steinbrenner and begin a career that had been his lifelong dream.

"He feels about baseball like I felt about football," said Billy Sr., then a Baton Rouge, La., orthodontist. "Baseball's always had a way of crowding the other things out."

"I think he will sign with the Yankees. Mr. Steinbrenner doesn't mind paying his athletes. He said he thought Billy was one of the three or four best players in the country."

But Toronto, Boston and two other clubs protested the selection immediately, charging tampering. Commissioner Bowie Kuhn conducted two days of hearings and ruled the Yankees illegally obtained Cannon's rights, violating rules by negotiating prior to the draft.

"The commissioner has decided the New York Yankees selection of Billy Cannon Jr. should be set aside," the official statement said. "The commissioner is satisfied that the clubs were misled by a telegram sent by Cannon's father saying that Cannon would not play professional baseball and would go to college instead."

Kuhn advised Cannon that he would not be permitted to sign with New York. Not then, or ever. It was a blow to the Cannon family, especially Billy Jr., who was packed and ready to report to short-season Oneonta as soon as the paperwork was out of the way.

"I'm very disappointed for my son," the elder Cannon said, "because after going up there and looking at the stadium and meeting the players, envisioning himself in that role, it's very disappointing for a young man.

"The commissioner admitted that he had no concrete evidence. He accused me of not dealing fairly but the fact is, I didn't break any rules. I might have bent them a little for the best interests of my son, but if legally trying to look after a player's welfare is construed as tampering, then maybe they better come up with a better definition of the word."

Kuhn proposed a special lottery, which took place in mid-August. Every team but the Yankees could bid, and at the cost of a third-round pick in the 1981 draft, the Cleveland Indians acquired Cannon's rights. The Indians could not satisfy his bonus demands, and a short time later Cannon ended another battle for his services by committing to Texas A&M—much to the dismay of fans at Louisiana State, his father's alma mater. He played baseball (outfielder) and football (defensive back), but didn't excel in either sport.

As a senior at Texas A&M, Cannon devoted his energy to football and became the first-round pick of the Dallas Cowboys in the 1984 NFL draft. He played one season as a linebacker, but was forced to quit when he injured his neck in his rookie season. Doctors advised him that he risked permanent injury if he continued playing.

## WORTH NOTING

■ The January draft marked the first time where an element of secrecy prevailed over the selection of players. At the behest of the commissioner's office, only names of players selected in the first two rounds of the regular phase were made public immediately. Names of remaining players were withheld for seven days. At a time when free agency was driving up salaries, clubs looked for ways to curb rising bonuses to amateur free agents. One means was to control the information flow to agents and college coaches, who were using the draft list to identify and recruit top players. By keeping agents and colleges in the dark for one week, clubs were able to make first contact with their draft picks and have a negotiating advantage. Another reason for tightening the privacy was to police clubs that were failing to notify players that they had been drafted within 15 days of selection. Some clubs, trying to limit a player's ability to negotiate, waited until the 15th day. Others waited beyond the deadline. Under the new system, the commissioner's office was obligated to notify all drafted players by mailgram within 24 hours of their selection. Players were informed which team drafted them, in what round and what their rights were. The embargo stiffened in 1986 when the names of first-rounders only were released publicly. A week later, an alphabetical listing of players only, by clubs, was made available.

■ One of the elite athletes in the 1980 draft was Texas high school quarterback **TURNER GILL,** who was drafted in the second round by the White Sox. Gill elected not to sign, and went off on a six-year quarterback odyssey that took him to the University of Nebraska for four years and the Canadian Football League's Montreal Concorde for two more. The $1.2 million contract he signed with Montreal in 1984 was the highest ever given a CFL rookie. When one too many

LARRY KINKER

**Teams overlooked Eric Davis at the top of the 1980 draft, but once he moved to the outfield and matured physically, his career took off**

first season at short-season Eugene, the lack of attention was simple.

"He couldn't play," Bender said. "And he didn't show us he really wanted to play baseball. His first love was basketball, and I think he looked at baseball as something to do in the summer. You had to question the future of the guy."

Greg Riddoch, who managed Davis his first season in pro ball, didn't see much hope, either. "I felt so bad for Eric," Riddoch said. "Defensively, he wasn't getting any better. Actually, he was regressing. He had lost quite a bit of confidence."

However, a year of maturity and hard work, along with a move to center field transformed Davis into a top-flight prospect.

"When we put him out there, it was like he had been there 50 years," Riddoch said. "He could do things that other kids who had played in the outfield all their lives could not do. You could drive the ball over his head and he had the ability to look away and run directly to where the ball was going to come down and be there when it did. Most players have to watch the ball the whole way. That's an instinct nobody taught him."

A year after hitting .219 and showing almost no power, Davis blossomed into a .322 hitter with 11 homers and 40 steals in a return to Eugene. From there, his development rivaled Strawberry's. He reached the big leagues with the Reds in 1984, and by 1987 hit 37 homers, stole 50 bases and won the first of three Gold Gloves.

"I've never seen a player that good at this stage of his career," Reds manager Pete Rose said. "Never. He can beat you with his bat, his legs, his glove. Eric is the one guy who can lead our league in home runs and stolen bases. Name me another cleanup hitter who can steal 100 bases. It's like having an atomic bomb sitting next to you in the dugout."

When Davis signed the richest contract in baseball history late in 1989, he was one of the best all-around talents in the game.

Strawberry and Davis became teammates back home in Los Angeles, for the Dodgers from 1992-93, after Strawberry left the Mets and inked a five-year, $22.25 million contract with that club as a free agent following the 1990 season. Davis followed suit a year later after leaving the Reds.

Both players proved to be disappointments in the two years they played together, though, and never came close to achieving the results they did with their former teams.

### STRIKEOUT ARTISTS GO EARLY

While the focus was on position players early in the draft, the Atlanta Braves and A's, selecting third and fourth, went a different route. They grabbed a pair of lefthanded strikeout kings from somewhat obscure college programs.

The Braves went for Portland's Ken Dayley, who led NCAA Division I pitchers with 138 strikeouts in 85 innings, an average of 14.6 per nine innings, while posting an 8-2, 1.58 record.

"Dayley was our first choice all the way across the board, even if we had the first pick," Braves West Coast scouting supervisor Bill Wight said.

Dayley never cut it as a starter for the Braves, going just 10-17, 4.48 in two-plus seasons. He later found a comfort zone pitching in relief for the St. Louis Cardinals, and went 33-45, 3.64 with 39 saves overall in an 11-year career.

The A's selected Mike King from Iowa's obscure Morningside College. King dominated the NCAA Division II ranks by leading in ERA (0.46) and strikeouts per nine innings (15.8). In his career at Morningside, King was 18-8, 1.09, but more remarkably struck out 304 in 174 innings, allowed only 49 hits and tossed seven no-hitters.

Oakland was ambitious in starting King off in Triple-A, and he was predictably overmatched

### Top 25 Bonuses

| | Player, Pos. | Drafted (Round) | Order | Bonus |
|---|---|---|---|---|
| 1. | *** Darryl Strawberry, of** | **Mets (1)** | **1** | **$152,500** |
| 2. | *** Billy Beane, of** | **Mets (1)** | **23** | **$125,000** |
| 3. | **Ricky Wright, lhp** | **Dodgers (Jan.-S/1)** | **(2)** | **$115,000** |
| 4. | Jeff Pyburn, of | Padres (1) | 5 | $103,500 |
| 5. | *** Ron Robinson, rhp** | **Reds (1)** | **19** | **$92,500** |
| 6. | **Ken Dayley, lhp** | **Braves (1)** | **3** | **$90,000** |
| | **Craig McMurtry, rhp** | **Braves (Jan.-R/1)** | **(4)** | **$90,000** |
| 8. | *** Darnell Coles, ss** | **Mariners (1)** | **6** | **$82,500** |
| 9. | *** Kelly Gruber, 3b** | **Indians (1)** | **10** | **$80,000** |
| | **Terry Francona, of** | **Expos (1)** | **22** | **$80,000** |
| 11. | *** Jay Reid, of** | **Giants (1)** | **7** | **$75,000** |
| | **Frank Wills, rhp** | **Royals (1)** | **16** | **$75,000** |
| 13. | *** Cecil Espy, of** | **White Sox (1)** | **8** | **$65,000** |
| | **Jim Acker, rhp** | **Braves (1)** | **21** | **$65,000** |
| 15. | *** Don Schulze, rhp** | **Cubs (1)** | **11** | **$62,500** |
| | **Glenn Wilson, 3b** | **Tigers (1)** | **18** | **$62,500** |
| 17. | **Ross Jones, ss** | **Dodgers (1)** | **9** | **$61,000** |
| 18. | *** Jeff Reed, c** | **Twins (1)** | **12** | **$60,000** |
| | * Jeff Horne, rhp | Pirates (2) | 33 | $60,000 |
| | * Wes Kent, 1b | White Sox (2) | 34 | $60,000 |
| 21. | * Garry Harris, ss | Blue Jays (1) | 2 | $58,000 |
| 22. | **Dennis Rasmussen, lhp** | **Angels (1)** | **17** | **$57,500** |
| 23. | * Lebo Powell, c | Phillies (1) | 13 | $55,000 |
| | *** John Gibbons, c** | **Mets (1)** | **24** | **$55,000** |
| 25. | **Tim Hulett, 2b** | **White Sox (Jan-S/1)** | **(3)** | **$52,500** |

*Major leaguers in bold. *High school selection*

## Largest Bonuses By Round

| | Player, Pos. | Club | Bonus |
|---|---|---|---|
| **1.** | ***Darryl Strawberry, of** | **Mets** | **$152,500** |
| 2. | *Wes Kent, 1b | White Sox | $60,000 |
| | *Jeff Horne, rhp | Pirates | $60,000 |
| 3. | Lindy Duncan, ss | Rangers | $37,500 |
| 4. | Craig Jones, rhp | Braves | $28,000 |
| | Jon Reelhorn, rhp | Phillies | $28,000 |
| 5. | *Brent Gjesdal, 3b | Yankees | $25,000 |
| 6. | *Mark Smith, of | Tigers | $25,000 |
| | *Richie Gaynor, of | Phillies | $25,000 |
| 7. | Dan Hanggie, ss | Yankees | $35,000 |
| **8.** | ***Eric Davis, ss** | **Reds** | **$18,000** |
| 9. | *Tim Howell, c | Pirates | $11,000 |
| 10. | Jerome Kovar, c | Phillies | $19,000 |
| **Jan/R.** | **Craig McMurtry, rhp** | **Braves (1)** | **$90,000** |
| **Jan/S.** | **Ricky Wright, lhp** | **Dodgers (1)** | **$115,000** |
| **Jun/S.** | **Bill Mooneyham, rhp** | **Angels (1)** | **$47,500** |

*Major leaguers in bold. *High school selection.*

in his first season. He struggled with a 0-4, 7.71 record, and was soon dispatched to the Chicago Cubs for veteran DH Cliff Johnson.

Despite being the fourth pick in the draft, King had suspected he was not an integral part of the A's future and would be trade bait. "Putting two and two together," he said, "that's the only thing I can think of."

King didn't last long with the Cubs, either, but later reached Triple-A with the Yankees. He never got a taste of life in the big leagues, and within four years of being drafted, his arm wore out.

Jeff Pyburn

University of Georgia outfielder Jeff Pyburn was drafted fifth overall by the San Diego Padres, but like Harris and King before him, he was out of the game within four years.

Pyburn had the physical gifts to run a 6.4-second 60-yard dash and start for three seasons in baseball (center field) and football (quarterback) at Georgia. He also hit .400 in 1980 and set school records with 15 home runs and 66 RBIs. His father Jim was a former major leaguer who earned a $40,000 bonus in 1954.

The Padres took Pyburn with a premium pick, though the Major League Scouting Bureau and other clubs rated him as a fifth-round talent, questioning his arm and bat speed. Padres general manager Bob Fontaine said Pyburn scared off most of those teams because of his football ability. The Buffalo Bills had taken him in the fifth round of the NFL draft earlier that year.

"He indicated to us that he preferred baseball," Fontaine said. "He was the player we were most anxious to get. He has great ability and is intelligent."

Deciding that baseball would offer a longer career, especially after he already had two knee surgeries, Pyburn signed with the Padres for a bonus of $103,500 and went on to hit .336 with 25 stolen bases in his first season at Class A Reno. In 1981, he hit .285 with eight home runs and 37 steals at Double-A Amarillo. But he regressed to .275 with just a single homer the next season at Triple-A Hawaii. When the Padres attempted to demote Pyburn to Amarillo late in the year, he quit.

San Diego traded Pyburn to Detroit during the offseason for minor league pitcher Larry Rothschild (later a major league manager), but he balked at another assignment to Double-A and was released in spring training. He subsequently signed a series of one-year contracts with the Bills to become a free safety, but never played in an NFL game as his knees failed him.

The failure of Harris, King and Pyburn to reach the majors cast a negative spin on the 1980 draft, though those players at least reached the upper minors. The same couldn't be said for Florida high school catcher Lebo Powell, the 13th overall pick, or the two players drafted right after him. None advanced beyond Class A.

Powell was a controversial player from the start, with wide disagreement in the Phillies organization over his value. "Biggest range I've ever seen, from top to bottom, on rating a player," Phillies scouting supervisor Jim Baumer said.

The Phillies liked Powell's power potential and impressive arm strength, but he hit .231 with 18 homers in three seasons in the organization, and was a liability in the field. They released him for a series of off-field indiscretions, including drug use.

"It was just a question of admitting a mistake," Baumer said. "He was just a bad character. I don't know if he was ever really in shape to see the ball or play like he could. He was a bad influence on the other players, so we got rid of him."

Indiana prep righthander Tim Maki, selected 14th by the Texas Rangers, won just nine games in five minor league seasons, while Don Collins, a righthander selected by the Cardinals from a Virginia high school, never made it out of spring training in 1983 after elbow surgery.

### GIFTS FROM OAKLAND

After winning the World Series from 1972-74 and finishing atop the American League West standings for five consecutive seasons, the Athletics

## One Team's Draft: Cincinnati Reds

| | Player, Pos. | Bonus | | Player, Pos. | Bonus | | Player, Pos. | Bonus |
|---|---|---|---|---|---|---|---|---|
| **1.** | ***Ron Robinson, rhp** | **$92,500** | 4. | Ken Scarpace, of | $20,000 | 9. | *Tim Hume, ss | $4,000 |
| 2. | *Jim Pettibone, rhp | $32,500 | 5. | Steve Leppert, c | $12,000 | 10. | Larry Simcox, ss | Did not sign |
| 2. | Ken Jones, rhp | $30,000 | 6. | *Miguel Salgueiro, rhp | $15,000 | **Other** | **Scott Terry (12), of** | **$3,000** |
| 2. | *Dave Miley, ss | $35,000 | 7. | Tom Wesley, 1b | Unavailable | | | |
| **3.** | ***Danny Tartabull, 2b** | **$30,000** | **8.** | ***Eric Davis, ss** | **$18,000** | | | |

*Major leaguers in bold. *High school selection.*

### WORTH NOTING

concussions knocked Gill's football career to the sidelines, he returned to baseball, joining the Indians organization for three seasons. But a bruising football career had taken a toll on his once-superior baseball tools and Gill never progressed above Double-A.

■ **DANNY TARTABULL,** a third-round pick of the Reds in 1980, was sculpted from an entirely different mold than his Cuban-born father Jose, who was one of the fastest players of his generation (1962-70) and stole 81 bases in his career, while homering just twice. By contrast, his son became one of the majors' top power hitters over the course of his 14-year career, hitting 262 homers, including more than 30 in a season on three occasions. He also stole just 37 bases.

■ Giants second-round pick **ERIC ERICKSON,** a lefthanded pitcher and outfielder from La Jolla, Calif., spent his first season at Rookie-level Great Falls performing in a dual role, going 3-1, 4.03 in 29 innings on the mound while hitting .269-4-24 in 171 at-bats. He became exclusively a hitter a year later, then only a pitcher the following season before abandoning the game to pursue a career at Utah as a quarterback. In 1985, he returned to the Giants organization as a pitcher, and remained in that role through 1988, when he worked briefly at the Triple-A level. In 102 pitching appearances, Erickson went 17-13, 5.43 and walked 295 in 287 innings, while striking out 266. His career totals as a hitter: .236-8-63 in 231 games.

■ Terry Francona's junior season for Arizona paled in comparison to the numbers posted by New Mexico first baseman **KEITH HAGMAN,** who set a pair of still-standing NCAA records for batting average (.551) and triples (17). Hagman also led the nation with 125 hits, while driving in 95 runs. He was selected in the seventh round by the Braves and never got past Class A.

**IN FOCUS: DARRYL STRAWBERRY**

The New York Mets celebrated the selection of the No. 1 overall pick in the 1980 draft by playing the Beatles' "Strawberry Fields Forever". How appropriate.

In acquiring 6-foot-6 Darryl Strawberry, the Mets went for a player with one of the most colorful names in the draft era. They envisioned Strawberry as a player who would, as the song said, patrol right field at Shea Stadium forever. Well maybe not forever, but for years to come.

"I know people are aware of my name, and I think that's going to help me throughout my career," Strawberry said. "I'm glad people notice me."

It took Strawberry three years to ripen into a major leaguer from the time he signed a $152,500 bonus as an 18-year-old out of Los Angeles' Crenshaw High. But he was one of the best-known players in the minor leagues until he reached the majors early in the 1983 season amidst one of the greatest fanfares ever for a rookie.

Once he reached New York, he sung his own No. 1 tune. Of all the No. 1 picks in the draft's first 20 years, none lived up to his billing quite like Strawberry. He helped the Mets to a World Series victory in 1986. The following year, his best in a 17-year career, he nearly became baseball's first 40-40 player, when he hit 39 homers and stole 36 bases.

bottomed out in 1979. The club's 54-108 record and attendance of 306,783 were the worst in club history, and they failed miserably in the draft, as well. They did not sign 36 of their 48 draft picks that year, including both first-rounders in the June regular phase and six of their first seven.

Because of Oakland's inability to sign its premium picks—in 1979 and prior years—the secondary phase of the January 1980 draft featured more talent than normal. Five of the first eight picks were previously drafted by the A's, including their first three selections from the previous June: shortstop Juan Bustabad, who was taken first by Boston and signed with the Red Sox for $50,000, and outfielders Mike Stenhouse (Harvard) and Tom Dodd (Oregon), who had dropped out of school to be eligible for the January draft. Stenhouse went fourth to the Montreal Expos and signed for $32,500, while Dodd went seventh to the Yankees, signing for $22,500.

Pitchers Ricky Wright (Dodgers, second) and Jeff Dedmon (Giants, eighth) were other unsigned Oakland picks snapped up in the January draft. Wright, a former Texas standout, received $115,000 from the Dodgers (a record for the January secondary phase), while Dedmon remained unsigned.

The A's outdid themselves in 1980, in the final year of Charles O. Finley's ownership, when they signed just seven of 39 players, spending a total of $74,500. The 1980 draft began the tenure of new farm director and scouting chief Walt Jocketty, 27, who joined the club in March after serving a brief stint as an assistant general manager with Triple-A Iowa. Finley was trying to unload his crumbling organization, and the A's were in disarray.

"It was pretty obvious Charlie let things go because he was planning to sell the club," Jocketty said. "Before I came out, I knew it wasn't good. People told me it was crazy to go out there. But it was an opportunity for a major league farm director's job."

Jocketty had less than three months to prepare for the 1980 draft, and he was running the show without a single full-time scout to help. Why pay a staff when a fresh kid from Des Moines, Iowa, could handle everything? "We had no scouts, no scouting secretary," Jocketty said. "All we had were the reports from the Scouting Bureau."

It was Jocketty's job to study the reports, plot the draft and build for the future—at the same time he was running the minor league system.

"That was it. I obviously didn't have the time to go out and look at players," he said. "The other teams call in all their national crosscheckers and top scouts for the draft. When we did it, it was different. If you can imagine a draft room where you have myself, my wife and (equipment manager) Steve Vucinich going over the list."

The A's drafted fourth, and Jocketty was told by Finley and manager Billy Martin that the organization's top need was for a lefthanded pitcher. Jocketty selected King, hardly a name destined for Cooperstown.

"I had a preferred list like anyone else," Jocketty said. "The first day my list went pretty fast. I had 50 names and thought that would be good for three days. I had to call the bureau and come up with some other names."

Jocketty scrambled to make 27 selections—26 in the regular phase, one in the secondary. Then came the hardest part, putting money on the table. Of the seven players he signed, third-rounder Rich Bordi was the only future major leaguer in the lot.

"It was tough putting a Rookie team together," said Jocketty, who became the director of baseball administration under new ownership, and later a general manager in St. Louis and Cincinnati. "We had to go out and hold open tryouts just to find players. We didn't have a lot to work with."

## Highest Unsigned Picks

**JUNE/REGULAR PHASE ONLY**

| Player, Pos., Team (Round) | College | Re-Drafted |
|---|---|---|
| Rhett Whisman, ss, Athletics (2) | Gulf Coast (Fla.) CC | Twins '81 (Jan.-S/1) |
| Turner Gill, ss, White Sox (2) | Nebraska | Yankees '83 (18) |
| Dan Plesac, lhp, Cardinals (2) | N.C. State | Brewers '83 (1) |
| Charles Reese, ss, Tigers (2) | Vanderbilt | Never |
| #Billy Cannon, ss, Yankees (3) | Texas A&M | Indians '81 (special draft) |
| Harry McCulla, c, Braves (4) | Delgado (La.) JC | Cardinals '81 (S/1) |
| Doug Drabek, rhp, Indians (4) | Houston | White Sox '83 (11) |
| Bob Sebra, rhp, Tigers (4) | Nebraska | Rangers '83 (5) |
| Steve Madden, of, Yankees (4) | None | Never |
| Matt Williams, rhp, Brewers (4)* | Rice | Blue Jays '81 (1) |

**TOTAL UNSIGNED PICKS:** Top 5 Rounds (15), Top 10 Rounds (54)

*# Selection forfeited. *Returned to same school.*

### FRANCONA DOMINANT COLLEGE PLAYER

The 1980 college season became the personal domain of Francona, the University of Arizona outfielder and son of ex-big leaguer Tito Francona. He was the college player of the year after hitting .395 with eight homers and 78 RBIs, MVP of the College World Series after leading Arizona to the title, and winner of the Golden Spikes Award as the nation's foremost amateur player.

Francona then was picked in the first round of the draft by the Expos, but a lack of speed and power, along with a pair of disabling knee injuries in 1982 and 1983, limited him to part-time duty much of a 10-year career in the big leagues. But he went on to a highly successful career as a manager.

Terry Francona

Many of the top college performers in 1980 were underclassmen not eligible for selection. Those players would make significant inroads on a 1981 draft that took on a college flavor of historical proportions.

The group included: Wichita State outfielder Joe Carter (.432, 91 RBIs, and NCAA records of 229 total bases and 34 doubles); Arkansas outfielder Kevin McReynolds (Southwest Conference triple-crown winner); Oral Roberts righthander Mike Moore (11-4, 1.55); and Yale righthander Ron Darling (11-2, 1.31). All went in the first 10 picks a year later.

# 1980 Draft List

**Did not sign. Major leaguers in bold, with first and last years noted. Order of selection indicated in parentheses. For the first five rounds of the June Regular Phase and the first round of all other phases, the peak level of each player is noted.*

## ATLANTA BRAVES

### January—Regular Phase (4)

1. **Craig McMurtry, rhp, McLennan (Texas) CC.—(1983-95)**
2. *David Chiono, rhp, Yuba (Calif.) CC.
3. Donald Haddock, 3b, Valencia (Fla.) CC.
4. *Tommy Blackmon, rhp, Spartanburg Methodist (S.C.) JC.

### January—Secondary Phase (12)

1. Scott Patterson, rhp, Long Beach (Calif.) CC.—(High A)
2. *Daniel McFadden, lhp, Spartanburg Methodist (S.C.) JC.

### June—Regular Phase (3)

1. **Ken Dayley, lhp, University of Portland.—(1982-93)**
1. **Jim Acker, rhp, University of Texas** (Choice from Expos as compensation for free agent Rowland Office)**—(1983-92)**
2. **Brian Fisher, rhp, Hinkley HS, Aurora, Colo.—(1985-92)**
3. *Harry McCulla, c, Central Arizona JC.—(AA)

DRAFT DROP *Attended Delgado (La.) JC; re-drafted by Cardinals, January 1981/secondary phase (1st round, 1st pick)*

4. Craig Jones, rhp, U.S. Military Academy.—(AAA)
5. Ralph Giansanti, 2b, South Windsor (Conn.) HS.—(Low A)
6. *Nicholas Brandt, lhp, Oroville (Calif.) HS.
7. Keith Hagman, 1b, University of New Mexico.
8. Tom Hayes, of, Texas Wesleyan College.
9. ***Darrel Akerfelds, rhp, Columbine HS, Lakewood, Colo.—(1986-91)**

DRAFT DROP *First-round draft pick (7th overall), Mariners (1983)*

10. Rick Siriano, of, University of Louisville.
11. George Hill, of, Santa Ana Valley HS, Santa Ana, Calif.
12. John Lee, 3b, Florida Southern College.
13. Quinton Lloyd, of, University of Texas.
14. Kevin Rigby, 2b, Duke University.
15. **Paul Zuvella, 2b, Stanford University.—(1982-91)**
16. Dale Weaver, ss, Southern Arkansas University.
17. Glen Germer, rhp, Texas Lutheran College.
18. Gary Wex, rhp, University of Alabama.
19. Andre Treadway, rhp, A.C. Reynolds HS, Asheville, N.C.
20. John Ayers, rhp, West Georgia College.
21. Russell Eagel, c-of, Georgia State University.
22. Mark Bonner, of, Oral Roberts University.
23. James Stefanski, c, Long Island University.
24. *Derek Edwards, rhp, Northern Kentucky Univ.

### June—Secondary Phase (5)

1. **Jeff Dedmon, rhp, West Los Angeles JC.—(1983-88)**
2. *Mike Hogan, rhp, Orange Coast (Calif.) JC.
3. *Timothy Greene, lhp, Middle Georgia JC.

## BALTIMORE ORIOLES

### January—Regular Phase (26)

1. George Dummar, 1b, Milford, Conn.—(High A)
2. *Chris Willsher, rhp, JC of San Mateo (Calif.).
3. Randall Duggan, c-of, Chipola (Fla.) JC.
4. Steven Gessell, rhp, San Jose (Calif.) CC.
5. *Lawrence Lewis, c, Cecil (Md.) CC.
6. ***Ed Wojna, rhp, Indian River (Fla.) CC.—(1985-89)**
7. *Joseph Malott, rhp, Murray State (Okla.) JC.
8. Michael Clarkson, of, St. Petersburg (Fla.) JC.
9. *David Maschino, lhp, Seminole (Okla.) JC.

### January—Secondary Phase (11)

1. **Mike Young, of, Chabot (Calif.) JC.–(1982-89)**
2. Michael Kreymborg, rhp, Bacone (Okla.) JC.
3. *Chuck Tomaselli, lhp, Manatee (Fla.) JC.
4. *Steven Davis, of, Middle Georgia JC.

### June—Regular Phase (26)

1. Jeff Williams, of, Princeton HS, Cincinnati.–(AAA)
2. **Al Pardo, c, Jefferson HS, Tampa.–(1985-89)**
3. **Ken Dixon, rhp, Amherst County HS, Monroe, Va.** (Choice from Dodgers as compensation for free agent Don Stanhouse)**—(1984-87)**
3. Andy Timko, ss, Kennedy HS, McDonald, Ohio.—(AA)
4. **Carl Nichols, c-ss, Compton (Calif.) HS.—(1986-91)**
5. Ron Dillard, ss, Norfolk State University.—(AA)
6. **Mark Brown, rhp, University of Massachusetts.—(1984-85)**
7. Neal Herrick, rhp, University of Maryland.
8. William Butler, ss, Cleveland State (Tenn.) CC.
9. Matt Tyner, of, University of Miami.
10. *Brian McDonough, rhp, Seminole (Okla.) JC.
11. ***Randy Asadoor, 3b, Bullard HS, Fresno, Calif.—(1986)**
12. *Joey Pursell, rhp, Tulane University.
13. *George Cook, 2b, Crenshaw HS, Los Angeles.
14. Rich Cratch, 2b, Bird HS, Chester, Va.
15. **Ricky Jones, ss, West Georgia College.—(1986)**
16. Dave Griggs, c, Sparrows Point HS, Baltimore.
17. *Robert Link, rhp, Brookwood Prep HS, Thomasville, Ga.
18. Joe Hughes, 3b, Florida International University.
19. Ron Cashore, of, San Joaquin Delta (Calif.) JC.
20. *Ron Kelly, 1b, Chamberlain HS, Lutz, Fla.
21. Scott Johnson, lhp, Montgomery (Md.) JC.
22. *Thomas Harrell, ss, Columbus (Ga.) College.
23. ***Tom Funk, lhp, Winnetonka HS, Gladstone, Mo.—(1986)**
24. *Michael Casha, of, Marina HS, San Leandro, Calif.
25. *Alan Sadler, ss, Crossland HS, Camp Springs, Md.
26. *Brent Worcester, lhp, Grant HS, Oklahoma City, Okla.

### June—Secondary Phase (24)

1. Chris Willsher, rhp, JC of San Mateo (Calif.).–(AAA)
2. Richard Marshall, rhp-of, Sharpsburg, Md.
3. Jeff Spencer, 2b, Lower Columbia (Wash.) JC.
4. *John Leonard, rhp, Yavapai (Ariz.) JC.

## BOSTON RED SOX

### January—Regular Phase (23)

1. ***Ray Krawczyk, rhp, Golden West (Calif.) JC.—(1984-89)**
2. *Michael Rosales, rhp, Lamar (Colo.) CC.
3. Brice Cote, rhp, Mercer County (N.J.) CC.
4. *Wallace Dulling, lhp, Columbia State (Tenn.) CC.
5. David Frank, ss-2b, Solano (Calif.) CC.
6. Nathan Banes, rhp, St. Johns River (Fla.) CC.
7. *Glen Davis, 1b-of, Middle Georgia JC.

### January—Secondary Phase (1)

1. Juan Bustabad, ss, Miami-Dade CC North.–(AAA)

DRAFT DROP *First-round draft pick (5th overall), Athletics (1979)*

2. Guy Burgess, lhp, Palm Beach (Fla.) JC.

### June—Regular Phase (24)

1. (Choice to Mets as compensation for free agent Skip Lockwood)
2. **Mike Brown, rhp, Clemson University** (Choice from Yankees as compensation for free agent Bob Watson)**—(1982-87)**
2. (Choice to Expos as compensation for free agent Tony Perez)
3. Mitch Johnson, rhp, Donegal HS, Mount Joy, Pa.—(AAA)
4. Jeff Hall, c, Rochester (N.Y.) Institute of Technology.—(AA)
5. Ronnie Hill, lhp, Dixie HS, Bloomington, Utah.—(High A)
6. **Pat Dodson, 1b, UCLA.—(1986-88)**
7. *Mark Margis, lhp, Culver City (Calif.) HS.
8. **Al Nipper, rhp, Northeast Missouri State University.—(1983-90)**
9. Michael Bryant, of, University of Lowell (Mass.).
10. Brian Zell, of, Cal Poly Pomona.
11. Timothy Duncan, ss, Christian Brothers (Tenn.) College.
12. ***Dave Magadan, 3b, Jesuit HS, Tampa.—(1986-2001)**
13. Simon Glenn, of, Texas A&M University.
14. Mark Weinbrecht, lhp, Clairemont HS, San Diego.
15. Tyrone Herman, rhp, Mankato State (Minn.) University.
16. **Oil Can Boyd, rhp, Jackson State University.—(1982-91)**
17. *Marcus Handley, rhp, Larue County HS, Hodgenville, Ky.
18. Robert Sandling, lhp, Crete-Monee HS, Park Forest, Ill.
19. Al Bowlin, lhp, Grace Davis HS, Modesto, Calif.
20. **Tom Bolton, lhp, Antioch HS, Brentwood, Tenn.—(1987-94)**
21. Parker Wilson, 3b, Livingston (Ala.) University.
22. George Mecerod, rhp, Adelphi (N.Y.) University.
23. *Bobby Falls, 2b, West Mecklenburg HS, Charlotte, N.C.
24. Mike Ciampa, of, Westfield State (Mass.) College.
25. Jeff Hunter, 3b, University of Nebraska.
26. *William Lowry, rhp, Santa Ynez HS, Goleta, Calif.
27. George Greco, lhp, Iona College.

### June—Secondary Phase (22)

1. *Clem Freeman, lhp, Manatee (Fla.) JC.—(AA)
2. Steve Garrett, rhp, Chabot (Calif.) JC.

## CALIFORNIA ANGELS

### January—Regular Phase (19)

1. Chris Ray, rhp, San Joaquin Delta (Calif.) JC.—(Rookie)
2. *Don Fenton, rhp, Lower Columbia (Wash.) JC.
3. ***Kevin Romine, ss-of, Orange Coast (Calif.) JC.—(1985-91)**

DRAFT DROP *Father of Andrew Romine, major leaguer (2010-15) • Father of Austin Romine, major leaguer (2011-14)*

4. *Timothy Arnold, lhp, Los Angeles Valley JC.
5. *Ryan Collier, of, Los Angeles CC.
6. *Steven Ray, lhp, Southwestern (Calif.) JC.
7. *Richard Diffine, 1b, Cerritos (Calif.) JC.
8. *David Wilder, of-ss, Contra Costa (Calif.) JC.
9. *Corey Zawadski, of, Broward (Fla.) CC.
10. *Greg Dees, c, Cosumnes River (Calif.) JC.
11. *James Tunell, rhp, Southwestern (Calif.) JC.
12. *Joseph Mehallow, lhp, Belleville Area (Ill.) JC.
13. *Billy Donathan, rhp, Edison (Fla.) CC.
14. *Mario Alos, 2b-3b, Miami-Dade CC North.

### January—Secondary Phase (21)

1. *Thomas McLaughlin, rhp, Los Angeles CC.—(Low A)
2. *George Page, of, Los Angeles Valley JC.

### June—Regular Phase (20)

1. **Dennis Rasmussen, lhp, Creighton University** (Choice from Astros as compensation for free agent Nolan Ryan)**—(1983-95)**
1. (Choice to Pirates as compensation for free agent Bruce Kison)
2. (Choice to Royals as compensation for free agent Fred Patek)
3. Jack McMahon, rhp, Cal State Dominguez Hills.—(AA)

DRAFT DROP *Son of Don McMahon, major leaguer (1957-74)*

4. Matt Gundelfinger, of-1b, University of Kansas.—(High A)
5. *Frank Marrero, rhp, Christopher Columbus HS, Miami.—(Low A)

DRAFT DROP *Attended Miami-Dade CC South; re-drafted by White Sox, January 1981/secondary phase (2nd round)*

6. Harry Francis, 3b, Texas A&M University.
7. **Mike Brown, of, San Jose State University.—(1983-88)**
8. Duffy Ryan, c, University of New Mexico.
9. Ron Sylvia, rhp, Cal State Los Angeles.
10. *David Mote, inf, El Segundo (Calif.) HS.
11. Chris Clark, of, Cal Poly Pomona.
12. John McGaffey, of-c, Point Loma Nazarene (Calif.) College.
13. Joe Brock, 1b, William Paterson (N.J.) College.
14. Bob Bastian, rhp, University of Miami.
15. Gregory Hammond, rhp, Phoenix.
16. Thomas Roen, lhp, Northern Illinois University.
17. Aldo Bagiotti, c, University of Fort Lauderdale (Fla.).
18. Goldie Wright, of, Rio Mesa HS, Camarillo, Calif.
19. *Jeff Salazar, rhp, Sylmar (Calif.) HS.
20. *Nelson Hayman, of, Belhaven (Miss.) College.
21. Thomas Schneider, rhp, Seton Hall University.
22. Dennis Valdes, of, Florida Southern College.
23. ***Orestes Destrade, 1b, Christopher Columbus HS, Miami.—(1987-94)**
24. ***Ricky Nelson, of, Arizona State University.—(1983-86)**
25. Ronald Hunt, 1b, UC Riverside.
26. Drew Steinbach, lhp, Illinois Institute of Technology.
27. James Christopher, of, Chapman (Calif.) College.
28. *Douglas Laufer, rhp, University of Texas.
29. *Steve Marlin, rhp, Miami HS, Claytool, Ariz.
30. Dave Burroughs, of-lhp, Phoenix (Ariz.) JC.

### June—Secondary Phase (10)

1. **Bill Mooneyham, rhp, Merced (Calif.) JC.—(1986)**

## CHICAGO CUBS

### January—Regular Phase (12)

1. *Mike Hogan, rhp, Orange Coast (Calif.) JC.–(AAA)
2. Gary Monroe, of, Seward County (Kan.) CC.
3. Scott Peterson, c, University of Fort Lauderdale (Fla.).
4. *Ralph Elpin, rhp, CC of Morris (N.J.).
5. *Mike Lambert, rhp, Citrus (Calif.) JC.
6. *Brian Peck, rhp, JC of Southern Idaho.
7. Kevin Schoendienst, of, St. Louis CC-Meramec.

DRAFT DROP *Son of Red Schoendienst, major leaguer (1945-63)*

8. Robert Gilles, c, Jefferson (Mo.) JC.
9. *Greg Braunwalder, 3b, Citrus (Calif.) JC.
10. Gary Young, rhp, Ferry, N.Y.
11. ***Jim Eppard, 1b, Citrus (Calif.) JC.–(1987-90)**

### January—Secondary Phase (24)

1. ***Tom Henke, rhp, East Central (Mo.) JC.—(1982-95)**
2. *Joseph Carter, rhp, San Diego Mesa JC.

### June—Regular Phase (11)

1. **Don Schulze, rhp, Lake Park HS, Roselle, Ill.—(1983-89)**
2. Dan Cataline, of, Archbishop Ryan HS, Philadelphia.—(AA)
3. David Pagel, ss, Central Michigan University.–(AA)
4. Bruce Seid, ss, Oak Park (Mich.) HS.—(Short-season A)

DRAFT DROP *Scouting director, Brewers (2008-14)*

5. James Walsh, of, Lewis (Ill.) University.—(AA)
6. Jeff Remo, c, Mahwah (N.J.) HS.
7. **Fritz Connally, 3b, Baylor University.—(1983-85)**
8. *Tom DiCeglio, ss, Lawrence HS, Cedarhurst, N.Y.
9. **Craig Lefferts, lhp, University of Arizona.—(1983-94)**
10. Brian Roerden, lhp, Adelphi (N.Y.) University.
11. Troy Chestnut, rhp, Marion (S.C.) HS.
12. *Dwayne Ellis, rhp, Pasadena (Calif.) CC.
13. *Mike Knox, rhp, College of Wooster (Ohio).
14. Rich Buonantony, rhp, Western HS, Las Vegas, Nev.
15. *Michael Winbush, rhp, Goldsboro (N.C.) HS.
16. Gary Wayne, c, Marion (La.) HS.
17. Mike Shulleeta, rhp, Yucaipa (Calif.) HS.
18. *Gerald McDermott, c, Fontana (Calif.) HS.
19. Jeff Burton, of, Brigham Young University.
20. *David Flattery, rhp, Iowa State University.
21. Ken Arnerich, ss, Alameda (Calif.) HS.
22. *Todd Schulte, lhp, Winfield HS, Old Monroe, Mo.
23. Rusty Piggott, 3b-ss, Rollins (Fla.) College.
24. *Thomas Corcoran, rhp, Miami-Dade CC North.
25. *Ken Scott, rhp, Fontana (Calif.) HS.
26. *Keith Turnbull, rhp, Winfield (Mo.) HS.
27. *Rob Amble, of, Bakersfield (Calif.) JC.
28. *Dick Seidel, rhp, Mira Costa (Calif.) JC.
29. Dwayne Tenney, ss, West Virginia Wesleyan College.
30. Jon MacMillan, of-1b, Azusa Pacific (Calif.) University.
31. *Gregg Goodman, rhp, Mississippi College.
32. Ken Pryce, rhp, Azusa Pacific (Calif.) University.
33. ***Bruce Tanner, rhp, Neshannock HS, New Castle, Pa.—(1985)**

DRAFT DROP *Son of Chuck Tanner, major leaguer (1955-62); major league manager (1970-88)*

**June—Secondary Phase (13)**

1. Darryl Banks, rhp, JC of Southern Idaho.—(AAA)
2. Joe Housey, rhp, University of New Orleans.
3. *Rick Thurman, rhp, Los Angeles Pierce JC.

## CHICAGO WHITE SOX

**January—Regular Phase (7)**

1. Bill Luzinski, of, Miami-Dade CC North.–(Low A)

DRAFT DROP *Brother of Greg Luzinski, first-round draft pick, Phillies (1968); major leaguer (1970-84)*

2. *Dave Malpeso, c, Miami-Dade CC North.
3. **Jim Siwy, rhp, University of Rhode Island.—(1982-84)**
4. *Allen Black, rhp, West Los Angeles JC.
5. *Billy Wiesler, of, Miami-Dade CC North.
6. *Mitchell Roe, rhp, Miami-Dade CC North.
7. *Dave Oliva, of, Los Angeles Valley JC.
8. *Rick Anderson, ss, Taft (Calif.) JC.
9. *Lamon Lawrence, lhp, JC of the Sequoias (Calif.).

**January—Secondary Phase (3)**

1. **Tim Hulett, 2b, Miami-Dade CC North.—(1983-95)**

DRAFT DROP *Father of Tug Hulett, major leaguer (2008-09)*

2. *Derek Tatsuno, lhp, University of Hawaii.

**June—Regular Phase (8)**

1. **Cecil Espy, of, Point Loma HS, San Diego.—(1983-93)**
2. Wes Kent, 1b, Sahuaro HS, Tucson, Ariz.—(AA)
2. *Turner Gill, ss, Arlington Heights HS, Fort Worth, Texas (Choice from Indians as compensation for free agent Jorge Orta).—(AA)

DRAFT DROP *Attended Nebraska; re-drafted by Yankees, 1983 (18th round); 3rd-round draft pick, New York Jets/National Football League (1984); quarterback, Canadian Football League (1984-85); head football coach, University at Buffalo (2006-09); head football coach, University of Kansas (2010-11); head football coach, Liberty University (2012-15)*

3. Allan Heath, lhp, Waukegan West HS, Waukegan, Ill. (Choice from Giants as compensation for free agent Milt May).—(High A)
3. Ronnie Perry, ss, Holy Cross College.—(AA)

DRAFT DROP *Third-round draft pick, Boston Celtics/National Basketball Association (1980)*

4. Mark Wiesler, 2b, Chaminade HS, Miramar, Fla.—(Rookie)
5. Len Bradley, rhp, Clemson University.—(AA)
6. David Nix, ss, DeSoto (Texas) HS.
7. Mike Morse, ss, South Plantation (Fla.) HS.

DRAFT DROP *Father of Mike Morse, major leaguer (2005-15)*

8. *Neil Reilly, c, Lake Forest HS, Lake Bluff, Ill.
9. Wayne Schuckert, lhp, Shaler HS, Pittsburgh.
10. *Larry McLane, lhp, Chapman (Calif.) College.
11. Mark Seeger, of, Northern Arizona University.
12. Roy Schumacher, rhp, Elgin (Ill.) CC.
13. Keith Flenoir, of, El Camino Real HS, Los Angeles.
14. Gary Robinette, 3b, East Tennessee State University.
15. Tom Mullen, rhp, University of Iowa.
16. Dave Wall, of, Iowa Western CC.
17. ***Calvin Schiraldi, rhp, Westlake HS, Austin, Texas.—(1984-91)**

DRAFT DROP *First-round draft pick (27th overall), Mets (1983)*

18. Terry McAnnally, rhp, Gardendale (Ala.) HS.
19. *Kevin House, of, Southern Illinois University.

DRAFT DROP *Wide receiver, National Football League (1980-87)*

20. *Mark Ridgik, rhp, Cherry Hill East HS, Cherry Hill, N.J.

**June—Secondary Phase (26)**

1. Jeff Barnard, rhp, Iowa Western CC.—(Low A)

## CINCINNATI REDS

**January—Regular Phase (20)**

1. Mark Bowden, lhp, San Jacinto (Texas) JC.–(AAA)
2. Michael Ferguson, rhp, Mount San Antonio (Calif.) JC.
3. *Todd Wheeler, lhp, Yakima Valley (Wash.) JC.
4. Andrew Barbee, of, JC of Southern Idaho.
5. *Dan Boever, ss, Westark (Ark.) CC.
6. *Harold Hatcher, c, Mesa (Ariz.) CC.
7. Leroy Wenzel, 1b, West Los Angeles JC.
8. *Jeffrey Adams, c, Saddleback (Calif.) CC.
9. *Broc Higgins, rhp, San Jacinto (Texas) JC.
10. Michael McCardell, c, Cecil (Md.) CC.

**January—Secondary Phase (22)**

1. *Scott Meier, c, San Joaquin Delta (Calif.) JC.–(AA)
2. Daniel Klosicki, rhp, Spokane Falls (Wash.) CC.

**June—Regular Phase (19)**

1. **Ron Robinson, rhp-ss, Woodlake (Calif.) HS.—(1984-92)**
2. Jim Pettibone, rhp, Saguaro HS, Scottsdale, Ariz. (Choice from Astros as compensation for free agent Joe Morgan).—(AA)
2. Ken Jones, rhp, Arizona State University.—(AA)
2. Dave Miley, ss-3b, Chamberlain HS, Tampa (Choice from Expos as compensation for free agent Fred Norman).—(AAA)

DRAFT DROP *Major league manager (2003-05)*

3. **Danny Tartabull, 2b, Carol City (Fla.) HS.—(1984-97)**

DRAFT DROP *Son of Jose Tartabull, major leaguer (1962-70)*

4. Ken Scarpace, of, Western Michigan University.—(AA)
5. Steve Leppert, c, Jacksonville State University.—(High A)

DRAFT DROP *Son of Don Leppert, major leaguer (1961-64)*

6. Miguel Salgueiro, rhp, South Miami HS.
7. Tom Wesley, 1b, Stillman (Ala.) College.
8. **Eric Davis, ss, Fremont HS, Los Angeles.—(1984-2001)**
9. Tim Hume, ss-2b, Gibbs HS, St. Petersburg, Fla.

DRAFT DROP *Brother of Tom Hume, major leaguer (1977-87)*

10. *Larry Simcox, ss, University of Mississippi.
11. Thomas Marino, c, McArthur HS, Pembroke Pines, Fla.
12. **Scott Terry, of-rhp, Southwestern (Texas) University.—(1986-91)**
13. Broderick Walker, of, Bellaire HS, Houston.
14. Dave Lochner, lhp-1b, Wright State University.
15. *Stan Edmonds, of, University of Southern California.
16. Anthony Threatt, rhp, Murray State University.
17. Bill Metil, 3b, Slippery Rock (Pa.) University.
18. Charles Smith, of, Lakewood HS, St. Petersburg, Fla.
19. Doug Barba, rhp, University HS, San Diego.
20. Anthony Delancey, ss, Astronaut HS, Titusville, Fla.
21. Brooks White, 2b, Canal Winchester HS, Winchester, Ohio.
22. Michael Murray, ss, Western Kentucky University.
23. *Coe Brier, c, Salisbury (N.C.) HS.
24. Scot Ender, rhp, Winona State (Minn.) University.
25. *Roger Lewis, rhp, Stevens HS, Rapid City, S.D.
26. *Calvin James, 1b-of, American HS, Carol City, Fla.
27. David Hall, of-3b, Gonzaga University.
28. Thomas Layton, rhp, Bacone (Okla.) JC.
29. T.J. Stout, of, Centralia (Wash.) JC.
30. Mike Foote, ss, University of New Mexico.
31. Sean Severns, c, Eastern Washington University.
32. Curt Heidenreich, rhp, Illinois State University.
33. *Willie Wilson, rhp, Wayne County HS, Jesup, Ga.
34. *David Carter, rhp, Edgewater HS, Orlando, Fla.

**June—Secondary Phase (3)**

1. Kevin Maroney, of, Miami Sinclair (Ohio) CC.—(Short-season A)
2. *Ed Schneider, lhp, Florida State University.
3. ***Randy O'Neal, rhp, Palm Beach (Fla.) JC.—(1984-90)**
4. Jeffrey Adams, c, Saddleback (Calif.) CC.
5. *Scott Meier, c, San Joaquin Delta (Calif.) JC.

## CLEVELAND INDIANS

**January—Regular Phase (9)**

1. Marlin Methven, ss, Edmonds (Wash.) CC.–(AA)
2. Alan Willis, rhp, Georgia Southern College.
3. *Tim Cannon, of, Chipola (Fla.) JC.
4. Angelo Gilbert, lhp, Laney (Calif.) JC.
5. Michael Dixon, lhp, Sacramento (Calif.) CC.
6. Charles Tillett, lhp-of, Brevard (Fla.) CC.
7. *Steve Giovacchini, ss, Modesto (Calif.) JC.
8. Darold Ellison, 3b, Mount Hood (Ore.) CC.
9. *Tom Gil, of, Miami-Dade CC South.
10. Florentino Gonzales, ss, Big Bend (Wash.) CC.
11. *Tracey Player, lhp, Florida JC.
12. Larry Swann, 1b-lhp, Chipola (Fla.) JC.
13. Dale Nichols, rhp, Central Florida CC.
14. *Phillip Jackson, of, San Joaquin Delta (Calif.) JC.
15. Michael Schwarber, rhp, Cleveland State (Tenn.) CC.
16. *Scott Brusse, rhp, Mount Hood (Ore.) CC.
17. *Michael Wilder, 2b, Contra Costa (Calif.) JC.
18. *Gordon Gradwohl, lhp, Edmonds (Wash.) CC.

**January—Secondary Phase (26)**

1. Mark Roberts, lhp, DeKalb (Ga.) JC.—(Short-season A)
2. Charles Hollowell, lhp, Hillsborough (Fla.) CC.
3. *Mitch Seoane, 2b, Hillsborough (Fla.) CC.

DRAFT DROP *Brother of Manny Seoane, major leaguer (1977-78)*

4. Darren Swanson, rhp, Green River (Wash.) CC.

**June—Regular Phase (10)**

1. **Kelly Gruber, ss, Westlake HS, Austin, Texas.—(1984-93)**
2. (Choice to White Sox as compensation for free agent Jorge Orta)
3. Greg Pope, rhp, Sacramento (Calif.) CC (Choice from Padres as compensation for free agent Rick Wise).—(High A)
3. Bart Mackie, c, Meadowdale HS, Lynwood, Wash.—(Low A)
4. ***Doug Drabek, rhp, St. Joseph's HS, Victoria, Texas.—(1986-98)**

DRAFT DROP *Attended Houston; re-drafted by White Sox, 1983 (11th round) • Father of Kyle Drabek, first-round draft pick, Phillies (2006); major leaguer (2010-14)*

5. Eric Jones, of, Luther Burbank HS, Sacramento, Calif.—(Low A)
6. **Jeff Moronko, 3b, Texas Wesleyan College.—(1984-87)**
7. *Norman Morton, lhp, McArthur HS, Hollywood, Fla.
8. **Rich Thompson, rhp, Amherst (Mass.) College.—(1985-90)**
9. Eddie Tanner, ss, Brookland-Cayce HS, West Columbia, S.C.
10. Lawrence Dotson, of, UC Irvine.
11. *Limbric Windham, of, Vigor HS, Prichard, Ala.
12. *Don Long, ss, Meadowdale HS, Edmonds, Wash.
13. **Mike Jeffcoat, lhp, Louisiana Tech.—(1983-94)**
14. Michael Kolodney, rhp, Brooklyn (N.Y.) College.
15. Richard Elkin, c, Tacoma (Wash.) CC.
16. ***Terry Steinbach, 3b, New Ulm (Minn.) HS.—(1986-99)**
17. Patrick Grady, of, Upsala (N.J.) College.
18. Gary Holden, of, Aragon HS, Burlingame, Calif.
19. William Holland, rhp, University of Louisville.
20. Anthony Freeman, of, Albany (Calif.) HS.
21. *Robert Gilchrist, rhp, Sandusky (Ohio) HS.
22. Richard Gebin, lhp, Monterey Peninsula (Calif.) JC.
23. Steven Jenter, rhp, University of Southwestern Louisiana.
24. Matt Minium, of, University of Miami.
25. Arthur Sullivan, of, Colby (Maine) College.
26. Thomas Stibora, lhp, Cleveland State University.
27. Dan McInerny, of, University of California.
28. *John Churlin, rhp, Meadowdale HS, Lynwood, Wash.
29. **Jack Fimple, ss-3b, Humboldt State (Calif.) University.—(1983-87)**
30. James Oros, 3b, St. Xavier (Ill.) College.
31. Michael Crowley, lhp, St. Mary's HS, Lynn, Mass.
32. *Timothy Kelly, c, College of Wooster (Ohio).
33. Andy Alvis, c-1b, Washington State University.

DRAFT DROP *Son of Max Alvis, major leaguer (1962-70)*

34. Richard Saavedra, rhp, Santa Clara (Calif.) HS.
35. Kevin Malone, 2b, University of Louisville.

DRAFT DROP *General manager, Expos (1994-95); general manager, Dodgers (1998-2001)*

36. Rickey Lintz, rhp, San Francisco State University.
37. Mark Wright, ss, Newberry (Fla.) HS.
38. *Rich Rice, rhp, Lake Worth (Fla.) HS.
39. *Harvey Heise, 3b, Brookland-Cayce HS, West Columbia, S.C.
40. *Thomas Smercynski, rhp, St. John's Prep, Peabody, Mass.
41. *William Schoenig, 2b, Montclair State (N.J.) College.
42. *Martin Writt, c, Livingston (N.J.) HS.
43. Luis Duarte, c-1b, Miami, Fla.
44. Shanie Dugas, ss, McNeese State University.

**June—Secondary Phase (8)**

1. **Dave Gallagher, of, Mercer County (N.J.) CC.—(1987-95)**
2. Gary Whisler, ss, Canada (Calif.) JC.
3. ***Steve Ellsworth, rhp, Fresno (Calif.) CC.—(1988)**

DRAFT DROP *Son of Dick Ellsworth, major leaguer (1958-71)*

4. *Glenn Edwards, of, Mercer County (N.J.) CC.
5. Tommy Blackmon, rhp, Spartanburg Methodist (S.C.) JC.
6. Winston Ficklin, 2b, Richmond, Calif.
7. *Nattie George, of, San Jose (Calif.) CC.
8. Ralph Elpin, rhp, CC of Morris (N.J.).
9. *Michael Wilder, 2b, Contra Costa (Calif.) JC.

**Special Draft**

* Billy Cannon, ss, Broadmoor HS, Baton Rouge, La.—DNP

DRAFT DROP *First-round draft pick, Dallas Cowboys/National Football League (1984); linebacker, NFL (1984) • Son of Billy Cannon, 1959 Heisman Trophy winner, running back/NFL (1960-70)*

## DETROIT TIGERS

**January—Regular Phase (17)**

1. **Mike Laga, 1b, Bergen (N.J.) CC.–(1982-90)**
2. *Paul Huyck, lhp, Yavapai (Ariz.) JC.
3. Kevin Young, of, Valencia (Fla.) CC.
4. Guy Hubert, ss, Delgado (La.) JC.
5. ***Randy Hunt, c, Chattahoochee Valley (Ala.) CC.—(1985-86)**
6. John Engen, lhp, University of Minnesota-Duluth.
7. James Doleski, rhp, Northern Virginia CC.
8. *Kenneth Merritt, c, Yavapai (Ariz.) JC.

**January—Secondary Phase (17)**

1. John Moller, lhp, Old Bridge, N.J.—(High A)
2. Nick O'Connor, rhp, Cumberland (Ky.) JC.

**June—Regular Phase (18)**

1. **Glenn Wilson, 3b, Sam Houston State University.—(1982-93)**
2. *Charles Reese, ss, Pequannock HS, Pompton Plains, N.J.—DNP

DRAFT DROP *Attended Vanderbilt; never re-drafted*

3. Roberto Casasnovas, of, Mahwah (N.J.) HS.—(High A)
4. ***Bob Sebra, rhp, Gloucester Catholic HS, Medford Lakes, N.J.—(1985-90)**

DRAFT DROP *Attended Nebraska; re-drafted by Rangers, 1983 (5th round)*

5. Lawrence Gilmore, 1b, West Covina (Calif.) HS.—(Low A)
6. Mark Smith, of, Fairfield (Ohio) HS.
7. Stan Younger, of, Brigham Young University.
8. Stine Poole, c, University of the Pacific.
9. Homer Moncrief, rhp, Jackson State University.
10. **Chuck Hensley, lhp, University of California.—(1986)**
11. **Dwight Lowry, c, University of North Carolina.—(1984-88)**
12. Carl Burns, 1b, Chadsey HS, Detroit.
13. Kevin Perrett, c, Madison HS, San Diego.
14. Michael Jones, ss, Rome (N.Y.) Free Academy.
15. Rondal Rollin, of, Cal State Northridge.
16. Howard Carter, of, Tuskegee (Ala.) Institute.
17. Thomas Merkle, of, Saginaw Valley State (Mich.) College.
18. *Jeff Morrison, lhp, University of Miami.
19. Norman Michaud, lhp, Northeastern University.
20. David Simononis, of, Penn State University.
21. James Clark, rhp, St. Peter's College.
22. Gary Nutter, rhp, Eckerd (Fla.) College.
23. Willie Ward, 1b, Barringer HS, Newark, N.J.

24. William Nash, of, Chadsey HS, Detroit.
25. *Mark Friedly, rhp, Glenn HS, Norwalk, Calif.
26. *David Hage, ss, Amsterdam (N.Y.) HS.
27. Robert Vavrock, rhp, Cal Poly San Luis Obispo.
28. *Walter Faber, lhp, Grand Rapids (Mich.) JC.
29. Robert Ruffus, rhp, Monmouth College.
**30. Ron Mathis, rhp, University of Missouri.—(1985-87)**
31. Mark Dacko, rhp, James Madison University.
32. *Dave Kopf, rhp, Kimball HS, Royal Oak, Mich.
33. *Mike Tanzi, lhp, Florida Southern College.
34. *Mark Recker, rhp, Oakland (Mich.) CC.
35. Mark Fellows, rhp, Central Michigan University.
36. George Foussianes, ss, University of Michigan.

### June—Secondary Phase (14)

1. *Joe McCarthy, of, University of South Carolina.—DNP
2. *Mitch Seoane, 2b, Hillsborough (Fla.) CC.

DRAFT DROP *Brother of Manny Seoane, major leaguer (1977-78)*

## HOUSTON ASTROS

### January—Regular Phase (18)

1. *Jeff Bair, rhp, CC of Morris (N.J.).—(Rookie)
2. Chris Buckley, of, CC of Morris (N.J.).

DRAFT DROP *Scouting director, Blue Jays (2001-03); scouting director, Reds (2006-15)*

3. *Pat Shortt, lhp, Eastern Arizona JC.
4. *Kelly Moore, of, San Diego Mesa JC.
**5. *Donnie Hill, ss, Orange Coast (Calif.) JC.—(1983-92)**

DRAFT DROP *First overall draft pick, June 1981/secondary phase, Athletics*

### January—Secondary Phase (14)

1. *Kevin Olson, rhp, Golden West (Calif.) JC.—DNP
**2. *Billy Hatcher, of-rhp, Yavapai (Ariz.) JC.—(1984-95)**

### June—Regular Phase (17)

1. (Choice to Angels as compensation for free agent Nolan Ryan)
2. (Choice to Reds as compensation for free agent Joe Morgan)
**3. Jeff Calhoun, lhp, University of Mississippi.—(1984-88)**
4. Ken Elsee, rhp, University of Nevada-Las Vegas.—(High A)
5. Tom Hawk, rhp, Arizona State University.—(High A)
6. Wes Clements, of-1b, University of Arizona.
7. Mike Sheppard, ss-3b, Seton Hall University.
8. *Tony Arias, rhp, Hialeah (Fla.) HS.
9. Scott Gardner, rhp, University of Oklahoma.
10. *James Miley, c, Tennant HS, Warminster, Pa.
11. David Sullivan, c, Oklahoma State University.
12. Tim Meckes, rhp, College of St. Francis (Ill.).
13. Gary D'Onofrio, ss, Oral Roberts University.
14. Neil Simons, of, Clemson University.
15. Jeff Morris, lhp, University of Arizona.
16. John Kolacki, lhp, Middletown South HS, Lincroft, N.J.
17. *Jose Rodiles, rhp, Lamar HS, Houston.
18. Roderick Shepard, c, Princeton University.
19. *Larry Kiesling, ss, Centenary College.
20. Billy Weems, of, Clemson University.
21. Joey Squilla, 1b, John Brown (Ark.) University.
22. Ken Babcock, lhp, Centenary College.
23. Dennis Cleveland, 3b, Jacksonville State University.
24. Gary Malinowski, rhp, Rutgers University.
25. Michael Cerefin, rhp, Burnt Hills (N.Y.) HS.

### June—Secondary Phase (1)

**1. Jeff Heathcock, rhp, Oral Roberts University.—(1983-88)**

## KANSAS CITY ROYALS

### January—Regular Phase (15)

1. *Tyson Hubbard, rhp, Spartanburg Methodist (S.C.) JC.—(High A)
**2. *Tim Crews, rhp, Valencia (Fla.) CC.—(1987-92)**

DRAFT DROP *Died as active major leaguer (March 23, 1993)*

3. Willie Neal, of, Chicago.
4. *Kevin Wiggins, of, San Diego Mesa JC.
5. Doug Potestio, rhp, Chabot (Calif.) JC.
6. *Kevin Kilstofte, rhp, Des Moines Area (Iowa) CC.
7. James Gleissner, c, Mount San Jacinto (Calif.) JC.
8. *Richard Turner, c, Santa Ana (Calif.) JC.

### January—Secondary Phase (5)

1. Steve Raine, rhp, Hartnell (Calif.) CC.—(AA)
2. *Richard Scott, 2b, Canada (Calif.) JC.
3. *Mark Hoffman, lhp, Chabot (Calif.) JC.

### June—Regular Phase (16)

**1. Frank Wills, rhp, Tulane University.—(1983-91)**
2. Roger Hansen, 3b, Rio Mesa HS, Camarillo, Calif.—(AAA)
2. Mike Olson, rhp, St. Louis Park (Minn.) HS (Choice from Angels as compensation for free agent Fred Patek).—(AA)
3. Doug Cook, rhp, Forest Hills HS, West Palm Beach, Fla.—(AA)
4. Lester Strode, lhp, Kentucky State University.—(AAA)
5. Cayetano Cadahia, c, Hialeah (Fla.) HS.—(AA)
**6. Rondin Johnson, 2b, University of Washington.—(1986)**
**7. Don Slaught, c, UCLA.—(1982-97)**
**8. Cliff Pastornicky, ss, Brigham Young University.—(1983)**

DRAFT DROP *Father of Tyler Pastornicky, major leaguer (2012-14)*

9. Bert Johnson, lhp, Cypress Lake HS, Fort Myers, Fla.
10. Ken Swank, lhp, Watsonville (Calif.) HS.
11. Francis Cutty, rhp, Pepperdine University.
**12. Butch Davis, of, East Carolina University.—(1983-94)**
13. Anthony Notaroberto, of, Trenton State (N.J.) College.
14. Aubrey Johnson, c, Castlemont HS, Oakland, Calif.
**15. Bob Hegman, ss, St. Cloud State (Minn.) University.—(1985)**
16. Theo Shaw, ss, Proviso East HS, Maywood, Ill.
**17. Tom Romano, of, Coastal Carolina College.—(1987)**
18. *Vince Beringhele, ss, Loyola HS, Los Angeles.
19. David Wong, rhp, Willamette (Ore.) University.
20. *Mitch Hawley, rhp, University of California.
21. *John Cox, lhp, Hueneme HS, Oxnard, Calif.
22. *Anthony Bartolomucci, lhp, Oak Forest (Ill.) HS.
23. Olice King, lhp-1b, Bradley University.
24. *Al Romero, c, San Diego State University.
25. *Dan Sehlhorst, c, Oak Hills HS, Cincinnati.
26. *Jeff Doerr, rhp, Aragon HS, San Mateo, Calif.
27. Billy Best, 2b, East Carolina University.
28. *Rich Poznanski, c-of, Eisenhower HS, Yakima, Wash.

### June—Secondary Phase (4)

**1. Keith Creel, rhp, University of Texas.—(1982-87)**
2. Bob Ferris, c-1b, Arizona State University.
3. Russ Stephans, c, Arizona State University.
4. *David Wilder, of-ss, Contra Costa (Calif.) JC.
5. *Andrew Pavlovic, rhp, Yavapai (Ariz.) JC.
6. Harold Hatcher, c, Mesa (Ariz.) CC.
7. *David Bailor, of, Yavapai (Ariz.) JC.

## LOS ANGELES DODGERS

### January—Regular Phase (10)

1. David Lesch, rhp, Central Arizona JC.—(Rookie)
**2. R.J. Reynolds, of, Sacramento (Calif.) CC.—(1983-90)**
**3. Larry See, 3b, Cerritos (Calif.) JC.–(1986-88)**
4. *Robbie Allen, ss, Clemson University.
5. Hollis Martin, ss, Potomac State (W.Va.) JC.
**6. *Ralph Bryant, of, Abraham Baldwin Agricultural (Ga.) JC.—(1985-87)**
7. *Mark Wenzel, rhp, Fresno (Calif.) CC.
8. *Damon Hunt, of, Sacramento (Calif.) CC.
9. *Paul Hagan, of, South Georgia JC.
10. *David Bailor, of, Yavapai (Ariz.) JC.
11. Brett Wise, rhp, Seminole (Fla.) CC.
12. *Richard Lucero, rhp, Phoenix (Ariz.) JC.
13. *Greg Hudson, rhp, DeKalb South (Ga.) CC.

### January—Secondary Phase (2)

**1. Ricky Wright, lhp, University of Texas.—(1982-86)**
2. *Jack Leonard, 3b, Louisburg (N.C.) JC.
3. *Harry Kazanjian, c-of, San Francisco CC.

### June—Regular Phase (9)

**1. Ross Jones, ss, University of Miami.—(1984-87)**
2. (Choice to Twins as compensation for free agent Dave Goltz)
3. (Choice to Orioles as compensation for free agent Don Stanhouse)
4. (Choice to Padres as compensation for free agent Jay Johnstone)
5. *Peter Beall, ss, Mater Dei HS, Santa Ana, Calif.—(High A)

DRAFT DROP *Attended UCLA; re-drafted by Angels, 1984 (16th round)*

6. Paul Bard, c, Tufts (Mass.) University.

DRAFT DROP *Father of Daniel Bard, first-round draft pick, Red Sox (2006); major leaguer (2009-13) • Father of Luke Bard, first-round draft pick, Twins (2012)*

7. Todd Gauntlett, c, UCLA.
8. *Kevin Sliwinski, of, Santiago HS, Garden Grove, Calif.
9. Steve Marsden, rhp, University of Wisconsin.
10. Ricky Thomas, of, University of La Verne (Calif.).
11. Curt Reade, rhp, Fresno State University.
12. Anthony Lachowetz, of, Springfield (Mass.) College.
13. Greg Smith, 1b, Southern University.
14. Thomas Robinson, 2b, Widener (Pa.) University.
15. Charles Jones, rhp, University of New Hampshire.
16. Frank Dente, rhp, Palm Beach (Fla.) JC.
17. Richard Lloyd, rhp, East Valley HS, Otis Orchards, Wash.
18. Pasquale Raimondo, 2b, SUNY-Buffalo.
**19. Tom Klawitter, lhp, University of Wisconsin.—(1985)**
20. Audie Cole, of, Eastern Michigan University.
21. Jon Debus, of, College of St. Francis (Ill.).
22. Francis McQuade, rhp, Elmhurst (Ill.) College.
23. Phillip Webber, of, San Bernardino Valley (Calif.) JC.
24. *Jerry Bendorf, ss, Gonzaga University.
25. Bobby Kenyon, rhp, Clemson University.
26. *Jim Pacanowski, c, Downers Grove South HS, Woodbridge, Ill.
27. *Con Ryan, rhp, Colorado State University.
28. *Todd Zacher, 2b, University of Arkansas.
29. *Gregory Hull, of, Hiram Johnson HS, Sacramento, Calif.
30. *Tom Woleslagel, ss, Ross HS, Fremont, Ohio.
31. Michael Strawberry, of, Los Angeles Southwest CC.

DRAFT DROP *Brother of Darryl Strawberry, major leaguer (1983-99); first overall draft pick, Mets (1980)*

32. *Hank DeMello, c, Roseville (Calif.) HS.

### June—Secondary Phase (9)

1. Robbie Allen, ss, Clemson University.—(AAA)
2. Rick Felt, lhp, DeKalb South (Ga.) CC.
3. *Michael Carringer, rhp, Bacone (Okla.) JC.

## MILWAUKEE BREWERS

### January—Regular Phase (25)

1. Michael Orlich, rhp, Central Arizona JC.—(Rookie)
2. Ronald Kollman, rhp, JC of Southern Idaho.
3. Terry Ragan, of, Chipola (Fla.) JC.
4. *Alan Haugen, ss-2b, Centralia (Wash.) JC.
5. *Ben Donisi, 3b, Broward (Fla.) CC.
6. *Frank Booker, 2b, Contra Costa (Calif.) JC.
7. Curt Watanabe, 3b, University of Hawaii.
8. *Garrett Nago, c, Pima (Ariz.) CC.
9. *Ralph Kennedy, rhp, Miami-Dade CC North.
10. David Jensen, rhp, Logan, Utah.
11. *Michael Burton, rhp, Enterprise State (Ala.) JC.
12. *Greg Cottrell, c, Los Angeles Valley JC.
13. *Rory Brown, lhp, Broward (Fla.) CC.
14. *Phil Smith, ss, Laney (Calif.) JC.
15. *John Whitt, of, Los Angeles Harbor JC.
16. *Kevin Lindsley, rhp, Linn-Benton (Ore.) CC.
17. *William Palmer, 3b, Laney (Calif.) JC.
18. *Michael Evans, lhp, Merced (Calif.) JC.
19. Ronnie Jones, of, Central Arizona JC.
20. Walt Steele, 3b, Pepperdine University.
21. *Robert Zima, rhp, Central Arizona JC.
22. Steven Mitchell, of, Clifton Park, N.Y.
23. *Joseph Mutt, rhp, Orange Coast (Calif.) JC.
24. *Gerrett Smith, of, Pasadena (Calif.) CC.
25. *Michael Mangold, c, Umpqua (Ore.) CC.

### January—Secondary Phase (19)

**1. *Herm Winningham, of, DeKalb South (Ga.) CC.—(1984-92)**
2. Craig Herberholz, rhp, Central Arizona JC.
**3. *Randy O'Neal, rhp, Palm Beach (Fla.) JC.—(1984-90)**
4. *James Jones, rhp, Corte Madera, Calif.
5. *Randy Poitevint, 3b, Central Arizona JC.
6. *Andrew Speck, rhp, Aloha, Ore.

### June—Regular Phase (25)

**1. Dion James, of, McClatchy HS, Sacramento, Calif.—(1983-96)**
2. Bob Schroeck, lhp, Southern Illinois University.—(AA)
3. Maury Ornest, 3b, UC Santa Barbara.—(High A)

DRAFT DROP *Son of Harry Ornest, owner, St. Louis Blues/ National Hockey League (1983-86)*

**4. *Matt Williams, rhp, Rice University** (Choice from Giants as compensation for free agent Jim Wohlford)**—(1983-85)**

DRAFT DROP *Returned to Rice; re-drafted by Blue Jays, 1981 (1st round)*

4. Butch Kirby, ss-2b, Arundel HS, Severna, Md.—(Low A)
5. Gerard Miller, 1b-of, Southern Illinois University.—(Low A)
**6. Randy Ready, 2b, Mesa (Colo.) College.—(1983-95)**
7. Ted Pallas, rhp, Pepperdine University.
8. *Billy Irions, lhp, Seminole (Okla.) JC.
**9. *Steve Engel, lhp, Reading HS, Cincinnati.—(1985)**
10. *Todd Soares, ss, Kingsburg (Calif.) HS.
11. *Dan Davidsmeier, ss, University of Southern California.
12. *Russ Kibler, rhp, Sandalwood HS, Jacksonville, Fla.
13. Sam Favata, 2b, Cal State Fullerton.
14. Johnson Wood, 1b-rhp, Oxnard (Calif.) JC.
15. Jeff Gilbert, lhp, Pasadena, Md.
16. *Audrey Robinson, of, Canada (Calif.) JC.
17. Ricki Bass, of, University of Hawaii.

DRAFT DROP *Son of Dick Bass, running back/National Football League (1960-69)*

18. *Gary Adams, lhp, Grass Lake (Mich.) HS.
19. *Bill Peltola, rhp, University of Southern California.
20. *Vic Woods, ss, Centennial HS, Compton, Calif.
21. *David Conte, ss, Lakewood HS, Long Beach, Calif.
22. *Richard Wiesner, of, Kennedy HS, Manchester, Mo.
23. *Duane Widner, rhp, Hueneme HS, Port Hueneme, Calif.
24. *Dean Naylor, rhp, Miami-Dade CC South.
25. *Terry Coates, 3b, Southern Wayne HS, Mount Olive, N.C.

### June—Secondary Phase (6)

1. Mark Effrig, rhp, Lower Columbia (Wash.) JC.—(AA)
2. *Garrett Nago, c, Pima (Ariz.) CC.
3. Bob Elliott, rhp, Georgia Southern College.

## MINNESOTA TWINS

### January—Regular Phase (11)

1. *Jeff Barnard, rhp-1b, Iowa Western CC.—(AAA)
2. *Timothy Greene, lhp, Middle Georgia JC.
3. Keith Silva, lhp, Lemoore, Calif.
4. Harold Jackson, rhp, Solano (Calif.) CC.
5. *Jeffrey Spencer, inf, Lower Columbia (Wash.) JC.
6. Al Arrieta, rhp, Pepperdine University.
**7. *Steve Ellsworth, rhp, Fresno (Calif.) CC.—(1988)**

DRAFT DROP *Son of Dick Ellsworth, major leaguer (1958-71)*

8. *Ricardo Moreyra, c, Palm Beach (Fla.) JC.
9. *Ernie Moya, rhp, Hillsborough (Fla.) CC.
10. *Luis Roche, c, Los Angeles CC.
11. *Mike Kasprzak, rhp, Manatee (Fla.) JC.

12. David Wilson, rhp, Montreat-Anderson (N.C.) JC.
13. *Mike Vanderburg, lhp-of, Orange Coast (Calif.) JC.
14. *Gary Klein, rhp, Pasadena (Calif.) CC.

**January—Secondary Phase (9)**

1. *Nattie George, of, San Jose (Calif.) CC.—(Low A)
2. *John Leonard, rhp, Yavapai (Ariz.) JC.
3. *Daniel Casey, lhp, Edison, N.J.
4. Brian Butera, of, Tulane University.

**June—Regular Phase (12)**

1. **Jeff Reed, c, Joliet West HS, Joliet, Ill.—(1984-2000)**
2. **Jim Weaver, of, Florida State University** (Choice from Dodgers as compensation for free agent Dave Goltz)**—(1985-89)**
2. **Tim Teufel, 2b, Clemson University.—(1983-93)**
3. **Scotti Madison, c, Vanderbilt University.—(1985-89)**
4. **Rod Booker, ss, University of California.—(1987-91)**
5. ***Mike Fuentes, of, Florida State University.—(1983-84)**

DRAFT DROP *Returned to Florida State; re-drafted by Expos, 1981 (2nd round)*

6. Lee Belanger, lhp, University of La Verne (Calif.).
7. Kirby Krueger, rhp, University of New Orleans.
8. **Andre David, of, Cal State Fullerton.—(1984-86)**
9. Tony Guerrero, lhp, Cleveland HS, Northridge, Calif.
10. Ken Foster, 1b, Cal Poly Pomona.
11. Kevin Williams, of, University of Hawaii.
12. *Mitch Ashmore, c, Centenary College.
13. Lyle Brackenridge, of, University of California.
14. *Dan Clark, ss, Glenn HS, La Mirada, Calif.
15. Tony Pilla, 2b, Long Island University.
16. **Jim Eisenreich, of, St. Cloud State University.—(1982-98)**
17. Jeffrey Martin, c, Louisa (Va.) County HS.
18. Mike Cole, 2b, San Diego CC.
19. Domingo Nunez, ss, Wagner College.
20. Michael Tirella, lhp, University of Rhode Island.
21. *Bryan Price, lhp, Tamalpais HS, Mill Valley, Calif.

DRAFT DROP *Major league manager (2014-15)*

22. *Reggie Wyatt, lhp, Santa Monica (Calif.) JC.
23. *Mark Bauer, rhp, Merced (Calif.) HS.
24. Scott Wilhelmy, c, Carleton-Northfield (Minn.) College.
25. *Rod Langston, of, Brevard (Fla.) CC.
26. **Rich Yett, rhp, Don Lugo HS, Chino, Calif.—(1985-90)**
27. William Price, 2b, Cal State Dominguez Hills.
28. *Kurt Reid, of, St. Louis CC-Meramec.
29. Mark Wright, rhp, Boise State (Idaho) University.
30. Frank Ramppen, c-3b, University of Tampa.
31. *Don Smith, rhp, Orange Coast (Calif.) JC.
32. *Chuck Lusted, rhp, Georgia Southern College.
33. (void) *Robert Elliott, rhp, Georgia Southern.
34. *Chuck Yaeger, lhp, Rio Mesa HS, Camarillo, Calif.
35. David Jackson, rhp, Hogan HS, Vallejo, Calif.
36. *Kenny Kohler, c, North Plainfield (N.J.) HS.
37. Brad Baker, ss, Gustavus Adolphus HS, St. Peter, Minn.

**June—Secondary Phase (25)**

1. John Palica, of, Los Angeles Harbor JC.—(AA)
2. *Steve Watson, rhp, Manatee (Fla.) JC.
3. *Dave Malpeso, c, Miami-Dade CC North.

## MONTREAL EXPOS

**January—Regular Phase (22)**

1. *Rick Felt, lhp, DeKalb South (Ga.) CC.—(AAA)
2. *Richard Marshall, of, Hagerstown (Md.) JC.
3. David Spriggs, of, Ohio University.
4. *Benny Melares, c, St. Clair County (Mich.) CC.
5. *Richard Vitato, ss, Merced (Calif.) JC.
6. *Rich DeVincenzo, lhp, Miami-Dade CC North.
7. *Steve Janousek, lhp, Middle Georgia JC.
8. ***Bryan Kelly, rhp, Valencia (Fla.) CC.—(1986-87)**
9. Mike Powers, rhp, Kentucky Wesleyan College.
10. Joe Emery, rhp, Garden City, Mich.

**January—Secondary Phase (4)**

1. **Mike Stenhouse, of, Harvard University.—(1982-86)**

DRAFT DROP *First-round draft pick (26th overall), Athletics (1979) • Son of Dave Stenhouse, major leaguer (1962-64)*

2. ***Mike Sharperson, ss, DeKalb South (Ga.) CC.—(1987-95)**

**June—Regular Phase (21)**

1. (Choice to Braves as compensation for free agent Rowland Office)
1. **Terry Francona, of, University of Arizona** (Choice from Yankees as compensation for free agent Rudy May)**—(1981-90)**

DRAFT DROP *Son of Tito Francona, major leaguer (1956-70) • Major league manager (1997-2015)*

2. (Choice to Reds as compensation for free agent Fred Norman)
2. **Joe Hesketh, lhp, SUNY-Buffalo** (Choice from Red Sox as compensation for free agent Tony Perez)**—(1984-94)**
3. **Greg Bargar, rhp, University of Arizona.—(1983-86)**
4. **Tom Gorman, lhp, Gonzaga University.—(1981-87)**
5. **Roy Johnson, of, Tennessee State University.—(1982-85)**
6. Bob Valliant, lhp, Oxbow HS, Wells River, Vt.
7. Ken Weislak, 3b, Lewis (Ill.) University.
8. David Hoeksema, ss, University of Iowa.
9. **Bryan Little, ss, Texas A&M University.—(1982-86)**

DRAFT DROP *Brother of Grady Little, major league manager (2003-07)*

10. *Phil Deriso, lhp, Auburn University.
11. Terry Eldridge, of, Anne Arundel (Md.) CC.
12. *Julius Anderson, 3b, Nichols (Ga.) HS.
13. Larry Groves, rhp-of, Emporia State (Kan.) University.
14. Pete Chapin, rhp, Cal State Fullerton.
15. *Mike Williams, 1b, Western Kentucky University.
16. *Kevin Sumuel, of, Rockdale (Texas) HS.
17. *Douglas Young, rhp, Glenbard West HS, Glen Ellyn, Ill.
18. Joel Lepel, c, Mankato State (Minn.) University.
19. Bob Baldrick, lhp, Hughes HS, Cincinnati.
20. Larry Glasscock, lhp, Western Kentucky University.
21. *Alvin Ruben, 1b, University of Houston.
22. Ken Westray, lhp, Eastern Illinois University.
23. Scott Hinson, rhp, Cox HS, Virginia Beach, Va.
24. Harry Jones, c, Newton County HS, Covington, Ga.
25. *Don DeLoach, ss, Florida State University.
26. Mark Schuler, rhp, Memphis State University.
27. Jeff Whelan, of, Xavier University.
28. Dane Rogers, of, Richland (Texas) JC.
29. Glen Stachiet, of, South Lake HS, St. Clair Shores, Mich.
30. ***Chris Sabo, 3b, Catholic Central HS, Detroit.—(1988-96)**
31. Steve Dawes, ss, Xavier University.
32. *Kendall Carter, rhp, Coronado HS, Scottsdale, Ariz.
33. Rod Nealeigh, 1b-of, Anderson (Ind.) College.

**June—Secondary Phase (15)**

1. ***Herm Winningham, of, DeKalb South (Ga.) CC.—(1984-92)**

## NEW YORK METS

**January—Regular Phase (2)**

1. Roger Frash, of, Oxnard (Calif.) JC.—(High A)
2. *Joe Anderson, rhp, Florida JC.
3. *Charles Nat, rhp, Solano (Calif.) CC.
4. *Robert Smart, of, Golden West (Calif.) JC.
5. *Michael Sims, rhp, Johnson County (Kan.) CC.
6. *Gary Dawson, of, Orange Coast (Calif.) JC.
7. *Eric Porter, c, Iowa Western CC.
8. *Michael Paul, 3b, JC of the Sequoias (Calif.).
9. *James Harris, of, Butte (Calif.) JC.

**January—Secondary Phase (16)**

1. *Chris Johnston, 3b, Costa Mesa (Calif.) JC.–(AAA)

**June—Regular Phase (1)**

1. **Darryl Strawberry, of, Crenshaw HS, Los Angeles.—(1983-99)**

DRAFT DROP *First 1980 high school draft pick to reach majors (May 6, 1983) • Brother of Michael Strawberry, 31st-round draft pick, Dodgers (1980)*

1. **Billy Beane, of, Mount Carmel HS, Rancho Bernardo, Calif.** (Choice from Pirates as compensation for free agent Andy Hassler)**—(1984-89)**

DRAFT DROP *General manager, Athletics (1997-2015)*

1. **John Gibbons, c, MacArthur HS, San Antonio, Texas** (Choice from Red Sox as compensation for free agent Skip Lockwood)**—(1984-86)**

DRAFT DROP *Major league manager (2004-15)*

2. **Jay Tibbs, rhp, Huffman HS, Birmingham, Ala.—(1984-90)**
3. Jody Johnston, rhp, Franklin Academy, Burke, N.Y.—(AA)
4. Mike Davis, 2b, Wichita State University.–(AAA)
5. **Ronn Reynolds, c, University of Arkansas.—(1982-90)**
6. *Jay Palma, 3b, Peterson HS, Sunnyvale, Calif.
7. **Jeff Bittiger, rhp, Secaucus (N.J.) HS.—(1986-89)**
8. **Lloyd McClendon, c, Valparaiso University.—(1987-94)**

DRAFT DROP *Major league manager (2001-15)*

9. *Anthony Kelley, rhp, Orr HS, Chicago.
10. *Otis Tramble, ss, Southern University.
11. Alex Delano, of, Florida Southern College.
12. Scott Merlack, rhp, North Hills HS, Pittsburgh.
13. **Rick Ownbey, rhp, Santa Ana (Calif.) JC.—(1982-86)**
14. *Carl Ehmann, of, Corona del Mar HS, Newport Beach, Calif.
15. *John Hennell, 1b, University of Arkansas.
16. Jim Woodward, ss-3b, Long Beach State University.
17. Kevin Teate, rhp, Jonesboro (Ga.) HS.
18. *Alan Maria, lhp, Pan American University.
19. Donald Magdzuik, rhp, Los Alamitos (Calif.) HS.
20. Mickey Replogle, rhp, Rose State (Okla.) JC.
21. *Mark Pingree, 2b, Lewis-Clark State (Idaho) College.
22. *Trey Brooks, ss, Texas Christian University.
23. *Anthony Beal, of, Mainland HS, Daytona Beach, Fla.
24. *Steve O'Donnell, ss, Connellsville (Pa.) HS.
25. Kenneth Stelly, lhp, Northwestern State University.
26. *Keith Jones, of, Wichita State University.
27. Chuck Schnoor, ss, Kearney State (Neb.) College.
28. *Thomas Saenz, lhp, Pacifica HS, Cypress, Calif.
29. *Anthony Malloy, lhp, Rider College.
30. Jessie Vann, 3b, Johnson County (Kan.) CC.
31. Shake Moore, of, Long Beach State University.
32. Duane Evans, 1b, Oklahoma State University.
33. Martin Brophy, c, St. Clair (Pa.) HS.
34. *Lance Hudson, ss, San Bernardino HS, Fremont, Calif.
35. *Darrel White, of, St. Louis CC-Meramec.
36. Bill Boone, 1b, LaSalle University.
37. Ricky Poe, 1b-of, Arkansas State University.
38. *Nick Esposito, rhp, Los Medanos (Calif.) JC.

**June—Secondary Phase (11)**

1. *Bill Worden, c, Stanford University.—(AA)
2. ***Al Newman, 2b, Chaffey (Calif.) JC.—(1985-92)**
3. *Derek Tatsuno, lhp, Aiea, Hawaii.

## NEW YORK YANKEES

**January—Regular Phase (21)**

1. *Clem Freeman, lhp, Manatee (Fla.) JC.—(AA)
2. Mark Cartwright, rhp, Yuba (Calif.) CC.
3. Reggie Bratton, rhp, Spartanburg Methodist (S.C.) JC.
4. Jeff Reynolds, 3b, Potomac State (W.Va.) JC.
5. *Randy Graham, rhp, Santa Rosa (Calif.) JC.
6. Daniel O'Regan, of, JC of San Mateo (Calif.).
7. Steve Toporek, rhp, JC of Lake County (Ill.).

**January—Secondary Phase (7)**

1. **Tom Dodd, of, University of Oregon.–(1986)**
2. *Tod Taylor, rhp, Citrus (Calif.) JC.
3. *Robert Jackowiak, rhp, Middle Georgia JC.

**June—Regular Phase (22)**

1. (Choice to Expos as compensation for free agent Rudy May)
2. (Choice to Red Sox as compensation for free agent Bob Watson)
3. *Billy Cannon, ss, Broadmoor HS, Baton Rouge, La.—DNP

DRAFT DROP *Selection voided; subject to special draft (1980), selected by Indians; attended Texas A&M, never re-drafted; first-round draft pick, Dallas Cowboys/National Football League (1984); linebacker, NFL (1984) • Son of Billy Cannon, 1959 Heisman Trophy winner, running back/ NFL (1960-70)*

4. *Steve Madden, of, New Hartford (N.Y.) HS.—DNP

DRAFT DROP *No school, never re-drafted • Brother of Andrew Madden, first-round draft pick, Red Sox (1977)*

5. Brent Gjesdal, 3b, Reynolds HS, Portland, Ore.—(AA)
6. ***Glenn Braggs, of, San Bernardino (Calif.) HS.—(1986-92)**
7. Dan Hanggie, ss, Cal State Fullerton.
8. *Dave Yobs, of, Oral Roberts University.
9. Steve Fincher, lhp, Jefferson HS, Tampa.
10. Mark Mendez, rhp, San Joaquin Delta (Calif.) JC.
11. Ken Martin, rhp, Burlington HS, Waterbury, Vt.
12. *Jeff L. Brown, c, Monache HS, Porterville, Calif.
13. David Bailey, 1b, Florida Southern College.
14. Kevin Shannon, c, University of Texas.
15. **Clay Christiansen, rhp, University of Kansas.—(1984)**
16. David Banes, 3b, University of Florida.
17. Glenn Robertson, ss, Cal State Fullerton.
18. *Todd Lamb, rhp, Cape Elizabeth (Maine) HS.
19. Michael Foster, lhp, Humboldt State (Calif.) University.
20. Don DeWitt, rhp, Ball State University.
21. Ken Smith, rhp, Florida State University.
22. John Gaston, rhp, University of Nevada.
23. Doug Latrenta, of, St. John's University.
24. Joe Perna, of, University of South Florida.
25. Jeffrey Marks, lhp, Pine Bush (N.Y.) HS.
26. Kevin Quirk, rhp, St. Joseph's University.
27. *David Myers, ss, Temple University.
28. Randy McDaniel, 2b, University of Tennessee.
29. Gerald Kennedy, rhp, Knoxville, Tenn.
30. *Jim Camacho, ss, Cal Poly Pomona.
31. **Ben Callahan, 1b-rhp, Catawba (N.C.) College.—(1983)**
32. ***Pat Clements, lhp, Pleasant Valley HS, Chico, Calif.—(1985-92)**
33. James D'Aloia, ss, St. Leo College.
34. Brad Bennett, of, Fresno State University.
35. James Gross, 3b, Miami (Ohio) University.
36. Randy Filkins, of, Cal State Stanislaus.

DRAFT DROP *Brother of Les Filkins, first-round draft pick, Tigers (1975)*

37. Darren Holt, 2b, Fresno State University.
38. *Don Montgomery, of, Proviso West HS, Bellwood, Ill.
39. Tim Knight, of, Florida International University.
40. *Joseph Portale, c, Baldwin-Wallace (Ohio) College.
41. Bob Raftice, lhp, Cape Elizabeth (Maine) HS.
42. *Gregory Eskra, rhp, Oak Glen HS, Chester, W.Va.

**June—Secondary Phase (20)**

1. John Milholland, ss, Louisburg (N.C.) JC.–(Low A)
2. Sheldon Andrews, rhp, Lower Columbia (Wash.) JC.
3. ***Randy Hunt, c, Chattahoochee Valley (Ala.) CC.—(1985-86)**
4. Joseph Stefani, rhp, Iowa Western CC.

## OAKLAND ATHLETICS

**January—Regular Phase (3)**

1. ***Dave Gallagher, of, Mercer County (N.J.) CC.—(1987-95)**
2. *Richard Ousman, rhp, Los Angeles Pierce JC.
3. *Rick Thurman, rhp, Los Angeles Pierce JC.
4. *Gail Arnold, rhp, Linn-Benton (Ore.) CC.
5. *Steven Garrett, rhp, Chabot (Calif.) JC.
6. *Greg McAnulty, of, Centralia (Wash.) JC.
7. *Gregory Mine, rhp, Green River (Wash.) CC.
8. *Greg Monda, 1b, Centralia (Wash.) JC.
9. *Eric Kuntz, rhp, Big Bend (Wash.) CC.
10. *Reggie Sells, rhp, Cochise County (Ariz.) CC.
11. *Michael Schreck, of, Antelope Valley (Calif.) JC.

### January—Secondary Phase (23)

1. *Larry Hernandez, of, Valencia (Fla.) CC.—DNP

### June—Regular Phase (4)

1. Mike King, lhp, Morningside (Iowa) College–(AAA)
2. *Rhett Whisman, ss, Fairfield (Ohio) HS.–(Low A)

DRAFT DROP *Attended Gulf Coast (Fla.) CC; re-drafted by Twins, January 1981/secondary phase (1st round)*

3. **Rich Bordi, rhp, Fresno State University.—(1980-88)**

DRAFT DROP *First player from 1980 draft to reach majors (July 16, 1980)*

4. Ken Johnson, ss, Garfield HS, Woodbridge, Va.—(Short-season A)
5. *Brian Myers, rhp, Lakewood (Calif.) HS.—DNP

DRAFT DROP *Attended Stanford; never re-drafted*

6. ***Terry Bell, c, Fairmont East HS, Kettering, Ohio.—(1986-87)**

DRAFT DROP *First-round draft pick (17th overall), Mariners (1983)*

7. John Horner, lhp, Warren Local HS, Belpre, Ohio.
8. *John Sullivan, ss, Grand Island (N.Y.) HS.
9. ***John Farrell, rhp, Short Regional HS, Monmouth Beach, N.J.—(1987-96)**

DRAFT DROP *Major league manager (2011-15)*

10. *Scott Parsons, of, Livingston (N.J.) HS.
11. *Scott Kimball, c, Skyline HS, Oakland, Calif.
12. *Robert Shannon, ss, Paul VI HS, Bellmawr, N.J.
13. *Randy Ward, 1b, University of Nevada-Las Vegas.
14. *Erik Sonberg, lhp, Bishop Kelley HS, Tulsa, Okla.

DRAFT DROP *First-round draft pick (18th overall), Dodgers (1983)*

15. *Eric Broersma, rhp, UCLA.
16. ***Scott Anderson, rhp, Newport HS, Bellevue, Wash.—(1987-95)**
17. Juan Cruz, ss, Davis HS, Yakima, Wash.
18. *Jim Teahan, rhp, University of Utah.
19. *David Couch, c, Asheboro (N.C.) HS.
20. Terry Byrum, 2b, University of Houston.
21. Joseph Soprano, of-1b, New York Tech.
22. *Barry Koch, rhp, Mesa (Ariz.) CC.
23. *David Peters, of, Northport, N.Y.
24. ***Danny Jackson, lhp, Aurora Central HS, Aurora, Colo.—(1983-97)**

DRAFT DROP *First overall draft pick, January 1982/ secondary phase, Royals*

25. *Bruce Kastelic, ss, Oklahoma State University.
26. *Don O'Connor, rhp, Sunset HS, Hayward, Calif.

### June—Secondary Phase (18)

1. *Chris Johnston, 3b, Orange Coast (Calif.) JC.–(AAA)

## PHILADELPHIA PHILLIES

### January—Regular Phase (14)

1. **Tony Ghelfi, rhp, Iowa Western CC.–(1983)**
2. Ron Richardson, rhp, Linn-Benton (Ore.) CC.
3. Jimmy Darnell, rhp, Seminole (Okla.) CC.
4. *Robin Dreizler, c, El Camino (Calif.) JC.
5. *Daniel Prine, lhp, Mott (Mich.) CC.
6. *David Vanderleen, rhp, Grand Rapids (Mich.) JC.
7. *Paul Perez, c, Lassen (Calif.) JC.
8. *Warren Oliver, ss, Belleville Area (Ill.) CC.
9. *Tommy George, ss, Bacone (Okla.) JC.
10. *Harlan Robertson, c, Hill (Texas) JC.
11. *Joe Dan Petty, rhp, Panola (Texas) JC.
12. *Kevin Bates, ss, Brevard (Fla.) CC.
13. *John Proctor, c, Allen County (Kan.) CC.
14. *Bryan Price, rhp, Ranger (Texas) JC.
15. *Douglas Scott, of, Grand Rapids (Mich.) JC.
16. Michael Befort, rhp, Allen County (Kan.) CC.
17. *Bradley Coker, c, McLennan (Texas) CC.
18. *Keith Kearney, c, Blinn (Texas) JC.
19. *Willie Briscoe, rhp, Blinn (Texas) JC.
20. *Kenneth Myrick, ss-2b, Blinn (Texas) JC.
21. Richard Yraguen, ss, Treasure Valley (Ore.) CC.
22. Dale Drew, rhp, Joliet (Ill.) JC.

### January—Secondary Phase (18)

1. *James Harris, lhp, Thomas Jefferson HS, Brooklyn, N.Y.—DNP
2. Steven True, lhp, Seminole (Okla.) JC.
3. *Bryon Henderson, c, Linn-Benton (Ore.) CC.
4. Edward Schiavo, rhp, Boyertown, Pa.

### June—Regular Phase (13)

1. Lebo Powell, c, Pine Forest HS, Pensacola, Fla.—(Low A)
2. Larry Knight, rhp, Lookout Valley HS, Chattanooga, Tenn.—(High A)
3. Doug Maggio, c, Shaler HS, Pittsburgh.—(Short-season A)
4. Jon Reelhorn, rhp, Fresno State University.–(AAA)
5. Yonis Rodriguez, rhp, Eastern District HS, Ozone Park, N.Y.—(High A)
6. Richie Gaynor, of, Bullard HS, Fresno, Calif.
7. *Bobby Hinson, rhp, LaMarque (Texas) HS.
8. *Greg Lorenzetti, ss, Fortuna (Calif.) HS.
9. **Steve Jeltz, ss-2b, University of Kansas.—(1983-90)**
10. Jerome Kovar, c, Southern Methodist University.
11. Craig Musick, ss-of, Seminole (Okla.) JC.
12. Johnny McAnally, lhp, Rogers HS, Tulsa, Okla.
13. Randy Salava, of, Indiana State University.
14. Bernardo Howard, 3b-ss, Wyandotte HS, Kansas City, Kan.
15. Tim Steverson, rhp, Umatilla (Fla.) HS.
16. ***Mike Brumley, ss, Union HS, Broken Arrow, Okla.—(1987-95)**

DRAFT DROP *Son of Mike Brumley, major leaguer (1964-66)*

17. *John Machin, lhp, Turner HS, Carrolton, Texas.
18. *Steve Smith, ss, Dallas (Ore.) HS.
19. *Andy Nossek, lhp, Waltrip HS, Houston.
20. Bryan Hoppie, ss-2b, Santa Ana (Calif.) HS.
21. **Rocky Childress, rhp, Santa Rosa (Calif.) HS.—(1985-88)**
22. Ron Ridling, of, Southeastern Oklahoma State University.
23. **Marty Decker, rhp, Point Loma Nazarene (Calif.) College.—(1983)**
24. ***Mike Capel, rhp, Spring (Texas) HS.—(1988-91)**
25. **Darren Daulton, c, Arkansas City (Kan.) HS.—(1983-97)**
26. *Douglas LaPlant, rhp, West Columbus HS, Brazoria, Texas.
27. Greg Money, rhp, W.W. Samuell HS, Dallas.
28. *Scott Wright, rhp, Vintage HS, Napa, Calif.
29. Andre Mallet, of, Madison HS, Houston.
30. Dale Cook, rhp, Winfield HS, Calvin, La.

### June—Secondary Phase (21)

1. ***Kevin Romine, of, Orange Coast (Calif.) JC.—(1985-91)**

DRAFT DROP *Father of Andrew Romine, big leaguer (2010-15) • Father of Austin Romine, major leaguer (2011-14)*

2. *Tim Lambert, rhp, Citrus (Calif.) JC.
3. **Ken Dowell, ss, Sacramento (Calif.) CC.—(1987)**
4. Paul Perez, c, Lassen (Calif.) JC.
5. **Ed Wojna, rhp, Indian River (Fla.) CC.—(1985-89)**
6. *John Whitt, of, Los Angeles Harbor JC.

## PITTSBURGH PIRATES

### January—Regular Phase (24)

1. *Darryl Banks, rhp, JC of Southern Idaho.—(AAA)
2. *Gerald Eckelberry, rhp, JC of Southern Idaho.
3. James Goff, rhp, Edmonds (Wash.) CC.
4. Scott Gibson, rhp, Seminole (Fla.) CC.
5. *Kyle Johnson, rhp, Seminole (Okla.) JC.
6. *Mark Andos, rhp, Cuyahoga (Ohio) CC.
7. Ray Jablonski, c, Canisius College.
8. *Robert Bailey, 3b-of, Louisburg (N.C.) JC.
9. *Matthew Shibner, 3b-rhp, Louisburg (N.C.) JC.
10. ***Bill Bathe, c, Fullerton (Calif.) JC.–(1986-90)**

### January—Secondary Phase (6)

1. ***Keith Creel, rhp, University of Texas.—(1982-87)**
2. *Sheldon Andrews, rhp, Lower Columbia (Wash.) JC.
3. ***Tom Nieto, c, Cerritos (Calif.) JC.–(1984-90)**
4. *Kevin Babb, rhp, Rose Lodge, Ore.
5. *Jeff Metz, rhp, Yavapai (Ariz.) JC.

### June—Regular Phase (23)

1. **Rich Renteria, ss, South Gate (Calif.) HS** (Choice from Angels as compensation for free agent Bruce Kison)**—(1986-94)**

DRAFT DROP *Major league manager (2014)*

1. (Choice to Mets as compensation for free agent Andy Hassler)
2. Jeff Horne, rhp, White Oak HS, Jacksonville, N.C. (Choice from Giants as compensation for free agent Rennie Stennett).—(High A)
2. **Tim Burke, rhp, University of Nebraska.—(1985-92)**
3. Keith Thibodeaux, rhp, Louisiana Tech.—(AA)
4. Mike Berger, c, Central Catholic HS, Pittsburgh.—(AAA)
5. Alec McCullock, rhp, Birmingham-Southern College.—(AA)
6. **Joe Orsulak, of-1b, Parsippany Hills HS, Parsippany, N.J.—(1983-97)**
7. Robert Adkins, rhp, Texas Wesleyan College.
8. Nick Castaneda, c, San Pedro (Calif.) HS.
9. Tim Howell, c, Lompoc (Calif.) HS.
10. Michael Allman, rhp, Forthill HS, Cumberland, Md.
11. John Schaive, 1b, University of New Orleans.

DRAFT DROP *Son of John Schaive, major leaguer (1958-63)*

12. *Chuck Mathison, rhp, Theodore HS, Mobile, Ala.
13. Christopher Edwards, rhp, Indiana (Pa.) HS.
14. Robert Nichols, lhp, Delmar (Del.) HS.
15. Chris Conroyd, lhp, North Carolina State University.
16. Pat McAlurney, lhp, Wagner College.
17. *Darryl Jones, 1b, Carver HS, Columbus, Ga.
18. Mark Isbell, of, Texas Lutheran College.
19. Jeff White, lhp, Northridge HS, Johnstown, Ohio.
20. *Michael Gray, 2b, Gallatin County HS, Warsaw, Ky.
21. *Robert Lackeby, rhp, Grants Pass (Ore.) HS.
22. Meredith Tingler, rhp, Clifton Forge HS, Eagle Rock, Va.
23. *Donald Lawson, of, Bridgeport (Ala.) HS.
24. *Mark Gabriel, ss, Niagara Catholic HS, Niagara Falls, N.Y.
25. *Joe Cipolloni, c, Phoenix (Ariz.) JC.
26. *Ricky Hunley, of, Petersburg (Va.) HS.

DRAFT DROP *Linebacker, National Football League (1984-89)*

27. *George Pugsley, rhp, Miraleste HS, Ranchos Palos Verdes, Calif.
28. Don Howard, lhp, Norfolk State University.
29. Rob O'Leath, of-1b, Butler University.
30. Barry Maxwell, c, Gallatin County HS, Glencoe, Ky.
31. *Richie Carter, of, Hood River (Ore.) HS.
32. *Randy Edwards, lhp, Bishop Walsh HS, Lavale, Md.
33. Bernie Bastian, rhp, Francis Marion (S.C.) College.
34. *Andrew Baranek, 3b, Central Catholic HS, Allentown, Pa.
35. *Hal Nurkka, lhp, Chaparral HS, Scottsdale, Ariz.
36. *Bill Merrifield, ss, Rocky Mount (N.C.) HS.
37. Larry Acker, lhp, Manatee (Fla.) JC.
38. *Scott Diez, lhp, Riverview HS, Sarasota, Fla.
39. Matthew Sinnen, c, Virginia Wesleyan College.
40. *Carl Vasquez, rhp, Marietta (Ohio) College.
41. *Charles Fonville, c, White Oak HS, Jacksonville, N.C.
42. *Joseph Cutler, of, Phoenix (Ariz.) JC.

### June—Secondary Phase (17)

1. *Dave Chiono, rhp, Yuba (Calif.) CC.—DNP
2. *Tyson Hubbard, rhp, Spartanburg Methodist (S.C.) JC.
3. *Richard Lucero, rhp, Phoenix (Ariz.) JC.
4. *Brian Peck, rhp, JC of Southern Idaho.

## ST. LOUIS CARDINALS

### January—Regular Phase (16)

1. Ken Spears, of, Stratford, Conn.—(High A)
2. Brian O'Donnell, lhp, Milroy, Pa.
3. Mitch Southern, of, Mount San Antonio (Calif.) JC.
4. **Kevin Hagen, rhp, Bellevue (Wash.) CC.—(1983-84)**
5. Donald Hughes, rhp, Pensacola (Fla.) JC.
6. *Edward McNamara, rhp, Edmonds (Wash.) CC.
7. James Gonzales, c, Edmonds (Wash.) CC.
8. *Barry Aden, rhp, Centralia (Wash.) JC.
9. *Dan Devers, rhp, Yavapai (Ariz.) JC.

### January—Secondary Phase (20)

1. *Joe Stefani, rhp, Iowa Western CC.—(Short-season A)

### June—Regular Phase (15)

1. Don Collins, rhp, Ferguson HS, Newport News, Va.—(High A)
2. ***Dan Plesac, lhp, Crown Point (Ind.) HS.—(1986-2003)**

DRAFT DROP *Attended North Carolina State; re-drafted by Brewers, 1983 (1st round)*

3. Dan Stryffeler, of, Fitch HS, Youngstown, Ohio.—(AAA)
4. **Ricky Horton, lhp, University of Virginia.—(1984-90)**
5. Brent Milligan, lhp, West Perry HS, Loysville, Pa.—(Low A)
6. Russ Davis, rhp, University of Mississippi.
7. **Jim Adduci, of, Southern Illinois University.—(1983-89)**
8. Jay North, rhp, Ygnacio Valley HS, Concord, Calif.
9. *Joe Wood, 2b, Herkimer (N.Y.) HS.
10. *David Page, 3b-rhp, Sunnyside HS, Tucson, Ariz.
11. *Dave Droschak, rhp, Pensacola (Fla.) JC.
12. *Mike Samuel, ss, Pacifica HS, Garden Grove, Calif.
13. *Steven Anderson, ss, Kennedy HS, Granada Hills, Calif.
14. Mike Gambeski, 3b, Hamden (Conn.) HS.
15. Rick Weems, c, Columbus (Ga.) College.
16. John Martin, rhp, University of Washington.
17. Paul Cherry, lhp, Monsignor Pace HS, Davie, Fla.
18. *Gary Jensen, c, Solano (Calif.) CC.
19. *Jim Jefferson, rhp, Marcos de Niza HS, Tempe, Ariz.
20. *James Allison, of, Ygnacio Valley HS, Concord, Calif.
21. Greg Dunn, rhp-of, Eisenhower HS, Yakima, Wash.
22. Mike Rhodes, lhp, Virginia Tech.
23. James Stevens, of-3b, Kecoughtan HS, Hampton, Va.
24. Perry Redmond, of, University City (Mo.) HS.
25. *Mike Santiago, lhp, Baldwin Park (Calif.) HS.
26. Barry Sayler, c, Seattle University.
27. *Jay Keeler, rhp, Florida State University.
28. Ken Mohler, lhp, University of South Florida.
29. Richard Reed, rhp, Lindbergh HS, St. Louis.
30. Keith Thrower, ss, Texas Wesleyan College.
31. Tom Epple, lhp, Memorial HS, Levittown, N.Y.
32. Kevin Fehr, rhp, University of Alabama-Birmingham.
33. *John Vela, lhp, Poly HS, Riverside, Calif.
34. *Joseph Hackett, of, Elon College.
35. *Todd Schulz, of, Tombstone HS, Huachuca City, Ariz.
36. Raymond Williams, 2b-of, Pinole HS, Richmond, Calif.
37. ***Rick Aguilera, rhp, Edgewood HS, West Covina, Calif.—(1985-2000)**

### June—Secondary Phase (23)

1. ***Ray Krawczyk, rhp, Golden West (Calif.) JC.—(1984-89)**
2. *Ric Wilson, c, Mesa (Ariz.) CC.

DRAFT DROP *Scouting director, Angels (2011-15)*

## SAN DIEGO PADRES

### January—Regular Phase (6)

1. ***Ken Dowell, ss, Sacramento (Calif.) CC.—(1987)**
2. ***Curt Wardle, lhp, San Bernardino Valley (Calif.) JC.—(1984-85)**
3. *George Sarkissian, 3b, Mount San Antonio (Calif.) JC.
4. *Anthony Wadley, rhp, Laney (Calif.) JC
5. *Stacy Morgan, rhp, JC of the Redwoods (Calif.).
6. *William Dees, 1b, Chipola (Fla.) JC.

### January—Secondary Phase (10)

1. Ricky McMullen, 2b, Slidell, La.—(AAA)
2. *Randy Newman, lhp, Cypress (Calif.) JC.

### June—Regular Phase (5)

1. Jeff Pyburn, of, University of Georgia.—(AAA)

DRAFT DROP *Fourth-round draft pick, Buffalo Bills/ National Football League (1980) • Son of Jim Pyburn, major leaguer (1955-57)*

2. (Choice to Giants as compensation for free agent John Curtis)
3. (Choice to Indians as compensation for free agent Rick Wise)
4. Neil Bryant, lhp, Los Angeles CC.—(AA)

4. Dave Christianson, 1b, Kennedy HS, Chicago (Choice from Dodgers as compensation for free agent Jay Johnstone).—(High A)
5. Steve Murray, of, Glassboro State (N.J.) College.—(AA)
**6. Gerry Davis, 3b, Howard University.—(1983-85)**
7. John White, rhp, Long Beach State University.
8. *John Tillema, rhp, San Jose State University.
9. *Sam Martin, ss, Louisburg (N.C.) JC.
10. Pat Casey, of, University of Portland.
DRAFT DROP *Baseball coach, Oregon State (1995-2015)*
**11. George Hinshaw, of, University of La Verne (Calif.).—(1982-83)**
12. *Gary Blaine, ss, Livingston HS, Smithland, Ky.
13. Pat Blamey, rhp, Santa Clara, Calif.
14. Andy Krzanik, rhp, Elmhurst (Ill.) College.
15. Rodney Bellamy, ss, University of Georgia.
16. Raymie Styons, c, East Carolina University.
**17. *Glen Cook, rhp, Ithaca (N.Y.) College.—(1985)**
18. Bruce Hines, 2b, University of La Verne (Calif.).
**19. Mike Couchee, rhp, University of Southern California.—(1983)**
20. Joe Wood, 3b, Emporia State (Kan.) University.
21. Brian Duffy, rhp, University of California.
22. Rick Witt, ss-3b, Gonzaga University.
23. James Coffman, rhp, Portland State University.
24. Mike Bertalot, of, Portland State University.
25. Michael Smith, lhp, University of Washington.
26. Joe Scherger, of, University of Nebraska.
27. *Jeff Walsh, rhp, Santa Clara University.
28. Jim Thomas, c, UCLA.
29. Mike Mahoski, rhp, Gonzaga University.
30. Mickey Britt, rhp, East Carolina University.
31. *Terry Raley, ss, St. Mary's (Texas) University.
32. Scott Lovekamp, rhp, Concordia (Ill.) College.
33. *Stan Williams Jr., rhp, University of Southern California.
DRAFT DROP *Son of Stan Williams, major leaguer (1958-72)*
34. David Kirk, rhp, University of North Carolina.
35. Daniel Wodrich, 2b, Washington State University.
36. Billy Ireland, of-c, Oklahoma State University.
37. *John Slaughter, of, Southern Alamance HS, Burlington, N.C.
38. *Chuck Hartenstein, 2b, Johnson HS, Austin, Texas.
DRAFT DROP *Son of Chuck Hartenstein, major leaguer (1966-77)*
39. *Brad Ditto, 2b-ss, Rio Hondo (Calif.) JC.
**40. *Jeff M. Robinson, rhp, Christian HS, El Cajon, Calif.—(1987-92)**

**June—Secondary Phase (7)**

**1. *Ron Romanick, rhp, Arizona State University.—(1984-86)**
2. Tim Cannon, of, Chipola (Fla.) JC.
3. *Michael Tolbert, rhp, Triton (Ill.) JC.

## SAN FRANCISCO GIANTS

**January—Regular Phase (8)**

1. Willie Hysaw, rhp, Compton (Calif.) JC.—(Rookie)
2. *Randy Ebersberger, ss, Los Angeles Pierce JC.
3. Mark McDonald, rhp, Santa Barbara (Calif.) CC.
4. Joseph Henderson, 3b, San Diego Mesa JC.
5. *Dennis Ivy, of, San Joaquin Delta (Calif.) JC.
6. *Pedro LaTorre, 2b, Miami-Dade CC North.
7. *Andrew Epping, rhp, Indian Hills (Iowa) CC.
8. *James Oxe, c, Grossmont (Calif.) JC.

**January—Secondary Phase (8)**

**1. *Jeff Dedmon, rhp, West Los Angeles JC.—(1987-88)**
2. Bill Hainline, ss, Spokane, Wash.

**June—Regular Phase (7)**

**1. Jessie Reid, 1b, Lynwood (Calif.) HS.—(1987-88)**
2. Eric Erickson, lhp, La Jolla (Calif.) HS (Choice from Padres as compensation for free agent John Curtis).—(AAA)
2. (Choice to Pirates as compensation for free agent Rennie Stennett)
3. (Choice to White Sox as compensation for free agent Milt May)
4. (Choice to Brewers as compensation for free agent Jim Wohlford)
5. Rollo Adams, c-of, Southern California College.—(AA)
**6. *Dave Hengel, of, Mission HS, Fremont, Calif.—(1986-89)**
7. Mike Wallace, 3b, University of Nevada.
8. Doran Perdue, 2b, Murray State University.
9. *Ross Kingsley, c, Craig HS, Janesville, Wis.
**10. Alan Fowlkes, rhp, Cal Poly Pomona.—(1982-85)**
**11. *Brick Smith, 1b, Wake Forest University.—(1987-88)**
12. *Mark Shiflett, lhp, Auburn University.
13. Kelly Smith, of, Washington State University.
14. *Mark Johnson, c, University of San Francisco.
15. Jerome Littman, ss, Milton (Wis.) College.
16. Ben Gallo, lhp, San Diego State University.
17. Joe Banach, lhp, Peabody HS, Pittsburgh.
18. Sean Toerner, 2b, Cal State Northridge.
19. Joe Olivas, inf-rhp, San Joaquin Delta (Calif.) JC.
20. Ken Frazier, c, Compton (Calif.) HS.
21. *Craig Stevenson, ss, Chatsworth HS, Northridge, Calif.
22. David Wilson, 3b, University of Southern California.
23. *Tommy Alexander, rhp, Gordon (Ga.) JC.
24. Jeff Trax, rhp, Oakland (Mich.) University.
**25. Randy Gomez, c, University of Utah.—(1984)**
**26. Mark Dempsey, rhp, Ohio State University.—(1982)**
27. Mark Sharpe, ss-2b, UC San Diego.
28. Billy Heimach, 2b, Western Michigan University.
**29. *Gary Green, ss, Taylor-Allderdice HS, Pittsburgh.—(1986-92)**
DRAFT DROP *Son of Fred Green, major leaguer (1959-64) • First-round draft pick, Padres (1984)*
**30. *Danny Clay, of, Los Angeles Pierce JC.—(1988)**
31. *Richard Belli, rhp, Terra Nova HS, Pacifica, Calif.
**32. *Colin Ward, lhp, Citrus (Calif.) JC.—(1985)**
33. *John Duval, rhp, San Luis Obispo (Calif.) HS.
34. *Jeff Anderson, rhp, Nampa (Idaho) HS.
35. James Smith, rhp, Western HS, Las Vegas, Nev.
36. David Cardwell, ss, East Tennessee State University.
37. *Bob Tumpane, 1b, Lewis (Ill.) University.
38. Mike Lenti, 2b, St. Xavier (Ill.) College.
39. *Louis Zanini, ss, Edison HS, Stockton, Calif.
40. *Monico Corral, ss, University of San Francisco.
41. *Marlon Warren, ss, Rancho Cotate HS, Rohnert Park, Calif.
42. Doug Wabeke, 2b, Central Michigan University.
43. Robert Spurlin, c, Northern Illinois University.

**June—Secondary Phase (19)**

1. Lance Junker, of, Loyola Marymount University.—(High A)
**2. *Donnie Hill, ss, Orange Coast (Calif.) JC.—(1983-92)**
DRAFT DROP *First overall draft pick, June 1981/secondary phase, Athletics*
3. Daniel McDonald, lhp, Penn State University.
4. *Harry Kazanjian, c-of, CC of San Francisco.
5. Thomas McLaughlin, rhp, Los Angeles CC.

## SEATTLE MARINERS

**January—Regular Phase (5)**

1. *Don Freeman, ss, West Los Angeles JC.–(High A)
2. *Mike Reddish, c, Indian River (Fla.) CC.
3. *Mark Effrig, rhp, Shoreline (Wash.) CC.
4. *Al Simmons, 2b, Fort Steilacoom (Wash.) CC.
5. *Ric Wilson, c, Mesa (Ariz.) CC.
DRAFT DROP *Scouting director, Angels (2011-15)*
6. Michael Howe, lhp, Rochester, Pa.
7. *Bret Elbin, ss, Hagerstown (Md.) JC.
8. Takashi Upshur, 2b, Glassboro State (N.J.) College.

**January—Secondary Phase (13)**

**1. *Bill Mooneyham, rhp, Merced (Calif.) JC.—(1986)**
**2. Dan Firova, c, Refugio, Texas.—(1981-88)**
3. *Chris Glass, rhp, Hagerstown (Md.) JC.

**June—Regular Phase (6)**

**1. Darnell Coles, ss, Eisenhower HS, Rialto, Calif.—(1983-97)**
**2. Matt Young, lhp, UCLA.—(1983-93)**
3. Bob Hudson, rhp, UC Riverside.—(AAA)
4. Steve Krueger, lhp, University of Arkansas.–(AA)
5. *Ken Lynn, rhp, Riverside HS, Greer, S.C.–(Low A)
DRAFT DROP *Attended Spartanburg Methodist (S.C.) JC; re-drafted by Pirates, June 1981/secondary phase (3rd round)*
6. *Kevin Dukes, lhp, Arizona State University.
7. Bill Crone, ss, West Chester University.
8. *Tim Kammeyer, rhp, University of Southern California.
9. *William Blair, c, Boone HS, Orlando, Fla.
**10. Donell Nixon, of-3b, West Columbus HS, Evergreen, N.C.—(1987-90)**
DRAFT DROP *Brother of Otis Nixon, major leaguer (1983-99)*
11. Glen Walker, of, Washington State University.
12. Don McKenzie, rhp, Newberry (S.C.) College.
**13. Ed Vande Berg, lhp, Arizona State University.—(1982-88)**
14. Clark Crist, ss, University of Arizona.
15. Kevin McGann, 3b, University of New Orleans.
**16. John Moses, of, University of Arizona.—(1982-92)**
**17. Rusty McNealy, of, Florida International University.—(1983)**
18. David Blume, 1b, Lewis-Clark State (Idaho) College.
19. *Stan Holmes, of, Arizona State University.
20. *Leo George, c, Southern Methodist University.
DRAFT DROP *Son of Bill George, linebacker/National Football League (1952-66)*
**21. *Ernest Riles, ss, Middle Georgia JC.—(19F85-93)**
22. *Darren Mazeroski, 2b, Hempfield HS, Greensburg, Pa.
DRAFT DROP *Son of Bill Mazeroski, major leaguer (1956-72)*
23. *Brian Rice, lhp, Bayside HS, Virginia Beach, Va.

**June—Secondary Phase (2)**

**1. Harold Reynolds, ss, Canada (Calif.) JC.—(1983-94)**
DRAFT DROP *Brother of Don Reynolds, major leaguer (1978-79)*
2. Mark Pedersen, rhp, Washington State University.
3. *Don Freeman, ss, West Los Angeles JC.

## TEXAS RANGERS

**January—Regular Phase (13)**

1. *Mike Carriger, rhp, Bacone (Okla.) JC.—DNP
**2. Billy Taylor, rhp, Abraham Baldwin Agricultural (Ga.) JC.—(1994-2001)**
**3. *Al Newman, 2b, Chaffey (Calif.) JC.—(1985-92)**
4. *Dewayne Ward, rhp, Murray State (Texas) JC.
5. *Hans Herzog, lhp, Louisburg (N.C.) JC.
**6. Daryl Smith, rhp, Essex (Md.) CC.—(1990)**
7. *Steve Watson, rhp, Manatee (Fla.) JC.
8. *James Casey, rhp, Miami-Dade CC North.
9. James Maxwell, ss, Mercer County (N.J.) CC.
10. *Ronald Caldwell, rhp, CC of Baltimore.
11. Jeffrey Simmons, rhp, Essex (Md.) CC.
12. *Glen Edwards, of, Valencia (Fla.) CC.

**January—Secondary Phase (25)**

**1. Tommy Dunbar, of, Middle Georgia JC.—(1983-85)**
2. *David McDonald, lhp, Penn State University.
3. *John Millholland, ss, Louisburg (N.C.) JC.
4. *Jeff Groth, of, Chagrin Falls, Ohio.
DRAFT DROP *Wide receiver, National Football League (1979-85)*

**June—Regular Phase (14)**

1. Tim Maki, rhp, Carroll HS, Huntertown, Ind.—(High A)
**2. Dwayne Henry, rhp, Middletown HS, Odessa, Del.—(1984-95)**
3. Lindy Duncan, ss, University of Missouri.—(AA)
**4. Curtis Wilkerson, ss, Dinwiddie HS, Sutherland, Va.—(1983-93)**
5. Brad Mengwasser, rhp, Southern Methodist University.—(AAA)
6. Al Hartman, rhp, Joliet West HS, Joliet, Ill.
7. Tony Hudson, rhp, Cal State Fullerton.
8. Craig Goodin, ss, Tulare Union HS, Tulare, Calif.
9. *Doug Shields, ss, Plant HS, Tampa.
10. Joe Roberts, c, University of Louisville.
11. Tim Henry, lhp, Texas Wesleyan College.
12. *Dion Lowe, of, Lakewood (N.J.) HS.
13. David Stokes, 3b, Tulane University.
14. Stan Haas, of, University of Nebraska.
15. Montye Mayfield, rhp, Bell HS, Hurst, Texas.
16. Dennis Long, rhp, University of Connecticut.
17. *Lorenzo Spencer, of, Tampa Bay Tech HS, Tampa.
18. Dan Murphy, of, University of Nevada-Las Vegas.
19. Randall Carter, 2b, University of Arkansas.
20. Brett Benza, of, University of Rhode Island.
21. Brooks Wallace, ss, Texas Tech.
22. Andrew Wright, c, Lincoln (R.I.) HS.
23. George Crum, of, Hillsborough HS, Tampa.
24. *Chris Joslin, lhp, Linden HS, Gaines, Mich.
25. Richard Wilkinson, 1b, University of Texas-Arlington.
26. Perry Cliburn, rhp, Mississippi State University.
27. Paul Ondo, 1b, Southern Illinois University.
28. *P.J. Gay, of, University of North Carolina.
29. *Chris Oleson, 3b, Hinkley HS, Aurora, Colo.
30. *Cameron Young, rhp, Texas Christian University.
31. Anthony Garcia, 3b, Plant HS, Tampa.
32. Gary Venner, c, Texas Wesleyan College.
**33. Walt Terrell, rhp, Morehead State University.—(1982-92)**
34. *Bill Lucas, ss, Florida A&M University.

**June—Secondary Phase (12)**

**1. Mike Mason, lhp, Oral Roberts University.—(1982-88)**
2. *Gail Arnold, rhp, Linn-Benton (Ore.) CC.
3. *Mark Ochal, rhp, University of North Carolina.
**4. Tom Henke, rhp, East Central (Mo.) JC.—(1982-95)**

## TORONTO BLUE JAYS

**January—Regular Phase (1)**

1. Colin McLaughlin, rhp, University of Connecticut.—(AAA)
**2. *Roger Samuels, lhp, San Jose (Calif.) CC.—(1988-89)**
3. *Steve Smith, c, JC of San Mateo (Calif.).
4. *Ronald Burns, rhp, Centralia (Wash.) JC.
5. *Michael Lazzeri, of, Bellevue (Wash.) CC.
6. *Raymond Brown, 3b-rhp, Enterprise State (Ala.) JC.

**January—Secondary Phase (15)**

1. *Cary Palmer, rhp, Mesa (Ariz.) CC.—DNP
2. *Andrew Pavlovic, rhp, Yavapai (Ariz.) JC.

**June—Regular Phase (2)**

1. Garry Harris, ss, Hoover HS, San Diego.—(AA)
2. Ken Kinnard, 1b, Claremore (Okla.) HS.—(AAA)
3. Rico Sutton, of, Lamar University.—(AA)
4. Bob McNair, 1b, Oregon State University.—(High A)
5. Dennis Howard, rhp, SUNY-Buffalo.—(AAA)
6. David Trimble, 2b, Davis HS, Yakima, Wash.
7. *John Stevens, rhp, Granada Hills HS, Northridge, Calif.
8. Matt Nawrocki, rhp, College of St. Francis (Ill.).
9. Kirk Richmond, c, Everett HS, Lansing, Mich.
10. Paul Langfield, rhp, Providence College.
11. Jim Baker, rhp, Bethel (Ind.) College.
12. Sean Everton, of, Santa Clara University.
13. Mike Hurdle, of, Texas A&M University.
14. *Ben Snyder, rhp, St. Mary's (Calif.) College.
15. *Robert Smith, rhp, Westchester HS, Houston.
16. *Pete Zeegers, 1b, Tallahassee (Fla.) HS.
17. *Tom Heckman, rhp, University of Missouri.
18. John Cosby, c, Portland State University.
19. *Dennis Tiefenthaler, ss, Armour, S.D.
20. *Doug Scherer, rhp, San Jose (Calif.) CC.
21. Steven Smith, rhp, Coastal Carolina College.
22. James Michalec, c, Rice University.
23. Tom Lukish, rhp, University of Houston.
24. *Thomas Penney, c, University of Houston.
25. David Goffena, rhp-of, Sidney (Ohio) HS.

**June—Secondary Phase (16)**

1. *Michael Jefferson, of, Laney (Calif.) JC.—(High A)

# 1981

# Moore, Carter lead shift to college focus

Some blamed a poor high school crop. Others cited the impact of major league free agency. More likely it was a sign that college baseball was coming of age as a development source.

Whatever the reason, the early rounds of the 1981 draft represented a sudden and dramatic swing in demographics to low-risk, quick-return college talent for the first time in the event's 16-year history.

Emphasis in the early rounds had always been on raw, untested high school talent, but 17 of 26 first-round picks in 1981 were from the college ranks. Never before had more than 10 collegians been taken in the first round. Moreover, 34 of the first 50 players selected were from college, double the previous record.

The reverberations were felt throughout the draft, as twice as many college as high school players were selected overall, and a record-low 113 prep players actually signed. The Houston Astros didn't select a single high school player, the only such occurrence in draft history.

The emphasis on college talent continued to grow in the draft in succeeding years and by 1985 had become so pronounced that 11 of the first 12 selections were from the college ranks. Coincidentally, the first round of that draft is acknowledged as the most-talented ever.

New York Mets general manager Frank Cashen tried to explain the draft's new philosophy: "For quicker dividends, you go for college players, especially pitchers, because they're more advanced than high school kids. It takes less time for them to develop. Consequently, it's better economically . . . it costs us less money."

Free agency also contributed, with an increasing number of teams reluctant to stick with high school players in the early rounds, typically spending four or five years developing them to then risk losing them to free agency once they hit the big leagues. Other clubs, seeking immediate replacements for players lost to free agency, were looking to the colleges to fill voids.

Of 26 first-round picks in 1981, 19 reached the majors, tying the mark set the preceding two years. Additionally, the first 10 selections succeeded—tying a mark set in 1978. That made it one of the most productive first rounds ever, but the real strength of the 1981 draft was the depth of talent secured in the second and third rounds, and even beyond.

Tony Gwynn, the only Hall of Famer to come from the 1981 draft, was a third-rounder, while some of the best arms like righthanders David Cone and Mark Gubicza (both Royals picks), and lefthanders Mark Langston (Mariners) and Frank Viola (Twins) were all premium second-rounders.

But not everyone was infatuated with the talent in the 1981 draft.

SEATTLE MARINERS

Picking first overall for the second time in three years, the Mariners took Oral Roberts righthander Mike Moore, deciding Yale righthander Ron Darling's price tag might be too expensive

"It's the leanest year I've ever seen," Atlanta Braves longtime scouting director Paul Snyder said on the eve of the draft. "I'm not trying to degrade the draft, but we've only listed 14 players who we feel are worthy of first-round money.

For the Braves, who had one pick in the first three rounds, it did prove to be the leanest year ever, as not a single one of their 39 selections in the regular or secondary phases in June advanced to the big leagues; only one reached Triple-A. The Braves had no more luck with nine selections in January, making it the only time in draft history that a team whiffed on all its picks.

With their top pick (12th overall), the Braves inexplicably rolled the dice on an obscure Washington high school outfielder, Jay Roberts, a University of Washington football recruit who didn't even play baseball his senior year while partaking instead in track and field.

Roberts proved to be one of the biggest busts in draft history, hitting .187 in four seasons with 249 strikeouts in 226 games, none above Class A, before being released.

### MARINERS OPT FOR MOORE

For the second time in three years, the Seattle Mariners had first pick in the June regular phase. They made it known early they were looking for pitching.

The Mariners had their mind set on Oral Roberts righthander Mike Moore most of the spring, especially after farm director Hal Keller saw the 6-foot-4, 205-pound righthander touch 97

## AT A GLANCE

### This Date In History
**WINTER DRAFT:** Jan. 13-14
**SUMMER DRAFT:** June 8-10

### Best Draft
**SAN DIEGO PADRES. KEVIN MCREYNOLDS** (1) never quite lived up to all the hype, despite a career that was at least equal to any 1981 first-rounder. The real catch for the Padres was landing Hall of Famer **TONY GWYNN** (3) two rounds later. **JOHN KRUK** (June/secondary, 3) and **GREG BOOKER** (10) were nice additions.

### Worst Draft
**ATLANTA BRAVES.** By almost any standard, the weakest draft in baseball history. The Braves selected 48 players; none played in the majors, one reached Triple-A.

### First-Round Bust
**JAY ROBERTS, OF, BRAVES.** The Braves went looking for the best athlete they could find, and went out on a limb in taking Roberts, who excelled at football and track in high school but played little baseball. He hit .187-9-68 over four seasons, none above low Class A, before being released during the 1984 season.

### Second To None
**MARK LANGSTON, LHP, MARINERS.** Langston posted a 6-7, 4.38 record as a junior at San Jose State. The Mariners took him in the second round, taught him some of the finer points of pitching and were rewarded when he led the American League in strikeouts three of his first four seasons in Seattle.

### Late-Round Find
**LENNY DYKSTRA, OF, METS (13TH ROUND).** Dykstra had legitimate top-of-the-order skills, but scouts were skeptical of his undersized frame. What Dykstra lacked physically he more than made up for with his fearless style of play. Dykstra played 12 years in the majors with

CONTINUED ON PAGE 244

## AT A GLANCE

CONTINUED FROM PAGE 243

the Mets and Phillies; in his best season, for the 1993 National League-champion Phillies, he hit .305-19-66 and led the league with 143 runs, 194 hits and 129 walks.

### Never Too Late

**DANA WILLIAMS, OF, REDS (34TH ROUND).** The Reds took an unsuccessful stab at Williams, an Alabama high school product. Two years later, he signed with the Red Sox for $15,000 as a nondrafted free agent out of Enterprise State (Ala.) CC. Though he got only one major league hit, in 1989, Williams had a lengthy career in the minors, hitting .291 over 10 seasons.

### Overlooked

**BOBBY BONILLA, OF, PIRATES.** The Pirates got a bargain when they signed Bonilla out of a New York City high school in 1981 for $3,000. He played 16 seasons in the majors from 1986-2001, hitting .279 with 287 home runs.

### International Gem

**STAN JAVIER, OF, CARDINALS.** Javier was the son of longtime Cardinals second baseman Julian Javier, and named for Cardinals great Stan Musial, a close friend of his father's. A Dominican prospect, Javier signed with the Cardinals at 17 for $12,500, but was packaged to the Yankees, along with **BOBBY MEACHAM** (the Cardinals' first-round pick in 1981), less than two years later. Overall, he played 17 seasons with eight clubs in the majors, hitting .269-57-503 with 246 stolen bases.

### Minor League Take

**KEVIN MCREYNOLDS, OF, PADRES.** McReynolds didn't play in the minors in 1981 while recovering from a serious knee injury, but dominated the minor leagues over the next two years. He hit a combined .368-33-137 in 1982 between Class A Reno and Double-A Amarillo, and then won a Pacific Coast

## 1981: THE FIRST ROUNDERS

| CLUB: PLAYER, POS., SCHOOL | HOMETOWN | B-T | HT. | WT. | AGE | BONUS | FIRST YEAR | LAST YEAR | PEAK LEVEL (YEARS) |
|---|---|---|---|---|---|---|---|---|---|
| **JUNE—REGULAR PHASE** | | | | | | | | | |
| **1. Mariners: Mike Moore, rhp, Oral Roberts** | **Eakly, Okla.** | **R-R** | **6-4** | **205** | **21** | **$100,000** | **1981** | **1995** | **Majors (14)** |
| Unsigned 1978 third-rounder became top pick after going 28-11, 2.64 in three years at ORU; went 161-176, 4.39 in majors, won two games for A's in '89 Series. | | | | | | | | | |
| **2. Cubs: Joe Carter, of, Wichita State** | **Oklahoma City** | **R-R** | **6-3** | **215** | **21** | **$125,000** | **1981** | **1998** | **Majors (16)** |
| Attended WSU for football, left as one of its best baseball players ever, hit .411-24-120 as JR; highlight of long MLB career was walkoff HR in '93 Series for Blue Jays. | | | | | | | | | |
| **3. Angels: Dick Schofield, ss, Griffin HS** | **Springfield, Ill.** | **R-R** | **5-11** | **177** | **18** | **$70,000** | **1981** | **1996** | **Majors (14)** |
| Remarkably similar career to that of father Ducky, 19-year utilityman; dad played in 1,321 games, hit .227; son played in 1,368 games, mostly for Angels, hit .230. | | | | | | | | | |
| **4. Mets: Terry Blocker, of, Tennessee State** | **Columbia, S.C.** | **L-L** | **6-2** | **185** | **20** | **$127,500** | **1981** | **1989** | **Majors (3)** |
| Hit .402 with 11 HRs, 34-of-35 SBs as a college JR, Mets thought they had another Willie Wilson; could never crack Mets OF, spent most of career in Triple-A, Mexico. | | | | | | | | | |
| **5. Blue Jays: Matt Williams, rhp, Rice** | **Clute, Texas** | **R-R** | **6-2** | **197** | **21** | **$83,000** | **1981** | **1986** | **Majors (2)** |
| College senior led NCAA in strikeouts much of '81 season with big fastball/slider; never clicked as a pro, went 3-2, 5.29 in majors, 43-53, 3.80 in minors. | | | | | | | | | |
| **6. Padres: Kevin McReynolds, of, Arkansas** | **Little Rock, Ark.** | **R-R** | **6-1** | **200** | **21** | **$115,000** | **1982** | **1994** | **Majors (12)** |
| Tore up knee a month before draft; returned to hit .372-65-253 over next two seasons in minors, but MLB career (.265-211-807) never lived up to expectations. | | | | | | | | | |
| **7. White Sox: Daryl Boston, of, Woodward HS** | **Cincinnati** | **L-L** | **6-4** | **185** | **18** | **$68,000** | **1981** | **1995** | **Majors (11)** |
| Recruited as QB by Notre Dame, other colleges, but White Sox loved his power-speed package; spent 11 seasons in majors but never fully realized potential. | | | | | | | | | |
| **8. Cardinals: Bobby Meacham, ss, San Diego State** | **Westminster, Calif.** | **R-R** | **6-1** | **185** | **20** | **$92,500** | **1981** | **1990** | **Majors (6)** |
| Hit .375-7-51 with 44 SBs as college teammate of Tony Gwynn, but showed limited offense in 10 years as a pro; hit .236 in majors with Yankees, same in minors. | | | | | | | | | |
| **9. Rangers: Ron Darling, rhp, Yale** | **Millbury, Mass.** | **R-R** | **6-3** | **205** | **20** | **$115,000** | **1981** | **1995** | **Majors (13)** |
| If not for use of an agent, would have been No. 1 pick; attended Yale as SS, took up pitching and made rapid strides; won 136 games in major league career. | | | | | | | | | |
| **10. Giants: Mark Grant, rhp, Catholic HS** | **Joliet, Ill.** | **R-R** | **6-2** | **195** | **17** | **$85,000** | **1981** | **1995** | **Majors (8)** |
| No. 1-ranked player by Scouting Bureau had 191 SO as prep SR, twice led league in wins in minors, but went 22-32, 4.31 in majors; longtime Padres broadcaster. | | | | | | | | | |
| **11. Twins: Mike Sodders, 3b, Arizona State** | **Westminster, Calif.** | **R-R** | **6-3** | **195** | **22** | **$42,500** | **1981** | **1984** | **Class AAA (2)** |
| Breakout senior year at ASU (.424-22-100) drew comparisons to Bob Horner, but engaged in bitter holdout with Twins, career never took off before tore rotator cuff. | | | | | | | | | |
| **12. Braves: # Jay Roberts, of, Centralia HS** | **Centralia, Wash.** | **R-R** | **6-3** | **210** | **18** | **$65,000** | **1981** | **1984** | **Class A (2)** |
| Braves gambled on best available athlete, but Washington football recruit failed miserably, hit .187-9-68 in minors; picked up football at UW after getting released. | | | | | | | | | |
| **13. Indians: George Alpert, of, Livingston HS** | **Livingston, N.J.** | **L-L** | **6-1** | **185** | **17** | **$80,000** | **1981** | **1983** | **Class A (2)** |
| Had 100 college football offers, chose baseball after hitting .510-8-35; hit just .216-10-59 as a pro, voluntarily retired in 1983 to become WR at Penn State. | | | | | | | | | |
| **14. Pirates: Jim Winn, rhp, John Brown (Ark.)** | **Clever, Mo.** | **R-R** | **6-4** | **185** | **21** | **$65,000** | **1981** | **1988** | **Majors (6)** |
| Hard thrower went 10-2, 1.56 (69 IP/93 SO) for NAIA school that promptly dropped baseball; went 12-17, 4.67 in majors before elbow surgery ended career. | | | | | | | | | |
| **15. Athletics: Tim Pyznarski, 3b/of, Eastern Illinois** | **Chicago Ridge, Ill.** | **R-R** | **6-2** | **190** | **21** | **$67,500** | **1981** | **1989** | **Majors (1)** |
| Big college season (.437-24-74) led to first-round opportunity; big minor league campaign in Triple-A in 1986 (.326-23-119, 25 SB) led to brief shot in majors. | | | | | | | | | |
| **16. Cubs: Vance Lovelace, lhp, Hillsborough HS** | **Tampa** | **L-L** | **6-5** | **190** | **17** | **$85,000** | **1981** | **1994** | **Majors (3)** |
| Big lefty played on same HS team as Dwight Gooden; chronic control issues in minors (23-58, 5.02, 729 BB in 793 IP) limited time in majors, walked 10 in 5 IP. | | | | | | | | | |
| **17. Tigers: Ricky Barlow, rhp, Woodville HS** | **Woodville, Texas** | **R-R** | **6-1** | **160** | **18** | **$67,500** | **1981** | **1987** | **Class AAA (1)** |
| Went 14-1 as prep senior, but 3-29, 6.96 in one two-year stretch in minors; went 23-58, 5.56 overall with 434 BB/386 SO ratio in seven seasons. | | | | | | | | | |
| **18. Expos: Darren Dilks, lhp, Oklahoma State** | **Upland, Calif.** | **L-L** | **6-3** | **204** | **20** | **$85,000** | **1981** | **1984** | **Class AAA (2)** |
| Led Cowboys to final game of CWS as two-way player in '81, went 16-3, 3.35 with 243 Ks in 187 IP on mound in two years; rotator-cuff injury ended career. | | | | | | | | | |
| **19. Red Sox: Steve Lyons, of/ss, Oregon State** | **Corvallis, Ore.** | **L-R** | **6-3** | **190** | **21** | **$55,000** | **1981** | **1993** | **Majors (9)** |
| Nicknamed "Psycho" for quirky personality, but made things happen on field with speed, hustle, arm strength, occasional power; hit .252-19-196 in majors. | | | | | | | | | |
| **20. Phillies: Johnny Abrego, rhp, Mission HS** | **San Jose, Calif.** | **R-R** | **5-11** | **175** | **18** | **$70,000** | **1981** | **1987** | **Majors (1)** |
| Arizona State signee blew out arm in final start in Rookie ball, sat out 1982 after elbow surgery; Rule 5 pick-up by Cubs a year later, saw brief service in majors. | | | | | | | | | |
| **21. Blue Jays: # John Cerutti, lhp, Amherst College** | **Albany, N.Y.** | **L-L** | **6-2** | **185** | **21** | **$40,000** | **1981** | **1992** | **Majors (7)** |
| Rare D-III first-rounder after elevating velocity to 90-91 mph, going 11-1, 2.30; spent six years in Toronto, died with heart issue in 2004 when club broadcaster. | | | | | | | | | |
| **22. Dodgers: Dave Anderson, ss, Memphis State** | **Memphis, Tenn.** | **R-R** | **6-2** | **185** | **20** | **$50,000** | **1981** | **1992** | **Majors (10)** |
| Didn't play baseball as college freshman, but surged into first round after hitting .397-14-61 with 39 SBs; after playing career, had extensive career as coach. | | | | | | | | | |
| **23. Royals: Dave Leeper, of, Southern California** | **Orange, Calif.** | **L-L** | **5-11** | **165** | **21** | **$70,000** | **1981** | **1988** | **Majors (2)** |
| Drafted in third round by Twins as pitcher in 1978, became OF at USC, hit .355 with 10 HRs as JR; spent bulk of career in minors, reached MLB briefly, hit .075-0-4. | | | | | | | | | |
| **24. Rangers: Al Lachowicz, rhp, Pittsburgh** | **McKees Rocks, Pa.** | **R-R** | **6-3** | **190** | **20** | **$52,500** | **1981** | **1986** | **Majors (1)** |
| Second of two Rangers first-rounders showed early promise, but often clashed with club officials over role/lack of opportunity, went winless in brief MLB career. | | | | | | | | | |
| **25. Red Sox: Kevin Burrell, c, Poway HS** | **Poway, Calif.** | **R-R** | **6-2** | **175** | **18** | **$60,000** | **1981** | **1991** | **Class AAA (4)** |
| Chased major league dream for 11 years as journeyman catcher, but came up short; peaked in Triple-A, hit .233-53-319 overall; became longtime scout. | | | | | | | | | |
| **26. Padres: Frank Castro, c, Miami** | **Hialeah, Fla.** | **R-R** | **6-0** | **180** | **21** | **$50,000** | **1981** | **1986** | **Class AA (4)** |
| Cuban-born player moved to U.S. at 11, hit 30 homers over three years at Miami; compensation to Padres for loss of Dave Winfield, hit .254-36-209 in minors. | | | | | | | | | |
| **JANUARY—REGULAR PHASE** | | | | | | | | | |
| **1. Cubs: Jim Rooney, lhp, CC of Morris (N.J.)** | **Stony Point, N.Y.** | **L-L** | **6-2** | **185** | **20** | **Unsigned** | **1981** | **1984** | **Class AA (1)** |
| Re-drafted by Orioles in June/secondary phase (7th overall), signed for $15,000, pitched four years in O's system, had extensive career since as coach/scout. | | | | | | | | | |
| **JANUARY—SECONDARY PHASE** | | | | | | | | | |
| **1. Cardinals: Harry McCulla, c, Delgado (La.) JC** | **Houma, La.** | **R-R** | **6-1** | **195** | **20** | **$34,000** | **1981** | **1986** | **Class AA (3)** |
| Won Midwest League batting title at .317 in 1985, but never cracked .300 again in six-year career; overall, hit .251-50-279 in 646 games. | | | | | | | | | |
| **JUNE—SECONDARY PHASE** | | | | | | | | | |
| **1. Athletics: Donnie Hill, ss, Arizona State** | **Pomona, Calif.** | **B-R** | **5-10** | **160** | **20** | **$35,000** | **1981** | **1992** | **Majors (9)** |
| Switch-hitting SS on '81 College World Series champions; spent nine seasons in majors in utility role with four clubs, hit .257-28-228 in 756 games. | | | | | | | | | |

*# Deceased.*

## How They Should Have Done It

Based on the career WAR (Wins Above Replacement, as calculated by Baseball-Reference.com) numbers achieved by all the players eligible for the 1981 draft, here's how the first round should have unfolded. Numbers in parentheses indicate the round when the player was actually drafted

| | Player, Pos. | Actual Draft | WAR | Bonus |
|---|---|---|---|---|
| 1. | Tony Gwynn, of | Padres (3) | 68.9 | $25,000 |
| 2. | David Cone, rhp | Royals (3) | 62.5 | $17,000 |
| 3. | Fred McGriff, 1b | Yankees (9) | 52.6 | $15,000 |
| 4. | Mark Langston, lhp | Mariners (2) | 50.7 | $38,500 |
| 5. | Frank Viola, lhp | Twins (2) | 47.4 | $25,000 |
| 6. | Devon White, of | Angels (6) | 47.0 | $12,500 |
| 7. | Lenny Dykstra, of | Mets (13) | 42.2 | $17,500 |
| 8. | Paul O'Neill, of | Reds (4) | 38.8 | $35,000 |
| 9. | Mark Gubicza, rhp | Royals (2) | 38.0 | $55,000 |
| 10. | Sid Fernandez, lhp | Dodgers (3) | 32.8 | $40,000 |
| 11. | Kevin McReynolds, of | Padres (1) | 30.0 | $115,000 |
| | Bobby Bonilla, of | Pirates (NDFA) | 30.0 | $3,000 |
| 13. | Mickey Tettleton, c | Athletics (5) | 29.3 | $18,000 |
| 14. | Mike Moore, rhp | Mariners (1) | 28.5 | $100,000 |
| 15. | Kevin Gross, rhp | Phillies (Jan.-S/1) | 28.0 | $18,000 |
| 16. | John Kruk, of | Padres (June-S/3) | 24.9 | $2,500 |
| 17. | John Franco, lhp | Dodgers (5) | 24.2 | $15,000 |
| 18. | Bob Tewksbury, rhp | Yankees (19) | 21.2 | $5,000 |
| 19. | Ron Darling, rhp | Rangers (1) | 20.2 | $115,000 |
| 20. | Glenn Davis, 1b | Astros (Jan.-S/1) | 19.5 | $23,500 |
| 21. | Joe Carter, of | Cubs (1) | 19.4 | $125,000 |
| 22. | Dick Schofield, ss | Angels (1) | 18.8 | $70,000 |
| 23. | Phil Bradley, of | Mariners (3) | 18.6 | $25,000 |
| 24. | Bill Wegman, rhp | Brewers (5) | 18.1 | $10,000 |
| 25. | Mike Gallego, 2b | Athletics (2) | 17.1 | $25,000 |
| 26. | Eric Plunk, rhp | Yankees (4) | 13.8 | $60,000 |

| | Top 3 Unsigned Players | | | Year Signed |
|---|---|---|---|---|
| 1. | Roger Clemens, rhp | Mets (12) | 140.3 | 1982 |
| 2. | Mark McGwire, rhp | Expos (8) | 62.0 | 1984 |
| 3. | Lance Johnson, of | Pirates (30) | 30.1 | 1984 |

mph in an outing against UCLA March 16.

"Once I saw him, he was on the top perch and someone had to knock him off," Keller said. "I liked his consistency and ability to hold his stuff a long time. A lot of pitchers can throw hard for four or five innings. There's a lot of five-inning pitchers. I think he's a nine-inning pitcher."

It took one of the most memorable pitching performances in NCAA playoff history, by Yale's Ron Darling, to suddenly make it a two-man entry the final two weeks. With Mariners scouts in attendance, Darling went head-to-head against St. John's Viola, with Viola winning in the 12th inning, 1-0.

Darling was spectacular in defeat. He had a no-hitter through 11, struck out 16, and lost when St. John's Steve Scafa hit a flare over the second baseman's head for his team's only hit and scored the game's only run when he stole second, third and home.

"I went back to see Darling in that game because I had heard so many good things," Keller said. "I had no idea we would seriously consider him, but he pitched so good, we had to consider him with Moore."

A key factor that swung support to Moore was Darling's decision to hire an agent, Steve Kaufman. The Mariners could never get a set bonus figure from Kaufman on what it would take to sign Darling, though it was later determined to be $150,000.

Moore, on the other hand, conducted his own negotiations. His $100,000 price tag was more in the Mariners' range, so they went for Moore, who was 12-3, 3.18 with 101 strikeouts in 124 innings as a junior for Oral Roberts.

"I knew I was either going to be the No. 1 pick or go real quick after that," said Moore, 28-11, 2.64 in three seasons in college. "Seattle called me on Saturday and told me I was going to be the first choice (on Monday). I guess I could have gotten more money, but Seattle is the team I wanted to be with. I didn't want to hold out. I was ready to play and didn't see any reason to wait."

Moore had mixed success in seven seasons with the Mariners, but became a key member of Oakland's 1989 World Series championship team after signing with the A's as a free agent.

When Seattle passed on Darling, other clubs followed suit and he lasted until the ninth pick. The Texas Rangers took him in that spot and signed him for $115,000—more than he would have gotten from the Mariners, but less than his asking price. Curiously, the Rangers pedaled Darling off to the Mets prior to the 1982 season in an ill-conceived trade.

Darling might never have become a first-rounder had he not attended an Ivy League institution.

"I went to college as a shortstop," he said. "If I had gone any other place except Yale (where there was a pitching shortage), I might still be in the infield."

The 6-foot-3, 195-pound Darling began pitching with a purpose in his sophomore season at Yale, and was an immediate hit, going 11-2, 1.31. He also set a school record by hitting .386. A year later though, he was overworked as he completed all 13 starts on the mound while taking a regular turn in the field when he wasn't pitching. His performance slipped slightly, to 9-4, 2.09, but his classic matchup against Viola, in his final outing, restored Darling's status as a first-round pick.

FRINZI STUDIO

Ron Darling

Viola, who went in the second round to the Minnesota Twins and later became a teammate of Darling's with the Mets, remained in awe of the game Darling pitched against him in college. "It's the best game I ever saw pitched," said Viola a decade later, and by then an established big-leaguer.

For all the notoriety that Darling received from that classic encounter, Viola went 10-0, 0.87 for St. John's in his final collegiate season and ended up becoming the better pitcher over the course of their careers. He reached the big leagues by 1982, a full 15 months before Darling, and by 1987 was the World Series MVP for the champion Twins; a year later, he went 24-7, 2.64 and was the American League's Cy Young Award winner—

### AT A GLANCE

League triple crown a year later, batting .377-32-116 for Triple-A Las Vegas.

### One Who Got Away

**ROGER CLEMENS, RHP, METS (12TH ROUND).** In one season at San Jacinto (Texas) JC, Clemens put himself on the radar by increasing the velocity on his fastball roughly 10 mph to the low 90s. He rejected a $30,000 offer from the Mets in favor of an opportunity to pitch for two seasons at Texas, and the decision paid off as he became the most celebrated player in the 1983 draft class.

### He Was Drafted?

**BUBBY BRISTER, SS, TIGERS (4TH ROUND).** Brister played on two Super Bowl championship teams as a quarterback in the NFL for 15 years, but before that played briefly in the Tigers system. Drafted out of a Louisiana high school, Brister got a $50,000 bonus to forgo a scholarship to Alabama. His first season at Rookie-level Bristol ended after 39 games when he broke his thumb. Brister chose not to return a year later and instead launched a college football career—first at Tulane, later at Northeast Louisiana—that led to his being picked in the 1986 NFL draft by the Pittsburgh Steelers.

### Did You Know . . .

The Astros became the only team in draft history in 1981 to select only college players in the June regular phase. None of the 26 players they drafted reached the majors.

### They Said It

Mets scouting director **JOE MCILVAINE**, who passed on outfielder **KEVIN MCREYNOLDS** in the first round of the 1981 draft, but later traded for him as a general manager: "I am disappointed with how McReynolds turned out. He should have been a superstar. He didn't use that talent as much as he should have."

## DRAFT SPOTLIGHT: TONY GWYNN

Tony Gwynn was an unheralded baseball player as an amateur but become one of the game's all-time greatest hitters

Tony Gwynn pulled off one of the rarest doubles in draft history on June 9, 1981. He was drafted that day by professional teams in baseball and basketball, by the San Diego Padres and San Diego Clippers, in the same city where he played the two sports as a collegiate star.

For three years, Gwynn had excelled as a point guard for San Diego State, and helped turn around a downtrodden program. He earned all-conference honors as a senior, while becoming the school's all-time assists leader. Basketball was his passion. But when the 5-foot-11 Gwynn was forced to make a decision on which sport to pursue professionally, it wasn't a tough call. It was baseball all the way.

Even though Gwynn didn't play baseball as a freshman, and joined the Aztecs baseball team only at the conclusion of basketball each of the next three springs, he excelled at his second sport. As a fourth-year junior, he hit .416 with 11 homers and 62 RBIs, in spite of missing the first 20 games of the season. "I thought I could play baseball for a long time," Gwynn said. "In the NBA, guys who are 5-11 usually only last one or two years. There is always someone coming out of the draft who is better than you are."

Gwynn excelled in both sports at Long Beach Poly High. He hit .563 as a senior, but was recruited almost exclusively to play basketball. He chose San Diego State because basketball coach Tim Vezie agreed to let him play baseball. But when an overweight Gwynn was a freshman, Vezie reversed course and forbade him from playing baseball, putting him on a conditioning program and get in better shape for basketball.

A year later, Bobby Meacham, a highly recruited freshman shortstop who remembered Gwynn as an outstanding hitter in high school, spotted him on campus and pushed Aztecs baseball coach Jim Dietz to give him a shot. A skeptical Dietz did, though only after two of his outfielders were injured. "There were flaws." Dietz recalled. "He was way behind in fundamentals. His throwing arm wasn't developed. I watched him in batting practice, though, and he had a short, compact swing. Within a few days, he was hitting everything thrown at him. So we hid him in left field and went from there."

Gwynn hit .301 in his first season, mostly in a reserve role. He spent two more seasons juggling basketball and baseball. By 1981, Meacham had emerged as a star and attracted droves of scouts, which also benefited Gwynn. By hitting in excess of .400 for a second straight season, Gwynn also convinced scouts he was a viable baseball prospect.

The Padres focused on Gwynn because general manager Jack McKeon was a regular at San Diego State games to watch his son Kelly. McKeon took a liking to Gwynn and pushed hard to draft him as early as the second round. They took him one round later, and signed him for $25,000.

Gwynn wasted little time in proving he could hit professional pitching. Assigned to short-season Walla Walla, he hit a league-best .331, and with 12 homers and 37 RBIs might have won a Northwest League triple crown had he not been promoted to Double-A Amarillo, where he hit .462 with four homers in 23 games. Of equal significance, Gwynn developed into more of a complete player.

"After a couple of weeks at Walla Walla, I felt my arm getting stronger and stronger," Gwynn said. "I didn't do anything special to work on it. I was just able to play and throw every day without worrying about basketball or my studies."

From there, it was just a matter of time until Gwynn joined the Padres. He did on July 19, 1982, and remained in San Diego for 20 years, winning eight batting titles while hitting .338 overall. By the time he finally hung it up after the 2001 season, Gwynn had built his Hall of Fame credentials with 3,141 hits and five Gold Glove Awards.

After his playing career, Gwynn succeeded Dietz as the baseball coach at San Diego State in 2002, and remained in the role until he died in 2014 of salivary gland cancer.

recognition the more celebrated Darling never achieved. Over a 15-year big league career, Viola went 176-150, 3.73; Darling went 136-116, 3.87 over 13 seasons.

### COLLEGES MAKE SIGNIFICANT IMPACT

Moore and Darling led the unprecedented wave of college selections in the first round. Of the 17 collegians who got top-round billing, eight were not drafted out of high school, a testament to the growing impact of college baseball in the game's player-development process.

Among those passed over out of high school was Wichita State outfielder Joe Carter, drafted second overall by the Chicago Cubs. He had a spectacular three-year career with the Shockers, setting several NCAA single-season and career records.

"I can understand why I didn't get drafted in high school," Carter said. "I was pretty raw. I didn't know much about baseball except throwing and hitting. Plus, no one really saw me play. We would get a game up with some school and just head over and play them. It was really no big deal."

Carter was better known in high school as a football player. He was an all-state quarterback, and yet was recruited by Wichita State to play wide receiver. He started several games for the Shockers as a freshman and appeared to have a bright future in football.

But he never played again, as he became such an overnight hit on the baseball diamond that he turned all his attention to that sport. He hit .450 with 19 homers and 101 RBIs as a freshman. Over his three-year career at Wichita State, Carter hit .436 with 58 homers and a college-record 312 RBIs.

Carter signed with the Cubs for $125,000 and went on to play 16 years in the majors for six clubs, and became best known for his walkoff home run in Game Six of the 1993 World Series, which propelled the Toronto Blue Jays to a second straight championship.

As talented as Carter was, Arkansas outfielder Kevin McReynolds was the most coveted talent in the 1981 draft. A triple crown winner in the Southwest Conference the previous year, he was an established power hitter with speed and superior defensive skills.

But little more than a week before that year's draft, McReynolds had surgery to repair a knee damaged that spring while sliding into second base. On D-Day, he was hobbling on crutches,

### Fastest To The Majors

| | Player, Pos. | Drafted (Round) | Debut |
|---|---|---|---|
| 1. | Mike Moore, rhp | Mariners (1) | April 11, 1982 |
| 2. | Frank Viola, lhp | Twins (2) | June 6, 1982 |
| 3. | Jeff Keener, rhp | Cardinals (7) | June 8, 1982 |
| 4. | Tony Gwynn, of | Padres (3) | July 19, 1982 |
| 5. | Neal Heaton, lhp | Indians (2) | Sept. 3, 1982 |

**FIRST HIGH SCHOOL SELECTION:** Dick Schofield, ss (AngelS/1, Sept. 8, 1983)

**LAST PLAYER TO RETIRE:** John Franco, lhp (July 1, 2005)

uncertain whether his knee would ever respond 100 percent. In 32 games as a junior, he hit .342 with eight home runs.

Most teams were skeptical that he would make a full recovery. But not the San Diego Padres, who took McReynolds with the sixth pick overall.

"Some clubs were unwilling to take the chance," Padres general manager Jack McKeon said. "In a way, I guess you could say he was damaged goods, but we talked to his doctors, we had our doctors talk to his doctors and we decided his chances for full recovery were good."

McReynolds, who signed with the Padres for $115,000, missed the balance of the 1981 season and was still not 100 percent the following spring. He was relegated to DH duties most of the 1982 season. "There are a few things I can't do as well as I did before the injury," he said. "I can't run the bases as well."

McReynolds' knee injury never enabled him to exploit the depths of his talent, but he played 12 major league seasons with the Padres, Mets and Kansas City Royals, before retiring in 1994.

## SPOTLIGHT ON CWS PLAYERS

The 1981 draft took place the same day that Arizona State beat Oklahoma State 7-4 to win the College World Series. The Sun Devils, with a first-round pick and three more in the second round, tied Pacific-10 Conference rival Southern California for most players drafted with 10.

Oddly, the three first-round picks who received exposure from playing in the World Series were the only college players who did not reach the big leagues.

The best known of the trio was ASU senior third baseman Mike Sodders, who hit .424 with 22 homers and 100 RBIs. He was drafted with the 11th pick overall by the Twins after being passed over as a junior a year earlier, and made such an impression as a power hitter in his breakout season that he was compared to Bob Horner, the record-setting ASU third baseman who three years earlier was taken with the No. 1 pick in the draft."

Kevin McReynolds

"Sodders has the best bat we've ever drafted," Twins farm director George Brophy said.

But Sodders was almost immediately at odds with the tight-fisted Twins, who initially offered him a bonus of $27,500 and later amended the amount to $42,500. The negotiations left a sour taste, and a disgruntled Sodders was traded by the Twins to the White Sox early in his career. His four-year career in the minors topped out in Triple-A.

A torn rotator cuff doomed the professional career of lefthander Darren Dilks, who led Oklahoma State to a berth in the College World Series championship game opposite ASU by going 7-2, 3.72 and striking out 153 in 121 innings, while also hitting .336 with nine home runs. He signed with the Expos for $85,000 as the 18th pick overall, but his career also peaked in Triple-A after just four seasons, during which time he went 15-26, 5.22.

Miami earned a trip to the 1981 College World Series largely behind the accomplishments of junior lefthander Neal Heaton, the top pitcher in the collegiate ranks. He followed up an 18-win season in 1980 with a 16-1, 2.16 campaign as a junior, with a national-high 172 strikeouts in 154 innings.

But it was catcher Frank Castro, Heaton's batterymate, who was taken in the first round, not Heaton. Castro hit .258 with 17 homers for the Hurricanes and was selected by the Padres with the second of their two first-round selections. His career peaked in Double-A.

Heaton was expected to fall in line behind Moore and Darling among college arms in the first round, but his price tag scared off teams and he slipped through to the second round. He was picked by the Indians with the 39th pick overall and signed for $90,000—the largest bonus in the second round, and the seventh-largest overall. Heaton went on to win 80 games in a 12-year career.

## YANKEES TAKE GAMBLE ON ELWAY

The most intriguing draft scenario in 1981 surrounded Stanford outfielder John Elway, who was drafted by the New York Yankees. He was chosen with the team's first pick, though that didn't occur until the last selection of the second round (52nd overall) as the Yankees had forfeited their first-round pick as compensation for signing Dave Winfield as a free agent.

### Top 25 Bonuses

| | Player, Pos. | Drafted (Round) | Order | Bonus |
|---|---|---|---|---|
| 1. | **Terry Blocker, of** | **Mets (1)** | **4** | **$127,500** |
| 2. | **Joe Carter, of** | **Cubs (1)** | **2** | **$125,000** |
| 3. | **Kevin McReynolds, of** | **Padres (1)** | **6** | **$115,000** |
| | **Ron Darling, rhp** | **Rangers (1)** | **9** | **$115,000** |
| 5. | **Mike Moore, rhp** | **Mariners (1)** | **1** | **$100,000** |
| 6. | **Bobby Meacham, ss** | **Cardinals (1)** | **8** | **$92,500** |
| 7. | **Neal Heaton, lhp** | **Indians (2)** | **39** | **$90,000** |
| 8. | Darren Dilks, lhp | Expos (1) | 18 | $85,000 |
| | ***Mark Grant, rhp** | **Giants (1)** | **10** | **$85,000** |
| | ***Vance Lovelace, lhp** | **Cubs (1)** | **16** | **$85,000** |
| 11. | **Matt Williams, rhp** | **Blue Jays (1)** | **5** | **$83,000** |
| 12. | *George Alpert, of | Indians (1) | 13 | $80,000 |
| 13. | ***Darrin Jackson, of** | **Cubs (2)** | **28** | **$77,000** |
| 14. | John Elway, of | Yankees (2) | 52 | $75,000 |
| | ***Phil Lombardi, c** | **Yankees (3)** | **78** | **$75,000** |
| 16. | ***Dick Schofield, ss** | **Angels (1)** | **3** | **$70,000** |
| | **Dave Leeper, of** | **Royals (1)** | **23** | **$70,000** |
| | ***John Abrego, rhp** | **Phillies (1)** | **20** | **$70,000** |
| 19. | ***Daryl Boston, of** | **White Sox (1)** | **7** | **$68,000** |
| 20. | **Orestes Destrade, 1b** | **Yankees (NDFA)** | | **$67,500** |
| | **Tim Pyznarski, 3b** | **Athletics (1)** | **15** | **$67,500** |
| 22. | *Jay Roberts, of | Braves (1) | 12 | $65,000 |
| | *Ricky Barlow, rhp | Tigers (1) | 17 | $65,000 |
| | **Jim Winn, rhp** | **Pirates (1)** | **14** | **$65,000** |
| 25. | *Bill Babcock, lhp | White Sox (3) | 59 | $60,000 |
| | ***Eric Plunk, rhp** | **Yankees (4)** | **104** | **$60,000** |
| | **Ron Romanick, rhp** | **Angels (Jan.-S/1)** | **(4)** | **$60,000** |

*Major leaguers in bold. *High school selection.*

## WORTH NOTING

Yale righthander **RON DARLING** made his mark on the 1981 draft as one of the first noteworthy players to hire an agent to navigate the draft process. In fact, it was Darling's decision to be represented by Steve Kaufman that tilted the Mariners toward **MIKE MOORE** and away from him with the No. 1 overall pick. Darling slipped to ninth overall. With rare exceptions, agents had not had a presence in the draft before because players lost their NCAA eligibility if they hired an agent. The Mariners contacted Kaufman before the draft but could not get a firm commitment on the bonus Darling sought. Moore, on the other hand, handled his own negotiations and agreed to a bonus of $100,000. The influence of agents grew over the years, of course, with all significant draft prospects, both high school and college, using their services as they went through the process. Hiring agents still violated NCAA rules, but baseball players worked around this by using agents as "advisers" before the draft and not technically hiring them. The NCAA generally looked the other way, with occasionally messy exceptions, until it finally decided in 2016 to allow representation in negotiations with major league teams.

Wichita State's potent 1-2 combo of **JOE CARTER** (Cubs, first round) and **PHIL STEPHENSON** (Expos, fifth) led an assault on the NCAA record book in 1981. Carter, a three-time All-American, hit .435 over his career and set records for hits (344), total bases (634) and RBIs (312), along with season records for doubles (34, set in 1980), total bases (229, set in 1980) and RBIs (120). Stephenson, the younger brother of Shockers coach Phil Stephenson, set NCAA records for runs (112) and hits (119), and reeled off a record 47-game hitting streak while hitting .447-16-92. Unlike Carter, Stephenson

CONTINUED ON PAGE 248

## WORTH NOTING

CONTINUED FROM PAGE 247

returned for his senior year and added to his impressive list of NCAA records.

■ In a year when every major college home run record was either broken or tied, the most publicized player in the country was Florida State senior outfielder **MIKE FUENTES**, who hit 27 homers to finish with 64 in his career. That broke Bob Horner's NCAA career mark of 58, set in 1978. Fuentes, who also hit .353 and drove in 83 runs, was drafted in the second round by the Expos, two rounds ahead of teammate **JEFF LEDBETTER**, who went unsigned and shattered every collegiate home run record himself a year later. Fuentes and Ledbetter, who hit 19, helped Florida State set an NCAA team record with 113, though the mark was later tied by Wichita State. Virginia Tech sophomore **FRANKLIN STUBBS**, a first-round pick in 1982, and Mississippi State's **BRUCE CASTORIA**, a Giants 19th-round pick, both hit 29 homers on the season to tie the single-season mark set by UCLA's Jim Auten in 1979. Fuentes became the third straight Expos draft pick to win the Golden Spikes Award, following in the footsteps of Cal State Fullerton first-rounder Tim Wallach in 1979 and Arizona first-rounder Terry Francona in 1980, but he played in just nine games in the majors for the Expos, eight as a pinch-hitter.

■ For the first time in draft history, every player picked in the first two rounds of the June regular phase was signed. The two headliners drafted in 1981 who did not sign were Texas junior-college product **ROGER CLEMENS** (Mets, 12th round) and righthanded pitcher-turned-first baseman **MARK MCGWIRE** (Expos, eighth round), a California high school product. Clemens went on to spend two seasons at Texas before resurfacing as a first-round pick of the Red Sox in 1983, while McGwire attended USC for three seasons before becom-

Wichita State outfielder Joe Carter was an all-state quarterback in high school but quickly showed that baseball was his true calling

A year earlier, the Yankees pulled a late coup by selecting Billy Cannon Jr., son of a former Heisman Trophy winner, with their top pick (third round), only for commissioner Bowie Kuhn to invalidate the selection after ruling that Yankees owner George Steinbrenner had tampered with Cannon before the draft.

Undeterred, Steinbrenner set his sights on Elway, who was finishing his sophomore year at Stanford and already was regarded as the best quarterback prospect in football history. Steinbrenner had an affinity for football players, and the pursuit of Elway began with the Yankees owner writing a long, detailed letter to the Elway family, extolling why it was great to be a Yankee.

Elway had been a top baseball prospect at a California high school in 1979 and could have been a first-round pick in that year's draft were it not for his football commitment to Stanford. The Royals took him in the 18th round and made a name-your-price offer, but it wasn't enough.

Two years later, after hitting .361 with nine homers as a draft-eligible sophomore at Stanford, Elway became an interesting dilemma again for baseball teams. No one bit on him through the first two rounds, but the Yankees showed no hesitation in jumping on him with their top pick—with the last selection on the first day of the three-day process.

"We felt we could have waited," said Gary Hughes, an area scout in 1981 who was charged with tracking Elway's every move that spring. "But Mr. Steinbrenner wanted to take him right away, with our first pick. His feeling was that people might sleep on it overnight and come back the next day saying, 'He's the best athlete available,' and somebody would get him before we did."

If there were doubts about Elway's signability, there were few regarding his raw ability.

"He has a well above-average arm, he runs well and he makes contact," Hughes said. "And this year, he started hitting with power. That's the big attraction. He still doesn't pull the ball as much as you'd like, especially for Yankee Stadium, but that should come in time."

Elway made it clear from the start that he wouldn't give up his blossoming college football career under any circumstance, and the Yankees responded with an arrangement that would enable him to spend his spring break in 1982 in training camp with the major league team, while playing for their short-season team in Oneonta, N.Y., from June 20-Aug. 1. The offer also included a $75,000 signing bonus.

"We want him," Yankees farm director Bill Bergesch said, "but we're willing to let baseball take a back seat until he's finished with his college football career. We just want to be in a position to go head-to-head for him with the NFL when the time comes."

Elway mulled over the Yankees' offer for more than three months, knowing that he would have to sign by Sept. 30, the day fall classes began at Stanford, or the Yankees would lose their rights to him. He finally signed on the same night that Stanford suffered an embarrassing 28-6 loss to San Jose State, coached by Elway's father Jack.

The next summer, playing in 42 games for Oneonta, Elway started slowly but finished strong to hit .318 with four homers, 25 RBIs and 13 stolen bases. He also gunned down eight runners with his powerful right-field arm.

"He showed up in Oneonta having not played for a year, had one hit in his first 19 at-bats," Hughes said, "and by the time he left the club to go back to school for football practice he was leading the team in every offensive category, including stolen bases."

After his six-week audition in the Yankees farm system, Elway was non-committal about whether he would pursue a career in football or baseball once he was finished with college.

DAVID MADISON

John Elway

"I feel fortunate to be in a position to have a choice," he said. "I've known that I'd have to make it for so long that I've been able to put it in the back of my mind. It hasn't affected my summer here and I don't want it to affect my last year at Stanford. I'll make the decision when the time comes. It's difficult to say right now what all the factors will be."

Elway didn't win a Heisman Trophy in his four years at Stanford, but was a near-automatic choice as the No. 1 pick in a 1983 NFL draft that was historic because of the star quarterbacks it produced.

To Elway's dismay, he was chosen by the Baltimore Colts, even though he had warned that club in advance that he would not sign with them, and would even consider a baseball career with the Yankees if they didn't trade him to an NFL team closer to his West Coast roots.

The Yankees stoked the brewing firestorm by

offering Elway an escalating five-year contract that would pay him $500,000 a year—easily the wealthiest contract in baseball history for a player whose professional experience amounted to 42 games in Class A.

The Colts, realizing they might lose Elway to baseball with no compensation, capitulated and traded his rights to the Denver Broncos, who signed him to the most lucrative contract in NFL history to that point, $5 million over five years. Elway lived up to his potential in 16 years with the Broncos, leading that team to two Super Bowl titles in a Hall of Fame career.

### MIXED BAG OF PREP PROSPECTS

For all the inroads that college players made in the first round in 1981, high school pitcher Mark Grant was actually the No. 1-rated player by the Major League Scouting Bureau.

Grant, who went 11-1, 0.97 with 191 strikeouts in 101 innings as a senior at Joliet (Ill.) Catholic High, lasted until the 10th pick, where he was selected by the San Francisco Giants.

A righthander with a blazing fastball, Grant quickly established himself as one of the top prospects in baseball. In his first full season, he was 16-5 for a Class A Midwest League team that was 63-75 overall. His 243 strikeouts in 199 innings were the most in professional baseball. He also won a league-best 14 games in the Triple-A Pacific Coast on his ascent to San Francisco.

From there on, though, it was a struggle for Grant. He wore out his welcome with the Giants after going just 2-7 over parts of three seasons in the majors, and over the course of an eight-year career, with six teams, won just 22 games.

The first high school player selected in 1981 was also from Illinois. He was Dick Schofield, a .488 hitter from Griffin High in Springfield selected third by the California Angels, and the son of Dick Schofield Sr., who signed a $40,000 bonus with St. Louis in 1953. The elder Schofield played 18 seasons in the big leagues, but scouts said there was no comparison between the two as hitters. Dick Jr. had a wide edge.

Mark Grant

"Dick Sr. was faster and quicker, and had a better arm," said longtime Cardinals scout Jim Belz, who was the athletic director at Griffin High. "Defensively, they were about even in high school. Both were good competitors. Dick Jr., though, has better power."

Among the nine high school players selected in the first round, only Schofield had a representative career. He played 14 years in the majors, and hit .230 with 56 homers.

No player in the 1981 draft failed quite like Roberts, selected 12th overall by the Braves. Unenthused with that year's crop, they were more intent in drafting the best athlete and took a leap of faith in selecting the 6-foot-3, 210-pound Roberts, who played little baseball in high school, while excelling in football, basketball and track.

His selection in the first round was the biggest surprise of the draft, considering that few other teams even had him on their prospect list a week before selections were made. But at the last minute, Roberts said he would consider playing baseball, and 22 scouts showed up for the only game he played that spring in an American Legion contest.

Roberts hit a home run, walked twice, stole three bases and pitched two perfect innings with three strikeouts. The performance left an even greater impression on the Braves, who shifted their allegiance to Roberts on the night before the draft. He gave up his football scholarship when the Braves unexpectedly drafted him and overwhelmed him with a $65,000 bonus offer.

"He has speed and power, and you don't always find that combination, so we thought we should go get him right away," Snyder said. "With all the young pitchers we got last year, we wanted to get a player this year and we think we did. Of course, any time you draft a high school player, it's a gamble."

Roberts reported to the Braves' Rookie-league team in West Palm Beach, Fla., saying, "After 18 years of it raining every other day, it will be nice

### Largest Bonuses By Round

| | Player, Pos. | Club | Bonus |
|---|---|---|---|
| **1.** | **Terry Blocker, of** | **Mets** | **$127,500** |
| **2.** | **Neal Heaton, lhp** | **Indians** | **$90,000** |
| **3.** | *** Phil Lombardi, c** | **Yankees** | **$75,000** |
| **4.** | *** Eric Plunk, rhp** | **Yankees** | **$60,000** |
| 5. | * Steve Phillips, ss | Mets | $43,000 |
| 6. | * Max Diaz, 3b | White Sox | $50,000 |
| **7.** | *** Jim Olander, of** | **Phillies** | **$20,000** |
| **8.** | *** Mark Carreon, of** | **Mets** | **$17,500** |
| 9. | * Troy Berry, 2b | Phillies | $18,000 |
| 10. | Scot Elam, rhp | Blue Jays | $16,000 |
| **Other** | **Orestes Destrade, 1b** | **Yankees (NDFA)** | **$67,000** |
| **Jan/R.** | **Greg Tabor, ss** | **Rangers (1)** | **$44,500** |
| **Jan/S.** | **Ron Romanick, rhp** | **Angels (1)** | **$60,000** |
| **Jun/S.** | **Donnie Hill, ss** | **Athletics (1)** | **$35,000** |

*Major leaguers in bold. *High school selection.*

### One Team's Draft: San Diego Padres

| | Player, Pos. | Bonus |
|---|---|---|
| **1.** | **Kevin McReynolds, of** | **$115,000** |
| 1. | Frank Castro, c | $50,000 |
| **2.** | **Bill Long, rhp** | **$35,000** |
| **3.** | **Tony Gwynn, of** | **$25,000** |
| 4. | * Scott Thompson, of | $22,500 |
| 5. | Burk Goldthorn, c | Did not sign |
| 6. | * Louis Langie, ss | $15,000 |
| 7. | * Craig Holthus, of | Did not sign |
| 8. | Craig Shumock, 3b/of | $8,000 |
| 9. | Larry Kiesling, 3b/of | $2,500 |
| **10.** | **Greg Booker, rhp** | **$10,000** |
| **Other** | **John Kruk (S/3), of** | **$2,500** |

*Major leaguers in bold. *High school selection.*

### WORTH NOTING

ing a first-round selection of the Athletics in 1984.

■ The only time in draft history that a team failed to pick even one future major leaguer in the traditional June, regular phase occurred in 1981—and it happened twice. Atlanta struck out on all 34 picks, plus 14 more selections it made in the other three phases. Houston went 0-for-26. In both cases, the Braves and Astros forfeited two premium picks due to major league free agency.

■ While Atlanta had only one pick in the first three rounds, the Angels had just one selection in the first five rounds, representing the greatest number of draft picks one team forfeited in a single draft. The Angels were penalized for signing John D'Acquisto, Geoff Zahn, Juan Beniquez and Bill Travers during the previous offseason as free agents. Between **DICK SCHOFIELD**, the third pick overall, and **DEVON WHITE**, their sixth-round selection, the Angels sat through a span of 130 selections without making a pick. But in White, an extremely raw, undisciplined youngster from New York City, the wait was worth it. "He was the rawest professional baseball player I had ever seen," said Gene Mauch, then California's director of player personnel. "He didn't know a thing about swinging a bat. He could throw the ball, but he didn't know where it was going. He could do only one thing like a big-league ballplayer, and that was run." White spent six years refining his skills in the minor leagues, but soon matured into a 17-year big-leaguer who hit .263 with 208 homers and 346 stolen bases, and also was a seven-time Gold Glover.

■ In a year when drafting college players was in vogue, the Reds stuck with an old tradition. Though they didn't have a first-round selection, they took a high school player with their first pick for the 17th year in a row.

**IN FOCUS: TERRY BLOCKER**

The New York Mets, for all their drafting acumen in the early 1980s, passed over both Arkansas outfielder Kevin McReynolds and Yale righthander Ron Darling in the 1981 draft with the fourth pick overall, and selected speedy outfielder Terry Blocker, a .402 hitter with 11 homers and 34 stolen bases for little-known Tennessee State. He received a bonus of $127,500, the largest paid out in 1981.

Blocker, described as a Lou Brock clone, had a difficult time cracking a talented Mets outfield and got only 15 at-bats with the club in 1985. He was traded to Atlanta, but played in only 110 games in an abbreviated big league career, hitting .205 with two home runs and 11 RBIs.

After a stint in Mexico to close out his career, Blocker was in the news in 1995 during spring training when as a replacement player with the Braves he befriended pitcher David Shotkoski, who was robbed and murdered near the team's hotel in West Palm Beach, Fla. Blocker ultimately tracked down Shotkoski's killer—even as it meant spending time in the worst areas of town and interacting with questionable individuals to gather details, which he subsequently provided to police. It led to a conviction, and Blocker later gave the reward money posted to Shotkoski's widow.

to go out there and catch a few rays, get a little tan and play pro ball."

Roberts never did get his priorities right. In four years of pro ball, none above Class A, Roberts hit .187 with nine home runs, 68 RBIs and 249 strikeouts in 226 games. After putting his ill-fated baseball career in his past, Roberts returned to the University of Washington to resume his football career. He was a backup linebacker for three seasons.

Just before the 1987 Sun Bowl, he revisited his baseball past in an interview, and explained his rationale for signing with the Braves in the first place: "Money! Money! Money! I love money! It's great! I wish I had more of it. Money is the root of all evil . . . and I am very evil."

Soon after playing in the 1988 Independence Bowl, Roberts was charged with rape in the assault of a Seattle woman. Though his trial was declared a mistrial, he dropped out of school and his otherwise undistinguished playing career ended. Roberts ran afoul of the law on repeated occasions through the years, before being killed in a 1998 car accident.

Until making their ill-advised switch to Roberts the night before the 1981 draft, the Braves' focus was on another high school outfielder with a football reputation, George Alpert, from Livingston, N.J. He hit .510 with eight homers as a senior, and went to the Cleveland Indians with the next pick.

"I love baseball, I've wanted to be a pro baseball player my whole life," said Alpert, who caught 25 touchdown passes his final two years in high school. "There was no decision between football and baseball."

But after Alpert struggled in his first three seasons in the Indians system, much like Roberts did with the Braves, he quit the Indians to pursue a football career at Penn State. He played there for three seasons, but never came close to the star-quality talent he had been as a high school recruit.

Another first-round pick from the prep ranks who found success in the pro ranks difficult to come by was righthander Ricky Barlow, selected by the Detroit Tigers with the 17th pick. Barlow went 14-1 in his senior year at a Texas high school, but learned all about losing in the minor leagues, going 23-58 in six seasons. He went through a drought at one point in his career, where he won just three games in 33 decisions over three seasons.

While the careers of Roberts, Alpert and Barlow were abject failures, and symbolized the overall disappointment of the high school crop in the first round, numerous prep players drafted in later rounds rose to the forefront.

If nothing else, the success enjoyed by players like Cone (Royals, second round), Lenny Dykstra (Mets, 13th round), Fred McGriff (Yankees, ninth round), Paul O'Neill (Reds, fourth round) and Devon White, (Angels, sixth round) pointed out the imperfections and inexactness in drafting high school talent—and provided graphic evidence why more clubs were beginning to draft college players, where there is less margin for error, with increasing regularity.

## Highest Unsigned Picks

**JUNE/REGULAR PHASE ONLY**

| Player, Pos., Team (Round) | College | Re-Drafted |
|---|---|---|
| Brad Powell, rhp, Giants (3) | North Carolina | Red Sox '84 (12) |
| John Marzano, c, Twins (3) | Temple | Red Sox '84 (1) |
| Nelson Santovenia, c, Expos (3) | Miami | Expos '82 (S/1) |
| Randy Whisler, ss, Cubs (4) | Oklahoma State | Blue Jays '85 (27) |
| Dan Penner, rhp, Giants (4) | Hawaii | Never |
| Jeff Ledbetter, 1b, Expos (4) | * Florida State | Red Sox '82 (1) |
| Jerry Holtz, ss, Phillies (4) | Villanova | Orioles '84 (4) |
| Shane Mack, of, Royals (4) | UCLA | Padres '84 (1) |
| David Ledbetter, rhp/1b, Orioles (4) | Florida State | Never |
| Burk Goldthorn, c, Padres (5) | * Texas | Pirates '82 (Jan.-S/1) |

**TOTAL UNSIGNED PICKS:** Top 5 Rounds (15), Top 10 Rounds (41)

**Returned to same school.*

Cone won 194 games over a 17-year career, McGriff slugged 493 homers over 19 seasons. Only Gwynn, the Hall of Famer, had a more productive career.

The high school talent who generated the greatest post-draft hype in 1981 wasn't even picked in the first two rounds. It was Hawaiian lefthander Sid Fernandez, who burst on the professional scene like few high school players in the draft era—and came along right on the heels of Fernando-mania, which was sweeping Los Angeles at the time.

Selected in the third round by the Dodgers, Fernandez debuted at Rookie-level Lethbridge, where he went 5-1, 1.54 with a Pioneer League-leading 128 strikeouts in 76 innings. He broke a 28-year old league record by striking out 21 in a game, sandwiched between others in which he struck out 18. A year later, at Class A Vero Beach, the hulking 6-foot-1, 230-pound Hawaiian was almost unhittable. In 85 innings, he fanned a Florida State League-leading 137 batters while allowing just 38 hits. He pitched a pair of no-hitters while racking up an 8-1, 1.91 record.

"He was the best-looking young lefthander I've ever seen," gushed Dodgers scouting director Ben Wade.

When Fernandez earned a midseason promotion to Triple-A Albuquerque in 1982, he was the rage of the Dodgers farm system, and only Fernando Valenzuela earned more acclaim among pitchers in the organization at the time.

But a 19-year-old Fernandez not only met his match in Albuquerque with a disastrous stint, but his portly figure also became a source of concern, especially when officials believed it began to affect his delivery.

The Dodgers were so convinced that Fernandez might never recover from his harrowing experience in Albuquerque and would eventually hurt his arm because of the strain his heavy physique put on it, that they shipped him to the Mets in a four-player deal following the 1983 season, even though he had led the Double-A Texas League in wins (13), strikeouts (209) and ERA (2.82) that season and made a late-season appearance in Los Angeles.

Fernandez went on to pitch 10 injury-free seasons with the Mets, and 15 years in the big leagues overall, posting a 114-96, 3.36 record with 1,743 strikeouts in 1,867 innings.

# 1981 Draft List

**Did not sign. Major leaguers in bold, with first and last years noted. Order of selection indicated in parentheses. For the first five rounds of the June Regular Phase and the first round of all other phases, the peak level of each player is noted.*

## ATLANTA BRAVES

**January—Regular Phase (11)**

1. Terry Cormack, c, Long Beach (Calif.) CC.—(AA)
2. Michael Hinton, lhp, Fenton, Mich.
3. *James McIntosh, rhp, Carl Albert (Okla.) JC.
4. *Muldrow Lloyd, rhp, Spartanburg Methodist (S.C.) JC.
5. *Dan Boever, ss, Westark (Ark.) CC.
6. Mark Lance, lhp, Joliet (Ill.) JC.
7. *Martin Dean, 1b-c, Carl Albert (Okla.) JC.

**January—Secondary Phase (13)**

1. Jon Soderberg, rhp, Gulf Coast (Fla.) CC.–(Low A)
2. Jay Palma, 3b, DeAnza (Calif.) JC.

**June—Regular Phase (12)**

1. Jay Roberts, of-rhp, Centralia (Wash.) HS.—(Low A)
2. (Choice to Mets as compensation for free agent Claudell Washington)
3. (Choice to Yankees as compensation for free agent Gaylord Perry)
4. Clint Brill, c, Humboldt State (Calif.) University.—(Low A)
5. Jerry Ragsdale, c, Turlock (Calif.) HS.—(Low A)
6. Paul Llewellyn, of-1b, Eastern Hills HS, Fort Worth, Texas.
7. Ken Clark, ss, Bradford HS, Starke, Fla.
8. Pat Hodge, of, Vintage HS, Napa, Calif.
9. Rudy Torres, rhp, Catalina HS, Tucson, Ariz.
10. *Manny Mantrana, ss, Jackson HS, Miami.

DRAFT DROP *Baseball coach, Texas-Pan American (2009-15)*

11. Carmine Sperto, rhp, Lincoln HS, Brooklyn, N.Y.
12. *Scott Tabor, rhp, University of Arkansas.
13. *Kevin Towers, rhp, Mira Costa (Calif.) JC.

DRAFT DROP *First overall draft pick, June 1982/ secondary phase, Padres; scouting director, Padres (1994-95); general manager, Padres (1996-2009); general manager, Diamondbacks (2011-14)*

14. *Steve Gay, rhp, Green River (Wash.) CC.
15. *Julius McDougal, ss, Callaway HS, Jackson, Miss.
16. *John Seitz, rhp, Shippensburg (Pa.) University.
17. Steve Chmil, ss, Vanderbilt University.
18. *Mike Leverette, 3b, Harlem HS, Appling, Ga.
19. Bruce Heiser, 2b, Oral Roberts University.
20. Bob Tumpane, 1b, Lewis (Ill.) University.
21. Bryan Neal, of, Southwestern (Texas) University.
22. Dave Clay, rhp, West Chester (Pa.) University.
23. *Frank DeSantis, c, University of Nevada-Las Vegas.
24. Al Sears, rhp, Old Dominion University.
25. Leonard Klaus, rhp, University of Missouri-St. Louis.
26. *Andy Sherkness, lhp, Catholic HS, McAdoo, Pa.
27. *Tony Leonardi, rhp, Aurora West HS, Aurora, Ill.
28. *Tom Wasilewski, rhp, Wyoming Valley HS, Kingston, Pa.
29. Jimmy Tompkins, rhp, University of Texas.
30. Mike Hamer, rhp, University of Texas.
31. Bill Lucas, 2b-ss, Florida A&M University.

DRAFT DROP *Nephew of Henry Aaron, major league (1954-76)*

32. Lary Aaron, of, Florida A&M University.

DRAFT DROP *Son of Henry Aaron, major leaguer (1954-76)*

33. Larry Moser, of, Parkland HS, Breinigsville, Pa.
34. Kyle Sanford, 1b, Texas Wesleyan College.
35. Brad Edlefsen, rhp, University of Montevallo (Ala.).
36. Jeff Wagner, of, Round Rock (Texas) HS.

**June—Secondary Phase (18)**

1. *John Wallace, of, Fresno (Calif.) CC.—DNP
2. *David Blair, c, Middle Georgia JC.
3. Keith Street, of, Middle Georgia JC.
4. Robyn Lynch, 1b, Garden City (Kan.) CC.
5. *Michael Fay, rhp, DeAnza (Calif.) JC.

## BALTIMORE ORIOLES

**January—Regular Phase (25)**

1. Dave Corman, 2b, Hagerstown (Md.) JC.—(AA)
2. Rocky Cusack, 3b, Florida JC.
3. David Gray, rhp, San Joaquin Delta (Calif.) JC.

**The third overall pick in the 1981 draft, Dick Schofield was the first prep pick to the majors**

4. Anthony Wadley, rhp, Laney (Calif.) JC.
5. *George Page, of, Los Angeles Valley JC.
6. Frank Ferroni, lhp, Canada (Calif.) JC.

DRAFT DROP *First overall draft pick, June 1977/secondary phase, Twins*

7. *Wayne Walker, ss, Florida JC.
8. *Brad Wheeler, lhp, Indian River (Fla.) CC.
9. *Michael Bayly, p, Florida JC.
10. Charles Guinn, rhp, Seminole (Okla.) JC.

**January—Secondary Phase (26)**

1. Tommy Alexander, rhp, Gordon (Ga.) JC.–(High A)
2. *Russ Kibler, 1b, Gulf Coast (Fla.) CC.
3. *Robert Link, rhp, Thomasville, Ga.
4. Brian McDonough, rhp, Seminole (Okla.) CC.

**June—Regular Phase (25)**

1. (Choice to Red Sox as compensation for free agent Jim Dwyer)
2. (Choice to Twins as compensation for free agent Jose Morales)
3. Jeff Lackie, lhp, McKinney (Texas) HS.—(High A)
4. *David Ledbetter, rhp-1b, Chipola (Fla.) JC.—(AA)

DRAFT DROP *Attended Florida State; never re-drafted • Brother of Jeff Ledbetter, 4th-round draft pick, Expos (1981); first-round draft pick, Red Sox (1982)*

5. Dave Falcone, 1b, University of Florida.—(AAA)
6. John Mitcheltree, rhp, Old Dominion University.
7. Mark Butler, lhp, California Lutheran University.
8. Johnny Tutt, of, Auburn University.
9. Don Cole, lhp, Columbus (Ga.) College.
10. **Tony Arnold, rhp, University of Texas.—(1986-87)**
11. Ron Cardieri, c, University of Florida.
12. **Jeff Schaefer, 2b, University of Maryland.—(1989-94)**
13. Rick Rembielak, ss, Miami (Ohio) University.

DRAFT DROP *Baseball coach, Kent State (1994-2004); baseball coach, Wake Forest (2005-09); baseball coach, Akron (2012-15)*

14. Tandy Charley, lhp, Hoquiam HS, Taholah, Wash.
15. *Jeff Roberts, rhp, Lake Havasu (Ariz.) HS.
16. Charles Bertucio, of-lhp, Laney (Calif.) JC.
17. *Alejandro Diaz, c, Jackson HS, Miami.
18. Brett Gold, rhp, LaSalle University.
19. *Mark Dougherty, 2b, Scottsdale (Ariz.) CC.
20. *DeWayne Rosenbaum, rhp, David Lipscomb College.
21. Ron Kelly, 1b, Miami-Dade CC South.
22. *Mike Snaidach, rhp, South Park HS, Library, Pa.
23. Ralph Albano, 2b, Jacksonville University.
24. *Mike Knox, rhp, Memorial HS, Tulsa, Okla.
25. Lee Granger, of, UC Irvine.
26. Oliver Maull, c, Cape Henlopen HS, Lewes, Del.
27. Tim Riche, of, Howard University.
28. *Ken Sinclair, rhp, St. Francis (N.Y.) College.
29. *Bart Bishop, rhp, Sunset HS, Miami.
30. Hubert Crumley, rhp, Edgewood (Md.) HS.
31. ***Cecil Fielder, 1b, Nogales HS, La Puente, Calif.—(1985-98)**

DRAFT DROP *Father of Prince Fielder, first-round draft pick, Brewers (2002); major leaguer (2005-15)*

32. *Larry Paskiewicz, 2b, Cochise County (Ariz.) JC.
33. *James Thomas, of, Boys Latin HS, Baltimore.

**June—Secondary Phase (7)**

1. Jim Rooney, lhp, CC of Morris (N.J.).—(AA)

DRAFT DROP *First overall draft pick, January 1981/ regular phase, Cubs*

2. Randy Boyd, lhp, Cochise County (Ariz.) CC.
3. *Rod Langston, of, Indian River (Fla.) CC.

## BOSTON RED SOX

**January—Regular Phase (20)**

1. **Danny Sheaffer, c, Harrisburg Area (Pa.) CC.—(1987-97)**
2. Joe Arfstrom, of, Miami-Dade CC New World Center.
3. David Scheller, lhp, Lewis & Clark (Ill.) CC.
4. *Robyn Lynch, 1b, Garden City (Kan.) CC.
5. *Joey Farrill, rhp, Gulf Coast (Fla.) CC.
6. *Robert Meyer, rhp, Golden West (Calif.) JC.
7. *John Wallace, of, Fresno (Calif.) CC.
8. John Sorensen, rhp, Joliet (Ill.) JC.
9. Steven Seaman, ss, CC of Beaver County (Pa.).
10. *Mark Wenzel, rhp, Fresno (Calif.) CC.

**January—Secondary Phase (22)**

1. Dave Malpeso, c, Miami-Dade CC North.—(AAA)
2. Scott Jefferson, of, Contra Costa (Calif.) JC.

**June—Regular Phase (19)**

1. **Steve Lyons, ss-of, Oregon State University.—(1985-93)**
1. Kevin Burrell, c, Poway (Calif.) HS (Choice from Orioles as compensation for free agent Jim Dwyer).—(AAA)
2. Chris Howard, 2b, William O. Boone HS, Orlando, Fla.—(High A)
3. **Rob Woodward, rhp, Lebanon (N.H.) HS.—(1985-88)**
4. **Todd Benzinger, 1b, New Richmond HS, Cincinnati.—(1987-95)**
5. Peter Gonzales, of, San Leandro (Calif.) HS.—(Short-season A)
6. Kevin Clinton, rhp, University of Kansas.

DRAFT DROP *Son of Lou Clinton, major leaguer (1960-67)*

7. *Kevin Fowler, ss, C.E. Donart HS, Stillwater, Okla.
8. John Key, rhp, Central HS, Muskogee, Okla.
9. Charles Fisher, of, Jacksonville State University.
10. Craig Walck, 3b, Ursinus (Pa.) College.
11. *Peter Mancini, 2b, Memorial HS, West New York, N.J.
12. Chuck Davis, rhp, Jacksonville State University.
13. Pat Castiglia, 1b, Eckerd (Fla.) College.
14. Willie Weston, rhp, Mississippi Valley State University.
15. Kevin Johnston, of, Logan HS, LaCrosse, Wis.
16. *Troy Howerton, lhp, Arkansas City (Kan.) HS.
17. Bruce Lockhart, lhp, Brunswick (Maine) HS.
18. *Jeff Achilles, rhp, University of Houston.
19. Bill Carpenter, ss, Brandeis (Mass.) University.
20. *Darryl Menard, rhp, Clear Lake HS, Seabrook, Texas.
21. *Brian Smith, rhp, South HS, Weymouth, Mass.

**June—Secondary Phase (9)**

1. **Steve Ellsworth, rhp, Cal State Northridge.—(1988)**

DRAFT DROP *Son of Dick Ellsworth, major leaguer (1958-71)*

2. Tony Beal, of, Seminole (Fla.) CC.

## CALIFORNIA ANGELS

**January—Regular Phase (4)**

1. Kevin Price, rhp, Cosumnes River (Calif.) JC.–(AAA)
2. *Mike Blair, c, Middle Georgia JC.
3. *David Velez, ss, Los Medanos (Calif.) JC.
4. Robert Gast, rhp, Clemson University.
5. Gary Robbins, of-rhp, Solano (Calif.) CC.
6. *Bruce Hamrick, 3b, Hiwassee (Tenn.) JC.
7. *Brian Hartsock, c, Riverside (Calif.) CC.
8. *Ken Rebiejo, rhp, Ohlone (Calif.) JC.
9. *Darrell Higgs, rhp, Pima (Ariz.) CC.
10. *Ronald Bachmeier, 2b, Glendale (Calif.) JC.
11. *Richard Henkemeyer, lhp, Brainerd (Minn.) CC.
12. *Jeff Mace, of, Scottsdale (Ariz.) CC.
13. *Jim Sharp, lhp, Gloucester County (N.J.) JC.
14. Curt Mathe, 1b-of, Des Moines Area (Iowa) CC.
15. *Bruce Miller, rhp-c, Des Moines Area (Iowa) CC.
16. *Kent Testerman, c, Los Angeles Valley JC.

**January—Secondary Phase (4)**

1. **Ron Romanick, rhp, Arizona State University.—(1984-86)**
2. *Mike Hogan, rhp, Orange Coast (Calif.) JC.
3. *George Cook, 2b, Los Angeles CC.
4. *Craig Stevenson, ss, Los Angeles Valley JC.

**June—Regular Phase (3)**

1. **Dick Schofield, ss, Griffin HS, Springfield, Ill.—(1983-96)**

DRAFT DROP *Son of Dick Schofield, major leaguer (1953-71) • Uncle of Jayson Werth, first-round draft pick, Orioles (1997); major leaguer (2002-15) • First 1981 high school draft pick to reach majors (Sept. 8, 1983)*

2. (Choice to Expos as compensation for free agent John D'Acquisto)
3. (Choice to Twins as compensation for free agent Geoff Zahn)
4. (Choice to Mariners as compensation for free agent Juan Beniquez)
5. (Choice to Brewers as compensation for free agent Bill Travers)
6. **Devon White, 3b, Park West HS, Manhattan, N.Y.—(1985-2001)**
7. Lonnie Garza, ss, Pan American University.
8. ***Joey Meyer, 1b, Punahou HS, Kailua, Hawaii.—(1988-89)**
9. Rick Turner, c, UC Riverside.
10. **Sap Randall, 1b, Grambling State University.—(1988)**
11. Rick Stromer, 3b, Grand Canyon College.
12. Tim Kammeyer, rhp, University of Southern California.
13. Buck Long, rhp, Texas Southern University.
14. Brad Withrow, rhp, University of Wyoming.
15. Doug Lindsey, rhp, University of La Verne (Calif.).
16. Rick Sundberg, c, Santa Clara University.
17. Jeff Kennedy, of, Lamar University.
18. Dave Morris, of, Grand Canyon College.
19. Bill Worden, c, Stanford University.
20. **Craig Gerber, ss, Cal Poly San Luis Obispo.—(1985)**
21. Mark Smelko, 1b, San Diego State University.
22. Lee Jones, rhp, University of Southern California.
23. Scott Oliver, rhp, Bellarmine (Ky.) College.
24. Steve Eakes, ss, Cal State Sacramento.
25. Joe King, rhp, University of La Verne (Calif.).
26. Darryl Stephens, of, Cal State Fullerton.
27. *Kendall Walling, ss, Canyon (Texas) HS.
28. Thomas Dowies, rhp, McNeese State University.
29. Jack Crawford, of, Seminole (Okla.) JC.
30. *Tony DeFrancesco, c, Suffern HS, Monsey, N.Y.

DRAFT DROP *Major league manager (2012)*

**June—Secondary Phase (26)**

1. *Reggie Montgomery, of, Orange Coast (Calif.) JC.—(AAA)
2. *Dick Seidel, rhp, University of Arizona.
3. *Jeff Mace, of, Scottsdale (Ariz.) CC.

4. *James Woods, ss, San Jacinto (Texas) JC.

## CHICAGO CUBS

**January—Regular Phase (1)**

1. *Jim Rooney, lhp, CC of Morris (N.J.).—(AA)
2. Greg Trotter, rhp, Westark (Ark.) CC.
3. *Craig Jenks, lhp, Butte (Calif.) JC.
4. *Tim Arnsberg, rhp, Merced (Calif.) JC.

DRAFT DROP *Brother of Brad Arnsberg, 19th-round draft pick, Indians (1981); major leaguer (1986-92)*

5. *Clay Carter, rhp, JC of Southern Idaho.
6. **Billy Hatcher, of, Yavapai (Ariz.) JC.—(1984-95)**

DRAFT DROP *Brother of Johnny Hatcher, third-round draft pick, January 1981/regular phase, Tigers*

7. *Robin Emerson, rhp, Bakersfield (Calif.) JC.
8. *George Martinez, rhp, Pasadena (Calif.) CC.

**January—Secondary Phase (7)**

1. *Nick Brandt, lhp, Merced (Calif.) JC.—(Rookie)
2. *Gary Jensen, c, Solano (Calif.) CC.
3. *Ken Scott, rhp, Chaffey (Calif.) JC.

**June—Regular Phase (2)**

1. **Joe Carter, of, Wichita State University.—(1983-98)**
1. **Vance Lovelace, lhp, Hillsborough HS, Tampa** (Choice from Reds as compensation for free agent Larry Biittner)**—(1988-90)**
2. **Darrin Jackson, of, Culver City (Calif.) HS.—(1985-99)**
3. Mitch Cook, rhp, New Hanover HS, Wilmington, N.C.—(AA)
4. *Randy Whisler, ss, Klamath Union HS, Klamath Falls, Ore.—(Low A)

DRAFT DROP *Attended Oklahoma State; re-drafted by Blue Jays, 1985 (27th round)*

5. Rob Schilling, rhp, University of the Pacific.—(AA)
6. Dave Rosenhahn, ss, SUNY-Buffalo.
7. *Steve Rousey, rhp, Crescenta Valley HS, La Crescenta, Calif.

DRAFT DROP *Baseball coach, Cal State Northridge (2002-10)*

8. Trey Brooks, 2b, Texas Christian University.
9. Tom Isgett, rhp, McBee HS, Hartsville, S.C.
10. Anthony Colbert, of, Murphy (N.C.) HS.
11. *Bill Hobbs, lhp, Arroyo HS, El Monte, Calif.
12. Ken Emmert, 3b, Arcadia (Calif.) HS.
13. Walter Beede, 1b, Fitchburg (Mass.) HS.

DRAFT DROP *Father of Tyler Beede, first-round draft pick, Blue Jays (2011); first-round draft pick, Giants (2014)*

14. Jim Adamczak, rhp, Arkansas Tech.
15. Allen Black, rhp, Arizona State University.
16. Stan Webb, rhp, Washington State University.
17. Ron Kaufman, rhp, Davis & Elkins (W.Va.) College.
18. Otis Tramble, ss, Southern University.
19. Lawrence Wilson, of-1b, Redlands (Calif.) HS.
20. *Jim Sherman, of, University of Delaware.

DRAFT DROP *Baseball coach, Delaware (2001-15)*

21. Robert Hook, lhp, Victor Valley (Calif.) CC.
22. Pat Tobin, 1b, University of the Pacific.
23. *Mark Walberg, of, Indiana State University.
24. Wendell Henderson, c, Grambling State University.
25. Jeff Andrews, rhp, East Tennessee State University.
26. Mark Nowlin, rhp, UC Santa Barbara.
27. Lawrence Tribble, c, South Point HS, Belmont, N.C.
28. *Derril Lewis, lhp, San Bernardino Valley (Calif.) JC.
29. *Lawrence McGee, 3b, Cal State Los Angeles.

**June—Secondary Phase (10)**

1. Jeff Rutledge, ss, Fresno (Calif.) CC.—(AA)
2. Ron Bachmeier, 2b, Glendale (Calif.) JC.
3. *Dean Naylor, rhp, Miami-Dade CC South.

## CHICAGO WHITE SOX

**January—Regular Phase (8)**

1. *Reggie Montgomery, of, Orange Coast (Calif.) JC.—(AAA)
2. *Greg Griffin, of, Texas Southmost JC.
3. *James Twardowski, 3b, Blinn (Texas) JC.
4. John Moses, lhp, Houston.
5. *Kevin Kollmansperger, rhp, McLennan (Texas) CC.
6. Ed Sedar, of-inf, JC of Lake County (Ill.).
7. *Bobby Joe Williams, ss, Panola (Texas) JC.
8. *Charlie Corbell, rhp, Blinn (Texas) JC.
9. *Mark Dennis, lhp, McLennan (Texas) CC.
10. *Dave Van Horn, 3b, McLennan (Texas) CC.

DRAFT DROP *Baseball coach, Nebraska (1998-2002); baseball coach, Arkansas (2003-15)*

11. *Gary Jones, of, Paris (Texas) JC.
12. *Curtis Dishman, 1b, Blinn (Texas) JC.
13. *Alceed Owens, rhp, Texas Southmost JC.
14. *Michael Edwards, ss, Blinn (Texas) JC.
15. *Doug Galloway, rhp, Paris (Texas) JC.
16. *Joe Petty, rhp, Panola (Texas) JC.

**January—Secondary Phase (20)**

1. Scott Meier, c, San Joaquin Delta (Calif.) JC.—(AA)
2. *Frank Marrero, rhp, Miami-Dade CC South.

**June—Regular Phase (7)**

1. **Daryl Boston, lhp-of, Woodward HS, Cincinnati.—(1984-94)**
2. (Choice to Athletics as compensation for free agent Jim Essian)
3. Bill Babcock, lhp, Grosse Point North HS, Grosse Point Woods, Mich.—(AA)
4. **Craig Smajstrla, ss, Pearland (Texas) HS.—(1988)**
5. *Greg McClain, 3b-of, Pasadena HS, Altadena, Calif.—(Low A)

DRAFT DROP *Attended California; re-drafted by Pirates, 1984 (8th round)*

6. Max Diaz, 3b-rhp, American HS, Fremont, Calif.
7. Mike Withrow, rhp, University of Texas.

DRAFT DROP *Father of Chris Withrow, first-round draft pick, Dodgers (2007)*

8. **Wade Rowdon, ss, Stetson University.—(1984-88)**
9. Greg Butler, rhp, Lodi HS, Lockeford, Calif.
10. Mike Tanzi, lhp, Florida Southern College.
11. Chuck Epperson, of, Jackson State University.
12. **Eddie Miles, of, University of Louisville.**
13. **Al Jones, rhp, Alcorn State University.—(1983-85)**
14. Dave Yobs, of, Oral Roberts University.
15. *Mike Bertotti, ss, Lassen HS, Susanville, Calif.
16. Kevin Jones, of, Lincoln HS, San Diego.
17. *Richard Smith, ss, Vallejo (Calif.) HS.
18. Michael Buggs, of, University of California.
19. Pat Adams, 1b, University of Detroit.
20. Donn Koch, c, Florida Southern College.
21. **Jack Hardy, rhp, Biscayne (Fla.) College.—(1989)**
22. Jim Harris, of, University of Nevada-Reno.
23. *Mark Heuer, rhp, Harper (Ill.) JC.
24. Jim Sutton, rhp, Cal State Fullerton.
25. Mike Ledna, 2b, Purdue University.
26. Mike Nagle, ss, UC Irvine.
27. *Steve Iannini, of, Colonial HS, Orlando, Fla.
28. Jason Costa, of, Castro Valley (Calif.) HS.
29. Roger Stevens, of, Elgin (Ill.) CC.
30. ***La Vel Freeman, 1b, Kennedy HS, Sacramento, Calif.—(1989)**
31. *Richie Hines, 1b, Hill HS, Jackson, Miss.
32. *Ed Vidmar, lhp, University of Arkansas.
33. Art Niemann, rhp, Louisiana Tech.
34. *Mark Johnson, c, North Boone HS, Poplar Grove, Ill.
35. *Roger Johnson, c, Parkway West HS, Ballwin, Mo.
36. John Walsh, 2b, Westmount HS, Campbell, Calif.
37. Billy Gayton, 3b, Indian Hills (Iowa) CC.

DRAFT DROP *Scouting director, Padres (2001-05)*

38. *Mike Toothman, of, Stanford University.

**June—Secondary Phase (3)**

1. *Norman Morton, rhp, Miami-Dade CC North.—DNP
2. *John Leonard, rhp, Yavapai (Ariz.) JC.

## CINCINNATI REDS

**January—Regular Phase (15)**

1. *Dan Durst, rhp, Iowa Western CC.—DNP
2. *Damon Farmar, of, West Los Angeles JC.
3. *Randy Romagna, rhp, Indian River (Fla.) CC.
4. *Terrell Ayo, 2b, Linn-Benton (Ore.) CC.
5. John Minyard, rhp, Des Moines Area (Iowa) CC.
6. Jackie Foley, of-1b, Edison (Fla.) CC.
7. William Kincanon, rhp, Triton (Ill.) JC.

**January—Secondary Phase (3)**

1. **Rob Murphy, lhp, Miami, Fla.—(1985-95)**
2. Tyron Hubbard, rhp, Spartanburg Methodist (S.C.) JC.
3. *Derek Tatsuno, lhp, Aiea, Hawaii.

**June—Regular Phase (16)**

1. (Choice to Cubs as compensation for free agent Larry Biittner)
2. Lanell Culver, of, Palmdale (Calif.) HS.—(High A)
3. Delwyn Young, ss, Belmont HS, Los Angeles.—(AAA)

DRAFT DROP *Father of Delwyn Young, major leaguer (2006-10)*

4. **Paul O'Neill, of, Brookhaven HS, Columbus, Ohio.—(1985-2001)**
5. Steve Padia, c, Wharton (Texas) HS.—(AA)
6. Guy Findeison, rhp, South Plantation (Fla.) HS.
7. Dexter Day, 3b-of, William Carey (Miss.) College.
8. **Terry McGriff, c, Westwood HS, Fort Pierce, Fla.—(1987-94)**
9. Richard Johns, rhp, Sebring (Fla.) HS.
10. Bubba Jennings, 2b, St. Edward's (Texas) University.
11. *Mark Brown, rhp, Mater Dei HS, Santa Ana, Calif.
12. Charlie Colclough, 1b, University of South Carolina-Aiken.
13. Joe Stalp, rhp, Portland State University.
14. ***Scott Ruskin, of-lhp, Sandalwood HS, Jacksonville, Fla.—(1990-93)**
15. Jeff Rhodes, of-rhp, Poly Tech HS, Fort Worth, Texas.
16. Tony Howell, of-1b, Central State (Ohio) University.
17. *Brian Blakely, 3b, Abingdon (Va.) HS.
18. John Grier, of, Central Cabarrus HS, Concord, N.C.
19. Mark Matzen, 3b, Seton Hall University.
20. Michael Manfre, ss, Kean (N.J.) College.
21. *Michael Darby, rhp-ss, Rock Island (Ill.) HS.
22. Tom Riley, ss, University of Washington.
23. *Dan Whelan, rhp, Catholic HS, Lexington, Ky.
24. Gerardo Macias, lhp, New Mexico State University.
25. *Vince Bargar, lhp, San Joaquin Memorial HS, Firebaugh, Calif.
26. John Groninger, c, University of Northern Colorado.
27. ***Jeff Datz, c, Glassboro State (N.J.) College.—(1989)**
28. Tom Pillar, 3b-of, University of Northern Colorado.
29. *Ronald Johnson, of, Garfield HS, Seattle.
30. Tim Dodd, rhp, Cleveland (Tenn.) HS.
31. Ron Carapezzi, 3b, Fairfield University.
32. *Alan Koonce, rhp, Robert E. Lee HS, Midland, Texas.
33. Gary Desa, ss, Damien HS, Honolulu.

DRAFT DROP *Brother of Joe Desa, major leaguer (1980-85)*

34. ***Dana Williams, ss, Davidson HS, Mobile, Ala.—(1989)**
35. *Greg Key, 2b, University of Montevallo (Ala.).
36. *Arthur Pigg, 2b, Garfield HS, Seattle.

**June—Secondary Phase (24)**

1. *Don Long, ss, Edmonds (Wash.) CC.—(AA)
2. Don Fenton, rhp, Lower Columbia (Wash.) JC.
3. *Randy Romagna, rhp, Indian River (Fla.) CC.

## CLEVELAND INDIANS

**January—Regular Phase (14)**

1. Steve Cushing, lhp, St. Leo (Fla.) College.–(Low A)
2. *Todd Wenberg, rhp, Waldorf (Iowa) JC.

DRAFT DROP *Baseball coach, Creighton (1982-83)*

3. *Dennis Van Loren, rhp, Cochise County (Ariz.) CC.
4. *Jim Opie, 3b-of, Valencia (Fla.) CC.
5. Dane Clark, rhp, Gloucester County (N.J.) JC.
6. *Anthony Virgo, rhp, Contra Costa (Calif.) JC.
7. James Pool, c, Kansas Newman College.

**January—Secondary Phase (10)**

1. John Tillema, rhp, San Jose, Calif.—(High A)
2. *James Miley, c, Montgomery (Md.) JC.
3. *Alan Peel, c, Sacramento (Calif.) CC.

**June—Regular Phase (13)**

1. George Alpert, of, Livingston (N.J.) HS.—(Low A)
2. **Neal Heaton, lhp, University of Miami—(1982-93)**

DRAFT DROP *First overall draft pick, January 1979/regular phase, Mets*

3. (Selection forfeited for right to select Billy Cannon in special 1980 draft)
4. Randy Washington, of, Amos Alonzo Stagg HS, Stockton, Calif.—(AAA)
5. Rich Doyle, rhp, Neff HS, La Mirada, Calif.—(AAA)
6. ***Matt Kinzer, rhp, Norwell HS, Ossian, Ind.—(1989-90)**

DRAFT DROP *Punter, National Football League (1987)*

7. **Dwight Taylor, of, University of Arizona.—(1986)**
8. Brian Silvas, rhp, University of Miami
9. ***Tommy Gregg, of, Reynolds HS, Winston-Salem, N.C.—(1987-97)**
10. Wayne Johnson, lhp, Orange Park (Fla.) HS.
11. ***Terry Wells, lhp, Westview HS, Kankakee, Ill.—(1990)**
12. *Jeff Bassett, of, Willoughby Hills (Ohio) HS.
13. *Steve Gelmine, lhp, New Providence (N.J.) HS.
14. ***Jim Paciorek, of, University of Michigan.—(1987)**

DRAFT DROP *Brother of John Paciorek, major leaguer (1963) • Brother of Tom Paciorek, major leaguer (1970-87)*

15. Scott Collins, 2b, University of Missouri.
16. *Stan Yagiello, ss, Livingston (N.J.) HS.
17. John Merchant, 1b, The Kings (N.Y.) College.
18. Phil Deriso, lhp, Auburn University.
19. ***Brad Arnsberg, rhp, Medford (Ore.) HS.—(1986-92)**

DRAFT DROP *Brother of Tim Arnsberg, fourth-round draft pick, Cubs January/regular phase (1981)*

20. Michael Poindexter, rhp, Jackson HS, Charleston, W.Va.
21. ***Chuck Jackson, ss, Ingraham HS, Seattle.—(1987-94)**

DRAFT DROP *Father of Justin Jackson, first-round draft pick, Blue Jays (2007)*

22. *James Warner, of, Friendly HS, Oxon Hill, Md.
23. *Bill Cutshall, rhp, Mayo HS, Rochester, Minn.
24. ***Keith Miller, ss, All Saints HS, Bay City, Mich.—(1987-95)**
25. *Jim O'Dell, 1b, Lower Columbia (Wash.) JC.
26. *Geoff Redgrave, lhp, Thomas Wooten HS, Rockville, Md.

**June—Secondary Phase (23)**

1. *Ted Perkins, of, El Cerrito, Calif.—DNP
2. Sam Martin, ss, Louisburg (N.C.) JC.

## DETROIT TIGERS

**January—Regular Phase (18)**

1. *Jeff Rutledge, ss, Fresno (Calif.) CC.—(AA)
2. *Everett Graham, of, Louisburg (N.C.) JC.
3. *Johnny Hatcher, of, Yavapai (Ariz.) JC.

DRAFT DROP *Brother of Billy Hatcher, fourth-round draft pick, January 1981/regular phase, Cubs; major leaguer (1984-95)*

4. ***Mike Sharperson, ss, DeKalb South (Ga.) CC.—(1987-95)**

DRAFT DROP *Died as active player (May 26, 1996)*

5. Laurence Berthelson, rhp, Los Angeles Valley JC.
6. James Ross, rhp, Henry Ford (Mich.) CC.
7. *Herb McManaway, of-1b, St. Clair County (Mich.) CC.

**January—Secondary Phase (2)**

1. **Bob Melvin, c, Canada (Calif.) JC.–(1985-94)**

DRAFT DROP *Major league manager (2003-15)*

2. Donald O'Connor, rhp, Chabot (Calif.) JC.

**June—Regular Phase (17)**

1. Ricky Barlow, rhp, Woodville (Texas) HS.—(AAA)
2. **Nelson Simmons, of, Madison HS, San**

**Diego.—(1984-87)**
3. Bob Williamson, c, Catholic Central HS, Redford, Mich.—(Rookie)
4. Bubby Brister, ss, Neville HS, Monroe, La.—(Rookie)
DRAFT DROP *Quarterback, National Football League (1986-2000)*
5. Stan Barker, of, Alcorn State University.—(Low A)
**6. Bryan Kelly, rhp, University of Alabama.—(1986-87)**
**7. Chuck Cary, lhp, University of California.—(1985-93)**
DRAFT DROP *Brother of Greg Cary, fourth-round draft pick, January 1981/regular phase, Mets*
8. Reggie Thomas, of, University of Arkansas.
9. George Miguel, lhp, Grady Vocational HS, Brooklyn, N.Y.
10. *David Flattery, rhp, Iowa State University.
11. Mark Lockenmeyer, rhp-of, Princeton University.
12. Albert Silva, 1b, Tampa Catholic HS, Tampa.
13. *Rob Clark, lhp, Southern Illinois University.
**14. Scotty Earl, 2b, Eastern Kentucky University.—(1984)**
15. *Tom Brassil, ss, Duke University.
16. Mark Jacob, rhp, University of Detroit.
17. Steve Haynes, of, Alabama Christian College.
18. Robert McFadden, rhp, College of Wooster (Ohio).
19. *Don Rowland, ss, Bishop Gallagher HS, St. Clair Shores, Mich.
DRAFT DROP *Scouting director, Angels (1999-2003)*
20. Bryon Horn, 2b, Eastern Michigan University.
21. Kraig Priessman, c, Northwest HS, Cincinnati.
22. Greg Norman, 1b, UCLA.
23. Chris Goodyear, 3b, Hillsborough (Fla.) CC.
24. *Robert Yeager, 3b, Piscataway (N.J.) HS.
**25. *Barry Lyons, c, Delta State (Miss.) University.—(1986-95)**
26. *Randal Gorgon, rhp, Eastern Michigan University.
27. Dan Phillip, c, Ashland (Ohio) College.
28. *Jim Phelps, rhp, Saline (Mich.) HS.
29. Bruce Franklin, 2b, Coastal Carolina College.
30. Jim Moriarty, of, South Weymouth (Mass.) HS.
31. *Billy DeWitt, rhp, Broadmoor HS, Baton Rouge, La.
32. Jon Zureich, 1b, Eastern Michigan University.

**June—Secondary Phase (15)**

**1. Randy O'Neal, rhp, University of Florida.—(1984-90)**
2. Ernie Moya, rhp, Hillsborough (Fla.) CC.
3. Tom Corcoran, rhp, Florida International University.

## HOUSTON ASTROS

**January—Regular Phase (23)**

1. *Trent Ferrin, rhp, JC of Southern Idaho.—(Short-season A)
2. *Michael Fay, rhp, DeAnza (Calif.) JC.
3. *John Salery, of, Indian River (Fla.) CC.
4. *John Bryant, of, Santa Ana (Calif.) JC.
5. *Joe Wendolowski, ss, CC of Morris (N.J.).

**January—Secondary Phase (5)**

**1. Glenn Davis, 1b-of, Manatee (Fla.) JC.—(1984-93)**
DRAFT DROP *Stepbrother of Storm Davis, major leaguer (1982-94)*
2. *Don Long, ss, Edmonds (Wash.) CC.
3. *Dean Naylor, rhp, Miami-Dade CC South.

**June—Regular Phase (24)**

1. (Choice to Rangers as compensation for free agent Dave Roberts)
2. (Choice to Dodgers as compensation for free agent Don Sutton)
3. Curtis Burke, of, Tennessee State University.—(AA)
4. Ben Snyder, rhp, St. Mary's (Calif.) College.–(AA)
5. Steve McAllister, ss, Bradley University.—(AA)
6. *Mike Rubel, 1b, Cal State Fullerton.
7. Gary Blaylock, 3b, University of Kansas.
DRAFT DROP *Son of Gary Blaylock, major leaguer (1959)*
8. Henry Janssen, c, Seton Hall University.
9. Larry Simcox, ss, University of Mississippi.

MORRIS FOSTOFF

**The Royals struck gold with a local pick in the third round with prep righthander David Cone**

10. Geoff Meadows, rhp, Slippery Rock (Pa.) University.
11. Don Berti, c, Pfeiffer (N.C.) College.
12. Randy Braun, of, Missouri Southern State College.
13. Phil Smith, 2b, Lewis-Clark State (Idaho) College.
14. *Stu Foulks, rhp, Mercer County (N.J.) CC.
15. Hank Clark, 3b, Cal State Northridge.
16. Mike Callahan, rhp, North Adams State (Mass.) College.
17. Mark Clinton, rhp, University of Michigan.
18. Mitch Coplon, rhp, Oklahoma State University.
19. David Malloy, lhp, Rider College.
20. Don Mundie, rhp, Mississippi State University.
21. *Jim Harkins, lhp, Eastern Kentucky University.
22. Greg Mize, rhp, Broward (Fla.) CC.
23. Rex Schimpf, rhp, Louisiana Tech.
24. Joe Ferrante, rhp, San Diego State University.
25. Glenn Carpenter, of, University of Florida.
26. Roger Godwin, rhp, Georgia Southern College.
27. Ed Reilly, rhp, Seton Hall University.
28. Ira Lane, of, Texas Southern University.

**June—Secondary Phase (20)**

**1. Eric Bullock, of, Los Angeles Harbor JC.—(1985-92)**
2. Bobby Falls, ss, Walters State (Tenn.) CC.

## KANSAS CITY ROYALS

**January—Regular Phase (24)**

1. Rick Rizzo, of, Mesa (Colo.) College.—(AAA)
2. Thomas McHugh, 1b, Iowa Western CC.
3. James Brittman, 1b, Chicago.
4. James Minor, rhp, Fullerton (Calif.) JC.
**5. *Dave Johnson, rhp, CC of Baltimore.—(1987-93)**
DRAFT DROP *Father of Steve Johnson, major leaguer (2012-15)*
6. Tracy Hall, of, Detroit.
**7. *Russ Morman, of, Iowa Western CC.—(1986-97)**
8. *Carl Davis, of, Detroit.
9. *Jeff Kobernus, lhp, Laney (Calif.) JC.
**10. Bill Pecota, 3b, DeAnza (Calif.) JC.–(1986-94)**
11. John Antonelli, c, CC of Baltimore.
12. David Spalt, ss, Patterson HS, Baltimore.
13. *Craig Stump, 3b, CC of Baltimore.

**January—Secondary Phase (24)**

1. Mitch Ashmore, c, Centenary College.—(AAA)
2. *Steven Anderson, 3b, West Los Angeles JC.
3. *John Stevens, rhp, Los Angeles Valley JC.

**June—Regular Phase (23)**

**1. Dave Leeper, of, University of Southern California.—(1984-85)**
**2. Mark Gubicza, rhp, Penn Charter HS, Philadelphia** (Choice from Cardinals as compensation for free agent Darrell Porter)—**(1984-97)**
**2. Tony Ferreira, lhp, North HS, Riverside, Calif.—(1985)**
**3. David Cone, rhp, Rockhurst HS, Kansas City, Mo.—(1986-2003)**
**4. *Shane Mack, ss, Gahr HS, Cerritos, Calif.—(1987-98)**
DRAFT DROP *Attended UCLA; re-drafted by Padres, 1984 (1st round)*
5. Marty Wilkerson, 3b, University of Southern California.—(AAA)
6. Nick Harsh, rhp, San Diego State University.
**7. John Davis, rhp, Centennial HS, Pueblo, Colo.—(1987-90)**
8. Warren Skelton, ss, Harrison HS, Evansville, Ind.
9. John Bryant, rhp, University of La Verne (Calif.).
10. Randy Smith, c, Vallejo (Calif.) HS.
11. Warren Oliver, ss, Texas Christian University.
**12. *Mark Williamson, rhp, San Diego State University.—(1987-94)**
13. *Lex Bleckley, ss, Pennsville (N.J.) HS.
14. *Robert Merenda, of, San Juan HS, Orangeville, Calif.
15. Stan Palmore, of, Vocational HS, Chicago.
16. Joe Citari, 1b, Oak Park (Ill.) HS.
**17. *Rich Rodriguez, lhp, Mountain View HS, El Monte, Calif.—(1990-2003)**
18. *Ken Spratke, rhp, Chippewa Valley HS, Mount Clemens, Mich.
19. Tom Mohr, of, Rib Lake (Wis.) HS.
20. Mitch Hawley, rhp, University of California.
21. Tommy Thompson, 1b, Georgia Tech.
22. Perry Swanson, rhp, Texas A&M University.
23. *Pat Saitta, rhp, Salesian HS, Bronx, N.Y.
24. Rick Plautz, of, Grand Canyon College.
25. Marty Martino, of, Indiana State University.
26. *Jay Phillips, 2b, Virginia Tech.
27. Mark Bloomfield, lhp, University of Nevada-Las Vegas.
28. *Mark Solz, of, Santana HS, Santee, Calif.
29. *Glen Gwaltney, of, Sylvan Hills HS, North Little Rock, Ark.
30. Meade Langhorne, of, University of Richmond.
31. Don Seeker, of, Miami (Ohio) University.
32. Bill Gaunce, c, William Carey (Miss.) College.
33. Allen Peake, 1b, Stafford (Va.) HS.
34. Richard Sielicki, rhp, Bothell HS, Seattle.

**June—Secondary Phase (21)**

1. Reggie Wyatt, rhp, Santa Monica (Calif.) JC.—(AA)

## LOS ANGELES DODGERS

**January—Regular Phase (21)**

1. *Kevin White, rhp, Cosumnes River (Calif.) JC.—DNP
2. Robert Seymour, of-3b, Sacramento (Calif.) CC.
3. Frederick Bass, 3b, Sacramento (Calif.) CC.
4. John Sylvia, ss, JC of the Sequoias (Calif.).
5. *Jack Lopp, 1b, Pasadena (Calif.) CC.
6. Eugene Steinbach, c, DeKalb South (Ga.) CC.
7. *Brad Harlow, ss-3b, Cosumnes River (Calif.) JC.
8. *Brett Ragland, rhp, Valencia (Fla.) CC.
9. *Jon Van Dort, of-1b, Chaffey (Calif.) JC.
10. *Larry Riddle, rhp, Alvin (Texas) CC.
11. *Andy Hargrove, rhp, Barstow (Calif.) CC.
12. *James Sewell, of, Sacramento (Calif.) CC.
13. *Ronnie Chapman, 2b, Louisburg (N.C.) JC.
14. *James Woods, ss, San Jacinto (Texas) JC.
15. *Charles Byers, 3b, Chaffey (Calif.) JC.
**16. *Benny Distefano, 1b, Alvin (Texas) CC.—(1984-92)**

**January—Secondary Phase (21)**

1. Shayne Hammond, lhp, Southeastern (N.C.) CC.—(AA)
2. *Tom DiCeglio, ss, Gulf Coast (Fla.) CC.

**June—Regular Phase (22)**

**1. David C. Anderson, ss, Memphis State University.—(1983-92)**
**2. Sid Bream, 1b, Liberty University.—(1983-94)**
**2. Lemmie Miller, of, Arizona State University** (Choice from Astros as compensation for free agent Don Sutton)—**(1984)**
**3. Sid Fernandez, lhp, Kaiser HS, Honolulu, Hawaii.—(1983-97)**
4. Steve Boncore, c, University of La Verne (Calif.).—(High A)
**5. John Franco, lhp, St. John's University.—(1984-2005)**
6. Brian Williams, of, South HS, Bakersfield, Calif.
7. Mike Beuder, lhp, Santa Clara University.
8. Greg Chinn, of, Cal State Sacramento.
**9. Stu Pederson, of, University of Southern California.—(1985)**
DRAFT DROP *Father of Joc Pederson, major leaguer (2014-15)*
10. *Mark Pirruccello, c, Cal State Fullerton.
11. Greg Carne, rhp, Redondo HS, Torrance, Calif.
12. Peyton Mosher, rhp, University of Georgia.
13. David L. Anderson, rhp, University of Nevada-Reno.
14. Dean Rennicke, rhp, University of Wisconsin.
15. Jimmy Guillen, rhp, Roosevelt HS, Los Angeles.
16. Harold Perkins, ss, Cal State Los Angeles.
17. Chris Chavez, ss, University of Nebraska.
18. Jerry Bendorf, ss, Gonzaga University.
19. Jeff Greene, ss, University of Vermont.
20. *Tim Criswell, rhp, Carrollton (Ga.) HS.
21. John Gregory, 1b, Lake Worth (Fla.) HS.
22. Craig Thompson, of, Dallas Baptist University.
23. Bill Murray, 2b, University of San Francisco.
24. Steve Young, of, Chambersburg (Pa.) HS.
25. *Robert Philps, rhp, Carmichaels (Pa.) HS.
26. Charles Beard, rhp-3b, Cal State Sacramento.
27. *David Dunlap, inf-of, Cal State Sacramento.
28. *Brett Davis, of, Pearland (Texas) HS.
29. *Jeff Carter, ss, Evanston (Ill.) Township HS.
30. *Ronnie Robbins, rhp, Louisiana State University JC-Alexandria.

**June—Secondary Phase (22)**

**1. Ralph Bryant, of, Abraham Baldwin Agricultural (Ga.) JC.—(1985-87)**
2. Mike Moore, c, Edmonds (Wash.) CC.
3. *Ethan McHenry, rhp, Yakima Valley (Wash.) JC.

## MILWAUKEE BREWERS

**January—Regular Phase (22)**

1. Dewey James, of, Central Arizona JC.—(Low A)
**2. Tim Crews, rhp, Valencia (Fla.) CC.—(1987-92)**
DRAFT DROP *Died as active major leaguer (March 23, 1993)*
**3. Mike Felder, 2b, Contra Costa (Calif.) JC.—(1985-94)**
4. *John Thornton, c, CC of Baltimore.
5. *Michael Hakala, rhp, Yakima Valley (Wash.) JC.
6. *Jeff Schultz, rhp, Athens, Pa.
7. *Bruce Kipper, 1b, Scottsdale (Ariz.) CC.
8. *Phillip Chilton, rhp, Scottsdale (Ariz.) CC.

9. *Gene Morgan, rhp, Middle Georgia JC.
10. *Phil Lane, 3b, Broward (Fla.) CC.
11. Gary Evans, rhp, Morrisville, Pa.
12. Chris Fedor, rhp, Cuyahoga (Ohio) CC.
13. *Scott Davis, c, Fullerton (Calif.) JC.
14. *Irvin Anderson, rhp-of, Mount Olive (N.C.) JC.
15. *Don Carfino, 3b, Bellflower, Calif.
16. *Wade Jannsen, rhp, Central Arizona JC.
17. *Jeffrey Hutchinson, rhp, Indian Hills (Iowa) JC.
18. *James Kelly, lhp, El Camino (Calif.) JC.
19. *Ethan McHenry, rhp, Yakima Valley (Wash.) JC.

**January—Secondary Phase (14)**

1. Mike Samuel, ss, Orange Coast (Calif.) JC.—(AA)
2. *Keith Mucha, 3b, Granada Hills, Calif.
3. **Ernest Riles, ss, Middle Georgia JC.—(1985-93)**
4. *Audrey Robinson, of, Foothill (Calif.) JC.
5. *Jeffrey Johnson, rhp, Pasadena, Calif.
6. *Richie Carter, of, Umpqua (Ore.) CC.

**June—Regular Phase (21)**

1. (Choice to Blue Jays as compensation for free agent Roy Howell)
2. Scott Roberts, rhp, University of Hawaii.—(AAA)
3. Dan Davidsmeier, ss, University of Southern California.—(AAA)
4. Bruce Williams, rhp, West Linn (Ore.) HS.—(High A)

DRAFT DROP *Brother of Mitch Williams, major leaguer (1986-97)*

5. Collin Tanabe, c, University of Hawaii / Choice from Angels as compensation for free agent Bill Travers).—(AA)
5. **Bill Wegman, rhp, Oak Hills HS, Cincinnati.—(1985-95)**
6. Rich Embser, lhp, Bloomfield (N.J.) College.
7. **Bryan Clutterbuck, rhp, Eastern Michigan University.—(1986-89)**
8. Dave Hoff, rhp-1b, University of Pittsburgh-Johnstown.
9. Dan Burns, rhp, Cal State Fullerton.
10. *Todd Morgan, lhp, Dinwiddie HS, Church Road, Va.
11. *Ron Sismondo, lhp, University of Arizona.
12. *Bobby Alexander, lhp, Cardinal Gibbons HS, Baltimore.
13. Randy McFarlen, of, Cal Poly Pomona.
14. *Dean Albany, rhp, Brooklyn Park (Md.) HS.
15. Mike Villegas, rhp, Grand Canyon College.
16. ***Jeff Ballard, lhp, Billings West HS, Billings, Mon.—(1987-94)**
17. *Jeff McNally, ss, Billings West HS, Billings, Mon.

DRAFT DROP *Son of Dave McNally, major leaguer (1962-75)*

18. Mike Myerchin, lhp, Cal State Dominguez Hills.
19. *Jim Teahan, rhp, University of Utah.
20. Stan Borosky, c, Buckeye South HS, Rayland, Ohio.
21. Barry McPherson, rhp, St. Louis CC-Meramec.
22. Charles Dinkins, lhp, Southern University.
23. Eric Peyton, of, Cal Poly San Luis Obispo.
24. Bart Brainard, c-of, University of San Diego.
25. *Scott Campbell, lhp, Los Angeles Pierce JC.
26. *Greg Brandenburg, rhp, Lafayette HS, Ballwin, Mo.
27. *Tom Rasinski, ss, Villa Park (Calif.) HS.
28. *Bart Elbin, rhp, Southern Fulton HS, Warfordsburg, Pa.
29. *Ken Cerf, of, Gilman HS, Baltimore.

**June—Secondary Phase (19)**

1. *John Thornton, 1b-c, CC of Baltimore.—(AA)
2. *Frank Marrero, rhp, Miami-Dade CC North.
3. *Rick Knapp, rhp, Indian River (Fla.) CC.

## MINNESOTA TWINS

**January—Regular Phase (12)**

1. *Pete Kutsukos, rhp, Seminole (Fla.) CC.—(AA)
2. Cedric Gray, of, Canada (Calif.) JC.
3. Talbot Aiello, inf-of, Miami-Dade CC North.
4. *Robin Thompson, rhp, Santa Monica (Calif.) JC.
5. *Dan Devers, rhp, Yavapai (Ariz.) JC.
6. *Steve Shields, of, Santa Monica (Calif.) JC.
7. Art Valencia, rhp, Cerritos (Calif.) JC.
8. Michael Kribell, lhp, Irene, S.D.

JOHN KLINE

**The Yankees drafted Fred McGriff, but he found big league success with six other franchises**

9. *Steve Davis, of, Middle Georgia JC.
10. *Jeff Sutterfield, rhp, Orange Coast (Calif.) JC.
11. *Brian Kubala, rhp-3b, Miami-Dade CC North.
12. *Ignacio Velazquez, inf-c, Miami-Dade CC North.
13. ***Ralph Bryant, of, Abraham Baldwin Agricultural (Ga.) JC.—(1985-87)**
14. *Ernie Moya, rhp, Hillsborough (Fla.) CC.

**January—Secondary Phase (25)**

1. Rhett Whisman, ss, Gulf Coast (Fla.) CC.—(Low A)
2. *Mike O'Hara, rhp, West Covina, Calif.

**June—Regular Phase (11)**

1. Mike Sodders, 3b, Arizona State University.—(AAA)
2. **Frank Viola, lhp, St. John's University.—(1982-96)**
2. Craig Henderson, lhp, University of Wisconsin-Oshkosh (Choice from Orioles as compensation for free agent Jose Morales).—(AAA)
3. ***John Marzano, c, Central HS, Philadelphia** (Choice from Angels as compensation for free agent Geoff Zahn)—**(1987-98)**

DRAFT DROP *Attended Temple; re-drafted by Red Sox, 1984 (1st round)*

3. **Curt Wardle, lhp, UC Riverside** (Choice from Mets as compensation for free agent Mike Cubbage)—**(1984-85)**
3. Eric Broersma, rhp, UCLA.—(AAA)
4. Paul Fleming, of, East St. John HS, Garyville, La.—(Low A)
5. **Dave Meier, ss, Stanford University.—(1984-88)**
6. George Skeens, c, Ramapo (N.J.) College.
7. Jeff Arney, rhp, UC Riverside.
8. Stan Holmes, of, Arizona State University.
9. **Steve Lombardozzi, ss, University of Florida.—(1985-90)**

DRAFT DROP *Father of Steve Lombardozzi, major leaguer (2011-15)*

10. Ken Proctor, of, Cal Poly Pomona.
11. *Tom Schubert, lhp, Peekskill (N.Y.) HS.
12. Steve Korczyk, rhp, Upsala (N.J.) College.
13. Herb Carter, of, East St. John HS, Garyville, La.
14. Mike Weiermiller, lhp, University of Rochester (N.Y.).
15. Sebby Borriello, c, St. John's University.
16. Mike McCain, 2b, Arizona State University.
17. Carson Carroll, 2b, UC Irvine.
18. David Hoyt, of, University of New Haven.
19. Jim Flores, ss, Fresno State University.
20. Mike Giordano, rhp, University of New Haven.
21. Albert Everett, rhp, Hillsborough HS, Tampa.
22. Gerry Lomastro, of, Louisiana Tech.
23. Dean Kappes, c, Breckenridge HS, Kent, Minn.
24. Randy Weibel, rhp, Eastern Illinois University.
25. *Bill Blount, lhp, Hoover HS, San Diego.
26. *George Flower, 3b, Calvert Hall HS, Baltimore.
27. Robert Heimerl, of, Sibley HS, West St. Paul, Minn.
28. *Rick Hazard, of, UC Riverside.
29. Gary Robertson, 1b, Cal State Stanislaus.
30. *Rob Vodvarka, lhp, Montclair HS, Upland, Calif.
31. Marc Page, rhp, Riverview HS, Sarasota, Fla.
32. Mike Piatnik, ss, Florida Southern College.
33. *Michael Watson, of, Delgado (La.) JC.
34. *Gary Jost, 2b, University of Minnesota.

**June—Secondary Phase (13)**

1. Johnny Salery, of, Indian River (Fla.) CC.—(AA)
2. *Jeff Salazar, rhp, Los Angeles Valley JC.

## MONTREAL EXPOS

**January—Regular Phase (17)**

1. *Bruce Crabbe, inf, Gulf Coast (Fla.) CC.—(AAA)
2. *Mark De LaTorre, lhp, Los Angeles Harbor JC.
3. *Glen Davis, 1b-of, Middle Georgia JC.
4. *Steve Oliverio, rhp, Cumberland (Ky.) JC.
5. Ricky Lemon, of, Paul Quinn (Texas) College.
6. *Cal Santarelli, rhp, Edison (Fla.) CC.
7. *Jeffrey French, of, Central Arizona JC.
8. Barry Branam, rhp, Cincinnati.
9. *John Olsen, of, St. Clair County (Mich.) CC.
10. *Albie Scoggins, of, Indian River (Fla.) CC.
11. *Steve Lusby, 1b, Manatee (Fla.) JC.
12. *Doug Birkoffer, 2b, Cumberland (Ky.) JC.
13. *Shane O'Shea, 3b, Indian River (Fla.) CC.
14. *Frank Russo, of, Indian River (Fla.) CC.
15. Thomas Fettig, 3b, Pensacola (Fla.) JC.
16. Paul LeMire, of-1b, Northeastern University.
17. Robert Graves, rhp, Cowley County (Kan.) CC.
18. ***Jeff Treadway, 2b, Middle Georgia JC.—(1987-95)**

**January—Secondary Phase (23)**

1. *Reggie Wyatt, lhp, Santa Monica (Calif.) JC.—(AA)
2. *Michael Winbush, rhp, Winston-Salem State (N.C.) University.

**June—Regular Phase (18)**

1. Darren Dilks, lhp, Oklahoma State University.—(AAA)
2. Jeff Carl, ss, University of Wisconsin-Oshkosh (Choice from Angels as compensation for free agent John D'Acquisto).—(AA)
2. **Mike Fuentes, of, Florida State University.—(1983-84)**
3. ***Nelson Santovenia, c, Miami-Dade CC South.—(1987-93)**

DRAFT DROP *Attended Miami; re-drafted by Expos, June 1982/secondary phase (1st round)*

4. *Jeff Ledbetter, 1b, Florida State University.—(AA)

DRAFT DROP *Returned to Florida State; re-drafted by Red Sox, 1982 (1st round) • Brother of David Ledbetter, 4th-round draft pick, Orioles (1981)*

5. ***Phil Stephenson, 1b, Wichita State University.—(1989-92)**

DRAFT DROP *Returned to Wichita State; re-drafted by Athletics, 1982 (3rd round) • Brother of Gene Stephenson, baseball coach, Wichita State (1978-2013)*

6. Bobby Doerrer, 2b, Southern Illinois University.
7. Steve Yenser, rhp, Northern Kentucky University.
8. ***Mark McGwire, rhp-1b, Damien HS, Claremont, Calif.—(1986-2001)**

DRAFT DROP *First-round draft pick (10th overall), Athletics (1984)*

9. ***Marvin Freeman, rhp, Vocational HS, Chicago.—(1986-96)**
10. Craig Corbett, of, Lenoir-Rhyne (N.C.) College.
11. Mike Norment, c, Middle Tennessee State University.
12. Don Carter, of, University of Arkansas.
13. Tom Ellis, of, Southeastern Oklahoma State University.
14. *Jose Pena, ss, Blair HS, Altadena, Calif.
15. Dan Hoskins, ss, Falmouth, Ky.
16. Mike Vaughn, c, University of Alabama-Birmingham.
17. *Gerry Melillo, c, Eckerd (Fla.) College.
18. *Craig Koslowski, rhp, St. Francis de Sales HS, Chicago.
19. John Damon, 2b, Pepperdine University.
20. Paul Hertzler, 1b, Cal Poly San Luis Obispo.
21. Derrell Baker, 3b, Georgia Southern College.
22. Randy Budd, rhp, University of Akron.
23. Ron Gilbreath, rhp, Southeastern Oklahoma State University.
24. Willie Cooley, of, Long Beach State University.
25. ***Gene Walter, lhp, Eastern Kentucky University.—(1985-88)**
26. Jerome Coleman, of, Jacksonville State University.
27. *Carlos Hidalgo, rhp, Pan American University.
28. Hardy Dotson, of, Texas Wesleyan College.
29. Dan Flattery, c, Iowa State University.
30. *Mike King, c, Jackson State University.
31. Tyris Suggs, c, Lane (Tenn.) College.
32. Kevin McDaniel, ss, Troy State University.
33. Fred Mitchell, rhp, Cal State Dominguez Hills.
34. *Allen Harp, c, Coronado HS, Lubbock, Texas.
35. Elliott Skorupa, rhp, Eastern Illinois University.

36. *David Czosek, rhp, University of South Alabama.
37. Charlie Scott, rhp, Jackson State University.
38. Chris Campbell, 1b, University of Texas.

**June—Secondary Phase (12)**

1. **Al Newman, 2b, San Diego State University.—(1985-92)**
2. Jim McIntosh, rhp, Carl Albert (Okla.) JC.
3. *Michael Winbush, rhp, Winston-Salem State University.

## NEW YORK METS

**January—Regular Phase (3)**

1. **Randy Milligan, of, San Diego Mesa JC.—(1987-94)**
2. Steve Ray, lhp, Southwestern (Calif.) JC.
3. *Rey Tolentino, rhp, Chaffey (Calif.) JC.
4. *Dodd Hook, 1b, Indian Hills (Iowa) CC.
5. Jim Cazet, ss, Modesto (Calif.) JC.
6. *Greg Cary, rhp, Chabot (Calif.) JC.

DRAFT DROP *Brother of Chuck Cary, 7th-round draft pick, January 1981/regular phase, Tigers; major league (1985-93)*

7. *Craig Walter, rhp, Waldorf (Iowa) JC.
8. Tim Hampton, rhp, Modesto (Calif.) JC.
9. *Brian Pate, 3b-of, Columbia State (Tenn.) CC.
10. *William Bankhead, 3b, Green River (Wash.) CC.
11. *Roger Lee, of-1b, Garden City (Kan.) CC.
12. Greg Shirley, c, Alabama Christian College.
13. Robert Smith, 2b-of, Sanford, Fla.

**January—Secondary Phase (9)**

1. **Herm Winningham, of, DeKalb South (Ga.) CC.—(1984-92)**
2. *Billy Irions, lhp, Seminole (Okla.) JC.
3. *Nick Esposito, rhp, Los Medanos (Calif.) JC.

**June—Regular Phase (4)**

1. **Terry Blocker, of, Tennessee State University.—(1985-89)**
2. (Choice to Rangers as compensation for free agent Rusty Staub)
2. **John Christensen, of, Cal State Fullerton** (Choice from Braves as compensation for free agent Claudell Washington)**—(1984-88)**
3. (Choice to Twins as compensation for free agent Mike Cubbage)
4. **Dave Cochrane, rhp-3b, Troy HS, Yorba Linda, Calif.—(1986-92)**
5. Steve Phillips, ss, De La Salle HS, Detroit.—(AA)

DRAFT DROP *General manager, Mets (1997-2003)*

6. Ken Harris, ss-of, University of La Verne (Calif.).
7. *Jeff Keeler, rhp, Florida State University.
8. **Mark Carreon, of, Salpointe HS, Tucson, Ariz.—(1987-96)**

DRAFT DROP *Son of Camilo Carreon, major leaguer (1959-66)*

9. Rich Webster, rhp, Memphis State University.
10. *Albert Candelaria, lhp, Yerba Buena HS, San Jose, Calif.
11. Steve Walker, rhp, Mount Carmel HS, San Diego.
12. ***Roger Clemens, rhp, San Jacinto (Texas) JC.—(1984-2005)**

DRAFT DROP *First-round draft pick (19th overall), Red Sox (1983)*

13. **Lenny Dykstra, of, Garden Grove (Calif.) HS.—(1985-96)**
14. *Gary Kanwisher, rhp, Pascack Valley HS, Hillsdale, N.J.
15. Larry McNutt, 1b, Jackson State University.
16. *Ron Woellert, rhp, Moeller HS, Cincinnati.
17. *Bryan Olden, 2b, Beaverton (Ore.) HS.
18. Ed Garton, 3b, University of Iowa.
19. **Lou Thornton, 3b, Jefferson Davis HS, Hope Hull, Ala.—(1985-90)**
20. *Mark Boyd, c, McEachern HS, Powder Springs, Ga.
21. Steve Slaton, rhp, Long Beach State University.
22. Matthew Fitts, rhp, Lompoc (Calif.) HS.
23. *Kurt Griffon, of, Plaquemine (La.) HS.
24. Bob Costello, c, New York Tech.
25. Russell Orrick, of, Vintage HS, Napa, Calif.
26. Randy Hoffman, of, Southeastern Louisiana University.
27. James Oates, lhp, Huntingdon (Ala.) College.
28. Joe Licata, of-3b, Florida State University.
29. *Gary Heien, rhp, O'Fallon (Ill.) HS.
30. Michael Franks, 2b, Loyola Marymount University.
31. Mike Harlander, rhp, University of Nebraska.
32. Steve DeMatties, c, Ithaca (N.Y.) College.
33. ***Luis Medina, of, Warren HS, Downey, Calif.—(1988-91)**
34. Bruce Kastelic, ss, Oklahoma State University.
35. Louis Martinez, c, DeWitt Clinton HS, Bronx, N.Y.
36. *Darrell Rodgers, rhp, Eisenhower HS, Lawton, Okla.
37. Larry Czeszewski, c, Midwestern State (Texas) University.
38. Scot Holliday, of, Middle Tennessee State University.

**June—Secondary Phase (14)**

1. John Felice, of, JC of the Canyons (Calif.).–(AAA)
2. Gail Arnold, rhp, Brigham Young University.
3. *Greg Griffin, of, Corpus Christi, Texas.
4. *Kevin Sliwinski, of, Orange Coast (Calif.) JC.
5. *Greg Cary, rhp, Chabot (Calif.) JC.

DRAFT DROP *Brother of Chuck Cary, 7th-round draft pick, January 1980/regular phase, Detroit Tigers; major leaguer (1985-93).*

## NEW YORK YANKEES

**January—Regular Phase (26)**

1. Mike Gatlin, of, Lurleen B. Wallace State (Ala.) JC.—(Short-season A)
2. Ed Darling, 1b, Millbury, Mass.

DRAFT DROP *Brother of Ron Darling, first-round draft pick, Rangers (1981); major leaguer (1983-95)*

3. *Kurt Eskildsen, rhp, Los Angeles Harbor JC.
4. Mark Blaser, 3b, Butte (Calif.) JC.
5. Johnny Hawkins, c, Pensacola (Fla.) JC.
6. Boyce Bailey, rhp, Pensacola (Fla.) JC.
7. *David Niemiec, rhp, San Jose (Calif.) CC.
8. Howard Maynor, 3b, Merced (Calif.) JC.
9. *Billy Williams, 1b, Solano (Calif.) CC.
10. *David Aragon, ss, Santa Barbara (Calif.) CC.
11. Mike Isherwood, c, JC of the Sequoias (Calif.).
12. *Eric Call, 1b-of, Palm Beach (Fla.) JC.
13. *Rick Knapp, rhp, Indian River (Fla.) CC.
14. *Keith Bragg, of, Lurleen B. Wallace State (Ala.) JC.
15. *Jeffrey Allen, rhp, Truman (Ill.) JC.
16. *Brent Main, rhp, JC of the Sequoias (Calif.).
17. *Kevin Bascue, of-1b, Garden City (Kan.) CC.
18. *Mike Costello, rhp, Centralia (Wash.) JC.
19. *Kelly Pfaller, of, Lane (Ore.) CC.

**January—Secondary Phase (16)**

1. *Rod Langston, of, Indian River (Fla.) CC.—DNP
2. *Todd Schulz, of, Central Arizona JC.
3. *Brian Peck, rhp, JC of Southern Idaho.
4. *Randy Edwards, lhp, Allegany (Md.) CC.

**June—Regular Phase (26)**

1. (Choice to Padres as compensation for free agent Dave Winfield)
2. John Elway, of, Stanford University.—(Short-season A)

DRAFT DROP *First overall draft pick, Baltimore Colts/ National Football League (1983); quarterback, NFL (1983-98)*

3. **Scott Bradley, c, University of North Carolina** (Choice from Braves as compensation for free agent Gaylord Perry)**—(1984-92)**

DRAFT DROP *Baseball coach, Princeton (2001-15)*

3. **Phil Lombardi, c, Kennedy HS, Granada Hills, Calif.—(1986-89)**
4. **Eric Plunk, rhp, Bellflower (Calif.) HS.—(1986-99)**
5. *Dennis Lubert, lhp, University of South Carolina.—(High A)

DRAFT DROP *Returned to South Carolina; re-drafted by Braves, 1982 (11th round)*

6. **Mike Pagliarulo, 3b, University of Miami.—(1984-95)**
7. Andy Swope, rhp, Otterbein (Ohio) College.
8. ***John Fishel, of, Loara HS, Anaheim, Calif.—(1988)**
9. **Fred McGriff, 1b, Jefferson HS, Tampa.—(1986-2004)**
10. Matt Gallegos, ss, San Francisco State University.
11. Tom Jones, of, University of North Carolina-Wilmington.
12. Scott Repass, lhp, Louisburg (N.C.) JC.
13. David Woodworth, lhp, Western Michigan University.
14. Mike Browning, rhp, University of Miami.
15. Mike Reddish, c-of, Florida International University.
16. Mike Speeney, ss, Council Rock HS, Holland, Pa.
17. **Dickie Scott, ss, Ellsworth (Maine) HS.—(1989)**
18. Pat Bone, of, Florida International University.
19. **Bob Tewksbury, rhp, St. Leo (Fla.) College.—(1986-98)**
20. **Logan Easley, rhp, JC of Southern Idaho.—(1987-89)**
21. Steve Swinney, of, Thornwood HS, Markham, Ill.
22. Steve Scafa, 2b, St. John's University.
23. Gary Kempton, c, Southern Illinois University.
24. ***Les Lancaster, rhp, Nimitz HS, Irving, Texas.—(1987-93)**
25. Mark Silva, rhp, Cal Poly San Luis Obispo.
26. Paul Doty, rhp, Brigham Young University.
27. Mark Shiflett, lhp, Auburn University.
28. Larry Mikesell, lhp, University of Florida.
29. Mike Siwiec, rhp, Triton (Ill.) JC.
30. *Ken Reed, rhp, Tuslaw HS, North Lawrence, Ohio.
31. Greg Zunino, of, University of California.

DRAFT DROP *Father of Mike Zunino, first-round draft pick, Mariners (2012); major leaguer (2013-15)*

32. Bob Bomerito, 3b, Wichita State University.
33. Larry Lewis, rhp, Prospect HS, Mount Prospect, Ill.
34. *Mark Baker, rhp, Palm Beach (Fla.) JC.
35. *Derek Vanacore, of, Sacramento (Calif.) HS.
36. *Bill Stevenson, 1b, St. Thomas Aquinas HS, Fort Lauderdale, Fla.
37. Meade Palmer, of, Philadelphia College of Pharmacy.
38. Stan Williams, rhp, University of Southern California.

DRAFT DROP *Son of Stan Williams Sr., major leaguer (1958-72)*

39. Scott Smith, of, Kent County HS, Chestertown, Md.

**June—Secondary Phase (5)**

1. *Phil Lane, 3b, Broward (Fla.) CC.—(High A)
2. Trent Ferrin, rhp, JC of Southern Idaho.
3. Billy Williams, 1b, Solano (Calif.) CC.
4. David Niemiec, rhp, West Valley (Calif.) JC.
5. Shane O'Shea, ss, Indian River (Fla.) CC.
6. John Hughes, 1b, JC of Southern Idaho.

## OAKLAND ATHLETICS

**January—Regular Phase (16)**

1. **Steven Kiefer, ss, Fullerton (Calif.) JC.—(1984-89)**

DRAFT DROP *Brother of Mark Kiefer, major leaguer (1993-96)*

2. Mark Jarrett, rhp, Riverside (Calif.) CC.
3. *Wayne Bonham, of, Yavapai (Ariz.) JC.
4. Gary Dawson, of, Fullerton (Calif.) JC.
5. *Ricky Daniels, ss, Los Angeles CC.
6. *Robert Feldhaus, 2b, Chaffey (Calif.) JC.
7. *Jeffrey Rojas, rhp, San Bernardino Valley (Calif.) JC.
8. *Lee Mays, rhp, Los Angeles CC.
9. ***Doug Baker, ss, Los Angeles Valley JC.—(1984-90)**

DRAFT DROP *Brother of Dave Baker, major leaguer (1982)*

10. Jay Schellin, of, Arcadia, Calif.
11. Gregory Mine, rhp, Green River (Wash.) CC.
12. Elton Hooker, of, Los Angeles CC.
13. *Carter Pittman, ss, Central Arizona JC.
14. *Paul Felix, of, Fullerton (Calif.) JC.
15. Gene Ransom, 2b, University of California.

DRAFT DROP *Ninth-round draft pick, Golden State Warriors/National Basketball Association (1979) • Brother of Jeff Ransom, major leaguer (1981-83)*

16. James Sanfilippo, 3b, Kearney, N.J.
17. *Marvin McWhirter, 1b, Los Angeles CC.

**January—Secondary Phase (6)**

1. *John Leonard, rhp, Yavapai (Ariz.) JC.—(Rookie)
2. *Robert Lackeby, rhp, Central Arizona JC.
3. John Vela, lhp, Saddleback (Calif.) CC.
4. Kelvin Hudson, 2b, San Bernardino Valley (Calif.) JC.

**June—Regular Phase (15)**

1. **Tim Pyznarski, 3b-of, Eastern Illinois University.—(1986)**
2. **Mike Gallego, 2b, UCLA** (Choice from White Sox as compensation for free agent Jim Essian)**—(1985-97)**
2. **Rick Rodriguez, rhp, UC Riverside.—(1986-90)**
3. John Hotchkiss, 3b, Cal Poly Pomona.—(AAA)
4. **Curt Young, lhp, Central Michigan University.—(1983-93)**
5. **Mickey Tettleton, c-of, Oklahoma State University.—(1984-97)**
6. ***Alvin Davis, 1b, Arizona State University.—(1984-92)**
7. *Don Smith, rhp, Orange Coast (Calif.) JC.
8. **Bill Bathe, c, Pepperdine University.—(1986-90)**
9. Jim Camacho, ss, Cal Poly Pomona.
10. Tony Herron, lhp, Fresno State University.
11. *Tom Siefert, c, Whitmer HS, Toledo, Ohio.
12. Tom Heckman, rhp, University of Missouri.
13. Dave Weatherman, rhp, Cal State Fullerton.
14. *Henry Gatewood, c, McClatchy HS, Sacramento, Calif.
15. Luis Rojas, of, Texas Christian University.
16. *Kevin Madden, rhp, Massanutten Academy, Westmont, N.J.
17. Thad Reece, 2b, University of Hawaii.
18. *Bo Jordan, rhp, Mississippi College.
19. Phil Strom, 1b, University of Utah.
20. Scot Mitchell, c, Cal State Northridge.
21. Chuck Kolotka, rhp, Northern Illinois University.
22. Tom Copeland, of, UC Riverside.
23. *Gary Weinberger, of, Cal State Sacramento.
24. Mike Ashman, 1b, Cal Poly Pomona.
25. Kevin Coughlin, of, Fresno State University.
26. Bruce Amador, 2b, Cal State Stanislaus.
27. Bryan Smith, 3b, Rio Hondo (Calif.) JC.
28. *Mike Correia, rhp-2b, University HS, San Diego.
29. Pat O'Hara, c, Covina HS, Hesperia, Calif.
30. John Michel, 1b, Evergreen HS, Vancouver, Wash.
31. *Steve Clark, of, San Diego CC.

**June—Secondary Phase (1)**

1. **Donnie Hill, ss, Arizona State University.—(1983-92)**
2. *Craig Fitzpatrick, rhp, Koeltztown, Mo.
3. *Damon Farmar, of, West Los Angeles JC.

## PHILADELPHIA PHILLIES

**January—Regular Phase (19)**

1. *Eric Schmidt, rhp, Antelope Valley (Calif.) JC.—DNP
2. Mark Frishman, of, Los Angeles Valley JC.
3. *Herbert Jordan, rhp, Blinn (Texas) JC.
4. Michael Sims, rhp, Johnson County (Kan.) CC.
5. *Joe Jordan, c, Seminole (Okla.) JC.

DRAFT DROP *Scouting director, Orioles (2005-11)*

6. Tommy George, ss, Bacone (Okla.) JC.
7. Kent Kaiser, of, Mineral Area (Mo.) JC.
8. *Kyle Johnson, rhp, Seminole (Okla.) JC.
9. John Proctor, c-of, Allen County (Kan.) CC.

DRAFT DROP *Brother of David Proctor, first-round draft pick, Mets (1988)*

10. *Ron Johnson, rhp, Mission (Calif.) JC.
11. *Marvin White, lhp, Seminole (Okla.) JC.
12. *Donald McCaleb, 2b, Angelina (Texas) JC.
13. Steve Giovacchini, rhp, Modesto (Calif.) JC.
14. *Billy Vinson, rhp, Ranger (Texas) JC.
15. *Tim Middleton, rhp, Bacone (Okla.) JC.

**January—Secondary Phase (11)**

1. **Kevin Gross, rhp, Oxnard (Calif.) JC.—(1983-97)**
2. *Doug Laufer, rhp, University of Texas.
3. *Andrew Nossek, lhp, Blinn (Texas) JC.

**June—Regular Phase (20)**

1. **Johnny Abrego, rhp, Mission HS, San Jose, Calif.—(1985)**
2. C.L. Penigar, of, Ontario (Calif.) HS.—(AAA)
3. Vinnie Soreca, c, Pace (N.Y.) University.–(High A)
4. *Jerry Holtz, ss, Atlantic City HS, Margate, N.J.—(AA)

DRAFT DROP *Attended Villanova; re-drafted by Orioles, 1984 (4th round)*

5. John Kanter, ss-2b, Camelback HS, Phoenix.—(High A)
6. Bill Currier, of, University of Vermont.

DRAFT DROP *Baseball coach, Vermont (1988-2009); baseball coach, Fairfield (2012-15)*

**7. Jim Olander, of, Sahuaro HS, Tucson, Ariz.—(1991)**
8. Dave Seiler, lhp, University of Texas.
9. Troy Berry, 2b, Benson HS, Portland, Ore.
10. Mel Williams, of, David Lipscomb College.
11. Bud Bartholow, rhp, Oral Roberts University.
**12. Charles Hudson, rhp, Prairie View A&M University.—(1983-89)**
13. Steve Witt, rhp, Servite HS, Buena Park, Calif.
14. Jim Reilly, rhp, Longview (Mo.) CC.
15. *Todd Simmons, rhp, Bellflower (Calif.) HS.
16. Joe Nemeth, 1b, Cal State Dominguez Hills.
17. *David Denny, ss, Humble (Texas) HS.
18. *Brooks Shumake, ss, Hartsville (S.C.) HS.
19. Todd Smith, c, Wingate (N.C.) College.
**20. *Vince Coleman, of, Florida A&M University.—(1985-97)**
21. *Ed Augustine, of, Brevard (Fla.) CC.
22. Jay Davisson, rhp, Eastern Michigan University.
23. Ace Oswell, rhp, Texas Wesleyan College.
**24. *Charlie Kerfeld, rhp, Carson HS, Carson City, Nev.—(1985-90)**
25. *Jerry Anderson, rhp, Violet Hill HS, Horseshoe Bend, Ark.
26. Adolph Crump, c, Prairie View A&M University.
27. Ron Mack, lhp, Crowder (Mo.) JC.
28. Al LeBoeuf, 1b, Eastern Connecticut State University.
29. Tim Finch, rhp, San Joaquin Delta (Calif.) JC.
30. *Jeff Brinson, 2b, Riverview Academy, Albany, Ga.
31. Frank Rubio, rhp, Midwestern State (Texas) University.
32. *Todd Ezold, c, Classical HS, Springfield, Mass.
33. *Mike Dennis, rhp, Wolfson HS, Jacksonville, Fla.

#### June—Secondary Phase (6)

1. Billy Irions, rhp, Seminole (Okla.) JC.—(Low A)
2. *John Bryant, of, Santa Ana (Calif.) JC.
3. *John Whitt, of, Cal State Dominguez Hills.

## PITTSBURGH PIRATES

#### January—Regular Phase (13)

1. Brian Reams, rhp, Long Beach (Calif.) CC.–(Low A)
2. Dick Scott, 2b, Canada (Calif.) JC.
**3. *John Kruk, of, Allegheny (Pa.) CC.—(1986-95)**
4. Tim Cassell, rhp, Sacramento (Calif.) CC.
5. *Paul Steinert, of, Dundalk (Md.) CC.
6. *Jeff Bernash, rhp, Yakima Valley (Wash.) JC.
7. *Scott Reckord, rhp, Bellevue (Wash.) CC.
8. William Daiker, rhp, CC of Baltimore.
9. *Randy Graham, rhp, Santa Rosa (Calif.) JC.
10. *Robert Kaser, rhp, Mount Hood (Ore.) CC.

#### January—Secondary Phase (19)

1. *Norman Morton, lhp, Miami-Dade CC North.—DNP
2. Todd Davidson, of, Wexford, Pa.
3. *Bobby Falls, ss, Walters State (Tenn.) CC.

#### June—Regular Phase (14)

**1. Jim Winn, rhp, John Brown (Ark.) University.—(1983-88)**
**2. Lee Tunnell, rhp, Baylor University.—(1982-89)**
3. Craig Brown, of, Goldsboro (N.C.) HS.—(AA)
4. Stacey Pettis, of, Castlemont HS, Oakland, Calif.—(High A)

DRAFT DROP *Brother of Gary Pettis, major leaguer (1982-92)*

**5. *Bip Roberts, ss-2b, Skyline HS, Oakland, Calif.—(1986-98)**

DRAFT DROP *Attended Chabot (Calif.) JC; re-drafted by Pirates, June 1982/secondary phase (1st round)*

6. Mike Zamba, rhp, University of New Haven.
7. *Scott Wade, of, Duval HS, Seabrook, Md.
8. Kevin Battle, 3b, North Lenoir HS, Grifton, N.C.
9. Ken Brown, ss, Grambling State University.
10. Richard Mott, rhp, Oscar Smith HS, Chesapeake, Va.
11. Steve Susce, rhp, Mississippi State University.
12. Jim Churchill, of, Texas Wesleyan College.

Seattle polished Mark Langston's ability and saw him lead the AL in strikeouts three times

13. Tom Gil, of, University of Miami.
14. Tony Burley, 2b, University of Iowa.
15. Keith Stafford, rhp, Wiley (Texas) College.
16. *Jeff Fruge, rhp, Menard HS, Alexandria, La.
**17. *Scott Bankhead, rhp, Reidsville (N.C.) HS.—(1986-95)**

DRAFT DROP *First-round draft pick (16th overall), Royals (1984)*

18. *Jim Thrift, ss, Oakton HS, Vienna, Va.

DRAFT DROP *Son of Syd Thrift, general manager, Pirates (1985-88); general manager, Orioles (1999-2002)*

19. Mark Veon, of-c, Point Park (Pa.) College.
20. Steve Kellam, c, Northern Kentucky University.
21. Larry Lamonde, rhp, University of Pittsburgh.
22. Marvin Parker, c, Baker County HS, MacClenny, Fla.
23. Bob Loscalzo, of, Villanova University.
24. *Mark Davis, lhp, Oconomowoc HS, Okawchee, Wis.
25. *Geoff Magnuson, of, Eastmont HS, East Wenatchee, Wash.
26. *Dale Hurst, rhp, Marietta (Ohio) College.
27. Danny Smith, ss, University of Texas-Arlington.
28. *Ray Krieger, of, Sayreville War Memorial HS, South Amboy, N.J.
**29. *Chris Bosio, rhp, Cordova HS, Rancho Cordova, Calif.—(1986-96)**
**30. *Lance Johnson, of, Cincinnati.—(1987-2000)**
31. *Michael Scarcella, rhp, Roxbury HS, Roxbury Township, N.J.
32. *Jim Balmer, rhp, Marple Newton HS, Newton Square, Pa.
33. *Gary Butler, rhp, Woodson HS, Annandale, Va.
34. *Steve McGuire, rhp, Bayley-Ellard HS, Morris Plains, N.J.
35. *James Lane, c, DeKalb South (Ga.) CC.
36. *Allan Peterson, c-of, Lower Columbia (Wash.) JC.
37. *Jerry Lillard, 1b, Glencoe (Ky.) HS.
38. *Ken Bender, of, Wilson HS, Tacoma, Wash.
39. *Steve Hallahan, inf, Penn Hills HS, Pittsburgh.
40. *Bill Drambel, rhp, University of Iowa.
41. *Brian Jones, 2b, Gallatin County HS, Warsaw, Ky.
42. *Charles Simpson, 3b, James Hunt HS, Wilson, N.C.
43. *Paul Westwood, ss, Peabody HS, Pittsburgh.

#### June—Secondary Phase (4)

**1. Ray Krawczyk, rhp, Oral Roberts University.—(1984-89)**
2. *Bruce Crabbe, ss-of, Gulf Coast (Fla.) CC.
3. *Ken Lynn, rhp, Spartanburg Methodist (S.C.) JC.
4. *Kelly Simon, rhp, Orange Coast (Calif.) JC.

## ST. LOUIS CARDINALS

#### January—Regular Phase (7)

1. Brad Luther, ss, JC of the Sequoias (Calif.).—(High A)
2. *Barry Aden, rhp, Centralia (Wash.) JC.
3. *Alan Griffin, 1b, Thornton (Ill.) CC.
**4. *Oddibe McDowell, of, Miami-Dade CC North.—(1985-94)**

DRAFT DROP *First overall draft pick, June 1983/secondary phase, Twins; first-round draft pick (11th overall), Rangers (1984); first player from 1984 draft to reach majors (May 19, 1985)*

5. John DiGioia, c, Mount San Antonio (Calif.) JC.
6. Robert Hayes, rhp, Onondaga (N.Y.) CC.
7. *Todd Oakes, rhp, Waldorf (Iowa) JC.
8. *Gregory Wirth, rhp, Glendale (Ariz.) CC.
9. *Jerry Eklund, rhp, Eastern Arizona JC.

#### January—Secondary Phase (1)

1. Harry McCulla, c, Delgado (La.) JC.—(AA)
2. *Jorge Reyes, lhp, Miami-Dade CC South.
3. *Mike Santiago, lhp, Mount San Antonio (Calif.) JC.

#### June—Regular Phase (8)

**1. Bobby Meacham, ss, San Diego State University.—(1983-88)**
2. (Choice to Royals as compensation for free agent Darrell Porter)
**3. Tom Nieto, c, Oral Roberts University.—(1984-90)**
**4. Curt Ford, 2b, Jackson State University.—(1985-90)**
5. Jeff Lauck, of-1b, McLane HS, Fresno, Calif.—(Low A)
**6. *Reggie Williams, of, Southern University.—(1985-88)**
**7. Jeff Keener, rhp, University of Kentucky.—(1982-83)**
8. Willy Finnegan, rhp, University of Nevada-Las Vegas.
9. Scott Young, rhp, University of Delaware.
**10. *Bruce Walton, rhp, North HS, Bakersfield, Calif.—(1991-94)**
11. Bobby Kish, rhp, University of South Carolina.
12. Greg Guin, 1b, Clemson University.
**13. Danny Cox, rhp, Troy State University.—(1983-95)**
14. *Greg Morhardt, of, Gilbert HS, Winsted, Conn.

DRAFT DROP *Son of Moe Morhardt, major leaguer (1961-62)*

15. *Todd Ostrominski, rhp, Hampton HS, Allison Park, Pa.
16. Alan Hunsinger, 1b, Oregon State University.
17. *Keith Gilliam, lhp, Austin Peay State University.
18. Brian Hopkins, of-rhp, Pottsville (Pa.) HS.
19. *Rich Rosemus, lhp, Madison HS, Portland, Ore.
20. John Adams, rhp, University of Mississippi.
21. *Jeff Edwards, lhp, DuPont HS, Old Hickory, Tenn.
22. *Juan Perkins, of, Newton-Conover HS, Conover, N.C.
23. *Ron Proctor, rhp, Los Altos HS, Hacienda Heights, Calif.
24. *Sal Vaccaro, lhp, Westmoor HS, Daly City, Calif.
25. David Reinhardt, 3b, Utica (N.Y.) Free Academy.
26. *Leland Maddox, c, Lincoln HS, San Diego.

DRAFT DROP *Scouting director, Pirates (1997-98)*

27. Dave Bear, rhp, Ben Davis HS, Indianapolis.
28. Chuck Menzhuber, 2b, University of Southern California.
29. *Bob Fingers, rhp, Saguaro HS, Scottsdale, Ariz.
30. Steven Roath, of, Manchester (Conn.) CC.
31. *David Osteen, ss-rhp, Anneville-Cleona HS, Anneville, Pa.

DRAFT DROP *Son of Claude Osteen, major leaguer (1957-75)*

32. *Jim Cecchini, c, University of Southern California.

#### June—Secondary Phase (2)

**1. Randy Hunt, c, University of Alabama.—(1985-86)**

## SAN DIEGO PADRES

#### January—Regular Phase (5)

**1. *Eric Bullock, of, Los Angeles Harbor JC.—(1985-92)**
2. *Michael Moore, c, Edmonds (Wash.) CC.
3. *Donald Fenton, rhp, Lower Columbia (Wash.) JC.
4. Pride Evans, inf, Citrus (Calif.) JC.
5. *Keith Street, of, Middle Georgia JC.
6. Paul Huyck, lhp, Hancock (Calif.) JC.
7. Fred Williams, lhp, Mountain View, Calif.
8. *Willard Medley, rhp, Gulf Coast (Fla.) CC.

#### January—Secondary Phase (15)

1. *Sam Martin, ss, Louisburg (N.C.) JC.—(AA)
2. *Marcus Handley, rhp, Cumberland (Ky.) JC.

#### June—Regular Phase (6)

**1. Kevin McReynolds, of, University of Arkansas.—(1983-94)**
1. Frank Castro, c, University of Miami / Choice from Yankees as compensation for free agent Dave Winfield).—(AA)
**2. Bill Long, rhp, Miami (Ohio) University.—(1985-91)**
**3. Tony Gwynn, of, San Diego State University.—(1982-2001)**

DRAFT DROP *Elected to Baseball Hall of Fame, 2007; baseball coach, San Diego State (2002-14) • Brother of Chris Gwynn, first-round draft pick, Dodgers (1985); major leaguer (1987-96) • Father of Tony Gwynn Jr., major leaguer (2006-14)*

4. Scott Thompson, of, Lower Dauphin HS, Grantville, Pa.—(AAA)
5. *Burk Goldthorn, c, University of Texas.—(AAA)

DRAFT DROP *No school; re-drafted by Pirates, January 1982/secondary phase (1st round)*

6. Louis Langie, ss, Gardena HS, Compton, Calif.
7. *Craig Holthus, of, Fruita Monument HS, Grand Junction, Colo.
8. Craig Shumock, 3b-of, University of North Carolina.
9. Larry Kiesling, 3b, Centenary College.
**10. Greg Booker, rhp, Elon College.–(1983-90)**
11. Mark Gillaspie, of, Mississippi State University.
12. Mark Ochal, rhp, University of North Carolina.
13. John Hennell, 1b, University of Arkansas.
**14. Paul Noce, ss, Washington State University.—(1987-90)**
15. Steve Schefsky, rhp, San Diego State University.
16. Jim Giacomazzi, rhp, Azusa Pacific (Calif.) College.
17. Lee Purchatzke, rhp, University of Wisconsin-Oshkosh.
18. Bobby Macias, rhp, Oral Roberts University.
19. *Jeff Morrison, lhp, University of Miami.
20. Bill Solomon, rhp, Iowa State University.
21. Steve Patterson, c, Long Beach State University.
22. Marty Kain, rhp, Washington State University.
23. Jeff Blood, of, Lewis-Clark State (Idaho) College.
24. Jamie Oberbruner, rhp, University of Wisconsin-Parkside.
25. Joey Balderston, rhp, Santa Clara University.
26. Mark Christy, rhp, University of New Orleans.
27. Jim Leopold, rhp-of, University of Kentucky.
28. Bob Gonsoulin, ss, Southeast Missouri State University.
29. Ray Etchebarren, 3b, Oklahoma State University.

DRAFT DROP *Son of Andy Etchebarren, major leaguer (1962-78)*

30. Mark Wedel, 2b, Long Beach State University.
31. Tom Cannon, 3b-rhp, Sayreville HS, Parlin, N.J.
32. *Lynn Morton, of, South Alamance HS, Graham, N.C.
33. Paul Grame, rhp, Stanford University.
34. Jeff Ronk, 2b, University of California.
35. Wes Smith, rhp, University of Portland.
36. Jim Stein, rhp, University of Washington.
37. *Wade Boccard, inf, Bloomfield (Colo.) HS.

**June—Secondary Phase (16)**

1. *Everett Graham, of, Louisburg (N.C.) JC.—(AAA)
2. Peter Kutsukos, rhp, Seminole (Fla.) CC.
3. **John Kruk, of, Allegheny (Pa.) CC.—(1986-95)**

## SAN FRANCISCO GIANTS

**January—Regular Phase (9)**

1. *Mel White, rhp, Fullerton (Calif.) JC.—DNP
2. Louis D'Amore, rhp, CC of Morris (N.J.).
3. Gene Lambert, lhp, Los Angeles Valley JC.
4. Daryl Pitts, of, Los Angeles CC.
5. *Chuck Bartlett, c, Cuyahoga (Ohio) CC.
6. *Al Cardwood, rhp-1b, Ranger (Texas) JC.
7. *Keith O'Day, rhp, West Valley (Calif.) JC.
8. *Bob Lockwood, of, Los Angeles Valley JC.
9. *Terry Quinn, 2b, Los Angeles Valley JC.
10. *Douglas Boren, rhp, Fresno (Calif.) CC.
11. *Chad Miltenberger, c, JC of the Sequoias (Calif.).
12. *James McCann, ss, San Diego Mesa JC.
13. Ted Ladd, ss, St. Andrews, Tenn.
14. *Orlando Blackwell, ss, Sacramento (Calif.) CC.
15. *Keith Davila, rhp, Sacramento (Calif.) CC.
16. *Michael Pintar, rhp, JC of Southern Idaho.
17. *Tony Laird, of-1b, Treasure Valley (Ore.) CC.
18. *Bradley Mettler, rhp, San Joaquin Delta (Calif.) JC.

**January—Secondary Phase (17)**

1. *John Duval, rhp, Cuesta (Calif.) JC.—(Rookie)
2. *Tony Beal, of, Seminole (Fla.) CC.
3. *Louis Lanini, inf, San Joaquin Delta (Calif.) JC.

**June—Regular Phase (10)**

1. **Mark Grant, rhp, Joliet Catholic HS, Joliet, Ill.—(1984-93)**
2. **Kelvin Torve, 1b, Oral Roberts University.—(1988-91)**
3. *Brad Powell, rhp, Ridge HS, Basking Ridge, N.J.—(Rookie)

DRAFT DROP *Attended North Carolina; re-drafted by Red Sox, 1984 (12th round)*

4. *Dan Penner, rhp, Rio Mesa HS, Camarillo, Calif.—DNP

DRAFT DROP *Attended Hawaii; never re-drafted*

5. *Dennis Livingston, lhp, North Reading (Mass.) HS.—(AAA)

DRAFT DROP *Attended Oklahoma State; re-drafted by Dodgers, 1984 (1st round)*

6. Bryan Snyder, of, East Tennessee State University.
7. Bob O'Connor, 2b, Rider College.
8. Randy Ebersberger, ss, Loyola Marymount University.
9. George Spiroff, c, Kent State University.
10. *Kevin Brown, lhp, Overlea HS, Baltimore.
11. Glenn Barling, inf-rhp, California Baptist College.
12. Marty Baier, of, Elk Grove HS, Sacramento, Calif.
13. Mike Brecht, lhp, Central Michigan University.
14. Glenn Jones, of, Morehead State University.
15. Marty Mathiesen, rhp, Cal State Chico.
16. Brian Murtha, lhp, Shippensburg (Pa.) University.
17. *Monico Corral, ss, University of San Francisco.
18. Kernan Ronan, rhp, Northern Arizona University.
19. *Bruce Castoria, 1b, Mississippi State University.
20. **Matt Nokes, c, Patrick Henry HS, San Diego.—(1985-95)**
21. Steve Malin, rhp, Elmhurst (Ill.) College.
22. Darrell Pride, of, Ector HS, Odessa, Texas.
23. Todd Zacher, 3b, University of Arkansas.
24. Steve Wilcox, rhp, Fresno State University.
25. Dean Kornacker, ss, St. Xavier (Ill.) College.
26. Chuck Lusted, rhp, Georgia Southern College.
27. Gary Davenport, 2b, Santa Clara University.

DRAFT DROP *Son of Jim Davenport, major leaguer (1958-70); major league manager (1985)*

28. *David Rhino, ss, Henderson HS, Atlanta.
29. *Tim Haller, 2b, San Mateo (Calif.) HS.

DRAFT DROP *Son of Tom Haller, major leaguer (1961-72)*

30. Mike Spinozzi, 2b, College of St. Francis (Ill.).
31. *Ricky Hester, of, Southeastern (N.C.) CC.
32. *Bill Gordon, 3b, Sylmar (Calif.) HS.
33. Randy Gleason, 3b, Cal State Chico.
34. *Mark Warren, of, American River (Calif.) JC.
35. *Clay Harbin, rhp, Johnson HS, Huntsville, Ala.
36. *Vince DeBono, rhp, Cupertino (Calif.) HS.
37. *Jim Rigby, 2b, McCaskey HS, Lancaster, Pa.
38. Don Pote, of, Juniata (Pa.) College.
39. *Curtis Zucco, lhp, Greensburg-Salem HS, Delmont, Pa.
40. *John Atkinson, lhp, Poly HS, Long Beach, Calif.
41. *Steve Stark, rhp, Chaminade HS, Canoga Park, Calif.
42. *Mark Michna, of, Blinn (Texas) JC.
43. *Terry Lawrence, of, Texas A&M University.
44. Mark Winters, lhp, Quaker Hill, Conn.

**June—Secondary Phase (8)**

1. *Craig Stevenson, ss, Los Angeles Valley JC.—(Low A)
2. ***Dave Leiper, lhp, Fullerton (Calif.) JC.—(1984-96)**
3. *Mike Hogan, rhp, Orange Coast (Calif.) JC.

## SEATTLE MARINERS

**January—Regular Phase (2)**

1. Bret McAfee, ss, Merced (Calif.) JC.—(Low A)
2. *Kelly Simon, rhp, Orange Coast (Calif.) JC.
3. *Jason Felice, of, JC of the Canyons (Calif.).
4. *Gary Parmenter, rhp, Middle Georgia JC.
5. *Dennis Werth, lhp-1b, Tacoma (Wash.) CC.
6. Jeff Eldridge, rhp, Olympic (Wash.) JC.
7. *Chris Mitchell, rhp, Jefferson State (Ala.) JC.
8. *John Hughes, 1b, JC of Southern Idaho.

**January—Secondary Phase (18)**

1. *Thor Edgell, rhp, Fullerton (Calif.) JC.—High A)
2. *Louis Burmester, rhp, Williston Park, N.Y.

**June—Regular Phase (1)**

1. **Mike Moore, rhp, Oral Roberts University.—(1982-95)**

DRAFT DROP *First player from 1981 draft to reach majors (April 11, 1982)*

2. Kevin Dukes, lhp, Arizona State University.–(AA)
2. **Mark Langston, lhp, San Jose State University** (Choice from Rangers as compensation for free agent Bill Stein)**—(1984-89)**
3. **Phil Bradley, of, University of Missouri.—(1983-90)**
4. **Ricky Nelson, of, Arizona State University.—(1983-86)**
4. **Lee Guetterman, lhp, Liberty University** (Choice from Angels as compensation for free agent Juan Beniquez)**—(1984-96)**
5. **Brick Smith, 1b, Wake Forest University.—(1987-88)**
6. *Brian Howard, ss, Rockville (Md.) HS.
7. Eric Parent, rhp, Anderson (Calif.) HS.
8. Vic Martin, 1b-rhp, San Diego State University.
9. *Eric Varoz, 2b, Hillcrest HS, Midvale, Utah.
10. Terry Hayes, lhp, Wichita State University.
11. Ronn Dixon, rhp, University of New Orleans.
12. Don Holland, rhp, Holy Family HS, Denver.
13. Dave Myers, ss, Temple University.
14. Frank Meraz, of, University of Oklahoma.
15. Kal Koenig, lhp, David Lipscomb College.
16. Stan Edmonds, of, University of Southern California.
17. Wayne Kinley, rhp, East Gaston HS, Mount Holly, N.C.
18. *Bob Hallas, rhp, Purdue University.
19. Clay Hill, c-3b, Washington State University.
20. Randy Meier, of, Central Michigan University.
21. ***Charlie O'Brien, c, Wichita State University.—(1985-2000)**
22. Howie Brodsky, of, University of New Orleans.
23. *Dan Griffin, ss, Niceville (Fla.) HS.
24. *Brian Rupe, of, Virginia Tech.
25. Jim Aulenbach, c, University of Massachusetts.

**June—Secondary Phase (25)**

1. Ric Wilson, c, Arizona State University.—(AA)

DRAFT DROP *Scouting director, Angels (2011-15)*

2. *Richie Carter, rhp, Umpqua (Ore.) CC.

## TEXAS RANGERS

**January—Regular Phase (10)**

1. **Greg Tabor, ss, Chabot (Calif.) JC.—(1987)**
2. ***Dave Leiper, lhp, Fullerton (Calif.) JC.—(1984-96)**
3. Barry Bass, of-rhp, Manatee (Fla.) JC.
4. Oscar Mejia, ss, El Camino (Calif.) JC.
5. *Brian Aviles, rhp, Rockland (N.Y.) CC.
6. *Calvin Gray, of, Angelina (Texas) JC.
7. *Craig Tice, lhp, Ocean County (N.J.) JC.
8. *Brian Farley, rhp, St. Petersburg (Fla.) JC.
9. *Paul Edwards, of, Solano (Calif.) CC.
10. *Randy Boyd, lhp, Cochise County (Ariz.) CC.

**January—Secondary Phase (8)**

1. *Ken Lynn, rhp, Spartanburg Methodist (S.C.) JC.—(Low A)
2. *Tony Arias, rhp, Miami-Dade CC North.
3. *Kevin Sliwinski, of, Orange Coast (Calif.) JC.
4. Joseph Hackett, of-1b, Greensboro, N.C.

**June—Regular Phase (9)**

1. **Ron Darling, rhp, Yale University.—(1983-95)**

DRAFT DROP *Brother of Ed Darling, 2nd-round draft pick, January 1981/regular phase, Yankees*

1. **Al Lachowicz, rhp, University of Pittsburgh** (Choice from Astros as compensation for free agent Dave Roberts)**—(1983)**
2. Chuckie Canady, of, North Carolina State University (Choice from Mets as compensation for free agent Rusty Staub).—(AAA)
2. (Choice to Mariners as compensation for free agent Bill Stein)
3. Brendan Hennessy, 3b, Bogota (N.J.) HS.—(Low A)
4. Doug Davis, c, Eastern Michigan University.—(AA)
5. Frank Brosious, rhp, Mansfield (Pa.) University.—(AA)
6. ***Barry Jones, rhp, Centerville (Ind.) HS.—(1986-93)**
7. Marty Leach, rhp, St. Leo (Fla.) College.
8. Mike Schmid, lhp, University of Lowell (Mass.).
9. Larry McLane, lhp, Chapman (Calif.) College.
10. Joe Benes, lhp, University of Nebraska-Omaha.
11. Mitch Zwolensky, rhp, Eastern Michigan University.
12. Tony Triplett, ss, Kansas State University.
13. Lew Surratt, 1b, Lamar University.
14. Chris Serazio, of, University of Southern Colorado.
15. Keith Jones, of, Wichita State University.
16. *Wayne Dale, c, Campbell University.
17. **Kevin Buckley, of, University of Maine.—(1984)**
18. Rod Hodde, 1b, Texas A&M University.
19. Bryan Harwell, 2b, Southeastern Oklahoma State University.
20. Gary Sharp, 3b, Southeastern Oklahoma State University.
21. Ray Warren, lhp, CC of Rhode Island.
22. Randy Thorpe, of, University of Texas-Arlington.
23. Curtis Kouba, lhp, University of Texas-Arlington.
24. **Glen Cook, rhp, Ithaca (N.Y.) College.—(1985)**
25. Scott Perry, 3b, CC of Rhode Island.
26. Jeff Barnes, rhp, University of Charleston (W.Va.).
27. Ken Gordon, ss, Upsala (N.J.) College.
28. *Robert Fannin, c-1b, Ranger (Texas) JC.
29. *Larry Long, of, University of Texas.
30. *Keith Hamilton, rhp, Broken Bow (Okla.) HS.
31. Mike Johnson, 2b, University of Connecticut.
32. *Tim Barker, 2b, Saint John Vianney HS, Aberdeen, N.J.
33. Jim Schult, of, Mercy (N.Y.) College.
34. Jim Jeffries, c-of, American University.

**June—Secondary Phase (17)**

1. *Doug Laufer, rhp, University of Texas.—DNP
2. ***Oddibe McDowell, of, Miami-Dade CC North.—(1985-94)**

DRAFT DROP *First overall draft pick, June 1983/secondary phase, Twins; first-round draft pick (11th overall), Rangers (1984)*

3. Todd Schulte, lhp, Old Monroe, Mo.

## TORONTO BLUE JAYS

**January—Regular Phase (6)**

1. *Ken Galloway, lhp, West Valley (Calif.) JC.—(High A)
2. Richard Fagnani, lhp, Westchester (N.Y.) CC.
3. Fred Mead, 1b-of, Stamford, Conn.
4. *Mark Hoffman, lhp, Chabot (Calif.) JC.
5. *Scott Simmons, lhp, Massasoit (Mass.) CC.
6. *Ed Augustine, lhp, Seminole (Fla.) CC.
7. *Dave Eichhorn, rhp, Watsonville, Calif.

DRAFT DROP *Brother of Mark Eichhorn, major leaguer (1982-96)*

8. Jeff Phillips, rhp, Lake Michigan JC.
9. Steve Stenquist, rhp, Norwalk (Conn.) CC.
10. Martin Pulley, c, Eastern Illinois University.
11. James Wahlig, of-2b, Iowa State University.

**January—Secondary Phase (12)**

1. Joey Pursell, rhp, Tulane University.—(High A)
2. Steve Reish, rhp, Union City, Ind.

**June—Regular Phase (5)**

1. **Matt Williams, rhp, Rice University.—(1983-85)**
1. **John Cerutti, lhp, Amherst (Mass.) College** (Choice from Brewers as compensation for free agent Roy Howell)**—(1985-91)**
2. Bill Pinkham, c, University of San Diego.—(AA)
3. Glenn Gallagher, of-rhp, Clemson University.—(AA)
4. Scott Pleis, c-2b, Wentzville HS, St. Louis.—(Low A)

DRAFT DROP *Son of Bill Pleis, major leaguer (1961-66)*

5. Jim Bishop, 3b, Lynwood (Calif.) HS.—(AA)
6. **Stan Clarke, lhp, University of Toledo.—(1983-90)**
7. ***Jeff Kaiser, lhp, Western Michigan University.—(1985-93)**
8. ***Alan Cockrell, of-c, Parkwood HS, Joplin, Mo.—(1996)**

DRAFT DROP *First-round draft pick (9th overall), Giants (1984)*

9. Mark Poole, c, Oklahoma State University.
10. Scot Elam, rhp, University of Michigan.
11. Tim Rodgers, rhp, Oklahoma State University.
12. Chuck Faucette, of, Willingboro (N.J.) HS.

DRAFT DROP *10th-round draft pick, New York Giants/ National Football League (1987)*

13. Greg Moore, rhp, Texas Christian University.
14. Gary Henderson, rhp, Mountain View, Ark.
15. Gerry Hool, c, University of Michigan.
16. *Jeff Szecinski, 2b, Long Island University.
17. Ed Schneider, lhp, Florida State University.
18. Myron Gilmore, of, St. Edward's (Texas) University.
19. Chris Phillips, rhp, Centenary College.
20. *Tom Willerson, rhp, Springfield (Mass.) College.
21. *Jeff Pries, rhp, Corona del Mar HS, Newport Beach, Calif.

DRAFT DROP *First-round draft pick (22nd overall), Yankees (1984)*

22. *Jack Del Rio, 1b, Hayward (Calif.) HS.

DRAFT DROP *Linebacker, National Football League (1985-95); head coach, Jacksonville Jaguars/ NFL (2004-11); head coach, Oakland Raiders/ NFL (2015)*

23. *Tim Dietz, rhp, Nathan Hale HS, Tulsa, Okla.
24. Terry Raley, ss, St. Mary's (Texas) University.

**June—Secondary Phase (11)**

1. **Mike Sharperson, ss, DeKalb South (Ga.) CC.—(1987-95)**

DRAFT DROP *Died as active player (May 26, 1996)*

2. ***Benny Distefano, 1b, Alvin (Texas) CC.—(1984-92)**
3. *Tim Arnsberg, rhp, Merced (Calif.) JC.

DRAFT DROP *Brother of Brad Arnsberg, 19th-round draft pick, Indians (1981); major leaguer (1986-92)*

4. *David Eichhorn, rhp, Cabrillo (Calif.) JC.

DRAFT DROP *Brother of Mark Eichhorn, major leaguer (1982-96)*

5. *Ken Galloway, lhp, West Valley (Calif.) JC.
6. *Mark Hoffman, lhp, Chabot (Calif.) JC.

# 1982

## AT A GLANCE

### This Date In History
**WINTER DRAFT:** Jan. 12-13
**SUMMER DRAFT:** June 7-9

### Best Draft
**NEW YORK METS.** The Mets drafted a record 17 future major leaguers, including **DWIGHT GOODEN** with the fifth pick in the June regular phase. They didn't sign seven of the 17, including Florida prep outfielder **RAFAEL PALMEIRO** (8).

### Worst Draft
**SAN FRANCISCO GIANTS.** The Giants identified the right players; they just didn't sign them. Eight of their top 10 selections in the June regular phase went unsigned—including Bay Area sluggers, **BARRY BONDS** (2) and **PETE INCAVIGLIA** (10). Bonds didn't sign over a difference of just $5,000 and went to Arizona State; Incaviglia went to Oklahoma State and set NCAA single-season (48) and career (100) marks for homers.

### First-Round Bust
**MARK SNYDER, RHP, INDIANS.** No first-round pitcher in draft history accomplished so little as Snyder, who failed to win a single game in four seasons in the minors. Elbow and shoulder injuries limited him to just 35 innings, none above low Class A.

### Second To None
**DAVID WELLS, LHP, BLUE JAYS.** Over a 21-year major league career, Wells was traded five times, released twice and granted free agency five times. Through it all, he won 239 games—45 more than any other pitcher drafted in 1982.

### Late-Round Find
**BRET SABERHAGEN, RHP, ROYALS (19TH ROUND).** Had Saberhagen, who missed most of his senior high school season because of a sore arm, pitched his no-hitter in the Los Angeles City championship at Dodger Stadium before the draft instead of after it, he would never

# Teams find big talent, but struggle to sign it

The 1985 draft is generally recognized for producing the single greatest talent haul in the event's history. The star power included the likes of Barry Bonds, Barry Larkin, Randy Johnson, Bo Jackson, Will Clark and Rafael Palmeiro.

The fruits of that draft were sown three years earlier, however, as all those players were products of a 1982 process that might have earned its own place as the most talent-filled draft of all—had those players signed out of high school. Bonds, Larkin and Jackson were all unsigned second-rounders; Johnson and Clark were fourth-rounders, Palmeiro an eighth-rounder.

B.J. Surhoff, the top pick in 1985, was an unsigned fifth-rounder in 1982; No. 3 overall pick Bobby Witt, a seventh-rounder. Five other 1985 first-round selections—Joe Magrane (third round), Mike Campbell (fifth), Chris Gwynn (fifth), Pete Incaviglia (10th) and Walt Weiss (10th)—were also premium unsigned picks out of high school.

In all, 11 players drafted in the 10 top rounds in 1982 became first-rounders three years later. Indeed, no draft in history was so changed by players who didn't sign.

In the end, the cumulative first-round WAR (Wins Above Replacement) value of 495.7 of the 1985 crop is easily better than the first round of any draft. But setting aside whether a player signed, the WAR of the players picked in the first five rounds in 1982 (845.3) is actually higher than 1985 (749.0). With Bonds, Larkin and Jackson as linchpins, the second round in 1982 is also the strongest on record, as is the fourth.

Among drafted players who did sign in 1982, Kansas City Royals righthander Bret Saberhagen, a lowly 19th-rounder, had the highest WAR (59.2). But his value doesn't even hold up among all amateurs signed that year as Puerto Rican third baseman Edgar Martinez, who signed with the Seattle Mariners for $4,000, had a career WAR of 68.3.

Overall, though, the 1982 draft crop ranked as one of the strongest ever. A total of 202 players who were drafted that year reached the majors, a record number to that point. The New York Mets alone contributed a record 17 players. They drafted 29 players in the June regular phase, with 14 reaching the majors—at 48.3 percent, the highest success rate of any draft in history.

Their first-round pick, righthander Dwight Gooden, could have made their draft remarkable on his own, as one of the elite talents ever produced in the draft. He was the National League's rookie of the year at age 19, Cy Young Award winner at 20 and the unquestioned ace of the Mets in 1986 when they captured the World Series.

Third-rounder Roger McDowell also played a key role in 1986, going 14-9 with a club-best 22 saves. Had they signed Palmeiro, their eighth-rounder, the Mets' '82 draft might have

ASSOCIATED PRESS

The Cubs found a longtime major league shortstop with the No. 1 pick in Shawon Dunston, but the 1982 draft became better known for all the high school talent that passed through unsigned

been hailed as the greatest individual draft ever.

In contrast to the record 17 college players who were taken in the first round in 1981, the 1982 draft saw a swing back to high school picks. Still, 11 college players went in the first round, the second-highest total in the draft's 18 years.

Every high school player drafted in the first round signed, but no draft in history produced so many premium high school players who went unsigned. The New York Yankees not only failed to sign Surhoff, but were also left empty-handed in their pursuit of Jackson. Like Surhoff, Jackson later became a No. 1 pick—in the 1986 NFL draft.

Bonds, who became the game's greatest single-season and career home run hitter, didn't sign with the San Francisco Giants, the team that had signed his father 18 years earlier. They were at odds over a difference of $5,000.

"Their final offer was $70,000," said Bonds, an outfielder at Serra High in San Mateo, Calif. "I only wanted $75,000. If they'd given me $75,000, I'd have been gone. They kept saying, 'Your dad only signed for so much ($8,000, in 1964).' Hey, this is 1982. I knew of other guys who were drafted lower by other organizations who were getting more."

Arizona State coach Jim Brock was delighted to land a player of Bonds' magnitude, especially after he slugged a school-record 11 homers as a freshman and was clocked in the 100-yard dash in 9.5 seconds.

"He's an exceptional talent," Brock said. "He's going to come in and start for us as a freshman,

## 1982: THE FIRST ROUNDERS

| CLUB: PLAYER, POS., SCHOOL | HOMETOWN | B-T | HT. | WT. | AGE | BONUS | FIRST YEAR | LAST YEAR | PEAK LEVEL (YEARS) |
|---|---|---|---|---|---|---|---|---|---|
| **JUNE—REGULAR PHASE** | | | | | | | | | |
| 1. Cubs: Shawon Dunston, ss, Thomas Jefferson HS | Brooklyn, N.Y. | R-R | 6-1 | 175 | 19 | $135,000 | 1982 | 2002 | Majors (18) |
| Strong-armed SS with 3.7-second speed to 1B hit .790 with 10 HRs, was 37-of-37 in steals as prep SR; played 18 years in majors, had 150 homers, 212 steals. | | | | | | | | | |
| 2. Blue Jays: Augie Schmidt, ss, New Orleans | Kenosha, Wis. | R-R | 6-2 | 185 | 20 | $92,500 | 1982 | 1986 | Class AAA (2) |
| Golden Spikes Award winner hit .372-14-56; hit wall in Triple-A at pro level, never reached majors; succeeded dad as longtime coach at Carthage (Wis.) College. | | | | | | | | | |
| 3. Padres: Jimmy Jones, rhp, Thomas Jefferson HS | Dallas | R-R | 6-1 | 180 | 18 | $102,500 | 1982 | 1993 | Majors (8) |
| Went 55-11 with 27 shutouts in HS, spun one-hit shutout for Padres in MLB debut in 1986, but lacked consistency/confidence, went just 43-39, 4.46 in majors. | | | | | | | | | |
| 4. Twins: Bryan Oelkers, lhp, Wichita State | St. Louis | L-L | 6-2 | 190 | 21 | $69,500 | 1982 | 1989 | Majors (2) |
| Had breakout 18-2, 2.07 season with national-best 166 Ks for CWS runner-up, was first '82 pick to reach majors, but career (3-8, 6.01) fell far short of expectations. | | | | | | | | | |
| 5. Mets: Dwight Gooden, rhp, Hillsborough HS | Tampa | R-R | 6-3 | 183 | 17 | $85,000 | 1982 | 2000 | Majors (16) |
| Emerged as prep senior with dynamic stuff/command, had unprecedented success in first two years in majors (41-14, 2.00, 544 SO/495 IP), before career unraveled. | | | | | | | | | |
| 6. Mariners: Spike Owen, ss, Texas | Cleburne, Texas | B-R | 5-9 | 160 | 21 | $100,000 | 1982 | 1996 | Majors (13) |
| Slick-fielding SS hit .336-4-32 with 39 SBs as JR, set NCAA record with 95 walks as SO; saw action for five clubs in majors, hit .246-46-439 with 96 SBs in 13 years. | | | | | | | | | |
| 7. Pirates: Sam Khalifa, ss, Sahuaro HS | Tucson, Ariz. | R-R | 5-11 | 170 | 18 | $100,000 | 1982 | 1989 | Majors (3) |
| Only Arab-American to play in majors; quickness/range were strengths; hit .237-2-37 for Pirates, quit game after father was murdered by Islamic extremists. | | | | | | | | | |
| 8. Angels: Bob Kipper, lhp, Central Catholic HS | Aurora, Ill. | R-L | 6-2 | 175 | 17 | $92,500 | 1982 | 1994 | Majors (8) |
| First of four Chicago-area players in top 28 picks; mid-90s lefty passed up offer from Nebraska, pitched only two games for Angels, went 27-37, 4.34 overall. | | | | | | | | | |
| 9. Braves: Duane Ward, rhp, Farmington HS | Farmington, N.M. | R-R | 6-4 | 185 | 18 | $85,000 | 1982 | 1996 | Majors (9) |
| Diamond in rough when signed by Braves; threw hard but didn't refine command until dealt to Toronto, became dominant reliever (45 SV in 1993) before injuries. | | | | | | | | | |
| 10. Royals: John Morris, of, Seton Hall | Bellmore, N.Y. | L-L | 6-1 | 180 | 21 | $95,000 | 1982 | 1993 | Majors (7) |
| Cape Cod League MVP in '81 hit .431-19-80 with 36 SBs for Seton Hall as JR; lacked outstanding tools, found going tougher in high minors, hit .238-8-63 in majors. | | | | | | | | | |
| 11. Giants: Steve Stanicek, 1b, Nebraska | Park Forest, Ill. | R-R | 6-3 | 185 | 20 | $90,000 | 1982 | 1990 | Majors (2) |
| Landed in first round after breakout '82 season (.448-20-70); hit in minors (293-108-519), debuted in majors 15 days after brother Pete, but got just 16 ABs. | | | | | | | | | |
| 12. Indians: Mark Snyder, rhp, Bearden HS | Knoxville, Tenn. | R-R | 6-5 | 210 | 18 | $85,000 | 1982 | 1985 | Class A (3) |
| Only first-rounder in draft history who didn't win game in pro ball; went 0-5, 7.20 in 35 innings over four seasons, career ravaged by elbow/shoulder woes. | | | | | | | | | |
| 13. Phillies: John Russell, c/of, Oklahoma | Norman, Okla. | R-R | 6-0 | 195 | 21 | $75,000 | 1982 | 1994 | Majors (10) |
| Held OU records for homers in season (20), career (48) at time of selection, but struggled to hit (.225-34-129) and find position in backup role in 10 years in majors. | | | | | | | | | |
| 14. White Sox: Ron Karkovice, c, Boone HS | Orlando, Fla. | R-R | 6-1 | 205 | 18 | $75,000 | 1982 | 1997 | Majors (12) |
| Teamed with fellow big leaguer Joe Oliver behind plate on HS team; played with White Sox entire career in majors, hit 96 HRs, threw out runners at 41 percent clip. | | | | | | | | | |
| 15. Astros: Steve Swain, of, Grossmont HS | El Cajon, Calif. | R-R | 6-2 | 180 | 18 | $65,000 | 1982 | 1985 | Class A (2) |
| Never escaped A-ball in four seasons in Astros system, but collarbone injury limited him to 143 games, hit .210-4-38; son Brett became NFL wide receiver. | | | | | | | | | |
| 16. Red Sox: Sam Horn, 1b, Morse HS | San Diego | L-L | 6-5 | 215 | 18 | $82,500 | 1982 | 1995 | Majors (8) |
| Willie McCovey clone with huge frame/raw power; hit 187 HRs in minors, 62 in majors, but had big swing, vulnerable to lefthanded pitching; best suited for DH role. | | | | | | | | | |
| 17. Cubs: Tony Woods, ss, Whittier (Calif.) College | Oakland, Calif. | R-R | 6-2 | 185 | 20 | $60,000 | 1982 | 1988 | Class AAA (2) |
| Showed early promise after switch to 3B, but never bounced back after breaking wrist in 1984; didn't hit for power in seven seasons (.254-48-295), erratic in field. | | | | | | | | | |
| 18. Red Sox: Rob Parkins, rhp, Cerritos HS | Cerritos, Calif. | R-R | 6-2 | 185 | 18 | $65,000 | 1983 | 1994 | Class AAA (1) |
| Cinch top-five pick before hurting arm just before draft, missed first pro season after surgery; struggled to get untracked, quit game for five years before returning. | | | | | | | | | |
| 19. Dodgers: Franklin Stubbs, 1b, Virginia Tech | Hamlet, N.C. | L-L | 6-2 | 200 | 21 | $75,000 | 1982 | 1995 | Majors (10) |
| Junior season (.310-17-64, 28 SB) didn't measure up to sophomore year (.417-29-83, 34 SB), but still picked in top round; hit .232-104-348 with four teams. | | | | | | | | | |
| 20. Tigers: Rich Monteleone, rhp, Tampa Catholic HS | Tampa | R-R | 6-2 | 220 | 19 | $73,000 | 1982 | 1996 | Majors (10) |
| Better known than Gooden in Tampa prep ranks after 39-4, 0.33 career mark; went 24-17, 3.87 in majors, holds record for games pitched (210) without start or save. | | | | | | | | | |
| 21. Cardinals: Todd Worrell, rhp, Biola (Calif.) College | Arcadia, Calif. | R-R | 6-5 | 200 | 22 | $66,000 | 1982 | 1997 | Majors (11) |
| Late bloomer didn't take pitching seriously in college until 22, didn't achieve success in pros until he became closer; won 50 games, saved 258 for Cardinals/Dodgers. | | | | | | | | | |
| 22. Reds: Scott Jones, lhp, Hinsdale South HS | Hinsdale, Ill. | R-L | 5-11 | 185 | 18 | $100,000 | 1982 | 1984 | Class A (2) |
| Led team to state title but never showed same velocity in pro ball; plagued by elbow problems first, then shoulder issues, released after going 10-9, 5.33. | | | | | | | | | |
| 23. Reds: Billy Hawley, rhp, Brookland-Cayce HS | West Columbia, S.C. | L-R | 6-2 | 190 | 18 | $45,000 | 1982 | 1987 | Class AA (2) |
| Lacked overpowering stuff, lasted six seasons in Reds system with plus control; went 42-33, 3.63 overall, but never capitalized on 18-5, 1.87 season in Class A in '86. | | | | | | | | | |
| 24. Orioles: Joe Kucharski, rhp, South Carolina | Clinton, Md. | R-R | 6-3 | 225 | 21 | $67,500 | 1982 | 1987 | Class AAA (4) |
| Clocked at 92-93 mph while going 11-3, 2.97 in junior season, but never flashed same velo with Orioles; went 47-62, 4.60 overall, last four seasons in Triple-A. | | | | | | | | | |
| 25. Brewers: Dale Sveum, ss, Pinole Valley HS | Pinole, Calif. | B-R | 6-2 | 185 | 18 | $107,500 | 1982 | 1999 | Majors (12) |
| Star athlete in HS, nearly quit Brewers after half season in Rookie ball to pursue QB opportunity at Arizona State; went on to long career in majors as player, coach. | | | | | | | | | |
| 26. Red Sox: Jeff Ledbetter, 1b/of, Florida State | Clearwater, Fla. | L-L | 6-3 | 200 | 22 | $55,000 | 1982 | 1986 | Class AA (3) |
| Shattered NCAA season (42) and career (97) HR records in final year at FSU, but never lived up to hype in pros; career peaked in Double-A, hit just .246-45-195. | | | | | | | | | |
| **JANUARY—REGULAR PHASE** | | | | | | | | | |
| 1. Blue Jays: Kash Beauchamp, of, Bacone (Okla.) JC | Grove, Okla. | R-R | 6-2 | 160 | 18 | $27,500 | 1982 | 1995 | Class AAA (6) |
| Dad spent 50 years as player/coach, was Jays' Triple-A manager when son drafted; hit .282-74-414 in 12 years in minors, had long coaching career. | | | | | | | | | |
| **JANUARY—SECONDARY PHASE** | | | | | | | | | |
| 1. Royals: Danny Jackson, lhp, Trinidad State (Colo.) JC | Aurora, Colo. | R-L | 6-0 | 175 | 20 | $55,000 | 1982 | 1997 | Majors (15) |
| Left Oklahoma after FR year, had immediate success in pro ball, going 17-3, 2.49 in 1982; led Royals to World Series title three years later, won 112 games in majors. | | | | | | | | | |
| **JUNE—SECONDARY PHASE** | | | | | | | | | |
| 1. Padres: Kevin Towers, rhp, Brigham Young | Oceanside, Calif. | R-R | 6-1 | 185 | 20 | $20,000 | 1982 | 1989 | Class AAA (1) |
| Went 29-40 in minors before arm injury ended career; within four years was Padres scouting director, a year later became GM; also served in Arizona. | | | | | | | | | |

## AT A GLANCE

have lasted until the 19th round. He considered a USC scholarship before signing for $20,000 and became the first high school player in the class to reach the big leagues in 1984, beating Gooden by three days. A year later, Saberhagen, 21, won the American League Cy Young; Gooden, 20, was the NL recipient.

### Never Too Late

**KENNY ROGERS, LHP, ROYALS (39TH ROUND).** Three Florida prep products, Rogers, outfielder **DAVE MARTINEZ** (Rangers, 40th round) and righthander **MIKE YORK** (Yankees, 40th round), were the latest 1982 draft picks to reach the majors, but Rogers' tale was the most compelling. He didn't play high school baseball until his senior year, after being spotted the previous summer by Rangers scout Joe Marchese in a rec league game, as a lefthanded-throwing shortstop. Marchese noted Rogers' easy arm action, and recommended that he be drafted as a pitcher; 17 years later Rogers had 167 big league victories.

### Overlooked

**JOE BOEVER, RHP, CARDINALS.** Boever was passed over despite going 14-8 for Nevada-Las Vegas and leading the NCAA in innings (168) and complete games (15). He signed as a free agent on June 25 (no bonus) and worked in 516 big league games over 12 seasons, going 34-45, 3.93 with 49 saves.

### International Gem

**EDGAR MARTINEZ, 3B, MARINERS.** Puerto Rican righthander **EDWIN CORREA** created all the buzz by signing with the White Sox for an international record $50,000 bonus; four months later, the New York-born, Puerto Rican-bred Martinez signed for $4,000. Over 18 seasons with the Mariners, Martinez

CONTINUED ON PAGE 260

## AT A GLANCE

CONTINUED FROM PAGE 259

upstaged every other player signed in 1982 by hitting .312-309-1,261 and leading the AL in batting twice.

### Minor League Take

**DWIGHT GOODEN, RHP, METS.** At 18, Gooden dominated the Class A Carolina League by going 19-4, 2.50 with 300 strikeouts in 191 innings, while allowing just 121 hits. He closed out the 1983 season by pitching the Mets' Tidewater club to a Triple-A World Series title.

### One Who Got Away

**BARRY BONDS, OF, GIANTS (2ND ROUND).** The first round of the 1985 draft was the most potent in history, thanks to Bonds, **WILL CLARK, BARRY LARKIN, RAFAEL PALMEIRO, B.J. SURHOFF** and **BOBBY WITT**—all premium unsigned picks out of high school in 1982. Bonds was the highest unsigned pick.

### He Was Drafted?

**DELL CURRY, RHP, RANGERS (37TH ROUND).** Now known as the father of NBA star Stephen Curry, Dell was a 1986 NBA first-round pick and the Charlotte Hornets' all-time leading scorer. He starred in baseball and basketball in high school and at Virginia Tech, and was a two-time baseball draft pick.

### Did You Know . . .

**DAVID WELLS** pitched a perfect game for the Yankees on May 17, 1998, 42 years after Don Larsen hurled the last perfecto by a Yankees pitcher in the 1956 World Series. Wells and Larsen were both alums of San Diego's Point Loma High.

### They Said It

Florida State slugger **JEFF LEDBETTER**, who hit 42 homers in 1982 on his way to being drafted in the first round by the Red Sox: "I'd compare myself to Reggie Jackson or Mike Schmidt in the way I can carry a team."—*Ledbetter's career fizzled out in Double-A.*

MICHAEL PONZINI

**Underappreciated righthander Bret Saberhagen lasted until the 19th round but had the most productive career of any 1982 draft pick**

and very few players do that. There will be times when he struggles, but he's going to be a very good player by the time he leaves here."

### DUNSTON GOES OFF BOARD FIRST

The 1982 draft represented the first big test for the Philadelphia Connection that new general manager Dallas Green brought to Chicago to restore dignity and order to a sad-sack Cubs franchise, which had the worst record in the strike-shortened 1981 National League season and a depleted farm system.

If the Cubs were to become contenders in the NL East, Green believed it would be built on astute drafting, the formula he used as farm and scouting director in Philadelphia. Green, who managed the Phillies to a World Series victory in 1980, joined the Cubs following the 1981 season and brought a large contingent of Phillies executives and scouts.

With the first overall pick, as well as two additional first-round selections in 1982, the Cubs had an opportunity to catch up in a hurry.

Shortstops Shawon Dunston and Augie Schmidt, and fireballing righthander Jimmy Jones were the clear-cut top three prospects, and the Cubs used their No. 1 selection on Dunston. They planned to move Dunston back to third base, his original position until moving to shortstop as a high school senior in Brooklyn.

"He may not be a bona fide shortstop," Green said, "but we feel he's the best athlete in the crop. He's the best hitter in the nation."

Gordon Goldsberry, the Cubs' director of minor leagues and scouting, concurred: "We feel that Shawon has the most physical potential of any player our scouting staff has seen this year. We had five of our people watch him play at various times."

What they saw was a shortstop with a rocket arm from the hole who hit .790 with 10 home runs, and stole 37 bases in as many attempts. In four years in high school, Dunston hit 25 homers.

### How They Should Have Done It

Based on the career WAR (Wins Above Replacement, as calculated by Baseball-Reference.com) numbers achieved by all the players eligible for the 1982 draft, here's how the first round should have unfolded. Numbers in parentheses indicate the round when the player was actually drafted

| Rank | Player, Pos. | Actual Draft | WAR | Bonus |
|---|---|---|---|---|
| 1. | Bret Saberhagen, rhp | Royals (19) | 59.2 | $20,000 |
| 2. | David Wells, lhp | Blue Jays (2) | 53.6 | $50,000 |
| 3. | Dwight Gooden, rhp | Mets (1) | 53.2 | $85,000 |
| 4. | Kenny Rogers, lhp | Rangers (39) | 51.4 | $1,500 |
| 5. | Kirby Puckett, of | Twins (Jan.-R/1) | 50.8 | $40,000 |
| 6. | Jimmy Key, lhp | Blue Jays (3) | 49.6 | $37,000 |
| 7. | Jose Canseco, 3b | Athletics (15) | 42.2 | $10,000 |
| 8. | Terry Pendleton, 3b | Cardinals (7) | 28.2 | $5,000 |
| 9. | Mike Greenwell, 3b | Red Sox (3) | 25.6 | $15,000 |
| 10. | Chris Bosio, rhp | Brewers (Jan.-S/2) | 24.8 | $9,000 |
| 11. | Zane Smith, lhp | Braves (3) | 21.0 | $30,000 |
| 12. | Tom Browning, lhp | Reds (9) | 20.5 | $3,500 |
|  | Bip Roberts, ss | Pirates (June-S/1) | 20.5 | $20,000 |
| 14. | Alvin Davis, 1b | Mariners (6) | 19.9 | $10,000 |
| 15. | Mark McLemore, ss | Angels (9) | 19.4 | $8,000 |
| 16. | Danny Jackson, lhp | Royals (Jan.-S/1) | 17.3 | $55,000 |
| 17. | Cecil Fielder, 1b | Royals (June-S/4) | 17.1 | $3,000 |
| 18. | Kal Daniels, of | Reds (June-S/1) | 16.8 | $45,000 |
| 19. | Steve Buechele, ss | Rangers (5) | 16.5 | $65,000 |
| 20. | Randy Myers, lhp | Mets (June-S/1) | 15.7 | $15,000 |
| 21. | Ron Karkovice, c | White Sox (1) | 14.7 | $75,000 |
| 22. | Kirk McCaskill, rhp | Angels (4) | 14.6 | $27,000 |
| 23. | Spike Owen, ss | Mariners (1) | 12.4 | $100,000 |
| 24. | Vince Coleman, of | Cardinals (10) | 12.2 | $5,000 |
| 25. | Jim Deshaies, lhp | Yankees (21) | 12.1 | $1,000 |
| 26. | Shawon Dunston, ss | Cubs (1) | 11.5 | $135,000 |

| Top 5 Unsigned Players | | | | Year Signed |
|---|---|---|---|---|
| 1. | Barry Bonds, of | Giants (2) | 162.5 | 1985 |
| 2. | Randy Johnson, lhp | Braves (4) | 102.1 | 1985 |
| 3. | Rafael Palmeiro, of | Mets (8) | 71.8 | 1985 |
| 4. | Barry Larkin, ss | Reds (2) | 70.2 | 1985 |
| 5. | Will Clark, 1b | Royals (4) | 56.2 | 1985 |

Dunston, 19, actually had a chance to make himself eligible for the January draft had he not been one class short of graduating. "The Blue Jays wanted to sign me early," Dunston said. "If I would have taken an extra class, I could've graduated the previous January and been eligible for the draft then, but I didn't want to because I wanted to play another season of high school ball."

Dunston signed with the Cubs for $135,000 and made a promise to be in Chicago by 1986—as a shortstop. "Four years exactly and I'll be there," Dunston predicted. "I should be ready to replace Larry Bowa at shortstop for the Cubs. He's pretty old, isn't he?"

Dunston actually displaced Bowa in 1985, but a .194 average and shoddy play in the field soon sent him packing for Triple-A and more seasoning. By 1986, he stepped in as the regular shortstop, right on schedule, and hit 17 homers that year. He didn't develop into a top-of-the-line, everyday shortstop until 1989, when he led the Cubs to their second NL East championship of the decade.

In 18 seasons in the majors, playing for six teams, Dunston had a .269 average, 150 homers (most by any first-rounder) and 212 stolen bases.

Neither of Chicago's other two first-round picks reached the big leagues. Shortstop Tony Woods, a .423 hitter from tiny Whittier (Calif.) College, peaked in Triple-A, while speedy outfielder Stan Boderick had a promising rookie season, but fizzled thereafter.

Foiled in their efforts to land Dunston with the top pick in January, and later by the Cubs in June, the Toronto Blue Jays settled for Schmidt, the best college shortstop available. He signed for $92,500 after hitting .372 with 14 homers and 73 RBIs as a junior at the University of New Orleans. He was the 1982 recipient of the Golden Spikes Award.

Even with Alfredo Griffin as the shortstop in Toronto, and prospect Tony Fernandez in the pipeline, Schmidt looked forward to a long career with the Jays—even if it meant switching positions.

"We thought a lot of Augie," Blue Jays farm director Bobby Mattick said. "We felt he was the best player available when we picked, and if not at shortstop, he'd make a fine major league second baseman or third baseman."

Between the grind of pro ball and changes the Blue Jays made to his swing and throwing mechanics, which led to shoulder problems, Schmidt never reached the majors. In two stints in Triple-A covering 106 games, he hit just .238 with no home runs.

Jones went third to the San Diego Padres, and signed for $102,500. His credentials may have been the equal of anyone's in the draft, and like Dunston, he enjoyed a storybook career at Thomas Jefferson High—in this case Dallas, not Brooklyn.

Augie Schmidt

Armed with a mid-90s fastball, the 6-foot-1, 185-pound Jones went 15-3, 0.63 and struck out 232 batters in 127 innings his senior year. That pushed his career win total to 55—still a Texas prep standard. Padres officials, though, were none too pleased with the way Jones was handled late in his high school career, when he was left in a playoff game for 16 innings, and threw 251 pitches. In the process, he struck out 28.

"He's the best high school pitcher I've ever seen," director of player development Bob Cluck said, "but his high school coach tried to use Jimmy as a ticket to the state title and almost ruined the kid. Can you believe he threw 251 pitches in a 16-inning game, then came back the next day and pitched in relief and the coach was ready to start him the next day? Thank goodness, Jimmy's team

## Fastest To The Majors

| | Player, Pos. | Drafted (Round) | Debut |
|---|---|---|---|
| 1. | Bryan Oelkers, lhp | Twins (1) | April 9, 1983 |
| 2. | Spike Owen, ss | Mariners (1) | June 25, 1983 |
| 3. | Danny Jackson, lhp | Royals (Jan.-S/1) | Sept. 11, 1983 |
| 4. | *Bret Saberhagen, rhp | Royals (19) | April 4, 1984 |
| 5. | *Dwight Gooden, rhp | Mets (1) | April 7, 1984 |

**LAST PLAYER TO RETIRE:** Kenny Rogers, lhp (Sept. 14, 2008)

**High school selection.*

## DRAFT SPOTLIGHT: KIRBY PUCKETT

ROBERT HANASHIRO

**Only one Twins official saw Kirby Puckett play in person before they took him in the January 1982 draft, and he became an organization icon**

It was the summer of 1981. With the game ground to a halt by an unprecedented 54-day strike, Minnesota Twins assistant farm director Jim Rantz found himself with a little extra time on his hands. In his mind, it was the perfect opportunity to pack up his family and see a game, in this case a Central Illinois Collegiate League encounter involving his son Mike.

"I wasn't on assignment," Rantz recalled, "but I guess when you're at a ball game, you're always working."

Rantz was one of a couple of dozen fans in attendance, and it wasn't long before his attention shifted to a player on the visiting team. "Lo and behold, they had this guy playing for Quincy," Rantz said. "He went 3-for-4, hit a home run, threw someone out at the plate and stole a couple of bases. I didn't know it at the time but he was leading the league in hitting, too."

The player was Kirby Puckett, a virtually unknown rising sophomore at Bradley. "What impressed me the most was the way he carried himself on and off the field," Rantz said. "It was like 90 degrees or more and everyone else was dragging around. He was the first one on the field and the first one off. You could see he enjoyed playing, he was having fun."

Because big league teams were trying to save money during the strike, they had pulled scouts off the road, so Rantz was certain no one else knew about Puckett. He was 5-foot-8 and 165 pounds when he graduated from Chicago's Calumet High two years earlier, and as the youngest of nine siblings had taken a year off school to work, installing carpets in Thunderbirds at a Ford factory, to help support his family. Bradley coach Dewey Kalmer spotted him at a major league tryout and offered him a scholarship. He hit .378 with eight homers, but when his father died unexpectedly, Puckett chose to transfer as a sophomore to Triton Junior College in suburban Chicago to be closer to his family.

That made him eligible for the January 1982 draft, and on Rantz' recommendation—he was the only person in the organization to see Puckett play—the Twins selected Puckett with the third pick. The Twins offered him $6,000, so he decided to stay at Triton for the spring semester. He led the Trojans to the Junior College World Series by hitting .472 with 16 homers and 78 RBIs, along with 28 doubles, eight triples and 42 stolen bases. He was named the national juco player of the year—and he was no longer an unknown.

"Thank God we had the rights to him," Rantz said.

The Twins knew it would be harder than ever to sign him, and with the June draft approaching, they upped their offer to $20,000. Puckett accepted.

That was the beginning of a brilliant career with the Twins, along with a special relationship with an adoring fan base. He had already established his Hall of Fame credentials after 12 seasons, when on March 27, 1996, at age 35, his career suddenly ended when he awoke with blurred vision, later diagnosed as glaucoma. Doctors attempted various treatments, to no avail, and Puckett announced his retirement in a tear-filled ceremony four months later. Puckett died in 2006, a day after suffering a stroke. "If ever there was a player who was identified more with an organization, and who exemplified more what an organization was all about, I don't know who that would be," said Andy MacPhail, the Twins' general manager in their 1987 and '91 championship seasons

To this day, Rantz shakes his head over how the Twins lucked into Puckett. "Call it fate if you want, but otherwise I would not have seen him. The one knock on him was his size; everyone thought he was too small. Again, as Kirby went along, he got a little bigger, but no one knew how big his heart was."

## WORTH NOTING

Edwin Correa

■ The White Sox made the biggest splash on the international stage in 1982 when they signed Puerto Rican righthander **EDWIN CORREA**, 16, for $50,000, the largest bonus ever given a foreign player. Five years later, Correa's younger brother Ramser set a new mark for international players by agreeing to a $125,000 deal with the Brewers. Edwin's career was short-lived because of arm trouble, but as a 20-year-old rookie with the Rangers, after being acquired by that club in a five-player deal with the White Sox a year earlier, won 12 games and struck out 189 in 202 innings.

■ Florida State's **JEFF LEDBETTER**, the third of three first-round picks by the Red Sox, made the 1982 college season his own personal showcase with his record-shattering 42 home runs on the season—16 more than runner-up Chris Cawthon, a teammate. He also set an NCAA record with 273 total bases and would have established a new standard for RBIs, with 124, had Wichita State's Russ Morman (a supplemental first-round pick of the White Sox in 1983) not had the advantage of playing in the College World Series and finished with 130. In addition to his career record 97 homers, Ledbetter established a still-standing career mark of 346 RBIs.

■ Wichita State, playing a college-record 87 games, led its own assault on the NCAA record book, shattering a number of team and individual records. First

lost. It may have saved his career."

Jones was bothered by nagging injuries all the way up the ladder in the Padres system, which delayed his arrival in San Diego. The longer it took him to get there, the more he agonized trying to emerge from the shadow cast by Gooden—a player drafted after Jones who had already achieved big league fame.

Jimmy Jones

"I thought about Dwight a lot, a whole lot," Jones said. "He was 19 and blowing people away, and I'm hurt. You see what he's doing, and I'm home with a cast on watching the All-Star Game. Golly, it got to me."

On Sept. 21, 1986, Jones made his long awaited debut with the Padres in spectacular fashion, beating the Houston Astros on a brilliant one-hit shutout. But in eight seasons with six teams, he went just 43-39, 4.36.

### GOODEN LEADS TAMPA CONTINGENT

If there was a defining feature about the 1982 draft crop, it was the depth of high school pitching.

"No question, the strength of this year's draft is high school pitching," said Mets scouting director Joe McIlvaine. "It's the best group of high school pitchers I've seen in some time. There could be as many as eight to 10 pitchers go in the first round."

In all, nine prep arms were claimed in the first round, but no one stood out quite like Gooden, who was a relative unknown to scouts at the outset of the 1982 season. Not only wasn't he regarded as the best high school pitcher in Tampa, he wasn't even considered among the best on his own team a year earlier.

But with the departure of Vance Lovelace and Al Everett in the 1981 draft, and Floyd Youmans, whose family moved to California, the spotlight shone on Gooden, who was primarily a third baseman/outfielder his first three years in high school.

The most acclaimed arms in Tampa were righthanders Rich Monteleone and Lance McCullers, who went 27-2 between them in leading Tampa Catholic to the state 3-A title. But the Mets bypassed both and went for the lesser-known Gooden, who posted a 7-4, 1.51 record.

His selection caught a number of teams off guard, but Gooden began to emerge as a legitimate talent in the weeks leading up to the draft, and the Mets astutely nabbed him.

"Gooden was a little bit of a projection," McIlvaine said. "We surprised a few people when we picked him fifth. I think, yes, it was somewhat of a gamble at that point. But I felt in my own mind, and I had scouted Florida for eight years, that he was the best pitching prospect I had ever seen in that state.

"I think you have to remember with Dwight is that he was a very, very young high school senior. He was only 16 when he began his senior year. I think much of his physical growth and development took place during his senior year."

Less than a year later, Gooden was the hottest prospect in the game. At Class A Lynchburg, in his first full season, Gooden went 19-4, 2.50 with a Carolina League-record 300 strikeouts in 191 innings. His blazing fastball made him spectacular to watch, but it was his mastery of a slow breaking ball that made him a strikeout pitcher supreme.

"No one person can take credit for Dwight Gooden, except maybe his folks," said Mets minor league director Steve Schryver. "His makeup is nothing short of exceptional, and I don't mean for a young pitcher. I mean for any pitcher. I think he's a pitcher for the millennium."

By 19, Gooden was the talk of the baseball world as he made one of the best debuts in major league history, winning 17 games and striking out 276 in 216 innings. In back-to-back late-season outings, he struck out 16 without walking a batter. A year later, Gooden won 24 games and the N.L. Cy Young Award. Though he would never again repeat the success he enjoyed in his first two seasons because of a string of off-field problems, mostly related to his newfound fame, no pitcher from the draft era—or any era in major league history—ever debuted in such spectacular fashion.

Led by Gooden, the talent level throughout the Florida high school ranks was exceptional in 1982.

The 6-foot-3, 200-pound Monteleone overshadowed Gooden by posting a 14-1, 0.33 record with a 20-138 walk-strikeout ratio, that pushed his career mark to 39-4, 0.33. He also led Hillsborough County hitters with a .535 average and drove in 34 runs. Monteleone was a first-round pick of the Detroit Tigers (20th overall), but it wasn't until 1989 that he finally won his first big league game.

### Top 25 Bonuses

| | Player, Pos. | Drafted (Round) | Order | Bonus |
|---|---|---|---|---|
| **1.** | *** Kenny Williams, of** | **White Sox (3)** | **68** | **$160,000** |
| **2.** | *** Shawon Dunston, ss** | **Cubs (1)** | **1** | **$135,000** |
| **3.** | *** Dale Sveum, ss** | **Brewers (1)** | **25** | **$107,500** |
| **4.** | *** Jimmy Jones, rhp** | **Padres (1)** | **3** | **$102,500** |
| **5.** | **Spike Owen, ss** | **Mariners (1)** | **6** | **$100,000** |
| | *** Sammy Khalifa, ss** | **Pirates (1)** | **7** | **$100,000** |
| | * Scott Jones, rhp | Reds (1) | 22 | $100,000 |
| | * Eddie Allen, of | Royals (3) | 64 | $100,000 |
| **9.** | **John Morris, of** | **Royals (1)** | **10** | **$95,000** |
| 10. | Augie Schmidt, ss | Blue Jays (1) | 2 | $92,500 |
| | *** Bob Kipper, lhp** | **Angels (1)** | **8** | **$92,500** |
| **12.** | **Steve Stanicek, 1b** | **Giants (1)** | **11** | **$90,000** |
| **13.** | *** Dwight Gooden, rhp** | **Mets (1)** | **5** | **$85,000** |
| | *** Duane Ward, rhp** | **Braves (1)** | **9** | **$85,000** |
| | * Mark Snyder, rhp | Indians (1) | 12 | $85,000 |
| **16.** | *** Sam Horn, 1b** | **Red Sox (1)** | **16** | **$82,500** |
| **17.** | **John Russell, c** | **Phillies (1)** | **13** | **$75,000** |
| | *** Ron Karkovice, c** | **White Sox (1)** | **14** | **$75,000** |
| | **Franklin Stubbs, 1b** | **Dodgers (1)** | **19** | **$75,000** |
| **20.** | *** Rich Monteleone, rhp** | **Tigers (1)** | **20** | **$73,000** |
| **21.** | **Bryan Oelkers, lhp** | **Twins (1)** | **4** | **$69,500** |
| **22.** | **Joe Kucharski, rhp** | **Orioles (1)** | **24** | **$67,500** |
| **23.** | **Todd Worrell, rhp** | **Cardinals (1)** | **21** | **$66,000** |
| 24. | * Steve Swain, of | Astros (1) | 15 | $65,000 |
| | * Rob Parkins, rhp | Red Sox (1) | 18 | $65,000 |
| | **Tim Birtsas, lhp** | **Yankees (2)** | **36** | **$65,000** |
| | **Steve Buechele, ss** | **Rangers (5)** | **122** | **$65,000** |
| | * Kevin Murray, of | Brewers (11) | 287 | $65,000 |

*Major leaguers in bold. *High school selection.*

## Largest Bonuses By Round

| | Player, Pos. | Club | Bonus |
|---|---|---|---|
| 1. | * **Shawon Dunston, ss** | **Cubs** | **$135,000** |
| 2. | * **Floyd Youmans, rhp** | **Mets** | **$62,500** |
| 3. | * **Kenny Williams, of** | **White Sox** | **$160,000** |
| 4. | Chris Johnston, 1b/3b | Blue Jays | $50,000 |
| 5. | **Steve Buechele, 3b** | **Rangers** | **$65,000** |
| 6. | * Kevin Stanley, lhp | Royals | $35,000 |
| 7. | * Don Timberlake, rhp | Angels | $22,500 |
| 8. | * **Jeff Sellers, rhp** | **Red Sox** | **$25,000** |
| 9. | Geoff Doggett, of | Cubs | $30,000 |
| 10. | Ronnie Chapman, 2b | Blue Jays | $14,000 |
| Other | * Kevin Murray, of | Brewers (11) | $65,000 |
| Jan/R. | Kash Beauchamp, of | Blue Jays (1) | $27,500 |
| **Jan/S.** | **Danny Jackson, lhp** | **Royals (1)** | **$55,000** |
| **Jun/S.** | **Charlie Kerfeld, rhp** | **Astros (1)** | **$50,000** |

*Major leaguers in bold. *High school selection.*

In 10 seasons, he went 24-17, 3.87.

McCullers (13-1) went in the second round to Philadelphia and also reached the big leagues, where he became a workhorse reliever. His son, Lance Jr., became a prominent high school player in the Tampa area a generation later, and also a second-round pick, in 2012.

Besides Gooden and Monteleone, Boderick (Cubs), a third Tampa product, and catcher Ron Karkovice (White Sox), from Orlando, were first-round picks. Somehow, talents like Palmeiro, third baseman Mike Greenwell (Red Sox, third round) and outfielder Jose Canseco (Athletics, 15th round) slipped through the cracks.

"Florida is usually good for a couple of No. 1 picks every year, but that was an exceptional year," recalled John Hart, who coached in the annual Florida high school all-star series that year, and later managed the Cleveland Indians on an interim basis before becoming a prominent big league executive. "I had a lot of fun with those kids. Every crosschecker and general manager or scouting director was there, because there was so much talent. It was fun to be in the middle of that."

Canseco was as noteworthy, and controversial, as any player to emerge from the Florida prep ranks in 1982. A skinny, obscure outfielder from Miami's Coral Park High, he wasn't selected to the high school all-star game, but that was just fine with Oakland A's scout Camilo Pascual, an 18-year big leaguer who knew all about Canseco and was certain no one else did—and wanted to keep it that way. Canseco and twin brother Ozzie played on the same high school team as Pascual's son.

The A's bided their time and waited until the 15th round, confident Canseco would still be available. "Two reasons, really," said A's scouting director Dick Wiencek. "First, he was a third baseman, and he was too tall and awkward for the position. Second, no one, except Camilo, knew about him.

"I remember Camilo came into our draft meeting, took out all the money he had in his wallet, and said he'd give it all to Canseco if we'd take him. I had not seen him myself, but Camilo was convinced he could play. So we agreed we'd take him about the middle. We drafted 31 players that year, and he was the 15th."

Canseco, Cuban-born like Pascual, didn't even make the varsity at Coral Park High until his senior year, and was the only prep player the A's signed in 1982. He agreed to a bonus of $10,000, and was assigned to Rookie-level Idaho Falls.

"The first day, we hit him 20 ground balls at third, and he didn't pick up one," Wiencek said. "That first month I was very nervous. Here we had invested $15,000 (including incentives) in a 15th-round pick and we were afraid he couldn't play. Eventually, we decided the answer was to try him at a different position. He ran too good and had too good an arm to play first base, so we decided to put him in the outfield."

Canseco's breakthrough came in 1985, when he hit .318 with 25 homers and 80 RBIs at Double-A Huntsville and was the Southern League's MVP despite playing only 58 games. Promoted to Triple-A Tacoma for the second half of the season, Canseco hit 348 with 11 home runs in 60 games and was Baseball America's Minor League Player of the Year. Not even Pascual, his biggest supporter, envisioned Canseco had that kind of potential.

"I thought he had all the tools to be a major league player, but I didn't know that he was going to be that great," Pascual said. "Nobody could prognosticate that good. I thought he might have a chance to hit about 20 homers in the big leagues, but, my goodness, he's become much better than I thought he would."

Jose Canseco

In 1988, Canseco became the first player in baseball history to steal 40 bases and hit 40 home runs in the same season.

Canseco transformed himself from a 165-pound weakling to a 230-pound hulk, though few actually saw him put in a lot of training time. Canseco left the impression that he was doing his training away from other players, and that his physique and development into a power hitter were a result of maturation and dedication to his training regimen.

"Really, I changed physically," Canseco said. "I got taller, I gained more weight. Plus I used a heavier bat. If you've got bat speed, a heavier bat will help you. It's also dedication and hard work. I liked what I saw in myself. It didn't just build strength and muscle, it built confidence."

It later turned out that the bombastic Canseco, by his own admission, used performance-enhancing drugs throughout his career, and that his transformation was largely a result of steroid use. He went on to play 17 seasons in the majors, hitting 462 homers with 1,407 RBIs, but it was a career rocked with controversy, particularly as he repeatedly leveled steroid allegations at other players, and ultimately his accomplishments, like many of the era, left fans with a hollow feeling.

### LEDBETTER BECOMES FLOP AS PRO

The most publicized player with a Florida heritage in 1982 was actually Florida State slugging sensation Jeff Ledbetter, who shattered every col-

### WORTH NOTING

baseman **PHIL STEPHENSON**, who had four outstanding seasons playing for his older brother Gene, the Shockers head coach, stole an NCAA-record 87 bases while hitting .399 with 23 homers and 115 RBIs. He also broke his own record for runs scored, though his total of 123 was topped by teammate **LOREN HIBBS**, who finished with 125. Stephenson, a second-round pick of the A's, also established career marks for runs (420), hits (418), total bases (730), walks (300) and stolen bases (300). The Shockers also were proficient on the mound. They had the three winningest pitchers in college baseball in 1982 in **BRYAN OELKERS** (18-2, 2.07), **DON HEINKEL** (16-5, 2.23) and Erik Sonberg (17-3, 2.22). Oelkers, who also led the nation with 166 strikeouts in 156 innings, was the fourth player selected overall in the draft (Twins) and the first member of the Class of 1982 to reach the big leagues. Sonberg became a first-round pick of the Dodgers in 1983. The soft-tossing Heinkel wasn't picked until the 30th round, despite setting an NCAA record with 51 wins, breaking the mark of 50 set by Texas' Rich Wortham in 1974. For all their multitude of individual accomplishments, the Shockers were shocked in the College World Series, losing to an underwhelming Miami team that had no players drafted in the first 17 rounds, and only three overall. The Hurricanes flourished despite losing their best prospect, outfielder **SCOTT PARSONS**, who dropped out of school after his freshman year at Miami in 1981, and was the second player taken in the January draft (secondary phase).

■ Arizona State, which was upset in NCAA regional play and did not even reach the national tournament, had more players drafted (14) than any college team in a single draft. Every Sun Devils regular was selected, with the exception of outfield-

CONTINUED ON PAGE 264

## WORTH NOTING

CONTINUED FROM PAGE 263

er-turned-quarterback Mike Pagel, who was selected in the NFL draft. Outfielder **KEVIN ROMINE** (Red Sox, second round) was ASU's highest selection, but first baseman **ALVIN DAVIS** (Mariners, sixth round) was the most productive big leaguer.

■ One of the key provisions of the 1981 baseball strike settlement was the reclassification of major league free agents into tiers, based on the relative strengths of the players. For purposes of the draft, the return for a Type A free agent (rated in the top 20 percent of players at his position) was a draft pick as well as an existing minor leaguer. Clubs losing Type B free agents (rated in the 20-30th percentile) were awarded the signing team's first-round pick, plus a bonus selection between the first and second rounds, which became known as "sandwich picks." The Cubs took Florida prep outfielder **STAN BODERICK** and the Reds selected Illinois prep first baseman **ROBERT JONES** with the first two sandwich picks in draft history. Neither player came close to reaching the major leagues.

■ **SAM KHALIFA**, Pittsburgh's first-round pick (seventh overall), had one of the more unusual backgrounds of any player in the draft era. Khalifa's father Rashad was an Egyptian exchange student who came to the U.S. in the early 1960s, when Sam was born. The family returned on occasion to the Middle East, where the young Khalifa was first introduced to baseball, only to return to the U.S. where the elder Khalifa eventually became a professor of Egyptian studies at the University of Arizona. Khalifa, who developed into a top prospect at Tucson's Sahuaro High, became the first Arab-American to play in the majors, when he ascended to the Pirates in 1985, but quit the game five years later when his father, by then a teacher of the Muslim faith, was murdered by Islamic extremists.

lege home run record in sight.

His 42 homers, including 12 in his first 24 at-bats, shattered the NCAA mark of 29, set in 1978 by UCLA's Jim Auten, and tied in 1981 by Virginia Tech's Franklin Stubbs and Mississippi State's Bruce Castoria. Ledbetter's 97 career homers also obliterated the record of 64 set a year earlier by FSU teammate Mike Fuentes. He also hit .389, drove in 124 runs and went 10-1 as a pitcher, making him the first college player with 20 homers and 10 wins in a season.

A fourth-round pick of the Expos in 1981, Ledbetter decided to return to Florida State as a senior because he wanted to play one season with his brother David, a transfer from Chipola (Fla.) Junior College. He also wanted to be a first-round pick, and accomplished that when the Boston Red Sox took him with the last pick in the first round.

Jeff Ledbetter

"I don't care how small a ballpark they have at Florida State, 42 homers is good in Little League," Red Sox owner Haywood Sullivan said.

Ledbetter didn't just let his bat do the talking. He was a colorful quote, too.

"I've got a bad reputation," he said. "People think I'm lackadaisical because I don't run out every ground ball. I'm not the type of player a younger guy should model himself after. I used to drink six beers a night and never get in before 2 a.m." A year later, he insisted, he "had cut down and I haven't had two six-packs since Christmas."

Ledbetter, for all his hype, was a disappointment from day one in professional baseball. Asked to start his career at Class A Winston-Salem, Ledbetter balked initially before agreeing on a $55,000 deal. But he sulked and never got untracked, and only a late-season surge lifted his average to .243 with seven homers. "Disappointment is not strong enough to describe my first season as a pro," Ledbetter said. "I couldn't wait for the season to end to get my act together."

The outspoken Ledbetter also created controversy when he was quoted in the Boston Globe saying, "I'd compare myself to Reggie Jackson or Mike Schmidt in the way I can carry a team," and predicted he'd be in Boston within a year.

When he struggled in 1983 and 1984, and the Red Sox wanted to ship Ledbetter back to Double-A in 1985, he had other ideas and asked for his release. Surprisingly, Boston gave it to him. He signed on with the St. Louis Cardinals, but failed in that organization as well.

"Jeff didn't do what we thought he would do," Red Sox director of player development Ed Kenney said. "We expected more from him. We would have liked for him to stay with it if we thought he could salvage something out of his baseball career. It just did not look like this was going to happen.

"He's a guy who suffered going from the aluminum bat to the wood bat, and his attitude wasn't the greatest. He blamed us. Then he went to the Cardinals, and it was their fault."

The Red Sox saw Ledbetter as part of a windfall draft, with five picks in the first two rounds. "It's almost like Christmas come early," Kenney said.

With the 16th pick overall, the Red Sox went for 6-foot-6, 215-pound slugger Sam Horn, described by scouts as another Willie McCovey. He was rated the best high school bat in the draft.

Horn hit some prodigious home runs in the minor leagues for the Red Sox, but his career was plagued by inconsistency at the plate, poor defense at first base and weight issues. He played in 103 games in Boston while hitting .232, though he played for three other big league clubs.

Horn at least reached the big leagues. Right-hander Rob Parkins, selected two picks later, never came close. He went 14-1 as a junior at Cerritos (Calif.) High and was expected to be among the first four or five players selected in 1982.

"Best-looking delivery I've ever seen on a high school kid," said Joe Stephenson, Boston's California-based scout.

But Parkins encountered arm problems in the weeks leading up to the draft, scaring off a number of teams. The Red Sox, who ranked Parkins as the third-best prospect available, were undaunted. Right after signing, however, Parkins had surgery to remove bone chips in his elbow and was lost for the year. He came back to pitch four seasons in the organization but never advanced above Class A while going 19-26, 4.11, and quit the organization out of frustration in the spring of 1987.

After five years away from the game, Parkins called the Red Sox, asking for a second chance. They gave it to him, but he didn't win a game in 10 appearances in his return to Class A. A year later, he hooked on with the Mariners and earned a brief trial in Triple-A—the only time in a career that spanned 14 years that he pitched above Class A.

### JACKSON HIGHIGHTS FOOTBALL CROP

First, it was Billy Cannon Jr., a wide receiver. Then came John Elway, the quarterback. Next, Bo Jackson, a running back. From 1980-82, the Yankees did their part to assemble the makings of an all-pro backfield. They failed with Cannon, had partial success with Elway, and struck out again with Jackson, the multi-sport Alabama high school star.

### One Team's Draft: New York Mets

| Player, Pos. | Bonus | Player, Pos. | Bonus | Player, Pos. | Bonus |
|---|---|---|---|---|---|
| 1. * **Dwight Gooden, rhp** | $85,000 | 5. * **Gerald Young, ss** | $20,000 | 9. **Joe Redfield, ss** | $10,200 |
| 2. * **Floyd Youmans, rhp** | $62,500 | 6. * Kyle Hartshorn, rhp | $17,000 | 10. * Troy Evers, rhp | Did not sign |
| 3. **Roger McDowell, rhp** | $32,500 | 7. **Greg Olson, c** | $16,000 | Other **Randy Myers (S/1), lhp** | $15,000 |
| 4. **Tracy Jones, 3b** | Did not sign | 8. * **Rafael Palmeiro, of** | Did not sign | | |

*Major leaguers in bold. *High school selection.*

It wasn't for lack of trying, as the Yankees made a reported $250,000 offer to Jackson, whose exploits became the stuff of scouting legend. He set a national prep record with 20 home runs in just 25 games, missing several games because of his participation on the track team. In his only pitching effort of his senior year (he went 9-1 as a junior), Jackson fanned 15 in the county championship game, a day after he won seven of 10 events in the county decathlon, a precursor to his winning the second of two state titles in that event. Over his three-year baseball career, Jackson also stole 90 bases in 91 attempts and twice blasted home runs that were measured in excess of 500 feet.

Despite the best combination of raw speed and power in the 1982 draft—or maybe any draft—Jackson did not sign and pursued a football career at Auburn. But it wouldn't be the last time that baseball would ever hear from Jackson, or the last time that he would turn his back on a lucrative payday in favor of a challenge from a second sport.

Jackson wasn't the only blue-chip football talent that major league teams pursued vigorously in the 1982 draft, and outfielders Kenny Williams and Kevin Murray would have commanded first-round attention had their ties to football not made them high-risk investments. In the end, both players signed baseball contracts—to the long-term satisfaction of one organization, to the short-term regret of the other.

Williams, an exceptional athlete from San Jose, Calif., was a third-round pick of the Chicago White Sox. He committed to playing football at Stanford, but signed with the White Sox for a $165,000 bonus—the highest paid out in 1982—with the understanding that he would be allowed to fulfill his football obligation to Stanford while playing summers in the White Sox system.

Kenny Williams

Williams did play his freshman season at Stanford as a backup wide receiver on an Elway-directed offense. He also returned 25 kickoffs for 568 yards. After that season, however, Williams decided to give up football and devote his full attention to baseball. Though he never fulfilled his exceptional promise as a player (hitting .218 with 27 home runs in six major league seasons, the first three with the White Sox), Williams returned to Chicago once his playing career was over, and enjoyed a long association with the team. He rose from the ranks of a scout, to a special assistant to team owner Jerry Reinsdorf, to the team's general manager and finally to executive vice president, a role that enabled him to oversee the entire organization.

Murray was also an exceptional baseball talent and one of the nation's elite quarterback recruits. He chose not to play baseball his senior year at Texas' North Dallas High while preparing for a football career at Texas A&M and slid to the 11th round of the 1982 draft, where he was picked by the Milwaukee Brewers. He signed for $65,000, but after playing a summer at Rookie-level Pikeville and a fall in instructional league, he enrolled in school at A&M the following January—a day after receiving the final instalment of his bonus from the Brewers.

When Murray reported to spring practice with the Aggies football team in 1983, instead of spring training with Milwaukee, the Brewers obtained a restraining order, claiming that Murray had violated the terms of his contract.

A court battle went against the Brewers. A Texas judge ruled that they could not prevent Murray from playing college football; furthermore, he would be entitled to keep all of his signing bonus.

"I testified that Murray told me he received a 1982 Buick Regal, gasoline credit cards and a Visa card, and $200 a week through A&M alumni and assistant coaches," Brewers scouting coordinator Dan Duquette said. "He cleaned up on everybody all year."

It wouldn't be the last time Murray's name was in the news. His younger brother Calvin was a first-round pick of the Indians in 1989, turned down a bonus offer approaching $300,000 in favor of playing baseball at Texas. He was re-drafted in the first round again in 1992, by the Giants.

Murray's son Kyler was cut from the same mold as his father. A top prospect in the 2015 baseball draft, he opted out because of his commitment to play quarterback at Texas A&M.

Interestingly, the Brewers were almost the victim of a double whammy in the 1982 draft as first-round pick Dale Sveum, another of the nation's top prep quarterbacks, had his own misgivings about a career in professional baseball after signing a $107,500 contract with the Brewers out of a California high school. He also considered reneging on his deal after becoming disenchanted with his performance while playing alongside Murray in his first pro season at Pikeville.

Sveum, an exceptional athlete at Pinole Valley High, passed up a scholarship offer from Arizona State to sign with the Brewers.

"After my rookie year I almost quit and went to Arizona State to play football," Sveum admitted a couple of years into his career. "I thought about it; I almost did it. But finally I got talked out of it."

Sveum went on to a long career in the majors as a player, coach and manager.

## Highest Unsigned Picks

**JUNE/REGULAR PHASE ONLY**

| Player, Pos., Team (Round) | College | Re-Drafted |
|---|---|---|
| Robert Jones, 1b, Reds (1-S) | Southern Illinois | Brewers '85 (27) |
| Barry Bonds, of, Giants (2) | Arizona State | Pirates '85 (1) |
| Scott Kamieniecki, rhp, Tigers (2) | Michigan | Brewers '85 (23) |
| Bo Jackson, of, Yankees (2) | Auburn | Angels '85 (20) |
| Barry Larkin, ss, Reds (2) | Michigan | Reds '85 (1) |
| Dave Otto, lhp, Orioles (2) | Missouri | Athletics '85 (2) |
| Joe Magrane, lhp, Pirates (3) | Arizona | Cardinals '85 (1) |
| Gil Villaneuva, lhp, Giants (3) | Arizona State | Athletics '85 (17) |
| Chad Squires, c, Indians (3) | Hawaii | Never |
| Tracy Jones, 3b, Mets (4) | None | Reds '83 (Jan.-S/1) |

**TOTAL UNSIGNED PICKS:** Top 5 Rounds (23), Top 10 Rounds (57)

## IN FOCUS: DWIGHT GOODEN

The Major League Scouting Bureau ranked Dwight Gooden as the 25th-best prospect in the country for the 1982 draft. So what did the Mets see that other teams apparently didn't see? "I think there were days in high school when he wouldn't throw as hard as he could," Mets scouting director Joe McIlvaine said. "It was because he was playing third base the day before, or the outfield some days. He wasn't just a pitcher."

There had been a reluctance on the part of Hillsborough High coach Billy Reed to use Gooden on the mound, but he had no choice once Floyd Youmans left the team.

"I had a good arm in the outfield," Gooden said, "but coach didn't want to pitch me that much because he wasn't too sure of my curveball. All I had was a fastball. I didn't really have any offspeed pitches until my senior year."

But after an offseason that included instruction from several Cincinnati Reds scouts, Gooden developed a better feel for a curve, and began to emerge as a legitimate pitching prospect.

"I figured that pitchers had a better chance of getting drafted than fielders, so I decided I should be a pitcher," Gooden said. "But I never expected to be picked in the first round. I wasn't even sure I'd get picked at all."

# 1982 Draft List

*Did not sign. Major leaguers in bold, with first and last years noted. Order of selection indicated in parentheses. For the first five rounds of the June Regular Phase and the first round of all other phases, the peak level of each player is noted.*

## ATLANTA BRAVES

**January—Regular Phase (10)**

1. Johnny Hatcher, of, Yavapai (Ariz.) JC.—(AAA)

DRAFT DROP *Brother of Billy Hatcher, major leaguer (1984-95)*

2. *Larry Riddle, rhp, Alvin (Texas) CC.
3. John Van Gennep, rhp, Thornton, Ill.
4. Gregory Mayse, ss-3b, Cecil (Md.) CC.
5. *Greg Laniban, lhp, Brevard (Fla.) CC.
6. James Thompson, of, Riverdale (Ga.) HS.
7. Gary Hall, of, Kings River (Calif.) JC.
8. *David Grams, rhp, Mount San Antonio (Calif.) JC.

**January—Secondary Phase (10)**

1. Al Candelaria, lhp, San Jose (Calif.) CC.—(High A)
2. *Mark Warren, of, American River (Calif.) JC.

**June—Regular Phase (9)**

1. **Duane Ward, rhp, Farmington (N.M.) HS.—(1986-95)**
2. **Joe Johnson, rhp, University of Maine.—(1985-87)**
3. **Zane Smith, lhp, Indiana State University.—(1984-96)**
4. ***Randy Johnson, lhp, Livermore (Calif.) HS.—(1988-2007)**

DRAFT DROP *Attended Southern California; re-drafted by Expos, 1985 (2nd round) • Elected to Baseball Hall of Fame, 2015*

5. ***Mike Campbell, rhp, Newport HS, Seattle.—(1987-96)**

DRAFT DROP *Attended Hawaii; re-drafted by Mariners, 1985 (1st round)*

6. Rich Thompson, of, University of Texas.
7. Mike Knox, ss, The Citadel.
8. Tracy Edwards, c, Mesquite (Texas) HS.
9. *Ron Robicheaux, 1b, Lafayette (La.) HS.
10. Dave Van Horn, 2b, University of Arkansas.

DRAFT DROP *Baseball coach, Nebraska (1998-2002); baseball coach, Arkansas (2003-15)*

11. Dennis Lubert, lhp, University of South Carolina.
12. Tom Willerson, rhp, Springfield (Mass.) College.
13. Urban Meyer, ss, St. John's HS, Ashtabula, Ohio.

DRAFT DROP *Head football coach, Utah (2003-04); head football coach, Florida (2005-10); head football coach, Ohio State (2012-15)*

14. *Doug Hodo, of, Churchill HS, San Antonio, Texas.
15. Jim Rivera, rhp, North Carolina State University.
16. Dave Griffin, 1b, Texas Wesleyan College.
17. Jeff Hentz, rhp, LaSalle University.
18. *Bill Anderson, ss, Point Loma Nazarene (Calif.) College.
19. Tony Neuendorff, c-3b, Southwestern (Texas) University.
20. Dale Chatham, lhp, William Carey (Miss.) College.
21. Kurt Moody, lhp, University of Missouri.
22. Chip Childress, ss-rhp, Lynchburg (Va.) College.
23. Rusty Uresti, c, University of Texas.
24. John Mortillaro, lhp, Jacksonville State University.
25. Tom Reynolds, 3b, Eastern Connecticut State University.
26. Preston Cash, of, Shorter (Ga.) College.
27. Allen Carden, 3b, Northwest Whitfield HS, Rocky Face, Ga.
28. *Steve Cranford, c-3b, DeKalb Central (Ga.) JC.
29. Charlie Morelock, rhp, Fayette County HS, Fayetteville, Ga.
30. David Morris, rhp, West Georgia College.
31. *Mark North, lhp, Huffman HS, Birmingham, Ala.

**June—Secondary Phase (11)**

1. *John Bryant, of, Santa Ana (Calif.) JC.—(AA)
2. Ken Lynn, rhp, Spartanburg Methodist (S.C.) JC.

## BALTIMORE ORIOLES

**January—Regular Phase (23)**

1. Jeff Doerr, 3b, JC of San Mateo (Calif.).—(AA)
2. Dennis Tiefenthaler, ss, Yavapai (Ariz.) JC.
3. *Robert Rase, rhp, Indian River (Fla.) CC.
4. *Romy Cucjen, ss, Southwestern (Calif.) JC.
5. Robert Karjalainen, 1b-of, Florida JC.
6. *Scott Russell, of, JC of Southern Idaho.
7. *Scott Hurst, rhp, Florida JC.
8. Thomas Banner, 3b, University of New Haven.
9. *Rick Hopkins, 2b, Orange Coast (Calif.) JC.

**January—Secondary Phase (5)**

1. John Leonard, rhp, Dawson, Pa.—(Rookie)
2. *Manny Mantrana, ss, Miami-Dade CC North.

DRAFT DROP *Baseball coach, Texas-Pan American (2009-15)*

**June—Regular Phase (24)**

1. Joe Kucharski, rhp, University of South Carolina.—(AAA)
2. ***Dave Otto, lhp, Elk Grove Village (Ill.) HS.—(1987-94)**

DRAFT DROP *Attended Missouri; re-drafted by Athletics, 1985 (2nd round)*

3. **John Habyan, rhp, St. John the Baptist HS, Brentwood, N.Y.—(1985-96)**
4. Manuel Miranda, 2b, Sweetwater HS, Chula Vista, Calif.—(High A)
5. **Ken Gerhart, of, Middle Tennessee State University.—(1986-88)**
6. Edward Mason, rhp, Boone HS, Orlando, Fla.
7. *Rick Lockwood, 3b, Georgia Tech.
8. Roger Wilson, rhp, Poly HS, Long Beach, Calif.
9. **Eric Bell, lhp, Beyer HS, Modesto, Calif.—(1985-93)**
10. ***Walt Weiss, ss, Suffern (N.Y.) HS.—(1987-2000)**

DRAFT DROP *First-round draft pick (10th overall), Athletics (1985); major league manager (2013-15)*

11. **Billy Ripken, rhp-ss, Aberdeen (Md.) HS.—(1987-98)**

DRAFT DROP *Son of Cal Ripken Sr., major league manager (1987-88) • Brother of Cal Ripken Jr., major leaguer (1981-2001)*

12. Randy Wilson, rhp, University of South Florida.
13. Gerry Melillo, c, Eckerd (Fla.) College.
14. Ron Salcedo, 3b, Arizona State University.
15. Mike Vanderburg, of, Cal State Fullerton.
16. Scott Lawrence, ss, Chopticon HS, Hollywood, Md.
17. *Marty Lanoux, 2b, Orange Park (Fla.) HS.
18. Chris Holmes, c, Durant (Okla.) HS.
19. Steve Spalt, ss, Patterson HS, Baltimore.
20. *Eric Hohn, lhp, Butler (Pa.) Area HS.
21. **Jim Traber, 1b, Oklahoma State University.—(1984-89)**
22. Greg Beucher, ss, Connellsville (Pa.) HS.
23. Bill Cowgill, of, North Carolina HS, Goldsboro, Md.
24. Carlos Concepcion, rhp, Charlotte, N.C.
25. *Chris Courtright, of, Highland Regional HS, Blackwood, N.J.
26. *Matthew Merriman, 3b, Roswell (Ga.) HS.
27. Gene Dudek, 2b, SUNY-Buffalo.
28. ***Jeff McKnight, ss, Westark (Ark.) CC.—(1989-94)**

DRAFT DROP *Son of Jim McKnight, major leaguer (1960-62)*

29. Michael Cain, 2b, Jackson State University.

**June—Secondary Phase (25)**

1. ***Brad Arnsberg, rhp, Merced (Calif.) JC.—(1986-92)**
2. ***Troy Afenir, c, Palomar (Calif.) JC.—(1987-92)**

## BOSTON RED SOX

**January—Regular Phase (17)**

1. **Mike Rochford, lhp, Santa Fe (Fla.) CC.—(1988-90)**
2. *Curt Kindred, rhp, Fullerton (Calif.) JC.
3. Scott Skripko, rhp, Middle Georgia JC.
4. **Charlie Mitchell, rhp, Columbia State (Tenn.) CC.—(1984-85)**

DRAFT DROP *Brother of John Mitchell, major leaguer (1986-90)*

5. John Roth, of, Cypress (Calif.) JC.
6. *Mike Gildehaus, rhp, Jefferson (Mo.) JC.
7. *Ted Langdon, rhp, Brevard (Fla.) CC.

DRAFT DROP *First overall draft pick, January 1983/regular phase, Reds*

8. *Irving Weston, c, Kingsborough (N.Y.) CC.
9. *Kevin Smith, rhp, Seminole (Fla.) CC.
10. *Gregory Haynes, 1b-c, Jackson State (Tenn.) CC.

**January—Secondary Phase (13)**

1. *Jose Rodiles, rhp, Seminole (Okla.) JC.—(AA)

**June—Regular Phase (18)**

1. **Sam Horn, 1b, Morse HS, San Diego** (Choice from Rangers as compensation for Type A free agent Frank Tanana)**—(1987-95)**
1. Rob Parkins, rhp, Cerritos (Calif.) HS.—(AAA)
1. Jeff Ledbetter, 1b-of, Florida State University (Choice from Athletics as compensation for Type A free agent Joe Rudi)—(AA)
2. **Kevin Romine, of, Arizona State University** (Choice from Cubs as compensation for Type A free agent Bill Campbell)**—(1985-91)**

DRAFT DROP *Father of Andrew Romine, major leaguer (2010-15) • Father of Austin Romine, major leaguer (2011-14)*

2. Steve Jongewaard, ss, Fountain Valley (Calif.) HS.—(High A)
3. **Mike Greenwell, 3b, North Fort Myers (Fla.) HS.—(1985-96)**
4. Tim Gordon, 3b, University of Maryland.–(High A)
5. Gary Miller-Jones, 2b, University of South Alabama.—(AAA)
6. Sam Nattile, 3b, University of Central Florida.
7. *Jay Grate, rhp-ss, East Noble HS, Avila, Ind.
8. **Jeff Sellers, rhp, Paramount HS, Long Beach, Calif.—(1985-88)**
9. *Fred Carter, of, Millwood HS, Oklahoma City, Okla.

DRAFT DROP *Brother of Joe Carter, major leaguer (1983-98)*

10. Dave Oliva, of, Santa Clara University.
11. *Don O'Toole, rhp, Moore Catholic HS, Staten Island, N.Y.
12. Rob Geels, c, Fresno State University.
13. Mike Mesh, ss, Southern Illinois University.
14. Scott Diez, lhp, Miami-Dade CC South.
15. Tom Bonk, 1b, LaSalle University.
16. Bruster Minor, rhp, Columbus, Miss.
17. *Ed Mondelli, lhp, Neshaminy HS, Hulmeville, Pa.
18. B.J. Richardson, c, Southern Illinois University.
19. *Scott Gay, rhp, Milford (N.H.) HS.

**June—Secondary Phase (20)**

No selection.

BERNARD TRONCALE

Sam Horn was one of three Red Sox first-round picks in June 1982, and the only big leaguer

## CALIFORNIA ANGELS

**January—Regular Phase (7)**

1. Jay Lewis, rhp, Eastern Oklahoma State JC.—(High A)
2. *Brian Phillips, rhp, Diablo Valley (Calif.) JC.
3. *Cedric Wright, of, Laney (Calif.) JC.
4. *Vince Woods, of, Long Beach (Calif.) CC.
5. *John Johnson, rhp, Mount San Antonio (Calif.) JC.
6. *Harold Littlejohn, ss-3b, Ranger (Texas) JC.
7. *Tom Duggan, 3b, Orange Coast (Calif.) JC.
8. John Hudson, rhp, Euless, Texas.
9. *Martin Rodriguez, rhp, San Bernardino Valley (Calif.) JC.
10. (void) *Ty Dabney, 2b, Riverside, Calif.
11. *Ed McCarter, rhp, Umpqua (Ore.) CC.
12. *Chip Dill, rhp, Cerritos (Calif.) JC.
13. *Kent Testerman, c, Los Angeles Valley JC.

**January—Secondary Phase (26)**

1. *Kendall Walling, ss, Santa Ana (Calif.) JC.–(Low A)

**June—Regular Phase (8)**

1. **Bob Kipper, lhp, Central Catholic HS, Aurora, Ill.—(1985-92)**
2. (Choice to Yankees as compensation for Type A free agent Reggie Jackson)
3. **Tony Mack, rhp, Lamar University.—(1985)**

4. **Kirk McCaskill, rhp, University of Vermont.—(1985-96)**
DRAFT DROP *Recipient, 1981 Hobey Baker Award/hockey (1981); fourth-round draft pick, Winnipeg Jets/ National Hockey League (1981)*
5. ***Chris Gwynn, of, Poly HS, Long Beach, Calif.—(1987-96)**
DRAFT DROP *Attended San Diego State; re-drafted by Dodgers, 1985 (1st round) • Brother of Tony Gwynn, major leaguer (1982-2001)*
6. David Brady, c, Southeastern Oklahoma State University.
7. Don Timberlake, rhp, South Granville HS, Butner, N.C.
8. Scott Suehr, rhp, William Carey (Miss.) College.
9. **Mark McLemore, ss, Morse HS, San Diego.—(1986-2004)**
10. Kevin Davis, ss, West Mecklenburg HS, Charlotte, N.C.
11. *Wade Phillips, rhp, West Orange Stark HS, Orange, Texas.
12. Dave Govea, 1b, Cal State Northridge.
13. Scott Glanz, rhp, University of Arkansas.
14. Billy Wiesler, of, Louisiana State University.
15. Kris Kline, ss-3b, Grand Canyon College.
DRAFT DROP *Scouting director, Nationals (2009-15)*
16. Greg Key, of, University of Montevallo (Ala.).
17. Doug McKenzie, rhp, Cal State Northridge.
18. Don Groh, lhp, University of Nevada-Reno.
19. Mike Madril, of, Grand Canyon College.
20. Bob Kilmer, rhp, University of La Verne (Calif.).
21. *Jeff Norwood, lhp, Northwood (Texas) Institute.
22. Mike Rizzo, 2b, St. Xavier (Ill.) College.
DRAFT DROP *Scouting director, Diamondbacks (2000-06); general manager, Nationals (2009-15)*
23. Kirk Knowles, rhp, Northeast Louisiana University.
24. Robert Ritchie, 1b, Triton (Ill.) JC.
25. Alex Christy, of, Indiana University.
26. Dave Heath, c, Auburn University.
27. Bert Adams, c, Hebert HS, Beaumont, Texas.

**June—Secondary Phase (14)**

1. *Mark Bauer, rhp, Merced (Calif.) JC.—(AAA)
2. *Paul Williams, of, Mesa (Ariz.) CC.
3. *Keith Bond, rhp, Rose State (Okla.) JC.
4. *Gerald McDermott, c, Fontana (Calif.) HS.
5. Jeff Salazar, rhp, Los Angeles Valley JC.
6. *Chip Dill, rhp, Cerritos (Calif.) JC.

## CHICAGO CUBS

**January—Regular Phase (2)**

1. ***Troy Afenir, c, Palomar (Calif.) JC.-(1987-92)**
2. ***Alex Madrid, rhp, Yavapai (Ariz.) JC.—(1987-89)**
3. *Mike Mazzocco, of, JC of the Canyons (Calif.).
4. *Michael Lozano, lhp, Sacramento (Calif.) CC.
5. *Frank Spear, lhp, Santa Ana (Calif.) JC.
6. *James Price, rhp, Ranger (Texas) JC.
7. *Charles Martin, rhp, Merced (Calif.) JC.
8. Steve Cordner, of, Gloucester County (N.J.) JC.
9. Jim Allen, 1b-3b, University of Southern California.

**January—Secondary Phase (24)**

1. Jeff Fruge, rhp, Panola (Texas) JC.—(AA)

**June—Regular Phase (1)**

1. **Shawon Dunston, ss, Thomas Jefferson HS, Brooklyn, N.Y.—(1985-2002)**
1. Tony Woods, ss, Whittier (Calif.) College (Choice from Expos as compensation for Type B free agent Tim Blackwell).—(AAA)
1. Stan Boderick, of, Robinson HS, Tampa (Supplemental choice—27th—as compensation for Blackwell).—(Low A)
2. (Choice to Red Sox as compensation for Type A free agent Bill Campbell)
3. Juan Velasquez, c, Miami Lakes HS, Hialeah, Fla.—(Low A)
4. C.J. Sciacca, ss, La Habra HS, Whittier, Calif.—(High A)
5. **Gary Varsho, 2b, University of Wisconsin-Oshkosh.—(1988-95)**
6. *Guy Normand, lhp, Gresham (Ore.) HS.
7. ***Eric Nolte, lhp, Hemet (Calif.) HS.—(1987-91)**

TYLER BOLDEN

**White Sox first-rounder Ron Karkovice spent 12 seasons in the big leagues as a catcher**

8. Frank DeSantis, c, University of Nevada-Las Vegas.
9. Geoff Doggett, of, University of South Alabama.
10. *Ken Harvey, ss, University of Richmond.
11. ***Mike Birkbeck, rhp, University of Akron.—(1986-95)**
12. Rudy Serafini, lhp, Shippensburg (Pa.) University.
13. Stephen Young, lhp, Amador HS, Pioneer, Calif.
14. *Joe Dunlap, ss, Haskell (Okla.) HS.
15. Larry Whelan, of, Kearney State (Neb.) College.
16. Joe Pantaleo, rhp, Lamar University.
17. Derrick Smith, 1b, Grambling State University.
18. Steve Roadcap, c, Francis Marion (S.C.) College.
19. Joe Holecek, c, Truman (Ill.) JC.
20. Steve Burton, of, Southwest State (Minn.) University.
21. *Jim Orsag, 1b, Thornton Fractional South HS, Lansing, Ill.
22. Jim Boudreau, lhp, Arizona State University.
DRAFT DROP *Son of Lou Boudreau, major leaguer (1938-52)*
23. Kevin Atwood, of, Cordova HS, Rancho Cordova, Calif.
24. **Jeff Schwarz, rhp, Fort Pierce West HS, Fort Pierce, Fla.—(1993-94)**
25. Charles Stewart, c, William Paterson (N.J.) College.
26. *Jonathon Baker, c, Valley HS, Sacramento, Calif.

**June—Secondary Phase (21)**

1. *Byron Kemmerling, rhp, Alvin (Texas) CC.—(High A)
2. Damon Farmar, of, West Los Angeles JC.
3. *Tim Englund, rhp, San Jacinto (Texas) JC.

## CHICAGO WHITE SOX

**January—Regular Phase (13)**

1. ***Rodney McCray, of, Santa Monica (Calif.) JC.—(1990-92).**
2. (void) *Stephen Clements, lhp, JC of Marin (Calif.).
3. *Tom Wallace, of, Glendale (Calif.) JC.
4. **John Cangelosi, of, Miami-Dade CC North.—(1985-99)**
5. *Randy Robertson, rhp, Citrus (Calif.) JC.
6. ***Chris Beasley, rhp, Orange Coast (Calif.) JC.—(1991)**
7. *Brian Kubala, rhp, Miami-Dade CC North.
8. *James Eurton, c, Long Beach (Calif.) CC.
9. *Larry Bentz, of, Kellogg (Mich.) CC.
10. *Ron Herring, rhp, Southwestern (Calif.) JC.
11. *Ronald Brown, of, Enterprise State (Ala.) JC.

**January—Secondary Phase (11)**

No selection.

**June—Regular Phase (14)**

1. **Ron Karkovice, c, Boone HS, Orlando, Fla.—(1986-97)**
2. Rolando Pino, 3b-ss, Miami Springs HS, Hialeah, Fla.—(AAA)
3. **Kenny Williams, of, Mount Pleasant HS, San Jose, Calif.—(1986-91)**
DRAFT DROP *General manager, White Sox (2000-12)*
4. *Scott Kannenberg, rhp, Wheat Ridge HS, Lakewood, Colo.—(High A)
DRAFT DROP *Attended San Diego State; re-drafted by Angels, January 1986/regular phase (2nd round)*
5. *Otis Green, lhp-1b, Carol City (Fla.) HS.—(AAA)
DRAFT DROP *Attended Miami-Dade CC North; re-drafted by White Sox, January 1983/secondary phase (1st round)*
6. *Todd Trafton, c, Elk Grove HS, Sacramento, Calif.
7. **Mike Trujillo, rhp, University of Northern Colorado.—(1985-89)**
8. Mike Hunsucker, 1b, DeSoto (Texas) HS.
9. Tom Moritz, of, University of Southern California.
10. *Terry Marshall, lhp, California Baptist College.
11. *Twain Freeman, rhp, Simeon Vocational HS, Chicago.
DRAFT DROP *Brother of Marvin Freeman, major leaguer (1986-96)*
12. Shawn Stacey, rhp, Granite Hills HS, El Cajon, Calif.
13. Mike Toothman, of, Stanford University.
14. Dave McLaughlin, of, Montclair State (N.J.) College.
15. Kim Christensen, 3b, Lamar University.
16. Gary Gonzales, rhp, Kerman (Calif.) HS.
17. Buster Sunde, rhp, Western Michigan University.
18. *Richard Alvarez, rhp, Blackford HS, San Jose, Calif.
19. Mark Ruckebeil, rhp, Zion-Benton HS, Winthrop Harbor, Ill.
20. *Matthew Warren, rhp, Mount Eden HS, Hayward, Calif.
21. Larry McGee, of, Cal State Los Angeles.
22. *Todd Oakes, rhp, University of Nebraska.
23. Bill Sandry, 1b, University of Kentucky.
24. Bobby Taylor, rhp, Texas A&M University.
25. *Dan Hamstra, rhp, University of Illinois.
26. Bryan Koch, c, Muhlenberg HS, Reading, Pa.
27. Garry Keeton, 2b, Middle Tennessee State University.
28. ***Tim Layana, rhp, Loyola HS, Culver City, Calif.—(1990-93)**
29. *Dan Davies, lhp, Bishop Gallagher HS, Mount Clemens, Mich.

**June—Secondary Phase (16)**

1. **Joel McKeon, lhp, Miami-Dade CC North.—(1986-87)**
2. *Wayne Stewart, rhp, San Jacinto (Texas) JC.

## CINCINNATI REDS

**January—Regular Phase (24)**

1. Orsino Hill, of, Los Angeles CC.—(AAA)
DRAFT DROP *Father of Derek Hill, first-round draft pick, Tigers (2014)*
2. Glenn Spagnola, rhp, Fullerton (Calif.) JC.
3. ***Randy Myers, lhp, Clark (Wash.) JC.—(1985-98)**
4. *Tom DiCeglio, ss, Gulf Coast (Fla.) CC.
5. Jay Munson, of, Shoreline (Wash.) CC.
6. Steven Stout, rhp, Arizona Western JC.
7. *Scott Obert, c, JC of Southern Idaho.
8. *Kent Schwartz, of, Cloud County (Kan.) CC.
9. *Louis Burmester, rhp, Nassau (N.Y.) CC.
10. *Glen Kuiper, ss, Indian Hills (Iowa) CC.
DRAFT DROP *Brother of Duane Kuiper, major leaguer (1974-85)*
11. Thomas Walker, of, Maple Woods (Mo.) CC.

**January—Secondary Phase (14)**

1. *Richie Carter, of, Umpqua (Ore.) CC.—(AA)
2. *Ron Johnson, of, University of Oregon.
3. *Ken Sinclair, rhp, Bronx, N.Y.

**June—Regular Phase (23)**

1. Scott Jones, lhp, Hinsdale South HS, Hillsdale, Ill. (Choice from Yankees as compensation for Type B free agent Dave Collins).—(High A)
1. Billy Hawley, rhp, Brookland-Cayce HS, West Columbia, S.C.—(AA)
1. *Robert Jones, 1b, Proviso East HS, Maywood, Ill. (Supplemental choice—28th—as compensation for Collins).—(High A)
DRAFT DROP *Attended Southern Illinois; re-drafted by Brewers, 1985 (27th round)*
2. ***Barry Larkin, ss, Moeller HS, Cincinnati.—(1986-2004)**
DRAFT DROP *Attended Michigan; re-drafted by Reds, 1985 (1st round); elected to Baseball Hall of Fame, 2012*
3. Mike Konderla, rhp, University of Texas.—(AAA)
4. Buddy Pryor, c, Arizona State University.—(AAA)
5. James Posillico, of, Clarke HS, Westbury, N.Y.—(High A)
6. Tony Evans, ss, University of Michigan.
7. ***Bobby Witt, rhp, Canton (Mass.) HS.—(1986-2001)**
DRAFT DROP *First-round draft pick (3rd overall), Rangers (1985)*
8. ***Mickey Brantley, of, Coastal Carolina College.—(1986-89)**
DRAFT DROP *Father of Michael Brantley, major leaguer (2009-15)*
9. **Tom Browning, lhp, Tennessee Wesleyan College.—(1984-95)**
10. Jeff Spisok, ss, Schlarman HS, Danville, Ill.
11. Darryl Wilks, of-1b, Auburn University.
12. ***Rick Luecken, rhp, Texas A&M University.—(1989-90)**
DRAFT DROP *First-round draft pick (18th overall), Giants (1979)*
13. Kevin Steinmetz, 3b, Portland State University.
14. *Robert Farnan, 2b, University of Texas-El Paso.
15. Michael Romano, c, Suffolk (Mass.) University.
16. *Ron Bianco, ss, Seminole (Fla.) HS.
17. Jeff Davis, ss, Newberry (S.C.) College.
18. Vin Rover, ss, Loyola Marymount University.
19. Greg Toler, c, Oak Ridge HS, Orlando, Fla.
20. William Albino, of, Fairfield University.
21. Tim R. Scott, rhp, C.W. Post (N.Y.) University.
22. Curt Culbertson, 2b, University of Texas-Arlington.
23. Scott Radloff, 1b, Valley City State (N.D.) College.
24. *Mark Hammond, rhp, Willibrord Catholic HS, Chicago.
25. *John Koontz, ss-2b, Petersburg (W.Va.) HS.
26. Louie Trujillo, rhp, Kansas State University.
27. *Steve Eager, c, Utah Technical JC.
28. Dave Keller, 1b-of, University of Northern Colorado.
29. Paul Farlow, of, Randleman HS, Sophia, N.C.
30. *Hector Limon, ss, Estacado HS, Lubbock, Texas.
31. *Brad Alvaro, 2b, Caldwell (Idaho) HS.
32. *Mike Mills, rhp, Trevecca Nazarene (Tenn.) College.
33. *Eric Boudreaux, rhp, Strake Jesuit HS, Houston.
34. *Larry Herrel, rhp, Rogers HS, Tulsa, Okla.

**June—Secondary Phase (7)**

1. **Kal Daniels, of, Middle Georgia JC.—(1986-92)**

**2. *Alex Madrid, rhp, Yavapai (Ariz.) JC.—(1987-89)**

## CLEVELAND INDIANS

**January—Regular Phase (11)**

1. *Tracy Echols, of, DeKalb South (Ga.) CC.–(Low A)
2. *James Jefferson, rhp, Palm Beach (Fla.) JC.
3. Rod Carraway, inf-of, University of South Carolina.
4. Craig Kiley, c, SUNY-Farmingdale JC.
5. Kelvin Stovall, of, DeKalb Central (Ga.) JC.
6. *Jeff Gyarmati, rhp, Mercer County (N.J.) CC.
7. Kerry Kohler, c, CC of Morris (N.J.).
8. *Steve White, rhp, Mercer County (N.J.) CC.
9. *Moses Coleman, 1b, Brewton Parker (Ga.) JC.
10. *Paul Williams, of, Mesa (Ariz.) CC.
11. *John Charboneau, of, Cuyahoga West (Ohio) CC.

DRAFT DROP *Brother of Joe Charboneau, major leaguer (1980-82)*

12. *James Hill, lhp, Alabama Christian College.
13. Richard Howroyd, c, St. Albans, W.Va.
14. *John Murray, 3b, DeKalb South (Ga.) CC.

**January—Secondary Phase (17)**

1. *Craig Holthus, of, Fruita Memorial HS, Grand Junction, Colo.—DNP
2. John Thornton, 1b, CC of Baltimore.
3. Robert Gilchrist, rhp, Sandusky, Ohio.

**June—Regular Phase (12)**

1. Mark Snyder, rhp, Bearden HS, Knoxville, Tenn.—(Low A)
2. **Jim Wilson, 1b, Oregon State University.—(1985-89)**
3. *Chad Squires, c, Gahr HS, Artesia, Calif.—DNP

DRAFT DROP *Attended Hawaii; never re-drafted*

4. Andrew Ortiz, lhp, Jersey City State College.—(AA)
5. Pookie Bernstine, of, Lewis-Clark State (Idaho) College.—(AAA)
6. Chris Cawthon, of, Florida State University.
7. ***Carlos Diaz, c, St. Mary of the Assumption HS, Elizabeth, N.J.—(1990)**
8. Wes Pierorazio, lhp, Long Island University.
9. Andre Holmes, of, Monrovia (Calif.) HS.
10. Rick Filippo, lhp, University of Illinois.
11. Jay Keeler, rhp, Florida State University.
12. (void—player previously selected)
13. **Jeff Barkley, rhp, The Citadel.—(1984-85)**
14. Rod Peters, 2b, George Washington University.
15. Charles Mitchell, 2b, West Chester (Pa.) University.
16. Dwight Madison, of, Georgetown University.
17. *Chris Knabenshue, of, Smoky Hill HS, Aurora, Colo.
18. Mark Fagan, rhp, Ithaca (N.C.) College.
19. Dave McCarthy, lhp, Amherst (Mass.) College.
20. *Casey Close, rhp-of, Worthington (Ohio) HS.
21. *Paul Beck, rhp, Murray (Utah) HS.
22. *Doug Little, rhp, North Shore HS, West Palm Beach, Fla.
23. *Steve Kordish, rhp, Princeton University.
24. Wayne Dale, c, Campbell University.
25. ***Bill McGuire, c, Creighton Prep HS, Omaha, Neb.—(1988-89)**

DRAFT DROP *First-round draft pick (27th overall), Mariners (1985)*

26. *Joseph Iafelice, ss, Euclid (Ohio) HS.
27. *Robbie Cobb, 2b, Ohio State University.
28. *Richard Burkett, lhp, Hartville (S.C.) HS.
29. Edward Clark, lhp, Charlottesville (Va.) HS.
30. Mike Connolly, rhp, East Bridgewater (Mass.) HS.
31. *Daniel Neal, lhp, University of Wyoming.

**June—Secondary Phase (2)**

1. *Brian Howard, ss-2b, Rockville, Md.—(Short-season A)
2. Edward Emmons, rhp, South Florida JC.
3. *Dennis Woods, of, Spartanburg Methodist (S.C.) JC.
4. *Ricky Hester, of, Clemson University.
5. Mark Barbagelata, ss, JC of Southern Idaho.

## DETROIT TIGERS

**January—Regular Phase (19)**

1. Thor Edgell, rhp, Fullerton (Calif.) JC.—(High A)
2. *Jody Ryan, rhp, Seminole (Fla.) CC.
3. Steve Caito, rhp, Northwest Mississippi JC.
4. Anthony Long, 2b-of, San Diego Mesa JC.
5. *Scott Whaley, rhp, Gadsden State (Ala.) JC.
6. Gary Whaley, of-1b, San Diego Mesa JC.
7. *Tod Schulz, of, Central Arizona JC.
8. *Cordell Ross, of-ss, Central Arizona JC.

**January—Secondary Phase (25)**

1. ***Dana Williams, ss, Enterprise State (Ala.) JC.—(1989)**

**June—Regular Phase (20)**

1. **Rich Monteleone, rhp, Tampa Catholic HS, Tampa.—(1987-96)**
2. ***Scott Kamieniecki, rhp, St. Mary's HS, Detroit.—(1991-2000)**

DRAFT DROP *Attended Michigan; re-drafted by Brewers, 1985 (23rd round)*

3. **Colin Ward, lhp, UCLA.—(1985)**
4. Marc Washington, of, Northwestern HS, Detroit.—(High A)
5. Benny Ruiz, ss, Midwestern State (Texas) University.—(AAA)
6. **Chris Pittaro, ss, University of North Carolina.—(1985-87)**
7. Kerry Cook, rhp, Bradley University.
8. Jon Furman, rhp, Pepperdine University.
9. **Doug Baker, ss, Arizona State University.—(1984-90)**

DRAFT DROP *Brother of Dave Baker, major leaguer (1982)*

10. Walter Faber, lhp, Western Michigan University.
11. Scott Tabor, rhp, University of Arkansas.
12. ***Steve Ziem, rhp, Cal Poly Pomona.—(1987)**
13. Randy Conte, rhp, University of Illinois.
14. ***Jeff D. Robinson, rhp, Cal State Fullerton.—(1984-92)**

DRAFT DROP *First player from 1982 draft to reach majors (April 7, 1984)*

15. Ronnie Whitmore, rhp, Covington (Va.) HS.
16. *Louis Blanco, c, Eastchester HS, Tuckahoe, N.Y.
17. *Steve Chumas, 3b, Western Michigan University.
18. Craig Mills, ss, Hamilton (Ohio) HS.
19. John Young, c, University of Michigan.
20. *Mark Novak, rhp, Middle Tennessee State University.
21. Kirk Anderson, rhp, Cal State Dominguez Hills.
22. Paul Sokolowski, 1b, San Diego State University.
23. *Bert Martinez, 2b, Arizona State University.
24. Glen Hobbie, rhp, Greenville (Ill.) College.

DRAFT DROP *Son of Glen Hobbie, major leaguer (1957-64)*

25. William Culver, rhp, Loyola Marymount University.
26. James Irwin, of, Eastern Michigan University.
27. *Jeff Jacobson, 2b, University of Michigan.
28. *Doug Starcher, rhp, Miramar (Fla.) HS.
29. Keith Traylor, of, Poly HS, Long Beach, Calif.
30. **Don Heinkel, rhp, Wichita State University.—(1988-89)**
31. **Don Gordon, rhp, University of South Carolina.—(1986-88)**
32. *Robert Nettles, rhp, Orange Coast (Calif.) JC.
33. William Granger, rhp, Alabama Christian College.

**June—Secondary Phase (4)**

1. *Doug Sheets, rhp-c, Saddleback (Calif.) CC.—DNP
2. *Tim McMannon, rhp, JC of Southern Idaho.
3. *Richard Helzer, rhp, JC of Marin (Calif.).

## HOUSTON ASTROS

**January—Regular Phase (16)**

1. *Mark Bauer, rhp, Merced (Calif.) JC.—(AAA)
2. ***Randy Kramer, rhp, San Jose (Calif.) CC.—(1988-92)**
3. *Jeff D. Brown, of-1b, Orange Coast (Calif.) JC.
4. *Andrea Eli, rhp, San Diego CC.
5. *Jeff Schassler, rhp, Highland Falls, N.Y.
6. Sam Moore, rhp, Walters State (Tenn.) CC.
7. Keith Morin, of, Middlesex County (N.J.) JC.
8. *Tim Englund, rhp, San Jacinto (Texas) JC.
9. *Harold Stewart, rhp, San Jacinto (Texas) JC.
10. Orlando Denis, inf, San Jacinto (Texas) JC.

MEL BAILEY

Cecil Fielder, a June secondary pick of the Royals, found major league success with the Tigers

**January—Secondary Phase (22)**

1. *Kevin Sliwinski, of, Orange Coast (Calif.) JC.—(AAA)

**June—Regular Phase (15)**

1. Steve Swain, of, Grossmont HS, El Cajon, Calif.—(Low A)
2. **Louie Meadows, 1b, North Carolina State University.—(1986-90)**
3. **Mark Knudson, rhp, Colorado State University.—(1985-93)**
4. Rick Thompson, ss, Purdue University.–(High A)
5. Mike Stellern, of, University of Missouri-St. Louis.—(AA)
6. **Mark Bailey, 2b, Southwest Missouri State University.—(1984-92)**
7. Bruce Castoria, 1b, Mississippi State University.
8. Jamey Shouppe, lhp, Florida State University.

DRAFT DROP *Baseball coach, Florida A&M (2014-15)*

9. Jimmy Thomas, 2b, Wichita State University.
10. Rich Bombard, rhp, University of Florida.
11. John Miller, 3b, Mission Bay HS, San Diego.
12. Mike Botkin, of, University of Kentucky.
13. Tracy Dophied, of, University of Texas.
14. Jim Sherman, of, University of Delaware.

DRAFT DROP *Baseball coach, Delaware (2001-15)*

15. *Andy Wortham, lhp, Pasadena (Calif.) HS.
16. Ray Perkins, rhp, Virginia Tech.
17. Jeff Jacobson, c-of, University of Houston.
18. Mike Kasprzak, rhp, University of Miami.
19. **Jeff Datz, c, Glassboro State (N.J.) College.—(1989)**
20. Arbrey Lucas, rhp, Grand Canyon College.
21. Richard Strasser, rhp, Florida International University.
22. Jim Ambrose, rhp, Old Dominion University.
23. Neil Lautaret, 3b, Sahuaro HS, Tucson, Ariz.
24. James Donnelly, c, Ocean County (N.J.) CC.
25. B.J. Hinson, 2b, East Tennessee State University.
26. Tom Roarke, c, Jacksonville University.
27. ***Rob Nelson, 1b, South Pasadena (Calif.) HS.—(1986-90)**
28. *Karl Dorrell, of, Helix HS, San Diego.

DRAFT DROP *Wide receiver, National Football League (1987); Head football coach, UCLA (2003-07)*

**June—Secondary Phase (5)**

1. **Charlie Kerfeld, rhp, Yavapai (Ariz.) JC.—(1985-90)**
2. Mike Hogan, rhp, Arizona State University.

## KANSAS CITY ROYALS

**January—Regular Phase (9)**

1. *Bob Ralston, 2b, Chabot (Calif.) JC.—(AAA)
2. *Eric Schmidt, rhp, Antelope Valley (Calif.) JC.
3. *Craig Reid, ss-2b, Panola (Texas) JC.
4. Jack Shuffield, of, Ventura (Calif.) JC.
5. *Scott Groot, ss, Orange Coast (Calif.) JC.
6. *Chris Schulz, c, Golden West (Calif.) JC.
7. Donald Sparling, 1b, Spokane Falls (Wash.) CC.
8. *George Cook, 2b, Los Angeles CC.
9. *Edward Bass, rhp, Chabot (Calif.) JC.
10. *James Mecate, of, Rio Hondo (Calif.) JC.
11. *Mark Berry, 3b, Oxnard (Calif.) JC.
12. Roscoe Palmer, of, Riverhead, N.Y.

**January—Secondary Phase (1)**

1. **Danny Jackson, lhp, Trinidad State (Colo.) JC.—(1983-97)**
2. *Damon Farmar, of West Los Angeles JC.
3. *Richard Smith, rhp, Diablo Valley (Calif.) JC.

**June—Regular Phase (10)**

1. **John Morris, of, Seton Hall University.—(1986-92)**
2. Joe Szekely, c, Texas A&M University.—(AAA)

DRAFT DROP *Son of Joe Szekely, major leaguer (1953)*

3. Ed Allen, of, Verbum Dei HS, Compton, Calif.—(AA)
4. ***Will Clark, 1b, Jesuit HS, New Orleans.—(1986-2000)**

DRAFT DROP *Attended Mississippi State; re-drafted by Giants, 1985 (1st round); first player from 1985 draft to reach majors (April 8, 1986)*

5. *Mike Ollom, rhp, Cascade HS, Everett, Wash.—(AA)

DRAFT DROP *Attended Arizona; re-drafted by Rangers, 1985 (14th round) • Son of Jim Ollom, major leaguer (1966-67)*

6. Kevin Stanley, lhp, Ocean View HS, Huntington Beach, Calif.
7. Doug Gilcrease, ss, Auburn University.
8. Art Martinez, rhp, Grand Canyon College.
9. **Israel Sanchez, lhp, Von Steuben HS, Chicago.—(1988-90)**
10. Jay Phillips, 2b, Virginia Tech.
11. Eric Monson, 3b, Pacific Lutheran University.
12. Mark Pirruccello, c, Cal State Fullerton.
13. Darren Sturdivant, c, Cherry Creek HS, Englewood, Colo.
14. John Serritella, rhp, Weber HS, Melrose Park, Ill.

15. Phillip George, lhp, Plum HS, Pittsburgh.
16. Bill Wilder, rhp, East Carolina University.
17. *Gary Bockhorn, rhp-of, Steeleville (Ill.) HS.
18. Michael Cusey, rhp, Wilson HS, Hacienda Heights, Calif.
**19. Bret Saberhagen, ss, Cleveland HS, Northridge, Calif.—(1984-2001)**
DRAFT DROP *First 1982 high school draft pick to reach majors (April 4, 1984)*
20. Rob Davis, c, Los Altos HS, Hacienda Heights, Calif.
21. Stan Oxner, c, Westark (Ark.) CC.
22. Jeff Neuzil, ss, University of Kansas.
23. Robert DeBord, rhp, University of Richmond.
24. Greg Moseley, rhp, Occidental (Calif.) College.
25. *Darryl Dixon, of, Michigan State University.
**26. *Andy Stankiewicz, ss, St. Paul HS, Cerritos, Calif.—(1992-98)**
DRAFT DROP *Baseball coach, Grand Canyon (2012-2015)*
27. Matt Hall, of, Mesa (Colo.) College.
28. Duane Ware, rhp, University of Washington.
29. Willis Whitehurst, ss, Pottstown (Pa.) HS.
30. *Loren Hoppes, ss, Wapato (Wash.) HS.
31. Dave Rooker, of, University of Arizona.
DRAFT DROP *Son of Jim Rooker, major leaguer (1968-80)*

**June—Secondary Phase (6)**

1. Tom Wallace, of, Glendale (Calif.) JC.—(Low A)
2. *Mark Berry, 3b, Oxnard (Calif.) JC.
3. *Robert Locke, of, Gordon (Ga.) JC.
**4. Cecil Fielder, 1b, La Puente, Calif.—(1985-98)**
DRAFT DROP *Father of Prince Fielder, first-round draft pick, Brewers (2002); major leaguer (2005-15)*

## LOS ANGELES DODGERS

**January—Regular Phase (20)**

1. Michael Kolb, rhp, Sacramento (Calif.) CC.—(Rookie)
2. *William Wilson, lhp, San Jacinto (Texas) JC.
3. *Mike Kolovitz, rhp, Triton (Ill.) JC.
4. *Joey Aragon, ss, Citrus (Calif.) JC.
5. *Jerald Phillips, c, Taft (Calif.) JC.
6. Mike Pinckard, rhp, Cerritos (Calif.) JC.
7. *Bill Geivett, 3b-1b, Sacramento (Calif.) CC.
8. *Riley Epps, c, McLennan (Texas) CC.
9. *Greg Wallace, c, Bee County (Texas) JC.

**January—Secondary Phase (12)**

1. Henry Gatewood, c, Sacramento (Calif.) CC.—(AA)
2. *Derril Lewis, lhp, San Bernardino Valley (Calif.) JC.
3. *Bart Elbin, rhp, Louisburg (N.C.) JC.

**June—Regular Phase (19)**

**1. Franklin Stubbs, 1b, Virginia Tech.—(1984-95)**
2. Richard Flores, ss, Coachella Valley HS, Thermal, Calif.—(High A)
**3. Ken Howell, rhp, Tuskegee (Ala.) Institute.—(1984-90)**
4. *Ron McCormack, rhp, Liberty HS, Renton, Wash.—(High A)
DRAFT DROP *Attended Green River (Wash.) CC; re-drafted by Royals, January 1983/secondary phase (2nd round)*
5. Bill White, 1b, The Citadel.—(AA)
6. Brian Innis, rhp, University of Illinois.
DRAFT DROP *Brother of Jeff Innis, major leaguer (1987-93)*
7. Tim Hill, of-3b, Elk Grove HS, Wilton, Calif.
8. Joe Vavra, ss, University of Wisconsin-Stout.
9. *Richard Jennings, 3b, Fenwick HS, Chicago.
10. Ron Burns, rhp, Eastern Washington University.
11. John Diehl, of, Shippensburg, Pa.
12. *Steve Gehrke, rhp, University of Nebraska.
**13. Reggie Williams, of, Southern University.—(1985-88)**
14. Gary Newsom, 2b, Georgia Tech.
15. Brian Piper, rhp, University of Texas-El Paso.
16. Mark Mangione, ss, University of Kentucky.
17. *Rich Medina, lhp, Lewis-Clark State (Idaho) College.
18. Greg Clark, of, North Carolina Wesleyan College.
19. Tim Meeks, rhp, Santa Rosa (Calif.) JC.
20. Bill Scudder, rhp, San Francisco State University.
21. Edward Williams, 2b-of, Cal State Los Angeles.
22. Gerald Cain, of, Zion-Benton HS, Zion, Ill.
23. Mike Gentle, lhp, University of North Alabama.
24. *Kurt Beamesderfer, c, Troy HS, Yorba Linda, Calif.
25. Joe Wesley, 3b-of, Silver Creek HS, San Jose, Calif.
26. *Stan Van Muyden, rhp, Elk Grove HS, Wilton, Calif.
27. *Gordie Hershiser, rhp, Birmingham Groves, HS, Bloomfield Hills, Mich.
DRAFT DROP *Brother of Orel Hershiser, major leaguer (1983-2000)*
28. Kirk Vucsko, rhp, Lewis (Ill.) University.
**29. Jeff Hamilton, ss-of, Flint Carman HS, Davison, Mich.—(1986-91)**

**June—Secondary Phase (3)**

1. Don Smith, rhp, Arizona State University.—(AAA)
2. *Matt Rowe, rhp, JC of Marin (Calif.).
3. *Jim O'Dell, of-1b, Lewis-Clark State (Idaho) College.

## MILWAUKEE BREWERS

**January—Regular Phase (25)**

1. Derek Tatsuno, lhp, Aiea, Hawaii.—(AAA)
2. Larry Jackson, of, Triton (Ill.) JC.
3. Robert Sullivan, rhp, Moorpark (Calif.) JC.
4. *Sherman Bennett, rhp, Miami-Dade CC South.
5. Mark Delgado, 3b, Alvin (Texas) CC.
6. Brian Finley, of, Contra Costa (Calif.) JC.
7. *Byron Kemmerling, rhp, Alvin (Texas) CC.
8. *Daniel Aruca, of, Miami-Dade CC North.
9. *Rex Perozo, rhp, Miami-Dade CC South.
10. *Joe Grayston, ss, Long Beach (Calif.) CC.
11. *Terry Repp, 2b-3b, St. Louis CC-Meramec.
12. *Tyrone Walker, c, Central Arizona JC.
13. *Brad Goodwin, of, Umpqua (Ore.) CC.
14. *David Williams, ss-2b, Central Arizona JC.
15. *Mark Michel, rhp, Ventura (Calif.) JC.
16. *Tony Blasucci, of-lhp, Broward (Fla.) CC.
17. James Culver, of, Antelope Valley (Calif.) JC.
18. Fred Williams, of, JC of Lake County (Ill.).
19. *Earl Frishman, 3b, Los Angeles Valley JC.
20. *Anthony Brown, rhp, Yakima Valley (Wash.) JC.
21. *Steve Arseneault, ss-2b, Glendale (Calif.) JC.
22. *Joseph Lozano, lhp, Ventura (Calif.) JC.
23. Billy Smith, rhp, Santa Ana (Calif.) JC.
**24. *Tom Pagnozzi, 3b, Central Arizona JC.—(1987-98)**
25. *Mark Stathas, ss, Linn-Benton (Ore.) CC.
26. *Fred Perez, c, Ventura (Calif.) JC.
27. *Michael Russell, rhp, Santa Barbara (Calif.) CC.

**January—Secondary Phase (21)**

1. *Curtis Zucco, lhp, Mount Olive (N.C.) JC.—(Short-season A)
**2. Chris Bosio, rhp, Sacramento (Calif.) CC.—(1986-96)**
3. *Frank Marrero, rhp, Miami-Dade CC North.

**June—Regular Phase (25)**

**1. Dale Sveum, ss, Pinole Valley HS, Pinole, Calif.—(1986-99)**
DRAFT DROP *Major league manager (2008-13)*
2. Bryan Duquette, lhp, University of Hawaii.—(AAA)
3. Dan Scarpetta, lhp, Auburn Senior HS, Rockford, Ill.—(AAA)
4. Alan Cartwright, of, Southeastern Oklahoma State University.—(AAA)
5. Bill Shamblin, rhp, Mojave HS, Riviera, Ariz.—(AA)
**6. Billy Jo Robidoux, 1b, Ware (Mass.) HS.—(1985-90)**
7. *Kevin Sheary, rhp, Roxbury HS, Flanders, N.J.
**8. Jim Paciorek, of, University of Michigan.—(1987)**
DRAFT DROP *Brother of John Paciorek, major leaguer (1963) • Brother of Tom Paciorek, major leaguer (1970-87)*
9. Brian Mignano, rhp, Stanford University.
**10. Jay Aldrich, rhp, Montclair State (N.J.) College.—(1987-90)**
11. Kevin Murray, of, North Dallas HS, Dallas.
DRAFT DROP *Brother of Calvin Murray, first-round draft pick, Indians (1989); first-round draft pick, Giants (1992); major leaguer (1999-2004)*
12. Hank Landers, of, Brown University.
13. *David Bailey, 1b, University of Montevallo (Ala.).
14. Ben Donisi, 3b, Florida International University.
15. *Greg Burlingame, lhp, Kingsway HS, Mullica Hill, N.J.
16. Rob Derksen, rhp, University of Wisconsin.
**17. Chuck Crim, rhp, University of Hawaii.—(1987-94)**
18. Gary Ream, rhp, Eastern Wayne HS, LaGrange, N.C.
19. Barry Koch, rhp, Arizona State University.
20. Joel Weatherford, of, Newberry (S.C.) College.
21. *Michael Parsons, rhp, St. Louis CC-Meramec.
22. Michael Meyer, 2b, Cal State Los Angeles.
23. Matt Sferrazza, of-3b, Cerritos (Calif.) JC.
24. *Stan Floyd, of, University of Houston.
25. *Greg Bartek, rhp, Roxbury HS, Succasunna, N.J.
26. *Paul Togneri, lhp, Nogales HS, La Puente, Calif.
**27. *Mark Ciardi, rhp, University of Maryland.—(1987)**
28. *Kevin Renz, rhp, Paris (Texas) JC.
29. Dave Klipstein, of, Mississippi State University.
30. *Ric Abbott, ss-2b, Santa Ana (Calif.) JC.

**June—Secondary Phase (12)**

1. Tim Utecht, 1b, Lower Columbia (Wash.) JC.—(High A)
2. Jeff Gyarmati, rhp, Mercer County (N.J.) CC.
3. *John Wallace, of, University of Southern California.
4. *Dean Albany, rhp, CC of Baltimore.
5. *Steve Oswald, lhp, Triton (Ill.) JC.
6. *Doug Givler, rhp, Frederick (Md.) CC.

## MINNESOTA TWINS

**January—Regular Phase (3)**

**1. Kirby Puckett, of, Triton (Ill.) JC.—(1984-95)**
DRAFT DROP *Elected to Baseball Hall of Fame, 2001*
2. *Doug Sheets, rhp-c, Saddleback (Calif.) CC.
3. *Steve Moses, of, Cerritos (Calif.) JC.
DRAFT DROP *Brother of John Moses, major leaguer (1982-92)*
4. *Matt Rowe, rhp, JC of Marin (Calif.).
5. *Brad Seehwaer, ss, Umpqua (Ore.) CC.
6. *Robert Locke, of, Gordon (Ga.) JC.
7. *Mark Friedly, rhp, Cerritos (Calif.) JC.
8. *Bob Grandstaff, 3b, Golden West (Calif.) JC.
**9. *Greg Mathews, lhp, Santa Ana (Calif.) JC.—(1986-92)**
10. *Marty Reed, lhp, Hillsborough (Fla.) CC.
11. *Troy Galloway, lhp, Modesto (Calif.) JC.
12. *Jeffrey Rojas, rhp, San Bernardino Valley (Calif.) JC.
13. *Steve Brueggeman, lhp-of, Kings River (Calif.) JC.

**January—Secondary Phase (8)**

1. *Mark Margis, lhp, Culver City, Calif.—DNP
2. *John Bryant, of, Santa Ana (Calif.) JC.
3. Ted Perkins, of, Richmond, Calif.

**June—Regular Phase (4)**

**1. Bryan Oelkers, lhp, Wichita State University.—(1983-86)**
DRAFT DROP *First player from 1982 draft to reach majors (April 19, 1983)*
**2. Allan Anderson, lhp, Lancaster (Ohio) HS.—(1986-91)**
3. Greg Howe, of, Eastern Michigan University.—(AAA)
4. Robert Ferro, ss, Muhlenberg HS, Reading, Pa.—(Low A)
5. Ken Klump, rhp, Southern Illinois University.—(AA)
6. Bob DeCosta, ss, Stanford University.
7. Brian Rupe, of, Virginia Tech.
8. Mike Tryon, c, Catholic University.
9. *Shell Scott, ss, Mount Carmel HS, Poway, Calif.
10. David Butters, c, Sutherland HS, Pittsford, N.Y.
**11. Mark Davidson, of, Clemson University.—(1986-91)**
12. *Scott Sabo, lhp, University of Wisconsin.
13. Erez Borowsky, c, Vanderbilt University.
14. Jeff Szczecinski, 2b, Long Island University.
15. Mike Moreno, ss, Lewis-Clark State (Idaho) College.
**16. *Lenny Webster, c, Lutcher (La.) HS.—(1989-2000)**
17. Kiel Higgins, rhp, University of New Mexico.
**18. Frank Eufemia, rhp, Ramapo (N.J.) College.—(1985)**
**19. Marty Pevey, c, Georgia Southern College.—(1989)**
20. Terrill Parham, lhp, Georgia Southern College.
21. Larry Hatley, of, South Stanley HS, Albemarle, N.C.
22. *Mark Cardaci, of, William Paterson (N.J.) College.
23. Andrew Lesnak, ss, Southeastern Louisiana University.
24. Brian Hobaugh, rhp, University of Iowa.
25. Thomas Cichon, 1b, John F. Kennedy HS, Utica, N.Y.
26. *Andre Crawford, of, Harding HS, Charlotte, N.C.
27. *David Turney, of-inf, Mount San Antonio (Calif.) JC.
28. Ronn Van Krevelen, of, University of Minnesota.
29. Doug Smith, rhp, Liberty University.
30. Alberto Zappala, 2b, Fairfield University.
31. Paul Mancuso, lhp, University of New Orleans.
32. *Eduardo Gonzalez, c, Jackson HS, Miami.
33. *Robert Cramer, lhp, Highland HS, Bakersfield, Calif.

**June—Secondary Phase (18)**

1. Curt Kindred, rhp, Fullerton (Calif.) JC.–(High A)

## MONTREAL EXPOS

**January—Regular Phase (18)**

1. Troy McKay, of-rhp, Des Moines Area (Iowa) CC.—(AA)
2. *Scott Prickett, lhp, Des Moines Area (Iowa) CC.
3. *Blaze Katich, of, Pensacola (Fla.) JC.
4. *Robert Wright, inf, San Joaquin Delta (Calif.) JC.
5. Julius Anderson, 3b, South Georgia JC.
6. Rodney Schnatz, rhp, Batavia, Ohio.
7. (void) *Roy Campbell, of, Columbia State (Tenn.) CC.
8. *Terrill Adams, rhp, Mission (Calif.) JC.
9. *Robert Thompson, of, JC of Southern Idaho.
10. *James Bettis, of, University of Cincinnati.
11. Rick Miller, rhp-1b, Richmond, Ky.
12. *Curran Hubbard, rhp, St. Louis CC-Meramec.
13. Terry Strickland, 3b, Campbell University.
14. *Jeffrey Edwards, 3b, Louisburg (N.C.) JC.

**January—Secondary Phase (6)**

1. *David Alores, rhp, Blinn (Texas) JC.—DNP
2. *Mark Baker, rhp, Palm Beach (Fla.) JC.
3. *David Flattery, rhp, Iowa State University.

**June—Regular Phase (17)**

1. (Choice to Cubs as compensation for Type B free agent Tim Blackwell)
**2. John Dopson, rhp, Delone Catholic HS, Finksburg, Md.—(1985-94)**
3. Tim Thiessen, ss, Fresno State University.—(AA)
4. *Lloyd Martin, lhp, Santa Clara University.—DNP
DRAFT DROP *Returned to Santa Clara; never re-drafted*
**5. Rene Gonzales, ss, Cal State Los Angeles.—(1984-97)**
6. Buck Belue, of, University of Georgia.
7. *Jeff Peterson, lhp, St. Mary's (Calif.) College.
8. *Wayne Able, of, Davidson HS, Mobile, Ala.
9. *Ron Jackson, c, McKinney (Texas) HS.
10. John Glidewell, rhp, Gorham (Ill.) HS.
11. Jim Cecchini, c, University of Southern California.
12. *Paul Quinzer, rhp, Castle HS, Newburgh, Ind.
13. *Darryl Stephens, of, Stanford University.
14. *Tom Thompson, 1b-of, Knoch HS, Renfrew, Pa.
15. Tom Krupa, 1b, Louisiana Tech.
16. Mark Hall, 2b, Bowling Green State University.
17. *Lou Brock Jr., ss, Ladue HS, St. Louis.
DRAFT DROP *Son of Lou Brock, major leaguer (1961-79) • Defensive back, National Football League (1987)*
18. *Tim Rypien, c, Shadle Park HS, Spokane, Wash.
DRAFT DROP *Brother of Mark Rypien, quarterback/ National Football League (1988-2001)*
19. Keith Washington, ss, Los Angeles CC.
20. *Scott Powers, ss, Middle Georgia JC.
**21. *Jeff Parrett, rhp, University of Kentucky.—(1986-96)**
22. Tim Nichting, c, Xavier University.

23. Shawn Mielke, rhp, Valley HS, Las Vegas, Nev.
24. Jim Lumpe, 2b, University of Missouri.
DRAFT DROP *Son of Jerry Lumpe, major leaguer (1956-67)*
25. *Kevin Pour, of-rhp, New Athens (Ill.) HS.
26. Corey Zawadski, of, Southern Illinois University.
27. Daniel Szajko, of, University of Notre Dame.
28. Mike Hocutt, 3b, Iowa State University.
29. Gary Weinberger, of, Cal State Sacramento.
30. Steve Shoemaker, of, Cumberland (Ky.) College.
31. David Duvnjak, c, Ball State University.

**June—Secondary Phase (19)**

1. **Nelson Santovenia, c, University of Miami.—(1987-93)**
2. *Norman Morton, lhp, Miami-Dade CC North.
3. David Flores, rhp, Texas A&M University.
4. Blaze Katich, of, Pensacola (Fla.) JC.
5. Curtis Zucco, lhp, Mount Olive (N.C.) JC.
6. *Jeffrey Edwards, 3b, Louisburg (N.C.) JC.

## NEW YORK METS

**January—Regular Phase (6)**

1. *Tim McMannon, rhp, JC of Southern Idaho.—DNP
2. *Bobby Estrada, rhp, San Jacinto (Texas) JC.
3. ***Kal Daniels, of, Middle Georgia JC.—(1986-92)**
4. *Greg Selecky, 1b, Brookdale (N.J.) CC.
5. Scott Adams, rhp, Alabama Christian College.
6. *Brett Harrison, ss, Bacone (Okla.) JC.
7. Kenneth Bodle, of, Orange Coast (Calif.) JC.
8. *Steven Oswald, lhp, Triton (Ill.) JC.
9. *Tim Utecht, 1b, Lower Columbia (Wash.) JC.
10. Edward Groves, rhp, Romulus (Mich.) HS.
11. *Timothy Lemons, 3b, Gulf Coast (Fla.) CC.
12. Michael Robair, rhp, Chipola (Fla.) JC.
13. Nick Brandt, lhp, Butte (Calif.) JC.
14. *Robert Voydat, ss, DeAnza (Calif.) JC.
15. *Keith Bond, lhp, Rose State (Okla.) JC.
16. David Wyatt, lhp, Alabama Christian College.
17. John Wilson, of, Bamberg, S.C.
DRAFT DROP *Brother of Mookie Wilson, major leaguer (1980-91)*
18. *Andrew Sanclers, of, Allen County (Kan.) CC.
19. Ed Pruitt, lhp, Blum, Texas.

**January—Secondary Phase (18)**

1. Steven Gay, rhp, Green River (Wash.) CC.—(High A)
2. ***Luis Medina, of, Cerritos (Calif.) JC.—(1988-91)**
3. Marvin Parker, c, Florida JC.

**June—Regular Phase (5)**

1. **Dwight Gooden, rhp, Hillsborough HS, Tampa.—(1984-2000)**
2. **Floyd Youmans, rhp, Fontana (Calif.) HS.—(1985-89)**
3. **Roger McDowell, rhp, Bowling Green State University.—(1985-96)**
4. ***Tracy Jones, 3b, Loyola Marymount University.—(1986-91)**
DRAFT DROP *No school; re-drafted by Reds, January 1983/secondary phase (1st round, 1st pick)*
5. **Gerald Young, ss, Santa Ana Valley HS, Santa Ana, Calif.—(1987-94)**
6. Kyle Hartshorn, rhp, Allentown HS, New Egypt, N.J.
7. **Greg Olson, c, University of Minnesota.—(1989-93)**
8. ***Rafael Palmeiro, of, Jackson HS, Miami.—(1986-2005)**
DRAFT DROP *First-round draft pick (23rd overall), Cubs (1985)*
9. **Joe Redfield, ss, UC Santa Barbara.—(1988-91)**
10. *Troy Evers, rhp, West HS, Appleton, Wis.
11. Alan Carmichael, c, Baylor HS, Signal Mountain, Tenn.
12. **Mickey Weston, rhp, Eastern Michigan University.—(1989-93)**
13. *David Jacas, of, Ramapo HS, Spring Valley, N.J.
14. *Scott Tidmore, rhp, Arab (Ala.) HS.
15. **Barry Lyons, c, Delta State (Miss.) University.—(1986-95)**
16. ***Doug Henry, rhp, Tennyson HS, Hayward, Calif.—(1991-2001)**
17. John Boyles, rhp, Gannon (Pa.) University.
18. Carl Hollis, ss, Stillman (Ala.) College.
19. ***Jeff Richardson, rhp, Northwest HS, Wichita, Kan.—(1990)**
20. **Steve Springer, of, University of Utah.—(1990-92)**
21. *Jim Phillips, rhp, University of Kansas.
22. **Wes Gardner, rhp, University of Central Arkansas.—(1984-91)**
23. Eugene Hawkins, c, Norfolk State University.
24. Rick Paul, rhp, St. Louis University.
25. John Metasavage, 3b, Auburn University.
26. *John Grier, of, Rye (N.Y.) HS.
27. *John Morgan, ss, Lee HS, Montgomery, Ala.
28. *Charles Higson, rhp, Columbia HS, Columbia Falls, Mon.
29. *Ricky Kyle, rhp, Northwest HS, Omaha, Neb.

**June—Secondary Phase (9)**

1. **Randy Myers, lhp, Clark (Wash.) JC.—(1985-98)**
2. Stu Foulks, rhp, Jacksonville University.
3. *Jim Benedict, rhp, Los Angeles Valley JC.

## NEW YORK YANKEES

**January—Regular Phase (21)**

1. George Freeman, rhp, Fresno (Calif.) CC.—DNP
2. *Charles Hardwick, lhp, Mount Olive (N.C.) JC.
3. Tony Russell, of, Middle Georgia JC.
4. Earl Nichols, rhp, Allen County (Kan.) CC.
5. *Tony Arias, rhp, Miami-Dade CC South.
6. *Brad Wheeler, lhp, Indian River (Fla.) CC.
7. *Tim Meacham, rhp, Lurleen B. Wallace (Ala.) JC.
8. *Harry Overton, of, Louisburg (N.C.) JC.
9. *George Pierce, of, Lurleen B. Wallace (Ala.) JC.
10. *Lee Boykin, c-of, Quinsigamond (Mass.) CC.
11. *Donald Johnson, rhp, Rock Valley (Ill.) JC.
12. *Joseph Orszulak, rhp, Quinsigamond (Mass.) CC.
13. *Marty Freeman, 2b-of, Indian River (Fla.) CC.
14. *Joe Fletcher, rhp, Illinois Valley CC.
15. *David Lenderman, rhp, Linn-Benton (Ore.) CC.
16. *Marvin White, 3b, JC of Marin (Calif.).
17. *Frank Russo, of, Indian River (Fla.) CC.
18. *Chad Miltenberger, c-dh, JC of the Sequoias (Calif.).
19. *John Smolski, rhp, Illinois Valley CC.
20. *Randy Howard, ss, Illinois Valley CC.
21. *Ronald Troester, rhp, JC of Southern Idaho.
22. *Jeffery Franks, c, Umpqua (Ore.) CC.
23. *Tracy Poulsen, rhp, JC of Southern Idaho.
24. *Scott Ninneman, rhp, Oxnard (Calif.) JC.
25. *Paul Osborne, c, DeKalb North (Ga.) JC.
26. *Ronald Marbrey, 2b, West Covina, Calif.

**January—Secondary Phase (9)**

1. ***Oddibe McDowell, of, Miami-Dade CC North.—(1985-94)**
DRAFT DROP *First overall draft pick, June 1983/secondary phase, Twins; first-round draft pick (12th overall), Rangers (1984); first player from 1984 draft to reach majors (May 19, 1985)*
2. *Ken Reed, rhp, Crowder (Mo.) JC.

**June—Regular Phase (22)**

1. (Choice to Reds as compensation for Type B free agent Dave Collins)
2. **Tim Birtsas, lhp, Michigan State University** (Choice from Angels as compensation for Type A free agent Reggie Jackson)**—(1985-90)**
2. ***Bo Jackson, ss, McAdory HS, Bessemer, Ala.—(1986-94)**
DRAFT DROP *Attended Auburn; re-drafted by Angels, 1985 (20th round); Heisman Trophy winner (1985); first overall draft pick, National Football League, Tampa Bay Buccaneers (1986); Running back, NFL (1987-90)*
3. **Dan Pasqua, of, William Paterson (N.J.) College.—(1985-94)**
4. Jim Riggs, 3b, Eastern Michigan University.–(AA)
5. ***B.J. Surhoff, ss, Rye (N.Y.) HS.—(1987-2005)**
DRAFT DROP *Attended North Carolina; re-drafted by Brewers, 1985 (1st round, 1st pick) • Brother of Rick Surhoff, 20th-round draft pick, Phillies (1982); major leaguer (1985) • Son of Dick Surhoff, Forward/National Basketball Association (1952-54)*
6. Herman Cunningham, of, Danville (Ill.) HS.
7. Rory Brown, lhp, Florida International University.
8. Bill Ruffner, of, Wake Forest University.
9. Joey MacKay, of, Villa Park HS, Orange, Calif.
10. Richard Gumbert, rhp, Lawrence HS, Mashpee, Mass.
11. Michael Fennell, c, LeMoyne College.
12. Charles Tomaselli, lhp, St. Leo (Fla.) College.
13. Kirk Bailey, rhp, Appalachian State University.
14. Ron Inman, lhp, University of North Carolina-Wilmington.
15. Stephen George, lhp, Florida Southern College.
16. Fredi Gonzalez, c, Southridge HS, Miami.
DRAFT DROP *Major league manager (2007-15)*
17. Tim Kubacki, ss, University of Toledo.
18. ***Jim Morris, lhp, Brownwood (Texas) HS.—(1999-2000)**
DRAFT DROP *Subject of hit movie, 'The Rookie.'*
19. Tim Byron, rhp, Seton Hall University.
20. Pete Adams, ss, University of Maine.
21. **Jim Deshaies, lhp, LeMoyne College.—(1984-95)**
22. John Bryant, rhp, Alma (Mich.) College.
23. Peter Post, of, Florida International University.
24. Greg Unger, lhp, University of the Pacific.
25. **Jim Corsi, rhp, St. Leo (Fla.) College.—(1988-99)**
26. **Tom Barrett, 2b, University of Arizona.—(1988-92)**
DRAFT DROP *Brother of Marty Barrett, major leaguer (1982-91)*
27. **Pete Dalena, 1b, Fresno State University.—(1989)**
28. Jeff Wiley, 2b, St. Clair County (Mich.) CC.
29. Dick Seidel, rhp, University of Wisconsin-LaCrosse.
30. Steve Compagno, lhp, Cal Poly San Luis Obispo.
31. *Richard Lewallen, of, University of Kansas.
32. Paul Peer, of, University of Toledo.
33. *Wayne Fugett, rhp, Valdosta State (Ga.) College.
34. Mark Chestna, of, St. Peters HS, Worcester, Mass.
35. ***Jeff Manto, rhp-3b, Bristol (Pa.) HS.—(1990-2000)**
36. Clayton Stidham, rhp, Central Catholic HS, Toledo, Ohio.
37. *Hilario Valdespino, 3b, Carol City HS, Miami.
DRAFT DROP *Son of Sandy Valdespino, major leaguer (1965-71)*
38. Craig Jobes, 3b, Lakeland Regional HS, Wanaque, N.J.
39. *David Poulos, ss, Middle Georgia JC.
40. **Mike York, rhp-of, Argo HS, Justice, Fla.—(1990-91)**
41. Randy White, lhp, Yakima Valley (Wash.) JC.
42. Stacy Morgan, rhp, Washington State University.
43. *Andrew Fava, 3b, Loyola HS, Towson, Md.
44. Glynn Perry, of, Kansas State University.
45. Daniel Gasparino, c, University of Vermont.
46. Paul LeSieur, c, St. Leo (Fla.) College.
47. Robert Woodcock, 2b, University of San Francisco.

**June—Secondary Phase (24)**

1. *Mark Stathas, ss, Linn-Benton (Ore.) CC.—DNP
2. Richie Carter, of, Umpqua (Ore.) CC.
3. ***Luis Medina, of, Cerritos (Calif.) JC.—(1988-91)**
4. Richard Borowski, 3b, Erie (N.Y.) CC.
5. Marvin White, 3b, JC of Marin (Calif.).
6. *Jeff Franks, c, Umpqua (Ore.) CC.
7. *Bob Grandstaff, 3b, Golden West (Calif.) JC.

## OAKLAND ATHLETICS

**January—Regular Phase (26)**

1. *Richard Helzer, rhp, JC of Marin (Calif.).—DNP
2. ***Robby Thompson, ss, Palm Beach (Fla.) JC.—(1986-96)**
3. *Chuck Spiegel, 1b, Golden West (Calif.) JC.
4. *Jerrald Muldrew, of, Contra Costa (Calif.) JC.
5. *Stevie Bowens, lhp, Compton (Calif.) CC.
6. *Larry Schofield, p, Laney (Calif.) JC.
7. *Jack Reinholtz, lhp, Orange Coast (Calif.) JC.
8. Clemente Oropeza, 3b-rhp, CC of San Francisco.
9. *Anthony Huff, rhp-of, Compton, Calif.
10. *Michael Fields, rhp, El Camino (Calif.) JC.
11. Robert Currie, of, Paterson, N.J.
12. Gary Pool, lhp, University of Redlands (Calif.).
13. *Fred Dalaine, of, Orange Coast (Calif.) JC.
14. *Robert Gray, of, Saddleback (Calif.) CC.
15. *Martin Alejos, 1b, Santa Rosa (Calif.) JC.

**January—Secondary Phase (23)**

1. **Dave Leiper, lhp, Fullerton (Calif.) JC.—(1984-96)**

**June—Regular Phase (26)**

1. (Choice to Red Sox as compensation for Type A free agent Joe Rudi)
2. **Steve Ontiveros, rhp, University of Michigan.—(1985-2000)**
3. **Phil Stephenson, 1b, Wichita State University.—(1989-92)**
DRAFT DROP *Brother of Gene Stephenson, baseball coach, Wichita State (1978-2013)*
4. Brian Graham, of, UCLA.—(AA)
5. **Charlie O'Brien, c, Wichita State University.—(1985-2000)**
6. Ray Thoma, ss, Western Michigan University.
7. Glenn Godwin, lhp, University of San Diego.
8. *Mike Dotterer, of, Stanford University.
DRAFT DROP *Eighth-round draft pick, Los Angeles Raiders/National Football League (1983) • Son of Dutch Dotterer, major leaguer (1957-61)*
9. *Pat Griffin, rhp, Northern Illinois University.
10. **Jeff Kaiser, lhp, Western Michigan University.—(1985-93)**
11. Bob Bathe, 1b, Cal State Fullerton.
12. Ed Myers, rhp, University of Arkansas.
13. **Jim Eppard, 1b, University of California.—(1987-90)**
14. Tony Laurenzi, of, Long Beach State University.
15. **Jose Canseco, 3b, Carol City HS, Miami.—(1985-2001)**
DRAFT DROP *Brother of Ozzie Canseco, major leaguer (1990-93)*
16. *Todd Welborn, rhp, East Wilkes HS, Ronda, N.C.
17. Russ Wortmann, c, University of Texas-El Paso.
18. Leon Baham, ss, Brigham Young University.
19. Pete Kendrick, lhp, Brigham Young University.
20. Eric Barry, lhp, Cal State Fullerton.
21. Mike Gorman, rhp, Oregon State University.
22. *Thomas Walsh, 2b-ss, California Baptist College.
23. Tim Lambert, rhp, San Diego State University.
24. Thomas Czuk, 3b, University of West Florida.
25. David Peterson, 1b-of, Western Michigan University.
26. Douglas Farrow, rhp, Pomona-Pitzer (Calif.) College.
27. Tom Conquest, rhp, Chapman (Calif.) College.
28. Bob Hallas, rhp, Purdue University.
29. *Matt Held, c, UC Riverside.
30. Mark Border, rhp, Cal Poly Pomona.
31. *Keith Mucha, 3b, Oral Roberts University.

**June—Secondary Phase (26)**

1. *Jose Rodiles, rhp, Seminole (Okla.) JC.—(AA)
2. ***Rodney McCray, of, Santa Monica (Calif.) JC.—(1990-92)**
3. *Rich Rosemus, lhp, Linn-Benton (Ore.) CC.

## PHILADELPHIA PHILLIES

**January—Regular Phase (14)**

1. *Jimmy King, ss, Colorado Springs, Colo.—DNP
DRAFT DROP *Brother of Jeff King, first overall draft pick, Pirates (1986); major leaguer (1989-99)*
2. Vaughn Calloway, c, Pratt (Kan.) CC.
3. Dan Odgers, 3b-ss, Chipola (Fla.) JC.
4. *Dodd Hook, 3b-1b, Indian Hills (Iowa) CC.
5. Ray Ortega, 3b, Bakersfield (Calif.) CC.
6. *Darren Loy, c, Seminole (Okla.) JC.
7. Kirk Burgess, rhp, Seminole (Okla.) JC.
8. *Alejandro Garcia, lhp, San Jacinto (Texas) JC.
9. *Alan Brown, c, San Jacinto (Texas) JC.
10. *Joe Jordan, c, Seminole (Okla.) JC.
DRAFT DROP *Scouting director, Orioles (2005-11)*
11. *Joe Neely, lhp, Bacone (Okla.) JC.
12. *Walt Stull, rhp, Sacramento (Calif.) CC.
13. Harris Campbell, of, Van Nuys, Calif.
14. *Jamie Doughty, ss, Seminole (Okla.) JC.
15. *Jamie Campbell, rhp, McBee HS, Bethune, S.C.
16. *Tony Faryniarz, rhp, Cordova HS, Rancho

Cordova, Calif.
17. Thomas Orsag, rhp, Triton (Ill.) JC.
18. *Robert McClanahan, lhp, Mount Olive (N.C.) JC.
19. *Matt Butcher, 2b, West Los Angeles JC.
**20. Rick Surhoff, rhp, St. Johns River (Fla.) CC.—(1985)**
DRAFT DROP *Brother of B.J. Surhoff, fifth-round draft pick, Yankees (1982); first overall draft pick, Brewers (1985); major leaguer (1987-2005) • Son of Dick Surhoff, Forward/National Basketball Association (1952-54)*

**January—Secondary Phase (16)**
1. John Machin, lhp, Austin (Texas) CC.—(High A)
2. *Mark Michna, of, Blinn (Texas) JC.
3. *Craig Fitzpatrick, rhp, Koeltztown, Mo.

**June—Regular Phase (13)**
**1. John Russell, c-of, University of Oklahoma.—(1984-93)**
DRAFT DROP *Major league manager (2008-10)*
**2. Lance McCullers, rhp, Tampa Catholic HS, Tampa.—(1985-92)**
DRAFT DROP *Father of Lance McCullers, first-round draft pick, Astros (2012); major leaguer (2015)*
3. Keith Ross, of, Newberry (Fla.) HS.—(Low A)
4. Gib Seibert, of, Arizona State University.—(AAA)
**5. Mike Maddux, rhp, University of Texas-El Paso.—(1986-2000)**
DRAFT DROP *Brother of Greg Maddux, major leaguer (1986-2007)*
**6. *Mike Cook, rhp, St. Andrews HS, Charleston, S.C.—(1986-93)**
DRAFT DROP *First-round draft pick (19th overall), Angels (1985)*
**7. Howard Nichols, 1b-c, Skyline HS, Oakland, Calif.**
**8. *Billy Bates, 2b-ss, Aldine HS, Houston.—(1989-90)**
9. Russell Morton, rhp, Kansas Newman College.
10. *Lance Lincoln, ss, Pullman (Wash.) HS.
DRAFT DROP *Son of Keith Lincoln, running back, National Football League (1961-68)*
11. Kevin Coker, rhp, North Brunswick HS, Leland, N.C.
12. Jerry Arnold, lhp, Baylor University.
13. Damon Dombek, lhp, Penney HS, East Hartford, Conn.
14. Frank Martinez, 1b, Selma (Calif.) HS.
15. Terry Dickerson, lhp, Forest Hill HS, West Palm Beach, Fla.
16. Henry Smith, 3b, Forest Brook HS, Houston.
17. Kevin Walters, c, Santa Clara University.
18. *Greg Lorenzetti, of, Stanford University.
19. Brant Weatherford, rhp, Muskogee (Okla.) HS.
20. *Steve Castleberry, 3b, Mount Carmel HS, Poway, Calif.
21. *Bernie Walker, of, Corsicana (Texas) HS.
**22. Greg Legg, ss, Southeastern Oklahoma State University.—(1986-87)**
23. Milo Choate, 3b, University of Texas.
24. James Vest, of, Holy Cross College.
25. David Vernon, c, Oxnard (Calif.) HS.
26. Greg Devone, of, Oak Park (Mich.) HS.
27. Rodger Cole, rhp, Wiley (Texas) College.
28. Byron Beal, rhp, Lewisville (Texas) HS.
**29. *Ken Patterson, lhp, McGregor (Texas) HS.—(1988-94)**
30. David Kennard, 2b-ss, Texas A&M University.
**31. *Bruce Ruffin, lhp, Hanks HS, El Paso, Texas.—(1986-97)**
DRAFT DROP *Father of Chance Ruffin, first-round draft pick, Tigers (2010)*
32. John Powell, rhp, Lewisville (Texas) HS.
33. Louis Lukes, of, Cajon HS, San Bernardino, Calif.
34. Paul Robinson, rhp, Sam Houston State University.
35. *Wayne Egbert, rhp, Sumner (Wash.) HS.

**June—Secondary Phase (17)**
**1. Ken Jackson, ss, Angelina (Texas) JC.—(1987)**
2. *Craig Reid, ss, Panola (Texas) JC.
3. *Brett Harrison, ss, Bacone (Okla.) JC.
4. Todd Johnson, of, Northwood (Texas) Institute.

## PITTSBURGH PIRATES

**January—Regular Phase (8)**
1. Chip Cunningham, 3b, Cumberland (Ky.) JC.—(High A)
2. *Dennis Woods, of, Spartanburg Methodist (S.C.) JC.
3. *Mark Barbagelata, ss, JC of Southern Idaho.
4. *Tim Grachen, lhp, Fullerton (Calif.) JC.
5. *Mike Santiago, lhp, Mount San Antonio (Calif.) JC.
6. *Jamie Brisco, rhp, Fresno (Calif.) CC.
7. *Michael Wood, rhp, Frederick (Md.) CC.
8. *Richard Borowski, 3b, Erie (N.Y.) CC.
9. *Al Hamilton, 3b, Crowder (Mo.) JC.
10. *Robert Kline, rhp, Hagerstown (Md.) JC.
11. Gary Grudzinski, rhp, Lackawanna (Pa.) JC.

**January—Secondary Phase (4)**
1. Burk Goldthorn, c, University of Texas.—(AAA)
**2. Benny Distefano, 1b, Alvin (Texas) CC.—(1984-92)**
3. *Tim Barker, 2b, Seminole (Fla.) CC.

**June—Regular Phase (7)**
**1. Sam Khalifa, ss, Sahuaro HS, Tucson, Ariz.—(1985-87)**
2. Jim Opie, 3b, University of New Orleans.—(AAA)
**3. *Joe Magrane, lhp, Rowan County HS, Morehead, Ky.—(1987-96)**
DRAFT DROP *Attended Arizona; re-drafted by Cardinals, 1985 (1st round)*
4. Charles Marty, rhp, Point Loma Nazarene (Calif.) College.—(Low A)
5. Shawn Stone, rhp, Grossmont (Calif.) JC.–(High A)
6. Mitch McKelvey, rhp, Groveton HS, Alexandria, Va.
7. Brian Devalk, of, University of New Orleans.
8. David Coss, of, Centenary College.
9. *Tom Bryant, 3b, Caldwell (N.J.) HS.
10. David Frederick, of, Anderson (Ind.) College.
11. Tony Bagwell, 3b-ss, Shorter (Ga.) College.
**12. *Ray Hayward, lhp, University of Oklahoma.—(1986-88)**
DRAFT DROP *First-round draft pick (10th overall), Padres (1983)*
13. *Barry Shiflett, 1b, Western Albemarle HS, Earlysville, Va.
**14. Shawn Holman, rhp, Ambridge HS, Sewickley, Pa.—(1989)**
15. *Bob D'Agostino, rhp, University of Southwestern Louisiana.
16. Andy Watson, inf, Centenary College.
17. *Bryant Robertson, of, Hillcrest HS, Country Club Hills, Ill.
18. Justin Catlett, rhp, Meridian (Miss.) HS.
19. Bernard Stanton, rhp, Stillman (Ala.) College.
20. *Mike Patton, rhp, Seton Hall University.
21. James Smith, c, Kelly HS, Wise, Va.
22. James Mims, c, Baptist (S.C.) College.
23. John Kenny, ss, Denison (Ohio) University.
24. *Fred Laningham, ss, West HS, Bakersfield, Calif.
25. *Michael Walker, ss, Cerritos (Calif.) HS.
26. *Mark Barron, rhp, JC of DuPage (Ill.).
27. *Ed Veres, ss, West Branch HS, Grassflat, Pa.
28. *Randy Foster, lhp, Oxford (N.Y.) HS.
29. *Jose DeLeon, rhp, Perth Amboy (N.J.) HS.
30. Tom Graziano, 1b-of, University of New Orleans.
31. *Mark Whitman, 3b, Erwin (N.C.) HS.
32. *Craig Conti, of, McDowell HS, Erie, Pa.
33. *Marshall Miller, 3b, Brashear HS, Pittsburgh.
34. *Tom Snowberger, of, Sylvania Northview HS, Pittsburgh.
35. *Allen Depew, of, Herculaneum HS, Pevely, Mo.

**June—Secondary Phase (13)**
**1. Bip Roberts, ss, Chabot (Calif.) JC.—(1986-98)**
2. *Frank Russo, 1b-3b, Indian River (Fla.) CC.
3. *Mike Mazzocco, of, JC of the Canyons (Calif.).
**4. Scott Bailes, lhp, St. Louis CC-Meramec.—(1986-98)**
5. *Marty Freeman, 2b-of, Indian River (Fla.) CC.

## ST. LOUIS CARDINALS

**January—Regular Phase (22)**
1. *Tom Mauch, of, Mount San Antonio (Calif.) JC.—(High A)
2. *David Bond, rhp, Pasadena (Calif.) CC.
3. *Brent Blum, 1b-lhp, Centralia (Wash.) JC.
4. *Doug Givler, rhp, Frederick (Md.) CC.
5. *Victor Walker, rhp, Chipola (Fla.) JC.
6. Ken Mills, lhp, Massasoit (Mass.) CC.
7. *Mark Turner, rhp, Louisburg (N.C.) JC.
8. Ron Morander, ss, Massasoit (Mass.) CC.

**January—Secondary Phase (20)**
**1. *Brad Arnsberg, rhp, Merced (Calif.) JC.—(1986-92)**
2. *Jerry McDermott, c, Fontana, Calif.

**June—Regular Phase (21)**
**1. Todd Worrell, rhp, Biola (Calif.) University.—(1985-97)**
DRAFT DROP *Brother of Tim Worrell, major leaguer (1993-2006)*
2. Tim Wallace, c, Wofford College.—(AAA)
3. John Young, lhp, Bradley University.—(AA)
4. Mike Shade, rhp, West Chester (Pa.) University.—(AAA)
**5. *Mark Davis, of, Herbert Hoover HS, San Diego.—(1991)**
DRAFT DROP *Attended Stanford; re-drafted by Padres, 1985 (9th round) • Brother of Mike Davis, major leaguer (1980-89)*
6. Brian Farley, rhp, Vanderbilt University.
**7. Terry Pendleton, of, Fresno State University.—(1984-98)**
8. Gary Gill, 1b, Slippery Rock (Pa.) University.
9. David Clements, ss, University of Mississippi.
**10. Vince Coleman, of, Florida A&M University.—(1985-97)**
**11. *Rob Dibble, rhp, Southington (Conn.) HS.—(1988-95)**
12. *Bobby Joe Edmonds, of, Lutheran North HS, St. Louis.
DRAFT DROP *Running back, National Football League (1986-95)*
13. Vince Russomagno, 1b-of, Brandeis (Mass.) University.
14. Pedro LaTorre, 2b, Troy State University.
15. Billy Donathon, rhp, Louisiana State University.
16. Dennis Seiple, lhp, University of South Carolina-Aiken.
17. Ted Carson, rhp, University of Tennessee.
18. Tom Rossi, of, University of Connecticut.
19. *John Healey, c, Warren Central HS, Indianapolis.
20. *Tim Thompson, rhp, Cal State Fullerton.
21. Jeff Pasquale, 3b, Slippery Rock (Pa.) University.
22. Kevin Moon, rhp, Oakland (Calif.) HS.
23. Brad Blunt, rhp, North County Tech HS, Desloge, Mo.
24. Mark Schulte, of, Marissa (Ill.) HS.
25. *Steve Routos, ss, Newport HS, Bellevue, Wash.
26. Pat Wallace, of, Hofstra University.
27. Tom Bocock, ss, James Madison University.
28. Bruce Dunn, rhp, Lewis-Clark State (Idaho) College.
**29. *Kevin Ward, of, University of Arizona.—(1991-92)**
30. Bill Packer, c, Sacred Heart University.
31. Paul Russell, c, Sacred Heart HS, San Francisco.
32. *Oliver Whitaker, lhp, Brookland-Cayce HS, West Columbia, S.C.

**June—Secondary Phase (23)**
1. *Tom Mauch, of, Mount San Antonio (Calif.) JC.—(High A)
2. Keith Turnbull, rhp, Mineral Area (Mo.) JC.

## SAN DIEGO PADRES

**January—Regular Phase (4)**
1. *John Yowler, lhp, Valencia (Fla.) CC.—(High A)
2. *Jim Benedict, rhp, Los Angeles Valley JC.
3. *Glenn Zielinski, of, Taft (Calif.) JC.
4. Craig Estrada, ss, Cuesta (Calif.) JC.
5. *Mike Kellog, ss, Spokane Falls (Wash.) CC.
6. *Randy Ardery, rhp, Allegheny (Pa.) CC.
7. Sam Daniels, rhp, Wanchese, N.C.
8. *Timmy Reid, rhp, Taft (Calif.) JC.

**January—Secondary Phase (2)**
1. Scott Parsons, of-rhp, University of Miami.—(AAA)
2. *Dean Albany, rhp, CC of Baltimore.
3. Ken Bender, of, Centralia (Wash.) JC.
4. *Jeff Salazar, rhp, Los Angeles Valley JC.

**June—Regular Phase (3)**
**1. Jimmy Jones, rhp, Thomas Jefferson HS, Dallas.—(1986-93)**
2. Joe Plesac, rhp, North Carolina State University.—(High A)
DRAFT DROP *Brother of Dan Plesac, first-round draft pick, Brewers (1983); major leaguer (1986-2003)*
**3. Mark Wasinger, 2b, Old Dominion University.—(1986-88)**
**4. Mark Williamson, rhp, San Diego State University.—(1987-94)**
5. Greg Raymer, rhp, Western Kentucky University.—(AA)
6. Tom Brassil, ss, Duke University.
7. Osbe Hoskins, of, Western Michigan University.
**8. Mitch Williams, lhp, West Linn (Ore.) HS.—(1986-97)**
9. John Frierson, c, Oakland (Calif.) HS.
10. Rigo Rodriguez, 3b, San Diego State University.
11. Al Simmons, 2b, Eastern Washington University.
12. Jeff Dean, rhp, Central Missouri State University.
13. Bob Allinger, of, Evergreen HS, Vancouver, Wash.
14. Bob Klusacek, lhp, Stetson University.
15. John Westmoreland, c, California Lutheran University.
16. *Chris Burgess, rhp, Delta State (Miss.) University.
17. Willie Anderson, of, Hoover HS, San Diego.
18. Greg Steffanich, lhp, JC of Southern Idaho.
19. Don Freeman, 2b, Oklahoma State University.
20. *Joe Sickles, of, Florida Southern College.
**21. Bob Patterson, lhp, East Carolina University.—(1985-98)**
22. Mark Poston, rhp, Appalachian State University.
23. Lawrence Pott, c, Cal Poly San Luis Obispo.
24. Dan Jones, 3b, Lewis & Clark (Ore.) College.
25. Greg Crabb, rhp, San Diego State University.
26. Kevin Wiggins, of, San Diego State University.
27. Frank Warner, rhp, Wake Forest University.
28. Jim Harkins, lhp, Eastern Kentucky University.
**29. Gene Walter, lhp, Eastern Kentucky University.—(1985-88)**

**June—Secondary Phase (1)**
1. Kevin Towers, rhp, Brigham Young University.—(AAA)
DRAFT DROP *General manager, Padres (1996-2009); general manager, Diamondbacks (2010-14)*
2. *Scott Groot, ss, Orange Coast (Calif.) JC.
3. Ray Nodell, of, Broward (Fla.) CC.

## SAN FRANCISCO GIANTS

**January—Regular Phase (12)**
1. Mike Jones, of, Arvonia, Va.—(AA)
2. *Dale Gehringer, inf, Los Angeles Pierce JC.
3. *Reggie Mosley, of, Laney (Calif.) JC.
**4. *Joel McKeon, lhp, Miami-Dade CC North.—(1986-87)**
5. David Miller, ss, Walters State (Tenn.) CC.
6. Scott Norman, rhp, Walters State (Tenn.) CC.
7. Terry Quinn, 2b, Los Angeles Valley JC.
8. Ethan Charles, of, Los Angeles Harbor JC.
9. *Dave Snell, rhp, Spokane Falls (Wash.) CC.
10. *Kenneth Schulz, rhp, Fort Steilacoom (Wash.) CC.
11. Orlando Blackwell, ss-2b, Sacramento (Calif.) CC.
12. Joseph Powell, of, Allegany (Md.) JC.
13. *Cesar Hooker, lhp, CC of San Francisco.
14. *Darrell Freter, 3b-rhp, JC of Southern Idaho.
15. *Tony Laird, of-1b, Treasure Valley (Ore.) CC.
16. Scott Rainey, c-rhp, Rose State (Okla.) JC.
17. Randy Saunier, ss-2b, Eastern Oklahoma State JC.
18. *Richard Belli, rhp, Canada (Calif.) JC.
19. *Mark Breining, lhp, CC of San Francisco.
20. *Lonnie Strickland, rhp, Utah Technical JC.
21. Mark Swenson, lhp, Costa Mesa, Calif.
22. Mickey Swenson, 2b, Costa Mesa, Calif.

**January—Secondary Phase (8)**
1. Everett Graham, of, Louisburg (N.C.) JC.—(AAA)
2. *Ken Lynn, rhp, Spartanburg Methodist (S.C.) JC.
3. *Bob Merenda, of, Sacramento (Calif.) CC.

#### June—Regular Phase (11)

**1. Steve Stanicek, 1b, University of Nebraska.—(1987-89)**
DRAFT DROP *Brother of Pete Stanicek, major leaguer (1987-88)*
**2. *Barry Bonds, of, Serra HS, San Carlos, Calif.—(1986-2007)**
DRAFT DROP *Attended Arizona State; re-drafted by Pirates, 1985 (1st round) • Son of Bobby Bonds, major leaguer (1968-81)*
3. *Gil Villaneuva, lhp, Tehachapi (Calif.) HS.—(High A)
DRAFT DROP *Attended Arizona State; re-drafted by Athletics, 1985 (17th round)*
4. *Mike Young, lhp, Rolling Hills HS, Rancho Palos Verdes, Calif.—(AA)
DRAFT DROP *Attended Los Angeles Harbor JC; re-drafted by Blue Jays, January 1983/secondary phase (1st round)*
5. *David McNeil, of, Narbonne HS, Los Angeles.—DNP
DRAFT DROP *Attended San Diego State; never re-drafted*
6. *Brian Guinn, ss, University of California.
7. Lester Mosley, of, Morningside HS, Inglewood, Calif.
8. *Will Schock, rhp, Tamalpais HS, Mill Valley, Calif.
9. *Andy Leonard, c, El Camino HS, South San Francisco.
**10. *Pete Incaviglia, 3b-1b, Monterey HS, Pebble Beach, Calif.—(1986-98)**
DRAFT DROP *First-round draft pick (8th overall), Expos (1985); first player from 1985 draft to reach majors (April 8, 1986)*
11. Randy Morse, lhp, Central Michigan University.
12. *Steve Cotter, rhp, Skyline (Calif.) JC.
13. Billy Cabell, ss, Amherst HS, Madison Heights, Va.
14. Matt Cimo, of, Eastern Illinois University.
15. Jeff Blobaum, rhp, Cal State Stanislaus.
16. Billy Loard, c, Norwalk (Calif.) HS.
17. Jim Stassi, c, University of Nevada-Reno.
DRAFT DROP *Father of Max Stassi, major leaguer (2013-14)*
18. *Tom Krause, ss, Diablo Valley (Calif.) JC.
19. John Hughes, lhp, Westlake HS, Westlake Village, Calif.
20. Steve Keeney, of, UC Davis.
21. *Daniel Morris, of-lhp, Hoover HS, Glendale, Calif.
22. Rob Brzezinski, 2b, University of the Pacific.
23. *Ken May, lhp, Los Angeles Pierce JC.
24. Mark Morton, 3b, Cal State Northridge.
25. *Mike Meyers, 3b, Narbonne HS, Carson, Calif.
26. Glenn Knudsen, c, California Baptist College.
27. *Charles Kane, rhp, El Camino (Calif.) JC.
28. *Rob Holbrook, rhp, Oregon State University.
29. Stan Baughn, of, Oklahoma State University.
30. Dean Hummel, lhp, Portland State University.
**31. *Carl Willis, rhp, University of North Carolina-Wilmington.—(1984-95)**
32. *Jeff Gilbert, rhp, Clemson University.
33. Mike Empting, c, University of Oklahoma.
**34. Randy Bockus, of, Kent State University.—(1986-89)**
35. Brice Proctor, 2b, Southwestern (Calif.) JC.
**36. *Jose Tolentino, 1b, Seminole (Okla.) JC.—(1991)**
37. *Buck Jackson, of, Banning HS, Carson, Calif.
38. *Michael Wilder, 2b, St. Mary's (Calif.) College.
39. *Mark Kane, 3b, Oregon Tech.
40. *James Doss, of, Cal State Chico.
41. Kelvin Smith, of-inf, Southwestern (Texas) University.
42. *Jeff Montgomery, of, Cuesta (Calif.) JC.
43. Kevin Bates, 2b, University of Oklahoma.
44. Brain Bargerhuff, rhp, Texas Wesleyan College.

#### June—Secondary Phase (15)

**1. *Jody Reed, ss, Manatee (Fla.) JC.–(1987-97)**

## SEATTLE MARINERS

#### January—Regular Phase (5)

1. Wray Bergendahl, rhp, Cerritos (Calif.) JC.—(AA)
2. Kevin Roy, rhp, Umpqua (Ore.) CC.
3. *Ray Nodell, of, Broward (Fla.) CC.
4. Michael Evans, lhp, Merced, Calif.
5. *Jeff Wilpon, c, Roslyn Heights, N.Y.
6. Scott Roebuck, 3b, Citrus (Calif.) JC.

#### January—Secondary Phase (3)

**1. *Charlie Kerfeld, rhp, Yavapai (Ariz.) JC.—(1985-90)**
2. *Rich Rosemus, lhp, Linn-Benton (Ore.) CC.
3. *Vince DeBono, lhp, DeAnza (Calif.) JC.

#### June—Regular Phase (6)

**1. Spike Owen, ss, University of Texas.—(1983-95)**
DRAFT DROP *Brother of Dave Owen, major leaguer (1983-88)*
2. Mike Wishnevski, of, Indiana Central University.—(AAA)
3. Renard Brown, of, Liberty University.—(AAA)
**4. Terry Taylor, rhp, Crestview (Fla.) HS.—(1988)**
5. Jeff McDonald, rhp, UCLA.—(AA)
**6. Alvin Davis, 1b, Arizona State University.—(1984-92)**
7. Joe Whitmer, rhp, Brigham Young University.
8. *Gary Parmenter, rhp, Middle Georgia JC.
9. John Duncan, c, St. Louis University.
10. Brian David, 2b, Cal State Fullerton.
11. Darrell Bickers, ss, Charlottesville (Va.) HS.
12. *Kirk Killingsworth, rhp, University of Texas.
13. Ron Sismondo, lhp, University of Arizona.
14. Roger Hill, of, University of Nebraska.
15. Eric Stewart, c, Cal Poly Pomona.
16. Randy Newman, lhp, Arizona State University.
17. Scott Barnhouse, rhp, Mercer University.
18. Robbie Vollmer, of, University of South Carolina.
19. Ken Briggs, of, Long Beach State University.
20. Randy Ramirez, rhp, Long Beach State University.
21. Greg Bartley, rhp, East Tennessee State University.
22. *Clay Daniel, lhp, Gulf Coast (Fla.) CC.
23. *Rich Rice, rhp, Palm Beach (Fla.) JC.
24. Dave Smith, 1b, University of Southern California.
25. *Greg Shirley, c, Huntington Beach (Calif.) HS.
26. Randy Faulconer, c, James Madison University.
27. *Brad Colton, of, University of Maine.
**28. *Mel Stottlemyre Jr., rhp, Davis HS, Yakima, Wash.—(1990)**
DRAFT DROP *Son of Mel Stottlemyre, major leaguer (1964-74) • Brother of Todd Stottlemyre, major leaguer (1988-2002)*
29. David Rodriguez, 2b, Lake View HS, Chicago.
30. Todd Francis, 1b, Beaverton (Ore.) HS.
**31. *Lance Johnson, of, Triton (Ill.) JC.—(1987-2000)**
32. *Terence Johnson, 1b, Kearny HS, San Diego.
33. *Scott DeMarrais, c, Emerson (N.J.) HS.
34. *Jeb Best, of, University of Washington.

#### June—Secondary Phase (8)

1. Tom Duggan, 3b, Orange Coast (Calif.) JC.—(AA)
2. *Jamie Doughty, 3b, Seminole (Okla.) JC.
3. Kevin Roy, rhp, Umpqua (Ore.) CC.
4. Larry Paskiewicz, of, University of Texas-El Paso.
5. Jeff Schassler, rhp, Francis Marion (S.C.) College.
**6. *Robby Thompson, ss, Palm Beach (Fla.) JC.—(1986-96)**

## TEXAS RANGERS

#### January—Regular Phase (15)

1. Jim Allison, rhp, Modesto (Calif.) JC.—(High A)
2. Larry McLin, lhp, DeKalb South (Ga.) CC.
**3. *Jody Reed, ss, Manatee (Fla.) JC.—(1987-97)**
4. *Keith Turnbull, rhp, Mineral Area (Mo.) JC.
5. *John Fryhoff, lhp, San Jose (Calif.) CC.
6. *Kent Cooper, of, West Valley (Calif.) JC.
**7. *Scott Bailes, lhp, St. Louis CC-Meramec.—(1986-98)**
8. *Mike Dotzler, c, DeAnza (Calif.) JC.
9. *James Mee, c, Seminole (Fla.) CC.
10. *Todd Johnson, of, Northwood (Texas) Institute.
11. *Barry Burham, c, Hampton, Va.

#### January—Secondary Phase (19)

1. Chris Joslin, lhp, Hillsborough (Fla.) CC.–(High A)
2. *Ed Augustine, of, Brevard (Fla.) CC.
3. *Michael Winbush, rhp, Winston-Salem State (N.C.) University.
4. *Alex Diaz, c, Miami-Dade CC North.

#### June—Regular Phase (16)

1. (Choice to Red Sox as compensation for Type A free agent Frank Tanana)
2. Mike Rubel, 1b, Cal State Fullerton.—(AAA)
3. Clint Curry, 3b, Turner Ashby HS, Bridgewater, Va.—(Short-season A)
4. Terry Johnson, lhp, Michigan State University.—(AA)
**5. Steve Buechele, 2b, Stanford University.—(1985-95)**
DRAFT DROP *First-round draft pick (9th overall), White Sox (1979)*
6. *Rob Walton, rhp, Rutherford (N.J.) HS.
DRAFT DROP *Baseball coach, Oral Roberts (2003-11)*
7. Kevin Stock, 3b, Stadium HS, Tacoma, Wash.
DRAFT DROP *Son of Wes Stock, major league (1959-67)*
8. *Eric Lane, c, Tulane University.
9. Eric Dersin, rhp, Frankfort HS, Fort Ashby, W.Va.
10. Bob Gergen, ss, Oklahoma City University.
11. *Mike Oglesbee, 1b, Alamogordo (N.M.) HS.
12. *Loren Hibbs, of, Wichita State University.
DRAFT DROP *Baseball coach, North Carolina-Charlotte (1993-2015)*
13. Eli Ben, of, Seton Hall University.
14. David Hopkins, rhp, University of Virginia.
15. Mark Swiski, of, LaSalle University.
16. Rob Clark, lhp, Southern Illinois University.
17. Barry Brunenkant, c, University of New Mexico.
18. Bob Hausladen, c, Stanford University.
19. Bobby Kohler, of, Texas Tech.
20. Mark Sutton, 2b, University of Maine.
21. *Regan Bass, rhp, Washington State University.
22. Joe Ambrosino, ss, Widener (Pa.) University.
23. *Bobby McKercher, ss, Serra HS, San Carlos, Calif.
24. Sam Sorce, rhp, University of Miami.
25. Ed Brennan, of, Arizona State University.
26. Jimmy Foit, ss, Virginia Tech.
27. Warren McReddie, 1b, University of Massachusetts.
28. Bill Porterfield, 1b, Murray State (Okla.) JC.
29. *Doug Shields, of, University of Miami.
30. *Rickey Darwin, rhp, Bonham (Texas) HS.
DRAFT DROP *Brother of Danny Darwin, major leaguer (1978-90)*
31. *Jordan Stanley, lhp, Sulphur Springs (Texas) HS.
32. *Jeff Colton, lhp, Bishop Moore HS, Longwood, Fla.
33. Cecil Brim, of, Drewry Mason HS, Ridgeway, Va.
34. *Woodrow Broussard, lhp, Loreauville HS, St. Martinville, La.
35. *Buddy Shaw, rhp, Hollywood Hills HS, Hollywood, Fla.
36. *Robert Williams, rhp, Hodge HS, Jonesboro, La.
37. *Dell Curry, rhp, Fort Defiance HS, Grottoes, Va.
DRAFT DROP *First-round draft pick, Utah Jazz/National Basketball Association (1986); guard/NBA (1986-2002) • Father of Stephen Curry, guard/NBA (2009-15)*
38. *Rodney Carter, of, Elizabeth (N.J.) HS.
**39. Kenny Rogers, lhp-of, Plant City HS, Dover, Fla.—(1989-2006)**
**40. *Dave Martinez, 1b-of, Lake Howell HS, Casselberry, Fla.—(1986-2001)**
41. Mike Esser, of, George Mason University.

#### June—Secondary Phase (10)

**1. Randy Kramer, rhp, San Jose (Calif.) CC.—(1988-92)**
2. *Manny Mantrana, ss, Miami-Dade CC North.
DRAFT DROP *Baseball coach, Texas-Pan American (2009-15)*
3. Jeff Mace, of, Lewis-Clark State (Idaho) College.
4. Michael Winbush, rhp, Winston-Salem State (N.C.) University.

## TORONTO BLUE JAYS

#### January—Regular Phase (1)

1. Kash Beauchamp, of, Bacone (Okla.) JC.—(AAA)
DRAFT DROP *Son of Jim Beauchamp, major leaguer (1963-73)*
2. Ronny Johnson, rhp, Los Angeles Pierce JC.
**3. *Ken Jackson, 3b-ss, Angelina (Texas) JC.—(1987)**
4. *Tim Owen, c, Palm Beach (Fla.) JC.
5. *David Hinnrichs, rhp, McLennan (Texas) CC.
6. *Shawn Holton, rhp, Allegheny (Pa.) CC.
7. *George Jones, of, JC of the Sequoias (Calif.).
8. *Leo Cardenas, 3b, Texas Southmost JC.
DRAFT DROP *Son of Leo Cardenas, major leaguer (1960-75)*
9. *Michael Voelkel, rhp, Centralia (Wash.) JC.
10. *Paul Scholer, c, Miami-Dade CC North.
11. *Scott Morris, c, Modesto (Calif.) JC.
12. *Edward Emmons, rhp, South Florida JC.
13. *Jack Dietrich, ss-2b, Valencia (Fla.) CC.
14. *Norman Bethel, 3b-1b, Fresno (Calif.) CC.

#### January—Secondary Phase (15)

1. Randy Romagna, rhp-3b, Indian River (Fla.) CC.—(High A)
2. *Norman Morton, lhp, Miami-Dade CC North.
3. *Dave Eichhorn, rhp, Cabrillo (Calif.) JC.
DRAFT DROP *Brother of Mark Eichhorn, major leaguer (1982-96)*

#### June—Regular Phase (2)

1. Augie Schmidt, ss, University of New Orleans.—(AAA)
**2. David Wells, lhp, Point Loma HS, San Diego.—(1987-2007)**
**3. Jimmy Key, lhp, Clemson University.—(1984-98)**
4. Chris Johnston, 1b-3b, Arizona State University.—(AAA)
5. Dave Stenhouse, c, Holy Cross College.—(AAA)
DRAFT DROP *Son of Dave Stenhouse, major leaguer (1962-64) • Brother of Mike Stenhouse, first-round draft pick, Athletics (1980); major leaguer (1982-86)*
**6. Pat Borders, 3b-of, Lake Wales (Fla.) HS.—(1988-2005)**
7. Vernon Rhodes, ss, University of Arkansas-Monticello.
8. Chris Shaddy, ss, University of Arkansas.
**9. Dave Walsh, lhp, UC Santa Barbara.—(1990)**
10. Ronnie Chapman, 2b, Florida International University.
**11. *Ed Vosberg, lhp, University of Arizona.—(1986-2002)**
12. Mark Gerard, 1b, Western Michigan University.
13. *Stan Hilton, rhp, Baylor University.
DRAFT DROP *First-round draft pick (5th overall), Athletics, 1983*
**14. *Ron Jones, of, Seguin (Texas) HS.—(1988-91)**
15. *Chuck Bartlett, c, Mississippi State University.
16. *Deric Ladnier, ss, Gonzalez Tate HS, Pensacola, Fla.
DRAFT DROP *Scouting director, Royals (2000-08); scouting director, Diamondbacks (2015)*
17. *Vince Lopez, ss, La Quinta HS, Santa Ana, Calif.
18. Keith Gilliam, lhp, Austin Peay State University.
19. Scott Kimball, c, UC Santa Barbara.
20. John Mason, of, Greenville, Texas.
**21. Steve Davis, lhp, Texas A&M University.—(1985-89)**
**22. *Randy Byers, of, Cumberland Regional HS, Bridgeton, N.J.—(1987-88)**
23. *Dan Boever, ss, University of Nebraska.
24. Rusty Rightmire, rhp, Louisiana Tech.
25. *Chris Sarmiento, rhp, MacArthur HS, Saginaw, Mich.
26. Michael Lavery, c, Amherst (Mass.) College.
**27. *Mike Henneman, rhp, Jefferson (Mo.) JC.—(1987-96)**
28. *James Jackson, 1b, Fremont HS, Oakland, Calif.
29. *Greg Simpson, lhp, Stuart (Okla.) HS.
30. Tim Phillips, rhp, Florida State University.
31. *James Hudson, 3b, Oklahoma State University.
32. *Jim St. Laurent, of, Manatee (Fla.) JC.

#### June—Secondary Phase (22)

1. *David Hinnrichs, rhp, McLennan (Texas) CC.—(High A)
2. *Jamie Brisco, rhp, Fresno (Calif.) CC.
3. Kevin Sliwinski, of, Orange Coast (Calif.) JC.
4. Greg Griffin, of, Midwestern State (Texas) University.
**5. *Oddibe McDowell, of, Miami-Dade CC North.—(1985-94)**
DRAFT DROP *First overall draft pick, June 1983/secondary phase, Twins; first-round draft pick (12th overall), Rangers (1984); first player from 1985 draft to reach majors (May 19, 1985)*
6. *Tony Blasucci, of, Broward (Fla.) CC.

# 1983

# Belcher rockets to top, as Clemens slips past

Tim Belcher was one of the great rags to riches stories in draft history.

A virtual unknown little more than six weeks before the 1983 draft, Belcher shot to the top of the charts with a newfound fastball and a series of stunning performances, and the Minnesota Twins took him No. 1 overall.

"One scout said he had been in the business more than 20 years and never saw a situation like mine," said Belcher, a 21-year-old righthander from Ohio's obscure Mount Vernon Nazarene College.

Belcher's was one of the more intriguing sagas of the draft era, but the more notable storyline of the 1983 process was the curious omission of one of the most celebrated draft picks of all time—not only by the Twins, but by every club in the top half of the first round.

It wasn't until the 19th pick that the Boston Red Sox finally took Roger Clemens, who was easily the best player from the 1983 draft crop. In fact, according to WAR (Wins Above Replacement), the separation between Clemens and the second-best talent in the draft was the widest gulf in draft history.

Clemens assembled a cumulative WAR of 140.3 in a brilliant 24-year career, while Wally Joyner, a third-round pick of the California Angels, was next among players selected in the June segment of the draft at 35.7. Among the 26 first-rounders that year, Belcher was a distant second, at 26.2.

Twins scouting director George Brophy had the foresight to select Belcher, if not Clemens, and astutely assessed the 1983 crop as one of the leanest ever.

"This is the worst draft I've seen since it began in 1965," Brophy said. "It's the weakest in both caliber of the first round and overall depth. If you draft No. 1, you're supposed to get a bell ringer, a franchise-type player.

"Belcher was pitching for a Bible college against no opposition. We saw him in the twilight, and he had the best arm. But no one knew what they were getting."

It made sense that Belcher's talent was slow to emerge, but there was almost no logic to the slight of Clemens, who was well known to all teams after starring for two years at the University of Texas. He put an exclamation point on his college career by pitching the championship game of the 1983 College World Series for the victorious Longhorns.

By contrast, Belcher went unnoticed most of his college career, even by area scouts. In high school he wanted to be a shortstop. "I hated pitching in high school," he said. "I wanted to play every day."

It wasn't until the summer of 1982, when he traveled to Columbus, Ohio, and tried out for the U.S. entry in the Pan American Games that Belcher was finally convinced that pitching was his

Tim Belcher quickly rose to the top of the 1983 draft and got the call from the Twins, but the two sides could not get together on a deal

ticket to playing baseball professionally. He flashed a 90 mph fastball, but after going an uninspiring 9-8, 4.65 in his first two years against NAIA competition, he began the 1983 college season in similar fashion by losing four of his first five decisions.

With the draft rapidly approaching, Belcher suddenly put himself on the map by ratcheting up his fastball consistently to 93-96 mph, and almost overnight attracted curious scouts in droves.

Belcher said the turning point came in a midseason game against Malone College, when he gave up six runs in the first two innings, then finished the game by retiring 15 straight. He lost 6-0 but didn't lose another game. In his last 31 innings, Belcher struck out 55, threw a no-hitter against Kenyon College and a pair of one-hitters.

Belcher finished with a 5-4, 2.86 record, but an eye-opening 95 strikeouts in 66 innings, a No. 1 rating from the Major League Scouting Bureau and the attention of the baseball world.

"A lot has happened to me in the last few months," Belcher said. "At the start of the season, I was hoping to get drafted. I wasn't thinking about the first round. As for being the first player taken, well, I didn't even dream about that."

## AT A GLANCE

### This Date In History

**WINTER DRAFT:** Jan. 11-12
**SUMMER DRAFT:** June 6-8

### Best Draft

**CINCINNATI REDS.** The Reds got at least six years of major league production from seven different picks, including 18 by **LENNY HARRIS** (5), whose 211 career pinch-hits are a major league record. **KURT STILLWELL** (1), **CHRIS SABO** (2), **JEFF MONTGOMERY** (13) and **ROB DIBBLE** (June/ secondary, 1)—appeared in All-Star Games. The Reds also signed their first 23 picks, then a draft record.

### Worst Draft

**MINNESOTA TWINS.** With the top picks in both the June regular and secondary phases, the Twins had a golden opportunity to boost their ailing franchise. But they lowballed **TIM BELCHER** and **ODDIBE MCDOWELL** and failed to sign either, as well as **BILLY SWIFT**, their second selection in the regular phase. None of their other 48 picks reached the big leagues.

### First-Round Bust

**RON DELUCCHI, OF, PIRATES.** DeLucchi positioned himself as a top power-hitting prospect in the 1983 draft by hitting 12 homers in 13 games in American Legion tournament play the previous summer. When he was released by the Pirates, DeLucchi had homered just 15 times in four minor leagues seasons.

### On Second Thought

**DAVE MAGADAN, 1B-3B, METS.** Magadan finished third in the National League batting race in 1990 with a .328 average, but his .288 career average in 16 major league seasons pales compared to his Southeastern Conference record .439 average in three seasons at Alabama and his .323 mark in four minor league seasons on his travels to New York.

CONTINUED ON PAGE 274

## AT A GLANCE

CONTINUED FROM PAGE 273

### Late-Round Find

**DOUG DRABEK, RHP, WHITE SOX (11TH ROUND).** The Sox unearthed Drabek, though he never won a game for them until 1997—in the 12th season of a 13-year big league career. Drabek was dealt to the Yankees before reaching Chicago, and in 1990 won a Cy Young while a member of the Pirates. Overall, he went 155-134, 3.73.

### Never Too Late

**SCOTT ARNOLD, RHP, YANKEES (40TH ROUND).** The Yankees made little effort to sign Arnold, a junior at Miami (Ohio). He resurfaced a year later as a fifth-round pick of the Cardinals, signed for $6,000 and played six big league games in 1988.

### Overlooked

**PAUL ASSENMACHER, LHP, BRAVES.** The Braves signed Assenmacher out of Aquinas (Mich.) College as a nondrafted free agent on July 10, 1983. Sixteen years later, he pitched the last of 884 big league games, finishing with a record of 61-44, 3.53 with 56 saves.

### International Gem

**TEDDY HIGUERA, LHP, BREWERS.** Puerto Rican lefthander **JUAN NIEVES** generated buzz by signing with the Brewers for a bonus of $110,000. But Higuera, purchased from the Mexican League, made the bigger splash. He went 94-64, 3.61 in nine seasons in Milwaukee, while Nieves went 32-25, 4.71 in three seasons before getting derailed by arm problems.

### Minor League Take

**EDDIE WILLIAMS, 3B, METS.** Williams was regarded as the best hitting prospect in the 1983 draft class, but he spent the bulk of his 20-year pro career in the minors, while also drifting to Mexico, Japan, Korea and the U.S. independent leagues. He hit more minor league home runs (178)

## 1983: THE FIRST ROUNDERS

| CLUB: PLAYER, POS., SCHOOL | HOMETOWN | B-T | HT. | WT. | AGE | BONUS | FIRST YEAR | LAST YEAR | PEAK LEVEL (YEARS) |
|---|---|---|---|---|---|---|---|---|---|
| **JUNE—REGULAR PHASE** | | | | | | | | | |
| 1. Twins: Tim Belcher, rhp, Mount Vernon Nazarene | Sparta, Ohio | R-R | 6-3 | 210 | 21 | Unsigned | 1984 | 2000 | Majors (14) |
| Small-college arm with 95 mph FB, burst on scene late; first draft client of agent Scott Boras, elected not to sign with Twins, picked by Yankees in January. | | | | | | | | | |
| 2. Reds: Kurt Stillwell, ss, Thousand Oaks HS | Thousand Oaks, Calif. | B-R | 5-11 | 165 | 18 | $135,000 | 1983 | 1996 | Majors (9) |
| Hit .562-6-27 as prep senior, opted for lucrative Reds bonus offer vs Stanford education; lost Reds SS job to Barry Larkin, but hit .249-34-310 in big leagues. | | | | | | | | | |
| 3. Rangers: Jeff Kunkel, ss, Rider College | Leonardo, N.J. | R-R | 6-2 | 175 | 21 | $100,000 | 1983 | 1994 | Majors (8) |
| Son of MLB umpire, ex-righthander Bill Kunkel; hit .399-6-37 as college JR, but only .221-18-73 in injury-plagued eight-year career in majors with Rangers, Cubs. | | | | | | | | | |
| 4. Mets: Eddie Williams, 3b, Herbert Hoover HS | San Diego | R-R | 6-0 | 170 | 18 | $130,000 | 1983 | 1999 | Majors (10) |
| Played for same school as namesake Ted Williams; pro career lasted 18 years, but never fulfilled potential, played in only 395 MLB games, hit .252 with 39 homers. | | | | | | | | | |
| 5. Athletics: Stan Hilton, rhp, Baylor | Hurst, Texas | R-R | 6-1 | 195 | 22 | $70,000 | 1983 | 1989 | Class AAA (2) |
| Upstaged big arms at Texas by going fifth overall; went 8-2, 2.74 as college SR, was on fast track to majors before career compromised by shoulder surgery in 1984. | | | | | | | | | |
| 6. Cubs: Jackie Davidson, rhp, Everman HS | Everman, Texas | R-R | 6-0 | 175 | 18 | $82,500 | 1983 | 1995 | Class AAA (2) |
| Went 16-2, 0.57 with 249 K's in 126 IP, but most often cited as victim of abuse in Texas prep ranks; began career with elbow strain, never regained form in minors. | | | | | | | | | |
| 7. Mariners: # Darrel Akerfelds, rhp, Mesa (Colo.) College | Lakewood, Colo. | R-R | 6-2 | 210 | 20 | $105,000 | 1983 | 1995 | Majors (5) |
| Spent two seasons as Arkansas linebacker, transferred home to play baseball at D-II school; went 9-10, 5.08 in majors; Padres coach when died of cancer in 2012. | | | | | | | | | |
| 8. Astros: Robbie Wine, c, Oklahoma State | Norristown, Pa. | R-R | 6-2 | 195 | 20 | $110,000 | 1983 | 1990 | Majors (2) |
| Son of ex-MLB SS Bobby Wine made switch to catcher as soph in college, hit. 364-19-70; never swung bat well as pro, but became an accomplished defender. | | | | | | | | | |
| 9. Blue Jays: Matt Stark, c, Los Altos HS | Hacienda Heights, Calif. | R-R | 6-4 | 220 | 18 | $130,000 | 1983 | 1992 | Majors (2) |
| Prime USC recruit as tight end, son of softball standout; had big arm, power to all fields, but ankle/shoulder injuries doomed career, hit .179-0-3 in 13 MLB games. | | | | | | | | | |
| 10. Padres: Ray Hayward, lhp, Oklahoma | Enid, Okla. | L-L | 6-1 | 190 | 22 | $100,000 | 1983 | 1991 | Majors (3) |
| Won 26 games, hit .381 with 30 HRs as two-way talent at OU; never won a game for Padres, went 4-8, 6.75 in big league career; had long career as coach/scout. | | | | | | | | | |
| 11. Indians: Dave Clark, of, Jackson State | Tupelo, Miss. | L-R | 6-2 | 200 | 20 | $75,000 | 1983 | 1999 | Majors (13) |
| Prepped for long career as manager/coach with 17 years in pros as player; hit .378-13-43 at Jackson State, .264-62-284 with six clubs over 13 years in majors. | | | | | | | | | |
| 12. Pirates: Ron DeLucchi, of, Campolindo HS | Moraga, Calif. | R-R | 6-1 | 180 | 18 | $92,500 | 1983 | 1986 | Class A (3) |
| 1982 American Legion player of year (.580, set record for homers in national play), but never advanced beyond Class A in Pirates system, hit .230-15-101 for career. | | | | | | | | | |
| 13. White Sox: Joel Davis, rhp, Sandalwood HS | Jacksonville, Fla. | R-R | 6-5 | 205 | 18 | $75,000 | 1983 | 1989 | Majors (4) |
| Fanned 190 in 100 IP while going 12-0, 0.72 as prep SR; pitched four years in majors with 93-96 mph FB, but career ended after major shoulder surgery in 1988. | | | | | | | | | |
| 14. Expos: Rich Stoll, rhp, Michigan | Attica, Ind. | R-R | 5-11 | 182 | 20 | $75,000 | 1983 | 1987 | Class AAA (4) |
| Pitched five years in Expos system, went 35-33, 3.77, but career compromised by torn labrum; was 30-5, 2.64 in college, later became Baptist minister, HS coach. | | | | | | | | | |
| 15. Tigers: Wayne Dotson, rhp, Estacado HS | Lubbock, Texas | R-R | 6-1 | 175 | 18 | $69,900 | 1983 | 1986 | Class AA (1) |
| Dominated as HS senior with 15-2, 0.93 record (113 IP/229 SO), but waived by Tigers after being caught stealing from teammate; went 14-23, 5.69. | | | | | | | | | |
| 16. Expos: Brian Holman, rhp, North HS | Wichita, Kan. | R-R | 6-4 | 185 | 18 | $100,000 | 1983 | 1988 | Majors (4) |
| Opening Day starter for Mariners in 1990, but arm trouble ended career (37-45, 3.71) year later; brother Brad, stepfather Dick LeMay also played in majors. | | | | | | | | | |
| 17. Mariners: Terry Bell, c, Old Dominion | Kettering, Ohio | R-R | 6-0 | 195 | 20 | $70,000 | 1983 | 1989 | Majors (2) |
| Hit .400-7-63 for ODU in '83 season, but strength of game was defense, big arm behind plate; went hitless in nine games in majors (.231-8-138 in minors). | | | | | | | | | |
| 18. Dodgers: Erik Sonberg, lhp, Wichita State | Tulsa, Okla. | R-L | 6-2 | 195 | 21 | $100,000 | 1983 | 1989 | Class AAA (2) |
| Banner college career with 37-8, 2.85 mark, 17-3, 2.22 as JR; control issues, major shoulder problems as pro led to release by Dodgers after going 19-38, 6.20. | | | | | | | | | |
| 19. Red Sox: Roger Clemens, rhp, Texas | Katy, Texas | R-R | 6-4 | 205 | 20 | $121,000 | 1983 | 2007 | Majors (24) |
| Obvious standout in maligned first-round crop; flashed dominant stuff/command in 13-5, 3.04 season for Longhorns, but inconsistency caused clubs to pass. | | | | | | | | | |
| 20. Mets: Stan Jefferson, of, Bethune-Cookman | Bronx, N.Y. | R-R | 6-0 | 175 | 20 | $50,000 | 1983 | 1991 | Majors (6) |
| Mets chose local product, speed merchant with second first-round pick; hit .408-4-20, 67-of-68 in SB attempts for B-C, but MLB career (.216-16-67, 60 SB) fizzled. | | | | | | | | | |
| 21. Royals: Gary Thurman, of, North Central HS | Indianapolis | R-R | 5-10 | 170 | 18 | $60,000 | 1983 | 1998 | Majors (9) |
| Top prep QB prospect focused on football in HS, struggled early to take advantage of raw speed but played nine years in majors, hit .243-2-64, stole 65 bags. | | | | | | | | | |
| 22. Phillies: Ricky Jordan, 1b, Grant Union HS | Sacramento, Calif. | R-R | 6-3 | 190 | 18 | $82,500 | 1983 | 1997 | Majors (8) |
| Aggressive hitter with good bat speed, but slow to take advantage of raw power potential; went deep 55 times in majors before shoulder surgery ended career. | | | | | | | | | |
| 23. Angels: Mark Doran, of, Wisconsin | South Holland, Ill. | R-R | 6-3 | 210 | 21 | $75,000 | 1983 | 1990 | Class A (1) |
| Better known as kicker/backup QB in college, but had speed, power, arm strength to excel in baseball; never got untracked as hitter, career peaked in A-ball. | | | | | | | | | |
| 24. Cardinals: Jim Lindeman, 3b, Bradley | Des Plaines, Ill. | R-R | 6-1 | 200 | 21 | $57,500 | 1983 | 1995 | Majors (9) |
| Single-season, career HR leader at Bradley, won Cards over in workout; spent nine years in majors, hit .244-21-89, but chronic back issues limited his power. | | | | | | | | | |
| 25. Orioles: Wayne Wilson, rhp, Redondo Union HS | Redondo Beach, Calif. | L-R | 6-3 | 180 | 17 | $40,000 | 1983 | 1987 | Class A (4) |
| Former outfielder impressed O's with lean frame, live arm, but had trouble commanding stuff in lower minors, posted 21-19, 4.90 record (192 BB/173 SO). | | | | | | | | | |
| 26. Brewers: Dan Plesac, lhp, North Carolina State | Crown Point, Ind. | L-L | 6-5 | 210 | 21 | $75,000 | 1983 | 2003 | Majors (18) |
| Went to N.C. State with eye on hoops career, never took baseball seriously until early in pro career with Brewers; pitched in 1,064 games over 18 years in majors. | | | | | | | | | |
| **JANUARY—REGULAR PHASE** | | | | | | | | | |
| 1. Reds: Ted Langdon, rhp, Brevard (Fla.) CC | Rockledge, Fla. | R-R | 6-4 | 250 | 19 | $30,000 | 1983 | 1987 | Class AA (1) |
| Reds had first pick in both January phases, encouraged Florida JC product to drop 40 pounds from big frame; reached Double-A and won 25 games. | | | | | | | | | |
| **JANUARY—SECONDARY PHASE** | | | | | | | | | |
| 1. Reds: Tracy Jones, 3b, Loyola Marymount | Hawthorne, Calif. | R-R | 6-3 | 180 | 21 | $27,500 | 1983 | 1991 | Majors (6) |
| Mets unsigned fourth-rounder in 1982, sat out fall after hitting .391 for LMU previous spring; spent six years in majors with Reds, four other clubs, hit .273-27-164. | | | | | | | | | |
| **JUNE—SECONDARY PHASE** | | | | | | | | | |
| 1. Twins: Oddibe McDowell, of, Arizona State | Hollywood, Fla. | L-L | 5-9 | 170 | 20 | Unsigned | 1985 | 1994 | Majors (7) |
| Unsigned for fifth time after .352-7-50, 36-SB season; rewarded in 1984 by winning Golden Spikes Award; played seven MLB seasons, hit .253-74-266. | | | | | | | | | |

*# Deceased.*

## How They Should Have Done It

Based on the career WAR (Wins Above Replacement, as calculated by Baseball-Reference.com) numbers achieved by all the players eligible for the 1983 draft, here's how the first round should have unfolded. Numbers in parentheses indicate the round when the player was actually drafted

| | Player, Pos. | Actual Draft | WAR | Bonus |
|---|---|---|---|---|
| 1. | Roger Clemens, rhp | Red Sox (1) | 140.3 | $121,000 |
| 2. | Ellis Burks, of | Red Sox (Jan.-R/1) | 49.5 | $35,000 |
| 3. | Wally Joyner, 1b | Angels (3) | 35.7 | $30,000 |
| 4. | Ron Gant, ss | Braves (4) | 33.8 | $26,000 |
| 5. | Robby Thompson, ss | Giants (June-S/1) | 33.7 | $15,000 |
| 6. | Doug Drabek, rhp | White Sox (11) | 29.8 | $13,000 |
| 7. | Kevin Seitzer, 3b | Royals (11) | 28.7 | $10,000 |
| 8. | Terry Steinbach, c | Athletics (9) | 28.0 | $14,000 |
| 9. | Rick Aguilera, rhp | Mets (3) | 22.4 | $27,500 |
| 10. | Dave Magadan, 3b | Mets (2) | 21.1 | $53,000 |
| 11. | Jeff Montgomery, rhp | Reds (9) | 20.9 | $9,000 |
| 12. | John Smiley, lhp | Pirates (12) | 20.2 | $1,000 |
| 13. | Dave Martinez, of | Cubs (Jan.-S/3) | 19.2 | $5,000 |
| 14. | John Burkett, rhp | Giants (6) | 19.1 | $12,500 |
| 15. | Dan Plesac, lhp | Brewers (1) | 17.6 | $75,000 |
| 16. | Chris Sabo, 3b | Reds (2) | 16.5 | $72,000 |
| 17. | Paul Assenmacher, lhp | Braves (NDFA) | 13.7 | $3,000 |
| 18. | Charlie Hayes, 3b | Giants (4) | 10.5 | $10,200 |
| 19. | Jack Howell, 3b | Angels (NDFA) | 9.7 | $13,500 |
| | Glenallen Hill, of | Blue Jays (9) | 9.7 | $32,500 |
| 21. | Rob Dibble, rhp | Reds (June-S/1) | 9.6 | $15,000 |
| | Eric King, rhp | Giants (NDFA) | 9.6 | $5,000 |
| 23. | Brian Holman, rhp | Expos (1) | 9.3 | $100,000 |
| 24. | Mike Aldrete, 1b | Giants (7) | 8.9 | $6,500 |
| 25. | Tom Pagnozzi, c | Cardinals (8) | 7.7 | $13,500 |
| 26. | Greg Cadaret, lhp | Athletics (11) | 6.7 | $15,000 |

| Top 3 Unsigned Players | | | | Year Signed |
|---|---|---|---|---|
| 1. | Matt Williams, 3b | Mets (27) | 46.5 | 1986 |
| 2. | Tim Belcher, rhp | Twins (1) | 26.2 | 1984 |
| 3. | Todd Stottlemyre, rhp | Yankees (5) | 23.2 | 1985 |

### CAREER TAKES CURIOUS TWISTS

The overnight emergence of Belcher was unique in draft annals, but it hardly told the whole story of his bizarre courtship by major league clubs. He had a fascinating professional career before throwing even a single pitch, and also introduced draft watchers to agent Scott Boras.

Initially, at least, Belcher was happy to be drafted by the Twins, the most tight-fisted team in the game.

"I'm happy to be drafted No. 1 and I know the Twins have a history of moving players up through their farm system rapidly," he said on the day he was picked. "I want to sign right now and get on with my baseball career. I still have the option of going back to school for my senior year, but for me not to sign now would not be beneficial for my career. I can't be drafted any higher than I was."

Almost immediately, though, Belcher and the Twins ran into discord.

"I talked to Brophy the night before the draft. I told him what I wanted," Belcher said. "What I was asking for wasn't out of line with what other first-round picks were getting."

Belcher's starting point was $135,000—the same figure Boras had suggested that Kurt Stillwell, another client, ask for in his negotiations with the Cincinnati Reds as the second pick. The Reds were amenable to that amount, and agreed on a deal the night before the draft.

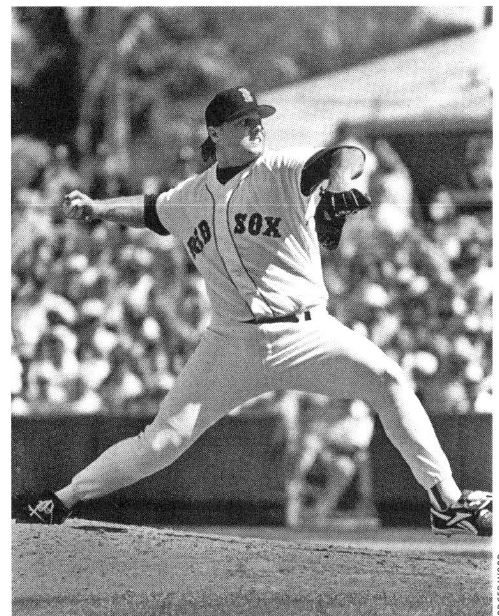


RODGER WOOD

Roger Clemens inexplicably fell to the 19th overall pick in 1983, but his career far outstripped that of any other player available that year

But the Twins, who had never paid a bonus in excess of $69,500, countered with a $90,000 offer. They eventually upped the amount to $120,000, but Belcher and Boras stuck to their guns. The negotiations then began to turn nasty.

"If you ask me," Brophy said, "I think Mr. Belcher has a fear of failure. When we got our offer up to $120,000 he still wouldn't sign. He pitches better with his tongue than his arm."

To stay active when negotiations stalled, Belcher joined Team USA and pitched that summer in Japan, at the Intercontinental Cup in Belgium and the Pan American Games in Venezuela. His performance was disappointing overall, and the Twins actually reduced their offer.

"After I got back from all that travel, I thought that maybe it would be best for me to compromise," Belcher said. "I directed my attorney to tell the Twins I was willing to accept $110,000, if the money was paid the right way.

"I thought we were close to wrapping up the details, then they cut the $110,000 bonus in half. I was left with no other choice except not to sign."

Belcher became the second player drafted No. 1 overall in June not to sign. He joined catcher Danny Goodwin, who jilted the Chicago White Sox in 1971.

Belcher also elected not to return to Mount Vernon Nazarene for his senior year, making him eligible for the secondary phase of the January draft. He was snapped up quickly by the New York Yankees with the first pick, and routinely signed a contract for $113,000.

The Yankees' exhilaration at landing a player of Belcher's stature turned to disbelief when they lost Belcher to the Oakland A's in baseball's short-lived compensation draft. The A's were entitled to compensation, under baseball's new free agent guidelines, for the loss of Type A free-

### AT A GLANCE

and drove in more runs (685) than any of his fellow first-rounders.

### One Who Got Away

**TIM BELCHER, RHP, TWINS (1ST ROUND).** Belcher and the Twins engaged in contentious negotiations and never agreed on a contract. The Yankees took Belcher the following January with the No. 1 pick—but then left him exposed in baseball's short-lived compensation draft, where he was snatched by the A's.

### He Was Drafted?

**CHRIS MILLER, SS, BLUE JAYS (17TH ROUND).** A first-round pick of the Atlanta Falcons in 1987, Miller played 10 years in the NFL. But his first exposure to professional sports came in the baseball draft. The Mariners drafted him again in 1985 and signed him. He spent 30 games in their system, hitting .148 with 31 strikeouts in 88 at-bats.

### Did You Know . . .

**JIM MORRIS,** whose story became the subject of a hit movie, "The Rookie," was the fourth pick in the regular phase of the January 1983 draft. He signed with the Brewers for $35,000, but never progressed beyond Class A with the Brewers or White Sox because of arm injuries. He attended a Devil Rays tryout a decade later, when he was a high school coach, and his fastball was clocked in the high 90s. He spent parts of the 1999 and 2000 seasons in the big leagues with the Devil Rays.

### They Said It

**EDDIE WILLIAMS,** picked fourth overall by the Mets: "I think I'm a good third baseman. Actually, with all due respect to Brooks Robinson, my goal is to be the best third baseman—ever. Some might call that cockiness, but you got to have a goal."—*Williams spent parts of 10 seasons in the majors, but washed out at third and moved to first base.*

## DRAFT SPOTLIGHT: ROGER CLEMENS

Roger Clemens started college at San Jacinto (Texas) JC before making his first national mark with a talented Texas staff

Roger Clemens had a distinguished college career at Texas and a brief, successful stint in the minors. His 24-year career in the majors, which included 354 wins and 4,672 strikeouts, may have been the best of any pitcher in baseball's draft era.

So how did 10 nondescript pitchers go before Clemens in the 1983 draft, in one of the weakest first rounds on record?

Part of it stemmed from the impression that he was the third-best pitcher on a talented Longhorns pitching staff; part of it was a result of a midseason lapse when he lost his rhythm and mechanics, and his confidence in the process, in an attempt to light up the radar guns for scouts.

The only scout who wasn't put off Clemens was Boston's Danny Doyle. "There was no doubt who the best pitcher on the Texas staff was in my mind," he said. "Roger had the best arm and the best makeup. It was a rare kind of makeup and intensity."

Clemens went 13-5, 3.04 as a junior for Texas in 1983, and struck out 151 while walking 22 in 166 innings. He won the championship game of the College World Series, a 4-3 Texas victory over Alabama. Over his two-year career at Texas, he went 25-7.

Still, Texas coach Cliff Gustafson continued to refer to and utilize Clemens as the No. 3 pitcher on his staff, behind fellow junior righthanders Calvin Schiraldi and Mike Capel. While it may have fooled a lot of scouts, it also stimulated Clemens' competitive nature.

Doyle got an insight into that after a game against college power Arizona State, a 3-2 loss in which the pitches were called from the Texas dugout.

"I saw Roger after that game," Doyle recalled. "He was hot because Arizona State beat him on three hits. They got them on changeups, and Roger knew that if he had thrown fastballs in those situations, they never would have gotten around on him."

Clemens was always supremely confident in his ability, especially when it came to throwing his fastball, but calling for changeups was a storied Texas way of teaching Clemens to use something other than the fastball to get hitters out in crucial situations.

Gustafson knew how and when to push Clemens' buttons. He later acknowledged that making him the No. 3 pitcher was a ploy to drive him. "They knew what to do to get the most out of me," Clemens said. "Gus didn't have to say a whole lot, but when he said something he meant business."

Gustafson also set Clemens straight after his only real on-field lapse as a Longhorn, when he stumbled over a three-start stretch midway through his junior year. It led to a rare loss of confidence, with Clemens fighting himself. Scouts saw it in his performance—and in his body language. With Gustafson's help, Clemens soon accepted his struggles as a challenge, responded with tenacity and quickly rediscovered his form down the stretch.

"All the talk out of Texas was about Calvin Schiraldi, and probably rightfully so," said Red Sox scouting director Eddie Kasko. "He had a good arm, good pitcher's body and was easy to project as a big leaguer. Well, when Danny Doyle's draft list came into the office, he had Clemens rated over Schiraldi.

"I called Danny and asked why, and he said, in his Oklahoma accent, 'Eddie, I like what that Clemens boy has behind his belt buckle.' "

Boston took Clemens with the 19th pick and never had reason to look back as he made a startling and immediate impact. He began his career at Class A Winter Haven, where he turned heads by working 29 innings and striking out 36, with no walks. Promoted to Double-A New Britain, Clemens went 4-1, 1.38, striking out 59 while walking 12 in 52 innings, then tossing a three-hit shutout in the Eastern League championship game.

Clemens arrived in Boston in 1984 amid fanfare seldom reserved for a rookie. Two years later, he pitched one of the greatest games in major league history, a 20-strikeout, no-walk masterpiece against Seattle on April 29, 1986. Two Cy Young Awards followed in short order.

As he continued to etch his name into big league history, everyone was only left to wonder how he could possibly have been an afterthought in the 1983 draft.

agent pitcher Tom Underwood and were free to draw the name of any player not on the 26-man protection lists of the other 25 clubs. They chose Belcher, who signed with the Yankees after their protection list was filed, but was still eligible for selection.

The turn of events left Belcher bewildered.

"I'm just shocked and caught by surprise," he said. "I feel like I'm back on the roller coaster I've been on since June. It seems now I'll have files on three teams and I haven't thrown my first pro pitch."

Belcher wasn't the only marquee player the Twins failed to sign in the 1983 draft. They also didn't reach agreement with Arizona State outfielder Oddibe McDowell, the first selection in the secondary phase, and Maine pitcher Billy Swift, their second-round pick in the regular phase.

McDowell, offered $32,500, was looking for something in the $50,000-$60,000 range, so he returned to Arizona State.

"If they had offered a little more," said McDowell, who was drafted for a fifth time, "I'd be out playing. I'm ready to play professional ball, but I'm definitely not going to play for what they're offering."

After a banner senior season for Arizona State, McDowell became a first-round pick of the Texas Rangers in 1984.

Swift also went back to school, but the Twins blew the whistle on his impermissible use of an agent in his negotiations and he was suspended for the first third of the 1984 college season by the NCAA. He was selected second overall in the 1984 draft by the Seattle Mariners.

Belcher, McDowell and Swift all enjoyed solid big league careers. Meanwhile, not a single player the Twins actually signed in their ill-fated 1983 draft ever played in the majors.

### CONTRAST IN STYLES

Minnesota and Cincinnati picked 1-2 in the 1983 draft after finishing with the poorest records in their respective leagues in 1982. Coincidence or not, the Twins and Reds were the two teams that had participated the least in major league free agency after it became a way of life after the 1976 season.

While the Twins continued to take a hardline approach in negotiations with their draft picks, the Reds engaged in a more aggressive approach to signing new talent.

They took no chances. If they were going to

### Fastest To The Majors

| | Player, Pos. | Drafted (Round) | Debut |
|---|---|---|---|
| 1. | Jeff Robinson, rhp | Giants (2) | April 7, 1984 |
| 2. | Roger Clemens, rhp | Red Sox (1) | May 15, 1984 |
| 3. | Carl Willis, rhp | Tigers (23) | June 9, 1984 |
| 4. | Jeff Kunkel, rhp | Rangers (1) | July 23, 1984 |
| 5. | Calvin Schiraldi, rhp | Mets (1) | Sept. 1, 1984 |

**FIRST HIGH SCHOOL SELECTION:** Bill Wilkinson, lhp (MarinerS/4, June 13, 1985)

**LAST PLAYER TO RETIRE:** Roger Clemens, rhp (Sept. 16, 2007)

## Top 25 Bonuses

| | Player, Pos. | Drafted (Round) | Order | Bonus |
|---|---|---|---|---|
| 1. | * **Kurt Stillwell, ss** | **Reds (1)** | **2** | **$135,000** |
| 2. | * **Eddie Williams, 3b** | **Mets (1)** | **4** | **$130,000** |
| | * **Matt Stark, c** | **Blue Jays (1)** | **9** | **$130,000** |
| 4. | **Roger Clemens, rhp** | **Red Sox (1)** | **19** | **$121,000** |
| 5. | **Robbie Wine, c** | **Astros (1)** | **8** | **$110,000** |
| 6. | **Darrel Akerfelds, rhp** | **Mariners (1)** | **7** | **$105,000** |
| 7. | **Jeff Kunkel, ss** | **Rangers (1)** | **3** | **$100,000** |
| | **Ray Hayward, lhp** | **Padres (1)** | **10** | **$100,000** |
| | * **Brian Holman, rhp** | **Expos (1)** | **16** | **$100,000** |
| | Erik Sonberg, lhp | Dodgers (1) | 18 | $100,000 |
| 11. | * Ron DeLucchi, of | Pirates (1) | 12 | $92,500 |
| 12. | * Jackie Davidson, rhp | Cubs (1) | 6 | $82,500 |
| | * **Ricky Jordan, 1b** | **Phillies (1)** | **22** | **$82,500** |
| 14. | **Calvin Schiraldi, rhp** | **Mets (1-S)** | **27** | **$77,500** |
| 15. | **Dave Clark, of** | **Indians (1)** | **11** | **$75,000** |
| | * **Joel Davis, rhp** | **White Sox (1)** | **13** | **$75,000** |
| | Rich Stoll, rhp | Expos (1) | 14 | $75,000 |
| | Mark Doran, of | Angels (1) | 23 | $75,000 |
| | **Dan Plesac, lhp** | **Brewers (1)** | **26** | **$75,000** |
| 20. | **Chris Sabo, 3b** | **Reds (2)** | **30** | **$72,000** |
| 21. | Stan Hilton, rhp | Athletics (1) | 5 | $70,000 |
| | **Terry Bell, c** | **Mariners (1)** | **17** | **$70,000** |
| | **Mike Brumley, ss** | **Red Sox (2)** | **33** | **$70,000** |
| 24. | * Wayne Dotson, rhp | Tigers (1) | 15 | $69,900 |
| 25. | **Marty Clary, rhp** | **Braves (3)** | **74** | **$63,000** |

*Major leaguers in bold. *High school selection.*

risk a premium pick on Stillwell, they would make every effort, including a club-record bonus, to sign him and steer him away from his Stanford commitment.

So when the Twins indicated a day before the draft that they were going for Belcher with the No. 1 pick, the Reds were on Stillwell's doorstep. Before the day was over, they had hashed out a tentative agreement with the slick-fielding shortstop from Thousand Oaks, Calif. Kurt was the son of ex-big leaguer Ron Stillwell, who had signed a $70,000 bonus deal with the Washington Senators out of the University of Southern California in 1961, and began his career in the big leagues.

Kurt Stillwell

The next day, Reds scout Dave Calaway was in the Stillwell home with contract in hand. As soon as the Reds announced the selection of Stillwell in the draft conference call, Calaway made it official less than a minute later by getting the youngster's name on the dotted line.

"I didn't expect this at all," said Stillwell, a .552 hitter with six homers and 25 stolen bases in 22 games for Thousand Oaks High. "We had thrown around some astronomical figures. I thought I'd scared all the teams away with what I wanted, but the money had to exceed the cost of a Stanford scholarship. I always wanted to be a major league baseball player, and thanks to a very generous offer by the Reds, I can start now."

The Reds became one of the few teams in the 1980s to steer a Stanford recruit to professional baseball. Most teams didn't even try to compete with Stanford's baseball/education package, the most attractive in the country.

"It wasn't a snap decision," said Stillwell, who went on to play nine years in the majors. "Some people may criticize me for passing up a Stanford education, but I can't worry about that. I didn't want to be a doctor or lawyer or dentist. I can't look back now. I don't regret it a bit."

The Reds also signed their first 23 selections in the June regular phase, to that point a draft record.

The Rangers, drafting third, also went for a shortstop with a big league lineage. In Jeff Kunkel's case, though, his dad Bill was still active in the game as an American League umpire.

Kunkel played three seasons at Rider College, earning All-America honors his junior year when he hit .399 with six homers in 39 games. His strong arm added to his appeal and he quickly became one of the top college prospects in the 1983 draft.

Understandably, his biggest supporter in the months leading up to the draft was his father, a former major league righthander who was on leave from his umpiring duties while recovering from a second cancer operation. Bill Kunkel got to see plenty of Jeff that spring and became convinced he could walk right into the big leagues.

"Not speaking as a father, but as one who has been active in baseball for 29 years," he said, "I think Jeff has the poise, the professionalism and whatever else it takes to be playing in the big leagues."

The elder Kunkel died on May 4, 1985—but he lived long enough to see his dream fulfilled.

### FIRST ROUND FULL OF HOLES

The controversy surrounding Belcher and the bewildering turn of events that preceded his first professional appearance was a bad omen for the 1983 draft.

With the notable exception of Clemens, few first-rounders turned out as hoped. In all, eight never even sniffed the big leagues. That included a pair of Texas schoolboy righthanders, Jackie Davidson (Cubs) and Wayne Dotson (Tigers), who each struck out more than 200 hitters in their senior years.

Davidson went 17-2, 0.57 for Everman High, while striking out an astonishing 246 in 126 innings, but often was cited in later years, along with Texas prep pitching stars like Jimmy Jones (1982) and Kerry Wood (1995), as classic cases of abuse by misguided high school coaches toward their star pitchers. Davidson pitched in 22 of his team's 28 games, and in one 15-day stretch, made seven starts. By mid-May, he had strained tendons in his elbow but continued to pitch to get his team into the Texas state high school tournament.

"At the time, the only thing on my mind was winning a state championship, so I kept throwing," Davidson said. "By the time we were finally eliminated in the state playoff, I was playing a position, not even pitching anymore. Things were moving pretty fast back then, and I was just a dumb kid who couldn't even figure out an ERA.

"I think the coach should have used better

### WORTH NOTING

Calvin Schiraldi

■ Led by a pitching staff that included **CALVIN SCHIRALDI** (14-2, 1.74), **ROGER CLEMENS** (13-5, 3.04), **MIKE CAPEL** (13-1, 2.98) and **KIRK KILLINGSWORTH** (12-3, 2.56), Texas set out to capture the 1983 College World Series title, and did so in convincing fashion. Clemens, Boston's first-round pick, beat Alabama 4-3 in the final. In five games, the vaunted Longhorns staff allowed just 13 runs. Schiraldi, not Clemens, was named the College World Series MVP. In 14 innings, he allowed just one run while striking out 16. A supplemental first-round pick of the Mets, he spent his first two major league seasons in that organization, before joining Clemens in Boston in 1986. Schiraldi went on to play eight seasons in the majors, posting a 32-39, 4.28 record. Capel, drafted in the 13th round by the Cubs, pitched three seasons in the majors, while Killingsworth, the only senior among the four pitchers, was drafted in the seventh round by the Rangers. His career in pro ball peaked in Triple-A.

■ One day in 1982, it dawned on Scott Boras, who received a $500 signing bonus from the Cardinals in 1974 as a nondrafted free agent and hit .288 over four minor league seasons, that baseball revenue had increased 10-fold since the draft began in 1965, but bonuses had stagnated.

"I was in law school," Boras said. "I hadn't played ball in years, but I started thinking of ways to help these kids."

In 1983, Boras agreed to

CONTINUED ON PAGE 278

## WORTH NOTING

CONTINUED FROM PAGE 277

represent **TIM BELCHER** and **KURT STILLWELL**, who became the first two picks in that year's draft. He set the bar for both players at $135,000, and while he was able to strike a deal with the Reds at that amount for Stillwell, his tactics did not work with Belcher, who was unable to secure a contract with the Twins. Soon the precocious, hard-driving agent was setting bonus records on a regular basis for the growing number of players he represented. "Teams were irate," he said. "They said to me, 'Don't get involved, come work for us.' I told them I didn't want to be a baseball executive, I wanted to be an advocate for players, that this was bad for baseball, bad for the system." Boras revolutionized the draft by getting players signed out of college and high school for exorbitant sums. He has advised roughly 100 first-round draft picks and negotiated more than $300 million in draft bonuses. He also has has negotiated more than $3 billion in major league contracts. Boras has been called both "the devil" and "the real commissioner of baseball," and there's little arguing that he has transformed careers, teams and the national pastime.

■ A total of 15 college players were selected in the first round of the 1983 draft, the second-most ever. But Alabama first baseman **DAVE MAGADAN** (.525-9-95) and Brigham Young first baseman **WALLY JOYNER** (.462-23-95), two of the more prominent college stars that year, were not among them. Magadan, a Mets second-rounder, led the NCAA Division I ranks in batting with his .525 average, while Joyner, an Angels third-rounder, was tops with 115 hits, 218 total bases and 32 doubles. In Joyner's case, his All-American performance turned out to be a more accurate indicator of his professional worth than his draft standing, and he enjoyed the best major league career among all the position players drafted in June. Joyner, who hit .290-

judgment, but 50 percent of it was my fault. I was doing well but I wanted to do better."

The Cubs were aware that Davidson had a sore elbow and that the velocity on his fastball had dipped from the low 90s to the low 80s when they drafted him with the sixth pick overall, but scouting director Gordon Goldsberry consulted two doctors who both assured him that Davidson's elbow issues were minor.

After signing with the Cubs for $82,500, though, Davidson made two ineffective starts in the Rookie-level Appalachian League before Cubs team physician Dr. Jacob Suker decided that his arm injury was more serious than originally thought. He said Davidson had an "overuse syndrome," and told Cubs officials to shut him down for the next seven months.

"When they sent me to Rookie ball," Davidson said, "I couldn't break a pane of glass. I was told if I kept on like I was, I might not be able to throw as hard or as good as I did."

Davidson bounced around the Cubs system for seven years, but never came close to realizing his potential. He appeared in 163 minor league games and went 51-62, 4.81 before being released in 1989.

Dotson, picked 15th by the Tigers, struck out 229 in 113 innings for Lubbock's Estacado High, while going 15-2, 0.93. He also played third base and shortstop when not pitching, and hit .529 as his team's leadoff hitter.

Dotson was ineffective from the start, but his problems stemmed from an inability to find the strike zone. He walked 197 while striking out 189 in 280 innings, which resulted in a 14-23, 5.69 career mark over three seasons. The Tigers released him in spring training 1986, after determining that Dotson stole stereo equipment from a teammate.

Among high school position players in the 1983 draft, the most obvious failure was California prep outfielder Ron DeLucchi. He had been the first player from the class to stamp himself as a sure first-rounder—and the first to be released.

Scouts became convinced DeLucchi was the real deal when he hit .580 and almost singlehandedly led his Lafayette, Calif., team to a second-place finish at the 1982 American Legion World Series. Along the way, he put on one of the greatest displays of power-hitting in Legion playoff history, hitting 12 homers in 13 postseason games.

"That's what made him," said Don Miller, DeLucchi's stepbrother and high school and Legion coach. "He went from being a middle-round selection to a first-round pick."

The 6-foot, 190-pound outfielder continued his hot hitting as a senior at Campolindo High, batting .493, and Pittsburgh used the 12th pick on him.

"He was the best player on the list when our turn came," Pirates scouting director Milt Graff said. "I think he can make it to the majors quick. We project him as a good power hitter."

DeLucchi soon discovered pro ball was a different story, and within three years he was looking for a new line of work. His career totals: a .229 average and 15 homers in 268 games, none above the Class A level.

### Largest Bonuses By Round

| | Player, Pos. | Club | Bonus |
|---|---|---|---|
| **1.** | *** Kurt Stillwell, ss** | **Reds** | **$135,000** |
| **2.** | **Chris Sabo, 3b** | **Reds** | **$72,000** |
| **3.** | **Marty Clary, rhp** | **Braves** | **$65,000** |
| **4.** | *** Mitch Lyden, c** | **Yankees** | **$50,000** |
| | *** Bill Wilkinson, lhp** | **Mariners** | **$50,000** |
| **5.** | *** Joey Meyer, 1b** | **Brewers** | **$35,000** |
| 6. | * Rex Blackwell, of | White Sox | $24,000 |
| 7. | Drex Roberts, of | Blue Jays | $60,000 |
| 8. | * Jeff Satzinger, rhp | Pirates | $25,000 |
| **9.** | *** Glenallen Hill, of** | **Blue Jays** | **$32,500** |
| 10. | Todd Lamb, rhp | Braves | $37,500 |
| **Other** | **Mike Capel, rhp** | **Cubs (13)** | **$25,000** |
| **Jan/R.** | **Javier Ortiz, 1b** | **Rangers (1)** | **$60,000** |
| Jan/S. | Kevin A. Brown, lhp | Mets (1) | $40,000 |
| Jun/S. | Three tied at | | $50,000 |

*Major leaguers in bold. *High school selection.*

"He just never caught fire," Pirates minor league director Branch Rickey III said. "He didn't show the power he was supposed to have had in high school, and he didn't grow any or get any stronger. We held on to him as long as we could."

Among college players drafted in the first round who fell short of expectations, Baylor senior righthander Stan Hilton (Athletics) and Wichita State lefthander Erik Sonberg (Dodgers) were the most notable.

As a senior with limited bargaining power, Hilton went fifth overall, a significant upgrade from a year earlier when he was taken in the 13th round by the Toronto Blue Jays. In the process, he stole some of the limelight from rival Texas and all the attention that was showered that spring on their quartet of standout hurlers, led by Clemens.

By adding a quality breaking ball and changeup to his repertoire as a senior to complement an above-average fastball, Holmes went 8-2, 2.74 and almost overnight was on the fast track to the big leagues.

But Hilton's pro career was on a downhill slide almost before it started, as he missed the 1984 season after surgery for a torn rotator cuff and most of the following season with resulting tendinitis. In seven minor league seasons in the A's and Cleveland Indians organizations, he went just 21-19, 4.89. His career peaked in Triple-A.

As the 18th pick overall, Sonberg was reminded repeatedly during a seven-year career in the minors that he was selected one spot ahead of Clemens. But at the time of his selection, Sonberg's credentials were at least the equal of his more celebrated counterpart, as he went 37-8, 2.85 in a stellar career at Wichita State, and outpitched Clemens as a junior while going 17-3, 2.22 with 142 strikeouts in 146 innings.

The Dodgers chose Sonberg over Clemens in part because they wanted a high-profile lefthander to cushion themselves amidst growing concerns over the viability of Steve Howe, and his drug problems that subsequently led to his being suspended for the 1984 season. Sonberg began the 1984 season in Triple-A, but it proved to be too much too soon for the young lefty and his promising career began to unravel.

He went a ghastly 7-19, 7.39 with 112 walks and just 105 strikeouts in a combined 188 innings in 1984 and 1985, in the only two seasons he pitched at the Triple-A level, before missing the 1986 season while undergoing the first of five shoulder surgeries that derailed his career. Sonberg never got untracked in 1987 and was released by the Dodgers a year later. He got trials with three other organizations but never regained his stellar college form. Sonberg was left to ponder what might have been after he went 19-38, 6.20 in 107 minor league appearances.

Not all the elite-level talent in the 1983 draft went unsigned or fell short of expectations. If nothing else, there was Clemens.

The Red Sox snagged the Texas fireballer with the 19th pick, after 10 pitchers had been taken before him, and in a gesture that suggested they recognized they might have gotten a steal, signed him for $121,000—the fourth-largest bonus paid out that year.

Clemens emerged almost immediately as the draft's dominant pick when he debuted at Class A Winter Haven and didn't walk a batter in 29 innings while striking out 36. Fourteen starts later, he was in Boston and taking the wraps off a career that quickly produced back-to-back Cy Young Awards in 1986-87.

Red Sox scouting director Eddie Kasko explained Clemens' availability: "It was one of those years when there was no clear-cut No. 1 choice and opinions were varied on a lot of players."

While clubs argued the merits of the then-record 13 pitchers drafted in the first round, there was little debating the credentials of Juan Nieves, a Puerto Rican lefthander who attended Avon Old Farms, a posh Connecticut prep school where he went 19-1, 1.05 with 288 strikeouts in 196 innings over a three-year career. He also hit .525 with 10 homers.

Had he been eligible for the 1983 draft, Nieves would undoubtedly have been a premium first-round selection. But because Puerto Ricans and all international players were not subject to the draft, even if they attended high school or college in the United States, Nieves became the subject of an intense bidding war involving 17 clubs.

The Yankees, Blue Jays, Atlanta Braves and Milwaukee Brewers were in it until the end, before the upstart Brewers, who had been tracking Nieves closely for two years, signed him on the strength of a $110,000 bonus—the largest in club history, and the largest ever paid a foreign player. The Brewers' willingness to let him play a position on days he didn't pitch weighed in Milwaukee's favor as well, though Nieves quickly abandoned that plan once he began his pro career.

Nieves signed on July 1, 1983, and immediately proved he was something special by going 7-1, 1.30 with 89 strikeouts in 69 innings with the Brewers' Class A Midwest League affiliate in Beloit. By the time he debuted in the majors in 1986, Nieves' minor league record was an exemplary 33-9.

Juan Nieves

The young lefthander reached the pinnacle of his career on April 15, 1987, when he hurled a no-hitter against Baltimore. But his promising major league career was over, little more than a year later, when a slight tear was detected in his rotator cuff. Surgery and repeated efforts at rehabilitating the injury proved fruitless.

The so-called Nieves Rule was subsequently adopted by Major League Baseball, making foreign players attending school in the U.S. eligible for the draft.

### METS GET UPPER HAND

If any team appeared to clean up on the 1983 draft, it was the New York Mets, who were already making significant waves in the game with all the talent they had assembled in recent drafts.

By allowing Pete Falcone, an eight-game winner in 1982, to sign with the Braves as a free agent prior to the 1983 season, they received two draft picks as compensation, giving them four of the first 32 selections. They corralled almost every big name in sight and spent liberally to sign the quartet. Their picks included:

- Eddie Williams (fourth overall). A third baseman from San Diego, he was rated the No. 2 high school player in the country by the Major League Scouting Bureau and the best hitter overall. He signed with the Mets for a bonus of $130,000.
- Stan Jefferson (20th). A fleet outfielder from Bethune-Cookman by way of the Bronx, Jefferson was the nation's top basestealer, swiping 67 bases in 68 attempts. He was signed for $50,000.
- Calvin Schiraldi (27th). He, not Clemens, was the ace righthander for College World Series champion Texas. Schiraldi posted a 14-2, 1.74 record as a junior and earned a $77,500 bonus.
- Dave Magadan (32nd). A .525 hitter with nine homers and 95 RBIs for CWS runner-up Alabama, Magadan was the 1983 Golden Spikes Award winner. He signed for $53,000.

"We're elated with the draft," Mets director of baseball operations Lou Gorman said. "It was a

## One Team's Draft: Cincinnati Reds

| Player, Pos. | Bonus | Player, Pos. | Bonus | Player, Pos. | Bonus |
|---|---|---|---|---|---|
| 1. ***Kurt Stillwell, ss** | **$135,000** | 4. Mike Goedde, rhp | $20,000 | 8. Dan Boever, of | $7,500 |
| 2. **Chris Sabo, 3b** | **$72,000** | 5. **Lenny Harris, 3b** | **$25,000** | 9. **Jeff Montgomery, rhp** | **$9,000** |
| 2. ***Joe Oliver, c** | **$55,000** | 6. James Petties, rhp | $10,000 | 10. Danny Smith, lhp | $10,000 |
| 3. Peter Grimm, rhp | $35,000 | 7. Ron Henika, 3b | $8,500 | Other **Rob Dibble (S/1), rhp** | **$15,000** |

*Major leaguers in bold. *High school selection.*

### WORTH NOTING

22-100 as a rookie with the Angels in 1996, initially committed to BYU to play basketball, but pursued baseball after he tore ligaments in his ankle as a high school senior. With their 95 RBIs, Magadan and Joyner finished tied for second nationally behind Wichita State slugger **RUSS MORMAN** (.439-23-105), the second of two first-round picks by the White Sox. Morman set an NCAA-record with his 130 RBIs a year earlier.

Nebraska, which won its first 26 games but failed to land its first-ever berth in the Omaha-based College World Series, had nine players drafted in June, more than any other college. The Cornhuskers, however, didn't approach the 15 players Sacramento (Calif.) City College had drafted in January, a record for a winter draft.

**JEFF TROUT**, the father of future Angels sensation Mike Trout, was a baseball star in his own right before his career, slowed by knee and foot injuries, peaked in Double-A. A switch-hitting second baseman, the elder Trout hit .519-14-63 as a senior at Delaware in 1983 on his way to being drafted in the fifth round by Minnesota. In four seasons in the Twins system, the last three in Double-A, Trout hit .303 with 22 homers. "I was kind of a Pete Rose-type hitter, a grinder," he said. "I wasn't a speed demon, I didn't have a good arm, and I wasn't the smoothest defensive player."

Outfielder **TONY LATHAM**, a fourth-round pick of the Red Sox from the University of Virginia, drowned in a boating accident in the Gulf of Mexico, north of Fort Myers, Fla., following the 1983 season, while participating in instructional league. Two of his Red Sox teammates survived a harrowing 22-hour experience at sea in choppy waters after the boat they were riding in capsized, but Latham was unable to swim.

**IN FOCUS: JEFF KUNKEL**

The scenario for an impending family feud was set when the Texas Rangers drafted Jeff Kunkel with the third pick overall in 1983. Jeff's father Bill was an American League umpire and former major league pitcher.

Sure enough, major league history was made in spring training the following year when dad umpired third base and son played shortstop in a Rangers exhibition game. Young Jeff even brought out the lineup card and gave it to his father.

"I would have rather been there that day than working home plate in the seventh game of the World Series," the proud father said.

Tragically, it was the only time the Kunkels would appear together in the same game. Bill was forced to retire a short time later because of a recurrence of intestinal cancer. Little more than a year later, he was dead.

Jeff, meanwhile, reached the big leagues in midseason 1984. Over the next six seasons he endured a multitude of injuries that cost him any shot of regular big league employment. His 1985 season, spent almost entirely at Triple-A Oklahoma City, was a lost season as he grieved the death of his father.

In eight major league seasons, Kunkel played in 357 games, hitting just .221 with 18 homers.

year in which the talent was a bit down by comparison with other years, but overall we came out fine and got what we went after. Joe McIlvaine, our scouting director, had ranked Williams No. 1 overall and we got him with the fourth pick."

All four players reached the majors, enabling the Mets to set the pace for the second year in a row for most draft picks matriculating to the majors. But in keeping with the general lack of talent in the 1983 draft, just 12 picks overall became future big leaguers—compared to a draft-record 17 a year earlier. Williams, Jefferson and Schiraldi never lived up to their potential and were all traded away before they saw significant time in the big leagues.

Schiraldi was dealt to the Red Sox after the 1985 season, where he was reunited with Clemens and was the losing pitcher in Games Six and Seven of the 1986 World Series, won by the Mets.

Of all the players the Mets drafted in 1983, Williams had the greatest upside. He also came with the most hype, and proved to be the biggest disappointment.

Like his predecessor at San Diego's Hoover High, Hall of Famer Ted Williams, the two shared the same surname and the same uniform number. They also destroyed high school pitching, though almost 50 years apart.

Williams knew just how good he was, without having to be told. "Cream of the crop," he said. He was so confident in his ability that he figured in one year, two at most, he would stabilize third base for the Mets, which had been a trouble position. In his mind, he wouldn't even have to work at it very hard. Or so he thought.

Eddie Williams

Dismayed with his poor work habits and .185 average at Class A Columbia, the Mets abruptly gave up on Williams just a year after drafting him, trading him to Cincinnati.

Williams played in 395 big league games, spread over 10 seasons, while hitting .252 with 39 homers. In three separate stints, he suited up with his hometown Padres.

"Once you get a label in baseball," he said to a reporter in 1990, in his first go-around with the Padres, "it sticks with you forever. I know I'm a big league player. Nobody can tell me anything different. But when you're a guy who has been with five teams, what can you say? You're thought of by everyone in baseball as having an attitude problem. I'm trying my damnedest to change it, but really, no matter what I do, that won't go away.

"But when you're 18 years old, never have struggled before in your life, and you run into adversity, I don't consider it strange that I didn't know how to handle it. But it didn't matter. That's a label that stuck with me."

## LIMITED DEMAND FOR CATCHERS

With the unqualified success of major league catchers like Johnny Bench, Gary Carter, Carlton Fisk, Thurman Munson and Ted Simmons in the 1970s, there was an unprecedented run on young catchers in the draft during the decade like no time in the event's history.

From 1970-79, 16 catchers were taken within the first 10 picks in those years, including the first pick overall in 1970, '71 and '75. But few panned out as hoped, and by the end of the decade catching, with its myriad of physical and mental demands, had evolved into the trickiest demographic among all positions for scouts to judge with any degree of accuracy

In the 1980s, it wasn't until 1983 that another catcher was claimed in the first 10 picks, and predictably neither the careers of Robbie Wine, drafted eighth overall by the Houston Astros, or Matt Stark, taken ninth by the Blue Jays, measured up as expected, though both reached the majors briefly.

Wine, son of ex-big leaguer Bobby Wine, had established himself in 1982 as a player to watch when he hit .364 with a school-record 19 homers and 70 RBIs as a sophomore at Oklahoma State. He slumped to .282 with 13 homers and 45 RBIs a year later, but in the process developed a reputation for defensive excellence behind the plate, and with his bloodlines, along with the publicity he generated in 1982, it carried him on a high into the 1983 draft.

In 23 major league games over parts of the 1986-87 seasons in the majors, Wine hit just .146 and didn't drive in a single run. He languished in the minors over most of his eight-year career as a pro, hitting .215 while drilling 61 homers.

The 6-foot-4, 230-pound Stark was one of the greatest tight ends in Southern California prep history, but he elected to pass up a scholarship to USC to cast his lot with the Blue Jays. Stark reached Toronto for five games in 1987, but a succession of shoulder injuries ruined his chances of more extensive big league service, though he resurfaced with the White Sox for eight more games in 1990. Overall, he hit .179 with no homers and three RBIs. Stark later spent eight years playing in the Mexican League.

Stark's father also had a claim to fame as he was a member of the International Softball Congress Hall of Fame, and once caught for legendary Eddie Feigner's King and His Court in the 1960s.

### Highest Unsigned Picks

**JUNE/REGULAR PHASE ONLY**

| Player, Pos., Team (Round) | College | Re-Drafted |
|---|---|---|
| Tim Belcher, rhp, Twins (1) | None | Yankees '84 (Jan.-S/1) |
| Billy Swift, rhp, Twins (2) | *Maine | Mariners '84 (1) |
| Gary Green, ss, Cardinals (2) | *Oklahoma State | Padres '84 (1) |
| Steve Bast, lhp, Angels (3) | USC | Red Sox '86 (5) |
| Mike Pavelka, lhp, Orioles (3) | Minnesota | Never |
| Todd Crosby, ss, Padres (4) | Hawaii | Phillies '86 (S/5) |
| Tom Powers, rhp, Pirates (4) | Triton (Ill.) JC | White Sox (S/1) |
| David Lynch, lhp, Phillies (4) | New Orleans | Rangers '87 (22) |
| Steve Browning, c, Mets (5) | Ga. Southern | Orioles '87 (21) |
| Randy Strijek, ss, Pirates (5) | W. Kentucky | Orioles '86 (17) |

**TOTAL UNSIGNED PICKS:** Top 5 Rounds (13), Top 10 Rounds (39)

**Returned to same school.*

*Did not sign. Major leaguers in bold, with first and last years noted. Order of selection indicated in parentheses. For the first five rounds of the June Regular Phase and the first round of all other phases, the peak level of each player is noted.

# 1983 Draft List

## ATLANTA BRAVES

### January—Regular Phase (19)

1. James Bartlett, rhp, Cuyahoga (Ohio) CC.—(Rookie)
2. Jay Reeves, rhp, Pearl River (Miss.) JC.
3. *Daryl Brown, rhp, CC of Morris (N.J.).
4. *Clarence Perry, 1b, Spartanburg Methodist (S.C.) JC.
5. Sal D'Alessandro, c, Orange Coast (Calif.) JC.
6. *Darryl Decker, rhp, Paris (Texas) JC.
7. ***Chris Cron, 1b, Santa Ana (Calif.) JC.—(1991-92)**

DRAFT DROP *Father of C.J. Cron, first-round draft pick, Angels (2011); major leaguer (2014-15)*

8. ***Tom Prince, c, Kankakee (Ill.) JC.—(1987-2003)**
9. *Wallace Moore, of, DeKalb (Ga.) JC.
10. *Melvin Webb, of, Brewton Parker (Ga.) JC.
11. *Charles Williams, 3b, DeKalb (Ga.) JC.
12. *David Grams, rhp, Mount San Antonio (Calif.) JC.

### January—Secondary Phase (19)

1. ***Rob Nelson, 1b, Mount San Antonio (Calif.) JC.—(1986-90)**
2. *Bryant Robertson, of, Triton (Ill.) JC.
3. *Steven Cotter, rhp, Skyline (Calif.) JC.

### June—Regular Phase (20)

1. (Choice to Mets as compensation for Type B free agent Pete Falcone)
2. (Choice to Dodgers as compensation for Type A free agent Terry Forster)
3. **Marty Clary, rhp, Northwestern University.—(1987-90)**
4. **Ronnie Gant, ss, Victoria (Texas) HS.—(1987-2003)**
5. *Dera Clark, rhp, Artesia (N.M.) HS.—(AAA)

DRAFT DROP *Attended Arkansas; never re-drafted*

6. *Chuck Oertli, c, Travis HS, Austin, Texas.
7. Joe Scime, 1b, University of Wisconsin.
8. **Steve Ziem, rhp, Cal Poly Pomona.—(1987)**
9. ***Jay Buhner, of, McLennan (Texas) CC.—(1987-2001)**
10. Todd Lamb, rhp, Duke University.
11. **Kevin Coffman, of-rhp, Victoria (Texas) HS.—(1987-90)**
12. Eric Shirley, rhp, Texas Tech.
13. Doug Bates, lhp, J.J. Kelly HS, Wise, Va.
14. David Lebeau, ss, UC Davis.
15. Kyle Reese, c, North Cobb HS, Acworth, Ga.
16. Mike Nipper, 2b, East Tennessee State University.
17. Troy Tomsick, rhp, Ranum HS, Denver.
18. Brian Aviles, rhp, Coastal Carolina College.
19. *Huck Hibberd, rhp, San Jose State University.
20. *Robert Huffman, of, Hamilton (Ohio) HS.
21. Ross Kingsley, ss, University of Wisconsin-Oshkosh.
22. David Camara, of, San Diego CC.
23. ***Jim Hunter, rhp, Brookdale (N.J.) CC.—(1991)**
24. Chris Baird, of, North Carolina State University.
25. Mike Nagle, rhp, Garrett (Md.) CC.
26. *Arned Hernandez, of, Sunnyside HS, Tucson, Ariz.
27. **Mark Lemke, 2b, Notre Dame HS, Whitesboro, N.Y.—(1988-98)**
28. D.J. Jones, rhp, King HS, Tampa.
29. Paul Daddario, 2b-ss, SUNY-Buffalo.
30. Louis Newsome, lhp, Cherokee (Ala.) HS.
31. Mac Rodgers, rhp, Texas Wesleyan College.
32. Warren Bachmann, 1b, Armstrong State (Ga.) College.
33. Wayne Harrison, of, Lynchburg (Va.) College.
34. *Gerald Wright, ss-of, Reagan HS, Austin, Texas.
35. *Wayne Stephens, rhp, Texas Southern University.
36. Bob Berry, 3b, Auburn University.
37. Ron Bunnell, c, University of Georgia.

### June—Secondary Phase (18)

1. *Kevin Williamson, rhp, Pima (Ariz.) CC.—(High A)
2. *Tim Englund, rhp, Rice University.
3. Mickey Ballou, of, Long Beach (Calif.) CC.
4. ***Tom Prince, c, Kankakee (Ill.) CC.—(1987-2003)**

## BALTIMORE ORIOLES

### January—Regular Phase (25)

1. ***Bill Fulton, rhp, Pensacola (Fla.) JC.—(1987)**
2. Nick Piazza, c-of, Scottsdale (Ariz.) CC.
3. Scott Ninneman, rhp, Oxnard (Calif.) JC.
4. **Mark Leiter, rhp, Connors State (Okla.) JC.—(1990-2001)**

DRAFT DROP *Brother of Al Leiter, major leaguer (1987-2005)*

5. *Frank Morrison, rhp, Lower Columbia (Wash.) JC.
6. Steve Morris, of, Fullerton (Calif.) JC.
7. Anthony Burroughs, rhp, CC of Baltimore.
8. *Derrick Richardson, 3b, Westark (Ark.) CC.
9. *Alan Sontag, rhp, Indian River (Fla.) CC.
10. *James Pruett, 2b, Florida JC.
11. *William Benfield, 1b, Florida JC.
12. *Jerome Rothman, lhp, Indian River (Fla.) CC.

### January—Secondary Phase (25)

1. ***Ken Patterson, lhp, McLennan (Texas) CC.—(1988-94)**
2. *Chris Courtright, of, CC of Baltimore.

### June—Regular Phase (25)

1. Wayne Wilson, rhp, Redondo HS, Redondo Beach, Calif.—(High A)
2. Mike Conley, lhp, Hamilton (Ohio) HS.—(Rookie)
3. *Mike Pavelka, lhp, Hopkins (Minn.) HS.—DNP

DRAFT DROP *Attended Minnesota; never re-drafted*

4. Rick Lockwood, 3b, Georgia Tech.—(AAA)
5. David Dahse, of, Texas Lutheran College.—(High A)
6. *Jim Howard, ss, Siena College.
7. *Bryan Price, lhp, University of California.

DRAFT DROP *Major league manager (2014-15)*

8. Mike Lopez, of, Eckerd (Fla.) College.
9. Marc Heyison, 3b, George Washington University.
10. Tim Smith, of, Mercer University.
11. Jeff Jacobson, 2b, University of Michigan.
12. Mike Skinner, rhp, CC of Morris (N.J.).
13. *James Colmer, rhp, University of Mississippi.
14. Keith Mucha, 3b, Oral Roberts University.
15. Randy King, rhp, Rogers HS, Tulsa, Okla.
16. Rich Medina, lhp, Lewis-Clark State (Idaho) College.
17. Ben Bianchi, rhp, Portland State University.
18. Gerald Adams, rhp, Howard University.
19. Louis Dichiaro, 2b, Seton Hall University.
20. *Chuck Baldwin, ss, Whiteville (N.C.) HS.
21. Jonathan Black, of, Widener (Pa.) College.
22. *Chris Bengel, rhp, Calvert Hall HS, Baltimore.
23. Jeff Leriger, ss, University of Georgia.
24. Ty Nichols, ss, Dodge City (Kan.) HS.
25. *Keith Felden, rhp, Clearwater (Fla.) HS.
26. Danny Fitzpatrick, c, CC of Baltimore.
27. *Bert Pascual, of, Miami-Dade CC South.

DRAFT DROP *Son of Camilo Pascual, major leaguer (1954-71) • Brother of Camilo Pascual, 28th-round draft pick, Athletics (1983)*

28. Ken Wilp, lhp, University of New Mexico.
29. *Robert Squires, c, Dekalb HS, Waterloo, Ind.

### June—Secondary Phase (3)

1. Rich Rice, rhp, University of Florida.—(AA)
2. **Bob Milacki, rhp, Yavapai (Ariz.) JC.—(1988-96)**
3. *Alan Sontag, rhp, Indian River (Fla.) CC.
4. *Chris Courtright, of, CC of Baltimore.

## BOSTON RED SOX

### January—Regular Phase (20)

1. **Ellis Burks, of, Ranger (Texas) JC.—(1987-2004)**
2. Michael Kane, 3b, Truman (Ill.) JC.
3. Dave Hall, 2b-3b, Columbia State (Tenn.) CC.
4. Richard Winfield, c, Truman (Ill.) JC.
5. ***Eric Hetzel, rhp, Eastern Oklahoma JC—(1989-90)**

DRAFT DROP *First overall draft pick, June 1985/secondary phase, Red Sox*

6. *Michael Adams, rhp, Garden City (Kan.) CC.
7. *Terry Selk, 3b, Las Vegas, Nev.

RON VESELY

Ron Gant was an obscure fourth-round pick but went on to be a Braves franchise cornerstone

8. Kevin Camilli, c, Polk (Fla.) CC.
9. Jason Jackson, of, Bethune, S.C.
10. *Craig Gutman, rhp, El Camino (Calif.) JC.

### January—Secondary Phase (22)

1. *Richard Helzer, rhp, JC of Marin (Calif.).—DNP

### June—Regular Phase (19)

1. **Roger Clemens, rhp, University of Texas.—(1984-2007)**
2. **Mike Brumley, ss, University of Texas** (Choice from Athletics as compensation for Type A free agent Tom Burgmeier)**—(1987-95)**

DRAFT DROP *Son of Mike Brumley, major leaguer (1964-66)*

2. John Toale, 3b, Taravella HS, Coral Springs, Fla.—(AA)
3. Paul Thoutsis, of, Holy Name Central HS, Worcester, Mass.—(AAA)
4. Tony Latham, of, University of Virginia.–(High A)

DRAFT DROP *Died as active player (Oct. 30, 1983)*

5. Tim Corder, rhp, Memphis State University.
6. Gary Tremblay, c, Coastal Carolina College.
7. **John Mitchell, rhp, Overton HS, Nashville, Tenn.—(1986-90)**

DRAFT DROP *Brother of Charlie Mitchell, major leaguer (1984-85)*

8. **Dana Kiecker, rhp, St. Cloud State (Minn.) University.—(1990-91)**
9. Chris Cannizzaro, 2b, San Diego State University.

DRAFT DROP *Son of Chris Cannizzaro, major leaguer (1960-74)*

10. Alvin Hamilton, 2b, Southwest Missouri State University.
11. *Steve Beer, rhp, Loara HS, Anaheim, Calif.
12. ***Kirt Manwaring, c, Horsehead Central HS, Horsehead, N.Y.—(1987-99)**
13. *Ray Revak, lhp, Key West (Fla.) HS.
14. *Billy Sheeks, rhp, Christian Brothers HS, Memphis, Tenn.
15. **Mike Dalton, lhp, DeAnza (Calif.) JC.—(1991)**
16. Jim Hines, rhp, Crane Hill, Ala.
17. DeMarlo Hale, 1b, Southern University.
18. *Blane Lockley, of, Franklin HS, Baldwin, La.
19. John Sanderski, rhp, St. John's HS, Oxford, Mass.

### June—Secondary Phase (11)

1. ***Randy Byers, of, CC of Baltimore.—(1987-88)**

## CALIFORNIA ANGELS

### January—Regular Phase (24)

1. Steve Lee, of, Seminole (Okla.) JC.—(Short-season A)
2. *Mark Scott, rhp, Southeastern Illinois JC.
3. *Ted Kockenmeister, lhp, Mercer County (N.J.) CC.
4. Terrence Spellmon, 2b, Hill (Texas) JC.
5. *James Gonzales, rhp, Pima (Ariz.) CC.
6. ***Mark Gardner, rhp, Fresno (Calif.) CC.—(1989-2001)**
7. Billy Mitchell, of, Howard (Texas) JC.
8. *Troy Dodd, 1b, El Reno (Texas) JC.
9. *David Chambers, rhp, Ohlone (Calif.) JC.
10. *Andre Toliver, of, Pima (Ariz.) CC.
11. *Saul Cortez, rhp, Riverside (Calif.) CC.
12. *Greg Sparks, 1b, Mesa (Ariz.) CC.

### January—Secondary Phase (6)

1. ***Brad Arnsberg, rhp, Merced (Calif.) JC.—(1986-92)**
2. *James Jackson, 1b, Laney (Calif.) JC.
3. *Jeff Franks, c, Ranger (Texas) JC.

### June—Regular Phase (23)

1. Mark Doran, of, University of Wisconsin.—(AAA)
2. Bill Merrifield, ss, Wake Forest University.—(AAA)
3. **Wally Joyner, 1b, Brigham Young University** (Choice from Yankees as compensation for Type A free agent Don Baylor)**—(1986-2001)**
3. *Steve Bast, lhp, Damien HS, Upland, Calif.—(AAA)

DRAFT DROP *Attended Southern California; re-drafted by Red Sox, 1986 (5th round)*

4. **Pat Clements, lhp, UCLA.—(1985-92)**
5. Mark Lynds, of, Los Medanos (Calif.) JC.—(Short-season A)
6. Steve Heatherly, 2b, Morehead State University.
7. Tom Alfredson, ss, Coral Springs (Fla.) HS.
8. Brian Migliore, rhp, Tulane University.
9. Charles Smith, 1b, Midwestern State (Texas) University.
10. Kenny Grant, ss-3b, Eastside HS, Paterson, N.J.
11. Bobby Buchanon, 1b-3b, Jackson State University.
12. Don Tinkey, rhp, Youngstown State University.
13. Scott Cannon, rhp, Pan American University.

R&R SPORTS GROUP

**The White Sox saw Doug Drabek's talent but ultimately did not benefit from it in the majors**

14. Steve Sciacca, c, University of San Diego.
15. Doug Reibel, 1b, St. Xavier (Ill.) College.
16. **Ray Chadwick, rhp, Winston-Salem State (N.C.) University.—(1986)**
17. *Matt Sexton, ss, Kansas Newman College.
18. Marty Cain, 3b, Anadarko (Okla.) HS.
19. Don Stanfield, rhp, Northview HS, Covina, Calif.
20. Fred Wilburn, rhp, University of Texas-Arlington.
21. Mike O'Hara, of, Cal State Northridge.
22. *Dirk Tidwell, rhp, Westlake HS, Austin, Texas.
23. *Michael Cutola, lhp, Secaucus (N.J.) HS.
24. Greg Steen, 2b, Arizona State University.
25. Reggie Montgomery, of, University of Southern California.
26. ***Shawn Hillegas, rhp, Middle Georgia JC.—(1987-93)**
27. ***Chris Beasley, rhp, Newport Beach, Calif.—(1991)**

**June—Secondary Phase (15)**

1. Byron Kemmerling, rhp, Lamar University.–(AA)
2. Alex Diaz, c, Middle Georgia JC.

## CHICAGO CUBS

**January—Regular Phase (5)**

1. *David Cortez, ss, Lower Columbia (Wash.) JC.—(AA)
2. *Derek Vanacore, of, Sacramento (Calif.) CC.
3. *Kevin Williamson, rhp, Pima (Ariz.) CC.
4. *Stanley Bryant, c, Modesto (Calif.) JC.
5. *David Stewart, 1b, Citrus (Calif.) JC.
6. *Paul Hartwig, p, Yavapai (Ariz.) JC.
7. Jim Doyle, rhp, Queensborough (N.Y.) CC.
8. *Carl Hamilton, lhp, Triton (Ill.) JC.
9. *Chris Ritter, rhp, CC of Baltimore.
10. Derrick Hardamon, of, Fresno (Calif.) CC.
11. *Dean Williams, 1b, Shasta (Calif.) JC.

**January—Secondary Phase (5)**

1. Jonathon Baker, c, Sacramento (Calif.) CC.—(Low A)
2. James Balmer, rhp, Delaware County (Pa.) CC.
3. **Dave Martinez, of, Valencia (Fla.) CC.—(1986-2001)**

**June—Regular Phase (6)**

1. Jackie Davidson, rhp, Everman (Texas) HS.—(AAA)
2. **Rich Amaral, 2b, UCLA.—(1991-2000)**
3. David Kopf, rhp, University of Michigan.—(AAA)
4. Terry Edwards, of, Central State (Ohio) University.—(Short-season A)
5. **Steve Engel, lhp, Eastern Kentucky University.—(1985)**
6. John Cox, lhp, University of California.
7. **Jacob Brumfield, of, Hammond (La.) HS.—(1992-99)**
8. Bob Glendening, c, St. Lawrence (N.Y.) University.
9. David Lenderman, rhp, Southern Utah State College.
10. Jeff Brewer, rhp, Eastern Connecticut State University.
11. Marty Tyson, ss, Ontario (Calif.) HS.
12. Hal Walck, rhp, Old Dominion University.
13. **Mike Capel, rhp, University of Texas.—(1988-91)**
14. Donnie Richardson, of, Campbellsville (Ky.) College.
15. Dean Holmes, rhp, Cal State Los Angeles.
16. John Turner, of, Xavier University.
17. *Billy Plante, 3b-of, Virginia Tech.
18. *Eric Bauer, lhp, Clackamas (Ore.) CC.
19. Jim Dickerson, of, University of North Carolina-Charlotte.
20. Jim Phillips, rhp, University of Kansas.
21. *Darrell Clifton, ss, Calallen HS, Corpus Christi, Texas.
22. *Robert Auth, rhp, Westminster Christian HS, Miami.
23. ***Jeff King, ss, Rampart HS, Colorado Springs, Colo.—(1989-99)**

**DRAFT DROP** *First overall draft pick, Pirates (1986)*

24. *Anthony Smith, of, East Ascension HS, Gonzales, La.
25. *Calvin James, 1b-of, University of Miami.
26. *Wade Tobin, rhp, Mineral County HS, Hawthorne, Nev.
27. Tad Slowik, rhp, Rollins (Fla.) College.
28. *Mark McMorris, 1b, Delgado (La.) JC.

**June—Secondary Phase (6)**

1. Gary Parmenter, rhp, University of South Carolina.—(AAA)
2. Carl Hamilton, lhp, Triton (Ill.) JC.

## CHICAGO WHITE SOX

**January—Regular Phase (18)**

1. *Don Dunster, rhp, Mission (Calif.) JC.—(AAA)
2. *Clark Lange, 3b, Miami-Dade CC North.
3. William Ottino, 3b, Los Angeles Pierce JC.
4. Don Devlin, ss, Des Moines Area CC.
5. *Bill Geivett, 3b, Sacramento (Calif.) CC.
6. *Kight Higgins, rhp, Seminole (Okla.) JC.
7. ***Steve Peters, lhp, Seminole (Okla.) JC.—(1987-88)**
8. *Robert Koopman, lhp, Harper (Ill.) JC.
9. *John Koenig, rhp, Blinn (Texas) JC.
10. Jesse Vasquez, of, Mount San Antonio (Calif.) JC.
11. *Michael McClear, rhp, Valencia (Fla.) CC.
12. Vincent Woods, of, Long Beach (Calif.) CC.
13. ***Damon Berryhill, c, Orange Coast (Calif.) JC.—(1987-97)**
14. *Jeff Farber, of, Long Beach (Calif.) CC.
15. *Patrick Dougherty, rhp, Los Angeles Harbor JC.
16. *Kirk Bates, 2b, Fullerton (Calif.) JC.

**January—Secondary Phase (24)**

1. Otis Green, 1b-lhp, Miami-Dade CC North.—(AAA)
2. *Matthew Warren, rhp, Chabot (Calif.) JC.

**June—Regular Phase (17)**

1. **Joel Davis, rhp, Sandalwood HS, Jacksonville, Fla.** (Choice from Yankees as compensation for Type A free agent Steve Kemp)**—(1985-88)**
1. (Choice to Mariners as compensation for Type A free agent Floyd Bannister)
1. **Russ Morman, of-1b, Wichita State University** (Supplemental choice—28th—for loss of Type B free agent Bill Almon)**—(1986-97)**
2. Roger Jensen, of, Sonoma State (Calif.) University.—(AA)
3. Mike Soper, ss, Palmetto HS, Miami.—(AAA)
4. **Bruce Tanner, rhp, Florida State University.—(1985)**

**DRAFT DROP** *Son of Chuck Tanner, major leaguer (1955); major league manager (1970-88)*

5. Tim Gourlay, ss, Western Michigan University.—(Short-season A)
6. Rex Blackwell, of, Colton HS, Grand Terrace, Calif.
7. Eric Schmidt, rhp, Oklahoma State University.
8. Charlie Moore, ss, Valdosta State (Ga.) College.
9. *Paul Fuller, c, St. Lee HS, Chicago.
10. Paul Imig, rhp, Florida Southern College.
11. **Doug Drabek, rhp, University of Houston.—(1986-98)**

**DRAFT DROP** *Father of Kyle Drabek, first-round draft pick, Phillies (2006); major leaguer (2010-14)*

12. Jeff O'Dell, of, University of Central Florida.
13. Jim Hickey, rhp, Pan American University.
14. Bob D'Agostino, rhp, University of Southwestern Louisiana.
15. Joe Sickles, of, Florida Southern College.
16. Richard Johnson, 2b, Harper (Ill.) JC.
17. Ken Henricks, of-3b, Garey HS, Ontario, Calif.
18. Pat Pomeranz, of, University of Mississippi.
19. Kirk Gilmore, 3b, Washington HS, Los Angeles.
20. Michael Taylor, of, Wagner College.
21. Jim Trevathan, c, Baylor University.
22. *Robert O'Hearn, c, Canada (Calif.) JC.
23. Kevin Kristan, rhp, Creighton University.
24. Kurt Walker, rhp, Fresno State University.
25. *Lawrence Samuel, ss, Eastern Hills HS, Fort Worth, Texas.
26. *Terry Brown, of, El Cerrito HS, Berkeley, Calif.
27. Darryl Rector, of, Compton (Calif.) HS.
28. *Tom Ard, of, Seton Hall Prep School, Springfield, N.J.
29. *Terry Winkelhake, c, Harper (Ill.) JC.

**June—Secondary Phase (13)**

1. *Mike Young, lhp, Los Angeles Harbor JC.—(AA)
2. Troy Thomas, of, Mount San Antonio (Calif.) JC.
3. *Robert Koopman, lhp, Harper (Ill.) JC.

## CINCINNATI REDS

**January—Regular Phase (1)**

1. Ted Langdon, rhp, Brevard (Fla.) CC.—(AA)
2. Jac Hein, rhp, Southeastern Illinois JC.
3. *Mike Duncan, 1b, JC of Southern Idaho.
4. *David Boston, of, Triton (Ill.) JC.

**DRAFT DROP** *Brother of Daryl Boston, first-round draft pick, White Sox (1981); major leaguer (1984-94)*

5. *Cordell Williams, of, Johnson County (Kan.) CC.
6. *Paul James, rhp, St. Louis CC-Meramec.
7. *Thomas Fulkerson, rhp, Rend Lake (Ill.) JC.
8. *Keith Reinhart, rhp, St. Louis CC-Florissant Valley.
9. *Mike Westbrook, ss, Johnson County (Kan.) CC.
10. *Douglas Miller, rhp, Des Moines Area (Iowa) CC.
11. *Larry Mims, 2b, Indian Hills (Iowa) CC.
12. Robbie Ergle, rhp, Santa Fe (Fla.) CC.
13. *Jimmy Franklin, rhp, Westark (Ark.) CC.
14. Andre Hamb, of, Thornton HS, Harvey, Ill.

**January—Secondary Phase (1)**

1. **Tracy Jones, 3b, Hawthorne, Calif.—(1986-91)**
2. ***Luis Medina, of, Cerritos (Calif.) JC.—(1988-91)**
3. Mark Hammond, rhp, Willibrord HS, Chicago.

**June—Regular Phase (2)**

1. **Kurt Stillwell, ss, Thousand Oaks (Calif.) HS.—(1986-96)**

**DRAFT DROP** *Son of Ron Stillwell, major leaguer (1961-62)*

2. **Chris Sabo, 3b, University of Michigan.—(1988-96)**
2. **Joe Oliver, c, Boone HS, Orlando, Fla.** (Choice from Yankees as compensation for Type A free agent Bob Shirley)**—(1989-2001)**
3. Peter Grimm, rhp, SUNY-Buffalo.—(AA)
4. Mike Goedde, rhp, University of Evansville.—(Low A)
5. **Lenny Harris, 3b, Jackson HS, Miami.—(1988-2005)**
6. James Petties, rhp, Tennessee State University.
7. Ron Henika, 3b, Oral Roberts University.
8. Dan Boever, of, University of Nebraska.
9. **Jeff Montgomery, rhp, Marshall University.—(1987-99)**
10. Danny Smith, lhp, University of Miami.
11. Scott Loseke, of, University of Arkansas.
12. Darren Riley, of, Patrick Henry HS, San Diego.
13. Hugh Kemp, rhp, University of Georgia.
14. Mark Calvert, rhp, University of South Carolina.
15. Greg Monda, 1b, Washington State University.
16. Ken Houp, c, Oral Roberts University.
17. Gary Denbo, ss, Oakland (Mich.) CC.
18. Ronnie Giddens, 2b, Union (Tenn.) University.
19. Scott Middleton, rhp, Southwest Missouri State University.
20. Robert Balaguer, of, Dartmouth College.
21. Steve Oliverio, rhp, University of South Alabama.
22. David Salmen, of, Geneva (Pa.) College.
23. *Tony Walker, of, Henry Ford HS, Detroit.
24. *Bill Blount, 1b, Proctor HS, Utica, N.Y.
25. Michael Mattern, of, University of New Haven.
26. *Tim Fernandez, 2b, Pima (Ariz.) CC.
27. Jordan Berge, of, University of Northern Colorado.
28. Larry Huggins, of, Mesa (Colo.) College.
29. *Anthony Blackmon, ss, West Side HS, Gary, Ind.
30. *Ron Marigny, ss, St. Augustine HS, New Orleans.
31. *William Humes, ss-of, Erwin HS, Asheville, N.C.
32. Manuel Correa, of, Fairleigh Dickinson University.
33. *Jeff Mons, c, Bolles School, Jacksonville, Fla.

**June—Secondary Phase (20)**

1. **Rob Dibble, rhp, Southington, Conn.—(1988-95)**
2. *Gregg Schiffelbein, of, Allen County (Kan.) CC.
3. *Derrick Richardson, 3b, Westark (Ark.) CC.
4. *Larry Mims, 2b, Indian Hills (Iowa) CC.

## CLEVELAND INDIANS

**January—Regular Phase (12)**

1. Glenn Simmons, rhp, DeKalb Central (Ga.) JC.—(High A)
2. Anthony Grande, ss, Rome, N.Y.
3. *Alex Diaz, c, Middle Georgia JC.
4. Robert Kowalski, 2b, Niagara Falls, N.Y.
5. Shawn Cisco, rhp, Cypress (Calif.) JC.
6. *Ralph Backes, rhp, Monroe (N.Y.) CC.
7. *Jeff Kitchens, lhp, DeKalb (Ga.) JC.
8. *Amin David, c, Fullerton (Calif.) JC.
9. *Richard Belli, of, Canada (Calif.) JC.
10. *Marion Frazier, c, DeKalb South (Ga.) JC.
11. *Robert Mortimer, lhp, Ferrum (Va.) JC.

**January—Secondary Phase (10)**

1. *Bob Grandstaff, 3b, Golden West (Calif.) JC.—(AA)
2. *Manny Mantrana, ss, Middle Georgia JC.

**DRAFT DROP** *Baseball coach, Texas-Pan American (2009-15)*

3. *Brad Powell, rhp, Basking Ridge, N.J.

**June—Regular Phase (11)**

1. **Dave Clark, of, Jackson State University.—(1986-98)**

**DRAFT DROP** *Major league manager (2009) • Brother of Louis Clark, wide receiver, National Football League (1987-92)*

2. **Andy Allanson, c, University of**

**Richmond.—(1986-95)**
3. Cal Santarelli, rhp, Louisiana State University.—(AA)
4. Glenn Edwards, of, Oklahoma State University.—(AA)
5. Mike Greer, rhp, Valley HS, Las Vegas, Nev.—(Low A)
6. Stephen Whitmyer, rhp, University of Notre Dame.
7. Paul Perry, rhp, Jacksonville University.
8. Rick Browne, lhp, University of Alabama.
9. Joe Kramer, of, Cleveland State University.
10. Michael Street, rhp, Rochester (N.Y.) Institute of Technology.
11. Steve Smith, of, Oregon State University.
12. Tom Reynolds, rhp, Chicago State University.
13. Kelly Robinette, ss, East Carolina University.
14. *Bruce Crabbe, ss-3b, University of Florida.
15. Vin Martelli, c, Harvard University.
**16. *John Farrell, rhp, Oklahoma State University.—(1987-96)**
DRAFT DROP *Major league manager (2011-15)*
17. Jeffery Killings, of, Haworth HS, Kokomo, Ind.
18. Mike Murphy, rhp, Manhattan College.
19. Kenneth Connerty, of, University of Lowell (Mass.).
20. *John Boling, lhp, St. Xavier (Ill.) College.
21. Steve Arbogast, rhp, American University.
22. Vic Madden, 1b, University of the Pacific.
**23. *John Ramos, c, Plant HS, Tampa.—(1991)**
24. *David Zapien, 1b, Nooksack Valley HS, Sumas, Wash.
25. *James Rockey, of, Fremont HS, Sunnyvale, Calif.
26. *Andy Leonard, c, Canada (Calif.) JC.
27. *Erick Rapp, rhp, Weatherwax HS, Aberdeen, Wash.

**June—Secondary Phase (19)**
1. *Richard Belli, rhp, Canada (Calif.) JC.—DNP

## DETROIT TIGERS

**January—Regular Phase (16)**
1. *Jon Leake, 3b, Sacramento (Calif.) CC.—(High A)
2. *Wallace Love, rhp, American River (Calif.) JC.
**3. *Joe Bitker, rhp, Sacramento (Calif.) CC.—(1990-91)**
4. *Kevin Brockway, rhp, West Los Angeles JC.
5. Larry Goodwin, of, Cleveland State (Tenn.) CC.
6. *Walt Stull, rhp, Sacramento (Calif.) CC.

**January—Secondary Phase (8)**
**1. *Randy Byers, of, CC of Baltimore.—(1987-88)**
2. *Gordie Hershiser, rhp, Indian River (Fla.) CC.
DRAFT DROP *Brother of Orel Hershiser, major leaguer (1983-2000)*

**June—Regular Phase (15)**
1. Wayne Dotson, rhp, Estacado HS, Lubbock, Texas.—(AA)
2. Rodney Poissant, rhp, Irvine (Calif.) HS.—(AA)
**3. Jeff M. Robinson, rhp, Azusa Pacific (Calif.) University.—(1987-92)**
4. Alan Dunn, rhp, University of Alabama.—(AA)
5. Bruce Hinz, rhp, University of Oklahoma.—(AA)
6. Rob Baker, of, Indiana State University.
7. Anthony Cunningham, of, Denton (Texas) HS.
**8. *Rob Mallicoat, lhp, Hillsboro (Ore.) HS.—(1987-92)**
**9. Jim Walewander, 2b, Iowa State University.—(1987-93)**
10. David McClure, c, Wichita State University.
11. *Scott Sadler, rhp, Radford HS, Hickam AFB, Hawaii.
12. *Don Cohoon, 3b, Braintree (Mass.) HS.
13. Alejandro Garcia, lhp, University of Houston.
14. Tim Bailey, c, East Tennessee State University.
15. *Richard Rumbold, rhp, Norland HS, Miami.
16. Joey Millis, of, Old Dominion University.
17. *Peter Mancini, 2b, Seton Hall University.
**18. *D.J. Dozier, ss-of, Kempsville HS, Virginia Beach, Va.—(1992)**
DRAFT DROP *First-round draft pick, Minnesota Vikings/ National Football League (1987); Running back, NFL (1987-91)*
19. Michael Patterson, rhp, Michigan State University.
20. Jim Scudero, lhp, New York Tech.
21. Thomas Held, rhp, Defiance (Ohio) College.
22. Brad Wheeler, lhp, St. Joseph, Mich.
**23. Carl Willis, rhp, University of North Carolina-Wilmington.—(1984-95)**
24. *Warren Dickey, rhp, Westmont (Calif.) College.
25. John Bauldry, rhp, Spring Arbor (Mich.) College.
26. Paul Embry, ss, Lincoln, Ala.
27. *Doug Duke, c, Central HS, Tuscaloosa, Ala.
28. *Mike Reitzel, lhp, Handy HS, Bay City, Mich.
29. *Kevin Gilles, rhp, Clio (Mich.) HS.
30. *Gary Peters, 2b, Royal Oak (Mich.) HS.
31. Tyrone Barnes, rhp, Mississippi Valley State University.
32. Michael Ward, 1b, Central Michigan University.

**June—Secondary Phase (17)**
1. Glenn Simmons, rhp, DeKalb (Ga.) JC.—(High A)
2. Scott Baker, rhp, Mesa (Ariz.) CC.
**3. *Chris Cron, 1b, Santa Ana (Calif.) JC.—(1991-92)**
DRAFT DROP *Father of C.J. Cron, first-round draft pick, Angels (2011); major leaguer (2014-15)*
4. *Cyrenius Phillips, 1b, Panola (Texas) JC.
5. *John Bryant, of, Cal State Fullerton.

## HOUSTON ASTROS

**January—Regular Phase (7)**
1. *Bob Vodvarka, lhp, Chaffey (Calif.) JC.—(Rookie)
2. Steve Verrone, rhp, CC of Morris (N.J.).
3. *Greg Edge, 2b, Sacramento (Calif.) CC.
4. *Robert Smith, rhp, Miami-Dade CC South.
5. *Scott Marsh, lhp, Golden West (Calif.) JC.
6. *Randy Robinson, lhp, Mercer (N.J.) CC.
7. *Dan Sullivan, 1b, Sacramento (Calif.) CC.
**8. *Brett Gideon, rhp, Bee County (Texas) JC.—(1987-90)**

**January—Secondary Phase (11)**
**1. Troy Afenir, c, Palomar (Calif.) JC.—(1987-92)**

**June—Regular Phase (8)**
**1. Robbie Wine, c, Oklahoma State University.—(1986-87)**
DRAFT DROP *Son of Bobby Wine, major leaguer (1960-72); major league manager (1985) • Baseball coach, Penn State (2005-13)*
2. (Choice to Pirates as compensation for Type A free agent Omar Moreno)
3. Mike Friederich, rhp, Fredericksburg (Texas) HS.—(AA)
4. Greg Dube, rhp, University of Portland.—(AA)
5. Rayner Noble, lhp, University of Houston.—(AAA)
DRAFT DROP *Baseball coach, Houston (1995-2010)*
6. Jim O'Dell, 1b, Lewis-Clark State (Idaho) College.
7. *Curtis Parham, of, Thornridge HS, Phoenix, Ill.
8. *David Carley, rhp, Campolindo HS, Moraga, Calif.
9. *David Hensel, of, Powers HS, Flint, Mich.
**10. Roger Samuels, lhp, Santa Clara University.—(1988-89)**
11. Charles Mathews, rhp, Texas Wesleyan College.
12. Randy Hammond, rhp, Mesa (Colo.) College.
13. Nelson Rood, ss, Florida Southern College.
14. Rodney Martin, of, Azusa Pacific (Calif.) University.
15. Steve Lipinski, of, Montclair State (N.J.) College.
16. Shane Fairbanks, of, University of Missouri.
17. Scott Houp, of, Long Beach State University.
18. Anthony Kelley, rhp, University of Nebraska.
19. Doug Snyder, of, Los Medanos (Calif.) JC.
20. Frank Talotta, 2b, Coastal Carolina College.
21. Glenn Sherlock, c, Rollins (Fla.) College.
22. *Jeff Hirsch, rhp, Broward (Fla.) CC.
23. Doug Shaab, lhp, University of Delaware.
24. Seth Richmond, of, Trevecca Nazarene (Tenn.) College.
25. Peter Mueller, 1b, Upsala (N.J.) College.
26. *Brian Brooks, lhp, El Cerrito HS, Hercules, Calif.
27. Jason Johnson, rhp, Altoona (Wis.) HS.
**28. Tom Funk, lhp, Northwest Missouri State University.—(1986)**
29. *David Lawson, of, University of Missouri.
30. *Michael Allen, 2b-of, Lincoln HS, San Diego.
31. Daraka Shaheed, ss, Contra Costa (Calif.) JC.
32. Ronald Russell, ss, Canoga Park HS, Reseda, Calif.
33. Robert Retz, lhp, Tucson, Ariz.

**June—Secondary Phase (22)**
1. *Paul Williams, of, University of Oklahoma.—DNP
2. *Scott Sempier, ss-3b, CC of Morris (N.J.).
3. *Robert Nettles, rhp, Orange Coast (Calif.) JC.

## KANSAS CITY ROYALS

**January—Regular Phase (22)**
1. Mark Van Blaricom, ss, Orange Coast (Calif.) JC.—(AAA)
2. *Brett Adams, rhp, Yakima Valley (Wash.) JC.
3. *Keith Peterson, of, Edmonds (Wash.) CC.
4. *Mike Clarkin, rhp, Normandale (Minn.) CC.
5. *Chris Stull, of, Northeastern Oklahoma JC.
6. *Larry Schofield, rhp, Laney (Calif.) JC.
7. Keith Williamson, of, Pasadena (Calif.) CC.
8. *Steve Echols, of, Sacramento (Calif.) CC.
9. Russell Powers, rhp, North Tarrytown, N.Y.
10. *Steve Vasquez, rhp, Chabot (Calif.) JC.
11. *Elmer Lewis, 2b, Pasadena (Calif.) CC.
12. *Tim Jester, of, JC of San Mateo (Calif.).
13. *David Miramontes, rhp, Butte (Calif.) JC.
14. *Craig Moe, rhp, Bellevue (Wash.) CC.
15. *Dexter McClendon, of, Los Angeles CC.
16. *Robert Bartlett, of, Citrus (Calif.) JC.
17. *Robert Orozco, of, Chabot (Calif.) JC.
18. *Michael David, rhp, Santa Barbara (Calif.) CC.
19. John Rubel, of, Cypress (Calif.) JC.
20. *Manny Salinas, ss, Southwestern (Calif.) JC.

**January—Secondary Phase (16)**
1. Ron McCormack, rhp, Green River (Wash.) CC.—(High A)
2. Glen Gwatney, of, North Little Rock, Ark.

**June—Regular Phase (21)**
**1. Gary Thurman, of, North Central HS, Indianapolis, Ind.—(1987-97)**
2. Todd Mabe, ss, Edison HS, Huntington Beach, Calif.—(AA)
3. Joe Jarrell, ss, Ramapo (N.J.) College.—(AAA)
4. Geoff Petersen, of, Clovis West HS, Fresno, Calif.—(High A)
**5. *Scott Hemond, c, Dunedin (Fla.) HS.—(1989-95)**
DRAFT DROP *Attended South Florida; re-drafted by Athletics (first round), 1986*
6. Mike Miller, 2b, Washington State University.
7. David Koller, rhp, Peabody HS, Pittsburgh.
8. Carey Ross, 3b, Central Michigan University.
9. *Montie Phillips, of, Davis HS, Yakima, Wash.
10. Jeff Hull, rhp, South Hills HS, Covina, Calif.
**11. Kevin Seitzer, 3b, Eastern Illinois University.—(1986-97)**
12. Dave Landrith, c, University of Arizona.
DRAFT DROP *Son of Hobie Landrith, major leaguer (1950-63)*
13. Tim Richardson, 1b, University of Illinois.
**14. Tom Edens, rhp, Lewis-Clark State (Idaho) College.—(1987-95)**
15. *Vince Shinholster, ss, Loara HS, Anaheim, Calif.
16. Gary Klein, rhp, Cal State Northridge.
17. Ed Bass, rhp, San Jose State University.
18. Kevin Tuck, rhp, University of Tennessee.
19. David Velez, of, St. Mary's (Calif.) College.
20. John Yowler, lhp, CC of Baltimore.
21. Charles Green, 2b, Wiley (Texas) College.
22. John Lutz, 3b, Thomas More HS, Milwaukee.
**23. Jeff Schulz, of, Indiana State University-Evansville.—(1989-91)**
24. Dennis Boatright, rhp, William Jewell (Mo.) College.
25. John Zelenka, 2b, Tulane University.
26. Jere Longenecker, 1b, Pepperdine University.
27. Floyd Smith, rhp, Dowagiac (Mich.) HS.
28. *Michael Van Mill, of, Bishop McNamara HS, Kankakee, Ill.
29. *Darwin Freeman, of, Birmingham HS, Inglewood, Calif.
**30. *Todd Zeile, c, William S. Hart HS, Valencia, Calif.—(1989-2004)**
31. Mike Conte, 3b, Cal State Los Angeles.
32. *Mark Dudenake, c, Clark HS, Las Vegas, Nev.
33. John Devich, of, Long Beach (Calif.) CC.
34. *Chris Morgan, of, Georgia Tech.

**June—Secondary Phase (25)**
1. *John Nero, of, Fullerton (Calif.) JC.—DNP
2. Robert Vodvarka, lhp, Chaffey (Calif.) JC.
3. *Robert Bartlett, of, Citrus (Calif.) JC.
4. Scott Campbell, of, Citrus (Calif.) JC.

## LOS ANGELES DODGERS

**January—Regular Phase (17)**
1. Derek Lee, rhp, Sacramento (Calif.) CC.—(High A)
2. Todd Cobbs, rhp, Vincennes University (Ind.) JC.
3. *Pat Sullivan, c, Sacramento (Calif.) CC.
4. *Mark Tindall, lhp, Sinclair (Ohio) JC.
5. *Victor Marin, rhp, Chaffey (Calif.) JC.
6. Randy Hamrick, lhp, Spartanburg Methodist (S.C.) JC.
7. *John Partridge, rhp, Alvin (Texas) CC.
8. *Rob Leary, rhp-c, JC of San Mateo (Calif.).
9. *Kenneth Boone, rhp, Citrus (Calif.) JC.
10. *Ted Parker, of, Spartanburg Methodist (S.C.) JC.
11. *Scott Campbell, of, Citrus (Calif.) JC.
12. Mark Reynolds, of, Austin (Texas) CC.
**13. Wayne Kirby, of, Newport News, Va.—(1991-98)**
DRAFT DROP *Brother of Terry Kirby, running back/ National Football League (1993)*
14. Karl Ciamaichelo, ss-3b, Havertown, Pa.
15. *Gerald Robinson, c, Easton, Md.

**January—Secondary Phase (23)**
1. *Dennis Woods, of, Spartanburg Methodist (S.C.) JC.—DNP
**2. *Rodney McCray, of, West Los Angeles JC.—(1990-92)**

**June—Regular Phase (18)**
1. Erik Sonberg, lhp, Wichita State University.—(AAA)
2. Mike Cherry, rhp, The Citadel (Choice from Padres as compensation for Type A free agent Steve Garvey).—(AA)
2. Bob Hamilton, rhp, Northeast HS, St. Petersburg, Fla.—(AA)
**2. Luis Lopez, c, Lafayette HS, Brooklyn, N.Y.** (Choice from Braves as compensation for Type A free agent Terry Forster)**—(1990-91)**
3. Mitchell Moran, of, Pan American University.—(High A)
4. Bert Flores, of, Mount Whitney HS, Visalia, Calif.—(High A)
5. Rick Thurman, rhp, Pepperdine University.—(High A)
**6. Scott May, rhp, University of Wisconsin-Oshkosh.—(1988-91)**
7. Tim Zapolski, 3b, Boulder City (Nev.) HS.
8. Dave Eichhorn, rhp, University of Miami.
DRAFT DROP *Brother of Mark Eichhorn, major leaguer (1982-96)*
9. Curtis Campbell, c, Gardena (Calif.) HS.
10. Chuck Bartlett, c, Mississippi State University.
11. Joe Karmeris, 3b, Reavis HS, Burbank, Ill.
12. Kevin Dotson, c, Memphis State University.
13. Ken Harvey, 2b, University of Richmond.
14. Barry Wohler, lhp, University of Minnesota.
15. *Richard Ross, 3b, North Park (Ill.) College.
16. Steve Shields, rhp, Cal State Los Angeles.
17. Michael Blair, c, Jacksonville State University.
18. *Fred LaGroue, rhp, Holy Cross HS, Chalmette, La.
19. Chris Chapman, of, Southern University.
20. *Mark Stevens, of-1b, Citrus (Calif.) JC.
**21. *Shawn Gilbert, ss, Agua Fria HS, Litchfield Park, Ariz.—(1997-2000)**
**22. *Mike Fetters, rhp, Iolani HS, Ewa Beach, Hawaii.—(1989-2005)**
DRAFT DROP *First-round draft pick (27th overall), Angels (1986)*
23. Rob Rowen, lhp, Lassen (Calif.) JC.
24. Vince Beringhele, of, UCLA.
25. John Rexrode, rhp, Dallas Baptist University.
26. *Scott Parrish, rhp, Clemson University.
27. *Dale Hamrick, 3b-c, Spartanburg Methodist (S.C.) JC.
28. Fernando Fernandez, 3b, Lennox (Calif.) HS.

29. *Kevin Monk, 1b, Fremont HS, Los Angeles.
30. *Danny Kapea, lhp-of, Waipahu (Hawaii) HS.

**June—Secondary Phase (24)**

1. *Jon Leake, 3b-1b, Sacramento (Calif.) CC.—(High A)
2. *Terence Guzman, lhp, Ferrum (Va.) JC.
3. Tim Criswell, rhp, DeKalb Central (Ga.) JC.

## MILWAUKEE BREWERS

**January—Regular Phase (26)**

1. **LaVel Freeman, of, Sacramento (Calif.) CC.—(1989)**
2. Steve Anderson, c, Cerritos (Calif.) JC.
3. Michael Serviente, rhp, Northwood (Texas) Institute.
4. *John Griswold, lhp, Mercer County (N.J.) CC.
5. *Tim Lemmons, rhp, Gulf Coast (Fla.) CC.
6. *Jeff Graham, of, Gadsden State (Ala.) JC.
7. ***Bobby Thigpen, of-rhp, Seminole (Fla.) CC.—(1986-94)**
8. Tom Kleean, lhp, Palm Beach (Fla.) JC.
9. *Mark Stone, p, Sierra (Calif.) JC.
10. Greg Simmons, rhp, Gadsden State (Ala.) JC.
11. *Rick Waltman, rhp, South Florida JC.
12. Troy Watkins, rhp, Sacramento (Calif.) CC.
13. *Herman Spera, rhp, Endwell, N.Y.
14. *Mark Leonette, rhp, Rio Hondo (Calif.) JC.
15. *Randy Poitevint, 3b, Sunland, Calif.
16. *Ken Longman, rhp, Sacramento (Calif.) CC.
17. Gary Appino, of, Sacramento (Calif.) CC.
18. *Henry Gonzalez, rhp, Mount San Antonio (Calif.) JC.
19. *Bret Williamson, of, Central Arizona JC.
20. *Michael Crawford, of, Moorpark (Calif.) JC.
21. *Alfred Sapp, of, East Los Angeles JC.

**January—Secondary Phase (4)**

1. **Jim Morris, lhp, Ranger (Texas) JC.—(1999-2000)**

DRAFT DROP *Subject of hit movie, 'The Rookie'*

2. *Wayne Egbert, rhp, Green River (Wash.) CC.
3. Gerald McDermott, 3b, San Bernardino Valley (Calif.) JC.
4. *Paul Togneri, lhp, Citrus (Calif.) JC.

**June—Regular Phase (26)**

1. **Dan Plesac, lhp, North Carolina State University.—(1986-2003)**
2. **Glenn Braggs, of, University of Hawaii.—(1986-92)**
3. Jeff Reece, lhp, Oregon State University.—(AA)
4. **Mike Birkbeck, rhp, University of Akron.—(1986-95)**
5. **Joey Meyer, 1b, University of Hawaii.—(1988-89)**
6. Kerry Everett, 3b, Point Loma Nazarene (Calif.) College.
7. Mike Gobbo, c, Midwestern State (Texas) University.
8. Derek Diaz, rhp, University of Hawaii-Hilo.
9. **Jeff Parrett, rhp, University of Kentucky.—(1986-96)**
10. Jeff Gilbert, rhp, Clemson University.
11. John Thompson, rhp, Willamette (Ore.) University.
12. *Darryl Stephens, of, Stanford University.
13. Bobby Fingers, rhp, Scottsdale (Ariz.) CC.

DRAFT DROP *Son of Rollie Fingers, major leaguer (1968-85)*

14. Kyle Selden, lhp, Cerritos (Calif.) HS.
15. **Mark Ciardi, rhp, University of Maryland.—(1987)**
16. Terry Derby, 3b, University of Hawaii.
17. *Alan Sadler, rhp, University of Maryland.
18. *Chris Kahler, rhp, University of North Carolina.
19. *Lindsay Meggs, 3b, UCLA.

DRAFT DROP *Baseball coach, Indiana State (2007-09); baseball coach, Washington (2010-15)*

20. *Phil Lane, of, University of Miami.
21. *Kendall Carter, rhp, Arizona State University.
22. *Jeff Glover, rhp, Farragut HS, Knoxville, Tenn.
23. *Pete Beall, 3b, UCLA.
24. Joe Mitchell, c, Morehead State University.
25. John Beuerlein, c, University of Arizona.
26. David Page, 3b-1b, Tucson, Ariz.
27. Tom Steinbach, of, Valley Stream South HS, Valley Stream, N.Y.
28. Michael Smith, c, Southern Connecticut State University.
29. Bo Shipp, 3b, Morehead State University.
30. *Todd Azar, rhp, Cherry Hill East HS, Cherry Hill, N.J.
31. ***Dan Gakeler, 1b-rhp, Mercer County (N.J.) CC.—(1991)**
32. *Jeff Pequignot, of, Stetson University.

**June—Secondary Phase (21)**

1. Rick Abbott, 2b, University of Texas-El Paso.—(High A)
2. **Alex Madrid, rhp, Yavapai (Ariz.) JC.—(1987-89)**
3. *Saul Cortez, rhp, Riverside (Calif.) CC.
4. *Bob Bernardo, of-3b, Allegheny (Pa.) CC.

Dan Plesac, the last pick of the first round, went on to appear in more than 1,000 games

## MINNESOTA TWINS

**January—Regular Phase (2)**

1. Kevin Hammond, rhp, St. Petersburg (Fla.) JC.—(Rookie)
2. *David Cohen, ss, Fullerton (Calif.) JC.
3. (void) Clark Lancet, 3b, Miami-Dade CC North.
4. *Troy Thomas, of, Mount San Antonio (Calif.) JC.
5. Donnie Iasparro, rhp, Fullerton (Calif.) JC.
6. Troy Galloway, lhp, Modesto (Calif.) JC.
7. *Faustino Diaz, 3b, Miami-Dade CC New World Center.
8. *Thomas Green, rhp, Fullerton (Calif.) JC.
9. *Octavio Marante, lhp, Miami-Dade CC New World Center.
10. *Eric Schou, lhp, JC of San Mateo (Calif.).
11. *John Saylor, rhp, JC of San Mateo (Calif.).
12. *Alfredo Perez, of, Miami-Dade CC New World Center.
13. *Hugo Carballoza, rhp, Miami-Dade CC New World Center.
14. *John Nero, of, Fullerton (Calif.) JC.
15. Leo Cardenas, ss, Taft (Calif.) JC.

DRAFT DROP *Son of Leo Cardenas, major leaguer (1960-75)*

**January—Secondary Phase (20)**

1. Coe Brier, c-1b, Salisbury, N.C.—(Low A)
2. *Chip Dill, rhp, Cerritos (Calif.) JC.
3. *Steve Iannini, of, Orlando, Fla.

**June—Regular Phase (1)**

1. ***Tim Belcher, rhp, Mount Vernon Nazarene College.—(1987-2000)**

DRAFT DROP *No school; re-drafted by Yankees, January 1984/secondary phase (1st round)*

2. ***Billy Swift, rhp, University of Maine.—(1985-98)**

DRAFT DROP *Returned to Maine; re-drafted by Mariners, 1984 (1st round)*

3. Chris Forgione, of, Salesianum HS, Wilmington, Del.—(AA)
4. Tim Wiseman, rhp, UC Riverside.—(AA)
5. Jeff Trout, 2b, University of Delaware.—(AA)

DRAFT DROP *Father of Mike Trout, first-round draft pick, Angels (2009); major leaguer (2011-15)*

6. *Steve Wiley, lhp, Myers Park HS, Charlotte, N.C.
7. Tim Thompson, rhp, Cal State Fullerton.
8. Mike Verkuilen, of, University of Wisconsin.
9. David Vetsch, of, St. Cloud State (Minn.) University.
10. *Dwayne Dahl, rhp, Rush City (Minn.) HS.
11. Jim Weiss, c, New York Tech.
12. Doug Palmer, of-rhp, Creighton University.
13. Greg Cottrell, c, Oral Roberts University.
14. Matt Butcher, ss, University of Nebraska.
15. *Matt Bergeron, ss, Nicholls State University.
16. *Ken Galloway, lhp, Fresno State University.
17. Jim Pancake, c, St. Cloud State (Minn.) University.
18. Jeff Schugel, 3b, Mankato State (Minn.) University.

DRAFT DROP *Father of A.J. Schugel, major leaguer (2015)*

19. *Kent McBride, of, UC Santa Barbara.
20. *Doug Emery, of, East Mecklenburg HS, Charlotte, N.C.
21. Mike Cloninger, rhp-1b, East Lincolnton (N.C.) HS.

DRAFT DROP *Son of Tony Cloninger, major leaguer (1961-72) • Brother of Darin Cloninger, 11th-round draft pick, Padres (1983)*

22. Craig Coppola, 1b, Nicholls State University.
23. Robert Calley, c, Chino HS, Ontario, Calif.
24. Tony Diaz, of, Garden Grove (Calif.) HS.
25. Jay Johnson, of, College of St. Thomas (Minn.).
26. *Ron Johnson, rhp, Fruita Memorial HS, Grand Junction, Colo.
27. Shawn Smith, ss, UC Riverside.
28. *Mark Brown, rhp, Garden Grove (Calif.) HS.
29. Scott Klingbeil, rhp, Cal State Chico.
30. Angel Garcia, of, Bell HS, Huntington Beach, Calif.
31. *Joe Giordanella, rhp, Lindenhurst (N.Y.) HS.

**June—Secondary Phase (1)**

1. ***Oddibe McDowell, of, Arizona State University.—(1985-94)**

DRAFT DROP *First overall draft pick, June 1983/secondary phase, Twins • First-round draft pick (12th overall), Rangers (1984) • First player from 1984 draft to reach majors (May 19, 1985)*

2. Henry Gonzales, rhp, Mount San Antonio (Calif.) JC.

## MONTREAL EXPOS

**January—Regular Phase (13)**

1. Steve Moran, lhp, Triton (Ill.) JC.—(AA)
2. *Chris Huchingson, rhp, Wharton County (Texas) JC.
3. Charles Hilton, rhp, Riverside (Calif.) CC.
4. *Joe Neely, lhp, Bacone (Okla.) JC.
5. Rick Smith, c, Antelope Valley (Calif.) JC.
6. *John Ackerman, rhp, Labette (Kan.) JC.
7. Tony Nicometi, lhp, Buffalo, N.Y.
8. *William Froelich, rhp, Indian Hills (Iowa) CC.
9. *Bob Bernardo, of, Allegany (Md.) JC.
10. *Scott Clemo, ss, Gulf Coast (Fla.) CC.
11. *Cyrenius Phillips, 1b, Panola (Texas) JC.
12. (void) Bret Allen, p, DeAnza (Calif.) JC.
13. *Tim Swab, lhp, Northeastern Oklahoma A&M JC.
14. *Cordell Ross, ss, Central Arizona JC.
15. *Patrick Cummings, c, Delgado (La.) JC.
16. James Hess, rhp, Western Kentucky University.
17. Kevin Birkoffer, inf, Western Kentucky University.
18. *Gary Wright, of, Alvin (Texas) CC.

**January—Secondary Phase (17)**

1. *Robert Nettles, rhp, Orange Coast (Calif.) JC.—(Short-season A)
2. ***Ron Jones, of, Wharton County (Texas) JC.—(1988-91)**
3. *Kevin Pour, of-rhp, Belleville Area (Ill.) JC.
4. Jeff Wilpon, c, Palm Beach (Fla.) JC.

**June—Regular Phase (14)**

1. Rich Stoll, rhp, University of Michigan.—(AAA)
1. **Brian Holman, rhp, North HS, Wichita, Kan.** (Choice from Giants as compensation for Type A free agent Joel Youngblood)**—(1988-91)**
2. Jim Jefferson, rhp, Arizona State University.—(AAA)
3. Randy Ray, c, Minden (La.) HS.–(Short-season A)
4. Cas Soma, rhp, UC Irvine.—(Low A)
5. **Cliff Young, lhp, Willis (Texas) HS.—(1990-93)**
6. **Bill Moore, of-1b, Cal State Fullerton.—(1986)**
7. ***Erik Hanson, rhp, Peddie Prep, Kennelon, N.J.—(1988-98)**
8. Don Montgomery, of, Creighton University.
9. *Tim Meacham, rhp, University of Alabama.
10. Robbie Cobb, 2b, Ohio State University.
11. Tom Traen, lhp, Creighton University.
12. Gary Mahler, 1b, Rider College.
13. *Bob Latmore, ss, Deland HS, Osteen, Fla.
14. Jeff DePiano, of, Jacksonville University.
15. Gary Page, rhp, Point Loma Nazarene (Calif.) College.
16. Alan DeVall, 2b, University of La Verne (Calif.).
17. Mike Rupp, c, UC Irvine.
18. Ralph Antone, 1b, Western Kentucky University.
19. Fred Blair, 1b, Wright State University.
20. *Eddie Delzer, lhp, Cal State Fullerton.
21. Norland Claxton, 3b, Jackson State University.
22. *Loren Hibbs, of, Wichita State University.

DRAFT DROP *Baseball coach, North Carolina-Charlotte (1993-2015)*

23. *Craig Howard, lhp, Iowa State University.
24. Gary Brahs, lhp, UC Irvine.
25. Michael Fisher, rhp, Wright State University.
26. Steven Graf, of, Northwestern State University.
27. H.J. Lopes, 2b, Temple University.
28. *Randy Riley, 1b, Jacksonville University.
29. David Pascho, rhp, University of Washington.

30. J.C. Batista, ss, Southridge HS, Miami.
31. John Dodd, lhp, Canyon HS, Canyon Country, Calif.
32. David Lucas, ss, Wichita State University.
33. Shane Reilly, ss, Plantation (Fla.) HS.

**June—Secondary Phase (10)**

1. Mark Tindall, lhp, Sinclair (Ohio) CC.—(Short-season A)

## NEW YORK METS

**January—Regular Phase (3)**

1. Ralph Adams, rhp, McKeesport, Pa.—(High A)
**2. *Joe Kraemer, lhp, Lower Columbia (Wash.) JC.—(1989-90)**
3. *Miles Schuler, rhp, Santa Ana (Calif.) JC.
4. *James Eurton, c, Citrus (Calif.) JC.
5. *Henry Robinson, rhp, Lower Columbia (Wash.) JC.
6. *Rocky Lambourne, rhp, Snow (Utah) JC.
7. *Kevin Ryan, rhp, Palm Beach (Fla.) JC.
8. Reggie Dobie, rhp, Triton (Ill.) JC.
9. *Jerry Mack, 2b, Iowa Western CC.
10. Michael Houston, of, East Los Angeles JC.
11. *Carl Coates, rhp, Utah Technical JC.
12. *Greg Mooneyham, 1b, Palm Beach (Fla.) JC.
13. *Jeffrey Hintz, of, Merced (Calif.) JC.
14. *Kenneth Reed, rhp, Crowder (Mo.) JC.
15. *Rob Jones, c, Yuba (Calif.) CC.
16. David Jarman, of, JC of the Redwoods (Calif.).
17. *Samuel Thielapape, ss, Northwood (Texas) Institute.
18. Dennis Glynn, 2b, Eastern Connecticut State University.
19. *Joseph Morris, rhp, Enterprise State (Ala.) JC.

**January—Secondary Phase (3)**

1. Kevin A. Brown, lhp, Ranger (Texas) JC.—(AA)
**2. Jeff McKnight, ss, Westark (Ark.) CC.—(1989-94)**
DRAFT DROP *Son of Jim McKnight, major leaguer (1960-62)*

**June—Regular Phase (4)**

**1. Eddie Williams, 3b, Herbert Hoover HS, San Diego.—(1986-98)**
**1. Stan Jefferson, of, Bethune-Cookman College** (Choice from Braves as compensation for Type B free agent Pete Falcone)**—(1986-91)**
**1. Calvin Schiraldi, rhp, University of Texas** (Supplemental choice—27th—as compensation for loss of Type B free agent Pete Falcone)**—(1984-91)**
**2. Dave Magadan, 1b, University of Alabama.—(1986-2001)**
**3. Rick Aguilera, rhp, Brigham Young University.—(1985-2000)**
**4. David West, lhp, Craigmont HS, Memphis, Tenn.—(1988-98)**
5. *Steve Browning, c, Cook County HS, Adel, Ga.—(Short-season A)
DRAFT DROP *Attended Georgia Southern; re-drafted by Orioles, 1987 (21st round)*
**6. Marcus Lawton, ss, Harrison Central HS, Gulfport, Miss.—(1989)**
DRAFT DROP *Brother of Matt Lawton, major leaguer (1995-2005)*
7. Eric Stampfl, rhp, St. John's University.
8. Kelvin Page, rhp, DeKalb County HS, Smithville, Tenn.
9. *Gar Millay, 2b, University HS, San Diego.
10. Erick Ricketts, of-c, Soddy Daisy (Tenn.) HS.
11. Jeff Ciszkowski, rhp, Brandywine (Del.) HS.
12. *Ryan Virgo, of, Madera (Calif.) HS.
**13. Jeff Innis, rhp, University of Illinois.—(1987-93)**
14. *Bob Caffrey, c, Cal State Fullerton.
DRAFT DROP *First-round draft pick (13th overall), Expos (1984)*
15. *Barry Dacus, rhp, UC Santa Barbara.
16. Jeff Dinkel, of, Grand Canyon College.
17. *Mark Gabriel, ss-of, Niagara University.
18. *John Martin, rhp, Morro Bay HS, Los Osos, Calif.
19. Rob Colescott, ss, Deerfield Beach (Fla.) HS.
20. Bill Stiles, rhp, Comsewogue HS, Port Jefferson, N.Y.
21. Scott Bardwell, rhp, Central Washington University.
22. Charles Huggins, of, Johnson HS, Huntsville, Ala.
23. *Ed West, rhp, University of Denver.
24. *Mike Shambaugh, 1b, Jay (Okla.) HS.
25. Charles Friedel, rhp, Glassboro State (N.J.) College.
26. *Frank Velleggia, c, University of Alabama.
**27. *Matt Williams, 3b, Carson City (Nev.) HS.—(1987-2003)**
DRAFT DROP *First-round draft pick (3rd overall), Giants (1986) • Major league manager (2014-15)*
28. Chris Hayes, rhp, Davis HS, Modesto, Calif.
29. Desmond Brooks, c, Far Rockaway HS, Queens, N.Y.
30. *Mike Santiago, lhp, University of Oklahoma.
31. *Jeff Kantnor, c, Reading (Pa.) HS.
32. Corky Swindell, 2b, University of Houston.
DRAFT DROP *Brother of Greg Swindell, first-round draft pick, Indians (1986); major leaguer (1986-2002)*
33. *Scott Sellner, ss, Cordova HS, Rancho Cordova, Calif.
34. Everton Johnson, of, Samuel Gompers HS, Bronx, N.Y.
35. *Roy Caso, ss-2b, Portland (Conn.) HS.
**36. Joe Klink, lhp, Biscayne (Fla.) College.—(1987-96)**
37. *Mike Young, of, UCLA.
DRAFT DROP *Wide receiver, National Football League (1985-94)*

**June—Secondary Phase (16)**

1. *Bob Grandstaff, 3b, Golden West (Calif.) JC.—(AA)
2. Kenneth Reed, rhp, Crowder (Mo.) JC.

## NEW YORK YANKEES

**January—Regular Phase (14)**

1. *Blaine Deabenderfer, rhp, Louisburg (N.C.) JC.—(Low A)
**2. Ozzie Canseco, rhp, Miami-Dade CC South.—(1990-93)**
DRAFT DROP *Brother of Jose Canseco, major leaguer (1985-2001)*
3. *Kevin Torlai, c, Lower Columbia (Wash.) JC.
4. Tim Williams, rhp, Butte (Calif.) JC.
5. Scott Todd, 3b, Brevard (Fla.) CC.
6. *Lynn Van Every, ss, JC of Southern Idaho.
7. *Tracy Poulsen, rhp, JC of Southern Idaho.
8. Steven Fingerlow, rhp, North Tonawanda, N.Y.
9. *Philip Laws, c, Blinn (Texas) JC.
10. *Todd Persico, rhp, Mesa (Ariz.) CC.
11. *Steve Rollings, of, Edison (Fla.) JC.

**January—Secondary Phase (26)**

1. *David Rhino, of, DeKalb Central (Ga.) JC.—DNP
2. *Ed Veres, rhp, Indian River (Fla.) CC.

**June—Regular Phase (13)**

1. (Choice to White Sox as compensation for Type A free agent Steve Kemp)
2. (Choice to Reds as compensation for Type A free agent Bob Shirley)
3. (Choice to Angels as compensation for Type A free agent Don Baylor)
**4. Mitch Lyden, c, Beaverton (Ore.) HS.—(1993)**
**5. *Todd Stottlemyre, rhp, Davis HS, Yakima, Wash.—(1988-2002)**
DRAFT DROP *Attended Nevada-Las Vegas; re-drafted by Cardinals, January 1985/secondary phase (1st round, 1st pick) • Son of Mel Stottlemyre Sr., major leaguer (1964-74) • Brother of Mel Stottlemyre Jr., major leaguer (1990)*
6. *John Savage, rhp, Reno (Nev.) HS.
DRAFT DROP *Baseball coach, UC Irvine (2002-04); baseball coach, UCLA (2005-15)*
7. *Elanis Westbrooks, 2b-ss, Bellaire HS, Houston.
8. David Smalley, lhp, Florida State University.
9. *Reggie Farmer, of, Madison HS, San Diego.
10. Sam Rebiejo, rhp, San Jose State University.
11. *Paul DeJaynes, rhp, Galesburg (Ill.) HS.
12. Anthony Sarno, rhp, CC of Morris (N.J.).
13. Richard Mattocks, 2b, North Carolina Wesleyan.
14. Steve O'Donnell, ss, Oklahoma State University.
**15. Steve Frey, lhp, Bucks County (Pa.) CC.—(1989-96)**
16. Fernando Davis, lhp, Chicago Vocational HS.
**17. *Brad Brink, rhp, Downey HS, Modesto, Calif.—(1992-94)**
DRAFT DROP *First-round draft pick (7th overall), Phillies (1986)*
18. *Turner Gill, ss, University of Nebraska.
DRAFT DROP *Third-round draft pick, New York Jets/ National Football League (1984) • Quarterback, Canadian Football League (1984-85)*
19. *Mark Ambrose, ss-rhp, Wyoming (Pa.) HS.
**20. *John Hoover, rhp, Fresno State University.—(1990)**
DRAFT DROP *First-round draft pick (25th overall), Orioles (1984)*
21. Isaac Washington, 2b, Albany HS, Berkeley, Calif.
22. *Scott Raziano, 3b, University of New Orleans.
23. Greg Funk, 2b, Fresno State University.
24. Jeffrey Smith, 1b, Central State (Ohio) University.
25. *Arnold Issac, lhp, Huntsville (Texas) HS.
26. *Tommy Gross, ss, Lanier HS, Jackson, Miss.
27. *Doug Torborg, lhp, Dayton Regional HS, Mountainside, N.J.
DRAFT DROP *Son of Jeff Torborg, major leaguer (1964-73); major league manager (1977-2003)*
28. Terry Gammage, rhp, Delray Beach, Fla.
29. Louis Monte, rhp, Bishop Turner HS, Buffalo, N.Y.
30. *Mike Dotterer, of, Stanford University.
DRAFT DROP *Eighth-round draft pick, Los Angeles Raiders/National Football League (1983) • Son of Dutch Dotterer, major leaguer (1957-61)*
31. Rick Molnar, 3b-ss, University of Toledo.
32. Doug Carpenter, of, Florida International University.
33. Stanley Johnson, ss, Texas Southern University.
34. Derrick Cunningham, of, Danville (Ill.) HS.
35. *Rob Livchak, lhp, Ohio University.
36. *Jesse Long, rhp, East Lyme (Conn.) HS.
37. Francis Corbin, c, Susquehanna Valley HS, Kirkwood, N.Y.
38. *Gus Torres, of, Temple Heights Christian HS, Tampa.
39. *Leonard Nichols, c, Temple Heights Christian HS, Tampa.
**40. *Scott Arnold, rhp, Miami (Ohio) University.—(1988)**
41. Frank Thomas, rhp, Morton East HS, Cicero, Ill.
42. *Donald Lewis, rhp, Balboa HS, San Francisco.
43. *Michael Dowdy, of, Marshall HS, Chicago.

**June—Secondary Phase (9)**

**1. Brad Arnsberg, rhp, Merced (Calif.) JC.—(1986-92)**
**2. Bill Fulton, rhp, Pensacola (Fla.) JC.—(1987)**
3. *Derek Vanacore, of, Sacramento (Calif.) CC.
4. *Greg Burlingame, lhp, CC of Baltimore.
5. *Blaine Deabenderfer, rhp, Louisburg (N.C.) JC.
6. *Rod Rush, of, Allen County (Kan.) CC.
7. *Lynn Van Every, ss, JC of Southern Idaho.
8. *Chris Ritter, rhp, CC of Baltimore.

## OAKLAND ATHLETICS

**January—Regular Phase (6)**

1. Oscar DeChavez, rhp, Fullerton (Calif.) JC.—(High A)
2. *William Dudek, rhp, Central Arizona JC.
3. Darel Hansen, rhp, Riverside (Calif.) CC.
4. *James Reschke, lhp, Imperial Valley (Calif.) JC.
5. *Dale Johnson, rhp, Citrus (Calif.) JC.
6. Steve Bowens, lhp, Compton (Calif.) JC.
**7. *Jerry Goff, 1b-c, JC of Marin (Calif.).—(1990-96)**
**8. Steve Howard, of, Laney (Calif.) JC.—(1990)**
9. *Philip Braase, ss, JC of Southern Idaho.
10. *William Anderson, rhp, Los Angeles Harbor JC.
11. Maurice Castain, of, Napa (Calif.) JC.

**January—Secondary Phase (2)**

1. *Todd Welborn, rhp, Ronda, N.C.—(AA)
2. *Twain Freeman, rhp, Utica (Miss.) JC.
DRAFT DROP *Brother of Marvin Freeman, major leaguer (1986-96)*
3. Mike Wilder, 2b, St. Mary's (Calif.) College.

**June—Regular Phase (5)**

1. Stan Hilton, rhp, Baylor University.—(AAA)
2. (Choice to Red Sox as compensation for Type A free agent Tom Burgmeier)
3. John Marquardt, ss, University of Missouri.—(AA)
4. Steve Chasteen, rhp, Patrick Henry HS, San Diego.—(Rookie)
5. Brian Guinn, ss, University of California.—(AAA)
**6. *John Leister, rhp, Michigan State University.—(1987-90)**
**7. Jose Tolentino, 1b, University of Texas.—(1991)**
8. *Jeff Peterson, lhp, St. Mary's (Calif.) College.
**9. Terry Steinbach, 3b, University of Minnesota.—(1986-99)**
DRAFT DROP *Brother of Tom Steinbach, 19th-round draft pick, Mariners (1983)*
**10. Brian Dorsett, c, Indiana State University.—(1987-96)**
**11. Greg Cadaret, lhp, Grand Valley State (Mich.) College.—(1987-98)**
12. Jim Jones, c, Pepperdine University.
13. Doug Scherer, rhp, University of Arizona.
14. Twayne Harris, ss, Poly HS, Long Beach, Calif.
15. Scott Whaley, rhp, Jacksonville State University.
16. Orlando Artilles, of, University of Miami.
17. *Robert Ryley, c, St. Francis De Sales HS, Beecher, Ill.
18. *David Karasinski, lhp, Utica (Mich.) HS.
19. *Roger Lewis, rhp, Oral Roberts University.
20. *Jeff Anderson, rhp, University of Nebraska.
21. Mike Fulmer, lhp, UC Santa Barbara.
22. Lawrence Smith, lhp, California Baptist College.
**23. *Gary Wayne, lhp, University of Michigan.—(1989-94)**
24. Steve Chumas, 3b, Western Michigan University.
25. Larry Beardman, of, Cal Poly Pomona.
26. Matt Held, c, UC Riverside.
27. *Brian Leighton, of, Loyola Marymount University.
28. Camilo Pascual, rhp, University of Miami.
DRAFT DROP *Son of Camilo Pascual, major leaguer (1954-71) • Brother of Bert Pascual, 27th-round draft pick, Orioles (1983)*
29. Bob Vantrease, lhp, University of Delaware.
30. Steve Gomez, rhp, Cal Poly Pomona.
31. *Scott Schultz, 3b, Mira Costa (Calif.) JC.
32. Mike Rantz, 2b-ss, College of St. Thomas (Minn.).
33. *Steven Maunakea, rhp-of, Balboa HS, San Francisco.
34. Ralph Sheffield, of, Pepperdine University.
35. Scott Wanzer, rhp, UC Riverside.
36. *Craig Amerkhanian, lhp, University of California.

**June—Secondary Phase (7)**

**1. Rob Nelson, 1b, Mount San Antonio (Calif.) JC.—(1986-90)**
2. Mark Bauer, rhp, University of Miami.
**3. *Luis Medina, of, Cerritos (Calif.) JC.—(1988-91)**
4. Mark Leonette, rhp, Rio Hondo (Calif.) JC.
5. Joe Odom, rhp, Laney (Calif.) JC.
6. James Jackson, 1b, Laney (Calif.) JC.

## PHILADELPHIA PHILLIES

**January—Regular Phase (21)**

1. *Danny Sheeley, rhp, Crowder (Mo.) JC.—DNP
2. Billy Ferguson, rhp, Angelina (Texas) JC.
3. *William Jose, rhp, Mineral Area (Mo.) JC.
4. *Bill Jester, lhp, Seminole (Okla.) JC.
5. *Rod Rush, of, Allen County (Kan.) CC.
6. *Greg Schiffelbein, of, Allen County (Kan.) CC.
7. *Herbert Darden, rhp, Jefferson (Mo.) CC.
8. *Roy Ellis, rhp, Indian Hills (Iowa) CC.
9. *Louis Kelly, of, Angelina (Texas) JC.
10. *Chris Moritz, ss, San Jacinto (Texas) JC.
11. *Arnold Garritano, c, Kalamazoo Valley (Mich.) CC.
12. *Jeff Stewart, 1b, Kalamazoo Valley (Mich.) CC.
13. *David Greene, c-3b, Fresno (Calif.) CC.
14. Gralyn Engram, ss, Hammond, La.

**January—Secondary Phase (9)**

1. Jeff Norwood, lhp, Northwood (Texas) Institute.—(Low A)
2. Darryl Menard, rhp, Austin (Texas) CC.
3. Wayne Stewart, rhp, San Jacinto (Texas) JC.
4. *Bernie Walker, of, Navarro (Texas) JC.
5. *Rich Rosemus, lhp, Taft (Calif.) JC.

**June—Regular Phase (22)**

1. **Ricky Jordan, 1b, Grant Union HS, Sacramento, Calif.—(1988-96)**
2. Mike Colpitt, ss, Okmulgee (Okla.) HS.—(High A)
3. Wayne Dannenberg, of, East Tennessee State University.—(High A)
4. *David Lynch, lhp, Sehome HS, Bellingham, Wash.—(AAA)

DRAFT DROP *Attended New Orleans; re-drafted by Rangers, 1987 (22nd round)*

5. Ken Lewis, ss-2b, Forest Brook HS, Houston.—(Short-season A)
6. **Kevin Ward, of, University of Arizona.—(1991-92)**
7. Prince Cousinard, of, Texas Southern University.
8. ***Jeff Bronkey, rhp, Klamath Union HS, Klamath Falls, Ore.—(1993-95)**
9. Steve Moses, of, Arizona State University.

DRAFT DROP *Brother of John Moses, major leaguer (1982-92)*

10. Brian Householder, lhp, Kofa HS, Yuma, Ariz.
11. *Sherman Collins, rhp, Paden (Okla.) HS.
12. Butch Baccala, rhp, San Francisco State University.
13. ***Kevin Campbell, rhp, Des Arc (Ark.) HS.—(1991-95)**
14. Max Floyd, c, University of Texas-El Paso.
15. Bruce Long, rhp, Southwest Baptist (Mo.) University.
16. *Greg Brinkman, rhp, University of Houston.
17. *Phillip Whitten, ss, Kimball HS, Dallas.
18. Todd Adkins, ss, Elmwood HS, Wayne, Ohio.
19. Tony Evetts, rhp, Iowa State University.
20. John McLarnon, rhp, San Jose State University.
21. *Lawrence Grubb, rhp, University of South Florida.
22. David Cram, rhp, Belmont College.
23. Steven Monson, c, Chesapeake HS, Pasadena, Md.
24. **Tom Newell, rhp, Lassen (Calif.) JC.—(1987)**
25. Danny Griffen, of, Hill (Texas) JC.
26. Randy Collier, lhp, Wabash Valley (Ill.) JC.
27. Timothy Meert, c, Garces Memorial HS, Bakersfield, Calif.
28. Randy Maples, c, Bakersfield (Calif.) JC.
29. ***Mike Jackson, rhp, Forest Brook HS, Houston.—(1986-2005)**
30. Stanley Strutz, rhp, Triton (Ill.) JC.
31. Daniel Siblerud, rhp, Kalispell (Mon.) HS.

**June—Secondary Phase (12)**

1. *David Hinnrichs, rhp, Rice University.—(High A)
2. ***Mike Henneman, rhp, Oklahoma State University.—(1987-96)**
3. ***Ken Patterson, lhp, McLennan (Texas) CC.—(1988-94)**
4. Ken Longman, rhp, Sacramento (Calif.) CC.

## PITTSBURGH PIRATES

**January—Regular Phase (11)**

1. *Bill Gilmore, rhp, Pasadena (Calif.) CC.—(Low A)
2. *Ronnie Gideon, 1b, Panola (Texas) JC.
3. *Van Evans, of, Grossmont (Calif.) JC.
4. Joe Dudek, 1b, St. Clairsville, Ohio.
5. *David Leonard, ss, Ferrum (Va.) JC.
6. *Todd Fraser, of, Chabot (Calif.) JC.
7. *John Shouse, c, Cumberland (Ky.) JC.
8. Peter Davila, of, Alexandria, Va.
9. Thomas Hartman, ss, Lancaster, Pa.
10. Pat Brown, of, CC of Baltimore.
11. ***Rich Sauveur, lhp, Manatee (Fla.) JC.—(1986-2000)**
12. **Tim Drummond, rhp, Charles County (Md.) CC.—(1987-90)**
13. *Terence Guzman, lhp, Ferrum (Va.) JC.
14. Dan Smith, ss, Grossmont (Calif.) JC.

**January—Secondary Phase (13)**

1. Brian Howard, ss-2b, Rockville, Md.—(Short-season A)
2. Dean Albany, rhp, CC of Baltimore.
3. *Michael Walker, ss, Cerritos (Calif.) JC.

**June—Regular Phase (12)**

1. Ron DeLucchi, of, Campolindo HS, Moraga, Calif.—(High A)

**The Giants took Charlie Hayes, a high school player from Mississippi, in the fourth round**

THE SPORTS GROUP

2. **Stan Fansler, rhp, Elkins (W.Va.) HS** (Choice from Astros as compensation for Type A free agent Omar Moreno)**—(1986)**
2. (Choice to Cardinals as compensation for Type A free agent Gene Tenace)
3. Andy Hall, c, El Cajon (Calif.) HS.—(AAA)
4. *Tom Powers, rhp, Mount Carmel HS, South Holland, Ill.—DNP

DRAFT DROP *Attended Triton (Ill.) JC; re-drafted by White Sox, June 1984/secondary phase (1st round)*

5. *Randy Strijek, ss, Draper HS, Schenectady, N.Y.—(AA)

DRAFT DROP *Attended Western Kentucky; re-drafted by Orioles, 1986 (17th round)*

6. Boris King, 1b, Palm Springs (Calif.) HS.
7. Thad Steele, of, Western Hills HS, Cincinnati.
8. Jeff Satzinger, rhp, Coon Rapids (Minn.) HS.
9. *Matt Siuda, ss, Muskegon (Mich.) HS.
10. Scott Walker, 1b, Pleasant Grove (Vt.) HS.
11. Jack Welch, rhp, Thornton HS, Riverdale, Ill.
12. **John Smiley, lhp, Perkiomen HS, Trappe, Pa.—(1986-97)**
13. *Steve Hecht, 2b, Tulsa Union HS, Tulsa, Okla.
14. Aaron Carlie, lhp, Jackson State University.
15. *Eric Opron, 3b, St. John's HS, Geneva, Ohio.
16. Larry Johnson, of, University of Alabama-Birmingham.
17. *Ivan Hyso, rhp, Palm Springs HS, Cathedral, Calif.
18. *Oscar Talley, of, Douglas Freeman HS, Richmond, Va.
19. *David Cross, of-1b, Perth Amboy (N.J.) HS.
20. *Howard Manzon, of, CC of Morris (N.J.).
21. ***Steve Carter, of, Albemarle HS, Charlottesville, Va.—(1989-90)**
22. *Ted Williams, of, Caldwell HS, Columbus, Miss.
23. Kevin Gordon, rhp, Eastern Illinois University.
24. Curtis Thurston, of, Henderson State (Ark.) University.
25. *Perry Franklin, 3b, Junction City (Ark.) HS.
26. *Brian Kopetsky, ss, Muhlenberg HS, Laureldale, Pa.
27. *Kendall Echols, rhp, University of Maryland.
28. Kevin Letwin, lhp, University of Maryland.
29. *Lyle Swepson, ss, Southern Alamance HS, Graham, N.C.
30. *Carlos Calderon, c, Narbonne HS, Torrance, Calif.
31. *David Hellman, ss, Covington Catholic HS, Edgewood, Ky.
32. Johnny Cortez, 2b, Oklahoma City University.
33. Bryan Burrows, 3b, University of Texas.
34. Charles Carr, 1b, West Virginia State College.
35. *Wayne Webb, rhp, Mansfield (Pa.) University.

**June—Secondary Phase (4)**

1. Tony Blasucci, lhp, Florida State University.—(AAA)
2. James Eurton, c, Citrus (Calif.) JC.
3. *Ronnie Gideon, 1b, Panola (Texas) JC.
4. *Dennis Wood, of, Spartanburg Methodist (S.C.) JC.
5. **Rich Sauveur, lhp, Manatee (Fla.) JC.—(1986-2000)**
6. *Michael Walker, ss, Cerritos (Calif.) JC.
7. *John Shouse, c, Cumberland (Ky.) JC.

## ST. LOUIS CARDINALS

**January—Regular Phase (23)**

1. Jeff Perry, rhp, JC of the Canyons (Calif.).—(AAA)
2. *Jordan Stevens, 1b, Merced (Calif.) JC.
3. *Tom Seyler, rhp, Antelope Valley (Calif.) JC.
4. *Deron Johnson Jr., 3b, Grossmont (Calif.) JC.

DRAFT DROP *Son of Deron Johnson, major leaguer (1960-76)*

5. *Ronald Vara, 3b, Indian River (Fla.) CC.
6. *Scott Baker, rhp, Mesa (Ariz.) CC.
7. *Mike Trapasso, lhp, Jefferson (Mo.) JC.

DRAFT DROP *Baseball coach, Hawaii (2001-15)*

8. *Robert Jensen, rhp, Bellevue (Wash.) CC.
9. *Chris Gaeta, of, New Milford, N.J.

**January—Secondary Phase (7)**

1. *Greg Burlingame, lhp, CC of Baltimore.—(High A)
2. Jamie Brisco, rhp, Fresno (Calif.) CC.

**June—Regular Phase (24)**

1. **Jim Lindeman, 3b, Bradley University.—(1986-94)**
2. Paul Oates, lhp, Alemany HS, Granada Hills, Calif. (Choice from Pirates as compensation for Type A free agent Gene Tenace).—(Low A)
2. ***Gary Green, ss, Oklahoma State University.—(1986-92)**

DRAFT DROP *Returned to Oklahoma State; re-drafted by Padres, 1984 (1st round) • Son of Fred Green, major leaguer (1959-64)*

3. John Rigos, of, Coastal Carolina College.—(AA)
4. Kevin Whitaker, lhp, Millikan HS, Long Beach, Calif.—(Low A)
5. Mike Robinson, of, University of Arkansas.—(AAA)
6. Mark Dougherty, 2b, Florida Southern College.
7. Ted Milner, of, Biola (Calif.) University.
8. **Tom Pagnozzi, c, University of Arkansas.—(1987-98)**
9. Kurt Kaull, 3b, George Washington University.
10. *Scott Madden, lhp, University of Arkansas-Little Rock.
11. James O'Connor, c, George Penney HS, East Hartford, Conn.
12. Charles Kinard, 3b, Newberry (S.C.) HS.
13. *E.L. Ittner, rhp, U.S. International University.
14. *Justin Gannon, lhp, James Madison University.
15. *Mike Ullian, lhp, Stetson University.
16. Mike Behrend, rhp-3b, Tennessee Tech.
17. Chuck McGrath, rhp, Brown University.
18. Mark Angelo, 1b, Florida Southern College.
19. George Vogel, of, Southern Illinois University-Edwardsville.
20. Jim Reboulet, 2b, Southern Illinois University.

DRAFT DROP *Brother of Jeff Reboulet, major leaguer (1992-2003)*

21. Glenn Harris, 1b, University of Virginia.
22. Sal Agostinelli, c, Slippery Rock University.
23. Tim Kavanaugh, ss, University of Missouri.
24. **John Costello, rhp, Mercyhurst (Pa.) College.—(1988-91)**
25. Jeffrey Gass, rhp, Murray State University.
26. *Allen Sigler, of, Memphis State University.
27. Phil Burwell, rhp, Cal State Los Angeles.
28. *David Smith, c, Shaw HS, New Orleans.
29. *Dennis Hummel, ss, Oak Park HS, Gladstone, Mo.

**June—Secondary Phase (8)**

1. Tom Mauch, of, Cal Poly Pomona.—(High A)
2. Jac Hein, rhp, Southeastern Illinois JC.
3. *Bobby Joe Edmonds, of, University of Arkansas.

DRAFT DROP *Running back, National Football League (1986-95)*

## SAN DIEGO PADRES

**January—Regular Phase (9)**

1. ***Bob Milacki, rhp, Yavapai (Ariz.) JC.—(1988-96)**
2. Jeff Stewart, rhp, Martin (Tenn.) JC.
3. *Richard Murdock, rhp, Merced (Calif.) JC.
4. ***Michael A. Smith, rhp, Ranger (Texas) JC.—(1989-90)**
5. *Robert Green, of, Cochise County (Ariz.) CC.
6. ***Dennis Cook, lhp, Angelina (Texas) JC.—(1988-2002)**
7. *Dennis Carter, rhp, Middle Georgia JC.

**January—Secondary Phase (15)**

1. *John Koontz, ss, Petersburg, W.Va.—DNP
2. *Robert Cramer, lhp, Bakersfield (Calif.) JC.

**June—Regular Phase (10)**

1. **Ray Hayward, lhp, University of Oklahoma.—(1986-88)**
2. (Choice to Dodgers as compensation for Type A free agent Steve Garvey)
3. **Ed Vosberg, lhp, University of Arizona.—(1986-2002)**
4. *Todd Crosby, ss, El Camino Real HS, Woodland Hills, Calif.—(AAA)

DRAFT DROP *Attended Hawaii; re-drafted by Phillies, 1986 (5th round)*

5. Henry Hubbard, of, Wofford College.—(High A)
6. Eric Hardgrave, 1b, Stanford University.
7. Mike Mills, rhp, Birmingham-Southern College.
8. Jeffrey Parks, rhp, Yakima Valley (Wash.) JC.
9. Jay Porter, c, Mississippi State University.
10. Ken Clawson, ss, Johnson HS, Sacramento, Calif.
11. Darin Cloninger, rhp, Campbell University.

DRAFT DROP *Son of Tony Cloninger, major leaguer (1961-72) • Brother of Mike Cloninger, 21st-round draft pick, Twins (1983)*

12. *Richard McIntyre, rhp, La Junta (Colo.) HS.
13. Steve Wolff, ss, Oral Roberts University.
14. Jeff Childers, rhp, Marshall HS, Portland, Ore.
15. Marlon Hubbard, rhp, Vanderbilt University.
16. Tim McLoughlin, rhp, Davis & Elkins (W.Va.) College.
17. David Dillard, 1b, University of Washington.
18. David James, rhp, Northern Kentucky University.

**June—Secondary Phase (14)**

1. Craig Reid, ss, University of Oklahoma.—(Low A)
2. Ted Kockenmeister, lhp, Mercer County (N.J.) CC.
3. *Bill Gillmore, rhp, Pasadena (Calif.) CC.

## SAN FRANCISCO GIANTS

**January—Regular Phase (15)**

**1. *Mike Fitzgerald, c, Middle Georgia JC.—(1983-92)**
2. *Ray Rosthenhausler, ss-2b, Pima (Ariz.) CC.
3. Jesse Brew, inf, Santa Monica (Calif.) JC.
4. *Tom Meagher, rhp, West Valley (Calif.) JC.
5. *Jeff Hughes, inf, JC of the Canyons (Calif.).
6. Brian Wood, lhp, Los Angeles Pierce JC.
7. *Peter Palermo, rhp, Monroe (N.Y.) CC.
8. *Bruce Morrison, 1b, Yavapai (Ariz.) JC.
9. *Hector Berrios, of-lhp, Connors State (Okla.) JC.
10. Bill Gordon, of, JC of the Canyons (Calif.).
11. *Bob Siegel, rhp, Scottsdale (Ariz.) CC.
12. *Charles Baumann, rhp, Skyline (Calif.) JC.
13. *Steve Wood, rhp, Skyline (Calif.) JC.
14. *Hector Cano, inf, Pasadena (Calif.) CC.
15. *Eric Pawling, 3b, Moorpark (Calif.) JC.

**January—Secondary Phase (21)**

1. *Tim Criswell, rhp, DeKalb Central (Ga.) JC.—(AA)
2. *Michael Meyers, 3b, Los Angeles Pierce JC.
3. *Mike Oglesbee, 1b, Yavapai (Ariz.) JC.
4. *Gayron Jackson, of, West Los Angeles JC.

**June—Regular Phase (16)**

1. (Choice to Expos as compensation for Type A free agent Joel Youngblood)
**2. Jeff D. Robinson, rhp, Cal State Fullerton.—(1984-92)**
DRAFT DROP *First player from 1983 draft to reach majors (April 7, 1984)*
3. Don Long, 3b, Washington State University.—(AA)
**4. Charlie Hayes, 3b, Forrest County Agricultural HS, Hattiesburg, Miss.—(1988-2001)**
DRAFT DROP *Father of Ke'Bryan Hayes, first-round draft pick, Pirates (2015)*
5. Steve Smith, rhp, Baylor University.
DRAFT DROP *Baseball coach, Baylor (1995-2015)*
**6. John Burkett, rhp, Beaver (Pa.) HS.—(1987-2003)**
**7. Mike Aldrete, 1b-of, Stanford University.—(1986-96)**
8. *Michael Fay, of, Bishop Montgomery HS, Manhattan Beach, Calif.
9. Eric Lane, c, Tulane University.
10. A.J. Jones, of, San Francisco State University.
11. Dan Yokubaitis, lhp, UC Santa Barbara.
12. Deron McCue, of, Hutchinson (Kan.) CC.
13. Steve Miller, ss, Hyattsville, Md.
14. *John Reilley, rhp, Westlake HS, Westlake Village, Calif.
15. Dave Allen, of, Oral Roberts University.
16. Kurt Lee, lhp, Brigham Young University.
17. *Bobby Ralston, 2b-ss, University of Arizona.
18. *Robert Fannin, 1b, Lubbock Christian (Texas) College.
19. *Mike Pitz, rhp, Colfax (Calif.) HS.
20. Todd Oakes, rhp, University of Nebraska.
21. Charlie Corbell, rhp, University of Arkansas.
22. Jim Spring, 2b, Wichita State University.
23. George Ferran, rhp, Granada Hills (Calif.) HS.
24. Phillip Arp, 1b, Georgia College.
25. Kirk Raithel, rhp, Cal State Stanislaus.
26. Brian Fabun, ss, Mission (Calif.) JC.
27. *Michael Rooney, of, St. Viator HS, Arlington Heights, Ill.
28. Wayne Bonham, of, University of Arizona.
29. *Joey Zellner, 2b, Yakima Valley (Wash.) JC.
30. David Webb, ss, Chatsworth HS, Canoga Park, Calif.
31. Todd Thomas, of, Oregon State University.
32. Steve Gehrke, rhp, University of Nebraska.
33. *Jack Pool, 3b-1b, Mercer University.
34. Ken Ritter, of, Kennedy HS, Granada Hills, Calif.
35. *John Paye, of, Menlo HS, Atherton, Calif.
DRAFT DROP *Tenth-round draft pick, San Francisco 49ers/National Football League (1987)*

**June—Secondary Phase (2)**

**1. Robby Thompson, ss, University of Florida.—(1986-96)**
2. *Steve Eagar, c, Brigham Young University.
3. *Kight Higgins, rhp, Seminole (Okla.) JC.

## SEATTLE MARINERS

**January—Regular Phase (8)**

1. Keith Komeiji, c, Orange Coast (Calif.) JC.—(Low A)
2. *Jeff Osterode, lhp, Orange Coast (Calif.) JC.
3. Sam Haley, of, Front Royal, Va.
4. *Ken Altona, lhp, Bellevue (Wash.) CC.
5. *Edward Clark, rhp, Golden West (Calif.) JC.
6. *Joe Mitchum, rhp, Yakima Valley (Wash.) JC.

**January—Secondary Phase (18)**

1. *Marty Lanoux, 2b, Santa Fe (Fla.) CC.—(AAA)

**June—Regular Phase (7)**

**1. Darrel Akerfelds, rhp, Mesa (Colo.) College.—(1986-91)**
DRAFT DROP *Brother of Duane Akerfelds, 22nd-round draft pick, Mariners (1983)*
**1. Terry Bell, c, Old Dominion University** (Choice from White Sox as compensation for Type A free agent Floyd Bannister)**—(1986-87)**
**2. Mickey Brantley, of, Coastal Carolina College.—(1986-89)**
DRAFT DROP *Father of Michael Brantley, major leaguer (2009-15)*
**3. Dave Hengel, of, University of California.—(1986-89)**
**4. Bill Wilkinson, lhp, Cherry Creek HS, Englewood, Colo.—(1985-88)**
DRAFT DROP *First 1983 high school draft pick to reach majors (June 13, 1985)*
5. Bob Hinson, rhp, Lubbock Christian (Texas) College.—(High A)
**6. Scott Nielsen, rhp, Brigham Young University.—(1986-89)**
7. John Wallace, of, University of Southern California.
8. *Mark Hamann, rhp, McNary HS, Salem, Ore.
9. Bob Gunnarsson, lhp, University of Southern California.
10. Billy Wrona, ss, University of Miami.
DRAFT DROP *Brother of Rick Wrona, major leaguer (1988-94)*
11. Mickey Meister, rhp, University of Southern California.
12. Frank Tunnell, ss, Grand Canyon College.
13. *Jay Hunt, lhp, Washington State University.
14. *Reggie Hammonds, of, Northwestern University.
DRAFT DROP *Brother of Jeffrey Hammonds, first-round draft pick, Orioles (1992); major leaguer (1993-2003)*
15. Bob Bruzik, ss, Quinnipiac College.
16. Ed Salazar, lhp, Lewis-Clark State (Idaho) College.
17. Oriol Perez, of, Florida International University.
18. James Bryant, rhp, William Carey (Miss.) College.
19. Tom Steinbach, of, University of Minnesota.
DRAFT DROP *Brother of Terry Steinbach, major leaguer (1986-99); ninth-round draft pick, Athletics (1983)*
20. Brad Colton, of, University of Maine.
21. Jeff Lawson, 1b, Phillips (Okla.) University.
22. *Duane Akerfelds, rhp, Columbine HS, Littleton, Colo.
DRAFT DROP *Brother of Darrel Akerfelds, first-round draft pick, Mariners (1983); major leaguer (1986-91)*
23. Doug Swearingen, lhp, Ohio State University.
24. Paul Smith, 1b, UC Santa Barbara.
25. *Jeff Kambak, c, Loyola Marymount University.
26. George Priftis, 2b, University of Virginia.
**27. Rick Luecken, rhp, Texas A&M University.—(1989-90)**
DRAFT DROP *First-round draft pick (18th overall), Giants (1979)*
28. Gary Balmer, 3b, Lewis-Clark State (Idaho) College.
29. *William King, ss, Proviso East HS, Maywood, Ill.
30. *Orlando Martinez, of-3b, Rockhurst HS, Castle City, Mo.
31. *Mike McIlvaine, rhp, University of Delaware.
32. *Randy Luciani, rhp, Windham HS, Willimantic, Conn.
33. Ben Amaya, 3b, University of Nebraska.
34. *Dan Ducusin, of, Chaparral HS, Scottsdale, Ariz.

**June—Secondary Phase (23)**

1. *Jose Rodiles, rhp, Arizona State University.—(AA)
2. *Dennis Carter, of, Chipola (Fla.) JC.
3. *Jerry Mack, 2b, Iowa Western CC.

## TEXAS RANGERS

**January—Regular Phase (4)**

**1. Javier Ortiz, 1b, Miami-Dade CC South.—(1990-91)**
2. Mike Soper, lhp, Winthrop, Mass.
3. *Mickey Ballou, of, Long Beach (Calif.) CC.
4. *Franklin Brandt, ss, Kankakee (Ill.) CC.
5. *Joe Odom, rhp, Laney (Calif.) JC.
6. *Bret Davis, lhp, DeAnza (Calif.) JC.
7. Robin Keathley, rhp, Modesto (Calif.) JC.
8. Brad Jones, c, Dallas.
9. *Charles Wood, rhp, Louisburg (N.C.) JC.
10. *Thomas Arrington, rhp, JC of Marin (Calif.).
11. *Kevin Hooper, rhp, Ranger (Texas) JC.
12. *Thomas Henderson, ss, Spartanburg Methodist (S.C.) JC.
**13. *Mark Higgins, 1b, Chipola (Fla.) JC.—(1989)**

**January—Secondary Phase (12)**

**1. *Alex Madrid, rhp, Yavapai (Ariz.) JC.—(1987-89)**
2. *Eduardo Gonzalez, c, Miami.

**June—Regular Phase (3)**

**1. Jeff Kunkel, ss, Rider College.—(1984-92)**
DRAFT DROP *Son of Bill Kunkel, major leaguer (1961-63); American League umpire (1968-84)*
2. George Threadgill, of, Whiteville (N.C.) HS.—(AAA)
**3. Randy Asadoor, 3b, Fresno State University.—(1986)**
4. Thomas Jackson, ss, Indio HS, Palm Desert, Calif.—(Low A)
**5. Bob Sebra, rhp, University of Nebraska.—(1985-90)**
6. Bill Hance, c, University of Missouri.
7. Kirk Killingsworth, rhp-of, University of Texas.
8. John Harrington, rhp, Alcorn State University.
9. Steve Kordish, rhp, Princeton University.
10. Bruce Kipper, lhp, Grand Canyon College.
11. *Tim Raley, c, Potomac Senior HS, Triangle, Va.
12. *Thomas Kelley, of, Marist HS, Chicago.
13. Kerry Burns, rhp, Oklahoma City University.
14. Greg Bailey, of, Washington State University.
15. *Eloy Gil, c, Miami Springs HS, Hialeah, Fla.
16. Anthony Carlucci, c, University of Rhode Island.
17. David Linton, lhp, Musselman HS, Inwood, W.Va.
18. Reggie Mosley, 1b, Arizona State University.
19. Dan Simpson, of, University of Southern Colorado.
20. Vince Sakowski, 3b, Stanford University.
21. Dennis Knight, rhp, James Madison University.
22. Mark Gile, 2b, University of Kansas.
23. *Mike Yastrzemski, of, Florida State University.
DRAFT DROP *Son of Carl Yastrzemski, major leaguer (1961-83)*
24. David Harman, rhp, University of New Orleans.
25. Ricky Hester, ss-of, Clemson University.
26. Ron Hansen, c, Santa Clara University.
27. John Andrade, 2b, Towson State University.
28. Mark Cipres, rhp, University of the Pacific.
29. Roger Lawrence, 1b, Dallas Baptist University.
30. Nick Esposito, rhp, University of California.
31. Bret Elbin, 3b, University of Alabama.
32. *Stu Rogers, lhp, Georgia Tech.
33. Regan Bass, rhp, Washington State University.
34. Jim Cesario, of, University of New Orleans.
35. Mark Novak, rhp, Middle Tennessee State University.
36. *William Warren, c, Connors State (Okla.) JC.
37. *Joe Heeney, 3b, University of Kansas.
38. James Mart, c, Texas Wesleyan College.
**39. *Les Lancaster, rhp, University of Arkansas.—(1987-93)**
40. Wayne King, 1b, Virginia Tech.
41. Rick Knapp, rhp, Virginia Tech.
42. Glen Davis, 1b, University of Georgia.
43. John Munley, rhp, James Madison University.
44. Marty Blair, ss, The Citadel.
45. *Clay Damon, 3b, Lewis & Clark HS, Spokane, Wash.
46. Mike Keehn, 2b, Kearney State (Neb.) College.
47. Fred Lovely, of, Central Florida CC.
48. *Kevin Penner, of, Wichita State University.
49. *Michael Reeves, of, James Madison University.
50. *Brad Hill, of, Emporia State (Kan.) University.

**June—Secondary Phase (26)**

1. *Ray Rosthenhausler, ss, Pima (Ariz.) CC.—(Class A)
**2. *Jody Reed, ss, Florida State University.—(1987-97)**
**3. *Mark Higgins, 1b, Chipola (Fla.) JC.—(1989)**
4. *Marty Lanoux, 2b, Santa Fe (Fla.) CC.

## TORONTO BLUE JAYS

**January—Regular Phase (10)**

1. Howard Akers, of, Gulf Coast (Fla.) CC.—(High A)
2. *Scott Hamilton, rhp, Seminole (Okla.) JC.
3. *Scott Sempier, 3b, CC of Morris (N.J.).
4. *John Baumgartner, lhp, CC of Morris (N.J.).
5. *William Cunningham, c, Chipola (Fla.) JC.
6. *Mark White, of, Laney (Calif.) JC.
7. *Eric Tutt, 1b, East Mississippi JC.
8. *John Hegwood, lhp, University of San Francisco.
9. Duane Miller, rhp, University of North Dakota.
10. *Keith Hoskison, c, St. Louis CC-Meramec.
11. *Todd Edwards, ss, Lake Michigan (Mich.) JC.
12. *Jeff Corbally, of, Lower Columbia (Wash.) JC.
13. *Paul Mason, of, Chabot (Calif.) JC.
14. Greg Ferlenda, rhp, Onondaga (N.Y.) CC.

**January—Secondary Phase (14)**

1. *Mike Young, lhp, Los Angeles Harbor JC.—(AA)
2. Rob Holbrook, rhp, Oregon State University.

**June—Regular Phase (9)**

**1. Matt Stark, c, Los Altos HS, Hacienda Heights, Calif.—(1987-90)**
**2. Webster Garrison, ss, Ehrat HS, Marrero, La.—(1996)**
**3. Jeff DeWillis, c, Pearland (Texas) HS.—(1987)**
**4. Jeff Hearron, c, University of Texas.—(1985-86)**
5. Alan McKay, lhp, Baylor University.—(AAA)
6. Tom Linkmeyer, ss, Marian (Ind.) College.
7. Drex Roberts, of, University of North Carolina.
8. Ken Whitfield, ss-of, Minden (La.) HS.
**9. Glenallen Hill, of, Santa Cruz (Calif.) HS.—(1989-2001)**
10. *Durrell Schoenly, lhp, Boyertown (Pa.) HS.
**11. *Mike Raczka, lhp, University of New Haven.—(1992)**
12. Rob Emerson, rhp, Fresno State University.
13. *Bruce Carter, of, East St. John HS, Mount Airy, La.
14. Ronnie Robbins, rhp, Louisiana State University.
15. Jeff Thompson, ss, Mercer University.
16. Denny Murray, rhp, Florida International University.
17. *Chris Miller, ss, Sheldon HS, Eugene, Ore.
DRAFT DROP *First-round draft pick, Atlanta Falcons/National Football League (1987); quarterback, NFL (1987-99)*
18. *Jim Van Houten, rhp, American International (Mass.) College.
19. Mark Clemons, rhp, Coastal Carolina College.
20. Mark Dickman, rhp, University of Houston.
21. Mike Werner, lhp, University of South Carolina.
22. *Tim Becker, ss, Manheim Central HS, Lititz, Pa.
23. *Don Enoch, rhp, Delran (N.J.) HS.

**June—Secondary Phase (5)**

1. Otis Green, of-1b, Miami-Dade CC North.—(AAA)
2. *Mike Clarkin, rhp, Normandale (Minn.) CC.
3. *Mike Trapasso, lhp, Jefferson (Mo.) CC.
DRAFT DROP *Baseball coach, Hawaii (2001-15)*
4. *Charlie Baumann, rhp, Skyline (Calif.) JC.
5. *Keith Hoskison, c, St. Louis CC-Meramec.

1984

AT A GLANCE

### This Date In History

**WINTER DRAFT:** Jan. 17-18
**SUMMER DRAFT:** June 4-6

### Best Draft

**CHICAGO CUBS.** Between them, **GREG MADDUX** (2) and **JAMIE MOYER** (6) had 48 years of major league service.

### Worst Draft

**MILWAUKEE BREWERS. ISAIAH CLARK** (1) hurt his knee playing basketball as a high school junior, and sure enough, he tore ligaments in the same knee 15 games into his pro career, needed reconstructive surgery and missed the next year and a half. He lasted only two more years in the Brewers system and never made it beyond Class A. **JOHN JAHA** (14) was the only return from 61 players the team drafted.

### First-Round Bust

**TOM HARTLEY, OF, WHITE SOX.** Hartley, the second of two first-round picks by the White Sox, hit just .218 in three minor league seasons. The Sox gave up on him on July 15, 1986, when they traded him to the Brewers in a deal for major leaguer Ray Searage, but he never reported to the Brewers.

### On Second Thought

**TOM GLAVINE, LHP, BRAVES/GREG MADDUX, RHP, CUBS.** The future Hall of Famers were overlooked in the first round—Glavine because of concerns he might pursue a hockey career; Maddux because of his undersized frame. Both went on to win 300 games in the majors.

### Late Round Find

**JEFF FASSERO, LHP, CARDINALS (22ND ROUND).** Fassero won 121 games over a 16-year major league career, a significant feat considering he signed with the Cardinals for just $1,500, and was released twice by other clubs before making his major league debut seven years later at age 28.

# Loaded Olympic team dominates first round

They were labeled the best amateur baseball team ever assembled in the United States. It was the original dream team.

For seven weeks in the summer of 1984, 20 of the nation's best college prospects, many of them recently minted first-round draft picks, were united on a team that barnstormed through the country on their way to Los Angeles for the Olympic Games, where baseball was a demonstration sport. The players enjoyed a wave of success and popularity never before seen in the U.S. beyond the major leagues.

While Team USA lost to Japan 6-3 in the gold-medal game, played before a capacity crowd at Dodger Stadium, there was little mistaking the talent on that 31-5-1 team.

"I think everyone knows that it was the best amateur baseball team ever put together," said first baseman Mark McGwire, an Oakland Athletics draft pick who later established the major league single-season home run record. "I don't think there ever has been, or ever will be a team to match it. If you ask anybody on the team, they'll say the same thing."

The impact the 1984 Olympic team had on the draft was underscored by the fact that 18 of the 20 players on the roster were first-round picks. Thirteen were drafted in 1984; the remaining five a year later.

A unique arrangement between Major League Baseball and the U.S. Baseball Federation, the governing body for amateur baseball, created the best Team USA possible. Big league clubs agreed to let drafted players selected to the Olympic squad spend the summer with Team USA before embarking on their professional careers. In some cases, players signed contracts before their participation in the Olympics; in other cases, they didn't.

"Baseball is an Olympic sport this summer," Texas Rangers minor league director Tom Grieve said, "and it's only fitting for the U.S. to put its best team on the field. If we had our choice, of course, we'd like to get all of our kids signed and playing immediately.

"But considering the circumstances, we can make the best of it. I don't think it's a bad situation, a group of young college kids with the opportunity to represent their country."

Grieve's Rangers, who signed 34 of their first 35 draft picks in the June regular phase, had two players on the team: outfielder Oddibe McDowell, a first-rounder, and pitcher Sid Akins, a third-rounder. Both delayed the start of their professional careers until 1985 in order to participate.

## MCGWIRE LEADS OLYMPIC CLASS

As talented as the 1984 Olympic squad was, success wasn't as easy to come by in the professional ranks for most of its players. Three members of the team didn't even reach the majors.

ASSOCIATED PRESS

Unable to agree on the parameters of a deal with Mark McGwire, the Mets took high school slugger Shawn Abner with the No. 1 overall pick, but he was never more than a big league journeyman

Of the 15 Olympians selected in the 1984 draft, only the University of Southern California's McGwire was an unqualified success—though fans discovered later that his career had been aided by the use of performance-enhancing drugs. Still, McGwire hit a major league rookie record of 49 homers in 1987 with the A's, and a major league record 70 in 1998 with the St. Louis Cardinals. Over a 16-year career, he went deep 583 times. McGwire led the college ranks in 1984 with 32 homers, shattering the USC record of 19 he had set a year earlier.

The New York Mets had the No. 1 selection in the 1984 draft and initially targeted McGwire. But the two sides couldn't agree on the parameters of a contract on the eve of the draft, and the Mets switched their choice away from McGwire to Pennsylvania prep outfielder Shawn Abner.

Abner was only too happy to sign with the Mets and was awarded the largest bonus paid out that year, $150,500, but his six-year career in the majors paled in comparison to McGwire, who received $145,000 from the A's as the 10th pick.

Beyond McGwire, the only Olympian in the 1984 draft class to play more than 10 years in the majors was righthander Billy Swift (Mariners, second overall). He spent 15 years in the big leagues and won 21 games for the San Francisco Giants in

## 1984: THE FIRST ROUNDERS

| CLUB: PLAYER, POS., SCHOOL | HOMETOWN | B-T | HT. | WT. | AGE | BONUS | FIRST YEAR | LAST YEAR | PEAK LEVEL (YEARS) |
|---|---|---|---|---|---|---|---|---|---|
| **JUNE—REGULAR PHASE** | | | | | | | | | |
| 1. Mets: Shawn Abner, of, Mechanicsburg HS | Mechanicsburg, Pa. | R-R | 6-0 | 185 | 17 | $150,500 | 1984 | 1995 | Majors (6) |
| Mets preferred Mark McGwire, compromised on prep product on signability issue; traded to Padres two years later, hit .227-11-71 in disappointing six-year career. | | | | | | | | | |
| 2. Mariners: Billy Swift, rhp, Maine | South Portland, Me. | R-R | 6-1 | 175 | 22 | $90,000 | 1985 | 1998 | Majors (13) |
| Second-rounder in 1983 became second pick a year later; won 27 college games, led Maine to 4 straight CWS trips, debuted in majors in 1985, went 94-78, 3.95. | | | | | | | | | |
| 3. Cubs: Drew Hall, lhp, Morehead State | Rush, Ky. | L-L | 6-5 | 200 | 21 | $119,000 | 1984 | 1994 | Majors (5) |
| Late bloomer surged up draft boards on strength of 94 mph fastball, 9-1, 2.18 season with 105 SO/70 IP; late Olympic team cut, went only 9-12, 5.21 in majors. | | | | | | | | | |
| 4. Indians: Cory Snyder, ss, Brigham Young | Canyon Country, Calif. | R-R | 6-3 | 175 | 21 | $137,700 | 1985 | 1995 | Majors (9) |
| Enrolled at BYU as pitcher, became three-time All-America SS with .429 career average, 73 HRs; never quite fulfilled early promise in majors, hit .247 with 149 HRs. | | | | | | | | | |
| 5. Reds: Pat Pacillo, rhp, Seton Hall | Rutherford, N.J. | R-R | 6-2 | 205 | 20 | $135,000 | 1985 | 1990 | Majors (2) |
| Better in college as OF (.356-27-156) than on mound (12-3, 11 SV, 97 IP/131 SO), but Reds preferred mid-90s FB; produced only 4-3, 5.90 big league mark. | | | | | | | | | |
| 6. Angels: Erik Pappas, c, Mount Carmel HS | Chicago | R-R | 6-0 | 185 | 18 | $110,000 | 1984 | 1996 | Majors (3) |
| Hit .487-7-30, threw out every basestealer as prep SR; spent 13 years in pro ball on strength of power, receiving skills, hit .242-1-35 in limited look with Cubs, Cards. | | | | | | | | | |
| 7. Cardinals: Mike Dunne, rhp, Bradley | Bartonville, Ill. | L-R | 6-4 | 195 | 21 | $116,000 | 1985 | 1994 | Majors (5) |
| Showed vast improvement in junior season (8-2, 2.44) at Bradley; had best big league season with Pirates in '93 (13-6, 3.03), but overall was 25-30, 4.08. | | | | | | | | | |
| 8. Twins: Jay Bell, ss, Gonzalez Tate HS | Pensacola, Fla. | R-R | 6-1 | 175 | 18 | $125,000 | 1984 | 2003 | Majors (18) |
| Played 18 seasons in majors, none with Twins, who traded him to Indians for Bert Blyleven in 1986; homered off Blyleven in first MLB AB, hit career .265-195-860. | | | | | | | | | |
| 9. Giants: Alan Cockrell, of, Tennessee | Knoxville, Tenn. | R-R | 6-2 | 210 | 21 | $82,500 | 1984 | 1996 | Majors (1) |
| Two-year starting QB for Volunteers chose Giants offer vs. returning for senior year; took 12 years to reach majors, played 1,414 games in minors, nine in MLB. | | | | | | | | | |
| 10. Athletics: Mark McGwire, 1b, Southern California | Claremont, Calif. | R-R | 6-5 | 215 | 20 | $145,000 | 1984 | 2001 | Majors (16) |
| Began college career as pitcher, twice set USC season records for HR (19 in 1983, 32 in 1984), MLB mark for rookies (49 in 1987) on way to historic career as slugger. | | | | | | | | | |
| 11. Padres: Shane Mack, of, UCLA | Cerritos, Calif. | R-R | 6-0 | 190 | 20 | $115,000 | 1985 | 1998 | Majors (9) |
| Career .361-29-142 mark at UCLA, consensus best college talent in '84 draft; struggled early with Padres, found his stride with Twins, hit .299-80-398. | | | | | | | | | |
| 12. Rangers: Oddibe McDowell, of, Arizona State | Hollywood, Fla. | L-L | 5-9 | 170 | 21 | $113,000 | 1985 | 1995 | Majors (7) |
| Hit .405-23-74 with 36 SBs for ASU before getting drafted for a sixth time, reached Rangers after just 31 games in minors; MLB totals: .253-74-266, 179 SB. | | | | | | | | | |
| 13. Expos: Bob Caffrey, c, Cal State Fullerton | Fullerton, Calif. | R-R | 6-1 | 185 | 22 | $95,000 | 1984 | 1988 | Class AA (1) |
| Three-year starter at QB for Titans, quit football as SR, led Titans to CWS title on strength of 28-HR, 90-RBI season; went from boom to bust as pro, hit .234-37-161. | | | | | | | | | |
| 14. Red Sox: # John Marzano, c, Temple | Philadelphia | R-R | 5-10 | 180 | 21 | $100,000 | 1985 | 1999 | Majors (10) |
| Unsigned Twins third-rounder in 1981 improved stock on strength of .448-15-61 season for Temple; backup catcher for 10 years in majors, hit .241-11-72. | | | | | | | | | |
| 15. Pirates: Kevin Andersh, lhp, New Mexico | Albuquerque, N.M. | R-L | 6-3 | 185 | 20 | $103,000 | 1984 | 1989 | Class AA (1) |
| Had live arm with 90-plus fastball, but plagued by control issues throughout career; set UNM career record with 17 losses, went 26-40, 4.18 in five pro seasons. | | | | | | | | | |
| 16. Royals: Scott Bankhead, rhp, North Carolina | Reidsville, N.C. | R-R | 5-10 | 170 | 20 | $95,000 | 1985 | 1995 | Majors (10) |
| Set UNC record with 20 straight wins (9-0 as SO, 11-0 as JR), pitched 10 years in majors for five clubs; went 57-48, 4.18, but career plagued by shoulder issues. | | | | | | | | | |
| 17. Astros: Don August, rhp, Chapman (Calif.) College | Mission Viejo, Calif. | R-R | 6-3 | 190 | 20 | $100,000 | 1985 | 1995 | Majors (4) |
| Division II All-American, Olympic team member after 16-4, 1.81 season; dealt to Brewers in '86, went 13-7, 3.09 as '87 rookie, but lost velo, sharpness on curve. | | | | | | | | | |
| 18. Brewers: Isaiah Clark, ss, Crockett HS | Crockett, Texas | R-R | 6-1 | 180 | 18 | $110,000 | 1984 | 1990 | Class AA (1) |
| Power-hitting SS hit .500-13-49 as prep SR; tore knee ligaments 15 games into first pro season, career stalled while brothers Phil and Jerald reached majors. | | | | | | | | | |
| 19. Braves: # Drew Denson, 1b/of, Purcell Marian HS | Cincinnati | B-R | 6-5 | 205 | 18 | $106,000 | 1984 | 1996 | Majors (2) |
| Top scorer in Cincinnati prep basketball ranks also known for tape-measure homers; won Gulf Coast League triple crown in pro debut, but career fizzled out. | | | | | | | | | |
| 20. White Sox: Tony Menendez, rhp, American HS | Carol City, Fla. | R-R | 6-2 | 195 | 19 | $90,000 | 1984 | 1995 | Majors (3) |
| Cuban-born hurler went 33-8, 0.51 in prep career but rarely displayed same fastball in 12-year pro career; went 3-1, 4.97 in 23 major league games. | | | | | | | | | |
| 21. Phillies: Pete Smith, rhp, Burlington HS | Burlington, Mass. | R-R | 6-2 | 170 | 18 | $92,500 | 1984 | 1999 | Majors (11) |
| Prep contemporary of Tom Glavine soon joined future Hall of Famer with Braves; career dented by arm problems, but pitched 11 MLB seasons, going 47-71, 4.55. | | | | | | | | | |
| 22. Yankees: Jeff Pries, rhp, UCLA | Newport Beach, Calif. | R-R | 6-5 | 200 | 21 | $92,500 | 1984 | 1987 | Class AAA (1) |
| Son of Scouting Bureau assistant director; two-way player for Bruins, spent six years as pitcher in Yankees system, went 24-21; torn rotator cuff ended career. | | | | | | | | | |
| 23. Dodgers: Dennis Livingston, lhp, Oklahoma State | North Reading, Mass. | L-L | 6-0 | 180 | 21 | $100,000 | 1984 | 1991 | Class AAA (3) |
| Went 33-8 in college, despite 229 BBs in 293 IP; control issues plagued pro career, walked 349 in 469 IP while going 24-36, 5.13, released by Dodgers in 1988. | | | | | | | | | |
| 24. Giants: Terry Mulholland, lhp, Marietta (Ohio) Coll. | Uniontown, Pa. | R-L | 6-3 | 200 | 21 | $65,000 | 1984 | 2006 | Majors (20) |
| Used 30-3, 2.37 record at Division III level to propel him to 20-year MLB career; played for 12 clubs, went 124-142, 4.41; known for all-time great pickoff move. | | | | | | | | | |
| 25. Orioles: # John Hoover, rhp, Fresno State | Fresno, Calif. | R-R | 6-3 | 200 | 21 | $87,500 | 1984 | 1990 | Majors (1) |
| Top college arm in 1984 (18-3, 2.09, 177 IP/205 SO), Olympic team ace, but heavy workload left him with dead arm; pitched two games in majors in 1990. | | | | | | | | | |
| 26. White Sox: Tom Hartley, of, Hudson's Bay HS | Vancouver, Wash. | R-R | 6-5 | 210 | 18 | $65,000 | 1984 | 1986 | Class A (1) |
| Compared by area scouts to Dale Murphy because of size, speed, power potential, athleticism, but pro career was big disappointment; hit .218-2-40 in 162 games. | | | | | | | | | |
| **JANUARY—REGULAR PHASE** | | | | | | | | | |
| 1. Mariners: Calvin Jones, rhp, Chaffey (Calif.) JC | Riverside, Calif. | R-R | 6-2 | 180 | 20 | $45,000 | 1984 | 1996 | Majors (2) |
| Left UC Riverside for juco; reached Seattle in eighth pro year, went 5-7, 4.33; hung on in minors until 1996, later pitched in Mexico, indy leagues through 2002. | | | | | | | | | |
| **JANUARY—SECONDARY PHASE** | | | | | | | | | |
| 1. Yankees: Tim Belcher, rhp, Mount Vernon Nazarene | Sparta, Ohio | R-R | 6-3 | 200 | 22 | $113,000 | 1984 | 2000 | Majors (14) |
| Top pick in 1983 by Twins went unsigned, became property of Yankees, then A's in extraordinary chain of events; went 146-140 overall with seven teams. | | | | | | | | | |
| **JUNE—SECONDARY PHASE** | | | | | | | | | |
| 1. Mets: Tommy Hinzo, 2b, Southwestern (Calif.) JC | Chula Vista, Calif. | R-R | 5-10 | 170 | 19 | Unsigned | 1986 | 1995 | Majors (2) |
| Unsigned as third pick in January (Indians), finally signed after leading Arizona to 1986 CWS title; had brief major league career, spent 10 years in minors. | | | | | | | | | |

*# Deceased.*

## AT A GLANCE

### Never Too Late

**DON WAKAMATSU, C, YANKEES (51ST ROUND).** The last player taken in the 1984 draft, Wakamatsu carved out a long career as a player, coach and manager, including an 18-game stint as a backup catcher for the White Sox in 1991.

### Overlooked

**BERNARD GILKEY, OF, CARDINALS.** Gilkey was better known for his basketball skills at St. Louis' University City High and had committed to playing that sport at Drake. But he spent the summer playing baseball in a local senior men's league and then in the National Baseball Congress World Series. He signed with the Cardinals for $15,000 on Aug. 22 and went on to play 12 years in the majors, hitting .275 with 118 homers.

### International Gem

**LARRY WALKER, OF, EXPOS.** The Dodgers signed shortstop **CRAIG SHIPLEY**, an Australian who played in college at Alabama, for $83,000, but the most noteworthy foreign player signed in 1984 was Walker. A native of Maple Ridge, B.C., Walker signed with the Expos for $1,500 and played 17 seasons in the majors, the first six in Montreal, while winning three batting titles. Overall, he hit .313 with 383 home runs.

### Minor League Take

**ALAN COCKRELL, OF GIANTS.** Cockrell gave up his senior year as the quarterback at Tennessee to sign with the Giants. On Sept. 7, 1996, at age 33, he finally made his big league debut—marking the longest time for a first-rounder to reach the majors to that point in draft history. Cockrell played in nine games with the Rockies and retired. In 1,414 games in the minors, including 10 seasons in Triple-A, Cockrell hit .278 with 141 homers.

CONTINUED ON PAGE 290

## AT A GLANCE

CONTINUED FROM PAGE 289

### Ones Who Got Away

**MIKE HARKEY, RHP, PADRES (18TH ROUND); JACK MCDOWELL, RHP, RED SOX (20TH ROUND).** Harkey and McDowell were California high school products deemed unsignable because of college commitments to Cal State Fullerton and Stanford. Three years later, they became the first two college selections in the draft. Harkey went to the Cubs with the fourth pick overall; McDowell to the White Sox with the fifth.

### He Was Drafted?

**RODNEY PEETE, SS, BLUE JAYS (30TH ROUND).** Peete was viewed as a potential first-round pick out of a Kansas high school in 1984 and during his college career at USC, but in the end baseball played second fiddle to football. He finished second in the 1988 Heisman Trophy balloting and played 16 years in the NFL. He was selected four times in the baseball draft from 1984-90, though never higher than the 13th round (1989).

### Did You Know . . .

**GREG MADDUX** and **TOM GLAVINE** were taken 16 picks apart in the second round—Maddux, by the Cubs with the 31st pick; Glavine, by the Braves with the 47th pick. Maddux wore uniform No. 31 with the Cubs (and later with the Braves), while Glavine had uniform No. 47 as a Brave.

### They Said It

Agent **BOB COHEN**, on the decision by the Mets to pass on his client, **MARK MCGWIRE**, with the No. 1 overall pick: "They put pressure on him the day before the draft to sign. They wanted him to do a contract that day, and he said, 'I'm not going to do a contract that day.' The Mets made a big mistake, period."

1993, but was more of a workmanlike pitcher over the balance of his career, going 73-70.

Catcher John Marzano (Red Sox, 14th overall) and righthander Scott Bankhead (Royals, 16th) played 10 years, while infielder Cory Snyder (Indians, fourth) and outfielder Shane Mack (Padres, 11th) played nine. Snyder and Mack, along with McGwire, were the highest-profile college talents in the 1984 class.

The lone member of the fabled Olympic team to achieve Hall of Fame status was University of Michigan shortstop Barry Larkin, the fourth overall pick in the 1985 draft. He spent most of the summer and Olympic tournament as a backup, playing behind second baseman Flavio Alfaro (Braves, fourth round) and shortstop Gary Green (Padres, supplemental first round). Larkin was one of the more vocal critics about the selection process itself and the way he was used.

"There were some politics in it, that's for sure," Larkin said. "It could have been done a lot better. I knew going in that there were a lot of good players, but I still thought I'd be playing almost every day. I don't know if that was optimistic or not, but I wasn't even given a chance."

The first four picks in the 1985 draft were Olympians, and they generally outplayed their 1984 counterparts—both for Team USA and later at the professional level. Mississippi State first baseman Will Clark led Team USA in hitting (.397) and home runs (16). Oklahoma righthander Bobby Witt topped the team with a 0.69 ERA while going 3-0. He had the best raw stuff on the staff and struck out 36 in 26 innings, but like Larkin was relegated to mostly a secondary role.

The only members of the Olympic team who didn't play in the big leagues were catcher Bob Caffrey (Expos, 13th overall), and the two non-first-rounders, Akins and Alfaro.

Caffrey's career was undermined by shoulder injuries, and he played only briefly in Double-A. Akins topped out in Triple-A, while Alfaro played only a single season of pro ball, in Class A. He was packaged by the Atlanta Braves to the Milwaukee Brewers in a deal involving major leaguers Ted Simmons and Rick Cerone following the 1985 season, but retired in a dispute with Brewers management over which level he would play.

### METS GO IN DIFFERENT DIRECTION

While most of the focus in the 1984 draft was on the Olympic team, the Mets had the first pick overall for the fourth time in draft history and elected to go for the 6-foot-1, 190-pound Abner. They made their final decision when they couldn't get a commitment from McGwire a night earlier, in a lengthy phone conversation with the player and his father.

Abner worked out with the Mets that afternoon at Shea Stadium, and had a feeling they would take him No. 1 when they called him that night to make sure he arrived home safely.

"I have watched Shawn play in the American Legion all-star game since his sophomore year," Mets scouting director Joe McIlvaine said. "He's a big, strong kid, physically mature for a 17-year-old. He has quickness, power, runs well, and is an above-average outfielder with a strong arm."

Abner was a .400-plus hitter in each of his first three years at Mechanicsburg High, but took his game to a new level as a senior by hitting .580 with 10 doubles, 10 triples, eight home runs and 31 RBIs in 28 games, breaking records his older brother Ben had set three years earlier. Ben, then a junior at Georgia Southern, was a finalist for the Olympic team and had his own hopes of becoming a first-round pick at the outset of the 1984 season. But he slipped to the fifth round, even as he slugged 27 homers as a college junior.

The Mets selected Shawn, an all-state quarterback who had committed to play football at the University of Georgia, with the intent of converting him to a shortstop. McIlvaine said Abner had the natural ability to make it to the big leagues as a center fielder, but the possibility of a shortstop with his offensive capabilities was too intriguing.

"He's got great movement and speed," McIlvaine said. "He's already a good center fielder, but it would be interesting to have a shortstop with his power."

Abner never played shortstop for the Mets, but at 19, as a non-roster player in major league spring training, he impressed club officials by slamming two homers (one off former Mets star Tom Seaver) and driving in seven runs in his first game. Overall he hit .350 for the spring, but he had a disap-

## How They Should Have Done It

Based on the career WAR (Wins Above Replacement, as calculated by Baseball-Reference.com) numbers achieved by all the players eligible for the 1984 draft, here's how the first round should have unfolded. Numbers in parentheses indicate the round when the player was actually drafted

| | Player, Pos. | Actual Draft | WAR | Bonus |
|---|---|---|---|---|
| 1. | Greg Maddux, rhp | Cubs (2) | 106.8 | $75,000 |
| 2. | Tom Glavine, lhp | Braves (2) | 81.4 | $80,000 |
| 3. | Mark McGwire, 1b | Athletics (1) | 62.0 | $145,000 |
| 4. | Jamie Moyer, lhp | Cubs (6) | 50.4 | $13,000 |
| 5. | Al Leiter, lhp | Yankees (2) | 40.2 | $85,000 |
| 6. | Jay Bell, ss | Twins (1) | 37.0 | $125,000 |
| 7. | Ken Caminiti, 3b | Astros (3) | 33.3 | $35,500 |
| 8. | Lance Johnson, of | Cardinals (6) | 30.1 | $18,000 |
| 9. | Tim Belcher, rhp | Yankees (Jan.-S/1) | 26.2 | $113,000 |
| 10. | Jeff Fassero, lhp | Cardinals (22) | 24.1 | $1,500 |
| 11. | Jay Buhner, of | Pirates (Jan.-S/2) | 22.8 | $33,000 |
| 12. | Shane Mack, of | Padres (1) | 21.6 | $115,000 |
| 13. | Bernard Gilkey, of | Cardinals (NDFA) | 21.5 | $15,000 |
| 14. | Billy Swift, rhp | Mariners (1) | 20.9 | $90,000 |
| | Jeff Blauser, ss | Braves (June-S/1) | 20.9 | $55,000 |
| 16. | Mike Jackson, rhp | Phillies (Jan.-S/2) | 19.4 | $7,500 |
| 17. | Jody Reed, 2b | Red Sox (8) | 15.7 | $15,000 |
| 18. | Jeff Nelson, rhp | Dodgers (22) | 15.2 | $7,500 |
| 19. | Mike Henneman, rhp | Tigers (4) | 13.2 | $20,000 |
| 20. | Bryan Harvey, rhp | Angels (NDFA) | 12.6 | $2,500 |
| 21. | John Jaha, 3b | Brewers (14) | 12.4 | $25,000 |
| 22. | Scott Bankhead, rhp | Royals (1) | 11.4 | $95,000 |
| 23. | Terry Mulholland, lhp | Giants (1) | 11.3 | $65,000 |
| 24. | Oddibe McDowell, of | Rangers (1) | 10.6 | $113,000 |
| 25. | Norm Charlton, lhp | Expos (1) | 8.4 | $85,000 |
| 26. | Darren Holmes, rhp | Dodgers (16) | 7.6 | $8,500 |

| | Top 3 Unsigned Players | | | Year Signed |
|---|---|---|---|---|
| 1. | Chuck Finley, lhp | Angels (15) | 58.4 | 1985 |
| 2. | Mark Grace, 1b | Twins (Jan.-R/15) | 46.1 | 1985 |
| 3. | Greg Vaughn, of | Brewers (June-S/4) | 30.6 | 1986 |

pointing 1986 season at Double-A Jackson (.266 with 14 home runs) that caused the Mets to sour on him.

After three years in the Mets system, Abner was packaged to the San Diego Padres in an eight-player deal that brought veteran outfielder Kevin McReynolds to New York. While he hit .281 with 41 homers in his minor league career with the Mets, Abner's long swing and lack of plate discipline had become a source of consternation to Mets officials, and they regarded him as no more than a fourth outfielder.

That proved true in San Diego as Abner fought a losing battle to hold a big league job. Playing parts of four seasons with the Padres, he hit .207 with eight homers and 46 RBIs in 254 games, and closed out an underwhelming six-year career with the California Angels and Chicago White Sox.

"Shawn was a very advanced 17-year-old," said McIlvaine, who inherited Abner when he became the Padres general manager. "He had everything you'd ever want. He had all the tools and that great makeup. Who wouldn't want him? But Shawn's problem is his swing got too long and he became his own worst enemy."

As Abner struggled, McGwire's star continued to rise until it peaked in 1998. He turned the baseball world on its ear that year with his slugging exploits while smashing one of the game's most sacred home run records.

### HIGH SCHOOL VS. COLLEGE

In a draft where a record-low 253 high school players were selected, the Mets went against the grain by drafting Abner first, and high school selections with their first eight picks and 16 of their first 17.

"It's pretty much been our philosophy to take high school players since I've been here," said McIlvaine, who became the Mets' scouting director in 1980. "We feel it is in our best interests to get players as young as we can so we can work them in our system longer."

"We feel we have much more to offer. We have a longer season than in college, and we feel we can offer them much better instruction within our own system. We don't necessarily set out to draft just high school players, but we do prefer to get a player as young as possible."

Seattle, picking right after the Mets, went for a heavy college emphasis. The Mariners took Swift, a college senior from Maine, with their first pick and college players with their first 21 selections.

Neither the Mets nor Mariners had much suc-

## Fastest To The Majors

| | Player, Pos. | Drafted (Round) | Debut |
|---|---|---|---|
| 1. | Oddibe McDowell, of | Rangers (1) | May 19, 1985 |
| 2. | Billy Swift, rhp | Mariners (1) | June 7, 1985 |
| 3. | Scott Bankhead, rhp | Royals (1) | May 25, 1986 |
| 4. | Greg Mathews, lhp | Cardinals (10) | June 3, 1986 |
| 5. | Terry Mulholland, lhp | Giants (1) | June 8, 1986 |

**FIRST HIGH SCHOOL SELECTION:** Greg Maddux, rhp (Cubs/2, Sept. 3, 1986)

**LAST PLAYER TO RETIRE:** Jamie Moyer, lhp (May 27, 2012)

### DRAFT SPOTLIGHT: MARK MCGWIRE

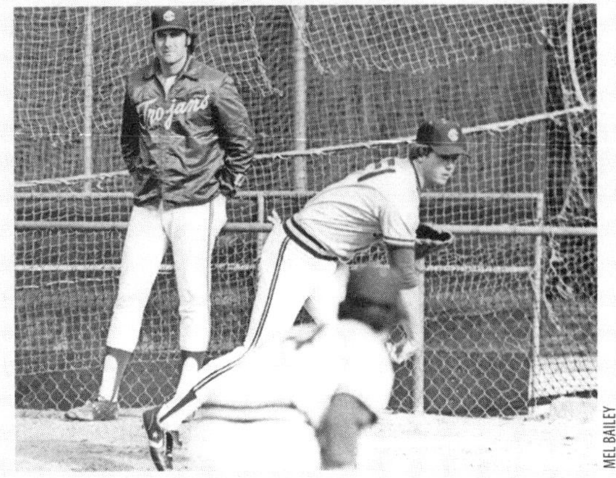


MEL BAILEY

Mark McGwire's path to standout major league slugger began with a stint as a pitcher at USC, and turned in the right direction in the Alaska League

Mark McGwire didn't just set home run records. He shattered them.

As a junior in 1984 at the University of Southern California, he hammered 32 homers—smashing his own record of 19, set a year earlier. As a rookie in 1987 with the Oakland Athletics, he bashed 49—easily toppling the major league first-year mark of 38. As a slugging first baseman in 1998 for the St. Louis Cardinals, he pounded 70—obliterating the single-season standard of 61, set 37 years earlier by Roger Maris.

But had McGwire not trekked off to Alaska in the summer of 1982, the baseball world may never have known about McGwire the slugger. As a high school player at Damien High in Claremont, Calif., as an eighth-round draft pick of the Montreal Expos in 1981 and as a freshman at USC, McGwire was a pitcher, first and foremost. Yet Trojans hitting coach Ron Vaughn would often watch the 6-foot-5 McGwire demonstrate his raw power during batting practice and wonder what he might accomplish as a hitter.

McGwire went 4-4, 3.04 on the mound and hit a feeble .200 with three homers in limited looks as a hitter in his freshman year. That summer Vaughn was an assistant coach with the Alaska League's Anchorage Glacier Pilots, and when the team lost two of its projected first basemen, Vaughn recommended that McGwire, who had been recruited to play for the team as a pitcher, fill the void. He not only convinced skeptical head coach Jim Dietz that the inexperienced McGwire would be a suitable replacement, but promised him that he would make McGwire his own personal project for the summer.

Vaughn sold McGwire on the merits of his plan, but before he had an opportunity to put it into practice, the fragile McGwire had second thoughts about playing in remote Alaska. "I was away from home for the first time in my life with a group of people I didn't know," McGwire recalled years later. "I didn't have the support of my family and girlfriend, and I went through a very bad period of homesickness."

McGwire was so distraught that he broke down and cried in front of Dietz, who had to work to keep McGwire from catching the next plane home. "He just wanted someone to cave and let him go home," said Dietz, who refused to accommodate his wish. "This was a make-or-break situation. There are always those defining moments in players' careers, and this was one of them."

Dietz, who had a long and successful career coaching summer-league teams in Alaska and at San Diego State, convinced McGwire that he had a future as a hitter. He reminded him that major league sluggers Dave Winfield and Dave Kingman had made the transition in Alaska in summers past. McGwire could relate to Kingman's situation as he also arrived on the USC campus, a dozen years earlier, as a hard-throwing righthander with the capability of driving the ball out of the park on occasion.

Vaughn tutored McGwire daily, spending hours on end with him in the batting cage. Slowly but surely, McGwire began to quicken his swing and maximize his power potential; he also became a more complete hitter by recognizing pitchers and working counts.

"He was a big, strapping kid who had a decent swing," Vaughn recalled. "But he needed a lot of work, which he was willing to put in no matter how much was asked of him."

McGwire had a breakout summer, hitting .403 with 13 home runs, and showered praise on Vaughn and Dietz for all their work with him. "(Dietz) never benched me for a game—even if I was playing poorly," McGwire said. "He let me work my way out of slumps. He also made a few adjustments in my swing which gave me a short, fast stroke."

Dietz deflected most of the credit for McGwire's emergence as one of the game's great sluggers to Vaughn, both in Alaska, and after the pair returned home to California.

"I can guarantee you that if Mark had stayed a pitcher, he wouldn't have anything close to the success he's had. He'd probably be out of baseball by now," said Dietz, retelling the McGwire story in the midst of his magical chase to 70 homers. "Because he had someone like Ron who championed him early on, Mark was really blessed."

## WORTH NOTING

The January draft, three years away from being abolished, got a new twist for junior-college players in 1984. In the past, big league clubs were permitted to sign juco talent prior to the start of their spring season, but an amendment to the draft rules prohibited such signings, in effect protecting junior-college programs from the willful signing of players until the team had completed play in the spring. "The old rule was ridiculous," said Miami-Dade North Community College coach Demie Mainieri, who had more players drafted over the life of the January draft than any coach in history. "It got to the point where I was losing two or three starters every year. In some cases, I'd lose them a day before the season started. I'll still lose some of them in June, but at least I can sleep before the season starts."

Cal State Fullerton beat Texas 3-1 to win the 1984 College World Series. The Titans tied Arizona State for most players drafted in June, with 13.

In both the January and June drafts, the team that selected first in the regular phase also had the No. 1 selection in the secondary phase. In January, the Reds had the top pick in both phases; the Mets followed suit in June. It was merely a coincidence that the same team ended up with the top pick in the secondary phase as the order in that phase was drawn randomly.

Shortstop **ISAIAH CLARK** was the first-round pick of the Brewers in 1984 out of Crockett (Texas) High; his older brother **JERALD**, an outfielder from Lamar University, was also drafted, by the Dodgers in the 23rd round though didn't sign until re-drafted by the Padres in the 12th round a year later; younger brother Phil, a catcher from Crockett High, was a first-round selection of the Tigers in 1986 (also 18th overall). Jerald played seven years in the majors and

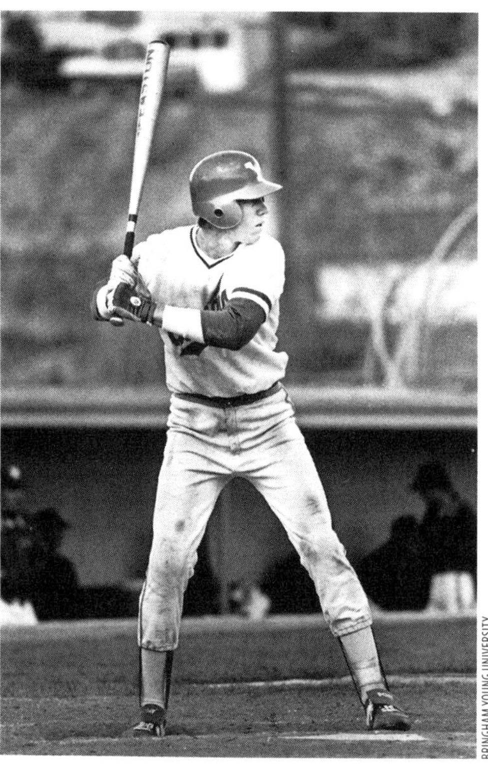

BRIGHAM YOUNG UNIVERSITY

**Cory Snyder was a record-setting hitter at Brigham Young, but after a fast start to his big league career he never fulfilled that promise**

## Top 25 Bonuses

| | Player, Pos. | Drafted (Round) | Order | Bonus |
|---|---|---|---|---|
| 1. | ***Shawn Abner, of** | **Mets (1)** | **1** | **$150,500** |
| 2. | **Mark McGwire, 1b** | **Athletics (1)** | **10** | **$145,000** |
| 3. | **Cory Snyder, 3b** | **Indians (1)** | **4** | **$137,000** |
| 4. | **Pat Pacillo, rhp** | **Reds (1)** | **5** | **$135,000** |
| 5. | ***Jay Bell, ss** | **Twins (1)** | **8** | **$125,000** |
| 6. | **Drew Hall, lhp** | **Cubs (1)** | **3** | **$119,000** |
| 7. | **Mike Dunne, rhp** | **Cardinals (1)** | **7** | **$116,000** |
| 8. | **Shane Mack, of** | **Padres (1)** | **11** | **$115,000** |
| 9. | **Tim Belcher, rhp** | **Yankees (Jan.-S/1)** | **(1)** | **$113,000** |
| | **Oddibe McDowell, of** | **Rangers (1)** | **12** | **$113,000** |
| 11. | ***Erik Pappas, c** | **Angels (1)** | **6** | **$110,000** |
| | *Isaiah Clark, ss | Brewers (1) | 18 | $110,000 |
| 13. | ***Drew Denson, of** | **Braves (1)** | **19** | **$106,000** |
| 14. | Kevin Andersh, lhp | Pirates (1) | 15 | $103,000 |
| 15. | **John Marzano, c** | **Red Sox (1)** | **14** | **$100,000** |
| | **Don August, rhp** | **Astros (1)** | **17** | **$100,000** |
| | Dennis Livingston, lhp | Dodgers (1) | 23 | $100,000 |
| 18. | **Scott Bankhead, rhp** | **Royals (1)** | **16** | **$95,000** |
| | Bob Caffrey, c | Expos (1) | 13 | $95,000 |
| 20. | Jeff Pries, rhp | Yankees (1) | 22 | $92,500 |
| | ***Pete Smith, rhp** | **Phillies (1)** | **21** | **$92,500** |
| 22. | ***Tony Menendez, rhp** | **White Sox (1)** | **20** | **$90,000** |
| | **Billy Swift, rhp** | **Mariners (1)** | **2** | **$90,000** |
| 24. | **John Hoover, rhp** | **Orioles (1)** | **26** | **$87,500** |
| 25. | **Norm Charlton, lhp** | **Expos (1-S)** | **28** | **$85,000** |
| | ***Al Leiter, lhp** | **Yankees (2)** | **50** | **$85,000** |

*Major leaguers in bold. *High school selection.*

cess with their approaches. Swift was the only player Seattle drafted in the June regular phase, among 40 selections overall, who reached the majors.

A record 20 first-rounders from 1984, including the top 12, reached the big leagues. None accomplished more than McGwire, though shortstop Jay Bell (Twins, eighth overall) and lefthander Terry Mulholland (Giants, 24th) had longer careers.

Bell, who hit .265 with 195 homers over 18 seasons, was traded to the Cleveland Indians little more than a year after being drafted by the Twins, in a package deal that included future Hall of Famer Bert Blyleven. A year later, Bell made big league history when he homered on the first pitch he saw, off none other than Blyleven. It was also the 47th homer Blyleven allowed in 1986, setting a new major league mark.

Mulholland's career lasted 20 years, during which he played for 12 different big league clubs.

But the careers of most of the other first-rounders, like Abner's, fell short of expectations.

Lefthander Drew Hall was drafted third overall by the Chicago Cubs after making significant strides as a junior at Morehead State. A big, gawky pitcher with major control issues when he entered college, Hall posted a 9-1, 2.10 record in 1984, while fanning 105 in 70 innings. In one outing against Eastern Kentucky, he struck out 19, overpowering his opponent with his newfound 94-mph fastball. Hall's career stalled out in Chicago as he went just 3-4, 6.41 over a three-year period from 1986-88.

### SNYDER ENDS UP DISAPPOINTING

Cory Snyder was Cleveland's first selection in the 1984 draft, the fourth pick overall. He was signed to a $137,700 bonus, the largest in club history.

His career began with as much promise as any player in the class, and some of his early home run exploits surpassed those of McGwire, though his career tapered off even more quickly.

Like McGwire, Snyder was primarily a pitcher at a California high school. He won 14 games as a senior with a fastball that peaked at 91 mph, and his intentions were to become primarily a pitcher in college at Brigham Young. But Snyder was also the kind of talent who changed opinions in a hurry, especially when it came to his true calling.

As a freshman in 1982 for BYU, Snyder hit the first three pitches he saw for home runs, all off Nevada-Las Vegas righthander Joe Boever, a future big leaguer. He abandoned pitching and went on to rewrite a number of NCAA batting records. As a junior at BYU, he hit .450 with 27 homers and 85 RBIs and set NCAA records for single-season (.900) and career slugging percentage (.844).

His 73 career homers were second all-time in the college ranks—and 19 more than McGwire hit at USC. Snyder also hit 22 homers in the summer of 1983, setting a still-standing Cape Cod League record, and 10 more homers the following summer for Team USA.

Because of the Olympics, it wasn't until instructional league that the Indians got their first close-up look at Snyder. That's when he really got Cleveland people talking. "He's the finest all-around athlete we've signed in my 12 years with the club," Indians farm director Bob Quinn said.

Snyder batted .390 with 14 homers and 53 RBIs, all instructional league bests by wide margins. "Head and shoulders above everyone else," Indians manager Pat Corrales said. "He's some-

## Largest Bonuses By Round

| | Player, Pos. | Club | Bonus |
|---|---|---|---|
| 1. | * **Shawn Abner, of** | **Mets** | **$150,500** |
| 2. | * **Al Leiter, lhp** | **Yankees** | **$85,000** |
| 3. | * **Greg Myers, c** | **Blue Jays** | **$68,000** |
| 4. | **Kent Anderson, ss** | **Angels** | **$37,500** |
| 5. | Ben Abner, of | Expos | $50,000 |
| 6. | * Larry Pardo, rhp | Rangers | $35,000 |
| 7. | Bill Jester, lhp | Phillies | $30,000 |
| 8. | * Chuck Donahue, ss | Reds | $30,000 |
| 9. | Four tied at | | $20,000 |
| 10. | * Brian Morrison, of | Blue Jays | $30,000 |
| **Other** | * **Zach Crouch, lhp** | **Red Sox (13)** | **$25,000** |
| | * **John Jaha, 3b** | **Brewers (14)** | **$25,000** |
| Jan/R. | Dave Martinez, rhp | Angels | $60,000 |
| **Jan/S.** | **Tim Belcher, rhp** | **Yankees (1)** | **$113,000** |
| **Jun/S.** | **Jeff Blauser, ss** | **Braves (1)** | **$55,000** |

*Major leaguers in bold. *High school selection.*

thing special."

So anxious were the downtrodden Indians to get Snyder's bat in the major league lineup that they gave him a crash course at second base. Though he had never played the position before, he went to spring training in 1985 as a candidate to be the Opening Day starter at the position. But the experiment quickly was aborted, and when Snyder reached Cleveland a month into the 1986 season, he had become a right fielder.

"He's the best prospect I've ever had as a manager," Corrales said after Snyder had been in the big leagues less than a month. "Nobody else is even close. You're not talking about just a good player, but a top quality player. A Mike Schmidt type."

"Arm-wise," said Indians coach Bobby Bonds, "there is nobody in either league that can throw with him."

Snyder did display major league power and an exceptional throwing arm over most of his first five seasons with the Indians, but his star began to fade in 1989 when pitchers exposed him as an undisciplined hitter obsessed with pulling the ball for power. A .244 average, with 652 strikeouts in 657 games, had a way of taking the shine off, and Snyder's career with the Indians ended with a thud. He lasted only four more seasons, playing with four different clubs.

If Snyder's career was viewed as a disappointment, then so were those of the two most decorated college performers in the 1984 class: McDowell, the Arizona State outfielder who won the 1984 Golden Spikes Award, and Fresno State righthander John Hoover, who led NCAA pitchers in wins and strikeouts.

Even Mack, the consensus best college talent at the outset of the 1984 season, was considered a disappointment during his time in San Diego until he resurrected his career with a change of scenery in Minnesota.

McDowell hit .405 with 23 homers and 74 RBIs and stole 36 bases for Arizona State—a significant uptick on his performance from a year earlier as a junior, when he was drafted first overall by the Twins in the June secondary phase, but went unsigned. Drafted for the sixth time in 1984 when the Rangers took him with the 12th pick, McDowell was the first of the Olympians to reach the big leagues. He became the Rangers' center fielder after a 31-game trial in Triple-A to start the 1985 season.

While the 5-foot-9, 160-pound McDowell energized a struggling Rangers club initially with his speed and surprising power for a player his size, his career fell short of expectations overall as he soon drifted from the Rangers to Cleveland to Atlanta. In seven big league seasons, he hit .253 with 74 homers and 169 stolen bases.

Hoover, a lowly 20th-round draft pick in 1983 after a modest 7-4 season for Fresno State, elevated himself to the first round in 1984 (Orioles, 25th overall) by going 18-3, 2.09 with 205 strikeouts in 177 innings for the Bulldogs as a senior. He was also anointed the ace of the Olympic squad, and worked a team-high 60 innings over the course of the summer, posting a 4-2, 1.62 record.

But Hoover, a breaking-ball specialist, absorbed the loss for the U.S. in the gold-medal game, and his career was never quite the same. Even with his heavy workload during the spring and summer, the Orioles assigned Hoover to Triple-A to close out the 1984 season, and he started four more games. He then participated in instructional league.

Hoover went a combined 12-21, 5.13 over the next two seasons, backtracking from Double-A in 1985 to Class A a year later. In 1986, he worked in just 61 innings for three teams in the O's system, walked 55 and struck out just 25. A year later, the Orioles traded him to Montreal. The Expos released him after a year.

Hoover saw his only big league service with the Rangers in 1990, amounting to two games and five innings, before that club also released him.

### MADDUX, GLAVINE COME IN SECOND

For all the emphasis on college talent in the first round, two players selected in the second round, future Hall of Fame pitchers Greg Maddux and Tom Glavine, gave clubs reason to remain open-minded on the viability of high school talent.

Maddux, an undersized righthander from Nevada, was selected by the Cubs, while Glavine, a Massachusetts-reared lefthander, went 16 picks later to the Braves. For 10 years in the heart of their careers, they were acclaimed teammates in Atlanta.

Greg Maddux

The Cubs discovered Maddux in 1983, while following one of his teammates at Valley High in Las Vegas, but even when they scouted him in earnest a year later, when he was a frail 5-foot-11 and 155 pounds, it took a discerning eye and a lot of conviction on the part of Cubs scouts to commit to a bonus of $75,000 for Maddux.

"I really believe this boy would possibly be the No. 1 player taken in the country if only he looked a bit more physical," read the report written by Cubs area scout Doug Mapson. "He throws

## WORTH NOTING

Phil played five, but a severe knee injury prevented Isaiah, generally regarded as the most talented of the three brothers, from achieving his big league dream.

■ Led by the contingent of Olympic team players, the 1984 draft had more college players selected in the first round (18) than any draft in history. That topped the previous record of 17, set in 1981. Even the Reds, who had never spent their first pick on a college player since the draft's inception in 1965, joined the converts by selecting Seton Hall's **PAT PACILLO**, a two-way talent, with the fifth pick overall. The Reds chose to develop Pacillo as a pitcher, even though he spent most of his college career as a hitter. As a junior at Seton Hall, Pacillo threw 35 innings, though he had 56 strikeouts. As a hitter, he slammed 27 homers and drove in 152 runs in his career. Pacillo also cracked the Olympic team as a pitcher, a tribute to his impressive raw stuff. But he pitched sparingly for the team and his pro career never took off. He spent parts of the 1987-88 seasons with the Reds, but went a combined 4-3, 5.90. Languishing in the minors in 1990, he expressed a desire to move back to the outfield, but that never came to pass. There were actually five college players selected in the round who did not make the Olympic roster. None had much success in their pro careers, though Morehead State lefthander **DREW HALL**, the third pick overall, pitched in the big leagues over parts of five seasons. Outfielder **ALAN COCKRELL** (Giants, ninth overall) played nine games in the majors—all in 1996, at the end of a nomadic career in the minors. New Mexico lefthander **KEVIN ANDERSH** (Pirates, 15th overall), UCLA righthander **JEFF PRIES** (Yankees, 22nd) and Oklahoma State lefthander **DENNIS LIVINGSTON** (Dodgers, 23rd) all failed to reach the majors—or even come close.

CONTINUED ON PAGE 294

## WORTH NOTING

CONTINUED FROM PAGE 293

■ Established on Sept. 1, 1974, the Major League Scouting Bureau achieved its goal of full membership by all major league clubs 10 years to the day later—after a resolution at the 1983 Winter Meetings requiring all 26 clubs to belong. "I've never been a supporter of the bureau," said Dodgers scouting director **BEN WADE**. "We were forced into it. "We've always been successful the way we've done it, so why change?"

■ The Blue Jays didn't have a first-round pick in 1984, but targeted Massachusetts prep lefthander **TOM GLAVINE** in the second round (48th overall). The Braves snatched the future Hall of Famer one pick earlier. The Jays decided to take little-known righthander **DANE JOHNSON**, who went 1-2, 6.89 that spring at Florida's St. Thomas University. The 6-foot-6 Johnson was much better known as a basketball player. "I played Little League baseball until I was 13, but I didn't play again until my freshman year in college," Johnson said. "I was just concentrating on basketball and track in high school. The whole thing is a little weird. I might have had a chance to get drafted by the NBA if I had finished my senior year, but right now baseball is my only interest." Johnson went 22-32, 6.17 with 252 walks and 211 strikeouts in 369 innings in his six seasons in the Blue Jays minor league system, all at the Class A level, before drawing his release. Undaunted, Johnson spent the next two seasons pitching in Taiwan, before signing with the Brewers as a free agent in 1993. Another year and another team later, Johnson's persistence paid off as he reached the majors with the White Sox, and two years after that played briefly with the Blue Jays—12 years after the club drafted him. Johnson hooked on with the Jays as a roving minor league pitching instructor once his playing career was finished and became Toronto's bullpen coach in 2015.

86-89 consistently with very good movement. His movement isn't a gradual tailing type, but a quick, explosive, bat-breaking kink. He has a big league curve right now, although he needs to be a little more consistent with it. He threw a couple this day that were 79 mph, tight, down-breaking well-located pitches. I don't think I've ever seen a 10 curve, but these several pitches come about as close as you are going to get."

Beyond the scouting report, Mapson was impressed with Maddux's flawless mechanics, unflappable demeanor, pitching intelligence and textbook approach, and the ease with which he carved up opposing hitters without overpowering stuff.

"He threw so easily," Mapson said. "Scouts would question his velocity. I'd get 85-87 on the slow gun, but one day in the eighth inning of a seven-inning game, he needed a strikeout. I swear the pitch hit 90. When he needed that extra something, it was always there."

Tom Glavine

Mapson knew the Cubs would never spend the third pick in the draft on a high school righthander with Maddux's build. But the Cubs, at Mapson's prompting, were committed to drafting Maddux. They simply had to keep their fingers crossed until their turn came around in the second round. When it did, they grabbed the unassuming righthander, who would go on to win more games than any high school pitcher in the draft era.

In Glavine's case, his talent and overall package were an easier sell in the first round, but he had a tricky career decision to make that caused clubs to take a cautious approach. Within five days in early June, he was drafted by both the Braves and the National Hockey League's Los Angeles Kings (fourth round).

Competition for his services enabled Glavine to extract an $80,000 signing bonus from the Braves, but it cost him any shot at going in the first round. He was the 52nd-ranked player by the NHL's Central Scouting Bureau, and his ties to hockey scared off several teams.

"It wasn't the money so much as the fear that he'd decide to turn around and play hockey if he had some adjustment problems," Braves scouting director Paul Snyder said.

But to Glavine, a two-time Massachusetts player of the year in both hockey and baseball, it was really no decision at all.

"It was a difficult decision as far as what was really best," Glavine said. "But I looked at the longevity of what a career would be, and baseball was the way to go. It would have been baseball anyway. I've dreamed of playing professionally for a long time.

"The decision never was whether to play hockey. The decision was whether to go to college. I had a full scholarship to the University of Lowell. That was the big thing. Four years of college for free."

Glavine had few problems adjusting to professional baseball and surfaced in the big leagues right on schedule in 1987. But the Braves were one of the weakest teams in the game his first two years, and he endured his share of growing pains. In 1988, he went 7-17 and led the National League in losses. By 1989, he developed into one of the game's top lefthanders, largely because of the implementation of his trademark circle changeup, a pitch he discovered almost by accident while shagging balls in the outfield one day during spring training. Two years later, when he won 20 games for the first of five times, he had established his reputation for his stoic approach and unflappable demeanor on the mound.

When Maddux joined Glavine in 1993, the two pitchers thrived with their uncanny ability to trick hitters and manipulate all points of the strike zone with their impeccable control. Their presence provided the resurgent Braves with a dynamic duo atop the rotation, enabling the club to win an unprecedented 13 division titles in 14 years.

### YANKEES TRIPPED UP BY RULING

The January draft took on a renewed interest in 1984 because of the inclusion of pitcher Tim Belcher, who was the first pick in the draft the previous June by the Twins, but went unsigned.

Belcher elected not to return for his senior season to Ohio's Mount Vernon Nazarene College, making him eligible for selection in the secondary phase in January. He was snapped up quickly by the New York Yankees, who by luck of the draw had first pick. Almost as a matter of routine, they signed Belcher to a contract for $113,000.

"Considering we didn't have a shot at him last June, we're obviously delighted to get him now," said Bill Bergesch, the Yankees vice president of baseball operations. "We, of course, knew about him last June and we had good reports on him then, but we knew we'd never get a shot at him. We were so pleasantly surprised just to even get a No. 1 pick. It's been several years since we've had a No. 1."

The Yankees exhilaration at landing a player of Belcher's stature, however, would soon turn to agony and disbelief when Belcher was lost almost immediately to the A's in baseball's short-lived compensation draft.

Oakland was entitled to compensation, under

### One Team's Draft: Atlanta Braves

| Player, Pos. | Bonus | Player, Pos. | Bonus | Player, Pos. | Bonus |
|---|---|---|---|---|---|
| **1. *Drew Denson, 1b/of** | **$106,000** | 5. *Bob Pfaff, c | $32,500 | 9. Vince Barger, lhp | $19,000 |
| **2. *Tom Glavine, lhp** | **$80,000** | 6. Rob Sepanek, 1b | $12,500 | 10. *Leon Wright, ss | $12,000 |
| 3. Matt Rowe, rhp | $30,000 | 7. Greg Johnson, rhp | $11,500 | **Other Jeff Blauser (S/1), ss** | **$55,000** |
| 4. Flavio Alfaro, ss | $13,000 | 8. Rick Siebert, rhp | $7,500 | | |

*Major leaguers in bold. *High school selection*

## Highest Unsigned Picks

**JUNE/REGULAR PHASE ONLY**

| Player, Pos., Team (Round) | College | Re-Drafted |
|---|---|---|
| Curt Krippner, rhp, Reds (2) | Texas | Brewers '87 (2) |
| Kurt Dempster, rhp, Indians (2) | Arizona State | Indians '87 (30) |
| Todd Brown, of, Indians (3) | * Arizona State | Brewers '85 (5) |
| John Verducci, ss, Twins (3) | * Stanford | Giants '85 (5) |
| Kevin Garner, rhp/of, Expos (3) | Texas | Padres '87 (1) |
| Mo Sanford, rhp, Yankees (3) | Alabama | Reds '88 (32) |
| Larry Melton, rhp, Padres (4) | * Portland | Pirates '85 (8) |
| Scott Ruskin, of/lhp, Rangers (4) | * Florida | Indians '85 (3) |
| Sean Berry, ss, Red Sox (4) | UCLA | Royals '86 (Jan.-S/1) |
| Scott Mackie, of, Pirates (4) | James Madison | Indians '87 (7) |

**TOTAL UNSIGNED PICKS:** Top 5 Rounds (13), Top 10 Rounds (38)

**Returned to same school.*

terms of the settlement of the 1981 strike, for the recent loss of Type A free-agent pitcher Tom Underwood to Baltimore and were free to draw the name of any player not on the 26-man protection list of the other 25 major league clubs, as filed on Jan. 12. They chose Belcher, who was drafted by the Yankees on Jan. 17 and signed with the team two weeks later.

The A's made their selection on Feb. 8 and without hesitation took an unprotected Belcher, much to the chagrin of New York officials.

The Yankees immediately filed a protest with baseball's Player Relations Committee, citing inequities in the compensation system. They contended that Belcher wasn't drafted until after they submitted their list of protected players, but the protest was denied by commissioner Bowie Kuhn, who said the dispute arose from the Collective Bargaining Agreement and would have to be resolved by the Players Association and Player Relations Committee. But Kuhn was at least sympathetic to the unintended consequence of the ruling, and compensated the Yankees to the tune of a first-round pick in the 1985 draft.

Tim Belcher

"The unfortunate result of this matter is that it is unfair to the Yankees," said Kuhn.

The sudden turn of events left Belcher bewildered.

"I'm just shocked and caught by surprise," he said. "I feel like I'm back on the roller coaster I've been on since June. It seems now I'll have files on three teams and I haven't thrown my first pro pitch."

"(The system) stinks. I think most people are trying to figure out if I'm bitter at one team or the other. I have nothing against the A's or Yankees. The system obviously has a flaw and that bothers me."

Even though Belcher was now A's property, the Yankees were obligated to pay him his signing bonus. In hindsight, they could have avoided losing the 21-year-old righthander had they signed him after the A's made their compensation selection. However, Belcher had indicated to Yankees officials that classes at Mount Vernon Nazarene began Feb. 1 and he would return to school if not signed by that date.

The mix-up had repercussions in the Yankees system. Owner George Steinbrenner was none too pleased about losing a player of Belcher's stature, regardless of the circumstances, and newly-installed general manager Murray Cook was one of two baseball operations officials disciplined. In Cook's case, he had his responsibilities sharply curtailed.

A new Basic Agreement in 1985 wiped out the compensation draft.

Belcher pitched four years in the Oakland system, impressing A's officials with his 94-mph fastball while trying to live down a reputation for wildness. He went 34-34, 4.37, walking 343 in 502 innings.

"I never considered myself wild," he said. "I just wasn't throwing strikes. But it seemed the Oakland organization got more and more anxious. They kept seeing the walks. Every walk was like another brick in a very large wall I was building in front of my career, and it was going to take a couple of years to tear down that wall."

The A's finally gave up on Belcher in August 1987, using his potential to fetch established lefthander Rick Honeycutt from the Dodgers.

Belcher considered the trade a career-saver. He immediately stepped his game up a notch, earning National League rookie pitcher of the year honors with the Dodgers in 1988 and led the NL with eight shutouts a year later.

"I'm not sure the results would have been the same if I stayed with Oakland," he said. "I was able to come here with a clean slate."

Over a 14-year career with seven clubs, Belcher won 146 games.

The Yankees also created a stir when they voided the contract of the first of two second-round picks, Keith Miller, after he had signed with the club for $60,000. Miller, a second baseman from Oral Roberts, had missed most of the 1984 season with a knee injury and the Yankees voided the contract on the grounds of a pre-existing injury—even though he was considered damaged goods at the time of the draft. Miller subsequently signed with the Mets on Sept. 6 for $44,500 and later recovered fully from his injury, though never played in the majors.

The Yankees other second-round pick, lefthander Al Leiter, made headlines of another sort in the spring of 1984 when he struck out 32 in a 14-inning high school game. He was signed to a bonus of $85,000, the highest paid out to a second-rounder.

Detroit and Toronto were the only two clubs to forfeit their first-round picks in 1984.

To compound their problem, the Tigers had the services of their second-round pick, University of Miami righthander Rob Souza, for only half a season as he lost his life in a car accident seven months after he was drafted. Souza had gone 30-16 with 366 strikeouts in three seasons at Miami.

### IN FOCUS: SHANE MACK

Shane Mack was a three-year star at UCLA and at one point was considered the best all-around talent in the 1984 college crop. The Padres drafted him with the 11th overall pick, but it looked like his pro career would be a bust after five seasons, when he was released. He had played in 161 games in San Diego, with a .245 average and four homers, along with a sore elbow, to show for his career. His tools were apparent, but Mack suffered from poor plate discipline and a lack of confidence.

As U.S. Olympic teammates like Mark McGwire, Will Clark and Barry Larkin were thriving, Mack had difficulty even cracking the Padres roster, and languished in the minors over much of his early career.

"What hurt most," Mack said, "was to see those other guys come up and start so well, while I'd play a few games, then be back on the bench. I never really felt like I got a chance to get comfortable, to settle in there. Those other first-rounders were allowed to show what they could do, but it was as if I was under the gun all the time."

The Twins plucked Mack from the Padres in the 1989 Rule 5 draft, and he thrived in five seasons as Minnesota's regular right fielder, hitting .309 with 67 homers, before accepting a lucrative offer to play in Japan.

# 1984 Draft List

*Did not sign. Major leaguers in bold, with first and last years noted. Order of selection indicated in parentheses. For the first five rounds of the June Regular Phase and the first round of all other phases, the peak level of each player is noted.*

## ATLANTA BRAVES

**January—Regular Phase (20)**

1. Jim Salisbury, rhp, Rio Hondo (Calif.) JC.—(High A)
2. *Scott Kershaw, rhp, Oxnard (Calif.) JC.
3. Bill Clossen, rhp, Rend Lake (Ill.) JC.
4. *James Massey, rhp, American River (Calif.) JC.
5. *Tim Peters, rhp, JC of Southern Idaho.
6. *Richard Browe, of, Central Arizona JC.
7. J.R. Turner, 2b, Diablo Valley (Calif.) JC.
8. *Jose Bennett, of, Arizona Western JC.
9. Keith Burke, of, Iowa Western CC.
10. *Edward McIvor, rhp, University of Texas.

**January—Secondary Phase (12)**

1. Steve Beer, rhp, Santa Ana (Calif.) JC.—(Rookie)
2. **Chris Cron, 1b, Santa Ana (Calif.) JC.—(1991-92)**

DRAFT DROP *Father of C.J. Cron, first-round draft pick, Angels (2011); major leaguer (2014-15)*

3. Mike Yastrzemski, of, Highland Beach, Fla.

DRAFT DROP *Son of Carl Yastrzemski, major leaguer (1961-83)*

4. *Arned Hernandez, of, Arizona Western JC.
5. Tony Leonardi, rhp, Aurora, Ill.

**June—Regular Phase (19)**

1. **Drew Denson, 1b-of, Purcell Marian HS, Cincinnati.—(1989-93)**
2. **Tom Glavine, lhp, Billerica HS, North Billerica, Mass.—(1987-2007)**

DRAFT DROP *Fourth-round draft pick, Los Angeles Kings/National Hockey League (1984); elected to Baseball Hall of Fame, 2014 • Brother of Mike Glavine, major leaguer (2003)*

3. Matt Rowe, rhp, Pepperdine University.—(Low A)
4. Flavio Alfaro, ss, San Diego State University.—(High A)
5. Bob Pfaff, c, Westwood HS, Round Rock, Texas.—(High A)
6. Rob Sepanek, 1b, Eastern Michigan University.
7. Greg Johnson, rhp, Southwest Missouri State University.
8. Rick Siebert, rhp, University Heights, Ohio.
9. Vince Barger, lhp, Fresno State University.
10. Leon Wright, ss, Woodward HS, Cincinnati.
11. *Bobby Green, of, Florida Southern College.
12. Dennis Hood, of, Muir HS, Altadena, Calif.
13. Kelly Guthrie, of, McLennan (Texas) CC.
14. Bob Posey, 3b, Campbell University.
15. Darrell King, 3b, East Los Angeles JC.
16. Jeff Groves, rhp, Glassboro State (N.J.) College.
17. Scott Powers, ss, Clemson University.
18. Tim Meacham, rhp, University of Alabama.
19. Chris Clawson, of, Kansas Newman College.
20. Mike Santiago, lhp, University of Oklahoma.
21. *Tony Bailey, rhp, Grambling State University.
22. **Greg Tubbs, of, Austin Peay State University.—(1993)**
23. Lyle Smith, c, Stanford University.
24. Chuck Martin, rhp, Santa Clara University.
25. *Mark Gabriel, ss-of, Niagara University.
26. *Ed Fulton, c, Tunstall HS, Dry Fork, Va.
27. Charles Williams, 2b, Augusta (Ga.) College.
28. Danny Weems, rhp, North Greene HS, Greeneville, Tenn.
29. *Tyrone Sims, c, Assumption HS, Belle Rose, La.
30. ***Joe Ausanio, rhp, Catholic HS, Kingston, N.Y.—(1994-95)**
31. Kyle O'Brien, 3b, Amherst (Mass.) College.
32. *Randy Ralstin, rhp, Foothill (Calif.) JC.
33. Scott James, c, West Chester University.

**June—Secondary Phase (5)**

1. **Jeff Blauser, ss, Sacramento (Calif.) CC.—(1987-99)**
2. *Doug Cox, lhp, DeKalb Central (Ga.) JC.
3. Franklin Hamrick, 3b-c, Spartanburg Methodist (S.C.) JC.
4. *David Potts, rhp, Broome (N.Y.) CC.
5. ***Steve Cummings, rhp, Blinn (Texas) JC.—(1989-90)**
6. *Scott Ayers, rhp, McLennan (Texas) CC.
7. *Blaine Deabenderfer, rhp, Louisburg (N.C.) JC.
8. *Jim Rockey, of, San Jose (Calif.) CC.
9. *Dodd Johnson, 1b, McLennan (Texas) CC.
10. *Kevin Williamson, rhp, Arizona State University.

Jamie Moyer was an unheralded sixth-round pick of the Cubs, but he pitched well into his 40s

## BALTIMORE ORIOLES

**January—Regular Phase (25)**

1. Pedro Llanes, rhp, Los Angeles Harbor JC.—(High A)
2. *Dana Smith, ss, Canada (Calif.) JC.
3. *William Thompson, lhp, Gloucester County (N.J.) JC.
4. *Mike Knaflec, lhp, Santa Fe (Fla.) CC.
5. ***Blaine Beatty, lhp, San Jacinto (Texas) JC.—(1989-91)**
6. Chris Egelston, rhp, Johnson County (Kan.) CC.
7. Chris Gaeta, of, CC of Morris (N.J.).
8. *James Kinnear, rhp, Central Arizona JC.
9. *Robert Collum, ss-2b, Mesa (Ariz.) CC.
10. *Barry Harper, rhp, Rose State (Okla.) JC.
11. Chris Mica, c, Alvin (Texas) CC.
12. Robert Ricciani, c, Mercer County (N.J.) JC.
13. *Ronald Aron, rhp, Camden County (N.J.) JC.
14. *Terry Moore, c, San Jacinto (Texas) JC.
15. *Chris Eaton, 1b, Longview (Mo.) CC.

**January—Secondary Phase (5)**

1. Kurt Beamesderfer, c, Fullerton (Calif.) JC.—(AA)
2. ***Jim Hunter, rhp, Brookdale (N.J.) CC.—(1991)**

**June—Regular Phase (25)**

1. **John Hoover, rhp, Fresno State University.—(1990)**
2. **Jeff Tackett, c, Camarillo (Calif.) HS.—(1991-94)**
3. Greg Talamantez, rhp, Idaho Falls (Idaho) HS.—(AA)
4. Gerry Holtz, ss-2b, Villanova University.—(AA)
5. **Mike Raczka, lhp, University of New Haven.—(1992)**
6. D.L. Smith, ss, UC Riverside.
7. Chris Padget, of, University of Mississippi.
8. *Rick Morris, of, Scottsdale (Ariz.) CC.
9. Alan Hixon, rhp, Old Dominion University.
10. Bill Lavelle, rhp, University of Portland.
11. *Randy Mazey, lhp, United HS, Seward, Pa.

DRAFT DROP *Baseball coach, Charleston Southern (1994-96); baseball coach, East Carolina (2003-05); baseball coach. West Virginia (2013-15)*

12. Jeff Hubbard, 3b, University of North Carolina.
13. ***Pete Stanicek, 2b, Stanford University.—(1987-88)**

DRAFT DROP *Brother of Steve Stanicek, first-round draft pick, Giants (1982); major leaguer (1987-89)*

14. *Steve Mumaw, lhp, University of Tampa.
15. *Raul Gutierrez, rhp, Mesa (Ariz.) CC.
16. Troy Howerton, lhp, Wichita State University.
17. *Jay Searcy, 3b, University of Oklahoma.
18. *Mike Prior, of, Illinois State University.

DRAFT DROP *Defensive back, National Football League (1985-94)*

19. Frank Velleggia, c, University of Alabama.
20. Randy Riley, 1b, Jacksonville University.
21. *Randy Butts, 1b, North Hagerstown (Md.) HS.
22. *Mike Montagnino, c, Harding HS, Charlotte, N.C.
23. *Lem Pilkinton, c, Overton HS, Nashville, Tenn.
24. Steven Colavito, of, Schuylkill HS, Bernville, Pa.

DRAFT DROP *Son of Rocky Colavito, major leaguer (1955-68)*

25. *Rich Bosley, rhp, Appalachian State University.
26. *Brian Thomas, ss, Lewis & Clark (Ore.) College.
27. ***Jeff Ballard, lhp, Stanford University.—(1987-94)**
28. ***David Haas, rhp, Truman HS, Independence, Mo.—(1991-93)**

**June—Secondary Phase (24)**

1. ***Blaine Beatty, lhp, San Jacinto (Texas) JC.—(1989-91)**
2. ***Jim Hunter, rhp, Brookdale (N.J.) CC.—(1991)**

## BOSTON RED SOX

**January—Regular Phase (13)**

1. *Greg Mayberry, rhp, Ferrum (Va.) JC.—(AAA)
2. *Mark Winner, rhp, Taft (Calif.) JC.
3. ***Daryl Irvine, rhp, Ferrum (Va.) JC.—(1990-92)**
4. Paul Slifko, rhp, DeKalb (Ga.) JC.
5. *Charles Bell, of, Nashville, Tenn.
6. *Pat Hewes, c, Bakersfield (Calif.) JC.
7. Tary Scott, 1b, Walters State (Tenn.) CC.
8. *Jimmy Hitt, rhp, Chipola (Fla.) JC.
9. *George Creekmore, rhp, JC of the Sequoias (Calif.)

**January—Secondary Phase (3)**

1. **Dan Gakeler, 1b-rhp, Mercer County (N.J.) CC.—(1991)**
2. *Larry Herrel, rhp, Tulsa, Okla.
3. **John Leister, rhp, Michigan State University.—(1987-90)**

DRAFT DROP *Quarterback, Michigan Panthers/United States Football League (1983)*

**June—Regular Phase (14)**

1. **John Marzano, c, Temple University.—(1987-98)**
2. Scott Wade, of, Oklahoma State University.—(AAA)
3. Brock Knight, rhp, American Fork (Utah) HS.—(Short-season A)
4. ***Sean Berry, ss, West Torrance (Calif.) HS.—(1990-2000)**

DRAFT DROP *Attended UCLA; re-drafted by Royals, January 1986/secondary phase (1st round)*

5. *Steve Boyd, c, Southern Illinois University.—(Short-season A)

DRAFT DROP *No school; re-drafted by Cardinals, January 1985/secondary phase (2nd round)*

6. *Larry Schwartz, lhp, Seton Hall University.
7. **Steve Curry, rhp, Manatee (Fla.) JC.—(1988)**
8. **Jody Reed, ss, Florida State University.—(1987-97)**
9. Tony DeFrancesco, c, Seton Hall University.

DRAFT DROP *Major league manager (2012)*

10. Odie Abril, rhp, Colton (Calif.) HS.
11. Mickey Fenn, rhp, David Lipscomb College.
12. *Brad Powell, rhp, University of North Carolina.
13. **Zach Crouch, lhp, Cordova HS, Rancho Cordova, Calif.—(1988)**
14. *Mickey Pina, of, Bridgewater (Mass.) HS.
15. ***Derek Lilliquist, lhp, Sarasota (Fla.) HS.—(1989-96)**

DRAFT DROP *First-round draft pick (6th overall), Braves (1987)*

16. ***Scott Jordan, of, Georgia Tech.—(1988)**
17. *Terry Griffin, rhp, Forrest HS, Jacksonville, Fla.
18. *Brian Nichols, c, El Cerrito HS, Richmond, Calif.
19. Larry Riddle, rhp, University of Texas-El Paso.
20. ***Jack McDowell, rhp, Notre Dame HS, Van Nuys, Calif.—(1987-99)**

DRAFT DROP *First-round draft pick (5th overall), White Sox (1987) • First player from 1987 draft to reach majors (Sept. 15, 1987)*

21. Mike Goff, 2b, University of Alabama-Birmingham.
22. Dan Sullivan, 1b, UCLA.
23. *Tim Weinfurtner, rhp, Palmetto HS, Miami.
24. Joe Stephenson, lhp, Sonoma State (Calif.) University.

**June—Secondary Phase (26)**

1. Chris Moritz, ss, San Jacinto (Texas) JC.—(AAA)

## CALIFORNIA ANGELS

**January—Regular Phase (5)**

1. Dave Martinez, rhp, Blinn (Texas) JC.—(AAA)
2. **Doug Jennings, 1b-of, Brevard (Fla.) CC.—(1988-93)**

3. *Billy Bartels, rhp, Fresno (Calif.) CC.
4. *Darin Mott, rhp, Fullerton (Calif.) JC.
5. *Gary Alexander, 3b, Laney (Calif.) JC.
6. *Todd Gedaminski, lhp, Lincoln Land (Ill.) CC.
7. Chris Horrell, rhp, Fullerton (Calif.) JC.
8. *Jeff Klukkert, rhp, Linn-Benton (Ore.) CC.
9. *Lee Stansbury, rhp, Linn-Benton (Ore.) CC.
10. *Brad Rohde, rhp, Brevard (Fla.) CC.
11. *Jim Osborne, 1b, Harford (Md.) CC.
12. *Jack Mayes, of-rhp, Brevard (Fla.) CC.
13. *Paul Migliore, ss, Delgado (La.) JC.
14. *Hector Cano, 3b, Pasadena (Calif.) CC.
15. *Michael Reyna, 3b, West Los Angeles JC.
16. *Michael Weglein, of, Essex (Md.) CC.

**January—Secondary Phase (26)**

1. *Robert Auth, rhp, Miami-Dade CC North.—(Low A)
2. *Thomas Thompson, of, Renfrew, Pa.
3. *Keith Felden, rhp, St. Petersburg (Fla.) JC.

**June—Regular Phase (6)**

**1. Erik Pappas, c, Mount Carmel HS, Chicago.—(1991-94)**
2. (Choice to Astros as compensation for Type A free agent Frank LaCorte)
**3. Sherman Corbett, lhp, Texas A&M University.—(1988-90)**
DRAFT DROP *Baseball coach, Texas-San Antonio (2001-12)*
**4. Kent Anderson, ss, University of South Carolina.—(1989-90)**
DRAFT DROP *Brother of Mike Anderson, first-round draft pick, Phillies (1969); major leaguer (1971-79)*
5. Todd Eggertsen, rhp, Brea-Olinda HS, Brea, Calif.—(AA)
**6. Brian Brady, of, New York Tech.—(1989)**
7. Mike Romanovsky, lhp, University of Maryland.
8. Bryan Price, lhp, University of California.
DRAFT DROP *Major league manager (2014-15)*
**9. Doug Davis, c, North Carolina State University.—(1988-92)**
10. Terry Jones, of-1b, San Diego State University.
**11. Pete Coachman, 3b, University of South Alabama.—(1990)**
12. Matt Sexton, ss, Kansas Newman College.
13. *Joe Lynch, rhp, William Paterson (N.J.) College.
14. Marty Reed, lhp, University of Tampa.
**15. *Chuck Finley, lhp, Northeast Louisiana University.—(1986-2002)**
16. Pete Beall, 1b, UCLA.
**17. Dante Bichette, of, Palm Beach (Fla.) JC.—(1988-2001)**
18. Allan Peterson, of, Lewis-Clark State (Idaho) College.
19. Gerald Baker, c, College of Boca Raton (Fla.).
20. Barry Dacus, rhp, UC Santa Barbara.
21. Eddie Delzer, lhp, Cal State Fullerton.
22. Mike Campbell, 3b, Cal State Los Angeles.
23. Michael Butler, lhp, Montclair State (N.J.) College.

**June—Secondary Phase (6)**

1. *Eric Tutt, of, Middle Georgia JC.—(Rookie)
2. *Tom Forrester, 1b, Miami-Dade CC North.
3. *Mark McMorris, 1b, Southeastern Louisiana University.
4. Jim Osborne, 1b, Harford (Md.) CC.
5. *Larry Allen, of, Laney (Calif.) JC.
6. *Robert Auth, rhp, Miami-Dade CC South.
7. *Todd Gedaminski, lhp, Lincoln Land (Ill.) CC.

## CHICAGO CUBS

**January—Regular Phase (4)**

**1. Damon Berryhill, c, Orange Coast (Calif.) JC.—(1987-97)**
2. *Chris Moritz, ss, San Jacinto (Texas) JC.
3. Todd Smith, of, Grossmont (Calif.) JC.
4. Mark Solz, 1b, Grossmont (Calif.) JC.
5. *Matt Crouch, rhp, Sacramento (Calif.) CC.
6. *Jeff Cook, rhp-of, Johnson County (Kan.) CC.
7. *Theodore Parker, of, Spartanburg Methodist (S.C.) JC.
8. Von Thayer, rhp, Grossmont (Calif.) JC.
9. Brent Casteel, c, Santa Fe (Fla.) CC.
10. *Jeff Yurtin, 3b, Sacramento (Calif.) CC.
11. Dennis Fortner, 2b, Bacone (Okla.) JC.
12. *Mike Stanford, rhp-inf, Citrus (Calif.) JC.

**January—Secondary Phase (24)**

1. *Rob Bartlett, of, Citrus (Calif.) JC.—DNP

**June—Regular Phase (3)**

**1. Drew Hall, lhp, Morehead State University.—(1986-90)**
**2. Greg Maddux, rhp, Valley HS, Las Vegas, Nev.—(1986-2007)**
DRAFT DROP *Elected to Baseball Hall of Fame (2014); first 1984 high school draft pick to reach majors (Sept. 3, 1986) • Brother of Mike Maddux, major leaguer (1986-2000)*
3. Julius McDougal, ss, Jackson State University.—(AAA)
**4. David Liddell, c, Rubidoux HS, Riverside, Calif.—(1990)**
5. Anthony Lee, rhp, Garner (N.C.) HS.—(Rookie)
**6. Jamie Moyer, lhp, St. Joseph's University.—(1986-2012)**
7. *Al Ashmont, rhp, Union Catholic HS, Winfield Park, N.J.
8. *Glenn Twardy, of, Wilson HS, Alhambra, Calif.
9. Bryan House, 2b, Illinois State University.
10. *Marshall Bliss, rhp, Palmyra (Pa.) HS.
11. *Bill Geivett, 3b-of, UC Santa Barbara.
12. Jimmie Gardner, rhp, Technical HS, Tampa.
**13. Jeff Pico, rhp, Antioch (Calif.) HS.—(1988-90)**
14. Michael O'Connor, c, Bentley (Mass.) College.
15. Myron Hunter, lhp, Springfield (Ill.) HS.
16. Rick Hopkins, ss-2b, Long Beach State University.
17. Bill Danek, rhp, St. John's University.
18. John Lewis, of, Grambling State University.
19. Bruce Crabbe, ss, University of Florida.
**20. *Alex Sanchez, of-rhp, Antioch (Calif.) HS.—(1989)**
DRAFT DROP *First-round draft pick (17th overall), Blue Jays (1987)*
21. Frank Spear, lhp, UC Santa Barbara.
22. Tim Rice, lhp, Clemson University.
23. Matthew Reed, rhp, University of New Haven.
24. David Amaro, 1b, Duke University.
DRAFT DROP *Son of Ruben Amaro Sr., major leaguer (1958-69) • Brother of Ruben Amaro Jr., major leaguer (1991-98); general manager, Phillies (2008-15)*
**25. Laddie Renfroe, rhp, University of Mississippi.—(1991)**
26. Robert Mandeville, ss-2b, Whitworth (Wash.) College.
27. Parnell Perry, of, Grant HS, Sacramento, Calif.
28. *Bill Blount, lhp, San Diego State University.
29. Jeff Sjoberg, ss, Mankato State (Minn.) University.
30. *Jim Kating, c-1b, Fremd HS, Rolling Meadows, Ill.

**June—Secondary Phase (15)**

1. Steve Maye, rhp, Los Angeles Harbor JC.—(AA)
2. *Derrick Richardson, 3b, University of Arkansas.
**3. Dwight Smith, of, Spartanburg Methodist (S.C.) JC.—(1989-96)**
DRAFT DROP *Father of Dwight Smith Jr., first-round draft pick, Blue Jays (2011)*
4. *Rob Tomberlin, 3b, Normandale (Minn.) CC.
5. *Mike Stanford, rhp, Citrus (Calif.) JC.

## CHICAGO WHITE SOX

**January—Regular Phase (26)**

1. *Tom Forrester, lhp-1b, Miami-Dade CC North.—(AAA)
2. *Keith Bennett, ss, Laney (Calif.) JC.
3. Tom Lahrman, rhp, Kishwaukee (Ill.) JC.
4. Norm Santiago, 3b, Mount San Antonio (Calif.) JC.
5. Jorge Alcazar, c, Miami-Dade CC North.
6. *Adrian Powell, 3b, West Los Angeles JC.
7. *Kevin Thomas, lhp, Spartanburg Methodist (S.C.) JC.
8. *Thomas Henderson, ss, Spartanburg Methodist (S.C.) JC.
9. *Tim Buddenbaum, of, Iowa Western CC.

**January—Secondary Phase (7)**

**1. *Jeff Richardson, rhp, Connors State (Okla.) JC.—(1990)**
2. *Mike Clarkin, rhp, Normandale (Minn.) CC.
3. Jim Phelps, rhp, Saline, Mich.

**June—Regular Phase (26)**

**1. Tony Menendez, rhp, American HS, Hialeah, Fla.** (Choice from Blue Jays as compensation for Type A free agent Dennis Lamp)**—(1992-94)**
1. Tom Hartley, of, Hudson's Bay HS, Vancouver, Wash.—(Low A)
2. Kevin Renz, rhp, Sam Houston State University.—(AAA)
3. Kent Torve, 3b-of, San Diego State University.—(AA)
DRAFT DROP *Brother of Kelvin Torve, major leaguer (1988-91)*
4. Todd Simmons, rhp, Cal State Fullerton.—(AAA)
**5. Adam Peterson, rhp, Timpview HS, Provo, Utah.—(1987-91)**
6. *Al Toledo, rhp, Brooklyn Technical HS, Brooklyn, N.Y.
7. Chris Jefts, rhp, Darlington HS, Rome, Ga.
**8. *Terry Wells, lhp, University of Illinois.—(1990)**
9. *Rob Swain, ss, Texas A&M University.
10. Bill Eveline, ss, Waukegan East HS, Waukegan, Ill.
11. *Antoine Pickett, of, El Cerrito HS, Oakland, Calif.
12. Jim Filippi, rhp, Florida International University.
13. Pete Venturini, ss, St. Peter's College.
14. *Ron Bianco, 2b, Duke University.
15. *John Von Ahnen, of, Wagner College.
16. Jeff Anderson, rhp, University of Nebraska.
17. Steve Oswald, lhp, University of New Orleans.
18. Dan Sehlhorst, c, University of Kentucky.
19. Manny Salinas, ss, U.S. International (Calif.) University.
20. *Dan Cronkright, 3b, Central Michigan University.
21. *John Selvitella, of-rhp, San Francisco HS, Fairfield, Calif.
22. Michael Murray, 3b, Kean (N.J.) College.
23. Darren Garrick, rhp, Southern Utah State College.
24. Jerry Bertolani, of, Los Medanos (Calif.) JC.
25. Eric Campbell, rhp-c, Creighton University.
26. *Don Samra, 2b, Florida Southern College.
27. Walter Lampkin, lhp, Iowa State University.
28. Scott Goss, 1b, Ball State University.
29. *Brian Osinski, rhp, Proviso West HS, Stone Park, Ill.
30. John Christy, of, Baylor University.
31. James Byrd, 2b, Florida Memorial College.
32. Darrell Pruitt, 3b, Southern Utah State College.
33. Larry Arrington, c, University of San Francisco.
34. James Markert, c, Western Michigan University.
35. Scott Nossek, lhp, University of Arizona.
DRAFT DROP *Son of Joe Nossek, major leaguer (1964-70)*
36. David White, rhp, College of St. Francis (Ill.).
37. *Mike Patterson, lhp, Mount San Antonio (Calif.) JC.
38. Joseph Martinez, of, Mount San Antonio (Calif.) JC.

**June—Secondary Phase (20)**

1. *Tom Powers, rhp, Triton (Ill.) JC.—DNP

## CINCINNATI REDS

**January—Regular Phase (6)**

1. Dusty Rogers, lhp, Utica (Miss.) JC.—(High A)
2. *Ron Bennett, rhp, Dundalk (Md.) CC.
3. *Jeff Marr, rhp, Brevard (Fla.) CC.
4. *Scott Hamilton, rhp, Seminole (Okla.) JC.
**5. Michael A. Smith, rhp, Ranger (Texas) JC.—(1989-90)**
6. *Jim Carroll, rhp, Mesa (Ariz.) CC.
7. Ernest Bacon, rhp, Bristol (Mass.) CC.
8. *Eddy Yanes, rhp, Brevard (Fla.) CC.
9. *William Avant, rhp, Blinn (Texas) JC.
10. *Paul James, rhp, St. Louis CC-Meramec.

**January—Secondary Phase (22)**

1. *Fred Carter, 3b, Millwood HS, Oklahoma City, Okla.—(High A)
DRAFT DROP *Brother of Joe Carter, first-round draft pick, Cubs (1981); major leaguer (1983-98)*

**June—Regular Phase (5)**

**1. Pat Pacillo, rhp, Seton Hall University.—(1987-88)**
2. *Curt Krippner, rhp, Cypress Creek HS, Houston.—(AA)
DRAFT DROP *Attended Texas; re-drafted by Brewers, 1987 (2nd round)*
**3. Chris Jones, 3b-1b, Liverpool (N.Y.) HS.—(1991-2000)**
4. Steve Kennelley, ss-2b, Golden West HS, Visalia, Calif.—(High A)
5. Brooks Shumake, 3b, Clemson University.—(AA)
6. Mark Berry, c, University of Arkansas.
7. *Allan Stallings, of, University of Alabama.
8. Charles Donahue, ss, Robinson HS, Tampa.
9. Doug Kampsen, rhp, University of Minnesota.
10. Leon Wilcox, ss, Westwood HS, Fort Pierce, Fla.
11. *Greg LaFever, rhp, Wichita State University.
12. Joel Lono, lhp, University of Hawaii.
13. Scott Reburn, rhp, University of Louisville.
14. Francesco Trasacco, lhp, Quinnipiac College.
15. George Pace, of-lhp, University of Richmond.
16. Frank Driver, rhp, Hampton (Va.) HS.
17. Scott Hughes, rhp, Old Dominion University.
18. Michael Torre, ss, Oak Ridge HS, Orlando, Fla.
19. Lalo Berezo, of, University of Cincinnati.
20. Clay Daniel, lhp, University of Florida.
21. Allen Sigler, of, Memphis State University.
22. Mark Germann, ss-2b, Rutgers University.
23. John Bryant, of, Cal State Fullerton.
24. Glenn Zielinski, of, University of Nevada-Las Vegas.
25. Tim Mirabito, rhp, LeMoyne College.
26. *Howie Freiling, 1b, Northeast HS, Philadelphia.

**June—Secondary Phase (11)**

No selection.

## CLEVELAND INDIANS

**January—Regular Phase (3)**

**1. *Tommy Hinzo, ss, Southwestern (Calif.) JC.—(1987-89)**
DRAFT DROP *First overall draft pick, June 1984/secondary phase, Mets*
2. Butch Garcia, c, Palm Beach (Fla.) JC.
3. *Michael Redding, rhp, Florida JC.
4. *Tom Duke, c, CC of Morris (N.J.).
5. *Wayne Higginbotham, rhp, Florida JC.
6. *Frank Taylor, of, DeKalb North (Ga.) JC.
7. *Kevin Badgett, of, Knoxville, Tenn.
8. *Douglas Parton, rhp, Spokane Falls (Wash.) CC.
9. *Robert Alexander, lhp, DeKalb Central (Ga.) JC.
**10. *Mike Fitzgerald, c-of, Middle Georgia JC.—(1988)**
11. *Eduardo Gonzalez, of, Chipola (Fla.) JC.
12. *Steven Polk, 1b, JC of the Canyons (Calif.).
13. Mark Barineau, 2b-ss, Tallahassee, Fla.

**January—Secondary Phase (17)**

1. *Blaine Deabenferter, rhp, Louisburg (N.C.) JC.—(Low A)
2. *Joe Giordanella, rhp, Lindenhurst (N.Y.) HS.
3. *Erick Rapp, rhp, Centralia (Wash.) JC.

**June—Regular Phase (4)**

**1. Cory Snyder, ss, Brigham Young University.—(1986-94)**
**2. John Farrell, rhp, Oklahoma State University.—(1987-96)**
DRAFT DROP *Major league manager (2011-15)*
2. *Kurt Dempster, rhp, Esperanza HS, Yorba Linda, Calif. (Choice from Athletics as compensation for Type A free agent Lary Sorensen).—(Low A)
DRAFT DROP *Attended Arizona State; re-drafted by Indians, 1987 (30th round)*
3. *Todd Brown, of, Arizona State University.—(AAA)
DRAFT DROP *Returned to Arizona State; re-drafted by Brewers, 1985 (5th round)*
4. Pete Carganilla, ss, Porterville (Calif.) HS.—(Low A)
5. Ken Galloway, lhp, Fresno State University.—(High A)
6. Andrew Robertson, rhp, St. Agatha HS, Detroit.
7. Chris Kahler, rhp, Winthrop College.
8. Rozier Jordan, of, Howard University.

**9. Chris Beasley, rhp, Arizona State University.—(1991)**
10. Bill Leslie, 3b, San Marino (Calif.) HS.
11. *Charles Hardwick, lhp, Wilmington, N.C.
12. Reggie Coker, of, Austin, Texas.
13. Joe Stephenson, rhp, Campbell University.
14. Mark Hopkins, c, Augusta (Ga.) College.
15. *Mark Hardy, of, UC Riverside.
**16. *Randy McCament, rhp, Grand Canyon College.—(1989-90)**
**17. *Mark Gardner, rhp, Fresno State University.—(1989-2001)**
18. Rick Sharp, rhp, Loyola Marymount University.
19. *Mark Malizia, of, Geneva (Ohio) HS.
20. Dain Syverson, ss-c, Oregon State University.
21. *Sean Grubb, rhp-1b, Norman (Okla.) HS.
22. James McMahan, ss-3b, Montreat-Anderson (N.C.) JC.
23. Mike Shellnut, rhp, Tennessee Wesleyan College.
24. *Ward Merdes, lhp, Santa Clara University.
25. *Brian Dodd, lhp, Greenway HS, Glendale, Ariz.
**26. *Mike Devereaux, of, Arizona State University.—(1987-98)**
27. *Bob Dombrowski, ss, Coronado HS, Scottsdale, Ariz.
28. *Chris Norman, rhp, University of South Carolina.
29. David Jenkins, of, Southern Tech (Ga.) Institute.
30. Michael Tolleson, of, Wofford University.
31. *Scott Fricks, c, Eastern Hills HS, Fort Worth, Texas.
**32. *Tommy Gregg, of, Wake Forest University.—(1987-97)**
33. *Steve Clinton, ss, San Jose (Calif.) CC.
34. *Rich Martig, 3b, Santa Clara University.
35. *Damon Tyson, ss, Cleveland Central HS, East Cleveland, Ohio.
36. *Paul List, of, North Hollywood HS, Hollywood, Calif.
37. *Rock Hurst, c, Furman University.
38. *Ken Rahming, 1b-3b, Miami-Dade CC North.
39. Lonnie Phillips, rhp, Cleveland State University.
40. Mark DiFrancisco, rhp, Cleveland State University.
41. Tommy Decker, c, Duke University.
42. *Charles Wacha, rhp, Edison (Fla.) CC.
43. *John Pust, ss, Western Carolina University.
44. Mark Reed, rhp, University of Bridgeport (Conn.).
**45. *Jeff Plympton, rhp, King Philip HS, Plainville, Mass.—(1991)**
46. *Kevin Chenail, rhp, Drury HS, North Adams, Mass.
47. David Lelievre, c, University of Lowell (Mass.).
48. *Brad DeJardin, 1b, St. Francis HS, Pasadena, Calif.

**June—Secondary Phase (8)**

**1. Mark Higgins, 1b, University of New Orleans.—(1989)**
2. *Joe Giordanella, rhp, Ocean County (N.J.) JC.
**3. *Tim Fortugno, lhp, Golden West (Calif.) JC.—(1992-95)**
4. *Tom Duke, c, CC of Morris (N.J.).
5. *Terence Guzman, lhp, Ferrum (Va.) JC.

## DETROIT TIGERS

**January—Regular Phase (23)**

1. Charles McHugh, rhp, Harford (Md.) CC.—(AA)
2. Kelly Burton, of, Grossmont (Calif.) JC.
3. *Marc D'Andrea, lhp, Southwestern (Calif.) JC.
4. *Dan Flores, rhp, Oxnard (Calif.) JC.
5. *Jordan Stevens, 1b-of, Merced (Calif.) JC.
6. *Joey Seaver, lhp, Walters State (Tenn.) CC.
7. *Johannes McFarlane, rhp, San Diego CC.
8. *Richard Solis, rhp, Merced (Calif.) JC.
9. *Doyle Wilson, c, Mesa (Ariz.) CC.
10. *Bernie Walker, of, Navarro (Texas) JC.

**January—Secondary Phase (23)**

1. Scott Schultz, 3b, Mira Costa (Calif.) JC.—(High A)
2. *Don Cohoon, 3b, Chipola (Fla.) JC.

**June—Regular Phase (24)**

1. (Choice to Giants as compensation for Type A free agent Darrell Evans)
2. Rob Souza, rhp, University of Miami.—(AA)

DRAFT DROP *Died as active player (Jan. 7, 1985)*
3. Marty Freeman, of, University of Maryland.—(AA)
**4. Mike Henneman, rhp, Oklahoma State University.—(1987-96)**
5. Al Labozetta, lhp, New York Tech.—(AA)
6. Steve Eagar, c, Brigham Young University.
7. *Damon Allen, rhp, Cal State Fullerton.

DRAFT DROP *Quarterback, Canadian Football League (1984-2006) • Brother of Marcus Allen, running back/National Football League (1982-97)*
8. Gerald Phillion, lhp, Central Michigan University.
9. Jeff Hermann, 1b, College of St. Francis (Ill.).
10. John Roddy, rhp, University of Southern California.
11. Chris Morgan, of, Georgia Tech.
12. *Kent Murphy, lhp, Western Illinois University.
13. *Miguel Ferradas, c, American HS, Hialeah, Fla.
14. *Fred Samson, ss, Cooper City HS, Miramar, Fla.
15. Kevin Creech, 3b, West Georgia College.
16. John Boling, lhp, St. Xavier (Ill.) College.
17. *Luis Cedeno, rhp, Memorial HS, West New York, N.J.
18. Ronald Stock, lhp, College of St. Francis (Ill.).
19. *Pete Schmidt, c, San Bernardino (Calif.) HS.
20. Tim Newsome, ss, St. Xavier (Ill.) College.
21. Jeff Peterson, 1b-lhp, St. Mary's (Calif.) College.
22. William Fuggatt, c, Tennessee Wesleyan College.
23. *Gary Pifer, rhp, Saddleback (Calif.) CC.
24. Allan Kline, rhp, Olivet Nazarene (Ill.) College.
25. *Rufus Ellis, rhp, Alabama State University.
26. Alan Goetz, rhp, Alma (Mich.) College.
27. Cary Colbert, 1b, Kansas State University.
28. David Minnema, rhp, Central Michigan University.
29. *Robert Moore, of, Purcell Marian HS, Cincinnati.
30. *William Kushmaul, of, Midland (Mich.) HS.
31. Donald Bulmer, c, Poly HS, Riverside, Calif.
32. *Greg Lotzar, of, Central Michigan University.
33. *Marc Wolever, of, Lewis Central HS, Council Bluffs, Iowa.
34. *Bill Shuta, rhp, University of Michigan.

**June—Secondary Phase (10)**

1. Ray Rosthenhausler, ss, Pima (Ariz.) CC.—(High A)
2. *Darryl Stephens, of, Stanford University.
3. Jerry Mack, 2b, Iowa Western CC.
4. Keith Nicholson, rhp, Mission (Calif.) JC.
5. *Larry Mims, 2b, Indian Hills (Iowa) CC.
6. *Jeff Forney, of, Roane State (Tenn.) CC.

## HOUSTON ASTROS

**January—Regular Phase (18)**

1. Anthony Hampton, of, Los Angeles Harbor JC.—(High A)
**2. *Russ Swan, lhp, Spokane Falls (Wash.) CC.—(1989-94)**
3. *Lamonte Bethea, rhp, Scottsdale (Ariz.) CC.
4. John Elliott, 2b, Long Beach (Calif.) CC.
5. *Jeff Sutter, rhp, Sacramento (Calif.) CC.
**6. Dave Meads, lhp, Middlesex County (N.J.) JC.—(1987-88)**
7. *Ed Ricks, 3b-of, Long Beach (Calif.) CC.
**8. *Greg Hibbard, lhp, Mississippi Gulf Coast JC.—(1989-94)**
9. Joe Mikulik, of, San Jacinto (Texas) JC.
10. *Anthony Ciccione, ss, Mission (Calif.) JC.
11. *Marc Lopez, rhp, Pasadena (Calif.) CC.
12. *Thomas Chermany, of, Arizona Western JC.
13. *Scott Winterburn, c, Citrus (Calif.) JC.
**14. *Jeff Gardner, 2b, Orange Coast (Calif.) JC.—(1991-94)**

**January—Secondary Phase (16)**

**1. Rob Mallicoat, lhp, Taft (Calif.) JC.—(1987-92)**
2. *Donald Enoch, rhp, Mercer County (N.J.) CC.
3. William King, ss, Chicago.

**June—Regular Phase (17)**

**1. Don August, rhp, Chapman (Calif.) College.—(1988-91)**
2. Terry Green, ss, Stringtown (Okla.) HS (Choice from Angels as compensation for Type A free agent Frank LaCorte).—(AA)
2. Karl Allaire, ss, Rhode Island College.—(AAA)

**3. Ken Caminiti, 3b, San Jose State University.—(1987-2001)**
4. Don Dunster, rhp, St. Mary's (Calif.) College.—(AAA)
**5. Dan Walters, c, Santana HS, Santee, Calif.—(1992-93)**
6. Clarke Lange, 3b, University of Miami.
**7. Chuck Jackson, of, University of Hawaii.—(1987-94)**

DRAFT DROP *Father of Justin Jackson, first-round draft pick, Blue Jays (2007)*
**8. *John Vander Wal, 1b, Hudsonville (Mich.) HS.—(1991-2004)**
9. *Mike Patton, rhp, Seton Hall University.
10. Mike Ullian, lhp, Stetson University.
11. Craig Stevenson, 3b, University of Southern California.
12. Gary Chesnoski, rhp, Slippery Rock (Pa.) University.
13. Chris Parker, rhp, Jacksonville State University.
14. Tony Metoyer, 3b, Texas A&M University.
15. Jeff Livin, rhp, Southwestern (Texas) University.
16. John Spazante, rhp, Ramapo (N.J.) College.
17. Norm Brock, of, Morehead State University.
18. Chris Huchingson, rhp, Texas A&M University.
19. *Ed Shea, c, Palm Beach (Fla.) JC.
20. *Ken Pennington, ss, Fairfax HS, Los Angeles.
21. Bob Parker, ss, Mississippi State University.
22. Steve Berlin, lhp, University of Denver.
23. Ray Paparella, 2b-3b, Villanova University.
24. Joe Kwolek, 3b, Orange Coast (Calif.) JC.
25. Alfredo Perez, of-c, Florida International University.

**June—Secondary Phase (9)**

**1. *Luis Medina, 1b, Arizona State University.—(1988-91)**
2. *Ed Ricks, 3b-of, Long Beach (Calif.) CC.
3. *Scott Lerner, lhp, Diablo Valley (Calif.) JC.
4. Mark Baker, rhp, Mineral Area (Mo.) JC.
**5. *Craig Worthington, 3b, Cerritos (Calif.) JC.—(1988-96)**

## KANSAS CITY ROYALS

**January—Regular Phase (15)**

1. Jeff Redus, of, Snead State (Ala.) JC.—(Short-season A)

DRAFT DROP *Brother of Gary Redus, major leaguer (1982-94)*
2. *Eric Hetzel, rhp, Eastern Oklahoma State JC.—(1989-90)

DRAFT DROP *First overall draft pick, June 1985/secondary phase, Red Sox*
3. *David S. Miller, rhp-of, Pensacola (Fla.) JC.
4. *Dirk Veldman, rhp, Moraine Valley (Ill.) CC.
5. *Peter Carey, of, Rockland (N.Y.) CC.
6. Roy Ellis, rhp, Indian Hills (Iowa) CC.
7. *Rob Tomberlin, 3b, Normandale (Minn.) CC.
8. *Greg Roscoe, rhp, Des Moines Area (Iowa) CC.
9. Rob Robinson, rhp, Lower Columbia (Wash.) JC.
10. *Louis Fuentes, c, Mission (Calif.) JC.
11. *Steven Purdy, rhp, Northeastern Oklahoma A&M JC.
12. *Scott Volz, rhp, Des Moines Area (Iowa) CC.
13. *James Sullivan, rhp, Fort Steilacoom (Wash.) CC.
14. Paul Howarth, of, Scottsdale (Ariz.) CC.
15. *Robert Fields, rhp, Pima (Ariz.) CC.
16. *Tim Swob, lhp, Northeastern Oklahoma A&M JC.
17. *Jeffrey D. Brown, of, Yucaipa, Calif.

**January—Secondary Phase (13)**

1. Andy Leonard, c, Canada (Calif.) JC.—(Low A)
**2. *Steve Carter, of, Hagerstown (Md.) JC.—(1989-90)**

**June—Regular Phase (16)**

**1. Scott Bankhead, rhp, University of North Carolina.—(1986-95)**
**2. Luis de los Santos, 3b-c, Newtown HS, Elmhurst, N.Y.—(1988-91)**
3. Bobby Bell, of, Gardena (Calif.) HS.—(Low A)
4. Jim Daniel, rhp, Wichita State University.—(AA)
5. Rob Van Vuren, rhp, Louisiana Tech.—(High A)
**6. Chito Martinez, of, Brother Martin HS, Metairie, La.—(1991-93)**
7. Darin Grimes, ss, North HS, Wichita, Kan.
8. Kurt Kunz, ss, University of Wisconsin-Parkside.

9. *Bill Cunningham, lhp, Ohio State University.
10. John Radtke, rhp, Stanford University.
11. Thomas Johnson, 1b, Taylor Allderdice HS, McKees Rock, Pa.
12. Jose Rodiles, rhp, Arizona State University.
13. Doug Konruff, rhp, University of Wisconsin.
14. Troy Brauchle, rhp, University of Alabama.
15. Lindsay Meggs, 3b, UCLA.

DRAFT DROP *Baseball coach, Indiana State (2007-09); baseball coach, Washington (2010-15)*
16. Carl Rogers, rhp, University of Central Arkansas.
17. Brian McCormack, rhp, San Clemente HS, Capistrano Beach, Calif.
18. Maurice Dorsey, c, Marshall HS, Chicago.
19. Jeffrey M. Brown, 1b, University of Richmond.
**20. Kevin Koslofski, of, Maroa-Forsyth HS, Maroa, Ill.—(1992-96)**
21. *Darrin Garner, 2b, Crenshaw HS, Los Angeles.
22. *Mike Blaskowski, c, Wausau (Wis.) West HS.

**June—Secondary Phase (12)**

1. Derek Vanacore, of, UC Santa Barbara.—(High A)
2. Matt Crouch, rhp, Sacramento (Calif.) CC.
3. Jeff Bedell, 3b, Montgomery (Md.) JC.

DRAFT DROP *Son of Howie Bedell, major leaguer (1962-68)*
4. Louis Fuentes, c, Mission (Calif.) JC.

## LOS ANGELES DODGERS

**January—Regular Phase (24)**

1. *John Alva, ss, Pima (Ariz.) JC.—(AAA)
2. *Keith Nicholson, rhp, Mission (Calif.) JC.
3. *Eddie Citronelli, c, Ranger (Texas) JC.
4. Jovon Edwards, of, SUNY Tech JC-Alfred.
5. *Kevin Phillips, rhp, Panola (Texas) JC.
6. *Tim McCoy, lhp, Mount San Antonio (Calif.) JC.
7. *Ted Brooks, of, Victor Valley (Calif.) CC.
8. *Brent Bolin, rhp, Central Arizona JC.
9. *Keith Sheldon, rhp, DeKalb South (Ga.) CC.
10. Daniel Robles, of, Mount San Antonio (Calif.) JC.
11. *Kelly Wilson, of, Paris (Texas) JC.

**January—Secondary Phase (4)**

**1. Shawn Hillegas, rhp, Middle Georgia JC.—(1987-93)**
2. *Vince Shinholster, ss, Santa Ana (Calif.) JC.

**June—Regular Phase (23)**

1. Dennis Livingston, lhp, Oklahoma State University.—(AAA)
**2. Tim Scott, rhp, Hanford (Calif.) HS.—(1991-97)**
**3. Tracy Woodson, 1b, North Carolina State University.—(1987-93)**

DRAFT DROP *Baseball coach, Valparaiso (2007-13); baseball coach, Richmond (2014-15)*
4. David Carlucci, c, Westfield State (Mass.) College.—(High A)
5. Jim Ward, 2b, University of Arkansas.—(High A)
6. Mike Pesavento, lhp, North Carolina State University.
7. Jeff Edwards, lhp, Vanderbilt University.
8. Jay Hornacek, 3b, Lyons Township HS, LaGrange, Ill.
9. Jeff L. Brown, of, University of Southern California.
10. Jimmy Williams, lhp, Choctaw County HS, Butler, Ala.
11. Ted Holcomb, ss-1b, Westchester HS, Playa del Rey, Calif.
12. Doug Treadway, rhp, Florida State University.
13. Jack Schlichting, of-c, University of Minnesota.
14. Bob Jacobsen, rhp, Fresno State University.
15. Jack Ritch, 2b, Georgia College.
**16. Darren Holmes, rhp, T.C. Roberson HS, Fletcher, N.C.—(1990-2003)**
17. *Greg Smith, of-1b, Baylor HS, Chattanooga, Tenn.
18. *Adrian Adkins, c-of, Jones County HS, Gray, Ga.
19. Craig Dorsey, of, CC of Baltimore.
20. *Brad Freking, lhp, Wauconda (Ill.) HS.
21. Eddie Jacobo, of, Fresno State University.
**22. Jeff Nelson, rhp, Catonsville HS, Baltimore.—(1992-2005)**
**23. *Jerald Clark, of, Lamar University.—(1988-95)**

DRAFT DROP *Brother of Phil Clark, first-round draft pick, Tigers (1986); major leaguer (1992-96) • Brother of Isaiah Clark, first-round draft pick, Brewers (1984)*

24. *John Cowan, of, Montclair State (N.J.) College.

**June—Secondary Phase (3)**

1. Greg Mayberry, rhp, Ferrum (Va.) JC.—(AAA)
2. Brian Kopetsky, ss-of, Dundalk (Md.) CC.
3. John Satnat, lhp, Modesto (Calif.) JC.
4. *Scott Clemo, 3b, Gulf Coast (Fla.) CC.

## MILWAUKEE BREWERS

**January—Regular Phase (17)**

1. Mathew Kent, 1b, Chipola (Fla.) JC.—(High A)
2. *Terence Johnson, of, San Diego Mesa JC.
3. *Steve Naegle, rhp, Diablo Valley (Calif.) JC.
4. *Russ Burk, lhp, Middle Georgia JC.
5. *Peter Davidson, rhp, Miami-Dade CC North.
6. *Robert Askew, of, Brookdale (N.J.) CC.
7. *Kevin Kirkman, rhp, JC of the Sequoias (Calif.).
8. Howard Bowens, 2b, Sacramento (Calif.) CC.
9. Reggie Dymally, 3b, Los Angeles.
10. *James Trafton, rhp, Riverside (Calif.) CC.
11. *Jaime Barragan, 1b, Southwestern (Calif.) JC.
12. *Gary Stacy, of, Southwestern (Calif.) JC.
13. *Gary Gorski, 3b, Los Angeles Harbor JC.
14. *Richard Brown, rhp, Brookdale (N.J.) CC.
15. Richard Sauer, of, Oxnard (Calif.) JC.
16. *Joseph McFarland, ss, Los Angeles CC.
17. *James Cook, of, Mount San Antonio (Calif.) JC.
18. *Craig Breaux, of, Yavapai (Ariz.) JC.
19. *Steven Mills, rhp, San Diego CC.
20. Scott Groot, ss, Yorba Linda, Calif.

**January—Secondary Phase (21)**

1. *Steve Wiley, lhp, Indian River (Fla.) CC.—DNP
2. *Kevin Monk, 1b, Los Angeles CC.
3. *Carlos Calderon, c, Santa Monica (Calif.) JC.
4. *Darwin Freeman, of, El Camino (Calif.) JC.

**June—Regular Phase (18)**

1. Isaiah Clark, ss, Crockett (Texas) HS.—(AA)

DRAFT DROP *Brother of Phil Clark, first-round draft pick, Tigers (1986); major leaguer (1992-96) • Brother of Jerald Clark, 23rd-round draft pick, Tigers (1984); major leaguer (1988-95)*

2. Bob Simonson, of, Taft (Calif.) JC.—(AA)
3. Warren Olson, c, Medford (Mass.) HS.—(High A)
4. Rod Zeratsky, c, Indiana State University.—(AA)
5. James Larsen, of, Eldorado HS, Las Vegas, Nev.—(Short-season A)
6. Mike Frew, rhp, Bradley University.
7. Rob DeWolf, of, Malone (Ohio) College.
8. Frank Mattox, 2b, University of California.

DRAFT DROP *Scouting director, Mariners (1998-2003)*

9. Tim Casey, of, University of Portland.
10. Mike Stanek, 2b, University of Delaware.
11. Alan Sadler, rhp, University of Maryland.
12. Gary Kanwisher, rhp, Oklahoma State University.
13. Greg Watkins, rhp, Shaw (N.C.) University.
14. **John Jaha, 3b-ss, Douglas HS, Portland, Ore.—(1992-2001)**
15. *Robin Torres, lhp-of, Culver City (Calif.) HS.
16. *Gary Grant, of, McKinley HS, Canton, Ohio.

DRAFT DROP *First-round draft pick, Los Angeles Clippers/ National Basketball Association (1988)*

17. *Mike Erb, rhp, Madison HS, San Diego.
18. Lloyd Schafer, 2b-ss, Ramona HS, Riverside, Calif.
19. Carl Gordon, of, Wingate (N.C.) College.
20. *Doug Gonring, c, Florida Atlantic University.
21. *Buddy Haney, 1b, Texas A&M University.
22. *Dan Nyssen, of, Eisenhower HS, Yakima, Wash.
23. Rick Ames, rhp, Florida Tech.
24. *John Keao, rhp, Waialua (Hawaii) HS.
25. *Herman Spera, rhp, Syracuse University.
26. *Joe Polubeski, 2b, Burbank HS, Sun Valley, Calif.
27. *James Gasser, rhp, Newbury Park (Calif.) HS.
28. *Bryan Luedtke, c, Potomac HS, Triangle, Va.
29. *Michael Stewart, of, Bakersfield (Calif.) JC.

DRAFT DROP *Defensive back, National Football League (1987-96)*

30. *Kenneth Greco, ss, Boys Latin HS, Timonium, Md.

**June—Secondary Phase (10)**

1. Darryel Walters, of, Miami-Dade CC North.–(AAA)
2. *Gary Alexander, rhp, Laney (Calif.) JC.
3. *Stephen Bowden, rhp, San Jacinto (Texas) JC.
4. ***Greg Vaughn, of, Sacramento (Calif.) CC.—(1989-2003)**
5. *Joey Seaver, lhp, Walters State (Tenn.) CC.
6. *Scott Hamilton, rhp, Seminole (Okla.) JC.
7. *Russ Burk, lhp, Middle Georgia JC.

Astros third-rounder Ken Caminiti became an NL MVP but struggled with steroids, drug use

## MINNESOTA TWINS

**January—Regular Phase (7)**

1. *Doug Cox, lhp, DeKalb Central (Ga.) JC.—(High A)
2. *Daryl Boyd, rhp, Palm Beach (Fla.) JC.
3. Greg Hill, c, Proctorville, Ohio.
4. *Dave Lawn, lhp, Laney (Calif.) JC.
5. Phil Wilson, of, Ehrhardt, S.C.

DRAFT DROP *Brother of Mookie Wilson, major leaguer (1980-91)*

6. ***Joe Bitker, rhp, Sacramento (Calif.) CC.—(1990-91)**
7. Jose Martinez, ss, Miami-Dade CC North.
8. Robert Lee, rhp, Normandale (Minn.) CC.
9. *Steve Janni, c, Allen County (Kan.) CC.
10. *Robert Cramer, lhp, Bakersfield (Calif.) JC.
11. *John Lastinger, 1b, University of Georgia.
12. *Craig Robison, p-of, Fullerton (Calif.) JC.
13. Joe Gherna, 2b, Three Rivers, Mich.
14. *Randall Comnick, rhp, Olympic (Wash.) JC.
15. ***Mark Grace, 1b, Saddleback (Calif.) CC.—(1988-2003)**
16. Ken DeGroot, 3b, Miami-Dade CC North.

**January—Secondary Phase (9)**

1. Alan Sontag, rhp, Indian River (Fla.) JC.—(AAA)
2. *Kenneth Shaw, rhp, Miami-Dade CC North.

**June—Regular Phase (8)**

1. **Jay Bell, ss, Gonzalez Tate HS, Pensacola, Fla.—(1986-2003)**
2. Greg Morhardt, 1b, University of South Carolina.—(AAA)

DRAFT DROP *Son of Moe Morhardt, major leaguer (1961-62)*

3. *John Verducci, ss, Stanford University.—(AAA)

DRAFT DROP *Returned to Stanford; re-drafted by Giants, 1985 (5th round)*

4. Larry Blackwell, ss, Dinwiddie (Va.) HS.—(AA)
5. Neil Landmark, rhp, North Central Bible (Minn.) College.—(High A)
6. Bob Ralston, 2b-ss, University of Arizona.
7. Mike Ryan, 1b-of, Florida Atlantic University.
8. Ray Velasquez, rhp, La Puente (Calif.) HS.
9. Chris Calvert, c, Chapman (Calif.) College.
10. Pat Crosby, of, Benjamin N. Cardozo HS, Springfield Gardens, N.Y.
11. Brian Leighton, of, Loyola Marymount University.
12. Joey Aragon, ss, Chapman (Calif.) College.
13. Brian Honeycutt, rhp, William Penn HS, New Castle, Del.
14. Jeff Smith, of, St. Petersburg Catholic HS, St. Petersburg, Fla.
15. Jeff Rojas, rhp, Chapman (Calif.) College.
16. Perry Husband, 2b, Cal State Northridge.
17. Tom Thomas, of, Cal State Fullerton.
18. Robert Richards, rhp, Onondaga (N.Y.) CC.
19. Juan Yancof, rhp, Miami.
20. **Gene Larkin, 3b-1b, Columbia University.—(1987-93)**
21. ***Clay Parker, rhp, Louisiana State University.—(1987-92)**
22. Anthony Lopez, c, La Puente (Calif.) HS.
23. James Dalton, ss, New York Tech.
24. Dave Williams, ss, Cal State Northridge.
25. Steve Riley, c, Tulane University.
26. Jose Dominguez, rhp, Cal State Northridge.
27. Dan Jones, c, Minot State (N.D.) College.
28. *Bill Voeltz, lhp, Broward (Fla.) CC.
29. *Dennis Bryant, rhp, Olympic (Wash.) JC.
30. Todd Budke, ss, Kirkwood (Iowa) CC.
31. *Dan Raley, ss, Potomac HS, Triangle, Va.
32. *Mel Houston, 3b, Laney (Calif.) JC.
33. *Jamie Acton, c, Foreman HS, Topeka, Ill.
34. *Jerome Santivasci, rhp, Patapsco HS, Baltimore.
35. Al Cardwood, 1b, Long Island University.
36. *Mickey Billmeyer, c, Hagerstown (Md.) JC.
37. *Billy Gardner Jr., 1b, Waterford (Conn.) HS.

DRAFT DROP *Son of Billy Gardner, major leaguer (1954-63); major league manager (1981-87)*

**June—Secondary Phase (22)**

1. Eddy Yanes, of, Brevard (Fla.) CC.—(AA)
2. *Mike Trapasso, lhp, Oklahoma State University.

DRAFT DROP *Baseball coach, Hawaii (2001-15)*

3. *Vince Shinholster, ss, Santa Ana (Calif.) JC.
4. *Mike Belanger, lhp, San Joaquin Delta (Calif.) JC.

## MONTREAL EXPOS

**January—Regular Phase (14)**

1. *Jim Willis, of, Triton (Ill.) JC.—(Low A)
2. *Thomas Green, rhp, Fullerton (Calif.) JC.
3. *John Power, rhp, Taft (Calif.) JC.
4. *Scott Lerner, lhp, Diablo Valley (Calif.) JC.
5. Anson Jones, 3b, Taft (Calif.) JC.
6. Mike Pierce, rhp, Bossier City, La.
7. *Mike Havers, lhp, Kirkwood (Iowa) CC.
8. *Mike Sims, ss, Seminole (Fla.) CC.
9. *Mike Veres, ss, Indian River (Fla.) CC.
10. *Colt Larson, rhp, JC of Marin (Calif.).
11. *Thomas Shurley, rhp, Edmonds (Wash.) CC.
12. *Keith Seifert, c, DeKalb South (Ga.) CC.
13. *Mitch Moen, rhp, Indian Hills (Iowa) CC.
14. *David Zech, ss, Central Arizona JC.
15. *James Gibbs, rhp-dh, Muscatine (Iowa) CC.
16. *Roy Calhoun, lhp, Mott (Mich.) CC.

**January—Secondary Phase (6)**

1. *Gregg Schiffelbein, of, Allen County (Kan.) CC.—(High A)
2. *James Rockey, of, San Jose (Calif.) CC.
3. *Marty Lanoux, 2b, Santa Fe (Fla.) CC.

**June—Regular Phase (13)**

1. Bob Caffrey, c, Cal State Fullerton.—(AA)
1. **Norm Charlton, lhp, Rice University** (Supplemental choice—28th—as compensation for Type B free agent Manny Trillo)—**(1988-2001)**
2. Dave Graybill, rhp, Arizona State University.—(AAA)
3. *Kevin Garner, rhp-of, Brazoswood HS, Lake Jackson, Texas.—(AAA)

DRAFT DROP *Attended Texas; re-drafted by Padres, 1987 (1st round)*

4. **Gary Wayne, lhp, University of Michigan.—(1989-94)**
5. Ben Abner, of, Georgia Southern College.—(AA)

DRAFT DROP *Brother of Shawn Abner, first overall draft pick, Mets (1985); major leaguer (1987-92)*

6. Scott Raziano, 3b, University of New Orleans.
7. *Tim Dulin, 2b, Memphis State University.
8. Kent Bachman, 2b-ss, Cal Poly San Luis Obispo.
9. Bob Slover, ss, Jacksonville University.
10. ***Anthony Young, rhp-of, Furr HS, Houston.—(1991-96)**
11. Bill Cutshall, rhp, University of Minnesota.
12. *Frank Dominguez, c, Southridge HS, Miami.
13. ***Jeff Brantley, rhp, Mississippi State University.—(1988-2001)**
14. ***Michael C. Walker, rhp, Hernando HS, Brooksville, Fla.—(1988-96)**
15. Todd Wilkinson, of, University of North Carolina.
16. Steve St. Claire, of, Whitehall (N.Y.) Central HS.

DRAFT DROP *Son of Ebba St. Claire, major leaguer (1951-54) • Brother of Randy St. Claire, major leaguer (1984-94)*

17. Kurt Brauckmiller, rhp, Portland State University.
18. Lex Bleckley, ss, University of Delaware.
19. *Oneri Fleita, lhp, Key West (Fla.) HS.
20. Dave Pregon, 1b, Georgia Southern College.
21. Pete Hardee, rhp, Appalachian State University.
22. *Mike Scott, rhp, St. Xavier (Ill.) College.
23. *Bob Bretwisch, lhp, Proviso HS, Westchester, Ill.
24. *Sal Vaccaro, lhp, Santa Clara University.

25. Jeff Cisco, c, Winthrop College.
26. Jeff LaMarr, c, Cordova HS, Rancho Cordova, Calif.
27. *Mike Darby, rhp, University of Iowa.
28. *Herman Boddy, rhp, Mississippi Valley State University.
29. Doug Shields, of, University of Miami.
30. *Jeff Atha, ss-3b, Central Gwinnett HS, Lawrenceville, Ga.
31. Ernie Pacheco, rhp-of, Providence College.
32. Greg Hudson, rhp, Southern Tech (Ga.) Institute.
33. Jeff Doorey, lhp, Baldwin-Wallace (Ohio) College.
34. *Mark Bond, rhp, St. Mary's (Texas) University.

**June—Secondary Phase (19)**

1. *Gordie Hershiser, rhp, Indian River (Fla.) CC.—(AA)

DRAFT DROP *Brother of Orel Hershiser, major leaguer (1983-2000)*

2. *Jose Alou, of, Canada (Calif.) JC.

DRAFT DROP *Son of Felipe Alou, major leaguer (1958-74); major league manager (1992-2006) • Brother of Moises Alou, major leaguer (1990-2008)*

## NEW YORK METS

**January—Regular Phase (2)**

1. *Garry Clark, rhp, St. Louis CC-Forest Park.—(High A)
2. **Kevin Elster, ss, Golden West (Calif.) JC.—(1986-2000)**
3. *Mike Westbrook, of-inf, Johnson County (Kan.) CC.
4. Bryant Robertson, of, Triton (Ill.) JC.
5. *Richard Yochem, c, Valencia (Fla.) CC.
6. ***Craig Worthington, 3b, Cerritos (Calif.) JC.—(1988-96)**
7. **Scott Little, of, Mineral Area (Mo.) JC.—(1989)**
8. *Paul Nicholson, rhp, Rockland (N.Y.) CC.
9. *Tim Williams, lhp, Crowder (Mo.) JC.
10. **Brian Givens, lhp, Trinidad State (Colo.) JC.—(1995-96)**
11. *Jeff Schneeberger, c, Indian Hills (Iowa) CC.
12. *John Sellick, 1b, Santa Rosa (Calif.) JC.
13. Dale Coles, 1b-of, Clairton, Pa.
14. Owen Moreland, rhp, Seminole (Okla.) JC.
15. *Mark Behny, rhp, Garden City (Kan.) CC.
16. *William Mulligan, lhp, Indian Hills (Iowa) CC.

**January—Secondary Phase (20)**

1. *Larry Mims, 2b, Indian Hills (Iowa) CC.—(AA)
2. *Jerry Mack, 2b, Iowa Western JC.

**June—Regular Phase (1)**

1. **Shawn Abner, of, Mechanicsburg (Pa.) HS.—(1987-92)**

DRAFT DROP *Brother of Ben Abner, fifth-round draft pick, Expos (1984)*

2. Lorenzo Sisney, c, Washington HS, Gardena, Calif.—(Low A)
3. Mark Brunswick, c, Coldwater (Ohio) HS.—(High A)
4. Jeff Howes, rhp, Plainville (Conn.) HS.—(Low A)
5. Brandon Bailey, 1b, Hanna HS, Anderson, S.C.—(High A)
6. David Sanders, rhp, Columbia (Miss.) HS.
7. Anthony Thompson, of, Marion (Ind.) HS.
8. Barry Hightower, lhp, Northview HS, Dothan, Ala.
9. **Rich Rodriguez, lhp, University of Tennessee.—(1990-2003)**
10. *Mike Goff, rhp, Red Bluff HS, Cottonwood, Calif.
11. Lorin Jundy, rhp, Palmdale HS, Saugus, Calif.
12. ***John Wetteland, rhp, Cardinal Newman HS, Santa Rosa, Calif.—(1989-2000)**
13. **Mauro Gozzo, rhp-ss, Berlin (Conn.) HS.—(1989-94)**
14. *Terrel Hansen, rhp, Bremerton (Wash.) HS.
15. Jeff Cooley, ss, El Camino HS, Sacramento, Calif.
16. *Dan Eskew, rhp, McGavock HS, Nashville, Tenn.
17. ***John Orton, c, Soquel HS, Santa Cruz, Calif.—(1989-93)**

DRAFT DROP *First-round draft pick (25th overall), Angels (1987)*

18. Bucky Autry, ss, University of Indiana.
19. *Wendell Harris, of, Pasadena HS, Altadena, Calif.
20. Marty Crews, 3b-rhp, Fernandina Beach HS, Yulee, Fla.
21. Shane Young, lhp, Memphis State University.
22. *Greg Johnson, rhp, Red Bank HS, Hixson, Tenn.
23. *Garrett Carter, 3b-of, Walterboro (S.C.) HS.
24. *George Fowler, c, Delano (Calif.) HS.
25. Ramon Pereira, ss, Concordia (N.Y.) College.
26. Mark Davis, rhp, Cal State Sacramento.
27. Angelo Cuevas, of, Aviation HS, Long Island City, N.Y.
28. *Dale Snyder, 3b, Soquel (Calif.) HS.
29. Lew Graham, of, San Diego State University.
30. Allen Wilson, c, Memphis State University.
31. *Steve Brueggemann, rhp, Cal State Sacramento.
32. ***Randy Veres, rhp, Cordova HS, Rancho Cordova, Calif.—(1989-97)**
33. Troy James, rhp, Tacoma (Wash.) CC.
34. *Gary Canfield, lhp, McLane HS, Fresno, Calif.
35. *Eddie Soto, rhp, Lincoln HS, Brooklyn, N.Y.

**June—Secondary Phase (1)**

1. ***Tommy Hinzo, 2b, Southwestern (Calif.) JC.—(1987-89)**
2. Terence Johnson, of, San Diego Mesa JC.
3. *John Alva, 3b, Pima (Ariz.) CC.
4. Mike Westbrook, 2b-3b, Johnson County (Kan.) CC.
5. *John Sellick, 1b-3b, Santa Rosa (Calif.) JC.

## NEW YORK YANKEES

**January—Regular Phase (21)**

1. William Smith, of-ss, Virginia Commonwealth University.—(Low A)
2. *Norman Gates, rhp, Broward (Fla.) CC.
3. *David Potts, rhp, Broome (N.Y.) CC.
4. *Dody Rather, rhp, San Jacinto (Texas) JC.
5. *Dom Atteo, 1b-c, Indian River (Fla.) CC.
6. Kevin Trudeau, rhp, Chabot (Calif.) JC.
7. Doug Armstrong, rhp, American River (Calif.) JC.
8. Derek Lane, rhp, Iowa Western CC.
9. *Ike Bradley, c, Beloit, Wis.
10. *Darrell Hughes, of, Paducah (Ky.) CC.
11. *Chuck Johnson, of, Laney (Calif.) JC.
12. ***Jerry Goff, 1b-c, JC of Marin (Calif.).—(1990-96)**
13. *Doug Hylton, rhp, Bakersfield (Calif.) JC.
14. *Tom Brousseau, ss, Butte (Calif.) JC.
15. *Darren Pearson, rhp, Laney (Calif.) JC.
16. Carl Jones, of, San Joaquin Delta (Calif.) JC.
17. *Tim Tucker, of-c, Gavilan (Calif.) JC.
18. *Michael Trapp, lhp, Richfield, Minn.

**January—Secondary Phase (1)**

1. **Tim Belcher, rhp, Mount Vernon Nazarene (Ohio) College.—(1987-2000)**

DRAFT DROP *First overall draft pick, Twins (1983)*

2. *Tom Bryant, 3b, Caldwell, N.J.
3. Donald Lewis, rhp, San Francisco.
4. *David Zapien, 1b, Centralia (Wash.) JC.
5. *Mark Dudenake, c, Orange Coast (Calif.) JC.

**June—Regular Phase (22)**

1. Jeff Pries, rhp, UCLA.—(AAA)
2. **Keith Miller, of, Oral Roberts University** (Choice from Padres as compensation for Type A free agent Rich Gossage)**—(1987-95)**
2. **Al Leiter, lhp, Central Regional HS, Pine Beach, N.J.—(1987-2005)**

DRAFT DROP *Brother of Mark Leiter, major leaguer (1990-2001)*

3. ***Mo Sanford, rhp, Starkville (Miss.) HS.—(1991-95)**

DRAFT DROP *Attended Alabama; re-drafted by Reds, 1988 (32nd round)*

4. ***Randy Hennis, rhp, Patrick Henry HS, San Diego.—(1990)**

DRAFT DROP *Attended UCLA; re-drafted by Astros, 1987 (2nd round)*

5. Corey Viltz, 1b, The Dalles (Ore.) HS.—(High A)
6. *Steve Iannini, of, Georgetown University.
7. Randy Foyt, 2b, Texas Wesleyan College.
8. Art Calvert, of, U.S. International (Calif.) University.
9. Matt Harrison, lhp, LeMoyne College.
10. *Hardin Brown, of, Red Springs (N.C.) HS.
11. Robbie Robinson, rhp, LaGrange (Ill.) HS.
12. Dennis Chastain, lhp, University of Georgia.
13. Keith Foley, c, Florida Atlantic University.
14. Tony Thomas, rhp, Hillsborough HS, Tampa.
15. *Gator Thiesen, ss-2b, Mississippi State University.
16. Phil Lane, of, University of Miami.
17. *Bean Stringfellow, lhp, Virginia Tech.
18. Jeff Franks, c, University of Texas-El Paso.
19. Frank Shamie, rhp, St. Patrick HS, Chicago.
20. Gordon Meyer, 2b, Nicholls State University.
21. Darren Mandel, c-1b, University of Miami.
22. Dan Greenleaf, rhp, Los Angeles Harbor JC.
23. Tom Woleslagel, ss, Ohio State University.
24. **Bob Davidson, rhp, East Carolina University.—(1989)**
25. Mark DeLaTorre, lhp, Brigham Young University.
26. James Starling, rhp, Delaware State College.
27. Chris Zink, 3b-2b, Lamar University.
28. Pat Dougherty, rhp, Universtiy of Nevada-Reno.
29. Kevin Blake, ss, Western Oregon State College.
30. *Jeff Livesey, c, Lakeland HS, Ringwood, N.J.
31. Todd Marston, c, Cal State Sacramento.
32. Ricardo Rivas, c, La Progresiva HS, Miami.
33. Gary Cathcart, of, Middle Tennessee State University.
34. *Braz Davis, rhp, Pearland (Texas) HS.
35. *Greg Kuzma, lhp, Indian Hills HS, Oakland, N.J.
36. *William Wolf, ss, Barron Collier HS, Naples, Fla.
37. *Scott Johnson, 3b, Rice University.
38. Jeff King, c, Ohio State University.
39. *Todd Persico, of, Triton (Ill.) JC.
40. *Todd Krumhever, rhp, Hemet (Calif.) HS.
41. *Kevin Ryan, rhp, Palm Beach (Fla.) JC.
42. *Al Quintero, of, Lewis-Clark State (Idaho) College.
43. Jeff Ott, rhp, University of Iowa.
44. Jay Burton, of, Lamar University.
45. *Ira Tieul, c, Grambling State University.
46. *Ray Graff, of, University of Detroit.
47. **Tom Gilles, 3b-rhp, Indiana State University.—(1990)**
48. *Greg Iavarone, c, University of Illinois.
49. *Frank Ricchey, c, Upper Moreland HS, Willow Grove, Pa.
50. *Ty Dabney, of, UC Riverside.
51. ***Don Wakamatsu, c, Arizona State University.—(1991)**

DRAFT DROP *Major league manager (2009-10)*

**June—Secondary Phase (16)**

1. Dody Rather, rhp, San Jacinto (Texas) JC.—(AA)
2. *Scott Kershaw, rhp, Oxnard (Calif.) JC.
3. **Darren Reed, c, Ventura (Calif.) JC.—(1990-92)**
4. Shell Scott, 3b-ss, JC of Southern Idaho.
5. Ike Bradley, c, University of Wisconsin.
6. *Steve Wiley, lhp, Indian River (Fla.) CC.
7. Fred Carter, of, Connors State (Okla.) JC.

DRAFT DROP *Brother of Joe Carter, first-round draft pick, Cubs (1981); major leaguer (1983-98)*

## OAKLAND ATHLETICS

**January—Regular Phase (9)**

1. ***Tim Fortugno, lhp, Golden West (Calif.) JC.—(1992-95)**
2. *Mike Belanger, lhp, San Joaquin Delta (Calif.) JC.
3. Darren Balsley, rhp, Palomar (Calif.) JC.
4. *Scott Clemo, 3b, Gulf Coast (Fla.) CC.
5. *Larry Allen, of-1b, Laney (Calif.) JC.
6. *Bill Bluhm, 3b, JC of the Canyons (Calif.).
7. Robert Gould, of, Fullerton (Calif.) JC.
8. *Reggie Attaway, rhp-inf, Laney (Calif.) JC.
9. *Melvin Sisney, rhp, Los Angeles CC.
10. ***Darren Reed, c, Ventura (Calif.) JC.—(1990-92)**

**January—Secondary Phase (25)**

1. Michael Walker, ss, Cerritos (Calif.) JC.—(Low A)
2. *Arnold Isaac, of, Wharton County (Texas) JC.

**June—Regular Phase (10)**

1. **Mark McGwire, 1b, University of Southern California.—(1986-2001)**
2. (Choice to Indians as compensation for Type A free agent Lary Sorensen)
3. Mark Howie, ss, Louisiana State University.—(AAA)
4. Russ Kibler, rhp, University of Florida.—(AAA)
5. Victor Figueroa, rhp, Mesa (Colo.) College.—(High A)
6. Pat Dietrick, of, Purdue University.
7. **Todd Burns, rhp, Oral Roberts University.—(1988-93)**
8. Tony Arias, 3b, Florida International University.
9. Greg Brake, lhp, Western Michigan University.
10. *David Denny, 3b, University of Texas.
11. Dan Winters, c, Indiana University.
12. Ed Puikunas, lhp, Chapman (Calif.) College.
13. Kevin Russ, of, Gonzalez Tate HS, Pensacola, Fla.
14. Tony Johnson, 3b, Gonzalez Tate HS, Pensacola, Fla.
15. **Joe Strong, rhp, UC Riverside.—(2000-01).**
16. Mike Eddington, 1b, Michigan State University.
17. Brian Criswell, lhp, Western Michigan University.
18. Cordell Ross, ss, Michigan State University.
19. ***John Fishel, of, Cal State Fullerton.—(1988)**
20. *Tom Scaletta, ss, Cal Poly Pomona.
21. Scott Parrish, rhp, Clemson University.
22. (void) Rod Brunelle, of, Grand Valley State (Mich.) College.
23. *Mac Siebert, lhp-1b, Gonzalez Tate HS, Pensacola, Fla.
24. *Wade Kosakowski, rhp, St. Francis de Sales HS, Calumet City, Ill.
25. John Gonzalez, rhp, Monroe HS, Sylmar, Calif.
26. Mike Cupples, c, Grand Valley State (Mich.) College.
27. Mark Gillespie, lhp, UC Riverside.
28. Jim Thrift, ss, Winthrop College.

DRAFT DROP *Son of Syd Thrift, general manager, Pirates (1985-88); general manager, Orioles (1999-2002)*

29. Eldridge Armstrong, of, University of Southern California.
30. *Joe Leahey, rhp, Western Michigan University.
31. Scott Lavander, rhp, St. Mary's (Calif.) College.
32. Mark Beaver, rhp, Winthrop College.
33. Andy Krause, of, Michigan State University.

**June—Secondary Phase (18)**

1. *Tim McCoy, lhp, Mount San Antonio (Calif.) JC.—(AAA)
2. *James Trafton, rhp, Riverside (Calif.) CC.

## PHILADELPHIA PHILLIES

**January—Regular Phase (22)**

1. *Jeff Mays, rhp, Crowder (Mo.) JC.—(AA)
2. *Dodd Johnson, 3b-of, McLennan (Texas) CC.
3. *Darryel Walters, of, Miami-Dade CC North.
4. *Keith Kerns, ss, Bacone (Okla.) JC.
5. Walter Nesbitt, rhp, Bishop State (Ala.) JC.
6. *Mark Baker, c, Mineral Area (Mo.) JC.
7. *Brian Duff, rhp, Bee County (Texas) JC.
8. *Mike Oglesbee, lhp-1b, Lee (Texas) JC.
9. *Steve Towey, rhp, Fort Steilacoom (Wash.) CC.
10. ***Jeff Wetherby, of-1b, JC of the Canyons (Calif.).—(1989)**
11. *Ken Altona, lhp, Bellevue (Wash.) CC.
12. *Fred Frazier, rhp, Delgado (La.) JC.
13. Rodney Wheeler, of-1b, Hill (Texas) JC.
14. *Scott Shaffer, lhp, Strasburg, Pa.
15. *Jon Beuder, of, El Camino (Calif.) JC.
16. *John Shea, lhp, Worcester Academy, Colchester, Conn.
17. *Rich Richardi, ss, Valencia (Fla.) CC.
18. *Carl Coates, rhp, Utah Technical JC.
19. Todd Herrenbruck, 1b, Rend Lake (Ill.) JC.

**January—Secondary Phase (18)**

1. Darrell Clifton, ss, Blinn (Texas) JC.—(Rookie)
2. **Mike Jackson, of-rhp, Hill (Texas) JC.—(1986-2004)**
3. *Rickey Darwin, rhp, Bonham, Texas.

DRAFT DROP *Brother of Danny Darwin, major leaguer (1978-98)*

**June—Regular Phase (21)**

1. **Pete Smith, rhp, Burlington (Mass.) HS.—(1987-98)**
2. **Marvin Freeman, rhp, Jackson State University.—(1986-96)**
3. Scott Hufford, of, Pacific Grove (Calif.) HS.—(High A)

4. Todd Soares, of, Fresno State University.—(AAA)
5. Jim Fortenberry, of, Wingate (N.C.) College.—(AAA)
6. Roger Johnson, c, University of Missouri.
7. Bill Jester, lhp, Seminole (Okla.) JC.
8. *David Johnson, rhp, Seminole (Okla.) JC.
9. Heath Frazier, 2b, Stringtown (Okla.) HS.
10. Guy Hardaker, 3b, Central State (Okla.) University.
11. Darren Loy, c, University of Texas.
12. Bradley Thomas, rhp, School of the Ozarks (Mo.).
**13. Todd Frohwirth, rhp, Northwest Missouri State University.—(1987-96)**
14. Scott Wright, rhp, Cal State Fullerton.
15. *David Havley, rhp, Bartlesville (Okla.) HS.
**16. N. Keith Miller, ss, Lubbock Christian (Texas) College.—(1988-89)**
17. Jeff Knox, rhp, Bothell (Wash.) HS.
18. *Ken Adams, rhp, Park Hill HS, Kansas City, Mo.
19. Mike Miller, lhp, Arkansas Tech University.
20. Isaac Johnson, ss, Cordova HS, Rancho Cordova, Calif.
**21. Shawn Barton, lhp, University of Nevada-Reno.—(1992-96)**
22. Daryl Evans, rhp, Newport (Wash.) HS.
23. Robert Gsellman, c, Culver City (Calif.) HS.
24. *Ken Morris, rhp, Whitehouse (Texas) HS.
**25. Bob Scanlan, rhp, Harvard HS, Beverly Hills, Calif.—(1991-2001)**
26. Eric Bennett, c, University of San Diego.
27. *Steven Harris, rhp, Paxon HS, Jacksonville, Fla.
28. Ray Roman, c, Cal State Fullerton.
29. *Ray Carter, ss, Western Oklahoma State JC.
30. *David Osteen, ss-rhp, Elon College.
DRAFT DROP *Son of Claude Osteen, major leaguer (1957-75)*
31. *Dean Douty, rhp, Ocean View HS, Fountain Valley, Calif.

**June—Secondary Phase (23)**

1. Ronnie Gideon, 1b, Panola (Texas) JC.—(AA)
2. *Chris Sarmiento, rhp, Seminole (Okla.) JC.
3. George Creekmore, rhp, JC of the Sequoias (Calif.).

## PITTSBURGH PIRATES

**January—Regular Phase (16)**

**1. *Gil Heredia, rhp, Pima (Ariz.) CC.—(1991-2001)**
2. Michael Edge, rhp, Brewton Parker (Ga.) JC.
3. *Floyd Rossom, rhp, Angelina (Texas) JC.
4. *James Warner, lhp, Allegany (Md.) CC.
5. Frank Klopp, of, San Diego Mesa JC.
6. *Steve Bowden, rhp, San Jacinto (Texas) JC.
7. *Oscar Valencia, lhp, Grossmont (Calif.) JC.
8. *Joe Schueller, of, Kansas City (Kan.) CC.
9. Anthony Stewart, of, Portland, Maine.
10. Van Evans, of, Grossmont (Calif.) JC.
**11. *Alex Cole, of, Manatee (Fla.) JC.—(1990-96)**
12. *Michael Campbell, rhp, Dundalk (Md.) CC.
13. Dan Clark, 2b, Grossmont (Calif.) JC.
14. *Darrell Smith, 2b, Paris (Texas) JC.
15. *Rob Russell, lhp, Allegany (Md.) CC.
16. *Damon Baldwin, 1b, San Jacinto (Texas) JC.
17. *Danny Wilson, of, Bucks County (Pa.) CC.
18. *Jeffrey Bonsall, rhp, Cecil (Md.) CC.
19. Carey Cheek, of, CC of Baltimore.
20. *Louis Kelly, of, Angelina (Texas) JC.
21. *Roy Mays, c, Angelina (Texas) JC.
22. *Mark Maultsby, c, Louisburg (N.C.) JC.
23. *Jeff Forney, of, Roane State (Tenn.) CC.
24. *David Miller, ss, Walters State (Tenn.) CC.
25. James Davins, of, University of Maine.

**January—Secondary Phase (10)**

1. *Ronnie Gideon, 1b, Panola (Texas) JC.—(AA)
**2. Jay Buhner, of, McLennan (Texas) CC.—(1987-2001)**
3. *John D. Martin, rhp, Golden West (Calif.) JC.
**4. Tom Prince, c, Kankakee (Ill.) CC.—(1987-2003)**
5. *Oscar Talley, of, Ferrum (Va.) JC.

**June—Regular Phase (15)**

1. Kevin Andersh, lhp, University of New Mexico.—(AA)
2. Tim McMillan, of, Oak Hill HS, Scarbro, W.Va.—(High A)
**3. Barry Jones, rhp, Indiana University.—(1986-93)**
4. *Scott Mackie, of, Elkton (Md.) HS.—(High A)
DRAFT DROP *Attended James Madison; re-drafted by Indians, 1987 (7th round)*
**5. *Wes Chamberlain, of, Simeon HS, Chicago.—(1990-95)**
DRAFT DROP *Attended Jackson State; re-drafted by Pirates, 1987 (4th round)*
6. Greg Stading, rhp, Central HS, Billings, Mon.
7. Kevin Helton, rhp, Carson-Newman (Tenn.) College.
8. Greg McClain, ss, University of California.
9. Ron Knotts, of, Southeastern Oklahoma State University.
10. *Gerald Ingram, of, Simeon HS, Chicago.
11. Terrance Smith, c, Simeon HS, Chicago.
12. Lance Belen, 3b, University of Hawaii.
13. Steve Brown, ss-of, South Florence HS, Effingham, S.C.
14. *Bob Orr, lhp, Los Medanos (Calif.) JC.
15. *Craig Repoz, ss, Katella HS, Anaheim, Calif.
DRAFT DROP *Son of Roger Repoz, major leaguer (1964-72)*
16. James Nicholson, ss, Muskingum (Ohio) College.
17. Todd Hansen, 1b-rhp, Idaho Falls (Idaho) HS.
18. Emmett Robinson, ss-2b, St. Augustine (N.C.) College.
**19. *Stu Cole, ss, South Mecklenburg HS, Charlotte, N.C.—(1991)**
20. *Mike Linskey, lhp, Loyola HS, Baltimore.
21. Lindsey Johnson, c, Oregon State University.
22. Eric Bolling, 3b-of, Rollins (Fla.) College.
23. Scott Neal, lhp, Southwestern (Texas) University.
24. Reggie Hammonds, of, Northwestern University.
DRAFT DROP *Brother of Jeffrey Hammonds, first-round draft pick, Orioles (1992); major leaguer (1993-2005)*
25. *Joel Smith, of, Jones County HS, Macon, Ga.
26. *Steven Trumbull, of, Pinellas Park (Fla.) HS.
27. John Johnson, of, Chicago State University.
28. (void) *Frank Thomas, rhp, Triton (Ill.) JC.
29. Reggie Barringer, ss, Cumberland (Tenn.) College.
30. Jeff Wayland, rhp, Rio Grande (Ohio) College.
31. Chris Hill, rhp, Cumberland (Tenn.) College.
32. *Larry Gryskevich, 1b-lhp, Brooke HS, Weirton, W.Va.
33. *William Savage, ss, Sussex HS, Georgetown, Md.
34. *Michael McHugh, lhp, Boonton (N.J.) HS.
35. *James Agemy, rhp, Divine Child HS, Dearborn Heights, Mich.
36. Stan Fabre, rhp, Nicholls State University.
37. *Tommy Kurczewski, rhp, Henry Ford HS, Sterling Heights, Mich.
38. *Darrell Rodgers, rhp, University of Oklahoma.
39. Belgee Falkner, of, Baylor University.
40. *Jeff Necessary, inf-of, Abingdon HS, Glade Spring, Va.
41. *Brent Pless, lhp, Brown HS, Kannapolis, N.C.
42. *Spencer Wilkinson, rhp, Muskogee (Okla.) HS.

**June—Secondary Phase (13)**

**1. *Eric Hetzel, rhp, Eastern Oklahoma State JC.—(1989-90)**
DRAFT DROP *First overall draft pick, June 1985/secondary phase, Red Sox*
2. Jon Kolb, rhp, Southwestern (Calif.) JC.
3. *Steve DeAngelis, of, Saddleback (Calif.) CC.
4. *Jim Willis, of, Triton (Ill.) JC.
5. *Billy Bartels, rhp, Fresno (Calif.) CC.
6. *Gregg Schiffelbein, of, Allen County (Kan.) CC.
**7. *Gordon Dillard, lhp, Connors State (Okla.) JC.—(1988-89)**
8. Rob Russell, lhp, Allegany (Md.) CC.

## ST. LOUIS CARDINALS

**January—Regular Phase (8)**

**1. *Jeff Blauser, ss, Sacramento (Calif.) CC.—(1987-99)**
2. *Dan Hickey, lhp, JC of Marin (Calif.).
**3. *Doug Piatt, rhp, Gulf Coast (Fla.) CC.—(1991)**
4. *Gordie Hershiser, rhp, Indian River (Fla.) CC.
DRAFT DROP *Brother of Orel Hershiser, major leaguer (1983-2000)*
**5. *Greg Vaughn, of, Sacramento (Calif.) CC.—(1989-2003)**
6. *Scott Willis, rhp, JC of the Sequoias (Calif.).
7. *Burt Beattie, c, Crowder (Mo.) JC.
8. John Haynes, rhp, Columbia State (Tenn.) CC.
9. *Robert Jensen, rhp, Bellevue (Wash.) CC.
10. Michael Robertson, rhp, Murray State (Okla.) JC.
11. *Theron Powell, of, Roane State (Tenn.) CC.
12. *Sammy Garcia, lhp, Los Angeles CC.
13. *Greg Bochesa, c, Los Angeles Harbor JC.
14. *Rene Isenhart, rhp, Citrus (Calif.) JC.
15. *Pete Roberts, lhp, Mira Costa (Calif.) JC.

**January—Secondary Phase (14)**

1. Dennis Carter, of, Chipola (Fla.) JC.—(AA)
2. *Shell Scott, 3b, JC of Southern Idaho.

**June—Regular Phase (7)**

**1. Mike Dunne, rhp, Bradley University.—(1987-92)**
**2. Matt Kinzer, rhp, Purdue University.—(1989-90)**
DRAFT DROP *Punter, National Football League (1987)*
3. Ron Johns, 1b-3b, Cal Poly Pomona.—(AAA)
4. Brett Harrison, ss, University of Arkansas.—(AA)
**5. Scott Arnold, rhp, Miami (Ohio) University.—(1988)**
**6. Lance Johnson, of, University of South Alabama.—(1987-2000)**
7. David Crossley, lhp, Eckerd (Fla.) College.
8. *Phil Goguen, rhp, Southwest HS, San Diego.
9. Jon Billinger, c, Long Beach State University.
**10. Greg Mathews, lhp, Cal State Fullerton.—(1986-92)**
11. *Billy Carver, c, Beech HS, Hendersonville, Tenn.
12. *Tim Sossamon, of, Louisiana State University.
13. *Carey Nemeth, 3b, James Madison University.
14. *John Rohde, lhp, Carson-Newman (Tenn.) College.
15. Tommy Mathews, 1b, Tulane University.
16. *Ron Rooker, lhp, San Jose State University.
17. *Joe Murtagh, rhp, Downers Grove HS, Woodridge, Ill.
18. Don Isner, c, Georgetown (Ky.) College.
19. Gary Blaine, of, Murray State University.
**20. Craig Wilson, ss-2b, Anne Arundel (Md.) CC.—(1989-93)**
21. Jim Van Houten, rhp, American International (Mass.) College.
**22. Jeff Fassero, lhp, University of Mississippi.—(1991-2005)**
23. John Murphy, 3b, The Citadel.
24. *Brad Bierley, of-3b, Pepperdine University.
25. Bill Wilson, of-lhp, Pan American University.
26. Steve Barnard, c, San Diego State University.

**June—Secondary Phase (21)**

**1. Mike Fitzgerald, c-of, Middle Georgia JC.—(1988)**
2. *Kevin Thomas, lhp, Spartanburg Methodist (S.C.) JC.

## SAN DIEGO PADRES

**January—Regular Phase (12)**

1. Larry Martin, of, Mississippi Gulf Coast JC.—(Short-season A)
2. Richard Scales, ss, Chipola (Fla.) JC.
3. *DeJon Watson, of, West Los Angeles JC.
DRAFT DROP *Scouting director, Reds (1998-2000)*
4. *Dave Satnat, lhp, Modesto (Calif.) JC.
5. Greg Sparks, 1b, Mesa (Ariz.) CC.
6. *Ernest May, rhp, Taft (Calif.) JC.
7. Robert Greenlee, lhp, Uniondale, N.Y.
8. Robert Perkins, c, Mesa (Ariz.) CC.
**9. Rodney McCray, of, West Los Angeles JC.—(1990-92)**

**January—Secondary Phase (8)**

**1. Randy Byers, 3b-of, CC of Baltimore.—(1987-88)**
2. *Lynn Van Every, ss, JC of Southern Idaho.

**June—Regular Phase (11)**

**1. Shane Mack, of, UCLA.—(1987-98)**
**1. Gary Green, ss, Oklahoma State University** (Supplemental choice—27th—as compensation for Type B free agent Ruppert Jones)**—(1986-92)**
2. (Choice to Yankees as compensation for Type A free agent Rich Gossage)
3. Brad Pounders, 3b, UC Riverside.—(AAA)
4. *Larry Melton, rhp, University of Portland.—(AAA)
DRAFT DROP *Returned to Portland; re-drafted by Pirates, 1985 (8th round)*
5. Eric Varoz, 2b, Brigham Young University.—(AA)
6. *Steve Allen, rhp, Central Valley HS, Veradale, Wash.
7. Randy Robertson, rhp, University of Southern California.
8. Mike DeButch, ss-2b, Bradley University.
9. Trace Czyzewski, rhp, Lewis & Clark (Ore.) College.
10. Mike Costello, rhp, Washington State University.
11. Mickey Kazmierski, rhp, Texas Christian University.
12. Joe Filandino, rhp, West Virginia University.
13. *Phil Williams, c, Seminole (Okla.) JC.
14. Michael Visor, rhp, Ballard HS, Seattle.
15. Terry Forbes, rhp, Long Beach State University.
16. Jeff Gray, of, Muir HS, Pasadena, Calif.
17. Russell Ford, rhp, Texas Wesleyan College.
**18. *Mike Harkey, rhp, Ganesha HS, Pomona, Calif.—(1988-97)**
DRAFT DROP *First-round draft pick (4th overall), Cubs (1987)*
19. *Kevin Gorczyca, c, Hoffman HS, South Amboy, N.J.
20. Mike Gildehaus, rhp, Missouri Southern State University.

**June—Secondary Phase (7)**

1. Bob Grandstaff, 3b, Arizona State University.—(AA)
**2. Joe Bitker, rhp, Sacramento (Calif.) CC.—(1990-91).**
3. *Larry Cratsenburg, inf, Orange Coast (Calif.) JC.

## SAN FRANCISCO GIANTS

**January—Regular Phase (10)**

**1. Greg Litton, 2b, Pensacola (Fla.) JC.—(1989-94)**
2. *Jose Alou, of, Canada (Calif.) JC.
DRAFT DROP *Son of Felipe Alou, major leaguer (1958-74); major league manager (1992-2006) • Brother of Moises Alou, major league (1990-2008)*
3. *Eric Tutt, of, Middle Georgia JC.
4. Greg Schmidt, rhp, Pomona, Calif.
**5. Mackey Sasser, c, Dothan, Ala.—(1987-95)**
6. *William Dudek, rhp, Central Arizona JC.
7. John Ackerman, rhp, Labette (Kan.) CC.
8. *Dick Canan, ss, Triton (Ill.) JC.
9. Brad Porter, c-1b, Mission (Calif.) JC.
10. *Jeff Schow, 2b, JC of Southern Idaho.
11. *Dion Beck, lhp, Cerritos (Calif.) JC.
12. David Hornsby, c, Chowan (N.C.) JC.

**January—Secondary Phase (2)**

1. Lyle Swepson, ss, Louisburg (N.C.) JC.—(Low A)
2. *Terence Guzman, lhp, Ferrum (Va.) JC.

**June—Regular Phase (9)**

**1. Alan Cockrell, of, University of Tennessee.—(1996)**
**1. Terry Mulholland, lhp, Marietta (Ohio) College** (Choice from Tigers as compensation for Type A free agent Darrell Evans)**—(1986-2004)**
2. Joe Olker, lhp, University of Illinois.—(AAA)
**3. Tony Perezchica, ss, Palm Springs (Calif.) HS.—(1988-92)**
4. Keith Silver, rhp, Lamar University.—(AA)
5. T.J. McDonald, of-3b, Pace (N.Y.) University.—(AA)
6. Greg Gilbert, rhp, Cal Poly San Luis Obispo.
7. John Grimes, c, Texas Tech.
**8. Stu Tate, rhp, Auburn University.—(1989)**
9. *Garrett O'Connor, rhp, University of Southwestern Louisiana.
10. Loren Hibbs, of, Wichita State University.
DRAFT DROP *Baseball coach, North Carolina-Charlotte (1993-2015)*

11. Darin James, of, Patrick Henry HS, San Diego.
12. Todd Moriarty, lhp, Southern Utah State College.
13. *Greg Ehmig, of-1b, Rhea County HS, Dayton, Tenn.
14. Steve Cottrell, rhp, Stanford University.
15. David Hinnrichs, rhp, Rice University.
16. Charles Culberson, of, Jacksonville State University.
17. Romy Cucjen, ss, Arizona State University.
18. *Chad Miltenberger, c, Lewis-Clark State (Idaho) College.
19. *John Skurla, of, Washington State University.
20. Tom Messier, lhp, University of Rhode Island.
21. *Michael Pirro, 3b, Henniger HS, Syracuse, N.Y.
22. Michael Cicione, 3b, Los Angeles Valley JC.
23. Kent Cooper, of, Santa Clara University.
24. James Utley, rhp, University of Texas-El Paso.
25. Jim Wasem, ss, Eastern Washington University.
26. *Aaron Marks, rhp, Glendale (Ariz.) CC.

#### June—Secondary Phase (17)

1. *Eric Bauer, lhp, Eastern Washington University.—(AAA)
2. ***Mike Blowers, 3b, Tacoma (Wash.) CC.—(1989-99)**
3. Rod Rush, of, Oklahoma City University.

## SEATTLE MARINERS

#### January—Regular Phase (1)

1. **Calvin Jones, rhp, Chaffey (Calif.) JC.—(1991-92)**
2. *Larry Cratsenburg, ss, Orange Coast (Calif.) JC.
3. *Rickie Vogt, rhp, Bellevue (Wash.) CC.
4. *Steve Maye, rhp, Los Angeles Harbor JC.
5. *Jeff Osterode, lhp, Orange Coast (Calif.) JC.
6. **(void) *Joe Kraemer, lhp, Lower Columbia (Wash.) JC.—(1989-90)**
7. *David Swolsky, c, Triton (Ill.) JC.
8. ***Mike Blowers, 3b, Tacoma (Wash.) CC.—(1989-99)**

#### January—Secondary Phase (11)

1. *Ray Rosthenhausler, ss, Pima (Ariz.) CC.—(High A)
2. *Robert Nettles, rhp, Orange Coast (Calif.) JC.

#### June—Regular Phase (2)

1. **Bill Swift, rhp, University of Maine.—(1985-98)**
2. Mike Christ, rhp, Jacksonville University.—(AAA)
3. Ken Spratke, rhp, Eastern Michigan University.—(AAA)
4. Steve Rousey, rhp, Cal State Fullerton.—(High A)
5. Ed West, rhp, University of Denver.—(Short-season A)
6. Don Neufelder, lhp, Murray State University.
7. Bob Gibree, c, St. Leo (Fla.) College.
8. Bob Siegel, rhp, University of Hawaii.
9. Bill Mendek, lhp, Temple University.
10. Steve Murray, 2b, Arizona State University.
11. Jim Walker, rhp, Cal State Northridge.
12. Brad Kinney, rhp, UC Santa Barbara.
13. Greg Brinkman, rhp, University of Houston.
14. Bregg Ray, ss, Texas Wesleyan College.
15. *Tim Schneider, 3b, Louisiana State University.
16. Scott Buss, of, Fresno State University.
17. Jack Reinholtz, lhp, Cal State Fullerton.
18. David Bresnahan, c, Grand Canyon College.
19. Nestor Valiente, c, Florida International University.
20. Darrell Higgs, rhp, Grand Canyon College.
21. *Anthony Buglione, c, University of New Haven.
22. Arvid Morfin, ss-3b, Beaverton (Ore.) HS.
23. Logan White, rhp, Western New Mexico University.

DRAFT DROP *Scouting director, Dodgers (2002-07)*

24. A.J. Anderson, of, St. Leo (Fla.) College.
25. Mike Solomon, of, Cal State Northridge.
26. Mike Carozza, of, Long Beach State University.
27. Paul Steinert, rhp, Florida International University.
28. Richard Hayden, c, El Dorado HS, Placentia, Calif.
29. William O'Leary, 3b, Northeastern University.
30. Tom Krause, ss, San Jose State University.
31. Dan Larson, 2b, University of Houston.
32. *Kraig Luckenbill, rhp, Trinity HS, Euless, Texas.
33. *Rex Peters, 1b, Cherry Creek HS, Denver.
34. Rich Middleton, 3b, Portland State University.
35. Mark Machalec, of, Rice University.
36. *Jim King, ss, Oklahoma Baptist University.

DRAFT DROP *Brother of Jeff King, first overall draft pick, Pirates (1986)*

37. Michael Wood, rhp, Francis Marion (S.C.) College.
38. Charlie Fonville, 1b, Western Carolina University.
39. A.D. Jackson, of, St. Thomas (Fla.) University.
40. Dan Clark, 2b, UC Santa Barbara.

#### June—Secondary Phase (4)

1. *Vince Lopez, ss, Orange Coast (Calif.) JC.—(Rookie)
2. ***Russ Swan, lhp, Spokane Falls (Wash.) CC.—(1989-94)**
3. *Jeff Marr, rhp, Brevard (Fla.) CC.
4. *Thomas Green, rhp, Fullerton (Calif.) JC.
5. (void) *David Miller, ss, Walters State (Tenn.) CC.

## TEXAS RANGERS

#### January—Regular Phase (11)

1. Kevin Bootay, of, Cerritos (Calif.) JC.—(AAA)
2. ***Gordon Dillard, lhp, Connors State (Okla.) JC.—(1988-89)**
3. *Jon Kolb, rhp, Southwestern (Calif.) JC.
4. Carmelo LoSauro, rhp, Miami-Dade CC North.
5. ***Steve Cummings, rhp, Blinn (Texas) JC.—(1989-90)**
6. John Schofield, rhp, Laney (Calif.) JC.
7. *Nathaniel Greene, of, Ranger (Texas) JC.
8. *Jeff Colton, lhp, Valencia (Fla.) CC.
9. *Patrick Rowe, 2b, Baltimore.
10. *Charles Todd, c, Rockland (N.Y.) CC.

#### January—Secondary Phase (19)

1. *Dale Hamrick, 3b-c, Spartanburg Methodist (S.C.) JC.—(Rookie)
2. *Darryl Stephens, of, Stanford University.

#### June—Regular Phase (12)

1. **Oddibe McDowell, of, Arizona State University.—(1985-94)**

DRAFT DROP *First overall draft pick, June 1983/secondary phase, Twins • First player from 1984 draft to reach majors (May 19, 1985)*

2. Jimmy Meadows, rhp, Walters State (Tenn.) CC.—(High A)
3. Sid Akins, rhp, University of Southern California.—(AAA)
4. ***Scott Ruskin, of-lhp, University of Florida.—(1990-93)**

DRAFT DROP *Returned to Florida; re-drafted by Indians, 1985 (3rd round)*

5. Dave Darretta, ss, Dunedin (Fla.) HS.—(High A)
6. Larry Pardo, rhp, Columbus HS, Miami.
7. **Scott Anderson, rhp, Oregon State University.—(1987-95)**
8. Huck Hibberd, rhp, San Jose State University.
9. Scott Russell, of, Mount Whitney HS, Visalia, Calif.
10. Riley Epps, c, University of Houston.
11. Kirk Bates, 2b-1b, Cal State Fullerton.
12. Larry Klein, ss, Emporia State (Kan.) University.
13. Jamie Doughty, ss, University of Texas.
14. Kendall Carter, rhp, Arizona State University.
15. Joe Grayston, ss, Azusa Pacific (Calif.) University.
16. Jeff Paul, 3b, University of Maine.
17. Bryan Dial, rhp, Middle Tennessee State University.
18. Jim St. Laurent, of, University of South Carolina.
19. E.L. Ittner, rhp, U.S. International (Calif.) University.
20. Michael Grouse, 1b, Phillips (Okla.) University.
21. James Bridges, lhp, Florida Southern College.
22. Mike Fay, rhp, UC Santa Barbara.
23. Jeff Melrose, 1b-of, Santa Clara University.
24. Rick Poznanski, c, Washington State University.
25. Rob Amble, of, Azusa Pacific (Calif.) University.
26. Steve Cullers, c, James Madison University.
27. Albert Farmer, 2b, William Carey (Miss.) College.
28. Neil Reilly, c, Phillips (Okla.) University.
29. Tim Owen, c, University of Florida.
30. Jim Jagnow, 2b, Louisiana Tech.
31. Billy Sheeks, rhp, Christian Brothers (Tenn.) College.
32. Ronnie King, of, Baylor University.
33. Dan Danelson, rhp, Lewis-Clark State (Idaho) College.
34. Darrell Whitaker, rhp, Dallas Baptist University.
35. Brad Hill, of, Emporia State (Kan.) University.

DRAFT DROP *Baseball coach, Kansas State (2004-15)*

36. *Greg Karpuk, rhp, South Glastonbury, Conn.
37. Matthew Baker, rhp, Jersey City State College.
38. John Schuessler, of, Northeastern University.
39. Rodney Covington, of, Cherokee County HS, Centre, Ala.
40. Dale Lanik, 1b, Emporia State (Kan.) University.
41. Mark Kramer, of, Bremen HS, Midlothian, Ill.
42. *Gregg Patterson, lhp, East Ascension HS, Gonzales, La.
43. **Paul Kilgus, lhp, University of Kentucky.—(1987-93)**
44. *Dave Alvis, 1b, University of Southwestern Louisiana.

DRAFT DROP *Son of Max Alvis, major leaguer (1962-70)*

45. *Walt Guillory, of, University of Southwestern Louisiana.
46. Ross Jones, rhp, Palatka (Fla.) HS.
47. *Rod Ehrhard, of, Manatee (Fla.) JC.

#### June—Secondary Phase (14)

1. Thomas Kelley, of, Triton (Ill.) JC.—(Low A)
2. Robert O'Hearn, c, St. Mary's (Calif.) College.
3. *Dave Lawn, lhp, Laney (Calif.) JC.

## TORONTO BLUE JAYS

#### January—Regular Phase (19)

1. **Eric Yelding, of-ss, Chipola (Fla.) JC.—(1989-93)**
2. *Scott Ayers, rhp, McLennan (Texas) CC.
3. ***Dwight Smith, of, Spartanburg Methodist (S.C.) JC.—(1989-96)**

DRAFT DROP *Father of Dwight Smith Jr., first-round draft pick, Blue Jays (2015)*

4. *Keith Swartzlander, rhp, Allegheny (Pa.) CC.
5. *Jeff Bedell, 3b, Montgomery (Md.) JC.

DRAFT DROP *Son of Howie Bedell, major leaguer (1962-68)*

6. Darryl Landrum, of, Calhoun (Ala.) CC.

DRAFT DROP *Brother of Ced Landrum, major leaguer (1991-93)*

7. *Robert Smith, rhp, Miami.
8. *Jack Peel, of, Northwest Mississippi JC.
9. *Steve DeAngelis, of, Saddleback (Calif.) CC.
10. Steve Lounello, rhp, Albany, N.Y.
11. *John Bornhop, of, East Central (Mo.) JC.
12. *Randy Usenick, rhp, Mishawaka, Ind.

#### January—Secondary Phase (15)

1. *Mark Hamann, rhp, Taft (Calif.) JC.—DNP
2. Tim Rypien, c, Spokane Falls (Wash.) CC.

DRAFT DROP *Brother of Mark Rypien, quarterback, National Football League (1988-2001).*

3. *Chris Miller, ss, University of Oregon.

DRAFT DROP *First-round draft pick, Atlanta Falcons/ National Football League (1987); quarterback, NFL (1987-99)*

#### June—Regular Phase (20)

1. (Choice to White Sox as compensation for Type A free agent Dennis Lamp)
2. **Dane Johnson, rhp, St. Thomas (Fla.) University.—(1994-97)**
3. **Greg Myers, c, Poly HS, Riverside, Calif.—(1987-2004)**
4. Pat Saitta, rhp, Concordia (N.Y.) College.—(High A)
5. Todd Provence, rhp, Anderson HS, Redding, Calif.—(High A)
6. ***Scott Livingstone, 3b, Lake Highlands HS, Dallas.—(1991-98)**
7. Rob Turano, rhp, Mansfield (Pa.) University.
8. Tim Englund, rhp, Rice University.
9. Tom Wasilewski, rhp, Vanderbilt University.
10. Brian Morrison, of, Oakland (Calif.) HS.
11. *William Stokes, 1b, Pasadena (Calif.) HS.
12. *Jeff Oswalt, lhp, Madison HS, San Diego.
13. *Robert Lipscomb (Muhammad), ss, Pasadena HS, Altadena, Calif.
14. Norm Tonucci, ss, Waterford (Conn.) HS.
15. *Mike C. Jones, of, Valdosta State (Ga.) College.
16. Mark Cooper, c, Louisiana State University.
17. Bruce Blake, lhp, Quinsigamond (Mass.) CC.
18. *Jeff Mott, ss, Merced (Calif.) HS.
19. Jim Howard, ss, Siena College.
20. Rick Moyer, rhp, Kent State University.
21. *Russ Elsberry, rhp, Monterey Peninsula (Calif.) JC.
22. ***Eric Fox, of, Fresno State University.—(1992-95)**
23. Willie Shanks, rhp, University of Missouri-St. Louis.
24. Thomas Winter, lhp, Siena College.
25. ***Rodney Brewer, lhp, Apopka HS, Zellwood, Fla.—(1990-93)**
26. *Anthony Newman, of, Beaverton HS, Portland, Ore.

DRAFT DROP *Second-round draft pick, Los Angeles Rams/ National Football League (1987); defensive back, NFL (1988-91)*

27. Greg Lorenzetti, of, Stanford University.
28. *Jerald Jones, lhp, Vallejo (Calif.) HS.
29. Lawrence Monaco, rhp, Siena College.
30. *Rodney Peete, ss, Shawnee Mission (Kan.) South HS.

DRAFT DROP *Quarterback, National Football League (1989-2004)*

#### June—Secondary Phase (25)

1. **Jeff Richardson, rhp, Wichita, Kan.—(1990)**
2. ***Daryl Irvine, rhp, Ferrum (Va.) JC.—(1990-92)**
3. *Paul James, rhp, St. Louis CC-Meramec.
4. Dan Hickey, lhp, JC of Marin (Calif.).
5. *Keith Felden, rhp, St. Petersburg (Fla.) JC.

# 1985

# Star quality makes '85 talent best in history

Best draft ever! That's what baseball's scouting fraternity began labeling the Class of 1985—even as the draft was still unfolding.

Normally, the relative merits of a class must stand the test of time, but it was obvious from the start that the 1985 draft was one for the ages.

With headliners like Barry Bonds, Barry Larkin, Rafael Palmeiro, Will Clark and B.J. Surhoff, the star-quality talent that came out of the first round of the 1985 draft is unmatched—though 2005, in time, could give it a run for its money.

The cumulative WAR (Wins Above Replacement) of 1985 first-rounders is 495.7—easily better than the first round of any draft. The talent didn't stop there, either, as Randy Johnson was taken in the second round and John Smoltz was a 22nd-round afterthought. Both were inducted into the Hall of Fame in 2015.

And that doesn't include the likes of Bobby Witt and Pete Incaviglia, the third and eighth overall picks, or Bo Jackson, an obvious first-round talent who lasted until the 20th round because of his football obligations at Auburn. None of those three displayed the sustained success as some of their peers, but Incaviglia hit 48 home runs that year at Oklahoma State to set an NCAA record that may never be broken, while Witt and Jackson showed flashes of brilliance—and are still the only players in draft history to earn perfect 80 grades on the Major League Scouting Bureau's 20-to-80 grading scale.

"The 1981 draft was pretty good, too," then-New York Mets vice president Joe McIlvaine said. "The first 10 guys drafted in '81 all played in the big leagues, but I don't think the caliber that year was equal to the caliber of 1985.

"And it's probably the fastest group to get to the big leagues. Whether that says something about the outstanding caliber of the players themselves, or the caliber of play in the major leagues, I don't know. But it's pretty amazing."

Pretty amazing is what they also said about a 1984 draft that yielded Mark McGwire, Cory Snyder, Oddibe McDowell, Billy Swift and Scott Bankhead from the U.S. Olympic team.

"A lot of people would have thought the talent group out of the Olympic year would never be duplicated," then-Texas Rangers general manager Tom Grieve said. "Well, 1985 came sooner than anyone thought."

Actually, the 1984 Olympic team also contributed heavily to the talent pool for the 1985 draft as Surhoff, Clark, Witt and Larkin—the first four players drafted—were all Olympians. As was Chris Gwynn, selected 10th overall.

"A lot of it was exposure," Surhoff said. "We got a lot of publicity from the Olympic team, and I think the teams that drafted us were willing to take a chance on us because of that. But we were also in the right place at the right time. Some of us just happened to be drafted by teams that needed players right away."

UNIVERSITY OF NORTH CAROLINA

In spite of all the elite talent available, the Brewers went for North Carolina's B.J. Surhoff with the No. 1 overall pick, favoring his all-around skills and positional versatility above other players

The seeds for the 1985 draft were planted in 1982 when numerous top high school players went unsigned. Three years later they matured into Grade A prospects, ripe for the picking.

Of the first 12 players drafted in 1985, an unprecedented 11 were from the college ranks. That included the five Olympic team players, plus Bonds, Incaviglia, shortstop Walt Weiss and pitcher Mike Campbell, all of whom were coveted prospects out of high school. Bonds and Larkin were unsigned second-round picks in 1982. Clark went in the fourth round. Surhoff, Gwynn and Campbell were selected in the fifth.

Then-Cleveland Indians general manager Joe Klein said, "None was quite at the level where a club would invest the kind of first-round money, $40,000 to $100,000, it took to keep them from going to college, because that would have been overpaying just to buy a player."

In all, 12 of the 17 college players selected in the first round of the 1985 draft had been picked in the first 10 rounds of the 1982 draft.

"Had they signed then," Grieve said, "they wouldn't have been in the 1985 draft, so you could make a case that it was luck. But no matter how you look at it, 1985 was a particularly good year."

Even the lesser phases of the 1985 draft contributed as lefthander Chuck Finley, a first-round pick

## AT A GLANCE

### This Date In History

**WINTER DRAFT:** Jan. 3-5
**SUMMER DRAFT:** June 3-5

### Best Draft

**CHICAGO CUBS.** The Cubs got significant mileage out of two picks, outfielder **RAFAEL PALMEIRO** (1), who hit .288 with 569 homers over 20 seasons, and first baseman **MARK GRACE** (24), who hit .303 with 175 homers in 16 years.

### Worst Draft

**MINNESOTA TWINS.** The Twins thought they were on to something special with hard-throwing prep righthanders **JEFF BUMGARNER** (1) and **STEVE GASSER** (2), but both pitchers were foiled by control issues. Bumgarner went 48-71, 4.26 in eight minor league seasons. Gasser was one of the best prospects in the game until suddenly losing the ability to throw strikes. In 24 innings in his final minor league season, he went 0-3, 11.25 with 55 walks, 23 strikeouts and 27 wild pitches.

### First-Round Bust

**TREY MCCALL, C, PHILLIES.** There was plenty of debate among Phillies scouts whether McCall merited first-round consideration. He was overmatched in a five-year career in the Phillies system and played in just 309 games—none above Class A. He had a cumulative .202 average.

### Second Time Around

**RANDY JOHNSON, LHP, EXPOS.** As one of the most dominating pitchers in history, it seems improbable Johnson wasn't snapped up in the first round. But he was nowhere close to the finished product he became once he streamlined his mechanics and grew into his 6-foot-10 frame.

### Late Round Find

**JOHN SMOLTZ, RHP, TIGERS (22ND ROUND).** It took first-round money

CONTINUED ON PAGE 304

## AT A GLANCE

**CONTINUED FROM PAGE 303**

($60,500) on the night before Smoltz was scheduled to enroll at Michigan State for the Tigers to finally snare a prized local product. They never reaped any long-term benefit from the future Hall of Famer, as he was packaged to Atlanta while still in Double-A.

### Never Too Late

**JIM ABBOTT, LHP, BLUE JAYS (36TH ROUND).** It wasn't a publicity stunt the Blue Jays pulled by drafting Abbott, who was born without a right hand. That became evident three years later when Abbott became a first-round pick of the Angels out of Michigan and led the U.S. to a gold medal in the 1988 Seoul Olympics.

### Overlooked

**KEN HILL, RHP, TIGERS.** The Tigers signed Hill for $1,500 out of Massachusetts' North Adams State College on Feb. 14, 1985. It wasn't until they dealt him to the Cardinals, who in turn sent him to Montreal in 1992, that he developed into a top-notch starting pitcher. In 14 big league seasons, Hill won 117 games.

### International Gem

**ROBERTO ALOMAR, SS, PADRES.** Not only was 1985 a banner year for the draft, but it also was a great year on the international front. Future Hall of Famer Alomar was the big catch, signing with the Padres for $52,500. Fellow Puerto Ricans **CARLOS BAERGA** and **BERNIE WILLIAMS** also signed—Baerga with the Padres for $40,500, Williams with the Yankees for $16,000. The Rangers signed Dominican outfielder **SAMMY SOSA** for $3,500.

### Minor League Take

**GREGG JEFFERIES, SS, METS.** Few players arrived in the big leagues with as much fanfare as Jefferies, a two-time Minor League Player of the Year. In 458 minor league games, the Mets first-rounder hit .333 with 47 home runs, 314

## 1985: THE FIRST ROUNDERS

| CLUB: PLAYER, POS., SCHOOL | HOMETOWN | B-T | HT. | WT. | AGE | BONUS | FIRST YEAR | LAST YEAR | PEAK LEVEL (YEARS) |
|---|---|---|---|---|---|---|---|---|---|
| **JUNE—REGULAR PHASE** | | | | | | | | | |
| 1. Brewers: B.J. Surhoff, c, North Carolina | Rye, N.Y. | L-R | 6-2 | 185 | 20 | $150,000 | 1985 | 2005 | Majors (19) |
| Versatile talent was high school shortstop, college catcher, C/3B/OF in 2,313 games in majors; hit .282-188-1,153, stole 141 bags for three different clubs. | | | | | | | | | |
| 2. Giants: Will Clark, 1b, Mississippi State | New Orleans | L-L | 6-1 | 170 | 21 | $160,000 | 1985 | 2000 | Majors (15) |
| Developed picturesque HR swing in college, won 1984 Golden Spikes Award; highly-competitive player hit .300-plus 10 times in majors, went deep 284 times. | | | | | | | | | |
| 3. Rangers: Bobby Witt, rhp, Oklahoma | Canton, Mass. | R-R | 6-1 | 185 | 21 | $179,000 | 1985 | 2001 | Majors (16) |
| Had explosive stuff regarded in same league as Nolan Ryan's; never quite learned to throw strikes consistently, harness ability, went just 142-157, 4.83. | | | | | | | | | |
| 4. Reds: Barry Larkin, ss, Michigan | Cincinnati | R-R | 6-0 | 175 | 21 | $165,000 | 1985 | 2004 | Majors (19) |
| Hall of Famer was slower to develop because of Northern upbringing, two-sport background, but soon passed peers in talented '85 crop, played 19 years with Reds. | | | | | | | | | |
| 5. White Sox: Kurt Brown, c, Glendora HS | Glendora, Calif. | R-R | 6-2 | 205 | 18 | $150,000 | 1985 | 1991 | Class AAA (1) |
| Improbable pick between Larkin and Bonds impressed scouts with power, arm, agility; struggled with bat (.243-23-206), as receiver in seven years in Sox system. | | | | | | | | | |
| 6. Pirates: Barry Bonds, of, Arizona State | San Carlos, Calif. | L-L | 6-1 | 175 | 20 | $125,000 | 1985 | 2007 | Majors (22) |
| Potential evident, but scouts said he hadn't put it all together; they also questioned abrasive attitude; unquestioned ability in spectacular/controversial MLB career. | | | | | | | | | |
| 7. Mariners: Mike Campbell, rhp, Hawaii | Bellevue, Wash. | R-R | 6-3 | 195 | 21 | $110,000 | 1985 | 1996 | Majors (6) |
| Mariners went for local product, were encouraged with results until injuries/mechanical flaws undermined career; went 8-16, 5.74 with M's, won just 12 games. | | | | | | | | | |
| 8. *Expos: Pete Incaviglia, of, Oklahoma State | Pebble Beach, Calif. | R-R | 6-1 | 225 | 21 | $175,000 | 1986 | 2002 | Majors (12) |
| One-dimensional slugger set NCAA season (48), career (100) HR records for Cowboys; manipulated draft to land with Rangers, hit 206 HRs in majors. | | | | | | | | | |
| 9. Indians: Mike Poehl, rhp, Texas | Houston | R-R | 6-4 | 195 | 20 | $125,000 | 1985 | 1991 | Class AA (4) |
| Lost in shuffle on talented Texas staff, went 7-1, 3.67 (61 IP/78 SO) with 93-94 mph FB; rarely flashed same velo in injury-plagued pro career, went 30-29, 3.62. | | | | | | | | | |
| 10. Dodgers: Chris Gwynn, of, San Diego State | Long Beach, Calif. | L-L | 6-0 | 170 | 20 | $135,000 | 1985 | 1996 | Majors (10) |
| Clone of famous older brother in college, hit .383-19-95 with NCAA-record 137 hits as soph; lacked Tony's extra-base power, speed, arm in unfulfilled MLB career. | | | | | | | | | |
| 11. Athletics: Walt Weiss, ss, North Carolina | Suffern, N.Y. | B-R | 6-0 | 175 | 21 | $95,000 | 1985 | 2000 | Majors (14) |
| Quality defender throughout college and pro career; got most out of ability, though he hit only .258-25-386 with four teams; current Rockies skipper. | | | | | | | | | |
| 12. Astros: Cameron Drew, of, New Haven | Yardville, N.J. | L-R | 6-5 | 210 | 21 | $100,000 | 1985 | 1991 | Majors (1) |
| D-II basketball All-American, late comer to baseball; became top prospect (.312-52-302), but career undermined by knee problems, played seven games in majors. | | | | | | | | | |
| 13. Twins: Jeff Bumgarner, rhp, Hanford HS | Richland, Wash. | R-R | 6-6 | 210 | 18 | $162,000 | 1985 | 1992 | Class AAA (1) |
| UCLA recruit went 11-0, 0.28 (78 IP/132 SO) as prep SR, took club-record bonus to sign; went 48-71, 4.26 in minors, struggled to change speeds/throw strikes. | | | | | | | | | |
| 14. Braves: Tommy Greene, rhp, Whiteville HS | Whiteville, N.C. | R-R | 6-5 | 225 | 18 | $162,000 | 1985 | 1997 | Majors (8) |
| Top prep arm in class went 15-2, 0.22 with 270 Ks in 124 IPs as SR; showed flashes in majors/minors, but career marked by poor breaking ball, inconsistency. | | | | | | | | | |
| 15. Angels: Willie Fraser, rhp, Concordia (N.Y.) College | Newburgh, N.Y. | R-R | 6-2 | 185 | 20 | $92,500 | 1985 | 1999 | Majors (8) |
| Small-college arm burst into first round on strength of 94 mph fastball, nasty forkball; first of two Angels first-rounders, went 38-40, 4.47 in majors with five clubs. | | | | | | | | | |
| 16. Phillies: Trey McCall, c, Abingdon HS | Abingdon, Va. | R-R | 6-3 | 200 | 17 | $92,500 | 1985 | 1989 | Class A (4) |
| Surprise first-rounder, even after .596-10-34 senior season; never advanced beyond Class A, hit .202-15-99 overall; coach at Emory & Henry (Va.) College. | | | | | | | | | |
| 17. Royals: Brian McRae, ss, Manatee HS | Bradenton, Fla. | B-R | 5-10 | 175 | 17 | $125,000 | 1985 | 1999 | Majors (10) |
| Son of Hal, Royals DH at time; two-sport talent, played baseball in Florida, football in Missouri; became quality CF, hit .261-103-532, 196 SBs in majors. | | | | | | | | | |
| 18. Cardinals: Joe Magrane, lhp, Arizona | Morehead, Ky. | R-L | 6-5 | 200 | 20 | $110,000 | 1985 | 1996 | Majors (8) |
| Went 13-8, 3.62 as college JR, quickly developed into premium lefty, led NL in ERA (2.18) in 1988, but promising career undone by reconstructive elbow surgery. | | | | | | | | | |
| 19. Angels: Mike Cook, rhp, South Carolina | Charleston, S.C. | L-R | 6-2 | 180 | 21 | $92,000 | 1985 | 1994 | Majors (5) |
| Led Carolina to CWS on strength of 16-2, 1.91 record, broke ankle in first pro season in golf-cart incident; pitched in majors a year later, but went 1-5, 5.55 overall. | | | | | | | | | |
| 20. Mets: Gregg Jefferies, ss, Serra HS | Millbrae, Calif. | B-R | 5-10 | 170 | 17 | $100,000 | 1985 | 2000 | Majors (14) |
| Two-time Baseball America Minor League POY struggled to find defensive home, live up to lofty expectations in majors; still hit .289-126-663 for five teams. | | | | | | | | | |
| 21. Red Sox: Dan Gabriele, rhp, Western HS | Walled Lake, Mich. | B-R | 6-4 | 190 | 18 | $100,000 | 1985 | 1989 | Class AA (2) |
| Compared to Jim Palmer with long, loose frame, fluid arm action; struggled to meet expectations with suspect control/breaking ball, went 42-40, 4.11 in minors. | | | | | | | | | |
| 22. Cubs: Rafael Palmeiro, of, Mississippi State | Miami | L-L | 6-0 | 170 | 20 | $100,000 | 1985 | 2005 | Majors (20) |
| Pure hitter projected as one of draft's top prospects after .415-29-94 soph season, but stock dropped after .300-20-67 junior year; had 569 HRs, 3,020 hits in majors. | | | | | | | | | |
| 23. Padres: Joey Cora, ss, Vanderbilt | Caguas, P.R. | B-R | 5-8 | 153 | 20 | $80,000 | 1985 | 1998 | Majors (11) |
| Poised, intelligent player emerged as first-rounder on strength of JR year (.403-7-33, 41 SB); overcame early injury issues to hit .277-30-294 with 117 SBs in majors. | | | | | | | | | |
| 24. Cubs: Dave Masters, rhp, California | Honolulu | R-R | 6-9 | 220 | 20 | $88,500 | 1985 | 1993 | Class AAA (5) |
| Atypical player, attended college for academics, but size, fastball landed him in first round; struggled to refine command/curve, career peaked in Triple-A. | | | | | | | | | |
| 25. Blue Jays: Greg David, of, Barron Collier HS | Naples, Fla. | L-R | 6-1 | 185 | 18 | $116,500 | 1985 | 1992 | Class AA (3) |
| Drafted as OF, later became C, 1B and 3B in five years in organization, none above Class A; also played in Padres, Royals systems, hit .240-67-357 overall. | | | | | | | | | |
| 26. Tigers: Randy Nosek, rhp, Chillicothe HS | Chillicothe, Mo. | R-R | 6-4 | 200 | 18 | $100,000 | 1986 | 1991 | Majors (2) |
| Played tennis as prep senior since HS didn't field baseball team (went 10-1, 0.83 in Legion ball); struggled in pros, went 29-47 in minors, 1-3 in majors. | | | | | | | | | |
| **JANUARY—REGULAR PHASE** | | | | | | | | | |
| 1. Giants: Ricky Nelson, of, Orange Coast (Calif.) CC | Oswego, Ill. | R-R | 6-5 | 220 | 20 | $20,000 | 1985 | 1990 | Class AA (2) |
| Played basketball two years at Southern Illinois; impressed scouts with raw power while working out for JC team; hit .247-53-192 in six minor league seasons. | | | | | | | | | |
| **JANUARY—SECONDARY PHASE** | | | | | | | | | |
| 1. Cardinals: Todd Stottlemyre, rhp, Yakima Valley (Wash.) CC | Yakima, Wash. | L-R | 6-3 | 185 | 19 | Unsigned | 1986 | 2002 | Majors (14) |
| Son of Mel Sr., brother of Mel Jr., drafted/signed by Blue Jays in June; Todd went on to pitch 14 years in majors, went 138-121, 4.28, played for five clubs. | | | | | | | | | |
| **JUNE—SECONDARY PHASE** | | | | | | | | | |
| 1. Red Sox: Eric Hetzel, rhp, Louisiana State | Crowley, La. | R-R | 6-4 | 170 | 21 | $50,000 | 1985 | 1991 | Majors (2) |
| Juco transfer, four-time draftee went 10-4, 3.77 (105 IP/99 SO) in only season at LSU; limited duty in majors (3-7, 6.12) because of shoulder issues. | | | | | | | | | |

**Signed to major league contract.*

## How They Should Have Done It

Based on the career WAR (Wins Above Replacement, as calculated by Baseball-Reference.com) numbers achieved by all the players eligible for the 1985 draft, here's how the first round should have unfolded. Numbers in parentheses indicate the round when the player was actually drafted.

| | Player, Pos. | Actual Draft | WAR | Bonus |
|---|---|---|---|---|
| 1. | Barry Bonds, of | Pirates (1) | 162.5 | $125,000 |
| 2. | Randy Johnson, lhp | Expos (2) | 102.1 | $60,000 |
| 3. | Rafael Palmeiro, of | Cubs (1) | 71.8 | $100,000 |
| 4. | Barry Larkin, ss | Reds (1) | 70.2 | $165,000 |
| 5. | John Smoltz, rhp | Tigers (22) | 69.5 | $60,500 |
| 6. | Chuck Finley, lhp | Angels (Jan.-S/1) | 58.4 | $3,500 |
| 7. | Will Clark, 1b | Giants (1) | 56.2 | $160,000 |
| 8. | Mark Grace, 1b | Cubs (24) | 46.1 | $30,000 |
| 9. | David Justice, of | Braves (4) | 40.4 | $30,000 |
| 10. | Brady Anderson, of | Red Sox (10) | 34.8 | $15,000 |
| 11. | B.J. Surhoff, c | Brewers (1) | 34.3 | $150,000 |
| 12. | Randy Velarde, ss | White Sox (19) | 25.0 | $1,500 |
| 13. | Ken Hill, rhp | Tigers (NDFA) | 23.8 | $1,500 |
| 14. | Todd Stottlemyre, rhp | Blue Jays (June-S/1) | 23.2 | $80,000 |
| 15. | Mike Stanley, 1b | Rangers (16) | 20.9 | $500 |
| 16. | John Wetteland, rhp | Dodgers (Jan.-S/2) | 19.6 | $20,000 |
| 17. | Gregg Jefferies, ss | Mets (1) | 19.3 | $100,000 |
| 18. | Walt Weiss, ss | Athletics (1) | 16.5 | $95,000 |
| 19. | Bobby Witt, rhp | Rangers (1) | 15.1 | $179,000 |
| 20. | Mike Macfarlane, c | Royals (4) | 14.7 | $15,000 |
| 21. | Mike Devereaux, of | Dodgers (5) | 14.6 | $20,000 |
| 22. | Brian McRae, ss | Royals (1) | 14.1 | $125,000 |
| 23. | Greg W. Harris, rhp | Padres (10) | 13.0 | $12,000 |
| 24. | Joe Magrane, lhp | Cardinals (1) | 12.2 | $110,000 |
| 25. | Jeff Brantley, rhp | Giants (6) | 11.6 | $8,000 |
| 26. | Dennis Cook, lhp | Giants (18) | 11.0 | $1,000 |

| | Top 3 Unsigned Players | | | Year Signed |
|---|---|---|---|---|
| 1. | Brian Jordan, of | Indians (20) | 32.7 | 1988 |
| 2. | Greg Vaughn, of | Pirates (Jan-S/1) | 30.6 | 1986 |
| 3. | Kevin Tapani, rhp | Cubs (9) | 29.4 | 1986 |

of the California Angels in the January secondary phase, was probably the most productive big-leaguer ever to come from that phase.

The pronounced emphasis on college talent in the 1985 draft also meant that a record-low 232 high school players were selected in the June regular phase.

### BREWERS SELECT SURHOFF NO. 1

With pick of the litter in a deep, talented pool, the Milwaukee Brewers went for Surhoff, a catcher and occasional shortstop from the University of North Carolina. Brewers general manager Harry Dalton said Surhoff was the most complete player available.

"Surhoff doesn't have the power of a Clark or Incaviglia, but he's better balanced," Dalton said. "Incaviglia has a good bat and good power, but doesn't have the defensive tools Surhoff has."

It was Surhoff's play in a rare game at shortstop in his junior year that persuaded Brewers officials to commit to him.

"In terms of one game," said Ray Poitevint, Milwaukee's director of player procurement, "I can't ever recall where I've seen a shortstop make so many difficult plays on defense and hit the ball so hard. He made one play, in particular, that most shortstops can't make. He went 4-for-4 and hit one ball farther than you ever expect a shortstop to hit it. It was only one game, but it was the kind you don't forget. Even though we drafted him as a catcher, we would have made him the first pick as a shortstop. He's that good."

Surhoff immediately went behind the plate as a freshman at North Carolina in part because the Tar Heels had also recruited Weiss (Oakland's first-round pick in 1985) to play shortstop. Surhoff took to catching like a duck to water. He also hit .392 with 32 home runs and 157 RBIs in three seasons for the Tar Heels, stole 84 bases and struck out just 24 times in 783 plate appearances. As a junior, he played five different positions, and it was his unique blend of speed, versatility and exceptional bat control that appealed to the Brewers.

To help Surhoff make a smooth transition to pro ball, the Brewers left him behind the plate in his first pro season and he had a vintage summer at Class A Beloit, hitting .336 with seven homers and 58 RBIs. From there, they would decide whether he'd make a position switch—ideally to shortstop, where in effect he would replace longtime Brewers shortstop Robin Yount, who moved to the outfield in 1985.

The switch never came off. Surhoff remained a catcher, opened the 1987 season behind the plate in Milwaukee and played there for several more seasons. He ended up playing more games in the outfield, with a heavy dose of games at third base, over the balance of his 19-year big league career.

### PLENTY OF ATTRACTIVE OPTIONS

Milwaukee settled on Surhoff with the No. 1 choice, even though several of the most desirable picks in draft history, all college talents ready to make an immediate impact, were available for the taking. Among them:

- Clark, a sweet-swinging first baseman from Mississippi State who went on to become baseball's first $4 million a year player. He was rated the best all-around hitter in the draft and claimed by the San Francisco Giants with the second pick.
- Witt, a fireballing righthander from Oklahoma who had the best pure arm in the draft, his control issues notwithstanding. He went third to the Rangers, and his $179,000 signing bonus was the largest paid out in 1985.
- Larkin, a future Hall of Fame shortstop from Michigan. He went fourth overall to the Cincinnati Reds.
- Bonds, an Arizona State product who became baseball's greatest home run hitter. He was chosen sixth overall by the Pittsburgh Pirates.
- Incaviglia, who established NCAA season and career records for homers. The Montreal Expos claimed him with the eighth pick, though he ended up becoming property of the Rangers in a landmark trade after signing with the Expos.

UNIVERSITY OF MICHIGAN

Barry Larkin

Clark was half of a prolific hitting tandem at Mississippi State, along with Palmeiro, who was

### AT A GLANCE

RBIs and 143 stolen bases.

#### One Who Got Away

**BO JACKSON, OF, ANGELS (20TH ROUND).** The Angels took what appeared to be a wild stab at Jackson with a late-round pick. But it wasn't so far-fetched a year later when Jackson, then a Heisman Trophy winner and the No. 1 pick in the NFL draft, stunned both the baseball and football industries by signing to play baseball after being drafted by the Royals.

#### He Was Drafted?

**MARK SEAY, OF, RANGERS (6TH ROUND).** Seay played five years in the NFL as a wide receiver for the San Diego Chargers and Philadelphia Eagles, after receiving a $25,500 bonus from the Rangers out of a California high school in the 1985 draft. He played three seasons of pro ball, hitting .133 with 116 strikeouts in 291 at-bats, before quitting to play football at Long Beach State.

#### Did You Know . . .

The Dodgers signed 34 of the 35 players they selected in the June regular phase—at 97.1 percent, the highest success rate ever (until 2015). The lone holdout was fourth-rounder **MIKE PRIOR**, an outfielder from Illinois State who hit .419-19-68. Prior was drafted in the seventh round earlier in the year by the NFL's Tampa Bay Buccaneers as a defensive back, chose a football career and played 13 seasons in the NFL.

#### They Said It

Angels scouting director **LARRY HIMES**, on his futile attempt to sign **BO JACKSON**: "We felt if Bo Jackson was not selected in this draft, professional baseball would not have the opportunity to get him. The NFL is a very high-powered operation and when the NFL draft comes next April, they will make sure Bo Jackson is signed, sealed and ready to play in the NFL."

## DRAFT SPOTLIGHT: PETE INCAVIGLIA

GARY LAWSON

**Pete Incaviglia set power marks in college that still stand, but his major league career didn't quite measure up**

Pete Incaviglia left an indelible mark everywhere he played. At Oklahoma State in 1985, he set still-standing NCAA single-season records with 48 home runs, 143 RBIs and a 1.140 slugging percentage, and established career marks for homers (100) and slugging (.915).

"The best college hitter I've seen since the advent of the aluminum bat," Oklahoma State coach Gary Ward said. "The only guy I've seen comparable was (Bob) Horner."

It didn't take Incaviglia long to make his mark on pro ball, either. In the first swing of spring batting practice in 1986, he hit a pitch from Texas Rangers manager Bobby Valentine so hard that it knocked a hole in the fence at the team's spring training headquarters in Pompano Beach, Fla. "I throw batting practice to a lot of guys, and it was only batting practice, I know that," Valentine said, "but I've never seen anything like it."

Incaviglia was so confident in his ability that he boasted he would go straight to the big leagues out of college—and he did, after an impressive showing in spring training.

The Montreal Expos were on the lookout for a power hitter in the 1985 draft, and were determined to land Incaviglia. They had the eighth pick and paid no heed to warnings by Incaviglia that he might be selective about the team he played for.

Incaviglia, a Monterey, Calif., native, was not wild about being drafted by Montreal because of the cold weather in Canada, and made no attempt to hide his displeasure.

So determined was Incaviglia that he wouldn't play for Montreal that he forced the Expos to do something that had never happened before: trade a draft pick to a team of his choice. After a summer of futile efforts to sign Incaviglia, they signed him on Nov. 2, to a bonus of $150,000, and traded him to the Rangers for minor league pitcher Bob Sebra and journeyman infielder Jim Anderson. The signing was contingent upon the trade, and the Expos and Rangers had to walk a fine line to avoid interference by the commissioner's office, which forbid the trading of draft picks.

The Incaviglia deal prompted Major League Baseball to revise its rules, prohibiting teams from trading drafted players until one year after they had signed. That rule held up until 2015, when the commissioner's office modified it to say the player must remain with the team that drafted him until the conclusion of the current major league season.

Incaviglia's ploy, followed by an explosive spring in 1986 in which he hit seven exhibition-season home runs, sent him straight to the big leagues and raised expectations sky high. He also gave the rest of the American League a full view of his swagger. That irritating swagger. Even after hitting 100 big league home runs, including 30 as a rookie, in his first four seasons everyone was left to wonder why he hadn't reached his full potential.

A barrel-chested free-swinger, Incaviglia suffered by being forced to hit cleanup, where his league-leading strikeout totals of 185 in 1986 and 153 in 1988 were magnified. Incaviglia also exasperated those who worked with him every day. No matter what he did with a bat, he always had to battle how people interpreted his body language.

Rick Leach knew Incaviglia from afar as a member of the Toronto Blue Jays and later got to know Incaviglia as a teammate in 1989. "After playing with Inky, I realize the way he carries himself is because he believes in himself," he said. "He has to play a certain way and feel a certain way to get the most out of his abilities. I have a great deal of respect for him. I know how hard he works and how he approaches the game."

For all of the attention he got with his power and his personality, Incaviglia never quite delivered as he was expected to in a 12-year major league career. He hit just .246 with 206 homers in 1,284 games, and also struck out on 1,277 occasions.

selected by the Chicago Cubs with the 22nd pick. Clark homered on his first swing in the minors and duplicated the feat with the Giants—off Nolan Ryan, no less—in San Francisco's Opening Day lineup in 1986.

"We figured he could hit line drives and be a good doubles hitter. And we thought he would hit to all fields," Giants manager Roger Craig said. "We didn't expect the power we've seen. His fly balls keep flying. He's got one of those beautiful swings, and the ball jumps off the bat. He's going to hit some home runs."

Giants hitting instructor Jim Lefebvre was even more effusive in his praise of a young Clark.

"Best pure hitter I've seen come along in a long time," Lefebvre said. "He's a natural hitter. He's got rhythm, timing and hitting instincts. You always wonder how they'll react to the curve. He can hit it. And he's got a good idea of the strike zone. You don't see that at his age and experience."

Clark's career got off to a fast start, but eventually leveled off, and he was passed by several of his peers in the hallowed class. Over 16 big league seasons, though, he hit .303 with 284 homers.

As special a hitting prospect as Clark was, Witt was his equal on the mound. He earned his unprecedented 80 grade from the Scouting Bureau after a victory over Texas, when he struck out 17 Longhorns, something no one else had ever done. He was also near-perfect in his domination of No. 1-ranked Miami, when he spun a three-hitter and fanned 12.

**Bobby Witt**

The 80 grade indicated that Witt had superstar potential, once-in-a-lifetime ability. Scouts said he was the spitting image of a young Nolan Ryan, complete with his outstanding fastball and slider, his instincts and poise.

But he also had a young Ryan's tendency to be wild, and that proved to be his undoing. Witt never consistently produced results that matched his pure stuff, or harnessed his control.

Witt never won a game in the minor leagues (0-6, 6.43) prior to opening the 1986 season in the Rangers rotation, and promptly led the American League with 143 walks and 22 wild pitches as a

### Fastest To The Majors

| | Player, Pos. | Drafted (Round) | Debut |
|---|---|---|---|
| 1. | Will Clark, 1b | Giants (1) | April 8, 1986 |
| | # Pete Incaviglia, of | Expos (1) | April 8, 1986 |
| 3. | Bobby Witt, rhp | Rangers (1) | April 10, 1986 |
| 4. | Chuck Finley, lhp | Angels (Jan.-S/1) | May 29, 1986 |
| 5. | Barry Bonds, of | Pirates (1) | May 30, 1986 |

**FIRST HIGH SCHOOL SELECTION:** Gregg Jefferies, ss (Mets/1, Sept. 6, 1987)

**LAST PLAYER TO RETIRE:** Randy Johnson, lhp (Oct. 4, 2009)

*#Debuted in major leagues (with Rangers).*

## Top 25 Bonuses

| | Player, Pos. | Drafted (Round) | Order | Bonus |
|---|---|---|---|---|
| 1. | **Bobby Witt, rhp** | **Rangers (1)** | **3** | **$179,000** |
| 2. | * Rick Balabon, rhp | Yankees (1-S) | 28 | $177,000 |
| 3. | **Barry Larkin, ss** | **Reds (1)** | **4** | **$165,000** |
| 4. | * Jeff Bumgarner, rhp | Twins (1) | 13 | $162,000 |
| | ***Tommy Greene, rhp** | **Braves (1)** | **14** | **$162,000** |
| 6. | **Will Clark, 1b** | **Giants (1)** | **2** | **$160,000** |
| 7. | **B.J. Surhoff, c** | **Brewers (1)** | **1** | **$150,000** |
| | * Kurt Brown, c | White Sox (1) | 5 | $150,000 |
| | **Pete Incaviglia, of** | **Expos (1)** | **8** | **#$150,000** |
| 10. | **Chris Gwynn, of** | **Dodgers (1)** | **10** | **$135,000** |
| 11. | **Barry Bonds, of** | **Pirates (1)** | **6** | **$125,000** |
| | Mike Poehl, rhp | Indians (1) | 9 | $125,000 |
| | ***Brian McRae, of** | **Royals (1)** | **17** | **$125,000** |
| 14. | * Greg David, c/of | Blue Jays (1) | 25 | $116,500 |
| 15. | **Mike Campbell, rhp** | **Mariners (1)** | **7** | **$110,000** |
| | **Joe Magrane, lhp** | **Cardinals (1)** | **18** | **$110,000** |
| 17. | **Cameron Drew, of** | **Astros (1)** | **12** | **$100,000** |
| | ***Gregg Jefferies, ss** | **Mets (1)** | **20** | **$100,000** |
| | * Dan Gabriele, rhp | Red Sox (1) | 21 | $100,000 |
| | **Rafael Palmeiro, of** | **Cubs (1)** | **22** | **$100,000** |
| | ***Randy Nosek, rhp** | **Tigers (1)** | **26** | **$100,000** |
| 22. | **Walt Weiss, ss** | **Athletics (1)** | **11** | **$95,000** |
| 23. | **Willie Fraser, rhp** | **Angels (1)** | **15** | **$92,500** |
| | * Trey McCall, c | Phillies (1) | 16 | $92,500 |
| 25. | **Mike Cook, rhp** | **Angels (1)** | **19** | **$92,000** |

*Major leaguers in bold. *High school selection. #Major league contract.*

rookie, though he struck out 174 in 158 innings and managed to win 11 games.

Over his major league career, Witt went 142-157, 4.83, lasting for parts of 16 seasons because every club he pitched for felt like it knew how to tap into his potential. In the end, Witt just never put it all together.

"I got to the big leagues so fast I never really learned how to pitch," he said.

With the fourth pick, the Reds drafted Larkin, an appealing player with his Cincinnati roots who had rejected their overtures three years earlier as a second-round pick. Larkin quickly signed for a club-record $165,000 bonus.

From there, Larkin went on to play 19 seasons with the Reds, and justified his selection as the first player from the Class of 1985 to be inducted into the Hall of Fame by hitting .295, slugging 198 homers and stealing 379 bases. He was a 12-time all-star, three-time Gold Glove winner and the National League's 1995 MVP. He was the first shortstop to become a 30-30 player.

### DUELING HOME RUN KINGS

Of all the players drafted in 1985, no two made louder statements—both with their brash personalities and prolific long-ball exploits—than Bonds and Incaviglia.

They were San Francisco Bay Area products who went unsigned by the Giants in 1982—Bonds as a second-rounder, Incaviglia as a 10th-rounder. Bonds ended up in college at Arizona State, Incaviglia at Oklahoma State.

The Pirates drafted Bonds, fully expecting him to display the same combination of power and speed his father became known for over a 14-year big league career. Bobby Bonds hit 30 homers and stole 30 bases in the same season five times, a record in his day. His son matched the feat over the duration of his career, though it took him five years to achieve his first 30-30 season.

Over the next 15 years in San Francisco, Bonds became the greatest home run hitter in big league history, hitting 73 homers in 2001 to eclipse Mark McGwire's single-season mark of 70, and 762 in his career, topping the mark of 755, set by Henry Aaron. Of course, those achievements came with accusations that Bonds' late-career power surge, at the height of the Steroid Era, was artificially aided. Over the course of his career, Bonds bulked up from 185 pounds during his tenure with the Pirates to a hulking 240 pounds with the Giants.

Incaviglia, the powerful Oklahoma State slugger, enjoyed the most phenomenal offensive year in college baseball history, hitting .464 with NCAA records for home runs (48) and RBIs (143). Those two figures, along with the 100 homers he smashed in his career, are still records.

"His bat is no fluke," Expos scouting director Jim Fanning said. "He can flat-out hit."

Incaviglia was determined to blaze his own trail to the big leagues. He aligned himself with hard-line agent Bucky Woy and demanded a two-year major league contract with a stipulation that he be placed on Montreal's roster. It was his way of saying he wasn't thrilled about being drafted by the Expos—or, more specifically, a cold-weather team.

Negotiations turned sour, and Incaviglia held out into the fall. Finally on Nov. 2, the Expos, realizing they could not sign Incaviglia and risking losing him in the January 1986 draft, negotiated a deal to send him to the Rangers. Because baseball rules prohibited the trading of draft picks, Montreal went through the formality of signing Incaviglia to a major league contract with a bonus of $150,000, then packaged him to the Rangers in a deal for pitching prospect Bob Sebra and journeyman infielder Jimmy Anderson.

Baseball later passed a rule restricting teams from trading players for one year from the date they signed.

### FIRST-ROUND TALENT RUNS DEEP

Most of the attention in the first round focused on the high-profile selections in the first 10 picks, but there was no shortage of talent later in the round. Two players with unusually advanced hitting skills also garnered attention: shortstop Gregg Jefferies, selected by the Mets with the 20th pick, and Palmeiro, taken two picks later by the Cubs.

For three years at Mississippi State, Palmeiro joined Clark to form the most-feared hitting duo in the college ranks. They were commonly referred to as Thunder (in the case of the more bombastic Clark) and Lightning (the softer-spoken Palmeiro). Palmeiro had the more dynamic season as a freshman, and hit .410 with 47 home runs over his first two years. But he fell off in 1985, hitting .300, although he did contribute 20 homers. It cost him in the draft. Projected as one of the top prospects at the start of the 1985 season, Palmeiro slipped to 22nd overall.

"I think it was because of the pressure I put on myself," Palmeiro said. "There was a lot of talk about Will and me being one and two in the draft,

### WORTH NOTING

■ Despite being placed on probation by the Pacific-10 Conference while suffering its first losing season in school history, Arizona State still had more players drafted in 1985 than any other school, 12. Meanwhile, Sacramento City College, which set a January draft record by having 15 players selected in 1983, almost matched that total when 14 Sac City players, twice as many as any other school, were selected.

■ Outfielder/first baseman **LUIS MEDINA** was overshadowed in his two seasons at Arizona State by first-rounders Oddibe McDowell and **BARRY BONDS**, but hit .318 with 17 homers as a junior, and .379 with 10 homers as a senior. When the Indians drafted him in the ninth round in 1985, it marked a record-tying seventh time he had been picked. He finally signed, for a bonus of $8,000, and went on to play three seasons with the Indians from 1988-91, hitting .205 with 10 homers in 51 games.

■ **RICK BALABON**, a Pennsylvania high school righthander, was regarded as one of the top prospects in the 1985 draft, but priced himself out of the first round with his bonus demands. The Yankees claimed him with the 28th pick and signed him for $177,000—second only to the $179,000 bonus **BOBBY WITT** received from the Rangers as the third pick overall. Balabon went 15-20, 4.35 in three-plus seasons in the Yankees system before being dealt to Seattle, but never reached the majors.

■ **ROB LEMLE**, a third-round pick of the Mets, was shot to death in a gang-related incident in 1989 near his Compton, Calif., home. Lemle, 22, had just enjoyed his best season of an injury-plagued career in the Mets system, hitting .279 with 38 stolen bases in 66 games. He was late reporting after recovering from gunshot wounds stemming from a different altercation that left

CONTINUED ON PAGE 308

## WORTH NOTING

CONTINUED FROM PAGE 307

two dead; his season ended when an errant pitch broke three bones in his hand.

■ As strong as the first round was, seven of 26 players didn't reach the majors. None failed quite like the two high school catchers selected: **KURT BROWN** (White Sox, fifth overall) and **TREY MCCALL** (Phillies, 16th overall). Brown played briefly in Triple-A, but he was always remembered as the player taken after **BARRY LARKIN** and before **BARRY BONDS**. McCall never advanced beyond Class A.

■ The Cape Cod League made a crucial decision in its evolution as a top summer college league in 1985 by returning to wood bats. The Cape soon became a destination for many of the nation's elite college players, a high percentage of whom had previously played in Alaska.

■ For the first time in 1985, foreign players attending school in the U.S. became subject to the draft, an outgrowth of the bidding war that took place in 1983 over Puerto Rican lefthander Juan Nieves, who attended prep school in Connecticut for three years. The first foreigner picked was shortstop **JORGE ROBLES**, who was enrolled at Miami-Dade New World Center CC and a member of Puerto Rico's 1984 American Legion World Series champions. Four Canadians, three at Arizona's Cochise Community College, were also selected in the January draft. In June, Puerto Rican shortstop **JOEY CORA**, attending school at Vanderbilt, was picked in the first round by San Diego. Second baseman **JOSE MOTA** (Manny's eldest son), from Cal State Fullerton by way of the Dominican Republic, went in the second round to the White Sox.

■ Some 125 players from the Dominican Republic were chosen in a special draft on March 1, 1985, the only such occasion players from that country were subject to a draft. It followed a six-month

BOB WIRZ

**Will Clark stood out with teammate Rafael Palmeiro at Mississippi State, and he made the smoother transition to the professional ranks**

and I just couldn't get going."

Palmeiro had a textbook swing, but unlike Clark had difficulty adjusting initially to wood bats in pro ball. He soon evolved into a steady .300 hitter, but never hit more than 14 homers in any of his first five seasons in the majors.

His home run production climbed to 26 in 1991, however, and he went on to hit 373 over a nine-year span. Toward the end of his career, Palmeiro faced allegations of steroid use and vehemently denied them. But he tested positive for a performance-enhancing substance in 2005 and was implicated in the Mitchell Report in 2007, casting a cloud over the end of his career. Despite compiling 3,020 hits and 569 home runs, his career ended with a whimper.

Just as Palmeiro asserted himself as one of the greatest hitters in college baseball history in his first two seasons at Mississippi State, Jefferies assembled one of the most enviable track records of success in modern minor league history in his first two full seasons in the Mets system. He hit .353 with 16 homers and 111 RBIs with 57 stolen bases at low Class A Columbia in 1986; a year later, he did a number on Double-A pitching to a similar tune: .367, 20 homers, 101 RBIs. He won back-to-back Baseball America Minor League Player of the Year awards, a feat matched only by Andruw Jones.

But it wasn't just his phenomenal hitting feats in the minor leagues that had Mets fans anxiously awaiting his arrival. What made Jefferies so intriguing was his intense work ethic and unusual training techniques. This was no ordinary ballplayer.

Jefferies' switch-hitting skills were so advanced for a young player that he had scouts and managers groping to find comparisons.

"You hate to make such heavy-handed comparisons, but Mickey Mantle is the only one who has come along with that kind of power from both sides," said Bobby Floyd, who managed Jefferies in the minor leagues "I've never seen a switch-hitter handle the bat and hit with power from both sides like Gregg."

Matching his swing was Jefferies' desire to be the best baseball player possible. He displayed such intensity that he was likened to a young Ty Cobb.

"God put me on this earth to play baseball," Jefferies said, "and I'm working as hard as I can to fulfill that."

Though Mets fans hoped Jeffereies would carry the team through the 1990s and help New Yorkers forget about the tragically flawed careers of Darryl Strawberry and Dwight Gooden, his days with the Mets never lived up to advance billing.

There was little mistaking his skills or drive, but Jefferies had difficulty accepting failure, and his tantrums wore thin on his teammates. Compounding his problem, he never found a home defensively.

Jefferies played 14 seasons in the majors, hitting .289 with 126 homers. He had his best season with the St. Louis Cardinals in 1993 (.342 with 16 home runs), while playing first base.

In contrast to Palmeiro and Jefferies, Brian McRae was a relative unknown in the 1985 draft. The Major League Scouting Bureau filed no reports on him. Neither did a number of big league clubs, even though he was the son of a big leaguer.

But McRae needed no introduction to the Royals, who jumped at the chance to draft him 17th overall. Brian had been part of the Royals family for nearly 10 years, having regularly tagged along with father Hal to Royals Stadium. He had taken batting practice and shagged flies in the outfield with Royals players.

His selection marked the first time in the draft's 20-year history a player was taken by the same team for which his father was an active player.

"It is a little like a dream come true," the younger McRae said. "I have grown up watching the Royals play. I used to work out with them all the time. I thought maybe someday I might be able to do this, but you think a lot of things."

McRae never got a chance to play alongside his father, who retired in 1987. By the time Brian reached the majors in 1990, he had moved from shortstop to center field. He played 10 years in the majors, the first five with Kansas City. He played with five clubs, hitting .261 with 103 homers and 196 stolen bases.

Bonds more than lived up to expectations as the son of a former big leaguer and McRae largely did the same, but outfielder Chris Gwynn, a third first-rounder with a big league lineage, did not.

He was selected 10th overall by the Los Angeles Dodgers and considered a superior prospect to his

### Largest Bonuses By Round

| | Player, Pos. | Club | Bonus |
|---|---|---|---|
| **1.** | **Bobby Witt, rhp** | **Rangers** | **$179,000** |
| **2.** | ***Greg Smith, ss** | **Cubs** | **$80,000** |
| 3. | *Glen Braxton, of | White Sox | $66,000 |
| 4. | Scott Marrett, rhp | Angels | $40,000 |
| 5. | *Billy St. Peter, 3b | Reds | $27,500 |
| 6. | *Mark Seay, of | Rangers | $25,500 |
| **7.** | ***Matt Maysey, rhp** | **Padres** | **$21,000** |
| 8. | *Cliff Gonzalez, of/ss | Mets | $32,500 |
| 9. | *Rodney Murrell, ss | Mets | $30,000 |
| **10.** | ***Jason Grimsley, rhp** | **Phillies** | **$27,000** |
| **Other** | ***John Smoltz, rhp** | **Tigers (22)** | **$60,500** |
| **Jan/R.** | **Jeff Small, ss** | **Mariners (1)** | **$55,000** |
| Jan/S. | Three tied at | | $60,000 |
| **Jun/S.** | **Todd Stottlemyre, rhp** | **Blue Jays (1)** | **$80,000** |

*Major leaguers in bold. *High school selection.*

older brother Tony, a fellow San Diego State product and third-round pick in 1981. But Tony went on to win eight National League batting titles on his way to the Hall of Fame, while Chris hit .261 with 17 homers in a disappointing 10-year career.

Unlike Tony, who divided his time between baseball and basketball in college, the younger Gwynn focused on baseball. As a result, he was more polished, though both brothers were near clones in their approach to hitting.

As a sophomore at San Diego State, Chris hit .395 and set NCAA records for most hits (137) and at-bats in a season (358), while also producing the second-highest mark for total bases (243). He missed 32 games early in his junior season with knee problems and never came close to duplicating his impressive 1984 season, although he still hit .403. More telling, he went deep only twice and struggled to find his power stroke in pro ball.

## IMPRESSIVE TALENT BEYOND FIRST

As talent-filled as the first round of the 1985 draft was, after that teams found two future Hall of Famers: Johnson, taken in the second round by the Expos, and Smoltz, who went in the 22nd round to the Detroit Tigers. And then there was Cubs 24th rounder Mark Grace, who had a stellar big league career.

Yet scouts generally agreed that the very best talent of all was Jackson, a player the Angels took a futile stab at in the 20th round. Jackson hit .401 with 17 homers for Auburn as a redshirt sophomore, and would have been a cinch first-round choice had he indicated he wanted to play baseball. Instead, Jackson returned to school and won the 1985 Heisman Trophy.

"Going into the draft we felt, athletically, he was the best talent in the draft," Angels scouting director Larry Himes said. "He has the potential to be the first player to steal 40 bases and hit 40 home runs in a major league season."

Though Jackson went on to become the No. 1 pick of the National Football League's Tampa Bay Buccaneers the following spring, it wasn't the last baseball saw of Jackson.

Like Jackson, a second-rounder in 1982, the 6-foot-10 Johnson was a premium unsigned selection in the same draft. He went in the fourth round to the Braves, but chose to attend Southern California. All angles and elbows when he pitched in those days, Johnson was an intimidating force on the mound but struggled to throw strikes. Heading into 1985, most experts believed he was ready for a breakout year. Instead, he succumbed to the pressure of the draft, didn't handle adversity well and went 6-9, 5.35 while leading the nation with 104 walks in 118 innings and striking out 99.

When the Expos drafted Johnson, they knew they would have to tighten up his long, gangly body. They convinced him that if he could get a handle on his emotions, they could get a handle on his mechanics, but he still alternated between wild and unhittable. In 400 innings in the minors with the Expos, he walked 318 and struck out 428, while producing a 27-25 record. In 818 big league innings through the 1992 season, he went 49-48 and walked 519 in 818 innings, while striking out 818.

But during the 1992 season, after Johnson had moved on to the Seattle Mariners, a tip from then-Rangers pitching coach—and USC alum—Tom House sent Johnson on his way to pitching immortality.

"Tom noticed that I was landing on the heel of my foot and spinning off toward third base," Johnson said. "As a result, my arm dropped, I was wide open, I became a sidearm pitcher and I was inconsistent with my release point and location."

Once he began landing on the ball of his right foot, it pulled his momentum toward the plate, and from then on Johnson became one of the most dominant pitchers in big league history.

MEL BAILEY
Randy Johnson

He ended his career by going 303-166, 3.29 with 1,497 walks and a staggering 4,875 strikeouts in 4,135 innings. He struck out 300 batters in five consecutive seasons from 1998-2002, and won five Cy Young Awards over a 22-year career.

Smoltz, a high school righthander from Lansing, Mich., was an afterthought in the 1985 draft. With teams convinced he was headed to Michigan State, he was passed over until the Tigers, his favorite team, took him with what appeared to be a token late-round pick.

On Sept. 22, with his first MSU class 10 hours away, everything finally came together. Smoltz signed a contract with the Tigers that provided for a bonus of $60,500 and other incentives.

"I'm the closest thing to being a Spartan that never attended a class," Smoltz said.

By that point, the minor league season had ended, but the Tigers, coming off their 1984 World Series title, were winding down the 1985 season, finishing a distant third to the Blue Jays and Yankees, and invited Smoltz to join the club before instructional league.

## One Team's Draft: Chicago Cubs

| | Player, Pos. | Bonus | | Player, Pos. | Bonus | | Player, Pos. | Bonus |
|---|---|---|---|---|---|---|---|---|
| **1.** | **Rafael Palmeiro, of** | **$100,000** | 4. | Roger Williams, rhp | $32,500 | 8. | Bob Bafia, 3b | $16,000 |
| 1. | Dave Masters, rhp | $88,500 | **5.** | **Rick Wrona, c** | **$22,500** | **9.** | **Kevin Tapani, rhp** | **Did not sign** |
| **2.** | ***Greg Smith, ss** | **$80,000** | 6. | *John Viera, of | Did not sign | 10. | Greg Kallevig, rhp | $14,500 |
| 3. | *Mike Miller, c | $32,500 | 7. | Joe Murphy, 1b/of | $20,000 | **Other** | **Mark Grace (24), 1b** | **$30,000** |

*Major leaguers in bold. *High school selection.*

### WORTH NOTING

moratorium the commissioner's office had placed on signing Dominican talent after reports that several teams had been hiding away young players in the hopes that they might gain the upper hand in signing them when they became old enough to play in the U.S.

■ **PETE INCAVIGLIA'S** assault on the NCAA record book overshadowed everything else that happened in a big year for talent at the college level. Home run records fell at a dizzying pace in one of the most wide-open years in college annals. Brigham Young (148), Florida State (146) and South Carolina (144) all eclipsed the record for homers in a season by a team held by Florida State, which hit 131 in 1982. Other offensive records fell that year as Central Florida outfielder **TIM BARKER** established a still-standing record for hits in a season (142), while also setting a mark for stolen bases (112), though that record would be toppled two years later. Barker, a 12th-round pick of the Expos who never reached the majors, set his records while playing 82 games. Many of the records set in 1985 stood the test of time as the NCAA enacted legislation to limit teams to 60 games, effective with the 1986 season. That number would eventually be reduced to 56.

■ Miami won the 1985 College World Series, beating Texas 3-1 in the championship game for its second title in four years. The Hurricanes had five players drafted, only one in the first 12 rounds. The most dominant pitcher of the 1985 season was Texas lefthander Greg Swindell, a sophomore who was not eligible for the draft. He went 19-2, 1.47 with three saves, and a school-record 189 strikeouts in 172 innings. A year later, he was taken second overall by Cleveland. That team's first pick in the 1985 draft was Swindell's teammate **MIKE POEHL**, who went 7-1, 3.67. Arm problems stalled Poehl and he never reached the majors.

## IN FOCUS: BARRY BONDS

As Barry Bonds struggled to come into his own with the Pirates, hitting just .256 while averaging 21 homers a season in his first four years, he gained a reputation as a player with unlimited, but unfulfilled potential and a prickly, abrasive personality.

The same description characterized his three-year career at Arizona State, where he was unpopular with teammates and hit just 11 homers in each of his first two seasons. ASU coach Jim Brock once called him "rude, inconsiderate and self-centered. He bragged about the money he turned down, and popped off about his dad. I don't think he ever figured out what to do to get people to like him."

As a junior at ASU in 1985, Bonds began to unleash some of his home run potential, going deep 23 times, but the Sun Devils were on probation and ineligible for postseason play. The Pirates signed him quickly for $125,000 and less than a year later was Pittsburgh's starting center fielder and leadoff hitter. Bonds played seven seasons for the Pirates, became a free agent and signed a six-year deal with the Giants for $43.75 million—the irony of which became quickly apparent because Bonds didn't sign with the team a decade earlier out of Serra High in nearby San Mateo over the difference of just $5,000.

"It was off the charts," Smoltz said. "You talk about the wildest, coolest experience of my life? Getting to see what the major leagues was like, to hang with the major league team I grew up idolizing and watching, it was unreal."

On Aug. 12, 1987, the Tigers traded Smoltz to the Braves in a deal that landed established righthander Doyle Alexander, who went 9-0 in 11 starts down the stretch and led the Tigers to a division title. At the time, Smoltz was 4-10, 5.68 for Double-A Glens Falls in the Eastern League.

Smoltz was crestfallen, his family devastated. He'd gone from a perennial contender, his hometown team, to one of baseball's worst franchises.

"I thought everything that was going good for me or could go good for me completely took a turn for the worst," Smoltz said. "Ultimately, I didn't realize what an opportunity this was going to be like for me. I was only stuck in the moment and couldn't believe I got traded. All I cared about is I wanted to play for the Tigers."

Braves coaches adjusted Smoltz's delivery at Triple-A Richmond, and he was in the big leagues less than a year later. He made his first all-star team in 1989, and along with Tom Glavine, and eventually Greg Maddux, formed a triumvirate atop the Braves rotation that enabled them to dominate the National League for more than a decade.

John Smoltz

Even after Smoltz had Tommy John surgery in 2000, causing him to miss that season, he returned to the Braves as a dominant closer, saving 204 games over a four-year period—including a National League-record 55 in 2002—before returning to the rotation. In 19 years with the Braves, he went 210-147, 3.26.

From a 24th-round pick in 1985 to National League rookie of the year in 1988, that's the unlikely route Grace traveled in three short years through the Cubs system.

Overlooked in the draft because he hit only two homers in 1985 at San Diego State, Grace spent that summer playing in Alaska and signed with the Cubs on Aug. 29 for a bonus of $30,000, and once in pro ball immediately displayed grace and agility around first base and pure hitting ability. Over 16 big league seasons, the first 13 with the Cubs, Grace hit .303 with 173 homers.

### BROTHER ACT HIGHLIGHTS JANUARY

A father-and-sons act took center stage in the January draft. The sons of ex-big leaguer Mel Stottlemyre, Todd and Mel Jr., became the first brothers of the draft era to be selected in the first round of the same draft. Todd went first overall in the secondary phase to the Cardinals, while his older brother went third to the Houston Astros.

While both managed to reach the majors, they combined to win 138 times—all by Todd, who went 138-121, 4.28 in a 14-year career with five clubs. Mel Jr. played briefly with the Royals in

### Highest Unsigned Picks

**JUNE/REGULAR PHASE ONLY**

| Player, Pos., Team (Round) | College | Re-Drafted |
|---|---|---|
| Michael Young, lhp, Phillies (2) | Arizona | Padres '86 (4) |
| Scott Servais, c, Mets (2) | Creighton | Astros '88 (3) |
| Lance Blankenship, 3b, Red Sox (2) | California | Athletics '86 (10) |
| Mark Cole, ss, Padres (2) | Oklahoma | Tigers '89 (15) |
| Joe Klancnik, rhp, Pirates (3) | Oral Roberts | Cubs '87 (9) |
| Scott Ruskin, lhp/of, Indians (3) | * Florida | Expos '86 (Jan.-S/1) |
| Mike Hensley, rhp, Astros (3) | Oklahoma | Cardinals '88 (2) |
| Tino Martinez, 1b, Red Sox (3) | Tampa | Mariners '88 (1) |
| Mike Prior, of, Dodgers (4) | None | Astros '86 (Jan.-S/4) |
| Greg Burlingame, lhp, Padres (4) | * Hawaii | Cubs '86 (31) |

**TOTAL UNSIGNED PICKS:** Top 5 Rounds (14), Top 10 Rounds (34)

**Returned to same school.*

1990. The Stottlemyres had played together at Nevada-Las Vegas during the 1984 college season, but had complained about being overworked as they threw 261 innings between them. Their father, then the pitching coach for the Mets, encouraged them to drop out of school, making them eligible for the January draft.

Todd, 19, spent that spring pitching for Yakima Valley College in his hometown of Yakima, Wash., and ultimately did not sign with the Cardinals upon conclusion of his junior-college season. He went back into the draft pool in June and again was selected in the first round by Toronto (third overall). He finally signed with the Blue Jays for $80,000 on Aug. 12, after a long holdout, but reached the big leagues with that club in 1988. Mel Jr. signed with the Astros for $60,000, but arm problems hampered his professional career.

The best talent to come out of the January draft was Finley, selected fourth overall in the secondary phase by the Angels, the same team that had selected him in the 15th round the previous June.

Finley would become one of baseball's top lefthanders, but his rise to prominence was one of the most unlikely success stories of the draft era.

Recruited by only one college out of a Louisiana high school in 1980, he attended Louisiana Tech as a freshman, walking 33 in 27 innings before he quit school and went to work on his family's 200-acre nursery, planting trees and laying sod. After a year of that, Finley realized he missed baseball and enrolled at nearby Northeast Louisiana, though he went 6-7 over his final two seasons.

He didn't sign with the Angels the first time they drafted him, even as he had exhausted his college options, but did so the following January, for $3,500. Finley had never strayed far from home when he signed with the Angels, and reluctantly agreed to join their short-season club in Salem, Ore. He so impressed the Angels there and in a short stint in the Class A Midwest League to open the following season that he was called up to the big leagues on May 29, 1986 after 41 minor league innings, all as a reliever.

Finley soon emerged as one the top starters in the majors, and posted a 200-173, 3.85 record over 17 seasons—the first 14 with the Angels, who took a leap of faith on a naïve 22-year-old with a limited track record of success.

# 1985 Draft List

**Did not sign. Major leaguers in bold, with first and last years noted. Order of selection indicated in parentheses. For the first five rounds of the June Regular Phase and the first round of all other phases, the peak level of each player is noted.*

## ATLANTA BRAVES

**January—Regular Phase (13)**

1. David Seitz, lhp, Birmingham, Ala.—(Low A)
2. *Lionel Gaston, lhp, Triton (Ill.) JC.
3. *Ken Sebree, rhp, Brevard (Fla.) CC.
4. David Shotkoski, rhp, Kishwaukee (Ill.) JC.
5. *Kendrick Bourne, of, Chaffey (Calif.) JC.
6. *Chris Hawkins, lhp, Anderson (S.C.) JC.
7. Adrian Wills, c, Walters State (Tenn.) CC.
8. Tom Cantrell, ss, DeKalb South (Ga.) CC.
9. *Mike Sander, rhp, Chipola (Fla.) JC.
10. *Stanley Cook, of, Walters State (Tenn.) CC.
11. **Paul Marak, rhp, Trinidad State (Colo.) JC.—(1990)**
12. *Barry Pearman, rhp, Brewer State (Ala.) JC.
13. *Tom Brock, of, Central Arizona JC.
14. *Duane Crow, rhp, Vincennes University (Ind.) JC.
15. *Douglas Willey, rhp, Essex (Md.) CC.

**January—Secondary Phase (23)**

1. John Alva, ss, Pima (Ariz.) CC.—(AAA)
2. James Rockey, of, San Jose (Calif.) CC.

**June—Regular Phase (14)**

1. **Tommy Greene, rhp, Whiteville (N.C.) HS.—(1989-97)**
2. (Choice to Cardinals as compensation for Type A free agent Bruce Sutter)
3. Tom Abrell, rhp, Central HS, Muncie, Ind.—(Low A)
4. **David Justice, 1b-of, Thomas More (Ky.) College.—(1989-2002)**
5. Ellis Roby, 2b, University of Arkansas.—(AAA)
6. Todd Dewey, c, California Lutheran University.
7. Chris Mullins, of, Yosemite HS, Oakhurst, Calif.
8. **Al Martin, 1b-of, Rowland HS, West Covina, Calif.—(1992-2003)**
9. Mike Scott, rhp, St. Xavier (Ill.) College.
10. ***Stan Royer, c, Charleston (Ill.) HS.—(1991-94)**

DRAFT DROP *First-round draft pick (16th overall), Athletics (1988)*

11. Jeff Greene, rhp, University of Toledo.
12. **Gary Eave, rhp, Grambling State University.—(1988-90)**
13. Jermaine Casey, of, Rich Central HS, Country Club Hills, Ill.
14. Steven Vasquez, rhp, San Jose State University.
15. Dave Ford, 1b, University of Connecticut.
16. Mike Trapasso, lhp, Oklahoma State University.

DRAFT DROP *Baseball coach, Hawaii (2002-15)*

17. Greg Marshall, of, Grant HS, Sacramento, Calif.
18. Michael Alfano, 3b, C.W. Post (N.Y.) University.
19. Robert Burke, rhp, University of Southern Colorado.
20. Roger Huff, rhp, Waterville (Maine) HS.
21. **Jeff Wetherby, of, University of Southern California.—(1989)**
22. Pat Gliha, rhp, University of Akron.
23. ***Milt Hill, rhp, DeKalb Central (Ga.) JC.—(1991-94)**
24. Bean Stringfellow, lhp, Virginia Tech.
25. ***Paul McClellan, rhp, Sequoia HS, Redwood City, Calif.—(1990-91)**
26. Roger Hackett, of, Southern Tech (Ga.) Institute.
27. *Ward Horton, 1b, Chamblee (Ga.) HS.
28. Monty Aldrich, of, Eastern Illinois University.
29. David Garrison, 2b, Samford University.

**June—Secondary Phase (14)**

1. Dodd Johnson, 3b, University of Texas.–(High A)
2. *John Clements, rhp, Chipola (Fla.) JC.
3. *Lionel Gaston, lhp, Triton (Ill.) JC.

## BALTIMORE ORIOLES

**January—Regular Phase (20)**

1. *Tom Gallagher, lhp, Sacramento (Calif.) CC.—DNP
2. *Mike Direnzo, c, Broome (N.Y.) CC.
3. *DeWayne Coleman, rhp, Chaffey (Calif.) JC.
4. *Arned Hernandez, of, Arizona Western JC.
5. ***Al Osuna, lhp, Cerritos (Calif.) JC.—(1990-96)**
6. ***Gil Heredia, rhp, Pima (Ariz.) CC.—(1991-2001)**
7. Ernie Young, of, Essex (Md.) CC.
8. *Stephen Kraiss, 1b, Orange Coast (Calif.) JC.
9. Michael Rossano, 1b, Chaffey (Calif.) JC.
10. *Patrick Murray, 3b-ss, Queensborough (N.Y.) CC.
11. *John Horsey, lhp, Essex (Md.) CC.
12. *Harlan Blackiston, rhp, Camden County (N.J.) JC.
13. *Orlando Guerra, rhp, Orange Coast (Calif.) JC.
14. *Jeff Simmelink, c, Lower Columbia (Wash.) JC.
15. *Vince Ogawa, rhp, El Camino (Calif.) JC.
16. *John Woodward, of, Santa Fe (Fla.) CC.
17. *Johannes McFarlane, rhp, Mesa (Ariz.) CC.
18. *John Marchbank, lhp, Centralia (Wash.) CC.

**January—Secondary Phase (25)**

1. *Terry Griffin, rhp, Florida JC.—(High A)
2. Bob Latmore, ss, Indian River (Fla.) CC.
3. *Vince Shinholster, ss, Santa Ana (Calif.) JC.
4. ***Mike Blowers, 3b, Tacoma (Wash.) CC.—(1989-99)**

**June—Regular Phase (19)**

1. (Choice to Angels as compensation for Type A free agent Fred Lynn)
2. (Choice to Pirates as compensation for Type A free agent Lee Lacy)
3. (Choice to Angels as compensation for Type A free agent Don Aase)
4. **Brian Dubois, lhp, Reed Custer HS, Briarwood, Ill.—(1989-90)**
5. Tim Dulin, 2b, Memphis State University.—(AAA)
6. Chuck Stanhope, rhp, Troy State University.
7. **Jeff Ballard, lhp, Stanford University.—(1987-90)**
8. Norm Roberts, of, University of Arkansas.
9. **Pete Stanicek, 2b, Stanford University.—(1987-88)**

DRAFT DROP *Brother of Steve Stanicek, first-round draft pick, Giants (1982); major leaguer (1987-89)*

10. Larry Kline, c, Archbishop Curley HS, Baltimore.
11. ***Mike Loynd, rhp, Florida State University.—(1986-87)**

DRAFT DROP *First player from 1986 draft to reach majors (July 24, 1986)*

12. *Ty Griffin, ss, King HS, Tampa.

DRAFT DROP *First-round draft pick (9th overall), Cubs (1988)*

13. Joe Gast, lhp, Calvert Hall HS, Baltimore.
14. *Dell Curry, rhp, Virginia Tech.

DRAFT DROP *First-round draft pick, Utah Jazz/National Basketball Association (1986); guard, NBA (1986-2002) • Father of Stephen Curry, guard, NBA (2010-15)*

15. Brad Powell, rhp, University of North Carolina.
16. Kinney Sims, of, Lower Columbia (Wash.) JC.
17. Peter Mancini, ss, Seton Hall University.
18. Jim Sullivan, of, Indiana State University.
19. Rob Santo, 1b, Flagler (Fla.) College.
20. Kevin Burke, 1b, George Mason University.
21. Ray Crone, 2b, Sam Houston State University.
22. *Joe Bradley, lhp, Batesburg-Leesville (S.C.) HS.
23. Steven St. Hill, of, Long Island University.
24. Robert Bellini, of, St. John's University.
25. Frank Bellino, of, Mount San Antonio (Calif.) JC.
26. Matt Skinner, c, University of Texas-Arlington.
27. *Steve Muh, lhp, Long Branch (N.J.) HS.
28. Tim Haller, 2b, Regis (Colo.) College.
29. Frederick Ludwig, rhp, Penfield (N.Y.) HS.
30. Terrell McCall, lhp, Enka HS, Asheville, N.C.
31. *John Albertson, c, Mainland HS, Northfield, N.J.
32. Robert Dromerhouser, c, Mercy (N.Y.) College.
33. **Rico Rossy, ss, Purdue University.—(1991-98)**
34. Mike Halasz, ss, Chapman (Calif.) College.
35. *Curry Harden, rhp, A&M Consolidated HS, College Station, Texas.
36. *Chaeho Chong, c, Chatsworth (Calif.) HS.
37. *Kevin Smith, of, Eastern Illinois University.

**June—Secondary Phase (11)**

1. **Craig Worthington, 3b, Cerritos (Calif.) JC.—(1988-96)**
2. Mickey Billmeyer, c, North Carolina State University.
3. *John Kohli, lhp, Mira Costa (Calif.) JC.
4. *Joey Seaver, lhp, University of Tennessee.
5. *Barry Griffin, lhp, North Idaho JC.

## BOSTON RED SOX

**January—Regular Phase (22)**

1. Tim Speakman, c, Fullerton (Calif.) JC.—(Short-season A)
2. *Rod Simon, rhp, Central Arizona JC.
3. *Oscar Murphy, rhp, Columbia State (Tenn.) CC.
4. Greg Bochesa, c, Los Angeles Harbor JC.
5. *Ricky Carriger, rhp, Northeastern Oklahoma A&M JC.
6. *Steven Meyer, rhp, Westark (Ark.) CC.
7. Dell Carter, of, Kings River (Calif.) JC.
8. *Tom Kane, rhp, Manatee (Fla.) JC.
9. *Steve Mrowka, 3b, Polk (Fla.) CC.

DRAFT DROP *Baseball coach, George Washington (2005-12)*

10. *Tim Good, c, Angelina (Texas) JC.
11. *Kevin Edwards, ss, Westark (Ark.) CC.

**January—Secondary Phase (20)**

1. **Daryl Irvine, rhp, Ferrum (Va.) JC.—(1990-92)**
2. *Ken Morris, rhp, Angelina (Texas) JC.

**June—Regular Phase (21)**

1. Dan Gabriele, rhp, Western HS, Walled Lake, Mich.—(AA)
2. ***Lance Blankenship, 3b, University of California.—(1988-93)**

DRAFT DROP *Returned to California; re-drafted by Athletics, 1986 (10th round)*

3. ***Tino Martinez, 1b, Jefferson HS, Tampa.—(1990-2005)**

DRAFT DROP *Attended Tampa; re-drafted by Mariners, 1988 (1st round)*

4. Donnie McGowan, rhp, Central Missouri State University.—(High A)
5. Mike Clarkin, rhp, University of Minnesota.—(AA)
6. **Todd Pratt, c, Hilltop HS, Chula Vista, Calif.—(1992-2006)**
7. Gary Gouldrup, 3b, Oliver Ames HS, North Easton, Mass.
8. *Scott Middaugh, rhp, Patrick Henry HS, San Diego.
9. Jim Orsag, 1b, University of Illinois.
10. **Brady Anderson, of, UC Irvine.—(1988-2002)**
11. Chris Bayer, rhp, Pace (N.Y.) University.
12. Greg Lotzar, of, Central Michigan University.
13. *Mike Bianco, c, Seminole (Fla.) HS.

DRAFT DROP *Baseball coach, McNeese State (1998-2000); baseball coach, Mississippi (2001-2015)*

14. Mike Carista, rhp, Saugus, Mass.
15. Derek Livernois, rhp, Lyman HS, Altamonte Springs, Fla.
16. *Ron Stephens, ss, Linsly Institute, Wheeling, W.Va.
17. *James Boehne, rhp, Louisiana Tech.
18. Kerman Williams, rhp Vanguard HS, Ocala, Fla.
19. *Gregg Magistri, lhp, Louisiana Tech.
20. Billy Plante, 3b, Virginia Tech.
21. James Cox, lhp, Harrisburg, Ohio.
22. *Tom Hostetler, rhp, East Mississippi JC.
23. *Cliff Suggs, rhp, Cooper HS, Abilene, Texas.
24. Erik Laseke, 2b, Columbia State (Tenn.) CC.
25. John Abbott, lhp, Visalia, Calif.
26. ***Ed Sprague, c, St. Mary's HS, Stockton, Calif.—(1991-2001)**

DRAFT DROP *First-round draft pick (25th overall), Blue Jays (1988) • Baseball coach, Pacific (2004-15) • Son of Ed Sprague, major league (1968-76)*

27. *Grady Hall, lhp, Northwestern University.

DRAFT DROP *First-round draft pick (20th overall), White Sox (1986)*

**June—Secondary Phase (1)**

1. **Eric Hetzel, rhp, Louisiana State University.—(1989-90)**
2. Bill Zupka, rhp, Queensborough (N.Y.) CC.

## CALIFORNIA ANGELS

**January—Regular Phase (16)**

1. *John Wilder, rhp, Walters State (Tenn.) JC.—(Rookie)
2. *John Hoffman, lhp, Glendale (Calif.) JC.
3. *Lyle Befort, rhp, Butler County (Kan.) CC.
4. *John Buss, lhp, Triton (Ill.) JC.
5. *Phillip Lieberher, lhp, Polk (Fla.) CC.
6. *Martin Robitaille, 1b-of, Cochise County (Ariz.) CC.
7. *Anthony Venneri, 1b, Dundalk (Md.) CC.
8. *Darren Peters, rhp, Triton (Ill.) JC.
9. *Gary Nalls, ss, Garden City (Kan.) CC.

**January—Secondary Phase (4)**

1. **Chuck Finley, lhp, West Monroe, La.—(1986-2002)**
2. *Bill Voeltz, lhp, Broward (Fla.) CC.

**June—Regular Phase (15)**

1. **Willie Fraser, rhp, Concordia (N.Y.) College.—(1986-95)**
1. **Mike Cook, rhp, University of South Carolina** (Choice from Orioles as compensation for Type A free agent Fred Lynn)**—(1986-93)**
2. Bob Sharpnack, rhp, Fountain Valley (Calif.) HS.—(AA)
3. Jerome Nelson, of, Pine Forest HS, Pensacola, Fla.—(AAA)
3. Chris Collins, rhp, Mercer University (Choice from Orioles as compensation for Type A free agent Don Aase).—(AA)
4. Scott Marrett, rhp, Pepperdine University.—(High A)
5. **Bobby Rose, ss, San Dimas HS, Glendora, Calif.—(1989-92)**
6. Tim Burcham, rhp, University of Virginia.
7. Michael Kesler, lhp, Western New Mexico University.
8. Richard Morehouse, rhp, South Dakota State University.
9. Jim McCollom, 1b, Clemson University.
10. Steve McGuire, rhp, University of North Carolina.
11. Kendall Walling, ss, Lubbock Christian (Texas) College.
12. Tim Arnold, c, University of Nevada-Las Vegas.
13. Bill Geivett, 3b, UC Santa Barbara.
14. **Jeff Manto, of, Temple University.—(1990-2000)**
15. **Frank DiMichele, lhp, CC of Philadelphia.—(1988)**
16. Reggie Lambert, of, Loyola Marymount University.
17. *Carlos Carrasco, rhp, Live Oak HS, Morgan Hill, Calif.
18. *Rick Raether, rhp, University of Miami.
19. *Freddie Davis, rhp, Auburndale (Fla.) HS.
20. ***Bo Jackson, of, Auburn University.—(1986-94)**

DRAFT DROP *Heisman Trophy winner (1985); first overall draft pick, Tampa Bay Buccaneers/National Football League (1986); running back, NFL (1987-90)*

21. *Charlie White, of, Woodham HS, Pensacola, Fla.
22. Mark Ban, of, Cal State Northridge.
23. Glenn Washington, of, Ramapo (N.J.) College.
24. *Toby Nivens, rhp, McAllen (Texas) HS.

DRAFT DROP *First overall draft pick, January 1986/ secondary phase, Twins*

25. *Scott Carter, rhp, Brandon (Fla.) HS.
26. *Dan Grunhard, of, Northwestern University.
27. *Kevin Kunkel, rhp, Stanford University.

DRAFT DROP *Son of Bill Kunkel, major leaguer (1961-63); umpire, Major League Baseball (1968-84) • Brother of Jeff Kunkel, first-round draft pick, Rangers (1983); major leaguer (1984-92)*

28. *Wade Phillips, rhp, University of Texas.

**June—Secondary Phase (21)**

1. Gary Nalls, ss, Lamar University.—(High A)
2. David Johnson, rhp, University of Oklahoma.
3. ***Greg Vaughn, of, Sacramento (Calif.) CC.—(1989-2003)**

## CHICAGO CUBS

**January—Regular Phase (23)**

1. Jeff Small, ss, Seattle.—(AAA)
2. Lee Grimes, of, Palm Beach (Fla.) JC.
3. *Daryl Boyd, rhp, Palm Beach (Fla.) JC.
4. *Ron Ewart, of, Cerritos (Calif.) JC.
5. *Doug Kline, rhp, Blue Mountain (Ore.) CC.

6. Michael Jones, of, Miami-Dade CC North.
7. *William O'Neal, 1b, Westark (Ark.) CC.
8. Scott Lochow, c, Edmonds (Wash.) CC.
9. *Tim Anderson, ss, Sacramento (Calif.) CC.
10. *Gary Geiger, 3b-rhp, Seminole (Okla.) JC.
DRAFT DROP *Son of Gary Geiger, major leaguer (1958-70)*
11. *Mike Siler, rhp, Edmonds (Wash.) CC.

**January—Secondary Phase (9)**

**1. *Craig Worthington, 3b, Cerritos (Calif.) JC.—(1988-96)**
2. *Phil Williams, c, Seminole (Okla.) JC.
3. *Glenn Twardy, of, Mount San Antonio (Calif.) JC.

**June—Regular Phase (24)**

**1. Rafael Palmeiro, of, Mississippi State University** (Choice from Padres as compensation for Type A free agent Tim Stoddard)—**(1986-2005)**
1. Dave Masters, rhp, University of California.—(AAA)
**2. Greg Smith, ss, Glenelg HS, Sykesville, Md.—(1989-91)**
DRAFT DROP *Scouting director, Tigers (1997-2004); scouting director, Pirates (2008-11)*
3. Mike Miller, c, Paradise Valley HS, Phoenix.—(AA)
4. Roger Williams, rhp, University of North Carolina.—(AAA)
**5. Rick Wrona, c, Wichita State University.—(1988-94)**
6. *John Viera, of, Southridge HS, Cutler Ridge, Fla.
7. Joe Murphy, 1b-of, Wagner College.
8. Bob Bafia, 3b, Fresno State University.
**9. *Kevin Tapani, rhp, Central Michigan University.—(1989-2001)**
10. Greg Kallevig, rhp, South Dakota State University.
11. Scott Anders, c, Ohio Dominican College.
**12. Doug Dascenzo, of, Oklahoma State University.—(1988-96)**
13. Dick Canan, 3b, University of Illinois.
14. Fernando Zarranz, rhp, St. Thomas HS, Miami.
15. *Sergio Espinal, 2b, Oklahoma State University.
**16. Joe Kraemer, lhp, Vancouver, Wash.—(1989-90)**
17. *Don Burke, of, Florida Southern College.
18. Robert Strickland, rhp, SUNY-Buffalo.
19. Mark McMorris, 1b, Southeastern Louisiana University.
**20. Kelly Mann, c, Santa Monica (Calif.) HS.—(1989-90)**
21. Len Damian, rhp, Canyon HS, Anaheim, Calif.
22. Jeff Hirsch, rhp, UCLA.
23. *Brent Addison, ss, Auburndale (Fla.) HS.
**24. Mark Grace, 1b, San Diego State University.—(1988-2003)**
25. Kris Roth, rhp, Southwestern Oklahoma State University.
26. *John Peet, 1b-of, Santa Monica (Calif.) HS.
27. Clint Hartwick, ss, Redlands HS, Glendora, Calif.
28. John Horn, lhp, Georgia Tech.
29. Mark Jefferson, lhp, North Marion HS, Carolina, W.Va.
30. *Bobby DeJardin, ss, Mater Dei HS, Huntington Beach, Calif.
31. *Tom Williams, 2b, Elkton (Md.) HS.
32. Tim Wallace, 2b, Cal State Hayward.

**June—Secondary Phase (12)**

1. Ron Ewart, 1b-of, Cerritos (Calif.) JC.—(High A)
2. *Robert Chadwick, lhp, Oxnard (Calif.) JC.
3. *Paul Kuzniar, rhp, Alvin (Texas) CC.

## CHICAGO WHITE SOX

**January—Regular Phase (6)**

1. *Louis Calvert, rhp, Blinn (Texas) JC.—DNP
2. *Jorge Robles, ss, Miami-Dade CC New World Center.
**3. Tony Scruggs, of, Mount San Antonio (Calif.) JC.—(1991)**
4. *Rob Wolkoys, 3b, Mount San Antonio (Calif.) JC.
5. Victor Heckman, rhp, Western Michigan University.
6. Chris Alvarez, of-3b, Miami-Dade CC South.

**Cubs first-rounder Rafael Palmeiro was a 20-year major league vet with more than 3,000 hits**

**January—Secondary Phase (22)**

1. Tom Forrester, lhp-1b, Miami-Dade CC North.—(AAA)
2. Larry Allen, of, Laney (Calif.) JC.

**June—Regular Phase (5)**

1. Kurt Brown, c, Glendora (Calif.) HS.—(AAA)
**2. Jose Mota, 2b, Cal State Fullerton.—(1991-95)**
DRAFT DROP *Son of Manny Mota, major leaguer (1962-82) • Brother of Andy Mota, sixth-round draft pick, January 1985/regular phase, Royals; major leaguer (1991)*
3. Glen Braxton, of, Idabel (Okla.) HS.—(High A)
**4. Bobby Thigpen, rhp, Mississippi State University.—(1986-94)**
5. Aubrey Waggoner, of, Eisenhower HS, Fontana, Calif.—(AAA)
**6. John Pawlowski, rhp, Clemson University.—(1987-88)**
DRAFT DROP *Baseball coach, College of Charleston (2000-08); baseball coach, Auburn (2009-13)*
7. James Bledsoe, of, Manual Arts HS, Los Angeles.
8. Marty Warren, rhp, Campbell University.
9. *Scott Nelson, lhp, Oak Park-River Forest HS, River Forest, Ill.
**10. Wayne Edwards, lhp, Azusa Pacific (Calif.) University.—(1989-91)**
11. Eric Milholland, c, Valparaiso University.
12. John Stein, rhp, University of Nevada-Las Vegas.
13. Dan Cronkright, 3b, Central Michigan University.
14. David Sheldon, of, University of San Francisco.
15. John Von Ahnen, of, Wagner College.
16. Steve Mehl, ss-2b, North Highlands (Calif.) HS.
**17. Tom Drees, lhp, Creighton University.—(1991)**
18. George Stone, rhp, Clemson University.
**19. Randy Velarde, ss, Lubbock Christian (Texas) College.—(1987-2002)**
20. Samuel Ruiz, 2b, Central State (Ohio) University.
21. Michael Moore, of, Cal State Los Angeles.
22. David Reynolds, ss, Northwestern State University.
**23. Donn Pall, rhp, University of Illinois.—(1988-98)**
24. Tom Hildebrand, 2b, Northwestern University.
25. David Lee, rhp, University of Florida.
26. *John Hairston, 3b, Grant HS, Portland, Ore.
27. Andre Toliver, of, Grand Canyon College.
28. *Matt Lagunas, ss, Mesa (Ariz.) HS.
29. *Dale Roder, rhp, Briar Cliff (Iowa) College.
30. Steve Ruzich, c, College of St. Francis (Ill.).

**June—Secondary Phase (9)**

1. Scott Kershaw, rhp, UCLA.—(Low A)
2. Vince Lopez, ss, UCLA.
3. Ken Rahming, of, Miami-Dade CC North.

## CINCINNATI REDS

**January—Regular Phase (3)**

1. Scott Willis, rhp, JC of the Sequoias (Calif.).—(High A)
2. Jack Smith, ss, Seminole (Fla.) CC.
3. *Jeff Moe, 3b, Clark (Wash.) CC.
4. Brad Brusky, rhp, Des Moines Area (Iowa) CC.
5. *William Parham, 1b, Walters State (Tenn.) CC.
6. *Mathias Butala, rhp, Willmar (Minn.) CC.
7. *Ray Schuyler, of, CC of Morris (N.J.).
8. *Kevin Pozniak, rhp, North Arkansas CC.
9. *David Suemnicht, rhp, Indian Hills (Iowa) CC.
10. *Gary Fonnesbeck, rhp, Lane (Ore.) CC.
11. *Randy St. Ward, of, Westark (Ark.) CC.
12. *Mike Grabliauskas, lhp, Rockland (N.Y.) CC.
13. *Jose Tartabull, of, Miami-Dade CC North.
DRAFT DROP *Son of Jose Tartabull Sr., major leaguer (1962-70) • Brother of Danny Tartabull, major leaguer (1984-97)*

**January—Secondary Phase (11)**

1. *Tom Powers, rhp, Triton (Ill.) JC.—DNP
**2. *Shawn Gilbert, ss, Golden West (Calif.) JC.—(1997-2000)**

**June—Regular Phase (4)**

**1. Barry Larkin, ss, University of Michigan.—(1986-2004)**
DRAFT DROP *Elected to Baseball Hall of Fame (2012)*
2. Steve Davis, of, Plano East, Plano, Texas.—(AA)
3. Ken Huseby, rhp, Rolling Meadows (Ill.) HS.—(High A)
4. Joe Dunlap, ss, Oral Roberts University.—(AAA)
5. *Billy St. Peter, 3b, Western HS, Bay City, Mich.—(AA)
DRAFT DROP *Attended Michigan; re-drafted by Cubs, 1988 (7th round)*
6. Tim Deitz, rhp, University of Arkansas.
7. Ricky Epps, of, Linden-Kildare HS, Linden, Texas.
8. Tim Watkins, rhp, Mississippi College.
9. Rich Sapienza, c, Ocala Forest HS, Ocala, Fla.
10. Pete Beeler, c, Middleburg (Fla.) HS.
**11. Don Wakamatsu, c, Arizona State University.—(1991)**
DRAFT DROP *Major league manager (2009-10)*
**12. Marty Brown, of-3b, University of Georgia.—(1988-90)**
13. Troy Girdner, rhp, St. Cloud HS, Kissimmee, Fla.
14. Larry Schwartz, lhp, Seton Hall University.
15. Don Brown, ss, Vernon (Fla.) HS.
16. Mike Ramsey, of, Texas Christian University.
**17. Mike Roesler, rhp, Ball State University.—(1989-90)**
18. Jeff Hayward, rhp, Jacksonville State University.
19. Tom Summers, lhp, University of Cincinnati.
20. Gary Curtis, ss, University of Arkansas.
21. *Keith Kaiser, rhp, MacArthur HS, San Antonio, Texas.
22. Cal Cain, of, Fresno State University.
23. *Mike Oglesbee, 1b, University of Nevada-Las Vegas.
24. Thomas Wilson, c, Jacksonville University.
25. Richard Beaupre, ss, North Carolina Wesleyan College.
26. *Everett Cunningham, rhp, Waterloo (Iowa) HS.
27. *James Johnston, rhp, Regis HS, Cedar Rapids, Iowa.
28. Rick Campbell, ss, University of Kentucky.

**June—Secondary Phase (18)**

1. Jeff Forney, of, Florida Atlantic University.—(AA)

## CLEVELAND INDIANS

**January—Regular Phase (10)**

1. *Rick Wharf, ss, Centralia (Wash.) JC.—DNP
2. *Jeff Smith, rhp, Cleveland State (Tenn.) CC.
3. Myron Gardner, rhp, Louisburg (N.C.) JC.
4. Mike Farr, rhp, Dundalk (Md.) CC.
5. *Frank Taylor, of, DeKalb North (Ga.) JC.
6. *Shawn Talbott, rhp, Cochise County (Ariz.) CC.
7. John Githens, rhp, Camden County (N.J.) JC.
8. *Ed Stockhousen, 2b, DeKalb North (Ga.) JC.
9. *James Ryerson, ss, Brookdale (N.J.) CC.
10. Charles Todd, 1b-c, Rockland (N.Y.) CC.
11. *Charles Bell, of, Aquinas (Tenn.) JC.

**January—Secondary Phase (6)**

1. *Doug Cox, lhp, DeKalb (Ga.) JC.—(High A)
2. *Kevin Thomas, lhp, Spartanburg Methodist (S.C.) JC.
3. *Anthony Newman, of, University of Oregon.
DRAFT DROP *Defensive back, National Football League (1988-99)*

#### June—Regular Phase (9)

1. Mike Poehl, rhp, University of Texas.—(AA)
2. Andy Ghelfi, rhp, Indiana State University.—(AA)

DRAFT DROP *Brother of Tony Ghelfi, major leaguer (1983)*

**3. *Scott Ruskin, of-lhp, University of Florida.—(1990-93)**

DRAFT DROP *Returned to Florida; re-drafted by Expos, January 1986/secondary phase (1st round)*

**4. Scott Jordan, of, Georgia Tech.—(1988)**
**5. Rod Nichols, rhp, University of New Mexico.—(1988-95)**
6. Charles Scott, rhp, Arizona State University.
7. Greg Williamson, rhp, Western New Mexico University.
8. Glenn Fairchild, ss, Cal State Los Angeles.
**9. Luis Medina, 1b, Arizona State University.—(1988-91)**
10. Mike Rountree, of, Claremont (Calif.) College.
11. Kent Murphy, lhp, Western Illinois University.
12. Manny Mercado, lhp, St. Mary's HS, Jersey City, N.J.
13. Don Lovell, of, Portland State University.
14. Greg LaFever, rhp, Wichita State University.
15. Rock Hurst, c, Furman University.
16. Troy Startoni, c, St. Thomas (Fla.) University.
17. Bill Wilkes, 1b, Campbell University.
18. Greg Karpuk, rhp, University of North Carolina.
19. John Power, 1b-lhp, Madison HS, Portland, Ore.
**20. *Brian Jordan, ss, Milford Mill HS, Baltimore.—(1992-2006)**

DRAFT DROP *Defensive back, National Football League (1989-91) • First-round draft pick (30th overall), Cardinals (1988)*

21. Rob Swain, ss, Texas A&M University.
22. Mike Bellaman, rhp, Penn State University.
23. *Brad Smith, rhp, Cleveland State (Tenn.) CC.
24. Casey Webster, 1b, Western Oregon State College.
25. Steve Johnigan, c, Texas A&M University.
26. Jules Franzen, c, Curry (Mass.) College.
27. Robert Link, rhp, St. Leo (Fla.) College.
28. *Russell Whittle, lhp, North Greenville (S.C.) JC.
29. Donaciano Santos, 1b, Shadle Park HS, Spokane, Wash.
**30. *Chris Nabholz, lhp, Pottsville (Pa.) HS.—(1990-95)**
31. Dave Alvis, 1b, University of Southwestern Louisiana.

DRAFT DROP *Son of Max Alvis, major leaguer (1962-70)*

32. *Kevin Shea, lhp, Lewis-Clark State (Idaho) College.
33. *Jay Semke, of, Cambridge (Ohio) HS.
**34. *Jeff Mutis, lhp, Allentown (Pa.) Catholic HS.—(1991-94)**

DRAFT DROP *First-round draft pick (27th overall), Indians (1988)*

35. *Josh Lowery, ss, Oakland (Calif.) Tech HS.
36. *Gary Zwolinski, lhp, Brother Wright HS, Farmington Hills, Mich.
37. Michael Vannucci, c, Ohlone (Calif.) JC.
38. Michael Workman, of, Florida Southern College.
39. *Clay Parrach, 1b-of, Aurora (Neb.) HS.

#### June—Secondary Phase (19)

1. *John Woodward, of, Santa Fe (Fla.) CC.—DNP
2. *John Vuz, c, Keystone (Pa.) JC.
**3. *Greg Briley, ss, Louisburg (N.C.) JC.—(1988-93)**
4. *Jorge Robles, ss, Miami-Dade CC New World Center.

## DETROIT TIGERS

#### January—Regular Phase (26)

1. Ken Williams, lhp, Live Oak, Fla.—(AAA)
2. Paul Jackson, rhp-ss, Citrus (Calif.) JC.
3. David Cooper, c, Macomb (Mich.) CC.
4. *Jerald Frost, ss, Ocean County (N.J.) JC.
5. Frank Masters, c, Scottsdale (Ariz.) CC.
6. *Craig Burns, of, Sacramento (Calif.) CC.
7. *Robert Fassold, c, Mira Costa (Calif.) JC.
8. *Tyrone Boseman, ss, Montreat-Anderson (N.C.) JC.
9. *Rodger Castner, rhp, Arizona Western JC.
10. *Daniel Cetnar, rhp, Thornton (Ill.) CC.
11. *Steve Kovensky, rhp, Palomar (Calif.) JC.
12. *Scott Spurgeon, c-3b, Labette (Kan.) CC.
13. *Gary Smith, lhp-1b, Brookdale (N.J.) CC.
14. *Donald Mire, c, Citrus (Calif.) JC.

#### January—Secondary Phase (8)

1. Gary Pifer, rhp, Santa Ana (Calif.) JC.—(High A)
2. *Ken Pennington, ss, El Camino (Calif.) JC.
3. *Larry Cratsenberg, inf, Orange Coast (Calif.) JC.

#### June—Regular Phase (26)

**1. Randy Nosek, rhp, Chillicothe (Mo.) HS.—(1989-90)**
2. Scott Carter, rhp, Havelock (N.C.) HS.—(High A)
**3. Steve Searcy, lhp, University of Tennessee.—(1988-92)**
4. Robert Friesen, rhp, Meridian HS, Boise, Idaho.—(Low A)
5. Gerry Wetherell, rhp, Mount Vernon Nazarene (Ohio) College.—(Low A)
**6. Scott Lusader, of, University of Florida.—(1987-91)**
**7. Doug Strange, 2b, North Carolina State University.—(1989-98)**
8. Donny Rowland, 2b, University of Miami.

DRAFT DROP *Scouting director, Angels (1999-2003)*

9. Derreck Bastinck, c, Ramapo (N.J.) College.
**10. *Lou Frazier, of, Scottsdale (Ariz.) CC.—(1993-98)**
11. Ruben Jackson, of, Cajon HS, San Bernardino, Calif.
12. Joe Slavik, lhp, Eastern Michigan University.
13. Alain Patenaude, rhp, University of Miami.
14. Doyle Balthazar, c, Los Angeles (Calif.) HS.
**15. Mark Lee, lhp, Florida International University.—(1988-95)**
16. *Jeff Henderson, lhp, Stetson University.
17. Allen Liebert, c, West HS, Waukegan, Ill.
**18. *Andy Stankiewicz, 2b, Pepperdine University.—(1992-98)**

DRAFT DROP *Baseball coach, Grand Canyon (2012-15)*

19. Ted Lawrence, c, Pace (N.Y.) University.
20. Ed Waylock, ss, Bradley University.
21. *Ted Wiesfuss, ss, Chatsworth (Calif.) HS.
**22. John Smoltz, rhp, Waverly HS, Lansing, Mich.—(1988-2009)**

DRAFT DROP *Elected to Baseball Hall of Fame (2015)*

23. Thelanious Prioleau, ss, Central State (Ohio) University.
24. *Craig Good, rhp, Rio Mesa HS, Camarillo, Calif.
25. Thomas Knapp, of, Ferris State (Mich.) College.
26. Tom Snowberger, of, University of Iowa.
27. *Dan Disher, rhp, University of Michigan.
28. Ken Gohmann, rhp, Northwestern University.
29. *Ken Deal, rhp, Trinidad State (Colo.) JC.
30. *Steve Kern, 3b, Durfee HS, Fall River, Mass.
31. Adam Dempsay, c, Bradley University.
32. Rob Thomson, c, Kansas University.
33. *Randy Kotchman, ss, Seminole (Fla.) HS.

#### June—Secondary Phase (26)

1. *Pete Roberts, lhp, Mira Costa (Calif.) JC.—(AAA)
2. *David Miller, rhp, Camden County (N.J.) JC.
3. *Rob Hartwig, of, Los Angeles Harbor JC.
**4. Kevin Ritz, rhp, Indian Hills (Iowa) CC.—(1989-98)**
5. *Gary Alexander, rhp, Laney (Calif.) JC.
6. *Mike Sisco, ss, St. Louis CC-Meramec.
7. *Tom Powers, rhp, Triton (Ill.) JC.

## HOUSTON ASTROS

#### January—Regular Phase (11)

1. *Pete Roberts, lhp, Mira Costa (Calif.) JC.—(AAA)
2. Randy Randle, ss, San Jacinto (Texas) JC.
3. *Jimmy Hitt, rhp, Chipola (Fla.) JC.
4. *Ken Sorensen, rhp, San Jacinto (Texas) JC.
5. *John Clements, rhp, Chipola (Fla.) JC.
6. *Mark Lundy, 1b, Mira Costa (Calif.) JC.
7. Carlo Colombino, 3b, Brookdale (N.J.) CC.
8. Robert Romo, rhp, Ventura (Calif.) JC.
9. John Sheehan, rhp, Ocean County (N.J.) JC.
10. *Mike Sisco, ss, St. Louis CC-Meramec.
11. *Flynn Carr, c, Cochise County (Ariz.) CC.
12. *Jeff Piland, lhp, Cerritos (Calif.) JC.
13. *Don Enoch, rhp, Mercer County (N.J.) CC.
**14. Jeff Baldwin, of, Camden County (N.J.) JC.—(1990)**

#### January—Secondary Phase (3)

**1. Mel Stottlemyre Jr., rhp, Yakima Valley (Wash.) JC.—(1990)**

DRAFT DROP *Son of Mel Stottlemyre Sr., major leaguer (1964-74) • Brother of Todd Stottlemyre, first overall draft pick, January 1985/secondary phase, Cardinals; major leaguer (1988-2002)*

2. *Anthony Blackmon, ss, Seminole (Okla.) JC.
3. *Paul James, rhp, St. Louis CC-Meramec.

#### June—Regular Phase (12)

**1. Cameron Drew, of, University of New Haven.—(1988)**
2. Bert Hunter, ss, Norte Vista HS, Riverside, Calif.—(AAA)
3. *Mike Hensley, rhp, Latta HS, Ada, Okla.–(Low A)

DRAFT DROP *Attended Oklahoma; re-drafted by Cardinals, 1988 (2nd round) • Father of Ty Hensley, first-round draft pick, Yankees (2014)*

**4. Blaise Ilsley, lhp, Indiana State University.—(1994)**
5. Troy Aleshire, c, Meadowbrook HS, Byesville, Ohio.—(Low A)
**6. Mike Simms, 1b, Esperanza HS, Yorba Linda, Calif.—(1990-99)**
7. Jeff Edwards, c, Cal Poly Pomona.
**8. Terry Wells, lhp, University of Illinois.—(1990)**
**9. John Fishel, of, Cal State Fullerton.—(1988)**
10. James Vike, rhp, Willamette (Ore.) University.
11. Joe Schultz, rhp, Southeast Missouri State University.
12. Wayne Rogalski, 2b, University of New Haven.
13. Calvin James, of, University of Miami.
14. Gary Murphy, rhp, University of Arkansas.
15. *Bryn Kosco, ss, Poland (Ohio) HS.

DRAFT DROP *Son of Andy Kosco, major leaguer (1965-74)*

16. *Craig Wilson, c, La Mirada (Calif.) HS.
17. Scott Gray, ss, Stetson University.
18. Tim Arnsberg, rhp, San Diego State University.

DRAFT DROP *Brother of Brad Arnsberg, major leaguer (1986-92)*

19. Tim Jester, of, University of California.
20. Ron Roebuck, lhp, University of Southern California.

DRAFT DROP *Son of Ed Roebuck, major leaguer (1955-66)*

21. Steve Gelmine, lhp, Florida State University.
22. Kevin Smith, rhp, Florida State University.
23. Tony Dineen, rhp, Lewis-Clark State (Idaho) College.
24. Stan Fascher, rhp, University of Florida.
25. *Keith Hamilton, rhp, University of Oklahoma.
**26. *Jeff Reboulet, ss, Louisiana State University.—(1992-2003)**
27. O.B. Hartman, rhp, Otterbein (Ohio) College.
28. Robert Shepis, of, Seton Hall University.
29. *Doug Fisher, 1b, Central Michigan University.
30. Rich Johnson, 1b, Sam Houston State University.
31. *Dewitt Cotton, of, Westchester (Calif.) HS.
32. *Isaac Elder, of, Westchester (Calif.) HS.
33. *Ron Moore, rhp, UC Riverside.
34. *Rick Hirtensteiner, of, Buena HS, Ventura, Calif.

#### June—Secondary Phase (20)

1. Gayron Jackson, of, El Camino (Calif.) JC.—(Short-season A)

DRAFT DROP *Son of Grant Jackson, major leaguer (1965-82)*

2. *Jim Willis, of, Triton (Ill.) JC.
3. *Scot Boudreaux, rhp, Wharton County (Texas) JC.
4. *Tim Lichty, of-3b, Moorpark (Calif.) JC.
5. Shawn Talbott, rhp, Cochise County (Ariz.) CC.
6. *Ed Shea, c, Palm Beach (Fla.) JC.

## KANSAS CITY ROYALS

#### January—Regular Phase (18)

1. *Scot Boudreaux, rhp, Wharton County (Texas) JC.—DNP
2. Peter Carey, of, Rockland (N.Y.) CC.
3. Dejon Watson, 1b, West Los Angeles JC.

DRAFT DROP *Scouting director, Reds (1998-2000)*

**4. *Kevin Brown, lhp, Sacramento (Calif.) CC.—(1990-92)**
5. *Joaquin Contreras, of, Miami-Dade CC South.
**6. *Andy Mota, 2b, Golden West (Calif.) JC.—(1991)**

DRAFT DROP *Son of Manny Mota, major leaguer (1962-82) • Brother of Jose Mota, major leaguer (1991-95)*

7. *Dennis King, ss, Riverside (Calif.) CC.
8. *Tim John, rhp, JC of Southern Idaho.
9. *Brad Noe, of, Edmonds (Wash.) CC.
10. *Mike Aspray, rhp, West Los Angeles JC.
**11. *Blas Minor, rhp, Merced (Calif.) JC.—(1992-97)**
12. Keith Sheldon, rhp, Brasstown, N.C.
13. *Mike Zuber, rhp, Centralia (Wash.) JC.
14. *Robert Bartlett, of, Citrus (Calif.) JC.
15. *Pat Waid, of, Oxnard (Calif.) JC.
16. *Scott Reaves, ss, JC of the Sequoias (Calif.).
17. *Jon Taylor, of, Cuesta (Calif.) JC.
18. *Steve Hansen, 3b, Kings River (Calif.) JC.
19. *Todd Nelms, lhp, Los Medanos (Calif.) JC.
20. Richard Day, 3b, Essex (Md.) CC.
21. Gerald Smith, c, Essex (Md.) CC.

#### January—Secondary Phase (16)

1. *Mike Reitzel, lhp, Seminole (Okla.) JC.—(High A)
2. *Darrin Garner, ss, Orange Coast (Calif.) JC.
3. *Charles Wacha, rhp, Edison (Fla.) CC.

#### June—Regular Phase (17)

**1. Brian McRae, ss, Manatee HS, Bradenton, Fla.—(1990-99)**

DRAFT DROP *Son of Hal McRae, major leaguer (1968-87); major league manager (1991-2002)*

**2. Chris Jelic, c, University of Pittsburgh.—(1990)**
3. Mike Loggins, of, University of Arkansas.—(AAA)
**4. Mike Macfarlane, c, Santa Clara University.—(1987-99)**
5. Ricky Rojas, rhp, Miami Lakes HS, Hialeah, Fla.—(AAA)
**6. *Deion Sanders, of, North Fort Myers (Fla.) HS.—(1989-2001)**

DRAFT DROP *First-round draft pick, Atlanta Falcons/National Football League (1989); defensive back, NFL (1989-2005).*

7. David Tinkle, ss, Ocean View HS, Huntington Beach, Calif.
8. Deric Ladnier, 3b, University of Mississippi.

DRAFT DROP *Scouting director, Royals (2000-08); scouting director, Diamondbacks (2015)*

9. Kevin Karcher, rhp, Oakland (Mich.) CC.
10. Randy Goodenough, lhp, Iowa Central CC.
11. *Greg S. Harris, lhp, Gonzaga University.
12. Ken Crew, rhp, Fresno State University.
13. Tim Lemons, 1b-rhp, Auburn University.
14. *Carl Shaw, rhp, Bellevue (Wash.) CC.
15. Albert Peluso, rhp, Point Park (Pa.) College.
16. Robert O'Hoppe, ss, Erskine (S.C.) College.
17. Linton Dyer, c, Grady Vocational HS, Brooklyn, N.Y.
18. Sal Vaccaro, lhp, Santa Clara University.
19. Dean Duane, rhp, University of New Mexico.
20. *Brett Roach, ss, Lakeview HS, St. Clair Shores, Mich.
21. *Tony Welborn, of, Appalachian State University.

DRAFT DROP *Twin brother of Todd Welborn, fourth-round draft pick, Mets (1985)*

22. Gene Morgan, rhp, Mississippi State University.
23. Abbie Woyce, rhp, Vanderbilt University.
24. Rufus Ellis, rhp, Alabama State University.
25. Jimmy Franklin, rhp, Arkansas Tech.
26. Hunter Hoffman, 3b, Hewitt-Trussville HS, Trussville, Ala.
27. *John Schilling, of, Santa Ana HS, Villa Park, Calif.
28. *Scott Shockey, 1b, El Toro (Calif.) HS.
29. Darren Watkins, rhp, Everett, Wash.
30. Russ Stachler, ss, Borah HS, Boise, Idaho.

#### June—Secondary Phase (23)

1. *Todd Ross, 3b-ss, Shasta (Calif.) JC.—DNP
2. *Joe Kemp, of, Citrus (Calif.) JC.
3. *Curtis Parham, of, Phoenix, Ill.

## LOS ANGELES DODGERS

#### January—Regular Phase (9)

1. Brad Zeinert, lhp-of, Tigerton, Wis.—(Rookie)

2. Darren Farley, 3b-of, San Jacinto (Texas) JC.
**3. *Greg Briley, ss, Louisburg (N.C.) JC.—(1988-93)**
4. *Mike Kitz, lhp, JC of San Mateo (Calif.).
5. *Paul Kuzniar, rhp, Alvin (Texas) CC.
6. *Lester Logan, c, Los Angeles CC.
7. *Gregory Martin, 2b-ss, Middle Georgia JC.
8. *Mike Fowler, 3b-c, Spartanburg Methodist (S.C.) JC.
9. *Bruce Powers, of, Skyline (Calif.) JC.
10. *Chris Graves, rhp, Middle Georgia JC.
11. Kevin Nelson, rhp, Yuba (Calif.) CC.
12. *Derek Keathley, rhp, Yuba (Calif.) CC.
13. *John McEntee, lhp, JC of Marin (Calif.).

**January—Secondary Phase (13)**

1. Eric Tutt, 1b-3b, Middle Georgia JC.—(Rookie)
**2. John Wetteland, rhp, JC of San Mateo (Calif.).—(1989-2000)**
3. *Adrian Adkins, c, Middle Georgia JC.

**June—Regular Phase (10)**

**1. Chris Gwynn, of, San Diego State University.—(1987-96)**
**DRAFT DROP** *Brother of Tony Gwynn, major leaguer (1982-2001)*
2. Mike Watters, 2b, University of Michigan (Choice from Rangers as compensation for Type A free agent Burt Hooton).—(AAA)
2. Dan Smith, c, Morehead State University.—(High A)
3. Pete Geist, of, Georgia Tech.—(High A)
4. *Mike Prior, of, Illinois State University.—DNP
**DRAFT DROP** *No school; re-drafted by Astros, January 1986/secondary phase (4th round) • Defensive back/National Football League (1985-94)*
**5. Mike Devereaux, of, Arizona State University.—(1987-98)**
6. Walt McConnell, 3b, Georgia Tech.
7. Rene Garcia, lhp, Hoover HS, Glendale, Calif.
**8. Jack Savage, rhp, University of Kentucky.—(1987-90)**
9. Walt Stull, rhp, UC Riverside.
10. Fred Farwell, lhp, University of Arkansas.
11. Mike Fiala, rhp, Princeton University.
12. Ken Lambert, c, University of Portland.
13. Andy Naworski, rhp, UCLA.
14. Mike Batesole, 3b, Oral Roberts University.
**DRAFT DROP** *Baseball coach, Cal State Northridge (1996-2002); baseball coach, Fresno State (2003-15)*
15. Jay Ray, rhp, University of Kentucky.
**16. Mike Huff, of, Northwestern University.—(1989-96)**
17. Bryan Smith, lhp, St. Mary's (Calif.) College.
18. Carl Thomas, lhp, Calhoun County HS, Edison, Ga.
19. Mike Burke, 1b, St. Xavier (Ill.) College.
20. Mike Lilly, rhp, West Georgia College.
21. Charles Hardwick, lhp, University of South Carolina.
22. Edwin Hart, lhp, Patrick Henry HS, Beaverdam, Va.
23. Jeff Hartman, ss, McCaskey HS, Lancaster, Pa.
24. Michael A. White, of, Valdosta State (Ga.) College.
25. Paul Moralez, 1b, UC Riverside.
26. Douglas Ames, lhp, Columbia, S.C.
27. Robert Tucker, c, West Virginia University.
28. Kevin Ayers, ss, University of North Carolina-Charlotte.
29. Brett Parker, ss, Sul Ross State (Texas) University.
30. Andrew Anthony, of, Valdosta State (Ga.) College.
31. James Garrison, ss-2b, Plant City (Fla.) HS.
32. Ron Jackson, c, Huston-Tillotson (Texas) College.
33. Bill Bluhm, 3b, JC of the Canyons (Calif.).

**June—Secondary Phase (24)**

1. Doug Cox, lhp, DeKalb (Ga.) JC.—(High A)
2. Marvin Newton, c, San Bernardino Valley (Calif.) JC.
3. *John McEntee, lhp, JC of Marin (Calif.).

## MILWAUKEE BREWERS

**January—Regular Phase (2)**

1. Oliver Nichols, rhp, Oxnard (Calif.) JC.—(Rookie)
2. *Harry Michael, of, Big Bend (Wash.) CC.

TOM DIPACE

**Gregg Jefferies sizzled as a minor leaguer but couldn't match the expectations of Mets fans**

**3. *Steve Carter, of, Hagerstown (Md.) JC.—(1989-90)**
4. John Ludy, rhp, Boyertown, Pa.
5. *John Chaffee, ss-2b, Grossmont (Calif.) JC.
6. *Everett Utter, c, Spartanburg Methodist (S.C.) JC.
7. Oscar Duran, lhp-1b, East Los Angeles JC.
**8. *Chris Howard, of-lhp, Miami-Dade CC South.—(1993-95)**
9. *Ernie Isaac, 2b, Sacramento (Calif.) CC.
10. *Brian Clark, 1b, Polk (Fla.) CC.
11. Armando Verdugo, c, East Los Angeles JC.
12. *Tim Fisher, c, Sacramento (Calif.) CC.
13. *William Schutt, rhp, Southwestern (Calif.) JC.
14. *Rusty Covington, rhp, Shelby State (Tenn.) CC.
15. *Eric Woods, of, Sacramento (Calif.) CC.
**16. *Jim Bowie, 1b, Sacramento (Calif.) CC.—(1994)**
17. *Brett Bohatuk, rhp, Macomb (Mich.) CC.

**January—Secondary Phase (2)**

**1. Randy Veres, rhp, Sacramento (Calif.) CC.—(1989-97)**
2. *Ed Shea, c, Palm Beach (Fla.) JC.
3. *Miguel Ferradas, c, Miami-Dade CC South.
4. *Steve Wiley, lhp, Indian River (Fla.) CC.
5. *Joe Palubeski, 2b, JC of the Canyons (Calif.).

**June—Regular Phase (1)**

**1. B.J. Surhoff, c-ss, University of North Carolina.—(1987-2006)**
**DRAFT DROP** *Brother of Rick Surhoff, major leaguer (1985) • Son of Dick Surhoff, forward/National Basketball Association (1952-54)*
2. Carl Moraw, rhp, Bowling Green State University.—(AA)
3. Shon Ashley, ss, Meridian HS, Boise, Idaho.—(AAA)
**4. Billy Bates, 2b, University of Texas.—(1989-90)**
5. Todd Brown, of, Arizona State University.—(AAA)
6. Robert Tinkey, 3b, West Liberty State (W.Va.) College.
7. Charles McGrew, c, Southeastern Oklahoma State University.
**8. Doug Henry, rhp, Arizona State University.—(1991-2001)**
9. *Anthony Hill, of, University of Rhode Island.
10. Rich Bosley, rhp, Appalachian State University.
11. Lance Lincoln, ss, Lewis-Clark State (Idaho) College.
**DRAFT DROP** *Son of Keith Lincoln, running back, National Football League (1961-68)*
12. Mario Monico, of, University of Hawaii.
13. Edward Greene, of, Swarthmore (Pa.) College.
**14. Russ McGinnis, 1b, University of Oklahoma.—(1992-95)**
**15. *Colby Ward, rhp, Brigham Young University.—(1990)**
16. *Bob Collum, 3b, University of Hawaii.
17. *Enoch Simmons, ss-of, North HS, Riverside, Calif.
18. Damon Oppenheimer, c, University of Southern California.
**DRAFT DROP** *Scouting director, Yankees (2005-15)*
19. Frank Fazzini, of, Florida State University.
20. *Russ Burk, lhp, Baltimore.
21. Eric Pilkington, lhp, Westmont (Calif.) College.
22. *Robert Clark, of, JC of the Desert (Calif.).
**23. *Scott Kamieniecki, rhp, University of Michigan.—(1991-2000)**
24. Don Bridges, c, Arlington HS, Riverside, Calif.
**25. *Nikco Riesgo, 3b, Poly HS, Long Beach, Calif.—(1991)**
26. *Bruce Wegman, rhp, Oak Hills HS, Cincinnati.
**DRAFT DROP** *Brother of Bruce Wegman, major leaguer (1985-95)*
27. *Robert Jones, of-1b, Southern Illinois University.
**DRAFT DROP** *First-round draft pick (28th overall), Reds (1982)*
28. *Steven Lee, ss, Fontana (Calif.) HS.
29. Buddy Haney, of, Texas A&M University.
30. *Mike Ross, ss, Fresno (Calif.) CC.
31. *Mike Gorman, ss, Bishop Amat HS, Azusa, Calif.
32. *Dave Dawson, rhp, Culver City (Calif.) HS.
33. *Don Arnold, lhp-1b, Hemet (Calif.) HS.
34. Gary Sanchez, of, University of Alabama, Birmingham.
**35. *Pedro Borbon Jr., lhp, Dewitt Clinton HS, Bronx, N.Y.—(1992-2003)**
**DRAFT DROP** *Son of Pedro Borbon, major leaguer (1969-80)*

**June—Secondary Phase (17)**

1. John Wilder, rhp, Walters State (Tenn.) CC.—(Rookie)
2. *Tom Gallagher, lhp, Sacramento (Calif.) CC.
**3. *Steve Carter, of, Hagerstown (Md.) JC.—(1989-90)**
4. *Joe Palubeski, 2b, JC of the Canyons (Calif.).
5. *Robert Bartlett, of, Citrus (Calif.) JC.
6. *Dennis King, ss, Riverside (Calif.) CC.
7. Jeff Smith, rhp, Cleveland State (Tenn.) CC.

## MINNESOTA TWINS

**January—Regular Phase (14)**

1. *Tony Faryniarz, rhp, Sacramento (Calif.) CC.—(Short-season A)
2. James Cook, rhp, Mount San Antonio (Calif.) JC.
3. Mike Redding, rhp, Manatee (Fla.) JC.
4. *Dan Paradoa, of, Indian River (Fla.) CC.
5. Scott Rohlof, of, Central Arizona JC.
6. *Jerald Higby, lhp, Modesto (Calif.) JC.
**7. *Mike Benjamin, 2b, Cerritos (Calif.) JC.—(1989-2002)**
8. *James Dodds, of, JC of the Sequoias (Calif.).
9. *Duane Walker, of, Santa Fe (Fla.) CC.
10. *James Winkle, c, Umpqua (Ore.) CC.
11. Gary Thomasson, of, Santa Ana (Calif.) JC.
12. *Craig McIver, rhp, Fullerton (Calif.) JC.

**January—Secondary Phase (26)**

1. *Garrett O'Connor, rhp, Lafayette, La.—(Short-season A)
2. *William Stokes, 1b, Glendale (Calif.) JC.

**June—Regular Phase (13)**

1. Jeff Bumgarner, rhp, Hanford HS, Richland, Wash.—(AAA)
2. Steve Gasser, rhp, New Philadelphia (Ohio) HS.—(AAA)
**3. Paul Abbott, rhp, Sunny Hills HS, Fullerton, Calif.—(1990-2004)**
4. Robbie Smith, rhp, Louisiana State University.—(AA)
5. Brad Bierley, 3b-of, Pepperdine University.—(AAA)
6. Gary Borg, of, University of Illinois.
7. Lee Swenson, c, Luther (Iowa) College.
8. Mark Davis, lhp, University of Nebraska.
9. Mike Adams, rhp, Phillips (Okla.) University.
10. Julio DeLancer, ss, Lehman (N.Y.) College.
11. Howard Manzon, of, Pace (N.Y.) University.
12. Tom Scaletta, ss, Cal Poly Pomona.
13. Marty Lanoux, 3b, Louisiana State University.
14. Joe Boyce, ss, Coon Rapids (Minn.) HS.
15. *Paul Burghardt, 1b-lhp, Normandale (Minn.) CC.
16. Robert Strube, lhp, Luther (Iowa) College.
17. *David Keating, lhp, North Salinas (Calif.) HS.
18. *Scott Wilkinson, of, Cerritos (Calif.) JC.
19. Henry Siemers, of-3b, St. John's University.
20. Robert Perry, 1b-3b, UC Irvine.
**21. Lenny Webster, c, Grambling State University.—(1989-2000)**
22. *Don Snowden, lhp-of, Fountain Valley (Calif.) HS.
23. Mark Casey, 2b, Iona College.
24. *Mark Hicks, of, Davis (Calif.) HS.
25. *Derk Madden, rhp, San Mateo (Calif.) HS.
26. William O'Connor, of, Adelphi (N.Y.) University.

27. Buddy Buzzard, c, University of La Verne (Calif.).
28. *Mike Owens, of, Notre Dame HS, Sauquoit, N.Y.
29. *Burt Beattie, 3b, University of Nebraska.
30. Harrison Sherman, of, Santa Monica (Calif.) JC.
31. Ted Miller, c, Newberry (S.C.) College.
32. Kenneth Wright, rhp, University of Central Florida.

**June—Secondary Phase (13)**

1. Dewayne Coleman, rhp, Chaffey (Calif.) JC.—(High A)
**2. *Shawn Gilbert, ss, Golden West (Calif.) JC.—(1997-2000)**
3. *Philip Price, rhp, Los Angeles Harbor JC.

## MONTREAL EXPOS

**January—Regular Phase (7)**

1. Maurice Bigden, ss, Cuesta (Calif.) JC.—(Short-season A)
2. *Gayron Jackson, of, West Los Angeles JC.
3. *Carl Rose, rhp-c, South Georgia JC.
4. *Frank Ward, lhp, Santa Rosa (Calif.) JC.
5. *Larry Walsh, lhp, Cabrillo (Calif.) JC.
6. Kenneth Fox, of, Lane (Ore.) CC.
7. *Luc Berube, ss, Cochise County (Ariz.) CC.
8. *Tim Lichty, of, Moorpark (Calif.) JC.
9. Mark Berghela, of, University of Albany.
10. *Eric Jacques, rhp, San Jose (Calif.) CC.
11. *George Bargfrede, of, CC of Morris (N.J.).
12. *Robert Hartley, of, Clark (Wash.) JC.
13. Sean Baker, 3b, CC of Morris (N.J.).
14. *Don Cohoon, inf, Indian River (Fla.) CC.
15. William DeBoever, rhp, Des Moines Area (Iowa) CC.
16. *Robert Slate, lhp, Ferrum (Va.) JC.
17. *Tim Demoonie, ss-2b, Middle Georgia JC.
18. *Kevin Brooks, c-rhp, Jackson State (Tenn.) CC.
19. *Kurt Soderholm, ss-of, Central Florida CC.

**January—Secondary Phase (15)**

**1. *Michael C. Walker, rhp, Seminole (Fla.) CC.—(1988-96)**
2. Mel Houston, ss, Laney (Calif.) JC.
3. *Jeff Atha, ss-3b, DeKalb South (Ga.) CC.

**June—Regular Phase (8)**

**1. Pete Incaviglia, of-3b, Oklahoma State University.—(1986-98)**
DRAFT DROP *First player from 1985 draft to reach majors (April 8, 1986)*
**2. Randy Johnson, lhp, University of Southern California.—(1988-2009)**
DRAFT DROP *Elected to Baseball Hall of Fame (2015)*
3. Jeff Oller, ss, Minden (La.) HS.—(AA)
4. Anthony Candelino, of, Elizabeth (N.J.) HS.—(Short-season A)
5. Leonard Kelly, rhp, Tennessee State University.—(High A)
6. Bill Cunningham, lhp, Ohio State University.
**7. Jeff Fischer, rhp, University of Florida.—(1987-89)**
**8. Mark Gardner, rhp, Fresno State University.—(1989-2001)**
9. Bob Sudo, rhp, Ramapo (N.J.) College.
10. Chan Galbato, rhp, SUNY-Fredonia.
11. Paul Martineau, 1b, Eastern Connecticut State University.
12. Tim Barker, of, University of Central Florida.
13. Mike Day, c, Oklahoma State University.
14. *Bobby Jones, of, El Campo HS, Citrus Heights, Calif.
15. Darren Travels, rhp, Contra Costa (Calif.) JC.
16. *Guy Normand, lhp, Washington State University.
17. Loren White, c, Illinois State University.
18. Robert Williams, rhp, Morehead State University.
19. Stu Stauffacher, lhp, University of Houston.
20. *Mike Adkisson, of, Interlake HS, Bellevue, Wash.
21. *David Dasch, ss, Ithaca (N.Y.) College.
22. *Barry Shifflett, 3b, University of North Carolina-Charlotte.
**23. *Frank Bolick, ss, Mount Carmel (Pa.) HS.—(1993-98)**
24. *Rick Parker, c, John Curtis HS, River Ridge, La.
25. *Randy Robinson, rhp, Woodlake (Calif.) HS.
26. *Mark Arndt, lhp, Spencer (Texas) HS.
27. *Mike Montagnino, c, North Greenville (S.C.) JC.

**June—Secondary Phase (10)**

**1. Jim Hunter, rhp, University of Georgia.—(1991)**
2. Scott Ayers, rhp, University of New Orleans.
3. *Louis Calvert, rhp, Blinn (Texas) JC.
4. *Frank Taylor, of-1b, DeKalb North (Ga.) JC.

## NEW YORK METS

**January—Regular Phase (19)**

1. Mike Anderson, rhp, Los Angeles Valley JC.—(High A)
2. Scott Jaster, of, Trinidad State (Colo.) JC.
DRAFT DROP *Son of Larry Jaster, major leaguer (1965-72)*
3. *Robert Doman, lhp, Allegheny (Pa.) CC.
4. *William Norwood, rhp, Jefferson Davis (Ala.) JC.
5. *Mark Howell, c, Howard (Texas) JC.
6. Geary Jones, c, Butte (Calif.) JC.
7. *Joe Warren, rhp, Scottsdale (Ariz.) CC.
8. *Shawn McAfee, ss, Angelina (Texas) JC.
9. *Andy Berg, lhp, Sacramento (Calif.) CC.
10. *Herbert Nauert, 2b, Angelina (Texas) JC.
11. *Steve Eckenrode, 1b, Panola (Texas) JC.
**12. *Jerry Nielsen, lhp, Sacramento (Calif.) CC.—(1992-93)**
13. Randy Tubbleville, of, Angelina (Texas) JC.

**January—Secondary Phase (5)**

1. Craig Repoz, ss, Fullerton (Calif.) JC.—(AA)
DRAFT DROP *Son of Roger Repoz, major leaguer (1964-72)*
2. *Steven Harris, rhp, Florida JC.
3. *John Sellick, 1b-3b, Santa Rosa (Calif.) JC.

**June—Regular Phase (20)**

**1. Gregg Jefferies, ss, Serra HS, Millbrae, Calif.—(1987-2000)**
DRAFT DROP *First 1985 high school draft pick to reach majors (Sept. 6, 1987)*
**2. *Scott Servais, c, Westby HS, Coon Valley, Wis.—(1991-2001)**
DRAFT DROP *Attended Creighton; re-drafted by Astros, 1988 (3rd round)*
3. Rob Lemle, of, Compton (Calif.) HS.—(Low A)
DRAFT DROP *Died as active player (Nov. 24, 1989)*
4. Todd Welborn, rhp, Appalachian State University.—(AA)
DRAFT DROP *Twin brother of Tony Welborn, 21st-round draft pick, Royals (1985)*
**5. *Tim Layana, rhp, Loyola Marymount University.—(1990-93)**
DRAFT DROP *Returned to Loyola Marymount; re-drafted by Yankees, 1986 (3rd round)*
6. *Dan Henley, 3b, University of Southern California.
**7. *Monty Fariss, ss, Leedey (Okla.) HS.—(1991-93)**
DRAFT DROP *First-round draft pick (6th overall), Rangers (1988)*
8. Cliff Gonzalez, of-ss, St. Raymond's HS, Bronx, N.Y.
9. Rodney Murrell, ss, Skyline HS, Dallas.
10. Kennedy Farmer, of, Harrison Central HS, Saucier, Miss.
11. *Chris Gallego, ss, Rowland HS, Walnut, Calif.
DRAFT DROP *Brother of Mike Gallego, major leaguer (1985-97)*
12. Ron Narcisse, c, Norfolk State University.
13. Mark Willoughby, lhp, Independence HS, Tickfaw, La.
14. Victor Garcia, lhp, Cardinal Hayes HS, Bronx, N.Y.
15. Chris Rauth, rhp, Ithaca (N.Y.) College.
16. *Reggie Garcia, rhp, Hanford (Calif.) HS.
17. David Gelatt, 2b, University of Washington.
18. Kevin Armstrong, rhp, Sam Houston State University.
19. Alan Hayden, of, Northern Kentucky University.
20. *David Jacas, of, University of San Diego.
21. John Tuozzo, rhp, University of Hartford.
22. Jaime Archibald, 1b, Lewis-Clark State (Idaho) College.
23. *Gary Bockhorn, rhp, Southern Illinois University.
24. *Shannon Jones, rhp, Live Oak HS, Watson, La.
25. *Carlton Cochrane, lhp, Central Arizona JC.
26. *Howard Williams, lhp, Texas Christian University.
27. Jeff Jones, ss, Washington HS, Los Angeles.
28. *Mark Hudson, rhp, West Valley (Calif.) JC.
29. Arthur Douglas, of, Robert E. Lee HS, Montgomery, Ala.
30. Mark Bohne, rhp, Buchholz HS, Gainesville, Fla.
31. Bruce McDonald, rhp, Vanguard HS, Ocala, Fla.
32. *Dan Monzon, ss, Cardinal Spellman HS, Bronx, N.Y.
DRAFT DROP *Son of Dan Monzon, major leaguer (1972-73)*
33. Maury Gooden, of, Huston-Tillotson (Texas) College.
34. *Erik Judson, 2b, Hemet (Calif.) HS.
35. Steve Brueggeman, lhp-of, Cal State Sacramento.
36. Kurt DeLuca, 3b, Ithaca (N.Y.) College.
37. Thomas Wachs, lhp, Huntington (Ind.) College.

**June—Secondary Phase (16)**

**1. *Jerry Nielsen, lhp, Sacramento (Calif.) CC.—(1992-93)**
**2. *Gordie Dillard, lhp, Oklahoma State University.—(1988-89)**
3. *Andy Berg, lhp, Sacramento (Calif.) CC.
4. Joaquin Contreras, of, Miami-Dade CC South.
5. *Jerald Higby, lhp, Modesto (Calif.) JC.

## NEW YORK YANKEES

**January—Regular Phase (24)**

1. David Clark, lhp, Laney (Calif.) JC.—(High A)
2. *Bill Zupka, rhp, Queensborough (N.Y.) CC.
3. *Bruce Charlesbois, rhp, Indian River (Fla.) CC.
4. *Paul Zack, rhp, CC of Morris (N.J.).
5. *Darrin Bartel, 3b, San Jacinto (Texas) JC.
6. Dino Johnson, 3b-of, Sacramento (Calif.) CC.
7. *Greg Vella, 1b, JC of San Mateo (Calif.).
8. *Scott Maxwell, of, Cochise County (Ariz.) CC.
9. *David Martin, rhp, Chaffey (Calif.) JC.
10. *Greg Wherry, rhp, Los Angeles Harbor JC.

**January—Secondary Phase (24)**

1. *Scott Lerner, lhp, Diablo Valley (Calif.) JC.—DNP
2. *Jeff Marr, rhp, Brevard (Fla.) CC.
3. *Todd Gedaminski, lhp, Lincoln Land (Ill.) CC.

**June—Regular Phase (23)**

1. (Choice to Padres as compensation for Type A free agent Ed Whitson)
1. Rick Balabon, rhp, Conestoga HS, Berwyn, Pa. (Supplemental choice—28th—as compensation for loss of Tim Belcher to Athletics in 1984 major league compensation draft).—(AAA)
2. Troy Evers, rhp, Iowa State University.—(AA)
**3. Ken Patterson, lhp, Baylor University.—(1988-94)**
4. Scott Gay, rhp, Western Carolina University.—(AA)
5. Bobby Green, of, Florida Southern College.—(AAA)
**6. Shane Turner, ss, Cal State Fullerton.—(1988-92)**
**7. Mike Christopher, rhp, East Carolina University.—(1991-96)**
8. *Brad Hildreth, ss, UMS Wright HS, Mobile, Ala.
9. Chris Lombardozzi, ss, University of Florida.
DRAFT DROP *Brother of Steve Lombardozzi, major leaguer (1985-90) • Uncle of Steve Lombardozzi Jr., major leaguer (2011-15)*
10. Jason Maas, of, Cal Poly San Luis Obispo.
DRAFT DROP *Brother of Jason Maas, major leaguer (1990-95)*
11. Scott Shaw, ss-3b, Eckerd (Fla.) College.
12. Neal Cargile, of, Gardner-Webb College.
13. Ed Stanko, 1b, College of William & Mary.
14. Greg Iavarone, c, University of Illinois.
15. Matt Mainini, of, University of South Florida.
16. Brent Blum, lhp, Eastern Washington University.
17. John Shane, rhp, University of Wisconsin.
18. Todd Ezold, c, University of Massachusetts.
19. John Pleicones, ss, Florida Southern College.
20. Rob Lambert, 2b, Cal Poly San Luis Obispo.
21. *Steve Taylor, of, Lincoln HS, Spring Valley, Calif.
22. *Mark Razook, ss, South Hills HS, West Covina, Calif.
23. Ted Higgins, 1b, University of Nevada-Reno.
**24. *Billy Bean, of, Loyola Marymount University.—(1987-95)**
25. David Banks, 1b, Troy State University.
26. Tim Reker, lhp, Florida International University.
27. Chris Carroll, rhp, University of Kentucky.
28. *Grant Feruto, of, Boulder (Colo.) HS.
29. *Jeff Ingram, c, Shawnee Mission HS, Overland Park, Kan.
30. *Preston Watson, rhp, Luling (Texas) HS.
31. Scott Cantrell, rhp, University of Toledo.
32. Ric Sisler, rhp, University of Tennessee.
33. Robert Kupfner, 3b, Bloomfield (Colo.) HS.

**June—Secondary Phase (15)**

1. *Mike Belanger, lhp, Cal State Fullerton.—DNP
2. Garrett O'Connor, rhp, University of Southwestern Louisiana.
3. *Scott Lerner, lhp, Diablo Valley (Calif.) JC.
4. *Jeff Marr, rhp, Brevard (Fla.) CC.
5. *Terry Griffin, rhp, Florida JC.

## OAKLAND ATHLETICS

**January—Regular Phase (12)**

1. *Allen Wisdom, lhp, San Jacinto (Texas) JC.—(High A)
2. *David Ray, c, DeKalb Central (Ga.) JC.
3. *Marty Newton, c, San Bernardino Valley (Calif.) JC.
4. *Robert Chadwick, lhp, Oxnard (Calif.) JC.
5. *Ralph Lusian, 2b, Mira Costa (Calif.) JC.
6. *Larry Oedewaldt, 3b, Grossmont (Calif.) JC.
7. *Phil Price, rhp, Los Angeles Harbor JC.
8. *Joe Kemp, of, Citrus (Calif.) JC.
9. *Rob DeYoung, rhp, Fullerton (Calif.) JC.
10. *Ron Dale, ss-of, Los Angeles Valley JC.

**January—Secondary Phase (12)**

1. Mark Gabriel, ss, Niagara Catholic HS, Niagara Falls, N.Y.—DNP
2. Rich Martig, 3b, Santa Clara University.

**June—Regular Phase (11)**

**1. Walt Weiss, ss, University of North Carolina.—(1987-2000)**
DRAFT DROP *Major league manager (2014-15)*
**2. Dave Otto, lhp-1b, University of Missouri.—(1987-94)**
**3. Wally Whitehurst, rhp, University of New Orleans.—(1989-96)**
4. Phil Cundari, rhp, Seton Hall University.—(AA)
5. Keith Wentz, 3b, York (Pa.) College.—(Short-season A)
6. Steve Iannini, of, Georgetown University.
7. Kirk McDonald, rhp, Otterbein (Ohio) College.
8. *Ray Williamson, of, Santa Clara University.
9. Pat Britt, c, UC Riverside.
10. Mike Duncan, 1b, University of Nebraska.
11. *David Richards, lhp, Grossmont HS, El Cajon, Calif.
12. Shannon Mendenhall, ss, Lake Worth (Fla.) HS.
13. Joe Xavier, ss, Fresno State University.
14. John Minch, c, Ohio State University.
15. *Mark Manering, 1b, Miami (Ohio) University.
**16. Bruce Walton, rhp, University of Hawaii.—(1991-94)**
17. *Gil Villanueva, lhp, Arizona State University.
18. Scott Hyde, c, University of Missouri-St. Louis.
19. Mark Tortorice, lhp, Grand Canyon College.
20. Kevin Williamson, rhp, Arizona State University.
21. Bryan Olden, 2b, University of Portland.
**22. Jeff Shaver, rhp, SUNY-Fredonia.—(1988)**
23. Gary Cullison, lhp, Portland State University.
**24. *Jim Pena, lhp, Cal State Dominguez Hills.—(1992)**
25. Bob Stocker, rhp, University of Wisconsin-Oshkosh.
**26. Larry Arndt, inf-of, Bowling Green State University.—(1989)**
27. Frank Groves, rhp, U.S. International University.
28. Martin Hall, rhp, Cochise County (Ariz.) CC.
29. Reese Lambert, lhp, Oklahoma State University.
**30. *Bob Malloy, rhp, University of Virginia.—(1987-90)**

**June—Secondary Phase (7)**

1. Blaine Deabenderfer, rhp, University of North Carolina.—(Low A)
2. *Ken Sebree, rhp, Brevard (Fla.) CC.
3. *Russ Elsberry, rhp, San Diego State University.
4. *James Hitt, rhp, Chipola (Fla.) JC.

**5. *Steve Wapnick, rhp, Moorpark (Calif.) JC.—(1990-91)**
6. *Mike Stanford, rhp, Citrus (Calif.) JC.

## PHILADELPHIA PHILLIES

### January—Regular Phase (15)

1. Scott Steen, 3b, Ventura (Calif.) JC.—(High A)
2. *Clyde Powell, of, Delgado (La.) JC.
3. *Bruce Carter, ss, Delgado (La.) JC.
4. *Darwin DeVaughan, rhp, Seminole (Okla.) JC.
5. *Chris Burgin, rhp, Tulsa, Okla.
6. Nathaniel Green, of-3b, Ranger (Texas) JC.
7. *Jason Bridges, 3b, McLennan (Texas) CC.
8. *Brian Shepherd, rhp, Angelina (Texas) JC.
9. *Joseph Bourque, ss, San Jacinto (Texas) JC.
10. *Jack Johnson, 3b-ss, Central Arizona JC.
11. *Mark Shiflett, rhp, McLennan (Texas) CC.
12. *Scotty George, of, Seminole (Okla.) JC.
13. *Kevin Ponder, rhp, McLennan (Texas) CC.
14. *Andrew Bourne, of, Citrus (Calif.) JC.
15. *Jimmy Carroll, rhp, Mesa (Ariz.) CC.
16. *Mike McLeod, rhp, Allen County (Kan.) CC.
**17. *John Barfield, lhp, Crowder (Mo.) JC.—(1989-91)**
**18. *Dann Howitt, rhp-of, Venice, Calif.—(1989-94)**
19. *Todd Ross, 3b-ss, Shasta (Calif.) JC.
20. Ryan Silva, c, North Idaho JC.
21. *Mike Domenick, 1b-of, Triton (Ill.) JC.

### January—Secondary Phase (7)

1. Eric Boudreaux, rhp, Austin (Texas) CC.—(AAA)
2. Steve DeAngelis, of, Dana Point, Calif.

### June—Regular Phase (16)

1. Trey McCall, c, Abingdon (Va.) HS.—(High A)
**2. Bruce Ruffin, lhp, University of Texas** (Choice from Pirates as compensation for Type A free agent Sixto Lezcano)**—(1986-97)**
2. *Mike Young, lhp, University of Arizona.—(AA)
DRAFT DROP *Returned to Arizona; re-drafted by Padres, 1986 (4th round)*
3. Vince Holyfield, of, Southern Arkansas University.—(AA)
**4. Wally Ritchie, lhp, Glendale (Calif.) JC.—(1987-92)**
5. *Darin Campbell, ss, DeMatha HS, Lanham, Md.—(Rookie)
DRAFT DROP *Attended North Carolina; re-drafted by Indians, 1988 (22nd round)*
6. Rick Lundblade, 1b, Stanford University.
7. Jeff Kaye, c, University of Oklahoma.
8. *Jimmy Long, rhp, Oklahoma State University.
9. Todd Howey, of, Texas Tech.
**10. Jason Grimsley, rhp, Tarkington HS, Cleveland, Texas.—(1989-2006)**
11. John McKinney, rhp, Marshall University.
12. Ben Blackman, 3b-ss, San Joaquin Delta (Calif.) JC.
**13. *Eric Fox, of, Fresno State University.—(1992-95)**
14. Clifton Walker, rhp, Northwestern State University.
15. Rod Brunelle, of, Grand Valley State (Mich.) College.
**16. Rick Parker, ss, University of Texas.—(1990-96)**
17. Steve Sharts, lhp, Cal State Northridge.
18. Tim Collins, rhp, Metropolitan State (Colo.) College.
19. Mario Perez, rhp, St. Mary's (Texas) University.
20. Scott McClanahan, rhp, Lubbock Christian (Texas) College.
21. Derrick Richardson, ss, University of Arkansas.
22. Robert Nazabal, rhp, Merced (Calif.) JC.
23. Dion Beck, lhp, Cal State Fullerton.
24. *Robert Hatcher, lhp, Twin Lake HS, West Palm Beach, Fla.
25. *Alex Alvarez, c, Garden Grove (Calif.) HS.
26. Bruce Luttrull, rhp, Arlington HS, Corona, Calif.
27. *Robbie Key, lhp, Broadmoor HS, Baton Rouge, La.
28. Kenley Graves, of-2b, North Idaho JC.
29. *Paul Skorupa, rhp, Eastern Illinois University.
30. Greg Suhajda, of-c, Grand Valley State (Mich.) College.
31. David Pruett, rhp, Anderson (Ind.) College.
32. *Mark Borcherding, p, Rock Island (Ill.) HS.
33. David Denny, 3b-of, University of Texas.

### June—Secondary Phase (8)

1. Allen Wisdom, lhp, San Jacinto (Texas) JC.—(High A)
2. Steve Bowden, rhp, San Jacinto (Texas) JC.
**3. *Kevin D. Brown, lhp, Sacramento (Calif.) CC.—(1990-92)**
4. Steven Harris, rhp, Florida JC.
**5. *Blas Minor, rhp, Merced (Calif.) JC.—(1992-97)**
6. Ernie Rodriguez, 2b, Sacramento (Calif.) CC.

## PITTSBURGH PIRATES

### January—Regular Phase (5)

1. *Pat Gilbert, of, Columbia State (Tenn.) CC.—(AA)
2. Steve Taylor, of, Henry Clay HS, Lexington, Ky.
3. *David R. Miller, rhp, Camden County (N.J.) JC.
4. Mike Stevanus, ss, Valencia (Fla.) CC.
5. *Troy Jackson, of, JC of San Mateo (Calif.).
6. *Mitchell Ferrick, rhp, Santa Rosa (Calif.) JC.
7. *Barry Griffin, lhp, North Idaho JC.
8. Craig Heakins, c, Triton (Ill.) JC.
**9. *Derek Lee, 3b, Manatee (Fla.) JC.—(1993)**
10. *James Warner, lhp, Allegany (Md.) CC.
11. Keith Swartzlander, rhp, Allegheny (Pa.) CC.
12. *Tom Hoffman, rhp, Pensacola (Fla.) JC.
13. *John Vuz, c, Keystone (Pa.) JC.
14. *Brian Warfel, of, Labette (Kan.) CC.

### January—Secondary Phase (19)

**1. *Greg Vaughn, of, Sacramento (Calif.) CC.—(1989-2003)**
2. *Ken Rahming, of, Miami-Dade CC North.
3. Chris Ritter, rhp, CC of Baltimore.

### June—Regular Phase (6)

**1. Barry Bonds, of, Arizona State University.—(1986-2007)**
DRAFT DROP *Son of Bobby Bonds, major leaguer (1968-81)*
2. (Choice to Phillies as compensation for Type A free agent Sixto Lezcano)
2. Damon Hansel, c, Granite Hills HS, El Cajon, Calif. (Choice from Orioles as compensation for Type A free agent Lee Lacy).—(Low A)
3. *Joe Klancnik, rhp, Niles (Ill.) West HS.—(High A)
DRAFT DROP *Attended Oral Roberts; re-drafted by Cubs, 1987 (9th round)*
4. Robin Vaughn, ss, Crenshaw HS, Los Angeles.—(Rookie)
5. Ondra Ford, of, Ontario (Calif.) HS.—(High A)
**6. Brett Gideon, rhp, University of Mary Hardin-Baylor (Texas).—(1987-90)**
**7. Tommy Gregg, of, Wake Forest University.—(1987-97)**
8. Larry Melton, rhp, University of Portland.
9. Terry Wakefield, of, Guthrie (Okla.) HS.
10. Jeff Cook, of, Phillips (Okla.) University.
11. Desmond Scieneaux, 1b, Montclair (Calif.) HS.
**12. Billy Sampen, rhp, MacMurray (Ill.) College.—(1990-94)**
13. *Brad Robinson, of-1b, Seminole (Okla.) JC.
14. Kyle Todd, 3b, Baylor University.
15. *Luis Ramos, ss, Georgia Southern College.
16. Ronnell Daniels, of, Utica (Miss.) JC.
17. *Brian Zanardelli, rhp, Robert Morris ((Ill.) College.
18. Juan McWilliams, 3b, Grambling State University.
19. Richard Kiluk, of, University of Lowell (Mass.).
20. John Shouse, c, Cumberland (Ky.) College.
21. Ray Gambino, ss, Point Park (Pa.) College.
22. Mark Koller, rhp, Peabody HS, Pittsburgh.
23. Ralph Denkenberger, of, Loch Raven HS, Baltimore.
24. Thomas Pierce, ss, Georgia College.
25. Robert Benkert, c, William Paterson (N.J.) College.
26. Mark Oberholtzer, rhp, Ohio Wesleyan University.
27. Tony Mealy, of, Fayetteville (W.Va.) HS.
28. Kyle Channing, lhp, Dallas Baptist University.
29. Lawrence Brady, of, Coastal Carolina College.
30. Brian Schaum, ss, California (Pa.) University.
31. *Buster Lopes, rhp, University of Notre Dame.
32. *Greg Shirley, c, Azusa Pacific (Calif.) University.
33. Scott Berry, of, Cumberland (Ky.) College.
34. Page Odle, of, Oral Roberts University.
35. Doug Smallwood, 3b, Thomas Johnson HS, Frederick, Md.
**36. *Tom Shields, ss, University of Notre Dame.—(1992-93)**

### June—Secondary Phase (4)

**1. *Tommy Hinzo, ss, University of Arizona.—(1987-89)**
DRAFT DROP *First overall draft pick, June 1984/secondary phase, Mets*
2. *Jason Bridges, ss-3b, McLennan (Texas) CC.
3. Kirk Barry, of, Mesa (Ariz.) CC.

## ST. LOUIS CARDINALS

### January—Regular Phase (17)

1. *Chris Lee, rhp, Edison (Fla.) CC.—(Low A)
**2. Alex Cole, of, Manatee (Fla.) JC.—(1990-96)**
**3. *Kip Gross, rhp, Murray State (Okla.) JC.—(1990-2000)**
4. *Jeff Burkhart, of, Vincennes University (Ind.) JC.
5. *Kirk Barry, of, Mesa (Ariz.) CC.

### January—Secondary Phase (1)

**1. *Todd Stottlemyre, rhp, Yakima Valley (Wash.) JC.—(1988-2002)**
DRAFT DROP *Son of Mel Stottlemyre Sr., major leaguer (1964-74) • Brother of Mel Stottlemyre Jr., first-round draft pick, January 1985/secondary phase, Astros; major leaguer (1990)*
2. Steve Boyd, c, Columbus, Ohio.

### June—Regular Phase (18)

**1. Joe Magrane, lhp, University of Arizona.—(1987-96)**
2. Jim Fregosi, ss-3b, University of New Mexico (Choice from Braves as compensation for Type A free agent Bruce Sutter).—(AA)
DRAFT DROP *Son of Jim Fregosi Sr., major leaguer (1961-78); major league manager (1978-2000)*
**2. Tim Jones, ss, The Citadel.—(1988-93)**
3. Mike Henry, rhp, Chamberlain HS, Lutz, Fla.—(Low A)
4. Nate Singletary, of, King HS, Tampa.—(High A)
**5. Steve Peters, lhp, University of Oklahoma.—(1987-88)**
**6. Ray Stephens, c, Troy State University.—(1990-92)**
7. *Doug Little, rhp, Florida State University.
8. Mark Jackson, of-inf, University of Arkansas.
**9. *Bryan Hickerson, lhp, University of Minnesota.—(1991-95)**
10. Gator Thiesen, 2b, Mississippi State University.
11. Carey Nemeth, 3b, James Madison University.
12. *Mike Tresemer, rhp, UC Santa Barbara.
13. Joe Farmer, rhp, University of Kentucky.
14. David DeCordova, lhp, UC San Diego.
15. Mike Robertson, of, Southern Illinois University-Edwardsville.
16. Kerry Griffith, rhp, University of Louisville.
17. Jim Puzey, c, University of Nevada-Reno.
18. Anthony Buglione, c, University of New Haven.
19. Shawn McGinnis, of, Chaparral HS, Las Vegas, Nev.
20. Rob Knowles, of, San Diego State University.
21. *Daven Bond, rhp, Mesa (Colo.) College.
**22. Howard Hilton, rhp, University of Arkansas.—(1990)**
23. *Darren Linden, 1b, Southwestern Oklahoma State University.
24. Alex Ojea, 2b, Florida International University.
25. *Brad Rhodes, lhp, North Davidson HS, Clemmons, N.C.
26. *John McClain, of, Clifton (N.J.) HS.
27. David Turney, ss, Southern California College.
28. *Jeff Bonacquista, 1b-of, South HS, Pueblo, Colo.
29. Ken Warmbier, of, University of Illinois.
30. *Kevin Sheary, rhp, University of Miami.
31. Mick Freed, rhp, Eastern Illinois University.
**32. *Larry Gonzales, c, Edgewood HS, West Covina, Calif.—(1993)**
33. *Ben Webb, rhp, Tate HS, Gonzalez, Fla.
34. Mike McNeely, rhp, Illinois Wesleyan University.

### June—Secondary Phase (6)

1. *Rick Morris, 2b, Arizona State University.—(AAA)
**2. *Blaine Beatty, lhp, Baylor University.—(1989-91)**

## SAN DIEGO PADRES

### January—Regular Phase (21)

1. *Rob Hartwig, of, Los Angeles Harbor JC.—DNP
**2. *Steve Wapnick, rhp, Moorpark (Calif.) JC.—(1990-91)**
3. *Robert Gomez, rhp, JC of the Sequoias (Calif.).
4. *Ken Garcia, 2b, JC of the Sequoias (Calif.).
**5. Jim Lewis, rhp, Citrus (Calif.) JC.—(1991)**
6. *Michael Herrera, rhp, Modesto (Calif.) JC.
**7. *Jim Bruske, of, Antelope Valley (Calif.) JC.—(1995-2000)**
8. *David Smith, of, Delgado (La.) JC.
9. Rodney Clark, 1b, Fullerton (Calif.) JC.

### January—Secondary Phase (17)

1. *Mike Stanford, rhp, Citrus (Calif.) JC.—DNP
2. *Tyrone Sims, c, Western Oklahoma State JC.

### June—Regular Phase (22)

1. (Choice to Cubs as compensation for Type A free agent Tim Stoddard)
**1. Joey Cora, ss, Vanderbilt University** (Choice from Yankees as compensation for Type A free agent Ed Whitson)**—(1987-98)**
2. *Mark Cole, ss, Kennedy HS, Sacramento, Calif.—(AA)
DRAFT DROP *Attended Oklahoma; re-drafted by Tigers, 1989 (15th round)*
**3. Jim Tatum, 3b, Santana HS, Santee, Calif.—(1992-98)**
4. *Greg Burlingame, lhp, University of Hawaii.—(High A)
DRAFT DROP *Returned to Hawaii; re-drafted by Cubs, 1986 (31st round)*
5. Chris Knabenshue, of, University of Northern Colorado.—(AAA)
**6. Eric Nolte, lhp, UCLA.—(1987-91)**
**7. Matt Maysey, rhp, Alief Hastings HS, Houston.—(1992-93)**
8. *Troy Cunningham, rhp, East Valley HS, Spokane, Wash.
**9. *Mark Davis, of, Stanford University.—(1991)**
DRAFT DROP *Brother of Mike Davis, major leaguer (1980-89)*
**10. Greg W. Harris, rhp, Elon College.—(1988-95)**
11. Jay Nieporte, c, Stetson University.
**12. Jerald Clark, 3b, Lamar University.—(1988-95)**
DRAFT DROP *Brother of Phil Clark, first-round draft pick, Tigers (1986), major leaguer (1982-96) • Brother of Isaiah Clark, first-round draft pick, Brewers (1985)*
13. Bill Blount, lhp, San Diego State University.
14. Bill Marx, rhp, Bradley University.
15. *Dana Schmerer, lhp, Eastern Washington University.
16. Carl Ferraro, lhp, Florida Southern College.
17. Eric Bauer, lhp, Eastern Washington University.
18. Tom Meagher, rhp, UC Santa Barbara.
19. *Willie Forbes, lhp, Gulf Coast (Fla.) CC.
20. *Bob Lutticken, c, Serra HS, San Mateo, Calif.
21. Joe Lynch, rhp, William Paterson (N.J.) College.
22. Maurice Morton, 1b, Elon College.
23. Greg Hall, c, University of New Mexico.
24. Adam Ging, ss, UC Irvine.
25. Bill Stevenson, c, Lewis-Clark State (Idaho) College.

### June—Secondary Phase (12)

1. *Tony Faryniarz, rhp, Sacramento (Calif.) CC.—(Short-season A)
**2. *Al Osuna, lhp, Cerritos (Calif.) JC.—(1990-96)**

## SAN FRANCISCO GIANTS

### January—Regular Phase (1)

1. Ricky Nelson, of, Orange Coast (Calif.) JC.—(AA)
2. Todd Miller, of, St. Petersburg (Fla.) JC.

3. *Randy Ryan, lhp, Harford (Md.) CC.
**4. *Kevin Ritz, rhp, Indian Hills (Iowa) CC.—(1989-98)**
5. Steve Santora, of, Ventura (Calif.) JC.
6. Timber Mead, rhp-3b, Mount Hood (Ore.) CC.
7. *John Cebuhar, lhp, Eastern Oklahoma State JC.
8. *Kelvin Dubose, c, Gordon (Ga.) JC.
9. Brian Petty, ss, Moorpark (Calif.) JC.
10. *Darryl Robinson, of, Los Angeles Valley JC.

**January—Secondary Phase (21)**

1. *Antoine Pickett, of, Contra Costa (Calif.) JC.—(High A)
2. *Sherman Collins, rhp, Seminole (Okla.) JC.

**June—Regular Phase (2)**

**1. Will Clark, 1b, Mississippi State University.—(1986-2000)**
DRAFT DROP *First player from 1985 draft to reach majors (April 8, 1986)*
2. Brian Ohnoutka, rhp, Texas Christian University.—(AAA)
3. Doug Robertson, rhp, Cal State Fullerton.—(AAA)
4. Bob Jackson, 3b, Galesburg (Ill.) HS.—(Short-season A)
5. John Verducci, ss, Stanford University.—(AAA)
**6. Jeff Brantley, rhp, Mississippi State University.—(1988-2001)**
7. Mike Whitt, 1b-c, Loyola Marymount University.
**8. Trevor Wilson, of-lhp, Oregon City, Ore.—(1988-98)**
9. Jeff Carter, of, University of Nebraska.
**10. Joe Kmak, c, UC Santa Barbara.—(1993-95)**
11. Lloyd Jackson, of, Douglass HS, Baltimore.
12. Darren Pearson, rhp, Cal Poly San Luis Obispo.
13. Ty Dabney, of, UC Riverside.
14. George Bonilla, lhp, UC Santa Barbara.
**15. Randy McCament, rhp, Grand Canyon College.—(1989-90)**
16. Darrell "Doc" Rodgers, rhp, University of Oklahoma.
17. Steven Vankempen, rhp, North Park (Ill.) College.
**18. Dennis Cook, of-lhp, University of Texas.—(1988-2002)**
19. Joe Jordan, c, University of Oklahoma.
DRAFT DROP *Scouting director, Orioles (2004-11)*
20. Lee Townsend, lhp, Long Beach State University.
21. Brad Bambee, rhp, Beaverton (Ore.) HS.
22. *Rob Hernandez, 1b-lhp, Los Angeles Valley JC.
23. Tommy Smith, 1b, Clemson University.
24. Mike Dandos, ss, University of Utah.
25. Billy Smith, of, Oklahoma State University.
26. *Brian Harrison, lhp-of, Ventura (Calif.) JC.
27. David Blakley, rhp, Santa Clara University.
28. *Andre London, of, Lithia Springs HS, Douglasville, Ga.
29. Paul Van Stone, 2b-ss, University of San Diego.
30. Tom Ealy, of, Chaparral HS, Las Vegas, Nev.

**June—Secondary Phase (2)**

1. *Pat Gilbert, of, Columbia State (Tenn.) CC.—(AA)
2. *Mike Reitzel, lhp, Seminole (Okla.) JC.
3. *Lance Davis, rhp, Connors State (Okla.) JC.

## SEATTLE MARINERS

**January—Regular Phase (8)**

1. *Dan Larsen, rhp, Citrus (Calif.) JC.—(High A)
2. *Pat Garman, 3b, JC of the Sequoias (Calif.).
3. Tony Woods, ss, Mount San Jacinto (Calif.) JC.
4. *Shane Flores, c, Golden West (Calif.) JC.
5. Chris Miller, ss, University of Oregon.
DRAFT DROP *First-round draft pick, Atlanta Falcons/National Football League (1987); quarterback, NFL (1987-99).*
6. Brad Rohde, rhp, Brevard (Fla.) CC.
7. *John Turner, of-inf, Walters State (Tenn.) CC.
8. *Tim McKercher, c, Orange Coast (Calif.) JC.

**January—Secondary Phase (18)**

1. *Steve Bowden, rhp, San Jacinto (Texas) JC.—(AA)
2. *Greg Ehmig, lhp, Walters State (Tenn.) CC.

**June—Regular Phase (7)**

**1. Mike Campbell, rhp, University of Hawaii.—(1987-96)**
**1. Bill McGuire, c, University of Nebraska** (Supplemental choice—27th—as compensation for loss of Type B free agent Steve Henderson)**—(1988-89)**
**2. Mike Schooler, rhp, Cal State Fullerton.—(1988-93)**
**3. Clint Zavaras, rhp, Mullen HS, Denver.—(1989)**
4. Nezi Balelo, ss, Pepperdine University.—(AA)
5. *Brad Mengel, ss, Eagle Rock (Calif.) HS.—(AA)
DRAFT DROP *Attended Cal State Los Angeles; re-drafted by Blue Jays, 1989 (43rd round)*
6. *Brad Eagar, c, Orem (Utah) HS.
7. Tim McLain, rhp, Auburn University.
8. Barrymore Greaves, of, Cassidy HS, Raynham, Mass.
9. Bret Davis, lhp, University of New Mexico.
10. Rich Slominski, 1b, Cal State Fullerton.
11. John Clem, of, Western Kentucky University.
12. Jeff Roberts, rhp, Arizona State University.
13. *Kevin Pearson, ss, University of Oklahoma.
14. Dave Stewart, 1b, UC Santa Barbara.
**15. Clay Parker, rhp, Louisiana State University.—(1987-92)**
16. Dave McCorkle, rhp, Florida Southern College.
17. George Lopez, 3b, Arizona State University.
18. Mike Simon, of, University of Texas.
19. Steve Oizumi, rhp, Western New Mexico University.
20. Dane Quince, rhp-1b, North Brunswick HS, Leland, N.C.
21. Doug Givler, rhp, University of Georgia.
22. Tom Eccleston, of, Cal State Chico.
23. *Scott Johnson, of, University of North Carolina.
24. *Mike Scanlin, of, Texas A&M University.
25. Bob Bernardo, of, West Virginia University.
26. Mike Darby, rhp, University of Iowa.
27. *Dewayne Jones, ss, Murphy HS, Mobile, Ala.
28. Brian Thomas, ss, Lewis-Clark State (Idaho) College.
29. Greg Fulton, ss, Atlantic Christian (N.C.) College.
30. *Michael Florak, 1b, Steubenville Central Catholic HS, Steubenville, Ohio.

**June—Secondary Phase (15)**

1. *Pat Garman, 3b, JC of the Sequoias (Calif.).—(AAA)
2. Don Cohoon, 3b, Indian River (Fla.) CC.
**3. *Jim Bruske, rhp-of, Antelope Valley (Calif.) JC.—(1995-2000)**

## TEXAS RANGERS

**January—Regular Phase (4)**

1. David Rolland, 3b-of, Orange Coast (Calif.) JC.—(High A)
2. *Lance Davis, rhp, Connors State (Okla.) JC.
3. Travis Sheffield, of, Los Angeles CC.
4. *Mike Papajohn, of, Gulf Coast (Fla.) CC.
5. *Scott Broadfoot, rhp, Allen County (Kan.) CC.
6. Anthony Clark, of, Los Angeles Harbor JC.
7. *Jay Fox, rhp, Spokane Falls (Wash.) CC.
8. *Michael Gianfrancesco, 3b, Nassau (N.Y.) CC.
9. *John Fleming, p, East Mississippi JC.
10. *Mel Sisney, rhp, Los Angeles CC.
**11. *Rafael Bournigal, ss, Canada (Calif.) JC.—(1992-99)**

**January—Secondary Phase (10)**

1. Ed Soto, rhp, Miami-Dade CC North.—(High A)
2. *Gary Alexander, rhp, Laney (Calif.) JC.

**June—Regular Phase (3)**

**1. Bobby Witt, rhp, University of Oklahoma.—(1986-2001)**
2. (Choice to Dodgers as compensation for Type A free agent Burt Hooton)
3. Jim Vlcek, rhp, Amos Alonzo Stagg HS, Palos Hills, Ill.—(High A)
**4. Steve Wilson, lhp, University of Portland.—(1988-93)**
**5. Chad Kreuter, c, Pepperdine University.—(1988-2003)**
DRAFT DROP *Baseball coach, Southern California (2007-10)*
6. Mark Seay, of, San Bernardino (Calif.) HS.
DRAFT DROP *Wide receiver, National Football League (1993-97)*
7. Dan Olsson, rhp, Montclair State (N.J.) College.
8. Mitch Thomas, rhp, Northeast Louisiana University.
9. Michael Jackson, of, Appomattox (Va.) HS.
10. Frank Bryan, rhp, Clovis (Calif.) HS.
**11. Kevin Reimer, 1b, Cal State Fullerton.—(1988-93)**
12. Terrill Adams, rhp, San Jose State University.
13. Mike Dotzler, c, Sunnyvale, Calif.
14. *Mike Ollom, rhp, Lewis-Clark State (Idaho) College.
DRAFT DROP *Son of Jim Ollom, major leaguer (1966-67)*
15. Warren Busick, rhp, Citrus (Calif.) JC.
**16. Mike Stanley, 1b, University of Florida.—(1986-2000)**
17. Rob Mortimer, lhp, James Madison University.
18. Tommy West, rhp, Old Dominion University.
19. Joseph Nannariello, rhp, Pace (N.Y.) University.
20. Steve Lankard, rhp, Long Beach State University.
21. Dan Van Cleve, of, Mississippi State University.
22. Jay Reynolds, rhp, University of Oklahoma.
23. Ron Russell, 1b, Brandeis (Mass.) University.
24. *Randy Snyder, c, Davis HS, Yakima, Wash.
25. William Booker, rhp, Texas Christian University.
**26. Gary Mielke, rhp, Mankato State (Minn.) University.—(1987-90)**
27. *Mark Potoshnik, rhp, Kennewick (Wash.) HS.
28. James Browne, 1b, Drexel University.
29. *Damon Allen, rhp, Cal State Fullerton.
DRAFT DROP *Quarterback, Canadian Football League (1984-2007) • Brother, Marcus Allen, running back, National Football League (1982-97)*
**30. *John Hudek, rhp, Plant HS, Tampa.—(1994-99)**
31. *Willie Tatum, 3b, Burbank HS, Sacramento, Calif.

**June—Secondary Phase (25)**

1. Darrin Garner, ss, Orange Coast (Calif.) JC.—(AAA)
2. Dan Larsen, rhp, Citrus (Calif.) JC.
3. *Tim McCoy, lhp, Oral Roberts University.
4. *Anthony Newman, of, University of Oregon.
DRAFT DROP *Defensive back, National Football League (1988-99)*
5. Paul James, rhp, University of Missouri.

## TORONTO BLUE JAYS

**January—Regular Phase (25)**

**1. *Howard Farmer, rhp, Utica (Miss.) JC.—(1990)**
DRAFT DROP *Brother of Mike Farmer, major leaguer (1996)*
2. *Brian Veilleux, lhp, Allen County (Kan.) CC.
3. *John Kohli, lhp, Mira Costa (Calif.) JC.
4. Jim Tracy, rhp, North Shore (Mass.) CC.
5. *Craig Bolton, lhp, Santa Fe (Fla.) CC.
6. *Joe Hollinshed, 1b, Lurleen B. Wallace State (Ala.) JC.
7. *Michael House, lhp, Bellevue (Wash.) CC.
8. Dennis Jones, lhp, Gadsden State (Ala.) JC.
9. *Marvin McBurrows, of, Chipola (Fla.) JC.
10. *Don Stanford, rhp, Onondaga (N.Y.) CC.
11. *Rey Vizcaino, rhp, Indian River (Fla.) CC.
12. *Travis Law, of, San Jose (Calif.) CC.
13. *Bernard Black, inf-c, Florida JC.
14. *James Bodace, of, Los Angeles Pierce JC.
15. *Dan Dondlinger, c, Kings Rivers (Calif.) JC.

**January—Secondary Phase (14)**

1. *Oneri Fleita, lhp, Miami-Dade CC North.—(High A)
2. *Wendell Harris, of, Pasadena HS, Altadena, Calif.
3. Keith Felden, rhp, St. Petersburg (Fla.) JC.
4. *Jim Willis, of, Triton (Ill.) JC.

**June—Regular Phase (25)**

1. Greg David, of, Barron Collier HS, Naples, Fla.—(AA)
**2. Kevin Batiste, of, Ball HS, Galveston, Texas.—(1989)**
3. Joe Humphries, rhp, Western Michigan University.—(AA)
4. Chris Jones, rhp, Ohio State University.—(AAA)
5. Jeff Mays, rhp, University of Nebraska.—(AA)
**6. Jeff Musselman, lhp, Harvard University.—(1986-90)**
**7. Shawn Jeter, of, Woodlawn HS, Shreveport, La.—(1992)**
8. Steve Mumaw, lhp, University of Tampa.
9. *Brian Johnson, c, Westfield HS, Houston.
10. *Erik Boddie, of, West HS, Waukegan, Ill.
11. Paul Rodgers, of, U.S. Grant HS, Oklahoma City, Okla.
12. Sterling Housley, 2b, Southeastern Louisiana University.
13. Mike Jones, of, Valdosta State (Ga.) College.
14. Walter Watford, ss, Troy State University.
**15. *Rich DeLucia, rhp, University of Tennessee.—(1990-99)**
16. Glen Kwiatkowski, rhp, Eastern Michigan University.
17. *Dewayne Martin, rhp, Sandpoint HS, Sagle, Idaho.
18. Roger Marquardt, c, Western Michigan University.
19. *Kight Higgins, rhp, Texas Christian University.
20. Joseph Schlieper, lhp, West Virginia University.
21. *Scott Runge, rhp, Sacramento (Calif.) CC.
22. *Tim McKinley, c, Southeastern Illinois JC.
23. *Blake Butterfield, rhp, Glendora (Calif.) HS.
24. Kerry St. Clair, of, University of Georgia.
25. *Alex Smith, ss, Indiana University.
26. John Rohde, lhp, Carson-Newman (Tenn.) College.
27. Randy Whisler, 2b, Oklahoma State University.
28. Richard Anderson, rhp, Florida Memorial College.
29. Dwayne Smith, of, South Young HS, Knoxville, Tenn.
30. *Steven Adams, rhp, Hartnell (Calif.) CC.
31. Pat Sullivan, c, University of Tennessee.
32. *Robert Cuff, rhp, St. Petersburg (Fla.) JC.
33. *Reggie Ramert, of, Dudley HS, Greensboro, N.C.
34. Doug Gonring, c, Florida Atlantic University.
35. Derek Ware, of, Christian Brothers HS, Sacramento, Calif.
**36. *Jim Abbott, lhp, Flint Central HS, Flint, Mich.—(1989-99)**
DRAFT DROP *First-round draft pick (8th overall), Angels (1988) • 1988 recipient of James E. Sullivan Award, symbolic of nation's outstanding amateur athlete*
37. Greg Dennis, ss, Baylor University.

**June—Secondary Phase (3)**

**1. Todd Stottlemyre, rhp, Yakima Valley (Wash.) JC.—(1988-2002)**
DRAFT DROP *First overall draft pick, January 1985/secondary phase, Cardinals • Son of Mel Stottlemyre Sr., major leaguer (1964-74) • Brother of Mel Stottlemyre Jr., first-round draft pick/January 1985 secondary phase, Astros; major leaguer (1990)*
2. *Craig Bolton, lhp, Santa Fe (Fla.) CC.
3. *Chris Lee, rhp, Edison (Fla.) CC.
4. *Antoine Pickett, 3b, Contra Costa (Calif.) JC.
5. *Joe Hollinshed, 1b, Lurleen B. Wallace State (Ala.) JC.
6. *Bruce Powers, of, Skyline (Calif.) JC.
7. *Oneri Fleita, lhp, Miami-Dade CC North.

# 1986

## AT A GLANCE

### This Date In History
**WINTER DRAFT:** Jan. 14-15
**SUMMER DRAFT:** June 2-4

### Best Draft
**CLEVELAND INDIANS.** The Indians drafted 16 future big leaguers—one short of the record, set by the Mets in 1982—and signed 11. They landed the likes of **GREG SWINDELL** (1) and **RUDY SEANEZ** (4), who spent 17 years in the majors; **TOM LAMPKIN** (11), a 13-year big leaguer; and **JEFF SHAW** (January/regular, 1), a 12-year player.

### Worst Draft
**NEW YORK METS.** The Mets identified 13 future major leaguers, but nine went unsigned—including three first-round picks in 1989, along with **JOHN OLERUD** and **SCOTT ERICKSON**, who had lengthy major league careers. None of the players they signed had meaningful careers with the Mets.

### First-Round Bust
**TERRY CARR, OF, ANGELS.** The third of five Angels picks in the first round, Carr had shoulder surgery in his first season. In his five-year pro career he never advanced past Class A, and hit .217 overall.

### Second Best
**KEVIN TAPANI, RHP, ATHLETICS.** Tapani, drafted as a senior out of Central Michigan, never won a game for the A's, but managed to win 143 over a 13-year career.

### Late-Round Find
**CHRIS HOILES, C, TIGERS (19TH ROUND).** The Tigers spent their first-round pick on a catcher, **PHIL CLARK**, who had defensive shortcomings and rarely caught in five seasons in the big leagues. They traded Hoiles, an Eastern Michigan product, to Baltimore in a deal for Fred Lynn before he ever caught a game for them. Hoiles played 10 seasons for the Orioles, hitting .262-151-449. Clark signed with Detroit for $83,000; Hoiles for just $2,000.

# Royals make history by grabbing Jackson

Bo Jackson's 1986 season at Auburn ended after 21 games, when he was declared ineligible by the Southeastern Conference. In 69 at-bats, he hit four home runs and struck out 29 times—hardly the kind of performance that would warrant a second look from major league clubs, under normal circumstances.

But Jackson was anything but normal, and his signing by the Kansas City Royals later that year represented the greatest coup in the 50-year history of the baseball draft.

In a bold move, the Royals snatched Jackson, the reigning Heisman Trophy winner and No. 1 overall pick of the Tampa Bay Buccaneers in that year's football draft, away from the NFL. With his exceptional power/speed package, Jackson became one of the greatest raw talents to play Major League Baseball in the draft era, and his impact on the game—even in a relatively brief, injury-riddled career—was substantial.

The defending World Series champion Royals selected Jackson in the fourth round, and after nearly a month of negotiating, Jackson shocked the sports world by signing a three-year, $1.066 million deal on June 21. The unprecedented contract, the richest ever signed by an amateur, included a $100,000 signing bonus, another $100,000 in salary for the balance of the 1986 season, plus $333,000 for 1987 and $383,000 for 1988. It also provided for an additional $150,000 incentive bonus once Jackson made it to the big leagues.

"I could have played football," Jackson said. "I could have signed a contract and become an instant millionaire. But this is the first day of summer, summer's the time for baseball and I'm ready to go. This is what Bo wants to do the rest of his life.

"People have thought Bo is using this as leverage to get more money from Tampa Bay. I'm always going to do the opposite of what the public thinks. I did this so people would swallow their Adam's apple. I didn't choose baseball over football because of the longevity or that the Royals are World Series champions. I've had my share of football."

Kansas City was the obvious beneficiary of Jackson's decision, but baseball insiders viewed his signing as an enormous victory for the game overall.

"Baseball has been complaining internally about how many good athletes we lose to other sports, especially football," Royals general manager John Schuerholz said. "This is one of the rare times baseball has been able to prevail. We feel very good about the fact that we were able to do something to turn it around."

The New York Mets' Joe McIlvaine, a proponent of signing the best athletes available, also saw it as a major breakthrough for baseball.

"I just think it's a good thing for baseball,

Most teams thought that Bo Jackson was destined to leave baseball behind for the NFL, but the Royals had inside information and signed him after waiting until the fourth round to draft him

particularly getting a high-class athlete," he said. "It's very important for baseball to corral the best talent it possibly can. What we're hoping is that something like this can make the youth of America realize that the best future and the best long-term gains are still in baseball.

"We hope that a young man can take a look at that instead of going for the short-term gains. We'll watch and see if it makes a difference."

San Diego Padres manager Jack McKeon may have summed Jackson's historic signing best: "What he is, is the best damn free-agent signing in the history of the game."

Jackson's landmark signing was the overriding development of the 1986 draft, considered a fairly mundane process otherwise. But from a historical perspective, a number of key developments affected the future of the draft.

Major League Baseball's player development subcommittee enacted several changes. Concerned with agents using draft lists to uncover prospective clients and college coaches using them as a recruiting vehicle, it elected to impose a news blackout on the draft. Outside of the names of players drafted in the first round of the regular phase, no other information was released for a week thereafter—and then only in alphabetical order, by clubs.

"Baseball believes the information is theirs, and they can do with it what they want," said a spokes-

## 1986: THE FIRST ROUNDERS

| CLUB: PLAYER, POS., SCHOOL | HOMETOWN | B-T | HT. | WT. | AGE | BONUS | FIRST YEAR | LAST YEAR | PEAK LEVEL (YEARS) |
|---|---|---|---|---|---|---|---|---|---|
| **JUNE—REGULAR PHASE** | | | | | | | | | |
| **1. Pirates: Jeff King, 3b, Arkansas** | **Colorado Springs, Colo.** | **R-R** | **6-0** | **165** | **21** | **$180,000** | **1986** | **1999** | **Majors (11)** |
| Set Arkansas season, career records for homers, RBIs, but started slowly in pro ball; finally rewarded Pirates patience in eighth MLB season (.271-30-111). | | | | | | | | | |
| **2. Indians: Greg Swindell, lhp, Texas** | **Houston** | **R-L** | **6-2** | **225** | **21** | **$165,000** | **1986** | **2003** | **Majors (17)** |
| Developed into three-year stalwart at Texas, went 43-8, spun NCAA record 14 shutouts; jumped to majors after three starts in minors, won 123 games in 17 years. | | | | | | | | | |
| **3. Giants: Matt Williams, ss, Nevada-Las Vegas** | **Carson City, Nev.** | **R-R** | **6-2** | **180** | **20** | **$157,500** | **1986** | **2003** | **Majors (17)** |
| Giants stuck neck out on UNLV SS who batted .351-25-89 as junior, correctly projecting he would evolve into all-star 3B with power (378 homers), Gold-Glove skills. | | | | | | | | | |
| **4. Rangers: Kevin Brown, rhp, Georgia Tech** | **McIntyre, Ga.** | **R-R** | **6-4** | **193** | **21** | **$174,500** | **1986** | **2005** | **Majors (19)** |
| Walked on at Georgia Tech, set school records for career wins (28), strikeouts (249); won 211 games over 19 years in majors, became game's first $100 million player. | | | | | | | | | |
| **5. Braves: Kent Mercker, lhp, Dublin HS** | **Dublin, Ohio** | **L-L** | **6-2** | **185** | **18** | **$100,000** | **1986** | **2008** | **Majors (18)** |
| Was 13-1, 0.33 (85 IP/190 SO) as prep senior, pitched 18 years in majors though he never had peaks of fellow Braves lefties Glavine/Avery; went 74-67, 4.16. | | | | | | | | | |
| **6. Brewers: Gary Sheffield, ss, Hillsborough HS** | **Tampa** | **R-R** | **6-0** | **190** | **17** | **$142,500** | **1986** | **2009** | **Majors (22)** |
| Entered game with similar fanfare as uncle Dwight Gooden; gifted young hitter, went on to hit 509 homers over 22 major league seasons, nine all-star games. | | | | | | | | | |
| **7. Phillies: Brad Brink, rhp, Southern California** | **Modesto, Calif.** | **R-R** | **6-1** | **185** | **21** | **$145,000** | **1986** | **1995** | **Majors (3)** |
| Impressed scouts with dominant stuff early in junior year at USC, but overworked, became plagued by arm issues in pro ball; never won a major league game. | | | | | | | | | |
| **8. Mariners: Patrick Lennon, ss, Whiteville HS** | **Whiteville, N.C.** | **R-R** | **6-2** | **200** | **18** | **$120,000** | **1986** | **2003** | **Majors (6)** |
| Back-to-back first-rounders from tiny eastern N.C. high school (after Tommy Greene); showed power (187 HRs), speed (141 SBs) in minors, struggled to find position. | | | | | | | | | |
| **9. Cubs: Derrick May, of, Newark HS** | **Newark, Del.** | **L-R** | **6-4** | **205** | **17** | **$100,000** | **1986** | **2000** | **Majors (10)** |
| Son of 12-year big leaguer Dave May; had best season for Cubs in '93 (.295-10-77), played 10 years in majors, but struggled to hit for power, match his father. | | | | | | | | | |
| **10. Twins: Derek Parks, c, Montclair HS** | **Upland, Calif.** | **R-R** | **6-0** | **190** | **17** | **$130,000** | **1986** | **1994** | **Majors (3)** |
| New to catching as prep senior, impressed scouts with raw power, arm, receiving skills, but became a tease in career impacted by injuries, inconsistent bat. | | | | | | | | | |
| **11. Padres: Thomas Howard, of, Ball State** | **Germantown, Ohio** | **B-R** | **6-1** | **198** | **21** | **$98,500** | **1986** | **2001** | **Majors (11)** |
| Ex-Ball State QB made huge strides with bat (.358-18-50 for Team USA in1985, .448-26-94 as JR), never quite hit his stride in 11 years in majors (.264-44-264). | | | | | | | | | |
| **12. Athletics: Scott Hemond, c, South Florida** | **Dunedin, Fla.** | **R-R** | **5-11** | **200** | **20** | **$125,000** | **1986** | **1996** | **Majors (7)** |
| Evolved into top college catcher with plus arm/agility, hit .335-9-55 as JR; moved around diamond to take advantage of athleticism, but bat became a liability. | | | | | | | | | |
| **13. Astros: Ryan Bowen, rhp, Hanford HS** | **Hanford, Calif.** | **R-R** | **6-2** | **185** | **18** | **$165,000** | **1987** | **1997** | **Majors (5)** |
| Top prep arm at outset of '86, went 11-1, 1.01 (76 IP/149 SO) as senior, signed day before set to enroll at USC; never quite clicked as big leaguer (17-28, 5.28). | | | | | | | | | |
| **14. Red Sox: Greg McMurtry, of, Brockton HS** | **Brockton, Mass.** | **L-R** | **6-2** | **195** | **18** | **Unsigned** | **Never played pro baseball** | | |
| Pirates targeted Willie Wilson clone as possible No. 1 pick before he made it clear he would play football at Michigan; played five years in NFL as wide receiver. | | | | | | | | | |
| **15. Expos: Kevin Dean, of, Hogan HS** | **Vallejo, Calif.** | **R-R** | **6-1** | **175** | **18** | **$112,500** | **1986** | **1992** | **Class AAA (4)** |
| Expos were attracted to his speed, CF skills, athleticism, hoped his line-drive bat would develop; it didn't, soon traded to Braves, hit .250-29-248 in seven seasons. | | | | | | | | | |
| **16. Angels: Roberto Hernandez, rhp, So. Carolina-Aiken** | **New York City** | **R-R** | **6-4** | **225** | **21** | **$90,000** | **1986** | **2007** | **Majors (17)** |
| Backup catcher at UConn, transferred to NAIA school to focus on pitching; hardest thower in '86 class, overcame early injuries to pitch in 1,010 games in majors. | | | | | | | | | |
| **17. Reds: Scott Scudder, rhp, Prairiland HS** | **Blossom, Texas** | **R-R** | **6-2** | **170** | **18** | **$125,000** | **1986** | **1995** | **Majors (5)** |
| Had the raw material needed to excel, including mid-90s fastball, three other pitches; lacked command/stamina; spent five years in majors, went 21-34, 4.80. | | | | | | | | | |
| **18. Tigers: Phil Clark, c, Crockett HS** | **Crockett, Texas** | **R-R** | **6-0** | **175** | **18** | **$83,000** | **1986** | **1996** | **Majors (5)** |
| Younger brother of Jerald, big leaguer; Isaiah, fellow first-rounder; offense-first player, hit .290 in minors, .276 in majors; moved to outfield early in career. | | | | | | | | | |
| **19. Dodgers: Mike White, of, Loudon HS** | **Loudon, Tenn.** | **L-R** | **6-2** | **180** | **18** | **$75,000** | **1986** | **1992** | **Class AAA (1)** |
| Hit .544-15-66 with 28 SBs as prep senior, quit midway through '87 season for personal reasons; never surfaced above Triple-A in seven seasons, hit .277-12-217. | | | | | | | | | |
| **20. White Sox: Grady Hall, lhp, Northwestern** | **Findlay, Ohio** | **R-L** | **6-2** | **200** | **22** | **$77,500** | **1986** | **1992** | **Class AAA (5)** |
| Set school record for wins by going 11-1, 2.31 (70 IP/94 SO) as SR; had poise, plus slider, began pro career in Triple-A, never went higher in seven pro seasons. | | | | | | | | | |
| **21. Mets: Lee May Jr., of, Purcell Marian HS** | **Cincinnati** | **R-R** | **6-2** | **175** | **18** | **$130,500** | **1986** | **1993** | **Class AAA (2)** |
| Son of 18-year big league slugger; game built around speed, but never learned to hit, tap into tools; played eight years in minors, hit just .226 with 8 homers. | | | | | | | | | |
| **22. Angels: Lee Stevens, of, Lawrence HS** | **Lawrence, Kan.** | **L-L** | **6-4** | **200** | **18** | **$80,500** | **1986** | **2003** | **Majors (10)** |
| Intriguing raw power in lanky frame, fluid lefthanded swing compared to a young Will Clark's; went deep 144 times in 10 years in majors, 146 times in minors. | | | | | | | | | |
| **23. Cardinals: Luis Alicea, 2b, Florida State** | **Guaynabo, P.R.** | **B-R** | **5-9** | **165** | **20** | **$82,500** | **1986** | **2002** | **Majors (13)** |
| Steady Puerto Rican product, hit .392-8-73 with 28 SBs as FSU junior, went on to play 13 seasons in majors for five clubs, mostly at 2B, hit .260-47-422. | | | | | | | | | |
| **24. Royals: Tony Bridges-Clements, ss, Don Lugo HS** | **Chino, Calif.** | **R-R** | **6-0** | **180** | **17** | **$80,000** | **1986** | **1992** | **Class AAA (1)** |
| Spent entire career in Royals system; always held his own in field with sound defensive skills, bat always a little light, hit .230-9-142 overall. | | | | | | | | | |
| **25. Angels: Terry Carr, of, Bennett HS** | **Salisbury, Md.** | **R-R** | **6-1** | **172** | **18** | **$78,000** | **1986** | **1990** | **Class A (4)** |
| Quick, live-bodied talent with excellent speed; hit .439-8-30 with 23 SBs as prep SR, but never made progress in pros with injuries, line-drive approach. | | | | | | | | | |
| **26. Blue Jays: Earl Sanders, rhp, Jackson State** | **Moss Point, Miss.** | **R-R** | **6-3** | **210** | **21** | **$90,000** | **1986** | **1992** | **Class AA (5)** |
| Two-way player in college (.432-17-60 as hitter; 11-2, 2.32 on mound), played both ways as first-year pro before settled in as pitcher; stalled out in Double-A. | | | | | | | | | |
| **JANUARY—REGULAR PHASE** | | | | | | | | | |
| **1. Indians: Jeff Shaw, rhp, Cuyahoga (Ohio) CC** | **Washington, Ohio** | **R-R** | **6-2** | **180** | **19** | **$50,000** | **1986** | **2002** | **Majors (12)** |
| Transfer from Ohio's University of Rio Grande; played for five major league teams, initially as set-up man, later as closer; saved 48 games in 1998, 203 overall. | | | | | | | | | |
| **JANUARY—SECONDARY PHASE** | | | | | | | | | |
| **1. Twins: Toby Nivens, rhp, San Jacinto (Texas) JC** | **McAllen, Texas** | **R-R** | **6-1** | **185** | **19** | **$75,000** | **1986** | **1991** | **Class AA (5)** |
| Led San Jac to national juco title in spring with 14-4, 1.72 record, went 9-2, 2.62 for Twins Rookie club in summer; career (40-46 overall) never took off from there. | | | | | | | | | |
| **JUNE—SECONDARY PHASE** | | | | | | | | | |
| **1. Mets: Al Jimenez, 1b, Miami-Dade CC South** | **Miami** | **L-L** | **6-1** | **170** | **19** | **$30,000** | **1986** | **1991** | **Class AAA (1)** |
| Evolved from ninth-round pick in January to No. 1 overall in June; spent six years in Mets system, but bat/power never developed; hit just .256-33-263. | | | | | | | | | |

## AT A GLANCE

### Never Too Late

**DOUG LINTON, RHP, BLUE JAYS (43RD ROUND).** The Jays took a flier on Linton, a UC Irvine product, and signed him on Sept. 5 for $10,000. He looked like a bargain a year later when he went 14-2, 1.73 in Class A, but ultimately played just one season in Toronto, going 1-4, 6.95. Overall, he played seven years in the majors, going 17-20, 5.78.

### Overlooked

**MIKE BORDICK, SS, ATHLETICS.** Passed over in the 1986 draft, Bordick was snapped up by the Athletics on July 10, signing for $15,000. He played seven of his 14 years in the majors at shortstop for the A's. Overall, he hit .260-91-626.

### International Gem

**JUAN GONZALEZ, OF, RANGERS.** The Rangers were the most aggressive team in signing international free agents in the mid-1980s, and two of the most noteworthy players they signed in 1986 were Gonzalez, a Puerto Rican signed for $75,000, and lefthander **WILSON ALVAREZ**, a Venezuelan signed for $30,500. Gonzalez won two MVP awards for the Rangers while hitting .295 with 434 homers in a 17-year big league career. Alvarez pitched one game for Texas before he was traded to the White Sox in 1989, but tossed a no-hitter in his second big league start. He played for 14 seasons, winning 103 games.

### Minor League Take

**GARY SHEFFIELD, SS, BREWERS.** Sheffield, 17, announced his arrival like few first-rounders in draft history. In his pro debut at Rookie-level Helena, he hit .365-15-71 in 57 games; two years later, splitting the 1988 season between Double-A El Paso and Triple-A Denver, he batted a combined .327-28-119.

CONTINUED ON PAGE 320

## AT A GLANCE

CONTINUED FROM PAGE 319

### One Who Got Away

**GREG MCMURTRY, OF, RED SOX (1ST ROUND).** The Red Sox were the best bet to sign McMurtry, a Brockton, Mass., product, but were left empty-handed when he pursued a college football career at Michigan, and later played in the NFL. McMurtry, picked 14th overall, became just one of six first-rounders never to play baseball professionally.

### He Was Drafted?

**KEVIN JOHNSON, SS, ATHLETICS (23RD ROUND).** Johnson played baseball in college at California, and two games in the A's system at Class A Modesto in 1986. But Johnson believed he might be risking a promising NBA career, so he quit almost immediately. He subsequently played 12 seasons in the NBA, becoming a three-year all-star, and later became the mayor of Sacramento.

### Did You Know . . .

For the second year in a row, the Rangers called up their first-round draft pick to the majors before he had won a single game in the minors. They promoted righthander Bobby Witt, their top selection in 1985, after he went 0-6 at Double-A Tulsa; righthander **KEVIN BROWN**, picked first in 1986, debuted after failing to post a decision in the Rookie-level Gulf Coast League and at Tulsa.

### They Said It

Renowned talent evaluator **HUGH ALEXANDER**, on baseball's historic signing of **BO JACKSON**: "Nothing surprises me anymore what that guy can do. He can run like hell, and he can hit the ball out of Yellowstone Park. What more do you want? You've got to go back to Mays and Mantle to find anyone with that kind of combination."

man for commissioner Peter Ueberroth, explaining the new policy.

California Angels scouting director Larry Himes was among those who pushed hard for the rule. "We spend as much as $1.5 million a year gathering information and making evaluations, and the result of that research should be private," he said. "The colleges have their own networks, but they often wait for our drafts to verify their own rankings. I see this as giving us a running start."

The policy also allowed clubs to contact their draft picks and negotiate with them without interference from outside forces likely to drive up bonus payments.

It appeared to achieve its desired effect, at least in the short term. Almost 90 percent (236 of 263) of the players selected in the first 10 rounds in 1986 elected to sign, the best ratio ever.

The committee also decided to phase out the January draft, effective in 1987. Because most players drafted in January were from junior colleges and not eligible to sign until the conclusion of their seasons, officials generally agreed that draft had outlived its usefulness. In addition, the secondary phase of the June draft would be eliminated. In the future the January and June drafts would become one, all-encompassing phase.

Teams also had a growing concern that with four separate draft phases annually, players selected in the first round of the other phases were equating their worth to the players selected in the first round of the mainstream June regular phase.

Of greater significance, teams felt bonuses to the top picks were escalating at an unacceptable rate, and that a new "get-tough" policy was necessary by Major League Baseball to help stem the tide. With top bonuses edging towards $200,000, MLB expressed a desire to draw the line at roughly half that amount, so they approved a rule to provide relief to clubs that did not sign their first-round picks. Beginning with 1986, teams that did not sign first-rounders got a special compensation selection in the following year's draft.

The Boston Red Sox became the initial beneficiary after failing to sign their top pick, outfielder Greg McMurtry, who elected to play football at the University of Michigan. They got a compensation pick at the end of the first round in 1987.

### WINDFALL OPPORTUNITY FOR ANGELS

Jackson was the showpiece, but it was evident that the talent overall in the 1986 draft ran unusually deep. More players selected that year (246) reached the major leagues than in any draft of the two-draft era, although it was somewhat skewed as 16 players were drafted in both January and June—and thus were counted twice, leaving the actual total at 230.

Moreover, the first 13 players selected became big leaguers (a draft first) and more players drafted in the first 10 rounds (96) of the June regular phase succeeded in reaching the big leagues than in any draft to date.

For the Angels, in particular, the 1986 draft provided a rare opportunity to get a leg up.

Having lost Type A free agents Al Holland and Juan Beniquez to the New York Yankees

## How They Should Have Done It

Based on the career WAR (Wins Above Replacement, as calculated by Baseball-Reference.com) numbers achieved by all the players eligible for the 1986 draft, here's how the first round should have unfolded. Numbers in parentheses indicate the round when the player was actually drafted. Asterisk denotes a player signed as a draft-and-follow.

| | Player, Pos. | Actual Draft | WAR | Bonus |
|---|---|---|---|---|
| 1. | Curt Schilling, rhp | Red Sox (Jan.-R/2) | 79.9 | $15,000 |
| 2. | Kevin Brown, rhp | Rangers (1) | 68.3 | $174,500 |
| 3. | Gary Sheffield, ss | Brewers (1) | 60.4 | $142,500 |
| 4. | Matt Williams, ss | Giants (1) | 46.5 | $157,500 |
| 5. | Moises Alou, of | Pirates (Jan.-R/1) | 39.7 | $75,000 |
| 6. | Tom Gordon, rhp | Royals (6) | 35.3 | $17,500 |
| 7. | Pat Hentgen, rhp | Blue Jays (5) | 32.7 | $35,000 |
| 8. | Greg Swindell, lhp | Indians (1) | 30.9 | $165,000 |
| 9. | Greg Vaughn, of | Brewers (June-S/1) | 30.6 | $25,000 |
| 10. | Kevin Tapani, rhp | Athletics (2) | 29.4 | $30,000 |
| 11. | Mike Bordick, ss | Athletics (NDFA) | 26.7 | $15,000 |
| 12. | Chris Hoiles, c | Tigers (19) | 23.5 | $2,000 |
| 13. | Erik Hanson, rhp | Mariners (2) | 22.4 | $90,000 |
| 14. | Rick Reed, rhp | Pirates (26) | 21.1 | $500 |
| 15. | Andy Ashby, rhp | Phillies (NDFA) | 21.0 | $18,000 |
| 16. | Rey Sanchez, ss | Rangers (13) | 20.5 | $8,000 |
| 17. | Roberto Hernandez, rhp | Angels (1) | 19.0 | $90,000 |
| 18. | Todd Zeile, c | Cardinals (2-S) | 18.9 | $45,000 |
| 19. | Jeff King, 3b | Pirates (1) | 16.8 | $180,000 |
| 20. | Darryl Hamilton, of | Brewers (11) | 16.6 | $11,000 |
| 21. | Omar Olivares, rhp | Padres (NDFA) | 15.7 | $16,000 |
| 22. | Mark Whiten, of | Blue Jays (Jan.-R/5) | 14.0 | $4,000 |
| * | Rick Wilkins, c | Cubs (23) | 14.0 | $126,000 |
| 24. | Jeff Shaw, rhp | Indians (Jan.-R/1) | 13.9 | $50,000 |
| 25. | Hal Morris, 1b | Yankees (8) | 13.3 | $12,000 |
| 26. | Dean Palmer, 3b | Rangers (3) | 13.2 | $50,000 |
| **Top 3 Unsigned Players** | | | | **Year Signed** |
| 1. | John Olerud, lhp/1b | Mets (27) | 58.0 | 1989 |
| 2. | Chuck Knoblauch, ss | Phillies (18) | 44.5 | 1989 |
| 3. | Steve Finley, of | Braves (11) | 44.1 | 1987 |

and Baltimore Orioles, respectively, following the 1985 season, the Angels got four extra draft picks as compensation under terms of the new Basic Agreement. That gave them five of the first 28 picks—a windfall opportunity never previously afforded a team in the draft's 21-year history.

"We're in a situation without precedent," a gleeful Himes said. "I think the draft this year is the strongest I've been involved with. There's enough talent that even the No. 28 selection is going to be someone with baseball ability who is interested in playing professional baseball as a career."

The Angels played it safe, selecting five players whose signability was not an issue. They agreed to terms with righthander Roberto Hernandez, their top pick (16th overall), for $90,000, and paid out bonuses of at least $70,000 to get their other four picks under contract.

"The draft did for us just about what we wanted it to," Himes said. "Our emphasis was on pitching. We got two college players to match up with the players we have in our system."

Their draft bonanza never panned out as expected. Himes left after the 1986 season to become general manager of the Chicago White Sox, and support for the players he drafted waned with a revamped development staff in place.

Hernandez and Mike Fetters (27th overall), the

two college righthanders they drafted, went on to pitch 1,630 games in the majors between them (all but nine in relief), but Hernandez encountered early arm problems and was acquired by the White Sox (in a deal executed by Himes) before ever pitching for the Angels. Fetters was also moved in another inconsequential transaction before establishing himself as a big league pitcher.

Among the other three players the Angels selected, all high school picks, only outfielder Lee Stevens (22nd overall) reached the majors. He slugged 144 homers over a 10-year career, though only 14 were hit while with the Angels. Outfielder Terry Carr (25th) and righthander Daryl Green (28th) never advanced beyond Class A.

The Angels were in prime position to gamble one of their extra selections on Jackson, whom they had drafted a year earlier in the 20th round.

"I can't risk (a draft pick) on Bo unless I get some type of commitment from him that he wants to play baseball," Himes said.

Four years later, when the Angels' quintet of first-rounders had combined to play one game in the big leagues, Jackson had not only become a budding star but was named MVP of the 1989 All-Star Game, which was played in Anaheim.

Like numerous other scouts who saw him play that spring at Auburn, Himes said Jackson would have been the No. 1 pick if he had committed to baseball. Himes and most others were convinced Jackson would play in the NFL, which had lost the previous three Heisman Trophy winners to the upstart United States Football League. In his mind, the NFL couldn't lose a player of Jackson's stature.

"I think it's almost cut-and-dried," Himes said. "He's going to the NFL. I don't think he's going to be able to resist the hoopla and the dollars that go with the NFL draft. I don't think the baseball team that drafts him is going to be able to compete.

"Our interest is as high as it was earlier. He's still right at the top talent-wise. I don't think you'd be taking a risk on his ability, but there would be a definite risk in drafting and signing him. I've got a chance to put a lot of good players in the system and I can't take that risk unless we were to get a commitment."

Kansas City, on the other hand, was not daunted by the prospect of steering Jackson away from football, and the Royals selected the two-sport star with the 104th pick in the draft. Jackson had visited with the Royals, Angels and Toronto Blue Jays before the draft, and directed his agent, Richard Woods, to telephone the Texas Rangers, Orioles, Padres and Mets to gauge their interest.

## Fastest To The Majors

| | Player, Pos. | Drafted (Round) | Debut |
|---|---|---|---|
| 1. | Mike Loynd, rhp | Rangers (7) | July 24, 1986 |
| 2. | Greg Swindell, lhp | Indians (1) | Aug. 21, 1986 |
| 3. | Bo Jackson, of | Royals (4) | Sept. 2, 1986 |
| 4. | Kevin Brown, rhp | Rangers (1) | Sept. 30, 1986 |
| 5. | Matt Williams, ss | Giants (1) | April 11, 1987 |

**FIRST HIGH SCHOOL SELECTION:** Gary Sheffield, ss (Brewers/1, Sept. 3, 1988)

**LAST PLAYER TO RETIRE:** Moises Alou, of (June 10, 2008)

## DRAFT SPOTLIGHT: BO JACKSON

Bo Jackson's football exploits were so well known that everyone just assumed he wouldn't play pro baseball, but one scout knew different

Kenny Gonzales remembers the first time he became aware of Vincent Jackson. Jackson was a junior at McAdory High in Bessemer, Ala., and his coach Terry Brasseale called Gonzales to tell him about his amazing multi-sport athlete.

"Terry called me about a youngster who was making headlines as a football halfback and breaking records in track, and said I ought to see him play baseball," said Gonzales, a scout for the Kansas City Royals who had been a graduate assistant on Brasseale's team at Montevallo (Ala.) University. "That's where it all started with us and Bo. And we spent the next five years scouting his head and his heart."

Gonzales watched Jackson hit a national-record 20 home runs in 25 games as a high school senior. He watched him hit 500-foot home runs. He saw him beat out two-hop ground balls to second base, and saw him make pinpoint throws from the warning track.

In Gonzales' scouting report, he rated Jackson's potential at 71 on a 20-80 scale, where anything over 70 is a superstar. He graded Jackson at 80 on power and speed. His arm rated a 70. It was obvious that Jackson had all the talent to be one of the greatest all-around players in baseball history. There was only one problem.

As good a prospect as Jackson was in baseball, he was even better at football. He rushed for more than 5,000 yards in four years at Auburn. He won the 1985 Heisman Trophy. He was the No. 1 pick of the Tampa Bay Buccaneers in the 1986 NFL draft.

With the Buccaneers offering a five-year, $7.5 million contract—the largest ever offered to a rookie—how could Major League Baseball compete? Jackson, after all, had turned down $250,000 out of high school as a second-round pick of the New York Yankees.

When he was declared ineligible to play baseball in the spring of 1986 by the NCAA because the Buccaneers paid for him to fly to Tampa for a physical, most people thought they'd seen the last of Jackson on a diamond.

"It would have been easy to write him off, and say he's going to play football," Gonzales said. "In fact, when scouts came around his senior year, they really were convinced of that. Bo had a lot on his mind, and wasn't playing anywhere near his potential. A lot of scouts were saying, 'Look at him. He don't want to play baseball. He's got football on his mind.'"

Gonzales was undeterred. He was hooked on Jackson from the beginning and nothing was going to change his mind now. He developed a special bond with Jackson, and his mother. Every time he went to Bessemer, he stayed at the Ramada Inn where Florence Bond worked as a maid. He went out of his way to befriend her, but never put on a hard sell.

Through that relationship, Gonzales gained valuable insight on Jackson's relationship with his mother and his own intentions. He gauged correctly that Jackson would attend college and not sign out of high school, so there was no point wasting a draft pick on him. When Jackson was eligible for the draft again in 1985, Gonzales again got the inside scoop that he wouldn't sign, that he was determined to finish college.

Finally in 1986, when all signs pointed to Jackson signing a lucrative contract to play in the NFL, Gonzales realized both his reluctance to sign with the Buccaneers and his willingness to consider baseball, under the right circumstances. The Royals were on the short list of teams that he would play for—information he quickly relayed to his bosses.

Royals general manager John Schuerholz was skeptical, but only until scouting director Art Stewart made an impassioned pitch on Gonzales' behalf.

"John, all I can tell you," Stewart said, "is that Kenny Gonzales has spent seven years on Bo Jackson, and knows him and his family better than anyone. They treat him like a member of the family. We have to believe in Kenny."

On the morning of the 1986 draft, Jackson called Schuerholz to tell him that if he was going to play baseball, he wanted to play for the Royals. The Royals took him in the fourth round, launching one of the most implausible, remarkable careers in sports annals.

And none of it would have been possible without the work of Gonzales, the scout who signed Bo Jackson.

## WORTH NOTING

■ With the abolishment of the January draft, effective in 1987, baseball adopted a "draft-and-follow" rule, which allowed clubs to retain the rights to players drafted in June until a week before the next year's draft—provided the players attended junior college. Once the player completed his junior-college season the following spring, he was eligible to sign with the team that controlled his rights; if he chose not to sign, he re-entered the draft pool. The first player who benefited most handsomely from the new draft-and-follow policy was catcher **RICK WILKINS**, a 23rd-round pick of the Cubs in 1986 who signed for $125,000 after a breakout 1987 season at Florida CC-Jacksonville.

■ Florida State's **MIKE LOYND** compiled one of the best pitching records in college baseball history in 1986, going 20-3 and striking out 223 in 166 innings. His 20 wins tied the NCAA Division I record set in 1979 by Hawaii's Derek Tatsuno, while his strikeout total fell 11 short of Tatsuno's mark. Yet Loynd, an outspoken senior righthander who lost twice to champion Arizona at the College World Series, wasn't drafted until the seventh round, by the Rangers. He was so upset after learning that he had not been selected in the first round that he blasted baseball's scouting fraternity as well as Georgia Tech's **KEVIN BROWN**, who was also drafted by the Rangers and later in the year became Loynd's teammate. "I couldn't believe they took Brown so high," Loynd said. "That kid is not a pitcher. I'm thinking of quitting baseball. This is ridiculous." Loynd was the first member of the Class of 1986 to reach the big leagues. He was promoted after five minor league appearances and won his debut on July 24, but a 3-7, 5.84 record in 35 appearances in 1986-87 sent him packing. He never returned to the big leagues.

■ Shortstop **PATRICK LENNON** became the second player in two years from tiny

"John Schuerholz of the Royals and Pat Gillick of the Blue Jays were the only general managers who kept an open mind," Woods said. "Skepticism was everywhere. People would wink at us, and say, 'C'mon, you guys. What's really the story?' The media, the public, football people, baseball people. Nobody believed us."

On the morning of the draft, Jackson telephoned Schuerholz and indicated his choice of baseball teams was the Royals. He also indicated he didn't have to be selected in the first round.

"Once we selected our first three players," Royals scouting director Art Stewart said, "it was then that we decided to go for Bo. We felt we could risk a fourth-round pick on him. We knew he had been honest with us in saying he wanted to play for Kansas City when California and Toronto didn't take him in the first round."

The Royals weren't flying blind when they selected Jackson. They had inside information. The source: Auburn baseball coach Hal Baird.

Several weeks before the draft, Schuerholz phoned Baird. "He wanted to know whether I thought Bo was serious about baseball," said Baird, who played seven seasons in the Royals organization. "So I asked Bo, point blank. Bo has never been anything but completely honest with me. He told me he was interested in looking at baseball."

Baird called Schuerholz back. "I told them they had an excellent chance at Bo," he said.

On draft day, the Royals were ready to make history.

"Did we think we had a chance to sign him? Yes," Schuerholz said. "Our scout, Kenny Gonzales, followed him closely for four years. His college coach played in our organization, and he was convinced baseball was a very real and viable option for Bo."

Little did anyone realize that Jackson would be in the big leagues later that year, and that it would take less than three years for Jackson to realize his superstar potential.

By then, though, his career had taken another unexpected turn. In the 1987 NFL draft, the Los Angeles Raiders took Jackson with what appeared to be a meaningless seventh-round pick. But Jackson, always looking for a challenge, worked out an agreement with the Raiders to join that club midway through the 1987 NFL season, once the major league season was over. Even without the advantage of training camp, he stepped in immediately and starred for the Raiders.

That dual arrangement persisted for three seasons until Jackson sustained a serious hip injury while playing for the Raiders that ended his NFL career and severely compromised his ability to play baseball. He did go through a difficult hip surgery and managed to continue playing until 1993.

In all or parts of eight big league seasons, Jackson hit .250 with 141 homers—modest numbers when put in the context of the immense mystique that he generated.

### SOUTHWEST CONFERENCE MONOPOLY

The two top picks in the regular phase of the June draft were Southwest Conference rivals: Arkansas third baseman Jeff King, drafted by the Pittsburgh Pirates, and Texas lefthander Greg Swindell, selected by the Cleveland Indians.

### Top 25 Bonuses

| | Player, Pos. | Drafted (Round) | Order | Bonus |
|---|---|---|---|---|
| 1. | **Jeff King, 3b** | **Pirates (1)** | **1** | **$180,000** |
| 2. | **Kevin Brown, rhp** | **Rangers (1)** | **4** | **$174,500** |
| 3. | **Greg Swindell, lhp** | **Indians (1)** | **2** | **$165,000** |
| | ***Ryan Bowen, rhp** | **Astros (1)** | **13** | **$165,000** |
| | **Matt Williams, 3b** | **Giants (1)** | **3** | **$165,000** |
| 6. | **Brad Brink, rhp** | **Phillies (1)** | **7** | **$145,000** |
| 7. | ***Gary Sheffield, ss** | **Brewers (1)** | **6** | **$142,500** |
| 8. | *Lee May Jr., of | Mets (1) | 21 | $130,500 |
| 9. | ***Derek Parks, c** | **Twins (1)** | **10** | **$130,000** |
| 10. | **Scott Hemond, c** | **Athletics (1)** | **12** | **$125,000** |
| | ***Scott Scudder, rhp** | **Reds (1)** | **17** | **$125,000** |
| | **†Rick Wilkins, c** | **Cubs (23)** | **582** | **$125,000** |
| 13. | ***Patrick Lennon, ss** | **Mariners (1)** | **8** | **$120,000** |
| 14. | *Kevin Dean, of | Expos (1) | 15 | $112,500 |
| 15. | ***Kent Mercker, lhp** | **Braves (1)** | **5** | **$100,000** |
| | ***Derrick May, of** | **Cubs (1)** | **9** | **$100,000** |
| | **Bo Jackson, of** | **Royals (4)** | **105** | **#$100,000** |
| | **†Jimmy Rogers, rhp** | **Blue Jays (16)** | **419** | **$100,000** |
| | ***Tom Quinlan, ss** | **Blue Jays (27)** | **686** | **$100,000** |
| 20. | **Thomas Howard, of** | **Padres (1)** | **11** | **$98,500** |
| 21. | **Roberto Hernandez, rhp** | **Angels (1)** | **16** | **$90,000** |
| | Earl Sanders, rhp | Blue Jays (1) | 26 | $90,000 |
| | **Erik Hanson, rhp** | **Mariners (2)** | **36** | **$90,000** |
| 24. | ***Phil Clark, c** | **Tigers (1)** | **18** | **$83,000** |
| 25. | **Luis Alicea, 2b** | **Cardinals (1)** | **23** | **$82,500** |

*Major leaguers in bold. *High school selection. #Major league contract. †Signed as draft-and-follow.*

Both players enjoyed productive three-year careers in college. King hit .372 overall at Arkansas, and set single-season records in home runs (17, in both 1985 and '86) and RBIs (82, in 1985), and career marks in the same categories (42 homers, 204 RBIs). Swindell was even more spectacular in going 43-8, 2.05 overall, with 501 strikeouts in 440 innings. He also spun an NCAA record 14 shutouts.

The Pirates selected King with the No. 1 pick, hoping that he might be ready to fill a void at third base with the big league club by 1987.

"His performance will dictate how fast he advances," Pirates scouting director Elmer Gray said. "I'm hoping, though, that Jeff will follow in the footsteps of Barry Bonds (the Pirates 1985 first-rounder, who reached the big leagues in less than a year)."

King, however, had trouble adjusting to pro ball and did not reach Pittsburgh until 1989—to the dismay of Pirates officials, prompting them to second-guess their decision to go for King.

"It was an organizational decision to take King," Gray said. "Several of our people, including general manager Syd Thrift, were in on the decision. Essentially we arrived at King by a process of elimination. We had to weigh taking a high school or college player, a position player or a pitcher. King was the player that we felt best suited our needs."

King had become a first baseman when he finally did arrive. He hit just .195 as a rookie and struggled to get untracked over the next three years while switching between first base and third. He showed flashes of brilliance on occasion, but didn't become a regular with the Pirates until 1993.

King played eight seasons in Pittsburgh, but it

wasn't until his final year in a Pirates uniform, in 1996, that he displayed the kind of performance they were expecting. He hit .271 while slugging 30 homers and driving in 111 runs. By then he had become eligible for free agency and signed with Kansas City, and closed out his career by playing three more seasons before abruptly retiring. Overall, he hit .256 with 154 homers and 709 RBIs.

After being drafted by Cleveland, Swindell looked like he might go directly to the big leagues, but Indians officials squelched the idea. Not only did Swindell have a heavy workload that spring, a factor in him losing his last three decisions, but he also held out for eight weeks before signing for $165,000. Once he did sign and made three appearances in the minor leagues, there was little doubt he was ready for the big leagues, and he made his debut on Aug. 21.

Swindell began his career by dropping a memorable 24-5 decision to Boston, but he recovered to finish with a 5-2 record. From there, his career was off and running, and he won 39 games through 1989. He likely would have become one of the American League's elite pitchers had arm injuries in 1987 and 1989 not hindered him. Overall, he went 123-122, 3.86 in a 17-year big league career.

### EMPHASIS ON PREP TALENT

The proliferation of elite-level college talent at the top of the 1985 draft drove home the point to the game's talent finders that they were doing an inadequate job of signing the best high school prospects.

In 1982, when most of the 1985 first-round picks were available for the first time, 45 of 110 high school selections in the first 10 rounds went unsigned—including a preponderance of the early selections in 1985.

Big league clubs did not do an about-face and suddenly draft every high school player in sight in 1986, but they made a more concerted effort to sign them, and inked 82 of 98 players in the first 10 rounds—an 84 percent success rate, easily the best to that point in the draft's evolution.

Teams also said the depth and quality of the high school crop was richer than in past years.

### Largest Bonuses By Round

| | Player, Pos. | Club | Bonus |
|---|---|---|---|
| **1.** | **Jeff King, 3b** | **Pirates** | **$180,000** |
| **2.** | **Erik Hanson, rhp** | **Mariners** | **$90,000** |
| 3. | * Chad Smith, lhp | Braves | $65,000 |
| **4.** | **Bo Jackson, of** | **Royals** | **$100,000** |
| 5. | Scott Morse, rhp | Rangers | $42,500 |
| 6. | * Steve Piskor, c | Mets | $39,000 |
| 7. | Doug Duke, c | Expos | $27,500 |
| 8. | Bill Melvin, rhp | Cubs | $35,000 |
| 9. | * Ralph Meister, rhp | Braves | $25,000 |
| | * Rich DePastino, rhp | Blue Jays | $25,000 |
| **10.** | *** Randy Knorr, c** | **Blue Jays** | **$16,000** |
| **Other** | **# Rick Wilkins, c** | **Cubs (23)** | **$125,000** |
| **Jan/R.** | **Moises Alou, of** | **Pirates (1)** | **$75,000** |
| Jan/S. | Toby Nivens, rhp | Twins (1) | $75,000 |
| **Jun/S.** | **Pat Garman, 3b** | **Rangers (1)** | **$70,000** |

*Major leaguers in bold. *High school selection. #Signed as draft-and-follow.*

FRED VUICH

Pittsburgh went for Jeff King with the No. 1 pick hoping for a quick return on its investment, but he struggled to reach the majors

"There's a larger number of high school kids in this year's draft than I've seen in a long time," said Dodgers scouting director Ben Wade, "and that's not to take anything away from the college field."

"Last year was a freak year where you had so many college kids who were advanced and could jump right into the big leagues," added Brewers scouting coordinator Dan Duquette. "That was the exception, rather than the rule. There's some depth to the high school players this year. There seems to be more depth to that group than there has been in years."

The high school talent was especially plentiful in Texas in 1986. Three schoolboy players from that state went in the first round; nine were taken in the first three rounds.

"I've been scouting Texas for 15 years," veteran Philadelphia scout Doug Gassaway said, "and this is the best crop of high school players I've seen yet."

Only three of the nine succeeded in reaching the big leagues, and none was more successful than righthander Roger Pavlik, a second-rounder drafted by the Rangers. He won 47 games in a seven-year career.

The sons of ex-big leaguers Lee May and Dave May (not related) were drafted in the first round, but only Derrick May (Dave's son) made his mark in the majors. He was drafted ninth overall by the Chicago Cubs and had a 10-year career, hitting .271 with 52 homers. His father played 12 seasons, hitting .251 with 96 homers.

Lee May Jr. was selected 21st overall by the Mets in 1986, and fell far short of duplicating the success of his father, who hit 354 homers in an 18-year career. The younger May's career peaked in Triple-A, and he had only a .226 average and eight homers to show for eight seasons in the minors.

While the 26 picks in the first round yielded 15 prep players, the first four off the board were still college players—same as 1985. But that was mostly a factor of the pressing need for immediate help on the part of clubs drafting early in the rotation.

Following the selection of King and Swindell, the San Francisco Giants selected Nevada-Las

### WORTH NOTING

Whiteville (N.C.) High to be drafted in the first round. Selected eighth overall by Seattle, Lennon followed in the footsteps of pitcher Tommy Greene, Atlanta's No. 1 pick in 1985. Lennon's drive to the big leagues stalled in 1989 at Double-A Williamsport, when he was arrested and charged with attempted murder. He subsequently pleaded guilty to lesser charges of reckless endangerment and a weapons violation, and was jailed for two months. He was one of three players drafted in the first two rounds in 1986 who ended up being imprisoned. Expos first-rounder **KEVIN DEAN** and Indians second-rounder **KEVIN WICKANDER** also ended up behind bars after their playing careers ended. Wickander pitched six years in the majors, but subsequently became heavily involved with drugs.

■ Righthander **TOBY NIVENS** was drafted first overall by the Twins in the January secondary phase, and signed for $75,000 after winning 14 games and posting a 1.72 ERA in leading San Jacinto (Texas) Junior College to its second straight Junior College World Series championship.

■ Michigan's **CASEY CLOSE** was one of the most-valuable two-way players in the college game in 1986. He hit .440-19-72 with 16 game-winning RBIs as an outfielder and went 6-1, 3.93 on the mound, but his performance did not make a big impression on scouts and he was relegated to the seventh round. Close spent five years as an outfielder in the Yankees and Mariners systems, hitting .264-33-255 overall, before calling it quits and becoming one of the most successful agents in the game.

■ The Blue Jays spent $100,000 on Sept. 23 to sign their 27th-round draft pick, third baseman **TOM QUINLAN**, who was also a

CONTINUED ON PAGE 324

## WORTH NOTING

CONTINUED FROM PAGE 323

fourth-round pick of the Calgary Flames in the 1986 NHL draft. Quinlan reached the big leagues, playing 42 games in four years with three different clubs, but hit a combined .155-1-5.

■ The Mets' 10th-round pick, **CURTIS PRIDE**, was legally deaf, but never let his handicap stand in the way of a distinguished athletic career. He played 11 seasons in the majors, while hitting .250-20-82 with 29 steals. Pride played basketball in college at William & Mary as the team's starting point guard, while playing in the Mets farm system. As a 15-year-old, Pride was rated one of the top youth soccer players in the world.

■ Arizona won its third College World Series title in 11 years in 1986, beating Florida State 10-2 in the championship game. The Wildcats had more players drafted (11) than any college, though their highest-drafted player, lefthander **MIKE YOUNG**, quit the team on March 1 after working only 15 innings. San Diego drafted Young in the fourth round. A year earlier, Young had suffered a serious eye injury when struck by a line drive off the bat of Stanford's Toi Cook, though he was still drafted by the Phillies in the second round in 1985, and his excellent raw ability prompted the Padres to pick him a year later. He was reluctant to sign, but finally relented and pitched in the short-season Northwest League. But the lingering effects of the accident overwhelmed him, and he went just 2-3, 7.58 in his first pro season. His control, which he had mastered in 1985, deserted him as he walked 26 batters in 19 innings. He struggled for two more seasons before suffering a nervous breakdown related to his accident and didn't pitch at all in 1988. He elected to give baseball one more shot in 1989, but when he went 0-1, 7.04 in Class A, the Padres released him.

Vegas shortstop Matt Williams, and the Rangers followed by going for Georgia Tech righthander Kevin Brown. Swindell and Brown were in the big leagues before the end of the 1986 major league season, while Williams was San Francisco's Opening Day shortstop in 1987.

Williams, who slammed 25 homers with 89 RBIs his junior year at UNLV, was not a consensus top pick entering the draft, but Giants president Al Rosen, himself a power-hitting third baseman in his day, locked in on Williams, envisioning he would fit the same profile one day.

Rosen had no hesitation in authorizing a $157,500 signing bonus for Williams, and he rewarded Rosen's faith by quickly asserting himself as one of the game's top power prospects, especially once he moved to his more natural position at third base. By 1990, Williams led the National League with 122 RBIs. In 1994, with 43 homers by mid-August, he was on pace to challenge the single-season home run record, before the lockout cut the season short. Williams never topped that figure again, but he completed a 17-year career with 378 homers.

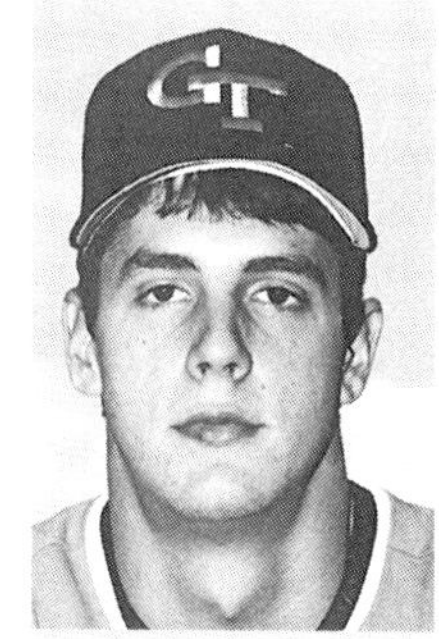

Kevin Brown

Brown's evolution into a top pitching prospect wasn't even a pipe dream while in high school. He wasn't recruited by any colleges while attending a rural Georgia high school, and rarely even pitched. A brilliant student, Brown was accepted into Georgia Tech's engineering program and had no intention of even playing baseball in college.

Three years later, after adding 8-10 mph in velocity to his fastball and setting school records for wins (28) and strikeouts (249), he was the fourth pick in the draft. He signed with the Rangers for $174,500.

Even as he floundered in his first two seasons in the Rangers system, winning just one game in the minors and one in the majors, Brown soon developed into one of the game's premier pitchers. By 1999, when he signed a landmark seven-year deal with the Dodgers, he became baseball's first $100 million player. Over a 19-year career, he won 211 games.

After Brown's selection by the Rangers, there was a sharp swing back to high school talent, and the 1986 draft marked the first time since 1982 that more high school players were selected in the first round than college players.

The first prep selection was lefthander Kent Mercker, who went 33-3, 0.45 and struck out 509 in 233 innings in three years at Dublin (Ohio) High. Despite his impressive record, Mercker was seen as somewhat of a compromise choice by the Atlanta Braves, who signed him for only $100,000—far less than what the top four picks received. Mercker overcame arm problems early in his pro career and reached Atlanta late in the 1989 season, though he was more of a complementary part of a blossoming young Braves staff. He went on to pitch 18 seasons in the majors, though he won just 74 games.

The Milwaukee Brewers, picking sixth, took shortstop Gary Sheffield, nephew of Mets pitching sensation Dwight Gooden. Sheffield, whose mother was Gooden's sister, was a blossoming star in his own right. He hit .500 with 14 home runs in 24 games his senior year at Tampa's Hillsborough High, the same school Gooden attended.

"He was the most dominant offensive player I ever coached," said Hillsborough coach Billy Reed, who also coached Gooden and several other first-round picks.

Sheffield cultivated his baseball skills growing up in the same house as his famous uncle. Gooden was 12, Sheffield 8, when they temporarily shared the same living quarters in Tampa.

"Really, we've been like brothers," Sheffield said. "When I was in high school, he trusted me with his car after he got drafted. Stuff like that. Since I can remember, we've always done a lot of things together."

As Gooden's nephew, Sheffield, 17, had an instant identity in the scouting community.

"When I signed, I knew it would be that way, that I would be Dwight's nephew, not just Gary Sheffield," he said. "That doesn't bother me because I'm proud to be related to Dwight. But one of my goals is to have a big name of my own."

Sheffield went hitless in his first 10 at-bats at Rookie-level Helena, then overwhelmed Pioneer League pitching, finishing the 1986 season with

### Highest Unsigned Picks

| Player, Pos., Team (Round) | | College | Re-Drafted |
|---|---|---|---|
| Greg McMurtry, of, Red Sox (1) | | Michigan | Tigers '90 (27) |
| Kraig Washington, ss, Cubs (2) | | UCLA | Cubs '88 (21) |
| Jack Armstrong, rhp, Giants (3) | | Oklahoma | Reds '87 (1) |
| Joe Lewis, c, Padres (3) | | Louisiana State | Never |
| Rob Richie, of, Rangers (4) | * | Nevada | Tigers '87 (2) |
| Mark Guthrie, lhp, Cardinals (4) | * | Louisiana State | Twins '87 (7) |
| David Lowe, rhp, Mariners (5) | | U.S. Naval Academy | Never |
| Eddie Zosky, ss, Mets (5) | | Fresno State | Blue Jays '89 (1) |
| Tom Goodwin, of, Pirates (6) | | Fresno State | Dodgers '89 (1) |
| Harold Milliken, rhp, Athletics (6) | | Miami-Dade North CC | Never |

**TOTAL UNSIGNED PICKS:** Top 5 Rounds (8), Top 10 Rounds (26)

**Returned to same school.*

### One Team's Draft: Kansas City Royals

| | Player, Pos. | Bonus | | Player, Pos. | Bonus | | Player, Pos. | Bonus |
|---|---|---|---|---|---|---|---|---|
| 1. | *Tony Bridges-Clements, ss | $80,000 | 5. | Pat Bailey, c | $22,500 | 8. | Mike Oglesbee, 1b | $7,000 |
| 2. | *Darryl Robinson, of | $50,000 | **6.** | **Tom Gordon, rhp** | **$17,500** | 10. | Mike Tresemer, rhp | $5,000 |
| **3.** | ***Harvey Pulliam, of** | **$47,500** | 7. | Rob Wolkoys, ss | $18,000 | **Other** | **Sean Berry (Jan.-S/1), ss** | **$35,000** |
| **4.** | **Bo Jackson, of** | **$100,000** | 9. | Paul Murphy, 3b | Did not sign | | | |

*Major leaguers in bold. *High school selection.*

Gary Sheffield

a .365 average, 15 homers and a league-leading 71 RBIs. Two years later he was in the big leagues, though his accomplishments as a teenager (.238 with four home runs in 24 games) didn't come close to matching those of Gooden at the same age.

Sheffield struggled to find a home defensively. He quickly played himself off shortstop, and eventually third base, and spent the bulk of his career as an outfielder. Sheffield also wore out his welcome, more often than not, with the eight clubs he played for.

But over a 22-year big league career, Sheffield hit .292, slugged 509 homers and drove in 1,676 runs—numbers that were the equal or better of any player drafted in 1986. He made $168 million over this career and was a nine-time all-star.

## FOOTBALL EVENS SCORE

While Major League Baseball threw a solid cross-body block at the NFL by luring Jackson away, baseball lost a battle when the Red Sox could not lure McMurtry away from Michigan's powerful football program.

McMurtry, a talented two-sport athlete from nearby Brockton, was a 6-foot-3, 195-pound wide receiver who had 22 touchdowns as a senior in leading Brockton High to its second straight Massachusetts Division I state title. As a center fielder, he hit .605 with 13 homers and 44 RBIs while leading a 22-1 Brockton team to a sectional title the following spring.

The Red Sox figured they had a better chance than any other team to sign McMurtry, so when he was available with the 14th pick, they jumped on him. "I'm very surprised I was drafted in the first round," McMurtry said. "I told the scouts I would be going to college. That's why I'm really surprised."

Ed Kenney, Boston's vice president for player development said: "He is a clone of Willie Wilson. Similar background. Wilson was a great football player. I know some will say we made a gamble. But we're not the kind of team that would waste a No. 1 draft choice. I know one thing. If we don't get him, we're not going to look back and say we made a mistake."

McMurtry was open-minded about signing with the Red Sox initially, but made up his mind that he would play football—especially when they wouldn't meet his asking price of $225,000.

"It was back and forth between football and baseball," said McMurtry, who declined the highest bonus offer in Red Sox history ($172,000, including a college education). "Part of me wanted the Red Sox and part of me wanted Michigan. In the end, football and tradition and the Big Ten won out."

McMurtry was a four-year starter for the Wolverines, and at one point was projected to be picked in the first round of the 1990 NFL draft. Had that occurred, he would have become the first athlete selected in the first round of two different professional drafts. But the New England Patriots didn't take him until the third round.

He played five years in the NFL, the first four with the Patriots, catching five touchdown passes. McMurtry said he never regretted his decision to pick football over baseball.

"I wanted to play college football to see how good I could be," he said. "That's the main reason why I turned down an offer to play baseball."

## SCHILLING HIGHLIGHTS JANUARY PHASE

The final January draft proved to be one of extremes, as more players were selected in the regular phase (366) than any previous January draft, and fewer selections than ever were made in the secondary phase (44). Accordingly, more future big leaguers than ever (44) were products of the regular phase.

The Indians started on the right foot when they selected Cuyahoga (Ohio) Community College righthander Jeff Shaw with the top pick, and the Pirates followed by selecting Canada (Calif.) College outfielder Moises Alou, son of former major league player and manager Felipe Alou. Shaw pitched for 12 seasons in the majors, saving 203 games, while Alou hit .303 over 17 seasons with 332 homers.

But the real prize in the January draft was righthander Curt Schilling, a second-round pick of the Red Sox from Yavapai (Ariz.) CC. He didn't truly hit his stride until he joined his fourth organization, the Philadelphia Phillies, in 1993. Prior to that, he was dogged by immaturity and poor work habits, and won just four games in parts of four major league seasons, miscast as a reliever.

Phillies pitching coach Johnny Podres recognized that Schilling had the raw stuff to be a starting pitcher, and his career was transformed in that role. He went 212-138 over the next 15 years, was a two-time 20-game winner and exceeded 300 strikeouts on three occasions. He also became one of the greatest postseason pitchers in baseball history by assembling an 11-2, 2.33 record in 19 appearances, while striking out 120 in 133 innings.

The overarching effect of the pending dissolution of the January draft, however, was the increasing emphasis on high school players. With the corresponding adoption of the "draft-and-follow" rule, clubs now had the liberty to select a junior college-bound high school player in June, follow his progress for almost a year and then determine prior to the following year's draft whether to sign him. Such draft-and-follow strategy became standard practice in future drafts.

### Largest Draft-And-Follow Bonuses

| | Player, Pos. | Club (Round) | Bonus |
|---|---|---|---|
| 1. | **Rick Wilkins, c** | **Cubs (23)** | **$125,000** |
| 2. | **Jimmy Rogers, rhp** | **Blue Jays (16)** | **$100,000** |
| 3. | **David Howard, of** | **Royals (32)** | **$50,000** |
| 4. | Jay Makemson, rhp | Yankees (June-S/1) | $25,000 |
| 5. | * Terry Marrs, of | Red Sox (11) | $20,000 |

*Major leaguers in bold. *High school selection.*

## IN FOCUS: GREG SWINDELL

Greg Swindell's final victory at Texas pretty much summed up his dazzling career as a Longhorns pitcher.

Working before more than 30 scouts with the Southwest Conference championship on the line, Swindell threw a three-hit shutout at Houston, striking out 16 and besting Mike Walker, a second-round pick, 1-0. The win was Swindell's 43rd at Texas and solidified his stature as the No. 2 pick in the 1986 draft.

That stood in stark contrast to 1983, when Swindell wasn't drafted out of Houston's Sharpstown High and wasn't even the No. 1 pitcher on the staff. Rusty Richards was the ace, and while both had committed to Texas, there were doubts that Swindell was good enough.

"When I came here," Swindell said, "I wasn't even a real good high school pitcher. I didn't have any idea I could have any kind of success here."

Swindell never had to worry about that. By his freshman year at Texas, he had added 5-8 mph to his fastball and went 14-2, 2.04. He became one of the dominant pitchers in Texas history a year later by going 19-2, 1.67 with 204 strikeouts in 172 innings. As a junior, he was used extensively as a starter and reliever, and chalked up seven saves and 10 wins. In 136 innings, he walked just 29 while striking out 180.

# 1986 Draft List

**Did not sign. Major leaguers in bold, with first and last years noted. Order of selection indicated in parentheses. For the first five rounds, the peak level of each player is noted. + Signed as draft-and-follow (Second school noted if applicable).*

## ATLANTA BRAVES

**January—Regular Phase (6)**

1. *Bob Jones, lhp, Citrus (Calif.) JC.--DNP
2. Richard Longuil, rhp, Iowa Western CC.
3. Brian Deak, c, Yavapai (Ariz.) JC.
4. *Brad Herrel, rhp, Northeastern Oklahoma A&M JC.
5. *Ed Banasiak, rhp, CC of Morris (N.J.).
6. Ken Pennington, 3b, El Camino (Calif.) JC.
7. *Edward Lamando, lhp, DeKalb Central (Ga.) JC.
8. *Tim Groner, inf, Walters State (Tenn.) CC.
9. Morris Bland, ss, Indian River (Fla.) CC.
10. Jesse Minton, 1b, Chaffey (Calif.) JC.
11. ***Jorge Pedre, c, West Los Angeles JC.—(1991-92)**

**January—Secondary Phase (2)**

1. **Kevin Brown, lhp, Sacramento (Calif.) CC.—(1990-92)**
2. *Carlos Carrasco, rhp, Gavilan (Calif.) JC.

**June—Regular Phase (5)**

1. **Kent Mercker, lhp, Dublin (Ohio) HS.—(1989-2006)**
2. Brian Champion, ss, Corvallis (Ore.) HS.—(AA)
3. Chad Smith, lhp, Sullivan HS, Kingsport, Tenn.—(High A)
4. **Mike Bell, 1b, Newton (N.J.) HS.—(1990-91)**
5. Andy Nezelek, rhp, Bucknell University.—(AAA)
6. Rick Morris, of, Arizona State University.
7. Robert Stuart, ss, Sonora HS, Brea, Calif.
8. Sean Ross, of, Hoggard HS, Wilmington, N.C.
9. Ralph Meister, rhp, Norman (Okla.) HS.
10. Jim LeMasters, rhp, West Liberty State (W.Va.) College.
11. ***Steve Finley, of, Southern Illinois University.—(1989-2007)**
12. Terry Sloan, c, The Masters (Calif.) College.
13. Rich Maloney, ss, Western Michigan University.

DRAFT DROP *Baseball coach, Ball State (1996-2002, 2013-15); baseball coach, Michigan (2003-12)*

14. *Steve Wilson, rhp, St. Xavier (Ill.) College.
15. Mark Clark, rhp, St. Mary's HS, St. Louis.
16. Alex Smith, ss, Indiana University.
17. Walt Williams, lhp, Western Michigan University.
18. ***Tim Salmon, of, Greenway HS, Phoenix.—(1992-2006)**
19. Jay Johnson, 2b, Dallas Baptist University.
20. Dave Butts, 3b, Murray State University.
21. George Naumczik, lhp, Northern Illinois University.
22. Steve Alexander, of, Southern Tech (Ga.) Institute.
23. Stan Scarborough, rhp, Parkview HS, Lilburn, Ga.
24. John Stewart, lhp, Georgia Tech.
25. Lynn Robinson, of, Chicago State University.
26. David Plumb, c, Auburn University.
27. ***Ben McDonald, rhp, Denham Springs (La.) HS.—(1989-97)**

DRAFT DROP *First overall draft pick, Orioles (1989)*

28. Jeff Weiss, of, University of California.
29. **Jim Czajkowski, rhp, University of North Alabama.—(1994)**
30. Steve O'Quinn, rhp, DeKalb (Ga.) JC.
31. Arthur Smith, of, Coastal Carolina College.
32. Phil Maldonado, c, Texas Tech.
33. *Byron Magee, lhp, Shippensburg (Pa.) HS.
34. *Richard Pfaff, c, Westwood HS, Round Rock, Texas.
35. Scott Kickbush, c, Iowa State University.
36. Randy Ralstin, rhp-1b, University of the Pacific.
37. Joe Datin, 1b, University of South Carolina.
38. *Todd Pennington, of, Roswell (Ga.) HS.
39. Ron Huntington, 2b, Western Carolina University.
40. *Ken Sirak, ss, Camarillo (Calif.) HS.
41. *Tim Lindsay, lhp, Arcadia (Calif.) HS.
42. David Karasinski, lhp, University of Michigan.
43. *Kerry Cahill, ss, Father Judge HS, Philadelphia.

**June—Secondary Phase (9)**

1. Carl Jones-Pointer, of, Mount San Antonio (Calif.) JC.—(Low A)
2. Jerald Frost, ss, Ocean County (N.J.) JC.
3. *Paul Keefer, 2b, Des Moines Area (Iowa) CC.

## BALTIMORE ORIOLES

**January—Regular Phase (15)**

1. *Glenn Twardy, of, Cerritos (Calif.) JC.—(Short-season A)
2. ***Jaime Navarro, rhp, Miami-Dade CC New World Center.—(1989-2000)**

DRAFT DROP *Son of Julio Navarro, major leaguer (1962-70)*

3. *Joel Smith, of, Middle Georgia JC.
4. *Paris Hayden, of, Indian River (Fla.) CC.
5. *Mike Taylor, rhp, McLennan (Texas) CC.
6. *Jeff Gidcumb, rhp, Florida JC.
7. Robert Williams, rhp, SUNY-Buffalo.
8. Ricky Carriger, rhp, Northeastern Oklahoma A&M JC.
9. *Todd Nash, of, Golden West (Calif.) JC.
10. ***Rafael Bournigal, ss, Canada (Calif.) JC.—(1992-99)**

**January—Secondary Phase (3)**

1. David Miller, rhp, Camden County (N.J.) JC.—(AAA)

**June—Regular Phase (16)**

1. (Choice to Angels as compensation for Type A free agent Juan Beniquez)
2. John Posey, c, Campbell University.—(AAA)
3. Mike Lehman, c, Vallivue HS, Caldwell, Idaho.—(AAA)
4. Doug Cinnella, rhp, Seton Hall University.—(AAA)
5. Craig Lopez, rhp, Virginia Commonwealth University.—(High A)
6. Tom Michno, rhp, Columbus (Ga.) College.
7. Bill Kler, of, Milwaukie (Ore.) HS.
8. Terry Crowley Jr., ss, Dulaney HS, Baltimore.

DRAFT DROP *Son of Terry Crowley, major leaguer (1969-83)*

9. **Blaine Beatty, lhp, Baylor University.—(1989-91)**
10. Ken Adderley, of, Florida International University.
11. Dale Barry, lhp, Texas A&M University.
12. Walt Harris, of, Stanford University.
13. Steve Sonneberger, rhp, Middle Tennessee State University.
14. **Gordie Dillard, lhp, Oklahoma State University.—(1988-89)**
15. *William Jones, rhp, Palatka (Fla.) HS.
16. Larry Mims, 2b, University of Nebraska.
17. Randy Strijek, ss, Western Kentucky University.
18. *Bill Narleski, ss, University of Virginia.
19. Steven Williams, rhp, Upsala (N.J.) College.
20. Walt Wallen, 3b, University of South Carolina-Aiken.
21. Richard Winzenread, rhp, Hanover (Ind.) College.
22. Mark Morawski, 2b, Eckerd (Fla.) College.
23. *Jim Huslig, rhp, Shawnee Mission East HS, Shawnee Mission, Kan.
24. *Daniel Bench, c, Northeast HS, St. Petersburg, Fla.
25. Rob Walton, rhp, Oklahoma State University.

DRAFT DROP *Baseball coach, Oral Roberts (2004-12)*

26. Tracey Pancoski, of, Brookdale (N.J.) CC.
27. *Dave Briggs, 1b-of, Rumson Fair Haven (N.J.) HS.
28. *Mike Shambaugh, 1b, Oral Roberts University.
29. *Charles Tanton, c, Lee (Texas) JC.
30. *Jim DePalo, c, Harvard University.
31. Robert Cox, of-1b, Anne Arundel (Md.) CC.
32. *Mark Bookmeyer, of, Lee (Texas) JC.
33. Chris Klyczek, 2b, St. Benedictine (Ill.) College.
34. *Tommy Raffo, lhp-1b, Bishop Kenny HS, Jacksonville, Fla.

DRAFT DROP *Baseball coach, Arkansas State (2009-15)*

35. Matthew Radzik, c, Indian Hills (Iowa) CC.
36. Matthew Nowak, 3b, Southwest Missouri State University.
37. ***Rob Lukachyk, ss, Henry Hudson HS, Highlands, N.J.—(1996)**
38. *John Fowler, ss, Brunswick (Md.) HS.
39. *Darren Villani, 3b, West Windsor HS, Lawrenceville, N.J.
40. *Craig Marshall, rhp, Pittsburg (Kan.) HS.
41. *Dell Ahalt, ss, Hagerstown (Md.) JC.
42. *Doug Shields, ss, LaSalle HS, Cincinnati.
43. +Franklin Martz, 2b, Frederick (Md.) CC / Hagerstown (Md.) JC.
44. *Eric Cox, c, Esperanza HS, Yorba Linda, Calif.
45. Phil Williams, c, University of Hawaii.
46. *Rod Steiner, 3b, Seminole (Okla.) JC.
47. *Casey Moore, c, Loyola Academy HS, Glencoe, Ill.
48. *David Arendas, ss, West Windsor HS, Lawrenceville, N.J.

DRAFT DROP *Brother of Dan Arendas, 17th-round draft pick, Yankees (1986)*

49. *Daniel Johnston, 2b, Manual HS, Indianapolis.

**June—Secondary Phase (26)**

1. +Paris Hayden, of, Indian River (Fla.) CC.—(AA)
2. ***Jaime Navarro, rhp, Miami-Dade CC New World Center.—(1989-2000)**

DRAFT DROP *Son of Julio Navarro, major leaguer (1962-70)*

3. *Ray Schuyler, of, CC of Morris (N.J.).

## BOSTON RED SOX

**January—Regular Phase (13)**

1. ***Alan Mills, rhp, Polk (Fla.) CC.—(1990)**
2. **Curt Schilling, rhp, Yavapai (Ariz.) JC.—(1988-2006)**
3. *Scott Boggs, 3b, Columbia State (Tenn.) CC.
4. *Bill Rawdon, rhp, Columbia State (Tenn.) CC.
5. *Michael Whiting, rhp, Eastern Utah JC.
6. *Michael Leland, c, San Joaquin Delta (Calif.) JC.
7. *Thomas McGee, of, San Jacinto (Texas) JC.
8. Glen O'Donnell, 3b, Quinsigamond (Mass.) CC.
9. *Charlie Holmes, rhp, Mount San Antonio (Calif.) JC.
10. *Andres Cruz, of, Laredo (Texas) JC.
11. Lem Pilkinton, c, Columbia State (Tenn.) CC.
12. Kendrick Bourne, of, Chaffey (Calif.) JC.

**January—Secondary Phase (7)**

1. Ray Revak, lhp, Key West, Fla.—(Low A)
2. *Mike Bianco, c, Indian River (Fla.) CC.

DRAFT DROP *Baseball coach, McNeese State (1998-2000); baseball coach, Mississippi (2001-15)*

**June—Regular Phase (14)**

1. *Greg McMurtry, of, Brockton (Mass.) HS.--DNP

DRAFT DROP *Attended Michigan; re-drafted by Tigers, 1990 (27th round); first-round draft pick, New England Patriots/National Football League (1990); wide receiver, NFL (1990-94)*

2. Paul Williams, c, M.B. Smiley HS, Houston.—(AA)
3. **Scott Cooper, 3b-rhp, Pattonville HS, St. Louis.—(1990-97)**
4. Charles Wacha, rhp, Columbus (Ga.) College.—(AA)
5. Steve Bast, lhp, University of Southern California.—(AAA)
6. Bart Haley, lhp, Grand Canyon College.
7. *Mike Garcia, rhp, North HS, Moreno Valley, Calif.
8. David Milstien, ss, Simi Valley (Calif.) HS.
9. *Joe Kelly, lhp, Notre Dame HS, Whitesboro, N.Y.
10. Jim Morrison, rhp, Anna-Jonesboro HS, Anna, Ill.
11. +Terry Marrs, of, Lake Worth (Fla.) HS / Palm Beach (Fla.) JC.
12. David Walters, rhp, Campbell University.
13. Joe Marchese, 2b, Mankato State (Minn.) University.
14. Anthony Hill, of, University of Rhode Island.
15. Brian Warfel, of, Labette (Kan.) CC.
16. *Steven Tucker, lhp, Riverview HS, Sarasota, Fla.
17. *Tony Kounas, c, San Gorgonio HS, Highland, Calif.
18. Ron Warren, lhp, Troy State University.
19. Tim Buheller, of, Virginia Tech.
20. Mike Baker, 2b, University of Nevada-Reno.
21. Tom Sepela, rhp, Lock Haven (Pa.) University.
22. Stu Weidie, of, University of New Orleans.
23. *Chris Hanks, c, Roaring Forks HS, Carbondale, Colo.

**June—Secondary Phase (20)**

1. +Ed Banasiak, rhp, CC of Morris (N.J.).—(Short-season A)

## CALIFORNIA ANGELS

**January—Regular Phase (21)**

1. Brandy Vann, rhp, Butler County (Kan.) CC.—(AAA)
2. Scott Kannenberg, rhp, San Diego State University.
3. *Keith James, of, Mount San Jacinto (Calif.) JC.
4. Bill VanDerwel, rhp, Seminole (Okla.) JC.
5. *Scott Henion, rhp, Crowder (Mo.) JC.
6. *Robert Cabello, ss, Moorpark (Calif.) JC.
7. *Richard Hochanadel, lhp, Labette (Kan.) CC.
8. *Edwin Alicea, 2b, Chipola (Fla.) JC.

DRAFT DROP *Brother of Luis Alicea, first-round draft pick, Cardinals (1986); major leaguer (1988-2002)*

9. *Marcus Trammell, 2b, Louisburg (N.C.) JC.
10. Tony Rasmus, ss, Enterprise State (Ala.) JC.

DRAFT DROP *Father of Colby Rasmus, first-round draft pick, Cardinals (2005); major leaguer (2009-15) • Father of Cory Rasmus, first-round draft pick, Braves (2006); major leaguer (2013-15)*

11. Greg Jackson, 1b, Polk (Fla.) CC.
12. *Greg Sims, of, Lee (Texas) JC.
13. *Israel Gonzales, rhp, Laredo (Texas) JC.
14. *Lane Mallett, lhp, Panola (Texas) JC.
15. *Jay Searcy, 3b, University of Texas.

**January—Secondary Phase (25)**

1. *Jeff Marr, rhp, Brevard (Fla.) CC.—DNP

**June—Regular Phase (22)**

1. **Roberto Hernandez, rhp, University of South Carolina-Aiken** (Choice from Orioles as compensation for Type A free agent Juan Beniquez)**—(1991-2006)**
1. **Lee Stevens, of, Lawrence (Kan.) HS.—(1990-2002)**
1. Terry Carr, of, Bennett HS, Salisbury, Md. (Choice from Yankees as compensation for Type A free agent Al Holland).—(High A)
1. **Mike Fetters, rhp, Pepperdine University** (Supplemental choice—27th—as compensation for Beniquez)**—(1989-2004)**
1. Daryl Green, rhp, Nacogdoches (Texas) HS (Supplemental choice—28th—as compensation for Holland).—(High A)
2. Jeff Gay, c, Santana HS, Santee, Calif.—(AA)
3. Chris Graves, of, Brenham (Texas) HS.—(AA)
4. **Paul Sorrento, of, Florida State University.—(1989-99)**
5. David Grilione, 1b, Selma (Calif.) HS.—(High A)
6. Colin Charland, lhp, Dallas Baptist University.
7. ***Tony Scruggs, of, UCLA.—(1991)**
8. Mike Anderson, of, University of Northern Colorado.
9. ***Jon Shave, ss, Fernandina Beach (Fla.) HS.—(1993-99)**
10. Greg Fix, lhp, Columbus (Ga.) College.
11. **Colby Ward, rhp, Brigham Young University.—(1990)**
12. Jim Bisceglia, lhp, St. John's University.
13. Scott Cerny, 2b, UC Santa Barbara.
14. Gary Gorski, 3b, UCLA.
15. Mike Knapp, c, University of California.
16. Troy Giles, of, Passaic (N.J.) HS.
17. *Mark Carper, rhp, Atholton HS, Highland, Md.
18. Luis Merejo, rhp, CC of Morris (N.J.).
19. *Stephen Mauldin, of, A.P. Leto HS, Tampa.
20. *Gary Forrester, ss, Sacramento (Calif.) CC.
21. Ken Bandy, of-rhp, Dallas Baptist University.

**June—Secondary Phase (8)**

1. **Alan Mills, rhp, Polk (Fla.) CC.—(1990-2001)**
2. *Richard Hochanadel, lhp, Labette (Kan.) CC.
3. Robert Cabello, ss, Moorpark (Calif.) JC.

## CHICAGO CUBS

**January—Regular Phase (10)**

1. **Shawn Boskie, rhp, Modesto (Calif.) JC.—(1990-98)**
2. **Jerome Walton, of, Enterprise State (Ala.) JC.—(1989-98)**
3. ***Ray Lankford, of, Modesto (Calif.) JC.—(1990-2004)**
4. Ken Taylor, c, San Bernardino Valley (Calif.) JC.
5. ***Derek Lee, of, Manatee (Fla.) JC.—(1993)**
6. ***Ken Ramos, of, Otero (Colo.) JC.—(1997)**
7. *Paul Aguirre, lhp, Grossmont (Calif.) JC.
8. *Mark Linden, 3b, Bellevue (Wash.) CC.

9. *John Kuehl, 3b, Scottsdale (Ariz.) CC.
DRAFT DROP *Son of Karl Kuehl, manager, Expos (1976)*
10. *Bobby Hill, inf, McLennan (Texas) CC.

**January—Secondary Phase (22)**

1. *Mike Ross, ss, Fresno (Calif.) CC.—(AAA)

**June—Regular Phase (9)**

**1. Derrick May, of, Newark (Del.) HS.—(1990-99)**
DRAFT DROP *Son of Dave May, major leaguer (1967-78)*
2. *Kraig Washington, ss, Diamond Bar (Calif.) HS.—(Low A)
DRAFT DROP *Attended UCLA; re-drafted by Cubs, 1988 (21st round)*
3. Eddie Williams, of, Vallejo (Calif.) HS.—(High A)
**4. Pat Gomez, lhp, San Juan HS, Citrus Heights, Calif.—(1993-95)**
**5. Joe Girardi, c, Northwestern University.—(1989-2003)**
DRAFT DROP *Major league manager (2006-15)*
6. Bill Kazmierczak, rhp, Lewis (Ill.) University.
7. Mike Reeder, 1b, Newark (Del.) HS.
8. Bill Melvin, rhp, Louisburg (N.C.) JC.
**9. Jimmy Bullinger, ss, University of New Orleans.—(1992-98)**
DRAFT DROP *Brother of Kirk Bullinger, major leaguer (1998-2004)*
10. Mike Curtis, lhp, Ohio State University.
11. Darren Eggleston, ss, Martinsville (Va.) HS.
12. Steve Parker, lhp, University of Arkansas.
13. Steve Hill, 2b, San Diego State University.
14. *Doug Peters, rhp, Shenango HS, New Castle, Pa.
15. *Mark Dawn, of, Sarasota (Fla.) HS.
16. Phil Harrison, lhp, University of Nebraska.
17. Harry Shelton, of, University of North Alabama.
18. *Al Jorajuria, ss, Kathleen HS, Lakeland, Fla.
19. Anthony LaPoint, rhp, Oral Roberts University.
20. *Mike Mahady, rhp, Manasquan HS, Brielle, N.J.
21. Martin Rivero, ss, Cal Poly Pomona.
22. Kent Alexander, rhp, Appalachian State University.
**23. +Rick Wilkins, c, Florida JC-Jacksonville.—(1991-2001)**
24. Sergio Espinal, 2b, Oklahoma State University.
25. Ray Mullino, rhp, Mississippi State University.
26. *Mike Noel, of, Clovis (Calif.) West HS.
27. David Sommer, rhp, Clark (Wash.) JC.
28. Greg Jackson, of, Tucson (Ariz.) HS.
29. Eric Woods, of, San Diego State University.
30. *Jon Anderson, c, North Shore HS, West Palm Beach, Fla.
31. *Greg Burlingame, lhp, University of Hawaii.
32. *Eric Hughes, rhp, Hug HS, Hawthorne, Nev.
33. *Tom Popplewell, rhp, Fairfield (Ohio) HS.

**June—Secondary Phase (13)**

1. Tony Faryniarz, rhp, San Diego State University.—(Short-season A)
2. *Mike Reitzel, lhp, University of Hawaii.

## CHICAGO WHITE SOX

**January—Regular Phase (19)**

1. Juan Adames, ss, Miami-Dade CC South.—(High A)
2. *Mike Todd, 1b, San Bernardino Valley (Calif.) JC.
3. Chris Cota, of, JC of the Canyons (Calif.).
4. Vincent Harris, of, Triton (Ill.) JC.
5. Jeff Greene, 1b, Seminole (Fla.) CC.
6. *Pete Kuld, c, JC of the Canyons (Calif.).
7. *Keith Kaub, 1b, Golden West (Calif.) JC.

**January—Secondary Phase (11)**

1. Randy Robinson, rhp, JC of the Sequoias (Calif.).—(Low A)

**June—Regular Phase (20)**

1. Grady Hall, lhp, Northwestern University.—(AAA)
2. Carl Sullivan, of, Brenham (Texas) HS.—(AA)
**3. Scott Radinsky, lhp, Simi Valley (Calif.) HS.—(1990-2001)**
4. Frank Potestio, rhp, UC Riverside.—(AAA)
5. Todd Trafton, 1b, University of Arizona.—(AAA)
6. Bo Kennedy, rhp, Central HS, Elvins, Mo.
**7. Matt Merullo, c, University of North Carolina.—(1989-95)**
DRAFT DROP *Grandson of Lenny Merullo, major leaguer (1941-47)*
8. Gil Villanueva, lhp, Cal State Fullerton.
9. Bryce Hulstrom, lhp, Oregon State University.
10. Doug Little, rhp, Florida State University.
11. *Terry Brown, of, University of Southern California.
**12. Mark Davis, of, Stanford University.—(1991)**
DRAFT DROP *Brother of Mike Davis, major leaguer (1980-89)*
13. *Mark Smith, lhp, Waltrip HS, Houston.
14. Todd Hall, lhp, Bowling Green State University.
15. Mike Ollom, rhp, Lewis-Clark State (Idaho) College.
DRAFT DROP *Son of Jim Ollom, major leaguer (1966-67)*
16. Dan Wagner, of, Tulane University.
17. John Becker, c, Arroyo HS, El Monte, Calif.
18. *Don Erickson, ss, JC of the Canyons (Calif.).
19. Kelly Maebe, lhp, Crescenta Valley HS, La Crescenta, Calif.
20. *Collin Wiley, rhp-c, Cal Poly Pomona.
21. *Brian Steiner, lhp, Seminole (Okla.) JC.

**June—Secondary Phase (24)**

**1. *Dan Rohrmeier, 3b, Miami-Dade CC North.—(1997)**

## CINCINNATI REDS

**January—Regular Phase (18)**

1. Ron Wenrich, of, University of Georgia.—(Rookie)
2. Bill Dodd, rhp, Saddleback (Calif.) CC.
3. Rainford Harris, of, Brooklyn, N.Y.
**4. *Mike Butcher, rhp, Northeastern Oklahoma A&M JC.—(1992-95)**
5. *Jesse Ybarra, of, Des Moines Area (Iowa) CC.
**6. Chris Hammond, lhp, Gulf Coast (Fla.) CC.—(1990-2006)**
7. *Mike Bosco, ss, DeAnza (Calif.) JC.
8. *Steve Meyer, rhp, Westark (Ark.) CC.
9. *Tony Floyd, rhp, Three Rivers (Mo.) CC.
**10. *Lonnie Maclin, of, St. Louis CC-Meramec.—(1993)**
11. *Paul Keefer, 2b, Des Moines Area (Iowa) CC.
12. *Scott Volz, rhp, Des Moines Area (Iowa) CC.

**January—Secondary Phase (16)**

1. *Rick Parker, c, Western Oklahoma State JC.—(Low A)

**June—Regular Phase (17)**

**1. Scott Scudder, rhp, Prairiland HS, Blossom, Texas.—(1989-93)**
2. Keith Thomas, of, Kenwood HS, Chicago.—(AA)
**3. Reggie Jefferson, 1b, Lincoln HS, Tallahassee, Fla.—(1991-99)**
4. Mike Moscrey, lhp, Thomas Jefferson HS, Dallas.—(AA)
5. Joe Lazor, lhp, Mount Vernon Nazarene (Ohio) College.—(AAA)
**6. Ed Taubensee, c, Lake Howell HS, Casselberry, Fla.—(1991-2001)**
**7. Jeff Richardson, ss, Louisiana Tech.—(1989-93)**
8. Kevin Pearson, ss, University of Oklahoma.
**9. Chuck Carr, of, Fontana (Calif.) HS.—(1990-97)**
10. Tom Novak, rhp, University of Central Florida.
**11. Keith Lockhart, 2b, Oral Roberts University.—(1994-2003)**
12. Kent Willis, rhp, University of Southern Mississippi.
13. *Derek Heyden, rhp, Corvallis (Ore.) HS.
14. Bernie Walker, of, Texas Christian University.
15. *Allen Rath, rhp, Highland HS, Riverside, Iowa.
16. John Savage, rhp, Santa Clara University.
DRAFT DROP *Baseball coach, UC Irvine (2002-04); baseball coach, UCLA (2005-15)*
17. Sean O'Hare, 1b, Old Dominion University.
18. *Tom Harms, of, Portland State University.
19. *Tony Terzarial, of, Highland (Ind.) HS.
20. Ken Sims, of, Jackson HS, Jenkinsburg, Ga.
**21. Keith Brown, rhp, Cal State Sacramento.—(1988-92)**
**22. *Pete Young, 3b-rhp, McComb HS, Summit, Miss.—(1992-93)**
23. Quinn Marsh, rhp, Utah Technical JC.
24. John Stewart, 2b, Northwestern University.
25. Doug Eastman, of, Cal State Sacramento.
26. Bret Williamson, of, Mesa (Colo.) College.
**27. *Paul Miller, rhp, Carthage (Wis.) College.—(1991-93)**
28. Charles McFadden, c, Lake City (S.C.) HS.
29. *Jesse Davis, of, Wooster HS, Reno, Nev.
30. *Robert Copeland, c, Waltrip HS, Houston.
**31. *James Byrd, ss, Lawton (Okla.) HS.—(1993)**
32. *Troy Hammell, ss, Lakewood (Calif.) HS.
33. *Todd Nace, of, Hattiesburg (Miss.) HS.
34. *Charles Thompson, 2b, Lawton (Okla.) HS.
35. *Tommy Youngblood, rhp, Auburn (Ala.) HS.
36. *Mike Taylor, ss, Waltrip HS, Houston.
37. *Ryan Jackson, rhp, Swansea (S.C.) HS.
38. *Brett Hendley, 1b, Stratford Academy HS, Macon, Ga.

**June—Secondary Phase (7)**

1. Greg Lonigro, ss, Florida JC-Jacksonville.—(AAA)
**2. *Jonathan Hurst, rhp, Spartanburg Methodist (S.C.) JC.—(1992-94)**

## CLEVELAND INDIANS

**January—Regular Phase (1)**

**1. Jeff Shaw, rhp, Cuyahoga (Ohio) CC.—(1990-2001)**
DRAFT DROP *Father of Travis Shaw, major leaguer (2015)*
**2. Michael C. Walker, rhp, Seminole (Fla.) CC.—(1988-96)**
3. Jim Baxter, c, Southwestern (Calif.) JC.
4. Anthony Scaglione, rhp, Morton (Ill.) JC.
5. *Benny Castillo, of, CC of Baltimore.
6. *Kevin Lawson, of, Florida JC.
7. *Andrew Bourne, of, Citrus (Calif.) JC.
8. *Randy Ryan, lhp, Miami-Dade CC North.
**9. Troy Neel, 1b, Howard (Texas) JC.—(1992-94)**
10. *Thomas Draper, rhp, Monroe (N.Y.) CC.
11. *Jeff Forgione, lhp, Cecil (Md.) CC.
12. *Winston Relaford, of, Florida JC.
**13. *Brian Drahman, rhp, Miami-Dade CC South.—(1991-94)**

**January—Secondary Phase (15)**

**1. *Lou Frazier, of, Scottsdale (Ariz.) CC.—(1993-98)**
2. Kraig Luckenbill, rhp, Tarrant (Texas) JC.

**June—Regular Phase (2)**

**1. Greg Swindell, lhp, University of Texas.—(1986-2002)**
**2. Kevin Wickander, lhp, Grand Canyon College.—(1989-96)**
**3. Joe Skalski, rhp, St. Xavier (Ill.) College.—(1989)**
**4. Rudy Seanez, rhp, Brawley Union HS, Brawley, Calif.).—(1989-2006)**
**5. Bruce Egloff, rhp, UC Santa Barbara.—(1991)**
6. Steve Bird, rhp, University of South Carolina-Aiken.
**7. Tommy Hinzo, 2b, University of Arizona.—(1987-89)**
DRAFT DROP *First overall draft pick, June 1984/secondary phase (1984)*
8. *Greg Fowble, ss, Granada Hills (Calif.) HS.
9. Ray Williamson, of, Santa Clara University.
10. Doyle Wilson, c, University of Arkansas.
**11. Tom Lampkin, c, University of Portland.—(1988-2002)**
12. Kent Maggard, rhp, Purdue University.
13. *Dan Davies, lhp, University of Miami.
14. Kerry Richardson, 3b, Lubbock Christian (Texas) College.
15. Jeff Battaglia, of, West Virginia University.
16. Kevin Kuykendall, rhp, Western Oregon State College.
17. Carl Chambers, lhp, Chicago State University.
18. Mark Pike, of, University of South Florida.
**19. *Steve Hosey, of, Fremont HS, Oakland, Calif.—(1992-93)**
DRAFT DROP *First-round draft pick (14th overall), Giants (1989)*
20. Jeff Simmelink, c, Lower Columbia (Wash.) JC.
21. Scott Johnson, of, Unversity of North Carolina.
22. Tom Gamba, 3b, Ithaca (N.Y.) College.
23. Jim Richardson, 3b, University of Oklahoma.
24. Keith Seifert, c, Columbus (Ga.) College.
25. Phil Dillmore, lhp, Florida Southern College.
26. Abraham Walker, 2b, Western Michigan University.
**27. *Kevin Bearse, lhp, Old Dominion University.—(1990)**
28. Riley Polk, 2b-ss, University of South Carolina.
29. Mike Twardoski, of, University of Alabama.
30. John Balis, 3b, North Park (Ill.) College.
31. James Hindulak, lhp, Cleveland State University.
32. Dana Schmerer, lhp, Eastern Washington University.
33. *Jonathan King, ss, York (Pa.) HS.
34. Brad Wolten, of, Washington State University.
35. Luis Martinez, of, Cleveland State University.
36. Lew Kent, c, Grand Canyon College.
37. *Reggie Farmer, of, University of Nevada-Las Vegas.
**38. *Tom McGraw, lhp, Battleground HS, Lake Center, Wash.—(1997)**
39. *Chad Allen, rhp, Richland (Wash.) HS.
40. *Shawn Rohrwild, rhp, Andrew Hill HS, San Jose, Calif.

**June—Secondary Phase (6)**

**1. Jim Bruske, rhp-of, Loyola Marymount University.—(1995-2000)**
2. Paul Kuzniar, rhp, University of Houston.
3. *Dan Eskew, rhp, Indian River (Fla.) CC.

## DETROIT TIGERS

**January—Regular Phase (17)**

1. *Jeff Cesari, rhp, Taft (Calif.) JC.—(Short-season A)
2. Henry Lott, lhp, Chicago.
3. *Ken Weatherby, of, Laney (Calif.) JC.
4. *Rick Christian, of, Hagerstown (Md.) JC.
**5. *Kevin Higgins, 2b, Los Angeles Harbor JC.—(1993)**
**6. *Mike Maksudian, of, CC of Morris (N.J.).—(1992-94)**
7. *Rocky Elli, lhp, Kishwaukee (Ill.) JC.
**8. Wayne Housie, of, Riverside (Calif.) CC.—(1991-93)**
9. *Roddy Wilburn, rhp, Southwestern (Calif.) JC.
10. *Allen Robbins, of, Columbia Basin (Wash.) CC.

**January—Secondary Phase (26)**

**1. *Jerry Nielsen, lhp, Sacramento (Calif.) CC.—(1992-93)**
2. *Lionel Gaston, lhp, Triton (Ill.) JC.

**June—Regular Phase (18)**

**1. Phil Clark, c, Crockett (Texas) HS.—(1992-96)**
DRAFT DROP *Brother of Jerald Clark, major leaguer (1988-95) • Brother of Isaiah Clark, first-round draft pick, Brewers (1984)*
**2. Milt Cuyler, of, Southwest Macon (Ga.) HS.—(1990-98)**
3. Zach Doster, of, T.R. Robinson HS, Tampa.—(High A)
**4. Billy Bean, of, Loyola Marymount University.—(1987-95)**
5. Pat Austin, ss, Wilmington (Ohio) College.—(AAA)
6. Richard Lacko, rhp, Long Island University.
7. Darryl Martin, of, Roberto Clemente HS, Chicago.
8. Ron Marigny, ss-2b, Tulane University.
9. Wade Phillips, rhp, University of Texas.
10. Russ Elsberry, rhp, San Diego State University.
11. Steve Parascand, lhp, Rider College.
12. *Brian Davis, of, Cleveland (Texas) HS.
13. *Dante Johnson, of, Academy of Physical Education, Cincinnati.
14. *Damon Saetre, 1b, Dowagiac Union HS, Dowagiac, Mich.
15. *Gary Peters, 2b, University of Detroit.
**16. Scott Aldred, lhp, Montrose (Mich.) HS.—(1990-2000)**
17. Darrin Hursey, lhp, Urbana (Ill.) HS.
18. Dan Dimascio, of, UC San Diego.

**19. Chris Hoiles, c, Eastern Michigan University.—(1989-98)**
20. *Mike Hansen, rhp, Central Michigan University.
21. *Brad Stoltenberg, rhp, Sacramento (Calif.) CC.
22. *Doug Noch, rhp, Central Michigan University.
23. *Robert Bleisch, c, Chula Vista (Calif.) HS.
24. *Florentino Lozano, of, San Marcos (Calif.) HS.
25. *Sam Drake, rhp, Charles Henderson HS, Troy, Ala.
26. Paul Foster, of, Auburn University.

#### June—Secondary Phase (14)

1. *Mike Jones, rhp, Cosumnes River (Calif.) JC.--DNP
2. *Robert Cuff, rhp, Florida Southern College.

## HOUSTON ASTROS

#### January—Regular Phase (14)

1. *Ervin Houston, of, Laney (Calif.) JC.—(Short-season A)
2. Sam August, rhp, Orange Coast (Calif.) JC.
3. Dan Lewis, of, El Camino (Calif.) JC.
4. *James Cartwright, rhp, Walters State (Tenn.) CC.
5. *Steve Cantu, lhp, San Jacinto (Texas) JC.
6. Bobby Simmons, inf, Louisburg (N.C.) JC.
7. *Dave Oropeza, rhp, Pima (Ariz.) CC.
8. *Jack Moore, inf, Itawamba (Miss.) JC.
9. *Joe Federico, of, Glendale (Calif.) JC.
10. Bryan King, ss, Los Angeles Harbor JC.
11. *Jorge Hernandez, inf, Laredo (Texas) JC.
12. *Gary Murdock, lhp, CC of Morris (N.J.).
13. *Paul Garrison, rhp, Los Medanos (Calif.) JC.
14. *Aaron Rico, rhp, Southwestern (Calif.) JC.
15. *David Haggard, rhp, Los Angeles Harbor JC.
16. *Larry Oedenwalt, inf, San Diego Mesa JC.
17. *Kevin Barker, rhp, Contra Costa (Calif.) JC.
18. *Frank Isbell, rhp, Alvin (Texas) CC.
19. *Jeff Massicotte, rhp, Florida JC.
20. *Gerald Cifarelli, c, Diablo Valley (Calif.) JC.
21. *Samuel Coston, of, Los Medanos (Calif.) JC.
22. *Thomas Siau, inf, Texarkana (Texas) CC.

#### January—Secondary Phase (20)

1. *Scott Carter, rhp, Manatee (Fla.) JC.--DNP
2. *Mark Potoshnik, rhp, Taft (Calif.) JC.
3. *Dewitt Cotton, of, West Los Angeles JC.
4. *Mike Prior, of, Chicago Heights, Ill.

DRAFT DROP *Defensive back, National Football League (1985-98)*

#### June—Regular Phase (13)

**1. Ryan Bowen, rhp, Hanford (Calif.) HS.—(1991-95)**
2. Mike Hook, lhp, Santana HS, Santee, Calif.—(AA)
**3. Tuffy Rhodes, of, Western Hills HS, Cincinnati.—(1990-95)**
4. Fred Costello, rhp, Oceana HS, San Bruno, Calif.—(AAA)
**5. David Rohde, ss, University of Arizona.—(1990-92)**
6. Rich Simon, rhp, St. Francis (N.Y.) College.
**7. Gary Cooper, of, Brigham Young University.—(1991)**
8. Kevin Hancock, of, Mira Mesa HS, San Diego.
9. Rusty Kryzanowski, 3b, University of Wisconsin-Oshkosh.
10. Mike Beams, of-ss, Lake Brantley HS, Altamonte Springs, Fla.
11. Matthew Stennett, of, University of Pittsburgh.
**12. Trent Hubbard, 2b, Southern University.—(1994-2003)**
13. Guy Normand, lhp, Washington State University.
14. Daven Bond, rhp, Mesa (Colo.) College.
15. Kevin Wasilewski, rhp, Stetson University.
**16. Brian Meyer, rhp, Rollins (Fla.) College.—(1988-90)**
17. Mike Boagni, of, Washington HS, Los Angeles.
**18. Ed Whited, 3b, Rider College.—(1989)**
19. James Olson, rhp, Eastern Washington University.
20. Carl Grovom, lhp, U.S. International University.
21. *Brian Fleury, c, Morristown HS, Morris Plains, N.J.
22. Tom Temrowski, 1b, Florida Southern College.
23. Joe Estes, lhp, University of Arizona.
24. John Murphy, c, University of Missouri-St. Louis.
25. *Steve Stowell, lhp, UCLA.

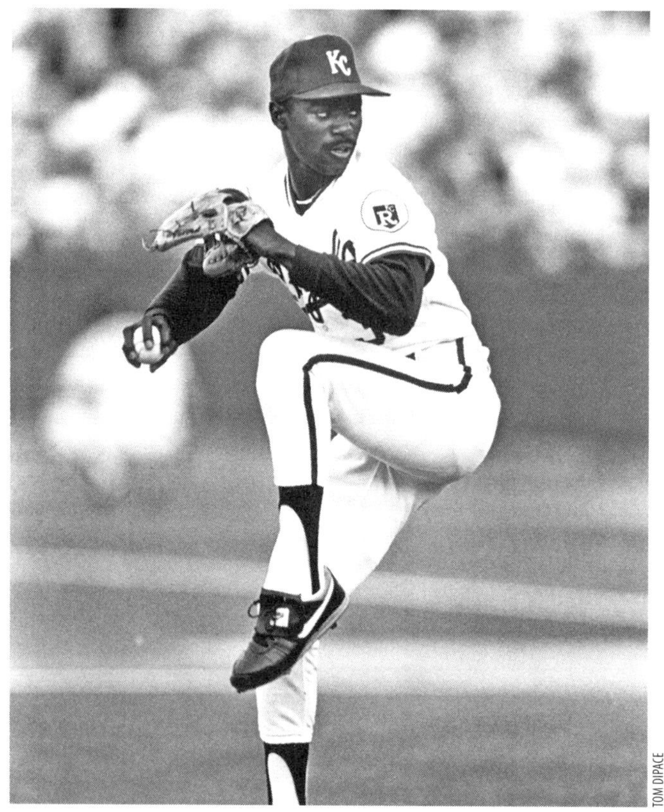

TOM DIPACE

**Tom Gordon was an unheralded Royals sixth-rounder who spent 21 years in the big leagues**

26. *Toncie Reed, of, Pleasant Grove HS, Texarkana, Texas.
27. *Randy Pryor, rhp, Pearland (Texas) HS.
28. Damon Brooks, of, University of Dayton.
29. *Bob Suggs, rhp, Horatio (Ark.) HS.
30. *Steven Glass, ss-3b, San Francisco State University.
31. *Jay Garrett, of, Banning HS, Carson, Calif.
32. *Gary Cameron, lhp-1b, Mountain View HS, Orem, Utah.
33. +Andy Ruscitto, c, Valencia HS, Placentia, Calif. / Fullerton (Calif.) JC.
**34. Eric Anthony, of, Sharpstown HS, Houston.—(1989-97)**
35. *Don Young, of, Mount Miguel HS, Spring Valley, Calif.
36. *Jose Fernandez, c, Palm Beach (Fla.) JC.
37. *Chris Basso, c, Taravella HS, Coral Springs, Fla.
38. *John Jackson, inf, Apopka HS, Tangerine, Fla.
39. *Paul Anderson, ss, Morse HS, San Diego.
40. *Brian Thornbury, inf, Southwestern (Calif.) JC.
41. *Eric Bridge, rhp, San Diego CC.
42. *George Fowler, 3b, Bakersfield (Calif.) JC.
43. *Tim MacNeil, rhp, Esperanza HS, Yorba Linda, Calif.
44. *Richard Lodding, rhp, Western HS, Cypress, Calif.
45. *Jose Lleneras, rhp, Patrick Henry HS, San Diego.
46. *Mike Contreras, rhp, Sweetwater HS, National City, Calif.
47. *Joe Bellezzo, c, Poway (Calif.) HS.
48. *Jason Brosnan, lhp, Arroyo HS, San Leandro, Calif.

#### June—Secondary Phase (5)

**1. Lou Frazier, of, Scottsdale (Ariz.) CC.—(1993-98)**
2. *Craig Wilson, c, Cerritos (Calif.) JC.
3. *Scott Carter, rhp, Manatee (Fla.) JC.
4. +Joe Ortiz, of, Scottsdale (Ariz.) CC.
5. *Brian Bennett, c, JC of the Desert (Calif.).
6. *David Haggard, rhp, Los Angeles Harbor JC.
7. *Mike Peters, rhp, Florida JC.
**8. *Mike Maksudian, of, CC of Morris (N.J.).—(1992-94)**
9. *Mike Pomeranz, lhp, Miami-Dade CC North.
10. *Julio Morales, 1b, Nassau (N.Y.) CC.
11. *Tim Lichty, of, Fresno State University.

## KANSAS CITY ROYALS

#### January—Regular Phase (23)

1. *Kevin Moynagh, rhp, Shelton State (Ala.) JC.--DNP
2. *Kevin Knutson, 1b, Big Bend (Wash.) CC.
3. Kenny Jackson, of, Miami-Dade CC North.
4. *John Buss, lhp, Triton (Ill.) JC.
5. *Brian Bennett, c, JC of the Desert (Calif.).
6. Eugenio Acevedo, rhp, Queensborough (N.Y.) CC.
7. *Harry Michael, of, Big Bend (Wash.) CC.
8. *Rex Barker, inf, Chabot (Calif.) JC.
9. *Eric Nelson, rhp, Chabot (Calif.) JC.
10. *Ron Tyson, of, Southwestern (Calif.) JC.
11. *Frank Halcovich, rhp, JC of the Canyons (Calif.).
12. *Rene Rivera, inf, Long Beach (Calif.) CC.
13. *Jerry Daniels, lhp, St. Louis CC-Meramec.
14. *Kevin Wrice, rhp, St. Louis CC-Forest Park.
15. *Lorenzo Lesky, inf, West Los Angeles JC.
16. *Anthony Peterson, rhp, San Joaquin Delta (Calif.) JC.
17. Brian Meyers, rhp, Essex (Md.) CC.
18. *Jon Seise, lhp, Essex (Md.) CC.
19. *John Horsey, lhp, Essex (Md.) CC.
20. *Jim Hoos, of, Essex (Md.) CC.

#### January—Secondary Phase (9)

**1. Sean Berry, ss, Torrance, Calif.—(1990-2000)**
2. *Carl Shaw, rhp, Bellevue (Wash.) CC.

#### June—Regular Phase (24)

1. Tony Bridges-Clements, ss, Don Lugo HS, Chino, Calif.—(AAA)
2. Darryl Robinson, of, Whitney Young HS, Chicago.—(AA)
**3. Harvey Pulliam, ss, McAteer HS, San Francisco.—(1991-97)**
**4. Bo Jackson, of, Auburn University.—(1986-94)**

DRAFT DROP *Heisman Trophy winner (1985); first overall draft pick, Tampa Bay Buccaneers/National Football League (1986); Running back, NFL (1987-90)*

5. Pat Bailey, c, University of Alabama.—(Low A)
**6. Tom Gordon, rhp, Avon Park (Fla.) HS.—(1988-2006)**

DRAFT DROP *Father of Dee Gordon, major leaguer (2011-15) • Father of Nick Gordon, first-round draft pick, Twins (2014)*

7. Rob Wolkoys, ss, Chapman (Calif.) College.
8. Mike Oglesbee, 1b, University of Nevada-Las Vegas.
9. *Paul Murphy, 3b, University of Delaware.
10. Mike Tresemer, rhp, UC Santa Barbara.
11. Brannon Champagne, rhp, University of Illinois.
12. Luke Nocas, rhp, Santa Ynez HS, Solvang, Calif.
13. Gary Blouin, rhp, University of Washington.
14. Pete Capello, ss, Pace (N.Y.) University.
15. Ben Lee, lhp, Gulfport (Miss.) HS.
**16. Greg Hibbard, lhp, University of Alabama.—(1989-94)**
**17. Dennis Moeller, lhp, Los Angeles Valley JC.—(1992-93)**
18. Tim Odom, rhp-1b, Hattiesburg (Miss.) HS.
19. *Rocky Ynclan, rhp, Tulare Union HS, Tulare, Calif.
20. Anthony Snypes, of, Sullivan East HS, Bristol, Tenn.
21. *Mike Skaggs, of, Henderson County (Ky.) HS.
22. Gus Jones, rhp, Tennessee Tech.
23. Tim Goff, c, Middle Tennessee State University.
24. Michael Davis, c, Lake Brantley HS, Longwood, Fla.
25. *Charles Scales, of, University of Pittsburgh.
26. John Joslyn, 1b, UCLA.
**27. *Torey Lovullo, 2b, UCLA.—(1988-99)**

DRAFT DROP *Major league manager (2015)*

28. *Miles Bowman, of, Crenshaw HS, Los Angeles.
29. Peter Alborano, of, Brooklyn College.
30. John Larios, of, Fresno State University.
31. *Chris Martin, ss, Hamilton HS, Los Angeles.
**32. +David Howard, of, Manatee (Fla.) JC.—(1991-99)**
**33. *Tom Urbani, 1b-lhp, Harbor HS, Santa Cruz, Calif.—(1993-96)**
34. *Pat Fetty, rhp, Soquel HS, Santa Cruz, Calif.
35. *Raymond Sanders, of, Skyline HS, West Pittsburg, Calif.
36. *Brad Davis, of, Morningside HS, Inglewood, Calif.
37. *Chris Schaefer, rhp, Mater Dei HS, Evansville, Ind.
38. *Tony Anderson, c, Tuscaloosa County HS, Northport, Ala.
39. *Matthew Gillis, c, Orange Coast (Calif.) JC.
40. *Javier Fimbres, c, Bell Gardens (Calif.) HS.
41. *Marvin Fight, of, Southwest HS, Kansas City, Mo.
42. *Chris Airey, c, Dulaney HS, Monkton, Md.
43. *Steven Day, of-rhp, Brooklyn Park HS, Baltimore.
44. *Richard Pfaff, 1b-of, Archbishop Curley HS, Baltimore.

#### June—Secondary Phase (10)

1. *Tim Herrmann, rhp, Blinn (Texas) JC.--DNP
**2. Mike Butcher, rhp, Northeastern Oklahoma A&M JC.—(1992-95)**
3. Antoine Pickett, of, Contra Costa (Calif.) JC.
4. Jim Willis, of, Cumberland (Tenn.) College.
5. Charles Mount, rhp, Northeastern Oklahoma A&M JC.
6. *Rex Barker, inf, Chabot (Calif.) JC.
7. *Steve Cantu, lhp, San Jacinto (Texas) JC.
8. *Jeff Cesari, rhp, Taft (Calif.) JC.
9. *Bobby Jones, of, Sacramento (Calif.) CC.
10. *Mark Linden, 3b, Bellevue (Wash.) CC.

DRAFT DROP *Brother of Todd Linden, major leaguer (2003-06)*

## LOS ANGELES DODGERS

#### January—Regular Phase (20)

1. Tim K. Anderson, ss, Sacramento (Calif.) CC.—(High A)
2. *Brian Flanagan, of, Citrus (Calif.) JC.
3. Lee Langley, lhp, Linn-Benton (Ore.) CC.
4. Adam Brown, c, DeKalb (Ga.) JC.
5. *Stephen Carmarda, rhp, San Jacinto (Texas) JC.
**6. *Darren Lewis, of, Chabot (Calif.) JC.—(1990-2002)**
7. *Mike Bundeson, lhp, Mott (Mich.) CC.
8. *Keith Hayes, c, Los Angeles CC.
9. *Brad Freking, lhp, Harper (Ill.) JC.
10. *Ranfred Johnson, rhp, Los Angeles Harbor JC.
11. *Mike Bledsoe, lhp, JC of the Sequoias (Calif.).
12. *Eliezer Quinones, of, Gulf Coast (Fla.) CC.

13. *Mike Ripplinger, of, Taft (Calif.) JC.
14. *Tim M. Anderson, of, DeKalb (Ga.) JC.
15. *David Downey, of, Muscatine (Iowa) CC.
16. *David Ray, c, DeKalb (Ga.) JC.

**January—Secondary Phase (12)**

1. Jim Kating, c, Triton (Ill.) JC.—(AA)
2. *Blake Butterfield, rhp, Mount San Antonio (Calif.) JC.
**3. *Pedro Borbon, lhp, Ranger (Texas) JC.—(1992-2003)**
DRAFT DROP *Son of Pedro Borbon Sr., major leaguer (1969-80)*

**June—Regular Phase (19)**

1. Mike White, of, Loudon (Tenn.) HS.—(AAA)
**2. Dave Hansen, ss, Rowland HS, Rowland Heights, Calif.—(1990-2004)**
**3. Mike Munoz, lhp, Cal Poly Pomona.—(1989-2000)**
4. Mike Pitz, rhp, University of the Pacific.—(AA)
**5. Kevin Campbell, rhp, University of Arkansas.—(1991-95)**
6. Mike Siler, rhp, University of Portland.
7. Dan Henley, ss, University of Southern California.
8. Joe Kesselmark, of, Pace (N.Y.) University.
9. Henry Goshay, of, Pacelli HS, Phenix City, Ala.
10. Ken Riensche, rhp, St. Mary's (Calif.) College.
11. Kenny King, rhp, University of North Carolina-Wilmington.
12. Daniel Pena, lhp, University of Texas.
13. Chris Cerny, lhp, University of New Mexico.
14. Danny Montgomery, 2b, University of North Carolina-Charlotte.
15. *Ted Dyson, 1b, Arizona State University.
16. Anthony Ciccone, 2b, Sonoma State (Calif.) University.
17. Eric Mangham, of, Florida State University.
18. *Clifton Smith, 3b, South San Francisco HS.
19. Billy Brooks, rhp, Georgia Southern College.
20. Stephen Wood, rhp, St. Mary's (Calif.) College.
21. Jeff D. Brown, of, Brigham Young University.
22. Donnie Poteet, 3b, Augusta (Ga.) College.
23. John Knapp, 3b, University of Iowa.
24. Billy Bartels, rhp, Fresno State University.
25. *Timothy Brown, of, Monroe (Ga.) HS.
**26. *Paul Quantrill, rhp, Okemos (Mich.) HS.—(1992-2005)**
27. Greg Hornsby, of, King HS, Tampa.
28. *Scott Longaker, rhp, Petaluma (Calif.) HS.
29. *David Proctor, rhp, Topeka (Kan.) HS.
30. *Craig Stiveson, rhp, Marin Catholic HS, Novato, Calif.
31. *Chris Dominque, rhp, Westchester HS, Los Angeles.
32. *Greg Reid, of, Poly HS, Long Beach, Calif.

**June—Secondary Phase (11)**

1. +Carlos Carrasco, rhp, Gavilan (Calif.) JC.—(High A)
**2. *Wade Taylor, rhp, Jefferson Davis (Ala.) JC.—(1991)**
3. Miguel Ferradas, c, Miami-Dade CC South.
4. *Adrian Adkins, c, Middle Georgia JC.
5. *Mike Bundesen, lhp, Mott (Mich.) CC.
6. *Keith Hayes, c, Los Angeles CC.
7. Andrew Bourne, of, Citrus (Calif.) JC.

## MILWAUKEE BREWERS

**January—Regular Phase (5)**

1. Edwin Anderson, rhp, DeKalb Central (Ga.) JC.—(Rookie)
2. *Reid Gunter, rhp, Sacramento (Calif.) CC.
**3. *John Briscoe, rhp, Texarkana (Texas) CC.—(1991-96)**
4. *Allen Rutledge, inf, Hillsborough (Fla.) CC.
5. Terry Brown, inf, Hillsborough (Fla.) CC.
6. Jose Samaniego, ss, South Mountain (Ariz.) CC.
7. *Byron Williams, of, Glendale (Calif.) JC.
8. Rob Sobczyk, c, Madison Area Tech (Wis.) JC.
9. William Rabb, of, San Joaquin Delta (Calif.) JC.
10. *Rich Bielski, inf, Miami-Dade CC North.
11. *Mike Kelly, of, St. Petersburg (Fla.) JC.
12. *Pat Mackey, inf, Central Arizona JC.
13. *James Matas, rhp, Modesto (Calif.) JC.
14. *Ed Beuerlein, c, Scottsdale (Ariz.) CC.
15. *Miguel Ferradas, c, Miami-Dade CC South.
16. *Clyde Keller, rhp, Sacramento (Calif.) CC.

**January—Secondary Phase (17)**

1. *Dan Eskew, rhp, Indian River (Fla.) CC.—(AAA)
2. *Don Arnold, lhp, Taft (Calif.) JC.
3. *Bruce Wegman, rhp, Central Arizona JC.
DRAFT DROP *Brother of Bill Wegman, major leaguer (1985-95)*

**June—Regular Phase (6)**

**1. Gary Sheffield, ss, Hillsborough HS, Tampa.—(1988-2006)**
DRAFT DROP *Nephew of Dwight Gooden, major leaguer (1984-2000) • First 1986 high school draft pick to reach majors (Sept. 3, 1988)*
2. Mark Ambrose, rhp, Vanderbilt University.–(AA)
**3. Tim McIntosh, c-of, University of Minnesota.—(1990-96)**
4. David Woodhouse, rhp, Bonita Vista HS, Chula Vista, Calif.—(Rookie)
5. Brian Stone, rhp, University of New Haven.—(AAA)
**6. George Canale, 1b, Virginia Tech.—(1989-91)**
7. Jamie Cangemi, rhp, Ithaca (N.Y.) College.
8. Bryan Foster, ss, North Central HS, Indianapolis.
9. Keith Fleming, rhp, Georgia Tech.
10. *Buddy Jenkins, lhp, Starmount HS, Hamptonville, N.C.
**11. Darryl Hamilton, of, Nicholls State University.—(1988-2001)**
12. A.J. Richardson, 3b, Eastern Michigan University.
13. *Chuck Baldwin, 1b, Clemson University.
14. Billy Walker, 1b, Connell (Wash.) HS.
15. Shane Ogawa, rhp, Hilo (Hawaii) HS.
16. David Carley, rhp, University of Arizona.
17. Joey Seaver, lhp, University of Tennessee.
18. James Falzone, c, Cumberland (Tenn.) College.
19. *Jeff Goodale, 3b, Palm Springs (Calif.) HS.
20. Robert Jones, of, Southern Illinois University.
DRAFT DROP *First-round draft pick (28th overall), 1982, Reds*
21. *Scott Drury, c, JC of the Canyons (Calif.).
22. *Gregory Brown, ss, Taravella HS, Coral Springs, Fla.
23. *Stephen Condon, rhp, Davidson College.
24. *Bob Vancho, rhp, Trumbull (Conn.) HS.
25. *Mitch McDowell, of, Madison Area Tech (Wis.) JC.
**26. *Charlie Montoyo, 3b, Louisiana Tech.—(1993)**
27. *Steve Cole, lhp, Englewood HS, Jacksonville, Fla.
**28. *Joe Grahe, rhp, Palm Beach (Fla.) JC.—(1990-99)**
29. Francis Boreffi, of, Union Endicott HS, Endicott, N.Y.
30. Troy Holland, of, Malabar HS, Mansfield, Ohio.
31. +Chris Cassels, of, Gonzalez Tate HS, Pensacola, Fla. / Enterprise State (Ala.) JC.
32. *Todd Azar, of, Old Dominion University.
33. *Craig Stefan, of, North Central (Ill.) College.
34. *Dennis Tafoya, rhp, Yuba (Calif.) CC.
35. *Mark Rubini, of, University of Delaware.
36. *Jarrod Dossen, rhp, Wayne HS, Fort Wayne, Ind.
37. *Michael Hawkins, of, Glenelg HS, Baltimore.
38. *Chip Duncan, rhp, Columbus (Ga.) College.

**June—Secondary Phase (4)**

**1. Greg Vaughn, of, University of Miami.—(1989-2003)**
**2. Brian Drahman, rhp, Miami-Dade CC South.—(1991-94)**
3. *Mike Taylor, rhp, McLennan (Texas) CC.
4. *Fred Riscen, lhp, Los Angeles Pierce JC.
5. *Jack Hollis, of, Los Angeles Harbor JC.
6. *Robert Chadwick, lhp, University of Arkansas.
7. *Scott Boggs, 3b, Columbia State (Tenn.) CC.
8. *John Kuehl, 3b, Scottsdale (Ariz.) CC.
DRAFT DROP *Son of Karl Kuehl, major league manager (1976)*
9. *Ed Beuerlein, c, Scottsdale (Ariz.) CC.

## MINNESOTA TWINS

**January—Regular Phase (9)**

**1. Jarvis Brown, of, Triton (Ill.) JC.—(1991-95)**
2. Eric Johnson, ss, Taft (Calif.) JC.
3. *Mike Pomeranz, lhp, Miami-Dade CC North.
**4. Mike Dyer, rhp, Citrus (Calif.) JC.—(1989-96)**
5. *John Grove, rhp, Ventura (Calif.) JC.
6. *Brent Hahn, c, San Jose, Calif.
7. Robert Hernandez, lhp, Fullerton (Calif.) JC.
**8. *Mike Schwabe, rhp, Rancho Santiago (Calif.) JC.—(1989-90)**
9. *Craig Stamey, c, Spartanburg Methodist (S.C.) JC.
10. Ken Davis, of, San Bernardino Valley (Calif.) JC.
11. *Clint Thompson, c, Gulf Coast (Fla.) CC.
12. *Wade Clark, rhp, Los Angeles CC.
13. *Ruben Gonzalez, 1b, Rancho Santiago (Calif.) JC.
14. Jorge Hoffner, rhp, Broward (Fla.) CC.

**January—Secondary Phase (1)**

1. Toby Nivens, rhp, San Jacinto (Texas) JC.—(AA)
2. *Antoine Pickett, of, Contra Costa (Calif.) JC.

**June—Regular Phase (10)**

**1. Derek Parks, rhp-c, Montclair HS, Upland, Calif.—(1992-94)**
**2. Jeff Bronkey, rhp, Oklahoma State University.—(1993-95)**
3. Fred White, rhp, Jordan HS, Long Beach, Calif.—(AA)
4. Park Pittman, rhp, Ohio State University.—(AAA)
5. Chris Martin, of, Nogales (Calif.) HS.—(High A)
6. Mike Randle, of, San Jacinto (Texas) JC.
**7. Bryan Hickerson, lhp, University of Minnesota.—(1991-95)**
8. John Eccles, c, Cal State Fullerton.
9. *Jeff Lynch, rhp, Tehachapi (Calif.) HS.
**10. Jeff Reboulet, ss, Louisiana State University.—(1992-2003)**
11. *Todd Wilson, lhp-1b, Billings (Mon.) HS.
12. *Paul DeJaynes, rhp, Bradley University.
**13. Scott Leius, ss, Concordia (N.Y.) College.—(1990-99)**
14. David Jacas, of, University of San Diego.
15. David Dasch, ss, Ithaca (N.Y.) College.
16. Ira Goldstein, c, New York Tech.
17. Kenny Morgan, of, University of North Carolina-Charlotte.
18. Dana Heinle, rhp, UC Riverside.
19. *Kurt Olson, 1b-of, Hinsdale Central HS, Clarendon Hills, Ill.
20. Kendall Snyder, 1b-3b, Eastern Illinois University.
21. Shawn Courtney, 2b, University of Northern Colorado.
22. *Sam Bland, c, Fenger HS, Chicago.
23. Mike Lexa, 2b, Indiana State University.
24. *Michael Gianfrancesco, 3b, C.W. Post University.
25. Michael Stolnick, of, University of Wisconsin-Parkside.
26. *Michael Stewart, of, Fresno State University.
DRAFT DROP *Defensive back, National Football League (1987-96)*
27. *Mike Parks, rhp, Miami-Dade CC North.
28. Vern Hildebrandt, ss, Gahr HS, Cerritos, Calif.
29. Mike Baer, inf, University of California.
30. Burt Beattie, c, University of Nebraska.

**June—Secondary Phase (25)**

1. *James McClellan, rhp, Ohlone (Calif.) JC.--DNP
2. *Eric Albright, c, Los Angeles Harbor JC.
**3. *Mike Schwabe, rhp, Rancho Santiago (Calif.) JC.—(1989-90)**
4. *Scott Hutson, rhp, Mesa (Ariz.) CC.

## MONTREAL EXPOS

**January—Regular Phase (16)**

1. Randy Bouman, rhp, Cypress (Calif.) JC.—(Rookie)
2. *Mark Helms, c, Panola (Texas) JC.
3. *Scott McMullen, rhp, Sacramento (Calif.) CC.
4. *Roy Westbrook, c, Angelina (Texas) JC.
5. *Brian Branigan, rhp, CC of Morris (N.J.).
6. *Brent Saclett, rhp, JC of the Siskiyous (Calif.).
7. *Willie Garza, rhp, Laney (Calif.) JC.
8. Kody Duey, 1b, Bakersfield (Calif.) JC.
9. *Leo Clouser, rhp, Los Angeles Pierce JC.
10. *Steve Gray, inf, Cuesta (Calif.) JC.
11. *Fred Riscen, lhp, Los Angeles Pierce JC.
12. *James McClellan, rhp, Ohlone (Calif.) JC.
13. *Fred Schweizer, rhp, Chabot (Calif.) JC.
14. *Guillermo Herrera, rhp, Laney (Calif.) JC.
15. *Joe Leonguerrero, rhp, Sacramento (Calif.) CC.
16. *Chris Morocco, 1b, Middle Georgia JC.
17. *Brian Lutes, rhp, Bakersfield (Calif.) JC.
18. *Orlando Cepeda, rhp, JC of the Canyons (Calif.).
DRAFT DROP *Son of Orlando Cepeda, major leaguer (1958-74)*
19. *Steve Eaton, inf, DeKalb Central (Ga.) JC.
20. *Greg Adelsbach, inf, JC of Southern Idaho.
21. *Lance Dorsey, ss, CC of Morris (N.J.).
22. *Jerald Frost, ss, Ocean County (N.J.) JC.
23. Greg Faught, of, Dallas Baptist University.

**January—Secondary Phase (8)**

**1. *Scott Ruskin, of-lhp, University of Florida.—(1990-93)**
2. *Bobby Jones, of, Sacramento (Calif.) CC.
3. *Andy Berg, lhp, Sacramento (Calif.) CC.

**June—Regular Phase (15)**

1. Kevin Dean, of, Hogan HS, Vallejo, Calif.—(AAA)
**2. Jeff Tabaka, lhp, Kent State University.—(1994-2001)**
3. Tony Welborn, of-rhp, Appalachian State University.—(AA)
**4. Kent Bottenfield, rhp, Madison HS, Portland, Ore.—(1992-2001)**
**5. Gene Harris, rhp, Tulane University.—(1989-95)**
6. John Howes, lhp, Indiana State University.
7. Doug Duke, c, University of Alabama.
8. Mike Dull, 3b, University of South Alabama.
9. Mark Hardy, of, UC Riverside.
**10. Mike Blowers, ss, University of Washington.—(1989-99)**
11. Paul Frye, of, Indiana State University.
12. Rob Leary, c, Louisiana State University.
13. Manuel Alvarez, of, George Washington HS, New York.
14. Scott Clemo, 2b, University of Florida.
15. Joe Sims, of, Northeast Louisiana University.
16. Russ Schueler, ss, University of Kentucky.
17. *Reggie Hubbard, ss, Hogan HS, Vallejo, Calif.
18. Dave Morrow, c, Brigham Young University.
19. *Chris Dorn, rhp, Cypress Creek HS, Houston.
20. Scott McHugh, 3b, University of Central Florida.
21. Don Burke, of, Florida Southern College.
22. Kevin Finigan, of, Claremont-Mudd (Calif.) College.
23. Randy Maville, c, Apollo HS, Glendale, Ariz.
24. Bobby Gaylor, ss, University of Tennessee.
25. Steven King, rhp, Mississippi State University.
26. Jim McDonald, rhp, University of Arizona.
27. Jeff Wedvick, c, Iowa State University.
28. Albert Foster, ss, Sandia HS, Albuquerque, N.M.
29. Robert Simmons, 1b, Rollins (Fla.) College.
30. Brad Brian, c, Eastern Kentucky University.
31. John Marino, lhp, Citrus (Calif.) JC.
32. Dean Rockweiler, lhp, University of Wisconsin-LaCrosse.
33. *Vince Fultz, rhp, Salinas (Calif.) HS.
34. *Johnny Johnson, of, Santa Cruz (Calif.) HS.
35. *Mike Briley, 2b, Cypress Creek HS, Houston.
**36. *Brian Johnson, c, Skyline HS, Oakland, Calif.—(1994-2001)**
37. *Mike Funk, of, Fries (Va.) HS.

**June—Secondary Phase (15)**

1. *Jeff Oswalt, lhp, San Diego Mesa JC.—(Rookie)
2. *Roy Westbrook, c, Angelina (Texas) JC.

## NEW YORK METS

**January—Regular Phase (22)**

1. *Mike Thompson, rhp, Mira Costa (Calif.) JC.--DNP
2. *Carl Jones-Pointer, of, Mount San Antonio (Calif.) JC.
3. Ronald Height, 2b, Citrus (Calif.) JC.
4. Steve Newton, rhp, Pensacola (Fla.) JC.
5. *Thomas Henderson, c, Citrus (Calif.) JC.
**6. Terry McDaniel, of, Kansas City, Mo.—(1991)**
7. *Kevin Ponder, rhp, Central Florida JC.
8. *William Norwood, rhp, Jefferson Davis (Ala.) JC.
9. *Jeff George, rhp, Waubonsee (Ill.) JC.
**10. *Dan Rohrmeier, 3b, Miami-Dade CC North.—(1997)**

11. *Gordon Farmer, rhp, JC of the Siskiyous (Calif.).
**12. *Dean Hartgraves, lhp, JC of the Siskiyous (Calif.).—(1995-98)**
13. Mark DiVincenzo, 3b, Mount San Antonio (Calif.) JC.

**January—Secondary Phase (18)**

1. Rob Hernandez, lhp, Los Angeles Valley JC.—(AA)
2. *Jerald Higby, lhp, Modesto (Calif.) JC.

**June—Regular Phase (21)**

1. Lee May, of-1b, Purcell Marian HS, Cincinnati.—(AAA)
DRAFT DROP *Son of Lee May, major leaguer (1965-82).*
2. Fritz Polka, c, Mankato State (Minn.) University.—(AA)
3. James Morrisette, of, Fairhope (Ala.) HS.—(High A)
**4. Kip Gross, rhp, University of Nebraska.—(1990-2000)**
**5. *Eddie Zosky, ss, St. Paul HS, Whittier, Calif.—(1991-2000)**
DRAFT DROP *Attended Fresno State; re-drafted by Blue Jays, 1989 (1st round)*
6. Steve Piskor, c, Plano East HS, Plano, Texas.
7. Rick Brown, rhp, William Paterson (N.J.) College.
8. Peter Bauer, rhp, St. Paul, Minn.
9. *Rob Fitzpatrick, c, Midland Park (N.J.) HS.
**10. Curtis Pride, of, Kennedy HS, Silver Spring, Md.—(1993-2004)**
11. Jaime Roseboro, of, Los Angeles CC.
DRAFT DROP *Son of John Roseboro, major leaguer (1957-70)*
12. David Crowson, rhp, Brenham (Texas) HS.
13. *Tom Peters, rhp, Santa Monica (Calif.) HS.
14. Jason Woods, c, West Orange-Stark HS, Orange, Texas.
15. Mark Fiedler, lhp, St. Thomas (Minn.) College.
**16. Archie Corbin, rhp, Charlton Pollard HS, Beaumont, Texas.—(1991-99)**
17. *Darryl Fry, lhp, Texas A&M University.
18. Richard Durant, rhp, Huntingdon (Ala.) College.
19. *Michael Hoog, 1b, Niwot HS, Longmont, Colo.
20. Andrew Taylor, rhp, Adelphi (N.Y.) University.
21. Richard Lundahl, ss-3b, Southern Utah State College.
22. *Kevin Miller, c, San Joaquin Delta (Calif.) JC.
23. Bill Robinson, rhp, University of North Carolina.
DRAFT DROP *Son of Bill Robinson, major leaguer (1966-83)*
24. *Titi Roche, of, Miami Lakes HS, Hialeah, Fla.
25. *John Thoden, rhp, Patchogue-Medford HS, Medford, N.Y.
**26. *Cal Eldred, rhp, Urbana Community HS, Center Point, Iowa.—(1991-2005)**
DRAFT DROP *First-round draft pick (17th overall), Brewers (1989)*
**27. *John Olerud Jr., 1b-lhp, Interlake HS, Bellevue, Wash.—(1989-2005)**
DRAFT DROP *First player from 1989 draft to reach majors (Sept. 3, 1989)*
28. Robert Olah, 1b, Notre Dame HS, Bridgeport, Conn.
29. *James Sloan, lhp, Casa Roble HS, Citrus Heights, Calif.
30. *Chris Stiltner, c, Vanden HS, Travis AFB, Calif.
**31. *Ever Magallanes, ss, Texas A&M University.—(1991)**
32. *Mike Richardson, inf, Glendale (Calif.) JC.
33. *Anthony Coleman, rhp, Leflore HS, Mobile, Ala.
34. Lee Johnson, rhp, Beaumont HS, St. Louis.
35. Cedric Hawkins, ss, Geneva (Pa.) College.
**36. *Scott Erickson, rhp, Homestead HS, Sunnyvale, Calif.—(1990-2004)**
37. *Ken Todd, of, Santana HS, Santee, Calif.
38. +Rodney Bond, 1b-of, Dixie Hollins HS, Pinellas Park, Fla.
39. *Todd Hawkins, c, Baylor University.
40. *Brian Beal, c, Harrisburg (Ill.) HS.
**41. *Todd Jones, rhp, Osborne HS, Marietta, Ga.—(1993-2006)**
DRAFT DROP *First-round draft pick (27th overall), Astros (1989)*
42. *Robert Sneed, rhp, Lassen (Calif.) JC.
43. *Phil Angelos, rhp, Waukegan (Ill.) HS.

**June—Secondary Phase (1)**

1. Alex Jimenez, 1b, Miami-Dade CC South.—(AAA)

GEORGE GOJKOVICH

**The Pirates took Moises Alou second in January; he played in 1,942 big league games**

2. Rocky Elli, lhp, Kishwaukee (Ill.) JC.
3. John Wenrick, rhp, Long Beach (Calif.) CC.
4. Scott Henion, rhp, Crowder (Mo.) JC.
5. *Thomas Henderson, c, Citrus (Calif.) JC.
6. +Tom Fine, rhp, Northeastern Oklahoma A&M JC.
7. +Kevin Ponder, rhp, Central Florida JC.
**8. *Jerry Nielsen, lhp, Sacramento (Calif.) CC.—(1992-93)**
9. +Jeff George, rhp, Waubonsee (Ill.) JC.

## NEW YORK YANKEES

**January—Regular Phase (25)**

1. *Jay Makemson, rhp, Orange Coast (Calif.) JC.—(High A)
**2. Dean Wilkins, rhp, San Diego Mesa JC.—(1989-91)**
3. Luc Berube, 3b, Cochise County (Ariz.) CC.
4. *Scott Miller, inf, Manatee (Fla.) JC.
5. *Reggie Glover, inf, Contra Costa (Calif.) JC.
**6. Darrin Chapin, rhp, Cuyahoga (Ohio) CC.—(1991-92)**
7. *Shawn Jenkins, 1b, Chabot (Calif.) JC.
8. *Gary Brown, 1b, Sacramento (Calif.) CC.
9. *Jeff Jones, of, San Joaquin Delta (Calif.) JC.
10. *Greg Roth, 3b, Cochise County (Ariz.) CC.
11. *Pete Robertson, of, San Jose (Calif.) CC.
12. *Andrew Nieman, rhp, Sinclair (Ohio) CC.
13. *Matt Gruver, of, Sacramento (Calif.) CC.

**January—Secondary Phase (13)**

1. Mark Manering, 1b, Miami (Ohio) University.—(AA)
2. *Jeff Oswalt, lhp, San Diego Mesa JC.

**June—Regular Phase (25)**

1. (Choice to Angels as compensation for Type A free agent Al Holland)
**2. Rich Scheid, lhp, Seton Hall University.—(1992-95)**
**3. Tim Layana, rhp, Loyola Marymount University.—(1990-93)**
**4. Steve Rosenberg, lhp, University of Florida.—(1988-91)**
**5. John Ramos, c, Stanford University.—(1991)**
6. Tim Becker, ss, University of South Alabama.
7. Casey Close, of, University of Michigan.
**8. Hal Morris, 1b, University of Michigan.—(1988-2000)**
9. Jerry Rub, rhp, University of South Alabama.
10. Ralph Kraus, of, University of Arkansas.
11. Chris Byrnes, lhp, Stetson University.
**12. Andy Stankiewicz, 2b, Pepperdine University.—(1992-98)**
DRAFT DROP *Baseball coach, Grand Canyon (2012-15)*
13. Bill Voeltz, lhp, St. Thomas (Fla.) University.
**14. Scott Kamieniecki, rhp, University of Michigan.—(1991-2000)**
**15. Steve Adkins, lhp, University of Pennsylvania.—(1990)**
16. Dana Ridenour, rhp, UCLA.
17. Dan Arendas, of, Princeton University.
DRAFT DROP *Brother of David Arendas, 48th-round draft pick, 1986, Orioles*
**18. Turner Ward, of, University of South Alabama.—(1990-2001)**
19. *Darius Gash, of, Roane State (Tenn.) CC.
20. Kevin Crofton, c, Hillsborough (Fla.) CC.
21. Mark Rose, rhp, University of South Florida.
**22. Kevin Maas, 1b, University of California.—(1990-95)**
23. Robert Hunter, of, Dunnellon (Fla.) HS.
24. Robert Ryan, rhp, Knox (Ill.) College.
25. *Dana Leibovitz, 1b, United Township HS, Silvis, Ill.
**26. *Scott Livingstone, 3b, Texas A&M University.—(1991-98)**
**27. *Erik Johnson, ss, UC Santa Barbara.—(1993-94)**
28. *Troy Paulsen, ss, La Quinta HS, Fountain Valley, Calif.
29. *Steven Livesey, 3b, Springstead HS, Spring Hill, Fla.
30. *Greg Torborg, of, Springfield HS, Mountainside, N.J.
DRAFT DROP *Son of Jeff Torborg, major leaguer (1964-73); major leaguer manager (1977-2003)*

**June—Secondary Phase (18)**

1. +Jay Makemson, rhp, Orange Coast (Calif.) JC / Cerritos (Calif.) JC.—(High A)
2. *Rich Bielski, of-1b, Miami-Dade CC North.
3. *William Norwood, rhp, Jefferson Davis (Ala.) JC.
4. *Scott Miller, rhp, Manatee (Fla.) JC.
5. *Brad Herrel, rhp, Northeastern Oklahoma A&M JC.
6. *Kevin Moynagh, rhp, Shelton State (Ala.) JC.

## OAKLAND ATHLETICS

**January—Regular Phase (11)**

1. *Tim Herrmann, rhp, Blinn (Texas) JC.—(Low A)
2. *Jeff Kipila, rhp, Brookdale (N.J.) CC.
3. *Scott Hutson, rhp, Mesa (Ariz.) CC.
**4. David Veres, rhp, Mount Hood (Ore.) CC.—(1994-2003)**
5. *Eric Albright, c, Los Angeles Harbor JC.—(AA)
6. *Anthony Toney, of, Orange Coast (Calif.) JC.
7. *Mark Stancel, rhp, Hinds (Miss.) JC.
8. *Greg Mannion, of, Cerritos (Calif.) JC.
9. *Alex Jimenez, 1b, Miami-Dade South CC.
DRAFT DROP *First overall draft pick, June 1986/secondary phase, Mets*
10. *David Cantrell, rhp, West Los Angeles JC.
11. *Paul Ellison, c, Orange Coast (Calif.) JC.
12. *Steven Pratt, c, Saddleback (Calif.) CC.
13. *William Kehoe, c, Scottsdale (Ariz.) CC.
14. *Joe Ortiz, of, Scottsdale (Ariz.) CC.

**January—Secondary Phase (21)**

1. Pat Gilbert, of, Columbia State (Tenn.) CC.—(AA)
2. *Thomas Gallagher, lhp, Sacramento (Calif.) CC.

**June—Regular Phase (12)**

**1. Scott Hemond, c, University of South Florida.—(1989-95)**
**2. Kevin Tapani, rhp, Central Michigan University.—(1989-2001)**
3. Darrin Duffy, ss, Grand Canyon College.—(AAA)
4. David Gavin, of, Central State (Ohio) University.—(AA)
5. Jeff Glover, rhp, University of Tennessee.—(High A)
6. *Harold Milliken, rhp, Key West (Fla.) HS.
7. *Ken Bowen, ss, Oregon State University.
8. Drew Stratton, of, Princeton University.
9. Vince Teixeira, 3b, UC Santa Barbara.
**10. Lance Blankenship, 3b, University of California.—(1988-93)**
11. Todd Hartley, of-rhp, Fort Hays State (Kan.) University.
12. Robbie Gilbert, rhp, Mississippi Valley State University.
**13. Rod Beck, rhp, Grant HS, Van Nuys, Calif.—(1991-2004)**
14. Mark Beavers, lhp, Brigham Young University.
15. Weston Weber, rhp, Mankato State (Minn.) University.
16. Jim Carroll, rhp, University of Arizona.
17. Kevin Kunkel, rhp, Stanford University.
DRAFT DROP *Son of Bill Kunkel, major leaguer (1961-63); umpire, Major League Baseball (1968-84) • Brother of Jeff Kunkel, first-round draft pick, Rangers (1983); major leaguer (1984-92)*
**18. Dann Howitt, of, Cal State Fullerton.—(1989-94)**
19. Billy Reynolds, c, University of Maine.
20. Jeff Kopyta, rhp, Creighton University.
21. Jamie Reiser, 2b, Bowling Green State University.
22. Glenn Hoffinger, of, University of Portland.
23. Kevin Johnson, ss, University of California.
DRAFT DROP *Guard, National Basketball Association (1987-2000) • Mayor, City of Sacramento (2008-15)*
24. *Anthony Johnson, c-ss, Lincoln HS, San Diego.
DRAFT DROP *Running back, National Football League (1990-2000)*
25. Larry Ritchey, rhp, Point Park (Pa.) College.

**June—Secondary Phase (22)**

**1. *Bret Barberie, 2b, Cerritos (Calif.) JC.—(1991-96)**
2. *Carlton Cochran, lhp, Central Arizona JC.
3. *Glenn Twardy, of, Cerritos (Calif.) JC.

## PHILADELPHIA PHILLIES

**January—Regular Phase (8)**

1. Jesse Allison, rhp, Labette (Kan.) CC.—(Short-season A)
**2. Steve Scarsone, 2b, Rancho Santiago (Calif.) JC.—(1992-99)**
3. *Dale DeVaughan, rhp, Seminole (Okla.) JC.
4. *Jonathan Dukes, rhp, Bacone (Okla.) JC.
**5. Chuck Malone, rhp, Three Rivers (Mo.)**

CC.—(1990)
6. *Charles Mount, rhp, Northeastern Oklahoma A&M JC.
**7. *Rusty Richards, rhp, Austin (Texas) CC.—(1989-90)**
8. *Darryl Rowley, lhp, Northeastern Oklahoma A&M JC.
9. *Gregory Carter, rhp, Seminole (Okla.) JC.
10. *Rodney Downey, rhp, McLennan (Texas) CC.
11. *Troy Garner, rhp, Delgado (La.) JC.
12. *Mike Peters, rhp, Florida JC.
13. *Joe Bourque, inf, San Jacinto (Texas) JC.
14. *Mike Seal, lhp, Delgado (La.) JC.
15. *Jimmy Wooly, rhp, Seminole (Okla.) JC.
16. *Rodney Sitton, of, Connors State (Okla.) JC.
17. *Anthony Ward, lhp, Seminole (Okla.) JC.
18. *Steve Barton, rhp, Connors State (Okla.) JC.
19. *Mickey House, of, Texarkana (Texas) CC.
20. *Anthony Miller, of, Aquinas (Tenn.) JC.
21. *Rob DeYoung, rhp, Fullerton (Calif.) JC.
22. *Jeff Gremillion, of, Blinn (Texas) JC.
23. *Todd Ashmore, inf, Carl Albert (Okla.) JC.
24. Joel Faulk, 3b, Merced (Calif.) JC.
25. *Daryn Lansdell, rhp, Cochise County (Ariz.) CC.
26. *Roger Quillen, rhp, Merced (Calif.) JC.
27. *Dino Ebel, ss, San Bernardino Valley (Calif.) JC.
28. *Wendell Harris, of, Citrus (Calif.) JC.
29. *David Lozano, inf, Cerritos (Calif.) JC.

### January—Secondary Phase (24)

**1. *Blas Minor, rhp, Merced (Calif.) JC.—(1992-97)**
2. *Alex Alvarez, c, Cypress (Calif.) JC.

### June—Regular Phase (7)

**1. Brad Brink, rhp, University of Southern California.—(1992-94)**
**2. Cliff Brantley, rhp, Port Richmond HS, Staten Island, N.Y.—(1991-92)**
3. Rod Robertson, ss, West Orange-Stark HS, Orange, Texas.—(AAA)
DRAFT DROP *Brother of Andre Robertson, major leaguer (1981-85)*
4. Dave Brundage, of-lhp, Oregon State University.—(AAA)
5. Todd Crosby, 2b, University of Hawaii.—(AAA)
6. Scott Ruckman, ss, Madera (Calif.) HS.
7. Chris Bennett, rhp, Cal State Sacramento.
DRAFT DROP *Brother of Erik Bennett, 17th-round draft pick, 1986, Phillies; major leaguer (1995-96)*
**8. Chuck McElroy, lhp, Lincoln HS, Port Arthur, Texas.—(1989-2001)**
9. Steve Blackshear, lhp, Rice University.
10. *Franklin Harris, c, Jackson State University.
11. *Greg Hunter, ss, Juanita HS, Kirkland, Wash.
12. Keith Greene, of, McNeese State University.
13. Harvey Brumfield, of, Fresno State University.
14. Doug Hodo, of, University of Texas.
15. Darrell Coulter, rhp, North County HS, Bonne Terre, Mo.
16. Martin Foley, ss, Grambling State University.
**17. *Erik Bennett, rhp, Eureka (Calif.) HS.—(1995-96)**
DRAFT DROP *Brother of Chris Bennett, 7th-round draft pick, 1986, Phillies*
**18. *Chuck Knoblauch, ss, Bellaire HS, Houston.—(1991-2002).**
DRAFT DROP *First-round draft pick (25th overall), Twins (1989)*
19. *Brad Gregory, rhp, Sarasota (Fla.) HS.
20. *Mitch DuPlantis, 3b, Vanderbilt HS, Houma, La.
21. Chris Limbach, lhp, Warren Central HS, Indianapolis, Ind.
22. *Jon Miller, rhp, McNeese State University.
23. Olen Parker, 2b, Grambling State University.
**24. Garland Kiser, lhp, Sullivan Central HS, Blountville, Tenn.—(1991)**
25. Leroy Vantress, ss, Shady Grove HS, Maringouin, La.
26. *Miah Bradbury, c, Mount Carmel HS, San Diego.
27. Glen Anderson, rhp, University of Southwestern Louisiana.
28. Kenny Miller, c, McNeese State University.
29. *Kevin Van de Brake, ss, Selah (Wash.) HS.
30. Jeff Stark, of, Fresno State University.
31. Jeff Myaer, rhp, University of Utah.
32. Mark Sims, lhp, Ouachita HS, Monroe, La.
33. Tim Peek, rhp, Memorial HS, Elkhart, Ind.
34. Ken Jarner, ss, Santa Rosa (Calif.) JC.
35. *Wayne Helm, rhp, Laguna Hills (Calif.) HS.
**36. *Jesse Levis, c, Northeast HS, Philadelphia.—(1992-2001).**
37. Steve Ochoa, of, San Jose State University.
38. Gary Berman, 1b-3b, UCLA.
39. *Ernie Johnson, lhp, El Dorado Springs HS, El Dorado, Mo.
40. Scott Church, ss, East Tennessee State University.

### June—Secondary Phase (17)

**1. *Derek Lee, of, Manatee (Fla.) JC.—(1993)**
2. *Mark Hudson, rhp, West Valley (Calif.) JC.
3. +Robert Jones, lhp, Citrus (Calif.) JC. / Cypress (Calif.) JC.
4. *Jorge Robles, ss, Miami-Dade CC New World Center.

## PITTSBURGH PIRATES

### January—Regular Phase (2)

**1. Moises Alou, of, Canada (Calif.) JC.—(1990-2008)**
DRAFT DROP *Son of Felipe Alou, major leaguer (1958-74); major league manager (1992-2006)*
2. Carl Rose, rhp, South Georgia JC.
3. Robert Harris, of, Sacramento (Calif.) CC.
4. *Mike Khoury, of, Brockton, Mass.
5. *Michael Patrick, c, Seminole (Okla.) JC.
6. *Darryl Knight, of, Seminole (Okla.) JC.
7. *Peter Drevline, 1b, Kishwaukee (Ill.) JC.
8. *Adrian Adkins, c, Middle Georgia JC.
9. *Rusty Crockett, ss, Seminole (Okla.) JC.
10. *David Vasquez, of, San Jacinto (Texas) JC.
**11. *Arci Cianfrocco, ss, Onondaga (N.Y.) CC.—(1992)**
12. *Mark Dover, rhp, Gavilan (Calif.) JC.
13. *Tim Sinicki, rhp, Broome (N.Y.) CC.
DRAFT DROP *Baseball coach, Binghamton (1993-2015)*
14. *Brandon Montler, 1b, University of Colorado.
15. *Ray Washington, of, Philadelphia CC.
16. *James Webb, rhp, Allegheny (Pa.) CC.
17. *Norman Bromley, 3b, Cecil (Md.) CC.

### January—Secondary Phase (10)

1. Scott Runge, rhp, Sacramento (Calif.) CC.—(AA)
2. *Jason Bridges, 1b, McLennan (Texas) CC.

### June—Regular Phase (1)

**1. Jeff King, 3b, University of Arkansas.—(1989-99)**
**2. Michael A. Walker, rhp, University of Houston.—(1992)**
3. Ray Doss, rhp, Mount Vernon (Texas) HS.–(Low A)
4. Joel Forrest, lhp, Mesa (Colo.) College.—(High A)
5. Steve Moser, 2b, University of Nevada-Las Vegas.—(High A)
**6. *Tom Goodwin, of, Central HS, Fresno, Calif.—(1991-2004)**
DRAFT DROP *First-round draft pick (22nd overall), Dodgers (1989)*
7. Bill Copp, lhp, Iowa State University.
**8. Tony Longmire, of, Hogan HS, Vallejo, Calif.—(1993-95)**
9. Tim Vaughn, ss, Gonzaga University.
**10. Stan Belinda, rhp, Allegheny (Pa.) CC.—(1989-2000)**
**11. Keith Shepherd, rhp, Wabash (Ind.) HS.—(1992-96)**
12. Dean Moran, 3b, Cumberland (Tenn.) College.
13. Blane Lockley, of-1b, Northeast Louisiana University.
14. Brian Lipscomb, of, LaPorte HS, Kingsford Heights, Ind.
**15. Tom Shields, ss, University of Notre Dame.—(1992-93)**
16. Randy Wilson, rhp, University of South Florida.
17. Doug Fisher, 1b, Central Michigan University.
18. +Andre Redmond, of, Roosevelt HS, Seattle / Bellevue (Wash.) CC.
19. Al Quintana, ss, Northwestern University.
20. Ed Hartman, ss, Indiana (Pa.) University.
21. Jeff Gurtcheff, c, University of Iowa.
22. Garland Slaughter, of, Culpeper (Va.) HS.
23. Peter Murphy, rhp-3b, Columbia University.
24. *Lonnie Walker, of, Lee (Texas) JC.
**25. Jeff Banister, c-1b, University of Houston.—(1991)**
DRAFT DROP *Major league manager (2015)*
**26. Rick Reed, rhp, Marshall University.—(1988-2003)**
27. Daryl Boyd, rhp, University of Florida.
28. *Scott Barczi, c, Northwestern University.
29. *Steve Culkar, rhp, University of Kentucky.
30. Tim Kirk, lhp, University of North Carolina.
31. *Torre Bowen, ss, Mount Lebanon HS, Pittsburgh.
32. Ron Robicheaux, of, University of Southwestern Louisiana.
**33. *Mike Mordecai, ss, Hewitt-Trussville HS, Birmingham, Ala.—(1994-2004)**
34. *Michael Olen, c, Crestwood HS, Wapwallopen, Pa.

### June—Secondary Phase (21)

1. *Harry Michael, of, Big Bend (Wash.) CC.—(High A)
2. +Norm Bromley, inf, Cecil (Md.) CC.
**3. Scott Ruskin, of-lhp, Jacksonville, Fla.—(1990-93)**
**4. *Arci Cianfrocco, ss, Onondaga (N.Y.) CC.—(1992-98)**
5. *James Webb, rhp, Allegheny (Pa.) CC.

## ST. LOUIS CARDINALS

### January—Regular Phase (24)

1. Stan Barrs, ss, Florida JC.—(Low A)
**2. *Bret Barberie, 2b, Cerritos (Calif.) JC.—(1991)**
3. *Robert Stiegele, ss, Brevard (Fla.) CC.
4. *Jack Hollis, of, Los Angeles Harbor JC.
5. Randy Butts, 1b, Hagerstown (Md.) JC.
6. *Andrew Schreiver, rhp, Louisburg (N.C.) JC.
7. Michael Alvarez, of, Fullerton (Calif.) JC.
8. *Michael Murrie, lhp, Southeastern Illinois JC.
9. *Baron Bower, c, Fresno (Calif.) CC.
10. *Joe Jones, of, San Diego CC.
11. Orlando Thomas, c, Aquinas (Tenn.) JC.

### January—Secondary Phase (14)

1. *Craig Wilson, c, Cerritos (Calif.) JC.—(AA)

### June—Regular Phase (23)

**1. Luis Alicea, 2b, Florida State University.—(1988-2002)**
DRAFT DROP *Brother of Edwin Alicea, 8th-round draft pick/January 1986 (Angels)*
2. Reed Olmstead, 1b-lhp, Blair HS, Pasadena, Calif.—(AA)
**2. Todd Zeile, c, UCLA** (Supplemental choice—55th—as compensation for Type C free agent Ivan DeJesus)**—(1989-2004)**
3. David Sala, lhp, University of Cincinnati.—(Low A)
**4. *Mark Guthrie, lhp, Louisiana State University.—(1989-2003)**
DRAFT DROP *Returned to Louisiana State; re-drafted by Twins, 1987 (7th round)*
**5. Bien Figueroa, ss, Florida State University.—(1992)**
6. *Mike Couture, c, Eastern Wayne HS, Goldsboro, N.C.
7. Vince Kindred, of, Troy State University.
8. Rob Glisson, lhp, Chapman (Calif.) College.
9. Greg Smith, ss, Central State (Ohio) University.
**10. Larry Carter, rhp, West Virginia State College.—(1992)**
11. Pat Hewes, c, University of Houston.
**12. Mike Perez, rhp, Troy State University.—(1990-97)**
13. Mark Behny, rhp, Wichita State University.
14. Mike Senne, of, University of Arizona.
15. William Hershman, rhp, Clarion (Pa.) University.
16. Ted Parker, of, University of South Carolina-Aiken.
17. Scott Hamilton, rhp, University of Oklahoma.
18. Steve Meyer, 1b, Southwest Missouri State University.
19. Scott Lawrence, rhp, San Diego State University.
20. Ernie Radcliffe, 1b, Central State (Ohio) University.
21. Eddie Looper, 3b, University of Alabama.
22. Stan Zaltsman, lhp, University of Oklahoma.
**23. Mark Grater, rhp, Florida International University.—(1991-93)**
24. Eric Hohn, lhp, Penn State University.
25. Bobby Nettles, rhp, Cal State Fullerton.
26. *Andrew Casano, rhp, St. John's University.
27. Ed Carter, of, Parker HS, Jacksonville, Fla.
28. Edward Lampe, of, Brentwood (N.Y.) HS.
29. Tom Baine, of, UC Irvine.
30. Steve Jeffers, 2b, Western Illinois University.

### June—Secondary Phase (19)

1. Rick Christian, of, Hagerstown (Md.) JC.—(AAA)
2. *Keith Kaub, 1b, Golden West (Calif.) JC.
**3. +Lonnie Maclin, of, St. Louis CC-Meramec.—(1993)**
4. *Pete Kuld, c, JC of the Canyons (Calif.).

## SAN DIEGO PADRES

### January—Regular Phase (12)

**1. Doug Brocall, rhp, Lamar (Colo.) CC.—(1992-2006)**
2. Brian Wood, rhp, Middle Georgia JC.
**3. *John Patterson, ss, Central Arizona JC.—(1992-95)**
**4. Warren Newson, of, Middle Georgia JC.—(1991-98)**
5. *John Spinapont, rhp, Brookdale (N.J.) CC.
6. *Hector Cotto, of, Miami-Dade CC New World Center.
7. *James Matoska, inf, Brookdale (N.J.) CC.
8. *Vince Herring, lhp, Santa Rosa (Calif.) JC.
**9. *Bob Ayrault, rhp, Moorpark (Calif.) JC.—(1992-93)**
10. *Ray Schuyler, of, CC of Morris (N.J.).

### January—Secondary Phase (4)

1. Brian Harrison, of, Ventura (Calif.) JC.—(AA)
2. Bob Lutticken, c, JC of San Mateo (Calif.).

### June—Regular Phase (11)

**1. Thomas Howard, of, Ball State University.—(1990-2000)**
2. Will Taylor, of, Alexandria (La.) HS.—(AAA)
3. *Joe Lewis, c, St. Amant (La.) HS.—(Low A)
DRAFT DROP *Attended Louisiana State; never re-drafted*
4. Mike Young, lhp, University of Arizona.—(AA)
5. Craig Cooper, 1b, Georgia Southern College.—(AAA)
**6. James Austin, rhp, Virginia Commonwealth University.—(1991-93)**
7. Carl Holmes, of, Magnolia HS, Anaheim, Calif.
8. Tom LeVasseur, 3b, San Diego State University.
9. Mike King, c, Middletown South HS, Lincroft, N.J.
10. Paul Quinzer, rhp, Indiana State University.
11. Jimmy Dean, 3b, Madison HS, San Diego.
12. Jeff Yurtin, 3b, Louisiana State University.
13. Greg S. Harris, lhp, Gonzaga University.
14. Mark Sampson, lhp, University of California.
15. Ron Moore, rhp, UC Riverside.
16. Brian Brooks, lhp, University of Southern California.
17. *Jeff Barns, ss, University of South Carolina.
18. Mike Basso, 3b, University of Houston.
19. Tony Pellegrino, ss, St. John's University.
20. *Mike Grimes, rhp, Jesuit HS, Dallas.
21. Keith Harrison, of, Gahr HS, Cerritos, Calif.
22. Jim Navilliat, lhp, Providence College.
**23. *Alan Zinter, c, Hanks HS, El Paso, Texas.—(2002-04)**
DRAFT DROP *First-round draft pick (24th overall), Mets (1989)*
24. *Mark Walker, lhp, Bellarmine Prep, Menlo Park, Calif.
25. *Woody Smith, ss, Andrews (S.C.) HS.
26. *Charles Chauvin, c, Vallejo (Calif.) HS.
27. Terry McDevitt, ss, Eastern Illinois University.

### June—Secondary Phase (3)

1. Pete Roberts, lhp, University of Alabama.—(AAA)
2. *Mike Ross, ss-2b, Fresno (Calif.) CC.

## SAN FRANCISCO GIANTS

### January—Regular Phase (4)

1. *Mike Jones, rhp, Cosumnes River (Calif.) JC.–(AA)
2. Jim Jones, of, Linn-Benton (Ore.) CC.
3. *Thayer Swain, of, San Jacinto (Texas) JC.
4. John Barry, ss, Agoura, Calif.

5. *Tom Fine, rhp, Northeastern Oklahoma A&M JC.
6. Jeff Hughes, of, Northridge, Calif.
7. *Mark Diefenderfer, rhp, Butte (Calif.) JC.
8. *James Gasser, rhp, Moorpark (Calif.) JC.
9. *John Cebuhar, lhp, Eastern Oklahoma JC.
10. Drew Richer, lhp, Los Angeles Valley JC.
11. *Damon Tyson, ss, Los Angeles CC.
12. *Chris Chavez, lhp, Santa Monica (Calif.) JC.
13. *John Gleason, rhp, Moorpark (Calif.) JC.

**January—Secondary Phase (6)**

**1. Paul McClellan, rhp, JC of San Mateo (Calif.).—(1990-91)**
2. *Jorge Robles, ss, Miami-Dade CC New World Center.

**June—Regular Phase (3)**

**1. Matt D. Williams, 3b, University of Nevada-Las Vegas.—(1987-2003)**
DRAFT DROP *Major league manager (2014-15)*
**2. Kirt Manwaring, c, Coastal Carolina College.—(1987-99)**
**3. *Jack Armstrong, rhp, Rider College.—(1988-94)**
DRAFT DROP *Attended Oklahoma; re-drafted by Reds, 1987 (1st round)*
4. Paul Meyers, of, University of Nebraska.—(AAA)
**5. Jim McNamara, c, North Carolina State University.—(1992-93)**
6. Tim McCoy, lhp, Oral Roberts University.
7. Greg Conner, of, University of Southern Mississippi.
8. Gregg Ritchie, of, George Washington University.
DRAFT DROP *Baseball coach, George Washington (2013-15)*
**9. Russ Swan, lhp, Texas A&M University.—(1989-94)**
10. Matthew S. Williams, c, Corvallis (Ore.) HS.
11. John Toal, 2b, University of Oklahoma.
12. *Gordon Douglas, rhp, University of North Carolina.
13. *Chris Haslock, rhp, Los Angeles Valley JC.
14. Dave Patterson, 1b, University of Arkansas.
15. Kevin Redick, of, Westmont (Calif.) College.
**16. Jim Pena, lhp, Cal State Dominguez Hills.—(1992)**
17. Dee Dixon, of, Norfolk State University.
18. *Lennie McGuire, rhp, Corvallis (Ore.) HS.
19. David Connelly, of-1b, North Hollywood (Calif.) HS.
**20. Craig Colbert, 3b, Oral Roberts University.—(1992-93)**
21. Charles Higson, rhp, Lewis-Clark State (Idaho) College.
22. Chuck Tate, rhp, Oklahoma State University.
23. Kevin Fitzgerald, 2b, George Washington University.
24. David Nash, of, Central Michigan University.
25. Chris Shultis, 3b, University of Utah.
26. *Carlos Robles, 1b, Pater Noster HS, Los Angeles.
27. *Derek Scholl, of, Los Angeles Harbor JC.
28. *Greg Roscoe, rhp, University of Nevada-Las Vegas.
**29. Mark Leonard, of, UC Santa Barbara.—(1990-95)**
30. John Rannow, c-of, Concordia (Ore.) College.
31. Keith Krafve, 3b, Oregon State University.
32. *Jeff Distasio, 1b, Georgia Tech.
33. Robin Riemer, lhp, Monroe (N.Y.) CC.

**June—Secondary Phase (23)**

1. *Jay Searcy, 3b, University of Texas.--DNP

## SEATTLE MARINERS

**January—Regular Phase (7)**

1. Jim Pritikin, of, San Diego Mesa JC.—(High A)
2. Jim Blueberg, rhp, Yuba (Calif.) CC.
3. *Rod Byerly, lhp, Brevard (Fla.) CC.
4. *Shawn Butler, lhp, Green River (Wash.) CC.
5. (void) *Danny Kapea, lhp, Central Arizona JC.
6. Rudy Webster, rhp, Central Iowa JC.
7. *Ken Shamburg, 1b-3b, Butte (Calif.) JC.
8. *Mike Beiras, rhp, El Camino (Calif.) JC.
**9. *Jonathan Hurst, rhp, Spartanburg Methodist (S.C.) JC.—(1992-94)**
10. *David Kandra, rhp, Butte (Calif.) JC.

**January—Secondary Phase (5)**

**1. Eric Fox, of, Fresno State University.—(1992-95)**
2. *Mike Montagnino, c, Palm Beach (Fla.) JC.

**June—Regular Phase (8)**

**1. Patrick Lennon, ss, Whiteville (N.C.) HS.—(1991-99)**
**2. Erik Hanson, rhp, Wake Forest University.—(1988-98)**
**3. Jerry Goff, c, University of California.—(1990-96)**
4. Mike McDonald, ss, Douglas County HS, Douglasville, Ga.—(AAA)
5. *David Lowe, rhp, Satellite HS, Satellite Beach, Fla.--DNP
DRAFT DROP *Attended Naval Academy; never re-drafted*
**6. Rich DeLucia, rhp, University of Tennessee.—(1990-99)**
7. Mark Wooden, rhp, Lewis-Clark State (Idaho) College.
8. Ted Williams, of, University of Alabama.
9. Michael Brandts, 3b-of, Marietta (Ohio) College.
10. Dan Disher, rhp, University of Michigan.
11. Troy Williams, 2b, Eastern Kentucky University.
**12. Jim Bowie, 1b, Louisiana State University.—(1994)**
13. Dru Kosco, of, Ball State University.
DRAFT DROP *Son of Andy Kosco, major leaguer (1965-74)*
14. Dave Hartnett, lhp, Creighton University.
15. Jody Ryan, rhp, Troy State University.
16. *Rusty Harris, ss, Lewis-Clark State (Idaho) College.
17. *Gary Young, rhp, Hoopa (Calif.) HS.
18. Jose Tartabull, of, Miami-Dade CC North.
DRAFT DROP *Son of Jose Tartabull, major leaguer (1962-70) • Brother of Danny Tartabull, major leaguer (1984-97)*
19. Wendell Bolar, 3b, Cal State Chico.
20. Tommy Little, rhp, Tulane University.
21. *Montie Phillips, 3b, Lewis-Clark State (Idaho) College.
22. Mike Thorpe, rhp, Arizona State University.
**23. *Jamie McAndrew, rhp, Ponderosa HS, Parker, Colo.—(1995-97)**
DRAFT DROP *First-round draft pick (28th overall), Dodgers (1989) • Son of Jim McAndrew, major leaguer (1968-74)*
24. Jose Bennett, of, Western New Mexico University.
25. *Kevin Sheary, rhp, University of Miami.
26. *Erick Bryant, rhp, Poly HS, Long Beach, Calif.
**27. *Paul Carey, 1b, Boston College HS, Weymouth, Mass.—(1993)**
28. *Anthony Carnavale, c, Trinidad (Colo.) HS.
29. Deron Johnson Jr., 1b, San Diego State University.
DRAFT DROP *Son of Deron Johnson, major leaguer (1960-76)*

**June—Secondary Phase (12)**

**1. Greg Briley, 2b, North Carolina State University.—(1988-93)**
2. *Larry Oedenwalt, inf, San Diego Mesa JC.
3. *Gary Alexander, rhp, University of Arizona.
4. *Paul Ellison, c, Orange Coast (Calif.) JC.
5. *Damon Allen, rhp, San Diego.
DRAFT DROP *Quarterback, Canadian Football League (1985-2007) • Brother of Marcus Allen, running back, National Football League (1982-97)*

## TEXAS RANGERS

**January—Regular Phase (3)**

1. Chris Shiflett, rhp, Rancho Santiago (Calif.) JC.—(AA)
2. *Heath Lane, rhp, San Joaquin Delta (Calif.) JC.
3. *David Boss, rhp, San Jose (Calif.) CC.
4. *John Wenrich, rhp, Long Beach (Calif.) CC.
5. *Michael Ferreira, rhp, Chabot (Calif.) JC.
6. *Brian McSwain, rhp, Spartanburg Methodist (S.C.) JC.
7. *Julio Morales, 1b, Nassau (N.Y.) CC.
8. *Angel Caceres, lhp, Arizona Western JC.
9. *John Burgos, lhp, Arizona Western JC.
10. *Wesley Holmes, rhp, Garden City (Kan.) CC.
11. *Dennis Karlin, rhp, Garden City (Kan.) CC.

**January--Secondary Phase (19)**

1. *Carlton Cochrane, lhp, Central Arizona JC.--DNP
2. *Damon Allen, rhp, San Diego.
DRAFT DROP *Quarterback, Canadian Football League (1985-2007) • Brother, Marcus Allen, running back, National Football League (1982-97)*
3. *Louis Cedeno, rhp, West New York, N.J.

**June—Regular Phase (4)**

**1. Kevin Brown, rhp, Georgia Tech.—(1986-2005)**
**2. Roger Pavlik, rhp, Aldine HS, Houston.—(1992-98)**
**3. Dean Palmer, ss, Florida HS, Tallahassee, Fla.—(1989-2003)**
**4. *Rob Richie, of, University of Nevada-Reno.—(1989)**
DRAFT DROP *Returned to Nevada-Reno; re-drafted by Tigers, 1987 (2nd round)*
5. Scott Morse, rhp, University of Maine.—(AA)
6. Rick Raether, rhp, University of Miami.
**7. Mike Loynd, rhp, Florida State University.—(1986-87)**
DRAFT DROP *First player from 1986 draft to reach majors (July 24, 1986)*
8. Brad Fontes, c, McLane HS, Fresno, Calif.
9. *David Howell, lhp, Swampscott (Mass.) HS.
10. *Mike Belanger, lhp, Cal State Fullerton.
**11. John Barfield, lhp, Oklahoma City University.—(1989-91)**
12. Rick Bernardo, 1b, University of Maine.
**13. Rey Sanchez, ss, Live Oak HS, Morgan Hill, Calif.—(1991-2004)**
14. Ron Jackson, c, Texas Christian University.
15. Mike Scanlin, of, Texas A&M University.
16. Joe Pearn, c, Fairleigh Dickinson University.
17. Paul Postier, ss, Southeastern Oklahoma State University.
18. James McCutcheon, of, Clovis (Calif.) HS.
**19. Bob Malloy, rhp, University of Virginia.—(1987-90)**
20. Jose Velez, 1b-of, Chipola (Fla.) JC.
21. *Mark Juhas, rhp, Arcadia (Calif.) HS.
22. *William Bomar, c, Coeur d'Alene HS, Hayden Lake, Idaho.
23. Gary Lang, ss, University of Kansas.
**24. Wayne Rosenthal, rhp, St. John's University.—(1991-92)**
25. *Luke Sable, of, Geoge Mason University.
26. *Dean Weese, rhp, U.S. International (Calif.) University.
27. *Glenn Abraham, of, Howard University.
28. Gar Millay, 2b, University of Arizona.
29. Lucius Cole, of, Monacan HS, Richmond, Va.
30. Mike Spear, of, Manchester HS, Richmond, Va.

**June—Secondary Phase (2)**

1. Pat Garman, 3b, Cal State Fullerton.—(AAA)
2. *David Boss, rhp, San Jose (Calif.) CC.
3. *Elliot Quinones, of, Gulf Coast (Fla.) CC.
4. *Allen Rutledge, inf, Hillsborough (Fla.) CC.
5. *Brian McSwain, rhp, Spartanburg Methodist (S.C.) JC.

## TORONTO BLUE JAYS

**January—Regular Phase (26)**

1. Morgan Roderick, rhp, DeKalb Central (Ga.) JC.—(Short-season A)
2. Lindsay Foster, ss, Louisburg (N.C.) JC.
3. *Pat Mehrtens, lhp, Faulkner State (Ala.) JC.
4. *David Black, rhp, St. Louis CC-Meramec.
**5. Mark Whiten, of, Pensacola (Fla.) JC.—(1990-2000)**
6. *Peter Brown, rhp, Chipola (Fla.) JC.
7. *Chuck Johnson, inf, Laney (Calif.) JC.
8. *Michael Ordez, rhp, Merced (Calif.) JC.
**9. *Wade Taylor, rhp, Jefferson Davis (Ala.) JC.—(1991)**
10. *Dean DeCillis, 3b, Miami-Dade CC South.
11. *Greg Lonigro, ss, Florida JC-Jacksonville.
12. *Doug DeKock, c, Santa Fe (Fla.) CC.
13. *Vincent Davis, of, Gulf Coast (Fla.) CC.
14. *Rodney Brooks, rhp, Lurleen B. Wallace State (Ala.) JC.
15. *Glenn Moore, inf, Indian River (Fla.) CC.

**January—Secondary Phase (23)**

1. *Charlie White, of, Jefferson Davis (Ala.) JC.—(AA)
2. *Bruce Powers, of, Skyline (Calif.) JC.

**June—Regular Phase (26)**

1. Earl Sanders, rhp, Jackson State University.–(AA)
**2. Steve Cummings, rhp, University of Houston.—(1989-90)**
3. Andy Dziadkowiec, c, Quigley South HS, Chicago.—(AAA)
**4. Xavier Hernandez, rhp, University of Southwestern Louisiana.—(1989-98)**
**5. Pat Hentgen, rhp, Fraser (Mich.) HS.—(1991-2004)**
6. Jerry Schunk, ss, University of Toledo.
**7. *Cris Carpenter, rhp, University of Georgia.--(1988-96)**
DRAFT DROP *First-round draft pick (14th overall), Cardinals (1987)*
8. *Jimmy Long, rhp, Oklahoma State University.
9. Rich DePastino, rhp, Riverview HS, Sarasota, Fla.
**10. Randy Knorr, c-3b, Baldwin Park (Calif.) HS.—(1991-2001)**
**11. Willie Blair, rhp, Morehead State University.—(1990-2001)**
12. *Jose Salva, rhp, University of Southwestern Louisiana.
13. *Ron Lewis, ss, Raines HS, Jacksonville, Fla.
**14. Carlos Diaz, c, Oklahoma State University.—(1990)**
15. *Demetrius Smith, of, Gardena HS, Los Angeles.
**16. +Jimmy Rogers, rhp, Seminole (Okla.) JC.—(1995)**
17. John Shea, lhp, University of Connecticut.
18. *Jason Younker, of, North Bend HS, Coos Bay, Ore.
19. *James Moran, c, St. Joseph's University.
20. *Steve Surico, lhp, Tustin (Calif.) HS.
21. Barry Shifflett, of, University of North Carolina-Charlotte.
22. Joseph Ward, rhp, University of Rhode Island.
23. *Tony Lewis, rhp, Pepperdine University.
24. Robert Watts, ss, West Virginia University.
25. Richard Ironside, c, Nassau (N.Y.) CC.
26. *Mark Beck, rhp, Mayfair HS, Lakewood, Calif.
**27. Tom Quinlan, ss, Hill Murray HS, Maplewood, Minn.—(1990-96)**
DRAFT DROP *Fourth-round draft pick, Calgary Flames/ National Hockey League (1986) • Brother of Robb Quinlan, major leaguer (2003-07)*
**28. Darren Hall, rhp, Dallas Baptist University.—(1994-98)**
29. Bob Cavanaugh, rhp, Central Michigan University.
30. Andy Wortham, lhp, University of California.
31. Pat Rosenbauer, rhp, University of Toledo.
32. Ray McDonald, 3b, University of San Francisco.
33. *Sherman Collins, rhp, University of Oklahoma.
34. *Chris Woodfin, rhp, South Iredell HS, Statesville, N.C.
35. Gary Bockhorn, rhp, Southern Illinois University.
36. *Warren Holt, rhp, Aptos (Calif.) HS.
37. *John Dolak, c, Palisades HS, Malibu, Calif.
38. *Brian Goodwin, rhp, Frankfort (Ind.) HS.
39. *Tommy Hardgrove, 1b, Arlington Heights HS, Fort Worth, Texas.
40. *Glenn Baxley, 3b, Moreau HS, Union City, Calif.
41. *Steve Balstad, of, St. John Bosco HS, Buena Park, Calif.
42. Barry Morphew, ss, Alexandria (Ind.) HS.
**43. Doug Linton, rhp, UC Irvine.—(1992-2003)**
44. *David Freese, of, Springboro (Ohio) HS.

**June—Secondary Phase (16)**

**1. *John Briscoe, rhp, Texarkana (Texas) CC.—(1991-96)**
2. *David Keating, of, UCLA.
3. *Pat Mehrtens, lhp, Faulkner State (Ala.) JC.
4. *Andrew Nieman, rhp, Sinclair (Ohio) CC.
5. *Charlie White, of, Jefferson Davis (Ala.) JC.
6. *Scott Lerner, lhp, St. Mary's (Calif.) College.

# 1987

# Mariners make right call on Griffey at No. 1

When the Seattle Mariners drafted Ken Griffey Jr. with the No. 1 pick in 1987, they made history. Never before had the first pick been the son of a big leaguer—an active big leaguer, no less.

Two years later, when Griffey, then 19, became Seattle's Opening Day center fielder, he and his father, Ken Sr., 38, became the only father-son act ever to play in the majors simultaneously. The elder Griffey spent the 1989 season as a first baseman/outfielder for the Cincinnati Reds.

That was hardly the last of their exploits as a father-son tandem. On Aug. 31, 1990, they earned the distinction of appearing together in the same game, in the same outfield for the Mariners.

And then to top it all off, the Griffeys homered in the same game, back-to-back in the first inning on Sept. 14, 1990. Senior went deep to left-center field at Anaheim Stadium, and Junior followed suit by driving a 3-0 pitch to almost the same spot, making for one of the most electrifying moments in major league history.

Over the balance of the 1990 season, Griffey Sr. hit .377 playing alongside his son, and he hit .296 overall in a 19-year major league career. Yet there was no doubt in his mind who was the best player in the family. "He's got more power than I'll ever have," he said. "He hits a lot harder. At his age now, he's a lot faster than I ever was.

"I'm very proud of my son because he accomplished this on his own. I really didn't get to see him develop very much because I was away. He learned and he watched me over the years and picked up a few things."

In 22 seasons in the majors, Griffey hit 630 home runs, won 10 Gold Glove Awards and played in 13 All-Star Games. With those accomplishments, he added to his notoreity by becoming the first No. 1 overall pick inducted to the Hall of Fame in 2016.

While Griffey and his father agreed to terms with the Mariners on a $160,000 bonus the night before the 1987 draft, before that there had been doubt that Seattle, selecting first overall for the third time in its undistinguished 10-year history, would pay enough to sign Griffey, or any high school player.

Mariners owner George Argyros had announced his intention to sell the club earlier in the spring. With the franchise still in limbo, there were questions whether Argyros was committed to paying top dollar to get the best player possible.

"We have sufficient funds to get the top player," assured club president Chuck Armstrong. "And I mean the top player, not the player we can sign."

The pending sale of the Mariners never came to pass, but Argyros, known for meddling in his team's affairs, wanted a player who could contribute in the short term. He was pushing for Cal State Fullerton righthander Mike Harkey.

TOM DIPACE

**After considerable internal debate, the Mariners settled on Ken Griffey Jr. with the No. 1 overall pick; he not only went on to a Hall of Fame career but also was instrumental in saving baseball in Seattle**

In the end, the wisdom of general manager Dick Balderson, scouting director Roger Jongewaard and chief scout Bob Harrison prevailed, and the Mariners were rewarded many times over. Griffey was even credited for saving baseball in Seattle as he soon evolved into a franchise player and the marquee talent in the game.

Griffey was the first of 1,263 players drafted in 1987. That topped the previous record of 1,169 for a June draft, set in 1967. The sharp increase stemmed from a streamlining of the draft process, from four phases to one, all-encompassing phase. Not only were both January drafts abolished, but the June secondary phase was wiped out as well.

"The new draft has simplified things," Milwaukee Brewers scouting director Dan Duquette said. "It's taken away some artificial bargaining power. The talent in the January draft never equated with the talent in the June draft, but it's part of the psychology: players think that because they're a first-round pick, they deserve first-round money."

The Kansas City Royals were the last team to stop drafting, bowing out in the 74th round. That was 16 rounds less than the record they set in 1969 for a June regular phase, but Royals scouting director Art Stewart was convinced there was worthwhile talent still on the board.

"We kept drafting," Stewart said, "because we

## AT A GLANCE

### This Date In History
June 2-4

### Best Draft
**TEXAS RANGERS.** The first nine players the Rangers drafted all reached the big leagues—a draft record. In all, the Rangers drafted 14 players who reached the majors. The best of the bunch was righthander **ROBB NEN**, a 32nd-rounder who won 45 games and saved 314 more in a 10-year career.

### Worst Draft
**PITTSBURGH PIRATES.** The Pirates got off on the wrong foot by taking outfielder **MARK MERCHANT** with the second pick overall. Five of the nine future big leaguers they drafted didn't sign; the four that did combined to play in just 39 games for the Pirates.

### First-Round Bust
**BILL HENDERSON, C, TIGERS.** Henderson set national prep records for career hits and RBIs, but labored with the bat in three seasons in the minors, none above Class A. He played in 217 games, hitting .228-8-64 before deciding to call it quits.

### On Second Thought
**ALBERT BELLE, OF, INDIANS.** Based on his production over a tumultuous 12-year career, Belle should have been an easy call for the first round—just as his talent indicated during a prolific college career at Louisiana State. But the temper tantrums and petulant acts that characterized his time at LSU caused every club to pass over him in the first round.

### Late-Round Find
**STEVE FINLEY, OF, ORIOLES (13TH ROUND).** With a 19-year career that included a .271 average, 304 home runs, 1,167 RBIs and 320 stolen bases, Finley demonstrated many times over that he was a bargain as a college senior who

**CONTINUED ON PAGE 334**

## AT A GLANCE

CONTINUED FROM PAGE 333

signed for $5,000.

### Never Too Late

**TOM MARSH, RHP, BLUE JAYS (70TH ROUND).** Drafted as a pitcher out of the University of Toledo, Marsh returned to school for his senior year and came back out a year later as a hitter, and an 18th-round pick of the Phillies. He played three years in that role in the majors, hitting .246-5-34.

### Overlooked

**JOE SIDDALL, C, EXPOS.** A Canadian from just across the Michigan border, Siddall had a football scholarship to Central Michigan, but before he played a down with the Chippewas, he attended an Expos tryout camp and ended up signing after being offered a bonus of $10,000. Siddall played four seasons in the majors, hitting .169-1-11.

### International Gem

**JAVY LOPEZ, C, BRAVES.** Lopez, a Puerto Rican, signed with the Braves for $45,500 and went on to play 12 of his 15 major league seasons with the club. His best was his last, in 2003, when he hit .328 with 43 homers and 109 RBIs—all career highs. Overall, he had a .287 average and 260 homers—a substantially better return than the Brewers received for the $125,000 bonus they invested in righthander **RAMSER CORREA**, another Puerto Rican. Correa's 11-year minor league career was plagued by arm problems.

### Minor League Take

**KEN GRIFFEY JR., OF, MARINERS/CRAIG BIGGIO, C, ASTROS.** Success in the minors isn't always a harbinger of major league success, but it was in the case of these two Hall of Famers. No other first-rounders in 1987 enjoyed comparable success on their march to the majors, brief as their time in the minors was. Griffey hit .313-14-40 with

## 1987: THE FIRST ROUNDERS

| CLUB: PLAYER, POS., SCHOOL | HOMETOWN | B-T | HT. | WT. | AGE | BONUS | FIRST YEAR | LAST YEAR | PEAK LEVEL (YEARS) |
|---|---|---|---|---|---|---|---|---|---|
| 1. Mariners: Ken Griffey Jr., of, Moeller HS | Cincinnati | L-L | 6-3 | 185 | 17 | $160,000 | 1987 | 2010 | Majors (22) |
| Made draft history as son of major leaguer, later played alongside dad in Seattle OF; hit 630 homers in 22-year career, first No. 1 pick to reach Hall of Fame. | | | | | | | | | |
| 2. Pirates: Mark Merchant, of, Oviedo HS | Oviedo, Fla. | B-R | 6-1 | 185 | 18 | $165,000 | 1987 | 1997 | Class AAA (4) |
| Considered equal of Griffey on eve of draft; skilled hitter with raw power, speed, CF skills, but injury-plagued career never took off; hit .260-84-414 in minors. | | | | | | | | | |
| 3. Twins: Willie Banks, rhp, St. Anthony HS | Jersey City, N.J. | R-R | 6-1 | 190 | 18 | $160,000 | 1987 | 2003 | Majors (9) |
| Dominant HS arm (12-2, 0.65, 103 IP/199 SO) showed stuff of Dwight Gooden, athleticism of Bob Gibson; career never clicked as expected, went 33-39, 4.75. | | | | | | | | | |
| 4. Cubs: Mike Harkey, rhp, Cal State Fullerton | Diamond Bar, Calif. | R-R | 6-5 | 185 | 20 | $160,000 | 1987 | 1997 | Majors (8) |
| With impressive frame, 95 mph fastball, was darling of scouts, but never quite put it all together as Titans junior, or in injury-plagued major league career. | | | | | | | | | |
| 5. White Sox: Jack McDowell, rhp, Stanford | Van Nuys, Calif. | R-R | 6-5 | 175 | 21 | $165,000 | 1987 | 1999 | Majors (12) |
| Black Jack had maturity, mound presence, long/lean frame, impressive raw stuff; won CWS championship game, '93 Cy Young Award, 127 games in 12-year career. | | | | | | | | | |
| 6. Braves: Derek Lilliquist, lhp, Georgia | Sarasota, Fla. | L-L | 6-0 | 190 | 21 | $160,000 | 1987 | 1996 | Majors (8) |
| Markedly improved draft stock in breakout season (14-3, 2.24, 137 IP, 30 BB/190 SO), but struggled to live up to expectations in pros, went 25-34, 4.13 in majors. | | | | | | | | | |
| 7. Orioles: Chris Myers, lhp, H.B. Plant HS | Tampa | L-L | 6-2 | 185 | 18 | $160,000 | 1987 | 1992 | Class AAA (2) |
| High expectations based on dominant prep record (10-1, 0.20, 68 IP, 13 BB/130 SO), tailing fastball, changeup, command, poise; never came together in pro ball. | | | | | | | | | |
| 8. Dodgers: Dan Opperman, rhp, Valley HS | Las Vegas, Nev. | R-R | 6-3 | 175 | 18 | $160,000 | 1989 | 1992 | Class AA (2) |
| Mechanically perfect delivery, dominant raw stuff in 26-1 HS career, but had two elbow surgeries before his first pro pitch, fastball never returned to form. | | | | | | | | | |
| 9. Royals: Kevin Appier, rhp, Antelope Valley (Calif.) JC | Lancaster, Calif. | R-R | 6-2 | 180 | 19 | $105,000 | 1987 | 2006 | Majors (16) |
| Surprise first-rounder won 169 games over 16-year major league career on strength of deceptive, herky-jerky delivery, lively 89-92 fastball, solid command. | | | | | | | | | |
| 10. Padres: Kevin Garner, rhp/of, Texas | Midland, Mich. | L-R | 6-2 | 185 | 21 | $150,000 | 1987 | 1994 | Class AAA (3) |
| Two-way threat in college (.289-24-127/15-4); Padres wanted him as pitcher, but elbow injury in 1988 made him hitter in career ravaged by illness/injury. | | | | | | | | | |
| 11. Athletics: Lee Tinsley, of, Shelby County HS | Shelbyville, Ky. | B-R | 5-11 | 175 | 18 | $125,000 | 1987 | 1999 | Majors (5) |
| Purdue football recruit had athleticsm, speed; overmatched early in career, finally reached majors in seventh pro season, hit .241-13-79 with 41 steals. | | | | | | | | | |
| 12. Expos: Delino DeShields, ss/2b, Seaford HS | Seaford, Del. | L-R | 6-2 | 180 | 18 | $125,000 | 1987 | 2002 | Majors (13) |
| High-profile Villanova basketball recruit spent 12 years in majors (.268-80-561, 463 SBs), traded in 1993 by Expos to Dodgers for Pedro Martinez; father of Delino Jr. | | | | | | | | | |
| 13. Brewers: Bill Spiers, ss, Clemson | Cameron, S.C. | L-R | 6-3 | 192 | 21 | $150,000 | 1987 | 2001 | Majors (13) |
| Punter/shortstop at Clemson, hit .320-17-119 with 60 SBs; played 12 years in majors with Brewers/Astros (.271-37-388, 97 SBs), initially as SS, later in utility role. | | | | | | | | | |
| 14. Cardinals: Cris Carpenter, rhp, Georgia | Gainesville, Ga. | R-R | 6-2 | 185 | 22 | $160,000 | 1988 | 1996 | Majors (8) |
| One of nation's top punters decided to cast lot with baseball as ace closer (18 wins, 25 saves in 1986-87), but became starter in pros, fell short of expectations. | | | | | | | | | |
| 15. Orioles: Brad DuVall, rhp, Virginia Tech | Silver Spring, Md. | R-R | 6-1 | 180 | 21 | Unsigned | 1988 | 1990 | Class A (2) |
| Second of two Orioles first-rounders went 9-2, 2.54 as Hokies JR, decided to return to school; drafted by Cardinals in first round in '88, arm injury limited pro career. | | | | | | | | | |
| 16. Giants: Mike Remlinger, lhp, Dartmouth | Plymouth, Mass. | L-L | 6-0 | 195 | 21 | $115,000 | 1987 | 2004 | Majors (14) |
| Dominant Ivy League pitcher (career mark: 22-12, 2.14, 239 IP/337 SO), spun shutout in big league debut, worked in set-up role over bulk of 14-year MLB career. | | | | | | | | | |
| 17. Blue Jays: Alex Sanchez, rhp, UCLA | Antioch, Calif. | R-R | 6-2 | 170 | 21 | $100,000 | 1987 | 1995 | Majors (1) |
| Went 16-3, 4.06 as college SO, 6-7, 5.92 as JR; followed same curious pattern in pros, going 37-18, 2.90 in minors prior to brief MLB stint in 1989, 22-36 after. | | | | | | | | | |
| 18. Reds: Jack Armstrong, rhp, Oklahoma | Neptune, N.J. | R-R | 6-5 | 215 | 22 | $112,500 | 1987 | 2000 | Majors (7) |
| Third round with Rider in 1986, first round after transfer to Oklahoma; high-water mark came in 1990, won 12 games, one in World Series, started All-Star Game. | | | | | | | | | |
| 19. Rangers: Brian Bohanon, lhp, North Shore HS | Houston | L-L | 6-3 | 210 | 18 | $137,000 | 1987 | 2002 | Majors (12) |
| Went 17-2, 1.19 as prep SR, but heavy workload took a toll; missed most of first two years with arm issues, though won 54 games in 12-year major league career. | | | | | | | | | |
| 20. Tigers: Bill Henderson, c, Westminster Christian HS | Miami | R-R | 6-3 | 200 | 18 | $125,000 | 1987 | 1989 | Class A (2) |
| Set national prep records for career hits (203), RBIs (219), never came close to duplicating success in pro ball (.228-8-64) before abruptly quitting game. | | | | | | | | | |
| 21. Tigers: Steve Pegues, of, Pontotoc HS | Pontotoc, Miss. | R-R | 6-2 | 170 | 19 | $80,000 | 1987 | 1998 | Majors (2) |
| Spent two years in majors, hit .266-6-18 in 100 games, but pro career never came together; flashed all tools in high school, hit .495 with 59 RBIs, 62 steals as SR. | | | | | | | | | |
| 22. Astros: Craig Biggio, c, Seton Hall | Kings Park, N.Y. | R-R | 5-11 | 185 | 21 | $110,000 | 1987 | 2007 | Majors (20) |
| Capitalized on big season in college (.407-14-68, 30 SBs) to hit .344-12-90 with 50 SBs in minors, .281-291-1,175 with 414 steals in Hall of Fame career in majors. | | | | | | | | | |
| 23. Rangers: Bill Haselman, c, UCLA | Saratoga, Calif. | R-R | 6-3 | 205 | 21 | $82,500 | 1987 | 2003 | Majors (13) |
| Back-up QB to Troy Aikman at UCLA chose career in pro baseball; spent 13 years in majors as reserve catcher, hit .259-47-210, later became longtime coach. | | | | | | | | | |
| 24. Mets: Chris Donnels, 3b, Loyola Marymount | Torrance, Calif. | L-R | 6-0 | 185 | 21 | $89,500 | 1987 | 2004 | Majors (8) |
| Benefited from aluminum bat in college to hit .366, set school records in homers (45), RBIs (211), but hit just .233-17-86 in 450 games in eight seasons in majors. | | | | | | | | | |
| 25. Angels: John Orton, c, Cal Poly San Luis Obispo | Santa Cruz, Calif. | R-R | 6-0 | 175 | 21 | $83,000 | 1987 | 1996 | Majors (5) |
| Top-notch defensive catcher hit .348-11-30 as college JR, but bat never translated to pros; played five years in majors, hit .200-4-29, had four stints on disabled list. | | | | | | | | | |
| 26. Red Sox: Reggie Harris, rhp, Waynesboro HS | Waynesboro, Va. | R-R | 6-2 | 195 | 18 | $92,500 | 1987 | 2000 | Majors (6) |
| Had chance to play basketball at Virginia Tech, just like cousin Dell Curry, ex-NBA star; had mid-90s fastball, spent six years in majors (2-3, 4.91), twice a Rule 5 pick. | | | | | | | | | |

felt there was a lot of depth to the draft. There were some legitimate players through 55 rounds."

Stewart's intuition proved correct as the Royals ended up drafting five future major leaguers, including first baseman Jeff Conine, after the 57th round—after all but two clubs had dropped out.

The streamlined draft was part of a growing effort by teams to get a better grip on rising costs. Just as major league salaries had been rising, signing bonuses were climbing as well.

Commissioner Peter Ueberroth had chided club owners about overspending, especially as it applied to handing out exorbitant long-term contracts to major league free agents, but the escalation in bonuses to amateur free agents was also part of his message. Clubs eventually were charged with

## How They Should Have Done It

Based on the career WAR (Wins Above Replacement, as calculated by Baseball-Reference.com) numbers achieved by all the players eligible for the 1987 draft, here's how the first round should have unfolded. Numbers in parentheses indicate the round when the player was actually drafted. Asterisks denote players signed as draft-and-follows.

| Rank | Player, Pos. | Actual Draft | WAR | Bonus |
|---|---|---|---|---|
| 1. | Ken Griffey Jr., of | Mariners (1) | 83.7 | $160,000 |
| 2. | Craig Biggio, c | Astros (1) | 64.9 | $110,000 |
| 3. | Kevin Appier, rhp | Royals (1) | 54.9 | $105,000 |
| 4. | Steve Finley, of | Orioles (13) | 44.1 | $10,000 |
| 5. | Albert Belle, of | Indians (2) | 39.8 | $80,000 |
| 6. | * Reggie Sanders, of | Reds (7) | 39.6 | $51,000 |
| 7. | Ray Lankford, of | Cardinals (3) | 37.9 | $30,000 |
| 8. | Travis Fryman, ss | Tigers (1-S) | 34.3 | $75,000 |
| 9. | Jack McDowell, rhp | White Sox (1) | 28.2 | $165,000 |
| 10. | Delino DeShields, ss/2b | Expos (1) | 24.3 | $125,000 |
| 11. | * Darryl Kile, rhp | Astros (30) | 20.4 | $100,000 |
| 12. | Mike Timlin, rhp | Blue Jays (5) | 19.6 | $22,000 |
| | Jeff Conine, 3b | Royals (58) | 19.6 | $7,500 |
| 14. | Pete Harnisch, rhp | Orioles (1-S) | 18.2 | $80,000 |
| 15. | Dave Hollins, 3b | Padres (6) | 17.7 | $24,500 |
| 16. | Dave Burba, rhp | Mariners (2) | 16.7 | $70,000 |
| 17. | Brad Ausmus, c | Yankees (48) | 16.4 | $20,000 |
| 18. | Scott Brosius, 3b | Athletics (20) | 15.8 | $10,000 |
| 19. | Robb Nen, rhp | Rangers (32) | 15.4 | $50,500 |
| 20. | Mike Stanton, lhp | Braves (13) | 14.9 | $15,000 |
| 21. | Derek Bell, of | Blue Jays (2) | 13.0 | $67,500 |
| 22. | Mike Remlinger, lhp | Giants (1) | 10.9 | $115,000 |
| 23. | Todd Hundley, c | Mets (2) | 10.8 | $75,000 |
| 24. | David Segui, 1b | Orioles (18) | 10.4 | $1,000 |
| 25. | Bill Spiers, ss | Brewers (1) | 10.3 | $150,000 |
| 26. | Steve Sparks, rhp | Brewers (5) | 10.1 | $13,000 |
| | Gil Heredia, rhp | Giants (9) | 10.1 | $1,500 |

| | Top 3 Unsigned Players | | | Year Signed |
|---|---|---|---|---|
| 1. | Mike Mussina, rhp | Orioles (11) | 83.0 | 1990 |
| 2. | Jeff Cirillo, 3b/rhp | Cubs (37) | 34.4 | 1991 |
| 3. | Scott Erickson, rhp | Astros (34) | 25.1 | 1989 |

collusion when the courts determined they had conspired with one another to limit the movement of free agents and suppress salaries. But those charges didn't fully come to light until after the 1987 draft. It was no coincidence that bonuses to the top players not only dipped from the previous two years, but were orchestrated in such a way that the top picks received almost identical amounts.

Griffey's $160,000 bonus was $20,000 less than what top pick Jeff King received in 1986, and $19,000 below the amount Bobby Witt received as the highest-paid player two years earlier. Each of the first eight picks in 1987 received amounts ranging from $160,000 to $165,000.

A year later, with collusion exposed, signing bonuses began moving to record levels and never stopped over the next two decades, as a period of inflation took the draft into a new realm.

### SWING BACK TO PREP TALENT

Unlike the previous two years when the first four players came from the college ranks, the 1987 draft saw a swing to high school talent. Led by Griffey, the first three selections were from the prep ranks.

The Pittsburgh Pirates, selecting second, went for outfielder Mark Merchant from Oviedo, Fla.; the Minnesota Twins followed by taking righthander Willie Banks from Jersey City, N.J.

In some quarters, the switch-hitting Merchant was considered Griffey's equal, and with his combination of raw power and speed even drew comparisons to Mickey Mantle. He hit .419 with five homers and 48 stolen bases in 49 attempts his senior year at Oviedo High. Like Griffey, Merchant agreed to terms with the Pirates prior to the draft, on a $165,000 bonus.

Merchant didn't reach the big leagues in a 12-year pro career—four of it spent in the Seattle system, oddly enough, after he was dealt to the Mariners in 1989.

Banks was regarded as the dominant arm in the 1987 class. He was compared to Bob Gibson and Dwight Gooden at St. Anthony High, while compiling a 12-2, 0.65 record with 199 strikeouts in 103 innings.

"Their ability to throw a good major league fastball, their ability to throw a good curveball and their composure are equal," Twins scout Herb Stein said. "I was there when Gooden broke the Carolina League strikeout record (300) at Lynchburg (in 1983) and it wouldn't surprise me if Willie does the same darn thing."

Banks pitched nothing like Gooden in his first two pro seasons, but he showed signs of putting it all together in 1989, throwing a no-hitter and leading the Class A California League with 173 strikeouts in 174 innings.

MEL BAILEY
Willie Banks

He always flashed impressive raw stuff, but Banks struggled to throw strikes consistently and ended up as a career journeyman. He played for seven different teams over nine big league seasons and went 33-39, 4.75 with 302 walks and 428 strikeouts in 610 innings. He pitched in the affiliated minors until 2003, had stints in Japan in 1999 and 2000, and pitched in independent ball in four seasons before hanging it up in 2010.

For Griffey, on the other hand, his road to greatness seemed like destiny.

He grew up in Cincinnati, the son of one of the Big Red Machine's main cogs. It was hard to impress a kid who had grown up with Pete Rose, Joe Morgan, Johnny Bench and Dave Concepcion and played against them in father-son games.

Everything came so easy, so naturally for Griffey—even when he became the Opening Day center fielder for the Mariners as a teenager.

"Anyone else who was 19," said Mike Cameron, his coach at Cincinnati's Moeller High, "I'd say for the benefit of the kid's future, not to throw him into the circus. Let him grow up a bit. But not Kenny. He's not in awe of the press, not in awe of the players."

Griffey did not play baseball his first two years at Moeller High, sitting out his freshman year because of poor grades then missing his sophomore season when he chose to attend spring training with his father in Florida.

### AT A GLANCE

49 stolen bases in 130 games; Biggio hit .344-12-90 with 50 steals in 141 games.

#### One Who Got Away

**MIKE MUSSINA, RHP, ORIOLES (11TH ROUND).** With a reported price tag of $350,000, Mussina went from a slam-dunk first-rounder to an 11th-rounder. After three years at Stanford, he established his rightful place in the first round of the 1990 draft. He was selected by the Orioles again out of college. He affirmed what all the fuss was about in high school by assembling a 270-153, 3.68 record in 18 major league seasons.

#### He Was Drafted?

**TOI COOK, OF, TWINS (38TH ROUND).** Cook was a four-year regular in both baseball and football at Stanford, and led the Cardinal to the 1987 College World Series in his role as the team's leadoff hitter. Over his career, he hit .317 with 157 RBIs and 85 stolen bases. But Cook chose to pursue a football career as a defensive back. An eighth-round pick of the New Orleans Saints in 1987, he played 11 years in the NFL.

#### Did You Know . . .

Nineteen of 26 second-round draft picks in 1987 reached the majors. At 73.1 percent, that was the highest success rate of any second round on record.

#### They Said It

Moeller High baseball coach **MIKE CAMERON** on **KEN GRIFFEY JR.**, when he showed up to play baseball as an 11th-grader: "I had heard all the rumors about what a great player Kenny was. And then he swings at the first 10 pitches and he misses every single one. He pulled his head. He looked awful. I said, 'That's terrible. You missed every pitch. That swing will have to go.' He said, 'Nah, that's the Griffey swing.' "

## DRAFT SPOTLIGHT: ALBERT BELLE

Scouts always said that Joey Belle had major league tools. The problem was, he also had a major league attitude problem.

In 1987 at Louisiana State University, Belle had a number of run-ins with fans and Tigers coach Skip Bertman. One day he went a step too far.

He left the field to charge after a fan who had hurled racial slurs at him during the Southeastern Conference tournament. Later in the game, Belle hit an apparent home run, but instead of running on contact, he stood at the plate, admiring it. When the ball bounced off the fence—not over it—he raced to first base for an extremely long single.

Known as Joey as an amateur and early in his pro career, Albert Belle balanced his temper with impressive on-field performance

Bertman suspended Belle for the rest of the season. It came at a critical juncture for LSU as it was about to embark on an appearance in the College World Series, and Belle's potent bat (.331-49-172 over three years) would leave a significant void. The 1987 draft was also right around the corner and Belle was projected as one of the top players in the country. When draft day came, Belle fell out of the first round. The Cleveland Indians took him in round two, 47th overall.

To Bertman, Belle was a classic case of Dr. Jekyll and Mr. Hyde during his productive, but stormy career at LSU. "The disparity in his on-field and off-field personality is the greatest of any player I've ever coached," Bertman said. "Except for that one flaw in his baseball personality, self-control after making an out, he's a great kid."

A good student at LSU with a major in accounting, Belle was friendly off the field. But on the field, failure could trigger a tantrum. He'd fail to run out ground balls. He was distracted easily by taunting fans. Scouts eying his every move magnified everything.

On ability, almost every club viewed Belle as the best everyday college player in the country. But none drafted him where his talent warranted because of his history of emotional outbursts and the negative backlash he generated. The Indians, who had no first-round selection, took him in the second round. It took them until Aug. 20 to sign him for $80,000, roughly half of what he would have received as an early first-rounder.

Belle repeated his temper tantrums and insubordination in the pro ranks. Twice during the 1988 season he was suspended. He was kicked off his winter league club. The Indians had a long talk with Belle when he reported for the 1989 season, and their message was cut-and-dried. "They told me they are not going to tolerate my actions any longer," Belle said. "They told me one more incident and my professional baseball career would probably be over. That will change your attitude real quick."

Belle became a model citizen at Double-A Canton, and after a productive season earned his first big-league promotion. But the bad behavior soon returned and he challenged the Cleveland organization time and again. In 1990, after being suspended yet again, he returned from a lengthy absence to announce that he had been treated for alcoholism. He also declared that he wanted to be known as Albert, his given name.

As Albert Belle, he was a destructive force. In eight seasons in Cleveland, Belle hit .295 with 242 homers and 751 RBIs. He homered 50 times on one occasion, led the league in RBIs three times.

Through all of his behavior issues at the college and minor league levels, and especially during his 12-year career in the majors, Belle was an intimidating presence at the plate, and his performance led to clubs working with him to help him exorcise his demons.

"At times you wonder why you want to keep paying the price for that behavior," said Dan O'Dowd, Indians assistant general manager at the time of Belle's departure from the club in 1996. "But this game is all about winning. And we began to see the ability that was there with Albert. We tried to see the positives."

The 6-foot-3, 190-pound lefthander hit .478 with 11 homers as a junior, then hit .484 with seven homers his senior year. His impressive high school record, coupled with his heritage, made Griffey a tough act for the Mariners to overlook in the 1987 draft.

"Ken has got great bloodlines and lots of talent," said Jongewaard, on whose recommendation the New York Mets took Darryl Strawberry with the No. 1 pick in 1980. "There's nothing he can't do above average. But what really sold us were his instincts for the game and his power potential."

### CHICAGO CLUBS GRAB COLLEGE ARMS

For all the emphasis on high school talent in the 1987 draft, 10 of the first 18 players taken were college pitchers. The first two college players drafted were 6-foot-5 righthanders from California who went to the two Chicago teams.

The Cubs, selecting fourth, went for Harkey (10-2, 2.72), while the White Sox took Jack McDowell (13-5, 4.13), who hurled Stanford to the first of consecutive College World Series titles. McDowell also became the first player from the Class of 1987 to reach the big leagues.

Mike Harkey

At the outset of the 1987 season, the 6-foot-5 Harkey was a favorite to be the No. 1 pick in the draft. He had size and a 95 mph fastball, and physically was everything scouts looked for in an elite prospect. But Harkey's mechanics and mental toughness were questioned the better part of the spring, and he slipped to fourth overall.

It didn't take long for Harkey to reach Chicago as he breezed through the minors, and he projected as a top rookie candidate in 1989. But he missed that season and most of two of the next three for the Cubs with an assortment of knee, elbow and shoulder injuries, and his career quickly became one of unfulfilled expectations. In eight seasons, he won just 36 games.

McDowell achieved a feat in 1987 matched only once before in draft history.

After pitching Stanford to the NCAA title, he was the top pick of the White Sox and capped his whirlwind success story by pitching in the big leagues that season—going an impressive 3-0,

### Fastest To The Majors

| | Player, Pos. | Drafted (Round) | Debut |
|---|---|---|---|
| 1. | Jack McDowell, rhp | White Sox (1) | Sept. 15, 1987 |
| 2. | Cris Carpenter, rhp | Cardinals (1) | May 14, 1988 |
| 3. | Jack Armstrong, rhp | Reds (1) | June 21, 1988 |
| 4. | Craig Biggio, c | Astros (1) | June 26, 1988 |
| 5. | Dave Eiland, rhp | Yankees (7) | Aug. 3, 1988 |

**FIRST HIGH SCHOOL SELECTION:** Ken Griffey Jr., of (Mariners/1, April 3, 1989)

**LAST PLAYER TO RETIRE:** Brad Ausmus, c (Oct. 3, 2010)

## Top 25 Bonuses

| | Player, Pos. | Drafted (Round) | Order | Bonus |
|---|---|---|---|---|
| 1. | * Mark Merchant, of | Pirates (1) | 2 | $165,000 |
| | **Jack McDowell, rhp** | **White Sox (1)** | **5** | **$165,000** |
| 3. | *** Ken Griffey Jr., of** | **Mariners (1)** | **1** | **$160,000** |
| | *** Willie Banks, rhp** | **Twins (1)** | **3** | **$160,000** |
| | **Mike Harkey, rhp** | **Cubs (1)** | **4** | **$160,000** |
| | **Derek Lilliquist, lhp** | **Braves (1)** | **6** | **$160,000** |
| | * Chris Myers, lhp | Orioles (1) | 7 | $160,000 |
| | * Dan Opperman, rhp | Dodgers (1) | 8 | $160,000 |
| | **Cris Carpenter, rhp** | **Cardinals (1)** | **14** | **$160,000** |
| 10. | Kevin Garner, rhp/of | Padres (1) | 10 | $150,000 |
| | **Bill Spiers, ss** | **Brewers (1)** | **13** | **$150,000** |
| 12. | *** Brian Bohanon, lhp** | **Rangers (1)** | **19** | **$137,000** |
| 13. | *** Delino DeShields, ss** | **Expos (1)** | **12** | **$125,000** |
| | *** Lee Tinsley, of** | **Athletics (1)** | **11** | **$125,000** |
| | * Bill Henderson, c | Tigers (1) | 20 | $125,000 |
| 16. | **Mike Remlinger, lhp** | **Giants (1)** | **16** | **$115,000** |
| 17. | * Vince Phillips, of | Yankees (13) | 341 | $113,000 |
| 18. | **Jack Armstrong, rhp** | **Reds (1)** | **18** | **$112,500** |
| 19. | * Donnie Carroll, of | Dodgers (2) | 40 | $112,000 |
| 20. | **Craig Biggio, c** | **Astros (1)** | **22** | **$110,000** |
| 21. | **Kevin Appier, rhp** | **Royals (1)** | **9** | **$105,000** |
| | Tyrone Kingwood, of | Expos (1-S) | 28 | $105,000 |
| 23. | **Alex Sanchez, rhp** | **Blue Jays (1)** | **17** | **$100,000** |
| | *** David Holdridge, rhp** | **Angels (1-S)** | **31** | **$100,000** |
| | **# Darryl Kile, rhp** | **Astros (30)** | **782** | **$100,000** |

*Major leaguers in bold. *High school selection. #Signed as draft-and-follow.*

1.93 in a four-game trial in September. Only Jim Gideon, who pitched Texas to victory in the 1975 College World Series, was drafted in the first round by the Texas Rangers and debuted with that club in September, duplicated McDowell's rare triple play.

Unlike Gideon, who pitched in only one game in his big league career, McDowell won 127 games over a 12-year period. He was a two-time 20-game winner, including 1993, when he won the American League Cy Young Award by going 22-10, 3.37. McDowell had a stormy relationship with the White Sox in his seven-year tenure in Chicago. He took his club to arbitration three times and repeatedly questioned the way he was handled.

The University of Georgia played in its first College World Series in 1987, on the strength of two pitchers who were drafted in the first round: lefthander Derek Lilliquist, selected sixth overall by the Atlanta Braves, and righthander Cris Carpenter, picked 14th by the St. Louis Cardinals. Both players held out until August before signing for the same amount, $160,000.

Lilliquist went 14-3, 2.24 overall and demolished Georgia's season strikeout record by fanning 190 in 137 innings. As the team's DH, he also contributed 19 home runs. He elevated himself from a projected third-round pick to a first-rounder—and became the first college pitcher the Braves drafted with their top pick since 1980.

As a pro Lilliquist thought he needed to throw harder, and he changed his delivery to generate more velocity, but struggled in the process and went just 10-18, 4.59 in two seasons with the Braves. He became a reliever with four other clubs over the balance of his eight-year career, going 25-34, 4.13 with 17 saves.

Carpenter, by contrast, was clearly a reliever at Georgia, saving a school-record 14 games in 1986 and 11 more as a redshirt junior, but became mostly a starter in pro ball. Carpenter also played eight years in the majors with a variety of clubs and went 27-22, 3.91 with seven saves.

Like Georgia, UCLA had two players drafted in the first round: righthander Alex Sanchez, who went 17th overall to the Toronto Blue Jays, and catcher Bill Haselman, taken 23rd by the Rangers.

The Jays were gambling that Sanchez, who felt the pressures of the draft and posted a 6-7, 5.92 record, would return to his sophomore form, when he set a school record by winning 16 games. He pitched impressively in three seasons in the minors, going 37-18, 2.90 with 484 strikeouts in 470 innings and was the most valuable pitcher in the Triple-A International League in 1989, which led to his big league debut late in the 1989 season.

But in four starts for Toronto, Sanchez went 0-1, 10.03, and that would be as good as it got. A power pitcher with control on his climb to the big leagues, Sanchez mysteriously lost velocity on his fastball and struggled to throw strikes thereafter.

Arm problems impacted the careers of most of the other college pitchers drafted in the first round.

Dartmouth lefthander Mike Remlinger became the top pick of the San Francisco Giants (16th overall) and only the fourth Ivy Leaguer to go in the first round after leading NCAA Division I pitchers with an average of 14.0 strikeouts per nine innings. Overall, he fanned 132 in 85 innings as a junior, while going 9-2, 2.44.

Remlinger maintained his strikeout touch in his first pro season, fanning 105 in 69 innings, but elbow problems for the better part of the next 10 years short-circuited his career—save for a shutout he pitched for the Giants in his major league debut in 1991. But at age 31, Remlinger suddenly blossomed. Beginning in 1997, he pitched in 588 games, winning 50 times, before retiring at 40.

Oklahoma righthander Jack Armstrong was drafted 18th overall by the Reds, a year after being taken in the third round out of New Jersey's Rider College. He had gambled that he could significantly improve his draft position as a senior by transferring to a bigger college program, and succeeded.

His shining moment came in 1990, when he started the All-Star Game for the National League on the strength of an 11-3, 2.28 record at midseason, and worked two scoreless innings. He won just one more game in 1990—though he did come out of the bullpen to win a game for the Reds in the World Series. He went 23-52 over the balance of his career, which ended in 1994, for all intents and purposes, when he tore the rotator cuff in his pitching shoulder.

Texas righthander Kevin Garner, drafted 10th overall by the San Diego Padres, lasted just one season as a pitcher after injuring his elbow, though he played for another 12 years as a position player. Virginia Tech righthander Brad DuVall, drafted 15th by the Baltimore Orioles, was the lone first-round pick who didn't sign. He was chosen in the first round again a year later by the Cardinals, but an arm injury ended his career after three seasons, none above Class A.

### WORTH NOTING

■ Puerto Rican righthander **RAMSER CORREA**, 16, set a bonus record for foreign talent in 1987 by signing with the Brewers for $125,000—part of an overall package that amounted to some $225,000, when the cost of a major league contract after three years in the minors, four airplane tickets a year for his family to see him pitch and two cars were factored in. As a Seventh-Day Adventist, Correa also dictated that he would not pitch between sundown Friday and sundown Saturday. The 6-foot-5 Correa spent 11 years in the minors with the Brewers, Indians and Dodgers, and won just 26 games. His career was plagued almost throughout by arm problems after he had elbow and shoulder surgery early in his tenure with the Brewers. In 1982, Correa's older brother Edwin had established a signing-bonus record of $50,000, when he signed with the White Sox. He played in the majors for three seasons, before arm problems ended his career.

■ Stanford won the 1987 College World Series, beating Oklahoma State 9-5 in the final. Righthander **JACK MCDOWELL**, a first-round choice of the White Sox, was the only Stanford player drafted in the first 10 rounds. In all, six Cardinal were selected, including outfielders **RUBEN AMARO JR.**, an 11th-rounder (Angels) who later became general manager of the Phillies, and

CONTINUED ON PAGE 338

**WORTH NOTING**

CONTINUED FROM PAGE 337

**TOI COOK**, a 38th-rounder (Twins) who passed up the opportunity to play baseball professionally for a long career in the NFL.

■ The NCAA Division I leaders in home runs and stolen bases in 1987 were not drafted. Brigham Young catcher Mike Willes was passed over despite hitting 31 home runs, to go with a .439 average and 108 RBIs. He returned as a college senior in 1988, and again topped the nation in homers, with 35. Texas-Pan American outfielder Don Guillot stole an NCAA record 107 bases, but also found no takers. Another collegian of note who was not drafted (because he was not eligible for selection) was Oklahoma State sophomore third baseman Robin Ventura, who went on a remarkable 58-game hitting streak that finally ended in the College World Series. Ventura, who was drafted in the first round by the White Sox in 1988, led the nation with 110 RBIs.

■ The Tigers drafted Georgia Tech two-sport star **RICCARDO INGRAM** in the fourth round after he hit .426-17-99 with 17 steals as a junior. They believed they had lost their rights to him when he elected to return to school for his senior year, to play both football and baseball. But Ingram was declared ineligible by the NCAA with two games remaining in the 1987 football season for accepting money from an agent. Because that indiscretion also disqualified him from playing baseball during his senior season, the commissioner's office ruled that the rights to sign Ingram would be restored to the Tigers. They were given until May 25, 1988, to sign him, or he would go back into the draft pool. Ingram had hoped to be picked in the NFL draft in April, but was passed over. He decided to sign with the Tigers on May 22, for a bonus of $40,000. He had a 10-year professional career but ended up playing in just 16 major league games over two seasons. After his playing

## BELLE ANTICS UPSTAGE DRAFT

With the notable exception of temperamental Louisiana State outfielder Joey Belle, the quality of position players in the 1986 college crop was thought to be substandard. The first such player drafted was Clemson shortstop Bill Spiers, selected 13th overall by the Brewers, and he went on to play 13 years in the majors.

In the end, college position players proved to be the strongest demographic in the draft.

Seton Hall catcher Craig Biggio, selected 22nd overall by the Houston Astros, became the first player from the class to be inducted into the Hall of Fame.

Belle lasted until the second round because of his behavior in a controversial three-year career at Louisiana State, but he had a significant major league career, as did outfielder Steve Finley, who wasn't drafted until the 13th round.

Had he not been suspended by LSU prior to NCAA regional play, Belle probably would have been one of the first handful of players drafted. He was hitting .349 with 21 home runs when he was suspended for leaving the field to chase a Mississippi State fan who shouted racial slurs at him during the championship game of the Southeastern Conference tournament in Athens, Ga.

The Cleveland Indians didn't have a first-round pick and rolled the dice by taking Belle in the second. They were able to sign him for a bonus of $80,000 after a lengthy holdout.

"We felt his ability outweighed some of the downside, and we felt that some of the downside was not as bad as reported," Indians scouting director Jeff Scott said. "But 46 people went ahead of him in the draft, and we had to treat him as such in negotiations."

Several more acts of defiance in the minor leagues almost ended Belle's career, but he eventually reached Cleveland in 1989. He became one of the game's most prolific power hitters in a 12-year career, though controversy continued to follow him.

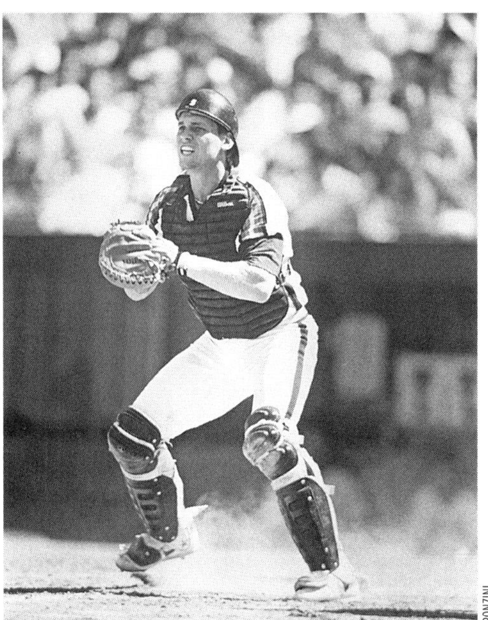

PONZINI

Craig Biggio started his Hall of Fame career as a catcher, later playing second base and center field and piling up more than 3,000 hits

### Largest Bonuses By Round

| | Player, Pos. | Club | Bonus |
|---|---|---|---|
| 1. | * Mark Merchant, of | Pirates | $165,000 |
| | **Jack McDowell, rhp** | **White Sox** | **$165,000** |
| 2. | * Donnie Carroll, of | Dodgers | $112,000 |
| 3. | * Tom Redington, ss | Braves | $92,000 |
| **4.** | *** Keith Mitchell, of** | **Braves** | **$80,000** |
| 5. | * Dennis Burlingame, rhp | Braves | $60,000 |
| **6.** | *** Greg Colbrunn, 3b** | **Expos** | **$85,000** |
| **7.** | ***# Donnie Elliott, rhp** | **Phillies** | **$50,000** |
| **8.** | **# James Byrd, ss** | **Red Sox** | **$40,000** |
| | * Kevin Shaw, rhp | Royals | $40,000 |
| 9. | Steve Wilson, rhp | Athletics | $30,000 |
| 10. | Brian Steiner, lhp | Rangers | $40,000 |
| 11. | * Ed Martel, rhp | Yankees | $80,500 |
| 12. | Winston Relaford, of | Braves | $40,000 |
| 13. | * Vince Phillips, of | Yankees | $133,000 |
| **14.** | *** David Nied, rhp** | **Braves** | **$75,000** |
| **15.** | *** Butch Henry, lhp** | **Reds** | **$60,000** |
| 16. | *# Billy Reed, lhp | Padres | $19,000 |
| 17. | *# Wayne Weinheimer, of | Cubs | $20,000 |
| 18. | Bill Losa, c | Rangers | $22,500 |
| 19. | * Scott Taylor, c | Cubs | $20,000 |
| 20. | Jose Munoz, ss | Dodgers | $15,000 |
| **21.** | **# Mark Kiefer, rhp** | **Brewers** | **$30,000** |
| 22. | * Scott Grove, rhp | Braves | $12,500 |
| 23. | * Joe Roebuck, 3b/ss | Brewers | $30,000 |
| 24. | * Stanton Cameron, of | Mets | $17,500 |
| 25. | # Virgil Cooper, rhp | White Sox | $20,000 |
| **Other** | **# Darryl Kile, rhp** | **Astros (30)** | **$100,000** |

*Major leaguers in bold. *High school selection. #Signed as draft-and-follow.*

Biggio, by contrast, was a franchise icon throughout his 20-year career, all spent with the Astros. He excelled by hitting .281 with 3,060 hits and 291 home runs—all while playing three diverse positions. His 668 doubles were the most by a righthanded hitter in big league history.

As a junior at Seton Hall, Biggio hit .407 with 14 homers and 30 stolen bases in 32 attempts. But he was nearly lost in the shuffle in a stacked Pirates lineup, as first baseman Marteese Robinson (.529-16-90, 58 SB) led the nation in batting and hits (126), and became a sixth-round pick in the 1987 draft, and freshman DH Mo Vaughn (.429-28-90) became a first-round pick in 1989.

Drafted as a catcher and signed for $110,000, Biggio excelled at that position in the minors for two years and four more in the majors, earning all-stars honors in 1991 before moving to second base in 1992. The Astros sold the 5-foot-11, 180-pound Biggio on the move, saying that his speed and quickness would become greater assets at his new position, while his career would be extended. Biggio adjusted to second base quickly and established himself as a five-time all-star. He later moved to center field. All the while, he was a hustling, consistent leadoff man with unusual power.

## JUNIOR COLLEGES PLAY KEY ROLE

The end of the January draft placed more emphasis on junior-college talent. One of the outgrowths of the consolidation of the draft into a single phase was a new "draft-and-follow" approach, which provided teams the opportunity to draft players headed for junior college and control their rights until a week before the following year's draft. If a player went unsigned, he simply became part of the next draft pool.

From the 1986 draft, 20 players signed the following spring as draft-and-follows. That included the likes of Florida CC-Jacksonville catcher Rick Wilkins, a 23rd-round pick of the Cubs who made significant progress as a sophomore and signed for $125,000. Had Wilkins gone back into the 1987 draft, he would have warranted first-round consideration. Seminole (Okla.) College righthander Jimmy Rogers, a 16th-round pick of the Blue Jays in 1986, also profited handsomely by waiting as he agreed to a $100,000 bonus.

From the 1987 draft, 48 players signed the next spring as draft-and-follows.

Most prominent was righthander Darryl Kile, an unheralded 30th-round pick of the Astros who returned to Chaffey (Calif.) JC as a sophomore and blossomed into a legitimate prospect. He secured a $100,000 bonus. Kile won 133 games in a 12-year big league career, including 20 in 2000, before he died suddenly as an active major leaguer in 2002 from coronary disease.

Outfielder Reggie Sanders, a product of Spartanburg Methodist (S.C.), signed with the Reds for $51,000 after being drafted in the seventh round in 1987. Like Kile, he proved to be a wise investment as he played 17 years in the majors, hitting .267 with 305 homers while stealing 304 bases.

Not every junior-college player drafted in 1987 waited to sign.

Antelope Valley (Calif.) JC righthander Kevin Appier signed with the Royals for $105,000 shortly after being selected with the ninth overall pick. He had spent his freshman year at Fresno State and would have been ineligible to be drafted had he remained in school there, but became eligible by transferring to a junior college. He signed for substantially less than all eight of the players drafted before him, but proved to be a bargain for the Royals as he won 169 games in his career, including 115 in a Kansas City uniform.

Outfielder Ray Lankford, drafted in the third round by the Cardinals out of Modesto (Calif.) JC, was another astute junior-college selection. Signed for $30,000, Lankford played 14 seasons in the majors, 13 with the Cardinals, and hit .272 with 238 homers, while stealing 258 bases.

### DIFFERENT PATHS FOR PREP STARS

Based on their performance for Team USA, the bronze medalists at the 1986 World Junior Championship, two must-see players for scouts heading into the 1987 draft were righthanders Mike Mussina, from Montoursville (Pa.) High, and Dan Opperman, from Valley High in Las Vegas.

Mussina shackled Cuba, the gold-medal-winning squad, in a dominating 1-0 win in pool play, allowing five hits, walking one and striking out 16. Opperman stood out in a two-way role, hitting a team-high .429 while going 0-1, 1.08 with 12 strikeouts in eight innings.

Both players were in the running to become the top pick in the 1987 draft until Griffey surged ahead of the field, but their talent certainly ranked with Merchant and Banks, who were chosen second and third. Opperman went eighth overall to the Los Angeles Dodgers, while Mussina tumbled all the way to the 11th round, where he was taken by the Orioles.

Dan Opperman

Opperman's stock dropped marginally because of concerns that he hurt his arm in his final pitching appearance for Valley High, while Mussina's $350,000 price tag scared off every team.

In Opperman's case, the concerns were well founded. After compiling a 26-1 record in four prep seasons with a 93-95 mph fastball, he developed pain in his right elbow. It was thought to be fatigue, but Opperman had it checked out by a physical therapist and a local orthopedic surgeon, and even flew to Los Angeles to have Dodgers team surgeon Dr. Frank Jobe assess it.

Jobe said everything looked OK, and the Dodgers took Opperman with their top pick. A $160,000 bonus persuaded him to give up a scholarship to the University of Texas, but he blew out his elbow in his first workout after reporting to Rookie-level Great Falls.

Jobe performed Tommy John surgery on Opperman's elbow on July 17, and he returned to Great Falls in 1988 with the hope he could pitch by late summer. But pain persisted when he threw in the bullpen, and for the second straight season he didn't work an inning as Jobe had to operate again to remove scar tissue.

Scouting director Ben Wade long defended the choice. "What would you have done if your doctor told you the kid was fine?" Wade asked. "I had no

## One Team's Draft: Montreal Expos

| Player, Pos. | Bonus | Player, Pos. | Bonus | Player, Pos. | Bonus |
|---|---|---|---|---|---|
| **1. *Delino DeShields, ss** | **$125,000** | **9. *Donovan Osborne, lhp** | **Did not sign** | **19. Jeff Carter, rhp** | **$1,000** |
| 1. Tyrone Kingwood, of | $105,000 | 10. Chris Pollack, lhp | $2,500 | 20. Matt Shiflett, rhp | $1,000 |
| **2. *Nate Minchey, rhp** | **$87,500** | 11. *Steve Lemuth, of | $14,000 | 21. Rob Mason, c | $1,000 |
| **2. Richie Lewis, rhp** | **$85,000** | 12. Chris Marchok, lhp | $4,000 | 22. Tom Giannelli, 1b | $1,000 |
| **3. John Vanderwal, of** | **$40,000** | **13. Rob Natal, c** | **$1,000** | 23. Kevin Cavalier, rhp | $2,000 |
| 4. Boi Rodriguez, 3b | $42,000 | 14. Terrel Hansen, rhp | $10,000 | 24. Jeff Atha, 2b | $1,000 |
| **5. Arci Cianfrocco, ss** | **$38,000** | 15. Kelvin Shepherd, of | $1,000 | 25. Mike Sodders, lhp | Did not sign |
| **6. *Greg Colbrunn, 3b** | **$85,000** | 16. *Robbie Orndorff, 2b | Did not sign | **Other Kevin Foster (29), rhp/3b** | **$30,000** |
| **7. Howard Farmer, rhp** | **$5,000** | 17. Javan Reagans, of | $2,000 | | |
| 8. Trevor Penn, 1b | $17,500 | 18. Tim Piechowski, of | $4,000 | | |

*Major leaguers in bold. *High school selection.*

### WORTH NOTING

career ended, he enjoyed a long career as an instructor and manager in the Twins minor league system. He was stricken with brain cancer in 2010 and died in April 2015 at age 48.

■ One top high school draft pick in 1987 who almost didn't sign was righthander **DAVID HOLDRIDGE**, selected by the Angels with a supplemental first-round pick (31st overall). Holdridge was a projected first-rounder when he entered his senior year at Ocean View High in Huntington Beach, Calif., but sustained a serious shoulder injury in November, while playing football with friends and ran into a goal post, crushing his right shoulder blade. It was almost a year before Holdridge pitched again. He still signed with the Angels for $100,000, and 11 years later, at age 29, after a long journey through the minors, he finally reached the big leagues, making seven relief appearance for the Mariners. Two of Holdridge's high school teammates also were drafted in 1987. Righthander **BRENT KNACKERT** was a second-round pick of the White Sox and had brief big league stints in 1990 and 1996. Catcher **ERIC CHRISTOPHERSON** wasn't taken until the 33rd round, but became a first-round pick of the Giants in 1990 after three years at San Diego State.

■ For all the emphasis on college pitching in the 1987 draft, the most dominant arm might have been Florida State's 5-foot-9 righthander **RICHIE LEWIS**, who lasted until the second round. He led the nation with 15 wins and 196 strikeouts, and over a three-year period with the Seminoles went 38-12, 3.22 while fanning 520 in 383 innings. Lewis was claimed in the second round by the Expos and pitched in parts of seven years in the majors, but his career was compromised by elbow problems, which Montreal officials attributed to being overused in college.

**IN FOCUS: MARK MERCHANT**

Mark Merchant was the second overall pick in the 1987 draft, going to the Pittsburgh Pirates. But he will always be remembered as the player selected right after Ken Griffey Jr.

Merchant played in just 125 games in the Pirates system before that organization gave up on him, shipping him to Seattle in a 1989 five-player trade. His arrival meant the Mariners owned the first two picks in the 1987 draft, but Merchant never came close to measuring up to the celebrated Griffey, or even played with him. He peaked in Double-A before being released in 1993, hooked on with the Reds and later reached Triple-A with the Royals and White Sox.

"When you look at Merchant, you can't believe clubs were torn between him and Griffey," said Doug Melvin in 1990, when he was Baltimore's farm director. "But I bet if you had asked most clubs who they would have taken, they would have been split."

Over 12 seasons with 14 teams, including stints with independent teams and in Mexico, Merchant hit .263 with 103 homers. Injuries plagued him from the outset—notably a separated shoulder in 1988 that sapped his arm strength, and a broken ankle in 1991 that took his speed.

"Things went how they were supposed to for (Griffey)," Merchant said. "They didn't for me."

## Highest Unsigned Picks

| Player, Pos., Team (Round) | College | Re-Drafted |
|---|---|---|
| Brad DuVall, rhp, Orioles (1) | * Virginia Tech | Cardinals '88 (1) |
| Brian Williams, rhp/of, Pirates (3) | South Carolina | Astros '90 (1) |
| Scott Livingstone, 3b, Athletics (3) | * Texas A&M | Tigers '88 (2) |
| Rick Lantrip, ss, Mariners (4) | Arizona | Yankees '90 (5) |
| Rey Noriega, ss, Cubs (4) | Miami (Fla.) | Yankees '89 (60) |
| Mike Ignasiak, rhp, Cardinals (4) | Michigan | Brewers '88 (8) |
| Dickie Dixon, lhp, Phillies (5) | Mississippi | Twins '90 (27) |
| Ricky Kimball, rhp, Mets (5) | Florida State | Cardinals '90 (17) |
| Joe Slusarski, rhp, Mariners (6) | * New Orleans | Athletics '88 (2) |
| John Kosenski, rhp, Braves (6) | Oklahoma | Never |

**TOTAL UNSIGNED PICKS:** Top 5 Rounds (8), Top 10 Rounds (34)

**Returned to same school.*

other choice but to sign him. I would have looked like a damn fool if I would have passed him and he turned up with no injury."

Opperman finally made his pro debut to open the 1989 season, starting and working two innings for Class A Vero Beach. The Dodgers brought him along slowly, limiting his innings, and he finished the season with a 0-7, 3.54 record. By that time, 11 first-rounders from the 1987 draft had already reached the major leagues, and yet Opperman was still looking for his first professional win.

In 1990, Opperman appeared to be on the comeback trail with a 12-8, 3.45 record in Double-A, but with a fastball that peaked at 89-90 mph it was apparent that his elbow would never be the same. While he didn't officially retire until the spring of 1993, Opperman's professional baseball career had become one interrupted journey after another. "I was a bitter, miserable person for a long time," he said. "After being hurt and knowing my baseball career was over, I was not a pleasant person to be around. I definitely had a chip on my shoulder."

Delino DeShields

Unlike previous years, teams became increasingly more mindful of a player's signability. In numerous situations, they avoided the temptation to gamble on a top prospect if they weren't confident he would sign for the price they wanted to pay. As a result, only one high school player selected in the first three rounds, outfielder/righthander Brian Williams, a third-round pick of the Pirates, went unsigned.

Mussina was a player every team in the game targeted, but subsequently avoided because he was unsignable. The Major League Scouting Bureau had stamped Mussina with one of its highest grades on record—75.5 on its 20-80 grading scale—so he was a hot topic leading up to the draft. But Mussina, a straight-A student, wasn't budging from his bonus demands to consider giving up a full ride to Stanford.

The Orioles made little attempt to sign him, but he became their first-round selection in 1990, after three years at Stanford, and went on to have a long, productive major league career.

Besides Griffey, the only other high school selection in 1987 whose career merited being picked in the first round was Delino DeShields, chosen 12th overall by the Expos. He had a successful 12-year career in the majors as a second baseman, hitting .268 with 80 homers while stealing 463 bases.

His selection was considered a gamble as DeShields, who hit .355 as a shortstop at Seaford (Del.) High, was a top basketball recruit with a college commitment to Villanova. The Expos signed him for $125,000, with the promise he could pursue his basketball career during the school year.

"We like him so much that we're willing to work something out so he can play both," Expos general manager Murray Cook said. "Naturally, we'd like to have him concentrate on baseball, but we're willing to have him play both. He's the best athlete in the country, according to our scouts."

Shortly after DeShields signed, he decided to forgo his commitment to Villanova and concentrate full time on baseball.

"I don't want to be behind the other players who can go to spring training," said the 5-foot-11 former guard who averaged 21 points, five rebounds and eight assists as a prep senior. "I'm going to miss basketball, but I feel this is the best for my future. It will benefit me in the long run."

Besides Mussina, outfielder Vince Phillips (Muir High, Pasadena, Calif.) was considered an unsignable first-round talent. Teams thought he would attend college at Southern California to play both football and baseball, but the New York Yankees took a run at Phillips in the 13th round and managed to sign him on Aug. 6, at a cost of $133,000—equivalent to first-round money.

Phillips hit .511 with four homers and 25 stolen bases as a senior at Muir High while also passing for 2,000 as a quarterback. He spent four years in the Yankees organization, hitting .266 with 27 homers, but never played again after leading the Double-A Eastern League in RBIs in 1991.

Two more high school players who fell due to signability were catcher Brad Ausmus, a 48th-round pick of the Yankees, and righthander Robb Nen, selected in the 32nd round by the Rangers. Ausmus planned to attend Dartmouth until the Yankees signed him on Aug. 29 to a $20,000 bonus, while Nen, the son of ex-big leaguer Dick Nen, jumped at the chance to sign with the Rangers when they overwhelmed him with a $50,500 bonus.

## Largest Draft-And-Follow Bonuses

| | Player, Pos. | Club (Round) | Bonus |
|---|---|---|---|
| 1. | **Darryl Kile, rhp** | **Astros (30)** | **$100,000** |
| 2. | John Latham, lhp | Pirates (30) | $60,000 |
| 3. | ***Mark Holzemer, lhp** | **Angels (4)** | **$55,000** |
| 4. | **Reggie Sanders, ss/of** | **Reds (7)** | **$51,000** |
| 5. | ***Donnie Elliott, rhp** | **Phillies (7)** | **$50,000** |
| | *Cullen Hartzog, rhp | Yankees (39) | $50,000 |
| | **Mike James, rhp** | **Dodgers (43)** | **$50,000** |
| 8. | *Ryan Richmond, rhp | Mets (34) | $45,000 |
| 9. | **James Byrd, ss** | **Red Sox (8)** | **$40,000** |
| | **Riccardo Ingram, of** | **Tigers (4)** | **$40,000** |

*Major leaguers in bold. *High school selection.*

# 1987 Draft List

**Did not sign. Major leaguers in bold, with first and last years noted. Order of selection indicated in parentheses. For the first five rounds, the peak level of each player is noted.*
*+ Signed as draft-and-follow (Second school noted if applicable).*

## ATLANTA BRAVES (6)

1. **Derek Lilliquist, lhp, University of Georgia.—(1989-96)**
2. Mike Urman, c, Canoga Park (Calif.) HS.—(Low A)
3. Tom Redington, ss, Esperanza HS, Anaheim, Calif.—(AA)
4. **Keith Mitchell, of, Lincoln HS, San Diego.—(1991-98)**

DRAFT DROP *Brother of Kevin Mitchell, major leaguer (1984-98)*

5. Dennis Burlingame, rhp, Kingsway HS, Mullica Hill, N.J.—(High A)

DRAFT DROP *Brother of Greg Burlingame, 24th-round draft pick, Mariners (1987)*

6. *John Kosenski, rhp, Fairview HS, Boulder, Colo.
7. Paulo Reis, ss-2b, Diamond Vocational HS, Fall River, Mass.
8. **Brian Hunter, 1b, Cerritos (Calif.) JC.—(1991-2000)**
9. Kevin Kelly, lhp, Wichita State University.
10. Lamar Hall, ss, Pinole Valley HS, San Pablo, Calif.
11. Anthony Baldwin, of, McLennan (Texas) CC.
12. Winston Relaford, of, Florida JC.

DRAFT DROP *Brother of Desi Relaford, major leaguer (1996-2004)*

13. **Mike Stanton, lhp, Alvin (Texas) CC.—(1989-2006)**
14. **David Nied, rhp, Duncanville (Texas) HS.—(1992-96)**

DRAFT DROP *First player selected, Major League Baseball expansion draft, Rockies (No. 17, 1992)*

15. Craig Gourlay, rhp, Wake Forest University.
16. Brian Cummings, rhp, Blinn (Texas) JC.
17. Rich Casarotti, 2b, Santa Rosa (Calif.) JC.
18. *Joey Chimelis, ss, Howard (Texas) JC.
19. Darren Cox, lhp, Triton (Ill.) JC.
20. *Marc Loeb, c, Eisenhower HS, Rialto, Calif.
21. Theron Todd, of, CC of Baltimore.
22. Scott Grove, rhp, Douglas County HS, Littleton, Colo.
23. Jeff Allison, of, Purdue University.
24. Richard Duke, c, Oregon State University.
25. *George Sells, of, Attleboro (Mass.) HS.
26. Pat Tilmon, rhp, University of South Carolina-Spartanburg.
27. Seth Reeser, rhp, Shippensburg (Pa.) University.
28. *Greg Randazza, rhp, Elizabeth (N.J.) HS.
29. John Albertson, c, Camden County (N.J.) JC.
30. Greg Harper, c, West Georgia College.
31. *Joseph Pagan, rhp, Chicago State University.
32. Kevin McNees, of, Western Michigan University.
33. John Mitchell, 1b, Mississippi State University.
34. Brian Wright, c, South Gate (Calif.) HS.
35. *Godfrey Knight, ss, Georgia Southern College.
36. Randy Ward, lhp, University of West Florida.
37. *Darrell Wyatt, of, Kishwaukee (Ill.) JC.
38. Steve Glass, ss-3b, San Francisco State University.
39. Greg Cloninger, ss, Campbell University.

DRAFT DROP *Son of Tony Cloninger, major leaguer (1961-72)*

40. Scott Bohlke, of, University of Georgia.
41. Jeff Dodig, of, Winthrop College.
42. *John Niekro, rhp, Shiloh HS, Lilburn, Ga.

DRAFT DROP *Son of Phil Niekro, major leaguer (1964-87) • Nephew of Joe Niekro, major leaguer (1978-88)*

43. *Roger Kinard, lhp, Georgia Tech.
44. *John Pappas, rhp, Crown Point (Ind.) HS.
45. +Paul Opdyke, rhp, Valley HS, Las Vegas, Nev. / Arizona Western JC.
46. *Shawn Buchanan, ss, Horace Mann HS, Gary, Ind.
47. Greg Ziegler, rhp, Morton (Ill.) JC.
48. *Steve Gill, lhp-of, El Dorado HS, Placentia, Calif.
49. *Paul Gogo, rhp, Kishwaukee (Ill.) JC.
50. *Herman Johnson, c, Skyline HS, Dallas.

## BALTIMORE ORIOLES (7)

1. Chris Myers, lhp, H.B. Plant HS, Tampa.—(AAA)
1. *Brad DuVall, rhp, Virginia Tech (Choice from Indians as compensation for Type A free agent Rick Dempsey).—(High A)

DRAFT DROP *Returned to Virginia Tech; re-drafted by Cardinals, 1988 (1st round)*

1. **Pete Harnisch, rhp, Fordham University** (Supplemental choice—27th—as compensation for Dempsey)**—(1988-2001)**
2. (Choice to Mets as compensation for Type B free agent Ray Knight)
3. **Anthony Telford, rhp, San Jose State University.—(1990-2002)**
4. **Chuck Ricci, rhp, Shawnee HS, Medford, N.J.—(1995)**
5. Tim Holland, ss, Rio Americano HS, Sacramento, Calif.—(AAA)
6. Sam Amarena, rhp, Tulane University.
7. Dan Simonds, c, Davidson College.
8. Mike Eberle, c, Indiana State University.
9. **Jack Voigt, of-3b, Louisiana State University.—(1992-98)**
10. Thomas Harms, of, Portland State University.
11. ***Mike Mussina, rhp, Montoursville (Pa.) HS.—(1991-2008)**

DRAFT DROP *First-round draft pick (20th overall), Orioles (1990)*

12. Bob Shoulders, of, Purdue University.
13. **Steve Finley, of, Southern Illinois University.—(1989-2007)**
14. Steve Culkar, rhp, University of Kentucky.
15. Chris Pinder, c, Virginia Commonwealth University.
16. Charles Elmore, of, Troy State University.
17. Terry Brown, of, University of Southern California.
18. **David Segui, 1b, Louisiana Tech.—(1990-2006)**

DRAFT DROP *Son of Diego Segui, major leaguer (1962-77) • Brother of Dan Segui, 47th-round draft pick, Mets (1987)*

19. George Wahlig, 2b, Southwest Missouri State University.
20. Dave Bettendorf, 3b, Kent State University.
21. Steve Browning, c, Valdosta State (Ga.) College.
22. ***Ray Gianelli, 3b, New York Tech.—(1991-95)**
23. Joe Hartline, of, Methodist (N.C.) College.
24. Steve Williams, lhp, Crescent City HS, Pomona Park, Fla.
25. *Longo Garcia, rhp, Cal State Fullerton.
26. Marcus Pilkinton, rhp, Troy State University.
27. *Malcolm Jordan, of, Montgomery HS, Santa Rosa, Calif.
28. *John Sipple, lhp, Oregon State University.
29. *Terry Melton, c, Charles Owen HS, Swannanoa, N.C.
30. Jeff Ahr, of, Xavier University.
31. David Esquer, ss, Stanford University.

DRAFT DROP *Baseball coach, California (2000-15)*

32. Paul Murphy, 3b, University of Delaware.
33. Scott Wallman, c, Sutherland HS, Pittsford, N.Y.
34. ***Kirk Dressendorfer, rhp, Pearland (Texas) HS.—(1991)**

DRAFT DROP *First-round draft pick (36th overall), Athletics (1990)*

35. *Matt Howard, rhp, Jersey Village HS, Houston.
36. *Reggie Robinson, of, Hogan HS, Vallejo, Calif.
37. *Steve Godin, of, Fauquier HS, Warrenton, Va.
38. *Mike Shebek, rhp, Ball State University.
39. *Mike Beall, 1b, St. Thomas (Fla.) University.
40. *Tim Seaton, 2b, Millard North HS, Omaha, Neb.
41. *Jimmy Crowley, 3b, Liberty Road HS, Cockeysville, Md.

DRAFT DROP *Son of Terry Crowley, major leaguer (1969-83)*

42. *Dan Martz, ss, Thomas Johnson HS, Frederick, Md.
43. *Gerald Santos, rhp, Christopher Columbus HS, Miami.
44. George Hildreth, of, Monroe (N.Y.) CC.
45. *Marc Imbasciani, of-c, C.W. Post University.
46. *Mike Brenner, of, Muscatine (Iowa) CC.
47. *Shawn Jenkins, of, Southwood HS, Shreveport, La.
48. *David Lucchino, c, Central Catholic HS, Pittsburgh.
49. *Kevin Pleasant, ss, Lake Park HS, Roselle, Ill.
50. *Jody Treadwell, rhp, Temple Christian HS, Jacksonville, Fla.
51. *Julio Morales, 1b, C.W. Post University.
52. *Mark Brockell, 3b, James Madison University.

## BOSTON RED SOX (26)

1. **Reggie Harris, rhp, Waynesboro (Va.) HS.—(1990-99)**
1. **Bob Zupcic, of, Oral Roberts University** (Supplemental choice—32nd—for failure to sign 1986 first-round pick Greg McMurtry)**—(1991-94)**
2. Paul Brown, lhp, University of Hawaii.—(AA)
3. Craig Wilson, c, Cerritos (Calif.) JC.—(AA)
4. Scott Powers, ss, Brandeis (Mass.) University.—(AA)
5. Harry Michael, of, Emporia State (Kan.) University.—(High A)
6. Ronnie Richardson, rhp, Lee HS, Columbus, Miss.
7. *Scott Vonderlieth, lhp, Mission Bay HS, San Diego.
8. **+James Byrd, ss, Seminole (Okla.) JC.—(1993)**
9. Mike Kelly, of, University of South Florida.
10. **Jeff Plympton, rhp, University of Maine.—(1991)**
11. **Phil Plantier, 3b, Poway (Calif.) HS.—(1990-97)**
12. Pedro Matilla, c, Southridge HS, Miami.
13. Peter Estrada, rhp, Irvington (N.J.) HS.
14. Sam Melton, 3b, Columbia State (Tenn.) CC.
15. ***Desi Wilson, 1b, Glen Cove (N.Y.) HS.—(1996)**
16. Larry Scannell, of, Lewis (Ill.) University.
17. Vince DeGifico, 1b, University of Southern Maine.
18. *Stewart Lee, 3b, Jacksonville State University.
19. *Scott Thompson, of, Westminster (Md.) HS.
20. *Kevin Digiacomo, c, Ithaca (N.Y.) HS.
21. *James Wray, lhp, Troy State University.
22. Anthony Mosley, lhp, Fort Meade (Fla.) HS.
23. *Richard Santiago, lhp, Palm Bay (Fla.) HS.
24. *Pat Pesavento, ss, University of Notre Dame.
25. ***Jayhawk Owens, c, Glen Este HS, Cincinnati.—(1993-96)**
26. ***Stan Spencer, rhp, Columbia River HS, Vancouver, Wash.—(1998-2000)**

DRAFT DROP *First-round draft pick (35th overall), Expos (1990)*

27. Greg McCollum, rhp, University of Illinois.
28. +Chris Hanks, c, JC of Southern Idaho.
29. *Don Redmond, of, Guilford (N.C.) College.
30. *Jesse Cross, rhp, Middle Georgia JC.
31. *Clint Creed, c, Triton HS, Dunn, N.C.

## CALIFORNIA ANGELS (25)

1. **John Orton, c, Cal Poly San Luis Obispo.—(1989-93)**
1. **Dave Holdridge, rhp, Ocean View HS, Huntington Beach, Calif.** (Supplemental choice—31st—as compensation for Type A free agent Reggie Jackson)**—(1998)**
2. Mike Erb, rhp, San Diego State University (Choice from Athletics as compensation for Jackson)—(AAA)
2. **Kevin Flora, ss, Bonita HS, La Verne, Calif.—(1991-95)**
3. Chris Threadgill, of, Whiteville (N.C.) HS.—(High A)
4. **+Mark Holzemer, lhp, Mullen HS, Littleton, Colo. / Seminole (Okla.) JC.—(1993-2000)**
5. Wiley Lee, 2b, Old Dominion University.—(AA)
6. Scott Randolph, rhp, Mount Hood (Ore.) CC.
7. Ramon Martinez, ss, Franklin HS, Highland Park, Calif.
8. Mike Musolino, c, Sacramento (Calif.) CC.
9. Mario Molina, of, Alhambra (Calif.) HS.
10. *Kyle Balch, rhp, Vanderbilt University.
11. **Ruben Amaro Jr., of, Stanford University.—(1991-98)**

DRAFT DROP *General manager, Phillies (2008-15) • Son of Ruben Amaro, major leaguer (1958-69)*

12. Reed Peters, of, University of Nevada-Las Vegas.
13. Ted Dyson, 1b, Arizona State University.
14. *Ray Harris, lhp, University of Arkansas.
15. Jeff Barns, ss, University of South Carolina.
16. Daniel Ward, rhp, St. Mary's (Calif.) College.
17. James Townsend, lhp, Ohio State University.
18. Jay Bobel, rhp, Michigan State University.
19. Cary Grubb, 3b, Clarion (Pa.) University.
20. Jim McAnany, c, Loyola Marymount University.

DRAFT DROP *Son of Jim McAnany, major leaguer (1958-62)*

21. Rob Wassenaar, rhp, Stanford University.
22. Mark Baca, of, Cal State Fullerton.
23. Frank Mutz, rhp, The Master's (Calif.) College.
24. Tony Mattia, 1b, Arizona State University.
25. Jimmy Long, rhp, Oklahoma State University.
26. *Brian Sajonia, lhp, Washington State University.
27. John Fritz, rhp, Beaver Falls (Pa.) HS.
28. *Perry Berry, ss, Cortez (Colo.) HS.
29. Lanny Abshier, 3b, University of Central Florida.
30. *Kevin McDonald, rhp, Deer Park (Texas) HS.
31. *Andrew McDonald, 2b, Riverview HS, Sarasota, Fla.
32. +Todd James, lhp, Sacramento (Calif.) CC.
33. *Scott Schanz, rhp, North HS, Riverside, Calif.
34. *Paul Gay, of, South Florida JC.
35. +Justin Martin, rhp, McKay HS, Salem, Ore. / Mount Hood (Ore.) CC.
36. *Kevin Brown, of, JC of the Sequoias (Calif.).
37. *Randy Vollmer, ss, Taravella (Fla.) HS.
38. *Woody Smith, ss, Spartanburg Methodist (S.C.) JC.

## CHICAGO CUBS (4)

1. **Mike Harkey, rhp, Cal State Fullerton.—(1988-97)**

DRAFT DROP *Father of Cory Harkey, running back/ National Football League (2012-14)*

2. (Choice to Expos as compensation for Type A free agent Andre Dawson)
3. **Alex Arias, 3b, George Washington HS, New York.—(1992-2002)**
4. *Rey Noriega, ss, Southwest HS, Miami.—(AAA)

DRAFT DROP *Attended Miami (Fla.); re-drafted by Yankees, 1989 (60th round)*

5. Gregg Patterson, lhp, Louisiana State University.—(High A)
6. **Frank Castillo, rhp, Eastwood HS, El Paso, Texas.—(1991-2004)**
7. **Matt Franco, 3b, Westlake HS, Thousand Oaks, Calif.—(1995-2003)**
8. **Matt Walbeck, c, Sacramento (Calif.) HS.—(1993-2003)**
9. *Joe Klancnik, rhp, Triton (Ill.) JC.
10. *Kevin O'Connor, ss, Mater Dei HS, Huntington Beach, Calif.
11. Jeff Massicotte, rhp, Florida JC.
12. *Billy Masse, of, Davidson College.
13. Horace Tucker, of, Lincoln HS, San Diego.
14. Gabby Rodriguez, lhp, UC Irvine.
15. Eric Perry, 1b, Dos Palos (Calif.) HS.
16. *Darin Campbell, ss, University of North Carolina.
17. +Wayne Weinheimer, of, Sacramento (Calif.) HS. / Sacramento (Calif.) CC.
18. Ray Williams, of, Northwestern State University.
19. Scott Taylor, c, Waukegan East HS, Waukegan, Ill.
20. *Steve Allen, rhp, University of Massachusetts.
21. Braz Davis, rhp, Baylor University.
22. Derek Stroud, lhp, Fresno State University.
23. Derek Moore, of, Santa Monica (Calif.) JC.
24. Lenny Bell, 1b-3b, University of Texas.
25. Steve Owens, 3b, St. Lawrence (N.Y.) University.

DRAFT DROP *Baseball coach, Le Moyne (2000-10); baseball coach, Bryant (2011-15)*

26. John Gardner, rhp, Indiana State University.
27. Warren Arrington, of, Troy State University.
28. +Sean Reed, lhp, Linn-Benton (Ore.) CC.
29. Glenn Sullivan, 1b, University of Oklahoma.
30. Danny Carpenter, of, Dallas Baptist University.
31. Michael Boswell, c-ss, Palm Beach (Fla.) JC.
32. *Mike Eastley, 3b, Lee (Texas) JC.
33. **Fernando Ramsey, of, New Mexico State University.—(1992)**
34. *Bob Brucato, of, Rancho Santiago (Calif.) JC.
35. *Bill Lantrip, lhp, Overton HS, Memphis, Tenn.
36. *David Zauner, ss, Berkley (Mich.) HS.
37. ***Jeff Cirillo, rhp, Providence HS, North Hollywood, Calif.—(1994-2006)**
38. **+Tom Thobe, lhp, Edison HS, Huntington Beach, Calif. / Golden West (Calif.) JC—(1995-96)**

DRAFT DROP *Brother of J.J. Thobe, major leaguer (1995)*

39. Anthony Whitson, rhp, Unicoi HS, Erwin, Tenn.

DRAFT DROP *Brother of Ed Whitson, major leaguer*

*(1977-91)*
40. *Tracy Smith, 3b-rhp, Miami (Ohio) University.
DRAFT DROP *Baseball coach, Miami (Ohio) (1997-2005); baseball coach, Indiana (2006-14); baseball coach, Arizona State (2015)*
41. *Kirk Goodson, rhp, Independence (Va.) HS.
DRAFT DROP *Son of Ed Goodson, major leaguer (1970-77)*
42. *Eric Crawford, of, Venice HS, Los Angeles.
43. *Johnny Walker, of, Holmes HS, San Antonio, Texas.
DRAFT DROP *Eighth-round draft pick, Green Bay Packers/ National Football League (1991)*
44. David Hellmann, 3b, Miami (Ohio) University.

## CHICAGO WHITE SOX (5)

**1. Jack McDowell, rhp, Stanford University.—(1987-99)**
DRAFT DROP *First player from 1987 draft to reach majors (Sept. 15, 1987)*
**2. Brent Knackert, rhp, Ocean View HS, Huntington Beach, Calif.—(1990-96)**
3. Kinnis Pledger, of, Garland County CC, Benton, Ark.—(AAA)
**4. Steve Schrenk, rhp, North Marion HS, Aurora, Ore.—(1999-2000)**
**5. Dan Rohrmeier, 3b, St. Thomas (Fla.) University.—(1997)**
**6. Jerry Kutzler, rhp, William Penn (Iowa) College.—(1990)**
7. Ed Smith, 3b, Pemberton HS, Brown Mills, N.J.
DRAFT DROP *Tight end, National Football League (1997-99)*
8. Bernardo Cruz, ss, Southview HS, Lorain, Ohio.
9. *Dan Gil, 3b, Polytechnic HS, North Hollywood, Calif.
**10. Rob Lukachyk, ss, Brookdale (N.J.) CC.—(1996)**
11. Ken Burroughs, rhp, Northeast HS, St. Petersburg, Fla.
**12. Buddy Groom, lhp, University of Mary Hardin-Baylor (Texas).—(1992-2004)**
**13. Dwayne Hosey, of, Altadena, Calif.—(1995-96)**
14. Ed Walsh, 1b, Providence College.
15. *Maurice Crum Sr., 1b, Hillsborough HS, Tampa.
DRAFT DROP *Linebacker, National Football League (1991)*
16. John Sabatino, rhp, Lewis (Ill.) University.
17. Paul Fuller, c, University of Southern California.
18. *Chris Hansen, rhp, Iona College.
19. Ray Payton, of-1b, Southern University.
20. Brad Fella, lhp, Indiana University.
21. Curt Hasler, rhp, Bradley University.
22. Jesus Merejo, ss, CC of Morris (N.J.).
23. *Brian Roberts, c, Loara HS, Anaheim, Calif.
24. Franklyn Harris, c, Jackson State University.
25. +Virgil Cooper, rhp, Labette (Kan.) CC.
26. Keith Harris, of, Queensborough (N.Y.) CC.
27. Shaun Doyle, of, Cal State Dominguez Hills.
28. Dwight Thomas, 1b, Dallas Baptist University.
29. *Kerry Valrie, of-2b, Robertsdale HS, Loxley, Ala.
30. +Mario Silva, 2b-3b, American HS, Miami.
31. *Derek Davis, of, Simeon HS, Chicago.
32. Kevin Murdock, c, University of Wisconsin-Oshkosh.
33. Randy Warren, of, Elon College.
34. Paul Colontino, of, Roosevelt HS, Brooklyn, N.Y.
35. *John Kroeger, c, Fairleigh Dickinson University.
36. John Morabito, of-inf, Wake Forest University.
37. *Brian Gennings, rhp, Queen City (Texas) HS.
38. *Jeff Buell, 1b, Indiana State University.
39. *Phil Doyle, ss, Huffman HS, Birmingham, Ala.
40. *Lawrence Smith, ss, Bethune-Cookman College.

## CINCINNATI REDS (18)

**1. Jack Armstrong, rhp, University of Oklahoma.—(1988-94)**
**2. Freddie Benavides, ss, Texas Christian University.—(1991-94)**
3. Brian Lane, ss, Midway HS, Waco, Texas.—(AAA)
4. Jeremy Mathews, ss, Sandalwood HS, Jacksonville, Fla.—(Low A)
5. Shane Letterio, ss, Lake Mary HS, Longwood, Fla.—(AAA)
6. *Bo Loftin, c, Jacksonville (Ala.) HS.

White Sox first-round pick Jack McDowell was in Chicago by September, the first 1987 draftee to reach the majors, and won 127 games

BERNARD TRONCALE

**7. +Reggie Sanders, ss-of, Spartanburg Methodist (S.C.) JC.—(1991-2007)**
**8. *Jim Kremers, 3b-of, University of Arkansas.—(1990)**
9. *Brian Nichols, c, University of Southern California.
10. Joe Turek, rhp, West Chester (Pa.) University.
11. Steve McCarthy, lhp, Brown University.
12. Eugene "Motorboat" Jones, 1b, Litchfield HS, Gadsden, Ala.
13. Steve Hester, rhp, Cedarville HS, Crozet, Va.
**14. Bill Risley, rhp, Truman (Ill.) JC.—(1992-98)**
**15. Butch Henry, lhp, El Paso (Texas) HS.—(1992-99)**
16. Scott Jeffery, rhp, Mansfield (Pa.) University.
17. Gary Sloan, of-inf, Long Beach State University.
18. Dante Johnson, of, Santa Fe (Fla.) CC.
19. Brad Robinson, of, Oral Roberts University.
20. Lavell Cudjo, of, Charlotte HS, Punta Gorda, Fla.
21. Scott Economy, rhp, James Madison University.
22. *John Cebuhar, lhp, University of Arkansas.
23. Ed Rush, ss, University of South Florida.
24. *Norman Villaneuva, c, Tehachapi (Calif.) HS.
25. Paul Kovarick, 1b, Broome (N.Y.) CC.
26. Scott Sellner, 3b, Cal State Sacramento.
27. Bryan Ganter, of, Oregon State University.
**28. Milt Hill, rhp, Georgia College.—(1991-94)**
29. Mike Stout, rhp, James Madison University.
30. Steve Storms, rhp, Fairborne (Ohio) HS.
31. Joey Vierra, rhp, University of Hawaii.
32. Mike Shepherd, of, Georgia Southern College.
33. Rick Keen, rhp, Colorado State University.
34. *Mike Virden, of, Ballinger (Texas) HS.
35. Tori Tomasino, c, University of Northern Colorado.
36. *Bob Gralewski, 1b, Salesianum HS, Wilmington, Del.
37. Keith Beam, of, Southern Arkansas University.
38. *Tom Mileski, 1b, Willis (Texas) HS.
39. *Tim Wells, rhp, Mineral Area (Mo.) JC.
40. *Scott McCarty, lhp, Converse HS, San Antonio, Texas.
**41. *Tim Costo, ss, Glenbard HS, Glen Ellyn, Ill.—(1992-93)**
DRAFT DROP *First-round draft pick (8th overall), Indians (1990)*
42. Brian Whitaker, 2b, Southern Utah State College.
43. *Mark Faile, of, Lancaster (S.C.) HS.
44. +Tony Terzarial, of, Triton (Ill.) JC.
**45. +Glenn Sutko, c, Spartanburg Methodist (S.C.) JC.—(1990-91)**
46. *Russell Williams, rhp, Bryan County HS, Pembroke, Ga.
47. *Richard Reisdorf, of, Winona (Minn.) HS.
48. *Todd Mercier, 1b, Manchester (Conn.) CC.
49. *Kevin Kirk, rhp, Lewisville (Texas) HS.
50. *Anthony Brown, of, Connellsville (Pa.) HS.
51. Carl Nordstrom, rhp, Allegheny (Pa.) CC.
52. *Anthony Fleming, of, Triton (Ill.) JC.
53. Scott Trochim, 3b, Rutgers University.
54. Brian Mershon, of-2b, University of Illinois.
55. Robert Riccio, ss-2b, University of New Haven.
56. Andy Alvey, 2b, Georgia College.
57. *Joe White, rhp, Mesa (Colo.) College.
58. Mike Mohr, of, Western Illinois University.
59. Reggie Brock, of, Chicago State University.
60. David Hamilton, 2b, Southwest Texas State University.
61. *Jimmy Armstrong, lhp, Wichita Falls (Texas) HS.

## CLEVELAND INDIANS (15)

1. (Choice to Orioles as compensation for Type A free agent Rick Dempsey)
**2. Albert Belle, of, Louisiana State University.—(1989-2000)**
3. Tom Kurczewski, rhp, Michigan State University.—(Low A)
4. Carl Keliipuleole, rhp, Brigham Young University.—(AA)
**5. Tom Kramer, rhp, Roger Bacon HS, Cincinnati.—(1991-93)**
6. Todd Ogden, rhp, Rice University.
7. Scott Mackie, of, James Madison University.
8. Chris Isaacson, c, Eastern Washington University.
9. Greg Roscoe, rhp, University of Nevada-Las Vegas.
**10. Ever Magallanes, ss, Texas A&M University.—(1991)**
11. Chuck Baldwin, 2b, Clemson University.
12. *Gordie Farmer, rhp, Arizona State University.
13. Pete Kuld, c, Pepperdine University.
14. Jamie Allison, of, Indiana State University.
15. Bill Narleski, ss, University of Virginia.
DRAFT DROP *Son of Ray Narleski, major leaguer (1954-59) • Grandson of Bill Narleski, major leaguer (1929-30)*
**16. Steve Olin, rhp, Portland State University.—(1989-92)**
DRAFT DROP *Died as active major leaguer (March 22, 1993)*
17. John Stitz, rhp, St. Joseph's (Ind.) College.
18. *Dan Eskew, rhp, University of Tennessee.
19. Chris Dunham, 1b, Stetson University.
20. Willie Garza, rhp, Laney (Calif.) JC.
21. Vince Barranco, of, Gonzaga University.
**22. Kevin Bearse, lhp, Old Dominion University.—(1990)**
23. Frank Sommerkamp, c, Hillsborough (Fla.) CC.
24. David Harwell, rhp, Dallas Baptist University.
**25. Beau Allred, of, Lamar University.—(1989-91)**
26. Sam Ferretti, 2b, Rutgers University.
27. *Kevin Dattola, of, Brevard (Fla.) CC.
28. *Kevin Farlow, ss, Kennedy HS, Northridge, Calif.
29. Robbie Rogers, ss, University of San Diego.
30. *Kurt Dempster, rhp, Arizona State University.
31. *David Ferrell, 2b, Palo Alto (Calif.) HS.
32. *Mark Smith, rhp, San Jacinto (Texas) JC.
33. Ivan McBride, ss, Baptist (S.C.) College.
34. Brent Roberts, of-3b, Snow (Utah) JC.
35. *Clyde Samuel, rhp, Mission (Calif.) JC.
36. *Scott Tedder, of, Ohio Wesleyan College.
37. Wayne Bell, of, Pasadena, Calif.

## DETROIT TIGERS (21)

1. Bill Henderson, c, Westminster Christian HS, Miami (Choice from Phillies as compensation for Type A free agent Lance Parrish).—(High A)
**1. Steve Pegues, of, Pontotoc (Miss.) HS.—(1994-95)**
**1. Travis Fryman, ss, Tate HS, Gonzalez, Fla.** (Supplemental choice—30th—as compensation for Parrish)**—(1990-2002)**
**2. Rob Richie, of, University of Nevada-Reno.—(1989)**
3. Jim Hayes, rhp, Topeka, Kan.—(Low A)
**4. +Riccardo Ingram, of, Georgia Tech.—(1994-95)**
**5. Torey Lovullo, 2b, UCLA.—(1988-99)**
DRAFT DROP *Major league manager (2015)*
6. Dean DeCillis, ss, Miami-Dade CC South.
7. Chris Harley, 3b, CC of Baltimore.
**8. *Derek Lee, of, University of South Florida.—(1993)**
9. Blaine Rudolph, rhp, Fresno (Calif.) CC.
10. Robert Shipman, of, Winter Haven (Fla.) HS.
11. Dave Dawson, rhp, Orange Coast (Calif.) JC.
12. Jody Supak, rhp, University of Houston.
13. Paul Nozling, lhp, Lakeland (Ohio) CC.
14. Don Vesling, lhp, Eastern Michigan University.
15. *Shane Jackson, rhp-c, Northern HS, Pontiac, Mich.
16. *Hernan Cortes, 1b, San Francisco State University.
17. Mike Wilkins, rhp, Lamar University.
18. Anthony Toney, of, Orange Coast (Calif.) JC.
19. *Sean Baron, 1b, University of San Diego.
20. Larry Coker, lhp, University of Houston.
**21. Mike Schwabe, rhp, Arizona State University.—(1989-90)**
22. Chris Schnurbusch, ss, Central Missouri University.
23. Ron Cook, lhp, St. Clair County (Mich.) CC.
24. Steve Strong, c, University of Arizona.
25. Doug Biggs, of, Auburndale (Fla.) HS.
26. *Mark Dawn, of, Manatee (Fla.) JC.
27. Dave Richards, lhp, Grossmont (Calif.) JC.
28. *Tim McDonald, rhp, Central Michigan University.
29. Jay Fox, rhp, Eastern Washington University.
30. *Eric Methner, rhp, Coleman (Mich.) HS.
31. *Jeff Tanderys, rhp, Novi (Mich.) HS.
32. Mike Koller, rhp, Glen Este HS, Cincinnati.
**33. +Rusty Meacham, rhp, Indian River (Fla.) CC.—(1991-2001)**
34. *John Johnson, rhp, Kellogg (Mich.) CC.
35. *Andy Postema, 3b, Grand Rapids (Mich.) JC.
36. *Joseph Frias, ss, Elizabeth (N.J.) HS.
37. *Greg Haeger, lhp, Catholic Central HS, Livonia,

Mich.

DRAFT DROP *Brother of Charlie Haeger, major leaguer (2006-07)*

38. +Edward Ferm, rhp, Long Beach (Calif.) CC.
39. *Damon Webb, of, MacKenzie HS, Detroit.
40. *Mario Linares, c, Colonial HS, Orlando, Fla.
41. *Terre Woods, c, West Side HS, Gary, Ind.

## HOUSTON ASTROS (22)

1. **Craig Biggio, c, Seton Hall University.—(1988-2006)**

DRAFT DROP *Elected to Baseball Hall of Fame, 2015*

2. **Randy Hennis, rhp, UCLA.—(1990)**
3. David Henderson, ss, McAlester (Okla.) HS.—(High A)
4. Roger Locke, rhp, Sparkman HS, Harvest, La.—(Low A)
5. Harold Allen, lhp, Indiana State University.—(AAA)
6. Billy Carver, c, University of Tennessee.
7. Dan Nyssen, of, University of Hawaii.
8. John Massarelli, c, University of Akron.
9. *Mike Ross, ss-2b, Cal State Fullerton.
10. Chris Small, rhp, Troy State University.
11. David Washington, of, Murrah HS, Jackson, Miss.
12. **Andy Mota, 2b-of, Cal State Fullerton.—(1991)**

DRAFT DROP *Son of Manny Mota, major leaguer (1962-82) • Brother of Jose Mota, major leaguer (1991-95)*

13. Rusty Harris, ss, Lewis-Clark State (Idaho) College.
14. Leo Clouser, rhp, Los Angeles Pierce JC.
15. Chris Hawkins, lhp, University of South Carolina-Spartanburg.
16. **Al Osuna, lhp, Stanford University.—(1990-96)**
17. Steve Polverini, rhp, Cal State Los Angeles.
18. Doug Royalty, rhp, San Diego State University.
19. Greg Johnson, rhp, Middle Tennessee State University.
20. **Dean Hartgraves, lhp, JC of the Siskiyous (Calif.).—(1995-98)**
21. Ken Dickson, 3b, University of South Carolina-Aiken.
22. Chris Lee, rhp, University of Miami.
23. Todd Newman, lhp, Brigham Young University.
24. *William Parrish, ss, Shorter (Ark.) JC.
25. Dennis Tafoya, rhp, Cal State Sacramento.
26. David Panizzi, of, Bradley Univeristy.
27. *Kevin Smothers, 3b, Lincoln HS, San Diego.
28. *Scott Kirk, of-1b, San Bernardino Valley (Calif.) JC.
29. *Michael Bible, c, JC of the Canyons (Calif.).
30. **+Darryl Kile, rhp, Chaffey (Calif.) JC.—(1991-2002)**

DRAFT DROP *Died as active major leaguer (June 22, 2002)*

31. +Toncie Reed, of, Seminole (Okla.) JC.
32. *Anthony Manahan, 2b, Horizon HS, Scottsdale, Ariz.

DRAFT DROP *First-round draft pick (38th overall), Mariners (1990) • Brother of Austin Manahan, first-round draft pick, Pirates (1988)*

33. *Tony Ochs, c, Southeastern Illinois JC.
34. ***Scott Erickson, rhp, San Jose (Calif.) CC.—(1990-2006)**
35. *Barry Earl, of, Columbus (Ga.) College.
36. *Sam Austin, of, Waukegan (Ill.) East HS.
37. ***Lance Dickson, lhp, Grossmont HS, La Mesa, Calif.—(1990)**

DRAFT DROP *First-round draft pick (23rd overall), Cubs (1990)*

38. *Rodney Windes, lhp, Cal State Los Angeles.
39. *Kevin Bumgarner, rhp, Cypress (Calif.) JC.
40. *Kevin Nielsen, lhp, JC of the Canyons (Calif.).
41. *Dusty Madsen, rhp, Bella Vista HS, Fair Oaks, Calif.
42. *Peter Hankinson, ss, University of Minnesota.
43. *Todd Pick, rhp, Lassen (Calif.) JC.
44. *Greg Gistlinck, c, Anaheim (Calif.) HS.
45. *Dan Donovan, rhp, Freehold Township (N.J.) HS.
46. *James Elliot, c, Glenbard West HS, Glen Ellen, Ill.

## KANSAS CITY ROYALS (9)

1. **Kevin Appier, rhp, Antelope Valley (Calif.) JC.—(1989-2004)**
2. **Terry Shumpert, 2b, University of Kentucky.—(1990-2003)**
3. **Stu Cole, ss, University of North Carolina-Charlotte.—(1991)**
4. Jon Alexander, lhp, University of South Florida.—(High A)
5. Bob Wellington, rhp, Elizabeth (N.J.) HS.—(Rookie)
6. Ken Bowen, ss, Oregon State University.
7. Trey Gainous, of, Auburn University.
8. Kevin Shaw, rhp, Katella HS, Yorba Linda, Calif.
9. Bud Adams, rhp, Vanderbilt University.
10. Richie LeBlanc, rhp, Louisiana Tech.
11. +Darron Johnson, of, Boone HS, Orlando, Fla. / Santa Fe (Fla.) CC.
12. Kevin Pickens, rhp, Louisiana Tech.
13. Archie Smith, lhp, Vanderbilt University.
14. *Javier Alvarez, ss, Sacred Heart HS, San Francisco.
15. Bill Drohan, rhp, Brewer State (Ala.) JC.
16. **Bobby Moore, of, Eastern Kentucky University.—(1991)**
17. *Greg Hammond, c, Chipola (Fla.) JC.
18. *John Seeburger, 1b, UC Irvine.
19. Doug Nelson, rhp, University of the Pacific.
20. Don Wright, 1b, San Jacinto (Texas) JC.
21. *Darnell Dickerson, of, King HS, Detroit.
22. Jim Hudson, rhp, Los Angeles Harbor JC.
23. Doug Bock, c, University of Missouri.
24. Ben Pierce, lhp, Birmingham-Southern College.
25. Luis Mallea, rhp, St. Francis (N.Y.) College.
26. Keith Shibata, lhp, UCLA.
27. Montie Phillips, 3b, Lewis-Clark State (Idaho) College.
28. *Kelly Boyer, rhp, Shadow Mountain HS, Phoenix.
29. Steve Hoeme, rhp, Pratt (Kan.) CC.
30. Juan Berrios, c-of, Long Island University.
31. *Jim Kosnik, lhp, Oakland University.
32. **Jim Campbell, lhp, San Diego State University.—(1990)**
33. **Jorge Pedre, c, Los Angeles Harbor JC.—(1991-92)**
34. Bobby Knecht, 2b, Hanover (Ind.) College.
35. *Scott Weiss, ss-rhp, Quartz Hill HS, Palmdale, Calif.
36. Darryl Hardwick, of, Redwood HS, Visalia, Calif.
37. Derek Sholl, of, Los Angeles Harbor JC.
38. Jeff Baum, 2b, Dallas Baptist University.
39. Brendan Haugh, of, Cloud County (Kan.) CC.
40. *Don Ray, c, University of Kentucky.
41. Tim Byrnes, ss, Adelphi (N.Y.) University.
42. Pat Bergquist, of, University of Minnesota-Duluth.
43. *Tim Ricks, rhp, Fayetteville HS, Childersburg, Ala.
44. Doug Hupke, of, University of San Francisco.
45. Jeff Cruse, rhp, Eastern Kentucky University.
46. Greg Karklins, rhp, Wright State University.
47. Kent Headley, of, Wichita State University.
48. *Damon Tyson, ss, Los Angeles CC.
49. ***Tim Laker, c, Simi Valley (Calif.) HS.—(1992-2006)**
50. Billy Gardner Jr., 1b, Mitchell (Conn.) JC.

DRAFT DROP *Son of Billy Gardner, major leaguer (1954-63); major league manager (1981-87)*

51. +Fred Russell, ss, Compton (Calif.) HS / Compton (Calif.) JC.
52. *Kim Cornist, of, Armijo HS, Suisun City, Calif.
53. *Jeff Joseph, 2b, Arizona State University.
54. Erwin Houston, of, Laney (Calif.) JC.
55. *Henry DeLeon, 1b-of, Lee (Texas) JC.
56. *Greg Blevins, c, Choctaw (Okla.) HS.
57. *Fred Maggard, rhp, Cumberland (Ky.) HS.
58. **Jeff Conine, 3b-1b, UCLA.—(1990-2006)**
59. ***Mark Small, rhp, West Seattle (Wash.) HS.—(1996)**
60. Jerry Bentley, lhp, Mason (Ohio) HS.
61. *Adam Mokres, of, Cuesta (Calif.) JC.
62. *Steve Gray, inf, Cuesta (Calif.) JC.
63. *Merle Gardner, of, Rockhurst HS, Kansas City, Mo.
64. *Fred Riscen, lhp, JC of the Canyons (Calif.).
65. ***Bret Barberie, 2b, Cerritos (Calif.) JC.—(1991-96)**
66. ***Erik Plantenberg, lhp, Newport HS, Bellevue, Wash.—(1993-97)**
67. *Mark Jones, rhp, Lee Davis HS, Mechanicsville, Va.
68. *Gary Hymel, c, Belaire HS, Baton Rouge, La.
69. *Chris Moock, ss, Baker HS, Greenwell Spring, La.

DRAFT DROP *Son of Joe Moock, major leaguer (1967)*

70. ***Kevin McGehee, rhp, Tioga HS, Pineville, La.—(1993)**
71. *Eric Kuhlman, of, Bradley University.
72. *Peter Hinkle, rhp, King HS, Tampa.
73. *Jerry Dean, rhp, Northeast HS, Little Rock, Ark.
74. *Stewart Anthony, ss, Sparrows Point HS, Baltimore.

## LOS ANGELES DODGERS (8)

1. Dan Opperman, rhp, Valley HS, Las Vegas, Nev.—(AAA)
2. Donnie Carroll, of, Granite Hills HS, El Cajon, Calif.—(High A)
3. **Chris Nichting, rhp, Northwestern University.—(1995-2002)**
4. Tom DeMerit, of, Dartmouth College.—(High A)
5. Luis Martinez, ss, Ohio Dominican College.—(AAA)
6. **Darrin Fletcher, c, University of Illinois.—(1989-2002)**
7. **Tony Barron, 3b-of, Willamette (Ore.) University.—(1996-97)**
8. Howard Freiling, 1b, University of North Carolina.
9. Ken Luckham, rhp, Los Amigos HS, Fountain Valley, Calif.
10. Doug Noch, rhp, Central Michigan University.
11. Larry Gonzales, rhp, Don Lugo HS, Chino, Calif.
12. *Barry Blackwell, c, Florida State University.
13. Sherman Collins, rhp, University of Oklahoma.
14. D.J. Floyd, c, Chino HS, Ontario, Calif.
15. Alan Lewis, ss, Davidson College.
16. John Wanish, rhp, Florida State University.
17. Bruce Dostal, of, William Paterson (N.J.) College.
18. Steve Green, of, Georgia Tech.
19. **Rafael Bournigal, ss, Florida State University.—(1992-99)**
20. **Jose Munoz, ss, Florida JC-Jacksonville.—(1996)**
21. **Dennis Springer, rhp, Fresno State University.—(1995-2002)**
22. *Mike Parks, rhp, University of Florida.
23. Dan Kreuder, rhp, Pace (N.Y.) University.
24. Randy Wadsworth, c-of, California (Pa.) University.
25. Frank Mustari, 3b, Illinois State University.
26. Brian Emmert, 1b, Pace (N.Y.) University.
27. Dan Piscetta, rhp, College of Wooster (Ohio).
28. David Martin, rhp, Phillips (Okla.) University.
29. **Zak Shinall, rhp, El Camino (Calif.) JC.—(1993)**
30. Todd Melisauskas, c, Shippensburg (Pa.) University.
31. Eric Johnson, of, Cal State Sacramento.
32. Bill Argo, of, Iowa State University.
33. *Chris Harding, of-3b, Clover HS, Moseley, Va.
34. ***Jim Poole, lhp, Georgia Tech.—(1990-2000)**
35. Brian Currie, lhp, University of South Carolina.
36. *Garrett Carter, 3b, University of South Carolina.
37. +Jeff Herman, of, DeAnza (Calif.) JC.
38. *Larry Rezny, lhp, Grand Haven (Mich.) HS.
39. +Brett Magnusson, of, Santa Rosa (Calif.) JC.
40. *Jerry Lutterman, rhp, Lafayette HS, Ellisville, Mo.
41. *Jim Robinson, rhp-c, Sullivan HS, Chicago.
42. *Joe Fernandez, of, Galileo HS, San Francisco.
43. **+Mike James, rhp, Lurleen B. Wallace State (Ala.) JC.—(1995)**
44. Chris Gettler, rhp, Jacksonville University.
45. ***Doug Simons, lhp, Pepperdine University.—(1991-92)**
46. Sam Bland, c, Kishwaukee (Ill.) JC.
47. +Albert Bustillos, rhp, Gavilan (Calif.) JC.
48. *Ken Woods, ss, Palisades HS, Pacific Palisades, Calif.
49. *Troy Arrington, rhp-ss, Jordan HS, Los Angeles.
50. *Vince Muldrew, of-lhp, Centennial HS, Compton, Calif.
51. *Andre Perkens, c, Blair HS, Altadena, Calif.

## MILWAUKEE BREWERS (13)

1. **Bill Spiers, ss, Clemson University.—(1989-2001)**
2. Chris Johnson, rhp, Red Bank HS, Hixson, Tenn.—(AA)
2. Curt Krippner, rhp, University of Texas (Choice from Yankees as compensation for Type B free agent Rick Cerone).—(High A)
3. **Jaime Navarro, rhp, Miami-Dade CC New World Center.—(1989-2000)**

DRAFT DROP *Son of Julio Navarro, major leaguer (1962-70)*

4. Larry Carter, rhp, Plant City (Fla.) HS.—(AA)
5. **Steve Sparks, rhp, Sam Houston State University.—(1995-2004)**
6. **Charlie Montoyo, 2b, Louisiana Tech.—(1993)**
7. Brad Kucera, lhp, Creighton University.
8. Joe Ortiz, c, University of the Pacific.
9. **Frank Bolick, 3b, Georgia Tech.—(1993-98)**
10. *Scott Kimball, rhp, Salem State (Mass.) College.
11. Rob Smith, of, Washington State University.
12. Mark Aguilar, 1b, Pima (Ariz.) CC.
13. **Troy O'Leary, of, Cypress (Calif.) HS.—(1993-2003)**
14. Tony Boze, of, Anderson (S.C.) College.
15. Mike Whitlock, lhp, Cuesta (Calif.) JC.
16. *Keith Krenke, of, Owatonna (Minn.) HS.
17. *Layne Lambert, ss, Arlington HS, Riverside, Calif.
18. Mark Chapman, rhp, Auburn University.
19. Todd Shiver, rhp, Georgia Tech.
20. ***Brian Turang, c-of, Long Beach (Calif.) CC.—(1993-94)**
21. **+Mark Kiefer, rhp, Fullerton (Calif.) JC.—(1993-96)**

DRAFT DROP *Brother of Steve Kiefer, major leaguer (1984-89)*

22. Dan Russell, 1b, Moorpark (Calif.) JC.
23. Joe Roebuck, 3b-ss, Bryan (Ohio) HS.
24. ***Jeromy Burnitz, c-of, Conroe (Texas) HS.—(1993-2006)**

DRAFT DROP *First-round draft pick (17th overall), Mets (1990)*

25. ***Chris Haney, lhp, Orange County HS, Barbourville, Va.—(1991-2002)**

DRAFT DROP *Son of Larry Haney, major leaguer (1966-78)*

26. *James Ingram, lhp, Lasanger HS, Hawthorne, Calif.
27. Tim Raley, c-of, Wichita State University.
28. *Alfred Mitchell, of, Cuesta (Calif.) JC.
29. *Odel Stewart, of, Buena HS, Sierra Vista, Ariz.
30. *Greg Knowles, rhp, Cardinal Gibson HS, Plantation, Fla.
31. *Doug Louden, rhp, Elmhurst HS, Fort Wayne, Ind.
32. Jeff Kinder, lhp, Randolph Southern HS, Lynn, Ind.
33. *James Henderson, c, Westlake HS, Agoura, Calif.
34. *Shane Espitia, rhp, Ventura (Calif.) HS.
35. *Bart Grubbs, rhp, Carbon HS, Price, Utah.
36. +Ron Jefferson, rhp, Kishwaukee (Ill.) JC.
37. *Steve Renard, lhp, Preble HS, Green Bay, Wis.
38. *Michael Bobala, lhp, Hudson (Fla.) HS.
39. *Mike Tosar, 2b, Christopher Columbus HS, Miami.
40. *Martin Durkin, 2b, Columbus HS/Miami-Dade CC South.
41. *Troy Chacon, lhp, Pima (Ariz.) CC.
42. *Kreg Gresham, rhp, Independence HS, Charlotte, N.C.
43. *Ethon Flowers, c, Central Arizona JC.
44. *Steve Peck, rhp, Mesa (Ariz.) CC.
45. *Robert Dampier, rhp, Arizona Western JC.
46. David Bates, ss, South Salem (Ore.) HS.
47. +Steve Albillar Diez, c, Righetti HS, Santa Maria, Calif. / Cuesta (Calif.) JC.

## MINNESOTA TWINS (3)

1. **Willie Banks, rhp, St. Anthony HS, Jersey City, N.J.—(1991-2002)**
2. **Terry Jorgensen, of, University of Wisconsin-Oshkosh.—(1989-2003)**
3. Wade Wacker, ss, Jackson (Minn.) HS.—(Rookie)
4. Mike Mathiot, c, Springfield (Ill.) HS.—(Low A)
5. David Smith, of, Tulane University.—(High A)
6. **Larry Casian, lhp, Cal State Fullerton.—(1990-98)**
7. **Mark Guthrie, lhp, Louisiana State University.—(1989-2003)**
8. *Mike Hinde, of, Brevard (Fla.) CC.
9. *Tom Lachmann, c, Kiona Benton HS, Benton City, Wash.
10. David Richardson, lhp, Lone Pine (Calif.) HS.

11. *Daren Burns, rhp, Birmingham-Southern College.
**12. Shawn Gilbert, ss, Fresno State University.—(1997-2000)**
13. Doug Kline, rhp, University of Portland.
14. Steve Stowell, lhp, UCLA.
15. *Lozzell Mongomery, ss, Roswell (Ga.) HS.
16. Jose Marzan, 1b-of, Florida State University.
**17. Chip Hale, 2b, University of Arizona.—(1989-97)**
DRAFT DROP *Major league manager (2015)*
18. Mark Ericson, c, University of Connecticut.
19. Ed Alvarez, of, American HS, Miami.
20. Mike Anthony, lhp, Rancho Santiago (Calif.) JC.
21. Charles Jones, 1b, University of North Carolina-Wilmington.
**22. *Dan Smith, lhp, Apple Valley (Minn.) HS.—(1992-94)**
DRAFT DROP *First-round draft pick (16th overall), Rangers (1990)*
23. *Dennis Burbank, rhp, Valencia HS, Anaheim, Calif.
24. Pat Bangston, rhp, Kent State University.
25. Dean Tartarian, ss, Cardozza HS, Bayside, N.Y.
26. *Dan DeVille, rhp, Mount San Antonio (Calif.) JC.
27. *Cord Corbitt, lhp, Leonard HS, West Palm Beach, Fla.
**28. *Bret Boone, ss, El Dorado HS, Villa Park, Calif.—(1992-2005)**
DRAFT DROP *Grandson of Ray Boone, major leaguer (1948-60) • Son of Bob Boone, major leaguer (1972-90); major league manager (1995-2003) • Brother of Aaron Boone, major leaguer (1997-2009)*
29. *Glen Dallmann, c, Bradley University.
30. Walter Watts, rhp, Independence HS, San Jose, Calif.
31. *Matt Bullock, of, Alta Loma (Calif.) HS.
32. Steve Scanlon, rhp, Pepperdine University.
33. +Richard Freeman, c, Dundalk (Md.) CC.
34. *Daryl Lancaster, lhp, Whittier Christian HS, Whittier, Calif.
35. *John Stewart, of, Horace Mann HS, Gary, Ind.
**36. *Craig Paquette, 3b, Rancho Alamitos HS, Garden Grove, Calif.—(1993-2003)**
37. Tom Marten, rhp, Long Island University.
38. *Toi Cook, of, Stanford University.
DRAFT DROP *Defensive back, National Football League (1987-97)*
39. *Charles Guetter, rhp, Pensacola (Fla.) JC.
40. *Chris Garrett, rhp, Westchester HS, Los Angeles.
41. *Matt Hattabaugh, c, Marina HS, Huntington Beach, Calif.
42. +Bryan Roskom, ss, Appleton (Wis.) HS / Indian Hills (Iowa) JC.

## MONTREAL EXPOS (12)

**1. Delino DeShields, ss, Seaford (Del.) HS.—(1990-2002)**
DRAFT DROP *Father of Delino DeShields Jr., first-round draft pick, Astros (2008); major leaguer (2015)*
1. Tyrone Kingwood, of, Imperial Valley (Calif.) JC (Supplemental choice—28th—as compensation for Type A free agent Andre Dawson).—(AA)
**2. Nate Minchey, rhp, Pflugerville (Texas) HS** (Choice from Cubs as compensation for Dawson).**—(1993-97)**
**2. Richie Lewis, rhp, Florida State University.—(1992-98)**
**3. John Vander Wal, of, Western Michigan University.—(1991-2004)**
4. Boi Rodriguez, 3b, Indiana State University.—(AAA)
**5. Arci Cianfrocco, ss, Purdue University.—(1992-98)**
**6. Greg Colbrunn, 3b, Fontana (Calif.) HS.—(1992-2004)**
**7. Howard Farmer, rhp, Jackson State University.—(1990)**
DRAFT DROP *Brother of Mike Farmer, major leaguer (1996)*
8. Trevor Penn, 1b, Cal State Los Angeles.
**9. *Donovan Osborne, lhp, Carson HS, Carson City, Nev.—(1992-2004)**
DRAFT DROP *First-round draft pick (13th overall), Cardinals (1990)*
10. Chris Pollack, lhp, Florida State University.
11. Steve Lemuth, of, Pentucket Regional HS, Groveland, Mass.
12. Chris Marchok, lhp, Harvard University.
**13. Bob Natal, c, UC San Diego.—(1992-97)**
14. Terrel Hansen, rhp, Washington State University.
15. Kelvin Shephard, of, University of Montevallo (Ala.).
16. *Robbie Orndorff, 2b, Connellsville HS, Millrun, Pa.
17. Javan Reagans, of, Dallas Baptist University.
18. Tim Piechowski, of, St. Mary's (Minn.) College.
**19. Jeff Carter, rhp, University of Tampa.—(1991)**
20. Matt Shiflett, rhp, Arizona State University.
21. Rob Mason, c, University of New Orleans.
22. Tom Giannelli, 1b, University of Redlands (Calif.).
23. Kevin Cavalier, rhp, Northeast Louisiana University.
24. Jeff Atha, 2b, Jacksonville State University.
25. *Mike Sodders, lhp, University of Alabama.
26. Bruce Wegman, rhp, Central Arizona JC.
DRAFT DROP *Brother of Bill Wegman, major leaguer (1985-95)*
27. Larry Doss, of, Southwest Missouri State University.
28. *Bret Davis, rhp, Sacramento (Calif.) CC.
**29. +Kevin Foster, rhp-3b, Evanston (Ill.) HS / Kishwaukee (Ill.) JC.—(1993-2001)**
30. Steve Overeem, rhp, Southern California College.
31. *Mike Lane, 1b, Ely HS, Coral Springs, Fla.
32. *Marty Posey, of, Mosley HS, Panama City, Fla.
33. *John McGinnis, lhp, Clackamas HS, Milwaukie, Ore.
34. *Greg Kennard, rhp, Leonard HS, West Palm Beach, Fla.
35. *Jon French, ss, St. Joseph HS, Alameda, Calif.
36. *Robert Wilkinson, of, Waukegan West HS, Waukegan, Ill.
37. *Kevin Johnson, of, Taft (Calif.) JC.
38. *Peter LeBlond, of, Mesa (Ariz.) HS.
39. Roosevelt Walker, of, Selma (Ala.) HS.
40. *Mike Seda, of, Shadow Mountain HS, Phoenix.
41. James Faulk, of, Louisburg (N.C.) JC.
42. *Arnold Williams, 1b-of, Southeast Guilford HS, Greensboro, N.C.
43. *Greg Brown, ss, Indian River (Fla.) CC.
44. *Bobby Magallanes, ss, Bell HS, Downey, Calif.
DRAFT DROP *Brother of Evar Magallanes, major leaguer (1991)*
45. *David Horine, ss-2b, Chandler (Ariz.) HS.
46. *Chris Grant, of, Crenshaw HS, Los Angeles.
47. *Hermie Brown, of-1b, Crenshaw HS, Los Angeles.
48. *Lash Bailey, c, Verbum Dei HS, Compton, Calif.
49. *Robert Small, 1b, Compton (Calif.) JC.

## NEW YORK METS (24)

**1. Chris Donnels, 3b, Loyola Marymount University.—(1991-2002)**
**2. Todd Hundley, c, Fremd HS, Palatine, Ill.** (Choice from Orioles as compensation for Type B free agent Ray Knight)**—(1990-2003)**
DRAFT DROP *Son of Randy Hundley, major leaguer (1964-77)*
**2. Pete Schourek, lhp, Marshall HS, Falls Church, Va.—(1991-2001)**
3. Tim Hines, c, Kishwaukee (Ill.) JC.—(AAA)
4. Mike Miller, rhp, St. Louis CC-Meramec.—(AA)
5. *Ricky Kimball, rhp, Redan HS, Lithonia, Ga.—(Low A)
DRAFT DROP *Attended Florida State; re-drafted by Cardinals, 1990 (17th round)*
6. Jim Tesmer, of, Fresno (Calif.) CC.
7. Terry Griffin, rhp, Tennessee Temple HS, Jacksonville, Fla.
**8. Tim Bogar, ss, Eastern Illinois University.—(1993-2001)**
DRAFT DROP *Major league manager (2014)*
**9. Pat Howell, of, Vigor HS, Prichard, Ala.—(1992)**
10. Steve LaRose, rhp, Crowder (Mo.) JC.
11. Monte Krogman, rhp, Quincy (Ill.) HS.
12. Derrick Young, of, Edmonds (Wash.) CC.
**13. Terry Bross, rhp, St. John's University.—(1991-93)**
14. *Robert Pickowitz, ss-of, Indio (Calif.) HS.
15. *Todd Krumm, rhp, Michigan State University.
**16. Eric Hillman, lhp, Eastern Illinois University.—(1992-94)**
17. *Robert Dodd, lhp, River City HS, Sacramento, Calif.
**18. Denny Harriger, rhp, Ford City (Pa.) HS.—(1998)**
19. Jim McAnarney, rhp, Fort Hays State (Kan.) University.
**20. John Johnstone, rhp, Bishop Ludden HS, Liverpool, N.Y.—(1993-2000)**
21. *Kyle Irvin, rhp, Oral Roberts University.
22. David Trautwein, rhp, University of North Carolina.
23. Pat Disabato, lhp, Lewis (Ill.) University.
24. Stanton Cameron, of, Palo HS, Powell, Tenn.
25. *Gary Forrester, ss, Sacramento (Calif.) CC.
**26. *Dan Wilson, c-rhp, Barrington (Ill.) HS.—(1992-2005)**
DRAFT DROP *First-round draft pick (7th overall), Reds (1990)*
27. Doug Myres, rhp, University of Texas-Arlington.
28. *Jon Martin, c-of, Edison HS, Huntington Beach, Calif.
29. Lonnie Walker, of, University of Houston.
30. James Echols, of, East Webster HS, Mantee, Miss.
31. +Craig Scott, rhp, Franklin County HS, Cowan, Tenn. / Motlow State (Tenn.) CC.
32. Titi Roche, of, Miami-Dade CC North.
33. *Andrew Lumsdon, lhp, Brazil (Ind.) HS.
34. +Ryan Richmond, rhp, Bradley-Bourbonnais HS, Bourbonnais, Ill. / Kishwaukee (Ill.) JC.
35. *Robbie Guzik, of, Latrobe (Pa.) HS.
36. Greg Turtletaub, of, JC of San Mateo (Calif.).
37. David Joiner, 3b-of, Vanderbilt University.
**38. Anthony Young, rhp, University of Houston.—(1991-96)**
39. *Brent Bartlett, 3b, Allen County (Kan.) CC.
40. *Rob Norman, lhp, Tullahoma (Tenn.) HS.
41. Marc Wiese, 3b, Wilson HS, Tacoma, Wash.
42. Chris Hill, lhp, Duncanville (Texas) HS.
43. *Barry Johnson, rhp, Joliet Catholic HS, Joliet, Ill.
44. *Darrin White, c, Cypress Fair HS, Cypress, Texas.
45. *Shaun Lesina, rhp, JC of the Redwoods (Calif.).
46. Scott Spoolstra, of-1b, Moraine Valley (Ill.) JC.
47. Dan Segui, rhp, Kansas City (Kan.) CC.
DRAFT DROP *Son of Diego Segui, major leaguer (1962-77) • Brother of David Segui, 18th-round draft pick, Orioles (1987); major leaguer (1990-2004)*
48. *Manny Cervantes, 1b, La Serna HS, Whittier, Calif.
49. *Jeff Borgese, of, Los Gatos HS, Los Angeles.
50. *Mike Cornelius, lhp, Fenger HS, Chicago.
51. +Richard Ostopowicz, lhp, Northwood Institute (Texas) JC.
52. *William Abernathy, rhp, Bowden (Ga.) HS.
53. *Keith Dunkel, ss, Topeka West HS, Topeka, Kan.
54. *Eric Bush, of, Quincy (Ill.) HS.
55. *Michael Kirk, of, West Valley HS, Cottonwood, Calif.
56. *Ryan Hundsdorfer, 3b, Monache HS, Porterville, Calif.
57. *Joe Magill, c, J.K. Mullen HS, Littleton, Colo.
58. *Ken Henderson, of-1b, Saratoga HS, Santa Clara, Calif.
59. *Scott Sorenson, rhp, Cloquet (Minn.) HS.
60. *Terence Harshaw, c, Northeast HS, North Little Rock, Ark.

## NEW YORK YANKEES (23)

1. (Choice to Rangers as compensation for Type A free agent Gary Ward)
2. (Choice to Brewers as compensation for Type B free agent Rick Cerone)
3. Bill DaCosta, rhp, New York Tech.—(High A)
4. Doug Gogoleski, rhp, Michigan State University.—(AAA)
5. Anthony Morrison, lhp, High Point College.—(AA)
6. Tom Popplewell, rhp, Miami-Dade CC North.
**7. Dave Eiland, rhp, University of South Florida.—(1988)**
8. *Doug Tegtmeier, rhp, Beatrice (Neb.) HS.
9. Lew Hill, of, Collingwood HS, Cleveland.
10. Dean Kelley, 2b, University of Tampa.
11. Ed Martel, rhp, De la Salle HS, New Baltimore, Mich.
12. *Mike Mahady, rhp, Brewton Parker (Ga.) JC.
13. Vince Phillips, of, Muir HS, Pasadena, Calif.
**14. Gerald Williams, of, Grambling State University.—(1992-2004)**
15. Darrell Tingle, ss, Louisburg (N.C.) JC.
16. Rodney Imes, rhp, Old Dominion University.
**17. *Terry Bradshaw, ss, Windsor HS, Zuni, Va.—(1995-96)**
18. Royal Clayton, rhp, UC Riverside.
DRAFT DROP *Brother of Royce Clayton, first-round draft pick, Giants (1988); major leaguer (1991-2007)*
19. Freddie Hailey, of, Western Carolina University.
20. *Robert Coffel, c, Bremen (Ind.) HS.
21. *Rob Bargas, 3b, Sacramento (Calif.) CC.
22. David Turgeon, 3b, Davidson College.
23. Bobby Dickerson, ss, Nicholls State University.
24. Steve Erickson, c, Pepperdine University.
25. Tom Weeks, 1b, Cal Poly Pomona.
26. +David Howell, lhp, Miami-Dade CC South.
27. Sean Gargin, rhp, John Jay (N.Y.) College.
28. *Paul Meade, ss, Urbandale (Iowa) HS.
29. Dennis Ryans, ss, LaSalle HS, South Bend, Ind.
30. *Steve Tucker, lhp, Manatee (Fla.) JC.
31. *Curtis Ralph, rhp, Sacramento (Calif.) CC.
32. *Brian Faw, rhp, DeKalb Central (Ga.) JC.
33. *David Sorokowski, rhp, Southridge HS, Miami.
34. *Todd Ingram, rhp, Sammamish HS, Bellevue, Wash.
35. +Ricky Rhodes, rhp, Navarro (Texas) JC.
36. *Joel Sealer, lhp, University of Nebraska.
37. Todd Brill, lhp, Allen County (Kan.) CC.
38. *Jeff Livesey, c, Auburn University.
39. +Cullen Hartzog, rhp, Mosley HS, Panama City, Fla. / Middle Georgia JC.
40. *Todd Neibel, rhp, Southern Illinois University. /
41. Rod Ehrhard, c, University of Tampa.
**42. *James Mouton, ss, Luther Burbank HS, Sacramento, Calif.—(1994-2001)**
43. *Mike Minix, ss, Paintsville (Ky.) HS.
44. Joey Blackwell, ss, Donithan (Miss.) HS.
45. *Richard Ayers, of, Donithan (Miss.) HS.
46. Dan Roman, ss, Indiana State University.
47. *Tom Breidenbach, rhp, Concordia (N.Y.) College.
**48. Brad Ausmus, c, Cheshire (Conn.) HS.—(1993-2010)**
DRAFT DROP *Major league manager (2014-15)*
49. *David Fitzgerald, lhp, Davidson College.
50. Ken Brown, ss, Northeast Louisiana University.
51. *Jim Agemy, rhp, University of Michigan.
52. *Kevin Parrish, rhp, Cleveland State University.
53. *David Taylor, of, Miami, Fla.
54. *Brent McCoy, ss, Howard University.
55. Steve Taddeo, of, Florida State University.
56. *Derrick Pedro, of, King HS, Tampa.

## OAKLAND ATHLETICS (11)

**1. Lee Tinsley, of, Shelby County HS, Shelbyville, Ky.—(1993-97)**
2. (Choice to Angels as compensation for Type A free agent Reggie Jackson)
**3. *Scott Livingstone, 3b, Texas A&M University.—(1991-98)**
DRAFT DROP *Returned to Texas A&M; re-drafted by Tigers, 1988 (2nd round)*
**4. Scott Chiamparino, rhp, Santa Clara University.—(1990-92)**
5. Jim Chenevey, lhp, Harvard University.—(Low A)
6. Marteese Robinson, 1b, Seton Hall University.
7. Joel Smith, of, University of Tennessee.
8. Mike Ryser, c, Southern Utah State College.
9. Steve Wilson, rhp, St. Xavier (Ill.) College.
10. Kevin MacLeod, lhp, University of Toledo.
**11. *Jerry Nielsen, lhp, Florida State University.—(1992-93)**
12. Rick Berg, rhp, LeMoyne College.
13. Trevor Eldridge, ss, Cerritos (Calif.) HS.
**14. Ron Coomer, 3b, Taft (Calif.) JC.—(1995-2003)**
15. Pat Wernig, lhp, Texas A&M University.
16. Brian Veilleux, lhp, Texas Christian University.
17. Keith Watkins, of, University of Southern California.
18. *Dan Penner, rhp, Cal State Northridge.
19. Rodney Williams, ss, Waukegan West HS, Waukegan, Ill.
**20. Scott Brosius, 3b, Linfield (Ore.) College.—**

**(1991-2001)**
21. *Jay Knoblauh, of, Rice University.
22. Will Schock, rhp, University of California.
23. Steven Hosinski, rhp, Bethel (Ind.) College.
24. Roy Hill, rhp, Alcorn State University.
25. *Howard Landry, lhp, Howard (Texas) JC.
26. Mike Dockery, lhp, Abingdon (Va.) HS.
27. David Finley, ss, UC Riverside.
28. *Chad Kuhn, 1b, University of New Mexico.
29. *Andrew Nieman, rhp, Holy Cross College.
30. *Eric Campa, ss, Colton (Calif.) HS.
31. Fred Hanker, 3b, Cal State Dominguez Hills.
32. Robert Parry, of, San Diego State University.
33. *Eric Christopherson, c, Ocean View HS, Huntington Beach, Calif.

DRAFT DROP *First-round draft pick (19th overall), Giants (1990)*

34. *Antonio Adams, 2b, Vanden HS, Vacaville, Calif.
35. *Jeff Cesari, rhp, UC Santa Barbara.

## PHILADELPHIA PHILLIES (20)

1. (Choice to Tigers as compensation for Type A free agent Lance Parrish)
2. Matt Rambo, lhp, Richland (Texas) JC.—(AA)
3. **Kim Batiste, ss, St. Amant HS, Prairieville, La.—(1991-96)**
4. **Ricky Trlicek, rhp, LaGrange (Texas) HS.—(1992-97)**
5. *Dickie Dixon, lhp, Antioch HS, Nashville, Tenn.—(High A)

DRAFT DROP *Attended Mississippi; re-drafted by Twins, 1990 (27th round)*

6. **Doug Lindsey, c, Seminole (Okla.) JC.—(1991-93)**
7. **+Donnie Elliott, rhp, Deer Park (Texas) HS / San Jacinto (Texas) JC.—(1994-95)**
8. Isaac Galloway, of, Alta Loma (Calif.) HS.
9. David Allen, rhp, Greece Athena HS, Rochester, N.Y.
10. *Robert Lefebre, of, Miami-Dade CC South.
11. *Marc Helms, c, Panola (Texas) JC.
12. *Kevin Castleberry, ss, Conroe (Texas) HS.
13. Dave Willes, 2b, Brigham Young University.
14. Mark Cobb, of, Franklin HS, Columbus, Ohio.
15. Gary Maasberg, 3b, Santa Clara University.
16. Scott Reaves, 3b, Cal Poly San Luis Obispo.
17. *Jeff Williams, rhp, Wichita North HS, Wichita, Kan.
18. Steve Dell'Amico, rhp, Pepperdine University.
19. Jimmy Barragan, 1b, Oklahoma State University.
20. **Jim Vatcher, of, Cal State Northridge.—(1990-92)**
21. Troy Zerb, 2b, Ephrata (Wash.) HS.
22. Jeff Scott, c, Butler County (Kan.) CC.
23. Robert Hurta, lhp, Angelina (Texas) JC.
24. *Anthony Ward, lhp, Seminole (Okla.) JC.
25. *Jeff Hilleshiem, rhp, Central (Iowa) College.
26. Marc Lopez, rhp, Alhambra, Calif.
27. **Toby Borland, rhp, Quitman (La.) HS.—(1994-2004)**
28. John LaRosa, lhp, Cal State Northridge.
29. Steve Bates, of, Fresno State University.
30. *Jon Degennaro, rhp, Moorpark (Calif.) JC.
31. Royal Thomas, rhp, Westbrook HS, Beaumont, Texas.
32. Joe Williams, of, University of San Francisco.
33. Shelby McDonald, rhp, Alvin (Texas) CC.
34. Matt Viggiano, rhp, Cousino HS, Warren, Mich.
35. Bob Chadwick, lhp, University of Nevada-Las Vegas.
36. **Greg McCarthy, lhp, Bridgeport (Conn.) HS.—(1996-98)**
37. **Andy Carter, lhp, Springfield HS, Erdenheim, Pa.—(1994-95)**
38. *Pete Schmidt, c, Oral Roberts Univeristy
39. Phil Fagnano, rhp, University of South Florida.
40. Tony Trevino, 2b, Cal State Fullerton.
41. Eric Enos, c, University of San Francisco.
42. Rodney Hampton, of, Fostoria (Ohio) HS.
43. *Ken Bean, of, Ranger (Texas) JC.
44. *Jason DeGroote, c, Granite Hills HS, Ramona, Calif.
45. *Bill Lucid, lhp, Alemany HS, Sylmar, Calif.
46. *Greg Bicknell, rhp, Bullard HS, Fresno, Calif.
47. *Matt Lundin, ss, Tustin (Calif.) HS.
48. *Troy Mentzer, c, Allen County (Kan.) CC.
49. Corey Smith, c, McCluer HS, Ferguson, Mo.

**A rare Ivy Leaguer, Giants first-rounder Mike Remlinger spent 14 years in the big leagues**

50. Robert Britt, of, Wilmington (Del.) College.
51. *Kurt Pfeffer, 3b, Drake HS, Forest Knolls, Calif.

## PITTSBURGH PIRATES (2)

1. Mark Merchant, of, Oviedo (Fla.) HS.—(AAA)
2. **Ben Shelton, lhp-1b, Oak Park (Ill.) HS.—(1993)**
3. ***Brian Williams, ss, Lewisville HS, Fort Lawn, S.C.—(1991-2000)**

DRAFT DROP *Attended South Carolina; re-drafted by Astros, 1990 (1st round)*

4. **Wes Chamberlain, of, Jackson State University.—(1990-95)**
5. Ben Webb, rhp, Chipola (Fla.) JC.—(AA)
6. Mark Thomas, of, Santa Rosa (Calif.) JC.
7. ***Mickey Morandini, ss, Indiana University.—(1990-2000)**
8. ***Kurt Knudsen, rhp, American River (Calif.) JC.—(1992-94)**
9. Jim Haywood, lhp-1b, Dundee-Crown HS, Carpentersville, Ill.
10. Scott Barczi, c-of, Northwestern University.
11. Jose Palos, of, Castle Park HS, Chula Vista, Calif.
12. Chip Duncan, rhp, Columbus (Ga.) College.
13. Jeff Griffith, 3b, Anderson (Ind.) College.
14. Rey Vizcaino, 1b-rhp, Valdosta State (Ga.) College.
15. Craig Lewis, rhp, JC of Southern Idaho.
16. Anthony Thompson, of, Selma (Ala.) HS.
17. **Steve Carter, of, University of Georgia.—(1989-90)**
18. Kevin Burdick, 2b-ss, University of Oklahoma.
19. ***Mike Fyhrie, ss-rhp, Ocean View HS, Westminster, Calif.—(1996-2002)**
20. Mike Wall, 3b, Norwood (Mass.) HS.
21. Pete Freeman, c-1b, University of Georgia.
22. Ron Downs, rhp, University of Wyoming.
23. Mickey Peyton, of-ss, Valdosta State (Ga.) College.
24. *Jeff Knepper, rhp, Mount Union (Pa.) Area HS.
25. Keith Raisanen, of, Birmingham-Southern College.
26. ***Bob Ayrault, rhp, University of Nevada-Las Vegas.—(1992-93)**
27. Doug Torborg, lhp, University of North Carolina.

DRAFT DROP *Son of Jeff Torborg, major leaguer (1964-73); major league manager (1977-2003)*

28. Lyle Befort, rhp, Fort Hays State (Kan.) University.
29. Ed Shea, c, University of Florida.
30. +John Latham, lhp, Spartanburg Methodist (S.C.) JC.
31. George Spriggs, 2b, Anne Arundel (Md.) CC.
32. Gary Schmitt, of, Allegheny (Pa.) CC.
33. Jody Williams, 2b-ss, Hampton-Sydney (Va.) College.
34. Troy Jackson, of-1b, Canada (Calif.) JC.
35. Tim Holmes, rhp, Valparaiso University.
36. *Anthony Lee, rhp, Kishwaukee (Ill.) JC.
37. Robert Barnwell, rhp, Henderson State (Ark.) College.
38. *Mike Persichni, lhp, Penn State University.
39. Frank Moore, lhp, North Carolina Wesleyan College.
40. Andrew Stewart, of, Austin Peay State University.
41. *Jeff Shore, c, University of North Carolina-Charlotte.
42. *Troy Trollope, of, Billings (Mon.) HS.
43. *Jessie Torres, c, Nampa (Idaho) HS.
44. *Todd McCray, rhp, Santa Fe (Fla.) CC.
45. *Steve Borris, of, Valencia (Fla.) CC.
46. *Shawn Purdy, rhp, Valencia (Fla.) CC.
47. *Alfonso Bryan, of, Dundalk (Md.) CC.
48. *David Silvernail, rhp, University HS, Spokane, Wash.
49. *Reggie Hubbard, ss, Santa Rosa (Calif.) JC.
50. Rodger Castner, rhp, University of Nevada-Las Vegas.
51. *Anthony Brown, ss-of, Highlands HS, North Highland, Calif.
52. *Steve Polewski, ss, Triton (Ill.) JC.
53. **Paul Miller, rhp, Carthage (Wis.) College.—(1991-93)**

## ST. LOUIS CARDINALS (14)

1. **Cris Carpenter, rhp, University of Georgia.—(1988-96)**
2. **Jeremy Hernandez, rhp, Cal State Northridge.—(1991-95)**
3. **Ray Lankford, of, Modesto (Calif.) JC.—(1990-2004)**
4. ***Mike Ignasiak, rhp, University of Michigan.—(1991-95)**

DRAFT DROP *Returned to Michigan; re-drafted by Brewers, 1988 (8th round)*

5. **Rodney Brewer, 1b-of, University of Florida.—(1990-93)**
6. Antron Grier, of, Faulkner (Ala.) University.
7. Dean Weese, rhp, U.S. International (Calif.) University.
8. Tim Redman, c, Georgetown (Ky.) College.
9. *David Tripp, rhp-of, Mount St. Joseph HS, Glen Burnie, Md.
10. *Paul Splatt, ss, CC of Baltimore.
11. Darren Nelson, of-1b, Chapman (Calif.) College.
12. Alan Biggers, ss, Stratford HS, Goose Creek, S.C.
13. Ken Sebree, rhp, University of Florida.
14. Brad Harvick, lhp, Oral Roberts University.
15. Jean-Paul Gentleman, ss, University of Mississippi.
16. Ed Fulton, c, Florida State University.
17. Kevin Robinson, of, U.S. International (Calif.) University.
18. **Tim Sherrill, lhp, University of Arkansas.—(1990-91)**
19. Chris Houser, rhp, University of Nevada-Reno.
20. Kris Huffman, ss, Catawba (N.C.) College.
21. Frank Moran, ss-2b, U.S. International (Calif.) University.
22. Shawn Hathaway, rhp, Washington State University.
23. John Balfanz, 1b, Cal State Northridge.
24. Mike Hinkle, rhp, Kansas State University.
25. Pat Moore, c, Louisiana Tech.
26. Joey Fernandez, of, University of Florida.
27. *Ken Deal, rhp, Florida International University.
28. John Sellick, 1b, UC Riverside.
29. Clint Horsley, rhp, Liberty University.
30. Ken Smith, rhp, West Virginia University.
31. Dan Hitt, lhp, St. Louis CC-Meramec.
32. Scott Halama, rhp, Florida Atlantic University.
33. Jim Gibbs, rhp, Southwest Missouri State University.
34. Tony Russo, rhp, University of Missouri.
35. Larry Pierson, rhp, University of Missouri.
36. *Brad Court, ss, Logan HS, Union City, Calif.
37. Jerry Daniels, lhp, St. Louis CC-Meramec.
38. *William Ramirez, of, Anderson HS, Cincinnati.
39. *David Williams, rhp, Marked Tree (Ark.) HS.
40. Ryan Johnston, of, George Mason University.

## SAN DIEGO PADRES (10)

1. Kevin Garner, rhp-of, University of Texas.—(AAA)
2. **Roger Smithberg, rhp, Bradley University.—(1993-94)**
3. Bob Sheridan, rhp, Upland (Calif.) HS.—(Short-season A)
4. Darrin Reichle, rhp, St. Leo (Fla.) College.—(AA)
5. David Bond, lhp, Troy State University.—(High A)
6. **Dave Hollins, 3b, University of South Carolina.—(1990-2002)**
7. Andy Skeels, c, University of Arkansas.
8. ***Marty Cordova, ss, Bishop Gorman HS, Las Vegas, Nev.—(1995-2003)**
9. Reggie Farmer, of, University of Nevada-Las Vegas.
10. Saul Soltero, rhp, Emporia State (Kan.) University.
11. *Steve Fitzgerald, ss, Brookdale (N.J.) CC.
12. *Ed Jones, rhp, W.T. White HS, Dallas.
13. *Glen Gardner, of, Rutgers University.
14. Rich Holsman, lhp, San Diego State University.
15. Charles Hillemann, of, Southern Illinois University.
16. +Billy Reed, lhp, Santana HS, Santee, Calif. / Grossmont (Calif.) JC.
17. *Gil Torres, of, Gulf Coast (Fla.) CC.
18. Tony Lewis, rhp, Pepperdine University.
19. Steve Loubier, rhp, University of Maine.
20. Terry Gilmore, rhp, Florida Southern College.
21. *Pedro Gonzalez, c, American HS, Hialeah, Fla.
22. Kevin Farmer, c, University of South Alabama.
23. **Paul Faries, ss, Pepperdine University.—(1990-93)**
24. Monte Brooks, of, San Jose State University.
25. *Nathan LaDuke, of, Alhambra HS, Phoenix.

DRAFT DROP *11th-round draft pick, Phoenix Cardinals/National Football League (1991)*

26. ***Alan Newman, lhp, La Habra (Calif.) HS.—(1999-2000)**
27. Mike Myers, rhp, UC Santa Barbara.
28. Steve Hendricks, of, U.S. International (Calif.)

University.
29. Jay Estrada, rhp, Metropolitan State (Colo.) College.
30. *Harry Perez, of, Olivet Nazarene (Ill.) College.
31. *William Neverr, rhp, Dimond HS, Anchorage, Alaska.
32. *Jason Thornburg, 3b, Golden West HS, Visalia, Calif.
33. *Eldridge Olmstead, rhp, Cate HS, Laguna Beach, Calif.
34. *Tony Spires, rhp, Anderson (S.C.) College.

## SAN FRANCISCO GIANTS (16)

1. **Mike Remlinger, lhp, Dartmouth College.—(1991-2006)**
2. **Eric Gunderson, lhp, Portland State University.—(1990-2000)**
3. **Mike Benjamin, ss, Arizona State University.—(1989-2002)**
4. Joe Speakes, of, Poly HS, Sun Valley, Calif.—(Rookie)
5. Steve Hecht, 2b, Oral Roberts University.–(AAA)
6. Jamie Cooper, of, Dallas Baptist University.
7. *Sylvester Love, of, University of Southern Mississippi.
8. Tom Hostetler, rhp, Delta State (Miss.) University.
9. **Gil Heredia, rhp, University of Arizona.—(1991-2000)**
10. John Vuz, c, Jacksonville University.
11. *David Westwood, 1b, University of Pittsburgh.
12. *Bill Gearhart, rhp, Armstrong State (Ga.) College.
13. Randy Lind, of, Portland State University.
14. *Dan Henrikson, lhp-of, Richland (Wash.) HS.
15. Tony Michalak, ss-2b, University of Illinois.
16. *Stan Loewer, rhp, Louisiana State University.
17. Doug Messer, lhp, Florida International University.
18. **Erik Johnson, ss, UC Santa Barbara.—(1993-94)**
19. Markus Owens, c-3b, University of Hawaii.
20. Kevin Meier, rhp, Georgia Southern College.
21. Ron McClintock, 1b-of, Concordia (Ore.) College.
22. Mike Greenwood, of, Moorpark (Calif.) JC.
23. **Mark Dewey, rhp, Grand Valley State (Mich.) College.—(1990-96)**
24. Mike Ham, c, Cal State Fullerton.
25. Jim Terrill, lhp, Lamar University.
26. Keith James, of, JC of the Desert (Calif.).
27. Andy Rohn, 2b, Central Michigan University.
28. *Robert Somerville, rhp, Charles County (Md.) CC.
29. Steve Lienhard, rhp, Overton HS, Memphis, Tenn.
30. *Adam Smith, c, Oklahoma State University.
31. Rich Aldrete, of, University of California.

DRAFT DROP *Brother of Mike Aldrete, major leaguer (1986-96)*

32. Reid Gunter, rhp, Sacramento (Calif.) CC.
33. Jim Malseed, of, Winthrop College.
34. *Lennie McGuire, rhp, Mount Hood (Ore.) CC.
35. **Jimmy Myers, rhp, Crowder (Okla.) HS.—(1996)**
36. *David Klinefelter, lhp, Allegheny (Pa.) CC.
37. *Mike Meyers, 1b, Washington State University.
38. Chris Kocman, 3b, Cal State Chico.
39. Donn Perno, 2b, University of Georgia.
40. Mike Wandler, ss-3b, Point Park (Pa.) College.
41. Rocco Buffolino, rhp, Cal State Sacramento.
42. Gary Geiger, rhp, Texas A&M University.

DRAFT DROP *Son of Gary Geiger, major leaguer (1958-70)*

43. Robert Wilson, 1b, Sonoma State (Calif.) University.
44. Kip Southland, ss, Central Michigan University.
45. Glenn Abraham, of, Howard University.
46. Todd Hawkins, c, Baylor University.
47. Elanis Westbrooks, ss, University of Texas.
48. *Mike Rooney, rhp, Alemany HS, Granada Hills, Calif.

## SEATTLE MARINERS (1)

1. **Ken Griffey Jr., of, Moeller HS, Cincinnati.—(1989-2006)**

DRAFT DROP *Son of Ken Griffey, major leaguer (1973-91) • First 1987 high school draft pick to reach majors (April 3, 1989) • Elected to Baseball Hall of Fame, 2016*

2. **David Burba, rhp, Ohio State University.—(1990-2004)**
3. Mike Goff, rhp, Fresno State University.—(AA)
4. *Rick Lantrip, ss, Golden West HS, Visalia, Calif.—(Low A)

DRAFT DROP *Attended Arizona; re-drafted by Yankees, 1990 (5th round)*

5. Brian Wilkinson, rhp, Cherry Creek HS, Englewood, Colo.—(High A)

DRAFT DROP *Brother of Bill Wilkinson, major leaguer (1985-88)*

6. ***Joe Slusarski, rhp, University of New Orleans.—(1991-2001)**
7. Mike McGuire, rhp, Sweeny HS, Old Ocean, Texas.
8. ***Eric Helfand, c, Patrick Henry HS, San Diego.—(1993-95)**
9. Ted Eldredge, rhp, University of California.
10. *Tookie Spann, 3b-of, Tulane University.
11. *Bob Bretwisch, lhp, Bradley University.
12. Brian Baldwin, rhp, Northeastern University.
13. *Jim Foley, rhp, Orange Coast (Calif.) JC.
14. Keith Helton, lhp, University of Arkansas.
15. Charlie Webb, lhp, Cal Poly Pomona.
16. Corey Paul, of, Belmont HS, Los Angeles.
17. +Ellerton Maynard, of, Miami-Dade CC New World Center.
18. **Mike Gardiner, rhp, Indiana State University.—(1990-95)**
19. Dorian Daughtry, of, Kingsborough (N.Y.) CC.
20. Mike Sisco, ss, University of Arkansas.
21. Daryl Burrus, 3b-c, Locke HS, Los Angeles.
22. Kevin Reichardt, 2b, University of Wisconsin-Oshkosh.

DRAFT DROP *Son of Rick Reichardt, major leaguer (1964-74)*

23. ***Pat Listach, ss, McLennan (Texas) CC.—(1992-97)**
24. *Greg Burlingame, lhp, Univeristy of Hawaii.

DRAFT DROP *Brother of Dennis Burlingame, 5th-round draft pick, Braves (1987)*

25. Otis Patrick, of, Edmonds (Wash.) CC.
26. +Little Anthony Gordon, lhp, Avon Park (Fla.) HS / Polk (Fla.) CC.

DRAFT DROP *Brother of Tom Gordon, major leaguer (1988-2009)*

27. *Randy Rivera, rhp, Ranger (Texas) JC.
28. Tony Cayson, of, Ocala Forest HS, Ocala, Fla.
29. *Brian Cisarik, of, University of Texas.
30. Gary Cameron, lhp-1b, Utah Technical JC.
31. *Keith Barrett, of-inf, Cal Poly Pomona.
32. Ranfred Johnson, rhp, El Camino (Calif.) JC.
33. *Justin Minton, ss, Trevor Brown HS, Phoenix.
34. +Scott Pitcher, rhp, Hillsborough (Fla.) CC.
35. Steve Hisey, of, UCLA.
36. Jeff Hooper, c, Washington State University.
37. Erick Bryant, rhp, Long Beach, Calif.
38. **Todd Haney, 2b, University of Texas.—(1992-98)**
39. Scott Stoerck, rhp, Orange Coast (Calif.) JC.
40. Steve Bieksha, rhp, University of Lowell (Mass.).
41. John Hoffman, c, Ballard HS, Seattle.
42. ***Gar Finnvold, rhp, Palm Beach (Fla.) JC.—(1994)**
43. Tom Peters, rhp, Santa Monica (Calif.) JC.
44. *Jeff Brouelette, 2b, Orange Coast (Calif.) JC.
45. *Emmitt Cohick, of, Fullerton (Calif.) JC.
46. ***Jeff Darwin, rhp, Bonham (Texas) HS.—(1994-97)**

DRAFT DROP *Brother of Danny Darwin, major leaguer (1978-98)*

47. *Corey Thomas, rhp, Pinole Valley HS, Pinole, Calif.
48. *Florentino Lozano, of, Palomar (Calif.) JC.
49. *Keith May, rhp, Bassett (Va.) HS.
50. *John Burton, rhp, Bonita HS, La Verne, Calif.
51. Ruben Gonzales, 1b, Pepperdine University.
52. ***James Hurst, lhp, South Florida JC.—(1994)**
53. *David Boss, rhp, San Jose (Calif.) CC.
54. +Jeff Keitges, 1b, American River (Calif.) JC.
55. Jeff Morrison, 1b, Chapman (Calif.) College.

## TEXAS RANGERS (19)

1. **Brian Bohanon, lhp, North Shore HS, Houston.—(1990-2001)**
1. **Bill Haselman, c, UCLA** (Choice from Yankees as compensation for Type A free agent Gary Ward)**—(1990-2003)**
1. **Mark Petkovsek, rhp, University of Texas** (Supplemental choice—29th—as compensation for Ward)**—(1991-2001)**
2. **Barry Manuel, rhp, Louisiana State University.—(1991-98)**
3. **Scott Coolbaugh, 3b, University of Texas.—(1989-94)**

DRAFT DROP *Brother of Mike Coolbaugh, major leaguer (2001-02)*

4. **Jonathan Hurst, rhp, Spartanburg Methodist (S.C.) JC.—(1992-94)**
5. **Terry Mathews, rhp, Northeast Louisiana University.—(1991-99)**
6. **Kevin Belcher, of, Navarro (Texas) JC.—(1990)**
7. **Tony Scruggs, of, UCLA.—(1991)**
8. Gary Alexander, of, University of Arizona.
9. ***Bert Heffernan, c, Clemson University.—(1992)**
10. Brian Steiner, lhp, Seminole (Okla.) JC.
11. *Bryant Winslow, of, Columbine HS, Littleton, Colo.
12. Mike Taylor, rhp, McLennan (Texas) CC.
13. Glen Bruckner, 2b, Georgetown University.
14. Spencer Wilkinson, rhp, University of Arkansas.
15. Todd Van Horn, ss, St. Edward's (Texas) University.
16. Darren Niethammer, c-of, Evansville, Ind.
17. Omar Brewer, of, University of Houston.
18. Bill Losa, c, San Jacinto (Texas) JC.
19. Wayne Ebarb, rhp, Zwolle (La.) HS.
20. Mike Rogers, of, University of Missouri.
21. Rod Lung, c, McNeese State University.
22. David Lynch, lhp, University of New Orleans.
23. Adam Lamle, lhp, University of Southwestern Louisiana.
24. *Mike Helm, ss, Carson (Calif.) HS.
25. Randy Boron, rhp, Cleveland State University.
26. *Greg Logan, rhp, Martin HS, Arlington, Texas.
27. Marv Rockman, rhp, Oklahoma State University.
28. Luke Sable, of George Mason University.
29. *John Morton, rhp, University of Texas.
30. Todd Schultz, ss, Ferris State (Mich.) College.
31. **Kevin Mmahat, lhp, Tulane University.—(1989)**
32. **Robb Nen, rhp, Los Alamitos HS, Seal Beach, Calif.—(1993-2002)**

DRAFT DROP *Son of Dick Nen, major leaguer (1963-70)*

33. +Thayer Swain, of, San Jacinto (Texas) JC.
34. *Manuel Molina, rhp, Arizona Western JC.
35. ***Ed Pierce, of, Glendora HS, San Dimas, Calif.—(1992)**
36. *Brad Hebets, rhp, University of Southwestern Louisiana.
37. Todd Kopczynski, rhp, Univeristy of North Carolina.
38. *Elgin Bobo, c, Monta Vista HS, Freedom, Calif.
39. *Brian Maize, 1b, Rolling Meadows HS, Arlington Heights, Ill.
40. *Michael Brady, rhp, Nassau (N.Y.) JC.
41. *Gary Ross, rhp, San Diequito HS, Olivehaim, Calif.
42. *Kevin Jones, 3b, Seminole (Okla.) JC.
43. *Eric Stone, rhp, Seminole (Okla.) JC.
44. *Charlton Lynch, inf-of, Lincoln HS, San Diego.
45. *Mike Burton, 1b, JC of the Sequoias (Calif.).
46. *Kevin Weik, rhp-ss, Trinity HS, Bedford, Texas.
47. ***Keith Osik, ss, Wading River (N.Y.) HS.—(1996-2004)**
48. *Ernie Carr, of, Jacksonville Unversity.
49. Angel Caceres, 1b, Arizona Western JC.
50. Brian Romero, lhp, East Los Angeles JC.
51. *Anthony Hicks, of, University of Maryland.

## TORONTO BLUE JAYS (17)

1. **Alex Sanchez, rhp, UCLA.--(1989)**
2. **Derek Bell, of, King HS, Tampa.—(1991-2001)**
3. Bob Wishnevski, rhp, Kishwaukee (Ill.) JC.—(AAA)
4. Ed Smith, of, Warrior (Ala.) HS.—(Low A)
5. **Mike Timlin, rhp, Southwestern (Texas) University.—(1991-2008)**
6. Matt Gilmore, ss, Reseda HS, Encino, Calif.
7. Jason Townley, rhp, Escambia HS, Pensacola, Fla.
8. Joe Newcomb, rhp, Memphis State University.
9. ***Kevin King, lhp, Braggs (Okla.) HS.—(1993-95)**
10. ***Darrell Whitmore, ss, Warren County HS, Front Royal, Va.—(1993-95)**
11. Nate Cromwell, lhp, Chaparral HS, Las Vegas, Nev.
12. Chris Lariviere, rhp, Cal State Los Angeles.
13. **Ryan Thompson, of, Kent County HS, Rock Hall, Md.—(1992-2002)**
14. Terrence Wilson, of, Clintondale HS, Clemens, Mich.
15. Brian Rollins, ss-2b, Crenshaw HS, Los Angeles.
16. Mark Young, of, UC Riverside.
17. *Anton Mobley, of, Fernandina Beach (Fla.) HS.
18. ***David Haas, rhp, Wichita State University.—(1991-93)**
19. **Rob MacDonald, lhp, Rutgers University.—(1990-96)**
20. Greg Vella, 1b, UC Santa Barbara.
21. Mike Chesney, c, New York Tech.
22. *Pierre Sylvain, rhp, Nicholls State University.
23. Jim Trahey, rhp, Eastern Michigan University.
24. ***Erik Schullstrom, rhp, Alameda HS, San Leandro, Calif.—(1994-95)**
25. Steve Baucom, 3b, Clemson University.
26. *Chris Butterfield, rhp-of, Merced (Calif.) JC.
27. +Shawn Scott, of-ss, El Camino HS, Pacifica, Calif. / San Mateo (Calif.) JC.
28. Rodney Richey, rhp, University of South Carolina.
29. Steven Roberts, of-1b, UC Davis.
30. **Steve Wapnick, rhp, Fresno State University.—(1990-91)**
31. Allan Silverstein, rhp, New York Tech.
32. *Greg Perschke, rhp, Southwestern Michigan JC.
33. Anthony Conliffe, rhp, West Virginia University.
34. *Joe Summers, of, Royal HS, Simi Valley, Calif.
35. *Allen Tyson, rhp, Glen Oak HS, Canton, Ohio.
36. *Todd Ross, ss, Lassen (Calif.) CC.
37. Dan Etzweiler, 3b, University of Maine.
38. Steve Berriatua, ss, University of San Francisco.
39. *Rodney Mills, of, Anderson (Ind.) HS.
40. *Bruce Bensching, rhp, Clarkston (Wash.) HS.
41. *Pat Rodgers, of, Pensacola (Fla.) JC.
42. +Todd Embry, rhp, Paris (Texas) HS / Paris (Texas) JC.
43. *David Atkinson, of-3b, Waukegan (Ill.) HS.
44. Bob Bevis, rhp, Western Michigan University.
45. ***Darren Lewis, of, Chabot (Calif.) JC.—(1990-2002)**
46. Darrin Wade, 1b, Jackson State University.
47. *Rick Nowak, rhp, UC San Diego.
48. *William Abare, 1b, St. Augustine (Fla.) HS.
49. *Michael Stewart, of, Fresno State University.

DRAFT DROP *Defensive back, National Football League (1987-96)*

50. *Mario Baker, ss, Thomasville (Ga.) HS.
51. *Jeff Burr, rhp, San Gorgonio HS, Highland, Calif.
52. Cisco Johnson, 2b, St. Leo (Fla.) College.
53. +Mike Taylor, ss, San Jacinto (Texas) JC.
54. *Wes Bliven, rhp, Santa Clara University.
55. *John Booth, rhp, Sullivan (Ind.) HS.
56. *Jeff Beck, rhp, El Camino (Calif.) JC.
57. ***Orlando Palmeiro, of, Southridge HS, Miami.—(1995-2007)**
58. *Doug McCoy, 2b, Laurel HS, New Castle, Pa.
59. *David Keating, of, UCLA.
60. *Matthew Barker, of, Taylor HS, DeLand, Fla.
61. Willy Fillard, 3b, Slippery Rock State (Pa.) University.
62. *Michael Roberts, of, North Florida JC.
63. *Thomas Strabazy, of, Bishop Noll HS, Whiting, Ind.
64. *Fausto Tejero, c, Miami-Dade CC New World Center.
65. *Eugene Nicholas, ss, Utica (Miss.) JC.
66. Terrence L. Wilson, rhp, Warren (Pa.) HS.
67. *Eric Cullens, ss, Hillsborough (Fla.) CC.
68. *Sergio Guasch, rhp, Miami-Dade CC North.
69. *Todd Hudson, rhp, Cardinal Mooney HS, Sarasota, Fla.
70. ***Tom Marsh, rhp, University of Toledo.—(1992-95)**
71. +Brian Dixon, of-2b, Clearwater (Fla.) HS / Manatee (Fla.) CC.

# 1988

# Teams go college early, find Piazza, Lofton late

Andy Benes' wife Jennifer helps him try on a Padres jersey for size after San Diego made him the No. 1 pick in the 1988 draft out of Evansville

Six days before the 1988 draft, the San Diego Padres still had not completely made up their minds to take Evansville pitcher Andy Benes with the No. 1 pick. They needed one more piece of evidence to convince them he was their man.

Benes provided it May 26, when he shut out No. 2 Arizona State 1-0 in the opening round of the NCAA regional in Tempe, Ariz. Six Padres officials were on hand to see Benes stop the Sun Devils on eight hits, while striking out eight.

"He was awesome," Padres scouting director Tom Romenesko said. "If Arizona State had been using wood bats, they could have started a bonfire with the broken ones."

The victory put Benes' record at 16-3 and capped a brilliant season for the 6-foot-5, 230-pound righthander, a relative unknown at the start of the 1988 college season.

San Diego had the No. 1 pick in the draft for the fourth time in its 20-year history. With the three previous picks (Mike Ivie in 1970, Dave Roberts in 1972 and Bill Almon in 1974) having achieved only marginal success, the Padres were committed to getting the right man this time.

A total of 14 Padres officials saw Benes at one point during the 1988 season. Almost as many saw Auburn's Gregg Olson. The decision came down to those two college righthanders, neither of whom was drafted out of high school three years earlier.

"They're two very similar pitchers," said general manager Jack McKeon, who had installed himself as manager of the struggling Padres four days before the draft but saw both pitchers several times. "About the only difference between the two is that Olson has a better curveball."

Benes began to open eyes when he struck out 21 against UNC Wilmington in March with a fastball clocked at 94 mph. By the time he beat ASU, he had struck out a national-best 188 in 146 innings. An NCAA-record eight shutouts contributed to a 1.42 ERA. Romenesko actually became convinced Benes was a candidate to be the No. 1 pick when he saw him in an early-season loss against Purdue.

"Every time I'd seen him before there were dozens of scouts," Romenesko said. "This time there was only a guy from Cleveland and myself. It was a real lousy day, and Andy lost the game when he jammed a guy and the wind blew (the ball) out of the park. He knocked the next guy on his ass. That's when I knew I wanted him."

Olson's progress, meanwhile, was inhibited by illness and injury. He pitched with a broken toe in February and battled mononucleosis in April and May, wearing a flak jacket to protect his infected spleen. Still, he went 7-3, 2.00 with 10 saves in his role as Auburn's closer. He also struck out 113 in

## AT A GLANCE

### This Date In History
June 1-3

### Best Draft
**HOUSTON ASTROS.** The Astros got no mileage out of **WILLIE ANSLEY**, a first-round pick who signed for $180,000, but drafted two players who had standout careers. **LUIS GONZALEZ** (4) played 19 seasons in the majors, hitting .283 with 354 homers, and **KENNY LOFTON** (17), who played 17 years (only one with the Astros), hit .299, scored 1,528 runs and stole 622 bases. Gonzalez' price tag was $35,000, Lofton's $12,000.

### Worst Draft
**CHICAGO CUBS. TY GRIFFIN** was a major disappointment as the top pick, but none of the team's next 13 selections ascended to the majors, either. The only players the club signed who became big leaguers were **KEVIN ROBERSON** (16), who hit .194 in 138 games with the Cubs, and **JESSIE HOLLINS** (40), who worked just five innings.

### First-Round Bust
**BILL BENE, RHP, DODGERS.** The Dodgers looked past Bene's history of wildness in college and paid the price as he walked 489 in 444 minor league innings, which resulted in a 15-30, 5.59 record in 10 seasons. In 1989 and 1990, Bene walked 152 and struck out only 58 in 84 innings, while going 1-14, 8.04.

### Second Time Around
**ARTHUR RHODES, LHP, ORIOLES.** Rhodes hung around the major leagues for 20 years, and pitched in 900 games with nine teams. He went 87-70, 4.08 with 33 saves, and most impressive struck out 1,152 batters in 1,188 innings.

### Late Round Find
**KENNY LOFTON, OF, INDIANS (17TH ROUND).** Lofton was a renowned basketball player at

CONTINUED ON PAGE 348

## AT A GLANCE

**CONTINUED FROM PAGE 347**

Arizona, setting school career records for assists and steals. He played in just five baseball games there, but the Astros were smitten with his speed and center-field skills, and astutely took a mid-round stab at him.

### Never Too Late

**MIKE PIAZZA, C, DODGERS (62ND ROUND).** The best late-round find in draft history, Piazza was selected only as a favor to his godfather Tommy Lasorda, then the Dodgers manager. Piazza defied long odds by becoming one of the greatest offensive catchers in history, winning election to the Hall of Fame in 2016.

### Overlooked

**BOB WELLS, RHP, PHILLIES.** Wells signed as a nondrafted free agent for $1,000, but pitched in just five innings in 1994 before being put on waivers. The Washington junior-college product was claimed by the home-state Mariners, and spent five seasons in that organization, winning 12 games in 1996. He played nine seasons in the majors.

### International Gem

**PEDRO MARTINEZ, RHP, DODGERS.** Puerto Ricans became subject to the draft in 1989, after sizeable bonuses were doled out in 1987 (Ramser Correa, $125,000) and 1988. Outfielder **MELVIN NIEVES** (Braves, $103,400), shortstop **WIL CORDERO** (Expos, $100,000), first baseman **CARLOS DELGADO** (Blue Jays, $90,000) and catcher **IVAN RODRIGUEZ** (Rangers, $20,000) were the most prominent signings, but Martinez, a Dominican who became a future Hall of Famer, trumped them all.

### Minor League Take

**TINO MARTINEZ, 1B, MARINERS.** Martinez was the best hitter in the NCAA Division II ranks and for the U.S. Olympic team in 1988, and put the final touches on a productive 16-year

## 1988: THE FIRST ROUNDERS

| CLUB: PLAYER, POS., SCHOOL | HOMETOWN | B-T | HT. | WT. | AGE | BONUS | FIRST YEAR | LAST YEAR | PEAK LEVEL (YEARS) |
|---|---|---|---|---|---|---|---|---|---|
| 1. Padres: Andy Benes, rhp, Evansville | Evansville, Ind. | R-R | 6-5 | 230 | 20 | $235,000 | 1989 | 2002 | Majors (14) |
| Concentrated on baseball only as college JR, improved dramatically (16-3, 1.42, 146 IP/188 SO); won 155 games in majors, joined brother Alan in Cards rotation. | | | | | | | | | |
| 2. Indians: Mark Lewis, ss, Hamilton HS | Hamilton, Ohio | R-R | 6-1 | 170 | 18 | $180,000 | 1988 | 2001 | Majors (11) |
| Hit .600-15-66 as prep SR, universally praised for SS actions/instincts at time, but suspect defense hurt prowess in pro ball; hit .263-48-306 in majors for six clubs. | | | | | | | | | |
| 3. Braves: Steve Avery, lhp, Kennedy HS | Taylor, Mich. | L-L | 6-4 | 185 | 18 | $211,500 | 1988 | 2003 | Majors (11) |
| On top of baseball world with pair of 1-0 wins in '91 NLCS, became key part of Braves rotation with Glavine/Maddux/Smoltz until shoulder issues killed career. | | | | | | | | | |
| 4. Orioles: Gregg Olson, rhp, Auburn | Omaha, Neb. | R-R | 6-4 | 210 | 21 | $188,000 | 1988 | 2001 | Majors (14) |
| Dominant college reliever (combined 18-4, 1.62, 20 SV, 150 IP/209 SO as SO/JR), had 160 saves from 1989-93 for Orioles before sore shoulder doomed his career. | | | | | | | | | |
| 5. Dodgers: Bill Bene, rhp, Cal State Los Angeles | Long Beach, Calif. | R-R | 6-4 | 190 | 20 | $150,000 | 1988 | 1997 | Class AAA (2) |
| Dodgers gambled on pitcher with mid-90s arm, history of wildness; got burned by 15-30, 5.59 record, 489 walks in 444 IP in career that peaked in Triple-A. | | | | | | | | | |
| 6. Rangers: Monty Fariss, ss, Oklahoma State | Leedey, Okla. | R-R | 6-4 | 180 | 20 | $156,000 | 1988 | 2005 | Majors (3) |
| Drafted as Cal Ripken-style SS after .397-30-114 season for Cowboys, but regressed in field as pro, never hit enough (.217-4-29 in majors) to support shift to 3B/OF. | | | | | | | | | |
| 7. Astros: Willie Ansley, of, Plainview HS | Plainview, Texas | R-R | 6-2 | 195 | 18 | $180,000 | 1989 | 1993 | Class AAA (1) |
| Considred a poor man's Bo Jackson; had same explosive tools, strong/powerful frame, acceleration out of box; career derailed by back, shoulder injuries. | | | | | | | | | |
| 8. Angels: Jim Abbott, lhp, Michigan | Flint, Mich. | L-L | 6-3 | 200 | 20 | $200,000 | 1989 | 1999 | Majors (10) |
| Ultimate human-interest story of draft era; thrived in college, won Olympic gold, made electrifying debut with Angels, hurled no-hitter for Yankees to cap career. | | | | | | | | | |
| 9. Cubs: Ty Griffin, 2b, Georgia Tech | Tampa | B-R | 6-0 | 180 | 20 | $152,500 | 1989 | 2005 | Class AA (5) |
| Thrived as 2B in college, on Olympic team; drafted as potential successor to Ryne Sandberg, but career flamed out when moved to new position, offense stalled out. | | | | | | | | | |
| 10. White Sox: Robin Ventura, 3b, Oklahoma State | Santa Maria, Calif. | L-R | 6-1 | 170 | 20 | $186,500 | 1989 | 2004 | Majors (16) |
| Hitting machine at Oklahoma State, compared to Wade Boggs in style/approach; developed from one-tool talent to complete player in 16 major league seasons. | | | | | | | | | |
| 11. Phillies: Pat Combs, lhp, Baylor | Houston | L-L | 6-3 | 200 | 21 | $145,000 | 1989 | 1995 | Majors (4) |
| Polished lefty with plus fastball, four pitches for strikes; made impressive debut, led Phils in wins in second year, but elbow/shoulder issues cut career short. | | | | | | | | | |
| 12. Red Sox: Tom Fischer, lhp, Wisconsin | West Bend, Wis. | L-L | 5-11 | 190 | 21 | $110,000 | 1988 | 1993 | Class AAA (2) |
| Hard-throwing lefty went 6-6, 5.00 as college JR, though had masterful 19-SO/7-IP game; nephew of Red Sox pitching coach Bill Fischer never reached majors. | | | | | | | | | |
| 13. Pirates: Austin Manahan, ss, Horizon HS | Phoenix | R-R | 6-1 | 175 | 18 | $115,000 | 1988 | 1995 | Class AA (3) |
| Younger brother of Anthony, Mariners 1990 first-rounder; pro career got off to rough start (.201 BA, 177 SOs, 61 errors in first 478 ABs), released by Pirates in '93. | | | | | | | | | |
| 14. Mariners: Tino Martinez, 1b, Tampa | Tampa | L-R | 6-2 | 190 | 20 | $135,000 | 1989 | 2005 | Majors (16) |
| Dominated D-II ranks (.452-25-76), powered Olympic team to gold, slugged 339 homers in majors, replaced Mattingly at 1B for Yankees, went deep 44 times in '97. | | | | | | | | | |
| 15. Giants: Royce Clayton, ss, St. Bernard HS | Playa del Rey, Calif. | R-R | 6-0 | 175 | 18 | $180,000 | 1988 | 2007 | Majors (17) |
| Soured Giants early with unimpressive bat, but turned corner when he developed plate discipline; became elite defender, played for 11 teams in majors. | | | | | | | | | |
| 16. Athletics: Stan Royer, 3b, Eastern Illinois | Charleston, Ill. | R-R | 6-3 | 195 | 20 | $110,000 | 1988 | 1994 | Majors (4) |
| A's projected him as power-hitting catcher, but never developed power and didn't take to position switch; sent to Cardinals, hit just .250-4-21 in 89 MLB games. | | | | | | | | | |
| 17. Indians: Charles Nagy, rhp, Connecticut | Fairfield, Conn. | R-R | 6-1 | 200 | 21 | $126,000 | 1989 | 2003 | Majors (14) |
| Played football as freshman at Cornell, but baseball career took off after transfer to UConn; twice Big East pitcher of year, won 15-plus games six times in majors. | | | | | | | | | |
| 18. Royals: Hugh Walker, of, Jacksonville HS | Jacksonville, Ark. | L-R | 6-1 | 190 | 18 | $116,000 | 1988 | 1994 | Class AAA (1) |
| Compared to Kirby Puckett because of small, powerful frame, speed, desire to excel, but career did not compare; hit just .248-48-306 in seven seasons in minors. | | | | | | | | | |
| 19. Expos: Dave Wainhouse, rhp, Washington State | Mercer Island, Wash. | R-R | 6-2 | 182 | 20 | $115,000 | 1989 | 2001 | Majors (7) |
| Born in Toronto, reconnected to Canadian heritage when drafted by Expos, became ace of Olympic squad; had five-pitch repertoire but modest MLB career. | | | | | | | | | |
| 20. Twins: Johnny Ard, rhp, Manatee (Fla.) JC | Hemingway, S.C. | R-R | 6-5 | 215 | 21 | $95,000 | 1988 | 1993 | Class AA (2) |
| Triumphed over adversity after father disabled in accident, created hardship for family; had promising start for Twins, shoulder issues hampered career with Giants. | | | | | | | | | |
| 21. Mets: Dave Proctor, rhp, Allen County (Kan.) CC | Topeka, Kan. | R-R | 6-3 | 200 | 20 | $100,000 | 1988 | 1992 | Class AA (2) |
| Nephew of ex-big leaguer Mike Torrez turned back on promising hoops career; got velocity to 97 mph in Mets system before five arm surgeries spelled end of career. | | | | | | | | | |
| 22. Cardinals: John Ericks, rhp, Illinois | Tinley Park, Ill. | R-R | 6-7 | 215 | 20 | $92,500 | 1988 | 1997 | Majors (3) |
| Intimidating with 6-7 frame, fastball that peaked at 97, but career plagued by wildness, arm trouble; cut by Cards after surgery, but reached majors with Pirates. | | | | | | | | | |
| 23. Cardinals: Brad DuVall, rhp, Virginia Tech | Silver Spring, Md. | R-R | 6-1 | 185 | 22 | $92,500 | 1988 | 1990 | Class A (2) |
| Fourth player in draft history to become two-time first-rounder; went 11-3, 3.82 as college SR, but pro career plagued by arm problems, never made it out of A-ball. | | | | | | | | | |
| 24. Brewers: Alex Fernandez, rhp, Monsignor Pace HS | Miami | R-R | 6-1 | 205 | 18 | Unsigned | 1990 | 2000 | Majors (10) |
| Brewers let decorated young talent get away; dominated Miami prep ranks, became college star, won Golden Spikes Award on way to becoming 1990 first-rounder. | | | | | | | | | |
| 25. Blue Jays: Ed Sprague, 3b, Stanford | Stockton, Calif. | R-R | 6-2 | 190 | 20 | $100,000 | 1989 | 2002 | Majors (11) |
| Celebrated career included playing for two-time CWS champs, gold-medal Team USA squad, two-time World Series champ Blue Jays; hit .247-152-558 in majors. | | | | | | | | | |
| 26. Tigers: Rico Brogna, 1b, Watertown HS | Watertown, Conn. | R-R | 6-2 | 190 | 18 | $100,000 | 1988 | 2001 | Majors (9) |
| Clemson QB recruit languished in Tigers system, played just nine games in Detroit; career took off with Phillies; hit 64 HRs, drove in 287 runs in three years. | | | | | | | | | |

72 innings.

"I haven't really pitched healthy this year," Olson said. "No one knows what I can do."

### OLSON FIRST TO REACH MAJORS

Benes and Olson, and two high school selections, shortstop Mark Lewis and lefthander Steve Avery, formed a clearly defined quartet at the top of the draft.

The Padres went for Benes, and the Cleveland Indians and Atlanta Braves followed suit by taking Lewis and Avery. The Baltimore Orioles selected fourth and were overjoyed that Olson was there. Like the Padres, the Orioles were seeking a polished college arm capable of pitching in the big leagues in short order, and they also believed there

## How They Should Have Done It

Based on the career WAR (Wins Above Replacement, as calculated by Baseball-Reference.com) numbers achieved by all the players eligible for the 1988 draft, here's how the first round should have unfolded. Numbers in parentheses indicate the round when the player was actually drafted. Asterisk denotes a player who signed as a draft-and-follow.

| | Player, Pos. | Actual Draft | WAR | Bonus |
|---|---|---|---|---|
| 1. | Kenny Lofton, of | Astros (17) | 68.1 | $12,000 |
| 2. | Jim Edmonds, of | Angels (7) | 60.3 | $22,500 |
| 3. | Mike Piazza, c | Dodgers (62) | 59.2 | $15,000 |
| 4. | Robin Ventura, 3b | White Sox (1) | 55.9 | $186,500 |
| 5. | Luis Gonzalez, 1b | Astros (4) | 51.5 | $35,000 |
| 6. | Tim Wakefield, 1b | Pirates (8) | 34.6 | $15,000 |
| 7. | Brian Jordan, of | Cardinals (1-S) | 32.7 | $92,500 |
| 8. | John Valentin, ss | Red Sox (5) | 32.5 | $40,000 |
| 9. | Andy Benes, rhp | Padres (1) | 31.7 | $235,000 |
| 10. | Woody Williams, rhp | Blue Jays (28) | 30.9 | $1,000 |
| 11. | Marquis Grissom, of | Expos (3) | 29.5 | $48,000 |
| 12. | Tino Martinez, 1b | Mariners (1) | 29.0 | $135,000 |
| 13. | Charles Nagy, rhp | Indians (1) | 25.3 | $126,000 |
| 14. | Darren Oliver, lhp | Rangers (3) | 22.5 | $50,000 |
| 15. * | Damion Easley, ss | Angels (30) | 20.4 | $40,000 |
| 16. | Jim Abbott, lhp | Angels (1) | 19.9 | $200,000 |
| 17. | Royce Clayton, ss | Giants (1) | 19.4 | $180,000 |
| 18. | Arthur Rhodes, lhp | Orioles (2) | 15.4 | $45,000 |
| 19. | Steve Avery, lhp | Braves (1) | 14.0 | $211,500 |
| 20. | Gregg Olson, rhp | Orioles (1) | 13.2 | $188,000 |
| 21. | Tim Naehring, ss | Red Sox (8) | 12.7 | $25,000 |
| 22. | Gary DiSarcina, ss | Angels (6) | 11.2 | $21,500 |
| 23. | David Weathers, rhp | Blue Jays (3) | 10.9 | $37,500 |
| 24. | Darren Lewis, of | Athletics (18) | 10.5 | $20,000 |
| 25. | Eric Karros, 1b | Dodgers (6) | 10.2 | $32,500 |
| 26. | Mickey Morandini, ss | Phillies (5) | 9.7 | $25,000 |
| | Rheal Cormier, lhp | Cardinals (6) | 9.7 | $15,000 |

| | Top 3 Unsigned Players | | | Year Signed |
|---|---|---|---|---|
| 1. | Alex Fernandez, rhp | Brewers (1) | 28.9 | 1990 |
| 2. | Scott Erickson, rhp | Blue Jays (44) | 25.1 | 1989 |
| 3. | Aaron Sele, rhp | Twins (37) | 20.6 | 1991 |

was little to distinguish between Benes and Olson.

Olson did get there first, on Sept. 2, 1988, after he passed on an opportunity to play with the U.S. Olympic team. He worked out of the Orioles bullpen over the final month of the season, while Benes and a handful of other first-round picks were winning gold at the Olympics in Seoul, South Korea.

The Orioles had been burned four years earlier when first-round pick John Hoover, ace of the 1984 Olympic staff, came down with a sore arm after being overworked and never fulfilled his potential. So they were reluctant to have Olson pitch for the 1988 Olympic squad, and a commitment that he would be in the big leagues by September persuaded him to drop off the team.

The Orioles were also in the midst of one of the worst periods in their storied history, having opened the 1988 season with a major league record 21 straight losses. They looked to Olson to change the club's fortunes, and by saving 27 games in 1989 he became the catalyst as the O's went from 54-107 in 1988 to 87-75 a year later. Over a five-year period, Olson saved 160 games before his career was beset by elbow problems.

Benes delayed his pro career until 1989 because of his involvement in the Olympics. He began the season in the minor leagues, though he was in San Diego's rotation by August.

Auburn righthander Gregg Olson fell to the Orioles with the No. 4 pick, and he quickly became a dominant closer before injuries struck

Benes' rise was more dramatic than Olson's as he wasn't even in early-round consideration at the start of his junior season at Evansville.

In his first two years in college, Benes played football and basketball, in addition to baseball. As a sophomore quarterback, he threw for 1,400 yards in six games; he also caught 30 passes in four other games as a tight end. He produced only a 7-5, 4.38 record that season for the baseball team.

It was apparent even then that Benes had the talent to emerge as an elite-level draft pick; he just had to channel all his efforts into pitching to realize it.

"When he came here, he was not a power pitcher because he played football, baseball and basketball," Evansville baseball coach Jim Brownlee said. "He thought he was going to be a Division I basketball player. But nobody (scouts) ever talked to him."

Benes recognized that he was spreading his considerable talents too thin and devoted all his attention to baseball as a junior.

"I realized my future was with baseball," Benes said. "If I was going to pursue a pro baseball career, I had to spend more time with it. I wouldn't have been a first-round pick had I stayed with football. I wanted to be a pro baseball player and a good one."

Once he made the decision, the results were sudden and dramatic. Benes started 3-0 as a junior, highlighted by his 21-strikeout masterpiece against UNC Wilmington. Scouts descended, and he went nearly 40 innings at one point without giving up a run. His fastball was clocked as high as 100 mph.

"At the beginning of the season, coach Brownlee told me how hard I needed to work to become a No. 1 draft pick," Benes said. "I knew I needed to get off to a good start. And I did."

Benes never slowed down and not only became the No. 1 pick but also went on to sign the richest bonus contract to that point in draft history.

### THREE PLAYERS TOP BONUS MARK

By agreeing with the Padres on a $235,000 bonus on June 20, Benes took bonus payments to new

**AT A GLANCE**

major league career by hitting .320-17-93 and .326-18-86 at Triple-A Calgary in 1990 and 1991.

### One Who Got Away

**ALEX FERNANDEZ, RHP, BREWERS (1ST ROUND).** Fernandez was no ordinary first-rounder who eluded the Brewers in 1988. He became the fourth overall pick two years later, drafted by the White Sox after going 15-2, 2.01 (148 IP/177 SO) as a freshman at Miami, and 12-2, 1.19 (121 IP/154 SO) at Miami-Dade CC South in 1990. He became the first juco player to win the Golden Spikes Award.

### He Was Drafted?

**TODD MARINOVICH, LHP, ANGELS (43RD ROUND).** Marinovich was a touted quarterback at Southern California, and later played in eight games for the NFL's Los Angeles Raiders. He was better known for his intense training regimen as a young athlete, orchestrated by his father Marv. Though drafted by the Angels as a lefthanded pitcher, he never played baseball in college.

### Did You Know . . .

Tim Stoddard and **KENNY LOFTON** are the only athletes to play for a Final Four team in the NCAA men's basketball tournament as well as in a World Series. Stoddard played for North Carolina State's 1974 championship hoops squad and appeared in the 1979 World Series for the Orioles. Lofton played in the 1988 Final Four for Arizona and in the 1995 World Series for the Indians. Coincidentally, Stoddard and Lofton attended the same high school, Washington High in East Chicago, Ind.

### They Said It

Angels scouting director **BOB FONTAINE JR.**, on **JIM ABBOTT**, the club's No. 1 pick: "This is the only kid I've ever signed that I'm 100 percent sure what kind of makeup he has."

## DRAFT SPOTLIGHT: JIM ABBOTT

In late May 1988, 10 California Angels front-office officials gathered to prepare for the draft. As they scanned their scouting reports, they kept coming to the same conclusion: Two hands are not necessarily better than one.

The Angels had the eighth pick overall, and they used it to get University of Michigan lefthander Jim Abbott, who had gained much notoriety in college and amateur circles as a one-handed pitching prospect. Abbott was not expected to be drafted so early, but the Angels either knew something that other clubs didn't or were gambling that Abbott would be a potential drawing card and divert attention from the organization's on-field struggles.

**The Angels had no misgiving in making Michigan's Jim Abbott their first-round pick, and he had a solid major league career**

The company line was that Abbott, who went 26-8, 3.03 in three seasons at Michigan, was chosen solely on his major league potential, and general manager Mike Port, scouting director Bob Fontaine Jr. and minor league director Bill Bavasi were unanimous in their belief that Abbott best suited their needs. Angels officials were convinced Abbott's 93 mph fastball outweighed any liabilities he might pose defensively.

"We looked very closely at the fielding aspect," said Angels scout George Bradley, who had followed Abbott since his high school days in Michigan. "We analyzed it and cross-checked it. We had a lot of people see him and the consensus was that he handles it well."

Abbott balanced his glove on the stub of his right arm during delivery, then stuffed his left hand into the glove on the follow-through. He had been adept at switching the ball from his glove to his bare hand and throwing it for years.

There was little urgency to sign Abbott because of his commitment to the U.S. Olympic team, but the sides agreed on a $200,000 bonus on Aug. 3. He pitched in and won the gold-medal game in Seoul for the victorious U.S. squad. His inspiring story led to his becoming the only baseball player ever to win the Sullivan Award, emblematic of the country's best amateur athlete.

The next spring, he pitched so impressively in spring training that he cracked the Opening Day rotation—becoming the 17th player in the draft era to make his professional debut in the big leagues.

Abbott became an instant gate attraction, and his initial appearance on April 8, 1989 not only drew a capacity crowd, but was one of the most electric debuts in major league history. It was also one of the most heavily scrutinized appearances, as well, as the Angels were questioned over their motivation to begin Abbot's career at the highest level.

"There are those who will say that he made the team for purely mercenary reasons," Port said, "and it is hard to fight that perception. We just have to hope that Jim's performance is good enough to substantiate the decision we made.

"I think we had in mind he would be in the big leagues sometime in 1989. But that came to quick revision once we got to know Jim and saw him against some pretty good major league hitters. We appraised it as accurately and realistically as we could."

Other Angels officials who had gotten to know Abbott while scouting him in college had little doubt that he could handle all the publicity surrounding his physical disability and would make a fairly easy transition to the major leagues.

"He's the only guy we ever drafted," Bavasi said, "where you knew going in what he had inside. Bob (Fontaine) said at the time, 'This is the only kid I've ever signed that I'm 100 percent sure what kind of makeup he has.'

"He has great ability and he has it right here," Bavasi added, pointing to his heart, "so you're going to get his best game every time out. And that's good enough to win at this level."

Abbott went on to pitch 10 years in the major leagues for four teams. He won 87 games and had a 4.25 career ERA, and pitched a no-hitter for the Yankees in 1993.

heights in 1988. He broke the mark of $208,000, set in 1979 by first baseman Todd Demeter, a second-round pick of the New York Yankees. Two high school pitchers—Avery and righthander Reid Cornelius—also surpassed the previous record.

Avery got a $211,500 bonus on June 30 from the Braves after going 13-0, 0.51 with 196 strikeouts in 88 innings, while also hitting .511 with eight homers and 44 RBIs as a senior at Kennedy High in Taylor, Mich. He had a Stanford University scholarship as an additional bargaining chip.

Success in the professional ranks came almost as easily for the 6-foot-4, 180-pound lefthander. In his first two seasons in the Braves system, Avery went 19-8, 1.93 and averaged better than a strikeout an inning, earning recognition as the best pitching prospect in baseball.

"He's the best major league prospect I've seen in the Braves organization (since 1975), no doubt," said Bobby Dews, the Braves director of player development. "The thing that stands out for me is his offspeed stuff is so advanced for his age. You see a lot of kids with great fastballs, but when they get to the big leagues if that's the only thing they can get over the plate, they are in trouble. He is able to get all his pitches over."

Avery seemed to have the world by the tail when he debuted in the Braves rotation at 20, and pitched alongside future Hall of Famers Tom Glavine and John Smoltz, and later Greg Maddux. In 1991, he won 18 games for the worst-to-first Braves, and a pair of 1-0 decisions over Pittsburgh in the National League Championship Series.

But almost as quickly as Avery rose, going 47-25, 3.17 from 1991-93, his career suddenly went into rapid decline, stemming initially from an injured muscle in his side and later arm problems. In his final three seasons, from 1997-99 after being let go by the Braves, he went 22-21, 5.26.

Avery's record bonus for a high school player just lasted until Aug. 8, when the Montreal Expos startled the baseball world by signing Cornelius, an 11th-round draft pick, to a $225,000 bonus. A straight-A student at Thomasville (Ala.) High, Cornelius likely would have been one of the first five players drafted had he not been viewed as a lock to attend college at Mississippi State.

"He and Steve Avery were the top two high school pitchers in the draft," Expos scouting director Gary Hughes said. "We decided, by (the 11th round), it was worth taking a chance on him.

"We were always led to believe he would sign.

### Fastest To The Majors

| Player, Pos. | Drafted (Round) | Debut |
|---|---|---|
| 1. Gregg Olson, rhp | Orioles (1) | Sept. 2, 1988 |
| 2. # Jim Abbott, lhp | Angels (1) | April 8, 1989 |
| 3. Andy Benes, rhp | Padres (1) | Aug. 11, 1989 |
| 4. Marquis Grissom, of | Expos (3) | Aug. 21, 1989 |
| 5. Pat Combs, lhp | Phillies (1) | Sept. 5, 1989 |

**FIRST HIGH SCHOOL SELECTION:** Steve Avery, lhp (Braves/1, June 13, 1990)

**LAST PLAYER TO RETIRE:** Darren Oliver, lhp (Sept. 29, 2013)

*#Debuted in major leagues.*

## Top 25 Bonuses

| | Player, Pos. | Drafted (Round) | Order | Bonus |
|---|---|---|---|---|
| 1. | **Andy Benes, rhp** | **Padres (1)** | **1** | **$235,000** |
| 2. | ***Reid Cornelius, rhp** | **Expos (11)** | **284** | **$225,000** |
| 3. | ***Steve Avery, lhp** | **Braves (1)** | **3** | **$211,500** |
| 4. | **Jim Abbott, lhp** | **Angels (1)** | **8** | **$200,000** |
| 5. | **Robin Ventura, 3b** | **White Sox (1)** | **10** | **$186,500** |
| 6. | ***Mark Lewis, ss** | **Indians (1)** | **2** | **$180,000** |
| | **Gregg Olson, rhp** | **Orioles (1)** | **4** | **$180,000** |
| | *Willie Ansley, of | Astros (1) | 7 | $180,000 |
| | ***Royce Clayton, rhp** | **Giants (1)** | **15** | **$180,000** |
| 10. | **Monty Fariss, ss** | **Rangers (1)** | **6** | **$156,000** |
| 11. | Ty Griffin, 2b | Cubs (1) | 9 | $152,500 |
| 12. | Bill Bene, rhp | Dodgers (1) | 5 | $150,000 |
| 13. | **Pat Combs, lhp** | **Phillies (1)** | **11** | **$145,000** |
| 14. | **Tino Martinez, 1b** | **Mariners (1)** | **14** | **$135,000** |
| 15. | **Charles Nagy, rhp** | **Indians (1)** | **17** | **$126,000** |
| 16. | *Hugh Walker, of | Royals (1) | 18 | $116,000 |
| 17. | *Austin Manahan, ss | Pirates (1) | 13 | $115,000 |
| | **David Wainhouse, rhp** | **Expos (1)** | **19** | **$115,000** |
| 19. | Tom Fischer, lhp | Red Sox (1) | 12 | $110,000 |
| | **Stan Royer, 3b** | **Athletics (1)** | **16** | **$110,000** |
| 22. | Dave Proctor, rhp | Mets (1) | 21 | $100,000 |
| | **Ed Sprague, 3b** | **Blue Jays (1)** | **25** | **$100,000** |
| | ***Rico Brogna, 1b** | **Tigers (1)** | **26** | **$100,000** |
| 24. | Johnny Ard, rhp | Twins (1) | 20 | $95,000 |
| | **Ted Wood, of** | **Giants (1-S)** | **29** | **$95,000** |

*Major leaguers in bold. *High school selection.*

Money was the factor. We kept getting tremendous reports on him, but nothing he did changed our minds. It was just a case of ownership deciding they wanted to spend the money."

Cornelius pitched three seasons in the majors, going 8-17, 4.91 with three clubs, but his career essentially ended when he developed arthritis in his pitching shoulder after surgery for a torn labrum.

In addition to Benes, Avery and Cornelius, Olympic-team hero Jim Abbott, drafted eighth overall by the California Angels, also cracked the $200,000 bonus barrier.

The Angels used their first-round pick on Abbott, winner of the 1988 Sullivan Award and 1987 Golden Spikes Award, and one of the great human-interest stories in baseball history. Born without a right hand, Abbott overcame his handicap, deploying a 93 mph fastball while demonstrating remarkable courage and poise in the face of a media blitz. Abbott spent 10 seasons in the majors, winning as many as 18 games for the Angels in 1991, but also going just 2-18, 7.48 for the same club in 1996. In between those extremes, he pitched a no-hitter with the Yankees in 1993.

In all, eight first-rounders and Cornelius earned bonuses of at least $180,000, a significant uptick from 1987, when $165,000 was the top mark and the first eight selections all earned between $160,000-$165,000. Overall, first-round bonuses jumped 10.9 percent—the fourth double-digit increase in five years. Bonus records were set in seven separate rounds.

Despite the record bonus payments, one first-round pick managed to slip through the cracks. Milwaukee took righthander Alex Fernandez with the 24th pick overall after he went 14-0, 0.45 at Miami's Monsignor Pace High. He turned down a reported $150,000 bonus to play at the University of Miami, becoming the first first-rounder since 1979 to spurn the pros for college baseball.

Few freshmen burst on the major college baseball scene as quickly as Fernandez, who went 15-2, 2.01 with 177 strikeouts in 148 innings for Miami. And few left as quickly as the 5-foot-11, 215-pound righthander transferred to Miami-Dade South Community College as a sophomore to become eligible for the 1990 draft. He was taken by the Chicago White Sox with the fourth pick overall that year and signed for $350,000.

### TEAM USA GOES FOR GOLD

The Olympics added baseball as a demonstration sport for the 1984 Los Angeles Games, and it retained that status four years later in Seoul.

In both years, major league clubs allowed drafted players—college players from the current year's crop—to participate in the Games, though consent came late in 1988. In keeping with Olympic guidelines in effect at the time, players could sign contracts but could not accept bonus money until after the Games. In all, 10 first-rounders delayed their debuts until 1989 in order to participate.

Unlike 1984, when the 20-man U.S. team featured 18 eventual first-round draft picks, the 1988 team had fewer headline performers and 11 first-rounders: nine from 1988 and two from 1989. Another first-round selection, Washington State righthander Dave Wainhouse, played for Team Canada after being drafted by Montreal.

The 1984 and 1988 drafts both yielded 18 college players in the first round, the most ever. But after the acclaimed 1984 squad could do no better than a silver medal, Team USA placed a premium on identifying the best present talent for '88, regardless of pro potential. It worked as the U.S., behind Abbott's seven-hitter, avenged its 1984 loss to Japan, winning 5-3 in the gold-medal game.

Benes (7-2, 3.29), Abbott (8-1, 2.55) and Louisiana State's Ben McDonald (8-2, 2.61), who became the No. 1 pick in the 1989 draft, formed a star-studded rotation for Team USA, which went 42-11 during a summer-long barnstorming tour leading up to the Olympics in September. All three debuted in the majors in 1989 and went on to win at least 78 major league games, with Benes leading the way with 155 wins.

Three first-round picks—first baseman Tino Martinez, second baseman Ty Griffin and third baseman Robin Ventura—were the team's key offensive cogs. Martinez, a University of Tampa product picked 14th overall by the Seattle Mariners, slammed two homers in the gold-medal game, and hit a robust .402 with 20 homers and 70 RBIs for the summer. In a 16-year major league career, spent mostly with the Mariners and Yankees, Martinez hit .271 with 339 homers and 1,271 RBIs.

Griffin (.416-16-52) and Ventura (.380-12-77) shared the offensive load much of the summer and created significant buzz in Chicago, as they were drafted back-to-back by the two Chicago teams. Griffin (Cubs) signed for $152,500 as the ninth pick overall pick; Ventura (White Sox) received $186,500 as the 10th selection.

Griffin, a three-year standout at second base for Georgia Tech, established himself as a top prospect

### WORTH NOTING

■ Like other players from the Caribbean region, Puerto Ricans were not subject to a restrictive draft process—at least not through 1988. But the wheels were set in motion to make players from the island territory draft-eligible going forward after three more Puerto Ricans received bonuses during the year of at least $90,000. Outfielder **MELVIN NIEVES** signed for a bonus of $103,400 on May 10 with the Braves; shortstop **WIL CORDERO** earned $100,000 from the Expos on May 24; and catcher **CARLOS DELGADO** commanded $90,000 from the Blue Jays on Oct. 9. All three players were just 16 years old at the time they signed, and all went on to play at least seven years in the majors. Though none topped the record of $125,000, set a year earlier by righthander Ramser Correa, 16, who signed with the Brewers, bonuses to Puerto Ricans were beginning to escalate at a rapid rate and Major League Baseball's response was to make Puerto Ricans subject to the draft for the first time in 1989. Correa himself had broken the record set a year earlier by outfielder Juan Gonzalez, who received $75,000 from the Rangers. The Rangers also signed another prominent Puerto Rican in 1988, future major league all-star catcher **IVAN RODRIGUEZ**, though his signing cost them only $20,000.

■ Ultimately, the most notable international signing in 1988 occurred when the Dodgers landed Dominican righthander **PEDRO MARTINEZ**, who would reach the Hall of Fame in 2015. Martinez signed for a bonus of just $6,000—an indication that bonus escalation had not yet become a factor elsewhere in the Caribbean. It would be another two years before Canadians became part of the formal draft process, though Canadians attend-

CONTINUED ON PAGE 352

## WORTH NOTING

CONTINUED FROM PAGE 351

ing colleges in the U.S., including Expos first-round pick **DAVE WAINHOUSE**, a righthander who was at Washington State, were subject to the draft, and 10 such players were selected in 1988.

■ **MARK LEWIS** is not likely to ever forget his first game of professional baseball. After being drafted second overall in 1988 and signing for a $180,000 bonus with the Indians, Lewis broke in with Rookie-level Burlington and promptly played all 27 innings of a game that took eight hours and 16 minutes to play. It ended at 3:27 a.m. Burlington lost 3-2 as Lewis went 1-for-12 and committed two errors at shortstop.

■ **PETE ROSE JR.** couldn't help but become a ballplayer. "My kid can hit because he's had more practice than anybody else," said his father Pete, the game's all-time hit leader. "He ought to be able to hit because I always brought him to the ballpark. Every day he was here, I worked with him. And you don't take infield every day with Buddy Bell and Mike Schmidt and Dave Concepcion and not have some of that rub off on you." Pete Jr. developed into a top third-base prospect under his father's care, but it was Baltimore, and not Cincinnati, that drafted him in 1988. The younger Rose, who hit .440 with four homers as a senior at Cincinnati's Oak Hills High, was selected in the 12th round by the Orioles and signed with that club late in August after leading his team to the American Legion World Series title. There was speculation that Rose's father, the Reds manager at the time, might put pressure on Cincinnati to take his son, possibly by as early as the third round. But that proved unfounded.
"You can't make a decision based on emotion," Reds scouting director John Cox said. "You have to divorce yourself from all that and consider the realities of who

for the 1988 draft when he hit a two-out, two-run ninth-inning homer at the 1987 Pan American Games in Indianapolis. The homer lifted Team USA to a 6-4 win over Cuba, that nation's first loss in Pan Am competition in 20 years. Griffin enjoyed more international heroics at the '88 Olympics, further raising expectations.

The Cubs were intent on drafting Griffin, even though he hadn't demonstrated in college that he could play any position but second base, and future Hall of Famer Ryne Sandberg was entrenched at the position for the Cubs. During his first professional season at Class A Peoria, Griffin moved to third base. The errors started to mount and his offensive game disappeared.

"I went up to the plate thinking about the plays I made at third base, and not concentrating fully on hitting," Griffin said. "It was a new position and I had to learn it, and it was a struggle."

Griffin eventually moved to the outfield, and even back to second base later in his career, but his hitting struggles continued. He batted .241 with 39 homers in five minor league seasons, none above Double-A, before he was released.

Ventura capped a brilliant three-year career at Oklahoma State in 1988 by hitting .391 with 26 homers and 96 RBIs. For his career, he hit .428 with 68 home runs and 302 RBIs and was Baseball America's College Player of the Decade.

He became arguably the most successful first-rounder in the Class of 1988 by spending 16 years in the majors, hitting .267 with 294 homers and 1,182 RBIs while developing into a Gold-Glove caliber third baseman.

It was during the 1987 college season that Ventura established himself as one of the great hitters in college history, with a record 58-game hitting streak that finally ended at the College World Series. Ventura added to his lore by playing with the Olympic team, and winning the Golden Spikes Award, given to the country's top amateur player.

As the 10th overall pick, Ventura was upstaged in the 1988 draft not only by his Olympic teammate Griffin but by his college teammate Monty Fariss, who hit .397 with 30 homers and led the nation with 114 RBIs and went sixth overall to the Texas Rangers.

Like Griffin, Fariss fell far short of expectations in pro ball. A tall, rangy shortstop in college, his footwork proved less than ideal for the position as a pro, and he was burdened by throwing problems. He divided most of his minor league and brief major league career between second base and the outfield, but his bat was never strong enough to carry him. In 104 major league games from 1991-93, he hit .217 with four homers.

### LOFTON, PIAZZA: WILD CARDS

Major league clubs continued to make a more concerted effort to bring in high school talent in 1988, picking 515 preps. That was in contrast to the record-low 234 taken just three years earlier. In 1986, that number jumped to 334; in 1987, 415. Of the 515 selections, 186 (or 36.1 percent) signed, the highest number in 11 years.

Still, 13 of the 14 most successful players out of the 1988 draft, at least according to WAR (Wins Above Replacement), were from the college or junior-college ranks. The noteworthy exception was outfielder Jim Edmonds, drafted in the seventh round out of a local high school by the Angels. He spent 17 years in the majors, hitting .284 with 393 homers, and winning eight Gold Gloves.

### Largest Bonuses By Round

| | Player, Pos. | Club | Bonus |
|---|---|---|---|
| **1.** | **Andy Benes, rhp** | **Padres** | **$235,000** |
| 2. | Brian Johnson, c | Indians | $85,000 |
| **3.** | *** Doug Saunders, 2b** | **Mets** | **$70,000** |
| 4. | * Eric Brooks, c | Blue Jays | $81,250 |
| 5. | * Willie Romay, of | Mariners | $50,500 |
| 6. | * Mike Ogliaruso, rhp | Blue Jays | $51,640 |
| **7.** | **Ron Witmeyer, 1b** | **Athletics** | **$78,000** |
| **8.** | *** Mark Wohlers, rhp** | **Braves** | **$45,000** |
| 9. | Edwin Alicea, 2b | Braves | $36,250 |
| 10. | Jon Martin, of | Pirates | $29,000 |
| **11.** | *** Reid Cornelius, rhp** | **Expos** | **$225,000** |
| **12.** | **Frank Seminara, rhp** | **Yankees** | **$33,000** |
| **13.** | **Jeff Darwin, rhp** | **Mariners** | **$30,000** |
| 14. | * Mike Anaya, rhp | Mets | $20,000 |
| **15.** | **Bobby Munoz, rhp** | **Yankees** | **$42,500** |
| 16. | * Steve Whitehead, rhp | Expos | $33,000 |
| **17.** | ***# Marcus Moore, rhp** | **Angels** | **$62,500** |
| 18. | Tom Mileski, rhp | Rangers | $25,000 |
| 19. | * Steve Perry, rhp | Yankees | $11,000 |
| 20. | Woody Smith, 3b | Cubs | $20,000 |
| 21. | Bruce Prybylinski, rhp | Yankees | $13,000 |
| 22. | * Matthew Current, c | Phillies | $22,000 |
| 23. | # Chris Keim, lhp | Reds | $18,000 |
| 24. | Jim Buccheri, of | Athletics | $20,000 |
| | * Bernard Doyle, of | Red Sox | $20,000 |
| 25. | * Chris Toney, 3b | Phillies | $12,500 |
| **Other** | **# Kerry Woodson, rhp** | **Mariners (29)** | **$80,000** |

*Major leaguers in bold. *High school selection. #Signed as draft-and-follow.*

In the final analysis, all the early-round selections in 1988 were upstaged by two of the more improbable success stories of the draft era as outfielder Kenny Lofton, chosen in the 17th round by the Houston Astros, and catcher Mike Piazza, a lowly 62nd-rounder of the Los Angeles Dodgers (1,389th pick overall), joined Edmonds in becoming the most productive players drafted.

Kenny Lofton

Lofton played baseball for four years at Washington High in East Chicago, Ill., and hit .414 as a senior. But he was also an all-state basketball player and went to the University of Arizona to play basketball in college. He became a prominent point guard for the Wildcats and eventually set school career records for assists and steals, and played on four NCAA tournament teams.

Lofton's commitment to basketball left little time for baseball, and he played in just five games at Arizona, all as a junior, with a single at-bat. But his speed and athleticism intrigued Astros scout Clark Crist, a former Arizona baseball player, and he persuaded his organization to draft Lofton even though he intended to play basketball as a senior.

Three years later, Lofton hit .308 with 17 triples and 40 stolen bases in Triple-A, which earned him a 20-game September cameo in Houston. With Steve Finley established as their center fielder, the Astros sent Lofton in trade to Cleveland, where he blossomed into one of the game's best leadoff hitters and center fielders. In 10 seasons with the Indians, Lofton hit .300, scored 975 runs and stole 452 bases. He led the American League in stolen bases five consecutive seasons while also winning four Gold Gloves in a row.

Mike Piazza

Piazza's emergence into a Hall of Famer was even more of a longshot, as he was drafted by the Dodgers with the last of their 61 picks—and then only as a favor to Dodgers manager Tommy Lasorda, a friend of Piazza's father Vince.

Two years earlier, Lasorda had also gone to bat for Piazza, a little-known Pennsylvania high school catcher, and recommended him to Ron Fraser, the coach at the University of Miami and also a friend of Lasorda's. After getting just nine at-bats for the Hurricanes as a freshman, Piazza transferred to Miami-Dade Community College North and would have gone undrafted had it not been for Lasorda.

Once Piazza landed in the Dodgers system, he made a steady rise through the ranks, hitting every step of the way. But it wasn't until 1992 that Dodgers management finally seemed convinced that Piazza was the real deal, and a year later he quieted all skeptics by hitting .318 with 25 homers and 112 RBIs while winning National League rookie of the year honors. By the time he finally retired in 2007, he was one of the best offensive catchers in baseball history, hitting .308 overall, with 427 homers and 1,335 RBIs.

Even though the Astros and Dodgers didn't fully appreciate the talents of either Lofton or Piazza initially, the unexpected emergence of both players into all-stars cushioned the disappointment the Astros and Dodgers experienced when their first-round picks fell far short of expectations.

Houston's choice (seventh overall) was Texas high school outfielder Willie Ansley, a promising University of Oklahoma football recruit described by scouts as a raw version of Bo Jackson. His career peaked in Triple-A, derailed by shoulder and back injuries.

Cal State Los Angeles righthander Bill Bene, selected by the Dodgers with the fifth pick overall, had a great arm but never harnessed his control.

"His arm is probably as strong as anybody's we've seen around the country in a good many years," Dodgers scout Eddie Bane said. "He's erratic, but there's nothing wrong with him that can't be corrected."

Bene tested the Dodgers player-development staff. In his first two full pro seasons, he went a combined 1-14, 8.04 and walked 152 in 84 innings, while striking out just 58. Things became so dire in 1989, at Class A Bakersfield, that pitching coach Guy Conti used a department-store mannequin in the batter's box rather than ask a live hitter to face Bene.

Bene never advanced beyond Triple-A in nine seasons and went just 15-30, 5.59 overall. In 444 innings, he walked 489 and struck out 422.

### LEWIS FALLS SHORT OF EXPECTATIONS

Among all players drafted in the first round in 1988, Lewis appeared most destined for stardom. His high school accomplishments dwarfed those of none other than Ken Griffey Jr., the No. 1 overall pick out of a rival high school a year earlier. Lewis, a slick-fielding shortstop out of Hamilton (Ohio) High, set national prep records for hits (222) and RBIs (212), and as a senior hit .600 with 15 homers and 66 RBIs. He had the highest Major League Scouting Bureau grade in his draft class.

"I've had some scouts tell me that if (Lewis) had been a senior last year, Griffey would've been the second player taken in the draft," said Dan Bowling, Lewis' high school coach.

After receiving a $180,000 bonus from the Indians, Lewis showed positive signs early, but he only flashed his considerable potential as he progressed through the system. As he continued to struggle to find consistency on both sides of the ball early in his major league career, he alienated some in the organization with a cocky attitude. In the process, he squandered numerous opportunities to secure a regular major league job.

"It's tough to adjust to the big league game and big league life," then-Indians manager Mike Hargrove said. "Some people do it very well and very gracefully, and other people struggle like a dog through it."

After waiting seven years for Lewis to live up to

## One Team's Draft: Baltimore Orioles

| Player, Pos. | Bonus | Player, Pos. | Bonus | Player, Pos. | Bonus |
|---|---|---|---|---|---|
| **1. Gregg Olson, rhp** | **$180,000** | 9. Mike Linskey, lhp | $2,000 | 18. *Joe Redman, 2b | $5,000 |
| **1. *Ricky Gutierrez, ss** | **$80,000** | 10. Doug Robbins, c | $7,500 | 19. Scott McNaney, ss | None |
| **2. *Arthur Rhodes, lhp** | **$45,000** | 11. Cris Allen, 3b | Did not sign | 20. Robert Doman, lhp | $2,500 |
| **3. Stacy Jones, rhp** | **$40,000** | **12. *Pete Rose Jr., 3b** | **$21,000** | 21. Rene Francisco, of | Did not sign |
| 4. *Aman Hicks, of | $22,500 | 13. Rodney Lofton, ss | $6,000 | 22. Roy Gilbert, of | $1,000 |
| 5. *Steve Nicosia, of | $19,500 | 14. Jim Robertson, rhp | Did not sign | 23. Chris Burgin, rhp | None |
| **6. *Tom Martin, lhp** | **$23,000** | 15. *Gustavo Miranda, 3b/ss | Did not sign | 24. Zach Kerr, rhp | None |
| 7. Keith Lee, of | $15,000 | 16. Bob Bretwisch, lhp | $1,000 | **25. Brian Barnes, lhp** | **Did not sign** |
| 8. Mike Deutsch, rhp | $15,000 | 17. Mike Richardson, 1b | $1,000 | **Other*Joey Hamilton (28), rhp** | **Did not sign** |

*Major leaguers in bold. *High school selection.*

**WORTH NOTING**

he is, where he is going and what's going on."

When the Expos drafted **MARQUIS GRISSOM** in the third round, they immediately began comparing him to former Expos great Andre Dawson, an 11th-round pick in 1975. Both were products of Florida A&M, both were center fielders who could run, hit with power and throw, and both were largely overlooked by scouts. Grissom hit .448 with 12 homers and went 9-3, 2.40 as a pitcher in 1988, but most clubs didn't bear down on him because of his sophomore standing. The Expos weren't fooled, and little more than a year later Grissom was in the big leagues.

The Red Sox showed no hesitation in going for one of their own in the first round (12th overall), taking University of Wisconsin junior lefthander **TOM FISCHER**. He was the nephew of Red Sox pitching coach Bill Fischer, who had never seen him pitch. Fischer impressed scouts a month before the draft, striking out 19 batters in a seven-inning game in a Big 10 Conference matchup against Iowa, but overall was an ordinary 6-6, 5.00 with 36 walks and 80 strikeouts in 77 innings on the season. In his three-year college career, he went just 19-16. "His uncle had practically no role in his drafting," Red Sox scouting director Eddie Kasko said. Fischer spent six seasons in the Red Sox system, reaching Triple-A. Overall, he went 41-42, 4.79.

No first-round pick from 1988 failed quite to the degree as Virginia Tech senior righthander **BRAD DUVALL**, who was drafted 23rd overall by the Cardinals. A year earlier, DuVall was also drafted in the first round—15th overall by the Orioles—but chose not sign. He went 7-11, 3.35 in three minor league seasons, none above Class A, and struggled with arm problems before being released.

## IN FOCUS: ROBIN VENTURA

Robin Ventura's prowess in college and pro ball was in stark contrast to his profile as a high school shortstop. He was not drafted, nor was he recruited by more than a few colleges.

The coaching staff at Oklahoma State had little idea what to expect from Ventura when he arrived on campus in the fall of 1985. They had never seen him play at Righetti High in Santa Maria, Calif., and scouts had said that Ventura couldn't run, had limited power and would need another position.

But the Cowboys had no hesitation in offering him a scholarship after bringing him to campus on a recruiting trip, an astute decision as Ventura turned into an immediate sensation. He hit .469 with 21 homers and a national-best 96 RBIs as a freshman. As a sophomore, he went on an NCAA-record 58-game hitting streak, and over his three-year career hit .428 while acknowledged as one of the greatest hitters in college baseball history. By the 1988 draft, scouts were calling the lefthanded-hitting Ventura the best hitting prospect around and were convinced he could play third base.

"He's the best pure hitter in the draft, and we need hitting," said White Sox personnel director Al Goldis, whose club selected him with the 10th pick. "His hitting fundamentals are excellent."

his promise, the Indians finally ran out of patience following the 1994 season and traded him to the Cincinnati Reds. Lewis spent parts of 11 seasons in the majors with six clubs, hitting .263 with 48 homers overall.

Righthander Johnny Ard, drafted 20th overall by the Minnesota Twins, also fell short of his bid to play in the majors, but the $95,000 bonus he received from the Twins went to a noble cause.

"This is going to sound greedy," Ard said, "but it is going to help me and my family out financially."

Twelve years earlier, Ard's father Jimmy, a former minor league catcher, sustained burns over 98 percent of his body in an auto accident and later spent 27 months in a hospital. Even though the elder Ard survived his ordeal, he was totally disabled. He raised three sons on his own, supporting them with disability and social-security checks.

"We've never been ones to live high on the hog, and I won't when I get into money," the younger Ard said. "But it's always nice to have a piece of money when you need it."

Ard's promising career never panned out as he hoped. In six minor league seasons, he went 49-33, 3.54 with a fastball that peaked at 95 mph, but never advanced beyond Double-A after shoulder reconstruction surgery.

### YANKEES TAKE RUN AT SANDERS

A total of 1,432 players were drafted in 1988, topping the record of 1,263 set in 1987. The Yankees were the final team to stop drafting, in the 75th round, though for the ninth time in 10 years, they did not have a first-round pick.

New York relinquished its first-round selection to St. Louis for signing free agent Jack Clark, as well as its picks in the second (John Candelaria) and third rounds (Jose Cruz), and didn't pick for the first time until 104 players were gone. Four teams had already drafted six players by that point. The Yankees still had a noteworthy draft as 15 of their picks reached the majors—more than any club in 1988, and just two shy of the record of 17 set by the Mets in 1982. They made draft history by signing each of their first 27 picks, topping the previous record of 23 (Cincinnati, 1983) for consecutive players signed at the start of a draft.

Among the players the Yankees signed was a prime-time football talent, All-American defensive back Deion Sanders, who had elected not to play baseball that season at Florida State. Sanders signed for $25,000 as a 30th-rounder and agreed to play that summer in the Yankees system. He briefly reached Triple-A before returning to Florida State for his final year of football.

"We wouldn't have agreed to it," Yankees scouting director Brian Sabean said, "unless we felt there were some long-term possibilities to it."

Sanders returned to the Yankees in 1989 and spent the early portion of the season at Double-A Albany. The Atlanta Falcons selected Sanders fifth overall in that year's National Football League draft, but he continued to play baseball in the minors after setting his asking price at $10 million to play in the NFL and negotiations predictably bogged down.

Deion Sanders

On June 1, the Yankees promoted Sanders to the big leagues, giving him more bargaining leverage with the Falcons. Sanders played in 14 games for the Yankees before he reached an agreement with the Falcons, and he left the Yankees in the middle of a game in Seattle to begin his NFL career.

Sanders returned to the Yankees in 1990 and played in another 57 games, but they released him on Sept. 24, deciding football would interfere with his ultimate success in baseball.

St. Louis, meanwhile, spent one of its three 1988 first-round picks on a two-sport star of its own in Brian Jordan, who played briefly in the Cardinals organization that summer before rejoining the football team at the University of Richmond. Jordan was subsequently drafted in the sixth round of the 1989 NFL draft by Buffalo, but was cut in training camp by the Bills. He also hooked on with the Falcons, however, and played alongside Sanders in the team's defensive backfield that fall.

Jordan remained with the Falcons through the 1991 season, leading the team in tackles in both 1990 and 1991, before signing a three-year contract with the Cardinals that stipulated he could no longer play football. Over a 15-year career in the majors, Jordan hit .282 with 141 homers and 821 RBIs.

### Highest Unsigned Picks

| Player, Pos., Team (Round) | College | Re-Drafted |
|---|---|---|
| Alex Fernandez, rhp, Brewers (1) | Miami | White Sox '90 (1) |
| Jeff Seale, rhp, Mets (2) | Texas | Indians '91 (32) |
| Tyler Green, rhp, Reds (3) | Wichita State | Phillies '91 (1) |
| Mike Harrison, c, Twins (3) | California | Reds '91 (5) |
| Derrick Warren, of, Mets (3) | Alabama | Never |
| Joe Ciccarella, 1b, Phillies (4) | Loyola Marymount | Red Sox '91 (4) |
| Terry Christopher, rhp, Astros (5) | None | Never |
| Joey Eischen, lhp, White Sox (5) | Pasadena (Calif.) CC | Rangers '89 (4) |
| Joe Grahe, rhp, Athletics (5) | * Miami | Angels '89 (2) |
| Steve Dean, of/rhp, Twins (5) | Oklahoma | Never |

**TOTAL UNSIGNED PICKS:** Top 5 Rounds (10), Top 10 Rounds (26)

**Returned to same school.*

### Largest Draft-And-Follow Bonuses

| Player, Pos. | Club (Round) | Bonus |
|---|---|---|
| 1. **Kerry Woodson, rhp** | **Mariners (29)** | **$80,000** |
| 2. *** Marcus Moore, rhp** | **Angels (17)** | **$62,500** |
| 3. Bob Hurlbutt, c | Astros (31) | $50,000 |
| **Jeff Patterson, rhp** | **Phillies (58)** | **$50,000** |
| 5. * Daryl Ratliff, of | Pirates (5) | $40,000 |
| **Damion Easley, ss** | **Angels (30)** | **$40,000** |
| *** Jessie Hollins, rhp** | **Cubs (40)** | **$40,000** |
| 8. Ronnie Plemmons, of | White Sox (46) | $36,000 |
| 9. * John Gross, rhp | Royals (43) | $32,500 |
| 10. William Abare, 1b | Blue Jays (60) | $30,000 |

*Major leaguers in bold. *High school selection.*

# 1988 Draft List

*Did not sign. Major leaguers in bold, with first and last years noted. Order of selection indicated in parentheses. For the first five rounds, the peak level of each player is noted. + Signed as draft-and-follow (Second school noted if applicable).*

## ATLANTA BRAVES (3)

1. **Steve Avery, lhp, Kennedy HS, Taylor, Mich.—(1990-2003)**

DRAFT DROP *First 1988 high school draft pick to reach majors (June 13, 1990)*

2. **Jim Kremers, c, University of Arkansas.—(1990)**
2. **Matt Murray, rhp, Loomis Chaffee HS, Windsor, Conn.** (Choice from Phillies as compensation for Type B free agent Dave Palmer)—**(1995)**
2. John Kupsey, 3b, Gloucester Catholic HS, Gibbstown, N.J. (Supplemental choice—57th—as compensation for Type C free agent Glenn Hubbard).—(AA)
3. Preston Watson, rhp, University of Texas.—(AA)
4. Kevin Tyson, c, Jefferson HS, Lafayette, Ind.—(Rookie)
5. **Turk Wendell, rhp, Quinnipiac College.—(1993-2004)**
6. Jimmie Pullins, of, Tyler (Texas) HS.
7. Lee Heath, of, LaSalle HS, Cincinnati.
8. **Mark Wohlers, rhp, Holyoke (Mass.) HS.—(1991-2002)**
9. Edwin Alicea, 2b, Florida State University.

DRAFT DROP *Brother of Luis Alicea, first-round draft pick, Cardinals (1986); major leaguer (1988-2002)*

10. *Tommy Adams, of, Capistrano Valley HS, Mission Viejo, Calif.
11. Sean Hutchinson, c, Northview HS, Covina, Calif.
12. *Fred Cooley, rhp, University of Southern Mississippi.
13. David Waldenberger, 3b, Rowland HS, Rowland Heights, Calif.
14. *Mike Hostetler, rhp, Sprayberry HS, Marietta, Ga.
15. **Tony Tarasco, of, Santa Monica (Calif.) HS.—(1993-2002)**
16. *Russell Brock, rhp, Lockland (Ohio) HS.
17. John Greenwood, 1b, San Francisco State University.
18. Tom Rizzo, ss, North Adams State (Mass.) College.
19. Randy Simmons, of, University of Delaware.
20. *Mike Lopez, rhp, Sheridan HS, Denver, Colo.
21. Steve Lopez, 3b-of, Vacaville (Calif.) HS.
22. Donovan Campbell, of, Texas Southern University.
23. *Greg Perschke, rhp, University of New Orleans.
24. Ramces Guerrero, 2b, Dominican (N.Y.) College.
25. *Marty Neff, of, Magnolia HS, Anaheim, Calif.
26. *Craig Bradshaw, lhp, Alexandria (La.) HS.
27. *Ron Hazl, of, Alhambra HS, Glendale, Ariz.
28. Rickey Rigsby, of, Angelina (Texas) JC.
29. *Scott Stice, rhp, Wake Forest University.
30. Gary Schoonover, ss, Brigham Young University.
31. *Mark Dressen, rhp, La Serna HS, Whittier, Calif.
32. James Kortright, rhp, Snow (Utah) JC.
33. *Chris Gaskill, rhp, Westfield HS, Houston.
34. *Adam Schulhofer, 3b, Canoga Park HS, Woodland Hills, Calif.
35. Alan Thomas, of, Ventura (Calif.) JC.
36. *Billy Morris, ss, St. Francis HS, Glendale, Calif.
37. William Lange, lhp, Rio Hondo (Calif.) JC.
38. Scott Goselin, 2b, Olivet Nazarene (Ill.) College.
39. *Scott Ruffcorn, rhp, Austin (Texas) HS.

DRAFT DROP *First-round draft pick (25th overall), White Sox (1991)*

40. *Mike Smith, of, Woodward HS, Cincinnati.
41. *Mike Solar, 1b, Covina HS, West Covina, Calif.
42. *John Keller, c, Westwood HS, Austin, Texas.
43. Calvain Culberson, of, Armstrong State (Ga.) University.
44. Wallace Gonzales, c, Rosemead (Calif.) HS.
45. Rodolfo Gardey, rhp, Canada (Calif.) JC.
46. *Steve Dailey, of, Ventura (Calif.) HS.
47. *Jason Gonzales, ss, Cuero (Texas) HS.
48. Mark Eskins, rhp, Jacksonville State University.
49. Chris Jones, 1b, Southern Tech (Ga.) Institute.
50. Pat Stivers, ss-2b, Mesa (Colo.) College.
51. Brent McCoy, ss, Howard University.
52. *Doug Kimball, ss-rhp, Shadow Mountain HS, Phoenix.
53. *David Cronin, of, LaSalle HS, Cincinnati.
54. David Piela, c, Western Carolina University.
55. *Craig Triplett, c-1b, Paradise Valley HS, Phoenix.
56. Marco Paddy, c, Southern University.

FRANK RAGSDALE

**Angels seventh-rounder Jim Edmonds was one of the most productive players in the '88 class**

57. *Jeff Blanks, ss, Del Rio (Texas) HS.
58. *Greg Viks, rhp, DeSoto (Texas) HS.
59. Glen Gardner, of, Rutgers University.
60. *Roy Gamez, c, Casa Grande (Ariz.) HS.
61. Joe Saccomanno, ss-2b, Bloomfield (N.J.) College.
62. Paul Bacosa, rhp, San Jose State University.
63. Eric Kuhlman, of, Bradley University.
64. *Drayton Reedy, 1b, Towers HS, Decatur, Ga.
65. *Mike Eiffert, of, Lewisville (Texas) HS.
66. *Kevin Thomas, rhp, Rockdale HS, Conyers, Ga.
67. Kevin Henry, 3b, Auburn University.

## BALTIMORE ORIOLES (4)

1. **Gregg Olson, rhp, Auburn University.—(1988-2001)**

DRAFT DROP *First player from 1988 draft to reach majors (Sept. 2, 1988)*

1. **Ricky Gutierrez, ss, American HS, Hialeah, Fla.** (Supplemental choice—30th—for failure to sign 1987 first-round draft pick Brad DuVall)**—(1993-2004)**
2. **Arthur Rhodes, lhp-of, La Vega HS, Waco, Texas.—(1991-2011)**
3. **Stacy Jones, rhp, Auburn University.—(1991-96)**
4. Aman Hicks, of, Gardena (Calif.) HS.—(Low A)
5. Steve Nicosia, of, Bishop Gallagher HS, St. Clair Shores, Mich.—(Low A)
6. **Tom Martin, lhp, Bay HS, Panama City, Fla.—(1997-2007)**
7. Keith Lee, of, Glassboro State (N.J.) College.
8. Mike Deutsch, rhp, Rider College.
9. Mike Linskey, lhp, James Madison University.
10. Doug Robbins, c, Stanford University.
11. *Cris Allen, 3b, Florida Southern College.
12. **Pete Rose Jr., 3b, Oak Hills HS, Cincinnati.—(1997)**

DRAFT DROP *Son of Pete Rose, major leaguer (1963-86); major league manager (1984-89)*

13. Rodney Lofton, ss, Grambling State University.
14. *Jim Robinson, rhp, Northwestern University.
15. *Gustavo Miranda, 3b-ss, Miami (Fla.) Senior HS.
16. Bob Bretwisch, lhp, Bradley University.
17. Mike Richardson, 1b, Portland State University.
18. Joe Redman, 2b, Paulsboro (N.J.) HS.
19. Scott McNaney, ss, Elizabethtown (Pa.) College.
20. Robert Doman, lhp, James Madison University.
21. *Rene Francisco, of, Indian River (Fla.) CC.
22. Roy Gilbert, of, Centenary College.
23. Chris Burgin, rhp, University of Oklahoma.
24. Zach Kerr, rhp, New Mexico State University.
25. ***Brian Barnes, lhp, Clemson University.—(1990-94)**
26. Carey Metts, c, Mars Hill (N.C.) College.
27. Chris Shebby, rhp, Georgetown University.
28. ***Joey Hamilton, rhp, Statesboro (Ga.) HS.—(1994-2003)**

DRAFT DROP *First-round draft pick (8th overall), Padres (1991)*

29. *Michael Place, rhp, Seminole (Fla.) HS.
30. Brian Janutolo, ss, Bluefield State (W.Va.) College.
31. Mark Withers, of, North Carolina State University.
32. *Baylor Alexander, c, Wolfson HS, Jacksonville, Fla.
33. Jeff Champ, c, San Diego State University.
34. Dell Ahalt, 3b, North Carolina State University.
35. *Bobby Lamm, of, Hunt HS, Wilson, N.C.
36. John Fowler, 3b, Frederick (Md.) CC.
37. *Mark Brockell, 3b, James Madison University.
38. *Aaron Van Scoyoc, ss, Norway (Iowa) HS.
39. Bob Block, of, Southern Arkansas University.
40. Chris LaFollette, of, Southview HS, Fayetteville, N.C.
41. *Brian Cornelius, of, Southern University.
42. *Jason Marshall, ss, Cooper HS, Abilene, Texas.

DRAFT DROP *Baseball coach, Texas-San Antonio (2013-15)*

43. *Chris Finley, of, Lamar HS, Houston.
44. Earl Williams, c, Catonsville (Md.) CC.
45. Don Marett, rhp, Owen HS, Black Mountain, N.C.

## BOSTON RED SOX (12)

1. Tom Fischer, lhp, University of Wisconsin.—(AAA)

DRAFT DROP *Nephew of Bill Fischer, major leaguer (1956-64)*

2. Andy Rush, rhp, Somerset (Pa.) HS.—(High A)
3. Mickey Rivers Jr., of, Bacone (Okla.) JC.—(High A)

DRAFT DROP *Son of Mickey Rivers, major leaguer (1970-84)*

4. Dan Kite, rhp, Louisiana State University.—(High A)
5. **John Valentin, ss, Seton Hall University.—(1992-2002)**
6. Ed Riley, lhp, St. Peter-Marien HS, Worcester, Mass.
7. Dave Owen, lhp, Carson-Newman (Tenn.) College.
8. **Tim Naehring, ss, Miami (Ohio) University.—(1990-97)**
9. Willie Tatum, 3b, University of the Pacific.
10. Sean Moore, of, Nogales HS, La Puente, Calif.
11. *David Stuart, rhp, Indian River (Fla.) CC.
12. Alan Sanders, rhp, Lower Columbia (Wash.) JC.
13. Richard Witherspoon, of, Nogales HS, La Puente, Calif.
14. Garrett Jenkins, of, Steubenville (Ohio) HS.
15. Howard Landry, lhp, University of Southwestern Louisiana.
16. Bernie Dzafic, rhp, Lincoln Land (Ill.) CC.
17. *Eric Slinkard, c, Chula Vista (Calif.) HS.
18. ***Hilly Hathaway, lhp, Sandalwood HS, Jacksonville, Fla.—(1992-93)**
19. Kevin Crowder, 2b-3b, Keene (N.H.) HS.
20. *Corey Powell, of, Patrick Henry HS, San Diego.
21. *Gary Kinser, rhp, Columbia State (Tenn.) CC.
22. Chris Whitehead, 3b, Middle Tennessee State University.
23. *Scott Bakkum, rhp, Aquinas HS, La Crosse, Wis.
24. Bernard Doyle, of, North Newton HS, Morocco, Ill.
25. **John Flaherty, c, George Washington University.—(1992-2005)**
26. *Joe Blasucci, ss, South Broward HS, Hollywood, Fla.
27. *Mark Mitchelson, lhp, Hillsborough (Fla.) CC.
28. **Scott Taylor, lhp, Bowling Green State University.—(1992-93)**
29. John Spencer, of, University of Lowell (Mass.).
30. *Andrew Flagler, 1b, Valencia (Fla.) CC.
31. *Dan Robinson, 3b, San Jacinto (Texas) JC.
32. *Michael Rebhan, rhp, Lake City (Fla.) CC.
33. **Peter Hoy, rhp, LeMoyne College.—(1992)**
34. Barton Moore, 2b, Jefferson State (Ala.) JC.
35. *Marty Posey, of, Gulf Coast (Fla.) CC.
36. *Jim Wiley, of-rhp, Westark (Ark.) JC.
37. *Steve Worrell, lhp, Lower Cape May Regional HS, Cape May, N.J.
38. *Roger Luce, c, San Jacinto (Texas) JC.

## CALIFORNIA ANGELS (8)

1. **Jim Abbott, lhp, University of Michigan.—(1989-99)**

DRAFT DROP *1988 recipient of James E. Sullivan Award, symbolic of nation's outstanding amateur athlete/United States*

2. (Choice to Giants as compensation for Type A free agent Chili Davis)
3. Glenn Carter, rhp, Triton (Ill.) JC.—(AAA)
4. **J.R. Phillips, lhp-of, Bishop Amat HS, Rowland Heights, Calif.—(1993-99)**
5. David Neal, lhp, Montgomery HS, Semmes, Ala.—(High A)
6. **Gary DiSarcina, ss, University of Massachusetts.—(1989-2000)**
7. **Jim Edmonds, of, Diamond Bar (Calif.)**

**HS.—(1993-2010)**
8. David Partrick, of, Tate HS, Cantonment, Fla.
9. Jeff Kelso, of, Missouri Western State College.
10. Dave Sturdivant, c, University of Nevada-Las Vegas.
**11. Scott Lewis, rhp, University of Nevada-Las Vegas.—(1990-94)**
12. Jeff Kipila, of, Elon College.
**13. *Mike Robertson, of, Servite HS, Placentia, Calif.—(1996-98)**
**14. *Damon Mashore, of, Clayton Valley HS, Concord, Calif.—(1996-98)**
DRAFT DROP *Son of Clyde Mashore, major leaguer (1969-73)*
15. Mike Sheehy, of, Penn State University.
16. *Dirk Skillicorn, of, St. Francis HS, Los Altos, Calif.
**17. +Marcus Moore, rhp, Kennedy HS, Richmond, Calif. / Sacramento (Calif.) CC.—(1993-96)**
18. *L.V. Powell, of, Poly HS, Long Beach, Calif.
19. *Tom Bates, ss, Paris (Texas) JC.
20. *Kirk Dulom, 3b, Miami.
21. +Paul Borse, of, Sacramento (Calif.) CC.
**22. Larry Gonzales, c, University of Hawaii.—(1993)**
23. *Bill Minnis, ss, Mesa (Ariz.) CC.
24. Jeff Oberdank, 2b, UC Irvine.
25. Gary Cooper, 3b, Scottsdale (Ariz.) CC.
26. Wes Bliven, rhp, Santa Clara University.
27. Bruce Vegely, lhp, Cal State Dominguez Hills.
28. Frank Dominguez, c, University of Miami.
29. John Marchese, rhp, Grand Canyon College.
**30. +Damion Easley, ss-2b, Long Beach (Calif.) CC.—(1992-2008)**
31. *Darrin Gleiser, ss, Sandpoint Legion HS, Sandpoint, Idaho.
32. *Robert Dodd, lhp, Sacramento (Calif.) CC.
33. *Michael Lloyd, ss, Miami-Dade CC New World Center.
34. *Jim Henry, lhp, Placer HS, Forest Hill, Calif.
35. Don Vidmar, rhp, Grand Canyon College.
36. Steve Kirwin, of, Lewis (Ill.) University.
37. *Mike Hartnett, c, Borah HS, Boise, Idaho.
38. *Raul Rodarte, ss, Ganesha HS, Diamond Bar, Calif.
39. Rodney Eldridge, 1b-of, Scottsdale (Ariz.) CC.
40. +Corey Kapano, ss, Azusa (Calif.) HS / Mount San Antonio (Calif.) JC.
41. *Mark Roberts, rhp, Brewton Parker (Ga.) JC.
42. *James Pedicaris, of, Lake Gibson HS, Lakeland, Fla.
43. *Todd Marinovich, lhp, Capistrano Valley HS, Mission Viejo, Calif.
DRAFT DROP *First-round draft pick, Oakland Raiders/ National Football League (1991); quarterback, NFL (1991-92)*
44. *Jon Anderson, c, Indian River (Fla.) CC.
45. William Jones, c, Triton (Ill.) JC.
46. *Brian Goodwin, rhp, Indian River (Fla.) CC.
47. *Rene Delgado, ss, Miami-Dade CC North.

## CHICAGO CUBS (9)

1. Ty Griffin, 2b, Georgia Tech.—(AA)
2. (Choice to Expos as compensation for Type B free agent Vance Law)
3. Roberto Smalls, rhp, St. Thomas, Virgin Islands.—(Low A)
4. Brad Huff, c, Monroe (Ga.) Area HS.—(High A)
5. John Salles, rhp, Fresno State University.—(AAA)
6. Troy Bailey, of, Williams HS, Alexandria, Va.
7. Billy St. Peter, 3b-ss, University of Michigan.
8. Rob Bonneau, ss, Gonzaga Prep HS, Spokane, Wash.
9. *Dennis Gray, lhp, Banning (Calif.) HS.
10. David Goodwin, rhp, Xavier University.
11. Billy Paynter, c, Coronado HS, Tempe, Ariz.
12. *Roger Burnett, ss, Broken Arrow (Okla.) HS.
13. James Murphy, of, Portland State University.
14. *Rick Hirtensteiner, of, Pepperdine University.
15. Todd Borders, c, Lake Wales (Fla.) HS.
DRAFT DROP *Brother of Pat Borders, major leaguer (1988-2004)*
**16. Kevin Roberson, of, Parkland (Ill.) JC.—(1993-96)**
17. Luis Sierra, of, Dupont HS, Wilmington, Del.
18. Daren Burns, rhp, Birmingham-Southern College.
19. *Andy Croghan, rhp, Servite HS, Yorba Linda, Calif.
20. Woody Smith, 3b, Spartanburg Methodist (S.C.) JC.
21. Kraig Washington, of, Rancho Santiago (Calif.) JC.
DRAFT DROP *Grandson of Kenny Washington, first black player in NFL (1946)*
22. Mathew Leonard, 3b, Benedictine (Kan.) College.
23. Jason Doss, rhp, Westwood HS, Fort Pierce, Fla.
24. George Browder, c, Zephyrhills (Fla.) HS.
25. Juan Figueroa, of, Laredo (Texas) JC.
26. Dan Johnston, rhp, Creighton University.
27. +Greg Kessler, rhp, North Idaho JC.
28. Tim Ellis, lhp, Rosemont (Calif.) JC.
29. Mike Sodders, lhp, University of Alabama.
30. John Jensen, of, University of Texas.
31. Albert Stacey, 1b, Cleveland State University.
32. Ronnie Rasp, rhp, University of Montevallo (Ala.).
33. Shannon Jones, rhp, Southeastern Louisiana University.
34. Ben Shreve, ss, West Virginia University.
35. *Rodney Pedraza, rhp, Cuero (Texas) HS.
36. Richard Mundy, c, Pattonville HS, Bridgeton, Mo.
**37. *Chris Pritchett, ss, Central Catholic HS, Modesto, Calif.—(1996-2000)**
38. *Bill Judge, 3b, Brother Rice HS, Oak Forest, Ill.
39. Tracy Smith, rhp, Miami (Ohio) University.
DRAFT DROP *Baseball coach, Miami, Ohio (1997-2005); baseball coach, Indiana (2006-14); baseball coach, Arizona State (2015)*
**40. +Jessie Hollins, rhp, Willis (Texas) HS / San Jacinto (Texas) JC.—(1992)**
41. Eric Williams, of, University of North Carolina-Charlotte.
42. Marvin Cole, ss, Alexandria (La.) HS.
43. Chris Lutz, rhp, University of Michigan.
44. *Mathew Johnson, ss, Arvada West HS, Arvada, Colo.
45. *Peter Gardere, 1b, Robert E. Lee HS, Houston.
46. Rusty Crockett, ss, University of Texas.

## CHICAGO WHITE SOX (10)

**1. Robin Ventura, 3b, Oklahoma State University.—(1989-2004)**
DRAFT DROP *Major league manager (2012-15)*
2. Lenny Brutcher, rhp, Cicero-North HS, Syracuse, N.Y.—(High A)
3. Mike Mitchener, rhp, Armstrong State (Ga.) College.--(Low A)
**4. Johnny Ruffin, rhp, Choctaw County HS, Butler, Ala.—(1993-2001)**
**5. *Joey Eischen, lhp, West Covina (Calif.) HS.—(1994-2006)**
DRAFT DROP *Attended Pasadena (Calif.) CC; re-drafted by Rangers, 1989 (4th round)*
6. Mark Chasey, 1b, Florida Southern College.
**7. *Rich Batchelor, rhp, University of South Carolina-Aiken.—(1993-97)**
8. Wayne Moye, of, Princeton HS, Cincinnati.
9. Jerome Wolak, of, South Hills HS, West Covina, Calif.
**10. John Hudek, rhp, Florida Southern College.—(1994-99)**
11. Dennis Walker, 3b-c, Grambling State University.
12. Scott Egan, c, Glen Ridge (N.J.) HS.
13. Scott Middaugh, rhp, San Diego State University.
14. John Zaksek, of, University of Cincinnati.
15. Fred Dabney, lhp, Seminole (Okla.) JC.
16. Frank Merigliano, rhp, University of Pittsburgh.
17. *Todd Hobson, of, Lawrence North HS, Indianapolis, Ind.
18. John Chafin, rhp, Marshall University.
19. Wayne Busby, ss, Mississippi College.
20. *James Pague, rhp, Central Florida CC.
21. Scott Tedder, of, Ohio Wesleyan University.
22. Michael Galvan, lhp, Louisiana Tech.
23. John Furch, 1b, Duke University.
24. *Brian Noack, ss, Pensacola (Fla.) JC.
25. Dwayne Harvey, rhp, Sherrills Ford, N.C.
26. Arthur Thigpen, rhp, Flagler (Fla.) College.
27. Patrick Hulme, rhp, Hanna HS, Anderson, S.C.
28. Chris Fruge, rhp, Mississippi Delta JC.
29. *Anthony Pritchett, c, Mobile County HS, Grand Bay, Ala.
**30. *John DeSilva, rhp, Brigham Young University.—(1993-95)**
31. James Garrett, rhp, Southern University.
32. Paul Abbatinozzi, c, Flagler (Fla.) College.
33. Craig Teter, of, Seminole (Okla.) JC.
34. *Lee Dorsey, lhp, Hanna HS, Anderson, S.C.
35. *Keith Morrison, rhp, North Gwinett HS, Suwanee, Ga.
36. *Brian Whittal, rhp-3b, Marysville, Wash.
37. Ron Stephens, rhp, University of Cincinnati.
38. Scott Fuller, rhp, University of Wisconsin.
**39. *Marvin Benard, of, Bell HS, Cudahy, Calif.—(1995-2003)**
40. *Jack Johnson, c, St. Rita HS, Chicago.
41. *Jeff Graff, of, Texarkana (Texas) CC.
**42. Derek Lee, of, University of South Florida.—(1993)**
43. Jeff Ingram, c, University of New Orleans.
**44. *Ozzie Timmons, of, Brandon HS, Tampa.—(1995-2000)**
45. Todd Bargman, 1b, Oklahoma State University.
46. +Ronnie Plemmons, of, Spartanburg Methodist (S.C.) JC.
47. Lane Mallet, of, University of Houston.
48. *Brian Cordero, lhp, St. John's University.
49. *Timothy Sheriff, ss, West Oak HS, Westminster, S.C.
50. Robert Fletcher, 3b, University of Alabama.
51. Robert Thompson, c-of, Indian River (Fla.) CC.
52. Steve James, 1b, Mississippi Valley State University.
53. Brett Berry, of, Emporia State (Kan.) University.
DRAFT DROP *Son of Ken Berry, major leaguer (1962-75)*
54. *Hart Lee Dykes, lhp, Oklahoma State University.
DRAFT DROP *First-round draft pick, New England Patriots/National Football League (1989); wide receiver, NFL (1989-90)*
55. Jeff Buell, 1b, Indiana State University.
56. *Alex Alvarez, rhp, Gulf Coast (Fla.) CC.
57. *Dwayne Wade, of, Washington HS, Greenville, Miss.
58. *Brian Stephens, of, Hillsborough (Fla.) CC.
59. *Wayne Johnson, ss, Leuzinger HS, Gardena, Calif.
60. +Brian Gennings, rhp, Texarkana (Texas) CC.
61. *Mike Carlsen, ss, St Anthony's HS, Jersey City, N.J.

## CINCINNATI REDS (15)

1. (Choice to Giants as compensation for Type B free agent Eddie Milner)
**2. Jeff Branson, ss, Livingston (Ala.) College.—(1992-2001)**
**3. *Tyler Green, rhp, Thomas Jefferson HS, Denver.—(1993-98)**
DRAFT DROP *Attended Wichita State; re-drafted by Phillies, 1991 (1st round)*
4. Gaetano Gianni, c, Gordon Tech HS, Chicago.—(Rookie)
5. K.C. Gillum, 3b, Westerville North HS, Westerville, Ohio.—(AA)
6. Kurt Dempster, rhp, Arizona State University.
7. Shane Coker, of, Asher (Okla.) HS.
8. Carl Stewart, rhp, Plano East HS, Plano, Texas.
9. *Kevin Digiacomo, c, Choate College HS, Ithaca, N.Y.
10. Roosevelt Williams, 3b, Tyler (Texas) HS.
11. Mark Arland, of, Central Valley HS, Spokane, Wash.
**12. Steve Foster, rhp, University of Texas-Arlington.—(1991-93)**
**13. *Paul Byrd, rhp, St. Xavier HS, Louisville, Ky.—(1995-2009)**
14. Johnny Almaraz, rhp, Southwest Texas State University.
DRAFT DROP *Scouting director, Phillies (2014-15)*
15. *Craig Rapp, lhp, Red Land HS, Lewisberry, Pa.
16. *Scott McCarty, lhp, San Jacinto (Texas) JC.
17. Benny Colvard, of, Southeastern Oklahoma State University.
18. Kyle Reagan, of, East Lyme (Conn.) HS.
**19. Jerry Spradlin, rhp, Fullerton (Calif.) JC.—(1993-2000)**
20. *Earl Coachman, 3b, George C. Wallace (Ala.) CC.
DRAFT DROP *Brother of Pete Coachman, major leaguer (1990)*
21. Brian Nichols, c, University of Southern California.
22. Doug Bond, 1b, Quinnipiac College.
23. +Chris Keim, lhp, Taft (Calif.) JC.
24. *Chris Hart, of, Harrisonburg (Va.) HS.
25. Duane Mulville, c, Bakersfield (Calif.) JC.
26. *Charles Sullivan, 3b, Greenwich (Conn.) HS.
27. Jason Satre, rhp, Abilene (Texas) HS.
28. +Augie Gonzalez, c, Orosi (Calif.) HS / Taft (Calif.) JC.
29. *Ted Klamm, lhp, Bishop Ludden HS, Syracuse, N.Y.
30. Trevor Weeks, c, University of Miami.
31. C.L. Thomas, rhp, Western Kentucky University.
**32. Mo Sanford, rhp, University of Alabama.—(1991-95)**
33. *Brett Roberts, rhp, South Webster (Ohio) HS.
DRAFT DROP *Second-round draft pick, Sacramento Kings/National Basketball Association (1992)*
34. Dwayne Van Horne, rhp-3b, University of South Carolina-Spartanburg.
35. *Derrick Copes, of, Angelina (Texas) JC.
36. Michael Malley, lhp, University of Connecticut.
37. *Issac Jackson, of, Victor Valley HS, Victorville, Calif.
38. Jon Fuller, c, Bellevue (Wash.) CC.
39. *Dan Cholowsky, ss, Bellarmine Prep, San Jose, Calif.
DRAFT DROP *First-round draft pick (39th overall), Cardinals (1991)*
40. John Edward, lhp, New Mexico State University.
41. Cary Moore, inf-of, Sulphur Springs (Texas) HS.
42. Brian Landy, lhp, Quinnipiac College.
43. *Glenn Osinski, 3b, Triton (Ill.) JC.
44. Mike Mulvaney, 1b, University of Wyoming.
45. *Jason Cornell, of, Iowa Western CC.
46. *Bo Siberz, rhp, Westark (Ark.) CC.
47. *Barry Leavell, of, Washington HS, Chicago.
48. *David Williams, rhp, Westark (Ark.) CC.
49. *Brian Carie, rhp, Vincennes University (Ind.) JC.
50. Lawrence Moore, of, Rend Lake (Ill.) JC.
51. *Adrian Jones, of-rhp, University of Missouri.
52. *Mark Healy, rhp-1b, Iowa Western CC.
53. *Dan Schwader, lhp, Kishwaukee (Ill.) JC.
54. *Ben Blake, c, Indianola (Ind.) HS.
55. *Phil Zimmerman, 2b, Regis HS, Denver.
56. *Tim Boge, c, Dyersville-Beckman HS, Dyersville, Ia.
57. *Rick Freehling, of, Regis HS, Denver.
58. *Sam Austin, of, Triton (Ill.) JC.
59. *Robert Robinson, rhp, Circleville (Ohio) HS.
**60. *Don Wengert, rhp, Heelan HS, Sioux City, Iowa.—(1995-2001)**
DRAFT DROP *Brother of Bill Wengert, 23rd-round draft pick, Dodgers (1988)*

## CLEVELAND INDIANS (2)

**1. Mark Lewis, ss, Hamilton (Ohio) HS.—(1991-2001)**
**1. Charles Nagy, rhp, University of Connecticut** (Choice from Giants as compensation for Type A free agent Brett Butler)—**(1990-2003)**
**1. Jeff Mutis, lhp, Lafayette College** (Supplemental choice—27th—as compensation for Butler)**—(1991-94)**
2. Brian Johnson, c, University of Texas.—(AAA)
3. Clyde Pough, rhp-ss, Avon Park (Fla.) HS.—(AAA)
4. Daren Epley, 1b, Bradley University.—(AAA)
5. Ty Kovach, rhp, Central Arizona JC.—(AA)
6. Don Young, of, Grossmont (Calif.) JC.
**7. Greg McMichael, rhp, University of Tennessee.—(1993-2000)**
8. Olonzo Woodfin, lhp, Sylmar (Calif.) HS.
**9. Brett Merriman, rhp, Grand Canyon College.—(1993-94)**
10. *Tom Duffin, 3b-of, Miami-Dade CC North.
**11. *Jorge Fabregas, c-1b, Christopher Columbus HS, Miami.—(1994-2002)**
DRAFT DROP *First-round draft pick (34th overall), Angels (1991)*
12. *Keith Millay, rhp, Apollo HS, Owensboro, Ky.
13. *Tommy Boudreau, rhp, Chaparral HS, Las Vegas, Nev.
14. *Josh Lowery, ss, Laney (Calif.) JC.
15. Charles Alexander, lhp, Western Michigan University.

16. Joey James, of, UCLA.
17. Barry Blackwell, c, Florida State University.
18. *Darrin Paxton, lhp, East HS, Wichita, Kan.
19. Sean Baron, 1b, University of San Diego.
20. Leonard Leger, rhp, Ventura (Calif.) JC.
21. *Jason Geis, of, Hudson's Bay HS, Vancouver, Wash.
22. Darin Campbell, 3b, University of North Carolina.
23. Bob Kairis, rhp, Northwestern State University.
24. Rick Falkner, of, University of Portland.
25. Javier Murillo, 2b, Azusa Pacific (Calif.) University.
26. Martin Eddy, of-1b, Dallas Baptist University.
27. Lawrence Smith, 2b, Bethune-Cookman College.
28. Randy Mazey, of, Clemson University.

DRAFT DROP *Baseball coach, Charleston Southern (1994-96); baseball coach, East Carolina (2003-05); baseball coach, West Virginia (2013-15)*

29. *Kraig Constantino, 1b-c, Branham HS, San Jose, Calif.
30. William Scarborough, rhp, Ferrum (Va.) College.
31. *David Keating, of, UCLA.
32. Rougnas Odor, ss, University of New Orleans.

DRAFT DROP *Uncle of Rougned Odor, major leaguer (2014-15)*

33. Alex Ferran, of, Coral Park HS, Miami.
34. Andrew Baker, rhp, Cook HS, Lenox, Ga.
35. *Troy Eklund, of, University of Arkansas.
36. Cecil Pettiford, rhp, Jackson State University.
37. Dan Williams, c, Western Oregon State College.
38. Lenny Gilmore, of, Cal State Northridge.
39. Mark Tepper, 1b, Lubbock Christian (Texas) College.
40. Keith Bevenour, lhp, Penn State University.
41. Brad Hebets, rhp, University of Southwestern Louisiana.
42. *John Abercrombie, c, Eisenhower HS, Houston.
43. Teryl Morrison, rhp, Contra Costa (Calif.) JC.
44. Jeff Bonchek, 3b, Michigan State University.
45. Steve Harrell, of, Hamilton (Ohio) HS.
46. Todd Mraz, c, University of Texas-Arlington.
47. Brian Cofer, ss, University of Montevallo (Ala.).
48. *Douglas Egloff, rhp, Denver.
49. *Greg Fowble, 2b, University of Arizona.
50. Dean Meddaugh, of-2b, Victor Valley (Calif.) CC.
51. *John Eierman, of, Leo HS, Chicago.
52. Michael Ashworth, rhp, Westmont (Calif.) College.
53. Bill Kull, of, Florida Southern College.
54. *David Ferrell, 2b, DeAnza (Calif.) JC.
55. *Jason Pfaff, 1b, St. Xavier HS, Cincinnati.
56. *Michael Bonetto, lhp, Big Bear HS, Big Bear Lake, Calif.
57. *Erik Young, of, Baldwin-Wallace (Ohio) College.
58. *Mark Smith, rhp, San Jacinto (Texas) JC.

## DETROIT TIGERS (26)

1. **Rico Brogna, 1b-lhp, Watertown (Conn.) HS.—(1992-2001)**
2. **Scott Livingstone, 3b, Texas A&M University.—(1991-98)**
3. Tookie Spann, of, Tulane University.—(AA)
4. Lance Shebelut, 1b, Fresno State University.—(Low A)
5. Mike Lumley, rhp, Eastern Michigan University.—(AAA)
6. Eric Stone, rhp, University of Texas.
7. Tim Brader, lhp, Shelton State (Ala.) JC.
8. Tom Aldrich, ss, Bowdoin (Mass.) College.
9. **Kurt Knudsen, rhp, University of Miami.—(1992-94)**
10. Chris Gollehon, rhp, Medical Lake HS, Fairchild, Wash.
11. *Michael Brown, of, Pensacola Catholic HS, Pensacola, Fla.
12. Mickey Delas, c, Eastern Michigan University.
13. Mike Rendina, 1b, Grossmont HS, El Cajon, Calif.
14. Linty Ingram, rhp, Arizona State University.
15. **David Haas, rhp, Wichita State University.—(1991-93)**
16. Brett Roach, c, Eastern Michigan University.
17. **Rich Rowland, c, Mendocino (Calif.) CC.—(1990-95)**
18. Ron Howard, 2b, Palomar (Calif.) JC.
19. *Todd Taylor, c, Lakeland (Fla.) HS.
20. Kurt Shea, rhp, Southwestern Michigan JC.
21. Robert Thomas, rhp, Sonoma State (Calif.) University.
22. *Willie Warrecker, lhp, University of California.
23. John Barton, rhp, University of Nevada-Reno.
24. Benny Castillo, of, Oklahoma State University.
25. Robert Frassa, of, CC of Morris (N.J.).
26. *Brian Dour, rhp, Bradley University.
27. *Michael Pfeifer, rhp, Stevens HS, Edison, N.J.
28. Eric Shoup, rhp, Point Park (Pa.) College.
29. Jimmy Hitt, rhp, Florida Southern College.
30. Mike Davidson, of, Michigan State University.
31. James Hill, ss, University of the Pacific.
32. Joe Niedinger, rhp, Catholic Central HS, Monroe, Mich.
33. *Craig Eubanks, rhp, Marysville (Calif.) HS.
34. *Ed Bustamonte, of, Fresno State University.
35. Mike Jones, rhp, Loyola Marymount University.
36. Travis Kinyoun, c, Royal HS, Simi Valley, Calif.
37. Duane Walker, of, University of South Florida.
38. Bert Patton, lhp, Eastern Michigan University.
39. *Todd Winston, c, Marysville (Mich.) HS.
40. *Bobby Holley, ss, UCLA.
41. +Don Pedersen, 1b-of, JC of the Canyons (Calif.).
42. *David Brink, rhp, Lake Michigan JC.
43. *Joe Arredondo, 1b, Bellflower (Calif.) HS.
44. *Derric Taylor, of, Muir HS, Altadena, Calif.
45. *Kirk Piskor, c, Plano East HS, Plano, Texas.
46. *James Wolfe, c, Spanish River HS, Boca Raton, Fla.
47. *Tony Muser Jr., 2b, Los Alamitos (Calif.) HS.

DRAFT DROP *Son of Tony Muser, major leaguer (1969-78); major league manager (1997-2002)*

48. *Robert Welch, c, Horizon HS, Scottsdale, Ariz.
49. *Andrew Watson, rhp, Vashon HS, St. Louis.
50. *Russ Gaston, rhp, Belleville Area (Ill.) CC.

## HOUSTON ASTROS (7)

1. Willie Ansley, of, Plainview (Texas) HS.—(AAA)
2. Mica Lewis, ss, Cal State Los Angeles.—(AA)
2. **Dave Silvestri, ss, University of Missouri** (Choice from Yankees as compensation for Type B free agent Jose Cruz)**—(1992-99).**
3. **Scott Servais, c, Creighton University.—(1991-2001)**
4. **Luis Gonzalez, 1b, University of South Alabama.—(1990-2008)**
5. *Terry Christopher, rhp, University of Kentucky.—(High A)

DRAFT DROP *No school; never re-drafted*

6. **Chris Gardner, rhp, Cuesta (Calif.) JC.—(1991)**
7. Bernie Jenkins, of, St. Francis (N.Y.) College.
8. Gordy Farmer, rhp, Arizona State University.
9. Brian Griffiths, rhp, Mount Hood (Ore.) CC.
10. David Klinefelter, lhp, Allegheny (Pa.) CC.
11. Maurice Jones, of, Edgewater HS, Orlando, Fla.
12. Dave Shermet, of, Arizona State University.
13. Bill Gearhart, rhp, Armstrong State (Ga.) College.
14. Larry Lamphere, of, Central Michigan University.
15. Wally Trice, lhp, U.S. International (Calif.) University.
16. Ed Quijada, 3b, Rio Vista (Calif.) HS.
17. **Kenny Lofton, of, University of Arizona.—(1991-2007)**
18. Rod Windes, lhp, Cal State Los Angeles.
19. ***Mike Durant, c, Watterson HS, Columbus, Ohio.—(1996)**
20. Eric Given, c, University of South Carolina-Spartanburg.
21. Rick Dunnum, rhp, William Penn (Iowa) College.
22. Ken Morris, rhp, Northwestern State University.
23. Jim Desapio, lhp, St. Francis (N.Y.) College.
24. +David Metheney, rhp, Dixie Hollins HS, Seminole, Fla. / South Florida CC.
25. *Kevin Schula, c, El Dorado HS, Placentia, Calif.
26. Rod Scheckla, rhp, Oregon State University.
27. Ben Gonzales, rhp, Cypress (Calif.) JC.
28. *Mark King, of, Mount Carmel HS, San Diego.
29. Anthony Gutierrez, lhp, Englewood HS, Littleton, Colo.
30. *Mike Kirk, of, Shasta (Calif.) JC.
31. +Bob Hurlbutt, c, Monroe (N.Y.) CC.
32. *Matthew Lackie, rhp, Rancho Santiago (Calif.) JC.
33. *Mark Rudis, c, Clear Creek HS, League City, Texas.
34. *Eric Gray, rhp, Bloomington HS, Rialto, Calif.
35. *Dan Tiumalu, 3b-of, Helix HS, Lemon Grove, Calif.
36. Scott Spurgeon, 3b, Northwest Missouri State University.
37. +Duane Brown, rhp, South Umpqua HS, Myrtle Creek, Ore. / JC of the Siskiyous (Calif.).
38. *Elgin Bobo, c, Cabrillo (Calif.) JC.
39. Mark Hudgins, ss, Plantation (Fla.) HS.
40. *Richard Czajkowski, ss, Haverling HS, Bath, N.Y.
41. ***Chris Tremie, c, South Houston (Texas) HS.—(1995-2004)**
42. *Billy Wissler, rhp, Central Dauphin HS, Harrisburg, Pa.
43. Troy Dovey, rhp, Miami-Dade CC South.
44. Luis Navarro, lhp, Southwest HS, Miami.
45. *Heath Daniel, of, Central HS, Phenix City, Ala.
46. *Craig Fairbanks, rhp, Morello Prep HS, Boulder Creek, Calif.
47. *Scott Mowl, 1b, Bellflower (Calif.) HS.
48. *David Lacroix, rhp-ss, Los Angeles Harbor JC.
49. *Placido Vicente, c, Southwest HS, Miami.
50. *Anthony Dunnahoe, 1b-of, Haines City (Fla.) HS.
51. *Ross Macaluso, ss, Hillsborough (Fla.) CC.
52. *James Simpson, of, Lake Worth (Fla.) HS.
53. *Steven Schuerman, rhp, Spokane Falls (Wash.) CC.
54. *Joe Burnett, of, Delgado (La.) JC.
55. *John Hercholcz, rhp, Miami-Dade CC North.
56. *Patrick King, of-inf, Don Lugo HS, Chino, Calif.
57. *Jose Rubiera, of, Howard (Texas) JC.
58. *Nelson Izquierdo, 2b, Monsignor Pace HS, Hialeah, Fla.
59. *Grady Garrow, rhp, Butte (Calif.) JC.
60. *Matthew Morgan, of, Creskill (N.J.) HS.
61. *Jon Newville, rhp, Bishop Montgomery HS, Palos Verdes Estates, Calif.
62. *Jim Greenlee, lhp, Pinole Valley HS, San Pablo, Calif.
63. *Joe Church, rhp, Santana HS, Santee, Calif.
64. *Michael Ballerelli, of, Castle Park HS, San Diego.

## KANSAS CITY ROYALS (18)

1. Hugh Walker, of, Jacksonville (Ark.) HS.—(AAA)
2. **Bob Hamelin, 1b, Rancho Santiago (Calif.) JC.—(1993-98)**
3. **Joel Johnston, rhp, West Chester, Pa.—(1991-95)**
4. Greg Harvey, rhp, Seminole (Okla.) JC.—(AA)
5. **Tim Spehr, c, Arizona State University.—(1991-99)**
6. Jim Smith, rhp, Jacksonville State University.
7. Frankie Watson, of, Longwood (Va.) College.
8. Randy Vaughn, rhp, Shelton State (Ala.) JC.
9. Jeff Hulse, c, Kansas State University.
10. Jeff Garber, 2b, James Madison University.
11. **Mike Magnante, lhp, UCLA.—(1991-2002)**
12. Steve Otto, rhp, St. Xavier (Ill.) College.
13. David Rolls, c, University of San Diego.
14. **Victor Cole, rhp, Santa Clara University.—(1992)**
15. Kyle Balch, rhp, Vanderbilt University.
16. **Kerwin Moore, of, King HS, Detroit.—(1996)**
17. John Conner, rhp, Rose State (Okla.) JC.
18. Stan Bowling, rhp, Desales HS, Louisville, Ky.
19. Marvin Mayberry, c, Cody HS, Detroit.
20. *John Cuda, rhp, Penn Hills HS, Verona, Pa.
21. Milt Richardson, of, Skyline (Calif.) JC.
22. Frank Halcovich, of-1b, University of Arizona.
23. Kyle Irvin, rhp, Oral Roberts University.
24. Kelvin Davis, ss, Longwood (Va.) College.
25. Zach Kimbell, rhp, Kansas State University.
26. Chad Stombaugh, c, Rend Lake (Ill.) JC.
27. *Rich Gonzales, of-1b, Rancho Santiago (Calif.) JC.
28. Gerald Ingram, of, Western Kentucky University.
29. Ronald Collins, 1b, Mount San Jacinto (Calif.) JC.
30. John Gilcrist, of, Indian River (Fla.) CC.
31. John McCormick, lhp, Ohio State University.
32. Stephen Osik, rhp, Long Island University.
33. Mike Beall, 1b, St. Thomas (Fla.) University.
34. *Mike Gillette, c, University of Michigan.
35. Steve Preston, 2b, Michigan State University.
36. Greg Prusia, of, Alfred (N.Y.) University.
37. *Brad Seitzer, ss-3b, Lincoln Land (Ill.) CC.

DRAFT DROP *Brother of Kevin Seitzer, major leaguer (1986-97)*

38. *Dean McMillin, lhp, Ventura (Calif.) HS.
39. Brad Hopper, rhp, Fullerton (Calif.) JC.
40. *Jim Austin, of, Mater Dei HS, Mission Viejo, Calif.
41. *Mickey Kerns, ss, Hancock (Md.) HS.
42. *Greg Blevins, c, Northeastern Oklahoma JC.
43. +John Gross, rhp, Clovis HS, Fresno, Calif. / Fresno CC.
44. *William Melvin, of, Pace HS, Milton, Fla.
45. *David Fletcher, rhp, Yucca Valley (Calif.) HS.'
46. +Jerome Byers, of, Washington HS, Kansas City, Kan. / Johnson County (Kan.) CC.
47. *Kim Cornist, of, Solano (Calif.) CC.
48. *Jose Fernandez, c, University of Florida.
49. +Jason Bryans, rhp, Macomb (Mich.) CC.

## LOS ANGELES DODGERS (5)

1. Bill Bene, rhp, Cal State Los Angeles.—(AAA)
2. (Choice to Athletics as compensation for Type A free agent Mike Davis)
3. **Billy Ashley, of, Belleville (Mich.) HS.—(1992-98)**
4. Anthony Collier, of, Muir HS, Pasadena, Calif.—(AA)
5. Paul Branconier, rhp, Covina (Calif.) HS.—(Low A)
6. **Eric Karros, 1b, UCLA.—(1991-2004)**
7. **Jeff Hartsock, rhp, North Carolina State University.—(1992)**
8. *Scott Erwin, rhp, Georgia Tech.
9. **Jim Poole, lhp, Georgia Tech.—(1990-2000)**
10. **Eddie Pye, ss, Middle Tennessee State University.—(1994-95)**
11. Brock McMurray, of, Southeastern Louisiana University.
12. **Jerry Brooks, of-3b, Clemson University.—(1993-96)**
13. Chris Morrow, of, Skyline (Calif.) JC.
14. ***Dana Allison, lhp, James Madison University.—(1991)**
15. Lance Rice, c, Oregon State University.
16. **Brian Traxler, 1b, University of New Orleans.—(1990)**
17. Mike Chiusano, c, Nazareth HS, Brooklyn, N.Y.
18. *Coleman Smith, of, Conestoga Valley HS, Talmage, Pa.
19. James Wray, lhp, Troy State University.
20. Sean McKamie, ss, Central HS, St. Paul, Minn.
21. Steve Finken, ss, University of Michigan.
22. Michael St. Estaben, lhp, Chino (Calif.) HS.
23. Bill Wengert, rhp, Iowa State University.

DRAFT DROP *Brother of Don Wengert, 60th-round draft pick, Reds (1988); major leaguer (1995-2001)*

24. Rod Harvell, of, Fairfield (Calif.) HS.
25. Mike Sampson, rhp, Holyoke (Mass.) CC.
26. Ernie Carr, 3b-of, Jacksonville University.
27. *Mike Munson, rhp, University of Illinois.
28. Eric Ganino, c, Fontana (Calif.) HS.
29. John Braase, rhp, College of Idaho.
30. Sean Snedeker, rhp, Texas A&M University.
31. Clayton Enno, lhp, Des Moines Area (Iowa) CC.
32. Bryan Beals, 2b-of, Chapman (Calif.) College.
33. Cam Biberdorf, rhp, Mayville State (N.D.) College.
34. Napoleon Robinson, rhp, Columbus (Ga.) College.
35. **Hector Ortiz, c, Ranger (Texas) JC.—(1998-2002)**
36. Jeff Castillo, rhp, Mesa (Colo.) College.
37. Brad Boggetto, rhp, Parkland (Ill.) JC.
38. Wendall Zink, 3b-ss, Dixie (Utah) JC.
39. K.G. White, of, Georgia Tech.
40. *Felix Rios, 3b, Sabana Seca, P.R.
41. *Todd Reische, c, Minooka (Ill.) HS.
42. +Eric Blackwell, of, Spartanburg Methodist (S.C.) JC.
43. ***Garey Ingram, c, Columbus (Ga.) HS.—(1994-97)**
44. *Brent Miller, 3b-1b, Jordan HS, Columbus, Ga.
45. *Brad Cohen, of, Starkville (Miss.) Academy.
46. *Wilfred Brown, ss, Lurleen B. Wallace State (Ala.) JC.
47. +Garrett Beard, of-3b, Spartanburg Methodist (S.C.) JC.
48. *Terry Miller, of, Compton (Calif.) CC.
49. *Deon Montgomery, ss, Compton (Calif.) CC.
50. *Jose Fernandez, of, CC of San Francisco.
51. *Daniel Hancock, rhp, Bremen HS, Midlothian, Ill.
52. *Gaither Bagsby, rhp, Dickson County (Tenn.) HS.
53. *Michael Emmons, rhp, Pensacola (Fla.) JC.

54. *Shannon Zerlang, of-3b, JC of the Redwoods (Calif.).
55. *Craig Thomas, of, Northside HS, Warner Robins, Ga.
56. *Dan Frye, ss-2b, Logansport (Ind.) HS.
DRAFT DROP *Twin brother of Dennis Frye, 57th-round draft pick, Dodgers (1988)*
57. *Dennis Frye, 1b-of, Logansport (Ind.) HS.
DRAFT DROP *Twin brother of Dan Frye, 56th-round draft pick, Dodgers (1988)*
58. *Mike Vdovkin, rhp, Merced (Calif.) HS.
59. *Chris Harding, of, Louisburg (N.C.) JC.
60. *Robert Hoffman, c, Kennedy HS, Richmond, Calif.
61. Erik Boddie, of, Creighton University.
**62. Mike Piazza, 1b-c, Miami-Dade CC North.—(1992-2007)**
DRAFT DROP *Elected to Baseball Hall of Fame, 2016*

## MILWAUKEE BREWERS (24)

**1. *Alex Fernandez, rhp, Monsignor Pace HS, Miami.—(1990-2000)**
DRAFT DROP *Attended Miami (Fla.); re-drafted by White Sox, 1990 (1st round); first player from 1990 draft to reach majors (Aug. 2, 1990)*
2. Randy Snyder, c, Washington State University.—(AAA)
3. Joe Andrzejewski, rhp, Chesapeake HS, Pasadena, Md.—(Low A)
4. Ken Kremer, 1b, Rider College.—(Low A)
**5. Pat Listach, ss, Arizona State University.—(1992-97)**
6. Greg Landry, rhp, University of Texas.
**7. Chris George, rhp, Kent State University.—(1991)**
**8. Mike Ignasiak, rhp, University of Michigan.—(1991-95)**
DRAFT DROP *Brother of Mike Ignasiak, major league (1973)*
**9. Bert Heffernan, c, Clemson University.—(1992)**
10. *Charlie Fiacco, of, UCLA.
11. Danny Kapea, lhp, University of Hawaii.
12. Don Meyett, of, Catonsville (Md.) CC.
13. Leon Glenn, 1b, East Central (Miss.) JC.
14. *Ken Hokuf, rhp, Golden West (Calif.) JC.
15. Sylvester Love, of, University of Southern Mississippi.
16. Heath Lane, rhp, University of Arizona.
17. Robert Scott, of, Mankato West HS, Mankato, Miss.
18. Stewart Lee, 3b, Jacksonville State University.
19. Dave Voit, rhp, University of Kentucky.
20. Ruben Rodriquez, of, University of Southwestern Louisiana.
21. *Brian Dodd, lhp, Arizona State University.
22. Robert Lipscomb (Muhammed), of, University of Hawaii.
23. Tim Snow, 2b, East Carolina University.
24. *Troy Bradford, rhp, Cochise County (Ariz.) CC.
25. Kevin Carmody, lhp, North Adams State (Mass.) College.
26. Javier Brown, ss-of, Morse HS, San Diego.
27. David Fitzgerald, lhp, Davidson College.
28. *Doug Vanderweele, rhp, Bonanza HS, Las Vegas, Nev.
29. Rich Pfaff, of, Essex (Md.) CC.
30. Larry Oedewaldt, c, U.S. International (Calif.) University.
31. Michael Grayson, rhp, Florida International University.
32. *Robert Jakubik, 1b, St. John Bosco HS, Cerritos, Calif.
33. *Chris Norton, c, Lake Howell HS, Maitland, Fla.
34. *Donald Culberson, of, Neshoba Central HS, Philadelphia.
35. *Dwayne Wilson, of, Oceanside (Calif.) HS.
36. Brad Tilly, 2b, Bradley University.
37. Mike Littlewood, 3b, Brigham Young University.
DRAFT DROP *Baseball coach, Brigham Young (2013-15)*
38. Bryan Parks, c, Catonsville (Md.) CC.
39. *Chris Tacik, rhp, Thomas Johnson HS, Frederick, Md.
40. *Bryan Hastings, rhp, East Forsyth HS, Kernersville, N.C.
41. *Edgar Anderson, of, Logan HS, Dolton, Ill.
42. *Scott Craven, 3b, Punahou HS, Kailua, Hawaii.

TOM DIPACE

Florida A&M was productive scouting ground for the Expos, yielding Marquis Grissom in '88

## MINNESOTA TWINS (20)

1. Johnny Ard, rhp, Manatee (Fla.) JC.—(AAA)
**2. Alan Newman, lhp, Fullerton (Calif.) JC.—(1999-2000)**
3. *Mike Harrison, c, Campolinda (Calif.) HS.—(AA)
DRAFT DROP *Attended California; re-drafted by Reds, 1991 (5th round)*
**4. Steve Dunn, 1b, Robinson HS, Fairfax, Va.—(1994-95)**
5. *Steve Dean, of-rhp, Ada (Okla.) HS.--DNP
DRAFT DROP *Attended Oklahoma; never re-drafted*
**6. Pat Mahomes, rhp, Lindale (Texas) HS.—(1992-2003)**
7. Doug Sutton, rhp, University of Kentucky.
8. Jay Kvasnicka, of, University of Minnesota.
**9. Doug Simons, lhp, Pepperdine University.—(1991-92)**
10. Jody Harrington, lhp, Armijo HS, Fairfield, Calif.
**11. J.T. Bruett, of, University of Minnesota.—(1992-93)**
12. Deryk Gross, of, University of the Pacific.
13. Mike Pomeranz, lhp, Clemson University.
14. Steve Muh, lhp, University of Georgia.
15. +Tony Tucker, of, Tate HS, Cantonment, Fla. / Pensacola (Fla.) JC.
16. *Gary Tatterson, rhp, Glendale (Ariz.) CC.
17. Gary Resetar, c, Rutgers University.
18. *Vince Palyan, of, University of Minnesota.
19. Carl Fraticelli, 2b, Loyola Marymount University.
20. Loy McBride, of, Cal State Los Angeles.
21. Jeff Milene, c, Mayo HS, Rochester, Minn.
22. Angel Lugo, ss, Grady HS, Brooklyn, N.Y.
23. *Jeff Edmunds, 1b, Plantation HS, Sunrise, Fla.
24. *Jody Hurst, of, Mississippi State University.
25. J.P. Wright, of, Washburn (Kan.) University.
26. *Steve Gill, lhp-of, Cypress (Calif.) JC.
**27. *Scott Stahoviak, rhp-1b, Carmel Mundelein HS, Grays Lake, Ill.—(1993-98)**
DRAFT DROP *First-round draft pick (27th overall), Twins (1991)*
28. *Peter Raether, rhp, Edina (Minn.) HS.
29. *Jon Bellamy, 3b, Lafayette (La.) HS.
30. *Will Vespe, 1b, University of Miami.
31. *Chris Hmielewski, lhp, Leyden HS, Franklin Park, Ill.
32. Dom Rovasio, rhp, Quinnipiac College.
33. *Pat Hope, rhp, Oklahoma State University.
34. *George Behr, of, Hill Murray HS, Maplewood, Minn.
35. Steve Morris, of, University of Hawaii.
36. *Michael Teron, rhp, Santa Clara HS, Oxnard, Calif.
**37. *Aaron Sele, rhp, North Kitsap HS, Poulsbo, Wash.—(1993-2007)**
DRAFT DROP *First-round draft pick (23rd overall), Red Sox (1991)*
38. *Marc Pak, of, Valley HS, Las Vegas, Nev.
39. *Sheldon Forehand, of, American HS, Fremont, Calif.
40. Pedro Oliva, of, Kennedy HS, Bloomington, Minn.
DRAFT DROP *Son of Tony Oliva, major leaguer (1962-76)*
41. *David Baine, lhp, San Marin HS, Novato, Calif.
42. Willie McKinnon, of, Nicholls (Ga.) HS.
43. *Jeremy Kendall, lhp, Towns Country HS, Hiwassee, Ga.
44. *Carl Johnson, rhp, North Thurston Johnson HS, Frederick, Md.
45. Troy Hoerner, of, Milaca (Minn.) HS.
DRAFT DROP *Son of Joe Hoerner, major leaguer (1963-77)*
46. *John Jackson, of, Washington State University.
47. *Jerome McGerry, of-rhp, Liberty Eylau HS, Texarkana, Texas.
48. *Frederick Smith, rhp, Venice HS, Culver City, Calif.

## MONTREAL EXPOS (19)

**1. Dave Wainhouse, rhp, Washington State University.—(1991-2000)**
2. Ben Howze, rhp, Washington HS, Pensacola, Fla. (Choice from Cubs as compensation for Type B free agent Vance Law).—(High A)
**2. Chris Nabholz, lhp, Towson State University.—(1990-95)**
**3. Marquis Grissom, of-rhp, Florida A&M University.—(1989-2005)**
DRAFT DROP *Brother of Antonio Grissom, 36th-round draft pick, Expos (1988)*
**4. Scott Davison, rhp-ss, Redondo Union HS, Redondo Beach, Calif.—(1995-96)**
5. Tyrone Woods, 3b, Hernando HS, Brooksville, Fla.—(AAA)
**6. Tim Laker, c, Oxnard (Calif.) JC.—(1992-2006)**
**7. Bret Barberie, ss, University of Southern California.—(1991-96)**
8. Bryn Kosco, 3b, North Carolina State University.
DRAFT DROP *Son of Andy Kosco, major leaguer (1965-74)*
9. +Martin Martinez, rhp, Cochise County (Ariz.) CC.
10. Joe Klancnik, rhp, University of Florida.
**11. Reid Cornelius, rhp, Thomasville (Ala.) HS.—(1995-2000)**
12. Isaac Elder, of, Cal State Los Angeles.
13. Rod Boddie, of, James Madison University.
14. Dan Archibald, rhp, San Jose State University.
15. +Rafael Adame, rhp, Bell HS, Maywood, Calif. / Cerritos (Calif.) JC.
16. Steve Whitehead, rhp, Brawley (Calif.) HS.
17. Dan Freed, rhp, Illinois State University.
**18. Darrin Winston, lhp, Rutgers University.—(1997-98)**
19. *Richard Busch, c, St. Petersburg (Fla.) HS.
20. Brian Sajonia, lhp, Washington State University.
21. Eric Nelson, 3b-rhp, San Jose State University.
22. *Brian Pease, lhp, Bonny Eagle HS, Cornish, Maine.
23. Pat Heiderscheit, rhp-c, Iowa State University.
24. Mike Farrell, rhp, LeMoyne College.
25. Dale Buzzard, rhp, University of La Verne (Calif.).
26. David Oropeza, rhp, University of Alabama.
27. *Scott Banton, of, Virginia Commonwealth University.
28. Keith Kaub, 1b, Cal State Fullerton.
29. *Robert Langer, ss, Carmel HS, Mundelein, Ill.
30. *Danny Parente, 1b-lhp, Los Angeles Harbor JC.
31. *Vernon Slater, of, Brandon HS, Tampa.
32. *Justin Heinold, lhp, Stroman HS, Victoria, Texas.
33. *Dan Stanley, ss, Lindberg HS, Renton, Wash.
34. *Marvin Cobb, rhp, University of Oklahoma.
35. +Mike Virden, of, Lee (Texas) JC.
36. *Antonio Grissom, of, Lakeshore HS, Red Oak, Ga.
DRAFT DROP *Brother of Marquis Grissom, third-round draft pick, Expos (1988); major leaguer (1989-2005).*
37. *Todd Manly, rhp, San Jose (Calif.) CC.
38. *Mike Lane, 1b, Indian River (Fla.) CC.
39. Ken Lake, of, University of Wyoming.
40. Ricardo Cartwright, of, Florida A&M University.
41. +Paul Hutto, rhp, Auburndale (Fla.) HS / Manatee (Fla.) JC.
42. *Brad Erdman, 3b, Douglas (Ariz.) HS.
43. *Gary Young, rhp, San Jacinto (Texas) JC.
44. *Jesus Molina, lhp, Pima (Ariz.) CC.
45. Jeff Tuss, rhp, Capital HS, Helena, Mont.
46. *Stephen Day, rhp, Indian River (Fla.) CC.
47. *Cord Corbitt, lhp, Palm Beach (Fla.) JC.
48. *Frank Giunta, 1b-lhp, Martin County HS, Palm City, Fla.
49. *Jared Snyder, c, Saugus (Calif.) HS.
50. *Norman Montoya, lhp, Newark Memorial HS, Newark, Calif.
51. +Jeff Ramsey, ss-of, Northampton East HS, Rich Square, N.C. / Louisburg (N.C.) JC.
52. *Robert Yonker, rhp, CC of Morris (N.J.).
53. *Doug DeKock, c, University of Miami.
54. *Keith Hopkins, of, Brandon HS, Tampa.
55. Marlon Correa, 2b, Carol City (Fla.) HS.
56. *James Wallkvist, rhp, Lincoln HS, San Francisco.
57. *John Fleischer, rhp, Benedictine HS, Richmond, Va.
58. *John Halverson, rhp, Brookwood HS, Snellville, Ga.

## NEW YORK METS (21)

1. Dave Proctor, rhp, Allen County (Kan.) CC.—(AA)
2. *Jeff Seale, rhp, Fairview HS, Boulder, Colo.--DNP
DRAFT DROP *Attended Texas; re-drafted by Indians, 1991 (32nd round)*
**3. Doug Saunders, 2b, Esperanza HS, Yorba Linda, Calif.—(1993)**
3. *Derrick Warren, of, Washington HS, Pensacola, Fla. (Choice from Yankees as compensation for Type B free agent John Candelaria).—(Short-season A)
DRAFT DROP *Attended Alabama; never re-drafted*
4. Dan Furmanik, rhp, Palm Beach (Fla.) JC.—(High A)
5. Tim Howard, 2b, Imperial Valley (Calif.) JC.—(AAA)
6. Kyle Washington, of, Kishwaukee (Ill.) JC.
**7. Kevin Baez, ss, Dominican (N.Y.) College.—(1990-93)**
8. Mike Lehnerz, rhp, Regis HS, Denver.
9. *Pat Leinen, lhp, University of Nebraska.
10. Andrew Fidler, lhp, Methacton HS, Audubon, Pa.
11. Greg Langbehn, lhp, Everest HS, Schofield, Wis.
12. *Doug Bennett, rhp, Hillcrest HS, Springfield, Mo.
13. Jeff Thompson, ss, Newnan (Ga.) HS.
14. Mike Anaya, rhp, Valley HS, Albuquerque, N.M.
15. Nicky Davis, 1b, Merritt Island (Fla.) HS.
16. Andy Reich, rhp, Louisburg (N.C.) JC.
17. Mason Rudolph, c, Dobson HS, Mesa, Ariz.
18. Mike Noelke, 2b, University of Wisconsin-La Crosse.
19. *Beau Campbell, c, Lindberg HS, Renton, Wash.
20. Jon Hudson, lhp, University of Kentucky.
21. Paul Johnson, rhp, Rutgers University.
22. Chris Butler, rhp, McEachern HS, Marietta, Ga.
23. Dale Plummer, rhp, University of Maine.
**24. *Mike Kelly, of, Los Alamitos (Calif.) HS.—(1994-99)**
DRAFT DROP *First-round draft pick (2nd overall), Braves (1991)*
25. Fred Brown, rhp, Navarro (Texas) JC.
**26. *Sean Lawrence, lhp, River Forest HS, Oak Park, Ill.—(1998)**
27. *Paul Perkins, rhp, Fairfield (Calif.) HS.
28. Deron Sample, rhp-of, Paris (Texas) JC.
29. Chris Dorn, rhp, San Jacinto (Texas) JC.
30. +Robbie Guzik, of, Allegheny (Pa.) CC.

31. *Phillip Essex, rhp, McLennan (Texas) CC.
32. Rich Bristow, rhp, Geneva (Ill.) HS.
33. Brian Zimmerman, lhp, North Central (Ill.) College.
34. David Parouse, c, Dominican (N.Y.) College.
**35. *Gary Wilson, ss-2b, Arcata (Calif.) HS.—(1995)**
36. *Scott Ellrich, lhp, Crystal Lake South HS, Crystal Lake, Ill.
37. Tony Moore, of, Madison HS, San Antonio, Texas.
**38. *Joe Vitko, rhp, Central Cambria HS, Ebensburg, Pa.—(1992)**
39. Bryan Rogers, rhp, Sonoma State (Calif.) University.
40. *Jeff Herrington, rhp, Northeastern Oklahoma A&M JC.
41. Reid Hartmann, 2b, St. Louis CC-Meramec.
42. *Steve Hinton, lhp, Elgin (Ill.) HS.
43. +Danny Auchard, lhp, Tracy (Calif.) HS / San Joaquin Delta (Calif.) JC.
44. *Brian Buzard, lhp, Neodesha (Kan.) HS.
45. James Harris, c, St. John the Baptist HS, North Babylon, N.Y.
46. Tom Becker, ss, Pratt (Kan.) CC.
47. +Joseph McCann, rhp, DeKalb (Ga.) JC.
48. *Alex Garces, rhp, Westminster Christian HS, Miami.
49. *Mark Moore, c, Shawnee Mission East HS, Overland Park, Kan.
50. +Nathaniel Benson, rhp, Leo HS, Country Club Hills, Ill. / Kishwaukee (Ill.) JC.
51. *John Bentley, rhp, Trinity HS, Weaverville, Calif.
52. *Mike Sell, 2b, Capital HS, Helena, Mon.
53. +Wayne Mathis, of, Cuero (Texas) HS / Ranger (Texas) JC.
54. *Mark Bonini, of, Pinole Valley (Calif.) HS.
55. *Pat Kokora, ss, Boulder (Colo.) HS.
56. *Mike Kundrat, rhp, Thornwood HS, Calumet City, Ill.
57. *Greg Akerman, 3b, Bradley-Bourbonnais HS, Bradley, Ill.
58. *Perry Amos, of-lhp, Orland HS, Willows, Calif.
59. *Chuck Foster, of, San Jacinto (Texas) JC.
60. *Jerome Tolliver, of, Lincoln Academy HS, Kansas City, Mo.

## NEW YORK YANKEES (22)

1. (Choice to Cardinals as compensation for Type A free agent Jack Clark)
2. (Choice to Astros as compensation for Type B free agent Jose Cruz)
3. (Choice to Mets as compensation for Type B free agent John Candelaria)
4. Todd Malone, lhp, Casa Robles HS, Citrus Heights, Calif.—(High A)
5. Don Sparks, 3b, Loyola Marymount University.—(AAA)
**6. Jeff Johnson, lhp, University of North Carolina-Charlotte.—(1991-93)**
7. Billy Masse, of, Wake Forest University.
8. Bobby DeJardin, ss, Loyola Marymount University.
**9. Pat Kelly, ss, West Chester (Pa.) University.—(1991-99)**
**10. Kenny Greer, rhp, University of Massachusetts.—(1993-95)**
**11. Andy Cook, rhp, Memphis State University.—(1993)**
**12. Frank Seminara, rhp, Columbia University.—(1992-94)**
13. Jeff Livesey, c, Auburn University.
14. Jeff Hoffman, rhp, Vanderbilt University.
**15. Bobby Munoz, rhp, Palm Beach (Fla.) JC.—(1993-2001)**
16. Herb Erhardt, inf-c, Pan American (Texas) University.
17. Jay Knoblauh, of, Rice University.
**18. Jerry Nielsen, lhp, Florida State University.—(1992-93)**
19. Steve Perry, lhp, Martin Luther King HS, Detroit.
20. Craig Brink, rhp, UC Irvine.
21. Bruce Prybylinski, rhp, Illinois State University.
22. Skip Nelloms, of, Western Carolina University.
23. Bob Zeihen, of, Indiana State University.
24. John Seeburger, 1b, UC Irvine.
25. Jason Bridges, of, University of Alabama.
**26. Mike Draper, rhp, George Mason University.—(1993)**
27. Curtis Ralph, rhp, Sacramento (Calif.) CC.
28. Michael Rhodes, of, University of Houston.
**29. Russ Davis, ss, Shelton State (Ala.) JC.—(1994-2001)**
**30. Deion Sanders, of, Florida State University.—(1989-2001)**
DRAFT DROP *First-round draft pick, Atlanta Falcons/ National Football League (1989); defensive back, NFL (1989-2005)*
**31. *Joe Vitiello, 1b-rhp, Stoneham (Mass.) HS.—(1995-2003)**
DRAFT DROP *First-round draft pick (7th overall), Royals (1991)*
**32. *John Cummings, lhp, Canyon HS, Anaheim, Calif.—(1993-97)**
33. *Todd Youngblood, ss, Farmington (N.M.) HS.
34. *David Tuttle, rhp, Los Gatos (Calif.) HS.
35. *Mark Kingston, of, Potomac HS, Dumphries, Va.
DRAFT DROP *Baseball coach, Illinois State (2010-14); baseball coach, South Florida (2015)*
36. *Troy Tallman, c, Napa (Calif.) HS.
37. *Pat Maloney, of, Lyons Township HS, LaGrange, Ill.
38. *Deshon Brown, of, Modesto (Calif.) HS.
39. *Thomas Quinn, rhp, South Florida JC.
40. *Matthew Barker, of, Brevard (Fla.) CC.
**41. *Chad Ogea, rhp, St. Louis HS, Lake Charles, La.—(1994-99)**
42. *Brian Faw, rhp, DeKalb (Ga.) JC.
**43. *Orlando Palmeiro, of, Miami-Dade CC South.—(1995-2007)**
44. *Donald Robinson, of, Killian HS, Miami.
45. Brad Stoltenberg, rhp, Cal State Sacramento.
46. Art Canestro, lhp, New York Tech.
47. *Brian Reimsnyder, of, University of Florida.
48. *Michael Gonzalez, rhp, Sul Ross State (Texas) University.
49. *Kurt Pfeffer, rhp, JC of Marin (Calif.).
50. *Allen Popowitz, rhp, Saddle River County HS, Upper Saddle River, N.J.
**51. *Fernando Vina, ss-2b, Cosumnes River (Calif.) JC.—(1993-2004)**
52. *Franklin Lacy, c-of, Laney (Calif.) JC.
53. *Alex Kuhn, c, Eldorado HS, Albuquerque, N.M.
54. *George Day, 2b, LaGrange HS, Lake Charles, La.
55. *Keiver Campbell, of, Greenville (Miss.) HS.
56. *Joe Smith, rhp, Paris (Texas) JC.
57. Mike Eckert, lhp, Pan American (Texas) University.
58. Cliff Broxton, rhp, Mercer University.
59. *Jeff Pickett, c, Blue Springs (Mo.) HS.
60. Matt Michael, lhp, Morehead State University.
DRAFT DROP *Son of Gene Michael, major leaguer (1966-75); major league manager (1981-87)*
61. *Rodney Huffman, rhp, Lake Highlands HS, Dallas.
62. *Phil Mendelson, rhp, Grand Junction (Colo.) HS.
63. *James Mauldin, rhp, Seminole (Okla.) JC.
64. Mark Ohlms, rhp, Grand View (Iowa) College.
65. *Jay Gravens, rhp, Dallas Baptist University.
66. *Mark Futrell, rhp, Miami-Dade CC South.
67. Mark Zeratsky, c, Grand View (Iowa) College.
68. (void) *Wayne Weinheimer, of, Sacramento (Calif.) CC.
69. Len Thigpen, of, Monticello, Fla.
70. *Rob Bargas, 3b, Sacramento (Calif.) CC.
71. *Scott Thoma, rhp, Texas Wesleyan College.
72. *Dan Rambo, rhp, Central Michigan University.
73. *Michael Boyan, rhp, Bradley University.
74. *Oscar Rivas, lhp, San Jacinto (Texas) JC.
75. *Robert LeFebre, of, Florida Southern College.

## OAKLAND ATHLETICS (16)

**1. Stan Royer, c-3b, Eastern Illinois University.—(1991-94)**
2. Wynn Beck, c, South Brunswick HS, Southport, N.C. (Choice from Dodgers as compensation for Type A free agent Mike Davis).—(AA)
**2. Joe Slusarski, rhp, University of New Orleans.—(1991-2001)**
**3. John Briscoe, rhp, Texas Christian University.—(1991-96)**
4. Enoch Simmons, of, Loyola Marymount University.—(AAA)
**5. *Joe Grahe, rhp, University of Miami.—(1990-99)**
DRAFT DROP *Returned to Miami (Fla.); re-drafted by Angels, 1989 (2nd round)*
6. Dan Eskew, rhp, University of Tennessee.
**7. Ron Witmeyer, 1b, Stanford University.—(1991)**
8. Rich Rozman, rhp, Michigan State University.
9. Nick Venuto, rhp, Kent State University.
10. Tom Carcione, c, Texas A&M University.
11. Joel Chimelis, ss, University of Texas.
12. James Lawson, rhp, Huntington (Ind.) College.
13. Mike Messerly, 1b, Middle Tennessee State University.
14. *Rodney Peete, 3b, University of Southern California.
DRAFT DROP *Quarterback, National Football League (1989-2004)*
**15. Rod Correia, ss, Southeastern Massachusetts University.—(1993-95)**
16. *Mike Butler, lhp, North Caroline HS, Denton, Md.
17. Gerard Rizza, rhp, Long Island University.
**18. Darren Lewis, of, University of California.—(1990-2002)**
19. William Love, of-lhp, Lassen (Calif.) JC.
20. Dean Borrelli, c, University of Massachusetts.
21. Tony Floyd, rhp, Southwest Missouri State University.
22. Ray Harris, lhp, University of Arkansas.
**23. Bronswell Patrick, rhp, Conley HS, Winterville, N.C.—(1998-99)**
24. Jim Buccheri, of, Golden West (Calif.) JC.
25. Joe Hillman, of, Indiana University.
26. Tony Ariola, lhp, Northwestern University.
27. Michael Mungin, rhp, Norfolk State University.
28. Greg Ferguson, lhp, Virginia Tech.
29. Dewayne Jones, 2b, University of South Alabama.
30. *Steve Whitaker, lhp, Atwater (Calif.) HS.
DRAFT DROP *First-round draft pick (33rd overall), Giants (1991)*
31. Jeff Webber, of, Merced (Calif.) JC.
32. *Lyndon Wright, c, Caesar Rodney HS, Camden, Del.
33. *Mike Raskind, rhp, Granite Hills HS, El Cajon, Calif.
34. *Tim McDonald, rhp, Central Michigan University.
35. *Bobby Jones, of, Cal State Fullerton.
36. *Chris Butterfield, of, Cal Poly Pomona.
37. *Eric Gruben, rhp, Citrus (Calif.) JC.
38. Brian Foster, 1b-of, Farragut HS, Knoxville, Tenn.
39. Tim Vannaman, of, Rice University.
40. Jim Foley, rhp, Cal State Fullerton.
41. Graham Miller, rhp, Laney (Calif.) JC.
42. *Clifford Jones, lhp-of, Oakland HS, Richmond, Calif.
43. Steven Peck, rhp, Mesa (Ariz.) CC.
44. *Randy Brown, ss, Alief Elsik HS, Houston.
45. *John Pricher, rhp, Winter Park HS, Orlando, Fla.
46. *Pat Tozier, Clayton Valley HS, Concord, Calif.
47. *Pat Sullivan, lhp, Notre Dame HS, Signal Mountain, Tenn.
48. *Blase Sparma, rhp, Watterson HS, Columbus, Ohio.
DRAFT DROP *Son of Joe Sparma, major leaguer (1964-70)*

## PHILADELPHIA PHILLIES (11)

**1. Pat Combs, lhp, Baylor University.—(1989-92)**
2. (Choice to Braves as compensation for Type B free agent David Palmer)
**3. Tim Mauser, rhp, Texas Christian University.—(1991-95)**
4. *Joe Ciccarella, 1b, Mater Dei HS, Huntington Beach, Calif.—(AA)
DRAFT DROP *Attended Loyola Marymount; re-drafted by Red Sox, 1991 (4th round)*
**5. Mickey Morandini, ss, Indiana University.—(1990-2000)**
6. Albert Bennett, of, Lee (Texas) JC.
7. Mike Owens, lhp, University of Massachusetts.
8. Gary Wilson, rhp, St. Mary's (Texas) University.
9. Anthony Lozinski, c, University of the Pacific.
10. Jeff Etheredge, of, Panola (Texas) JC.
11. +Mike Sullivan, rhp, North Lake (Texas) JC / Seminole (Okla.) JC.
**12. *Scott Hatteberg, c, Eisenhower HS, Yakima, Wash.—(1995-2008)**
13. Chris Lowe, of, University HS, Johnson City, Tenn.
14. Nick Santa Cruz, 2b-ss, Rancho Santiago (Calif.) JC.
15. Tim Churchill, 1b-of, Cypress (Calif.) JC.
**16. Tom Marsh, of-rhp, University of Toledo.—(1992-95)**
17. *Brian Walker, lhp, Capistrano Valley HS, Mission Viejo, Calif.
18. Eric Bratlien, rhp, Cal Poly San Luis Obispo.
19. *Sam Colarusso, rhp, Orange Coast (Calif.) JC.
20. Todd Goergen, rhp, Trinidad State (Colo.) JC.
21. *David Boss, rhp, UC Santa Barbara.
22. Mathew Current, c, Middletown (Ohio) HS.
23. *Mark Steffens, of, Germantown Academy HS, Fort Washington, Pa.
24. Calvin Talford, of, Castlewood HS, Dante, Va.
25. Chris Toney, 3b, Hiram Johnson HS, Sacramento, Calif.
26. *Jamie Allen, lhp, Hillsborough (Fla.) CC.
27. *James Short, 1b, Esperanza HS, Yorba Linda, Calif.
28. Tim Dell, rhp, Huntington (Ind.) College.
29. *Greg Rehkow, lhp, Blue Springs (Mo.) HS.
30. Brian Harper, lhp, Southeast Missouri State University.
31. Craig Johnston, lhp, Napa (Calif.) HS.
32. Ray Walker, ss, Madison HS, Houston.
33. John Marshall, 1b-3b, University of Kentucky.
34. *Darryl Vice, 2b, University of California.
35. Michael Dafforn, rhp, Fort Wayne, Ind.
36. *Brian Archer, rhp, Kearny HS, San Diego.
37. *Rod Klopfer, 3b, Fullerton (Calif.) JC.
38. Darrell Lindsey, rhp, University of Southern Mississippi.
39. *Tom Crowley, 2b, Deptford (N.J.) HS.
**40. Paul Fletcher, rhp, West Virginia State College.—(1993-96)**
41. Andrew Barrick, 2b-3b, Elizabethtown (Pa.) College.
42. Joe Tenhunfeld, of, University of Cincinnati.
43. *Paul Anderson, rhp, San Diego Mesa JC.
44. Reggie Garcia, rhp, JC of the Sequoias (Calif.).
45. *Todd Pick, rhp, Lassen (Calif.) JC.
46. Troy Kent, rhp, UC Riverside.
47. Greg Breaux, 2b, Waltrip HS, Houston.
48. *David Willman, c, Hill HS, Boyertown, Pa.
49. Nick Macaluso, 2b, University of New Orleans.
50. Brian Cummings, 1b-of, Panola (Texas) JC.
51. Thomas Doyle, 1b, Redondo Beach (Calif.) HS.
52. *Gary Balderas, 3b, Madison HS, Houston.
**53. *Steve Cooke, lhp, Tigard (Ore.) HS / JC of Southern Idaho.—(1992-98)**
54. Chris Walker, 1b, University of Montevallo (Ala.).
55. *Rodd Hairston, rhp, Angelina (Texas) JC.
56. *Willie Navarette, lhp, Rancho Santiago (Calif.) JC.
57. *Dallas Monday, lhp, Jefferson County HS, Strawberry Plains, Tenn.
**58. +Jeff Patterson, rhp, Cypress (Calif.) JC.—(1995)**
59. *Bubba Smith, rhp, Rubidoux HS, Riverside, Calif.
60. *Carey Newton, rhp, Christian Brothers HS, West Sacramento, Calif.
61. *James Davis, c, University HS, Johnson City, Tenn.
62. *Juan Price, c, Sweetwater HS, San Diego.
63. *David Richison, ss, Spiro (Okla.) HS.
64. *Randy Graves, ss, Poly HS, Riverside, Calif.
65. +Gil Valencia, of, Camarillo (Calif.) HS / Oxnard (Calif.) JC.

## PITTSBURGH PIRATES (13)

1. Austin Manahan, ss, Horizon HS, Scottsdale, Ariz.—(AA)
DRAFT DROP *Brother of Anthony Manahan, first-round draft pick, Mariners (1990)*
2. Keith Richardson, rhp, Georgia Southern College.—(AA)
3. Glen McNabb, 2b-ss, Millikan HS, Long Beach, Calif.—(High A)
4. Steve Buckholz, rhp, Fresno State University.—(AA)
5. +Daryl Ratliff, of, Santa Cruz (Calif.) HS / Cabrillo (Calif.) JC.—(AAA)
**6. Blas Minor, rhp, Arizona State University.—(1992-97)**
**7. John Wehner, 3b, Indiana University.—(1991-2001)**

**8. Tim Wakefield, 1b, Florida Institute of Technology.—(1992-2011)**
9. Jeff Payne, lhp, University HS, Morgantown, W.Va.
10. Jon Martin, of, Golden West (Calif.) JC.
**11. Joe Ausanio, rhp, Jacksonville University.—(1994-95)**
12. Chris Estep, of, University of Kentucky.
13. Mike Huyler, 2b, Golden West (Calif.) JC.
14. *Deryk Hudson, 3b, Fullerton (Calif.) JC.
15. *Mitchell Burke, c, Florida A&M University.
16. *Jim Heins, rhp, Vanderbilt University.
17. Bobby Underwood, lhp, University of South Carolina.
**18. Randy Tomlin, lhp, Liberty University.—(1990-94)**
**19. Mandy Romero, c, Brevard (Fla.) CC.—(1997-2003)**
20. *Lawrence Gilligan, ss, Lakeland HS, Ringwood, N.J.
21. Val Henderson, of, Bellevue (Wash.) CC.
**22. *David Staton, 1b, Orange Coast (Calif.) JC.—(1993-94)**
23. Renald Datcher, 1b, Lackey HS, Laplata, Md.
24. Scott Cowley, of, St. Leo (Fla.) College.
25. Greg Sims, of, St. Leo (Fla.) College.
26. *Chris Sheffield, 2b, Pine Forest HS, Pensacola, Fla.
27. Paul McGhay, of, Montana State University.
28. Jeff Osborne, c, Kent State University.
29. Matthew Udell, rhp, Southwestern Michigan JC.
30. Jeff Kuder, lhp, Mount Vernon Nazarene (Ohio) College.
31. Troy Clemens, c, Foothill (Calif.) JC.
32. *Brian Purvis, of, Noblesville (Ind.) HS.
33. Paul Spalt, ss, North Carolina State University.
34. Steve Roeder, rhp, Penn HS, Mishiwaka, Ind.
35. Derek Tinnin, of-ss, Anderson (Ind.) College.
36. Al Molina, ss, Pan American (Texas) University.
37. Darwin Pennye, of, Southwest Texas State University.
38. Mike Thompson, 1b, North Texas State University.
39. Ken Buksa, c-of, St. Xavier (Ill.) College.
40. Mike Fortuna, of, Coastal Carolina College.
41. Richard Haupt, lhp, Bald Eagle Area HS, Milesburg, Pa.
42. Ronald Way, lhp, Henry Ford (Mich.) CC.
43. *Mark Hummell, 3b, Arizona Western JC.
44. Richard Wilson, lhp, Columbus (Ga.) College.
45. *Ben Burlingame, rhp, Newton South HS, Newton, Mass.
46. Fernando Arguellas, c, Florida Southern College.
47. Craig Juran, lhp, Colorado State University.
48. *Steve O'Donnell, 3b, LaSalle University.
49. Wade Lytle, 3b, Bellmont HS, Decatur, Ind.
50. Keith Mays, rhp, Louisburg (N.C.) JC.
51. *Mike LeBlanc, rhp, University of Maine.
52. Joe Pagan, rhp, Chicago State University.
53. Bryan Arnold, c-1b, Florida Southern College.
54. Dan Nielson, rhp, Western Michigan University.
55. *Cary Elston, rhp, Green River (Wash.) CC.
56. *Scott Sharts, 1b, Simi Valley (Calif.) HS.
57. Bobby West, of, Brewton Parker (Ga.) College.
58. *Ken Baurle, rhp, North Allegheny HS, Pittsburgh.
59. *Troy Trollope, of, Bellevue (Wash.) CC.
60. *Thomas Owen, c, Brewton Parker (Ga.) JC.
61. *Jon Fisher, c, Brenham (Texas) HS.
62. *Jerry Summers, of, Beaver County (Pa.) CC.
63. *David Silvernail, rhp, Columbia Basin (Wash.) CC.
64. +Jessie Torres, c, JC of Southern Idaho.
65. *Burk Cromer, 3b, Lexington (S.C.) HS.
**DRAFT DROP** *Brother of Tripp Cromer, major leaguer (1993-2003) • Brother of D.T. Cromer, major leaguer (2000-01)*
66. *Randy Martin, ss-of, Godby HS, Tallahassee, Fla.

## ST. LOUIS CARDINALS (23)

**1. John Ericks, rhp, University of Illinois** (Choice from Yankees as compensation for Type A free agent Jack Clark)**—(1995-97)**
1. Brad DuVall, rhp, Virginia Tech.—(High A)
**DRAFT DROP** *First-round draft pick (15th overall), Orioles (1988)*
**1. Brian Jordan, of, University of Richmond** (Supplemental choice—29th—as compensation for Clark)**—(1992-2006)**

MORRIS FOSTOFF

Less heralded than some other two-sport stars, Brian Jordan played 15 big league seasons

**DRAFT DROP** *Defensive back, National Football League (1989-90)*
2. Mike Hensley, rhp, University of Oklahoma.—(Low A)
**DRAFT DROP** *Father of Ty Hensley, first-round draft pick, Yankees (2014)*
3. Charlie White, of, University of New Orleans.—(AA)
4. Mike Ross, 2b, Cal State Fullerton.—(AAA)
5. Lee Plemel, rhp, Stanford University.—(AA)
**6. Rheal Cormier, lhp, CC of Rhode Island.—(1991-2007)**
7. Steve Fanning, ss, Troy State University.
8. Jerry Davis, ss, Lincoln HS, San Diego.
**9. Mark Clark, rhp, Lincoln Land (Ill.) CC.—(1991-2000)**
**10. Joe Hall, 3b, Southern Illinois University.—(1994-97)**
11. Rod Brooks, rhp, Troy State University.
12. Tom Malchesky, 3b, Western Carolina University.
13. Bill Decker, rhp, Iowa Central CC.
14. John Cebuhar, lhp, University of Arkansas.
15. Mike Fiore, of, University of Miami.
16. Delynn Corry, rhp, Cedar City (Utah) HS.
17. David Richardson, lhp, Middle Tennessee State University.
18. Julio Mendez, ss, University of Florida.
19. Mark Battell, c, Mercy (N.Y.) College.
20. *Steve Callahan, lhp, Lewis-Clark State (Idaho) College.
21. Fred Langiotti, c, University of Tampa.
22. Tim Pettengill, c, University of Nebraska.
23. Jeff Shireman, ss, Georgia Southern College.
24. John Lepley, lhp, University of Nebraska.
25. Randy Berlin, 1b-3b, Virginia Tech.
26. Cory Satterfield, rhp, Campbell University.
27. Sean Grubb, rhp, Oral Roberts University.
28. John Stephens, 3b, The Citadel.
29. *David D. Adams, rhp, Auburn University.
30. Joe Federico, 1b-of, University of Nebraska.
31. Richard Hoffman, rhp, Long Island University.
32. Dave Grimes, rhp, Arkansas Tech University.
33. Steve Graham, of, Ithaca (N.Y.) College.
34. Brian Golden, rhp, Gettysburg (Pa.) College.
35. John Kroeger, c, Fairleigh Dickinson University.
36. *David C. Adams, rhp, Ohio University.
37. *William Henderson, rhp, Volunteer State (Tenn.) CC.
38. +David Bell, of, Volunteer State (Tenn.) CC.
39. *Scott Buchheit, lhp, St. Dominic HS, St. Peters, Mo.
40. *Ken Phillips, of, Pasadena (Calif.) CC.
41. *Steve DiBartolomeo, rhp, University of New Haven (Conn.).
42. *Jerry Lutterman, rhp, St. Louis CC-Meramec.
43. *Ray Calhoun, rhp, Spartanburg Methodist (S.C.) JC.
44. +Derron Spiller, lhp, Rio Mesa HS, Camarillo, Calif. / Ventura (Calif.) CC.
45. *Joe Philpot, rhp, Volunteer State (Tenn.) CC.
46. *David King, 1b-3b, Northeastern Oklahoma A&M JC.

## SAN DIEGO PADRES (1)

**1. Andy Benes, rhp, University of Evansville.—(1989-2002)**
**DRAFT DROP** *Brother of Alan Benes, first-round draft pick, Cardinals (1993); major leaguer (1995-2003)*
2. Kelly Lifgren, rhp, Glendale (Ariz.) CC.—(AA)
**3. Ray Holbert, ss, Jordan HS, Long Beach, Calif.—(1994-2000)**
**DRAFT DROP** *Brother of Aaron Holbert, first-round draft pick, Cardinals (1990); major leaguer (1996)*
4. Squeezer Thompson, rhp, Mount Dora (Fla.) HS.—(Low A)
**5. Bryce Florie, rhp, Hanahan (S.C.) HS.—(1994-2001)**
6. Bob Brucato, rhp, Northwestern University.
**7. *Mike Grace, rhp, Joliet Catholic HS, Joliet, Ill.—(1995-99)**
**8. Nikco Riesgo, 3b-of, San Diego State University.—(1991)**
9. Matt Witkowski, ss, Deer Valley HS, Glendale, Ariz.
**10. A.J. Sager, rhp, University of Toledo.—(1994-98)**
11. Scott Welish, 1b-of, San Diego Mesa JC.
12. *Chris Ebright, of-1b, University of Oklahoma.
13. J.D. Noland, of, Central Florida CC.
14. Eric Harris, ss, Roosevelt HS, Dallas.
**15. Mike Humphreys, of, Texas Tech.—(1991-93)**
16. Brian Cisarik, 1b-of, University of Texas.
17. Vance Tucker, rhp, Seminole (Okla.) JC.
18. Joe Murdock, lhp, Southern Arkansas University.
19. *Greg Ebbert, lhp, Lake Brantley HS, Longwood, Fla.
20. Brian Span, of, Seminole (Fla.) CC.
21. Pedro Lopez, c, Arizona Western JC.
22. Scott Bingham, ss, Willamette (Ore.) University.
23. David Briggs, 3b, Brookdale (N.J.) CC.
24. Brad Hoyer, lhp, Cal Poly Pomona.
25. Renay Bryand, lhp, UC Santa Barbara.
26. Greg Conley, c, Rollins (Fla.) College.
27. Chris Haslock, rhp, Cal State Dominguez Hills.
28. Stanley Tukes, rhp, Broward (Fla.) CC.
29. Darrin Hart, ss, Harding HS, Charlotte, N.C.
30. Rob Cantwell, lhp, North Idaho JC.
31. Chad Kuhn, 1b-of, University of New Mexico.
32. +Craig Pueschner, of, Sahuaro HS, Tucson, Ariz. / Yavapai (Ariz.) CC.
33. John Kuehl, 1b-3b, University of California.
**DRAFT DROP** *Son of Karl Kuehl, major league manager (1976)*
34. *Randy Tanner, of, University of Southern California.
35. Bob Curnow, c, Cal Poly Pomona.
36. Craig Proctor, 2b, Cal Poly Pomona.
37. *Jason Farrell, rhp, Kennedy HS, Granada Hills, Calif.
38. *Heath Jones, c, El Segundo HS, Hawthorne, Calif.
39. Walter Wilkerson, rhp, Clermont (Fla.) HS.
40. *Ramey Brooks, c, Blanchard (Okla.) HS.
41. Richard Peacock, of, Ernest Ward HS, Walnut Hill, Fla.
42. Jeff Hart, rhp, University of Central Arkansas.
**43. *Brian Looney, lhp, Cunnery HS, Cheshire, Conn.—(1993-95)**
44. *Mike Basse, of, Mater Dei HS, San Juan Capistrano, Calif.

## SAN FRANCISCO GIANTS (17)

**1. Royce Clayton, ss, St. Bernard HS, Playa del Rey, Calif.** (Choice from Reds as compensation for Type B free agent Eddie Milner)**—(1991-2007)**
1. (Choice to Indians as compensation for Type A free agent Brett Butler)
**1. Ted Wood, of, University of New Orleans** (Supplemental choice—28th—as compensation for Type A free agent Chili Davis)**—(1991-93)**
2. Scott Ebert, rhp, Edmond Memorial HS, Edmond, Okla. (Choice from Angels as compensation for Davis).—(Low A)
2. Chris Hancock, lhp, Fontana (Calif.) HS.—(AAA)
3. R.J. Smiley, of, Los Angeles CC.—(AAA)
4. Carl Hanselman, rhp, Merritt Island (Fla.) HS.—(AAA)
**5. Scooter Tucker, c, Delta State (Miss.) University.—(1992-95)**
6. Jeff Kaiser, ss, Southwest Missouri State University.
7. David Horan, rhp, Eastern Oklahoma State JC.
8. Gary Sharko, rhp, Grand Canyon College.
**9. Kevin Rogers, lhp, Mississippi Delta JC.—(1992-94)**
10. *Turtle Zaun, 1b, North Carolina State University.
11. Longo Garcia, rhp, Cal State Fullerton.
12. *Moose Adams, rhp, Juanita HS, Kirkland, Wash.
13. Andre George, 2b, Mount Hood (Ore.) CC.

14. Adam Smith, c, Oklahoma State University.
15. Shannon Coppell, of, Eastern Illinois University.
16. Mark Standiford, 2b, Wichita State University.
17. Mitchell Ferrick, rhp, UC Riverside.
18. Adell Davenport, 3b, Southern University.
19. David Slavin, c, University of Missouri.
20. Shane Durham, lhp, Wichita State University.
**21. Steve Decker, c, Lewis-Clark State (Idaho) College.—(1990-99)**
22. Steven Gray, ss, Cuesta (Calif.) JC.
**23. John Patterson, 2b, Grand Canyon College.—(1992-95)**
24. George Penrod, of, Florida Atlantic University.
**25. Reggie Williams, of, University of South Carolina-Aiken (1992-99).**
26. Bill Gibbons, rhp, University of Delaware.
27. David Wuthrich, lhp, Troy State University.
28. Adam Hilpert, ss, Cal State Stanislaus.
29. Ken Brauckmiller, rhp, Portland State University.
30. Glenn Warren, of, Mount Olive (N.C.) College.
31. William Berry, lhp, Glendale (Calif.) JC.
32. Mike Sanderson, of, University of Alabama.
33. David Cantrell, rhp, Chapman (Calif.) College.
34. Pat Brady, of, St. Marys (Calif.) College.
35. Jerry Brock, rhp, University of South Carolina-Spartanburg.
36. Brett Hewatt, 1b-of, Seward County (Kan.) CC.
37. David Booth, of, West Virginia State College.
38. *Rod Billingsley, c, George Mason University.
39. Lance Burnett, of, Crowder HS, McAlester, Okla.
40. Sean Thompson, of-3b, Los Angeles Valley JC.
41. Greg Lee, ss, Allan Hancock (Calif.) JC.
42. *Basilio Ortiz, of, Buckley HS, Hartford, Conn.
43. *Michael Scialo, ss, Saguero HS, Scottsdale, Ariz.
44. *Jason Hendricks, rhp, Kincaid HS, Houston.
45. *Danny Lane, inf, Laguna Beach (Calif.) HS.

## SEATTLE MARINERS (14)

**1. Tino Martinez, 1b, University of Tampa.—(1990-2005)**
**2. Greg Pirkl, c, Los Alamitos (Calif.) HS.—(1993-96)**
3. Jim Campanis, c, University of Southern California.—(AA)
DRAFT DROP *Grandson of Al Campanis, major leaguer (1943); general manager, Dodgers (1968-87) • Son of Jim Campanis, major leaguer (1966-73)*
**4. Lee Hancock, lhp, Cal Poly San Luis Obispo.—(1995-96)**
5. Willie Romay, of, Maimi (Fla.) Senior HS.—(High A)
6. Kelvin Thomas, of, Smiley HS, Houston.
DRAFT DROP *Twin brother of Delvin Thomas, 18th-round draft pick, Mariners (1988)*
7. Julio Reyan, of, Southridge HS, Miami.
8. *Mike Smedes, rhp, Laguna Hills (Calif.) HS.
**9. *Steve Chitren, rhp, Stanford University.—(1990-91)**
10. *Ted Devore, rhp, University of Portland.
11. *Ronnie Allen, rhp, Lake Washington HS, Kirkland, Wash.
12. Nick Felix, lhp, Texas A&M University.
**13. Jeff Darwin, rhp, Alvin (Texas) CC.—(1994-97)**
DRAFT DROP *Brother of Danny Darwin, major leaguer (1978-98)*
14. Mike Beiras, rhp, Texas Tech University.
**15. Scott Taylor, rhp, University of Kansas.—(1995)**
16. Mark Razook, ss, Cal State Fullerton.
17. James Kosnik, lhp, Oakland University.
18. Delvin Thomas, ss, Smiley HS, Houston.
DRAFT DROP *Twin brother of Kelvin Thomas, sixth-round draft pick, Mariners (1988)*
19. *James Clifford, 1b, Ingraham HS, Seattle.
20. Tom Liss, lhp, University of Detroit.
21. Michael McLaughlin, ss, Glassboro State (N.J.) College.
22. Jeff Miller, c, Normandale (Minn.) CC.
23. Joe White, rhp, Mesa (Colo.) College.
24. *Todd Krumm, of-rhp, Michigan State University.
DRAFT DROP *Defensive back, National Football League (1988)*
25. *Jim Price, rhp, Stanford University.

Tino Martinez went from an NCAA Division II school to major league standout quickly

26. Jorge Robles, 2b, University of Miami.
27. Doug Davis, 1b-3b, Grossmont (Calif.) JC.
28. *Scott Cline, 3b, UCLA.
**29. +Kerry Woodson, rhp, San Jose (Calif.) CC.—(1992)**
30. *Scott Bibee, rhp, Carson City (Nev.) HS.
31. *Joel Wolfe, 3b, Chatsworth HS, Northridge, Calif.
32. *Dusty Madsen, rhp, Sacramento (Calif.) CC.
33. Tim Stargell, 2b, Southern University.
34. Ben Burnau, lhp, Miami (Ohio) University.
35. *Mike Cloutier, of, University of Detroit.
36. *Mike Kerber, c, Canoga Park HS, West Hills, Calif.
37. *Shawn Brown, of, Granada Hills HS, Los Angeles.
38. John Kohli, lhp, University of Nebraska.
39. *Glen Raasch, c, Mount San Antonio (Calif.) JC.
40. *Felix Gurruchaga, lhp, Miami-Dade CC New World Center.
**41. Chris Howard, c, University of Southwestern Louisiana.—(1991-94)**
42. *Dean Haskins, c-3b, Montgomery HS, Santa Rosa, Calif.
43. +Rob Callistro, rhp, Concord (Calif.) HS / Diablo Valley (Calif.) JC.
44. *Damian Torino, c, North Marion HS, Sparr, Fla.
45. *John Burton, rhp, Mount San Antonio (Calif.) JC.
46. Tom Brock, of, University of Michigan.
47. *Mark Ringkamp, rhp, Palomar (Calif.) JC.
48. *Eddie Christian, of, Salesian HS, San Pablo, Calif.
49. *Arthur Bass, of, Westfield HS, Houston.
50. *Daniel Donovan, rhp, Brookdale (N.J.) CC.
51. Keith Barrett, of-inf, Cal Poly Pomona.
52. *Brent Lutz, 3b, Issaquah (Wash.) HS.

## TEXAS RANGERS (6)

**1. Monty Fariss, ss, Oklahoma State University.—(1991-93)**
2. Timmie Morrow, of, South Alamance HS, Graham, N.C.—(AAA)
**3. Darren Oliver, lhp, Rio Linda (Calif.) HS.—(1993-2013)**
DRAFT DROP *Son of Bob Oliver, major leaguer (1965-75).*
4. Everett Cunningham, rhp, Northwestern University.—(AA)
5. Cliff Williams, c, East St. Louis HS, Fairview Heights, Ill.—(High A)
**6. Rob Maurer, 1b, University of Evansville.—(1991-92)**
7. Dom Pierce, 3b, Skyline (Calif.) JC.
8. Travis Law, of, Oklahoma State University.
9. Trey McCoy, of, Virginia Tech.
10. Eric McCray, lhp, Farmerville (La.) HS.
11. *David Wallace, ss-of, Brandeis HS, New York.
12. Cedric Shaw, lhp, Grambling State University.
13. Tim MacNeil, rhp, Rancho Santiago (Calif.) JC.
14. Mike Patrick, c-3b, University of Texas.
15. *Peter Lawrence, of, Logan HS, Union City, Calif.
16. John Sipple, lhp, Oregon State University.
17. Carl Randle, rhp, Huston-Tillotson (Texas) College.
18. Tom Mileski, rhp, San Jacinto (Texas) JC.
19. Jim Hvizda, rhp, Old Dominion University.
20. Joey Wardlow, 2b, University of Tampa.
21. *Mark Bowlan, rhp, Memphis State University.
22. Doug Cronk, 1b, University of Southern Mississippi.
23. Mike Reitzel, lhp, Northeastern Oklahoma State University.
24. *Mark Tolbert, rhp, Dixie (Utah) JC.
25. Rod Morris, of, Southeastern Louisiana University.
26. Kyle Spencer, rhp, Missouri Valley (Mo.) College.
27. Jeff Shore, c, University of North Carolina-Charlotte.
28. Todd DeVaughan, rhp, Seminole (Okla.) JC.
29. Robert Gamez, lhp-1b, Chabot (Calif.) JC.
**30. Jeff Frye, 2b, Southeastern Oklahoma State University.—(1992-2001)**
31. Jonathan Huth, rhp, Waldorf (Iowa) JC.
32. Lindsey Robinson, 3b, University of South Carolina-Spartanburg.
33. *Shawn Wills, of, Hanford (Calif.) HS.
**34. *Tom Urbani, 1b, Cabrillo (Calif.) JC.—(1993-96)**
35. *David Schmidt, 2b, Montgomery HS, San Diego.
36. Tony Berry, of, Rust (Miss.) College.
37. Steve Allen, rhp, University of Massachusetts.
38. Jeff Simmons, rhp, Rend Lake (Ill.) JC.
39. Brian Evans, rhp, Jacksonville University.
40. Ken Penland, lhp, University of South Carolina-Spartanburg.
41. *Anthony Peeler, lhp, Paseo HS, Kansas City, Mo.
DRAFT DROP *First-round draft pick, Los Angeles Lakers/ National Basketball Association (1992); guard, NBA (1992-2003).*
42. Greg Kuzma, lhp, Princeton University.
43. William Schorr, rhp, Nicholls State University.
44. *Fred Collins, lhp, Manatee (Fla.) JC.
45. (void) *Americo Loera, rhp, Dallas Baptist University.
46. Ed Ohman, rhp, Auburn University.
47. *Donald Parker, of, Rangeview HS, Aurora, Colo.
48. +Brian Mouton, of, Hayward HS, Oakland, Calif. / Laney (Calif.) JC.
49. *Pat Underhill, rhp, Valencia (Fla.) CC.
50. *Shannon Albright, rhp, Fruita HS, Grand Junction, Colo.
51. (void) *Mike Easley, 1b, Texas A&M University.
52. Jeff Hainline, 1b, Gonzaga University.
53. *Dan Robinson, of, Crossett (Ark.) HS.
54. *Henderson Mosley, ss, H.D. Woodson HS, Washington, D.C.
55. *Paul Spyhalski, of, Howard (Texas) JC.
56. *Brett Snyder, rhp, Rancho Santiago (Calif.) JC.
57. *Tony Tijerina, c, Long Beach (Calif.) CC.
**58. +Shannon Penn, ss, Lakeland (Ohio) CC.—(1995-96)**
59. *Joe Caruso, rhp, Casa Grande HS, Petaluma, Calif.

## TORONTO BLUE JAYS (25)

**1. Ed Sprague, 3b-c, Stanford University.—(1991-2001)**
DRAFT DROP *Son of Ed Sprague, major leaguer (1968-76) • Baseball coach, Pacific (2004-15)*
2. Tim Hodge, c, Callaway HS, Jackson, Miss.—(AA)
**3. David Weathers, rhp, Motlow State (Tenn.) CC.—(1991-2009)**
4. Eric Brooks, c, LaMirada (Calif.) HS.—(AAA)
5. B.J. Parese, ss, Owasso (Okla.) HS.—(High A)
6. Mike Ogliaruso, rhp, Countryside HS, Palm Harbor, Fla.
7. Rob Montalvo, ss, Memorial HS, West New York.
**8. *Tim Pugh, rhp, Oklahoma State University.—(1992-97)**
9. *Brent Gilbert, rhp, Blinn (Texas) JC.
10. Anthony Ward, lhp, Oral Roberts University.
11. *Pat Pesavento, ss, University of Notre Dame.
12. *William Fuller, rhp, Eau Gallie HS, Melbourne, Fla.
13. Curtis Johnson, rhp, University of Washington.
14. *Eric Persinger, rhp, Marion (Ind.) HS.
15. *Greg Kobza, 1b, Blinn (Texas) JC.
16. *Matthew Wilke, ss, Beaver Dam (Wis.) HS.
17. Mike Brady, rhp, Nassau (N.Y.) CC.
18. Rick Vaughn, c, Oral Roberts University.
19. Tim Bruzdewicz, lhp, Allegheny (Pa.) CC.
20. *Dan Berthel, of, El Camino (Calif.) JC.
21. Rickey Holifield, of, Ganesha HS, Montclair, Calif.
22. *Mario Baker, of, Gulf Coast (Fla.) CC.
23. Terrance Jones, ss, Monroe (N.Y.) CC.
24. *Mike Daniel, c, Connors State (Okla.) JC.
25. Tim Brown, rhp, St. Petersburg (Fla.) JC.
26. Rick Nowak, rhp, UC San Diego.
27. Greg McCutcheon, rhp, Kent State University.
**28. Woody Williams, rhp, University of Houston.—(1993-2007)**
29. Greg Harding, 1b, University of Richmond.
30. Scott Hutson, rhp, Arizona State University.
**31. *Mike Matheny, c, Reynoldsburg (Ohio) HS.—(1994-2006)**
DRAFT DROP *Major league manager (2012-15)*
**32. Greg O'Halloran, c, Orange Coast (Calif.) JC.—(1994)**
**33. *George Tsamis, lhp, Stetson University.—(1993)**
34. *Jeff Lawrence, lhp, Fallbrook (Calif.) HS.
35. *Michael Harris, 1b, Tates Creek HS, Lexington, Ky.
36. Chris Kerr, rhp, California Baptist College.
37. Jeff Mooney, rhp, Chapman (Calif.) College.
**38. Ray Giannelli, 3b, New York Tech.—(1991-95)**
39. *Eric Reichenbach, rhp, Sachem HS, Farmingville, N.Y.
40. Eric Bradley, rhp, Laney (Calif.) JC.
41. +Andrew Carlton, 1b-rhp, Providence HS, Frankfort, Ill. / Kishwaukee (Ill.) JC.
42. *Brian Brazier, inf, Hanford (Calif.) HS.
43. *Matt Sines, rhp, Hillsborough (Fla.) CC.
**44. *Scott Erickson, rhp, San Jose (Calif.) CC.—(1990-2006)**
45. +Wayne Williams, c, Chesapeake HS, Pasadena, Md. / Middle Georgia JC.
46. *Thomas Irwin, rhp, Victor Valley HS, Victorville, Calif.
47. Eric Carter, rhp, Louisburg (N.C.) JC.
48. *Greg Gousha, c, Orange Glen HS, Escondido, Calif.
**49. *Dax Jones, of, Waukegan (Ill.) West HS.—(1996)**
50. *Greg Davis, rhp, North Torrance HS, Gardena, Calif.
51. *Michael Boyd, ss, Clearwater Catholic HS, Largo, Fla.
52. *Gordon Purvis, rhp-ss, Berrien County HS, Ray City, Ga.
53. *Jeff Kidwiler, ss, Chapman (Calif.) College.
54. *Terre Woods, of-3b, Utica (Miss.) JC.
55. *Anthony Mills, inf-of, Taft (Calif.) HS.
**56. *Jason Wood, ss, McLane HS, Fresno, Calif.—(1998-2008)**
57. *David Edwards, of, East St. Louis HS, Brooklyn, Ill.
**58. *Darrell Whitmore, ss, West Virginia University.—(1993-95)**
59. *Michael Lustyk, 1b, Interlake HS, Bellevue, Wash.
60. +William Abare, 1b, St. Petersburg (Fla.) JC.
61. *Brad Raulston, of, La Jolla (Calif.) HS.
62. Jesse Cross, rhp, Middle Georgia JC.
63. *Thomas Hamilton, of, Forest Hills HS, Marshville, N.C.
64. *Warren Holt, rhp, Cabrillo (Calif.) JC.
65. *Walter Heckel, 2b, St. John's University.
66. *Jeff Borgese, ss, San Jose (Calif.) CC.
67. *Ross Urshan, rhp, Lyman HS, Altamonte Springs, Fla.
68. *Louis Williams, rhp, Benton Harbor (Mich.) HS.
69. *Jerry Worley, of, Miami Springs (Fla.) HS.
70. *James Lewis, rhp, Terry Parker HS, Jacksonville, Fla.
71. *Kenneth Koon, of, Orange Park (Fla.) HS.
72. *Dennis Stachura, c, Downers Grove North HS, Downers Grove, Ill.
73. Anton Mobley, of, Yule, Fla.

# 1989

**AT A GLANCE**

### This Date In History
June 2-4

### Best Draft
**MINNESOTA TWINS.** The Twins got solid production from three of their first four picks: second baseman **CHUCK KNOBLAUCH** (1), who hit .289 with 98 homers and 403 stolen bases in 12 big league seasons, and pitchers **DENNY NEAGLE** (3), who won 124 games in 13 years, and **SCOTT ERICKSON** (4), who won 142 games in 15 years.

### Worst Draft
**CHICAGO CUBS.** The Cubs dropped the ball on first-rounder **EARL CUNNINGHAM**, who didn't advance beyond Class A, and second-rounder **GARY SCOTT**, the team's Opening Day third baseman in 1991 and 1992 who quickly lost the job both years by hitting a combined .160 with three homers in 67 games. None of the other 52 players they drafted played a game in a Cubs uniform.

### First-Round Bust
**JEFF JACKSON, OF, PHILLIES.** The Chicago prep generated considerable hype in a breakout senior season, but that appeared to be an aberration as Jackson never came close to fulfilling expectations in six seasons in the Phillies system, hitting .223-36-222 with 664 strikeouts before being released.

### Second Best
**BRIAN HUNTER, OF, ASTROS.** Hunter had a modest 10-year major league career, hitting .264-25-241, though he stole 260 bases and twice led the American League in steals. In a draft deep in high school outfielders, he had the best career among the players from that demographic selected in the first two rounds.

### Late-Round Finds
**JIM THOME, SS, INDIANS (13TH ROUND); TREVOR HOFFMAN, SS, REDS (11TH ROUND).** Thome became

# Bonus spending marks dawn of new draft era

In its 25th year, the baseball draft proved more popular—and more expensive—than ever. A record 1,490 players were selected in the 1989 draft, and several clubs claimed a record number of players, led by the Houston Astros, who didn't stop drafting until 87 rounds were complete.

Bonuses also continued to rise, with the average first-round bonus reaching $176,008—a jump of 23.5 percent from 1988. New signing bonus standards were set three times: first by catcher Tyler Houston, the second overall pick who signed with the Atlanta Braves on June 19 for $241,500. He eclipsed the mark of $235,000, set a year earlier by No. 1 overall pick Andy Benes.

Houston's record stood for two months before the Baltimore Orioles agreed to terms with holdout righthander Ben McDonald, the No. 1 pick, for a bonus of $350,000. Less than a week later, the Toronto Blue Jays reached agreement with first baseman John Olerud, a third-round pick, on a bonus of $575,000. Both McDonald and Olerud signed unprecedented three-year major league deals worth more than $800,000.

Record bonuses were rampant in 1989, with new marks established in 13 of the top 25 rounds.

The Orioles became the first team to reside in first place when they made the No. 1 overall pick. McDonald, a two-time Louisiana State All-American and 1988 U.S. Olympic team star, was so dominant as an amateur talent that scouts pegged him as the No. 1 pick in '89 as much as a year before the draft.

Expectations for Olerud were more tempered, and his unexpected signing was seen as more of a shot in the dark.

Because of a near-fatal aneurysm near his brain just five months before the draft that required a six-hour operation, Olerud, a lefthanded pitcher/first baseman from Washington State, fell to the third round. Olerud had expressed a reluctance to sign until he was 100 percent healthy, but the Blue Jays drafted him anyway, bided their time and secured a deal on Aug. 25—just days before he was slated to return to college for his senior year.

Olerud became the first player from the Class of '89 to reach the big leagues, debuting with a base hit in his first at-bat on Sept. 3. In the process, he became just the 18th player in draft history to bypass playing in the minors.

McDonald wasn't far behind as he made two minor league starts, then was promoted to Baltimore. He made his first appearance with the Orioles on Sept. 6 and won his only decision on the final day of the regular season.

### SLAM-DUNK SELECTION

McDonald was in a class of his own as the 1989 draft unfolded. With his strapping 6-foot-7, 215-pound frame, a mid-90s fastball and hammer curve that highlighted a four-pitch repertoire, along with the ability to throw all his pitches consistently for strides, he combined a blend of velocity and command rarely seen in a draft pick.

**Scouts had targeted LSU righthander Ben McDonald as the top prospect in the 1989 draft class for months, but his major league career did not live up to expectations, mostly due to injury**

After playing a dominant role for Team USA as it won the gold medal in the 1988 Olympics, McDonald only tightened his grip on the draft's No. 1 slot at the midway point of the the 1989 college season by working 45 consecutive innings without allowing a run.

"It's a goal I set last year, and I'm glad I could attain it," said McDonald, who went 14-4, 3.49 and struck out 202 in 152 innings as a junior.

McDonald was Baltimore's payback for a dreadful 107-loss season in 1988, and the Orioles showed no hesitation in drafting him, even though he was ineffective in several late-season appearances. In his last 22 innings for LSU, he gave up 27 runs and 38 hits, and was the losing pitcher in both his team's losses at the College World Series.

McDonald went to LSU on a basketball scholarship and missed 26 baseball games as a freshman because of his commitment to that sport, but soon quit basketball—to the regret of LSU basketball coach Dale Brown.

"He was a really good prospect," Brown said. "He's the best athlete I've ever seen in the state of Louisiana, and that's overall—basketball, baseball, football. There's been no one to compare to him."

As a sophomore, with his focus only on baseball, McDonald became a complete pitcher, going 13-7, 2.65 while allowing just 27 walks and striking out 144 in 119 innings. He gained command of

## 1989: THE FIRST ROUNDERS

| CLUB: PLAYER, POS., SCHOOL | HOMETOWN | B-T | HT. | WT. | AGE | BONUS | FIRST YEAR | LAST YEAR | PEAK LEVEL (YEARS) |
|---|---|---|---|---|---|---|---|---|---|
| 1. *Orioles: Ben McDonald, rhp, Louisiana State | Denham Springs, La. | R-R | 6-7 | 215 | 21 | $350,000 | 1989 | 1997 | Majors (9) |
| Acclaimed pitcher had it all (size, stuff, control, poise, amateur resume), but college workload played role in early elbow problems, unfulfilled expectations. | | | | | | | | | |
| 2. Braves: Tyler Houston, c, Valley HS | Las Vegas, Nev. | L-R | 6-2 | 210 | 18 | $225,000 | 1989 | 2003 | Majors (8) |
| Hit .485-13-66 as prep senior, but couldn't get out of own way early in pro career with confrontational attitude; settled into utility role, hit .265-63-253 for six clubs. | | | | | | | | | |
| 3. Mariners: Roger Salkeld, rhp, Saugus HS | Saugus, Calif. | R-R | 6-5 | 210 | 18 | $225,000 | 1989 | 2000 | Majors (3) |
| Can't miss prospect entering 1992 season; had size, 95-98 mph FB, but hurt his arm, had major shoulder surgery and never fully recovered, won 10 games. | | | | | | | | | |
| 4. Phillies: Jeff Jackson, of, Simeon Academy | Chicago | R-R | 6-3 | 180 | 17 | $185,000 | 1989 | 1998 | Class AA (3) |
| Unknown prospect until breakout prep season (.504-16-72, 52 SBs); compared to Eric Davis for power/speed/arm, but burdened by draft status, never developed. | | | | | | | | | |
| 5. Rangers: Donald Harris, of, Texas Tech | Lubbock, Texas | R-R | 6-1 | 180 | 21 | $150,000 | 1989 | 1995 | Majors (3) |
| Rangers made calculated gamble on best athlete in draft, potential NFL first-rounder; speed, CF skills evident, flashed raw power, but never learned to hit. | | | | | | | | | |
| 6. Cardinals: Paul Coleman, of, Frankston HS | Frankston, Texas | R-R | 5-11 | 200 | 18 | $160,000 | 1989 | 1993 | Class AA (1) |
| Elicited Bo Jackson comps with tape-measure power, raw speed, plus arm, but never reached potential because of injuries, force-fed approach by Cards. | | | | | | | | | |
| 7. White Sox: Frank Thomas, 1b, Auburn | Columbus, Ga. | R-R | 6-5 | 240 | 21 | $175,000 | 1989 | 2008 | Majors (19) |
| Played freshman football with Bo Jackson at Auburn, but had sense to focus on baseball thereafter, became star in college, minors and in Hall of Fame MLB career. | | | | | | | | | |
| 8. Cubs: Earl Cunningham, of, Lancaster HS | Lancaster, S.C. | R-R | 6-2 | 225 | 19 | $185,000 | 1989 | 1996 | Class A (7) |
| High expectations coming out of HS, but overmatched as pro; career burdened by injuries, weight issues, prone to strikeouts, never fully tapped into raw power. | | | | | | | | | |
| 9. Angels: Kyle Abbott, lhp, Long Beach State | Mission Viejo, Calif. | L-L | 6-4 | 190 | 21 | $182,500 | 1989 | 1996 | Majors (4) |
| Went to D-III college to play water polo, career took off after transfer to Long Beach, led team to CWS; second straight Abbott drafted by Angels, won just 4 games. | | | | | | | | | |
| 10. Expos: Charles Johnson, c, Westwood HS | Fort Pierce, Fla. | R-R | 6-3 | 185 | 17 | Unsigned | 1993 | 2005 | Majors (12) |
| Power-hitting catcher with Gold Glove skills; chose college career at Miami, snubbing Expos and their $195,000 offer; came back out as first-rounder in '92 draft. | | | | | | | | | |
| 11. Indians: Calvin Murray, of, W.T. White HS | Dallas | R-R | 5-11 | 180 | 17 | Unsigned | 1993 | 2005 | Majors (5) |
| Most deemed him unsignable, but Indians never got message; stole 170 straight bags in HS, set Texas career mark with 139 SBs, bat became a burden. | | | | | | | | | |
| 12. Astros: Jeff Juden, rhp, Salem HS | Salem, Mass. | R-R | 6-7 | 240 | 18 | $193,325 | 1989 | 2001 | Majors (8) |
| Dominant prep pitcher (30-4, 0.44, 254 IP/488 SO in career), but alternately inspired Astros with mid-90s FB, exasperated them with control, makeup issues. | | | | | | | | | |
| 13. Royals: Brent Mayne, c, Cal State Fullerton | Costa Mesa, Calif. | L-R | 6-2 | 195 | 21 | $138,000 | 1989 | 2004 | Majors (15) |
| Stretch for first round because of limitations as hitter, but polished receiver, capable of moving quickly; spent 15 years in majors, seven with Royals, hit .263-38-403. | | | | | | | | | |
| 14. Giants: Steve Hosey, of, Fresno State | Inglewood, Calif. | R-R | 6-3 | 215 | 20 | $167,600 | 1989 | 1998 | Majors (2) |
| First of 3 FSU drafts in first round, despite dip from SO (.365-13-73) to JR season (.302-6-41); impressive specimen with power/speed package, but holes in swing. | | | | | | | | | |
| 15. Dodgers: Kiki Jones, rhp, Hillsborough HS | Tampa | R-R | 5-11 | 170 | 17 | $175,000 | 1989 | 2001 | Class AA (1) |
| Power pitcher in small, athletic frame; began pro career at 11-0, but arm problems soon zapped fastball velocity; immaturity, off-field issues also took a toll. | | | | | | | | | |
| 16. Red Sox: Greg Blosser, of, Sarasota HS | Sarasota, Fla. | L-L | 6-3 | 190 | 18 | $180,000 | 1989 | 2000 | Majors (2) |
| One-tool player, but more promising bat than Boggs/Greenwell, ex-Sox picks from Tampa prep ranks; struggled making contact, overcoming shortcomings in field. | | | | | | | | | |
| 17. Brewers: Cal Eldred, rhp, Iowa | Urbana, Iowa | R-R | 6-4 | 210 | 21 | $188,750 | 1989 | 2005 | Majors (14) |
| Struggled in minors because of sore shoulder, but quickly emerged as quality major league starter before elbow injury, illness impacted middle/end of career. | | | | | | | | | |
| 18. Pirates: Willie Greene, ss, Jones County HS | Haddock, Ga. | L-R | 5-11 | 160 | 17 | $132,000 | 1989 | 2000 | Majors (9) |
| Hit .564-17-55 with 32 SBs as prep senior, impressed scouts with bat speed/swing; surfaced in majors at 20 with Reds (third organization), hit .234-86-307 overall. | | | | | | | | | |
| 19. Blue Jays: Eddie Zosky, ss, Fresno State | Whittier, Calif. | R-R | 6-0 | 170 | 21 | $170,000 | 1989 | 2000 | Majors (5) |
| Slick fielder with big arm, became perennial Blue Jays SS of future but never swung bat when it counted, hit .160-0-3 in limited looks; spent seven years in Triple-A. | | | | | | | | | |
| 20. Reds: Scott Bryant, of/rhp, Texas | San Antonio, Texas | R-R | 6-2 | 215 | 21 | $168,000 | 1989 | 1996 | Class AAA (6) |
| Power bat/arm, led nation with 118 RBIs, started CWS final on mound; Reds looked at him both ways, but never pitched in pros, plate discipline became obstacle. | | | | | | | | | |
| 21. Tigers: Greg Gohr, rhp, Santa Clara | Campbell, Calif. | R-R | 6-3 | 200 | 21 | $155,000 | 1989 | 1997 | Majors (4) |
| Became pitcher as college soph, hardest thrower in Tigers system until rash of injuries took toll; in 1996, gave up 31 HRs in 116 IP—worst ratio in MLB history. | | | | | | | | | |
| 22. Dodgers: Tom Goodwin, of, Fresno State | Fresno, Calif. | L-R | 6-0 | 170 | 20 | $157,500 | 1989 | 2004 | Majors (14) |
| Led NCAA in steals in 1988-89, got down line in 3.3 seconds on drag bunt; played 14 MLB seasons, but suspect on-base skills limited the utility of his speed. | | | | | | | | | |
| 23. Red Sox: Mo Vaughn, 1b, Seton Hall | Norwalk, Conn. | L-R | 6-1 | 220 | 21 | $126,000 | 1989 | 2003 | Majors (12) |
| Set school career HR mark as freshman (28); had storied eight-year career with Red Sox, 1995 AL MVP; career took immediate nosedive after he left as free agent. | | | | | | | | | |
| 24. Mets: Alan Zinter, c, Arizona | El Paso, Texas | B-R | 6-2 | 190 | 21 | $123,000 | 1989 | 2006 | Majors (2) |
| Offense-first player with suspect catching skills, persevered 14 years in minors, finally reached majors in 2002; slugged 250 HRs in minors, 13 seasons in Triple-A. | | | | | | | | | |
| 25. Twins: Chuck Knoblauch, ss, Texas A&M | Houston | R-R | 5-9 | 170 | 20 | $120,000 | 1989 | 2002 | Majors (12) |
| Became standout big leaguer with speed, defensive skills at 2B, dependable bat, defense suddenly became liability with Yankees, developed irreversible case of yips. | | | | | | | | | |
| 26. Mariners: Scott Burrell, rhp, Hamden HS | Hamden, Conn. | R-R | 6-5 | 195 | 18 | Unsigned | 1990 | 1991 | Class A (1) |
| Chose basketball at UConn over $110,000 offer from Mariners; later signed with Blue Jays, pitched 61 innings in minors before elbow injury, NBA came calling. | | | | | | | | | |

**Signed to major league cintract.*

four pitches and confidence in his ability, and the big payoff came when he became the ace of the victorious U.S. Olympic squad. He pitched complete-game victories over host South Korea in the opener and Puerto Rico in the semifinals.

Veteran scouts who watched him mature with the Olympic team and then dominate college hitters the following spring said unequivocally that, barring a major setback, he was a lock to be the first pick in the June draft.

The Orioles knew getting McDonald under contract might be a long and drawn-out affair. McDonald's father Larry handled all negotiations with the Orioles, with input from hardline agent Scott Boras, and the team's first offer of $255,000 was rejected out of hand. Negotiations broke off

## AT A GLANCE

one of the game's most prolific power-hitting first basemen, after beginning his career as an obscure junior-college shortstop. Hoffman had an equally unlikely rise to stardom after also being drafted as a shortstop, converting to a reliever after two seasons and going on to set the all-time saves record.

### Never Too Late

**DESI WILSON, OF, ASTROS (87TH ROUND).** The 6-foot-7 Wilson, the last of 1,490 players drafted in 1989, chose not to sign as he was in the midst of a record-breaking basketball career at Fairleigh Dickinson. He never played baseball until his senior year in 1991, when he was drafted in the 30th round by the Rangers and signed with that club. His lone major league season, in 1996, came in a Giants uniform.

### Overlooked

**STEVE SHIFFLETT, RHP, ROYALS.** Righthander **KERRY TAYLOR** received $70,000 from the Twins as a Minnesota high school product; Shifflett got no bonus from the Royals as a 23-year-old Emporia State (Kan.) signee. Neither player distinguished himself in brief major league careers, but a slight edge goes to Shifflett (1-4, 2.60 in 34 relief appearances). Taylor went 0-5, 6.56 in two seasons with the Padres.

### International Gem

**MATT STAIRS, OF, EXPOS.** Canadians were still exempt from the draft, and the Expos made the most astute signing of the year in getting Stairs, a New Brunswick product, to agree to a $12,500 bonus. He played 19 years in the majors, hit .262-265-899 overall and established the standard for most pinch-hit home runs in a career (23). He played for 12 clubs—more than any position player in big league history.

**CONTINUED ON PAGE 364**

## AT A GLANCE

CONTINUED FROM PAGE 363

### Minor League Take

**ALAN ZINTER, C, METS.** Zinter played 13 seasons in the minors before making his big league debut on June 18, 2002. No other first-rounder in big league history played so long before achieving his goal. He played in just 67 games in the majors between 2002-04, but otherwise spent 19 seasons in the minors and hit 250 homers.

### Ones Who Got Away

**CALVIN MURRAY, OF, INDIANS (1ST ROUND); CHARLES JOHNSON, C, EXPOS (1ST ROUND).** Even as bonuses rose substantially in 1989, three first-round picks went unsigned. Murray and Johnson, the 11th and 12th picks overall, rejected significant offers in favor of attending college and became first-rounders again in 1992.

### He Was Drafted?

**MARCUS ROBERTSON, OF, INDIANS (19TH ROUND).** Six future NFL players and two future NBA first-rounders were selected in the '89 baseball draft. Robertson, an Iowa State product, played 11 years in the NFL as a defensive back and was a two-time Pro Bowler.

### Did You Know . . .

**SCOTT BURRELL**, an unsigned first-round pick of the Mariners, is the only athlete in American professional sports to be taken in the first round in two different sports. He was also drafted by the NBA's Charlotte Hornets in 1993.

### They Said It

**SCOTT BORAS**, agent of No. 1 pick **BEN MCDONALD**, on his stance in negotiations with the Orioles: "You can't expect Ben to sign for a figure comparable to what high school players are getting. It's more like an NFL or NBA situation, because he's so close to being an impact player in the big leagues. He's a very, very unique talent."

several times, and his price continued to rise.

"You can't expect Ben to sign for a figure comparable to what high school kids are getting," Boras said. "It's more like an NFL or NBA situation because he's so close to being an impact player in the big leagues. He's a very, very unique talent."

The threat of a new baseball league to begin play in 1990, backed by New York businessman Donald Trump, complicated things further. Rumors surfaced of McDonald signing a $2 million contract with the new circuit.

In the end, the rival league never panned out and McDonald signed a deal with the Orioles worth a guaranteed $824,300—a $350,000 signing bonus, plus $24,300 in pro-rated salary for 1989, $125,000 for 1990 and an additional $350,000 for 1991. With incentives, McDonald was in line to earn as much as $1.1 million.

Fans and even team officials saw McDonald as the club's savior, something he had trouble living up to, especially as his early days were plagued by injuries.

"There was so much pressure," McDonald recalled. "I still remember in 1991 when (manager) Frank Robinson said in spring training, 'We're only going to go as far as McDonald takes us. If he wins 20 or 21 games, we have a chance.' "I'm thinking, 'Wow. I had only won eight games in my career. I don't even know what I'm doing."

McDonald's career was a disappointment. He went 78-70, 3.91 in nine major league seasons, but was troubled by injuries, leading to six stints on the disabled list. His career ended on Feb. 26, 1998, when he had rotator-cuff surgery for a third time.

Six days after McDonald signed his record deal, Olerud agreed on a similar contract, and his career outstripped McDonald's. Olerud hit an American League-best .363 with 54 doubles in 1993, producing career highs in homers (24) and RBIs (107). He was a steady first baseman for 17 seasons, and finished his career with a .295 average, 255 homers and 1,230 RBIs. He won three Gold Gloves and made two All-Star Game appearances.

Though McDonald was the only college righthander drafted in the top half of the first round, teammate Russell Springer, along with Cal State Fullerton's Mark Beck and Iowa's Cal Eldred, all ranked right behind McDonald before they were all slowed by arm injuries to varying degrees.

Eldred's problems weren't serious enough to knock him out of the first round, and he went on to be selected by the Milwaukee Brewers with the 17th pick; he won 88 games over 14 seasons in the majors. Springer slipped to the seventh round after arthroscopic surgery and his strikeout total dipped from 156 in 119 innings as a sophomore, to just 89 in 90 innings as a junior. He signed with the New York Yankees for $70,000 (the largest bonus paid to a seventh-rounder), and pitched for 18 seasons in the majors, going 36-45, 4.52.

Beck, meanwhile, was second in the nation in strikeouts as a sophomore, but had rotator-cuff surgery on the eve of the 1989 season and didn't pitch at all as a junior. The Braves took a stab at him in the 16th round and signed him for $55,000, but the 6-foot-5 Beck never pitched an inning professionally.

## How They Should Have Done It

Based on the career WAR (Wins Above Replacement, as calculated by Baseball-Reference.com) numbers achieved by all the players eligible for the 1989 draft, here's how the first round should have unfolded. Numbers in parentheses indicate the round when the player was actually drafted.

| | Player, Pos. | Actual Draft | WAR | Bonus |
|---|---|---|---|---|
| 1. | Jeff Bagwell, 3b | Red Sox (4) | 79.5 | $32,500 |
| 2. | Frank Thomas, 1b | White Sox (1) | 73.6 | $175,000 |
| 3. | Jim Thome, ss | Indians (13) | 72.8 | $15,000 |
| 4. | John Olerud, 1b/lhp | Blue Jays (3) | 58.0 | $575,000 |
| 5. | Jeff Kent, 2b | Blue Jays (20) | 55.2 | $15,000 |
| 6. | Brian Giles, of | Indians (17) | 50.8 | $20,000 |
| 7. | Chuck Knoblauch, ss | Twins (1) | 44.5 | $120,000 |
| 8. | Tim Salmon, of | Angels (3) | 40.6 | $60,000 |
| 9. | Trevor Hoffman, 3b | Reds (11) | 28.4 | $3,000 |
| 10. | Mo Vaughn, 1b | Red Sox (1) | 27.1 | $126,000 |
| 11. | Ryan Klesko, lhp/1b | Braves (5) | 26.9 | $110,000 |
| 12. | Scott Erickson, rhp | Twins (4) | 25.1 | $49,000 |
| 13. | Denny Neagle, lhp | Twins (3) | 22.7 | $50,000 |
| 14. | Ben McDonald, rhp | Orioles (1) | 20.9 | $350,000 |
| 15. | Eric Young, of | Dodgers (43) | 18.7 | $3,000 |
| 16. | Paul Quantrill, rhp | Red Sox (6) | 18.1 | $30,000 |
| 17. | Shane Reynolds, rhp | Astros (3) | 17.9 | $40,000 |
| 18. | Cal Eldred, rhp | Brewers (1) | 16.2 | $188,750 |
| 19. | Chad Curtis, of | Angels (45) | 14.0 | $5,000 |
| 20. | Gregg Zaun, c | Orioles (17) | 13.7 | $40,000 |
| 21. | Curtis Leskanic, rhp | Indians (8) | 12.4 | $30,000 |
| 22. | J.T. Snow, 1b | Yankees (5) | 11.0 | $57,800 |
| 23. | Todd Jones, rhp | Astros (1-S) | 10.9 | $75,000 |
| 24. | Pat Rapp, rhp | Giants (15) | 9.5 | $1,000 |
| 25. | Mike Trombley, rhp | Twins (14) | 9.2 | $51,000 |
| 26. | Tom Goodwin, of | Dodgers (1) | 8.6 | $157,500 |

| | Top 3 Unsigned Players | | | Year Signed |
|---|---|---|---|---|
| 1. | Jason Giambi, ss | Brewers (43) | 51.6 | 1992 |
| 2. | Jorge Posada, ss | Yankees (43) | 42.7 | 1990 |
| 3. | Mark Grudzielanek, ss | Mets (17) | 26.4 | 1991 |

### ATHLETIC OUTFIELDERS IN DEMAND

Even though 14 of the 26 first-round picks came from the college ranks, the 1989 draft stood out for its exceptional high school talent. The Major League Scouting Bureau's list had McDonald at the top, followed by nine high school players. Of the bureau's top 128 prospects, 79 were from the prep ranks.

Scouts generally rated the crop of athletic high school outfielders the best in years—maybe even the best in the draft era. The harvest included the likes of Jeff Jackson (Phillies), Paul Coleman (Cardinals) and Earl Cunningham (Cubs), all snapped up in the first 10 picks. Two others (Calvin Murray, Indians; Greg Blosser, Red Sox) were taken in the first round, and the list could have been expanded to include Kenny Felder (Padres, second round), Michael Moore (Blue Jays, second) and Todd Steverson (Cardinals, sixth) had signability not been an issue. Along with Murray, all ended up in college and became first-round picks three years later.

Bo Jackson, the ultimate athletic outfielder of his era, was the all rage of baseball in 1989. Every major league team was mesmerized by Jackson's combination of raw speed and power, as well as his ability to accomplish almost anything in baseball after temporarily abandoning an even more promising career in football.

The St. Louis Cardinals seemed more intrigued than most clubs. They had the sixth pick in the draft and targeted Coleman, a powerfully built Texan. In their minds, they believed that they had just landed the second coming of Bo Jackson.

Coleman never came close to reminding anyone of Jackson. In five seasons, peaking at Double-A in 1993, he hit .225 and went deep just 19 times. Injuries, mostly to Coleman's legs, contributed to the demise of the former Texas prep standout. As a last resort, the Cardinals converted him to a pitcher in instructional league following the 1993 season, but an arm injury wiped out his entire 1994 season and ended his career.

Like Coleman, the careers of the other highly touted prospects like Jackson and Cunningham—and even Donald Harris, a raw but talented two-sport athlete from Texas Tech, drafted fifth overall by the Texas Rangers—all fizzled, and none of the record nine outfielders drafted in the first round came close to leaving a mark on the game.

Jeff Jackson

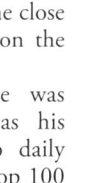

Jackson's demise was almost as rapid as his ascent. A Chicago daily featured the area's top 100 players at the outset of the 1989 season, and Jackson was notably absent—though in fairness, he was a pitcher through his sophomore year at Simeon High, and actually came close to quitting.

Even when he moved to the outfield as a junior, Jackson was still just 5-foot-8. But his outlook changed dramatically over the next 12 months when he sprouted seven inches and became a hot commodity as a senior by hitting .504 with 22 doubles, nine triples and 16 home runs, while driving in 72 runs and stealing 54 bases.

The Philadelphia Phillies didn't hesitate to select him with the fourth pick and sign him for a $185,000 signing bonus.

Jackson's career never took off. In eight minor league seasons, none above Double-A, he hit .225 and went deep just 32 times. Scouts wrote him off as a one-year wonder who came on the scene overnight and disappeared just as quickly. As he struggled, Jackson had a difficult time living down the attention he received for being drafted before

## Fastest To The Majors

| Player, Pos. | Drafted (Round) | Debut |
|---|---|---|
| 1. #John Olerud, 1b/lhp | Blue Jays (3) | Sept. 3, 1989 |
| 2. Ben McDonald, rhp | Orioles (1) | Sept. 6, 1989 |
| 3. Scott Erickson, rhp | Twins (4) | June 25, 1990 |
| 4. Rafael Novoa, lhp | Giants (9) | July 31, 1990 |
| 5. Frank Thomas, 1b | White Sox (1) | Aug. 2, 1990 |

**FIRST HIGH SCHOOL SELECTION:** Jeff Juden, rhp (Astros/1, Sept. 15, 1991)

**LAST PLAYER TO RETIRE:** Jim Thome, 1b (Oct. 3, 2012)

*#Debuted in major leagues.*

## DRAFT SPOTLIGHT: JOHN OLERUD

TOM DIPACE

**John Olerud was a two-way standout at Washington State and would have been a first-round pick if not for a brain aneurysm**

John Olerud did a lot of amazing things on the baseball diamond as a sophomore in 1988 at Washington State. As the team's first baseman/DH, he hit .464 with 23 homers; as the No. 1 starter in the Cougars rotation, he went 15-0, 2.49.

But Olerud's most amazing accomplishment may have occurred a year later, on April 15 when he made his season debut—three months after collapsing during a preseason workout, and two months after undergoing high-risk surgery to repair a near-fatal aneurysm at the base of his brain.

Olerud was projected as the second-best prospect in the college crop for the 1989 draft before being felled by his injury, and would have been one of the top players selected in June had he not voluntarily taken himself out of the draft with an announcement that he intended to return to WSU for his senior year.

"I decided it would be best for me to stay here another year," said Olerud, who hit .359 with five homers and 30 RBIs in 78 at-bats in his abbreviated junior season, while going just 3-2, 6.68 on the mound. "If I hadn't had the aneurysm and I would have had a good year, I would have turned pro. But I really need another year to get my strength back. There probably isn't enough first-round draft money out there to set me up for life."

Every major league club heeded Olerud's request by not drafting him in the first round, but the Toronto Blue Jays grabbed him in the third—even with little or no intention of trying to sign him in the short term.

"We would like him to get to 100 percent," Blue Jays general manager Pat Gillick said. "We hope over the next few weeks he not only feels 100 percent, but he feels 100 percent about himself. I don't think he feels completely up to par. I think when he's healthy, he might be more acceptable to talking."

Olerud spent the summer playing for the local Palouse Empire Cougars of the far-flung Alaska League, and starred in his customary two-way role. Gillick met with the Olerud family nine times over the course of the summer, not to sign Olerud but to monitor his progress. Other members of the Jays organization kept tabs on him, as well.

Satisfied with his health and duly impressed by his summer-league performance, Toronto made its first firm offer in early August. The proposal, about $400,000, would have been the highest bonus in baseball history. Olerud declined, but the Blue Jays persisted and at one point asked him what it would take; he responded that his stance had not changed, that he really wanted to return to school for his senior year.

Ben McDonald, the first overall pick in June, signed with Baltimore on Aug. 19 for an unprecedented $824,300, including a three-year, guaranteed major league contract, plus incentives. A week later, almost six months to the day after the aneurysm was removed, Olerud agreed to a similar pact with Toronto, though the amount earmarked as a signing bonus in his deal, $575,000, made it the richest bonus contract in draft history.

The Oleruds said the money didn't make the deal, though the security certainly didn't hurt. They placed more importance on signing with an organization they knew and trusted, and on the opportunity to play immediately in the big leagues. In the process, Olerud became the 18th player in draft history to advance directly to the majors.

His first big league at-bat came against Minnesota on Sept. 3. Admittedly nervous, the sweet-swinging Olerud grounded a 2-0 fastball by the second baseman for a single. By 1993, Olerud became an instrumental part of the World Series champion Blue Jays lineup, hitting an American League-best .363 while leading the league with 54 doubles, 33 intentional walks and a .473 on-base percentage. He went on to play 17 seasons in the majors.

## WORTH NOTING

■ Among the more noteworthy second-rounders who fell short of expectations were lefthander **RUSTY RUGG** (Brewers) and **TOM ENGLE** (Mets), whose amazing pitching feats in high school are still recognized as national records. Rugg spun a remarkable 19 no-hitters, along with 14 one-hitters, during his career at Downsville (La.) High. Unfortunately, he developed arm problems shortly after signing with the Brewers for a bonus of $80,000. Though he hung on for five seasons while enduring two surgeries, he pitched in just 18 pro games, none above Rookie ball. Engle earned his place in the record books as a senior at Fairfield Union High in Lancaster, Ohio, by throwing six consecutive no-hitters during the 1989 season. Engle spent eight seasons in the minors, peaking in Triple-A in 1995, but two elbow surgeries ended his career.

■ While Rugg and Engle earned national acclaim for their no-hit feats, the best known prep pitcher of 1989 was **JON PETERS**, a righthander from Brenham (Texas) High. He became the nation's most celebrated high school pitcher since fellow Texan David Clyde in 1973. Peters won a national-record 53 consecutive games from 1986-89 before dropping his first and only decision in his next to last high school appearance, and was featured in Sports Illustrated in consecutive years, gracing the publication's cover on May 8, 1989. He also became the subject of television features and intense scrutiny after completing his career with a 54-1 record, 22 shutouts, five no-hitters and 612 strikeouts in 370 innings. Peters never threw hard enough in the eyes of scouts to justify being drafted in 1989, nor did he ever play pro ball. Before enrolling at Texas A&M and subsequently transferring to Blinn (Texas) Junior College, Peters hurt his right elbow in a summer all-star game and later had a succession of arm operations.

future Hall of Famer Frank Thomas.

The 6-foot-2, 225-pound Cunningham was more established than Jackson. He set a South Carolina career home run record (34) while at Lancaster High, and might even have had more raw power than Coleman. Had he not struck out four times in three games with Braves general manager Bobby Cox in attendance, Cunningham might well have been drafted right after McDonald; he slipped six spots to the Chicago Cubs, who were in the market for a power hitter.

Like Jackson and Coleman, Cunningham's pro career fell far short of expectations. He never escaped Class A in eight seasons, hitting just .224 with 84 homers. He battled injury issues early in his career, weight issues later on and overall never developed any plate discipline. He spent four seasons at low Class A Peoria, and in the 1991-92 seasons alone, he walked just 29 times as compared to 297 strikeouts.

"The Cunninghams, the Colemans, the Judens and Jacksons, those kids had a lot of talent. A lot of ability," said Chicago Cubs scouting director Dick Balderson, several years after drafting Cunningham. "Of course, if you saw them today, you'd go out and do your work all over again. That shows the scientific basis of the game, or the lack thereof. I really have no answer for why it happened."

In Cunningham's case specifically, though, Balderson had a ready explanation.

"Some kids just don't understand the work it takes to get to the big leagues," he said. "Earl Cunningham didn't know what work is. He's a great kid and person. But he had limitations. We'd say, 'Earl, this is what you need to do,' and 'Earl, try this,' and he didn't know what to do. He was bewildered."

The Rangers pulled the biggest surprise early in the first round by drafting Harris, an all-Southwest Conference free safety whose stock rose sharply as a draft-eligible sophomore. At the time, the athletic Harris was also touted as a potential first-rounder in the NFL draft, though the contract he signed with the Rangers, which included a $150,000 bonus, prohibited him from playing football.

Nonetheless, after Harris reached the big leagues briefly with the Rangers in 1991, the hometown Dallas Cowboys selected him in the 12th round of the 1992 NFL draft. The Rangers debated whether to open the 1992 season with Harris in center field or ship him to Double-A for more seasoning, and when they opted for the latter Harris never reported and instead signed on with the Cowboys.

By then, his football skills had eroded from three years of inactivity and he was cut after three weeks in Cowboys camp. He was welcomed back to the Rangers, but his big league career never materialized. In 82 games, he hit just .205.

### FIRST BASEMEN STEAL GLORY

For all the emphasis on McDonald and high school outfielders in the 1989 draft, by far the most distinguishing feature was an exceptional crop of college first basemen. Based on Wins Above Replacement, the four most productive players drafted were Jeff Bagwell, Thomas, Jim Thome and Olerud, all of whom carved out lengthy major league careers. Only Thomas was actually picked in the first round.

### Top 25 Bonuses

| | Player, Pos. | Drafted (Round) | Order | Bonus |
|---|---|---|---|---|
| 1. | **John Olerud, 1b/lhp** | **Blue Jays (3)** | **79** | **#$575,000** |
| 2. | **Ben McDonald, rhp** | **Orioles (1)** | **1** | **#$350,000** |
| 3. | ***Tyler Houston, c** | **Braves (1)** | **2** | **$225,000** |
| | ***Roger Salkeld, rhp** | **Mariners (1)** | **3** | **$225,000** |
| 5. | ***Jeff Juden, rhp** | **Astros (1)** | **12** | **$193,325** |
| 6. | **Cal Eldred, rhp** | **Brewers (1)** | **17** | **$188,750** |
| 7. | *Jeff Jackson, of | Phillies (1) | 4 | $185,000 |
| | *Earl Cunningham, of | Cubs (1) | 8 | $185,000 |
| 9. | ***Greg Blosser, of** | **Red Sox (1)** | **16** | **$180,000** |
| 10. | **Frank Thomas, 1b** | **White Sox (1)** | **7** | **$175,000** |
| | *Kiki Jones, rhp | Dodgers (1) | 15 | $175,000 |
| 12. | **Eddie Zosky, ss** | **Blue Jays (1)** | **19** | **$170,000** |
| 13. | Scott Bryant, of/rhp | Reds (1) | 20 | $168,000 |
| 14. | **Steve Hosey, of** | **Giants (1)** | **14** | **$167,600** |
| 15. | *Paul Coleman, of | Cardinals (1) | 6 | $160,000 |
| | ***Andy Fox, 3b** | **Yankees (2)** | **45** | **$160,000** |
| 17. | **Tom Goodwin, of** | **Dodgers (1)** | **22** | **$157,500** |
| 18. | **Greg Gohr, rhp** | **Tigers (1)** | **21** | **$155,000** |
| 19. | **Donald Harris, of** | **Rangers (1)** | **5** | **$150,000** |
| | **Aaron Small, rhp** | **Blue Jays (22)** | **575** | **$150,000** |
| 21. | **Brent Mayne, c** | **Royals (1)** | **13** | **$138,000** |
| 22. | **Kyle Abbott, lhp** | **Angels (1)** | **9** | **$136,500** |
| 23. | ***Willie Greene, 3b** | **Pirates (1)** | **18** | **$132,000** |
| 24. | †Joe Norris, rhp | Expos (26) | 670 | $130,625 |
| 25. | **Mo Vaughn, 1b** | **Red Sox (1)** | **23** | **$126,000** |

*Major leaguers in bold. *High school selection. #Major league contract. †Signed as draft-and-follow.*

First basemen Mo Vaughn (Red Sox, first round) and Ryan Klesko (Braves, fifth round) ranked as the 10th- and 11th-best players in the class, while J.T. Snow (Yankees, fifth round), was 22nd. Yet another first baseman of note drafted in 1989, Jason Giambi (Brewers, 43rd round), has the highest WAR among players who didn't sign.

Thome (612), Thomas (521), Bagwell (449) and Giambi (440) are also the four leading home run hitters in the Class of 1989, and seven of the top 11 were first basemen.

Mo Vaughn

The first basemen won five MVP awards and combined to lead their league in walks 12 times and on-base percentage six times.

The Chicago White Sox took Thomas seventh overall, though few teams believed he belonged among the top 10 picks—or even the top half of the first round. While the 6-foot-5, 240-pound Thomas had unmistakable power, led the Southeastern Conference with a .403 batting average and posted a 73-25 walk-strikeout ratio as a junior at Auburn, numerous clubs believed the college numbers he posted were deceiving, and projected he'd strike out too frequently to ever tap into his power.

Not only did scouts misjudge how well Thomas knew the strike zone or understood the finer points

## Largest Bonuses By Round

| | Player, Pos. | Club | Bonus |
|---|---|---|---|
| 1. | **Ben McDonald, rhp** | **Orioles** | **$350,000** |
| 2. | ***Andy Fox, 3b** | **Yankees** | **$160,000** |
| 3. | **John Olerud, 1b** | **Blue Jays** | **$575,000** |
| 4. | *Kyle Duke, lhp | Mariners | $116,000 |
| 5. | ***Ryan Klesko, 1b/lhp** | **Braves** | **$110,000** |
| 6. | *Mark Charbonnet, of | Indians | $67,000 |
| 7. | **Russ Springer, rhp** | **Yankees** | **$70,000** |
| 8. | Six tied at | | $30,000 |
| 9. | ***Sterling Hitchcock, lhp** | **Yankees** | **$50,000** |
| 10. | David Williams, rhp | Braves | $35,000 |
| | *John Dempsey, c | Cardinals | $35,000 |
| 11. | **Kelly Stinnett, c** | **Indians** | **$55,000** |
| 12. | Jim Wiley, rhp | Yankees | $40,000 |
| 13. | *Jeremy McGarity, rhp | Cardinals | $27,500 |
| 14. | *Gus Santiago, 3b | Expos | $20,000 |
| 15. | James Dennison, lhp | Red Sox | $24,000 |
| 16. | Steve Martin, of | Padres | $58,000 |
| 17. | ***Gregg Zaun, c** | **Orioles** | **$40,000** |
| 18. | ***#Matt Whisenant, lhp** | **Phillies** | **$60,000** |
| 19. | *James Heilgeist, of | Expos | $25,000 |
| 20. | ***#David Stevens, rhp** | **Cubs** | **$50,000** |
| 21. | **Gerald Alexander, rhp** | **Rangers** | **$25,000** |
| 22. | ***Aaron Small, rhp** | **Blue Jays** | **$150,000** |
| 23. | **Mike Thomas, lhp** | **Mets** | **$20,000** |
| 24. | *Sean Hearn, of | Blue Jays | $22,000 |
| 25. | *Javier Puchales, of | Dodgers | $10,000 |
| | *Duane Ashley, rhp | Expos | $10,000 |
| Other | #Joe Norris, rhp | Expos (26) | $130,625 |

*Major leaguers in bold. *High school selection.*

of hitting, but they also did not accurately gauge his overall baseball ability or desire to improve.

As a three-sport star at Columbus (Ga.) High, Thomas yearned for a chance to play professional baseball but was passed over in the 1986 draft. "The scouts didn't like me, I guess," he said. "They said I was a football player just playing baseball. Sure, I had some extra weight, but it was just baby fat."

Thomas was a hit from the start in pro ball. In 1990, his first full season, he hit .323 with 18 home runs in 109 games in Double-A, while walking 112 times. The White Sox called him up to Chicago in August, and he hit at a .318 clip the remainder of the 1990 season. Over 16 seasons with the White Sox, he hit .307 with 448 homers and 1,465 RBIs. He also drew 1,466 walks against 1,165 strikeouts.

The Boston Red Sox targeted New England talent in 1989, and astutely drafted two homegrown products—Vaughn in the first round, and Bagwell in the fourth. They got significant mileage out of Vaughn, a Seton Hall product who hit .300 with 39 home runs and 126 RBIs in 1995 and won the American League MVP before departing Boston after eight seasons as a free agent. Injuries short-circuited his career shortly thereafter.

Bagwell, a University of Hartford product, had significant offensive upside in his own right and hit .418 with 24 home runs in his final two college seasons, but was overlooked early in the draft because of his defense. At best, Bagwell was an average third baseman with a decent arm and limited range, but after being dealt by the Red Sox to Houston in a 1990 trade-deadline deal for veteran pitcher Larry Andersen, the Astros quickly found a home for him at first base, and his career blossomed. Over 15 years in an Astros uniform, Bagwell hit .297 with 1,529 RBIs, in addition to his 449 homers.

Thome proved to be the biggest surprise among the group, especially after being taken in the 13th round by the Cleveland Indians as a shortstop out of an Illinois junior college. He hit 26 homers in his first four minor league seasons before busting loose for 25 at Triple-A Charlotte in 1993. He eventually drilled 334 homers in 12 seasons in an Indians uniform, including 52 in 2002. It's safe to say that Thome quickly made the Indians forget that they had wasted their first-round pick on someone named Calvin Murray.

Jeff Bagwell

### BLUE JAYS GO ON SPENDING SPREE

No club pursued the talent in the 1989 draft as aggressively as the Blue Jays, who moved into the brand new SkyDome on June 3. With the record string of sellouts that followed, the Jays had more available cash than ever to pour into the draft.

Said one observer of the Blue Jays draft: "It could be one of the great drafts ever if they sign everybody, but it could cost them $2 million to do it. They really stuck their necks out."

The Jays spent a record $1,311,770 on their 1989 picks, $575,000 of which went to Olerud; $170,000 to first-rounder Eddie Zosky; and another $150,000 to 22nd rounder Aaron Small, a California high school righthander and a record for that round.

As aggressive as the Blue Jays were, they still allowed several premium prospects to go unsigned, including three players in the top 10 rounds: second-rounder Michael Moore, fourth-rounder Troy Bradford and ninth-rounder Jeffrey Hammonds. Moore was the son of a wealthy Beverly Hills businessman and nephew of ex-NFL star Ahmad Rashad (formerly known as Bobby Moore), and elected to play football and baseball at UCLA. Bradford, the nation's most sought-after junior college pitcher, decided to attend college at Arizona, while Hammonds, a top-rated high school outfielder from New Jersey, followed through on a commitment to Stanford (and later became the fourth overall pick in the 1992 draft).

For all the money spent in 1989, three first-rounders and a handful of prominent second-rounders went unsigned—the greatest number of unsigned picks in the first two rounds since 1979.

The Montreal Expos, picking 10th, never came to terms with Florida high school catcher Charles Johnson, who passed up their $197,500 offer and instead attended college at Miami. The Expos paid the price for shelling out the richest signing bonus ever given a high school draft pick a year earlier.

### WORTH NOTING

■ An interesting twist to the 1989 draft was the inclusion of the Northwest League's independent Boise Hawks franchise. The Hawks chose two players, starting in the fourth round. Draft rules provided unaffiliated minor league clubs the opportunity to draft, and the Hawks exercised it, becoming the first club since Bend (Northwest) in 1971 to do so. The rule has since been changed.

"It was not done for publicity," Hawks director of baseball operations Mal Fichman said. "It was done to help the ball club. Reaction from major league clubs was 99 percent good. A couple of clubs weren't sure what we were doing initially. They were concerned we would draft 30-40 players and resell them. You can't sell or trade drafted players, so obviously that was not our intent at all."

■ A significant development in the 1989 draft was the inclusion of players from U.S. territories, most notably Puerto Ricans. Previously only players of Puerto Rican nationality who attended college in the U.S. were eligible, while all others 16 and older were free to sign on the open market. The new regulation required Puerto Ricans to complete at least their third year of high school or reach age 17. The change was aimed at curbing bonus payments to Puerto Ricans, and while it accomplished that goal in the short term, many in the game cited it as a reason for a decline in the talent Puerto Rico produced in future years. A total of 55 Puerto Ricans were selected in 1989, though none in the first five rounds, as most of the best 16-year-olds on the island were signed a year earlier as free agents.

■ A second draft change approved at the 1988 Winter Meetings affected baseball's college scholarship plan. In the past, clubs could offer high school draft picks no more than $1,500 a semester, or $12,000 over four years, to offset the cost of attending

CONTINUED ON PAGE 368

## WORTH NOTING

CONTINUED FROM PAGE 367

college. Those parameters often hampered a player who planned to attend a more expensive college, and clubs often would have to increase their bonus offer to entice the player into pro ball. The rule change enabled clubs to negotiate the amount of scholarship money earmarked for college. "That figure could be $10,000 or more a semester," said Bill Murray, administrator for the commissioner's office. "It all depends on where a player decides to go to school."

■ The Reds signed their second-round pick, Owasso (Okla.) High outfielder and three-sport star **AARON GOINS**, to a $93,000 bonus, but Goins never played a game of pro ball. He suffered a stress fracture in his foot after reporting to the Reds' Rookie-level club in the Gulf Coast League. After rehabbing the injury without seeing game action, Goins became so disillusioned with baseball and life in the minors that he turned his attention back to football. He had committed to playing that sport in college at Oklahoma prior to signing with the Reds, but ended up playing sparingly for the Sooners in 1990.

■ Righthander **KIKI JONES**, selected 15th overall by the Dodgers, was the fourth player from Tampa's Hillsborough High to crack the first round in the 1980s. He followed in the footsteps of lefthander Vance Lovelace (Cubs/1981), righthander Dwight Gooden (Mets/1982) and shortstop Gary Sheffield (Brewers/1986), all of whom reached the majors. Though the 5-foot-10 Jones went 8-3, 1.14 as a senior, walking 14 and striking out 100 in 61 innings, his career peaked in Double-A. "Kiki isn't as fluid or advanced as Dwight was at the same stage," said Hillsborough coach Billy Reed, "but velocity-wise, he threw just as hard. He faced more publicity than any athlete I've ever had—I mean it was a media zoo every time we played."

Johnson based his worth on the $225,000 bonus the Expos paid 11th-rounder Reid Cornelius, plus $10,000 for inflation.

Cleveland, selecting 11th, lost Texas prep infielder Murray to the University of Texas, despite a final offer in excess of $200,000. It's unclear whether all clubs, notably the Indians, got the message, but Murray's high school coach, at Murray's request, had sent word to the industry, via the Major League Scouting Bureau, prior to the draft that Murray was unsignable at any price.

"There's no way in the world we would have drafted him," said Indians scouting director Chet Montgomery, "if we'd gotten word those were his intentions. You never want to waste a draft pick, but it was an especially important pick to us because we didn't have a second-round pick."

After three years in college, both Johnson and Murray resurfaced as first-round picks in 1992.

The Seattle Mariners also failed to sign the second of their two first-round picks, Connecticut two-sport high school star Scott Burrell, who chose to play both baseball and basketball at the University of Connecticut over a $110,000 bonus from the Mariners.

The 6-foot-5, 195-pound Burrell didn't play baseball for UConn as a freshman, which made him eligible for the 1990 draft, and he was selected by the Blue Jays—though not until the fifth round. He ended up accepting the Blue Jays' $150,000 offer, but only played a single season in their farm system—in 1991 in Class A, where he went 2-6, 3.71 in 14 games—because of a combination of injuries and an overriding commitment to basketball.

Burrell played basketball for four years at UConn, becoming the first player in NCAA history to accumulate 1,500 points, 750 rebounds, 275 assists and 300 steals, before pursuing an eight-year career in the NBA. As a first-round pick of the Charlotte Hornets in 1993, he became the only athlete in American professional sports history to be drafted in the first round in two sports.

### MIXED BAG OF FIRST-ROUNDERS

McDonald and Olerud, along with Houston, set the tone for the 1989 with their record bonuses, while righthander Roger Salkeld, chosen third by the Seattle Mariners, also eclipsed the $200,000 barrier. In the process, numerous other players set club-record signing bonuses.

Houston's career with the Braves was a case of déjà vu because his father, Sam, played seven seasons in the organization, before being released in 1974."He didn't make it. I want to make it," the younger Houston said after learning he'd been drafted by Atlanta.

"Houston was probably the safest decision we could have made," said Braves scouting director Paul Snyder. "He is an above-average receiver with an above-average arm, and there's true thunder in his bat."

Snyder said Houston, who hit .485 with 13 home runs as a high school senior, was such an advanced prospect that he was one of two players he scouted who was ready to turn pro after the 10th grade. Besides his obvious physical tools, Houston's tenacity also appealed to the Braves.

"I play hard, because that's the way the game should be played," said Houston, who patterned his game after his namesake, Ty Cobb, a noted antagonist. "If other players don't like that, then they shouldn't be playing. I don't have any problem with guys who play hard. Why should they?"

Houston didn't enjoy the most auspicious beginning to his pro career, and his attitude and work habits were frequently blamed for his stagnation in the Braves system. In 703 minor league games, he hit .236 with 54 home runs. Signed as a lefthanded-hitting catcher with speed and power, Houston never asserted himself behind the plate and moved to third base before settling into mostly a utility role over eight major league seasons. In 700 big league games, he hit .265 with 63 homers.

Tyler Houston

Salkeld, who signed with the Mariners for $210,000, was the grandson of ex-big leaguer Bill Salkeld, who once caught Hall of Famer Warren Spahn during their days with the Boston Braves. He went 13-1, 0.51 with 174 strikeouts in 109 innings as a senior at Saugus (Calif.) High, and continued to pitch impressively early in his career, with 402 strikeouts in his first 368 minor league innings on the strength of a fastball that reached 98 mph and two superior breaking pitches.

Salkeld was never the same after he tore his rotator cuff and had reconstructive shoulder surgery before the 1992 season, however, just as he was on the verge of cracking the Mariners rotation. In 45 major league appearances over three seasons,

## One Team's Draft: Cleveland Indians

| Player, Pos. | Bonus | Player, Pos. | Bonus | Player, Pos. | Bonus |
|---|---|---|---|---|---|
| **1. *Calvin Murray, of** | **Did not sign** | 10. John Cotton, 2b | $12,000 | 19. Marcus Robertson, of | $17,500 |
| 2. Selection to Dodgers | | **11. #Kelly Stinnett, c** | **$55,000** | 20. Dennis Kluss, of | $5,000 |
| **3. Jerry Dipoto, lhp** | **$50,000** | 12. *Von Wechsburg, rhp | $20,000 | 21. Avery Johnson, ss | None |
| **4. Jesse Levis, c** | **$40,000** | **13. Jim Thome, ss** | **$15,000** | 22. Charles Davis, 1b | $1,500 |
| **5. *Alan Embree, lhp** | **$30,000** | 14. Nolan Lane, of | $12,000 | 23. #Miguel Flores, ss | $10,000 |
| 6. *Mark Chabonnet, of | $67,000 | 15. Tom Lachmann, c | $7,000 | 24. Jeffrey Hancock, 2b | $1,000 |
| 7. *John Martinez, c | $30,000 | **16. *Mike Potts, lhp** | **Did not sign** | **25. Robert Person, ss/of** | **$1,000** |
| **8. Curtis Leskanic, rhp** | **$30,000** | **17. *Brian Giles, of** | **$20,000** | **Other James Hurst (32), lhp** | **$12,500** |
| 9. Chad Allen, rhp | $12,000 | 18. *Stacy Hamm, of | $8,000 | | |

*Major leaguers in bold. *High school selection. #Signed as draft-and-follow.*

## Highest Unsigned Picks

| Player, Pos., Team (Round) | College | Re-Drafted |
|---|---|---|
| Charles Johnson, c, Expos (1) | Miami (Fla.) | Marlins '92 (1) |
| Calvin Murray, of, Indians (1) | Texas | Giants '92 (1) |
| Scott Burrell, rhp, Mariners (1) | Connecticut | Blue Jays '90 (5) |
| Chris Roberts, lhp/of, Phillies (2) | Florida State | Mets '92 (1) |
| Kenny Felder, of, Padres (2) | Florida State | Brewers '92 (1) |
| Michael Moore, of, Blue Jays (2) | UCLA | Dodgers '92 (1-S) |
| Stan Payne, lhp, Dodgers (2) | Georgia | Athletics '92 (12) |
| Phil Nevin, ss, Dodgers (3) | Cal State Fullerton | Astros '92 (1) |
| Jon Farrell, of/c, Cardinals (4) | Florida CC | Pirates '91 (1) |
| Jason Evans, ss, Cubs (4) | Oklahoma | White Sox '92 (12) |

**TOTAL UNSIGNED PICKS:** Top 5 Rounds (18), Top 10 Rounds (39)

Salkeld went 10-10, 5.61.

Despite the draft's aim to spread the wealth and level the playing field among big league clubs, the 1989 draft became more a case of the rich getting richer as the defending World Series champion Los Angeles Dodgers had five selections in the first two rounds, stemming from compensation for the loss of free agents. They secured more premium picks than any other club, and their fifth selection was made before the Oakland A's, the team the Dodgers beat to win the title, had made their first pick. The Dodgers owned five of the first 52 selections.

At a time when runaway inflation drove the draft, it was also noteworthy that the Dodgers spent at least $100,000 on each of their first four picks—though, curiously, were unable to sign the second of their second-rounders or their third-round selection.

Only outfielder Tom Goodwin (22nd overall), who twice led the NCAA ranks in stolen bases at Fresno State and was one of the fastest players in the draft, had a significant big league career among their premium selections. He hit .263 over 14 seasons and stole 365 bases.

The team's top pick, prep righthander Kiki Jones (15th overall), a power pitcher in a small, athletic package, began his career with considerable promise as he won his first 11 pro decisions. He got sidetracked by a combination of immaturity, off-field problems and injuries. Though he hung around pro ball until 2001, Jones spent only one season as high as Double-A, and won just 19 minor league games overall.

Goodwin, who hit a career-high .369 as a junior and stole 164 bases over his three-year college career, also had the distinction of being the last of three Fresno State players drafted in the first round, a feat that had been achieved only once before—in 1979, when three Michigan players, including lefthander Steve Howe, turned the trick.

Besides Goodwin and Zosky, drafted 19th overall by the Blue Jays, outfielder Steve Hosey was selected 14th overall by the San Francisco Giants.

Hosey not only had the highest upside among the three Fresno State first-rounders because of his imposing 6-foot-3, 220-pound frame, but his combination of above-average power and speed also made him one of the most attractive talents in the entire draft. He was also seen as one of the riskier first-rounders because his skills were not fully developed. He hit just .302 with six home runs as a junior after batting .365 with 13 homers as a sophomore. Hosey rarely asserted himself as a pro, and spent just 24 games in the majors.

Zosky's career was only marginally better, as he spent parts of five seasons in the big leagues and played in just 44 games. A top-notch defender with an outstanding throwing arm, Zosky also had great difficulty solving major league pitching.

Alan Zinter, selected 24th overall by the Mets as a switch-hitting catcher out of the University of Arizona, also had a brief big league career. He gained the distinction of taking 13 years to get there, longer than any first-rounder on record. He was called up by Houston in 2002, and played in only 67 games over two seasons while hitting just .167, but persevered in the minors for 19 seasons with nine different organizations, and slugged 250 homers. He spent 13 years of his career in Triple-A.

Meanwhile, Zinter's college teammate, Trevor Hoffman, went on to set the major league record for career saves—even after being drafted in the 11th round by the Cincinnati Reds as a light-hitting shortstop, signing for just $3,000 and playing his first two professional seasons at that position. Hoffman recognized his career was going nowhere fast as an everyday player after he hit just .227 with three homers in his first two pro seasons, but had the foresight to persuade the Reds to give him a chance on the mound to better utilize his superior arm strength.

That he did during the 1991 season, with positive results, as Hoffman went 2-1, 2.27 with 20 saves in 41 appearances at two stops in the Reds system, while also striking out 75 in 49 innings. Unfortunately, the Reds never benefited from Hoffman's startling transformation into a premier closer as he was lost to the Florida Marlins in the 1992 expansion draft. The Marlins then made the mistake of almost immediately trading him to San Diego, where his career blossomed.

Hoffman initially thrived on the strength of a mid-90s fastball, but an injury after the 1994 season forced him to reinvent himself and he subsequently developed one of the best changeups in the game. Over 16 seasons with the Padres, he saved 552 games. He finished his career with the Brewers and stretched his career saves total to 601—a major league record until Mariano Rivera eclipsed the mark in 2011.

## Largest Draft-And-Follow Bonuses

| | Player, Pos. | Club (Round) | Bonus |
|---|---|---|---|
| 1. | Joe Norris, rhp | Expos (26) | $130,625 |
| 2. | Keith Morrison, rhp | Braves (38) | $80,000 |
| **3.** | **Steve Cooke, lhp** | **Pirates (35)** | **$65,000** |
| **4.** | ***Matt Whisenant, lhp** | **Phillies (18)** | **$60,000** |
| | Randy Brown, ss | Red Sox (28) | $60,000 |
| | **Hilly Hathaway, lhp** | **Angels (35)** | **$60,000** |
| **7.** | **Kelly Stinnett, c** | **Indians (11)** | **$55,000** |
| 8. | *Corey Powell, of | Expos (64) | $40,000 |
| 9. | *Ned Darley, rhp | Blue Jays (11) | $35,000 |
| | **Garey Ingram, c** | **Dodgers (44)** | **$35,000** |
| | Terrance Tewell, c | Phillies (51) | $35,000 |

*Major leaguers in bold. *High school selection.*

### IN FOCUS: FRANK THOMAS

BILL NICHOLS

Rebuffed by baseball scouts and undrafted out of Columbus (Ga.) High in 1986, Frank Thomas accepted a football scholarship to Auburn and played briefly as a freshman tight end alongside Bo Jackson, the 1986 Heisman Trophy winner. When Thomas hit 22 homers as a freshman in the Southeastern Conference, he soon focused all his efforts on baseball. By 1989, there was no overlooking his considerable ability—or his aptitude for the game.

On a predraft psychological test administered by the Chicago White Sox, Thomas scored so high that Sox officials initially believed someone had taken the test for him. The New York Mets had him take a similar test and arrived at a similar conclusion, saying it was the highest score they had ever seen. Karl Kuehl, a special assistant for the Oakland A's, says he was among many evaluators who rated Thomas as a second- or third-round talent, and was quick to praise the White Sox.

"Chicago just did a hell of a job, getting to know a lot about him personally," Kuehl said. "They had an idea about his aptitude. The difference is Thomas' intelligence. My God, this guy never puts a bad at-bat out there. Capacity to improve: How do you scout that? You see the actions. But ability to improve is in the head and heart."

# 1989 Draft List

*Did not sign. Major leaguers in bold, with first and last years noted. Order of selection indicated in parentheses. For the first five rounds, the peak level of each player is noted. + Signed as draft-and-follow (Second school noted if applicable).

## ATLANTA BRAVES (2)

1. **Tyler Houston, c, Valley HS, Las Vegas, Nev.—(1996-2003)**
2. Tab Brown, rhp, St. Xavier HS, Louisville, Ky.—(Low A)
2. Brian Boltz, lhp, Catawba (N.C.) College (Supplemental choice—57th—as compensation for Type C free agent Rick Mahler).—(AA)
3. Kevin Castleberry, 2b, University of Oklahoma.—(AAA)
4. George Virgilio, 2b, Elizabeth (N.J.) HS.—(AA)
5. **Ryan Klesko, lhp-1b, Westminster (Calif.) HS.—(1992-2007)**
6. **Mike Mordecai, ss, University of South Alabama.—(1994-2005)**
7. Stuart McMillan, of, Withrow HS, Cincinnati.
8. Troy Hughes, of, Mount Vernon (Ill.) HS.
9. Nathan Fults, of-c, Franklin County HS, Decherd, Tenn.
10. David Williams, rhp, Westark (Ark.) CC.
11. Vincent Jiminez, c-ss, Rockdale (Texas) HS.
12. Brett Grebe, rhp, Westminster (Calif.) HS.
13. Tony Valle, rhp, Southwest Texas State University.
14. *Bo Siberz, rhp, Westark (Ark.) CC.
15. *Billy Morris, ss, Los Angeles Pierce JC.
16. Mark Beck, rhp, Cal State Fullerton.
17. Dickey Marze, of-2b, Northwestern State University.
18. **Joe Roa, rhp, Hazel Park (Mich.) HS.—(1995-2004)**
19. Darren Ritter, rhp, University of Maryland-Baltimore County.
20. *John Slate, lhp, Glenn HS, Winston-Salem, N.C.
21. *Chris Castro, rhp, Baldwin Park (Calif.) HS.
22. Tony Gallaher, rhp, Waite HS, Toledo, Ohio.
23. Jose Olmeda, ss, Oklahoma Baptist University.
24. *Thomas Niles, rhp, University of Southern Maine.
25. *Chris Kughn, of, University of Virginia.
26. Earl Steinmetz, rhp, Converse Judson HS, San Antonio, Texas.
27. ***Todd Greene, 3b, Evans HS, Martinez, Ga.—(1996-2006)**
28. Chris Burton, of, Sam Houston State University.
29. *Gilbert Johnson, of, Fairfax HS, Los Angeles.
30. *Jason Johnson, rhp, Williamsport (Pa.) HS.
31. Jason Ellis, c, Newton County HS, Conyers, Ga.
32. Earl Jewett, rhp, Wagner College.
33. Barry Chiles, rhp, East Wake HS, Raleigh, N.C.
34. *James Dillon, rhp, University of Maine.
35. *Clint Compton, rhp, Liberty Eylau HS, Texarkana, Texas.
36. *David Simon, of, Joplin (Mo.) HS.
37. Daniel Sims, of, Birmingham-Southern College.
38. +Keith Morrison, rhp, Middle Georgia JC.
39. +Kevin Walling, 1b, Kankakee (Ill.) CC
40. *Brett Misavage, rhp, Allegany (Pa.) CC.
41. *Joel Heath, ss-rhp, Tarkington HS, Cleveland, Texas.

DRAFT DROP *Twin brother of Jason Heath, 49th-round draft pick, Braves (1989)*

42. *John Harris, ss, Southwest HS, Fort Worth, Texas.
43. *William Noweck, rhp, Catonsville (Md.) CC.
44. *Jared Baker, rhp, Stratford HS, Goose Creek, S.C.
45. *Trent Petrie, ss, Menomonee (Wis.) HS.
46. *David Rollen, c, Panola (Texas) JC.
47. *Reginald Jackson, of-rhp, Atlanta (Texas) HS.
48. *Victor McCraney, of, Basic HS, Henderson, Nev.
49. *Jason Heath, ss, Tarkington HS, Cleveland, Texas.

DRAFT DROP *Twin brother of Joel Heath, 41st-round draft pick, Braves (1989)*

50. *Leron Rogers, 2b, Lutheran HS, Milwaukee.
51. Kevin Haeberle, rhp, Glendale (Ariz.) CC.
52. Travis Dunlap, rhp, Calallen, HS, Corpus Christi, Texas
53. *Walter Dunson, of, Central HS, Carrollton, Ga.
54. *David Hollingsworth, rhp, Memorial Day HS, Savannah, Ga.
55. *Willie Brown, of, Calhoun County HS, Edison, Ga.
56. Anthony Maye, rhp, Withrow HS, Cincinnati.
57. *Ken Musacchio, c, Great Bridge HS, Chesapeake, Va.
58. *Turner Williams, of, Bayside HS, Virginia Beach, Va.
59. *Kevin Cockrell, ss, Montreat-Anderson (N.C.) JC.
60. Gene Martin, of, Imperial Valley (Calif.) JC.
61. *Bryan White, of, Tri Cities HS, Hapeville, Ga.

## BALTIMORE ORIOLES (1)

1. **Ben McDonald, rhp, Louisiana State University.—(1989-97)**
2. Keith Schmidt, of, Burton (Texas) HS.—(Low A)
2. Tommy Taylor, rhp, Louisa County HS, Mineral, Va. (Choice from Mariners as compensation for Type B free agent Tom Niedenfuer).—(AA)
3. Eric Alexander, rhp, University HS, Los Angeles.—(Rookie)
4. T.R. Lewis, 3b, Sandalwood HS, Jacksonville, Fla.—(AAA)
5. Matt Anderson, lhp, Buena HS, Ventura, Calif.—(High A)
6. Allen Davis, of, Lee County HS, Sanford, N.C.
7. *Dan Melendez, 1b, St. Bernard HS, Mar Vista, Calif.
8. Shawn Heiden, rhp, Hillcrest HS, Sandy, Utah.
9. ***Mike Lansing, ss, Wichita State University.—(1993-2001)**
10. ***Chad Mottola, of, St. Thomas Aquinas HS, Pembroke Pines, Fla.—(1996-2006)**

DRAFT DROP *First-round draft pick (5th overall), Reds (1992)*

11. Gary Shingledecker, 2b, North Carolina State University.
12. **Brad Pennington, lhp, Vincennes University (Ind.) JC.—(1993-98)**
13. **Mike Oquist, rhp, University of Arkansas.—(1993-99)**
14. Aaron Norwood, of, Cerritos (Calif.) HS.

DRAFT DROP *Son of Willie Norwood, major leaguer (1977-80)*

15. Ed Horowitz, c, Rider College.
16. Dan Berthel, of, Long Beach State University.
17. **Gregg Zaun, c, St. Francis HS, Glendale, Calif.—(1995-2010)**

DRAFT DROP *Nephew of Rick Dempsey, major leaguer (1969-92)*

18. Brad Hildreth, ss, Mississippi State University.
19. Tony Beasley, ss-2b, Liberty University.
20. David Riddle, rhp, San Diego State University.
21. James Roso, c, Linn-Benton (Ore.) CC.
22. Pat Hedge, of, University of Hartford.
23. Chris Bastiste, of, Roosevelt HS, San Bernardino, Calif.
24. *Brad Gore, rhp, Taloga (Okla.) HS.
25. Mel Wearing, 1b, Norfolk State University.
26. +Michael Egelston, rhp, Johnson County (Kan.) CC.
27. *Henderson Mosley, of, Central State (Ohio) University.
28. ***Brian Bark, of-lhp, North Carolina State University.—(1995)**
29. Pat Leinen, lhp, University of Nebraska.
30. Mark Rupp, rhp, New Mexico State University.
31. *Greg D'Alexander, 3b-c, University of Arkansas.
32. Robert Wheatcroft, rhp, Cal State Northridge.
33. Doug Reynolds, c, Liberty University.
34. ***John Burke, rhp, Cherry Creek HS, Englewood, Colo.—(1996-97)**

DRAFT DROP *First-round draft pick (6th overall), Astros (1991); first-round draft pick (27th overall), Rockies (1992)*

35. *Vincent Jones, 1b, Nemo Vista HS, Center Ridge, Ark.
36. **Keith Kessinger, ss, University of Mississippi.—(1993)**

DRAFT DROP *Son of Don Kessinger, major leaguer (1964-79); major league manager (1979)*

37. *Sean Spellecy, of, Mesa (Ariz.) CC.
38. +Shawn O'Connell, rhp, Campolindo HS, Moraga, Calif. / Diablo Valley (Calif.) JC.
39. ***Brian Sackinsky, rhp, South Park HS, Library, Pa.—(1996)**
40. John Hemmerly, lhp, San Diego State University.
41. +Michael Wiley, lhp, Conway (Ark.) HS / Connors State (Okla.) JC.
42. David Brown, rhp, American International (Mass.) College.
43. *Anthony Bonifazio, of, Bishop Gorman HS, Las Vegas, Nev.
44. *Byron Mathews, of, Lafayette HS, Ballwin, Mo.
45. Richard Meek, of, Linn-Benton (Ore.) CC.
46. ***Brian Banks, c, Mountain View HS, Mesa, Ariz.—(1996-2003)**

## BOSTON RED SOX (23)

1. **Greg Blosser, of, Sarasota (Fla.) HS** (Choice from Padres as compensation for Type A free agent Bruce Hurst)**—(1993-94)**
1. **Mo Vaughn, 1b, Seton Hall University.—(1991-2003)**

DRAFT DROP *Son of Leroy Vaughn, running back, National Football League (1955)*

1. **Kevin Morton, lhp, Seton Hall University** (Supplemental choice—29th—as compensation for Hurst)**—(1991)**
2. **Jeff McNeely, of, Spartanburg Methodist (S.C.) JC.—(1993)**
3. **Eric Wedge, c, Wichita State University.—(1991-94)**

DRAFT DROP *Major league manager (2003-13)*

4. **Jeff Bagwell, 3b, University of Hartford.—(1991-2005)**
5. Tim Mitchell, 1b, Culver City HS, Los Angeles.—(Rookie)
6. **Paul Quantrill, rhp, University of Wisconsin.—(1992-2005)**
7. +Paul Anacki, rhp, Sandwich (Mass.) HS / Wilbraham (Mass.) Academy.
8. *Stoney Burke, c, Avon HS, Danville, Ind.
9. Cedric Santiago, lhp, Central Juvenil HS, Yauco, P.R.
10. **Greg Hansell, rhp, Kennedy HS, La Palma, Calif.—(1995-99)**
11. Jason Freidman, of-1b, Cypress (Calif.) JC.
12. *Peter Janicki, rhp, El Dorado HS, Placentia, Calif.

DRAFT DROP *First-round draft pick (8th overall), Angels (1992)*

13. *Chris Wimmer, 2b, East HS, Wichita, Kan.
14. *Fred Starks, rhp-of, Rockledge (Fla.) HS.
15. James Dennison, lhp, Jacksonville State University.
16. Tim Graham, of, Lancaster (Ohio) HS.
17. Colin Dixon, 1b, Southeastern Louisiana University.
18. Lawrence Grant, ss, Ballard HS, Seattle.
19. H.B. Awkard, of, Nelson County HS, Faber, Va.
20. *B.J. Wallace, lhp, Monroe Academy HS, Monroeville, Ala.

DRAFT DROP *First-round draft pick (3rd overall), Expos (1992)*

21. Ernie Brown, rhp, Catonsville (Md.) CC.
22. Brian Conroy, rhp, University of Massachusetts.
23. *Dom DeSantis, rhp, Miami-Dade CC North.
24. Troy Vann, of, San Francisco CC.
25. Terre Woods, c, Hinds (Miss.) JC.
26. *Sean Darrock, of, Mission Bay HS, San Diego.
27. *Mark Williams, of, Patrick Henry (Ala.) JC.
28. +Randy Brown, ss, San Jacinto (Texas) JC.
29. *Tracy Wildes, rhp, Sandalwood HS, Jacksonville, Fla.
30. David Ring, rhp, Columbia Central HS, Columbia, Tenn.
31. *Jerald Shelton, 3b, Shelton State (Ala.) JC.
32. *Sean Hickman, lhp, Linn-Benton (Ore.) CC.
33. +John Lammon, c, Solano (Calif.) CC.
34. Bryan Niemeyer, of, Minster (Ohio) HS.
35. *Michael Hickey, ss, Edmond Memorial HS, Edmond, Okla.
36. Willie Dukes, of, Mississippi Delta JC.
37. *Michael Canton, ss, San Augustine (Texas) HS.
38. Melvin Gonzales, rhp, Camuy Arenas HS, Arecibo, P.R.
39. John Malzone, of, North Adams State (Mass.) College.

DRAFT DROP *Son of Frank Malzone, major leaguer (1955-66)*

40. John Locker, rhp, University of Michigan.
41. *Roberto Santa, 1b, Arecibo (P.R.) HS.

## CALIFORNIA ANGELS (9)

1. **Kyle Abbott, lhp, Long Beach State University.—(1991-96)**
2. **Joe Grahe, rhp, University of Miami.—(1990-99)**
3. **Tim Salmon, of, Grand Canyon College.—(1992-2006)**
4. **Erik Bennett, rhp, Cal State Sacramento.—(1995-96)**
5. Terry Taylor, 2b, Texas A&M University.—(AA)
6. David Staydohar, of, American River (Calif.) JC.
7. Marvin Cobb, rhp, University of Oklahoma.
8. Rick Hirtensteiner, of, Pepperdine University.
9. Fili Martinez, lhp, Cal State Northridge.
10. Ron Lewis, of, Florida State University.

DRAFT DROP *Wide receiver, National Football League (1990-94)*

11. *Jeff Rhein, of, Sacramento (Calif.) CC.
12. *Mike Couture, c, Clemson University.
13. Clifton Garrett, lhp-of, Roberto Clemente HS, Chicago.
14. Kent Williams, of, University of South Alabama.
15. Wayne Helm, rhp, Pepperdine University.
16. Eric Martinez, rhp, Mira Mesa HS, San Diego.
17. Ricky Goode, rhp, Porterville (Calif.) JC.
18. Dave Adams, rhp, Ohio University.
19. Rick Parker, c, Tulane University.
20. Brian Specyalski, 2b-ss, University of Connecticut.
21. Jewell Walker, rhp, University HS, Los Angeles.
22. David Rice, rhp, Cal Poly Pomona.
23. Bob Jones, of, Cal State Fullerton.
24. Willy Warrecker, lhp, University of California.
25. Chris Allen, 1b, Florida Southern College.
26. *Brian Dodd, lhp, Arizona State University.
27. Matt Lasher, ss, James Madison University.
28. +Norman Montoya, lhp, Chabot (Calif.) JC.
29. **Paul Swingle, rhp, Grand Canyon College.—(1993)**
30. ***Joe Randa, ss, Delafield, Wis.—(1995-2006)**
31. Ron Tallent, c, Wooster Prep, Winthrop, Mass.
32. Tim Pinkowski, rhp, Lewis (Ill.) University.
33. Jeff Kilpatrick, of, Florida Southern College.
34. Henry Threadgill, 2b, Clemson University.
35. **+Hilly Hathaway, lhp, Manatee (Fla) JC.—(1992-93)**
36. Les Haffner, rhp, University of South Florida.
37. ***Chris Gomez, ss, Lakewood (Calif.) HS.—(1993-2008)**
38. +Ken House, 3b, Cabrillo (Calif.) JC.
39. Douglas Canney, lhp, Salem (Mass.) HS.
40. Bryan Street, c, Simeon HS, Chicago.
41. Jose Santana, of, Martin Methodist (Tenn.) College.
42. James Jones, rhp, University of Connecticut.
43. Drew Peterson, 3b, Brighton HS, Sandy, Utah.
44. *Glenn Osinski, ss, Triton (Ill.) JC.
45. **Chad Curtis, of, Grand Canyon College.—(1992-2001)**
46. *John Jackson, of, University of Southern California.

DRAFT DROP *Wide receiver, National Football League (1990-96)*

47. *Allen Rath, rhp, University of Iowa.
48. *Jon Anderson, c, Georgia Tech.
49. Chris Rios, of, College of the Southwest (N.M.).
50. *James Mason, c, Liberty University.
51. *Carlton Davenport, 2b, UC Santa Barbara.

## CHICAGO CUBS (8)

1. Earl Cunningham, of, Lancaster (S.C.) HS.—(High A)
2. **Gary Scott, 3b, Villanova University.—(1991-92)**
3. Billy White, ss, University of Kentucky.—(AAA)
4. *Jason Evans, ss, Chatsworth (Calif.) HS.—(AAA)

DRAFT DROP *Attended Oklahoma; re-drafted by White Sox, 1992 (12th round)*

5. *Darrick Duke, 1b-of, Reagan HS, Houston, Texas.—(Low A)

DRAFT DROP *Attended Texas; re-drafted by Padres, 1993 (12th round)*

6. Calvin Ford, of, Ontario (Calif.) HS.
7. Edgardo Larregui, of, Villa Carolina HS, Carolina, P.R.
8. Travis Willis, rhp, University of California.
9. **Dave Swartzbaugh, rhp, Miami (Ohio) University.—(1995-97)**
10. *Gordon Sanchez, c, San Marcos (Calif.) HS.
11. Richie Grayum, of, Mississippi State University.
12. Timothy Moore, ss, La Habra HS, Whittier, Calif.
13. *David DeMoss, of, North Marion HS, Fairmont,

W.Va.
14. *Jamie Sepeda, rhp, Sinton (Texas) HS.
15. Aaron Taylor, rhp, Wooster HS, Reno, Nev.
16. Mike Little, 1b-of, Biloxi (Miss.) HS.
17. Brad Erdman, c, Cochise County (Ariz.) CC.
18. Chris Ebright, of, University of Oklahoma.
19. (void) *Edwin Corps, rhp, Ciem HS, Carolina, P.R.
**20. +David Stevens, rhp, La Habra (Calif.) HS / Fullerton (Calif.) JC.—(1994-2000)**
21. Steve DiBartolomeo, rhp, University of New Haven.
22. Dale Craig, c, Hancock (Calif.) JC.
23. Freddie Hill, rhp, Hinds (Miss.) JC.
24. Kalani Bush, rhp, Loyola Marymount University.
25. Ray Mack, rhp, Sumter (S.C.) HS.
26. Kevin Dalson, ss, Michigan State University.
27. *Tony Pena, rhp, Mater Dei HS, Santa Ana, Calif.
28. Scott Teague, lhp, University of North Carolina-Asheville.
29. Eric Jaques, lhp, Indiana University.
30. Micah Murphy, 1b, Lee (Texas) JC.
31. Mark Linden, 3b, Whitworth (Wash.) College.
DRAFT DROP *Brother of Todd Linden, major leaguer (2003-07)*
32. Doug Welch, of, Lubbock Christian (Texas) University.
33. Don Gillespie, lhp, Eisenhower HS, Rialto, Calif.
34. *Matthew Hess, 3b, Dixon (Ill.) HS.
35. Randy Sodders, 2b, Hillsborough (Fla.) CC.
36. +Charlie Fiacco, 2b, UCLA.
37. *Joe Wise, rhp, Georgia Tech.
38. Rene Francisco, of, Jacksonville University.
39. Amilcar Correa, rhp, San Sebastian (P.R.) HS.
40. *Felix Holguin, rhp, Deming (N.M.) HS.
41. *Angel Allende, c, Papa Juan XXIII HS, Bayamon, P.R.
42. *Raymon Martinez, ss, Superior Catholic HS, Bayamon, P.R.
43. *Juan Debrand, ss, Chipola (Fla.) CC.
44. *Shawn Gift, of, Gilbert (Ariz.) HS.
45. *Axel Ortiz, 3b, Luis Verone HS, Loiza, P.R.
46. *Bennie Mayberry, of, Pima (Ariz.) CC.
47. Clinton White, of, JC of the Desert (Calif.).
48. *Edwin Zayas, rhp, Isidro Sanchez HS, Luquillo, P.R.
49. *Robert Boisvert, of, Housatonic (Conn.) CC.
50. *Michael Barber, rhp, Elsinore HS, Lake Elsinore, Calif.
51. *Lonnie Webb, 3b, South Georgia JC.
52. *Hector Reyes, rhp, Francisco Morales HS, Naranijito, P.R.
53. *Gary Goldsmith, rhp, Alamogordo (N.M.) HS.
54. *Timothy Sharp, rhp, Three Rivers (Mo.) CC.

## CHICAGO WHITE SOX (7)

**1. Frank Thomas, 1b, Auburn University.—(1990-2008)**
DRAFT DROP *Elected to Baseball Hall of Fame, 2014*
2. Don Sheppard, of, Pittsburg (Calif.) HS.—(AAA)
3. Todd Martin, ss, Morehead HS, Eden, N.C.—(Short-season A)
4. Dan Matznick, rhp, Sterling (Ill.) HS.—(High A)
5. Mike Eatinger, 3b, UC Riverside.—(High A)
6. John Smith, rhp, Garrett (Md.) CC.
7. Mike Mongiello, rhp, Fairleigh Dickinson University.
8. *John Sutherland, rhp, UCLA.
**9. Kevin Tolar, lhp, Mosley HS, Panama City, Fla.—(2000-03)**
10. *Scotty Pugh, 1b, Cooper HS, Abilene, Texas.
11. Gregory Kobza, 1b, Texas Tech.
12. David Van Winkle, rhp, Northwestern University.
13. Adam Sanders, ss, Hanover (Ind.) College.
**14. *Keith Johns, ss, Sandalwood HS, Jacksonville, Fla.—(1998)**
15. *Doug Shields, of, Southern Illinois University.
16. *Rollie Caridad, rhp, Westminster Christian HS, Miami.
17. Scott Stevens, rhp, Brookdale (N.J.) CC.
**18. Richard Long, lhp, Eastern Washington University.**
**19. Brian Keyser, rhp, Stanford University.—(1995-96)**
20. Scott Thoma, rhp, Texas Christian University.
21. Jorge Ruiz, rhp, University Gardens HS, Rio Piedras, P.R.
22. James Robinson, rhp, Northwestern University.
23. Scott Cepicky, 1b, University of Wisconsin.
24. Greg Perschke, rhp, University of New Orleans.
25. Kevin Conover, lhp, Rutgers University.
26. Randy Norris, of, High Point College.
27. Bobby Hunter, rhp, Mainland HS, South Day, Fla.
28. Thomas Borgula, rhp, Northwestern University.
29. *David Geeve, rhp, Oakton (Ill.) CC.
30. *John Reece, of, Jersey Village HS, Houston.
31. *Michael Potter, rhp, Potterville HS, Dimondale, Mich.
**32. Joe Borowski, rhp, Bayonne (N.J.) HS.—(1995-2008)**
33. *T.J. O'Donnell, 2b-ss, Hazlet (N.J.) HS.
34. *Dean Locklear, lhp, Seminole (Okla.) JC.
35. *Chris Gump, 3b, Westwood HS, Tempe, Ariz.
36. *Jon French, ss-2b, Modesto (Calif.) JC.
37. *Richard Paschal, lhp, Coronado HS, Phoenix.
38. *Harry Durkin, ss-2b, Cardinal Gibbons HS, Fort Lauderdale, Fla.
DRAFT DROP *Brother of Marty Durkin, 38th-round draft pick, Indians (1989)*
39. Horace Gaither, ss-2b, Southern University.
40. *Matt Klusener, lhp, Shawnee Heights HS, Topeka, Kan.
41. *Bobby Reed, rhp, Mississippi State University.
42. Michael Davino, rhp, University of South Carolina-Aiken.
43. Dan Monzon Jr., 3b-2b, Pace (N.Y.) University.
DRAFT DROP *Son of Dan Monzon, major leaguer (1972-73)*

## CINCINNATI REDS (20)

1. Scott Bryant, of-rhp, University of Texas.—(AAA)
2. Aaron Goins, of, Owasso (Okla.) HS.--DNP
**3. Ross Powell, lhp, University of Michigan.—(1993-95)**
4. *Paul Jackson, of, Oldham County HS, LaGrange, Ky.--DNP
DRAFT DROP *Attended Western Kentucky; never re-drafted*
**5. Darron Cox, c, University of Oklahoma.—(1999)**
**6. Tim Pugh, rhp, Oklahoma State University.—(1992-97)**
7. *Bert Inman, rhp, Westwood HS, Austin, Texas.
8. Charles Wyatt, rhp, Pflugerville HS, Manor, Texas.
9. Rafael Diaz, lhp, Escuela Superior Catolica HS, Bayamon, P.R.
10. Rick Allen, 3b, Loyola Marymount University.
**11. Trevor Hoffman, ss, University of Arizona.—(1993-2007)**
DRAFT DROP *Brother of Glenn Hoffman, major leaguer (1980-89); major league manager (1998)*
12. Jamie Dismuke, 1b, Corcoran HS, Syracuse, N.Y.
13. Steve Vondran, 3b-c, Fresno State University.
14. Todd Watson, 3b, Howard University.
15. Noel Velez, 3b-1b, Alcides Figueroa HS, Anasco, P.R.
16. *J.J. Picollo, c, Cherry Hill West HS, Cherry Hill, N.J.
17. *Kenneth Neal, of, Memphis Catholic HS, Memphis, Tenn.
18. Bob Dombrowski, 3b, Arizona State University.
19. Sean Doty, rhp, Linn-Benton (Ore.) CC.
20. Harry Henderson, 1b, San Diego State University.
21. Bob Blankenship, rhp, Cal State Sacramento.
22. Mark Borcherding, rhp, Bradley University.
23. Frank Kremblas, c, Eastern Kentucky University.
24. Dale Stevens, rhp, Seminole (Fla.) CC.
25. Jack Hollis, of, Stanford University.
26. Mark Cerny, of, University of Houston.
27. Gilbert Galloway, rhp, Northwestern State University.
28. Carlos Molina, c, Vega Baja (P.R.) HS.
29. *Darrin Glenn, 2b, Howard (Texas) CC.
30. Torin Berge, 1b, Metropolitan State (Colo.) College.
31. Eric Bates, rhp, Cal State Sacramento.
32. Brian Fry, lhp, Monroe (N.Y.) CC.
33. *Bruce Smolen, ss, Kishwaukee (Ill.) JC.
**34. Scott Pose, of, University of Arkansas.—(1993-2000)**
35. James Burns, of, Crockett (Texas) HS.
36. *John Kostro, of, Thomas Jefferson HS, Denver.
37. *Todd Unrein, lhp, University of Southwestern Louisiana.
38. Andy Duke, of, Texas A&M University.
39. Thomas Aubertin, rhp, St. Louis CC-Meramec.
40. +Chris Vasquez, of, Hart HS, Newhall, Calif. / JC of the Canyons (Calif.)
41. *Julian Velez, rhp, Mets de Guaynabo HS, Bayamon, P.R.
42. *Jerry Grider, rhp, Cooper HS, Abilene, Texas.
**43. *Sean Lowe, rhp, Mesquite (Texas) HS.—(1997-2003)**
DRAFT DROP *First-round draft pick (15th overall), Cardinals (1992)*
44. *Jonathan Bates, ss, Arlington (Texas) HS.
45. *Scott Dodd, lhp, Glendale (Ariz.) CC.
46. *Jason Carroll, rhp, Putnam HS, Milwaukie, Ore.
47. *Tim Boge, c, Muscatine (Iowa) CC.
48. *James Nix, ss, Brenham (Texas) HS.
49. *Donnie Carlisle, rhp, Brewer HS, Fort Worth, Texas.
50. Mark Roberts, ss, Dixie (Utah) JC.
51. *Thomas Yerly, rhp, Hall HS, Spring Valley, Ill.
52. Shawn Ledet, lhp, H.L. Bourgeois HS, Houma, La.
53. *Tim Grieve, rhp, Martin HS, Arlington, Texas.
DRAFT DROP *Son of Tom Grieve, major leaguer (1970-79); general manager, Rangers (1985-94) • Brother of Ben Grieve, first-round draft pick, Athletics (1994); major leaguer (1997-2004)*
54. *Jeffery Leftin, of, Beechwood HS, Fort Mitchell, Ky.
55. *Lee Reiber, c, Meridian (Idaho) HS.

## CLEVELAND INDIANS (11)

**1. *Calvin Murray, 3b-of, W.T. White HS, Dallas.—(1999-2004)**
DRAFT DROP *Attended Texas; re-drafted by Giants, 1992 (1st round)*
2. (Choice to Dodgers as compensation for Type B free agent Jesse Orosco)
**3. Jerry Dipoto, lhp, Virginia Commonwealth University.—(1993-2000)**
DRAFT DROP *General manager, Angels (2011-15)*
**4. Jesse Levis, c, University of North Carolina.—(1992-2001)**
**5. Alan Embree, lhp, Prairie HS, Vancouver, Wash.—(1992-2009)**
6. Mark Charbonnet, of, Gahr HS, Cerritos, Calif.
7. John Martinez, c, Juana Diaz (P.R.) HS.
**8. Curtis Leskanic, rhp, Louisiana State University.—(1993-2004)**
9. Chad Allen, rhp, Gonzaga University.
10. John Cotton, 2b, Angelina (Texas) JC.
**11. +Kelly Stinnett, c, Seminole (Okla.) JC.—(1994-2007)**
12. Von Wechsberg, rhp, Camarillo (Calif.) HS.
**13. Jim Thome, ss, Illinois Central JC.—(1991-20012)**
14. Nolan Lane, of, St. Xavier (Ill.) College.
15. Tom Lachmann, c, Columbia Basin (Wash.) CC.
**16. *Mike Potts, lhp, Lithonia (Ga.) HS.—(1996)**
**17. Brian Giles, of, Granite Hills HS, El Cajon, Calif.—(1995-2009)**
18. Stacy Hamm, of, Valhalla HS, El Cajon, Calif.
19. Marcus Robertson, of, Iowa State University.
DRAFT DROP *Defensive back, National Football League (1991-2002)*
20. Dennis Kluss, of, Veneta, Ore.
21. Avery Johnson, ss, Texas Southern University.
22. Charles Davis, 1b, West Georgia College.
23. +Miguel Flores, ss, Burbank HS, San Antonio, Texas / Laredo (Texas) CC.
24. Jeffrey Hancock, 2b, Dallas Baptist University.
**25. Robert Person, ss-of, Seminole (Okla.) JC.—(1995-2003)**
**26. *Billy Brewer, lhp, Dallas Baptist University.—(1993-99)**
27. Tommy Tillman, lhp, University of North Carolina-Wilmington.
28. Joseph Perez, of, James Monroe HS, Bronx, N.Y.
29. Alan Walden, rhp, Cleveland State (Tenn.) CC.
30. *Kraig Constantino, 1b, Mission (Calif.) JC.
**31. Bill Wertz, rhp, Ohio State University.—(1993-94)**
**32. James Hurst, lhp, Florida Southern College.—(1994)**
**33. *Andy Sheets, ss, St. Amant (La.) HS.—(1996-2002)**
34. Ronald Young, of, UC Riverside.
35. *Jeffrey Weibel, c, North Kitsap HS, Poulsbo, Wash.
36. *Jeff Martin, c, Goodpasture HS, Godlettsville, Tenn.
37. Michael Soper, rhp, University of Alabama.
38. Marty Durkin, 2b, Georgia Tech.
DRAFT DROP *Brother of Harry Durkin, 38th-round draft pick, White Sox (1989)*
39. Gene Mirabella, rhp, Brookdale (N.J.) CC.
40. *David Norwood, rhp, Lehigh University.
41. *Barry Sheperd, rhp, Angelina (Texas) JC.
42. +Dickie Brown, rhp, Connors State (Okla.) JC.
43. *Chris Johnson, rhp, Red Oak (Texas) HS.
44. *James Walker, rhp, Connors State (Okla.) JC.
45. +Michael Shirley, of, Southwestern Michigan JC.
46. Scott Johnson, 1b, Allegheny (Pa.) JC.
47. *Cary Conklin, rhp, University of Washington.
48. *R.D. Long, ss, Webster HS, Penfield, N.Y.
49. *Ken Kaveny, 1b, Linn-Benton (Ore.) CC.
50. *Gavin Saladino, 3b, McClancy HS, Howard Beach, N.Y.
51. *Michael Strobel, 3b, Bonanza HS, Las Vegas, Nev.
52. *Eric Snell, of, Hamilton West HS, Trenton, N.J.
53. *Darrin Kotch, lhp, Rutgers University.
54. Erik Young, of, Baldwin-Wallace (Ohio) College.
55. +Barry O'Neil, of, Lower Columbia (Wash.) JC.

## DETROIT TIGERS (21)

**1. Greg Gohr, rhp, Santa Clara University.—(1993-96)**
2. Brad Wilson, c, Towns County HS, Hiawassee, Ga.—(High A)
3. Gino Tagliaferri, ss, Kennedy HS, Granada Hills, Calif.—(Low A)
**4. *Paul Carey, of, Stanford University.—(1993)**
DRAFT DROP *Returned to Stanford; re-drafted by Miami/Florida State League, 1990 (4th round)*
5. David Keating, of, UCLA.—(AA)
**6. *Doug Mirabelli, c, Valley HS, Las Vegas, Nev.—(1996-2007)**
7. Eric Albright, c, Texas A&M University.
**8. John DeSilva, rhp, Brigham Young University.—(1993-95)**
9. Kelley O'Neal, 2b, Belleville (Mich.) HS.
10. Jody Hurst, of, Mississippi State University.
11. Bub Maietta, rhp, Dubois Area (Pa.) HS.
12. Keith Langston, rhp, Texas A&M University.
13. Jeff Goodale, of, UC Riverside.
14. Robert Davis, of, Colerain HS, Cincinnati.
15. Mark Cole, ss, University of Oklahoma.
16. Frank Gonzales, lhp, Colorado State University.
17. Pat Pesavento, ss, University of Notre Dame.
18. Chris Hall, ss, Don Lugo HS, Chino, Calif.
**19. John Doherty, rhp, Concordia (N.Y.) College.—(1992-96)**
20. Keith Kimberlin, ss, Missouri Baptist College.
21. Ken Lewis, of, Cosumnes River (Calif.) JC.
22. Michael Bowman, rhp, Montreat-Anderson (N.C.) JC.
23. Jim Heins, rhp, Vanderbilt University.
24. Daniel Cruz, of, Papa Juan XXIII HS, Bayamon, P.R.
25. Tim Herrmann, rhp, Texas A&M University.
26. *Derrick Copes, of, Angelina (Texas) JC.
27. Doug Marcero, lhp, Western Michigan University.
**28. Ivan Cruz, 1b, Jacksonville University.—(1997-2002)**
29. Craig Middlekauff, of-1b, Santa Clara University.
30. Bob Reimink, 2b, Western Michigan University.
31. David Wilson, rhp, Cal Poly San Luis Obispo.
32. Freddie Gamble, ss, Manning (S.C.) HS
**33. Mark Ettles, rhp, University of West Florida.—(1993)**
34. Kasey McKeon, c, San Diego State University.
DRAFT DROP *Scouting director, Reds (2001-02) • Son of Jack McKeon, major league manager (1973-2005)*
35. Stephen Matchett, rhp, Pembroke State (N.C.) University.
36. Mac Seibert, 1b, Jacksonville State University.
37. *Bradley Lamont, rhp, Michigan State University.
38. *Joel Shapiro, rhp, Jacksonville University.
39. Matt Coleman, rhp, University of Kentucky.
40. *Mike Bianco, c, Lousiana State University.
DRAFT DROP *Baseball coach, McNeese State (1998-*

*2000); baseball coach, Mississippi (2001-15)*
41. Brian Rountree, rhp, University of South Carolina.
42. *Randy Rivera, rhp, Oklahoma State University.
43. Brian Cornelius, of, Southern University.
44. Mario Moccia, 1b, New Mexico State University.
45. +Jim Henry, lhp, Sacramento (Calif.) CC.
46. Matt Logue, rhp, Coastal Carolina University.
47. *Kevin Taylor, rhp, Waukegan East HS, Waukegan, Ill.
48. *Marcus Ortiz, lhp, Fajardo Raiders, Bayamon, P.R.
49. *Chris Bailey, ss, Garfield HS, Seattle.
50. *Michael Bond, ss, Walbrook HS, Baltimore.
51. *Michael Parker, rhp, North Hagerstown (Md.) HS.
52. Samuel Ubinas, c, Aguas Buenas HS, Caguas, P.R.
53. Brian Dubose, 1b, Redford St. Mary's HS, Detroit.
54. *Tony Muser, 2b, Cerritos (Calif.) JC.
DRAFT DROP *Son of Tony Muser, major leaguer (1969-78); major league manager (1997-2002)*
**55. Mike Garcia, rhp, Riverside (Calif.) JC.—(1999-2000)**
56. Lance Daniels, of, Clayton Valley HS, Concord, Calif.
**57. *Scott Klingenbeck, rhp, Oak Hills HS, Cincinnati.—(1994-98)**
58. *Todd Kelly, 1b, Bethel HS, Hampton, Va.
59. *Scott Simmons, lhp, Three Rivers (Mo.) CC.

## HOUSTON ASTROS (12)

**1. Jeff Juden, rhp, Salem (Mass.) HS.—(1991-99)**
DRAFT DROP *First 1989 high school draft pick to reach majors (Sept. 15, 1991)*
**1. Todd Jones, rhp, Jacksonville State University** (Supplemental choice—27th—as compensation for Class A free agent Nolan Ryan)**—(1993-2008)**
**2. Brian Hunter, of, Fort Vancouver HS, Vancouver, Wash.** (Choice from Rangers as compensation for Ryan)**—(1994-2003)**
2. Jermaine Swinton, of, Fort Hamilton HS, Brooklyn, N.Y.—(High A)
**3. Shane Reynolds, rhp, University of Texas.—(1992-2004)**
4. Tyrone Scott, lhp, Leuzinger HS, Palmdale, Calif.—(Low A)
5. *Jack Stanczak, 1b-3b, LaSalle HS, Philadelphia.—(High A)
DRAFT DROP *Attended Villanova; re-drafted by Mariners, 1992 (17th round)*
6. Scott Makarewicz, c, Michigan State University.
7. Gershon Dallas, of, Hillsborough (Fla.) CC.
8. Craig Curtis, of, North Kansas City (Mo.) HS.
9. Cole Hyson, rhp, University of Arkansas.
10. Mark Hampton, rhp, Southwest Mississippi JC.
11. Ken Wheeler, rhp, Chillicothe (Ohio) HS.
12. Lance Madsen, of, University of Utah.
13. Glen Reyes, ss, Orange Glen HS, Escondido, Calif.
14. *Robert Ferguson, rhp, Glendale (Ariz.) CC.
15. P.J. Riley, of, Southern Illinois University.
16. Corey Diggs, 3b, Hogan HS, Vallejo, Calif.
**17. Mark Small, rhp, Washington State University.—(1996)**
**18. Donne Wall, rhp, University of Southwestern Louisiana.—(1995-2002)**
19. *Mike Condon, c, Harris County HS, Pine Mountain, Ga.
20. *Marcus Lee, of, Mount Carmel HS, San Diego.
21. Anthony Lucin, c, Morton (Ill.) JC.
**22. *Ricardo Jordan, lhp, Miami-Dade CC South.—(1995-98)**
23. *Jeffrey Slider, lhp, San Bernardino Valley (Calif.) JC.
24. +David Wallace, of, Howard (Texas) CC.
25. *Brian Fontes, rhp, McLane HS, Fresno, Calif.
26. *Paul Dalzochio, rhp, DeAnza (Calif.) JC.
27. *Geoff Grenert, rhp, Coronado HS, Scottsdale, Ariz.
28. *Michael Houck, rhp, Redondo HS, Redondo Beach, Calif.
29. David Richison, ss-2b, Texarkana (Texas) CC.
30. *Dominic Herness, rhp, San Bernardino Valley (Calif.) JC.
31. Howard Prager, of, University of Texas-Arlington.
32. Kevin Scott, c, Washington State University.
33. +Steve Veit, 1b, Mesa (Ariz.) CC.

MORRIS FOSTOFF

**Brewers first-round righthander Cal Eldred spent more than a decade in the major leagues**

34. *Frank Castillo, rhp, North HS, Denver.
35. *Gerardo Diaz, of, Inter American HS, Carolina, P.R.
36. *David Angotti, c, Valhalla HS, El Cajon, Calif.
37. *Greg Almond, c, Bay HS, Panama City, Fla.
38. *Rob Henkel, rhp, Irving (Texas) HS.
39. *David Duplessis, lhp-of, Los Medanos (Calif.) JC.
40. *Mike Bailey, of, Eisenhower HS, Yakima, Wash.
41. *Rod McCall, 1b, Rancho Alamitos HS, Stanton, Calif.
42. Steve Boatman, rhp, Coppell (Texas) HS.
43. *Shawn Wills, of, UCLA.
44. *Matt Ruoff, 3b, Casa Grande HS, Petaluma, Calif.
45. Ruben Cruz, of, Cidra HS, Salinas, P.R.
46. +Bryan Smith, of, Texarkana (Texas) CC.
47. *Clarke Rea, c, Scottsdale (Ariz.) CC.
48. *Andre Earthly, c, Smiley HS, Houston.
49. *Chris Gies, rhp, Temple University.
50. *James Henderson, of, Los Angeles Harbor JC.
51. *Richard Williams, rhp, Lamar HS, Houston.
52. *John Elder, rhp, Terry Parker HS, Jacksonville, Fla.
53. Mike McDowell, rhp, Eastern Washington University.
54. *Donald Strayer, of, Plant HS, Tampa.
55. *Carl Stall, ss, Paragould (Ark.) HS.
56. *Alan Walania, rhp, Notre Dame HS, Derby, Conn.
57. *Bradley West, of, Dansville (N.Y.) HS.
58. *David Maice, c, Weber HS, Chicago.
59. *Jeff Boatner, of, Columbus (Ga.) HS.
60. *Darrell McMillin, 3b, Ventura (Calif.) JC.
61. *Alfred Kermode, rhp, Chandler (Ariz.) HS.
62. +John Vandemark, lhp, Lockport (N.Y.) HS / Florida CC-Jacksonville.
63. *Marc Claus, ss, Cardinal Gibbons HS, Fort Lauderdale, Fla.
64. *William Brockschmidt, rhp, Mater Dei HS, Tustin, Calif.
65. *Chad Phillips, rhp, Orange Coast (Calif.) JC.
66. *Craig Fairbrother, of, Cerritos (Calif) JC.
67. *Rollie Jacobson, of-1b, Palm Desert HS, Rancho Mirage, Calif.
68. *Brian Carpenter, rhp, Marble Falls (Texas) HS.
69. *Floyd White, 1b-of, Jones County HS, Gray, Ga.
70. *Clark Cole, 1b, Columbus (Ga.) HS.
71. *Steve Cromwell, of, Spencer HS, Columbus, Ga.
72. *Todd Jarvis, lhp, Drury HS, North Adams, Mass.
**73. *Ryan Karp, of-lhp, Los Angeles Harbor JC.—(1995-97)**
74. *Steven Hernandez, ss, Ocean View HS, Huntington Beach, Calif.
75. +Gary Christopherson, 3b, Ocean View HS, Huntington Beach, Calif. / Orange Coast (Calif.) JC.
76. *James Short, 1b, Cypress (Calif.) JC.
77. *Jason Dailey, 1b-3b, Anderson HS, Austin, Texas.
78. *Scott Mowl, 1b, Cerritos (Calif.) JC.
79. *William Fitzgerald, rhp, Katella HS, Anaheim, Calif.
80. *John Parr, rhp, JC of the Redwoods (Calif.).
81. *Kevin Schula, c, Cypress (Calif.) JC.
82. *Matthew Lackie, rhp, Rancho Santiago (Calif.) JC.
83. *John DeRicco, 3b, University of Nevada-Reno.
84. *Michael Petrich, of, University of Minnesota-Duluth.
85. Mario Prats, lhp, Coral Park HS, Miami.
86. *Dean Haskins, c, Santa Rosa (Calif.) JC
**87. *Desi Wilson, 1b, Fairleigh Dickinson University.—(1996)**

## KANSAS CITY ROYALS (13)

**1. Brent Mayne, c, Cal State Fullerton.—(1990-2004)**
2. Rick Tunison, 1b, Brevard (Fla.) JC.—(AA)
2. Lance Jennings, c, El Rancho HS, Pico Rivera, Calif. (Supplemental choice—58th—as compensation for Type C free agent Jamie Quirk).—(AA)
3. Ed Gerald, of, St. Paul's (N.C.) HS.—(AA)
4. *Ray Suplee, of, Sarasota (Fla.) HS.—(High A)
DRAFT DROP *Attended Georgia; re-drafted by Yankees, 1992 (6th round)*
5. Brian Ahern, rhp, University of Central Florida.—(AAA)
6. Bubba Dunn, rhp, Volunteer State (Tenn.) JC.
**7. Ed Pierce, of-lhp, Orange Coast (Calif.) JC.—(1992)**
**8. Matt Karchner, rhp, Bloomsburg State (Pa.) University.—(1995-2000)**
9. *Keith Adaway, of, Parkway South HS, Ballwin, Mo.
10. Chris Schaefer, rhp, Indiana State University.
11. Clint Foster, rhp, Frankston (Texas) HS.
12. Gary Caraballo, 3b, Luis Munoz Marin HS, Yauco, P.R.
13. Sean Collins, of, Kansas State University.
14. Colin Ryan, c, University of Maine.
15. Scott Centala, rhp, Texas A&M University.
16. David King, 1b, University of Southwestern Louisiana.
17. Chris Jones, 3b, Serra HS, Lawndale, Calif.
18. Kirk Thompson, of, Texas A&M University.
19. Michael Webster, lhp, Grand Canyon College.
20. Kirk Baldwin, lhp, Central Missouri State University.
21. David Ritchie, ss, East Carolina University.
22. Donald Lindsey, lhp, Michigan State University.
23. Ben Pardo, lhp, University of Houston.
24. Louis Talbert, rhp, Lassen (Calif.) JC.
25. *Kevin Nielsen, lhp, San Diego State University.
26. *Jay Hassel, rhp, El Dorado HS, Placentia, Calif.
**27. Andres Berumen, rhp, Banning (Calif.) HS.—(1995-96)**
28. Darnell Dickerson, of, University of Pittsburgh.
29. Patrick Murphy, 3b, Hanover (Ind.) College.
30. David Solseth, c, Grand View (Iowa) College.
31. Kevin Long, of, University of Arizona.
32. Herbert Milton, rhp, Smiley HS, Houston.
33. Javier Alvarez, ss, Marin (Calif.) JC.
34. *Enoc Rosado, c, Humacao (P.R.) HS.
35. *George Liebert, of, Zion Benton HS, Zion, Ill.
36. *Arnie Sambel, of, University of San Francisco.
37. Eric West, rhp, West Orange-Stark HS, Orange, Texas.
38. Rodney Rodgers, rhp, University of Iowa.
39. +Gabriel Pineda, rhp, San Bernardino Valley (Calif.) JC.
40. *Torreahno Sweet, of, Serra HS, Los Angeles.
41. *Jackie Kellogg, of, Clover Park HS, Tacoma, Wash.
42. *Conrad Colby, 1b, Rancho Santiago (Calif.) JC.
43. Jay Andrews, ss, Smiley HS, Houston.
44. *Shawn Purdy, rhp, Indian River (Fla.) CC.
45. *Reginal Ricketts, c, Soddy-Daisy HS, Hixon, Tenn.
46. *Cristobal Rodriguez, rhp, Manuela Toro Morice HS, Caguas, P.R.
47. *Joel Cartagena, rhp, Rio Piedras (P.R) HS.
48. *Sean Drinkwater, ss, El Toro (Calif.) HS.
49. +Ricky Moser, rhp-3b, Lakeland (Fla.) HS / Polk State (Fla.) CC.
50. *Chris Coulter, lhp, Beech HS, Goodlettsville, Tenn.
51. *Randall Parks, rhp, Northeastern Oklahoma A&M JC.
52. *Kevin Ashworth, 1b, Pacifica HS, Garden Grove, Calif.
**53. *Victor Darensborg, lhp, Westchester HS, Los Angeles.—(1998-2005)**
54. +George Day, ss, Northeastern Oklahoma A&M JC.
55. *Robert Mosser, rhp, Oley Valley HS, Oley, Penn.
56. *David Toth, c, Brookdale (N.J.) CC.
57. *Javier Robles, rhp, La Cumbre-Micke HS, Cantera Santurce, P.R.
58. *Kenny Marrero, c, University of Politecnica HS, Dorado, P.R.
59. *John Dean, of, Topeka (Kan.) HS
60. Rod Stillwell, ss, University of Arkansas.
DRAFT DROP *Son of Ron Stillwell, major leaguer (1961-62) • Brother of Kurt Stillwell, first-round draft pick, Reds (1983); major leaguer (1986-96)*

## LOS ANGELES DODGERS (22)

1. Kiki Jones, rhp, Hillsborough HS, Tampa (Choice from Yankees as compensation for Type A free

agent Steve Sax).—(AA)

**1. Tom Goodwin, of, Fresno State University.—(1991-2004)**

**1. Jamie McAndrew, rhp, University of Florida** (Supplemental pick—28th—as compensation for Sax)—**(1995-97)**

DRAFT DROP *Son of Jim McAndrew, major leaguer (1968-74)*

2. Bill Lott, of, Petal HS, Hattiesburg, Miss (Choice from Indians as compensation for Type B free agent Jesse Orosco).—(AAA)

DRAFT DROP *Son of Billy Rex Lott, running back/National Football League (1958-63)*

2. *Stan Payne, lhp, Clarke Central HS, Athens, Ga.—(Short-season A)

DRAFT DROP *Attended Georgia; re-drafted by Athletics, 1992 (12th round)*

**3. *Phil Nevin, ss, El Dorado HS, Placentia, Calif.—(1995-2006)**

DRAFT DROP *Attended Cal State Fullerton; re-drafted by Astros, 1992 (1st round, 1st pick)*

4. Javier DelaHoya, rhp, Grant HS, Van Nuys, Calif.—(AAA)
5. John Deutsch, 1b, Montclair State (N.J.) University.—(AA)
6. Tim Barker, ss, Virginia Commonwealth University.
7. Bryan Baar, c, Western Michigan University.
8. Jason Brosnan, lhp, Fresno State University.
9. Barry Parisotto, rhp, Gonzaga University.

**10. *Kevin Jordan, 2b, Canada (Calf.) JC.—(1995-2001)**

11. *Dennis Burbank, rhp, Cypress (Calif.) JC.
12. Garrett Teel, c, William Paterson (N.J.) College.
13. Lee DeLoach, ss-2b, Rutgers University-Camden.
14. Michael Wismer, of, Villanova University.
15. Keith Daniel, rhp, Pender HS, Currie, N.C.
16. Frank Humber, lhp, Wake Forest University.
17. Pedro Gonzalez, c, Miami-Dade CC North.
18. Audelle Cummings, rhp, Ohio Dominican College.
19. Mike Potthoff, rhp, University of Missouri.
20. Gary Forrester, ss, University of Nevada-Las Vegas.
21. Mike Galle, 3b, Purdue University.
22. Billy Miller, of, San Diego State University.
23. Craig White, ss-2b, Slippery Rock State (Pa.) University.
24. Rex Peters, 1b, Cal State Fullerton.
25. Javier Puchales, of, Caguas (P.R.) Skill Center.
26. Craig Bishop, lhp, Erie (N.Y.) CC.
27. Raymond Bielanin, rhp, Niagara University.
28. Ray Calhoun, rhp, Spartanburg Methodist (S.C.) JC.
29. Tim Patrick, lhp, Sacramento (Calif.) CC.
30. *Jerome Santivasci, rhp, Clemson University.
31. Darnell Whims, of, Thomas Johnson HS, Frederick, Md.
32. Yale Fowler, of-1b, Cal State San Bernardino.
33. *John Farren, c, Villanova University.

**34. Matt Howard, 2b, Pepperdine University.—(1996)**

35. *Albert Drumheller, lhp-of, Shenandoah Area (Pa.) HS.
36. Steve O'Donnell, 1b, La Salle University.
37. Helmut Bohringer, 3b, Adelphi (N.Y.) University.
38. Daniel Stupur, 2b-3b, George Fox (Ore.) College.
39. Joe Seals, c, Belmont (Tenn.) College.
40. Jimmy Brown, ss-2b, Carlos Escobar Lopez HS, Loiza, P.R.
41. +Ross Farnsworth, lhp, Pinole (Calif.) HS / Diablo Valley (Calif.) JC.
42. *Roger Sweeney, of, San Rafael (Calif.) HS.

**43. Eric Young, of, Rutgers University.—(1992-2006)**

DRAFT DROP *Father of Eric Young Jr., major leaguer (2009-15)*

**44. +Garey Ingram, c, Middle Georgia JC.—(1994-97)**

45. *Melvin Warren, of, Fairfield (Calif.) HS.
46. *Ray Bowen, lhp, San Diego Mesa JC.
47. *Martin Kilian, rhp, San Jose (Calif) CC.
48. *Mark Lundeen, lhp, Napa (Calif.) HS.
49. *Daniel Poulton, rhp, Minidoka HS, Heyburn, Idaho.
50. *Brannon Veal, of, Middle Georgia JC.
51. *Patrick Reed, ss, Castlemont HS, Oakland, Calif.
52. +Don Meyers, 1b-3b, Sacramento (Calif.) CC.
53. *Gaither Bagsby, rhp, Roane State (Tenn.) CC.
54. +Robert Hoffman, c, Contra Costa (Calif.) JC.
55. *Timothy McDermott, c, Millard South HS, Omaha, Neb.
56. *Brian Van Horn, lhp, Pinconning HS, Bentley, Mich.
57. *Richard Josepher, 1b-3b, St. Rita HS, Chicago.
58. *Bradley Cohen, of, Meridian (Miss.) JC.
59. *Charles Williams, of, Lumberton (Miss.) HS.
60. *Pete Altenberger, rhp, Purdue University.
61. *Brent Prudhomme, 1b, Kaplan (La.) HS.
62. Rich Crane, lhp, Fresno State University.

## MILWAUKEE BREWERS (17)

**1. Cal Eldred, rhp, University of Iowa.—(1991-2005)**

1. Gordon Powell, 3b, Hughes HS, / Cincinnati (Supplemental choice—30th—for failure to sign 1988 first-round draft choice Alex Fernandez).—(High A)
2. Rusty Rugg, lhp, Downsville (La.) HS.—(Rookie)
3. Bo Dodson, 1b, Christian Brothers HS, Sacramento, Calif. (Choice from Mariners as compensation for Type B free agent Jeffrey Leonard).—(AAA)
3. John Byington, 3b, Texas A&M University.—(AAA)
4. Bill Brakeley, lhp, University of Delaware.—(Low A)
5. Jason Zimbauer, rhp, Andrew HS, Orland Hills, Ill.—(Low A)
6. Tony Diggs, 2b, University of North Florida.

**7. *Danny Perez, of, Hanks HS, El Paso, Texas.—(1996)**

8. Brant McCreadie, rhp, Kaiser HS, Honolulu, Hawaii.
9. Eric Patton, rhp, Saddleback (Calif.) CC.
10. John Finn, 3b, Arizona State University.
11. Timothy Wilson, rhp, St. Andrew's (N.C.) College.
12. Daren Cornell, ss, Cal Lutheran University.
13. *Steven Hegan, of, South Pontotoc (Miss.) HS.
14. Darrin White, c, Blinn (Texas) JC.
15. Kenneth Harris, of, Taft (Calif.) JC.
16. Mitch Hannahs, 2b, Indiana State University.

DRAFT DROP *Baseball coach, Indiana State (2014-15)*

17. Geoff Kellogg, rhp, Mead HS, Spokane, Wash.
18. Scott Muscat, rhp, University of North Carolina-Charlotte.
19. Kevin Tannahill, c, San Jose State University.
20. Arthur Butcher, of, University of Texas.
21. David Weldin, of, Bakersfield (Calif.) JC.
22. *Brian Gore, ss, Sterling HS, Baytown, Texas.
23. Bob Vancho, rhp, Housatonic (Conn.) CC.
24. Sam Drake, rhp, Georgia Tech.
25. *Manny Gagliano, ss, Crawford HS, San Diego.
26. *Scott Cline, 3b, UCLA.
27. Michael Johnson, c, University of Wisconsin-Milwaukee.
28. *Demerius Pittman, of, Workman HS, La Puente, Calif.
29. *Derek January, lhp, Bridgeton Academy HS, Swampscott, Mass.
30. *Charles Walker, of, Starmount HS, Booneville, N.C.
31. *Timothy Smith, rhp, Boston College.
32. *Bill Barber, lhp, St. Petersburg (Fla.) JC.
33. *Shane Smith, lhp, W.C. Hinkley HS, Aurora, Colo.
34. *Jay Patterson, of, Cabrillo (Calif.) JC.
35. William Robertson, of, Mesa State (Colo.) College.
36. Rocky Ynclan, rhp, University of Hawaii.
37. *Jesse Villanueva, rhp, Evergreen HS, Vancouver, Wash.
38. Rusty Charpia, ss, Clemson University.
39. *Marc Tsitouris, 3b, Wingate (N.C.) College.

DRAFT DROP *Son of John Tsitouris, major leaguer (1957-68)*

40. James Walker, of, Rio Piedras (P.R.) JC.
41. Justin McCray, ss-3b, Cal Poly San Luis Obispo.
42. *Donald Culberson, of, East Central (Miss.) JC.

**43. *Jason Giambi, ss, South Hills HS, Covina, Calif.—(1995-2014)**

DRAFT DROP *Brother of Jeremy Giambi, major leaguer (1998-2003)*

44. *Jason Grabosch, 1b-3b, Coronado HS, Tucson, Ariz.
45. *Fausto Tejero, c, Florida International University.
46. *Scott Rose, rhp, Hillsborough (Fla.) CC.

**47. *Sean Whiteside, 1b-of, West Davidson HS, Lexington, N.C.—(1995)**

## MINNESOTA TWINS (25)

**1. Chuck Knoblauch, ss, Texas A&M University.—(1991-2002)**

2. John Gumpf, of, Poly HS, Riverside, Calif.—High A)

**3. Denny Neagle, lhp, University of Minnesota.—(1991-2003)**

**4. Scott Erickson, rhp, University of Arizona.—(1990-2006)**

5. *Jay Richardson, of, Northside HS, Fort Smith, Ark.--DNP

DRAFT DROP *Attended Westark (Ark.) JC; never re-drafted*

6. Ken Norman, of, Sweetwater (Texas) HS.
7. Ray Ortiz, of, Oklahoma State University.
8. Jeff Thelen, rhp, Craig HS, Janesville, Wis.
9. Troy Buckley, c, Santa Clara University.

DRAFT DROP *Baseball coach, Long Beach State (2011-15)*

**10. Marty Cordova, 3b, Orange Coast (Calif.) JC.—(1995-2003)**

**11. Dan Masteller, 1b, Michigan State University.—(1995)**

12. Alvin Brown, c, Los Angeles CC.
13. Timmy Moore, of, Rose HS, Greenville, N.C.

**14. Mike Trombley, rhp, Duke University.—(1992-2002)**

**15. George Tsamis, lhp, Stetson University.—(1993)**

16. David Krol, rhp, University of Toledo.
17. *Chad McConnell, of, Ogorman HS, Sioux Falls, S.D.

DRAFT DROP *First-round draft pick (13th overall), Phillies (1992)*

18. Mike House, 1b, Hawaii Pacific College.
19. Bob McCreary, rhp, Villanova University.
20. Javier Fimbres, 1b, Cerritos (Calif.) JC.
21. Tim Nedin, lhp, Florida State University.
22. Rex Delanuez, of, Cal State Los Angeles.

**23. *Derrick White, 3b, Santa Rosa (Calif.) JC.—(1993-98)**

24. Ken Briggs, c, Chapman (Calif.) College.
25. Phil Wiese, lhp, University of New Orleans.
26. *Jeff Pearce, of, JC of Marin (Calif.).
27. Tom Houk, ss, Lincoln Land (Ill.) CC.
28. *Ben Lindsey, c, Lakeland HS, Croton, N.Y.

**29. *Tom Urbani, lhp, Long Beach State University.—(1993-96)**

30. Jody Bryant, of, Twin Falls (Idaho) HS.
31. Mike Lloyd, ss, St. Leo (Fla.) College.
32. Francisco Ramirez, c, Vega Alta (P.R.) HS.
33. +Allen Hayes, of, Forestbrook HS, Houston / Angelina (Texas) JC.
34. *Gregory Bowles, of, Cleveland State (Tenn.) JC.
35. *Todd Johnson, c, Bullard HS, Fresno, Calif.
36. Bradley Brooks, 1b-rhp, Western New Mexico University.
37. Randy Gentile, 3b, Illinois State University.
38. *Richard Faulks, lhp, Cal State Fullerton.
39. David Bigham, lhp, West HS, Rogers, Minn.
40. Jon Pittenger, 3b, University of Missouri.
41. Robert Schiel, ss, St. Cloud State (Minn.) University.
42. John Howard, of, Pasadena (Calif.) CC.
43. Joe Siwa, c, Auburn University.
44. Bryan Asp, rhp, North Hennepin (Minn.) CC.
45. *James Dorough, lhp, Lafayette HS, Lexington, Ky.
46. *Steve Stuart, lhp, Prairie HS, Ridgefield, Wash.
47. *Michael Jewell, rhp, Sacramento (Calif.) CC
48. *Reggie Jackson, lhp-of, Lake Wales (Fla.) HS.
49. +Charles Wallgren, c, Sacramento (Calif.) CC.
50. *Scotty Smith, rhp, Baylor HS, Chattanooga, Tenn.
51. +Todd Blakeman, 1b, Lakeland (Ohio) CC

**52. +Denny Hocking, c, El Camino (Calif.) JC.—(1993-2005)**

53. *Scott Shell, 3b, Red Bank HS, Hixon, Tenn.
54. *Anthony Spaan, ss, Saddleback (Calif.) CC.
55. *Mark Burke, rhp, West HS, Rockford, Ill.
56. *Sam Vranjes, c, University of Southern California.
57. Todd Logan, c, Eastern Washington University.
58. Karl King, c, Mount St. Mary's HS, Oklahoma City, Okla.
59. *Timothy Leppert, c, Brown County HS, Nineveh, Ind.

DRAFT DROP *Son of Don Leppert, major leaguer (1861-64)*

## MONTREAL EXPOS (10)

**1. *Charles Johnson, c, Westwood HS, Fort Pierce, Fla.—(1994-2005)**

DRAFT DROP *Attended Miami (Fla.); re-drafted by Marlins, 1992 (1st round)*

**2. Glenn Murray, c, Manning (S.C.) HS.—(1996)**

3. Ron Krause, ss, North HS, Eastlake, Ohio.—(AA)

**4. Brian Barnes, lhp, Clemson University.—(1990-94)**

5. Dan Hargis, c, Eastern Illinois University.—(High A)

**6. Pete Young, rhp-3b, Mississippi State University.—(1992-93)**

7. *Jeff Brohm, ss, Trinity HS, Louisville, Ky.

DRAFT DROP *Quarterback, National Football League (1996-97)*

8. *Walter Camp, rhp, Leonard HS, Lake Worth, Fla.

**9. Doug Bochtler, rhp, Indian River (Fla.) CC.—(1995-2000)**

10. Mike Fier, lhp, Mankato State (Minn.) University.
11. John Thoden, rhp, University of North Carolina.
12. Paul Ciaglo, lhp, University of Massachusetts.
13. *James Martin, of, Eufaula (Okla.) HS.
14. Gus Santiago, 3b, Buena (N.J.) HS.
15. Buck Atwater, ss, Southern Alamance HS, Graham, N.C.
16. *Greg Margheim, lhp, Virginia Tech.
17. Andrew Swain, rhp, Purdue University.
18. *Kelton Jacobson, rhp, Kennedy HS, Seattle.
19. James Heilgeist, of, Liberty HS, Issaquah, Wash.

**20. F.P. Santangelo, ss, University of Miami.—(1995-2001)**

21. *Craig Stiveson, rhp, Pepperdine University.
22. Rusty Kilgo, lhp, Arizona State University.
23. Michael Regira, rhp, Nicholls State University.
24. *Hector Rodriguez, 3b, Arroyo (P.R.) HS.
25. Duane Ashley, rhp, Yerba Buena HS, San Jose, Calif.
26. +Joe Norris, rhp, Bakersfield (Calif.) JC.
27. Bill Cramer, c, Cal State Sacramento.
28. Joseph Logan, rhp, Florida Southern College.
29. Pressley Herron, ss-of, West Mecklenburg HS, Charlotte, N.C.
30. Charles Smith, 1b, Tennessee State University.
31. *Harold Williams, 1b, East St. John HS, Garyville, La.
32. Todd Mayo, of, University of California.
33. Gary Pipik, of, Florida Southern College.
34. Deryk Hudson, 3b, Long Beach State University.
35. Robert Small, c, Cal State Chico.
36. *Ronnie Quijada, rhp, Mount Pleasant HS, San Jose, Calif.
37. *John Rodgers, c, Waxahachie (Texas) HS.
38. James Eddy, rhp, Marietta (Ohio) College.
39. *Chris Stewart, rhp, Christian Brothers HS, Memphis, Tenn.
40. *James Bell, c, Mesa (Ariz.) CC.
41. *Shane Warenski, lhp, Granger HS, West Valley, Utah.
42. *Gary Adams, of, Science Hill HS, Johnson City, Tenn.
43. James Wallkvist, rhp, San Francisco CC.
44. Tyrone Horne, of, West Montgomery HS, Troy, N.C.
45. *Todd A. Taylor, c, South Florida JC.
46. *Todd H. Taylor, lhp, Millikan HS, Long Beach, Calif.
47. Michael Romberg, rhp, U.S. International (Calif.) University.
48. Chris Etheridge, c, Whitevllle (N.C.) HS.
49. *Shawn Henrichs, rhp, Hermiston (Ore.) HS.
50. Hector Rivera, of, Banonguitas (P.R.) HS.
51. Gary Young, rhp, San Jacinto (Texas) JC.
52. *Richard Greenwell, c, Shelby County HS, Shelbyville, Ky.
53. Fernando Torres, rhp, Las Piratas HS, Rio Piedras, P.R.
54. *Troy Kopp, c, Mission Viejo HS, Dana Point, Calif.

DRAFT DROP *Quarterback, Canadian Football League (1998-2000)*

55. *Heath Altman, of-ss, Richmond HS, Hamlet, N.C.

56. *Alan Beavers, rhp, Scottsdale (Ariz.) CC.
57. *Todd Hall, ss, El Dorado HS, Placerville, Calif.
58. *Corey McCormick, lhp-of, Burbank HS, Sacramento, Calif.
59. +Matt Conley, rhp, Moreno Valley (Calif) HS / San Jacinto (Texas) JC.
60. *Riley McKelvey, ss, North Greenville (S.C.) JC.
61. *Michael Bieger, rhp, JC of the Desert (Calif.).
62. *Michael Morland, c, Canada (Calif.) JC.
63. *Paul Carpentier, 3b, Montclair (Calif.) HS.
64. +Corey Powell, of, Grossmont HS, San Diego / Grossmont (Calif.) JC.
65. *Chad Dembisky, rhp, Lassen (Calif.) JC.
66. *Kevin Cerveny, rhp, Palomar (Calif.) JC.
67. *Cornell Caldwell, of, Independence HS, Charlotte, N.C
68. Christopher Ellis, c-of, Cave Spring HS, Roanoke, Va.
69. Abimael Rodriguez, ss, Hatillo (P.R.) HS.

## NEW YORK METS (24)

1. **Alan Zinter, c, University of Arizona.—(2002-04)**

DRAFT DROP *Brother of Ed Zinter, 38th-round draft pick, Padres (1989)*

2. Tom Engle, rhp, Fairfield Union HS, Lancaster, Ohio.—(AAA)
3. **Brook Fordyce, c, St. Bernards HS, Old Lyme, Conn.—(1995-2004)**
4. Tim McClinton, of, Downers Grove North HS, Woodridge, Ill.—(High A)
5. Paul Meyer, c, Patrick Henry HS, Minneapolis.—(Rookie)
6. Rob Rees, rhp, Lake Washington HS, Kirkland, Wash.
7. **Butch Huskey, 3b, Eisenhower HS, Lawton, Okla.—(1993-2000)**
8. Derek Henderson, ss, Tennesee State University.
9. *Nathaniel Florell, of-rhp, Sullivan HS, Chicago.
10. *Scot McCloughan, rhp-ss, Loveland (Colo.) HS.

DRAFT DROP *Son of Kent McCloughan, wide receiver/ National Football League (1965-70)*

11. *Ritchie Moody, lhp, Brookville (Ohio) HS.
12. Jay Davis, lhp, Orr HS, Chicago.
13. Ed Vazquez, rhp, Baruch (N.Y.) College.
14. Chris Butterfield, of, Cal Poly Pomona.
15. *Sean Hogan, lhp, Bishop Rosecrans HS, Nashport, Ohio.
16. *Kendall Rhine, rhp, Parkview HS, Lilburn, Ga.

DRAFT DROP *First-round draft pick (37th overall), Astros (1992)*

17. ***Mark Grudzielanek, ss, Hanks HS, El Paso, Texas.—(1995-2007)**
18. Omar Garcia, 1b, Concepcion de Gracia HS, Carolina, P.R.
19. *Clint Whitworth, rhp, Frederick (Okla.) HS.
20. Tim Buhe, ss, Northwestern University.
21. *Jason Angel, rhp, Hermitage HS, Glen Allen, Va.
22. Marcel Johnson, 1b, Fremont HS, Oakland, Calif.
23. **Mike Thomas, lhp, Labette (Kan.) JC.—(1995)**
24. **Joe Vitko, rhp, St. Francis (Pa.) College.—(1992)**
25. *Jeff Hostetler, lhp, Science Hill HS, Johnson City, Tenn.
26. *David Hutcheson, rhp, Chamberlain HS, Tampa.
27. *Todd Harris, lhp, Taft (Calif.) CC.
28. *Thomas Bates, ss, Paris (Texas) JC.
29. *Will Hunt, lhp, Asher HS, Byars, Okla.
30. *Joseph Petcka, rhp, Everest HS, Clintonville, Wis.
31. **Dave Telgheder, rhp, University of Massachusetts.—(1993-98)**
32. *Ronald Miller, ss, Ruskin HS, Kansas City, Mo.
33. Steven Graves, c, University of Southern Mississippi.
34. *Robert Dodd, lhp, Sacramento (Calif.) CC.
35. Jerome Tolliver, 1b, Bacone (Okla.) JC.
36. Arness Rittman, 3b-2b, Shanks HS, Quincy, Fla.
37. +Joe Arredondo, 3b, Cerritos (Calif.) JC.
38. Joe Delli Carri, ss, University of Pennsylvania.

DRAFT DROP *Scouting director, Pirates (2012-15)*

39. *Leon Clay, of, Texas Christian University.
40. Eric Thornton, of, Faulkner (Ala.) University.
41. Michael Hemmerich, lhp, Marian (Ind.) College.
42. *Clayton Klavitter, 3b, Glendale (Ariz.) CC.
43. *Kevin Magers, of, Nettleton (Miss.) HS.
44. *Clifford Hamilton, of, Diablo Valley (Calif.) JC.
45. James Scheffler, rhp, Joliet (Ill.) JC.
46. *Craig Gienger, of, Douglas County HS, Castle Rock, Colo.
47. *Erskine Kelley, ss, Freeport (N.Y.) HS.
48. +Ottis Smith, lhp, Goodrich HS, Fond du lac, Wis. / Kishwaukee (Ill.) JC.
49. *Ronald Ollison, 2b-ss, Malvern (Ark.) HS.
50. Michael Freitas, rhp, Sacramento (Calif.) CC.
51. *Clifford Krull, rhp-of, Bonduel (Wis.) HS.
52. *Brian Thompson, of, Sunset HS, Hayward, Calif.
53. Jaime Hoffner, 1b, Mankato State (Minn.) University.
54. +Tim Sandy, 1b-of, Fargo, N.D. / Kishwaukee (Ill.) JC.

## NEW YORK YANKEES (15)

1. (Choice to Dodgers as compensation for Type A free agent Steve Sax)
2. **Andy Fox, 3b, Christian Brothers HS, Sacramento, Calif.—(1996-2004)**
3. Jason Robertson, of, Hillcrest HS, Country Club Hills, Ill.—(AAA)
4. Adin Lohry, c-3b, Winter Park (Fla.) HS.—(AA)
5. **J.T. Snow, 1b, University of Arizona.—(1992-2008)**

DRAFT DROP *Son of Jack Snow, wide receiver, National Football League (1965-75)*

6. Larry Stanford, rhp, Florida International University.
7. **Russ Springer, rhp, Louisiana State University.—(1992-2010)**
8. Scott Romano, 3b, Hillsborough HS, Tampa.
9. **Sterling Hitchcock, lhp, Armwood HS, Seffner, Fla.—(1992-2004)**
10. Richard Turrentine, rhp, Arkansas HS, Texarkana, Ark.
11. James Mauldin, rhp, Texas Tech.
12. Jim Wiley, rhp, Westark (Ark.) JC.
13. Mike Gardella, lhp, Oklahoma State University.
14. ***Ricky Greene, rhp, Coral Gables (Fla.) HS.—(1999)**

DRAFT DROP *First-round draft pick (16th overall), Tigers (1992)*

15. *Ernie Yaroshuk, of-1b, Christopher Columbus HS, Miami.
16. **Brian Johnson, 3b-of, Stanford University.—(1994-2001)**
17. Richard Barnwell, of, Pepperdine University.
18. *Keith Seiler, lhp, University of Virginia.
19. Tim Cooper, 3b-ss, Hiram Johnson HS, Sacramento, Calif.
20. Rich Polak, rhp, University of Central Florida.
21. Aaron Van Scoyoc, ss, Westark (Ark.) JC.
22. Jose Vazquez, 2b, Florida International University.
23. Peter Gietzen, lhp, Florida International University.
24. James Haller, lhp, Kansas State University.
25. Joel Petlick, rhp, Pfeiffer (N.C.) College.
26. *Chris Martin, ss, Pepperdine University.
27. *Tony Khoury, c, Bowsher HS, Toledo, Ohio.
28. ***Dennis Konuszewski, rhp, Bridgeport (Mich) HS.—(1995)**
29. *Marty Posey, of, Gulf Coast (Fla.) CC.
30. *Troy Penix, 1b, Tokay HS, Stockton, Calif.
31. *Jeff Asnicar, lhp, Enterprise HS, Redding, Calif.
32. John Jarvis, c, University of Southwestern Louisiana.
33. Todd Devereaux, of, University of Arizona.
34. Ricky Strickland, of, Austin Peay State University.
35. *Bob Baxter, lhp, Harvard University.
36. Paul Oster, of, University of Oklahoma.
37. *Agusto Padilla, 1b, Camuy (P.R.) HS.
38. **Rich Batchelor, rhp, University of South Carolina-Aiken.—(1993-97).**
39. James Moody, rhp, Huntingdon (Ala.) College.
40. Brian Turner, of, Grand Valley HS, Orwell, Ohio.
41. *Daniel Heidman, rhp, Hoban HS, Akron, Ohio.
42. *Arthur Johnson, ss, Denham Springs (La.) HS.
43. ***Jorge Posada, ss, Rio Piedras (P.R.) HS.—(1995-2011)**
44. **+Mike Figga, c, Central Florida CC.—(1997-99)**
45. *Robert Glenn, lhp, George Wallace (Ala.) CC.
46. *Timothy Jones, rhp-of, American River (Calif.) JC.
47. *Shad Mix, 3b, Mission (Calif.) JC.
48. Tim Garland, of, Pensacola (Fla.) JC.
49. *Joel Schaedler, rhp, Holy Name HS, Berea, Ohio.
50. *Joseph Finley, c, Columbia (Miss.) HS.
51. +Tim Demerson, of, Howard (Texas) JC.
52. *Bruce Freeman, c, Clarksdale HS, Meridian, Miss.
53. *Jeffrey Stych, of, Southeast HS, Lincoln, Neb.
54. *Malcolm Jordan, of, Santa Rosa (Calif.) JC.
55. *Scott Pace, lhp, Roosevelt Roads HS, Fajardo, P.R.
56. *Eric Ford, ss, Brandon (Miss.) HS.
57. Gerald Davis, of, Chadsey HS, Detroit.
58. *Brian Jackson, rhp, Bonner Springs (Kan.) HS.
59. *Jeff Pickett, c, Allen County (Kan.) CC.
60. Rey Noriega, of, University of Miami.
61. Bo Gilliam, of, Florida A&M University.

## OAKLAND ATHLETICS (26)

1. (Choice to Mariners as compensation for Type B free agent Mike Moore)
2. **Scott Lydy, of, South Mountain (Ariz.) CC.—(1993)**
3. Mike Grimes, rhp, University of Michigan.—(High A)
4. Darin Kracl, rhp, Brigham Young University.—(High A)
5. Scott Erwin, rhp, Georgia Tech.—(AA)
6. **Steve Chitren, rhp, Stanford University.—(1990-91)**
7. Scott Shockey, 1b, Pepperdine University.
8. **Craig Paquette, 3b, Golden West (Calif.) JC.—(1993-2003)**
9. Gavin Osteen, lhp, Allegany (Md.) CC.

DRAFT DROP *Son of Claude Osteen, major leaguer (1957-75)*

10. Todd Smith, rhp, Lassen (Calif.) JC.
11. *Levon Largusa, lhp, Mount Eden HS, Hayward, Calif.
12. Russ Cormier, rhp, Northeastern University.
13. *Rodney Peete, 3b, University of Southern California.

DRAFT DROP *Quarterback, National Football League (1989-2004)*

14. Brett Hendley, 1b, Georgia Southern College.

DRAFT DROP *Son of Bob Hendley, major leaguer (1961-67)*

15. **Kurt Abbott, ss, St. Petersburg (Fla.) JC.—(1993-2001)**
16. Darryl Vice, 2b, University of California.
17. *Andy Beasley, c, Virginia Military institute.
18. Scott McCarty, lhp, San Jacinto (Texas) JC.
19. Mike Conte, of, Virginia Tech.
20. ***Matt Mieske, of, Western Michigan University.—(1993-2000)**
21. **Dana Allison, lhp, James Madison University.—(1991)**
22. *Walter Rivera, rhp, Chipola (Fla.) JC.
23. *John Tejeck, ss, Mount Carmel HS, San Diego.
24. Russell Miller, rhp, Anderson (S.C.) JC.
25. Doug Twitty, of-1b, University of Nebraska.
26. Lee Sammons, of, Augusta (Ga.) College.
27. *Charles McCray, rhp, University of Florida.
28. Todd Russell, rhp, Pearl River (Miss) JC.
29. Trent Weaver, 3b-2b, Baylor University.
30. *James Wilkie, rhp, Portage (Ill.) HS.
31. Brad Brimhall, rhp, Ricks (Idaho) JC.
32. Ed Tredway, c, Flagler (Fla.) College.
33. David Latter, rhp, University of Southern California.
34. *Sean Hardwick, rhp, North Myrtle Beach (S.C.) HS.
35. *Dallas Rhinehart, rhp, Sullivan Central HS, Kingsport, Tenn.
36. *Richard Lovan, lhp, Lakewood HS, Long Beach, Calif.
37. Fred Cooley, rhp-3b, University of Southern Mississippi.
38. Jim Gibbs, rhp, San Diego State University.
39. Mario Lyons, of, Eastern Washington University.
40. Jeffrey Lynch, rhp, UC Santa Barbara.
41. Brad Eager, c, Brigham Young University.
42. **Mike Mohler, lhp, Nicholls State University.—(1993-2001)**
43. Eric Campa, ss, San Bernadino Valley (Calif.) JC.
44. James Waggoner, ss, Austin Peay State University.
45. Daniel Orr, rhp, Glendale (Ariz.) CC.
46. Hugh Gulledge, rhp, Enterprise State (Ala.) JC.
47. Kevin Lofthus, 1b, University of Nevada-Las Vegas.
48. Sean Krokroskia, of, Southwest Oklahoma State University.
49. Scott Henry, c, University of South Florida.
50. Gary Ross, rhp, Grossmont (Calif.) JC.
51. Ruben Lardizabal, rhp, Cochise County (Ariz.) CC.
52. *Clifford Jones, lhp-of, Laney (Calif.) JC.
53. *Roderick Walker, c, Morristown West HS, Morristown, Tenn.
54. *Christopher Lohman, 3b-of, Notre Dame HS, Northridge, Calif.
55. *Todd Breyfogle, rhp, Scottsdale (Ariz.) CC.
56. *Chris Kelley, rhp, Lurleen B. Wallace (Ala) JC.
57. *Jason Davis, rhp, Upland (Calif.) HS
58. (void) *William Rose, rhp, Hillsborough (Fla.) CC.
59. *Robert Richter, of, Arcadia (Calif.) HS.
60. *Jamie Anderson, of, Hillsborough HS, Tampa.
61. +Anthony Pritchett, of, Faulkner State (Ala.) JC.

## PHILADELPHIA PHILLIES (4)

1. Jeff Jackson, of, Simeon HS, Chicago.—(AA)
2. *Chris Roberts, lhp, Middleburg (Fla.) HS.—(AAA)

DRAFT DROP *Attended Florida State; re-drafted by Mets, 1992 (1st round)*

3. Lamar Foster, 3b, Bibb County HS, Brent, Ala.—(Short-season A)
4. Julio Vargas, c, Santa Ana (Calif.) HS.—(High A)
5. **Steve Parris, rhp, College of St. Francis (Ill.).—(1995-2003)**
6. *Miah Bradbury, c, Loyola Marymount University.
7. Corey Thomas, of, Don Lugo HS, Chino, Calif.
8. Darrell Goedhart, rhp, Mount San Jacinto (Calif.) JC.
9. Paul Carson, of, Woodinville (Wash.) HS.
10. Cary Williams, of, University of Alabama.
11. Casey Waller, 3b, Virginia Tech.
12. Tommy Hardgrove, 1b, Texas Christian University.
13. Robert Mendonca, 3b, Modesto (Calif.) JC.
14. Sam Taylor, of, University of Kentucky.
15. Steven Avent, c, Oklahoma City University.
16. +James Savage, 3b, Hillsborough (Fla.) CC.
17. Joe Urbon, of, Washington State University.
18. **+Matt Whisenant, lhp, La Canada (Calif) HS / Glendale (Calif.) JC.—(1997-2000)**
19. Bill Smith, c, Sacramento (Calif.) CC.
20. *Steve Campos, rhp, Venice HS, Los Angeles.
21. Ismael Cruz, ss, Eckerd (Fla.) College.
22. David Ross, lhp, Saddleback (Calif.) CC.
23. Mark Randall, rhp, Saddleback (Calif.) CC.
24. *Joseph Davis, ss-rhp, Central Arizona JC.
25. *Sean Teague, c, Judson HS, Converse, Texas.
26. *Ted Corbin, ss, Barron Collier HS, Naples, Fla.
27. David Agado, rhp, Tarleton State (Texas) University.
28. *Thomas Neff, of, Rancho Santiago (Calif.) JC.
29. Matt Stevens, rhp, Le Moyne College.
30. Josh Lowery, ss, University of Portland.
31. Brian Adams, c, Otero (Colo.) JC.
32. **Steve Bieser, of-c, Southeast Missouri State University.—(1997-98)**

DRAFT DROP *Baseball coach, Southeast Missouri State (2013-15)*

33. (void) *Rafael Charriez, lhp, Rexville Superior HS, Bayamon, P R.
34. *Scott Corliss, rhp, Mater Dei HS, Chino Hills, Calif.
35. Dana Brown, of, Seton Hall University.

DRAFT DROP *Scouting director, Expos/Nationals (2002-09)*

36. John Douglas, of, University of Oklahoma.
37. Steven Stocker, c, University of Washington.

DRAFT DROP *Brother of Kevin Stocker, major leaguer (1993-2000)*

38. Ken Sirak, ss, University of Nebraska.
39. +Gary Morgan, 3b, JC of the Canyons (Calif.).
40. Charles Shive, rhp, University of Southern Mississippi.
41. Robert Gaddy, lhp, University of Tennessee.
42. James Cosman, c, University of Mississippi.
43. Elliot Gray, rhp, Wiley (Texas) College.
44. Daniel Welch, of, Christian Brothers (Tenn.) College.
45. Scott Wiegandt, lhp, Bellarmine (Ky.) College.
46. *Larry Maddox, of, Saddleback (Calif.) CC.
47. Robby Corsaro, rhp, Long Beach State University.
48. *Leon Whaley, of, St. Cloud (Fla.) HS.
49. *Coy Baskin, lhp, Cypress Creek HS, Cypress, Texas.

50. *Thomas Heming, lhp, Aquinas (Tenn.) JC.
51. +Terrance Tewell, c, Cypress (Calif.) JC.
52. *Gregory Phillips, ss-of, Rutledge HS, Bean Station, Tenn.
53. *Alexis Santana, rhp, Universidad HS, Caguas, P.R.

## PITTSBURGH PIRATES (18)

1. **Willie Greene, ss, Jones County HS, Gray, Ga.—(1992-2000)**
2. **Rich Aude, 3b, Chatsworth (Calif.) HS.—(1993-96)**
2. **John Hope, rhp, Stranahan HS, Fort Lauderdale, Fla.** (Supplemental choice—59th—as compensation for Type C free agent Dave LaPoint)**—(1993-96)**
3. Rob Bailey, of, Fullerton (Calif.) JC.—(AA)

DRAFT DROP *Son of Bob Bailey, major leaguer (1962-78)*

4. *Patrick Hicks, c, Overland HS, Aurora, Colo.--DNP

DRAFT DROP *Attended Mesa (Ariz.) CC; re-drafted by Orioles, 1991 (36th round)*

5. Michael Brown, 1b, Vacaville (Calif.) HS.—(AA)
6. Kevin Rychel, rhp, Midland (Texas) HS.
7. Tim Williams, of, Springboro (Ohio) HS.
8. Ricardo Ufret, ss, Aquinas (Tenn.) JC.
9. Joe Ronca, of, Tate HS, Cantonment, Fla.
10. David Bird, lhp, Chapman (Calif.) College.
11. Joe McLin, 1b, Riverside HS, Milwaukee.
12. **Paul Wagner, rhp, Illinois State University.—(1992-99)**
13. *Brian Arntzen, c, American River (Calif.) JC.
14. Ashley Scoates, rhp, Evans HS, Martinez, Ga.
15. *Joe Russo, 3b, Santa Fe (Fla.) CC.
16. *Steve Gill, of, Cypress (Calif.) JC.
17. Scott Arvesen, rhp, St. Xavier (Ill.) College.
18. Marcus Hanel, c, Horlick HS, Racine, Wis.
19. *Darren Hedley, of, American River (Calif.) JC.
20. ***Jeff McCurry, rhp, San Jacinto (Texas) JC.—(1995-99)**
21. Dean Hinson, c-1b, Bloomfield (N.M.) HS.
22. Eric Parkinson, rhp, Kellogg (Mich.) CC.
23. Luis Garcia, ss, Francisco Oller HS, Levittown, P.R.
24. David Howard, c-1b, Siena College.
25. David Watson, lhp, Yavapai (Ariz.) JC.
26. Bill Holmes, 1b, Marietta (Ohio) College.
27. Ken Trusky, of, University of Maryland.
28. Michael Hayes, of, Edmonds (Wash.) CC.
29. *Steve Young, of, Van Horn HS, Kansas City, Mo.
30. Mike Brewington, of, Methodist (N.C.) College.
31. *Chris Abbe, c-ss, Sycamore HS, Cincinnati.
32. Robert Peterson, c, College of Wooster (Ohio).
33. Nelson Caraballo, c, Florida International University.
34. Tony Mitchell, c, Mumford HS, Detroit.
35. **+Steve Cooke, lhp, JC of Southern Idaho.—(1992-98)**
36. ***Derek Wallace, rhp, Chatsworth (Calif.) HS.—(1996-99)**

DRAFT DROP *First-round draft pick (11th overall), Cubs (1992)*

37. *Robert Hinds, ss, Cerritos (Calif.) HS.
38. *Casey Burrill, c, Hart HS, Newhall, Calif.
39. Kimberly Broome, lhp, Columbus (Ga.) College.
40. Tom Deller, rhp, University of Kentucky.
41. Troy Mooney, rhp, Ashland (Ohio) College.
42. ***Mark Johnson, 1b-rhp, Dartmouth College.—(1995-2002)**
43. Shane Sparks, rhp, Campbell County HS, Jacksboro, Tenn.
44. *Chad Trahan, rhp, Tecumseh (Okla.) HS.
45. *Randy Martin, of, Palm Beach (Fla.) JC.
46. *David Pearlman, rhp, Los Amigos HS, Fountain Valley, Calif.
47. *Todd Johnson, rhp, Cal State Los Angeles.
48. *William Bates, rhp, Eastern Michigan University.

## ST. LOUIS CARDINALS (6)

1. Paul Coleman, of, Frankston (Texas) HS.—(AA)
2. **Mike Milchin, lhp-1b, Clemson University.—(1996)**
3. **Tripp Cromer, ss, University of South Carolina.—(1993-2003)**

DRAFT DROP *Brother of D.T. Cromer, major leaguer (2000-01)*

4. *Jon Farrell, of-c, Sandalwood HS, Jacksonville, Fla.—(AA)

DRAFT DROP *Attended Florida CC-Jacksonville; re-drafted by Pirates, 1991 (1st round)*

5. Tony Ochs, c, Memphis State University.—(High A)
6. ***Todd Steverson, of, Culver City HS, Venice, Calif.—(1995-96)**

DRAFT DROP *First-round draft pick (25th overall), Blue Jays (1992)*

7. Tracey Ealy, of, Chaparral HS, Las Vegas, Nev.
8. Anthony Lewis, of, Rancho HS, Las Vegas, Nev.
9. Jeff Fayne, of, Munford HS, Brighton, Tenn.
10. John Dempsey, c, Crespi HS, Agoura, Calif.

DRAFT DROP *Son of Rick Dempsey, major leaguer (1969-92)*

11. *Kevin Legault, rhp, Watervliet (N.Y.) HS.
12. David Boss, rhp, UC, Santa Barbara.
13. Jeremy McGarity, rhp, El Capitan HS, Lakeside, Calif.
14. Jose Fernandez, c, University of Florida.
15. Donald Green, lhp, Iowa State University.
16. Ben Ellsworth, ss, Orem (Utah) HS.
17. Danny Davis, of, Rustburg (Va.) HS.
18. Joseph Turvey, c, Roxborough HS, Philadelphia.
19. Mark Bowlan, rhp, Memphis State University.
20. **+Bill Hurst, rhp, Central Florida CC.—(1996)**
21. James Allen, of, Otterbein (Ohio) College.
22. Jeff Oswalt, lhp, U.S. International (Calif.) University.
23. Alan Botkin, lhp, Clemson University.
24. Tremayne Donald, 2b, Tilghman HS, Paducah, Ky.
25. Michael Campas, of, University of San Francisco.
26. Jose Trujillo, 2b, University of Miami.
27. Albert Pacheco, rhp, Florida International University.
28. Dennis Fletcher, rhp, University of Arkansas.
29. Cliff Brannon, rhp-of, Kennesaw (Ga.) College.
30. Denny Wiseman, rhp, Florida International University.
31. **Steve Dixon, lhp, Paducah (Ky.) CC.—(1993-94)**
32. Clyde Keller, rhp, Florida State University.
33. Manuel Rodriguez, rhp, Universidad HS, Rio Piedras, P.R.
34. Millard Hammond, rhp, Wellston (Ohio) HS.
35. Anthony Hicks, of, Florida International University.
36. Tim Lata, rhp, University of Michigan.
37. **Frank Cimorelli, rhp, Dominican (N.Y.) College.—(1994)**
38. David Cassidy, lhp, Arizona State University.
39. John Corona, lhp, Cerritos (Calif.) JC.
40. Bill Espinal, rhp, Pace (N.Y.) University.
41. *Bill Meury, ss, University of Maryland.
42. Bill Fielitz, c, Birmingham-Southern College.
43. Kevin Tahan, 1b-of, U.S. International (Calif.) University.
44. Larry Merrill, 3b-2b, Vestavia Hills (Ala.) HS.
45. Tim Jordan, of, Fernandina Beach HS, Yulee, Fla.
46. Scott Banton, of, Virginia Commonwealth University.
47. Ron French, of, Fernandina Beach HS, Yulee, Fla.
48. *Steven Jackson, c, Sullivan (Mo.) HS.
49. Mark Tolbert, rhp, Dixie (Utah) JC.
50. *Brian Cavalli, c, St. Joseph HS, Alameda, Calif.
51. *Tim Costa, rhp, LeMoore (Calif.) HS.
52. *Steve Harelson, lhp, Hempfield HS, Landisville, Pa.
53. Greg Glover, rhp, Junction City (Ark.) HS.
54. +Sean Page, of, Volunteer State (Tenn.) JC.
55. *Stanley Hurt, lhp-of, Jefferson Forest HS, Forest, Va.
56. *Algerian Williams, rhp, King HS, Tampa.

SIMON GRIFFITHS

Yankees fifth-rounder J.T. Snow reached the big leagues quickly and stayed there 15 years

## SAN DIEGO PADRES (16)

1. (Choice to Red Sox as compensation for Type A free agent Bruce Hurst)
2. *Kenny Felder, of, Niceville (Fla.) HS.—(AAA)

DRAFT DROP *Attended Florida State; re-drafted by Brewers, 1992 (1st round)*

3. Scott Bream, ss, Millard South HS, Omaha, Neb.—(AAA)
4. Russell Garside, lhp, Douglas HS, Garnerville, Nev.—(Low A)
5. **Dave Staton, 1b, Cal State Fullerton.—(1993-94)**
6. **Darrell Sherman, of, Long Beach State University.—(1993)**
7. Rick Davis, rhp, Cal State Dominguez Hills.
8. Billy Johnson, rhp, South Georgia JC.
9. **+Ray McDavid, of, Clairemont HS, San Diego, Calif. / Arizona Western JC—(1994-95)**
10. Lee Henderson, c, West Covina (Calif.) HS.
11. *Pat Clougherty, c, Broughton HS, Raleigh, N.C.
12. **Kevin Higgins, 2b, Arizona State University.—(1993)**
13. Ted Devore, rhp, University of Portland.
14. Brian McKeon, rhp, Madison (Wis.) Tech JC.
15. Shawn Whalen, of, Warner Pacific (Wash.) College.
16. Steve Martin, of, Arizona State University.
17. Terry Rupp, 1b, University of Tampa.
18. Kerry Knox, lhp, Texas Christian University.
19. Tony McGee, c, Jacksonville University.
20. **+Tim Worrell, rhp, Biola (Calif.) University.—(1993-2006)**

DRAFT DROP *Brother of Todd Worrell, first-round draft pick, Cardinals (1982); major leaguer (1985-97)*

21. Samuel Shannon, 2b, South Mecklenburg HS, Charlotte, N.C.
22. John Phelan, rhp, Eastern Washington University.
23. *James Hallinan, rhp, Snow (Utah) JC.
24. Jeff Barton, of, Princeton University.
25. *Scott Vorderlieth, lhp, San Diego Mesa JC.
26. Steve Bethea, ss, University of Texas.

DRAFT DROP *Son of Bill Bethea, major leaguer (1964)*

27. +Jeffrey Huber, lhp, Chaparral HS, Scottsdale, Ariz. / Miami-Dade CC North.
28. Rod Billingsley, c, George Mason University.
29. Dan Deville, rhp, Cal State Fullerton.
30. Matt Toole, ss, Santa Clara University.
31. ***Joel Adamson, lhp, Artesia HS, Lakewood, Calif.—(1996-98)**
32. ***Rich Robertson, lhp, San Jacinto (Texas) JC.—(1993-98)**
33. Charles Thompson, rhp, South Johnson HS, Four Oaks, N.C.
34. *Douglas McConathy, 3b, Western HS, Buena Park, Calif.
35. Mark Gieseke, 1b-lhp, Cal State Sacramento.
36. Rico Coleman, of, Grambling State University.
37. Brian Beck, of, Hidden Valley HS, Grants Pass, Ore.
38. Ed Zinter, rhp, Brigham Young University.

DRAFT DROP *Brother of Alan Zinter, first-round draft pick, Mets (1989); major leaguer (2002-04)*

39. Rafael Santiago, lhp, San Lorenzo (P.R.) HS.
40. James Joyce, c, Seminole HS, Sanford, Fla.
41. Jose Davila, rhp, Edep (P.R.) College.
42. *Alfredo Suarez, c, Cottana HS, San Juan, P.R.
43. Troy Cunningham, rhp, Gonzaga University.

## SAN FRANCISCO GIANTS (14)

1. **Steve Hosey, of, Fresno State University.—(1992-93)**
2. **Clay Bellinger, ss, Rollins (Fla.) College.—(1999-2002)**
3. Jason McFarlin, of, Pensacola (Fla.) HS.—(AAA)
4. Mike Grahovac, c-1b, Chapman (Calif.) College.—(Low A)
5. Brian Dour, rhp, Bradley University.—(High A)
6. *Renaldo Bullock, of, Proviso West HS, Bellwood, Ill.
7. *Matt Watson, rhp, Cal State Fullerton.
8. Frank Carey, 2b, Stanford University.
9. **Rafael Novoa, lhp, Villanova University.—(1990-93)**
10. +Ricky Ward, ss, Chemeketa (Ore.) JC.
11. **Greg Brummett, rhp, Wichita State University.—(1993)**
12. John Carrico, lhp, Purdue University.
13. *Jeff Gidcumb, rhp, University of Florida.
14. Roger Miller, c, University of Georgia.
15. **Pat Rapp, rhp, University of Southern Mississippi.—(1992-2001)**
16. Dan Rumsey, of, Arizona State University.
17. Steve Callahan, lhp, Lewis-Clark State (Idaho) College.
18. Ed Gustafson, rhp, Washington State University.
19. Steve Willis, 1b, Arizona State University.
20. Kelly Ahrens, c, Newberry (S.C.) College.
21. Daniel Stenz, lhp, Grand Canyon College.
22. Dave Hocking, lhp, Oklahoma Baptist University.
23. Stewart Hillman, rhp, University of Detroit.
24. Greg Lund, rhp, Kutztown (Pa.) University.
25. Steve Rolen, 3b, West Virginia University.
26. Jeff Brauning, ss-2b, Oregon State University.
27. Jon Schiller, rhp, Central Washington University.
28. Dan Rambo, rhp, Central Michigan University.
29. Mike McDonald, of, Wichita State University.
30. Darren Garrison, lhp, Southwest Missouri State

University.
31. *Eugene Thomas, of, Montgomery (Md.) JC.
32. Clark Huntey, c, Central Michigan University.
**33. +Dan Carlson, rhp, Mount Hood (Ore.) CC.—(1996-99)**
34. Shawn May, ss-2b, Mansfield (Pa.) University.
35. *Danny Jenkins, 3b, South Torrance HS, Torrance, Calif.
36. John Chiaramonte, rhp, Moorpark (Calif.) JC.
37. Gus Vollmer, of, University of South Florida.
38. Ronald Crowe, ss-rhp, Cal Poly San Luis Obispo.
39. *Cyrus Crosby, rhp, Seminole (Okla.) JC.
40. Darren Musselwhite, rhp, University of Mississippi.
41. Daniel Henrikson, lhp, Clark (Wash.) JC.
42. Vince Palyan, of, University of Minnesota.
43. *Tyler Williams, c, North HS, Davenport, Iowa.
44. +Brian McLeod, rhp, Orange Coast (Calif.) CC.
45. +Lenny Ayres, rhp, Kennewick (Wash.) HS / Lower Colunbia (Wash.) JC.
**46. *Albie Lopez, rhp, Westwood HS, Mesa, Ariz.—(1993-2003)**
47. Heath Jones, 1b, El Camino (Calif.) JC.
48. Matt Harr, 2b, Briar Cliff (Iowa) College.
49. Jon Pattin, c, Johnson County (Kan.) JC.
DRAFT DROP *Son of Marty Pattin, major leaguer (1968-80)*
50. *Michael Sambito, 1b, Seminole (Fla.) HS.
DRAFT DROP *Brother of Joe Sambito, major leaguer (1976-87)*

## SEATTLE MARINERS (3)

**1. Roger Salkeld, rhp, Saugus (Calif.) HS.—(1993-96)**
DRAFT DROP *Grandson of Bill Salkeld, major leaguer (1945-50)*
1. *Scott Burrell, rhp, Hamden (Conn.) HS (Choice from Athletics as compensation for Type B free agent Mike Moore).—(High A)
DRAFT DROP *Attended Connecticut; re-drafted by Blue Jays, 1990 (5th round); first-round draft pick, Charlotte Hornets/National Basketball Association (1993); guard, NBA (1993-2001)*
2. (Choice to Orioles as compensation for Type B free agent Tom Niedenfuer)
3. (Choice to Brewers as compensation for Type B free agent Jeffrey Leonard)
4. Kyle Duke, lhp, Newman Smith HS, Carrollton, Texas.—(AA)
5. Jim Gutierrez, rhp, Burlington-Edison HS, Burlington, Wash.—(AAA)
6. David Evans, rhp, San Jacinto (Texas) JC.
7. Scott Lodgek, rhp, University of North Carolina.
8. Sean Twitty, of, McClancy Memorial HS, Astoria, N.Y.
9. Bill Kostich, lhp, Taylor Center HS, Taylor, Mich.
10. Fred McNair, ss, Bleckley County HS, Cochran, Ga.
DRAFT DROP *Quarterback, Canadian Football League (1991) • Brother of Steve McNair, quarterback, National Football League (1995-2007)*
**11. *Charlie Greene, c, Killian HS, Miami.—(1996-2000)**
12. Jim Newlin, rhp, Wichita State University.
13. Mark Brakebill, 3b, Glendale (Ariz.) CC.
14. Valentine Ballesteros, lhp, Southwestern Michigan JC.
15. Lash Bailey, 1b, Long Beach (Calif.) CC.
16. Richard Lodding, rhp, Cypress (Calif.) JC.
17. Oscar Rivas, lhp, Arizona State University.
18. *Keith Tippett, ss, Ocala Forest HS, Ocala, Fla.
19. Matthew Kluge, c, Hillsborough HS, Tampa.
20. *Pat Russo, rhp, University of Tampa.
21. Damon Saetre, 1b, Western Michigan University.
22. Mike LeBlanc, rhp, University of Maine.
**23. *David Mlicki, rhp, Oklahoma State University.—(1992-2002)**
24. Melvin DeJesus, rhp, Stella Marquez HS, Salinas, P.R.
25. Richard Hanlin, of, Cal State San Bernardino.
26. Darin Loe, rhp, Valley City State (N.D.) University.
27. David Smith, of, University of Southwestern Louisiana.
28. *Philip Black, lhp, University of North Florida.
29. Winston LeBlanc, ss, Mississippi Delta JC.
30. Tom Duffin, 3b, University of South Alabama.
31. *Jason Ogden, rhp, San Jacinto (Calif.) JC.
32. +Kelly Hartman, 1b, Turner HS, Leon, Okla. / Murray State (Okla.) JC.
33. *Darryl Boyd, rhp, JC of the Siskiyous (Calif.).
34. Israel Seda, 2b, Cabo Ojo HS, Puerto Real, P.R.
35. *Gaylon Johnson, c, Central Valley HS, Redding, Calif.
36. *David Hobbs, rhp, Westwood HS, Fort Pierce, Fla.
37. *Steve Surico, lhp, Loyola Marymount University.
38. +Todd Youngblood, ss, Cochise County (Ariz.) CC.
39. Keith Bryant, rhp, Mount Vernon Nazarene (Ohio) College.
40. *James Schultz, c, Cooper HS, Crystal, Minn.
41. *Cedric Allen, lhp, Johnston HS, Austin, Texas.
42. *Joey Madden, ss-of, Salesian HS, Richmond, Calif.
**43. *Larry Mitchell, rhp, Charlottesville (Va.) HS.—(1996)**
44. *Andy Small, 3b, San Bernardino Valley (Calif.) JC.
45. +L.V. Powell, of, Cerritos (Calif.) JC.
46. *Jesus Gonzalez, c, Triton (Ill.) JC.
47. Tommy Boudreau, of, Cerritos (Calif.) JC.
48. Alvin Rittman, ss, Bethune-Cookman College.
49. Landon Williams, ss, Grambling State University.
50. Bobby Magallanes, ss, Cerritos (Calif.) JC.
DRAFT DROP *Brother of Ever Magallanes, major leaguer (1991)*
51. Mark Czarkowski, lhp, University of Hartford.
**52. Brian Turang, of, Loyola Marymount University.—(1993-94)**
53. *Brian Morrow, of, El Dorado (Kan.) HS.
54. +John Johnson, ss, Channel Islands HS, Oxnard, Calif. / Ventura (Calif.) JC.
55. *Brian McGlone, ss, Leto HS, Tampa.
56. *Andre Keene, 1b, Duval HS, Lanham, Md.
57. *Thomas Wilson, of, Troy HS, Yorba Linda, Calif.
58. James Terrell, of, Hogan HS, Vallejo, Calif.
59. *Ryan Lefebvre, of, Loyola HS, Los Angeles.
DRAFT DROP *Son of Jim Lefebvre, major leaguer (1965-72); major league manager (1989-99)*
60. *James Beauchamp, rhp, Modesto (Calif.) JC.
61. *David Utz, rhp, Ocean Springs (Miss.) HS.
62. *D.J. Boston, 1b-of, Woodward HS, Cincinnati.
DRAFT DROP *Brother of Daryl Boston, first-round draft pick, White Sox (1981); major leaguer (1984-94)*
63. *Marcus Urban, rhp, Procter Hug HS, Reno, Nev.
64. *Matthew Winton, of, Merced (Calif.) JC.
65. +Clem Barlow, of, Southern Union State (Ala.) JC.
66. (void) *Walter Rivera, rhp, Chipola (Fla.) JC.
67. *Dusty Madsen, of, Sacramento (Calif.) CC.
68. +Paul Perkins, rhp, Solano (Calif.) CC.
69. *Del Marine, 3b, El Camino Real HS, Woodland Hills, Calif.
70. *Dexter St. George, of, Lanett (Ala.) HS.
71. *Sidney Stigall, ss, Eau Gallie HS, Melbourne, Fla.

## TEXAS RANGERS (5)

**1. Donald Harris, of, Texas Tech.—(1991-93)**
DRAFT DROP *12th-round draft pick, Dallas Cowboys/ National Football League (1992)*
2. (Choice to Astros as compensation for Type A free agent Nolan Ryan)
**3. Dan Peltier, of, University of Notre Dame.—(1992-96)**
**4. Joey Eischen, lhp, Pasadena (Calif.) CC.—(1994-2006)**
5. Jason Ayala, rhp, Brighton HS, Sandy, Utah.—(Rookie)
6. Ken Powell, of, Poly HS, Long Beach, Calif.
7. Dave Giberti, lhp, Alhambra HS, Martinez, Calif.
8. Jay Franklin, rhp, Oral Roberts University.
9. Randy Marshall, of-1b, LeMoyne College.
10. Steve Rowley, rhp, Tulane University.
**11. *Chris Snopek, ss, Harrison County HS, Cynthiana, Ky.—(1995-98)**
12. Barry Winford, c, Mississippi State University.
13. Michael Arner, rhp, Clearwater (Fla.) HS.
14. Geoff Flinn, ss, University of Indiana.
15. George Kerfut, rhp, Pace (N.Y.) University.
16. Rob Brown, rhp, San Diego State University.
17. Mike Burton, 1b, Fresno State University.
18. Kevin Keon, rhp, LeMoyne College.
19. Keith McGough, rhp, Neville HS, Monroe, La.
20. *Ron Rico, of, La Mirada (Calif) HS.
**21. Gerald Alexander, rhp, Tulane University.—(1990-92)**
22. Bryan Gore, lhp, Oklahoma State University.
23. Tyrone Washington, rhp, Southern University.
24. Travis Buckley, rhp, Johnson County (Kan.) CC.
25. Troy Eklund, of, University of Arkansas.
26. Trevor Haughney, of, St. Raymonds HS, New York.
27. David Perez, rhp, St. Mary's (Texas) University.
28. Todd Abell, ss-3b, Lynchburg (Va.) College.
29. Roberto Camarillo, ss, Magnolia HS, Anaheim, Calif.
30. Brian Crowley, of, University of Hartford.
31. James Clinton, ss-2b, University of Illinois-Chicago.
32. *Mark Slobonik, c, Oakton (Ill.) CC.
33. Brian Roper, c, Texas Tech.
34. Jose Texidor, of, Juana Diaz (P.R.) HS.
35. *David Lavallee, 3b-1b, University of Rhode Island.
36. *Gilbert Cleveland, rhp, University of North Alabama.
37. Kevin Fowler, rhp, University of Montevallo (Ala.).
38. Daren Hays, of, Lubbock Christian University.
39. John Graves, rhp, Oklahoma City University.
40. Scott Asche, lhp, Cleveland State University.
41. *Ben O'Connor, lhp, University of Maryland-Baltimore.
42. Stacy Parker, of, UC Irvine.
43. *Jason Beauchamp, rhp, Cordova HS, Rancho Cordova, Calif.
44. Brian Scheetz, rhp, University of Illinois-Chicago.
45. Eric Bickhardt, rhp, St Joseph's University.
46. *Bertland Watson, of, Mount San Jacinto (Calif.) JC.
**47. +Danny Patterson, rhp, San Gabriel HS, Rosemead, Calif. / Cerritos (Calif.)—(1996-2004)**
48. Dick Phillips, rhp, Vernon (Texas) JC.
49. Victor Reyes, c, Juayanilla (P.R.) HS.
50. *Jeff Gyselman, c, Inglemoor HS, Bothell, Wash.
51. *Ron Reams, of, Laney (Calif.) JC.
52. *Dan Madsen, c, Newbury Park HS, Thousand Oaks, Calif.
53. *Bryan Leiser, rhp, Ventura (Calif.) JC.
54. +Avery Duval, rhp, Hernando HS, Brooksville, Fla. / Manatee (Fla.) JC.
55. Brandon Devereaux, lhp, American Fork (Utah) HS.
56. *Gabriel Angulo, of, Miami-Dade CC South.
57. *David Eggert, lhp, Ventura (Calif.) JC.
58. *Tory Winrow, ss-3b, Helix HS, Lemon Grove, Calif.
59. *Michael Weisenberg, c, St Francis HS, Pasadena, Calif.

## TORONTO BLUE JAYS (19)

**1. Eddie Zosky, ss, Fresno State University.—(1991-2000)**
2. *Michael Moore, of, Beverly Hills (Calif.) HS.—(AAA)
DRAFT DROP *Attended UCLA; re-drafted by Dodgers, 1992 (1st round)*
**2. Brent Bowers, of, St. Lawrence HS, Burbank, Ill.** (Supplemental choice—60th—as compensation for Type C free agent Rick Leach)**—(1996)**
**3. John Olerud, 1b-lhp, Washington State University.—(1989-2005)**
DRAFT DROP *First player from 1989 draft to reach majors (Sept. 3, 1989)*
4. *Troy Bradford, rhp, Cochise County (Ariz.) CC.—(AA)
DRAFT DROP *Attended Arizona; re-drafted by Cubs, 1990 (2nd round)*
5. Ricky Steed, rhp, Covina (Calif.) HS.—(AAA)
6. Marc Loeb, c, San Bernardino Valley (Calif.) JC.
7. Jeff Irish, c, Milford HS, Highland, Mich.
8. Lonell Roberts, of, Bloomington (Calif.) HS.
**9. *Jeffrey Hammonds, of, Scotch Plains-Fanwood HS, Scotch Plains, N.J.—(1993-2005)**
DRAFT DROP *First-round draft pick (4th overall), Orioles (1992); first player from 1992 draft to reach majors (June 25, 1993)*
10. Shawn Holtzclaw, of, Auburn University.
11. +Ned Darley, rhp, Manning (S.C.) HS / Spartanburg Methodist (S.C.) JC.
12. Walter Heckel, 2b, St John's University.
13. Michael Taylor, lhp, Hillsborough HS, Tampa.
14. Robert Blumberg, lhp, Nicholls State University.
15. Scott Gordon, rhp, Xavier University.
16. *Pat Leahy, rhp, Eisenhower HS, Yakima, Wash.
17. Dante Reid, of-lhp, Geneva (N.Y.) HS.
18. *Kipp Jeffries, ss, Etiwanda HS, Rialto, Calif.
19. Gerald Crump, of, Upland HS, Fontana, Calif.
**20. Jeff Kent, ss, University of California.—(1992-2007)**
21. Gregg Martin, rhp, Northwestern University.
**22. Aaron Small, rhp, South Hills HS, West Covina, Calif.—(1994-2006)**
23. *Angel Reyes, lhp-of, Ramon Jose Davila HS, Coamo, P.R.
24. Sean Hearn, of, Worthing HS, Houston.
25. Scott Fritz, rhp, Southside HS, Muncie, Ind.
26. *C.J. Kerr, lhp, Cerritos (Calif.) JC.
27. Andrew Rooney, 1b, Ocean County (N.J.) JC.
28. Sterling Stock, rhp, Pacific Lutheran (Wash.) University.
29. Daren Brown, rhp, Southeastern Oklahoma State University.
DRAFT DROP *Major league manager (2010)*
30. Allen Tyson, rhp, Gulf Coast (Fla.) CC.
31. *Douglas Hekking, rhp, Ohlone (Calif) JC.
32. Norbert Wilson, of, Renaissance HS, Detroit.
33. *Eric Johnson, c, Chatsworth (Calif.) HS.
34. +Keith Hines, of, Chipola (Fla.) JC.
35. +Morgan Adams, rhp, Olustee (Okla.) HS
36. Kris Harmes, c, Donegal HS, Mount Joy, Pa.
37. Darren Kizziah, rhp, Western Kentucky University.
38. Kenny Kulina, lhp, Jacksonville University.
39. Greg Bicknell, rhp, Fresno (Calif.) CC.
40. Chris Beacom, 2b-1b, Northwestern University.
41. Kevin Meyers, ss, University of Southwestern Louisiana.
42. *Jason Miller, 3b, Plattsburg (N.Y.) HS.
43. Brad Mengel, 3b, Cal State Los Angeles.
44. *Gracia Martinez, ss, Bayamon Military Academy, Toa Baja, P.R.
45. *Vic Merritt, 1b, Nicholls State University.
46. *Shannon Jackson, lhp, Shelton State (Ala.) CC.
47. *Thomas Leahy, rhp, Howard (Texas) JC.
48. *Bob Aylmer, lhp, Fordham University.
49. *Jason DeLeon, of, Burroughs HS, Ridgecrest, Calf.
50. *Robert Moose, 1b Lake Howell HS, Maitland, Fla.
51. *Robert Barber, c, Sommers, Mon.
52. *Thomas Froning, lhp, Sidney (Ohio) HS.
53. *Randy Powers, rhp, University of Southern California.
54. *Jose Flores, ss, Colegio Notre Dame HS, Cidra, P.R
55. *Mike Daniel, c, Connors State (Okla.) JC
**56. *Jon Shave, 2b, Mississippi State University.—(1993-99)**
57. *Thomas Brown, lhp, Delaware Tech JC.
58. *David Gray, rhp, Banning (Calif.) HS.
59. *Ricardo Serpo, of, Rexville Superior HS, Bayamon, P.R
60. *Leland Patterson, rhp, Riverside (Calif.) CC.
61. *Travis Sexton, c-of, Taylor HS, Kokomo, Ind.
62. +David Fletcher, rhp, Mount San Jacinto (Calif.) JC.
63. *Gregory Lewis, of, Newburgh Free Academy, Newburgh, N.Y.
64. *Thomas Irwin, rhp, Orange Coast (Calif.) JC.
**65. *Ricky Otero, of, Vega Baja, P.R.—(1995-97)**
66. *Jeff Lawrence, lhp, Palomar (Calif.) JC.
67. *Jeffery Cheek, rhp, Pensacola (Fla.) JC.
68. +Lee Daniels, ss-3b, Wilcox County HS, Rochelle, Ga. / Itawamba (Miss.) JC.
69. *Peter Stacey, c, Granite Hills HS, El Cajon, Calif.
70. *LaBradford Smith, rhp, University of Louisville.
DRAFT DROP *First-round draft pick, Washington Bullets/National Basketball Association (1991); guard, NBA (1991-94)*
71. *Robert Tucker, c, Santee, Calif.
72. *James Bostock, 2b-ss, De la Salle Collegiate HS, New Baltimore, Mich.
73. *Marc Palmieri, rhp, Chaminade HS, Melville, NY.
74. *Mark St. Claire, c, Whitehall (N.Y.) HS.
75. *Bert Emanuel, of, Langham Creek HS, Houston.
DRAFT DROP *Defensive back, National Football League (1994-2001)*

## BOISE HAWKS NORTHWEST LEAGUE (A)

1-3. No selections
4. Paul Cluff, 2b, Brigham Young University.—(Short-season A)
5. Darrell MacMillan, c, Kennesaw (Ga.) College.—(Short-season A)

# 1990

# Braves' fallback thrives as spending takes off

Major league teams went on a spending spree in 1990.

Triggered by a lucrative new television deal, clubs spent freely at the big league level, signing a wave of players to unprecedented multiyear, multimillion-dollar contracts that inflated payrolls for years to come. They also spent freely to sign amateur talent, paying out some of the largest bonuses in draft history.

The biggest jackpot of the 1990 draft went to Texas schoolboy Todd Van Poppel, who signed a major league deal with the defending World Series champion Oakland Athletics that included a $500,000 bonus and was worth a total of $1.2 million. It was the first major league contract signed by a high school player in 13 years, and the seven-figure amount was the largest ever committed to a draft choice at the time.

Van Poppel's record-setting deal, agreed to on July 16, highlighted a dramatic escalation of bonuses and climaxed a spending spree in which the 10 largest bonuses to that point of the draft era were paid out in a 12-month period, beginning with 1989 draftees Ben McDonald and John Olerud, who signed multiyear deals in excess of $800,000 in August 1989.

The average bonus for first-round picks in 1990 was $252,577, up 43.5 percent from the 1989 average of $176,008 and the largest year-to-year percentage increase in draft history. Every 1990 first-round pick received a bonus of at least $175,000, and for the first time since 1985 every first-round pick signed.

Major league clubs committed more bonus money than ever on 1990 draft choices, and they came away with more future big leaguers (237) than in any other draft to date. The only draft to top 1990 came in 2008, when 247 players reached the major leagues. Twenty-two of the 26 first-round picks in 1990 reached the majors; the only drafts with better success rates were 2004 and '08, when 27 of 30 first-rounders reached the majors.

Just nine college players were taken in the first round in 1990, the lowest total in any draft after 1980. The first college player selected was University of Minnesota catcher Dan Wilson, seventh overall by the Cincinnati Reds, the latest a college player had been drafted since 1971, when the entire first round was comprised of high school players.

Van Poppel was identified as the top prospect in the 1990 draft early in the process, but he said he did not want to sign a pro contract, preferring instead to attend the University of Texas and pitch in the 1992 Olympics.

The Atlanta Braves held the first pick and made little secret of their preference for Van Poppel, but they were repeatedly informed by the Van Poppel family that Todd planned to attend college. A day before the draft, Braves general manager Bobby Cox and scouting director Paul Snyder met with the family and reportedly offered a contract worth more than $1 million. The family declined it.

PETER BAUER

Larry Wayne Jones, better known as Chipper, gets the call that he's the No. 1 selection, setting him on a career all spent in Atlanta that saw him become one of the best switch-hitters in baseball history

"There were no negotiations at all with the young man," Snyder said. "I went out to Texas twice and didn't get to talk to him. (Scout) Red Murff tried to talk to him but couldn't. So Bobby went out there and (Van Poppel) didn't show for that meeting, either. We talked to his mother and father, but never to him."

At that point, the Braves decided to move on to Plan B: Larry Wayne Jones, a high school shortstop from Pierson, Fla., better know as Chipper Jones.

"When you have a ballplayer of Chipper's caliber and the other guy doesn't want to play," Cox said, "there was no debate after we determined (Van Poppel) was unsignable. That's not to say we would have taken Van Poppel over Chipper. But he wouldn't talk with us."

With the draft little more than 12 hours away, Cox sent Braves scouts Tony DeMacio and Dean Jongewaard to meet with Jones and his father. They offered $250,000 as a signing bonus; Jones' father countered at $300,000. The sides agreed to split the difference at $275,000, with the Braves sweetening the offer to more than $400,000 by agreeing to pay about $60,000 for college should Jones decide he wanted to attend at some point and a life insurance annuity.

The deal was in place by the time the Braves led off the draft by selecting Jones.

## AT A GLANCE

### This Date In History
June 4-6

### Best Draft
**NEW YORK YANKEES.** Sixteen Yankees picks reached the majors, one short of the draft record of 17, set in 1982 by the Mets. The key was a pair of late-round draft-and-follows: lefthander **ANDY PETTITTE** (22) and shortstop-turned-catcher **JORGE POSADA** (24), who both played instrumental roles on five World Series championship teams from 1996-2009.

### Worst Draft
**CHICAGO CUBS.** The Cubs earned this dubious distinction for the third straight draft, no small reason why they had losing records in eight seasons from 1990-2000. Only three of 46 picks made the majors, including pitchers **LANCE DICKSON** (1), whose career amounted to three games in 1990, and **RYAN HAWBLITZEL** (2), who made eight relief appearances in 1996.

### First-Round Bust
**RONNIE WALDEN, LHP, DODGERS.** Walden began his pro career by going 3-0, 0.42 in three starts at Rookie-level Great Falls. But he had two elbow surgeries, causing him to miss all of 1991 and '92. He made three appearances in Class A in 1993 before torn ligaments in his pitching shoulder ended his career.

### Second Best
**BOB WICKMAN, RHP, WHITE SOX.** Wickman lost the tip of his index finger on his right hand in a childhood farming accident, which worked to his advantage when pitching because it enabled him to grip the ball differently and get sink on his fastball. In 15 big league seasons (none with the White Sox), including his last 10 as a closer, he went 63-61, 3.57 with 267 saves in 835 appearances.

CONTINUED ON PAGE 378

## AT A GLANCE

CONTINUED FROM PAGE 377

### Late-Round Find
**ANDY PETTITTE, LHP, YANKEES (22ND ROUND).** The Yankees took maximum advantage of the draft-and-follow rule in 1990, selecting both Pettitte and **JORGE POSADA** (24), along with five others, before signing them the following spring. Pettitte, a San Jacinto (Texas) JC product, pitched 18 years in the majors, all but three with the Yankees, and won 256 games.

### Never Too Late
**DANNY YOUNG, LHP, ASTROS (83RD ROUND).** By pitching in four games for the Cubs in 1990, Young earned the distinction (since surpassed) of becoming the highest-round draft pick to reach the majors.

### Overlooked
**CORY LIDLE, RHP, TWINS.** Lidle signed for $10,000 out of a California high school and was released two years later. He signed on to play for independent Pocatello in the Rookie-level Pioneer League in 1993, and his contract was later purchased by the Brewers. Lidle found his way to the majors, pitching for seven clubs in nine years with an 82-72, 4.57 record.

### International Gem
**MARIANO RIVERA, RHP, YANKEES.** Signed out of Panama for just $2,500, Rivera became the game's dominant closer over a 19-year career with the Yankees, saving a major league record 652 games.

### Minor League Take
**ADAM HYZDU, OF, GIANTS.** Hyzdu reached the majors with the Pirates and played parts of seven years in the big leagues, but not before spending 11 seasons in the minors with five other organizations. He hit .229-19-61 in 221 major league games, but had 273 homers and 1,010 RBIs in 1,703 games in the minors over 17 seasons.

## 1990: THE FIRST ROUNDERS

| CLUB: PLAYER, POS., SCHOOL | HOMETOWN | B-T | HT. | WT. | AGE | BONUS | FIRST YEAR | LAST YEAR | PEAK LEVEL (YEARS) |
|---|---|---|---|---|---|---|---|---|---|
| 1. Braves: Chipper Jones, ss, The Bolles School | Pierson, Fla. | B-R | 6-4 | 185 | 18 | $275,000 | 1990 | 2012 | Majors (19) |
| Compromise pick when Todd Van Poppel looked unsignable; went on to stellar career as cornerstone of Braves' long playoff run, 1999 MVP, eight-time all-star. | | | | | | | | | |
| 2. Tigers: Tony Clark, of, Christian HS | El Cajon, Calif. | B-R | 6-7 | 195 | 17 | $500,000 | 1990 | 2009 | Majors (15) |
| Elite prep basketball talent, played hoops in college before committing full-time to Tigers; hit 251 homers in MLB career, became leader of players union. | | | | | | | | | |
| 3. Phillies: Mike Lieberthal, c, Westlake HS | Westlake Village, Calif. | R-R | 6-0 | 170 | 19 | $225,000 | 1990 | 2007 | Majors (14) |
| Unusually high draft for small-bodied prep catcher but fulfilled projection in 14-year MLB career, capped by .300-31-96 all-star season in 1999, also won Gold Glove. | | | | | | | | | |
| 4. White Sox: Alex Fernandez, rhp, Miami-Dade CC South | Hialeah, Fla. | R-R | 6-0 | 205 | 20 | $350,000 | 1990 | 2000 | Majors (10) |
| Rejected Brewers in 1988, had big frosh/soph years at Miami (15-2, 2.01), in JC (12-2, 1.19), won 107 games in majors before shoulder issues ended career. | | | | | | | | | |
| 5. Pirates: Kurt Miller, rhp, West HS | Bakersfield, Calif. | R-R | 6-5 | 195 | 17 | $232,000 | 1990 | 1999 | Majors (5) |
| First prep pitcher drafted, traded twice before 21; ideal mechanics with plus velocity, but career plagued by injuries, inconsistency; went 2-7, 7.48 in 44 MLB games. | | | | | | | | | |
| 6. Mariners: Marc Newfield, 1b, Marina HS | Huntington Beach, Calif. | R-R | 6-4 | 210 | 17 | $220,000 | 1990 | 1999 | Majors (6) |
| Best prep power threat in draft with size/strength, quick hands/wrists, but hit just .249-22-132 in 355 games for three clubs; other tools were short. | | | | | | | | | |
| 7. Reds: Dan Wilson, c, Minnesota | Barrington, Ill. | R-R | 6-3 | 185 | 21 | $250,000 | 1990 | 2005 | Majors (14) |
| Hit .370-8-49, threw out 17 of 21 runners, went 4-3, 4.20 on mound as college junior; hit .262 with 88 HRs in majors, defensive stalwart in 12 seasons for Mariners. | | | | | | | | | |
| 8. Indians: Tim Costo, ss, Iowa | Glen Ellyn, Ill. | R-R | 6-5 | 205 | 21 | $300,000 | 1990 | 1998 | Majors (2) |
| Moved to 1B in pros, traded to Reds in 1991; best power in college ranks, hit record 41 HRs at Iowa, 96 in minors, but long swing proved undoing in majors. | | | | | | | | | |
| 9. Dodgers: Ronnie Walden, lhp, Blanchard HS | Blanchard, Okla. | L-L | 6-3 | 180 | 17 | $215,000 | 1990 | 1993 | Class A (1) |
| Injury-riddled career never got off ground; hurt elbow four starts into pro career, sat out 1991-92 seasons, shoulder zapped 1993 comeback; worked 31 IPs as pro. | | | | | | | | | |
| 10. Yankees: Carl Everett, of, Hillsborough HS | Tampa | B-R | 6-0 | 190 | 18 | $250,000 | 1990 | 2006 | Majors (14) |
| Yanks gave up on raw athlete, picked by Marlins in '92 expansion draft; MLB career marked by occasional brilliance (.300-34-108 in 2000), plenty of controversy. | | | | | | | | | |
| 11. Expos: Shane Andrews, 3b, Carlsbad HS | Carlsbad, N.M. | R-R | 6-2 | 210 | 18 | $175,000 | 1990 | 2003 | Majors (7) |
| Man among boys as power-hitting SS/strong-armed RHP in New Mexico prep ranks; moved to 3B, struggled to make contact, went deep 86 times in seven seasons. | | | | | | | | | |
| 12. Twins: Todd Ritchie, rhp, Duncanville HS | Duncanville, Texas | R-R | 6-3 | 180 | 18 | $252,500 | 1990 | 2008 | Majors (8) |
| Went 15-1, 0.69 as prep SR, beat Todd Van Poppel 1-0 in Texas playoff game; reached majors in eighth season, won 15 games for Pirates in 1999, but only 43 overall. | | | | | | | | | |
| 13. Cardinals: Donovan Osborne, lhp, Nevada-Las Vegas | Carson City, Nev. | L-L | 6-2 | 180 | 20 | $235,000 | 1990 | 2006 | Majors (9) |
| Three-year workhorse at UNLV (35-12, 4.21, 402 IP/358 SO), lively low-90s FB, control, went 49-46 from 1992-2004, but missed four seasons with shoulder woes. | | | | | | | | | |
| 14. *Athletics: Todd Van Poppel, rhp, James W. Martin HS | Arlington, Texas | R-R | 6-5 | 195 | 18 | $500,000 | 1990 | 2004 | Majors (11) |
| Top talent based on size/velocity, slid because of bonus demands; signed record $1.2 million deal, straight fastball led to mediocre MLB career (40-52, 5.58) | | | | | | | | | |
| 15. Giants: Adam Hyzdu, of, Moeller HS | Cincinnati | R-R | 6-3 | 210 | 18 | $250,000 | 1990 | 2006 | Majors (7) |
| Broke Ken Griffey Jr. season/career HR records at Moeller High, went deep 273 times in minors, finally reached majors in 2000, homered 19 times in seven seasons. | | | | | | | | | |
| 16. Rangers: Dan Smith, lhp, Creighton | Apple Valley, Minn. | L-L | 6-5 | 190 | 21 | $220,000 | 1990 | 2000 | Majors (2) |
| Dominant arm for Team USA in 1989, Creighton in 1990 (14-3, 1.96, 120 IP/134 SO), but rushed to majors by Rangers, his career never took off (1 MLB win). | | | | | | | | | |
| 17. Mets: Jeromy Burnitz, of, Oklahoma State | Conroe, Texas | B-R | 6-0 | 195 | 21 | $192,500 | 1990 | 2006 | Majors (14) |
| AVG dipped from .403 as freshman to .288 as junior, but hit 47 HRs; played for seven big league clubs, had most success with Brewers in 1998 (38 HRs, 125 RBIs). | | | | | | | | | |
| 18. Cardinals: Aaron Holbert, ss, David Starr Jordan HS | Long Beach, Calif. | R-R | 6-0 | 170 | 17 | $195,000 | 1990 | 2006 | Majors (2) |
| Nine years, 124 days between first MLB game (in 1996) and second (in 2005), longest in game's history; slick defender, played 17 years with eight organizations. | | | | | | | | | |
| 19. Giants: Eric Christopherson, c, San Diego State | Westminster, Calif. | R-R | 6-1 | 190 | 21 | $175,000 | 1990 | 1999 | Class AAA (5) |
| Sound defender with arm strength, soft hands, quick feet; improved at plate from .256-0-24 as soph to .341-6-51 as junior; pro career peaked in Triple-A. | | | | | | | | | |
| 20. Orioles: Mike Mussina, rhp, Stanford | Montoursville, Pa. | R-R | 6-2 | 185 | 21 | $250,000 | 1990 | 2008 | Majors (18) |
| Drafted by O's in '87, again in '90 after going 31-16, 3.89 in three years at Stanford; won AL-record 11-plus games for 17 straight years, 20-win season in final year. | | | | | | | | | |
| 21. Astros: Tom Nevers, ss, Edina HS | Edina, Minn. | R-R | 6-1 | 185 | 18 | $250,000 | 1990 | 2002 | Class AAA (4) |
| Chose Astros over Pittsburgh Penguins ('89 NHL draft); 13-year career in minors peaked in Triple-A, hit .259-119-620; related to NFL Hall of Famer Ernie Nevers. | | | | | | | | | |
| 22. Blue Jays: Steve Karsay, rhp, Christ The King HS | College Point, N.Y. | R-R | 6-3 | 185 | 18 | $350,000 | 1990 | 2006 | Majors (11) |
| Won 14 games as prep SR, scared teams off with LSU commitment; acquired by A's in Rickey Henderson trade, reached MLB at 21, but career marked by injuries. | | | | | | | | | |
| 23. Cubs: Lance Dickson, lhp, Arizona | La Mesa, Calif. | R-L | 6-1 | 185 | 20 | $180,000 | 1990 | 1995 | Majors (1) |
| Went 17-17, 4.41 at Arizona, dominated in first pro season (7-3, 0.94 76 IP/111 SO) and reached majors; never returned, plagued by injuries and loss of curveball. | | | | | | | | | |
| 24. Expos: Rondell White, of, Jones County HS | Gray, Ga. | R-R | 6-1 | 185 | 18 | $175,000 | 1990 | 2007 | Majors (15) |
| Second straight Jones County High first-rounder, joining Willie Greene (Pirates '89); all tools (except arm) average or better, hit .284-198-768 in 15 MLB seasons. | | | | | | | | | |
| 25. Padres: Robbie Beckett, lhp, McCallum HS | Austin, Texas | L-L | 6-6 | 225 | 17 | $175,000 | 1990 | 2000 | Majors (2) |
| Big, hard-throwing lefty could never throw strikes; walked 846 in 857 minor league IPs, plus 10 more in 7 MLB innings, went 34-61, 6.13 in 10 seasons in minors. | | | | | | | | | |
| 26. Athletics: Don Peters, rhp, College of St. Francis (Ill.) | Crestwood, Ill. | R-R | 5-11 | 180 | 20 | $175,000 | 1990 | 1999 | Class AAA (2) |
| NAIA player of year in 1989 (15-2, 2.83); had mid-90s fastball, but pro career never took off because of spotty control, arm injury that sidelined him from 1992-94. | | | | | | | | | |

**Signed to major league cintract.*

"I know there are some people who will say I was the Braves' second choice," Jones said, "but that's better than being the ninth or 10th. If Todd Van Poppel doesn't want to play for the Atlanta Braves, I'm more than happy to take his place."

Other teams also had concerns about signing Van Poppel. He was not selected until the Athletics made him the 14th pick in the first round.

### JONES BECOMES BETTER PLAYER

Jones proved to be a Hall of Fame-worthy player, and Van Poppel had a disappointing career. Jones played 19 seasons in the major leagues, all with the Braves, and established himself as one of the best switch-hitters in baseball history. In 2,499 games, most of them as a third baseman, he batted .303 and hit 468 home runs.

Van Poppel spent 11 seasons in the major leagues, compiling a 40-52 record and 5.58 ERA in 359 games for six teams, mostly as a middle reliever. He was out of the game by 2005, burdened from the outset of his career by oversized expectations and the fast-track status that came with his major league contract, which stipulated that he had to be in the big leagues by 1994, or the A's had to place him on waivers and risk losing him.

Cox saw Jones play three times as an amateur and was his manager for all but the final two years of Jones' distinguished career. Cox never had reason to second-guess his draft-day decision.

"It wasn't a case of settling for Chipper," Cox said at the time. "We liked him very much. In fact, it was not an easy decision deciding between Chipper and Van Poppel. Van Poppel simply helped us make that decision.

"Good middle infielders are hard to find. I think we have found a good one. About eight people in our organization have seen him, and they all came to the same conclusion: He's pretty much a polished ballplayer at this time."

Jones was both an all-state football and baseball player at The Bolles School, a private school in Jacksonville, Fla. The day before his high school team played in the Florida 2-A baseball championship game, Jones got into a scuffle with a teammate and broke his hand. The hand was still in a cast a couple of weeks later when the Braves drafted him.

Jones didn't distinguish himself that summer in the Rookie-level Gulf Coast League, batting only .229 and playing shaky defense.

"I knew coming out of high school that I was capable and worthy of the No. 1 pick," Jones said. "I was just trying so hard to impress everybody that it cost me."

A year later, he asserted himself as an elite prospect and continued to thrive as he climbed through the Braves system, although 131 errors in three seasons raised concerns about his viability as a shortstop. The Braves moved Jones to left field and expected him to be a regular in 1994, but he sustained a serious knee injury in spring training and missed the season. Upon returning in 1995, Jones became the Braves' third baseman and developed into one of baseball's best players. He retired after the 2012 season, long after establishing himself as the most productive player to come out of the 1990 draft.

When Jones agreed to a $275,000 bonus with the Braves, it was the most lucrative contract ever for high school player. But bonuses escalated at such a fast rate during the next few weeks that Jones' bonus was surpassed by six other draft picks, most notably Van Poppel.

### BONUSES CONTINUE ON DIZZYING PACE

Five days before the A's agreed to pay Van Poppel a $500,000 bonus as part of his $1.2 million deal, the Detroit Tigers spent $500,000 of their own to sign Tony Clark, a two-sport player from a San Diego high school and the second overall pick in the draft.

In addition to their generous outlay to Clark, the Tigers agreed that he could play basketball at the University of Arizona, meaning that he would be available to the Tigers only from mid-May to mid-August for the next few years.

"Basketball was the sport I loved and it was what I did year-round," said Clark, a 6-foot-8 athlete who averaged 43.7 points as a high school senior. "Baseball was just something I did because I could hit the ball far and loved watching it go."

Bo Schembechler was the Tigers president at the time, having taken the position in January 1990 after resigning as the football coach at the University of Michigan. He was impressed by Clark's raw athleticism and cared little that Clark had played baseball sparingly in high school. Schembechler ignored the input of Tigers general manager Bill Lajoie and the scouting staff, who were concerned that Clark's development would be compromised by his commitment to basketball.

"We went for talent, not the safe pick, somebody who may be able to help us sooner," said Joe McDonald, Detroit's director of player development. "The biggest thing is that Clark has that ability to hit a baseball with exceptional power."

Clark endured recurring back spasms at Arizona and spent only a semester at the school before transferring to San Diego State, where he played basketball for two years after undergoing back surgery. Clark played in just 88 games over his

## How They Should Have Done It

Based on the career WAR (Wins Above Replacement, as calculated by Baseball-Reference.com) numbers achieved by all the players eligible for the 1990 draft, here's how the first round should have unfolded. Numbers in parentheses indicate the round when the player was actually drafted. Asterisks denote players who signed as draft-and-follows.

| | Player, Pos. | Actual Draft | WAR | Bonus |
|---|---|---|---|---|
| 1. | Chipper Jones, ss | Braves (1) | 85.1 | $275,000 |
| 2. | Mike Mussina, rhp | Orioles (1) | 83.0 | $250,000 |
| 3. | * Andy Pettitte, lhp | Yankees (22) | 60.8 | $85,000 |
| 4. | * Jorge Posada, ss | Yankees (24) | 42.7 | $30,000 |
| 5. | Ray Durham, 2b | White Sox (5) | 33.7 | $30,000 |
| 6. | Mike Hampton, lhp | Mariners (6) | 29.0 | $40,000 |
| 7. | Alex Fernandez, rhp | White Sox (1) | 28.9 | $350,000 |
| 8. | Rondell White, of | Expos (1) | 28.1 | $175,000 |
| 9. | Garret Anderson, of | Angels (4) | 25.7 | $60,000 |
| 10. | Bret Boone, 2b | Mariners (5) | 22.6 | $62,500 |
| 11. | Rusty Greer, of | Rangers (10) | 22.3 | $15,000 |
| 12. | Carl Everett, of | Yankees (1) | 20.4 | $250,000 |
| 13. | Jeromy Burnitz, of | Mets (1) | 19.6 | $192,500 |
| 14. | Troy Percival, c/rhp | Angels (6) | 17.5 | $25,000 |
| 15. | Bob Wickman, rhp | White Sox (2) | 17.2 | $70,000 |
| 16. | David Bell, 3b | Indians (7) | 15.3 | $50,000 |
| 17. | Mike Lieberthal, c | Phillies (1) | 15.2 | $225,000 |
| 18. | Tony Graffanino, ss | Braves (10) | 15.1 | $77,500 |
| 19. | * Eddie Guardado, lhp | Twins (21) | 13.7 | $36,500 |
| 20. | Dan Wilson, c | Reds (1) | 13.0 | $250,000 |
| 21. | Tony Clark, 1b | Tigers (1) | 12.5 | $500,000 |
| 22. | Fernando Vina, 2b | Mets (9) | 12.1 | $27,000 |
| 23. | Steve Karsay, rhp | Blue Jays (1) | 11.2 | $350,000 |
| 24. | Cory Lidle, rhp | Twins (NDFA) | 10.7 | $10,000 |
| 25. | Mike Lansing, ss | Miami Miracle (6) | 9.8 | $11,000 |
| 26. | James Baldwin, rhp | White Sox (4) | 9.2 | $40,000 |

| | Top 3 Unsigned Players | | | Year Signed |
|---|---|---|---|---|
| 1. | Jason Varitek, c | Astros (23) | 24.3 | 1994 |
| 2. | Rick Helling, rhp | Mets (50) | 20.6 | 1992 |
| 3. | Marvin Benard, of | Giants (20) | 8.6 | 1992 |

## AT A GLANCE

### Ones Who Got Away

**TIM SCHWEITZER, LHP, PHILLIES (2ND ROUND); MIKE SCHIEFELBEIN, RHP, RANGERS (2ND ROUND).** The highest unsigned picks in 1990 ended up as college teammates at Arizona. Schweitzer became a seventh-round pick of the Mariners three years later and never pitched a game in pro ball because of injuries. Schielfelbein was a 15th-round pick of the Giants in 1994 and won just two games in two years.

### They Were Drafted?

Michigan football coach Bo Schembechler had a short tenure as president of the Tigers, and his team's 1990 draft had a pronounced football flavor. **KERRY COLLINS** (26), **GREG MCMURTRY** (27) and **RODNEY PEETE** (28) all were selected with consecutive picks. McMurtry, who would play five years in the NFL as a wide receiver, was recruited to Michigan by Schembechler in 1986, the same year the Red Sox made him a first-round pick.

### Did You Know . . .

**BRET BOONE** (Mariners, fifth round) and **DAVID BELL** (Indians, seventh) were the third links in baseball's first three-generation families. Boone reached the majors in 1992, following his grandfather Ray and father Bob. Bell made it in 1995, following his grandfather Gus and father Buddy. Younger brothers Aaron Boone and Mike Bell would also become big leaguers.

### They Said It

**TODD VAN POPPEL**, expressing his displeasure at being drafted by the Athletics: "If they think they can buy me, they're wrong. Money's not everything. The things I want to do, money can't buy. I've got to mature as a person and as a ball player. I think I can do that in college."—*The A's signed Van Poppel to a major league contract valued at $1.2 million.*

## DRAFT SPOTLIGHT: TODD VAN POPPEL

Todd Van Poppel looked like a can't-miss prospect in high school, but a major league deal retarded his development

Oakland A's general manager Sandy Alderson took one of the biggest gambles of the draft era when he called Texas high school pitcher Todd Van Poppel's name with the 14th selection in the 1990 draft.

Van Poppel was the big catch in the Class of 1990. A 6-foot-5 righthander armed with an explosive fastball, he had as much potential as any pitching prospect selected in the first quarter-century of the draft, according to scouts. He was highly regarded by every team, including the Atlanta Braves, who had the first pick.

Yet Van Poppel was passed over by the Braves, and the next 12 teams in the draft rotation as well. Next up were the A's, the defending World Series champions. Alderson felt he was in a position to gamble on a player of Van Poppel's rare ability because the A's had seven picks in the first two rounds. If Van Poppel held firm on his commitment to the University of Texas, the A's still could have a fruitful draft.

Van Poppel and his father, Hank, expressed displeasure that the A's had drafted the 18-year-old pitcher. "If they think they can buy me, they're wrong," an irritated Van Poppel said. "Money's not everything. The things I want to do, money can't buy."

Alderson decided it was best to take a low-pressure approach with the Van Poppels and agent Scott Boras. Two weeks after the draft, Alderson, farm director Karl Kuehl and instructor Harvey Dorfman met with the Van Poppels for three hours in their Texas home.

"It was a very positive discussion," Alderson said. "The focus of our discussion was that Todd was in a very enviable position. We stressed that he had a choice among positives."

Van Poppel agreed to a deal with the A's on July 16. In addition to a $500,000 bonus, he would be paid $100,000 in salary for the 1990 season, $200,000 for 1991 and $400,000 for 1992. At the time, the $1.2 million deal was the richest ever signed by a draft pick.

In his first pro game, Van Poppel combined on a one-hit shutout in the short-season Northwest League. After several more impressive outings that drew large throngs of curious fans, Van Poppel was promoted to the Class A Midwest League. In eight appearances between the two stops, he went 3-2, 2.15, struck out 49 and allowed 18 hits in 38 innings.

Van Poppel spent the next season in the Double-A Southern League and impressed with a mid-90s fastball and big-breaking curve. He made his major league debut on Sept. 11, 1991, little more than a year after signing. It was a chance for the A's and their fans to take a sneak peek at the future.

Under the terms of his contract, Van Poppel could be optioned to the minor leagues three times, beginning with the 1991 season. That meant he would have to be in the major leagues by 1994 for good or be subject to waivers, free for another club to claim him at minimal cost. It didn't help that injuries limited him to nine games in 1992.

By the time he had exhausted his minor league options, his breaking pitches and changeup remained inconsistent. He had pitched only 294 innings in the minors, going 17-25, 4.01, and was in the untenable position of having to learn on the job in the majors.

"It was very foolish, a jump like that," A's pitching coach Bob Cluck said. "He was under constant scrutiny and did not have the time to build the skills to be successful in the major leagues."

Van Poppel remained with the A's through the 1994 and '95 seasons, struggling to justify his spot on the roster while showing flashes of his potential. He continued to scuffle in 1996, and was 3-9, 9.06 when the A's designated him for assignment on Aug. 1. Over the next 10 months, he twice was placed on waivers and twice released.

"It's hard to analyze what went wrong," Alderson said. "There were tremendous pressures that come from those kinds of expectations. But as time went on, he was no longer considered to be the best. Right to the end, Todd was trying to justify a position on our team at a time when we needed him to be competitive and to contribute."

After leaving the A's, Van Poppel played for five teams before retiring after failing to make the New York Mets in spring training 2005. The curse of unfulfilled potential is played out time and again in baseball, and Van Poppel had become the latest example.

first four seasons in the Tigers system and rarely displayed his power potential, hitting only seven home runs.

But with basketball behind him once and for all by 1994, he began to progress as a baseball player. Clark made it to the Tigers in 1995 and spent 15 years in the major leagues, hitting 251 home runs. In 2014, Clark became the executive director of the Major League Baseball Players Association.

The same day that Jones signed with the Braves, the Chicago White Sox agreed on a $350,000 deal with righthander Alex Fernandez, the fourth overall pick and the only non-high school player among the first six picks. Two years earlier, Fernandez had turned down $150,000 from the Milwaukee Brewers as their first-round pick in favor of playing at the University of Miami. After going 15-2, 2.01 with 177 strikeouts in 148 innings as a freshman, Fernandez transferred to Miami-Dade Community College South in order to become eligible for the 1990 draft.

Fernandez went 12-2, 1.19 with 154 strikeouts in 121 innings at Miami-Dade and became the first junior college player to win the Golden Spikes Award, emblematic of the nation's best amateur player. (Bryce Harper became the second junior college player to win the award when he was at the College of Southern Nevada in 2010.)

Fernandez was promoted to the White Sox on Aug. 2, becoming the first player from the class of 1990 to reach the majors. He joined the White Sox on the same day as first baseman Frank Thomas, the team's 1989 first-round pick. Add in 1987 first-rounder Jack McDowell and 1988 first-rounder Robin Ventura, and the White Sox arguably had the best four-year run of first-round picks in draft history. Fernandez had a productive 10-year career, winning 107 games, before shoulder issues forced him to retire.

The only other player drafted in 1990 to make it to the majors that year was lefthander Lance Dickson, selected by the Chicago Cubs with the 23rd pick out of the University of Arizona. Dickson went 0-3, 7.24 in three September starts for the Cubs and never got back to the big leagues. Plagued by an assortment of injuries and an ineffective curveball, which had been his signature pitch, Dickson won just eight games over the next five years in the minors.

In addition to Clark, Fernandez and Van Poppel, two other 1990 first-round picks received bonuses of at least $300,000: University of Iowa shortstop Tim Costo, regarded as the top power hitter in the college ranks; and New York high

### Fastest To The Majors

| | Player, Pos. | Drafted (Round) | Debut |
|---|---|---|---|
| 1. | Alex Fernandez, rhp | White Sox (1) | Aug. 2, 1990 |
| 2. | Lance Dickson, lhp | Cubs (1) | Aug. 9, 1990 |
| 3. | Kirk Dressendorfer, rhp | Athletics (1-S) | April 13, 1991 |
| 4. | Chris Haney, lhp | Expos (2) | June 21, 1991 |
| 5. | Mike Mussina, rhp | Orioles (1) | Aug. 4, 1991 |

**FIRST HIGH SCHOOL SELECTION:** Todd Van Poppel, rhp (Athletics/1, Sept. 11, 1991)

**LAST PLAYER TO RETIRE:** Andy Petttte, lhp (Sept. 28, 2013)

## Top 25 Bonuses

| Player, Pos. | Drafted (Round) | Order | Bonus |
|---|---|---|---|
| 1. * **Tony Clark, of** | Tigers (1) | 2 | $500,000 |
| * **Todd Van Poppel, rhp** | Athletics (1) | 14 | #$500,000 |
| 3. *†**Frankie Rodriguez, rhp/ss** | Red Sox (2) | 41 | $420,000 |
| 4. * Chris Weinke, 3b | Blue Jays (2) | 62 | $375,000 |
| 5. **Alex Fernandez, rhp** | White Sox (1) | 4 | $350,000 |
| * **Steve Karsay, rhp** | Blue Jays (1) | 22 | $350,000 |
| 7. **Tim Costo, ss** | Indians (1) | 8 | $300,000 |
| 8. * **Chipper Jones, ss** | Braves (1) | 1 | $275,000 |
| 9. * **Todd Ritchie, rhp** | Twins (1) | 12 | $252,500 |
| 10. **Mike Mussina, rhp** | Orioles (1) | 20 | $250,000 |
| **Dan Wilson, c** | Reds (1) | 7 | $250,000 |
| * Tom Nevers, ss | Astros (1) | 21 | $250,000 |
| * **Carl Everett, of** | Yankees (1) | 10 | $250,000 |
| * **Adam Hyzdu, of** | Giants (1) | 15 | $250,000 |
| 15. **Donovan Osborne, lhp** | Cardinals (1) | 13 | $235,000 |
| 16. * **Kurt Miller, rhp** | Pirates (1) | 5 | $232,000 |
| 17. * **Mike Lieberthal, c** | Phillies (1) | 3 | $225,000 |
| 18. * **Marc Newfield, 1b** | Mariners (1) | 6 | $220,000 |
| **Dan Smith, lhp** | Rangers (1) | 16 | $220,000 |
| 20. * Ronnie Walden, lhp | Dodgers (1) | 9 | $215,000 |
| 21. * **Aaron Holbert, ss** | Cardinals (1) | 18 | $195,000 |
| 22. **Jeromy Burnitz, of** | Mets (1) | 17 | $192,500 |
| 23. **Lance Dickson, lhp** | Cubs (1) | 23 | $180,000 |
| 24. * **Shane Andrews, 3b** | Expos (1) | 11 | $175,000 |
| * **Rondell White, of** | Expos (1) | 24 | $175,000 |
| * **Robbie Beckett, lhp** | Padres (1) | 25 | $175,000 |
| Eric Christopherson, c | Giants (1) | 19 | $175,000 |
| Don Peters, rhp | Athletics (1) | 26 | $175,000 |

*Major leaguers in bold. *High school selection. #Major league contract. †Signed as draft-and-follow.*

school righthander Steve Karsay, who insisted he was firm on attending Louisiana State.

The Cleveland Indians, drafting eighth, spent $300,000 to sign Costo, who had only five homers in his first 108 games in the Indians system and was traded to the Reds on June 14, 1991. The trouble was, the deal occurred six days shy of the one-year anniversary of Costo signing with the Indians, a violation of a major league rule that prohibited the trading of a draft pick within a year of the player's signing date. Major League Baseball essentially looked the other way and approved the trade anyway.

"We tried to take into consideration Costo himself," said Bill Murray, director of baseball operations for the commissioner's office. "The kid had been told he was traded. What do we do, make him go back? You have to try and be equitable, not just with the clubs, but the player, too."

The Toronto Blue Jays drafted Karsay with the 22nd pick, and a month later signed him with a $350,000 bonus offer. The Jays didn't hesitate on another high-risk pick, using their second-round choice on third baseman Chris Weinke, one of the nation's best high school quarterbacks at Cretin High in St. Paul, Minn. Weinke had started fall football practice at Florida State when the Jays signed him for a $375,000 bonus on Aug. 20.

Weinke didn't make it to the big leagues in a career that peaked in Triple-A. He returned to Florida State in 1997 to play football, led the Seminoles to a national championship in 1999, won the Heisman Trophy in 2000 at the age of 28 and went on to play in the NFL for seven years, mostly as a backup quarterback.

The Blue Jays committed $1,672,450 to sign their draft picks, breaking a record they had set a year earlier. In addition to large outlays to Karsay and Weinke, they signed fifth-round pick Scott Burrell, a righthanded pitcher, to a $150,000 bonus. Burrell also was a rising basketball star at the University of Connecticut, and he became a first-round NBA draft choice in 1993. He pitched one season in the Jays system, in part because of injury, but mostly because of his overriding commitment to basketball.

### WINDFALL DRAFTS FOR A'S, EXPOS

The Athletics had seven selections in the first two rounds of the 1990 draft, gaining five extra picks because they lost free agents Dave Parker, Storm Davis and Tony Phillips to other clubs after the 1989 season.

The A's appeared to get off to a spectacular start in the draft, landing Van Poppel with the 14th choice, one of two compensation picks for losing Parker. They followed up by selecting college pitchers Don Peters, Kirk Dressendorfer, David Zancanaro and Curtis Shaw, and then chose college catcher Eric Helfand and high school outfielder Gary Hust—all among the first 66 players drafted.

None of the seven lived up to expectations. Only Van Poppel, Dressendorfer and Helfand played in the major leagues. Dressendorfer, who went 45-8 over three seasons at the University of Texas, was plagued throughout his pro career by back and arm problems. He went 3-3, 5.45 in 1991, his only year in the majors. Helfand played in just 53 major league games.

The Montreal Expos had 10 selections in the first two rounds. They gained two picks each for the loss of free agents Hubie Brooks, Pascual Perez and Mark Langston, one for Bryn Smith and an additional pick for failing to sign Charles Johnson,

DAVID SEELIG

**Tony Clark was an underappreciated baseball prospect because of his basketball prowess, but he went on to play 15 years in the majors**

### WORTH NOTING

■ Led by **TONY CLARK** (Tigers, second overall) and **TODD VAN POPPEL** (A's, 14th), who established a bonus record for first-round picks by signing for $500,000, new round records were set all over the baseball landscape in 1990. At least a dozen new marks were set, including the second (**FRANKIE RODRIGUEZ**, $420,000), fourth (**JOHNNY WALKER**, $170,000), fifth (**SCOTT BURRELL**, $150,000), eighth (**JOHN CUMMINGS**, $80,000) and 10th rounds (**TONY GRAFFANINO**, $77,500).

■ The Major League Scouting Bureau warned clubs before the 1990 draft that Oklahoma high school lefthander **RONNIE WALDEN'S** arm might be suspect, but the Dodgers drafted him anyway with the ninth pick overall. Walden made four appearances with Rookie-level Great Falls before missing the next two seasons because of elbow surgery, the latest in an all-too-familiar Dodgers script where seven first-rounders over an eight-year stretch met with disaster, mainly because of injury. It was the final straw for longtime Dodgers scouting director Ben Wade, who lost his job.

■ The Royals didn't have picks in the first or second rounds in 1990, and made a curious selection in the third round by drafting Henry Ford (Mich.) CC righthander **SHAYNE REA**, a former high school dropout whose weight once had ballooned to 320 pounds and who had been in jail for drug use. Rea turned his life around, got into shape and made considerable progress as a pitching prospect in junior college. But back problems hampered his career, and he was released after going 18-20, 4.31 in four seasons in the Royals system. A year later, Rea committed suicide.

■ Former Michigan football coach Bo Schembechler took over the presidency of the Tigers just months before the

CONTINUED ON PAGE 382

## WORTH NOTING

CONTINUED FROM PAGE 381

1990 draft, and his imprint was apparent in the way the Tigers approached the draft. He mandated the selection of slugging first baseman **TONY CLARK** with the No. 2 pick overall, overruling his own scouting staff, and was influential in the drafting of three future NFL players with consecutive picks: 26th-rounder **KERRY COLLINS**, a Penn State recruit; 27th-rounder **GREG MCMURTRY**, who Schembechler had recruited himself to play both football and baseball at Michigan; and 28th-rounder **RODNEY PEETE**, a two-sport star at Southern California.

■ University of Minnesota catcher **DAN WILSON**, selected seventh by the Reds, and Iowa shortstop **TIM COSTO**, chosen eighth by the Indians, were the first college players drafted. Within a year, Costo was traded to the Reds, and the two became teammates in Cincinnati in 1992 and '93. Oddly, both players played in 12 games for the Reds in 1992; a year later, Wilson participated in 36 games, Costo in 31. That's when their paths diverged as Wilson was traded to the Mariners and played 12 years with that club during the greatest era in Seattle's checkered baseball history. Costo was dealt back to the Indians, never to see the big leagues again.

■ As a junior at Cincinnati's Moeller High, **ADAM HYZDU** broke the school's season (13) and career (22) home run records, set two years earlier by Ken Griffey Jr. The Giants spent the first of their two first-round picks in 1990 on Hyzdu, a 6-foot-3, 210-pound outfielder. Ten years later, after a noteworthy minor league career, Hyzdu reached the big leagues with the Pirates. Over parts of seven seasons with four major league clubs, he homered 19 times in 221 games. In 1,703 games as a minor leaguer, Hyzdu homered 273 times. San Francisco's other 1990 first-rounder, San Diego State catcher **ERIC CHRISTOPHERSON**, fell short of playing in the majors.

their No. 1 pick in the 1989 draft.

The Expos spent $1.252 million to sign all 10 picks, seven of whom reached the majors. They signed all of their draft choices through the first 14 rounds, 22 players in all. The most notable success story was outfielder Rondell White, the 24th overall selection, who played 15 seasons in the major leagues, batting .284 with 198 homers.

The Yankees didn't have extra draft choices, but they did have a first-round selection for only the second time in 12 years, having given up the others as the penalty for signing major league free agents. The Yankees' first pick in 1990 was outfielder Carl Everett, who had a long major league career (with other teams) and was among 16 future big leaguers in New York's draft haul, a record in the one-draft era. The group included lefthander Andy Pettitte in the 22nd round and catcher Jorge Posada in the 24th, both key players in the Yankees' return to glory in the mid-1990s.

### FIRST-ROUND FALLOUT

Teams drafted a total of 1,489 players in 1990, one fewer than the record 1,490 selected in 1989. The Houton Astros made a record 100 picks, topping their own record of 87 selections a year earlier.

A majority of the Astros selections were junior-college players or players who were headed to junior college, and seven signed the following spring. The group included 83rd-round choice Danny Young, a lefthanded pitcher who signed after spending his freshman year at Aquinas (Tenn.) Junior College. Young surfaced briefly in the majors in 2000, becoming the highest-round draft choice ever to reach the big leagues.

The Astros' first-round selection, Minnesota high school shortstop Tom Nevers, failed to make the major leagues, despite playing professionally until 2002. Prior to accepting a $250,000 bonus from the Astros, Nevers was drafted in 1989 by the NHL's Pittsburgh Penguins (fifth round). He played hockey at the University of Minnesota from 1995-97 and spent the summers playing baseball in the minor leagues. Nevers was a great-great nephew of football Hall of Fame player Ernie Nevers, who also pitched briefly for the St. Louis Browns.

Besides Nevers, the only high school first-rounder who fell short of the majors was lefthander Ronnie Walden, drafted by the Los Angeles Dodgers out of an Oklahoma high school with the ninth overall pick. His promising career barely got off the ground before it was ravaged by injuries.

After going 3-0, 0.42 in his first three starts at Rookie-level Great Falls, and showing a fastball in the mid- to high-90s, Walden felt a twinge in his elbow in his fourth start. He missed the balance of the season and subsequently had two elbow surgeries that sidelined him for all of the 1991 and '92 seasons. A year later, he had shoulder surgery, prompting his retirement from baseball after just 31 minor league innings.

Stanford righthander Mike Mussina, chosen 20th by the Baltimore Orioles, had the longest and most distinguished career among pitchers drafted in the first round. He won 270 games over 18 major league seasons, 10 with the Orioles and eight with the Yankees. Mussina set an American League record by winning at least 11 games for 17 years in a row. In 2008, he became the second pitcher to retire from baseball after a 20-win season, joining Sandy Koufax, who did it in 1966.

### RODRIGUEZ ADDS DRAFT DRAMA

Pitcher/shortstop Frankie Rodriguez, selected by the Boston Red Sox with the first pick in the second round, was the highest-drafted player in 1990 who did not sign. He sought a $200,000 bonus, and the Red Sox countered at $145,000.

Rodriguez, a New York high school product, elected to attend Howard (Texas) Junior College, so he remained under control to the Red Sox through the 1991 junior-college season under terms of baseball's draft-and-follow rule. Rodriguez

## Largest Bonuses By Round

| | Player, Pos. | Club | Bonus |
|---|---|---|---|
| **1.** | ***Tony Clark, of** | **Tigers** | **$500,000** |
| | ***Todd Van Poppel, rhp** | **Athletics** | **$500,000** |
| **2.** | ***#Frankie Rodriguez, rhp/ss** | **Red Sox** | **$420,000** |
| 3. | *Mike Thomas, of | Orioles | $137,000 |
| 4. | Johnny Walker, of | Braves | $170,000 |
| 5. | Scott Burrell, rhp | Blue Jays | $150,000 |
| 6. | *Wade Fyock, rhp | Royals | $75,000 |
| **7.** | **Jalal Leach, of** | **Yankees** | **$92,500** |
| **8.** | **John Cummings, lhp** | **Mariners** | **$80,000** |
| **9.** | **Brian Kowitz, of** | **Braves** | **$45,000** |
| **10.** | ***Tony Graffanino, ss** | **Braves** | **$77,500** |
| 11. | Terry Powers, rhp | Red Sox | $20,000 |
| 12. | *Craig Sides, rhp | Indians | $25,000 |
| | **Rod Myers, rhp** | **Royals** | **$25,000** |
| 13. | Kip Yaughn, rhp | Orioles | $30,000 |
| **14.** | **#Jeff McCurry, rhp** | **Pirates** | **$125,000** |
| 15. | *Sean Smith, rhp | Yankees | $50,000 |
| **16.** | ***Jim Converse, rhp** | **Mariners** | **$60,000** |
| **17.** | ***Brian Daubach, 1b** | **Mets** | **$25,000** |
| 18. | *#Keith Kimsey, of | Tigers | $42,000 |
| 19. | *Derrick Bottoms, lhp | Astros | $30,000 |
| 20. | *Ralph Garr Jr., of | Braves | $20,000 |
| | Matthew Wilke, ss | Blue Jays | $20,000 |
| **21.** | **#Eddie Guardado, lhp** | **Twins** | **$36,500** |
| **22.** | ***#Andy Pettitte, lhp** | **Yankees** | **$90,000** |
| **23.** | **#Tom Wilson, of** | **Yankees** | **$90,000** |
| 24. | #Shawn Kennedy, rhp | Rangers | $35,000 |
| 25. | Bill Norris, 3b | Red Sox | $15,000 |
| Other | #Jeff Johnson, rhp | Red Sox (31) | $115,000 |

*Major leaguers in bold. *High school selection. #Signed as draft-and-follow.*

## Highest Unsigned Picks

| Player, Pos., Team (Round) | College | Re-Drafted |
|---|---|---|
| Tim Schweitzer, lhp, Phillies (2) | Arizona | Mariners '93 (7) |
| Mike Schiefelbein, rhp, Rangers (2) | Arizona | Padres '93 (26) |
| Keith Grunewald, ss, Tigers (2) | North Carolina | Rockies '93 (12) |
| Jose Prado, rhp, Giants (2) | Miami | Dodgers '93 (8) |
| Eric Maloney, rhp, White Sox (2) | Creighton | Dodgers '93 (19) |
| Silvio Censale, lhp, Twins (4) | Miami | Phillies '93 (10) |
| Greg Thomas, of, Red Sox (4) | Vanderbilt | Indians '93 (9) |
| Chris West, 1b/3b, Orioles (4) | Louisburg (N.C.) JC | Dodgers '91 (43) |
| Jimmy Lewis, rhp, Cardinals (5) | Florida State | Astros '91 (2) |
| Doug Creek, lhp, Angels (5) | *Georgia Tech | Cardinals '91 (7) |

**TOTAL UNSIGNED PICKS:** Top 5 Rounds (10), Top 10 Rounds (30)

**Returned to same school.*

was eligible to sign with Boston between the completion of Howard's season and a week prior to the 1991 draft.

The situation became complicated when Howard won the Junior College World Series and Rodriguez struck out 17 in the title game and was the tournament MVP. Howard's season didn't end until less than 48 hours before the 1991 draft, and by then Rodriguez's stock had soared. Featuring a fastball that reached 96-98 mph, he went 14-1, 3.14, and hit .450 with 26 home runs and 93 RBIs, leading the nation's junior-college players in both strikeouts by a pitcher (139) and home runs.

The Red Sox, anxious to strike a deal with Rodriguez and keep him out of the 1991 draft, agreed on a bonus of $425,000 about nine hours before the deadline. At the time, it was the largest bonus ever paid to a second-round pick.

Despite his impressive credentials on the mound and a preponderence of opinion that he should be developed as a pitcher, Rodriguez preferred playing shortstop and insisted the Red Sox allow him to play that position. He hit .271 with six home runs and 31 RBIs in his first pro season.

A year later, realizing that pitching might be his quickest ticket to the majors, Rodriguez moved to the mound and reached the majors as a pitcher with the Red Sox in 1995. After he went 0-2, 10.57 in nine appearances, the Red Sox traded Rodriguez to the Minnesota Twins. He spent seven years in the majors with four clubs and went 29-39, 5.53.

TYLER-TRAVIS BOLDEN

Frankie Rodriguez

Under draft rules in place at the time, two minor league clubs without major league affiliations took part in the 1990 draft, beginning with the fourth round. The New York-Penn League's Erie Sailors chose one player, and the Florida State League's Miami Miracle claimed 16, including Stanford outfielder Paul Carey in the fourth round and Wichita State second baseman Mike Lansing in the sixth. The Miracle focused almost exclusively on drafting college seniors, though the players were legitimate prospects and paid bonuses accordingly. The Miracle signed 15 of their 16 picks, paying bonuses totaling $104,000.

Carey broke Mark McGwire's Pacific-10 Conference record by hitting 56 homers in his four-year career at Stanford, including 16 as both a junior and a senior. After signing for a $37,500 bonus, he hit .327 with four home runs and 20 RBIs in 49 games with Miami. The following year, Carey's contract was purchased by the Orioles.

Most major league clubs were wary of the Miracle's tactics. Team owner Marv Goldklang said he was having difficulty getting enough talent from major league clubs to become competitive in the Florida State League, so he took advantage of existing provisions in the Rule 4 draft.

"It was absolutely a last resort," Goldklang said. "If the help was forthcoming, there's a good chance we would not have participated in the draft."

Under the existing Professional Baseball Agreement between the major and minor leagues, Carey would have been required to stay with the Miracle for a minimum of a year. But under terms of a new PBA that went into effect on Dec. 15, 1990, Major League Baseball acquired the rights to Miracle players for $300,000 and in turn sold players to interested major league organizations at a minimum cost of $65,000. The Orioles won a bidding war among eight to 10 clubs for Carey's services, acquiring him for $150,000. The new PBA also forbid independent clubs from participating in the draft.

Carey played only the 1993 season in the major leagues. Lansing, who received an $11,000 bonus from Miami, was much more successful. His contract was purchased by the Expos following the 1991 season on the recommendation of new Expos manager Felipe Alou, who had watched Lansing in the Florida State League while he was managing at West Palm Beach in 1990-91. Lansing played nine years in the majors, hitting .271 with 84 homers.

## Largest Draft-And-Follow Bonuses

| | Player, Pos. | Club (Round) | Bonus |
|---|---|---|---|
| **1.** | ***Frank Rodriguez, rhp/ss** | **Red Sox (2)** | **$420,000** |
| **2.** | **Jeff McCurry, rhp** | **Pirates (14)** | **$125,000** |
| 3. | Jeff Johnson, rhp | Red Sox (31) | $115,000 |
| **4.** | **Tom Wilson, of** | **Yankees (23)** | **$90,000** |
| 5. | Fred Starks, rhp | White Sox (14) | $80,000 |
| | ***Andy Pettitte, lhp** | **Yankees (22)** | **$80,000** |
| **7.** | **Ben Blomdahl, rhp** | **Tigers (14)** | **$67,000** |
| 8. | Renaldo Bullock, of | Mariners (30) | $50,000 |
| 9. | David Chisum, of | Indians (43) | $45,000 |
| 10. | *Keith Kimsey, of | Tigers (18) | $42,000 |

*Major leaguers in bold. *High school selection.*

## One Team's Draft: New York Yankees

| Player, Pos. | Bonus | Player, Pos. | Bonus | Player, Pos. | Bonus |
|---|---|---|---|---|---|
| **1. *Carl Everett, of** | **$250,000** | 10. Darren Hodges, rhp | $15,000 | 19. Brent Gilbert, rhp | $1,000 |
| **2. Robert Eenhoorn, ss** | **$100,000** | 11. Richard Hines, lhp | $15,000 | **20. Kevin Jordan, 2b** | **$7,500** |
| 3. *Tate Seefried, 1b | $92,500 | 12. Ron Frazier, rhp | $20,000 | 21. Keith Seiler, lhp | $1,000 |
| **4. Kirt Ojala, lhp** | **$50,000** | 13. *Jeff Motuzas, c | $20,000 | **22. #Andy Pettitte, lhp** | **$80,000** |
| 5. Rick Lantrip, ss | $33,000 | 14. Bo Siberz, rhp | $25,000 | **23. #Tom Wilson, c/of** | **$90,000** |
| **6. Sam Militello, rhp** | **$40,000** | 15. *Sean Smith, rhp | $50,000 | **24. #Jorge Posada, ss** | **$30,000** |
| **7. Jalal Leach, of** | **$92,500** | **16. *Ricky Ledee, of** | **$19,500** | **25. Matt Dunbar, lhp** | **$2,500** |
| 8. Tim Rumer, lhp | $15,000 | 17. Bryan Faw, rhp | $1,000 | **Other Shane Spencer (28), of** | **$15,000** |
| 9. Matt Terrell, of | Did not sign | 18. Bob Deller, rhp | $12,500 | | |

*Major leaguers in bold. *High school selection. #Signed as draft-and-follow.*

## IN FOCUS: MIKE MUSSINA

STANFORD BASEBALL

The Orioles were delighted to land Stanford righthander Mike Mussina with the 20th pick in 1990. Orioles owner Larry Lucchino said: "Somewhere, Mr. Williams is smiling now."

The late Edward Bennett Williams, the team owner before Lucchino, had tried in vain to sign Mussina to a six-figure contract in 1987, when the Orioles drafted him in the 11th round out of a Pennsylvania high school. Mussina was the top prep pitching prospect in that draft. The Major League Scouting Bureau had awarded him a 76 grade on the 20-80 scouting scale, and he would have been among the top two or three picks had he been amenable to signing. But Mussina was committed to attending Stanford, and teams refused to meet his $350,000 price tag.

Three years later, Mussina was available again when the Orioles picked 20th. Some scouts said he had not made much progress at Stanford, where he went 31-16, 3.89, including a 16-2 loss to Georgia in the College World Series on the eve of the 1990 draft. The O's finally got their man when Mussina agreed to a $250,000 bonus, signing on July 28, the latest signing date for a 1990 first-rounder.

Over 18 major league seasons, Mussina won 270 games with the Orioles and Yankees.

# 1990 Draft List

**Did not sign. Major leaguers in bold, with first and last years noted. Order of selection indicated in parentheses. For the first five rounds, the peak level of each player is noted. + Signed as draft-and-follow (Second school noted if applicable).*

## ATLANTA BRAVES (1)

**1. Chipper Jones, ss, The Bolles School, Jacksonville, Fla.—(1993-2012)**
2. (Choice to Red Sox as compensation for Type B free agent Nick Esasky)
3. Lance Marks, of, Dana Hills HS, Dana Point, Calif.—(High A)
4. Johnny Walker, of, University of Texas.—(Rookie)
DRAFT DROP *Eighth-round draft pick, Green Bay Packers/ National Football League (1991)*
**5. Joe Ayrault, c, Sarasota (Fla.) HS.—(1996)**
6. *Ken Reed, 3b-1b, Hamilton (Ohio) HS.
**7. Ed Giovanola, ss, Santa Clara University.—(1995-99)**
8. *Armando Rodriguez, of, JC of San Mateo (Calif.).
**9. Brian Kowitz, of, Clemson University.—(1995)**
**10. Tony Graffanino, ss, East Islip (N.Y.) HS.—(1996-2009)**
**11. *Phil Stidham, rhp, University of Arkansas.—(1994)**
**12. Brian Bark, lhp-of, North Carolina State University.—(1995)**
13. *Damon Lembi, 3b-1b, Burlingame (Calif.) HS.
14. Kian Sly, of-1b, San Diego (Calif.) HS.
15. Adrian Garcia, c, Elizabeth (N.J.) HS.
16. *Michael Tarter, c, Walton HS, Marietta, Ga.
17. Jerome Koller, rhp, Martinsville (Ind.) HS.
**18. Mike Potts, lhp, Gordon (Ga.) JC.—(1996)**
19. Juan Williams, of, Ramona HS, Riverside, Calif.
20. Ralph Garr Jr., of, Bellaire HS, Missouri City, Texas.
DRAFT DROP *Son of Ralph Garr, major leaguer (1968-80)*
21. *Richard King, rhp, Gordon (Ga.) JC.
22. Stewart Ford, lhp, Ranger (Texas) JC.
**23. *Matt Wagner, rhp, Cedar Falls (Iowa) HS.—(1996)**
24. Jason Kempfer, rhp, Sparta HS, Baldwin, Ill.
25. Cory Mathis, of, Gonzales (Texas) HS.
26. Michael Place, rhp, St. Petersburg (Fla.) JC.
27. Larry Owens, lhp, Armstrong State (Ga.) University.
28. Loren Gress, 1b, Hutchinson (Kan.) JC.
29. Scott Ryder, rhp, Georgia Southern College.
30. *David Hollingsworth, rhp, Middle Georgia JC.
31. Gerald Trevino, ss, Pleasanton (Texas) HS.
32. Kevin O'Connor, of, University of Illinois.
33. Doyle Moore, of, Madison Heights HS, Anderson, Ind.
34. *Dustin Longenecker, of, Parkview HS, Stone Mountain, Ga.
**35. *Scott Watkins, lhp, Seminole (Okla.) JC.—(1995)**
36. Brian Dare, lhp, University of Texas.
37. *Adrian Jones, of-rhp, Universtiy of Missouri-St. Louis.
38. Don Robinson, of, Haynesville (La.) HS.
**39. *Jason Wood, ss, Fresno (Calif.) CC.—(1998-2008)**
40. *Chris Chandler, ss, Beverly Hills (Calif.) HS.
41. Amauri Rodriguez, 2b, Edison (Fla.) CC.
42. John Wilder, rhp-ss, South Florence HS, Florence, S.C.
43. *Billy Maitland, rhp, Dinwiddie County HS, Sutherland, Va.
44. *Christopher Robbins, rhp, Union County HS, Blairsville, Ga.
45. *Ja'Rad Hunt, 2b-3b, McNair HS, Atlanta.
46. Samuel Rutter, rhp, Abingdon (Va.) HS.
47. Shannon Ledwick, rhp, Ranger (Texas) JC.
48. *Jake Green, ss-rhp, Suwannee HS, Live Oak, Fla.
49. *Adan Garcia, rhp, Gadsden HS, Anthony, N.M.
50. *Joe Hiller, rhp, Stratford Academy HS, Macon, Ga.
51. *Reed Garwood, 1b, Deerfield Winds HS, Albany, Ga.
52. *Mark Beeman, 3b, Carlsbad (N.M.) HS.
53. *Ricky Freeman, 3b, Bellaire HS, Houston.
**54. *Kelly Wunsch, lhp, Bellaire HS, Houston.—(2000-05)**
DRAFT DROP *First-round draft pick (26th overall), Brewers (1993)*
55. Tommy Owen, c, University of Georgia.
56. *Jason Gonzales, ss, Blinn (Texas) JC.
57. *Gary Herrmann, lhp, Blinn (Texas) JC.
58. +Brad Riddle, of, Morton (Ill.) JC.
59. *Darrett Robinson, of, Bellaire HS, Houston.
60. James Arendt, of, Montezuma (Iowa) HS.
61. *Jamine Adams, of, Canyon Springs HS, Moreno Valley, Calif.
62. Mark Chambers, of, University of Northern Iowa.
63. Anthony Johnson, of, Huston-Tillotson (Texas) College.
64. *Doug Valdez, lhp, El Dorado HS, Albuquerque, N.M.
65. *Greg Quinn, of, Shadow Mountain HS, Phoenix.
66. *Victor McCraney, of, Taft (Calif.) JC.
67. *James Richardson, of, Westark (Ark.) JC.
68. *Robert Hooker, ss, Norland HS, Miami.

## BALTIMORE ORIOLES (20)

**1. Mike Mussina, rhp, Stanford University.—(1991-2008)**
**2. Erik Schullstrom, rhp, Fresno State University.—(1994-95)**
2. Jeff Williams, rhp, Wichita State University (Supplemental choice—69th—for loss of Type C free agent Dave Schmidt).—(AAA)
3. Mike Thomas, of, Richmond County HS, Rockingham, N.C.—(High A)
4. *Chris West, 1b-3b, Eastern Wayne HS, Goldsboro, N.C.—Low A)
DRAFT DROP *Attended Louisburg (N.C.) JC; re-drafted by Dodgers, 1991 (43rd round)*
**5. Bobby Chouinard, rhp, Forest Grove (Ore.) HS.—(1996-2001)**
6. Brad Tyler, ss, University of Evansville.
7. Shane Hale, lhp, University of South Alabama.
8. *Mike Daniel, c, Oklahoma State University.
9. Roy Hodge, of, Charles E. Shea HS, St. Thomas, Virgin Islands.
**10. Damon Buford, 2b-of, University of Southern California.—(1993-2001)**
DRAFT DROP *Son of Don Buford, major leaguer (1963-72)*
11. Gordon Graham, 1b, Hershey (Pa.) HS.
12. Jason Alstead, of, St. Cloud State (Minn.) University.
13. Kip Yaughn, rhp, Arizona State University.
14. Scott Miley, of, Mission HS, San Jose, Calif.
15. *Duane Page, rhp, Ocean View HS, Westminster, Calif.
16. *Willie Speakman, c, Fullerton (Calif.) JC.
17. Steve Godin, of, East Carolina University.
18. Brett Benge, rhp, Rend Lake (Ill.) JC.
19. Brent Miller, 1b, Middle Georgia JC.
20. Steve DiMarco, 3b, C.W. Post (N.Y.) College.
21. Daniel Ramirez, ss, University of Tennessee.
**22. Scott McClain, 3b-rhp, Atascadero (Calif.) HS.—(1998-2008)**
23. Justin Evans, of, Bethany (Okla.) HS.
24. Scott Sprick, ss, Jacksonville State University.
25. Michael Hebb, rhp, Anne Arundel (Md.) CC.
26. David Paveloff, rhp, Chapman (Calif.) College.
27. Michael Lamitola, 2b, Seton Hall University.
28. *Dom DeSantis, rhp, University of New Orleans.
29. *Jason Hutchins, rhp, Golden West (Calif.) JC.
**30. *Robin Jennings, of, Annandale HS, Alexandria, Va.—(1996-2001)**
31. Todd Unrein, lhp, University of Southwestern Louisiana.
32. Greg Hays, rhp, Long Beach State University.
**33. Jim Dedrick, rhp, Southern California College.—(1995)**
34. +Matt Jarvis, lhp, La Cueva HS, Albuquerque, N.M. / Mesa (Ariz.) CC.
**35. *Bill Simas, rhp, St. Joseph HS, Santa Maria, Calif.—(1995-2000)**
36. *Kyle Allred, ss, Murray State (Okla.) JC.
37. Ihosvany Marquez, rhp, Miami Springs HS, Hialeah, Fla.
38. Jose Millares, 3b, Azusa Pacific (Calif.) University.
**39. *Jon Nunnally, c, Hargrave Military Academy, Pelham, N.C.—(1995-2000)**
40. +Kevin Ryan, rhp, Seminole (Okla.) JC.
41. *David McLaughlin, ss, Milwaukie (Ore.) HS.
42. *Dennis Van Pelt, of-1b, Long Branch (N.J.) HS.
43. +Doug McConathy, 1b-3b, Cypress (Calif.) JC.
44. Doug Flowers, c, North Carolina Wesleyan College.

## BOSTON RED SOX (18)

1. (Choice to Cardinals as compensation for Type A free agent Tony Pena)
**2. +Frankie Rodriguez, rhp-ss, Eastern District HS, Brooklyn, N.Y. / Howard (Texas) JC** (Choice from Braves as compensation for Type B free agent Nick Esasky)**—(1995-2001)**
2. (Choice to Twins as compensation for Type A free agent Jeff Reardon)
**3. Walt McKeel, c, Greene Central HS, Snow Hill, N.C.—(1996-2002)**
4. *Greg Thomas, of, Lake Brantley HS, Altamonte Springs, Fla.—(AAA)
DRAFT DROP *Attended Vanderbilt; re-drafted by Indians, 1993 (9th round)*
5. Tim Tackett, c, Waverly (Ohio) HS.—(High A)
**6. Gar Finnvold, rhp, Florida State University.—(1994)**
7. Todd Miller, rhp, Temple University.
8. *Aaron Knieper, rhp, Nouvel Catholic HS, Saginaw, Mich.
9. *Mike Collett, rhp, Citrus (Calif.) JC.
10. Richie Borrero, c, Segundo Ruiz Belvis HS, Hormigueros, P.R.
11. Terry Powers, rhp, Volunteer State (Tenn.) CC.
12. David Schmidt, 2b, Southwestern (Calif.) CC.
13. Greg Graham, ss, University of Louisville.
14. Quinn Feno, 1b-of, New Bedford (Mass.) HS.
15. Bruce Chick, of, University of Georgia.
**16. Erik Plantenberg, lhp, San Diego State University.—(1993-97)**
17. *Evan Pratte, 2b-ss, Southwest Missouri State University.
18. +Robert Henkel, lhp, San Jacinto (Texas) JC.
19. Brian Young, rhp, Ohio University.
20. Mike DeKneef, ss, Lewis-Clark State (Idaho) College.
21. *Chad Trahan, rhp, Seminole (Okla.) JC.
22. David Klvac, lhp, San Jacinto (Texas) JC.
23. Ryan Maloney, lhp, Lancaster (Ohio) HS.
24. Timothy Smith, rhp, Boston College.
25. Bill Norris, 3b, Eckerd (Fla.) College.
**26. *Les Norman, of, College of St. Francis (Ill.).—(1995-96)**
27. Chris Davis, rhp, JC of the Sequoias (Calif.).
28. John Crimmins, c, Norwood (Mass.) HS.
29. Scott Bethea, ss, Louisiana State University.
30. *Jerry Burns, rhp, Napa Valley (Calif.) JC.
31. +Jeff Johnson, rhp, Fresno (Calif.) CC.
32. *Joseph Mondello, c, San Jacinto (Texas) JC.
33. *James Young, of, Weaver (Ala.) HS.
34. Nick Ortiz, 3b-ss, Cidra (P.R.) HS.
35. (void) Jorge Posada, ss, Calhoun (Ala.) CC.—(1995-2011)
36. Tim Davis, 2b, Southern Illinois University.
37. *Greg Sorrell, lb-of, Poway HS, San Diego.

## CALIFORNIA ANGELS (24)

1. (Choice to Expos as compensation for Type A free agent Mark Langston)
**2. Phil Leftwich, rhp, Radford University.—(1993-96)**
3. Brandon Markiewicz, ss, Dixie Hollins HS, St. Petersburg, Fla.—(High A)
**4. Garret Anderson, of, Kennedy HS, Granada Hills, Calif.—(1994-2010)**
**5. *Doug Creek, lhp, Georgia Tech.—(1995-2003)**
DRAFT DROP *Returned to Georgia Tech; re-drafted by Cardinals, 1991 (7th round)*
**6. Troy Percival, c-rhp, UC Riverside.—(1995-2009)**
DRAFT DROP *Baseball coach, UC Riverside (2015)*
7. Randy Powers, rhp, University of Southern California.
8. Danny Gil, c, University of Southern California.
9. Mark Simmons, 3b, Morgan Park HS, Chicago.
10. J.R. Showalter, ss, University of Georgia.
11. Mike Pineiro, 3b, West Covina (Calif.) HS.
12. Joe Bertucci, 3b, Ridgewood HS, Port Richey, Fla.
**13. *Ryan Hancock, rhp, Monta Vista HS, Cupertino, Calif.—(1996)**
14. Fausto Tejero, c, Florida International University.
**15. *Jermaine Allensworth, ss, Madison Heights HS, Anderson, Ind.—(1996-99)**
DRAFT DROP *First-round draft pick (34th overall), Pirates (1993)*
16. Wayne Johnson, ss, Oklahoma Christian College.
17. Todd McCray, rhp, University of Florida.
**18. Mark Dalesandro, c, University of Illinois.—(1994-2001)**
19. Brian Grebeck, ss, San Diego State University.
DRAFT DROP *Brother of Craig Grebeck, major leaguer (1990-2001)*
**20. P.J. Forbes, 2b, Wichita State University.—(1998-2001)**
**21. Ken Edenfield, rhp, Western Kentucky University.—(1995-96)**
22. Brian Guzik, ss, Greater Latrobe (Pa.) HS.
23. Joe Williams, 3b, New Mexico State University.
24. Don Barbara, 1b, Long Beach State University.
25. *Drew Christman, of, Midwest City (Okla.) HS.
26. Britt Craven, rhp, Pepperdine University.
27. Vladimiro Alcaraz, 1b, West Valley HS, Spokane, Wash.
28. *Brian Toney-Gay, of, Morritton (Ark.) HS.
29. *Mark Ledinsky, lhp-of, JC of Lake County (Ill.).
30. *Kevin Lewis, c, Indian River (Fla.) CC.
31. Louis Pakele, rhp, University of Hawaii-Hilo.
**32. *David Berg, 2b, Sacramento (Calif.) CC.—(1998-2004)**
33. Jeff Ball, rhp, University of Hawaii.
34. *Todd Hall, ss, Sacramento (Calif.) CC.
35. Theron Heusman, lhp, El Reno (Okla.) JC.
36. Joseph Hardwick, of, Nashua (N.H.) HS.
37. Ronald Watson, rhp, Eckerd (Fla.) College.
38. Elgin Bobo, 1b-c, Sonoma State (Calif.) University.
39. *Todd Blyleven, rhp, Villa Park (Calif.) HS.
DRAFT DROP *Son of Bert Blyleven, major leaguer (1970-92)*
40. *John Deremer, rhp, San Jose (Calif.) CC.
41. *Joshua Hurst, ss, Glendale (Ariz.) CC.
42. *Jay Hassel, rhp, Rancho Santiago (Calif.) JC.
43. *Tony Gonzales, ss, Rubidoux HS, Mira Loma, Calif.
44. Todd Refnes, rhp, Cal Poly San Luis Obispo.
45. *Freddie Diaz, ss, El Monte (Calif.) HS.
46. *Steven Morgan, of, Tate HS, Gonzales, Fla.
47. *Earl Partrick, c, Tate HS, Gonzales, Fla.
**48. *Marty Malloy, ss-2b, Trenton (Fla.) HS.—(1998-2002)**
49. Eric Buechele, c, Fresno State University.
DRAFT DROP *Brother of Steve Buechele, first-round draft pick (1979); major leaguer (1985-95)*
50. *Tony Rice, c, Notre Dame University.
DRAFT DROP *Quarterback, Canadian Football League (1990)*
51. *Jerry McLemore, of, Waxahachie (Texas) HS.
52. *Brian Duva, 2b-of, Oak Hall HS, Gainesville, Fla.
53. *Joe Davis, ss, Central Arizona JC.
54. *Bimbo Coles, ss, Virginia Tech.
DRAFT DROP *Guard, National Basketball Association (1990-2003)*

## CHICAGO CUBS (23)

**1. Lance Dickson, lhp, University of Arizona.—(1990)**
**2. Ryan Hawbiltzel, rhp, John I. Leonard HS, West Palm Beach, Fla.—(1996)**
2. Troy Bradford, rhp, University of Arizona (Supplemental choice—72nd—as compensation for Type C free agent Scott Sanderson).—(High A)
3. Tim Parker, rhp, Clemson University.—(AA)
4. Sean Cheetham, rhp, Woodbridge (Va.) HS.—(High A)
5. Tyson Godfrey, rhp, Aberdeen (Wash.) HS.—(Low A)
6. *Ronnie Brown, of, Manatee (Fla.) JC.
7. Adrian Sanchez, rhp, Rio Grande HS, Albuquerque, N.M.
8. Phil Dauphin, of, Indiana University.
9. Jim Wolff, c, Palm Beach (Fla.) JC.
10. *Randy Ortega, c, Lincoln HS, Stockton, Calif.
11. Michael Young, rhp, Anderson (Ind.) University.
**12. Pedro Valdes, lhp, Carlos Escobar Lopez HS, Loiza, P.R.—(1996-2000)**
13. *Steve Gurtner, rhp, Holy Cross HS, Chalmette, La.
14. Scott Gardner, rhp, Imperial Valley (Calif.) JC.
15. Joe Porcelli, lhp, Iona College.

16. *Travis Woods, of, Santa Monica (Calif.) CC.
17. Willie Gardner, of, Tupelo (Miss.) HS.
18. Mike Gabbani, c, Cal State Dominguez Hills.
19. Ken Krahenbuhl, rhp, San Bernardino Valley (Calif.) JC.
20. Steve Coffey, ss, University of Massachusetts.
21. Jim Robinson, c, Mississippi State University.
22. Joe Biasucci, 2b, Palm Beach (Fla.) JC.
23. Brian Wilson, ss, Modesto (Calif.) JC.
24. *Wil Delafield, of, Denham Springs (La.) HS.
25. John DeRicco, 1b, University of Nevada-Reno.
26. *Kurt Bierek, 3b, Glencoe HS, Hillsboro, Ore.
27. +Patrick Huston, 3b, Los Angeles Pierce JC.
28. *Angel Abreu, rhp, Josefina Barcelo HS, Guaynabo, P.R.
29. +Jay Meyer, lhp, Johnson County (Kan.) CC.
30. Andy Hartung, 3b, University of Maine.
31. Charles Kirk, rhp, Jacksonville University.
32. *Benjamin Bryant, rhp, San Jacinto (Texas) JC.
33. J.P. Postiff, 3b, Fresno State University.
34. +Steven Walker, of, Lee County HS, Leesburg, Ga. / Lurleen B. Wallace (Ala.) JC.
35. *Jorge Santiago, 3b, Tomas C. Ongay HS, Bayamon, P.R.
**36. *Ramon E. Martinez, ss, Superior Catolica HS, Toa Alta, P.R.—(1998-2009)**
37. *Edwin Zayas, rhp, Luquillo (P.R.) HS.
38. *Darren Stumberger, 3b-1b, Spanish River HS, Boca Raton, Fla.
39. *Mike Schmitz, 1b, Coconut Creek (Fla.) HS.
40. *James Riggio, rhp, Chamberlain HS, Tampa.
41. *Ricardo Serpa, of-lhp, Polytechnic University HS, Bayamon, P.R.
42. Tommy Helms, 2b, Western Hills HS, Cincinnati.
DRAFT DROP *Son of Tommy Helms, major leaguer (1964-77); major league manager (1988-89)*
43. *Travis Champion, of, Hibriten HS, Lenoir, N.C.
44. *Jeff Mapson, c, Pairndale (Calif.) HS.
45. Rolando Fernandez, of, Northwestern State University.

## CHICAGO WHITE SOX (4)

**1. Alex Fernandez, rhp, Miami-Dade CC South.—(1990-2000)**
DRAFT DROP *First-round draft pick (24th overall), Brewers (1988); first player from 1990 draft to reach majors (Aug. 2, 1990)*
**2. Bob Wickman, rhp, University of Wisconsin-Whitewater.—(1992-2007)**
2. *Eric Maloney, rhp, Carmel HS, Mundelein, Ill. (Supplemental choice—67th—as compensation for Type C free agent Richard Dotson).--DNP
DRAFT DROP *Attended Creighton; re-drafted by Dodgers, 1993 (19th round)*
**3. Robert Ellis, rhp, Panola (Texas) JC.—(1996-2003)**
**4. James Baldwin, rhp, Pinecrest HS, Southern Pines, N.C.—(1995-2005)**
**5. Ray Durham, 2b, Harding HS, Charlotte, N.C.—(1995-2008)**
6. Charles Poe, of, West Covina (Calif.) HS.
7. Mike Vogel, c-of, Cretin HS, Brooklyn Park, Minn.
8. Nathaniel James, of, Lake Mary HS, Altamonte Springs, Fla.
9. Doug McGraw, rhp, Duncanville (Texas) HS.
10. Jonathon Taylor, c, Alcorn Central HS, Corinth, Miss.
11. Keith Strange, c, Oregon Tech.
**12. +Jimmy Hurst, of, Central HS, Tuscaloosa, Ala. / Three Rivers (Mo.) JC.—(1997)**
**13. Rod Bolton, rhp, University of Kentucky.—(1993-95)**
14. +Fred Starks, rhp, Brevard (Fla.) CC.
15. Mike Bradish, 1b, Christ College-Irvine (Calif.).
16. Jeff DiNuzzo, rhp, Seton Hall University.
17. Larry Gilligan, 2b, Brookdale (N.J.) CC.
18. Brandon Wilson, ss, University of Kentucky.
19. Kerry Valrie, of, University of Southern Mississippi.
20. Jonathan Jenkins, rhp, East Carolina University.
21. Muzzy Jackson, 1b, Mercer University.
22. Ted Marshall, lhp, Sweet Water HS, Nanafalia, Ala.
23. Todd Altaffer, lhp, Jacksonville State University.
24. *Mark Gilreath, rhp, Brevard (Fla.) JC.
25. Jonathan Story, ss-2b, Southern University.
26. Vince Zarate, of, John F. Kennedy HS, New York.
27. James Coachman, 1b, Troy State University.
DRAFT DROP *Brother of Pete Coachman, major leaguer (1990)*
28. *Dennis McCaffery, of, Villanova University.
29. *Bo Magee, lhp, Jackson State University.
30. Roosevelt Smith, rhp, Southern University.
31. Todd Hotz, lhp, University of Texas.
32. +Corey Austin, 1b-of, Faulkner State (Ala.) JC.
33. *Jason Hisey, rhp, University of Arizona.
34. +Billy Warner, rhp, Central Private HS, Greenwell Springs, La. / Southwest Mississippi JC.
35. *Cedrick Thomas, lhp, Gulf Coast (Fla.) CC.
**36. Jason Bere, rhp, Middlesex (Mass.) CC.—(1993-2003)**
37. *Ron Scott, lhp, Sarasota (Fla.) HS.
38. Tim Green-Shornock, 1b, Marlboro HS, Morganville, N.J.
39. Mike Potter, rhp, Central Arizona JC.
40. Greg McGough, c, Northeast Louisiana University.
**41. *Matt Skrmetta, rhp, Satellite Beach (Fla.) HS.—(2000)**
42. *Brian Hancock, lhp, Volunteer State (Tenn.) CC.
43. Donald Culberson, rhp, East Central (Miss.) JC.
44. *Karun Jackson, ss, Bishop State (Ala.) JC.
**45. *Allen Battle, of, University of South Alabama.—(1995-96)**
46. *Eric Chapman, of, Garrett (Md.) CC.
**47. *Chad Zerbe, lhp, Gaither HS, Tampa.—(2000-03)**
48. *Emanuel Hayes, ss, Forest Brook HS, Houston.
49. Andrew Hoey, rhp, Central Washington University.
50. *John Timko, c, Clearwater (Fla.) HS.
51. *Clemente Gordon, c, Grambling State University.
52. *Steve Davis, rhp, Angelina (Texas) JC.
53. *Chris Hitt, lhp, Jersey Village HS, Houston.
54. *Brad Kantor, 3b-c, Manatee (Fla.) JC.
55. *Mike Badorek, rhp, Olivet Nazarene (Ill.) College.
56. *Greg Elliott, ss, Pearl River (Miss.) JC.
57. *Anthony Box, ss-of, Brookwood (Ala.) HS.

## CINCINNATI REDS (7)

**1. Dan Wilson, c, University of Minnesota.—(1992-2005)**
**2. Keith Gordon, ss, Wright State University.—(1993)**
3. Dan Tobin, rhp, Dowagiac Union HS, Dowagiac, Mich.—(Rookie)
4. Mike Ferry, rhp, Auburn University.—(AAA)
5. Kevin Aubin, c, Drury HS, Stamford, Vt.—(Rookie)
**6. Steve Gibralter, of, Duncanville (Texas) HS.—(1995-96)**
7. Juan Loyola, of, Pablo Avila Gonzalez HS, Camuy, P.R.
**8. Larry Luebbers, rhp, University of Kentucky.—(1993-2000)**
9. *Ken Carlyle, rhp, University of Mississippi.
10. *Clifton Foster, rhp, Angelina (Texas) JC.
11. *Shannon Jones, ss, Aurora Central HS, Aurora, Colo.
**12. John Roper, rhp, Hoke County HS, Raeford, N.C.—(1993-95)**
13. Derrick Graham, of, Hoke County HS, Raeford, N.C.
14. Bobby Perna, 3b, Cumberland (Tenn.) University.
15. *Randy Albaladejo, c, Colegio Nuestra HS, Vega Alta, P.R.
**16. *Shane Halter, ss, Seminole (Okla.) JC.—(1997-2004)**
17. Tucker Hammargren, 1b-c, Arizona State University.
18. *Brian Carlin, of, Angelina (Texas) JC.
19. Kevin Berry, rhp, Northwestern State University.
**20. *Marc Valdes, rhp, Jesuit HS, Tampa.—(1995-2001)**
DRAFT DROP *First-round draft pick (27th overall), Marlins (1993)*
21. *Mark Fields, of, Washington HS, Los Angeles.
22. *Martis Aviles, lhp, Pedro Albeus HS, Levittown, P.R.
23. *Joe Wallace, c, Granite City (Ill.) HS.
24. *Ryan Towns, rhp, Gonzales (Texas) HS.
25. Greg Margheim, lhp, Virginia Tech.
26. *Brian Hierholzer, c, Blue Valley North HS, Overland Park, Kan.
27. *Scott Connor, rhp, Gateway HS, Aurora, Colo.
28. Kevin Riggs, 2b, East Carolina University.
29. *Mark Mann, rhp, McNicholas HS, Cincinnati.
30. *Craig Bolcerek, c, Brenham (Texas) HS.
31. *Jorge Ortiz, rhp, Baptist HS, Carolina, P.R.
32. *Edwin Corps, rhp, Centro Servicio HS, San Juan, P.R.
33. Charles McClain, rhp, University of Tennessee.
34. *John Gast, 3b, East Carolina University.
35. Bo Loftin, c, University of New Orleans.
36. *Chad Hodge, of, Marcus HS, Flower Mound, Texas.
37. *Michael Carlton, c, Texas City (Texas) HS.
38. *Jim Rushworth, rhp, Panola (Texas) JC.
39. Pierre Burris, of-3b, Kansas City (Kan.) CC.

## CLEVELAND INDIANS (8)

**1. Tim Costo, ss, University of Iowa.—(1992-93)**
1. Sam Hence, of, Stone County HS, Wiggins, Miss. (Supplemental choice—39th—for failure to sign 1989 first-round draft pick Calvin Murray)—(High A)
**2. Darrell Whitmore, of, West Virginia University** (Choice from Mariners as compensation for Type B free agent Pete O'Brien)—**(1993-95)**
2. Pat Bryant, of, Cleveland HS, Reseda, Calif.—(AAA)
**3. Jason Hardtke, ss, Leland HS, San Jose, Calif.—(1996-98)**
4. Jeff Brohm, ss, University of Louisville.--DNP
DRAFT DROP *Quarterback, National Football League (1996-97)*
**5. Oscar Munoz, rhp, University of Miami.—(1995)**
**6. *Paul Bako, c, Lafayette (La.) HS.—(1998-2009)**
**7. David Bell, 3b, Moeller HS, Cincinnati.—(1995-2006)**
DRAFT DROP *Grandson of Gus Bell, major leaguer (1950-64) • Son of Buddy Bell, major leaguer (1972-89); major league manager (1996-2007) • Brother of Mike Bell, major leaguer (2000)*
8. Shawn Bryant, lhp, Oklahoma City University.
9. Rod McCall, 1b, Orange Coast (Calif.) JC.
10. Robert Smith, 2b, Allen County (Kan.) CC.
11. Carl Johnson, rhp, Lassen (Calif.) JC.
12. Craig Sides, rhp, Jefferson Davis HS, Montgomery, Ala.
13. Todd Whitehurst, rhp, North Monterey HS, Salinas, Calif.
14. Dino Philyaw, of, Southern Wayne HS, Dudley, N.C.
15. Samuel Baker, rhp, Hill (Texas) JC.
16. James Morgan, of, North Marion HS, Sparr, Fla.
**17. Dave Mlicki, rhp, Oklahoma State University.—(1992-2002)**
**18. Steve Gajkowski, rhp, Bellevue (Wash.) CC.—(1998)**
19. Ricky Powell, of, Tioga HS, Alexandria, La.
20. Bobby Schultz, of, Walton HS, Marietta, Ga.
21. *Matt Carpenter, c, Euclid Senior HS, Euclid, Ohio.
22. Jerry Ashford, 3b-c, Everman (Texas) HS.
23. *Baylor Alexander, c, Florida JC.
24. +Ronnie Coleman, of, Kishwaukee (Ill.) JC.
25. Timothy Thomas, 1b-of, Ohio University.
26. Scott Morgan, rhp, Middle Tennessee State University.
27. +Oscar Resendez, rhp, Texas Southmost JC.
28. Bart Peterson, rhp, Brigham Young University.
29. *David Vindivich, of, Mount Tahoma HS, Tacoma, Wash.
30. *Eric Trice, of, LaGrande (Ore.) HS.
31. Omar Ramirez, of, Hill (Texas) JC.
32. Pete Guerra, c, Laredo (Texas) JC.
33. Kenneth Day, rhp, Washington State University.
34. Larry Minter, of, Harlan HS, Chicago.
35. Nick Sued, c, Hill (Texas) JC.
36. Edwin Couvertier, of, King (Tenn.) College.
37. *Cesar Ramirez, of, Phoenixville Area (Pa.) HS.
38. Joseph Fleet, rhp, Southeastern Louisiana University.
39. Tim Langdon, lhp, East Carolina University.
40. +Michael Zollars, ss, Western Oklahoma State JC.
41. *Joseph Frias, 2b, Oklahoma City University.
42. *Mark Martin, of, Connors State (Okla.) JC.
43. +David Chisum, of, Laredo (Texas) JC.
44. *John Rodgers, c, Panola (Texas) JC.
45. *Efrain Montero, lhp, Mount Vernon Nazarene (Ohio) College.
46. *Braxton Hickman, 1b, San Jacinto (Texas) JC.
47. (void) Allen Hayes, of-rhp, Forest Brook HS, Houston, Texas.
48. *Jay Vaught, rhp, Deer Park (Texas) HS.
49. *Joseph Chastain, lhp, Florida JC.
50. DeWayne Wilson, 2b, Lockhart HS, Sharon, S.C.
**51. Carlos Crawford, rhp, Montreat-Anderson (N.C) JC.—(1996)**
52. *Chad Brown, lhp, North Gaston HS, Gastonia, N.C.
53. *James Warwick, ss, Colfax (Wash.) HS.
54. *Lance Martin, of, Tumwater (Wash.) HS.
55. *Brian Coleman, rhp, Bainbridge Island (Wash.) HS.
56. Aaron Morris, of-1b, Lakeland (Ohio) CC.
57. John Lorms, c, Eastern Kentucky University.
58. Tracy Sanders, of, Limestone (S.C.) College.
59. Frank Monastero, 2b, West Chester (Pa.) University.

## DETROIT TIGERS (2)

**1. Tony Clark, of, Christian HS, El Cajon, Calif.—(1995-2009)**
2. (Choice to Athletics as compensation for Type B free agent Tony Phillips)
2. *Keith Grunewald, ss, Walton HS, Marietta, Ga. (Choice from Padres as compensation for Type B free agent Fred Lynn).—(AA)
DRAFT DROP *Attended North Carolina; re-drafted by Rockies, 1993 (12th round)*
3. Vince Bradford, of, Malvern (Ark.) HS.—(Rookie)
4. Jimmy Alder, 3b, Dobyns-Bennett HS, Kingsport, Tenn.—(AA)
**5. Shannon Withem, rhp, Willow Run HS, Ypsilanti, Mich.—(1998)**
6. Steve Wolf, rhp, Fresno State University.
7. *Randy Curtis, of, Riverside (Calif.) CC.
8. Dan Rogers, 1b, Missouri Southern University.
9. Greg Coppeta, lhp, University of Southern Maine.
10. *Roger Luce, c, University of Texas.
11. Sean Sadler, 3b, Missouri Baptist College.
12. Aaron Seja, of, Millikan HS, Long Beach, Calif.
**13. *Charlie Greene Jr., c, Miami-Dade CC South.—(1996-2000)**
**14. +Ben Blomdahl, rhp, Riverside (Calif.) CC.—(1995)**
15. *Toby McFarland, lhp, Petoskey (Mich.) HS.
16. Brian Nelson, rhp, George Mason University.
17. Tom Drell, rhp, Florida Southern College.
18. +Keith Kimsey, of, Santa Fe HS, Lakeland, Fla. / Polk (Fla.) CC.
19. Michael Guilfoyle, lhp, St. Peter's College.
20. Warren Sawkiw, 2b, Wake Forest University.
21. Greg Haeger, 1b-lhp, University of Michigan.
22. David Mastropietro, of, LaSalle University.
23. Douglas Kimbler, ss, College of St. Rose (N.Y.).
24. Brian Saltzgaber, of-2b, Western Michigan University.
25. Gregg Radachowsky, rhp, Boston College.
26. *Kerry Collins, ss-3b, Wilson HS, West Lawn, Pa.
DRAFT DROP *First-round draft pick, Carolina Panthers/ National Football League (1995); quarterback, NFL (1995-2011)*
27. *Greg McMurtry, of, University of Michigan.
DRAFT DROP *First-round draft pick (14th overall), Red Sox (1986); wide receiver, National Football League (1990-94)*
28. *Rodney Peete, 3b, Marina Del Ray, Calif.
DRAFT DROP *Quarterback, National Football League (1989-2004)*
29. *Darwin Traylor, of, Poly HS, Riverside, Calif.
30. *John Rosengren, lhp, Rye (N.Y.) HS.
31. Paul Reinisch, 1b, Wake Forest University.
32. Brian Schubert, rhp, Kent State University.
33. Bob Undorf, rhp, University of South Florida.
34. *Thomas Paskievitch, rhp, Central Michigan University.
35. Dennis McNamara, of, Central Michigan University.
36. Kirk Mendenhall, ss, Westminster (Mo.) College.
37. Kevin Miller, c, Cal State Chico.

38. Rob Fazekas, rhp, Rutgers University.
39. Robert Riker, rhp, Central Michigan University.
40. Eric Leimeister, rhp, St. John's University.
41. Tim Kirt, of, Missouri Baptist College.
42. Keith Roberts, of, West Nassau HS, Callahan, Fla.
43. Brian Warren, rhp, New Mexico State University.
44. *Matthew Hammett, lhp, Macomb (Mich.) JC.
45. *David Bowden, c, Martin Luther King HS, Detroit.
46. *Rodney Tisdale, of, University Christian HS, Jacksonville, Fla.
47. *Steven Hughart, lhp, Brevard (Fla.) JC.
48. +Arthur Johnson, ss, Texarkana (Texas) CC.
49. *Gregory Steele, rhp, Homer (Mich.) HS.
50. *Karry Riley, rhp, Suwannee HS, Live Oak, Fla.
51. *Dan Ruff, of, University of Michigan.
**52. *Willie Adams, rhp, La Serna HS, La Mirada, Calif.—(1996-97)**

DRAFT DROP *First-round draft pick (36th overall), Athletics (1993)*

53. *Tim Goodwin, of, Burlington (Iowa) HS.
54. *Doug Newstrom, rhp, Woodson HS, Fairfax, Va.
55. John Sutey, of, Kentwood HS, Kent, Wash.
**56. *Willie Morales c, Tucson (Ariz.) HS.—(2000)**

## HOUSTON ASTROS (15)

1. (Choice to Giants as compensation for Type B free agent Ken Oberkfell)
1. Tom Nevers, ss, Edina (Minn.) HS (Choice from Giants as compensation for Type A free agent Kevin Bass).—(AAA)

DRAFT DROP *Fifth-round draft pick, Pittsburgh Penguins/ National Hockey League (1989)*

**1. Brian Williams, rhp, University of South Carolina** (Supplemental choice—31st—as compensation for Type A free agent Kevin Bass)**—(1991-2000)**
2. Gary Mota, of, Fullerton (Calif.) JC.—(AA)

DRAFT DROP *Son of Manny Mota, major leaguer (1962-82) • Brother of Domingo Mota, 31st-round draft pick, Dodgers (1990) • Brother of Andy Mota, major leaguer (1991) • Brother of Jose Mota, major leaguer (1991-95)*

**3. Chris Hatcher, of, University of Iowa.—(1998)**
4. Perry Berry, 2b, University of Southwestern Louisiana.—(High A)
5. Al Harley, of, Sheldon HS, Eugene, Ore.—(AA)
6. Jimmy White, of, Brandon HS, Tampa.
7. David Nix, lhp, Harrison HS, Evansville, Ind.
8. Tony Gilmore, c, University of Arkansas.
9. Jorge Correa, rhp, Miami (Fla.) Senior HS.
**10. *Brian Boehringer, rhp, University of Nevada-Las Vegas.—(1995-2004)**
11. Fletcher Thompson, 2b, Nicholls State University.
**12. Jeff Ball, 3b, San Jose State University.—(1998)**
**13. Ray Montgomery, of, Fordham University.—(1996-98)**

DRAFT DROP *Scouting director, Diamondbacks (2010-14); scouting director, Brewers (2014-15)*

14. +James Evans, rhp, Allan Hancock (Calif.) JC.
15. Layne Lambert, 3b, University of Nevada-Las Vegas.
16. Marsalis Basey, ss, Martinsburg (W.Va.) HS.
17. Jon Quaid, lhp, Chabot (Calif.) JC.
18. *Frank Jacobs, 1b, University of Notre Dame.
19. Derrick Bottoms, lhp, Overton HS, Nashville, Tenn.
20. Luis Martinez, rhp, Huston-Tillotson (Texas) College.
21. *Anthony Griffin, 1b, Washington HS, Hawthorne, Calif.
22. Dennis Reed, rhp, Cal Poly San Luis Obispo.
**23. *Jason Varitek, c, Lake Brantley HS, Longwood, Fla.—(1997-2011)**

DRAFT DROP *First-round draft pick (21st overall), Twins (1993); first-round draft pick (14th overall), Mariners (1994)*

24. *Johnny Mitchell, of, Sprayberry HS, Marietta, Ga.
25. *Dillard Martin, of, Seminole (Okla.) JC.
**26. *Jim Dougherty, rhp, University of North Carolina.—(1995-99)**
27. Lincoln Gumbs, ss, Clarke (Miss.) JC.
28. Douglas Ketchen, rhp, Cal State Fullerton.
**29. *Bret Hemphill, c, Cupertino HS, Santa Clara, Calif.—(1999)**
**30. *Chris Singleton, of, Pinole Valley HS, Hercules, Calif.—(1999-2005)**
31. Michael Irwin, rhp, University of Portland.
32. Lance Smith, c, McNeese State University.
33. *Robert Baldwin, of, DeLand HS, Lake Helen, Fla.
34. *Joe Gonzalez, rhp, Miami (Fla.) Senior HS.
35. *Dax Winslett, rhp, Plano Senior HS, Plano, Texas.
36. Scott Black, rhp, University of Missouri.
37. *Rodney Foster, of-2b, Midwest City (Okla.) HS.
38. Jose Flores, ss, Universidad HS, Cidra, P.R.
39. Jason Wall, lhp, Louisiana State University.
40. Vincent Roman, of, Ithaca (N.Y.) College.
41. Scott Bullard, rhp, Florida JC.
42. Stephen McCumiskey, c, University of Rhode Island.
43. +Donnie Dault, rhp, Austin (Texas) HS / Blinn (Texas) JC.
44. +Robert McCloud, rhp, Palomar (Calif.) JC.
45. *Steve Williams, of, Santa Cruz HS, Arizona City, Ariz.
46. *Christopher Milton, ss, Wilson HS, Hacienda Heights, Calif.
47. *Derek Davis, of, Ellison HS, Fort Hood, Texas.
48. *Greg Almond, c, Middle Georgia JC.
49. *Cleveland Ladell, 2b-of, Texarkana (Texas) HS.
50. *Mark Prather, of, McLennan (Texas) CC.
51. *Malcolm Huckaby, 3b, Bristol Central HS, Bristol, Conn.
52. *James Davis, 3b, Lincoln HS, San Diego.
53. +Brian McGlone, ss, Hillsborough (Fla.) CC.
54. *Todd Coburn, c, Wooster HS, Carson City, Nev.
55. *Scott Smith, of, Coppell (Texas) HS.
56. *Michael Belcher, c, Broad Run HS, Sterling, Va.
57. *Carey Lundstrom, rhp, Los Angeles Harbor JC.
58. *David Maize, c, Triton (Ill.) JC.
59. *William Paragin, c, Hamilton (Ohio) HS.
60. *Bernard Bellard, rhp, Acadiana HS, Lafayette, La.
61. *Johnny Booker, of, Tucson (Ariz.) HS.
62. *David Angotti, c, Grossmont (Calif.) JC.
63. *Kevin Ehl, rhp, Cypress (Calif.) JC.
64. *Kevin Cook, of, Cypress (Calif.) JC.
65. *Steven Hernandez, ss, Orange Coast (Calif.) JC.
66. +Brian Thompson, of, Chabot (Calif.) JC.
67. *Jason Rathburn, rhp, Westlake HS, Austin, Texas.
68. +Ron Cacini, ss, Triton (Ill.) JC.
69. *Donald Miller, rhp, Sprayberry HS, Marietta, Ga.
70. *Michael Lustyk, rhp-3b, Interlake HS, Bellevue, Wash.
71. *Joseph Miller, of, Los Angeles Harbor JC.
72. *Todd Mancini, of, LaSalle Academy, Cranston, R.I.
73. *Mike Condon, c, Southern Union State (Ala.) JC.
74. *William Adams, of, John Jay HS, San Antonio, Texas.
75. *Jeffrey Brown, rhp, Schenectady (N.Y.) CC.
**76. *Travis Driskill, rhp, Anderson HS, Austin, Texas.—(2002-2007)**
77. *Anastoshio Navarro, 3b, El Rancho HS, Pico Rivera, Calif.
78. *Darious Carter, ss, Glenn Oaks HS, Baton Rouge, La.
79. Dennis Colon, ss, Colegio Maristas HS, Manati, P.R.
80. *Kenneth Jackson, 1b, Polk (Fla.) CC.
81. *Eric Mooney, lhp, St. Anthony HS, Long Beach, Calif.
82. *Jose Matos, rhp, Timote HS, Rio Piedras, P.R.
**83. +Danny Young, lhp, Cannon County HS, Woodbury, Tenn. / Aquinas (Tenn.) JC.—(2000)**
84. *Patrick Bettancourt, 3b, Mission Bay HS, San Diego.
85. *Marc Claus, ss, Broward (Fla.) CC.
86. *George Wyles, c, Permian HS, Odessa, Texas.
87. *Daniel Pagan, 3b-1b, Trina Padilla DeSanz HS, Rio Piedras, P.R.
88. *Greg Guell, lhp, Miami-Dade CC South.
89. *Adam West, of, Hudson Valley (N.Y.) CC.
90. *Sean Garrison, lhp, Berlin HS, Kensington, Conn.
91. *Geoff Grenert, rhp, Mesa (Ariz.) CC.
92. *Brian Whyburn, rhp, Ukiah (Calif.) HS.
93. *Scott Mowl, rhp, Cerritos (Calif.) JC.
94. *Matthew Martinez, 2b, Sacramento (Calif.) CC.
95. *Chad Phillips, rhp, Orange Coast (Calif.) JC.
96. *Michael Houck, rhp, El Camino (Calif.) JC.
97. *Floyd White, 1b-of, Middle Georgia JC.
98. *Cedric Moore, of, Westwood HS, Port Pierce, Fla.
99. *Jeff Caldwell, of, Bogalusa (La.) HS.

## KANSAS CITY ROYALS (25)

1. (Choice to Padres as compensation for Type A free agent Mark Davis)
2. (Choice to Athletics as compensation for Type A free agent Storm Davis)
3. Shayne Rea, rhp, Henry Ford (Mich.) CC.—(High A)
4. Doug Harris, rhp, James Madison University.—(AAA)
5. Darren Burton, of, Pulaski County HS, Somerset, Ky.—(AAA)
6. Wade Fyock, rhp, Somerset (Pa.) HS.
7. Tom Smith, rhp, Avon Park (Fla.) HS.
**8. Philip Hiatt, 3b, Louisiana Tech.—(1993-2001)**
9. Anthony Lee, rhp, El Dorado HS, Las Vegas, Nev.
10. Robert Toth, rhp, Pacifica HS, Cypress, Calif.
11. *Chad Drown, ss, La Mirada HS, Placentia, Calif.
**12. Rod Myers, rhp, University of Wisconsin.—(1996-2004)**
13. Chad Strickland, c, Carl Albert HS, Oklahoma City, Okla.
14. Damon Pollard, rhp, University of Southern Mississippi.
15. Thomas Lee, rhp, Los Angeles CC.
16. David Haber, of, Catonsville (Md.) CC.
**17. Raul Gonzalez, 3b-of, Gilberto Concepcion de Gracia HS, Carolina, P.R.—(2000-04)**
18. Donnie Harrel, c, Taft (Calif.) JC.

DRAFT DROP *Baseball coach, Seattle University (2009-15)*

19. Doug Shields, of, Southern Illinois University.
20. Doug Peters, rhp, Indiana University.
21. Brady Stewart, ss, Ohio State University.
22. Tony Long, lhp, Montgomery (Md.) JC.
23. Vernon Slater, of, Polk (Fla.) CC.
24. Andre Newhouse, ss, Sterling HS, Houston.
25. Raymie Brooks, c, El Reno (Okla.) JC.
26. Alan Budnick, rhp, University of Detroit.
27. Rafael Gutierrez, rhp, East Los Angeles JC.
28. Arnie Sambel, of, University of San Francisco.
29. Charles Frederick, rhp, Parkland (Ill.) JC.
**30. +Brian Bevil, rhp, Angelina (Texas) JC.—(1996-98)**
31. Weddison Ebanks, of, Utah Valley CC.
32. *Marcello Hansen, lhp, Olympic (Wash.) JC.
33. Scott Davis, rhp, Adelphi (N.Y.) University.
34. Sean Franceschi, lhp, Univeristy of New Orleans.
**35. Brad Holman, rhp, Auburn University.—(1993)**

DRAFT DROP *Brother of Brian Holman, first-round draft pick, Expos (1983); major leaguer (1988-91)*

36. *Damon Daniels, of, Texarkana (Texas) CC.
37. John Schreiner, 1b, Penn State University.
38. David Hierholzer, rhp, Kansas State University.
39. *Kevin Sisk, 3b, James Madison University.
40. *Mitch Simons, 2b, Oklahoma State University.
41. Shannon Strong, of, Treasure Valley (Ore.) CC.
42. Terrance Mays, of, Kaskaskia (Ill.) CC.
43. Scott Hennessey, of, Johnson County (Kan.) CC.
44. *Tyres Blackburn, c-of, Bryan Adams HS, Dallas.
45. *Scott Moten, rhp, Bellflower (Calif.) HS.
46. *Brian Gelzheiser, rhp, Baldwin HS, Pittsburgh.
47. *Sean Strade, rhp, Grant HS, Portland, Ore.
48. *Reggie Ingram, of, Coffee HS, Douglas, Ga.
49. *Craig Tucker, rhp, Klamath HS, Klamath Falls, Ore.
50. *Richard Parker, rhp, Los Angeles CC.
51. *Gerald Sharko, 1b, Phoenix (Ariz.) JC.
52. *Brian Parks, rhp, Skagit Valley (Wash.) CC.
53. *Shane Gilder, 2b, San Jacinto (Texas) JC.
**54. *Lyle Mouton, of, Louisiana State University.—(1995-2001)**
55. John Jacobs, rhp, Chino (Calif.) HS.
56. +Nick Kaiser, 2b-ss, Cuesta (Calif.) JC.
57. *Jon Mathews, 1b-of, Centerville (Iowa) HS.

## LOS ANGELES DODGERS (9)

1. Ronnie Walden, lhp, Blanchard (Okla.) HS.—(High A)
2. (Choice to Expos as compensation for Type A free agent Hubie Brooks)
2. Leroy Williams, ss, East St. John HS, Reserve, La. (Supplemental choice—68th—as compensation for Type C free agent Dave Anderson).—(High A)
2. Scott Freeman, rhp, University of Wyoming (Supplemental choice—73rd—as compensation for Type C free agent John Tudor).—(High A)
3. (Choice to Pirates as compensation for Type A free agent Jim Gott)
**4. Mike Busch, 1b, Iowa State University.—(1995-96)**
5. Frank Smith, of, Poly HS, Riverside, Calif.—(AA)
6. Alton Pinkney, of, Glynn Academy, Brunswick, Ga.
7. Daniel Gray, c, SUNY Binghamton.
8. C.J. Kerr, lhp, Cerritos (Calif.) JC.
9. Jake Botts, rhp, North Monterey HS, Salinas, Calif.
10. Kenneth Hamilton, rhp, Patrick Henry (Ala.) JC.
11. *Eric Mapp, of, Natrona County HS, Casper, Wyo.
12. Keoki Farrish, of, Ohlone (Calif.) JC.
13. Greg Davis, rhp, El Camino (Calif.) CC.
14. Jimmy Daspit, rhp, Cal State Sacramento.
15. Tim Griffin, 3b, Stanford University.
16. *Donn Cunnigan, of, Gahr HS, Los Angeles.
**17. Steve Mintz, c-rhp, Mount Olive (N.C.) College.—(1995-99)**
18. Lonnie Webb, ss, South Georgia JC.
19. Burgess Watts, 3b-rhp, JC of Du Page (Ill.).
20. Peter Nurre, c, Cabrillo (Calif.) JC.
21. *Wayne Lindemann, lhp, Lower Columbia (Wash.) JC.
22. Michael Racobaldo, rhp, Pennsauken (N.J.) HS.
23. Ron Maurer, ss, University of North Carolina.
**24. Mike Mimbs, lhp, Mercer University.—(1995-97)**

DRAFT DROP *Twin brother of Mark Mimbs, 25th-round draft pick, Dodgers (1990)*

25. Mark Mimbs, lhp, Mercer University.

DRAFT DROP *Twin brother of Mike Mimbs, 24th-round draft pick, Dodgers (1990)*

26. Gordie Tipton, rhp, Oklahoma State University.
27. Jody Treadwell, rhp, Jacksonville University.
28. Randall Graves, ss, Riverside (Calif.) CC.
29. David Baumann, rhp, Western New England College.
30. Ben O'Connor, lhp, University of Maryland.
31. Domingo Mota, of, Cal State Fullerton.

DRAFT DROP *Son of Manny Mota, major leaguer (1962-82) • Brother of Gary Mota, second-round draft pick, Astros (1990) • Brother of Andy Mota, major leaguer (1991) • Brother of Jose Mota, major leaguer (1991-95)*

32. Anthony Rodriguez, c, Jose De Diego HS, Aguadilla, P.R.
33. Albert Maldonado, lhp, Barringer HS, Yauco, P.R.
34. *Kurt Ehmann, ss, Mendocino (Calif.) CC.
35. *Steve Matos, c, Chaminade-Madonna HS, Hollywood, Fla.
36. Mike Brady, lhp, Florida State University.
37. Ira Smith, of-2b, University of Maryland-Eastern Shore.
**38. *Brady Raggio, rhp, San Ramon HS, Danville, Calif.—(1997-2003)**
**39. *Mark Sweeney, of, University of Maine.—(1995-2008)**
40. Larry Jacinto, rhp, Southern California College.
41. *John Cranford, 2b, Middle Georgia JC.
42. +Clint Minear, lhp, East Mississippi JC.
43. *Charles Williams, of, Meridian (Miss.) JC.
44. Ed Lund, c, Notre Dame University.
45. *Jason Sengbusch, rhp, Westfield HS, Oxford, Wis.
46. Thomas Matthews, thp, University of Edinboro (Pa.).
47. *Joseph Jacobsen, rhp, Clovis West HS, Clovis, Calif.
48. Robert Sweeney, 3b, Waukesha County (Wis.) Technical JC.
49. Dirk Gorman, of, SUNY Binghamton.
50. *Ismael Castaneda, lhp, Hanford (Calif.) HS.
51. *Mario Johnson, ss, Simmons HS, Hollandale, Miss.
52. *Gordon Hockett, 1b, Union HS, Tulsa Okla.
53. *Robert Calton, lhp, Lehi (Utah) HS.
**54. +Todd Williams, rhp, Onondaga (N.Y.) CC.—(1995-2007)**
55. Brett Kim, 3b, JC of Marin (Calif.).
56. *Joe Wagner, rhp, Adams Friendship HS, Friendship, Wis.

DRAFT DROP *First-round draft pick (39th overall), Brewers (1993)*
57. +Patrick Reed, ss, Mount Hood (Ore.) CC.
58. +Melvin Warren, of, Solano (Calif.) CC.
59. Daniel Andrews, of, Cal Poly Pomona.
60. *David Madsen, 3b, Murray (Utah) HS.
61. *Greg Raisola, c, Nogales HS, Walnut, Calif.
62. +Roger Sweeney, of, JC of Marin (Calif.).
63. ***Andy Abad, of, Jupiter (Fla.) HS.—(2001-06)**

## MILWAUKEE BREWERS (14)

1. (Choice to Athletics as compensation for Type A free agent Dave Parker)
2. LaRue Baber, of, Grant HS, Sacramento, Calif.—(High A)
3. Michael Carter, ss, Livingston (Ala.) University.—(AAA)
4. Donnie Blair, rhp, Wabash (Ind.) HS.—(High A)
5. **Duane Singleton, of, McKee Vocational Tech, Staten Island, N.Y.—(1994-96)**
6. **Tom McGraw, lhp, Washington State University.—(1997)**
7. Bobby Benjamin, 1b-of, University of Nebraska.
8. Tim Clark, of, Louisiana State University.
9. Kevin McDonald, rhp, University of Southwestern Louisiana.
10. Kurt Archer, rhp, San Diego State University.
11. Brian Souza, rhp, University of Hawaii.
12. **Marshall Boze, rhp, Southwestern (Calif.) CC.—(1996)**
13. Dave Wrona, ss, Southern Illinois University.

DRAFT DROP *Brother of Rick Wrona, major leaguer (1988-94)*
14. Tim Carter, 1b, Miami (Ohio) University.
15. John Tatum, 3b, Grossmont HS, Santee, Calif.
16. Mike Couture, c, Clemson University.
17. Mark Stephens, lhp, Central Arizona JC.
18. Orlando Barrios, of, High Point College.
19. Patrick Miller, rhp, University of Detroit.
20. David White, rhp, University of South Florida.
21. Michael Norris, of, Richland (Texas) CC.
22. Charles Rambadt, c, Dominican (N.Y.) College.
23. Don Pruitt, rhp, University of Arizona.
24. Orlando Griego, rhp, New Mexico State University.
25. Christopher Wheat, ss, Monmouth College.
26. *Brendt Newbill, lhp, McNary HS, Salem, Ore.
27. *Michael Killimet, of, Fort Walton Beach (Fla.) HS.
28. Anthony Coble, of, Wingate (N.C.) College.
29. Todd Edwards, of, University of Arizona.
30. *Sam Taylor, of, El Cerrito HS, Richmond, Calif.
31. Mike Lynch, rhp, Rollins (Fla.) College.
32. Julian Salazar, ss, Pasadena (Calif.) CC.
33. Vince Castaldo, 3b, University of Kentucky.
34. *Alonso Beltran, rhp, Socorro HS, El Paso, Texas.
35. *Bobby Dickerson, of, Harrison Central HS, Gulfport, Miss.
36. Carlos Flores, ss, Sierra Vista HS, Baldwin Park, Calif.
37. *Luis Melendez, 3b, Inter American HS, Ponce, P.R.
38. *Steve Boyd, rhp, Central Arizona JC.
39. *David Repass, 1b-lhp, Forest HS, Ocala, Fla.
40. *Ernie Nietzke, of, Saddleback (Calif.) JC.
41. David Acevedo, rhp, Moca Central HS, San Sebastian, P.R.
42. *Reid Mizuguchi, rhp, Univeristy of Southern California.
43. Steven Sigloch, 2b, University of Utah.
44. *Clinton Brown, rhp, Taft (Calif.) CC.

## MINNESOTA TWINS (12)

1. **Todd Ritchie, rhp, Duncanville (Texas) HS.—(1997-2004)**
1. **Midre Cummings, of, Edison HS, Miami** (Supplemental choice—29th—as compensation for Type A free agent Jeff Reardon)—**(1993-2005)**
2. **Jayhawk Owens, c, Middle Tennessee State University.—(1993-96)**
2. Ron Caridad, rhp, Westminster Christian HS, Miami (Choice from Red Sox as compensation for Reardon).—(AA)
3. Jamie Ogden, 1b, White Bear Lake (Minn.) HS (Choice from Pirates as compensation for Type B free agent Wally Backman).—(AAA)
3. **Richie Becker, of, Aurora West HS, Aurora, Ill.—(1993-2000)**
4. *Silvio Censale, lhp, Catholic HS, Paramus, N.J.—(AA)

DRAFT DROP *Attended Miami (Fla.); re-drafted by Phillies, 1993 (10th round)*
5. **Brent Brede, of, Wesclin HS, Trenton, Ill.—(1996-98)**
6. Craig Hawkins, 2b, Simeon HS, Chicago.
7. Tim Persing, rhp, Mansfield (Pa.) University.
8. ***James Mouton, of, St. Mary's (Calif.) College.—(1994-2001)**
9. *Trevor Humphry, rhp, Delight (Ark.) HS.
10. Andrew Prater, c, Travis HS, Austin, Texas.
11. Mark Swope, rhp, University of Arkansas.
12. **Pat Meares, 3b, Wichita State University.—(1993-2001)**
13. *Steve Whitaker, lhp, Merced (Calif.) JC.
14. ***Jeff Granger, lhp, Orangefield (Texas) HS.—(1993-97)**

DRAFT DROP *First-round draft pick (5th overall), Royals (1993)*
15. Jon Henry, rhp, University of Central Florida.
16. Paul Russo, c-1b, University of Tampa.
17. *Fred Smith, rhp, Roosevelt HS, Brooklyn, N.Y.
18. *Scott Weiss, rhp, Stanford University.
19. Matt Morse, 2b, University of Michigan.
20. **Damian Miller, c, Viterbo (Wis.) College.—(1997-2007)**
21. **+Eddie Guardado, lhp, San Joaquin Delta (Calif.) CC.—(1993-2009)**
22. John Cohen, of, Mississippi State University.

DRAFT DROP *Baseball coach, Kentucky (2005-08); baseball coach, Mississippi State (2009-15)*
23. *David Schwartz, rhp, University of California.
24. Tom Gavin, 3b, Rider College.
25. *Clint Jensen, of, Naperville Central HS, Naperville, Ill.
26. *Robby Welles, rhp, Beverly Hills (Calif.) HS.
27. Dicky Dixon, lhp, University of Mississippi.
28. Devin Peppers, of, JC of the Desert (Calif.).
29. *Steve Kimble, of, Mount Zion HS, Decatur, Ill.
30. *Charles MacKendrick, rhp, Grand Junction (Colo.) HS.
31. Glenn Evans, ss, Harlan HS, Chicago.
32. Brian Ewing, of, College of Idaho.
33. *Geoff Edsell, rhp, Montoursville (Pa.) HS.
34. Kurt Pfeffer, rhp, CC of Marin (Calif.).
35. +Jay Belcher, rhp, Spring Hill HS, Olathe, Kan. / Allen County (Kan.) CC.
36. *Alex Pereira, lhp, Southwest HS, Miami.
37. *Brian Klepper, lhp, Iola (Kan.) HS.
38. Richard Portu, of, Westminster Christian HS, Miami.
39. Paul Bruno, c, New York Tech.
40. Matt Brown, c, San Jose State University.
41. **Brian Raabe, 2b, University of Minnesota.—(1995-97)**
42. Derrell Rumsey, of, Sonoma State (Calif.) University.
43. *Mike Neal, ss, Hammond (La.) HS.
44. *Greg Stephens, rhp, South HS, Fargo, Mo.
45. *Hiram Ramirez, c, F.D. Roosevelt HS, Ensenada, P.R.
46. *Jason Luttges, of, DeAnza (Calif.) CC.
47. *Chris Gump, 2b, Mesa (Ariz.) CC.
48. +David Garrow, ss, South Mountain (Ariz.) CC.
49. *Clarke Rea, c, Scottsdale (Ariz.) CC.
50. *Anthony Lacy, of-ss, Foothill HS, Sacramento, Calif.
51. *Larry Lucchetti, rhp, San Joaquin Delta (Calif.) CC.
52. *Kevin Rawitzer, lhp, Diablo Valley (Calif.) CC.
53. *Brian Henderson, of, Boone HS, Orlando, Fla.
54. *Blake Byers, c, Seabreeze HS, Daytona Beach, Fla.

RHONA WISE

The White Sox selected Miami junior college righthander Alex Fernandez fourth overall

## MONTREAL EXPOS (11)

1. **Shane Andrews, 3b, Carlsbad (N.M.) HS.—(1995-2002)**
1. **Rondell White, of, Jones County HS, Gray, Ga.** (Choice from Angels as compensation for Type A free agent Mark Langston)—**(1993-2007)**
1. **Gabe White, lhp, Sebring (Fla.) HS** (Supplemental choice—28th—as compensation for Langston)—**(1994-2005)**
1. **Stan Spencer, rhp, Stanford University** (Supplemental choice—35th—as compensation for Type A free agent Hubie Brooks)—**(1998-2000)**
1. **Ben Van Ryn, lhp, East Noble HS, Kendallville, Ind.** (Supplemental choice—37th—as compensation for Type A free agent Pascual Perez)—**(1996-98)**
1. Stan Robertson, of, Plainview (Texas) HS (Supplemental choice—40th—for failure to sign 1989 first-round draft pick Charles Johnson)—(Low A)
2. Michael Hardge, ss, Ellison HS, Killeen, Texas (Choice from Dodgers as compensation for Brooks).—(AA)
2. **Tavo Alvarez, rhp, Tucson (Ariz.) HS** (Choice from Yankees as compensation for Type A free agent Pascual Perez)—**(1995-96)**
2. **Chris Haney, lhp, University of North Carolina-Charlotte.—(1991-2002)**

DRAFT DROP *Son of Larry Haney, major leaguer (1966-78)*
2. Chris Martin, ss, Pepperdine University (Choice from Cardinals as compensation for Type B free agent Bryn Smith).—(AAA)
3. Mike Mathile, rhp, Wright State University.—(AAA)
4. **Jeff Barry, of, San Diego State University.—(1995-99)**
5. Ricky Clelland, rhp, Buckeye North US, Brilliant, Ohio.—(High A)
6. Steve Long, rhp, St. Xavier (Ill.) College.
7. Rob Fitzpatrick, c, Georgia Southern College.
8. Javier Pages, c, Stranahan HS, Fort Lauderdale, Fla.
9. Craig Clow, 1b, Western Oregon University.
10. Todd Samples, of, Liberty University.
11. Brian Jones, of, Barstow (Calif.) HS.
12. Bob Baxter, lhp, Harvard University.
13. Ted Ciesla, ss, Rutgers University.
14. Robbie Katzaroff, of, UCLA.
15. *Troy Kopp, c, University of the Pacific.

DRAFT DROP *Quarterback, Canadian Football League (1998-2000)*
16. Randy Wilstead, 1b, Brigham Young University.
17. *Jackie Ross, of, Edison HS, Miami.
18. *Frederick Collier, 1b, Abbeville (S.C.) HS.
19. Thomas Philips, c, Fresno State University.
20. Perry Sanchez, c, Long Beach State University.
21. *Scott Brocail, rhp, Lamar (Colo.) HS.

DRAFT DROP *Brother of Doug Brocail, major leaguer (1992-2009)*
22. *David Bingham, ss-of, Walla Walla (Wash.) CC.
23. Steve Renko, rhp, University of Kansas.

DRAFT DROP *Son of Steve Renko, major leaguer (1969-83)*
24. Marc Tsitouris, 1b-c, Wingate (N.C.) College.

DRAFT DROP *Son of John Tsitouris, major leaguer (1957-68)*
25. *Matt Haas, c, St. Mary's HS, Paducah, Ky.

DRAFT DROP *Son of Eddie Haas, major leaguer (1957-60); major league manager (1985)*
26. Ranbir Grewal, rhp, Fresno State University.
27. Darrin Kotch, lhp, Rutgers University.
28. ***Billy Brewer, lhp, Dallas Baptist University.—(1993-99)**
29. *Kenya Hunt, 1b, Oceanside (Calif.) HS.
30. Brian Sheehan, thp, University of North Carolina-Asheville.
31. *Dean Madsen, of, Yuba (Calif.) JC.
32. *Kelton Jacobson, rhp, Bellevue (Wash.) CC.
33. *Rick Navarro, rhp, Pomona (Calif.) HS.
34. *Trenton Hauswirth, c, Palm Desert (Calif.) HS.
35. Ryan Whitman, rhp, Jupiter HS, Lake Park, Fla.
36. *Mike Morland, c, University of Texas.
37. *Ben Boulware, of, Los Gatos (Calif.) HS.
38. John Polasek, lhp, Rice University.
39. *Jose Diaz, of, Rafael Lopez Landron HS, Guayama, P.R.
40. *David Schultz, of, Marina HS, Huntington Beach, Calif.
41. Doug Noce, c, Cal Poly San Luis Obispo.

DRAFT DROP *Brother of Paul Noce, major leaguer (1987-90)*
42. *Jacob Benz, lhp, College Park HS, Pleasant Hill, Calif.
43. *John Rogers, lhp, East Los Angeles HS.
44. *Todd Anderson, of, Lewis-Clark State (Idaho) College.
45. *Alex Miranda, 1b, Christopher Columbus HS, Miami.
46. *Victor Llanos, 3b, Gilberto Concepcion de Gracia HS, Carolina, P.R.
47. *Jason Jensen, of, McLane HS, Fresno, Calif.
48. *Mark Palfalvi, 1b, Chabot (Calif.) JC.
49. *Ronald Jones, of, San Diego Mesa CC.
50. *Jorge Adame, c, Bell HS, Maywood, Calif.
51. *Archie Jean, of, Mendocino (Calif.) CC.
52. *Allen Gallagher, ss, Centennial HS, Gresham, Ore.
53. +Charles Lee, of, Currituck County HS, Poplar Branch, N.C. / Louisburg (N.C.) JC.
54. *Clinton Oltjenbruns, 1b, Willits (Calif.) HS.

55. *Gregg Press, rhp, Cabrillo (Calif.) JC.
56. *Stephen Mitchell, rhp, Saratoga HS, Los Gatos, Calif.
57. *Brett Brown, c, San Diego Mesa CC.
58. *Randy Collins, c, Mount San Jacinto (Calif.) JC.
59. *Christopher Lowen, rhp, Moreno Valley (Calif.) HS.
60. *Paul Carpentier, rhp, Chaffey (Calif.) JC.
61. *Martin Colunga, c, Colton (Calif.) HS.
62. *Matthew Jones, 1b, Red Land HS, Lewisberry, Pa.
63. *Benji Grigsby, rhp, Lassen (Calif.) JC.

DRAFT DROP *First-round draft pick (20th overall), Athletics (1992)*

## NEW YORK METS (17)

1. **Jeromy Burnitz, of, Oklahoma State University.—(1993-2006)**
2. **Aaron Ledesma, ss, Chabot (Calif.) JC.—(1995-2000)**
3. **Micah Franklin, ss, Lincoln HS, San Francisco.—(1997)**
4. Mike Patrizi, c, Pennsauken (N.J.) HS.—(High A)
5. Darwin Davis, 3b, Simeon HS, Chicago.—(Rookie)
6. Demond Smith, of, Eisenhower HS, Rialto, Calif.
7. **Pete Walker, rhp, University of Connecticut.—(1995-2003)**
8. **Raul Casanova, c, Ponce (P.R.) HS.—(1996-2008)**
9. **Fernando Vina, 2b, Arizona State University.—(1993-2004)**
10. Ty Quillin, of, Nickerson HS, Buhler, Kan.
11. ***Darren Dreifort, of-rhp, Wichita (Kan.) Heights HS.—(1994-2004)**

DRAFT DROP *First-round draft pick (2nd overall), Dodgers (1993)*

12. Caspar Van Rynbach, rhp, Iowa Western CC.
13. *Tom Hamilton, of, South Fork HS, Indiantown, Fla.
14. Todd Douma, lhp, Arizona State University.
15. ***Steve Soderstrom, rhp, Turlock (Calif.) HS.—(1996)**

DRAFT DROP *First-round draft pick (6th overall), Giants (1993)*

16. Eric Corbell, rhp, Incarnate Word (Texas) College.
17. **Brian Daubach, 1b, Belleville Township HS, Belleville, Ill.—(1998-2005)**
18. *Trey Cheek, rhp, Broughton HS, Raleigh, N.C.
19. *Tony Phillips, rhp, University of Southern Mississippi.
20. Steven Steele, c, Millikan HS, Long Beach, Calif.
21. Jason King, ss, Washington State University.
22. Brad Schorr, rhp, Columbus (Ga.) HS.
23. Mike Sciortino, lhp, Central Connecticut State University.
24. Steven Seymour, rhp, Ocean County (N.J.) CC.
25. Steve Thomas, rhp, University of Alabama.
26. Robert Carpentier, rhp, University of New Hampshire.
27. +Bert Bull, of, Fairfax HS, Los Angeles / Los Angeles CC.
28. Terrell Williams, 3b, Harlan HS, Chicago.
29. ***Will Brunson, lhp, Eastfield (Texas) JC.—(1998-99)**
30. Philip Scott, ss, Wittenberg (Ohio) University.
31. *Joseph Sewell, rhp, UC Irvine.
32. ***Mike Holtz, lhp, Central Cambria HS, Ebensburg, Pa.—(1996-2006)**
33. *James Northeimer, c, Sacramento (Calif.) HS.
34. *Aaron Richards rhp-ss, Westlake HS, Austin, Texas.
35. James Manfred, rhp, Indian Hills (Iowa) CC.
36. *Maceo Mitchell, of, Fresno (Calif.) CC.
37. *Anthony Richardson, 1b, Simeon HS, Chicago.
38. ***Andrew Lorraine, lhp, Hart HS, Valencia, Calif.—(1994-2002)**
39. *Thomas King, of, Albany (Ga.) HS.
40. *Todd Pridy, 1b, Napa Valley (Calif.) JC.
41. +Shaun Watson, rhp, Southwestern HS, Brighton, Ill. / Rend Lake (Ill.) JC.
42. *Shane Bushard, 3b, North Idaho JC.
43. *Karl Carswell, 2b, Shawnee Mission HS, Overland Park, Kan.
44. *Douglas Yartz, lhp, Yuba (Calif.) CC.
45. **Ricky Otero, of, Lano Padro Rivera HS, Vega Baja, P.R.—(1995-97)**
46. Scotty Williams, rhp, Morristown (Tenn.) HS.
47. *Thomas Daniel, of, Prairie HS, Vancouver, Wash.
48. Tom Allison, 2b, Chapman (Calif.) College.

DRAFT DROP *Scouting director, Diamondbacks (2007-11)*

49. *Claude Allen, rhp, Hogan HS, Vallejo, Calif.
50. ***Rick Helling, rhp, Kishwaukee (Ill.) JC.—(1994-2006)**

DRAFT DROP *First-round draft pick (22nd overall), Rangers (1992)*

51. *Christopher Eckley, of-1b, Burke HS, Omaha, Neb.
52. +Randy Farmer, 2b-ss, Meridian (Miss.) JC.

## NEW YORK YANKEES (10)

1. **Carl Everett, of, Hillsborough HS, Tampa.—(1993-2006)**
2. **Robert Eenhoorn, ss, Davidson College** (Choice from Pirates as compensation for Type B free agent Walt Terrell).**—(1994-97)**
2. (Choice to Expos as compensation for Type A free agent Pascual Perez)
3. Tate Seefried, 1b, El Segundo (Calif.) HS.—(AAA)
4. **Kirt Ojala, lhp, University of Michigan.—(1997-99)**
5. Rick Lantrip, 3b, Fresno State University.—(Low A)
6. **Sam Militello, rhp, University of Tampa.—(1992-93)**
7. **Jalal Leach, of, Pepperdine University.—(2001)**
8. Tim Rumer, lhp, Duke University.
9. *Matthew Terrell, of, Sturgis (Mich.) HS.
10. Darren Hodges, rhp, Ferrum (Va.) College.
11. Richard Hines, thp, University of Mississippi.
12. Ron Frazier, rhp, Clemson University.
13. Jeff Motuzas, c, Nashua (N.H.) HS.
14. Bo Siberz, rhp, Texas A&M University.
15. Sean Smith, rhp, Seekonk HS, Pawtucket, R.I.
16. **Ricky Ledee, of, Colegio Nuestra Sonora Valvanara HS, Salinas, P.R.—(1998-2007)**
17. Bryan Faw, rhp, Clemson University.
18. Bob Deller, of, Texas Wesleyan University.
19. Brent Gilbert, rhp, Texas A&M University.
20. **Kevin Jordan, 2b, University of Nebraska.—(1995-2001)**
21. Keith Seiler, lhp, University of Virginia.
22. **+Andy Pettitte, lhp, Deer Park (Texas) HS / San Jacinto (Texas) JC.—(1995-2013)**
23. **+Tom Wilson, c-of, Fullerton (Calif.) JC.—(2001-04)**
24. **+Jorge Posada, ss, Calhoun (Ala.) CC.—(1995-2011)**
25. **Matt Dunbar, lhp, Florida State University.—(1995)**
26. *Shannon Knighton, 1b, Bleckley County HS, Cochran, Ga.
27. *Jim Musselwhite, rhp-1b, Apopka (Fla.) HS.
28. **Shane Spencer, of, Granite Hills HS, El Cajon, Calif.—(1998-2004)**
29. *Corey Hayes, of, Pattonville HS, Florissant, Mo.
30. *Brad Stuart, rhp, University of New Orleans.
31. *Kent Donnelly, rhp, Foothill HS, Santa Ana, Calif.
32. Mike Hankins, ss, UCLA.
33. John Sutherland, rhp, UCLA.
34. Pat Morphy, rhp, Northeastern Louisiana University.
35. ***Kevin Ohme, lhp, Indian River (Fla.) CC.—(2003)**
36. *Brett King, ss, Apopka (Fla.) HS.
37. *Ernie Yaroshuk, of-1b, Miami-Dade CC South.
38. John Thibert, rhp, San Diego Mesa CC.
39. ***Mike Heathcott, rhp, Creighton University.—(1998)**
40. *Wesley Hawkins, of, Mansfield (La.) HS.
41. ***John Wasdin, rhp, Godby HS, Tallahassee, Fla.—(1995-2007)**

DRAFT DROP *First-round draft pick (25th overall), Athletics (1993)*

42. Barry Smith, 2b, Cumberland (Ky.) College.
43. *Daniel Redovian, rhp, Brevard (Fla.) JC.
44. *William Lawrence, lhp, Gulf Breeze (Fla.) HS.
45. +Albert Perez, rhp, Ohlone (Calif.) JC.
46. +Matt Ruoff, 3b, Santa Rosa (Calif.) JC.
47. *James Ramminger, 1b, Goodrich HS, Fond du Lac, Wis.
48. *James Spero, of, Santa Rosa (Calif.) JC.
49. *Tim Kester, rhp, Coral Springs (Fla.) HS.
50. *Alex McCoy, of, Culver Military HS, Wilmington, N.C.
51. *Rich Haley, of, Codrova HS, Rancho Cordova, Calif.
52. *Kurt Alderman, c, Sacramento (Calif.) CC.
53. *Scott Patrick, rhp, Indian River (Fla.) CC.
54. +Jeff Cindrich, rhp, Edison (Fla.) CC.
55. *Franklyn Johnson, 1b, Howard (Texas) JC.
56. *Mark Saugstad, ss-3b, University of California.
57. *Sean Palmer, of, Ganesha HS, Diamond Bar, Calif.
58. *Andres Texidor, c, Centro de Instructico HS, Canovanas, P.R.
59. *Tracy Latimer, rhp, Westwood HS, Fort Pierce, Fla.
60. Scott Kendall, lhp, Central HS, Fort Pierce, Fla.
61. *Joe Smith, rhp, Cardinal Newman HS, West Palm Beach, Fla.
62. *Anthony Crueger, lhp, Texarkana (Texas) CC.
63. *Kortney Paul, c, Southwest HS, Fort Worth, Texas.
64. *Derek January, lhp, Miami-Dade CC South.
65. +Joseph Long, rhp, Citrus (Calif.) JC.
66. *Joel Grimes, 1b, Barbers Hill HS, Mount Bellvieu, Texas.
67. *Kevin Bosse, 3b-1b, Navasota (Texas) HS.
68. *Eric Methner, rhp, Michigan State University.
69. *Rodd Kelley, ss, Brandon (Fla.) HS.
70. *Pedro Lewis, 3b, McClatchy HS, Sacramento, Calif.
71. *Terry Vaughn, of, Oceanside (Calif.) HS.
72. ***Danny Rios, rhp, Monsignor Pace HS, Hialeah, Fla.—(1997-98)**
73. *Ray Gossett, lhp, Glendora HS, San Dimas, Calif.
74. *Eric Taylor, lhp, Mingo HS, Mingo Junction, Ohio.

## OAKLAND ATHLETICS (26)

1. **Todd Van Poppel, rhp, James W. Martin HS, Arlington, Texas** (Choice from Brewers as compensation for Type A free agent Dave Parker).**—(1991-2004)**

DRAFT DROP *First 1990 high school draft pick to reach majors (Sept. 11, 1991)*

1. Don Peters, rhp, College of St. Francis (Ill.).—(AAA)
1. David Zancanaro, lhp, UCLA (Supplemental choice—34th—as compensation for Type A free agent Storm Davis).—(AAA)
1. **Kirk Dressendorfer, rhp, University of Texas** (Supplemental choice—36th—as compensation for Parker).**—(1991)**
2. Curtis Shaw, lhp, University of Kansas (Choice from Tigers as compensation for Type B free agent Tony Phillips).—(AAA)
2. **Eric Helfand, c, Arizona State University** (Choice from Royals as compensation for Type A free agent Storm Davis).**—(1993-95)**
2. Gary Hust, of, Petal (Miss.) HS.—(AA)
3. Chaon Garland, rhp, Haverford (Pa.) College.—(AA)
4. Jeff Duncan, 3b, Jackson State (Tenn.) CC.—(Low A)
5. Chris Hart, of, Auburn University.—(AA)
6. **Creighton Gubanich, c, Phoenixville (Pa.) Area HS.—(1999)**
7. Dan Vizzini, lhp, Francis Marion (S.C.) College.
8. *Andy Bruce, 3b, Georgia Tech.
9. Mike Kennedy, c, Elon College.

DRAFT DROP *Baseball coach, Elon (1997-2015)*

10. **Ernie Young, of, Lewis (Ill.) University.—(1994-2004)**
11. Mark Craft, rhp, Virginia Military Institute.
12. Bill Picketts, 2b Cal State Los Angeles.
13. Eric Myers, rhp, Seminole (Okla.) JC.
14. Jim Dillon, rhp, University of Maine.
15. Kevin Dattola, of, University of South Florida.
16. **Doug Johns, lhp, University of Virginia.—(1995-99)**
17. *Scott Dodd, lhp, Glendale (Ariz.) CC.
18. Greg Reid, of, Cal State Los Angeles.
19. Carlos Salazar, 1b-c, Azusa Pacific (Calif.) University.
20. Chris Olofson, of, Bakersfield (Calif.) JC.
21. Rick Miller, lhp, Grand Canyon College.
22. **Izzy Molina, c, Christopher Columbus HS, Miami.—(1996-2002)**
23. **Tanyon Sturtze, rhp, Quinsigamond (Mass.) CC.—(1995-2008)**
24. *Dwayne Fowler, rhp, Long Beach State University.
25. David Tripp, rhp-of, Clemson University.
26. *Shawn Purdy, rhp, University of Miami.
27. Eric Booker, of, San Jose State University.
28. Glenn Osinski, ss, University of New Orleans.
29. Craig Connolly, rhp, University of Pennsylvania.
30. Mike Newson, rhp, Crenshaw HS, Los Angeles.
31. Scott Rose, rhp, Hillsborough (Fla.) CC.
32. Craig Sudbury, rhp, University of Utah.
33. Jeff Clifford, rhp, Assumption (Mass.) College.
34. Tony Gechter, rhp, Trinidad State (Colo.) JC.
35. ***T.J. Mathews, rhp, St. Louis CC-Meramec.—(1995-2002)**

DRAFT DROP *Son of Nelson Mathews, major leaguer (1960-65)*

36. Tony Scharff, rhp, Oklahoma City University.
37. **Todd Revenig, rhp, Mankato State (Minn.) University.—(1992)**
38. Reggie Bailey, 1b, Coffee HS, Douglas, Ga.
39. Mike Muhlethaler, 3b, University of California.
40. *Chris Oscar, lhp, Valley HS, Las Vegas, Nev.
41. Tony Fults, lhp, Franklin County HS, Decherd, Tenn.
42. *Carlos James, of, Pine Bluff (Ark.) HS.
43. ***Sean Lowe, rhp, McLennan (Texas) CC.—(1997-2004)**

DRAFT DROP *First-round draft pick (15th overall), Cardinals (1992)*

44. *Marcus Maple, of, Central HS, Beaumont Texas.
45. *Michael Bumpers, of, McCrory (Ark.) HS.
46. *Marcus Miller, rhp, Bay HS, Panama City, Fla.
47. *Oscar Draper, rhp, Johnson HS, Huntsville, Ala.
48. +Robert Pierce, rhp, Dixie (Utah) JC.
49. *John White, 3b, Long Beach (Calif.) CC.

## PHILADELPHIA PHILLIES (3)

1. **Mike Lieberthal, c, Westlake HS, Westlake Village, Calif.—(1994-2007)**
2. *Tim Schweitzer, lhp, Reedsport (Ore.) HS.--DNP

DRAFT DROP *Attended Arizona; re-drafted by Mariners, 1993 (7th round)*

3. Dan Larson, of, Birmingham (Calif.) HS.—(Low A)
4. John Ingram, lhp, Los Angeles Harbor JC.—(Short-season A)
5. Tom Nuneviller, of, West Chester (Pa.) University.—(AAA)
6. Mike Murphy, of, St. Pius X HS, Albuquerque, N.M.
7. **Joel Adamson, lhp, Cerritos (Calif.) JC.—(1996-98)**
8. Ron Lockett, 1b, Jackson State University.
9. ***Derrick White, 3b, Santa Rosa (Calif.) JC.—(1993-98)**
10. Jorge Pascual, 2b-3b, Aquinas (Tenn.) JC.
11. **Gary Bennett, c, Waukegan East HS, Waukegan, Ill.—(1995-2008)**
12. Chad Anderson, rhp, Roseburg (Ore.) HS.
13. Jay Edwards, of, Jackson State University.
14. **Mike Williams, rhp, Virginia Tech.—(1992-2003)**
15. Scott Coleman, lhp, Orange Glen HS, Valley Center, Calif.
16. *Eric Spann, of, Stamford (Conn.) HS.
17. Maurice Hines, 1b, Rose HS, Greenville, N.C.
18. Darren Hedley, of, American River (Calif.) CC.
19. Antonio Grissom, of, South Georgia JC.

DRAFT DROP *Brother of Marquis Grissom, major leaguer (1989-2005)*

20. ***Marvin Benard, of, Los Angeles Harbor JC.—(1995-2003)**
21. ***B.J. Waszgis, c, Fort Scott (Kan.) CC.—(2000)**
22. *Robert Lamb, rhp, Central HS, Tuscaloosa, Ala.
23. *James Koehler, 1b, De Anza (Calif.) JC.
24. R.A. Neitzel, 2b, Oregon State University.
25. Steve McGovern, rhp, Cal State Los Angeles.
26. *Omar Washington, rhp, Samuell HS, Dallas.
27. Terrell Smith, ss, Stanhope Elmore HS, Millbrook, Ala.
28. *Mark Graham, lhp, Santa Monica (Calif.) CC.
29. Gary Lance, rhp, American River (Calif.) CC.
30. Ryan Ridenour, c, Oregon Tech.
31. Erik Judson, ss-2b, UC San Diego.
32. Samuel Edwards, rhp, Gateway HS, Kissimmee,

Fla.
33. Thomas Jones, rhp-of, Sam Houston State University.
34. *Danny Miller, rhp, Poway (Calif.) HS.
35. *John Salamon, rhp, Sto-Rox HS, McKees Rocks, Pa.
36. Bill Higgins, lhp, Clinch Valley County HS, Castlewood, Va.
37. Mike Montgomery, rhp, East Tennessee State University.
38. Sean Ryan, 1b, Rutgers University.
39. Troy Paulsen, ss, Stanford University.
40. Jeff Borgese, of, Fresno State University.
41. Steven Hollins, ss, Appalachian State University.
42. Chadwick Silvers, of, Carson Newman (Tenn.) College.
43. Eric Hill, rhp, Walters State (Tenn.) CC.
44. Troy Rusk, c-1b, University of South Florida.
45. Jeffery Gunn, of, Grambling State University.
46. Pat Cheek, 3b, U.S. International (Calif.) University.
47. *Patrick Garrigan, ss, Miami (Ohio) University.
48. +Eric Maudlin, of, American River (Calif.) JC.
49. +Julio Cruz, c, American River (Calif.) JC.
50. *Lawrence Novey, c, Grant HS, Sacramento, Calif.
51. *Jeff Richardson, 3b, St. Bernards HS, Culver City, Calif.
52. *Jeffrey Wagner, 3b, Federal Way (Wash.) HS.
53. *Scott Eggleston, rhp, Maple Woods (Mo.) CC.
54. *Demetrius Comeaux, of, Gahr HS, Cerritos, Calif.
55. *Manuel Evans, of, Pasadena (Calif.) HS.
56. +Ron Ollison, 2b, Angelina (Texas) JC.
57. *Michael Myers, of, Donegal HS, Mount Joy, Pa.

## PITTSBURGH PIRATES (5)

1. **Kurt Miller, rhp, West HS, Bakersfield, Calif.—(1994-99)**
1. Mike Zimmerman, rhp, University of South Alabama (Supplemental choice—27th—as compensation for Type A free agent Jim Gott).—(AAA)
2. (Choice to Yankees as compensation for Type B free agent Walt Terrell)
3. (Choice to Twins as compensation for Type B free agent Wally Backman)
3. John Schulte, of, Brenham (Texas) HS (Choice from Dodgers as compensation for Gott).—(Low A)
4. Mitch House, c, Castlewood (Va.) HS.—(High A)
5. Glenn Coombs, rhp, Cypress Creek HS, Houston.—(Low A)

DRAFT DROP *Son of Danny Coombs, major leaguer (1963-71)*

6. Tim Edge, c, Auburn University.
7. **Kevin Young, 3b, University of Southern Mississippi.—(1992-2003)**
8. Jeff Conger, lhp-of, Charlotte Latin HS, Charlotte, N.C.
9. **Rich Robertson, lhp, Texas A&M University.—(1993-98)**
10. Cedrick Peppers, of, Hughes Springs HS, Avinger, Texas.
11. *Artis Johnson, of, Delray Beach (Fla.) HS.
12. Wes Grisham, of, Louisiana State University.
13. **Brian Shouse, lhp, Bradley University.—(1993-2009)**
14. **+Jeff McCurry, rhp, San Jacinto (Texas) CC.—(1995-99)**
15. **Rick White, rhp, Paducah (Ky.) JC.—(1994-2007)**
16. Lynn Carlson, rhp, Greenville (Ill.) College.
17. John Douris, rhp, Orange Coast (Calif.) CC.
18. Charles Tooch, ss, Forest Hill HS, West Palm Beach, Fla.
19. *Jason Leto, of-2b, St. Petersburg (Fla.) JC.
20. **Mark Johnson, 1b, Dartmouth College.—(1995-2002)**
21. Shelton Simpson, rhp, Eastern Kentucky University.
22. *Ben Murray, of, Beaver Dam (Wis.) HS.
23. *Robin Tumble, of-rhp, Carthage (Texas) HS.
24. **Keith Osik, c-3b, Louisiana State University.—(1996-2005)**
25. Troy Hooper, rhp, Shorter (Ga.) College.
26. Cory Schaefer, of, University of Wisconsin-Oshkosh.
27. Brad Davis, c, Columbus (Ga.) College.
28. Dave Tellers, rhp, San Jose State University.
29. Ben Johnson, 3b, Oregon State University.
30. Tom Green, of, Georgia Tech.
31. *Mark LaRosa, lhp, Louisiana State University.
32. *Aaron Wofford, ss, Lindhurst HS, Olivehurst, Calif.
33. David Pike, rhp, Riverview HS, Sarasota, Fla.
34. *Shawn Buchanan, of, University of Nebraska.
35. *Angel Delgado, ss-3b, East Chicago Central HS, East Chicago, Ill.
36. *Mike Russell, rhp, Fort Vancouver HS, Vancouver, Wash.
37. +John Carter, rhp, Simeon HS, Chicago / Kishwaukee (Ill.) JC.
38. Tim French, rhp, Northern Kentucky University.
39. Joe Sondrini, 2b, North Adams State (Mass.) College.
40. Steven Polewski, ss-2b, Chicago State University.
41. Javier Martinez, ss, Inter American HS, Levittown, P.R.

## ST. LOUIS CARDINALS (13)

1. **Donovan Osborne, lhp, University of Nevada-Las Vegas.—(1992-2004)**
1. **Aaron Holbert, ss, Jordan HS, Long Beach, Calif.** (Choice from Red Sox as compensation for Type A free agent Tony Pena).**—(1996-2005)**

DRAFT DROP *Brother of Ray Holbert, major leaguer (1994-2000).*

1. Paul Ellis, c, UCLA (Supplemental choice—30th—as compensation for of Pena).—(AAA)
2. (Choice to Expos as compensation for Type B free agent Bryn Smith)
3. **Marc Ronan, c-of, Florida State University.—(1993)**
4. Andy Beasley, c, Virginia Military Institute.—(High A)
5. *Jimmy Lewis, rhp, Florida JC.—(AAA)

DRAFT DROP *Attended Florida State; re-drafted by Astros, 1991 (2nd round)*

6. George Sells, lhp, Old Dominion University.
7. **Scott Baker, lhp, Taft (Calif.) JC.—(1995)**
8. Mark MacArthur, ss, The Master's (Calif.) College.
9. **Terry Bradshaw, of, Norfolk State University.—(1995-96)**
10. Mark Smith, of-rhp, University of Texas.
11. Jose Velez, of, Eugenio Maria de Hostos HS, Mayaguez, P.R.
12. Jimmy Davenport, of, Jackson State University.
13. **Tom Urbani, lhp, Long Beach State University.—(1993-96)**
14. *Keith Adaway, 2b-of, St. Louis CC-Meramec.
15. Brad Beanblossom, ss, Oklahoma State University.
16. *Pat Treend, rhp, El Camino Real HS, West Hills, Calif.
17. *Ricky Kimball, rhp, Florida State University.
18. David Norris, lhp, St. Mary's (Calif.) College.
19. Jimmy Marchesi, rhp, El Capitan HS, Lakeside, Calif.
20. Don Prybylinski, c, Illinois State University.
21. Troy Salvior, rhp, Hillsdale (Mich.) College.
22. Steve Dudek, of, Rancho HS, Las Vegas, Nev.
23. Kevin Carpenter, c, West Virginia University.
24. **Duff Brumley, rhp, Cleveland (Tenn.) State CC.—(1994)**
25. Skeets Thomas, of, University of South Carolina.
26. *Joe Wise, rhp, Georgia Tech.
27. Bill Gale, of, Central Connecticut State University.
28. Lorenzo Meza, ss, Sweetwater HS, National City, Calif.
29. Anthony Jenkins, of, The Citadel.
30. Harry Ball, 2b, Rollins (Fla.) College.
31. Brian Sullivan, lhp, Cumberland (Tenn.) Univeristy.
32. Rich Gonzalez, of, Cal State Fullerton.
33. Brian Avram, rhp, JC of Southern Idaho.
34. John Kelly, rhp, Kennesaw State (Ga.) College.
35. Frank Speek, rhp, Liberty University.
36. ***Kevin Morgan, 2b, Southeastern Louisiana University.—(1997)**
37. Tom Fusco, lhp, Long Island Univeristy.
38. Darryl Meek, rhp, Parkway South HS, St. Louis.
39. Michael Jolley, rhp, Dixie (Utah) JC.
40. Beto Rodriguez, 1b, U.S. International (Calif.) University.
41. Andy Petersen, rhp, San Diego State University.
42. Kevin Nielsen, lhp, San Diego State University.
43. ***Chris Turner, 3b-of, Western Kentucky University.—(1993-2000)**
44. Craig Ruyak, rhp, College of William & Mary.
45. Joe Aversa, ss, Southern California College.
46. *Ryan Martindale, c, Creighton University.
47. *Doak Wishon, of, Seminole (Okla.) JC.
48. *John Coletti, lhp, Seminole (Okla.) JC.
49. Sydney Lowman, c, Draughon's (Tenn.) JC.
50. Gilberto Torres, of, Florida International University.
51. Matthew Tomso, rhp, Mount Olive (Ill.) HS.
52. Jonas Hamlin, 1b, JC of Southern Idaho.
53. ***Bart Evans, rhp, Three Rivers (Mo.) CC.—(1998)**
54. Victor Vargas, 2b, University of Wyoming.
55. *Tom Afenir, c, Escondido HS, San Marcos, Calif.

DRAFT DROP *Brother of Troy Afenir, major leaguer (1987-92)*

56. +Joseph Merritt, c, Volunteer State (Tenn.) CC.
57. *Travis Hunter, rhp, JC of Southern Idaho.
58. +Keith Jones, of, Southeastern Illinois JC.
59. *Jackie Sosa, 1b-of, Castle Park Heights HS, Chula Vista, Calif.
60. *Nicholas DeLuca, ss, Taylorsville HS, Salt Lake City.

## SAN DIEGO PADRES (19)

1. (Choice to Giants as compensation tor Type A free agent Craig Lefferts)
1. **Robbie Beckett, lhp, McCallum HS, Austin, Texas** (Choice from Royals as compensation for Type A free agent Mark Davis).**—(1996-97)**
1. **Scott Sanders, rhp, Nicholls State University** (Supplemental choice—32nd—as compensation for Davis).**—(1993-99)**
2. (Choice to Tigers as compensation tor Type B free agent Fred Lynn)
3. Jerrey Thurston, c, Lake Brantley HS, Altamonte Springs, Fla.—(AAA)
4. Rusty Silcox, rhp, Arizona State University.—(AA)
5. Mark Anthony, 3b, Lancaster (S.C.) HS.—(High A)
6. Jeff Pearce, of, Pepperdine University.
7. Craig Bullock, 3b, Aldine HS, Houston.
8. Keith McKoy, 2b, Southeastern (N.C.) CC.
9. Tyrone Narcisse, rhp, Lincoln HS, Port Arthur, Texas.
10. Paul Gonzalez, 3b, Texas Christian University.
11. ***Jay Powell, rhp-3b, West Lauderdale HS, Collinsville, Miss.—(1995-2005)**

DRAFT DROP *First-round draft pick (19th overall), Orioles (1993)*

12. David Mowry, 1b, Glendora (Calif.) HS.
13. Steve Gill, of, University of Arizona.
14. **Scott Frederickson, rhp, University of Texas.—(1993)**
15. Kevin Farlow, ss, Cal State Fullerton.
16. Brent Bish, ss, Cal State Los Angeles.
17. **Matt Mieske, of, Western Michigan University.—(1993-2000)**
18. *Todd Evers, rhp, University of Wisconsin.
19. *Keith Stafford, ss-2b, Swainsboro (Ga.) HS.
20. Billy Meury, ss, University of Maryland.
21. *Scott Emerson, lhp, Shadow Mountain HS, Phoenix.
22. ***Jon Ratliff, rhp, Liverpool Central HS, Clay, N.Y.—(2000)**

DRAFT DROP *First-round draft pick (24th overall), Cubs (1993)*

23. James Elliott, c, University of Denver.
24. **Jay Gainer, 1b, University of South Alabama.—(1993)**
25. **Lance Painter, lhp, University of Wisconsin.—(1993-2003)**
26. Bruce Bensching, rhp, Lewis-Clark State (Idaho) College.
27. Jon Bellamy, 3b, Lassen (Calif.) JC.
28. Reginald Stephens, 2b, St. Louis CC-Forest Park.
29. *Greg Cushman, 3b, Monterey HS, Lubbock, Texas.
30. Ryan Ivie, lhp, Tumwater HS, Olympia, Wash.
31. Mike Bradley, rhp, University of Texas.
32. Darius Gash, of, Middle Tennessee State University.
33. Lawrence Hawks, 1b-c, Central Missouri State University.
34. Paul Martin, rhp, Florida CC.
35. *Thomas Quinn, rhp, Mississippi State University.
36. Joe Waldron, lhp, Southwestern Oklahoma State University.
37. *Shawn Pagee, c, JC of San Mateo (Calif.).
38. James West, c, University of San Francisco.
39. *Aaron Frederickson, lhp, University of Portland.
40. *Aldren Sadler, rhp, Rockdale County HS, Conyers, Ga.
41. David Adams, of, Cal State Los Angeles.
42. *Stephen Grack, of, Rancho Santiago (Calif.) JC.
43. Thomas DeCareau, of, Harvard University.
44. German Carion, 2b, Dra Conchita Cuevas HS, Gurabo, P.R.
45. Steve Siebert, 2b-of, Georgia Southern College.
46. Jeffrey Brown, lhp, Navarro (Texas) JC.
47. *Phillip Haney, c, Radford University.
48. Tim Ploeger, rhp, Western HS, Las Vegas, Nev.
49. ***Alan Benes, rhp, Lake Forest (Ill.) HS.—(1995-2003)**

DRAFT DROP *First-round draft pick (16th overall), Cardinals (1993) • Brother of Andy Benes, first overall draft pick, Padres (1988); major leaguer (1989-2002)*

50. *Gary Frank, 2b, La Jolla (Calif.) HS.
51. Robert Hays, rhp, Cal State Chico.
52. Jeffrey Ordway, ss-2b, Oregon Tech.
53. ***Al Levine, rhp, Southern Illinois University.—(1996-2004)**

## SAN FRANCISCO GIANTS (21)

1. **Adam Hyzdu, of, Moeller HS, Cincinnati** (Choice from Astros as compensation for Type B free agent Ken Oberkfell).**—(2000-06)**
1. Eric Christopherson, c, San Diego State University (Choice from Padres as compensation for Type A free agent Craig Lefferts).—(AAA)
1. (Choice to Astros as compensation for Type A free agent Kevin Bass)
1. **Marcus Jensen, c-rhp, Skyline HS, Oakland** (Supplemental choice—33rd—as compensation for Lefferts).**—(1996-2002)**
2. *Jose Prado, rhp, Coral Gables (Fla.) HS.—(AA)

DRAFT DROP *Attended Miami (Fla.); re-drafted by Dodgers, 1993 (8th round)*

2. **Joey Roselli, lhp, Bishop Alemany HS, Mission Hills, Calif.** (Supplemental choice—70th—as compensation for Type C free agent Candy Maldonado).**—(1995)**
3. **Rick Huisman, rhp, Lewis (Ill.) University.—(1995-96)**

DRAFT DROP *Brother of Justin Huisman, major leaguer (2004)*

4. **Mike Myers, lhp, Iowa State University.—(1995-2007)**
5. Julio Vega, of, Shoreham-Wading River HS, Shoreham, N.Y.—(Short-season A)
6. John Jackson, of, University of Southern California.

DRAFT DROP *Wide receiver, National Football League (1990-96)*

7. ***Greg Norton, ss, Bishop O'Dowd HS, Orinda, Calif.—(1996-2009)**
8. **Kevin McGehee, rhp, Louisiana Tech.—(1993)**
9. *Nate Holdren, of, Richland (Wash.) HS.
10. Derek Reid, of, Triton (Ill.) JC.
11. Kurt Peltzer, lhp, University of Wisconsin.
12. Shelby Hart, of, Golden West (Calif.) JC.
13. +Shawn Henrichs, rhp, Linn-Benton (Ore.) JC.
14. *Stacy Hollins, rhp, Willis (Texas) HS.

DRAFT DROP *Brother of Jesse Hollins, major leaguer (1992)*

15. Mark Yockey, lhp, Lewis-Clark State (Idaho) College.
16. **+Rikkert Faneyte, of, Miami-Dade CC South.—(1993-96)**
17. Jason Sievers, c, Lee's Summit (Mo.) HS.
18. Matt Borgogno, 2b, Cal State Fullerton.
19. *John Davis, rhp, Georgia Tech.
20. Tony Spires, ss, Coastal Carolina College.
21. Daniel Flanagan, rhp, Virginia Commonwealth University.
22. *Craig Bauer, rhp, Grand Canyon College.
23. Jim Huslig, rhp, University of Oklahoma.

24. *Jarrod Smith, 3b-of, Winter Haven (Fla.) HS.
25. *Alan Dosty, c, Grant HS, Sacramento, Calif.
26. *Lance Chambers, ss-3b, St. Petersburg (Fla.) JC.
27. Michael Helms, ss-of, University of Oregon.
28. Rodney Huffman, rhp, McLennan (Texas) CC.
**29. +Lou Pote, lhp, Kishwaukee (Ill.) JC.—(1999-2004)**
30. *Shawn Ramion, c, Lakeland (Ohio) CC.
31. *Vince Beall, of, Sacramento (Calif.) HS.
32. +Andre Keene, 1b, Lanham, Md. / Essex (Md.) JC.
33. *Marcus Lee, of, U.S. Naval Academy Prep School, San Diego.
34. Daniel Varnell, of, Foothill (Calif.) JC.
35. *Matt Castles, lhp, Davis (Calif.) HS.
36. Brian Dakin, c-inf, University of San Francisco.

## SEATTLE MARINERS (6)

**1. Marc Newfield, 1b, Marina HS, Huntington Beach, Calif.—(1993-98)**
1. Anthony Manahan, ss, Arizona State University (Supplemental choice—38th—for failure to sign 1989 first-round draft pick Scott Burrell).—(AAA)

DRAFT DROP *Brother of Austin Manahan, first-round draft pick, Pirates (1988)*

2. (Choice to Indians as compensation for Type B free agent Pete O'Brien)
**3. Dave Fleming, lhp, University of Georgia.—(1991-95)**
4. Paul Brannon, of, Kings Mountain (N.C.) HS.—(High A)
**5. Bret Boone, 2b, University of Southern California.—(1992-2005)**

DRAFT DROP *Grandson of Ray Boone, major leaguer (1948-60) • Son of Bob Boone, major leaguer (1972-90); major league manager (1995-03) • Brother of Aaron Boone, major leaguer (1997-2009)*

**6. Mike Hampton, lhp, Crystal River (Fla.) HS.—(1993-2010)**
**7. Kevin King, lhp, University of Oklahoma.—(1993-95)**
**8. John Cummings, lhp, University of Southern California.—(1993-97)**
9. David Lawson, 1b-of, West Covina (Calif.) HS.
10. Reese Wallace, rhp, Lufkin (Texas) HS.
11. Tommy Robertson, of, Fairfield Central HS, Ridgeway, S.C.
12. *Luis Victoria, rhp, Centro de Instructico, Isla Verde, P.R.
13. *Kekoa Kaluhiokalani, rhp, Waianae (Hawaii) HS.
14. Lipso Nava, ss, Miami-Dade CC New World Center.
15. Scott Schanz, rhp, UCLA.
**16. Jim Converse, rhp, Casa Roble HS, Orangevale, Calif.—(1993-97)**
17. Lee Russell, rhp, Campbell University.
18. David Adam, rhp, Central Connecticut State University.
**19. *Albie Lopez, rhp, Mesa (Ariz.) CC.—(1993-2003)**
20. Jim Neugent, lhp, Mustang HS, Yukon, Okla.
21. Tony Kounas, of, Loyola Marymount University.
22. *Pat Bojcun, rhp, Central Michigan University.
23. Greg Hunter, 2b, Washington State University.
24. Willie Wilder, of, Murray State University.
25. Douglas Fitzer, lhp, University of Detroit.
26. *Jeff Tucker, rhp, Allen County (Kan.) CC.
27. *Christopher Terry, ss, Tokay HS, Stockton, Calif.
28. *Brad Gay, c, Dixie Hollins HS, St. Petersburg, Fla.
29. David McDonald, lhp, Brandeis (Mass.) University.
30. +Renaldo Bullock, of, Triton (Ill.) JC.
31. *Damon Bihm, of, University HS, Los Angeles.
32. *Ron Rico, 1b, Cerritos (Calif.) JC.
33. Dion Gargagliano, lhp, CC of Morris (N.J.).
34. +Michael Bond, ss, Allegany (Md.) CC.
35. Clay Klavitter, 3b, Glendale (Ariz.) CC.
36. Salvy Urso, lhp, Plant HS, Tampa.
37. *Alfred Rivers, of, Tallassee (Ala.) HS.
38. *Miguel Nolasco, ss, Lely HS, Naples, Fla.
39. *Kenny Williams, rhp, Elk Grove (Calif.) HS.
40. +Bernard Erhard, ss-2b, Spartanburg Methodist (S.C.) JC.
41. *Gary Miller, rhp, Penn State University.
42. *Armando Morales, rhp, Indian Hills (Iowa) CC.
43. *Anthony Maisano, 1b, Georgia Tech.
44. *Kale Gilmore, of-1b, Broomfield (Colo.) HS.
45. *Brian Fontes, rhp, Fresno (Calif.) CC.
46. Charles Wiley, rhp, Johnson County (Kan.) CC.
47. *Scott Bedford, c, Edmonds (Wash.) CC.
48. *Rodney Mazion, ss, Hillsborough HS, Tampa.
**49. *George Glinatsis, rhp, University of Cincinnati.—(1994)**
50. *Richard Wrobel, of, Upland (Calif.) HS.
51. *Daniel Stanley, ss, Yakima Valley (Wash.) CC.
52. Jon Halland, 2b, Arizona State University.
53. *Brian Klomp, rhp, McLane HS, Fresno, Calif.
54. Rob Nichols, 1b, Washington State University.
55. *Roger Johnson, c, San Pedro (Calif.) HS.
56. *Eddie Miller, rhp, Compton (Calif.) CC.
57. *Dennis Shrum, 3b, Bullard HS, Fresno, Calif.
58. *Jim Bonnici, ss, Adams HS, Rochester, Mich.
59. *Robert Lewis, c, Los Angeles Harbor JC.
60. *Marcus Drake, of, Arroyo Grande HS, Oceano, Calif.
61. *Ron Stanford, rhp, Crisp County HS, Cordele, Ga.
62. *Hector Hernandez, rhp, Colegio Bautista HS, Carolina, P.R.
63. *Thomas Borio, rhp, Plainville (Conn.) HS.
64. *Brandon Newell, 3b, Nooksack Valley HS, Everson, Wash.
65. *Matt Pontbriant, lhp, St. Bernards HS, Norwich, Conn.
66. *Bryan Lundberg, rhp, Glendale (Ariz.) CC.
67. *Carl Grinstead, c, Cardinal Neumann HS, Lake Worth, Fla.
68. *Tim Cornish, of-ss, Camarillo (Calif.) HS.
69. *Keith Tippett, ss, Indian River (Fla.) CC.
70. *Dan Ricabal, rhp, San Gabriel HS, Rosemead, Calif.
71. *Shawn Sanderfer, 3b, Upland (Calif.) HS.
72. *Toraino Golston, of, Gateway HS, Aurora, Colo.
73. *Craig Gienger, 1b, Otero (Colo.) JC.
74. *Michael Bruce, c, Canoga Park (Calif.) HS.
75. Tim Roberts, lhp, Duke University.

## TEXAS RANGERS (16)

**1. Dan Smith, lhp, Creighton University.—(1992-94)**
2. *Mike Schiefelbein, rhp, Chatfield HS, Littleton, Colo.—(Low A)

DRAFT DROP *Attended Arizona; re-drafted by Padres, 1993 (26th round)*

3. Bobby Reed, rhp, Mississippi State University.—(AA)
4. Mickey Henson, rhp, South Point HS, Belmont, N.C.—(Low A)
**5. Jon Shave, ss, Mississippi State University.—(1993-99)**
6. Kevin Woodall, ss, Georgetown (S.C.) HS.
**7. Terry Burrows, lhp, McNeese State University.—(1994-97)**

DRAFT DROP *Baseball coach, McNeese State (2008-13)*

**8. Steve Dreyer, rhp, University of Northern Iowa.—(1993-94)**
9. Tim Wells, rhp, Southwest Missouri State University.
**10. Rusty Greer, of, University of Montevallo (Ala.).—(1994-2002)**
11. Efrain Gonzalez, of, Margarita River HS, Gurabo, P.R.
12. Andy Watson, rhp, Crowder (Mo.) CC.
**13. David Hulse, of, Schreiner (Texas) College.—(1992-96)**
14. Brian Mercado, rhp-3b, Eastern Connecticut State University.
15. Greg Blevins, c, University of Southwestern Louisiana.
16. *Harry Berrios, of, Ottawa Hills HS, Grand Rapids, Mich.
17. Frank Turco, ss, Barry (Fla.) University.
18. Rodney Busha, rhp, University of North Alabama.
19. Todd Guggiana, 3b, Long Beach State University.
**20. *Tim Kubinski, lhp, San Luis Obispo (Calif.) HS.—(1997-99)**
21. *Jarod Juelsgaard, rhp, Waldorf (Iowa) CC.
22. Marty Posey, c-of, Tulane University.
23. Keith Murray, of, University of South Alabama.
24. +Shawn Kennedy, rhp, El Monte (Calif.) HS / Cerritos (Calif.) JC.
**25. Matt Whiteside, rhp, Arkansas State University.—(1992-2001)**
26. Johnny Johnson, rhp, Birmingham-Southern College.
27. Troy Rhoades, rhp, Greenwood (Ark.) HS.
28. Chris McMullan, c, University of Richmond.
29. Steve Ramharter, lhp, Rice University.
30. *Noe Najera, lhp, Cypress (Calif.) CC.
31. Scott Erickson, lhp, Kearney State (Neb.) College.
32. *Bryan Judice, of, Poly HS, Riverside, Calif.
33. Mark Finney, rhp, Glendale (Ariz.) CC.
34. Greg Wiseman, of, Crowder (Mo.) CC.
35. Junior Antoine, of, Frederiksted HS, St. Croix, Virgin Islands.
36. Lee Hodge, 2b, University of Mississippi.
37. *Chris Alexander, c, Southside HS, Memphis, Tenn.
38. Chris Gies, rhp, Seminole (Okla.) JC.
39. Tim Cain, rhp, University of Connecticut.
40. *Damian Grossie, 3b, University of Southwestern Louisiana.
41. Tim Stafford, rhp, McNeese State University.
42. *Brad Haley, 3b-of, El Toro (Calif.) HS.
43. *Donavon Hopper, rhp, Goldendale (Wash.) HS.
44. *Reggie Moore, ss, UCLA.
45. Sidney Holland, of, University of Texas-Pan American.
46. Lance Jones, of, University of Texas.
47. George Evangelista, ss, Merrimack (Mass.) College.
48. Peter Laake, lb-of, University of Maryland.
49. Devin Kunz, lhp, Brigham Young University.
50. Steve Surico, lhp, Loyola Marymount University.
51. Anthony Bouton, rhp, University of South Carolina.
52. Paul Matachun, 3b-2b, Eastern Connecticut State University.
**53. *Joe Dawley, rhp, Canyon Springs HS, Moreno Valley, Calif.—(2002-2004)**
54. *Ryan Hepworth, of, North Florida CC.
55. *Richard Juarez, lhp, Fresno (Calif.) CC.
56. *Donald Aslaksen, of, Clear Creek HS, League City, Texas.
57. *Gary Beashore, 3b-rhp, Kansas City (Mo.) CC.
58. *Mark Lummus, lhp, Cleburne (Texas) HS.
59. *Quran Strane, of, Westmoore HS, Oklahoma City, Okla.
60. *Jerry Garrett, of, Oceanside (Calif.) HS.

## TORONTO BLUE JAYS (22)

**1. Steve Karsay, rhp, Christ the King HS, Queens, N.Y.—(1990-2006)**
2. Chris Weinke, 3b, Cretin HS, St. Paul, Minn.—(AAA)

DRAFT DROP *Heisman Trophy winner, 2000; quarterback, National Football League (2001-06).*

**2. Tim Hyers, lb-of, Newton County HS, Covington, Ga.** (Supplemental choice—71st—as compensation for free agent Lloyd Moseby).**—(1994-99)**
**3. Felipe Crespo, of, Notre Dame HS, Caguas, P.R.—(1996-2001)**

DRAFT DROP *Brother of Cesar Crespo, major leaguer (2001-04)*

**4. Howard Battle, of, Mercy Cross HS, Ocean Springs, Miss.—(1995-99)**
5. Scott Burrell, rhp, University of Connecticut.—(High A)

DRAFT DROP *First-round draft pick (26th overall), Mariners (1989); first-round draft pick, Charlotte Hornets, National Basketball Association (1993); forward/NBA (1993-2001)*

6. David Tollison, 2b, University of Texas.
**7. Scott Brow, rhp, University of Washington.—(1993-98)**
**8. Paul Menhart, rhp, Western Carolina University.—(1995-97)**
**9. Huck Flener, lhp, Cal State Fullerton.—(1993-97)**
10. Tom Singer, lhp, St. John's University.
11. Daniel Vittala, of, Northern Michigan University.
12. Mark Choate, ss, North HS, Bakersfield, Calif.
13. *Craig Holman, rhp, Jacksonville State University.
14. Matt Watson, rhp, Cal State Fullerton.
15. Travis Burley, rhp, Miramar HS, Hollywood, Fla.
**16. Mike Coolbaugh, ss, Roosevelt HS, San Antonio, Texas.—(2001-02)**

DRAFT DROP *Brother of Scott Coolbaugh, major leaguer (1989-94) • Died after being struck by batted ball while coaching first base in minor league game (July 22, 2007)*

17. Allen Rhea, lhp, Milligan (Tenn.) College.
18. Ron Reams, of, Laney (Calif.) JC.
19. Carlos Santiago, of, Escuelas Superior HS, Comerio, P.R.
20. Matthew Wilke, ss, University of North Dakota.
21. Raphael Garcia, rhp, Southern California College.
22. Sam Mandia, rhp, Seton Hall University.
23. Jason Reese, rhp, UC Riverside.
24. *Deron Pointer, of, Curtis HS, Tacoma, Wash.
25. Matthew Hudik, 2b, Ohio University.
26. David Marcon, lhp, Oral Roberts University.
27. Tom Hotchkiss, rhp, Santa Clara University.
28. Robert Adkins, rhp, Manatee HS, Bradenton, Fla.
29. Dale Kistaitis, lhp, University of Nebraska.
30. Ciro Ambrosio, ss, Long Island University.
31. Greg Wilcox, rhp, Davidson College.
32. Kyle Duey, rhp, University of Portland.
33. Bob Aylmer, lhp, Fordham University.
34. Scott Miller, ss-rhp, Elon College.
35. Rusty Filter, rhp, San Diego State University.
36. John Gilligan, rhp, University of Southern Mississippi.
**37. Ricardo Jordan, lhp, Miami-Dade CC South.—(1995-98)**
38. Frank Kower, rhp, University of North Carolina-Charlotte.
39. D.J. Boston, 1b, San Jacinto (Texas) JC.

DRAFT DROP *Brother of Daryl Boston, first-round draft pick, White Sox (1981); major leaguer (1989-94)*

40. *Darian Hagan, ss, University of Colorado.

DRAFT DROP *Ninth-round draft pick, San Francisco 49ers, National Football League (1992)*

41. Joe Ganote, rhp, University of North Carolina-Charlotte.
42. Roberto Duran, of, Seward Park HS, New York.
43. *Patrick Valero, lhp, Kent State University.
44. *Todd Weinberg, lhp, Somerset (Mass.) HS.
**45. Travis Baptist, lhp, Hillsboro HS, Aloha, Ore.—(1998)**
46. *Robert Barber, c, American River (Calif.) JC.
47. *John Allan, lhp, Yakima Valley (Wash.) CC.
48. *Chris Laiche, lhp, St. Martin's Episcopal HS, Metairie, La.
49. *Ryan Henderson, rhp, Citrus (Calif.) JC.
50. +David Pearlman, rhp, Fullerton (Calif.) JC.
51. *Jonathan Holsgrove, ss, Mineola HS, Williston Park, N.Y.
52. *Martin Thomas, 1b, Kendrick HS, Columbus, Ga.
53. *David Burke, rhp, Clay HS, Green Cove Springs, Fla.
54. *Jeffery Gatland, rhp, Northport HS, East Northport, N.Y.
55. *Bob Ippolito, rhp, Helix HS, La Mesa, Calif.

## ERIE SAILORS NEW YORK-PENN LEAGUE (SS)

1-3. No selections
4. Gary Daniels, of, Brigham Young University.—(Short-season A)

## MIAMI MIRACLE FLORIDA STATE LEAGUE (A)

1-3. No selections
**4. Paul Carey, of, Stanford University.—(1993)**
5. Miah Bradbury, c, Loyola Marymount University.—(AA)
**6. Mike Lansing, ss, Wichita State University.—(1993-2001)**
7. Greg D'Alexander, 3b, University of Arkansas.
8. Tommy Raffo, 1b, Mississippi State University.

DRAFT DROP *Baseball coach, Arkansas State (2009-15)*

9. Brad Gregory, rhp, Florida State University.
10. Ken Whitworth, rhp, UC Irvine.
11. Mike Czarnetski, of, UC Santa Barbara.
12. Rod Nettnin, lhp, University of Nevada.
13. Tim Rigsby, ss, Clemson University.
14. *Todd Pick, rhp, University of New Orleans.
15. John Urcioli, ss, New York Tech.
16. Mike Ericson, rhp, Michigan State University.
17. Joe Burnett, of, University of Southwestern Louisiana.
18. Charlie Rogers, lhp, University of North Alabama.
19. Billy Walker, rhp, Gonzaga University.

# Yankees sign Taylor to record-crushing bonus

The Yankees and GM Gene Michael gave lefthander Brien Taylor a $1.55 million bonus, but a shoulder injury kept Taylor from fulfiliing his promise

The 1991 draft is remembered for a North Carolina schoolboy, his steadfast mother and their California agent, and how the three sent shockwaves through the baseball industry by extracting a record-shattering $1.55 million signing bonus from the deep pockets of the New York Yankees.

Brien Taylor, a 6-foot-4, 205-pound lefthander from Beaufort, N.C., was the first pick in the draft. His bonus easily was the richest in the 26-year history of the process, nearly triple the $575,000 that John Olerud received from the Toronto Blue Jays in 1989 and Mike Kelly got from the Atlanta Braves earlier in 1991. The total value of Taylor's deal also eclipsed the previous high paid to a draft pick—$1.2 million to Todd Van Poppel a year earlier in the form of a major league contract by the Oakland Athletics.

Taylor's deal accelerated a wave of double-digit bonus inflation that didn't slow down for the better part of two decades. Average first-round bonuses jumped 43.5 percent from 1989 to 1990, and another 44.7 percent in 1991, from $252,577 to $365,396. The latter surge came even though the 1991 crop of college and high school talent was considered subpar—though Taylor was almost singlehandedly responsible for the increase.

For all the money that teams spend on signing bonuses, some players fall by the wayside. That was the case with Taylor, who suffered a severe shoulder injury after the 1993 season in an altercation in his hometown. He had reached Double-A and was continuing to show great promise to that point, but his shoulder was never the same. Taylor missed the 1994 season, never fully recovered from the injury and was released by the Yankees after the 1998 season.

The tradition-rich Yankees had limited experience in dealing with No. 1 draft picks, or first-rounders of any kind. The only other time they had the first pick was in 1967. And in the 12 drafts prior to 1991, they had just two first-round picks, forfeiting the others for signing major league free agents. In the 1980s alone, the Yankees forfeited 18 draft selections.

Every time the Yankees signed a free agent, it cost them a premium draft choice, part of the reason they declined and by 1990 were the worst team in the American League, a dubious distinction that earned them the first pick in the 1991 draft.

"All those years we finished second or came close, we thought we were just a player away, so we felt we had to take that chance," said Brian Sabean, the Yankees vice president for player development and scouting. "Obviously, it didn't work out. Now we've renewed a philosophy to draft and develop our own players."

Most industry observers thought the Yankees would sign the 19-year-old Taylor for an amount near their original offer of $350,000. But it turned out to be a protracted negotiation between the two sides, who at times exchanged heated words.

# 1991

## AT A GLANCE

### This Date In History
June 3-5

### Best Draft
**CLEVELAND INDIANS.** The Indians landed **MANNY RAMIREZ** with the 13th pick in the first round and also chose future major leaguers **HERBERT PERRY** (2), **CHAD OGEA** (3), **PAUL BYRD** (4), **ALBIE LOPEZ** (20) and **DAMIAN JACKSON** (44).

### Worst Draft
**HOUSTON ASTROS.** The Astros had seven of the first 50 picks, and they drafted a record 101 players. But all they got out of it were two undistinguished major leaguers: **JAMES MOUTON** (7), who spent eight seasons in the majors; and **ALVIN MORMAN** (39), who won six big league games. The Astros also failed to sign top pick **JOHN BURKE**.

### First-Round Bust
**AL SHIRLEY, OF, METS.** For pure athleticism, there might not have been a better talent in the draft than Shirley, a four-sport high school star and University of Virginia football recruit. He showed flashes of raw speed and power in six seasons in the Mets system, but never advanced beyond Class A because he was overmatched at the plate. In 1,294 at-bats, Shirley hit .198 and struck out 613 times.

### Second Down
**KEVIN STOCKER, SS, PHILLIES.** Just 11 second-rounders reached the major leagues. Stocker, a University of Washington product, had as good a career as any, batting .254 with 23 homers over eight seasons and fielding at a .969 clip.

### Late-Round Find
**MIKE CAMERON, OF, WHITE SOX (18TH ROUND).** Cameron had first-round tools as a Georgia high school player, but lasted deep into the

CONTINUED ON PAGE 392

## AT A GLANCE

CONTINUED FROM PAGE 391

1991 draft because of concerns about his hitting ability. He signed for $12,000. Five years into his career he began to hit with power, and soon he was an everyday center fielder in the major leagues. Cameron hit .249 with 278 homers and 297 stolen bases over 17 seasons and won three Gold Glove Awards.

### Never Too Late

**SCOTT WATKINS, LHP, EXPOS (70TH ROUND).** The Expos made a fruitless attempt to sign Watkins, a 12-game winner at Oklahoma State. A year later, he was drafted in the 23rd round by the Twins. He made 27 relief appearances for the Twins in 1995.

### Overlooked

**ESTEBAN LOAIZA, RHP, PIRATES.** The Mexican-born Loaiza attended high school in San Diego and went undrafted in 1991. Nine months later, he signed with the Pirates and blossomed with a 93-95 mph fastball. Loaiza won 126 games over 14 major league seasons. He went 21-9, 2.90 with a league-best 207 strikeouts for the White Sox in 2003 and started the All-Star Game.

### International Gem

**MAGGLIO ORDONEZ, OF, WHITE SOX.** Ordonez, a Venezuela native, signed with the White Sox at age 17 for $3,500. His talent never fully emerged until he reached the big leagues six years later. In 664 minor league games, Ordonez hit .270 with 62 homers; in 1,848 games over 14 seasons with the White Sox and Tigers, he hit .309 with 294 homers.

### Minor League Take

**SCOTT RUFFCORN, RHP, WHITE SOX.** Ruffcorn had a 66-25, 3.18 record in the minor leagues, along with good command of a 92-93 mph fastball. Scouts thought he would be a solid major league starter, but Ruffcorn had an 0-8,

## 1991: THE FIRST ROUNDERS

| CLUB: PLAYER, POS., SCHOOL | HOMETOWN | B-T | HT. | WT. | AGE | BONUS | FIRST YEAR | LAST YEAR | PEAK LEVEL (YEARS) |
|---|---|---|---|---|---|---|---|---|---|
| 1. Yankees: Brien Taylor, lhp, East Carteret HS | Beaufort, N.C. | L-L | 6-3 | 195 | 19 | $1,550,000 | 1992 | 2000 | Class AA (1) |
| Stunning $1.55M bonus seemed like sound investment; dominated with lively arm, upper-90s fastball but hurt shoulder in offseason fight, never recovered. | | | | | | | | | |
| 2. Braves: Mike Kelly, of, Arizona State | Los Alamitos, Calif. | R-R | 6-4 | 195 | 21 | $575,000 | 1991 | 2004 | Majors (6) |
| Career .350-46-194 hitter at ASU; had tools to be dominant big leaguer, but struggled with breaking balls, hit .258-123-424 in minors, .241-22-86 in majors. | | | | | | | | | |
| 3. Twins: David McCarty, 1b, Stanford | Houston | R-L | 6-5 | 205 | 21 | $395,000 | 1991 | 2005 | Majors (11) |
| BA College POY had big power surge as junior, hit .420-24-66; power never materialized in majors, hit just .242-36-175 in 632 games over parts of 11 seasons. | | | | | | | | | |
| 4. Cardinals: Dmitri Young, 3b, Rio Mesa HS | Oxnard, Calif. | R-R | 6-2 | 215 | 17 | $385,000 | 1991 | 2009 | Majors (13) |
| Switch-hitting SS, most advanced prep bat in draft; hit .292 with 171 HRs in 13 MLB seasons, playing mostly OF and DH; brother Delmon became No. 1 pick in 2003. | | | | | | | | | |
| 5. Brewers: Kenny Henderson, rhp, Ringgold HS | Ringgold, Ga. | R-R | 6-7 | 180 | 18 | Unsigned | 1995 | 1997 | Class A (2) |
| Turned down Brewers to attend Miami, went 29-12, 3.17 there; finally signed with Padres as fifth-rounder in 1995, pro career lasted two years, peaked in Class A. | | | | | | | | | |
| 6. Astros: John Burke, rhp, Florida | Littleton, Colo. | B-R | 6-4 | 210 | 21 | Unsigned | 1992 | 1998 | Majors (2) |
| Draft-eligible soph, bothered by sore shoulder in 1990 (2-5, 4.78), tired arm in 1991 (9-5, 2.25), chose not to sign; selected in first round by Rockies in '92. | | | | | | | | | |
| 7. Royals: Joe Vitiello, 1b/of, Alabama | Stoneham, Mass. | R-R | 6-3 | 210 | 21 | $345,000 | 1991 | 2004 | Majors (7) |
| Best power bat in college, hit .395-15-67 for Tide; drilled 154 more homers in minors, but power never evolved in majors, hit .248 with 26 HRs in seven seasons. | | | | | | | | | |
| 8. Padres: Joey Hamilton, rhp, Georgia Southern | Statesboro, Ga. | R-R | 6-4 | 215 | 20 | $385,000 | 1992 | 2004 | Majors (10) |
| Led NCAA D-I ranks with 18 wins as SO, went 12-6, 3.85 as JR on strength of dominant change, plus fastball; spent 10 seasons in majors, went 74-73, 4.44. | | | | | | | | | |
| 9. Orioles: Mark Smith, of, Southern California | Arcadia, Calif. | R-R | 6-2 | 215 | 21 | $350,000 | 1991 | 2004 | Majors (8) |
| Undrafted out of HS, made huge strides in all phases at USC, hit .336-16-80 as junior; eight-year MLB career never took off, hit .243-32-130 with five clubs. | | | | | | | | | |
| 10. Phillies: Tyler Green, rhp, Wichita State | Denver | R-R | 6-5 | 185 | 21 | $325,000 | 1991 | 2000 | Majors (4) |
| Pitched Shockers to CWS title as freshman, went 11-2 (116 IP/134 SO) as junior; showed flashes in pro ball, but career ravaged by shoulder/elbow surgeries. | | | | | | | | | |
| 11. Mariners: Shawn Estes, lhp, Minden HS | Douglas, Nev. | R-L | 6-2 | 175 | 18 | $332,500 | 1991 | 2009 | Majors (13) |
| Stanford recruit known for tantalizing curve; career plagued by shoulder issues, but turned corner when traded to Giants in 1995, went on to 101-93, 4.71 record. | | | | | | | | | |
| 12. Cubs: Doug Glanville, of, Pennsylvania | Teaneck, N.J. | R-R | 6-2 | 180 | 20 | $325,000 | 1991 | 2004 | Majors (9) |
| Rare Ivy League first-rounder hit .414-6-36 as JR, had speed, CF skills, hit .325-11-73 with 34 SBs for Phillies in 1999—best season in nine-year MLB career. | | | | | | | | | |
| 13. Indians: Manny Ramirez, of, George Washington HS | New York | R-R | 6-1 | 185 | 18 | $250,000 | 1991 | 2014 | Majors (19) |
| Hit .650 with 14 HRs as prep senior; quirky personality but became one of majors' best hitters, hit .312-555-1,831 in 19 seasons, slammed record 29 postseason HRs. | | | | | | | | | |
| 14. Expos: Cliff Floyd, 1b, Thornwood HS | South Holland, Ill. | L-R | 6-4 | 220 | 18 | $290,000 | 1991 | 2009 | Majors (17) |
| Hit .508 as prep JR/SR, drove in 130 runs, drew comparisons to Willie McCovey; injuries compromised MLB career, though he still hit .278 with 233 homers. | | | | | | | | | |
| 15. Brewers: Tyrone Hill, lhp, Yucaipa HS | Yucaipa, Calif. | L-L | 6-5 | 195 | 19 | $280,000 | 1991 | 1998 | Class AA (1) |
| Tall, angular lefty showed early promise in Brewers system, struck out 306 in 287 IP, but career undone by arm injuries, never advanced beyond Double-A. | | | | | | | | | |
| 16. Blue Jays: Shawn Green, of, Tustin HS | Tustin, Calif. | L-L | 6-3 | 170 | 18 | $580,000 | 1992 | 2007 | Majors (15) |
| California prep career hits leader/Stanford recruit, steered to pros by huge bonus; cracked 40-HR barrier three times, set single-game MLB record with 19 total bases. | | | | | | | | | |
| 17. Angels: Eduardo Perez, 1b, Florida State | Santurce, P.R. | R-R | 6-4 | 205 | 21 | $310,000 | 1991 | 2006 | Majors (13) |
| Son of Hall of Famer Tony, Puerto Rico bred, hit .370-11-58 with 30 SBs as FSU junior; played parts of 13 MLB seasons with six clubs, hit .247-79-294 as 1B/3B/OF. | | | | | | | | | |
| 18. Mets: Al Shirley, of, George Washington HS | Danville, Va. | R-R | 6-1 | 210 | 17 | $245,000 | 1991 | 1998 | Class AA (2) |
| Mets lured prep football star, but he hit woeful .197 with 613 SOs in 1,294 ABs in five years in system, none above Class A; never tapped into speed/power package. | | | | | | | | | |
| 19. Rangers: Benji Gil, ss, Castle Park HS | Chula Vista, Calif. | R-R | 6-2 | 180 | 18 | $312,000 | 1991 | 2005 | Majors (8) |
| Mexican-born player had advanced two-way skills at San Diego-area HS, became first '91 pick to reach majors before career leveled off; hit .237 in eight seasons. | | | | | | | | | |
| 20. Reds: Pokey Reese, ss, Lower Richland HS | Hopkins, S.C. | R-R | 5-9 | 160 | 17 | $200,000 | 1991 | 2008 | Majors (8) |
| On track to become future star with Gold Glove skills, emerging offensive ability, flair for game before career suddenly hit skids; hit .248 over eight MLB seasons. | | | | | | | | | |
| 21. Cardinals: Allen Watson, lhp, New York Tech | Middle Village, N.Y. | L-L | 6-3 | 190 | 20 | $225,000 | 1991 | 2000 | Majors (8) |
| Second of Cardinals' three first-rounders; success in minors (25-19, 2.42, 439 IP, 117 BB/393 SO) never translated to sustained outcome in majors (51-55, 5.03). | | | | | | | | | |
| 22. Cardinals: Brian Barber, rhp, Dr. Phillips HS | Orlando, Fla. | R-R | 6-1 | 175 | 18 | $200,000 | 1991 | 1999 | Majors (4) |
| Went 11-0 as senior for national prep power, moved quickly through Cardinals system before career stalled out in majors (5-8, 6.77), ended by arm problems. | | | | | | | | | |
| 23. Red Sox: Aaron Sele, rhp, Washington State | Poulsbo, Wash. | R-R | 6-4 | 195 | 20 | $210,000 | 1991 | 2007 | Majors (15) |
| Elevated himself into first-rounder after shutting out Cuba at 1990 Goodwill Games, developing dynamite breaking ball; won 148 games in majors with six clubs. | | | | | | | | | |
| 24. Pirates: Jon Farrell, c/of, Florida CC-Jacksonville | Jacksonville, Fla. | R-R | 6-2 | 180 | 19 | $220,000 | 1991 | 1996 | Class AA (1) |
| Cardinals '89 fourth-rounder spent one year at Miami, one year at juco; career as catcher never materialized, also hit just .246-58-237 in six seasons in minors. | | | | | | | | | |
| 25. White Sox: Scott Ruffcorn, rhp, Baylor | Austin, Texas | R-R | 6-4 | 210 | 21 | $185,000 | 1991 | 1999 | Majors (5) |
| Contrast between success in college (20-7, 3.23), minors (66-25, 3.18) vs. majors (0-8, 8.57) attributed to pitching tentatively, inability to develop offspeed stuff. | | | | | | | | | |
| 26. Athletics: Brent Gates, ss, Minnesota | Grandville, Mich. | B-R | 6-1 | 175 | 21 | $205,000 | 1991 | 1999 | Majors (7) |
| Hit .412-8-60 as Gophers JR, .319-15-138 in impressive minor league run-up, .290-7-69 (all MLB career-highs) as A's rookie, but never built on that success. | | | | | | | | | |

"The Yankees have to ask themselves if they can afford to let a No. 1 pick get away over the issue of a market value contract," said agent Scott Boras, who was advising the Taylor family. "The market for an American League player of like ability (Van Poppel) has already been established, and it's substantially more than they've offered."

The Yankees drafted Taylor on June 3 and did not sign him until Aug. 28, just hours before he was slated to start attending classes at Louisburg (N.C.) Junior College. Under the draft-and-follow rule in place at the time, had Taylor not signed and attended junior college, the Yankees would have retained his rights until just before the 1992 draft.

Taylor's patience, his mother Bettie's dogged determination and Boras' expert negotiating skills

## How They Should Have Done It

Based on the career WAR (Wins Above Replacement, as calculated by Baseball-Reference.com) numbers achieved by all the players eligible for the 1991 draft, here's how the first round should have unfolded. Numbers in parentheses indicate the round when the player was actually drafted. Asterisk denotes player who signed as a draft-and-follow.

| | Player, Pos. | Actual Draft | WAR | Bonus |
|---|---|---|---|---|
| 1. | Manny Ramirez, of | Indians (1) | 69.1 | $250,000 |
| 2. | Mike Cameron, of | White Sox (18) | 46.4 | $12,000 |
| 3. | Brad Radke, rhp | Twins (8) | 45.5 | $70,000 |
| 4. | Shawn Green, of | Blue Jays (1) | 34.5 | $580,000 |
| | Derek Lowe, rhp | Mariners (8) | 34.5 | $35,000 |
| 6. | Jeff Cirillo, rhp | Brewers (11) | 34.4 | $8,500 |
| 7. | Jason Schmidt, rhp | Braves (8) | 29.6 | $125,000 |
| 8. | Mark Grudzielanek, ss | Expos (11) | 26.4 | $15,000 |
| 9. | Cliff Floyd, 1b | Expos (1) | 25.8 | $290,000 |
| 10. | Steve Trachsel, rhp | Cubs (8) | 25.4 | $42,500 |
| 11. | Mike Sweeney, c | Royals (10) | 24.7 | $30,000 |
| 12. | Esteban Loaiza, rhp | Pirates (NDFA) | 23.0 | None |
| 13. | Joe Randa, 3b | Royals (11) | 21.2 | $25,000 |
| 14. | Aaron Sele, rhp | Red Sox (1) | 20.6 | $210,000 |
| 15. | LaTroy Hawkins, rhp | Twins (7) | 17.7 | $28,000 |
| 16. | Kirk Rueter, lhp | Expos (18) | 16.7 | $10,000 |
| 17. | Paul Byrd, rhp | Indians (4) | 16.3 | $70,000 |
| 18. | Matt Lawton, 2b | Twins (13) | 15.0 | $30,000 |
| 19. | Joey Hamilton, rhp | Padres (1) | 14.6 | $385,000 |
| 20. | * Jason Isringhausen, rhp | Mets (44) | 13.2 | $7,500 |
| 21. | Justin Thompson, lhp | Tigers (1-S) | 12.9 | $160,000 |
| 22. | Dmitri Young, 3b | Cardinals (1) | 12.1 | $385,000 |
| 23. | Shawn Estes, lhp | Mariners (1) | 11.1 | $332,500 |
| | Alex Gonzalez, ss | Blue Jays (14) | 11.1 | $145,000 |
| 25. | Doug Glanville, of | Cubs (1) | 10.8 | $325,000 |
| 26. | Scott Hatteberg, c | Red Sox (1-S) | 10.0 | $142,500 |

| | Top 3 Unsigned Players | | | Year Signed |
|---|---|---|---|---|
| 1. | Nomar Garciaparra, ss | Brewers (5) | 44.2 | 1994 |
| 2. | Jon Lieber, rhp | Cubs (9) | 24.3 | 1992 |
| 3. | Bobby Higginson, of | Phillies (18) | 23.0 | 1992 |

were principal factors in getting the Yankees to pony up the record contract. Yankees owner George Steinbrenner weakened his club's bargaining position by pressuring general manager Gene Michael into signing Taylor. But even Steinbrenner expressed shock at the size of the bonus.

"Never in my wildest dreams would I have paid that kid a million and a half," Steinbrenner said. "No damn way! On a high school kid? No way! I'm getting damned tired of people spending my money like this."

The draft system, which was instituted to curb bonus inflation, was now producing deals that were spiraling ever higher in value. Taylor's bonus was about 10 times what Ken Griffey Jr. had received four years earlier as the first pick in the 1987 draft.

"For some bizarre reason, teams are paying people $1.5 million just to come into an industry where they can make more millions," said Steve Greenberg, Major League Baseball's deputy commissioner. "I can't figure it out. First-round bonuses are up across the board. For some reason over the past two years, things have gone haywire and nobody's been able to figure out why."

"This is not a smart thing," said San Diego Padres general manager Joe McIlvaine. "We've got a workable, fair system that is equitable to clubs and players, and a few teams are trying to jeopardize it. If other clubs use these deals as a barometer, we'll all go out of business."

### FALLOUT FELT IN FIRST ROUND

Taylor's huge bonus continued an upward trend. Ben McDonald and Van Poppel, the marquee talents in the two previous drafts, also had received record deals that were negotiated by Boras. Industry officials had hoped those contracts, along with the one signed by Olerud, would be seen as aberrations. That proved not to be the case.

The repercussions of Van Poppel's $1.2 million, major league contract in 1990 (which included a $500,000 signing bonus) were evident a year later, when each of the top 12 picks received a bonus of at least $325,000, far more than any draft pick received before 1989.

"For years, we had been able to hold signing bonuses to $100,000 for the top guys, but not anymore," Houston Astros general manager Bill Wood said. "Agents have gotten into the picture, and clubs have responded by not wanting to lose their pick."

The threat of players attending or returning to college, and teams losing rights to those players if they didn't meet bonus demands, drove the sharp rise in bonuses. Even the threat of Taylor attending a junior college while remaining under their control was enough to push the Yankees into spending almost three times more than any team previously had spent on a signing bonus.

Many clubs were in favor of a rule change proposed at the 1991 Winter Meetings aimed at curtailing bonuses. The rule would have allowed clubs to keep the rights to high school players for four years after they were drafted, which would have eliminated much of the players' leverage. But the proposal failed to gained universal support and was not adopted.

Taylor's record bonus had a trickle-down effect as deadlines for signing 1991 draft choices neared. The Padres agreed to terms with Georgia Southern righthander Joey Hamilton, the eighth overall pick, on a $385,000 bonus the day he was scheduled to begin classes for his senior year. Hamilton was another Boras client, and it took the intervention of Padres owner Tom Werner to get the deal done after negotiations between McIlvaine and the Hamilton family reached an impasse.

The Padres initially offered Hamilton $350,000, commensurate with the amounts Joe Vitiello (seventh pick) and Mark Smith (ninth) received from the Kansas City Royals and Baltimore Orioles, respectively. The Padres had that offer on the table until Sept. 1, when they scaled it back to $325,000. On Sept. 18, McIlvaine withdrew the club's offer altogether. Warner then stepped in and worked out a compromise with Hamilton's stepmother, Janet, who had become embroiled in the often bitter stalemate with McIvaine. The Hamiltons went against the advice of Boras, who had told them to hold firm at $500,000.

The Milwaukee Brewers and the Astros refused to participate in the rampant spending and didn't sign their first-round picks, both Boras clients. The Brewers took Georgia high school righthander Kenny Henderson with the fifth pick, but would

### AT A GLANCE

8.57 record in 30 big league appearances from 1993-97. In 70 innings, he walked 70 and struck out 46. Few first-rounders have shown such a gap between minor league success and major league failure.

### Ones Who Got Away

**DUSTIN HERMANSEN, RHP, PIRATES (39TH ROUND); PAUL WILSON, RHP, PIRATES (57TH ROUND).** The Pirates made little effort to sign either pitcher out of high school. Three years later, Wilson was the No. 1 overall pick by the Mets, and Hermansen was the third player chosen, by the Padres.

### They Were Drafted?

**KERRY COLLINS, SS, TIGERS (60TH ROUND); STEVE MCNAIR, SS, MARINERS (35TH ROUND).** McNair was the third overall pick in the 1995 NFL draft and Collins was the fifth selection. McNair, a quarterback from Alcorn State, played 13 seasons in the NFL. Collins, a Penn State product, played 17 seasons.

### Did You Know . . .

The selection of **EDUARDO PEREZ** by the Angels marked the fifth time a son of a member of Cincinnati's Big Red Machine became a first-round pick. Perez's father, Tony, was the Reds first baseman from 1964-76. The others: Ken Griffey and Ken Griffey Jr. (Mariners, 1987); Lee May and Lee May Jr. (Mets, 1986); Hal McRae and Brian McRae (Royals, 1985); and Ed Sprague and Ed Sprague Jr. (Blue Jays, 1988).

### They Said It

Padres general manager **JOE MCILVAINE** on the record $1.55 million bonus paid by the Yankees to lefthander **BRIEN TAYLOR**: "This is not a smart thing. We've got a workable, fair system, and a few teams are trying to jeopardize it. If other clubs use these deals as a barometer, we'll all go out of business."

## DRAFT SPOTLIGHT: BRIEN TAYLOR

STAN DENNY

Brien Taylor was the complete package and lived up to his billing until an offseason altercation cut him down

The New York Yankees had the No. 1 pick in the draft for the second time ever, and scouting director Bill Livesey didn't need to be reminded of the significance of the selection. He was well aware that the Yankees had tumbled to the bottom of the American League standings a year earlier.

Livesey had a plan to pick a player who he hoped would change his team's fortunes, hopefully sooner than later.

"We had a meeting at a hotel in Arizona in January of 1991," Livesey said. "We brought in all our cross-checkers. Mike Kelly was a great outfielder at Arizona State at the time. We told our guys, 'This is the top college player in the country. Your job this year is to find somebody better. If we don't, Kelly will be our pick.'

"Our North Carolina scout, Jeff Taylor, called (a few weeks later) and said, 'I'm following up on our conversation in Arizona.' I said, 'What have you got?' He said, 'I've got a lefthanded pitcher in North Carolina.' Wow, he started to rave about him."

It wasn't long before everyone knew about Brien Taylor, a 6-foot-4, 205-pound lefthander from Beaufort, a small community on the North Carolina coast. On April 2, 1991, Taylor thrust himself into consideration for the No. 1 pick with a sterling performance in an Easter tournament. In a two-inning relief appearance, with a large group of scouts watching, he threw 19 pitches, 18 for strikes, and fanned the side in both innings with fastballs clocked at 94 mph. The next day, he struck out 17 in the championship game. Taylor racked up impressive numbers for East Carteret High during his senior season, going 8-2, 0.46 with 24 walks and 203 strikeouts in 84 innings.

"He had everything you are looking for: size, strength, athleticism, body type, loose, live arm, the ability to spin the ball," Livesey said. "He was the total package."

Taylor didn't know he would be a Yankee until he stepped out of a classroom on the afternoon of June 3 and saw his parents and others gathered to congratulate him. He was the second high school player selected first in the draft, after lefthander David Clyde (Rangers, 1973), and there would not be another until lefthander Brady Aiken in 2014.

Agent Scott Boras encouraged Taylor and his mother, Bettie, to remain firm on a contract that at least would equal the record $1.2 million deal that Boras had negotiated for Texas high school righthander Todd Van Poppel a year earlier. The Yankees' first offer was $350,000. Mrs. Taylor responded by saying the team was trying to lowball the family because it was black and poor. The two sides remained at odds for weeks.

As August wound down, with Taylor set to enroll at Louisburg (N.C.) Junior College, Yankees general manager Gene Michael met with Mrs. Taylor and worked out a contract for a draft-record $1.55 million signing bonus, almost $1 million more than the previous high. The baseball industry howled in disbelief.

For two years, at high Class A in 1992 and at Double-A in 1993, Taylor was everything he was cracked up to be, a pitcher capable of controlling a game. But Taylor's life took a cruel turn on a winter evening after the 1993 season. He was at home in North Carolina when he received a telephone call that his brother was in a fight at a local bar. Taylor went to the bar, and someone swung a fist at him. He put up his left arm to ward off the blow, and it was pushed awkwardly behind his head.

"I take him to (orthopedic surgeon) Dr. Frank Jobe," said Boras, "and Jobe looks at me: 'This is the worst rotator cuff tear I've ever seen. It is completely off the bone.' "

Taylor had surgery and missed all of the 1994 season. From 1995-98, he pitched 109 innings, all in Class A, going 3-15, 10.82 and walking 175. The Yankees released him after the 1998 season, and he spent two more years in baseball, with the Mariners and Indians organizations, pitching sparingly. Taylor faded away after that, getting back in the news in November 2012, when he was sentenced to 38 months in prison for selling crack cocaine.

not meet his reported $1 million asking price. They offered $500,000, but Henderson held firm and enrolled in college at Miami, just as Alex Fernandez had done in 1988, when the Brewers failed to sign him after drafting him in the first round. Four years later, Henderson signed with the Padres for $75,000 as a fifth-round pick, and his brief pro career fizzled in Class A.

The Astros held the sixth pick and selected University of Florida righthander John Burke, who had just become the sixth pitcher to throw a no-hitter in an NCAA playoff game. Burke wanted a $500,000 bonus, but the Astros refused. Burke, a draft-eligible sophomore, returned to school and was drafted in the first round a year later by the expansion Colorado Rockies.

Small-market franchises such as the Brewers and Astros failing to sign their top picks was viewed as a red flag by the industry, and raised concerns that wealthy clubs like the Yankees would price other teams out of the market for top talent. Wood blamed players and agents alike.

"It's a lack of backbone on the clubs' part, in not being able to show some common sense," he said. "They've convinced themselves that the money doesn't matter and that it's a one-time thing. But these contracts become base points. I don't want to become part of these matters of insanity."

### BLUE JAYS REMAIN BIG SPENDERS

The Yankees spent upward of $2.25 million in bonuses on 1991 draft picks, supplanting the Blue Jays as the industry's biggest spender in the draft. The Blue Jays, leaders in 1989 and '90, topped their club record in 1991 by spending $1.976 million, including more than $100,000 on each of five players. (The Yankees reached that threshold only with Brien Taylor.)

The Blue Jays gave $580,000 to their top pick, California high school outfielder Shawn Green, and signed Old Dominion righthander Jeff Ware, a supplemental first-round pick, for $337,500, the richest bonus in that round. They also paid the largest bonus to a player selected after the 10th round, giving $145,000 to Florida high school shortstop Alex Gonzalez, a 14th-round pick.

Green was the 16th pick in the draft, yet his bonus was the second-largest overall, behind only Taylor's. Green didn't sign until Sept. 25, days before he was slated to enroll at Stanford. A provision in the contract allowed Green to attend Stanford for two semesters in each of his first three years before reporting to spring training.

Green made it to the big leagues for good in 1995 and became an all-star outfielder, first with

### Fastest To The Majors

| Player, Pos. | Drafted (Round) | Debut |
|---|---|---|
| 1. * Benji Gil, ss | Rangers (1) | April 5, 1993 |
| 2. Tyler Green, rhp | Phillies (1) | April 9, 1993 |
| 3. Brent Gates, ss | Athletics (1) | May 5, 1993 |
| 4. David McCarty, 1b | Twins (1) | May 17, 1993 |
| 5. Scott Ruffcorn, rhp | White Sox (1) | June 19, 1993 |

**LAST PLAYER TO RETIRE:** LaTroy Hawkins (Oct. 20, 2015)

**High school selection.*

## Top 25 Bonuses

| | Player, Pos. | Drafted (Round) | Order | Bonus |
|---|---|---|---|---|
| 1. | * Brien Taylor, lhp | Yankees (1) | 1 | $1,550,000 |
| **2.** | *** Shawn Green, of** | **Blue Jays (1)** | **16** | **$580,000** |
| **3.** | **Mike Kelly, of** | **Braves (1)** | **2** | **$575,000** |
| **4.** | **David McCarty, 1b** | **Twins (1)** | **3** | **$395,000** |
| **5.** | *** Dmitri Young, 3b** | **Cardinals (1)** | **4** | **$385,000** |
| | **Joey Hamilton, rhp** | **Padres (1)** | **8** | **$385,000** |
| **7.** | **Mark Smith, of** | **Orioles (1)** | **9** | **$350,000** |
| **8.** | **Joe Vitiello, 1b/of** | **Royals (1)** | **7** | **$345,000** |
| **9.** | **Jeff Ware, rhp** | **Blue Jays (1-S)** | **35** | **$337,500** |
| **10.** | **Tyler Green, rhp** | **Phillies (1)** | **10** | **$325,000** |
| | **Doug Glanville, of** | **Cubs (1)** | **12** | **$325,000** |
| **12.** | *** Shawn Estes, lhp** | **Mariners (1)** | **11** | **$322,500** |
| **13.** | *** Benji Gil, ss** | **Rangers (1)** | **19** | **$312,000** |
| **14.** | **Eduardo Perez, 1b** | **Angels (1)** | **17** | **$310,000** |
| **15.** | *** Cliff Floyd, 1b** | **Expos (1)** | **14** | **$290,000** |
| 16. | * Scott Pisciotta, rhp | Expos (2) | 58 | $289,500 |
| 17. | * Tyrone Hill, lhp | Brewers (1) | 15 | $280,000 |
| **18.** | *** Manny Ramirez, of** | **Indians (1)** | **13** | **$250,000** |
| 19. | * Al Shirley, of | Mets (1) | 18 | $245,000 |
| **20.** | **Allen Watson, lhp** | **Cardinals (1)** | **21** | **$225,000** |
| 21. | Jon Farrell, c/of | Pirates (1) | 24 | $220,000 |
| **22.** | **Aaron Sele, rhp** | **Red Sox (1)** | **23** | **$210,000** |
| **23.** | **Brent Gates, 2b** | **Athletics (1)** | **26** | **$205,000** |
| **24.** | *** Pokey Reese, ss** | **Reds (1)** | **20** | **$200,000** |
| | *** Brian Barber, rhp** | **Cardinals (1)** | **22** | **$200,000** |

*Major leaguers in bold. *High school selection.*

the Blue Jays and then with the Los Angeles Dodgers. In 15 seasons, he hit .283 with 328 homers, including four in one game for the Dodgers in 2002, when he set a major league record for total bases in a game (19).

Another contributing factor to the bonus inflation in 1991 was the signing of Frankie Rodriguez, a shortstop/righthander from Howard (Texas) Junior College who agreed to terms with the Boston Red Sox less than 24 hours before the Yankees drafted Taylor. Rodriguez became the first big money, draft-and-follow pick of the draft era, signing for $425,000.

The Red Sox had selected Rodriguez in the second round in 1990. Instead of signing, he attended junior college, which meant the Red Sox retained his rights until the eve of the 1991 draft. Had he entered the 1991 draft pool, Rodriguez was considered a first-round lock, and he might have been picked as high as second overall.

The draft-and-follow approach had become popular since it came into play in 1987 as a result of the consolidation of the draft into one phase. The most expensive draft-and-follow in 1991 turned out to be Chad Tredaway, a shortstop from Seminole (Okla.) Junior College, a 16th-round pick who signed with the Chicago Cubs prior to the 1992 draft for $75,000.

### KELLY FALLS SHORT OF EXPECTATIONS

Kelly, an outfielder from Arizona State, was considered the top prospect in 1991, at least until Taylor emerged in the final weeks before the draft. Kelly hit .376 with 21 home runs and 82 RBIs and stole 20 bases as a sophomore, and followed it up with a solid junior season (.373-15-56, 23 SB), despite being pitched around extensively.

The Braves selected Kelly with the second pick in the 1991 draft, and he was in an enviable bargaining position. The Braves had passed on Olerud with the second pick in 1989 and on Van Poppel with the first pick in 1990, believing neither player would sign. Both did sign, and the Braves felt some pressure to strike a deal with Kelly. It cost them a $575,000 signing bonus, the same amount Olerud had received and a draft record until later that summer when Taylor signed.

The athletic Kelly showed the speed, power and center-field traits to become a dominant big leaguer, but his six-year career in the majors fell far short of expectations. He struggled to make contact against breaking pitches, and hit a meager .241 with 22 homers, along with 30 stolen bases in 327 games for four clubs.

Stanford outfielder David McCarty was a marginal first-round prospect entering his junior season, but he bolstered his stock with a highly productive year for the Cardinal (.420-24-66). The Minnesota Twins, holding the third pick, selected McCarty and signed him for a $395,000 bonus.

"The big question mark on me was power," said McCarty, one of the few first-rounders in draft history who threw lefthanded and batted righthanded. "I didn't put up the home run numbers as a sophomore, but I knew I could. I kind of questioned how the scouts doubted my power when I hit 12 home runs (in 1990), and none of them were cheap. Coming into the season, I knew that's what the scouts wanted to see. All I did was adjust my swing to get the ball in the air a little more—that, and I started pulling the ball a little more."

McCarty hit 136 home runs in the minor leagues, but wasn't much of a threat in the major leagues, hitting .242 with 36 home runs and 175 RBIs over 11 seasons.

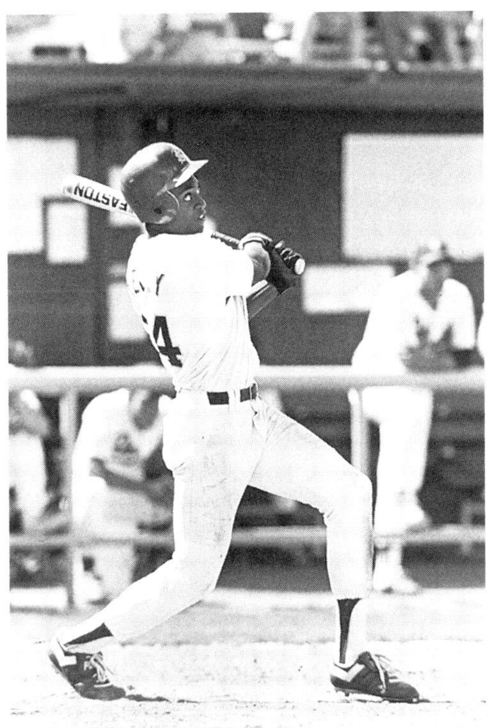


KEN AKERS

**Arizona State outfielder Mike Kelly was a solid all-around prospect, but he never hit enough to be a productive major leaguer**

**WORTH NOTING**

JOHN SPEAR

Five 1991 first-rounders did not reach the major leagues, among them Virginia high school outfielder **AL SHIRLEY**, who was selected 18th overall by the Mets. Shirley was an all-state defensive back who was expected to play linebacker in college, but New York lured him away from a football scholarship to the University of Virginia with a bonus of $245,000. The 6-foot-4, 240-pound Shirley hit .475 with eight homers in 12 games as a high school senior and was regarded as the best hitting prospect in the prep ranks, with the ability to play center field. But he struggled mightily in five seasons in the Mets system, including three at the Rookie level, hitting just .198 with 42 homers and striking out 613 times in 1,294 at-bats. The Mets traded him to the Royals after the 1995 season for catcher Brent Mayne. Shirley then played three seasons in the Royals organization, peaking in Double-A, before being released in 1998. He made an aborted attempt at age 25 to resume his football career at Virginia.

Louisiana State (55-18) won the first of five College World Series titles over a 10-year stretch in 1991, beating Wichita State, the 1989 champion, 6-3 in the championship game. The Tigers had six players drafted, the highest being righthander **CHAD OGEA** (14-5, 3.08) in the third round by the Indians. Arizona State (35-27) didn't reach postseason play, but had more players drafted (11) than any college, includ-

CONTINUED ON PAGE 396

## WORTH NOTING

CONTINUED FROM PAGE 395

ing outfielder **MIKE KELLY**, the second overall pick.

■ Canadians became fully vested in the draft process for the first time in 1991. Previously, Canadians who were not attending college in the United States were subject to bidding on the open market. Twenty-four Canadians were drafted, though none before the 10th round. The highest selection was Leamington, Ontario, first baseman **JASON WUERCH**, picked in the 11th round by the Yankees, who drafted seven Canadian players. Canada's influence might have been greater had two Vancouver-based prospects, shortstop David Chavarria (Rangers) and lefthander Bob MacDonald (Blue Jays), not signed just before major league owners approved the inclusion of Canadians in the draft on March 7, 1991.

■ Baseball owners also decided that Puerto Ricans, who became draft-eligible for the first time in 1989, wouldn't be eligible for selection any longer until their high school class graduated. Previously, Puerto Ricans were eligible for the draft at 17. With the adjustment, just 21 players were drafted out of Puerto Rican high schools in 1991, none higher than the sixth round.

■ Georgia Tech righthander **MARC PISCIOTTA** and his younger brother **SCOTT**, a righthander from Walton High in Marietta, Ga., both were drafted in 1991. Marc went 13-3 as a college junior and unexpectedly slipped to the Pirates in the 19th round. Scott went 14-1 as a prep senior and was selected in the second round by the Expos. Marc signed for $23,400 and spent parts of three seasons in the majors. Scott, who had a Stanford scholarship as a bargaining chip, received a $289,500 bonus, 16th-richest in the draft. He went 24-27 in five minor league seasons and did not make the major leagues.

Dmitri Young, a California high school shortstop, was the fourth player drafted and received a $385,000 bonus from the St. Louis Cardinals. Prior to the 1991 season, Young was the top-rated high school player in the country. He had begun his career in Alabama as a seventh-grader on the varsity, hitting .564. He moved to Oxnard, Calif., as a ninth grader and continued to be a hitting machine at Rio Mesa High. Young set a California high school career record for hits and batted .502 over his final three years. He hit .425 as a senior, along with 11 home runs.

Dmitri Young

The 6-foot-2, 215-pound Young drew comparisons with San Francisco Giants outfielder Kevin Mitchell. Young moved to third base as a pro and eventually settled in at first base. He had a solid career, hitting .292 with 171 homers over 13 major league seasons. A decade later, Young's younger brother Delmon was an even more accomplished hitter in high school, and he was the No. 1 pick in the 2003 draft. That made the Youngs and the Uptons (B.J. in 2002, Justin in 2005) the only sets of brothers to be selected among the first four picks in draft history.

Young was the first of five Cardinals picks before the second round of the 1991 draft. The extra choices came from losing major league free agents after the 1990 season. Lefthander Allen Watson (21st overall) and righthander Brian Barber (22nd) were among the extra selections, and both pitched in the major leagues.

The Astros had seven of the first 50 picks, but didn't take advantage of the windfall. Burke, their first pick, did not sign, and none of their following six choices made it to the big leagues.

Houston set a record for most players drafted with 101, one more than they had taken in the previous draft. It was the third year in a row the Astros selected the most players. A record 1,600 players were drafted, including a record 942 from the college ranks. Those marks would stand for at least a year as the draft was limited to 50 rounds in 1992.

### Highest Unsigned Picks

| Player, Pos., Team (Round) | College | Re-Drafted |
|---|---|---|
| Kenny Henderson, rhp, Brewers (1) | Miami | Expos '94 (2) |
| John Burke, rhp, Astros (1) | * Florida | Rockies '92 (1) |
| Dante Powell, of, Blue Jays (1-S) | Cal State Fullerton | Giants '94 (1) |
| Antone Williamson, 3b, Padres (3) | Arizona State | Brewers '94 (1) |
| Todd LaRocca, ss, Dodgers (3) | Stanford | Orioles '94 (5) |
| Blake Bentley, of, Reds (4) | Howard (Texas) JC | Cubs '95 (24) |
| Nomar Garciaparra, ss, Brewers (5) | Georgia Tech | Red Sox '94 (1) |
| Steve Verduzco, ss, Phillies (5) | Notre Dame | Astros '93 (4) |
| Doug Carroll, of, Red Sox (5) | South Florida | Mariners '94 (10) |
| Mickey Kerns, of, Pirates (6) | * Alabama | Angels '92 (9) |

**TOTAL UNSIGNED PICKS:** Top 5 Rounds (9), Top 10 Rounds (20)

**Returned to same school.*

### Largest Bonuses By Round

| | Player, Pos. | Club | Bonus |
|---|---|---|---|
| 1. | * Brien Taylor, lhp | Yankees | $1,550,000 |
| 2. | * Scott Pisciotta, rhp | Expos | $289,500 |
| **3.** | **Chad Ogea, rhp** | **Indians** | **$130,000** |
| **4.** | *** Chris Seelbach, rhp** | **Braves** | **$130,000** |
| **5.** | **Lyle Mouton, of** | **Yankees** | **$80,000** |
| 6. | * Mike Iglesias, rhp | Dodgers | $92,500 |
| 7. | * Bert Gerhart, rhp | Rangers | $71,000 |
| **8.** | *** Jason Schmidt, rhp** | **Braves** | **$125,000** |
| 9. | * Dennis Winicki, ss | Dodgers | $47,000 |
| 10. | * Josh Spring, rhp | Astros | $40,000 |
| 11. | * Adam Meinershagen, rhp | Blue Jays | $65,000 |
| 12. | Scott Eggleston, rhp | Padres | $50,000 |
| | Bert Inman, rhp | Yankees | $50,000 |
| 13. | Alonso Beltran, rhp | Blue Jays | $42,500 |
| **14.** | *** Alex Gonzalez, ss** | **Blue Jays** | **$145,000** |
| 15. | * Eric Lairsey, rhp | Braves | $25,000 |
| 16. | # Chad Tredaway, ss | Cubs | $75,000 |
| **17.** | **Shad Williams, rhp** | **Angels** | **$50,000** |
| 18. | # Brian Teeters, of | Royals | $50,000 |
| **19.** | *** Rick Gorecki, rhp** | **Dodgers** | **$110,000** |
| 20. | * Billy Stephens, rhp | Dodgers | $40,000 |
| 21. | * Kevin Zahner, c | Dodgers | $35,000 |
| **22.** | **Ken Huckaby, c** | **Dodgers** | **$25,000** |
| 23. | *# Kirk Larson, ss | Astros | $35,000 |
| 24. | * Kevin Smith, lhp | Dodgers | $20,000 |
| 25. | * Brandon Bluhm, lhp | Indians | $60,000 |
| Other | # Michael Hermanson, rhp | Padres (30) | $60,000 |

*Major leaguers in bold. *High school selection. #Signed as draft-and-follow.*

### GIL FIRST, RAMIREZ BEST

The Texas Rangers set a draft record by signing their first 28 picks, eclipsing the mark of 27 set by the 1988 Yankees. The Rangers' first-round selection was California high school shortstop Benji Gil (19th overall), who was the first in his draft class to reach the major leagues. The only other high school players to be the first in their class to get to the big leagues were Brian Greer in 1977 with the Padres and Mike Morgan in 1978 with the A's.

Gil was 20 when he made his major league debut on April 5, 1993. He had all of a year and a half in the minors and had yet to advance past Class A. Gil, though, had a lot of experience before he got to pro ball. He grew up in Tijuana, Mexico, just across the border from San Diego, and played year-round in semi-pro leagues south of the border. He attended Castle Park High in Chula Vista, Calif., to gain more exposure for the draft.

Gil played well in spring training in 1993, and both of the Rangers shortstops were injured when the season was about to start. He became the youngest player in the majors, and one of his teammates, 46-year-old Nolan Ryan, was the oldest.

"This is not Jeff Kunkel, where we rushed somebody who hadn't play much to the big leagues," Rangers general manager Tom Grieve said. "It's not some scared kid who hasn't played much baseball. The key for me is Benji is not afraid. He thinks he should be in the big leagues."

Gil spent the first six weeks of the season with the Rangers, hitting .123 and struggling in the field. He returned to the minors and went through a long period of readjustment, and his career took many twists and turns. He played parts of eight seasons in the majors with the Rangers and California Angels, hitting .237 with 32 home runs and 171 RBIs, but spent the bulk of his career in the minors and the Mexican League.

Outfielder Manny Ramirez proved to be the most productive first-rounder in 1991. He was the 13th pick, going to the Cleveland Indians and signing for $250,000, one of the smaller bonuses in the first round. Ramirez hit .322 with 80 homers and 320 RBIs in 358 minor league games before making his major league debut little more than two years after being drafted. He became one of baseball's elite hitters, batting .312 with 555 home runs over 19 seasons.

As prolific an offensive player as Ramirez was, he became equally known for his quirky, often irrational behavior that led to the catchphrase, "Manny being Manny." His career, which once had a Hall of Fame trajectory, took a downward spiral toward the end. Ramirez abruptly retired on May 30, 2011, rather than accept a 100-game suspension for use of performance-enhancing drugs.

The Montreal Expos drafted first baseman Cliff Floyd with the pick after Ramirez. Floyd was as highly regarded as Ramirez in the minor leagues and early in his big league career.

Cliff Floyd

"He's going to be a great major league player. Not a good one, a great one," said Jim Tracy, who was Floyd's manager in both Double-A and Triple-A. "This guy goes a little beyond anything you can possibly imagine from a baseball player. He's got the complete package. There's nothing he can't do, and he's going to get better. That's scary."

Expos scouting director Gary Hughes compared Floyd to a young Willie McCovey for his raw power potential. Floyd, however, suffered a career-threatening left wrist injury while playing for the Expos on May 15, 1995. He had three surgeries and missed the balance of the 1995 season. Floyd recovered, but never showed as much power as he had before the injury. He played 17 seasons in the majors, hitting .278 with 233 homers.

Three players who had prominent college basketball careers were drafted in the top four rounds. All had expectations of playing in the NBA, but pursued baseball instead.

## Largest Draft-And-Follow Bonuses

| | Player, Pos. | Club (Round) | Bonus |
|---|---|---|---|
| 1. | Chad Tredaway, ss | Cubs (16) | $75,000 |
| 2. | Michael Hermanson, rhp | Padres (30) | $60,000 |
| 3. | Greg Sinner, rhp | Indians (45) | $52,000 |
| 4. | Brian Teeters, of | Royals (18) | $50,000 |
| | ***Bob Henley, c** | **Expos (26)** | **$50,000** |
| 6. | Daren Hobson, rhp | Red Sox (31) | $42,500 |
| 7. | *Brian Holter, rhp | Indians (59) | $40,000 |
| | Joe Jacobsen, rhp | Dodgers (70) | $40,000 |
| | Lyle Barwick, c | Angels (29) | $40,000 |
| | Chris Moten, rhp | Twins (29) | $40,000 |

*Major leaguers in bold. *High school selection.*

Terrell Lowery averaged 28.5 points (fifth in NCAA Division I) and 9.1 assists (third) as a junior at Loyola Marymount in 1991. That didn't stop him from trying out for the baseball team, even though he had failed to make the squad the previous two years. He not only made the team, but showed so much promise as a center fielder that the Rangers selected him in the second round of the baseball draft and signed him for $75,000.

Lowery spent the 1991 season at Rookie-level Butte, where he hit .299 and stole 23 bases. Despite averaging a West Coast Conference-best 26 points per game during his senior year at Loyola Marymount, he wasn't selected in the 1992 NBA draft. He returned to baseball and played four years in the major leagues with three clubs, hitting .282 with three homers and 23 RBIs in 123 games.

The Twins took prominent basketball players in the third and fourth rounds: shortstop Keith Legree from Statesboro (Ga.) High and righthander Brett Roberts from Morehead State.

Legree, a top recruit as a point guard, accepted a $78,000 bonus from the Twins and showed promise in the Rookie-level Gulf Coast League in 1991, hitting .297 with 16 stolen bases. He played basketball for two years at Louisville and two years at Cincinnati. The 6-foot-7, 225-pound Roberts signed after his junior year at Morehead State and spent the summer at Rookie-level Elizabethton. He returned to college as a senior, was the NCAA's leading scorer (28.1 points per game) and was selected by the Sacramento Kings in the second round of the 1992 NBA draft. Roberts bypassed pro basketball and resumed his career in the Twins system.

Both Legree and Roberts played in the Twins system, from 1991-97. Legree hit .252 with 28 homers in a career that peaked in Double-A. Roberts' career topped out in Triple-A, and he went 42-44, 4.58.

## One Team's Draft: Toronto Blue Jays

| | Player, Pos. | Bonus |
|---|---|---|
| **1.** | ***Shawn Green, of** | **$580,000** |
| **1.** | **Jeff Ware, rhp** | **$337,500** |
| **1.** | ***Dante Powell, of** | **Did not sign** |
| 2. | *Trevor Mallory, rhp | $110,000 |
| 2. | Dennis Gray, lhp | $120,000 |
| **3.** | ***Chris Stynes, ss** | **$60,000** |
| 4. | *Roger Doman, rhp | $55,000 |
| **5.** | ***Rickey Cradle, of** | **$78,500** |
| **6.** | ***Jose Silva, rhp** | **$72,500** |
| **7.** | ***Carlton Loewer, rhp** | **Did not sign** |
| 8. | Stoney Briggs, of | $25,000 |
| 9. | *Pat Thacker, c | $42,500 |
| **10.** | **Kenny Robinson, rhp** | **$25,000** |
| 11. | *Adam Meinershagen, rhp | $65,000 |
| 12. | Keiver Campbell, of | $10,000 |
| 13. | Alonso Beltran, rhp | $42,500 |
| **14.** | ***Alex Gonzalez, ss** | **$145,000** |
| 15. | Sharnol Adriana, 2b | $20,000 |
| 16. | John Tsoukalas, 3b | $20,000 |
| 17. | Mike Carlsen, 2b | $14,000 |
| 18. | *Ryan Griffin, of | $32,500 |
| 19. | Brent Lutz, c | $25,000 |
| **20.** | **Ben Weber, rhp** | **$15,000** |
| 21. | Tim Lindsay, rhp | $2,000 |
| 22. | Andrew Dolson, lhp | $8,000 |
| 23. | Chris Kotes, rhp | $1,000 |
| 24. | Al Montoya, lhp | $1,000 |
| **25.** | ***Ryan Franklin, rhp** | **Did not sign** |
| Other | *Thomas Vaught (36), 3b | $25,000 |

*Major leaguers in bold. *High school selection.*

## IN FOCUS: MANNY RAMIREZ

Manny Ramirez was obsessed with baseball when he moved with his parents from the Dominican Republic to the Washington Heights neighborhood in Manhattan in 1985. It provided him a refuge from the drug culture of his new neighborhood, and he often practiced baseball from 6 a.m. until school started and from after school until dark.

As a senior at George Washington High, Ramirez hit .650 with 14 homers in just 63 at-bats, while also stealing 31 bases. "He was a man among boys," said Steve Mandl, his high school coach. Drafted by the Indians with the 13th pick in 1991, Ramirez was an immediate hit in the pro ranks, making his major league debut little more than two years after being drafted. He quickly became one of the elite hitters in the game, and over 19 seasons in the majors hit the ball at a .312 clip with 555 homers. In 1999 with the Indians, he drove in a staggering 165 runs.

"You can watch Manny in batting practice and just see the fluidity of his swing and see how natural everything was," Tribe manager Mike Hargrove said. "As far as hitting was concerned, you could see that he was something special. He had probably the prettiest righthanded power swing that I've ever seen. He had power to all fields, tremendous bat speed and bat control."

# 1991 Draft List

**Did not sign. Major leaguers in bold, with first and last years noted. Order of selection indicated in parentheses. For the first five rounds, the peak level of each player is noted.*
*+ Signed as draft-and-follow (Second school noted if applicable).*

## ATLANTA BRAVES (2)

1. **Mike Kelly, of, Arizona State University.—(1994-99)**
2. (Choice to Cardinals as compensation for Type A free agent Terry Pendleton)
3. Blase Sparma, rhp, Ohio State University.—(AA)
DRAFT DROP *Son of Joe Sparma, major leaguer (1964-70)*
4. **Chris Seelbach, rhp, Lufkin (Texas) HS.—(2000-01)**
5. Vince Moore, of, Alief Elsik HS, Alief, Texas.–(AA)
6. Jose Rodriquez, c, Miguel Melendez HS, Cayey, P.R.
7. Earl Nelson, lhp, Clark HS, San Antonio, Texas.
8. **Jason Schmidt, rhp, Kelso (Wash.) HS.—(1995-2009)**
9. Brad Rippelmeyer, c-rhp, Kansas State University.
DRAFT DROP *Son of Ray Rippelmeyer, major leaguer (1962)*
10. *Jerome Jones, 3b, Carthage HS, Beckville, Texas.
11. Ken Giard, rhp, Toll Gate HS, Warwick, R.I.
12. Andre Johnson, of, Norfolk State University.
13. Byron Woods, of, Northeastern Oklahoma A&M JC.
14. **Kevin Lomon, rhp, Westark (Ark.) CC.—(1995-96)**
15. Eric Lairsey, lhp, Pierce County HS, Blackshear, Ga.
16. Willie Havens, rhp, Holmes HS, San Antonio, Texas.
17. Bill Shafer, rhp-1b, South Grand Prairie HS, Grand Prairie, Texas.
18. +Jason Noel, of, Edison (Fla.) CC / North Florida JC.
19. *Jes Rathke, rhp, Brownwood (Texas) HS.
20. Javier Rivas, of, Los Angeles CC.
21. Mike Hostetler, rhp, Georgia Tech.
22. ***Ryan Karp, lhp, University of Miami.—(1995-97)**
23. *Don Denbow, of-1b, Corsicana (Texas) HS.
DRAFT DROP *Son of Donnie Denbow, first-round draft pick, Dodgers (1967)*
24. Sequinn Leichmon, ss, Strong (Ariz.) HS.
25. Brad James, of, Illinois State University.
26. **Pedro Swann, of, Delaware State University.—(2000-03)**
DRAFT DROP *Baseball coach, Maryland-Eastern Shore (2013-15)*
27. *William Maier, c, Raritan Valley (N.J.) CC.
28. Paul Kelliher, c, University of Maine.
29. Kevin Grijak, of, Eastern Michigan University.
30. *Jason Cash, 1b, Newbury Park HS, Simi Valley, Calif.
31. *Alton Huffstetler, rhp, Adairsville (Ga.) HS.
32. Jimmy Armstrong, lhp, Dallas Baptist University.
33. *Phil Hollis, ss, Purdue University.
34. Rick O'Neill, ss, Illinois State University.
35. Craig Rapp, lhp, North Carolina State University.
36. Dirk Blair, rhp, Southeastern Oklahoma State University.
37. Ben Weeks, rhp, Butte (Calif.) JC.
38. Dwayne Fowler, rhp, Long Beach State University.
39. Augie Vivenzio, c, College of Boca Raton (Fla.).
40. *Darnell Hendricks, of, Taft HS, Los Angeles.
41. Thomas Coates, of, Austin Peay State University.
42. Scott Behrens, rhp, Illinois State University.
43. *Leland Macon, of, Kirkwood (Mo.) HS.
44. *Greg Granger, rhp, Edgewood HS, Elletsville, Ind.
45. Michael Weiser, of-3b, Fargo (N.D.) HS.
46. *Rinker Robinson, lhp, Tavares HS, Mount Dora, Fla.
47. *Kurt Bierek, 3b-1b, Modesto (Calif.) JC.
48. *Kevin Willingham, rhp, DeSoto (Texas) HS.
49. Ronald York, of, South Carolina State College.
50. Yves Martineau, rhp, Therise Martin HS, Pointe-aux-Trembles, Quebec.
51. *Matt Sherwood, rhp, Blinn (Texas) JC.
52. *Phil Doyle, 3b-of, University of Alabama.
53. Robert Grob, c, Frederick (Md.) CC.
54. Carlos Lara, c, New Mexico Highlands University.
55. *Rodney Close, of, Bainbridge (Ga.) HS.
56. *Earl Wheeler, rhp, Oklahoma State University.
57. *Jason Garrett, 3b, Bowie HS, Manchaca, Texas.
58. *Jason Gunter, rhp, Sulphur (La.) HS.
59. *Jeremy Woods, rhp, Midwest City (Okla.) HS.
60. Ron Lloyd, of, Judson HS, Schertz, Texas.
61. *Derek Berschaminski, 1b, University of North Dakota.
62. *Robert Valdez, lhp, Central Arizona JC.
63. *Frank Watts, of, Baker HS, Columbus, Ga.

## BALTIMORE ORIOLES (9)

1. **Mark Smith, of, University of Southern California.—(1994-2003)**
2. Shawn Curran, c, Corona (Calif.) HS.—(Rookie)
3. **Alex Ochoa, of, Miami Lakes HS, Hialeah, Fla.—(1995-2002)**
4. **Vaughn Eshelman, lhp, University of Houston.—(1995-97)**
5. Jim Wawruck, of, University of Vermont.–(AAA)
6. Danny Fregoso, rhp, Catalina HS, Tucson, Ariz.
7. **Jimmy Haynes, rhp, Troup County HS, LaGrange, Ga.—(1995-2004)**
8. Terry Farrar, lhp, Missouri Baptist College.
9. Chris Lemp, rhp, Sacramento (Calif.) CC.
10. **B.J. Waszgis, c, McNeese State University.—(2000)**
11. Brad Seitzer, 3b, Memphis State University.
DRAFT DROP *Brother of Kevin Seitzer, major leaguer (1986-97)*
12. **Curtis Goodwin, of, San Leandro (Calif.) HS.—(1995-99)**
13. Jim Audley, of, Wichita State University.
14. Glenn Coleman, of, JC of the Desert (Calif.).
15. Lamann Washington, ss, Beaufort (S.C.) HS.
16. Derek Adams, ss, Louisburg (N.C.) JC.
17. *Joel Franklin, rhp, Coronado (Calif.) HS.
18. *Aaron Lane, lhp, Lincoln Land (Ill.) CC.
19. Troy Tallman, c, Stanford University.
20. Allen Plaster, rhp, University of North Carolina-Charlotte.
21. Jeremy Winget, 1b, Murray (Utah) HS.
22. Chris Chatterton, rhp, High Point College.
23. **Rick Krivda, lhp, California (Pa.) University.—(1995-98)**
24. Glenn Tatro, of, Bryant (R.I.) College.
25. Steven Firsich, rhp, Grossmont (Calif.) JC.
26. Rick Forney, rhp, Anne Arundel (Md.) CC.
27. Jamie Conner, ss, Hedgesville HS, Martinsburg, W.Va.
28. *Angelo Stutts, of, Hammond (La.) HS.
29. *Orrett Bennett, of, Evanston (Ill.) HS.
30. Basillo Ortiz, of, Eastern Connecticut State College.
31. *Kyle Kennedy, rhp, Quitman (Miss.) HS.
32. *Erick Mapp, of, Cochise County (Ariz.) CC.
33. Kris Gresham, c, University of North Carolina-Charlotte.
34. Scott Conner, rhp, New Mexico JC.
35. *Shane Shallenberger, of, Portales (N.M.) HS.
36. *Patrick Hicks, c, Mesa (Ariz.) CC.
37. *Johnny Walker, of, Hillsborough HS, Tampa.
38. Mat Sanders, rhp, University of Portland.
39. *Terry Hawke, of, Putnam City West HS, Oklahoma City, Okla.
40. +Scott Emerson, lhp, Scottsdale (Ariz.) JC.
41. +Hector Castenada, c, Laredo (Texas) JC.
42. *Ryan Creek, of, Jefferson HS, Martinsburg, W.Va.
DRAFT DROP *Brother of Doug Creek, major leaguer (1995-2003)*
43. *Jeff Ferguson, ss, La Serna HS, La Mirada, Calif.
44. *Brett Ames, lhp, Tucson (Ariz.) HS.
45. *Tom Szimanski, rhp, Catonsville (Md.) CC.
46. *Torn Clarkson, 2b, The Bolles School, Jacksonville, Fla.
47. *Chris Pageau, ss, Schenectady (N.Y.) JC.
48. +Matthew Riemer, ss, Patapsco HS, Baltimore / Allegany (Md.) CC.

## BOSTON RED SOX (23)

1. **Aaron Sele, rhp, Washington State University.—(1993-2007)**
1. J.J. Johnson, of, Pine Plains (N.Y.) HS (Supplemental choice–37th–as compensation for Type A free agent Larry Andersen).—(AAA)
1. **Scott Hatteberg, c, Washington State University** (Supplemental choice—43rd—as compensation for Type A free agent Mike Boddicker).**—(1995-2008)**
2. Terry Horn, rhp, Yukon (Okla.) HS (Choice from Royals as comp. for Boddicker).—(Rookie)
2. Chad Schoenvogel, rhp, Blinn (Texas) JC.—(High A)
3. Joe Caruso, rhp, Loyola Marymount University.—(AAA)
4. Joe Ciccarella, 1b-lhp, Loyola Marymount University.—(AAA)
5. *Doug Carroll, of, Holliston (Mass.) HS.–(High A)
DRAFT DROP *Attended South Florida; re-drafted by Mariners, 1994 (10th round)*
6. Donny Jones, of, Poway (Calif.) HS.
DRAFT DROP *Brother of Jaime Jones, first-round draft pick, Marlins (1995)*
7. Dan Collier, of, Enterprise State (Ala.) JC.
8. **Luis Ortiz, 3b, Union (Tenn.) University.—(1993-96)**
9. *Dan McDonald, 3b, Evans HS, Orlando, Fla.
10. **Tony Rodriguez, ss, University of Charleston (W.Va.).—(1996)**
11. Jimmy Crowley, 3b, Clemson University.
DRAFT DROP *Son of Terry Crowley, major leaguer (1969-83)*
12. Craig Bush, rhp, Lancaster (Ohio) HS.
13. John Eierman, of, Rice University.
14. Dana LeVangie, c, American International (Mass.) College.
15. **Cory Bailey, rhp, Southeastern Illinois JC.—(1993-2002)**
16. Tony Ferreira, 2b, Manatee (Fla.) CC.
17. **Tim Van Egmond, rhp, Jacksonville State University.—(1994-96)**
18. **Ron Mahay, of-lhp, South Suburban (Ill.) JC.—(1995-2010)**
19. Brian Bright, of, University of Massachusetts.
20. Cesar Martinez, lhp, Chula Vista HS, San Diego.
21. **Joel Bennett, rhp, East Stroudsburg (Pa.) University.—(1998-99)**
22. Jim Lentz, c, Columbia State (Tenn.) CC.
23. Bryan Brown, of, Tulane University.
24. *Ryan Beeney, ss, Newark (Ohio) HS.
25. *Melvin Walker, of, McNair HS, Atlanta.
26. *Jesus Armendariz, lhp, Howard (Texas) JC.
27. *Jake Austin, of, Wake Forest University.
28. *Rafael Gutierrez, of, Sandalwood HS, Jacksonville, Fla.
29. *Lance Davis, lhp, Mary Montgomery HS, Semmes, Ala.
30. *Chris Wiggs, ss, Santa Fe Catholic HS, Lakeland, Fla.
31. +Daren Hobson, rhp, Meridian (Miss.) CC.
32. *Joshua Stough, rhp, Walker County HS, Jasper, Ala.
33. Diogenes Baez, of, Connors State (Okla.) JC.
34. Kevin Becker, rhp, Hilliard HS, Galloway, Ohio.
35. *Jerry Taylor, c-of, Goliad (Texas) HS.
36. *Richie Wyman, of, Central Florida CC.
37. *Marc Albarado, of, Woodlawn HS, Baton Rouge, La.
38. *Steve Carver, ss, The Bolles School, Jacksonville, Fla.
39. +Chris Davis, rhp, Northwest Mississippi CC.

## CALIFORNIA ANGELS (17)

1. **Eduardo Perez, 1b, Florida State University.—(1993-2006)**
DRAFT DROP *Son of Tony Perez, major leaguer (1964-86)*
1. **Jorge Fabregas, 3b-c, University of Miami** (Supplemental choice—34th—as compensation for Type A free agent Chili Davis).**—(1994-2002)**
2. **Chris Pritchett, 1b, UCLA.—(1996-2000)**
3. Mark Ratekin, rhp, Point Loma Nazarene (Calif.) College.—(AAA)
4. John Donati, 1b, De la Salle HS, Concord, Calif.—(High A)
5. David Kennedy, rhp-of, Montclair State (N.J.) College.—(AAA)
6. Brian Williard, rhp, Dixie Hollins HS, St. Petersburg, Fla.
7. **Chris Turner, 3b-c, Western Kentucky University.—(1993-2000)**
8. *Kurt Ehmann, ss, Arizona State University.
9. **Mark Sweeney, of, University of Maine.—(1995-2008)**
10. Gary Hagy, ss, UCLA.
11. Jeff Knox, rhp, Deltona (Fla.) HS.
12. *Ken Maire, rhp, Eureka (Calif.) HS.
13. Kyle Sebach, rhp, Grossmont (Calif.) JC.
14. Fred Young, rhp, Hillsborough HS, Tampa.
15. Korey Keling, rhp, University of Oklahoma.
16. Shawn Purdy, rhp, University of Miami.
17. **Shad Williams, rhp, Fresno (Calif.) CC.—(1996-97)**
18. Chance Gledhill, rhp, Oklahoma City University.
19. Dennis McCaffery, of, Villanova University.
20. *Kevin Kloek, rhp, Citrus (Calif.) CC.
21. *Keith Stafford, ss, South Georgia JC.
22. Ron Martin, of, Downey HS, Compton, Calif.
23. Robbie Saitz, rhp, Fresno State University.
24. James Ruocchio, 3b, C.W. Post (N.Y.) College.
25. *J.D. McGuirt, 1b, McIntosh HS, Peachtree City, Ga.
26. *Scott Schultz, rhp, Broad Run HS, Sterling, Va.
27. Mark Mammola, lhp, Pace (N.Y.) University.
28. *Frank Greely, of, Lassen (Calif.) JC.
29. +Lyall Barwick, c, Delgado (La.) JC.
30. *Mike Parisi, rhp, Arcadia (Calif.) HS.
31. +Michael Monday, c, Orange Coast (Calif.) JC.
DRAFT DROP *Son of Rick Monday, first overall draft pick, Athletics (1965); major leaguer (1966-84)*
32. John Wylie, rhp, Jacksonville University.
33. **Orlando Palmeiro, of, University of Miami.—(1995-2007)**
34. *Mike Halperin, lhp, Barron Collier HS, Naples, Fla.
35. *Glenn Duckett, ss, Carthage (Mo.) HS.
36. *Rob Plarski, c, Poway (Calif.) HS.
37. *Dee Dalton, ss, Cave Spring HS, Roanoke, Va.
38. *Richie Blackwell, lhp, Whiteville (N.C.) HS.
39. *Enrique Ramos, rhp, Luquillo (P.R.) HS.
40. *David Vindivich, of, Edmonds (Wash.) CC.
41. *O.J. McDuffie, of, Penn State University.
DRAFT DROP *First-round draft pick, Miami Dolphins/ National Football League (1993); wide receiver/ NFL (1993-2000)*
42. +Freddie Diaz, ss, Pasadena (Calif.) CC / Cerritos (Calif.) JC.
43. ***Aaron Boone, ss-3b, Villa Park (Calif.) HS.—(1997-2009)**
DRAFT DROP *Grandson of Ray Boone, major leaguer (1948-60) • Son of Bob Boone, major leaguer (1972-90); major league manager (1995-2003) • Brother of Bret Boone, major leaguer (1992-2005)*
44. *Eric Morgan, rhp, Cocoa (Fla.) HS.
45. ***Jacob Cruz, of, Channel Islands HS, Oxnard, Calif.—(1996-2005)**
DRAFT DROP *First-round draft pick (32nd overall), Giants (1994)*
46. Mike Butler, lhp, North Carolina State University.
47. +Eric Mayo, rhp, Cherokee HS, Canton, Ga. / DeKalb (Ga.) JC.
48. *Rudolph Stroud, ss-3b, Brandon (Fla.) HS.
49. Mark Ledinsky, lhp-of, Jacksonville University.
50. *Allan Parker, ss, Polk (Fla.) CC.
51. *Browning Nagle, rhp, University of Louisville.
DRAFT DROP *Quarterback, National Football League (1991-96)*
52. *Travis Exum, rhp, Lake Weir HS, Ocklawaha, Fla.
53. *John Foran, rhp, Marianna HS, Alford, Fla.

## CHICAGO CUBS (12)

1. **Doug Glanville, of, University of Pennsylvania.—(1996-2004)**
2. (Choice to Blue Jays as compensation for Type A free agent George Bell)
3. Bill Bliss, lhp, Villanova University.—(High A)
4. **Terry Adams, rhp, Mary Montgomery HS, Semmes, Ala.—(1995-2005)**
5. **Ozzie Timmons, of, University of Tampa.—(1995-2000)**
6. Hector Trinidad, rhp, Pioneer HS, Whittier, Calif.
7. Maceo Houston, of, Galileo HS, San Francisco.
8. **Steve Trachsel, rhp, Long Beach State University.—(1993-2008)**
9. ***Jon Lieber, rhp, University of South Alabama.—(1994-2008)**
10. Scott Weiss, rhp, Stanford University.
11. *Sean Drinkwater, 2b-ss, Cypress (Calif.) JC.
12. Michael Reeves, of, Arizona State University.
13. Carl Schramm, rhp, Illinois Benedictine College.
14. Ben Burlingame, rhp, University of Maine.

15. Devin Chavez, 3b-1b, Riverview HS, Kennewick, Wash.
16. +Chad Tredaway, ss, Seminole (Okla.) JC.
17. Mitchell Root, ss, Chatsworth (Calif.) HS.
DRAFT DROP *Grandson of Charlie Root, major leaguer (1923-41)*
18. *Trevor Humphry, rhp, Westark (Ark.) CC.
19. Thomas Walker, 1b, Walla Walla (Wash.) CC.
20. *Bryan Garrett, of, Odessa (Texas) JC.
**21. *Chris Clemons, rhp, McGregor (Texas) HS.—(1997)**
DRAFT DROP *First-round draft pick (33rd overall), White Sox (1994)*
22. Kirk Goodson, rhp, Bluefield State (W.Va.) College.
DRAFT DROP *Son of Ed Goodson, major leaguer (1970-77)*
23. Joe Szczepanski, lhp, California Baptist College.
24. Joe Terilli, of, Northwood (Texas) Institute.
25. Michael Tidwell, lhp, Lenoir-Rhyne (N.C.) College.
26. *Frank Sanders, of, Dillard HS, Fort Lauderdale, Fla.
DRAFT DROP *Wide receiver, National Football League (1995-2003)*
27. +Orlando Lopez, lhp, Francisco Mendoza HS, Isabella, P.R. / Lake City (Fla.) CC.
28. Randy Belyeu, c, Jacksonville State University.
29. Rudy Gornez, ss, California Baptist College.
30. Brian Kenny, rhp, Villanova University.
31. Steven Davis, rhp, Lenoir-Rhyne (N.C.) College.
32. Frank Sample, rhp, College of the Ozarks (Mo.).
**33. +Robin Jennings, of, Manatee (Fla.) JC.—(1996-2001)**
34. *Jonathan Cornelius, of, Charter Oak HS, Covina Calif.
35. +Robert Nutting, c, Riverton HS, Galena, Kan. / Northeastern Oklahoma A&M JC.
**36. *Ramon E. Martinez, ss, Vernon Regional (Texas) JC.—(1998-2009)**
37. *Chad Richardson, rhp, JC of Southern Idaho.
38. *Curtis Hall, ss, Pocatello (Idaho) HS.
39. *David Skeels, c, Thousand Oaks (Calif.) HS.
40. *Kevin Lydon, lhp, Mission HS, Fremont Calif.
41. *Daron Mooneyham, ss, Mammoth HS, Mammoth Lakes, Calif.
42. *Doug Webb, 3b-rhp, Alta HS, Draper, Utah.
43. *Traver Hunter, rhp, JC of Southern Idaho.
44. Perry Amos, lhp, Butte (Calif.) JC.
45. *Eluid Barreto, of, Benito Cerezo HS, Agua Dilla, P.R.
46. *Orlando Portalatin, of, Luis Pales Matos HS, Bayamon, P.R.
47. +Roque Colon, of-1b, Fernando Callejo HS, Manati, P.R. / Paris (Texas) JC.

## CHICAGO WHITE SOX (25)

**1. Scott Ruffcorn, rhp, Baylor University.—(1993-97)**
**2. Larry Thomas, lhp, University of Maine.—(1995-97)**
**3. Mike Robertson, 1b, University of Southern California.—(1996-98)**
**4. Brian Boehringer, rhp, University of Nevada-Las Vegas.—(1995-2004)**
5. Eric Richardson, of, Brenham (Texas) HS.–(High A)
6. Harold Henry, of, Northeast Louisiana University.
7. Steve Olsen, rhp, Eastern Kentucky University.
8. *Demond Thomas, ss-of, Elizabethtown (Ky.) HS.
9. Troy Fryman, 1b, Jefferson Davis State (Ala.) JC.
DRAFT DROP *Brother of Travis Fryman, first-round draft pick, Tigers (1987); major leaguer (1990-2002)*
10. Juan Thomas, of, Paul Blazer HS, Ashland, Ky.
**11. Al Levine, rhp, Southern Illinois University.—(1996-2005)**
**12. Doug Brady, ss, Liberty University.—(1995)**
**13. Mike Heathcott, rhp, Creighton University.—(1998)**
14. Glenn DiSarcina, ss, Universiiy of Massachusetts.
DRAFT DROP *Brother of Gary DiSarcina, major leaguer (1989-2000)*
15. *Charles Frontera, rhp, Bishop Ford HS, Brooklyn, N.Y.
16. Marc Kubicki, rhp, University of Southern Mississippi.
17. Demarcus Harris, ss, Caesar Rodney HS, Camden, Del.
**18. Mike Cameron, of, LaGrange (Ga.) HS.—(1995-2011)**
DRAFT DROP *Father of Daz Cameron, first-round draft pick, Astros (2015)*
19. *Denis Pujals, rhp, Southwest HS, Miami.
20. Michael Call, rhp, University of Washington.
21. Matt Hattabaugh, c, Cal State Fullerton.
22. David Martorana, 3b-ss, Flagler (Fla.) College.
23. Tony Milledge, of, Palmetto (Fla.) HS.
DRAFT DROP *Brother of Lastings Milledge, first-round draft pick, Mets (2003); major leaguer (2006-11)*
**24. *Dean Crow, rhp, San Jacinto (Texas) JC.—(1998)**
25. Shawn Buchanan, of, University of Nebraska.
26. Essex Burton, 2b-of, San Francisco State University.
27. Richard Bowrosen, 2b, Flagler (Fla.) College.
28. *Clay Hill, of, South Grand Prairie HS, Grand Prairie, Texas.
29. John Herrholz, rhp, University of New Orleans.
30. *Carmine Cappuccio, of, Rollins (Fla.) College.
**31. Mike Bertotti, lhp, Iona College.–(1995-97)**
32. Dean Haase, c, University of Wisconsin-Oshkosh.
33. Julio Vinas, c, American HS, Hialeah, Fla.
34. *David Marrero, 3b, Miami Lakes HS, Hialeah, Fla.
35. *John MacCauley, rhp, University of Evansville.
36. *Jason Jordan, 1b, Jefferson Davis HS, Montgomery, Ala.
37. *Sean Duncan, of, Martin HS, Arlington, Texas.
38. *Brandon Wilhite, rhp, Mississippi Delta JC.
39. *Darin Dreasky, 2b, Central Michigan University.
40. *Mike Schmitz, 1b, Brevard (Fla.) JC.
41. *Robert Perry, 3b, Sacramento (Calif.) CC.
42. *Derek Bullock, rhp, Chaparral HS, Las Vegas, Nev.
43. *Michael Eaglin, ss-2b, DeAnza HS, San Pablo, Calif.
44. *Tyler Borup, 1b, Sammamish HS, Bellevue, Wash.
45. *Shannon Coulter, ss, Grand Prairie HS, Cedar Hill, Texas.
46. *Bill King, rhp, Carrol HS, Ozark, Ala.
47. *Deloren Corbett, rhp, St. Augustine (Fla.) HS.
48. *Greg McGraw, rhp, Mortimer-Jordan HS, Gardendale, Ala.
49. *Brian Jones, of, St. Augustine (Fla.) HS.
50. *Bobby Langer, ss, Creighton University.
51. *Robert Lamb, rhp, Mississippi Delta JC.
52. *Shawn McGinn, ss, University of Nebraska-Omaha.
53. *Chris Mader, c, Rollins (Fla.) College.
54. *Lovett Purnell, of, Seaford (Del.) HS.

## CINCINNATI REDS (20)

**1. Pokey Reese, ss, Lower Richland HS, Hopkins, S.C.—(1997-2004)**
2. Toby Rumfield, c, Belton (Texas) HS.—(AAA)
3. Joe DeBerry, 1b, Clemson University.—(AAA)
DRAFT DROP *Son of Fisher DeBerry, head football coach, Air Force Academy (1984-2006)*
4. *Blake Bentley, of, Mansfield (Texas) HS.–(High A)
DRAFT DROP *Attended Howard (Texas) JC; re-drafted by Cubs, 1995 (24th round)*
5. Mike Harrison, c, University of California.—(AA)
6. Dave Tuttle, rhp, Santa Clara University.
7. Chris Reed, rhp, Katella HS, Anaheim, Calif.
**8. John Courtright, lhp, Duke University.—(1995)**
9. Damon Montgomery, of, Fremont HS, Los Angeles.
10. Armando Morales, rhp, University of New Orleans.
11. Scott Dodd, lhp, Arizona State University.
12. Rodney Steph, rhp, Texas Tech.
13. *Jason Heath, 3b-of, Seminole (Okla.) JC.
**14. Brian Koelling, ss, Bowling Green State University.—(1993)**
15. Ken Cavazzoni, of, Columbia University.
16. *Bubba Hardwick, lhp, Polk (Fla.) CC.
17. Mike Jones, c-3b, Wichita State University.
18. Mike Coletti, lhp, Oklahoma City University.
19. Gene Taylor, of, Lubbock Christian (Texas) University.
20. *Jeff Stephens, 3b, University of Texas-Arlington.
**21. Kevin Jarvis, rhp, Wake Forest University.—(1994-2006)**
22. *Cliff Foster, rhp, Angelina (Texas) JC.
23. *James Ritchey, c, Copperas Cove (Texas) HS.
24. Rodney Thomas, of, North Marion HS, Reddick, Fla.
25. John Gast, 3b, East Carolina University.
26. Wayne Wilkerson, of, Norfolk State University.
27. *Isaac Burton, 3b, Washington HS, Los Angeles.
28. John Hrusovsky, rhp, Indian River (Fla.) CC.
29. Scott Snead, ss, North Carolina State University.
30. *Brian Carlin, of, Northwestern State University.
31. Bill Dreisbach, c, West Liberty State (W.Va.) College.
32. *Matt Cesare, ss, Pearce HS, Richardson, Texas.
33. *Kevin Zellers, ss-2b, Holy Name HS, Maple Heights, Ohio.
34. Elijah Robinson, of-1b, Joliet Central HS, Joliet, Ill.
35. *Doyle Preston, of, Mount Vernon HS, Saltillo, Texas.
36. Matt Martin, 2b, Lubbock Christian (Texas) University.
37. Rossi Morris, of, Madison HS, Houston.
38. *John Sherbert, c, Whiteville (N.C.) HS.
39. Yamil Concepcion, 3b, Juan Ponce de Leon HS, Florida, P.R.
**40. *Stephen Larkin, 1b, Moeller HS, Cincinnati.—(1998)**
DRAFT DROP *Brother of Barry Larkin, first-round draft pick, Reds (1985); major leaguer (1986-2004)*
**41. *Aaron Fultz, lhp, Munford (Tenn.) HS.—(2000-07)**
42. Dee Jenkins, ss, Dreher HS, Columbia, S.C.
43. *Jimmy Rice, ss-2b, McLean County HS, Owensboro, Ky.
44. *Brett Backlund, rhp, University of Iowa.
45. +James Etheridge, lhp, Marengo Academy, Linden, Ala. / Meridian (Miss.) CC.
46. *Curt Lowry, of, Paris (Texas) HS.
47. *Saul Bustos, 3b, Odessa (Texas) JC.
48. John Gildon, c, Pleasant Grove HS, Texarkana, Texas.
49. Rod Sanders, of, Wilson HS, Florence, S.C.
50. Derbe Pearson, rhp, Dayton (Texas) HS.
51. Stephen Claybrook, ss, Calallen HS, Robstown, Texas.
52. Stuart Downing, of, Fairport (N.Y.) HS.

## CLEVELAND INDIANS (13)

**1. Manny Ramirez, 3b-of, George Washington HS, New York.—(1993-2011)**
**2. Herbert Perry, 3b, University of Florida.—(1994-2004)**
DRAFT DROP *Brother of Chan Perry, major leaguer (2000-02)*
**3. Chad Ogea, rhp, Louisiana State University.—(1994-99)**
**4. Paul Byrd, rhp, Louisiana State University.—(1995-2009)**
5. Kevin Logsdon, lhp, Linn-Benton (Ore.) CC.—(AAA)
6. Tom Vantiger, of, Iowa State University.
**7. Pep Harris, rhp, Lancaster (S.C.) HS.—(1996-98)**
8. Chris Coulter, lhp, Pensacola (Fla.) JC.
9. Paul Meade, ss, Oral Roberts University.
10. Scott Sharts, 1b-rhp, Cal State Northridge.
11. Brad Kantor, 2b, Manatee (Fla.) JC.
12. Jeff Whitaker, ss, Martinsville (Va.) HS.
DRAFT DROP *Nephew of Lou Whitaker, major leaguer (1977-95)*
13. Ryan Martindale, c, Creighton University.
14. Mike Jewell, rhp, Sacramento (Calif.) CC.
15. Tommy Bates, ss, University of Southwestern Louisiana.
16. Rod Koller, rhp, Southern Arkansas University.
17. Denny Key, rhp, Spartanburg Methodist (S.C.) JC.
18. Michael Burritt, 3b-rhp, Oak Grove HS, San Jose, Calif.
19. Chris Maffett, rhp, Southport HS, Indianapolis, Ind.
**20. Albie Lopez, rhp, Mesa (Ariz.) CC.—(1993-2003)**
**21. *Jed Hansen, ss, Capitol HS, Olympia, Wash.—(1997-99)**
22. Grady Davidson, lhp, Southern University.
23. Greg Knapland, lhp, University of Washington.
24. Andre White, of, Laney (Calif.) JC.
25. Brandon Bluhm, lhp, West HS, Chehalis, Wash.
26. *Rufus Boykin, of, Oviedo (Fla.) HS.
27. *Denny Vigo, 1b-3b, Cal State Northridge.
28. *Warren Frierson, 2b, Hartsville HS, Lydia, S.C.
29. Patrick Maxwell, 2b, Western New Mexico University.
30. Rodd Hairston, 1b, Stephen F. Austin University.
31. Ian Doyle, rhp, Cuyahoga (Ohio) CC.
32. *Jeff Seale, rhp, San Jacinto (Texas) JC.
33. Dave Duplessis, 1b, St. Mary's (Calif.) College.
34. *Dave Majeski, of, University of Florida.
35. Gary Tatterson, rhp, Arizona State University.
36. Jorge Santiago, 3b, Tomas C. Ongay HS, Bayamon, P.R.
37. Michael Moore, c, West Virginia University.
38. *Robert Sherwood, c, Burroughs HS, Burbank, Calif.
39. *Jason Elders, rhp, Rocky River (Ohio) HS.
40. Michael Taylor, c, Brookdale (N.J.) CC.
41. Brian Buzard, lhp, Wichita State University.
42. *Erik Lane, ss, Russellville (Ark.) HS.
43. *Damien Crabtree, lhp, Ballard HS, Seattle.
**44. +Damian Jackson, ss, Ygnacio Valley HS, Concord, Calif. / Laney (Calif.) JC.—(1996-2006)**
45. +Greg Sinner, rhp, Kishwaukee (Ill.) JC.
46. *James Gatlin, c, Cedar Hill (Texas) HS.
47. *William Duffie, c, Irmo (S.C.) HS.
48. *Shannon Jones, ss, New Mexico JC.
**49. *Steven Bourgeois, rhp, Delgado (La.) CC.—(1996)**
50. *Ryan Post, rhp, Wilson HS, Tacoma, Wash.
51. *Jonathan Stephany, of, Spanaway Lake HS, Tacoma, Wash.
52. *Jay Giardina, rhp, Delgado (La.) CC.
53. *Dale Dolejsi, rhp, Lindbergh HS, Renton, Wash.
54. *John Waters, of, Eastern Wayne HS, LaGrange, N.C.
55. *Jamie Hanson, c, Kentwood HS, Kent, Wash.
56. *Erasmo Velasco, of, Laredo (Texas) JC.
57. +Rob Augustine, rhp, Cowley County (Kan.) CC / Western Oklahoma State JC.
58. *Damon Sims, rhp, Belaire HS, Baton Rouge, La.
59. +Brian Holter, rhp, Benton (Ark.) HS / Connors State (Okla.) JC.
60. *Ryan Stofer, rhp, Victoria, B.C.
61. Andy Stemler, lhp, Lewis (Ill.) University.
62. *Tim Thompson, ss, Harding HS, Charlotte, N.C.

## DETROIT TIGERS (15)

1. (Choice to Brewers as compensation for Type A free agent Rob Deer)
**1. Justin Thompson, lhp, Klein Oak HS, Spring, Texas** (Supplemental choice—32nd—as compensation for Type A free agent Jack Morris).**—(1996-2005)**
**1. Trever Miller, lhp, Trinity HS, Louisville, Ky.** (Supplemental choice—41st—as compensation for Type A free agent Mike Heath).**—(1996-2011)**
**2. Tarrik Brock, of, Hawthorne (Calif.) HS.—(2000)**
**3. Brian Edmondson, rhp, Norte Vista HS, Riverside, Calif.** (Choice from Brewers as compensation for Type B free agent Edwin Nunez).**—(1998-99)**
3. Justin Mashore, of, Clayton Valley HS, Concord, Calif.—(AAA)
DRAFT DROP *Son of Clyde Mashore, major leaguer (1969-73) • Brother of Damon Mashore, ninth-round draft pick, Athletics (1991); major leaguer (1996-98)*
**4. Sean Bergman, rhp, Southern Illinois University.—(1993-2000)**
5. Paul Magrini, rhp, Wallington (N.J.) HS.—(Short-season A)
6. Jason Pfaff, rhp, University of Michigan.
7. Arthur Adams, rhp, Laney (Calif.) JC.
8. Joe Perona, c, Northwestern University.
**9. Clint Sodowsky, rhp, Connors State (Okla.) JC.—(1995-99)**
10. Thomas Gibson, of, Mission (Calif.) JC.
11. Brian Sullivan, of, Fordham University.
12. Clarke Rea, c, Arizona State University.
13. Evan Pratte, ss, Southwest Missouri State University.
14. Brian Prichard, c, Cincinnati Academy of Physical

Education.
**15. Phil Stidham, rhp, University of Arkansas.—(1994)**
16. Todd Bussa, rhp, Palm Beach Gardens (Fla.) HS.
17. *Todd Ruyak, lhp, University of Virginia.
18. Peter Feeley, of, University of Lowell (Mass.).
19. Robin Higginbotham, of, Mississippi Gulf Coast JC.
20. Rich Kelley, lhp, Jacksonville University.
21. Mark Tillman, of, Loyola Marymount University.
22. Tom Schwarber, rhp, Ohio State University.
23. Robert Grable, 3b, St. John's University.
24. Matt Bauer, lhp, Central Michigan University.
25. Scott Durussel, rhp, Western Michigan University.
26. John Reid, rhp, Stanford University.
27. *Victor Rodriguez, ss, Woodham HS, Pensacola Fla.
28. Bob Lemay, lhp, St. Andrews (N.C.) College.
29. Dan Ruff, of, University of Michigan.
**30. Kevin Morgan, ss, Southeastern Louisiana University.—(1997)**
31. Jim Givens, 2b-ss, Kent State University.
32. *Drew Christman, of, University of Oklahoma.
33. *Ray Ricken, rhp, Notre Dame HS, Warren, Mich.
34. Kenny Marrero, c, Arizona Western JC.
35. *Scott Kennedy, rhp, Plymouth-Canton HS, Plymouth, Mich.
36. *James Gordon, rhp, Turner HS, Burneyville, Okla.
37. +Del Marine, c, Moorpark (Calif.) JC.
38. (void) Demond Thomas, ss-of, Elizabethtown (Ky.) HS.
39. *Ryan Dedmon, 1b, Gaither HS, Lutz, Fla.
40. +Ricky Martinez, ss, JC of the Desert (Calif.).
41. *Joshua Kirtlan, 1b, Sacramento (Calif.) CC.
42. *Sean Hugo, 1b, Westmoore HS, Oklahoma City, Okla.
43. *Troy Wachter, of, Miller Place (N.Y.) HS.
44. Doug Martin, rhp, Eastern Michigan University.
45. Dennis Walsh, lhp, University of Alabama.
46. Greg Raffo, rhp, Middle Tennessee State University.
**47. *Bobby Hughes, c-3b, Los Angeles Valley JC.—(1998-99)**
48. *Tristan Paul, ss, Rolling Hills HS, Rolling Hills Estates, Calif.
49. *Brian Shumard, 1b, JC of the Redwoods (Calif.).
50. *Michael Jenkins, rhp, Moorpark (Calif.) JC.
51. *Reggie Jackson, lhp, Hillsborough (Fla.) CC.
52. *Chris McCarter, of, Gulf Coast (Fla.) CC.
53. +Curt Bell, c, Indian River (Fla.) CC.
54. +Robert Dickerson, of, Mississippi Gulf Coast JC.
55. *Ken Tipton, of, Texarkana (Texas) CC.
56. *Sean Davisson, c-of, Sacramento (Calif) CC.
57. +John Tirnko, c, Polk (Fla.) CC.
58. *Steven Breland, lhp, Mosley HS, Panama City, Fla.
59. +Toby McFarland, lhp, Riverside (Calif.) CC.
60. *Kerry Collins, ss-3b, Penn State University.
DRAFT DROP *First-round draft pick, Carolina Panthers/ National Football League (1995); quarterback, NFL (1995-2007)*
61. Rob Yelton, c, Miami (Ohio) University.
62. Greg Frey, of, Ohio State University.

## HOUSTON ASTROS (6)

**1. *John Burke, rhp, University of Florida.—(1996-97)**
DRAFT DROP *Returned to Florida; re-drafted by Rockies, 1992 (1st round)*
1. Shawn Livsey, ss, Simeon HS, Chicago (Supplemental choice–29th–as compensation for Type A free agent Danny Darwin).—(AA)
1. Jim Gonzalez, c, East Hartford (Conn.) HS (Supplemental choice—40th—as compensation for Type A free agent Dave Smith).—(AAA)
1. Mike Groppuso, 3b, Seton Hall University (Supplemental choice–44th–as compensation for Type A free agent Franklin Stubbs).—(AAA)
2. Buck McNabb, of, Fort Walton Beach (Fla.) HS (Choice from Cardinals as compensation for Type B free agent Juan Agosto).—(AAA)
2. Jimmy Lewis, rhp, Florida State University (Choice from Brewers as compensation for Stubbs).—(AAA)
2. Eddy Ramos, 3b, American HS, Hialeah, Fla.—(High A)
3. Chris Durkin, of, Youngstown State University.—(AA)
4. Brian Holliday, rhp, San Diego State University.—(High A)
5. Dan Grapenthien, 1b-of, Thornton Fractional South HS, Lansing, Ill.—(Low A)
6. Todd Hobson, of, Indiana State University.
**7. James Mouton, of, St. Mary's (Calif.) College.—(1994-2001)**
8. Tom Anderson, rhp, University of Iowa.
9. Angelo Lee, of, Simeon HS, Chicago.
10. Joshua Spring, rhp, Lebanon (Ohio) HS.
11. Kevin Webb, 3b, UCLA.
12. Rod Biehl, lhp, University of Louisville.
13. Anthony Miller, lhp, University of Dayton.
14. Bryant Winslow, 1b, UC Irvine.
15. Rich Schulte, of, Central (Iowa) College.
16. Michael Murphy, c, U.S. International (Calif.) University.
17. Randy Albaladejo, c, Colegio Nuestro HS, Vega Alta, P.R.
18. Mario Linares, c, University of Florida.
19. *Carlos Perez, 1b-of, Ellison HS, Killeen, Texas.
20. Chris White, rhp, Cleveland State University.
21. James Waring, rhp, Stetson University.
22. Roger Rumsey, of, Dallas Baptist University.
23. +Kirk Larson, ss, Homestead HS, Sunnyvale, Calif. / DeAnza (Calif.) JC.
24. Joe Sewell, rhp, UC Irvine.
**25. *Jose Flores, ss-2b, Brandeis HS, New York.—(2002-04)**
26. *Anthony Dermendziev, of, Santa Teresa HS, San Jose, Calif.
27. *Kyle Wagner, c, Red Land HS, New Cumberland, Pa.
28. *Aldren Sadler, rhp, Middle Georgia JC.
29. Mark Loughlin, lhp, Providence College.
30. *Michael Machado, of, Antioch (Calif.) HS.
31. *Matt Williams, rhp, Edmond Memorial HS, Edmond, Okla.
**32. *Bobby Howry, rhp, Deer Valley HS, Glendale, Ariz.—(1998-2010)**
33. *Craig Castellanos, lhp, Victor Valley HS, Victorville, Calif.
34. *Tony Pruett, c-of, El Camino (Calif.) JC.
35. *Jamine Adams, of, Riverside (Calif.) CC.
36. *Keith Davenport, lhp, Michigan State University.
37. Jeffrey Miller, rhp, Missouri Baptist College.
38. *Marion Gardinera, of, Mission Bay HS, San Diego.
**39. Alvin Morman, lhp, Wingate (N.C.) College.—(1996-99)**
**40. *Mike Metcalfe, ss, Colonial HS, Orlando, Fla.—(1998-2000)**
41. Heath Rose, lhp, MacMurray (Ill.) College.
42. Ricky Blest, lhp, Missouri Baptist College.
43. *Roy Nieto, rhp, Southwestern (Texas) University.
44. *Todd Coburn, c, Butte (Calif.) JC.
45. *Marty Henry, rhp, Treasure Valley (Ore.) CC.
46. *Donald Smith, rhp, Orange Coast (Calif.) JC.
47. *Eduardo Fuentes, 2b, Santurce (P.R.) HS.
48. *Paul Barber, ss, Queen City (Texas) HS.
49. *James Davis, 3b, San Diego CC.
50. *Michael Keenan, rhp, Allan Hancock (Calif.) JC.
51. *Johnny Mitchell, of, Middle Georgia JC.
52. *Jason Reed, lhp, El Capitan HS, El Cajon, Calif.
53. *Sean Tyler, of, Texarkana (Texas) CC.
54. *Kraig Kupiec, of, Durfee HS, Fall River, Mass.
55. *D.C. Olsen, c, Fullerton (Calif.) HS.
**56. *Lou Collier, rhp-ss, Vocational HS, Chicago.—(1997-2004)**
**57. *Andy Abad, of, Middle Georgia JC.—(2001-06)**
58. *Jamie Falconer, lhp, LaGrand (Ore.) HS.
59. *Johnny Isom, of, Crowley HS, Fort Worth, Texas.
60. *Joch Martin, of, Loves Park-Harlem HS, Rockford, Ill.
61. Sean Fesh, lhp, Bethel (Conn.) HS.
62. *Jeff Henry, of, Glenwood HS, Phenix City, Ala.
**63. *Jay Witasick, rhp, Brevard (Fla.) CC.—(1996-2007)**
64. *Luis Victoria, rhp, Centro de Instructico HS, Catano, P.R.
65. *Kerry Bertrand, of, Berwick HS, Morgan City, La.
66. *Eric Dumas, of, Covington HS, Madisonville, La.
67. *Chad Dunavan, of, Everman HS, Fort Worth, Texas.
68. *Trevin Smith, rhp-c, West Mecklenburg HS, Denver, N.C.
69. *Alfonso Montoya, of, San Marino (Calif.) HS.
70. *Chris Briones, c, Brea (Calif.) HS.
71. *Jeff Beck, c, Mount Vernon HS, Alexandria, Va.
72. *Matthew Maffei, 1b, Laguna Hills HS, Dana Point, Calif.
73. *Brett Baptist, rhp, Jacksonville (Ill.) HS.
74. *Matt Beaumont, lhp, Rittman (Ohio) HS.
75. *Donald Shump, 3b, Northeast HS, Pasadena, Md.
76. *Rahasal Buggs, c, Morgan Park HS, Chicago.
77. *Robert Giannola, c, Ohlone (Calif.) JC.
78. *Scott Martyka, of-lhp, Incline HS, Incline Village, Nev.
79. *Robert Medel, 3b, Waukegan (Ill.) HS.
80. *Thomas Uptegrove, of, Clear Creek HS, League City, Texas.
81. *Jeff Latimore, 3b, Vocational HS, Chicago.
82. *Robert Klemme, 1b, Niles North HS, Skokie, Ill.
83. *Koby Stovall, lhp, Skyview HS, Billings, Mon.
84. *David Vergara, lhp, Westminster (Calif.) HS.
85. *Anthony Spivey, rhp, Pacelli HS, Phenix City, Ala.
86. *Rodney Ruelas, lhp, Niles North HS, Skokie, Ill.
87. *Evan Bailey, rhp, Escambia HS, Pensacola, Fla.
88. *Britt Gusmus, of, Cherry Creek HS, Englewood, Colo.
89. *Pat Harter, of, Fernandina Beach (Fla.) HS.
90. *Danny Harris, 3b, Henry County HS, Stockbridge, Ga.
91. *Brook Holding, 3b, Blanchard (Okla.) HS.
92. *Mike Hammer, ss, Willowbrook HS, Villa Park, Ill.
93. *Craig Everett, of, Northeast HS, Pasadena, Md.
94. *Jose Avina, of, East Union HS, Lathrop, Calif.
95. *Daniel Pagan, 3b-1b, Howard (Texas) JC.
96. *Brian Hudson, rhp, Mater Del HS, Fountain Valley, Calif.

## KANSAS CITY ROYALS (7)

**1. Joe Vitiello, of-1b, University of Alabama.—(1995-2003)**
1. Jason Pruitt, rhp, Rockingham County HS, Wentworth, N.C. (Supplemental choice–30th–as compensation for Type A free agent Steve Farr).—(Low A)
**2. Ryan Long, 3b, Dobie HS, Pasadena, Texas** (Choice from Yankees as compensation for Type A free agent Steve Farr).**—(1997)**
2. (Choice to Red Sox as compensation for Type A free agent Mike Boddicker)
3. (Choice to Dodgers as compensation for Type B free agent Kirk Gibson)
4. Dwayne Gerald, ss, St. Paul's (N.C.) HS.—(Short-season A)
**5. Shane Halter, ss, University of Texas.—(1997-2004)**
**6. Mike Bovee, rhp, Mira Mesa HS, San Diego.—(1997)**
7. *Paul Failla, ss, North Allegheny HS, Wexford, Pa.
**8. Kevin Hodges, rhp, Klein Oak HS, Spring, Texas.—(2000)**
9. Steve Hinton, of, Creighton University.
**10. Mike Sweeney, c, Ontario (Calif.) HS.—(1995-2010)**
**11. Joe Randa, 3b, University of Tennessee.—(1995-2006)**
**12. Mike Fyhrie, rhp, UCLA.—(1996-2002)**
**13. Roderick Myers, of, Conroe (Texas) HS.—(1996-97)**
14. Angel Macias, rhp, East Los Angeles JC.
15. Chris Connolly, lhp, Radford University.
16. Michael Bailey, rhp, Tallahassee (Fla.) CC.
17. Mark Johnson, of, University of Arkansas.
18. +Brian Teeters, of, Bakersfield (Calif.) JC.
19. +Michael Currier, rhp, North Harris (Texas) CC / San Jacinto (Texas) JC.
20. John Downs, rhp, Muscatine (Iowa) CC.
21. David Farsaci, rhp, High Point College.
22. Matthew Bennett, rhp, Davis HS, Modesto, Calif.
23. Andy Brookens, 2b, Shippensburg (Pa.) University.
24. *Joe Carrillo, lhp, Southwestern (Calif.) JC.
**25. Les Norman, of, College of St. Francis (Ill.).—(1995-96)**
26. Joel Johnson, rhp, Simpson (Iowa) College.
27. Kris Glaser, rhp, Olney Central (Ill.) JC.
28. Daniel Servello, of, West Virginia University.
29. *Justin Craig, rhp, Peabody HS, Pittsburgh.
30. *Michael McLain, rhp, Sacramento (Calif.) CC.
31. Troy Babbitt, 3b, Cypress (Calif.) JC.
32. Paul Sanders, c, Oregon State University.
33. Ryan Towns, rhp, Blinn (Texas) JC.
34. Roger Landress, rhp, Augusta (Ga.) College.
35. Kevin Kobetitsch, lhp, Concordia (N.Y.) College.
36. Paul West, rhp, Garland County (Ark.) CC.
37. Rodney Williams, of, Palmdale (Calif.) HS.
38. *Shandel Curris, of, Cass HS, Detroit.
39. *Jim Miller, rhp, Michigan State University.
40. +Trenton Hauswirth, c, JC of the Desert (Calif.).
41. *Dax Winslett, rhp, McLennan (Texas) CC.
42. +Jarrod Smith, of-3b, Polk (Fla.) CC.
43. Chris Medrick, lhp, Emporia State (Kan.) University.
44. Jeff Smith, rhp, Oregon State University.
45. *Ramon Smith, of, Encinal HS, Alameda, Calif.
46. *Twaino Moss, of, Hancock Central HS, Sparta, Ga.
47. *James Reinecker, rhp, Northview HS, Covina, Calif.
48. *Jorge Ortiz, rhp, Baptist HS, Carolina, P.R.
49. *Jason Chandler, lhp, Burbank (Calif.) HS.
50. *Chad Bumgamer, rhp, Palm Desert (Calif.) HS.
51. *Michael Blang, rhp, Monona Grove HS, Monona, Wis.
52. *Rex Crosnoe, c, Cape-Central HS, Cape Girardeau, Mo.
53. *Darek Robinson, 3b, Pleasant Grove (Utah) HS.
54. *Edgar Orta, lhp, San Gabriel HS, Alhambra, Calif.
55. Thomathon Good, of, Brazoswood HS, Clute, Texas.
56. *Scott Harrison, rhp, University of Texas.
57. *Roy Marsh, of, Perry Hall HS, Baltimore.
58. *Michael Mitchell, 1b, Rio Mesa HS, Camarillo, Calif.
59. *Jason Guyton, of, Caruthersville (Mo.) HS.
60. *Ron Rivera, rhp, Miguel Melendez HS, Cayey, P.R.
61. *Francis Rosa, rhp, Trina Padilla de Sanz HS, Arecibo, P.R.
62. *Kenneth Phillips, of, University of Oregon.

## LOS ANGELES DODGERS (18)

1. (Choice to Mets as compensation for Type A free agent Darryl Strawberry)
2. (Choice to Expos as compensation tor Type B free agent Kevin Gross)
**3. Todd Hollandsworth, of, Newport HS, Bellevue, Wash.** (Choice from Royals as compensation for Type B free agent Kirk Gibson).**—(1995-2006)**
3. *Todd LaRocca, ss, The Lovett School, Atlanta.—(High A)
DRAFT DROP *Attended Stanford; re-drafted by Orioles, 1994 (5th round)*
4. Mike Walkden, lhp, Lake Stevens (Wash.) HS.—(High A)
5. Doug Bennett, rhp, University of Arkansas.—(Short-season A)
6. Mike Iglesias, rhp, Hayward (Calif.) HS.
7. Brandon Watts, lhp, Ruston (La.) HS.
8. Vince Jackson, of, Central HS, Davenport, Iowa.
9. Dennis Winicki, ss, Mona Shores HS, Muskegon, Mich.
10. Lonnie Jackson, of, Washington HS, Oakland.
**11. Chris Latham, ss, Basic HS, Las Vegas, Nev.—(1997-2003)**
12. Carlo Walton, c, East Side HS, Newark, N.J.
13. David Fitzpatrick, rhp, Sullivan South HS, Kingsport, Tenn.
14. Robert Legendre, rhp, Cypress (Calif.) JC.
15. Erik Zammarchi, of, JC of Marin (Calif.).
16. Chris Sinacori, rhp, Florida International University.
**17. Chad Zerbe, lhp, Hillsborough (Fla.) CC.—(2000-03)**
18. JoJo Smith, lhp, Vanderbilt University.
**19. Rick Gorecki, rhp, Oak Forest (Ill.) HS.—(1997-98)**
20. Billy Stephens, rhp, Ringgold (Ga.) HS.
21. Kevin Zahner, c, Ellington HS, Rockville, Conn.
**22. Ken Huckaby, c, San Joaquin Delta (Calif.) JC.—(2001-06)**
23. *David Carroll, lhp, Chantilly HS, Fairfax, Va.
24. Kevin Smith, lhp, Columbus (Ga.) HS.
25. Murph Proctor, 1b, University of Southern California.
26. Chris Crabtree, lhp, Middle Tennessee State University.
27. Todd Soares, of, New Bedford (Mass.) HS.
28. *Tito Landrum, of, Jacksonville State University.
29. Vern Spearman, of, Fresno State University.

30. Jack Johnson, c, University of Arizona.
31. Chris Demetral, 2b, Western Michigan University.
32. *Travis Hall, lhp, Middle Georgia JC.
33. Jay Kirkpatrick, c, Methodist (N.C.) College.
34. *Cedric Allen, lhp, McLennan (Texas) CC.
35. *Eduardo Acosta, ss, Rock Falls (Ill.) HS.
36. *Kenneth Sikes, 1b-rhp, Perry (Ga.) HS.
37. *Alejandro Periera, lhp, Miami-Dade CC New World Center.
38. Gary Cope, lhp, Motlow State (Tenn.) CC.
39. Clifton Joyce, lhp, South Stokes HS, Walnut Cove, N.C.
40. Michael Sube, lhp, West Virginia University.
41. Carlos Castillo, rhp, Cypress (Calif.) JC.
42. Carlos Thomas, rhp, Tennessee State University.
43. *Chris West, 3b, Louisburg (N.C.) JC.
44. Eric Vorbeck, of, Cal State Sacramento.
45. Marc Tramuta, ss, St. Bonaventure University.
46. *Mario Moody, ss, Glynn Academy, Brunswick, Ga.
47. *Ken Jones, 1b, Pelham (Ga.) HS.
48. *Matthew Svoboda, rhp, El Dorado HS, Placentia, Calif.
49. Richard Ware, 2b, Greenville (Ill.) College.
50. German Gonzalez, 3b, JC of the Desert (Calif.).
51. +Dustin Rennspies, c, Mosley HS, Panama City, Fla. / George C. Wallace (Ala.) JC.
52. Cam Aronetz, lhp, Simon Fraser (B.C.) University.
53. *Chris Vaughn, lhp, John A. Logan (Ill.) JC.
54. *Javier Ortiz, rhp, Manuela Toro HS, Caguas, P.R.
55. *Brian Clark, c, Armijo HS, Fairfield, Calif.
56. *Brian Wise, lhp, El Segundo (Calif.) HS.
57. *Roger Cropper, of, Central HS, St. Croix, Virgin Islands.
58. *William Belcher, of, Fairfax HS, Los Angeles.
59. *Jon Goodnch, rhp, Sonoma (Calif.) HS.
**60. *Steve Kline, lhp, Allegheny (Pa.) CC.—(1997-2007).**
61. *Jareld Dunkin, c, Capitol Hill HS, Oklahoma City, Okla.
62. *Kevin Clark, 3b, Basic HS, Henderson, Nev.
63. +Rich Linares, rhp, Cerritos (Calif.) JC.
64. *Shawn Buhner, 1b, Clear Creek HS, Nassau Bay, Texas.
DRAFT DROP *Brother of Jay Buhner, major leaguer (1987-2001)*
65. *David Silvas, ss, San Jacinto HS, Pearland, Texas.
66. Jason Bobb, rhp, Chippewa Falls (Wis.) HS.
67. *Derek Ornalas, of, Sylmar (Calif.) HS.
68. *Chris Kenady, of, Westonka HS, Mound, Minn.
69. *Richard Heineman, c, Culver City (Calif.) HS.
70. +Joe Jacobsen, rhp, Fresno (Calif.) CC.
71. *Mark Fraser, rhp, LaSalle HS, Sudbury, Ontario.
72. *Kerry Cosgrove, of, Palm Desert (Calif.) HS.
73. *Stephane DiLauro, ss, Academy Laval, Montreal, Quebec.
74. *Eric Ontiveros, rhp, Bakersfield (Calif.) JC.
75. *Joshua Hamik, c, Mount Si HS, Fall City, Wash.
76. *Brent Crowther, rhp, Capilano (B.C.) JC.
77. +Rich Haley, of, Sacramento (Calif.) CC.
78. *Chip Glass, of, Santa Rosa (Calif.) JC.
79. *Stephen Matyczyk, ss, Southington (Conn.) HS.
80. *Ismael Castaneda, lhp, Fresno (Calif.) CC.
81. *Gar Vallone, ss, El Dorado HS, Placentia, Calif.
82. *Michael Sanburn, rhp, JC of San Mateo (Calif.).
83. *Aaron Wofford, ss, Yuba (Calif.) JC.
84. *Jose Martinez, rhp, Los Angeles CC.
85. *Darrell Sutton, rhp, Beverly Hills (Calif.) HS.
86. *Brett Schafer, 3b, Santa Monica HS, Malibu, Calif.
87. *Andy Saltsman, c, Crescenta Valley HS, La Crescenta, Calif.
88. *Junaane Leach, of, San Marin HS, Novato, Calif.
89. *Martin Meza, rhp, Cerritos (Calif.) JC.
90. *Todd Blyleven, rhp, Cypress (Calif.) JC.
DRAFT DROP *Son of Bert Blyleven, major leaguer (1970-92)*
91. *Steven Arffa, lhp, Glendora (Calif.) HS.
92. *Derek Gauthier, 2b, East York College HS, Toronto.
93. *William Stroud, c-1b, Dunwoody HS, Atlanta.
94. *Shawn McNally, ss, Winder Barrow HS, Winder, Ga.

## MILWAUKEE BREWERS (5)

1. *Kenny Henderson, rhp, Ringgold (Ga.) HS.—(High A)
DRAFT DROP *Attended Miami (Fla.); re-drafted by Expos, 1994 (2nd round)*
1. Tyrone Hill, lhp, Yucaipa (Calif.) HS (Choice from Tigers as compensation for Type A free agent Rob Deer).—(AA)
2. (Choice to Astros as compensation for Type A free agent Franklin Stubbs)
2. Judd Wilstead, rhp, Dixie HS, St. George, Utah (Supplemental choice—71st—as compensation for Type C free agent Bill Krueger).—(AA)
3. (Choice to Tigers as compensation for Type B free agent Edwin Nunez)
4. Mike Harris, 1b, University of Kentucky.—(AAA)
**5. *Nomar Garciaparra, ss, St. John Bosco HS, Whittier, Calif.—(1996-2009)**
DRAFT DROP *Attended Georgia Tech; re-drafted by Red Sox, 1994 (1st round)*
6. Cecil Rodrigues, of, Indian River (Fla.) CC.
7. Derek Wachter, of, Iona College.
**8. Mike Matheny, c, University of Michigan.—(1994-2006)**
DRAFT DROP *Major league manager (2012-15)*
9. Bill Dobrolsky, c, Shippensburg (Pa.) University.
10. Jim Wilkie, rhp, Triton (Ill.) JC.
**11. Jeff Cirillo, 3b, University of Southern California.—(1994-2007)**
12. Paul Arredondo, ss, Colton HS, Grand Terrace, Calif.
13. Byron Browne, rhp, Grand Canyon University.
14. John Trisler, rhp, Indiana State University.
15. Scott Talanoa, 1b, Long Beach State University.
16. David Preikszas, of, Miami (Ohio) University.
17. Charles O'Laughlin, lhp, Southwestern (Calif.) JC.
18. Tim Albert, of, University of Hawaii.
19. Mike Basse, of, University of Tennessee.
20. Brian Hancock, lhp, Volunteer State (Tenn.) CC.
21. Rob Gorrell, rhp, Arizona State University.
22. *Scott Morgan, 3b, Lompoc (Calif.) HS.
23. Brian Dennison, lhp, University of Arkansas.
24. Andy Fairman, 1b, University of Michigan.
25. *Michael Swenson, lhp, Chamberlain HS, Tampa.
26. Derek Ghostlaw, c, Bentley (Mass.) College.
27. Mark Stillwell, 1b, Kaiser HS, Honolulu, Hawaii.
28. *Antonio Valdez, rhp, Miami Beach (Fla.) HS.
29. *Steven Brown, rhp, Central Arizona JC.
30. *Mark Sobolewski, c-3b, Florida Southern College.
31. *Brent Simonian, of, Fowler (Calif.) HS.
32. Howard House, of, Howard University.
33. *Ossie Garcia, rhp-of, American HS, Hialeah, Fla.
34. Mike Lawn, of, University of California.
35. *Geoff Hughes, of, Naperville North HS, Naperville, Ill.
36. *Bobby L. Jones, of, Arlington HS, Riverside, Calif. / Riverside (Calif.) CC.
37. *Pete Harvell, lhp, San Jose (Calif.) CC.
38. Jason Imperial, 3b, Rutgers University.
39. *Maurice Crum Sr., c-1b, University of Miami.
DRAFT DROP *Linebacker, National Football League (1991)*
40. Mike Stefanski, c, University of Detroit.
41. +Brad Gay, c, Hillsborough (Fla.) CC.
42. *Jerry Fisher, rhp, Southern HS, Baltimore.
43. *Michael Mace, rhp, Gulf Coast (Fla.) CC.
**44. +Bobby M. Jones, lhp, Chipola (Fla.) JC.—(1997-2004)**
45. Jackie Ross, of, Miami-Dade CC North.
46. *Charles Payne, rhp, Battle Ground Academy, Brenton, Tenn.
47. +Francisco Gonzalez, rhp, Inter American (P.R.) University.
48. +Tommy Schenbeck, rhp, Palm Beach (Fla.) JC.
49. *Scott Wayne, c, Englewood (Colo.) HS.

## MINNESOTA TWINS (3)

**1. David McCarty, 1b, Stanford University.—(1993-2005)**
**1. Scott Stahoviak, 3b, Creighton University** (Supplemental choice–27th–as compensation for Type A free agent Gary Gaetti).**—(1993-98)**
**2. Mike Durant, c, Ohio State University.—(1996)**
3. Keith LeGree, ss, Statesboro (Ga.) HS.—(AA)
4. Brett Roberts, rhp, Morehead State University.—(AAA)
DRAFT DROP *Second -round draft pick, Sacramento Kings/National Basketball Association (1992)*
5. Shawn Miller, rhp, Beyer HS, Modesto, Calif.—(High A)
6. Pedro Grifol, c, Florida State University.
**7. LaTroy Hawkins, rhp, West Side HS, Gary, Ind.—(1995-2015)**
**8. Brad Radke, rhp, Jesuit HS, Tampa.—(1995-2006)**
9. Neil Stevens, rhp-c, Beekmantown Central HS, Plattsburg, N.Y.
10. Tony Banks, of, Hoover HS, San Diego.
DRAFT DROP *Quarterback, National Football League (1995-2004)*
11. Bill Wissler, rhp, University of Pennsylvania.
12. Jeff Mansur, lhp, University of Portland.
**13. Matt Lawton, 2b, Mississippi Gulf Coast JC.—(1995-2006)**
DRAFT DROP *Brother of Marcus Lawton, major leaguer (1989)*
14. *Rob Neal, of, Westlake HS, Thousand Oaks, Calif.
15. *Travis Huenfeld, of, Rockhurst HS, Olathe, Kan.
16. *Rob Johnson, rhp, El Toro HS, Mission Viejo, Calif.
DRAFT DROP *Quarterback, National Football League (1995-2003)*
17. *Eric Kunz, rhp, Keller HS, Wautauga, Texas.
18. David Sartain, lhp, Virginia Commonwealth University.
19. Mike Fernandez, of-3b, New York Tech.
20. Steve Hazlett, of, University of Wyoming.
21. Michael Lewis, lhp, UCLA.
22. *Reid Hensley, rhp, Marian HS, Lansing, Ill.
23. Dennis Sweeney, lhp, Seton Hall University.
24. David Schwartz, rhp, University of California.
25. Bob Robinson, rhp, Ohio University.
26. *Kraig Hawkins, of, Mississippi Gulf Coast JC.
27. Rafael Pina, rhp, East Los Angeles JC.
28. Chad Baucom, c, Hibbing (Minn.) HS.
29. +Chris Moten, rhp, Cerritos (Calif.) JC.
30. *Ryan Kjos, rhp, Hopkins (Minn.) HS.
31. *Steven Friedrich, c, Troy HS, Yorba Linda, Calif.
32. *Matt Petersen, rhp, Iowa State University.
33. *David Baine, lhp, Sonoma State (Calif.) University.
**34. *Tim Davis, lhp, Florida State University.—(1994-97)**
35. *Myron Glass, of, St. Joseph HS, Kenosha, Wis.
36. +Troy Doezie, c, Brighton HS, Sandy, Utah / JC of Southern Idaho.
37. *Cesar Barrera, 3b, Ontario (Calif) HS.
**38. *T.J. Mathews, rhp, University of Nevada-Reno.—(1995-2002)**
DRAFT DROP *Son of Nelson Mathews, major leaguer (1960-65)*
39. *Jon Hillis, c, Alvin (Texas) CC.
40. *Cory Simpson, 3b-of, Red Bank HS, Chattanooga, Tenn.
41. *Brad Niedermeier, rhp, Niles West HS, Niles, Ill.
42. *German Casillas, lhp, Los Angeles Harbor JC.
43. *Joe Bergen, c, Mesa (Ariz.) CC.
44. +Tom Gourdin, c, Murray (Utah) HS / New Mexico JC.
45. *Kevin Allen, rhp, Mountain View HS, Mesa, Ariz.
46. James Kohl, rhp, Rutgers University.
47. Pat Wright, of, University of Minnesota.

## MONTREAL EXPOS (14)

**1. Cliff Floyd, 1b, Thornwood HS, South Holland, Ill.—(1991-2009)**
2. Scott Pisciotta, rhp, Walton HS, Marietta, Ga.—(AA)
DRAFT DROP *Brother of Marc Pisciotta, 19th-round draft pick, Pirates (1991); major leaguer (1997-99)*
2. Rodney Pedraza, rhp, University of Texas (Choice from Dodgers as compensation for Type B tree agent Kevin Gross).—(AAA)
3. Jeff Hostetler, rhp, Cleveland State (Tenn.) JC.—(High A)
4. Jim Austin, 3b-of, Arizona State University.—(High A)
5. Mike Daniel, c, Oklahoma State University.–(AA)
**6. Derrick White, 1b, University of Oklahoma.—(1993-98)**
7. Doug O'Neill, of, Cal Poly San Luis Obispo.
8. Mark LaRosa, rhp, Louisiana State University.
9. Brett Jenkins, 2b, University of Southern California.
DRAFT DROP *Brother of Geoff Jenkins, first-round draft pick, Brewers (1995); major leaguer (1998-2007)*
**10. Brian Looney, lhp, Boston College.—(1993-95)**
**11. Mark Grudzielanek, ss, Trinidad State (Colo.) JC.—(1995-2010)**
12. *Shawn Wills, of, UCLA.
13. Khary Heidelberg, of, Princess Anne HS, Virginia Beach, Va.
14. Gary Hymel, c, Louisiana State University.
15. James Ferguson, rhp, University of San Diego.
16. Buddy Jenkins, lhp, Wake Forest University.
17. Pete Tarutis, rhp, University of Scranton (Pa.).
**18. Kirk Rueter, lhp, Murray State University.—(1993-2005)**
19. Matt Allen, c, University of Alabama.
20. Jamal Easterling, rhp, Vintage HS, Vallejo, Calif.
21. John White, of, Wagner College.
22. *Lance Calmus, rhp, Jenks (Okla.) HS.
23. Mitch Simons, 2b, Oklahoma State University.
24. *Allen Gallagher, rhp, Lower Columbia (Wash.) CC.
25. *Craig Mattson, rhp, Belvidere (Ill.) HS.
**26. +Bob Henley, c, Mobile County HS, Grand Bay, Ala. / Okaloosa-Walton (Fla.) JC.—(1998)**
27. Jim Wynne, rhp, Oklahoma City University.
28. *Darrell O'Brien, ss-2b, Ontario (Calif.) HS.
29. Nick Sproviero, rhp, University of New Haven.
30. Scott Campbell, of, University of Oklahoma.
31. *Omar Fernandez, rhp, Gulliver Prep HS, Coral Gables, Fla.
32. *Matt Copp, rhp, Green Mountain HS, Golden, Colo.
33. *Dan DeStefano, rhp, Santaluces HS, Boynton Beach Fla.
34. Scott Dennison, 2b, San Diego State University.
35. +Shane McCubbin, c, Western Oklahoma State JC.
36. *Brian Sosa, 3b, Yucaipa (Calif.) HS.
37. *Maurio Hanson, of, Spartanburg Methodist (S.C.) JC.
38. *Ryan Duffy, lhp, Wallaceburg District HS, Sombra, Ontario.
39. Darrin Paxton, thp, Wichita State University.
40. +Kevin Galart, rhp, American River (Calif.) JC.
41. *Bill Brabec, of, Glenbard East HS, Lombard, Ill.
42. *Mike Cavanaugh, c, Linfield (Ore.) College.
43. Fernando DaSilva, rhp, Champlain Regional HS, Brossard, Quebec.
44. *Vincent Guay, of, Le Cegep de Sherbrooke, Sherbrooke, Quebec.
45. *Rocky Murray, lhp, North Bend (Ore.) HS.
46. Jason Thorsteinson, 1b, Steveston HS, Richmond, B.C.
47. *Jon Valenti, ss, Highland HS, Bakersfield, Calif.
48. *Matt Splawn, rhp-1b, Waxahachie (Texas) HS.
49. *Ron Lewis, rhp, El Molino HS, Forestville, Calif.
50. *Swindell Flowers, of, Greene Central HS, Hookerton, N.C.
51. *Jeffery Sommer, 1b, Moorpark (Calif.) JC.
52. *Eduardo Payan, 3b, Fairfax HS, Los Angeles.
53. *Marlin Hamilton, 1b, Jordan HS, Long Beach, Calif.
54. *Craig Peterson, of, McMinn Central HS, Etowah, Tenn.
55. *Jody Crump, lhp, Harrison County HS, Sadieville, Ky.
56. *Russ White, ss, Nathan Hale HS, Tulsa, Okla.
57. *Daniel Chastain, c, Fort Collins (Colo.) HS.
58. *Scott Wulfing, 2b, Poly HS, Riverside, Calif.
59. *Rodney Weary, 1b, St. Louis CC-Meramec.
60. *Jason Myers, lhp, Fontana (Calif) HS.
61. *Eric White, 2b, Mount San Antonio (Calif.) JC.
62. *Michael Clayton, c, Mount San Antonio (Calif) JC.
63. *Jason Vanheerde, c, Eisenhower HS, Rialto, Calif.
64. *Jay Sissener, rhp-1b, Mohave HS, Bullhead City, Ariz.
65. *Jason Jenkins, rhp, Henry Clay HS, Lexington, Ky.
66. *James Jennings, lhp, George Washington HS, Danville, Va.
67. *Robert Hughes, of, Western Oklahoma State JC.
68. *Dan DiPace, ss, Martin County HS, Palm City, Fla.
69. *Troy Walsh, of, Bellport HS, East Patchogue, N.Y.
**70. *Scott Watkins, lhp, Oklahoma State University.—(1995)**
71. *Shawn Moore, of, University of Virginia.
DRAFT DROP *Quarterback, National Football League (1991-94)*

## NEW YORK METS (22)

1. Al Shirley, of, George Washington HS, Danville, Va. (Choice from Dodgers as compensation for

Type A free agent Darryl Strawberry).—(AA)
1. (Choice to Cardinals as compensation for Type B free agent Vince Coleman)
**1. Bobby J. Jones, rhp, Fresno State University** (Supplemental choice—36th—as compensation for Strawberry).**—(1993-2002)**
**2. Bill Pulsipher, lhp, Fairfax (Va.) HS.—(1995-2005)**
**2. Marc Kroon, rhp, Shadow Mountain HS, Phoenix** (Supplemental choice—72nd—as compensation for Type C free agent Pat Tabler).**—(1995-2004)**
3. Jeff Kiraly, 1b, La Cueva HS, Albuquerque, N.M.—(Low A)
**4. Erik Hiljus, rhp, Canyon HS, Santa Clarita, Calif.—(1999-2002)**
5. Jared Osentowski, 3b, Kearney (Neb.) HS.—(Low A)
6. Eric Reichenbach, rhp, St. John's University.
7. Frank Jacobs, 1b, University of Notre Dame.
8. Randy Curtis, of, Riverside (Calif.) CC.
9. Dave Swanson, lhp, Berlin HS, Kensington, Conn.
10. Dwight Robinson, 3b, Middle Tennessee State University.
11. Todd Fiegel, lhp, University of Virginia.
**12. Jason Jacome, lhp, Pima (Ariz.) CC.—(1994-98)**
13. Tony Tijerina, c, Texas Tech.
14. Jeff Henderson, rhp, Golden West (Calif.) JC.
15. *Chris Petrocella, rhp, Fort Scott (Kan.) CC.
16. Donald White, of, Southeastern (Ill.) CC.
**17. Joe Crawford, lhp, Kent State University.—(1997)**
18. Tyson Young, 1b, Hardin Jefferson HS, Kountze, Texas.
19. *James White, of, Florida HS, Tallahassee, Fla.
20. Andrew Cotner, lhp, Illinois State University.
21. Greg Beals, c, Kent State University.
DRAFT DROP *Baseball coach, Ball State (2003-10); baseball coach, Ohio State (2011-15)*
22. Ervin Collier, rhp, County Central HS, New Madrid, Mo.
23. Cliff Jones, lhp, Hawaii Pacific University.
24. James McCready, rhp, Bentley (Mass.) College.
25. *Kyle Harris, of, Ridgecrest HS, Paragould, Ark.
26. *Todd Jackson, rhp, Arizona Western JC.
27. Ed Hokhanson, rhp, Joliet (Ill.) JC.
28. Mark Wipf, of, San Marcos HS, Santa Barbara, Calif.
**29. *Mark Lukasiewicz, lhp, Secaucus (N.J.) HS.—(2001-02)**
DRAFT DROP *First-round draft pick (41st overall), Blue Jays (1993)*
30. Chris George, lhp, Mississippi State University.
31. *Jerry Hiraldo, of, Gilberto Concepcion De Gracia HS, Carolina, P.R.
32. Brett Rossler, c-3b, Pearl River (Miss.) JC.
33. *Owen Johnson, rhp, St. Pius X HS, Houston.
34. *Travis Ryan, ss-2b, Labette (Kan.) CC.
35. *Robert Cardera, lhp, Chabot (Calif.) JC.
36. *Armando Fernandez, of, Hawthorne (Calif.) HS.
37. *Brad Talley, rhp, Jefferson Davis HS, Montgomery, Ala.
38. *Chris Prater, rhp, Three Rivers (Mo.) CC.
39. *Jesus Maldonado, rhp, Roosevelt HS, San Antonio, Texas.
40. *Robert Conway, rhp, Northwestern State University.
41. *Richard Towers, rhp, Paris (Texas) HS.
42. +Kenneth Bradley, ss, Dollarway HS, Pine Bluff, Ark. / Connors State (Okla.) JC.
43. *Brandon Ford, of, Golden West HS, Visalia, Calif.
**44. +Jason Isringhausen, rhp, Lewis & Clark (Ill.) JC.—(1995-2012)**
45. +Eric Harris, 1b, Laney (Calif.) JC.
46. *Brian Fassbender, rhp, West HS, Appleton, Wis.
47. *Trevor Blake, of, Greenway HS, Glendale, Ariz.
48. *Todd Abbott, rhp, North Little Rock (Ark.) HS.
49. *Cory Buck, c, Neligh-Oakdale HS, Oakdale, Neb.
50. *Ken Copeland, of, Otero (Colo.) JC.
51. *Anthony Richardson, 1b, Kishwaukee (Ill.) JC.

## NEW YORK YANKEES (1)

1. Brien Taylor, lhp, East Carteret HS, Beaufort, N.C.—(AA)
2. (Choice to Royals as compensation for Type A free agent Steve Farr)
3. Tim Flannelly, 3b, University of Michigan.—(AA)
3. Mark Hubbard, rhp-of, University of South Florida (Choice from Giants as compensation for Type B free agent Dave Righetti).—(AA)
4. Marc Gipner, c, Dunedin (Fla.) HS.—(Low A)
**5. Lyle Mouton, of, Louisiana State University.—(1995-2001)**
6. Eric Knowles, ss, St. Brenden HS, Miami.
7. Tommy Carter, lhp, Auburn University.
8. Grant Sullivan, thp, University of Mississippi.
**9. Keith Garagozzo, lhp, University of Delaware.—(1994)**
10. *Mike Muncy, ss, Camarillo (Calif.) HS.
11. Jason Wuerch, of, Kingsville HS, Leamington, Ontario.
12. Bert Inman, rhp, McLennan (Texas) CC.
13. Andy Albrecht, of, Auburn University.
14. Ben Short, rhp, University of Alabama.
15. Steven Munda, rhp, University of Illinois.
16. Andy Croghan, rhp, Long Beach State University.
**17. *Brad Rigby, rhp, Lake Brantley HS, Longwood, Fla.—(1997-2000)**
18. Billy Coleman, rhp, Northwood (Texas) Institute.
19. Roger Burnett, ss, Stanford University.
20. Brian Lewis, of, Virginia HS, Bristol, Va.
21. Scott Gully, rhp, Elon College.
22. *Scott Baldwin, lhp, Lewis-Clark State (Idaho) College.
23. Steve Anderson, ss, San Jose State University.
24. John Quintell, c, Cal State Sacramento.
25. *Terry Harvey, rhp, Dacula (Ga.) HS.
26. Dennis Burbank, rhp, Oklahoma State University.
27. Whitney Floren, rhp, University of South Florida.
28. Chris Heaps, ss, Gadsden State (Ala.) CC.
**29. *Fred Rath, rhp, Jefferson HS, Tampa.—(1998)**
DRAFT DROP *Son of Fred Rath, major leaguer (1968-69)*
30. *Michael Beresh, rhp, Cardinal Gibbons HS, Lighthouse Point, Fla.
31. +Charlie Brown, rhp, John Carroll HS, Fort Pierce, Fla. / Indian River (Fla.) JC.
32. *Arnaldo Espada, of, Colegio University HS, Coamo, P.R.
33. *Todd Harrell, rhp, Gulf Coast (Fla.) CC.
34. *Matt Parker, rhp, Jesuit HS, Temple Terrace, Fla.
35. Steve Livesey, 3b-1b, Davidson College.
36. *Marty Winchester, 1b, Long Beach (Calif.) CC.
37. *Ron Hollis, ss-rhp, Brighton HS, South Lyon, Mich.
38. *Paul Reynolds, 1b, East Lake HS, Tarpon Springs, Fla.
39. +David Renteria, ss, Riverside (Calif.) CC.
40. *Major Hudson, of, St. John's HS, Darlington, S.C.
41. *Chris Shafer, rhp, St. Petersburg (Fla.) HS.
42. *Will Green, 1b-3b, Chipola (Fla.) JC.
43. *Chris Plonk, rhp, Manatee (Fla.) JC.
44. *Nick Skuse, rhp, West Valley (Calif.) JC.
**45. *Bronson Heflin, rhp, Central Florida CC.—(1996)**
46. *William Lawrence, lhp, Pensacola (Fla.) JC.
47. *Chad Plonk, rhp, Manatee (Fla.) JC.
48. *Jason Flexen, of, Chabot (Calif.) JC.
49. *Matt Friedman, rhp, Eastern Hills HS, Fort Worth, Texas.
50. *Danny Larivee, of, Rio Americano HS, Sacramento, Calif.
51. *Jon Boddy, 1b-3b, Woodham HS, Pensacola, Fla.
52. *Michael Cutler, rhp, Orange Coast (Calif.) JC.
53. *Eric Taylor, lhp, St. Petersburg (Fla.) JC.
54. *Jason Crum, rhp, Indian River (Fla.) CC.
55. *Marco Contreras, rhp, Citrus (Calif.) JC.
56. *Mark Dean, ss, Florida CC.
57. *Michael Caldwell, rhp, Columbia Falls (Mon.) HS.
58. *Lawrence Markham, 2b, Okeechobee (Fla.) HS.
59. *Tim Kester, rhp, Miami-Dade CC South.
60. *Kelvin Washington, ss, Westwood HS, Fort Pierce, Fla.
61. *David Vance, of, Indian River (Fla.) CC.
62. *Scott Sorenson, rhp, Palm Beach Lakes HS, West Palm Beach, Fla.
63. *Jason Birmingham, ss, St. Patricks's HS, Sarnia, Ontario.
64. *Rob Berryman, rhp, York HS, Yorktown, Va.
65. *Jeremy Lewis, c, Jefferson HS, Cedar Rapids, Iowa.
66. *Alain Fernandez, of, Arroyo HS, San Lorenzo, Calif.
67. +Kory Kiper, ss, Wellington HS, West Palm Beach, Fla. / Indian River (Fla.) JC.
68. *Michael McKenna, rhp, Kishwaukee (Ill.) JC.
69. *Mariano Borges, of, Baronquita HS, Arecibo, P.R.
70. *Bert Martinez, 1b-c, Marian HS, Chula Vista, Calif.
71. *Jesse Kerr, rhp, Clear Lake HS, Houston.
72. +Howard Ferguson, rhp, St. Clair (Mich.) CC.
73. *Chris Targac, rhp, Sacred Heart HS, Weimer, Texas.
74. *Joel Irvine, c, Des Moines Area (Iowa) CC.
75. *Brent Hall, ss, Willow Creek HS, Claresholm, Alberta.
76. *Tim Borys, lhp, Princess Margaret HS, Surrey, B.C.
77. *Robert Nicholson, of, William Aberhart HS, Calgary, Alberta.
78. *Brandon Ford, rhp, John Carroll HS, Vero Beach, Fla.
79. *Chris Moock, 3b, Louisiana State University.
DRAFT DROP *Son of Joe Moock, major leaguer (1967)*
80. *Rex Pritchard, 3b, Whittier Christian HS, Fullerton, Calif.

## OAKLAND ATHLETICS (26)

**1. Brent Gates, ss, University of Minnesota.—(1993-99)**
1. Mike Rossiter, rhp, Burroughs HS, Burbank, Calif. (Supplemental choice–38th–as compensation for Type A free agent WIllie McGee).—(AAA)
**2. Mike Neill, of, Villanova University** (Choice from Giants as compensation for Type A free agent Willie McGee).**—(1998)**
2. Russ Brock, rhp, University of Michigan.—(AAA)
3. Joel Wolfe, of, UCLA.—(AAA)
**4. Steve Wojciechowski, lhp, St. Xavjer (Ill.) College.—(1995-97)**
5. Tim Smith, rhp, Ohio State University.—(AAA)
6. Tim Doyle, lhp, Cal State Sacramento.
7. Ricky Kimball, rhp, Florida State University.
**8. Scott Sheldon, ss, University of Houston.—(1997-2001)**
**9. Damon Mashore, of, University of Arizona.—(1996-98)**
DRAFT DROP *Son of Clyde Mashore, major leaguer (1969-73) • Brother of Justin Mashore, third-round draft pick, Tigers (1991)*
10. Zach Sawyer, rhp, Clinton (Mass.) HS.
**11. Jason Wood, ss, Fresno State University.—(1998-2008)**
**12. Miguel Jimenez, rhp, Fordham University.—(1993-94)**
13. Jeff Light, c-rhp, Stanford University.
**14. *Darrell May, lhp, Sacramento (Calif.) CC.—(1995-2005)**
**15. Brent Cookson, of, Long Beach State University.—(1995-99)**
16. Kurt Endebrock, 2b, Southern Illinois University.
17. Chris Thomson, 1b, Texas Christian University.
18. Rick Norton, 3b, University of Kentucky.
19. *James Henderson, rhp, Purdue University.
20. *Ivan Montane, rhp, Killian HS, Miami.
21. Todd Ingram, rhp, University of Arizona.
22. *William Kingsbury, rhp, Villanova University.
23. *Sean Gavaghan, rhp, University of Richmond.
**24. George Williams, 3b, University of Texas-Pan American.—(1995-2000)**
25. Daniel Nerat, rhp, William Penn (Iowa) College.
26. Brian McArn, of, University of Nebraska.
27. Robert Leary, 1b, Louisburg (N.C.) JC.
28. Greg Smock, lhp, Austin Peay State University.
29. Joe Misa, rhp, Lewis-Clark State (Idaho) College.
30. Brad Stowell, rhp, The Citadel.
31. *Craig Wagner, of-1b, Broken Arrow (Okla.) HS.
32. Michael Evans, rhp, St. Leo (Fla.) College.
33. Michael Thees, rhp, Carson-Newman (Tenn.) College.
34. Brad Parker, 3b, Auburn University.
35. Keith Millay, rhp, Gulf Coast (Fla.) CC.
36. Dane Walker, of, Portland State University.
37. Brandon Smith, c, Roswell (Ga.) HS.
38. Sean Scott, of, Pace (N.Y.) University.
39. Tom Myers, lhp, UC Santa Barbara.
40. Raymond Sutch, rhp, James Madison University.
41. Steven Shoemaker, rhp, Muscatine (Iowa) JC.
42. Mark Buckler, of, University of Vermont.
43. *William Bishop, c, Mississippi Gulf Coast JC.
44. Tod Frick, c, Florida Southern College.
45. *Leland McAfee, of, Mira Mesa HS, San Diego.
46. *Tom Hamilton, of, Indian River (Fla.) CC.
47. *Clinton Koppe, rhp, Brazoswood HS, Lake Jackson, Texas.
48. *David Boone, of, Hickory (N.C.) HS.
49. *Antonio Fant, of, El Cerrito HS, Richmond, Calif.
50. *Rick Braisted, of, Dixie Hollins HS, St. Petersburg, Fla.
51. *William Cornish, rhp, Northeast Lauderdale HS, Merion, Miss.
52. *Donald Aslasken, of, San Jacinto (Texas) JC.
53. *Carlos James, of, Seminole (Okla.) JC.
54. +Adrian Yots, 1b-3b, Columbia State (Tenn.) CC.
55. *Frank Campbell, 1b-of, Pasadena (Calif.) CC.
56. *Jim Bonds, rhp-c, UCLA.

## PHILADELPHIA PHILLIES (10)

**1. Tyler Green, rhp, Wichita State University.—(1993-98)**
DRAFT DROP *Son of Charlie Green, quarterback, National Football League (1966)*
**2. Kevin Stocker, ss, University of Washington.—(1993-2000)**
3. Ronnie Allen, rhp, Texas A&M University.-(AAA)
**4. Gene Schall, of, Villanova University.—(1995-96)**
5. *Steve Verduzco, ss, Bellarmine Prep HS, Scotts Valley, Calif.—(AA)
DRAFT DROP *Attended Notre Dame; re-drafted by Astros, 1993 (4th round)*
6. Tommy Eason, c, East Carolina University.
7. Dave Tokheim, of, UCLA.
8. Dave Hayden, ss, University of Tennessee.
9. Phil Geisler, of, University of Portland.
**10. Mike Grace, rhp, Bradley University.—(1995-99)**
11. Patrick Ruth, c, Cal State Stanislaus.
12. John Mallee, ss, University of Illinois-Chicago.
13. Brent Bell, 1b-3b, St. John Bosco HS, Downey, Calif.
14. *Andrew Martin, 3b-1b, The Master's (Calif.) College.
15. *Demond Thompkins, of, Elsenhower HS, Rialto, Calif.
16. Pat Bojcun, rhp, Central Michigan University.
17. Joe Jelinek, 2b, Maple Woods (Mo.) CC.
**18. *Bobby Higginson, of, Temple University.—(1995-2005)**
19. John Salamon, rhp, Allegheny (Pa.) CC.
20. Dom DeSantis, rhp, University of New Orleans.
21. Greg Brown, rhp, University of Tennessee.
22. Craig Holman, rhp, Jacksonville State University.
23. Tom Vilet, of, University of Wisconsin.
24. *Chad Sweitzer, rhp, American River (Calif.) JC.
25. *Jerry Whittaker, of, Poly HS, Long Beach, Calif.
26. Thane Page, rhp, Crowder (Mo.) JC.
27. Andrew Sallee, 1b, Claremont-McKenna (Calif.) College.
**28. *Curtis Schmidt, rhp, University of Kansas.—(1995)**
29. +Tim Pugh, lhp, Cecil (Md.) CC.
30. John Whisonant, lhp, U.S. International (Calif.) University.
31. Glenn Nevill, lhp, Baylor University.
32. *Allan Hebbert, rhp, Alta Loma (Calif.) HS.
33. Joel Gilmore, rhp, Dallas Baptist University.
34. *Aaron Edwards, of, Ontario (Calif.) HS.
35. Dean Hopp, c, Northeastern Oklahoma A&M JC.
36. *Paul Reynolds, 3b, Snowflake (Ariz.) HS.
37. Carlton Hardy, 3b-rhp, Grambling State University.
DRAFT DROP *Baseball coach, Savannah State (2006-15)*
38. *Dan Vetter, of, Del Campo HS, Fair Oaks, Calif.
39. Wayne Johnson, of, Compton (Calif.) CC.
40. *Tom Afenir, c, Palomar (Calif.) JC.
DRAFT DROP *Brother of Troy Afenir, major leaguer (1987-92)*
41. Jason Urbanek, 2b, Westby HS, Coon Valley, Wis.
42. Bruce Smolen, 3b, Bradley University.
43. Craig Billeci, 1b, St. Mary's (Calif.) College.
44. *Nathan LaDuke, of, Arizona State University.
DRAFT DROP *11th-round draft pick, Phoenix Cardinals/ National Football League (1991)*
45. *James Gwaltney, lhp, Rancho Santiago (Calif.) JC.

46. *John Lockett, of, Jordan HS, Long Beach, Calif.
47. *Don Hill, rhp, Westlake HS, Westlake Village, Calif.
48. Michael Merthie, of, Lake Mary HS, Sanford, Fla.
49. *Marion McKinney, 3b, Poly HS, Sun Valley, Calif.
50. *Chris Lee, rhp, Tooele (Utah) HS.
51. *Chris Witt, rhp, Roger Bacon HS, Cincinnati.
52. *Bobby Waits, lhp, Fresno (Calif.) CC.
53. *Michael White, 2b, Anderson (Calif.) HS.
54. *Alex Figueroa, c, Hawthorne (Calif.) HS.

## PITTSBURGH PIRATES (24)

1. Jon Farrell, c-of, Florida CC-Jacksonville.—(AA)
2. Dave Doorneweerd, rhp, Ridgewood HS, Port Richey, Fla.—(AA)
2. Dan Jones, rhp, Northwestern University (Supplemental choice—73rd—as compensation for Type C free agent Sid Bream).—(AA)
**3. Matt Ruebel, lhp, University of Oklahoma.—(1996-98)**
4. Benjamin Boka, c, Barrington (Ill.) HS.—(AAA)
5. Marty Neff, of, University of Oklahoma.—(AA)
6. *Mickey Kerns, of, University of Alabama.
**7. Tony Womack, ss, Guilford (N.C.) College.—(1993-2006)**
8. Matt Pontbriant, lhp, Brevard (Fla.) CC.
9. Deon Danner, lhp, University of North Carolina-Charlotte.
**10. *Chance Sanford, ss-2b, San Jacinto (Texas) JC.—(1998-99)**
11. Jason Bullard, rhp, Texas A&M University.
12. *Stacy Hollins, rhp, San Jacinto (Texas) JC.
DRAFT DROP *Brother of Jessie Hollins, major leaguer (1992)*
13. Chris Edmondson, 3b, Alcorn Central HS, Corinth, Miss.
14. Jacob Payne, c, Don Lugo HS, Ontario, Calif.
**15. *Jason McDonald, of, Sacramento (Calif.) CC.—(1997-2000)**
16. Dan Gernand, rhp, Arizona Western JC.
17. Todd Schroeder, 1b, Illinois State University.
18. +Brian Pelka, rhp, Allegheny (Pa.) CC.
**19. Marc Pisciotta, rhp, Georgia Tech.—(1997-99)**
DRAFT DROP *Brother of Scott Pisciotta, second-round draft pick, Expos (1991)*
20. Don Garvey, 2b, University of Wisconsin-Oshkosh.
21. Victor Bogan, of, Linn-Benton (Ore.) CC.
22. Mike Maguire, lhp, Northeastern University.
23. Sean Evans, rhp, University of South Carolina.
24. *Ivory Jones, of, Vallejo (Calif.) HS.
25. Ken Fairfax, rhp, Geibel HS, Uniontown, Pa.
26. *Tim Merrick, of, University of South Florida.
27. Michael Taylor, lhp, Admiral King HS, Lorain, Ohio.
28. James Martin, lhp, Eastern Michigan University.
29. Ron Ducksworth, ss, Mississippi Gulf Coast JC.
30. Craig Shotton, of, Florida Atlantic University.
31. *Ricardo Hermida, rhp, Coral Park HS, Miami.
32. Michael Teich, lhp, Cal State Sacramento.
33. *Felix Merced, ss, Florida Air Academy, Melbourne, Fla.
34. Marcus Ponder, of, South Georgia CC.
35. *Jason Green, rhp, Pinole Valley HS, Hercules, Calif.
36. *Neil James, 3b, Lake Mary HS, Altamonte Springs, Fla.
37. Jim Krevokuch, 3b, Old Dominion University.
38. *Steve Shoemaker, rhp, Phoenixville (Pa.) HS.
**39. *Dustin Hermanson, rhp, Kenton Ridge HS, Springfield, Ohio.—(1995-2006)**
DRAFT DROP *First-round draft pick (3rd overall), Padres (1994); first player from 1994 draft to reach majors (May 8, 1995)*
40. *Colin Hinds, of, Hamilton HS, Los Angeles.
41. *Todd Boulanger, lhp, Lord Tweedsmuir HS, Surrey, B.C.
42. *Terry Mitchum, 1b, Fairfield (Ohio) HS.
43. *Andrew Noffke, rhp, Northwestern HS, Springfield, Ohio.
44. *Jason Moore, c, Sacramento (Calif.) CC.
45. Gene Knapp, lhp, Osceola HS, Kissimmee, Fla.
46. *Brian Brewer, lhp, Armijo HS, Fairfield, Calif.
47. Jeff Leatherman, 1b, Auburn University.
48. *Scott May, c, Manatee HS, Bradenton, Fla.
DRAFT DROP *Grandson of Pinky May, major leaguer (1939-43) • Son of Milt May, major leaguer (1970-84)*
49. Ken Bonifay, 1b-of, Georgia Tech.
50. Clyde Earl, ss, Chicago State University.
51. *Kenneth Vike, rhp, DeSoto (Texas) HS.
52. O'Brien Cunningham, of, Lancaster (S.C.) HS.
DRAFT DROP *Brother of Earl Cunningham, first-round draft pick, Cubs (1989)*
53. Trace Ragland, of, Belmont College.
54. *Ryan Huffman, of, Clear Lake HS, Houston.
55. *Terrance Goree, 2b, Carthage (Texas) HS.
**56. *Jim Brower, rhp, Minnetonka (Minn.) HS.—(1999-2007)**
**57. *Paul Wilson, rhp, Boone HS, Orlando, Fla.—(1996-2005)**
DRAFT DROP *First overall draft pick, Mets (1994)*
58. *Scott Krause, ss, North HS, Willowick, Ohio.

## ST. LOUIS CARDINALS (4)

**1. Dmitri Young, 3b-of, Rio Mesa HS, Oxnard, Calif.—(1996-2008)**
DRAFT DROP *Brother of Delmon Young, first overall draft pick, Devil Rays (2003); major leaguer (2006-15)*
1. **Allen Watson, lhp, New York Tech** (Choice from Blue Jays as compensation for Type A free agent Ken Dayley).**—(1993-2000)**
1. **Brian Barber, rhp, Dr. Phillips HS, Orlando, Fla.** (Choice from Mets as compensation for Type B free agent Vince Coleman).**—(1995-99)**
1. Tom McKinnon, rhp, Jordan HS, Long Beach, Calif. (Supplemental choice—28th—as compensation for Type A free agent Terry Pendleton).—(High A)
1. Dan Cholowsky, 3b, University of California (Supplemental choice—39th—as compensation for Dayley).—(AAA)
2. Eddie Williams, c, Edison HS, Miami (Choice from Braves as compensation for Pendleton).—(High A)
2. (Choice to Astros as compensation for Type B free agent Juan Agosto)
3. Basil Shabazz, of, Pine Bluff (Ark.) HS.—(AA)
4. Andy Bruce, 3b, Georgia Tech.—(AA)
**5. Da Rond Stovall, of, Althoff HS, East St. Louis, Ill.—(1998)**
**6. John Mabry, of, West Chester (Pa.) University.—(1994-2007)**
**7. Doug Creek, lhp, Georgia Tech.—(1995-2005)**
DRAFT DROP *Brother of Ryan Creek, 42nd-round draft pick, Orioles (1991)*
8. Antoine Henry, of, Clairemont HS, San Diego.
9. Dennis Slininger, rhp, Largo (Fla.) HS.
**10. Allen Battle, of, University of South Alabama.—(1995-96)**
**11. Mike Difelice, c, University of Tennessee.—(1996-2008)**
12. Michael Badorek, rhp, Olivet Nazarene (Ill.) University.
13. Scott Simmons, lhp, Southwest Missouri State University.
**14. Mike Busby, rhp, Banning HS, Wilmington, Calif.—(1996-99)**
15. Victor Llanos, 3b, Gilberto Concepcion de Gracia HS, Carolina, P.R.
16. Kevin Lucero, lhp, Florida International University.
17. Ron Warner, ss, University of Wyoming.
18. Darrel Deak, 2b, Loyola Marymount University.
19. *Terrence McClain, of, Cape HS, Cincinnati.
20. Jason Hisey, rhp, University of Arizona.
21. *Jeff Meszar, ss, Butler County (Kan.) CC.
22. Scott Longaker, rhp, UC Santa Barbara.
23. Don Slattery, 1b, JC of Southern Idaho.
**24. John Frascatore, rhp, C.W. Post (N.Y.) College.—(1994-2001)**
25. Garrett Blanton, of, Florida State University.
**26. Rigo Beltran, lhp-1b, University of Wyoming.—(1997-2004)**
27. Rick Mediavilla, of, Loyola Marymount University.
28. Robert Strehlow, of-2b, Basic HS, Henderson, Nev.
29. Tim DeGrasse, rhp, UC Santa Barbara.
30. Curt Callicot, 3b, Riverside (Calif.) CC.
31. Larry Lucchetti, rhp, University of Nevada-Las Vegas.
32. Michael Cantu, 1b, Tarleton State (Texas) University.
33. Antonio Boone, rhp, Norfolk State University.
34. John O'Brien, 1b, Oral Roberts University.
35. *Dan Heideman, rhp, Florida CC.
36. Alan Robinson, of, Widener (Pa.) University.
37. Chris Vlasis, of-3b, Virginia Commonwealth University.
38. Paul Romanoli, lhp, Memphis State University.
39. Jerry Santos, rhp, Florida International University.
40. Eric Miller, rhp, JC of Southern Idaho.
41. Steven Jones, rhp, Memphis State University.
42. Steve Cerio, c, University of Nevada-Las Vegas.
43. David Chasin, of, St. Louis CC-Meramec.
44. *Earnest Fisher, rhp, Rider College.
45. Chad Smith, rhp, Lynchburg (Va.) College.
46. Jeff Dillman, rhp, Rider College.
47. Duffy Guyton, rhp, Dallas Baptist University.
48. Doug Radziewicz, 1b, University of Georgia.
49. Clint Davis, rhp, Dallas Baptist University.
50. Mike Eicher, of, University of Wyoming.
51. Curtis Underwood, 1b, Central State (Okla.) University.
52. Dirk Lindauer, rhp, Southwest Missouri State University.
53. Chad Sumner, 3b-2b, Georgia Southern University.
54. Keith Black, 2b, Troy State University.
55. Gary Taylor, of, University of Maine.
56. *Jeff Twist, c, Highland HS, Bakersfield, Calif.
57. *Aaron Gerteisen, of, Leon HS, Tallahassee, Fla.
58. *Colby Neal, rhp, North Mecklenburg HS, Davidson, N.C.
59. *Jaime Sanjurjo, of, Pedro Falu HS, Rio Grande, P.R.
60. *Shawn Lopez, of, Fort Scott (Kan.) CC.
61. Ray Davis, rhp, Palatka (Fla.) HS.
62. *Daniel Rude, rhp, Skyview HS, Billings, Mon.
63. *Hank Crosby, 3b-2b, Kanab (Utah) HS.
64. *Jason Shanahan, 3b, Sentinel HS, Missoula, Mon.
65. *Sean Centeno, 3b, Kelly Walsh HS, Casper, Wyo.
66. *Paul Williams, lhp, Mountain Home (Idaho) HS.
67. *Bryan Donnelly, rhp, St. Louis CC-Meramec.

## SAN DIEGO PADRES (8)

**1. Joey Hamilton, rhp, Georgia Southern University.—(1994-2003)**
1. Greg Anthony, rhp-of, Tavares (Fla.) HS (Supplemental choice—31st—as compensation for Type A free agent Jack Clark).—(Low A)
2. Jon Barnes, rhp, Lancaster (S.C.) HS.—(AA)
**3. *Antone Williamson, 3b, Torrance (Calif.) HS.—(1997)**
DRAFT DROP *Attended Arizona State; re-drafted by Brewers, 1994 (1st round)*
**4. Sean Mulligan, c, University of Illinois.—(1996)**
**5. Joey Long, lhp, Kent State University.—(1997)**
6. Mike Grohs, rhp, Old Dominion University.
**7. Homer Bush, ss, East St. Louis (Ill.) HS.—(1997-2004)**
8. Manny Cora, ss, Pedro Arbizu HS, Levittown, P.R.
9. Craig Hanson, rhp, Triton (Ill.) JC.
10. John Roberts, of, Watson Chapel HS, Pine Bluff, Ark.
11. Scott Pugh, 1b, University of Texas.
12. Scott Eggleston, rhp, Maple Woods (Mo.) CC.
13. Reginald Stewart, of, Fernandina Beach HS, Yulee, Fla.
14. Derek Valenzuela, c, St. John Bosco HS, Anaheim, Calif.
**15. *Justin Atchley, lhp, Sedro Wooley (Wash.) HS.—(2001)**
16. Alex Rivera, of, Benjamin Harrison HS, Cayey, P.R.
17. Billy Hall, 2b, Wichita State University.
18. Clint Compton, rhp, Seminole (Okia.) JC.
**19. Charlie Greene, c, Miami-Dade CC South.—(1996-2000)**
20. Paul Thompson, 1b, Blinn (Texas) JC.
21. *Michael Weston, lhp, Lower Richland HS, Eastover, S.C.
22. Joe Grygiel, lhp, University of Lowell (Mass.).
23. Dwight Wyatt, of, Halifax County HS, Scottsburg, Va.
24. +Darrell White, rhp, Bolton HS, Alexandria, La. / Texarkana (Texas) JC.
25. John Biancamano, 3b, Fairleigh Dickinson University.
26. *Alex Andreopoulos, c, Harbor Collegiate Institute, Toronto.
27. Derek Vaughn, of, Santa Monica (Calif.) JC.
28. *Greg Kennedy, lhp, Meridian (Miss.) CC.
**29. *Bryan Ward, lhp, Morris (N.J.) CC.—(1998-2000)**
30. +Michael Hermanson, rhp, Kishwaukee (Ill.) JC.
31. Tim Hall, c, Cumberland (Tenn.) University.
32. *James Garcia, of, San Bernardino Valley (Calif.) JC.
33. Randall Fjeld, rhp, Liberty HS, Renton, Wash.
34. *Sandy McKinnon, of, Coffee HS, Nicholls, Ga.
35. Brian D'Amato, rhp, Pilgrim HS, Warwick, R.I.
36. David Lebak, of, Trenton State (N.J.) College.
37. *Matt Bentke, of, Brenham (Texas) HS.
**38. Rich Loiselle, rhp, Odessa (Texas) JC.—(1996-2001)**
39. *Casey Kirkman, rhp, Exeter (Calif.) HS.
40. Joe Frias, 2b, Oklahoma City University.
**41. *John Dettmer, rhp, University of Missouri.—(1994-95)**
42. Mel Edwards, 2b-1b, Rider College.
43. Arthur Vazquez, rhp, Miami-Dade CC North.
44. Ralph Perez, of, Southwest HS, Miami.
45. Kevin Johnson, c, Mayville State (N.D.) University.
46. +Kyle White, 1b, Laney (Calif.) JC.
47. *Leon Bertsch, rhp, Morris (N.J.) CC.
48. Kyle Moody, 2b, University of Texas.
49. *Scott Shores, of, Phoenix JC.
50. Jerrold Rountree, of, UC Santa Barbara.
51. *Torri Allen, of, John Jay HS, San Antonio.
52. *Matthew Spade, rhp, Boyertown (Pa.) HS.
53. *Danan Hughes, of, University of Iowa.
DRAFT DROP *Wide receiver, National Football League (1993-98)*
54. Tim Goins, c, St. Mary's (Texas) University.
55. Jerry Creer, 2b, East St. Louis (Ill.) HS.
56. John Nash, of, Princeton University.
57. Jerry Burns, rhp, Napa Valley (Calif.) JC.

## SAN FRANCISCO GIANTS (16)

1. (Choice to Blue Jays as compensation for Type A free agent Bud Black)
1. Steve Whitaker, lhp, Long Beach State University (Supplemental choice—33rd—as compensation for Type A free agent Brett Butler).—(AAA)
2. (Choice to Athletics as compensation for Type A free agent Willie McGee)
3. (Choice to Yankees as compensation for Type B free agent Dave Righetti)
4. Chris Gambs, rhp, Monte Vista HS, Danville, Calif.—(AA)
5. William Vanlandingham, rhp, University of Kentucky.—(1994-97)
6. D.J. Thielen, 3b, Mount Hood (Ore.) CC.
7. Julian Frazier, of, Smackover (Ark.) HS.
**8. Dax Jones, of, Creighton University.—(1996)**
9. Doug Vanderweele, rhp, University of Nevada-Las Vegas.
10. Jeff Martin, rhp, Hazen HS, Renton, Wash.
11. *Tim Kraus, rhp, Colerain HS, Cincinnati.
12. Tim Luther, rhp, Missouri Southern State University.
13. Marcial Gornez, rhp, Columbus HS, Hialeah, Fla.
14. Ray Jackson, of, University of Tennessee.
15. Randy Swank, ss, American River (Calif.) JC.
16. *David Rosato, ss, South HS, Torrance, Calif.
**17. Frank Charles, c-of, Cal State Fullerton.—(2000)**
18. Kevin Brown, rhp, North Salem HS, Salem, Ore.
19. Matt Brewer, of, Southwest Missouri State University.
20. Eric Stonecipher, rhp, University of Kansas.
**21. *George Arias, 3b, Pima (Ariz.) CC.—(1996-99)**
22. *Gary Phillips, 3b, Motlow State (Tenn.) CC.
**23. *Craig Wilson, ss, Kansas State University.—(1998-2000)**
24. Charles Peysar, rhp, Atascadero (Calif.) HS.
25. Tim Flores, 2b, Grand Canyon University.
26. Hiram Ramirez, c, Franklin D. Roosevelt HS,

Ensenada, P.R.
27. Jarod Juelsgaard, rhp, Iowa State University.
28. Derek Dana, c, University of Massachusetts.
29. Al Benavides, rhp, University of Houston.
30. Rich Hyde, rhp, University of Illinois.
31. Thurman Williams, of, Chatsworth (Calif.) HS.
32. Adam Benschoter, c, Siena Heights (Mich.) College.
33. Ken Feist, of, Portland State University.
34. +Juan Johnson, ss, Thomas Stone HS, Waldorf, Md. / Essex (Md.) JC.
35. Rico Bolivar, 1b-of, Umpqua (Ore.) CC.
36. Vince Towns, rhp, Suitland HS, Forestville, Md.
37. +Herbert Baxter, lhp, Spartanburg Methodist (S.C.) JC.
38. *John Fullford, of, Douglas County HS, Castle Rock, Colo.
39. *Darvin Traylor, of, Riverside (Calif.) CC.
40. Scott Stroth, rhp, Kansas State University.
41. Don Montgomery, c, Lewis-Clark State (Idaho) College.
42. *Maurice Taylor, of, Thornwood HS, Calumet City, Ill.
43. *J.T. Messick, ss, Union HS, Tulsa, Okla.
44. Brett McGonnigal, of, University of Maryland.
45. Darren Wittcke, rhp, Portland State University.
46. Dan Calcagno, c, Sonoma State (Calif.) University.
47. *Chris Kelly, rhp, University of Tennessee.
48. *Noe Najera, lhp, Cypress (Calif.) JC.
49. *Leron Golden, of, American River (Calif.) JC.
50. *Stephen Gurtner, rhp, Butler County (Kan.) CC.
51. *Faruq Darcuiel, of, Hoover HS, Fresno, Calif.
52. *Scott Boyle, lhp, San Marin HS, Novato, Calif.
**53. Ken Grundt, lhp, Missouri Southern State University.—(1996-97)**
54. Jeff Locklear, lhp, Pembroke State (N.C.) University.
55. Tim Casper, 2b, Missouri Southern State University.
56. Kevin Bellomo, of, Western Carolina University.
57. *Craig Gee, rhp, Fontana HS, Bloomington, Calif.
58. Ronald Foster, 3b, Indian Hills (Iowa) CC.
59. *Lorenzo Hidalgo, rhp, San Joaquin Delta (Calif.) JC.
60. Ken Henderson, of, San Jose State University.
61. *Jason Beeler, rhp, Farmington (Ark.) HS.
62. *Chad Breashears, of, Malvern HS, Donaldson, Ark.
63. *Douglas Cecil, lhp, Fresno (Calif.) HS.
64. *Anthony Lacy, of, Sacramento (Calif.) CC.
65. *Shawn Everett, of, Cosumnes River (Calif.) JC.
66. *Craig Marcelin, c, St. Louis CC-Forest Park.
67. *Matthew Meier, 2b-ss, Washington HS, Cedar Rapids, Iowa.
68. *Sammie Mathis, rhp, El Dorado (Ark.) HS.
69. Demetris Jones, of, Motlow State (Tenn.) CC.

## SEATTLE MARINERS (11)

**1. Shawn Estes, lhp, Douglas HS, Minden, Nev.—(1995-2008)**
2. Tommy Adams, of, Arizona State University.—(AA)
**3. Jim Mecir, rhp, Eckerd (Fla.) College.—(1995-2005)**
**4. Desi Relaford, ss, Sandalwood HS, Jacksonville, Fla.—(1996-2007)**
5. Sean Rees, lhp, Arizona State University.—(High A)
6. Craig Clayton, rhp-1b, Cal State Northridge.
7. *Bruce Thompson, of, Brandon (Fla.) HS.
**8. Derek Lowe, rhp, Ford HS, Dearborn, Mich.—(1997-2013)**
9. Trey Witte, rhp, Texas A&M University.
10. Jeff Borski, rhp, University of South Carolina-Aiken.
11. Peter Weinbaum, rhp, Nassau (N.Y.) CC.
12. David Lisiecki, rhp, Lake Michigan (Mich.) JC.
13. Kevin Jenkins, rhp, Riverview (Mich.) HS.
14. Raul Rodarte, ss, Rancho Santiago (Calif.) JC.
15. Doug Anderson, lhp, University of North Florida.
16. Dan Sullivan, rhp, Indian River (Fla.) CC.
17. Kenny Winzer, rhp, Southern University.
18. Craig Bryant, ss, University of North Alabama.
19. Tony Phillips, rhp, University of Southern Mississippi.
20. Erik O'Donnell, rhp, University of Portland.
21. Toby Foreman, lhp, St. Mary's (Calif.) College.
**22. Darren Bragg, of, Georgia Tech.—(1994-2004)**
23. *Marty Gazarek, of, North Baltimore (Ohio) HS.
24. *Paul London, ss, Bethel HS, Hampton, Va.
**25. Matt Mantei, rhp, River Valley HS, Sawyer, Mich.—(1995-2005)**
26. Bubba Smith, 1b, University of Illinois.
27. *Todd Cady, c, Grossmont HS, La Mesa, Calif.
28. *Jimmy Riggio, rhp, Hillsborough (Fla.) CC.
29. *Chad Soden, lhp, Tuckerman (Ark.) HS.
30. *Edward Odom, ss, Atlantic HS, Delray Beach, Fla.
31. *Ryan Black, of, Sam Houston HS, Arlington, Texas.
**32. George Glinatsis, rhp, University of Cincinnati.—(1994)**
33. Byron Thomas, of, Catonsville (Md.) CC.
34. *Mike Martin Jr., ss, Maclay HS, Tallahassee, Fla.
35. *Steve McNair, ss, Mount Olive (Miss.) HS.
DRAFT DROP *Quarterback, National Football League (1995-2007)*
36. *Andrew Schope, lhp, Hempstead HS, Dubuque, Iowa.
37. *Daniel Scutchfield, lhp, Saline (Mich.) HS.
38. *Damian Cox, of, Victor Valley HS, Victorville, Calif.
39. *Kevin Faircloth, ss, Glenn HS, Winston-Salem, N.C.
40. *Lance Scott, rhp, Carmel (Calif.) HS.
41. *Lenny Weber, rhp, Jeanerette (La.) HS.
42. Craig Griffey, of, Ohio State University.
DRAFT DROP *Son of Ken Griffey, major leaguer (1973-91) • Brother of Ken Griffey Jr., major leaguer (1989-2010)*
**43. *Ryan Nye, rhp, Cameron (Okla.) HS.—(1997-98)**
44. *Chris Gorr, ss, Rancho Buena Vista HS, Vista, Calif.
45. +John Thompson, ss, Shadle Park HS, Spokane, Wash. / Scottsdale (Ariz.) JC.
46. *Federico Warner, of, Oceanside (Calif.) HS.
47. *William Lewis, c, East Carteret HS, Smyrna, N.C.
48. *Nicholas Williams, c, Hastings (Mich.) HS.
49. *Tyson Kimm, ss, Norway HS, Amana, Iowa.
DRAFT DROP *Son of Bruce Kimm, major leaguer (1976-80); major league manager (2002)*
50. *Jelani Lewis, of, Logan HS, Union City, Calit.
51. *Mark Fields, of, Southwestern (Calif.) JC.
52. *Bryan Pfeifer, lhp, Kennedy HS, Taylor, Mich.
53. *Jeff Tucker, rhp, Allen County (Kan.) CC.
54. +Greg Theron, rhp, Dobson HS, Mesa, Ariz. / Phoenix JC.
**55. *Jason Beverlin, rhp, Dondero HS, Royal Oak, Mich.—(2002)**
56. Jose Cruz, 3b, San Jacinto (Texas) JC.
57. *Francisco Antunez, c, Papa Juan XXIII HS, Bayamon, P.R.
58. Scott Bosarge, c, University of South Alabama.
59. *Chris Schmitt, lhp, Manatee (Fla.) JC.
60. *Rudolph Sasina, c, Overland HS, Aurora, Colo.
61. *Eddie Davis, of, Cerritos (Calif.) JC.
62. *James Lezeau, of, Prescott (Ariz.) HS.
**63. +Charles Gipson, of, Loara HS, Anaheim, Calif. / Cypress (Calif.) JC.—(1998-2005)**
64. +Brian Klomp, rhp, King's River (Calif.) JC.
65. *Shane Ziegler, rhp, Howard (Texas) JC.
66. *Brian Fontes, rhp, Fresno (Calif.) CC.
67. *Darian Hagan, ss, University of Colorado.
DRAFT DROP *Fourth-round draft pick, San Francisco 49ers/National Football League (1992); defensive back, Canadian Football League (1993-96)*

## TEXAS RANGERS (19)

**1. Benji Gil, ss-of, Castle Park HS, Chula Vista, Calif.—(1993-2003)**
DRAFT DROP *First player from 1991 draft to reach majors (April 5, 2003)*
**2. Terrell Lowery, of, Loyola Marymount University.—(1997-2000)**
3. Larry Hanlon, ss, University of Texas-Arlington.—(AAA)
4. Chris Curtis, rhp, Blinn (Texas) JC.—(AAA)
5. Mark O'Brien, lhp, Deering HS, Portland, Maine.—(High A)
6. Steve Sadecki, rhp, Vanderbilt University.
DRAFT DROP *Son of Ron Sadecki, major leaguer (1960-77)*
7. Bert Gerhart, rhp, New Hope HS, Columbus, Miss.
8. Roger Luce, c-rhp, University of Texas.
**9. Scott Eyre, lhp, JC of Southern Idaho.—(1997-2009)**
10. Dave Geeve, rhp, Bradley University.
11. Lance Schuermann, lhp, University of Nevada-Las Vegas.
12. Lanny Williams, c, Henderson State (Ark.) University.
13. Mike Edwards, 3b, University of Utah.
14. Jon Pitts, c, Esperanza HS, Anaheim, Calif.
**15. Kerry Lacy, rhp, Chattanooga State (Tenn.) Tech CC.—(1996-97)**
16. Chris Starr, rhp, Muskingum (Ohio) College.
17. Todd Gates, of, Loyola Marymount University.
18. Bo Magee, lhp, Jackson State University.
19. Jamie Bethke, c, Oak Park HS, Kansas City, Mo.
20. Brian Roberts, of, University of Illinois.
21. Paul Dalzochio, rhp, Long Beach State University.
22. James Koehler, 1b, University of Oklahoma.
23. Steve Burton, 1b, University of Richmond.
24. Mark Ringkamp, rhp, San Jose State University.
25. Billy Seaton, rhp, Mohave HS, Riviera, Ariz.
26. David Gandolph, lhp, Indiana University.
27. Charles Sullivan, 2b, Vanderbilt University.
28. Tom Migliozzi, rhp, St. John's University.
29. *Tim Beard, lhp, Grace King HS, Metairie, La.
**30. Desi Wilson, of, Fairleigh Dickinson University.—(1996)**
31. Joe Brownholtz, lhp, University of the Pacific.
32. Scott Buchheit, lhp, Southwest Missouri State University.
**33. *J.J. Thobe, rhp, Rancho Santiago (Calif.) JC.—(1995)**
DRAFT DROP *Brother of Tom Thobe, major leaguer (1995-96)*
34. Shelby Shaw, rhp, McNeese State University.
35. *Daniel Ortiz, lhp, Hoboken (N.J.) HS.
36. Brad Stuart, rhp, University of New Orleans.
37. Darryl Kennedy, c, University of North Florida.
38. +J.R. Lesch, rhp, Clackamas (Ore.) CC.
39. Kevin Sisk, ss-3b, James Madison University.
40. Jeff Carew, rhp, Kimberly (Wis.) HS.
41. *James Smith, rhp, Boyle County HS, Danville, Ky.
42. Darin Haddock, lhp, Oklahoma Baptist University.
43. *Joe Raineri, of, Smithtown East HS, Smithtown, N.Y.
44. Eric Vargas, c, Long Beach State University.
45. Joey Vallot, rhp, University of Arkansas.
46. Tim Minik, rhp, Austin Peay State University.
47. Keith Nalepka, c-1b, Montgomery (Md.) JC.
48. Heath Vaughn, rhp, Crowder (Mo.) CC.
49. +Jerry Martin, rhp, Shelby State (Tenn.) CC.
50. Patrick Underhill, rhp, University of West Florida.
**51. *Todd Walker, ss, Airline HS, Bossier City, La.—(1996-2007)**
DRAFT DROP *First-round draft pick (8th overall), Twins (1994)*
52. *David Ullan, c, La Grande (Ore.) HS.
53. Daryl Henderson, lhp, Elgin (Ill.) CC.
**54. *Raul Ibanez, of, Sunset HS, Miami.—(1996-2014)**
**55. *Trey Moore, lhp, Keller HS, Southlake, Texas.—(1998-2001)**
56. *Brian Wisler, of, Lynnwood HS, Alderwood Manor, Wash.
57. *Teddy Warrecker, c, Allan Hancock (Calif.) JC.
58. *Kevin Bradley, rhp, San Jose (Calif.) CC.
59. *Brian Davis, rhp, Corcoran (Calif.) HS.
60. *Lawrence Vrtiska, rhp, Iowa Western CC.
61. *Steve Maltaglaiti, rhp, East Islip (N.Y.) HS.
62. *Jason Rogers, lhp, McQueen HS, Reno, Nev.
63. *Pat Flury, rhp, Reed HS, Sparks, Nev.

## TORONTO BLUE JAYS (21)

1. **Shawn Green, of, Tustin (Calif.) HS** (Choice from Giants as compensation for Type A free agent Bud Black).**—(1993-2007)**
1. (Choice to Cardinals as compensation for Type A free agent Ken Dayley)
1. **Jeff Ware, rhp, Old Dominion University** (Supplemental choice—35th—as compensation for loss of Type A free agent George Bell).**—(1995-96)**
1. ***Dante Powell, ss, Millikan HS, Long Beach, Calif.** (Supplemental choice—42nd—as compensation for Type A free agent Bud Black).**—(1997-2001)**
DRAFT DROP *Attended Cal State Fullerton; re-drafted by Giants, 1994 (1st round)*
2. Trevor Mallory, rhp, Lakewood HS, St. Petersburg, Fla. (Choice from Cubs as compensation for Bell).—(High A)
2. Dennis Gray, lhp, Long Beach State University.—(AAA)
**3. Chris Stynes, ss, Boca Raton (Fla.) HS.—(1995-2004)**
4. Roger Doman, rhp, Joplin (Mo.) HS.—(AAA)
**5. Rickey Cradle, of, Cerritos (Calif.) HS.—(1998)**
**6. Jose Silva, rhp, Hilltop HS, Chula Vista, Calif.—(1996-2002)**
**7. *Carlton Loewer, rhp, St. Edmund HS, Eunice, La.—(1998-2003)**
DRAFT DROP *First-round draft pick (23rd overall), Phillies (1994)*
8. Stoney Briggs, of, Delaware Tech.
9. Pat Thacker, c, Millikan HS, Long Beach, Calif.
**10. Kenny Robinson, rhp, Florida State University.—(1995-97)**
DRAFT DROP *Died as active player (Feb. 28, 1999)*
11. Adam Meinershagen, rhp, Oakville HS, St. Louis.
12. Keiver Campbell, of, Alcorn State University.
13. Alonso Beltran, rhp, New Mexico JC.
**14. Alex Gonzalez, ss, Killian HS, Miami.—(1994-2006)**
15. Sharnol Adriana, 2b, Martin Methodist (Tenn.) College.
16. John Tsoukalas, 3b, Gonzaga University.
17. Mike Carlsen, 2b, Fairleigh Dickinson University.
18. Ryan Griffin, of, Dunedin (Fla.) HS.
19. Brent Lutz, c, University of Washington.
**20. Ben Weber, rhp, University of Houston.—(2000-05)**
21. Tim Lindsay, rhp, UCLA.
22. Andrew Dolson, lhp, Troy State University.
23. Chris Kotes, rhp, Columbia University.
24. Al Montoya, lhp, New Mexico State University.
**25. *Ryan Franklin, rhp, Spiro (Okia.) HS.—(1999-2011)**
26. *Jason Maloney, rhp, Bullard HS, Fresno, Calif.
DRAFT DROP *Son of Jim Maloney, major leaguer (1960-71)*
27. Paul Barton, lhp, University of Utah.
**28. Steve Sinclair, lhp, Kwantlen (B.C.) JC.—(1998-99)**
29. *Scott Bartucca, 1b, Onondaga (N.Y.) CC.
30. Joe Lis, 2b, University of South Florida.
DRAFT DROP *Son of Joe Lis, major leaguer (1970-77)*
31. Jim O'Connor, rhp, New York Tech.
32. *Mark Voisard, rhp, Mount Vernon Nazarene (Ohio) College.
33. Kurt Heble, 1b, McNeese State University.
34. Ted Langowski, 1b, University of San Francisco.
35. Darin Nolan, rhp, Washington State University.
36. Craig Vaught, 3b, Tallassee (Ala.) HS.
37. Gary Miller, rhp, Penn State University.
38. Alan Ford, rhp, San Francisco State University.
39. Chris Ermis, rhp, San Antonio (Texas) JC.
40. *Steve Marr, rhp, Western Kentucky University.
41. *Angel Abreu, rhp, Josefina Barcelo HS, Guaynabo, P.R.
42. *Andrew Srebroski, ss, Anne Arundel (Md.) CC.
43. Louis Benbow, 2b, Saddleback (Calif.) JC.
44. Craig Quinlan, 1b, St. Thomas (Minn.) University.
DRAFT DROP *Brother of Tom Quinlan, major leaguer (1990-96)*
45. Mike Morland, c, University of Texas.
46. *Ray Ragland, of, Chipola (Fla.) JC.
47. Peter Polis, c, New York Tech.
48. *Ryan Adamo, rhp, Reedsport (Ore.) HS.
49. +Emanuel Hayes, ss, Odessa (Texas) JC.
50. *Toraino Golston, of, New Mexico JC.
51. *Symmion Willis, ss, Mays HS, Atlanta.
52. *Pete Ambrosina, 2b, Berrien Springs, Mich.
53. *Vick Brown, ss, Grand Ridge HS, Cypress, Fla.
54. *Cuba Gregory, ss, Southeastern HS, Detroit.
55. *Gregg Rinaldi, rhp, Memorial HS, New Hyde Park, N.Y.
56. *Les Dennis, ss, West Linn (Ore.) HS.
57. *Ronald Mason, of, Martin Methodist (Tenn.) College.
58. *Patrick Guerrero, 3b, Middle Georgia JC.

## 1992

# Jeter slips, signability enters baseball jargon

The 1992 draft introduced a new buzzword to the baseball industry: signability. After several years of rapid bonus inflation, major league clubs began drafting players based on the likelihood they would sign and the amount they would sign for, not just on their baseball ability.

The concept was hardly new, but with bonus records being broken on an annual basis and rising at what team executives deemed an unacceptable rate, clubs reached a new level of resolve in 1992, beginning with the first pick.

The Houston Astros had the first choice, and owner John McMullen set a bonus limit of $700,000, a far cry from the $1.55 million the New York Yankees gave North Carolina high school lefthander Brien Taylor as the No. 1 pick in 1991. McMullen's stance might have cost his team Michigan high school shortstop Derek Jeter, the best talent to come out of the 1992 class, or Stanford outfielder Jeffrey Hammonds, the top-rated prospect entering the draft. The Astros settled on Cal State Fullerton third baseman Phil Nevin, the 1992 Golden Spikes Award winner.

Nevin, a third-round pick of the Los Angeles Dodgers out of high school, was participating in the College World Series on draft day, but had given the Astros assurances that his demands were in their range. He quickly signed for a $700,000 bonus. In addition to Nevin, the Astros considered Hammonds, Jeter, righthander Rick Greene of Louisiana State, outfielder Chad Mottola of Central Florida and Texas high school outfielder Shea Morenz. All except Morenz went in the first round.

Morenz was the nation's top quarterback recruit, and compared by some scouts to Mickey Mantle. His reported $1.4 million price tag put him well out of reach for the Astros. Every other club passed on Morenz until the Toronto Blue Jays selected him in the sixth round. He didn't sign, instead going to the University of Texas to play football and baseball. The Yankees picked Morenz in the first round of the 1995 draft and signed him, but he did not reach the major leagues.

Astros general manager Bill Wood maintained that Nevin was the club's preferred choice all along.

"Signability this year was a factor, but it has been for the last 15 years I've been watching drafts for the Astros," said Wood, who didn't sign John Burke, the club's first-round pick in 1991, because of his asking price. "We wanted to get a feel for what some players wanted so we knew things could get worked out on a reasonable basis."

Jeter was the sixth pick in the draft, going to the Yankees and forging a dynamic, 20-year career as one of the franchise's all-time great players.

Hall of Fame pitcher Hal Newhouser was a Michigan area scout for the Astros at the time, and he lobbied hard for his team to draft Jeter.

**No. 1 overall pick Phil Nevin eventually developed into a solid major leaguer, but had nowhere near the impact of Derek Jeter, who signed with the Yankees for the same amount that Nevin got from the Astros**

Jeter had a scholarship offer to the University of Michigan, and many scouts said it would take $1 million to sign him. Newhouser, however, claimed he could deliver Jeter for $750,000. That was $50,000 more the Astros' self-imposed limit, and the club ignored Newhouser, who quit in protest.

Jeter later signed for a bonus of $700,000, the same amount that Nevin received.

### NEVIN HAS CHECKERED CAREER

Nevin played 12 years in the majors, but only 18 games in an Astros uniform. His brief career in Houston was punctuated by run-ins with management. He refused to play in exhibition games with replacement players before the 1994-95 work stoppage was settled, and he engaged in a profanity-laced shouting match with general manager Bob Watson and manager Terry Collins when he was sent to the minors in July 1995. Nevin was traded to the Detroit Tigers a month later.

Nevin blamed others for his early failings as a pro, and it wasn't until 1999 when he landed with the San Diego Padres that his career took a turn for the better. He hit .288 with 156 homers over seven seasons with the Padres.

"I wish I had done some things differently and matured a little quicker than I did," Nevin said. "I'm never a person to look back and say I wish I had done different. But the situation with

### AT A GLANCE

**This Date In History**
June 1-3

**Best Draft**
**KANSAS CITY ROYALS.** The Royals had two first-round picks, outfielder **MICHAEL TUCKER** (10th overall) and righthander **JIM PITTSLEY** (17th). But outfielder **JOHNNY DAMON** (35th) ended up becoming their biggest catch, and **JON LIEBER**, a second-rounder, the most productive pitcher, although none of his 14-year career was spent with the Royals.

**Worst Draft**
**LOS ANGELES DODGERS.** The Dodgers drafted 53 players and spent more bonus money than anyone in 1992, but only **KEITH JOHNSON** (4) reached the majors; he got four at-bats for the Angels in 2000.

**First-Round Bust**
**PETE JANICKI, RHP, ANGELS.** The Angels worried about Janicki's durability and signed him to a major league deal with a bonus of just $90,000. Janicki injured his elbow in his final start for UCLA and again in his first pro start a year later. In 154 games in a five-year minor league career, he went 19-36, 6.25.

**On Second Thought**
**JASON GIAMBI, 3B, ATHLETICS.** Giambi was drafted for his prolific bat and hit .277 with 440 homers and 1,441 RBIs, while drawing 1,366 walks over a 20-year career in the majors.

**Late Round Find**
**CRAIG COUNSELL, SS, ROCKIES (11TH ROUND).** Counsell signed for $5,000 and spent 16 seasons in the majors, dividing his time between second base, third base and shortstop, while hitting .255-42-390, along with 103 stolen bases. He had the good fortune to be on base when both the Marlins in 1997 and Diamondbacks in 2001 won

CONTINUED ON PAGE 406

## AT A GLANCE

CONTINUED FROM PAGE 405

the World Series in walkoff fashion.

### Never Too Late

**CRAIG DINGMAN, RHP, TWINS (50TH ROUND).** One of two players drafted in the 50th and final round in 1992 who made the majors, Dingman didn't sign with the Twins out of a Wichita high school and attended Hutchinson (Kan.) CC. The Yankees took him in the 32nd round a year later, and it would be seven more years before he reached the big leagues. In four seasons, he went 4-5, 6.10.

### Overlooked

**MIKE REDMOND, C, MARLINS.** Signed as a free agent out of Gonzaga University, Redmond spent the first seven seasons of a 13-year career with the Marlins, hitting .284-13-243 in 485 games for the Fish. He was the Marlins manager from 2013-2015.

### International Gem

**DAVID ARIAS, 1B, MARINERS.** The player known throughout his major league career as David Ortiz, and more affectionately as Big Papi, went by the name Arias when he signed with the Mariners in 1992 for $3,500. He progressed through their system before being traded in 1996 to the Twins, and it was at that point that he wanted to be known as Ortiz. His career blossomed a few years later—much to the regret of the Twins, who non-tendered him in 2002, prompting him to sign with the Red Sox. He quickly developed into a franchise icon in Boston. Brazilian righthander **JOSE PETT** signed for $675,000 with the Blue Jays, and produced just a 23-36, 4.53 record in six minor league seasons.

### Minor League Take

**CHAD MOTTOLA, OF, REDS.** Mottola played in just 59 major league games in a 16-year professional career. That provided him plenty

## 1992: THE FIRST ROUNDERS

| CLUB: PLAYER, POS., SCHOOL | HOMETOWN | B-T | HT. | WT. | AGE | BONUS | FIRST YEAR | LAST YEAR | PEAK LEVEL (YEARS) |
|---|---|---|---|---|---|---|---|---|---|
| **1. Astros: Phil Nevin, 3b, Cal State Fullerton** | **Placentia, Calif.** | **R-R** | **6-2** | **185** | **21** | **$700,000** | **1993** | **2006** | **Majors (12)** |
| Astros passed on Derek Jeter due to firm $700K ownership-dictated bonus for pick; Nevin hit .402-22-86 as Fullerton JR, had solid MLB career (.270-208-743). | | | | | | | | | |
| **2. Indians: Paul Shuey, rhp, North Carolina** | **Raleigh, N.C.** | **R-R** | **6-3** | **210** | **21** | **$650,000** | **1992** | **2007** | **Majors (11)** |
| Came from era when reliever could be second pick overall; classic mid-90s power arm, compared to Rob Dibble; 11-year MLB career compromised by hip injury. | | | | | | | | | |
| **3. Expos: B.J. Wallace, lhp, Mississippi State** | **Monroeville, Ala.** | **R-L** | **6-3** | **195** | **21** | **$550,000** | **1993** | **1996** | **Class AA (1)** |
| Stood out as college JR (9-3, 2.69, school-record 145 SO), on Team USA Olympic squad, but pro career compromised by shoulder surgery, went 15-15 in minors. | | | | | | | | | |
| **4. Orioles: Jeffrey Hammonds, of, Stanford** | **Scotch Plains, N.J.** | **R-R** | **6-0** | **180** | **21** | **$975,000** | **1993** | **2005** | **Majors (13)** |
| Consensus best talent in draft, but bonus demands drove him down; speed was his best tool, but also advanced approach with bat; hit .272-110-423 in majors. | | | | | | | | | |
| **5. Reds: Chad Mottola, of, Central Florida** | **Pembroke Pines, Fla.** | **R-R** | **6-3** | **200** | **20** | **$400,000** | **1992** | **2007** | **Majors (5)** |
| Dale Murphy comps with size/power/arm/instincts; hit .331-23-148 at UCF, but became career journeyman in pros, played 59 games in majors, 1,800 in minors. | | | | | | | | | |
| **6. Yankees: Derek Jeter, ss, Central HS** | **Kalamazoo, Mich.** | **R-R** | **6-3** | **170** | **17** | **$700,000** | **1992** | **2013** | **Majors (18)** |
| Generation-defining player on/off field, fell to Yankees for signability reasons; resume includes 3,465 hits (sixth all-time), 14 all-star games, five World Series rings. | | | | | | | | | |
| **7. Giants: Calvin Murray, of, Texas** | **Dallas** | **R-R** | **5-11** | **185** | **20** | **$825,000** | **1993** | **2005** | **Majors (5)** |
| Two-time first-rounder stood out for top of scale speed, CF defense; concerns about hitting ability proved warranted, reached MLB in seventh season, hit just .231. | | | | | | | | | |
| **8. *Angels: Pete Janicki, rhp, UCLA** | **Placentia, Calif.** | **R-R** | **6-4** | **190** | **21** | **$90,000** | **1993** | **1998** | **Class AAA (3)** |
| Hurt arm in final college start, prompting Angels to slash bonus offer; concerns warranted as he broke his elbow in second pro inning, went 19-36, 6.25 in minors. | | | | | | | | | |
| **9. Mets: Preston Wilson, of, Bamberg-Ehrhardt HS** | **Bamberg, S.C.** | **R-R** | **6-3** | **190** | **17** | **$500,000** | **1993** | **2007** | **Majors (10)** |
| Emerged from nowhere as prep SR (.530-22-86; 13-0, 1.98); stepson of Mookie, but totally different tools as game built on power; hit .264-189-668 in 10 seasons. | | | | | | | | | |
| **10. Royals: Michael Tucker, ss, Longwood (Va.)** | **Chase Cirt, Va.** | **L-R** | **6-2** | **185** | **20** | **$450,000** | **1993** | **2007** | **Majors (12)** |
| Top pure bat in class hit .489-22-74 for D-II program; moved to OF in pros, hit .256-125-528 in MLB, but largely relegated to platoon role when struggled vs LHP. | | | | | | | | | |
| **11. Cubs: Derek Wallace, rhp, Pepperdine** | **Oxnard, Calif.** | **R-R** | **6-3** | **190** | **20** | **$550,000** | **1992** | **1999** | **Majors (2)** |
| Played secondary role (4-2, 3.20) for CWS champs because of midseason car accident; two-pitch guy with mid-90s FB, used as closer, but pro career never took off. | | | | | | | | | |
| **12. Brewers: Kenny Felder, of, Florida State** | **Niceville, Fla.** | **R-R** | **6-3** | **225** | **21** | **$525,000** | **1992** | **1996** | **Class AAA (1)** |
| Juggled football/baseball at FSU, but failed to win QB job, hit .268-4-15 as JR; had serious raw pop but hit only .243-57-216 in five injury-riddled pro seasons. | | | | | | | | | |
| **13. Phillies: Chad McConnell, of, Creighton** | **Sioux Falls, S.D.** | **R-R** | **6-1** | **180** | **20** | **$475,000** | **1993** | **1996** | **Class AA (3)** |
| Rare South Dakota product was one of best college bats in '92 draft (.400-14-73, 29 SB); pro career hurt by shoulder/back issues, peaked in Double-A (.254-39-199). | | | | | | | | | |
| **14. Mariners: Ron Villone, lhp, Massachusetts** | **Bergenfield, N.J.** | **L-L** | **6-3** | **230** | **22** | **$550,000** | **1993** | **2010** | **Majors (15)** |
| All-conference tight end at UMass became pitcher-only last two years, fanned 139 in 108 IP with mid-90s fastball; spent 15 years with 12 clubs in set-up role. | | | | | | | | | |
| **15. Cardinals: Sean Lowe, rhp, Arizona State** | **Mesquite, Texas** | **R-R** | **6-2** | **200** | **21** | **$300,000** | **1992** | **2003** | **Majors (7)** |
| Emerged as first-rounder by adding 10 mph to fastball during college years; struggled with consistency, mechanics in minors (58-58, 4.05), majors (23-15, 4.95). | | | | | | | | | |
| **16. Tigers: Rick Greene, rhp, Louisiana State** | **Miami** | **R-R** | **6-5** | **200** | **21** | **$470,000** | **1993** | **2000** | **Majors (1)** |
| Intimidating closer at LSU (3 years: 13-8, 3.57, 29 SV), on Olympic team with size, arm angle, but struggled with release point in pros, pitched in one MLB game. | | | | | | | | | |
| **17. Royals: Jim Pittsley, rhp, DuBois Area HS** | **DuBois, Pa.** | **R-R** | **6-7** | **220** | **18** | **$410,000** | **1992** | **1999** | **Majors (4)** |
| First prep arm drafted on basis of frame, 92-95 FB with explosive life, feel for pitching, but game never same after '95 elbow surgery, went 7-12, 6.02 in MLB. | | | | | | | | | |
| **18. Mets: Chris Roberts, lhp/of, Florida State** | **Middleburg, Fla.** | **R-L** | **6-0** | **186** | **20** | **$365,000** | **1993** | **2001** | **Class AAA (4)** |
| Near equal ability as pitcher and hitter, but developed on mound after going 8-4, 2.34 as JR; change best pitch, fastball a little light, went 46-53, 4.16 in minors. | | | | | | | | | |
| **19. Blue Jays: Shannon Stewart, of, Southridge HS** | **Miami** | **R-R** | **6-1** | **185** | **18** | **$450,000** | **1992** | **2008** | **Majors (14)** |
| Athletic player with speed/CF skills, developing power, though subpar arm from football injury; spent 14 years in majors (nine with Jays), hit .297-115-580, 196 SBs. | | | | | | | | | |
| **20. Athletics: Benji Grigsby, rhp, San Diego State** | **Lafayette, La.** | **R-R** | **6-1** | **195** | **21** | **$380,000** | **1992** | **1998** | **Class AAA (1)** |
| Became dominant closer for SDSU, his third college, but overworked, had dead arm by draft; underwent labrum surgery in 1992-93, never regained velocity. | | | | | | | | | |
| **21. Braves: Jamie Arnold, rhp, Osceola HS** | **Kissimmee, Fla.** | **B-R** | **6-2** | **185** | **18** | **$380,000** | **1992** | **2002** | **Majors (2)** |
| Top strikeout artist in Florida prep ranks (11-5, 1.21, 110 IP/166 SO), never developed into elite arm because of average fastball, lack of command/consistency. | | | | | | | | | |
| **22. Rangers: Rick Helling, rhp, Stanford** | **West Fargo, N.D.** | **R-R** | **6-3** | **215** | **21** | **$397,000** | **1992** | **2006** | **Majors (12)** |
| Rare Stanford JC transfer became first-rounder after 9-4, 4.43 season, development of FB/SL; played for two World Series winners with Marlins, won 20 with Rangers. | | | | | | | | | |
| **23. Pirates: Jason Kendall, c, Torrance HS** | **Torrance, Calif.** | **R-R** | **6-0** | **180** | **17** | **$336,000** | **1992** | **2012** | **Majors (15)** |
| Hit .549-3-39 as prep SR, but bat considered weakest tool when signed; strengths of game were sound defensive skills, instincts, competitive approach. | | | | | | | | | |
| **24. White Sox: Eddie Pearson, 1b, Bishop State (Ala.) JC** | **Mobile, Ala.** | **B-R** | **6-3** | **225** | **18** | **$354,000** | **1992** | **2000** | **Class AAA (2)** |
| Took GED in December, became draft-eligible as 18-year-old JC talent; huge raw power appealed to Sox, hit 188 HRs in minors/Mexico, but never reached majors. | | | | | | | | | |
| **25. Blue Jays: Todd Steverson, of, Arizona State** | **Inglewood, Calif.** | **R-R** | **6-2** | **194** | **20** | **$450,000** | **1992** | **1998** | **Majors (2)** |
| Centerpiece of talented '89 prep crop chose to go to ASU; five-tool ability, but struggled to make contact in college, minors (.241-49-203), brief look in majors. | | | | | | | | | |
| **26. Twins: Dan Serafini, lhp, Serra HS** | **San Bruno, Calif.** | **B-L** | **6-3** | **175** | **18** | **$350,000** | **1992** | **2007** | **Majors (7)** |
| Followed in footsteps of Fregosi, Bonds, Jefferies at Serra High, but never developed consistency for regular MLB work; lingered in minors, other leagues until 2013. | | | | | | | | | |
| **27. Rockies: John Burke, rhp, Florida** | **Littleton, Colo.** | **B-R** | **6-4** | **220** | **22** | **$336,000** | **1992** | **1998** | **Majors (2)** |
| Expansion Rockies went for local product/two-time first-rounder with initial draft pick; boasted mid-90s fastball, but never overcame history of wildness/injuries. | | | | | | | | | |
| **28. Marlins: Charles Johnson, c, Miami** | **Fort Pierce, Fla.** | **R-R** | **6-2** | **209** | **20** | **$585,000** | **1993** | **2005** | **Majors (12)** |
| Turned down first-round offer from Expos in 1989, signed late with Marlins; top-notch defender with raw power, hit .245 with 167 HRs in 12 MLB seasons. | | | | | | | | | |

**Signed to major league contract.*

Houston, yeah, I wish I had done that different. I wish I hadn't expressed my feelings the way I did. But that was the way I felt. I felt they were screwing me around, and I let them know that."

Nevin failed to make the Team USA squad that played in the Pan American Games in the summer of 1991, and came back for his junior season at Fullerton stronger and with a renewed sense of

## How They Should Have Done It

Based on the career WAR (Wins Above Replacement, as calculated by Baseball-Reference.com) numbers achieved by all the players eligible for the 1992 draft, here's how the first round should have unfolded. Numbers in parentheses indicate the round when the player was actually drafted. Asterisk denotes player who signed as a draft-and-follow.

| | Player, Pos. | Actual Draft | WAR | Bonus |
|---|---|---|---|---|
| 1. | Derek Jeter, ss | Yankees (1) | 71.8 | $700,000 |
| 2. | Johnny Damon, of | Royals (1-S) | 56.3 | $250,000 |
| 3. | Jason Giambi, 3b | Athletics (2) | 50.8 | $150,000 |
| 4. | Jason Kendall, c | Pirates (1) | 41.5 | $336,000 |
| 5. | Shannon Stewart, of | Blue Jays (1) | 24.7 | $450,000 |
| 6. | Jon Lieber, rhp | Royals (2) | 24.3 | $80,000 |
| 7. | Bobby Higginson, of | Tigers (12) | 23.0 | $10,000 |
| 8. | Charles Johnson, c | Marlins (1) | 22.5 | $585,000 |
| 9. | Craig Counsell, ss | Rockies (11) | 22.4 | $5,000 |
| 10. | Rick Helling, rhp | Rangers (1) | 20.6 | $397,000 |
| 11. | Raul Ibanez, of | Mariners (36) | 20.2 | $15,000 |
| 12. | Rich Aurilia, ss | Rangers (24) | 18.1 | $5,000 |
| 13. | Jose Vidro, 2b | Expos (6) | 17.2 | $30,000 |
| 14. | Phil Nevin, 3b | Astros (1) | 15.9 | $700,000 |
| 15. | Frank Catalanotto, 2b | Tigers (10) | 14.5 | $20,000 |
| 16. | * Ryan Franklin, rhp | Mariners (23) | 11.8 | $67,500 |
| 17. | Scott Karl, lhp | Brewers (6) | 8.8 | $35,000 |
| 18. | Jeffrey Hammonds, of | Orioles (1) | 8.7 | $975,000 |
| 19. | Marvin Benard, of | Giants (50) | 8.6 | $1,000 |
| 20. | Michael Tucker, ss | Royals (1) | 8.2 | $450,000 |
| 21. | Brendan Donnelly, rhp | White Sox (27) | 7.9 | $5,000 |
| 22. | Paul Shuey, rhp | Indians (1) | 7.0 | $650,000 |
| 23. | Mike Redmond, c | Marlins (NDFA) | 6.4 | $10,000 |
| 24. | Preston Wilson, of | Mets (1) | 6.3 | $500,000 |
| | Matt Herges, rhp | Dodgers (NDFA) | 6.3 | $4,000 |
| 26. | Roger Bailey, rhp | Rockies (3) | 5.3 | $95,000 |
| | Billy Simas, rhp | Angels (6) | 5.3 | $44,000 |
| 28. | Jon Nunnally, of | Indians (3) | 5.1 | $120,000 |

| | Top 3 Unsigned Players | | | Year Signed |
|---|---|---|---|---|
| 1. | Todd Helton, 1b | Padres (2) | 61.2 | 1995 |
| 2. | Darin Erstad, of | Mets (13) | 32.4 | 1995 |
| 3. | Casey Blake, 3b | Phillies (11) | 24.9 | 1996 |

purpose, batting .402 with 22 homers and 86 RBIs. He hit .526 in the College World Series, leading the Titans to a runner-up finish.

"A big reason why I've had success this year is that I stayed focused on playing baseball," Nevin said. "The other things that come with it I've been able to put aside when I stepped on the field."

"His personality is a blessing and a burden," said Augie Garrido, Nevin's coach at Cal State Fullerton. "It motivates him to be the best. He sees himself as the dominant person in any environment. He means well, but sometimes, like when he thinks he's being treated unfairly, he overreacts."

Nevin hit .270 with 208 homers in his 12 years in the major leagues and had three 100-RBI seasons, playing for seven teams. Initially a third baseman, he also played first base, catcher and in the outfield. It was a good career, though considerably short of Jeter's.

"People talk about the five guys who were picked ahead of Derek as if we were failures compared to what Derek has done," Nevin said. "But I'm proud of what I did. The other guys would tell you the same thing. But Derek Jeter is the class of our era. He really is."

### UNCERTAINTY REIGNS AT TOP

The 1992 draft was one of the most confusing ever. Small-market teams at the top of the order were reluctant to pay the prevailing market value for bonuses, and the draft lacked a consensus No. 1 prospect. Fallout from the unprecedented Taylor deal in 1991 was evident and put many clubs on the defensive.

"It's the Yankees business if they feel they can invest a million and a half dollars in a 19-year-old pitcher," said John Hart, general manager of the Cleveland Indians, whose club picked second in 1992. "But as a small-market team, we're not in a position to do that. We will not make the same mistake other teams have made. Even if it's the 30th player on our list, he'll be signed before the draft."

The 1992 class was not a particularly strong one, which made teams more reluctant to shell out big bonuses. "It's the weakest talent in seven or eight years," said scouting director Gary Hughes of the expansion Florida Marlins, who had the 28th and last pick in the first round.

Teams at the top of the order looked for talent that was both cheap and agreeable to sign. The budget-burdened Astros bypassed Hammonds and Jeter and settled on Nevin. The Indians and Montreal Expos, the next two teams to pick, also had deals in place. The Indians took North Carolina righthander Paul Shuey and signed him for $650,000. The Expos picked Mississippi State lefthander B.J. Wallace and signed him for $550,000.

Shuey, the first of six predominantly college relievers who populated the first round, was the hardest thrower in the country, with a fastball consistently clocked at 95 mph. He went 5-2, 3.13 with 87 strikeouts in 69 innings as a college junior. In 11 seasons in the majors as a reliever, Shuey went 45-28, 3.87. He was plagued by a hip injury and proved more effective in a set-up role than as a closer, saving only 23 games.

Wallace did not reach the majors in an injury-plagued pro career that lasted just four years. He was regarded as the premier lefthander in the draft after striking out a school-record 145 as a junior at Mississippi State. But an assortment of shoulder injuries, beginning in 1994 in Double-A, doomed Wallace's career.

Jeffrey Hammonds

The Baltimore Orioles, selecting fourth, were under no financial constraints and went for Hammonds, the top-rated prospect according to the Major League Scouting Bureau. He hit .380 with six homers and 33 RBIs, and stole 33 bases while striking out only six times as a junior at Stanford, and generally impressed scouts with his power potential, contact-oriented approach, superior speed and deft base-running skills.

Hammonds agreed to a $925,000 bonus on July 11, the richest in 1992 and the largest ever for a college player. He played 13 seasons in the majors and hit .272 with 110 homers.

### AT A GLANCE

of opportunity to build a stout minor league resume (.280-249-1,034, with 183 stolen bases in 1,800 games).

#### One Who Got Away

**TODD HELTON, 1B/LHP, PADRES (2ND ROUND).** Helton was passed over in the first round, despite legitimate baseball credentials. As a two-way player at Knoxville's Central High, he hit .655-10-39 with 18 steals and went 11-0, 0.32 on the mound. Helton left no doubt he was a first-round talent in three college seasons at Tennessee and was the eighth overall pick in 1995.

#### He Was Drafted?

**JOHN LYNCH, RHP, MARLINS (2ND ROUND).** Lynch accepted a $150,000 bonus from the Marlins and threw the first pitch in franchise history, a 95 mph fastball for short-season Erie. Lynch, a two-sport standout at Stanford, gave up on a promising baseball career a year later after the Tampa Bay Buccaneers took him in the third round of the 1993 NFL draft. He played 15 seasons in the NFL as a strong safety.

#### Did You Know . . .

The Dodgers didn't have a first-round pick in 1992, but still spent a then-draft record $2.483 million on their draft picks. Their payoff? Four major league at-bats from fourth-rounder Johnson, playing for the Angels.

#### They Said It

First overall pick **PHIL NEVIN**, on the significance of the Astros and four other clubs passing on **DEREK JETER**, enabling Jeter to land with the Yankees: "You hear people say things happen for a reason, but Derek Jeter was the perfect guy for that organization at that time. There was a reason the Yankees drafted sixth: They weren't very good. In a short time, they became the New York Yankees again."

## DRAFT SPOTLIGHT: DEREK JETER

Derek Jeter was the unqualified star of the 1992 draft class. Selected sixth overall by the New York Yankees, he became a 14-time all-star and five-time World Series champion. He had 3,456 hits and a .310 average, and was the team captain for his final 12 seasons.

But he became a Yankee through a twist of fate. The Houston Astros had the No. 1 pick in 1992 and narrowed their choice to Jeter and Cal State Fullerton third baseman Phil Nevin, the college player of the year.

Two veteran Michigan-based scouts, the Astros' Hal Newhouser and the Yankees' Dick Groch, both had tracked Jeter through high school in Kalamazoo, traveling hundreds of miles on blustery early-spring days to watch him. Both had a strong conviction that Jeter was going to be a great player and desperately wanted their clubs to draft him.

Five teams passed on Derek Jeter in the 1992 draft, before the Yankees took him in what seemed like fate

Newhouser, a Hall of Fame pitcher, had the inside track. He just needed to convince his bosses in Houston that a skinny high school shortstop from Michigan should be the first pick. Astros owner John McMullen mandated the club would spend no more than $700,000. Jeter's asking price, thought to be $1 million, was actually $750,000, according to Newhouser. That was still $50,000 over budget, though, so the Astros passed on Jeter in favor of Nevin, who had no qualms with the Astros' offer.

Scouting director Dan O'Brien broke the news to Newhouser, who immediately resigned. "Any scout that has followed a player and had the feelings that he did toward Derek was going to be greatly disappointed," O'Brien said.

Groch, too, was drawn to Jeter from the time he first saw him at a baseball camp in Michigan in the summer of 1990. Groch still had concerns about his wiry frame and inside-out swing, and wondered whether power pitchers would knock the bat out of his hands. He changed his mind on a cold day when Jeter turned on an inside fastball and drove it over the left-field fence, nearly reaching his home adjacent to the ballpark.

Most scouts believed Jeter intended to attend the University of Michigan, but Groch knew the family and determined that Jeter wanted to play pro ball.

"His mother and father both said, 'He wants to play professional baseball,'" Groch said. "I was certain about his signability. His father, Charles, was very candid: 'We have our price. If you meet our price, he is going to play professional baseball.'" When Yankees officials met before the draft, scouting director Bill Livesey cited the prevailing sentiment. Groch shot back, "He's not going to Michigan. The only place he's going is to Cooperstown."

The Astros, Cleveland Indians (picking second) and Montreal Expos (third) all were under strict budget constraints and passed on Jeter. The Baltimore Orioles, picking fourth, selected Stanford outfielder Jeffrey Hammonds, the highest-ranked player on their list.

The Cincinnati Reds had keen interest in Jeter based on the recommendation of scout Gene Bennett, who was as passionate as Newhouser and Groch. But scouting director Julian Mock made a last-minute decision to take Central Florida outfielder Chad Mottola.

"I felt like I was going to have a heart attack," Bennett said. "I was shocked when we didn't take him. There were no words to use. The damage was done."

The Yankees had the next pick. "We were an awfully happy room," Livesey said. They quickly called Jeter's name and signed him for a bonus of $700,000.

Jeter struggled early, hitting .210 in his first season and committing 56 errors in his second. From that point on, he made a beeline for Yankee Stadium, arriving late in 1995. A year later, he was the first rookie shortstop in 34 years to play regularly for the Yankees, became rookie of the year and played a pivotal role as the Yankees won their first World Series in 15 years. An historic career soon unfolded.

Jeter seemed destined to play shortstop for the Yankees. He was born in New Jersey, and even after he moved to Michigan at age 4, he stayed loyal to the Yankees. He spent summers with his grandparents in West Milford, N.J., and his grandmother often took him to Yankee Stadium. Childhood photographs feature young Derek in Yankees pinstripes.

Jeter's eighth-grade yearbook includes predictions of what each kid would be doing in 10 years. The forecast for Jeter: playing shortstop for the Yankees.

Though Jeter was available with the fifth pick, the Cincinnati Reds selected Mottola, largely because he agreed to a $400,000 bonus. Mottola hit .329 with 14 homers and 62 RBIs as a junior at Central Florida and drew comparisons with Dale Murphy for his size, power potential, arm strength and instincts. Mottola, though, played in just 59 games in the majors in a pro career than spanned 16 years. He hit 249 homers in the minors.

### THE BORAS FACTOR

None of the first six players drafted were represented by Scott Boras, the California-based agent who had drawn the rancor of baseball executives in the previous three drafts. Boras represented Andy Benes in 1988, Ben McDonald in 1989 and Taylor in 1991, each the No. 1 overall pick, in addition to top prospect Todd Van Poppel in 1990. Boras' negotiating tactics gained each player a record deal at the time it was signed.

Boras' prominent clients in the 1992 draft were college players, Texas outfielder Calvin Murray, Florida righthander John Burke and Miami catcher Charles Johnson, all of whom previously had been drafted in the first round and gone unsigned. Murray and Johnson were represented by Boras in the 1989 draft, and Burke in 1991.

Murray was the seventh player drafted in 1992, by the San Francisco Giants. Burke and Johnson slid to the expansion Colorado Rockies and Marlins with the final two picks in the first round.

Burke, a Colorado high school product, signed quickly with the Rockies for a $336,000 bonus. Murray and Johnson both held out until November before reaching agreements. Murray got $825,000, and Johnson received $575,000. Murray's bonus was the second-highest overall; Johnson's the sixth-highest.

Murray had agreed with the Giants on a $500,000 bonus prior to the draft, but changed his mind once he found out the Orioles gave Hammonds a $925,000 bonus. Murray claimed he was at least the equal of Hammonds, and Boras took over from there. At the same time, Boras engaged the Marlins in drawn-out and often contentious negotiations on behalf of Johnson. Marlins general manager Dave Dombrowski and Hughes also drafted Johnson in 1989 when they were in similar positions with the Expos. Johnson turned down a reported $197,500 bonus offer at that time and went to college.

This time, Johnson insisted on a contract that matched Taylor's record-setting $1.55 million deal. Negotiations dragged until Dombrowski and Hughes went to the Johnson home in Fort

### Fastest To The Majors

| | Player, Pos. | Drafted (Round) | Debut |
|---|---|---|---|
| 1. | Jeffrey Hammonds, of | Orioles (1) | June 25, 1993 |
| 2. | Chris Gomez, ss | Tigers (3) | July 19, 1993 |
| 3. | Tim Davis, lhp | Mariners (6) | April 4, 1994 |
| 4. | Rick Helling, rhp | Rangers (1) | April 10, 1994 |
| 5. | Rod Henderson, rhp | Expos (2) | April 19, 1994 |

**FIRST HIGH SCHOOL SELECTION:** Jim Pittsley, rhp (Royals/1, May 23, 1995)

**LAST PLAYER TO RETIRE:** Derek Jeter, ss (Sept. 28, 2014)

## Top 25 Bonuses

| | Player, Pos. | Drafted (Round) | Order | Bonus |
|---|---|---|---|---|
| 1. | **Jeffrey Hammonds, of** | **Orioles (1)** | **4** | **$975,000** |
| 2. | **Calvin Murray, of** | **Giants (1)** | **7** | **$825,000** |
| 3. | **Phil Nevin, 3b** | **Astros (1)** | **1** | **$700,000** |
| | ***Derek Jeter, ss** | **Yankees (1)** | **6** | **$700,000** |
| 5. | **Paul Shuey, rhp** | **Indians (1)** | **2** | **$650,000** |
| 6. | **Charles Johnson, c** | **Marlins (1)** | **28** | **$585,000** |
| 7. | B.J. Wallace, lhp | Expos (1) | 3 | $550,000 |
| | **Derek Wallace, rhp** | **Cubs (1)** | **11** | **$550,000** |
| | **Ron Villone, lhp** | **Mariners (1)** | **14** | **$550,000** |
| 10. | Michael Moore, of | Dodgers (1-S) | 36 | $537,500 |
| 11. | Kenny Felder, of | Brewers (1) | 12 | $525,000 |
| 12. | ***Preston Wilson, of** | **Mets (1)** | **9** | **$500,000** |
| | *Ryan Luzinski, c | Dodgers (1-S) | 32 | $500,000 |
| 14. | Chad McConnell, of | Phillies (1) | 13 | $475,000 |
| 15. | **Rick Greene, rhp** | **Tigers (1)** | **16** | **$470,000** |
| 16. | **Michael Tucker, ss** | **Royals (1)** | **10** | **$450,000** |
| | ***Shannon Stewart, of** | **Blue Jays (1)** | **19** | **$450,000** |
| | **Todd Steverson, of** | **Blue Jays (1)** | **25** | **$450,000** |
| 19. | ***Jim Pittsley, rhp** | **Royals (1)** | **17** | **$410,000** |
| 20. | **Chad Mottola, of** | **Reds (1)** | **5** | **$400,000** |
| | *Jamie Howard, rhp | Braves (2) | 59 | $400,000 |
| 22. | **Rick Helling, rhp** | **Rangers (1)** | **22** | **$397,000** |
| 23. | Benji Grigsby, rhp | Athletics (1) | 20 | $380,000 |
| | ***Jamie Arnold, rhp** | **Braves (1)** | **21** | **$380,000** |
| 25. | Chris Roberts, lhp | Mets (1) | 18 | $365,000 |

*Major leaguers in bold. *High school selection.*

Pierce, Fla., on Nov. 5—a revised signing deadline to accommodate players who had played in that year's Olympics. Talks between Johnson's father and Marlins officials broke off about 9:30 p.m. Dombrowski and Hughes returned home, but 90 minutes later Johnson told Boras he wanted to sign. Johnson made a call to Dombrowski, and they agreed on $575,000.

STEWART SMITH
Charles Johnson

Boras was such a polarizing figure that the father of top prospect Michael Tucker contacted every club when rumors surfaced on the eve of the draft that his son was linked to Boras, to make it clear that Boras was not representing his son. He feared an association with Boras could hurt Tucker's position in the draft. Tucker went 10th overall to the Royals and signed for $450,000.

In spite of efforts by clubs to hold the line on bonuses, the average bonus paid to 1992 first-round picks was $481,893, an increase of 31.9 percent over the 1991 average of $365,396. The Dodgers did not have a first-round choice, but still spent a draft-record $2.483 million to sign their picks. Only fourth-rounder Keith Johnson reached the majors, getting four at-bats with the Angels.

The Blue Jays again were among the big spenders. They gave out more bonus money than any other club in both 1989 and 1990, were second in 1991 and second again in 1992 with $2,249,500. Unlike the Dodgers, the Blue Jays had to pay two first-round picks, outfielders Shannon Stewart and Todd Steverson, and would have spent more than the Dodgers had they come to terms with Morenz, their sixth-round pick who opted for Texas.

The Blue Jays also gained the big prize in the international market, signing 16-year-old Brazilian righthander Jose Pett for $675,000, the largest bonus ever given an international amateur. The previous high was $125,000, given to Puerto Rican righthander Ramser Correa in 1987.

The Jays won a bidding war with the Atlanta Braves, Astros, Dodgers and Marlins for the 6-foot-6, 195-pound Pett, who was believed to be the first player ever signed out of Brazil. Because Pett's bonus was paid by a Canadian corporation, it was tax-free to Pett under Brazilian-Canadian taxation laws. Pett never justified the investment, going 23-36, 4.52 in a six-year career that peaked in Triple-A.

Prior to the 1992 draft, team owners tried to implement new rules to limit players' negotiating leverage. At a meeting in Chicago on March 5, owners approved a rule that gave teams exclusive negotiating rights to a player until a year after his college class graduated. Another provision reduced the draft to 50 rounds.

The Players Association filed a grievance in mid-April over the unilateral changes. The case was not heard until a week before the June 1 draft, and independent arbitrator George Nicolau sided with the union in his ruling on July 17, determining that Major League Baseball could not make changes to the draft without negotiating with the union. Even though amateur players were not members of the union, the arbitrator ruled the union had a say in the draft because draft picks were awarded as compensation to teams losing free agents, thus affecting the value of major league players.

The changes were reversed. After a one-year limit of 50 rounds, there was no limit again in 1993.

### OLYMPICS TAP DRAFT TALENT

Baseball became a medal sport in the Olympics for the first time in 1992, after winning favor as a demonstration sport in 1984 and '88. The U.S. teams featured college players from the current year's draft. The 1992 squad, which included 11 first-round picks, went 5-2 in round-robin play, lost to Cuba in the semifinals and dropped the bronze-medal game to Japan.

Cuba, which had boycotted the '84 and '88 Olympics, won the tournament in Barcelona, Spain, by going 9-0, its 13th straight major international tournament title. The Cubans had a 72-game winning streak in those events.

Nevin led Team USA during its 38-game summer schedule, hitting .347 with a team-best nine homers and 31 RBIs. Hammonds (.315-5-22, 11 SB), Murray (.307-0-18, 23 SB) and Tucker (.321-4-29, 28 SB) also played well. In the Olympic competition, Hammonds went 16-for-37, leading the team in hits and RBIs.

First-rounders Wallace (4-3, 4.06, team-high 54 strikeouts) and Greene (2-0, 1.69, team-high four saves) were on the pitching staff, but the most effective U.S. pitcher was lefthander Jeff Alkire (5-0, 1.90), a fifth-round pick of the St. Louis Cardinals who had only a brief pro career.

### WORTH NOTING

■ Due to the 50-round limit that was mandated for the 1992 draft (and rescinded after one year after the Players Association successfully argued to have it reversed), teams selected 1,411 players, the fewest since 1987. The record at the time was 1,533 in 1991, which was passed in 1993 when 1,721 players were selected. The signing rate of 66.7 percent for players drafted in 1992 was considerably higher than in 1991 (58.0 percent), 1993 (56.1 percent), and 1994 (53.3 percent).

■ Aside from the arbitrator's decision that reversed the unilateral imposition of a 50-round draft along with several other changes, the ruling established an important precedent that major league teams could not unilaterally change draft rules, a lesson they struggled to take to heart in the coming years.

■ Stanford had the most players drafted (11) and at the same time recruited the most drafted players who chose to enroll in school (10). The Cardinal, which fell short of the College World Series, had two first-round picks (outfielder **JEFF HAMMONDS**, righthander **RICK HELLING**) and two second-rounders (righthanders **BRIAN SACKINSKY** and **JOHN LYNCH**). Of its recruits, the Cardinal lost only second-rounder **BOB WOLCOTT** (Mariners) to the pro ranks. The most talented of the incoming players was Oklahoma high school catcher **A.J. HINCH**, a second-round pick of the White Sox.

■ Outfielder **SHON WALKER**, a supplemental first-round pick of the Pirates (33rd overall), set the national single-season high school home run record in 1992, hitting 29 for Harrison County High in Cynthiana, Ky. Walker did not rise above Class A in seven seasons in the Pirates system, hitting .254 with 57 homers, including a season high of 15.

CONTINUED ON PAGE 410

## WORTH NOTING

CONTINUED FROM PAGE 409

The second round of the 1992 draft was noteworthy for the football players that were selected. The Marlins drafted Lynch out of Stanford with the 66th pick overall. After signing for $150,000, Lynch made seven starts in the short-season New York-Penn League before quitting baseball and going on to spend 15 years in the NFL as a safety. The Braves spent $400,000 to sign Louisiana high school righthander **JAMIE HOWARD** (59th overall). It was the largest bonus paid to a second-round choice, and more than the Braves paid their first-round pick, righthander **JAMIE ARNOLD**. The Braves agreed that Howard would not have to report for almost a year while he was establishing a football career at Louisiana State. Howard became LSU's starting quarterback three games into his freshman year, and finished his four-year career as the second-leading passer in school history in both yards (6,158) and touchdowns (34). Compromised by a shoulder injury at LSU, however, Howard spent just three seasons in the Braves system, going 4-9, 5.10. The Padres also drafted **TODD HELTON** (55th overall), who did not agree to a deal and went to the University of Tennessee, where he became the backup quarterback to Peyton Manning and the star first baseman on the baseball team. Helton hit .370 with 38 homers and 238 RBIs over three seasons in college before becoming the Rockies' 1995 first-round draft choice and the best player in franchise history.

In one of many arbitration rulings that impacted the 1992 draft, the Twins won a battle with the Mariners over the No. 26 overall pick. Minnesota originally lost the pick to Seattle for signing Type B free agent pitcher Bill Krueger, but the Twins argued successfully that Krueger had signed a minor league contract before making the Mariners out of spring training, which negated the compensation.

Upstart Pepperdine won the 1992 College World Series, beating Cal State Fullerton. Though Nevin was the star of the tournament, Pepperdine had a first-round pick of its own, righthander Derek Wallace, who was drafted 11th overall by the Chicago Cubs. Wallace suffered a hairline leg fracture in a car accident prior to the season, but he came back and went 4-2, 3.20, mostly as a starter. Wallace pitched in 27 games as a reliever in the majors.

In addition to Wallace, other college first-rounders destined for relief roles as pros were Shuey, lefthander Ron Villone (Mariners, 14th overall), righthander Sean Lowe (Cardinals, 15th), Greene (Tigers, 16th) and righthander Benji Grigsby (Athletics, 20th). None enjoyed significant success in the majors, combining for 37 saves, 23 by Shuey. Greene, a dominant college closer for three years at LSU, struggled with his mechanics throughout his pro career and pitched in one major league game. Grigsby did not reach the majors, his career impacted by labrum surgery in both 1992 while at San Diego State and in 1993 after signing with the A's.

Every 1992 first-round pick received a bonus of at least $300,000 except for UCLA righthander Pete Janicki, who was drafted eighth overall by the California Angels. After summer-long negotiations, he got a $90,000 bonus.

Janicki, a teammate of Nevin's at El Dorado High in Placentia, Calif., injured his arm in the final start of his college career in NCAA regional play. He threw 89 pitches in the game, two days after throwing 148, understandably concerning the Angels about his long-term health.

Pete Janicki

Instead of a minor league contract, the Angels signed Janicki to a major league deal that stipulated he would receive a salary of $125,000 in 1993, and if he stayed healthy, $155,000 and $215,000 the following two years. It added up to a $585,000 deal, including bonus—the amount Janicki agreed to before suffering what was later determined to be a stress fracture in his elbow.

Janicki missed his 1992 pro season because of the injury, then had a recurrence of the injury a year later in the second inning of his first professional game. He pitched in six seasons, including three in Triple-A, but did not make the major leagues.

Injuries also had a profound effect on the career of outfielder Kenny Felder, drafted 12th overall by the Milwaukee Brewers. Felder turned down a $243,000 bonus offer from the Padres in 1989 as a second-round pick, opting to play football and baseball at Florida State. With a chance to win the starting quarterback job during spring practice as a redshirt sophomore, Felder temporarily abandoned baseball to focus on football, but when he failed to win the QB job, he turned his attention back to baseball. Felder didn't produce much in the Seminoles' remaining games but showed enough promise that the Brewers signed him for $525,000.

Felder's pro career was impacted by shoulder and elbow injuries, and his career ended during spring training 1998 when he hit a ball during batting practice that ricocheted off the batting cage and struck him flush in the face. He broke the orbital bone in his left eye and was left with 20-400 vision.

### DAMON REBOUNDS FROM DRAFT SLIGHT

Fourteen of the first 16 picks in the 1992 draft and 20 overall came from the college ranks, a record that wasn't matched until the 2005 and '08 drafts. One player was taken from junior college, leaving seven high school selections in the first round, the fewest ever.

The top prep talent acquitted itself well, though. In addition to Jeter, outfielder Shannon Stewart (Blue Jays, 19th overall) and catcher Jason Kendall (Pirates, 23rd), the son of former big leaguer catcher Fred Kendall, ranked among the five most

### Largest Bonuses By Round

| | Player, Pos. | Club | Bonus |
|---|---|---|---|
| **1.** | **Jeffrey Hammonds, rhp** | **Orioles** | **$975,000** |
| 2. | * Jamie Howard, rhp | Braves | $400,000 |
| 3. | * Dwight Maness, of | Dodgers | $170,000 |
| **4.** | *** Tom Evans, 3b** | **Blue Jays** | **$95,000** |
| 5. | Chris Abbe, c | Dodgers | $92,500 |
| 6. | * Emilio Mendez, ss | Cubs | $67,000 |
| **7.** | *** Anthony Sanders, of** | **Blue Jays** | **$100,000** |
| 8. | * Brian Doughty, rhp | Mariners | $80,000 |
| 9. | * Tim Adkins, lhp | Blue Jays | $52,500 |
| 10. | * David Post, 3b | Dodgers | $50,000 |
| 11. | * Jeff Hairston, of | Pirates | $75,000 |
| 12. | Derrick Cantrell, of | Brewers | $45,400 |
| 13. | * Richard Halbruner, 1b | Blue Jays | $38,000 |
| **14.** | *** Jason Phillips, rhp** | **Pirates** | **$102,000** |
| 15. | * Doug Meiners, rhp | Blue Jays | $75,000 |
| 16. | * Brian Darwin, of | Athletics | $35,000 |
| 17. | * Scott Lair, rhp | Cardinals | $30,000 |
| | Keith Troutman, rhp | Dodgers | $30,000 |
| 18. | * David Becker, c | Blue Jays | $32,500 |
| **19.** | **Mike Grzanich, rhp** | **Astros** | **$25,000** |
| 20. | *# Andreus Lewis, of | Rangers | $42,500 |
| **21.** | **# Aaron Guiel, of** | **Angels** | **$255,000** |
| 22. | * Richard Werner, rhp | Brewers | $30,500 |
| **23.** | **# Ryan Franklin, rhp** | **Mariners** | **$67,500** |
| 24. | Bob Juday, ss | Red Sox | $33,000 |
| 25. | # Lyle Prempas, lhp | Brewers | $120,000 |
| Other | # Russell Handy, rhp | Expos (50) | $150,000 |

*Major leaguers in bold. *High school selection. #Signed as draft-and-follow.*

### Highest Unsigned Picks

| Player, Pos., Team (Round) | College | Re-Drafted |
|---|---|---|
| Jon Ward, rhp, Mets (1) | Cal State Fullerton | Cardinals '95 (8) |
| Chad Alexander, of, Reds (2) | Texas A&M | Astros '95 (3) |
| Todd Helton, 1b, Padres (2) | Tennessee | Rockies '95 (1) |
| A.J. Hinch, c, White Sox (2) | Stanford | Twins '95 (3) |
| Brian Powell, rhp, Angels (3) | Georgia | Tigers '95 (2) |
| Gabe Alvarez, 3b, Athletics (3) | USC | Padres '95 (2) |
| Chad Sheffer, ss, Astros (4) | Florida State | Mariners '95 (14) |
| Brett Laxton, rhp, Padres (4) | Louisiana State | Mariners '95 (24) |
| Ryan Wilson, c, Cubs (4) | Cerritos (Calif.) JC | Never |
| Jeff Liefer, of, Indians (6) | Long Beach State | White Sox '95 (1) |

**TOTAL UNSIGNED PICKS:** Top 5 Rounds (9), Top 10 Rounds (28)

productive players in the 1992 class, according to Wins Above Replacement.

Outfielder Preston Wilson, selected ninth overall by the New York Mets and the stepson of former Mets star Mookie Wilson, wasn't far behind. A relative unknown entering the 1992 season at South Carolina's Bamberg-Ehrhardt High, the 6-foot-3, 195-pound Wilson, then a shortstop/pitcher, batted .530 and set state records for runs (71), hits (62), home runs (22) and RBIs. He also went 13-0, 1.98 on the mound.

Aside from Jeter, no 1992 draft choice had a better career than outfielder Johnny Damon, selected with a supplemental first-round pick (35th overall) by the Royals. .

The Royals made five of the first 44 picks in the 1992 draft, and Damon was the fourth. Tucker, a second baseman from Longwood (Va.) College, was their first selection (10th) and Pennsylvania high school righthander Jim Pittsley their second (17th overall).

Tucker, who led NCAA Division II with a .489 average and 22 homers, was considered the best pure hitter available. He played 12 seasons in the majors as an outfielder, hitting .256 with 125 homers.

The 6-foot-4 Pittsley, who went 10-3, 0.90 with 166 strikeouts in 85 innings as a senior at DuBois Area High, generally was recognized as the best prep arm. He was the first high school player in the class to reach the majors, although elbow issues impacted Pittsley's career and he won just seven games. The Royals, who had been lean spenders in recent drafts, committed a total of $1.873 million this time, third-highest among all clubs.

The Dodgers ended up with virtually nothing to show for their big spending. They spent heavily on their first two picks, Pennsylvania high school catcher Ryan Luzinski (31st overall, $500,000) and UCLA outfielder Michael Moore (36th, $537,000), and spent at least $150,000 on each of their next four selections. Luzinski, son of ex-big leaguer Greg Luzinski, played eight seasons and Moore 10, but neither could get higher than Triple-A.

The Pittsburgh Pirates earned special commendation for both signing the most consecutive picks (26) and also the most future big leaguers, though only Jason Kendall had a noteworthy career in the major leagues. In 15 years, he hit .288 with 75 homers.

### ROCKIES, MARLINS ENTER FRAY

Expansion teams in Denver and Miami were set to begin play in the National League in 1993, and they were afforded their first opportunity to draft talent in 1992. The teams were given the last two picks in each round.

The Rockies, picking 27th, selected Burke, who pitched at Cherry Creek High in suburban Denver before attending college at Florida. Burke was drafted by the Astros with the sixth overall pick in 1991 as a draft-eligible sophomore and didn't sign. He went 8-5, 3.31 with 65 walks and 97 strikeouts in 104 innings as a junior.

The Rockies signed Burke for $336,000 on the same day they drafted him. He featured a mid-90s fastball and a big-breaking curve, but battled control problems during the 1992 season at Florida, and his inability to throw strikes carried over to his pro career. He pitched in only two seasons for the Rockies.

The Marlins, picking 28th, took Johnson, who attended college at nearby Miami. The Marlins didn't get Johnson under contract until the last day possible, and it cost them $249,000 more in bonus money than what the Rockies gave Burke. But Johnson was worth the price. He spent 12 seasons in the majors, including seven with the Marlins, and was a four-time Gold Glove winner, in addition to hitting 167 home runs.

In the second round, the Marlins drafted John Lynch, a righthander from Stanford with a 95 mph fastball. He signed for $150,000 and had the distinction of throwing the first pitch in organization history, in the 1992 season opener for short-season Erie of the New York-Penn League. Lynch went 0-3, 2.15 in seven starts before returning to Stanford to play his senior year of football. He quit baseball the next year after being drafted in the third round of the 1993 NFL draft by the Tampa Bay Buccaneers. He spent 15 years in the NFL as a safety and appeared in nine Pro Bowls.

## Largest Draft-And-Follow Bonuses

| | Player, Pos. | Club (Round) | Bonus |
|---|---|---|---|
| 1. | *Russell Handy, rhp | Expos (50) | $150,000 |
| 2. | Ryan Creek, rhp | Astros (34) | $140,843 |
| 3. | *Lyle Prempas, lhp | Brewers (25) | $120,000 |
| 4. | Keith Heberling, lhp | Yankees (46) | $83,000 |
| 5. | Scott Norman, rhp | Tigers (26) | $72,500 |
| **6.** | **Ryan Franklin, rhp** | **Mariners (23)** | **$67,500** |
| **7.** | **Lou Collier, ss** | **Pirates (31)** | **$65,000** |
| 8. | Ken Sikes, 1b/rhp | Dodgers (33) | $62,500 |
| 9. | Kevin Pitts, of | Dodgers (26) | $60,000 |
| | Chris Cumberland, lhp | Yankees (48) | $60,000 |

*Major leaguers in bold. *High school selection.*

## IN FOCUS: JOHNNY DAMON

Entering his senior year of high school in Orlando, Fla., Johnny Damon was rated the top prep player in the 1992 draft class on the strength of his superior bat, speed and athleticism. Every time he came to the plate that spring, the PA blared: "Now batting, the No. 1 player in the country, Johnny Damon."

It was a lot for any kid to live up to, and Damon hit just .305, which caused him to tumble out of the first round. The Royals took him with the 35th pick overall and gave him $250,000 to sign. Though disappointed, Damon handled the adversity well, saying, "I don't know what happened. I know I can play with any of these guys getting drafted ahead of me."

The 6-foot-2, 190-pound outfielder quickly reasserted himself in pro ball, hitting .349 in the Rookie-level Gulf Coast League, and never stopped performing. He hit .318 with 152 stolen bases and an assortment of extra-base hits in four season in the minors, and took over Kansas City's center-field job in the latter half of the 1995 season. He went on to play 18 seasons in the majors, hitting .284 with 235 homers and 408 stolen bases.

Outside of Derek Jeter, the first high school player drafted in 1992, no prep pick—or draft selection of any kind—had a better career than Damon, in spite of his down senior year.

## One Team's Draft: Kansas City Royals

| | Player, Pos. | Bonus |
|---|---|---|
| **1.** | **Michael Tucker, ss** | **$450,000** |
| **1.** | ***Jim Pittsley, rhp** | **$410,000** |
| 1. | Sherard Clinkscales, rhp | $180,000 |
| **1.** | ***Johnny Damon, of** | **$250,000** |
| **2.** | **Jon Lieber, rhp** | **$80,000** |
| **3.** | **Chris Eddy, lhp** | **$80,000** |
| 4. | Steve Murphy, of | $70,000 |
| 5. | Jeff Haas, lhp | $45,000 |
| 6. | *Jelani Brandon, of | $60,000 |
| 7. | *Justin Adam, rhp | $30,000 |
| 8. | *Mike Kern, of | $44,000 |
| **9.** | **Bart Evans, rhp** | **$25,000** |
| 10. | John Dickens, rhp | $30,000 |
| 11. | *Ken Fitzpatrick, rhp | $24,000 |
| 12. | David Bladow, rhp | $2,000 |
| 13. | Jason Marshall, ss | $3,000 |
| 14. | Brian Harrison, rhp | $3,000 |
| **15.** | **Melvin Bunch, rhp** | **$20,000** |
| **16.** | **Steve Sisco, 2b** | **$3,000** |
| 17. | David Cornell, of | $3,000 |
| 18. | *Paul Vidivich, c | $15,000 |
| 19. | *Jeff Parsons, ss | Did not sign |
| 20. | Tom Heming, lhp | $2,000 |
| **21.** | **Larry Sutton, of** | **$2,000** |
| 22. | *Clemente Saiten, of | Did not sign |
| 23. | Sean Delaney, c | $2,000 |
| 24. | Paul Fletcher, lhp | $2,000 |
| 25. | *Jamie Splittorff, rhp | Did not sign |

*Major leaguers in bold. *High school selection.*

# 1992 Draft List

**Did not sign. Major leaguers in bold, with first and last years noted. Order of selection indicated in parentheses. For the first five rounds, the peak level of each player is noted. + Signed as draft-and-follow (Second school noted if applicable).*

## ATLANTA BRAVES (21)

1. **Jamie Arnold, rhp, Osceola HS, Kissimmee, Fla.—(1999-2000)**
2. Jamie Howard, rhp, St. Thomas More HS, Lafayette, La.—(Low A)
3. Carey Paige, rhp, Cooper HS, Abilene, Texas.—(AA)
4. **Damon Hollins, of, Vallejo (Calif.) HS.—(1998-2006)**
5. Sean Smith, c, Oconomowoc (Wis.) HS.—(High A)
6. ***Justin Atchley, lhp, Walla Walla (Wash.) CC.—(2001)**
7. Ken Warner, ss, St. Helena Central HS, Amite, La.
8. Maurice Christmas, rhp, Lexington Christian Academy, Lexington, Mass.
9. Anthony Diieso, of, Copiague HS, Lindenhurst. N.Y.
10. **Brad Clontz, rhp, Virginia Tech.—(1995-2000)**
11. **Bobby Smith, of-3b, Fremont HS, Oakland, Calif.—(1998-2002)**
12. **Chris Brock, of-rhp, Florida State University.—(1997-2002)**
13. ***Mark Hendrickson, lhp, Mount Vernon (Wash.) HS.—(2002-11)**

DRAFT DROP *Forward, National Basketball Association (1996-2000)*

14. Shane Bryant, rhp, Proctor Hug HS, Reno, Nev.
15. ***Jose Cruz Jr., of, Bellaire HS, Houston.—(1997-2008)**

DRAFT DROP *Son of Jose Cruz, major leaguer (1970-88) • First-round draft pick (3rd overall), Mariners (1995)*

16. Clint Gagnon, rhp, South Suburban (Ill.) JC.
17. Richard Williams, of, Hesperia (Calif.) HS.
18. ***Shane Monahan, of, Wheeler HS, Marietta. Ga.—(1998-99)**

DRAFT DROP *Great grandson of Howie Morenz, member/Hockey Hall of Fame; forward/National Hockey League (1923-37) • Grandson of Bernie "Boom Boom" Geoffrion, member/Hockey Hall of Fame; forward/National Hockey League (1951-68) • Son of Hartland Monahan, forward/National Hockey League (1975-81)*

19. Tyrone Domingo, ss, Los Angeles (Calif.) HS.
20. Jason Shelley, 1b, Vallejo (Calif.) HS.
21. Shawn Brennan, of, Moeller HS, Cincinnati.
22. Mike Warner, of, Florida International University.
23. Tony Stoecklin, lhp, Southern Illinois University-Edwardsville.

DRAFT DROP *Baseball coach, SIU-Edwardsville (2013-15)*

24. Aaron Turnier, lhp, University of Nevada-Las Vegas.
25. Dan Teran, lhp, Mesa (Ariz.) CC.
26. Bryan Spetter, ss-2b, Anderson (Ind.) University.
27. *Mike McKenna, rhp, Kishwaukee (Ill.) JC.
28. *Chris Wyrick, ss, University of Missouri.
29. Doug Wollenburg, ss, Ohio State University.
30. Phil Zimmerman, ss, Regis (Colo.) College.
31. Derrick Calvin, rhp, Southern University.
32. *Fernando Benitez, c, Lindsay (Calif.) HS.
33. Ryan Jacobs, lhp, Glenn HS, Kernersville, N.C.
34. *Cedric Williams, ss, Western Hills HS, Fort Worth, Texas.
35. *Brian Cravey, rhp, Silsbee (Texas) HS.
36. William Paragin, c, John A. Logan (Ill.) CC.
37. Anthony Ruff, of, Moreno Valley (Calif.) HS.
38. Terrell Buckley, of, Florida State University.

DRAFT DROP *First-round draft pick, Green Bay Packers/National Football League (1992); defensive back, NFL (1992-2005)*

39. James Stutts, of, San Jacinto (Texas) JC.
40. James Blaine, rhp, McLennan (Texas) CC.
41. David Bingham, of, Lewis-Clark State (Idaho) College.
42. *Corey Ehlers, rhp-3b, Sharpstown HS, Houston.
43. *Monty Means, of Union (S.C) HS.
44. *Mark Brunell, lhp, University of Washington.

DRAFT DROP *Quarterback, National Football League (1994-2006)*

45. *John Webb, c, McLennan (Texas) CC.
46. **Darrell May, lhp, Sacramento (Calif.) CC.—(1995-2005)**
47. Chris Church, lhp, Penn State University.
48. Ted Hassan, rhp, Jackson State University.
49. Kevin Nalls, 3b, Grambling State University.
50. John Simmons, lhp, St. Xavier (Ill.) College.

## BALTIMORE ORIOLES (4)

1. **Jeffrey Hammonds, of, Stanford University.—(1993-2005)**

DRAFT DROP *First player from 1992 draft to reach major leagues (June 25, 1993)*

2. **Brian Sackinsky, rhp, Stanford University.—(1996)**
3. Billy Owens, 1b, University of Arizona.—(AAA)
4. Hut Smith, rhp, A.L. Brown HS, Kannapolis, N.C.—(AA)
5. **Scott Klingenbeck, rhp, Ohio State University.—(1994-98)**
6. Robert Chancey, of, Stanhope Elmore HS, Millbrook, Ala.
7. Keith Eaddy, of, William Paterson (N.J.) College.
8. Cory Brown, rhp-of, Gibbs HS, St. Petersburg, Fla.
9. Calvin Lee, rhp, East St. John HS, Garvyille, La.
10. *Roberto Lopez, rhp, Wilcox HS, Santa Clara, Calif.
11. Angel Pagan, ss, Dra Maria Cadilla de Martinez HS, Arecibo, P.R.
12. Michael Porter, rhp, Centenary College.
13. Tobias Price, lhp, Lincoln HS, San Diego.
14. Adam Burton, 2b, Florida CC.
15. ***Ryan Minor, ss, Hammon (Okla.) HS.—(1998-2001)**

DRAFT DROP *Twin brother of Damon Minor, major leaguer (2000-04) • Second-round draft pick, Philadelphia 76ers/National Basketball Association (1996)*

16. ***Bubba Trammell, 3b, Cleveland State (Tenn) CC.—(1997-2003)**
17. Carlos Chavez, rhp, New Mexico JC.
18. **Garrett Stephenson, rhp, Ricks (Idaho) JC.—(1996-2003)**
19. *Korey Burkhart, rhp, Barton County (Kan.) CC.
20. *James Esparza, lhp, Cedar Valley (Texas) JC.
21. *Chris Bauer, ss, Jenks HS, Tulsa, Okla.
22. Keivi Baker, c, Shanks HS, Gretna, Fla.
23. Paul Jones, 1b, Cumberland (Ky.) College.
24. Aaron Lane, lhp, University of New Orleans.
25. *Ron Wallech, rhp, Hagerstown (Md.) JC.
26. *Brian Scutero, rhp, Valencia (Fla.) CC.
27. **Howie Clark, 1b, Huntington Beach (Calif.) HS.—(2002-08)**
28. **+Joe Dawley, rhp, Riverside (Calif.) CC.—(2002-04)**
29. Gregg Castaldo, ss, University of Central Florida.
30. *Dean Kent, of, Jesuit HS, Oldsmar, Fla.
31. *Ledowick Johnson, of, Louisburg (N.C.) JC.
32. Joe Lantrip, lhp, Memphis State University.
33. *Scott Schroeffel, of, North Allegheny HS, Pittsburgh.
34. *Tony Enard, rhp, Sparks (Nev.) HS.
35. ***Brian Simmons, of, Peters Township HS, McMurray, Pa.—(1998-2001)**
36. *Jose Santiago, ss, Dr. Phillips HS, Orlando, Fla.
37. *Rob Gardner, rhp, Carlmont HS, Belmont, Calif.
38. ***George Arias, 3b, Pima (Ariz.) CC.—(1996-99)**
39. Kyle Yeske, of, St. Mary's (Minn.) College.
40. George Freeberger, c, Polytechnic HS, Baltimore.
41. *Anthony Marnell, c, Bishop Gorman HS, Las Vegas, Nev.
42. *Scott Tanksley, rhp, Kemp (Texas) HS.
43. *Mario Iglesias, rhp, Hayward (Calif.) HS.
44. *Brad Crede, 3b, Fatima HS, Westphalia, Mo.

DRAFT DROP *Brother of Joe Crede, major leaguer (2000-09)*

45. *Mike Drumright, rhp, Valley Center (Kan.) HS.

DRAFT DROP *First-round draft pick (11th overall), Tigers (1995)*

46. *Robert Costello, rhp, Watson Chapel HS, Pine Bluff, Ark.
47. +Jarvis White, of, Polk (Fla.) CC.
48. *Marvin Perkins, of, Lake City (Fla.) CC.
49. *Joe Goodwin, c, South Carroll HS, New Windsor, Md.
50. *Michael Thompson, of, Clovis (N.M.) HS.

## BOSTON RED SOX (18)

1. (Choice to Mets as compensation for Type A free agent Frank Viola)
2. Tony Sheffield, of, Tullahoma (Tenn.) HS.—(High A)
3. Doug Hecker, 1b, University of Tennessee.—(AA)
4. Joe Hamilton, 3b, Dighton-Rehobeth HS, Rehobeth, Mass.—(AA)
5. **Steve Rodriguez, 2b, Pepperdine University.—(1995)**

DRAFT DROP *Baseball coach, Pepperdine (2003-15)*

6. Derek Vinyard, of, San Diego State University.
7. **Joe DePastino, lhp-of, Riverview HS, Sarasota, Fla.—(2003)**
8. J.B. Bowles, 3b, Montgomery HS, Rockville, Md.
9. Todd Carey, ss, Brown University.
10. Mark Senkowitz, c, Ohio Wesleyan University.
11. Aaron Rounsifer, ss, Vista (Calif.) HS.
12. Chad Amos, rhp, Ohio State University.
13. **Bill Selby, ss, University of Southern Mississippi.—(1996-2003)**
14. Jim Tyrrell, lhp, Dutchess (N.Y.) CC.
15. Gettys Glaze, rhp, The Citadel.
16. *Rick Gama, 2b, Southridge HS, Miami.
17. *Chris McCranie, ss, Colquitt County HS, Moultrie, Ga.
18. Eric Norman, ss, Jones County HS, Haddock, Ga.
19. Brent Hansen, rhp, University of California.
20. Rob Berryman, rhp, Yorktown, Va.
21. Leif McKinley, rhp, Chemeketa (Ore.) CC.
22. Jeff Martin, c, Vanderbilt University.
23. Wes Brooks, rhp, Belleville Area (Ill.) CC.
24. Bob Juday, ss-2b, Michigan State University.
25. Jeff Faino, lhp, Florida Tech.
26. Eric Cormier, rhp, Milford (Mass.) HS.
27. **Joe Hudson, rhp, West Virginia University.—(1995-98)**
28. Rick Milligan, of, San Joaquin Delta (Calif.) JC.
29. Ricky Craig, rhp, Webb City HS, Jasper, Mo.
30. Scott Bakkum, rhp, University of Minnesota.
31. (void) *Wilredo Rivera, of, Lino Padron Rivera HS, Vega Alta, P.R.
32. Randy Lawrence, rhp, Ferrum (Va.) College.
33. Ethan Faggett, of, Dunbar HS, Burleson, Texas.
34. *Marcus Cuper, lhp, Voorhees HS, High Bridge, N.J.
35. Andrew Moore, 2b, Bridgewater (Va.) College.
36. ***Lou Merloni, ss, Providence College.—(1998-2006)**
37. Jason Smith, c, University of West Florida.
38. T.J. O'Donnell, ss, Old Dominion University.
39. +Joe Barksdale, rhp, Southern Union State (Ala.) JC.
40. *Adam McCollough, c, Eisenhower HS, Lawton, Okla.
41. *Reggie Hightower, of, George C. Wallace (Ala.) CC.
42. *Gresham Fortune, of, East Central (Miss.) JC.
43. *Kevin Gibbs, ss, St. John's HS, Davidsonville, Md.
44. *Eric DeMoura, ss, Taunton (Mass.) HS.
45. *Chris Wagner, rhp, Santa Fe (Fla.) CC.
46. *Allen Williams, 3b, University of Arkansas.
47. *Brian Johnson, 1b, Lee County HS, Albany, Ga.
48. *Lewis Spencer, ss, Hampton (Va.) HS.
49. *Rico Wood, 2b, Southern Union State (Ala.) JC.
50. *Michael Linenberger, of, Mississippi Gulf Coast JC.

## CALIFORNIA ANGELS (8)

1. Pete Janicki, rhp, UCLA.—(AAA)
1. **Jeff Schmidt, rhp, University of Minnesota** (Supplemental choice—29th—as compensation for Type A free agent Wally Joyner).—**(1996)**
2. DeShawn Warren, lhp, Choctaw County HS, Butler, Ala.—(Low A)
2. Chris Smith, ss-of, Vallejo (Calif.) HS (Choice from Royals as compensation for Joyner).—(AA)
2. Marquis Riley, of, Central Arkansas University (Supplemental choice—67th—as compensation for Type C free agent Kirk McCaskill).—(AAA)
3. ***Brian Powell, rhp, Bainbridge (Ga.) HS.—(1998-2004)**

DRAFT DROP *Attended Georgia; re-drafted by Tigers, 1995 (2nd round)*

4. Shawn Holcomb, rhp, El Dorado HS, Placentia. Calif.—(Rookie)
5. Paxton Briley, rhp, Clemson University.—(Short-season A)
6. **Bill Simas, rhp, Fresno (Calif.) CC.—(1995-2000)**
7. Larry Hingle, lhp, Stetson University.
8. John Lloyd, rhp, Englewood HS, Jacksonville, Fla.
9. Mickey Kerns, of, University of Alabama.
10. Travis Thurmond, rhp, Beaverton (Ore.) HS.
11. ***Travis Driskill, rhp, Blinn (Texas) JC.—(2002-07)**
12. Morisse Daniels, of, Florida A&M University.
13. **John Snyder, rhp, Westlake HS, Thousand Oaks, Calif.—(1998-2000)**
14. Jay Simpson, of, University of South Alabama.
15. Dallas Rinehart, rhp, East Tennessee State University.
16. Michael Wolff, of, Georgia Tech.
17. +Ted Tiffany, of, Cactus HS, Glendale, Ariz. / Phoenix JC.
18. David Kessler, c, UC Riverside.
19. *Moe McWhite, of, Florida CC.
20. Kekoa Dafun, rhp, Baldwin HS, Kihei, Hawaii.
21. **+Aaron Guiel, of, Kwantlen (B.C.) JC.—(2002-06)**
22. John Pricher, rhp, University of Florida.
23. *Luis Ducasse, of, John F. Kennedy HS, Bronx, N.Y.
24. Ronald Davis, of, Simeon HS, Chicago.
25. ***Benny Agbayani, of, Hawaii Pacific University.—(1998-2002)**
26. *Charles Beale, rhp, Dublin (Ga.) HS.
27. +Juan Henderson, ss, Gulf Coast (Fla.) CC.
28. *David Krug, rhp, Concordia (N.Y.) College.
29. +Aaron Mayer, c, California HS, San Ramon, Calif. / Modesto (Calif.) JC.
30. *Manuel Mendez, lhp, Washington Union HS, Fresno, Calif.
31. *Seth Brizek, ss, Oley Valley HS, Fleetwood, Pa.
32. *Alvie Shepherd, rhp-of, Proviso West HS, Bellwood, Ill.

DRAFT DROP *First-round draft pick (21st overall), Orioles (1995)*

33. *Casey Kirkman, rhp, JC of the Sequoias (Calif.).
34. *Todd Singelyn, rhp, Loyola HS, Whittier, Calif.
35. *Erik Plaisted, rhp, Minnetonka (Minn.) HS.
36. *Chad Baker, rhp, Polk (Fla.) CC.
37. *Felix Merced, ss, Brevard (Fla.) CC.
38. *James Johnson, of, San Bernardino Valley (Calif.) JC.
39. *Brandy Bengoechea, ss, Lewis-Clark State (Idaho) College.
40. *Brian Ussery, c. Bloomingdale HS, Brandon, Fla.
41. *Dan Ladehoff, ss, Central HS, Davenport, Iowa.
42. *Michael Cole, of, Monterey (Calif.) HS.
43. Bill Blanchette, lhp, University of Hawaii.
44. Marcus Garcia, of, Mount San Antonio (Calif.) JC.
45. Greg Biley, ss, California Baptist College.
46. *Ben Duncan, of, Palomar (Calif.) JC.
47. *David Vindivich, of, Edmonds (Wash.) CC.
48. *Brad Buenconsejo, rhp, Hawaii Pacific University.
49. Joe Urso, 2b, University of Tampa.
50. **Anthony Chavez, rhp, San Jose State University.—(1997)**

## CHICAGO CUBS (11)

1. **Derek Wallace, rhp, Pepperdine University.—(1996-99)**
2. (Choice to Dodgers as compensation for Type A free agent Mike Morgan)
3. **Brant Brown, 1b, Fresno State University.—(1996-2000)**
4. Brandon Pico, of, Rogers HS, Newport, R.I.—(High A)
5. *Ryan Wilson, c, Cerritos (Calif.) HS.--DNP

DRAFT DROP *Attended Cerritos (Calif.) JC; never re-drafted*

6. Emilio Mendez, ss, Miami Beach (Fla.) HS.
7. Darren Dreyer, rhp, Southwest Texas State University.
8. **Mike Hubbard, c, James Madison University.—(1995-2001)**
9. ***Chris Petersen, ss, Georgia Southern University.—(1999)**
10. *Kris Hanson, rhp, University of Wisconsin-Stevens Point.
11. Kevin Booker, of, University of Central Arkansas.
12. **Kennie Steenstra, rhp, Wichita State University.—(1998)**
13. Adam Schulhofer, rhp, UCLA.

14. David DeMoss, of, West Virginia University.
15. Byron Bradley, 3b, Indiana University.
16. *Joel Galarza, c, Teodoro Aguilar HS, Yabucoa, P.R.
17. +Brent Woodall, lhp, University of California.
18. Billy Childress, lhp, Chowan (N.C.) JC.
19. Scott Barton, c, Marion County HS, Jasper, Tenn.
20. Chuck Daniel, rhp, Mississippi State University.
21. Dan Madsen, of, University of Nevada-Las Vegas.
22. Kevin Kessinger, of, University of Mississippi.

DRAFT DROP *Son of Don Kessinger, major leaguer (1964-79); major league manager (1979) • Brother of Keith Kessinger, major leaguer (1993)*

23. Paul Stojsavjevic, c, Southwestern (Calif.) JC.
24. *Shane White, rhp, Jay County HS, Redkey, Ind.
25. Dan Gustavson, rhp, Mount San Antonio (Calif.) JC.
26. Chris Plonk, 3b, Manatee (Fla.) JC.
27. Jason Boehlow, 1b, St. Louis University.
28. Joshua Simmons, ss, Cuesta (Calif.) CC.
29. J.J. Jarolimek, rhp, University of Nevada-Las Vegas.
30. Joe Rino, rhp, New Mexico Highlands University.
31. Coleman Smith, of, University of Tennessee.
32. *Mark Taylor, lhp, Northeast HS, St. Petersburg, Fla.
33. *David Caldwell, lhp, Canarsie HS, Brooklyn, N.Y.
34. Daryle Gavlick, lhp, Armstrong State (Ga.) College.
35. Jay Hassel, rhp, San Diego State University.
36. *Rich Crowe, of, Ocean View HS, Huntington Beach, Calif.
37. *Antonio Leonardi, rhp, Lee HS, Houston.
38. David Dark, lhp, Louisiana Tech.
39. Andrew Elsbecker, rhp, Des Moines Area CC-Boone.
40. Luis Matos, rhp, Monserrate Leon HS, Cabo Rojo, P.R.
41. +Dion Knighten, of, Los Angeles Harbor JC.
42. ***Justin Baughman, ss, Bellarmine Prep HS, San Jose, Calif.—(1998-2000)**
43. *Charles Leckie, 3b, La Quinta HS, Garden Grove, Calif.
44. *Jacob Steinkemper, c, Brophy Prep HS, Phoenix.
45. *Matt Schafer, c, Northeast HS, St. Petersburg, Fla.
46. *Robert Vargas, of, Irvington HS, Fremont, Calif.
47. *Andrew Marquardt, of, Kennewick (Wash.) HS.
48. Tim Stutheit, ss-3b, Bellevue (Neb.) College.
49. *Chad Schroeder, rhp, Larkin HS, Elgin, Ill.
50. *David Schmidt, c, Kennewick (Wash.) HS.

## CHICAGO WHITE SOX (24)

1. Eddie Pearson, 1b, Bishop State (Ala.) JC.—(AAA)
2. ***A.J. Hinch, c, Midwest City (Okla.) HS.—(1998-2004)**

DRAFT DROP *Attended Stanford; re-drafted by Twins, 1995 (3rd round); major league manager (2009-15)*

3. Byron Mathews, of, University of Oklahoma.—(High A)
4. Scott Patton, of, Capistrano Valley HS, Mission Viejo, Calif.—(Low A)
5. Tim Moore, rhp, Stanford University.—(AA)
6. **Chris Snopek, 3b, University of Mississippi.—(1995-98)**
7. Mickey McKinion, rhp, Montgomery HS, Wilmer, Ala.
8. Robert Theodile, rhp, San Jacinto (Texas) JC.
9. Carmine Cappuccio, of, Rollins (Fla.) College.
10. Andres Levias, of, El Camino (Calif.) JC.
11. *David Hutcheson, rhp, University of South Florida.
12. Jason Evans, 3b, University of Oklahoma.
13. **Craig Wilson, ss, Kansas State University.—(1998-2000)**
14. Phil Giese, lhp, Joliet (Ill.) JC.
15. Sean Johnston, lhp, Harvard University.
16. *Irven Stacy, 3b, Winter Haven (Fla.) HS.
17. David Elsbernd, rhp, Baylor University.
18. Steve Worrell, lhp, Stanford University.
19. Bob Mumma, c, University of Maryland-Baltimore County.
20. Wayne Lindemann, lhp, Washington State University.
21. Eugene Faircloth, c, University of North Carolina-Asheville.
22. *Tom Luke, rhp, University of Mississippi.
23. ***Jose Flores, ss-2b, New Mexico JC.—(2002-04)**
24. Jason Ogden, of, Rice University.
25. Jason Pierson, lhp, University of Delaware.
26. Ty Lynch, 2b-3b, University of Central Florida.
27. **Brendan Donnelly, rhp, Mesa State (Colo.) College.—(2002-10)**
28. Ted Rich, 2b, University of Florida.
29. *Geoff Grenert, rhp, University of Nevada-Reno.
30. *Kevin Chabot, of, Dr. Phillips HS, Orlando, Fla.
31. Yusef Ford, lhp, Cal State Fullerton.
32. *Kristren Detmer, lhp, Nokomis (Ill.) HS.
33. Scot Hollrah, rhp, Southeast Missouri State University.
34. ***Shayne Bennett, rhp, Parkland (Ill.) JC.—(1997-99)**
35. *Joel Colgrove, rhp, Warrior Academy HS, Boligee, Ala.
36. *John Reece, of, University of Nebraska.
37. *Jay Veniard, lhp, The Bolles School, Jacksonville, Fla.
38. Jim McDermott, rhp, Fordham University.
39. **Chris Tremie, c, University of Houston.—(1995-2004)**
40. Nelson Izquierdo, 3b, St. Thomas (Fla.) University.
41. Toby Lehman, rhp, Frank Phillips (Texas) JC.
42. *Jason Bell, rhp, Boone HS, Orlando, Fla.
43. *Hoby Mork, 3b, Minnetonka HS, Excelsior, Minn.
44. *Joe Freitas, of, Hanford (Calif.) HS.
45. *Josh Klimek, ss, Vianney HS, Kirkwood, Mo.
46. Tyres Blackburn, of, New Mexico JC.
47. *Jason Santoro, of, El Toro (Calif.) HS.
48. ***Mike Lowell, 2b, Coral Gables (Fla.) HS.—(1998-2010)**
49. Chris Mader, c-3b, Rollins (Fla.) College.
50. Efrain Ventura, of, Florida International University.

## CINCINNATI REDS (5)

1. **Chad Mottola, of, University of Central Florida.—(1996-2006)**
2. *Chad Alexander, of, Lufkin (Texas) HS.—(AAA)

DRAFT DROP *Attended Texas A&M; re-drafted by Astros, 1995 (3rd round)*

2. Rick Magdaleno, ss, Baldwin Park (Calif.) HS (Choice from Phillies as compensation for Type B free agent Mariano Duncan).—(AAA)
3. Todd Etler, rhp, Catholic HS, Covington, Ky.—(AAA)
4. **Eric Owens, ss, Ferrum (Va.) College.—(1995-2003)**
5. Jason Angel, rhp, Clemson University.—(High A)
6. **Curt Lyons, rhp, Madison Central HS, Richmond. Ky.—(1996)**
7. Martin Lister, lhp, Jefferson Davis (Ala.) JC.
8. Mike Meggers, of, University of Mary Hardin-Baylor (Texas).
9. Brian Silvia, c, University of Mississippi.
10. Dan Kopriva, 3b, University of Louisville.
11. Brad Keenan, lb, Concordia (Minn.) College.
12. Justin Towle, c, Inglemoor HS, Bothell, Wash.
13. Danny Oyas, of-rhp, San Bernardino Valley (Calif.) JC.
14. Cleveland Ladell, of, Northwood (Texas) Institute.
15. **Tim Belk, 1b, Lubbock Christian (Texas) College.—(1996)**
16. Jeff Ashton, 2b, Wright State University.
17. Jason Kummerfeldt, rhp, University of Wyoming.
18. Jeff Ramey, of, Indiana University.
19. James Nix, rhp, Texas A&M University.
20. Dan Frye, ss, Indiana State University.
21. **Will Brunson, lhp, Southwest Texas State University.—(1998-99)**
22. Johnny Bess, c, Mesa State (Colo.) College.
23. **Chad Fox, rhp, Tarleton State (Texas) University.—(1997-2009)**
24. *Sean Hogan, lhp, Morehead State University.
25. Ray Moon, of, Vincennes University (Ind.) JC.
26. Jeff Manship, of, University of Nevado-Reno.
27. *Will Roland, ss, Miller HS, Corpus Christi, Texas.
28. **Ricky Pickett, lhp, Northeastern Oklahoma A&M JC.—(1998)**
29. Jeff Nagy, of, University of Findlay (Ohio).
30. Todd Ruyak, lhp, University of Virginia.
31. Michael Collins, ss-2b, Central Florida CC.
32. Denny Fussell, lhp, University of Mary Hardin-Baylor (Texas).
33. Rodriguez Sanders, 2b, Spartanburg Methodist (S.C.) JC.
34. *Fletcher Austin, lhp, Tehachapi (Calif.) HS.
35. *Tony Darden, ss, Gilmer (Texas) HS.
36. *Ben Fay, c, Brewer HS, Fort Worth, Texas.
37. *Jeff Keppen, rhp, Central Gwinnett HS, Lawrenceville, Ga.
38. William Sullivan, rhp, North Florida JC.
39. *Steve Schneider, rhp, North Florida JC.
40. *Charles McQuaig, c, Milledge Academy, Milledgeville, Ga.
41. *Mike Henke, rhp, Corning East HS, Big Flats, N.Y.
42. *Peter Della Ratta, rhp, Gulf Breeze (Fla.) HS.
43. ***Kevin Beirne, rhp, McCullough HS, The Woodlands, Texas.—(2000-02)**
44. Louis Maberry, rhp, Abilene Christian (Texas) University.
45. *Brandon Stanley, ss, Clark HS, San Antonio, Texas.
46. *Brad Mulvaney, c, Arvada West HS, Arvada, Colo.
47. *David Miller, rhp, Lee County HS, Sanford, N.C.
48. *Robbie Mclver, ss, Lee County HS, Sanford, N.C.
49. *Doug Anderson, rhp, Waubonsie Valley HS, Naperville, Ill.
50. *Mark Mapes, c, Corning-Painted Post West HS, Painted Post, N.Y.

## CLEVELAND INDIANS (2)

1. **Paul Shuey, rhp, University of North Carolina.—(1994-2007)**
2. **Mike Matthews, lhp, Montgomery-Rockville (Md.) CC.—(2000-04)**
3. **Jon Nunnally, of, Miami-Dade CC South.—(1995-2000)**
4. **Matt Williams, lhp, Virginia Commonwealth University.—(2000)**
5. Jamie Taylor, 3b, Ohio State University.—(AAA)
6. ***Jeff Liefer, of, Upland (Calif.) HS.—(1999-2005)**

DRAFT DROP *First-round draft pick (25th overall), White Sox (1995)*

7. **J.J. Thobe, rhp, Rancho Santiago (Calif.) JC.—(1995)**

DRAFT DROP *Brother of Tom Thobe, major leaguer (1995-96)*

8. *Greg Gregory, lhp, Millikan HS, Long Beach, Calif.
9. *Larry Schneider, c, Tulane University.
10. *Ryan Ritter, ss, Wheeler HS, Marietta, Ga.
11. Terry Miller, ss, Lincoln HS, Port Arthur, Texas.
12. **Mitch Meluskey, c, Eisenhower HS, Yakima, Wash.—(1998-2003)**
13. *Chris Westcott, rhp, Delgado (La.) JC.
14. Chad Townsend, 1b, UC Riverside.
15. *Cerleston Bargman, 3b, Southridge HS, Miami.
16. Fred Smith, rhp, Connors State (Okla.) JC.
17. *Cale Carter, of, Mater Dei HS, Orange, Calif.
18. Curtis George, ss, Florida A&M University.
19. Noe Najera, lhp, North Carolina State University.
20. Damian Leyva, lhp, Miami-Dade CC Wolfson.
21. Jon Zubiri, rhp, Hanford (Calif.) HS.
22. *Joe Parks, of, Pike County HS, Concord, Ga.
23. Derek Hacopian, of, University of Maryland.
24. ***Stephen Randolph, lhp-1b, Bowie HS, Austin, Texas.—(2003-07)**
25. Leroy Thompson, of, Fernandina Beach (Fla.) HS.
26. Mike Neilson, lhp, Willamette (Ore.) University.
27. Eric White, 3b, Mount San Antonio (Calif.) JC.
28. David Welch, rhp, Tulane University.
29. *Lawyer Milloy, of, Lincoln HS, Tacoma, Wash.

DRAFT DROP *Defensive back, National Football League (1996-2010)*

30. Allen Gallagher, rhp, Lower Columbia (Wash.) CC.
31. John Lewandowski, c, South Suburban (Ill.) JC.
32. Ben Blake, rhp, Simpson (Iowa) College.

DRAFT DROP *Brother of Casey Blake, major leaguer (1999-2007)*

33. *Jason Langolis, lhp, Sanderson HS, Raleigh, N.C.
34. Epi Cardenas, 2b, Laredo (Texas) JC.
35. *Gregg Bitner, rhp, Euclid (Ohio) HS.
36. +Brian Wisler, rhp, Walla Walla (Wash.) CC.
37. *Kiko Palacios, c, Castle Park HS, San Diego.
38. Germaine Mayberry, of, Arizona State University.
39. *Jason Myers, lhp, Chaffey (Calif.) JC.
40. *Milton Anderson, of, Pasco Hernando (Fla.) CC.
41. +Johnathan Oram, ss, Tumwater HS, Olympia, Wash. / Edmonds (Wash.) CC.
42. +Mack Chambers, ss-2b, Seminole (Okla.) JC.
43. *Rodney Tisdale, of, Florida CC.
44. *Allan Hebbert, rhp, Chaffey (Calif.) JC.
45. *Claude Love, of, Plantation HS, Sunrise, Fla.
46. *Andy Pierce, rhp, Twin Falls (Idaho) HS.
47. *Matt Braughler, c, Lafayette HS, Lexington, Ky.
48. Roberto Garza, rhp, Laredo (Texas) JC.
49. *Jason Rooker, rhp, Edmonds (Wash.) CC.
50. *Joey Malone, rhp, Tennessee HS, Bristol, Tenn.

## COLORADO ROCKIES (27)

1. **John Burke, rhp, University of Florida.—(1996-97)**

DRAFT DROP *First-round draft pick (6th overall), Astros (1991)*

2. **Mark Thompson, rhp, University of Kentucky.—(1994-2000)**
3. **Roger Bailey, rhp, Florida State University.—(1995-97)**
4. Lloyd Peever, rhp, Louisiana State University.—(AAA)
5. Ryan Freeburg, 3b-of, Grand Canyon University.—(High A)
6. Will Scalzitti, c, Miami-Dade CC North.
7. **Jason Bates, ss, University of Arizona.—(1995-98)**
8. Chris Henderson, rhp, Brevard (Fla.) CC.
9. Mike Eiffert, lhp, University of Texas-Pan American.
10. **Garvin Alston, rhp, Florida International University.—(1996)**
11. **Craig Counsell, ss, University of Notre Dame.—(1995-2011)**

DRAFT DROP *Major league manager (2015)*

12. James Hovey, lhp, Indian Hills (Iowa) CC.
13. Mark Voisard, rhp, Mount Vernon Nazarene (Ohio) College.
14. **Juan Acevedo, rhp, Parkland (Ill.) JC.—(1995-2003)**
15. Danny Figueroa, of, Gabriela Mistral HS, Rio Piedras, P.R.
16. Greg Boyd, of, Essex (Md.) CC.
17. **Angel Echevarria, of, Rutgers University.—(1996-2002)**
18. Jason Hutchins, rhp, Texas A&M University.
19. Eric Wulf, c, Washington State University.
20. Mike Kotarski, lhp, Duke University.
21. Randy Edwards, of, Bishop Amat HS, West Covina, Calif.
22. Mike Oakland, 1b, Cal Poly San Luis Obispo.
23. Chris Neier, rhp, Cal State Chico.
24. Tom Schmidt, 3b, Brevard (Fla.) CC.
25. **Quinton McCracken, 2b, Duke University.—(1995-2006)**
26. *Thomas Waterman, lhp, Saddleback (Calif.) CC.
27. *Charles Whitehead, 2b, Pleasure Ridge Park HS, Louisville, Ky.
28. **Mark Strittmatter, c, Virginia Commonwealth University.—(1998)**
29. Keith Krenke, of, University of Minnesota.
30. Richard Hatfield, c, Pineville HS, Marianna, W.Va.
31. Jeff Sobkoviak, rhp, Kankakee (Ill.) CC.
32. Jay Holland, rhp, University of Hawaii.
33. Mike Case, of, Long Beach State University.
34. *Ken Copeland, of, Trinidad State (Colo.) JC.
35. *James Dixon, rhp, Trinidad State (Colo.) JC.
36. Tim Scott, 3b, University of Maine.
37. Mike Machado, of, Diablo Valley (Calif.) JC.
38. Greg Tafoya, lhp, Holbrook (Ariz.) HS.
39. Keith Barnes, lhp, Red Bank HS, Hixson, Tenn.
40. Neil Garrett, rhp, Joliet West HS, Joliet, Ill.
41. *Matt Chamberlain, rhp, Louisiana State University.
42. *Jason Weiss, rhp, Nevada Union HS, Gass Valley, Calif.
43. Bill Metzinger, rhp, University of Cincinnati.
44. +Anthony Dermendziev, of, San Jose (Calif.) CC.
45. *Jayson Sessoyeff, c, Clovis (Calif.) HS.
46. Jonathan Goodrich, rhp, Santa Rosa (Calif.) JC.
47. +Matt Pridgen, of, Hayden HS, Phoenix / Cochise County (Ariz.) CC.
48. *Dan Butcher, rhp, Diablo Valley (Calif.) JC.

49. Lamarr Rogers, 2b, Long Beach State University.
50. Torry Zerilla, ss, Youngstown State University.

## DETROIT TIGERS (16)

1. **Rick Greene, rhp, Louisiana State University.—(1999)**
2. Yuri Sanchez, ss, Lynn (Mass.) Tech HS.—(AAA)
3. **Chris Gomez, ss, Long Beach State University.—(1993-2008)**
4. Kenny Carlyle, rhp, University of Mississippi.—(AAA)
5. David Mysel, rhp, University of Maryland.—(AA)
6. Malvin DeJesus, ss, William Penn (Iowa) College.
7. **Pat Ahearne, rhp, Pepperdine University.—(1995)**
8. *David Reinfelder, lhp, Vassar (Mich.) HS.
9. Mike Lopez, rhp, University of Wyoming.
10. **Frank Catalanotto, 2b, East HS, Smithtown, N.Y.—(1997-2010)**
11. **Sean Whiteside, lhp, University of North Carolina-Charlotte.—(1995)**
12. **Bobby Higginson, of, Temple University.—(1995-2005)**
13. Rick Navarro, rhp, San Diego State University.
14. Mike Berlin, rhp, University of South Carolina.
15. Corey Parker, 1b, UC Irvine.
16. Scott Pagano, of, St. Francis (N.Y.) College.
17. Casey Mendenhall, rhp, University of Oklahoma.
18. Tim Jones, rhp, University of Texas-Pan American.
19. Darren Milne, of, Brigham Young University.
20. **Brian Maxcy, rhp, University of Mississippi.—(1995-96)**
21. Moises Ayala, c, Blanca Malaret HS, Sabana Grande, P.R.
22. *Luke Wilcox, 1b, St. Johns (Mich.) HS.
23. John Rosengren, lhp, University of North Carolina.
24. Kevin Lidle, c, Mount San Antonio (Calif.) JC.

DRAFT DROP *Brother of Cory Lidle, major leaguer (1997-2006)*

25. *Scott Timmerman, 2b, University of Michigan.
26. +Scott Norman, rhp, Pasco Hernando (Fla.) CC.
27. John Grimm, rhp, Kent State University.
28. *Beau Campbell, c, Washington State University.
29. *Derek Kraemer, rhp, Madison HS, Madison Heights, Mich.
30. Bart Greene, of, Sacramento (Calif.) CC.
31. *Thomas Wolff, rhp, Hillsdale (Mich.) HS.
32. *Rene Justiniano, 1b, Roberto Clemente HS, Chicago.
33. Jeff Brown, rhp, St. John's University.
34. Kenny Valdez, of, King HS, Tampa.
35. David Verduzco, rhp, Yale University.
36. John Lamar, of, Indiana State University.
37. *Wynter Phoenix, of, Grossmont HS, El Cajon, Calif.
38. *Gary Morris, rhp, St. Mary's HS, Orchard Lake, Mich.
39. *Javier Mejia, rhp, University HS, Los Angeles.
40. Eric Weber, rhp, Swan Valley HS, Saginaw, Mich.
41. ***Mark Redman, lhp, Escondido (Calif.) HS.—(1999-2008)**

DRAFT DROP *First-round draft pick (13th overall), Twins (1995)*

42. Matt Evans, 1b, Grand Canyon University.
43. *Scott Kapla, rhp, Catholic Central HS, Redford, Mich.
44. *Brian Jacobson, rhp, Perris (Calif.) HS.
45. *James Castro, rhp, Riverside (Calif.) CC.
46. *Chris Gonzalez, 3b, Harry Doss HS, Louisville, Ky.
47. *Brian Casey, lhp, East Montgomery HS, Biscoe, N.C.
48. *Carlos Yedo, 1b, Christopher Columbus HS, Miami.
49. ***David Newhan, 2b, Cypress (Calif.) JC.—(1999-2008)**
50. ***Eddie Gaillard, rhp, Florida Southern College.—(1997-99)**

## FLORIDA MARLINS (28)

1. **Charles Johnson, c, University of Miami.—(1994-2005)**

DRAFT DROP *First-round draft pick (10th overall), Expos (1989)*

2. John Lynch, rhp, Stanford University.—(Low A)

DRAFT DROP *Defensive back, National Football League (1993-2007)*

3. Rich Ireland, lhp, Crater HS, Central Point, Ore.—(Rookie)
4. Willie Brown, of, Florida A&M University.—(High A)
5. Alex Aranzamendi, ss, University Gardens HS, Rio Piedras, P.R.—(Low A)
6. Pat Leahy, rhp, University of Notre Dame.
7. Reynol Mendoza, rhp, Incarnate Word (Texas) College.
8. Dan Roman, lhp, Brooklyn (N.Y.) College.
9. Scott Samuels, of, Arizona State University.
10. Chris Sheff, of, Pepperdine University.
11. Tony Torres, ss, University of Nevada-Reno.
12. Mike Veneziale, rhp, Camden County (N.J.) JC.
13. Jerry Stafford, lhp, San Diego State University.
14. Jason Tidwell, rhp, Jacksonville State University.
15. Jim Patterson, rhp, Fresno State University.
16. Eddie Christian, of, Long Beach State University.
17. Gavin Baugh, ss, JC of San Mateo (Calif.).
18. Mark Skeels, c, Stanford University.
19. *John Codrington, rhp, Bowie HS, Austin, Texas.
20. *Rob Steinert, rhp, North Carolina State University.
21. *Chris Clark, of, Smackover (Ark.) HS.
22. Matt Donahue, rhp, North Caroline State University.
23. Todd Pridy, 1b, Long Beach State University.
24. +Marcus Mays, lhp, McNair HS, Decatur, Ga. / Middle Georgia JC.
25. **Andy Larkin, rhp, South Medford HS, Medford, Ore.—(1996-2000)**
26. *Brian Loyd, c, El Dorado HS, Placentia, Calif.
27. Matt Petersen, rhp, Iowa State University.
28. Kenny Kendrena, rhp, Cal State Northridge.
29. Anthony Bonifazio, of, Fresno State University.
30. *Mark Leber, 1b, Archbishop Mitty HS, San Jose, Calif.
31. Erick Strickland, of, West HS, Bellevue, Neb.

DRAFT DROP *Guard, National Basketball Association (1996-2003)*

32. Lou Lucca, 3b, Oklahoma State University.
33. *Tim Lanier, c, Catholic HS, Baton Rouge, La.
34. Bruce Nolte, ss, Pennsauken (N.J.) HS.
35. Rick Freehling, of, Creighton University.
36. *Matt Furrey, of, Hilliard (Ohio) HS.
37. Hiram Fantauzzi, of, Carmen B. Huyke HS, Arroyo, P.R.
38. Jason Frazier, c, Hilton Head HS, Bluffton, S.C.
39. Sean Gousha, c, University of San Diego.
40. Brad Frazier, lhp, Clarion (Pa.) University.
41. Doug Pettit, rhp, University of Texas.
42. *Matt Wood, rhp, Canyon HS, Anaheim, Calif.
43. Greg Reeder, rhp, Christian HS, Panama City, Fla.
44. Scott Johnson, rhp, Central HS, Greeley, Colo.
45. *Dan Lyons, rhp, Mullen HS, Littleton, Colo.
46. *Heath Altman, rhp, University of North Carolina-Wilmington.
47. Scott Englehart, rhp, George Fox (Ore.) College.
48. Mitchel Bowen, rhp, JC of the Canyons (Calif.).
49. *Robert Hernandez, c, San Jose (Calif.) CC.
50. *James Woods, of, San Fernando HS, Pacoima, Calif.

## HOUSTON ASTROS (1)

1. **Phil Nevin, 3b, Cal State Fullerton.—(1995-2006)**
1. Kendall Rhine, rhp, University of Georgia (Supplemental choice—37th—for failure to sign 1991 first-round draft pick John Burke).—(AAA)

DRAFT DROP *Son of Kendall Rhine, center, American Basketball Association (1967-69)*

2. David Landaker, ss, Royal HS, Simi Valley, Calif.—(High A)
3. **Chris Holt, rhp, Navarro (Texas) JC.—(1996-2001)**
4. *Chad Sheffer, ss, Bloomingdale HS, Valrico, Fla.—(Low A)

DRAFT DROP *Attended Florida State; re-drafted by Mariners, 1995 (14th round)*

5. **Sean Runyan, lhp, Urbandale (Iowa) HS.—(1998-2000)**
6. Jeff Tenbarge, rhp, University of Evansville.
7. Mike Rennhack, of, Leland HS, San Jose, Calif.
8. Chris Thomas, of, Boise State (Idaho) University.
9. Greg Elliott, 3b, Southeastern Louisiana University.
10. **Jamie Walker, lhp, Austin Peay State University.—(1997-2009)**
11. R.J. Bowers, of, West Middlesex (Pa.) Area HS.
12. Doug Mlicki, rhp, Ohio University.

DRAFT DROP *Brother of Dave Mlicki, major leaguer (1992-2002)*

13. **Hector Mercado, lhp, Jose Alegria HS, Dorado, P.R.—(2000-03)**
14. Donovan Mitchell, 2b, University of North Carolina-Charlotte.
15. *Cade Gaspar, rhp, Saddleback (Calif.) JC.

DRAFT DROP *First-round draft pick (18th overall), Tigers (1994) • Son of Rod Gaspar, major leaguer (1969-74)*

16. Joey Witt, 1b, Richfield (Minn.) HS.
17. Alan Probst, c, Mansfield (Pa.) University.
18. *Edwin Rodriguez, 2b, Cristo Rey HS, Ponce, P.R.
19. **Mike Grzanich, rhp, Parkland (Ill.) JC.—(1998)**
20. Marvin Billingsley, lhp-of, Odessa (Texas) JC.
21. Destry Westbrook, rhp, Texas Wesleyan University.
22. Dwayne Dawson, rhp, Cleveland State University.
23. Zak Krislock, rhp, University of Oklahoma.
24. Brett Wyngarden, c, Northwestern University.
25. *Scott Conant, ss, Western Michigan University.
26. *Aaron Wooley, 1b, Fresno (Calif.) CC.
27. *Chandler Martin, rhp, Sprague HS, Salem, Ore.
28. *Jeff Hook, rhp, Newbury Park (Calif.) HS.
29. ***Bobby Howry, rhp, Yavapai (Ariz.) JC.—(1998-2010)**
30. *Julio Colon, rhp, Los Angeles CC.
31. ***Rob Ramsay, lhp, Mountain View HS, Vancouver, Wash.—(1999-2000)**
32. *Joel Garber, lhp, Mira Costa HS, Manhattan Beach, Calif.
33. *Darold Brown, of, Laney (Calif.) JC.
34. +Ryan Creek, rhp, Louisburg (N.C.) JC.

DRAFT DROP *Brother of Doug Creek, major leaguer (1995-2003)*

35. *Teddy Warrecker, rhp, Allan Hancock (Calif.) JC.
36. *Robert Wiemer, 1b, Odessa (Texas) JC.
37. *Ryan Reynolds, rhp, Tumwater HS, Olympia, Wash.
38. Anthony Ross, of, St. Pius X HS, Kansas City, Mo.
39. *Brook Holding, 3b, Texarkana (Texas) CC.
40. *Flint Wallace, rhp, Weatherford (Texas) HS.
41. *Chris Hitt, lhp, Seminole (Okla.) JC.
42. *Travis Biggs, c, Northside HS, Barling, Ark.
43. *Rafael Graner, rhp, Buen Samaritano HS, Guayama, P.R.
44. +Brett Baptist, rhp, Lincoln Land (Ill.) CC.
45. *Andy Weltlinger, lhp, Calvert Hall HS, Randallstown, Md.
46. *Steven Martin, rhp, Bridge City (Texas) HS.
47. *Brian Aylor, of, Midwest City (Okla.) HS.
48. +Gary Trammell, 2b, Texarkana (Texas) CC.
49. *Fred Little, ss, Biloxi (Miss.) HS.
50. *Irving Smith, of, University of Notre Dame.

DRAFT DROP *First-round draft pick, New Orleans Saints/ National Football League (1993); Tight end, NFL (1993-99)*

## KANSAS CITY ROYALS (10)

1. **Michael Tucker, ss, Longwood (Va.) College.—(1995-2006)**
1. **Jim Pittsley, rhp, Dubois (Pa.) Area HS** (Choice from Padres as compensation for Type A free agent Kurt Stillwell).**—(1995-99)**

DRAFT DROP *First 1992 high school draft pick to reach majors (May 23, 1995)*

1. Sherard Clinkscales, rhp, Purdue University (Supplemental choice—31st—as compensation for Type A free agent Danny Tartabull).—(Low A)
1. **Johnny Damon, of, Dr. Phillips HS, Orlando, Fla.** (Supplemental choice—35th—as compensation for Stillwell).**—(1995-2012)**
2. **Jon Lieber, rhp, University of South Alabama** (Choice from Yankees as compensation for Tartabull).**—(1994-2008)**
2. (Choice to Angels as compensation for Type A free agent Wally Joyner)
3. **Chris Eddy, lhp, Texas Christian University.—(1995)**
4. Steve Murphy, of, Birmingham-Southern College.—(AA)
5. Jeff Haas, lhp, University of Houston.—(Low A)
6. Jelani Brandon, of, Lloyd Memorial HS, Erlanger, Ky.
7. Justin Adam, rhp, Holy Names HS, Windsor, Ontario.
8. Mike Kern, of, Culver City (Calif.) HS.
9. **Bart Evans, rhp, Southwest Missouri State University.—(1998)**
10. John Dickens, lhp, University of Texas.
11. Ken Fitzpatrick, rhp, Bell Gardens (Calif.) HS.
12. David Bladow, rhp, UC Irvine.
13. Jason Marshall, ss, Texas A&M University.

DRAFT DROP *Baseball coach, Texas-San Antonio (2013-15)*

14. Brian Harrison, rhp, Texas A&M University.
15. **Melvin Bunch, rhp, Texarkana (Texas) CC.—(1995-99)**
16. **Steve Sisco, 2b, Cal State Fullerton.—(2000)**
17. David Cornell, of, Stanford University.
18. Paul Vindivich, c, Mount Tahoma HS, Tacoma, Wash.
19. *Jeff Parsons, ss, Dale HS, Shawnee, Okla.
20. Tom Heming, lhp, University of Tennessee.
21. **Larry Sutton, of, University of Illinois.—(1997-2004)**
22. *Clemente Sainten, of, Arroyo Grande (Calif.) HS.
23. Sean Delaney, c, North Central (Ill.) College.
24. Paul Fletcher, lhp, University of Tennessee.
25. *Jamie Splittorff, rhp, Blue Springs (Mo.) HS.

DRAFT DROP *Son of Paul Splittorff, major leaguer (1970-84)*

26. Troy McAllister, ss, William Paterson (N.J.) College.
27. Chris Sheehan, rhp, Washington State University.
28. Jeff Antoon, 1b-3b, UC Santa Barbara.
29. Julius Alfonzo, 2b, Kingsborough (N.Y.) CC.
30. John Weglarz, rhp, Lamar University.
31. Eric Walls, of, Kaskaskia (Ill.) JC.
32. Aaron Dorlarque, rhp, Stanford University.
33. Richard Bacon, rhp, Cuesta (Calif.) JC.
34. James Hodgson, rhp, University of North Dakota.
35. *Steven Ashton, of, Sunny Hills HS, Fullerton, Calif.
36. Ray Solomon, rhp, Kwantlen (B.C.) JC.
37. Scott Abell, c, Longwood (Va.) College.
38. *Brent Coon, of, Troy HS, Yorba Linda, Calif.
39. *Mike Muncy, ss, Moorpark (Calif.) JC.
40. *Brandon Hoalton, rhp, Garden Grove (Calif.) HS.
41. *Steve Spille, lhp, Purcell Marian HS, Cincinnati.
42. *Charles Winters, lhp, St. Martin Deporres HS, Detroit.
43. *Sherroid Blake, of, Kashmere HS, Houston.
44. *Mike Williamson, 1b, Gilbert HS, Tempe, Ariz.
45. *Jason LeBlanc, rhp, La Serna HS, Whittier, Calif.
46. *David Brooks, ss, Blinn (Texas) JC.
47. *Casey Brookens, rhp, Chambersburg Area HS, Fayetteville, Pa.

DRAFT DROP *Son of Ike Brookens, major leaguer (1975)*

48. *Jared Janke, rhp, Diamond Bar (Calif.) HS.
49. *Carlos Williams, of, Colegio Santiago HS, Rio Grande, P.R.
50. *Lamont Williams, of, Georgetown (Texas) HS.

## LOS ANGELES DODGERS (19)

1. (Choice to Blue Jays as compensation for Type A free agent Tom Candiotti)
1. Ryan Luzinski, c, Holy Cross HS, Delran, N.J. (Supplemental choice—32nd—as compensation for Type A free agent Eddie Murray).—(AAA)

DRAFT DROP *Son of Greg Luzinski, first-round draft pick, Phillies (1968); major leaguer (1970-84)*

1. Michael Moore, of, UCLA (Supplemental choice—36th—as compensation for Type A free agent Mike Morgan).—(AAA)

DRAFT DROP *Nephew of Ahmad Rashad, first-round draft pick, St. Louis Cardinals/National Football League (1972); wide receiver/NFL (1972-82)*

2. Dwain Bostic, ss, Morse HS, San Diego (Choice

from Cubs as compensation for Morgan).—(Rookie)
2. Dan Melendez, 1b, Pepperdine University.—(AAA)
3. Dwight Maness, of, William Penn HS, New Castle, Del. (Choice from Mets as compensation for Murray).—(AAA)
3. David Spykstra, rhp, Cherry Creek HS, Englewood, Colo.—(High A)
**4. Keith Johnson, ss, University of the Pacific.—(2000)**
5. Chris Abbe, c, University of Texas.—(AA)
6. Jon Graves, rhp, Long Beach State University.
7. Brian Richardson, 3b, St. Bernard HS, Walnut, Calif.
8. Dan Markham, lhp, Diablo Valley (Calif.) JC.
9. Ryan Henderson, rhp, University of Southern California.
10. David Post, 3b, Kingston (N.Y.) HS.
11. Brent Colson, lhp, Georgia Tech.
12. Juan Hernaiz, of, Colegio Maria Auxiliadora HS, Carolina, P.R.
13. Jason Butcher, rhp, Albertson (Idaho) College.
14. Reggie Johnson, 3b, Georgia Tech.
15. Brandon White, rhp, Eastern Michigan University.
16. James Martin, of, Oklahoma State University.
17. Keith Troutman, rhp, Spartanburg Methodist (S.C.) JC.
18. Ervan Wingate, ss, Redlands (Calif.) HS.
19. David Pyc, lhp, University of Charleston (W.Va.).
20. *Widd Workman, rhp-of, Gilbert (Ariz.) HS.
21. Paul Wittig, c, Bremerton (Wash.) HS.
22. Tyrone Lewis, ss-2b, Waco Christian HS, Waco, Texas.
23. *Will Schleuss, lhp, Mussellman HS, Martinsburg, W.Va.
24. *Ryan Duffy, lhp, Northeastern Oklahoma A&M JC.
25. *Matt Powell, rhp, Southridge HS, Miami.
26. +Kevin Pitts, of, Kishwaukee (Ill.) JC / Triton (Ill.) JC.
27. Daniel Sarmiento, lhp, Tempe (Ariz.) HS.
28. *Jeff Velez, rhp, Greenwich (Conn.) HS.
29. *Sean Watkins, 1b-of, Notre Dame HS, Peoria Heights, Ill.
30. *Kyle Evans, 1b, Katella HS, Anaheim.
31. Kenny Cook, rhp, Spartanburg Methodist (S.C.) JC.
32. James Breuer, of, Century HS, Bismarck, N.D.
33. +Ken Sikes, 1b-rhp, Middle Georgia JC.
34. *Ryan Topham, of, Portage Central HS, Portage, Mich.
35. Joe Vogelgesang, rhp, Eastern Kentucky University.
36. *John Collins, rhp, Thompson HS, Alabaster, Ala.
37. Michael Serbalik, 2b, Siena College.
38. *Sheldon Anderson, of, Washington HS, Los Angeles.
39. Cliff Anderson, ss, Chapman (Calif.) College.
40. *Twaino Moss, of, Middle Georgia JC.
41. *Greg Ziesemer, rhp, Larkin HS, Elgin, Ill.
42. Ken Chapman, 1b, Florida Southern College.
43. *David Hayman, of, Hillcrest Christian HS, Jackson, Miss.
44. *Chris Apodaca, rhp, Lynwood (Calif.) HS.
45. +Brian Clark, c, Napa (Calif.) JC.
46. *Dimas Padilla, lhp, Rio Piedras (P.R.) HS.
47. *Jeff Poor, c, El Segundo (Calif.) HS.
48. *Stephen Munroe, of, Crescent HS, Thornhill, Ontario.
49. Nathan Dunn, ss, East Tennessee State University.
50. *Tyler Boulo, 3b, St. Paul's Episcopal HS, Mobile, Ala.

## MILWAUKEE BREWERS (12)

1. Kenny Felder, of, Florida State University.—(AAA)
1. Gabby Martinez, ss, Luchetti HS, Santurce, P.R. (Supplemental choice—38th—for failure to sign 1991 first-round draft pick Kenny Henderson).—(AAA)
**2. Bobby Hughes, c, University of Southern California.—(1998-99)**
3. Danan Hughes, of, University of Iowa.—(Rookie)

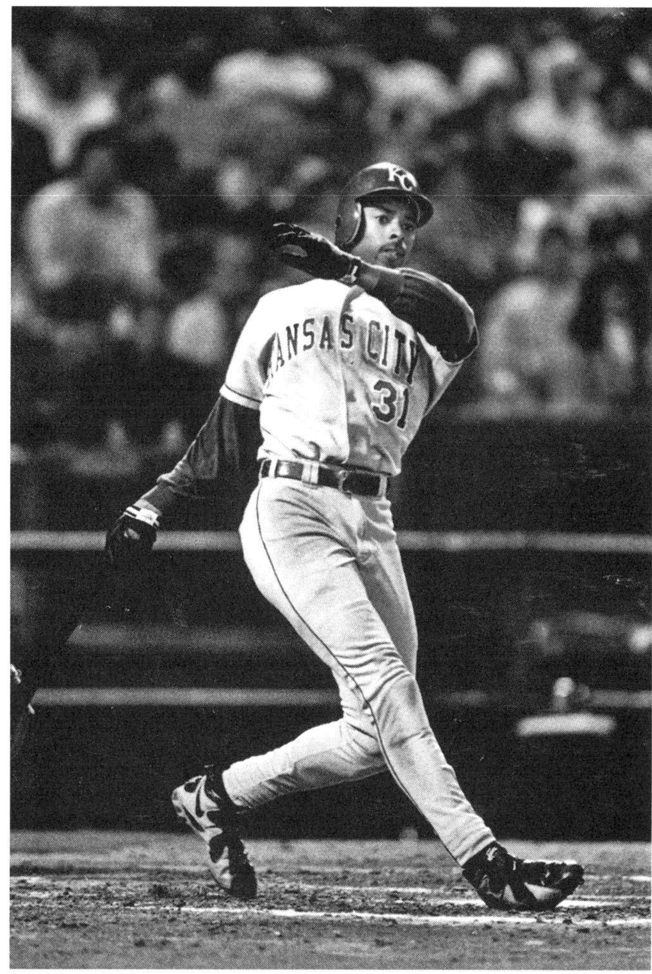


Royals first-rounder Michael Tucker found big league success out of tiny Longwood College

DRAFT DROP *Wide receiver, National Football League (1993-98)*
4. Kevin Kloek, rhp, Cal State Northridge.—(AAA)
5. Dan Kyslinger, rhp, Western Carolina University.—(High A)
**6. Scott Karl, lhp, University of Hawaii.—(1995-2000)**
7. *Chris Mayfield, of, McNeese State University.
8. Jeff Droll, rhp, Allegany (Md.) CC.
9. Wes Weger, ss, Stetson University.
10. *Travis Wilson, c, Rancho Buena Vista HS, Vista, Calif.
11. Ryan Maloney, rhp, Central HS, Butte, Mon.
12. Derrick Cantrell, of, Edison (Fla.) CC.
13. *Rayon Reid, rhp, North Miami (Fla.) HS.
14. Scott Richardson, 2b, Cal State Northridge.
15. Ron Rico, lhp, Cerritos (Calif.) JC.
16. *Guy Smith, rhp, Northern HS, Brunswick, Md.
17. Anthony Pridgen, of, Hallsboro (N.C.) HS.
18. George Behr, 1b, University of Minnesota.
19. *Danny Kanell, 3b, Westminster Academy HS, Fort Lauderdale, Fla.
DRAFT DROP *Quarterback, National Football League (1996-2004)*
20. Gerry Salzano, 3b, Steinert HS, Trenton, N.J.
**21. Danny Perez, of, Oklahoma State University.—(1996)**
22. Richard Werner, rhp, Oviedo (Fla.) HS.
23. Bubba Hardwick, lhp, Polk (Fla.) CC.
24. Brian Hostetler, c, Western Michigan University.
25. +Lyle Prempas, lhp, Fenwick HS, Westchester, Ill. / Triton (Ill.) JC.
**26. *Matt Morris, rhp, Valley Central HS, Montgomery, N.Y.—(1997-2008)**
DRAFT DROP *First-round draft pick (12th overall), Cardinals (1995)*
27. Ruben Cephas, of, Delaware Tech & CC.
**28. Tim Unroe, ss, Lewis (Ill.) University.—(1995-2000)**
**29. Sid Roberson, lhp, University of North Florida.—(1995)**
30. Aldren Sadler, rhp, Middle Georgia JC.
31. Craig Smith, ss, New Mexico State University.
32. David England, rhp, Augusta (Ga.) College.
33. Kevin Krause, rhp, West Genesee HS, Syracuse, N.Y.
34. David Majeski, of, University of Florida.
35. *Kelvin Barnes, ss-of, North Edgecombe HS, Battleboro, N.C.
36. Steve Maltagliati, rhp, East Islip, N.Y.
37. Chris Petrocella, rhp, Western Kentucky University.
38. Gary Rhoda, East Bladen HS, Elizabethtown, N.C.
**39. *Scott Sullivan, rhp, Auburn University.—(1995-2004)**
40. Sean Holub, 3b-1b, Johns Hopkins (Md.) University.
41. Mark Kingston, 1b, University of North Carolina.
DRAFT DROP *Baseball coach, Illinois State (2010-14); baseball coach, South Florida (2015)*
42. Walter Figueroa, of, Jose Benitez HS, Caguas, P.R.
43. Derrick Torres, of, Franklin D. Roosevelt HS, Guanica, P.R.
44. Chris Thomas, c, Stetson University.
45. *Scott Morgan, rhp, Allan Hancock (Calif.) JC.
46. *Todd Woodaz, rhp, King HS, Tampa.
47. Derek Gaskill, rhp, Manor HS, Portsmouth, Va.
48. *Kevin Horton, of, West Carteret HS, Morehead City, N.C.
49. *B.J. Stanley, 2b, Horizon HS, Scottsdale, Ariz.
50. Robert Powers, 2b, Marist HS, Bayonne, N.J.

## MINNESOTA TWINS (26)

**1. Dan Serafini, lhp, Serra HS, San Mateo, Calif.—(1996-2007)**
2. Chad Roper, ss-rhp, Belton-Honea Path HS, Belton, S.C.—(AA)
2. Tom Knauss, 3b, Hersey HS, Arlington Heights, Ill. (Supplemental choice—68th—as compensation for Type C free agent Dan Gladden).—(High A)
**3. Gus Gandarillas, rhp, University of Miami.—(2001)**
4. Kevin Pearson, ss, Fergus Falls (Minn.) HS.—(Low A)
5. Aaron Thatcher, lhp, Mountain Crest HS, Hyrum, Utah.--DNP
6. Keith Linebarger, rhp, Columbus (Ga.) College.
7. Armann Brown, of, Johnston HS, Austin, Texas.
8. *Chad Cooley, ss-of, Barbe HS, Lake Charles, La.
9. Rene Lopez, c, Los Angeles Harbor JC.
10. Ben Jones, of, Alexandria (La.) HS.
11. Anthony Byrd, of, Georgia Tech.
12. *Steve Rosga, ss, Cretin HS, Roseville, Minn.
DRAFT DROP *Seventh-round draft pick, New York Jets/ National Football League (1997)*
13. *Dexter McCleon, c, Meridian (Miss.) HS.
DRAFT DROP *Defensive back, National Football League (1997-2006)*
**14. Dan Naulty, rhp, Cat State Fullerton.—(1996-99)**
15. Todd A. Taylor, c, Florida Southern College.
16. Sean Gavaghan, rhp, University of Richmond.
17. Javi DeJesus, lhp, University of Southwestern Louisiana.
18. Jeff Crick, rhp, Sandalwood HS, Jacksonville, Fla.
19. Todd H. Taylor, lhp, Long Beach State University.
20. Ted Corbin, ss, Clemson University.
21. Ken Tirpack, 1b, Ohio State University.
22. Tom Horincewich, ss, Pace (N.Y.) University.
**23. Scott Watkins, lhp, Oklahoma State University.—(1995)**
24. Trevor Cobb, lhp, Cascade HS, Marysville, Wash.
25. *Jeff Cermak, 3b, Riverside-Brookfield HS, Brookfield, Ill.
26. Rob DeBrino, rhp, Northern Valley Regional HS, Northvale, N.J.
27. Andrew Kontorinis, 1b, University of South Alabama.
28. Paul Saccavino, rhp, University of Richmond.
29. Adrian Gordon, of, Alexandria (La.) HS.
30. Jason Tatar, rhp, Rantoul (Ill.) HS.
31. Marc Claus, 2b, University of North Florida.
32. Joe Miller, of, Los Angeles Harbor JC.
33. Kevin Legault, rhp, Seton Hall University.
34. Butch Burrough, rhp-of, Concordia (N.Y.) College.
35. *Chris Piggott, of, Stevenson HS, Long Grove, Ill.
36. Tim Costic, of, Fresno State University.
37. Luis Alvarado, rhp, Miguel Melendez HS, Cayey, P.R.
**38. *Gary Matthews Jr., 2b, Granada Hills HS, Northridge, Calif.—(1999-2010)**
DRAFT DROP *Son of Gary Matthews, first-round draft pick, Giants (1968); major leaguer (1972-87)*
39. *Chris Tolbert, of, Enterprise State (Ala.) JC.
40. *Dwayne Walters, rhp, Hibbing (Minn.) HS.
41. +George Johnson, ss, Lowndes HS, Quitman, Ga. / Middle Georgia JC.
42. Jason Baker, of, Motlow State (Tenn.) CC.
43. *Brent Nichols, lhp, Clayton Valley HS, Concord, Calif.
44. *Dave Bies, of, Como Park HS, St. Paul, Minn.
45. *John Box, lhp, Waltrip HS, Houston.
46. Hiram Cruz, ss, Southwest HS, Miami.
47. Jeff Horn, c, University of Wyoming.
48. Paul Gomez, c, North Florida JC.
49. *Bryan Zollman, 3b, Hill-Murray HS, Oakdale, Minn.
**50. *Craig Dingman, rhp, North HS, Wichita.—(2000-05)**

## MONTREAL EXPOS (3)

1. B.J. Wallace, lhp, Mississippi State University.—(High A)
**2. Rod Henderson, rhp, University of Kentucky.—(1994-98)**
**3. Everett Stull, rhp, Tennessee State University.—(1997-2002)**
4. Scott Gentile, rhp, Western Connecticut State University.—(AA)
5. Jon Saffer, of, Amphitheater HS, Tucson, Ariz.—(AAA)
**6. Jose Vidro, 2b, Blanca Malaret HS, Sabana**

**Grande, P.R.—(1997-2008)**
7. Luis Martinez, c, John F. Kennedy HS, Santa Isabel, P.R.
**8. Tommy Phelps, lhp, Robinson HS, Tampa.—(2003-05)**
9. *John Geis, 1b, Moore HS, Central Square, N.Y.
**10. Steve Falteisek, rhp, University of South Alabama.—(1997-99)**
11. Al Kermode, rhp, Grand Canyon University.
12. *Kevin Rawitzer, lhp, Arizona State University.
13. Matt Rundels, 2b, Kent State University.
14. Matt Raleigh, 3b, Western Carolina University.
**15. *Scott Schoeneweis, lhp, Lenape Valley HS, Mount Laurel, N.J.—(1999-2010)**
16. Vincent LaChance, of, Academie du Baseball Canada, Charlesbourg, Quebec.
17. Marc Niethammer, c, Lake Wales (Fla.) HS.
18. Jim Rushworth, rhp, Florida State University.
19. Arce Vializ, rhp, Martin Hernandez HS, Aguana, P.R.
20. Tom Doyle, 1b, University of Minnesota.
21. David Eggert, lhp, Cal State Northridge.
22. Todd Dreifort, of, Wichita State University.
DRAFT DROP *Brother of Darren Dreifort, first-round draft pick, Dodgers (1993); major leaguer (1994-2004)*
23. *Logan Miller, c, Sir Francis Drake HS, Fairfax, Calif.
24. Danny Lane, ss-3b, UC Santa Barbara.
25. +Andy Markham, rhp, Scottsdale (Ariz.) CC.
26. *Barry Lunney, lhp, Southside HS, Fort Smith, Ark.
27. Scott Harrison, rhp, University of Texas.
28. *Charles Bivens, of, Anson HS, Wadesboro, N.C.
29. *Lance Calmus, rhp, Seminole (Okla.) JC.
30. James Hylton, rhp, Diablo Valley (Calif.) JC.
31. Kevin Northrup, of, Clemson University.
32. *Brett Weinberger, of, Arizona State University.
33. Rocky Ray, rhp, California State University.
**34. *Jonathan Johnson, rhp, Forest HS, Ocala, Fla.—(1998-2003)**
DRAFT DROP *First-round draft pick (7th overall), Rangers (1995)*
35. *Craig Mattson, rhp, Kishwaukee (Ill.) JC.
36. *Eric Berthelot, lhp, Brother Martin HS, Metairie, La.
37. *Chaad Stewart, lhp, Elgin (Ill.) HS.
38. *Steve Beard, rhp, Woodstock HS, Hebron, Ill.
**39. +Kris Foster, rhp, Riverdale HS, Lehigh Acres, Fla. / Edison (Fla.) CC—(2001)**
40. *Jon Valenti, 3b, Bakersfield (Calif.) JC.
**41. Curt Schmidt, rhp, University of Kansas.—(1995)**
42. *Quentin Stone, 3b, Sparks (Nev.) HS.
43. *James Motte, ss, Trinidad State (Colo.) JC.
44. Brad Aurila, 1b-of, Edinboro (Pa.) University.
45. *Jerome Robinson, of, Anson HS, Wadesboro, N.C.
46. *Brandon Anderson, c, Imperial Valley (Calif.) JC.
47. *Andrew McCormick, of, Scottsdale (Ariz.) CC.
48. *Eric Harris, 1b, Columbia State (Tenn.) JC.
49. *Russ Shiels, lhp, Maple Ridge (B.C.) HS.
50. +Russell Handy, rhp, Arvin HS, Bakersfield, Calif. / Bakersfield (Calif.) JC.

## NEW YORK METS (9)

**1. Preston Wilson, ss, Bamberg Ehrhardt HS, Bamberg, S.C.—(1998-2007)**
DRAFT DROP *Stepson of Mookie Wilson, major leaguer (1980-91)*
1. Chris Roberts, lhp-of, Florida State University (Choice from Red Sox as compensation for Type A free agent Frank Viola).—(AAA)
1. *Jon Ward, rhp, Huntington Beach (Calif.) HS (Supplemental choice—30th—as compensation for Viola).—(Short-season A)
DRAFT DROP *Attended Cal State Fullerton; re-drafted by Cardinals, 1995 (8th round)*
2. (Choice to Pirates as compensation for Type A tree agent Bobby Bonilla)
3. (Choice to Dodgers as compensation for Type A free agent Eddie Murray)
4. Steve Lyons, rhp, Old Dominion University.—(High A)
5. Joe Petcka, rhp, Bradley University.—(High A)
6. *David Sumner, of, Northport HS, East Northport, N.Y
7. Chris Saunders, 3b, Fresno (Calif.) CC.
8. R.J. Spang, rhp, Horlick HS, Racine, Wis.
9. Andy Trumpour, rhp, Cypress (Calif.) JC.
10. Derek Baker, rhp, Glendale (Calif.) CC.
11. James Knott, rhp, Cowley County (Kan.) CC.
12. Eric Morales, c, Efrain Sanchez HS, Moca, P.R.
**13. *Darin Erstad, of, Jamestown (N.D.) HS.—(1996-2009)**
DRAFT DROP *First overall draft pick, Angels (1995)*
14. *Jeff Fry, lhp, Bellwood-Antis HS, Tyrone, Pa.
15. Scott Williams, rhp, Panola (Texas) JC.
16. Steve Lackey, ss, Norte Vista HS, Riverside, Calif.
17. Jonathen Smith, of, University of Miami.
18. *Toby Smith, rhp, Connors State (Okla.) JC.
19. *Bill Mobilia, ss, University of Minnesota.
**20. Allen McDill, lhp, Arkansas Tech.—(1997-2001)**
21. Andy Beckerman, rhp, Lubbock Christian (Texas) University.
22. Josh Haggas, 3b, Virginia Tech.
23. Tyril Sherman, rhp, San Jose (Calif.) CC.
24. *Chris Gobert, lhp, Northside HS, Lafayette, La.
25. *Karl Thompson, c, Diamond Bar (Calif.) HS.
26. *Chris Gump, 2b, University ot Arizona.
27. James Popoff, rhp, Cal State Fullerton.
28. Al Hammell, c, LeMoyne College.
29. *Clint Hendry, of, Hardee HS, Wauchula, Fla.
30. *Mike Biehle, lhp, Kings HS, South Lebanon, Ohio.
31. Brent Hayward, rhp, Henry Ford (Mich.) CC.
32. *Brad Schmeh, of, Eaton HS, Greeley, Colo.
33. Tripp Keister, of, University of Delaware.
34. John Harris, rhp, Columbus HS, Duncan, Neb.
35. *Justin Rayment, lhp, Sedro Woolley (Wash.) HS.
36. Greg Stark, rhp, Texas Wesleyan University.
37. Michael Farrell, ss, Grossmont (Calif.) JC.
38. Mark McGinn, rhp, Millard North HS, Omaha.
39. Jerry Hiraldo, of, Carolina Regional (P.R.) CC.
40. Chad Epperson, c, Seminole (Fla.) CC.
41. Travis Shaffer, rhp, Pittsburg State (Kan.) University.
42. Tom Pinson, lhp, Valdosta State (Ga.) College.
43. *Brian Cox, of, Grossmont (Calif.) JC.
44. *Tom Baird, lhp, Carthage (Mo.) HS.
45. *Dominic Demark, of, Prescott (Ariz.) HS.
46. Jose Flores, of, St. Mary's (Texas) University.
47. *Keith Bradley, ss, Connors State (Okla.) JC.
48. *Brian Parten, rhp, Thomasville (Ala.) HS.
49. +Steven Pack, rhp, Fallbrook (Calif.) HS / Los Angeles Pierce JC.
50. *Beau Champoux, ss, San Diego Mesa JC.

## NEW YORK YANKEES (6)

**1. Derek Jeter, ss, Central HS, Kalamazoo, Mich.—(1995-2014)**
2. (Choice to Royals as compensation for Type A free agent Danny Tartabull)
3. (Choice to Athletics as compensation for Type A free agent Mike Gallego)
**4. Mike Buddie, rhp, Wake Forest University.—(1998-2002)**
5. Don Leshnock, c, University of North Carolina.
DRAFT DROP *Son of Don Leshnock, major leaguer (1972)*
6. Ray Suplee, of, University of Georgia.
7. Carlton Fleming, 2b, Georgia Tech.
**8. Matt Luke, of, University of California.—(1996-99)**
**9. Ryan Karp, lhp, Florida International University.—(1995-97)**
10. Robert Hinds, 2b, UCLA.
11. Mike Gordon, rhp, Shanks HS, Quincy, Fla.
12. Kraig Hawkins, of, University of South Alabama.
13. Jim Thomforde, rhp, Trinity (Conn.) College.
14. Kent Wallace, rhp, Murray State University.
15. Jeff Antolick, rhp, Lafayette College.
16. Blaise Kozeniewski, ss, University of Georgia.
17. Bill Underwood, rhp, Kent State University.
18. Ernie Yaroshuk, of, Stetson University.
19. Gordon Sanchez, c, Long Beach State University.
20. Glenn Delafield, of, Panola (Texas) JC.
21. Travion Nelson, of, South Hills HS, Covina, Calif.
22. Bruce Pool, lhp, University of Texas-Arlington.
23. Cody Samuel, 1b, Washington HS, Redondo Beach, Calif.
**24. Mike DeJean, rhp, Livingston (Ala.) University.—(1997-2006)**
25. Nick Delvecchio, of, Harvard University.
26. *Eric Trice, of, University of Oregon.
27. *Francis Fucile, ss, St. Thomas Aquinas HS, Hollywood, Fla.
28. +Chris Ashby, c, Spanish River HS, Boca Raton, Fla. / Edison (Fla.) CC.
29. Brian McLamb, ss, Florida CC.
30. *Anthony Shelby, lhp, Lockport (Ill.) HS.
31. *Joshua Gregson, 1b, Dale HS, Shawnee, Okla.
32. *Mel Motley, of, Poly HS, Riverside, Calif.
33. *Mike Robbins, lhp, Skyline HS, Oakland.
34. *Greg Dean, rhp-3b, Ada (Okla.) HS.
35. *Drew Pearce, rhp, St. Francis HS, Mountain View, Calif.
36. *Victor Rodriguez, rhp, Okaloosa-Walton (Fla.) CC.
37. +Vick Brown, ss, Okaloosa-Walton (Fla.) CC.
38. R.D. Long, ss, University of Houston.
39. *Bryan Richardson, of, Lowe HS, Windsor, Ontario.
40. *Brad Tayles, rhp, Western Michigan University.
41. Tibor Brown, lhp, Stetson University.
42. *Sean McClellan, rhp, Seminole (Fla.) HS.
43. *John Ziegelman, of, Placer HS, Auburn, Calif.
44. *Andrew Stenger, of, Indian River (Fla.) JC.
45. *Dale Brandt, lhp, Vero Beach (Fla.) HS.
46. +Keith Heberling, lhp, Indian River (Fla.) JC.
47. *Sean Duncan, of, McLennan (Texas) CC.
48. +Chris Cumberland, lhp, Pasco Hernando (Fla.) CC.
DRAFT DROP *Son of John Cumberland, major leaguer (1968-74)*
49. *Reginald Coleman, of, Frankston (Texas) HS.
50. *Damon Lembi, c-1b, JC of San Mateo (Calif.).

## OAKLAND ATHLETICS (20)

1. Benji Grigsby, rhp, San Diego State University.—(AAA)
**2. Jason Giambi, 3b, Long Beach State University.—(1995-2014)**
DRAFT DROP *Brother of Jeremy Giambi, major leaguer (1998-2003)*
**3. *Gabe Alvarez, ss, Bishop Amat HS, Santa Ana, Calif.** (Choice from Yankees as compensation for Type A free agent Mike Gallego).—**(1998-2000)**
DRAFT DROP *Attended Southern California; re-drafted by Padres, 1995 (2nd round)*
3. Scott Miller, rhp, Clemson University.--DNP
**4. Don Wengert, rhp, Iowa State University.—(1995-2001)**
**5. Steve Cox, 1b, Monache HS, Porterville, Calif.—(1999-2005)**
6. Cliff Foster, rhp, University of Oklahoma.
7. Bob Bennett, rhp, Dartmouth College.
8. Troy Penix, 1b, University of California.
9. Marcel Galligani, of, Iona University.
10. William Urbina, rhp, Pueblo HS, Tucson, Ariz.
**11. D.T. Cromer, of, University of South Carolina.—(2000-01)**
DRAFT DROP *Brother of Tripp Cromer, major leaguer (1993-2003) • Brother of Brandon Cromer, first-round draft pick, Blue Jays (1992)*
12. Stan Payne, lhp, University of Georgia.
13. Brian Eldridge, 2b, University of Oklahoma.
14. Tim Killeen, c, University of Iowa.
**15. *Chris Michalak, lhp, University of Notre Dame.—(1998-2006)**
16. Brian Darwin, of, Gahr HS, Cerritos, Calif.
DRAFT DROP *Son of Bobby Darwin, major leaguer (1962-77)*
17. *Kip Schaefer, of, Redwood HS, Greenbrae, Calif.
18. Richard King, rhp, University of Tennessee.
19. Brian Domenico, rhp, Dean (Mass.) JC.
20. Mark Sobolewski, 3b, Florida Southern College.
21. +Skye Leibee, of-lhp, Taft (Calif.) JC.
**22. Gary Haught, rhp, University of Southwestern Louisiana.—(1997)**
23. David Keel, of, Motlow State (Tenn.) CC.
24. Terance Frazier, 3b, Fresno State University.
**25. Brian Lesher, 1b, University of Delaware.—(1996-2002)**
26. Trent Montgomery, rhp, Baker HS, Mobile, Ala.
27. *Mike Salazar, lhp, Fresno State University.
28. Jason White, 1b, Wichita State University.
29. Shawn Sanderfer, c, Riverside (Calif.) CC.
30. Larry Kingsbury, rhp, Villanova University.
31. Geoff Loomis, 2b, University of Portland.
32. Craig Gienger, rhp, Brigham Young University.
33. *Harold Williams, of, Livingston (Ala.) University.
34. Herman Johnson, c, Northwood (Texas) Institute.
35. *Martin Meza, rhp, Los Angeles Harbor JC.
36. Tim Bojan, rhp, College of St. Francis (Ill.).
37. Brendan Hause, 1b-lhp, Mira Mesa HS, San Diego.
38. *Bryan Evans, rhp, Brevard (Fla.) JC.
39. James Banks, rhp, Shelby State (Tenn.) CC.
40. James Byerly, rhp, Montclair State (N.J.) College.
41. *Jerrod Wong, 1b, Boise (Idaho) HS.
42. *Ramon Medina, of, American HS, Miami.
43. Stacy Hollins, rhp, San Jacinto (Texas) JC.
DRAFT DROP *Brother of Jessie Hollins, major leaguer (1992)*
44. *Donald Machacon, 2b, American HS, Miami.
**45. *Robert Fick, c, Newbury Park HS, Thousand Oaks, Calif.—(1998-2007)**
46. *Matt Curtis, c, Golden West HS, Visalia, Calif.
47. John Jones, 3b, Laney (Calif.) JC.
48. *Michael Jackson, of, San Rafael HS, Tiburon, Calif.
49. Lauro Felix, ss, New Mexico State University.
50. Mark Moore, c, Oral Roberts University.

## PHILADELPHIA PHILLIES (13)

1. Chad McConnell, of, Creighton University.–(AA)
2. (Choice to Reds as compensation for Type B free agent Mariano Duncan)
3. Trevor Humphry, rhp, Westark (Ark.) CC.—(High A)
4. Jason Moler, c, Cal State Fullerton.—(AAA)
**5. Larry Mitchell, rhp, James Madison University.—(1996)**
6. Jamie Sepeda, rhp, Stanford University.
7. Steve Solomon, of, Stanford University.
8. Jon McMullen, 1b, Rio Mesa HS, Oxnard, Calif.
DRAFT DROP *Son of Ken McMullen, major leaguer (1962-77)*
9. *Nate Brown, lhp, University of California.
10. Stan Evans, of, Seminole (Fla.) CC.
**11. *Casey Blake, ss, Indianola (Iowa) HS.—(1999-2011)**
**12. Jon Zuber, lhp-1b, University of California.—(1996-98)**
13. Alan Burke, 1b-3b, Long Beach State University.
14. Mike Gomez, 2b, University of Delaware.
15. Shawn Wills, of, UCLA.
16. Tim Costa, rhp, West Hills (Calif.) JC.
17. *Grant Hohman, ss, St. Bernard HS, Westchester, Calif.
18. *Jon Morris, c, Northeastern Oklahoma A&M JC.
19. Scott Haws, c, Bucks County (Pa.) CC.
20. Michael Thompson, of, Gulf Coast (Fla.) CC.
21. *Joe Scopio, 2b, Gloucester County (N.J.) JC.
22. Tim Cornish, of, Ventura (Calif.) JC.
**23. +Bobby Estalella, c, Cooper City HS, Pembroke Pines, Fla. / Miami-Dade CC South.—(1996-2004)**
DRAFT DROP *Grandson of Bobby Estalella, major leaguer (1935-49)*
24. Steven Nutt, lhp, Centenary College.
25. *Brian Brewer, lhp, Sacramento (Calif.) CC.
26. Jeremy Kendall, of, Winona State (Minn.) University.
27. Dell Allen, c-1b, Black Hawk (Ill.) JC.
**28. Tony Fiore, rhp, Triton (Ill.) JC.—(2000-03)**
29. David Fisher, 2b, Missouri Southern State College.
30. Eric Smith, rhp, Brigham Young University.
31. Chris Phipps, rhp, Tennessee HS, Bristol, Tenn.
32. *Clint Whitworth, rhp, Oklahoma City University.
33. Blake Doolan, rhp, Northeast Louisiana University.
34. *Bo Gray, rhp, Cherry Hill West HS, Cherry Hill, N.J.
35. Mark Tranberg, rhp, Cal State Dominguez Hills.
36. Thomas Irwin, rhp, California State University.
37. E.J. Brophy, c, University of Alabama-Birmingham.
38. Ronald Kratz, ss-3b, Kutztown (Pa.) University.
39. Phil Romero, 2b, Fresno State University.
40. Ryan McWilliams, rhp, Southern Illinois University.
41. Ben Martinez, of, Central HS, St. Paul, Minn.
42. Shane Hobbs, c, Santana HS, Santee, Calif.
43. *Matthew Kilgore, c, Dobyns Bennett HS, Kingsport, Tenn.
44. +Dan McDonald, of, Sarasota (Fla.) HS / Manatee (Fla.) JC.
45. *Matt Rosemeyer, of, Eldorado HS, Las Vegas

46. Charlton Moore, of, Chicago State University.
47. Michael Shipman, c, Dexter (Mo.) HS.
48. *Charles Burns, of, Grapevine (Texas) HS.
49. *Chris Freeman, rhp, Walters State (Tenn.) CC.
50. *Angel Aragon, rhp, Channel Islands HS, Oxnard, Calif.

## PITTSBURGH PIRATES (23)

1. **Jason Kendall, c, Torrance (Calif.) HS.—(1996-2010)**
**DRAFT DROP** *Son of Fred Kendall, major leaguer (1969-80)*
1. Shon Walker, of, Harrison County HS, Cynthiana, Ky. (Supplemental choice—33rd—as compensation for Type A free agent Bobby Bonilla).—(High A)
2. **Danny Clyburn, of, Lancaster (S.C.) HS** (Choice from Mets as compensation for Bonilla).**—(1997-99)**
2. **Trey Beamon, of, W.T. White HS, Dallas.—(1996-98)**
3. Jamie Keefe, ss, Spaulding HS, Rochester, N.H.—(AAA)
4. Tim Leger, of, Acadiana HS, Lafayette, La.—(Short-season A)
5. Brett Backlund, rhp, University of Iowa.—(AAA)
6. **Sean Lawrence, lhp, College of St. Francis (Ill.).—(1998)**
7. **Dennis Konuszewski, rhp, University of Michigan.—(1995)**
8. Aaron Cannaday, c, Elon College.
9. Rod Davidson, lhp, Rustburg (Va.) HS.
10. John Turlais, c, Illinois Math & Science Academy, Flora, Ill.
11. Jeff Hairston, of, Grant HS, Portland, Ore.
12. Larry Stahlhoefer, c, Chapman (Calif.) College.
13. Brian Wolf, 1b, Minster (Ohio) HS.
14. **Jason Phillips, rhp, Hughesville HS, Muncy, Pa.—(1999-2003)**
15. Ted Klamm, lhp, Seton Hall University.
16. Travis Palmer, of, Camp Verde (Ariz.) HS.
17. Jake Austin, of, Wake Forest University.
18. **Gary Wilson, rhp, Cal State Sacramento.—(1995)**
19. Rico Gholston, 1b, McNeese State University.
20. John Dillinger, rhp, Manatee (Fla.) JC.
21. Jay Cranford, 3b, University of Georgia.
22. G.G. Harris, 1b, Lancaster (S.C.) HS.
23. Sean Nolan, ss, Edison HS, Miami.
24. Michel Laplante, rhp, Academie du Baseball Canada, East Montreal, Quebec.
25. ***Steve Connelly, rhp, Woodrow Wilson HS, Long Beach.—(1998)**
26. Marc Mesewicz, lhp, Ohio State University.
27. **Chance Sanford, ss, San Jacinto (Texas) JC.—(1998-99)**
28. Matt Jones, 1b, Florida Atlantic University.
29. Stan Wiltz, 1b, Northeast Louisiana University.
30. **Kevin Polcovich, ss, University of Florida.—(1997-98)**
31. **+Lou Collier, ss, Kishwaukee (Ill.) JC / Triton (Ill.) JC—(1997-2004)**
32. *Jeff Meszar, ss, North Carolina State University.
33. *Stephen Bosch, rhp, Norwood (Ohio) HS.
34. Jamie Mackert, c, Community HS, West Chicago, Ill.
35. Jack Ford, lhp, Southwest Texas State University.
36. Erskine Kelly, of, University of Richmond.
37. *Trey Rutledge, rhp, Seminole (Okla.) JC.
38. Jon Gendron, rhp, Bishop Kelley HS, Tulsa, Okla.
39. *Phillip King, of, American River (Calif.) JC.
40. Mark Fabela, rhp, Santa Clara University.
41. *Jason Imrisek, c, Andrew HS, Orland Park, Ill.
42. Rich Townsend, lhp, Florida Southern College.
43. *Dan Destefano, rhp, Palm Beach (Fla.) CC.
44. Riegal Hunt, of, Old Dominion University.
45. *Tim Cossins, c, University of Oklahoma.
46. *Mickey Dutil, rhp, University of Southern Mississippi.
47. **Marc Wilkins, rhp, University of Toledo.—(1996-2001)**
48. **Adrian Brown, of, McComb (Miss.) HS.—(1997-2006)**
49. *Bert Emanuel, of-ss, Rice University.
**DRAFT DROP** *Wide receiver, National Football League (1994-2001)*
50. *James Rudolph, rhp, American River (Calif.) JC.

Pirates first-rounder Jason Kendall had a major league career that bested that of his father

## ST. LOUIS CARDINALS (15)

1. **Sean Lowe, rhp, Arizona State University.—(1997-2003)**
2. **Mike Gulan, 3b, Kent State University.—(1997-2001)**
3. **Steve Montgomery, rhp, Pepperdine University.—(1996-2000)**
4. Mark Williams, c, Coral Springs (Fla.) HS.—(Low A)
5. Jeff Alkire, lhp, University of Miami.—(AA)
6. **Keith Johns, ss, University of Mississippi.—(1998)**
7. *Mike Corominas, lhp, Diamond Bar (Calif.) HS.
8. Brian Carpenter, rhp, Baylor University.
9. Donnie Bellum, of, Albertson (Idaho) College.
10. **+Scarborough Green, ss, Lafayette HS, Ballwin, Mo. / St. Louis CC-Meramec—(1997-2000)**
11. Alan Beavers, rhp, Ohio University.
12. Glenn Bowen, c, Chesnee HS, Mayo, S.C.
13. Jamie Sailors, lhp, Parkland (Ill.) JC.
14. ***Todd Greene, of, Georgia Southern University.—(1996-2006)**
15. Rongie Dicken, ss, Volunteer State (Tenn.) JC.
16. Brad Owens, 2b, Western Illinois University.
17. Scott Lair, rhp, Parkway Central HS, Chesterfield, Mo.
18. ***Frank Lankford, rhp, University of Virginia.—(1998)**
19. Jeff Murphy, c, University of Nebraska.
20. **Brady Raggio, rhp, Chabot (Calif.) JC.—(1997-2003)**
21. *Mike Pasqualicchio, lhp, McClancy HS, Astoria, N.Y.
22. Joe Carrillo, lhp, University of Wyoming.
23. Todd Henderson, of, Carson-Newman (Tenn.) College.
24. *Michael Blais, rhp, University of Connecticut.
25. Darren Doucette, 1b, Ulster (N.Y.) CC.
26. *Mark Hamlin, of, Evans HS, Augusta, Ga.
27. Randy Bledsoe, rhp, Angelina (Texas) JC.
28. **Joe McEwing, of-ss, CC of Morris (N.J.).—(1998-2006)**
29. John Stutz, 3b, St. Andrews Presbyterian (NC.) College.
30. Andy Martin, 1b, The Master's (Calif.) College.
31. Jeff Matranga, rhp, Arizona State University.
32. **Kirk Bullinger, rhp, Southeastern Louisiana University.—(1998-2004)**
**DRAFT DROP** *Brother of Jim Bullinger, major leaguer (1992-98)*
33. Victor Pellot, of, Berkshire HS, Guaynabo, P.R.
34. Jason Stoppello, lhp, JC of Southern Idaho.
35. David Oehrlein, lhp, St. Cloud State (Minn.) University.
36. **T.J. Mathews, rhp, University of Nevada-Las Vegas.—(1995-2002)**
**DRAFT DROP** *Son of Nelson Mathews, major leaguer (1960-65)*
37. Trey Ritz, ss, Southern Arkansas University.
38. *Micah Stovall, lhp, Cypress (Calif.) HS.
39. *Bryan Garrett, of, Odessa (Texas) JC.
40. Dennis Milius, lhp, Cameron (Okla.) University.
41. Joe Larson, lhp, Bridgewater State (Mass.) College.
42. Jose Vazquez, of, University of Tennessee.
43. Brian Rupp, ss, University of Missouri-St. Louis.
44. Charlie Anderson, 2b, Mississippi State University.
45. Todd Blake, lhp-1b, Catawba (N.C.) College.
46. *John Cappelmann, rhp, Northern Valley Regional HS, Demarest, N.J.
47. *Paul Williams, lhp, Treasure Valley (Ore.) CC.
48. *Theopolis Frost, of, Wellington (Kan.) HS.
49. +Derrick Robinson, 3b, JC of Southern Idaho / Dixie (Utah) JC.
50. +Aaron Gerteisen, of, Tallahassee (Fla.) CC.

## SAN DIEGO PADRES (17)

1. (Choice to Royals as compensation for Type A free agent Kurt Stillwell)
2. ***Todd Helton, of, Central HS, Knoxville, Tenn.—(1997-2013)**
**DRAFT DROP** *Attended Tennessee; re-drafted by Rockies, 1995 (1st round)*
3. Jared Baker, rhp, University of South Carolina.—(AA)
4. ***Brett Laxton, rhp, Audubon (N.J.) HS.—(1999-2000)**
**DRAFT DROP** *Attended Louisiana State; re-drafted by Mariners, 1995 (24th round) • Son of Bill Laxton, major leaguer (1970-77)*
5. Jimmy Baron, lhp, Humble (Texas) HS.—(AAA)
6. Brad Gennaro, of, San Diego State University.
7. Tom Kindler, rhp, Kent State University.
8. *Rich Lawrence, ss, Barron Collier HS, Naples, Fla.
9. **Todd Erdos, rhp, Meadville (Pa.) HS.—(1997-2001)**
10. Ricky Talbott, 3b, Northview HS, Covina, Calif.
11. John Fantauzzi, 1b, Florida International University.
12. Troy Gillis, ss, Curtis HS, Tacoma, Wash.
13. Aaron Roques, of, Canyon Springs HS, Moreno Valley, Calif.
14. Marcus McCoy, of, Meridian (Miss.) HS.
15. Brian McLain, rhp, Mountain View HS, Vancouver, Wash.
16. Luis Arroyo, lhp, Inter American (P.R.) University.
17. Sean Drinkwater, ss, North Carolina State University.
18. Bobby Bonds, Jr., of, Canada (Calif.) JC.
**DRAFT DROP** *Son of Bobby Bonds, major leaguer (1968-81) • Brother of Barry Bonds, major leaguer (1986-2007)*
19. Chris Murphy, rhp, Elon College.
20. *Brent Bearden, rhp, Texarkana (Texas) CC.
21. Joe Bowden, ss, Simeon HS, Chicago.
22. Gabby Martinez, c, Odessa (Texas) JC.
23. Ken Grzelaczyk, rhp, St. John's University.
24. ***Geoff Jenkins, 3b, Cordova HS, Rancho Cordova, Calif.—(1998-2008)**
**DRAFT DROP** *First-round draft pick (9th overall), Brewers (1995)*
25. Joe Jumonville, rhp, Bishop Noll HS, Hammond, Ind.
26. *Rico Lagattuta, lhp, Westlake HS, Thousand Oaks, Calif.
27. Jeff Jones, rhp, Vincent Massey HS, Windsor, Ontario.
28. *Mark Davis, rhp, Sterling HS, Baytown, Texas.
29. Zaven Luckett, of, Westbury HS, Houston.
30. Erick Corps, ss, Berwind Superior HS, Carolina, P.R.
31. *Jeff Gyselman, c, Portland State University.
32. Bill Robbs, of, Grand Canyon University.
33. Michael Sanders, of, James Monroe HS, Bronx, N.Y.
34. Marty Winchester, lhp, Long Beach (Calif.) CC.
35. Mike Stadler, c, El Cajon Valley HS, El Cajon, Calif.
36. *Todd Bartels, rhp, Millard North HS, Omaha,

Neb.
**37. *Mark Bellhorn, ss, Oviedo (Fla.) HS.—(1997-2007)**
38. Roberto DeLeon, 2b, University of Texas.
39. *Justin Long, of-ss, Claremont HS, Pomona, Calif.
40. Scott Singleton, rhp, Westlake HS, Thousand Oaks, Calif.
41. Britton Scheibe, of, Mira Costa (Calif.) JC.
42. Brett Malekovic, 1b, Stagg HS, Palos Hills, Ill.
43. Hector Fargas, rhp, Rio Piedras (P.R.) HS.
44. *Karl Goins, c, Mira Mesa HS, San Diego.
45. Kevin Minchk, 1b, University of Iowa.
46. +Marcus Willis, rhp, W.T. White HS, Dallas / San Jacinto (Texas) JC.
47. *Adam Frost, rhp, Ocean Springs (Miss.) HS.
48. *Robert Myers, rhp, Long Beach (Calif.) CC.
49. Matt Goebel, of, Royal HS, Simi Valley, Calif.
50. *Shane Gunderson, c, Faribault (Minn.) HS.

## SAN FRANCISCO GIANTS (7)

**1. Calvin Murray, of, University of Texas.—(1999-2004)**
DRAFT DROP *First-round draft pick (11th overall), Indians (1989)*
2. Jim Rosenbohm, rhp, Hutchinson (Kan.) JC.—(Low A)
3. Benji Simonton, of, Diablo Valley (Calif.) JC.—(AAA)
4. Kurt Ehmann, ss, Arizona State University.–(AAA)
**5. Doug Mirabelli, c, Wichita State University.—(1996-2007)**
**6. Aaron Fultz, lhp, North Florida JC.—(2000-07)**
7. Mark Pooschke, 3b, Madison HS, Portland, Ore.
8. Chris Wimmer, ss, Wichita State University.
9. Petie Roach, 1b-of, University of Nevada-Reno.
**10. Jamie Brewington, rhp-of, Virginia Commonwealth University.—(1995-2000)**
**11. Chad Fonville, ss, Louisburg (N.C.) JC.—(1995-99)**
12. Armond Anderson, ss, East St. John HS, La Place, La.
13. Mark Peterson, lhp, Portland State University.
14. Jeff Myers, lhp, Pepperdine University.
15. Kenny Woods, ss, Lewis-Clark State (Idaho) College.
16. *Everard Griffiths, rhp, North Miami (Fla.) HS.
17. *Robby Welles, 3b, Los Angeles Pierce JC.
18. Kumandae Miller, rhp, Grant HS, Sacramento, Calif.
19. Mark Saugstad, 3b, UC Riverside.
20. Keith Stafford, ss, South Georgia JC.
21. *Josh Deakman, rhp, Beaverton (Ore.) HS.
**22. *Bryant Nelson, rhp-ss, Crossett (Ark.) HS.—(2002)**
23. Papo Ramos, of, University of Southwestern Louisiana.
24. Clay King, 3b, University of Texas.
25. Kendrick Mitchell, rhp, Madison HS, Portland, Ore.
26. *Dietrich Evans, c, Cibola HS, Yuma, Ariz.
27. Tom O'Neill, 2b, Northern Illinois University.
28. Craig Mayes, c, Michigan State University.
29. *John Licea, of, Lindsay (Calif.) HS.
30. *William Johnson, ss-of, Freedom HS, Morganton, N.C.
31. David Baine, lhp, Sonoma State (Calif.) University.
32. Andy Heckman, lhp, University of North Carolina-Charlotte.
33. Bobby Gorham, rhp, Howard University.
34. *Jason Maloney, rhp, Fresno (Calif.) CC.
DRAFT DROP *Son of Jim Maloney, major leaguer (1960-71)*
35. Charles Hicks, rhp, Birmingham-Southern College.
36. *Darian Hagan, ss, University of Colorado.
DRAFT DROP *Fourth-round draft pick, San Francisco 49ers/National Football League (1992); defensive back, Canadian Football League (1993-96)*
37. Jorge Vazquez, rhp, Juana Colon HS, Comerio, P.R.
38. *Dwayne Crawley, of-lhp, Douglas HS, Upper Marlboro, Md.
39. Chris Pinder, rhp, Woodbridge (Va.) HS.
40. James Poyner, c, DeKalb (Ga.) JC.
41. Jeff Richey, rhp, Louisiana Tech.
42. Dennis Szczechowski, rhp, Siena Heights (Mich.) College.
43. *Clay Crossan, rhp, American River (Calif.) JC.
44. Todd Harris, of, Spartanburg Methodist (S.C.) JC.
45. *Dan Reed, lhp, Gonzaga HS, McLean, Va.
46. *Tista Perri, rhp, Oak Ridge HS, Cameron Park, Calif.
47. *Shawn Bowders, of, Martinsburg HS, Kerneysville, W.Va.
**48. *Cody McKay, ss, Horizon HS, Scottsdale, Ariz.—(2002-04)**
DRAFT DROP *Son of Dave McKay, major leaguer (1975-82)*
49. Michael Cavanagh, c, Linfield (Ore.) College.
**50. Marvin Benard, of, Lewis-Clark State (Idaho) College.—(1995-2003)**

## SEATTLE MARINERS (14)

**1. Ron Villone, lhp, University of Massachusetts.—(1995-2009)**
**2. Bob Wolcott, rhp, North HS, Medford, Ore.—(1995-99)**
**3. Chris Widger, c, George Mason University.—(1995-2006)**
**4. Andy Sheets, ss, Louisiana State University.—(1996-2002)**
5. Dave Vanhof, lhp, Southgate Anderson HS, Southgate, Mich.—(High A)
**6. Tim Davis, lhp, Florida State University.—(1994-97)**
7. Chris Dessellier, rhp, Ypsilanti (Mich.) HS.
8. Brian Doughty, rhp, Juanita HS, Kirkland, Wash.
9. Ivan Montane, rhp, Miami-Dade CC South.
10. Joe Pomierski, 3b, Biloxi (Miss.) HS.
11. *Chris Dean, of, Hayward (Calif.) HS.
12. Mike Hickey, 2b, Texas A&M University.
13. Oscar Rivera, rhp, San Jose (Calif.) CC.
14. Brian Wallace, 3b, University of Delaware.
15. *Todd Johnson, c, Fresno State University.
**16. Brett Hinchliffe, rhp, Bishop Gallagher HS, Detroit.—(1999-2001)**
17. *Jack Stanczak, 3b, Villanova University.
18. Jackie Nickell, rhp, University of Southern California.
19. *Brent Smith, rhp, Arizona State University.
20. Bobby Worley, rhp, Ohio State University.
21. *Ray Farmer, of, Glenn HS, Kernersville, N.C.
DRAFT DROP *Linebacker, National Football League (1996-98); general manager, Cleveland Browns/NFL (2014-15)*
**22. *Ryan Nye, rhp, Westark (Ark.) CC.—(1997-98)**
**23. +Ryan Franklin, rhp, Seminole (Okla.) JC.—(1999-2011)**
24. James Clifford, 1b, University of Washington.
25. Derek Bieniasz, rhp, West Toronto Collegiate HS, Toronto.
26. *Chris Sturgeon, rhp, Grant HS, Portland, Ore.
27. *Josh Potter, rhp, Rose HS, Greenville, N.C.
28. Marcus Sturdivant, of, West Stanly HS, Oakboro, N.C.
29. Stacey Davis, 1b, Southwest DeKalb HS, Decatur, Ga.
30. *Eric Poullard, of, Sacred Heart HS, Ville Platte, La.
31. Richard Graham, rhp, University of Massachusetts.
32. *Jason Haynie, lhp, Lakewood HS, St. Petersburg, Fla.
33. *Raymond Miller, 3b, Dobson HS, Chandler, Ariz.
**34. Tim Harikkala, rhp, Florida Atlantic University.—(1995-2007)**
35. Ron Cody, rhp, UC Riverside.
**36. Raul Ibanez, of, Miami-Dade CC South.—(1996-2014)**
37. *Christian Shewey, c, Redmond (Wash.) HS.
38. Jamon Deal, rhp, University of North Carolina-Asheville.
39. Jerry Aschoff, lhp, Pepperdine University.
40. +Michael Brady, of, Glasgow HS, Newark, Del. / Spartanburg Methodist (S.C.) JC.
41. *Philip Olson, rhp, Riverview HS, Sarasota, Fla.
42. +Brian Williams, rhp, Phoenix JC.
43. *Dennis Regan, c, Loomis Chaffee HS, Windsor, Conn.
44. *Jeff Martin, lhp, Mahomet (Ill.) HS.
45. Stan Golden, rhp, Opelika (Ala.) HS.
46. *Randall Wilson, rhp, Esperanza HS, Yorba Linda, Calif.
47. *Chad Soden, lhp, Westark (Ark.) CC.
48. *Dax Winslett, rhp, McLennan (Texas) CC.
49. Kevin Stock, lhp, University of Virginia.
50. *Mike Martin, ss, Manatee (Fla.) JC.

## TEXAS RANGERS (22)

**1. Rick Helling, rhp, Stanford University.—(1994-2006)**
2. Ritchie Moody, lhp, Oklahoma State University.—(AAA)
**3. David Manning, rhp, Palm Beach (Fla.) JC.—(2003)**
4. Ramiro Martinez, lhp, Los Angeles CC.—(AA)
5. Mike Smith, ss, Indiana University.—(AAA)
6. Cory Pearson, of, Logan (W.Va.) HS.
7. Jeff Runion, rhp, Riverdale (Ga.) HS.
8. Kevin Dunivan, rhp, Captain Shreve HS, Shreveport, La.
9. Scott Malone, of, Texas Christian University.
DRAFT DROP *Baseball coach, Texas A&M-Corpus Christi (2008-15)*
10. Scot Sealy, c, University of South Alabama.
**11. John Dettmer, rhp, University of Missouri.—(1994-95)**
12. John Tomasello, of, University of San Francisco.
13. Del Eggleston, 2b-3b, Pfeiffer (N.C.) College.
14. David Hieb, c, University of South Carolina-Aiken.
15. Rod Seip, rhp, Egyptian HS, Tamms, Ill.
16. Mike Welch, of, George Washington University.
17. *Adam Danner, rhp, King HS, Tampa.
18. Chris Kelley, rhp, University of Tennessee.
19. Brent Evans, lhp, Southwest Missouri State University.
20. +Andreaus Lewis, of, McNair HS, Decatur, Ga. / Gordon (Ga.) JC.
21. Deshon Brown, of, Biola (Calif.) University.
22. Chris Newcomb, rhp, Indiana University.
23. Daniel Mascia, rhp, Adelphi (N.Y.) University.
**24. Rich Aurilia, ss, St. John's University.—(1992-2009)**
25. Chad Wiley, rhp, Kansas City (Kan.) JC.
**26. Mark Brandenburg, rhp, Texas Tech.—(1995-97)**
27. *Craig Bolcerek, c, Blinn (Texas) JC.
28. Wes Shook, of, Texas Tech.
29. Terry Rosenkranz, lhp, Morton (Ill.) JC.
30. +Whitney Shanklin, of, Crenshaw HS, Los Angeles / Fresno (Calif.) CC.
31. Ray Williams, 2b, Skyline HS, Dallas.
32. Jack Kimel, lhp, Western Carolina University.
33. *Antawan Smith, of, Madison County HS, Madison, Fla.
34. Michael Anderson, rhp, Northampton (Pa.) CC.
35. Chris Burr, 1b-of, George Mason University.
36. *Ted Rose, rhp, St. Clairsville (Ohio) HS.
**37. *Brian Dallimore, ss, Clark HS, Las Vegas, Nev.—(2004-05)**
38. *Michael Fox, rhp, Cameron (Okla) HS.
39. *Tripp Mackay, ss-2b, Mount Pleasant (Texas) HS.
40. *Frederick Barnes, lhp, Van Horn HS, Kansas City, Mo.
41. +Jason Farmer, rhp, Jones HS, Midwest City, Okla. / Seminole (Okla.) JC.
42. *Jason Smith, rhp, Canton Academy HS, Canton, Miss.
**43. *Jermaine Dye, rhp, Wood HS, Vacaville, Calif.—(1996-2009)**
44. *Matt Jones, ss, Rose HS, Greenville, N.C.
45. *Bob St. Pierre, rhp, DeMatha HS, Huntingtown, Md.
**46. *Britt Reames, c-rhp, Seneca (S.C.) HS.—(2000-06)**
47. *Larry Ephan, c, Lewis-Clark State (Idaho) College.
48. *Brian Basteyns, rhp, Enumclaw (Wash.) HS.
49. *Stan Stewart, rhp, North Florida JC.
50. *Darious Carter, of, Southwest Mississippi JC.

## TORONTO BLUE JAYS (25)

**1. Shannon Stewart, of, Southridge HS, Miami** (Choice from Dodgers as compensation for Type A free agent Tom Candiotti).**—(1995-2008)**
**1. Todd Steverson, of, Arizona State University.—(1995-96)**
1. Brandon Cromer, ss, Lexington (S.C.) HS (Supplemental choice—34th—as compensation for Candiotti).—(AAA)
DRAFT DROP *Brother of Tripp Cromer, major leaguer (1993-2003) • Brother of D.T. Cromer, 11th-round draft pick, Athletics (1992); major leaguer (2000-01)*
**2. Tim Crabtree, rhp, Michigan State University.—(1995-2001)**
3. Levon Largusa, lhp, University of Hawaii.—(High A)
**4. Tom Evans, rhp-3b, Juanita HS, Kirkland, Wash.—(1997-2000)**
5. Jeff Patzke, ss, Klamath Union HS, Klamath Falls, Ore.—(AAA)
6. *Shea Morenz, of, Central HS, San Angelo, Texas.
DRAFT DROP *First-round draft pick (27th overall), Yankees (1995) • Great grandson of Howie Morenz, member/Hockey Hall of Fame; forward, NHL (1923-37)*
**7. Anthony Sanders, 3b-of, Santa Rita HS, Tucson, Ariz.—(1999-2001)**
8. *Mike Kendzierski, rhp, Union HS, Endicott, N.Y.
9. Tim Adkins, lhp, Wayne HS, Huntington, W.Va.
DRAFT DROP *Brother of Jon Adkins, major leaguer (2003-08)*
10. Scot McCloughan, 3b, Wichita State University.
DRAFT DROP *Son of Kent McCloughan, defensive back, National Football League (1965-70)*
11. Scott Kennedy, rhp, Palm Beach (Fla.) JC.
**12. *Doug Mientkiewicz, c, Westminster Christian HS, Miami.—(1998-2009)**
13. Richard Halbruner, 1b, Providence HS, Matthews, N.C.
14. Pat Moultrie, of, Edison HS, Fresno, Calif.
15. Doug Meiners, rhp, Curtis HS, Staten Island, N.Y.
16. *Brian McClure, ss, Glenwood HS, Chatham, Ill.
17. Mike Stefanoff, rhp, Rowland HS, Rowland Heights, Calif.
18. David Becker, c, Elder HS, Cincinnati.
19. Chad Brown, lhp, North Greenville (S.C.) JC.
20. Ben Candelaria, of, Lorenzo Coballes Gandia HS, Hatillo, P.R.
21. *Terry Adams, 3b, Eastern Commerce HS, Toronto.
22. *Stanley Sanders, of, Stanhope Elmore HS, Millbrook, Ala.
23. Matt Johnson, ss, University of Iowa.
24. Randy Phillips, rhp, Arkansas State University.
25. *Aaron France, rhp, Loara HS, Anaheim, Calif.
26. Chris Chandler, 3b-ss, Moorpark (Calif.) JC.
27. *Matt Jones, 3b, Grossmont HS, El Cajon, Calif.
28. *John Knight, ss, Leland (Miss.) HS.
29. Derek Brandow, rhp, Oklahoma State University.
30. Jonathan Rivers, 1b, Tallassee (Ala.) HS.
31. *Deron Pointer, of, Washington State University.
32. *Tremayne Noles, 1b, Westchester HS, Los Angeles.
33. *Colin Mattiace, rhp, Jefferson HS, Cedar Rapids, Iowa.
34. *Carlton Washington, of, Eisenhower HS, Houston.
35. Aaron Hightower, of, Opp (Ala.) HS.
36. Keilan Smith, rhp, Frayser HS, Memphis, Tenn.
37. *Neil James, 3b, Broward (Fla.) CC.
38. *Peter Durkovic, lhp, Trinity-Pawling HS, Flushing, N.Y.
39. *Darrin Babineaux, rhp, Rayne (La) HS.
40. *Michael Schroeder, 3b, Yosemite HS, North Fork, Calif.
41. Jeff Ladd, c, University of Toledo.
42. Kevin King, of, Central HS, St. Croix, Virgin Islands.
43. Aaron Jersild, lhp, Clemson University.
44. *Steven Hacker, of-1b, Mehlville HS, St, Louis.
**45. *Jeff DaVanon, 2b, Bellaire HS, Houston.—(1999-2007)**
DRAFT DROP *Son of Jerry DaVanon, major leaguer (1969-77)*
46. Sy Dorsey, rhp, Dorsey HS, Los Angeles.
47. *Todd Abbott, rhp, Westark (Ark.) CC.
DRAFT DROP *Son of Glenn Abbott, major leaguer (1973-84)*
48. *Jason Uhlman, ss, Redondo HS, Redondo Beach, Calif.
49. Wade Norris, 1b, University of South Florida.
50. *Martin Jones, of, Aiken HS, Cincinnati.

1993

# Mariners get one right again, take Rodriguez

In 1987, the pick was Ken Griffey Jr. Six years later, it was Alex Rodriguez.

As arguably the two greatest No. 1 overall picks in draft history, Griffey and Rodriguez were coincidentally both selected by the Seattle Mariners. They played together as teammates for six years, with Griffey winning an American League MVP in 1997 and Rodriguez two years later. The resemblances hardly stopped there, as both signed at 17 and made their big league debuts as teenagers.

The Mariners scouting director in both cases was Roger Jongewaard, and it was his scouting acumen and persuasive skills that were influential in both players ending up in a Mariners uniform. In Griffey's case, Jongewaard had to convince a short-sighted owner, George Argyros, that a young high school outfielder was the more prudent choice than an experienced college pitcher, Cal State Fullerton righthander Mike Harkey. As for Rodriguez, Jongewaard was put to the test again as manager Lou Piniella made a pitch to draft another college arm, in this case Wichita State righthander Darren Dreifort, to provide short-term relief to his beleaguered pitching staff.

"If anything, I learned that you don't go the safe way," Jongewaard said. "You don't worry about who will get there quickly. You don't worry about agents. You take the best guy available. We knew Alex would be a difficult sign, and he was, but he was the best player out there."

Being right on previous No. 1 picks gave Jongewaard latitude in picking Rodriguez. It was actually the third time he had been involved with making the first pick in the June draft. He was the West Coast scouting coordinator for the New York Mets in 1980 and pushed for high school outfielder Darryl Strawberry, who like Griffey and Rodriguez became the most productive big leaguer in his draft class.

The Major League Scouting Bureau graded Dreifort as a 71 on the 20-80 scale and Rodriguez a 69. No other player in the 1993 draft had a grade higher than 62.

"There's nothing wrong with Dreifort," Jongewaard said. "Most years with the No. 1 pick you'd feel lucky he was out there. But a guy like Rodriguez doesn't come along very often."

Piniella eventually shared Jongewaard's high opinion of A-Rod. "I originally wanted us to go for the college relief pitcher. Then I saw films of the shortstop. He's a man among boys out there. Wow! No way we could pass on him."

Rodriguez debuted in the big leagues at age 18 and was there to stay by 1995 at 19. He soon was on his way to becoming one of the best players in major league history. His combination of power, speed and defensive excellence made him a franchise cornerstone until he left after the 2000 season

JOHN WILLIAMSON

**Though controversy dogged him through much of his major league career, few players in draft history were so highly touted as Alex Rodriguez and actually lived up to all the hype**

as a free agent, signing a 10-year, $252 million contract with the Texas Rangers, the richest deal in baseball history at the time.

Rodriguez spent three years with the Rangers, leading the American League in homers all three seasons, including a career-best 57 in 2002. But the club did not make the playoffs and traded him to the New York Yankees. Rodriguez then opted out of the final three years of his existing contract and signed another 10-year deal, this time for $275 million, another record.

The Yankees had Derek Jeter at shortstop, so Rodriguez agreed to play third base. He won two MVP awards with the Yankees and for the first time played on a World Series-winning team, but his career in pinstripes also had its share of controversy. After years of denying that he had used performance-enhancing drugs, Rodriguez admitted in 2009 to using steroids, saying he did from 2001-03 when playing for Rangers.

Rodriguez was linked to PEDs again in 2013 when his name showed up as a client of the Biogenesis clinic in Florida that was under investigation for providing athletes with illegal substances. Major League Baseball suspended A-Rod in August 2013 for 211 games, but he was allowed to play until his appeal was heard. The suspension was reduced to 162 games, keeping him off the field for the 2014 season.

**AT A GLANCE**

### This Date In History
June 3-5

### Best Draft
**SAN DIEGO PADRES.** The Padres signed six future big leaguers among the 91 players they drafted, but they included **DERREK LEE** (1), **MATT CLEMENT** (3) and **GARY MATTHEWS JR.** (13), all ranked among the 17 best players to come from the 1993 draft.

### Worst Draft
**NEW YORK YANKEES.** The Yankees signed three future big leaguers, all pitchers, none of whom won a game in pinstripes.

### First-Round Bust
**KIRK PRESLEY, RHP, METS.** Elvis may have had his third cousin in mind when he sang his 1956 classic, "Heartbreak Hotel." Beyond his name, Presley appeared to have the ingredient to become a star in his own right coming out of Tupelo (Miss.) High. He impressed scouts with his 6-foot-3 frame, easy delivery, poise and command of a three-pitch mix. But Presley encountered shoulder problems almost from the outset of his pro career, had rotator-cuff surgery in 1995 and never was the same pitcher he was in high school, when he went 37-1, 0.60. In a five-year career that peaked in Class A, he went just 8-10, 4.04.

### On Second Thought
**SCOTT ROLEN, 3B, PHILLIES.** Only **ALEX RODRIGUEZ**, the first overall pick, had a more productive career than Rolen, who played 17 seasons, hit .281-316-1,287 and won eight Gold Gloves. In his best season, 2004 for the Cardinals, he hit .314-34-124.

### Late-Round Find
**KEVIN MILLWOOD, RHP, BRAVES (11TH ROUND).** Millwood won 169 games in a 16-year big league career, including at least 17 on three occasions in his six

**CONTINUED ON PAGE 420**

## AT A GLANCE

CONTINUED FROM PAGE 419

years with the Braves.

### Never Too Late

**JASON CONTI, OF, PADRES (74TH ROUND).** An afterthought out of a Pittsburgh high school, Conti turned down the Padres in favor of the University of Pittsburgh. The Diamondbacks took him in the 32nd round in 1996, and he went on to play five seasons in the majors, hitting .238-6-47.

### Overlooked

**KEVIN MILLAR, 3B, MARLINS.** Millar played two seasons at Lamar and was not drafted in 1992 or 1993. He signed with the St. Paul Saints of the independent Northern League and showed enough promise that the Marlins signed him after the 1993 season. Claimed on waivers by the Red Sox after the 2002 season, Millar had the two best seasons of his 12-year major league career and provided a significant clubhouse presence in Boston's drive to its first World Series title since 1918.

### International Gem

**ANDRUW JONES, OF, BRAVES.** Australian shortstop **GLENN WILLIAMS** received an international bonus record of $925,000 from the Braves in 1993, but Jones, a center fielder from Curacao, proved to be a much better bargain at $40,000. Jones earned back-to-back Baseball America Minor League Player of the Year honors, hit 434 homers over a 17-year career and won 10 Gold Glove Awards.

### Minor League Take

**BROOKS KIESCHNICK, OF/RHP, CUBS.** Kieschnick starred for three years in a dual role at Texas, hitting a school-record 43 homers while also winning 34 games as a starting pitcher. Most of the eight organizations he played for professionally believed he had a greater upside with the bat, though he never established himself as an

## 1993: THE FIRST ROUNDERS

| | CLUB: PLAYER, POS., SCHOOL | HOMETOWN | B-T | HT. | WT. | AGE | BONUS | FIRST YEAR | LAST YEAR | PEAK LEVEL (YEARS) |
|---|---|---|---|---|---|---|---|---|---|---|
| 1. | *Mariners: Alex Rodriguez, ss, Westminster Christian HS | Miami | R-R | 6-3 | 190 | 17 | $1,000,000 | 1994 | Active | Majors (21) |
| | Considered the most complete prep position player ever drafted; reached MLB at 18, looked like all-time great as power-hitting SS, but career clouded by PED issues. | | | | | | | | | |
| 2. | Dodgers: Darren Dreifort, rhp, Wichita State | Wichita, Kan. | R-R | 6-2 | 205 | 21 | $1,300,000 | 1994 | 2004 | Majors (9) |
| | Best pure arm in draft with high-90s sinking fastball, slider as prime weapons, but endured 14 operations during 11-year MLB career, went only 48-60, 4.36. | | | | | | | | | |
| 3. | Angels: Brian Anderson, lhp, Wright State | Geneva, Ohio | B-L | 6-1 | 195 | 21 | $675,000 | 1993 | 2005 | Majors (13) |
| | Finesse lefty with masterful control of four-pitch mix, went 10-1, 1.14 (95 IP, 6 BB/98 SO) as college JR; 82-83, 4.74 mark in majors before second TJ surgery. | | | | | | | | | |
| 4. | Phillies: Wayne Gomes, rhp, Old Dominion | Hampton, Va. | R-R | 6-2 | 215 | 20 | $750,000 | 1993 | 2005 | Majors (6) |
| | Dominant college closer (55 SO/7 hits in 26 IP as JR); with mid-90s fastball/nasty curve, initially compared to Lee Smith, but career doomed by control issues. | | | | | | | | | |
| 5. | Royals: Jeff Granger, lhp, Texas A&M | Orange, Texas | R-L | 6-4 | 193 | 21 | $695,000 | 1993 | 2000 | Majors (4) |
| | Great athlete, started at QB for A&M, also went 31-9, 2.98 (347 IP/401 SO) in three years; rushed to majors, never again displayed same stuff/poise in pro ball. | | | | | | | | | |
| 6. | Giants: Steve Soderstrom, rhp, Fresno State | Turlock, Calif. | R-R | 6-3 | 220 | 21 | $750,000 | 1994 | 2000 | Majors (1) |
| | Drafted on basis of 92-94 mph arm strength/athleticism; went 6-5, 3.80 (107 IP/114 SO) as junior, slowed by tendinitis; pro career plagued by arm issues. | | | | | | | | | |
| 7. | Red Sox: Trot Nixon, of, New Hanover HS | Wilmington, N.C. | L-L | 6-2 | 195 | 19 | $890,000 | 1994 | 2008 | Majors (12) |
| | Excelled as hitter (.519-12-56), pitcher (12-0, 0.40) in HS, also premium QB recruit; considered best pure hitter in draft, prototype RF with superior arm, instincts. | | | | | | | | | |
| 8. | Mets: Kirk Presley, rhp, Tupelo HS | Tupelo, Miss. | R-R | 6-3 | 192 | 18 | $900,000 | 1994 | 1998 | Class A (5) |
| | Earned notoreity as third cousin of Elvis; dominant HS pitcher, went 37-1, 0.60 with 22 shutouts; hurt shoulder in first year, won just eight games as a pro. | | | | | | | | | |
| 9. | Tigers: Matt Brunson, ss, Cherry Creek HS | Englewood, Colo. | B-R | 5-11 | 160 | 18 | $800,000 | 1994 | 1996 | Class A (3) |
| | Dynamic athlete with speed to burn; hit .200-4-75 in three pro seasons, career also hurt by off-field problems; later played football at Colorado, baseball in Taiwan. | | | | | | | | | |
| 10. | Cubs: Brooks Kieschnick, of/rhp, Texas | Caldwell, Texas | L-R | 6-4 | 228 | 21 | $650,000 | 1993 | 2005 | Majors (6) |
| | Most celebrated college player in draft (.374-19-81/16-4, 3.25), but not a consensus first-rounder because of slow-twitch actions; struggled to crack MLB lineup. | | | | | | | | | |
| 11. | Indians: Daron Kirkreit, rhp, UC Riverside | Norco, Calif. | R-R | 6-6 | 225 | 20 | $600,000 | 1993 | 2001 | Class AAA (1) |
| | Went 10-5, 2.21 as college SO, 6-6, 3.15 as JR; power arm with 95 mph sinker/hard slider, but never returned to form after rotator-cuff surgery in '95. | | | | | | | | | |
| 12. | Astros: Billy Wagner, lhp, Ferrum (Va.) College | Tannersville, Va. | L-L | 5-11 | 180 | 21 | $550,000 | 1993 | 2010 | Majors (16) |
| | Polarizing player due to small/raw-boned frame, D-III competition, but electric arm capable of reaching 98; set NCAA SO records, averaged 11.9 SO/9 IP in majors. | | | | | | | | | |
| 13. | Yankees: Matt Drews, rhp, Sarasota HS | Sarasota, Fla. | R-R | 6-8 | 210 | 18 | $625,000 | 1994 | 2000 | Class AAA (5) |
| | Grandson of Karl (RHP on Yankees '47 W/S champs); went 22-13, 2.21 in first two pro years, 16-58, 6.56 in last six after dead nerve discovered in shoulder. | | | | | | | | | |
| 14. | Padres: Derrek Lee, 1b, El Camino HS | Granite Bay, Calif. | R-R | 6-5 | 195 | 17 | $600,000 | 1993 | 2011 | Majors (15) |
| | Nephew of Leron, 1966 first-rounder, son of Leon, ex-Japanese star; excellent athlete, best raw power in prep crop, hit 331 homers in 15-year MLB career. | | | | | | | | | |
| 15. | Blue Jays: Chris Carpenter, rhp, Trinity HS | Raymond, N.H. | R-R | 6-5 | 220 | 18 | $580,000 | 1994 | 2013 | Majors (15) |
| | Released by Jays in 2002 because of injuries/ineffectiveness, also had six arm surgeries in career; yet won 144 MLB games, became key playoff arm for Cardinals. | | | | | | | | | |
| 16. | Cardinals: Alan Benes, rhp, Creighton | Lake Forest, Ill. | R-R | 6-4 | 205 | 21 | $500,000 | 1993 | 2006 | Majors (8) |
| | Along with Andy (top pick in 1988), became fourth first-round brother act; justified status with size, low-90s sinker, feel, though won just 29 MLB games. | | | | | | | | | |
| 17. | White Sox: Scott Christman, lhp, Oregon State | Tualatin, Ore. | L-L | 6-3 | 190 | 21 | $475,000 | 1993 | 1997 | Class AA (2) |
| | Surged into first round on strength of breakout 14-1, 2.20 season for Beavers, but rarely showed same stuff/command in pros; went 16-29, 4.84 in minors. | | | | | | | | | |
| 18. | Expos: Chris Schwab, of, Cretin-Derham Hall HS | Eagan, Minn. | L-R | 6-3 | 215 | 18 | $425,000 | 1993 | 1999 | Class AA (2) |
| | Three-sport athlete in HS, but big lefthanded power only legitimate tool on baseball field; hit .220-73-315 in seven seasons, fanned 898 times in 699 games. | | | | | | | | | |
| 19. | Orioles: Jay Powell, rhp, Mississippi State | Collinsville, Miss. | R-R | 6-4 | 221 | 21 | $492,800 | 1993 | 2005 | Majors (11) |
| | One of elite closers in college ranks, though only modest success in draft year (3-6, 3.56, 7 SV); worked in 512 games in majors, won Game Seven for Marlins in '97. | | | | | | | | | |
| 20. | Twins: Torii Hunter, of, Pine Bluff HS | Pine Bluff, Ark. | R-R | 6-1 | 190 | 17 | $452,500 | 1993 | 2015 | Majors (19) |
| | High-risk/high-return prospect with multi-sport background, rode athleticism on defense as he learned to hit, won nine Gold Gloves, topped 350 HRs, 1,300 RBIs. | | | | | | | | | |
| 21. | Twins: Jason Varitek, c, Georgia Tech | Longwood, Fla. | B-R | 6-2 | 207 | 21 | Unsigned | 1995 | 2011 | Majors (15) |
| | Switch-hitting catcher with raw power, arm strength, leadership skills; rejected Twins offer, chose to return as senior, drafted in first round again a year later. | | | | | | | | | |
| 22. | Pirates: Charles Peterson, of, Laurens HS | Laurens, S.C. | R-R | 6-4 | 200 | 19 | $420,000 | 1993 | 1998 | Class AAA (1) |
| | Excelled in football/baseball with speed/strength, but power potential never developed in minors, hit .234-41-350; also played eight years of independent ball. | | | | | | | | | |
| 23. | Brewers: Jeff D'Amico, rhp, Northeast HS | Pinellas Park, Fla. | B-R | 6-6 | 235 | 17 | $525,000 | 1995 | 2004 | Majors (8) |
| | Size, arm strength intrigued teams, went in first round after missing most of 1993 with stress fracture; plagued by shoulder issues but still won 45 games in majors. | | | | | | | | | |
| 24. | Cubs: Jon Ratliff, rhp, LeMoyne College | Clay, N.Y. | R-R | 6-5 | 195 | 21 | $355,000 | 1993 | 2002 | Majors (1) |
| | One-look wonder; payoff for 10-1, 2.04 record as college JR, uninspiring 57-79, 4.60 mark in 10 minor league seasons was 1 IP stint (12 pitches) with A's in 2000. | | | | | | | | | |
| 25. | Athletics: John Wasdin, rhp, Florida State | Tallahassee, Fla. | R-R | 6-2 | 190 | 20 | $365,000 | 1993 | 2008 | Majors (12) |
| | After winning two games in first two years at FSU, propelled himself into first round with improved slider, 10-1, 3.15 mark as JR; went 39-39, 5.28 in majors. | | | | | | | | | |
| 26. | Brewers: Kelly Wunsch, rhp, Texas A&M | Houston | L-L | 6-5 | 192 | 20 | $400,000 | 1993 | 2006 | Majors (6) |
| | Spun his wheels in minors with injuries/inconsistent performance, before adopting sidearm delivery; led to six-year MLB career (11-6, 3.76) as situational reliever. | | | | | | | | | |
| 27. | Marlins: Marc Valdes, rhp, Florida | Tampa | R-R | 6-0 | 165 | 21 | $415,000 | 1993 | 2005 | Majors (6) |
| | Overcame small stature with advanced feel for pitching, hard/sinking fastball; went 31-14, 3.14 at UF, spent six years in majors (12-15, 4.95) with four clubs. | | | | | | | | | |
| 28. | Rockies: Jamey Wright, rhp, Westmoore HS | Oklahoma City, Okla. | R-R | 6-6 | 205 | 18 | $395,000 | 1993 | 2014 | Majors (19) |
| | Panic pick after Rockies' targeted college arms got snapped up; worked out as big righty constructed 19-year MLB career spanning 719 appearences/10 teams. | | | | | | | | | |

**Signed to major league contract.*

Like Griffey, Rodriguez once was on pace to become baseball's all-time home run leader. He was the youngest player to reach 500 home runs, and by the 2009 season he had 613. He fell off pace over the next five years because of injuries and his suspension. Rodriguez had 687 through the 2015 season. Griffey had 438 by age 30, but injuries slowed his pace and he finished with 630.

## How They Should Have Done It

Based on the career WAR (Wins Above Replacement, as calculated by Baseball-Reference.com) numbers achieved by all the players eligible for the 1993 draft, here's how the first round should have unfolded. Numbers in parentheses indicate the round when the player was actually drafted. Asterisk denotes player who signed as a draft-and-follow.

| | Player, Pos. | Actual Draft | WAR | Bonus |
|---|---|---|---|---|
| 1. | Alex Rodriguez, ss | Mariners (1) | 115.9 | $1,000,000 |
| 2. | Scott Rolen, 3b | Phillies (2) | 70.0 | $250,000 |
| 3. | Torii Hunter, of | Twins (1) | 50.0 | $452,500 |
| 4. | Chris Carpenter, rhp | Blue Jays (1) | 34.5 | $580,000 |
| 5. | Derrek Lee, 1b | Padres (1) | 34.1 | $600,000 |
| 6. | Kevin Millwood, rhp | Braves (11) | 29.4 | $35,000 |
| 7. | Billy Wagner, lhp | Astros (1) | 28.1 | $550,000 |
| 8. | Bill Mueller, 3b | Giants (15) | 23.8 | $2,500 |
| 9. | Trot Nixon, of | Red Sox (1) | 21.2 | $890,000 |
| 10. | Jermaine Dye, of | Braves (17) | 20.2 | $35,000 |
| 11. | Mark Loretta, ss | Brewers (7) | 19.2 | $32,500 |
| 12. | Richie Sexson, 1b | Indians (24) | 17.9 | $35,000 |
| | Paul LoDuca, c | Dodgers (25) | 17.9 | $27,000 |
| 14. | Jeff Suppan, rhp | Red Sox (2) | 17.4 | $190,000 |
| 15. | * Gary Matthews Jr., of | Padres (13) | 14.2 | $60,000 |
| | Kevin Millar, 3b | Marlins (NDFA) | 14.2 | None |
| 17. | Matt Clement, rhp | Padres (3) | 12.4 | $140,000 |
| 18. | John Thomson, rhp | Rockies (7) | 12.3 | $35,000 |
| 19. | Brian Moehler, rhp | Tigers (6) | 10.9 | $33,000 |
| 20. | Bengie Molina, c | Angels (NDFA) | 10.6 | $2,500 |
| 21. | Brian Anderson, lhp | Angels (1) | 10.4 | $675,000 |
| 22. | Steve Kline, lhp | Indians (8) | 10.2 | $35,000 |
| 23. | Mike Sirotka, lhp | White Sox (15) | 9.8 | $3,000 |
| 24. | Chris Singleton, of | Giants (2) | 9.7 | $207,500 |
| 25. | Jamey Wright, rhp | Rockies (1) | 9.6 | $395,000 |
| 26. | Scott Spiezio, 1b | Athletics (6) | 8.8 | $50,000 |
| 27. | Darren Dreifort, rhp | Dodgers (1) | 7.9 | $1,300,000 |
| 28. | Scott Sullivan, rhp | Reds (2) | 6.7 | $156,000 |

| | Top 3 Unsigned Players | | | Year Signed |
|---|---|---|---|---|
| 1. | Placido Polanco, 2b | White Sox (49) | 40.7 | 1994 |
| 2. | Jason Varitek, c | Twins (1) | 24.3 | 1994 |
| 3. | Keith Foulke, rhp | Tigers (14) | 20.9 | 1994 |

### LONG NEGOTIATIONS FOR TOP TWO

Close to 100 scouts attended some of Rodriguez's games during his senior season at Miami's Westminster Christian High in 1993.

"It was the Alex Rodriguez Sweepstakes," said Rich Hofman, his high school coach. "You can't imagine the pressure he had to go through. We had big crowds everywhere just to see him play. And every pitcher pitched to him like it was the last out of the World Series. I've never seen a player command so much attention."

Virtually everyone agreed that Rodriguez and Dreifort were the top prospects for the 1993 draft, and A-Rod preferred the Los Angeles Dodgers with the No. 2 pick. When it became evident that the Mariners would choose him first, Rodriguez fired his agent, Ron Shapiro, and informed Seattle that he wanted a $2.5 million signing bonus and a major league contract. He also hired Scott Boras.

Undeterred, the Mariners drafted Rodriguez, who also had a scholarship from the University of Miami as leverage. Seattle's first offer provided Rodriguez the option of a $1 million bonus or a three-year, major league contract with a $500,000 bonus and a guaranteed callup in September 1993 worth an additional $500,000.

Rodriguez quickly dismissed the offer through his 24-year-old half-sister, Susy Dunand, who was acting as his spokesperson.

MICKI & RICHARD LEWIS

Darren Dreifort had a dominant college career and was major league ready, but injuries dented his impact during his major league career

"At this point, I don't trust them," Dunand said. "This is not a negotiation. I was up-front with them before the draft and after."

There was little contact between the Mariners and the Rodriguez family until days before he was scheduled to attend his first college class on Aug. 26, after which he would be ineligible to sign. Three things swung the negotiations in favor of the Mariners: Rodriguez broke his cheekbone on an errant throw during infield practice at the U.S. Olympic Festival and didn't play again that summer; Mariners president Chuck Armstrong became involved; and Rodriguez decided that he wanted to start his professional career. He signed hours before he was set to start classes at Miami, agreeing to a $1 million bonus as part of a three-year, major league contract that had a total value of about $1.3 million.

"I'm glad the negotiations are over," Rodriguez said. "It's been a long process. I never wanted this to be a bad thing, a summer-long thing. One day I'll get my market value, when I prove myself as an impact player. I just want to get started."

It took even longer for the Dodgers to sign Dreifort, who agreed to a $1.3 million bonus on Sept. 8. He had sought a major league contract worth about $2 million. The bonus was second highest in draft history, trailing only the $1.55 million contract Brien Taylor received from the Yankees in 1991.

John Dreifort, Darren's father, handled the negotiations with input from Boras. "The negotiations weren't easy," John Dreifort said. "I think this really could have been one of the highlights of Darren's life, and one of the highlights of our whole family. But I'm not sure if I feel that way. I think Darren frankly was just tired of the whole thing."

Dreifort went 11-1, 2.48 with 120 strikeouts in 102 innings as a junior at Wichita State, and batted .327 with 22 homers while winning the 1993 Golden Spikes Award. He opened the 1994 season with the Dodgers, becoming the 19th player in draft history to debut in the majors without minor league experience.

The 6-foot-2, 215-pound Dreifort threw a hard,

### AT A GLANCE

everyday player, getting just 306 at-bats over six seasons. In 3,347 minor league at-bats, he slammed 164 homers. The Brewers used him mostly as a pitcher from 2003-05, but he fell short there as well, going 2-2, 4.59 in 74 appearances. In 87 minor league games, he went 3-5, 4.77.

#### One Who Got Away

**JASON VARITEK, C, TWINS (1ST ROUND).** Varitek went unsigned as the second of the Twins' two first-round picks in 1993, and was selected in the first round again in 1994 by the Mariners, who signed him but let him slip away before he reached the big leagues. Varitek spent 15 years in the majors, all with the Red Sox, and played a key role on two World Series champions.

#### SHE Was Drafted?

**CAREY SCHUELER, LHP-1B, WHITE SOX (43RD ROUND).** The White Sox made history by selecting Schueler, the daughter of general manager, Ron Schueler. The only woman ever drafted, she didn't sign, instead playing college basketball at DePaul and Saint Mary's (Calif.).

#### Did You Know . . .

The Brewers selected Florida high school righthander **JEFF C. D'AMICO** in the first round, and the A's chose Washington prep shortstop/righthander **JEFF M. D'AMICO** in the second round. They are not related.

#### They Said It

Mariners scouting director **ROGER JONGEWAARD**, on drafting **ALEX RODRIGUEZ**, a high school player, with the top pick in the draft: "If anything, I learned that you don't go the safe way. You don't worry about who will get there quickly. You don't worry about agents. You take the best guy available. We knew Alex would be a difficult sign, and he was, but he was the best player out there."

## DRAFT SPOTLIGHT: ALEX RODRIGUEZ

MORRS FIOSTOFF

Alex Rodriguez's production is unmatched, but performance-enhancing drug use may jeopardize his Hall of Fame candidacy

No one else in the draft era entered professional baseball with greater expectation and eventually produced as much as Alex Rodriguez—not Barry Bonds, not Roger Clemens, not Ken Griffey Jr.

An immensely talented high school shortstop from Miami, Rodriguez was the first player drafted in 1993 and was in the major leagues a year later at age 18. He was still playing in 2016, with more than 3,000 hits and nearly 700 home runs on his glittering resume with the Mariners, Rangers and Yankees.

Rodriguez was almost a perfect prospect, showing power and speed, an excellent glove and a great work ethic at a premium position. Many veteran scouts called him the best position player they had ever evaluated.

"A guy like Rodriguez doesn't come around very often," Mariners scouting director Roger Jongewaard said. "Some guys stand in the field, and you look at them and know they can play. He's one of them. His body language is so good. His actions, his tools, everything. It just comes so naturally to him."

In his last scouting report on Rodriguez, dated May 5, 1993, Jongewaard wrote: "Similar to (Derek) Jeter, only bigger and better—better at 17 now than all the superstars in baseball were when they were seniors in high school."

The maturation of Rodriguez into a mega-talent began between his sophomore and junior seasons at Miami's Westminster Christian High. As a sophomore, he was a good hitter with little power, and could bench-press little more than 100 pounds. Then he took up weight training, making great strides in his physical development and transforming from a skinny shortstop into a sculpted star on the U.S. 16-and-under team.

"The summer between his sophomore and junior years, the change was incredible," said J.D. Arteaga, a close friend and teammate and later a pitcher in pro ball. "He was always a good shortstop, but he didn't have much of an arm, although he could hit. But when he came back, he was bench-pressing 275 pounds and hitting the ball 400 feet."

As a junior, the 6-foot-3, 190-pound Rodriguez hit .477 with six homers and 42 stolen bases. As a senior, he hit .505 with nine home runs, reached base 89 times in 125 plate appearances as a leadoff man and stole 35 consecutive bases. His powerful bat, along with his quickness, arm and hands made him a potential all-star shortstop.

"The next Cal Ripken," a scout said before the draft. "He's not just a field-and-throw guy; he's got all of the tools."

Rodriguez by age 20 had established himself as the game's brightest young star. In 1996, he led the major leagues in doubles with 54, hit 36 home runs, batted .358, and finished second in the American League MVP voting.

A-Rod continued to perform at a high level, and along with his success came accusations that he was using performance-enhancing drugs. After years of denial, he acknowledged using PEDs and served a yearlong suspension in 2014 as a penalty. Despite impeccable on-field achievement, he may never be enshrined in the Baseball Hall of Fame.

Rodriguez was a magnet for attention long before he made 14 all-star teams, won three MVP awards, led the American League in home runs five times and won two Gold Glove Awards as a shortstop. When he stepped onto the field for the first game of his senior season at Westminster Christian, 68 scouts were watching, and the number increased as the spring wore on. Before a two-game road trip in April to St. Petersburg, a local newspaper ran the headline, "Superman is Coming to Town." Sports Illustrated devoted a two-page spread to Rodriguez.

"If you were to sit in front of a computer," said Augie Garrido, then the baseball coach of Cal State Fullerton, "and say, 'How would I construct the perfect shortstop?' You'd put all the data in, and then you would see Alex Rodriguez."

sinking fastball that peaked at 97 mph, along with a nasty, biting slider. Wichita State coach Gene Stephenson said he was a "franchise player who would set the tone for the Dodgers for a long time."

Dreifort had a star-crossed career, spending about as much time rehabbing from injuries as he did pitching during 11 major league seasons. In 113 starts and a total of 161 appearances, he compiled a 48-60 record and notched 11 saves. The Dodgers gave him a five-year, $55 million contract before the 2001 season, but he won only nine games in that span and missed two seasons entirely.

Dreifort retired at age 32, pitching in his final game on Aug. 16, 2004. By that time, he had endured elbow, hip, knee, shoulder and ankle issues and 22 surgeries related to baseball injuries.

### COLLEGE PITCHING DOMINATES

While the Rodriguez and Dreifort bonuses were not the huge spikes paid in the previous few years, they were substantial enough to spark a 27.2 percent rise in the average bonus for 1993 first-round picks, increasing to $613,037 after a 1992 average of $481,193. The 22 highest bonuses went to first-rounders, but not without considerable negotiations; only one player among the first 18 picks signed prior to July 19.

The Dodgers spent $2.504 million on their draft picks, breaking the record of $2.483 million they set a year earlier. The Milwaukee Brewers ($2.266 million), Toronto Blue Jays ($2.2615 million), Chicago Cubs ($2.135 million) and Boston Red Sox ($2.0275 million) also broke $2 million.

Nineteen pitchers went in the first round, and a record 14 came from the college ranks, marking a trend away from high school arms.

"If they don't have good arm action—and Dwight Gooden was an exception—high school pitching is too risky," one scouting director said. "A college pitcher will at least get to the big leagues faster, which will hold the job of the scouting director. They don't get rid of managers anymore. They fire the general manager and the scouting director."

Selected in order after Dreifort were Wright State lefthander Brian Anderson by the California Angels; Old Dominion righthander Wayne Gomes (Phillies); Texas A&M lefthander Jeff Granger (Royals); and Fresno State righthander Steve Soderstrom (Giants). All signed during a four-day stretch from July 27-30.

Anderson and Granger were polished lefties who accepted bonuses of less than $700,000 in return for being guaranteed a callup to the big leagues in September, making them the first players to debut in the majors in the year they were drafted since Cubs lefthander Lance Dickson and Chicago White

### Fastest To The Majors

| Player, Pos. | Drafted (Round) | Debut |
|---|---|---|
| 1. Brian Anderson, lhp | Angels (1) | Sept. 10, 1993 |
| 2. Jeff Granger, lhp | Royals (1) | Sept. 16, 1993 |
| 3. # Darren Dreifort, rhp | Dodgers (1) | April 7, 1994 |
| 4. * Alex Rodriguez, ss | Mariners (1) | July 8, 1994 |
| 5. Andrew Lorraine, lhp | Angels (4) | July 17, 1994 |

*#Debuted in major leagues. *High school selection.*

## Top 25 Bonuses

| | Player, Pos. | Drafted (Round) | Order | Bonus |
|---|---|---|---|---|
| 1. | **Darren Dreifort, rhp** | **Dodgers (1)** | **2** | **$1,300,000** |
| 2. | ***Alex Rodriguez, ss** | **Mariners (1)** | **1#** | **$1,000,000** |
| 3. | *Kirk Presley, rhp | Mets (1) | 8 | $900,000 |
| 4. | ***Trot Nixon, of** | **Red Sox (1)** | **7** | **$890,000** |
| 5. | *Matt Brunson, ss | Tigers (1) | 9 | $800,000 |
| 6. | **Wayne Gomes, rhp** | **Phillies (1)** | **4** | **$750,000** |
| | **Steve Soderstrom, rhp** | **Giants (1)** | **6** | **$750,000** |
| | **Brooks Kieschnick, of/rhp** | **Cubs (1)** | **10** | **$750,000** |
| 9. | **Jeff Granger, lhp** | **Royals (1)** | **5** | **$695,000** |
| 10. | **Brian Anderson, lhp** | **Angels (1)** | **3** | **$675,000** |
| 11. | *Matt Drews, rhp | Yankees (1) | 13 | $625,000 |
| 12. | Daron Kirkreit, rhp | Indians (1) | 11 | $600,000 |
| | ***Derrek Lee, 1b** | **Padres (1)** | **14** | **$600,000** |
| 14. | ***Chris Carpenter, rhp** | **Blue Jays (1)** | **15** | **$580,000** |
| 15. | **Billy Wagner, lhp** | **Astros (1)** | **12** | **$550,000** |
| 16. | ***Jeff D'Amico, rhp** | **Brewers (1)** | **23** | **$525,000** |
| 17. | **Alan Benes, rhp** | **Cardinals (1)** | **16** | **$500,000** |
| 18. | **Jay Powell, rhp** | **Orioles (1)** | **19** | **$492,800** |
| 19. | Scott Christman, lhp | White Sox (1) | 17 | $475,000 |
| 20. | ***Torii Hunter, of** | **Twins (1)** | **20** | **$452,500** |
| 21. | *Chris Schwab, of | Expos (1) | 18 | $425,000 |
| 22. | *Charles Peterson, rhp | Pirates (1) | 22 | $420,000 |
| 23. | ***Brad Fullmer, 3b** | **Expos (2)** | **60** | **$417,500** |
| 24. | **Marc Valdes, rhp** | **Marlins (1)** | **27** | **$415,000** |
| 25. | **Kelly Wunsch, lhp** | **Brewers (1)** | **26** | **$400,000** |

*Major leaguers in bold. *High school selection. #Major league contract.*

Sox righthander Alex Fernandez in 1990. Gomes and Soderstrom signed standard contracts and didn't reach the majors until at least 1996.

Anderson went 10-1 with an NCAA-leading 1.14 ERA as a junior at Wright State; in 95 innings, he walked six and struck out 98. He came within two outs of a shutout in his first major league win before settling into a mediocre career, posting an 82-83, 4.74 record. Anderson left baseball in 2007 after his second Tommy John surgery.

Granger went 15-3, 2.62 and struck out 150 in 124 innings as a junior at Texas A&M. He made seven impressive starts in short-season ball to begin his pro career. But his career soon unraveled, and he got shelled in three appearances for the Kansas City Royals, one in September 1993 and two early in the 1994 season. He struggled to find consistency with his pitches and rarely displayed the poise that was evident in college. In 27 major league appearances (25 in relief) over four seasons, Granger went 0-1, 9.09 in 31 innings.

Gomes had been a dominant closer at Old Dominion, working with a 95 mph fastball and a knee-buckling curve. He struggled at times to throw strikes in college, and his control issues lingered as a pro. In six major league seasons, all as a reliever, he went 30-23, 4.60 with 29 saves.

Soderstrom was an excellent athlete and showed impressive arm strength, but there were concerns about his heavy workload at Fresno State. He missed several starts leading up to the draft because of elbow tendinitis, but the San Francisco Giants were not scared off. He endured shoulder and elbow problems early in his pro career, and battled inconsistent command, and had a brief major league career, making three starts for the Giants in 1996.

None of the college arms drafted ahead of him came close to the success of lefthander Billy Wagner, the 12th overall pick by the Houston Astros out of Ferrum College, an NCAA Division III school in Virginia. The 5-foot-9, 170-pound Wagner went 17-3, 1.58 with 46 hits allowed and 327 strikeouts in 182 innings over his three college seasons, overwhelming batters with a 95-98 mph fastball and a hard curve. He spent 16 seasons in the major leagues, almost exclusively in the closer's role, and went 47-40, 2.31 with 422 saves, 601 hits allowed and 1,196 strikeouts in 903 innings.

### TWINS HAVE CURIOUS DRAFT

Georgia Tech catcher Jason Varitek and Texas outfielder/pitcher Brooks Kieschnick were the only college position players selected in the first round, the fewest since 1976.

Varitek was highly regarded for his defense, leadership qualities and switch-hitting skills, but many teams did not want to deal with his agent, Boras. Varitek lasted until the 21st pick, going to the Minnesota Twins, and he became the only first-round pick to not sign. The Twins also had the 20th selection and took Arkansas high school outfielder Torii Hunter and signed him for a $452,500 bonus. They didn't budge from their initial $450,000 offer to Varitek, breaking off contact after July 31 except to send a memo in mid-September reiterating their original offer.

Varitek spent the summer in the Cape Cod League, hitting a league-high .371 and winning MVP honors. He returned to college and was picked in the first round of the 1994 draft by the Mariners. He again engaged in a lengthy holdout before signing on April 20, 1995, for $650,000, a substantial amount for a college senior.

The Twins had four extra picks over the first three rounds as compensation for losing Greg Gagne and John Smiley to free agency. They failed to reach agreements with 12 of their first 19 selections, yet still spent a club-record $1.6955 million. The Twins' draft included 14 players who reached the majors, more than any other club, but only Hunter became an impact big leaguer.

The Cubs drafted Kieschnick with the 10th pick. He was the most celebrated player in the college ranks in 1993, going 16-4 as a pitcher for Texas and hitting 19 homers with 81 RBIs as the team's cleanup hitter. Scouts had mixed opinions on whether Kieschnick profiled best as a pitcher or position player in pro ball, or if he was even first-round material. He lacked overpowering stuff on the mound, and his only above-average tool was lefthanded power.

**Brooks Kieschnick**

The Cubs first tried Kieschnick as an outfielder, and he played in 113 big league games in that role through 2001, hitting.220 with eight homers. He was primarily a pitcher over the final four years of his career, going 2-2, 4.59 in 74 relief appearances.

## WORTH NOTING

The Padres drafted high school lefthander **MATT LACHAPPA** in the second round. A Native American, LaChappa grew up on the Barona Reservation just east of San Diego, and his father was chief of the Barona tribe. LaChappa was considered one of the Padres' top prospects, but he suffered a heart attack while warming up before an April 6, 1996, game in the Class A California League, and a second heart attack after being admitted to the hospital that left him in a coma for two months and unable to speak or walk for several more months. LaChappa gained limited use of his legs and arms, but had difficulty communicating and was confined to a wheelchair. The Padres continued to offer him a minor league contract every year, however, in order to provide him with insurance benefits, and often invited him to the ballpark, calling him a "Padre for life."

Major League Baseball made its first attempt in 1993 at establishing a signing deadline, setting a date of Aug. 15. It was seen as a goodwill gesture to college coaches, giving them a clearer indication on which players would turn pro and affording them the opportunity to find replacements before the start of the school year. The existing rule, in place since the outset of the draft in 1965, gave major league teams rights to a player until he entered his first college class. The Players Association objected to the change, arguing that the proposal was subject to bargaining, and an arbitrator ruled in favor of the union.

In a rare twist, the Athletics lost their 15th-round pick, Long Beach State righthander **DANIEL CHOI**, to South Korea's professional league for a reported $200,000 bonus. Choi, a Korean-American who grew up in Southern California, went 17-2 for Long Beach State in 1993, leading the NCAA Division I ranks in wins.

CONTINUED ON PAGE 424

## WORTH NOTING

CONTINUED FROM PAGE 423

■ The Brewers drafted **JEFF CHARLES D'AMICO**, a 6-foot-7 righthander from St. Petersburg, Fla., in the first round, while the Athletics drafted **JEFFREY MICHAEL D'AMICO**, a shortstop from Redmond, Wash., in the second. The two players knew each other from a recruiting trip both took to Stanford while in high school. Jeff C. signed with the Brewers for $525,000, while Jeff A. received a $190,000 bonus from the A's. Both had careers that were hampered by injuries, but still reached the big leagues, with Jeff C. D'Amico going 45-52, 4.61 with four clubs from 1996-2004.

■ The Pirates got a supplemental first-round pick (42nd overall) as compensation for the loss of free agent Barry Bonds to the Giants after the 1992 season. Initially, the Pirates weren't slated to receive compensation of any kind because they didn't offer Bonds arbitration before the Dec. 7 deadline. Pittsburgh called foul because the terms of Bonds' deal with the Giants were agreed to on Dec. 5, though not officially announced until Dec. 8. Major League Baseball held a hearing and ruled that the Pirates would receive the last supplemental first-round pick, but not the Giants second-round pick. "We have concluded that awarding some sort of compensation to the Pirates is justified," said Bill Murray, director of baseball operations for the commissioner's office.

■ A record total of 1,721 players were drafted in 1993, led by the Marlins, who continued picking for 91 rounds. One of the players drafted was **CAREY SCHUELER**, an 18-year-old lefthander picked by the White Sox in the 43rd round and the only woman ever drafted. Her father Ron was the White Sox general manager. Carey played on the boys' junior varsity baseball team as a 10th grader at Campolindo High in Moraga, Calif. She did not sign and played college basketball at DePaul.

## HIGH SCHOOL TALENT SHINES

Despite the emphasis on college players in the draft, the high school talent ended up being better. Based on Wins Above Replacement, the six most productive players were all preps: Rodriguez, Hunter, first baseman Derrek Lee (Padres, 14th overall), righthander Chris Carpenter (Blue Jays, 15th), second-round third baseman Scott Rolen (Phillies) and 11th-round righthander Kevin Millwood (Braves).

Carpenter, a rare first-rounder from New Hampshire, became the best pitcher drafted in 1993, even though the 6-foot-6 righthander missed the equivalent of five seasons in the majors because of injuries and endured three elbow surgeries, two shoulder surgeries and a rib-cage surgery. Carpenter resurrected his career with the St. Louis Cardinals after sitting out the 2003 season. He went 144-94, 3.76 for his career, won 10 postseason games while playing on two World Series champions, and won the 2005 National League Cy Young Award.

The 6-foot-5, 200-pound Lee, a product of a Sacramento, Calif., high school, had to choose between a basketball scholarship to North Carolina and a $600,000 bonus offer from the San Diego Padres. Not surprisingly, baseball won out as his father Leon and uncle Leron, a former first-rounder and big leaguer, both had extensive baseball backgrounds—principally as two of the foremost import sluggers in Japanese baseball history. Lee himself was the top power threat in the 1993 draft and went on to hit 331 homers and drive in 1,078 runs over a productive major league career. He also won a batting title, was a two-time all-star and three-time Gold Glover.

MORRIS FOSTOFF

Derrek Lee

Rolen turned down a basketball offer from the University of Georgia in favor of baseball. Compared with Hall of Famer Mike Schmidt as he progressed through the Phillies system, Rolen did not match Schmidt's production but had a good career in his own right with the Phillies and Cardinals, hitting .281 with 316 homers and winning eight Gold Gloves in his 17-year career.

After Rodriguez and the run of college pitchers, the next three players drafted were outfielder Trot Nixon (Red Sox), righthander Kirk Presley (Mets) and shortstop Matt Brunson (Tigers), all exceptional two-sport athletes with commitments to play college football. Nixon hit .519 with 12 homers and went 12-0, 0.40 with 120 strikeouts in 71 innings at Wilmington's New Hanover High, leading his team to the North Carolina 4-A championship. Also a highly rated quarterback, Nixon was attending football practice at North Carolina State when he agreed to sign with the Red Sox for an $890,000 bonus.

Nixon might have been the best pure hitting prospect in the draft, and he was a prototypical right fielder. He had a solid major league career, hitting .274 with 137 homers over 12 seasons.

Presley, a 6-foot-3, 190-pound righthander from Tupelo (Miss.), was a third cousin of music icon Elvis Presley. He had rotator-cuff surgery in 1995 and was out of baseball two years later. Presley pitched in 30 minor league games, none above Class A, going 8-10, 4.04 in 147 innings.

Brunson, a son of former NFL wide receiver and return specialist Larry Brunson, had a football scholarship to Texas Tech, but was swayed to baseball by an $800,000 bonus offer from the Detroit Tigers. Like Presley, Brunson failed to get past Class A. He spent two years in the Tigers system and another in the Marlins organization, and was released after the 1996 season with a career average of .200 in 1,059 at-bats. Brunson played two seasons as a wide receiver at the University of Colorado, and then played baseball in Taiwan for three seasons and in U.S. independent leagues for three more years.

### Largest Bonuses By Round

| | Player, Pos. | Club | Bonus |
|---|---|---|---|
| **1.** | **Darren Dreifort, rhp** | **Dodgers** | **$1,300,000** |
| **2.** | *** Brad Fullmer, 3b** | **Expos** | **$417,500** |
| 3. | * Troy Carrasco, lhp | Twins | $165,000 |
| **4.** | *** Nathan Bland, lhp** | **Dodgers** | **$125,000** |
| 5. | * Scott Hunter, of | Dodgers | $250,000 |
| **6.** | ***# Peter Munro, rhp** | **Red Sox** | **$300,000** |
| 7. | * Brandon Cain, rhp | Braves | $90,000 |
| 8. | Jose Prado, rhp | Dodgers | $85,000 |
| 9. | Rayon Reid, rhp | Pirates | $60,000 |
| | Jason Green, rhp | Braves | $60,000 |
| 10. | * John Vukson, rhp | Dodgers | $60,000 |
| 11. | * Josh Rath, of | Dodgers | $85,000 |
| 12. | * Jerrod Miller, rhp | Braves | $35,000 |
| 13. | * Wes Culp, of | Braves | $100,000 |
| 14. | * Peter Benny, rhp | Brewers | $45,000 |
| 15. | * Tyson Hartshorn, rhp | Blue Jays | $60,000 |
| 16. | * David Crafton, c | Tigers | $100,000 |
| **17.** | **Jermaine Dye, of** | **Braves** | **$35,000** |
| **18.** | *** John Rocker, lhp** | **Braves** | **$50,000** |
| **19.** | ***# Rocky Coppinger, rhp** | **Orioles** | **$200,000** |
| 20. | Three tied at | | $20,000 |
| 21. | Eric Chapman, of | Indians | $10,000 |
| 22. | # Kris Detmers, lhp | Cardinals | $110,000 |
| 23. | Eddie Davis, of | Dodgers | $25,000 |
| 24. | * Carl South, rhp | Dodgers | $100,000 |
| **25.** | **Paul LoDuca, c** | **Dodgers** | **$27,000** |
| **Other** | **# Vance Wilson, c** | **Mets (44)** | **$100,000** |

*Major leaguers in bold. *High school selection. #Signed as draft-and-follow.*

### Highest Unsigned Picks

| Player, Pos., Team (Round) | College | Re-Drafted |
|---|---|---|
| Jason Varitek, c, Twins (1) | * Georgia Tech | Mariners '94 (1) |
| Macey Brooks, of, Giants (2) | James Madison | Royals '96 (55) |
| Tucker Barr, c, Athletics (3) | Georgia Tech | Astros '96 (5) |
| Billy Koch, rhp, Mets (4) | Clemson | Blue Jays '96 (1) |
| Tim Miller, rhp, Padres (4) | Florida State | Never |
| Darrell Nicholas, of, Cardinals (4) | * New Orleans | Brewers '94 (4) |
| Dennis Twombley, c, White Sox (4) | San Diego State | Yankees '96 (40) |
| Toby Dollar, rhp, Twins (4) | Texas Christian | Dodgers '96 (29) |
| Thad Busby, c/of, Blue Jays (4) | Florida State | Never |
| Matt Miller, lhp, Cubs (5) | Texas Tech | Tigers '96 (2) |

**TOTAL UNSIGNED PICKS:** Top 5 Rounds (11), Top 10 Rounds (34)

**Returned to same school.*

Perhaps no player was more excited about being drafted than Sarasota (Fla.) High righthander Matt Drews when the Yankees called his name with the 13th overall pick. His grandfather, Karl Drews, pitched for the 1947 World Series champion Yankees and spent eight years in the major leagues.

"This is the greatest thing that could have happened," said the 6-foot-8 Drews, who went 10-2, 1.27 as a senior, helping his team to the state 4-A title. "A lot of people get drafted by the Yankees, but I don't think it could have meant more to them than it meant to me."

Drews went 15-7, 2.27 at Class A Tampa in 1995, but regressed the following season after being promoted to Triple-A Columbus. He continued to falter after being demoted to Double-A and then Class A. He was traded that summer to the Tigers and continued to struggle, going a disastrous 1-14, 5.56 on the season. A year later, Drews was diagnosed with a dead nerve in his pitching shoulder. His career ended on a 16-58, 6.56 downslide.

## MORE FOOTBALL CONNECTIONS

Two of the best players in college football, Florida State quarterback Charlie Ward (Brewers, 59th round) and San Diego State running back Marshall Faulk (Angels, 43rd round), were drafted, though neither had played college baseball. Ward was drafted in baseball and basketball, but not football, despite being the 1993 Heisman Trophy winner. A 1994 NBA first-round pick of the New York Knicks, he played in the NBA for 11 seasons as a point guard. Faulk was the second overall pick in the 1994 NFL draft and played 11 standout seasons of pro football.

University of Washington quarterback Billy Joe Hobert, the 1992 Rose Bowl MVP and a central figure in an extra benefits scandal that rocked the Huskies football program, was drafted by the White Sox in the 16th round. Hobert, who also didn't play baseball in college, signed with the White Sox for a $90,000 bonus and played 15 games in the Rookie-level Gulf Coast League before bolting to the NFL's Los Angeles Raiders, who had selected him in the third round earlier in the year. Hobert played eight years in the NFL.

Five Cuban defectors gained eligibility for the 1993 draft through a special agreement with Major League Baseball. Lefthander Ivan Alvarez, 22, was the first Cuban selected, going to the Giants in the ninth round. He was one of three Cubans who defected together in October 1992 while at a tournament in Mexico. None of the players reached the big leagues.

Beyond the traditionally fertile Caribbean, baseball began to aggressively mine talent in other parts of the world in the 1990s. Signing bonuses jumped in 1992 and continued to escalate in 1993. The Braves set the tone by signing Glenn Williams, a highly regarded, 16-year-old Australian shortstop for a $925,000 bonus, the most ever given to an international player, topping the $675,000 given to Brazilian righthander Jose Pett by the Blue Jays a year earlier. The 6-foot-2, 175-pound Williams was considered the top international player in 1993, and the Braves outbid the Blue Jays, among others, for his services.

"He's a switch-hitter with power ability from both sides of the plate, and we think he has a chance to be an offensive shortstop," said Chuck Lamar, the Braves director of player development and scouting. Williams did not live up to expectations, failing to advance past Double-A, and was released after six seasons. He batted .222 with 40 home runs.

The Mariners made a hefty investment in Japanese native Makoto Suzuki, who was pitching for a co-op team at Class A San Bernardino in the California League. Suzuki, whose fastball was clocked at 97 mph, normally would have been off limits to American teams because of an agreement between Major League Baseball and Japan. However, he had come to the United States in 1992 to play for a Cal League team with Japanese ownership, and was considered a free agent.

"We treated him like a first-round draft pick because that's what he would have been if he'd been in the draft," said Jongewaard, the Mariners scouting director.

### Largest Draft-And-Follow Bonuses

| | Player, Pos. | Club (Round) | Bonus |
|---|---|---|---|
| 1. | ***Peter Munro, rhp** | **Red Sox (6)** | **$300,000** |
| 2. | ***Rocky Coppinger, rhp** | **Orioles (19)** | **$200,000** |
| 3. | Kris Detmers, lhp | Cardinals (22) | $110,000 |
| 4. | **Vance Wilson, c** | **Mets (44)** | **$100,000** |
| 5. | *Brett Schlomann, rhp | Yankees (42) | $72,000 |
| 6. | ***Troy Mattes, rhp** | **Expos (16)** | **$65,000** |
| 7. | ***Gary Matthews Jr., of** | **Padres (13)** | **$60,000** |
| | Chris Weidert, rhp | Expos (38) | $60,000 |
| 9. | ***Mario Valdez, 1b** | **White Sox (48)** | **$52,500** |
| 10. | *Marc D'Allesandro, lhp | Rockies (47) | $50,000 |

*Major leaguers in bold. *High school selection.*

### One Team's Draft: Milwaukee Brewers

| | Player, Pos. | Bonus |
|---|---|---|
| 1. | ***Jeff D'Amico, rhp** | **$525,000** |
| 1. | **Kelly Wunsch, lhp** | **$400,000** |
| 1. | **Todd Dunn, of** | **$240,000** |
| 1. | Joe Wagner, rhp | $210,000 |
| 2. | **Brian Banks, c/of** | **$180,000** |
| 2. | ***Danny Klassen, ss** | **$180,000** |
| 3. | *George Preston, rhp | $75,000 |
| 4. | Shane Sheldon, rhp | $55,000 |
| 5. | Steve Duda, rhp | $35,000 |
| 6. | *Josh Zwisler, c | $35,000 |
| 7. | **Mark Loretta, ss** | **$32,500** |
| 8. | Tano Tijerina, rhp | $65,000 |
| 9. | Jon Hillis, rhp | $30,000 |
| 10. | Chris McInnes, ss | $16,000 |
| 11. | *Chris Junghans, c | Did not sign |
| 12. | *Brian Blessie, rhp | Did not sign |
| 13. | Brian Luna, 1b | $20,000 |
| 14. | *Peter Benny, rhp | $45,000 |
| 15. | Scott Perkins, rhp | $22,500 |
| 16. | *Jim Wallace, rhp | Did not sign |
| 17. | Chad Kopitzke, rhp | $10,000 |
| 18. | Gabriel Mercado, rhp | $7,500 |
| 19. | **Sean Maloney, rhp** | **$2,000** |
| 20. | *Pedro Fuentes, 3b | $10,000 |
| 21. | Chris Schmitt, lhp | $2,500 |
| 22. | Ricky Gutierrez, 2b | Did not sign |
| 23. | Ron Wallech, rhp | Did not sign |
| 24. | **Greg Martinez, of** | **$7,500** |
| 25. | Jarod Fryman, 3b | $20,000 |

*Major leaguers in bold. *High school selection.*

### IN FOCUS: KIRK PRESLEY

MORRIS FOSTOFF

Kirk Presley attracted attention in the 1993 draft as the third cousin of Elvis Presley, though he also made a name for himself in high school as both a quarterback and pitcher.

As a senior at Tupelo (Miss.) High, the 6-foot-3 righthander went 15-0, 0.58 with 15 walks and 161 strikeouts in 97 innings, while hitting .422 with nine homers and 49 RBIs. He almost singlehandedly led his team to a second straight state 5-A title. Over his career, he went 37-1, 0.60 with 22 shutouts.

Because of his desire to play both football and baseball at Mississippi State, Presley was considered the most difficult sign in the first round, though the Mets satisfied his bonus demands by coming up with a $900,000 offer. "Baseball is my career," said Presley. "There was no need for me to beat around the bush and play football. I'd just be wasting my time."

Despite being the most polished prep pitcher in the 1993 draft, with an ideal delivery and command of three pitches, Presley encountered shoulder problems immediately and never threw as hard in pro ball as he did in high school. He eventually had rotator-cuff surgery in 1995 in an unsuccessful attempt to salvage a fading career.

Presley pitched in just 30 minor league games, none above Class A, in his abbreviated five-year career.

# 1993 Draft List

**Did not sign. Major leaguers in bold, with first and last years noted. Order of selection indicated in parentheses. For the first five rounds, the peak level of each player is noted. + Signed as draft-and-follow (Second school noted if applicable).*

## ATLANTA BRAVES (24)

1. (Choice to Cubs as compensation for Type A free agent Greg Maddux)
2. Andre King, of, Stranahan HS, Fort Lauderdale, Fla.—(AA)

DRAFT DROP *Wide receiver, National Football League (2001-04)*

**3. Carl Schutz, lhp, Southeastern Louisiana University.—(1996)**
4. James Franklin, of, Larue County HS, Hodgenville, Ky.—(Rookie)
5. Del Mathews, 1b-lhp, Fernandina Beach (Fla.) HS.—(AAA)
6. Danny Magee, ss, Denham Springs (La.) HS.
7. Travis Cain, rhp, T.L. Hanna HS, Anderson, S.C.
**8. Micah Bowie, lhp, Kingwood (Texas) HS.—(1999-2008)**
9. Jason Green, rhp, Contra Costa (Calif.) JC.
**10. Rob Sasser, of, Oakland (Calif.) HS.—(1998)**
**11. Kevin Millwood, rhp, Bessemer City (N.C.) HS.—(1997-2012)**
12. Jerrod Miller, rhp, Ferris HS, Spokane, Wash.
13. Wes Culp, of, Anderson HS, Austin, Texas.
14. Brett Brewer, of, Snowflake (Ariz.) HS.
**15. John LeRoy, rhp, Sammamish HS, Bellevue, Wash.—(1997)**
16. John Reece, of, University of Nebraska.

DRAFT DROP *Defensive back, National Football League (1995)*

**17. Jermaine Dye, of, Cosumnes River (Calif.) CC.—(1996-2009)**
**18. John Rocker, lhp, First Presbyterian Day HS, Macon, Ga.—(1998-2003)**
19. David Wells, rhp, Wabash Valley (Ill.) JC.
**20. Roosevelt Brown, of, Vicksburg (Miss.) HS.—(1999-2002)**
21. *David Knoerr, of, Mesquite (Texas) HS.
22. Andrew Tolbert, of, John Jay HS, San Antonio, Texas.
23. Darold Brown, lhp, Laney (Calif.) JC.
24. *Jarod Erdody, c, Gladstone (Mich.) HS.
25. *Darren Grass, c, University of Minnesota.
26. Rich Betti, lhp, Quinsigamond (Mass.) CC.
27. Casey Burrill, c, University of Southern California.
28. Ralph Denman, of, Dallas Baptist University.
29. Michael Warner, rhp, Bellaire HS, Houston.
30. Wayne Newman, of, American River (Calif.) JC.
31. Bennie Tillman, of, Jackson State University.
32. Eric Olszewski, rhp, Concordia Lutheran HS, Spring, Texas.
33. Jason Dailey, of, Lee (Texas) JC.
34. Chris Cox, 3b, University of North Carolina.
35. *Gregory Feris, rhp, Plainview (Texas) HS.
36. Bill Faile, rhp, Greenwich (N.Y.) HS.
37. Gator McBride, 2b, John A. Logan (Ill.) JC.
38. Charlie Gann, rhp, Jurupa Valley HS, Mira Loma, Calif.
39. Rickey Carter, 3b, North Marion HS, Sparr, Fla.
40. Andrew Lollie, rhp, Windsor HS, Kirkwood, N.Y.
41. Brian Cruz, c, Anderson (Ind.) University.
42. *Shane Wooten, lhp, Davidson Academy, Goodlettsville, Tenn.
43. David Catlett, 1b, Laney (Calif.) JC.
44. Justin Rigney, lhp, Tallahassee (Fla.) JC.
45. Marcus Tyner, rhp, Laney (Calif.) JC.
46. Cam Browder, of, University of North Carolina-Charlotte.
47. Jason Simmons, rhp, Bradley University.
48. *Brent Moore, lhp, Midland Valley HS, Clearwater, S.C.
**49. *Scott Mullen, lhp, Beaufort (S.C.) HS.—(2000-03)**
50. Wonderful Monds III, of, Tennessee State University.

DRAFT DROP *Son of Wonderful Monds, Jr., defensive back, National Football League (1978)*

51. (void) *Pat Murphy, 2b, University of South Alabama.
52. *Steven Lay, rhp, Roane County HS, Kingston, Tenn.
53. *John Morris, 1b, Valley Christian HS, Lakewood, Calif.
54. *Reginald Swilley, rhp, Santa Teresa HS, San Jose, Calif.
55. +Ryan Martin, c, Highland HS, Pierron, Ill. / John A. Logan (Ill.) JC.
56. *Brian Steinbach, rhp, Arrowhead HS, Pewaukee, Wis.
57. *Andre Shaw, of, Lufkin (Texas) HS.

## BALTIMORE ORIOLES (19)

**1. Jay Powell, rhp, Mississippi State University.—(1995-2005)**
**2. David Lamb, ss, Newbury Park (Calif.) HS.—(1999-2002)**
3. Jimmy Walker, rhp, University of Kansas.—(High A)
4. Jason Hackett, lhp, Caravel Academy, Bear, Del.—(High A)
5. Mike Gargiulo, c, Bishop McDevitt HS, Harrisburg, Pa.—(High A)
6. Brian Brewer, lhp, Sacramento (Calif.) CC.
7. John Lombardi, rhp-of, Central Arizona JC.
8. Harry Berrios, of, Louisiana State University.
9. Edwon Simmons, ss, Leo HS, Chicago.
10. Wes Hawkins, of, Louisiana Tech.
11. Tim Karns, rhp, Regis (Colo.) College.
12. *Eric Mooney, lhp, St. Mary's (Calif.) College.
13. Brandon Bridgers, of, Methodist (N.C.) College.
**14. Kimera Bartee, of, Creighton University.—(1996-2001)**
15. Kevin Curtis, of, Long Beach State University.
16. Delshon Bowman, of, Brandon (Fla.) HS.
17. Lincoln Martin, 2b, Birmingham-Southern College.
18. Kenny Reed, 1b, Ball State University.
**19. +Rocky Coppinger, rhp, Coronado HS, El Paso, Texas / Hill (Texas) JC.—(1996-2001)**
20. *Mike McKinlay, rhp, Marriott HS, White Rock, B.C.
21. Alex Pena, rhp, New Mexico JC.
22. Jim Foster, c, Providence College.
23. Jeff Michael, ss, University of Kentucky.
24. Michael Lane, rhp, Belmont College.
25. *John Batts, 2b, Penn Charter HS, Philadelphia.
**26. Jesse Garcia, 2b, Lee (Texas) JC.—(1999-2005)**
27. Trovin Valdez, of, New Mexico JC.
28. Ron Shankle, ss, Essex (Md.) CC.
29. *Robert Conway, rhp, Tallahassee (Fla.) CC.
30. Rocco Cafaro, rhp, Polk (Fla.) CC.
31. Michael Trimarco, rhp, Aurora (Ill.) University.
32. Bryan Link, of, Austin Peay State University.
33. *Paul Barry, rhp, Sacramento (Calif.) CC.
34. *Jim Fritz, c, North Eugene (Ore.) HS.
35. *Michael Sak, 1b, West Leyden HS, Melrose Park, Ill.
36. *Jacques Landry, 3b, San Jacinto North (Texas) JC.
37. *Dennis Gilich, rhp, Peninsula HS, Gig Harbor, Wash.
38. *Jeff Westerman, rhp, Kennedy HS, La Palma, Calif.
39. *Aaron France, rhp, Meridian (Miss.) JC.
40. *Josh Itzoe, ss, Calvert Hall HS, Towson, Md.
41. *Mike Bohny, 3b, Baylor University.
42. Kendrick Singleton, rhp, Chamberlain HS, Tampa.
43. *Tim Giles, 1b, Arundel HS, Gambrills, Md.
44. *James Esparza, lhp, Cedar Valley (Texas) CC.

## BOSTON RED SOX (7)

**1. Trot Nixon, of, New Hanover HS, Wilmington, N.C.—(1996-2008)**
**2. Jeff Suppan, rhp, Crespi HS, Encino, Calif.—(1995-2012)**
**3. Ryan McGuire, 1b, UCLA.—(1997-2002)**
4. Shawn Senior, lhp, North Carolina State University.—(AAA)
5. Kevin Clark, 3b, Cypress (Calif.) JC.—(AA)
**6. +Peter Munro, rhp, Cardoza HS, Bayside, N.Y. / Okaloosa-Walton (Fla.) JC.—(1999-2004)**
7. David Gibralter, 3b, Duncanville (Texas) HS.

DRAFT DROP *Brother of Steve Gibralter, major leaguer (1995-96)*

**8. *Sean DePaula, rhp, Cardinal Cushing Central HS, Derry, Mass.—(1999-2002)**
9. Dean Peterson, rhp, Allegheny (Pa.) JC.
**10. Lou Merloni, ss, Providence College.—(1998-2006)**
11. Kurt Bogott, lhp, St. Xavier (Ill.) University.
12. Pat Murphy, 2b, University of South Alabama.
13. Willie Rivera, of, Lino Padron Rivera HS, Vega Alta, P.R.
14. David Smith, ss, LeMoyne College.
15. Jacob Cook, rhp, Greenville (Ohio) HS.
**16. Andy Abad, of, Middle Georgia JC.—(2001-06)**
17. Greg Patton, ss, George Washington University.
**18. *Keith McDonald, c, Cypress (Calif.) JC.—(2000-01)**
19. Courtney Arrollado, ss, Valhalla HS, El Cajon, Calif.
20. *Allan Westfall, rhp, Deltona (Fla.) HS.
21. John Graham, of, University of Massachusetts.
22. Craig Phillip, rhp, Aurora (Ill.) University.
23. *Mark Ballard, rhp, University of Maine.
24. Gregg Kennedy, lhp, University of Southern Mississippi.
**25. Shayne Bennett, rhp, JC of Du Page (Ill.).—(1997-99)**
26. *Christian McCarter, of, Northeast Louisiana University.
27. *Scotty Hartfield, of, Hattiesburg (Miss.) HS.
28. Steve Hayward, rhp, Seton Hall University.
29. *Jeff Belcher, of, Calhoun (Ala.) CC.
30. Jim Larkin, 3b, Holy Cross College.
31. Aaron Fuller, 2b, University of California.
32. Nathan Tebbs, 2b, JC of Southern Idaho.
33. *Ricky Rodriguez, ss, Miami Springs (Fla.) HS.
34. James Fernandes, rhp, Brandeis (Mass.) University.
35. John Walker, 2b, Grand Rapids (Mich.) JC.
36. Gavin Jackson, ss, Chipola (Fla.) JC.
37. Mark Dewalt, rhp, Upper Arlington (Ohio) HS.
38. *Wayne Slater, of, Franklin D. Roosevelt HS, Brooklyn, N.Y.
39. Tony Brannon, 2b, Johnstown-Monroe HS, Johnstown, Ohio.
40. *Patrick McLendon, c, Lee HS, Baytown, Texas.
**41. *Danny Ardoin, c, Texarkana (Texas) CC.—(2000-08)**
42. *Chad Helmer, rhp, East Bay HS, Ruskin, Fla.
43. Eric Ford, of, Jacksonville State University.
44. *Kenneth Davis, lhp, Chipola (Fla.) JC.
45. Joseph Hayward, of, Boston College.
46. *Scott Brewer, rhp, Southern Union State (Ala.) JC.
47. *Alphonso Johnson, ss, Hollandale Simmons HS, Hollandale, Miss.
48. *Ricky Joe Redd, of, Mississippi State University.
49. *Michael Davis, rhp, Northwest Whitfield HS, Rocky Face, Ga.
50. *Chris Ciraulo, c, Cardinal Newman HS, Santa Rosa, Calif.

## CALIFORNIA ANGELS (3)

**1. Brian Anderson, lhp, Wright State University.—(1993-2005)**

DRAFT DROP *First player from 1993 draft to reach majors (Sept. 10, 1993)*

**2. Ryan Hancock, rhp, Brigham Young University.—(1996)**
**3. Matt Perisho, lhp, McClintock HS, Tempe, Ariz.—(1997-2005)**
**4. Andrew Lorraine, lhp, Stanford University.—(1994-2002)**
5. Jose Cintron, rhp, Alfonso Martinez HS, Yabucoa, P.R.—(High A)
6. Geoff Edsell, rhp, Old Dominion University.
**7. George Arias, 3b, University of Arizona.—(1996-99)**
8. Tim Harkrider, ss, University of Texas.
**9. Jamie Burke, 3b, Oregon State University.—(2001-10)**
10. Willard Brown, rhp, Stetson University.
11. *Greg Romo, rhp, Wasco Union HS, Wasco, Calif.
**12. Todd Greene, of, Georgia Southern University.—(1996-2006)**
13. Kevin Ham, of, Eastwood HS, El Paso, Texas.
14. *John Pollard, of, Jersey Village HS, Houston.
15. *Terrance Freeman, 2b, Bloomingdale HS, Brandon, Fla.
16. *Sidney Newman, ss, Cordova HS, Rancho Cordova, Calif.
17. Derrin Doty, of, University of Washington.
18. Bryan Harris, lhp, Florida State University.
19. Jeffrey Bawlson, lhp, Hillsborough (Fla.) CC.
20. Geoff Grenert, rhp, University of Nevada-Reno.
21. Aaron Iatarola, of, Stetson University.
22. Aaron Puffer, rhp, Creighton University.
23. Brooks Drysdale, rhp, Santa Clara University.
24. John Bushart, lhp, Cal State Northridge.
25. *Carl Caddell, lhp, Wyatt HS, Fort Worth, Texas.
26. Shawn Slade, rhp, University of Tampa.
27. *Kevin Culmo, rhp, Sacramento (Calif.) CC.
28. *Casey Snow, c, Crespi HS, Encino, Calif.
29. *Tim Moran, 1b, Chabot (Calif.) JC.
30. *Steven Goodell, ss, Chabot (Calif.) JC.
31. +Daniel Petroff, rhp, Gulf Coast (Fla.) CC.
32. Carlos Pagan, c, Lino Padron Rivera HS, Vega Baja, P.R.
**33. +Keith Luuloa, ss, Modesto (Calif.) JC.—(2000)**
34. +Brendon Cowsill, 3b, Crescenta Valley HS, La Crescenta, Calif. / Los Angeles CC.
35. *Scott Rivette, rhp, Citrus (Calif.) JC.
36. *Todd Stubblefield, rhp-1b, Cooper City (Fla.) HS.
37. *Bryan Smithson, lhp, Santa Barbara (Calif.) HS.
38. *Everard Griffiths, rhp, Miami-Dade CC North.
39. *Adam Brick, c, Brandon (Fla.) HS.
40. *D.J. Johnson, rhp, Baxter Springs (Kan.) HS.
41. *Gary Stevenson, rhp, Hart HS, Valencia, Calif
42. *Howard Pride, of, Butler HS, Huntsville, Ala.
43. *Marshall Faulk, of, San Diego State University.

DRAFT DROP *First-round draft pick, Indianapolis Colts/ National Football League (1994); running back, NFL (1994-2005)*

44. *Ricky Gonzalez, c, Indian River (Fla.) CC.
45. *Richard Nadeau, of, Kennedy HS, Granada Hills, Calif.
46. *Ryan Folmar, c, Chambersburg (Pa.) Area HS.

DRAFT DROP *Baseball coach, Oral Roberts (2013-15)*

47. *Brian Boeth, rhp, Pensacola (Fla.) JC.
46. *Kyle Richardson, 3b, Casa Grande (Ariz.) HS.
49. *Randi Mallard, c-of, Gainesville (Ga.) HS.
50. *Alvin Casillas, rhp, Patillas HS, Caguas, P.R.
51. *William Perusek, rhp, Hillsborough (Fla.) CC.
52. *David Robinson, of, Gulf Coast (Fla.) CC.
53. *Rafael Gutierrez, of, Comerio HS, Levittown, P.R.
54. +Matt Schafer, c, Hillsborough (Fla.) CC.
55. *Shawn Coolidge, of, Dunedin (Fla.) HS.
56. *Daryl Porter, of, St. Thomas Aquinas HS, Fort Lauderdale, Fla.
57. *David Supple, c, Notre Dame HS, Northridge, Calif.

## CHICAGO CUBS (10)

**1. Brooks Kieschnick, of-rhp, University of Texas.—(1996-2004)**
**1. Jon Ratliff, rhp, LeMoyne College** (Choice from Braves as compensation for Type A free agent Greg Maddux).**—(2000)**
**1. Kevin Orie, ss, Indiana University** (Supplemental choice—29th—as compensation for Maddux).**—(1997-2002)**
2. (Choice to Rangers as compensation for Type A free agent Jose Guzman)
3. Vee Hightower, of, Vanderbilt University.—(AA)
4. Mike Montilla, ss, North Bergen (N.J.) HS.—(High A)
**5. *Matt Miller, lhp, Monterey HS, Lubbock, Texas.—(2001-02)**

DRAFT DROP *Attended Texas Tech; re-drafted by Tigers, 1996 (2nd round)*

6. Pat Cline, c, Manatee HS, Bradenton, Fla.
7. Scott Kendrick, rhp, Monroe-Woodbury HS, Central Valley, N.Y.
8. Chris Bryant, lhp, Brandon (Fla.) HS.
9. Bob Morris, 3b, University of Iowa.

DRAFT DROP *Brother of Hal Morris, major leaguer (1988-2000)*

10. *Jamey Price, rhp, Texarkana (Texas) CC.
**11. Steven Rain, rhp, Walnut (Calif.) HS.—(1999-2000)**
12. Gabe Whatley, of, Vanderbilt University.
13. Tony Locey, rhp, Columbus (Ga.) College.
**14. Jose Molina, c, Maestro Ladislao Martinez HS, Vega Alta, P.R.—(1999-2014)**

DRAFT DROP *Brother of Bengie Molina, major leaguer (1998-2010) • Brother of Yadier Molina, major leaguer (2004-15)*

15. Brad Chambers, of-rhp, Midlothian (Va.) HS.
16. Wade Walker, rhp, Northeast Louisiana University.
17. *Robert Duncan, 3b, Central Florida CC.
18. *Nathan Dunn, ss, Vestavia Hills HS, Birmingham, Ala.
19. Alfredo Garcia, rhp, Buena Park (Calif.) HS.
20. Nate Thomas, lhp-1b, First Colonial HS, Virginia Beach, Va.
21. David Hutcheson, rhp, University of South Florida.
22. *Gary Burnham, of, South Windsor (Conn.) HS.
23. Gilbert Avalos, ss, Alvin (Texas) CC.
24. John Rodgers, c, Rice University.
25. *Jimmy Hamilton, lhp, Turner Ashby HS, Weyers Cove, Va.
26. Andy Devries, lhp, Manatee (Fla.) JC.
27. Ronald Smith, 1b, Southern University.
28. John Sauer, of, Patterson HS, Baltimore.
29. Greg Hillman, lhp, University of Texas.
30. David Weber, rhp, Marist HS, Jersey City, N.J.
31. Kenneth Jones, of, Middle Georgia JC.
32. Gabe Duross, 1b-of, University of Maine.
33. Doug Alongi, of, Rutgers University.
34. Sean Fric, of, Alvin (Texas) CC.
35. Jared Snyder, c, Nicholls State University.
36. Frank Cicero, c, La Mirada (Calif.) HS.
37. *Adam Robinson, 2b, West Morris Central HS, Long Valley, N.J.
38. Daniel Gil, of, Mission Bay HS, San Diego.
39. +Kelvin Barnes, ss-of, Lake City (Fla.) CC.
**40. Bo Porter, of, University of Iowa.—(1999-2001)**
**DRAFT DROP** *Major league manager (2013-14)*
41. Gary Beashore, rhp, Missouri Western State College.
42. Jose DeJesus, 3b, Cecilio Lebron Ramos HS, Patillas, P.R.
43. Jason Dunn, rhp, Raritan Valley (N.J.) CC.
44. Mark Lavenia, lhp, University of South Carolina-Aiken.
45. James Young, of, Valdosta State (Ga.) College.
46. *Jose Peraza, lhp, Norwalk (Calif.) HS.
47. Shawn Hill, rhp, Nicholls State University.
48. Billy Vielleux, ss, Hartford HS, White River Junction, Vt.
49. Gabby Castro, lhp, Jose De Diego HS, Aguadilla, P.R.
50. Thomas Ball, lhp, Cal State Dominguez Hills.
51. Sean Hogan, lhp, Morehead State University.
52. Dee Dowler, 2b-of, Indiana State University.
53. Rodd Kurtz, lhp, University of Texas-Pan American.
54. Greg Twiggs, lhp, Brewton-Parker (Ga.) College.
55. Stephen Kulpa, ss, Quinnipiac College.
56. *Javier Herrera, rhp, Miami (Fla.) Senior HS.
57. Michael Gibson, of-2b, Bowie State (Md.) University.
58. Artis Johnson, of, Florida A&M University.
59. Ralph Eusebio, of, Brevard (Fla.) CC.
60. Joe Biernat, ss, University of South Carolina.
61. Brett McCabe, 1b, Centenary College.
62. Thomas King, of, Valdosta State (Ga.) College.
63. Tony Khoury, c-rhp, Ohio State University.
64. Sean Davisson, 2b-of, Long Beach State University.
65. *Dustin Wilkinson, 3b, Shaw HS, Columbus, Ga.
66. *Rob Carpenter, of, University of Southern Maine.
67. *Gregory Denly, rhp, Valdosta (Ga,) HS.
68. *Scott Stephens, lhp, Eau Gallie HS, Melbourne, Fla.
69. *Anthony Dellamano, rhp, Los Angeles Pierce JC.
70. *Chris Price, rhp, Goddard HS, Roswell, N.M.
71. *Cory Lima, 1b-of, Redan HS, Stone Mountain, Ga.
72. *Danier Anderson, of, Tioga HS, Pineville, La.
73. *Jose Castillo, lhp, Falfurrias (Texas) HS.
**74. Jason Maxwell, ss, Middle Tennessee State University.—(1998-2001)**
75. *Shawn Knight, ss, College of William & Mary.
76. James Farrow, rhp, Brewton-Parker (Ga.) College.
77. Jamil Cunningham, ss, Bethune-Cookman College.
78. *Steve Everson, of, Valdosta (Ga.) HS.
79. *Robert Baldwin, of, Duke University.
80. *Clarence Williams, c-1b, Crescent City (Fla.) HS.
**DRAFT DROP** *Running back, National Football League (1998)*
81. *Anthony Rich, ss, Rollins (Fla.) College.
82. +James Huntley, ss, West Mecklenburg HS, Charlotte, N.C. / Spartanburg Methodist (S.C.) JC.

RODGER WOOD

Angels first-rounder Brian Anderson was the first 1993 draft pick to reach the majors

## CHICAGO WHITE SOX (17)

1. Scott Christman, lhp, Oregon State University.—(AA)
**2. Greg Norton, 3b, University of Oklahoma.—(1996-2009)**
3. Joe Bales, rhp, Reed HS, Sparks, Nev.—(Low A)
4. *Dennis Twombley, c, Patrick Henry HS, San Diego.—(High A)
**DRAFT DROP** *Attended San Diego State; re-drafted by Yankees, 1996 (40th round)*
**5. David Lundquist, rhp, Cochise County (Ariz.) CC.—(1999-2002)**
6. Craig McClure, of, Columbine HS, Littleton, Colo.
7. Ben Boulware, 2b-of, Cal Poly San Luis Obispo.
8. Jason Goligoski, ss, Western Montana College.
9. Rich Pratt, lhp, University of South Carolina.
10. *Zane Leiber, rhp, Central Arizona JC.
**11. Tom Fordham, lhp, Grossmont (Calif.) JC.—(1997-98)**
12. Sandy McKinnon, of, Middle Georgia JC.
13. Steve Friedrich, of, Fullerton (Calif.) JC.
14. Bill Proctor, rhp, Western Oregon State College.
**15. Mike Sirotka, lhp, Louisiana State University.—(1995-2000)**
16. Billy Joe Hobert, of, University of Washington.
**DRAFT DROP** *Quarterback, National Football League (1995-99)*
17. Scott Vollmer, c, Pepperdine University.
18. *Bill Mobilia, ss, University of Minnesota.
19. Rich Carone, c, University of Mississippi.
20. Brian Woods, rhp, Fairleigh Dickinson University.
21. Andy McCormack, lhp, University of South Florida.
22. Curtis Broome, rhp, University of Evansville.
23. John Quirk, lhp, Westchester (N.Y.) CC.
24. Jim Dixon, rhp, New Mexico State University.
25. *Joel Peters, ss, Lincoln HS, Vincennes, Ind.
26. Harold Williams, of, Livingston (Ala.) University.
27. *Chris Olson, lhp, Alvin (Texas) HS.
28. +Alex Prejean, rhp, Clear Lake HS, Houston / San Jacinto (Texas) JC.
29. *Travis Rapp, c, Sebring (Fla.) HS.
30. *Tim Fuhrman, rhp, Casa Roble HS, Orangevale, Calif.
31. *Jory Diamond, rhp, Tallahassee (Fla.) CC.
**32. *Jeff Abbott, of, University of Kentucky.—(1997-2001)**
33. Jim Schlotter, rhp, Rider College.
34. David Moore, 3b, Dr. Phillips HS, Orlando, Fla.
35. *Ricky Garcia, rhp, Mesa (Ariz.) CC.
36. *Brad Harker, 1b, Lawrence (Kan.) HS.
37. Will Baldwin, rhp, Florida Memorial College.
38. *Jim Gargiulo, c, Coconut Creek (Fla.) HS.
39. *Ryan Roberts, ss, Utah Valley CC.
40. *Joshua Whittenton, 3b, Auburndale (Fla.) HS.
**41. *Brandon Berger, c, Beechwood HS, Fort Mitchell, Ky.—(2001-04)**
42. *Anthony Guerra, c, North Miami (Fla.) HS.
43. *Carey Schueler, lhp-1b, Campolindo HS, Moraga, Calif.
**DRAFT DROP** *Daughter of Ron Schueler, major leaguer (1972-79); general manager, White Sox (1991-2000)*
44. Todd Hall, ss, Cal State Sacramento.
**45. Frank Menechino, 2b, University of Alabama.—(1999-2005)**
46. *Marty Patterson, c, Croswell-Lexington HS, Croswell, Mich.
47. *Gorky Estrella, 3b, George Washington HS, New York.
**48. +Mario Valdez, 1b, Miami (Fla.) Senior HS / Miami-Dade North CC—(1997-2001)**
**49. *Placido Polanco, 2b, Miami-Dade CC Wolfson.—(1998-2013)**

## CINCINNATI REDS (20)

1. (Choice to Twins as compensation for Type A free agent John Smiley)
**1. Pat Watkins, of, East Carolina University** (Supplemental choice—32nd—as compensation for Type A free agent Greg Swindell).—**(1997-99)**
**2. Scott Sullivan, rhp, Auburn University.—(1995-2004)**
3. Steve Wilkerson, rhp, Grand Canyon University (Choice from Astros as compensation for Swindell).—(Low A)
3. Brad Tweedlie, rhp, Western Carolina University.—(AA)
4. Samuel Osorio, of, Jesus Vizcarondo HS, Loiza, P.R.--DNP
**5. Paul Bako, c, University of Southwestern Louisiana.—(1998-2009)**
6. *David Caldwell, lhp, Northeast Texas CC.
7. Darran Hall, of, Lincoln HS, San Diego.
8. Pete Harvell, lhp, University of Tennessee.
9. *John Ambrose, rhp, Memorial HS, Evansville, Ind.
**10. Chris Sexton, of-2b, Miami (Ohio) University.—(1999-2000)**
11. Joel Franklin, rhp, Southwestern (Calif.) JC.
12. Doug Durrwachter, ss, University of Texas-Arlington.
**13. James Lofton, ss, Los Angeles CC.—(2001)**
14. *J.J. Picollo, c, George Mason University.
15. *Jason Ruskey, lhp, Triton (Ill.) JC.
16. Jackie McCroskey, of, Male HS, Louisville, Ky.
17. *Matt Purkiss, 3b, Redwood HS, Visalia, Calif.
18. *Jeff Niemeier, c, University of Kansas.
19. Trey Rutledge, rhp, Louisiana State University.
20. Peter Magre, rhp, St. Mary's (Texas) University.
21. *Jamie Emiliano, rhp, Odessa (Texas) JC.
22. Scott McKenzie, rhp, Northwood (Texas) Institute.
23. *Anthony Johnson, of, Brookdale (N.J.) CC.
24. Stephen Gann, 2b, Dallas Baptist University.
25. Jason Chandler, rhp, Morehead State University.
26. Donald Broach, of, Cincinnati.
27. *Alejandro Sanchez, rhp, Ontario (Calif.) HS.
28. Jason Baker, of, Allegany (Md.) CC.
29. Jon Hebel, rhp, Auburn University.
30. *Scott Shores, of, Arizona State University.
31. Michael Moses, lhp, University of Wyoming.
32. Cobi Cradle, of, Long Beach State University.
**DRAFT DROP** *Brother of Rickey Cradle, major leaguer (1998)*
33. Steven Eddie, ss, University of Iowa.
34. Chad Akers, ss, West Virginia State College.
35. *Scott Wilson, 3b, San Dieguito HS, Carlsbad, Calif.
36. *Brian Jergenson, of-1b, La Crescent (Minn.) HS.
37. *Michael Bauder, lhp, Western HS, Las Vegas, Nev.
**38. *Chad Allen, of, Duncanville (Texas) HS.—(1999-2005)**
39. *Mel Motley, of, Riverside (Calif.) CC.
40. Jonathon Dold, of, St. John's (Minn.) University.
41. *James Debruin, rhp, Calhoun HS, Seadrift, Texas.
42. *Damon Miller, c, Washington HS, Cherokee, Iowa.
43. Danny Hagan, lhp, Louisville, Ky.

## CLEVELAND INDIANS (11)

1. Daron Kirkreit, rhp, UC Riverside.—(AAA)
2. Casey Whitten, lhp, Indiana State University.—(AAA)
3. J.J. Done, rhp, Monsignor Pace HS, Miami.—(Low A)
**4. Travis Driskill, rhp, Texas Tech.—(2002-07)**
5. Kris Hanson, rhp, University of Wisconsin-Whitewater.—(High A)
6. Matt Hobbie, of, Sarasota (Fla.) HS.
**7. *Seth Greisinger, rhp, McLean HS, Falls Church, Va.—(1998-2004)**
**DRAFT DROP** *First-round draft pick (6th overall), Tigers (1996)*
**8. Steve Kline, lhp, West Virginia University.—(1997-2007)**

9. Greg Thomas, 1b, Vanderbilt University.
10. *Derrick Cook, rhp, Robert E. Lee HS, Staunton, Va.
11. Jason Mackey, lhp, Lower Columbia (Wash.) JC.
12. Jeffrey Haag, c, Florida Southern College.
13. Steven Soliz, c, Cal State Los Angeles.
14. Todd Betts, 3b, Northeastern Oklahoma A&M JC.
**15. Roland De la Maza, rhp, Cal State Sacramento.—(1997)**
16. Mike Neal, 3b-ss, Louisiana State University.
17. Robert Lewis, c, Texas A&M University.
18. Todd Johnson, c, Fresno State University.
19. Blair Hodson, 1b, Yale University.
20. Brett Palmer, lhp, Idaho Falls (Idaho) HS.
21. Eric Chapman, of, University of South Carolina-Aiken.
22. Chris Plumlee, rhp, Arkansas State University.
23. *Steve Hagins, c, University HS, Irvine, Calif.
**24. Richie Sexson, 1b, Prairie HS, Brush Prairie, Wash.—(1997-2008)**
25. Robert Kulle, of, LeMoyne College.
26. Norman Williams, of, Chipola (Fla.) JC.
27. *Ryan Lefebvre, of, University of Minnesota.
DRAFT DROP *Son of Jim Lefebvre, major leaguer (1965-72); major league manager (1989-99)*
28. Rick Prieto, 2b-ss, Carmel, Calif.
29. Richard King, ss, Concordia (Texas) College.
30. *Greg Tippin, 1b, Cypress (Calif) JC.
31. *Jamie Coons, of, Edgewood (Md.) HS.
32. Richard Lemons, of, University of Arizona.
33. Gerad Cawhorn, 3b, San Jose State University.
34. *Ken Westmoreland, rhp, Austin HS, Decatur, Ala.
35. *Randy Woodall, rhp, Sheffield (Ala.) HS.
36. Rodney Holland, of, Schriener (Texas) College.
37. *Teddy Warrecker, c, Allan Hancock (Calif) JC.
38. *Michael Rodriguez, c-of, Brandeis HS, New York.
39. *David Townsend, rhp, Hinds (Miss.) CC.
40. *Ara Petrosian, rhp, Fountain Valley (Calif.) HS.
41. Jason Lyman, 2b, Cal State San Bernardino.
42. *Nisam Bean, ss, Kennedy HS, Richmond, Calif.
43. Wesley Dempsey, lhp, Southwest Texas State University.
44. Andy Pierce, rhp, Lassen (Calif.) CC.
45. Darnell Batiste, of, Sam Houston HS, Arlington, Texas.
46. *Jeff Bell, ss, Pinson Valley (Ala.) HS.
**47. *David Roberts, of, UCLA.—(1999-2008)**
48. *David Stevenson, of-1b, Los Angeles Valley JC.
49. *Larry Dobson, of, Putnam City HS, Oklahoma City, Okla.
50. *Poncho Ruiz, 2b, Esperanza HS, Placentia, Calif.
51. *Dean Mitchell, rhp, Navarro (Texas) JC.
52. *Bret Soverel, rhp, Martin County HS, Palm City, Fla.
53. *Aaron Gentry, ss, Claremore (Okla.) HS.
54. Kevin Dinnen, rhp, Barry (Fla.) University.
55. *Robert Kinnee, rhp, Marshall HS, Portland, Ore
56. +Carlos Arellano, rhp, Granada HS, Livermore, Calif. / Chabot (Calif.) JC.
57. *Angel Rodriguez, rhp, Isabella, P.R.
58. Tony Runion, rhp, Duke University.
59. *Brian Basowski, of, Los Angeles Pierce JC.
60. *Vincent Griffin, of, South Suburban (Ill.) JC.
61. *Brian Norris, rhp, Stephen F. Austin HS, Port Arthur, Texas.
**62. *Ken Vining, lhp, Cardinal Newman HS, Columbia, S.C.—(2001)**
63. *Jeffrey Kober, lhp, Jefferson (Wis.) HS.
64. *Roger Walker, c, Florida CC.
65. *Casey Swingley, rhp, Lower Columbia (Wash.) JC.
66. *Jason Vorhauer, 1b, Fairfield HS, Suisun City, Calif.
67. Bryan Garrett, of, Florida International University.
68. *Keith Cowley, 3b, Westminster (Calif.) HS.
69. *Joseph Adams, rhp, Freeman HS, Richmond, Va.
70. *Travis Peterson, of, Edmonds (Wash.) CC.
71. Pedro Marte, 2b-of, Florida Memorial College.
72. Jason Marshall, c, Baylor University.

## COLORADO ROCKIES (28)

**1. Jamey Wright, rhp, Westmoore HS, Oklahoma City, Okla.—(1996-2014)**
**2. Bryan Rekar, rhp, Bradley University.—(1995-2002)**
3. Joel Moore, rhp, Bradley University.—(AAA)
4. Doug Walls, rhp, Muscatine (Iowa) CC.—(AAA)
5. Mike Zolecki, rhp, St. Mary's (Texas) University.—(AA)
6. Chad Gambill, of, Clearwater (Fla.) HS.
**7. John Thomson, rhp, Blinn (Texas) JC.—(1997-2007)**
8. Kyle Houser, ss, Duncanville (Texas) HS.
9. John Myrow, of, UCLA.
**10. Edgard Clemente, of, Colegio Hostos HS, Guaynabo, P.R.—(1998-2000)**
DRAFT DROP *Nephew of Roberto Clemente, major leaguer (1955-72)*
11. Jacob Viano, rhp, Long Beach (Calif.) CC.
12. Keith Grunewald, ss, University of North Carolina.
**13. Derrick Gibson, of, Haines City (Fla.) HS.—(1998-99)**
14. Bob Lasbury, rhp, Manhattanville (N.Y.) College.
15. *Casey Davis of, Corsicana (Texas) HS.
DRAFT DROP *Son of Willie Davis, major leaguer (1960-79)*
16. Nate Holdren, 1b, University of Michigan.
17. Kevin Wehn, rhp, Florida International University.
18. Morgan Burdick, rhp, Clovis HS, Dunlap, Calif.
19. Jason Johnson, rhp, Auburn University.
DRAFT DROP *Great-grandson of Rankin Johnson, major leaguer (1914-18) • Grandson of Rankin Johnson, major leaguer (1941)*
20. John Giudice, of, Eastern Connecticut State University.
21. Derrick Calvin, rhp, Southern University.
22. Mike Higgins, c, Rutgers University.
23. Martin Dewitt, lhp, Mesa (Ariz.) CC.
24. Jason Smith, c, University of Texas-Arlington.
25. Jamie Anderson, ss, Hanover (Ind.) College.
26. Curt Conley, lhp, Ball State University.
27. Will Hoover, c, Cedar Cliff HS, Camp Hill, Pa.
28. Mario Munoz, 3b, Mesa State (Colo.) College.
29. Dan Barry, lhp, West Virginia University.
**30. +Mark Brownson, rhp, Wellington (Fla.) Community HS / Palm Beach (Fla.) JC.—(1998-2000)**
31. Pat McClinton, lhp, Bellarmine (Ky.) College.
32. Dennis McAdams, rhp, Palomar (Calif.) JC.
33. +Dominic Demark, of, Mesa (Ariz.) CC.
34. Ben Ortman, of, University of Portland.
35. *Philip Davis, rhp, Yuma (Ariz.) HS.
36. Dan Butcher, rhp, Diablo Valley (Calif.) JC.
37. Enrique Melendez, ss, Aurea E. Quiles Claudio HS, Ensenada, P.R.
38. *Darin Baugh, ss, Serra HS, San Mateo, Calif.
39. *Brandon Nickens, rhp, Los Angeles Pierce JC.
**40. Terry Jones, of, University of North Alabama.—(1996)**
41. *Justin Liniak, of, San Dieguito HS, Encinitas, Calif.
42. Brian Culp, c, Kansas State University.
43. *Larry Green, c, Utah Valley JC.
44. *Johnathan Delya, rhp, Crescent-Iroquois HS, Onarga, Ill.
45. +Andrew Keehn, rhp, Central Arizona JC.
46. *Joshua Jensen, rhp, Mountain Crest HS, Providence, Utah.
47. +Marc D'Allessandro, lhp, St. John Vianney HS, Hazlet, N.J. / Brookdale (N.J.) CC.
48. *Bradley Molcak, ss, Cardston (Alberta) HS.
49. Philip Schneider, lhp, Rutgers University.
50. +Bill Eden, lhp, Motlow State (Tenn.) CC.
51. *Michael Dewitt, rhp, Pine Plains (N.Y.) HS.
52. *Ryan Ware, ss, Jersey Village HS, Houston.
53. *Marty Remmers, rhp, Riverbank HS, Modesto, Calif.
54. *Brett Bibeau, rhp, Bishop Kelly HS, Boise, Idaho.
**55. *Brandon Knight, 2b, Buena HS, Oxnard, Calif.—(2001-08)**
56. *Chris Cooper, 2b, Mesa (Ariz.) CC.
57. *David Melendez, rhp, Blinn (Texas) JC.
58. +Anders Stahl, c, Anderson (Calif.) HS / Shasta (Calif.) JC.
59. *Frank Chelbian, lhp, Middlesex (N.J.) CC.
60. David Mineer, rhp, Utah State University.

## DETROIT TIGERS (9)

1. Matt Brunson, ss, Cherry Creek HS, Englewood, Colo.—(High A)
DRAFT DROP *Son of Larry Brunson, wide receiver, National Football League (1974-80)*
2. Tony Fuduric, rhp, Cardinal HS, Middlefield, Ohio.—(Short-season A)
3. Cameron Smith, rhp, Ithaca (N.Y.) College.—(AAA)
4. Michael Wilson, rhp, Blinn (Texas) JC.—(Low A)
5. Jayson Bass, of, O'Dea HS, Seattle.—(AAA)
**6. Brian Moehler, rhp, University of North Carolina-Greensboro.—(1996-2010)**
7. Greg Granger, rhp, Lake City (Fla.) CC,
8. Drew Christmon, of, University of Oklahoma.
9. Lonny Landry, of, Flagler (Fla.) College.
**10. *R.A. Dickey, rhp, Montgomery Bell Academy, Nashville, Tenn.—(2001-15)**
DRAFT DROP *First-round draft pick (18th overall), Rangers (1996)*
**11. Glen Barker, of, College of St. Rose (N.Y.).—(1999-2001)**
**12. Bryan Corey, ss-rhp, Los Angeles Pierce JC.—(1998-2008)**
**13. Eddie Gaillard, rhp, Florida Southern College.—(1997-99)**
**14. *Keith Foulke, rhp, Galveston (Texas) JC.—(1997-2008)**
15. Bobby L. Jones, of, Riverside (Calif.) CC.
16. David Crafton, c, Lyons Township HS, LaGrange Park, Ill.
17. Mike Salazar, lhp, Fresno State University.
**18. Shawn Wooten, c, Mount San Antonio (Calif.) JC.—(2000-05)**
**19. *Javier Cardona, c, Jose Alegria HS, Dorado, P.R—(2000-02)**
20. *Brandon Kent, rhp, Duncanville (Texas) HS.
21. Chris Wyrick, ss, University of Missouri.
22. Billy Thompson, c, University of Kentucky.
23. Corey Broome, c, University of North Carolina-Wilmington.
**24. *Matt Beech, lhp, University of Houston.—(1996-98)**
25. Shawn Brown, 2b, Rider College.
**26. Matt Skrmetta, rhp, Jacksonville University.—(2000)**
27. Eric Danapilis, of, University of Notre Dame.
28. Steve Dietz, ss, San Diego State University.
29. Jason Hamilton, 1b, St Joseph's University.
30. Joshua Neese, rhp, Southwestern Oklahoma State University.
31. Will Hunt, lhp, Louisiana State University.
32. Roderick Jackson, rhp, Jackson State University.
33. Craig Tupper, c, Cal State Hayward.
34. Mike Wiseley, of, Eastern Michigan University.
35. *Matt Abernathy, of, Pensacola (Fla.) JC.
36. Kirk Ordway, 2b, Portland State University.
37. *Michael Goralczyk, lhp, Niles (Mich.) HS.
38. Gabe Sollecito, rhp, UCLA.
39. *David Malenfant, rhp, Kearsley HS, Flint, Mich.
40. Samuel Arguto, rhp, Jacksonville University.
41. Adam Rodriguez, c, Oklahoma City University.
42. Scott Conant, ss, Western Michigan University.
43. Michael Richardson, rhp, San Diego State University.
44. *Joel Hillebrand, rhp, Roosevelt HS, Wyandotte, Mich.
45. Brandon Reed, rhp, West HS, Lapeer, Mich.
46. *Brian Rios, ss, Riverside (Calif.) CC.
47. Tyrone Dixon, of, University of South Alabama.
48. +Justin Bettencourt, lhp, Cabrillo (Calif.) JC.
49. *Anthony Jackson, of, Louisburg (N.C.) JC.
50. *Brian Wilkes, c, Bishop Kenny HS, Jacksonville, Fla.
51. *Michael Martino, rhp, Grand Blanc (Mich.) HS.
52. *Rich Hartmann, rhp, Long Island University.
53. Gary Goldsmith, rhp, New Mexico State University.
54. *Kiko Palacios, c, Southwestern (Calif.) JC.
55. *Chip Wade, c, Escambia HS, Pensacola, Fla.
56. *Brad Lee, lhp, Delaware Tech & CC.
57. +Jeffrey Barker, rhp, Riverside (Calif.) CC.
58. *Anthony Williams, rhp, Fort Walton Beach (Fla.) HS.
59. Robby Welles, 1b, Pepperdine University.
**60. Graham Koonce, of, Julian (Calif.) HS.—(2003)**
61. *Carlton Washington, of, University of Texas-El Paso.
62. *Nathan Smith, ss-of, Bonanza HS, Las Vegas, Nev.
63. *Adam Finnieston, of, Gulf Coast (Fla.) CC.
64. *Justin Duckwiler, c, Bonanza HS, Las Vegas, Nev.
65. *Terry Tripp, ss, Harrisburg (Ill.) HS.

## FLORIDA MARLINS (27)

**1. Marc Valdes, rhp, University of Florida.—(1995-2001)**
**2. John Roskos, c, Cibola HS, Rio Rancho, N.M.—(1998-2000)**
3. Dan Ehler, rhp, South Hills HS, Covina, Calif.—(High A)
4. Thomas Howard, lhp, Titusville (Fla.) HS.—(AA)
5. Ernie Delgado, rhp, Sunnyside HS, Tucson, Ariz.—(AAA)
6. Paul Thornton, rhp, Georgia Southern University.
**7. Todd Dunwoody, of, Harrison HS, West Lafayette, Ind.—(1997-2002)**
**8. Billy McMillon, of, Clemson University.—(1996-2004)**
9. Brady Babin, ss, St. Amant HS, Gonzales, La.
10. Ryan Filbeck, rhp, Rancho Santiago (Calif.) JC.
11. Damon Johnson, 3b, Crossett (Ark.) HS.
12. *Jason Fawcett, rhp, Robert E. Lee HS, Montgomery, Ala.
13. David Jefferson, of, Palo Alto (Calif.) HS.
14. Mike Sims, c, Cal State Northridge.
15. *Erik Robinson, of, West Orange HS, Winter Park, Fla.
16. Scott Southard, ss, University of South Alabama.
17. Don Matthews, rhp, Lower Columbia (Wash.) JC.
18. Tommy Giles, lhp, Thomas Jefferson HS, Carter Lake, Iowa.
19. Rich Seminoff, lhp, Grand Canyon University.
**20. Bryan Ward, lhp, University of South Carolina-Aiken.—(1998-2000)**
21. Greg Mix, rhp, Stanford University.
22. Dan Chergey, rhp, Cal Poly San Luis Obispo.
23. *Ivory Jones, of, Contra Costa (Calif.) JC.
24. Ronnie Brown, of, Mississippi State University.
25. *Richard Dishman, rhp, Archbishop Molloy HS, Jamaica, N.Y.
26. Matt Martinez, 2b, Cal State Sacramento.
27. Andy Small, 3b, Cal State Northridge.
28. *Tony Darden, ss, Northeast Texas CC.
29. Samuel Minyard, lhp, The Master's (Calif.) College.
30. +Justin Long, ss, Riverside (Calif.) CC / Chaffey (Calif.) JC.
31. *Justin Mark, rhp, Lassen (Calif.) JC.
32. *Matthew Wells, rhp, Quincy (Calif.) HS.
33. Zac Stark, lhp, David Lipscomb College.
34. Jeffrey Lewis, of, Dundalk (Md.) CC.
35. Eric Genden, of, Taravella HS, Coral Springs, Fla.
36. *Brett Ames, lhp, Pima (Ariz.) CC.
**37. *Brandon Villafuerte, rhp, Live Oak HS, Morgan Hill, Calif.—(2000-04)**
**38. Dave Berg, 2b, University of Miami.—(1998-2004)**
39. +James Merritt, rhp, South Georgia JC.
40. *Derrick Johnson, of, Ewing HS, Trenton, N.J.
41. *Eric Sees, ss, Santa Margarita HS, San Juan Capistrano, Calif.
42. *Chad Phillips, thp, Clemson University.
43. *Ian Roberts, of, Mountain View HS, Vancouver, Wash.
44. Greg Hubley, of, JC of San Mateo (Calif.).
**45. *Bobby Howry, rhp, Yavapai (Ariz.) JC.—(1998-2010)**
46. Jon Van Zandt, rhp, UCLA.
47. (void) *Rafael Corrales, rhp, Niles West HS, Skokie, Ill.
48. *Josh Deakman, rhp, Riverside (Calif.) CC.
49. *Michael Reyes, of, Wayland Baptist (Texas) University.
50. +Mark Creelman, 1b, Ulster (N.Y.) CC.
51. *Leslie Sean, lhp, Mendocino (Calif.) CC.
52. *Ward White, 1b, Proctor Hug HS, Reno, Nev.
53. *Jason Russell, rhp, Chattahoochee Valley (Ala.) CC.
54. *Charles Bivens, of, Taft (Calif.) JC.
55. *Diallo Banks, rhp, West Point (Miss.) HS.
56. *David Harper, rhp, Mansfield (Texas) HS.
57. *Michael Myers, c, Gaithersburg (Md.) HS.
58. *Marc Lee, of, Calvert HS, Tiffin, Ohio.
59. *Chad Ricketts, rhp, East Lake HS, Palm Harbor, Fla.
60. *Daniel Sousa, of, Mendocino (Calif.) CC.
61. *Michael Rios, rhp, University of the Pacific.

62. *Casey Baker, of, McLane HS, Fresno, Calif.
63. *Chris Sauritch, ss, Southern Illinois University.
64. *Robert Cowan, rhp, Saugus (Calif.) HS.
65. *Jamie Gann, rhp, Norman (Okla.) HS.
66. *Todd Teeter, c, West Orange HS, Winter Park, Fla.
67. *Chris Hendrix, c, Oakland HS, Murfreesboro, Tenn.
68. *Tony Longueira, ss, Cooper City (Fla.) HS.
**69. *Larry Barnes, 1b, Bakersfield (Calif.) JC.—(2001-03)**
70. Casey Deskins, lhp, University of Nebraska.
71. *Cameron Jones, ss, Millwood HS, Oklahoma City, Okla.
72. Franklin Roberts, rhp, Seaford (Del.) HS.
73. *Brent Yarrow, of, Chemainus (B.C.) HS.
74. *Brian Reid, 2b, Corona del Sol HS, Phoenix.
75. *Eric Johnson, of, South Georgia JC.
76. *David Bernhard, rhp, Monterey Peninsula (Calif.) JC.
77. *Kenny Williams, of, Independence HS, San Jose, Calif.
78. *Allen Stalvey, of, Columbia HS, Lake City, Fla.
79. *Charles Roberson, rhp, Franklin HS, Seattle.
80. *Dustin Spencer, ss, Santa Barbara (Calif.) HS.
81. *Michael Logan, rhp, Dougherty HS, Albany, Ga.
82. *Richard Bell, rhp, Crater HS, Central Point, Ore.
83. *John Woodard, rhp, Cartersville (Ga.) HS.
84. *Theron Truitt, of, LaGrange (Ga.) HS.
85. *Jerry Whaley, c, McIntosh County Academy, Darien, Ga.
86. *Stephen Haggard, rhp, Southern Arkansas University.
87. *Jason Mann, rhp, First Colonial HS, Virginia Beach, Va.
88. *Cabott Woods, rhp, Princeton (Ind.) Community HS.
89. *Jason Dyer, of, Shawnee (Okla.) HS.
90. *Tom Buckman, rhp, Broward (Fla.) CC.
91. *Shawn Summers, of, University of Tennessee.

## HOUSTON ASTROS (12)

**1. Billy Wagner, lhp, Ferrum (Va.) College.—(1995-2010)**
2. (Choice to Pirates as compensation for Type A free agent Doug Drabek)
3. (Choice to Reds as compensation for Type A free agent Greg Swindell)
4. Steve Verduzco, ss, San Jose, Calif.—(AA)
5. Derek Root, 1b, St. Edward HS, Lakewood, Ohio.—(AAA)
6. Jamie Saylor, ss, North Garland HS, Garland, Texas.
**7. *Jaime Bluma, rhp, Wichita State University.—(1996)**
8. Mike Diorio, rhp, Seward County (Kan.) CC.
9. Brett Callan, c, San Diego Mesa JC.
10. Kary Bridges, 3b, University of Mississippi.
11. Eddie Lewis, rhp, Central Missouri State University.
12. Billy Hartnett, rhp, Northeastern University.
13. *Rolo Avila, of, Los Angeles Harbor JC.
14. Tim Forkner, 3b, Seward County (Kan.) CC.
15. Troy Schulte, rhp, Creighton University.
16. Grant Gosch, of, Serra HS, San Mateo, Calif.
17. Mark Dorencz, ss, Illinois State University.
18. Tim Kester, rhp, Florida International University.
19. Jon Phillips, lhp, St. Bonaventure University.
20. John Vindivich, of, Southeastern Louisiana University.
21. Jason Turley, rhp, Brighton HS, Sandy, Utah.
22. *Jay Vaught, rhp, University of Texas.
23. *Landon Hessler, rhp, Brooksville-Hernando HS, Brooksville, Fla.
24. *Jon Cannon, lhp, Gunn HS, Los Altos, Calif.
25. Michael Walter, rhp, Palomar (Calif.) JC.
26. Tom Czanstkowski, rhp, University of Arkansas.
27. Trevor Froschauer, 1b-c, Lincoln Land (Ill.) CC.
28. Klint Klaas, 2b, Iowa Western CC.
29. *Steven Keen, rhp, Baldwin (Fla.) HS.
**30. +Jason Green, rhp, Port Hope & District HS, Port Hope, Ontario / Chipola (Fla.) JC.—(2000)**
31. Brock Steinke, rhp, Washington HS, Cedar Rapids, Iowa.
32. *Duane Eason, rhp, Hackensack (N.J.) HS.
33. Ted Wieczorek, 1b-3b, Southern California College.
34. *Joseph Painich, rhp, West Monroe (La.) HS.
35. *Jerry Brandon, 2b, Airline HS, Bossier City, La.
36. *Ryan Kelly, rhp, Amarillo (Texas) HS.
37. *Rafael Corrales, rhp, Niles West HS, Skokie, Ill.
38. +Joshua Halemanu, of, Mission (Calif.) JC.
39. Daniel Dolney, c, New Trier HS, Wilmette, Ill.
40. *Todd Cook, rhp, Tavares (Fla.) HS.
41. *Jonathan Lawrence, ss-2b, Columbus (Ga.) HS.
42. Terry Beyna, 3b, Illinois State University.
43. *Anthony Mack, of, Los Angeles Harbor JC.
**44. Bryant Nelson, ss, Texarkana (Texas) JC.—(2002)**
45. *Ryan O'Toole, rhp, Irvine (Calif.) HS.
46. *Mike Bustamonte, lhp, Eisenhower HS, Rialto, Calif.
47. *Chris Bowker, rhp, Dillon (Mon.) HS.
48. *Jeremy Miller, ss, Connelsville HS, Mill Run, Pa.
49. *James Sapp, of, Geneva (N.Y.) HS.
50. Ryan Campbell, rhp, Hoover HS, Fresno, Calif.
51. *Paul Powell, lhp, Denison (Texas) HS.
52. *Nassim Hijazi, lhp, Downey HS, Bellflower, Calif.
53. Scott Eidle, of, Yale University.
54. *Patrick Bell, rhp, Asheboro (N.C.) HS.
55. Shawn Bartle, rhp, McLennan (Texas) CC.
56. Chad White, of, University of Maine.
57. Richard Humphrey, rhp, Liberty University.
58. Yamil Lopez, ss, Puerto Nuevo, P.R.
59. Chad Crossley, rhp, University of South Florida.
60. *Pat Maxwell, c, Cherry Creek HS, Englewood, Colo.
61. *Dwayne Crawley, of-lhp, Prince George's (Md.) CC
62. *Eric Plooy, rhp, Hanford (Calif.) HS.
63. *Michael Myro, rhp, West Torrance HS, Torrance, Calif.
64. +Jeffrey Hook, rhp, Ventura (Calif.) JC.
65. *Trey Poland, lhp, Southwood HS, Shreveport, La.
66. *Carl Franzten, c, Fredericksburg (Texas) HS.
67. *Leo Nunez, ss, Fresno (Calif.) CC.
68. *Shaw Casey, ss-3b, Green Valley HS, Henderson, Nev.
69. *Colland Felts, c, Brighton HS, Sandy, Utah.
70. *Robert Slomkowski, rhp, Rutherford (N.J.) HS.
71. *Jermaine Timberlake, 2b, Louisa County HS, Louisa, Va.
72. *Anthony Sciola, c, Bullard HS, Fresno, Calif.
73. *Aaron Martin, lhp, Angelina (Texas) JC.
74. *Kiwane Garris, of, Westinghouse HS, Chicago.
75. *Jack Jones, ss, Downey HS, Modesto, Calif.
76. *Anthony Peters, c, Cardinal HS, Middlefield, Ohio.
77. *Aaron Baker, rhp, Bellmont HS, Decatur, Ind.
78. *Raphael Baro, lhp, LaSalle HS, Miami.
79. +John Anderson, rhp, Chaffey (Calif.) JC.
80. *Raul Plasencia, rhp, Jordan HS, Long Beach, Calif.
81. *Chad Pittman, of, Haltom City (Texas) HS.
82. *Kelvin Parker, of, Montgomery (Md.) JC.
83. *Jason Meier, of, Bluevale HS, Waterloo, Ontario.

## KANSAS CITY ROYALS (5)

**1. Jeff Granger, lhp, Texas A&M University.—(1993-97)**
2. (Choice to Blue Jays as compensation for Type A free agent David Cone)
3. (Choice to Twins as compensation for Type A free agent Greg Gagne)
4. Phil Grundy, rhp, Western Carolina University.—(AAA)
5. Phil Brassington, rhp, Lamar University.—(Short-season A)
6. Tyrone Frazier, of-ss, Woodlawn HS, Shreveport, La.
7. Pat Flury, rhp, JC of Southern Idaho.
8. O.J. Rhone, of, Central Missouri State University.
9. *Chad Green, of, Mentor (Ohio) HS.

DRAFT DROP *First-round draft pick (8th overall), Brewers (1996)*

10. *Tom Buchman, c, Shawnee Mission South HS, Lenexa, Kan.
11. Larry Smith, of, Broomfield (Colo.) HS.
12. Kevin Rawitzer, lhp, Arizona State University.
13. Malcolm Cepeda, 1b, Solano (Calif.) CC.

DRAFT DROP *Son of Orlando Cepeda, major leaguer (1958-74)*

14. Braxton Hickman, 1b, University of Texas.
15. Bill Dunn, 2b, Arizona State University.
16. Dustin Brixey, rhp, Northeastern Oklahoma A&M JC.
**17. Glendon Rusch, lhp, Shorecrest HS, Seattle.—(1997-2009)**
**18. Ken Ray, rhp, Roswell (Ga.) HS.—(1999)**
19. Jimmie Byington, of, Seminole (Okla.) JC.
20. Eric Anderson, rhp, Blue Springs (Mo.) HS.
21. Kris Ralston, rhp, Central Missouri State University.
22. Michael Evans, c-of, Lubbock Christian (Texas) College.
23. Jeremy Carr, 2b, Cal State Fullerton.
24. Nevin Brewer, rhp, Southeastern (N.C.) CC.
25. Leonard Weathersby, of, Hamilton HS, Los Angeles.
26. Luke Oglesby, of-2b, University of New Mexico.
27. Jason Huffman, rhp, Southeastern (N.C.) CC.
28. *Gadiel Medero, rhp, Medardo Carazo HS, Trujillo Alto, P.R.
29. Justin McCoy, c, Bingham HS, South Jordan, Utah.
30. Lino Diaz, 3b, University of Nevada-Las Vegas.
**31. *Jacque Jones, of, San Diego (Calif.) HS.—(1999-2008)**
32. Toby Smith, 1b-rhp, Wichita State University.
33. *Brian Meyers, rhp, George Fox (Ore.) College.
34. Stephen Wojtkowski, 3b, Montgomery (Md.) JC.
35. Neil Atkinson, lhp, St. Mary's (Texas) University.
36. Jeff Ramos, c, Power-St. Joseph's HS, Toronto.
**37. Sal Fasano, c, University of Evansville.—(1996-2008)**
38. Daron Dondero, ss, Mount San Jacinto (Calif.) JC.
39. *Derek Dubois, lhp, Fort William Collegiate HS, Murillo, Ontario.
40. *Ryan Stover, 1b, Winter Haven (Fla.) HS.
41. Matt Aminoff, rhp, George Washington University.
42. Cody Kosman, rhp, University of Nevada-Reno.
43. *Frank Stewart, of, Julian (Calif.) HS.
44. *Thornton Davis, 3b, Liberty County HS, Bristol, Fla.
45. +Donnie Delaney, of, Bossier Parish (La.) CC.
46. *Jeff Terrell, ss, Tri-City Christian HS, Blue Springs, Mo.

DRAFT DROP *Son of Jerry Terrell, major leaguer (1973-80)*

47. *Ricardo Calderon, 1b, Inter American HS, Carolina, P.R.
48. *Howard Rosenberry, lhp, Hagerstown (Md.) JC.
49. *Montrell Pride, 1b, Oak Ridge HS, Orlando, Fla.
50. *Brian Paluk, rhp, Catholic Central HS, Plymouth, Mich.
51. *Jess Utecht, of, Kamiakin HS, Richland, Wash.
52. +Will Roland, 3b, Galveston (Texas) JC.
53. *Toussaint Waterman, of, Country Day HS, Pontiac, Mich.
54. *Patrick Johnson, c, Taylorsville HS, Salt Lake City.
55. *Jeff Peck, lhp, Ryan HS, Denton, Texas.
56. *Jason Hueth, rhp, Norte Vista HS, Riverside, Calif.
57. *David Trentine, rhp, Foothill HS, Santa Ana, Calif.
58. *Christopher Jackson, of, Brownsboro HS, Chandler, Texas
59. *Sal McCullough, Muir HS, Pasadena, Calif.
60. *Bubba Dixon, lhp, Seminole (Okla.) JC.
61. *Mike Klostermeyer, 1b, Seminole (Okla.) JC.
62. *Tremain Mack, of, Chapel Hill HS, Tyler, Texas.

DRAFT DROP *Defensive back, National Football League (1997-2000)*

63. *Andrew Bernard, rhp, Highland HS, Bakersfield, Calif.
64. *Anthony Barrett, rhp, Athens (Texas) HS.
65. *Jeff Phipps, rhp, Palo Verde Valley HS, Blythe, Calif.
66. *Scott Seal, of, Irvine (Calif.) HS.
67. *Gordon Hegeman, 2b, Bakersfield (Calif.) JC.

## LOS ANGELES DODGERS (2)

**1. Darren Dreifort, rhp, Wichita State University.—(1994-2004)**
2. (Choice to Cardinals as compensation tor Type B free agent Todd Worrell)
3. Dax Winslett, rhp, Arizona State University.—(AA)
**4. Nathan Bland, lhp, Mountain Brook (Ala.) HS.—(2003)**
5. Scott Hunter, c-of, Northeast HS, Philadelphia.—(AAA)
6. *Nate Yeskie, rhp, Carson HS, Carson City, Nev.
7. Doug Newstrom, 1b, Arizona State University.
8. Jose Prado, rhp, University of Miami.
9. Matt Schwenke, c, UCLA.
10. John Vukson, rhp-3b, Sanger HS, Fresno, Calif.
11. Josh Rash, of, Lamar HS, Arlington, Texas.
12. Craig Scheffler, lhp, University of Wisconsin-Milwaukee.
13. Brian Rolocut, rhp, Miami-Dade CC Wolfson.
14. Brett Binkley, lhp, Georgia Tech.
15. David Steed, c, Meridian (Miss.) CC.
16. Dan Hubbs, rhp, University of Southern California.

DRAFT DROP *Baseball coach, Southern California (2013-15)*

17. Mike Biltimier, 1b, Purdue University.
18. Joe LaGarde, rhp, East Forsyth HS, Winston-Salem, N.C.
19. Eric Maloney, rhp, Creighton University.
20. Michael Kinney, of, Texas Tech.
**21. *Mark Watson, lhp, Marist HS, Atlanta.—(2000-03)**
22. *Charlie Nelson, of, University of Minnesota.
23. Eddie Davis, of, Long Beach State University.
24. Carl South, rhp, Marist HS, Atlanta.
**25. Paul LoDuca, c, Arizona State University.—(1998-2008)**
26. *Corey Coggburn, of, Ada (Okla.) HS.
27. +Bryan Coyle, rhp, Hudson's Bay HS, Vancouver, Wash. / Lower Columbia (Wash.) JC.
28. *Jeffrey Astgen, 2b, El Camino Real HS, Canoga Park, Calif.
29. *Anthony Cellars, of, Texas HS, Texarkana, Texas.
30. *Adrian Black, of, North Brunswick HS, Leland, N.C.
**31. *Doug Davis, lhp, North Gate HS, Pleasant Hill, Calif.—(1999-2011)**
**32. *Jordan Zimmerman, lhp, Brenham (Texas) HS.—(1999)**

DRAFT DROP *Brother of Jeff Zimmerman, major leaguer (1999-2001)*

33. *Raul Correa, rhp, Carmen Belen Viega HS, Juana Diaz, P.R.
34. *Dwayne McCray, of, Sumter (S.C.) HS.
35. *Tracy Johnson, of, Deer Valley HS, Phoenix.
**36. *Matt Wagner, rhp, Iowa State University.—(1996)**
37. *Richard Shaw, rhp, Sandwich HS, LaSalle, Ontario.
38. *Mark Manbeck, rhp, Round Rock (Texas) HS.
39. *David Propst, of, West Charlotte HS, Charlotte, N.C.
40. *Dion Rhodes, of, Hudson's Bay HS, Vancouver, Wash.
41. *Eric Yanz, rhp, Arvada West HS, Golden, Colo.
42. Bruce Yard, ss, Indiana (Pa.) University.
43. *Thomas Cody, c, Fort Vancouver HS, Vancouver, Wash.
44. *Bruce Piddington, rhp, Southwestern HS, Hazel Green, Wis.
45. *Ben Padilla, ss, Carson (Calif.) HS.
46. *Gustavo Rubio, 1b-c, Leuzinger HS, Lawndale, Calif.
47. *Jason Smith, rhp, Meridian (Miss.) CC.
48. *Jeff Falardeau, lhp, Notre Dame HS, Welland, Ontario.
49. Julio Colon, rhp, Long Beach State University.
50. *Richard Condon, 2b, Crossroads HS, Culver City, Calif.
51. *Kendall Hill, rhp, Escambia HS, Pensacola, Fla.
52. Nathan Rasmussen, 1b, Lakeville (Minn.) HS.
53. *Victor Sobieraj, rhp, Catholic Central HS, Windsor, Ontario.
54. *David Wease, 1b, Chesnee HS, Gaffney, S.C.
55. *Jaymie Bane, lhp, Paradise Valley HS, Phoenix.

DRAFT DROP *Son of Eddie Bane, first-round draft pick, Twins (1973); major leaguer (1973-76)*

56. *Steve Huls, ss, Rocori HS, Cold Spring, Minn.
57. Brian Carpenter, rhp, University of Texas.
58. *Matthew Powell, rhp, Miami-Dade CC Wolfson.

## MILWAUKEE BREWERS (23)

**1. Jeff C. D'Amico, rhp, Northeast HS, St. Petersburg, Fla.—(1996-2004)**
**1. Kelly Wunsch, lhp, Texas A&M University** (Choice from Blue Jays as compensation for Type A free agent Paul Molitor).**—(2000-05)**

1. **Todd Dunn, of, University of North Florida** (Supplemental choice—35th—as compensation for Type A free agent Chris Bosio).**—(1996-97)**
1. Joe Wagner, rhp, University of Central Florida (Supplemental choice—39th—as compensation for Molitor).—(AA)
2. **Brian Banks, c-of, Brigham Young University** (Choice from Mariners as compensation for Bosio).**—(1996-2003)**
2. **Danny Klassen, ss, John Carroll HS, Port St. Lucie, Fla.—(1998-2003)**
3. George Preston, rhp, Brenham (Texas) HS.—(Low A)
4. Shane Sheldon, rhp, Gordon (Ga.) JC.—(Rookie)
5. Steve Duda, rhp, Pepperdine University.—(AA)
6. Josh Zwisler, c, St. Vincent-St. Mary HS, Akron, Ohio.
7. **Mark Loretta, ss, Northwestern University.—(1995-2009)**
8. Tano Tijerina, rhp, Navarro (Texas) JC.
9. Jon Hillis, rhp, Rice University.
10. Chris McInnes, ss, Ricks (Idaho) JC.
11. *Chris Junghans, c, McDonough HS, Waldorf, Md.
12. *Brian Blessie, rhp, Burke HS, Omaha.
13. +Brian Luna, 1b, Craigmont HS, Memphis, Tenn. / Shelby State (Tenn.) CC.
14. Peter Benny, rhp, Wooster HS, Carson City, Nev.
15. Scott Perkins, rhp, University of Southwestern Louisiana.
16. *Jim Wallace, rhp, Kellenberg Memorial HS, Wantagh, N.Y.
17. Chad Kopitzke, rhp, University of Wisconsin-Oshkosh.
18. Gabriel Mercado, rhp, Indian Hills (Iowa) CC.
19. **Sean Maloney, rhp, Georgetown University.—(1997-98)**
20. Pedro Fuertes, 3b, Academia San Jorge, Carolina, P.R.
21. Chris Schmitt, lhp, University of West Florida.
22. *Ricky Gutierrez, 2b, University of Oklahoma.
23. *Ron Wallech, rhp, Hagerstown (Md.) JC.
24. **Greg Martinez, of, Barstow (Calif.) JC.—(1998)**
25. Jarod Fryman, 3b, Jefferson Davis (Ala.) JC.
26. Allen Mealing, of, Strom Thurmond HS, Edgefield, S.C.
27. James Cole, rhp, Mercer University.
28. Matt Murphy, lhp, University of Vermont.
29. *Todd Cutchins, lhp, Westlake (La.) HS.
30. Chris Carter, c, Clemson University.
31. Todd Landry, 1b, University of Arizona.
32. *Jay Reames, rhp, Seneca (S.C.) HS.

DRAFT DROP *Brother of Britt Reames, major leaguer (2000-06)*

33. Jim Hodge, of, Mercer County (N.J.) CC.
34. *Michael Kimbrell, lhp, Jefferson Davis (Ala.) CC.
35. *Mark Wasikowski, 3b, Pepperdine University.
36. Clayton Hill, of, McLennan (Texas) JC.
37. *Julio Ayala, lhp, Academia Monanita HS, Guaynabo, P.R.
38. *Jamie Bass, 2b, Pine Bluff (Ark.) HS.
39. *Brian Conley, ss, Glen Este HS, Cincinnati.
40. *Ronald Fawley, c-of, Santaluces HS, Lantana, Fla.
41. *Chris Ciaccio, rhp, University of Georgia.
42. *Lorne Rosas, of, Hilo (Hawaii) HS.
43. *Peter Jenkins, c, Redlands (Calif.) HS.
44. *John Cromwell, rhp, Lake Howell HS, Winter Park, Fla.
45. Jose Calderon, rhp, Gabriela Mistral HS, San Juan, P.R.
46. *Mandy Jacomino, c, Westminster Christian HS, Miami.
47. *Joseph Wails, rhp, La Sierra HS, Hesperia, Calif.
48. Eduardo Acosta, ss-of, Muscatine (Iowa) CC.
49. *Jason Greuel, rhp, South HS, Waukesha, Wis.
50. *Kerry Mikulski, of, Pope John Paul HS, Boca Raton, Fla.
51. Miguel Villaran, ss, Miguel Such HS, Loiza, P.R.
52. Francisco Garcia, c, Pedro Albizo Campos HS, Lewistown, P.R.
53. *Daniel Jordan, ss, Thomasville (Ga.) HS.
54. *Ken Wagner, rhp, Palm Beach (Fla.) JC.
55. *Anthony Pavlovich, rhp, Thomasville HS, Pavo, Ga.
56. ***Bret Hemphill, c, Cal State Fullerton.—(1999)**
57. *Michael Ribaudo, of, Sarasota (Fla.) HS.
58. *Marty Bourgon, c, Central Florida CC.
59. *Charlie Ward, ss-of, Florida State University.

DRAFT DROP *Heisman Trophy winner (1993) • First-round draft pick, New York Knicks, National Basketball Association (1994); guard, NBA (1994-2005)*

60. *Cameron Andrews, 1b, Milton (Fla.) HS.
61. *Brian Scutero, rhp, Valencia (Fla.) CC.

## MINNESOTA TWINS (21)

1. **Torii Hunter, of, Pine Bluff (Ark.) HS** (Choice from Reds as compensation for Type A free agent John Smiley).**—(1997-2015)**
1. ***Jason Varitek, c, Georgia Tech.—(1997-2011)**

DRAFT DROP *Returned to Georgia Tech; re-drafted by Mariners, 1994 (1st round)*

1. Marc Barcelo, rhp, Arizona State University (Supplemental choice—33rd—as compensation for Smiley).—(AAA)
1. Kelcey Mucker, of, Lawrenceburg (Ind.) HS (Supplemental choice--38th—as compensation for Type A free agent Greg Gagne).—(AA)
2. **Dan Perkins, rhp, Westminster Christian HS, Miami.—(1999)**
3. Troy Carrasco, lhp, Jesuit HS, Tampa (Choice from Royals as compensation for Gagne).—(AA)
3. **Javier Valentin, 3b, Fernando Callejo HS, Manati, P.R.—(1997-2008)**

DRAFT DROP *Brother of Jose Valentin, major leaguer (1992-2007)*

4. *Toby Dollar, rhp, Graham (Texas) HS.—(AAA)

DRAFT DROP *Attended Texas Christian; re-drafted by Dodgers, 1996 (29th round)*

5. *Jesse Ibarra, 1b, Loyola Marymount University.—(AAA)

DRAFT DROP *Returned to Loyola Marymount; re-drafted by Giants, 1994 (6th round)*

6. **Benj Sampson, lhp, Ankeny (Iowa) HS.—(1998-99)**
7. ***Kelly Dransfeldt, ss, Morris (Ill.) HS.—(1999-2004)**
8. Ryan Lane, ss, Bellefontaine (Ohio) HS.
9. **Kevin Ohme, lhp, University of North Florida.—(2003)**
10. *Mark Merila, 2b, University of Minnesota.
11. Troy Fortin, c, Lundar (Manitoba) HS.
12. ***Alex Cora, ss, Colegio Bautista, Caguas, P.R.—(1998-2011)**

DRAFT DROP *Brother of Joey Cora, first-round draft pick, Padres (1985); major leaguer (1987-98)*

13. +Pete Forster, lhp, Oak Park HS, Kansas City, Mo.
14. **Ryan Radmanovich, of, Pepperdine University.—(1998)**
15. *Mike Torti, ss, Newman Smith HS, Carrollton, Texas.
16. *Wylie Campbell, ss, Southwest HS, Fort Worth, Texas.
17. ***Danny Kolb, rhp, Walnut (Ill.) HS.—(1999-2007)**
18. *L.J. Yankosky, rhp, West Springfield HS, Springfield, Va.
19. *Chris Granata, rhp, Ohio State University.
20. Aaron Santini, ss, University of New Mexico.
21. **Shane Bowers, rhp, Loyola Marymount University.—(1997)**
22. **+Rob Radlosky, rhp, Central Florida CC.—(1999)**
23. Scott Stricklin, c, Kent State University.

DRAFT DROP *Baseball coach, Kent State (2005-13); baseball coach, Georgia (2014-15)*

24. *Rico Harris, of, Englewood HS, Jacksonville, Fla.
25. Brian O'Brien, lhp, Creighton University.
26. *Mauricio Estavil, lhp, Pepperdine University.
27. Russ Lehoisky, rhp, University of New Haven.
28. Mike Stadelhofer, rhp, Calistoga (Calif.) HS.
29. *Javier Encina, rhp, North Mesquite HS, Mesquite, Texas.
30. *Doug Rheaume, rhp, Santana HS, Lakeside, Calif.
31. Jacob Patterson, 1b, Neosho County (Kan.) CC.
32. *Andre Thompson, of, Wingfield HS, Jackson, Miss.
33. *Kenny Harrison, c, University of Hawaii.
34. Deron Dowhower, rhp, University of Virginia.

DRAFT DROP *Son of Rod Dowhower, head coach, Indianapolis Colts/National Football League (1985-86)*

35. James Motte, ss, University of Arizona.
36. Daniel Venezia, ss, Concordia (N.Y.) College.
37. ***Emil Brown, of, Harlan HS, Chicago.—(1997-2009)**
38. *Jason Ford, lhp, North Idaho JC.
39. *Stephen Watson, rhp, Westwood HS, Austin, Texas.
40. *Douglas Beddinger, rhp, Manatee (Fla.) JC.
41. *Jason Adge, rhp, Sacramento (Calif.) CC.
42. ***Lance Carter, rhp, Manatee HS, Bradenton, Fla.—(1999-2006)**
43. *Rob Landstad, of, Indian Hills (Iowa) CC.
44. Chad Rupp, 1b, University of Miami.
45. *Matt Freeman, c, Seminole (Fla.) HS.
46. Justin Tomberlin, 3b, University of Maine.

DRAFT DROP *10th-round draft pick, Toronto Maple Leafs/National Hockey League (1989)*

47. *Spencer McIntyre, lhp, Texas A&M University.
48. Eric Anderson, lhp, Parkland (Ill.) JC.
49. *Matthew Gondini, rhp, Green Valley HS, Henderson, Nev.
50. +Aaron Sellner, rhp, Naugatuck (Conn.) HS / CC of Morris (N.J.).
51. *Sandy Lopez, rhp, CC of Morris (N.J.).
52. Chris Phillips, 2b, Western Kentucky University.
53. *J.T. Messick, ss, Seminole (Okla.) JC.
54. *Anthony Lucca, lhp, South San Francisco (Calif.) HS.
55. *William Stone, lhp, Delight (Ark.) HS.
56. *Eddie Medlin, c, Billings (Mon.) HS.
57. *Andrew Burt, rhp, University of Wisconsin.
58. *Christopher Kilen, lhp, Janesville, Wis.
59. *Danny Peoples, 1b, Round Rock (Texas) HS.

DRAFT DROP *First-round draft pick (28th overall), Indians (1996)*

60. Aaron Schooler, rhp, Columbia Basin (Wash.) CC.

## MONTREAL EXPOS (18)

1. Chris Schwab, of, Cretin-Derham Hall, Eagan, Minn.—(AA)
1. Josue Estrada, of, Rio Piedras, P.R. (Supplemental choice—31st—as compensation for Type A free agent Spike Owen).—(Low A)
2. Martin Mainville, rhp, Ecole Pere Marquette HS, Montreal (Choice from Yankees as compensation for Owen).—(High A)
2. **Brad Fullmer, 3b, Montclair Prep HS, Chatsworth, Calif.—(1997-2004)**
3. Jason Baker, rhp, Robert E. Lee HS, Midland, Texas.—(AAA)
4. Ronnie Hall, of, Tustin (Calif.) HS.—(AA)
5. Nate Brown, lhp, University of California.—(High A)
6. Jeff Foster, 3b, University of Tennessee.
7. *Donnie Fowler, rhp, Spring (Texas) HS.
8. **Neil Weber, lhp, Cuesta (Calif.) CC.—(1998)**
9. **Jayson Durocher, rhp, Horizon HS, Scottsdale, Ariz.—(2002-03)**
10. **Trace Coquillette, of, Sacramento (Calif.) CC.—(1999-2000)**
11. *Richard Giannola, rhp, Boca Raton Community HS, Boca Raton, Fla.
12. Aaron Knieper, rhp, Central Michigan University.
13. Randy Culp, c, Ellison HS, Killeen, Texas.
14. Tom Schneider, lhp, Centenary College.
15. *Jason Bond, lhp, St. Mary's HS, Glendale, Ariz.
16. **+Troy Mattes, rhp, Riverview HS, Sarasota, Fla. / Miami-Dade CC South.—(2001)**
17. Angelo Thompson, of-1b, Shaw (N.C.) University.
18. *Ricardo Spears, of, University of California.
19. *Scott Needham, c, Bentonville (Ark.) HS.
20. *Kevin Nykoluk, c, Simi Valley (Calif.) HS.
21. *Darryl Monroe, of, University of Kansas.
22. *Peter Bezeredi, 1b, Seminole (Fla.) CC.
23. *Dirk Lewallen, 1b, Hesperia (Calif.) HS.
24. Matt Harrell, c, Duke University.
25. ***Donzell McDonald, of, Cherry Creek HS, Englewood, Colo.—(2001-02)**

DRAFT DROP *Brother of Darnell McDonald, first-round draft pick, Orioles (1997); major leaguer (2004-13)*

26. *Jason Romine, rhp, Omak (Wash) HS.
27. *Shane Gift, c, Gilbert (Ariz) HS.
28. *Stephan Neill, rhp, John Carroll HS, Port St. Lucie, Fla.
29. *Ryan Fisher, lhp, Unity HS, Milltown, Wis.
30. **+David Moraga, lhp, Armijo HS, Suisun City, Calif. / Sacramento (Calif.) CC.—(2000)**
31. Chris Grubb, of, Elizabethtown (Pa.) College.
32. *Daniel Albrecht, lhp, Butler County (Kan.) CC.
33. Brian Detwiler, c, William Paterson (N.J.) College.
34. Scott Quade, ss, Austin Peay State University.
35. *Jason Elmore, rhp, Louisburg (N.C.) JC.
36. *Robert Lentz, ss, Bloomingdale HS, Brandon, Fla.
37. *Shawn Lopez, rhp, Lewis-Clark State (Idaho) College.
38. +Chris Weidert, rhp, Butler County (Kan.) CC.
39. *Walter Owens, of, Odessa (Texas) JC.
40. *Nole Elizer, c, Cape Coral (Fla.) HS.
41. *Scott Kidd, ss, DeAnza (Calif.) JC.
42. *Steve Kokinda, ss, Cardinal Newman HS, Palm Beach, Fla.
43. *Shawn Painter, of, Beaconsfield (Quebec) HS.
44. Jeff Mitchell, rhp, Harvard University.
45. *Brett Rapozo, rhp, American River (Calif.) JC.
46. *John Portugal, rhp, Oceanside (Calif.) HS.
47. *Logan Miller, c, CC of Marin (Calif.).
48. *Richard Matteson, rhp, Diablo Valley (Calif.) JC.
49. *Orin Hirschkorn, rhp, Kerman (Calif.) HS.
50. *Brian Cummings, rhp, Iona Prep HS, East Chester, N.Y.
51. ***Mike Lincoln, rhp, Casa Roble HS, Orangevale, Calif.—(1999-2010)**
52. *Ryan Gause, ss, Temecula (Calif.) HS.
53. *Brian Downs, c, Don Lugo HS, Chino, Calif.
54. *Nason Beckett, c, Port Angeles (Wash.) HS.
55. *John O'Brien, of, Malvern HS, Chester, Pa.
56. *Jeffrey Howard, rhp, Spartanburg Methodist (S.C.) JC.
57. *Brett Lockwood, 3b, Mesa (Ariz.) CC.
58. Jason Woodring, rhp, Trinidad State (Colo.) JC.
59. Michael Leon, lhp, Western New Mexico University.
60. *Greg Morris, 3b, UC Davis.
61. Joseph Tosone, of, Dartmouth College.
62. *Adam Housley, rhp, Pepperdine University.

## NEW YORK METS (8)

1. Kirk Presley, rhp, Tupelo (Miss.) HS.—(Low A)
2. **Eric Ludwick, rhp, University of Nevada-Las Vegas.—(1996-99)**

DRAFT DROP *Brother of Ryan Ludwick, major leaguer (2002-15)*

3. **Mike Welch, rhp, University of Southern Maine.—(1998)**
4. ***Bill Koch, rhp, West Babylon (NY.) HS.—(1999-2004)**

DRAFT DROP *Attended Clemson; re-drafted by Blue Jays, 1996 (1st round)*

5. Fletcher Bates, of, New Hanover HS, Wilmington, N.C.—(AAA)
6. Matt Terrell, of, Western Michigan University.
7. Scott Adair, rhp, Norte Vista HS, Riverside, Calif.
8. Paul Petrulis, ss, Mississippi State University.
9. Joe Atwater, lhp, South Alamance HS, Graham, N.C.
10. Derek Sutton, lhp, Indian Hills (Iowa) CC.
11. *Jared Camp, rhp, East HS, Huntington, W.Va.
12. Ethan McEntire, lhp, Habersham Central HS, Cornelia, Ga.
13. *John Powell, rhp, Auburn University.
14. Jeff Cosman, rhp, University of Mississippi.
15. Rodney Mazion, of, University of Nevada-Las Vegas.
16. Paul Bowman, rhp, Garrett (Md.) CC.
17. Sean Kenny, rhp, Eastern Michigan University.
18. ***Jason Middlebrook, rhp Grass Lake (Mich.) HS.—(2001-03)**
19. ***Ryan Rupe, rhp, Northbrook HS, Houston.—(1999-2003)**
20. **Jarrod Patterson, 1b, Jefferson Davis (Ala.) JC.—(2001-03)**
21. *Billy Oliver, rhp-3b, Monte Vista HS, Cupertino, Calif.
22. Kevin Lewis, c, Florida Atlantic University.
23. David Zuniga, ss, San Jose State University.
24. Brian Mast, rhp, David Lipscomb College.
25. *Brandon Welch, of-1b, Butler County (Kan.) CC.
26. Thomas Wolff, rhp, Kellogg (Mich.) CC.
27. Robert Gontkosky, lhp, Rider College.

28. Tad Smith, 1b, Eastern Illinois University.
29. Scott Winterlee, c, University of Michigan.
**30. Benny Agbayani, of, Hawaii Pacific University.—(1998-2002)**
31. David Fellhauer, 1b, Gaither HS, Tampa.
32. *Burdette Greeny, rhp, Port Angeles (Wash.) HS.
33. Jesus Morales, ss, East Los Angeles JC.
34. Ross Ferrier, of, University of Waterloo (Ontario).
35. Gary Collum, of, Pace (N.Y.) University.
36. *Ken Harrell, c, Alamogordo (N.M.) HS.
37. *Joe Robinson, ss, Burlington (Iowa) HS.
38. *Carlos Morrison, of, Cimarron Memorial HS, Las Vegas.
39. *Keith Maxwell, of, Liberty County HS, Bristol, Fla.
40. +Santiago Sanchez, ss, Lodi (Calif.) HS / Cosumnes River (Calif.) JC.
41. +Barrett Short, rhp, Three Rivers (Mo.) CC.
42. *Michael Ruhmann, lhp, St. Louis CC-Meramec.
43. Brandon Newell, rhp, University of Washington.
**44. +Vance Wilson, c, Mesa (Ariz.) CC.—(1999-2006)**
45. Michael Johnson, 2b, Union (N.Y.) College.

## NEW YORK YANKEES (13)

1. Matt Drews, rhp, Sarasota (Fla.) HS.—(AAA)
DRAFT DROP *Grandson of Karl Drews, major leaguer (1947-54)*
2. (Choice to Expos as compensation for Type A free agent Spike Owen)
3. (Choice to Blue Jays as compensation for Type A free agent Jimmy Key)
4. Sloan Smith, of, Northwestern University.—(AA)
**5. Mike Jerzembeck, rhp, University of North Carolina.—(1998)**
6. Kurt Bierek, 1b, University of Southern California.
7. Jim Musselwhite, rhp, University of Georgia.
8. Rob Trimble, c-rhp, Texas A&M University.
9. Clint Whitworth, rhp, Oklahoma City University.
10. Derek Shumpert, of, Aquinas-Mercy HS, St. Louis.
11. Jason Rathbun, rhp, Baylor University.
12. Anthony Shelby, lhp, Triton (Ill.) JC.
13. Shawn Alazaus, lhp, Mount Vernon Nazarene (Ohio) College.
14. Jim Palmer, 3b, St. Thomas Aquinas HS, Fort Lauderdale, Fla.
15. Greg Resz, rhp, Southwest Missouri State University.
16. *Brannon Peters, lhp, Texarkana (Texas) JC.
**17. Frank Lankford, rhp, University of Virginia.—(1998)**
18. Joe Wharton, rhp, Baylor University.
19. *Terry Harvey, rhp, North Carolina State University.
20. Casey Mittauer, rhp, Florida International University.
21. *Andrew Remala, ss, El Dorado HS, Placentia, Calif.
22. Mike Schmitz, 1b-of, Florida State University.
23. *Jason Dietrich, rhp, Rancho Santiago (Calif.) JC.
24. Scott Standish, rhp, Bellevue (Neb.) College.
**25. *Chad Moeller, c, Upland (Calif.) HS.—(2000-10)**
26. Kent Donnelly, rhp, University of Southern California.
27. *Jason Clark, 1b, Poly HS, Riverside, Calif.
28. *Chris Druckrey, rhp, Kankakee HS, St. Anne, Ill.
29. +Frisco Parotte, rhp, Pedro Albizu Campos HS, Toa Baja, P.R. / Miami-Dade CC New World Center.
30. *Jay Evans, lhp, Indian River (Fla.) CC.
31. *Jason Smithberger, rhp, Watkins Mill HS, Gaithersburg, Md.
32. *Craig Dour, ss, Tarpon Springs HS, Palm Harbor Fla.
33. *Jarred McAlvain, 1b, Stigler (Okla.) HS.
34. *Tom Bernhardt, of, Columbus HS, Miami.
35. +Jim Kerr, ss, Coral Springs (Fla.) HS / Indian River (Fla.) CC.
**36. +Craig Dingman, rhp, Hutchinson (Kan.) CC.—(2000-05)**
37. *Matthew Aden, of, Northwest HS, Omaha, Neb.
38. Jason Berry, rhp, Miami-Dade CC Wolfson.
39. *Cade Gaspar, rhp, Saddleback (Calif.) CC.
DRAFT DROP *First-round draft pick (18th overall), Tigers (1994) • Son of Rod Gaspar, major leaguer (1969-74)*
40. *Joe Victery, rhp, Ninnekah (Okla.) HS.
41. *Eric Knutson, ss-2b, Benson HS, Omaha, Neb.
42. +Brett Schlomann, rhp, Owasso HS, Collinsville, Okla. / Seminole (Okla.) JC.
43. *Dietrich Johnson, of, South Dorchester HS, Cambridge, Md.
**44. *Eddie Yarnall, lhp, St. Thomas Aquinas HS, Fort Lauderdale, Fla.—(1999-2000)**
45. +Dale Brandt, lhp, Indian River (Fla.) CC.
46. *John Strasser, ss, Greenway HS, Glendale, Ariz.
47. *Shawne Ware, of, Sacramento (Calif.) CC.
48. *Phil Haigler, rhp, Faulkner Stale (Ala.) JC.
49. *Brandon Marsters, c, Sarasota (Fla.) HS.
50. *Javier Flores, c, Christopher Columbus HS, Miami.
51. *Roy Reis, c, Diman Vocational Tech HS, Fall River, Mass.
52. *Oliver Harwas, rhp, Okeechobee (Fla.) HS.
53. *Brent Southall, 1b-of, Manatee (Fla.) JC.
54. *Isreal Barnes, rhp, King HS, Tampa.
55. *Michael Massey, c, Indian River (Fla.) CC.
56. *Greg Smitherman, of, Hartshorne (Okla.) HS.
57. *Chris Wright, c, West Jones HS, Laurel, Miss.
58. *Ken Shelly, ss, Ely HS, Pompano Beach, Fla.
59. *Chris Dickerson, ss, Alvin (Texas) HS.
60. *Wyley Steelmon, c, Enid (Okla.) HS.
61. *Chris Halliday, c, Evans HS, Martinez, Ga.
62. *Nolan Lofgren, c, East HS, Rockford, Ill.
63. *Scott Carley, rhp, Crescent City HS, Milford, Ill.
64. *Matt Dornfeld, of, Harding HS, St. Paul, Minn.

**Astros first-rounder Billy Wagner emerged from a small college into a standout closer**

## OAKLAND ATHLETICS (25)

**1. John Wasdin, rhp, Florida State University.—(1995-2007)**
**1. Willie Adams, rhp, Stanford University** (Supplemental choice—36th—as compensation for Type A free agent Dave Stewart).—**(1996-97)**
**2. Jeff M. D'Amico, ss-rhp, Redmond (Wash.) HS.—(2000)**
2. Mike Moschetti, ss, La Mirada (Calif.) HS (Choice from Blue Jays as compensation for Stewart).—(High A)
3. *Tucker Barr, c, Maclay HS, Tallahassee, Fla.—(AA)
DRAFT DROP *Attended Georgia Tech; re-drafted by Astros, 1996 (5th round)*
**4. Jason McDonald, ss, University of Houston.—(1997-2000)**
5. Andy Smith, rhp, A.L. Brown HS, Kannapolis, N.C.—(AA)
**6. Scott Spiezio, 1b, University of Illinois.—(1996-2007)**
DRAFT DROP *Son of Ed Spiezio, major leaguer (1964-72)*
**7. Tim Kubinski, lhp, UCLA.—(1997-99)**
8. Leon Hamburg, of, Casa Roble HS, Orangevale, Calif.
9. Damon Newman, rhp, Fullerton (Calif.) JC.
10. *John Phillips, rhp, Bullard HS, Fresno, Calif.
11. Jason Rajotte, lhp, University of Maine.
**12. Chris Michalak, lhp, University of Notre Dame.—(1998-2006)**
13. Scott Baldwin, lhp, Lewis-Clark State (Idaho) College.
**14. Willie Morales, c, University of Arizona.—(2000)**
15. *Daniel Choi, rhp, Long Beach State University.
16. Mat Reese, of, Indiana State University.
17. *Steve Fuller, rhp, St. Charles (Ill.) HS.
18. Brian Whatley, c, Long Beach State University.
19. Pat Sanders, 1b, Cumberland (Tenn.) University.
20. Aaron Huber, rhp, Panola (Texas) JC.
21. Tony Banks, of, Cal State Fullerton.
22. Jeff Richardson, of, Long Beach State University.
23. Eric Harris, of, Columbia State (Tenn.) CC.
24. *Toby Larson, rhp, Lassen (Calif.) JC.
25. *Joe Montelongo, rhp, Truett-McConnell (Ga.) JC.
26. Derek Manning, lhp, University of North Carolina.
27. Ryan Whitaker, rhp, University of Arkansas.
28. Jason Lowe, rhp, University of Mississippi.
29. *Felix Martinez, ss, Juan Ponce deLeon HS, Rio Piedras, P.R.
30. *Jeff Poor, c, Los Angeles Harbor JC.
31. Brandy Bengoechea, ss, Lewis-Clark State (Idaho) College.
32. Michael McLeod, of, University of South Carolina.
33. Randy Ortega, c, Santa Clara University.
34. *Jon Farmer, 1b-lhp, Porterville (Calif.) JC.
35. *Peter Cervantes, of, Lincoln HS, Los Angeles.
36. Thomas Luft, rhp, Warner Southern (Fla.) College.
37. *Robert Moore, rhp, Lassen (Calif.) JC.
**38. *Brandon Kolb, rhp, Chabot (Calif.) JC.—(2000-01)**
39. Matthew Weisbruch, rhp, Bradley University.
40. *Bryan Warner, of, Monrovia (Calif.) HS.
41. Matt Walsh, rhp, Boston College.
42. Jeff Carr, c, Mission Viejo (Calif.) HS.
43. Chad Griffin, 2b, Garinger HS, Charlotte, N.C.
44. *Santos Cortez, of, Millikan HS, Long Beach, Calif.
45. *Tal Light, 3b, Seminole (Okla.) JC.
46. *Eric Fuller, ss, West HS, Bakersfield, Calif.
47. *Frank Harmer, c-rhp, Lake Brantley HS, Altamonte Springs, Fla.
48. *Jay Wiebe, of, Foothill HS, Bakersfield, Calif.

## PHILADELPHIA PHILLIES (4)

**1. Wayne Gomes, rhp, Old Dominion University.—(1997-2002)**
**2. Scott Rolen, 3b, Jasper (Ind.) HS.—(1996-2012)**
3. Josh Watts, of, Ironwood HS, Glendale, Ariz.—(High A)
4. Jeffrey Key, of, Newton County HS, Covington, Ga.—(AA)
5. Tom Franek, rhp, Mesa State (Colo.) College.—(High A)
6. *Blair Fowler, rhp, Everett (Wash.) HS.
7. *Scott Sladovnik, of, Westside HS, Omaha, Neb.
8. Bo Hamilton, rhp, Cleveland (Texas) HS.
9. Nelson Metheney, rhp, Clinch Valley (Va.) College.
10. Silvio Censale, lhp, University of Miami.
11. *Jarrod Mays, rhp, El Dorado Springs (Mo.) HS.
12. Chris Mayfield, of, McNeese State University.
13. Brian Costello, of, Dr. Phillips HS, Orlando, Fla.
**14. Rich Hunter, rhp, The Linfield School, Temecula, Calif.—(1996)**
15. Tom Danulevith, lhp, St. John's University.
16. Doug Angeli, ss, University of New Orleans.
17. *Eric Ekdahl, ss, Pepperdine University.
18. *Mark Gardner, lhp, Fountain Valley (Calif.) HS.
19. Jeff Gyselman, c, Portland State University.
20. Charles Tinsley, of, Cumberland HS, Lynch, Ky.
21. Nate Rodriquez, ss, Cal State Fullerton.
22. Andrew Szarko, rhp, University of Richmond.
23. Mark Foster, lhp, University of Richmond.
24. Tyrone Swan, rhp, University of La Verne (Calif.).
25. Matthew Brainard, c-3b, Wilmington (Del.) College.
26. Derek Stingley, of, Triton (Ill.) JC.
DRAFT DROP *Son of Darryl Stingley, wide receiver, National Football League (1973-77)*
**27. David Doster, 2b, Indiana State University.—(1996-99)**
28. Neal Murphy, c, Iona College.
29. Brian O'Connor, rhp, Creighton University.
DRAFT DROP *Baseball coach, Virginia (2004-15)*
30. Mike Muncy, ss, Ventura (Calif.) CC.
31. Danton Pierre-Louis, 1b, Dwight HS, New York.
32. Joey Madden, of, Cal State Hayward.
**33. Kevin Sefcik, ss, St. Xavier (Ill.) College.—(1995-2001)**
34. *Shawn Fouch, rhp, Virginia HS, Bristol, Va.
35. *Mike Boucher, rhp, Saddleback (Calif.) CC.
36. *Larry Karpinski, rhp, Eisenhower HS, Rialto, Calif.
37. *Darin Wood, c, Redwood HS, Visalia, Calif.
38. *Jake Esteves, rhp, Placer HS, Auburn, Calif.
39. Barry Fitzgerald, c, West Hills HS, Santee, Calif.
40. *Karl Chatman, of, Nacogdoches (Texas) HS.
41. *Michael Neal, rhp, Seymour (Tenn.) HS.
42. Dan Held, c, Waukesha County HS, Neosho, Wis.

## PITTSBURGH PIRATES (22)

1. Charles Peterson, of, Laurens (S.C.) HS.—(AAA)
**1. Jermaine Allensworth, of, Purdue University** (Supplemental choice—34th—as compensation for Type A free agent Doug Drabek).**—(1996-99)**
1. Andy Rice, 1b, Parker HS, Birmingham, Ala. (Supplemental choice—42nd—as compensation for Type A free agent Barry Bonds).—(High A)
**2. Kevin Pickford, lhp, Clovis West HS, Clovis, Calif.** (Choice from Astros as compensation for Drabek).**—(2002)**
2. Jose Delgado, ss, Luz A. Calderon HS, Carolina, P.R.—(AA)
3. Derek Swafford, of-2b, Ventura (Calif.) HS.—(High A)
4. Kerry Ward, rhp, Edison (Fla.) CC.—(Rookie)
5. Jason Temple, rhp, Woodhaven (Mich.) HS.—(AA)
6. *Shane McGill, rhp, Campbell HS, Smyrna, Ga.
7. Akili Smith, of, Lincoln HS, San Diego.
DRAFT DROP *First-round draft pick, Cincinnati Bengals, National Football League (1999); quarterback, NFL (1999-2002)*
8. Sean Hagen, ss, Brighton HS, Sandy, Utah.
9. Rayon Reid, rhp, Miami-Dade CC North.
10. T.J. Staton, 1b-lhp, Elyria West HS, Elyria, Ohio.
11. Matt Chamberlain, rhp, Louisiana State University.
12. Joseph Serna, rhp-c, Mount San Antonio (Calif.) JC.
**13. Kane Davis, rhp, Spencer HS, Reedy, W.Va.—(2000-07)**
14. Craig Mattson, rhp, Triton (Ill.) JC.
15. Kevin Keener, lhp, Arkansas HS, Texarkana, Ark.
16. Rich Luna, ss, Cosumnes River (Calif.) JC.
17. *Jake Eye, rhp, Windham (Ohio) HS.
18. Jeff Isom, lhp, Purdue University.
19. *Francisco Lebron, 1b, American Military Academy, Toa Baja, P.R.
20. Alan Purdy, ss, Vanderbilt University.
21. *Heath Henderson, rhp, Huffman HS, Birmingham, Ala.
22. Jeff Pickich, rhp, Southern Mississippi University.
23. Anthony Sharer, rhp, Tyrone Area (Pa.) HS.
24. *Matt Brown, rhp, Boone HS, Orlando, Fla.
25. Matt Ryan, rhp, University of Mississippi.
26. Matt Torres, c-3b, American River (Calif.) JC.
27. Ben Goldman, rhp, Sacramento (Calif.) CC.
28. Ryan Cunningham, 3b, Lancaster (S.C.) HS.
29. *Trevor Leppard, rhp, Simi Valley (Calif.) HS.
30. John Yselonia, 1b, University of Georgia.
31. Jeffery Henry, rhp, George C. Wallace (Ala.) CC.
32. Trevor Skjerpen, rhp, University of North Dakota.
33. *J.D. Brammer, rhp, Logan HS, West Logan, W.Va.
34. Joel Williamson, c, University of Texas.
35. *Ron Ricks, rhp, Florida HS, Tallahassee, Fla.
36. *Pete Pryor, 1b, Sacramento (Calif.) CC.
**37. Chris Peters, lhp, Indiana University.—(1996-2001)**
38. *Michael Butts, ss-2b, Hillsborough HS, Tampa.
39. Johnny Mitchell, of, University of South Carolina-Aiken.
40. *Nate Coleman, c, Northwest HS, Omaha, Neb.
41. *Bruce Stanley, rhp, Shenandoah HS, Middletown, Ind.
42. *Keith Finnerty, 2b, Rockland (N.Y.) CC.
43. *Robert Matlack, c, Madill (Okla.) HS.
44. Jeff Lutt, rhp, Wayne State (Neb.) College.
45. *Brian Harris, ss, Carmel (Ind.) HS.
46. *Robert Dulli, rhp, Fairfield (Ohio) HS.
47. *Tonka Maynor, of-lb, University of North Carolina-Greensboro.
48. *Freddy Perez, c, Miami (Fla.) Senior HS.
49. *Brandon Griffith, rhp, Sibley HS, Heflin, La.
50. *Derek Mitchell, ss, Waukegan HS, Gurnee, Ill.
51. *Justin Ludington, rhp, Sacramento (Calif.) CC.
52. Patrick Gosselin, ss, Montmorency HS, Sherbrooke, Quebec.
53. *Steve Hueston, rhp, Skyline (Calif.) JC.

## ST. LOUIS CARDINALS (16)

**1. Alan Benes, rhp, Creighton University.—(1995-2003)**
DRAFT DROP *Brother of Andy Benes, first overall draft pick, Padres (1989); major leaguer (1989-2002)*
2. Nate Dishington, 1b, Hoover HS, Glendale, Calif. (Choice from Dodgers as compensation for Type B free agent Todd Worrell).—(AAA)
**2. Jay Witasick, rhp, University of Maryland-Baltimore County.—(1996-2007)**
**3. Eli Marrero, c, Coral Gables (Fla.) HS.—(1997-2006)**
4. *Darrell Nicholas, of, University of New Orleans.—(AAA)
DRAFT DROP *Returned to New Orleans; re-drafted by Brewers, 1994 (4th round)*
5. Marc Ottmers, rhp, University of Texas-Pan American.—(Low A)
6. David Carroll, lhp, Manatee (Fla.) JC.
**7. Jeff Berblinger, 2b, University of Kansas.—(1997)**
8. Rantie Harper, of, Point Loma HS, San Diego.
9. Mike Windham, rhp, University of North Florida.
10. Mike Martin, rhp, Walters State (Tenn.) CC.
11. Scott Marquardt, rhp, Galveston (Texas) JC.
12. Chris Christopher, of, Auburn University.
13. Anton French, of, Lafayette (La.) HS.
14. Dave Madsen, 3b, Brigham Young University.
15. Dee Dalton, ss, Virginia Tech.
16. *Tom McMillan, of, Colegio El Buen Pastor HS, Guaynabo, P.R.
17. Travis Welch, rhp, Sacramento (Calif.) CC.
18. Jeremy Current, of, Mount Zion (Ill.) HS.
19. Steven Santucci, of, Assumption (Mass.) College.
20. Ossie Garcia, of, Miami-Dade CC Wolfson.
**21. Armando Almanza, lhp, New Mexico JC.—(1999-2005)**
22. +Kris Detmers, lhp, Lincoln Land (Ill.) CC.
23. Keith Conway, lhp, Gloucester County (N.J.) JC.
24. Greg Almond, c, North Carolina State University.
25. *Bo Johnson, lhp, Rice University.
26. Greg Deares, of, George Mason University.
27. *Jeremy Ross, rhp, Dixie (Utah) JC.
28. Rich Lopez, of, Mount San Antonio (Calif.) JC.
29. Joe Jumonville, 3b, University of Southwestern Louisiana.
30. Cory Corrigan, rhp, Ohio University.
31. Dan Pontes, rhp, Long Island University.
32. Michael Matvey, ss, Berry (Ga.) College.
33. Freddie Parker, rhp, Northeast HS, Clarksville, Tenn.
34. Ron Scott, lhp, University of Florida.
35. Matt Arrandale, rhp, University of Illinois.
36. Mark Dean, ss-of, Georgia Southern University.
37. Anthony Magnelli, rhp, Dominican (N.Y.) College.
38. Kevin Herde, c, University of San Diego.
39. Jeff Battles, rhp, Southern (Ga.) Tech.
40. Sheldon Cain, rhp, Berry (Ga.) College.
41. Eric Alexander, rhp, Florida International University.
42. Joe Henson, 1b-of, David Lipscomb College.
43. *Kurt Grashaw, rhp, University of Hartford.
44. Troy Barrick, rhp, North Carolina Wesleyan College.
45. Mark Cruise, rhp, Fresno State University.
46. Curtis Williams, of, Connors State (Okla.) JC.
47. Tighe Curren, lhp, Ventura (Calif.) JC.
48. *Kortney Paul, c, University of Arkansas.
49. Chris Stewart, rhp, Memphis State University.
50. Ed Kehrli, rhp, Pace (N.Y.) University.
51. *Alfred Hughes, 1b, Vernon Regional (Texas) JC.
52. *Brad Gore, rhp, Oklahoma State University.
53. *Matthew Leach, rhp, Long Island University.
54. *Josh Bradford, rhp, Hutchinson (Kan.) CC.
55. *Keith Bradley, ss, Connors State (Okla.) JC.
56. *Matt Johnson, 2b, South Park HS, Library, Pa.
57. *Tim Bradley, rhp, Dixie (Utah) JC.
58. *Anthony Fisher, of, Cretin HS, Oakdale, Minn.
59. *Mark Cridland, rhp, Ball HS, Galveston, Texas.
60. *Phillip Bailey, of, Westark (Ark.) CC.
61. Eric Iverson, of, Woodrow Wilson HS, Fargo, N.D.

## SAN DIEGO PADRES (14)

**1. Derrek Lee, 1b, El Camino HS, Sacramento, Calif.—(1997-2011)**
DRAFT DROP *Nephew of Leron Lee, first-round draft pick (1966); major leaguer (1969-76)*
2. Matt LaChappa, lhp, El Capitan HS, Lakeside, Calif.—(High A)
**3. Matt Clement, rhp, Butler (Pa.) Area HS.—(1998-2006)**
4. *Tim Miller, rhp, Williamsport (Pa.) HS.--DNP
DRAFT DROP *Attended Florida State; never re-drafted*
5. Hal Garrett, rhp, Brentwood (Tenn.) Academy.—(AAA)
**6. Greg Keagle, rhp, Florida International University.—(1996-98)**
7. Jason Schlutt, lhp, University of Central Florida.
8. Derek Mix, rhp, San Bernardino Valley (Calif.) JC.
**9. Jason Thompson, 1b, University of Arizona.—(1996)**
10. *Stacy Kleiner, c-3b, Taft HS, Tarzana, Calif.
11. *Faruq Darcuiel, of, Fresno (Calif.) CC.
12. Darrick Duke, of, University of Texas.
**13. +Gary Matthews Jr., of, Mission (Calif.) CC.—(1999-2010)**
DRAFT DROP *Son of Gary Matthews, first-round draft pick, Giants (1968); major leaguer (1972-87)*
14. DeVohn Duncan, rhp, Marist HS, Jersey City, N.J.
15. *Jose Colon, of, Eau Gallie HS, Melbourne, Fla.
16. Brad Kaufman, rhp, Iowa State University.
17. Daniel Harpe, rhp, Serra HS, San Diego.
18. Bryan Wolff, rhp, Oral Roberts University.
19. +Chris Logan, c, University of Southern Mississippi.
20. *Dan Cey, ss, El Camino Real HS, Woodland Hills, Calif.
DRAFT DROP *Son of Ron Cey, major leaguer (1971-87)*
**21. *Mark Hendrickson, lhp, Washington State University.—(2002-11)**
DRAFT DROP *Forward, National Basketball Association (1996-2000)*
22. Dan Zanolla, ss, Purdue University.
23. *Chris Humphries, rhp, Cochise County (Ariz.) CC.
**24. Chris Prieto, of, University of Nevada-Reno.—(2005)**
25. Santiago Rivera, ss, Arizona State University.
26. *Mike Schiefelbein, rhp, University of Arizona.
27. *Frankie Sanders, ss, Riverview HS, Sarasota, Fla.
28. Alan Meyer, rhp, Edison HS, Huntington Beach, Calif.
29. Chris West, 3b, East Carolina University.
30. *Nathan Koepke, 1b, Millikan HS, Long Beach, Calif.
31. Dickie Woodridge, 2b, LeMoyne College.
32. Leroy McKinnis, c, Jackson State University.
33. James Bostock, 2b, Eastern Michigan University.
34. *Corey Dillon, of, Franklin HS, Seattle.
DRAFT DROP *Running back, National Football League (1997-2006)*
35. *Dietrich Evans, c, Arizona Western JC.
36. *Travis Boyd, ss, UCLA.
37. *Kelan Washington, of, Lanier HS, Austin, Texas.
38. *Carlos Smith, ss, Anson County HS, Wadesboro, N.C.
39. *Chris Havens, rhp, Central HS, Elkhart, Ind.
40. *Ivan Loochkartt, of, Jordan HS, Long Beach, Calif.
41. Daniel Drewien, rhp, San Diego State University.
42. Obed Martinez, of, Josefina Barcelo HS, Rio Piedras, P.R.
43. *Brian Baklik, ss, El Campo (Texas) HS.
44. *Brent Bearden, rhp, Baylor University.
45. *Brent Stentz, rhp, Hernando HS, Brooksville, Fla.
46. *Etienne Hightower, of, Mount Lebanon (Pa.) HS.
47. *Brian Thompson, rhp, Northwest HS, Omaha, Neb.
48. *Robbie Reid, lhp, Spanish Fork (Utah) HS.
49. *William Bland, of, Dr. Phillips HS, Orlando, Fla.
50. *Oscar Hirschkorn, rhp, Kerman (Calif.) HS.
51. *Dexter Davis, ss, Jordan HS, Long Beach, Calif.
52. *Ken Wilson, c, South Mecklenburg HS, Charlotte, N.C.
53. *Brian Bejarano, ss, Alhambra HS, Laveen, Ariz.
54. *Jason Kendler, rhp, Corona del Sol HS, Tempe, Ariz.
55. *Greg Aiken, rhp, Temecula Valley HS, Temecula, Calif.
56. *Rodrick Meyer, c, Stanford University.
57. *Justin McConico, ss, Burke HS, Omaha, Neb.
58. *Gary Paul, 3b, Buena HS, Ventura, Calif.
59. *Jonas Armenta, rhp, Bloomfield (N.M.) HS.
60. *Jeff Van Every, lhp, Benson HS, Omaha, Neb.
61. *Kyle Griffiths, c, Lake Michigan JC.
62. *Ryan Van de Weg, rhp, Grand Rapids (Mich.) JC.
63. *Kevin Coe, of, Simeon HS, Chicago.
64. *Russ Chambliss, of, Tucker HS, Glen Allen, Va.
DRAFT DROP *Son of Chris Chambliss, first overall draft pick, January 1970/regular phase; major leaguer (1971-88)*
65. *Terry Adams, 3b, Eastern Commerce HS, Toronto.
66. *James Moore, ss, Sweetwater (Texas) HS.
67. *Byron Tribe, rhp, St. Thomas HS, Katy, Texas.
68. *Keith Dilgard, rhp, Raritan HS, Bridgewater, N.J.
69. *Roger Main, 3b, Dundalk (Md.) CC.
70. *Larry Smith, c, DeMatha HS, Lanham, Md.
71. *Donald Whitney, of, Cahokia (Ill.) HS.
72. *Scott Keithley, 2b, Alvin (Texas) HS.
73. *Isaac Byrd, of, Parkway Central HS, St. Louis.
DRAFT DROP *Wide receiver, National Football League (1997-2002)*
**74. *Jason Conti, of, Seneca Valley HS, Mars, Pa.—(2000-04)**
75. *Keith Whitner, of, Lincoln HS, Los Angeles.
76. *David Yocum, lhp, Christopher Columbus HS, Miami.
DRAFT DROP *First-round draft pick (20th overall), Dodgers (1995)*
77. *Donn Cunnigan, of, University of Southern California.
78. *Terrence Johnson, 1b-of, Guilford HS, Rockford, Ill.
79. Byron Clark, lhp, Western New Mexico University.
80. *Chris Corn, rhp, University of Kansas.
81. *Joshua Gibbons, rhp, Lincoln Way HS, New Lenox, Ill.
82. *Rob Bonanno, rhp, University of Florida.
83. *Larry Husted, 1b-of, Chaffey (Calif.) JC.
84. *Ted Persell, of, East Los Angeles JC.
85. *Michael Brown, ss, Hazelwood West HS, Florissant, Mo.
86. *Tim Farris, rhp, Newbury Park (Calif.) HS.
87. *Keith Evans, rhp, Crespi HS, Encino, Calif.
88. *Eric Skaife, rhp, South Torrance HS, Torrance Calif.
89. *Jesse Shanon, 1b, Dos Pueblos HS, Goleta, Calif.
90. *Mark Harriger, rhp, St. John Bosco HS, Lakewood, Calif.
91. *Trevor Preston, rhp, Temecula Valley HS, Temecula, Calif.

## SAN FRANCISCO GIANTS (6)

**1. Steve Soderstrom, rhp, Fresno State University.—(1996)**
**2. Chris Singleton, of, University of Nevada-Reno.—(1999-2005)**
2. *Macey Brooks, of, Kecoughtan HS, Hampton, Va. (Supplemental choice—71st—as compensation for Type C free agent Mike Felder).--DNP
DRAFT DROP *Attended James Madison; re-drafted by Royals, 1996 (55th round) • Wide receiver, National Football League (1998-2000)*
2. Brett King, ss, University of South Florida (Supplemental choice—72nd—as compensation for Type C free agent Chris James).—(AAA)
3. Don Denbow, of, Blinn (Texas) JC.—(AA)
DRAFT DROP *Son of Donnie Denbow, first-round draft pick, Dodgers (1967)*
**4. Jay Canizaro, ss, Blinn (Texas) JC.—(1996-2002)**
5. Heath Altman, rhp, University of North Carolina-Wilmington.—(High A)
6. *Pat Ryan, rhp, Apopka (Fla.) HS.
**7. Keith Williams, of, Clemson University.—(1996)**
8. Brent Smith, rhp, Arizona State University.
9. Ivan Alvarez, lhp, Canoga Park, Calif.
10. Jason Myers, lhp, Chaffey (Calif.) JC.
11. Brook Smith, lhp, Bradley University.
12. Kris Franko, lhp, Ohio University.
13. Joel Galarza, c, Yabucoa, P.R.
14. Michael McMullen, rhp, Glendale (Calif.) JC.
DRAFT DROP *Son of Ken McMullen, major leaguer (1962-77)*
**15. Bill Mueller, ss, Southwest Missouri State University.—(1996-2006)**
**16. *Mickey Callaway, rhp, Germantown (Tenn.) HS.—(1999-2004)**
17. Chris Gump, 2b, University of Arizona.
18. Doug Drumm, rhp, Rensselaer Polytechnical (N.Y.) Institute.
19. Mark Gulseth, 1b, University of New Mexico.
20. *Bobby Rector, rhp, Southwestern (Calif.) JC.
**21. Steve Bourgeois, rhp, Northeast Louisiana University.—(1996)**

22. Steven Day, lhp, Mesa State (Colo.) College.
23. Scott Barrett, c, Purdue University.
24. *Tim Conklin, rhp, Madison HS, Portland, Ore.
25. +Chris Ratliff, rhp, Laney (Calif.) JC.
26. *Tim Hicks, ss, Southwest HS, Macon, Ga.
27. *Rodney Bonds, rhp, Union City (Tenn.) HS.
28. +Jason Grote, rhp, Centennial HS, Gresham, Ore. / Mount Hood (Ore.) CC.
29. +Notorris Bray, of, Central Alabama CC.
30. *Chaad Stewart, lhp, Triton (Ill.) JC.
31. David Tessicini, ss, University of Vermont.
32. Brian Lootens, of, Arizona State University.
33. Matt Baumann, rhp, University of Maryland.
34. Clark Anderson, rhp, George Fox (Ore.) College.
35. Brian Zaletel, 3b, University of Tampa.
36. *Andrew Kalcounos, ss, DeMatha HS, Silver Spring, Md.
37. *Dan Fagley, c, Holy Cross HS, Riverton, N.J.
38. *Jeff Tagliaferri, 1b, Kennedy HS, Granada Hills, Calif.
39. Brian Benner, of, Capistrano Valley HS, Mission Viejo, Calif.
40. *Chad Dube, rhp, Cambridge, Ontario.
41. *Anthony Hilde, of, Pendleton (Ore.) HS.
42. *Duane Stewart, of, Chino HS, Ontario, Calif.
43. Leonard McMillan, rhp, Crowder (Mo.) JC.
44. *Ryan Miller, ss-2b, JC of the Sequoias (Calif.).
45. *William Dicken, ss, Bloomington (Ill.) HS.
46. *Tio Beall, rhp, South Salem HS, Salem, Ore.
47. *Kyle Logan, 3b, Oak Grove HS, Hattiesburg, Miss.
48. *David Russell, c, Bishop McGuinness HS, Lewisville, N.C.
49. Jon Sbrocco, 2b, Wright State University.
50. Todd Petering, of, Kansas State University.
51. *Micah Terrell, ss, Mitchell (Ind.) HS.
52. Chris Stasio, 1b, Barry (Fla.) University.
53. Michael Cecere, c, Rollins (Fla.) College.
54. Chance Reynolds, c, University of North Florida.
55. Andrew Mason, of, University of Washington.

## SEATTLE MARINERS (1)

1. **Alex Rodriguez, ss, Westminster Christian HS, Miami.—(1994-2013)**
DRAFT DROP *First 1993 high school draft pick to reach majors (July 8, 1994)*
2. (Choice to Brewers as compensation for Type A free agent Chris Bosio)
3. Ed Randolph, 3b-of, Roosevelt HS, Dallas.—(High A)
4. Mike Collett, rhp, University of Southern California.—(Short-season A)
5. David Cooper, rhp, Hesperia (Calif.) HS.—(Short-season A)
6. **Ken Cloude, rhp, McDonough HS, Baltimore.—(1997-99)**
7. Tim Schweitzer, lhp, University of Arizona.
8. Greg Hillengas, of, Seminole (Fla.) HS.
9. Rob Krueger, lhp, Western Michigan University.
10. **Dean Crow, rhp, Baylor University.—(1998)**
11. Casey Craig, rhp, Napoleon HS, Jackson, Mich.
12. Randy Jorgensen, 1b, University of Washington.
13. **Rafael Carmona, rhp, Indian Hills (Iowa) CC.—(1995-99)**
14. Brian Sosa, rhp, San Bernardino Valley (Calif.) JC.
15. Chris Green, rhp, Grossmont (Calif.) JC.
16. John Daniels, rhp, Mount San Antonio (Calif.) JC.
17. Chad Dunavan, of, Howard (Texas) JC.
18. Tim Bruce, rhp, University of Detroit.
19. *Doug Forde, lhp, Riverview HS, Sarasota, Fla.
20. +Chris Dean, 2b, Seminole (Okla.) JC.
21. Chris Dumas, of, Alabama Southern JC.
22. Matt Apana, rhp, University of Hawaii.
23. Mike Barger, of, Saint Louis University.
24. Joe Berube, c, Presbyterian (S.C.) College.
25. Daleon Isom, of, Benton Harbor (Mich.) HS.
26. Russell Jacobs, rhp, Winter Haven (Fla.) HS.
27. Joe Mathis, ss-of, Strom Thurmond HS, Johnston, S.C.
28. Jon Updike, rhp, Pensacola (Fla.) JC.
29. Andy Augustine, c, Triton (Ill.) JC.
30. Manny Patel, 2b, Yale University.
31. *Brandon Hoalton, rhp, Rancho Santiago (Calif.) JC.
32. John Tejcek, of, University of Arizona.
33. *Chris Parker, rhp, Gonzalez Tate HS, Pensacola, Fla.
34. *Grant Jondahl, rhp, Amador Valley HS, Pleasanton, Calif.
35. *John White, c, University Christian HS, Jacksonville, Fla.
36. Willie Wilkins, of, Atlantic HS, Boynton Beach, Fla.
37. *Brad Brasser, rhp, Grand Rapids Christian HS, Grand Rapids, Mich.
38. Kelvin Mitchell, lhp, Choctaw County HS, Butler, Ala.
39. *Brandon Kleitch, of, Cibola HS, Rio Rancho, N.M.
40. +Anibal Ramirez, ss, Miami-Dade CC Wolfson.
41. *Chris Champanois, c, Columbia Central HS, Brooklyn, Mich.
42. *Heath Webster, rhp, Peninsula HS, Rancho Palo Verde, Calif.
43. *Matt Wimmer, of, University of Washington.
44. *Thomas Redd, of, El Camino (Calif.) JC.
45. *Jeremy Morris, c, Monroe HS, Quincy, Fla.
46. Johnny Cardenas, c, Texas Christian University.
DRAFT DROP *Baseball coach, Stephen F. Austin University (2009-15)*
47. ***Marcus Jones, rhp, Esperanza HS, Yorba Linda, Calif.—(2000)**
48. *Bryan Belflower, rhp, Oak Ridge HS, Orlando, Fla.
49. *Jeremy Reeves, lhp, Lincoln Trail (Ill.) JC.
50. *Jeff Harris, rhp, Contra Costa (Calif.) JC.
51. Roy Miller, ss, Washington State University.
52. *Ryan Mullen, rhp, Boca Ciega HS, St. Petersburg, Fla.
53. *Kevin McCoy, rhp, Triton (Ill.) JC.
54. ***Matt Wise, rhp, Bonita HS, La Verne, Calif.—(2000-08)**
55. Jason Cook, ss, University of Virginia.
56. *Chris Knowles, 1b, Blinn (Texas) JC.
57. *John Romero, rhp, San Fernando HS, Sylmar, Calif.
58. *Chris Kelly, lhp, Hamilton HS, Inglewood, Calif.
59. *Ricky Tutson, of, Willow Run HS, Ypsilanti, Mich.
60. *Barret Markey, rhp, St. Petersburg (Fla.) HS.
61. *Robert Coddington, c, Grossmont HS, El Cajon, Calif.
62. *Michael Rodgers, lhp, Olney (Ill.) HS.
63. *Arnold Brathwarte, ss, St. Joseph's HS, Frederiksted, Virgin Islands.
64. *Justin Bice, rhp, Kentwood HS, Kent, Wash.
65. Scott Smith, of, Texas A&M University.
66. *Aaron Keal, rhp, Labette County (Kan.) CC.
67. *George Rayborn, rhp, Purvis (Miss.) HS.
68. *Cirilo Cruz, 3b, Miami-Dade CC North.
DRAFT DROP *Son of Tommy Cruz, major leaguer (1973-77)*
69. Rob Ippolito, rhp, University of Arizona.
70. *Jon Choate, of, Blinn (Texas) JC.

## TEXAS RANGERS (15)

1. (Choice to Blue Jays as compensation for Type A free agent Tom Henke)
1. **Mike Bell, 3b, Moeller HS, Cincinnati** (Supplemental choice—30th—as compensation for Type A free agent Jose Guzman).—**(2000)**
DRAFT DROP *Grandson of Gus Bell, major leaguer (1950-64) • Son of Buddy Bell, major leaguer (1972-89); major league manager, (1996-2006) • Brother of David Bell, major leaguer (1995-2006)*
2. **Edwin Diaz, 2b, Ladislao Martinez Maestro HS, Vega Alta, P.R.** (Choice from Cubs as compensation for Guzman).—**(1998-99)**
2. (Choice to Blue Jays as compensation for Type B free agent Manny Lee)
3. Andrew Vessel, of, Kennedy HS, Richmond, Calif.—(AA)
4. Toure Knighton, rhp, Tucson (Ariz.) HS.—(High A)
5. Rod Walker, ss, Hyde Park HS, Chicago.—(Short-season A)
6. Mark Ocasio, rhp, Gilberto Concepcion HS, Carolina, P.R.
7. **Dan Smith, rhp, Girard (Kan.) HS.—(1999-2003)**
8. Jack Stanczak, 3b, Villanova University.
9. Pete Hartman, lhp, Oklahoma City University.
10. Brian Thomas, of, Texas A&M University.
11. James Franklin, rhp, Carson-Newman (Tenn.) College.
12. Osmani Estrada, ss, Canoga Park, Calif.
13. **Marc Sagmoen, of, University of Nebraska.—(1997)**
14. Alexis Cabreja, of, Canoga Park, Calif.
15. Chris Unrat, c, Arkansas State University.
16. Tim Cossins, c, University of Oklahoma.
17. Brian Clark, of, University of Houston.
18. Ryan Falmier, rhp, Goreville HS, Tunnel Hill, Ill.
19. Wesley Sims, 2b, Austin Peay State University.
20. *Cesar Cerda, c, Southridge HS, Miami.
21. Leland Macon, of, St. Louis CC-Meramec.
22. Michael Jackson, rhp, Texas HS, Texarkana, Texas.
23. *Jason Dyess, rhp, McLaurin HS, Florence, Miss.
24. **Eric Moody, rhp, Erskine (S.C.) College.—(1997)**
25. Larry Ephan, c, Hawaii Pacific University.
26. Eric Dominow, 1b, Western Michigan University.
27. Lonnie Goldberg, 2b, George Mason University.
DRAFT DROP *Scouting director, Royals (2010-15)*
28. Jeffrey Davis, rhp, Massasoit (Mass.) CC.
29. *Cam Spence, rhp, South Gwinnett HS, Lithonia, Ga.
30. Steve Ouimet, 1b, North Shore HS, Glenwood Landing, N.Y.
31. Michael Hill, of, Harvard University.
32. *Scott Smith, rhp, University of Kentucky.
33. *Richard Collins, rhp-1b, Stockbridge (Ga.) HS.
34. *Jamie Phillips, c, Redan HS, Stone Mountain, Ga.
35. Gardner O'Flynn, lhp, University of New Hampshire.
36. Robert Kell, lhp, Temple University.
37. Gregory Lewis, of, University of New Hampshire.
38. Dom Gatti, of, Adelphi (N.Y.) University.
39. *Ivan Zweig, rhp, Tulane University.
40. Ray DeSimone, ss, Long Island University.
41. **Mike Cather, rhp, University of California.—(1997-99)**
42. Greg Willming, rhp, University of Evansville.
43. Joe Morvay, rhp, Ohio University.
44. *Cajen Rhodes, 1b, Berkmar HS, Lilburn, Ga.
45. Matt Huff, of, Northwestern University.
DRAFT DROP *Brother of Mike Huff, major leaguer (1989-96)*
46. *Bryan Cunningham, rhp, Monte Vista HS, Spring Valley, Calif.
47. *Rex Stevens, rhp, Wheeler HS, Marietta, Ga.
48. *Michael Jackson, of, JC of Marin (Calif.).
49. *Nick Caiazzo, c, Deering HS, Portland, Maine.
50. *Brian Tickell, rhp, Grand Prairie (Texas) HS.
51. +Juan Veras, ss, Palm Beach (Fla.) JC.
52. *Stephen Cardona, rhp, San Joaquin Delta (Calif.) JC.
53. *Daniel Schourek, rhp, Montgomery (Md.) CC.
DRAFT DROP *Brother of Pete Schourek, major leaguer (1991-2001)*
54. *William Pepper, 1b, Houston (Miss.) HS.
55. +Kenny Payne, 1b, St. Louis CC-Meramec.
56. *Robert Tucker, 1b, Robert E. Lee HS, Huntsville, Ala.
57. *Steve Frascatore, rhp, C.W. Post (N.Y.) College.
DRAFT DROP *Brother of John Frascatore, major leaguer (1994-2001)*
58. *Rayvon McGriff, of, Del Mar HS, San Jose, Calif.
59. *Frank Chapman, rhp, MacArthur HS, San Antonio.

## TORONTO BLUE JAYS (26)

1. **Chris Carpenter, rhp, Trinity HS, Manchester, N.H.** (Choice from Rangers as compensation for Type A free agent Tom Henke).—**(1997-2012)**
1. (Choice to Brewers as compensation for Type A free agent Paul Molitor)
1. Matt Farner, of, East Pennsboro HS, Enola, Pa. (Supplemental choice—37th—as compensation for Type A tree agent David Cone).—(Low A)
1. **Mark Lukasiewicz, lhp, Brevard (Fla.) CC** (Supplemental choice—40th—as compensation for Type A free agent Jimmy Key).—**(2001-02)**
1. Jeremy Lee, rhp, Galesburg (Ill.) HS (Supplemental choice—41st—as compensation for Henke).—(AA)
2. Anthony Medrano, ss, Jordan HS, Long Beach, Calif. (Choice from Royals as compensation for Cone).—(AAA)
2. Ryan Jones, 1b, Irvine (Calif.) HS (Choice from Rangers as compensation for Type B free agent Manny Lee).—(AAA)
2. (Choice to Athletics as compensation for Type A free agent Dave Stewart)
3. **Mike Romano, rhp, Tulane University** (Choice from Yankees as compensation for Key).—**(1999)**
3. Joe Young, rhp, Harry Ainlay HS, Fort McMurray, Alberta.—(AA)
4. *Thad Busby, c-of, Pace (Fla.) HS.—DNP
DRAFT DROP *Attended Florida State; never re-drafted*
5. Charles Bourne, ss, Muir HS, Altadena, Calif.—(Short-season A)
6. *Rob DeBoer, c, University of South Carolina.
7. *Donny Barker, rhp, Leander (Texas) HS.
8. Matt Stone, lhp, Vista (Calif.) HS.
9. Oreste Volkert, rhp, La Habra (Calif.) HS.
10. Ruben Corral, rhp, Arroyo HS, El Monte, Calif.
11. *Larry Mohs, rhp, Nutley (N.J.) HS.
12. Brent Coe, lhp, Franklin Central HS, Indianapolis, Ind.
13. **Adam Melhuse, 3b, UCLA.—(2000-08)**
14. *Chris Freeman, rhp, University of Tennessee.
15. Ty Hartshorn, rhp, Lamar (Colo.) HS.
16. *Shane Dennis, lhp, Wichita State University.
17. **Mike Johnson, rhp, Salisbury Composite HS, Edmonton, Alberta.—(1997-2001)**
18. David Morgan, c, Harvard University.
19. David Sinnes, rhp, University of Notre Dame.
20. *Aaron Gardin, of, Chaparral HS, Scottsdale, Ariz.
21. *Danny Crawford, rhp, Jersey Village HS, Houston.
22. *Steve Johnson, of, Michigan State University.
23. Rob Steinert, rhp, North Carolina State University.
24. Brian Grant, lhp, Diablo Valley (Calif.) JC.
25. Willie Daunic, 1b, Vanderbilt University.
26. Victor Davila, ss, Westchester (N.Y.) CC.
27. Michael Toney, rhp, Cochise County (Ariz.) CC.
28. *John Nape, rhp, Lewis (Ill.) University.
29. Rob Mummau, ss, James Madison University.
30. Richard Lutz, c, Elizabethtown (Pa.) College.
31. *Brad Feldewerth, rhp, Fort Zumwalt North HS, Wentzville, Mo.
32. *James Bowman, lhp, Highline HS, Seattle.
33. *Jon Phillips, rhp, South Cobb HS, Austell, Ga.
34. *Eric Booth, of, Bassfield (Miss.) HS.
35. *Michael Diebolt, lhp, Mayfield HS, Mayfield Village, Ohio.
36. *Scott Henderson, rhp, Villa Park (Calif.) HS.
37. Kip Roggendorf, 1b, Dowling (N.Y.) College.
38. *Ryan Brannan, rhp, Huntington Beach (Calif.) HS.
39. *James Smith, of, Greensboro HS, Quincy, Fla.
40. *Adrian Poindexter, ss, Caldwell HS, Columbus, Miss.
41. *David Sumner, of, University of Pittsburgh.
42. *Mane Gavric, of, Mather HS, Chicago.
43. Ivan Nobles, of, Brandon (Fla.) HS.
44. *David Meyer, lhp, University of Kansas.
45. *Brian Haebig, lhp, Sahuaro HS, Tucson, Ariz.
46. *Mark Macias, rhp, Ridgewood HS, Norridge, Ill.
47. +Herman Gordan, of, El Camino HS, Oceanside, Calif. / Arizona Western JC.
48. *Ronald Dempsey, of, Lufkin (Texas) HS.
49. *Jason Monk, rhp, Mississippi Gulf Coast JC.
50. *David Fogle, rhp, Torrance HS, Lomita, Calif.
51. *Brian Thomas, rhp, Mount Pleasant (Texas) HS.
52. ***Joe Nelson, ss, Notre Dame HS, Alameda, Calif.—(2001-10)**
53. *Jaime Roque, 2b, Vernon Regional (Texas) JC.
54. **+Jim Mann, rhp, Massasoit (Mass.) CC.—(2000-03)**
55. *Mike Hannah, of, Bremen (Ga.) HS.
56. Victor Rodriguez, rhp, Okaloosa-Walton (Fla.) CC.

# 1994

## AT A GLANCE

### This Date In History
June 2-4

### Best Draft
**MINNESOTA TWINS.** Second baseman **TODD WALKER** (1), catcher **A.J. PIERZYNSKI** (3) and third baseman **COREY KOSKIE** (26) each played regularly in the majors for at least seven seasons.

### Worst Draft
**PITTSBURGH PIRATES.** Lefthander **JIMMY ANDERSON** (9) was the only player the Pirates signed who reached the majors. In four seasons in a Pittsburgh uniform, he went 24-42, 5.17. None of the eight players the Pirates took ahead of Anderson advanced beyond Double-A, including first-rounder **MARK FARRIS**, who quit after five underachieving years to play football at Texas A&M. In three straight years, 1993-95, the Pirates drafted fewer big leaguers than any other team.

### First-Round Bust
**JACOB SHUMATE, RHP, BRAVES.** Move over Bill Bene, who walked 489 in 444 innings in a 10-year minor league career, and Robbie Beckett, who walked 846 in 850 innings in 11 seasons in the minors. Both former first-rounders had nothing on Shumate, who issued 436 walks in 312 innings in an eight-year career that peaked in Double-A. He went 14-30, 7.10.

### Second Best
**MIKE DARR, OF, TIGERS. TROY GLAUS** was the best player picked, but he shunned the Padres in favor of a three-year college career at UCLA. That left Darr as the most productive second-rounder, even though his career was cut short when he died of injuries sustained in a car accident on Feb. 15, 2002, while a member of the Mariners organization. In a three-year career with the Padres spanning 188 games, Darr hit .273-5-67.

# Work stoppage can't slow bonus inflation

The 1994 strike shut down baseball for 232 days and prompted cancellation of the World Series. Club owners were intent on putting a drag on rising salaries and trying to level the economic playing field among big-market and small-market clubs. However, signing bonuses for players selected in the draft continued to escalate at a prolific pace.

Righthander Paul Wilson of Florida State, the first pick in the draft, received a $1.55 million bonus from the New York Mets, equaling the record amount for a draft choice, set by Brien Taylor in 1991. A month later, Louisiana high school shortstop Josh Booty, the fifth pick, got $1.6 million from the Florida Marlins.

The Mets spent $3.697 million on their draft picks, and the Marlins spent $2.9845 million, breaking the record of $2.504 million the Los Angeles Dodgers spent in 1993. All told, 16 clubs spent more on bonuses than ever before. First-round bonuses rose to an average of $790,357, a 28.9 percent increase over 1993 and a 615 percent leap from 1987. Five first-round picks in 1994 got $1 million or more, and all but two first-rounders earned bonuses of at least $500,000. A total of 64 drafted players received $200,000 or more.

The Atlanta Braves and Boston Red Sox also spent liberally. The Braves gave George Lombard, their second-round pick, a $425,000 bonus to forgo a football scholarship to the University of Georgia. They landed their eighth-round pick, Billy Blythe, a top-rated Kentucky high school prospect who did not pitch that spring because of a sore arm, with a $300,000 bonus. Both were record amounts for those rounds. The Red Sox spent $365,000 to sign third-rounder Brian Rose and $338,000 for fourth-rounder Robb Welch.

Even with the strike in full blaze, the Toronto Blue Jays gave $355,000 to Andy Thompson, their 23rd-round pick, and the Seattle Mariners signed Matt Sachse, a 25th-round selection, for $300,000. Both those deals were struck in September, just as the two players were set to enroll in college—Thompson at Minnesota, Sachse at Stanford. The Mariners also signed Jordan Zimmerman, a 32nd-round draft-and-follow from Blinn (Texas) Junior College, the following spring for $325,000.

Spending on the international market went unchecked as well. The Dodgers paid $1.2 million for Korean pitcher Chan Ho Park, at the time the richest bonus ever for an international player.

All but two first-round choices were under contract by the time the strike hit on Aug. 12. For all the money spent, talent from the 1994 draft proved to be some of the leanest ever. According to Wins Above Replacement, the most productive player signed in 1994 was Puerto Rican righthander Javier Vazquez, a fifth-round pick of the Montreal Expos.

CLIFF WELCH

**No. 1 overall pick Paul Wilson (right) tied the record for the largest bonus in draft history at $1.55 million, only for it to be broken a few weeks later by Josh Booty, the fifth pick who got $1.6 million**

## WILSON PEGGED EARLY AS NO. 1

There was little suspense about who would be the No. 1 pick in the 1994 draft. "I'm going to the Big Apple, baby," Wilson said as the selection was announced in Omaha before the College World Series.

Wilson went 13-5, 2.08 with 161 strikeouts (second in the nation) in 143 innings in his junior season at Florida State. The 6-foot-5 righthander's biggest attributes were a 95 mph fastball and excellent makeup.

"He has what you look at for a guy you're projecting to be a major league pitcher," Mets scouting director John Barr said. "He's got size, he's got strength, he's got a good arm. I think he's going to be a very good pitcher in the big leagues."

After two weeks of negotiations, the Mets signed Wilson to his record-tying contract. Even after he went 0-7 in his first summer, it didn't temper expectations that he would reach Shea Stadium quickly.

Other than Wilson, the Mets' considerations were Texas high school outfielder Ben Grieve and Kent State righthander Dustin Hermanson, who went to the Oakland Athletics and San Diego Padres with the second and third picks in the draft.

The A's initially targeted Hermanson, but passed on him at the last minute in favor of Grieve, whose

## 1994: THE FIRST ROUNDERS

| CLUB: PLAYER, POS., SCHOOL | HOMETOWN | B-T | HT. | WT. | AGE | BONUS | FIRST YEAR | LAST YEAR | PEAK LEVEL (YEARS) |
|---|---|---|---|---|---|---|---|---|---|
| 1. Mets: Paul Wilson, rhp, Florida State | Orlando, Fla. | R-R | 6-5 | 220 | 21 | $1,550,000 | 1994 | 2006 | Majors (7) |
| Best combination of power stuff/command, size/rhythm in draft; made encouraging debut with Mets in '96, but career quickly unraveled with major injuries. | | | | | | | | | |
| 2. Athletics: Ben Grieve, of, James Martin HS | Arlington, Texas | L-R | 6-4 | 205 | 18 | $1,200,000 | 1994 | 2005 | Majors (9) |
| Along with Tom (Senators/1966), became first father/son first-round act; fulfilled potential as best HS power bat early but collapsed under immense expectations. | | | | | | | | | |
| 3. Padres: Dustin Hermanson, rhp, Kent State | Springfield, Ohio | R-R | 6-2 | 195 | 21 | $960,000 | 1994 | 2006 | Majors (12) |
| Pegged as closer to take advantage of power sinker/slider, spent bulk of career as starter; saved 34 games for W/S champ White Sox in 2005 before hurting back. | | | | | | | | | |
| 4. Brewers: Antone Williamson, 3b, Arizona State | Torrance, Calif. | L-R | 6-0 | 190 | 20 | $895,000 | 1994 | 1999 | Majors (1) |
| Brewers GM Sal Bando was ex-ASU 3B, so pushed for selection; big mistake as shoddy defense/lack of speed pushed him to 1B, never fulfilled potential with bat. | | | | | | | | | |
| 5. Marlins: Josh Booty, ss, Evangel Christian HS | Shreveport, La. | R-R | 6-3 | 215 | 19 | $1,600,000 | 1994 | 1998 | Majors (3) |
| Marlins used record bonus to buy record-setting prep QB away from football, but he hit .198-62-252 in five years in minors, reached MLB only to justify investment. | | | | | | | | | |
| 6. Angels: McKay Christensen, of, Clovis West HS | Fresno, Calif. | L-L | 5-11 | 175 | 18 | $700,000 | 1996 | 2004 | Majors (4) |
| Intriguing two-sport athlete with speed, missed first two years while on Mormon mission, never played for Angels; MLB career (.250-2-14) never got going. | | | | | | | | | |
| 7. Rockies: # Doug Million, lhp, Sarasota HS | Sarasota, Fla. | L-L | 6-3 | 175 | 19 | $905,000 | 1994 | 1997 | Class AA (2) |
| BA High School POY (12-2, 1.21, 87 IP/149 SO), ace of nation's No. 1 team; career started well but stalled by command issues; died in 1997 of asthma attack. | | | | | | | | | |
| 8. Twins: Todd Walker, 2b, Louisiana State | Bossier City, La. | L-R | 6-0 | 170 | 21 | $815,000 | 1994 | 2007 | Majors (12) |
| Best 2B in college history hit .396-52-246 in three years at LSU; mediocre defense impacted pro career, but advanced hitting led to productive 12-year MLB run. | | | | | | | | | |
| 9. Reds: C.J. Nitkowski, lhp, St. John's | Suffern, N.Y. | L-L | 6-2 | 185 | 21 | $675,000 | 1994 | 2012 | Majors (10) |
| Big East pitcher of year (5-4, 1.59, 74 IP/80 SO) showed polish/poise, command of four pitches, debuted in majors in 1995; went 18-32, 5.37 with eight clubs. | | | | | | | | | |
| 10. Indians: Jaret Wright, rhp, Katella HS | Anaheim, Calif. | R-R | 6-2 | 218 | 18 | $1,150,000 | 1994 | 2007 | Majors (11) |
| Son of ex-big leaguer Clyde, best HS arm in draft; fastball peaked at 98 in debut with Indians, but never met expectations (68-60, 5.09), doomed by shoulder issues. | | | | | | | | | |
| 11. Pirates: Mark Farris, ss, Angleton HS | Angleton, Texas | L-R | 6-2 | 190 | 19 | $820,000 | 1994 | 1998 | Class AA (1) |
| Considered a reach, rarely hit with power in minors (.244-14-126), missed 1995 with torn ACL; quit to play QB at Texas A&M, became prolific passer in 2000-01. | | | | | | | | | |
| 12. Red Sox: Nomar Garciaparra, ss, Georgia Tech | Whittier, Calif. | R-R | 6-0 | 165 | 20 | $895,000 | 1994 | 2009 | Majors (14) |
| Defense-first SS initially, but emerged as top all-around player in college, won AL batting titles in 1999-2000; family soccer background, married to Mia Hamm. | | | | | | | | | |
| 13. Dodgers: Paul Konerko, c, Chaparral HS | Scottsdale, Ariz. | R-R | 6-2 | 195 | 18 | $830,000 | 1994 | 2014 | Majors (18) |
| Natural hitter with suspect speed/catching skills; stung ball at .578-15-56 clip as prep SR, .307-106-419 in minors, became force at plate for White Sox over 16 years. | | | | | | | | | |
| 14. Mariners: Jason Varitek, c, Georgia Tech | Altamonte Springs, Fla. | B-R | 6-2 | 215 | 22 | $650,000 | 1995 | 2011 | Majors (15) |
| Second go-around as first-round pick, still held out until April 1995; career got off to slow/contentious start, but became Red Sox icon over 15-year MLB career. | | | | | | | | | |
| 15. Cubs: Jayson Peterson, rhp, East HS | Denver | B-R | 6-3 | 175 | 18 | $712,500 | 1994 | 1998 | Class A (4) |
| Dominant prep arm (8-0, 0.86, 49 IP/95 SO) alienated Cubs with immaturity, went 11-21, 4.89 in three seasons before dealt to Reds, never pitched above A-ball. | | | | | | | | | |
| 16. Royals: Matt Smith, lhp/1b, Grants Pass HS | Grants Pass, Ore. | L-L | 6-4 | 225 | 18 | $1,000,000 | 1994 | 1998 | Class AA (1) |
| Equal parts power bat/arm in HS, installed as hitter (.243-17-165) first by Royals, then pitcher (0-3, 3.81), eventually quit to play football at Oregon. | | | | | | | | | |
| 17. Astros: Ramon Castro, c, Lino Padron Rivera HS | Vega Baja, P.R. | R-R | 6-3 | 195 | 18 | $450,000 | 1994 | 2011 | Majors (13) |
| Highest Puerto Rican draft until fellow Astros pick Carlos Correa (2012); solid defender with raw power, 13-year MLB career as consummate backup catcher. | | | | | | | | | |
| 18. Tigers: Cade Gaspar, rhp, Pepperdine | Mission Viejo, Calif. | R-R | 6-3 | 185 | 20 | $825,000 | 1994 | 1996 | Class A (3) |
| Son of Rod, ex-MLB OF; had desire to be SS, but greater upside on mound, finally consented to pitch for Pepperdine, in pro ball, before derailed by arm issues. | | | | | | | | | |
| 19. Cardinals: Bret Wagner, lhp, Wake Forest | New Cumberland, Pa. | L-L | 5-11 | 190 | 21 | $525,000 | 1994 | 1997 | Class AA (3) |
| Teamed with twin Kyle in HS, as two-way star in college, early in pro career with Cards, before dealt to A's; had upside with 92-95 FB, but abruptly quit in mid-1997. | | | | | | | | | |
| 20. Mets: Terrence Long, 1b, Stanhope Elmore HS | Millbrook, Ala. | L-L | 6-1 | 180 | 18 | $500,000 | 1994 | 2006 | Majors (8) |
| Mets saw 30-30 potential; looked like he might achieve it by hitting .288-18-80 as A's rookie outfielder in 2000, before career quickly leveled off, hit .269-69-376. | | | | | | | | | |
| 21. Expos: Hiram Bocachica, ss, Rexville HS | Bayamon, P.R. | R-R | 5-11 | 168 | 18 | $635,000 | 1994 | 2007 | Majors (8) |
| Second Puerto Rican in first round, flashed early promise with all tools (except power), but became erratic at bat and in field, spent most of career in utility role. | | | | | | | | | |
| 22. Giants: Dante Powell, of, Cal State Fullerton | Long Beach, Calif. | R-R | 6-2 | 185 | 20 | $507,500 | 1994 | 2002 | Majors (4) |
| Unsigned first-rounder in 1991, first-round tools (speed/CF skills, power) still evident three years later; played well in Giants system, career stalled in majors. | | | | | | | | | |
| 23. Phillies: Carlton Loewer, rhp, Mississippi State | Eunice, La. | B-R | 6-4 | 205 | 20 | $590,000 | 1995 | 2003 | Majors (4) |
| No. 1 on scouting bureau list at outset of '94 season, went 7-5, 4.63; took 82 days to sign, underachieving MLB career (10-18, 6.13) impacted by injuries. | | | | | | | | | |
| 24. Yankees: Brian Buchanan, 1b/of, Virginia | Clifton, Va. | R-R | 6-4 | 215 | 20 | $500,000 | 1994 | 2009 | Majors (5) |
| Made huge strides as power/speed prospect in college (hit .392-22-66 as JR); overcame horrific 1995 ankle injury to play five years in majors, hit .258-32-103. | | | | | | | | | |
| 25. Astros: Scott Elarton, rhp, Lamar HS | Lamar, Colo. | R-R | 6-8 | 225 | 18 | $750,000 | 1994 | 2012 | Majors (10) |
| Astros spent big to lure lanky, three-sport prep standout away from Stanford; FB topped at 98 in checkered MLB career impacted by multiple shoulder surgeries. | | | | | | | | | |
| 26. White Sox: Mark Johnson, c, Warner Robins HS | Warner Robins, Ga. | L-R | 6-0 | 185 | 18 | $520,000 | 1994 | 2010 | Majors (8) |
| Impressed scouts as prep with defensive skills, leadership ability, power, plate discipline while hitting .489-13-44; spent eight years in majors, hit .218-16-83. | | | | | | | | | |
| 27. Braves: Jacob Shumate, rhp, Hartsville HS | Hartsville, S.C. | R-R | 6-1 | 185 | 18 | $500,000 | 1994 | 2001 | Class AA (4) |
| Two-sport prep star with moving 94 mph fastball; dogged by control issues throughout career, went 14-30, 7.10, walked 436, had 125 wild pitches in 312 IP overall. | | | | | | | | | |
| 28. Blue Jays: Kevin Witt, ss, Bishop Kenny HS | Jacksonville, Fla. | L-R | 6-4 | 185 | 18 | $470,000 | 1994 | 2006 | Majors (5) |
| Oversized SS with raw lefty power, became 1B/DH in 14-year pro career; spent bulk of time in minors, twice hit 36 homers in season in Triple-A on way to 269 total. | | | | | | | | | |

*# Deceased.*

father, Tom, was general manager of the Texas Rangers at the time. The Grieves became the first father-son duo drafted in the first round. Tom was the sixth overall pick in 1966 by the Washington Senators. The Rangers' first pick in 1994 was No. 56, so they had no shot at their GM's son.

"He's bigger and stronger, and has a beautiful natural swing that I didn't have," Tom Grieve said

## AT A GLANCE

### Late-Round Find

**PLACIDO POLANCO, SS, CARDINALS (19TH ROUND).** Polanco, a Dominican Republic native who was draft-eligible because he attended Miami-Dade CC North, had one of the best careers of any player drafted in 1994. Over 16 seasons, he hit .297-104-723 and won three Gold Gloves.

### Never Too Late

**MIKE GLAVINE, 1B, ASTROS (93RD ROUND).** Hall of Famer Tom Glavine's younger brother was the latest pick among 215 players drafted in 1994 who made it to the big leagues. He returned to Northeastern for his senior year and was a 22nd-round pick of the Indians in 1995. Eight years later, he played in six games with the Mets, with his brother as a teammate.

### Overlooked

**ARMANDO RIOS, OF, GIANTS.** Rios wasn't drafted in 1993, even after playing key roles in Louisiana State's College World Series titles in 1991 and '93. The Giants signed the Puerto Rican native prior to the 1994 season, and he played in the majors from 1998-2003, hitting .269-36-167 in 419 games. Just three players signed as free agents after the 1994 draft made it to the major leagues.

### International Gem

**ADRIAN BELTRE, 3B, DODGERS.** South Korean righthander **CHAN HO PARK** got a $1.2 million contract with the Dodgers, an international record. The Dodgers also signed Beltre, a Dominican native who proved to be the most productive amateur signed in 1994. Still active, Beltre has more than 400 home runs and multiple Gold Gloves.

### Minor League Take

**KEVIN WITT, SS, BLUE JAYS.** Witt had modest big league success, hitting .233-15-41 in 146 games

CONTINUED ON PAGE 436

**AT A GLANCE**

CONTINUED FROM PAGE 435

for four clubs. He made his mark in 12 years in the minors, hitting 269 homers with 885 RBIs.

## One Who Got Away

**TIM HUDSON, RHP/OF, ATHLETICS (35TH ROUND).** Hudson didn't sign out of Chattahoochee Valley (Ala.) JC. The A's drafted him again three years later in the sixth round out of Auburn University, and he emerged as the most productive big league pitcher drafted in 1994.

## They Were Drafted?

**CHARLIE WARD, SS, YANKEES (18TH ROUND); HINES WARD, OF, MARLINS (73RD ROUND).** Neither Ward gave much consideration to baseball, as other sports were a higher priority. Charlie won the 1993 Heisman Trophy as a quarterback for Florida State, and played with the New York Knicks. Hines turned down a $25,000 offer from the Marlins and became a star wide receiver at the University of Georgia on the way to a stellar career with the Pittsburgh Steelers.

## Did You Know . . .

Three first-rounders—**JOSH BOOTY** (Marlins), **MARK FARRIS** (Pirates) and **MATT SMITH** (Royals)—had greater success after quitting baseball and playing college football. Booty (LSU) and Farris (Texas A&M) became starting quarterbacks, and Smith (Oregon) was a three-year starter at linebacker.

## They Said It

Rangers general manager **TOM GRIEVE**, on his son **BEN** making the Grieves the first father-son first-round picks: "When it comes to fielding, throwing and hitting, 99 out of 100 scouts would recognize Ben had superior talent. And, of course, Ben had the advantage of growing up at the ballpark and being around major league players. He won't be awed by anything."

LARRY GOREN

Ben Grieve's professional career got off to a fast start, and he was the 1998 AL rookie of the year, but he could not sustain the success

of his son. "The only thing I could do was run a little faster. When it comes to fielding, throwing and hitting, 99 out of every 100 scouts would recognize Ben had superior talent. And, of course, Ben had the advantage of growing up at the ballpark and being around major league players."

Ben Grieve had a trying senior season at Martin High in Arlington, Texas. He was arrested along with two teammates for possession of alcohol and suspended five games, and he later contracted mononucleosis and missed several games. Grieve got just 38 at-bats for the season, yet was the first high school player drafted. He signed for $1.2 million and excelled, hitting .329 with seven homers and 50 RBIs in the short-season Northwest League. "We took a potential impact player, an everyday player, versus a guy (Hermanson) who throws hard and could one day be a closer," A's general manager Sandy Alderson said.

Grieve's older brother Tim, a righthander from Texas Christian, also was drafted in 1994, picked in the 23rd round by the Kansas City Royals.

Hermanson was a starter at Kent State as a junior, but most clubs viewed him as a closer in pro ball. He went to Double-A after signing and posted a 0.43 ERA, eight saves and 30 strikeouts in 21 innings before being promoted to Triple-A. Hermanson became the first player from the class to reach the majors, getting there after the strike was settled on April 2, 1995.

Unlike previous years when negotiations with top picks often were drawn out and contentious, Wilson, Grieve and Hermanson all had signed by June 20. Sixteen of the 28 first-rounders had signed by the end of June. Every first-rounder ultimately signed, and only righthander Carlton Loewer (Phillies) and catcher Jason Varitek (Mariners) didn't have deals before the onset of the strike.

## How They Should Have Done It

Based on the career WAR (Wins Above Replacement, as calculated by Baseball-Reference.com) numbers achieved by all the players eligible for the 1994 draft, here's how the first round should have unfolded. Numbers in parentheses indicate the round when the player was actually drafted. Asterisks denote players who signed as draft-and-follows.

| | Player, Pos. | Actual Draft | WAR | Bonus |
|---|---|---|---|---|
| 1. | Javier Vazquez, rhp | Expos (5) | 46.0 | $60,500 |
| 2. | Nomar Garciaparra, ss | Red Sox (1) | 44.2 | $895,000 |
| 3. | Placido Polanco, ss | Cardinals (19) | 41.4 | $10,000 |
| 4. | Paul Konerko, c | Dodgers (1) | 27.6 | $830,000 |
| 5. | A.J. Pierzynski, c | Twins (3) | 24.6 | $140,000 |
| | Corey Koskie, 3b | Twins (26) | 24.6 | $7,000 |
| 7. | Jason Varitek, c | Mariners (1) | 24.3 | $650,000 |
| 8. | Keith Foulke, rhp | Giants (9) | 20.9 | $40,000 |
| 9. | Ronnie Belliard, 2b | Brewers (8) | 20.7 | $60,000 |
| 10. | Carl Pavano, rhp | Red Sox (13) | 16.9 | $150,000 |
| 11. | Jay Payton, of | Mets (1-S) | 15.4 | $350,000 |
| 12. * | Julio Lugo, ss | Astros (43) | 13.6 | $60,000 |
| 13. | Aaron Boone, 3b | Reds (3) | 13.5 | $115,000 |
| 14. | Dustin Hermanson, rhp | Padres (1) | 11.4 | $960,000 |
| | Russell Branyan, 3b | Indians (7) | 11.4 | $60,000 |
| 16. | Bobby Howry, rhp | Giants (5) | 11.1 | $77,500 |
| 17. | Todd Walker, 2b | Twins (1) | 10.5 | $815,000 |
| 18. | Jose Rosado, lhp | Royals (12) | 10.4 | $20,000 |
| 19. * | Joe Mays, rhp | Mariners (6) | 9.4 | $45,000 |
| 20. | Dave Roberts, of | Tigers (28) | 9.0 | $1,000 |
| 21. | Ben Grieve, of | Athletics (1) | 8.4 | $1,200,000 |
| 22. | Scott Podsednik, of | Rangers (3) | 6.9 | $155,000 |
| 23. | Kyle Farnsworth, rhp | Cubs (47) | 6.4 | $20,000 |
| 24. | Danny Graves, rhp | Indians (4) | 5.9 | $80,000 |
| | John Halama, lhp | Astros (23) | 5.9 | $2,500 |
| 26. | Scott Sauerbeck, lhp | Mets (23) | 5.3 | $1,000 |
| 27. | Terrence Long, 1b | Mets (1) | 5.1 | $500,000 |
| 28. | Jaret Wright, rhp | Indians (1) | 4.7 | $1,150,000 |

| | Top 3 Unsigned Players | | | Year Signed |
|---|---|---|---|---|
| 1. | Tim Hudson, rhp | Athletics (35) | 58.7 | 1997 |
| 2. | J.D. Drew, of | Giants (20) | 44.8 | 1998 |
| 3. | Troy Glaus, 3b | Padres (2) | 37.9 | 1997 |

### MARLINS GAMBLE ON BOOTY

Booty was the highest-profile talent in 1994, and not just because he signed a record-breaking contract. He was arguably the nation's most talented player in both baseball and football. As a senior at Evangel Christian High in Shreveport, La., he hit .429 with 12 homers and 25 stolen bases, and he set national career high school records for passing yardage (11,700) and touchdown passes (126), despite missing the final four games of his senior year because of a broken hand. He was headed for Louisiana State as a shortstop and a quarterback, until signing with the Marlins on July 14.

"You'd better be good," said Marlins owner Wayne Huizenga, smiling at Booty at a news conference soon after he signed.

Booty was not good enough. In fact, he became one of the biggest busts of the draft era. He reached Miami, but only because his contract guaranteed that he would be a September callup in the 1995, '96 and '97 seasons. His big league career amounted to seven hits in 26 at-bats.

Frustrated with his lack of progress, Booty abandoned his baseball career after the 1998 season and enrolled at LSU to resurrect his football career at age 23. He had mixed success in two seasons as a quarterback, completing less than 50 percent of his passes. The Seattle Seahawks took him in the sixth round of the 2001 NFL draft, but he never played a down in an NFL game.

The four players selected ahead of Booty in the baseball draft also disappointed to varying degrees. Wilson's career was waylaid by injuries.

Grieve showed every indication of becoming a star when he hit a combined .350 with 31 homers and 136 RBIs in Double-A and Triple-A in 1997. That earned him a September promotion to Oakland, and he hit three doubles and drove in five runs in his debut game. Grieve hit .312 in 24 September games, and a year later was the American League rookie of the year and an all-star.

Grieve's smooth lefthanded swing reminded some of Ted Williams, but his career hit an early plateau. Oakland traded him to Tampa Bay after the 2000 season, but his decline continued, and he was out of the big leagues by 2005. In nine major league seasons, he hit .269 with 118 homers.

"I think he suffered a little bit from immense expectations," said Tom Grieve. "You look at that '97 season and everyone was thinking this kid was going to be the greatest player ever to come along."

Hermanson pitched in 12 major league seasons, working in 180 games as a starter and 177 as a reliever, and finished with a 73-78, 4.21 record with 56 saves. His best season was 2005, when he posted a 2.04 ERA and 34 saves for the Chicago White Sox. Hermanson injured his back late that season, essentially ending his career.

The Milwaukee Brewers selected Arizona State third baseman Antone Williamson with the fourth overall pick and thought he could be their third baseman by 1996. Williamson had a .378 average, 14 homers and 78 RBIs as a college sophomore, and he was equally prolific as a junior (.371-15-74). He was regarded as the most advanced hitter in the college ranks.

He played in just 23 major league games during his six seasons in the Brewers organization, hitting .204 with no home runs and six RBIs.

## VARITEK'S LONG, WINDING ROAD

Nomar Garciaparra (Red Sox), Paul Konerko (Dodgers) and Varitek proved to be the most successful first-round picks in 1994.

Garciaparra, an unsigned fifth-rounder in 1991 out of a California high school, hit .427 with 16 home runs and 33 stolen bases as a junior at Georgia Tech. After signing, he quickly became one of the best shortstops in baseball, along with Derek Jeter and Alex Rodriguez, and was a five-time all-star. Garciaparra won American League batting titles in 1999 and 2000 before injuries cut him down.

Georgia Tech teammates Garciaparra, Varitek,

### Fastest To The Majors

| | Player, Pos. | Drafted (Round) | Debut |
|---|---|---|---|
| 1. | Dustin Hermanson, rhp | Padres (1) | May 8, 1995 |
| 2. | C.J. Nitkowski, lhp | Reds (1) | June 3, 1995 |
| 3. | Paul Wilson, rhp | Mets (1) | April 4, 1996 |
| 4. | Matt Wagner, rhp | Mariners (3) | June 5, 1996 |
| 5. | Jose Rosado, lhp | Royals (12) | June 12, 1996 |

**FIRST HIGH SCHOOL SELECTION:** Josh Booty, ss (Marlins/1, Sept. 24, 1996)

## DRAFT SPOTLIGHT: JOSH BOOTY

MEL BAILEY

**Louisiana prep star Josh Booty had standout ability in both baseball and football, but could not find professional success in either sport**

At Evangel Christian High in Shreveport, La., Josh Booty became the first high school quarterback to pass for more than 10,000 yards. He was a recruit on the same level as Peyton Manning, another Louisiana QB in the class of 1994.

Booty also excelled in baseball and was a first-round draft choice of the Florida Marlins in 1994. When the Marlins' offered a $1.6 million signing bonus, Booty took the money.

Though he was a local hero and heavily committed to Louisiana State, the Marlins got an agreement from Booty that he would not play football for the duration of his six-year deal. They insisted on those terms after John Lynch, their second-round pick in 1992, abruptly quit baseball to pursue a pro football career.

"I would miss baseball if I played football a lot more than I would miss football if I played baseball," said Booty after signing. "Baseball is where I want to be."

The Marlins were as impressed with Booty's character as they were with his skills, which included raw power, a cannon arm and quick reflexes, all in a chiseled 6-foot-3, 215-pound frame. So they may have overlooked some other unsettling coincidences.

Booty's idol was John Elway, who once spurned the New York Yankees—and Gary Hughes, the scout who signed Elway and the scouting director who drafted Booty—to join the NFL in 1983. Booty and Lynch also shared the same agent, Jeff Moorad.

Marlins scout Bill Singer, however, had a relationship with Booty and his family and felt he knew Booty truly favored baseball. Singer was convinced Booty would excel at baseball and never give football a second thought.

But Booty's baseball career never panned out. He struggled in all facets of his game, hitting just .198 over five seasons in the minor leagues. He hit 62 home runs, but had 621 strikeouts in 1,745 at-bats. Drafted as a shortstop, Booty didn't have the range for the position and moved to third base, where he also proved to be a marginal defender.

Booty spent time in the big leagues from 1996-98, playing in 13 games and going 7-for-26. His first two appearances were a condition of his contract, though the Marlins were also trying to justify their investment. His last, on Opening Day 1998, was an effort to light a fire under Booty, but it didn't work and he quickly returned to the minors.

It was obvious that Booty was light years from ever playing regularly in the majors. The more Booty failed, the more he yearned for the spotlight and thought about football.

"I've always played better in bigger settings," Booty said. "The minor leagues, I just don't get into it too much. I just don't enjoy minor league baseball. Maybe I would enjoy Triple-A more than Double-A, but the 12-hour bus rides are horrible."

Booty was bound to the Marlins by his contract, and the Marlins would hold him to it—unless he returned his $1.6 million bonus. So Booty continued to plod along, his misery deepening with his constant struggles and a baseball career going nowhere.

Finally in 1998, Booty got the break he was looking for when the Marlins dropped him from their 40-man roster and exposed him to waivers. At 23, he returned to LSU, intent on resurrecting a football career that once held enormous promise.

But after years away from football, Booty's passing skills had regressed and he completed less than half his passes over two seasons as LSU's primary signal caller. He still had another year of eligibility, but he determined it was time to take his shot at the NFL, before it was too late. Booty quietly slipped to the sixth round in the 2001 NFL draft. He then spent three years in the NFL as a backup, but never threw a pass in an NFL game.

In the end, Booty had not only failed at baseball, but also at football. He was uniquely proficient at two sports, yet didn't thrive in either because of his divided loyalty. His biggest regret? He quit baseball too early and returned to football too late.

**WORTH NOTING**

■ In response to spiraling bonuses, major league teams discussed several changes to the draft with the Players Association as part of the negotiation of a new Collective Bargaining Agreement. The most significant proposal was a signing bonus structure for players drafted in the first five rounds, or a cap on the total amount of bonus money a team could spend annually. The owners also wanted to extend the draft to include all players worldwide, not just those playing in the United States, Canada and Puerto Rico. Continuing a theme that was common during baseball's extended period of labor strife, none of the proposed changes were made at the time because ownership and the union had more significant issues to deal with. But 17 years later, in the 2011 renewal of the CBA and after an extended period of labor peace, the two sides addressed the issues again and made significant changes to the draft process, including caps on bonus spending and a standard signing date. The international draft, however, remained a favored concept that presented significant logistical problems, and still had not been implemented.

■ The 1994 draft was notable for its lack of black players in the first round, at a time when the number of African-American players in Major League Baseball overall was declining. The first 16 players drafted were white, and the 17th pick, **RAMON CASTRO**, was a native of Puerto Rico. The first black player drafted was Alabama high school first baseman **TERRENCE LONG**, taken with the 21st pick by the Mets. One other black player, outfielder **DANTE POWELL**, drafted 22nd by the Giants, was selected in the first round.

■ The Mets had eight of the first 98 picks in the draft. However, they did not retain rights to Auburn righthander **JOHN POWELL**, the new NCAA career strikeout leader

outfielder Jay Payton and righthander Brad Rigby were among the first 40 picks in the draft—a record unmatched by any college team. Payton went 29th overall to the Mets, and Rigby went 40th to the A's. Tech made a run at a College World Series title, finishing second to an overachieving Oklahoma team that had only one draft pick in the first six rounds.

Varitek was a 1993 first-round choice of the Minnesota Twins as a junior and turned down a $450,000 offer. A year later, he became the 10th player to twice be a first-round draft choice, but was in a less favorable bargaining position because his college eligibility had expired.

The Mariners offered Varitek $400,000. He wanted $800,000, noting that Konerko, drafted just ahead of him, got $830,000, and Colorado high school righthander Jayson Peterson, taken right after him, received $712,500 from the Chicago Cubs. The stalemate continued as the strike put negotiations on hold for several months.

Varitek signed a contract with the St. Paul Saints of the independent Northern League with the intent of becoming a free agent if the Mariners didn't sign him before the 1995 draft. Major League Baseball, however, ruled that Varitek would be subject to the draft again if he didn't sign.

The Mariners again found themselves dealing with Scott Boras, Varitek's agent, who also represented the team's first-round choices the previous two years, Ron Villone and Alex Rodriguez. Both players signed after lengthy and contentious negotiations. Boras also had a pending grievance filed with the Players Association, contending that Rodriguez was misled by the Mariners before he signed a $1.3 million deal in August 1993.

"It's hard to go to ownership with the ceiling falling down (because of the strike) and ask for more money," said Mariners scouting director Roger Jongewaard. "And to say we have to get the money for Scott Boras is hard."

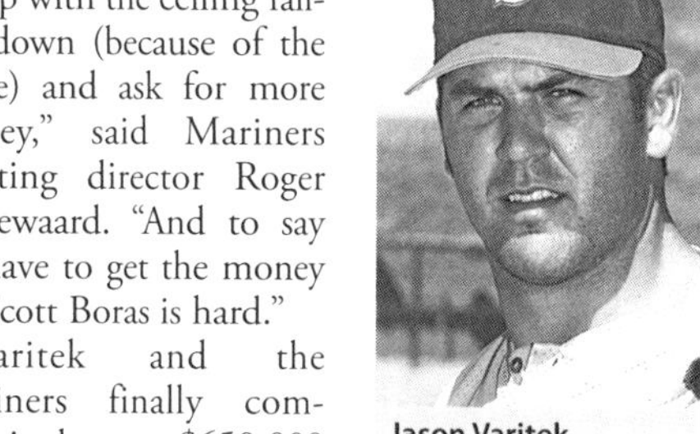

Jason Varitek

Varitek and the Mariners finally compromised on a $650,000 bonus in April 1995. Just before the 1997 trade deadline, the Mariners sent Varitek and pitcher Derek Lowe to the Red Sox for pitcher Heathcliff Slocumb. It proved to be a one-sided trade as Varitek became a fixture behind the plate for the Red Sox and was a key member of the team's World Series championships in 2004 and 2007.

Konerko was the first catcher drafted in 1994, selected by the Dodgers out of an Arizona high school. He made his mark as a first baseman over an 18-year major league career, the last 16 with the White Sox. The Dodgers traded Konerko to the Cincinnati Reds in 1998 after he had hit .331 with 43 homers and 153 RBIs in 154 games at Triple-A. The Reds later traded him to the White Sox. He hit .279 with 438 homers for his career.

There were more sad stories than successes among the 1994 first-round draft choices. Lefthander Doug

## Top 25 Bonuses

| | Player, Pos. | Drafted (Round) | Order | Bonus |
|---|---|---|---|---|
| 1. | ***Josh Booty, ss** | **Marlins (1)** | **5** | **$1,600,000** |
| 2. | **Paul Wilson, rhp** | **Mets (1)** | **1** | **$1,550,000** |
| 3. | ***Ben Grieve, of** | **Athletics (1)** | **2** | **$1,200,000** |
| 4. | ***Jaret Wright, rhp** | **Indians (1)** | **10** | **$1,150,000** |
| 5. | *Matt Smith, 1b | Royals (1) | 16 | $1,000,000 |
| 6. | **Dustin Hermanson, rhp** | **Padres (1)** | **3** | **$960,000** |
| 7. | *Doug Million, lhp | Rockies (1) | 7 | $905,000 |
| 8. | **Antone Williamson, 3b** | **Brewers (1)** | **4** | **$895,000** |
| | **Nomar Garciaparra, ss** | **Red Sox (1)** | **12** | **$895,000** |
| 10. | ***Paul Konerko, c** | **Dodgers (1)** | **13** | **$830,000** |
| 11. | Cade Gaspar, rhp | Tigers (1) | 18 | $825,000 |
| 12. | *Mark Farris, ss | Pirates (1) | 11 | $820,000 |
| 13. | **Todd Walker, 2b** | **Twins (1)** | **8** | **$815,000** |
| 14. | ***Scott Elarton, rhp** | **Astros (1)** | **25** | **$750,000** |
| 15. | *Jay Peterson, rhp | Cubs (1) | 15 | $712,500 |
| 16. | ***McKay Christensen, of** | **Angels (1)** | **6** | **$700,000** |
| 17. | **C.J. Nitkowski, lhp** | **Reds (1)** | **9** | **$675,000** |
| 18. | **Jason Varitek, c** | **Mariners (1)** | **14** | **$650,000** |
| 19. | ***Hiram Bocachica, ss** | **Expos (1)** | **21** | **$635,000** |
| 20. | **Carlton Loewer, rhp** | **Phillies (1)** | **23** | **$590,000** |
| 21. | Bret Wagner, lhp | Cardinals (1) | 19 | $525,000 |
| 22. | ***Mark Johnson, c** | **White Sox (1)** | **26** | **$520,000** |
| 23. | **Dante Powell, of** | **Giants (1)** | **22** | **$507,500** |
| 24. | ***Terrence Long, 1b** | **Mets (1)** | **20** | **$500,000** |
| | **Brian Buchanan, 1b** | **Yankees (1)** | **24** | **$500,000** |
| | *Jacob Shumate, rhp | Braves (1) | 27 | $500,000 |

*Major leaguers in bold. *High school selection.*

Million, the seventh overall selection, died on Sept. 24, 1997, due to complications from an asthma attack. He had a 26-32 record and 4.12 ERA in four seasons in the Colorado Rockies organization.

Outfielder Brian Buchanan, a first-round pick of the New York Yankees (24th overall), was hustling down the first-base line during a 1995 game at Class A Greensboro and hit the bag at an awkward angle. He collapsed, with his foot dangling grotesquely from his leg, having sustained a compound ankle fracture and dislocation. Doctors told Buchanan the damage to his ligaments and nerves was so severe that they considered amputation. The 6-foot-6 Buchanan, who had been a top power-hitting prospect, missed the balance of the 1995 season but came back to play professionally for 15 seasons, including five in the majors.

Loewer, selected 23rd overall by the Philadelphia Phillies out of Mississippi State, had his career compromised by a similar injury. He fell 10 feet out of a duck blind in 2000 and sustained a compound fracture and dislocation, costing him the season. Doctors said the unstable ankle contributed to elbow and shoulder problems in 2001 and '02 that essentially ended his career. In 48 big league appearances over four seasons, he went 10-18, 6.13.

Two first-rounders didn't get beyond Class A. Righthander Cade Gaspar, drafted 18th overall by the Detroit Tigers out of Pepperdine, was sidetracked by an arm injury. The Cubs sent Jayson Peterson home from spring training in 1995 for insubordination. He played four years before being traded to the Reds and had a 28-35, 4.93 record to show for his underwhelming career.

Righthander Jacob Shumate, selected by the Braves with the 27th pick out of a South Carolina high school, got no further than Double-A and

## Largest Bonuses By Round

| | Player, Pos. | Club | Bonus |
|---|---|---|---|
| 1. | * **Josh Booty, ss** | **Marlins** | **$1,600,000** |
| 2. | * **George Lombard, of** | **Braves** | **$425,000** |
| 3. | * **Brian Rose, rhp** | **Red Sox** | **$365,000** |
| 4. | * Robb Welch, rhp | Red Sox | $338,000 |
| 5. | * **Brian Barkley, lhp** | **Red Sox** | **$200,000** |
| | * Keith Smith, of | Tigers | $200,000 |
| 6. | * Michael Peeples, ss | Blue Jays | $200,000 |
| 7. | Jamie Jaye, lhp | Dodgers | $125,000 |
| 8. | * Billy Blythe, rhp | Braves | $300,000 |
| 9. | * **Jimmy Anderson, lhp** | **Pirates** | **$100,000** |
| 10. | * **Wes Helms, ss** | **Braves** | **$100,000** |
| 11. | * **Jake Robbins, rhp** | **Yankees** | **$80,000** |
| 12. | Eric Clifford, rhp | Mariners | $60,000 |
| 13. | * **Carl Pavano, rhp** | **Red Sox** | **$150,000** |
| 14. | *# Rodney Getz, rhp | Marlins | $220,000 |
| 15. | * **Gary Glover, rhp** | **Blue Jays** | **$62,500** |
| 16. | *# Pete Paciorek, 1b | Padres | $40,000 |
| 17. | * Mark Roettgen, rhp | Cardinals | $30,000 |
| 18. | Stephen Fuller, rhp | Astros | $86,000 |
| 19. | * Cy Simonton, of | Mariners | $40,000 |
| 20. | # Brady Wuestenhoefer, rhp | Rockies | $35,000 |
| 21. | **Lance Carter, rhp** | **Royals** | **$30,000** |
| 22. | * **John Riedling, rhp** | **Reds** | **$20,000** |
| 23. | * **Andy Thompson, ss** | **Blue Jays** | **$350,000** |
| 24. | * Dwayne Jacobs, rhp | Braves | $20,000 |
| 25. | * Matt Sachse, lhp | Mariners | $300,000 |
| Other | # **Jordan Zimmerman, lhp** | **Mariners (32)** | **$325,000** |

*Major leaguers in bold. *High school selection. #Signed as draft-and-follow.*

finished an eight-year minor league career with a 14-30, 7.10 record, 436 walks and 125 wild pitches in 312 innings.

Tragedy also struck outfielder Mike Darr, a second-round pick of the Tigers and the son of former major leaguer Mike Darr Sr. The younger Darr died on Feb. 15, 2002, from injuries sustained in a single-car accident in Peoria, Ariz., where he was attending spring training with the Mariners.

### TWO-SPORT STARS FILL FIRST ROUND

Multi-sport athletes had not particularly embraced pro baseball in recent years, but money talked louder than ever in 1994. Four top high school football/baseball athletes went in the first round, and all signed contracts: Booty, outfielder McKay Christensen (Angels, sixth overall), shortstop Mark Farris (Pirates, 11th) and first baseman/pitcher Matt Smith (Royals, 16th).

Christensen was one of the nation's top running back prospects, and he intended to pursue a football career at Brigham Young after serving a two-year Mormon mission. But once his baseball stock soared—Christensen hit .500 and stole 62 consecutive bases in his final high school season—some clubs decided it would be worth buying him out of his BYU commitment. The California Angels offered him a $700,000 bonus and agreed that he could fulfill his planned mission to Japan and delay the start of his pro career until 1996.

Christensen never played a game in the Angels organization. The team traded him to the White Sox on July 27, 1995. He made his major league debut with the White Sox in 1999, but wasn't much of a player. He had a .250 average, two homers and six stolen bases in 99 games over four seasons.

Farris passed for 1,831 yards and 21 touchdowns as a senior at Angleton (Texas) High, and planned to play quarterback at Texas A&M. But he also showed great promise in baseball and agreed to quit football when the Pirates offered him $820,000. Farris suffered a knee injury that kept him out of the 1995 season and troubled him throughout his four-year career in the minors. He didn't have enough range to play shortstop, or enough power to be a frontline third baseman.

Texas A&M football coach R.C. Slocum persuaded Farris in 1998 to give up baseball and return to football. Farris left with a career .244 average, 14 homers and 126 RBIs. At A&M, he passed for more than 2,000 yards in both 2000 and 2001.

Smith, an Oregon high school product, committed to Stanford to play linebacker for the football team, and both hit and pitch for the baseball team. He changed his mind when the Royals offered a $1 million bonus. Most clubs thought his future was as a pitcher, but the Royals likened him to pitcher-turned-power hitter Ryan Klesko. The 6-foot-4, 220-pound Smith never hit more than six homers in a season, though, prompting the Royals to try him as a pitcher in 1998. He was out of the game after going 0-3, 3.81. Smith, too, returned to football and became a starting linebacker for three seasons at Oregon (1998-2000).

Lombard was one of the nation's top running back recruits at the Lovett School in Atlanta and committed to play football at Georgia. He was a second-round draft choice of the hometown Braves, and chose baseball when the Braves offered a $425,000 bonus, the richest ever for a second-rounder. It was a significant gamble, considering that Lombard had played 35 baseball games over his last three years in high school.

Lombard showed promise as a power/speed threat, but didn't hit well enough to establish himself as a major league regular, batting .220 in parts of six seasons. He stuck with baseball until 2009, long after Jamie Howard and Andre King, the Braves' second-round picks in 1992 and 1993, who gave up on baseball and returned to football.

Keith Smith set numerous California high school career passing records at Newbury Park High, and accepted a football scholarship from Arizona. The Tigers picked Smith in the fifth round of the baseball draft and signed him for a $200,000 bonus. Smith lasted only a year in baseball before

## Highest Unsigned Picks

| Player, Pos., Team (Round) | College | Re-Drafted |
|---|---|---|
| Troy Glaus, 3b, Padres (2) | UCLA | Angels '97 (1) |
| Kenny Henderson, rhp, Expos (2) | *Miami | Brewers '91 (5) |
| Matthew LeCroy, c, Mets (2) | Clemson | Twins '97 (1-S) |
| Brad Freeman, 3b, Blue Jays (4) | Mississippi State | Indians '97 (12) |
| Brian Kuklick, rhp, Mets (5) | Wake Forest | Mets '97 (55) |
| Ryan Drese, rhp, Athletics (5) | California | Athletics '97 (14) |
| Eric DuBose, lhp, Dodgers (6) | Mississippi State | Athletics '97 (1) |
| Brett Nista, ss, Mets (7) | UCLA | Never |
| Tim Spindler, rhp/ss, Cubs (7) | Orange Co. (N.Y.) CC | Yankees '95 (32) |
| Scott Brand, rhp, Reds (8) | McLennan (Texas) CC | Yankees '95 (8) |

**TOTAL UNSIGNED PICKS:** Top 5 Rounds (6), Top 10 Rounds (25)

*Returned to same school.

### WORTH NOTING

whom they had drafted in the 13th round in 1993 after he led NCAA pitchers in strikeouts with 191. Powell returned to college, but the Mets kept his rights because he was a fifth-year senior. The team had until seven days before the 1994 draft to sign Powell, but that window closed when Auburn advanced to the College World Series. Powell, who had 602 strikeouts in his college career, was selected by the Rangers in the ninth round and, with no bargaining leverage, agreed to a $17,500 signing bonus.

■ The Brewers selected Arizona State third baseman **ANTONE WILLIAMSON** with the fourth pick overall. Brewers general manager Sal Bando also played third base for the Sun Devils in his collegiate days, but said the connection to Williamson was purely coincidental. While Williamson was generally regarded as the most advanced hitter in the collegiate ranks, there were concerns about Williamson's other tools, notably his defense. Bando ill-advisedly pushed for his selection, and not long after it was evident that the Brewers had made a mistake—that Williamson would never be the impact player they hoped he would be. He was a below-average runner and didn't hit for the power expected—especially after he was moved to first base midway through his career. Moreover, Williamson let his body get soft, became injury-prone and appeared to lose his drive. He played in just 23 major league games during his six seasons in the organization, hitting just .204-0-6. The Brewers closed one of the most unfortunate chapters in their draft history by cutting Williamson loose from minor league camp in spring training of 2000.

■ Just 68.4 percent of the college players drafted in 1994 signed pro contracts, the lowest percentage since 1978. A total of 286 high school players signed, the most in draft history at the time.

**IN FOCUS: PAUL WILSON**

Even after righthander Paul Wilson went 0-7 in his first summer as a professional, Mets fans still expected the top pick in the 1994 draft to reach Shea Stadium in short order and blossom into a frontline pitcher.

But Wilson's career was dented by injuries. He went 5-12, 5.38 in 1996, his only season with the Mets, before surgery to repair a torn labrum cost him most of the 1997 and '98 seasons. He then tore a ligament in his pitching elbow, and Tommy John surgery sidelined him all of 1999.

"I bawled my eyes out after the second surgery," Wilson said. "I couldn't believe it had happened again. But it made me want it even more. It was another challenge."

While Wilson worked his way back in 2000, the Mets became impatient and dealt him to the Devil Rays. He had a few productive, mostly injury-free years with the Rays and later the Reds, but compiled a 40-58, 4.86 record overall in seven major league seasons. On only one occasion did he post a winning record.

"There was so much hype, it was scary not to be good," Wilson said. "I was afraid of failing at Shea. I wanted to live up to those expectations, and when I didn't, it compounded the problems and made it worse. The pressure just built and built, and it consumed me."

quitting, giving back his bonus money and heading to Arizona. He passed for 5,829 yards and 41 touchdowns over four years, including the 1998 season, in which the Wildcats posted a 12-1 record, best in school history.

There also was a basketball player of note in the 1994 baseball draft: Trajan Langdon, who played guard for his Anchorage, Alaska, basketball team and was an infielder on the baseball team. The Padres selected Langdon in the sixth round, aware that he had committed to play basketball at Duke. Rather than try to talk him out of playing basketball, the Padres offered Langdon a deal that allowed him to spend as little as one month each summer playing baseball. It cost them about $230,000—a $75,000 bonus and the balance to cover the scholarship Langdon forfeited under NCAA rules by accepting a pro baseball contract.

Langdon played in just 50 games over three summers in the Padres system, hitting .156 with three homers. Basketball served him much better. He played four years at Duke, was the 11th player selected in the 1999 NBA draft, played three years with the Cleveland Cavaliers, and spent most of the next decade playing professionally in Europe.

Other basketball players of note selected in the 1994 baseball draft were Eric Montross (Cubs) and Charlie Ward (Yankees), who were picked a few weeks before becoming first-round selections in the NBA draft.

### PUERTO RICANS PLAY PROMINENT ROLE

A record-tying 1,721 players were drafted in 1994, the same number as in the previous year. The 1994 draft didn't end until the Houston Astros made a pick in the 98th round, their 100th selection overall. The Rangers were the last team to make their first pick (No. 56 overall) and the first team to drop out, in the 40th round.

Puerto Ricans were not subject to the draft until 1989, but played a greater role in the 1994 process than any draft ever, producing two first-rounders for the only time ever, as well as a record 34 picks and record-tying seven future major leaguers.

The Astros selected catcher Ramon Castro with the 17th overall pick, making him the first Puerto Rican ever drafted in the first round. Shortstop Hiram Bocachica soon became the second, going to the Expos four picks later. All three San Juan newspapers carried the developments on their front pages.

"The phone hasn't stopped ringing all day," said Ramon Castro Sr. "For us, this is a holiday. I knew since he was 5 years old that he would play in the major leagues. And now it looks like he is on his way."

Castro played 13 seasons in the majors, but none in an Astros uniform. He was traded to the Marlins in 1998 while still in the minors. Castro was one of four catchers drafted in the first round, three from the prep ranks and Varitek from the college ranks.

Three sons of former major leaguers were selected in the first round: Grieve, Cade Gaspar (son of Rod) and Jaret Wright (son of Clyde). Wright, selected by the Indians, was the hardest-throwing pitcher in the 1994 prep class, and shared the distinction with Hermanson of being the highest-rated player, according to the Major League Scouting Bureau. Wright's fastball eventually reached 98 mph, but he was plagued throughout his 11-year major league career by shoulder injuries and never quite fulfilled his potential, going 68-60, 5.09.

Gaspar's career in the Tigers organization was short-lived after he injured his right shoulder while lifting weights. Altering his pitching mechanics to compensate, he injured his right elbow. Gaspar lasted just three seasons, going 15-13, 4.65 and peaking in Class A.

Infielder Aaron Boone was selected in the third round by the Reds, who at the time employed his brother Bret as their second baseman and his father Bob as a coach. The Boones had become baseball's first three-generation family in 1992, when Bret reached the majors with the Mariners. Bret and Aaron's grandfather, Ray, and father also played in the big leagues.

In another potential three-generation scenario, UCLA righthander Brian Stephenson, son of Jerry and grandson of Joe, both former major leaguers, was drafted by the Cubs in the second round. Brian's career did not advance beyond Double-A.

## Largest Draft-And-Follow Bonuses

| | Player, Pos. | Club (Round) | Bonus |
|---|---|---|---|
| **1.** | **Jordan Zimmerman, lhp** | **Mariners (32)** | **$325,000** |
| 2. | * Rodney Getz, rhp | Marlins (14) | $220,000 |
| 3. | * Alex Fajardo, lhp | Dodgers (11) | $70,000 |
| **4.** | **Julio Lugo, ss** | **Astros (43)** | **$60,000** |
| | Jaime Malave, 1b | Dodgers (69) | $60,000 |
| 6. | Scott DeWitt, lhp | Marlins (52) | $50,000 |
| | Jason Romine, rhp | Rockies (59) | $50,000 |
| **8.** | ***Joe Mays, rhp** | **Mariners (6)** | **$45,000** |
| | Greg Romo, rhp | Tigers (25) | $45,000 |
| 10. | * Pete Paciorek, 1b | Padres (16) | $40,000 |
| | * J.D. Pretash, lhp | Astros (50) | $40,000 |
| | Brian Tickell, rhp | Astros (88) | $40,000 |

*Major leaguers in bold. *High school selection.*

## One Team's Draft: Boston Red Sox

| | Player, Pos. | Bonus |
|---|---|---|
| **1.** | **Nomar Garciaparra, ss** | **$895,000** |
| 2. | Selection to Braves | |
| **3.** | ***Brian Rose, rhp** | **$365,000** |
| 4. | * Robb Welch, rhp | $338,000 |
| **5.** | ***Brian Barkley, lhp** | **$200,000** |
| 6. | Joe Mamott, rhp | $65,000 |
| 7. | Denis McLaughlin, rhp | $54,000 |
| 8. | Chad Barnhardt, c | $46,000 |
| 9. | Chris Allison, 2b | $30,000 |
| 10. | * Damian Sapp, c | $28,000 |
| **11.** | ***Donnie Sadler, ss** | **$32,000** |
| 12. | * Antonio Santiago, lhp | $25,000 |
| **13.** | ***Carl Pavano, rhp** | **$150,000** |
| 14. | Mike Jacobs, rhp | $19,000 |
| 15. | Matt Bazzani, c | $20,000 |
| 16. | Chuck Malloy, rhp | $5,000 |
| 17. | Robert Moore, rhp | Did not sign |
| **18.** | ***Michael Coleman, of** | **$40,000** |
| 19. | * Tony DeRosso, 1b | $35,000 |
| 20. | Bartt Carney, of | Unavailable |
| 21. | Chris Westcott, rhp | $10,000 |
| 22. | Shawn Rogers, of | Did not sign |
| 23. | * Casey Child, of | Did not sign |
| 24. | Robert Butler, lhp | $17,500 |
| 25. | Marc Lewis, of | $15,000 |

*Major leaguers in bold. *High school selection.*

# 1994 Draft List

*Did not sign. Major leaguers in bold, with first and last years noted. Order of selection indicated in parentheses. For the first five rounds, the peak level of each player is noted. + Signed as draft-and-follow (Second school noted if applicable).*

## ATLANTA BRAVES (27)

1. **Jacob Shumate, rhp, Hartsville (S.C.) HS.—(AA)**
2. Corey Pointer, c, Waxahachie (Texas) HS (Choice from Red Sox as compensation for Type B free agent Otis Nixon)—(AA).
2. **George Lombard, of, Lovett HS, Atlanta.—(1998-2006)**
3. Joe Giuliano, rhp, Baden HS, Hamilton, Ohio.—(Low A)
4. Eric Pickett, 1b-of, Independence HS, San Jose, Calif.—(Short-season A)
5. Mike Russell, lhp, Nacogdoches (Texas) HS.—Rookie)
6. Derek Foote, c, Wake Forest-Rolesville HS, Wake Forest, N.C.

DRAFT DROP *Son of Barry Foote, first-round draft pick, Expos (1970); major leaguer (1973-82)*

7. **Ron Wright, 1b, Kamiakin HS, Kennewick, Wash.—(2002)**
8. Billy Blythe, rhp, Bryan Station HS, Lexington, Ky.
9. Jayson Bass, of, Fayette County HS, Fayette, Ala.
10. **Wes Helms, ss-rhp, Ashbrook HS, Gastonia, N.C.—(1998-2011)**
11. Joaquin Johnson, 1b-of, Oakland Tech HS, Oakland.
12. ***Scott Downs, lhp, Pleasure Ridge Park HS, Louisville, Ky.—(2000-14)**
13. William Wise, rhp, Sumter County HS, Plains, Ga.
14. Robert Duncan, of, Ellison HS, Killeen, Texas.
15. Kendall Hill, rhp, Jefferson Davis (Ala.) JC.
16. *Scott McAllister, lhp, Lovett HS, Atlanta.
17. Bennie Robbins, rhp, Pine Forest HS, Pensacola, Fla.
18. **Derrin Ebert, lhp, Hesperia (Calif.) HS.—(1999)**
19. Chris Gobert, lhp, Lee (Texas) JC.
20. Ray McWhite, c-3b, St. Thomas (Fla.) University.
21. Chris Gongora, lhp, Glendale (Ariz.) CC.
22. Rich Spiegel, c, Anne Arundel (Md.) CC.
23. Brett Newell, ss, University of Washington.
24. Dwayne Jacobs, rhp, First Coast HS, Jacksonville, Fla.
25. Tony Wood, 2b, Eastern Oregon State College.
26. *Jeff Garff, rhp, Viewmont HS, Bountiful, Utah.
27. *Jason Pozo, ss, Central Regional HS, Bayville. N.J.
28. *Skip Ames, rhp, Howard (Texas) JC.
29. *Matt Herr, rhp, Hotchkiss HS, New Windsor, N.Y.
30. Adam Mullen, c, Beaufort (S.C.) HS.
31. Gus Kennedy, of, University of Nevada-Reno.
32. ***Mark Hendrickson, lhp, Washington State University.—(2002-11)**

DRAFT DROP *Forward, National Basketball Association (1996-2000)*

33. *Jeremy Salyers, rhp, Pound (Va.) HS.
34. *Doug Bridges, lhp, Spring Valley HS, Columbia, S.C.
35. Antonio Williams, of, Tampa Bay Technical HS, Tampa.
36. Ken Raines, lhp, Western Michigan University.
37. Sadiel Suarez, ss, Miami (Fla.) Senior HS.
38. *Jim Egan, c, Champlin Park HS, Brooklyn Center, Minn.
39. Brandon Hoalton, rhp, Rancho Santiago (Calif.) JC.
40. Dwight Lewis, of, Long Beach (Calif.) CC.
41. Colby Weaver, c, Florida State University.
42. Angel Espada, 2b, Puerto Rico Technical Deportiva HS, Salinas, P.R.
43. *Jim Sipkovich, lhp, Marina HS, Huntington Beach, Calif.
44. Zach Collins, lhp, Essex (Md.) CC.
45. *Matt Lubozynski, lhp, Choctawhatchee HS, Fort Walton Beach, Fla.
46. *Drew Chaney, rhp, South HS, Springfield, Ill.
47. *Pete Cuellar, lhp, Poly HS, Long Beach, Calif.
48. *Rich Hills, ss, University of Oklahoma.
49. *Fred Knox, of, Eldorado HS, Albuquerque, N.M.
50. *Bryan Senior, of, Brookstone HS, Columbus. Ga.
51. ***Larry Barnes, 1b, Bakersfield (Calif.) JC.—(2001-03)**
52. *Derrick Langford, of, Contra Costa (Calif.) JC.
53. Wilton Person, of, Florida A&M University.
54. *Troy Silva, rhp, Cuesta (Calif.) JC.
55. Charles Fritz, lhp, West Chester (Pa.) University.
56. *Jason Cook, of, Jefferson Davis (Ala.) JC.
57. *Marlin Hardy, of, Anderson HS, Austin, Texas.

**First-round pick Nomar Garciaparra blossomed into a batting champion with the Red Sox**

## BALTIMORE ORIOLES (20)

1. (Choice to Mets as compensation for Type A free agent Sid Fernandez)
2. **Tommy Davis, 1b, University of Southern Mississippi.—(1999)**
3. Roger Worley, rhp, Quartz Hill (Calif.) HS.—(Rookie)
4. **Jason Rogers, lhp, University of Nevada-Reno.—(AAA)**
5. Todd LaRocca, rhp-ss, Stanford University.—(High A)
6. Brandon Huntsman, rhp, Pleasant Grove (Utah) HS.
7. Noel Ramos, 1b, Dr. Juan Alejo de Arizmendi HS, Isabela, P.R.
8. *Richard Welsh, ss, Germanton Academy, Blue Bell, Pa.
9. **Chris Fussell, rhp, Clay HS, Oregon, Ohio.—(1998-2000)**
10. *Jason Hairston, c, Jefferson HS, Portland, Ore.

DRAFT DROP *Grandson of Sam Hairston, major leaguer (1951) • Son of John Hairston, major leaguer (1969)*

11. Brian Kerr, of, Farmington (N.M.) HS.
12. Todd Dyess, rhp, Tulane University.
13. Sean Hugo, 1b-of, Oklahoma State University.
14. Kedric Porter, of, Hillsborough HS, Tampa.
15. Chris Kirgan, 1b, University of Northern Colorado.
16. Chaad Stewart, lhp, Triton (Ill.) JC.
17. Mike Nadeau, 2b, George Fox (Ore.) College.
18. *John Sneed, rhp, Westfield HS, Houston.
19. *Matt Leviton, lhp, De Matha Catholic HS, Adelphi, Md.
20. Rolo Avila, of, Long Beach State University.
21. Mike Wolff, 1b, Miami (Ohio) University.
22. *Ryan Young, rhp, University of Mississippi.
23. Tom D'Aquila, of, North Carolina Wesleyan University.
24. Shawn Bates, lhp, New Mexico JC.
25. ***Michael Young, ss-of, Bishop Amat HS, Covina, Calif.—(2000-13)**
26. Brad Crills, rhp, Mansfield (Pa.) University.
27. Matt Marenghi, rhp, Stanford University.
28. Frank Harmer, c, Brevard (Fla.) CC.
29. Craig Daedelow, ss, Huntington Beach (Calif.) HS.
30. Pedro Ortiz, of, Pedro Albizu Campos HS, Levittown, P.R.
31. Chris Sauritch, 2b, Southern Illinois University.
32. Tim Daigle, lhp, Nicholls State University.
33. **Rick Short, 3b, Western Illinois University.—(2005)**
34. *Robert Conway, rhp, Tulane University.
35. *Bradley Wagers, rhp, Parkland (Ill.) JC.
36. *Billy Oliver, rhp, Greenwood HS, Bowling Green, Ky.
37. *Ryan Kennedy, rhp, Quitman HS, Shubuta, Miss.
38. Ryan Hendricks, 1b, St. Andrews (N.C.) College.

DRAFT DROP *Son of Elrod Hendricks, major leaguer (1968-79)*

39. Todd Brown, of, University of Florida.
40. Derek Brown, 2b, South Hagerstown HS, Hagerstown, Md.
41. *Steven Cook, rhp, Blair (Neb.) HS.
42. *Allen Sebold, c, Northern Garrett HS, Grantsville, Md.
43. *Chris Blue, ss, Easton (Md.) HS.
44. *Brian August, ss, St. Marks HS, Wilmington, Del.

## BOSTON RED SOX (12)

1. **Nomar Garciaparra, ss, Georgia Tech.—(1996-2009)**
2. (Choice to Braves as compensation for Type B free agent Otis Nixon)
3. **Brian Rose, rhp, Dartmouth (Mass.) HS.—(1997-2001)**
4. Robb Welch, rhp, Twin Falls (Idaho) HS.—(High A)
5. **Brian Barkley, lhp, Midway HS, Waco, Texas.—(1998)**
6. Joe Mamott, rhp, Canisius College.
7. Denis McLaughlin, rhp, Old Dominion University.
8. **Chad Barnhardt, c, Lake Wales (Fla.) HS.**
9. Chris Allison, 2b, Bradley University.
10. Damian Sapp, c, Pleasant Grove (Utah) HS.
11. **Donnie Sadler, ss, Valley Mills (Texas) HS.—(1998-2007)**
12. Antonio Santiago, lhp, Colegio Mercy Soto HS, Carolina, P.R.
13. **Carl Pavano, rhp, Southington (Conn.) HS.—(1998-2012)**
14. Mike Jacobs, rhp, East Carolina University.
15. Matt Bazzani, c, UC Santa Barbara.
16. Chuck Malloy, rhp, St. Joseph's University.
17. *Robert Moore, rhp, University of Hawaii.
18. **Michael Coleman, of, Stratford HS, Nashville, Tenn.—(1997-2001)**
19. Tony DeRosso, 1b, Colquitt County HS, Moultrie, Ga.
20. Bartt Carney, of, Indian Hills (Iowa) CC.
21. Chris Westcott, rhp, University of New Orleans.
22. *Shawn Rogers, of, University of Hawaii.
23. *Casey Child, of, Mountain View HS, Orem, Utah.
24. Robert Butler, lhp, Rend Lake (Ill.) JC.
25. Marc Lewis, of, Calhoun (Ala.) CC.
26. Jayson Black, rhp, Crestview HS, Convoy, Ohio.
27. Keith Goodwin, of, Sulphur (La.) HS.
28. *Torrance Miller, of, South Georgia JC.
29. Nathan Barns, of, Central HS, Rapid City, S.D.
30. *John McNeese, lhp, University of Mississippi.
31. *Dave Elliott, of, Western Michigan University.
32. *Wayne Montgomery, rhp, Stratford Academy, Macon, Ga.
33. John Raifstanger, 2b, Springfield (Mass.) College.
34. ***David Maurer, lhp, Howard (Texas) JC.—(2000-04)**
35. *Derrick Lewis, rhp, Lanier HS, Montgomery, Ala.
36. *Angel Diaz, c, Lake Gibson HS, Lakeland, Fla.
37. *Jack Koch, rhp, Osceola HS, Kissimmee, Fla.
38. *Joe Robinson, ss, Indian Hills (Iowa) CC.
39. ***Tim Palmer, c, Fresno (Calif.) CC.**
40. ***Pat Daneker, rhp, Loyalsock Township HS, Williamsport, Pa.—(1999)**
41. *Andre Thompson, of, Hinds (Miss.) CC.
42. *Ken Arnold, 3b, Chipola (Fla.) JC.
43. *Dexter Battle, 1b, Hillsborough HS, Tampa.
44. *Mike Whitley, rhp, Southwest Missouri State University.
45. Rene Justiniano, rhp, Triton (Ill.) JC.
46. Chris Kurek, c, St. Bonaventure University.
47. *Jamey Price, rhp, University of Mississippi.

## CALIFORNIA ANGELS (6)

1. **McKay Christensen, of, Clovis West HS, Fresno, Calif.—(1999-2002)**
2. Norm Hutchins, of, Lincoln HS, Yonkers, N.Y.—(AAA)
3. Paul Failla, ss, University of Notre Dame.—(High A)
4. Matt Beaumont, lhp, Ohio State University.—(AAA)
5. Greg Morris, ss, UC Davis.—(AA)
6. **Jason Dickson, rhp, Northeastern Oklahoma A&M JC.—(1996-2000)**
7. Rich Stuart, of, Dra Maria Cadilla Martinez HS, Arecibo, P.R.
8. Nick Skuse, rhp, Sonoma State (Calif.) University.
9. Jayson Sears, c, Henderson (Texas) HS.
10. Rob Bonanno, rhp, University of Florida.
11. Kevin Young, 3b-of, Central Michigan University.
12. *Derek Baker, 3b, Tustin (Calif) HS.
13. Ariel Delgado, of, Lorenzo Vizcarrondo HS, Carolina, P.R.
14. **Bret Hemphill, c, Cal State Fullerton.—(1999)**
15. Mike Freehill, rhp, San Diego State University.
16. Allan Parker, ss, Tennessee State University.
17. **Mike Holtz, lhp, Clemson University.—(1996-2006)**

18. Keith Coe, rhp, Old Dominion University.
**19. *Todd Sears, 1b-rhp, Ankeny (Iowa) HS.—(2002-03)**
**20. *Dustan Mohr, of, Oak Grove HS, Hattiesburg, Miss.—(2001-07)**
21. +Brian Riley, rhp, Miami-Dade CC South.
22. Keith Volkman, lhp, Glen Burnie HS, Pasadena, Md.
**23. *Corky Miller, c, Yucaipa (Calif.) HS.—(2001-13)**
24. *Gilbert Vidal, c, Miami-Dade CC Wolfson.
25. Denny Van Pelt, 1b, Radford University.
26. *Paul Mintz, lhp, North Brunswick HS, Leland, N.C.
27. Saul Rodriguez, ss, Southwestern (Calif.) JC.
28. *Adam Walker, lhp, La Cueva HS, Albuquerque, N.M.
29. *Brian Blessie, rhp, Butler County (Kan.) CC.
30. *Garrett Lee, rhp, Crescenta Valley HS, La Crescenta, Calif.
31. Ryan Wheeler, ss-2b, Penn State University.
32. Mike Fontana, rhp, Long Beach State University.
33. *Rudy Rosales, rhp, Tucson (Ariz.) HS.
34. Dave Sick, rhp, San Jose State University.
35. *Michael Leach, rhp, Osceola HS, Seminole, Fla.
36. *Tim Logan, of, John F. Kennedy HS, Richmond, Calif.
37. *Gary Thompson, of, Morse HS, San Diego.
38. Jeremy Ruby, 1b-lhp, Valley View HS, Eynon, Pa.
39. *Brian Nelson, c, Sarasota (Fla.) HS.
40. Don Nestor, rhp, University of South Florida.
41. *Ryan Hammons, 1b, San Diego Mesa JC.
**42. *Eric Knott, lhp, Edison (Fla.) CC.—(2001-03)**
**43. *Kevin Nicholson, ss, Queen Elizabeth HS, Surrey, B.C.—(2000)**
DRAFT DROP *First-round draft pick (26th overall), Padres (1997)*
44. +Steve Quinteros, rhp, Montgomery HS, San Diego / Southwestern (Calif.) JC.
45. Joey Jackson, 2b, Wichita State University.

## CHICAGO CUBS (15)

1. Jay Peterson, rhp, East HS, Denver.—(High A)
2. Brian Stephenson, rhp, UCLA.—(AA)
DRAFT DROP *Grandson of Joe Stephenson, major leaguer (1943-47) • Son of Jerry Stephenson, major leaguer (1963-70)*
**3. Javier Martinez, rhp, Liceo Hispano Americano HS, Bayamon, P.R.—(1998)**
4. Jason Kelley, rhp, Suwanee HS, Live Oak, Fla.—(Low A)
5. Barry Fennell, lhp, Holy Cross HS, Pennsauken, N.J.—(AA)
6. Neal Faulkner, rhp, Northwest Shoals (Ala.) CC.
7. *Tim Spindler, rhp-ss, Washingtonville (N.Y.) HS.
8. Sean Bogle, rhp, Indiana State University.
**9. Jason Ryan, rhp, Immaculata HS, Somerville, N.J.—(1999-2000)**
10. Shawn Box, rhp, Schreiner (Texas) College.
11. David Crutchfield, of, Montgomery HS, Rockville, Md.
12. Marty Gazarek, of, Indiana University.
13. Michael McGehee, c, Browne HS, Phoenix.
14. Kevin Coe, of, Laredo (Texas) JC.
15. Ryan Casey, rhp, Virginia Wesleyan College.
16. *Joey Cranford, ss-2b, Stratford Academy, Macon, Ga.
17. Jason Stevenson, rhp, Chattahoochee Valley (Ala.) CC.
18. Roark Birsner, rhp, Edgewood Regional HS, Berlin, N.J.
19. Ricky Freeman, 1b, University of Houston.
20. Andy Holin, c, Jacksonville University.
21. Jeff Havens, rhp, San Jacinto (Texas) JC.
22. *Martin Barnett, rhp, Iowa Western CC.
23. Christian Jackson, of, Riverdale Baptist HS, Bowie, Md.
24. *Brad Hastings, lhp, South Georgia JC.
25. Joe Montelongo, rhp, Truett-McConnell (Ga.) JC.
26. Cortez Wyatt, rhp, West Georgia College.
27. *Courteney Stewart, of, Westlake HS, Atlanta.
28. Keith Pelatowski, lhp, Yale University.
29. Troy Ormonde, rhp, Taft (Calif.) JC.
30. Saul Bustos, ss, Texas Tech.
31. Michael Hartung, rhp, Brookdale (N.J.) CC.
32. Rob Rehkopf, lhp, Northwood (Texas) Institute.
33. David Blevins, of, University of Mississippi.
34. Alex Barylak, rhp, University of Georgia.
35. *Derek Mitchell, ss, Triton (Ill.) JC.
36. Chad Olinde, 2b-ss, Northeast Louisiana University.
**37. Richie Barker, rhp, Quinsigamond (Mass.) CC.—(1999)**
38. *Chad Helmer, rhp, Hillsborough (Fla.) CC.
39. *Robert Delpriore, rhp, Brookdale (N.J.) CC.
40. Ryan Opatkiewicz, ss-2b, Mount San Antonio (Calif.) JC.
41. *Widd Workman, of, Gilbert, Ariz.
42. *Dave Phillips, 2b, Washington Township (N.J.) HS.
43. Eric Hamm, rhp, University of California.
44. *Kelly Armstead, ss-3b, Harlan HS, Chicago.
45. Larry Edens, of, North Carolina State University.
46. *Matt Williams, rhp, Lincoln-Sudbury HS, Sudbury, Mass.
**47. +Kyle Farnsworth, rhp, Milton HS, Roswell, Ga. / Abraham Baldwin (Ga.) JC.—(1999-2014)**
48. *Allen Davis, lhp, Red Oak (Texas) HS.
49. *Jonathan Castro, rhp, Athens Christian HS, Athens, Ga.
50. *John Subranni, rhp, St. Raymonds HS, Bronx, N.Y.
51. Michael Micucci, c, Montclair State (N.J.) College.
52. *Dean Vinson, ss, Valdosta (Ga.) HS.
53. *Rafael Rivera, rhp, Superior Vocational HS, Arecibo, P.R.
54. *Jeffrey Astgen, 2b-of, Los Angeles Pierce JC.
55. +Rafael Corrales, rhp, Miami-Dade CC South.
56. Mike Lauterhahn, of, William Paterson (N.J.) College.
57. *Diego Rico, of, Sunnyside HS, Tucson, Ariz.
58. *Brian Logan, c, Troy HS, Yorba Linda, Calif.
59. *Galen Reeder, 1b-lhp, Shiloh HS, Snellville, Ga.
60. *Travis Rapp, c, Polk (Fla.) CC.
61. *Doug Forde, lhp, Pasco Hernando (Fla.) CC.
62. *Eric Montross, rhp, University of North Carolina.
DRAFT DROP *First-round draft pick, Boston Celtics, National Basketball Association (1994); center, NBA (1994-2002)*
63. *David Bittler, lhp, Bridgewater Raritan HS, Bridgewater, N.J.
64. +Jose Colon, of, Santa Fe (Fla.) CC / Indian River (Fla.) CC.
65. *Lance Shannon, of, Newton County HS, Covington, Ga.
66. *Donny Leon, ss, Doctor Pila HS, Ponce, P.R.
67. *Dustin Brundage, c, Valley Central HS, Walden, N.Y.
68. *Jamie Wise, lhp, Effingham County HS, Springfield, Ga.
69. *Eric Fuller, ss-rhp, La Mirada HS, Brea, Calif.
70. *Ray Johnson, 1b-2b, Bayonne (N.J.) HS.
71. *Ryan Fuller, rhp, Corning East HS, Beaver Dams, N.Y
72. *Marcus Pearson, of, Hardaway HS, Columbus, Ga.
73. *Theo Fefee, of, Lincoln Land (Ill.) CC.
74. *Steve Skrocki, lhp, Christian Brothers Academy, Howell, N.J.
75. *Rodney Stevenson, rhp, Southern Union State (Ala.) JC.

## CHICAGO WHITE SOX (26)

**1. Mark Johnson, c, Warner Robins (Ga.) HS.—(1998-2008)**
**1. Chris Clemons, rhp, Texas A&M University** (Supplemental choice—33rd—as compensation for Type A free agent Ellis Burks).**—(1997)**
2. John Ambrose, rhp, John A. Logan (Ill.) JC (Choice trom Rockies as compensation for Burks).—(AAA)
2. Jerry Whittaker, of, University of Oklahoma.—(AA)
**3. Carlos Castillo, rhp, Southwest HS, Miami.—(1997-2001)**
**4. Jeff Abbott, of, University of Kentucky.—(1997-2001)**
5. Doug Bearden, ss, Lexington (S.C.) HS.—(AA)
6. Shane Buteaux, rhp, University of Houston.
7. Dennis Crine, rhp, Saddleback (Calif.) JC.
8. Ryan Helms, ss, Western Hills HS, Cincinnati.
DRAFT DROP *Son of Tommy Helms, major leaguer (1964-77)*
9. Sean Bagley, c, Gig Harbor (Wash.) HS.
10. Tom McCaskey, rhp, San Marcos (Calif.) HS.
11. Russ Herbert, rhp, Ohio University.
12. Carlos Chantres, rhp, Christopher Columbus HS, Miami.
13. Brian Drent, of, Indian Hills (Iowa) CC.
14. David Cancel, of, Indian Hills (Iowa) CC.
15. Sean Duncan, lhp, University of Miami.
16. Rashad Albert, of, Fernandina Beach (Fla.) HS.
17. Brandon Moore, ss, Auburn University.
**18. *Sam McConnell, lhp, La Salle HS, Fairfield, Ohio.—(2004)**
**19. *Luis Garcia, of, Miami (Fla.) Senior HS.—(2002)**
20. Jeremy Griffith, rhp, Etowah HS, Atalla, Ala.
21. *Stephen Leonard, 3b-of, MacArthur HS, San Antonio, Texas.
22. *Charley Carter, 1b, Mount Pleasant (Texas) HS.
23. +Marvin Horn, 1b, El Camino (Calif.) JC.
**24. *Adam Bernero, rhp, John F. Kennedy HS, Sacramento, Caiif.—(2000-06)**
25. *Conan Horton, c, Sacramento (Calif.) CC.
26. Tom Koerick, c-3b, Villanova University.
27. Jamie Nichols, rhp, St. Mark's HS, Bear, Del.
28. *Todd Johannes, c, Westminster Christian HS, Miami.
29. *David Harden, lhp, Shawnee Mission West HS, Overland Park, Kan.
**30. *Eric Gagne, rhp, Eduardo Montpetit HS, Mascouche, Quebec.—(1999-2008)**
31. *Robert Hicks, of, Milby HS, Houston.
32. *James Molina, of, Southridge HS, Miami.
33. *Kerron Bradford, of, Rancocas Valley HS, Mount Holly. N.J.
**34. *Chad Bradford, rhp, Hinds (Miss.) CC.—(1998-2009)**
35. *Ryan Nicks, rhp, Gahr HS, Cerritos, Calif.
36. +Clayton Stevens, of, Faulkner State (Ala.) JC.
37. *Darren Merrill, ss, Los Altos HS, Hacienda Heights, Calif.
38. *Miles Campbell, lhp, Los Alamitos (Calif.) HS.
39. *Randy Hamilton, lhp, Simon Kenton HS, Independence, Ky.
40. *John Pollard, of, Houston.
41. *Nate Forbush, 1b, Bingham HS, West Jordan, Utah.
42. *Eliot Montijo, 3b, Benson HS, Ponerene, Ariz.
43. *Dustin Wright, rhp, Itawamba (Miss.) JC.
44. +Jason Olsen, rhp-3b, Napa Valley (Calif.) JC.
45. *Kevin Culmo, rhp, Sacramento (Calif.) CC.
46. *Tom Sullivan, rhp, Indian Hills (Iowa) CC.
47. Mike Tidick, of, Western Carolina University.
48. *Brian Horner, c-1b, Washington HS, Wenona, Md.
49. *Nathan Koepke, 1b, Long Beach (Calif.) CC.
50. Edgar Malin, of, Memorial HS, West New York, N.J.
51. *Daniel McCluskey, c, King HS, Metairie, La.
52. *Brett Bredensteiner, of, Duchesne HS, St. Charles, Mo.
53. *Michael Bova, lhp, American HS, Miami.
54. *Chris Simonson, 1b, Claremont (Calif.) HS.

## CINCINNATI REDS (9)

**1. C.J. Nitkowski, lhp, St. John's University.—(1995-2005)**
2. Tony Terry, of, Abbeville (S.C.) HS.—Short-season A)
**3. Aaron Boone, 3b, University of Southern California.—(1997-2009)**
DRAFT DROP *Grandson of Ray Boone, major leaguer (1948-60) • Son of Bob Boone, major leaguer (1972-90); major league manager (1995-2005) • Brother of Bret Boone, major leaguer (1992-2005)*
4. Mike Hampton, 3b, Clemson University.—(Low A)
5. Clay Caruthers, rhp, Texas Christian University.—(AA)
6. Clint Koppe, rhp, University of Texas.
7. Decomba Conner, of, North Greenville (S.C.) JC.
8. *Scott Brand, rhp, Monterey HS, Lubbock, Texas.
**9. Eddie Priest, lhp, Southern Union (Ala.) JC.—(1998)**
10. *Dustin Dabbs, c, Tupelo (Miss.) HS.
11. *Bryant Dickinson, ss-2b, Millbrook HS, Raleigh, N C.
12. Darron Ingram, of, Bryan Station HS, Lexington, Ky.
13. Brian Lott, rhp, McNeese State University.
14. *Clint Fair, lhp, Georgia Southern University.
15. Jay Sorg, 3b, Morehead State University.
**16. *Kevin Gryboski, rhp, Wilkes (Pa.) College.—(2002-06)**
17. Tony Boyette, c, Santa Fe HS, Alachua, Fla.
18. Dan Masse, rhp, Northeastern Oklahoma A&M JC.
19. Justin Smith, rhp, Gulf Coast (Fla.) CC.
20. Wayne Ennis, 1b, Millbrook HS, Raleigh, N.C.
21. Scott Savary, of, Clarke (Iowa) College.
**22. John Riedling, rhp, Ely HS, Pompano Beach, Fla.—(2000-05)**
23. *Terry Weaver, 3b, Liberty University.
24. *Andy Zwirchitz, rhp-ss, East HS, Appleton, Wis.
25. Scott Sharp, c, George Washington University.
26. Marc Weiss, rhp, California Lutheran University.
27. Adam Bryant, rhp, Virginia Commonwealth University.
28. Ray Brown, 1b, Cal State Sacramento.
DRAFT DROP *Brother of Keith Brown, major leaguer (1988-92)*
29. Tony Nieto, rhp, University of Southern California.
30. Nick Morrow, of, Vanderbilt University.
31. Jeff Andrews, c, Auburn University-Montgomery.
32. Cedric Allen, lhp, University of Mary Hardin-Baylor (Texas).
33. Brian Wilson, ss, University of Texas-San Antonio.
**34. *Paul Rigdon, rhp, Florida CC.—(2000-01)**
35. Doyle Preston, 3b-1b, University of Arkansas.
36. *Ed Flores, c, South HS, Bakersfield, Calif.
37. Damon Callahan, rhp, Bradley Central HS, Cleveland, Tenn.
38. *Brandon Credeur, of, University of Southwestern Louisiana.
39. *Jeff Hutzler, rhp, University of Texas-San Antonio.
40. Marlon Allen, 1b, Columbus (Ga.) College.
41. *David Guthrie, ss, Southern Union State (Ala.) JC.
42. *Isaac Burton, of, Arizona State University.
43. *Kevin Shipp, rhp, Meridian (Miss.) CC.
44. +Chad Angerhofer, lhp, Oak Hall Prep HS, Gainesville, Fla. / Seminole (Fla.) CC.
45. *Patrick Zicka, rhp, Indian Hill HS, Cincinnati, Ohio.
46. *Tim Bell, rhp, Bakersfield (Calif.) HS.
47. *Malcolm King, 1b-of, Oak Hall Prep HS, Gainesville, Fla.

## CLEVELAND INDIANS (10)

**1. Jaret Wright, rhp, Katella HS, Anaheim, Calif.—(1997-2007)**
DRAFT DROP *Son of Clyde Wright, major leaguer (1966-75)*
2. (Choice to Expos as compensation for Type A free agent Dennis Martinez).
**3. Rick Heiserman, rhp, Creighton University.—(1999)**
**4. Danny Graves, rhp, University of Miami.—(1996-2006)**
5. Pepe McNeal, c, Armwood HS, Seffner, Fla.—(High A)
6. Gonzalo Mojica, rhp, Teodora Aguilar Mora HS, Yabucoa, P.R.
**7. Russell Branyan, 3b, Stratford Academy, Warner Robins, Ga.—(1998-2011)**
8. David Caldwell, lhp, Northeast Texas CC.
9. Brad Tiller, ss, Sheldon Clark HS, Inez, Ky.
10. Jay Vaught, rhp, University of Texas.
11. Blair Jensen, ss-3b, Kingsburg (Calif.) HS.
12. Bob Oldham, rhp, Odessa (Texas) JC.
13. Scott Kramer, rhp, Emory (Ga.) University.
14. Bryan Warner, of, Glendale (Calif.) JC.
15. Quinn Murphy, ss, Assumption HS, Davenport, Iowa.
**16. Julius Matos, ss-2b, South Suburban (Ill.) JC.—(2002-03).**
17. *Tom Bennett, rhp, Alameda (Calif.) HS.
18. *Ron Wallech, rhp, North Carolina State University.

19. Darren Stumberger, 1b, University of South Florida.
20. Jim Betzsold, of, Cal State Fullerton.
21. Patrick Evans, c, Oklahoma Baptist University.
22. *Micah Stovall, lhp, Rancho Santiago (Calif.) JC.
23. Lenny Weber, rhp, University of New Orleans.
24. Teddy Warrecker, rhp, University of Arizona.
25. Jonathan Choate, of, Blinn (Texas) JC.
26. Arnold Santiago, 1b, Indian Hills (Iowa) CC.
**27. *Christian Parker, rhp, Eldorado HS, Albuquerque, N.M.—(2001)**
28. Ricky Gutierrez, 2b, University of Oklahoma.
29. Brian Duva, of, University of Florida.
**30. Bruce Aven, of, Lamar University.—(1997-2002)**
31. Heath Hayes, 3b, San Diego State University.
32. Scot Donovan, rhp, Armstrong State (Ga.) College.
33. *Brad O'Malley, rhp, Canevin Catholic HS, Carnegie, Pa.
34. Chris Granata, rhp, Ohio State University.
35. *William Hill, 2b, Muir HS, Altadena, Calif.
36. Tony Dougherty, rhp, Slippery Rock (Pa.) University.
37. Chip Glass, of, University of Oklahoma.
38. *Todd Abbott, rhp, University of Arkansas.
DRAFT DROP *Son of Glenn Abbott, major leaguer (1973-84)*
**39. *Danny Ardoin, c, Texarkana (Texas) CC.—(2000-08)**
40. *Marty Heminger, rhp, Mira Mesa HS, San Diego.
41. *Mike Skeeles, lhp, McKinley HS, Canton, Ohio.
42. Matt Culp, 1b, Murray State University.
43. *Nick De la Cruz, ss, Evergreen HS, Seattle.
**44. Chan Perry, 1b, University of Florida.—(2000-02)**
DRAFT DROP *Brother of Herbert Perry, major leaguer (1994-2004)*
45. Walter Owens, of, University of Miami.
46. Mike Mastrullo, 2b, Billerica (Mass.) HS.
47. *Denny Wagner, rhp, Castlewood (Va.) HS.
DRAFT DROP *First-round draft pick (42nd overall), Athletics (1997)*
48. *Zane Gamewell, rhp, Tenino (Wash.) HS.
49. +Gary Anderson, rhp, Blinn (Texas) JC.
50. *Jimmy Jones, rhp, Irmo HS, Columbia, S.C.
51. Steven Ortiz, lhp, McLennan (Texas) CC.
52. Elliot Lowry, lhp, Southeastern (N.C.) CC.
53. Tyler Cheff, c, University of Hawaii.
54. Jason Walker, lhp, Western Illinois University.
55. *Brian Wagner, c, Tokay HS, Lodi, Calif.
56. *Joel Gallimore, rhp, Batavia (Ohio) HS.
57. *Brad Thomas, rhp, Northeast Texas CC.
58. *Jason Morones, lhp, Lower Columbia (Wash.) CC.
59. *Chris Enochs, rhp, Oak Glen HS, Newell, W.Va.
DRAFT DROP *First-round draft pick (11th overall), Athletics (1997)*
60. *Robert O'Brien, 1b, Arcadia (Calif.) HS.
61. *Randy Crane, rhp, Linn-Benton (Ore.) CC.
62. *Juan Mussenden, 1b-of, Lake City (Fla.) CC.
63. *Brian Hincy, rhp, Federal Way (Wash.) HS.
64. Sean Murphy, 3b, St. Ambrose (Iowa) University.
65. *Jason Gooding, lhp, Seminole (Okla.) JC.

## COLORADO ROCKIES (7)

1. Doug Million, lhp, Sarasota (Fla.) HS.—(AA)
DRAFT DROP *Died as active player (Sept. 24, 1997)*
2. (Choice to White Sox as compensation for Type A free agent Ellis Burks)
3. (Choice to Marlins as compensation for Type B free agent Walt Weiss)
4. (Choice to Mets as compensation for Type B free agent Howard Johnson)
5. John Slamka, lhp, Glendale (Ariz.) JC.—(Low A)
**6. Luther Hackman, rhp, Columbus (Miss.) HS.—(1999-2003)**
7. John Hallead, of, Ellensburg (Wash.) HS.
8. Mike Kusiewicz, lhp, St. Pius HS, Nepean, Ontario.
9. Arnie Gooch, rhp, Neshaminy HS, Levittown, Pa.
10. Brent Crowther, rhp, Simon Fraser (B.C.) University.
11. Mark Wells, of, North Carolina State University.
**12. Mike Saipe, rhp, University of San Diego.—(1998)**
13. Rasheed Rushdan, of, Cheraw (S.C.) HS.
14. Pookie Jones, of, University of Kentucky.
DRAFT DROP *Quarterback, Canadian Football League (1997)*
15. Matt Carpenter, c, Cleveland State University.
16. Matt Pool, rhp, UC Davis.
17. Aaron Myers, ss-3b, Righetti HS, Santa Maria, Calif.
18. Arthur Waldrep, rhp, Union (Tenn.) University.
19. Jason Dietrich, rhp, Pepperdine University.
20. +Brady Wuestenhoefer, rhp, Mississippi Delta JC.
21. David Niles, of, Key West HS, Big Pine, Fla.
22. Link Jarrett, ss, Florida State University.
DRAFT DROP *Baseball coach, UNC Greensboro (2013-15)*
23. Jeff Twist, c, Oklahoma City University.
24. Chris Howard, lhp, Mobile (Ala.) University.
25. *Joe Germaine, rhp, Mountain View HS, Mesa, Ariz.
DRAFT DROP *Quarterback, National Football League (1999)*
26. Brian Rose, rhp, Cortland HS, Potsdam, N.Y.
27. *Ben Thomas, 1b-lhp, Central HS, Rapid City, S.D.
28. Scott Warembourg, rhp, Fresno State University.
29. Scott Larock, rhp, University of Hartford.
30. Jim Lezeau, of, Mesa State (Colo.) College.
31. Gary Jones, 2b, Ohio State University.
32. Mudcat Brewer, of, Middle Tennessee State University.
33. Joey DeAngelis, 1b, University of North Carolina-Greensboro.
34. *Rusty Loflin, c, Porterville (Calif.) JC.
35. *Brian Passini, lhp, Parkland (Ill.) JC.
36. *Jarret Daniel, of, Robinson HS, Tampa.
37. Chan Mayber, ss, Metro State (Colo.) College.
38. *Johnny Hunter, ss, Navarro (Texas) JC.
39. *Mike Sanchez, rhp, Chaffey (Calif.) JC.
40. *Jeffery Hallock, c, La Mirada (Calif.) HS.
41. *James Slaughter, of, Lincoln HS, Stockton, Calif.
42. Jon Mathews, 1b, University of New Orleans.
43. *Brandon Hearn, ss, Beverly Hills (Calif.) HS.
44. *Caleb Brown, lhp, Wylie HS, Abilene, Texas.
45. +James Podjan, rhp, Lake Michigan JC.
46. Efrain Alamo, of, Luis Hernaiz Verone HS, Canovanas, P.R.
47. *Todd Vickhammer, 3b, Flathead Christian HS, Kalispell, Mon.
48. *William Peters, rhp, Palatine (Ill.) HS.
**49. *Bart Miadich, rhp, Lakeridge HS, Lake Oswego, Ore.—(2001-03)**
50. *Jerson Perez, ss, Lynn Tech HS, Lynn, Mass.
**51. *Brandon Knight, 2b, Ventura (Calif.) CC.—(2001-08)**
52. *Danny Delk, ss, Franklin-Simpson HS, Franklin, Ky.
53. *Griffin Moore, ss, San Luis Obispo (Calif.) HS.
54. *Philip Davis, rhp, Central Arizona JC.
55. *Rusty Puffinbarger, c, Leedey HS, Camargo, Okla.
56. *Freddie Jackson, of, Central Arizona JC.
57. *Gabriel Foster, rhp, Yuba City (Calif.) HS.
58. *Darren Baugh, ss, JC of San Mateo (Calif.).
59. +Jason Romine, rhp, Mendocino (Calif.) CC.

## DETROIT TIGERS (18)

1. Cade Gaspar, rhp, Pepperdine University.—(High A)
DRAFT DROP *Son of Rod Gaspar, major leaguer (1969-74)*
**2. Mike Darr Jr., of, Corona (Calif.) HS.—(1999-2001)**
DRAFT DROP *Died as active player (Feb. 15, 2002) • Son of Mike Darr, major leaguer (1977)*
3. Greg Whiteman, lhp, James Madison University.—(AA)
4. Trad Sobik, rhp, Central Catholic HS, Clearwater, Fla.—(High A)
5. Keith Smith, of, Newbury Park (Calif.) HS.—(Low A)
DRAFT DROP *Quarterback, Canadian Football League (2001)*
6. Dave Kauflin, rhp, Chippewa Valley HS, Mount Clemens, Mich.
7. Neil Garcia, c, University of Nevada-Reno.
8. Ryan Balfe, ss, Central HS, Cornwall, N.Y.
9. Darryl Monroe, of, University of Kansas.
10. *Ryan Kjos, rhp, University of Texas.
**11. Bubba Trammell, of, University of Tennessee.—(1997-2003)**
12. Michael Bajda, rhp, Sacred Heart University.
13. Chad Stevenson, c, Green Valley HS, Henderson, Nev.
14. *Matt King, rhp, Start HS, Toledo, Ohio.
**15. Daryle Ward, 1b, Rancho Santiago (Calif.) JC.—(1998-2008)**
DRAFT DROP *Son of Gary Ward, major leaguer (1979-90)*
**16. *Scott Winchester, rhp, Clemson University.—(1997-2001)**
17. Jason Jordan, rhp, Wichita State University.
18. *Rob Hauswald, ss-2b, Lafayette HS, Lexington, Ky.
19. Kirk Hagge, ss, Crescenta Valley HS, La Crescenta, Calif.
20. Mac White, of, University of South Carolina.
21. *Joshua Farrow, lhp, Dadeville HS, Camp Hill, Ala.
22. Robert Balint, c, Valencia (Fla.) CC.
**23. Javier Cardona, c, Lake Land (Ill.) JC.—(2000-02)**
24. *Erik Desrosiers, rhp, Mesa (Ariz.) CC.
25. +Greg Romo, rhp, Bakersfield (Calif.) JC.
26. *Brian Winders, rhp, Louisiana State University.
27. Chris Newton, lhp, University of Michigan.
**28. Dave Roberts, of, UCLA.—(1999-2008)**
29. Jamie Borel, of, East Carolina University.
30. *Jeff Fryar, rhp, Fort Gibson (Okla.) HS.
31. Rivers Mitchell, of, Manatee (Fla.) CC.
32. *Steven Elkins, rhp, Chesterton HS, Porter, Ind.
33. +Brent Stentz, rhp, Pasco Hernando (Fla.) CC.
34. Mark Persails, rhp, Millington HS, Vassar, Mich.
35. +Bryan Jones, ss, Plantation (Fla.) HS / Edison (Fla.) JC.
36. Kelton Jacobson, rhp, Gonzaga University.
37. *Brent Sagedahl, rhp, Carthage (Wis.) College.
38. Matt Ruess, rhp, Iowa State University.
39. *Jacob Freeman, 3b, Bakersfield (Calif.) JC.
40. *John Hayduk, rhp, Broken Arrow (Okla.) HS.
**41. *Kiko Calero, rhp, Miami-Dade CC South.—(2003-09)**
42. *Derek Kopacz, of, Joliet (Ill.) JC.
43. Sean Freeman, 1b, Kent State University.
44. *Brian Fuller, c, Northwestern University.
45. *Manny Lutz, 3b, Monte Vista HS, Spring Valley, Calif.
46. *DeAndre Cooper, of, St. Francis Cabrini HS, Detroit.
47. Andy Kruger, of, Central Michigan University.
48. Eric Dinyar, rhp, University of Pittsburgh.
49. *Michael Goralczyk, lhp, Lake Michigan JC.
50. Mike Martin, 2b, Boston College.
51. Dale Dolejsi, rhp, University of the Pacific.
52. *John White, c, Gulf Coast (Fla.) CC.
53. *Derek Dixon, rhp, Chickasha (Okla.) HS.
54. *Aaron Anthony, 3b, Winder-Barrow HS, Winder, Ga.
55. Dan Driskill, rhp, Kansas Newman College.
56. *Michael Kujawa, rhp, Bowsher HS, Toledo. Ohio.
57. *Joe Eisen, of, Northmont HS, Englewood, Ohio.
58. *Dwayne Landry, ss, Gulf Coast (Fla.) CC.
59. *Rodney Archer, of, Allan Hancock (Calif.) JC.
60. *Joel Hillebrand, rhp, Henry Ford (Mich.) CC.
61. *John Perry, rhp, Brazoswood HS, Lake Jackson, Texas.
62. *Stephen Berger, of, Clay HS, Oregon, Ohio.
63. *Nole Elizer, c, Seminole (Fla.) CC.
64. *Steven Williams, rhp, Seaholm HS, Birmingham, Mich.
65. *Chris Champanois, c, Henry Ford (Mich.) CC.
66. *Reid Beucler, lhp, Georgetown Prep HS, Washington, D.C
67. *Brian Rios, ss, Riverside (Calif.) CC.
68. *Luis Rodriguez, of, Riverside (Calif.) CC.

## FLORIDA MARLINS (5)

**1. Josh Booty, ss, Evangel Christian HS, Shreveport, La.—(1996-98)**
DRAFT DROP *Quarterback, National Football League (2002-03) • First 1994 high school draft pick to reach majors (Sept. 24, 1996)*
2. Victor Rodriguez, ss, Rafael Lopez Landron HS, Guayama, P.R.—(AA)
3. Todd Cady, c, Arizona State University.—(High A)
**3. Brian Meadows, rhp, Henderson HS, Troy, Ala.** (Choice from Rockies as compensation for Type B free agent Walt Weiss).**—(1998-2006)**
4. Chad Miles, lhp, Washington State University.—(AA)
5. Jason Garrelts, rhp, Olivet Nazarene (Ill.) University.—(Rookie)
6. Mike Parisi, rhp, Cal State Fullerton.
**7. Ryan Jackson, of, Duke University.—(1998-2002)**
8. Hector Kuilan, c, Maestro Ladislao Martinez HS, Vega Alta, P.R.
9. Hayward Cook, of, UC Davis.
10. Abdul Cole, of, CC of San Francisco.
11. Jon Farmer, lhp, Porterville (Calif.) JC.
**12. Rob Stanifer, rhp, Anderson (S.C.) College.—(1997-2000)**
13. Jose Camilo, of, Jose M. Rivera Solis HS, Trujillo Alto, P.R.
14. +Rodney Getz, rhp, East Central HS, Lawrenceburg, Ind. / John A. Logan (Ill.) JC.
15. Allan Hebbert, rhp, Cal State Los Angeles.
**16. *Seth Etherton, rhp, Dana Hills HS, Laguna Niguel, Calif.—(2000-06)**
DRAFT DROP *First-round draft pick (18th overall), Angels (1998)*
17. Kenyon West, rhp, Central HS, Miami.
18. Jeremy Ross, rhp, Dixie (Utah) JC.
19. *Kevin Tolan, rhp, Citrus (Calif.) JC.
20. Mark Gugino, of, University of South Carolina.
**21. *Brian Shackelford, lhp, McAlester (Okla.) HS.—(2005-06)**
22. *James Smith, rhp, Winston Churchill HS, San Antonio, Texas.
23. Lionel Hastings, 2b, University of Southern California.
24. *Wally Maynard, rhp, University of South Carolina.
25. Dan Vardijan, rhp, Glenbrook South HS, Glenview, Ill.
26. Michael Reyes, of, Wayland Baptist (Texas) University.
27. Sommer McCartney, c, UC Riverside.
28. *Tim McClaskey, rhp, Wilton (Iowa) HS.
29. *Mark Hale, rhp, Central Arizona JC.
30. *Shawn O'Dell, 1b, Indian River HS, Chesapeake, Va.
31. *Kirk Pierce, c, Long Beach State University.
32. *Terry Bishop, lhp, Schenectady County (N.Y.) CC.
33. *Derrick Johnson, of, Mercer County (N.J.) CC.
34. Walter White, ss, Sonoma State (Calif.) University.
35. *Chad Mead, rhp, West Valley (Calif.) JC.
36. *Ali Samadini, rhp, Marin Catholic HS, Hamilton, Ga.
37. +Derek Santiago, rhp, Aurora West HS, Aurora, Ill. / Waubonsee (Ill.) JC.
38. *Mark Greenlee, lhp, Buffalo Grove HS, Arlington Heights, Ill.
39. *Jay Gospodarek, rhp, Canyon Del Oro HS, Tucson, Ariz.
40. *Jeremy Blaylock, rhp, Northeastern Oklahoma A&M JC.
41. *Quincy Foster, of, Hendersonville (N.C.) HS.
42. *Heath Askew, rhp, Connors State (Okla.) JC.
43. *Darren Mills, 3b, Key West (Fla.) HS.
44. *Aaron Cames, rhp, Woodland (Calif.) HS.
45. *Mike Evans, lhp, Wellington Community HS, Wellington, Fla.
46. +Theron Truitt, of, Gordon (Ga.) JC.
47. *Randy Niles, rhp, Key West (Fla.) HS.
48. Randy Shagena, rhp, Aquinas (Mich.) College.
49. Joel Holland, lhp, Linfield (Ore.) College.
50. *Gaylon Dixon, lhp, Seminole (Okla.) JC.
51. *Sonny Cortez, of, Cerritos (Calif.) JC.
52. +Scott Dewitt, lhp, Lassen (Calif.) JC.
53. *John Arnold, c, Seward County (Kan.) CC.
54. *Shane Phillips, of, Culpepper County HS, Rixeyville, Va.
55. *Chris Gorrell, rhp, Eldorado HS, Las Vegas, Nev.
56. *Justin Fenus, rhp, Colorado Northwestern CC.
57. *Chris Windsor, rhp, Garden City (Kan.) CC.
58. *Philip Henderson, rhp, Ringgold (Ga.) HS.
59. *Peter Quitner, of, San Jose (Calif.) CC.
60. *Todd Moser, lhp, St. Thomas Aquinas HS, Davie, Fla.
61. *Ryan Roberts, lhp, Chaffey (Calif.) JC.
62. *Tom Buckman, rhp, Edison (Fla.) CC.
63. *Curtis Hall, 3b, Orem, Utah.
64. *Tim Hicks, of-1b, Gordon (Ga.) JC.
65. *Greg McNeill, rhp, East Montgomery HS, Biscoe, N.C.
66. *John Payne, rhp, Athens Drive HS, Raleigh, N.C.
67. Jonathan Moores, rhp, Ithaca (N.Y.) College.

68. *Josh Deakman, rhp, Riverside (Calif.) CC.
69. *Ross Atkins, rhp, Wake Forest University.
DRAFT DROP *General manager, Blue Jays (2015)*
70. *Anthony Poindexter, of, Jefferson Forest HS, Forest, Va.
71. *Beau Payne, rhp, Edmonds (Wash.) CC.
72. *Glenn Foley, 1b, Boston College.
DRAFT DROP *Quarterback, National Football League (1994-99)*
73. *Hines Ward, of, Forest Park HS, Rex, Ga.
DRAFT DROP *Wide receiver, National Football League (1998-2011)*
74. *Troy Rauer, of, Arizona State University.
75. *Tyler Nicol, of, Southern Arkansas University.
76. *Douglas Bossert, rhp, Pitman (N.J.) HS.
77. *Brian Benefield, ss, Mesquite (Texas) HS.
78. *Ward White, c, Modesto (Calif.) JC.
79. *Peter Jezerinac, ss, Walton HS, Marietta, Ga.
80. *Michael Howes, rhp, Jenks HS, Tulsa, Okla.

## HOUSTON ASTROS (17)

1. **Ramon Castro, c, Lino Padron Rivera HS, Vega Baja, P.R.—(1999-2011)**
1. **Scott Elarton, rhp, Lamar (Colo.) HS** (Choice from Giants as compensation for Type A free agent Mark Portugal).**—(1998-2008)**
1. **Russ Johnson, ss, Louisiana State University** (Supplemental choice—30th—as compensation for Portugal).**—(1997-2005)**
2. Dan Lock, lhp, Yale University.—(AA)
3. **Oscar Robles, ss, Montgomery HS, San Diego.—(2005-07)**
4. Paul O'Malley, rhp, Illinois State University.—(AA)
5. Mike Gunderson, rhp, North Dakota State University.—(High A)
6. Shane Barksdale, of, Etowah HS, Gallant, Ala.
7. **Tony Mounce, lhp, Kamiakin HS, Kennewick, Wash.—(2003)**
8. Derek Dace, lhp, Sullivan (Mo.) HS.
9. Wes Pratt, of, North Carolina Wesleyan College.
10. Roy Marsh, of, Ohio State University.
11. *Bob Pailthorpe, rhp, Santa Clara University.
12. Hassan Robinson, of, Springfield (Mass.) College.
13. Victor Sanchez, c, University of the Pacific.
14. Anthony Rich, ss, Rollins (Fla.) College.
15. Billy Hall, rhp, Crowder (Mo.) JC.
16. Chris Crawford, rhp, Marquette University.
DRAFT DROP *Forward, National Basketball Association (1997-2003)*
17. ***Donzell McDonald, of, Trinidad State (Colo.) JC.—(2001-2002)**
DRAFT DROP *Brother of Darnell McDonald, first-round draft pick, Orioles (1997); major leaguer (2004-13)*
18. Stephen Fuller, rhp, Triton (Ill.) JC.
19. Mark Sacharko, rhp, Lancaster (Texas) HS.
20. *Rich Rodrigues, 3b, De Anza (Calif.) JC.
21. Johnny Smith, 3b, Auburn (N.Y.) HS.
22. Donald Scolaro, 2b, Florida Southern College.
23. **John Halama, lhp, St. Francis (N.Y.) College.—(1998-2006)**
24. *Ruben Jurado, rhp, Chino HS, Ontario, Calif.
25. Anthony Shaver, rhp, Jacksonville State University.
26. +Chris McFerrin, rhp, McLane HS, Fresno, Calif. / Fresno (Calif.) CC.
27. *Rad Weaver, rhp, Clark HS, San Antonio, Texas.
28. James Lynch, rhp, Harrison HS, Evansville, Ind.
29. *Braxton Whitehead, c, Franklin HS, Roxie, Miss.
30. *Rosario Ortiz, rhp, Globe (Ariz.) HS.
31. *Ben Smith, rhp, Glebe Collegiate HS, Nepean, Ontario.
32. *Joe Valenti, 1b, Mendon HS, Pittsford, N.Y.
33. *Joe Painich, rhp, Panola (Texas) JC.
34. +Kevin Burns, 1b, Texarkana (Texas) CC.
35. Stacy Chupailo, rhp, Mona Shores HS, Norton Shores, Mich.
36. *Michael Fee, rhp, Gibbs HS, St. Petersburg, Fla.
37. *Cory Lusk, rhp, Dundee Crown HS, Carpentersville, Ill.
38. *Rob Aronson, rhp, Eastern Connecticut State University.
39. *Shane Gift, rhp, Central Arizona JC.
40. *Prenenyer Rodriguez, rhp, McCutcheon HS, Lafayette, Ind.
41. *Peter Cervantes, rhp, East Los Angeles JC.
42. *Ralph Cadima, rhp, Mount San Antonio (Calif.) JC.
43. **+Julio Lugo, ss, Connors State (Okla.) JC.—(2000-11)**
44. *Michael Eikenberry, rhp, Lincoln Trail (Ill.) JC.
45. *Erik Augustin, of, Norristown (Pa.) HS.
46. ***Jay Spurgeon, rhp, Yosemite HS, Madera, Calif.—(2000)**
47. *Kelly Johnson, rhp, Walla Walla (Wash.) CC.
48. *Robert Mills, 3b, Henderson (Texas) HS.
49. *Jonathan Black, rhp, Texarkana (Texas) CC.
50. +J.D. Prestash, lhp, West Branch HS, Phillipsburg, Pa. / Gulf Coast (Fla.) CC.
51. *Casey Baker, of, Fresno (Calif.) CC.
52. *Trevor Zwaan, rhp, Prince Andrew HS, Dartmouth, N.S.
53. *John Rodriguez, of, Connors State (Okla.) JC.
54. *Scott Bronowicz, c, Shaler HS, Pittsburgh.
55. *Dustin Spencer, rhp, Cuesta (Calif.) JC.
56. *Stephen Dye, rhp, Butler HS, Augusta, Ga.
57. *Petey Watts, of, Pike County HS, Molena, Ga.
58. (void) *Dale Davis, lhp, Trinity HS, Bedford, Texas.
59. *Clint Weibl, rhp, Odessa (Texas) JC.
60. *Elvin Nina, rhp, Northeastern Oklahoma A&M JC.
61. *Kevin Parker, ss, Texarkana (Texas) CC.
62. *Chad Berryman, rhp, A.L. Brown HS, Kannapolis, N.C.
63. *Reed Goemann, lhp, Elk Grove HS, Sacramento, Calif.
64. ***Paul Hoover, ss, Steubenville (Ohio) HS.—(2001-10)**
65. *Mark Manbeck, rhp, Galveston (Texas) JC.
66. *Justin Bowser, rhp, Seward County (Kan.) CC.
67. *Jeffrey Conner, c, Colonial HS, Orlando, Fla.
68. *Barney Albritton, rhp, Parklane Academy, McComb, Miss.
69. *Brad Hardtke, 3b, Leland HS, San Jose, Calif.
70. *Daryl Jones, of, Bossier City (La.) HS.
71. ***Johnny Estrada, c, Roosevelt HS, Fresno, Calif.—(2001-08)**
72. *Brent Husted, ss, Santa Teresa HS, San Jose, Calif.
73. ***Jim Chamblee, rhp-3b, Odessa (Texas) JC.—(2003)**
74. *Brian Thompson, rhp, Howard (Texas) JC.
75. *Jason Middleton, rhp, Fort Myers (Fla.) HS.
76. *Ryan Anschuetz, rhp, Edison (Fla.) CC.
77. *Tim Worthen, 1b, Limestone Community HS, Peoria, Ill.
78. *Canaan Price, ss, Palm Desert (Calif.) HS.
79. Jay Wright, rhp, New Mexico Highlands University.
80. *Derek Ballard, 1b, Moon Valley HS, Phoenix.
81. *Jeff Mathews, rhp, Vassar (Mich.) HS.
82. *Javier Encinia, rhp, Blinn (Texas) JC.
83. *Jonathan Echols, c, Connors State (Okla.) JC.
84. *Matt Reed, 2b, Mississippi Delta JC.
85. *Shane Howell, 1b, Andrew Hill HS, San Jose, Calif.
86. *Michael Constantino, rhp, Manatee HS, Bradenton, Fla.
87. *Brian Slatkin, rhp, Lassen (Calif.) JC.
88. +Brian Tickell, rhp, McLennan (Texas) CC.
89. *Paul Powell, lhp, Texarkana (Texas) CC.
90. *James Sapp, of, Monroe (N.Y.) CC.
91. *Marcus Scott, of, Palm Springs HS, Desert Hot Springs, Calif.
92. *Tyler Steketee, rhp, Jenison (Mich.) HS.
93. ***Mike Glavine, 1b, Northeastern University.—(2003)**
DRAFT DROP *Brother of Tom Glavine, major leaguer (1987-2008) • Baseball coach, Northeastern (2015-)*
94. *Jeremie Durden, of, Huntington HS, Greenwood, La.
95. *Karl Chatman, of, Galveston (Texas) JC.
96. *Juan Rivera, ss, Cypress Creek HS, Orlando, Fla.
97. *Doug Rummel, rhp, Lake Travis HS, Austin, Texas.
98. *Cameron Saska, lhp, Granite Hills HS, El Cajon, Calif.

## KANSAS CITY ROYALS (16)

1. Matt Smith, lhp-1b, Grants Pass (Ore.) HS.—(AA)
2. **Jed Hansen, 2b, Stanford University.—(1997-99)**
3. **Jaime Bluma, rhp, Wichita State University.—(1996)**
4. **Matt Treanor, c, Mater Dei HS, Santa Ana, Calif.—(2004-12)**
DRAFT DROP *Husband of 3-time U.S. Olympic beach volleyball gold medalist Misty May*
5. **Tim Byrdak, lhp, Rice University.—(1998-2013)**
6. Blaine Mull, rhp, Freedom HS, Morganton, N.C.
7. Javier Gamboa, rhp, Cuesta (Calif.) JC.
8. ***Todd Belitz, lb-lhp, Edison HS, Huntington Beach, Calif.—(2000-01)**
9. *Kris Didion, 3b, Poly HS, Riverside, Calif.
10. Gary Coffee, 1b, Grady HS, Atlanta.
11. *Jacob Kringen, lhp, Elma (Wash.) HS.
12. **Jose Rosado, lhp, Galveston (Texas) JC.—(1996-2000)**
13. Eric Mooney, lhp, St. Mary's (Calif.) College.
14. ***Ryan Bradley, rhp, Ayala HS, Chino, Calif.—(1998)**
DRAFT DROP *First-round draft pick (40th overall), Yankees (1997)*
15. Ken Winkle, rhp, St. Leo (Fla.) College.
16. Sean McNally, 3b, Duke University.
DRAFT DROP *Baseball coach, Duke (2006-12)*
17. Tyler Williamson, c, Biola (Calif.) University.
18. Dan Dillingham, of, Polk (Fla.) CC.
19. Wayne Upchurch, rhp, University of Texas-Arlington.
20. Scott Pinoni, 1b, Duke University.
21. **Lance Carter, rhp, Manatee (Fla.) JC.—(1999-2006)**
22. *Nathan Ruhl, rhp, Lee's Summit (Mo.) HS.
23. Tim Grieve, rhp, Texas Christian University.
DRAFT DROP *Son of Tom Grieve, first-round draft pick, Senators (1966); major leaguer (1970-79); general manager, Rangers (1985-94) • Brother of Ben Grieve, first-round draft pick, Athletics (1994); major leaguer (1997-2005)*
24. Coby Welch, c, Tallahassee (Fla.) CC.
25. Manny Burciaga, rhp, Northwest Nazarene (Idaho) College.
26. Todd Thorn, lhp, Northwestern HS, Stratford, Ontario.
27. Jason Ritter, rhp, Connors State (Okla.) JC.
28. +Jaime Burton, lhp, Chemeketa (Ore.) CC.
29. Brent Kaysner, rhp, Green River (Wash.) CC.
30. Mike Kurnik, rhp, Cal Poly Pomona.
31. Shannon Coulter, ss, Texas Christian University.
32. Marc Phillips, lhp, Virginia Military Institute.
33. Kortney Paul, c, Arkansas State University.
34. Rick Pitts, of, Franklin HS, Seattle.
35. *Brian Scott, rhp, Ramona (Calif.) HS.
36. Ray Roberts, lhp, Napa Valley (Calif.) JC.
37. *Tom Stanton, c, Middleburg (Fla.) HS.
38. Duane Darby, lhp, West Middlesex Area HS, Grove City, Pa.
39. Victor Moreno, 3b, Flushing HS, Queens, N.Y.
40. *Stephen Rosen, rhp, Blue Springs (Mo.) HS.
41. *Steve Spille, lhp, Cincinnati.
42. *George Fergusson, of, Bronx (N.Y.) CC.
43. +Kimani Stafford, c, Swett HS, Richmond, Calif. / San Francisco CC.
44. *Eric Cole, 3b, Antelope Valley (Calif.) JC.
45. *Stephen Watson, rhp, Galveston (Texas) JC.
46. *J.J. Thomas, of, Wheeler HS, Marietta, Ga.
47. *Derek Anderson, lhp, Lynwood (Wash.) HS.
48. *Dale Hill, lhp, Trinity HS, Bedford, Texas.
49. *Vincent Wells, 2b, MacKenzie HS, Detroit.
50. *Brandon Stanley, 3b-rhp, Texarkana (Texas) CC.
51. *Charles Schoenfeldt, 1b, Victor Valley (Calif.) CC.
52. *Dustin Wilson, rhp, Kiona Benton HS, Benton City, Wash.
53. *Torrie Pinkins, c-2b, Mitchell-Baker HS, Camilla, Ga.
54. *Will Schleuss, lhp, Hagerstown (Md.) JC.
55. *Dale Slater, rhp, Muscatine (Iowa) CC.
56. *Matt Montgomery, rhp, Western HS, Anaheim, Calif.
57. *Dimitric Murph, rhp, Caldwell (Texas) HS.
58. *Michael Custer, rhp, Linn-Benton (Ore.) CC.
59. *Mario Olsen, rhp, Rowan (N.J.) College.
60. ***Kit Pellow, of, Johnson County (Kan.) CC.—(2002-04)**
61. *Matt Bailie, rhp, HIllsboro HS, Aloha, Ore.
62. *Demond Thompkins, of, University of Nevada-Las Vegas.
63. *Brett Schafer, of, UCLA.
64. *Patrick Machado, 1b, Clovis West HS, Fresno, Calif.
65. Ken Tipton, of, Dallas Baptist University.
66. *Eric Marks, 3b, Victor Valley (Calif.) CC.
67. Juan Rocha, of, Cerritos (Calif.) JC.
68. *Justin Bowles, of, Galveston (Texas) JC.
69. *Richard Igou, lhp, Notre Dame HS, Sherman Oaks. Calif.
70. **Jose Santiago, rhp, Carlos Escobar Lopez HS, Loiza, P.R.—(1997-2005)**
71. *Casey Martin, c, Lakewood (Calif.) HS.

## LOS ANGELES DODGERS (13)

1. **Paul Konerko, c, Chaparral HS, Scottsdale, Ariz.—(1997-2014)**
2. **Gary Rath, lhp, Mississippi State University.—(1998-99)**
3. **Mike Metcalfe, ss, University of Miami.—(1998-2000)**
4. **Ricky Stone, rhp, Hamilton (Ohio) HS.—(2001-07)**
5. Chris Ochsenfeld, lhp, Bethel HS, Hampton, Va.—(High A)
6. ***Eric DuBose, lhp, Patrician Academy, Butler, Ala.—(2002-06)**
DRAFT DROP *First-round draft pick (21st overall), Athletics (1997)*
7. Jamie Jaye, lhp, University of South Alabama.
8. *Jason Huisman, ss, Thornwood HS, Thornton. Ill.
DRAFT DROP *Brother of Rick Huisman, major leaguer (1995-96) • Brother of Justin Huisman, major leaguer (2004)*
9. *C.J. Ankrum, of, Saratoga (Calif.) HS.
10. Ron Hollis, rhp, University of Michigan.
11. +Alex Fajardo, lhp, Coral Gables HS, Miami / Miami-Dade CC Wolfson.
12. Greg Thompson, rhp-of, Goddard HS, Roswell, N.M.
13. Brian Harmon, of, Marist HS, Palos Heights, Ill.
14. **Eddie Oropesa, lhp, Canoga Park, Calif.—(2001-04)**
15. *Alex Andreopoulos, c, Seton Hall University.
16. *Ken Kilian, of, Wheaton Warrenville South HS, Warrenville Ill.
17. Kevin Zellers, ss-2b, Kent State University.
18. J.P. Roberge, 1b, University of Southern California.
19. Kyle Cooey, c, University of Connecticut.
20. ***Brett Tomko, rhp, Mount San Antonio (Calif.) JC.—(1997-2011)**
21. *Brock Rumfield, ss-3b, Belton (Texas) HS.
22. **Adam Riggs, 2b, University of South Carolina-Aiken.—(1997-2004)**
23. Johnny Hilo, of, Cal State Los Angeles.
24. *Zachary Hines, ss, DeKalb (Ga.) JC.
25. ***Randy Wolf, lhp, El Camino Real HS, Canoga Park, Calif.—(1999-2015)**
26. Jason Reed, lhp, Grossmont (Calif.) JC.
27. *George Dearborn, lhp, Mountain View HS, Vancouver, Wash.
28. *Ben Butkus, ss, Dr. Phillips HS, Orlando, Fla.
29. Jeff Paluk, rhp, Saginaw Valley State (Mich.) University.
30. Eric Stuckenschneider, of, Central Missouri State University.
31. *Michael Wood, c, San Clemente (Calif.) HS.
32. Brian Majeski, of, University of Connecticut.
33. Chip Sell, of, University of the Pacific.
34. Kevin Faircloth, ss, North Carolina State University.
35. +Robert Meyer, 2b, Kirkwood (Iowa) CC.
36. Ryan Sowards, 3b, Walla Walla (Wash.) CC.
37. *Leonardo Matos, lhp, Luis Munoz Rivera HS, Utuado, P.R.
38. ***Eric Byrnes, c, St. Francis HS, Portola Valley, Calif.—(2000-10)**
39. *Kirby Drube, of-rhp, Campbell County HS, Gillette, Wyo.
40. *Aaron Miller, lhp, Middletown (Del.) HS.
41. +Jeff Bramlett, lb, Bradley Central HS, Cleveland, Tenn.
42. *Ryan Roskowski, 3b, Clovis West HS, Fresno, Calif.
43. *Mark Shephard, rhp, Strathroy (Ontario) HS.
44. ***Jermaine Clark, ss-2b, Wood HS, Vacaville, Calif.—(2001-05)**
45. *Brad Block, rhp, Portage Central HS, Portage, Mich.

46. *Chuck Koone, of, McDowell HS, Marion, N.C.
47. *Keith Graffagnini, of, De la Salle HS, New Orleans, La.
48. +Marc Charbonneau, lhp, Kwantlen (B.C.) JC.
49. *David Sloan, c, York Community HS, Elmhurst, Ill.
**50. *Jim Parque, lhp, Crescenta Valley HS, La Crescenta, Calif.—(1998-2003)**
DRAFT DROP *First-round draft pick (46th overall), White Sox (1997)*
51. Elias Tapia, rhp, South Gate, Calif.
52. *Clint Lawrence, lhp, White Oaks HS, Oakville, Ontario.
**53. *Justin Atchley, lhp, Texas A&M University.—(2001)**
54. *Frank Hinojosa, c, Ayala HS, Chino, Calif.
55. *Thomas Cody, c, Lower Columbia (Wash.) JC.
56. *Adam Kiehl, of, East HS, Wauwatosa, Wis.
57. *Tracy Johnson, of, Glendale (Ariz.) CC.
58. *Hector Esparza, 3b, Independence HS, San Jose, Calif.
59. *Anthony Cellers, of, Seminole (Okla.) CC.
60. *Jaime Decker, c, Fort Madison (Iowa) HS.
61. *Luke Quaccia, 1b, Modesto (Calif.) JC.
62. *Josh Osborn, rhp, Butte (Calif.) JC.
63. +Joel Manfredi, 3b, Lincoln HS, Stockton, Calif. / Sacramento (Calif.) CC.
64. *Brandon Bowe, rhp, San Joaquin Delta (Calif.) JC.
65. *Calvin Tanton, c, Strathmore (Alberta) HS.
66. *Jesse Zepeda, ss, Cuesta (Calif.) JC.
67. *Eric Boisjoly, ss, Edouard Montpetit HS, Boucherville, Quebec.
68. +Lance Backowski, 2b, Fresno (Calif.) CC.
69. +Jaime Malave, 1b, Southeastern Illinois JC.
70. *Cordell Farley, of, Louisburg (N.C.) JC.
71. Greg Morrison, of, Kwantlen (B.C.) JC.
72. *Shawn Painter, of, John Abbott (Quebec) JC.
73. *Chris Vollaro, rhp, Oak Ridge HS, Spring, Texas.
74. *Jeremy Meccage, rhp, West HS, Billings, Mon.
75. *Otis Jasper, rhp, Quesnel (B.C.) HS.
76. *Justin Elsey, of, Casa Grande HS, Petaluma, Calif.
77. *Ovidio Zepeda, of, Richard King HS, Corpus Christi, Texas.

MORRIS FOSTOFF

Dodgers first-rounder Paul Konerko spent 17 seasons in the majors, most with the White Sox

## MILWAUKEE BREWERS (4)

**1. Antone Williamson, 3b, Arizona State University.—(1997)**
2. Doug Webb, rhp, San Diego State University.—(AA)
3. Larry Barnes, rhp, Englewood HS, Jacksonville, Fla.—(Low A)
4. Darrell Nicholas, of, University of New Orleans.—(AAA)
**5. Steve Woodard, rhp, Hartselle (Ala.) HS.—(1997-2003)**
6. Roberto Lopez, 2b, Oklahoma State University.
7. Chris Burt, rhp, Northern Illinois University.
**8. Ron Belliard, ss, Central HS, Miami.—(1998-2010)**
9. Ed Collins, rhp, Union (N.J.) HS.
10. Scott Krause, of, University of New Orleans.
11. *Jason Franklin, ss-of, Winter Haven (Fla.) HS.
12. *Tom Johnson, of, Elizabeth (N.J.) HS.
13. Shane Moses, rhp, Riverside (Calif.) CC.
14. Marc Fink, 1b, Memorial HS, Jackson, N.J.
15. Scott Nate, lhp, Lake Michigan JC.
**16. Robinson Cancel, 3b-c, Leonides Morales HS, Lajas, P.R.—(1999-2011)**
17. Adrian Wilkerson, of, Coffee HS, Douglas, Ga.
18. Joe Hiller, rhp, Columbus (Ga.) College.
**19. *Mike Kinkade, c-of, Washington State University.—(1998-2003)**
20. *Trent Brown, lhp, San Manuel HS, Oracle, Ariz.
21. Scott Huntsman, rhp, Wright State University.
22. Stephen Pritchard, ss, Western Carolina University.
23. Brian Titus, lhp, St. Bonaventure University.
24. Josh Tyler, 3b, University of Pittsburgh.
25. Alfredo Gutierrez, rhp, Norte Vista HS, Riverside, Calif.
26. *Ben McGarvey, rhp, Indian Hills (Iowa) CC.
27. *Paul Chiaffredo, c, Leland HS, San Jose, Calif.
28. *David Therneau, rhp, Denton (Texas) HS.
29. Robert Snook, c, Illinois Valley JC.
30. Jeffrey Kramer, rhp, Emory (Ga.) University.
31. *Jamold Little, ss, Southeastern Iinois JC.
32. Mac Norris, rhp, Dobson HS, Mesa, Ariz.
33. Anthony Iapoce, of, Lamar University.
34. Greg Beck, rhp, University of West Florida.
35. Ruberto Escalet, 2b, University of Mary Hardin-Baylor (Texas).
36. Brian Dalton, rhp, Florida Southern College.
37. *Mark Doubleday, ss, Faulkner State (Ala.) JC.
38. *Will Rushing, lhp, Georgia Southern University.
39. *Blair Murphy, rhp, Los Gatos (Calif.) HS.
40. *Corey Richardson, rhp, Millbrook HS, Raleigh, N.C.
41. *Deion Daniels, rhp, Seminole HS, Sanford, Fla.
42. *Elliott Brown, rhp, George C. Wallace (Ala.) CC.
43. *Doug Wakefield, lhp, Apple Valley (Calif.) HS.
44. +Anthony Allen, of, Jefferson City HS, Keaneysville, W.Va. / Potomac State (W.Va.) CC.
45. +Anthony Peters, c, Miami-Dade CC North.
46. *Beau Johnson, 1b-of, Ukiak (Calif.) HS.
47. +Bruce Lenhardt, rhp, Lake Michigan JC.
48. +David Glick, lhp, Palmdale (Calif.) HS/Antelope Valley (Calif.) JC.
49. *Tim Mullen, lhp, Malden Catholic HS, Reading, Mass.
50. *Jorge Santiago, c, Maestro Ladislao Martinez HS, Vega Alta, P.R.
51. *Javier Gomez, 1b, University HS, Moca, P.R.
52. *Chris Donohoo, lhp, Notre Dame HS, Chattanooga, Tenn.
53. +Rico Harris, of, Florida CC.
54. Anthony Pavlovich, rhp, Middle Georgia JC.
55. *Jeff Solomon, ss, Jackson HS, Miami.
56. *Ray Hughes, rhp-of, Aucilla Christian Academy, Monticello, Fla.
**57. *Matt Erickson, ss, West HS, Appleton, Wis.—(2004)**
58. *Bill Eaton, ss-rhp, Leonard HS, Lake Worth, Fla.
59. *Etienne Hightower, of, Okaloosa-Walton (Fla.) CC.
60. *Greg Cooper, rhp, Florida CC.
61. *Javil Byron, 2b, Carol City HS, Miami.

## MINNESOTA TWINS (8)

**1. Todd Walker, 2b, Louisiana State University.—(1996-2007)**
**1. Travis Miller, lhp, Kent State University** (Supplemental choice—34th—for failure to sign 1993 first-round draft pick Jason Varitek).**—(1996-2002)**
**2. Cleatus Davidson, ss, Lake Wales (Fla.) HS.—(1999)**
**3. A.J. Pierzynski, c, Dr. Phillips HS, Orlando, Fla.—(1998-2015)**
4. Tom Mott, rhp, Santa Clara University.—(AA)
5. John Schroeder, of, Coeur d'Alene (Idaho) HS.—(High A)
6. Walker Chapman, rhp, Beall HS, Frostburg, Md.
7. Antuan Bunkley, 1b, Palm Beach Lakes HS, West Palm Beach, Fla.
8. Jerome Brown, ss, Smithville (Okla.) HS.
9. Jeff Ferguson, 2b, Cal State Fullerton.
10. Marcus Starling, lhp, Florida CC.
**11. *David Dellucci, of, University of Mississippi.—(1997-2009)**
12. Paul Pavicich, lhp, San Jose State University.
13. Jim McCalmont, 2b, Grand Canyon University.
14. Brian Colburn, of, Central HS, La Crosse, Wis.
15. Eli Herdman, ss, Central Kitsap HS, Bremerton, Wash.
16. Kasey Richardson, lhp, Northern HS, Huntingtown, Md.
17. Robert Ruch, rhp, Millikin (Ill.) University.
18. *Glenn Davis, 1b, Malvern Prep HS, Aston, Pa.
DRAFT DROP *First-round draft pick (25th overall), Dodgers (1997) • Brother of Ben Davis, first-round draft pick, Padres (1995); major leaguer (1998-2004)*
19. Paul Morse, rhp, University of Kentucky.
20. Jason Meyhoff, lhp, University of Missouri.
21. Rodney McBride, rhp, White Station HS, Memphis, Tenn.
22. Damon Irvis, of, Lake Wales (Fla.) HS.
23. *Rob Neal, of, Cal Poly San Luis Obispo.
24. Nathan Craigue, ss, Concord (N.H.) HS.
25. *Brian Tokarse, rhp, Fullerton (Calif.) JC.
**26. Corey Koskie, 3b, Kwantlen (B.C.) JC.—(1998-2006)**
**27. Brandon Puffer, rhp, Capistrano Valley HS, Mission Viejo, Calif.—(2002-05)**
28. Matt Leach, rhp, Long Island University.
29. Scott Hilt, c, University of Hartford.
30. *Robert Quarnstrom, lhp, Hersey HS, Mount Prospect, Ill.
31. *Frankie Sanders, rhp, Pasco Hernando (Fla.) CC.
32. Jim Champion, 1b, Oregon State University.
33. Joe Correia, lhp, St. Louis HS, Pearl City, Hawaii.
34. Michael Raymondi, c, Watertown (S.D.) HS.
35. *Richard Rowe, ss, Lake Wier HS, Summerfield, Fla.
36. +Mike Narkter, rhp, Kent State University.
37. *Jacob Schaffer, ss, Holy Angels HS, Bloomington, Minn.
38. Brannon Peters, lhp, University of Texas.
**39. *Brian Lawrence, rhp, Carthage (Texas) HS.—(2001-07)**
40. *Brad Winget, 1b, Murray (Utah) HS.
41. *Justin Lamber, lhp, Hackensack (N.J.) HS.
42. *Mark Gardner, lhp, Orange Coast (Calif.) JC.
43. *Landon Hessler, rhp, Pasco Hernando (Fla.) CC.
44. *Linus Williams, lhp, Stigler (Okla.) HS.
45. *Chris Traylor, lhp, Bartlesville (Okla.) HS.
46. *Ajani Carter, of, Oakland (Calif.) HS.
47. Erick Thompson, rhp, Dallas Baptist University.
48. +Julio Ayuso, of, Interamericano HS, Carolina, P.R. / Gulf Coast (Fla.) CC.
49. *Kelly Gage-Cole, lhp, Centennial HS, Coquitlam, B.C.
50. *Billy Munoz, of, Kofa HS, Yuma, Ariz.
51. *Jose Marrero, 1b, Ponce Regional HS, Ponce, P.R.
52. *Ray Ragland, rhp, Clemson University.

## MONTREAL EXPOS (21)

**1. Hiram Bocachica, ss, Rexville HS, Bayamon, P.R.—(2000-07)**
**1. Mike Thurman, rhp, Oregon State University** (Supplemental choice—31st—as compensation for Type A free agent Dennis Martinez).**—(1997-2002)**
2. Jason Camilli, ss, Thunderbird HS, Phoenix (Choice from Indians as compensation for Martinez).—(AAA)
2. *Kenny Henderson, rhp, University of Miami.—(High A)
DRAFT DROP *Returned to Miami (Fla.); re-drafted by Padres, 1995 (5th round); first-round draft pick (5th overall), Brewers (1991)*
3. Paul Ottavinia, of, Seton Hall University.—(AAA)
**4. Jeremy Powell, rhp-of, Highlands HS, Sacramento, Calif.—(1998-2000)**
**5. Javier Vazquez, rhp, Colegio Ponceno HS, Ponce, P.R.—(1998-2011)**
**6. Scott Forster, lhp, James Madison University.—(2000)**
**7. Geoff Blum, ss, University of California.—(1999-2012)**
**8. Simon Pond, ss, Argyle HS, North Vancouver, B.C.—(2004)**
9. *Brian Hervey, rhp, Spanish River HS, Boca Raton, Fla.
10. Jason McCommon, rhp, Memphis State University.
11. Carl Hall, of, Wichita State University.
12. Jerald Stubbs, rhp, University of Alabama.
13. Jake Benz, lhp, Oklahoma State University.
14. Mark Lewis, ss, University of Nevada-Reno.
15. Kurt Alderman, c, Albertson (Idaho) College.
16. *Dan McKinley, of, Dobson HS, Mesa, Ariz.
DRAFT DROP *First-round draft pick (49th overall), Giants (1997)*
17. *Brent Peck, rhp, Gulf Coast (Fla.) CC.
18. Bob Hughes, of, University of Arkansas.
19. *Jason Ryan, lhp, St. Thomas Aquinas HS, Davie, Fla.
20. *Matt Jeckell, rhp, DeAnza (Calif.) JC
21. *Jason Welch, of, Bishop Verot HS, Fort Myers, Fla.
22. *Toby McDermott, lhp, Decatur HS, Federal Way, Wash.
23. Cary Fenton, 2b, Memphis State University.
24. *Jason Walker, ss, Springville (Utah) HS.
25. +Jeremy Ware, of, Centennial Collegiate HS, Guelph, Ontario / Indian Hills (Iowa) CC.
26. *Philip Derryman, rhp, Royal HS, Simi Valley, Calif.
27. *Robert Everett, rhp, Monroe Area (Ga.) HS.
28. *Stephan Neill, rhp, Indian River (Fla.) CC.
29. *Damon Warren, rhp, Hudson's Bay HS, Vancouver, Wash.

30. *Michael Young, lhp, Port Moody (B.C.) HS.
31. Ed Bady, of, Talledega (Ala.) JC.
32. *Michael Davis, rhp, Tallahassee (Fla.) CC.
33. *Joel Young, lhp, Ulster (N.Y.) CC.
34. Jay Cole, rhp, University of Alabama-Birmingham.
35. *Raul Torres, of, Hialeah (Fla.) HS.
36. Ben Fleetham, rhp, Rollins (Fla.) College.
37. Thad Chaddrick, 3b, Oklahoma State University.
38. *Mike Brandley, lhp, Wichita State University.
39. *Robert Price, rhp, Deer Valley HS, Glendale. Ariz.
40. *Rob Vael, rhp, North Delta (B.C.) HS.
41. Matt Haas, c, University of Notre Dame.
42. *Dennis Machado, lhp, Kenai Central HS, Kenai, Alaska.
43. *Ben Phillips, rhp, Sheridan (Wyo.) HS.
44. *Jonathan Zumwalt, rhp, South Kitsap HS, Port Orchard, Wash.
45. *James Berger, rhp, Immanuel HS, Dinuba. Calif.
46. *Kyle Duncan, rhp, Kalama (Wash.) HS.
47. *Garrett Neubart, of, Columbia University.

## NEW YORK METS (1)

1. **Paul Wilson, rhp, Florida State University.—(1996-2005)**
1. **Terrence Long, 1b-of, Stanhope Elmore HS, Millbrook, Ala.** (Choice from Orioles as compensation for Type A free agent Sid Fernandez).**—(1999-2006)**
1. **Jay Payton, of, Georgia Tech** (Supplemental choice—29th—as compensation for Fernandez).**—(1998-2010)**
2. Sean Johnston, lhp, Highland Park (Ill.) HS.—(High A)
2. ***Matthew LeCroy, c, Belton-Honea Path HS, Belton, S.C.** (Supplemental choice—63rd—as compensation for Type C free agent Charlie O'Brien).**—(2000-07)**
DRAFT DROP *Attended Clemson; re-drafted by Twins, 1997 (1st round)*
3. Bryon Gainey, 1b, Davidson HS, Mobile, Ala.—(AA)
4. Kevin McCarthy, of, North Allegheny HS, Wexford, Pa.—(Low A)
4. Kenny Pumphrey, rhp, Old Mill HS, Millersville, Md. (Choice from Rockies as compensation for Type B free agent Howard Johnson).—(AAA)
5. *Brian Kuklick, rhp, Hatboro Horsham HS, Horsham, Pa.--DNP
DRAFT DROP *Attended Wake Forest; re-drafted by Mets, 1997 (55th round)*
6. David Sanderson, of, University of Missouri.
7. *Brett Nista, ss, Laguna Hills (Calif.) HS.
8. Kevin Manley, rhp, Frostproof (Fla.) HS.
9. Robert Cox, 3b, Santa Monica (Calif.) JC.
10. ***Adam Piatt, ss, Bishop Verot HS, Fort Myers. Fla.—(2000-03)**
11. John Kelly, rhp, University of Connecticut.
12. Jeramie Simpson, of, Seward County (Kan.) CC.
13. Steve Arffa, lhp, University of Arizona.
14. ***Travis Harper, rhp, Circleville HS, Riverton, W.Va.—(2000-06)**
15. Melvin Poupart, rhp, Ana Roque HS, Humacao, P.R.
16. Craig Cope, lhp, F.J. Brennan HS, Windsor, Ontario.
17. ***Jason Dellaero, ss, Brewster (N.Y.) HS.—(1999)**
DRAFT DROP *First-round draft pick (15th overall), White Sox (1997)*
18. Toby Larson, rhp, University of Alabama-Birmingham.
19. Sammy Rodriguez, c, Mount St. Michaels HS, New York.
20. Craig Jelsovsky, ss, Monte Vista HS, Spring Valley, Calif.
21. Don Spingola, rhp, Chabot (Calif.) JC.
22. *Scott Haij, rhp, Columbia River HS, Vancouver, Wash.
23. **Scott Sauerbeck, lhp, Miami (Ohio) University.—(1999-2006)**
24. Matt Koenig, rhp, Brookdale (N.J.) CC.
25. Joe Lisio, rhp, New York Tech.
26. *Matt Lytle, lhp, Wyomissing Area (Pa.) HS.
DRAFT DROP *Quarterback, National Football League (2000-01)*
27. Bill Santamaria, rhp, Lakewood (N.J.) HS.
28. Roscoe Wicks, rhp, North Eugene HS, Eugene, Ore.
29. *Brad Kennedy, 2b, Neosho County (Kan.) CC.
30. Ryan Miller, ss, Long Beach State University.
31. Robert Borkowski, rhp, St. Mark's HS, Wilmington, Del.
32. Rocky Turner, of, University of Texas-Arlington.
33. Luis Hernandez, 2b, University of Miami.
34. Bo Haley, 1b, University of Wyoming.
35. Ethan Burke, rhp, Baker HS, Baker City, Ore.
36. *Joe Mattingly, rhp, Indian River (Fla.) JC.
37. *Nate Laufer, rhp, Los Angeles Baptist HS, Sylmar, Calif.
38. *Matt Simpson, c, California HS, Whittier, Calif.
39. Noah Peery, rhp, Arizona State University.
40. Mark Guerra, rhp, Jacksonville University.
41. ***Bryan Hebson, rhp, Central HS, Phenix City, Ala.—(2003)**
DRAFT DROP *First-round draft pick (44th overall), Expos (1997)*
42. *Calvin Whitekiller, rhp, Hulbert (Okla.) HS.
43. +Tracy Edmondson, 2b, Riverside (Calif.) CC.
44. *Sammie Mathis, rhp, Southern Arkansas University.
45. Daniel Engle, c, Western Oklahoma State JC.
46. *Darren Nordlund, of, Tacoma (Wash.) CC.
47. *Scott Schultz, rhp, Louisiana State U
48. *John Batts, 2b, University of Delaware.
49. *Mel Melehes, lhp, St. James HS, Guelph, Ontario.
50. Brian Mifflin, of, Lewes, Del.
51. *David Meng, rhp, University of New Mexico.
52. *Taylor Harris, 1b, DeKalb (Ga.) JC.
53. *Shawn McNally, rhp, Auburn University.
54. *Maurice Bruce, ss, Connors State (Okla.) JC.
55. *Anthony Roossien, 3b-1b, Trinity Christian Academy, Plano, Texas.
56. *Carlos Morrison, of, Central Arizona JC.
57. Tim Bishop, of, Valparaiso (Ind.) HS.
58. *John Garrison, rhp, San Joaquin Delta (Calif.) JC.
59. *Darren Dyt, of, Golden West HS, Tulare, Calif.
60. Kyle Kessel, lhp, Mundelein (Ill.) HS.
61. *Richard Lee, ss, Jackson (Miss.) Academy.
62. *Jeff Sonsoucie, lhp, Lebanon HS, Summerfield, Ill.
63. *Harold Zdziarski, rhp, Lackawanna (Pa.) CC.
64. David Leonhart, lhp, Oklahoma Christian College.
65. ***Kris Wilson, rhp, Tarpon Springs HS, Palm Harbor, Fla.—(2000-06)**
66. **+Brandon Villafuerte, rhp, West Valley (Calif.) JC.—(2000-04)**
67. *Matt Hopper, ss, Winder-Barrow HS, Winder, Ga.
68. *David Benham, 3b-of, Garland Christian Academy, Garland, Texas.
69. *Ted Cheatham, ss, Spring Hill (Kan.) HS.
70. *Heath Schesser, ss, Manhattan (Kan.) HS.
71. Hans Beebe, lhp, Camden County (N.J.) CC.
72. *Gregg Smyth, lhp, Rollins (Fla.) College.
73. *Michael Terry, 1b-lhp, Edison HS, Tulsa, Okla.
74. Paul LeClair, of, Livingston (Ala.) University.
75. *Jeromy Thomas, rhp, Kalama (Wash.) HS.

## NEW YORK YANKEES (24)

1. **Brian Buchanan, 1b-of, University of Virginia.—(2000-04)**
2. Rod Smith, of, Lafayette HS, Lexington, Ky.—(AA)
3. Garrett Butler, of, Northwest HS, Miami.—(AA)
4. Steve Shoemaker, rhp, University of Alabama.—(AAA)
5. Ray Ricken, rhp, University of Michigan.—(AAA)
6. Jose Velazquez, 1b, Rafael Lopez Landron HS, Guayama, P.R.
7. David Meyer, lhp, University of Kansas.
8. Ryan Beeney, ss, Kent State University.
9. Mike Mitchell, 1b, UCLA.
10. Eric Kofler, 1b, Central Catholic HS, Clearwater, Fla.
11. **Jake Robbins, rhp, Myers Park HS, Charlotte, N.C.—(2004)**
12. Marty Robinson, lhp, Cape Coral (Fla.) HS.
13. Jason Jarvis, rhp, Bellevue (Neb.) College.
14. Eric Schaffner, rhp, Frank Phillips (Texas) JC.
15. Dwaine Edgar, rhp, Southern University.
16. Brian Binversie, rhp, Iowa State University.
17. ***Jason Grabowski, c, The Morgan School, Clinton, Conn.—(2002-05)**
18. *Charlie Ward, ss, Florida State University.
DRAFT DROP *Heisman Trophy winner (1993) • First-round draft pick, New York Knicks, National Basketball Association (1994); guard, NBA (1994-2003)*
19. Derek Dukart, 3b, University of Nebraska.
20. **Ben Ford, rhp, Indian Hills (Iowa) CC.—(1998-2004)**
21. Chris Corn, rhp, University of Kansas.
22. Felix Mejia, rhp, American HS, Hialeah, Fla.
23. *Barry Patton, c, Kosciusko (Miss.) HS.
24. ***Jason Grilli, rhp, Baker HS, Baldwinsville, N.Y.—(2000-15)**
DRAFT DROP *First-round draft pick (4th overall), Giants (1997) • Son of Steve Grilli, major leaguer (1975-79)*
25. James Franklin, ss, Sarasota (Fla.) HS.
26. *Pat Dunham, rhp, Portage Central HS, Portage, Mich.
27. Jeremy Benson, lhp, University of Delaware.
28. *Corey Brittan, rhp, Hutchinson (Kan.) CC.
29. *Mitchell Henderson, of, Culver Military Academy, Lexington, Ky.
30. *Michael Hughes, ss, Caruthers Union HS, Fresno, Calif.
31. *Michael Karow, lhp, Tyler (Texas) JC.
32. *Fernando Rivero, 1b, Jackson HS, Miami.
33. *Mike Schnautz, lhp, Bryan (Texas) HS.
34. *Scott Jones, rhp, Miami (Ohio) University.
35. *Chris Halliday, c, Florida CC.
36. *Sidney Newman, ss, Cosumnes River (Calif.) JC.
37. ***Matt Blank, lhp, Martin HS, Arlington, Texas.—(2000-01)**
38. +Aaron Horton, lhp, Gulf Coast (Fla.) CC.
39. *Ben Tucker, rhp, University of Southern California.
40. *David Harper, rhp, McLennan (Texas) CC.
41. Carlos Yedo, 1b, Miami-Dade CC South.
42. *David Trentine, c, Cypress (Calif.) JC.
43. *Casey Cunningham, lhp, Santa Rosa (Calif.) JC.
44. *Casey Hensley, 1b, Fort Scott (Ky.) CC.
45. *Steven Keen, rhp, Florida CC.
46. *Darryl Craig, 1b, Kwantlen (B.C.) JC.
47. *Mitch Schardt, rhp, Lake Brantley HS, Longwood, Fla.
48. *Jason Deyell, rhp, Montcalm HS, London, Ontario.
49. *John Adams, of, Olathe South HS, Olathe, Kan.
50. *Jeremy Lee, rhp, Apache (Okla.) HS.
51. *Todd Martin, rhp, South Florence HS, Florence, S.C.
52. *Eric Carlisle, of, Sam Rayburn HS, Pasadena, Texas.
53. *Zack McWhirter, rhp, Plano (Texas) HS.
54. *Jason Jordan, 1b, University of Alabama.
55. *Eddy Furniss, 1b, Nacogdoches (Texas) HS.
56. *Dan DeYoung, rhp, Lisbon (Iowa) HS.
57. *Clint Chrysler, lhp, Boca Ciega HS, St. Petersburg, Fla.
58. *Jarred McAlvain, 1b, Eastern Oklahoma State JC.
59. *Shawn Onley, rhp, Northeast Texas CC.
60. *Jose Sevillano, of, Maestro Ladi HS, Vega Alta, P.R.
61. *Gerald Butt, c, Kwantlen (B.C.) JC.
62. +Erik Keech, c, Manatee (Fla.) JC.
63. *Erik Mattern, ss, Mater Dei HS, Fountain Valley, Calif.
64. *Goefrey Tomlinson, of, Everman (Texas) HS.
65. *Michael Gil, c, Miami-Dade CC South.
66. *Kyle Heine, c, Scarborough HS, Houston.
67. *Jason Elmore, rhp, Louisburg (N.C.) JC.
68. *Anthony Edwards, rhp, Bartlesville (Okla.) HS.
69. *Dusty Rhodes, of, Madison (N.J.) HS.
70. *David Aldrich, rhp, Jefferson State (Ala.) CC.
71. *Keith Dilgard, rhp, Florida CC.
72. *Clint Sauls, rhp, Evans HS, Martinez. Ga.
73. *Chris Dickerson, 3b, Blinn (Texas) JC.
74. *Ryan Anholt, of, Moose Jaw (Sask.) HS.
75. *Brandon James, 1b, Sacramento CC.
76. *Vernon Williams, of, Solano (Calif.) JC.
77. *Darren Bowleg, lhp, Indian River (Fla.) CC.
78. *Jose Cepeda, 2b-ss, Linn-Benton (Ore.) CC.
79. *Mike Schwamel, of, Holy Name HS, Seven Hills, Ohio.
80. *Jason Clark, 1b, Riverside (Calif.) CC.
81. *Matt Carnes, rhp, Miami (Okla.) HS.
82. *Tyler Bain, 2b, Seward County (Kan.) CC.
83. *Derek Adair, rhp, Neosho County (Kan.) CC.
84. Monte Barnes, lhp, Indian River (Fla.) JC.
85. *Jimmie Slaton, 3b, Barton County (Kan.) CC.
86. *Nate Dighera, 3b, Hilltop HS, Chula Vista, Calif.
87. *Wyley Steelmon, c, Cowley County (Kan.) CC.

## OAKLAND ATHLETICS (2)

1. **Ben Grieve, of, Martin HS, Arlington, Texas.—(1997-2005)**
DRAFT DROP *Son of Tom Grieve, first-round draft pick, Senators (1966); major leaguer (1970-79); general manager, Rangers (1985-94) • Brother of Tim Grieve, 23rd-round draft pick, Royals (1994)*
2. **Brad Rigby, rhp, Georgia Tech.—(1997-2000)**
3. Bill King, rhp, Birmingham-Southern College.—(AAA)
4. **Jason Beverlin, rhp, Western Carolina University.—(2002)**
DRAFT DROP *Baseball coach, Bethune-Cookman (2012-15)*
5. ***Ryan Drese, rhp, Bishop O'Dowd HS, Oakland.—(2001-06)**
DRAFT DROP *Attended California; re-drafted by Athletics, 1997 (14th round)*
6. **Emil Brown, of, Indian River (Fla.) CC.—(1997-2009)**
7. Mike Maurer, rhp, Iowa State University.
8. Rob DeBoer, c, University of South Carolina.
9. Robert Harris, ss, Texas A&M University.
10. ***Stephen Randolph, lhp, Galveston (Texas) JC.—(2003-07)**
11. *Bubba Scarce, rhp, Tunstall HS, Danville, Va.
DRAFT DROP *Son of Mac Scarce, major leaguer (1972-78)*
12. *Todd Weinberg, lhp, CC of Rhode Island.
13. Al Gogolin, rhp, Georgia Tech.
14. Chris Cochrane, rhp, Rutgers University.
15. Jon Valenti, 3b, Oklahoma City University.
16. Matt McDonald, lhp, Parkland (Ill.) JC.
17. Eric Martins, 2b, Long Beach State University.
18. Manny DaSilva, c, University of North Carolina.
19. Chad Rolish, lhp, Cal State Fullerton.
20. John Smith, lhp, Old Dominion University.
21. Alex Miranda, 1b, University of Miami.
22. Michael Rios, rhp, University of the Pacific.
23. Khris Law, of, Tunstall HS, Danville, Va.
24. Dock McDonald, of, Columbia State (Tenn.) CC.
25. Stacy Kelley, rhp, Milford Academy, Glastonbury, Conn.
26. Mike Stamison, ss, Cumberland (Tenn.) University.
27. Jason Holden, rhp, Shelby State (Tenn.) CC.
28. *Damond Nash, rhp, Arkansas HS, Texarkana, Ark.
29. *Cam Spence, rhp, Gordon (Ga.) JC.
30. *Aaron Gardin, of, Yavapai (Ariz.) JC.
31. +Terrance Freernan, ss, Edison (Fla.) CC.
32. *Danny Crawford, rhp, San Jacinto (Texas) JC.
33. *Frank Chapman, rhp, San Jacinto (Texas) JC.
34. +David Plant, rhp, Davis HS, Modesto, Calif. / Modesto (Calif.) JC.
35. ***Tim Hudson, rhp, Chattahoochee Valley (Ala.) JC.—(1999-2015)**
36. Chris Helfrich, rhp, University of Evansville.
37. *Brent Whitlock, c, Jackson State (Tenn.) CC.
38. *Richard Collins, rhp, Southern Union State (Ala.) JC.
39. *Victor Chambers, 2b, Vallejo (Calif.) HS.

## PHILADELPHIA PHILLIES (23)

1. **Carlton Loewer, rhp, Mississippi State University.—(1998-2003)**
2. **Ryan Nye, rhp, Texas Tech.—(1997-98)**
DRAFT DROP *Brother of Richard Nye, 47th-round draft pick, Giants (1994)*
3. Larry Wimberly, lhp, West Orange HS, Winter Garden, Fla.—(AAA)
4. **Jason Sikes, rhp, Warner Robins (Ga.) HS.—(Low A)**
5. Scott Shores, of, Arizona State University.—(AA)
6. Eric Schreimann, c, Jefferson City (Mo.) HS.
7. **Matt Beech, lhp, University of Houston.—(1996-98)**
8. **Jason Boyd, rhp, John A. Logan (Ill.) JC.—(1999-2004)**
9. Joel Zamudio, rhp, Monroe HS, Sepulveda, Calif.
10. Rob Burger, rhp, Lampeter-Strasburg HS,

Lampeter, Pa.
11. Mauricio Estavil, lhp, Pepperdine University.
**12. Wendell Magee, of, Samford University.—(1996-2002)**
13. Torrey Pettiford, 2b, Pembroke State (N.C.) University.
**14. Robert Dodd, lhp, University of Florida.—(1998)**
15. Peter Nyari, rhp, Edinboro (Pa.) University.
16. Adrian Antonini, rhp, Louisiana State University.
17. James Northeimer, c, University of Tennessee.
18. Jeff Jensen, 1b, Sam Houston State University.
19. John Torok, of, University of Toledo.
20. Matt Guiliano, ss, Iona College.
21. Matt Williamson, 2b-ss, Rice University.
22. Brett Legrow, rhp, University of Southern Mississippi.
23. Luis Andino, of, Carolina, P.R.
24. Bill Mobilia, ss, University of Minnesota.
25. *Bobby Kahlon, rhp, University of California.
26. Shane Pullen, of, University of Southern Mississippi.
27. Jason Valley, rhp, Washington State University.
28. Adan Millan, c, Cal State Fullerton.
29. Stephan Paasch, rhp, University of Maryland.
30. Ken Reed, rhp, Rolla (Mo.) HS.
31. Kyle Karvala, lhp, University of Wisconsin-Whitewater.
32. Larry Huff, ss, Cal State Los Angeles.
33. *Ryan Hankins, 3b, Simi Valley (Calif.) HS.
**34. Jose Flores, 3b, University of Texas.—(2002-04)**
35. Aaron Royster, of, Northeast Missouri State University.
36. Courtney Mitchell, lhp, Grambling State University.
**37. Bronson Heflin, rhp, University of Tennessee.—(1996)**
38. Samuel Wampler, c, Allan Hancock (Calif.) JC.
**39. *Brian Cooper, rhp, Citrus (Calif.) JC.—(1999-2005)**
40. *Rob Gaiko, rhp, Oklahoma State University.
41. David Stewart, lhp, Tulane University.
42. *Matt Kastelic, of, Rancho Santiago (Calif.) JC.
43. Johnny Beck, lhp, East Carolina University.
44. Len Manning, lhp, University of Wisconsin.
45. Brian Stumpf, rhp, Delaware County CC.
46. Chad Kearney, of, Brentwood HS, Central Islip, N.Y.
**47. *Joe Winkelsas, rhp, University of South Carolina-Salkehatchie.—(1999-2006)**
48. *Jeff Newkirk, of, Taft (Calif.) JC.
49. Jake Russell, 3b, Northeastern Oklahoma A&M JC.
50. *Cameron Flower, of, Rincon HS, Tucson, Ariz.
51. *Neal Presley, rhp, Opp (Ala.) HS.
52. *Jeff Andra, lhp, Northwest HS, Lenexa. Kan.
53. *Blair Fowler, rhp, Walla Walla (Wash.) JC.

## PITTSBURGH PIRATES (11)

1. Mark Farris, ss, Angleton (Texas) HS.—(AA)
**2. Roger Goedde, rhp, Reitz HS, Evansville, Ind.—(Short-season A)**
3. Aaron France, rhp, Cypress (Calif.) JC.—(AA)
4. Bryan Farson, lhp, Kent State University.—(AA)
5. Eddie Brooks, 2b, University of Kentucky.—(High A)
6. Mike Asche, ss, Kearney State (Neb.) College.
7. Randy Viegas, lhp, Oakmont HS, Roseville, Calif.
8. Bo Springfield, of, Denison (Texas) HS.
**9. Jimmy Anderson, lhp, Western Branch HS, Chesapeake, Va.—(1999-2004)**
10. *Jason Fry, rhp, Grand Island (Neb.) HS.
11. Richard Watts, c, UC Davis.
12. Cordell Dunn, rhp-ss, Rosa Fort HS, Tunica, Miss.
13. *Thomas Hunter, of-1b, Eagan (Minn.) HS.
14. Anthony Robinson, ss, Diamond Bar (Calif.) HS.
15. Jeff Kelly, lhp, McKee Tech HS, Staten Island, N.Y.
16. *Jason Krafft, rhp, Edison HS, Tulsa, Okla.
17. Richie Blackwell, lhp, East Carolina University.
18. Steve Thobe, 1b-of, Cal State Sacramento.
19. Jonathan Sweet, c, Ohio State University.
20. *Andrew Van Wyk, rhp, Heritage HS, Littleton, Colo.
21. Aaron Edwards, of, Cal Poly Pomona.
22. Leotis Warren, 3b, Conroe (Texas) HS.
23. *Minor Bond, rhp, Vanguard HS, Ocala. Fla.
24. *Mark Dobson, rhp, Heritage HS, Littleton, Colo.
25. *Pete Zamora, lhp, Capistrano Valley HS, Mission Viejo, Calif.
26. Stan Schreiber, ss, Kimberly HS, Appleton, Wis.
27. Tonka Maynor, of-1b, University of North Carolina-Greensboro.
28. Matt Spade, rhp, Marshall University.
29. Paul McSparin, c, Southeastern Illinois JC.
30. Matt Amman, c, University of Central Florida.
31. *Matthew Noe, lhp, San Gorgonio HS, Highland, Calif.
32. Richard Venezia, ss, California (Pa.) University.
33. +Jason Adamson, of, Moorpark (Calif.) HS / Moorpark (Calif.) JC.
34. *Kendrick Wallace, of, Carson (Calif.) HS.
35. +Kemuel Shipp, c, North Cobb HS, Kennesaw, Ga. / Gordon (Ga.) JC.
36. *Clark Odom, of, Maclay HS, Quincy, Fla.
37. Joe Maskivish, rhp, West Liberty State (W.Va.) College.
38. *Wayne Montgomery, ss-2b, Laney (Calif.) JC.
39. Albert Davis, of, Alcoa (Tenn.) HS.
40. Leland McAfee, ss, Grossmont (Calif.) JC.
41. *Jason Wright, rhp, Palomar (Calif.) JC.
42. Greg Chew, rhp, Gloucester (N.J.) CC.
43. Curry Deutsch, lhp, Winona State (Minn.) University.
44. *Bryan Barber, lhp, Nogales HS, West Covina, Calif.
45. Rick Paugh, lhp, Marshall University.
**46. *Brandon Larson, ss, Holmes HS, San Antonio.—(2001-04)**
DRAFT DROP *First-round draft pick (14th overall), Reds (1997)*

## ST. LOUIS CARDINALS (19)

1. Bret Wagner, lhp, Wake Forest University.—(AA)
DRAFT DROP *Twin brother of Kyle Wagner, 21st-round draft pick, Cardinals (1994)*
**2. Carl Dale, rhp, Winthrop College.—(1999)**
3. Corey Avrard, rhp, Archbishop Rummel HS, Metairie, La.—(AA)
4. Yates Hall, rhp, University of Virginia.—(AA)
**5. Curtis King, rhp, Philadelphia College of Textiles.—(1997-99)**
**6. Blake Stein, rhp, Spring Hill (Ala.) College.—(1998-2002)**
7. Richard Mear, lhp, Rowland HS, Rowland Heights, Calif.
8. Ryan Foderaro, rhp, Brigham Young U,
9. Tony Abell, of, Meade County HS, Ekron, Ky.
10. *Bruce Thompson, of, University of Miami.
**11. *Dan Reichert, rhp Turlock (Calif.) HS.—(1999-2003)**
DRAFT DROP *First-round draft pick (7th overall), Royals (1997)*
**12. *John Bale, lhp, Jefferson Davis (Ala.) JC.—(1999-2009)**
**13. *Ryan Freel, ss, Englewood HS, Jacksonville, Fla.—(2001-09)**
14. Pete Ambrosina, 2b, Lincoln Memorial (Tenn.) University.
15. *Brandon Parker, rhp, Long Beach (Miss.) HS.
16. Sean Garman, 1b-3b, JC of Southern Idaho.
DRAFT DROP *Son of Mike Garman, first-round draft pick, Red Sox (1967); major leaguer (1969-78)*
17. Mark Roettgen, rhp, Jefferson City (Mo.) HS.
18. Marcus Logan, rhp, Murray State University.
**19. Placido Polanco, ss, Miami-Dade CC Wolfson.—(1998-2013)**
20. *Jerome Robinson, of, Taft (Calif.) JC.
21. *Kyle Wagner, c, Wake Forest University.
DRAFT DROP *Twin brother of Bret Wagner, first-round draft pick, Cardinals (1994)*
**22. Jose Leon, 3b, Alberge Olimpico HS, Cayey, P.R.—(2002-04)**
23. Ryan Hall, c, Brigham Young University.
**24. Keith McDonald, c, Pepperdine University.—(2000-01)**
25. Kevin Lovingier, lhp, University of Oklahoma.
26. Steve Reed, rhp, Palm Beach Lakes HS, North Palm Beach, Fla.
27. Manuel Mendez, lhp, Fresno (Calif.) CC.
28. Richard Hartmann, rhp, Long Island University.
29. Steve Frascatore, rhp, C.W. Post (N.Y.) University.
DRAFT DROP *Brother of John Frascatore, major leaguer (1994-2001)*
30. Adam West, lhp, Los Angeles Pierce JC.
31. Mike McDougal, 1b, Taft (Calif.) JC.
32. Miguel Rivera, ss, Lincoln Memorial (Tenn.) University.
33. Hector Rodriguez, 3b, Florida Memorial College.
34. Kevin McNeill, lhp, McNeese State University.
35. Jody Crump, lhp, Volunteer State (Tenn.) CC.
36. Efrain Contreras, of, Texas A&M University.
37. Scott Cunningham, rhp, University of Arkansas.
38. Tommy Minor, rhp, Fresno State University.
39. Darren Tawwater, c, Texas Christian University.
40. Bo Johnson, lhp, Rice University.
41. Rob Helvey, lhp, Missouri Baptist College.
**42. Keith Glauber, rhp, Montclair State (N.J.) University.—(1998-2000)**
43. +Rodger Harris, 2b-of, Tulare Union HS, Tulare, Calif. / JC of the Sequoias (Calif.).
44. Chris Arambula, 1b, University of Utah.
45. Steve Abbs, of, University of Wyoming.
46. Matt Golden, rhp, Princeton University.
47. Dennis McCaffrey, rhp, Pemberton Township HS, Browns Mills, N.J.
48. *Jacob Whitfield, lhp, Florida HS, Tallahassee, Fla.
49. *Nakia Hill, 2b, Crawford HS, San Diego.
50. *Andre Hall, c, St. Augustine HS, New Orleans, La.
51. *Robert Smoker, c, Manheim Central HS, Manheim, Pa.
52. Calvin Coach, of, University of South Carolina-Aiken.
53. *Mike Wolger, lhp, University of California.
54. *Mark McWilliams, rhp, University of North Carolina-Charlotte.
55. Clarence Johns, rhp, Southern University.
56. Christian Reinheimer, lhp, University of the Pacific.
57. *Jack Moore, lhp, Zapata (Texas) HS.
58. *Jason Riley, c, Lee HS, Baytown, Texas.
59. *Duston Atkinson, c-of, Dixie (Utah) JC.
60. *Jarrod DeGeorgia, rhp, Santa Barbara (Calif.) CC.
61. *Eric Fuller, ss, Bakersfield (Calif.) JC.
62. *Michael Glendenning, 3b-of, Crespi HS, West Hills, Calif.
63. *Gene Moseley, rhp, Deer Park (Texas) HS.

## SAN DIEGO PADRES (3)

**1. Dustin Hermanson, rhp, Kent State University.—(1995-2006)**
DRAFT DROP *First player from 1994 draft to reach majors (May 8, 1995)*
**2. *Troy Glaus, 3b, Carlsbad (Calif.) HS.—(1998-2007)**
DRAFT DROP *Attended UCLA; re-drafted by Angels, 1997 (1st round)*
**3. Heath Murray, lhp, University of Michigan.—(1997-2002)**
4. Gordon Amerson, of, San Gorgonio HS, San Bernardino, Calif.—(High A)
5. Eric Newman, rhp, Texas Tech.—(AAA)
6. Trajan Langdon, 3b-rhp, East HS, Anchorage, Alaska.
DRAFT DROP *First-round draft pick, Cleveland Cavaliers, National Basketball Association (1999); guard, NBA (1999-2002)*
7. Shane Dennis, lhp, Wichita State University.
DRAFT DROP *Son of Don Dennis, major leaguer (1965-66)*
8. David Ullan, c, Portland State University.
9. Jake Remington, rhp, Broken Arrow (Okla.) HS.
**10. Greg LaRocca, ss, University of Massachusetts.—(2000-03)**
11. Keith Davis, rhp, Nicholls State University.
12. Rod Jackson, ss, Fairview HS, Camden, Ark.
13. Shawn Knight, ss, College of William & Mary.
14. Bubba Dixon, lhp, Delta State (Miss.) University.
15. James Johnson, of, University of Nevada-Reno.
16. +Pete Paciorek, 1b, San Marino HS, San Gabriel, Calif. / Glendale (Calif.) CC.
DRAFT DROP *Son of John Paciorek, major leaguer (1963)*
17. Jon Morris, c, Northeastern Oklahoma State University.
18. *Kurt Blackmon, rhp, Northwestern HS, Rock Hill, S.C.
19. *Matt Hyers, ss, Newton County HS, Covington, Ga.
DRAFT DROP *Brother of Tim Hyers, major leaguer (1994-99)*
20. Scott Schroeder, rhp, Mount Hood (Ore.) CC.
21. Jason Tyrus, of, University of Washington.
22. Josh Davis, c, Locust Grove (Okla.) HS.
DRAFT DROP *Son of Bob Davis, major leaguer (1973-81)*
23. Luis Torres, rhp, Jose Severo Quinones HS, Manati, P.R.
24. Erik Martinez, ss, Pepperdine University.
**25. *Rocky Biddle, rhp, Temple City HS, San Gabriel, Calif.—(2000-04)**
DRAFT DROP *First-round draft pick (51st overall), White Sox (1997)*
26. *Rusty Sarnes, lhp, Havana (Ill.) HS.
27. Darren Grass, c, University of Minnesota.
28. *Tim Jorgensen, ss, University of Wisconsin-Oshkosh.
DRAFT DROP *Brother of Terry Jorgensen, major leaguer (1989-93)*
29. *Alan Goudy, of, Kokomo (Ind.) HS.
30. *Jesse Coronado, rhp, Foothill HS, Bakersfield, Calif.
31. A.J. Jenkins, rhp, Texas Southern University.
32. Dwain Koscielniak, 3b, Ferris State (Mich.) University.
33. Mark Merila, 2b, University of Minnesota.
**34. *Gabe Molina, rhp, Trinidad State (Colo.) JC.—(1999-2003)**
35. Kenya Hunt, 1b, The Master's (Calif.) College.
36. *Aaron Bass, lhp, Crowder (Mo.) JC.
37. Jeff Conway, of, University of Texas.
38. Jarman Leach, lhp, San Diego State University.
**39. Rod Lindsey, of, Opelika (Ala.) HS.—(2000)**
40. *David Robinson, of, Santa Fe (Fla.) CC.
41. Chris Clark, rhp, Otero (Colo.) JC.
42. +Daryl Rutherford, 2b-of, Union (S.C.) HS.
43. *Tim Harrington, 1b, Glens Falls HS, Queensbury, N.Y.
44. Mark Barrett, lhp, University of Maryland.
45. Eliezer Rosario, ss, Cayey (P.R.) HS.
46. *Oscar Hirschkorn, rhp, Kings River (Calif.) JC.
47. Antonio Fernandez, 3b, University of New Mexico.
48. *Adam Sisk, rhp, Riverdale HS, Mitchellville, Md.
**49. *Jason Michaels, of, Jesuit HS, Tampa.—(2001-11)**
50. +Steve Chavez, 3b, Carlsbad (N.M.) HS / Yavapai (Ariz.) JC.
51. *Kevin Workman, ss, North Central HS, Spokane, Wash.
52. Mark Desabrias, 3b-rhp, Lake Howell HS, Casselberry, Fla.
53. *Kevin Durham, rhp, Pendleton (S.C.) HS.
54. *Derek Mickelson, rhp, Arizona State University.

## SAN FRANCISCO GIANTS (25)

**1. Dante Powell, of, Cal State Fullerton** (Choice from Rangers as compensation for Type A free agent Will Clark).**—(1997-2001)**
1. (Choice to Astros as compensation for Type A free agent Mark Portugal)
**1. Jacob Cruz, of, Arizona State University** (Supplemental choice—32nd—as compensation for Clark).**—(1996-2005)**
2. Andy Taulbee, rhp, Clemson University.—(AAA)
**3. Alberto Castillo, 1b-lhp, Miami-Dade CC Wolfson.—(2008-11)**
**4. Troy Brohawn, lhp, University of Nebraska.—(2001-03)**
**5. Bobby Howry, rhp, McNeese State University.—(1998-2010)**
6. Jesse Ibarra, 3b-rhp, Loyola Marymount University.
7. Pete Prater, rhp, Southwest Missouri State University.
8. Chad Frontera, rhp, Seton Hall University.
**9. Keith Foulke, rhp, Lewis-Clark State (Idaho) College.—(1997-2008)**
10. *Mike Littlefield, rhp, Mohave HS, Bullhead City, Ariz.
11. Chad Dillon, rhp, Boone County HS, Florence, Ky.
12. Jeff Poor, c, Los Angeles Harbor JC.
13. Ricardo Calderon, 1b, Iowa Western CC.
14. Luis Rodriguez, lhp, Gilberto Concepcio de Gracia HS, Carolina, P.R.
15. Mike Schiefelbein, rhp, University of Arizona.
16. Kevin Watson, of, George Fox (Ore.) College.
17. Ryan Hornbeck, lhp, El Camino (Calif.) JC.
18. Kevin Lake, lhp, University of Nevada-Reno.
19. Cory Lintern, rhp, Cal State Dominguez Hills.

**20. *J.D. Drew, of, Lowndes HS, Hahira. Ga.—(1998-2011)**
DRAFT DROP *First-round draft pick (2nd overall), Phillies (1997); first-round draft pick (5th overall), Cardinals (1998) • Brother of Tim Drew, first-round draft pick, Indians (1997); major leaguer (2000-04) • Brother of Stephen Drew, first-round draft pick, Diamondbacks (2004); major leaguer (2006-15)*
21. Chad Hartvigson, lhp, University of Washington.
22. Greg Keifer, of, University of Toledo.
23. *Jacob Esteves, rhp, Sacramento (Calif.) CC.
24. Todd Wilson, 3b, Lewis-Clark State (Idaho) College.
25. Mike Villano, c, Saginaw Valley State (Mich.) University.
26. Scott Cook, rhp, Central Michigan University.
27. Dennys Gomez, rhp, William Penn (Iowa) College.
28. Tony Mattos, rhp, Elon College.
29. Eric Martin, of, Cal State Dominguez Hills.
30. *Greg White, rhp, Waynesboro (Pa.) Area HS.
DRAFT DROP *Brother of Matt White, first-round draft pick, Giants (1996)*
31. *Tristan Paul, 3b, Los Angeles Harbor JC.
32. *Jack Witt, rhp, Hutchinson (Kan.) CC.
33. James Apicella, of, C.W. Post (N.Y.) College.
34. Brian Shepherd, c, Mesa State (Colo.) College.
35. *Angel Melendez, of, Labette (Kan.) CC.
36. Dan Schneider, c, University of North Carolina-Greensboro.
**37. *Mike Lincoln, rhp, American River (Calif.) JC.—(1999-2010)**
38. *Tim Conklin, rhp, Mount Hood (Ore.) JC.
39. *Daniel Sweet, rhp, Shasta HS, Redding, Calif.
40. *Joel Greene, lhp, Madison HS, Portland, Ore.
41. *Leroy McCauley, of, Central HS, Cape Girardeau, Mo.
42. *Matt Schuldt, c, Washington HS, Sioux Falls, S.D.
43. *Todd Eastin, c, South Mountain (Ariz.) CC.
44. *Brad Seare, lhp, West Jordan HS, Salt Lake City.
45. *Matt Woodward, 1b, Redmond (Wash.) HS.
DRAFT DROP *Son of Woody Woodward, major leaguer (1963-71); general manager, Yankees (1987); general manager, Mariners (1989-99)*
46. *David Rivera, rhp, Adelfina Irizarry HS, Toa Baja, P.R.
47. *Richie Nye, rhp, Westark (Ark.) CC.
DRAFT DROP *Brother of Ryan Nye, second-round draft pick, Phillies (1994); major leaguer (1997-98)*
48. *Eric Smith, rhp, Butler County (Kan.) CC.
49. *Matt McGuire, c, Parkway West HS, Chesterfield, Mo.
50. *Cody Barney, 3b, Chemeketa (Ore.) CC.
51. *Bryan Huie, lhp, Westark (Ark.) CC.
52. *Jake Thrower, ss, Yuma (Ariz.) HS.
53. *Brian Sailor, rhp, Marina HS, Huntington Beach, Calif.
54. *Geoff Wilson, of, Fountain Valley (Calif.) HS.
55. *Alan Paisano, rhp, Burroughs HS, Ridgecrest, Calif.
56. Dan Topping, c, St. Petersburg (Fla.) HS.
57. *Geoff Williamson, rhp, West Jones HS, Laurel, Miss.
58. *Robert Dillard, lhp, Huntington Beach (Calif.) HS.

## SEATTLE MARINERS (14)

**1. Jason Varitek, c, Georgia Tech.—(1997-2011)**
DRAFT DROP *First-round draft pick (21st overall), Twins (1993)*
**2. Trey Moore, lhp, Texas A&M University.—(1998-2001)**
**3. Matt Wagner, rhp, Iowa State University.—(1996)**
4. Mike Burrows, of, American Fork (Utah) HS.—(High A)
5. Tom Szimanski, rhp, Florida Southern College.—(High A)
**6. +Joe Mays, rhp, Southeast HS, Bradenton, Fla. / Manatee (Fla.) CC.—(1999-2006)**
7. Chris Beck, rhp, The Master's (Calif.) College.
8. *Dwayne Dobson, rhp, Clearwater (Fla.) HS.
9. James Rowson, lhp, Mount St. Michaels HS, Bronx, N.Y.
10. Doug Carroll, of, University of South Florida.
11. +Carlos Rose, of, Cleveland (Miss.) HS / Mississippi Delta JC.
12. Eric Clifford, rhp, Mesa (Ariz.) CC.
**13. Roy Smith, rhp, Dixie Hollins HS, Pinellas Park, Fla.—(2001-02)**
14. *Frank Sanders, of, Auburn University.
DRAFT DROP *Wide receiver, National Football League (1995-2003)*
15. Jason Ruskey, lhp, Arizona State University.
16. *Anthony Southern, of, Whiteville (N.C.) HS.
17. *Mike Martin Jr., c, Florida State University.
18. Collin Hinds, of, Loyola Marymount University.
19. Cy Simonton, of, Pittsburg (Calif.) HS.
20. *Gus Ornstein, 1b, Fieldston HS, Bronx. N.Y.
21. Eric Morgan, rhp, University of Miami.
22. Osvaldo Fernandez, lhp, Mission (Calif.) JC.
23. *Kevin Trimble, of, Mattoon (Ill.) HS.
24. +Adonis Harrison, ss, Muir HS, Pasadena, Calif. / Los Angeles CC.
25. Matt Sachse, lhp-1b, Ferris HS, Spokane, Wash.
26. Rick Ladjevich, 3b, Central Missouri State University.
27. Shane Thomason, ss, Chattanooga State (Tenn.) CC.
28. Kyle Towner, of, University of Alabama-Birmingham.
29. Shawn Buhner, 1b, Lewis-Clark State (Idaho) College.
DRAFT DROP *Brother of Jay Buhner, major leaguer (1987-2001)*
30. Marcus Williams, rhp, Henry Ford HS, Detroit.
31. Randy Vickers, ss, Glendale (Calif.) JC,
**32. +Jordan Zimmerman, lhp, Blinn (Texas) JC.—(1999)**
DRAFT DROP *Brother of Jeff Zimmerman, major leaguer (1999-2001)*
33. *Jason Hill, c, Cerritos (Calif.) JC.
34. *Todd Ozias, rhp, Taravella HS, Tamarac, Fla.
35. *Chris Hayes, 3b, Jacksonville University.
**36. *Scott Atchison, rhp, McCollough HS, The Woodlands, Texas.—(2004-15)**
37. *Johnathan Rose, lhp, Eastern Alamance HS, Haw River, N.C.
38. *James Bowman, lhp, Green River (Wash.) CC.
39. *Michael Rooney, rhp, North Rockland HS, Stony Point, N.Y.
40. *Matt Garrick, c, Duncanville (Texas) HS.
41. +Shane Hearns, of, Bedford HS, Lambertville, Mich. / Parkland (Ill.) JC.
42. *Brian Saltarelli, of, El Toro HS, Lake Forest, Calif.
43. *Gus Rubio, c, El Camino (Calif.) CC.
44. *Greg Scheer, lhp, Jacksonville University.
45. *Kyle Kennedy, rhp, Mississippi State University.
46. Marvin Fowler, of, Palatka (Fla.) HS.
47. *Greg Goligoski, of, Prescott (Ariz.) HS.
48. *Richard Nunez, rhp, Gulliver Prep HS, Miami.
49. *Brandon Butler, of, Hardin County HS, Selmer, Tenn.
50. *Derek Nicholson, c, Torrance (Calif.) HS.
51. *Stephen Bagby, of, Glen Oaks (Ind.) CC.
52. *Brad Smith, 3b, Marina HS, Huntington Beach, Calif.
53. *Saladin McCullough, of, Pasadena, Calif.
54. +Warren Tisdale, rhp, Mandarin HS, Jacksonville, Fla. / Pasco Hernando (Fla.) CC.
55. *Brad Marshall, of, JC of San Mateo (Calif.).
56. *Jermain Jordan, of, Vidalia (Ga.) HS.
57. +Scott Needham, c, Butler County (Kan.) CC / Westark (Ark.) CC.
**58. *Tim Hill, rhp, John A. Logan (Ill.) JC.**
59. *Ramon Arias, 1b, Lompoc (Calif.) HS.
60. +Albert Derenches, lhp, Gaither HS, Tampa / Hillsborough (Fla.) CC.
**61. *Morgan Ensberg, ss, Redondo Union HS, Hermosa Beach, Calif.—(2000-08)**
62. *Lucas Solomon, rhp, Canyon HS, Canyon Country, Calif.
63. *Kevin High, of, Palm Desert (Calif.) HS.
64. +Richard Mora, rhp, Cypress Creek HS, Orlando, Fla. / Valencia (Fla.) CC.
65. Shelby Johnson, c-rhp, Holmes (Miss.) JC.
66. *David Waites, rhp, McCullough HS, Spring, Texas.
67. *Jose Gonzales, c, Seminole (Okla.) JC.
68. *Juan Romero, of, Berwind Superior HS, Carolina, P.R.
69. *Kyle Rask, of, Redmond (Wash.) HS.
70. *Gerald Eady, of, Robert E. Lee HS, Jacksonville, Fla.
71. *John Lauderdale, c, Tustin (Calif.) HS.
72. *Toby Sanchez, of, Rancho Santiago (Calif.) JC.
73. *Jose Montenegro, ss, South Gate (Calif.) HS.
74. *Leron Cook, of, Roosevelt HS, Fresno, Calif.
75. *Steve Rawson, 3b, Redondo HS, Redondo Beach. Calif.

## TEXAS RANGERS (22)

1. (Choice to Giants as compensation for Type A free agent Will Clark)
**2. Kevin Brown, c, University of Southern Indiana.—(1996-2002)**
**3. Scott Podsednik, of, West (Texas) HS.—(2001-12)**
4. Dan Hower, lhp, Creighton University.—(High A)
5. Jason Johnson, of, Hogan HS, Vallejo, Calif.—(Low A)
**6. Jim Brower, rhp, University of Minnesota.—(1999-2007)**
7. Bucky Buckles, rhp, University of Oklahoma.
**8. Mark Little, of, Memphis State University.—(1998-2004)**
9. John Powell, rhp, Auburn University.
**10. Stephen Larkin, 1b-of, University of Texas.—(1998)**
DRAFT DROP *Brother of Barry Larkin, first-round draft pick, Reds (1985); major leaguer (1986-2004)*
11. *Terry Harvey, rhp, North Carolina State University.
12. Matt Bokemeier, ss, UC Santa Barbara.
13. Kevin Millican, c, University of Southeastern Louisiana.
14. Carlos Simmons, rhp, Prince George (Md.) CC.
15. Chris Gogolewski, lhp, St. Mary's (Minn.) University.
DRAFT DROP *Son of Bill Gogolewski, major leaguer (1970-75)*
16. Craig McLendon, c, Jonesboro (Ga.) HS.
17. Reid Ryan, rhp, Texas Christian University.
DRAFT DROP *Son of Nolan Ryan, major leaguer (1966-93); president, Astros (2013-15)*
18. *Trey Salinas, c, Moody HS, Corpus Christi, Texas.
19. Erik Sauve, 2b, Virginia Commonwealth University.
**20. Scott Stewart, lhp, East Gaston HS, Stanly, N.C.—(2001-04)**
21. Asbel Ortiz, ss, Ana J. Candelas HS, Cidra, P.R.
22. *Gerald Johnson, of, Menlo HS, Atherton, Calif.
23. Ryan Rutz, 2b, University of Washington.
24. Jason Miller, c, College of St. Rose (N.Y.).
25. Rodney Cook, rhp, Stephen F. Austin University.
26. Eddie Comeaux, of, University of California.
27. Danny Vasquez, of, Rockland (N.Y.) CC.
28. Jaime Escamilla, lhp, Point Loma Nazarene (Calif.) College.
29. Mike Mortimer, rhp, Northwest Nazarene (Idaho) College.
30. *Gary MacKinlay, lhp, Hylton HS, Dumphries, Va.
31. Joe Kail, 3b, Johns Hopkins (Md.) University.
32. Matthew Pauls, rhp-of, Odessa (Texas) JC.
33. Joe Keusch, rhp, Eastern Illinois University.
34. Janos Briscoe, rhp, Western Kentucky University.
35. Matthew Buhs, lhp, Southern Illinois University.
36. Michael-Sean Ryan, rhp, Broadneck HS, Annapolis, Md.
37. *Jesse Brown, rhp, Kalaheo HS, Kailua, Hawaii.
38. *Buck Hall, lhp, Georgia Tech.
39. *James Matan, 1b, Gonzaga HS, Kensington, Md.

## TORONTO BLUE JAYS (26)

**1. Kevin Witt, ss, Bishop Kenny HS, Jacksonville, Fla.—(1998-2006)**
2. John Crowther, rhp, Coker (S.C.) College.—(High A)
3. Chris McBride, rhp, University of North Carolina-Wilmington.—(AA)
4. *Brad Freeman, ss, Oxford (Miss.) HS.—(High A)
DRAFT DROP *Attended Mississippi State; re-drafted by Indians, 1997 (12th round)*
**5. Tom Davey, rhp, Henry Ford (Mich.) JC.—(1999-2002)**
6. Michael Peeples, ss, Clay HS, Green Cove Springs, Fla.
7. Jose Maysonet, ss, Dra Maria Cadilla Martinez HS, Arecibo, P.R.
8. Chris Pettiet, rhp, San Ramon Valley HS, Danville, Calif.
9. Don Morris, c, North Clayton HS, Riverdale, Ga.
10. Mike Halperin, lhp, University of Central Florida.
11. Billy Hibbard, rhp, Colonial HS, Orlando, Fla.
12. *Tommy Fambrough, ss, South Florence HS, Florence, S.C.
**13. Joe Davenport, rhp, Santana HS, Santee, Calif.—(1999-2001)**
14. Robby Hampton, of, Mount Pleasant (Texas) HS.
**15. Gary Glover, rhp, De Land (Fla.) HS.—(1999-2008)**
16. Willie Villa, of, Kamehameha HS, Nanakuli, Hawaii.
17. *Ryan Cummings, rhp, Walton HS, Marietta, Ga.
18. Mason Smith, rhp, Oregon State University.
19. Chris Freeman, rhp, University of Tennessee.
20. *Matt Freeman, c, Indian River (Fla.) CC.
21. Shayne Timmons, c, Concord (W.Va.) College.
22. *Brandon Ward, rhp, Fontana (Calif.) HS.
**23. Andy Thompson, ss, Sun Prairie (Wis.) HS.—(2000)**
DRAFT DROP *World champion racquetball player/12 & under age group*
24. Brent Bearden, rhp, Baylor University.
25. Randy Smith, rhp, Northeastern Oklahoma State University.
26. Terry Adams, 3b, Eastern HS, Toronto.
**27. Brian Smith, rhp, University of North Carolina-Wilmington.—(2000)**
28. Mark Landers, 1b, West Virginia University.
29. *Brian Dahl, rhp, University of Connecticut-Avery Point JC.
30. *Preston White, of, Boys and Girls HS, Brooklyn, N.Y.
31. Steve Soper, 2b, University of Tennessee.
32. *Michael Pageler, rhp, Red Mountain HS, Mesa, Ariz.
33. *Ryan Golisano, rhp, Fullerton (Calif.) HS.
34. *Jimmy Turman, rhp, Gordo (Ala.) HS.
35. Lester Henderson, lhp, University of Redlands (Calif.).
36. David Mendoza, rhp, El Camino HS, Oceanside, Calif.
37. Andy Shatley, 1b, Nettleton HS, Jonesboro, Ark.
38. Edward Budz, rhp, St. Xavier (Ill.) College.
39. Sean Strade, rhp, University of Portland.
40. *Mike Kleckner, rhp, Sentinel HS, Missoula, Mon.
41. Battle Holley, 3b, University of North Carolina-Wilmington.
42. Michael Zavershnik, lhp, St. Michael's HS, Mississauga, Ontario.
43. Benny Lowe, lhp, Indian River (Fla.) CC.
44. Eric Horton, rhp, Talladega (Ala.) JC.
45. *Tracy Evridge, of, Midland Valley HS, North Augusta. S.C
46. *Jonathan Shank, rhp, Chaparral HS, Scottsdale, Ariz.
47. Michael Strange, 2b, Santa Fe (Fla.) CC.
48. *Kerry Collins, rhp, Penn State University.
DRAFT DROP *First-round draft pick, Carolina Panthers, National Football League (1995); quarterback, NFL (1995-2011)*
49. *Dustyn Edler, of, Elsenhower HS, Yakima, Wash.
DRAFT DROP *Son of Dave Edler, major leaguer (1980-83)*
**50. Brian Bowles, rhp, Peninsula HS, Manhattan Beach, Calif.—(2001-03)**
51. *David Steffler, rhp, St. Peter's HS, Keene, Ontario.
52. *Reginald Amos, ss, Grenada (Miss.) HS.
53. *D'Wayne Bates, of, Silver Bluff HS, Jackson, S.C.
**54. +Chris Woodward, ss, Northview HS, Covina, Calif. / Mount San Jacinto (Calif.) JC.—(1999-2011)**
55. *Edward Taylor, rhp, Early County HS, Blakely, Ga.
56. *Charles Mitchell, rhp, Jordan HS, Long Beach, Calif.
**57. *Joe Nelson, ss, Seminole (Okla.) JC.—(2001-10)**
58. *Jaime Alvarez, c, Franklin HS, Los Angeles.
59. *Michael Cochran, rhp, Brandon (Miss.) HS.
60. *Sidney Harden, rhp, Harris County HS, Hamilton, Ga.
61. *Mike Hannah, of, Gordon (Ga.) JC.
62. *Rodney Hall, 2b, Clover (S.C.) HS.
63. *Alex Barbosa, of, Eloisa Pascual HS, Caguas, P.R.
64. *William Carroll, rhp, Tallahassee (Fla.) CC.

# 1995

# Cuban arm spices up draft in wake of strike

For the first time in the draft's 30-year history, the most discussed player wasn't from the United States, but rather was a Cuban refugee.

Ariel Prieto, a hard-throwing righthander who had pitched with distinction for Cuba's fabled national team, arrived in the United States on April 7, 1995, eight weeks before the draft. He pitched brilliantly for the Palm Springs Suns of the independent Western League, and some organizations saw him as worthy of the No. 1 overall pick.

The California Angels, who had the first choice, stayed with the player they long had favored, University of Nebraska outfielder Darin Erstad. Prieto, who featured a 93-96 mph fastball and an 88 mph slider, went to the Oakland Athletics with the fifth overall pick. He signed for a $1.2 million bonus and became the 20th player of the draft era to bypass the minor leagues on his way to the majors.

Aside from Prieto, the first round unfolded with few surprises, beginning with Erstad. The 1995 draft pool was considered one of the deepest ever, perhaps even comparable to the 1985 class that included Barry Bonds, Barry Larkin, Randy Johnson, Rafael Palmeiro, John Smoltz and a host of other future standouts. It turned out to be a big disappointment, however, considering that just 18 of the 28 first-round selections made it to the major leagues, the fewest since 1986. Just 86 players taken in the first 10 rounds reached the big leagues, the fewest of any draft after 1984.

Erstad's signing bonus of $1.575 million fell short of the record $1.6 million the Florida Marlins gave third baseman Josh Booty a year earlier. Many baseball executives expected bonuses to decrease, given that the industry was coming off the 1994 strike that drained millions of dollars in revenue from the game. However, that proved not to be the case. First-round bonuses averaged $918,019, a 16.1 percent hike. The annual surges since bonuses began escalating in 1988 had been between 23-45 percent.

"If ever there was a year for bonuses to level off or go down, this was it," Seattle Mariners scouting director Roger Jongewaard said. "But I don't see it happening. The big-market clubs still are in position to give more money, and that's the biggest reason bonuses will remain high."

### PRIETO ADDS ELEMENT OF INTRIGUE

The air of mystery surrounding Prieto and his overnight emergence as a top prospect in the 1995 draft made him one of the most intriguing selections in draft history.

He was one of 20,000 Cubans with family ties to the United States who were allowed to leave the island and enter the U.S. as part of a 1994 treaty engineered by the two nations' governments. Through connections with baseball agent Gus Dominguez, he joined the Palm Springs team and made six starts leading up to the 1995 draft.

The Angels held fast to their plan to take Nebraska outfielder Darin Erstad with the No. 1 overall pick, and he rewarded them with a quick ascent and 11 seasons as a fixture in center field

Prieto was a star on the Cuban national team from 1990-94 and won 76 games in international competition. Determined to play in the United States, he faked an arm injury and intentionally pitched poorly in Cuba's Serie Nacional in the winter of 1994-95. Once out of the public eye, Prieto had the paperwork processed for him and his wife to leave the country largely unnoticed.

"Ariel used his wife's name first on the visa application," Dominguez said. "His name was also on the second line. He kept a very low profile on all this. Because of that, he was able to slip by the Cuban officials. And when they found out, believe me, they weren't pleased."

Prieto, much like Cuban pitcher Rene Arocha before him, left his homeland with the express purpose of signing with a major league organization. Arocha had defected in 1991, becoming the first member of the Cuban national baseball team to escape the country and play in the U.S.

"I did this because this is what I have dreamed of doing for years," said Prieto, who claimed to be 25 years old, but was believed to be 28 or older.

Dominguez, who facilitated the departure of numerous Cuban defectors through the years, arranged for Prieto and Euclides Rojas, who had defected a year earlier on a makeshift raft and spent five days on the open ocean, to hook on with Palm Springs, where Al Campanis, the former general manager of the Los Angeles Dodgers, served as the club's director of player development. Dominguez had a long association with former Dodgers all-star

### AT A GLANCE

**This Date In History**
June 1-3

**Best Draft**
**CALIFORNIA ANGELS.** The Angels landed two of the five most productive major leaguers: outfielder **DARIN ERSTAD** in the first round and lefthander **JARROD WASHBURN** in the second.

**Worst Draft**
**LOS ANGELES DODGERS.** The Dodgers got two minor league seasons out of lefthander **DAVID YOCUM** (1) before his shoulder gave out, and two uneventful major league seasons, all in relief, out of a second lefthander, **ONAN MASAOKA** (3). None of the other 83 players they drafted played a game in L.A.

**First-Round Bust**
**RYAN JARONCYK, SS, METS.** After playing in 134 games in three seasons in the Mets farm system, Jaroncyk decided he didn't like baseball and quit the game. The Mets got a .238 batting average and one home run in Class A for their $850,000 investment.

**On Second Thought**
**CARLOS BELTRAN, OF, ROYALS.** If the Royals didn't get their money's worth for the $650,000 they spent on first-rounder **JUAN LEBRON**, a Puerto Rican outfielder who didn't rise above Class A in four seasons, they certainly did with the $300,000 they paid second-rounder Beltran, another Puerto Rican outfielder. Beltran spent the first seven years of his big league career with the Royals, hitting .287-123-516 with 164 stolen bases.

**Late Round Find**
**MIKE LOWELL, 3B, YANKEES (20TH ROUND).** The Yankees took Lowell after he hit .355-12-119 in three seasons at Florida International. He spent four years in the organization, playing eight games in the majors in 1998, before

CONTINUED ON PAGE 450

## AT A GLANCE

CONTINUED FROM PAGE 449

going on to a 13-year career with the Marlins and Red Sox.

### Never Too Late

**ROBBY HAMMOCK, C, MARLINS (66TH ROUND).** Three years after rejecting the Marlins out of a Georgia high school, Hammock hit .322-12-46 as a catcher at the University of Georgia. He signed with the Diamondbacks for $12,500 as a 23rd-round selection in 1998 and played 14 years of pro ball, including six in the majors (.254-12-48).

### Overlooked

**ERIC GAGNE, RHP, DODGERS.** Gagne was drafted by the White Sox after his freshman year at Seminole (Okla.) Junior College in 1994, but passed over after his sophomore season. The Dodgers signed him for $75,000 as a free agent, and he became a dominant closer in the big leagues from 2002-04, converting a record 84 straight save opportunities and winning the 2003 National League Cy Young Award.

### International Gem

**JOHAN SANTANA, LHP, ASTROS.** The Astros signed Santana, a 16-year-old Venezuelan, for $10,000 in 1995. They did not put him on their 40-man roster after he went 8-8, 4.66 in low Class A for the 1999 season, and this Twins grabbed him in the Rule 5 draft. He went 93-44, 3.22 over the next eight seasons, and won two American League Cy Young Awards and three ERA titles.

### Minor League Take

**TODD HELTON, 1B, ROCKIES.** Success in the minors is not always an indicator of major league stardom, but it was in the case of Helton, who hit .330-26-175 in 276 minor league games prior to his 17-year career with the Rockies.

### One Who Got Away

**CHAD HUTCHINSON, RHP, BRAVES (1ST ROUND).** The Braves didn't meet

## 1995: THE FIRST ROUNDERS

| CLUB: PLAYER, POS., SCHOOL | HOMETOWN | B-T | HT. | WT. | AGE | BONUS | FIRST YEAR | LAST YEAR | PEAK LEVEL (YEARS) |
|---|---|---|---|---|---|---|---|---|---|
| 1. Angels: Darin Erstad, of, Nebraska | Jamestown, N.D. | L-L | 6-2 | 205 | 21 | $1,575,000 | 1995 | 2009 | Majors (14) |
| Punter/kicker on national champ football team, hit .410-19-76 for baseball team; got most out of all-around ability, hit .355-25-100 in 2000, best MLB season. | | | | | | | | | |
| 2. Padres: Ben Davis, c, Malvern Prep | Aston, Pa. | B-R | 6-3 | 195 | 18 | $1,300,000 | 1996 | 2008 | Majors (7) |
| With defensive skills, power from both sides, was proclaimed as best prep catching prospect in 20 years; bat wasn't there, though, hit just .237-38-204 in majors. | | | | | | | | | |
| 3. Mariners: Jose Cruz Jr., of, Rice | Houston | B-R | 6-0 | 190 | 21 | $1,285,000 | 1995 | 2008 | Majors (12) |
| Set Rice career records for AVG (.375), HR (43), RBIs (203), switch-hitting skills/instincts rated best in draft; joined father, two uncles in majors, hit 204 homers. | | | | | | | | | |
| 4. Cubs: Kerry Wood, rhp, Grand Prairie HS | Grand Prairie, Texas | R-R | 6-4 | 185 | 17 | $1,265,000 | 1995 | 2012 | Majors (14) |
| Best prep arm in draft, went 14-0, 0.77 (82 IP/152 SO) as SR; landmark 1-hit/20-SO game as rookie one of best ever pitched, but career compromised by 14 DL trips. | | | | | | | | | |
| 5. *Athletics: Ariel Prieto, rhp, Palm Springs (Ind.) | Marianao, Cuba | R-R | 6-3 | 220 | 25 | $1,200,000 | 1995 | 2005 | Majors (6) |
| Rare Cuban draft set off frenzy when became eligible in late spring; with mid-90s FB/slider, went straight to MLB but career marked by lack of success/injuries. | | | | | | | | | |
| 6. Marlins: Jaime Jones, of, Rancho Bernardo HS | Poway, Calif. | L-L | 6-3 | 190 | 18 | $1,337,000 | 1995 | 2005 | Class AAA (2) |
| Picturesque swing highlighted complete package; dominated as prep (.475-10-30, 26 SBs, 4-0, 0.00), career never developed in minors, though injuries a factor. | | | | | | | | | |
| 7. Rangers: Jonathan Johnson, rhp, Florida State | Ocala, Fla. | R-R | 6-0 | 180 | 20 | $1,100,000 | 1995 | 2007 | Majors (6) |
| Overcame physical stature with advanced skills/bulldog approach; went 34-5, 2.63 at FSU, but just 2-4, 6.66 in majors, spent most of 13-year pro career in minors. | | | | | | | | | |
| 8. Rockies: Todd Helton, 1b/lhp, Tennessee | Powell, Tenn. | L-L | 6-2 | 190 | 21 | $892,500 | 1995 | 2013 | Majors (17) |
| Backup QB to Peyton Manning at Tennessee also excelled at plate (.370-38-238), on mound (19-5, 2.24, 23 SV); spent 17 years with Rockies, 2,519 hits, 369 HRs. | | | | | | | | | |
| 9. Brewers: Geoff Jenkins, of, Southern California | Rancho Cordova, Calif. | L-R | 6-1 | 200 | 20 | $911,000 | 1995 | 2008 | Majors (11) |
| Best hitting mechanics in college ranks with power to all fields; hit .399-23-78, became USC career RBI leader; hit .275-221-733 in 11 seasons, 10 with Brewers. | | | | | | | | | |
| 10. Pirates: Chad Hermansen, ss, Green Valley HS | Henderson, Nev. | R-R | 6-2 | 185 | 17 | $1,150,000 | 1995 | 2007 | Majors (6) |
| Set club bonus record, on fast track with 81 HRs/277 RBIs in minors before age 21, but MLB career (.195-13-34) compromised by free swinging, defensive struggles. | | | | | | | | | |
| 11. Tigers: Mike Drumright, rhp, Wichita State | Valley Center, Kan. | L-R | 6-4 | 215 | 21 | $970,000 | 1995 | 2003 | Class AAA (7) |
| Workhorse with plus fastball/curve, won 21 games as SO/JR at Wichita, moved quickly through lower minors but hit wall in Triple-A; went 49-83, 5.17 in 11 seasons. | | | | | | | | | |
| 12. Cardinals: Matt Morris, rhp, Seton Hall | Montgomery, N.Y. | R-R | 6-5 | 210 | 20 | $850,000 | 1995 | 2008 | Majors (11) |
| Took up pitching as prep SR, evolved into top prospect as college JR (10-3, 2.68); career interrupted by TJ surgery in '99, had best season (22-8, 3.16) two years later. | | | | | | | | | |
| 13. Twins: Mark Redman, lhp, Oklahoma | Del Mar, Calif. | L-L | 6-5 | 220 | 20 | $830,000 | 1995 | 2008 | Majors (10) |
| Transferred to OU, led team to CWS title in '94 with 14 wins, won school-record 15 a year later; led Marlins to World Series crown in '03 with career-best 14 wins. | | | | | | | | | |
| 14. Phillies: Reggie Taylor, of, Newberry HS | Newberry, S.C. | L-R | 6-1 | 185 | 18 | $970,000 | 1995 | 2008 | Majors (5) |
| Fastest player/best athlete in class had elite CF skills, big bat speed; rarely hit or walked enough to tap into speed/power package; hit .231-14-58 in majors. | | | | | | | | | |
| 15. Red Sox: Andy Yount, rhp, Kingwood HS | Kingwood, Texas | R-R | 6-2 | 180 | 18 | $986,000 | 1995 | 2006 | Class A (5) |
| Flashed 98 mph FB, but derailed in 1996 when he severed tendons in pitching hand; came back (3-6, 5.38) three years later, also tried OF, never got out of Class A. | | | | | | | | | |
| 16. Giants: Joe Fontenot, rhp, Acadiana HS | Lafayette, La. | R-R | 6-2 | 180 | 18 | $900,000 | 1995 | 1999 | Majors (1) |
| Had best stuff in Giants system when sent to Marlins in 1997 for closer Robb Nen; had shoulder issues a year later while going 0-7, 6.28, never salvaged career. | | | | | | | | | |
| 17. Blue Jays: Roy Halladay, rhp, Arvada West HS | Golden, Colo. | R-R | 6-5 | 200 | 18 | $895,000 | 1995 | 2013 | Majors (16) |
| Reinvented himself after early struggles with Jays, became two-time Cy Young winner on strength of cut fastball/command; spun PG, playoff no-hitter in 2010. | | | | | | | | | |
| 18. Mets: Ryan Jaroncyk, ss, Orange Glen HS | Escondido, Calif. | R-R | 6-1 | 170 | 18 | $850,000 | 1995 | 2000 | Class A (3) |
| Best pure middle infielder in draft abruptly quit in 1997 while in low A; sat out '98, later resurfaced briefly with Dodgers as Rule 5 pick; hit .237-1-47 in 154 games. | | | | | | | | | |
| 19. Royals: Juan Lebron, of, Carmen Huyke HS | Arroyo, P.R. | R-R | 6-4 | 185 | 18 | $650,000 | 1995 | 2002 | Class AA (3) |
| Rangy athlete with power potential; made steady progress through four seasons (.258-32-192), but injured shoulder after trade to Mets, career was never the same. | | | | | | | | | |
| 20. Dodgers: David Yocum, lhp, Florida State | Miami | L-L | 6-1 | 180 | 20 | $825,000 | 1995 | 1996 | Class A (2) |
| Fourth straight year FSU had first-round arm; went 12-3, 2.61 as draft-eligible soph, but pro career (2-3, 4.07) lasted just 15 games after three shoulder surgeries. | | | | | | | | | |
| 21. Orioles: Alvie Shepherd, rhp, Nebraska | Bellwood, Ill. | R-R | 6-7 | 235 | 21 | $650,000 | 1996 | 1999 | Class AA (2) |
| More success at plate (.343-12-70) than on mound (2-5, 6.57) in college, but O's loved big frame/95-98 FB, saw a future closer; peaked in Double-A (17-16, 5.58). | | | | | | | | | |
| 22. Astros: Tony McKnight, rhp, Arkansas HS | Texarkana, Ark. | L-R | 6-5 | 210 | 17 | $500,000 | 1995 | 2003 | Majors (2) |
| Signability pick threw 250 pitches in prep game as senior; overuse hindered early development, but eventually reached majors, went 7-7, 4.65 in 2000-01. | | | | | | | | | |
| 23. Indians: David Miller, 1b, Clemson | Philadelphia | L-L | 6-4 | 200 | 21 | $620,000 | 1996 | 2002 | Class AAA (3) |
| Recruited as pitcher, became hitter in college because of sore arm; hit .380-9-78 as junior, but power never showed itself in six minor league seasons (.264-32-254). | | | | | | | | | |
| 24. Red Sox: Corey Jenkins, of, Dreher HS | Columbia, S.C. | R-R | 6-2 | 195 | 18 | $575,000 | 1995 | 1999 | Class AA (1) |
| Two-sport star with speed/power/arm strength; struggled to make contact in minors (.206-33-138), quit to pursue football career at South Carolina, briefly in NFL. | | | | | | | | | |
| 25. White Sox: Jeff Liefer, 3b, Long Beach State | Upland, Calif. | L-R | 6-3 | 185 | 20 | $575,000 | 1996 | 2008 | Majors (7) |
| Set numerous offensive records while hitting .332-30-160 in three years for Dirtbags; shoulder/elbow injuries hurt pro career, hit .230-31-113 in seven MLB seasons. | | | | | | | | | |
| 26. Braves: Chad Hutchinson, rhp, Torrey Pines HS | Encinitas, Calif. | R-R | 6-6 | 230 | 18 | Unsigned | 1998 | 2001 | Majors (1) |
| With big frame, fastball that topped at 97, might have been first HS pitcher drafted, but teams scared off by Stanford commitment, potential NFL skills as QB. | | | | | | | | | |
| 27. Yankees: Shea Morenz, of, Texas | San Angelo, Texas | L-R | 6-2 | 205 | 21 | $650,000 | 1995 | 1999 | Class AAA (1) |
| Rejected $1.4 million offer from Blue Jays in 1992 for chance to play QB at Texas; power/speed/arm evident in baseball, but raw tools never translated in minors. | | | | | | | | | |
| 28. Expos: Michael Barrett, ss, Pace Academy | Alpharetta, Ga. | R-R | 6-2 | 185 | 18 | $500,000 | 1995 | 2010 | Majors (12) |
| Hit .624-10-58 as prep shortstop, but destined for position switch because of lack of speed; moved to third in minors, but spent bulk of career in majors as catcher. | | | | | | | | | |

**Signed to major league contract.*

Ron Cey, who obviously knew Campanis from their days together with the Dodgers. Cey put Dominguez in touch with Campanis.

In his first two starts with Palm Springs, Prieto allowed three hits and no runs, walked one and struck 16 in 10 innings. Upward of 50 scouts soon were flocking to his starts. In his six outings, he went 4-0, 0.97.

## How They Should Have Done It

Based on career WAR (Wins Above Replacement, as calculated by Baseball-Reference.com) achieved by players eligible for the 1995 draft through the 2015 season, here's how the first round should have unfolded. Numbers in parentheses indicate the round when the player was drafted. Asterisk denotes player who signed as a draft-and-follow.

| | Player, Pos. | Actual Draft | WAR | Bonus |
|---|---|---|---|---|
| 1. | Carlos Beltran, of | Royals (2) | 68.3 | $300,000 |
| 2. | Roy Halladay, rhp | Blue Jays (1) | 64.6 | $895,000 |
| 3. | Todd Helton, 1b/lhp | Rockies (1) | 61.2 | $892,500 |
| 4. | Darin Erstad, of | Angels (1) | 32.3 | $1,575,000 |
| 5. | A.J. Burnett, rhp | Mets (8) | 29.2 | $60,000 |
| 6. | Jarrod Washburn, lhp | Angels (2) | 28.5 | $355,000 |
| 7. | Kerry Wood, rhp | Cubs (1) | 27.7 | $1,265,000 |
| 8. | Randy Winn, of | Marlins (3) | 27.5 | $160,000 |
| 9. | Joe Nathan, rhp | Giants (6) | 26.8 | $60,000 |
| 10. | Bronson Arroyo, rhp | Pirates (3) | 26.5 | $125,000 |
| 11. | Mike Lowell, 2b | Yankees (20) | 24.8 | $20,000 |
| 12. | Geoff Jenkins, of | Brewers (1) | 21.9 | $911,000 |
| 13. | Matt Morris, rhp | Cardinals (1) | 20.5 | $850,000 |
| 14. | Jose Cruz Jr., of | Mariners (1) | 19.5 | $1,285,000 |
| 15. | Ryan Dempster, rhp | Rangers (3) | 19.3 | $200,000 |
| 16. | Sean Casey, 1b | Indians (2) | 16.3 | $223,000 |
| 17. | Russ Ortiz, rhp | Giants (4) | 13.6 | $97,000 |
| 18. | Doug Mientkiewicz, 1b/lhp | Twins (5) | 11.9 | $87,500 |
| | Eric Gagne, rhp | Dodgers (NDFA) | 11.9 | $75,000 |
| 20. | Brett Tomko, rhp | Reds (2) | 11.0 | $200,000 |
| 21. | * Brian Fuentes, lhp | Mariners (25) | 10.7 | $90,000 |
| 22. | Mark Redman, lhp | Twins (1) | 9.5 | $830,000 |
| 23. | Jason LaRue, c | Reds (5) | 8.8 | $45,000 |
| | Ryan Freel, 2b | Blue Jays (10) | 8.8 | $79,500 |
| | Gabe Kapler, of | Tigers (57) | 8.8 | $10,000 |
| 26. | Mark Bellhorn, ss | Athletics (2) | 8.0 | $280,000 |
| 27. | Marlon Anderson, 2b | Phillies (2) | 7.2 | $225,000 |
| 28. | Brian Schneider, c | Expos (5) | 6.7 | $60,000 |

| | Top 3 Unsigned Players | | | Year Signed |
|---|---|---|---|---|
| 1. | Ted Lilly, lhp | Blue Jays (13) | 27.0 | 1996 |
| 2. | Casey Blake, 3b | Yankees (45) | 24.9 | 1996 |
| 3. | Aaron Rowand, of | Mets (40) | 20.8 | 1998 |

Initially believing that Prieto would be a free agent, Dominguez claimed before the draft that several clubs had offered him a bonus of $2.3 million. Major League Baseball rules stipulated that independent league players were subject to the draft, however, if they had not yet gone through the process. A's general manager Sandy Alderson was ecstatic when the four clubs drafting ahead of the A's passed on Prieto.

"Our orthopedist said he is in the best shape of any of our pitchers, and he has extraordinary pitching instincts," Alderson said. "People in this game are so bound by history and tradition that someone pops up late, particularly someone who isn't 18 or 21, and they dismiss him. When you draft a young player, you can hide behind the developmental shield for years and hardly anyone notices if you were wrong. Well, we'll find out right away if we're right or wrong."

They were wrong.

The oldest first-round draft choice ever, Prieto had a 2-6, 4.97 record with the A's in 1995. He won just 15 major league games in five seasons with Oakland, and later played one season with the Tampa Bay Devil Rays. He spent the majority of his career in Triple-A, with his last season in 2005.

The Marlins, with a large Cuban community, would have been tempted to draft Prieto, but with the No. 6 pick, they did not have the opportunity. They took Cuban defectors Michael Tejara and Hansel Izquierdo, both pitchers for Miami's Southwest High, in the sixth and seventh rounds, respectively. The pair were members of Cuba's junior national team before defecting to the U.S. in the summer of 1994 at Miami International Airport while en route to the World Junior Championship in Canada. Both players received signing bonuses of $56,000 and never made the majors.

DAVID SEELIG

Oakland took Cuban defector Ariel Prieto with the fifth pick in hopes of a quick fix, but he got just 15 major league wins in 70 appearances

The Marlins also chose Rojas, Prieto's Palm Springs teammate and a former closer for Cuba's national team, though not until the 30th round. He received a bonus of $7,800 and pitched for two seasons in the Marlins system before injuries ended his career.

### ANGELS STICK WITH PRIMARY TARGET

The Angels targeted Erstad all spring and didn't let Prieto's late presence dissuade them. Erstad batted .410 with 19 home runs and 76 RBIs as a junior and set several Nebraska career records. He had also served as the punter for Nebraska's national championship football team the previous fall, averaging 42.6 yards.

Erstad's athletic feats were the stuff of legend in his home state of North Dakota. He was all-state in hockey and football, and a state champion in the 110- and 330-yard hurdles in track. His high school did not have a baseball team, but he starred in American Legion competition as both a hitter and pitcher, showing five-tool ability.

After two months of negotiations, Erstad signed with the Angels and received the second-largest bonus in draft history.

"It's just going to go into the bank, and I'll surprise my family one day," said Erstad, who was

### AT A GLANCE

Huchinson's reported $1.7 million bonus demand, leaving him as the only unsigned first-rounder in 1995. Hutchinson, one of the nation's top baseball and football recruits, went 25-11, 4.81 over three years for Stanford's baseball team, and passed for 4,235 yards in two seasons as the school's starting quarterback. He played briefly in the majors and the NFL.

### He Was Drafted?

**TOM BRADY, C, EXPOS (18TH ROUND).** The Expos knew Brady, from Serra High in San Mateo, Calif., was headed to Michigan to play football, but they tried to sign him anyway. He impressed scouts with his receiving and throwing skills, along with his lefthanded pull power. Without football, Brady might have been tabbed as high as the fifth round. He would have had to achieve a lot in baseball to match his four Super Bowl titles as an NFL quarterback.

### Did You Know . . .

Yankees first-rounder **SHEA MORENZ** and Mariners second-rounder **SHANE MONAHAN** were great-grandsons of Hockey Hall of Famer Howie Morenz, one of the greatest NHL players in the first half of the 20th century. Monahan's grandfather was Bernie "Boom Boom" Geoffrion, another NHL legend, who was Howie Morenz's son-in-law.

### They Said It

Mets first-round pick **RYAN JARONCYK,** attempting to explain a few years later why he quit the game midway through his third pro season: "Everyone makes mistakes and I learned from mine. It's easy to criticize someone who's 18 or 20 years old. There's big decisions to be made, and maybe I didn't make the right ones. But I've grown since then. At 18, you have a lot of talent, but you never know how things are going to pan out."

## DRAFT SPOTLIGHT: KERRY WOOD

Kerry Wood peaked early. On May 6, 1998, at age 20, he pitched one of the most dominating games in major league history, shutting out the Houston Astros on one hit, walking no one and striking out 20. It was the fifth start of his major league career for the Chicago Cubs.

MEL BAILEY

Unfortunately for the Cubs, Kerry Wood's greatness appeared only in flashes due to persistent injuries

Wood dominated from start to finish, showing command of a live 95-96 mph fastball and a devilish slider that buckled the knees of batter after batter. About the only surprise was that the Astros managed a hit.

"There's no one in the National League who has a better arm," said Cubs manager Jim Riggleman. "That game was one for the memory banks. The best I've ever seen pitched by anybody."

Some believe the 122-pitch game by Wood had something to do with what happened next. He developed a sore right elbow as the summer wore on, and by September was done for the season. He had struck out 233 in 167 innings and was the National League rookie of the year, but the following spring Wood would need Tommy John surgery.

The setback was the beginning of a long history of injuries that adversely affected Woods' career. He recovered from his elbow injury and showed flashes of brilliance in 98 mph doses, but never won 15 games in a season or contended for a Cy Young Award. Wood won just 86 games over 14 seasons. He retired in 2012, falling far short of the accomplishments that had been predicted for him.

There was something special about Wood on the pitcher's mound in high school. Like fellow Texans Nolan Ryan and Roger Clemens, he seemed destined to excel. Cubs scouting director Al Goldis was among the first to recognize the potential in the Texas prodigy.

"When I first started scouting, I saw Dwight Gooden in Tampa at the same age, and if Gooden were in this draft, I would've taken Wood ahead of Gooden," Goldis said. "I think he's the best pitcher in the draft, and maybe the best player in the draft. I haven't seen a guy throw like this in 10 years.

"A lot of college guys don't have deliveries like this guy. They might be older, but Wood is more advanced than most college guys talent-wise and mechanically. Even though he's only 17, his poise and mound presence are similar to those of a college pitcher."

The 6-foot-5, 195-pound Wood generated more buzz than any other high school prospect. Throwing from a loose, easy delivery, he had a fastball that projected as a well above-average pitch, both for velocity and late action. As a senior at Grand Prairie High in the Dallas-Fort Worth Metroplex, Wood went 14-0, 0.77 with 159 strikeouts in 81 innings. The Cubs drafted him with the fourth overall pick, and they expected him to be ready to dominate major league hitters within a few years.

"It would be nice to be in the majors two years from now, and I think I can," Wood said. "I'd like to get there as quickly as possible, but I'll do my job however the club wants me to and try to zip through as fast as I can."

For all the attention Wood received for spinning one of the best games in major league history as a 20-year-old, he was in the spotlight for a complete game prior to signing for all the wrong reasons. Two days after being drafted by the Cubs, Wood started both ends of a doubleheader in the Texas state playoffs. His Grand Prairie team needed to win both games to advance. Wood threw a 146-pitch, two-hitter to win the opener, and came back 30 minutes later and started the second game, throwing 29 pitches before being relieved after his team took a big lead and won handily.

That was 175 pitches in the same day for a high school pitcher. The Cubs were outraged. "That's unfathomable," Cubs general manager Ed Lynch said. "It's hard to imagine a coach would allow that to happen, especially to someone who's only 17."

Two contrasting complete games, thrown two years apart on two different stages, did much to both stoke the Kerry Wood legend, and in the end contribute to its demise.

highly regarded not only for his talent and competitive fire, but also for his professional and friendly demeanor. "I'm not going to change who I am or what kind of life I lead."

Erstad was in the big leagues by 1996 and became a fixture in the Angels outfield for 11 seasons. His best season came in 2000, when he set career highs in batting (.355), runs (121), doubles (39), homers (25), RBIs (100) and stolen bases (28). After a 14-year, major league career, Erstad returned to Nebraska and became the school's head baseball coach.

Like the Angels, the San Diego Padres got the player they wanted: Ben Davis, considered the best high school catcher in years. They took him with the second overall pick and had an agreement in place before the draft for a $1.3 million bonus. The Padres had drafted first baseman Todd Helton and outfielder Geoff Jenkins out of high school in 1992, and had a second chance at both in 1995, but chose Davis instead.

"Great catchers don't come along very often," Padres scouting director Kevin Towers said. "I felt we had to pick Ben. He is the best young catcher I've ever seen."

The 6-foot-3, 195-pound Davis, a switch-hitter, batted .507 with six home runs as a senior at Malvern Prep in Pennsylvania. He reached the big leagues in 1998, but his career stalled quickly, and the Padres gave up on Davis, trading him to the Mariners after the 2001 season. In 1,598 at-bats over seven seasons in the major leagues, Davis hit .237 with 38 homers. He was done in the major leagues by 2004 but continued to play professionally for another six, abandoning the catching position at one point in favor of pitching.

The Mariners were prepared to draft Prieto with the third pick, but their $900,000 offer, made a day before the draft, was countered with a demand of $1.9 million. So they turned to Rice University center fielder Jose Cruz Jr., a son of former major league all-star outfielder Jose Cruz and the best power-hitting prospect in the college ranks.

Cruz broke into the majors in 1997 and played 49 games for the Mariners before being traded to the Toronto Blue Jays. He played 12 seasons for nine teams, hitting .247 with 204 homers.

The Chicago Cubs, drafting fourth, took Texas high school righthander Kerry Wood, the consensus top pitching prospect in the draft pool. It marked the first time since 1978 that the first pitcher off the board went as low as No. 4. Wood quickly became a premier power pitcher, and his 20-strikeout, one-hit, no-walk masterpiece against

### Fastest To The Majors

| Player, Pos. | Drafted (Round) | Debut |
|---|---|---|
| 1. # Ariel Prieto, rhp | Athletics (1) | July 2, 1995 |
| 2. Darin Erstad, of | Angels (1) | June 14, 1996 |
| 3. Matt Morris, rhp | Cardinals (1) | April 4, 1997 |
| 4. Brett Tomko, rhp | Reds (2) | May 27, 1997 |
| 5. Jose Cruz Jr., of | Mariners (1) | May 31, 1997 |

**FIRST HIGH SCHOOL SELECTION:** Jeff Wallace, lhp (Royals/17, Aug. 21, 1997)

*#Debuted in major leagues.*

## Top 25 Bonuses

| | Player, Pos. | Drafted (Round) | Order | Bonus |
|---|---|---|---|---|
| 1. | **Darin Erstad, of** | **Angels (1)** | **1** | **$1,575,000** |
| 2.* | Jaime Jones, of | Marlins (1) | 6 | $1,337,000 |
| 3.* | **Mark Davis, c** | **Padres (1)** | **2** | **$1,300,000** |
| 4. | **Jose Cruz Jr., of** | **Mariners (1)** | **3** | **$1,285,000** |
| 5.* | **Kerry Wood, rhp** | **Cubs (1)** | **4** | **$1,265,000** |
| 6. | **Ariel Prieto, rhp** | **Athletics (1)** | **5** | **#$1,200,000** |
| 7.* | **Chad Hermansen, ss** | **Pirates (1)** | **10** | **$1,150,000** |
| 8. | **Jonathan Johnson, rhp** | **Rangers (1)** | **7** | **$1,100,000** |
| 9.* | Andy Yount, rhp | Red Sox (1) | 15 | $986,000 |
| 10. | Mike Drumright, rhp | Tigers (1) | 11 | $970,000 |
| 11. | **Geoff Jenkins, of** | **Brewers (1)** | **9** | **$911,000** |
| 12.* | **Joe Fontenot, rhp** | **Giants (1)** | **16** | **$900,000** |
| 13.* | **Roy Halladay, rhp** | **Blue Jays (1)** | **17** | **$895,000** |
| 14. | **Todd Helton, 1b** | **Rockies (1)** | **8** | **$892,500** |
| 15. | **Matt Morris, rhp** | **Cardinals (1)** | **12** | **$850,000** |
| * | **Reggie Taylor, of** | **Phillies (1)** | **14** | **$850,000** |
| * | Ryan Jaroncyk, ss | Mets (1) | 18 | $850,000 |
| 18. | **Mark Redman, lhp** | **Twins (1)** | **13** | **$830,000** |
| 19. | David Yocum, lhp | Dodgers (1) | 20 | $825,000 |
| 20.*† | Jorge Carrion, rhp | Rangers (7) | 178 | $700,000 |
| 21.* | Juan Lebron, of | Royals (1) | 19 | $650,000 |
| | Alvie Shepherd, rhp | Orioles (1) | 21 | $650,000 |
| | Shea Morenz, of | Yankees (1) | 27 | $650,000 |
| 24.* | **Nate Rolison, 1b** | **Marlins (2)** | **36** | **$610,000** |
| 25. | David Miller, 1b | Indians (1) | 23 | $600,000 |

*Major leaguers in bold. *High school selection. #Major league contract. †Signed as draft-and-follow.*

the Houston Astros on May 6, 1998—in his fifth career start—remains one of the great single-game pitching performances in baseball history.

Wood seemed destined to be an all-time great until injuries struck. After eight years as a starter, he moved to the bullpen in 2008 in an effort to avoid injuries. He retired in 2012 after returning to the Cubs, after pitching in 14 seasons and finishing with a 86-75, 3.67 career mark.

Two San Diego high school players, outfielder Jaime Jones and pitcher Chad Hutchinson, were both regarded as top-of-the-draft prospects, but each reportedly wanted a $1.7 million bonus. Jones went to the Marlins with the sixth overall pick, while Hutchinson slid to the Atlanta Braves with the 26th selection. Jones signed for $1.337 million, the second-highest bonus in 1995, while Hutchinson went to college.

### TRIO OF PICKS HIGHLIGHT CROP

The best players to come out of the 1995 draft were not among the first few selections. The Colorado Rockies, picking eighth, found a franchise cornerstone in Helton, a first baseman from the University of Tennessee. The Blue Jays got righthander Roy Halladay, a Colorado high school product, with the 17th pick. The Kansas City Royals found outfielder Carlos Beltran in the second round. All three players have a major league WAR (Wins Above Replacement) score of 60 or better. Erstad's WAR is 32.3.

Helton spent 17 seasons with the Rockies, hitting .316 with 369 homers, making five All-Star Game appearances and winning three Gold Glove Awards.

The 6-foot-6, 200-pound Halladay went 25-2 in his three-year high school career, featuring a mid-90s fastball and tantalizing knuckle-curve. He became an elite pitcher over the course of his 16 years in the major leagues, the first 12 with Toronto and the last four with Philadelphia.

Halladay reached the majors in 1998, but did not establish himself until 2002 after undergoing a mechanical makeover in Class A the previous season. His achievements included the 2003 American League Cy Young Award; the 20th perfect game in major league history, on May 29, 2010; and four months later, a no-hitter in the National League Division Series. Halladay went 203-105, 3.38 before retiring in 2013 because of a persistent back injury.

Before taking Beltran in the second round, the Royals selected another Puerto Rican outfielder, Juan LeBron, with the 19th pick in the first round. The 6-foot-4, 185-pound LeBron reminded some scouts of Juan Gonzalez, then a rising star with the Texas Rangers. "Juan is a real impact player," Royals scouting director Art Stewart said. "He's got tremendous power for a kid that just turned 19. He's a pure right fielder. He runs very well."

Carlos Beltran

LeBron's career never got back on track after he injured his shoulder during spring training in 1999. Beltran played seven seasons with the Royals, hitting .287 with 123 home runs, 516 RBIs and 164 stolen bases. He was still active after 18 seasons, entering the 2016 season with a career .280 average, 392 homers and 311 steals.

### THE CURIOUS CASE OF RYAN JARONCYK

With 10 first-round picks falling short of the major leagues, the failure rate in the 1995 draft was unusually high. The toll included five college selections and three players who didn't advance beyond Class A. Two of the most notable were Texas high school righthander Andy Yount, selected 15th by the Boston Red Sox, and California prep shortstop Ryan Jaroncyk, selected 18th by the New York Mets.

Yount and righthander Jeff Austin were a dominant 1-2 tandem on a Kingwood High pitching staff that also included sophomore righthander Mark Mangum. Austin lasted until the 10th round in 1995 because of a commitment to Stanford; he did not sign but became the fourth pick overall in the 1998 draft. Mangum was a first-round pick in 1997.

The 6-foot-2, 185-pount Yount, whose father played for the NFL's St. Louis Cardinals, was a converted shortstop who began pitching in earnest in the summer after his junior year. By the following spring, he was routinely touching 95 mph.

"We were pleased to get a quality arm like Yount at No. 15," Red Sox scouting director Wayne Britton said. "We've done a lot of homework on the kid. We've been in the home a lot. We probably saw him pitch as a scouting unit seven times. He

### WORTH NOTING

■ **DOUG BLOSSER,** a 1995 third-round pick of the Royals, died Jan. 24, 1998, from injuries in a car wreck in his hometown of Sarasota, Fla. Blosser was the younger brother of Greg Blosser, a 1989 first-round pick of the Red Sox. In three seasons in the Royals system, Doug Blosser hit .251-30-130. His death came four months to the day after Rockies 1994 first-rounder Doug Million, a former teammate at Sarasota High, died of an asthma attack. Blosser delivered the eulogy at Million's funeral.

■ Cal State Fullerton went 57-9 on its way to winning the 1995 College World Series, though its highest draft pick was eighth-rounder **JON WARD**. The Titans had a secret weapon in outfielder **MARK KOTSAY**, who hit .422-18-75 and doubled as the team's primary closer, going 2-1, 0.38 with nine saves. Kotsay, a sophomore, almost singlehandedly led the Titans to a national title by going 9-for-16 with three homers and 10 RBIs in four games. In an 11-5 championship game win over Southern California, he homered his first two times up and came on to record the last five outs. Kotsay was a first-round pick of the Marlins a year later.

■ **JOEL STEPHENS**, an Orioles ninth-round pick in 1995, died from colon cancer on Sept. 30, 1998, at age 22, after playing three seasons in the O's system and hitting .231-2-24. A three-sport high school star in Elmira, N.Y., Stephens broke the 37-year-old city rushing records of Ernie Davis, who starred at Syracuse, won the 1960 Heisman Trophy and was the No. 1 pick in the 1961 NFL draft. Davis died of leukemia at age 35. Syracuse had offered Stephens a scholarship to play football, prior to his signing with the Orioles for a bonus of $50,000.

■ University of Richmond first baseman **SEAN CASEY** led NCAA Division I with a

CONTINUED ON PAGE 454

## WORTH NOTING

CONTINUED FROM PAGE 453

.461 average and had 26 doubles, 14 homers and 70 RBIs. A second-round pick of the Indians, Casey went on to hit .302-130-735 in a 12-year big league career, including eight seasons with the Reds. Southwest Missouri State slugger **STEVE HACKER** led the NCAA with 37 homers and batted .409. The Braves took him in the 14th round. Hacker played six seasons in the minors, hitting .281 with 97 homers.

■ **SHAWN GALLAGHER**, a first baseman from New Hanover High in Wilmington, N.C., homered four times in an early-season game, and less than a month later tied a national record by hitting five homers in a game. He also tied a national mark by hitting safely in 51 straight games. Gallagher hit .591-16-61 as a senior, and was drafted in the fifth round by the Rangers. He went on to play seven seasons in the minor leagues but could not get past Double-A, batting .273 with 100 home runs.

■ Of all players drafted in 1995 with notable relatives in the game, the most significant and best-known was **JOSE CRUZ JR.**, the third pick overall. His father, Jose Cruz, was a former all-star, and his uncles Hector and Tommy, also had significant big league careers. Outfielder **RICHARD BROWN** was drafted in the second round by the Yankees, and his older brother **BILLY**, also an outfielder, went in the third round to the A's, making them the highest-drafted brothers in the same June draft. The Abners previously owned that distinction in 1984, when the Mets took Shawn in the first round and the Expos picked Ben in the fifth round. The Stottlemyre brothers, Todd and Mel Jr., went first and third in the January 1985 secondary phase. Billy Brown was a year older than Richard, but they were in the same academic year. Richard accepted a $389,500 bonus from the Yankees, and Billy passed up signing to play

has a free and easy delivery, and a power arm."

Yount went 1-3, 5.15 in his first two seasons in the Red Sox system, occasionally flashing a triple-digit fastball. But then he severed tendons in his pitching hand while visiting the gravesite of a high school friend. In his angst, Yount shattered a glass he was clutching in his right hand. "It was one of those things that doctors say you don't realize what you're doing," Yount said. "I was squeezing the glass so hard it shattered in my hand."

Yount had nine surgical procedures on his hand, and missed the 1997 and '98 seasons before the Red Sox released him. Looking for another chance, Yount got it with the Detroit Tigers. His mid-90s fastball returned, but he struggled to command his secondary pitches and had marginal success (2-3, 6.14) in Class A in 1999 and 2000. He then became an outfielder and hit .215 with eight home runs and 50 RBIs over two seasons before drawing his release. After three years out of baseball, Yount signed with the Reds in 2006 as a pitcher and lasted just six innings before calling it a career.

Some scouts regarded Jaroncyk, out of Orange Glen High in Escondido, Calif., as the best pure middle infielder in the 1995 crop. He seemed intent on attending Stanford, but changed his mind and signed with the Mets on the day he was drafted for $850,000.

BILL SETLIFF

Ryan Jaroncyk

Jaroncyk abruptly retired on May 8, 1997, while playing in the Class A South Atlantic League, giving his reasons for leaving in a letter to Mets general manager Joe McIlvaine. Jaroncyk wrote that he never had liked playing baseball and did so only at the urging of his father. He also disliked the frat-house culture prevalent in the minor leagues.

Jaroncyk's puzzling departure became unique in draft history as one of the few highly rated players to walk away from the game while completely healthy. The Mets, while disappointed, never sought to retrieve the bonus money they paid Jaroncyk. He hit just .207 with a single homer in 134 games before pulling the plug.

After sitting out the balance of the 1997 season and all of 1998, Jaroncyk was unexpectedly selected by the Dodgers in the 1998 Rule 5 draft. He decided to play again, only to suffer a disabling arm injury 20 games into his comeback. He subsequently played football in 2001 at Claremont-Mudd-Scripps, an NCAA Division III college.

"Everyone makes mistakes and I learned from mine," Jaroncyk said. "It's easy to criticize someone who's 18 or 20 years old. There's big decisions to be made, and maybe I didn't make the right ones sometimes. But I've grown since then. At 18, you have a lot of talent, but you never know how things are going to pan out with injuries and being in the wrong place at the wrong time."

Jones was regarded as the best high school hitter in the draft. At San Diego's Rancho Bernardo High, he hit .475 with 10 home runs and 26 stolen bases as a senior. "Jaime is the best high school hitter I've seen in San Diego in the last 30 years," said one of the area's most respected scouts.

"He's got a great swing. He's got plus power. He's at least an average hitter. He's a plus baserunner with average speed. And he's got great instincts," said Marlins scouting director Gary Hughes. "He's a baseball player, period."

Jones played 10 seasons of pro ball but did not make it to the major leagues. He never hit better than .284 or hit more than 10 homers in any of seven seasons in the Marlins system. He quit in 2001, but later played three seasons in the Arizona and Kansas City farm systems.

Injuries were a major factor in Jones' downfall as they limited him to less than 100 games in every season except one, but he simply never developed as most scouts thought he would.

Three college pitchers selected in the first round fell far short of expectations. Florida State lefthander David Yocum's injury-riddled career with the Dodgers ended in Class A after two seasons. Wichita State righthander Mike Drumright, selected with the 11th overall pick by the Tigers, and Nebraska righthander Alvie Shepherd, chosen 21st by the Baltimore Orioles, both struggled to throw strikes and develop reliable secondary stuff.

The Dodgers, who had gone two seasons without a lefthander in their rotation, tried to address that by taking Yocum with the 20th overall pick, believing he would reach the majors in short order. He developed a sore shoulder in his second pro season, and after three surgeries, he was released, showing a 2-3, 4.07 record for 15 pro appearances.

The 6-foot-7, 230-pound Shepherd routinely threw his fastball at 97-98 mph. He also played

### Largest Bonuses By Round

| | Player, Pos. | Club | Bonus |
|---|---|---|---|
| **1.** | **Darin Erstad, of** | **Angels** | **$1,575,000** |
| **2.** | ***Nate Rolison, 1b** | **Marlins** | **$610,000** |
| 3. | *Jeff Yoder, rhp | Cubs | $365,000 |
| **4.** | ***Jimmy Osting, lhp** | **Braves** | **$375,000** |
| **5.** | ***#Kevin McGlinchy, rhp** | **Braves** | **$425,000** |
| 6. | *Caleb Martinez, lhp | Phillies | $170,000 |
| 7. | *#Jorge Carrion, rhp/ss | Rangers | $700,000 |
| 8. | *Ricky Williams, of | Phillies | $70,000 |
| 9. | *Kyle Burchart, rhp | Blue Jays | $160,000 |
| 10. | *David Moore, rhp | Royals | $192,700 |
| 11. | *Craig Taczy, lhp | Dodgers | $100,000 |
| 12. | Cam Spence, rhp | Yankees | $240,000 |
| 13. | Frankie Sanders, rhp | Indians | $60,000 |
| **14.** | **Scott Winchester, rhp** | **Indians** | **$30,000** |
| 15. | *#Steve Hoff, lhp | Padres | $60,000 |
| 16. | Jeremy Williamson, lhp | Royals | $45,000 |
| 17. | #Michael Hughes, rhp | Angels | $227,000 |
| 18. | James O'Shaughnessy, rhp | Dodgers | $100,000 |
| **19.** | ***Aaron Miles, 2b** | **Astros** | **$75,000** |
| 20. | Phil Olson, rhp | Mets | $20,000 |
| | **Mike Lowell, 3b** | **Yankees** | **$20,000** |
| 21. | Dan Reed, lhp | Orioles | $20,000 |
| **22.** | **Donzell McDonald, of** | **Yankees** | **$90,000** |
| 23. | *#Alex Morris, rhp | Marlins | $175,000 |
| **24.** | ***Jeriome Robertson, lhp** | **Astros** | **$50,000** |
| **25.** | **#Brian Fuentes, lhp** | **Mariners** | **$90,000** |
| Other | #Ben Phillips, rhp | Yankees (36) | $250,000 |

*Major leaguers in bold. *High school selection. #Signed as draft-and-follow.*

first base at Nebraska, hitting .343 with 12 homers as a junior. The Orioles were confident that Shepherd would progress quickly once he concentrated on pitching, but he had little success, going 17-16, 5.58 in four seasons, none above Double-A.

Drumright threw his fastball in the mid-90s and was a workhorse, but he often had command problems. He made it to Triple-A and stayed there for seven seasons, going 34-67, 5.76 at that level.

## BONUS GROWTH REMAINS UNCHECKED

While most clubs initially took a cautious approach to the 1995 draft, especially coming off a crippling 232-day strike that led to cancellation of the 1994 World Series, three clubs spent in excess of $3 million on bonuses. The spending spree was led by the Red Sox with a tab of $3.044 million, followed closely by the Marlins ($3.0353 million) and New York Yankees ($3.021 million).

Boston justified its spending because it was the only team with multiple first-round picks—Yount ($986,000) and South Carolina high school outfielder Corey Jenkins ($575,000)—but also spent at least $225,000 on its next three selections. None of the five picks reached the majors.

In addition to the $1.337 million bonus the Marlins gave Jones, they spent $610,000 on Mississippi high school first baseman Nate Rolison, the largest bonus ever given to a second-round draft choice. Jones didn't make it to the major leagues, and Rolison got there for eight games.

The Yankees spent $650,000 on top pick Shea Morenz (27th overall), but more than $100,000 on seven other picks. None reached the big leagues.

In all, eight players became instant millionaires, including Nevada high school shortstop Chad Hermansen, the 10th overall pick, who reached agreement with the Pittsburgh Pirates in advance of the draft on a $1.15 million deal.

"The draft doesn't appear to have been affected at all by the strike," Orioles scouting director Gary Nickels said. "It seems to be operating independent of the other problems the strike has created."

Several players chosen after the first round received significant bonuses. Perhaps the most surprising was $700,000 to Jorge Carrion, drafted in the seventh round by the Rangers out of DeWitt Clinton High in the Bronx.

The team initially believed it had a deal in place with Carrion for $100,000, but he changed his mind and attended Northeast Texas Community College to pitch and play shortstop. The Rangers retained Carrion's rights until shortly before the 1996 draft. He continued to improve, and they upped their offer to $300,000 before more than doubling it to sign him. Had Carrion gone unsigned, he almost certainly would have been selected in the upper half of the first round.

Carrion wanted to play shortstop, but the Rangers wanted him for his 97 mph fastball. The two sides agreed he would both pitch and be a DH in his first two pro seasons, getting 50 at-bats a month, and then concentrate on pitching in 1998. Carrion abruptly quit during his third season after going 5-5, 5.65 at Class A Savannah. "I wasn't having fun anymore," he said. "I lost my love for baseball because I wasn't playing every day. I wasn't having fun pitching and sitting on the bench."

MEL BAILEY
Jorge Carrion

Sixteen months later, Carrion asked the Rangers for a second chance. They agreed, hopeful of getting some return on their $700,000 investment. But he never pitched another inning for the Rangers or any other pro team, showing a 12-10, 4.86 record for his short career.

The Braves spent $425,000 on a draft-and-follow, righthander Kevin McGlinchy, a fifth-round choice. In all, five draft-and-follow players received bonuses of at least $200,000.

## HUTCHINSON GOES UNSIGNED

The 6-foot-5, 225-pound Hutchinson, one of the nation's top prep quarterbacks, likely would have increased the average first-round signing bonus had he agreed to a deal. The Braves chose Hutchinson with the 26th overall pick. He declined a $1.5 million offer and enrolled at Stanford to play both football and baseball, becoming the only 1995 first-rounder not to sign.

Hutchinson threw a 97 mph fastball in high school and would have been one of the top 10 picks had he been more amenable to signing. In two years at California's Torrey Pines High, Hutchinson went 23-2, 1.33 with 182 strikeouts in 152 innings.

He said his decision to choose college was influenced by his mother, Martha, who had watched Chad's father, Lloyd, once a top prospect himself, struggle in the Philadelphia Phillies farm system.

"After talking with my mom, it was a pretty easy decision," Hutchinson said. "She's seen minor

### One Team's Draft: Texas Rangers

| Player, Pos. | Bonus | Player, Pos. | Bonus | Player, Pos. | Bonus |
|---|---|---|---|---|---|
| **1. Jonathan Johnson, rhp** | **$1,100,000** | 10. *Julio Mercado, of | $30,000 | 19. Chuck Bauer, rhp | $2,000 |
| 2. *Phil Lowery, lhp | Did not sign | 11. Brian Martineau, rhp | $25,000 | 20. Joe Goodwin, c | $10,000 |
| **3. *Ryan Dempster, rhp** | **$200,000** | 12. Bryan Link, lhp | $5,000 | 21. Ted Silva, rhp | $18,000 |
| **4. Ryan Glynn, rhp** | **$110,000** | **13. Cliff Brumbaugh, 3b** | **$17,000** | 22. *Bobby Styles, rhp | $7,500 |
| 5. *Shawn Gallagher, 1b | $90,000 | **14. Brandon Knight, rhp** | **$30,000** | 23. Robert Moore, rhp | $2,000 |
| **6. Dan Kolb, rhp** | **$42,000** | 15. Ryan Gorecki, 2b | $2,500 | 24. *Manny Torres, rhp | Did not sign |
| 7. *Jorge Carrion, rhp/ss | $700,000 | 16. Nathan Vopata, 3b/2b | $2,000 | 25. Mike McHugh, lhp | $3,000 |
| **8. *Craig Monroe, ss** | **$35,000** | 17. *Brian Llibre, c | $6,000 | **Other Mike Venafro (29), lhp** | **$2,000** |
| 9. *Juan Rivera, c | $32,000 | 18. *Damian Rose, of | $21,000 | | |

*Major leaguers in bold. *High school selection.*

### WORTH NOTING

baseball for Florida Atlantic University. Billy was drafted out of college by the Blue Jays and eventually played alongside his brother in the Yankees organization for two years. Neither of the Brown brothers reached the majors.

Besides being a first-round pick of the Yankees and a football-baseball star at Texas, **SHEA MORENZ** came from a significant hockey lineage as he was a great-grandson of hockey immortal Howie Morenz, the first Montreal Canadiens player to have his jersey retired (7) and one of the original nine inductees to the Hockey Hall of Fame in 1945. Outfielder **SHANE MONAHAN**, drafted in the second round by the Mariners out of Clemson, was also a great-grandson of Morenz and his hockey connection was even more significant as his grandfather was 14-year NHL veteran Bernie "Boom Boom" Geofffrion, the player generally credited with introducing the slap shot to the NHL, while his father, Hartland Monahan, played seven seasons in the NHL. Monahan focused his talents on baseball and starred for three years in college at Clemson, hitting .388-12-52 as a junior. He spent two seasons in the majors with the Mariners, hitting .235-4-28.

Catcher **A.J. HINCH**, drafted in the third round by the Twins, decided to return to Stanford for his senior year so he could play on the 1996 U.S. Olympic team. He turned down a $250,000 bonus. "When I'm 45 and retired and look back, I think I'm going to be very happy that I stuck it out and played in the Olympics," Hinch said. "Add to that I'm going to graduate, and it seems like an easy decision to me."

The Yankees drafted Virginia outfielder Brian Buchanan in the first round in 1994, and Florida high school lefthander **BRIAN BUCHANAN** in the second round a year later.

## IN FOCUS: TODD HELTON

JOHN WILLIAMSON

Todd Helton did it all in three years at Tennessee, especially in 1995 when he hit .407 with 20 home runs and 92 RBIs. He was a stalwart on the pitching staff, going 8-2, 1.66 with 12 saves.

For added measure he spent three seasons as a quarterback for the Volunteers, first as a backup to Heath Shuler, the runner-up in the 1993 Heisman Trophy balloting. In 1994, Helton became the starter when senior Jerry Colquitt injured his knee in the season opener.

Three weeks later, he suffered a knee injury himself and was replaced by freshman Peyton Manning, who went on to break numerous school records over four seasons, was the runner-up in the 1997 Heisman balloting and eventually was selected first overall by the Indianapolis Colts in the 1998 NFL draft.

Baseball was Helton's game, and he was selected with the eighth pick in the 1995 draft by the Rockies.

By 1997, he was in the majors. Over 17 seasons, he did it all with the Rockies, hitting .316 overall with 369 homers. He had five All-Star Game appearances and three Gold Gloves to his credit. In his best season, 2000, he led the National League in batting (.372), hits (216), doubles (59) and RBIs (147), as well as both slugging (.698) and on-base percentage (.463), while also slamming 42 homers.

### Highest Unsigned Picks

| Player, Pos., Team (Round) | College | Re-Drafted |
|---|---|---|
| Chad Hutchinson, rhp, Braves (1) | Stanford | Cardinals '98 (2) |
| Phill Lowery, lhp, Rangers (2) | Arizona State | Marlins '98 (6) |
| Billy Brown, of, Athletics (3) | Florida Atlantic | Blue Jays '97 (3) |
| Chuck Crowder, lhp, Tigers (3) | Georgia Tech | Pirates '98 (8) |
| A.J. Hinch, c, Twins (3) | * Stanford | Athletics '96 (3) |
| J.J. Putz, rhp, White Sox (6) | Michigan | Twins '98 (17) |
| Adam Everett, ss, Cubs (4) | N.C. State | Red Sox '98 (1) |
| Jay Hood, ss, Twins (4) | Georgia Tech | Angels '98 (6) |
| Gary Kinnie, rhp, Mariners (5) | Michigan State | Never |
| Cody McKay, 3b, Cardinals (5) | * Arizona State | Athletics '96 (9) |

**TOTAL UNSIGNED PICKS:** Top 5 Rounds (12), Top 10 Rounds (28)

**Returned to same school.*

league baseball firsthand and knows how hard it is. At Stanford, I'm away from home, but I'm kind of sheltered. It's a good starting point for me."

The St. Louis Cardinals drafted Hutchinson in the second round in 1998 and signed him for $2.3 million. He reached the major leagues briefly, but eventually gave up baseball and played briefly in the NFL for the Dallas Cowboys.

Other 1995 draft choices better known as football players than baseball players included quarterbacks Morenz, Tom Brady, Daunte Culpepper and Danny Kanell, and running back Ricky Williams. Yankees owner George Steinbrenner was a longtime admirer of talented football players, and his team drafted Morenz, Culpepper and Kanell.

Shea Morenz

Morenz, a lefthanded-hitting outfielder, was on the Astros' short list for the No. 1 pick in the 1992 draft. He was the top-ranked high school quarterback in the country and reportedly wanted $1.4 million to sign. He lasted until the sixth round in 1992, when the Blue Jays were unable to buy him out of his commitment to Texas.

Morenz's football career was plagued by injuries. He turned his focus to baseball in the spring of 1995, and flashed enough ability that the Yankees selected him in the first round.

"He's probably about as raw a college first-round pick as you'll ever come across," Texas assistant baseball coach Tommy Harmon said. "Football was pretty much his life until this year. He's kind of fun to look at and project because everything to know about baseball is in front of him."

Morenz spent five seasons in the minors, three with the Yankees and two with the Padres. He got to Triple-A for 13 games, but no higher, and hit .251 with 26 homers and 180 RBIs for his career.

Corey Jenkins gave up a chance to play quarterback at South Carolina and signed with the Red Sox. He spent five seasons in pro ball, peaking in Double-A, and hit just .206 with 33 home runs. Released at age 22, Jenkins resumed his football career, playing two years at Garden City (Kan.) Community College and then two years at South Carolina as a quarterback and then a defensive back. He played two seasons in the NFL.

Williams was an eighth-round pick of the Phillies out of a San Diego high school. He signed for a bonus of $70,000 and spent four seasons in the Phillies organization, from 1995-98, hitting .211 with four home runs and 46 stolen bases.

Williams fared much better in football, becoming one of the best running backs in college football history at Texas, winning the 1998 Heisman Trophy and setting an NCAA career rushing record of 6,279 yards. He played 11 seasons in the NFL.

### STRIKE'S IMPACT ON DRAFT

A total of 1,666 players were drafted in 1995. The process lasted 87 rounds, with Oakland the first team to drop out, in the 45th round, and Florida the last to quit picking.

Teams had just two compensation picks between the first and second rounds (tying the record low set every year from 1982-86), a reflection of the low number of free agents who were offered arbitration following the 1994 season. With the strike in full bloom, few clubs were willing to offer arbitration to departing free agents, in spite of it costing them the chance at compensation.

The only Type A free agents switching clubs that required compensation were lefthander Danny Jackson, who went from the Phillies to the Cardinals; and infielder Gregg Jefferies, who went from the Cardinals to the Phillies. Both those clubs ended up with an extra pick.

The Reds forfeited their first-round pick to the Red Sox for signing the lone Type B free agent, Damon Berryhill, a significant cost for a backup catcher who played in only 34 games in 1995.

In an attempt to slow the upward spiral of signing bonuses, team owners proposed a cap on what a team could spend to sign both drafted and international players during a calendar year. The plan called for the team with the No. 1 pick in the draft to have a limit of $1.302 million. The second team's limit would be $1.290 million, with caps decreasing down the line. In addition, teams would have spending limits for picks in the first five rounds. The first overall pick would receive $370,000, the second $365,000, and continue to decrease. Major League Baseball planned to negotiate the issue as part of the labor agreement with the union, but it never got to the bargaining table.

### Largest Draft-And-Follow Bonuses

| Player, Pos. | Club (Round) | Bonus |
|---|---|---|
| 1. * Jorge Carrion, rhp/ss | Rangers (7) | $700,000 |
| **2. * Kevin McGlinchy, rhp** | **Braves (5)** | **$425,000** |
| 3. Ben Phillips, rhp | Yankees (36) | $250,000 |
| 4. Michael Hughes, rhp | Angels (17) | $227,000 |
| 5. * Jeff Alfano, c | Brewers (4) | $200,000 |
| 6. * Alex Morris, rhp | Marlins (23) | $175,000 |
| 7. Richard Cremer, lhp | Yankees (34) | $120,000 |
| 8. Todd Cutchins, lhp | Mets (6) | $100,000 |
| * Denton McDaniel, lhp | Royals (48) | $100,000 |
| **10. Brian Fuentes, lhp** | **Mariners (25)** | **$90,000** |

*Major leaguers in bold. *High school selection.*

# 1995 Draft List

**Did not sign. Major leaguers in bold, with first and last years noted. Order of selection indicated in parentheses. For the first five rounds, the peak level of each player is noted. + Signed as draft-and-follow (Second school noted if applicable).*

## ATLANTA BRAVES (26)

1. ***Chad Hutchinson, rhp, Torrey Pines HS, San Diego.—(2001)**

DRAFT DROP *Attended Stanford; re-drafted by Cardinals, 1998 (2nd round); quarterback, National Football League (2002-04)*

2. Jim Scharrer, 1b, Cathedral Prep, Erie, Pa.—(AA)
3. **Rob Bell, rhp, Marlboro Central HS, Marlboro, N.Y.—(2000-07)**
4. **Jimmy Osting, lhp, Trinity HS, Louisville, Ky.—(2001-02)**
5. **+Kevin McGlinchy, rhp, Malden (Mass.) HS / Central Florida CC.—(1999-2000)**
6. *Matt Middleton, ss, Graham HS, Conover, Ohio.
7. Gerald Vecchioni, ss, Patapsco HS, Baltimore.
8. *Chad Mead, lhp-1b, Woodward (Okla.) HS.
9. Ben Wyatt, lhp, J.A. Fair HS, Little Rock, Ark.
10. Ryan Schurman, rhp, Tualatin (Ore.) HS.
11. Antone Brooks, lhp, Norfolk State University.
12. Joe Bauldree, rhp, Wake Forest-Rolesville HS, Wake Forest, N.C.
13. Charlie Cruz, lhp, Florida State University.
14. Steve Hacker, 1b, Southwest Missouri State University.
15. Matt McWilliams, rhp, University of North Carolina-Charlotte.
16. *Casey Crawford, of, O'Connell HS, Falls Church, Va.
17. Jason Shy, c, Butte (Calif.) JC.
18. Brian Rust, 3b, Lewis & Clark (Ore.) College.
19. Ben Fowler, rhp, Pace Academy, Alpharetta, Ga.
20. ***Jason Hart, ss, Fair Grove (Mo.) HS.—(2002)**
21. *David Noyce, lhp, Marietta (Ga.) HS.
22. Oscar Otero, 3b, Benjamin Harrison HS, Cayey, P.R.
23. Keith Dougherty, 3b, Columbus (Ga.) College.
24. Skeeter Ellison, of, Dixie (Utah) JC.
25. Jamie Wise, lhp, Abraham Baldwin (Ga.) CC.
26. Jeremy McMullen, lhp, Portland State University.
27. Matt Taylor, ss, Cal State Hayward.
28. Yan LaGrandeur, rhp, Cegep Montmorency HS, Granby, Quebec.
29. *Jacob Ruotsinoja, of, Seminole (Fla.) HS.
30. Ariel Colon, 1b, Dr. Jose M. Lazaro HS, Carolina, P.R.
31. Keith Mayhew, rhp, Ferrum (Va.) College.
32. Phillip Smith, of, Phillipsburg (N.J.) HS.
33. Corey Walker, of, Teikyo Westmar (Iowa) College.
34. Randy Hodges, of, Florida State University.
35. Curt Schnur, rhp, University of Delaware.
36. *Mike Goldstein, of, Cherry Creek HS, Englewood, Colo.
37. *Donnie Thomas, lhp, Andrew (Ga.) JC.
38. *Troy Satterfield, lhp, Jonesboro (Ga.) HS.
39. **Mike Mahoney, c, Creighton University.—(2000-05)**
40. *Nathan Bennett, lhp, Coastal Christian HS, Arroyo Grande, Calif.
41. Walker Reynolds, rhp, Berry (Ga.) College.
42. *Craig Cozart, rhp, University of Central Florida.

DRAFT DROP *Baseball coach, High Point (2009-15)*

43. *Darren Blakely of, Pensacola (Fla.) HS.
44. Eric White, rhp, Enrico Fermi HS, Enfield, Conn.
45. Toby Anglen, 2b, Arkansas State University.
46. ***Craig House, rhp, Christian Brothers HS, Memphis, Tenn.—(2000)**
47. Pooh Hines, ss, DeKalb (Ga.) JC.
48. **Jason Shiell, rhp, Windsor-Forest HS, Savannah, Ga.—(2002-06)**
49. *Luther Salinas, rhp-1b, La Verne Lutheran HS, Whittier, Calif.
50. *Robert Fishel, lhp, Pflugerville (Texas) HS.
51. Andrew Cochrane, lhp, Pacific Lutheran (Wash.) University.
52. Kevin Loewe, lhp, University of Maryland-Baltimore County.
53. *Jamel McAdory, 1b, Jackson State University.
54. *Craig Owens, of, Chowan (N. C.) College.
55. *Charlie Curry, ss-2b, Centennial HS, Portland, Ore.
56. Brian Jolliffe, lhp, University of Maine.

## BALTIMORE ORIOLES (21)

1. Alvie Shepherd, rhp, University of Nebraska.—(AA)
2. Chip Alley, c, Palm Beach Lakes HS, West Palm Beach, Fla.—(AA)
3. Darrell Dent, of, Montclair Prep, Panorama City, Calif.—(AAA)
4. Lou Fisher, rhp, Fremont HS, Oakland.—(AA)
5. ***Luke Hudson, rhp, Fountain Valley (Calif.) HS.—(2002-07)**

DRAFT DROP *Attended Tennessee; re-drafted by Rockies, 1998 (4th round)*

6. ***John Bale, lhp, University of Southern Mississippi.—(1999-2009)**
7. *Kevin Miller, 3b, Ballard HS, Seattle.
8. Scott Eibey, lhp, University of Northern Iowa.
9. Joel Stephens, of, Notre Dame HS, Elmira, N.Y.

DRAFT DROP *Died as active player (Oct. 1, 1998)*

10. **David Dellucci, of, University of Mississippi.—(1997-2009)**
11. Greg Dean, rhp, Oklahoma State University.
12. Carlos Akins, of, Western Kentucky University.
13. Bob O'Toole, c, Providence College.
14. Chris Bryant, 3b, North Carolina Wesleyan College.
15. Tim Olszewski, rhp, Triton (Ill.) JC.
16. ***Zach Sorensen, ss, Highland HS, Salt Lake City.—(2003-05)**
17. Jason LeCronier, of, McNeese State University.
18. *Lawrence Adams, 1b, Creekside HS, Fairburn, Ga.
19. Brion King, of, Oviedo (Fla.) HS.
20. *Carlos Casillas, 1b, Santa Monica HS, Los Angeles.
21. Dan Reed, lhp, Stanford University.
22. *Doug Thompson, rhp, Mississippi Gulf Coast JC.
23. +Matthew Achilles, rhp, Black Hawk (Ill.) JC.
24. *Jason Albert, 2b, Central Connecticut State University.
25. *Gaylon Dixon, lhp, Seminole (Okla.) JC.
26. Joaquin Serra, ss, Beverly Hills, Calif.
27. Bob Morseman, lhp, Salem-Teikyo (W.Va.) University.
28. Johnny Isom, of, Texas Wesleyan University.
29. Tom Russin, 1b, Eckerd (Fla.) College.
30. Chris Bray, rhp, Mount Olive (N.C.) College.
31. *A.J. Marquardt, of, Columbia Basin (Wash.) CC.
32. *William Morstad, 3b, Windsor Academy, Macon, Ga.
33. *Mike Cosgrove, rhp, Cypress (Calif.) JC.
34. *Darin Moore, rhp, Lodi HS, Acampo, Calif.
35. **Calvin Pickering, of-1b, King HS, Temple Terrace, Fla.—(1998-2005)**
36. *John Santos, rhp, Corcoran HS, Tulare, Calif.
37. Avery Taylor, ss, Long Beach (Miss.) HS.
38. +Kenny Sims, rhp, New Mexico JC.
39. *Craig Jones, rhp, La Quinta HS, Westminster, Calif.
40. *Cory Scott, rhp, Currituck County HS, Knott's Island, N.C.
41. *Josh Taylor, ss, Shawnee (Okla.) HS.
42. ***Jerry Hairston, 2b, Naperville North HS, Naperville, Ill.—(1998-2013)**

DRAFT DROP *Grandson of Sammy Hairston, major league r (1951) • Son of Jerry Hairston, major leaguer (1973-89) • Brother of Scott Hairston, major leaguer (2004-07)*

43. *Jason Glover, of, Georgia State University.
44. *Mike Wooden, rhp, North County HS, Baltimore.
45. Chris Paxton, c, Palmdale (Calif.) HS.
46. *Dan Keller, rhp, Fountain Valley (Calif.) HS.
47. *Corey Coil, rhp, Francis Scott Key HS, Taneytown, Md.
48. Wess Winn, ss, University of Texas-Arlington.
49. *Robert Williams, c, Edgewater HS, Winter Park, Fla.

## BOSTON RED SOX (15)

1. Andy Yount, rhp, Kingwood (Texas) HS.—(High A)
1. Corey Jenkins, of, Dreher HS, Columbia, S.C. (Choice from Reds as compensation for Type B free agent Damon Berryhill).—(AA)

DRAFT DROP *Linebacker, National Football League (2003-04)*

2. Jose Olmeda, ss, Santiago Veve Carzada HS, Fajardo, P.R.—(High A)
3. Jay Yennaco, rhp, Pinkerton Academy, Windham, N.H.—(AAA)
4. Mike Spinelli, lhp, Revere (Mass.) HS.—(High A)
5. **Steve Lomasney, c, Peabody (Mass.) HS.—(1999)**
6. **Matt Kinney, rhp, Bangor (Maine) HS.—(2000-05)**
7. **Cole Liniak, ss, San Dieguito HS, Encinitas, Calif.—(1999-2000)**
8. Luis Cardona, c, Manuel Mendez Liciaga HS, San Sebastian, P.R.
9. **Paxton Crawford, rhp, Carlsbad (N.M.) HS.—(2000-01)**
10. Kevie Austin, rhp, Emmanuel (Ga.) College.
11. Jeff Sauve, rhp, Clemson University.
12. **Jim Chamblee, ss, Odessa (Texas) JC.—(2003)**
13. Andy Noffke, rhp, Ohio State University.
14. *Andrew Beinbrink, 3b, Scripps Ranch HS, San Diego.
15. Kevan Cannon, lhp, Ohio State University.
16. **Rontrez Johnson, of, Marshall (Texas) HS.—(2003)**
17. Bobby Rodgers, rhp, Wake Forest University.
18. Felipe Roman, of, Metropolitana Universidad HS, Rio Piedras, P.R.
19. Ben Stallings, rhp, Apollo HS, Owensboro, Ky.
20. Dwight Ferguson, of, Miami-Dade Christian HS, Carol City, Fla.
21. Curtis Romboli, lhp, Boston College.
22. Pete Prodanov, 3b-of, Oklahoma State University.
23. *Chuck Lopez, of, Gahr HS, Cerritos, Calif.
24. *Chris Toomey, of-rhp, Dana Hills HS, Dana Point, Calif.
25. Scott Jones, rhp, Miami (Ohio) University.
26. Moises Rojas, of, Brito Miami Private HS, Hialeah, Fla.
27. **Juan Pena, rhp, Miami-Dade CC Wolfson.—(1999)**
28. *Kaleb Harp, c, DeKalb (Texas) HS.
29. Bob Rauch, rhp-ss, Lamar University.
30. Mark Varriano, c, University of North Dakota.
31. *Cliff Brand, rhp, Central Gwinnett HS, Lawrenceville, Ga.
32. *Cordele Mincey, rhp, Dodge County HS, Milan, Ga.
33. *Matt Burch, rhp, Thomas Edison HS, Horseheads, N.Y.

DRAFT DROP *First-round draft pick (30th overall), Royals (1998)*

34. *Bart Vaughn, rhp, Mount Dora Bible HS, Orlando, Fla.
35. Nick Gruber, c, Haddon Township HS, Westmont, N.J.
36. *Derrick Lewis, rhp, Central Alabama CC.
37. *Angel Diaz, c, Hillsborough (Fla.) JC.
38. *Tim Boeth, ss, Leon HS, Tallahassee, Fla.
39. *Jason Wilson, rhp, South Broward HS, Hollywood, Fla.
40. Jim Farrell, rhp, Kent State University.
41. *Brian Messer, rhp, Northwest HS, Shawnee, Kan.
42. +Juan Chaidez, c, Miami-Dade Christian HS, Hialeah, Fla. / Miami-Dade CC North.
43. ***Pat Burrell, 3b, Bellarmine Prep, San Jose, Calif.—(2000-2011)**

DRAFT DROP *First overall draft pick, Phillies (1998)*

44. *Bryan Wright, ss, Escambia HS, Pensacola, Fla.
45. *Kris Brown, of, Central HS, Kalamazoo, Mich.

## CALIFORNIA ANGELS (1)

1. **Darin Erstad, of, University of Nebraska.—(1996-2009)**

DRAFT DROP *Baseball coach, Nebraska (2011-15)*

2. **Jarrod Washburn, lhp, University of Wisconsin-Oshkosh.—(1998-2009)**
3. Jeremy Blevins, rhp, Sullivan East HS, Bristol, Tenn.—(AAA)
4. **Brian Cooper, rhp, University of Southern California.—(1999-2005)**
5. **Justin Baughman, ss, Lewis & Clark (Ore.) College.—(1998-2000)**
6. Ryan Kane, 3b, Presbyterian (S.C.) College.
7. *Chris Pine, rhp, Tualatin (Ore.) HS.
8. Brian Scutero, rhp, University of Central Florida.
9. Jason Stockstill, lhp, Katella HS, Anaheim, Calif.
10. Brandon McGuire, rhp-ss, Coahoma HS, Big Spring, Texas.
11. Danny Buxbaum, 1b, University of Miami.
12. Kyle Wagner, c, Wake Forest University.

DRAFT DROP *Twin brother of Bret Wagner, first-round draft pick, Cardinals (1994)*

13. Jon Vander Griend, of, University of Washington.
14. Josh Deakman, rhp, Arizona State University.
15. *Daren Hooper, of, Aragon HS, San Mateo, Calif.
16. *Mario Iglesias, rhp, Stanford University.
17. +Michael Hughes, rhp, Fresno (Calif.) CC.
18. ***Greg Jones, c-rhp, Seminole (Fla.) HS.—(2003-07)**
19. Jed Dalton, 3b-of, University of Nebraska.
20. Bryan Graves, c, Southern University.
21. *Donnell Tate, ss-c, Oakland (Calif.) HS.
22. Jim O'Quinn, lhp, Florida CC-Jacksonville.
23. *Greg Millichap, of, Serra HS, Woodside, Calif.
24. Gar Vallone, ss, UCLA.
25. John Romero, rhp, Mission (Calif.) JC.
26. Randy Betten, 2b, Arizona State University.
27. Tommy Darrell, rhp, Garrett (Md.) CC.
28. Alex Llanos, 2b, Lola Rodriguez de Tio HS, Carolina, P.R.
29. *Scott Prather, lhp, Lassiter HS, Marietta, Ga.
30. John McAninch, c, Lewis-Clark State (Idaho) College.
31. Ty Bilderback, of, University of Arkansas.
32. +E.J. t'Hoen, ss, Indian River (Fla.) CC.
33. ***Robb Quinlan, ss, Hill-Murray HS, Maplewood, Minn.—(2003-10)**

DRAFT DROP *Brother of Tom Quinlan, major leaguer (1990-96)*

34. *David Bittler, lhp, Florida CC.
35. *Derrick Vargas, lhp, Newark Memorial HS, Newark, Calif.
36. *Doug Hurst, rhp, Okaloosa-Walton (Fla.) CC.
37. *Mike Gauger, lhp, Wakulla HS, St. Marks, Fla.
38. *Bobby Bystrowski, 3b-of, Jesuit HS, Fair Oaks, Calif.
39. *Jake Jensen, ss-2b, Washington Union HS, Fresno, Calif.
40. Steve Mikesell, c, Glendale (Calif.) JC.
41. *Doug Blackman, c, Warren Easton HS, New Orleans, La.
42. *John Opina, ss, La Sierra HS, Riverside, Calif.
43. *Michael Clarke, rhp, St. Petersburg (Fla.) JC.
44. Esteban Barrios, of, Miami-Dade CC New World Center.
45. *Widd Workman, rhp-of, Brigham Young University.
46. *Antonio Diaz, ss, Gulf Coast (Fla.) CC.
47. *Sterling Bullock, 3b, Carson HS, Compton, Calif.
48. *Matt Koziara, rhp, Franklin (Pa.) HS.
49. Derek Ryder, c, Penn State University.
50. David Farfan, rhp, Fresno State University.
51. *Stanisles James, of, Shanks HS, Quincy, Fla.
52. Joel Katte, 3b, North HS, Sheboygan, Wis.
53. *Khalif Jefferson, ss, Serra HS, Compton, Calif.
54. *Javier Baretti, c, Elisa Pascual HS, Caguas, P.R.
55. *Fernando Sordo, rhp, Spanish River HS, Boca Raton, Fla.
56. *Eddie Marquez, 2b-ss, Pasco-Hernando (Fla.) CC.
57. *Steve Maris, ss-2b, Oak Hall HS, Gainesville, Fla.

DRAFT DROP *Grandson of Roger Maris, major leaguer (1957-68)*

58. *Moses Herrera, rhp, Colton (Calf.) HS.
59. *Jason Townsell, rhp, Marianna (Fla.) HS.
60. *Kurt Bultmann, ss-2b, Seminole HS, Largo, Fla.

## CHICAGO CUBS (4)

1. **Kerry Wood, rhp, Grand Prairie (Texas) HS.—(1998-2012)**
2. **Brian McNichol, lhp, James Madison University.—(1999)**
3. Jeff Yoder, rhp, Pottsville Area (Pa.) HS.—(AA)
4. ***Adam Everett, ss, Harrison HS, Marietta, Ga.—(2001-11)**

DRAFT DROP *Attended North Carolina State; re-drafted by Red Sox, 1998 (1st round)*

5. **Ismael Villegas, rhp, Margarita Janer HS, Guaynabo, P.R.—(2000)**
6. Tony Ellison, of, North Carolina State University.
7. Dorian Speed, of, Florida International University.

DRAFT DROP *Son of Horace Speed, major leaguer (1975-79)*

8. Denny Bair, rhp, Northeast Louisiana University.

9. Chad Ricketts, rhp, Polk (Fla.) CC.
10. Kasey Pressley, 1b, Dr. Phillips HS, Orlando, Fla.
11. Matt Hammons, rhp, Mission Bay HS, San Diego.
12. Barret Markey, rhp, St. Petersburg (Fla.) HS.
13. Terry Joseph, of, Northwestern State University.
14. Don Kinnie, of, Livingston (Ala.) University.
15. Kris Stading, lhp, Trevor G. Browne HS, Phoenix.
16. Brian Conley, ss-2b, Volunteer State (Tenn.) JC.
17. *Chris Moller, 1b, University of Alabama.
18. Jerry Connell, of, Colonial HS, Avenel, N.J.
19. Buck Gordon, c, Bridgewater (Va.) College.
**20. Chris Booker, rhp, Monroe County HS, Monroeville, Ala.—(2005-07)**
21. Brandon Hammack, rhp, University of Texas-San Antonio.
22. +Andrew Mallory, rhp, Dixie Hollins HS, St. Petersburg, Fla. / Edison (Fla.) CC.
23. Jim Putko, 1b, University of Akron.
24. Kevin Bentley, of, University of Southern Mississippi.
25. *Dax Norris, c, University of Alabama.
26. Brian Greene, rhp, Indiana University.
27. Tim Mosley, rhp, University of Arkansas.
28. Scott Vieira, c, University of Tennessee.
29. Ashanti McDonald, ss-of, Olivet Nazarene (Ill.) University.
30. John McNeese, lhp, University of Mississippi.
31. Ron Licciardi, lhp, University of Connecticut-Avery Point JC.
32. Tom Maleski, 3b-c, University of Houston.
33. Jason Martino, rhp, Voorhees HS, Pittstown, N.J.
34. Ryan Seidel, of, Southern California College.
35. *Chris Humpert, of, Arcadia (Calif.) HS.
36. *Robert Kern, of, Central HS, Cape Girardeau, Mo.
37. *Mark Taylor, lhp, Rice University.
38. *Casey Burns, rhp, Hopewell Valley Central HS, Trenton, N.J.
39. *Greg Strickland, of, Volunteer State (Tenn.) CC.
40. +Brandon Ward, rhp, Cerro Coso (Calif.) JC.
41. *Daniel Mooney, c, Monsignor Donovan HS, Forked River, N. J.
42. *Michael Smosna, rhp, Burroughs HS, Ridgecrest, Calif.
43. *Dave Phillips, 2b, Gloucester (N.J.) CC.
44. *David Kelly, rhp, Leon HS, Tallahassee, Fla.
45. *Tim Currens, of, Volunteer State (Tenn.) CC.
46. *Lance Haver, c, Molalla Union HS, Molalla, Ore.
47. Mickey Perez, 2b, University of Texas-San Antonio.
48. *Brett Cornwell, rhp, Hobbs (N.M.) HS.
49. *Jerry Zaffis, rhp, Eustis HS, Mount Dora, Fla.
50. *Aaron Anthony, 3b, Middle Georgia JC.
51. +Chris Grubbs, c, West Orange HS, Ocoee, Fla. / Okaloosa-Walton (Fla.) CC.
52. *Jack Koch, rhp, Miami-Dade CC North.
53. *John Ogden, c, Palm Beach (Fla.) JC.
54. *Arturo Mata, ss-2b, New Mexico JC.
**55. Justin Speier, c, Nicholls State University.—(1998-2009)**

DRAFT DROP *Son of Chris Speier, major leaguer (1971-89)*

56. *Scott Stephens, lhp, Manatee (Fla.) JC.
57. *Steven Bechard, rhp, Onieda (N.Y.) HS
58. *Seth Spiker, c, Blinn (Texas) JC.
59. *Bobby Sprague, c, Queen of Peace HS, North Arlington, N.J.
60. *Ryan Fuller, rhp, Monroe (N.Y.) CC.
61. *Kris Williams, rhp, Westfield (N. J.) HS.

## CHICAGO WHITE SOX (25)

**1. Jeff Liefer, 3b, Long Beach State University.—(1999-2005)**
**2. Brian Simmons, of, University of Michigan.—(1998-2001)**
**3. *J.J. Putz, rhp, Trenton (Mich.) HS.—(2003-14)**

DRAFT DROP *Attended Michigan; re-drafted by Twins, 1998 (17th round)*

4. Ryan Topham, of, University of Notre Dame.—(AA)
5. Tighe Brown, rhp, St. Xavier HS, Louisville, Ky.—(AA)
6. Craig Hunt, lhp, Ohio University.
7. Jason Lakman, rhp, Woodinville (Wash.) HS.
8. Adam Virchis, rhp, San Diego State University.
9. Jason Secoda, rhp, Cal State Los Angeles.
10. Chuck Klee, ss, Cardinal Gibbons HS, Fort Lauderdale, Fla.

TENNESSEE BASEBALL

Todd Helton became a Rockies franchise cornerstone, spending his entire career in Colorado

**11. Kevin Beirne, rhp, Texas A&M University.—(2000-02)**
12. Daron Hollins, of, Sierra (Calif.) JC.
13. Brian Downs, c, Riverside (Calif.) CC.
14. Tom Buckman, rhp, Edison (Fla.) CC.
15. *Eric Stanton, 1b, Newberry (S.C.) HS.
16. Erik Desrosiers, rhp, Grand Canyon University.
17. Derek Hasselhoff, rhp, Towson State University.
18. Mike Vota, rhp, Towson State University.
19. Jeff Johnson, ss, University of Mississippi.
20. *Chris Beck, of, El Dorado HS, Placentia, Calif.
21. Barry Shelton, 3b, West Virginia State College.
22. Jason Gray, rhp, Coconut Creek (Fla.) HS.
23. Frank Anderson, c, Southern Union State (Ala.) JC.
24. Tim Kraus, rhp, University of Notre Dame.
25. John Strasser, ss, Mesa (Ariz.) CC.
26. Josh Fauske, c, Central Washington University.
27. *Aaron Gentry, ss, Labette (Kan.) CC.
28. Brent Wilhelm, 3b, University of Kansas.
29. Kelly Kruse, rhp, Southwest Missouri State University.
30. Allen Halley, rhp, University of South Alabama.
31. +Brian Bullock, rhp, Itawamba (Miss.) JC.
32. Joel Garber, lhp, University of Nevada-Las Vegas.
33. *Chris Weekly, ss, Highland HS, Gilbert, Ariz.
34. *Eric LeBlanc, rhp, College of St. Rose (N.Y.).
**35. *Nate Robertson, lhp, Maize (Kan.) HS.—(2002-10)**
36. *Aaron Randle, 2b-ss, Northeast HS, Fort Lauderdale, Fla.
37. Darren Hayes, of, Wingate (N.C.) College.
**38. *Steve Sparks, rhp, Faulkner State (Ala.) JC.—(2000)**
39. *Andrew Tellez, of, Fullerton (Calif.) JC.
40. *Matt Howe, ss, Mayde Creek HS, Houston.

DRAFT DROP *Son of Art Howe, major leaguer (1974-85); major league manager (1989-2004)*

41. *Keeron Clarke, of-2b, South Plantation HS, Plantation, Fla.
42. Pete Demorejon, rhp, University of Miami.
43. *Justin Rayment, lhp, San Diego State University.
44. *David Harden, lhp, Allen County (Kan.) CC.
45. Jason Fennell, of, Baldwin HS, Pittsburgh.
46. *Nestor Gonzales, c, Rio Grande HS, Albuquerque, N.M.
47. *David Hostetter, of, Fannett Metal HS, Fort Loudoun, Pa.
48. *Brian Thrash, of, Rising Sun HS, Elkton, Md.
49. *Kris Conrad, rhp, Killian HS, Miami.
50. *Wade Sterling, c, Allen County (Kan.) CC.
51. Brian Bowness, 1b-3b, Villanova University.
52. *Peter Rodriguez, of, Broward (Fla.) JC.
53. Manny Lutz, 3b, Southwestern (Calif.) JC.
54. *Mike Biasucci, 2b, South Broward HS, Hollywood, Fla.

## CINCINNATI REDS (24)

1. (Choice to Red Sox as compensation for Type B free agent Damon Berryhill)
**2. Brett Tomko, rhp, Florida Southern College.—(1997-2011)**
3. Andre Montgomery, ss, Pleasure Ridge Park HS, Louisville, Ky.—(Low A)
**4. Mark Corey, rhp, Edinboro (Pa.) University.—(2001-04)**
**5. Jason LaRue, c, Dallas Baptist University.—(1999-2010)**
6. Andy Burress, c, Telfair County HS, McRae, Ga.
7. Herb Goodman, of, North Greenville (S.C.) JC.
**8. Ray King, lhp, Lambuth (Tenn.) University.—(1999-2008)**
9. *Bobby Walters, of, Sallisaw (Okla.) HS.
10. Ben Bailey, rhp, Glen Oaks (Mich.) CC.
11. Rich Lawrence, rhp, University of Central Florida.
**12. Justin Atchley, lhp, Texas A&M University.—(2001)**
13. *Michael Daniel, rhp, John A. Calhoun (Ala.) CC.
14. *Larfayette Stanley, rhp, Jordan HS, Columbus, Ga.
15. Anthony Patellis, 3b, Kent State University.
**16. Lance Davis, lhp, Lake Gibson HS, Lakeland, Fla.—(2001)**
17. Todd Fehrenbach, c, Citrus HS, Inverness, Fla.
18. Justin Marine, rhp, Moorpark (Calif.) JC.
19. Eric Mapp, of, Lamar University.
20. James Davis, c, Western Kentucky University.
21. *Jason Johnson, of, Montclair (Calif.) HS.
22. Gene Mattox, rhp, Florida CC.
23. Tony Cloud, rhp, Spartanburg Methodist (S.C.) JC.
**24. Jeff Sparks, rhp, St. Mary's (Texas) University.—(1999-2000)**
25. Stephen Claybrook, of, Texas A&M University.
26. David Guthrie, ss, North Carolina State University.
27. Steve Goodhart, 2b, Ohio Wesleyan University.
**28. *Andy Tracy, 1b, Bowling Green State University.—(2000-09)**
29. Jason Parsons, 1b, Dallas Baptist University.
**30. *Rob Mackowiak, ss-2b, South Suburban (Ill.) JC.—(2001-08)**
31. *Brian Willman, rhp, University of North Carolina.
**32. Scott MacRae, rhp, Valdosta State (Ga.) University.—(2001)**
33. *Zach Frachiseur, rhp, Rockdale County HS, Conyers, Ga.
34. Lamont Mason, 2b-ss, Lubbock Christian (Texas) University.
35. *Jeffery Juarez, of, New Braunfels (Texas) HS.
36. Will Schleuss, lhp, University of Alabama.
37. Tom Scott, of, Linfield (Ore.) College.
38. *Jason Hubbard, lhp, Angelina (Texas) JC.
39. *Brian Loyd, c, Cal State Fullerton.
40. Chris Murphy, lhp, University of Cincinnati.
41. Scott Wright, rhp, Missouri Southern State University.
42. Joe Montgomery, rhp, Jacksonville State University.
43. *Chad Truby, 3b, Yavapai (Ariz.) JC.
44. Dwayne Cushman, rhp, Valdosta State (Ga.) University.

## CLEVELAND INDIANS (23)

1. David Miller, 1b, Clemson University.—(AAA)
**2. Sean Casey, 1b, University of Richmond.—(1997-2008)**
3. Chad Whitaker, of, St. Thomas Aquinas HS, Fort Lauderdale, Fla.—(AA)

DRAFT DROP *Son of Steve Whitaker, major leaguer (1966-70)*

4. Scott Harrison, rhp, John Swett HS, Pinole, Calif.—(Low A)
5. Scott Schultz, rhp, Louisiana State University.—(Short-season A)
6. Jake Messner, of, Rio Americana HS, Sacramento, Calif.
7. Scott Morgan, of, Gonzaga University.
8. Tim Jorgensen, ss, University of Wisconsin-Oshkosh.

DRAFT DROP *Brother of Terry Jorgensen, major leaguer (1989-93)*

**9. Mike Edwards, ss, Mechanicsburg (Pa.) Area HS.—(2003-06)**
10. Jason Bennett, rhp, Shippensburg (Pa.) University.
11. Jewell Williams, of, Las Vegas (Nev.) HS.
12. Brett Merrick, lhp, University of Washington.
13. Frankie Sanders, rhp, Pasco Hernando (Fla.) CC.
**14. Scott Winchester, rhp, Clemson University.—(1997-2001)**
15. Darren Loudermilk, rhp, Oklahoma City University.
16. *Luis Estrella, rhp, Rancho Santiago (Calif.) JC.
17. Terry Harvey, rhp, North Carolina State University.
18. Keith Horn, rhp, Arkansas State University.
19. Jason Minici, of, Long Beach State University.
20. Marc Deschenes, ss, University of Massachusetts-Lowell.
**21. Mark Budzinski, of, University of Richmond.—(2003)**
**22. Mike Glavine, 1b, Northeastern University.—(2003)**

DRAFT DROP *Brother of Tom Glavine, major leaguer*

*(1987-2008) • Baseball coach, Northeastern (2015)*
23. Jon Edwards, rhp, Whitman (Wash.) College.
24. Ken Wagner, rhp, Florida Atlantic University.
**25. Jason Rakers, rhp, New Mexico State University.—(1998-2000)**
26. *Frank Chapman, rhp, San Jacinto (Texas) CC.
27. +Gary Rodriguez, of, Seminole (Okla.) JC.
28. *Michael Bishop, of-c, Willis (Texas) HS.
DRAFT DROP *Quarterback, National Football League (2000)*
29. *Corey Richardson, of, Daingerfield HS, Lone Star, Texas.
30. Jason Adge, rhp, University of Miami.
31. Richy Gonzalez, c, University of Miami.
32. *Michael Custer, rhp, Linn-Benton (Ore.) CC.
33. Nathan Coats, c, San Francisco CC.
**34. *Jamie Brown, rhp, West Lauderdale HS, Meridian, Miss.—(2004)**
35. Bryan Hardy, 1b, Martin HS, Arlington, Texas.
36. Jerry Taylor, of, University of Texas.
37. Chad Thornhill, ss, Cal State Northridge.
38. Ross Atkins, rhp, Wake Forest University.
DRAFT DROP *General manager, Blue Jays (2015)*
39. *Thomas Blythe, c, North Little Rock (Ark.) HS.
**40. *Randy Keisler, lhp, Navarro (Texas) JC.—(2000-07)**
41. +Mike Spiegel, lhp, Sacramento (Calif.) CC.
42. *Dennis Martinez Jr., rhp, St. Thomas (Fla.) University.
DRAFT DROP *Son of Dennis Martinez, major leaguer (1976-98)*
**43. Cody Ransom, ss, South Mountain (Ariz.) CC.—(2001-13)**
44. +Albert Garza, rhp, Wapato (Wash.) HS / Walla Walla (Wash.) CC.
45. *Kirk Irvine, rhp, Rancho Santiago (Calif.) JC.
46. *Rex Crosnoe, c, Southeast Missouri State University.
47. Sammie Mathis, rhp, Southern Arkansas University.
48. *Ryan Bailey, rhp, Rancho Bernardo HS, San Diego.
49. *Brian Anderson, rhp, East Tennessee State University.
50. *Peter Lopez, rhp, Central HS, Manchester, N.H.
51. Tony Fleetwood, lhp, Oklahoma State University.
52. *Michael Ploharz, rhp, Clovis (Calif.) HS.
53. *Kevin Eberwein, rhp, Green Valley HS, Henderson, Nev.
54. *Damien Kolb, of, Capital HS, Olympia, Wash.
55. *Brandon Driggers, rhp, Whitehouse (Texas) HS.

## COLORADO ROCKIES (8)

**1. Todd Helton, 1b-lhp, University of Tennessee.—(1997-2013)**
**2. Ben Petrick, c, Glencoe HS, Hillsboro, Ore.—(1999-2003)**
3. Chris Macca, rhp, St. Leo (Fla.) College.—(AA)
4. John Clark, ss, Samuel Clemens HS, Schertz, Texas.—(Short-season A)
5. Mike Vavrek, rhp, Lewis (Ill.) University.—(AAA)
6. Chandler Martin, rhp, University of Portland.
7. Cristy Rosa, rhp, Aurea E. Quiles HS, Guanica, P.R.
8. Tal Light, 3b, Oklahoma State University.
9. Jamie Emiliano, rhp, Florida International University.
10. Gary Gordon, of, Willingboro (N.J.) HS.
**11. Scott Randall, rhp, Santa Barbara (Calif.) CC.—(2003)**
12. Brian Kirkpatrick, ss, King City (Calif.) HS.
**13. John Lindsey, 1b, Hattiesburg (Miss.) HS.—(2010)**
14. Pat Williams, rhp, Mount San Antonio (Calif.) JC.
15. John Mahlberg, rhp, Douglas HS, Dillard, Ga.
16. Chris Druckery, rhp, Kankakee (Ill.) JC.
17. Garrett Neubart, of, Columbia University.
18. Heath Bost, rhp, Catawba (N.C.) College.
19. John Clifford, c, Villanova University.
20. Bobby Bevel, lhp, Xavier University.
21. Blake Barthol, c, Eastern Kentucky University.
22. David Groseclose, ss, Virginia Military Institute.
**23. David Lee, rhp, Mercyhurst (Pa.) College.—(1999-2004)**
24. Gilbert Vidal, c, Miami-Dade CC New World Center.
25. Reggie Douglas, rhp, Dorsey HS, Los Angeles.
26. Matt Whitley, ss, University of Tennessee.
27. *J.J. Moore, rhp, Burnsville (Minn.) HS.
28. *Rodney Nye, 3b, Cameron (Okla.) HS.
29. Marc Brzozoski, of, Shorter (Ga.) College.
30. Brett Elam, ss, McNeese State University.
31. Sean Murphy, rhp, University of North Carolina.
32. Brad Reitzenstein, rhp, University of Portland.
33. David Feuerstein, of, Yale University.
**34. *Ryan Kohlmeier, rhp, Chase County HS, Cottonwood Falls, Kan.—(2000-01)**
35. *Brian Bowman, c, Garces Memorial HS, Bakersfield, Calif.
36. *Jeremy Jones c, Raymore Peculiar HS, Raymore, Mo.
37. *Josh Kalinowski, lhp, Natrona County HS, Casper, Wyo.
38. *Scott Brent of, Linden (Calif.) HS.
39. *Matt Montgomery, rhp, Rancho Santiago (Calif.) CC.
40. *Brandon Lenox, ss, Red Mountain HS, Mesa. Ariz.
41. *Jason Pozo, rhp, Ocean County (N.J.) CC.
42. *Terrell Merriman, of, Cheraw (S.C.) HS.
43. *Anthony Taylor, rhp, Pueblo HS, Tucson, Ariz.
44. *Derek Corbett, rhp, Highland HS, Higley, Ariz.
45. *Mike Medina, c, Moody HS, Corpus Christi, Texas.
46. +Brad Schwartzbauer, c-3b, White Bear Lake (Minn.) Area HS / Iowa Central CC.
47. *Ali Samadani, rhp, CC of Marin (Calif.).
48. +Kent Zweifel, 1b, Henley HS, Klamath Falls, Ore. / Mount Hood (Ore.) CC.
49. Justin Drizos, 1b, University of Nevada-Reno.
50. +Andres Mitchell, ss, Motlow State (Tenn.) CC.
51. *Roddy Friar, c, Temecula Valley HS, Temecula, Calif.
52. +Chris Rodriguez, c, Modesto (Calif.) JC.
53. *Casey Kelley, 1b, Ellensburg (Wash.) HS.
54. *Dan Ledesma, ss, Moody HS, Corpus Christi, Texas.
55. *Derek Sawyer, ss, Paradise Valley HS, Phoenix.
56. *James Slaughter, of, San Joaquin Delta (Calif.) JC.
57. *John Garrison, rhp, San Joaquin Delta (Calif.) JC.
58. *Gabriel Foster, rhp, Santa Rosa (Calif.) JC.

## DETROIT TIGERS (11)

1. Mike Drumright, rhp, Wichita State University.—(AAA)
**2. Brian Powell, rhp, University of Georgia.—(1998-2004)**
3. *Chuck Crowder, lhp, Crestwood HS, Mantua, Ohio.—(AA)
DRAFT DROP *Attended Georgia Tech; re-drafted by Pirates, 1998 (8th round)*
4. Clay Bruner, rhp, Weatherford (Okla.) HS.—(AA)
5. Rosario Ortiz, rhp, Arizona Western JC.—(Short-season A)
6. Jeremiah Lignitz, c, Davison (Mich.) HS.
7. Chris Manser, rhp-of, Hillsborough HS, Tampa.
8. Scott Weaver, of, University of Michigan.
9. *Ron Marietta, lhp, Bishop Ford Central Catholic HS, Brooklyn, N.Y.
10. John Foran, rhp, University of Central Florida.
**11. Dave Borkowski, rhp, Sterling Heights (Mich.) HS.—(1999-2008)**
12. Jason Lawrie, rhp, Independence HS, San Jose, Calif.
13. *Kevin Jordan, ss, Robert E. Lee HS, Midland, Texas.
14. *Steve Hartsburg, ss, Schaumburg (Ill.) HS.
**15. *Justin Lehr, rhp-c, West Covina (Calif.) HS.—(2004-09)**
**16. *Mark Hendricksen, lhp, Washington State University.—(2002-11)**
DRAFT DROP *Forward, National Basketball Association (1996-2000)*
17. Craig Caballero, c, Grand Canyon University.
18. Brian Fuller, c, Northwestern University.
19. *Lawyer Milloy, of, U of Washington.
DRAFT DROP *Defensive back, National Football League (1996-2010)*
20. Ron Rojas, 2b, Northwestern University.
21. *Clint Bryant, 3b, Texas Tech.
22. *J.P. Webb, c, University of Texas.
23. Jay Waggoner, 1b-of, Auburn University.
24. Peter Durkovic, lhp, Fordham University.
25. Richard Gray, of, Embry-Riddle Aeronautical (Fla.) University.
**26. *Eric Valent, of, Canyon HS, Anaheim, Calif.—(2001-05)**
DRAFT DROP *First-round draft choice (42nd overall), Phillies (1998)*
**27. *Matt Thornton, lhp, Centerville HS, Sturgis, Mich.—(2004-15)**
DRAFT DROP *First-round draft choice (22nd overall), Mariners (1998)*
28. Clausel Milord, of, New York Tech.
29. Mike Miller, 3b, Hofstra University.
30. *Jason Haynie, lhp, University of South Carolina.
31. *Darrell Hussman, rhp, Quartz Hill HS, Lancaster, Calif.
32. Derek Mitchell, ss, Triton (Ill.) JC.
33. Derek Kopacz, 3b, Triton (Ill.) JC.
34. *Luke Bonner, rhp, Divine Child HS, Dearborn, Mich.
35. *Chris Clark, of, University of Arkansas.
36. Nate Shipman, c, River Ridge HS, New Port Richey, Fla.
37. *Greg Sprehn, rhp, Bangor (Wis.) HS.
38. *John Kremer, rhp, Bishop Chatard HS, Indianapolis, Ind.
39. *Josh Davis, rhp, Pensacola (Fla.) Catholic HS.
40. *Mike Davis, ss, Vocational HS, Chicago.
41. *Phil Rosengren, rhp, Rye Day HS, Rye, N.Y.
42. *Mike Whiteman, lhp, Potomac State (W.Va.) JC.
**43. *Robert Fick, c, Cal State Northridge.—(1998-2007)**
**44. *Jeremy Giambi, of, Cal State Fullerton.—(1998-2003)**
DRAFT DROP *Brother of Jason Giambi, major leaguer (1995-2014)*
45. *Errick Lowe, of, Lake Worth (Fla.) HS.
46. Doug Engleka, ss, Ohio University.
47. *Pedro Flores, lhp, Sierra Vista HS, Baldwin Park, Calif.
48. *Brian Justine, lhp, William T. Dwyer HS, Palm Beach Lakes, Fla.
49. +Judd Van Winkle, lhp, Spartanburg Methodist (S.C.) JC.
50. *Jose Nunez, 2b, Northeast Texas CC.
51. *Greg Ryan, lhp, Divine Child HS, Dearborn, Mich.
52. *Maurice Watkins, rhp, Prosser HS, Chicago.
53. *Bryan Houston, of, Escambia HS, Pensacola, Fla.
54. *Chad Cook, rhp, Fallbrook (Calif.) HS.
**55. *Mark Mulder, 1b-lhp, Thornwood HS, South Holland, Ill.—(2000-08)**
DRAFT DROP *First-round draft pick (2nd overall), Athletics (1998)*
56. Joe McFarlane, rhp, Anacortes (Wash.) HS.
**57. Gabe Kapler, 3b, Moorpark (Calif.) JC.—(1998-2010)**
58. Brian Cummins, lhp, Northwestern University.
59. David Reinfelder, lhp, Michigan State University.

## FLORIDA MARLINS (6)

1. Jaime Jones, of, Rancho Bernardo HS, San Diego.—(AAA)
**2. Nate Rolison, 1b, Petal (Miss.) HS.—(2000)**
**3. Randy Winn, of, Santa Clara University.—(1998-2010)**
4. Mike Marriott, rhp, Spring (Texas) HS.—(High A)
5. Rene Rascon, of, Sonoma State (Calif.) University.—(High A)
**6. Michael Tejera, lhp, Southwest HS, Miami.—(1999-2005)**
**7. Hansel Izquierdo, rhp, Southwest HS, Miami.—(2002)**
**8. *Mark Watson, lhp, Clemson University.—(2000-03)**
9. Tony Enard, rhp, Fresno State University.
10. Bob Pailthorpe, rhp, Santa Clara University.
**11. +Gary Knotts, rhp, Brewer HS, Somerville, Ala. / Northwest Shoals (Ala.) CC.—(2001-04)**
12. Jon Widerski, rhp, Academy of the Holy Angels, Richfield, Minn.
**13. *Jerrod Riggan, rhp, San Diego State University.—(2000-03)**
14. David Miller, rhp, University of North Carolina-Wilmington.
15. Rick Garcia, rhp, Oklahoma City University.
**16. Gabe Gonzalez, rhp, Long Beach State University.—(1998)**
17. Steve Goodell, ss, Arizona State University.
18. Rex Burgus, lhp, University of San Diego.
**19. Mike Duvall, lhp, Potomac State (W.Va.) JC.—(1998-2001)**
20. Mat Erwin, c, University of Nevada-Reno.
21. Joe Funaro, 2b, Eastern Connecticut State College.
22. Swan Austin, rhp, Douglasville, Ga.
23. +Alex Morris, rhp, Westlake HS, Austin, Texas / San Jacinto (Texas) JC.
24. *Jim Detwiler, lhp, Valley Forge Military Academy, Pottsville, Pa.
25. *Kevin Fitzmaurice, rhp, Silver Creek HS, San Jose, Calif.
26. *Ryan Tack, rhp, Durango HS, Las Vegas, Nev.
27. *David Therneau, rhp, Navarro (Texas) JC.
28. *Jorge Rodriguez, ss, Adolfo Gram Rivera HS, Penuelas, P.R.
29. Gary Santoro, rhp, Flagler (Fla.) College.
30. Euclides Rojas, rhp, Palm Springs/Western League.
31. *Mike Rose, rhp, Southwood HS, Shreveport, La.
32. *George Oleksik, rhp, Middle Tennessee State University.
33. *Todd Bramble, ss, Sprague HS, Salem, Ore.
34. *Kevin Green, of, Mohawk Valley (N.Y.) CC.
35. Jason Shanahan, 3b, Cal State Northridge.
36. +Tim McClaskey, rhp, Muscatine (Iowa) CC.
**37. *Brian Dallimore, 2b, Stanford University.—(2004-05)**
38. *Ken Duebelbeis, lhp, De Anza (Calif.) JC.
39. *Dion Battee, of, St. Bernard HS, Los Angeles.
**40. *Matt Blank, lhp, Galveston (Texas) JC.—(2000-01)**
41. *Dwaine Neal, of, Norland HS, Miami.
42. *Letarvius Copeland, of, Jackson HS, Miami.
43. Shannon Stephens, rhp, Cal Poly San Luis Obispo.
44. Jason Garrett, 1b, University of Texas-Arlington.
DRAFT DROP *Son of Adrian Garrett, major leaguer (1966-76)*
45. Rob Hernandez, c, Oklahoma State University.
46. *Jeff Cermak, of, Mesa (Ariz.) CC.
47. *Rhett Ingerick, rhp, Davidson College.
48. Raymond Green, c, Sonoma State (Calif.) University.
49. *Rafael Riguiero, rhp, North HS, Riverside, Calif.
50. *William Reed, of, Westchester HS, Inglewood, Calif.
51. +Aaron Cames, rhp, Sacramento (Calif.) CC.
52. *Scott McKee, c, Riverdale Baptist HS, Bowie, Md.
53. *Kerthatis Lovely, of, Glades Central HS, South Bay, Fla.
54. *Howard Bell, rhp, Westchester HS, Los Angeles.
55. *Darin Baker, of, Fallon (Nev.) HS.
56. *Carl Jones, of, Andress HS, El Paso, Texas.
57. *Joel Atwater, of, Southern Alamance HS, Graham, N.C.
58. *Richard Circuit, ss, La Jolla (Calif.) HS.
59. *Mark Greenlee, lhp, Triton (Ill.) JC.
60. *Will Fleck, rhp, Mercer County (N.J.) CC.
61. *Scott Esker, 3b, JC of the Redwoods (Calif.).
62. *Michael Laine, rhp, Connally HS, Waco, Texas.
63. *Druen Mahony, ss, Hillcrest HS, Fountain Inn, S.C.
64. +Quincy Foster, of, Spartanburg Methodist (S.C.) JC.
65. *James Nederostek, lhp, St. Mary's HS, Lodi, Calif.
**66. *Robby Hammock, c, South Cobb HS, Marietta, Ga.—(2003-11)**
67. *Matt Pidgeon, ss, Eureka (Calif.) HS.
68. Andy Bair, lhp, Calvert Hall HS, Towson, Md.
69. *Jason Berry, rhp, Mountain View HS, Orem, Utah.
70. *Bill Tull, rhp, Gloucester County (N.J.) CC.
71. *Derek Rowen, of, Mesa (Ariz.) CC.
72. *William Boughey, rhp, Berkmar HS, Lawrenceville, Ga.
73. *Jay Gospodarek, rhp, Pima (Ariz.) JC.
74. *Stephen Blevins, 1b, Spotsylvania (Va.) HS.
75. *Kevin Tolan, rhp, Citrus (Calif.) JC.
76. *Dusty Keppen, rhp, Central Gwinnett HS, Lawrenceville, Ga.
77. *Eric Kalie, ss, Martin County HS, Stuart, Fla.
78. *Brett Schreyer, rhp, Paul VI HS, Waterford, N.J.
79. *Joel Sajiun, of, Miami Springs HS, Hialeah, Fla.
80. *Timothy Hicks, of, Gordon (Ga.) JC.
81. *Shannon Carter, rhp, Gate City (Va.) HS.

82. *Brian Bush, of, Howland HS, Warren, Ohio.
83. (selection voided)
84. *Ryan Roberts, ss, Brigham Young University.
85. *Andrew Lecrone, 3b, Downers Grove North HS, Downers Grove, Ill.
86. *John Schmitz, of, JC of San Mateo (Calif.).
87. *Brian Haught, ss, Jesuit HS, Tampa.

## HOUSTON ASTROS (22)

1. **Tony McKnight, rhp, Arkansas HS, Texarkana, Ark.—(2000-01)**
2. Eric Ireland, rhp, Millikan HS, Long Beach, Calif.—(AAA)
3. Chad Alexander, of, Texas A&M University.—(AAA)
4. **Brian Sikorski, rhp, Western Michigan University.—(2000-06)**
5. **Mike Rose, c, Jesuit HS, Sacramento, Calif.—(2004-06)**
6. Scott Chapman, c, Alexander HS, Albany, Ohio.
7. Jason McCarter, rhp, Monterey Peninsula (Calif.) JC.
8. Eric Smith, rhp, Butler County (Kan.) CC.
9. Jason Adams, ss, Wichita State University.
10. Jeremy DeShazer, of, Lake Washington HS, Kirkland, Wash.
11. Ric Johnson, of, Indiana State University.
12. Eric Stachler, rhp, Bowling Green State University.
13. Marlon Mejia, ss, Westchester (N.Y.) CC.
14. **Barry Wesson, of, Brandon HS, Pearl, Miss.—(2002-03)**
15. Mike Corominas, lhp, Arizona State University.
16. *Aaron Vincent, rhp, Porterville (Calif.) JC.
17. *Charles Wheeler, lhp, Connors State (Okla.) JC.
18. *Derek Wallace, of, Neville HS, Monroe, La.
19. **Aaron Miles, 2b, Antioch (Calif.) HS.—(2003-11)**
20. Eric Cole, 3b, Antelope Valley (Calif.) JC.
21. *David Huggins, rhp, Galveston (Texas) CC.
22. *Shawn Sonnier, rhp, Chipola (Fla.) JC.
23. Nelson Ubaldo, of, University of Massachusetts.
24. **Jeriome Robertson, lhp, Exeter Union HS, Exeter, Calif.—(2002-04)**
25. Andy Bovender, 3b, University of North Carolina-Charlotte.
26. *Jimmy Alarcon, rhp, Jupiter (Fla.) Community HS.
27. +Aaron McNeal, 1b, Castro Valley (Calif.) HS / Chabot (Calif.) JC.
28. *Adrian Taylor, ss, Oakland Tech HS, Oakland.
29. *Troy Stoppa, lhp, Havre (Mon.) HS.
30. *Robert Porter, lhp, McComb (Miss.) HS.
31. *Caleb Brown, lhp, Howard (Texas) JC.
32. **+Tim Hamulack, of-lhp, Edgewood (Md.) HS / Montgomery (Md.) CC.—(2005-06)**
33. Gregg Smyth, lhp, Rollins (Fla.) College.
34. *Bryan King, rhp, Brawley Union HS, Brawley, Calif.
35. ***Eric Eckenstahler, lhp, Antioch HS, Lindenhurst, Ill.—(2002-03)**
36. *Brian Moon, c, Newton County HS, Mansfield, Ga.
37. *Javier Contreras, rhp, La Providencia HS, Rio Piedras, P.R.
38. *Scott Sandusky, c, Seward County (Kan.) CC.
39. Corbett Leonard, c, Spring Grove (Pa.) HS.
40. Ryan Coe, c, Kennesaw State College.
41. *Marty Godwin, of, Osceola HS, Kissimmee, Fla.
42. *Jason Welch, of, Edison (Fla.) CC.
43. Brett Brown, lhp, Delaware Tech & CC.
44. *Stephen Schwartz, rhp, Aurora (Ill.) University.
45. *Brock Ashby, of, St. Francis Xavier HS, Edmonton, Alberta.
46. *Troy Norrell, c, Brazoswood HS, Lake Jackson, Texas.
47. *Mark Burnett, ss, Bryant HS, Benton, Ark.
48. *Luis Ramos, rhp, La Providencia HS, Rio Piedras, P.R.
49. *Walter Harrington, rhp, Palomar (Calif.) JC.
50. *Ryan Channel, lhp, Satellite Beach (Fla.) HS.
51. *Jorge Mesa, c, Braddock HS, Miami.
52. *Ryan Block, rhp, Walla Walla (Wash.) HS.
53. *Corey Hart, 2b, Connors State (Okla.) JC.
54. *Mark Chambers, of, Navarro (Texas) JC.
55. *Stephen Dye, rhp, Middle Georgia JC.
56. *Brian Berryman, rhp, Redford Union HS, Redford, Mich.
57. *Chris Hargett, 1b, Jeffersonville (Ind.) HS.
58. *Juan Rivera, ss, Palm Beach (Fla.) JC.
59. *Chris Meyer, rhp, Dakota Collegiate HS, Winnipeg, Manitoba.
60. *Frank Bludau, rhp, Hallettsville (Texas) HS.
61. *Mark Tomse, lhp, Aurora Central Catholic HS, Aurora, Ill.
62. +Josh Pascarella, rhp, Rancho Bernardo HS, San Diego / Palomar (Calif.) JC.
63. *Adam Bell, c, Helena (Mon.) HS.
64. *James Crossley, 3b, Chabot (Calif.) JC.
65. +Gabe Garcia, c-rhp, James Logan HS, Union City, Calif. / Chabot (Calif.) JC.
66. James Hawkins, rhp, Santa Margarita HS, Laguna Niguel, Calif.
67. *Chris Oldham, c, Sullivan (Mo.) HS.
68. *Brian Jordan, rhp, Gordon (Ga. ) JC.
69. *Blake Ricken, lhp, Fresno (Calif.) CC.
70. *Josh Maloney, rhp, Butte Central HS, Butte, Mon.
71. *Chris Hill, rhp, Long Beach (Calif.) CC.
72. *Mike Meyers, rhp, Annandale HS, Tillsonburg, Ontario.
73. *Chris Castleberry, c, Americus (Ga.) HS.
74. *Peter Fukuhara, of, Canada (Calif.) JC.
75. *Brian Fritz, 1b, Santa Ynez HS, Solvang, Calif.
76. *Roger Foltynowicz, 3b, Lakeside HS, Evans, Ga.
77. *Wayne Chinapen, rhp-of, York Mills Collegiate Institute, Willowdale, Ontario.
78. *Scott Pasonage, rhp, Fullerton (Calif.) JC.
79. *Jason Von Haefen, rhp, Blinn (Texas) JC.
80. *Chris Sheldon, of, Glendale (Calif.) HS.
81. *Darren Brown, rhp, Brophy Prep, Scottsdale, Ariz.
82. *Shawn Jacob, c, Brandon (Miss.) HS.
83. *Bill Eaton, ss-rhp, Indian River (Fla.) CC.
84. *Brain Issett, of, Kimball HS, Royal Oak, Mich.
85. *Charley Carter, 1b, McLennan (Texas) CC.
86. *George Pickard, 1b, Hill (Texas) JC.

## KANSAS CITY ROYALS (19)

1. Juan Lebron, of, Carmen B. Huyke HS, Arroyo, P.R.—(AA)
2. **Carlos Beltran, of, Fernando Callejo HS, Manati, P.R.—(1998-2015)**
3. Doug Blosser, 1b, Sarasota (Fla.) HS.—(Low A)

DRAFT DROP *Died as active player (Jan. 24, 1998) • Brother of Greg Blosser, first-round draft pick, Red Sox (1989); major leaguer (1993-94)*

4. Vic Radcliff, ss, North Augusta (S.C.) HS.—(High A)
5. Steve Medrano, ss, Bishop Amat HS, La Puente, Calif.—(AA)
6. Melvin Dasher, of, Palatka (Fla.) HS.
7. Allen Sanders, rhp, Lee (Texas) JC.
8. Jeff Martin, rhp, Bishop Gorman HS, Las Vegas, Nev.
9. Mike Robbins, lhp, Stanford University.
10. David Moore, rhp, Northeast HS, Oakland Park, Fla.
11. **Mark Quinn, dh-rhp, Rice University.—(1999-2002)**
12. Todd Meady, rhp, Milford Academy, Middlebury, Conn.
13. *Steve Donaghey, rhp, Woburn (Mass.) HS.
14. Tony Penny, rhp, Newberry (S.C.) HS.
15. Matt Saier, rhp, Georgia Tech.
16. Jeremy Williamson, lhp, University of Southern Mississippi.
17. Mark Melito, ss, Wake Forest University.
18. Patrick Hallmark, c, Rice University.
19. *Chad Schroeder, rhp, Northwestern University.
20. Stephen Prihoda, lhp, Sam Houston State University.
21. Alonzo Aguilar, rhp, East Los Angeles JC.
22. James Vida, 1b, Florida Southern College.
23. Randy Paulin, c, University of the Pacific.
24. Tony Miranda, of, Cal State Fullerton.
25. **Jeff Wallace, lhp, Minerva (Ohio) HS.—(1997-2001)**

DRAFT DROP *First 1995 high school draft pick to reach majors (Aug. 21, 1997)*

26. Jon Albrecht, lhp, Kansas State University.
27. Steven Mullis, lhp, Brevard (N.C.) JC.
28. William Hodge, lhp, Jacksonville State University.
29. Emiliano Escandon, ss, Pomona-Pitzer (Calif.) College.
30. Taylor Bales, c, Lee (Texas) JC.
31. Scott Kortmeyer, of, Grand Canyon University.
32. Bret Schafer, of, UCLA.
33. Scott Key, rhp, Pensacola (Fla.) JC.
34. Jesus Liz, lhp, Miami-Dade CC North.
35. Craig Sanders, rhp, University of Nebraska.

DRAFT DROP *Son of John Sanders, major leaguer (1965)*

36. Adam Finnieston, of, University of Miami.
37. Bobby Shannon, lhp, Shippensburg Area (Pa.) HS.
38. *Jeremy Albritton, c, Parklane Academy, Bogue Chitto, Miss.
39. *Brian Wiese, rhp, Central HS, Baton Rouge, La.
40. *Cliff Wilson, 3b, Byrnes HS, Lyman, S.C.
41. *Seth Tate, ss, Wenatchee (Wash.) HS.
42. *Jamison Powers, rhp, Sullivan East HS, Bluff City, Tenn.
43. *Alan Bundy, rhp, E.O. Smith HS, Mansfield, Conn.
44. *Adam Bolthouse, lhp, Spring Lake (Mich.) HS.
45. *Brandon Buckley, c, San Ramon HS, Danville, Calif.
46. *James Scarborough of, Elkins HS, Fort Bend, Texas.
47. *Dustin Wilson, rhp, Columbia Basin (Wash.) CC.
48. +Denny McDaniel, lhp, Lake Travis HS, Austin, Texas / Blinn (Texas) JC.
49. *Greg Arnold, lhp, Smithtown HS, Nesconset, N.Y.
50. *Glen School, of, Brookdale (N.J.) CC.
51. *Rudy Bulgar, of, New Bedford (Mass.) HS.
52. *Brian Starcich, rhp, Blinn (Texas) JC.
53. *Paul Stryhas, 3b, Sarasota (Fla.) HS.
54. *Michael Cabales, rhp, East Islip (N.Y.) HS.
55. +Merrell Ligons, 2b, Palisades HS, Culver City, Calif. / El Camino (Calif.) JC.
56. *Stephen Watson, rhp, Galveston (Texas) JC.
57. *Andy Lynch, of, Bridgton Academy, North Bridgton, Maine.
58. *Lance Awbrey, c, Sinagua HS, Flagstaff, Ariz.
59. ***Paul Phillips, c, West Lauderdale HS, Bailey, Miss.—(2004-10)**
60. *Tommy Worthy, ss, Etowah HS, Attalla, Ala.
61. *Jaime Bonilla, lhp, Zayas Santana HS, Villalba, P.R.
62. *Michael Rodriguez, ss, Chaffey HS, Ontario, Calif.
63. *Courtney Thornton, rhp, Tallassee (Ala.) HS.
64. *Scott Ham, c, Palestine (Ill.) HS.
65. *Adam Reikowski, rhp, Providence HS, Charlotte, N.C.
66. Brian Winders, rhp, Louisiana State University.
67. *Michael Degruy, rhp, Harrison Central HS, Gulfport, Miss.
68. *Rob Shabansky, lhp, Bishop Gorman HS, Las Vegas, Nev.
69. *Ralph Cadima, of, Mount San Antonio (Calif.) JC.
70. *Jason Van Curen, rhp, Monte Vista HS, San Ramon, Calif.

## LOS ANGELES DODGERS (20)

1. David Yocum, lhp, Florida State University.—(High A)
2. Darrin Babineaux, rhp, University of Southwestern Louisiana.—(AAA)
3. **Onan Masaoka, lhp, Waiakea HS, Hilo, Hawaii.—(1999-2000)**
4. Judd Granzow, of, Faith Baptist HS, Granada Hills, Calif.—(Short-season A)
5. Sef Soto, rhp, Palomar (Calif.) JC.—(Low A)
6. Kevin Gibbs, of, Old Dominion University.
7. Trent Cuevas, ss, El Dorado HS, Placentia, Calif.
8. Jon Tucker, 1b, Chatsworth (Calif.) HS.
9. Eric Brown, ss, East St. John HS, LaPlace, La.
10. Mike Carpentier, ss, Cal State Sacramento.
11. Craig Taczy, lhp, Shepard HS, Crestwood, Ill.
12. *Kenny Miller, ss, Providence Catholic HS, New Lenox, Ill.
13. ***Brad Wilkerson, lhp, Apollo HS, Owensboro, Ky.—(2001-08)**

DRAFT DROP *First-round draft pick (33rd overall), Expos (1998)*

14. *Spencer Micunek, rhp, Henry Ford (Mich.) CC.
15. J.J. Pearsall, lhp, University of South Carolina.
16. Eric Flores, ss, Rio Mesa HS, Oxnard, Calif.
17. Tony Mota, of, Miami Springs HS, Miami.

DRAFT DROP *Son of Manny Mota, major leaguer (1962-82) • Brother of Andy Mota, major leaguer (1991) • Brother of Jose Mota, major leaguer (1991-95)*

18. Jay O'Shaughnessy, rhp, Northeastern University.
19. ***David Ross, c, Florida HS, Tallahassee, Fla.—(2002-15)**
20. *Jeffrey Rodriguez, c, Coral Gables HS, Miami.
21. Dennis Mauch, c, Cosumnes River (Calif.) JC.
22. A.J. Walkanoff, c, Creighton University.
23. Brett Illig, 3b, Phoenixville (Pa.) HS.
24. Travis Meyer, c, East Carolina University.
25. Peter Cervantes, rhp, East Los Angeles JC.
26. *Peyton Warren, rhp, West Florence HS, Florence, S.C.
27. Mike Sanchez, rhp, Chaffey (Calif.) JC.
28. Ken Morimoto, of, University of Hawaii.
29. *Greg Clark, c, Paradise Valley HS, Phoenix.
30. Mitch McNeely, lhp, Centenary College.
31. **Pedro Feliciano, lhp, Jose S. Alegria HS, Dorado, P.R.—(2002-13)**
32. Andy Owen, of, UC Riverside.
33. *Lazaro Gutierrez, lhp, Brito Miami Private HS, Hialeah, Fla.
34. Scott Chambers, lhp, John A. Logan (Ill.) JC.
35. Jeff Keppen, rhp, Georgia Southern University.
36. *Trevor Bishop, rhp, Assiniboia Composite HS, Assiniboia, Sask.
37. *David Schmidt, c, Oregon State University.
38. Terrence McClain, ss, Cumberland (Tenn.) University.
39. *Chad Roney, c, Jacksonville University.
40. +Bobby Cripps, c, Cameron HS, Powell River, B.C. / Central Arizona JC.
41. John Davis, rhp, Bethune-Cookman College.
42. ***Jason Smith, ss, Demopolis HS, Coatopa, Ala.—(2001-09)**
43. *Saul Rivera, ss, Rafael Cordero HS, Las Lomas, P.R.
44. *Jeffrey Deno, lhp, Franklin HS, Los Angeles.
45. *Brad Block, rhp, Lake Michigan (Mich.) JC.
46. Michael Bourbakis, rhp, Franklin D. Roosevelt HS, Brooklyn, N.Y.
47. ***Steve Green, rhp, Eduoard Montpetit HS, Longueuil, Quebec.—(2001)**
48. *Xavier Curley, 3b, Marshall County HS, Lewisburg, Tenn.
49. *Andrew Dougherty, c, Glassboro (N.J.) HS.
50. *Kevin Hodge, ss, Bryan (Texas) HS.
51. *Mark Paschal, of, Fontana HS, Bloomington, Calif.
52. *Maurice Hightower, lhp, Arlington (Texas) HS.
53. *Christian Keating, rhp, Brother Rice HS, Country Club Heights, Ill.
54. *Cesar Acosta, of, Yuma (Ariz.) HS.
55. *Brock Rumfield, ss-3b, McLennan (Texas) CC.
56. *Vance Cozier, rhp, Pickering HS, Ajax, Ontario.
57. *Joel Ainsworth, lhp, Sarnia Collegiate Institute, Sarnia, Ontario.
58. *Cesar Castenada, 3b, Lincoln HS, Los Angeles.
59. *Jose Rijo-Berger, of, Walla Walla (Wash.) CC.
60. *Chuck Koone, of, Spartanburg Methodist (S.C.) JC.
61. Cash Riley, of, Trinity Christian Academy, Irving, Texas.
62. *Brian Oliver, ss, Antioch (Calif.) HS.
63. *Chris Vollaro, rhp, Alvin (Texas) CC.
64. *Mark Vallecorsa, lhp, Damien HS, San Dimas, Calif.
65. *Stephen Dupont, rhp, Nicholls State University.
66. *Gregory Conley, c, Sequim (Wash.) HS.
67. *Paul Auton, c, Harry S. Ainlay HS, Edmonton, Alberta.
68. *Brian Dawson, rhp, San Bernardino Valley (Calif.) JC.
69. *Tim Hackman, rhp, Vernon (B.C.) HS.
70. *Brian Wagner, c, Sacramento (Calif.) CC.
71. *Joseph Thomas, rhp, West Covina HS, La Puente, Calif.
72. *Tony James, 2b, Chaffey (Calif.) JC.
73. *Ryan Cail, rhp, Kwantlen (B.C.) College.
74. +Craig Allen, rhp, University of Notre Dame.
75. *Todd Sutton, of, Angola HS, Pleasant Lake, Ind.
76. *Neal Atchison, rhp, Central Huron HS, Clinton, Ontario.
77. *Scott Oliver, rhp, Richland Northeast HS, Columbia. S.C.
78. *Deron Featherstone, rhp, Hendersonville (N.C.) HS.
79. Larry Bethea, 1b, Red Springs (N.C.) HS.
80. *Brandon Bowe, rhp, San Joaquin Delta (Calif.)

CC.
81. *Michael Tablit, rhp, Yuba (Calif.) CC.
82. +C.D. Stover, rhp, American River (Calif.) JC.
83. *Brad Brewer, ss, Sacramento (Calif.) CC.
84. *Mathew Randel, rhp, Ridgefield (Wash.) HS.
85. *Ryan Moskau, 1b-lhp, Sabino HS, Tucson, Ariz.
**DRAFT DROP** *Son of Paul Moskau, major leaguer (1977-83)*

## MILWAUKEE BREWERS (9)

1. **Geoff Jenkins, of, University of Southern California.—(1998-2008)**
2. Mike Pasqualicchio, lhp, Lamar University.—(AAA)
3. Greg Schaub, rhp, Solanco HS, Oxford, Pa.—(High A)
4. +Jeff Alfano, c, Mount Whitney HS, Visalia, Calif. / Fresno (Calif.) CC.—(AA)
5. Jared Camp, rhp, Indian River (Fla.) JC.—(AAA)
6. Toby Kominek, of, Central Michigan University.
7. Sam Singleton, as, DuPont HS, Rand, W.Va.
8. Ryan Ritter, 2b-of, Georgia Tech.
9. **Mike Kinkade, c-of, Washington State University.—(1998-2003)**
10. Jason Dawsey, lhp, Clemson University.
11. Darren Berninger, rhp, Nicholls State University.
12. Chris Walther, of, Gaither HS, Tampa.
13. **Mickey Lopez, 2b, Florida State University.—(2004)**
14. Shawn Miller, rhp, Northeastern Illinois University.
15. Jonathan Guzman, lhp, Pedro Albizu Campos HS, Levittown, P.R.
16. Donnie Moore, of, Dallastown HS, York, Pa.
17. Alex Andreopoulos, c, Seton Hall University.
18. Ledowick Johnson, of, North Carolina State University.
19. **Travis Smith, rhp, Texas Tech.—(1998-2006)**
20. Sergio Guerrero, 2b, Laredo (Texas) JC.
21. Brian Hommel, lhp, University of Louisville.
22. *Brad Pautz, rhp, Reedsville (Wis.) HS.
23. Dave Elliott, of, Western Michigan University.
24. Jesse Richardson, lhp, Northern Illinois University.
25. Michael Roche, 2b, Brevard (Fla.) JC.
26. Derek Torres, rhp, Miami-Dade CC North.
27. *Beau Johnson, 1b-of, Mendocino (Calif.) CC.
28. Rick Smith, 1b, Central Michigan University.
29. Ryan Arevalos, ss, University of Texas-San Antonio.
30. +Scott Kirby, 3b, Lake Gibson HS, Lakeland, Fla. / Polk (Fla.) CC.
31. Jerry Parent, of, Merrimack (Mass.) College.
32. *Travis Bailey, ss, Wellington Community HS, West Palm Beach, Fla.
33. *Anthony Rodriguez, rhp, Cooper City HS, Pembroke Pines, Fla.
34. *Eric Leiser, of, Antioch (Calif.) HS.
35. *Jonathan Rose, lhp, Brevard (N.C.) JC.
36. *Migues Rodriguez, ss, Sonora HS, Brea, Calif.
37. *Doug Wakefield, lhp, Victor Valley (Calif.) CC.
38. Josh Bishop, rhp, University of Missouri.
39. *Zane Curry, c, Ball HS, Galveston, Texas.
40. *Austin Lawes, of, North Miami HS, Miramar, Fla.
41. ***Andy Phillips, ss, Demopolis (Ala.) HS.—(2004-08)**
42. *Carlos Barbosa, c, Dinuba (Calif.) HS.
43. *Mark Cridland, of, Galveston (Texas) JC.
44. *Walter Ward, of, Northern HS, Chesapeake Beach, Md.
45. *Blair Murphy, rhp, De Anza (Calif.) JC.
46. *Byron Tribe, rhp, Galveston (Texas) JC.
47. *Rick Cercy, rhp, Seabreeze HS, Ormond Beach, Fla.
48. *Edward French, of, Seabreeze HS, Ormond Beach, Fla.
49. *Mike Leach, rhp, Palm Beach (Fla.) CC.
50. *James Landingham, of, South Miami HS, Miami.
51. *Stanford Woods, of, Boone HS, Orlando, Fla.
52. *Alain Cruz, c, Miami-Dade CC North.
53. *Eric Armour, of, Palm Beach (Fla.) CC.
54. *Kenny Avera, rhp, Pace (Fla.) HS.
55. *Robert Cornett, c, North Hall HS, Gainesville, Ga.
56. *Monty Ward, rhp, Monterey HS, Lubbock, Texas.
57. *Paul Turco, ss, Sarasota (Fla.) HS.
58. ***Kip Wells, rhp, Elkins HS, Fort Bend, Texas.—(1999-2012)**
**DRAFT DROP** *First-round draft pick (16th overall), White Sox (1998)*
59. *Charlie Hunter, rhp, Notre Dame HS, Ooltewah, Tenn.
60. *Steven Lawson, rhp, Damien HS, La Verne, Calif.
61. *Lance Jordan, rhp, Whittier Christian HS, La Habra, Calif.
62. *James Leary, rhp, South Grand Prairie HS, Grand Prairie, Texas.
63. *Dirk Lewallen, 1b, Victor Valley (Calif.) JC.
64. *Ara Petrosian, rhp, Cypress (Calif.) JC.
65. *Jason Ross, of, University of Hawaii.
66. *Richard Jennings, ss, Overland HS, Aurora, Colo.
67. *Kevin McDougal, of, Arvada West HS, Arvada, Colo.
68. *Eric McMaster, 2b, Arvada West HS, Arvada, Colo.

MORRIS FOSTOFF

A.J. Burnett was a Mets eighth-rounder who first found big league success with the Marlins

## MINNESOTA TWINS (13)

1. **Mark Redman, lhp, University of Oklahoma.—(1999-2008)**
2. Jason Bell, rhp, Oklahoma State University.—(AAA)
3. ***A.J. Hinch, c, Stanford University.—(1998-2004)**
**DRAFT DROP** *Returned to Stanford; re-drafted by Athletics, 1996 (3rd round); major league manager (2009-15)*
4. *Jay Hood, ss, Germantown (Tenn.) HS.—(AA)
**DRAFT DROP** *Attended Georgia Tech; re-drafted by Angels, 1998 (6th round)*
5. **Doug Mientkiewicz, 1b, Florida State University.—(1998-2009)**
6. Shane Gunderson, c-1b, University of Minnesota.
7. **Mike Moriarty, ss, Seton Hall University.—(2002)**
8. Will Rushing, lhp, Georgia Southern University.
9. Joe McHenry, of, Oakland HS, Murfreesboro, Tenn.
10. *Kyle Kane, of, Linfield HS, Temecula Valley, Calif.
**DRAFT DROP** *First-round draft pick (33rd overall), White Sox (1997)*
11. Jamaal Harrison, 1b, Palo Alto (Calif.) HS.
12. Jason McKenzie, rhp, University of Mississippi.
13. Jamie Splittorff, rhp, University of Kansas.
**DRAFT DROP** *Son of Paul Splittorff, major leaguer (1970-84)*
14. *Josh Holliday, c, Stillwater (Okla.) HS.
**DRAFT DROP** *Baseball coach, Oklahoma State (2013-15) • Brother of Matt Holliday, major leaguer (2004-15)*
15. Brad Neidermaier, rhp, Northwestern University.
16. Alan Mahaffey, lhp, University of Arkansas.
17. ***Robert Ramsay, lhp, Washington State University.—(1999-2000)**
18. Freddy Reyes, 1b-3b, Jefferson (Ind.) HS.
19. Carlisle Johnson, ss-of, DeWitt Taylor HS, Pierson, Fla.
20. Jeff Smith, c, Stetson University.
21. David Orndorff, c, Shippensburg Area (Pa.) HS.
22. Scott Tanksley, rhp, Mississippi State University.
23. +Jamie Vallis, lhp, Charles P. Allen HS, New Bedford, Nova Scotia / Vanier (Quebec) College.
24. Dave Blank, lhp, William Carey (Miss.) College.
25. Kevin Nelson, 1b, Bryant (Ark.) HS.
26. Tim Peters, lhp, Baylor University.
27. Joe Fraser, 2b, Cal State Fullerton.
28. **Jeff Harris, rhp, University of San Francisco.—(2005-06)**
29. Sean Reilly, lhp, Aldershot HS, Burlington, Ontario.
30. Travis Johnson, of, University of North Dakota.
31. Todd Bartels, rhp, Stanford University.
32. Lee Marshall, rhp, Enterprise (Ala.) HS.
33. *Javier Mejia, rhp, University of Southern California.
34. *Matt Noe, lhp, Riverside (Calif.) CC.
35. Ivory Jones, of, San Francisco State University.
36. Harold Boggs, rhp, West Virginia State College.
37. *Adam Danner, rhp, University of South Florida.
38. *Jake Chapman, lhp, St. Joseph's (Ind.) College.
39. *Scott Dobson, rhp, West Potomac HS, Alexandria, Va.
40. Matt Vanderbush, lhp, William Paterson (N.J.) College.
41. *Leo Torres, lhp, Cibola HS, Somerton, Ariz.
42. +Deion Daniels, rhp, Polk (Fla.) CC.
43. *Gary Forster, rhp, Montesano (Wash.) HS.
44. Jeff Garff, rhp, Dixie (Utah) JC.
45. *Toby Wilmot, lhp, University of Oklahoma.
46. Andres Cruz, c, Stella Marquez HS, Salinas, P.R.
47. *Brian Mitchell, 3b, Iowa City (Iowa) HS.
48. *Edgar Oropeza, rhp, CC of San Francisco.
49. *Brian Bodwell, rhp, Ocosta HS, Westport, Wash.
50. *Nelson Correa, 1b, Florida Air Academy HS, Melbourne, Fla.
51. (selection voided)
52. *Michael Brunet, lhp, Land O'Lakes (Fla.) HS.
53. Bryan Malko, rhp, Piscataway (N.J.) HS.
54. *Craig Black, 2b, Palm Beach Lakes HS, West Palm Beach, Fla.
55. *Paul Boykin, of, Columbine HS, Littleton, Colo.

## MONTREAL EXPOS (28)

1. **Michael Barrett, ss, Pace Academy, Atlanta.—(1998-2009)**
2. **Henry Mateo, ss, Escuela Central HS, Santurce, P.R.—(2001-06)**
3. Kenny James, of, Sebring (Fla.) HS.—(AAA)
4. **J.D. Smart, rhp, University of Texas.—(1999-2001)**
5. **Brian Schneider, c, Northampton HS, Cherryville, Pa.—(2000-12)**
6. Ronney Daniels, of-lhp, Lake Wales (Fla.) HS.
7. Peter Fortune, lhp, Rockland (N.Y.) CC.
8. Trey Martin, rhp, Arcadia HS, Phoenix.
9. Bienvenido Sanchez, rhp, Pajuil HS, Arecibo, P.R.
10. ***Jeff Austin, rhp, Kingwood (Texas) HS.—(2001-03)**
**DRAFT DROP** *First-round draft pick (4th overall), Royals (1998)*
11. +Jimmy Turman, rhp, Shelton State (Ala.) CC.
12. Rob Marquez, rhp, McNeese State University.
13. David Herr, rhp, Villanova University.
14. Tim Dixon, lhp, Cal State Fullerton.
15. D.C. Olsen, 1b, Cal State Fullerton.
16. **Pierre Luc LaForest, ss-3b, Edouard Montpetit HS, Gatineau, Quebec.—(2003-07)**
17. Wes Denning, of, University of Minnesota.
18. *Tom Brady, c, Serra HS, San Mateo, Calif.
**DRAFT DROP** *Quarterback, National Football League (2000-15)*
19. Jake Steinkemper, c, Arizona State University.
20. Mike Bell, lhp, Florida State University.
21. *Stan Baston, of-3b, North Florida Christian HS, Tallahassee, Fla.
22. Scott Mitchell, rhp, University of the Pacific.
23. Mo Blakeney, of, Elon College.
24. Mike Wolger, of-lhp, University of California.
25. Jaime Garcia, c, University of New Mexico.
26. Ryan Van Oeveren, ss, University of Michigan.
27. +Noah Hall, of, Aptos (Calif.) HS / West Valley (Calif.) JC.
28. *Jarrett Shearin, of, Wake Forest-Rolesville HS, Wake Forest, N C.
29. Jeremiah Colson, of, St. Paul's (N.C.) HS.
30. James Lacey, rhp, Coconut Creek (Fla.) HS.
31. *Toby McDermott, lhp, Tacoma (Wash.) CC.
32. *Joe Kerrigan Jr., ss, Radnor HS, Rosemont, Pa.
**DRAFT DROP** *Son of Joe Kerrigan, major leaguer (1976-80); major league manager (2001)*
33. *Shawn Peterson, c-of, Orem (Utah) HS.
34. *Scott Porter, rhp, Middleburg (Fla.) HS.
35. *Mitch Wylie, rhp, North Scott HS, Princeton, Iowa.
36. *Aaron Underwood, rhp, Lehigh HS, Lehigh Acres, Fla.
37. *Matt Dehner, 3b, El Dorado HS, Las Vegas, Nev.
38. *Brandon Gadke, of, Orange (Ohio) HS.
39. *Bruno Vaillancourt, lhp, Cegep Montmorency HS, Le Gardeur, Quebec.
40. *Shane Wright, rhp, Hayden HS, Topeka, Kan.
41. *Robert Everett, rhp, Lake City (Fla.) CC.
42. Torrance Davis, of, Liberty Eylau HS, Texarkana, Texas.
43. *Jesse Crespo, c, Camuy (P.R.) HS.
44. *Phil Derryman, rhp, Moorpark (Calif.) JC.
45. *Adam Huxhold, lhp, Lindbergh HS, Maple Valley, Wash.
46. *Daniel Prata, lhp, Kells Academy, Repentigny, Quebec.

## NEW YORK METS (18)

1. Ryan Jaroncyk, ss, Orange Glen HS, Escondido, Calif.—(High A)
2. Brett Herbison, rhp-ss, Central HS, Burlington, Ill.—(AA)
3. Ryan Bowers, c, Pine View HS, St. George, Utah.—(Rookie)
4. Corey Erickson, ss, Lanphier HS, Springfield, Ill.—(AAA)
5. Jeff Parsons, ss, University of Arkansas.—(High A)
6. +Todd Cutchins, lhp, Tallahassee (Fla.) CC.
7. ***Ryan Minor, 1b-rhp, University of Oklahoma.—(1998-2001)**
**DRAFT DROP** *Second-round draft pick, Philadelphia 76ers/National Basketball Association (1996) • Twin brother of Damon Minor, 19th-round draft pick, Mets (1995); major leaguer (2000-04)*
8. **A.J. Burnett, rhp, Central Arkansas**

**Christian HS, North Little Rock, Ark.—(1999-2015)**
9. *Tydus Meadows, of, Evans (Ga.) HS.
**10. Dan Murray, rhp, San Diego State University.—(1999-2000)**
**11. Grant Roberts, rhp, Grossmont HS, El Cajon, Calif.—(2000-04)**
12. Mark Pileski, ss, University of Massachusetts.
13. Erik Torres, rhp, Segundo Ruiz Belvis HS, Mayaguez, P.R.
14. *Eric McQueen, c, North Cobb HS, Acworth, Ga.
15. +Anthony Johnson, c-of, Oakland (Calif.) HS / Odessa (Texas) JC.
16. Lindsay Gulin, lhp, Issaquah (Wash.) HS.
**17. *Scott Proctor, rhp, Martin County HS, Stuart, Fla.—(2004-11)**
18. *Chris Adolph, of, Clovis West HS, Fresno, Calif.
**19. *Damon Minor, 1b, University of Oklahoma.—(2000-04)**
DRAFT DROP *Brother of Ryan Minor, seventh-round draft pick, Mets (1995); major leaguer (1998-2001)*
20. Phil Olson, rhp, Florida State University.
21. Joey Pyrtle, rhp, University of North Carolina-Wilmington.
22. +Andy Zwirchitz, rhp, Okaloosa-Walton (Fla.) CC.
23. *Brooks Stephens, 1b, Florida HS, Tallahassee, Fla.
24. Jeff Howatt, rhp, UCLA.
25. *Ben Hickman, rhp, Bryant (Ark.) HS.
26. P.J. Yoder, of, Alvernia (Pa.) College.
27. Preston Ballew, lhp, Carlsbad (N.M.) HS.
28. Chadwick Cooper, rhp, Potomac State (W.Va.) JC.
29. Mark Enloe, lhp, Tarkington HS, Cleveland, Texas.
**30. Nelson Figueroa, rhp, Brandeis (Mass.) University.—(2000-11)**
31. Matt Ferullo, rhp, University of Michigan.
32. Brandon Copeland, of, Washburn Rural HS, Topeka, Kan.
33. Mike Blang, rhp, Southern Illinois University.
34. Brandon Black, of, Pensacola (Fla.) JC.
35. *John Mattson, rhp, South Kitsap HS, Port Orchard, Wash.
36. *Jacob Handy, rhp, Arvin HS, Bakersfield, Calif.
37. Ryan Morrison, of, Onondaga (N.Y.) CC.
38. *Cliff Wren, c, Petal (Miss.) HS.
39. Richard Martinez, c, St. Mary's (Texas) University.
**40. *Aaron Rowand, ss, Glendora (Calif.) HS.—(2001-11)**
DRAFT DROP *First-round draft pick (35th overall), White Sox (1998)*
41. Tim Tessmar, lhp, Eastern Michigan University.
42. *Donald Loland, rhp, Ascension Catholic HS, Donaldsonville, La.
43. Casey Patterson, rhp, Fresno (Calif.) CC.
44. *Randy Young, of, Wichita State University.
45. Sean Gill, of, Wright State University.
46. *Taylor More, of, East HS, Cheyenne, Wyo.
47. *Steve Minus, rhp-c, Judson HS, San Antonio, Texas.
48. +Cory Patton, of, Olney Central (Ill.) JC.
49. *Jacob Bailey, rhp, Hutchinson (Kan.) CC.
50. *Clint Johnston, 1b, John Carroll HS, Vero Beach, Fla.
DRAFT DROP *First-round draft pick (15th overall), Pirates (1998)*
51. *Jaime Rodgers, rhp, Friendship Christian HS, Mount Juliet, Tenn.
52. Chris Dewitt, rhp, St. Andrews Presbyterian (N.C.) College.
53. *Shawn Hannah, rhp, Clovis (Calif.) HS.
54. *Luis Castillo, c, American HS, Miami Lakes, Fla.
55. *Chris Reinike, rhp, Long Beach (Miss.) HS.
56. Corey Brittan, rhp, Hutchinson (Kan.) CC.
57. *Derek Daugherty, of, Kingfisher (Okla.) HS.
58. *Quinn Cravens, of, Valley Center (Kan.) HS.
59. *Jerrell Carver, 1b, Northeastern HS, Elizabeth City, N.C.
60. *Tony Moreno, c, Riverside HS, El Paso, Texas.
61. *Brad Piercy, c, Crest HS, Shelby, N.C.
62. *Hector Esparza, 3b, San Jose (Calif.) CC.
63. *Darren Dyt, of, Porterville (Calif.) JC.

## NEW YORK YANKEES (27)

1. Shea Morenz, of, University of Texas.—(AAA)
DRAFT DROP *Great-grandson of Howie Morenz, Hockey Hall of Famer; forward, National Hockey League (1923-37)*
2. Richard Brown, of, Nova HS, Fort Lauderdale, Fla.—(AAA)
DRAFT DROP *Brother of Billy Brown, third-round draft pick, Athletics (1995)*
2. Brian Buchanan, lhp, Oviedo (Fla.) HS (Supplemental choice—59th—as compensation for Type C free agent Matt Nokes).—(AA)
3. Luke Wilcox, of, Western Michigan University.—(AAA)
4. Eric Boardman, rhp, Cerritos (Calif.) JC.—(Short-season A)
5. Jason Wright, rhp, Martinsville (Ind.) HS.—(Rookie)
6. Brad Williams, lhp, Sabino HS, Tucson, Ariz.
7. Bob St. Pierre, rhp, University of Richmond.
8. Scott Brand, rhp, McLennan (Texas) JC.
**9. Mike Judd, rhp, Grossmont (Calif.) JC.—(1997-2001)**
10. Jeff Saffer, of, Pima (Ariz.) CC.
**11. Darrell Einertson, rhp, Iowa Wesleyan College.—(2000)**
12. Cam Spence, rhp, Lake City (Fla.) CC.
13. *Ryan Mills, lhp, Horizon HS, Scottsdale, Ariz.
DRAFT DROP *First-round draft pick (6th overall), Twins (1998) • Son of Dick Mills, major leaguer (1970)*
14. Cesar Verdin, lhp, Crawford HS, San Diego.
15. *Josh Hochgesang, ss, Sunny Hills HS, Fullerton, Calif.
16. *Dana Davis, rhp, Rice University.
17. Denny Lail, rhp, Wingate (N.C.) College.
**18. Stephen Randolph, lhp, University of Texas.—(2003-07)**
**19. Jay Tessmer, rhp, University of Miami.—(1998-2002)**
**20. Mike Lowell, 2b, Florida International University.—(1998-2010)**
21. Scott Emmons, c, University of California.
**22. Donzell McDonald, of, Yavapai (Ariz.) JC.—(2001-02)**
DRAFT DROP *Brother of Darnell McDonald, first-round draft pick, Orioles (1997); major leaguer (2004-13)*
23. Cody McCormick, c, University of California.
24. *Ryan Snellings, lhp, Seminole HS, Largo, Fla.
25. *Danny Kanell, rhp, Florida State University.
DRAFT DROP *Quarterback, National Football League (1996-2004)*
26. *Daunte Culpepper, of, Vanguard HS, Ocala, Fla.
DRAFT DROP *First-round draft pick, Minnesota Vikings, National Football League (1999); quarterback, NFL (1999-2009)*
27. Pat Antrim, ss, Saddleback (Calif.) CC.
28. Les Dennis, ss, University of Portland.
29. *Jason Ryan, lhp, Indian River (Fla.) CC.
30. +Michael Schnautz, lhp, San Jacinto (Texas) JC.
31. *Chris Crawford, rhp, Wheeler HS, Marietta, Ga.
32. +Tim Spindler, rhp-ss, Orange County (N.Y.) CC.
33. *Brian Aylor, of, Oklahoma State University.
34. +Rick Cremer, lhp, West Frankfort (Ill.) HS / John A. Logan (Ill.) JC.
35. +Orlando Carey, of, Motlow State (Tenn.) CC.
36. +Ben Phillips, rhp, Howard (Texas) JC.
37. *Travis Brummitt, rhp, Cleveland State (Tenn.) CC
38. *Barry Brown, of, Grossmont (Calif.) JC.
39. *Raul DeCastro, 1b-of, Florida Bible Christian HS, Sunrise, Fla.
40. *Lateef Vaughn, ss, Southwestern (Calif.) JC.
41. *Ben Chestnut, of, Sacramento (Calif.) CC.
**42. *Joe Horgan, lhp, Cordova HS, Rancho Cordova, Calif.—(2004-05)**
43. Jason Imrisek, c, University of Evansville.
44. *Jared Hoerman, rhp, Plainview HS, Ardmore, Okla.
**45. *Casey Blake, 3b, Wichita State University.—(1999-2011)**
46. *Denis Pujals, rhp, University of Miami.
47. +Jason Ellison, rhp, Navarro (Texas) JC.
48. *Scott Kingston, 1b, Columbus (Ga.) HS.
49. *Philip Haigler, rhp, Vanderbilt University.
50. *Lance Hawkins, of, Lake Charles-Boston HS, Lake Charles, La.
51. *Brandon James, of, Sacramento (Calif.) CC.
52. *Brian Hervey, rhp, Tallahassee (Fla.) CC.
53. *Chad Clements, ss, Centreville HS, Fairfax, Va.
54. *Jason Becker, 2b, Bremen HS, Midlothian, Ill.
55. *Michael Hamm, c, Northwest Shoals (Ala.) CC.
56. *Darryl Craig, lhp-1b, Douglas (B.C.) College.
57. *Dorian Cameron, ss, Northern HS, Durham, N.C.
58. *Jude Campbell, of, Chabot (Calif.) JC.
59. *Daniel Thomas, rhp, Poway (Calif.) HS.
60. *Nathan Koepke, of, Long Beach (Calif.) CC.
61. *Scott Hemmings, of, Columbus (Ga.) HS.
62. *Charles Shipp, of, Vocational HS, Chicago.
63. *Jeremiah Johnson, rhp, Homer (Mich.) HS.
64. *Doug Dixon, rhp, Northside HS, Belhaven, N.C.
65. *Scott Hardesty, rhp, University of Illinois-Chicago.
66. *Jake Zajc, rhp, Bradley-Bourbonnais HS, Bourbonnais, Ill.
67. *Justin Carpenter, rhp, Prague (Okla.) HS.
68. *Charles Thomas, of, Harlan (Ky.) HS.
69. *Peter Fisher, rhp, Stoneham (Mass.) HS.
70. *Daniel Washburn, rhp, Nova HS, Pembroke Pines, Fla.
71. *William Duncan, c, Burlington-Edison HS, Burlington, Wash.

## OAKLAND ATHLETICS (5)

**1. Ariel Prieto, rhp, Palm Springs / Western League.—(1995-2001)**
DRAFT DROP *First player from 1995 draft to reach majors (July 2, 1995)*
**2. Mark Bellhorn, ss, Auburn University.—(1997-2007)**
3. *Billy Brown, of, St. Thomas Aquinas HS, Fort Lauderdale, Fla.—(High A)
DRAFT DROP *Attended Florida Atlantic; re-drafted by Blue Jays, 1997 (3rd round) • Brother of Richard Brown, second-round draft pick, Yankees (1995)*
4. Wayne Nix, rhp, Monroe HS, North Hills, Calif.—(AA)
**5. Danny Ardoin, c, McNeese State University.—(2000-08)**
6. Jamey Price, rhp, University of Mississippi.
7. Tim Jones, of, Buena Park (Calif.) HS.
8. Tom Bennett, rhp, Ohlone (Calif.) JC.
9. Tom Knickerbocker, of, Kirkwood (Iowa) JC.
**10. Ryan Christensen, of, Pepperdine University.—(1998-2003)**
11. Scott Rivette, rhp, Long Beach State University.
12. Troy Rauer, of, Arizona State University.
13. Willy Hilton, rhp, Eastern Illinois University.
14. Kevin Mlodik, rhp, University of Wisconsin-Oshkosh.
15. *David Shepard, rhp, Mansfield (Pa.) University.
16. Robert Harris, ss, Texas A&M University.
**17. David Newhan, of, Pepperdine University.—(1999-2008)**
18. Mike Klostermeyer, 1b, Louisiana State University.
19. *Jason Hill, c, Monte Vista HS, Danville, Calif.
20. David Slemmer, ss-2b, Southwest Missouri State University.
21. Bill Knight, of, University of Massachusetts.
22. T.J. Costello, lhp, Montclair State (N.J.) College.
23. Duane Filchner, of, Radford University.
**24. Steve Connelly, rhp, University of Oklahoma.—(1998)**
25. *Brian Callahan, rhp, The Citadel.
**26. Jeff DaVanon, of-2b, San Diego State University.—(1999-2007)**
DRAFT DROP *Son of Jerry DaVanon, major leaguer (1969-77)*
27. Ryan Kjos, rhp, University of Texas.
28. Victor Hernandez, of, Maria Pimeiro HS, Ciales, P.R.
29. *Stephen Bess, rhp, Montgomery Bell Academy, Nashville, Tenn.
30. Bill Batchelder, rhp, University of New Hampshire.
31. Kevin Gunther, rhp, Fresno State University.
32. Jace Johnson, of, Scottsdale (Ariz.) CC.
33. *Byron Embry, rhp, Madison Central HS, Richmond, Ky.
34. Chris Morrison, rhp, Auburn University.
35. J.D. French, rhp, Arkansas State University.
36. *Ryan Gill, rhp, Woodlawn HS, Baton Rouge, La.
37. +Rodney Clifton, of, Elgin (Ill.) HS / Triton (Ill.) JC.
38. *Greg Halvorson, c, Canyon Del Oro HS, Tucson, Ariz.
39. *Matthew Dornfeld, of, Arizona Western JC.
40. *Robert Norman, rhp, Columbia Academy, Mount Pleasant, Tenn.
41. Chris Nelson, rhp, Oklahoma State University.
42. Brandon Welch, of, Texas Tech.
43. Victor Chambers, 2b-of, CC of San Francisco.
44. Todd Abbott, rhp, University of Arkansas.
DRAFT DROP *Son of Glenn Abbott, major leaguer (1973-84)*

## PHILADELPHIA PHILLIES (14)

**1. Reggie Taylor, of, Newberry (S.C.) HS.—(2000-05)**
**1. David Coggin, rhp, Upland (Calif.) HS** (Supplemental choice—39th—as compensation for Type A free agent Danny Jackson).—**(2000-02)**
**2. Marlon Anderson, 2b, University of South Alabama** (Choice from Cardinals as compensation for Jackson).—**(1998-2009)**
2. (Choice to Cardinals as compensation for Type A free agent Gregg Jefferies)
3. Randy Knoll, rhp-3b, Corona (Calif.) HS.—(High A)
DRAFT DROP *Brother of Brian Knoll, 16th-round draft pick, Phillies (1995)*
4. Steve Carver, 3b, Stanford University.—(AAA)
5. *Pee Wee Lopez, c, Westminster Christian HS, Miami.—(AAA)
DRAFT DROP *Attended Miami-Dade CC South; re-drafted by Mets, 1996 (8th round)*
6. Caleb Martinez, lhp, Florida Christian HS, Miami.
7. *Chris Bauer, rhp-ss, Wichita State University.
8. Ricky Williams, ss, Patrick Henry HS, San Diego.
DRAFT DROP *Heisman Trophy winner, 1998; first-round draft pick, New Orleans Saints, National Football League (1999); running back, NFL (1999-2005)*
9. Kirk Pierce, c, Long Beach State University.
10. Brian Mensink, rhp, University of Minnesota.
11. *Jason Wallace, of, Callaway HS, Jackson, Miss.
**12. Jason Kershner, lhp, Saguaro HS, Scottsdale, Ariz.—(2002-04)**
13. Mark Raynor, ss, Barton (N.C.) College.
14. Marty Barnett, rhp, University of South Alabama.
15. Walter Dawkins, of, University of Southern California.
16. Melvin Pizarro, lhp, Luz A. Calderon HS, Carolina, P.R.
17. *Ryan Lentz, 3b, Woodinville (Wash.) HS.
DRAFT DROP *Son of Mike Lentz, first-round draft pick, Padres (1975)*
18. Matt Buckles, c, Palatka (Fla.) HS.
19. Chris Snusz, c, Mercyhurst (Pa.) College.
20. Brian Miller, rhp, Marian (Wis.) College.
21. Tyson Kimm, ss, Creighton University.
DRAFT DROP *Son of Bruce Kimm, major leaguer (1976-80); major league manager (2002)*
22. Brian Ford, lhp, Methodist (N.C.) College.
**23. Anthony Shumaker, lhp, Cardinal Stritch (Wis.) College.—(1999)**
24. Jared Janke, 1b, UC Santa Barbara.
25. Tim Walton, rhp, University of Oklahoma.
26. Todd Crane, of, University of Georgia.
27. Gary Yeager, rhp, Elizabethton (Pa.) College.
28. *Casey Brookens, rhp, James Madison University.
DRAFT DROP *Son of Ike Brookens, major leaguer (1975)*
29. Zachary Elliott, 2b-ss, UC Santa Barbara.
30. Kyle Kawabata, rhp, Washington State University.
31. Kevin Hooker, 2b, Oregon State University.
32. Kory Kosek, rhp, Mankato State (Minn.) University.
33. Brian Dunne, lhp, Kansas Newman College.
34. Richard O'Connor, ss, Valparaiso University.
35. Charles Cox, c, University of Texas-Pan American.
36. Scott Tebbetts, rhp, UC Riverside.
37. Bill Noone, rhp, Wilkes (Pa.) University.
38. Jed Kennedy, of, Bastrop (La.) HS.
39. David Robinson, of, University of Rio Grande (Ohio).
40. *Courtney Moore, of, Northwest Shoals (Ala.) CC.
41. Rob Gaiko, rhp, Oklahoma State University.
42. Jonathon Cornelius, of, Cal State Los Angeles.
43. Jeff Leaman, 3b, Indiana State University.
44. Clyde Livingston, c, Newberry (S.C.) College.
45. *Bryan Williamson, rhp, Kamiakin HS, Kennewick, Wash.
46. Jaime Mendes, rhp, New Mexico State University.
47. *Josh Glenn, rhp, Riley HS, South Bend, Ind.
48. *Marques Meshack, rhp, Lincoln HS, San Diego.

49. *Jason Bell, of, Atwater (Calif.) HS.
50. *Charles Marino, of, John F. Kennedy HS, La Palma, Calif.
51. *Jose Sandoval, ss, Poly HS, Sun Valley, Calif.
52. *Benito Lemos, c, Royal HS, Simi Valley, Calif.
53. *Mike Heidemann, 1b, Yavapai (Ariz.) JC.

DRAFT DROP *Son of Jack Heidemann, first-round draft pick, Indians (1967); major leaguer (1969-77)*

## PITTSBURGH PIRATES (10)

**1. Chad Hermansen, ss, Green Valley HS, Henderson, Nev.—(1999-2004)**
2. Garrett Long, 1b, Bellaire HS, Houston.—(AA)
**3. Bronson Arroyo, rhp, Brooksville-Hernando HS, Brooksville, Fla.—(2000-14)**
**4. Alex Hernandez, of, Pedro Albizo Campos HS, Levittown, P.R.—(2000-01)**
5. Dawan Elliott, of, Long Branch (N.J.) HS.—(Low A)
6. O.J. Cook, rhp, Liberty HS, Bethlehem, Pa.
7. *Josh Loggins, c, Harrison HS, West Lafayette, Ind.
8. *Brad Weber, of, DeKalb HS, Auburn, Ind.
9. Freddy May, of, John F. Kennedy HS, Seattle.
10. Daniel Delgado, ss, Killian HS, Miami.
**11. Brian O'Connor, lhp, Redding (Ohio) HS.—(2000)**
12. +Al Benjamin, of, Charles H. Milby HS, Houston / San Jacinto (Texas) JC.
13. Brian Settle, rhp, Woodrow Wilson HS, Portsmouth, Va.
14. Travis Gaerte, rhp, Fremont (Ind.) HS.
15. Elton Pollock, of, Presbyterian (S.C.) College.
16. *Ian Rauls, of, Ewing HS, Trenton, N.J.
17. *Jason Saenz, lhp, Mater Dei HS, Santa Ana, Calif.
18. Ryan Gillispie, rhp, Rancho Bernardo HS, San Diego.
19. Mike Symmonds, lhp, Old Dominion University.
20. Derek Bullock, rhp, Briar Cliff (Iowa) College.
21. Steven Flanigan, c, California (Pa.) University.
22. Chris Miyake, ss, UC San Diego.
23. Cory Bigler, rhp, University of Wisconsin-Milwaukee.
24. Tim Collie, rhp, University of North Carolina-Charlotte.
25. John Canetto, 3b, Coastal Carolina College.
26. *Chris Heck, lhp, Northeast Catholic HS, Philadelphia.
27. Jason Farrow, rhp, University of Houston.
28. +George Hlodan, rhp, Forward HS, Elizabeth, Pa. / Gulf Coast (Fla.) CC.
29. +Neal McDade, rhp, Florida CC.
30. +Brock Hundt, 3b, John A. Logan (Ill.) JC.
31. *Chris Miller, rhp-3b, Winter Haven (Fla.) HS.
32. *Ronald Brooks, rhp, Leon HS, Tallahassee, Fla.
33. *Travis Siegel, of, Choctaw HS, Midwest City, Okla.
34. *Jake Whitfield, lhp, Tallahassee (Fla.) CC.
35. *Matt Hoffman, rhp, Claremore (Okla.) HS.
36. *Ron Ricks, rhp, Tallahassee (Fla.) CC.
37. *Michael Carney, lhp, Merritt Island (Fla.) HS.
**38. *Brandon Larson, ss, Blinn (Texas) JC.—(2001-04)**

DRAFT DROP *First-round draft pick (14th overall), Reds (1997)*

39. *Joseph Wroble, lhp, South Suburban (Ill.) College.
40. *Arthur Young, of, New Rochelle (N.Y.) HS.
41. +Jason Wright, rhp, Palomar (Calif.) JC.
42. Scott Beach, rhp, Pittsburg State (Kan.) College.
43. Rob Thomas, lhp, Texas A&M University.
44. *Jason Shelley, ss, Plainfield (Ill.) HS.

## ST. LOUIS CARDINALS (12)

**1. Matt Morris, rhp, Seton Hall University.—(1997-2008)**
1. Chris Haas, 3b, St. Mary's HS, Paducah, Ky. (Supplemental choice—29th—as compensation for Type A free agent Gregg Jefferies).—(AAA)

DRAFT DROP *Nephew of Eddie Haas, major leaguer (1957-60); major league manager (1985)*

2. (Choice to Phillies as compensation for Type A free agent Danny Jackson)
2. Jason Woolf, ss, American HS, Hialeah, Fla. (Choice from Phillies as compensation for Jefferies)
3. Billy Deck, 1b, Potomac HS, Dumfries, Va.—(AA)
4. Brian Barfield, rhp, DeKalb (Ga.) JC.—(Rookie)
**5. *Cody McKay, 3b, Arizona State University.—(2002-04)**

DRAFT DROP *Returned to Arizona State; re-drafted by Athletics, 1996 (9th round) • Son of Dave McKay, major leaguer (1975-82)*

6. Joe Freitas, of, Fresno State University.
7. Matt King, rhp, Galveston (Texas) JC.
8. Jon Ward, rhp, Cal State Fullerton.

DRAFT DROP *First-round draft pick (30th overall), Mets (1992)*

9. Ryan McHugh, of, Florida Southern College.
**10. Matt DeWitt, rhp-3b, Valley HS, Las Vegas, Nev.—(2000-02)**
11. Robert Cooke, rhp, Mount Olive (N.C.) College.
12. Kevin Miedreich, rhp, St. Thomas Aquinas (N.Y.) College.
13. Shawn McNally, of-ss, Auburn University.
14. Ken Cameron, of, Washington State University.
15. Jason Lee, of, Burlington (Iowa) HS.
16. Andy Hall, 2b, Cal Poly San Luis Obispo.
**17. Britt Reames, rhp, The Citadel.—(2000-06)**
18. Lou Deman, c, Long Island University.
**19. Chris Richard, of-1b, Oklahoma State University.—(2000-09)**
20. Adam Benes, rhp, University of Evansville.

DRAFT DROP *Brother of Andy Benes, first overall draft pick, Padres (1989); major leaguer (1989-2002) • Brother of Alan Benes, first-round draft pick, Cardinals (1993); major leaguer (1995-2003)*

21. Tom Truselo, rhp, Delcastle HS, New Castle, Del.
22. Travis McClendon, c, University of Nevada-Las Vegas.
23. Jorge Roque, rhp, University of Puerto Rico.
24. Andy Schofield, of, Illinois State University.
25. *Mike Kimbrell, lhp, Southeastern Louisiana University.
26. Darrell Betts, ss, Ball State University.
27. Matt Wagner, rhp, Lewis-Clark State (Idaho) College.
**28. *Junior Spivey, 2b, Cowley County (Kan.) CC.—(2001-05)**
29. *Bryan Mazur, lhp, East Bladen HS, Elizabethtown, N.C.
30. *Rusty Sarnes, lhp, Lincoln Land (Ill.) CC.
31. Miguel Insunza, ss, Lewis-Clark State (Idaho) College.
32. *Gavin Brown, of, University of California.
33. Juan Munoz, of, Florida International University.
**34. Kerry Robinson, of, Southeast Missouri State University.—(1998-2006)**
35. *Dean Brueggemann, lhp, Belleville Area (Ill.) JC.
36. *Jeff Ryan, ss, Grand Prairie (Texas) HS.
37. Tony Falciglia, c, Fairleigh Dickinson University.
38. Jose Villafana, rhp, Mission (Calif.) JC.
39. Mike Swenson, lhp, University of South Florida.
40. *Bryce Darnell, c, Missouri Southern State University.
41. Scott Spaulding, rhp, Eastern Connecticut State University.
42. *Kyle West, ss, Pine View HS, St. George, Utah.
43. *Wade Jackson, 2b, University of Nevada-Reno.
44. Jason Lariviere, of-2b, University of Southern Maine.
45. +Brian Clark, lhp, Mississippi State University.
46. Bret Mueller, of, Cal Poly San Luis Obispo.
47. *Michael Gray, rhp, North Florida JC.
48. Nick Deluca, ss, Bellevue (Neb.) College.
49. Ruben Cardona, 2b, Belhaven (Miss.) College.
50. *Brandon Folkers, 1b, Pasco-Hernando (Fla.) JC.
51. +Todd Hogan, of, Middle Georgia JC.
52. *George Burgos, of, American HS, Miami.
53. *Brian Jorgensen, 3b, University of Missouri.
**54. Cliff Politte, rhp, Jefferson (Mo.) JC.—(1998-2006)**
55. *Cheron Farley, 2b, Lincolnton (N.C.) HS.
56. *Nick Roberts, rhp, South Sevier HS, Annabella, Utah.
57. *Michael Delano, lhp, North Hollywood (Calif.) HS.
58. *Nolan Vincent, 3b-of, Hollister (Mo.) HS.
59. *Ryan Gladwin, of, Martin County HS, Stuart, Fla.
60. Nick Kast, lhp, Oral Roberts University.
61. Rob Donnelly, rhp, Fresno State University.
62. *James Birr, ss, University of North Florida.
63. *Ryan Pene, lhp, Grand County HS, Moab, Utah.
64. *Michael Glendenning, 3b-of, Los Angeles Pierce JC.
65. *Craig Moore, 3b, Bergail HS, Freemont, Neb.

## SAN DIEGO PADRES (2)

**1. Ben Davis, c, Malvern Prep, Aston, Pa.—(1998-2004)**

DRAFT DROP *Brother of Glenn Davis, first-round draft pick, Dodgers (1997)*

**2. Gabe Alvarez, ss, University of Southern California.—(1998-2000)**
3. Ryan Van de Weg, rhp, Western Michigan University.—(AA)
**4. Brandon Kolb, rhp, Texas Tech.—(2000-01)**
5. Kenny Henderson, rhp, University of Miami.—(High A)

DRAFT DROP *First-round draft pick (5th overall), Brewers (1991)*

**6. Kevin Walker, lhp, Grand Prairie (Texas) HS.—(2000-05)**
7. Jason Totman, 2b, Texas Tech.
8. Sean Watkins, 1b, Bradley University.
9. Mike Martin Jr., c, Florida State University.
10. James Sak, rhp, Illinois Benedictine College.
11. Mark Wulfert, of, University of New Mexico.
12. Curt Lowry, of, McNeese State University.
13. Rick Gama, 2b, University of Miami.
14. Andy Hammerschmidt, lhp, University of Minnesota.
15. +Steven Hoff, lhp, Mills HS, San Bruno, Calif. / Canada (Calif.) JC.
16. John Rodriguez, ss, Miller HS, Corpus Christi, Texas.
17. Michael Irvine, rhp, University of Northern Iowa.
18. *Don Kirkendoll, lhp, Bacone (Okla.) JC.
19. Brandon Pernell, of, St. Bernard HS, Torrance, Calif.
20. Rich Hills, ss, University of Oklahoma.
**21. *Aaron Looper, rhp, Byng HS, Ada, Okla.—(2003)**

DRAFT DROP *Cousin of Braden Looper, major leaguer (1998-2009)*

22. Anthony Marnell, c, University of Arizona.
23. Matt Abernathy, of, University of Mississippi.
24. James Moore, of, Ranger (Texas) JC.
25. *Anthony Felston, of, Mississippi Delta JC.
26. *Damon Minor, of, Green River (Wash.) CC.
27. *Enrique Lazu, rhp, Santa Cruz HS, Trujillo Alto, P.R.
28. Carmen Bucci, ss, Northwestern University.
29. *Clint Weibl, rhp, Odessa (Texas) JC.
**30. Dusty Allen, of-1b, Stanford University.—(2000)**
31. *Joe Victery, rhp, Eastern Oklahoma State University.
32. Damond Nash, rhp, Texarkana (Texas) JC.
33. Ken Jones, c, Western Michigan University.
34. *Ryan Brown, rhp, Grapevine HS, Colleyville, Texas.
35. Andy Hunter, of, Arlington (Texas) HS.
36. *Jesse Cornejo, lhp, Wellington (Kan.) HS.
37. *Brandon Brown, lhp, Ranger (Texas) JC.
38. *Robb Gorr, ss, Rancho Buena Vista HS, Vista, Calif.
39. *Chuck Crumpton, rhp, Poteet HS, Mesquite, Texas.
40. Brian Jacobus, of, John R. Rogers HS, Puyallup, Wash.
41. *Scott Pratt, ss, Tooele (Utah) HS.
42. *William Alexander, rhp, Northwest Shoals (Ala.) CC.
43. *Rico Lagattuta, lhp, University of Nevada-Reno.
44. *John Robertson, rhp, Rockdale (Texas) HS.
45. *Brett Kondro, lhp, Fort Saskatchewan (Alberta) HS.
46. *Davis Kile, rhp, Friday Harbor (Wash.) HS.

DRAFT DROP *Brother of Darryl Kile, major leaguer (1991-2002)*

**47. +Wil Nieves, c, Eloisa Pascual HS, Santurce, P.R. / Lake City (Fla.) CC.—(2002-15)**
48. *Allen Goudy, of, Lake Michigan JC.
49. *Joel Vega, lhp, Academia Milagrosa HS, Cidra, P.R.
50. *Chad Reynolds, rhp, Friendship HS, Lubbock, Texas.
51. +Justin Sellers, rhp, Evergreen HS, Vancouver, Wash. / Green River (Wash.) CC.
52. +Adrian Stewart, 1b, Claremont (Calif.) HS / Fullerton (Calif.) JC.

DRAFT DROP *Son of Dave Stewart, major leaguer (1981-95); general manager, Diamondbacks (2014-15)*

## SAN FRANCISCO GIANTS (16)

**1. Joe Fontenot, rhp, Acadiana HS, Lafayette, La.—(1998)**
2. Jason Brester, lhp, Burlington-Edison HS, Burlington, Wash.—(AA)
3. Darin Blood, rhp, Gonzaga University.—(AAA)
**4. Russ Ortiz, rhp, University of Oklahoma.—(1998-2010)**
5. Jim Woodrow, rhp, Flagler (Fla.) College.—(Short-season A)
**6. Joe Nathan, rhp, SUNY Stony Brook.—(1999-2015)**
7. Alex Morales, of, University of Central Florida.
8. Ben Tucker, rhp, University of Southern California.
9. Manny Bermudez, rhp, Antioch (Calif.) HS.
10. Jeff Hutzler, rhp, University of Texas-San Antonio.
11. Ian Rand, of, Helix HS, La Mesa, Calif.
12. Bruce Thompson, of, University of Miami.
13. Philip Bailey, lhp, University of Central Arkansas.
14. Jon Watson, 2b, Fairleigh Dickinson University.
15. *Nate Forbush, c-1b, Central Arizona JC.
16. Brian Knoll, rhp, Brigham Young University.

DRAFT DROP *Brother of Randy Knoll, third-round draft pick, Phillies (1995)*

17. *Duane Eason, rhp, Brookdale (N.J.) CC.
18. *Rogelio Colon, rhp, Jose Gautier Benitez HS, Caguas, P.R.
19. Kurt Takahashi, rhp, Fresno (Calif.) CC.
20. Andy Norton, c, Gonzaga University.
21. Terry Weaver, ss, Liberty University.
22. *Danny Harmon, rhp, Midland HS, Floral, Ark.
23. *Mark Peer, of, St. Louis CC-Meramec.
**24. *Toby Hall, c, American River (Calif.) JC.—(2000-08)**
25. Marc Mosman, rhp, Cal State Dominguez Hills.
26. +Jeff Pohl, rhp, Three Rivers (Mo.) CC.
27. *Billy Coleman, rhp, Davidson (Okla.) HS.
28. *Jeremy Jackson, of, Indian Hills (Iowa) CC.
29. *Kelly Ireland, of, Mount Hood (Ore.) CC.
30. *John McMurray, 3b, Monticello (Ark.) HS.
31. *Shawn Lindsey, of, Franklin HS, Portland, Ore.
32. *Brian Phelan, c, East Denver HS, Denver.
33. *Brian Little, 3b, Tulare Union HS, Tulare, Calif.
**34. *Justin Miller, rhp, Torrance (Calif.) HS.—(2002-10)**
35. *Matt Schuldt, c, Howard (Texas) JC.
36. *Brandon Hayes, rhp, McLane HS, Fresno, Calif.
37. *Jason Dewey, c, Brandon HS, Valrico, Fla.
38. *LaJuan Rice, of, McNair HS, Atlanta.
39. +Tom Topaum, c, Centennial HS, Gresham, Ore. / Mount Hood (Ore.) CC.
**40. *Mike Lincoln, rhp, American River (Calif.) JC.—(1999-2010)**
41. *Mike Littlefield, rhp, Central Arizona JC.

DRAFT DROP *Son of John Littlefield, major leaguer (1980-81)*

**42. *Brad Lidge, rhp, Cherry Creek HS, Englewood, Colo.—(2002-12)**

DRAFT DROP *First-round draft pick (17th overall), Astros (1998)*

43. *Jason Huth, ss, Cherry Creek HS, Englewood, Colo.
44. *Mike Davis, rhp, Tallahassee (Fla.) CC.
45. *Eric Thompson, rhp, Greenon HS, Fairborn, Ohio.
46. *Casey Bookout, 1b, Stroud (Okla.) HS.
47. Joe Blasingim, rhp, Southwest Missouri State University.
48. *Kirk Boiling, rhp, West Torrance HS, Torrance, Calif.
49. *David Townsend, rhp, Delta State (Miss.) University.
**50. Edwards Guzman, 3b, Interamericana (P.R.) University.—(1999-2003)**

## SEATTLE MARINERS (3)

**1. Jose Cruz Jr., of, Rice University.—(1997-2008)**

DRAFT DROP *Son of Jose Cruz Sr., major leaguer (1970-*

88) • *Nephew of Hector Cruz, major leaguer (1973-82) • Nephew of Tommy Cruz, major leaguer (1973-77).*

**2. Shane Monahan, of, Clemson University.—(1998-99)**

DRAFT DROP *Great-grandson of Howie Morenz, Hockey Hall of Famer (1923-37) • Grandson of Boom Boom Geoffrion, Hockey Hall of Famer (1950-68) • Son of Hartland Monahan, forward, National Hockey League (1973-81)*

3. Greg Wooten, rhp, Portland State University.—(AAA)
4. Duan Johnson, ss, St. Paul's (N.C.) HS.—(Low A)
5. *Gary Kinnie, rhp, Chippewa Valley HS, Clifton Township, Mich.—(Rookie)

DRAFT DROP *Attended Michigan State; never re-drafted*

6. Karl Thompson, c, Santa Clara University.
7. Brandan Nogowski, lhp, Hood River Valley HS, Hood River, Ore.
8. Seth Brizek, ss, Clemson University.
9. Marty Weymouth, rhp, Brother Rice HS, Bloomfield Hills, Mich.
10. Ernest Tolbert, of, Lincoln HS, San Diego.
11. Russ Koehler, rhp, Chemeketa (Ore.) CC.
12. Dan Kurtz, rhp, LeMoyne College.
13. Andy Collett, rhp-1b, Loyola Marymount University.
14. Chad Sheffer, ss, University of Central Florida.
15. *Lance Severence, c, Bryan HS, Archbold, Ohio.
**16. Kevin Gryboski, rhp, Wilkes (Pa.) University.—(2002-06)**
**17. *Aaron Myette, rhp, Johnston Heights HS, Surrey, B.C.—(1999-2004)**
18. *Wynter Phoenix, of, UC Santa Barbara.
**19. Justin Kaye, rhp, Bishop Gorman HS, Las Vegas, Nev.—(2002)**
20. Greg Scheer, lhp, Jacksonville University.
21. Chad Soden, lhp, Arkansas State University.
22. Scott Maynard, c, Dana Hills HS, Laguna Niguel, Calif.
23. *Robbie Morrison, rhp, Wellington Community HS, Loxahatchee, Fla.
**24. *Brett Laxton, rhp, Louisiana Slate University.—(1999-2000)**

DRAFT DROP *Son of Bill Laxton, major leaguer (1970-77)*

**25. +Brian Fuentes, lhp, Merced (Calif.) JC.—(2001-12)**
26. *Keith Law, ss, East Paulding HS, Hiram, Ga.
**27. Ramon Vazquez, ss, Indian Hills (Iowa) CC.—(2001-09)**
28. *Greg Donahue, c, Rockland (N.Y.) CC.
29. +Robby Christianson, rhp, Chaffey (Calif.) JC.
**30. *Juan Pierre, of, Alexandria (La.) HS.—(2000-13)**
31. *Adam Walker, lhp, Yavapai (Ariz.) JC.
32. *Harold Frazier, rhp, Oral Roberts University.
33. *Yusef Hamilton, of, St. Martin Deporres HS, Detroit.
34. *Richard Sundstrom, rhp, John F. Kennedy HS, La Palma, Calif.
35. *Nathan Burnett, rhp, Rutherford HS, Panama City, Fla.
36. Todd Niemeier, lhp, University of Southern Indiana.
37. *Anthony Rice, 3b, CC of San Francisco.
38. *Joe Hunt, of, Santa Fe (Fla.) CC.
39. +Brian Nelson, c, Edison (Fla.) CC.
40. *Michael Campbell, of, Coronado HS, Mesa, Ariz.
41. *Shaylar Hatch, rhp, Gilbert (Ariz.) HS.
42. *Brian Grubbs, lhp, Cooper HS, Abilene, Texas.
43. *Travis Ray, rhp, Cairo (Ga.) HS.
44. *Leron Cook, of, Fresno (Calif.) CC.
45. *Joe DeVisser, ss, Mattawan HS, Schoolcraft, Mich.
46. *O.J. Burton, rhp, St. Thomas Aquinas HS, Fort Lauderdale, Fla.
47. Jeremy Palki, rhp, Clackamas (Ore.) CC.
48. *James Pietraszko, c, Forest Heights HS, Kitchener, Ontario.
49. +Brian Smith, of, Granite Hills HS, El Cajon, Calif. / Grossmont (Calif.) JC.
50. *Zachary Tharp, 1b, Boone HS, Orlando, Fla.
51. *Jacob Hermann, lhp, Eagle Point (Ore.) HS.
52. *Joel Greene, lhp, Linn-Benton (Ore.) CC.
53. *Brandon McNab, 1b, Boerne HS, Fair Oaks Ranch, Texas.
54. *Jeffrey Hammond, of, Flomaton (Ala.) HS.
55. *Jason Balcom, of, Mount De Sales Academy, Macon, Ga.
56. *Brian Cawaring, of, Alhambra HS, Martinez, Calif.
57. *Roy Roundy, c, Coronado HS, Scottsdale, Ariz.
58. *Todd Ozias, rhp, Miami-Dade CC Kendall.
59. *Jason Marr, rhp, Cerritos (Calif.) JC.
60. +Rafael Rivera, rhp, Miami-Dade CC New World Center.
61. *Ray Farmer, of, Duke University.

DRAFT DROP *Defensive back, National Football League (1996-98); general manager, Cleveland Browns/NFL (2014-15)*

62. *Eric Moten, of, Grant HS, Portland, Ore.
63. *Joseph Seymour, c, Southside HS, Elmira, N.Y.
64. *Damon Warren, rhp, Lower Columbia (Wash.) CC.
65. *Sean Hansen, 1b, Norco (Calif.) HS.
66. Isaac Burton, rhp, Arizona State University.
67. *Sean Kelley, rhp, Miramar HS, Miami.
68. +Steve Kokinda, 3b, Palm Beach (Fla.) JC.
69. +Gerald Eady, of, Seminole (Fla.) CC.
70. *Sean Hamilton, rhp, Dunedin (Fla.) HS.
71. *Eric Lloyd, rhp, Charlton County HS, Folkston, Ga.
72. *Brian Shultz, of, Blinn (Texas) JC.
73. *Travis Knight, 2b, Kent-Meridian HS, Kent, Wash.
74. *Tim Henley, of, Eastside HS, Gainesville, Fla.
75. *Wendell Simmons, rhp, Southwest HS, Macon, Ga.
76. *Michael Anderson, of, Jones County HS, Gray, Ga.
77. *Shane Roland, of, Cook County HS, Adel, Ga.

STAN DENNY

**Blue Jays first-rounder Roy Halladay struggled early before winning 203 big league games**

## TEXAS RANGERS (7)

**1. Jonathan Johnson, rhp, Florida State University.—(1998-2003)**
2. *Phill Lowery, lhp, Casa Grande HS, Petaluma, Calif.—(Low A)

DRAFT DROP *Attended Arizona State; re-drafted by Marlins, 1996 (6th round)*

**3. Ryan Dempster, rhp, Elphinstone SS, Gibson's, B.C.—(1998-2013)**
**4. Ryan Glynn, rhp, Virginia Military Institute.—(1999-2005)**
5. Shawn Gallagher, 1b, New Hanover HS, Wilmington, N.C.—(AAA)
**6. Danny Kolb, rhp, Sauk Valley (Ill.) CC.—(1999-2007)**
7. +Jorge Carrion, rhp-ss, DeWitt Clinton HS, Bronx, N.Y. / North Central (Texas) CC.
**8. Craig Monroe, ss, Texas HS, Texarkana, Texas.—(2001-09)**
9. Juan Rivera, c, Dr. Jose M. Lazaro HS, Rio Grande, P.R.
10. Julio Mercado, of, Brook Pointe HS, Stafford, Va.
11. Brian Martineau, rhp, Rancho Santiago (Calif.) JC.
12. Bryan Link, lhp, Winthrop University.
**13. Cliff Brumbaugh, 3b, University of Delaware.—(2001)**
**14. Brandon Knight, rhp, Ventura (Calif.) JC.—(2001-08)**
15. Ryan Gorecki, 2b, Seton Hall University.
16. Nathan Vopata, 3b-2b, Lewis-Clark State (Idaho) College.
17. Brian Llibre, c, West Covina (Calif.) HS.
18. Damian Rose, of, Overfelt HS, San Jose, Calif.
19. Chuck Bauer, rhp, College of St. Rose (N.Y.).
20. Joe Goodwin, c, George Mason University.
21. Ted Silva, rhp, Cal State Fullerton.
22. Bobby Styles, rhp, East Henderson HS, Hendersonville, N.C.
23. Robert Moore, rhp, University of Hawaii.
24. *Manny Torres, rhp, St. Joseph's HS, Trumbull, Conn.
25. Mike McHugh, lhp, Penn State University.
26. Chris Briones, c, University of Nevada-Reno.
27. *Spencer Brazeal, c, Mustang (Okla.) HS.
28. *Gary Johnson, of, East Los Angeles JC.
**29. Mike Venafro, lhp, James Madison University.—(1999-2006)**
30. Scott Mudd, rhp, Indiana University.
31. Kelly Stratton, of, University of Utah.
32. Scooter Bryant, lhp, Sulphur (La.) HS.
33. *Joe Garibaldi, lhp, Terra Nova HS, Pacifica, Calif.
34. John McAulay, c, William Carey (Miss.) College.
35. Bobby Kahlon, rhp, University of California.
36. *Joseph Williams, 3b, Chaffey HS, Ontario, Calif.
37. +Emar Fleming, rhp, Allegany (Md.) CC.
38. *Russell Bratton, rhp, Central HS, Columbia, Tenn.
**39. *D.J. Carrasco, rhp, Hayward (Calif.) HS.—(2003-12)**
40. Billy Reed, ss, Auburn University.
41. Mandell Echols, of, William Carey (Miss.) College.
42. Brent Sagedal, rhp, Carthage (Wis.) College.
43. *Amury Leon, ss, Tucson (Ariz.) HS.
44. Tom Smith, rhp, Petaluma (Calif.) HS.
45. Mark Draeger, rhp, Slippery Rock (Pa.) University.
46. Tim Codd, rhp, Edinboro (Pa.) University.
47. *Ryan Haley, rhp, Loxahachee, Fla.

## TORONTO BLUE JAYS (17)

**1. Roy Halladay, rhp, West HS, Arvada, Colo.—(1998-2013)**
**2. Craig Wilson, c, Marina HS, Huntington Beach, Calif.—(2001-07)**
3. Jeff Maloney, ss, Ridge HS, Basking Ridge, N.J.—(High A)
4. Mike Whitlock, 1b, San Lorenzo (Calif.) HS.—(High A)
5. Jay Veniard, lhp, University of Central Florida.—(AA)
6. Blaine Fortin, c, Lundar (Manitoba) HS.
7. Jeremi Rudolph, of, Apopka (Fla.) HS.
8. *Dave Marciniak, ss, Woodbridge (N.J.) HS.
9. Kyle Burchart, rhp, Bixby (Okla.) HS.
**10. Ryan Freel, 2b, Tallahassee (Fla.) CC.—(2001-09)**
**11. *Allen Levrault, lhp, Westport (Mass.) HS.—(2000-03)**
12. John Curl, 1b, Texas A&M University.
**13. *Ted Lilly, lhp, Fresno (Calif.) CC.—(1999-2013)**
14. *Jason Pomar, rhp, Vero Beach (Fla.) HS.
15. *Robert Corraro, rhp, Xavier HS, Madison, Conn.
16. Bill Brabec, rhp, Illinois State University.
17. *Johnny Byrd, rhp, University Christian HS, Jacksonville, Fla.
18. *Doug Dent, rhp, San Juan HS, Citrus Heights, Calif.
19. Jaron Seabury, rhp, Bellevue (Wash.) CC.
20. *Braxton Whitehead, 1b-c, Meridian (Miss.) CC.
21. Logan Miller, c, Texas Tech.
22. Scott Fitterer, rhp, Louisiana State University.
23. Brian Bejarano, 3b, Central Arizona JC.
24. *Mark Curtis, lhp, Bellerose HS, St. Albert, Alberta.
25. John Mitchell, rhp, Cal State Fullerton.
26. John Kehoe, 2b, Cumberland (Tenn.) University.
27. Robert Medina, c, Eloisa Pascual HS, Caguas, P.R.
28. Chris Hayes, 3b, Jacksonville University.
29. Brian Williams, c, Southwest Texas State University.
**30. *Brandon Duckworth, rhp, JC of Southern Idaho.—(2001-08)**
31. John Douglas, ss, Catholic (Washington, D.C.) University.
32. *Stanley Gay, lhp, Covington (Tenn.) HS.
33. *Todd Moser, lhp, Manatee (Fla.) JC.
34. Andrew McCormick, of, Grand Canyon University.
35. Jon Herring, lhp, Alabama Christian Academy, Montgomery, Ala.
36. +Randy Albaral, of, Jesuit HS, River Ridge, La. / Delgado (La.) CC.
37. *Seth Taylor, ss, Tate HS, Gonzales, Fla.
38. *Tyrone Gracia, 3b, Yarmouth Regional HS, Dennis, Mass.
39. *Eduardo Marquez, of, Mater Dei HS, Orange, Calif.
40. *B.J. Leach, rhp, Osceola HS, Seminole, Fla.
41. *Jesse Bechard, ss, Washington HS, Massillon, Ohio.
42. Thomas Peck, of, Rollins (Fla.) College.
43. *Justin Johnson, of, Diamond Bar (Calif.) HS.
44. *Brian Fitts, rhp, Gallatin (Tenn.) HS.
45. *Joe Pierson, ss, Huntington, (W.Va.) HS.
46. Ryan Cisar, ss, Magnolia HS, New Martinsville, W.Va.
47. *Antonio Jackson, of, Parker HS, Birmingham, Ala.
48. Paxton Stewart, 1b, Florida International University.
49. *Derek Hines, of, Arvada West HS, Arvada, Colo.
50. +Jeremy Satterfield, rhp, JC of Southern Idaho / Rancho Santiago (Calif.) JC.
51. *Kyle Adams, lhp, Creighton Prep, Omaha, Neb.
52. *Albert Colon, of, Apopka (Fla.) HS.
53. *Ryan Bundy, c, Lake Stevens HS, Everett, Wash.
54. *Claude Greene, 1b, O'Dea HS, Seattle.
55. *Travis Grant, rhp, Skyline HS, Salt Lake City.
56. *Sidney Harden, rhp, Middle Georgia JC.
57. *Pat Schultz, of, CC of Rhode Island.
58. *Doug Franklin, 2b, Pensacola (Fla.) JC.
59. *Andy Tarpley, rhp, University of California.

# Loophole free agents set new bonus records

It was a seemingly innocuous paragraph in the Professional Baseball Agreement, but in 1996 it cost four teams nearly $30 million and made four prospects rich beyond their dreams.

Rule 4(E) mandated that teams make formal contract offers to every draft pick within 15 days of their selection. Clubs generally were not strict about observing the rule, and in 1996 players discovered the loophole and exploited it to the fullest.

Four clubs had missed the deadline, and Major League Baseball had little recourse but to grant free agency to the players involved, touching off bidding wars for their services.

The four players were San Diego State first baseman Travis Lee, selected No. 2 overall by the Minnesota Twins; Texas high school righthander John Patterson (Expos, No. 5), Pennsylvania high school righthander Matt White (Giants, No. 7) and Florida high school lefthander Bobby Seay (White Sox, No. 12). Most scouts agreed that Lee was the top position player in the draft, and the other three were the top high school pitching prospects.

It was an opportune time for a top prospect to be on the open market, considering that two new expansion clubs, the Arizona Diamondbacks and Tampa Bay Devil Rays, were stocking their rosters and had no big-money contracts on their books.

"These guys were in the right place at the right time," Oakland Athletics president and general manager Sandy Alderson said. "This situation was a unique convergence of circumstances."

Lee ($10 million) and Patterson ($6.075 million) signed with the Diamondbacks, and White ($10.2 million) and Seay ($3 million) signed with the Devil Rays. The four clubs that lost the rights to their first-round picks were left to lament an obscure rule that previously had not been challenged or enforced.

"They found a chink in the armor, a technicality, that they could exploit and they took advantage of it," Montreal Expos scouting director Ed Creech said. "Baseball has shot itself in the foot again."

### BENSON OVERSHADOWED AS TOP PICK

The Pittsburgh Pirates, holding the first pick, selected Clemson righthander Kris Benson. He signed on Aug. 11, following his participation with the bronze-medal-winning U.S. team in the Atlanta Olympics. Benson's signing bonus of $2 million was a draft record, surpassing the $1.6 million the Florida Marlins gave third baseman Josh Booty in 1994.

Earlier in the year, the Marlins had signed righthander Livan Hernandez, a 20-year-old Cuban defector, to a $4.5 million contract, including a $2.5 million bonus. That was the largest contract ever for an amateur player.

"We've heard a lot about the Cuban players possibly driving up the bonus price," Pirates scouting director Paul Tinnell said. "But their situation was unique. It was a combination of ability, experience and marketability."

No. 1 overall pick Kris Benson signed for a relatively modest $2 million bonus, and his career was stunted by Tommy John surgery

Benson's bonus soon was overshadowed by the four players who became free agents on the basis of Rule 4(E), which had been in place since the first draft in 1965. The rule required that an offer—verbal or written, formal or informal—be made to all players within 15 days after the draft. The rule was revised in December 1990, mandating a written contract. Many baseball officials were unaware of the change and others ignored it, assuming it would never be enforced.

As bonuses started rising in the 1990s and players began holding out more, teams felt less urgency to tender contracts to formally begin the negotiation process. In 1996, most of the top college players had agreed to play in the Olympics, and many clubs delayed contract talks until the Olympics were over. By some estimates, only half of the 30 major league teams made proper offers to their draft picks. None of the four teams that lost their first-round picks claimed they followed the rule to the letter.

Credit (or blame) the California Angels and agent Scott Boras for the loophole coming to the forefront.

The Angels had failed to offer a major league contract to lefthander Brian Anderson by the Dec. 15, 1995, tender deadline. Anderson might have become a free agent, but agreed instead to be traded to the Cleveland Indians. His case prompted officials from both ownership and the union to

# 1996

## AT A GLANCE

### This Date In History
June 4-6

### Best Draft
**TEXAS RANGERS.** The Rangers learned after they drafted **R.A. DICKEY** (1) that he was damaged goods and reduced his signing bonus accordingly, but Dickey was the last active player among 1996 first-rounders. **DOUG DAVIS** (10) and **TRAVIS HAFNER** (31) also enjoyed long careers, giving the Rangers three of the top 11 performers in the draft.

### Worst Draft
**CINCINNATI REDS. BUDDY CARLYLE** (2) was one of the few 1996 draft picks still active in 2015, but he departed the Reds in 1998 without pitching in a single big league game. The Reds missed entirely on each of their other 42 selections, including **JOHNNY OLIVER** (1), whose four-year pro career peaked in Class A.

### First-Round Bust
**PAUL WILDER, 1B, DEVIL RAYS.** The expansion Devil Rays got one big league win to show for their $13.2 million splurge on loophole free-agent pitchers **MATT WHITE** and **BOBBY SEAY**. They did no better with Wilder. In five seasons, he hit .204-28-108 with 353 strikeouts in 851 at-bats.

### Second To None
**JIMMY ROLLINS, SS, PHILLIES.** In a 15-year career with the Phillies, Rollins outperformed every 1996 first-rounder. He hit .267-216-887 RBIs with 465 stolen bases, and won four Gold Gloves. In 2007, his best season, he earned National League MVP honors by hitting .296-30-94 with 41 stolen bases.

### Late Round Find
**ROY OSWALT, RHP, ASTROS (23RD ROUND).** At a slight 5-foot-11 and 150 pounds, Oswalt was overlooked by everyone except the Astros as a freshman

CONTINUED ON PAGE 466

## AT A GLANCE

CONTINUED FROM PAGE 465

at Holmes (Miss.) CC. His fastball jumped to 97-98 mph in 1997 and the Astros signed him to a bonus of $475,000. He became a two-time 20-game winner and three-time all-star. In 10 seasons with the Astros, Oswalt went 143-82, 3.24.

### Never Too Late

**CLAY CONDREY, RHP, YANKEES (93RD ROUND); TRAVIS PHELPS, RHP, DEVIL RAYS (89TH ROUND).** The Yankees drafted players for a record 100 rounds in 1996, including Condrey, who became the latest draft pick ever to play in the big leagues. He didn't sign and didn't agree to a pro deal for six years, when he was signed by the Padres as a free agent out of McNeese State. He pitched six years in the majors. Phelps is the latest draft pick to reach the big leagues with the team that drafted and signed him. He played three years in the major leagues, the first two with the Rays.

### Overlooked

**ROD BARAJAS, C, DIAMONDBACKS.** The expansion Diamondbacks, looking for catching depth, found Barajas at a tryout camp on Dec. 23, 1996. It turned into an opportunity of a lifetime for Barajas, who had exhausted his eligibility at Cerritos (Calif.) JC in 1995 and was hanging around the program as a bullpen catcher. Barajas played 14 seasons in the majors for seven clubs, hitting .235 with 136 homers.

### International Gem

**RAFAEL FURCAL, SS, BRAVES.** Cuban righthander **LIVAN HERNANDEZ** signed a record $4.5 million deal with the Marlins in early 1996. He debuted in the major leagues later that season and had a 17-year career, posting a 178-177, 4.44 record with nine clubs. But Furcal actually had a more productive career after signing out of the Dominican for $5,000.

## 1996: THE FIRST ROUNDERS

| CLUB: PLAYER, POS., SCHOOL | HOMETOWN | B-T | HT. | WT. | AGE | BONUS | FIRST YEAR | LAST YEAR | PEAK LEVEL (YEARS) |
|---|---|---|---|---|---|---|---|---|---|
| **1. Pirates: Kris Benson, rhp, Clemson** | **Kennesaw, Ga.** | **R-R** | **6-4** | **190** | **21** | **$2,000,000** | **1997** | **2010** | **Majors (9)** |
| Breakout season (14-2, 2.02, 156 IP, 27 BB/204 SO) led to easy choice as No. 1 pick; MLB career (70-74, 4.42) never met expectations, first two years were his best. | | | | | | | | | |
| **2. Twins: †Travis Lee, 1b, San Diego State** | **Olympia, Wash.** | **L-L** | **6-3** | **210** | **21** | **$10,000,000** | **1997** | **2006** | **Majors (9)** |
| Unrecruited as prep but evolved into elite prospect in college/summer ball; had swing/quick hands, grace around bag but never justified $10M investment. | | | | | | | | | |
| **3. Cardinals: Braden Looper, rhp, Wichita State** | **Mangum, Okla.** | **R-R** | **6-4** | **220** | **21** | **$1,675,000** | **1997** | **2009** | **Majors (12)** |
| Dominant college closer (4-1, 2.09, 12 SV) with 95-98 mph FB, traded to Marlins after four games with Cards, had penchant for blowing saves (72-65, 4.15, 103 SV). | | | | | | | | | |
| **4. Blue Jays: Billy Koch, rhp, Clemson** | **West Babylon, N.Y.** | **R-R** | **6-3** | **195** | **21** | **$1,450,000** | **1997** | **2004** | **Majors (6)** |
| No. 2 starter behind Benson at Clemson (10-5, 3.14, 112 IP/152 SO); suited to close with triple-digit fastball, temperament, struggled to command secondary stuff. | | | | | | | | | |
| **5. Expos: †John Patterson, rhp, West Orange-Stark HS** | **Orange, Texas** | **R-R** | **6-6** | **185** | **18** | **$6,075,000** | **1997** | **2007** | **Majors (6)** |
| Had size, loose arm, mid-90s velo to excel, but career tripped up by Tommy John surgery in 2000, other injuries; lasted just six years in majors, went 18-25, 4.32. | | | | | | | | | |
| **6. Tigers: Seth Greisinger, rhp, Virginia** | **Falls Church, Va.** | **R-R** | **6-4** | **190** | **20** | **$1,415,000** | **1997** | **2005** | **Majors (4)** |
| Made huge strides as college JR (12-2, 1.76 vs 6-7, 4.70 as soph), dominant arm on Olympic team, but string of elbow issues derailed professional career. | | | | | | | | | |
| **7. Giants: ^Matt White, rhp, Waynesboro Area HS** | **Waynesboro, Pa.** | **R-R** | **6-5** | **230** | **17** | **$10,200,000** | **1997** | **2003** | **Class AAA (2)** |
| "Best high school arm ever" had size, poise, delivery, command of three plus pitches, but hurt shoulder on cusp of majors, got stuck in minors over entire career. | | | | | | | | | |
| **8. Brewers: Chad Green, of, Kentucky** | **Mentor, Ohio** | **B-R** | **5-10** | **185** | **20** | **$1,060,000** | **1996** | **2005** | **Class AAA (4)** |
| Fastest player in college game excelled in CF, profiled as ideal leadoff type; never learned to bunt/put ball on ground to maximize speed, career stalled in Triple-A. | | | | | | | | | |
| **9. Marlins: Mark Kotsay, of, Cal State Fullerton** | **Sante Fe Springs, Calif.** | **L-L** | **6-0** | **180** | **20** | **$1,125,000** | **1996** | **2013** | **Majors (17)** |
| Ultimate blue-collar player; led Fullerton to CWS title, won Golden Spikes Award (.422-20-90; 2-1, 0.31, 11SV), overcame lack of speed/power to build long career. | | | | | | | | | |
| **10. Athletics: Eric Chavez, 3b, Mount Carmel HS** | **San Diego** | **B-R** | **6-1** | **190** | **18** | **$1,140,000** | **1997** | **2014** | **Majors (17)** |
| Best hitting prospect in class enjoyed most productive career (.268-260-902; 6 Gold Gloves) among first-rounders, despite losing most of '06-10 seasons to injury. | | | | | | | | | |
| **11. Phillies: Adam Eaton, rhp, Snohomish HS** | **Snohomish, Wash.** | **R-R** | **6-2** | **180** | **18** | **$1,100,000** | **1997** | **2009** | **Majors (10)** |
| Earned largest bonus in club history, but traded to Padres before reaching majors; later hooked on with Phils as free agent, was part of 2008 World Series team. | | | | | | | | | |
| **12. Giants: ^Bobby Seay, lhp, Sarasota HS** | **Sarasota, Fla.** | **L-L** | **6-2** | **190** | **17** | **$3,000,000** | **1997** | **2009** | **Majors (8)** |
| Third Sarasota High first-round arm in four years; set loophole free agency in motion over contract squabble with Sox; had modest MLB career (11-6, 4.16). | | | | | | | | | |
| **13. Mets: Robert Stratton, of, San Marcos HS** | **Santa Barbara, Calif.** | **R-R** | **6-2** | **220** | **18** | **$975,000** | **1996** | **2006** | **Class AAA (6)** |
| Compared to Dave Kingman throughout 11-year career in minors because of all-or-nothing approach; had 197 HRs with 1,151 strikeouts in 798 games. | | | | | | | | | |
| **14. Royals: Dermal Brown, of, Marlboro Central HS** | **Marlboro, N.Y.** | **L-R** | **6-1** | **210** | **18** | **$1,000,000** | **1996** | **2009** | **Majors (8)** |
| Best power/speed package signed by Royals since Bo Jackson; never turned promise into production in parts of eight MLB seasons (.231-14-89, 8 SBs in 271 games). | | | | | | | | | |
| **15. Padres: Matt Halloran, ss, Chancellor HS** | **Fredericksburg, Va.** | **R-R** | **6-2** | **185** | **18** | **$1,000,000** | **1996** | **2001** | **Class AA (1)** |
| Had prototype SS tools, size/athleticism, hit .493-7-28 as prep SR; bat never played after Rookie ball (.219-4-23 in six years), quickly fell out of favor with Padres. | | | | | | | | | |
| **16. Blue Jays: Joe Lawrence, ss, Barbe HS** | **Lake Charles, La.** | **R-R** | **6-1** | **190** | **19** | **$907,500** | **1996** | **2003** | **Majors (1)** |
| Spent seven seasons in minors (.256-44-239) before only MLB season in 2002 (.180-2-15); retired to play football at LSU, but plan scuttled by knee injury. | | | | | | | | | |
| **17. Cubs: Todd Noel, rhp, North Vermillion HS** | **Maurice, La.** | **R-R** | **6-4** | **185** | **17** | **$900,000** | **1996** | **2000** | **Class A (3)** |
| New to pitching as prep SR, stock skyrocketed with fresh arm/clean delivery, mid-90s FB; career compromised by shoulder problems, went 16-16, 4.15. | | | | | | | | | |
| **18. Rangers: R.A. Dickey, rhp, Tennessee** | **Nashville, Tenn.** | **R-R** | **6-1** | **205** | **21** | **$75,000** | **1997** | **Active** | **Majors (13)** |
| Went 38-10 in college, but bonus shaved to 10 cents on dollar over elbow issue; then jumpstarted fading career with knuckleball in 2005, won NL Cy Young in 2012. | | | | | | | | | |
| **19. Astros: Mark Johnson, rhp, Hawaii** | **Lebanon, Ohio** | **R-R** | **6-3** | **215** | **21** | **$775,000** | **1997** | **2005** | **Majors (1)** |
| Considered safe pick because of polished approach, but pitched in only nine major league games in 2000 (0-1, 7.50) with Tigers, his fourth club. | | | | | | | | | |
| **20. Yankees: Eric Milton, lhp, Maryland** | **Bellefonte, Pa.** | **L-L** | **6-3** | **200** | **20** | **$775,000** | **1997** | **2009** | **Majors (11)** |
| First-round gamble because of 10-19, 4.59 college record, but proved value in Cape Cod League (5-1, 0.21) before signing with Yankees; won 89 games in majors. | | | | | | | | | |
| **21. Rockies: Jake Westbrook, rhp, Madison County HS** | **Danielsville, Ga.** | **R-R** | **6-3** | **180** | **18** | **$750,000** | **1996** | **2013** | **Majors (13)** |
| Traded three times before age 22; found home with Indians, went on to win 105 major league games on strength of 90-91 mph sinking fastball, dominant change. | | | | | | | | | |
| **22. Mariners: Gil Meche, rhp, Acadiana HS** | **Lafayette, La.** | **R-R** | **6-3** | **185** | **17** | **$820,000** | **1996** | **2010** | **Majors (10)** |
| Went 12-1, 0.36 in 1994, also led Team USA to World junior title; down senior year due to viral infection, but recovered to pitch 10 years in majors, win 84 games. | | | | | | | | | |
| **23. Dodgers: Damian Rolls, 3b, Schlagel HS** | **Kansas City, Kan.** | **R-R** | **6-2** | **205** | **18** | **$695,000** | **1996** | **2006** | **Majors (5)** |
| Unknown at start of spring, but impressed Dodgers with athleticism, speed, power potential; spent five years in majors with Rays (.248-9-73) at six positions. | | | | | | | | | |
| **24. Rangers: Sam Marsonek, rhp, Tampa Jesuit HS** | **Lutz, Fla.** | **R-R** | **6-6** | **225** | **17** | **$834,000** | **1997** | **2005** | **Majors (1)** |
| Long journey to majors impacted by injuries, multiple arrests; pitched 1 inning for Yankees in 2004, then promptly blew out knee in wake-boarding accident. | | | | | | | | | |
| **25. Reds: John Oliver, of, Lake-Lehman HS** | **Lehman, Pa.** | **R-R** | **6-3** | **190** | **18** | **$672,000** | **1996** | **1999** | **Class A (2)** |
| Hit .625-11-43 as prep SR, patrolled CF with 6.4 speed, but pro career derailed by night-vision problem, repeated hamstring pulls; hit .208-14-75 in four seasons. | | | | | | | | | |
| **26. Red Sox: Josh Garrett, rhp, South Spencer HS** | **Richland, Ind.** | **R-R** | **6-4** | **190** | **18** | **$665,900** | **1996** | **2001** | **Class AA (2)** |
| Red Sox bought two-sport star away from basketball at Vanderbilt; had dominant breaking ball, but inconsistent fastball velocity doomed career (31-48, 5.23). | | | | | | | | | |
| **27. Braves: A.J. Zapp, 1b, Center Grove HS** | **Greenwood, Ind.** | **L-R** | **6-3** | **190** | **18** | **$650,000** | **1996** | **2006** | **Class AAA (3)** |
| All-state tennis player caught Braves' eye by hitting .507-14-46 as SR; one-dimensional talent rarely displayed same form in injury-plagued 11-year career. | | | | | | | | | |
| **28. Indians: Danny Peoples, 1b, Texas** | **Round Rock, Texas** | **R-R** | **6-0** | **210** | **21** | **$400,000** | **1996** | **2001** | **Class AAA (2)** |
| Bargain pick hit .375-17-86 as junior for Longhorns, but other tools short; struggled to make contact, find a true position in injury-riddled career in minors. | | | | | | | | | |
| **29. Devil Rays: Paul Wilder, of, Cary HS** | **Cary, N.C.** | **L-R** | **6-4** | **235** | **18** | **$650,000** | **1996** | **2001** | **Class A (3)** |
| First pick in Rays history had huge power, fell far short of expectations; never advanced past Class A in career beset by injuries, empty contact (353 SO/851 at-bats). | | | | | | | | | |
| **30. Diamondbacks: Nick Bierbrodt, lhp, Millikan HS** | **Long Beach, Calif.** | **L-L** | **6-4** | **180** | **18** | **$1,045,997** | **1996** | **2011** | **Majors (3)** |
| Unique provision in contract nearly doubled his bonus, but never justified it in short-lived MLB career (6-9, 6.64); was victim of shooting in minors in 2002. | | | | | | | | | |

*†Declared free agent because of improperly tendered contract; signed by Diamondbacks. ^Declared free agent because of improperly tendered contract; signed by Devil Rays.*

## How They Should Have Done It

Based on career WAR (Wins Above Replacement, as calculated by Baseball-Reference.com) achieved by players eligible for the 1996 draft through the 2015 season, here's how the first round should have unfolded. Numbers in parentheses indicate the round when the player was drafted. Asterisks denote players who signed as draft-and-follows.

| Player, Pos. | Actual Draft | WAR | Bonus |
|---|---|---|---|
| 1. * Roy Oswalt, rhp | Astros (23) | 50.2 | $475,000 |
| 2. Jimmy Rollins, ss | Phillies (2) | 46.0 | $340,000 |
| 3. Eric Chavez, 3b | Athletics (1) | 37.4 | $1,140,000 |
| 4. Ted Lilly, lhp | Dodgers (23) | 27.0 | $71,000 |
| 5. Casey Blake, 3b | Blue Jays (7) | 24.9 | $38,000 |
| 6. * Travis Hafner, 1b | Rangers (31) | 24.8 | $75,000 |
| 7. Mark Kotsay, of | Marlins (1) | 21.5 | $1,125,000 |
| 8. R.A. Dickey, rhp | Rangers (1) | 21.3 | $75,000 |
| 9. * Kyle Lohse, rhp | Cubs (29) | 20.5 | $110,000 |
| 10. Brad Penny, rhp | D'backs (5) | 19.2 | $60,000 |
| 11. Doug Davis, lhp | Rangers (10) | 18.5 | $25,000 |
| 12. Gil Meche, rhp | Mariners (1) | 17.1 | $820,000 |
| 13. * Marcus Giles, 2b | Braves (53) | 16.8 | $45,000 |
| 14. Jamey Carroll, ss | Expos (14) | 16.7 | $1,000 |
| 15. Milton Bradley, of | Expos (2) | 16.7 | $363,000 |
| 16. Eric Milton, lhp | Yankees (1) | 16.6 | $775,000 |
| 17. Wade Miller, rhp | Astros (20) | 14.8 | $7,500 |
| 18. Joe Crede, 3b | White Sox (7) | 14.7 | $80,000 |
| 19. Nick Johnson, 1b | Yankees (3) | 14.6 | $175,000 |
| 20. Jake Westbrook, rhp | Rockies (1) | 13.3 | $750,000 |
| 21. Kris Benson, rhp | Pirates (1) | 13.0 | $2,000,000 |
| 22. Jacque Jones, of | Twins (2) | 11.5 | $360,000 |
| 23. Chad Bradford, rhp | White Sox (13) | 10.3 | $12,500 |
| 24. Justin Duchscherer, rhp | Red Sox (8) | 10.1 | $47,500 |
| 25. Mark DeRosa, ss | Braves (7) | 9.8 | $60,000 |
| 26. Braden Looper, rhp | Cardinals (1) | 8.8 | $1,675,000 |
| 27. Jason Marquis, rhp | Braves (1-S) | 8.5 | $600,000 |
| 28. Junior Spivey, 2b | D'backs (36) | 8.2 | $5,000 |
| 29. * Dan Wheeler, rhp | Devil Rays (34) | 8.1 | $125,000 |
| 30. David Riske, rhp | Indians (56) | 7.5 | $75,000 |

| Top 3 Unsigned Players | | | Year Signed |
|---|---|---|---|
| 1. Barry Zito, lhp | Mariners (59) | 33.0 | 1999 |
| 2. Orlando Hudson, 2b | Blue Jays (33) | 30.9 | 1997 |
| 3. Aaron Harang, rhp | Red Sox (22) | 19.7 | 1999 |

discuss tightening the rules that applied to tendering offers. Union lawyers brought Rule 4(E) to the attention of agents who specialized in representing draft choices.

Boras said he was drawn to the tendering rule when he was revising a draft guidebook he prepared for his clients. Boras advised Seay that the Chicago White Sox were late in tendering an offer, and that he could challenge whether the team still held his rights. The White Sox did not contest the assertion and relinquished their rights to Seay on Aug. 15, making him a free agent. Seay wanted a $2 million bonus from the White Sox.

"I still contend that the grievance would not have held up," White Sox vice president Larry Monroe said. "But it would have been a hollow feeling to gather all the information for the hearing, go to New York and defend ourselves, win and find out that we still don't get the player. We're still very far apart on money, and we don't think we'll get him signed anyway."

Six other players appealed for free agency. Wichita State righthander Braden Looper (Cardinals, third overall), Maryland lefthander Eric Milton (Yankees, 20th) and Stanford catcher A.J. Hinch (Athletics, third round) all signed before

Travis Lee was the No. 2 overall pick by the Twins, but an overlooked rule allowed him to become a free agent and sign a record-breaking $10 million deal with the expansion Diamondbacks

MLB ruled on their cases, but Lee, Patterson and White carried through with their grievances. They became free agents on Sept. 24, becoming the first U.S. players in the draft era to gain unrestricted freedom during the summer when they had been drafted. Previous snafus involving Tom Seaver (1966), Bill Bordley (1979) and Billy Cannon (1980) afforded those players either limited free agency or access to a special lottery.

Boras, who represented Seay and White, said the ruling was a clear illustration of how the draft unfairly restricted the earning power of players.

"Baseball has made an admission that they're not paying for talent, they're paying for jurisdiction," Boras said, noting that most foreign players can sign with any club while American players are limited to one team. "With what has happened this year, now the draft is exposed. It shows that there is a small group of players who do have a very dominant market value—and are getting a third or a fifth of what the free market would bear. That's where the draft is wrong."

Major League Baseball closed the loophole after the 1996 season, but by then the horse was out of the barn.

### COURTING OF TRAVIS LEE

Lee was the first of the free agents to sign, getting a $10 million deal on Oct. 11.

"I think it's insanity to pay that to an unproven college player," Baltimore Orioles assistant general manager Kevin Malone said. "It's another sign the game is in trouble, and another sign that the industry can't control spending."

Lee said he chose the Diamondbacks, an expansion team not scheduled to begin play until 1998, because of the money and the chance to be part of building a franchise.

Lee hit .355 with 14 home runs and 33 stolen bases as a junior at San Diego State, and won the Golden Spikes Award. That summer he hit .416 with 17 home runs for USA Baseball's college

### AT A GLANCE

He hit .281-113-587 with 314 stolen bases over 14 seasons.

### Minor League Take

**ERIC CHAVEZ, 3B, ATHLETICS.** Chavez was one of the best hitting prospects in the 1996 draft class and won Minor League Player of the Year honors in his second pro season, hitting .327-33-126 at Double-A Huntsville and Triple-A Edmonton.

### One Who Got Away

**ERIC MUNSON, C, BRAVES (2ND ROUND).** Munson and Oakland first-rounder Chavez were a powerful 1-2 punch at San Diego's Mount Carmel High. Both players were recruited to play at Southern California, but only Munson honored the commitment. Three years later, he was the first college player drafted.

### He Was Drafted?

**QUINCY CARTER, OF, CUBS (2ND ROUND).** Carter was an NFL quarterback from 2001-05, but not before accepting a $450,000 bonus from the Cubs in the 1996 draft and playing four seasons as an outfielder. He did not advance beyond Class A, hitting .217-7-85.

### Did You Know . . .

**MIKE HESSMAN**, a 15th-round pick of the Braves, set the minor league career home run record on Aug. 4, 2015. He went deep for the 433rd time in his 19-year career, playing for Triple-A Toledo in the Tigers organization. Hessman hit 14 homers in a brief big league career.

### They Said It

Expos scouting director **ED CREECH**, reacting to a ruling that made his team's top pick, **JOHN PATTERSON**, and three other first-rounders free agents: "They found a chink in the armor, a technicality, that they could exploit and they took advantage of it. Baseball has shot itself in the foot again."

## DRAFT SPOTLIGHT: MATT WHITE

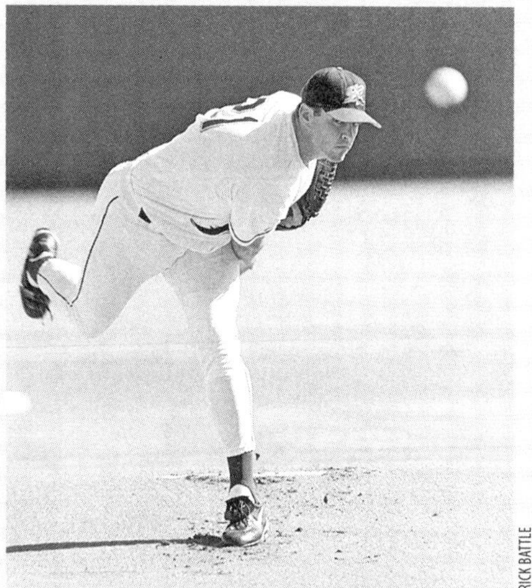


Matt White looked like the prototypical pitching prospect, but injuries and inconsistency left his career short of the big leagues

Matt White had big dreams. How could he not, when some scouts said he was the best high school righthander they had ever seen? How could he not when his agent found a loophole in the draft rules, and a brand new big league team labeled him a foundation player and gave him a record $10.2 million bonus?

On Nov. 17, 1996, White, a 6-foot-5, 235-pounder from Waynesboro (Pa.) High School, stunned the baseball world by signing a record deal with the Tampa Bay Devil Rays.

"It's like hitting a gold mine you never expected to hit," said Devil Rays managing general partner Vince Naimoli.

Since the summer of 1995, when he starred for the U.S. junior national team, White had carried the burden of great expectations. "Yeah, it was pretty pressure filled in order to perform up to my capability," he said, "but I worked hard to prepare for it."

It was easy to be impressed with White. With his big, powerful frame, he was capable of throwing a fastball 96 mph, along with an excellent changeup and a hard slider. The Devil Rays envisioned him at the front of their rotation for years to come.

"There's no question in our mind he was the most-talented player in this year's draft and a lot of drafts," Devil Rays general manager Chuck Lamar said.

White wasn't taken with the No. 1 pick in the draft, but it wasn't for lack of talent. Rather, White made it clear that his asking price was $2.5 million, and told teams not to bother drafting him unless they were prepared to meet his demands. Six teams passed on White before the San Francisco Giants drafted him seventh.

"God hates a coward," Giants general manager Bob Quinn said hours after selecting White. "If we don't want to be aggressive, we shouldn't be in this business."

The two sides barely spoke all summer. In mid-September, the Giants offered $1.625 million, a record amount at the time for a high school player. The White camp, advised by agent Scott Boras, countered with a four-year, major league deal worth $4.75 million.

"We're on different planets—except theirs is undiscovered," Giants senior vice president Brian Sabean said.

White defended his position. "Going into the draft, the Giants and most of the teams knew what we wanted," he said. "You're up front with people, and then they turn on you."

The stalemate ended on Sept. 24 when White became one of four first-round picks declared free agents by Major League Baseball because they had not been tendered contracts by their drafting teams within the required 15-day window after the draft. Suddenly, they were free to sell their services to any of the 30 major league clubs.

First baseman Travis Lee and righthander John Patterson soon signed unprecedented contracts with the Arizona Diamondbacks, and lefthander Bobby Seay signed with the Devil Rays, the other expansion team set to begin play in 1998.

White had no obvious suitors on Nov. 8, when he was in Tampa for a meeting with the Yankees. Seay's introductory news conference was the same day, and White attended to show support for his friend from the U.S. junior national team and a fellow Boras client.

The Devil Rays had shown only casual interest, but before he left the ceremony, White met Naimoli and Lamar for the first time, and his chance encounter put the wheels in motion for him to become a Devil Ray himself. Two weeks later, he signed his record deal.

White's career never panned out. He stalled from the start because of a back injury and inconsistent performance. Just as it looked like he was getting his career in gear in 2000 in Double-A and Triple-A, he injured his shoulder during trials for the U.S. Olympic team.

Despite several surgeries and months of rehabilitation, his shoulder never fully healed. He did not pitch in a big league game, and had a 4-15, 5.56 record over his final three seasons in the Devil Rays organization. By the time he was designated for assignment and retired at age 24, his fastball was rarely touching 90 mph.

"This really wasn't how we planned it to work out," White said.

national team that participated in the Olympics. Lee wasn't drafted or recruited out of high school in Olympia, Wash., and ended up at San Diego State because he sent a video of his swing to Aztecs coach Jim Dietz, who offered him a scholarship.

Lee's deal specified a $5 million bonus and $5 million in major league salary over three years, beginning in November 1997 when the Diamondbacks assembled their first 40-man roster. Major league rules later required that the payments be restructured, calling for all $10 million be paid in the form of a signing bonus within a year of Lee signing.

"To the people who say we're ruining baseball," said Diamondbacks general manager Joe Garagiola Jr., "there were other teams out there prepared to do what we did."

Patterson signed with the Diamondbacks on Nov. 7, and a day later Seay agreed to terms with the Devil Rays. On Nov. 25, White got a $10.2 million bonus deal from the Devil Rays.

### BURDENED BY EXPECTATIONS

The Devil Rays and Diamondbacks got little production for the substantial investments they made.

Lee made it to the big leagues first and had the longest and most productive career, lasting nine seasons. After a promising start with the Diamondbacks, he tailed off and was traded to the Philadelphia Phillies. In 1,099 games, he hit .256 with 115 homers and 488 RBIs.

Patterson endured injuries and made the Diamondbacks rotation in 2003, but he ended up with just 18 wins over parts of six seasons. Seay made 261 appearances over eight seasons as a middle reliever, most of them with the Detroit Tigers, and went 11-6, 4.16. White did not reach the major leagues as inconsistency and injuries stalled his career. In 122 minor league games, all as a starter in the Devil Rays system, he went 35-47, 4.64.

The rest of the draft became almost an afterthought. While there was a consensus that the overall talent wasn't as strong as it had been in previous years, particularly in position players, it unfolded pretty much as expected.

From the start, the emphasis was on pitching. Seven of the first eight players drafted were pitchers, along with 17 of the 30 first-round picks. The first four choices were from the college ranks, and 19 of the first-rounders were high school players.

Benson was a clear No. 1 choice. He emerged as Baseball America's College Player of the Year by going 14-2, 2.02 with 204 strikeouts in 156 innings. His two losses came at the College World Series.

### Fastest To The Majors

| | Player, Pos. | Drafted (Round) | Debut |
|---|---|---|---|
| 1. | Mark Kotsay, of | Marlins (1) | July 11, 1997 |
| 2. | Travis Lee, 1b | Twins (1) | March 31, 1998 |
| | Braden Looper, rhp | Cardinals (1) | March 31, 1998 |
| | *Mike Caruso, ss | Giants (2) | March 31, 1998 |
| 5. | A.J. Hinch, c | Athletics (3) | April 1, 1998 |

*High school selection.

## Top 25 Bonuses

| Player, Pos. | Drafted (Round) | Order | Bonus |
|---|---|---|---|
| 1. * Matt White, rhp | # Giants (1) | 7 | $10,200,000 |
| **2. Travis Lee, 1b** | **# Twins (1)** | **2** | **$10,000,000** |
| **3. * John Patterson, rhp** | **# Expos (1)** | **5** | **$6,075,000** |
| **4. * Bobby Seay, lhp** | **# White Sox (1)** | **12** | **$3,000,000** |
| **5. Kris Benson, rhp** | **Pirates (1)** | **1** | **$2,000,000** |
| **6. Braden Looper, rhp** | **Cardinals (1)** | **3** | **$1,675,000** |
| **7. Billy Koch, rhp** | **Blue Jays (1)** | **4** | **$1,450,000** |
| **8. Seth Greisinger, rhp** | **Tigers (1)** | **6** | **$1,415,000** |
| **9. * Eric Chavez, 3b** | **Athletics (1)** | **10** | **$1,140,000** |
| **10. Mark Kotsay, of** | **Marlins (1)** | **9** | **$1,125,000** |
| **11. * Adam Eaton, rhp** | **Phillies (1)** | **11** | **$1,100,000** |
| 12. Chad Green, of | Brewers (1) | 8 | $1,060,000 |
| **13. * Nick Bierbrodt, lhp** | **Diamondbacks (1)** | **30** | **$1,045,997** |
| **14. * Dermal Brown, of** | **Royals (1)** | **14** | **$1,000,000** |
| * Matt Halloran, ss | Padres (1) | 15 | $1,000,000 |
| 16. * Rob Stratton, of | Mets (1) | 13 | $975,000 |
| **17. * Joe Lawrence, ss** | **Blue Jays (1)** | **16** | **$907,500** |
| 18. * Todd Noel, rhp | Cubs (1) | 17 | $900,000 |
| **19. * Sam Marsonek, rhp** | **Rangers (1)** | **24** | **$834,000** |
| **20. * Gil Meche, rhp** | **Mariners (1)** | **22** | **$820,000** |
| **21. Mark Johnson, rhp** | **Astros (1)** | **19** | **$775,000** |
| **Eric Milton, lhp** | **Yankees (1)** | **20** | **$775,000** |
| **23. Jason Middlebrook, rhp** | **Padres (9)** | **260** | **$755,000** |
| **24. * Jake Westbrook, rhp** | **Rockies (1)** | **21** | **$750,000** |
| **25. * Damian Rolls, 3b** | **Dodgers (1)** | **23** | **$695,000** |

*Major leaguers in bold. *High school selection.*
*#Declared free agents and signed with other teams.*

"He's just the very best that I've ever seen in terms of consistency, focus and concentration," Clemson coach Jack Leggett said. "He has tremendous mental attributes that separate him from any other pitcher that I've ever seen at the college level. I know that's strong, but that's the way he is."

Benson spent nine mostly mediocre seasons in the majors, winning in double digits on five occasions, but posting a 70-75, 4.42 record. He showed promise in 1999 and 2000 before his career was derailed first by Tommy John surgery and later by rotator-cuff surgery.

The Twins, drafting second, chose Lee, considered by most clubs to be the best hitter in the draft. The St. Louis Cardinals followed by picking Looper, the nation's most dominant college closer. Neither Benson, Lee nor Looper had been drafted three years earlier out of high school.

The 6-foot-5, 235-pound White, who went 10-1, 0.66 with 131 strikeouts in 74 innings as a senior at Waynesboro (Pa.) Area High, was regarded by some scouts as one of the elite high school pitching prospects of the draft era. But his steep bonus demands and cavalier approach to the draft turned away numerous clubs. The Toronto Blue Jays, picking fourth, seriously considered White but took Benson's college teammate, hard-throwing Clemson righthander Billy Koch.

White, at the direction of Boras, advised at least 10 teams that they shouldn't draft him because they couldn't afford him. His leverage was a scholarship to Georgia Tech. The Giants stepped up and drafted White with the seventh overall pick.

"It's got to stop," one scouting director said of White's strategy of trying to manipulate the draft. "The draft is supposed to help the worst teams. Now agents are saying, 'Don't pick this guy.' We have to start calling their bluff."

### BONUSES HIT NEW STANDARD

Even without the loophole free agents, the average first-round bonus in 1996 was $944,404, the 10th consecutive year for an increase, although it was just 2.9 percent more than 1995. With the four free agents factored in, the average was $1,794,317, a 95.4 percent increase.

The Diamondbacks spent more than $18 million on bonuses for domestic players, giving $16.075 million to Lee and Patterson, and $2.3635 million to their own picks. Additionally, they paid out two of the six largest bonuses to international talent, signing Cuban righthanders Vladimir Nunez ($1.696 million) and Larry Rodriguez ($1.304 million).

The Diamondbacks paid their first-round pick, California prep lefthander Nick Bierbrodt, a $1,045,997 bonus, almost double the $525,000 he initially was guaranteed. He got more because a provision in his contract tied his bonus to the percentage increase in first-round bonuses from 1995 to 1996. It was the first—and last—time a draft pick's bonus was determined by how much teams spent. The commissioner's office quickly quashed the ploy for future draft picks.

The Devil Rays spent close to $16 million, giving $13.2 million to White and Seay, and $2.6865 million to their own picks. The Blue Jays led all spenders on draft choices with a record outlay of $4.505 million, topping the previous mark of $3.697 million by the Mets in 1994. The Pirates were the only other team to spend more than $3 million on draft choices, paying out $3.31 million.

The 22 richest bonuses in 1996 went to players taken in the first round, but record amounts also went to players selected in later rounds. The San Diego Padres gave Stanford righthander Jason Middlebrook, their ninth-round choice, a $755,000 bonus, easily the largest amount ever given to a player not selected in the first round.

The 6-foot-3, 215-pound Middlebrook, highly touted coming out of a Michigan high school in 1993, went 7-2, 2.34 with a no-hitter as a college freshman. His fastball was clocked at 97 mph, and he quickly became a leading candidate to be the top pick in the 1996 draft. But Middlebrook was limited to nine appearances as a sophomore because of a sore elbow that needed surgery, and he made just two starts in 1996 before a second surgery on the elbow. Teams shied away from him in the early rounds because of his medical history and his leverage as a redshirt sophomore.

Jason Middlebrook

Middlebrook showed flashes of his old form in pro ball, but continued to be plagued by elbow and shoulder injuries. He made 24 major league appearances over three seasons from 2001-03, going 4-4, 5.33. When Barry Bonds hit a record

## WORTH NOTING

■ The 1996 draft was noteworthy for the four loophole free agents and their record domestic bonus figures, but there also was a surge in bonuses on the international market, with six players getting deals of more than $1 million. None compared in size or significance with the $2.5 million bonus—and $4.5 million total outlay—given to Cuban righthander **LIVAN HERNANDEZ**. The Marlins signed the 20-year-old Hernandez on Jan. 11, topping the previous international record of $2 million, paid by the Dodgers to Japanese righthander Hideo Nomo in 1995. Armed with a 95 mph fastball, Hernandez was considered the best prospect among several Cuban defectors. Miami-based agent Joe Cubas helped Hernandez defect, as he did most of the Cubans of that era. Hernandez left the Cuban national team on Sept. 27, 1995, in Monterrey, Mexico, while training for the Intercontinental Cup. He was granted residency in the Dominican Republic. Since Dominicans weren't subject to the draft, Major League Baseball ruled that Hernandez was free to cut a deal with any team.

■ Other international signings of note included two by the Yankees: Venezuelan outfielder **JACKSON MELIAN**, for $1.6 million, and Japanese righthander **KATS MAEDA**, for $1.5 million. Melian's bonus was a record for a Venezuelan, as was the $950,000 bonus paid by the Dodgers to Panamanian outfielder **OMAR MORENO**. The Blue Jays also established a mark with the $750,000 bonus they paid to lefthander **DIEGOMAR MARKWELL**, from the Netherlands Antilles.

■ Louisiana State second baseman **WARREN MORRIS** hit the most dramatic home run in college baseball history, a two-run, two-out shot in the bottom of the ninth inning of the championship game of the 1996 College

CONTINUED ON PAGE 470

## WORTH NOTING

CONTINUED FROM PAGE 469

World Series that lifted the Tigers to a 9-8 win over Miami. Morris' homer was his first of the season; he missed most of the campaign because of a broken hamate bone. He was a fifth-round pick of the Rangers and spent five seasons in the major leagues. Miami had more players drafted (13) than any other college team, led by shortstop **ALEX CORA**, selected in the third round by the Dodgers.

■ Cuba won the baseball gold medal at the 1996 Olympics in Atlanta, beating Japan 13-9 as outfielder **OMAR LINARES** homered three times. It was the second straight Olympic triumph for Cuba; by going undefeated (9-0), the Cubans stretched their winning streak in major international competition to 126 straight games. The U.S. squad went 6-1 in round-robin play to earn the No. 2 seed in medal play, but lost in the semifinals to Japan and had to settle for bronze. The American team featured eight first-rounders from the 1996 draft, including pitchers **KRIS BENSON**, **BRADEN LOOPER**, **BILLY KOCH** and **SETH GREISINGER**; first baseman **TRAVIS LEE;** and outfielders **CHAD GREEN** and **MARK KOTSAY**—the first seven collegians selected.

■ Outfielder **DERNELL STENSON**, a third-round pick of the Red Sox, was murdered in Arizona in 2003, less than three months after making his major league debut with the Reds. Stenson was playing in the Arizona Fall League at the time. Four men were arrested for the random crime, with robbery stated as the motive.

■ Righthander **CHRIS REITSMA** was a supplemental first-round pick by the Red Sox (34th overall), making him the highest-drafted Canadian to date. Reitsma spent seven seasons in the majors, going 32-46, 4.70 with three clubs, but never threw as hard as 97 mph again after breaking his elbow early in his career.

## Highest Unsigned Picks

| Player, Pos., Team (Round) | College | Re-Drafted |
|---|---|---|
| Matt McClendon, rhp, Reds (1) | Florida | Braves '99 (5) |
| Eric Munson, c, Braves (2) | USC | Tigers '99 (1) |
| Josh Hancock, rhp, Brewers (4) | Auburn | Red Sox '98 (5) |
| Tom Graham, rhp, Athletics (4) | Fresno State | Never |
| Jeff Rizzo, 3b, Cardinals (5) | Stanford | Padres '99 (35) |
| Tony Lawrence, of, Expos (5) | *Louisiana Tech | Padres '97 (4) |
| Bobby Hill, ss, Angels (5) | Miami | White Sox '99 (2) |
| Kevin Burford, of, Phillies (6) | Rancho Santiago (Calif.) JC | Padres '97 (15) |
| Jason Verdugo, rhp, Angels (6) | *Arizona State | Giants '97 (12) |
| Mike Paradis, rhp, Athletics (7) | Clemson | Orioles '99 (1) |

**TOTAL UNSIGNED PICKS:** Top 5 Rounds (7), Top 10 Rounds (25)

**Returned to same school.*

73 home runs in 2001, Middlebrook gave up Nos. 65, 66 and 68.

The Houston Astros found a gem late in the draft, selecting righthander Roy Oswalt, an undersized Mississippi junior-college product, in the 23rd round. The Astros waited until the following spring to sign Oswalt, who by then had added 20 pounds to his slight frame and increased his velocity from the mid-90s to 97-98 mph. He received a $485,000 bonus.

According to WAR (Wins Above Replacement), Oswalt was the most productive player to emerge from the class of 1996. He posted a 163-102, 3.36 record over 13 major league seasons.

RICH ABEL

Roy Oswalt

Oswalt was one of numerous draft-and-follows in the 1996 class to have a noteworthy career. Others included righthander Kyle Lohse, a 29th-round pick of the Chicago Cubs; first baseman Travis Hafner, a 31st-round pick of the Texas Rangers; and infielder Marcus Giles, a 53rd-round selection of the Atlanta Braves. Hafner signed for $75,000 after leading Cowley County (Kan.) to two consecutive Junior College World Series titles. Seven draft-and-follows received bonuses of $200,000 or more.

### DICKEY OVERCOMES SLIGHT

The most successful position players selected in the first round proved to be Cal State Fullerton outfielder Mark Kotsay and California high school third baseman Eric Chavez, taken by the Marlins and Athletics with the ninth and 10th picks, respectively.

Kotsay batted .404 with 45 homers and 216 RBIs in college. Most scouts believed his power, speed and arm strength were a bit short, but they loved his intensity and baseball instincts. He became the first player from the 1996 class to reach the majors and enjoyed a 17-year career, hitting .276 with 127 homers for eight clubs.

Chavez had a short, compact stroke from the left side and most closely rivaled Lee as the top hitting prospect in the draft. Chavez batted .268 with 260 homers and won six Gold Glove awards in an injury-plagued, 17-year career. Shortstop Jimmy Rollins, from the California high school ranks, was the best position player to come out of the 1996 class. He played 15 seasons for the Phillies, winning the 2007 National League MVP award, hitting 229 home runs, stealing 465 bases and earning four Gold Glove Awards.

One of the strangest developments in draft history involved University of Tennessee righthander R.A. Dickey, selected by the Rangers with the 18th overall pick. His hopes for a healthy signing bonus were squelched by a magazine cover.

Dickey had agreed in principle with the Rangers on an $810,000 bonus, but the deal had not been signed when Rangers orthopedic consultant Dr. John Conway saw a picture of Dickey on the cover of Baseball America, along with the four other members of the U.S. Olympic team's projected rotation. Conway noticed that Dickey's right arm didn't hang naturally, and he suspected an injury.

Noted orthopedist Dr. James Andrews of Birmingham, Ala., examined Dickey after the Olympics and found that he was missing the ulnar collateral ligament in his elbow that provides stability to the joint. According to Andrews, Dickey had either torn the ligament so badly years before that it had vanished, or he was born without one.

The Rangers reduced their bonus offer to $75,000. Dickey signed and made it to the Rangers as a middle reliever, starting a long career in the major leagues that was still active entering the 2016 season. Dickey reinvented himself as a knuckleball pitcher after the 2009 season, and won 78 games over the next six seasons. In 2012, he was

## Largest Bonuses By Round

| | Player, Pos. | Club | Bonus |
|---|---|---|---|
| 1. | *^ Matt White, rhp | Giants | $10,200,000 |
| 2. | * Quincy Carter, of | Cubs | $450,000 |
| 3. | * Junior Brignac, ss | Braves | $415,000 |
| **4.** | ***Blaine Neal, rhp** | **Marlins** | **$350,000** |
| 5. | * Nick Leach, 1b | Dodgers | $215,000 |
| 6. | * Paul Stewart, rhp | Brewers | $275,000 |
| 7. | * Chris Moore, rhp | Marlins | $215,000 |
| 8. | Pee Wee Lopez, c | Mets | $105,000 |
| **9.** | **Jason Middlebrook, rhp** | **Padres** | **$755,000** |
| 10. | * Jeff Auterson, of | Dodgers | $97,500 |
| 11. | # Jason Walters, rhp | Dodgers | $225,000 |
| 12. | * Greg Ward, of | Braves | $52,500 |
| 13. | * Ben Norris, lhp | Diamondbacks | $175,000 |
| **14.** | **Ryan Kohlmeier, rhp** | **Orioles** | **$80,000** |
| **15.** | ***Mike Hessman, 1b** | **Braves** | **$115,000** |
| 16. | Kaipo Spenser, rhp | Indians | $100,000 |
| 17. | Derek Wallace, of | White Sox | $60,000 |
| **18.** | ***Mike Bacsik, lhp** | **Indians** | **$150,000** |
| 19. | * Ryan Ledden, rhp | Devil Rays | $75,000 |
| 20. | # Ismael Gallo, ss | Dodgers | $75,000 |
| **21.** | **# Jamie Brown, rhp** | **Indians** | **$285,000** |
| 22. | Dan Ferrell, lhp | Marlins | $20,000 |
| **23.** | **# Roy Oswalt, rhp** | **Astros** | **$475,000** |
| 24. | * Brad Farizo, rhp | Marlins | $43,500 |
| 25. | *# Kevin Dougherty, lhp | Mets | $30,000 |
| **Other** | ***# Kyle Lohse, rhp** | **Cubs (29)** | **$110,000** |

*Major leaguers in bold. *High school selection. #Signed as draft-and-follow. ^Signed with Devil Rays as free agent.*

a 20-game winner for the Mets and the National League Cy Young Award winner.

The Indians did not think any of the players available when they picked 28th overall were legitimate first-round material. They said they would pay their first pick no more than $400,000 and would select the first player remaining on their draft board willing to accept that amount. University of Texas first baseman Danny Peoples agreed and signed the day he was drafted. Peoples' career amounted to 573 games in the minor leagues (.250, 104 homers).

The Devil Rays and Diamondbacks got their first choices at the end of the first round. The Devil Rays selected North Carolina high school outfielder Paul Wilder, and the D-backs chose Bierbrodt. Wilder was considered second- to fourth-round material by most clubs, but Chuck Lamar, the Devil Rays general manager, said his club targeted the 6-foot-5, 230-pound outfielder from the start.

"This guy fits the profile of a power hitter," Lamar said.

Wilder flamed out after five years in the minors. He hit .204 with 28 home runs, 108 RBIs and 353 strikeouts in 851 at-bats, never advancing past Class A. Bierbrodt pitched three seasons in the majors, going 6-9, 6.66 in 38 appearances.

### RECORD NUMBER OF PICKS

A record 1,740 players were selected in the 1996 draft, surpassing the previous high of 1,719 in 1993. The process lasted 100 rounds, with the Padres dropping out first, in the 40th round, and the Yankees last.

The Orioles used their 33rd pick to draft third baseman Ryan Minor, who also was a second-round pick of the NBA's Philadelphia 76ers that year. The 6-foot-7 Minor starred at the University of Oklahoma, leading the Sooners to the 1994 College World Series title and earning All-America honors in basketball. He signed with the Orioles for a $100,000 bonus and spent the summer in the Rookie-level Appalachian League.

Minor attended training camp with the 76ers in the fall and did not make the roster, so he decided to pursue baseball full-time. The Orioles thought Minor could develop into a potential successor at third base to Cal Ripken Jr., but Minor hit just .177 with five home runs in parts of four major league seasons.

Washington State lefthander Mark Hendrickson also was selected in the MLB and NBA drafts. The 6-foot-10 Hendrickson was a 19th-round selection of the Rangers and a second-round pick by the 76ers. He played a season for the 76ers before being drafted again in baseball, by the Blue Jays in 1997, and subsequently pitched 10 seasons in the majors.

Two-sport stars were evident throughout the draft. The second round included outfielder Quincy Carter (Cubs), a Georgia Tech quarterback recruit; third baseman Doug Johnson (Devil Rays), a Florida quarterback recruit; outfielder Vernon Maxwell (Padres), a Tennessee defensive back recruit; and 6-foot-10 righthander Ryan McDermott (Indians), who had committed to play basketball at Arizona State. The Braves drafted outfielder Junior Brignac, a University of Washington wide receiver recruit, in the third round. All five signed baseball contracts. Brignac received $500,000, Carter got $450,000, Maxwell accepted $425,000 and Johnson got $400,000. None reached the major leagues; Carter and Johnson later played five seasons each in the NFL.

Athletes with multi-sport options were much less evident in the first round than they had been in recent drafts. The most heralded were outfielder Dermal Brown, selected with the 14th pick by the Kansas City Royals, and righthander Josh Garrett, chosen 26th overall by the Boston Red Sox.

Brown was a Maryland running back recruit and had not played a lot of baseball in high school, but he accepted a $1 million bonus from the Royals. He was regarded as the best power-hitting prospect signed by the team in nearly a decade. Brown played in parts of eight big league seasons, but never turned his promise into big results, hitting .233 with 14 home runs. The 6-foot-5 Garrett was an Indiana prep basketball star and had committed to Vanderbilt to play that sport. He signed with the Red Sox for a $665,000 bonus, and did not advance higher than Double-A in six seasons, going 31-48, 5.23.

## Largest Draft-And-Follow Bonuses

| | Player, Pos. | Club (Round) | Bonus |
|---|---|---|---|
| **1.** | **Roy Oswalt, rhp** | **Astros (23)** | **$475,000** |
| **2.** | **Jamie Brown, rhp** | **Indians (21)** | **$285,000** |
| 3. | * Roger Carter, rhp | Devil Rays (69) | $275,000 |
| **4.** | **Jason Smith, ss** | **Cubs (23)** | **$250,000** |
| 5. | Jason Walters, rhp | Dodgers (11) | $225,000 |
| 6. | Josh Kalinowski, lhp | Rockies (33) | $215,000 |
| 7. | Aaron Bond, rhp | Rangers (30) | $150,000 |
| **8.** | **Dan Wheeler, rhp** | **Devil Rays (34)** | **$125,000** |
| | Mark Curtis, lhp | Blue Jays (34) | $125,000 |
| **10.** | *** Kyle Lohse, rhp** | **Cubs (29)** | **$110,000** |

*Major leaguers in bold. *High school selection.*

## One Team's Draft: San Diego Padres

| | Player, Pos. | Bonus |
|---|---|---|
| 1. | * Matt Halloran, ss | $1,000,000 |
| 2. | * Vernon Maxwell, of | $425,000 |
| 3. | Widd Workman, rhp | $150,000 |
| 4. | Nathan Dunn, 3b | $105,000 |
| 5. | Brian Loyd, c | $90,000 |
| 6. | Tom Szymborski, rhp | $60,000 |
| 7. | Brian Carmody, lhp | $55,000 |
| 8. | * Chance Capel, rhp | Did not sign |
| **9.** | **Jason Middlebrook, rhp** | **$755,000** |
| 10. | Tim Lanier, c | Did not sign |
| 11. | Brian McClure, 2b | $4,000 |
| 12. | Ben Reynoso, ss | $4,000 |
| 13. | Brennan Hervey, 1b | Did not sign |
| 14. | * Francisco Gonzalez, rhp | $15,000 |
| **15.** | *** Steve Watkins, rhp** | **Did not sign** |
| 16. | * Sandro Garcia, 2b | $15,000 |
| 17. | * Craig Patterson, c | Did not sign |
| 18. | Jacob Ruotsinoja, of | $40,000 |
| 19. | Kyle Holle, rhp | Did not sign |
| 20. | Jimmy Alarcon, rhp | $2,000 |
| 21. | John Powers, 2b | $1,000 |
| 22. | * Dominic Marino, rhp | $15,000 |
| 23. | Ryan Thomas, rhp | $1,000 |
| 24. | * Jesse Cornejo, lhp | Did not sign |
| 25. | * Chris Speith, of | Did not sign |

*Major leaguers in bold. *High school selection.*

### IN FOCUS: KRIS BENSON

Kris Benson's emergence as the top pick in the 1996 draft was somewhat unexpected a year earlier, when he was cut from the U.S. college national team. But it provided Benson the motivation to get bigger and stronger, and he responded with a dominant junior season for Clemson.

"It gave me time off to go work out in the weight room," he said. "That's probably my main point of success. It gave me 15 pounds of muscle, and I've been strong all season. Last year I kind of ran out of gas after pitching about 80 innings. I've held up strong this year."

Benson ranked first among NCAA Division I pitchers in innings and was second in strikeouts, fourth in wins and sixth in ERA. His stuff, command and makeup were so dominant that by March the Pirates focused on him for the first pick overall, even if they wouldn't tip their hand.

"I know people will expect a lot, me being the No. 1 pick and all," Benson said. "But I've had to deal with that this season, too. I put a lot of great expectations on myself. I expect a lot out of myself, so it doesn't bother me if other people expect a lot from me."

Benson spent nine mostly unspectacular years in the majors, winning in double digits on five occasions, but overall finished his career at 70-75, 4.42.

# 1996 Draft List

**Did not sign. Major leaguers in bold, with first and last years noted. Order of selection indicated in parentheses. For the first five rounds, the peak level of each player is noted. + Signed as draft-and-follow (Second school noted if applicable).*

## ARIZONA DIAMONDBACKS (30)

1. **Nick Bierbrodt, lhp, Millikan HS, Long Beach, Calif.—(2001-04)**
2. Jerry Proctor, of, Muir HS, Pasadena, Calif.—(Short-season A)
3. Mark Osborne, c, Lee County HS, Sanford, N.C.—(AA)
4. Josh McAffee, c, Farmington (N.M.) HS.—(AAA)
5. **Brad Penny, rhp, Broken Arrow (Okla.) HS.—(2000-14)**
6. Eric Putt, rhp, Deltona (Fla.) HS.
7. ***Casey Fossum, lhp, Midway HS, Waco, Texas.—(2001-09)**

DRAFT DROP *First-round draft pick (48th overall), Red Sox (1999)*

8. Joe Verplancke, rhp, Cal State Los Angeles.
9. Marc Van Wormer, rhp, Prescott (Ariz.) HS.
10. George Oleksik, rhp, Middle Tennessee State University.
11. Ron Hartman, 3b, University of Maryland.
12. Michael Boughton, ss, Northwood (Texas) Institute.
13. Ben Norris, lhp, Westwood HS, Austin, Texas.
14. Jamie Gann, of, University of Oklahoma.
15. Reggie Davis, c, Augusta (Ga.) College.
16. *Kevin Johnson, ss, St. Joseph's HS, Alameda, Calif.

DRAFT DROP *Twin brother of Curtis Johnson, 38th-round draft pick, Diamondbacks (1996)*

17. Jackie Rexrode, ss, Riverdale Baptist HS, Laurel, Md.
18. David Chapman, of, Alta Loma (Calif.) HS.
19. *Jacob Brooks, rhp, East Lake HS, Palm Harbor, Fla.
20. John Fleming, rhp, Bonita Vista HS, Chula Vista, Calif.
21. *Brian Crisorio, 3b, East Lake HS, Clearwater, Fla.
22. *Jeffrey Nichols, rhp, Duncanville (Texas) HS.
23. Michael McCutchen, lhp, Modesto (Calif.) JC.
24. **+Eric Knott, lhp, Stetson University.—(2001-03)**
25. Scott Glasser, 2b, Rancho Santiago (Calif.) JC.
26. **Rob Ryan, of, Washington State University.—(1999-2001)**
27. Justin Bice, rhp, Grand Canyon University.
28. Beau Baltzell, c, Purdue University.
29. Kevin Sweeney, of, Mercyhurst (Pa.) College.
30. *Michael Pesci, of, University of Detroit.
31. Jose Nunez, 3b-2b, Northeast Texas CC.
32. **Jason Conti, of, University of Pittsburgh.—(2000-04)**
33. Dallas Anderson, rhp, Lethbridge (Alberta) CC.
34. *Corey Hart, 2b, Connors State (Okla.) JC.
35. Brett Hardy, of, UC Santa Barbara.
36. **Junior Spivey, 2b, Cowley County (Kan.) CC.—(2001-05)**
37. Jason Moore, c-1b, West Virginia State College.
38. *Curtis Johnson, of, St. Joseph's HS, Oakland.

DRAFT DROP *Twin brother of Kevin Johnson, 16th-round draft pick, Diamondbacks (1996)*

39. Bert Hudson, c, Jay (Fla.) HS.
40. Travis McCall, lhp, Ayala HS, Chino Hills, Calif.
41. Brad Allison, c, Morehead State University.
42. **Eric Sabel, rhp, Tennessee Tech.—(1999-2002)**
43. *Charles Chungu, rhp, University of New Hampshire.
44. *James Harrison, rhp, William Penn HS, New Castle, Del.
45. *Brett DeBoer, lhp, Lakeland HS, Rathdrum, Idaho.
46. Matt Bell, rhp, Joplin (Mo.) HS.
47. *Ryan Evans, c, Tuscaloosa County HS, Northport, Ala.
48. Jorge Martinez, c, Newtown HS, New York.
49. *Brent Wagler, rhp, Florida Southern College.
50. *Casey Rowe, rhp, Bullard HS, Fresno, Calif.
51. *Patrick Coogan, rhp, Louisiana State University.
52. *Jeff Remillard, rhp, Memorial HS, Manchester, N.H.
53. David Harper, rhp, Lubbock Christian (Texas) University.
54. ***Jason Jennings, rhp, Poteet HS, Mesquite, Texas.—(2001-09)**

DRAFT DROP *First-round draft pick (16th overall), Rockies (1999)*

LARRY GOREN

**Marlins first-rounder Mark Kotsay was the first player from '96 draft to reach the big leagues**

55. *Blake Ricken, lhp, Fresno (Calif.) CC.
56. *Andy McCulloch, rhp, Western HS, Las Vegas, Nev.
57. *Eric O'Brien, rhp, Alton (N.H.) HS.
58. Bryce Darnell, c, Missouri Southern State University.
59. Carmen Panaro, c, Niagara University.
60. Mark Chavez, rhp, Cal State Fullerton.
61. ***Brandon Duckworth, rhp, JC of Southern Idaho.—(2001-08)**
62. *George Otero, 3b-c, Monsignor Pace HS, Miami.

## ATLANTA BRAVES (27)

1. A.J. Zapp, 1b, Center Grove HS, Greenwood, Ind.—(AAA)
1. **Jason Marquis, rhp, Tottenville HS, Staten Island, N.Y.** (Supplemental choice—35th—for failure to sign 1995 first-round draft pick Chad Hutchinson).**—(2000-13)**
2. ***Eric Munson, c, Mount Carmel HS, San Diego.—(2000-09)**

DRAFT DROP *Attended Southern California; re-drafted by Tigers, 1999 (1st round); first player from 1999 draft to reach majors (July 18, 2000)*

3. Junior Brignac, of, Cleveland HS, Reseda, Calif.—(AA)
4. **Joe Nelson, rhp, University of San Francisco.—(2001-10)**
5. Josh Pugh, c, Henry Clay HS, Lexington, Ky.—(High A)
6. Shawn Onley, rhp, Rice University.
7. **Mark DeRosa, 3b, University of Pennsylvania.—(1998-2013)**
8. A.D. Thorpe, ss, Southern HS, Durham, N.C.
9. Nathan Harden, rhp, Dripping Springs (Texas) HS.
10. Garrett Lee, rhp, Glendale (Calif.) JC.
11. **Aaron Taylor, rhp, Lowndes HS, Hahira, Ga.—(2002-04)**
12. Greg Ward, of, Avon (Conn.) HS.
13. Jason Ross, of, University of Hawaii.
14. *John Alkire, rhp, University of Tennessee.
15. **Mike Hessman, 1b-rhp, Mater Dei HS, Westminster, Calif.—(2003-10)**
16. Earl Beasley, lhp, Lake City (Fla.) CC.
17. *Dana Davis, rhp, Rice University.
18. Donald Ceasar, rhp, LaGrange HS, Lake Charles, La.
19. Adam Milburn, lhp, University of Kentucky.
20. John Arnold, c, Eastern New Mexico University.
21. Jesse Crespo, c, Colegio Regional HS, Camuy, P.R.
22. *Aaron Melebeck, ss, Clear Brook HS, Webster, Texas.
23. Dax Norris, c, University of Alabama.
24. *Pat Collins, rhp, Union (N.J.) HS.
25. Anthony Brooks, ss, Gulf Coast (Fla.) CC.
26. Jason Katz, ss, New Mexico JC.
27. Aaron Strangfeld, 1b, Grossmont (Calif.) JC.
28. *Miguel Garcia, rhp, Cerritos (Calif.) JC.
29. Galen Reeder, lhp, DeKalb (Ga.) JC.
30. ***Freddy Sanchez, ss, Burbank (Calif.) HS.—(2002-11)**
31. *Adam Love, rhp, Westlake HS, Austin, Texas.
32. *Dustin Franklin, lhp, Permian HS, Odessa, Texas.
33. Jerrod Wong, 1b, Gonzaga University.
34. *Adam Springston, rhp, Oxnard (Calif.) JC.
35. +Byron Embry, rhp, Indian Hills (Iowa) CC.
36. +Scott Frawley, c, South Suburban (Ill.) JC.
37. *Hunter Wenzel, lhp, Boerne HS, Fair Oaks Ranch, Texas.
38. +Randy Phillips, lhp, Olney Central (Ill.) JC.
39. Jeff Lindemann, rhp, Andrew HS, Lockport, Ill.
40. *Anthony Barrow, 1b, Blazer HS, Ashland, Ky.
41. Justin Willoughby, lhp, Princeton (N.C.) HS.
42. George Snead, rhp, Albany State (Ga.) University.
43. +Cory Simpson, rhp, Sumner HS, Kentwood, La. / Southwest Mississippi CC.
44. *Nate Fernley, rhp, Long Beach (Calif.) CC.
45. John Zydowsky, ss, Portage HS, Pardeeville, Wis.
46. +Joe Holzbauer, rhp, Palomar (Calif.) JC.
47. *Patrick Fuentes, ss, Logan HS, South San Francisco.
48. *Greg Dukeman, rhp, Millikan HS, Long Beach, Calif.
49. Michael Jones, lhp, UC Riverside.
50. *Travis Richo, of, Fernandina Beach (Fla.) HS.
51. *Daniel Bell, of, University HS, Los Angeles.
52. +Brett Pierce, ss, Citrus (Calif.) JC.
53. **+Marcus Giles, 2b, Granite Hills HS, El Cajon, Calif. / Grossmont (Calif.) JC.—(2001-07)**

DRAFT DROP *Brother of Brian Giles, major leaguer (1995-2009)*

54. Jeff Champion, of, Florida Memorial College.
55. Adam Johnson, of, University of Central Florida.
56. *Bradley Green, ss, South Pittsburg (Tenn.) HS.
57. Juan Galban, lhp, Miami.
58. *Baylor Moore, lhp, Friendswood (Texas) HS.

DRAFT DROP *Son of Balor Moore, first-round draft pick, Expos (1969); major leaguer (1970-80)*

59. *Hector Gonzales, c, Scottsdale (Ariz.) CC.
60. *Ray Plummer, lhp, Point Loma Nazarene (Calif.) College.

## BALTIMORE ORIOLES (16)

1. (Choice to Blue Jays as compensation for Type A free agent Roberto Alomar)
2. **Brian Falkenborg, rhp, Redmond (Wash.) HS.—(1999-2008)**
3. Daren Hooper, of, University of Arizona.—(Low A)
4. Mark Seaver, rhp, Wake Forest University.—(High A)
5. Franky Figueroa, 1b-of, Florida Bible HS, Hialeah, Fla.—(AAA)
6. Josh McNatt, lhp, Motlow State (Tenn.) CC.
7. *Brent Schoening, rhp, Columbus (Ga.) HS.
8. **Chad Paronto, rhp, University of Massachusetts.—(2001-09)**
9. Luis Ramirez, 1b, Carmen B. Huyke HS, Arroyo, P.R.
10. **Luis Matos, of, Discipulos de Cristo HS, Bayamon, P.R.—(2000-06)**
11. *Bruce Stanley, rhp, Ball State University.
12. +Simeon Theodile, rhp, Acadiana HS, Lafayette, La. / Galveston (Texas) JC.
13. **Augie Ojeda, ss, University of Tennessee.—(2000-10)**
14. **Ryan Kohlmeier, rhp, Butler County (Kan.) CC.—(2000-01)**
15. **Josh Towers, rhp, Oxnard (Calif.) JC.—(2001-09)**
16. *Josh Morris, ss, Motlow State (Tenn.) CC.
17. Tim DeCinces, c, UCLA.

DRAFT DROP *Son of Doug DeCinces, major leaguer (1973-87)*

18. *Andrew Cheek, lhp, Beaver Creak HS, West Jefferson, N.C.
19. *Gabe Crecion, rhp, Chaminade Prep, West Hills, Calif.
20. Ashanti Davison, of, St. Mary's HS, Stockton, Calif.
21. **Gabe Molina, rhp, Arizona State University.—(1999-2003)**
22. ***Mike MacDougal, rhp, Mesa (Ariz.) HS.—(2001-12)**

DRAFT DROP *First-round draft pick (25th overall), Royals (1999)*

23. Jesse Perez, ss, Eugenio Maria de Hostos HS, Mayaguez, P.R.
24. *Jay Gehrke, rhp, North HS, Fargo, N.D.

DRAFT DROP *First-round draft pick (32nd overall), Royals (1999)*

25. **John Parrish, lhp, McCaskey HS, Lancaster, Pa.—(2000-10)**
26. Maleke Fowler, of, Nicholls State University.
27. *Robbie Baker, rhp, Westwood HS, Austin, Texas.
28. *Dell Lindsey, 3b, North Shore HS, Houston.
29. *Jason Johnson, lhp, Sacred Heart Academy, Winn, Mich.
30. +Johnny Morales, lhp, Central Arizona JC.
31. Jeff Phipps, rhp, San Joaquin Delta (Calif.) JC.

32. Todd Morgan, of, Deerfield Beach (Fla.) HS.
**33. Ryan Minor, 3b-1b, University of Oklahoma.—(1998-2001)**
DRAFT DROP *Second-round draft pick, Philadelphia 76ers, National Basketball Association (1996) • Brother of Damon Minor, 12th-round draft pick, Giants (1996); major leaguer (2000-04)*
34. +DeShawn Ziths, of, Columbia-Greene (N.Y.) CC.
35. Jeremiah Johnson, rhp, Kellogg (Mich.) CC.
36. +Jimmy Escalante, c, Hagerstown (Md.) JC.
37. Craig Ratliff, rhp, Paintsville HS, West Van Lear, Ky.
38. *Randall Benge, lhp, Fort Vancouver HS, Yacolt, Wash.
39. *Eric Drew, rhp, Montello (Wis.) HS.
40. *Ben Christensen, rhp, Goddard HS, West Goddard, Kan.
DRAFT DROP *First-round draft pick (26th overall), Cubs (1999)*
41. *Vanshan Renfroe, ss, McGavock HS, Hermitage, Tenn.
42. Michael Kirkpatrick, of, St. Elizabeth HS, New Castle, Del.
43. *Tyson Martinez, rhp, Fort Madison (Iowa) HS.
44. *Daniel Allen, of, Perry (Okla.) HS.
45. *Josh Taylor, ss, Seminole (Okla.) JC.
46. *Sean Gilchrist, of, Bigfork (Mon.) HS.
47. *Chad Anderson, of, Bigfork (Mon.) HS.

## BOSTON RED SOX (26)

1. Josh Garrett, rhp, South Spencer HS, Richland, Ind.—(AA)
**1. Chris Reitsma, rhp, Calgary (Alberta) Christian HS** (Supplemental choice—34th—as compensation for Type A free agent Erik Hanson).**—(2001-07)**
2. Gary LoCurto, 1b, University HS, San Diego (Choice from Blue Jays as compensation for Hanson).—(Low A)
2. Jason Sekany, rhp, University of Virginia.—(AAA)
**3. Dernell Stenson, of, LaGrange (Ga.) HS.—(2003)**
DRAFT DROP *Died as active player (Nov. 4, 2003)*
**4. John Barnes, of, Grossmont (Calif.) CC.—(2000-01)**
5. Bobby Brito, c, Cypress (Calif.) HS.—(Rookie)
6. Mike Perini, of, Carlsbad (N.M.) HS.
**7. Robert Ramsay, lhp, Washington State University.—(1999-2000)**
**8. Justin Duchscherer, rhp, Coronado HS, Lubbock, Texas.—(2001-10)**
9. +Marcus Martinez, lhp, Monterey HS, Lubbock, Texas / McLennan (Texas) JC.
**10. Shea Hillenbrand, ss, Mesa (Ariz.) CC.—(2001-07)**
11. Scott Musgrave, lhp, Appalachian State University.
12. Dion Ruecker, ss, Texas Tech.
13. Skipp Benzing, rhp, Indian Hills (Iowa) CC.
14. *Justin Lynch, rhp, Marina HS, Huntington Beach, Calif.
15. *Mark Robbins, 3b, Derry (Kan.) HS.
16. Jeff Keaveney, 1b-of, University of Southern Maine.
17. *Justin Crisafulli, rhp, Arizona Western JC.
18. Mike McKinley, of, Scottsdale (Ariz.) CC.
19. Mike Rupp, rhp, Monte Vista HS, Spring Valley, Calif.
20. Chuck Beale, rhp, Stetson University.
21. Javier Fuentes, ss-2b, Arizona State University.
**22. *Aaron Harang, rhp, Patrick Henry HS, San Diego.—(2002-15)**
23. *Paul McCurtain, rhp, Mesa (Ariz.) CC.
24. *Robert Brandt, rhp, A&M Consolidated HS, College Station, Texas.
25. *Dominic Barrett, of, Trimble Tech HS, Fort Worth, Texas.
26. Chris Thompson, rhp, St. Leo (Fla.) College.
27. *Ryan Murray, rhp, Tampa Bay Tech HS, Tampa.
28. Erik Metzger, c, Samford University.
**29. *Josh Stewart, lhp, Livingston Central HS, Ledbetter, Ky.—(2003-04)**
30. *William Whitaker, lhp, First Coast HS, Jacksonville, Fla.
31. *Matt Frick, c, Yavapai (Ariz.) JC.
**32. *Mike Bynum, lhp, Middleburg (Fla.) HS.—(2002-04)**
DRAFT DROP *First-round draft pick (49th overall), Padres (1999)*
33. +Adam Roller, rhp, Lakeland (Fla.) HS / Hillsborough (Fla.) CC.
34. *Jaime Bonilla, lhp, Lake City (Fla.) CC.
35. *Kasey Kuhlmeyer, lhp, San Pasqual HS, Escondido, Calif.
36. *Ken Sarna, ss, Durango HS, Las Vegas, Nev.
37. *Jeremy Swindell, lhp, Clear Lake HS, Houston.
38. *Travis McRoberts, ss, El Capitan HS, El Cajon, Calif.
39. Andre Thompson, of, Delta State (Miss.) University.
40. *Curtis Anthony, ss, Bishop Gorman HS, Las Vegas, Nev.
41. (Selection voided)
42. *Wesley Warren, of, Arcadia HS, Scottsdale, Ariz.
43. *Jamaon Halbig, c, Southwestern (Calif.) JC.
44. *Bart Vaughn, rhp, Manatee (Fla.) CC.

## CALIFORNIA ANGELS (20)

1. (Choice to Yankees as compensation for Type B free agent Randy Velarde)
2. Chuck Abbott, ss, Austin Peay State University.—(AAA)
**3. Scott Schoeneweis, lhp, Duke University.—(1999-2010)**
4. Brandon Steele, rhp, Huntington Beach (Calif.) HS.—(Rookie)
**5. *Bobby Hill, ss, Leland HS, San Jose, Calif.—(2002-05)**
DRAFT DROP *Attended Miami (Fla.); re-drafted by White Sox, 1999 (2nd round)*
6. *Jason Verdugo, rhp, Arizona State University.
7. Marcus Knight, of, Miramar HS, Pembroke Pines, Fla.
**8. Jerrod Riggan, rhp, San Diego State University.—(2000-03)**
9. Jason Stephens, rhp, University of Arkansas.
10. Eric Gillespie, 3b, Cal State Northridge.
11. Pat Johnson, c, Brigham Young University.
12. *Mark Richards, rhp, Winthrop University.
13. *Ken Polk, c, Howard (Texas) JC.
14. *Jaeme Leal, 1b, Poly HS, Riverside, Calif.
15. Theo Fefee, of, Bethune-Cookman College.
16. Nate Murphy, of, University of Massachusetts.
17. *Jason Cly, rhp, Arcadia (Calif.) HS.
18. Mark Harriger, rhp, San Diego State University.
19. Brian Ussery, c, University of Tampa.
20. Cale Carter, of, Stanford University.
21. Scott Byers, 1b, Georgia Tech.
22. Nathan Starkey, 3b-c, Modesto (Calif.) JC.
23. John Margaritis, of, Treasure Valley (Ore.) CC.
24. Eddie Ferrer, 2b, Florida International University.
25. Jose Ortiz, rhp, Hayward (Calif.) HS.
26. +Jason Dewey, c, Indian River (Fla.) CC.
27. Rob Neal, of, Cal Poly San Luis Obispo.
28. Matt Curtis, c, Fresno State University.
29. Wade Jackson, 2b, University of Nevada-Reno.
30. James Leach, lhp, Gibbs HS, Pinellas Park, Fla.
31. *William Robbins, rhp, Gulf Breeze (Fla.) HS.
32. *Greg Blum, c, Chino (Calif.) HS.
33. *Richard Stegbauer, c, Seminole (Fla.) HS.
34. *Kirk Asche, of, Edison (Fla.) CC.
35. Eric Plooy, rhp, JC of the Sequoias (Calif.).
36. *Jeremy Freitas, of, Fresno (Calif.) CC.
**37. *Jack Taschner, lhp, William Horlick HS, Racine, Wis.—(2005-10)**
38. *Michael Carney, lhp, Indian River (Fla.) CC.
39. *Gary Forrester, rhp, Centralia (Wash.) JC.
40. *Dominic Repetti, ss, DeAnza (Calif.) JC.
41. +Kris Williams, rhp, Brevard (Fla.) CC.
**42. +Greg Jones, c-rhp, Pasco-Hernando (Fla.) CC.—(2003-07)**
43. Marc Collier, ss, Lower Dauphin HS, Hummelstown, Pa.
44. *Richard Shaw, rhp, Marquette University.
45. *Nathan Burnett, rhp, Gulf Coast (Fla.) CC.
46. *Michael Gauger, lhp, Tallahassee (Fla.) CC.
47. *Adrian Merkey, ss, Polk (Fla.) CC.
48. *Chris Finnegan, c, Millard North HS, Omaha, Neb.
49. *Kenny Avera, rhp, Pensacola (Fla.) JC.
50. *Anthony Lopresti, c, University HS, San Diego.
51. *Michael Abate, of, Norwalk (Conn.) HS.
52. *Elvis Hernandez, of, Aurora West HS, Montgomery, Ill.
53. +Ryan Snellings, lhp, Pasco-Hernando (Fla.) CC.
54. *Paul Poplin, rhp, South Stanly HS, Norwood, N.C.
55. *Kevin Davis, ss, South Spencer HS, Rockport, Ind.
56. *Orlando Sloan, of, Santa Monica HS, Westchester, Calif.

## CHICAGO CUBS (17)

1. Todd Noel, rhp, North Vermillion HS, Maurice, La.—(High A)
2. Quincy Carter, of, Southwest DeKalb HS, Ellenwood, Ga.—(High A)
DRAFT DROP *Quarterback, National Football League (2001-04)*
3. Skip Ames, rhp, University of Alabama.—(Low A)
**4. Chris Gissell, rhp, Hudson's Bay HS, Vancouver, Wash.—(2004)**
**5. Chad Meyers, 2b-of, Creighton University.—(1999-2003)**
6. Doug Hall, of, University of Alabama.
7. Jon Cannon, lhp, Canada (Calif.) JC.
8. Brian Connell, lhp, Dunedin (Fla.) HS.
9. Nate Manning, 3b, Austin Peay State University.
**10. Phil Norton, lhp, Texarkana (Texas) JC.—(2000-04)**
11. *Steve Sanberg, c, Midlothian (Texas) HS.
12. *Mark Ernster, ss, Ironwood HS, Glendale, Ariz.
13. *Johnny Whitesides, rhp, Sarasota (Fla.) HS.
14. *Tim Lavery, lhp, Naperville Central HS, Naperville, Ill.
15. *Freddie Young, of, Lyman HS, Longwood, Fla.
16. Byron Tribe, rhp, University of Alabama.
17. Brad King, c, University of Central Florida.
18. Jim Crawford, rhp, Cowley County (Kan.) CC.
19. Marcel Longmire, c-of, Vallejo (Calif.) HS.
**20. Courtney Duncan, rhp, Grambling State University.—(2001-02)**
21. Ryan Anderson, 2b, Dallas Baptist University.
22. John Nall, lhp, University of California.
**23. +Jason Smith, ss, Meridian (Miss.) CC.—(2001-09)**
24. +Ron Payne, of, Pitt (N.C.) CC.
25. *Doug Young, rhp, Sierra (Calif.) JC.
26. Courteney Stewart, of, DeKalb (Ga.) JC.
27. Matthew Perry, rhp, Allegheny (Pa.) CC.
28. Jeff Velez, rhp, University of Connecticut.
**29. +Kyle Lohse, rhp, Hamilton Union HS, Glenn, Calif. / Butte (Calif.) CC.—(2001-15)**
30. Casey Brookens, rhp, James Madison University.
DRAFT DROP *Son of Ike Brookens, major leaguer (1975)*
31. Randy Crane, rhp, Linn-Benton (Ore.) CC.
32. *Mike Miller, rhp-3b, Manatee (Fla.) CC.
33. *Nicholas Lee, rhp, Brockton (Mass.) HS.
34. +Rick Powalski, lhp, Central Catholic HS, Clearwater, Fla.
35. *Keola Delatori, rhp, Schaumburg (Ill.) HS.
36. *David Regan, of, Brockton (Mass.) HS.
37. Len Hart, lhp, East Tennessee State University.
38. *Justin Lee, of, McLennan (Texas) CC.
39. +Brad Ramsey, c, Gulf Coast (Fla.) CC.
40. *Jeremy Smith, rhp, Needles (Calif.) HS.
41. Daniel Hodges, lhp, Liberty University.
42. Derrick Bly, 3b, Concordia (Calif.) University.
43. *Cameron Newitt, rhp, Northwest Shoals (Ala.) CC.
44. *John Guilmet, rhp, Merrimack (Mass.) College.
45. Keith Lewis, 2b, University of Mississippi.
46. *Mike Mainella, of, West Fairmont (W.Va.) HS.
47. *Joseph Tillmon, ss, Chatsworth HS, Winnetka, Calif.
48. Dax Kiefer, of, Texas Lutheran College.
49. *Jacob Sutter, rhp, Celina (Ohio) HS.
50. *Rob Holmes, rhp, Creighton Prep, Omaha, Neb.
51. *Rahman Corbett, of, Princeton HS, Cincinnati.
52. *Harris Stanton, of, Spartanburg Methodist (S.C.) JC.
53. *Chris Bentley, rhp, Molalla Union HS, Mulino, Ore.
54. *Cory Cattaneo, lhp, Sequoia HS, Redwood City, Calif.
55. +Shane Sullivan, rhp, Serrano HS, Pinon Hills, Calif. / Cerritos (Calif.) JC.
56. *Ryan Blackmum, c, Mater Dei HS, Garden Grove, Calif.
57. *John Halliday, 1b, Clearwater (Fla.) HS.
58. *Franklyn Bencosme, rhp, Miami-Dade CC North.
59. *Gene Richardson, rhp, Edison (Fla.) CC.
60. *Joseph Ortiz, c, Edison HS, San Antonio.
61. *Daniel Zisk, 3b, Pine Crest HS, Lighthouse Point, Fla.
DRAFT DROP *Son of Richie Zisk, major leaguer (1971-83)*
62. *Michael Thomson, rhp, Sulphur (La.) HS.
63. *Ryan Fien, rhp, University of Idaho.

## CHICAGO WHITE SOX (12)

**1. *Bobby Seay, lhp, Sarasota (Fla.) HS.—(2001-09)**
DRAFT DROP *Loophole free agent; signed with Devil Rays (1996)*
**2. Josh Paul, of-c, Vanderbilt University.—(1999-2007)**
3. Jimmy Terrell, ss, Tri-City Christian HS, Blue Springs, Mo.—(AA)
DRAFT DROP *Son of Jerry Terrell, major leaguer (1973-80)*
4. Mark Roberts, rhp, University of South Florida.—(AAA)
**5. Joe Crede, 3b, Fatima HS, Westphalia, Mo.—(2000-09)**
6. Dan Olson, of, Indiana State University.
7. *Kevin Knorst, rhp, Lake Howell HS, Winter Park, Fla.
**8. *Marcus Jones, rhp, Long Beach State University.—(2000)**
9. Edwin Cochran, 2b, Carmen B. Huyke HS, Arroyo, P.R.
10. Gene Forti, lhp, Del Valle HS, El Paso, Texas.
11. Steve Schorzman, rhp, Gonzaga University.
12. Darren Baugh, ss, University of Nevada-Reno.
**13. Chad Bradford, rhp, University of Southern Mississippi.—(1998-2009)**
14. Joe Farley, lhp, Susquehanna (Pa.) University.
15. Tom Reimers, rhp, Stanford University.
16. Jeff Inglin, of, University of Southern California.
17. Derek Wallace, of, Bossier Parish (La.) CC.
18. Joe Sutton, c, West Virginia Wesleyan College.
**19. Chris Heintz, 3b, University of South Florida.—(2005-07)**
20. Mario Iglesias, rhp, Stanford University.
21. *Kevin Sadowski, rhp, Joliet Catholic Academy, Joliet, Ill.
22. Reid Hodges, rhp, Columbus (Ga.) College.
23. *Mike Holmes, rhp, Wake Forest University.
24. Sean Connolly, c, Rollins (Fla.) College.
25. Elvis Perez, lhp, Miami Lakes HS, Hialeah, Fla.
26. Pete Pryor, 1b, University of Kentucky.
27. *Kenneth Ferguson, of, Issaquah (Wash.) HS.
28. Eloy Tellez, rhp, El Paso (Texas) CC.
29. *Robert Hatcher, lhp, Miami-Dade CC North.
30. *Marcos Munoz, rhp, North Rockland HS, Pomona, N.Y.
31. *Juan Mendoza, lhp, Miami-Dade CC Wolfson.
32. Rick Heineman, rhp, UCLA.
33. Kevin Stinson, rhp, Bellevue (Wash.) CC.
34. +Chris Delgado, 1b, St. Thomas Aquinas HS, Fort Lauderdale, Fla. / Okaloosa-Walton (Fla.) JC.
35. *Ray Goirigoizarri, 3b, Christopher Columbus HS, Miami.
36. *Anthony Lofink, of, Salesianum HS, Bear, Del.
37. *Tim McGhee, of, Crenshaw HS, Los Angeles.
38. *Michael Lindgren, rhp, Sandpoint (Idaho) HS.
39. Marcus Rodgers, lhp, Vigor HS, Saraland, Ala.
40. *Jose Arrieta, rhp, El Paso (Texas) CC.
**41. *Marshall McDougall, 2b, Buchholz HS, Gainesville, Fla.—(2005)**
42. *Ken Trapp, rhp, Texas City (Texas) HS.
43. *Kenard Lang, 1b, University of Miami.
DRAFT DROP *First-round draft pick, Washington Redskins, National Football League (1997); defensive end, NFL (1997-2006)*
44. *Johnnie Thibodeaux, 3b, Alfred M. Barbe HS, Lake Charles, La.
45. Allen Thomas, of, Wingate (N.C.) University.
46. Kirk Irvine, rhp, Cal State Fullerton.
**47. *Matt Watson, 3b-2b, McCaskey HS, Lancaster, Pa.—(2003-10)**
48. *Levy Duran, 3b, George Washington HS, New York.
49. *Andres Martinez, c, St. Brendan HS, Miami.
50. *Mario Gianfortune, of, Elmwood Park (Ill.) HS.
51. *William Mauer, c, East HS, Mission Hills, Kan.
52. Mike McDermott, 3b, University of Idaho.
53. *Elio Borges, ss, American HS, Miami.

## CINCINNATI REDS (25)

1. Johnny Oliver, of, Lake-Lehman HS, Lehman, Pa.—(Low A)
1. *Matt McClendon, rhp, Dr. Phillips HS, Orlando (Supplemental choice—33rd—as compensation for Type A free agent Ron Gant).—(AAA)

DRAFT DROP *Attended Florida; re-drafted by Braves, 1999 (5th round)*

2. **Buddy Carlyle, lhp, Bellevue (Neb.) East HS** (Choice from Cardinals as compensation for Gant).—**(1999-2015)**
2. Randi Mallard, rhp, Hillsborough (Fla.) CC.—(AA)
3. David Shepard, rhp, Clemson University.—(AAA)
4. Phil Merrell, rhp, Nampa (Idaho) HS.—(AAA)
5. Nick Presto, ss, Florida Atlantic University.—(AA)
6. Carl Caddell, lhp, Northwood (Texas) Institute.
7. Wylie Campbell, 2b, University of Texas.
8. Kevin Marn, of, Kent State University.
9. Desi Herrera, rhp, San Diego State University.
10. ***Mike Vento, of, Cibola HS, Albuquerque, N.M.—(2005-06)**
11. *Kris Lambert, lhp, Baylor University.
12. Corey Price, ss, North Central Texas JC.
13. Chris Ward, c, Lubbock Christian (Texas) College.
14. Teddy Rose, rhp, Kent State University.
15. *Drew Roberts, lhp, Kent State University.
16. Jason Williams, ss, Louisiana State University.
17. Bubba Dresch, 1b-of, St. Mary's (Texas) University.
18. *Keith Dilgard, rhp, Mississippi State University.
19. Bryan Zwemke, rhp, Trinidad State (Colo.) JC.
20. Gene Altman, rhp, Hudgens Academy, Lynchburg, S.C.
21. *Travis Young, 2b, University of New Mexico.
22. Kevin Needham, lhp, Northwestern State University.
23. Scott Garrett, c, Appalachian State University.
24. Jeremy Keller, 3b-1b, Winthrop University.
25. Matt Buckley, rhp, Campbell University.
26. Josh Harris, rhp, Smithson Valley HS, Canyon Lake, Texas.
27. Doug Kirby, of, Victor Valley (Calif.) CC.
28. Daniel Jenkins, of, Sam Houston State University.
29. Demond Denman, 1b, Dallas Baptist University.
30. Rod Griggs, of, Lambuth (Tenn.) University.
31. Brian Hucks, c, University of South Carolina.
32. Brian Horne, rhp, Limestone (S.C.) College.
33. Jeremy Skeens, of, Lakota HS, Middletown, Ohio.
34. Eric LeBlanc, rhp, College of St. Rose (N.Y.).
35. ***Doug Devore, lhp, Dublin (Ohio) HS.—(2004)**
36. *David Ferres, 2b, JC of the Redwoods (Calif.).
37. John Clark, 2b, Jacksonville State University.
38. Brandon O'Hearn, of, Columbus (Ga.) College.
39. Stephan Smith, rhp, Southwest Texas State University.
40. Jon Phillips, rhp, Georgia Southern University.

DRAFT DROP *Son of Taylor Phillips, major leaguer (1956-63)*

41. *Nicholas Prater, c, Judson HS, Converse, Texas.

## CLEVELAND INDIANS (28)

1. Danny Peoples, 1b, University of Texas.—(AAA)
2. Ryan McDermott, rhp, Alamogordo (N.M.) HS.—(Rookie)
3. Jarrod Mays, rhp, Southwest Missouri State University.—(AA)
4. J.D. Brammer, rhp, Stanford University.—(AAA)
5. Grant Sharpe, 1b, Watkins HS, Laurel, Miss.—(Low A)
6. **Paul Rigdon, rhp, University of Florida.—(2000-01)**
7. Jimmy Hamilton, lhp, Ferrum (Va.) College.
8. Rob Stanton, of, Rollins (Fla.) College.
9. **Sean DePaula, rhp, Wake Forest University.—(1999-2002)**
10. William Jackson, of, Collin County (Texas) CC.
11. **Joe Horgan, lhp, Sacramento (Calif.) CC.—(2004-05)**
12. **John McDonald, ss, Providence College.—(1999-2014)**
13. Cody Allison, c, Arkansas State University.
14. Troy Kent, ss-3b, Stanford University.
15. *Tonayne Brown, of, Godby HS, Tallahassee, Fla.
16. Kaipo Spenser, rhp, Arizona State University.
17. Mark Taylor, lhp, Rice University.
18. **Mike Bacsik, lhp, Duncanville (Texas) HS.—(2001-07)**

DRAFT DROP *Son of Mike Bacsik, major leaguer (1975-80)*

19. ***Dan Wright, rhp, Sullivan South HS, Kingsport, Tenn.—(2001-04)**
20. Mike Huelsmann, of, St. Louis University.
21. **+Jamie Brown, rhp, Okaloosa-Walton (Fla.) CC / Meridian (Miss.) CC.—(2004)**
22. *Tim Palmer, c, Fresno (Calif.) CC.
23. Adam Taylor, c, University of New Mexico.
24. Aurelio Rodriguez, ss, Mesa State (Colo.) College.

DRAFT DROP *Son of Aurelio Rodriguez, major leaguer (1967-83)*

25. *David Willis, c-1b, UC Santa Barbara.
26. Dennis Konrady, ss, Pepperdine University.
27. Bob Reichow, rhp, Bowling Green State University.
28. Brian Whitlock, ss, University of North Carolina.
29. Mel Motley, of, University of Nebraska.
30. Matt Koeman, rhp, Kansas State University.
31. *Chad Darnell, rhp, Carthage (Texas) HS.
32. *Jonathan McDonald, rhp, Edgewater HS, Orlando, Fla.
33. *Mitch Johnson, rhp, Meridian (Miss.) CC.
34. *Samuel Moses, rhp, Sacramento (Calif.) CC.
35. *Humberto Vargas, rhp, Connors State (Okla.) JC.
36. *Robert Aaron, rhp, McCallie HS, Chattanooga, Tenn.
37. *Josh Walker, rhp, Lassen (Calif.) JC.
38. *Jeremy Jones, c, Mesa (Ariz.) CC.
39. ***Marcus Gwyn, rhp, McCullough HS, The Woodlands, Texas.—(2007)**
40. *Byron Watson, of, North Central (Texas) JC.
41. *Miles Bryant, of, Woodham HS, Pensacola, Fla.
42. *Travis Veracka, lhp, Nashoba Regional HS, Stow, Mass.
43. *Alfred Leatherwood, 1b, Woodham HS, Pensacola, Fla.
44. Bryon Bosch, c, University of Washington.
45. *Scott Krause, 2b, Centralia (Wash.) HS.
46. *Brad Brenneman, rhp, Lane (Ore.) CC.
47. *Mark Zenk, ss, Mountlake Terrace HS, Edmonds, Wash.
48. Ryan Siponmaa, c, University of Massachusetts-Lowell.
49. *Chris Hesse, of, University of Southern Mississippi.
50. *Anthony Wright, of, Hooks (Texas) HS.
51. Casey Smith, c, Hill (Texas) JC.
52. *Mark Cridland, of, University of Texas.
53. *Joey Cole, rhp, Nacogdoches (Texas) HS.
54. Matt Minter, lhp, Lassen (Calif.) JC.
55. Charles Roberson, rhp, Green River (Wash.) CC.
56. **David Riske, rhp, Green River (Wash.) CC.—(1999-2010)**
57. ***Randy Keisler, lhp, Navarro (Texas) JC.—(2000-07)**
58. *Ovid Valentin, of, Oak Park-River Forest HS, Oak Park, Ill.

## COLORADO ROCKIES (21)

1. **Jake Westbrook, rhp, Madison County HS, Danielsville, Ga.—(2000-13)**
2. John Nicholson, rhp, Episcopal HS, Houston.—(High A)
3. **Shawn Chacon, rhp, Greeley Central HS, Greeley, Colo.—(2001-08)**
4. Steve Matcuk, rhp, Indian River (Fla.) CC.—(AA)
5. Jeff Sebring, lhp, Iowa State University.—(Short-season A)
6. Dean Brueggeman, lhp, Belleville Area (Ill.) CC.
7. Clint Bryant, 3b, Texas Tech.
8. Alvin Rivera, rhp, Luis Munoz Marin HS, Yabucoa, P.R.
9. Ryan Kennedy, rhp, Jones County (Miss.) JC.
10. Tom Stepka, rhp, Le Moyne College.
11. **Tim Christman, lhp, Siena College.—(2001)**
12. Travis Thompson, rhp, Madison (Wis.) Area Tech JC.
13. Don Schmidt, rhp, Portland State University.
14. *Denny Gilich, rhp, University of Portland.
15. Scott Schroeffel, rhp-of, University of Tennessee.
16. Rod Bair, of, Grand Canyon University.
17. Doug Livingston, 2b, Clemson University.
18. Brian Keck, ss, Fort Hays State (Kan.) University.
19. *Steve Scarborough, rhp, Duncanville (Texas) HS.
20. *Jonathan Storke, ss, Douglas HS, Minden, Nev.
21. Brian Hinchy, rhp, Green River (Wash.) CC.
22. Bernard Hutchison, of, University of Montevallo (Ala.).
23. Blake Anderson, c, Mississippi State University.

DRAFT DROP *Son of Donny Anderson, running back, National Football League (1966-74)*

24. Mark Hamlin, of, Georgia Southern University.
25. Brian Anthony, 1b, University of Nevada-Las Vegas.
26. Mike Petersen, 1b, San Jacinto (Texas) JC.
27. *Lucas Anderson, rhp, Green Valley HS, Henderson, Nev.
28. Jason Ford, lhp, University of Arizona.
29. *Melvin Rosario, of, Antonio Sarriera HS, Carolina, P.R.
30. +Steven Iannacone, rhp, Washington Township HS, Sicklerville, N.J. / Gloucester County (N.J.) CC.
31. *Les Graham, 3b, Latta HS, Ada, Okla.
32. +Jake Kidd, rhp, Hesperia (Calif.) HS / Chaffey (Calif.) JC.
33. +Josh Kalinowski, lhp, Indian Hills (Iowa) CC.
34. *Emmett Giles, ss, North Side HS, Jackson, Tenn.
35. +Brad Woodard, rhp, Palatka HS, San Mateo, Fla. / Santa Fe (Fla.) CC.
36. *Alex Fernandez, of, Hope HS, Providence, R.I.
37. *Eric Burris, of-1b, Carson (Calif.) HS.
38. ***Adam Bernero, rhp, Sacramento (Calif.) CC.—(2000-06)**
39. *Daniel Viveros, rhp, JC of the Sequoias (Calif.).
40. +Ryan Price, rhp, Goddard HS, Roswell, N.M. / Howard (Texas) JC.
41. *Robby Shoults, rhp, Chaffey (Calif.) JC.
42. *Martin Rankin, lhp, Hill (Texas) JC.
43. *James Carroll, rhp, North Shore HS, Houston.
44. *David Christy, ss, Mount Hood (Ore.) CC.
45. *Ben Cortez, rhp, Santa Fe Springs (Calif.) HS.
46. *Jose Vasquez, lhp, Cerritos (Calif.) JC.
47. *Chris Robert, c, Soquel HS, Capitola, Calif.
48. *James Munday, rhp, Hudson's Bay HS, Vancouver, Wash.
49. *Mathew Bobo, ss, Longview (Texas) HS.
50. *Damon Thames, ss, San Jacinto (Texas) JC.
51. *Jeremiah Harrington, of, Lowry HS, Winnemucca, Nev.

## DETROIT TIGERS (6)

1. **Seth Greisinger, rhp, University of Virginia.—(1998-2005)**
2. **Matt Miller, lhp, Texas Tech.—(2001-02)**
3. Antonio McKinney, of, Jefferson HS, Portland, Ore.—(High A)
4. **Kris Keller, rhp, Fletcher HS, Neptune Beach, Fla.—(2002)**
5. **Robert Fick, c, Cal State Northridge.—(1998-2007)**
6. Chris Bauer, rhp, Wichita State University.

DRAFT DROP *Brother of Greg Bauer, 35th-round draft pick, Tigers (1996)*

7. Scott Sollmann, of, University of Notre Dame.
8. Craig Quintal, rhp, Southern University.
9. Keith Whitner, of, Los Angeles CC.
10. Justin Hazleton, of, Philipsburg-Osceola HS, Philipsburg, Pa.
11. Aaron Alvord, rhp, Canton-Galva HS, Canton, Kan.
12. Jacques Landry, 3b, Rice University.
13. *Jeff Heaverlo, rhp, Ephrata (Wash.) HS.

DRAFT DROP *First-round draft pick (33rd overall), Mariners (1999) • Son of Dave Heaverlo, major leaguer (1975-81)*

14. *Dan Kelly, lhp, Niceville (Fla.) HS.
15. **Chris Wakeland, of, Oregon State University.—(2001)**
16. Rick Kirsten, rhp-of, Rolling Meadows (Ill.) HS.
17. George Restovich, c, University of Notre Dame.

DRAFT DROP *Brother of Michael Restovich, major leaguer (2002-07)*

18. Brian Rios, ss, Oral Roberts University.
19. Derrick Neikirk, c, Mesa (Ariz.) CC.
20. Don DeDonatis, ss, Eastern Michigan University.
21. David Lindstrom, c, Texas Tech.
22. Jeff Tagliaferri, 1b, Long Beach State University.
23. Jesse Zepeda, 2b, University of Oklahoma.
24. Chris Mitchell, rhp, Allentown (Pa.) College.
25. Tom Browning, lhp, Indiana State University.
26. David Darwin, lhp, Duke University.
27. *Matt Schuldt, rhp, Howard (Texas) JC.
28. *Drew Topham, 2b, Alfred M. Barbe HS, Lake Charles, La.
29. Kurt Airoso, of, Cal State Northridge.
30. Chad Schroeder, rhp, Northwestern University.
31. Nick Jamison, of, Center Grove HS, Greenwood, Ind.
32. *John Ogiltree, rhp, Kennedy HS, Mississauga, Ontario.
33. *Joe Kalczynski, c, Brother Rice HS, Farmington, Mich.
34. *Daniel Cole, rhp, Monroe (Mich.) HS.
35. *Greg Bauer, rhp-ss, Jenks HS, Tulsa, Okla.

DRAFT DROP *Brother of Chris Bauer, sixth-round draft pick, Tigers (1996)*

36. +T.J. Runnells, ss, Greeley West HS, Greeley, Colo. / Howard (Texas) JC.

DRAFT DROP *Son of Tom Runnells, major leaguer (1985-86); major league manager (1991-92)*

37. *Michael Garner, lhp, Fullerton (Calif.) HS.
38. *K.O. Wiegandt, rhp, Westminster Christian HS, Miami.
39. *Harry Kenoi, rhp, Los Angeles Pierce JC.
40. *Brian Justine, lhp, Broward (Fla.) CC.
41. *Bryan Houston, rhp, Lake City (Fla.) CC.
42. Mike Seebode, lhp, Ichabod Crane HS, Valatie, N.Y.
43. Dave Malenfant, rhp, Central Michigan University.
44. +Ian Herweg, rhp, Redondo Union HS, Redondo Beach, Calif. / Los Angeles Harbor JC.
45. Tris Moore, of, University of Miami.
46. Mike Ciminiello, 1b, Princeton University.
47. *Kevin Robles, c, Jose Alegria HS, Dorado, P.R.
48. *Durendell Daniels, of, Gulf Coast (Fla.) CC.
49. *Greg Sprehn, rhp, Triton (Ill.) JC.
50. Bruce Johnston, rhp, Nassau (N.Y.) CC.
51. *Brandon Wheeler, rhp, Countryside HS, Clearwater, Fla.

## FLORIDA MARLINS (9)

1. **Mark Kotsay, of, Cal State Fullerton.—(1997-2013)**

DRAFT DROP *First player from 1996 draft to reach majors (July 11, 1997)*

2. (Choice to Blue Jays as compensation for Type B free agent Devon White)
3. (Choice to Blue Jays as compensation for Type B free agent Al Leiter)
4. **Blaine Neal, rhp, Bishop Eustace HS, Pennsauken, N.J.—(2001-05)**
5. **Brent Billingsley, lhp, Cal State Fullerton.—(1999)**
6. David Townsend, rhp, Delta State (Miss.) University.
7. Chris Moore, rhp, Harlan Community HS, Chicago.
8. Quantaa Jackson, of, Wharton (Texas) HS.
9. *Vaughn Schill, ss, Audubon (N.J.) HS.
10. Cory Washington, of, Westover HS, Fayetteville, N.C.
11. Travis Wyckoff, lhp, Wichita State University.
12. *Skip Browning, rhp, Lakeview HS, Fort Oglethorpe, Ga.
13. *Ryan Owens, ss, Sonora HS, La Habra, Calif.
14. ***Brian Tallet, lhp, Putnam City West HS, Bethany, Okla.—(2002-11)**
15. David Wesolowski, rhp, Williamsville North HS, Williamsville, N.Y.
16. *Simon Tafoya, 1b, Pittsburg (Calif.) HS.
17. Larry Kleinz, ss, Villanova University.
18. *Bryan Farkas, lhp, Varina HS, Sandston, Va.
19. Shaw Casey, rhp, University of Nevada-Las Vegas.
20. Steve Gagliano, rhp, Rolling Meadows (Ill.) HS.
21. Matt Braughler, c, Indiana University.
22. Dan Ferrell, lhp, Indiana University.
23. Stephen Morales, c, Pedro Perez Fajardo HS, Mayaguez, P.R.
24. Brad Farizo, rhp, Shaw HS, Marrero, La.
25. Jeff Venghaus, 2b, Rice University.
26. ***Scott Dunn, rhp, Winston Churchill HS, San**

**Antonio, Texas.—(2004-06)**
27. *Brian Matzenbacher, rhp, Belleville Area (Ill.) CC.
28. *Justin Linquist, rhp, Palma HS, Salinas, Calif.
29. Pete Arenas, ss, University of Georgia.
30. Scott Conway, 1b, Lenape HS, Mount Laurel, N.J.
31. *Josh Laxton, rhp, Audubon (N.J.) HS.

DRAFT DROP *Son of Bill Laxton, major leaguer (1970-77)* • *Brother of Brett Laxton, 24th-round draft pick, Athletics (1996); major leaguer (1999-2000)*

32. Alain Diaz, of, Barry (Fla.) University.
33. *Rafael Rigueiro, rhp, Riverside (Calif.) CC.
34. Zak Ammirato, 3b-c, UCLA.
35. Justin Foerter, 1b, Holy Cross HS, Bordentown, N.J.
36. Jay Jones, c, University of Alabama-Birmingham.
37. Jason Alaimo, c, University of South Florida.
38. *Jason Sharp, ss, Owen County HS, Owenton, Ky.
39. *Jeff Bloomer, rhp, County HS, Pueblo, Colo.
40. *Simon Young, lhp, West Hall HS, Flowery Branch, Ga.
41. *Brian Forystek, lhp, Carl Sandburg HS, Palos Park, Ill.
42. *Edwin Erickson, 1b, Eisenhower HS, Yakima, Wash.
43. *Jimmy Frush, rhp, Texas Tech.
44. Patrick Pass, of, Tucker (Ga.) HS.

DRAFT DROP *Running back, National Football League (2000-06)*

45. *Mike Rose, rhp, Texarkana (Texas) CC.
46. *Steven Merrill, lhp, Sandy Union HS, Gresham, Ore.
47. Mike Evans, lhp-1b, Palm Beach (Fla.) JC.
48. *Harry Anderson, of, Virginia HS, Bristol, Va.
49. *Kevin Kurilla, rhp, Virginia Tech.
50. *Eric Abshor, of, Heritage HS, Littleton, Colo.
51. Kevin Zaleski, rhp, Indiana University.
52. *Daniel Torres, ss, Lenape HS, Mount Laurel, N.J.
53. *David White, of, Water of Life Christian HS, Douglasville, Ga.
54. *Joseph Hart, lhp, Walkersville (Md.) HS.
55. *Craig Lewis, rhp, Wallace State (Ala.) CC.
56. +Reece Borges, rhp, Lassen (Calif.) JC.
57. *Letarvius Copeland, of, Miami-Dade CC Wolfson.
58. *Travis Johnson, rhp, Snowflake HS, Taylor, Ariz.
59. *Israel Pope, ss, Virginia HS, Bristol, Va.
60. *Clayton Thomas, of, Central Senior HS, Victoria, Va.
61. *Darius Gill, rhp, Columbia HS, Decatur, Ga.
62. *Charles Walter, c, Lansdowne HS, Baltimore.
63. *Joel Sajiun, of, Miami-Dade CC North.
64. *Devon Younger, rhp, Lakota HS, West Chester, Ohio.
65. *Jorge Soto, c, Cecilio Lebron Ramos HS, Patillas, P.R.
66. *Dustin Brisson, 1b, Wellington Community HS, West Palm Beach, Fla.
67. *Juan Torres, rhp, Elvira M. Colon HS, Isabel, P.R.
68. *Brian Partenheimer, lhp, Indiana University.
69. Geoff Duncan, rhp, Georgia Tech.
70. *Josh Hoffpauir, ss, Vidalia (La.) HS.
71. *Gerald Perkins, 1b, Royalton Hartlant HS, Lockport, N.Y.
72. *Dwayne Webb, of, Gallatin County HS, Warsaw, Ky.
73. *Brian Pirazzi, ss, South San Francisco HS.
74. +Matt Pidgeon, ss, JC of the Redwoods (Calif.) / Sierra (Calif.) JC.
75. *Scott Eskra, 3b, Lassen (Calif.) JC.

## HOUSTON ASTROS (19)

1. **Mark Johnson, rhp, University of Hawaii.—(2000)**
2. John Huber, rhp, Lakota HS, Cincinnati.—(Short-season A)
3. Brandon Byrd, 3b, Trinity Presbyterian HS, Montgomery, Ala.—(Short-season A)
4. Bryan Braswell, lhp, University of Toledo.—(AA)
5. Tucker Barr, c, Georgia Tech.—(AA)
6. Michael Wheeler, ss, Oak Hills HS, Cincinnati.
7. Esteban Maldonado, rhp, Lambuth (Tenn.) University.
8. Jason Hill, c, Mount San Antonio (Calif.) JC.
9. **Brian Dallimore, 2b, Stanford University.—(2004-05)**
10. John Blackmore, rhp, Plainville (Conn.) HS.
11. Jay Mansavage, 2b, Southern Illinois University.
12. +Jeff Cermak, of, Arizona State University.
13. *Joey Hart, c, Round Rock (Texas) HS.
14. *Ryan Oase, 3b-rhp, Lake Stevens HS, Everett, Wash.
15. Jim Reeder, of, Northwestern University.
16. Randy Young, of, Wichita State University.
17. Matt Hyers, ss, Middle Georgia JC.

DRAFT DROP *Brother of Tim Hyers, major leaguer (1994-99)*

18. David Bernhard, rhp, University of San Francisco.
19. *Jake Eye, rhp-of, Ohio University.
20. **Wade Miller, rhp, Topton, Pa.—(1999-2007)**
21. Geoff Robertson, of, Landrum (S.C.) HS.
22. *Joe DiSalvo, of, University of New Orleans.
23. **+Roy Oswalt, rhp, Holmes (Miss.) JC.—(2001-13)**
24. *Matt Dailey, lhp, Castro Valley (Calif.) HS.
25. ***Paul Phillips, c, Meridian (Miss.) CC.—(2004-10)**
26. *Bryan Grace, rhp, Mississippi Delta JC.
27. *Michael Meyers, rhp, Black Hawk (Ill.) JC.
28. *Jurrian Lobbezoo, lhp, Indian River (Fla.) CC.
29. **Tom Shearn, rhp, Briggs HS, Columbus, Ohio.—(2007)**
30. *Kevin Tillman, 3b, Leland HS, San Jose, Calif.

DRAFT DROP *Brother of Pat Tillman, linebacker, National Football League (1998-2001)*

31. *Jed Fuller, rhp, St. Joseph Catholic HS, Renfrew, Ontario.
32. ***Trey Hodges, rhp, Klein Oak HS, Spring, Texas.—(2002-03)**
33. Dru Nicely, 3b, Burley (Idaho) HS.
34. *Brian Bishop, rhp, Crescenta Valley HS, La Crescenta, Calif.
35. *Kevin Duck, 1b, Rancho Santiago (Calif.) JC.
36. *Eric Cooper, rhp, Chabot (Calif.) JC.
37. *Jason Davis, c, Woodbury (N.J.) HS.
38. *James Igo, rhp, West Columbia (Texas) HS.
39. *Chris Youmans, c, Seminole HS, Lake Mary, Fla.
40. *Matt Gawer, lhp, Sullivan (Mo.) HS.
41. *James Hostetler, rhp, Fullerton (Calif.) JC.
42. *Jason Sinatra, of, Silver Creek HS, San Jose, Calif.
43. *Joseph Morrell, c, Elmira (N.Y.) Free Academy.
44. *Randy Brunette, ss, South Dade HS, Homestead, Fla.
45. *Brad Payne, ss, Stephen Leacock HS, Agincourt, Ontario.
46. *Bruce Sutton, of, Seminole (Okla.) JC.
47. *Derrick Vargas, lhp, Chabot (Calif.) JC.
48. *Chaz Eiguren, 1b, Seward County (Kan.) CC.
49. *Nathan King, of, Livingston (Texas) HS.
50. *Anthony Garcia, rhp, Belen Jesuit HS, Miami.
51. *Jason Chaney, lhp, Sacramento (Calif.) CC.
52. *Mark Burnett, ss, Northeast Texas CC.
53. *Resh Bondi, ss, Monterey HS, Seaside, Calif.
54. *Damon Edelen, c, Eastern Oklahoma State JC.

DRAFT DROP *Son of Joe Edelen, first-round draft pick, Cardinals (1973); major leaguer (1981-82)*

55. *Jerymane Beasley, of, Kamiakin HS, Kennewick, Wash.
56. *Rich Terwilliger, rhp, Corning East HS, Corning, N.Y.
57. *Charles Harrington, rhp, Oxnard (Calif.) JC.
58. *Ferdinand Rivera, ss, Ranger (Texas) JC.
59. *Brian Jensen, lhp, St. Vincent's HS, Petaluma, Calif.
60. *Steven Knotts, of, Parkway HS, Bossier City, La.
61. *Stephen Neal, 1b, Pine Bluff (Ark.) HS.
62. *Todd Uzzell, rhp, Coronado HS, El Paso, Texas.
63. *Troy Norrell, c, Navarro (Texas) JC.
64. *Alexander Stencel, of, Mount San Antonio (Calif.) JC.
65. *Greg Peterson, of, CC of Morris (N.J.).
66. *George Johnson, 1b-of, Connors State (Okla.) JC.
67. *Ben Keats, c, Faulkner State (Ala.) CC.
68. *Tyler Dunlap, ss, Pleasant Grove HS, Texarkana, Texas.
69. *Chris Hargett, 1b, Rend Lake (Ill.) JC.
70. *Johnnie Wheeler, lhp, Skiatook (Okla.) HS.
71. *Mike Rosamond, ss, Madison Central HS, Madison, Miss.

DRAFT DROP *First-round draft pick (42nd overall), Astros (1999)*

72. *Robbie White, lhp, Trinidad (Texas) HS.
73. *Daniel Duke, c, Leland HS, San Jose, Calif.
74. *Marcos Rios, c, Moreau HS, Hayward, Calif.
75. *Jason Cox, c, Northeast Texas CC.
76. *Richard Roberts, 2b, Texarkana (Texas) CC.
77. +Mike Janssen, rhp, Phoenix JC.
78. *Noah Sweeters, rhp, Los Gatos (Calif.) HS.
79. *Bobby Porter, lhp, Texarkana (Texas) JC.
80. *Jeremy Cunningham, rhp, Monte Vista HS, Cupertino, Calif.
81. *Tim Neumark, of, Allegany (Md.) CC.
82. *Shawn Hancock, rhp, Monte Vista HS, Cupertino, Calif.
83. *Luis Perez, rhp, Rancho Santiago (Calif.) JC.

## KANSAS CITY ROYALS (14)

1. **Dee Brown, of, Marlboro Central HS, Marlboro, N.Y.—(1998-2007)**
2. Taylor Myers, rhp, Green Valley HS, Henderson, Nev.—(Low A)
3. **Chad Durbin, rhp, Woodlawn HS, Baton Rouge, La.—(1999-2013)**
4. **Corey Thurman, rhp, Texas HS, Wake Village, Texas.—(2002-03)**
5. **Jeremy Hill, c-rhp, W.T. White HS, Dallas.—(2002-03)**
6. **Jeremy Giambi, of, Cal State Fullerton.—(1998-2003)**

DRAFT DROP *Brother of Jason Giambi, major leaguer (1995-2014)*

7. **Scott Mullen, lhp, Dallas Baptist University.—(2000-03)**
8. *Javier Flores, c, University of Oklahoma.
9. *Jeremy Morris, of, Florida State University.
10. Steve Hueston, rhp, Long Beach State University.
11. Mike Brambilla, c, Rancho Santiago (Calif.) JC.
12. Ethan Stein, rhp, University of North Carolina.
13. Cory Kyzar, rhp, South Jones HS, Ellisville, Miss.
14. **Brandon Berger, of, Eastern Kentucky University.—(2001-04)**
15. Eric Sees, ss, Stanford University.
16. Mike Torres, rhp, Fontana (Calif.) HS.
17. Roman Escamilla, c, University of Texas.
18. Kris Didion, 3b, Riverside, Calif.
19. Brett Taft, ss, University of Alabama.
20. Aaron Lineweaver, rhp, Dallas Baptist University.
21. **Jason Simontacchi, rhp, Albertson (Idaho) College.—(2002-07)**
22. **Kit Pellow, of, University of Arkansas.—(2002-04)**
23. Richie Benes, 2b, Christopher Columbus HS, Bronx, N.Y.
24. Brandon Baird, lhp, Wichita State University.
25. Scott Harp, 2b, Dallas Baptist University.
26. Jake Chapman, lhp, St. Joseph's (Ind.) College.
27. **Kiko Calero, rhp, St. Thomas (Fla.) University.—(2003-09)**
28. Jordy Alexander, lhp, Burnaby, B.C.
29. *Bob Spangler, ss, Allegany (Md.) CC.
30. *Bryan Bealer, lhp, North Medford (Ore.) HS.
31. +Steven Walsh, rhp, Cairine Wilson SS, Orleans, Ontario / Triton (Ill.) JC.
32. Donald Quigley, rhp, Sonoma State (Calif.) University.
33. ***Matt Guerrier, rhp, Shaker Heights (Ohio) HS.—(2004-14)**
34. Richard Boring, rhp, Texas A&M University.
35. *Gus Ornstein, 1b, Michigan State University.
36. ***Ryan Rupe, rhp, Texas A&M University.—(1999-03)**
37. *Bryan Welch, rhp, Central Catholic HS, Salem, Mass.
38. *Caleb Parmenter, of, Dinuba (Calif.) HS.
39. *John Janek, rhp, West HS, Abbott, Texas.
40. *Bill Cornish, rhp, A.B. Lucas HS, London, Ontario.
41. *Brent Gutierrez, of, Clovis West HS, Fresno, Calif.
42. *Brent Cook, rhp, Sprague HS, Salem, Ore.
43. *Ken Thomas, c, Pennsauken (N.J.) HS.
44. George Kauffman, rhp, Stetson University.
45. *Matt Ward, lhp, Rancho Santiago (Calif.) JC.
46. *Dennis Melendi, of, Monsignor Pace HS, Miami.
47. *Daniel Fernandez, 3b, Braddock HS, Miami.
48. ***Mario Ramos, lhp, Pflugerville (Texas) HS.—(2003)**
49. *Nikki Moses, of, Doyline HS, Minden, La.
50. *Michael Bender, rhp, Vanden HS, Vacaville, Calif.
51. *Tim Pittsley, rhp, Allegany (Md.) CC.

DRAFT DROP *Brother of Jim Pittsley, first-round draft pick, Royals (1992); major leaguer (1995-99)*

52. *David Meliah, ss, Walla Walla (Wash.) CC.
53. *Bret Halbert, lhp, Western HS, Buena Park, Calif.
54. *James Blanchard, ss, Grants Pass (Ore.) HS.
55. *Macey Brooks, of, James Madison University.

DRAFT DROP *Wide receiver, National Football League (1999-2000)*

56. *Daniel Williams, 2b, Grand Canyon University.

## LOS ANGELES DODGERS (23)

1. **Damian Rolls, 3b, Schlagel HS, Kansas City, Kan.—(2000-04)**
2. Josh Glassey, c, Mission Bay HS, San Diego.—(AAA)
3. **Alex Cora, ss, University of Miami.—(1998-2011)**

DRAFT DROP *Brother of Joey Cora, first-round draft pick, Padres (1985); major leaguer (1987-98)*

4. **Peter Bergeron, of, Greenfield (Mass.) HS.—(1999-2004)**
5. Nick Leach, 1b, Madera (Calif.) HS.—(AA)
6. Jack Jones, ss, Cal State Fullerton.
7. Ben Simon, rhp, Eastern Michigan University.
8. Chris Karabinus, lhp, Towson State University.
9. David Falcon, c, Tomas C. Ongay HS, Bayamon, P.R.
10. Jeff Auterson, of, Norte Vista HS, Riverside, Calif.
11. +Jason Walters, rhp, Meridian (Miss.) CC.
12. Randy Stearns, of, University of Wisconsin-River Falls.
13. Derrick Peoples, of, Ryan HS, Denton, Texas.
14. Willie King, 1b, Roosevelt HS, Brooklyn, N.Y.
15. Casey Snow, c, Long Beach State University.
16. Matt Kramer, rhp, Moorpark (Calif.) JC.
17. Mikal Richey, of, Columbia HS, Decatur, Ga.
18. Pedro Flores, lhp, East Los Angeles JC.
19. Mickey Maestas, rhp, George Mason University.
20. +Ismael Gallo, ss, Mount San Antonio (Calif.) JC.
21. Kimani Newton, of, St. Joseph HS, St. Croix, Virgin Islands.
22. Elvis Correa, rhp, South Division HS, Milwaukee.
23. **Ted Lilly, lhp, Fresno (Calif.) CC.—(1999-2013)**
24. +Pat Kelleher, of, Paradise Valley, Ariz. / Cypress (Calif.) JC.
25. Scott Morrison, ss, Baylor University.
26. Monte Marshall, 2b, Birmingham-Southern College.
27. Steve Wilson, c, Georgia Southern University.
28. Brian Zaun, of, Butler University.
29. Toby Dollar, rhp, Texas Christian University.
30. Rick Saitta, 2b-ss, Rutgers University.
31. Brian Foulks, of, Benedict (S.C.) College.
32. Brian Sankey, 1b, Boston College.
33. Brian Jacobson, lhp, California Baptist College.
34. *Brad Cresse, c, Marina HS, Huntington Beach, Calif.
35. *Donnie Thomas, lhp, Andrew (Ga.) JC.
36. **Wayne Franklin, lhp, University of Maryland.—(2000-06)**
37. *Jim Fritz, c, University of Tennessee.
38. **Jeff Kubenka, lhp, St. Mary's (Texas) University.—(1998-99)**
39. *Bryan Cranson, lhp, Bronson (Mich.) HS.
40. Frank Thompson, rhp, Embry-Riddle Aeronautical (Fla.) University.
41. Jason Weekley, of, St. Mary's (Calif.) College.
42. +Jacob Allen, c, Southeastern Illinois JC.
43. Kevin Culmo, rhp, Cal State Sacramento.
44. Eddie Sordo, rhp, Jacksonville University.
45. Erik Lazerus, ss, Cal State Chico.
46. *Bradley Turner, c, Belton (Texas) HS.
47. Eric Lovinger, rhp, Oregon State University.
48. Mike Hannah, rhp, Mercer University.
49. *Peter Brinjak, rhp, Power St. Josephs HS, Etobicoke, Ontario.
50. Brian Paluk, rhp, Saginaw Valley State (Mich.) University.
51. *Doug Straight, rhp, Buckhannon-Upshur HS, Buckhannon, W.Va.
52. Dean Mitchell, rhp, Texas A&M University.
53. Blake Mayo, rhp, University of Alabama-Birmingham.
54. *James Jackson, of, Kankakee (Ill.) HS.
55. *Adam Flohr, lhp, Spokane Falls (Wash.) CC.
56. *Spencer Micunek, rhp, Kalamazoo Valley (Mich.) CC.
57. *Ryan Anholt, 2b, Kwantlen (B.C.) JC.
58. *Brian Little, 3b, JC of the Sequoias (Calif.).
59. *Juan Huguet, c, Coral Park HS, Miami.

60. *Craig Jarvis, of, Claremont HS, Victoria, B.C.
61. *Kevin Sullivan, c, Pacelli HS, Stevens Point, Wis.
62. *Mark Paschal, of, Chaffey (Calif.) JC.
63. *George Bailey, 3b, St. Joseph HS, St. Croix, Virgin Islands.
64. *Joseph Thomas, rhp, Mount San Antonio (Calif.) JC.
65. *Devin Helps, lhp, McClung Collegiate HS, Manitou, Manitoba.
66. *Travis Bolton, c, West Valley HS, Anderson, Calif.
67. *Graig Merritt, c, Terry Fox HS, Pitt Meadows, B.C.
68. *Samuel Shelton, rhp, Durango (Colo.) HS.
69. *Mike Meyer, ss, Sabino HS, Tucson, Ariz.
70. *Matt Mason, c, J.L. Crowe HS, Trail, B.C.
71. *Kevin Huff, rhp, Horizon HS, Scottsdale, Ariz.
**72. *Eric Bruntlett, ss, Harrison HS, Lafayette, Ind.—(2003-09)**
73. *Edwin Rodriguez, 1b, Academia Cristo Rey HS, Ponce, P.R.
74. *Ryan Withey, ss, Mainland HS, Daytona Beach, Fla.
75. *Paul Sirant, rhp, River East Collegiate HS, Winnipeg, Manitoba.
76. *Chad Zaniewski, of, John I. Leonard HS, West Palm Beach, Fla.
77. *Richard Garner, c, Wade Hampton HS, Taylors, S.C.
78. *Jim Davis, 1b, Berrien County HS, Nashville, Ga.
79. *Saul Rivera, ss, Lake Land (Ill.) JC.

## MILWAUKEE BREWERS (8)

1. Chad Green, of, University of Kentucky.—(AAA)
2. Jose Garcia, rhp, Baldwin Park (Calif.) HS.—(AA)
**3. Kevin Barker, of, Virginia Tech.—(1999-2009)**
**4. *Josh Hancock, rhp, Vestavia Hills (Ala.) HS.—(2002-07)**
DRAFT DROP *Attended Auburn; re-drafted by Red Sox, 1998 (5th round); died as active major leaguer (April 29, 2007)*
5. Philip Kendall, c, Jasper (Ind.) HS.—(High A)
6. Paul Stewart, rhp, Garner (N.C.) HS.
7. Mike Wetmore, ss, Washington State University.
8. Brian Passini, lhp, Miami (Ohio) University.
9. Doug Johnston, rhp, Millard South HS, Omaha, Neb.
10. Josh Klimek, ss, University of Illinois.
**11. *Val Pascucci, rhp, Richard Gahr HS, Cerritos, Calif.—(2004-11)**
12. Garret Osilka, 3b, Edison (Fla.) CC.
**13. Allen Levrault, rhp, CC of Rhode Island.—(2000-03)**
14. *Shawn Sonnier, rhp, Panola (Texas) JC.
15. Al Hawkins, rhp, Elizabeth (N.J.) HS.
16. John Fulcher, lhp, George Mason University.
17. *Samone Peters, 1b, McKinleyville (Calif.) HS.
18. Maney Leshay, rhp, Palm Beach Atlantic (Fla.) College.
19. John Boker, rhp, Mount Vernon Nazarene (Ohio) College.
20. Jay Arnold, rhp, Glendale (Ariz.) CC.
21. *Danny Bogeajis, rhp, Lyman HS, Longwood, Fla.
22. Dan Thompson, of, Yale University.
23. *Monsantos Armstrong, of, Calhoun City (Miss.) HS.
24. Ross Parmenter, ss, Santa Clara University.
25. *Jeremy Ward, lhp, CC of Rhode Island.
26. Gio Cafaro, of, University of South Florida.
27. +Derek Lee, lhp, Texas Christian University.
28. *Kevin Candelaria, c, Page (Ariz.) HS.
29. *Tyler Van Patten, c, Seabreeze HS, Ormond Beach, Fla.
30. Jason Glover, of, Georgia State University.
31. *Antonio Garris, 3b-of, Anson County HS, Wadesboro, N.C.
32. Travis Tank, rhp, University of Wisconsin-Whitewater.
33. *Steven Truitt, 2b, Elkins HS, Missouri City, Texas.
34. Jesse Richardson, lhp, Hill (Texas) JC.
35. Mick Fieldbinder, rhp, University of Montevallo (Ala.).
**36. *Brandon Backe, ss, Ball HS, Galveston, Texas.—(2002-09)**
37. *Jay Sitzman, of, Horizon HS, Scottsdale, Ariz.
38. Adam Faurot, 3b-ss, Florida State University.
39. Brian Hedley, rhp, St. Mary's (Calif.) College.
40. *Greg Freetly, rhp, Orange Glen HS, San Marcos, Calif.
41. Jason Washam, c, University of New Orleans.
42. Ramon Fernandez, of, Miguel Melendez Munoz HS, Cayey, P.R.
43. *Frank Valois, of, Good Counsel HS, Ashton, Md.
44. *Michel Dubreuil, rhp, Miami-Dade CC North.
45. *Todd Ludwig, c, Thomas More HS, Franklin, Wis.
46. *James Morgan, rhp, Central HS, Chattanooga, Tenn.
47. *Jack Keene, rhp, Gulf Coast (Fla.) CC.
48. +Brian Moon, c, Southern Union State (Ala.) JC.
49. *Tim Boeth, 3b-ss, Tallahassee (Fla.) CC.
50. *Brent Kelley, rhp, Texarkana (Texas) JC.
51. *Kelley Love, rhp, Laredo (Texas) JC.
52. *Jose Camilo, ss, San Juan, P.R.
53. *Danny Prata, lhp, Seminole (Okla.) JC.
54. *Brian Steinbach, rhp, University of Michigan.
55. *Robert Cornett, c, Young Harris (Ga.) JC.
56. *John Cornette, rhp, Seabreeze HS, Ormond Beach, Fla.
57. *Eric McMaster, 2b, Seward County (Kan.) CC.

## MINNESOTA TWINS (2)

**1. *Travis Lee, 1b, San Diego State University.—(1998-2006)**
DRAFT DROP *Loophole free agent; signed by Diamondbacks (1996)*
**2. Jacque Jones, of, University of Southern California.—(1999-2008)**
3. Dan Cey, ss, University of California.—(AAA)
DRAFT DROP *Son of Ron Cey, major leaguer (1971-87)*
**4. Chad Allen, of, Texas A&M University.—(1999-2005)**
DRAFT DROP *Son of Jackie Allen, defensive back, National Football League (1969-72)*
**5. Mike Ryan, ss, Indiana (Pa.) HS.—(2002-10)**
6. Tommy LaRosa, rhp, University of Nevada-Las Vegas.
**7. Chad Moeller, c, University of Southern California.—(2000-10)**
8. Corey Spiers, lhp, University of Alabama.
9. Nate Yeskie, rhp, University of Nevada-Las Vegas.
10. Joe Cranford, 2b, University of Georgia.
11. Tommy Peterman, 1b, Georgia Southern University.
12. Ryan Lynch, lhp, UCLA.
**13. Mike Lincoln, rhp, University of Tennessee.—(1999-2010)**
14. David Hooten, rhp, Mississippi State University.
15. Steve Huls, ss, University of Minnesota.
16. Eric Brosam, 1b, Redwood Valley HS, Redwood Falls, Minn.
17. *William Gray, ss, Liberty Eylau HS, Texarkana, Texas.
18. Chris Garza, lhp, University of Nevada-Reno.
19. *Tyler Martin, ss, Melbourne (Fla.) HS.
**20. *Matt Kata, rhp-ss, St. Ignatius HS, Willoughby Hills, Ohio.—(2003-09)**
21. Jake Jacobs, rhp, Pine Forest HS, Pensacola, Fla.
22. Mike Bauder, lhp, University of Nevada-Las Vegas.
23. Richie Nye, rhp, University of Arkansas.
24. Marcus Smith, of, Valencia (Fla.) CC.
25. Phil Haigler, rhp, Vanderbilt University.
26. Charlie Gillian, rhp, Virginia Tech.
27. *Shaun Berrow, lhp, Tumwater HS, Olympia, Wash.
28. Brian Kennedy, of, Harrison HS, Lafayette, Ind.
29. *D.J. Johnson, rhp, Kansas State University.
30. *Dwayne Jones, c, Rockledge (Fla.) HS.
**31. *Mike Lamb, c, Cal State Fullerton.—(2000-10)**
32. C.J. Thieleke, 2b, University of Iowa.
33. Rick Loonam, rhp, Regis (Colo.) University.
34. Anthony Felston, of, University of Mississippi.
**35. *Josh Bard, c, Cherry Creek HS, Englewood, Colo.—(2002-11)**
36. *Andy Persby, 1b, Hill Murray HS, North St. Paul, Minn.
37. *Richard Durrett, c, Farmington (N.M.) HS.
38. Tom Buchman, c, University of Missouri.
39. *Ryan Brown, rhp, Northeast Texas CC.
40. *Anthony Denard, of, Emeryville HS, Oakland.
41. *Chris Shores, rhp, Beardstown (Ill.) HS.
42. Tony Gholar, rhp, William Carey (Miss.) College.
43. *Clinton Bailey, of, Chemainus (B.C.) HS.
44. Rick Moss, 3b, Lewis (Ill.) University.
45. +Barry Lunney, lhp, University of Arkansas.
46. *Craig Munroe, 1b, The Crescent School, Thornhill, Ontario.
47. +Toby Franklin, of, Westwood HS, Fort Pierce, Fla.
48. *Justin Pederson, rhp, University of Minnesota.
49. *Ryan Ferrell, rhp, Daviess County HS, Philpot, Ky.
50. *Jacob Schaffer, ss, Bradley University.
51. *Wilson Romero, of, Miami (Fla.) Senior HS.
52. *Adam Robinson, 2b, University of Virginia.
53. Mario Opipari, rhp, University of Kansas.
54. *Chris Alexander, rhp, Indian River (Fla.) CC.
55. John Mundine, rhp, Luling (Texas) HS.
56. *Chris Adams, rhp, McGregor (Texas) HS.

## MONTREAL EXPOS (5)

**1. *John Patterson, rhp, West Orange (Texas) Stark HS.—(2002-07)**
DRAFT DROP *Loophole free agent; signed by Diamondbacks (1996)*
**2. Milton Bradley, of, Poly HS, Long Beach, Calif.—(2000-11)**
3. Joe Fraser, rhp, Katella HS, Anaheim, Calif.—(Short-season A)
**4. Christian Parker, rhp, University of Notre Dame.—(2001)**
5. *Tony Lawrence, of, Louisiana Tech.—(AA)
DRAFT DROP *Returned to Louisiana Tech; re-drafted by Padres, 1997 (4th round)*
6. Karl Chatman, of, Dallas Baptist University.
7. Luis Rivera, c, Maria Vazquez HS, Bayamon, P.R.
8. Keith Evans, rhp, University of California.
9. Brian Matz, lhp, Clemson University.
10. Paul Blandford, 2b, University of Kentucky.
11. Jeremy Salyers, rhp, Walters State (Tenn.) CC.
12. *Greg Workman, lhp, Saddleback (Calif.) CC.
13. *Ricky Casteel, rhp, Liberty Eylau HS, Texarkana, Texas.
**14. Jamey Carroll, ss, University of Evansville.—(2000-07)**
15. Tripp MacKay, 2b, Oklahoma State University.
**16. Andy Tracy, 1b, Bowling Green State University.—(2000-09)**
**17. Chris Stowers, of, University of Georgia.—(1999)**
18. Matt Buirley, c, Ohio State University.
**19. Tim Young, lhp, University of Alabama.—(1998-2000)**
20. Rod Stevenson, rhp, Columbus (Ga.) College.
21. *Kevin Jordan, 2b-ss, Blinn (Texas) JC.
22. *Jason Hoffman, of, Monte Vista HS, Danville, Calif.
23. *Keith Dunn, rhp, Rosa Fort HS, Tunica, Miss.
24. Shannon Swaino, c, Kent State University.
25. *Thomas Pace, of, Mesa (Ariz.) HS.
26. Ethan Barlow, of, University of Vermont.
27. *Ryan Luther, ss, Olympic (Wash.) JC.
28. Michael Rahilly, rhp, North Fort Myers HS, Cape Coral, Fla.
29. +Kevin Forbes, of, American River (Calif.) JC.
30. Eric Sparks, lhp, SUNY Cortland.
31. Adam Martin, lhp, Merritt Island HS, Melbourne, Fla.
32. Darrick Edison, rhp, Cal Poly Pomona.
33. *Mike Shwam, rhp, Edison HS, Huntington Beach, Calif.
**34. Carl Sadler, lhp, Taylor County HS, Perry, Fla.—(2002-03)**
**35. *Eric Cyr, lhp, Edouard Montpetit HS, Montreal.—(2002)**
36. *Rafael Erazo, rhp, Marza Tereza Pineiro HS, Sabana Seca, P.R.
37. *Joe Fretwell, c, Cardinal Gibbons HS, Overland Park, Fla.
38. *Javier Sein, 1b, Benito Cerezo HS, Aguadilla, P.R.
39. *Jeremy Cook, rhp, Yuba City (Calif.) HS.
40. *Nathan Cook, 3b, Oakland (Calif.) HS.
41. *Robert Cope, rhp, JC of the Siskiyous (Calif.).
42. *Daniel Custer, 3b, Dewey HS, Copan, Okla.
43. *Jacob Smith, rhp, East Coweta HS, Newnan, Ga.
44. *Jason Huth, ss, Howard (Texas) JC.
45. *Michael Brown, of, Saguaro HS, Scottsdale, Ariz.
46. *Mike Sikorski, of, Knoch HS, Saxonburg, Pa.

## NEW YORK METS (13)

1. Rob Stratton, of, San Marcos HS, Santa Barbara, Calif.—(AAA)
2. Brendan Behn, lhp, Merced (Calif.) JC.—(Low A)
**3. Eddie Yarnall, lhp, Louisiana State University.—(1999-2000)**
4. Ray Lovingood, lhp, McMinn County HS, Riceville, Tenn.—(Low A)
5. Pat Burns, of, Ryan HS, Denton, Texas.—(High A)
6. Tom Johnson, of, Brookdale (N.J.) HS.
7. *Tony Milo, lhp, Laguna Hills (Calif.) HS.
8. Pee Wee Lopez, c, Miami-Dade CC South.
9. Willie Suggs, rhp, Mount Vernon (Ill.) HS.
10. Scott Comer, lhp, Mazama HS, Klamath Falls, Ore.
11. Garrick Haltiwanger, of, The Citadel.
12. *Geoff Linville, rhp, Redmond (Wash.) HS.
13. *David Walling, rhp, El Capitan HS, Lakeside, Calif.
DRAFT DROP *First-round draft pick (27th overall), Yankees (1999)*
14. Tom Stanton, c, Florida CC.
15. *Jeff Rook, of, Badin HS, Fairfield, Ohio.
**16. Dicky Gonzalez, rhp, Adolfina Irizarry HS, Toa Baja, P.R.—(2001-04)**
17. *Kregg Talburt, rhp, Tahlequah (Okla.) HS.
18. *Eric Schmitt, rhp, W.T. Woodson HS, Fairfax, Va.
19. Bailey Chancey, of, University of Alabama-Huntsville.
20. Mike Lyons, rhp, Stetson University.
21. John Tamargo, ss, University of Florida.
DRAFT DROP *Son of John Tamargo, major leaguer (1976-80)*
22. Jerson Perez, ss-2b, CC of Rhode Island.
23. Chase Mulvehill, of, Pell City (Ala.) HS.
24. *Kendall Prather, rhp, Sweetwater HS, Erick, Okla.
25. Kevin Dougherty, lhp, Eastern HS, Voorhees, N.J.
26. *Dennis Anderson, c, Canyon Del Oro HS, Tucson, Ariz.
27. *Jason Navarro, lhp, Tulane University.
28. *Paul Ciofrone, of, Stony Brook HS, Nesconset, N.Y.
29. *Todd Meldahl, lhp, Butte (Mon.) HS.
30. Mike Queen, lhp, Gravette (Ark.) HS.
31. +Joaquin Montada, rhp, Hialeah (Fla.) HS / Miami-Dade North CC.
32. Mike Meadows, 3b, Seminole (Fla.) HS.
33. *Jim Magrane, rhp, Ottumwa (Iowa) HS.
34. *Aaron Vincent, rhp, Bakersfield (Calif.) JC.
35. Tim Carr, rhp, Westlake HS, Westlake Village, Calif.
**36. *Randy Ruiz, 1b, James Monroe HS, Bronx, N.Y.—(2008-10)**
37. Adam Garmon, rhp, St. Augustine (Fla.) HS.
38. Jeff Hafer, rhp, James Madison University.
39. *Zackery Usry, 1b, Hokes Bluff HS, Piedmont, Ala.
**40. *Josh Pearce, rhp, West Valley HS, Yakima, Wash.—(2002-04)**
41. *Andrew Watt, of, St. Francis HS, Los Altos, Calif.
42. *Daniel Nelson, rhp, Lackawanna (Pa.) CC.
43. +John Mattson, rhp, Tacoma (Wash.) CC.
**44. +Tim Corcoran, rhp, Jackson HS, Slaughter, La. / Mississippi Gulf Coast JC.—(2005-07)**
45. +Pat Gorman, rhp, Rockland (N.Y.) CC / Lackawanna (Pa.) CC.
46. Tony Payne, lhp, Rutherford HS, Panama City, Fla.
47. *Brian Holden, lhp, Palm Beach Lakes HS, West Palm Beach, Fla.
48. B.J. Huff, of, University of Alabama-Birmingham.
49. *Jason Gronert, c, Lyman HS, Longwood, Fla.
50. *Michael Fierro, rhp, Merritt Island (Fla.) HS.
51. Mike Davis, rhp, Florida State University.
52. *Aaron Abram, of, Valley HS, West Des Moines, Iowa.
53. Matt Splawn, rhp, University of Texas.
54. *Ryan O'Toole, rhp, UCLA.
55. Jason Bohannon, lhp, Oklahoma City University.

## NEW YORK YANKEES (24)

**1. Eric Milton, lhp, University of Maryland** (Choice from Angels as compensation for Type B free agent Randy Velarde).**—(1998-2009)**
1. (Choice to Rangers as compensation for Type A free agent Kenny Rogers)
2. Jason Coble, lhp, Lincoln County HS, Fayetteville, Tenn.—(Low A)
**3. Nick Johnson, 1b, McClatchy HS, Sacramento, Calif.—(2001-12)**
DRAFT DROP *Nephew of Larry Bowa, major leaguer*

*(1970-85)*
4. Vidal Candelaria, c, Fernando Callejo HS, Manati, P.R.—(Short-season A)
**5. Zach Day, rhp, LaSalle HS, Cincinnati.—(2002-06)**
**6. Brian Reith, rhp, Concordia Lutheran HS, Fort Wayne, Ind.—(2001-04)**
7. Brian Aylor, of, Oklahoma State University.
8. Allen Butler, 3b, Lincoln Memorial (Tenn.) University.
9. *Chris Fulbright, rhp, Libertyville (Ill.) HS.
10. Rudy Gomez, 2b, University of Miami (Fla).
11. *Brant Ust, ss, Eastlake HS, Redmond, Wash.
12. Eric Krall, lhp, Birmingham-Southern University.
13. *Andrew Helmer, rhp, Bishop Dwenger HS, New Haven, Ind.
14. Yoiset Valle, lhp, Monsignor Pace HS, Miami Lakes, Fla.
15. *Nick Stocks, rhp, Jesuit HS, Tampa.
DRAFT DROP *First-round draft pick (36th overall), Cardinals (1999)*
16. Justin Rayment, lhp, San Diego State University.
**17. *Matt Ginter, rhp, Clark HS, Winchester, Ky.—(2000-08)**
DRAFT DROP *First-round draft pick (22nd overall), White Sox (1999)*
18. *Chuck Hazzard, 1b, University of Florida.
19. *Brian Gilman, c-ss, Westview HS, Portland, Ore.
20. Brandon Hendrikx, rhp, Rancho Santiago (Calif.) JC.
21. *Kyle Brunen, of, Delisle Composite HS, Vanscoy, Sask.
22. *Joe Pourron, rhp, Chattahoochee Valley (Ala.) CC.
23. *Kevin Overcash, ss, Collierville (Tenn.) HS.
24. *Fontella Jones, of, Mississippi Gulf Coast JC.
25. *Adam Ramos, of, Lehman HS, Bronx, N.Y.
26. *Joshua Hawes, rhp, Toll Gate HS, Warwick, R.I.
27. Jason McBride, rhp, Pensacola (Fla.) JC.
28. +Clay Eavenson, rhp, Loganville, Ga. / DeKalb (Ga.) JC.
29. *Ryan Tack, rhp, Saddleback (Calif.) CC.
**30. +Marcus Thames, of, East Central (Miss.) CC.—(2002-11)**
31. Ryan Huffman, of, Texas A&M University.
32. Ryan Wheeler, 2b, Lincoln Memorial (Tenn.) University.
33. Blaine Phillips, c, University of Southwestern Louisiana.
34. *Jared Hoerman, rhp, Eastern Oklahoma State JC.
35. *Dan Kerrigan, c, Northeast HS, St. Petersburg, Fla.
DRAFT DROP *Son of Joe Kerrigan, major leaguer (1976-80); major league manager (2001)*
36. *Noel Manley, c-1b, Louisburg (N.C.) JC.
37. +Justin Carpenter, rhp, Seminole (Okla.) JC.
38. *Jarvis Larry, of, Parkway HS, Bossier City, La.
39. *Eunique Johnson, 3b, Centennial HS, Compton, Calif.
40. Dennis Twombley, c, Pepperdine University.
41. *Gavin Hare, c, Eastlake HS, Redmond, Wash.
42. Alain Cruz, 3b, Miami-Dade CC North.
43. *Migues Rodriguez, ss, Cypress (Calif.) JC.
44. *William Pieper, 3b, Kamehameha HS, Honolulu, Hawaii.
45. *Mark Hamilton, lhp, Bell HS, Hurst, Texas.
46. *Daryl Grant, 1b-lhp, Florin HS, Sacramento, Calif.
47. *Nathan Dighera, of-c, Southwestern (Calif.) JC.
48. *Sam Norris, 1b, San Francisco CC.
49. *Robert Simpson, c, Christian HS, El Cajon, Calif.
50. *Charles Armstrong, lhp, Oakland.
51. *Caesar Castaneda, 3b, East Los Angeles JC.
52. *Russ Chambliss, of, Washington (Pa.) University.
DRAFT DROP *Son Chris Chambliss, major leaguer (1971-88)*
53. *Felix Lopez, 1b, Plant HS, Tampa.
54. *Jason Halper, of, Columbia University.
55. *Derek Bauer, 2b, Clarkstown North HS, New City, N.Y.
56. Bob Meier, c, Cinnaminson (N.J.) HS.
57. *Hector Rivera, 3b, Jesuit HS, Tampa.
58. *Trevor Bishop, rhp, Lethbridge (Alberta) CC.
59. *Jay Foster, rhp, Birch Hills Composite HS, Birch Hills, Sask.
60. *Nathan Cadena, ss, Cerritos (Calif.) JC.
61. *Cedrick Harris, of, Ashdown (Ark.) HS.
62. Jason Tisone, rhp, Seton Hall University.
63. *Tony Gomes, rhp, Lodi HS, Galt, Calif.
**64. *Matt Wise, rhp, Cal State Fullerton.—(2000-08)**
65. *Mitchell Roth, c, Cleveland HS, Reseda, Calif.
66. *Fred Smith, of, Bryan Station HS, Lexington, Ky.
67. *Craig Hann, c, F.P. Walshe HS, Fort MacLeod, Alberta.
68. *Avante Rose, of, Centennial HS, Compton, Calif.
69. *Ryan Suyama, ss, Sprague HS, Salem, Ore.
70. *Amir Taylor, of, Lincoln HS, San Diego.
71. *Adrian Mora, 2b-ss, Southwestern (Calif.) JC.
72. *Aaron Kramer, rhp, Grand Canyon University.
73. Harold Frazier, lhp, Northeastern Oklahoma State JC.
74. *William Duncan, c, Big Bend (Wash.) CC.
75. Mike Biehle, lhp, Ohio State University.
76. Adam Danner, rhp, University of South Florida.
77. Rhett Ingerick, rhp, Davidson College.
78. *Bryan Green, 1b, Jasper (Texas) HS.
79. *Richard Bottomley, c, Ramona (Calif.) HS.
80. *Garry Templeton, ss, Poway (Calif.) HS.
DRAFT DROP *Son of Garry Templeton, major leaguer (1976-91)*
81. *Nick Herz, c, Poway (Calif.) HS.
82. *Corey Ward, of, Skyline HS, Dallas.
83. *Gustavo Alonso, c, Jordan HS, Long Beach, Calif.
84. *Chris Small, c, Punahou HS, Honolulu, Hawaii.
85. *Matt Martinez, ss, Big Bend (Wash.) CC.
86. *Adam Wilson, ss, Mission Bay HS, San Diego.
87. *Nathan Kaup, 3b, Camarillo (Calif.) HS.
**88. Scott Seabol, 3b, West Virginia University.—(2001-05)**
89. *Damion Malott, of, Cosumnes River (Calif.) JC.
90. *Brad Gorrie, ss, University of Massachusetts.
91. *Michael Myers, c, Allentown (Pa.) College.
92. *Ben Hickman, rhp, Northeast Texas CC.
93. *Errol Smith, of, St. Augustine HS, San Diego.
**94. *Clay Condrey, rhp, Angelina (Texas) CC.—(2002-09)**
95. *Gregg Donohue, c, Rockland (N.Y.) CC.
96. *Jose Garcia, lhp, Southwestern (Calif.) JC.
97. *Mark Copeland, rhp, Muscatine (Iowa) CC.
98. Todd Trunk, rhp, North Central (Ill.) JC.
99. *Mike Amrhein, 3b, University of Notre Dame.
100. *Aron Amundson, 3b, Eastern Oklahoma State JC.

Eric Chavez proved to be a professional hitter, collecting 1,477 hits in 17 big league seasons

## OAKLAND ATHLETICS (10)

**1. Eric Chavez, 3b, Mount Carmel HS, San Diego.—(1998-2014)**
2. Josue Espada, ss, University of Mobile (Ala.).—(AAA)
**3. A.J. Hinch, c, Stanford University.—(1998-2004)**
DRAFT DROP *Major league manager (2009-15)*
4. *Tom Graham, rhp, Beyer HS, Modesto, Calif.—(AAA)
DRAFT DROP *Attended Fresno State; never re-drafted*
5. Julian Leyva, rhp, Arlington HS, Riverside, Calif.—(AAA)
6. Nick Sosa, 1b, Lake Mary (Fla.) HS.
7. *Mike Paradis, rhp, Auburn (Mass.) HS.
DRAFT DROP *First-round draft pick (13th overall), Orioles (1999)*
8. Brad Blumenstock, rhp, Southern Illinois University.
**9. Cody McKay, c-3b, Arizona State University.—(2002-04)**
DRAFT DROP *Son of Dave McKay, major leaguer (1975-82)*
10. *Eric Lee, of, Clear Lake HS, Houston.
11. Jake O'Dell, rhp, University of Texas.
12. Todd Mensik, 1b, University of Mississippi.
13. Doug Robertson, rhp, Bradley University.
14. *Chad Hawkins, rhp, Grapevine HS, Euless, Texas.
**15. Kevin Gregg, rhp, Corvallis (Ore.) HS.—(2003-15)**
16. Justin Bowles, of, Louisiana State University.
17. *Derek Rix, 3b, Bishop Kenny HS, Jacksonville, Fla.
18. *Joel Colgrove, rhp, University of Alabama.
19. *Joe Caruso, 2b, University of Alabama.
20. Eric Faulk, rhp, New Hanover HS, Wilmington, N.C.
21. Brian Luderer, c, Crespi HS, Tarzana, Calif.
22. *Scott Skeen, of, Mountain View HS, Bend, Ore.
23. +Frankey Jacobs, rhp, Jordan HS, Durham, N.C. / Louisburg (N.C.) JC.
**24. Brett Laxton, rhp, Louisiana State University.—(1999-2000)**
DRAFT DROP *Son of Bill Laxton, major leaguer (1970-77) • Brother of Josh Laxton, 31st-round draft pick, Marlins (1996)*
25. *Randy Eversgerd, rhp, Kaskaskia (Ill.) CC.
26. Rico Lagattuta, lhp, University of Nevada-Reno.
27. Flint Wallace, rhp, Texas Christian University.
28. T.R. Marcinczyk, 1b, University of Miami.
29. Monty Davis, 3b, Indian Hills (Iowa) CC.
30. Peter Dellaratta, rhp, University of South Alabama.
31. Ray Noriega, lhp, New Mexico Highland University.
32. Bryan Garcia, rhp, Quartz Hill (Calif.) HS.
33. *Ryan Gill, rhp, Galveston (Texas) JC.
34. *Joe Dusan, of, Bend (Ore) HS.
35. *Ian Perio, lhp, Castle HS, Kaneohe, Hawaii.
36. *Danny Chavers, ss, Riverview HS, Sarasota, Fla.
37. *Brent Spooner, c, Godby HS, Tallahassee, Fla.
38. *Bryan King, rhp, Yavapai (Ariz.) JC.
39. *Anthony Taylor, rhp, Central Arizona JC.
40. *Gary Burnham, of-1b, Clemson University.
41. *Graeme Brown, rhp, Avon Old Farms (Conn.) Prep School.
42. *Brent Miller, 3b, Butte (Calif.) JC.
43. *Michael Knight, of, Oakland (Calif.) HS.

## PHILADELPHIA PHILLIES (11)

**1. Adam Eaton, rhp, Snohomish (Wash.) HS.—(2000-09)**
**2. Jimmy Rollins, ss, Encinal HS, Alameda, Calif.—(2000-15)**
3. Kris Stevens, lhp, Fontana (Calif.) HS.—(AA)
4. Ryan Brannan, rhp, Long Beach State University.—(AAA)
5. Ira Tilton, rhp, Siena College.—(Low A)
6. *Kevin Burford, of, Fountain Valley (Calif.) HS.
7. B.J. Schlicher, c-1b, North Montgomery HS, Crawfordsville, Ind.
8. David Francia, of, University of South Alabama.
9. Brandon Marsters, c, Oral Roberts University.
10. Evan Thomas, rhp, Florida International University.
11. Sal Molta, rhp, Brookdale (N.J.) CC.
12. Jason Johnson, of, Chaffey (Calif.) JC.
13. Jason Knupfer, ss, Long Beach State University.
14. Mike Torti, 3b, Arizona State University.
15. *Brett Egan, ss, Royal HS, Simi Valley, Calif.
16. Brandon Allen, lhp, University of Illinois-Chicago.
17. Bob Van Iten, c, Truman HS, Independence, Mo.
18. Joe Cotton, rhp, Bowling Green State University.
19. Brad Crede, 1b, Central Missouri State University.
DRAFT DROP *Brother of Joe Crede, major leaguer (2000-09)*
20. Jason Wesemann, ss, University of Wisconsin.
21. *Greg Gregory, lhp, Pepperdine University.
22. Rodney Batts, 2b, Delta State (Miss.) University.
23. Marty Crawford, 2b, Baylor University.
24. Shannon Cooley, of, Northeast Louisiana University.
25. Adam Shadburne, rhp, University of Kentucky.
26. Javier Mejia, rhp, University of Southern California.
27. Skip Kiil, of, Cal State Fullerton.
28. Kevin Nichols, 1b-3b, University of Alabama.
29. Nick Thompson, c, Elon College.
30. Jason Davis, lhp, San Jose State University.
31. Terry Bishop, lhp, College of St. Rose (N.Y.).
32. Kirby Clark, c, Auburn University.
33. *Brad Philley, of, Rogers HS, Puyallup, Wash.
34. Tommy Ferrand, of, Southeastern Louisiana University.
35. Richard Estep, rhp, Grand Canyon University.
36. Justin Fenus, rhp, University of North Alabama.
37. Matt Buczkowski, c-3b, Butler University.
38. *Jude Voltz, 1b, Jesuit HS, Metairie, La.
39. Tommy Worthy, ss, Gadsden State (Ala.) CC.
40. Greg Taylor, ss, University of Arkansas-Little Rock.
41. Jason Cafferty, rhp, Hastings (Neb.) College.
42. John Crane, lhp, Rider University.
43. Eddie Rivero, of, University of Miami.
44. *David Campos, lhp, Kerman (Calif.) HS.
45. *Stephen Murphy, rhp, El Camino HS, South San Francisco.
46. *Lee Molaison, c, Terrebonne HS, Theriot, La.
47. Keith Shockley, lhp, Allen County (Kan.) CC.
48. *Clarence Hargrave, ss, Southern Union State (Ala.) JC.
49. *Chuck Crumpton, rhp, Northeast Texas CC.
50. *Rich Rodrigues, c, DeAnza (Calif.) JC.

## PITTSBURGH PIRATES (1)

1. **Kris Benson, rhp, Clemson University.—(1999-2010)**
2. Andy Prater, rhp, McCluer North HS, Florissant, Mo.—(Low A)
3. Luis Lorenzana, ss, Montgomery HS, San Diego.—(AAA)
4. Lee Evans, c, Tuscaloosa County HS, Northport, Ala.—(AAA)
5. **Tike Redman, of, Tuscaloosa (Ala.) Academy.—(2000-2007)**

DRAFT DROP *Brother of Prentice Redman, major leaguer (2003)*

6. Yustin Jordan, ss, Monticello (Ark.) HS.
7. Andy Hohenstein, rhp, Norte Vista HS, Riverside, Calif.
8. Bobby Vogt, lhp, Armwood HS, Tampa.
9. Jess Siciliano, rhp, Rockland (N.Y.) CC.
10. **Carlos Rivera, 1b, Academia Adventista HS, Rio Grande, P.R.—(2003-04)**
11. Jason Haynie, lhp, University of South Carolina.
12. Jeremy Rockow, of, Fort Myers (Fla.) HS.
13. Xavier Burns, 3b, Central State (Ohio) University.
14. Ali Brooks, ss-of, Laney (Calif.) JC.
15. *Nick Day, of, Green Valley HS, Las Vegas, Nev.
16. Michael Chaney, lhp, Bowling Green State University.
17. ***Mike Gonzalez, lhp, Faith Christian Academy, Pasadena, Texas.—(2003-13)**
18. Jason Elmore, rhp, Lucama, N.C.
19. Garrett Larkin, ss, Merrimack (Mass.) College.
20. Jacob Jensen, ss, Fresno (Calif.) CC.
21. Paul Ah Yat, lhp, University of Hawaii.
22. Luis Gonzalez, rhp, University of New Mexico.
23. Morgan Walker, 1b, Lamar University.
24. *Mark Freed, lhp, Pennsville (N.J.) HS.
25. Michael Gresko, lhp, Mercer County (N.J.) CC.
26. Daniel Tobias, rhp, Oregon, Ohio.
27. *Kendall Rhodes, rhp, Crockett (Texas) HS.
28. ***Willie Harris, 2b-ss, Cairo (Ga.) HS.—(2001-12)**
29. Ender Classen, ss, Antonio Lucchetti HS, Arecibo, P.R.
30. Wyatt Brooks, lhp, University of North Florida.
31. *Makani Lum, c-3b, Kamehameha HS, Kaneohe, Hawaii.

DRAFT DROP *Son of Mike Lum, major leaguer (1967-81)*

32. *Chad Ciccone, c, Hopewell HS, Aliquippa, Pa.
33. Carlton McKenzie, of-3b, Raritan Valley (N.J.) CC.
34. *Mo Douglas, 1b, Eureka HS, Glencoe, Mo.
35. Joe Hunt, of, Sante Fe (Fla.) CC.
36. *Barry Johnson, lhp-1b, Hales Franciscan HS, Chicago.
37. *Brandon Schliinz, 3b-c, Orono HS, Loretto, Minn.
38. ***Jamal Strong, of-ss, Pasadena HS, Altadena, Calif.—(2003-05)**
39. *Josh Bonifay, ss-2b, T.C. Roberson HS, Arden, N.C.

DRAFT DROP *Son of Cam Bonifay, general manager, Pirates (1993-2001)*

40. *Jesse Daggett, c, Crescenta Valley HS, La Crescenta, Calif.
41. Scott May, c, Carson-Newman (Tenn.) College.

DRAFT DROP *Grandson of Pinky May, major league (1939-43); son of Milt May, major leaguer (1970-84)*

42. *Jim McAuley, c, H.B. Plant HS, Tampa.
43. *Jeremy Sickles, c, Millikan HS, Long Beach, Calif.
44. *Frank Moore, 2b, Coffee HS, Douglas, Ga.
45. ***Chris Capuano, lhp, Cathedral HS, West Springfield, Mass.—(2003-15)**
46. Ricardo Finol, rhp, Navarro (Texas) JC.
47. *Ian Rauls, of, Mercer County (N.J.) CC.
48. *Duane Eason, rhp, Troy State University.
49. *Kevin Chapman, of, Bernards HS, Peapack, N.J.
50. *Jason Bowers, ss, Laurel Highlands HS, Uniontown, Pa.
51. *Francisco Lebron, 1b, Florida International University.
52. *Dwight Edge, of, Apopka (Fla.) HS.
53. **Rob Mackowiak, ss-2b, South Suburban (Ill.) JC.—(2001-08)**
54. *J.D. Arteaga, lhp, University of Miami.
55. *Nathan Shepperson, 1b, Virginia Military Institute.
56. *Steven Yeager, c, Thousand Oaks (Calif.) HS.

DRAFT DROP *Son of Steve Yeager, major leaguer (1972-86)*

## ST. LOUIS CARDINALS (3)

1. **Braden Looper, rhp, Wichita State University.—(1998-2009)**
2. (Choice to Reds as compensation for Type A free agent Ron Gant)
3. **Brent Butler, ss, Scotland County HS, Laurinburg, N.C.—(2001-03)**
4. Bryan Britt, of, University of North Carolina-Wilmington.—(High A)
5. *Jeff Rizzo, 3b, La Jolla (Calif.) HS.—(Rookie)

DRAFT DROP *Attended Stanford; re-drafted by Padres, 1999 (35th round)*

6. Jim Gargiulo, c, University of Miami.
7. Kevin Sheredy, rhp, UCLA.
8. Dave Schmidt, c, Oregon State University.
9. Shawn Hogge, rhp, Western HS, Las Vegas, Nev.
10. Cordell Farley, of, Virginia Commonwealth University.
11. Isaac Byrd, of, University of Kansas.

DRAFT DROP *Wide receiver, National Football League (1997-2002)*

12. *Rodney Eberly, 3b, Highland (Kan.) CC.
13. *Lance Smith, rhp, Dickinson (Texas) HS.
14. Steve Norris, lhp, Tyler (Texas) JC.
15. Greg Heffernan, rhp, St. Andrews Presbyterian (N.C.) College.
16. Stacy Kleiner, c, University of Nevada-Las Vegas.
17. Keith Gallagher, rhp, Murray State University.
18. *William Goodson, lhp, Troup County HS, LaGrange, Ga.
19. Keith Finnerty, 2b, St. John's University.
20. Ryan Darr, ss, Corona (Calif.) HS.

DRAFT DROP *Son of Mike Darr, major leaguer (1977) • Brother of Mike Darr Jr., major leaguer (1999-2001)*

21. ***Randy Flores, lhp, University of Southern California.—(2002-10)**

DRAFT DROP *Brother of Ron Flores, major leaguer (2005-07); scouting director, Cardinals (2015)*

22. Paul Tanner, ss, University of Nevada-Las Vegas.
23. *Nathan Rice, lhp, Cal State Northridge.
24. Jason Pollock, rhp, West Liberty State (W.Va.) College.
25. Andrew Gordon, rhp, James Madison University.
26. *Pat Driscoll, lhp, University of Nebraska.
27. Greg Montgomery, rhp, University of Central Arkansas.
28. Tim Onofrei, rhp-of, Albertson (Idaho) College.
29. Mark Nussbeck, rhp, Bellevue (Neb.) College.
30. *Orvin Matos, c, Luis Munoz Rivera HS, Utuado, P.R.
31. Brian Mazurek, 1b, College of St. Francis (Ill.).
32. *Steven Doherty, ss, Los Angeles CC.
33. Brad Kennedy, 3b, Southwest Missouri State University.
34. Ryan Kritscher, 2b-of, UC Santa Barbara.
35. Paul Wilders, 3b, Siena College.
36. **Stubby Clapp, 2b, Texas Tech.—(2001)**
37. Clint Weibl, rhp, University of Miami.
38. *Greg Johnson, rhp, Okeechobee (Fla.) HS.
39. *Daniel Pierce, of, Jurupa Valley HS, Mira Loma, Calif.
40. *Clay Hawkins, c-of, Seminole (Okla.) JC.
41. John Tuttle, rhp, San Marino (Calif.) HS.
42. Ryan Roberts, 3b, Brigham Young University.

## SAN DIEGO PADRES (15)

1. Matt Halloran, ss, Chancellor HS, Fredericksburg, Va.—(AA)
2. Vernon Maxwell, of, Midwest City (Okla.) HS.—(High A)
3. Widd Workman, rhp, Arizona State University.—(AA)
4. Nathan Dunn, 3b, Louisiana State University.—(High A)
5. Brian Loyd, c, Cal State Fullerton.—(AAA)
6. Tom Szymborski, rhp, University of Illinois-Chicago.
7. Brian Carmody, lhp, Santa Clara University.
8. *Chance Capel, rhp, Carroll HS, Southlake, Texas.

DRAFT DROP *First-round draft pick (30th overall), Cardinals (1999)*

9. **Jason Middlebrook, rhp, Stanford University.—(2001-03)**
10. *Tim Lanier, c, Louisiana State University.
11. Brian McClure, 2b, University of Illinois.
12. Ben Reynoso, ss, Fresno State University.
13. *Brennan Hervey, 1b, Florida Atlantic University.
14. Francisco Gonzalez, rhp, Antonio Lucchetti HS, Arecibo, P.R.
15. ***Steve Watkins, rhp, Lubbock Christian HS, Lubbock, Texas.—(2004)**
16. Sandro Garcia, 2b, Pope John Paul II HS, Deerfield Beach, Fla.
17. *Craig Patterson, c, El Dorado HS, Placentia, Calif.
18. Jacob Ruotsinoja, of, Manatee (Fla.) CC.
19. *Kyle Holle, rhp, Blinn (Texas) JC.
20. Jimmy Alarcon, rhp, Jupiter, Fla.
21. John Powers, 2b, University of Arizona.
22. Dominic Marino, rhp, Walnut (Calif.) HS.
23. Ryan Thomas, rhp, Houston Baptist University.
24. *Jesse Cornejo, lhp, Seward County (Kan.) CC.

DRAFT DROP *Son of Mardie Cornejo, major leaguer (1978) • Brother of Nate Cornejo, first-round draft pick, Tigers (1998); major leaguer (2001-04)*

25. *Chris Spieth, of, Garfield HS, Seattle.
26. Brendan Sullivan, rhp, Stanford University.
27. Nick Witte, rhp, Ball State University.
28. Trey Dunham, c, Shattuck (Okla.) HS.
29. Robbie Kent, 1b-2b, Arizona State University.
30. *Rufus French, of, Amory (Miss.) HS.
31. Danny Conroy, of, Fairleigh Dickinson University.
32. Shane Cronin, 1b-3b, Green River (Wash.) CC.
33. *Keith Kubiak, c, Giddings (Texas) HS.
34. *Jake Epstein, 1b-c, Mount Carmel HS, San Diego.

DRAFT DROP *Son of Mike Epstein, major leaguer (1966-74)*

35. Tyler Boulo, c, University of South Alabama.
36. *Rich Park, rhp, Norman (Okla.) HS.
37. Travis Jones, lhp, Asher (Okla.) HS.
38. *Al Thielemann, lhp, Vista HS, Oceanside, Calif.
39. *Davis Kile, rhp, Tacoma (Wash.) CC.

DRAFT DROP *Brother of Darryl Kile, major leaguer (1991-2002)*

40. *Paul Boykin, of, Odessa (Texas) JC.

## SAN FRANCISCO GIANTS (7)

1. *Matt White, rhp, Waynesboro (Pa.) Area HS.—(AAA)

DRAFT DROP *Loophole free agent; signed by Devil Rays (1996)*

2. **Mike Caruso, ss, Stoneman Douglas HS, Parkland, Fla.—(1998-2002)**

DRAFT DROP *First 1996 high school draft pick to reach majors (March 31, 1998)*

3. David Kenna, c, North Fort Myers (Fla.) HS.—(Short-season A)
4. **Ken Vining, lhp, Clemson University.—(2001)**
5. Matt Wells, lhp, University of Nevada-Reno.—(AA)
6. Bill Malloy, rhp, Rutgers University.
7. Brandon Leese, rhp, Butler University.
8. **Ryan Jensen, rhp, Southern Utah University.—(2001-05)**
9. Brian Manning, of, Allentown (Pa.) College.
10. Mike Glendenning, 3b, Los Angeles Pierce JC.
11. Tony Zuniga, ss, Rancho Santiago (Calif.) JC.
12. **Damon Minor, 1b, University of Oklahoma.—(2000-04)**

DRAFT DROP *Brother of Ryan Minor, second-round draft pick, Philadelphia 76ers, National Basketball Association (1996); 12th-round draft pick, Giants (1996); major leaguer (1998-2001)*

13. *Wynter Phoenix, of, UC Santa Barbara.
14. Paul Galloway, 3b, Clemson University.
15. Mick Pageler, rhp, Odessa (Texas) JC.
16. Mike Riley, lhp, West Virginia University.
17. +Eric Johnson, rhp, Mount Hood (Ore.) CC.
18. *Jeff Munster, rhp, Fresno (Calif.) CC.
19. Levi Miskolczi, of, Rider College.
20. Luis Estrella, rhp, Cal State Fullerton.
21. Robbie Crabtree, rhp, Cal State Northridge.
22. *Kevin Tommasini, of, Arizona State University.
23. *Tom Bartosh, of, Duncanville (Texas) HS.
24. +Joel Fuentes, ss, Southeastern (Iowa) CC.
25. *Lance Woodcock, ss, Ponderosa HS, Shingle Springs, Calif.
26. *Chris Curry, c, Conway (Ark.) HS.

DRAFT DROP *Baseball coach, Arkansas-Little Rock (2015)*

27. Art Baeza, 3b, Lewis-Clark State (Idaho) College.
28. *Craig Cozart, rhp, University of Central Florida.

DRAFT DROP *Baseball coach, High Point (2009-15)*

29. Michael Sorrow, of, Georgia Tech.
30. +Mark Hutchings, rhp, Mineral Area (Mo.) CC.
31. +Richard Clark, of, Countryside HS, Clearwater, Fla. / Indian River (Fla.) JC.
32. *Michael Wright, lhp, Crete-Monee HS, Crete, Ill.
33. *Michael Stevenson, rhp, Orange Coast (Calif.) JC.
34. *Jake Joseph, rhp, San Juan HS, Citrus Heights, Calif.
35. *Brad Garrett, of, Mountain View HS, Orem, Utah.
36. *Billy Coleman, rhp, North Central Texas JC.
37. *Donald Pearson, rhp, Foothill HS, Highlands, Calif.
38. *Charles Lopez, of, Cerritos (Calif.) JC.
39. *Matt Dempsey, 1b, Cypress (Calif.) JC.
40. *Andrew Beattie, ss, Clearwater (Fla.) HS.
41. *Chad Baum, c, Golden West (Calif.) JC.
42. *Chaz Johnson, of, Dr. Phillips HS, Orlando, Fla.
43. *Thomas Gessner, 3b, Thomas More HS, Milwaukee.
44. ***Brandon Larson, ss, Blinn (Texas) JC.—(2001-04)**

DRAFT DROP *First-round draft pick (14th overall), Reds (1997)*

45. *Don Gierke, of, Dr. Phillips HS, Orlando, Fla.
46. *Richard Dishman, rhp, Duke University.
47. *Mark Williams, rhp, Cal State Sacramento.
48. *Justin Sherrod, ss, Santaluces HS, Lake Worth, Fla.
49. *Rob Purvis, rhp, Tipton (Ind.) HS.

DRAFT DROP *First-round draft pick (45th overall), White Sox (1999)*

50. Angel Melendez, of, Caguas, P.R.

## SEATTLE MARINERS (22)

1. **Gil Meche, rhp, Acadiana HS, Lafayette, La.—(1999-2010)**
2. **Jeff Farnsworth, rhp, Okaloosa-Walton (Fla.) CC.—(2002)**
3. Tony DeJesus, lhp, Havelock (N.C.) HS.—(Short-season A)
4. **Denny Stark, rhp, University of Toledo.—(1999-2009)**
5. **Chris Mears, rhp, Lord Byng HS, Vancouver, B.C.—(2003)**
6. Peanut Williams, c, Nacogdoches (Texas) HS.
7. Danny Garey, rhp, St. Joseph (Mich.) HS.
8. ***Willie Bloomquist, ss, South Kitsap HS, Port Orchard, Wash.—(2002-15)**
9. Rob Luce, rhp, University of Nevada-Las Vegas.
10. Matt Noe, lhp, Riverside (Calif.) CC.
11. Julio Ayala, lhp, Georgia Southern University.
12. Joe Victery, rhp, University of Oklahoma.
13. Orin Kawahara, rhp, Rancho Santiago (Calif.) JC.
14. *Dwayne Dobson, rhp, Manatee (Fla.) CC.
15. Greg Beaver, rhp, East Rowan HS, Rockwell, N.C.
16. Mark Carroll, c, Coxsackie-Athens HS, Athens, N.Y.
17. Jason Bond, lhp, Arizona State University.
18. Allan Westfall, rhp, University of Miami.
19. +Larry Haynes, of, Nogales HS, West Covina, Calif. / Mount San Antonio (Calif.) JC.
20. **Brian Fitzgerald, lhp, Virginia Tech.—(2002)**
21. Kyle Kennison, rhp, University of Southern Maine.
22. Brian Lindner, ss, William Paterson (N.J.) College.
23. *Devlon Davis, c, Pittsburg (Calif.) HS.
24. *Jeremy Pierce, rhp, Ventura (Calif.) JC.
25. *Matt Vincent, lhp, Floyd Central HS, Floyd's Knob, Ind.
26. +Jacob Underwood, c, Hillsboro (Ore.) HS / Mount Hood (Ore.) JC.
27. +Josue Matos, rhp, Eugenio Maria de Hostos HS, Cabo Rojo, P.R. / Miami-Dade CC New World Center.
28. *Donovan Ross, 3b, Columbia State (Tenn.) CC.
29. *Karmen Randolph, ss, Los Angeles CC.
30. *Jason Wilson, rhp, Broward (Fla.) CC.
31. *Duncan McAdoo, rhp, Winnsboro (Texas) HS.
32. *Kevin Stewart, 3b, Corona HS, Newport Beach, Calif.
33. P.J. Williams, of, Blinn (Texas) JC.
34. *Joe Barnes, of, Old Mill HS, Severna, Md.

35. Dallas Mahan, lhp, Greeley West HS, Greeley, Colo.
36. *Scott Harrison, lhp, Dixie (Utah) JC.
37. *Steven Rivera, lhp, Dundalk (Md.) CC.
38. *Laron McGee, ss-2b, Morse HS, San Diego.
39. *James McCoy, of, South Dade HS, Homestead, Fla.
**40. Sean Spencer, lhp, University of Washington.—(1999-2000)**
41. *William Allison, rhp, Central Florida CC.
42. *Brett Anderson, rhp, University HS, San Diego.
43. *Scott Starkey, lhp, Vista HS, Oceanside, Calif.
44. *Noel Pelekoudas, 2b, Eastlake HS, Redmond, Wash.
45. *Adam Walker, lhp, Yavapai (Ariz.) CC.
46. *Michael Campbell, of, Mesa (Ariz.) CC.
47. +Bret Nielsen, of, Grossmont HS, El Cajon, Calif. / Grossmont (Calif.) JC.
**48. *Juan Pierre, of, Galveston (Texas) JC.—(2000-13)**
49. *Richard Sundstrom, rhp, Cypress (Calif.) JC.
50. *Jason Sutherland, c, Chuckey-Doak HS, Afton, Tenn.
51. Jason Regan, 3b-2b, Blinn (Texas) JC.
52. *Michael Albert, of, Carlsbad (Calif.) HS.
**53. *Greg Dobbs, 3b, Canyon Springs HS, Moreno Valley, Calif.—(2004-14)**
54. *Rich Snider, rhp, Byng HS, Ada, Okla.
55. *Chad Schmidt, of, Skidmore Tynan HS, Skidmore, Texas.
56. *Brandon Barnaby, rhp, Citrus (Calif.) JC.
57. *Tamar Turner, of, Liberty (Texas) HS.
58. *Brian Beinfest, lhp, Clayton (Calif.) Valley HS.
**59. *Barry Zito, lhp, University HS, San Diego.—(2000-15)**
DRAFT DROP *First-round draft pick (9th overall), Athletics (1999)*
60. *Ryan Grimmett, of, University of Miami.

## TAMPA BAY DEVIL RAYS (29)

1. Paul Wilder, of, Cary (N.C.) HS.—(High A)
2. Doug Johnson, 1b-ss, Buchholz HS, Gainesville, Fla.—(Rookie)
DRAFT DROP *Quarterback, National Football League (2000-04)*
3. Ed Kofler, rhp, Tarpon Springs HS, Palm Harbor, Fla.—(AA)
**4. Cedrick Bowers, lhp, Chiefland (Fla.) HS.—(2008-10)**
**5. Alex Sanchez, of, Miami-Dade CC Wolfson.—(2001-05)**
6. Elliot Brown, rhp, Auburn University.
**7. Mickey Callaway, rhp, University of Mississippi.—(1999-2004)**
8. Matt Quatraro, c, Old Dominion University.
9. Denis Pujals, rhp, University of Miami.
10. Chie Gunner, of, Grand View (Mo.) HS.
11. Robert Cafaro, rhp, Southern Connecticut State University.
12. Scott Madison, lhp, Rutgers University.
13. Shawn Stutz, rhp, Florida International University.
**14. Delvin James, rhp, Nacogdoches (Texas) HS.—(2002)**
15. John Kaufman, lhp, University of Florida.
**16. Jared Sandberg, 3b, Capital HS, Olympia, Wash.—(2001-03)**
DRAFT DROP *Nephew of Ryne Sandberg, major leaguer (1981-97); major league manager (2013-15)*
17. Michael DeCelle, of, University of Miami.
18. Brad Weber, lhp, Indiana University.
19. +Ryan Ledden, rhp, Parkview HS, Lilburn, Ga. / DeKalb (Ga.) JC.
20. Jamie Ebling, 2b, Florida Southern College.
21. Trey Salinas, c, University of Texas.
22. Luke Owens-Bragg, 2b, UC Riverside.
23. *Russ Jacobson, c, Horizon HS, Scottsdale, Ariz.
24. Matt Kastelic, of, Texas Tech.
25. James Manias, lhp, Fairfield University.
26. *Jeff Jankowiak, rhp, Wayzata HS, Plymouth, Minn.
**27. *Kyle Snyder, rhp, Riverview HS, Sarasota, Fla.—(2003-08)**
DRAFT DROP *First-round draft pick (7th overall), Royals (1999)*
28. *Donny Barker, rhp, University of Texas.
29. R.J. Howerton, rhp, Southeastern Oklahoma State University.
30. Kyle Whitley, rhp, Southeastern Oklahoma State University.
31. Mark Hale, rhp, Carefree, Ariz.
32. Michael Brown, rhp, Walters State (Tenn.) CC.
33. *Aaron Bouie, rhp, Albion (N.Y.) Central HS.
**34. +Dan Wheeler, rhp, Central Arizona JC.—(1999-2012)**
35. *Brian Packin, 1b, Randolph HS, Mendham, N.J.
36. *Kevin Kay, c, Forest Park HS, Morrow, Ga.
37. Derek Mann, ss, Columbus (Ga.) HS.
38. *Walter Ward, of, Edison (Fla.) CC.
39. *Ryan Mottl, rhp, McCluer North HS, Florissant, Mo.
40. Jared Verrall, 1b, Eastern Oregon State College.
41. Lance Severence, c, John A. Logan (Ill.) CC.
42. *Dayle Campbell, of, Lynwood HS, Carson, Calif.
43. *Jason Smith, rhp, Palm Beach Lakes HS, West Palm Beach, Fla.
**44. *Jason Michaels, of, Okaloosa-Walton (Fla.) CC.—(2001-11)**
45. Michael Kimbrell, lhp, Southeastern Louisiana University.
46. *Rob Henkel, rhp, Monte Vista HS, La Mesa, Calif.
47. *Jeremy Robinson, lhp, St. Amant (La.) HS.
48. *Michael Barraza, lhp, Gladstone HS, Azusa, Calif.
49. *Edward Lubbers, lhp, Forest Hill HS, West Palm Beach, Fla.
50. *Bret Stewart, lhp, Leesburg HS, Fruitland Park, Fla.
51. *Jason Briggs, rhp, Smithville (Texas) HS.
52. *Chris Lagrone, of, Seward County (Kan.) CC.
53. Scott Leon, rhp, University of Texas.
54. *L.J. Yankosky, rhp, Georgia Tech.
55. *Ron Merrill, ss, Jesuit HS, Tampa.
56. *Joel De los Santos, 2b, Burncoat HS, Worcester, Mass.
57. *Adrian Yother, rhp, Middle Georgia JC.
58. *Clint Kinsey, rhp, Fairland (Okla.) HS.
59. *Nathan Hilton, rhp, Boone (Iowa) HS.
60. *John Hensley, rhp, Fountain Central HS, Kingman, Ind.
61. Nathan Ruhl, rhp, Johnson County (Kan.) CC.
62. Mike King, of-2b, Duke University.
63. Tim Hill, rhp, St. Leo (Fla.) College.
64. Tony McCladdie, 2b, Middle Georgia JC.
65. *Don Kivinemi, rhp, Bellevue (Neb.) College.
66. Chris Anderson, c, Southeastern Oklahoma State University.
67. *Matt Hoffman, rhp, Seminole (Okla.) JC.
68. Spencer Young, rhp, Mingus Union HS, Cottonwood, Ariz.
69. +Roger Carter, rhp, Fort Gibson (Okla.) HS / Seward County (Kan.) CC.
70. *Juan Cruz, 3b, Jefferson HS, Lafayette, Ind.
71. *Jason Kirk, of, Altus (Okla.) HS.
72. *Brad Smith, 1b, Edmond Memorial HS, Edmond, Okla.
73. *Nicholas Rhodes, c, Danbury (Conn.) HS.
74. *Chad Pyle, ss, Christian County HS, Hopkinsville, Ky.
75. *Michael O'Brien, 1b, Old Bridge (N.J.) HS.
76. *Zack Roper, 3b, Tarpon Springs (Fla.) HS.
77. *Keith Brice, rhp, Westminster Christian HS, Miami.
78. *Rashard Casey, of, Hoboken (N.J.) HS.
79. *Emory Brock, of, Parkway West HS, St. Louis.
DRAFT DROP *Son of Lou Brock, major leaguer (1961-79)*
80. *Adrian Espino, 1b-of, Laredo (Texas) JC.
81. *David DeMarco, 1b, Marple Newtown HS, Newtown Square, Pa.
82. *Victor Sauceda, 2b-ss, Laredo (Texas) JC.
83. *Layne Meyer, rhp, Parkway West HS, Ballwin, Mo.
84. *Scott Diorio, rhp, Seward County (Kan.) CC.
85. *Justin Clements, ss, Manatee (Fla.) CC.
86. +Scott Neuberger, of, Tallahassee (Fla.) CC.
87. *David Taylor, rhp, Crossroads HS, Pacific Palisades, Calif.
88. *Shannon Lovan, rhp, Christian County HS, Crofton, Ky.
**89. +Travis Phelps, rhp, Crowder (Mo.) JC.—(2001-04)**
90. *Jack Koch, rhp, Miami-Dade CC North.
91. *David Hoffman, lhp, Danville (Ill.) HS.
92. *Brian Newton, lhp, Juanita HS, Kirkland, Wash.
93. *Willie Marin, rhp, Coral Gables (Fla.) HS.
94. *Blair Barbier, rhp, Brother Martin HS, Harvey, La.
95. *Ryan Gripp, ss, Indianola (Iowa) HS.
96. *Jerrod Harris, c, Labelle (Fla.) HS.
97. *Michael Rose, of, Alter HS, Dayton, Ohio.

## TEXAS RANGERS (18)

**1. R.A. Dickey, rhp, University of Tennessee.—(2001-2015)**
**1. Sam Marsonek, rhp, Jesuit HS, Tampa** (Choice from Yankees as compensation for Type A free agent Kenny Rogers).**—(2004)**
**1. Corey Lee, lhp, North Carolina State University** (Supplemental choice—32nd—as compensation for Rogers).**—(1999)**
2. Derrick Cook, rhp, James Madison University.—(AA)
3. Derek Baker, 3b, Rancho Santiago (Calif.) JC.—(AA)
**4. Kelly Dransfeldt, ss, University of Michigan.—(1999-2004)**
**5. Warren Morris, 2b, Louisiana State University.—(1999-2003)**
6. Tony Fisher, of, University of St. Thomas (Minn.).
7. Juan Pinella, of, North Stafford (Va.) HS.
8. Luis Acevedo, ss, Francisco Mendoza HS, Isabella, P.R.
9. *Randy Rodriguez, lhp, Florida Air Academy HS, Melbourne, Fla.
**10. Doug Davis, lhp, CC of San Francisco.—(1999-2011)**
11. *Quenten Patterson, rhp, Killeen (Texas) HS.
12. Tony Dellamano, rhp, UC Davis.
13. Justin Siegel, lhp, Long Beach State University.
14. *Chris Combs, 1b, North Carolina State University.
15. *Alex Vazquez, of, Westminster HS, Anaheim.
16. Ron Nelson, rhp, Ohio State University.
17. John Kertis, rhp, Miami.
18. *Brian Jackson, rhp, San Diego Mesa JC.
**19. *Mark Hendrickson, lhp, Washington State University.—(2002-11)**
DRAFT DROP *Forward, National Basketball Association (1996-2000)*
20. John Ellis, c, University of Maine.
21. Adrian Myers, of, William Carey (Miss.) College.
22. Tony Shourds, rhp, Norwalk (Conn.) CC.
23. *Casey Davis, of, Wichita State University.
DRAFT DROP *Son of Willie Davis, major leaguer (1960-79)*
24. Mike Zywica, of, University of Evansville.
25. *John Santos, rhp, Cuesta (Calif.) JC.
**26. *Joe Beimel, lhp, Alleghany (Pa.) CC.—(2001-15)**
27. *Todd Periou, lhp, Lassen (Calif.) JC.
28. Steve Smella, of, Indiana University.
29. *Grant Dorn, rhp, Derry Area (Pa.) HS.
30. +Aaron Bond, rhp, JC of Southern Idaho.
**31. +Travis Hafner, 3b, Cowley County (Kan.) CC.—(2002-13)**
32. *Danny Meier, of, Northeast Texas CC.
33. Ryan Smith, lhp, San Diego State University.
34. *Kevin Smith, rhp, Martin HS, Arlington, Texas.
35. *Ali Cepeda, of, Canada (Calif.) JC.
DRAFT DROP *Son of Orlando Cepeda, major leaguer (1958-74)*
36. *Ryan Christenson, rhp, Normandale (Minn.) CC.
37. *Mike Wombacher, lhp, Mingus Union HS, Clarkdale, Ariz.
38. *Scott Green, rhp, Navarro (Texas) JC.
39. *Craig Petulla, rhp, Philipsburg-Osceola HS, Philipsburg, Pa.
40. *Jesse Smith, ss-of, American River (Calif.) JC.
41. *Fehlendt Lentini, of, Napa (Calif.) JC.
42. *Kyle Skinner, ss, Mount St. Joseph's HS, Baltimore.
43. *Justin Wise, of, West Brook HS, Beaumont, Texas.
44. *Jose Pimentel, 1b, Indio HS, Palm Springs, Calif.
45. Francisco Jaramillo, ss, Southern Illinois University.
46. Rowan Richards, of, University of Notre Dame.
47. *Curtis Young, of, Purvis (Miss.) HS.
48. *David Wigley, c, Pensacola (Fla.) HS.
49. *Kevin Colbourn, lhp, Hagerstown (Md.) JC.
50. *Ron Chiavacci, rhp, Lackawanna (Pa.) CC.
51. *Greg Horton, of, El Paso (Texas) CC.
52. *Anthony Perlozzo, 1b, Athens HS, Sayre, Pa.

## TORONTO BLUE JAYS (4)

**1. Billy Koch, rhp, Clemson University.—(1999-2004)**
**1. Joe Lawrence, ss, Barbe HS, Lake Charles, La.** (Choice from Orioles as compensation for Type A free agent Roberto Alomar).**—(2002)**
1. Pete Tucci, 1b-of, Providence College (Supplemental choice—31st—as compensation for Alomar).—(AA)
2. (Choice to Red Sox as compensation for Type A free agent Erik Hanson)
**2. Brent Abernathy, ss, The Lovett School, Atlanta** (Choice from Marlins as compensation for Type B free agent Devon White).**—(2001-05)**
3. Yan Lachapelle, rhp, Cegep de St. Laurent HS, Montreal.—(High A)
**3. Clayton Andrews, lhp, Seminole HS, Largo, Fla.** (Choice from Marlins as compensation for Type B free agent Al Leiter).**—(2000)**
4. Ryan Stromsborg, 2b, University of Southern California.—(AA)
**5. John Bale, lhp, University of Southern Mississippi.—(1999-2009)**
6. Mike Rodriguez, c, Tarleton State (Texas) University.
**7. Casey Blake, 3b, Wichita State University.—(1999-2011)**
8. Davan Keathley, lhp, Johansen HS, Turlock, Calif.
9. Sam Goure, lhp, County HS, Pueblo, Colo.
**10. Josh Phelps, c, Lakeland HS, Rathdrum, Idaho.—(2000-08)**
11. Stan Baston, ss, Tallahassee (Fla.) CC.
12. Ryan Meyers, rhp, University of Tennessee.
13. *Lorenzo Ferguson, of, St. Martin de Porres HS, West Bloomfield, Mich.
14. Sean McClellan, rhp, Oklahoma State University.
15. Josh Bradford, rhp, Xavier University.
16. Lorenzo Bagley, of, University of Central Florida.
17. Jason Koehler, c, Rider College.
18. *Gary Johnson, of, East Los Angeles JC.
19. *Jason Ball, rhp, Los Alamitos (Calif.) HS.
20. Tim Giles, 1b, University of North Carolina-Greensboro.
21. Will Skett, of, Long Beach State University.
22. David Bleazard, rhp, Oklahoma City University.
23. Brad Moon, of, Hunting Hills HS, Red Deer, Alberta.
24. *Darold Butler, 2b, Simeon HS, Chicago.
25. *Stephen Wood, 1b, Bishop Amat HS, West Covina, Calif.
26. +Lawrence Adams, 1b, Lake City (Fla.) JC.
27. *Gary Peete, of, Munford HS, Brighton, Tenn.
28. *B.J. Leach, rhp, Palm Beach (Fla.) JC.
29. Ryan Zeber, c, Foothill HS, Tustin, Calif.
DRAFT DROP *Son of George Zeber, major leaguer (1977-78)*
30. *Ryan Webb, 3b, Upland (Calif.) HS.
31. +Clarence Watley, ss, Redan HS, Stone Mountain, Ga. / DeKalb (Ga.) JC.
32. *Justin Brager, ss, Wenatchee Valley (Wash.) CC.
**33. *Orlando Hudson, ss, Darlington (S.C.) HS.—(2002-12)**
34. +Mark Curtis, lhp, Pensacola (Fla.) JC.
35. +James Landingham, of, Miami-Dade CC Wolfson.
36. *Justin Montalbano, lhp, Mendocino (Calif.) CC.
37. *Craig Lariz, 1b, Key West (Fla.) HS.
38. *Cody Hartshorn, rhp, Lamar (Colo.) HS.
39. *Kyle Adams, lhp, Allen County (Kan.) CC.
40. +Orlando Woodards, rhp, Franklin HS, Stockton, Calif. / Sacramento (Calif.) CC.
41. *Anthony Novelli, rhp, Oak Grove HS, San Jose, Calif.
42. *Michael Galati, rhp, University of Connecticut.
43. *Derek Hines, of, Yavapai (Ariz.) CC.
44. *Greg Ferrell, of, Saddleback (Calif.) CC.
45. *Kevin Covington, of, Cherokee County HS, Centre, Ala.
46. *Robert Gonzales, c, Castle Park HS, Chula Vista, Calif.
47. *Michael Duperron, lhp, South Grenville HS, Prescott, Ontario.
48. *Harold Betts, c, Lakewood (Calif.) HS.
49. *Shaw Scovel, 3b, Foothill HS, Villa Park, Calif.
50. *Joshua Glober, rhp, Upper Canada College HS, Toronto.
51. *Steven Lacy, rhp, Alhambra HS, Glendale, Ariz.
52. *Michael Lopez, ss, Maryvale HS, Phoenix.

# 1997

## AT A GLANCE

### This Date In History
June 2-4

### Best Draft
**TORONTO BLUE JAYS.** The Blue Jays drafted **VERNON WELLS** fifth overall and added **MIKE YOUNG** (5) and **ORLANDO HUDSON** (43), three of the top big leaguers from the 1997 class, and secured **MARK HENDRICKSON** (20), who had gone unsigned in the previous five drafts while pursuing a basketball career at Washington State and the Philadelphia 76ers.

### Worst Draft
**MONTREAL EXPOS.** With eight selections before the second round, the Expos had an opportunity to bring fresh talent into their organization. But six of the eight, including top pick **DONNIE BRIDGES**, never reached the big leagues. **BRYAN HEBSON** pitched in two innings in the majors, and **T.J. TUCKER** won 13 games over five years.

### First-Round Bust
**AARON AKIN, RHP, MARLINS.** Seven pitchers drafted in the first round didn't reach the big leagues, but none missed as badly as Akin, a surprise junior-college selection who didn't advance beyond Class A in four minor league seasons.

### Second Best
**RANDY WOLF, LHP, PHILLIES.** The Phillies didn't sign **J.D. DREW** (1), but Wolf proved to be the most productive major league player among the second-round selections. He won 133 games over a 16-year big league career, the first eight with the Phillies.

### Late Round Find
**ORLANDO HUDSON, 2B, BLUE JAYS (43RD ROUND).** The Blue Jays selected Hudson after his first year of junior college with the intent of tracking his progress as a draft-and-follow. They signed him the next spring for $90,000, and he played 11 years in the

# Teams prefer caution after turbulence of '96

Fearful of more fallout from a draft system that was derailed a year earlier, major league teams took a cautious approach in 1997, routinely choosing players on the basis of signability. Several first-round talents were passed over because of their bonus demands, and others reached contractual agreements before the draft. Still, bonus payments again reached record levels.

No one better symbolized the state of affairs than Florida high school lefthander Rick Ankiel, who was selected with the 72nd overall pick by the St. Louis Cardinals and signed on Aug. 28 for $2.5 million, a record for a player signing with the team that drafted him.

All teams had passed on Ankiel because they couldn't get a handle on his bonus demands. Two other elite high school players, lefthander Ryan Anderson and outfielder Darnell McDonald, also fell because of signability issues. Anderson went 19th overall and McDonald 26th.

Some sense of order was restored when Rice University righthander Matt Anderson, the No. 1 overall pick, trumped Ankiel's bonus when he signed with the Detroit Tigers for $2.505 million, after holding out for more than six months.

"The key to this draft was price-committing," said agent Scott Boras, who represented Ankiel, along with Florida State outfielder J.D. Drew, the consensus best talent in the draft. "Ankiel, Anderson and McDonald all were considered top-five picks, but they got removed from the process. Teams are promoting average players to sign, and they're promoting greatness to go to college."

Bonuses for first-round picks averaged $1,325,536, a 44.3 percent jump from 1995.

The process was complicated by the volatility of the 1996 draft, when four premium picks were declared free agents because of a draft rule loophole and signed for record bonus amounts. Though Major League Baseball fixed the loophole to make sure the situation wouldn't repeat itself in 1997, clubs found themselves having to defend against the precedent of paying $10 million bonuses.

"Those were special circumstances involving expansion teams," Tigers general manager Randy Smith said. "Two million dollars is a lot of money. We're not interested in signing any of these players for $10 million. If we're going to spend that kind of money, we're going to spend it on a proven major leaguer, not on someone who is unproven."

Boras, who orchestrated Matt White's record $10.2 million bonus from the Tampa Bay Devil Rays in 1996 after White was declared a free agent, said the developments of 1996 proved the draft stunts bonuses.

"What we've seen happen in the last two years, first internationally and then domestically, has given us a great barometer on the true worth of a select number of quality amateur players," Boras

JEFF GOLDEN

Florida State outfielder J.D. Drew was regarded as the top talent in the 1997 draft class, but he wasn't the top pick (and didn't sign) in a draft that was defined by players' bonus demands

said. "The market has changed. I know from experience that there are many teams willing to pay optimum dollars for a premium talent."

## EYE OF THE STORM

Drew, who became the first 30-30 player in college baseball history during his junior season at Florida State, was a focal point of the 1997 draft. Even before the Philadelphia Phillies took him with the No. 2 pick overall, he was adamant that his rights were being stifled under a system that allowed him to negotiate with only one team.

Drew set his price tag at a reported $10 million and informed every club not to draft him unless it was prepared to pay that amount. The Phillies ignored the directive, setting off one of the most contentious negotiations in draft history.

"We made it very clear to the Phillies the day before the draft, and even an hour before the draft, and they still picked me," said Drew, who hit .455 with 31 home runs, 100 RBIs and 32 stolen bases for the 1997 college season, and led the NCAA in runs (110) and walks (84). "We had other things on the table that other teams would offer. And we let the Phillies know that if they weren't willing to match that, then don't draft us."

The Phillies maintained that Kris Benson's $2 million bonus as the No. 1 overall pick in the 1996 draft, was the benchmark, no matter how much the four loophole free agents received.

## 1997: THE FIRST ROUNDERS

| CLUB: PLAYER, POS., SCHOOL | HOMETOWN | B-T | HT. | WT. | AGE | BONUS | FIRST YEAR | LAST YEAR | PEAK LEVEL (YEARS) |
|---|---|---|---|---|---|---|---|---|---|
| 1. Tigers: Matt Anderson, rhp, Rice | Louisville, Ky. | R-R | 6-4 | 195 | 20 | $2,505,000 | 1998 | 2008 | Majors (7) |
| Landed record bonus for player signing with team that drafted him after six-month holdout; regularly hit triple digits until torn muscle injury in '02, never the same. | | | | | | | | | |
| 2. Phillies: J.D. Drew, of, Florida State | Hahira, Ga. | L-R | 6-1 | 200 | 21 | Unsigned | 1998 | 2011 | Majors (14) |
| Only 30-30 season in college history (.455-31-100, 32 SBs) led to contentious holdout; took five-tool talent to independent ball, became first-rounder again in '98. | | | | | | | | | |
| 3. Angels: Troy Glaus, 3b, UCLA | Oceanside, Calif. | R-R | 6-5 | 225 | 20 | $2,250,000 | 1998 | 2010 | Majors (13) |
| Padres' unsigned '94 second-rounder elevated stock after big college season (.409-34-91); led AL with 47 homers in 2000, four-time all-star, '02 World Series MVP. | | | | | | | | | |
| 4. Giants: Jason Grilli, rhp, Seton Hall | Baldwinsville, N.Y. | R-R | 6-5 | 185 | 20 | $1,875,000 | 1998 | Active | Majors (13) |
| Became elite pick with size, raw stuff, poise, bloodlines (son of Steve); persevered through early stretch of injuries/ineffectiveness to have long big league career. | | | | | | | | | |
| 5. Blue Jays: Vernon Wells, of, Bowie HS | Arlington, Texas | R-R | 6-0 | 195 | 18 | $1,600,000 | 1997 | 2013 | Majors (15) |
| Five-tool talent with power to all fields, elite CF skills; dynamic '03 season (.317-33-117, AL leader in H, TB, 2B) highlighted 12 years in Blue Jays uniform. | | | | | | | | | |
| 6. Mets: Geoff Goetz, lhp, Tampa Jesuit HS | Lutz, Fla. | L-L | 6-0 | 170 | 18 | $1,700,000 | 1997 | 2004 | Class AA (4) |
| Scott Kazmir clone with nasty mid-90s FB, power curve; traded to Marlins for Mike Piazza within year, but shoulder surgery doomed career, became reliever. | | | | | | | | | |
| 7. Royals: Dan Reichert, rhp, Pacific | Turlock, Calif. | R-R | 6-3 | 165 | 20 | $1,450,000 | 1997 | 2008 | Majors (5) |
| Put himself on map as college JR with 22-SO game; big arm on slender body, MLB career impacted by control problems, coping with juvenile diabetes. | | | | | | | | | |
| 8. Pirates: J.J. Davis, 1b/rhp, Baldwin Park HS | Pomona, Calif. | R-R | 6-6 | 230 | 18 | $1,675,000 | 1997 | 2005 | Majors (4) |
| Legit two-way talent in Dave Winfield mold with raw power at plate, 96 mph fastball on mound; moved to OF, struggled to make contact, career never blossomed. | | | | | | | | | |
| 9. Twins: Michael Cuddyer, ss, Great Bridge HS | Chesapeake, Va. | R-R | 6-3 | 195 | 18 | $1,850,000 | 1998 | Active | Majors (15) |
| Signed franchise-record bonus, quickly developed into professional hitter; was lacking in field at SS/3B in minors, found home in outfield in long MLB career. | | | | | | | | | |
| 10. Cubs: Jon Garland, rhp, Kennedy HS | Granada Hills, Calif. | R-R | 6-5 | 200 | 17 | $1,325,000 | 1997 | 2013 | Majors (13) |
| Youngest player in draft moved to crosstown White Sox at '98 trade deadline; became dependable starter over 13 MLB seasons with 90-93 mph sinking fastball. | | | | | | | | | |
| 11. Athletics: Chris Enochs, rhp, West Virginia | Newell, W.Va. | R-R | 6-3 | 210 | 21 | $1,204,000 | 1997 | 2005 | Class AAA (4) |
| Went 12-1, 3.03 as college JR, made impressive debut with mid-90s FB, plus curve, before career adversely impacted by hip surgery, shoulder tendinitis. | | | | | | | | | |
| 12. Marlins: Aaron Akin, rhp, Cowley County (Kan.) CC | Manhattan, Kan. | L-R | 6-2 | 190 | 19 | $1,050,000 | 1997 | 2000 | Class A (3) |
| Missouri transfer led Cowley County to Juco World Series title, went 12-0, 2.03 as juco player of year; never performed same magic in four pro seasons (9-20, 4.43). | | | | | | | | | |
| 13. Brewers: Kyle Peterson, rhp, Stanford | Elkhorn, Neb. | R-R | 6-3 | 210 | 21 | $1,400,000 | 1997 | 2001 | Majors (2) |
| Lacked overpowering fastball, but became first-rounder with secondary stuff, command, poise; went 5-9, 4.70 in majors, retired at 25 due to multiple arm injuries. | | | | | | | | | |
| 14. Reds: Brandon Larson, ss, Louisiana State | San Antonio, Texas | R-R | 5-11 | 190 | 21 | $1,330,000 | 1997 | 2007 | Majors (4) |
| JC transfer had unexpected breakout season (.381-40-118) for CWS champs at height of gorilla-ball era; never adapted to wood in pros, hit .179-8-37 in majors. | | | | | | | | | |
| 15. White Sox: Jason Dellaero, ss, South Florida | Brewster, N.Y. | B-R | 6-2 | 195 | 20 | $1,052,500 | 1997 | 2003 | Majors (1) |
| Earned first seven-figure bonus in Sox history as power-hitting SS; struggled to hit as a pro (.214 in minors, .091 in majors), best known for rocket arm. | | | | | | | | | |
| 16. Astros: Lance Berkman, 1b, Rice | New Braunfels, Texas | B-L | 6-1 | 205 | 21 | $1,000,000 | 1997 | 2013 | Majors (15) |
| Undrafted HS talent became elite hitter in college (.431-41-134 as JR); continued to hit at prolific clip for hometown Astros while making seamless transition to OF. | | | | | | | | | |
| 17. Red Sox: John Curtice, lhp, Great Bridge HS | Chesapeake, Va. | L-L | 6-4 | 210 | 17 | $975,000 | 1997 | 2000 | Class A (2) |
| Along with Cuddyer, second pair of HS teammates picked in first round; showed early promise, but shoulder unraveled; quit after two surgeries, 12-22, 4.78 record. | | | | | | | | | |
| 18. Rockies: Mark Mangum, rhp, Kingwood HS | Kingwood, Texas | R-R | 6-2 | 165 | 18 | $875,000 | 1997 | 2002 | Class AA (2) |
| Became first-rounder with velocity spike to mid-90s; couldn't hold up to pro workload with slender build, velocity regressed, went 37-49, 4.19 in minors. | | | | | | | | | |
| 19. Mariners: Ryan Anderson, lhp, Divine Child HS | Westland, Mich. | L-L | 6-10 | 210 | 17 | $2,175,000 | 1998 | 2005 | Class AAA (1) |
| Big lefty bent on becoming second coming of Big Unit with same style, stuff as Randy Johnson; more advanced at same age, but shoulder issues ruined career. | | | | | | | | | |
| 20. Cardinals: Adam Kennedy, ss, Cal State Northridge | Riverside, Calif. | L-R | 6-1 | 180 | 21 | $650,000 | 1997 | 2012 | Majors (14) |
| Signed smallest first-round bonus, enabling Cards to pursue Rick Ankiel; prolific bat, hit .482-26-99 as college JR, .272 in 14 MLB seasons, led Angels to '02 W/S title. | | | | | | | | | |
| 21. Athletics: Eric DuBose, lhp, Mississippi State | Gilbertown, Ala. | L-L | 6-3 | 215 | 21 | $860,000 | 1997 | 2008 | Majors (5) |
| Struck out school record 472 in three years, but not as dominant in 9-4, 4.32 JR season; inconsistent in 12-year pro career, went 9-15, 5.22 in 5 MLB seasons. | | | | | | | | | |
| 22. Orioles: Jayson Werth, c, Glenwood HS | Chatham, Ill. | R-R | 6-5 | 190 | 18 | $885,000 | 1997 | Active | Majors (13) |
| Rich background as grandson of Dick Schofield Sr., stepson of Dennis Werth; idled four years as catcher before move to OF, trade to Phillies jumpstarted career. | | | | | | | | | |
| 23. Expos: Donnie Bridges, rhp, Oak Grove HS | Purvis, Miss. | R-R | 6-4 | 195 | 18 | $870,000 | 1997 | 2005 | Class AAA (2) |
| First of eight Expos picks before second round; made steady rise through system with 94-95 FB, dominant curve before he was felled by a sore shoulder. | | | | | | | | | |
| 24. Yankees: Tyrell Godwin, of, East Bladen HS | Council, N.C. | L-R | 5-11 | 190 | 17 | Unsigned | 2001 | 2007 | Majors (1) |
| Speed-oriented player passed up $1.9M to play football/baseball at North Carolina; signed four years later for $480,000 after hitting skills regressed in college. | | | | | | | | | |
| 25. Dodgers: Glenn Davis, 1b, Vanderbilt | Aston, Pa. | B-L | 6-1 | 205 | 21 | $825,000 | 1997 | 2003 | Class AA (6) |
| Older brother of Ben, No. 2 pick in '95; rare switch-hitter/LH thrower, set Vandy career record with 43 homers, but prone to strikeouts, power never emerged in pros. | | | | | | | | | |
| 26. Orioles: Darnell McDonald, of, Cherry Creek HS | Englewood, Colo. | R-R | 5-10 | 185 | 18 | $1,900,000 | 1998 | 2013 | Majors (7) |
| Elite prep football/baseball talent scared teams off with bonus demands; took years to translate power/speed into performance, played in 331 MLB games. | | | | | | | | | |
| 27. Padres: Kevin Nicholson, ss, Stetson | Surrey, B.C. | B-R | 5-10 | 190 | 20 | $830,000 | 1997 | 2004 | Majors (1) |
| First Canadian first-rounder hit .360-33-162 at Stetson; had legit swing from both sides, arm for SS, never got second shot after hit .216-1-8 for Padres in 2000. | | | | | | | | | |
| 28. Indians: Tim Drew, rhp, Lowndes County HS | Hahira, Ga. | R-R | 6-2 | 200 | 18 | $1,600,000 | 1997 | 2005 | Majors (5) |
| Joined J.D./Stephen as draft's only three-brother first-round act; lively 94 mph FB, other legit stuff but hurt by Indians rushing him to majors (2-4, 6.99). | | | | | | | | | |
| 29. Braves: Troy Cameron, ss, St. Thomas Aquinas HS | Plantation, Fla. | B-R | 5-11 | 185 | 18 | $825,000 | 1997 | 2005 | Class AAA (1) |
| Offensive-oriented SS hit 43 HRs in first two pro seasons; big swing became detriment over nine-year career; hit .226-88-345, had 774 SOs in 707 games. | | | | | | | | | |
| 30. Diamondbacks: Jack Cust, 1b, Immaculata HS | Flemington, N.J. | L-R | 6-1 | 195 | 18 | $825,000 | 1997 | 2012 | Majors (10) |
| Hung on for 16 pro seasons because of power (330 combined HRs in majors/minors), on-base ability (1,519 walks), also fanned 2,236 times, lacked position. | | | | | | | | | |
| 31. Devil Rays: Jason Standridge, rhp, Hewitt Trussville HS | Trussville, Ala. | R-R | 6-4 | 205 | 18 | $700,000 | 1997 | 2009 | Majors (7) |
| Elite QB recruit passed up offer from Auburn to sign with Rays; had 92-94 mph FB, went 3-9, 5.81 in seven major league seasons, also played six years in Japan. | | | | | | | | | |

## AT A GLANCE

majors, hitting .273-93-542 with 85 stolen bases.

### Never Too Late

**WILLIE HARRIS, 2B, DEVIL RAYS (90TH ROUND).** The Rays drafted catcher **ROBBY HAMMOCK** in the 89th round and Harris a round later, making them the lowest selections in 1997 to eventually play in the majors. Both were Georgia juco products and went unsigned. Hammock was drafted by the Diamondbacks in 1998 (23rd round), and Harris by the Orioles in 1999 (24th round).

### Overlooked

**MATT MILLER, RHP, RANGERS.** Miller was 25 when he signed in December 1997 after two seasons in the independent Big South League. Released during spring training in 1998, he returned to the Big South League before the Rangers re-signed him. He played two seasons in the Texas organization before getting big league time with the Rockies and Indians, going 6-1, 2.72 in five seasons from 2003-07.

### International Gem

**CARLOS ZAMBRANO, RHP, CUBS.** The hard-throwing and temperamental Venezuelan righthander pitched 12 years in the majors (11 with the Cubs) and went 132-91, 3.66. Zambrano was one of the better hitting pitchers in major league history and homered 24 times.

### Minor League Take

**RYAN ANDERSON, LHP, MARINERS.** Anderson, a 6-foot-10 lefthander, often was compared with Randy Johnson and fell to the Mariners with the 19th pick overall. He went 20-26, 3.95 in three minor league seasons before a succession of shoulder surgeries ended his career. Anderson struck out 460 in 349 innings for his career, and was ranked the best prospect in the

CONTINUED ON PAGE 482

## AT A GLANCE

CONTINUED FROM PAGE 481

Seattle organization for five consecutive years.

### One Who Got Away

**J.D. DREW, OF, PHILLIES (1ST ROUND).** Drew, the second overall pick, and agent Scott Boras engaged the Phillies in contentious negotiations and never came close to an agreement. A year later, Drew was selected fifth overall by the Cardinals and signed.

### They Were Drafted?

**KELLEY WASHINGTON, SS, MARLINS (10TH ROUND); JAVON WALKER, OF, MARLINS (12TH ROUND).** Washington spent four years in the Marlins system, hitting .213-9-48 with 45 stolen bases, before heading to Tennessee to play football. He was a 2003 NFL draft choice of the Cincinnati Bengals. Walker was in the Marlins system for three years (.169-2-10, 4 SB) before quitting to play football at Florida State. He was a first-round draft choice of the Green Bay Packers in 2002. Both spent eight seasons in the NFL as wide receivers.

### Did You Know . . .

Rockies first-round pick **MARK MANGUM** was the No. 3 starter for Kingwood (Texas) High as a sophomore in 1995, behind senior Jeff Austin and junior Andy Yount. Austin and Yount also became first-round selections, Austin by the Royals in 1998 out of Stanford, and Yount by the Red Sox in 1995.

### They Said It

**GUS ANDERSON**, the father of **RYAN ANDERSON**, responding to the Tigers on whether his son would sign if they picked him first overall in the draft: "You tell your owner (Little Caesars Pizza founder and owner Mike Ilitch) that if he thinks he'll sign Ryan for $2.5 million, he can stick it. It'd be like someone offering him $10 million for a pizza franchise worth hundreds of millions."

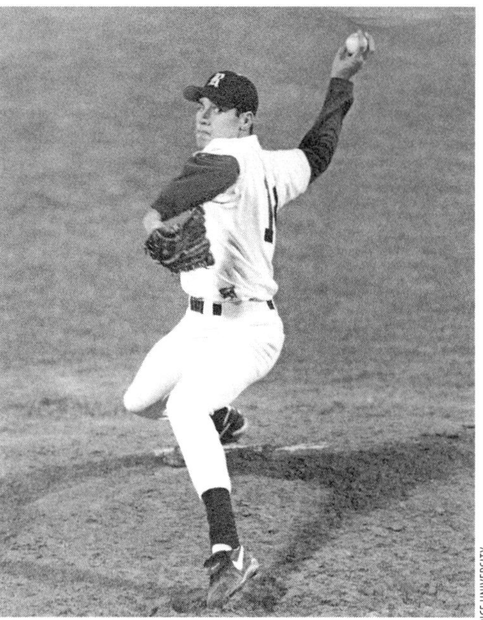

RICE UNIVERSITY

**Rice closer Matt Anderson became the No. 1 pick on the strength of a blazing fastball, but he never put it to consistent use in the majors**

"This kid is not a free agent," Phillies owner Bill Giles said. "There is a number we think is right, and it's more than Benson got. We're willing to go above that, but not a whole lot more."

Negotiations went nowhere, and Boras sought to have Drew declared a free agent on at least two occasions. He filed a grievance with MLB contending that the Phillies sent Drew's initial contract offer to his parents' home in Hahira, Ga., not his college address in Tallahassee, Fla., and thus failed to meet the 15-day deadline for teams to contact their draft choices. It failed.

The second grievance came after Drew signed with the independent Northern League's St. Paul Saints five weeks after being drafted, which Boras contended made him a professional and no longer subject to rules as they applied to amateurs. Drew lost that grievance as well.

The Phillies made their final offer on April 2, 1998, a $2.6 million bonus that would be a record for a drafted player, and a four-year major league contract that would have guaranteed Drew $3 million and paid him up to $6 million through various incentives. Boras rejected the offer, countering with a proposal for a $5 million signing bonus as part of a four-year deal that would have guaranteed Drew an additional $6.2 million. The Phillies dismissed it, and the sides never spoke again.

Drew went back into the draft pool in 1998, and the Cardinals selected him with the fifth overall pick. He signed for a bonus of $3 million, plus a major league contract, and was in the majors after a brief minor league apprenticeship and played 14 seasons in the big leagues.

### TIGERS CONSIDER TWO ANDERSONS

The Tigers, who gained the No. 1 pick in 1997 because of their 53-109 record a year earlier, focused their final scouting on four players: Matt Anderson, Ryan Anderson, Drew and McDonald. The latter three all said they wanted bonuses in excess of $3 million. Matt Anderson, who threw an explosive 98-100 mph fastball, did not state any demands and became the first player drafted.

"We felt that Matt had the best arm in the draft," Tigers GM Smith said. "He has a terrific arm and terrific makeup. We really didn't get involved in figures. We just talked with him and the family, and felt comfortable with him."

The Tigers initially offered Anderson $2.2 million and raised the ante to $2.51 million once Ankiel signed his record deal. Anderson, who went 10-2, 2.05 with nine saves and 105 strikeouts in 79 innings at Rice, was in no hurry to sign, preferring that the market establish itself.

Teams normally lost their rights to drafted players when the players enrolled in college in the fall, so both Anderson and Drew kept their options open by not returning for their senior years. Anderson finally signed on Dec. 23.

Anderson made 30 relief appearances in the minors to begin the 1998 season before being promoted to the Tigers. He went 5-1, 3.27 in 42 appearances, showing a 96-100 mph fastball that was clocked as high as 103.

The Tigers were grooming Anderson as their next closer, but he struggled early in the 1999 season, was sent back to the minors and never

## How They Should Have Done It

Based on career WAR (Wins Above Replacement, as calculated by Baseball-Reference.com) achieved by players eligible for the 1997 draft through the 2015 season, here's how the first round should have unfolded. Numbers in parentheses indicate the round when the player was drafted. Asterisk denotes player who signed as a draft-and-follow.

| | Player, Pos. | Actual Draft | WAR | Bonus |
|---|---|---|---|---|
| 1. | Tim Hudson, rhp | Athletics (6) | 58.7 | $22,500 |
| 2. | Lance Berkman, 1b | Astros (1) | 51.7 | $1,000,000 |
| 3. | Troy Glaus, 3b | Angels (1) | 37.9 | $2,250,000 |
| 4. * | Orlando Hudson, 2b | Blue Jays (43) | 30.9 | $90,000 |
| 5. | Jayson Werth, c | Orioles (1) | 29.4 | $885,000 |
| 6. | Vernon Wells, of | Blue Jays (1) | 28.7 | $1,600,000 |
| 7. | Michael Young, ss | Blue Jays (5) | 24.2 | $92,500 |
| 8. | Randy Wolf, lhp | Phillies (2) | 23.1 | $356,000 |
| 9. | Jon Garland, rhp | Cubs (1) | 22.4 | $1,325,000 |
| 10. | Chone Figgins, ss | Rockies (4) | 22.0 | $92,500 |
| 11. | Adam Kennedy, 2b | Cardinals (1) | 21.0 | $650,000 |
| 12. | David Eckstein, 2b | Red Sox (19) | 20.8 | $1,000 |
| 13. | Michael Cuddyer, 3b | Twins (1) | 16.7 | $1,850,000 |
| 14. | Aaron Cook, rhp | Rockies (2) | 15.9 | $309,500 |
| 15. | Jerry Hairston, ss | Orioles (11) | 13.6 | $30,000 |
| 16. | Joel Piniero, rhp | Mariners (12) | 13.4 | $30,000 |
| 17. | Scot Shields, rhp | Angels (38) | 12.4 | $2,000 |
| 18. | Scott Downs, lhp | Cubs (3) | 11.0 | $185,000 |
| 19. | Jeremy Affeldt, lhp | Royals (3) | 10.6 | $216,000 |
| 20. | Scott Linebrink, rhp | Giants (2) | 9.6 | $322,500 |
| 21. | Jack Cust, 1b | Diamondbacks (1) | 9.3 | $825,000 |
| 22. | Scott Williamson, rhp | Reds (9) | 8.7 | $40,000 |
| 23. | Rick Ankiel, lhp/of | Cardinals (2) | 8.6 | $2,500,000 |
| 24. | J.C. Romero, lhp | Twins (21) | 8.1 | $13,000 |
| | Mike Gonzalez, lhp | Pirates (30) | 8.1 | $15,000 |
| 26. | Michael Wuertz, rhp | Cubs (11) | 5.3 | $200,000 |
| 27. | Jason Grilli, rhp | Giants (1) | 4.8 | $1,875,000 |
| | Toby Hall, c | Devil Rays (9) | 4.8 | $37,500 |
| 29. | D.J. Carrasco, rhp | Orioles (26) | 4.6 | $25,000 |
| | Randy Choate, lhp | Yankees (5) | 4.6 | $150,000 |

| | Top 3 Unsigned Players | | | Year Signed |
|---|---|---|---|---|
| 1. | Chase Utley, 2b | Dodgers (2) | 62.3 | 2000 |
| 2. | J.D. Drew, of | Phillies (1) | 44.9 | 1998 |
| 3. | Cliff Lee, lhp | Marlins (8) | 44.3 | 2000 |

established himself on a consistent basis. He converted 22 of 24 save opportunities in 2001 and got a three-year, $9.3 million contract with the Tigers, but soon suffered an arm injury and was out of the major leagues by 2005. He went 15-7, 5.18 with 26 saves in 257 appearances.

## LITTLE UNIT FALTERS, TOO

Except for the Phillies, most clubs decided not to gamble in the first round. As a result, premium players like Ryan Anderson, McDonald and Ankiel were passed over.

Anderson, a 6-foot-10 lefthander from the Detroit suburb of Dearborn, slipped to the Seattle Mariners with the 19th selection overall. He never reached the majors because of three shoulder surgeries.

Ankiel ranked alongside Ryan Anderson as the premier high school pitchers in the draft, even as Ankiel slipped out of the first round because of reports that his asking price was upward of $5 million. The Cardinals picked Ankiel in the second round, after selecting Cal State Northridge shortstop Adam Kennedy with the 20th overall pick and signing him for $650,000, the smallest bonus in the first round.

Ankiel had a star-crossed career. He quickly fulfilled his potential as a pitching prospect and had all the makings of becoming a star, but just as quickly was afflicted by a severe bout of wildness that saw his career on the mound crash and burn. He resurrected himself as a hitter and outfielder, and played another seven years in the majors in that role.

McDonald, a football/baseball star at Cherry Creek High in suburban Denver, was considered the best athlete in the draft. He had a football scholarship from Texas, and lasted deep into the first round because of concerns about his signability. The Baltimore Orioles gambled the second of their two first-round picks on McDonald, who held out until the day before he was scheduled to begin football practice at Texas, signing a $1.9 million deal.

McDonald, Baseball America's 1997 High School Player of the Year, did not fulfill expectations. He didn't make it to the major leagues until 2004, and when he retired after the 2013 season, McDonald had a .250 batting average with 20 homers in 331 big league games.

The New York Yankees made a gamble of their own, selecting two-sport star Tyrell Godwin from a North Carolina high school with the 24th overall pick. Godwin opted for the University of North Carolina, where he played both baseball and foot-

### Fastest To The Majors

| | Player, Pos. | Drafted (Round) | Debut |
|---|---|---|---|
| 1. | Jim Parque, lhp | White Sox (1-S) | May 26, 1998 |
| 2. | Mike Frank, of | Reds (7) | June 19, 1998 |
| 3. | Matt Anderson, rhp | Tigers (1) | June 25, 1998 |
| 4. | Troy Glaus, 3b | Angels (1) | July 31, 1998 |
| 5. | Ryan Bradley, rhp | Yankees (1-S) | Aug. 22, 1998 |

**FIRST HIGH SCHOOL SELECTION:** Rick Ankiel, lhp (Cardinals/2, Aug. 23, 1999)

## DRAFT SPOTLIGHT: RICK ANKIEL

STAN DENNY

Rick Ankiel was a masterful pitcher in the minors and majors until a playoff start in 2000 when he lost his control, and it never returned

As talented a pitching prospect as Rick Ankiel was when he burst onto the major league scene as a precocious 20-year-old in 2000, it was his ability to overcome adversity that might have been his best quality. He faced hurdles throughout his life and career, especially in his transformation from a failed pitcher into a productive major league outfielder.

Growing up in Port St. Lucie, Fla., Ankiel developed into the best high school pitching prospect in the country. With three potential big league pitches, the 6-foot-1, 210-pound lefthander enjoyed unqualified success in his final year of high school, going 11-1, 0.47 with 22 walks and 162 strikeouts in 74 innings, yet was hard-pressed to please his father, Rick Sr. "My dad was hard on me all the time," Ankiel said. "If I swung at a bad pitch in Little League, he'd make me run wind sprints when I got home. It was always I could have done better."

Rick Sr. attended all of his son's games, sitting in the stands and flashing signs indicating what pitch to throw. He was constantly arguing with umpires and often at odds with coaches. "To some people, it's just a game," Rick Sr. once said. "To us, baseball is life."

The elder Ankiel had more than baseball in his life, though. He was arrested in 1999 and sentenced to six years in prison for his part in a drug-smuggling operation. He previously had been arrested 14 times and convicted on six occasions for offenses such as burglary, carrying a concealed weapon and fleeing police. Ankiel's stepbrother also had been arrested 28 times for assorted crimes.

Through all the turmoil around him, the younger Ankiel soldiered on and drew increased attention for his pitching feats. Ankiel Sr. aligned his son with agent Scott Boras, who advised the family to seek a signing bonus in the range of $5 million-$10 million. Scared off by Ankiel's contract demands, teams bypassed him in the 1997 draft until the St. Louis Cardinals selected him in the second round, 72nd overall. Ankiel had a scholarship from the University of Miami, but the Cardinals were undeterred.

"The system really got out of whack last year when those free agents signed (in 1996)," general manager Walt Jocketty said. "We're trying to take an aggressive approach to acquiring quality talent. We told him all along we would approach him like a first-round pick."

The Cardinals agreed not to initiate negotiations with Ankiel until he was finished pitching for USA Baseball's junior national team. On Aug. 28, they signed Ankiel to a bonus of $2.5 million, the largest awarded to a player signing with the team that drafted him—until Rice righthander Matt Anderson, the No. 1 pick in 1997, topped it by $5,000 when he signed with the Detroit Tigers nearly four months later.

Ankiel spent less than two years in the minors, going 25-9, 2.49. In 299 innings, he walked 112 and struck out 416. His major league debut, on Aug. 23, 1999, coincided with the beginning of his father's prison sentence. He went 11-7, 3.50 with 194 strikeouts in 175 innings in 2000, his first full major league season, throwing a fastball that peaked at 97 mph and a knee-buckling curve. But his career as a pitcher would never be the same after his start in a 2000 National League Division Series against the Braves.

Ankiel pitched two scoreless innings, but then lost all control with his pitches, walking four batters in the third inning and throwing five wild pitches, often missing his target by several feet. He had another meltdown in a second playoff start a few days later, and had major control problems at the outset of the 2001 season. He tried for four years to regain what he had lost, but to no avail. It didn't help that he missed the 2002 season while recovering from Tommy John surgery.

Ankiel won just two games after the 2000 season, and in spring 2005 he announced that he was going to become an outfielder. Two years later, he hit 32 homers for Triple-A Memphis, and his comeback became complete when the Cardinals called him up on Aug. 9, 2007. Ankiel homered in his first game back, had 11 homers by the end of the season, and a year later hit 25 homers. His career as a major league outfielder lasted seven years.

Ankiel wrote one of the most fascinating chapters in draft history, an epic story that ultimately was a tale about untapped potential on the pitching mound.

## WORTH NOTING

Marlins third-rounder **CHRIS AGUILA** tied the national single-season, high school home run record of 29, playing for McQueen High in Reno, Nev. He hit .580 and drove in 81 runs in 119 at-bats. Aguila spent 10 years in the Marlins system, and hit three home runs in 149 major league games.

One of the more intriguing signings of the 1997 proceedings involved 6-foot-9 lefthander **MARK HENDRICKSON**, a 20th-rounder of the Blue Jays, who agreed to a $300,000 bonus (or $100,000 a year, so long as he continued to play baseball) after being drafted for the sixth year in a row. That was a record for a player drafted after 1986, when the January draft was abolished. Hendrickson was first drafted in 1992 by the Braves, but his main focus was basketball, first as a two-time all-Pacific-10 Conference player at Washington State and then with the Philadelphia 76ers after being a second-round pick in the 1996 NBA draft. Hendrickson played in 114 games with four different NBA teams from 1996-2000, and eventually combined a career in pro basketball with one in the Blue Jays system before choosing to focus on baseball. From that point on, his baseball career flourished, as he reached the big leagues with the Blue Jays in 2002 and went on to pitch 10 seasons in the majors, first as a starter and then as a lefthanded relief specialist. In 328 career appearances, he went 58-74, 5.03.

Canadians factored into the draft like never before in 1997. Shortstop **KEVIN NICHOLSON**, chosen 27th overall by the Padres, was the first Canadian ever to be selected in the first round. He grew up in Surrey, British Columbia, and attended Stetson University. Outfielder **NTEMA NDUNGIDI** (36th overall, Orioles) and righthander **AARON MYETTE** (43rd, White Sox), another Surrey product who

ball. It marked the first time in draft history that the Yankees failed to sign their first-round pick.

Godwin, a good student who said he wanted to be a doctor, turned down a $1.9 million bonus. "Obviously it was not an economic decision," Yankees director of player development Mark Newman said. "The desire to play professional baseball was of lower priority to him."

Several clubs didn't want to become bogged down in tedious negotiations or risk losing their first-round pick altogether, and instead struck pre-draft deals. In most cases, a player was drafted earlier than his talent warranted, or he signed for less than the going rate.

The Toronto Blue Jays were the first club to arrange such a deal. Selecting fifth, the Jays signed Texas high school outfielder Vernon Wells to a relatively modest $1.6 million deal, and were rewarded many times over. Wells made it to the big leagues by 1999 and established himself as one of the best outfielders in the game for the next decade before injuries started taking a toll. In 2003, his best season, he hit .317 with 33 homers and 117 RBIs, and led the American League in hits (215), doubles (49) and total bases (373).

MEL BAILEY

Vernon Wells

With the eighth pick, the Pittsburgh Pirates chose J.J. Davis, a pitcher/outfielder from a California high school. After signing him for $1.675 million, the Pirates developed Davis as an outfielder, even though his fastball had been clocked up to 96 mph. In 63 big league games, Davis hit .179 with one home run and nine RBIs.

The Florida Marlins, Colorado Rockies and Devil Rays signed their first-round picks for below-market amounts agreed to before the draft. The Kansas City Royals thought they had a deal worked out with righthander Dan Reichert, the seventh pick overall, but he held out for six weeks before agreeing on a $1.415 million bonus.

### OFFENSIVE EXPLOSION HITS COLLEGES

The 1997 college season featured two players who hit at least 40 home runs, Rice first baseman Lance Berkman (42) and LSU shortstop Brandon Larson (41), who both were first-round draft choices. Seven other players topped 30 homers, including Drew and UCLA third baseman Troy Glaus, the second and third players drafted.

Glaus, who hit .409 with 34 home runs and 91 RBIs as a college junior, held out until mid-September before signing with the Anaheim Angels for a $2.25 million bonus. The 6-foot-5, 225-pound Glaus spent 13 seasons in the majors, playing for five clubs and hitting .254 with 320 homers.

Berkman, selected with the 16th pick overall by his hometown Houston Astros, had one of the greatest seasons in college history. In addition to his national-best 42 homers, six short of the record set in 1985 by Oklahoma State's Pete Incaviglia,

### Top 25 Bonuses

| | Player, Pos. | Drafted (Round) | Order | Bonus |
|---|---|---|---|---|
| **1.** | **Matt Anderson, rhp** | **Tigers (1)** | **1** | **$2,505,000** |
| **2.** | ***Rick Ankiel, lhp** | **Cardinals (2)** | **72** | **$2,500,000** |
| **3.** | **Troy Glaus, 3b** | **Angels (1)** | **3** | **$2,250,000** |
| 4. | *Ryan Anderson, lhp | Mariners (1) | 19 | $2,175,000 |
| **5.** | ***Darnell McDonald, of** | **Orioles (1)** | **26** | **$1,900,000** |
| **6.** | **Jason Grilli, rhp** | **Giants (1)** | **4** | **$1,875,000** |
| **7.** | ***Michael Cuddyer, ss** | **Twins (1)** | **9** | **$1,850,000** |
| 8. | *Geoff Goetz, lhp | Mets (1) | 6 | $1,700,000 |
| **9.** | ***J.J. Davis, of/rhp** | **Pirates (1)** | **8** | **$1,675,000** |
| **10.** | ***Vernon Wells, of** | **Blue Jays (1)** | **5** | **$1,600,000** |
| | ***Tim Drew, rhp** | **Indians (1)** | **28** | **$1,600,000** |
| **12.** | **Dan Reichert, rhp** | **Royals (1)** | **7** | **$1,450,000** |
| **13.** | **Kyle Peterson, rhp** | **Brewers (1)** | **13** | **$1,400,000** |
| **14.** | **Brandon Larson, ss** | **Reds (1)** | **14** | **$1,330,000** |
| **15.** | ***Jon Garland, rhp** | **Cubs (1)** | **10** | **$1,325,000** |
| 16. | Chris Enochs, rhp | Athletics (1) | 11 | $1,204,000 |
| **17.** | **Jason Dellaero, ss** | **White Sox (1)** | **15** | **$1,052,500** |
| 18. | Aaron Akin, rhp | Marlins (1) | 12 | $1,050,000 |
| **19.** | **Lance Berkman, 1b** | **Astros (1)** | **16** | **$1,000,000** |
| 20. | *John Curtice, lhp | Red Sox (1) | 17 | $975,000 |
| **21.** | ***Jayson Werth, c** | **Orioles (1)** | **22** | **$885,000** |
| 22. | *Mark Mangum, rhp | Rockies (1) | 18 | $875,000 |
| 23. | *Donnie Bridges, rhp | Expos (1) | 23 | $870,000 |
| **24.** | **Eric DuBose, lhp** | **Athletics (1)** | **21** | **$860,000** |
| **25.** | **Kevin Nicholson, ss** | **Padres (1)** | **27** | **$830,000** |

*Major leaguers in bold. *High school selection.*

Berkman drove in 134 runs (nine shy of Incaviglia's RBI mark), led the nation with 263 total bases and hit .409. Berkman followed with a fine major league career. In 15 seasons, including the first 12 with the Astros, he hit .293 with 366 homers.

The Cincinnati Reds selected Larson with the 14th overall pick. Some scouts questioned whether he was first-round material, despite Larson batting .381 with 41 homers and 118 RBIs as a junior at LSU—and they were right. He struggled to adapt to wood bats and batted .179 with eight homers in parts of four big league seasons.

Another college player with loud numbers but dubious first-round credentials was Kennedy, who hit .482 with 26 homers and 99 RBIs as a college junior, and led NCAA Division I in hits (134) for a second straight season. He forged a 14-year, big-league career as a second baseman, hitting .272 with 80 homers.

Several college pitchers, in addition to Matt Anderson, enhanced their draft standing with dominating performances. Righthander Jason Grilli, drafted fourth by the San Francisco Giants, struck out 125 in 81 innings for Seton Hall. Grilli, a son of former big leaguer Steve Grilli, was among the few 1997 draft picks still active in 2016. Used in a variety of roles while pitching for eight different teams, Grilli had a 25-36 record with 74 saves in 482 appearances.

Reichert burst onto the scene as a junior for Pacific with a 22-strikeout game against Washington State. He went 13-4, 2.30 with 169 strikeouts (second in the nation) in 133 innings for his junior season. A year after signing with the Royals, he was diagnosed with diabetes, struggled to maintain weight on his slender frame, lost velocity on his fastball, and struggled with command issues. In 124 major league appearances over five

## Largest Bonuses By Round

| | Player, Pos. | Club | Bonus |
|---|---|---|---|
| **1.** | **Matt Anderson, rhp** | **Tigers** | **$2,505,000** |
| **2.** | *** Rick Ankiel, lhp** | **Cardinals** | **$2,500,000** |
| **3.** | *** Cesar Crespo, ss** | **Mets** | **$775,000** |
| 4. | * Alan Webb, lhp | Tigers | $180,000 |
| 5. | * Peter Blake, lhp | Twins | $425,000 |
| 6. | * Will McCrotty, c | Dodgers | $150,000 |
| 7. | * Bry Ewen, c | Braves | $150,400 |
| 8. | * Ryan Lehr, 3b | Braves | $95,000 |
| 9. | * Jamie Goudie, 2b | Dodgers | $100,000 |
| 10. | * Kelley Washington, ss | Marlins | $100,000 |
| | Jamie Smith, rhp/c | White Sox | $100,000 |
| **11.** | *** Michael Wuertz, rhp** | **Cubs** | **$200,000** |
| 12. | * Doug Kohl, rhp | Diamondbacks | $65,000 |
| 13. | # Doug Dent, rhp | Braves | $250,000 |
| 14. | * Wes Anderson, rhp | Marlins | $400,000 |
| 15. | Kevin Burford, of | Padres | $80,000 |
| 16. | * Dustin Seale, lhp | Blue Jays | $30,000 |
| 17. | Deon Eaddy, ss | Cubs | $20,000 |
| 18. | * Terry McCormick, lhp | Devil Rays | $100,000 |
| **19.** | **# Travis Hughes, rhp** | **Rangers** | **$50,000** |
| **20.** | **# Mark Hendrickson, lhp** | **Blue Jays** | **$300,000** |
| 21. | * Tutu Moye, ss | Diamondbacks | $25,000 |
| 22. | # Derek Rix, 1b | Red Sox | $100,000 |
| 23. | * Jared Moon, rhp | Dodgers | $350,000 |
| 24. | # Melvin Rosario, of | Rockies | $50,000 |
| 25. | *# David Detienne, 3b | Dodgers | $65,000 |
| Other | *# Matt Bruback, rhp | Cubs (47) | $685,000 |

*Major leaguers in bold. *High school selection. #Signed as draft-and-follow.*

seasons, Reichert went 21-25, 5.56.

Righthander Kyle Peterson, drafted 13th overall by the Milwaukee Brewers, retired in 2002 after just 20 major league appearances because of shoulder problems. He went 5-9, 4.70 in two seasons with the Brewers, a far cry from his success at Stanford. He won 35 games over three seasons, and as a junior led the nation in innings (144) and was among the strikeout leaders (156).

Tim Hudson

Fresno State righthander Jeff Weaver lasted until the second round, when the Chicago White Sox drafted him. Weaver was as dominant as any college pitcher in 1997, striking out 21 against Texas A&M in his final outing to push his national-leading total to 181. Weaver, a draft-eligible sophomore and represented by Boras, did not sign. He was a first-round pick of the Tigers a year later.

The most successful player to come from the 1997 draft, according to WAR (Wins Above Replacement), was unheralded college senior Tim Hudson, who wasn't even drafted a year earlier. Hudson, a pitcher/outfielder for Auburn, signed for $22,500 after being drafted in the sixth round by the Oakland Athletics. The A's developed him as a pitcher, and Hudson won 222 games in a 17-year major league career.

### BONUS RECORDS CONTINUE TO FALL

With Drew and Godwin going unsigned, it marked the first draft since 1991 that two first-rounders did not reach an agreement. A total of 16 players in the top five rounds and 39 in the top 10 did not sign, the highest rates in eight years. Among those were second-rounder Chase Utley and eighth-rounder Cliff Lee. Those two, along with Drew, were three of the five most successful major league players from the class of 1997.

The Minnesota Twins went to the 11th hour before signing their top three picks, first-rounder Michael Cuddyer, supplemental first-rounder Matthew LeCroy and second-rounder Mike Restovich. Cuddyer signed for $1.85 million, LeCroy for $775,000 and Restovich for $650,000. The Twins spent $4,516,500 on their draft picks, double what they had ever spent previously.

The Twins' outlay topped the previous record of $4,505,000 that one team had spent on its draft picks, set in 1996 by the Blue Jays. Two other small-market franchises, the Montreal Expos and Orioles, blew past that mark as well. The Expos, with eight picks prior to the second round, spent $5,045,500, and the Orioles $4,976,500.

The Expos were still in the process of dismantling their powerful 1994 club and were awarded three picks each as compensation for losing righthander Mel Rojas and outfielder Moises Alou as free agents. Each of Montreal's first eight picks received bonuses of at least $400,000, but only two reached the major leagues.

The White Sox and Athletics also were compensated with three bonus picks apiece for the loss of free agents. The first of Oakland's three selections came with the 21st pick in the first round, the position immediately ahead of the Orioles. That effectively meant the first round had 31 picks.

Two of the first-rounders, Cuddyer and lefthander John Curtice (Red Sox), became the

## One Team's Draft: Baltimore Orioles

| | Player, Pos. | Bonus |
|---|---|---|
| **1.** | ***Jayson Werth, c** | **$885,000** |
| **1.** | ***Darnell McDonald, of** | **$1,900,000** |
| 1. | *Ntema Ndungidi, of | $500,000 |
| **2.** | ***Sean Douglass, rhp** | **$315,000** |
| **3.** | ***Matt Riley, lhp** | **$750,000** |
| 4. | *Shannon Carter, of | $125,000 |
| **5.** | **Rick Bauer, rhp** | **$75,000** |
| 6. | Caleb Balbuena, rhp | Did not sign |
| 7. | Ricky Casteel, rhp | $77,500 |
| **8.** | **Jay Spurgeon, rhp** | **$55,000** |
| 9. | Logan Cuellar, rhp | Did not sign |
| 10. | *David Zwirchitz, rhp | $12,500 |
| **11.** | **Jerry Hairston, ss** | **$30,000** |
| 12. | Darren Murphy, lhp | $15,000 |
| 13. | Mack Haman, of | $17,500 |
| 14. | *Sean Jones, rhp | $25,000 |
| 15. | Jordan Romero, rhp | $10,000 |
| 16. | Cliff Wilson, 3b | $15,000 |
| 17. | *Chris Thogersen, rhp | Did not sign |
| 18. | Lance Surridge, rhp | Did not sign |
| 19. | *Jason Ryba, rhp | $15,000 |
| **20.** | ***Joe Borchard, 1b** | **Did not sign** |
| 21. | *Antoine Ide, of | $10,000 |
| 22. | Juan Pacheco, ss | $5,000 |
| 23. | Tod Lee, c | $5,000 |
| 24. | *Jason Taylor, of | Did not sign |
| 25. | *Roy Wells, rhp | Did not sign |
| Other | Matt Schwager (34), rhp | $70,000 |

*Major leaguers in bold. *High school selection.*

### WORTH NOTING

attended Central Arizona Junior College, were supplemental first-round picks. Both Nicholson and Myette reached the majors. Ndungidi, who was born in the Congo, emigrated to Canada from Zaire as a toddler, and was raised in Montreal, did not play in the majors, despite high opinions of his potential. "He's the best high school position player I've seen in Canada since **LARRY WALKER**," said **WAYNE NORTON**, the Orioles' Canadian-based scout. Ndungidi began to display bizarre behavior in the fall of 2000, was jailed for running afoul of the law, and later spent time in a psychiatric facility.

■ The Marlins won the 1997 World Series and then dismantled their club, trading off established players for younger, less expensive talent, including a bounty of first-round draft picks. Among them were two players from the 1997 draft: righthander **JASON GRILLI**, the fourth pick overall who was acquired from the Giants; and lefthander **GEOFF GOETZ**, the sixth pick who was obtained from the Mets as part of a three-for-one deal for future Hall of Fame catcher Mike Piazza. Goetz ended up being the highest pick from the 1997 draft not to reach the majors. His career was sidetracked by shoulder problems, and he peaked at Double-A.

■ The highest-rated player in the 1997 draft, according to Major League Scouting Bureau grades (on the 20-80 scouting scale), was Florida State outfielder **J.D. DREW** with a 66. Michigan high school lefthander **RYAN ANDERSON**, Mississippi State lefthander **ERIC DUBOSE**, California high school righthander **JON GARLAND**, and Florida high school outfielder **J.R. MOUNTS** each had a grade of 65. Anderson, DuBose and Garland were first-round picks, and Mounts went in the third round. No 1 overall pick **MATT ANDERSON** had a grade of 60.

**IN FOCUS: RYAN ANDERSON**

MEL BAILEY

The Tigers narrowed their choice for the top pick in the 1997 draft to the Andersons—Matt and Ryan, unrelated—but dismissed Ryan as a candidate because of his exorbitant bonus demands.

Anderson was attractive to the Tigers on several counts, not the least of which that he was a local kid from the Detroit suburb of Dearborn. On two occasions at Divine Child High, he struck out all 21 hitters he faced in a game. But the Tigers made it clear they were going to use Kris Benson's bonus record of $2 million from 1996 as their starting point in negotiations, and Anderson's father Gus let the Tigers know that his son would want much more if he was the first pick.

So the Mariners drafted Anderson with the 19th overall selection, and the 6-foot-10 lefthander, nicknamed the Little Unit, agreed to a $2.175 million bonus. Anderson had said he hoped to be drafted by the Mariners to perhaps be on the same team as his idol Randy Johnson, the Big Unit.

Anderson never got the chance. He was in Triple-A by 2000, and averaged 12.6 strikeouts per nine innings that season, throwing a fastball that peaked at 100 mph. But he didn't pitch for four seasons while recovering from three shoulder surgeries, and never made it to the major leagues.

## Highest Unsigned Picks

| Player, Pos., Team (Round) | College | Re-Drafted |
|---|---|---|
| J.D. Drew, of, Phillies (1) | None | Cardinals '98 (1) |
| Tyrell Godwin, of, Yankees (1) | North Carolina | Rangers '00 (1) |
| Dane Sardinha, c, Royals (2) | Pepperdine | Reds '00 (2) |
| Jeff Weaver, rhp, White Sox (2) | *Fresno State | Tigers '98 (1) |
| Patrick Boyd, of, Mariners (2) | Clemson | Pirates '00 (4) |
| Chase Utley, ss, Dodgers (2) | UCLA | Phillies '00 (1) |
| Greg Withelder, lhp, Twins (3) | Virginia | Dodgers '00 (6) |
| Scott Barrett, lhp, Astros (3) | Texas | Astros '98 (5) |
| Kevin McGerry, rhp, Giants (4) | St. John's | Athletics '00 (4) |
| Eric Byrnes, of, Astros (4) | *UCLA | Athletics '98 (8) |

**TOTAL UNSIGNED PICKS:** Top 5 Rounds (16), Top 10 Rounds (39)

**Returned to same school.*

second set of high school teammates drafted in the first round in the same year. The two had played on the same youth teams since they were 7 years old and were teammates at Great Bridge High in Chesapeake, Va. California's Cordova High produced first-rounders Jerry Manuel (Tigers) and Mike Ondina (White Sox) in 1972. It would happen again three times over the next 20 years.

Michael Cuddyer

Cuddyer moved from shortstop to third base and eventually to right field as a pro. No matter where he played in the field, his bat was an asset in a 15-year major league career, highlighted by a National League batting title in 2013. Curtice had two shoulder surgeries by 2000 and did not advance beyond Class A.

It was the first draft when two brothers were selected in the first round. Drew went to the Phillies with the second pick, and younger brother Tim, a righthander at Georgia's Lowndes County High, went to the Cleveland Indians with the 28th pick. (A third Drew brother, Stephen, became a first-rounder of the Diamondbacks in 2004.)

Tim received a $1.6 million bonus, almost double the amount paid to the players selected right before him, Kevin Nicholson ($830,000), and after him, Troy Cameron ($825,000).

The previous year, the Indians had signed their first-round pick, first baseman Danny Peoples, also the 28th overall pick, for $400,000.

The Boones and Bells became three-generation professional baseball families in the 1990s, and another family followed suit in 1997. First-rounder Jayson Werth was the grandson of former major league shortstop Dick Schofield. Werth's stepfather Dennis, a former big league catcher, was married to Schofield's daughter. Werth's uncle, Dick Schofield Jr., also had a lengthy major league career.

Two-sport stars in the early rounds weren't as prevalent as in past years. In the first round, the most noteworthy were Godwin, who spent two years as a kick returner at North Carolina; McDonald; and Jason Standridge, a highly rated Auburn quarterback recruit who chose to pursue a baseball career with the Devil Rays. The Rays also picked Kenny Kelly, a prominent Miami quarterback recruit, in the second round.

Thomas Pittman, one of the Expos' seven supplemental first-round picks, and Alvin Morrow, a second-round pick of the Brewers, earned NFL training-camp trials with the Cleveland Browns after abandoning unsuccessful careers in the minors. Neither played in the NFL.

The junior colleges played a more significant role in the draft than in past years. Sophomore righthander Aaron Akin, who attended the University of Missouri as a freshman and went 12-0, 2.03 as a sophomore while leading Cowley County (Kan.) to the Junior College World Series title, was the first juco player taken in the first round in five years. He went to the Marlins with the 12th pick; his four-year pro career did not progress beyond Class A. The White Sox took two juco pitchers with supplemental first-round picks, Saddleback (Calif.) JC righthander Kyle Kane and Central Arizona JC righthander Aaron Myette.

The jucos would have played an even greater role in the 1997 draft if righthanders Roy Oswalt (Holmes, Miss.) and Dan Wheeler (Central Arizona), who ranked 1-2 nationally in ERA, and Cowley County first baseman Travis Hafner, MVP of the Junior College World Series, were not siphoned off as draft-and-follows from the previous year's draft. Oswalt received a $475,000 bonus from the Astros, one of 11 draft-and-follows who earned a six-figure bonus.

Several unsigned juco players who were part of the 1997 class and signed the following spring also made a substantial impact. Lefthander Matt Riley, an Orioles third-rounder, signed for a draft-and-follow record of $750,000 following a year at Sacramento (Calif.) CC, topping the record of $700,000 set by Rangers seventh-rounder Jorge Carrion in 1995. Riley endured three Tommy John surgeries in his career and went 5-4, 5.99 in parts of four major league seasons. Righthander Matt Bruback, a 47th-round choice of the Chicago Cubs out of a Texas high school, spent a season at Manatee (Fla.) JC before getting $685,000 from the Cubs.

The most successful juco draft pick in 1997 was Spartanburg Methodist (S.C.) infielder Orlando Hudson. A 43rd-round pick of the Blue Jays, he signed the following spring for $90,000 and had an 11-year career in the majors, hitting .273 with 93 homers and 543 RBIs.

## Largest Draft-And-Follow Bonuses

| | Player, Pos. | Club (Round) | Bonus |
|---|---|---|---|
| **1.** | ***Matt Riley, lhp** | **Orioles (3)** | **$750,000** |
| 2. | *Matt Bruback, rhp | Cubs (47) | $685,000 |
| **3.** | **Mark Hendrickson, lhp** | **Blue Jays (20)** | **$300,000** |
| 4. | Doug Dent, rhp | Braves (13) | $250,000 |
| **5.** | **Michael Vento, rhp** | **Yankees (40)** | **$135,800** |
| 6. | Keith Dunn, rhp | Yankees (30) | $130,000 |
| 7. | Derek Rix, 1b | Red Sox (22) | $100,000 |
| | *Pat Santoro, ss | Red Sox (35) | $100,000 |
| 9. | Luis Suarez, ss | White Sox (39) | $92,500 |
| **10.** | **Orlando Hudson, ss** | **Blue Jays (43)** | **$90,000** |

*Major leaguers in bold. *High school selection.*

# 1997 Draft List

**Did not sign. Major leaguers in bold, with first and last years noted. Order of selection indicated in parentheses. For the first five rounds, the peak level of each player is noted. + Signed as draft-and-follow (Second school noted if applicable).*

## ANAHEIM ANGELS (3)

1. **Troy Glaus, 3b, UCLA.—(1998-2010)**
2. (Choice to Mariners as compensation for Type B free agent Dave Hollins)
3. Heath Timmerman, rhp, Northeastern Oklahoma A&M JC.—(Low A)
4. Joe Gangemi, lhp, Seton Hall University.—(High A)
5. Michael Brunet, rhp, Pasco-Hernando (Fla.) CC.—(AAA)
6. **Matt Wise, rhp, Cal State Fullerton.—(2000-08)**
7. Matt Garrick, c, Texas A&M University.
8. Ryan Cummings, rhp, Georgia Southern University.
9. Dwayne Dobson, rhp, University of South Florida.
10. **Steve Green, rhp, Fort Scott (Kan.) CC.—(2001)**
11. Brian Tokarse, rhp, Cal State Fullerton.
12. *Felipe Alou Jr., of, Canada (Calif.) JC.

DRAFT DROP *Son of Felipe Alou, major leaguer (1958-74); major league manager (1992-2006) • Brother of Moises Alou, major leaguer (1990-2008)*

13. **Doug Nickle, rhp, University of California.—(2000-02)**
14. Adam Leggett, 2b, Georgia Tech.
15. *Brent Wagler, rhp, Florida Southern College.
16. Casey Child, of, University of Utah.
17. Keith Medosch, ss, University of North Florida.
18. *Michael O'Keefe, of, Notre Dame HS, Hamden, Conn.
19. Bo Donaldson, rhp, University of Tampa.
20. Jaymie Bane, lhp, Arizona State University.

DRAFT DROP *Son of Eddie Bane, first-round draft pick, Twins (1973); major leaguer (1973-76)*

21. **Mike Colangelo, of, George Mason University.—(1999-2002)**
22. Steve Fish, rhp, University of Nebraska.
23. +Jake Brooks, rhp, Polk (Fla.) CC.
24. Ernie Miller, lhp, Methodist (N.C.) College.
25. Jeb Dougherty, of, University of San Diego.
26. Tim Adams, 1b, UC Davis.
27. *David Walling, rhp, Grossmont (Calif.) JC.

DRAFT DROP *First-round draft pick (27th overall), Yankees (1999)*

28. *Rogier Vandepohl, ss, Indian River (Fla.) CC.
29. Mike Condon, ss, Seton Hall University.
30. Oscar Betancourt, 3b, Cal Poly Pomona.
31. Steve Hagins, of, San Diego State University.
32. Ben Talbott, 3b, Lehigh University.
33. +Eric Easton, rhp, East Lake HS, Tarpon Springs, Fla. / St. Petersburg (Fla.) CC.
34. Peter Quittner, of, University of San Francisco.
35. *Graham McAllister, c-1b, Lyons (Kan.) HS.
36. Casey Martin, c, Long Beach State University.
37. *Richard Stegbauer, c, Edison (Fla.) CC.
38. **Scot Shields, rhp, Lincoln Memorial (Tenn.) University.—(2001-10)**
39. *Ben Saxon, rhp, Chipola (Fla.) JC.
40. +Jullian Harris, lhp, West Valley (Calif.) JC.
41. ***Josh Pearce, rhp, Centralia (Wash.) JC.—(2002-04)**
42. Jay Nunley, of, University of North Florida.
43. +Ryan Bast, ss-2b, Sierra (Calif.) JC.
44. Brad Brewer, ss, University of Miami.
45. *Wesley Crawford, lhp, Polk (Fla.) CC.
46. *Matt Steele, rhp, Chipola (Fla.) JC.
47. *Jeff Kaita, rhp, Colfax HS, Applegate, Calif.
48. Aaron Porter, rhp, St. Mary's (Calif.) College.
49. *Daniel Kerrigan, c, Manatee (Fla.) CC.
50. Sheldon Philip-Guide, of, Glendale (Calif.) CC.
51. *William Hays, of, Garrett (Md.) CC.
52. *Ben Margalski, c, Northwest HS, High Ridge, Mo.
53. Steve Ahlers, ss, Livermore (Calif.) HS.
54. *Shamar Cotton, rhp, Skyline HS, Oakland.
55. *Brian Sullivan, lhp, Booker HS, Sarasota, Fla.
56. Gil Pichardo, of, South Shore HS, Brooklyn, N.Y.
57. Ron Ricks, rhp, University of West Florida.
58. *Lamar Harvey, rhp, Fremont HS, Sunnyvale, Calif.
59. *Jake Mapes, c, Hemet (Calif.) HS.
60. *Alexis Acosta, ss, Polk (Fla.) CC.

## ARIZONA DIAMONDBACKS (29)

1. **Jack Cust, 1b, Immaculata HS, Flemington, N.J.—(2001-11)**

Troy Glaus reached the major leagues within a year and hit 320 home runs in 13 seasons

2. Jason Royer, rhp, Del City (Okla.) HS.—(High A)
3. Jeff Brooks, 1b-3b, Solanco HS, Quarryville, Pa.—(High A)
4. *Chase Voshell, ss, Milford (Ohio) HS.—(High A)

DRAFT DROP *Attended Wake Forest; re-drafted by Cardinals, 2000 (3rd round)*

5. *Matt Riethmaier, rhp, Arkadelphia (Ark.) HS.—(Low A)

DRAFT DROP *Attended Arkansas; re-drafted by Phillies, 2000 (5th round)*

6. Mike Rooney, rhp, St. John's University.
7. **Brian Gordon, of, Round Rock (Texas) HS.—(2008-11)**
8. **Ron Calloway, of, Canada (Calif.) JC.—(2003-04)**
9. *Justin Singleton, ss, St. Paul's HS, Lutherville, Md.

DRAFT DROP *Son of Ken Singleton, major leaguer (1970-84)*

10. Casey Cuntz, ss, Louisiana State University.
11. Jamie Sykes, of, Valparaiso University.
12. Doug Kohl, rhp, Green Valley HS, Henderson, Nev.
13. *Peter Nystrom, of, Dunedin (Fla.) HS.
14. Alvin Montilla, of, St. Raymond's HS, Bronx, N.Y.
15. Brian Fox, c, Grayson County (Texas) JC.
16. David Haverstick, rhp, Bethel (Ind.) College.
17. *Steve Rowell, ss, Ridgewood HS, Kenner, La.
18. Jason Jensen, lhp, University of Southern Maine.
19. *Tony Hausladen, 1b, St. Louis University.
20. *Derek Michaelis, 1b, Midway HS, Waco, Texas.
21. Tutu Moye, ss, Rose HS, Greenville, N.C.
22. Keith Jones, 3b, Fullerton (Calif.) JC.
23. Jared Martin, ss, University of Southern Mississippi.
24. Jason Martines, rhp, Siena Heights (Mich.) College.
25. *Andrew Friedberg, lhp, Middleton (Wis.) HS.
26. *Ben Mitchell, rhp, Horizon HS, Scottsdale, Ariz.
27. John Adams, of, Wichita State University.
28. *Jared Hoerman, rhp, Eastern Oklahoma State JC.
29. Jeff Wilson, lhp, Elon College.
30. *Dan Hall, rhp, Plymouth (N.C.) HS.
31. Seth Tate, rhp, Wenatchee Valley (Wash.) CC.
32. Scott Abeyta, lhp, Contra Costa (Calif.) JC.
33. Lance Downing, 3b, Watson Chapel HS, Pine Bluff, Ark.
34. *Phillip McKaig, rhp, Corona Del Sol HS, Tempe, Ariz.
35. Jeremy Quire, c, Murray State University.
36. **Alex Cintron, ss, Mech-Tech College, Yabucoa, P.R.—(2001-09)**
37. Julio Guzman, of, Carson-Newman (Tenn.) College.
38. Charlie Jones, rhp, Florida Atlantic University.
39. *Kelly Martin, rhp, Arcadia HS, Phoenix.
40. Wyley Steelmon, 1b, Oklahoma State University.
41. *Jeremy Dameworth, of, Ramona (Calif.) HS.
42. *Jason Scobie, rhp, Westwood HS, Austin, Texas.
43. Jamie Puorto, lhp, Northeastern Illinois University.
44. *Jason Wiedmeyer, lhp, West Bend East HS, West Bend, Wis.
45. Steve Doherty, 2b, Long Beach State University.
46. Chris Bloomer, rhp, Purdue University.
47. Jeff Santa, lhp, Winthrop University.
48. *Bryce Terveen, c, JC of the Desert (Calif.).
49. *John Meyers, rhp, W.E. Boswell HS, Dallas.
50. ***Tommy Murphy, rhp-ss, Charlotte HS, Port Charlotte, Fla.—(2006-07)**
51. *George Dixon, of, Stamford Catholic HS, Stamford, Conn.
52. *Brandon Wells, lhp, Bagdad (Ariz.) HS.
53. *Ronnie Goodwin, rhp, North Little Rock HS, Sherwood, Ark.
54. *Aaron Rifkin, 1b, Etiwanda HS, Fontana, Calif.
55. *Stuart Hunt, lhp, Edmond Memorial HS, Edmond, Okla.
56. *Samuel Mendoza, rhp, Highland HS, Gilbert, Ariz.
57. *Anthony Denard, of, Laney (Calif.) JC.
58. *Anthony Pena, rhp, Dallas Christian HS, Red Oak, Texas.
59. *Ronnie Corona, rhp, Victor Valley HS, Victorville, Calif.
60. *Robert Pierce, 2b, Green Valley HS, Henderson, Nev.

## ATLANTA BRAVES (28)

1. Troy Cameron, ss, St. Thomas Aquinas HS, Fort Lauderdale, Fla.—(AAA)
2. **Joey Nation, lhp, Putnam City HS, Oklahoma City, Okla.—(2000)**
3. Juan Velazquez, ss, Jose Campeche HS, San Lorenzo, P.R.—(AAA)
4. **Cory Aldridge, of, Cooper HS, Abilene, Texas.—(2001-10)**
5. **Horacio Ramirez, lhp, Inglewood (Calif.) HS.—(2003-11)**
6. *Brett Groves, ss, Tampa Bay Tech, Tampa.
7. Bry Ewen, c, Belton (Texas) HS.
8. Ryan Lehr, c-3b, Grossmont HS, La Mesa, Calif.

DRAFT DROP *Brother of Justin Lehr, major leaguer (2004-09)*

9. ***Ryan Snare, lhp, East Lake HS, Palm Harbor, Fla.—(2004)**
10. *Gary Loudon, rhp, Shippensburg (Pa.) University.
11. Greg Strickland, of, Cumberland (Tenn.) University.
12. *Manny Crespo, of, Westminster Christian HS, Miami.
13. Doug Dent, rhp, Citrus Heights, Calif.
14. *Chris Frazier, rhp, Salado HS, Belton, Texas.
15. Jon Ciravolo, rhp, Kean (N.J.) College.
16. Jason Hairston, c, Washington State University.

DRAFT DROP *Grandson of Sam Hairston, major leaguer (1951) • Son of John Hairston, major leaguer (1969)*

17. Richard Thieme, lhp, Georgia Tech.
18. *Brad Drew, lhp, Waterloo Collegiate Institute, Waterloo, Ontario.
19. Stewart Smothers, of, San Diego State University.
20. Derrick Lewis, rhp, Florida A & M University.
21. Mike Roberts, rhp, Siena College.
22. Pat Schmidt, lhp, Bellefontaine (Ohio) HS.
23. Richard Dishman, rhp, Duke University.
24. *Bill Scott, of, Bishop Alemany HS, Mission Hills, Calif.
25. Robert Porter, lhp, Southwest Mississippi CC.
26. Mark Burke, 1b, Portland State University.
27. Jason Bowers, lhp, Central Cabarrus HS, Concord, N.C.
28. Troy Allen, of, George Washington University.
29. *John Wright, lhp, Walton HS, DeFuniak Springs, Fla.
30. *Tyler Kemhus, 3b, Oregon City (Ore.) HS.
31. David Lebejko, rhp, Central Connecticut State University.
32. Collin Wissen, of, Southwest Texas State University.
33. *Craig Carter, ss, Lake Havasu (Ariz.) HS.
34. *Patrick Hannaway, rhp, Monsignor Farrell HS, Staten Island, N.Y.
35. *Jeremy Hale, rhp, Lafayette HS, St. Joseph, Mo.
36. Tim Lyons, rhp, University of Kansas.
37. *Mike Dolan, rhp, Chattahoochee (Fla.) HS.
38. *Robert Medeiros, of, University of Hawaii.
39. *Sean Vann, of, Chaparral HS, Las Vegas, Nev.
40. *Charlie Thames, rhp, Humble (Texas) HS.
41. Will Fleck, rhp, La Salle University.
42. Paul Shanklin, rhp, West Virginia State College.
43. *Anthony Limbrick, of, Skyline HS, Oakland.
44. *Matt Price, lhp, Greater Atlanta Christian HS, Norcross, Ga.
45. +Justin Dansby, rhp, Eastern Oklahoma State JC / Cowley County (Kan.) CC.
46. *Daniel Wright, of, Dixie HS, St. George, Utah.
47. *Cameron Hardy, rhp, Lake City (Fla.) CC.
48. Prinz Milton, of, West Torrance (Calif.) HS.
49. +Michael Gray, lhp, Cuesta (Calif.) JC.
50. *Mike Robinson, rhp, Canby (Ore.) HS.

51. *Jason Westemeir, 3b-rhp, Bishop Alemany HS, Mission Hills, Calif.
52. *Tyler Shelton, ss, Hillsboro HS, Donnellson, Ill.
53. *Robert Coley, c, Irwin County HS, Fitzgerald, Ga.
54. *Travis Wessel, lhp, Morningside (Iowa) College.
55. *Shannon Royal, lhp, Mariner HS, Fort Myers, Fla.
56. +Greg Dukeman, rhp, Long Beach (Calif.) CC.
57. *Anthony Purkiss, ss, Golden West HS, Visalia, Calif.
58. *Jorge Guerrero, ss, A.B. Miller HS, Fontana, Calif.
59. *Tony Piccotti, 1b, Capital HS, Boise, Idaho.
60. *Tyler Van Patten, 1b, Polk (Fla.) CC.
61. *Travis Harrington, ss, Columbia HS, Lake City, Fla.
62. *Jerel Johnson, 3b, McNair HS, Decatur, Ga.
63. *Joey Alvarez, c, Temple (Texas) HS.
64. *Lonnie Jaquez, c, Carlsbad (N.M.) HS.
65. *Daniel Bell, of, Los Angeles CC.
66. *Darryl Stephens, of, St. Pius X HS, Decatur, Ga.
67. *Chris Carmichael, of, McNair HS, Decatur, Ga.
68. *Adam Kepler, of, Riverwood International HS, Atlanta.
69. *Justin Echols, of, Thatcher (Ariz.) HS.

## BALTIMORE ORIOLES (21)

1. **Jayson Werth, c, Glenwood HS, Chatham, Ill.—(2002-15)**
DRAFT DROP *Stepson of Dennis Werth, major leaguer (1979-82) • Grandson of Dick Schofield, major leaguer (1953-71) • Nephew of Dick Schofield, first-round draft pick, Angels (1981); major leaguer (1983-96)*
1. **Darnell McDonald, of, Cherry Creek HS, Englewood, Colo.** (Choice from Yankees as compensation for Type A free agent David Wells).**—(2004-13)**
DRAFT DROP *Brother of Donzell McDonald, major leaguer (2001-02)*
1. Ntema Ndungidi, of, Edouard Montpetit HS, Montreal (Supplemental choice—36th—as compensation for Wells).—(AA)
2. **Sean Douglass, rhp, Antelope Valley HS, Lancaster, Calif.—(2001-05)**
3. **+Matt Riley, lhp, Liberty Union HS, Oakley, Calif. / Sacramento (Calif.) CC.—(1999-2005)**
4. Shannon Carter, of, El Reno (Okla.) HS.—(AAA)
5. **Rick Bauer, rhp, Treasure Valley (Ore.) CC.—(2001-08)**
6. *Caleb Balbuena, rhp, Cuesta (Calif.) JC.
7. Ricky Casteel, rhp, Northeast Texas CC.
8. **Jay Spurgeon, rhp, University of Hawaii.—(2000)**
9. *Logan Cuellar, rhp, Wharton County (Texas) JC.
10. David Zwirchitz, rhp, East HS, Appleton, Wis.
11. **Jerry Hairston, ss, Southern Illinois University.—(1998-2013)**
DRAFT DROP *Grandson of Sam Hairston, major leaguer (1951) • Son of Jerry Hairston, major leaguer (1973-89) • Brother of Scott Hairston, major leaguer (2004-14)*
12. Darren Murphy, lhp, Grossmont (Calif.) JC.
13. Mack Haman, of, Coastal Carolina University.
14. Sean Jones, rhp, Barton HS, Hamilton, Ontario.
15. Jordan Romero, rhp, De Anza (Calif.) JC.
16. Cliff Wilson, 3b, Spartanburg Methodist (S.C.) JC.
17. *Chris Thogersen, rhp, Newbury Park HS, Thousand Oaks, Calif.
18. *Lance Surridge, rhp, University of North Carolina-Greensboro.
19. Jason Ryba, rhp, Cuyahoga Heights HS, Brooklyn Heights, Ohio.
20. ***Joe Borchard, 1b, Camarillo (Calif.) HS.—(2002-2007)**
DRAFT DROP *First-round draft choice (12th overall), White Sox (2000)*
21. Antoine Ide, of, Madison HS, Portland, Ore.
22. Juan Pacheco, ss, Rutgers University.
23. Tod Lee, c, Georgia Southern University.
24. *Jason Taylor, of, Ryan HS, Denton, Texas.
25. *Roy Wells, rhp, Perry County Central HS, Hazard, Ky.
26. **D.J. Carrasco, rhp, Pima (Ariz.) CC.—(2003-12)**
27. *Brian Harper, of, Hershey (Pa.) HS.
28. *Erick Eigenhuis, rhp-1b, Central Valley HS, Veradale, Wash.
29. *Anthony Reed, rhp, Eisenhower HS, Walters, Okla.
30. *Brian Schmitt, 1b, Monterey HS, Lubbock, Texas.
31. *Terry Byron, 3b, St. Joseph HS, St. Croix, Virgin Islands.
32. *Gavin Wright, of, Lufkin (Texas) HS.
33. *Andy Beal, lhp, Reidland HS, Paducah, Ky.
34. +Matt Schwager, rhp, Indian Hills (Iowa) CC.
35. *Austin Bilke, 3b, Beaver Dam (Wis.) HS.
36. +Juan Bonilla, c, Crestview (Fla.) HS / Chipola (Fla.) CC.
37. *Rod Perry, of, Mater Dei HS, Irvine, Calif.
38. *Sam Emerick, rhp, Lincoln Land (Ill.) CC.
39. *Bill Duplissea, c, San Mateo (Calif.) JC.
40. Tommy Martin, ss, Hillsdale (Mich.) College.
41. Shawn Curtis, rhp, Lexington, Ky.

## BOSTON RED SOX (17)

1. John Curtice, lhp, Great Bridge HS, Chesapeake, Va.—(High A)
1. Mark Fischer, of, Georgia Tech (Supplemental choice—35th—as compensation for Type A free agent Roger Clemens).—(AA)
2. Aaron Capista, ss, Joliet Catholic HS, Joliet, Ill. (Choice from Blue Jays as compensation for Clemens).—(AA)
2. Eric Glaser, rhp, Highlands HS, Fort Thomas, Ky.—(AAA)
3. **Travis Harper, rhp, James Madison University.—(2000-06)**
4. **Angel Santos, ss, Miguel Melendez HS, Cayey, P.R.—(2001-03)**
5. Greg Miller, lhp, Aurora West HS, Aurora, Ill.—(AAA)
6. *Kris Wilken, c, Eldorado HS, Albuquerque, N.M.
7. Jeff Taglienti, rhp, Tufts (Mass.) University.
8. Andy Hazlett, lhp, University of Portland.
9. ***Justin Wayne, rhp, Punahou HS, Honolulu, Hawaii.—(2002-04)**
DRAFT DROP *First-round draft choice (5th overall), Expos (2000)*
10. **Marty McCleary, rhp, Mount Vernon Nazarene (Ohio) College.—(2004-07)**
11. Tom Miller, lhp, Ohio University.
12. *Billy Rich, of, University of Connecticut.
13. Chaz Terni, ss, Montville HS, Uncasville, Conn.
14. Chad Alevras, c, University of New Mexico.
15. Rick O'Dette, lhp, St. Joseph's University.
16. Jorge DeLeon, 3b, University of South Florida.
17. Kenny Rayborn, rhp, University of South Alabama.
18. Danny Haas, of, University of Louisville.
DRAFT DROP *Son of Eddie Haas, major leaguer (1957-60); major league manager (1985)*
19. **David Eckstein, 2b, University of Florida.—(2001-10)**
20. Brian Partenheimer, lhp, Indiana University.
21. Joe Thomas, lhp, Marietta (Ohio) College.
22. +Derek Rix, 1b, Florida CC.
23. ***Nate Bump, rhp, Penn State University.—(2003-05)**
DRAFT DROP *First-round draft choice (25th overall), Giants (1998)*
24. *Jason Fingers, rhp, Torrey Pines HS, San Diego.
DRAFT DROP *Son of Rollie Fingers, major leaguer (1968-85)*
25. *Chris Domurat, c, Sandwich HS, Forestdale, Mass.
26. *Heath McMurray, rhp, Splendora (Texas) HS.
27. *Justin Fry, rhp, Ohio State University.
28. *David Stickel, ss, Temple Heights HS, Tampa.
29. *Ryan Yeager, ss, Port St. Joe (Fla.) HS.
30. ***Bret Prinz, rhp, Phoenix JC.—(2001-07)**
31. *Matt Kamalsky, rhp, Somerset (Pa.) HS.
32. *Robert Hardy, rhp, Countryside HS, Clearwater, Fla.
33. +Patrick Santoro, ss, Fenwick HS, Elmwood Park, Ill. / Triton (Ill.) CC.
34. *Layne Meyer, rhp, Polk (Fla.) CC.
35. *Jason Berni, rhp, Rancho Bernardo HS, San Diego.
36. *Ryan Atkinson, rhp, Bellarmine Prep, San Jose, Calif.
37. *Donovan Marbury, rhp, University of Southern Mississippi.
38. ***Dennis Tankersley, rhp, St. Charles (Mo.) HS.—(2002-04)**
39. *Shawn Weaver, rhp, Bald Eagle-Nittany HS, Loganton, Pa.
40. *Chad Zaucha, of, Mount Pleasant (Pa.) HS.
41. *Matthew Slagter, rhp, Jefferson HS, Tampa.
42. *Scott Candelaria, ss, La Cueva HS, Albuquerque, N.M.
43. *Nicholas Gray, ss, Florida HS, Tallahassee, Fla.
44. *Todd Smith, 3b, Apopka (Fla.) HS.
45. ***Joe Thurston, ss, Vallejo (Calif.) HS.—(2002-11)**

## CHICAGO CUBS (10)

1. **Jon Garland, rhp, Kennedy HS, Granada Hills, Calif.—(2000-13)**
2. (Choice to White Sox as compensation for Type A free agent Kevin Tapani)
3. **Scott Downs, lhp, University of Kentucky.—(2000-14)**
4. **Nathan Teut, lhp, Iowa State University.—(2002)**
5. Jaisen Randolph, of, Hillsborough HS, Tampa.—(AA)
6. Matt Mauck, 3b, Jasper (Ind.) HS.—(Low A)
DRAFT DROP *Quarterback, National Football League (2005)*
7. Paul Vracar, rhp, Orchard Park HS, Stoney Creek, Ontario.
8. Ron Walker, 3b, Old Dominion University.
9. Gary Johnson, of, University of Nevada-Reno.
10. Mike Amrhein, c, University of Notre Dame.
11. **Michael Wuertz, rhp, Austin (Minn.) HS.—(2004-11)**
12. **Randy Williams, lhp, Lamar University.—(2004-11)**
13. *Tanner Ericksen, rhp, Bullard HS, Fresno, Calif.
14. *Antwaan Randle el, of, Thornton HS, Riverdale, Ill.
DRAFT DROP *Wide receiver, National Football League (2002-10)*
15. T.P. Waligora, rhp, College of William & Mary.
16. Matt Magers, lhp, South Dakota State University.
17. Deon Eaddy, ss, Norfolk State University.
18. *John Massey, c, Adamsville (Tenn.) HS.
19. **Chris Piersoll, rhp, Fullerton (Calif.) JC.—(2001)**
20. ***Gary Johnson, of, Atherton, Calif.—(2003)**
21. Kevin Waldrum, rhp, Millsap HS, Weatherford, Texas.
22. *Cameron Likely, of, Port St. Joe (Fla.) HS.
23. *Greg Jacobs, of, Cypress (Calif.) JC.
24. *Kevin Hodge, ss, Blinn (Texas) JC.
25. Nathan Batts, lhp, Souhegan HS, Amherst, N.H.
26. Mike Meyers, rhp, Black Hawk (Ill.) JC.
27. Michael Delano, lhp, Los Angeles CC.
28. *Brad Love, lhp, Meridian (Miss.) CC.
29. ***Ryan Rupe, rhp, Texas A&M University.—(1999-2003)**
30. *George Arnott, c, Cabrillo (Calif.) JC.
31. *Anthony Calabrese, ss, Brunswick HS, Riverside, Conn.
32. *Andrew Perry, rhp, Claremont (Calif.) HS.
33. *Ryan McKinley, rhp, Scottsdale (Ariz.) CC.
34. *Chris Williamson, of-1b, Westfield HS, Houston.
35. +Ken Conroy, rhp, East Gaston HS, Gastonia, N.C. / Pitt (N.C.) CC.
36. Todd Fereday, 3b, Kansas State University.
37. *Brad Tucker, rhp, Fresno State University.
38. *Clark Todd, c, Lufkin (Texas) HS.
39. *Peter Selden, rhp, Holley (N.Y.) HS.
40. *Robert Mitchell, lhp, Dixie Heights HS, Erlanger, Ky.
41. ***Jeff Duncan, of, Lamont HS, Frankfort, Ill.—(2003-04)**
DRAFT DROP *Baseball coach, Kent State (2014-15)*
42. *Daren Bartula, rhp, McLennan (Texas) CC.
43. *Josh Benedict, lhp, South Salem HS, Keizer, Ore.
44. *John Halliday, 1b, Pasco-Hernando (Fla.) CC.
45. *Tim Whitfield, rhp, Leland HS, San Jose, Calif.
46. Tom Bernhardt, of, Louisiana State University.
47. +Matt Bruback, rhp, Samuel Clements HS, Schertz, Texas / Manatee (Fla.) CC.
48. *John Janek, of, McLennan (Texas) CC.
49. Brad Hargreaves, c, Okaloosa-Walton (Fla.) CC.
50. +Matt Gunderson, rhp, Walla Walla (Wash.) CC / Lower Columbia (Wash.) CC.
51. +Coby Robinson, of, Enterprise State (Ala.) JC.
52. *Lester Galer, rhp, Acalanes HS, Lafayette, Calif.
53. *Jeremy Taylor, rhp, Ankeny (Iowa) HS.
54. *Jeremy Smith, rhp, Cerro Coso (Calif.) CC.
55. +Matt Murphy, lhp, Wallace State (Ala.) CC.
56. *Joshua Latimer, lhp, Kishwaukee (Ill.) JC.
57. Morey Aldrup, ss, La Quinta HS, Santa Ana, Calif.
58. *Michael Joyce, lhp, Fitch HS, Groton, Conn.
59. *Shane Kelly, of, Meridian (Miss.) CC.

## CHICAGO WHITE SOX (15)

1. **Jason Dellaero, ss, University of South Florida.—(1999)**
1. Kyle Kane, rhp, Saddleback (Calif.) CC (Supplemental choice—33rd—as compensation for loss of service-time free agent Alex Fernandez).—(AAA)
1. Brett Caradonna, of, El Capitan HS, San Diego (Supplemental choice—34th—as compensation for Type A free agent Kevin Tapani).—(AAA)
1. **Aaron Myette, rhp, Central Arizona JC** (Supplemental choice—43rd—as compensation for Fernandez).**—(1999-2004)**
1. **Jim Parque, lhp, UCLA** (Supplemental choice—46th—as compensation for Fernandez).**—(1998-2003)**
DRAFT DROP *First player from 1997 draft to reach majors (May 26, 1998)*
1. **Rocky Biddle, rhp, Long Beach State University** (Supplemental choice—51st—for failure to sign 1996 first-round draft pick Bobby Seay).**—(2000-2004)**
2. ***Jeff Weaver, rhp, Fresno State University** (Choice from Cubs as compensation for Tapani).**—(1999-2010)**
DRAFT DROP *Returned to Fresno State; re-drafted by Tigers, 1998 (1st round) • Brother of Jered Weaver, first-round draft pick, Angels (2004); major leaguer (2006-15)*
2. (Choice to Indians as compensation for Type A free agent Albert Belle)
3. J.R. Mounts, of, Key West (Fla.) HS.—(High A)
4. Curtis Whitley, lhp, Mount Olive (N.C.) College.—(AA)
5. **Pat Daneker, rhp, University of Virginia.—(1999)**
6. Brian Scott, rhp, San Diego State University.
7. Jake Meyer, rhp, UCLA.
8. Tim Currens, rhp, Lindsey Wilson (Ky.) College.
9. Rolando Garza, ss, Coachella Valley HS, Coachella, Calif.
10. Jamie Smith, rhp-c, Texas A&M University.
11. Kevin Connacher, 2b, Florida Atlantic University.
12. Andrew Jacobson, rhp, Alma (Mich.) College.
13. Ryan Hankins, 2b, University of Nevada-Las Vegas.
14. Chad Durham, 2b-of, Surry (N.C.) CC.
DRAFT DROP *Brother of Ray Durham, major leaguer (1990-2008)*
15. Travis Rapp, c, University of North Florida.
16. *Adrean Acevedo, of, Miami-Dade CC Kendall.
17. *Shawn Barksdale, rhp, Etowah HS, Gallant, Ala.
18. Tom Williams, rhp, Southern University.
19. *Jason Bernard, rhp, Rutherford HS, Panama City, Fla.
20. *Tyson Boston, 3b, Burlington-Edison HS, Burlington, Wash.
21. Jay Kvasnicka, rhp, Northeastern Illinois University.
22. +Stuart Rohling, rhp, Northwest Shoals (Ala.) JC.
23. Matt Berger, 1b, University of Louisville.
24. *Cormac Joyce, lhp, Burke HS, Washingtonville, N.Y.
25. *Eric Thompson, 1b, Gardner Edge HS, Gardner, Kan.
26. *Joshua Johnston, rhp, JC of Eastern Utah.
27. +Anthony Garcia, c, Miami-Dade CC Wolfson.
28. Ricardo Ramon, of, Miami Senior HS, Hialeah, Fla.
29. *Matthew Goldsmith, rhp, Rockwall (Texas) HS.
30. *Ray Goirgolzarri, 3b, Miami-Dade CC South.
31. *Michael Mallonee, lhp, Southwestern (Calif.) JC.
32. *Chadd Clarey, rhp, Des Moines Area (Iowa) CC.
33. *Mark Floersch, rhp, New Trier HS, Winnetka, Ill.
34. *Jason Moates, rhp, Central HS, Columbia, Tenn.
35. *Nelson Carreno, c-of, Miami Christian HS, Miami.
36. *Edward Scott, ss-of, Dominguez HS, Compton, Calif.

37. *Kevin Provencher, rhp, Forest Hill HS, West Palm Beach, Fla.
38. *John Newman, rhp-ss, Skyline HS, Idaho Falls, Idaho.
39. +Luis Suarez, ss, Miami-Dade CC North.
40. *Darryl Rogue, rhp, Miami-Dade CC Kendall.
41. Michael Hill, 3b-of, Bentley (Mass.) College.
42. *Richard Clover, rhp, Central Missouri State University.
43. *Jeff Radziewicz, 1b, Easton (Md.) HS.
**44. *Matt Smith, lhp, Bishop Gorman HS, Las Vegas, Nev.—(2006-07)**
45. *Jason Aspito, ss, Driscoll Catholic HS, Itasca, Ill.
46. Francisco De Armas, c, Southridge HS, Miami.
47. *David Siemon, 3b, Forest Hills HS, West Palm Beach, Fla.
48. *Jackie Pettigrew, rhp, Sperry HS, Skiatook, Okla.
49. J.J. Newkirk, of, Long Beach State University.
50. *James Lunsford, c, Central HS, San Angelo, Texas.
51. *Luke Albert, c, Chaminade Madonna College HS, Hollywood, Fla.
52. Elio Borges, ss, Miami.

## CINCINNATI REDS (14)

**1. Brandon Larson, ss, Louisiana State University.—(2001-04)**
**2. Travis Dawkins, ss, Newberry (S.C.) HS.—(1999-2003)**
3. Thad Markray, 3b-rhp, Springhill (La.) HS.—(AAA)
4. Monte Roundtree, lhp, Rose HS, Greenville, N.C.—(Rookie)
**5. DeWayne Wise, of, Chapin (S.C.) HS.—(2000-13)**
6. Toby Sanchez, 1b, Long Beach State University.
**7. Mike Frank, lhp-of, Santa Clara University.—(1998)**
8. *Matt Borne, rhp, University of Kentucky.
**9. Scott Williamson, rhp, Oklahoma State University.—(1999-2007)**
10. David Runk, rhp, Tussey Mountain HS, Saxton, Pa.
11. Clint Brewer, rhp, Blanchard HS, Dibble, Okla.
12. Dustin Robinson, rhp, Oklahoma Baptist University.
13. Fernando Rios, of, Glendale (Calif.) HS.
14. Daniel Timm, rhp, University of Denver.
15. Braxton Whitehead, c-1b, University of Southern Mississippi.
16. David Tidwell, of, U of Alabama.
17. Tye Levy, lhp, Juniata Valley HS, Alexandria, Pa.
18. Wesley Stumbo, rhp, Georgetown (Ky.) College.
19. Benny Craig, of, Loyola Marymount University.
20. Kevin Baderdeen, ss, Glen Oaks (Mich.) CC.
21. Robert Averett, rhp, Florida A&M University.
22. Eric Welsh, 1b, Northern Illinois University.
23. *Brian Kirby, c, North Little Rock (Ark.) HS.
24. +Terence Senegal, of, Ovey Comeaux HS, Lafayette, La. / Angelina (Texas) JC.
25. +Samone Peters, 1b, Mendocino (Calif.) CC / Laney (Calif.) JC.
26. *Antjuan Mitchell, 1b, Mount Carmel HS, Chicago.
27. *Josh Holbrook, c-1b, San Marcos (Calif.) HS.
28. *Scott Sandusky, c, Texas A&M University.
29. Zay Brown, rhp, Midland Valley HS, Warrenville, S.C.
30. Marc Suarez, c, Cumberland (Tenn.) University.
31. +Cody Stanley, rhp, Clark HS, San Antonio, Texas / Northeast Texas CC.
32. *Todd Holt, of, Manchester HS, Chesterfield, Va.
33. *Chad Rogers, rhp, Pine Forest HS, Pensacola, Fla.
34. *Mke Bomar, lhp, Prairie HS, Brush Prairie, Wash.
35. Johnny Whitesides, rhp, Santa Fe (Fla.) CC.
36. *Jason Hubbard, lhp, White HS, Jacksonville, Fla.
37. *Cade Allison, rhp, Odessa (Texas) JC.
38. +Tim Godfrey, ss, Bacone (Okla.) JC.
39. *Brian Kennedy, c, North HS, Riverside, Calif.
40. *Luis Munne, c, Miami Springs HS, Hialeah, Fla.

## CLEVELAND INDIANS (27)

**1. Tim Drew, rhp, Lowndes County HS, Hahira, Ga.—(2000-04)**
DRAFT DROP *Brother of J.D. Drew, first-round draft pick, Phillies (1997); first-round draft pick, Cardinals (1998); major leaguer (1998-2011) • Brother of Stephen Drew, first-round draft pick, Diamondbacks (2004); major leaguer (2006-15)*
1. Jason Fitzgerald, of, Tulane University (Supplemental choice—41st—as compensation for Type A free agent Albert Belle).—(AAA)
2. Edgar Cruz, c, Vocational Tech, Juncos, P.R. (Choice from White Sox as compensation for Belle).—(AA)
2. Rob Vael, rhp, JC of Eastern Utah.—(AA)
3. Rob Pugmire, rhp, Cascade HS, Snohomish, Wash.—(AA)
4. Eric Thompson, of, Westover HS, Fayetteville, N.C.—(Short-season A)
5. Jon Hamilton, of-lhp, Ohlone (Calif.) JC.—(AAA)
6. Brian Benefield, 2b, Texas A&M University.
7. Mark Turnbow, rhp, Hardin County HS, Saltillo, Tenn.
8. Johnnie Wheeler, lhp, Connors State (Okla.) JC.
**9. Dustan Mohr, of, University of Alabama.—(2001-07)**
10. Joe Kilburg, 2b-of, Stanford University.
11. *Daniel Jahn, lhp, Franklin HS, Seattle.
12. *Brad Freeman, ss, Mississippi State University.
13. *Chad Hawkins, rhp, Navarro (Texas) JC.
DRAFT DROP *First-round draft pick (39th overall, Rangers (2000)*
14. Mike Hughes, lhp, St. John's University.
15. Tyler Swinburnson, rhp, Oregon State University.
16. *Denny New, lhp, Panola (Texas) JC.
**17. *Brian Shackelford, lhp, University of Oklahoma.—(2005-06)**
18. Troy Silva, rhp, Lewis-Clark State (Idaho) College.
19. *Devon Nicholson, rhp, Sacramento (Calif.) CC.
20. *Nicholas Waak, rhp, Chugiak (Alaska) HS.
21. Erick Rosa, c, Western Kentucky University.
22. Kelly Dampeer, ss, Radford University.
23. Heath Bender, 1b, University of Memphis.
24. *Reggie Nelson, ss, Mission Bay HS, San Diego.
25. Ryan Upshaw, of, New Mexico State University.
26. Chris Jackson, c, Mountain Brook (Ala.) HS.
27. Todd Harding, 2b, Lane (Ore.) CC.
28. *Derek Wigginton, of, Father Ryan HS, Antioch, Tenn.
29. *Courtney Hall, rhp, Meadowdale HS, Edmonds, Wash.
30. *Francis Paiso, lhp, Encinal HS, Alameda, Calif.
31. *Brandon Smith, 1b, Canyon HS, Anaheim, Calif.
32. *Jason Basil, c, St. Xavier HS, Westchester, Ohio.
33. *Anthony Jackson, of, Wilde Lake HS, Ellicott City, Md.
34. *Jon Rouwenhorst, lhp, Brethren Christian HS, Anaheim, Calif.
35. *Kris McWhirter, rhp, Davidson Academy, Goodlettsville, Tenn.
36. *Danny Borrell, lhp, Lee County HS, Sanford, N.C.
37. *Ryan Satterwhite, c, Tate HS, Cantonment, Fla.
38. *Austin Roberts, rhp, Elma (Wash.) HS.
39. *Brandon Wheeler, rhp, Hillsborough (Fla.) CC.
40. *Brandon Mauer, c, Lake Stevens HS, Everett, Wash.
41. *Brad Drummond, rhp, Liberty HS, Renton, Wash.
42. Ryan Haley, 2b, University of Central Oklahoma.
43. Danny Alvarez, rhp, Florida International University.
44. *Joey Cole, rhp, Howard (Texas) JC.
45. *Brian Seever, of, Sacramento (Calif.) CC.
46. *Jeff Parker, rhp, Martin HS, Arlington, Texas.
47. *Justin Hutton, c, Tyee HS, Tukwila, Wash.
48. *Mark Hamilton, lhp, Panola (Texas) JC.
49. *Richard Booth, of, Whiteville (N.C.) HS.
50. *Darnell Sanders, 1b, Warrensville HS, Twinsburg, Ohio.

## COLORADO ROCKIES (18)

1. Mark Mangum, rhp, Kingwood (Texas) HS.—AA)
**2. Aaron Cook, rhp, Hamilton (Ohio) HS.—(2002-12)**
**3. Todd Sears, 1b, University of Nebraska.—(2002-03)**
**4. Chone Figgins, ss, Brandon (Fla.) HS.—(2002-14)**
**5. Justin Miller, rhp, Los Angeles Harbor JC.—(2002-10)**
6. Sam Smith, ss, Jasper (Texas) HS.
7. Jake Kringen, lhp, University of Washington.
8. Jeremy Jackson, of, University of Arkansas.
9. D.J. Johnson, rhp, Kansas State University.
10. Derrick Vargas, lhp, Chabot (Calif.) JC.
11. Tino Sanchez, of, Luis Munoz Marin HS, Yauco, P.R.
12. Ryan Seifert, rhp, Iowa State University.
13. Roger Little, rhp, Perry Central HS, Hazard, Ky.
DRAFT DROP *Twin brother of Rodney Little, 15th-round draft pick, Rockies (1997)*
14. Jose Gonzales, c, Southeastern Louisiana University.
15. Rodney Little, rhp, Perry Central HS, Hazard, Ky.
DRAFT DROP *Twin brother of Roger Little, 13th-round draft pick, Rockies (1997)*
16. Jason Franklin, 3b, Cumberland (Tenn.) University.
17. Jerome Alviso, ss, Cal State Fullerton.
18. Ara Petrosian, rhp, Long Beach State University.
19. Michael Johns, ss, Tulane University.
**20. *Mark Woodyard, 1b, Grand Bay (Ala.) HS.—(2005)**
21. Armando Gonzalez, rhp, Cerritos (Calif.) JC.
22. *Kendall Rhodes, rhp, Angelina (Texas) JC.
23. *Jacob Minter, 1b, Blanchet HS, Edmonds, Wash.
24. +Melvin Rosario, of, Indian Hills (Iowa) CC.
25. *Trevor Kitsch, c, Kelowna (B.C.) SS.
26. *Jeremy Schultz, rhp, Mason City (Iowa) HS.
27. *Justin Lombardi, lhp, Coyle-Cassidy HS, Taunton, Mass.
28. *Rocky Kirk, lhp, Viewmont HS, Casper, Wyo.
29. *Dan Kelly, lhp, Okaloosa-Walton (Fla.) CC.
30. +J.J. Easter, of, Mount Union (Pa.) HS / Potomac State (W.Va.) CC.
31. *Brian Putnam, rhp, Indianola (Miss.) HS.
32. *Braxton Batson, lhp, Mississippi Gulf Coast JC.
33. +Cody Trask, rhp, Riverside (Calif.) CC.
34. *Mark Scates, of, Coeur D'Alene (Idaho) HS.
35. *James McCoy, of, Miami-Dade CC Kendall.
**36. *Alfredo Amezaga, ss, Miami Senior HS, Miami.—(2002-11)**
37. *Ronny Marmol, c, Southridge HS, Miami.
38. Ryan Price, rhp, Eastern New Mexico University.
39. *Walcott Richardson, of, Dracut (Mass.) HS.
40. *Brandon Roberson, rhp, Hill (Texas) JC.
41. *Yamilke Ulloa, lhp, Hialeah (Fla.) HS.
42. *Matt Ortiz, c, Grossmont (Calif.) JC.
43. *Shaun Wooley, lhp, Rancho Santiago (Calif.) JC.
44. *Chad Elliott, lhp, Rancho Santiago (Calif.) JC.
45. *Casey Lopez, 3b, Los Altos (Calif.) HS.
46. *Matt Thomas, rhp, Weatherford (Texas) HS.
47. *Bobby Bass, of, Livermore (Calif.) HS.

## DETROIT TIGERS (1)

**1. Matt Anderson, rhp, Rice University.—(1998-2005)**
**2. Shane Loux, rhp, Highland HS, Gilbert, Ariz.—(2002-12)**
3. Matt Boone, 3b, Villa Park (Calif.) HS.—High A)
DRAFT DROP *Grandson of Ray Boone, major leaguer (1948-60) • Son of Bob Boone, major leaguer (1972-90); major league manager (1995-2003) • Brother of Bret Boone, major leaguer (1992-2005) • Brother of Aaron Boone, major leaguer (1994-2009)*
4. Alan Webb, lhp, Durango HS, Las Vegas, Nev.—(AAA)
5. Heath Schesser, ss, Kansas State University.—(Low A)
6. Chris Parker, c, Westlake HS, Westlake Village, Calif.—(High A)
7. Mike Diebolt, lhp, University of Minnesota.
DRAFT DROP *Died as active player (Sept. 5, 1997)*
8. Dan Lauterhahn, 2b, William Paterson (N.J.) College.
**9. *Bud Smith, of-lhp, St. John Bosco HS, Lakewood, Calif.—(2001-02)**
10. Rick Roberts, lhp, Forest Hills HS, Summerhill, Pa.
11. +Leo Daigle, 1b, Monte Vista HS, Spring Valley, Calif. / Southwestern (Calif.) CC.
12. Darrell Pender, of, Miami Northwestern HS, Miami.
13. John Alkire, rhp, Cal State Fullerton.
14. Brennan Hervey, 1b, Florida Atlantic University.
15. Jason Howard, rhp, Purdue University.
16. Alex Steele, of, SUNY Cortland.
17. *Chris Curry, c, Meridian (Miss.) CC.
DRAFT DROP *Baseball coach, Arkansas-Little Rock (2015)*
18. Ryan Grimmett, of, University of Miami.
19. Jeremy Sassanella, c, DeKalb HS, Auburn, Ind.
20. Craig Johnson, rhp, Siena College.
21. Neil Alvarez, 1b, North Rockland HS, Haverstraw, N.Y.
22. Mandy Jacomino, of, University of Miami.
23. Kevin Mobley, rhp, Georgia College.
24. *Doyle Washington, of, Inglewood (Calif.) HS.
25. *Kelly Crosby, of, Wheaton Warrenville HS, Wheaton, Ill.
**26. Maxim St. Pierre, c, College de Levis HS, Montreal.—(2010)**
27. Bill Snyder, rhp, Rensselaer Polytechnic (N.Y.) Institute.
28. Jacob Schaffer, ss, Bradley University.
29. *Joseph Hall, of, Artesia HS, Lynwood, Calif.
30. Richard Ozarowski, ss, Florida Atlantic University.
31. *Scott Martines, 1b, Punahou HS, Honolulu, Hawaii.
32. +Steve Rodriguez, of, East Los Angeles JC.
33. Joel Greene, lhp, William Penn (Iowa) College.
34. John Guilmet, rhp, Merrimack (Mass.) College.
35. Matt Beck, rhp, Bradley University.
36. *Brian Cole, ss, Meridian (Miss.) HS.
DRAFT DROP *Died as active player (March 31, 2001)*
37. Antonio Hasbun, ss, Briarcliff (N.Y.) JC.
38. *Curtis Wickwire, 1b, Clovis West HS, Fresno, Calif.
39. Bernie Pedersoli, c, University of Illinois-Chicago.
40. Clark Parker, 2b, Cal State Northridge.
41. +Matthew Altagen, 1b, University HS, Malibu, Calif. / Los Angeles CC.
42. *Carlos Hernandez, rhp, Christopher Columbus HS, Bronx, N.Y.

## FLORIDA MARLINS (12)

1. Aaron Akin, rhp, Cowley County (Kan.) CC.—(High A)
**2. Jeff Bailey, c, Kelso (Wash.) HS.—(2007-09)**
**3. Chris Aguila, 3b, McQueen HS, Reno, Nev.—(2004-08)**
**4. Brandon Harper, c, Dallas Baptist University.—(2006)**
5. *Paul Avery, lhp, Fresno (Calif.) CC.—(High A)
DRAFT DROP *Attended Pepperdine; re-drafted by Dodgers, 1998 (15th round)*
6. Brian Reed, of, Green Valley HS, Henderson, Nev.
**7. Matt Erickson, 3b, University of Arkansas.—(2004)**
**8. *Cliff Lee, lhp, Benton (Ark.) HS.—(2002-14)**
9. Jon Heinrichs, of, UCLA.
10. Kelley Washington, ss, Shenandoah HS, Stephens City, Va.
DRAFT DROP *Wide receiver, National Football League (2003-10)*
11. Jesus Medrano, 2b, Bishop Amat HS, La Puente, Calif.
12. Javon Walker, of, St. Thomas More HS, Lafayette, La.
DRAFT DROP *First-round draft pick, Green Bay Packers, National Football League (2002); wide receiver, NFL (2002-09)*
**13. Ross Gload, 1b, University of South Florida.—(2000-11)**
14. Wes Anderson, rhp, Pine Bluff (Ark.) HS.
15. *Travis Bailey, ss, Palm Beach (Fla.) CC.
16. *James Shook, rhp, Columbia-Greene (N.Y.) CC.
17. Rhodney Donaldson, of, Troy State University.
18. Drew Shields, rhp, Pima (Ariz.) CC.
19. Robert Garvin, rhp, St. Andrew's Parish HS, Charleston, S.C.
20. *Howard Beard, of, Watkins HS, Laurel, Miss.
21. *Eric Bernhardt, rhp, Pittsburg (Kan.) HS.
22. Alex Melconian, c, Seton Hall University.
**23. *Andres Torres, of, Miami-Dade (Fla.) CC Wolfson.—(2002-13)**
24. *Jason Harrison, c, Allegany (Md.) CC.
25. Cory Lima, rhp, North Carolina A&T University.
26. Scott Henderson, rhp, University of Southern California.
27. Matt Schnabel, of-1b, Southwest Texas State University.
28. James McGowan, rhp, Queensborough (N.Y.) CC.
29. Blair Fowler, rhp, University of Washington.
30. Gaige Thomas, rhp, Brenham (Texas) HS.

31. *Jason Farmer, rhp, Indio (Calif.) HS.
32. *Bryant Hodges, rhp, Seminole County HS, Donaldsonville, Ga.
33. *Ronald Dorsey, of, Hammonton (N.J.) HS.
34. Chris Clark, of, University of Arkansas.
35. *Joshua Higgins, rhp, El Capitan HS, Santee, Calif.
36. +Antwoine Anderson, lhp, Withrow HS, Cincinnati / Columbia State (Tenn.) CC.
37. +Chris Louwsma, ss, Seminole HS, Sanford, Fla. / Seminole (Fla.) CC.
38. *Eric Absher, of, Howard (Texas) JC.
39. *Adam Spiker, 1b, Marina HS, Huntington Beach, Calif.
40. *Brad Weis, lhp, Chipola (Fla.) JC.
41. *Billy Nofsinger, rhp, King HS, Tampa.
42. *Nicholas Carlson, rhp, Madison (Wis.) Area Tech JC.
43. *Glenn Myers, lhp, South Charleston (W.Va.) HS.
44. *Steve Elzy, c, Cochise County (Ariz.) CC.
45. *Jimmy Barndollar, rhp, Pacifica HS, Garden Grove, Calif.
46. *Michael Wenger, lhp, Potomac State (W.Va.) JC.
47. *Michael Shumaker, 1b, Meyersdale (Pa.) Area HS.
48. *Aaron Lough, c, Potomac State (W.Va.) JC.
49. *Michael Nall, rhp, Schaumburg (Ill.) HS.
50. *Kyle Jenkins, rhp, Deptford HS, Woodbury, N.J.
51. *Frank Valois, of, Montgomery (Md.) JC.
52. *Tim Strange, c, Eau Gallie HS, Melbourne, Fla.
53. *Brian Middleton, rhp, Woodbury (N.J.) HS.
54. *Adrian Earles, of, Austin East HS, Knoxville, Tenn.
55. *Nicholas Huntsman, rhp, Pleasant Grove (Utah) HS.
56. *William Baber, 3b, Western Albemarle HS, Crozet, Va.
57. *Michael Kalchuk, rhp, Broward (Fla.) CC.
58. *Carl Lafferty, c, Pine Bluff (Ariz.) HS.

## HOUSTON ASTROS (16)

**1. Lance Berkman, 1b, Rice University.—(1999-2013)**
2. Camron Hahn, c, Male HS, Louisville.—(Rookie)
3. *Scott Barrett, lhp, Mayde Creek HS, Houston.—(Short-season A)
DRAFT DROP *Attended San Jacinto (Texas) JC; re-drafted by Astros, 1998 (5th round)*
**4. *Eric Byrnes, of, UCLA.—(2000-10)**
DRAFT DROP *Returned to UCLA; re-drafted by Athletics, 1998 (8th round)*
5. +Derek Stanford, rhp, Temple (Texas) HS / McLennan (Texas) CC.—(Low A)
6. Joe Messman, rhp, Oregon State University.
7. Rob Bystrowski, of, Sacramento (Calif.) CC.
8. Ryan Dunn, of, Texas Christian University.
9. Don Thomas, lhp, Kennesaw State (Ga.) College.
10. *Scott Fredericks, rhp, Saguaro HS, Scottsdale, Ariz.
11. *Javier Pamus, rhp, San Jose State University.
12. Peter Sullivan, rhp, Limestone (S.C.) College.
13. *Barton Leahy, of, Ohio University.
**14. *Trey Hodges, rhp, Blinn (Texas) JC.—(2002-03)**
15. J.J. Thomas, 1b, Georgia Tech.
16. Jim Wallace, rhp, University of North Carolina.
17. Pat Cutshall, ss, Mercyhurst (Pa.) College.
18. *Simon Mitchell, of, West Seattle HS, Seattle.
19. Brian Hecht, rhp, University of Illinois.
**20. +Tim Redding, rhp, Monroe (N.Y.) CC.—(2001-09)**
21. *Neal Maybin, of, Lake Howell HS, Casselberry, Fla.
**22. Jason Alfaro, rhp, Hill (Texas) JC.—(2004)**
23. Kyle Logan, of-3b, University of Southern Mississippi.
24. *Tim Judd, rhp, Dixon (Calif.) HS.
**25. *Charlton Jimerson, of, Mount Eden HS, Hayward, Calif.—(2006-08)**
26. *Jared Wood, rhp, St. Louis CC-Meramec.
27. *Derek Brewster, rhp, Carthage (Texas) HS.
28. *Graham Travis, rhp, Ballard HS, Seattle.
29. Joe Cathey, ss, Rice University.
30. *Chris Ross, rhp, Ringgold (Ga.) HS.
31. *Kris Clute, ss, Killian HS, Miami.
32. *Eric Armbruster, 1b, Central HS, Kalamazoo, Mich.
33. *Lamont Matthews, of, Kishwaukee (Ill.) JC.
34. *John Skinner, rhp, Chabot (Calif.) JC.

Lance Berkman quickly became a fixture in Houston and compiled 1,905 major league hits

35. *Kevin Marzion, rhp, Elk Grove (Calif.) HS.
36. *Jason Dill, 1b, Charlotte HS, Punta Gorda, Fla.
37. *Jerymane Beasley, of, Olympic (Wash.) JC.
38. *John Colon, rhp, Molokai HS, Maunaloa, Hawaii.
39. *Marcos Rios, c, Chabot (Calif.) JC.
40. *Garreth Perry, c, Service HS, Anchorage, Alaska.

## KANSAS CITY ROYALS (7)

**1. Dan Reichert, rhp, University of the Pacific.—(1999-2003)**
**2. *Dane Sardinha, c, Kamehameha HS, Kahuku, Hawaii.—(2003-11)**
DRAFT DROP *Attended Pepperdine; re-drafted by Reds, 2000 (2nd round)*
**3. Jeremy Affeldt, lhp, Northwest Christian HS, Spokane, Wash.—(2002-15)**
4. Goefrey Tomlinson, of, University of Houston.—(AAA)
5. Jason Gooding, lhp, Texas Tech.—(AAA)
**6. *Jason Anderson, rhp, Danville (Ill.) HS.—(2003-05)**
DRAFT DROP *Baseball coach, Eastern Illinois (2013-15)*
**7. Joe Dillon, 1b, Texas Tech.—(2005-09)**
8. Eric Yanz, rhp, Kansas State University.
**9. Kris Wilson, rhp, Georgia Tech.—(2000-06)**
10. David Willis, 1b, UC Santa Barbara.
11. Joe Caruso, 2b, University of Alabama.
**12. Jason Gilfillan, rhp, Limestone (S.C.) College.—(2003)**
13. Ryan Douglass, rhp, Canevin Catholic HS, Pittsburgh.
14. Tony Mancha, rhp, Las Cruces (N.M.) HS.
15. Justin Pederson, rhp, University of Minnesota.
16. *Rolando Geigel, rhp, Georgina Vaquero HS, Canovanas, P.R.
17. Justin Lamber, lhp, University of Richmond.
18. *Bruce Stanley, rhp, Ball State University.
19. Tarik Graham, of, Edgewater HS, Orlando, Fla.
20. Carlos Pagan, c, University of Mobile (Ala.).
21. Rod Metzler, 2b, Purdue University.
22. James Woods, c, Muskegon (Mich.) HS.
23. Rickey Crutchley, lhp, Etowah HS, Acworth, Ga.
24. Rashad Tillis, of, Lurleen B. Wallace State (Ala.) CC.
25. *Ryan Hutchison, rhp, Vincennes (Ind.) HS.
26. *Michael Perkins, rhp, Charlotte HS, Punta Gorda, Fla.
27. *Fontella Jones, rhp, Mississippi Gulf Coast JC.
28. Aaron Carter, rhp, St. Mary's (Texas) University.
29. David Ullery, c, Indiana State University.
30. *Robert Balazentis, rhp, Mercyhurst (Pa.) College.
31. *George Petticrew, rhp, Lakeside HS, Nine Mile, Wash.
32. +Kyle Turner, lhp, Antioch (Calif.) HS / Los Medanos (Calif.) CC.
33. *Nelson Bellido, rhp, Brooklyn, N.Y.
34. *Freddie Fincher, c, Galveston (Texas) JC.
35. *John Hale, rhp, Robert E. Lee HS, Midland, Texas.
36. *Donny Davis, rhp, El Cerrito HS, San Pablo, Calif.
37. *John Majors, rhp, Flomaton HS, Brewton, Ala.
38. *John Raymer, rhp, West Orange-Stark HS, Orange, Texas.
39. *Aaron Melebeck, ss, Galveston (Texas) JC.
40. *Kendall Thomas, c, Gloucester County (N.J.) JC.
**41. *Chris Sampson, ss-rhp, Lon Morris (Texas) JC.—(2006-10)**
42. *Chris Tallman, of, Rancho Santiago (Calif.) JC.
43. *Quentin Elder, rhp, Castlemont HS, Oakland.
44. *Daniel Martinez, lhp, Sweetwater HS, National City, Calif.
45. *Bret Halbert, lhp, Cypress (Calif.) JC.
46. *Gary Schulz, lhp, Montgomery (Texas) HS.
47. *Mark Villarreal, c, John Foster Dulles HS, Missouri City, Texas.
48. *Matthew Williams, 3b, Millikan HS, Long Beach, Calif.
49. *Carlos Spikes, of, North Florida Christian HS, Tallahassee, Fla.

## LOS ANGELES DODGERS (24)

1. Glenn Davis, 1b, Vanderbilt University.—(AA)
DRAFT DROP *Brother of Ben Davis, first-round draft pick, Padres (1995); major leaguer (1998-2004)*
**2. *Chase Utley, ss, Poly HS, Long Beach, Calif.—(2003-15)**
DRAFT DROP *Attended UCLA; re-drafted by Phillies, 2000 (1st round)*
**2. +Steve Colyer, lhp, Fort Zumwalt South HS, St. Peters, Mo. / St. Louis CC-Meramec** (Supplemental choice—83rd—as compensation for Type C free agent Delino DeShields).—**(2003-07)**
3. Ricky Bell, ss, Moeller HS, Cincinnati.—(AAA)
DRAFT DROP *Grandson of Gus Bell, major leaguer (1950-64) • Son of Buddy Bell, major leaguer (1972-89); major league manager (1996-2007) • Brother of David Bell, major leaguer (1995-2006) • Brother of Mike Bell, major leaguer (2000)*
4. John Hernandez, c, Nogales HS, La Puente, Calif.—(AAA)
5. Kip Harkrider, ss, University of Texas.—(AA)
6. Will McCrotty, c, Russellville (Ark.) HS.
DRAFT DROP *Twin brother of Wes McCrotty, 21st-round draft pick, Cardinals (1997)*
7. *Miles Durham, of, Cooper HS, Abilene, Texas.
8. Beau Parker, rhp, Prairie HS, Brush Prairie, Wash.
9. Jamie Goudie, ss, Hardaway HS, Columbus, Ga.
10. Joe Patterson, of, Ontario (Calif.) HS.
**11. *Cory Vance, lhp, Butler HS, Vandalia, Ohio.—(2002-03)**
12. *David Lamberth, ss, Macon County HS, Montezuma, Ga.
13. Matt Bornyk, rhp, Esquimalt HS, Victoria, B.C.
14. Brent Husted, rhp, University of Nevada-Reno.
15. *David Mittauer, rhp, Dade Christian HS, Cooper City, Fla.
16. *Scott Walter, c, Loyola HS, Manhattan Beach, Calif.
17. *Chad Cislak, rhp, Sabino HS, Tucson, Ariz.
18. Michael Balbuena, 3b, Key West (Fla.) HS.
19. Shane Allen, of, Glenns Ferry (Idaho) HS.
20. Peter Zamora, 1b-lhp, UCLA.
21. Stephen Verigood, lhp, Spartanburg Methodist (S.C.) JC.
22. Matt Montgomery, rhp, Long Beach State University.
23. Jared Moon, rhp, Redondo Union HS, Redondo Beach, Calif.
24. Michael Rawls, lhp, Bethune-Cookman College.
25. +David Detienne, 3b, Auburn Drive HS, Dartmouth, Nova Scotia / Indian River (Fla.) CC.
26. Bill Everly, rhp, West Virginia Wesleyan College.
27. Aaron Dean, 1b, Lamar University.
28. Richard Bell, lhp, California Lutheran University.
29. Darin Schmalz, rhp, University of Notre Dame.
30. *Sam Lopez, ss, Dinuba (Calif.) HS.
31. Wayne Slater, of, Bethune-Cookman College.
32. *Shaylar Hatch, rhp, Gilbert, Ariz.
33. *Shaun Benzor, lhp, Redlands (Calif.) HS.
34. *Blake McGinley, lhp, North HS, Bakersfield, Calif.
35. *Adam Thomas, of, Hazel Park HS, Troy, Mich.
**36. +Jesus Feliciano, of, Academia Discipulos de Cristo HS, Bayamon, P.R. / Miami-Dade JC.—(2010)**
37. *Tyler Renwick, rhp, New Mexico JC.
38. *Eliot Joyner, of, Mount San Antonio (Calif.) JC.
39. *Jahseam George, lhp, Buchanan HS, Clovis, Calif.
**40. *John Nelson, ss, Denton (Texas) HS.—(2006)**
41. *Ryan Beaver, rhp, Millikan HS, Long Beach, Calif.
42. Carlos Orozco, of, Montgomery HS, San Diego.
43, *Michael Hernandez, lhp, Carson (Calif.) HS.
44. *Graig Merritt, c, JC of Southern Idaho.
**45. *Shane Youman, lhp, New Iberia (La.) HS.—(2006-07)**
46. +Ryan Kellner, c, Spartanburg Methodist (S.C.) JC.
47. *Jean Emard, lhp, Edouard Montpetit HS, Montreal.
48. *Luis DeJesus, c, Miguel De Cervantes HS, Bayamon, P.R.
49. Lance Warren, c, Richmond Hill (Ga.) HS.
50. *Chris Howay, rhp, New Westminster (B.C.) HS.
51. *Eric Burris, 1b, Los Angeles Harbor JC.
52. *Russell Ivory, of, Grossmont (Calif.) JC.
53. +Ismael Garcia, 2b, Mount San Antonio (Calif.) JC.
54. *Michael Ford, of, Elk Grove (Calif.) HS.
55. *Melvin Anderson, 3b, North Iberville HS, Baton Rouge, La.
56. *Reggie Laplante, rhp, Edouard Montpetit HS,

Montreal.
57. *George Bailey, 3b, Indian River (Fla.) CC.
58. *James Howard, rhp, Orange Park, Fla.
59. *Joshua Ridgway, ss, Delta SS, Ladner, B.C.
60. *Jason Ware, 1b, Long Beach (Calif.) CC.
61. *Javier Gonzalez, rhp, Mount San Antonio (Calif.) JC.
**62. *Steve Holm, ss, McClatchy HS, Sacramento, Calif.—(2008-11)**
63. +Cedric Hebert, rhp, Grayson County (Texas) JC.
64. *Jeremy Loftice, rhp, Truett McConnell (Ga.) JC.
65. *Luis Fontanez, c, Juana Colon HS, Bayamon, P.R.
66. +John Castellano, c, Indian River (Fla.) CC.
67. *Cory Stephen, c, Martin Collegiate HS, Regina, Sask.
68. *Matt Ybarra, c, Encinal HS, Alameda, Calif.
69. Luis Medina, c, Pedro P. Casa Blanca HS, Bayamon, P.R.
70. *Ryan Withey, of, Seminole (Fla.) CC.

## MILWAUKEE BREWERS (13)

**1. Kyle Peterson, rhp, Stanford University.—(1999-2001)**
2. Alvin Morrow, of, Kirkwood (Mo.) HS.—(High A)
3. Jeff Deardorff, 3b, South Lake HS, Clermont, Fla.—(AAA)
4. Tommy Warren, of, Westchester HS, Inglewood, Calif.—(Rookie)
5. Frank Candela, of, Peabody (Mass.) HS.—(Low A)
6. Jake Eye, rhp, Ohio University.
**7. Bucky Jacobsen, of, Lewis-Clark State (Idaho) College.—(2004)**
8. Todd Incantalupo, lhp, Providence College.
**9. Matt Childers, rhp, Westside HS, Augusta, Ga.—(2002-05)**
DRAFT DROP *Brother of Jason Childers, major leaguer (2006)*
10. Chris Patten, ss, McClintock HS, Tempe, Ariz.
11. Jim Miller, rhp, Carthage (Wis.) College.
12. Kendal Guthrie, c, Northwood (Texas) Institute.
13. *Brent Kelley, rhp, Arkansas State University.
14. Chris Rowan, 3b, Mount Vernon (N.Y.) HS.
15. *Romaro Miller, ss, Shannon (Miss.) HS.
DRAFT DROP *Quarterback, National Football League (2001)*
16. Andy Cavanagh, rhp, Young Harris (Ga.) JC.
17. Mark Kirst, rhp, St. Norbert's (Wis.) College.
18. Jay Akin, lhp, Arkansas State University.
19. Shane Wooten, lhp, Birmingham-Southern College.
**20. Doug Clark, of, University of Massachusetts.—(2005-06)**
21. +Mark Cridland, of, University of Texas.
**22. *Charlie Manning, lhp, Winter Haven (Fla.) HS.—(2008)**
23. Kevin Priebe, lhp, Bradley University.
24. *Robbie Baker, rhp, Blinn (Texas) JC.
25. Steve Beller, rhp, West Virginia University.
26. Trad Sokol, lhp, Frederick (Md.) CC.
**27. Brian Mallette, rhp, Columbus (Ga.) College.—(2002)**
28. Marty Patterson, c, Michigan State University.
29. *Al Corbeil, c, Plantation HS, Margate, Fla.
30. *Brian Fields, lhp, East Carolina University.
31. Chauncey Jones, rhp, Briar Cliff (Iowa) College.
32. +Gary McConnell, rhp, North Florida CC.
33. *Arthur Garland, of-rhp, Magnolia HS, Anaheim, Calif.
34. *James Igo, rhp, Galveston (Texas) JC.
35. *Ryan Costello, lhp, Eastern HS, Voorhees, N.J.
36. Chad Helmer, rhp, Florida Southern College.
37. *Landon Jacobsen, rhp, Howard HS, Canova, S.D.
38. *Randy Rodriguez, lhp, Indian River (Fla.) CC.
39. Joel Arroyo, rhp, St. Leo (Fla.) College.
40. Bob Riggio, 3b, Lehman (N.Y.) College.
**41. *Geoff Geary, rhp, University of Oklahoma.—(2003-07)**
42. *Justin Ames, lhp, Moorpark (Calif.) HS.
43. Ryan Pearson, of, Troy State University.
44. *Marcus Quinones, rhp, Lee (Texas) JC.
45. Nick Caiazzo, c, University of Maine.
46. *Eric Tomlinson, of, Granbury (Texas) HS.
47. *Jeff Savage, rhp, Palm Beach Gardens (Fla.) HS.
48. *Oscar Ramirez, ss, Southridge HS, Miami.
49. *Nick Quinn, of, Atlantic HS, Boynton Beach, Fla.
50. *Jimmy Smith, of, Lake Mary HS, Longwood, Fla.
51. *Jose Camilo, 2b, North Florida CC.
52. *Michael Oiler, ss, Watertown (Wis.) HS.
53. *Bennie Harris, of, Myers Park HS, Charlotte, N.C.

## MINNESOTA TWINS (9)

**1. Michael Cuddyer, ss, Great Bridge HS, Chesapeake, Va.—(2001-15)**
**1. Matthew LeCroy, c, Clemson University** (Supplemental choice—50th—for failure to sign 1996 first-round draft pick Travis Lee).—**(2000-07)**
**2. Michael Restovich, of, Mayo HS, Rochester, Minn.—(2002-07)**
3. *Greg Withelder, lhp, Strath Haven HS, Wallingford, Pa.—(High A)
DRAFT DROP *Attended Virginia; re-drafted by Dodgers, 2000 (6th round)*
4. Bob Davies, lhp, Marietta (Ohio) College.—(High A)
5. Peter Blake, lhp, Indianola (Iowa) HS.—(Low A)
DRAFT DROP *Brother of Casey Blake, major leaguer (1999-2011)*
6. Nate Melson, rhp, Rogers (Ark.) HS.
7. Matt Carnes, rhp, University of Arkansas.
8. Ben Thomas, lhp, Wichita State University.
9. Jon Schaeffer, c, Stanford University.
10. Josh Gandy, lhp, University of Georgia.
11. Matt Jurgena, rhp, Hastings (Neb.) College.
12. Lateef Vaughn, ss, Long Beach State University.
13. DeShawn Southward, of, Pasco Comprehensive HS, Dade City, Fla.
14. *Eddy Furniss, 1b, Louisiana State University.
15. *Jake Weber, of, North Carolina State University.
16. *Jordan Gerk, lhp, KLO SS, Kelowna, B.C.
**17. *Kevin Frederick, rhp-3b, Creighton University.—(2002-04)**
18. Ray Underhill, rhp, Deland (Fla.) HS.
19. *Kevin Stuart, rhp, Golden West (Calif.) JC.
20. Billy Coleman, rhp, Western Michigan University.
**21. J.C. Romero, lhp, University of Mobile (Ala.).—(1999-2012)**
22. *Daniel Boyd, 3b, Pasco Comprehensive HS, Dade City, Fla.
23. Tim Sturdy, rhp, La Cueva HS, Albuquerque, N.M.
24. *Creston Whitaker, of, Jesuit Collegiate HS, Dallas.
**25. *Adam Johnson, rhp, Torrey Pines HS, San Diego.—(2001-03)**
DRAFT DROP *First-round draft pick (2nd overall), Twins (2000)*
26. *Dan Morris, lhp, Ayersville HS, Defiance, Ohio.
27. *Daylan Holt, of, Mesquite (Texas) HS.
28. *David Shank, rhp, Miramonte HS, Orinda, Calif.
29. Aaron Jaworowski, 1b, University of Missouri.
30. Tony Stevens, ss, Keystone (Fla.) HS.
31. Mike Cosgrove, rhp, University of Tennessee.
32. *Trevor Mote, ss, Kingman (Ariz.) HS.
**33. *Nick Punto, ss, Saddleback (Calif.) CC.—(2001-14)**
34. *Marques Tuiasosopo, 3b, Woodinville (Wash.) HS.
DRAFT DROP *Quarterback, National Football League (2001-08) • Son of Manu Tuiasosopo, defensive end, National Football League (1979-86) • Brother of Matt Tuiasosopo, major leaguer (2008-13)*
35. *Craig Hawkins, rhp, Notre Dame HS, Burlington, Ontario.
36. Brian Fitts, rhp, Volunteer State (Tenn.) CC.
37. Pat Stenger, rhp, St. Ignatius HS, Mentor, Ohio.
38. Bryant Melson, c, University of North Florida.
39. *Isaiah Haynes, of, Vanden HS, Fairfield, Calif.
40. *Casey Fuller, lhp, Dixon (Calif.) HS.
41. *Corey Richardson, of, Northeast Texas CC.
42. *Russell Bratton, rhp, University of Memphis.
43. *Justin Smith, lhp, Seward County (Kan.) CC.
44. *Josh Reese, rhp, Lincoln County HS, Fayetteville, Tenn.
45. *Matt Booth, lhp, Henry Clay HS, Lexington, Ky.
46. Aaron Miller, lhp, Campbell University.
47. Joe Foote, rhp, Park View HS, Sterling, Va.
48. Jason McConnell, 2b, University of Arkansas.
49. *David Justice, ss, Washington HS, Pensacola, Fla.
50. *Tagg Bozied, c, Arvada West HS, Arvada, Colo.
51. *Clint Bailey, rhp, Chemainus, B.C.
52. *Richard Durrett, 1b, El Paso (Texas) CC.
53. *Shawn Stiffler, lhp, Somerset (Pa.) HS.
DRAFT DROP *Baseball coach, Virginia Commonwealth (2013-15)*

## MONTREAL EXPOS (22)

1. Donnie Bridges, rhp, Oak Grove HS, Hattiesburg, Miss.—(AAA)
1. Chris Stowe, rhp, Chancellor HS, Fredericksburg, Va. (Supplemental choice—37th—as compensation for loss of service-time free agent Mel Rojas).—(Rookie)
1. Scott Hodges, ss, Henry Clay HS, Lexington, Ky. (Supplemental choice—38th—as compensation for loss of service-time free agent Moises Alou).—(AAA)
**1. Bryan Hebson, rhp, Auburn University** (Supplemental choice—44th—as compensation for Rojas).—**(2003)**
1. Thomas Pittman, 1b, East St. John HS, Garyville, La. (Supplemental choice—45th—as compensation for Alou).—(High A)
**1. T.J. Tucker, rhp, River Ridge HS, New Port Richey, Fla.** (Supplemental choice—47th—as compensation for Rojas).—**(2000-05)**
1. Shane Arthurs, rhp, Westmoore HS, Oklahoma City (Supplemental choice—48th—as compensation for Alou).—(AA)
1. Tootie Myers, of, Petal (Miss.) HS (Supplemental choice—52nd—for failure to sign 1996 first-round draft pick John Patterson).—(AA)
2. Kris Tetz, rhp, Lodi (Calif.) HS.—(High A)
3. Josh Reding, ss, Rancho Santiago (Calif.) JC.—(AAA)
4. *Ronte Langs, of, Whitehaven HS, Memphis, Tenn.—(High A)
DRAFT DROP *Attended Gulf Coast (Fla.) CC; re-drafted by Angels, 1998 (30th round)*
5. Julio Perez, rhp, Brito Private HS, Miami.—(High A)
6. Scott Ackerman, c, Oregon City (Ore.) HS.
7. Anthony Caracciolo, ss, Basic HS, Henderson, Nev.
8. Ryan Becks, lhp, West Valley (Calif.) JC.
**9. Talmadge Nunnari, 1b, Jacksonville University.—(2000)**
**10. Scott Strickland, rhp, University of New Mexico.—(1999-2010)**
**11. Matt Blank, lhp, Texas A&M University.—(2000-01)**
12. Ryan Van Gilder, rhp, Mankato State (Minn.) University.
13. Luis Rivera, c, Florida Southern College.
14. Scott Zech, 2b, Florida State University.
15. Lance Burkhart, c-3b, Southwest Missouri State University.
DRAFT DROP *Brother of Morgan Burkhart, major leaguer (2000-03)*
16. Ryan Saylor, rhp, Eastern Kentucky University.
17. *Spencer Nemer, rhp, Klein Forest HS, Houston.
18. *Josh Merrigan, lhp, Vermillion (S.D.) HS.
19. *Jonathan Boyett, 2b, Modesto (Calif.) JC.
20. *Marcus Bell, rhp, Pace (Fla.) HS.
21. Ray Plummer, lhp, Point Loma Nazarene (Calif.) College.
22. Michael Edge, of, North Brunswick HS, Winnabow, N.C.
23. *Matt Coleman, lhp, Centennial HS, Boring, Ore.
24. Tobin Lanzetta, rhp, Santa Clara University.
25. *Shaun Poole, lhp, Hudson HS, Spring Hill, Fla.
26. *Jim Harrelson, rhp, Davis HS, Modesto, Calif.
27. *Jason Hoffman, of, Ohlone (Calif.) JC.
28. Joe Fretwell, rhp, Valencia (Fla.) CC.
29. *Nathan Cook, 3b, Chabot (Calif.) JC.
30. *Derek Smith, ss, Tulare Union HS, Tulare, Calif.
31. *Jeff Lincoln, rhp, American River (Calif.) JC.
32. *Cory Vandegriff, ss, Halls HS, Knoxville, Tenn.
33. *Brandt Hayden, ss, South Salem HS, Salem, Ore.
34. +Joe Baldassano, rhp, Alta Loma (Calif.) HS / Riverside (Calif.) CC.
35. *Arthur Anderson, ss, East St. John HS, La Place, La.
36. *Sam Anderson, c, Mesquite (Texas) HS.
37. *David Vonah, 3b, Hoover HS, Fresno, Calif.
38. *Edwin Gomez, of, Teodoro Aguilar Mora HS, Yabucoa, P.R.
39. *James McKnight, c, Washington HS, Phoenix.
40. John White, c, Jacksonville University.
41. *Luis Martinez, c, Jose Campeche HS, San Lorenzo, P.R.
42. *Kevin Harmon, c, Palmdale HS, Acton, Calif.
43. *Josh Laidlaw, of, Cheyenne HS, North Las Vegas, Nev.
44. *Matthew Baird, of, North Central Texas JC.
45. *Mechel Elam, of, Eisenhower HS, San Bernardino, Calif.
46. *Brian Oxley, ss, Los Medanos (Calif.) JC.
47. *Matthew Cody, c, Woodlawn HS, Baton Rouge, La.
48. *Chris Herman, ss, South Hills HS, Covina, Calif.
49. *Dean Harper, c, Peoria, Ariz.

## NEW YORK METS (6)

1. Geoff Goetz, lhp, Jesuit HS, Tampa.—(AA)
**2. Tyler Walker, rhp, University of California.—(2002-10)**
**3. Cesar Crespo, ss, Notre Dame HS, Caguas, P.R.—(2001-04)**
DRAFT DROP *Brother of Felipe Crespo, major leaguer (1996-2001)*
4. Michael Yancy, of, Morse HS, San Diego.—(Low A)
5. Brian Jenkins, c, Port St. Joe (Fla.) HS.—(AA)
6. Matt Lowe, rhp, Walhalla (S.C.) HS.
7. Robert Weslowski, rhp, Marcellus Central HS, Marcellus, N.Y.
8. Vicente Rosario, of, George Washington HS, New York.
9. Kenny Miller, ss, University of Kentucky.
**10. *Garrett Atkins, 3b, University HS, Irvine, Calif.—(2003-10)**
11. John Mangieri, rhp, St. Francis (N.Y.) College.
12. Nick Maness, rhp, North Moore HS, Robbins, N.C.
**13. Eric Cammack, rhp, Lamar University.—(2000)**
14. *Craig Kuzmic, c, Cypress (Calif.) JC.
**15. *Jeremy Guthrie, rhp, Ashland (Ore.) HS.—(2004-15)**
DRAFT DROP *First-round draft pick (22nd overall), Indians (2002)*
16. Mark Proctor, ss, Courtland HS, Fredericksburg, Va.
17. Bobby Hill, ss, Gainesville HS, Waldo, Fla.
18. *Dominic Rich, 2b, Line Mountain HS, Herndon, Pa.
19. Nick Rains, of, John Carroll HS, Fort Pierce, Fla.
**20. Jason Roach, rhp-3b, University of North Carolina-Wilmington.—(2003)**
21. Jason Brett, ss, South Georgia JC.
22. *Marcellus Presley, of, Hiram Johnson HS, Sacramento, Calif.
23. *Seth Davidson, ss, University HS, San Diego.
**24. Jason Phillips, c, San Diego State University.—(2001-07)**
25. *Brandon Mayfield, rhp, Jefferson State (Ala.) CC.
26. J.D. Arteaga, lhp, University of Miami.
27. *Matt Ardizzone, 2b, University of Delaware.
28. *Anthony Brown, of, Alexis DuPont HS, Hockessin, Del.
29. Jose Rio-Berger, of, Lewis-Clark State (Idaho) College.
30. Jason Shuck, ss, Carl Albert State (Okla.) JC.
DRAFT DROP *Great nephew of Mickey Mantle, major leaguer (1951-68)*
31. Randy Hamilton, lhp, Northern Kentucky University.
32. Jorge Santiago, ss, Marist College.
33. Shaun Mikkola, rhp, Largo (Fla.) HS.
34. *Barry Paulk, of, Southridge HS, Miami.
35. *Miguel Miranda, ss, Academy HS, Rio Piedras, P.R.
36. *Greg White, 1b, James Madison University.
DRAFT DROP *Brother of Matt White, first-round draft pick, Giants (1996)*
**37. *Brandon Lyon, rhp, Taylorsville HS, Salt Lake City.—(2001-13)**
38. *Barry Wichert, lhp, Seminole State (Okla.) JC.
39. *Robert Scott, 2b, Cowley County (Kan.) CC.
**40. *Randy Keisler, lhp, Navarro (Texas) JC.—(2000-07)**
41. *David Benham, c, Liberty University.
42. David Lohrman, rhp, Rensselaer Polytechnic (N.Y.) Institute.
**43. *David DeJesus, of, Manalapan (N.J.) HS.—(2003-15)**
44. *Kevin Zaug, rhp, Carmel HS, Stormville, N.Y.
45. Tony Valentine, 2b, University of New

Hampshire.

DRAFT DROP *Son of Bobby Valentine, first-round draft pick, Dodgers (1968); major leaguer (1971-79); major league manager (1985-2012)*

46. Jason Bowring, 3b, Riverside (Calif.) CC.
47. *Tanner Brock, rhp, Lake Brantley HS, Altamonte Springs, Fla.
48. *Matt Whitehead, rhp, Athens (Texas) HS.
49. *Jeremy Jackson, lhp, Mississippi State University.
50. Mark Maberry, rhp, Tennessee Tech.
51. *Elvin Cannon, of, Northland HS, Columbus, Ohio.
**52. *Mike Tonis, c, Elk Grove (Calif.) HS.—(2004)**
53. Mathias Fafard, 3b, Indian River (Fla.) CC.
54. *Anthony Sutter, ss, Brookdale (N.J.) CC.
55. *Brian Kuklick, rhp, Wake Forest University.
56. Joshua Taylor, ss, Cowley County (Kan.) CC.
57. Clark Lambert, c, Lipscomb (Tenn.) University.
58. *Ryan Lamattina, lhp, St. Bonaventure University.

## NEW YORK YANKEES (25)

1. *Tyrell Godwin, of, East Bladen HS, Elizabethtown, N.C. (Choice from Rangers as compensation for Type A free agent John Wetteland).—(2005)

DRAFT DROP *Attended North Carolina; re-drafted by Rangers, 2000 (1st round)*

1. (Choice to Orioles as compensation for Type A free agent David Wells)
**1. Ryan Bradley, rhp, Arizona State University** (Supplemental choice—40th—as compensation for Wetteland).**—(1998)**
2. (Choice to Rangers as compensation for Type A free agent Mike Stanton)
2. Jason Henry, rhp, University of Illinois-Chicago (Supplemental choice—84th—as compensation for Type C free agent Jimmy Key).—(Short-season A)
3. Mike Knowles, rhp, Palatka (Fla.) HS.—(AA)
4. Dion Washington, of, JC of Southern Idaho.—(High A)
**5. Randy Choate, lhp, Florida State University.—(2000-15)**
6. John Darjean, of, Dallas Baptist University.
**7. Scott Wiggins, lhp, Northern Kentucky University.—(2002)**
8. Jeremy Morris, of, Florida State University.
**9. Randy Flores, lhp, University of Southern California.—(2002-10)**

DRAFT DROP *Scouting director, Cardinals (2015) • Brother of Ron Flores, major leaguer (2005-07)*

10. *David Parrish, c, Esperanza HS, Yorba Linda, Calif.

DRAFT DROP *First-round draft pick (28th overall), Yankees (2000) • Son of Lance Parrish, major leaguer (1977-95)*

11. Cody Klein, lhp, Andrews (Texas) HS.
12. *Ernie Villegas, of, Irving (Texas) HS.
**13. *Brian Tallet, lhp, Hill (Texas) JC.—(2002-11)**
14. Chris Wallace, rhp, Wright State University.
15. Marc Mirizzi, ss, University of Southern California.
16. Matt Purkiss, 3b, University of San Francisco.
17. *Albert Jones, of, Pasco Comprehensive HS, Dade City, Fla.
18. Brian August, 3b, University of Delaware.
19. *Michael Shelley, lhp, Ashford (Ala.) HS.
20. *Paul Manning, of, Hunting Hills HS, Red Deer, Alberta.

DRAFT DROP *Third-round draft pick, Calgary Flames, National Hockey League (1998); defenseman, NHL (2002-03)*

21. Bill Bronikowski, c, University of Toledo.
22. *Beau Hale, rhp, Little Cypress HS, Mauriceville, Texas.

DRAFT DROP *First-round draft pick (14th overall), Orioles (2000)*

23. Mike Langston, rhp, Ringgold (Ga.) HS.
24. Jack Koch, rhp, University of Tampa.
25. Stanton Wood, rhp, El Camino (Calif.) JC.
26. Aaron Jones, 1b, Southern Illinois University.
27. *Robert Fischer, ss, Lyons Township HS, LaGrange, Ill.
28. *Adam Huddleston, 1b, Mississippi Gulf Coast JC.
29. *Matt Vincent, lhp, John A. Logan (Ill.) JC.
30. +Keith Dunn, rhp, Grayson County (Texas) JC.
31. *Digno Torres, of, Jaime Collazo HS, Morovis, P.R.
32. *Brandon Davis, c, George County HS, Lucedale, Miss.
33. *Carlos Arvizu, 1b, Tucson (Ariz.) HS.
34. *Jarrod Douglass, rhp, Briarcliff (N.Y.) JC.
35. *Dustin Franklin, lhp, Odessa (Texas) JC.
36. *Chris Parrish, c, Jackson State (Tenn.) CC.
**37. *Marshall McDougall, ss, Santa Fe (Fla.) CC.—(2005)**
38. *Nathan Kent, rhp, Motlow State (Tenn.) CC.
39. *Jeremy Lyon, of, Donelson Christian Academy, Old Hickory, Tenn.
**40. +Mike Vento, of, New Mexico JC / Santa Ana (Calif.) CC.—(2005-06)**
**41. +Chris Spurling, rhp, Sinclair (Ohio) CC.—(2003-07)**
42. *Robert Mapp, lhp, Turner HS, Burneyville, Okla.
43. *David Rodriguez, of, Southridge HS, Miami.
44. Andy Smith, rhp, Bowling Green State University.
45. Jason Halper, of, Columbia University.
46. *Chad Conner, rhp, South Bend, Ind.
47. * Matthew Berry, rhp, Christian HS, Lakeside, Calif.
48. *Dylan Putnam, rhp, St. Mary's Prep, Ann Arbor, Mich.
49. *Dan Seimetz, 1b, Ohio State University.
50. *Blake Wilsford, 3b, Collierville (Tenn.) HS.
51. *Chad Harris, rhp, Jasper (Texas) HS.
52. *Anthony McNeal, 3b, Cosumnes River (Calif.) JC.
53. *Robert Fletcher, c, Southland Academy, Americus, Ga.
54. Russ Chambliss, of, Washington (Mo.) University.

DRAFT DROP *Son of Chris Chambliss, major leaguer (1971-88)*

**55. *Aaron Heilman, rhp, Logansport (Ind.) HS.—(2003-11)**

DRAFT DROP *First-round draft pick (31st overall), Twins (2000); first-round draft pick (18th overall), Mets (2001)*

56. *Corey Ward, of, Dallas.
57. *Mark Gilliam, 1b, Grundy County HS, Pelham, Texas.
58. *Jeffrey Rossi, lhp, Skyline HS, Salt Lake City.
59. *Adam Manley, of, Clover Park HS, Tacoma, Wash.
60. *David Clark, of, Denham Springs (La.) HS.
61. *Eric Rodriguez, rhp, Aurea E. Quiles HS, Guanica, P.R.
62. *Paul Schlosser, 3b, McCoy HS, Medicine Hat, Alberta.
63. *John Phillips, rhp, UCLA.
64. *Nicolas Alvarez, rhp, Socorro HS, El Paso, Texas.
65. +Javier Sein, 1b, Palm Beach (Fla.) CC.
66. *Nick Herz, c, Palomar (Calif.) JC.
67. *Roddy Friar, c, Mount San Jacinto (Calif.) JC.
68. *Scott Glaser, lhp, University of South Florida.

## OAKLAND ATHLETICS (11)

1. Chris Enochs, rhp, West Virginia University.—(AAA)
**1. Eric DuBose, lhp, Mississippi State University** (Special compensation—21st—for loss of service-time free agent Mike Bordick).**—(2002-06)**
**1. Nathan Haynes, of, Pinole Valley HS, Hercules, Calif.** (Supplemental choice—32nd—as compensation for Bordick).**—(2007-08)**
1. Denny Wagner, rhp, Virginia Tech (Supplemental choice—42nd—as compensation for Bordick).—(AAA)
**2. Chad Harville, rhp, University of Memphis.—(1999-2006)**
**3. Marcus Jones, rhp, Long Beach State University.—(2000)**
4. Jason Anderson, lhp, Radford University.—(AA)
5. Andy Kimball, rhp, University of Wisconsin-Oshkosh.—(AA)
**6. Tim Hudson, rhp, Auburn University.—(1999-2015)**
7. Roberto Vaz, of, University of Alabama.
**8. Adam Piatt, 3b, Mississippi State University.—(2000-03)**
9. Jared Jensen, rhp, Brigham Young University.
10. Javier Flores, c, University of Oklahoma.
11. Mike Koerner, of, Louisiana State University.
12. Adam Robinson, ss, University of Virginia.
13. *Jonathan Winterrowd, rhp, Germantown (Tenn.) HS.
**14. *Ryan Drese, rhp, University of California.—(2001-06)**
15. Eric Meeks, rhp, West Orange HS, Orlando, Fla.
16. Jamie Porter, of, University of Washington.
17. Elvin Nina, rhp, Oklahoma State University.
18. Mike Holmes, rhp, Wake Forest University.
19. *Josh Canales, ss, Carson (Calif.) HS.
20. Randy Niles, rhp, Florida State University.
21. Brad Gorrie, ss, University of Massachusetts.
22. *Forrest Johnson, c, Rialto (Calif.) HS.
23. Gary Thomas, 3b-of, Vanderbilt Catholic HS, Houma, La.
24. Jeremy Crawford, lhp, Glenwood HS, Chatham, Ill.
25. *Ronnie Williams, of, Booker HS, Sarasota, Fla.
26. David Waites, rhp, University of New Mexico.
27. Miguel Declet, ss, Eloisa Pascual HS, Caguas, P.R.
28. Ed Farris, 1b, Ball State University.
29. *Stephen Murphy, rhp, Canada (Calif.) JC.
30. Tim Manwiller, rhp, Radford University.
31. *Jonathan Weber, of, Los Angeles Harbor JC.
32. *Tim Newman, rhp, Davis HS, Yakima, Wash.
33. *Ian Perio, lhp, Laney (Calif.) JC.
34. *Keith Foxton, of, Kirkwood (Iowa) CC.
35. *Brandon Pack, c, Esperanza HS, Yorba Linda, Calif.
36. Jason Faust, lhp, University of New Orleans.
37. *Marshall Rubens, rhp, Del Campo HS, Citrus Heights, Calif.
38. *Matt Carlock, rhp, Armijo HS, Suisun City, Calif.
39. *Tony Dawson, rhp, Laney (Calif.) JC.
40. *Will Lewis, of, Rialto HS, Adelanto, Calif.

## PHILADELPHIA PHILLIES (2)

**1. *J.D. Drew, of, Florida State University.—(1998-2011)**

DRAFT DROP *Played for St. Paul/Northern League (1998); re-drafted by Cardinals, 1998 (1st round); first player from 1997 draft to reach majors (Sept. 8, 1988) • Brother of Tim Drew, first-round draft pick, Indians (1997); major leaguer (2000-04) • Brother of Stephen Drew, first-round draft pick, Diamondbacks (2004); major leaguer (2006-15)*

**2. Randy Wolf, lhp, Pepperdine University.—(1999-2015)**
3. Shomari Beverly, of, Encinal HS, Alameda, Calif.—(Low A)
4. Nick Marchant, of, Capital HS, Boise, Idaho.—(Rookie)
**5. Derrick Turnbow, rhp, Franklin (Tenn.) HS.—(2000-08)**
**6. Tom Jacquez, lhp, UCLA.—(2000)**

DRAFT DROP *Son of Pat Jacquez, major leaguer (1971)*

7. Derek Adair, rhp, St. John's University.
8. Brian Harris, ss, Indiana University.
**9. *Mike Schultz, rhp, Grover Cleveland HS, Reseda, Calif.—(2007)**
10. Bennie Bishop, of, Westchester HS, Inglewood, Calif.
11. Kevin Kurilla, ss, Virginia Tech.
12. Mark Rutherford, rhp, Eastern Michigan University.
**13. *Lance Niekro, ss, Jenkins HS, Lakeland, Fla.—(2003-07)**

DRAFT DROP *Son of Joe Niekro, major leaguer (1967-88) • Nephew of Phil Niekro, major leaguer (1964-87)*

14. Geoff Zawatski, rhp, University of Virginia.
15. Troy Norrell, c, Navarro (Texas) JC.
16. *Brett Weber, rhp, University of Illinois.
**17. Johnny Estrada, c-1b, JC of the Sequoias (Calif.).—(2001-08)**
18. Duane Johnson, of, Earl Wooster HS, Reno, Nev.
19. Jimmy Frush, rhp, Texas Tech.
20. Jeff Terrell, 2b, University of Missouri.

DRAFT DROP *Son of Jerry Terrell, major leaguer (1973-80)*

21. Rusty McNamara, of-3b, Oklahoma State University.
22. Gary Burnham, of, Clemson University.
23. Brett Black, rhp, North Carolina State University.
24. Pat Driscoll, lhp, University of Nebraska.
25. Jerry Valdez, c, Fort Hays State (Kan.) University.
**26. Andy Dominique, 3b, University of Nevada-Reno.—(2004-05)**
27. Adam Walker, lhp, University of Mississippi.
28. Kevin Shipp, rhp, Louisiana State University.
29. Chad Albaugh, rhp, William Penn (Iowa) College.
30. *Kevin Leighton, c, Brewster (N.Y.) HS.

DRAFT DROP *Baseball coach, Fordham (2012-15)*

31. Mark Manbeck, rhp, University of Houston.
32. Chris Humphries, rhp, University of Nevada-Las Vegas.
33. Ed Fitzpatrick, c, Freed-Hardeman (Tenn.) University.
34. Lamonte Collier, ss, Southeast Missouri State University.
35. Calvin Key, rhp, Arkansas State University.
36. Jeff Hootselle, lhp, Mary Washington (Va.) College.
37. Uriel Casillas, ss, Cal State Los Angeles.
38. Clay Eason, rhp, North Carolina State University.
39. Peter Mondello, rhp, Nicholls State University.
40. Ryan Cody, c, Fort Vancouver (Wash.) HS.
41. Jim Fritz, c, University of Southwestern Louisiana.
42. +John Marifan, lhp, Cerritos (Calif.) JC.
43. *David Walther, 2b, DeSmet Jesuit HS, St. Louis.
44. Jonathan Bushman, of, Lindbergh HS, St. Louis.

## PITTSBURGH PIRATES (8)

**1. J.J. Davis, 1b-rhp, Baldwin Park HS, Pomona, Calif.—(2002-05)**
2. Jose Nicolas, of, Westminster Christian HS, Miami.—High A)
**3. John Grabow, lhp, San Gabriel (Calif.) HS.—(2003-11)**
4. Maurice Washington, of, Chaparral HS, Las Vegas, Nev.—(Short-season A)
5. Chris Combs, rhp-of, North Carolina State University.—(High A)
6. Andy Bausher, lhp, Kutztown (Pa.) University.
**7. Kory DeHaan, of, Morningside (Iowa) College.—(2000-02)**
8. Paul Stabile, lhp, Brookdale (N.J.) CC.
9. Michael Parkerson, lhp, Columbus (Ga.) HS.
**10. Rico Washington, ss, Jones County HS, Gray, Ga.—(2008)**
**11. Sam McConnell, lhp, Ball State University.—(2004)**
12. *Jeff Leuenberger, rhp, Canyon HS, Anaheim, Calif.
13. Kris Lambert, lhp, Baylor University.
14. *Ryan Carter, lhp, Beyer HS, Modesto, Calif.
15. *Jason Moore, ss, Westminster Christian HS, Miami.
16. Jason Hardebeck, lhp, Carl Sandburg (Ill.) JC.
17. Chris Luttig, lhp, University of Evansville.
18. *Shawn Schumacher, c-3b, Panola (Texas) JC.
19. A.J. Jones, of, Mountain Pointe HS, Phoenix.
20. Kevin Haverbusch, ss-rhp, University of Maryland.
21. Keith Maxwell, of-c, Florida A&M University.
22. Alex Tolbert, 1b, Western Carolina University.
23. *Michael Smalley, lhp, Bishop Moore HS, Maitland, Fla.
24. *Jeff Carlsen, rhp, North Kitsap HS, Poulsbo, Wash.
25. +Jesse Daggett, c, JC of the Canyons (Calif.).
26. *Michael Wiggs, ss, Mount Olive (N.C.) College.
27. Brad Guy, rhp, Cal State Los Angeles.
28. *Matt Wood, rhp, Cary (N.C.) HS.
29. *Ryan Earey, 3b, Laney HS, Wilmington, N.C.
**30. Mike Gonzalez, lhp, San Jacinto (Texas) JC.—(2003-13)**
31. *Jeff LaRoche, lhp, Blinn (Texas) JC.

DRAFT DROP *Son of Dave LaRoche, major leaguer (1970-83) • Brother of Adam LaRoche, major leaguer (2004-15) • Brother of Adam LaRoche, major leaguer (2007)*

32. *Marcus Harris, lhp, Cabrillo HS, Lompoc, Calif.
**33. *Bill White, lhp, Benjamin Russell HS, Alexander City, Ala.—(2007-08)**
34. *C.J. Steele, ss, Spiro (Okla.) HS.
**35. *Jamal Strong, of-ss, Citrus (Calif.) JC.—(2003-05)**
36. *Jeff Phelps, ss, Kofa HS, Yuma, Ariz.
37. Chris Clark, of, Stanford University.
38. *Mike Scarborough, of, University of Texas.
39. *Josh Newton, rhp, Springhill (La.) HS.
40. Peter Austin, of, Millsaps (Miss.) College.
41. *Kevin Brown, 3b, North Fort Myers (Fla.) HS.
42. Derrick Lankford, 3b, Carson-Newman (Tenn.)

College.
43. Brett Kaplan, of, University of North Carolina.

## ST. LOUIS CARDINALS (20)

1. **Adam Kennedy, ss, Cal State Northridge.—(1999-2012)**
2. **Rick Ankiel, lhp-of, Port St. Lucie (Fla.) HS.—(1999-2013)**

DRAFT DROP *First 1997 high school draft pick to reach majors (Aug. 23, 1999)*

3. Patrick Coogan, rhp, Louisiana State University.—(AAA)
4. ***Xavier Nady, ss, Salinas (Calif.) HS.—(2000-14)**

DRAFT DROP *Attended California; re-drafted by Padres, 2000 (2nd round); first player from 2000 draft to reach majors (Sept. 30, 2000)*

5. Jason Navarro, lhp, Tulane University.—(AA)
6. Bryan Rupert, c, Limestone (S.C.) College.
7. Joe Secoda, 2b, Rancho Santiago (Calif.) JC.
8. **Jason Karnuth, rhp, Illinois State University.—(2001-05)**
9. ***Seth Etherton, rhp, University of Southern California.—(2000-06)**

DRAFT DROP *First-round draft pick (18th overall), Angels (1998)*

10. Finley Woodward, rhp, Auburn University.
11. Reynaldo Torres, 1b, Aurea E. Quiles HS, Guanica, P.R.
12. Aaron Gentry, ss, Berry (Ga.) College.
13. Derek Feramisco, of, Fresno State University.
14. Rob Macrory, 2b, Auburn University.
15. ***Jason Michaels, of, University of Miami—(2001-11)**
16. Jeremy Lambert, rhp, Kearns (Utah) HS.
17. Tim Davis, of, Atkinson County HS, Pearson, Ga.
18. David Kim, of, Seton Hall University.
19. *Jeff Munster, rhp, Fresno (Calif.) CC.
20. **Justin Brunette, lhp, San Diego State University.—(2000)**
21. *Wes McCrotty, lhp, Russellville (Ark.) HS.

DRAFT DROP *Twin brother of Will McCrotty, sixth-round draft pick, Dodgers (1997)*

22. Tristan Jerue, rhp, University of Georgia.
23. Chris Martine, c, George Mason University.
24. **Jose Rodriguez, lhp, Florida International University.—(2000-2002)**
25. Michael Huffaker, rhp, Birmingham-Southern College.
26. Craig Hopson, rhp, Boylan Catholic HS, Rockford, Ill.
27. Luke Quaccia, 1b, Stanford University.
28. Neal Arnold, rhp, University of Nebraska-Kearney.
29. Derek Gooden, rhp, Brewton-Parker (Ga.) College.
30. T.J. Maier, ss, Cal Poly San Luis Obispo.
31. Brady Gick, c, Ohio University.
32. *Andy Kroneberger, 2b, Camarillo (Calif.) HS.
33. Blake Ledbetter, c, Bertrand, Mo.
34. Michael Speckhardt, of, Marist College.
35. Robert Vazquez, 3b, Westmar (Iowa) University.
36. Andy Bevins, of, San Diego State University.
37. *Stephen Schaub, of, Cowley County (Kan.) CC.
38. Carl Gooden, of, MacArthur HS, Houston.
39. Remer McIntyre, of, Hillsborough HS, Tampa.
40. Scott Wilson, 3b-rhp, Tulane University.
41. *Doug Gant, lhp, Central HS, Macon, Ga.
42. *Jeremy Weinburg, 3b, Sonora HS, La Habra, Calif.
43. *Cody Getz, lhp, Wooster HS, Reno, Nev.
44. ***Willie Eyre, rhp, Snow (Utah) JC.—(2006-11)**
45. *Lionel Rogers, rhp, Fresno (Calif.) CC.
46. *Josh Dorminy, 1b, Middle Georgia JC.

## SAN DIEGO PADRES (26)

1. **Kevin Nicholson, ss, Stetson University.—(2000)**
2. **Ben Howard, rhp, Central Merry HS, Jackson, Tenn.—(2002-04)**
3. Jay Darr, rhp, Glen Rose HS, Malvern, Ark.—(Low A)
4. Tony Lawrence, c, Louisiana Tech.—(Low A)
5. ***Tim Hummel, ss, Burke HS, Montgomery, N.Y.—(2003-04)**

DRAFT DROP *Attended Old Dominion; re-drafted by White Sox, 2000 (2nd round)*

6. Brittan Motley, of, Hickman Mills HS, Kansas City, Mo.
7. Doug Young, rhp, Sierra (Calif.) JC.
8. Jason Dunaway, ss, Seward County (Kan.) CC.
9. **Junior Herndon, rhp, Moffat County HS, Craig, Colo.—(2001)**
10. Tony Cosentino, c, West Torrance HS, Torrance, Calif.
11. **Dave Maurer, lhp, Oklahoma State University.—(2000-04)**
12. Pat Ryan, rhp, University of South Florida.
13. Brent Horsman, of, Solano (Calif.) CC.
14. +Brian Dowell, rhp, Alvin (Texas) CC / McLennan (Texas) JC.
15. Kevin Burford, of, Rancho Santiago (Calif.) JC.
16. **Shawn Camp, rhp, George Mason University.—(2004-14)**
17. *Michael Tejada, c, Provo (Utah) HS.
18. Scott Hemmings, of, Abraham Baldwin Agricultural (Ga.) JC.
19. Karl Ryden, of, Alvin (Texas) CC.
20. *Jonathon Stone, 2b, Lodi (Calif.) HS.
21. Johnny Hunter, of, Texas A&M University.
22. Ricky Guttormson, rhp, Edmonds (Wash.) CC.
23. Scott Seal, 1b, Cal State Fullerton.
24. Clay Snellgrove, ss, Middle Tennessee State University.
25. Brian Jergenson, of-1b, University of Northern Iowa.
26. *Patrick Bourland, ss, Durango (Colo.) HS.
27. +Ron French, c, Northgate HS, Concord, Calif. / Sacramento (Calif.) CC.
28. Joe DeMarco, ss, University of Kansas.
29. +Shawn Garrett, ss, South Central HS, Kinmundy, Ill. / Olney Central (Ill.) CC.
30. Todd Naff, rhp, St. Edward's (Texas) University.
31. Jon Oisseth, lhp, Kansas State University.
32. *Ryan O'Donnell, c, Casa Grande (Ariz.) HS.
33. *Chad Olszanski, ss, San Pasqual HS, Escondido, Calif.
34. Jason Rakers, 3b, Quincy (Ill.) University.

DRAFT DROP *Brother of Aaron Rakers, major leaguer (2004-07)*

35. Bryan DeLeon, rhp, Trujillo Alto, P.R.
36. Dustin Viator, rhp, Nicholls State University.
37. *Greg Bochy, rhp, Mount Carmel HS, Poway, Calif.

DRAFT DROP *Son of Bruce Bochy, major leaguer (1978-87); major league manager (1995-2015) • Brother of Brett Bochy, major leaguer (2014-15)*

38. *Josh France, c, Brophy Jesuit Prep, Phoenix.
39. Jesse Curry, 1b, Gresham Union HS, Gresham, Ore.
40. Gus Ornstein, 1b, Michigan State University.
41. *Ryan Quinn, 3b, Brother Rice HS, Chicago.
42. Bryce Trudeau, rhp, San Bernardino Valley (Calif.) JC.

Adam Kennedy wasn't a consensus first-round talent but spent 14 years in the major leagues

## SAN FRANCISCO GIANTS (4)

1. **Jason Grilli, rhp, Seton Hall University.—(2000-15)**

DRAFT DROP *Son of Steve Grilli, major leaguer (1975-79)*

1. Dan McKinley, of, Arizona State University (Supplemental choice—49th—for failure to sign 1996 first-round draft pick Matt White).—(AAA)
2. **Scott Linebrink, rhp, Southwest Texas State University.—(2000-11)**
3. Jeff Andra, lhp, University of Oklahoma.—(AAA)
4. *Kevin McGerry, rhp, Father Judge HS, Philadelphia.—(High A)

DRAFT DROP *Attended St. John's; re-drafted by Athletics, 2000 (4th round)*

5. Giuseppe Chiaramonte, c, Fresno State University.—(AAA)
6. **Kevin Joseph, rhp, Rice University.—(2002)**
7. Joe Farley, lhp, Capital HS, Olympia, Wash.
8. Brett Casper, of, Oral Roberts University.
9. *Todd Bellhorn, lhp, University of Central Florida.

DRAFT DROP *Brother of Mark Bellhorn, major leaguer (1997-2007)*

10. *Joe Holland, lhp, Bowling Green State University.
11. Travis Young, 2b, University of New Mexico.
12. Jason Verdugo, rhp, Arizona State University.
13. C.J. Ankrum, 1b, Cal State Fullerton.
14. William Otero, ss, Ohio Dominican College.
15. Mike Byas, of, Southwest Missouri State University.
16. Tom Nielsen, lhp, Fordham University.
17. *Scott Goodman, of, Cuesta (Calif.) JC.
18. Darin Cissell, of, St. Louis University.
19. Nathan Rice, lhp, Cal State Northridge.
20. Jesse Travis, rhp, University of Portland.
21. *Paul Stryhas, 3b, Manatee (Fla.) CC.
22. +Mark Hills, lhp, Chemeketa (Ore.) CC.
23. Bryan Guse, c, University of Minnesota.
24. Will Malerich, lhp, College of William & Mary.
25. *Justin Lincoln, ss, Sarasota (Fla.) HS.
26. *Todd Uzzell, rhp, El Paso (Texas) CC.
27. Shawn Austin, lhp, Florida Southern College.
28. *George Crawford, of, Madison HS, Portland, Ore.
29. Zachary Wells, of, Diablo Valley (Calif.) JC.
30. Tim Flaherty, c, East Carolina University.
31. Clay Greene, 2b-of, University of Tennessee.
32. *Luis Santiago, rhp, Adolfo Rivera HS, Penuelas, P.R.
33. *Mike Stevenson, rhp, Orange Coast (Calif.) JC.
34. *Ty Burch, of, Cosumnes River (Calif.) JC.
35. +Shawn Lindsey, of, Lower Columbia (Wash.) JC.
36. *Dennis Anderson, c, Pima (Ariz.) CC.
37. *Jonathan Storke, ss, Cuesta (Calif.) JC.
38. *Lance Woodcock, ss, American River (Calif.) JC.
39. *Justin Thurman, lhp, Blue Mountain (Ore.) CC.
40. *Andy Neufeld, ss, Oviedo HS, Winter Springs, Fla.
41. *Clifton Bowie, of, Alba HS, Bayou La Batre, Ala.
42. *John Tatum, c, Forest Hill HS, West Palm Beach, Fla.
43. Mark Mosier, 3b, University of Chicago.
44. +Jeremy Luster, 3b-1b, DeKalb (Ga.) JC.
45. Chad Faircloth, of, University of North Carolina-Asheville.

## SEATTLE MARINERS (19)

1. Ryan Anderson, lhp, Divine Child HS, Westland, Mich.—(AAA)
2. Brandon Parker, rhp, University of Southern Mississippi (Choice from Angels as compensation for Type B free agent Dave Hollins).—(High A)
2. *Patrick Boyd, of, Central Catholic HS, Clearwater, Fla.—(AA)

DRAFT DROP *Attended Clemson; re-drafted by Pirates, 2000 (4th round)*

3. Patrick Dunham, rhp, Auburn University.—(AA)
4. Scott Prouty, rhp, Pekin HS, Marquette Heights, Ill.—(Rookie)
5. **Jermaine Clark, 2b, University of San Francisco.—(2001-05)**
6. Harvey Hargrove, 2b, Cal State Sacramento.
7. Sam Walton, lhp, W.W. Samuel HS, Dallas.
8. **Allan Simpson, rhp, Taft (Calif.) JC.—(2004-06)**
9. *Frank Corr, c, Father Lopez HS, Deltona, Fla.
10. Peter Duprey, lhp, Forest HS, Ocala, Fla.
11. Cip Garcia, c, La Cueva HS, Rio Rancho, N.M.
12. **Joel Pineiro, rhp, Edison (Fla.) CC.—(2000-11)**
13. Bret Soverel, rhp, Florida International University.
14. *Peter Bauer, rhp, Paint Branch HS, Silver Springs, Md.
15. *Richard Sundstrom, rhp, Cypress (Calif.) JC.
16. Danny Delgado, rhp, Monsignor Pace HS, Miami.
17. Clint Chrysler, lhp, Stetson University.
18. +Ryan Oase, rhp-1b, Edmonds (Wash.) CC.
19. +Jamie Clark, of, Brandon (Fla.) HS / Indian River (Fla.) CC.
20. Mike Marchiano, of, Fordham University.
21. Enmanuel Ulloa, rhp, George Washington HS, Bronx, N.Y.
22. Hubert Parker, ss-2b, Eisenhower HS, Rialto, Calif.
23. *Jim Abbott, rhp, Caledonia (Mich.) HS.
24. *Jason Farren, rhp, Karns City (Pa.) Area HS.
25. *Ryan Reynolds, 3b, The Woodlands (Texas) HS.
26. *Glenn Murphy, lhp, Madison County HS, Madison, Fla.
27. *John Gabaldon, rhp, La Cueva HS, Albuquerque, N.M.
28. *Kirk Bolling, rhp, Saddleback (Calif.) CC.
29. *Matt Huntingford, of, West Vancouver (B.C.) HS.
30. **+Aaron Looper, rhp, Westark (Ark.) CC / Indian Hills (Iowa) CC.—(2003)**

DRAFT DROP *Cousin of Braden Looper, first-round draft pick, Cardinals (1996); major leaguer (1998-2006)*
31. *Matt Woodward, 1b, Florida State University.
DRAFT DROP *Son of Woody Woodward, major leaguer (1963-71); general manager, Yankees (1987); general manager, Phillies (1988); general manager, Mariners (1989-99)*
32. *Dave Garley, rhp, Glendale (Calif.) CC.
33. *Dell Lindsey, 3b, Blinn (Texas) JC.
34. *Eric Mitchell, c, DuBois (Pa.) Area HS.
35. *Israel Torres, lhp, Dominguez HS, Compton, Calif.
36. *Brian Ferreira, of, Barron Collier HS, Naples, Fla.
37. *Mario Jackson, of, Pasadena (Calif.) CC.
38. *Ryan Webb, 3b, Citrus (Calif.) JC.
39. *Brian Spottsville, ss, Compton (Calif.) HS.
40. *Joseph Reyes, ss, Farmington (N.M.) HS.
41. *Kaazim Summerville, of, Burlingame (Calif.) HS.
42. *Andrew Padilla, ss, Highland HS, Bakersfield, Calif.
43. *Bryan Krill, rhp, Rancho Santiago (Calif.) JC.
44. *Peter Graham, rhp, Brookdale (N.J.) CC.
45. *Shaun Stokes, rhp, Jefferson Township HS, Oak Ridge, N.J.
46. *Barry Hawkins, rhp, Saddleback (Calif.) CC.
47. *Thomas Cunningham, c, Leesburg (Fla.) HS.
48. *Nick Padilla, rhp, St. Paul HS, Whittier, Calif.
49. *Joe Barnes, of, Indian River (Fla.) CC.
50. *Jonathan Brandt, rhp, Palo Alto (Calif.) HS.
51. *Chris Silva, lhp, Queensborough (N.Y.) CC.
52. *Shah Bobonis, rhp, Southridge HS, Miami.
53. *Scott Starkey, lhp, Palomar (Calif.) JC.
54. *Kie Polard, of, Crenshaw HS, Los Angeles.
**55. *D.J. Houlton, rhp, Servite HS, Yorba Linda, Calif.—(2005-07)**
56. *Kevin Bice, rhp, Rancho Santiago (Calif.) JC.
57. *Kyle Albright, of, Palomar (Calif.) JC.
58. *Chris Mayberry, 3b, Saugus (Calif.) HS.
59. *Jamel White, of, Antelope Valley (Calif.) JC.
60. *Desmond Dailey, of, Eastern Arizona JC.

## TAMPA BAY DEVIL RAYS (30)

**1. Jason Standridge, rhp, Hewitt Trussville HS, Trussville, Ala.—(2001-07)**
**2. Kenny Kelly, of, Tampa Catholic HS, Tampa.—(2000-05)**
3. Barrett Wright, rhp, Myers Park HS, Charlotte, N.C.—(High A)
**4. Todd Belitz, lhp, Washington State University.—(2000-01)**
5. Marquis Roberts, lhp-of, McLane HS, Fresno, Calif.—(Short-season A)
6. Doug Mansfield, of, Jacksonville HS, Sherwood, Ark.
7. Eddy Reyes, rhp, University of Miami.
8. Jack Joffrion, ss, Lamar University.
**9. Toby Hall, c, University of Nevada-Las Vegas.—(2000-08)**
10. *Carl Hutchens, rhp, L.C. Anderson HS, Austin, Texas.
11. Chris Wright, rhp, Cowley County (Kan.) CC.
12. Carlos Vazquez, c, Caribbean HS, Ponce, P.R.
13. Kevin Price, rhp, Bingham HS, Riverton, Utah.
14. Casey Davis, lhp, Boyd County HS, Ashland, Ky.
15. Jason Guerrero, ss, Pittsburg (Calif.) HS.
16. *Lazaro Gutierrez, lhp, University of Miami.
**17. *Chris Bootcheck, rhp, La Porte (Ind.) HS.—(2003-13)**
DRAFT DROP *First-round draft pick (20th overall), Angels (2000)*
18. Terry McCormick, lhp, Jesuit HS, Tampa.
19. *Lavar Johnson, of, North Shore HS, Houston.
20. *Matt Kaffel, rhp, Blinn (Texas) JC.
21. Damian Scioneaux, of, Mississippi State University.
22. Dustin Carr, 2b, University of Houston.
**23. Paul Hoover, ss, Kent State University.—(2001-10)**
24. Travis Miller, of, Dallas Baptist University.
25. *Josh Davis, rhp, Tallahassee (Fla.) CC.
26. *Coty Cooper, rhp, Seward County (Kan.) CC.
27. Anthony Pigott, of, Elon College.
**28. Jason Jimenez, lhp, San Jose State University.—(2002)**
**29. *Ryan Jorgensen, c, Kingwood (Texas) HS.—(2005-08)**
30. Jon Cummins, rhp, Indiana (Pa.) University.
31. +Michael Meseberg, of, Royal HS, Othello, Wash. / Edmonds (Wash.) CC.
32. +Jeremy Murch, lhp, Sarasota (Fla.) HS / Manatee (Fla.) CC.
33. *Daniel Firlit, ss, Rend Lake (Ill.) JC.
34. *Kris Ehmke, rhp, Thomas Stewart HS, Peterborough, Ontario.
35. *Ben Peterson, rhp, East Lake HS, Tarpon Springs, Fla.
36. Chris Mason, rhp, University of Alabama-Birmingham.
37. Heath McKoin, lhp, Watson Chapel HS, Pine Bluff, Ark.
38. Ryan Pandolfini, 1b, Rider University.
39. *Jim Munroe, rhp, Servite HS, Orange, Calif.
40. *David Cash, rhp, Davis HS, Modesto, Calif.
41. *John Hutchens, rhp, Fort Gibson (Okla.) HS.
42. *Lee Southard, rhp, Westmoore HS, Oklahoma City, Okla.
43. +Nicholas Rhodes, c, Norwalk (Conn.) CC.
44. *Alan Lowden, lhp, Hays HS, Kyle, Texas.
45. *Adam Luczycky, rhp, Labette (Kan.) CC.
46. *Marlyn Tisdale, rhp, Florida CC.
47. *Freddie Mitchell, of, Kathleen HS, Lakeland, Fla.
DRAFT DROP *Wide receiver, National Football League (2001-04)*
48. *Josh Long, 3b, Northview HS, McDavid, Fla.
49. *Jason Balkcom, rhp, Young Harris (Ga.) JC.
50. Chris Reynolds, rhp, North Lake (Texas) CC.
51. *Ivar Wentzel, lhp, Flagler Palm Coast HS, Palm Coast, Fla.
52. *Kyle Evans, rhp, Eldorado HS, Albuquerque, N.M.
53. *Dustin McKey, of, John Carroll HS, Alabaster, Ala.
54. *Alan Keller, c, Mendocino (Calif.) CC.
55. *Tyler Tiesing, c, Butler County (Kan.) CC.
56. *Nick Lyon, of, Monroe (Wash.) HS.
57. +Jeremy Robinson, lhp, Okaloosa-Walton (Fla.) CC.
58. *David Berry, c, Pearce HS, Richardson, Texas.
59. *Cedric Razor, 2b, Pitt (N.C.) CC.
60. *Richard McCabe, rhp, Camden HS, St. Mary's, Ga.
61. *Ron Brooks, rhp, Tallahassee (Fla.) CC.
62. *Tavaris Keyes, rhp, Central HS, Fort Pierce, Fla.
63. *Steve Gause, rhp, George Jenkins HS, Lakeland, Fla.
64. *Chris Wood, ss, Vanguard HS, Ocala, Fla.
65. *Zack Roper, 3b, Pasco-Hernando (Fla.) CC.
66. *Ray Nevels, of, Sarasota (Fla.) HS.
67. *Rafael Erazo, rhp, Labette (Kan.) CC.
68. *Dusty Hall, ss, Lincoln HS, Gahanna, Ohio.
**69. *Heath Bell, rhp, Rancho Santiago (Calif.) JC.—(2004-14)**
70. *Kenny Baugh, rhp, Lamar HS, Houston.
DRAFT DROP *First-round draft pick (11th overall), Tigers (2001)*
71. *Carlos Perez, 2b, Franklin D. Roosevelt HS, Brooklyn, N.Y.
72. *Julio Fortuna, rhp, Bushwick HS, Brooklyn, N.Y.
73. *John Gillespie, rhp, Lake Washington HS, Redmond, Wash.
74. *Jarrod Reineke, rhp, Grove HS, Joplin, Mo.
75. *Brian Brown, ss, Olney Central (Ill.) JC.
76. *Brandon Brewer, rhp, Greely HS, North Yarmouth, Maine.
77. *Jeff Dragg, of, Covington HS, Madisonville, La.
78. *Rob Meyers, rhp, De La Salle HS, Concord, Calif.
79. *Jon Smith, lhp, Ferris HS, Nuevo, Calif.
80. *Clint Kinsey, rhp, Allen County (Kan.) CC.
81. *Jonny Williams, c, Fox HS, Imperial, Mo.
82. *Zach Lekse, ss, Sacramento (Calif.) CC.
83. *Blake Williams, rhp, San Marcos (Texas) HS.
DRAFT DROP *First-round draft pick (24th overall), Cardinals (2000)*
84. *Mark Madsen, rhp, Quartz Hill HS, Lancaster, Calif.
85. *Chad Ashlock, rhp, Seward County (Kan.) CC.
86. *Bryan Edwards, rhp, Bowie HS, Austin, Texas.
87. *Jon Benick, c, Greater Nanticoke HS, Glen Lyon, Pa.
88. Bart Carter, 1b, William Carey (Miss.) College.
**89. *Robby Hammock, c, DeKalb (Ga.) JC.—(2003-11)**
**90. *Willie Harris, 2b-ss, Middle Georgia JC.—(2001-12)**
91. *Beau Barcus, 3b, San Lorenzo HS, Ben Lomond, Calif.
92. *Andy Baxter, ss, Unicoi County HS, Erwin, Tenn.

## TEXAS RANGERS (23)

1. (Choice to Yankees as compensation for Type A free agent John Wetteland)
**1. Jason Romano, 3b, Hillsborough HS, Tampa** (Supplemental choice—39th—as compensation for Type A free agent Mike Stanton).**—(2002-05)**
**2. Jason Grabowski, c, University of Connecticut.—(2002-05)**
2. Chris Tynan, rhp, Hudson's Bay HS, Vancouver, Wash. (Choice from Yankees as compensation for Stanton).—(Low A)
3. Brandon Warriax, ss, Purnell Swett HS, Pembroke, N.C.—(AA)
**4. David Elder, rhp, Georgia Tech.—(2002-03)**
5. Trey Poland, lhp, University of Southwestern Louisiana.—(AA)
6. Dan DeYoung, rhp, University of Mississippi.
**7. Mike Lamb, c, Cal State Fullerton.—(2000-10)**
8. Billy Diaz, rhp, Academia Adventista HS, Caguas, P.R.
9. Carlos Figueroa, lhp, Jose Lazaro HS, Carolina, P.R.
10. Kay-Jay Harris, of, Tampa Bay Tech HS, Tampa.
DRAFT DROP *Running back, National Football League (2005-06)*
11. Tom Sergio, 2b, North Carolina State University.
12. Corey Wright, of, Workman HS, La Puente, Calif.
13. *Robbie Milner, rhp, Deer Valley HS, Phoenix.
14. Jason Torres, c, John Carroll HS, Vero Beach, Fla.
15. *Karl Jernigan, ss, Milton HS, Navarre, Fla.
16. *Kevin Ruedi, rhp, Sacramento (Calif.) CC.
17. Geronimo Cruz, of, Alfred (N.Y.) University.
**18. *Jaime Bubela, of, Cypress Falls HS, Houston.—(2005)**
**19. +Travis Hughes, rhp, Cowley County (Kan.) CC.—(2004-06)**
20. *Jay Signorelli, rhp, Lake Brantley HS, Altamonte Springs, Fla.
21. Jeff Ridenour, rhp, Southern Illinois University.-Edwardsville.
22. *Curtis Gay, 1b, Cowley County (Kan.) CC.
23. *Quenten Patterson, rhp, Blinn (Texas) JC.
24. *Brian Shipp, ss, Central HS, Baton Rouge, La.
25. Alex Vazquez, of, Montgomery (Md.) JC.
26. Spike Lundberg, rhp, San Diego Mesa JC.
27. *Tanner Herrick, 1b, Show Low (Ariz.) HS.
28. *Mike Eskildsen, rhp, Maple Ridge (B.C.) HS.
**29. *Jason Young, rhp, Berkeley (Calif.) HS.—(2003-04)**
30. *Derek Hines, of, Yavapai (Ariz.) JC.
31. *David Curtiss, ss, Havre (Mon.) HS.
32. *Jeff Fields, c, Alamogordo (N.M.) HS.
**33. *Mitch Jones, 3b, Utah Valley State JC.—(2009)**
34. *Devon Younger, rhp, Meridian (Miss.) CC.
35. *Kelley Gulledge, c, Mansfield HS, Arlington, Texas.
36. *David Wigley, c, George C. Wallace (Ala.) CC.
37. *Blake Allen, rhp, Benjamin Russell HS, Alexander City, Ala.
38. Jason Beitey, rhp, Olympic (Wash.) JC.
**39. *Pete Orr, ss, New Market HS, Hamilton, Ontario.—(2005-13)**
40. *Craig Mosher, lhp, McRoberts HS, Richmond, B.C.
41. *Josh Hawes, rhp, CC of Rhode Island.

## TORONTO BLUE JAYS (5)

**1. Vernon Wells, of, Bowie HS, Arlington, Texas.—(1999-2013)**
2. (Choice to Red Sox as compensation for Type A free agent Roger Clemens)
3. Billy Brown, of, Florida Atlantic University.—(High A)
4. Woody Heath, rhp, Green River (Wash.) CC.—(High A)
**5. Michael Young, ss, UC Santa Barbara.—(2000-13)**
6. Paul Chiaffredo, c, Santa Clara University.
7. Matt McClellan, rhp, Oakland University.
8. Joe Casey, rhp, Twin Valley HS, Elverson, Pa.
9. Carlos Ortiz, c, Loara HS, Anaheim, Calif.
10. *Matt Bowser, 1b, Tarpon Springs HS, Palm Harbor, Fla.
11. Ron Bost, lhp, Central Cabarrus HS, Harrisburg, N.C.
12. Randy Eversgerd, rhp, Eastern Illinois University.
DRAFT DROP *Brother of Bryan Eversgerd, major leaguer (1994-98)*
13. Travis Hubbel, rhp, East Glen Composite HS, Edmonton, Alberta.
14. *Cam Reimers, rhp, Sentinel HS, Missoula, Mon.
15. Colin Brackeen, lhp, St. Olaf (Minn.) College.
16. Dustin Seale, lhp, Safford (Ariz.) HS.
17. Brian Barnett, ss, Linfield (Ore.) College.
18. Matt Weimer, rhp, Penn State University.
19. Erik Lorenz, rhp, University of Wisconsin-Whitewater.
**20. +Mark Hendrickson, lhp, Mount Vernon, Wash.—(2002-11)**
DRAFT DROP *Forward, National Basketball Association (1996-2000)*
21. David Huggins, rhp, McNeese State University.
22. John Sneed, rhp, Texas A&M University.
23. *Derek DeVaughan, rhp, Seminole State (Okla.) JC.
24. Anthony Salley, lhp, Wofford College.
25. Perfecto Gaud, lhp, Luis Munoz Marin HS, Yauco, P.R.
26. *Floyd Mack, of, Mays HS, Fairburn, Ga.
27. +Fred Smith, of, Volunteer State (Tenn.) CC.
28. Andy Barrett, ss, Stadium HS, Tacoma, Wash.
29. Juan Santos, c-1b, Florida CC.
30. Tim Lacefield, rhp, Harding (Ark.) University.
31. Jermaine Davis, of, Chesnee (S.C.) HS.
**32. *Sean Green, rhp, Male HS, Louisville, Ky.—(2006-11)**
33. Taylor Smith, rhp, Green Valley HS, Henderson, Nev.
34. *Jamie Jenkins, rhp, Hill HS, Miramichi, New Brunswick.
35. +Josh Stevens, rhp, Jurupa Valley HS, Mira Loma, Calif. / Riverside (Calif.) CC.
36. *Simon Stoner, rhp, Duchess Park HS, Prince George, B.C.
37. *Jason Burkley, c-3b, Lexington Catholic HS, Lexington, Ky.
38. Chivas Clark, of, Northeast HS, Macon, Ga.
39. *Matt Easterday, 2b, Newton County HS, Covington, Ga.
40. *Michael Ramsey, of, Columbus (Ga.) HS.
41. *Patrick Versluis, rhp, Saddleback (Calif.) CC.
42. *Andrew Beattie, ss, Pasco-Hernando (Fla.) CC.
**43. +Orlando Hudson, ss, Spartanburg Methodist (S.C.) JC.—(2002-12)**
44. *Todd Thompson, rhp, Indian Hills (Iowa) CC.
45. *Brandon Long, lhp, Central Alabama CC.
**46. *Brad Hawpe, lhp, Boswell HS, Fort Worth, Texas.—(2004-13)**
47. Jesus Lebron, of, Orlando, Fla.
48. *David Siboda, rhp, Southeast Missouri State University.
49. *Anthony Novelli, rhp, West Valley (Calif.) JC.
50. *Michael Albert, ss, Grossmont (Calif.) JC.
51. *Chad Schmidt, of, Blinn (Texas) JC.
**52. *Chad Qualls, rhp, Los Angeles Harbor JC.—(2004-15)**
53. *Jeff Nettles, 3b, Palomar (Calif.) JC.
DRAFT DROP *Son of Graig Nettles, major leaguer (1967-88)*
54. *Craig Lariz, 1b, Indian River (Fla.) CC.
55. *Rashard Casey, of, Penn State University.
56. *Arlyn Dozier, of, Vermillion Catholic HS, Abbeville, La.
57. *Travis Cole, rhp, Lakeridge HS, Lake Oswego, Ore.
**58. *Billy Traber, lhp, El Segundo (Calif.) HS.—(2003-09)**
DRAFT DROP *First-round draft pick (16th overall), Mets (2000)*
59. *Michael Willetts, rhp, Abraham Baldwin Agricultural (Ga.) JC.
60. *Brandon Tellis, of, Charleston (Miss.) HS.
61. *Gary Peete, of, Itawamba (Miss.) JC.
62. *Matthew Dempsey, 1b, Cypress (Calif.) JC.
63. *Charles Lawrence, of, Lakeside HS, Decatur, Ga.
64. *Jeremiah Barnes, rhp, Downey (Calif.) HS.
65. *William Wagner, of, Elmore County HS, Eclectic, Ala.
66. *Cameron Newitt, rhp, Northwest Shoals (Ala.) JC.
67. *Dave Steffler, rhp, Winthrop University.

# Phillies dig deep to get deal done for top pick

The Philadelphia Phillies picked an unfortunate year to make the No. 1 selection in the draft for the first time in franchise history. Not only did it come at a time of great upheaval in the draft's evolution, but circumstances seemed to conspire against the Phillies on numerous fronts.

Most scouts agreed the talent in 1998 was above-average, but one player stood above the rest: outfielder J.D. Drew. That created a predicament for the Phillies, who had drafted Drew a year earlier with the second overall pick, only to become engaged in the most contentious negotiations in draft history. The Phils were not about to go down that road again, even if he did have the power-hitting credentials they wanted.

With Drew out of the equation, the Phillies' quest for power shifted to University of Miami third baseman Pat Burrell, but his situation also was complicated. Burrell had missed the latter half of the 1998 college season because of a stress fracture in his lower back, leaving his status in doubt. The Phillies also had young star Scott Rolen at third base.

Further complicating matters, Phillies scouting director Mike Arbuckle couldn't get a consensus among his staff on the best prospect available not named Drew. Each of his four crosscheckers favored a different player.

In addition to Burrell, Philadelphia's short list included lefthanders Ryan Mills of Arizona State and Mark Mulder of Michigan State, and California high school third baseman Sean Burroughs.

Mills and Mulder were mature college pitchers who scouts believed could help the beleaguered Phillies staff quickly. Mills had the better raw stuff, and Mulder was more polished. Mills was the son of Dick Mills, who had pitched two games in the major leagues, and Burroughs, an elite hitting prospect from Long Beach, was the son of former American League MVP Jeff Burroughs, the No. 1 pick in the 1969 draft.

"From all the work we've done," Arbuckle said, "we think all the players we are considering want to play. We've heard nothing out of the ordinary. We don't foresee another situation like last year."

Burrell made the decision relatively easy for the Phillies by returning to the Miami lineup a week before the draft, hitting five homers in NCAA regional play and unloading a blast estimated at 500 feet in the first game of the College World Series.

"He has a power bat, which is one of the needs we had identified for the draft," Arbuckle said. "We felt all along that he was the player we wanted. His health was a concern, but we've seen all the CAT scans and MRIs and been at every practice and game he's played in. We think he's fine."

Burrell hit .432 with 17 homers in 118 at-bats in his junior season. Over his three-year career with the Hurricanes, he hit .442 with 61 homers and an

BILL SETLIFF

While a back injury clouded his status for much of the spring, Pat Burrell came back in time to show his stuff in the college postseason and nail down his status as the No. 1 overall pick of the Phillies

.886 slugging percentage that ranked second-best in NCAA history. Limited defensively at third base, Burrell moved to first base and later to the outfield.

Getting Burrell under contract, at a time of rampant inflation in the draft, was no easy matter for the Phillies, who were under considerable pressure to sign him after failing to secure Drew the previous year.

The St. Louis Cardinals drafted Drew with the fifth overall pick and gave him a record-setting deal on July 3 that provided a $3 million bonus and a four-year, major league contract with a total guarantee of $7 million.

The Phillies felt they were backed into a corner after Drew signed and had little leverage with Burrell. They negotiated a five-year, major league deal with Burrell that included a $3.15 million bonus and guarantees that brought the total value to $8 million. They ended up paying Burrell, by consensus a lesser player than Drew, significantly more than they had offered Drew less than two months earlier, when they still held his rights.

### DREW'S DRAFT GRIEVANCE LURKS

In a year of increasingly complex contracts, it was difficult to determine how many times the record for the largest signing bonus was broken, or who actually held the mark by the time all players in the 1998 draft were accounted for.

Led by Drew ($3 million) and then by Burrell

## AT A GLANCE

### This Date In History
June 2-4

### Best Draft
**CHICAGO WHITE SOX.** The White Sox got 12 big-league seasons from **KIP WELLS** (1) and 11 from **AARON ROWAND** (2), but the player that made the biggest mark was **MARK BUEHRLE**, a 38th-round draft-and-follow from Jefferson (Mo.) College. He was the best player to come out of the 1998 draft, according to WAR.

### Worst Draft
**ANAHEIM ANGELS. SETH ETHERTON** (1) was the only draft choice the Angels signed who played in the big leagues. He spent one season (11 games) in an Angels uniform before being traded to the Reds.

### First-Round Bust
**RYAN MILLS, LHP, TWINS.** Despite being the sixth overall pick and getting a $2 million signing bonus, Mills did not reach the major leagues, joining seven other first-rounders. Derailed by elbow problems, Mills went 17-40, 5.79 in seven seasons.

### Second Time Around
**BRANDON INGE, SS/RHP, TIGERS.** One of the most versatile talents in the draft, Inge generated interest as a shortstop (.330-15-61, 21 SB) and closer (5-2, 2.09 ERA, 11 saves) for Virginia Commonwealth. He spent his 13-year, big league career as a position player—1,083 games as a third baseman, 376 as a catcher—and hit .233-152-648.

### Late-Round Find
**MARK BUEHRLE, LHP, WHITE SOX (38TH ROUND).** The White Sox took a flier on Buehrle after he went 7-0 as a junior college freshman. They signed him 11 months later for $150,000, after he went 8-4, 1.45 as a sophomore. In a 16-year major league career, Buehrle won at

CONTINUED ON PAGE 496

## AT A GLANCE

CONTINUED FROM PAGE 495

least 10 games every year from 2001-2015, pitched two no-hitters, including a perfect game, started an All-Star Game, earned two Gold Gloves and won a World Series ring.

### Never Too Late

**MITCH JONES, 3B, ORIOLES (49TH ROUND).** With the draft reduced to 50 rounds, Jones became the latest 1998 pick to reach the majors. A Utah junior college product, he declined an offer from the Orioles and went to Arizona State. After hitting .357-27-92 as a senior in 2000, he was drafted by the Yankees in the seventh round, and he played in nine games for the Dodgers in 2009.

### Overlooked

**ERUBIEL DURAZO, 1B, DIAMONDBACKS.** Durazo left his native Mexico to play high school baseball in Arizona and then hit .434 in two years at Arizona's Pima CC, but went undrafted. He went to the Mexican League for two years, and after hitting .350-19-98 in 1998, was signed by the Diamondbacks. After less than a year in the minor leagues, Durazo started a seven-year major league career in which he hit .281-94-330.

### International Gem

**ALFONSO SORIANO, SS, YANKEES.** The Yankees signed Soriano, a 22-year-old Dominican playing in Japan, for $3.1 million; 16-year-old Dominican outfielder **WILY MO PENA** for $3.7 million; 16-year-old Dominican righthander **RICARDO ARAMBOLES** for $1.52 million; and 32-year-old Cuban right-hander **ORLANDO HERNANDEZ** to a four-year, $6.6 million contract. All but Aramboles played in the majors. Soriano had a 16-year career with four clubs, hitting .270-412-1,159.

### Minor League Take

**CHIP AMBRES, OF, MARLINS.** Ambres reached

## 1998: THE FIRST ROUNDERS

| CLUB: PLAYER, POS., SCHOOL | HOMETOWN | B-T | HT. | WT. | AGE | BONUS | FIRST YEAR | LAST YEAR | PEAK LEVEL (YEARS) |
|---|---|---|---|---|---|---|---|---|---|
| 1. *Phillies: Pat Burrell, 3b/1b, Miami | Boulder Creek, Calif. | R-R | 6-4 | 225 | 21 | $3,150,000 | 1998 | 2011 | Majors (12) |
| BA College Freshman of Year (.484-23-64), hit .442-61-187 over three years in college; signed record $8M MLB contract, had most success in majors with Phils. | | | | | | | | | |
| 2. Athletics: Mark Mulder, lhp, Michigan State | South Holland, Ill. | L-L | 6-6 | 200 | 20 | $3,200,000 | 1999 | 2008 | Majors (9) |
| Agreed to largest bonus for player signing standard contract; part of dominant A's trio with Hudson/Zito, promising career undone by rotator-cuff problems. | | | | | | | | | |
| 3. Cubs: Corey Patterson, of, Harrison HS | Kennesaw, Ga. | L-R | 5-10 | 175 | 18 | $3,700,000 | 1999 | 2013 | Majors (12) |
| Prep football star's contract included dual-sport provision; hit .528-22-61/38 SBs as prep SR; rushed to majors, never maximized five-tool potential due to approach. | | | | | | | | | |
| 4. Royals: Jeff Austin, rhp, Stanford | Kingwood, Texas | R-R | 6-0 | 185 | 21 | $2,700,000 | 1999 | 2004 | Majors (3) |
| Royals had signability in mind with top college arm, took six months to get deal done; never had raw stuff to sustain success, went 2-3, 6.78 in MLB career. | | | | | | | | | |
| 5. *Cardinals: J.D. Drew, of, St. Paul (Independent) | Hahira, Ga. | L-R | 6-1 | 200 | 22 | $3,000,000 | 1998 | 2011 | Majors (14) |
| Controversial '97 holdout went in first round after unsuccessfully trying to become free agent; five-tool talent never quite lived up to purported 30-30 potential. | | | | | | | | | |
| 6. Twins: Ryan Mills, lhp, Arizona State | Scottsdale, Ariz. | R-L | 6-5 | 200 | 20 | $2,000,000 | 1998 | 2004 | Class AAA (2) |
| Son of major leaguer had polished arm, on fast track to majors until beset immediately by elbow issues; went 17-40, 5.79 in seven minor league seasons. | | | | | | | | | |
| 7. Reds: Austin Kearns, of, Lafayette HS | Lexington, Ky. | R-R | 6-3 | 215 | 18 | $1,950,000 | 1998 | 2013 | Majors (12) |
| Considered equal as position player/pitcher out of HS, but developed as hitter because of raw power, suspect mechanics on mound; enjoyed solid MLB career. | | | | | | | | | |
| 8. Blue Jays: Felipe Lopez, ss, Lake Brantley HS | Kissimmee, Fla. | B-R | 6-0 | 175 | 18 | $2,000,000 | 1998 | 2011 | Majors (11) |
| Puerto Rico native overcame turbulent childhood to become elite talent with pure SS skills, but MLB career relegated to journeyman status due to limited bat. | | | | | | | | | |
| 9. Padres: Sean Burroughs, 3b, Woodrow Wilson HS | Long Beach, Calif. | L-R | 6-1 | 200 | 17 | $2,100,000 | 1999 | 2013 | Majors (7) |
| Success came early for ex-Little League star, son of big leaguer; became best hitting prospect in game, but career/life unraveled after he didn't hit enough in majors. | | | | | | | | | |
| 10. Rangers: Carlos Pena, 1b, Northeastern | Haverhill, Mass. | L-L | 6-2 | 210 | 20 | $1,850,000 | 1998 | 2014 | Majors (14) |
| Moved to U.S. from Dominican at 12, opened eyes with breakout '97 summer on Cape Cod; carved out 14-year MLB career with LH power, deft 1B skills, intangibles. | | | | | | | | | |
| 11. Expos: Josh McKinley, ss, Malvern Prep | Downingtown, Pa. | B-R | 6-2 | 190 | 18 | $1,250,000 | 1998 | 2004 | Class AA (3) |
| Budget pick for cash-strapped Expos; switch-hitting SS with power potential, but game never really developed, hit .254-48-358 in seven minor league seasons. | | | | | | | | | |
| 12. Red Sox: Adam Everett, ss, South Carolina | Kennesaw, Ga. | R-R | 6-1 | 165 | 21 | $1,725,000 | 1998 | 2011 | Majors (11) |
| Elite defender with range, actions, instincts; hit .375-13-63 as college JR, but bat limited him in pro game; spent bulk of career with Astros as player, coach. | | | | | | | | | |
| 13. Brewers: J.M. Gold, rhp, Toms River North HS | Toms River, N.J. | R-R | 6-5 | 225 | 18 | $1,675,000 | 1998 | 2003 | Class A (4) |
| Classic power pitcher with big frame, 91-95 mph fastball, but blew out elbow in 2000, had TJ surgery, never bounced back; went 13-17, 4.94, released in '04. | | | | | | | | | |
| 14. Tigers: Jeff Weaver, rhp, Fresno State | Simi Valley, Calif. | R-R | 6-5 | 220 | 21 | $1,750,000 | 1998 | 2010 | Majors (11) |
| Passed on White Sox as '97 second-rounder, even after leading D-I arms with 181 strikeouts; same style pitcher as brother Jered, went 104-119, 4.71 in majors. | | | | | | | | | |
| 15. Pirates: Clint Johnston, lhp/of, Vanderbilt | Vero Beach, Fla. | L-L | 6-3 | 200 | 20 | $1,000,000 | 1998 | 2005 | Class AA (1) |
| Hit .424-19-74 for Vandy, but Pirates preferred power in left arm, potential as future reliever; went 10-12, 4.26 before Blue Jays converted Rule 5 pick back to hitter. | | | | | | | | | |
| 16. White Sox: Kip Wells, rhp, Baylor | Sugar Land, Texas | R-R | 6-3 | 195 | 21 | $1,495,000 | 1999 | 2013 | Majors (12) |
| Modest success in college career (21-14, 5.17), but Sox saw upside in big, hard thrower; holdout until December, pitched for nine MLB clubs, went 69-103, 4.71. | | | | | | | | | |
| 17. Astros: Brad Lidge, rhp, Notre Dame | Englewood, Colo. | R-R | 6-4 | 200 | 21 | $1,070,000 | 1998 | 2012 | Majors (11) |
| Had more elbow operations (3) than wins (2) early in pro career, but rebounded to become dominant closer with 95-98 fastball, sharp slider, saved 225 MLB games. | | | | | | | | | |
| 18. Angels: Seth Etherton, rhp, Southern California | Monarch Beach, Calif. | R-R | 6-1 | 200 | 21 | $1,075,000 | 1998 | 2010 | Majors (4) |
| Passed up $75,000 offer as 9th-rounder in '97 to lead USC to CWS title, earn big bonus as SR; didn't have superior stuff to thrive in majors, went only 9-7, 6.28. | | | | | | | | | |
| 19. Giants: Tony Torcato, 3b, Woodland HS | Woodland, Calif. | L-R | 6-1 | 200 | 18 | $975,000 | 1998 | 2006 | Majors (4) |
| Hit .449-13-40 at NorCal HS with line-drive stroke; expected to add power as got stronger but three shoulder surgeries impacted swing, prompted move to OF. | | | | | | | | | |
| 20. Indians: C.C. Sabathia, lhp, Vallejo HS | Vallejo, Calif. | L-L | 6-6 | 240 | 17 | $1,300,000 | 1998 | Active | Majors (15) |
| Oversized lefty had D-I football offers, intimidating presence on mound, but also 97-98 FB, feel for pitching; became dominant arm in class with 200-plus MLB wins. | | | | | | | | | |
| 21. Mets: Jason Tyner, of, Texas A&M | Beaumont, Texas | L-L | 6-1 | 170 | 21 | $1,070,000 | 1998 | 2009 | Majors (8) |
| Speed was only standout tool, but adept CF, baserunner, bunter; mastered inside-out swing, knack for soft contact: no homers in college, 3 in minors, 1 in majors. | | | | | | | | | |
| 22. Mariners: Matt Thornton, lhp, Grand Valley State (Mich.) | Centreville, Mich. | L-L | 6-6 | 210 | 21 | $925,000 | 1998 | Active | Majors (12) |
| Surprise first-rounder played primarily basketball at D-II school; had limited success as starter in minors, made MLB debut as reliever at age 27, excelled in role. | | | | | | | | | |
| 23. Dodgers: Bubba Crosby, of, Rice | Houston | L-L | 5-11 | 185 | 21 | $995,000 | 1998 | 2007 | Majors (4) |
| Stung ball at .370-47-179 clip as SO/JR at Rice; struggled adjusting to wood in pros before developing a new approach, finally reached majors in 2003. | | | | | | | | | |
| 24. Yankees: Andy Brown, of, Richmond HS | Richmond, Ind. | L-L | 6-6 | 195 | 18 | $1,050,000 | 1998 | 2005 | Class AA (2) |
| Yanks eyed risky HS talents Mark Prior/Mark Teixeira, settled for more signable player; had frame/swing to develop plus power, but too prone to strikeouts. | | | | | | | | | |
| 25. Giants: Nate Bump, rhp, Penn State | Monroeton, Pa. | R-R | 6-3 | 185 | 21 | $750,000 | 1998 | 2011 | Majors (3) |
| Wisely returned to school as SR (7-3, 2.62, 106 IP/135 SO) after subpar JR year; traded within year, 6-7, 4.68 MLB career impacted by shoulder problems. | | | | | | | | | |
| 26. Orioles: Rick Elder, of/1b, Sprayberry HS | Marietta, Ga. | L-L | 6-6 | 230 | 18 | $950,000 | 1998 | 2003 | Class A (3) |
| Hit .509-17-44 as prep SR, .299-14-48 as first-year pro, but missed 2000 (TJ surgery), 2002 seasons (shoulder surgery), never showcased power/athleticism. | | | | | | | | | |
| 27. Marlins: Chip Ambres, of, West Brook HS | Beaumont, Texas | R-R | 6-1 | 190 | 18 | $1,500,000 | 1999 | 2009 | Majors (3) |
| Signed away from Texas A&M as multi-threat QB; knee/hamstring issues negated speed (best tool), bat also slow to develop, hit .233-4-10 in 189 MLB ABs. | | | | | | | | | |
| 28. Rockies: Matt Roney, rhp, Edmond North HS | Edmond, Okla. | R-R | 6-3 | 225 | 18 | $1,012,500 | 1998 | 2007 | Majors (2) |
| Rockies considered fellow Oklahoman Matt Holliday with top pick, ended up with both; reached MLB with Tigers, career essentially ended with '07 drug suspension. | | | | | | | | | |
| 29. Giants: Arturo McDowell, of, Forest Hill HS | Jackson, Miss. | L-L | 6-1 | 175 | 18 | $937,500 | 1998 | 2002 | Class AA (1) |
| Uncharacteristic Giants draft with raw baseball skills; speed was only tool that played, hit .215 in five seasons before release; later walked on for Alabama football. | | | | | | | | | |
| 30. Royals: Matt Burch , rhp, Virginia Commonwealth | Horseheads, N.Y. | R-R | 6-3 | 185 | 21 | $975,000 | 1998 | 2003 | Class AA (1) |
| SS/closer Brandon Inge (Tigers, second round) was higher-profile VCU talent; 12-4, 2.59 record as college junior masked modest stuff, control issues. | | | | | | | | | |

*Signed to major league contract.

## How They Should Have Done It

Based on career WAR (Wins Above Replacement, as calculated by Baseball-Reference.com) achieved by players eligible for the 1998 draft through the 2015 season, here's how the first round should have unfolded. Numbers in parentheses indicate the round when the player was drafted. Asterisk denotes player who signed as a draft-and-follow.

| Player, Pos. | Actual Draft | WAR | Bonus |
|---|---|---|---|
| 1. * Mark Buehrle, lhp | White Sox (38) | 58.5 | $150,000 |
| 2. C.C. Sabathia, lhp | Indians (1) | 55.8 | $1,300,000 |
| 3. J.D. Drew, of | Cardinals (1) | 44.9 | $3,000,000 |
| 4. Matt Holliday, 3b/1b | Rockies (7) | 44.1 | $842,500 |
| 5. Carlos Pena, 1b | Rangers (1) | 25.1 | $1,850,000 |
| 6. Jack Wilson, ss | Cardinals (9) | 23.5 | $40,000 |
| 7. Aaron Rowand, of | White Sox (1-S) | 20.8 | $575,000 |
| 8. Aubrey Huff, 3b/1b | Devil Rays (5) | 20.2 | $130,000 |
| 9. Mark Mulder, lhp | Athletics (1) | 20.0 | $3,200,000 |
| 10. Brandon Inge, ss/rhp | Tigers (2) | 19.0 | $450,000 |
| 11. Pat Burrell, 3b/1b | Phillies (1) | 18.8 | $3,150,000 |
| 12. Adam Dunn, of | Reds (2) | 16.9 | $772,000 |
| Juan Pierre, of | Rockies (13) | 16.9 | $20,000 |
| 14. Jeff Weaver, rhp | Tigers (1) | 15.5 | $1,750,000 |
| 15. Nick Punto, ss | Phillies (21) | 15.3 | $20,000 |
| 16. Matt Thornton, lhp | Mariners (1) | 14.2 | $925,000 |
| 17. Morgan Ensberg, 3b | Astros (9) | 13.8 | $25,000 |
| 18. Austin Kearns, of | Reds (1) | 12.8 | $1,950,000 |
| 19. Adam Everett, ss | Red Sox (1) | 12.6 | $1,725,000 |
| 20. B.J. Ryan, lhp | Reds (17) | 11.8 | $2,000 |
| 21. Brad Wilkerson, of | Expos (1-S) | 11.0 | $1,000,000 |
| 22. Ryan Madson, rhp | Phillies (9) | 10.7 | $325,000 |
| 23. Eric Byrnes, of | Athletics (8) | 10.5 | $15,000 |
| 24. Corey Patterson, of | Cubs (1) | 9.6 | $3,700,000 |
| Bill Hall, ss | Brewers (6) | 9.6 | $90,000 |
| 26. Erubiel Durazo, 1b | Diamondbacks (NDFA) | 9.1 | None |
| 27. Javier Lopez, lhp | Diamondbacks (4) | 8.5 | $130,000 |
| 28. David Ross, c | Dodgers (7) | 8.4 | $72,500 |
| 29. Kip Wells, rhp | White Sox (1) | 8.3 | $1,495,000 |
| 30. Brad Lidge, rhp | Astros (1) | 8.2 | $1,070,000 |
| Eric Hinske, 3b | Cubs (17) | 8.2 | $40,000 |

| Top 3 Unsigned Players | | | Year Signed |
|---|---|---|---|
| 1. Mark Teixeira, 1b/3b | Red Sox (9) | 52.4 | 2001 |
| 2. Cliff Lee, lhp | Orioles (20) | 44.3 | 2000 |
| 3. Barry Zito, lhp | Rangers (3) | 32.6 | 1999 |

($3.15 million), the record for a player signing with the team that drafted him fell twice in rapid order, though the size of the bonus was clouded by the nature of the major league contracts each player signed. Such deals allowed the Cardinals and Phillies to spread out the value of the contract over a period of years, in contrast to the standard minor league contract that mandated bonus payments be paid in full by the end of the second calendar year.

The record appeared to fall again with contracts signed by Mulder, the second pick overall, and Georgia high school outfielder Corey Patterson, the third selection, though there was a difference in interpretation in the actual value of those bonuses.

Patterson agreed with the Chicago Cubs on a bonus contract worth $3.7 million, topping Burrell's $3.15 million bonus. But the present value of Patterson's contract was calculated as $2.895 million because it was scheduled to be paid out over five years with provisions of Patterson's status as a two-sport athlete. The difference of $805,000 was calculated based on the deferred payments in Patterson's deal.

Mulder signed a contract with the Oakland Athletics with a value of $3.2 million, although the A's maintained it was not a record-setting amount because the bonus, due to be paid in full by December 1999, was backloaded and the present value was $2.944 million.

Historically, the value of a bonus had been established by the face value of the contract, with no regard to when the payments were made, so Patterson's $3.7 million bonus was determined to be a record. So for historical purposes, three bonus records were set in 1998.

For players signed by the team that drafted them, the 1998 draft established the six richest bonuses in draft history to that point. In addition to Drew, Burrell, Patterson and Mulder, the Kansas City Royals paid $2.7 million to Stanford righthander Jeff Austin, the fourth overall pick.

The Cardinals agreed with righthander Chad Hutchinson, their second-round pick, on a $3.4 million, major league deal that included a $2.3 million bonus. "This is an area we can compete in, getting quality young talent like J.D.," Cardinals general manager Walt Jocketty said. "I'm sure there will be other clubs upset by what we've done. I'm sure they'll be upset because they wish they had these players."

MORRIS FOSTOFF

Chad Hutchinson

The average first-round bonus jumped to a record $1,637,667 in 1998, an increase of 23.1 percent over the 1997 average of $1,325,536. Factoring in the $5.3 million in bonuses they spent on Drew and Hutchinson, the Cardinals set a record by spending $6,983,500 on all their draft picks, topping the mark of $5,045,500 set by the Montreal Expos in 1997. Six other clubs also surpassed the old mark: Royals ($6.54 million), Phillies ($5.6935 million), New York Yankees ($5.687 million), Cubs ($5.6489 million), Colorado Rockies ($5.628 million), San Francisco Giants ($5.5575 million) and A's ($5.0914 million).

The record spending came against the backdrop of a grievance initiated by Boras on behalf of Drew. They challenged a change Major League Baseball made to the draft rules. After Drew ended his amateur status by signing with the St. Paul Saints of the independent Northern League in 1997, MLB responded by changing the official name of the process to the "First-Year Player Draft." MLB said it was simply an effort to make clear that players in independent or other professional leagues, like Drew, who had never signed a standard minor league contract, were subject to the draft. The Players Association took up the cause, and the case went to arbitrator Dana Eischen.

In his ruling, delivered two weeks before the 1998 draft, Eischen determined that MLB had violated terms of the Basic Agreement with the Players Association by altering the draft rules. While he sided with the union, it was a Pyrrhic victory because Eischen refused to grant Drew free agency. He acknowledged that Drew was the main party

### AT A GLANCE

the big leagues briefly but played in more minor league games (1,136), and had more homers (125) and RBIs (524) than any other 1998 first-rounder.

### Ones Who Got Away

**MARK PRIOR, RHP, YANKEES (1ST ROUND); MARK TEIXEIRA, 3B, RED SOX (9TH ROUND).** Both players sought bonuses out of high school that were roughly one-fifth the amounts they received three years later. Prior spent a year at Vanderbilt and two at Southern California, and Teixeira attended Georgia Tech.

### He Was Drafted?

**DREW HENSON, 3B, YANKEES (3RD ROUND).** Henson spent three years as a quarterback at the University of Michigan and four more in the NFL, and he appeared in nine games with the Yankees over two major league seasons.

### Did You Know . . .

**MATT THORNTON**, a first-round pick of the Mariners, didn't win a game at NCAA Division II Grand Valley State, where he was primarily a basketball player, or in his first two seasons in the Mariners system. But he and lefthander **C.C. SABATHIA** were the only 1998 first-round picks still active in 2016.

### They Said It

Cardinals first baseman **MARK MCGWIRE**, on **J.D. DREW**, who declined a huge bonus in 1997 and signed with the Cardinals a year later: "You've got to get your head examined if you're going to turn down $6 million out of college. I hope he means what he says when he says he wants to play baseball. It's absolutely ridiculous what some of these young kids are getting. They don't even know what it takes to be a big league ballplayer. I guess we'll see how badly he wants to play. Let's face it, he's burned some bridges for a whole year."

## DRAFT SPOTLIGHT: J.D. DREW

JOHN WILLIAMSON

Outfielder J.D. Drew was a reliable contributor for the Cardinals, but he never achived the stardom foretold by his amateur career

The baseball draft has had its share of noteworthy holdouts and controversial signings, but few players struck a chord that reverberated through the game quite like outfielder J.D. Drew. Though he was not the No. 1 overall pick in either 1997 or '98, and the bonus record he established was short-lived, Drew not only dominated the chatter around two drafts, but led to a renaming of the process.

A talented junior outfielder at Florida State in 1997 who became the first and only 30-30 player in college history, Drew was drafted second overall by the Phillies. He and agent Scott Boras caused furor and consternation with a contentious negotiation that resulted in no deal being struck. Rather than return to college for his senior season, Drew gave up his amateur status and signed to play in the independent Northern League for the balance of the 1997 season and the following spring.

Drew's intent was not to prepare himself for the 1998 draft as much as it was to be declared a free agent, on the grounds that he no longer was an amateur. Major League Baseball moved quickly to counteract the maneuver by renaming the process the "First-Year Player Draft." The Players Association filed a grievance, contending that MLB couldn't unilaterally make changes to the draft. Arbitrator Dana Eischen ruled against MLB, but also determined he had no jurisdiction to grant Drew free agency.

Once the arbitrator ruled, the Phillies had about a week to get Drew under contract, but the sides remained at a stalemate. "We got no read from J.D. that he was ready to make a deal," Phillies scouting director Mike Arbuckle said. "It's just the same old rhetoric with Scott—that the system is so unfair."

Drew continued to dominate the predraft discussion in 1998. The Phillies had the first pick, but steered clear. Drew went to the Cardinals with the fifth pick overall and soon signed for a record $3 million bonus that was part of a four-year, major league contract that guaranteed him $7 million.

Cardinals players had mixed reactions to Drew's signing. First baseman Mark McGwire, who was chasing Roger Maris' single-season mark of 61 home runs, said: "You've got to get your head examined if you're going to turn down $6 million out of college. I hope he means what he says when he says he wants to play baseball. I'm from the old school—that you've got to prove yourself in the big leagues, and that's where you make your money. It's absolutely ridiculous what some of these young kids are getting."

Drew quickly proved himself. After batting .386 with nine home runs and 33 RBIs in 30 games with St. Paul of the independent Northern League to begin the 1998 season, he hit a combined .321 with seven home runs in 45 games at Double-A Arkansas and Triple-A Memphis. The Cardinals called him to the big leagues on Sept. 7, the same day that McGwire hit his 62nd homer and broke Maris' record.

"I took a little heat at the beginning because of the deal with Philadelphia," Drew said. "I have no hard feelings. It was just one of those things where they read me wrong. I was being up-front and honest with them, and they didn't think I would take it that far."

Drew had a relatively successful 14-year, major league career, but he remains best remembered for his efforts to circumvent the draft system. Fans and the media alike never particularly warmed to Drew because of a perception that he was a soft player who missed too much time because of injuries and compromised his vast baseball talent.

But in Drew's defense, he was a quiet country boy from rural Georgia who never embraced the limelight. He played on an even keel, and was not one for throwing his helmet in disgust after striking out. Nor was he the kind of player who gave a fist bump after hitting a home run. He rarely flashed a smile, let alone celebrated an impressive play. His trademark tranquility became interpreted as apathy. Drew was a very good player, but he never attained the heights expected of a player generally regarded as the best amateur prospect in the country for two years.

affected by the ruling, but said he did not have jurisdiction to make a ruling on Drew because he was not a member of the union.

Where did Drew stand as the draft unfolded? Right where most predicted, in the No. 5 slot held by the Cardinals, the team that had paid Boras client Rick Ankiel, a second-round choice in 1997, a record $2.5 million bonus. The Cardinals quickly came to terms with Drew, avoiding the rancor that characterized the negotiations with the Phillies.

Drew made three-week stops in both Double-A and Triple-A before making his major league debut for the Cardinals on Sept. 8, in the same game that Mark McGwire hit his record 62nd home run. In 36 at-bats before the end of the season, Drew hit .417 with five home runs and 13 RBIs, one of the best major league debuts in recent memory. Despite enduring numerous injuries, Drew established himself as a solid player in 14 major league seasons with four teams, although he fell short of being the star that many expected him to be.

## HENSON, HUTCHINSON SET NEW BAR

On the same day that Burrell signed, the Yankees gave a $2 million bonus to third-round selection Drew Henson, more than double the previous record for a third-rounder. Henson's deal allowed him to play football at the University of Michigan, but would give him an additional $2.7 million if he quit football after his freshman year, or an additional $1.9 million if he played football for four years and then pursued baseball full time.

Henson had spectacular credentials coming out of Brighton (Mich.) High. He was the nation's No. 1-ranked quarterback, had a 95 mph fastball, and set national high school career records for home runs (70), RBIs (290) and runs (259). As a senior, he hit .608 with 22 home runs and 83 RBIs, and had a 14-1, 0.86 record with 174 strikeouts in 82 innings. He undoubtedly would have been one of the first picks in the draft if football wasn't also a factor.

The 6-foot-5, 220-pound Henson made strides in his first three seasons in the Yankees organization, hitting .287 with 22 home runs while rising to Double-A. But the Yankees could not persuade him to give up football, so they traded him to the Cincinnati Reds on July 12, 2000. Henson returned to school for his junior year, and with Tom Brady no longer ahead of him on the Michigan football depth chart, he completed 131 of 217 passes for 1,852 yards and 16 touchdowns, positioning himself as a potential first overall pick in the 2002 NFL draft.

The Reds were in no position financially to

### Fastest To The Majors

| | Player, Pos. | Drafted (Round) | Debut |
|---|---|---|---|
| 1. | J.D. Drew, of | Cardinals (1) | Sept. 8, 1998 |
| 2. | Jeff Weaver, rhp | Tigers (1) | April 14, 1999 |
| 3. | Ryan Rupe, rhp | Devil Rays (6) | May 5, 1999 |
| 4. | Kip Wells, rhp | White Sox (1) | Aug. 2, 1999 |
| 5. | Mark Mulder, lhp | Athletics (1) | April 18, 2000 |

**FIRST HIGH SCHOOL SELECTION:** Corey Patterson, of (Cubs/1, Sept. 18, 2000) satisfy Henson's desire to give up football and play baseball only, so they traded him back to the Yankees the following spring. New York quickly signed him to a six-year, $17 million deal that prohibited him from playing football. Rather than bringing Henson along slowly, the Yankees pushed him to Triple-A in 2001, and he hit .222 with 11 home runs in 71 games and struck out 85 times. He wasn't much more productive the next two years, hitting .237 with 32 home runs and 143 RBIs in 261 games, striking out 273 times and committing 63 errors at third base.

Henson made token appearances with the Yankees in 2002 and '03, getting nine at-bats, but it was apparent the big investment in Henson wasn't going to pay off. Some scouts said the team's biggest mistake was pushing him along too quickly, which seemed to rob Henson of confidence in his hitting ability. He left baseball after the 2003 season, forfeiting the three years and $12 million remaining on his contract.

The expansion Houston Texans took Henson in the sixth round of the 2003 NFL draft on the chance he might return to football, and they traded his rights to the Dallas Cowboys in March 2004. He played for the Cowboys and two other clubs over the next four years as a seldom-used backup and was out of the NFL by 2009.

Henson's script was similar to that of the 6-foot-5, 230-pound Hutchinson, a top pitching prospect in 1998 who slid to the second round (No. 48 overall) because of his desire to continue playing quarterback for Stanford. Hutchinson had gone to college after turning down a $1.6 million bonus offer as a 1995 first-round pick of the Atlanta Braves.

Hutchinson went 25-11, 4.81 in three years at Stanford. After signing the largest contract ever given to a second-rounder, he struggled with his command in four seasons in the Cardinals system, going 17-25, 5.63 with 266 walks in 352 innings. Hutchinson made three appearances for the Cardinals early in the 2001 season, was sent back to the minor leagues, and by the end of the year had decided to return to football. Like Henson, he languished in the NFL as a backup, his career lasting for three years.

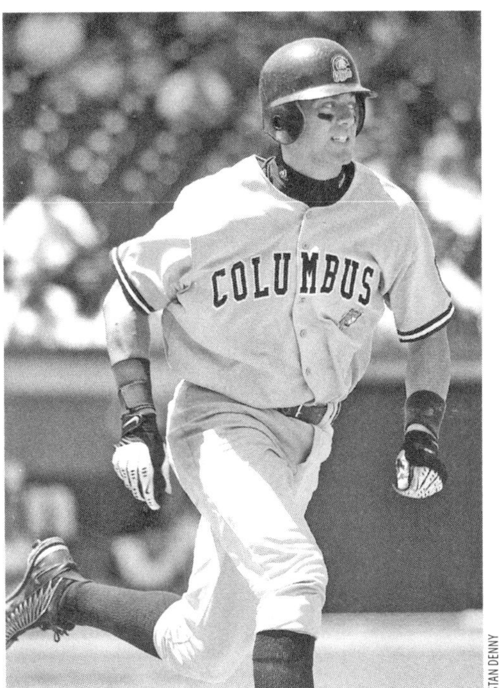

Drew Henson collected millions of dollars from the Yankees to steer him away from football, but he never fulfilled his baseball promise

## Top 25 Bonuses

| Player, Pos. | Drafted (Round) | Order | Bonus |
|---|---|---|---|
| **1. * Corey Patterson, of** | **Cubs (1)** | **3** | **$3,700,000** |
| **2. Mark Mulder, lhp** | **Athletics (1)** | **2** | **$3,200,000** |
| **3. Pat Burrell, 3b/1b** | **Phillies (1)** | **1** | **#$3,150,000** |
| **4. J.D. Drew, of** | **Cardinals (1)** | **5** | **#$3,000,000** |
| **5. Jeff Austin, rhp** | **Royals (1)** | **4** | **$2,700,000** |
| **6. Chad Hutchinson, rhp** | **Cardinals (2)** | **48** | **#$2,300,000** |
| **7. * Sean Burroughs, 3b** | **Padres (1)** | **9** | **$2,100,000** |
| 8. Ryan Mills, lhp | Twins (1) | 6 | $2,000,000 |
| *** Felipe Lopez, ss** | **Blue Jays (1)** | **8** | **$2,000,000** |
| *** Drew Henson, 3b/rhp** | **Yankees (3)** | **97** | **$2,000,000** |
| **11. * Austin Kearns, of** | **Reds (1)** | **7** | **$1,950,000** |
| **12. Carlos Pena, 1b** | **Rangers (1)** | **10** | **$1,850,000** |
| **13. Jeff Weaver, rhp** | **Tigers (1)** | **14** | **$1,750,000** |
| *** Matt Belisle, rhp** | **Braves (2)** | **52** | **$1,750,000** |
| 15. * J.M. Gold, rhp | Brewers (1) | 13 | $1,700,000 |
| **16. * Chip Ambres, of** | **Marlins (1)** | **27** | **$1,500,000** |
| **17. Kip Wells, rhp** | **White Sox (1)** | **16** | **$1,495,000** |
| **18. * Choo Freeman, of** | **Rockies (1-S)** | **38** | **$1,400,000** |
| **19. * C.C. Sabathia, lhp** | **Indians (1)** | **20** | **$1,300,000** |
| 20. * Josh McKinley, ss | Expos (1) | 11 | $1,250,000 |
| **21. * Chris George, lhp** | **Royals (1-S)** | **31** | **$1,162,500** |
| **22. Seth Etherton, rhp** | **Angels (1)** | **18** | **$1,075,000** |
| **23. Brad Lidge, rhp** | **Astros (1)** | **17** | **$1,070,000** |
| **Jason Tyner, of** | **Mets (1)** | **21** | **$1,070,000** |
| 25. * Andy Brown, of | Yankees (1) | 24 | $1,050,000 |

*Major leaguers in bold. *High school selection. #Major league contract.*

Bonus records weren't limited to premium picks or to players like Hutchinson and Henson who had options in two sports. Two 1998 draft-and-follows, a nondrafted free agent and several international players also received record bonuses.

Catcher Gerald Laird, a second-round pick of the A's, and outfielder Ivan Reyes, a fourth-round selection of the Yankees, signed the following spring for bonuses of $1 million, the first draft-and-follows to get seven-figure deals. Laird significantly enhanced his stock during his freshman year at Cypress (Calif.) JC. Reyes, a Puerto Rican high school product, also improved his status after a year at Miami-Dade North CC.

Outfielder Bobby Kielty, who had been passed over in the draft four times, including in 1998 as a fourth-year junior at the University of Mississippi, became the subject of a bidding war after his performance in the summer Cape Cod League, where he nearly won the triple crown and earned MVP honors. Kielty, free to negotiate with anyone, eventually signed with the Minnesota Twins for $500,000, the largest bonus ever for a nondrafted free agent. He played seven years in the majors, hitting .254 with 53 home runs and 253 RBIs.

The Yankees also spent big money on the international market, signing four players to seven-figure bonuses: outfielder Wily Mo Pena ($3.7 million), shortstop Alfonso Soriano ($3.1 million) and righthander Ricardo Aramboles ($1.52 million),

## WORTH NOTING

■ The expansion Arizona Diamondbacks and Tampa Bay Devil Rays stunned the industry by signing four loophole free agents to bonuses that totaled $29.275 million in 1996, but those clubs were hardly a factor in the 1998 draft, in the year they began play in the major leagues. The Diamondbacks forfeited their first two picks for signing free agents **JAY BELL** and **WILLIE BLAIR**, and spent just $1,689,500 on all their selections. The only team that spent less was the Devil Rays, who sacrificed their first three picks as the cost for signing free agents **ROBERTO HERNANDEZ**, **WILSON ALVAREZ** and **DAVE MARTINEZ**, and spent $1,589,500. The Devil Rays spent $160,000 to sign their 50th and last pick, Hill (Texas) Junior College outfielder **LUIS CANDELARIA**.

■ Outfielder **J.D. DREW**, selected by the Cardinals with the fifth pick overall from the Northern League's St. Paul Saints, became the first American player drafted in the first round out of an independent league. Cuban righthander **ARIEL PRIETO** was the fifth overall pick in 1995, coming out of the independent Western League. Including Drew, a record 11 first-rounders in the 1998 draft played in an independent league at some point in their professional career.

■ Three players from the 1998 draft died while they were active in pro ball, including major league righthanders **JOSH HANCOCK** and **STEVE BECHLER**. Hancock, a fifth-round pick of the Red Sox who pitched for four teams over six major league seasons, was killed in a car wreck April 29, 2007, in St. Louis. He was determined to be intoxicated when his vehicle hit a parked truck. Bechler, a third-round choice of the Orioles out of an Oregon high school, died on Feb. 17, 2003, at age 23. Bechler collapsed while running during spring training in Fort Lauderdale,

CONTINUED ON PAGE 500

**WORTH NOTING**

CONTINUED FROM PAGE 499

Fla., and died a week later of organ failure caused by heatstroke. His death was linked to the use of the dietary supplement Xenadrine. Bechler had made his major league debut with the Orioles the previous September, going 0-0, 13.50 in three appearances. **BRIAN COLE**, 22, a promising outfielder in the Mets farm system, was killed March 31, 2001, in an auto accident near Marianna, Fla. An 18th-round pick in 1998 out of Navarro (Texas) Junior College, Cole was named Baseball America's Junior College Player of the Year that year after hitting .524 with 27 homers, 82 RBIs and 49 stolen bases in 60 games. At Class A St. Lucie and Double-A Binghamton in 2000, Cole hit .306 with 19 homers, 86 RBIs and 69 stolen bases. "He was a player we were going to build around as an organization," said **JIM DUQUETTE**, the Mets farm director at the time of Cole's death. Cole's family was later awarded $131 million to settle a lawsuit against the Ford Motor Company.

■ The Orioles drafted **TIM RAINES JR.** in the sixth round. Three years later, on Oct. 4, 2001, he played center field for the Orioles in a 5-4 loss to the Red Sox, while his father, Tim Raines Sr., played left field. The only other father-son combo to play in the same major league game was the Griffeys, Ken Sr. and Ken Jr., who did it late in the 1990 season with the Mariners. The elder Raines wrapped up a 23-year career in the majors a year later, while Tim Jr. continued to play with the Orioles through the 2004 season. The Raines would reunite in 2011, when Tim Jr. played for the Newark Bears of the independent Can-Am League, who were managed by his father.

■ San Diego's selection of **SEAN BURROUGHS** with the ninth overall pick marked the second time in draft history that a father and son became first-round picks. Burroughs' father, Jeff, was the No. 1

all from the Dominican Republic; and Cuban righthander Orlando "El Duque" Hernandez, who received a $1 million bonus as part of a major league contract valued at $6.6 million.

## BURRELL CAPS HUGE COLLEGE CAREER

Burrell's rise to the No. 1 overall pick was somewhat meteoric, considering he was a 43rd-round selection of the Boston Red Sox in 1995 out of a California high school. He decided to attend college at Miami after the Red Sox refused to include a signing bonus as part of their offer.

As a freshman at Miami, Burrell hit .484, best in NCAA Division I, with 23 homers. He also excelled as a sophomore and in summer competition, and even his back injury as a junior wasn't enough to knock him out of the top spot in the 1998 draft or as the Golden Spikes Award winner.

Burrell spent 12 seasons in the majors as an outfielder, including nine in Philadelphia, and hit .253 with 292 homers. His two best seasons in a Phillies uniform came in 2002 (.282-37-116) and 2005 (.281-32-117).

With the second pick, the A's considered Drew as a potential outfield bookend to Ben Grieve, the second pick in the 1994 draft. But Oakland decided to let another team deal with the demands of Drew and Boras, and chose Mulder.

"We're confident of Mulder's intentions and desire to play pro ball," said A's scouting director Grady Fuson. "I think everyone in the organization was willing to fight it out with Drew, but that wasn't in the best interests of the organization."

The 6-foot-6, 200-pound Mulder was an unheralded high school player who was recruited by Michigan State primarily as a first baseman. After declining a token offer from the Detroit Tigers as a 55th-round pick in 1995 and redshirting as a freshman, he developed into a top-flight pitching prospect, going 6-6, 3.40 with 19 walks and 113 strikeouts in 85 innings in 1998.

Oakland refused to give on Mulder's demand for a major league contract. After several months of haggling, Mulder reached an agreement on the largest signing bonus ever for a player signing a standard minor league contract. Mulder led the American League in wins in 2001 (21) and had 103 victories over a nine-year major league career that was compromised by shoulder issues.

KEVIN FOWLER

Mark Mulder

Despite a deep and talented pool of college pitchers, the Cubs spent the third pick on Patterson, the only high school player among the first six players drafted. A center fielder with speed and power, Patterson was considered the top prep athlete available. He hit .528 with 22 home runs and 37 stolen bases in as many attempts as a senior at Harrison High in suburban Atlanta. The Cubs reached agreement on Patterson's historic contract shortly before he was scheduled to begin classes at Georgia Tech.

### Largest Bonuses By Round

| | Player, Pos. | Club | Bonus |
|---|---|---|---|
| **1.** | *** Corey Patterson, of** | **Cubs** | **$3,700,000** |
| **2.** | **Chad Hutchinson, rhp** | **Cardinals** | **$2,300,000** |
| **3.** | *** Drew Henson, 3b/rhp** | **Yankees** | **$2,000,000** |
| 4. | *# Ivan Reyes, ss | Yankees | $1,000,000 |
| 5. | * Ryan Dittfurth, rhp | Rangers | $400,000 |
| 6. | * Ric Riccobono, rhp | Red Sox | $500,000 |
| **7.** | *** Matt Holliday, 3b** | **Rockies** | **$842,500** |
| 8. | # Justin Lincoln, 3b/rhp | Rockies | $215,000 |
| **9.** | *** Ryan Madson, rhp** | **Phillies** | **$325,000** |
| 10. | *# Pedro Zazueta, rhp | Cardinals | $72,500 |
| | * Larnell Hamm, of | Mets | $72,500 |
| 11. | * Jon Pridie, rhp | Twins | $150,000 |
| 12. | * Russ Cleveland, c | Tigers | $50,000 |
| 13. | * Ben Levesque, rhp | Pirates | $120,000 |
| **14.** | ***John Ennis, rhp** | **Braves** | **$125,000** |
| 15. | * Johnny Hernandez, of | Cardinals | $175,000 |
| 16. | *# Neal Frendling, rhp | Devil Rays | $82,500 |
| 17. | * Reuben St. Amand, rhp | Blue Jays | $50,000 |
| 18. | *# David Brous, lhp | Giants | $225,000 |
| 19. | Kevin Hodge, ss/3b | Twins | $28,000 |
| 20. | * John Egly, 3b | Diamondbacks | $25,000 |
| **21.** | **Nick Punto, ss** | **Phillies** | **$20,000** |
| | * Mike Bumatay, lhp/of | Pirates | $20,000 |
| 22. | # Brian Shipp, ss | Mets | $180,000 |
| 23. | *# J.J. Sherrill, of | Indians | $425,000 |
| 24. | # Jason Willis, rhp | Yankees | $90,000 |
| 25. | * Eric Sandberg, 1b | Twins | $162,000 |
| Other | *# Josh Schaffer, 3b | Angels (26) | $300,000 |

*Major leaguers in bold. *High school selection. #Signed as draft-and-follow.*

Patterson played in 12 major league seasons but never developed into a star, hitting .252 with 118 homers and 218 stolen bases.

The Royals, with ownership issues, a tight budget and three selections among the first 31 picks, chose Austin, Baseball America's College Player of the Year, with the fourth pick. Austin was a polished college product close to being major league ready, but many scouts did not consider him a premium prospect. The Royals hoped to sign him quickly for a modest bonus, but Austin and Boras took a hard-line negotiating stance.

"This is not a J.D. Drew situation," Royals scouting director Terry Wetzel said. "Austin is a very good pitching prospect whom we'd very much like to sign, but there's no way his value goes up by sitting out. He'll never see another offer as good as the one that we've made him just by the nature of his age and the type of pitcher that he is."

Austin decided not to return to Stanford for his senior year, which allowed negotiations to continue. He signed with the Royals the following February for a $2.7 million bonus. It was money poorly spent by the Royals, considering that Austin's major league career amounted to a 2-3, 6.75 record in 38 appearances for the Royals and Reds.

Baylor University righthander Kip Wells, who was picked 16th overall by the Chicago White Sox, followed Austin's lead and did not return to college after negotiations with the White Sox bogged down. Wells signed on Dec. 23 for a bonus of $1.495 million.

Only 10 of the 30 first-round picks had signed before the end of June. Burroughs and Florida prep shortstop Felipe Lopez were also among those who engaged in drawn-out negotiations.

Lopez circulated a letter before the draft asking teams not to select him unless they were prepared to offer a $3 million bonus. The Toronto Blue Jays, who had a history of getting their first-round picks signed quickly, selected Lopez with the eighth overall pick. With few college options and a difficult home life, Lopez relented and signed on Aug. 11 for a bonus of $2 million.

Burroughs was encouraged by his family to accept a scholarship to Southern California, something his father, Jeff, passed on when he was the No. 1 overall pick in the 1969 draft. The San Diego Padres, picking ninth, viewed Burroughs as the best pure high school hitter in the country and couldn't resist drafting him. They signed him on Sept. 2 for a $2.1 million bonus.

Though he reached San Diego in 2002 at age 21, the 6-foot-1, 195-pound Burroughs never hit for power in the minor leagues, and homered just 11 times in 432 games over four years with the Padres. By 29, he was out of the game, though he returned to the majors briefly in 2011 and '12, hitting .252 with one homer in 127 at-bats.

### PREDRAFT DEALS PROLIFERATE

With signing bonuses skyrocketing, several teams chose to negotiate deals before the 1998 draft, contingent on the player being available. Such prearranged deals were technically prohibited by draft rules, but they became part of the process for teams looking for cost certainty. The first player who struck an agreement before the draft was Mills, selected sixth by the Twins. He agreed to a $2 million signing bonus while still pitching for Arizona State in the College World Series.

Other first-rounders who agreed to deals: Expos shortstop Josh McKinley (No. 11, $1.25 million), Pittsburgh Pirates lefthander Clint Johnston (No. 15, $1 million), Giants third baseman Tony Torcato (No. 19, $975,000), Giants righthander Nate Bump (No. 25, $750,000) and Yankees outfielder Andy Brown (No. 24, $1.05 million).

The Giants had the unenviable task of signing three first-rounders and seven of the first 72 selections. They not only managed to get all seven in the fold, but also signed their first 23 picks. Even with predraft deals for Torcato and Bump, the Giants spent upward of $5.5 million on their picks, considerably more than they had ever spent.

One of two college seniors drafted in the first round, Bump was targeted by the Giants because of his limited leverage, and his $750,000 bonus was the smallest in the first round. The California Angels signed the other college senior, Southern Cal righthander Seth Etherton (18th overall), giving him a bonus of $1.075 million.

Another factor that affected the 1998 draft more than any previous draft was contracts for two-sport athletes. Before 1995, a player's signing bonus had to be paid out before the end of the second calendar year following the player's contract date. A rule change that year enabled clubs to spread out payments over a period of five years if the player was a two-sport talent. The rule was designed to give teams protection against athletes who received their entire signing bonuses, only to subsequently quit baseball to pursue their other sport, usually football.

Hutchinson and Henson were the highest profile dual-sport athletes in the 1998 draft, and Henson was one of seven high-round picks affected by the new contract language. Hutchinson's deal also was spread out over a number of years, but under terms of the major league contract he signed.

Patterson was the highest pick to take advantage of the two-sport rule, even though he did not play football his senior year in high school and had accepted a baseball scholarship to Georgia Tech. He had been considered one of the top wide receivers in the country by prep football analysts as a junior, and his letter of intent with Georgia Tech specifically mentioned that he was welcome to join the football team at any time.

RODGER WOOD

Corey Patterson

Other athletes who took advantage of the two-sport rule included Florida Marlins first-rounder Chip Ambres ($1.5 million), Rockies supplemental first-rounder Choo Freeman ($1.4 million), Reds second-rounder Adam Dunn ($772,000), Cardinals second-rounder Tim Lemon ($650,000) and Rockies seventh-rounder Matt Holliday ($885,000). Only Dunn had an agreement that allowed him to play football in college; he played one season as a quarterback at Texas.

The most surprising first-round selection was probably Matt Thornton, a lefthander from NCAA Division II Grand Valley State (Mich.) who was selected by the Seattle Mariners with the 22nd pick.

## One Team's Draft: Colorado Rockies

| Player, Pos. | Bonus | Player, Pos. | Bonus | Player, Pos. | Bonus |
|---|---|---|---|---|---|
| **1. *Matt Roney, rhp** | **$1,012,500** | 8. Justin Lincoln, 3b/rhp | $215,000 | 18. Jase Wrigley, rhp | $1,000 |
| **1. *Choo Freeman, of** | **$1,400,000** | 9. Justin Carter, lhp | $50,000 | 19. Doug Thompson, rhp | $1,000 |
| 1. *Jeff Winchester, c | $537,500 | 10. Andrew Beinbrink, 3b | Did not sign | 20. Tom Whitehurst, of | $8,000 |
| **2. *Jermaine Van Buren, rhp** | **$375,000** | 11. Ryan Cameron, rhp | $27,500 | 21. Erik Johnson, c | $7,500 |
| **2. Jody Gerut, of** | **$450,000** | 12. Brian Brantley, rhp | $25,000 | 22. Ryan LaMattina, lhp | $1,000 |
| 3. Kevin Gordon, rhp | $270,000 | **13. Juan Pierre, of** | **$20,000** | 23. Richy Leon, 2b | $1,000 |
| **4. Luke Hudson, rhp** | **$150,000** | 14. *Vernand Morency, of | $30,000 | 24. Michael Mundy, rhp | $1,000 |
| **5. *Ryan Shealy, 1b** | **Did not sign** | **15. Mark DiFelice, rhp** | **$1,000** | 25. Kevin Duck, 1b | $5,000 |
| 6. *Javier Guzman, of | $85,000 | 16. *Brandon Garner, rhp | $25,000 | Other Frank Haase (45), lhp | $46,000 |
| **7. *Matt Holliday, 3b** | **$842,500** | 17. Josh Etherdge, 1b/of | $1,000 | | |

*Major leaguers in bold. *High school selection.*

### WORTH NOTING

overall pick in 1969 out of Woodrow Wilson High in Long Beach, Calif., the same school that Sean attended. The other first-round, father-son combo: father Tom Grieve in 1966 (sixth overall) and son Ben in 1994 (second overall). **BEN KNAPP** was a 1998 second-round pick of the Orioles; his father, Chris, was a first-rounder in 1975.

■ Like many aspects of the draft, college baseball was in a state of flux in 1998 after Southern California out-slugged Arizona State, 21-14, in the championship game of the College World Series, capping a season dominated by hitting and offense like none before it. "I'll never get used to the era of the aluminum bat," said Rod Dedeaux, the former USC head coach who had led the Trojans to 11 national titles before retiring in 1986. "Something needs to be done to change the game. This was exciting, and not to take anything away from the game, but this was not baseball." Less than two months after the College World Series, the NCAA rules committee recommended changes aimed at reducing the impact aluminum bats had on the game and ended the so-called "gorilla ball" era. The recommendations, effective with the 2000 college season, would force bat-makers to produce aluminum bats that performed more like wood bats.

■ For all the emphasis on offense in the college game, the most significant NCAA record set in 1998 was for saves. USC righthander **JACK KRAWCZYK** had 23, the last coming in the CWS championship game. Krawczyk's primary pitch was a knuckleball, explaining why he wasn't drafted until the 25th round by the Brewers. His pro career peaked at Triple-A. USC senior righthander **SETH ETHERTON**, the Trojans ace, led the nation in strikeouts, with 182 in 137 innings. A year earlier, he had been a ninth-round draft choice of the Cardinals, but this time he was selected in the first round by the Angels.

## IN FOCUS: SEAN BURROUGHS

From his days as a celebrated Little Leaguer, Sean Burroughs' future as a major league star seemed to be mapped out. He was a first-round pick of the Padres, a member of the 2000 U.S. Olympic team, and by the time he reached San Diego in 2002, at age 21, he was considered one of the game's top young hitters.

But he never hit for much power in the minor leagues, and homered just 11 times in 432 games over four years with the Padres. Tired of waiting for his power to emerge, the Padres traded him after the 2005 season, and his career—and life—soon spiraled downward.

Burroughs was out of baseball by age 29 and living on the edge. He said he wandered the streets of Las Vegas at all hours, abusing any substance he could ingest and eating cheeseburgers that he found in garbage cans. For more than a year, he lived as a vagabond. "I was doing a lot of things that were morally not correct and physically not correct," he said. "I was knocking at death's door. I was flirting with going to jail and getting locked up someplace. It was scary. Some people kind of came to my rescue. It was pure insanity."

Burroughs got his personal life straightened out and gave baseball another shot, first in the Diamondbacks organization. He returned to the majors briefly in 2011 and 2012, but hit just .252 with one homer in 127 at-bats.

## Highest Unsigned Picks

| Player, Pos., Team (Round) | College | Re-Drafted |
|---|---|---|
| Ben Diggins, 1b/rhp, Cardinals (1-S) | Arizona | Dodgers '00 (1) |
| Mark Prior, rhp, Yankees (1-S) | Vanderbilt | Cubs '01 (1) |
| Jeff Verplancke, rhp, Mariners (2) | * Cal State L.A. | Giants '99 (11) |
| Alex Hart, rhp, Orioles (2) | Florida | Pirates '02 (5) |
| Greg Porter, ss, Reds (3) | Texas A&M | Angels '01 (45) |
| Beau Craig, c, Padres (3) | USC | Athletics '00 (6) |
| Barry Zito, lhp, Rangers (3) | USC | Athletics '99 (1) |
| Kevin Kelly, 3b, Expos (3) | Duke | Giants '02 (5) |
| Paul French, rhp, Angels (3) | Arizona State | Never |
| Brad Busbin, rhp, Astros (3) | Georgia Tech | Phillies '02 (27) |

**TOTAL UNSIGNED PICKS:** Top 5 Rounds (17), Top 10 Rounds (43)

**Returned to same school.*

Thornton primarily was a basketball player in college; he pitched just 20 innings for the baseball team in 1998. Few teams projected him as a first-rounder simply because he had not pitched enough to be effectively scouted. Thornton did not win a game in college or in his first two seasons in the Mariners system, missed the 2002 season while recovering from Tommy John surgery, and was disabled much of the following year because of a herniated disk in his neck. But he eventually developed into an effective reliever over a dozen seasons in the majors, and along with C.C. Sabathia, was one of only two 1998 first-rounders still active in 2016.

Sabathia, a California prep product taken 20th overall by the Cleveland Indians, achieved the highest WAR (55.8) among first-rounders and the second-best score overall.

At one point in high school, the 6-foot-7 Sabathia weighed 270 pounds and appeared to be leaning toward a college football career as a tight end. In addition to pitching for the baseball team, he also played first base and flashed prodigious power. The Indians liked his upside on the mound and developed him as a pitcher after signing him to a $1.3 million bonus. After 15 major league seasons—eight in Cleveland and seven with the Yankees—Sabathia had won 212 games.

The career WAR leader for the class of 1998 was nowhere to be found in the early stages of the draft. Lefthander Mark Buehrle, a 38th-round pick of the White Sox out of Jefferson (Mo.) College, achieved the highest score over his 16-year, major league career. Buehrle signed in the spring of 1999 as a draft-and-follow for a $150,000 bonus. He won 214 games and pitched two no-hitters in the major leagues.

The three highest-ranked players entering the 1998 draft, according to the Major League Scouting Bureau's 20-80 grading system, were righthander J.M. Gold (67), outfielder Rick Elder (66) and Mills (66), none of whom reached the major leagues. Gold, a hard-throwing New Jersey high school product drafted 13th overall by the Milwaukee Brewers, did not advance past Class A in six seasons in the minors. Elder's career also topped out in Class A. An unpolished, 6-foot-6, 230-pound slugger from a Georgia high school, he proved to be an all-or-nothing gamble in five seasons in the minors, hitting just 40 homers and striking out at an accelerated rate. Mills went 17-40, 5.79 in seven minor league seasons.

The Pirates also came up short with their top pick. Selecting 15th overall, they drafted Johnston, who was one of the leading hitters in the college ranks that spring for Vanderbilt (.424-19-74) and also showed promise as a lefthanded pitcher in 20 innings of work. Most teams viewed Johnston's future as a hitter, but the Pirates liked him as a pitcher. "There's a lot of upside to this kid as a starting pitcher," scouting director Leland Maddox said. "He has a fastball that's 90-94 mph and could gain velocity since he hasn't pitched a whole lot."

Johnston, hampered by elbow problems, didn't advance past Class A as a pitcher and later flamed out as a hitter in the Blue Jays organization. None of the first 14 players the Pirates drafted in 1998 reached the major leagues.

### CHANGES IN THE WORKS

The overall mood of the industry toward the draft in 1998 was not positive. As bonuses continued to skyrocket, there was an overwhelming feeling among clubs that nothing could be done to refine the process, which most observers felt had evolved from a method of distributing talent to the most needy clubs into a high stakes poker game dominated by agents and money. Even members of the players union were questioning the wisdom of paying college and high school players with no track record as much as $3 million in bonuses.

Sandy Alderson, MLB's newly appointed vice president of baseball operations, addressed the issue during his first day on the job.

"It's definitely an issue that needs to be addressed," said Alderson, formerly the president and general manager of the Athletics. "There are a number of ways the draft is no longer serving its original purpose. We're not redistributing the talent the way that is was intended. Even major league players are beginning to wonder if the money that is going to amateur players is being distributed the right way."

Rangers scouting director Chuck McMichael said, "We just need to overhaul the draft, plain and simple. I know better than to think that we'll be able to roll back the type of money that we're spending, but there just has to be a better way of doing things."

A change that did occur in time for the 1998 draft was a rollback in the number of rounds to a maximum of 50, spread over two days. Previously, there had been no limit on rounds and the draft was spread over three days.

## Largest Draft-And-Follow Bonuses

| | Player, Pos. | Club (Round) | Bonus |
|---|---|---|---|
| 1. | ***Gerald Laird, c** | **Athletics (2)** | **$1,000,000** |
| | *Ivan Reyes, ss | Yankees (4) | $1,000,000 |
| 3. | *J.J. Sherrill, of | Indians (23) | $425,000 |
| 4. | *Josh Schaffer, 3b | Angels (26) | $300,000 |
| 5. | *Richard Lane, of | Expos (28) | $275,000 |
| 6. | Cam Reimers, rhp | Blue Jays (35) | $250,000 |
| | *David Brous, lhp | Giants (18) | $225,000 |
| | Gavin Wright, of | Astros (33) | $225,000 |
| | Mario Mendoza, rhp | Angels (46) | $225,000 |
| 10. | Justin Lincoln, 3b/rhp | Rockies (8) | $215,000 |

*Major leaguers in bold. *High school selection.*

# 1998 Draft List

*Did not sign. Major leaguers in bold, with first and last years noted. Order of selection indicated in parentheses. For the first five rounds, the peak level of each player is noted. + Signed as draft-and-follow (Second school noted if applicable).

## ANAHEIM ANGELS (18)

1. **Seth Etherton, rhp, University of Southern California.—(2000-06)**
2. Brandon Emanuel, rhp, Northwestern State University.—(AAA)
3. *Paul French, rhp, Northgate HS, Concord, Calif.—DNP

DRAFT DROP *Attended Arizona State; never re-drafted*

4. Brian Oliver, ss, University of California.—(AA)
5. Darren Blakely, of, University of Hawaii.—(AAA)
6. Jay Hood, ss, Georgia Tech.
7. Jeff Hundley, lhp, Bowling Green State University.
8. Jason Hill, c, University of California.
9. Kevin McClain, rhp, Central Florida CC.
10. ***Justin Lehr, rhp-c, UC Santa Barbara.—(2004-09)**
11. Bill Mott, of, Santa Clara University.
12. Ed Welch, of, Point Grey HS, Vancouver, B.C.
13. Greg Jacobs, lhp, Cal State Fullerton.
14. Jason Huisman, ss, University of Mississippi.

DRAFT DROP *Brother of Justin Huisman, major leaguer (2004) • Brother of Rick Huisman, major leaguer (1995-96)*

15. *Jaime Germain, 3b, Jose Campeche HS, San Lorenzo, P.R.
16. Justin Ross, of, University of Tennessee.
17. Doug Bridges, lhp, Embry-Riddle Aeronautical (Fla.) University.
18. Casey Kelley, 1b, Washington State University.
19. *Justin Stine, lhp, University of Missouri.
20. Ed Hurtado, rhp, UC Riverside.
21. Oliver Harwas, rhp, Warner Southern (Fla.) College.
22. Chad Berryman, rhp, Virginia Commonwealth University.
23. ***Ryan Braun, c-rhp, Edison HS, Fresno, Calif.—(2006-11)**
24. Chris Demouy, lhp, Louisiana State University.
25. Tommy Bond, rhp, University of Florida.
26. +Josh Shaffer, 3b, Esperanza HS, Yorba Linda, Calif. / Santa Ana (Calif.) JC.
27. *Simon Stoner, rhp, Pasco Hernando (Fla.) CC.
28. +Greg Moore, rhp, Ohlone (Calif.) JC.
29. Angel Diaz, c, University of Tampa.
30. *Ronte Langs, of, Gulf Coast (Fla.) CC.
31. Mike Leach, rhp, Florida Southern College.
32. *Ryan Flanagan, rhp, Gulf Coast (Fla.) CC.
33. Kenny Corley, 1b, University of Arizona.
34. ***Bobby Crosby, ss, La Quinta HS, Cypress, Calif.—(2003-10)**

DRAFT DROP *Son of Ed Crosby, major leaguer (1970-76)*

35. *Ben Margalski, c, Belleville Area (Ill.) CC.
36. Mike Christensen, 3b, Florida Southern College.
37. *Matt Tucek, rhp, Waxahachie (Texas) HS.
38. Chris Aronson, rhp, George Mason University.
39. Brad Downing, of, Cal Poly Pomona.

DRAFT DROP *Son of Brian Downing, major leaguer (1973-92)*

40. Will Croud, of, University of Central Florida.
41. Doug Wakefield, lhp, Cal State Dominguez Hills.
42. Matt Lubozynski, lhp, University of Central Florida.
43. +Josh Warren, rhp, Polk (Fla.) CC.
44. *Jon Steitz, rhp, Hopkins School, New Haven, Conn.
45. *Cam Esslinger, rhp, Seton Hall University.
46. +Mario Mendoza, rhp, Central Arizona JC.

DRAFT DROP *Son of Mario Mendoza, major leaguer (1974-82)*

47. Rudy Arguelles, of, Arizona State University.
48. *Brian Ferreira, of, Manatee (Fla.) JC.
49. Bryn Wade, 2b, Biola (Calif.) University.
50. *Edgardo Salgado, c, Florida Air Academy, Melbourne, Fla.

## ARIZONA DIAMONDBACKS (30)

1. (Choice to Royals as compensation for Type A free agent Jay Bell)
2. (Choice to Tigers as compensation for Type A free agent Willie Blair)
3. Darryl Conyer, of, Mission Bay HS, San Diego.—(Rookie)
4. **Javier Lopez, lhp, University of Virginia.—(2003-15)**
5. **J.D. Closser, c, Monroe HS, Alexandria, Ind.—(2004-06)**
6. Brock McCarty, of, Ouachita Parish HS, Monroe, La.
7. Jeff Pass, lhp, Chrysler HS, New Castle, Ind.
8. **Andrew Good, rhp, Rochester HS, Rochester Hills, Mich.—(2003-05)**
9. *Brendan Fuller, rhp, Clearwater (Fla.) HS.
10. Tom Kail, of, Baldwin HS, Pittsburgh.
11. Hector Cruz, ss, Florida College.

DRAFT DROP *Son of Hector "Heity" Cruz, major leaguer (1973-82)*

12. Victor Hall, of, Monroe HS, Arleta, Calif.
13. *Brian Sager, rhp, Branford (Conn.) HS.
14. Dan Meier, of, Arizona State University.
15. Chris Cervantes, lhp, Pima (Ariz.) CC.
16. Heath Corbett, of, McMinn County HS, Athens, Tenn.
17. Lamar Sturdivant, of, Woodbury (N.J.) HS.
18. **Bret Prinz, rhp, Phoenix JC.—(2001-07)**
19. Jeff Barndollar, rhp, Saddleback (Calif.) CC.
20. John Egly, 3b, Mountain View HS, Liberty, Mo.
21. Paul Giambalvo, rhp, University of South Florida.
22. *Ryan Blake, c, Glenn HS, Kernersville, N.C.
23. **Robby Hammock, c, University of Georgia.—(2003-11)**
24. Troy Niehaus, lhp, Eastern Michigan University.
25. Steven Neal, 1b, Pratt (Kan.) CC.
26. *Jason Reuss, 1b, Canyon HS, Anaheim, Calif.

DRAFT DROP *Son of Jerry Reuss, major leaguer (1969-90)*

27. Mario Knorr, of, El Capitan HS, Lakeside, Calif.
28. Justin Santonocito, ss, Mercyhurst (Pa.) College.
29. **Mike Koplove, rhp-ss, University of Delaware.—(2001-07)**
30. ***Charlie Manning, lhp, Polk (Fla.) CC.—(2008)**
31. *Carl Makowsky, rhp, Conroe (Texas) HS.
32. *Mario Glaser, rhp, Edmonds (Wash.) CC.
33. *Horace Lawrence, lhp, El Cerrito HS, Richmond, Calif.
34. Justin Kees, rhp, Southern Illinois University.
35. *Russ Bayer, lhp, Naperville Central HS, Naperville, Ill.
36. James Rinne, of, Illinois Wesleyan University.
37. Matt White, rhp, Western Oregon University.
38. Justin Crivello, lhp, Edmonds (Wash.) CC.
39. Kirk Bolling, rhp-3b, Saddleback (Calif.) CC.
40. *John Gouzd, rhp, Fairmont (W.Va.) Senior HS.
41. Justin Beasley, c, Butler University.
42. Jody Fuller, rhp, University of Tennessee-Martin.
43. Adam Neubart, of, Rutgers University.
44. *Courtney Hall, rhp, Edmonds (Wash.) CC.
45. *Wilton Reynolds, of, Monte Vista HS, Spring Valley, Calif.
46. *Ben Mitchell, rhp, Scottsdale (Ariz.) CC.
47. *Cole Saben, rhp, Portland Lutheran HS, Portland, Ore.
48. *Bryon Gribbons, rhp, Cooper City (Fla.) HS.
49. *Joseph Bunton, 3b, Bell HS, Cudahy, Calif.
50. *Lucas Gruner, c, Mayfair HS, Long Beach, Calif.

## ATLANTA BRAVES (28)

1. (Choice to Rockies as compensation for Type A free agent Andres Galarraga)
2. **Matt Belisle, rhp, McCallum HS, Austin, Texas** (Choice from Padres as compensation for Type B free agent Greg Myers).**—(2003-15)**
2. (Choice to Rockies as compensation for Type A free agent Walt Weiss)
3. **Ryan Langerhans, of, Round Rock (Texas) HS.—(2002-13)**
4. Johnny McGinnis, rhp, Dacula (Ga.) HS.—(Short-season A)
5. Damien Jones, of, Vigor HS, Whistler, Ala.—(AA)
6. *Victor Menocal, ss, Gainesville (Ga.) HS.
7. **Scott Sobkowiak, rhp, University of Northern Iowa.—(2001)**
8. *Josh Karp, rhp, Bothell (Wash.) HS.

DRAFT DROP *First-round draft pick (6th overall), Expos (2001)*

9. Matt Targac, lhp, Sacred Heart HS, Hallettsville, Texas.
10. *Charlie Bilezikjian, of, Port Richmond HS, Staten Island, N.Y.
11. L.J. Yankosky, rhp, Georgia Tech.
12. Greg Donato, 3b, Clovis (Calif.) HS.
13. ***Steve Smyth, lhp, Cypress (Calif.) JC.—(2002)**
14. **John Ennis, rhp, Monroe HS, Panorama City, Calif.—(2002-07)**
15. Tommy Clark, of, Brunswick (Ga.) HS.
16. *Rob Moravek, rhp, Simsbury (Conn.) HS.
17. Dan Curtis, rhp, Central HS, Chattanooga, Tenn.
18. Colin Stewart, of, Sonoma State (Calif.) University.
19. Zach Frachiseur, rhp, University of Georgia.
20. Gregg Maluchnik, c, Duke University.
21. Aaron Garmong, lhp, Wayne State (Neb.) College.
22. *Sean Bischofberger, c, Granite Hills HS, El Cajon, Calif.
23. +Jason Mikels, rhp, Rio Linda (Calif.) HS / Sacramento (Calif.) CC.
24. Derrick Truitt, rhp, Columbia State (Tenn.) JC.
25. *Kregg Jarvais, c, University of Maine.
26. Brian Cox, of, Florida State University.
27. Bubba Scarce, rhp, North Carolina State University.
28. Louis Angulo, lhp, Miami-Dade CC North.
29. **+Tim Spooneybarger, of, Pine Forest HS, Pensacola, Fla. / Okaloosa-Walton (Fla.) CC.—(2001-03)**
30. Drue James, c, Southeastern Oklahoma State University.
31. *Tim Lemke, c-3b, Immaculata HS, Belle Meade, N.J.
32. **+Nick Green, 2b, DeKalb (Ga.) JC.—(2004-13)**
33. +Derek Clifton, rhp, Clear Creek HS, League City, Texas / Tyler (Texas) CC.
34. Paul Burke, c, Bellarmine (Ky.) College.
35. +Marcus Hambrick, of, Robert E. Lee HS, Montgomery, Ala. / Central Alabama CC.
36. *Phil Rosengren, rhp, Northwestern University.
37. *Adrian Walker, lhp, Mission Bay HS, San Diego.
38. *Kevin Benson, of, Century HS, Bismarck, N.D.
39. Casey Cheshier, 3b, San Jose State University.
40. Jerry Simmons, of, The Citadel.
41. *Michael Perez, c, Palm Beach Lakes HS, West Palm Beach, Fla.
42. *Eric Wise, rhp, Basic HS, Henderson, Nev.
43. *Greg Birch, lhp, McArthur HS, Davie, Fla.
44. ***Dallas McPherson, rhp-3b, Randleman (N.C.) HS.—(2004-11)**
45. **Brad Voyles, rhp, Lincoln Memorial (Tenn.) University.—(2001-03)**
46. *Josh Carter, 3b, Fallbrook (Calif.) HS.
47. *Mike Gleason, rhp, Santa Fe Trail HS, Carbondale, Kan.
48. +Jason King, ss, Englewood HS, Jacksonville / Florida CC-Jacksonville.
49. *Micah Nodah, rhp, Columbia HS, Live Oak, Fla.
50. Shaun Harper, of, Frederick Douglas HS, Atlanta.

## BALTIMORE ORIOLES (26)

1. Rick Elder, of, Sprayberry HS, Marietta, Ga.—(High A)
1. Mamon Tucker, of, Stephen F. Austin HS, Austin, Texas (Supplemental choice—39th—as compensation for Type A free agent Randy Myers).—(AA)
2. Ben Knapp, rhp, Oviedo (Fla.) HS (Choice from Blue Jays as compensation for Myers).—(High A)

DRAFT DROP *Son of Chris Knapp, first-round draft pick, White Sox (1975); major leaguer (1975-80)*

2. *Alex Hart, rhp, Chambersburg (Pa.) Area HS.—(High A)

DRAFT DROP *Attended Florida; re-drafted by Pirates, 2002 (5th round)*

3. **Steve Bechler, rhp, South Medford HS, Medford, Ore.—(2002)**

DRAFT DROP *Died as active major leaguer (Feb. 17, 2003)*

4. Chris Davidson, rhp, Western Carolina University.—DNP
5. Josh Yarno, rhp, Moscow (Idaho) HS.—(Rookie)
6. **Tim Raines Jr., of, Seminole HS, Sanford, Fla.—(2001-04)**

DRAFT DROP *Son of Tim Raines, major leaguer (1979-2002)*

7. Tim Nelson, 3b, Allan Hancock (Calif.) JC.
8. Randy Perez, lhp, El Capitan HS, Lakeside, Calif.
9. Francisco Monzon, c, Lorenzo Vizcarrondo HS, Carolina, P.R.
10. *Dustin Emberley, rhp, Composite HS, Weyburn, Sask.
11. Eliot Tomaszewski, rhp, Sandia HS, Albuquerque, N.M.
12. Derrick Gutierrez, ss, Sandalwood HS, Jacksonville, Fla.
13. *John Kremer, rhp, University of Evansville.
14. *Jason Bellamy, rhp, Conway (S.C.) HS.
15. *Josh Doud, rhp, Round Rock, Texas.
16. Jason Pruitt, lhp, View Marana HS, Tucson, Ariz.
17. ***Mike MacDougal, rhp, Wake Forest University.—(2001-12)**

DRAFT DROP *First-round draft pick (25th overall), Royals (1999)*

18. Denis Gratton, rhp, Kitchener, Ontario.
19. *Ryan Smith, rhp, Lake Howell HS, Longwood, Fla.
20. ***Cliff Lee, lhp, Meridian (Miss.) CC.—(2002-14)**
21. Tony Mack, of, Boone HS, Orlando, Fla.
22. Dustin Brewer, rhp, Granite City (Ill.) HS.
23. Sam Berrien, 1b, Fort Meade (Fla.) HS.
24. Billy Whitecotton, rhp, North County HS, Linthicum, Md.
25. Joey Hammond, ss, University of North Carolina-Charlotte.
26. *Jason Mandryk, rhp, Valley Heights HS, Langton, Ontario.
27. *Jared Jones, of, Walla Walla (Wash.) HS.
28. ***Jason Botts, 1b, Paso Robles (Calif.) HS.—(2005-08)**
29. ***Doug Slaten, lhp, Venice (Calif.) HS.—(2006-12)**
30. Ricky Green, c, Coffee County HS, Tullahoma, Tenn.
31. Sean Fischer, lhp, Grand Rapids (Mich.) CC.
32. *Troy Roberson, rhp, King's Academy, Boynton Beach, Fla.
33. *Fred Brassfield, of, Bryan Station HS, Lexington, Ky.
34. Phillip Cullen, rhp, Chelan (Wash.) HS.
35. *Jeffrey Gatch, rhp, Aquinas (Mich.) College.
36. *Scott Moore, rhp, Cowley County (Kan.) CC.
37. Jason Benham, 3b, Liberty University.

DRAFT DROP *Brother of David Benham, 12th-round draft pick, Red Sox (1998)*

38. *Mike Smith, lhp, Fletcher (Okla.) HS.
39. Marc Houle, rhp, Des Moines Area (Iowa) CC.
40. *Matt Crandall, rhp, Allan Hancock (Calif.) JC.
41. *Cory Acklus, of, Cascade HS, Everett, Wash.
42. *Matt Blethen, lhp-of, Havre de Grace (Md.) HS.
43. *Derek Eddie, c, Seward County (Kan.) CC.
44. (Selection voided)
45. *Brock Ralph, of, Raymond (Alberta) HS.

DRAFT DROP *Wide receiver, Canadian Football League (2003-11)*

46. *Zach Lush, c, Florida Tech.
47. Sonny Garcia, rhp, Texas Southern University.
48. *Kevin Fox, lhp, Citrus (Calif.) JC.
49. ***Mitch Jones, 3b, Utah Valley State JC.—(2009)**
50. *Scott Ridenour, rhp, Potomac State (W.Va.) JC.

## BOSTON RED SOX (12)

1. **Adam Everett, ss, University of South Carolina.—(2001-11)**
2. (Choice to Cardinals as compensation for Type A free agent Dennis Eckersley)
3. **Mike Maroth, lhp, University of Central Florida.—(2002-07)**
4. Jerome Gamble, rhp, Benjamin Russell HS, Alexander City, Ala.—(AAA)
5. **Josh Hancock, rhp, Tupelo, Miss.—(2002-07)**

DRAFT DROP *Died as active major leaguer (April 30, 2007)*

6. Ric Riccobono, rhp, Commack (N.Y.) HS.
7. *Keto Anderson, 2b, Prattville (Ala.) HS.

DRAFT DROP *Brother of Marlon Anderson, major leaguer (1998-2009)*

8. Will Silverthorn, lhp, J.J. Pearce HS, Richardson, Texas.

**9. *Mark Teixeira, 3b, Mount St. Joseph HS, Severna Park, Md.—(2003-15)**
DRAFT DROP *First-round draft pick (5th overall), Rangers (2001)*
**10. *Lenny DiNardo, lhp, Santa Fe HS, High Spring, Fla.—(2004-09)**
11. Carlos Rodriguez, of, Louisville, Ky.
12. David Benham, c, Liberty University.
DRAFT DROP *Brother of Jason Benham, 37th-round draft pick, Orioles (1998)*
**13. *Mike Rabelo, c, Ridgewood HS, New Port Richey, Fla.—(2006-08)**
14. Matt Phillips, rhp, University of Delaware.
15. Lance Surridge, rhp, University of North Carolina-Greensboro.
16. Jason Norton, rhp, University of South Alabama.
17. Benny Flores, lhp, Cal State Fullerton.
18. Terrance Hill, lhp, Southern University.
19. Shon Norris, rhp, University of North Carolina-Asheville.
20. Tony James, 2b, San Jose State University.
21. Andrew Checketts, rhp, Oregon State University.
DRAFT DROP *Baseball coach, UC Santa Barbara (2012-15)*
22. Tom Linarelli, rhp, University of Washington.
23. Andrew Larned, c, Fairfield University.
24. Josh Adeeb, of, Vanderbilt University.
**25. John Hattig, ss, Southern HS, Santa Rita, Guam.—(2006)**
**26. *Ben Kozlowski, lhp, Seminole (Fla.) HS.—(2002)**
27. *James Gates, of, Butler HS, Huntsville, Ala.
28. *Jason Blanton, rhp, Brevard (Fla.) CC.
29. *Ryan Siebert, rhp, Germantown (Tenn.) HS.
30. *James Garcia, of, West Torrance HS, Torrance, Calif.
31. *Robert Floyd, lhp, Satsuma (Ala.) HS.
32. Keith Hart, 1b, Lubbock Christian (Texas) University.
33. *Heath Heiberger, lhp, Putnam County HS, Hennepin, Ill.
34. Chad Johnson, c, Bradley University.
35. *Mark Younk, c, Texas HS, Wake Village, Texas.
36. Tonayne Brown, of, Lurleen B. Wallace (Ala.) JC.
37. Tony Caridi, c, Klein HS, Spring, Texas.
**38. +Dennis Tankersley, rhp, St. Louis CC-Meramec.—(2002-04)**
39. *Rob Shabansky, lhp, University of Arizona.
40. Phil Ledesma, of, Rider University.
41. *Jason Fingers, rhp, Central Arizona JC.
DRAFT DROP *Son of Rollie Fingers, major leaguer (1968-85)*
42. +Bryan Barnowski, c, Southwick-Tolland HS, Granville, Mass. / St. Petersburg (Fla.) CC.
43. *Ron Bohinski, ss, Lakeland (Fla.) HS.
44. *John Parrado, c, Miami Lakes (Fla.) HS.
45. *Jon Smithers, 3b, Florida College.
46. *Chris Hart, c, Central Catholic HS, Clearwater, Fla.
47. *Richie Smith, 2b, Liberty County HS, Marianna, Fla.
48. *Darry Burgess, rhp, Alvin (Texas) HS.

## CHICAGO CUBS (3)

**1. Corey Patterson, of, Harrison HS, Kennesaw, Ga.—(2000-11)**
DRAFT DROP *First 1998 high school draft pick to reach majors (Sept. 18, 2000) • Son of Don Patterson, defensive back, National Football League (1979-80) • Brother of Eric Patterson, major leaguer (2011)*
**2. David Kelton, ss, Troup County HS, La Grange, Ga.—(2003-04)**
2. Jeff Goldbach, c, Princeton (Ind.) Community HS (Choice from Astros as compensation for Type B free agent Dave Clark).—(AA)
3. Kevin Bass, 3b, Fayette County HS, Fayette, Ala.—(High A)
DRAFT DROP *Brother of Bryan Bass, first-round draft pick, Orioles (2001)*
4. Jeramy Gomer, lhp, Durant HS, Plant City, Fla.—(High A)
5. Aaron Sams, lhp, James Madison University.—(High A)
6. Tony Schrager, 2b, Stanford University.
7. Keola De la Tori, rhp, Triton (Ill.) JC.
**8. Will Ohman, lhp, Pepperdine University.—(2000-12)**
9. *Steven Reba, rhp, Concordia Lutheran HS, Fort Wayne, Ind.
10. Nate Frese, ss, University of Iowa.
11. Dustin Krug, rhp, Lassen (Calif.) JC.
12. Tony Zamarripa, rhp, Texas A&M University.
13. David Ericks, rhp, Illiana Christian HS, Lansing, Ill.
14. *Tom Lipari, lhp, Indian Hills (Iowa) JC.
15. *Casey Grzecka, c, Santa Margarita HS, Laguna Niguel, Calif.
16. Omar Rohena, 3b, Casiano Cepeda HS, Rio Grande, P.R.
**17. Eric Hinske, 3b, University of Arkansas.—(2002-13)**
18. *Carlton Wells, lhp, King HS, Tampa.
19. Joe Ohm, rhp, University of Wisconsin-La Crosse.
20. *Dennis Cervenka, rhp, La Vernia (Texas) HS.
21. Larry Dant, rhp, Dana (Neb.) College.
22. Mikel Moreno, of, Arizona State University.
23. *Michael Carey, rhp, Westminster (Calif.) HS.
24. *Charles Redmond, of, Liberty Eylau HS, Texarkana, Texas.
25. *Nick Moran, rhp, Elk Grove (Calif.) HS.
26. *Eric Arnold, ss, La Porte (Texas) HS.
27. Tydus Meadows, of, Vanderbilt University.
28. *Adam Cox, of, Thomas County Central HS, Thomasville, Ga.
29. Larry Alvarez, rhp, Nogales HS, Walnut, Calif.
30. *Justin Smith, c, Lake Brantley HS, Longwood, Fla.
31. Leo Torres, lhp, Metro State (Colo.) College.
32. Matt Griffin, ss, Southern Tech (Ga.) Institute.
33. Chris Brown, rhp, Northwestern State University.
34. *Dustin Brentz, rhp, Moss Point HS, Pascagoula, Miss.
35. *Matt Whitehead, rhp, Northeast Texas CC.
36. *Ben Johanning, 1b, Osceola HS, Kissimmee, Fla.
**37. *Trey Lunsford, c, Grayson County (Texas) CC.—(2002-03)**
38. *Chris Wood, ss, Central Florida CC.
39. *Keith Whatley, lhp, Atlanta (Texas) HS.
40. *Jonathan Macklin, lhp, Hallandale (Fla.) HS.
41. *Nate Beucler, rhp, Huntington Beach (Calif.) HS.
42. Kevin Boles, c, University of South Florida.
DRAFT DROP *Son of John Boles, major league manager (1996-2001)*
43. *Jacob Pierce, rhp, Longview (Texas) HS.
44. *Juston Olson, rhp, Oak Park-River Forest HS, Oak Park, Ill.
45. Chris Connally, of, Texas Christian University.
46. *Dustin Matthews, ss, Whitney Young HS, Chicago.
DRAFT DROP *Son of Gary Matthews, major leaguer (1972-87) • Brother of Gary Matthews Jr., major leaguer (1999-2010)*
47. +Jon-Mark Sprowl, ss, Bay HS, Panama City Beach, Fla. / Shelton State (Ala.) JC.
DRAFT DROP *Son of Bobby Sprowl, major leaguer (1978-81)*
48. *Chris Kellett, c, Deltona HS, Orange City, Fla.
49. *Greg Eubanks, rhp, Wellington (Fla.) HS.
50. *Daniel Jackson, rhp, South Suburban (Ill.) JC.

## CHICAGO WHITE SOX (16)

**1. Kip Wells, rhp, Baylor University.—(1999-2012)**
**1. Aaron Rowand, of, Cal State Fullerton** (Supplemental choice—35th—as compensation for Type A free agent Dave Martinez).—**(2001-2011)**
**2. Gary Majewski, rhp, St. Pius X HS, Houston.—(2004-10)**
**3. Josh Fogg, rhp, University of Florida.—(2001-09)**
3. Daniel Mozingo, lhp, Ashtabula Harbor HS, Ashtabula, Ohio (Choice from Devil Rays as compensation for Martinez).—(AA)
4. Juan Santamarina, 3b, Gulliver Prep, Miami.—(High A)
5. *Steve Kelly, rhp, Fairfield HS, Hamilton, Ohio.—(AAA)
DRAFT DROP *Attended Georgia Tech; re-drafted by Reds, 2001 (4th round)*
6. Matt Borne, rhp, University of Kentucky.
7. Eric Fischer, lhp, Moeller HS, Cincinnati.
8. Mitch Wylie, rhp, St. Ambrose (Iowa) University.
9. Kelly Mosley, of, Wakulla HS, Crawfordville, Fla.
10. *Steve Bess, rhp, Rice University.
11. Mike Williams, rhp, Galveston (Texas) JC.
12. Kai Freeman, rhp, University of Minnesota.
13. Gerald McCall, c, Meridian (Miss.) HS.
14. Solomon Johnson, lhp, Navarro (Texas) JC.
**15. *Nate Robertson, lhp, Wichita State University.—(2002-10)**
16. Ernesto Lowe, of, American HS, Miami.
17. Brannon Whatley, rhp, Kennesaw State (Ga.) University.
18. *Chris Hamblen, c, Highlands HS, Fort Thomas, Ky.
19. +Jason Stovall, lhp, Battiest HS, Bethel, Okla.
20. *Erik Lohse, rhp, Hamilton Union HS, Glenn, Calif.
DRAFT DROP *Brother of Kyle Lohse, major leaguer (2001-15)*
21. Andre Simpson, rhp, Mount Miguel HS, Lemon Grove, Calif.
22. *Carlos Castillo, 2b, Miami-Dade CC North.
23. *Todd Johannes, c, University of Florida.
24. *Caleb Reger, 1b, Bradshaw Mountain HS, Prescott, Ariz.
25. +Mark Cochrane, c, Stoneman Douglas HS, Coral Springs, Fla. / Broward (Fla.) CC.
**26. Edwin Almonte, rhp, St. Francis (N.Y.) College.—(2003)**
27. Eric Battersby, lhp-of, St. Mary's (Texas) University.
28. *Travis Edwards, of, Woodrow Wilson HS, Long Beach, Calif.
29. *Nelson Lopez, 3b, Monsignor Pace HS, Miami.
30. *Jason Abreu, ss, Hialeah Miami Lakes HS, Miami Lakes, Fla.
31. Carlos Cline, 1b, Brookdale (N.J.) CC.
32. *Todd Eames, rhp, JC of Eastern Utah.
33. *Paul Reuer, of, Schaumburg (Ill.) HS.
34. Terrell Merriman, of, Averett (Va.) College.
35. *Scott Atwood, 1b, North Florida CC.
36. *Dan Wells, c, Columbine HS, Littleton, Colo.
37. *Jason Bernard, rhp, Gulf Coast (Fla.) CC.
**38. +Mark Buehrle, lhp, Jefferson (Mo.) CC.—(2000-15)**
39. *Curtis Young, rhp, Grand Junction (Colo.) HS.
40. *Michael Baetzel, ss, Kishwaukee (Ill.) JC.
41. *Mike Mallonee, lhp, Southwestern (Calif.) JC.
**42. *Kevin Cameron, rhp, Joliet Catholic HS, Joliet, Ill.—(2007-09)**
43. *Mike Scioletti, 3b, U.S. Military Academy.
44. *Julio Guerrero, of, San Angelo (Texas) HS.
45. *John Gusich, 3b, Deer Valley HS, Glendale, Ariz.
46. *Vince Serafini, 1b, Lockport (Ill.) HS.
47. *Nathan Boyd, rhp, Allen Academy, Bryan, Texas.
48. *Ryan Costello, lhp, Milford Academy, Voorhees, N.J.
49. *Ricardo Suarez, of, Miami-Dade CC North.
50. *Justin Hairston, 2b, JC of DuPage (Ill.).
DRAFT DROP *Grandson of Sam Hairston, major leaguer (1951) • Son of Jerry Hairston, major leaguer (1973-89) • Brother of Jerry Hairston Jr., major leaguer (1998-2013) • Brother of Scott Hairston, major leaguer (2004-14)*

## CINCINNATI REDS (7)

**1. Austin Kearns, of, Lafayette HS, Lexington, Ky.—(2002-13)**
**2. Adam Dunn, of, New Caney (Texas) HS.—(2001-14)**
3. *Greg Porter, ss, Keller (Texas) HS.—(AAA)
DRAFT DROP *Attended Texas A&M; re-drafted by Angels, 2001 (45th round)*
4. Darrell Hussman, rhp, University of Arizona.—(Low A)
5. Jayson Larman, rhp, Wayne (Okla.) HS.—(Rookie)
**6. Bobby Madritsch, lhp, Point Park (Pa.) College.—(2004-05)**
**7. Josh Hall, rhp, E.C. Glass HS, Lynchburg, Va.—(2003)**
8. Clint Vaughn, 1b, Oklahoma Christian University.
9. David Therneau, rhp, Bellevue (Neb.) University.
10. Jacob Wallis, c, Paschal HS, Joshua, Texas.
11. Casey DeHart, lhp, Texarkana (Texas) CC.
**12. John Koronka, lhp, South Lake HS, Clermont, Fla.—(2005-09)**
13. Damien Hart, lhp, Coastal Carolina University.
14. Dennis Russo, rhp, Santa Fe Catholic HS, Auburndale, Fla.
15. Blane Layton, of, Jacksonville University.
16. Casey McEvoy, rhp, University of Cincinnati.
**17. B.J. Ryan, lhp, University of Southwestern Louisiana.—(1999-2009)**
18. Gary Loudon, rhp, Shippensburg (Pa.) University.
19. Glen Joseph, rhp, King HS, Tampa.
20. Duane Price, of, Texas Tech.
21. *Alex Kellner, c, Freedom HS, Morganton, N.C.
22. *Jason France, lhp, Chandler (Ariz.) HS.
23. Travis Copley, c, University of Tennessee.
24. Eric Cooper, rhp, Texas Tech.
25. Randy Stegall, ss, Cumberland (Tenn.) University.
26. *Vince LaCorte, rhp, Gavilan (Calif.) JC.
DRAFT DROP *Son of Frank LaCorte, major leaguer (1975-84)*
27. Cory Stewart, lhp, Boerne (Texas) HS.
28. *Humberto Aguilar, 1b, Odessa (Texas) HS.
29. *John Nix, rhp, Kingwood (Texas) HS.
30. Tim Birdsong, rhp, Southeastern Oklahoma State University.
**31. *Brad Salmon, rhp, Tate HS, Gonzalez, Fla.—(2007)**
32. Roger Sellers, rhp, North Central Texas JC.
33. *Paul Sanchez, of, Hubbard HS, Chicago.
34. James Matan, of, University of North Carolina-Charlotte.
35. Andrew Beattie, ss, St. Petersburg (Fla.) JC.
36. Chris Toomey, of, Long Beach State University.
37. *Donald Caldwell, of, Jefferson HS, Tampa.
38. *David Jensen, 1b, Green Valley HS, Henderson, Nev.
39. Randy Woodrum, lhp, Middle Tennessee State University.
**40. *Lance Cormier, rhp, Lafayette (La.) HS.—(2004-11)**
**41. Todd Coffey, rhp, Chase HS, Forest City, N.C.—(2005-12)**
42. Robert Jenkins, of, Valparaiso University.
43. *David Carr, of, Marquette HS, Milwaukee.
44. *David Martin, c, Katy (Texas) HS.
**45. *Terrmel Sledge, of, Long Beach State University.—(2004-07)**
46. *John Whiteside, rhp, Sunset HS, Beaverton, Ore.
47. *Michael Grant, lhp, Charlotte Christian HS, Charlotte, N.C.
48. *Gerald Butt, rhp, Mayville State (N.D.) University.

## CLEVELAND INDIANS (20)

**1. C.C. Sabathia, lhp, Vallejo (Calif.) HS.—(2001-15)**
**2. Zach Sorensen, ss, Wichita State University.—(2003-05)**
3. Scott Pratt, ss, Auburn University.—(AAA)
4. Ron Marietta, lhp, St. John's University.—(Low A)
**5. Ryan Drese, rhp, University of California.—(2001-06)**
6. Tyler Minges, of, Ross HS, Hamilton, Ohio.
7. Brody Percell, lhp, Oregon State University.
8. Chris Reinike, rhp, Mississippi State University.
9. Paul Day, 3b, Long Beach State University.
10. Michael McPadden, rhp, Port St. Lucie (Fla.) HS.
11. Jacob Reynolds, rhp, Giles County HS, Pulaski, Tenn.
12. Donnie Suttles, rhp, Western Carolina University.
13. Matt Wade, rhp, Parkview HS, Lilburn, Ga.
14. Brian Jackson, rhp, University of Southern Colorado.
**15. Matt White, lhp, Clemson University.—(2003-05)**
16. Rick Matsko, rhp, Shippensburg (Pa.) University.
17. Mark Koeth, rhp, Brookhaven (Texas) JC.
18. T.T. Gallaher, of, University of New Haven.
19. *David Raymer, of, Sacramento (Calif.) CC.
20. Barry Patton, c, Mississippi State University.
21. *Mike DiRosa, c, Coral Gables (Fla.) HS.
22. Carey Novits, lhp, Cal State Northridge.
23. +J.J. Sherrill, of, Monterey HS, Seaside, Calif. / Sacramento (Calif.) CC.
24. Tommy Bost, of, Louisiana Tech.
25. Eric Mileski, rhp, Benedictine (Ill.) University.
26. Chris MacMillan, 3b, Cal State Northridge.
27. Jeff DiPippo, c, University of Southern California.
28. Rudy Rosales, rhp, Pima (Ariz.) CC.
29. Ruben Escobar, rhp, The Master's (Calif.) College.

30. Mike Pursell, 2b, Tulane University.
31. Marques Esquerra, ss, Point Loma Nazarene (Calif.) College.
32. Craig Brown, lhp, Tulane University.
33. *Brian Strelitz, rhp, Temple City (Calif.) HS.
34. *James Jurries, 3b, Brazoswood HS, Lake Jackson, Texas.
35. *Randon Ho, lhp, University of Hawaii.
36. *Matt Ramie, 1b, Castle HS, Kanoehe, Hawaii.
37. *Micah Simmons, ss, Paxon School, Jacksonville, Fla.
38. *Brian Minks, lhp, Neosho County (Kan.) CC.
39. Darrel Berck, rhp, Palomar (Calif.) JC.
40. Dan Guillory, rhp, Louisiana State University.
41. *Brian Sullivan, rhp, Port St. Lucie (Fla.) HS.
42. *Blake Whealy, ss, Oak Park-River Forest HS, Oak Park, Ill.
43. *Dana Thomas, rhp, Fork Union (Va.) Military Academy.
44. *Miguel Hernandez, 3b, Nuestra Senora HS, Bayamon, P.R.
45. *Eric Bush, lhp, Booker T. Washington HS, Pensacola, Fla.
46. Brandon Mauer, c, Bellevue (Wash.) CC.
47. *Kevin Spaulding, rhp, Anacortes (Wash.) HS.
48. *Garth Blumberg, of, Hoquiam (Wash.) HS.
**49. *Kevin Hooper, 2b, Wichita State University.—(2005-06)**
50. Omar Moraga, 3b, University of Arizona.

## COLORADO ROCKIES (17)

1. (Choice to Astros as compensation for Type A free agent Darryl Kile)
**1. Matt Roney, rhp, Edmond North HS, Edmond, Okla.** (Choice from Braves as compensation for Type A free agent Andres Galarraga).**—(2003-06)**
**1. Choo Freeman, of, Dallas Christian HS, Mesquite, Texas** (Supplemental choice—36th—as compensation for Galarraga).**—(2004-06)**
1. Jeff Winchester, c, Archbishop Rummel HS, Metairie, La. (Supplemental choice—40th—as compensation for Type A free agent Walt Weiss).—(AA)
**2. Jermaine Van Buren, rhp, Hattiesburg (Miss.) HS.—(2005-06)**
**2. Jody Gerut, of, Stanford University** (Choice from Braves as compensation for Weiss).**—(2003-10)**
3. Kevin Gordon, rhp, University of Central Florida.—(Low A)
**4. Luke Hudson, rhp, University of Tennessee.—(2002-07)**
**5. *Ryan Shealy, 1b, Cardinal Gibbons HS, Fort Lauderdale, Fla.—(2005-10)**
DRAFT DROP *Attended Florida; re-drafted by Rockies, 2002 (11th round)*
6. Javier Guzman, of, University Garden HS, Rio Piedras, P.R.
**7. Matt Holliday, 3b, Stillwater (Okla.) HS.—(2004-15)**
8. +Justin Lincoln, 3b-rhp, Manatee (Fla.) JC.
9. Justin Carter, lhp, University of South Alabama.
10. *Andrew Beinbrink, 3b, Arizona State University.
11. Ryan Cameron, rhp, University of Massachusetts.
12. Brian Brantley, rhp, Old Dominion University.
**13. Juan Pierre, of, University of South Alabama.—(2000-13)**
14. Vernand Morency, of, Northwestern HS, Miami.
DRAFT DROP *Running back, National Football League (2005-07)*
**15. Mark DiFelice, rhp, Western Carolina University.—(2008-11)**
16. Brandon Garner, rhp, Central Merry HS, Jackson, Tenn.
17. Josh Etheredge, 1b-of, Auburn University.
18. Jase Wrigley, rhp, Georgia Tech.
19. Doug Thompson, rhp, Louisiana State University.
20. Tom Whitehurst, of, University of South Alabama.
21. Erik Johnson, c, University of Central Florida.
22. Ryan LaMattina, lhp, St. Bonaventure University.
23. Richy Leon, 2b, Arizona State University.
24. Michael Mundy, rhp, Rutgers University.
25. Kevin Duck, 1b, Cal State Fullerton.
26. *J.J. Durmanich, rhp, Merced (Calif.) JC.
27. *Manases Pabon, of, Hato Rey, P.R.
28. *Michael Johnson, of, Westark (Ark.) CC.
29. +Aaron Geralds, of, Madison Central HS, Madison, Miss. / Meridian (Miss.) JC.
30. *James Hymon, ss, Leo HS, Chicago.
**31. *Mark Woodyard, 1b-rhp, Okaloosa-Walton (Fla.) JC.—(2005)**
32. *Greg Colburn, rhp, Skyview HS, Billings, Mon.
33. *Rocky Kirk, lhp, Cochise County (Ariz.) CC.
34. *Paul Miller, of, Pleasure Ridge Park HS, Louisville, Ky.
35. *Ryan Truxall, rhp, Miami-Dade CC North.
36. *Geoff Boutelier, rhp, Cypress (Calif.) JC.
37. *Ryan Wardinsky, ss, Flathead HS, Kalispell, Mon.
38. *T.J. Bird, of, Cloverdale (Calif.) HS.
39. *David Bernstine, c, Vallejo (Calif.) HS.
40. +Joe Simpson, rhp, Southeastern Illinois JC.
41. *Bryce Coppieters, of, Raymond (Alberta) HS.
**42. *Nyjer Morgan, of, Storefront HS, St. Albert, Alberta.—(2007-14)**
43. *Doug Baylor, of, John H. Reagan HS, Austin, Texas.
**44. *Alfredo Amezaga, ss, St. Petersburg (Fla.) JC.—(2002-11)**
45. +Frank Haase, lhp, Merced (Calif.) JC.
46. *John McCanne, 3b, Mammoth HS, Mammoth Lakes, Calif.

## DETROIT TIGERS (14)

**1. Jeff Weaver, rhp, Fresno State University.—(1999-2010)**
DRAFT DROP *Brother of Jered Weaver, first-round draft pick, Angels (2004); major leaguer (2006-15)*
**1. Nate Cornejo, rhp, Wellington (Kan.) HS** (Supplemental choice—34th—as compensation for Type A free agent Willie Blair).**—(2001-04)**
DRAFT DROP *Son of Mardie Cornejo, major leaguer (1978)*
**2. Brandon Inge, ss-rhp, Virginia Commonwealth University.—(2001-13)**
**2. Adam Pettyjohn, lhp, Fresno State University** (Choice from Diamondbacks as compensation for Blair).**—(2001-08)**
3. Tommy Marx, lhp, Brother Rice HS, West Bloomfield, Mich.—(High A)
**4. Andres Torres, of, Miami-Dade CC North.—(2002-13)**
5. Greg Peterson, rhp-of, St. John's University.—DNP
6. Bobby Sismondo, lhp, Ohio University.
7. Clint Smith, rhp, University of Oklahoma.
8. Barry Tolli, of, Newbury Park HS, Thousand Oaks, Calif.
9. *Donny Sevieri, of, El Dorado HS, Albuquerque, N.M.
10. Billy Rich, of, University of Connecticut.
11. *Seth Taylor, ss, University of South Alabama.
12. Russ Cleveland, c, Chaparral HS, Las Vegas, Nev.
13. Laz Gutierrez, lhp, University of Miami.
14. Calvin Chipperfield, rhp, Mount San Antonio (Calif.) JC.
15. *Doc Brooks, c, Central HS, Phenix City, Ala.
16. *Greg Sain, 3b, West Torrance HS, Torrance, Calif.
17. Reggie Nelson, ss, Santa Ana (Calif.) JC.
18. *Andrew Earley, rhp, Shaker Heights (Ohio) HS.
19. Galen Shea, rhp, Houston Baptist University.
20. Jim Hostetler, rhp, Fullerton (Calif.) JC.
21. Nate Forbush, c, University of Utah.
22. Ryan Earl, lhp, Thousand Oaks (Calif.) HS.
23. Bill Madson, rhp, Carthage (Wis.) College.
24. Thomas Koutrouba, lhp, University of Maine.
25. Derek Besco, of, University of Michigan.
26. Craig DaLuz, 3b, Fresno State University.
27. Jason Colquitt, c, East Carolina University.
28. Lacarlo Moore, of, St. Xavier (Ill.) University.
29. *Scott Lawson, lhp, John A. Logan (Ill.) JC.
30. Keith Law, ss, DeKalb (Ga.) JC.
31. *Mack Paciorek, 3b, Los Angeles CC.
DRAFT DROP *Son of John Paciorek, major leaguer (1963)*
32. Ron Bush, ss, College of William & Mary.
33. Brian McGowan, rhp, Queens (N.Y.) College.
34. *Robert Stiehl, c, West Torrance HS, Torrance, Calif.
DRAFT DROP *First-round draft pick (27th overall), Astros (2000)*
35. Joe Yingling, c, Camarillo (Calif.) HS.
36. *Scott Stuck, rhp, Climax-Scotts HS, Climax, Mich.
37. *Antoine Cameron, of, Ayala HS, Chino Hills, Calif.
38. *Edgar Varela, 3b, San Gabriel (Calif.) HS.
39. *Ryan Cox, rhp, Southern Illinois University-Edwardsville.
40. *David Mendez, of, Lehman HS, Bronx, N.Y.
41. *Chris Tiller, rhp, Panola (Texas) JC.
42. *Kevin Estrada, ss, El Segundo (Calif.) HS.
43. *Keith Perez, rhp, Holly (Mich.) HS.
44. *Craig Bowser, of, Lufkin (Texas) HS.
45. *Miles Luuloa, ss, Molokai HS, Kaunakakai, Hawaii.
46. *Patrick Gill, rhp, Grandville (Mich.) HS.
47. *Warren Trott, ss, West Torrance HS, Torrance, Calif.
48. *Chris Curry, c, Meridian (Miss.) CC.
DRAFT DROP *Baseball coach, Arkansas-Little Rock (2015)*

## FLORIDA MARLINS (27)

**1. Chip Ambres, of, West Brook HS, Beaumont, Texas.—(2005-08)**
2. Derek Wathan, ss, University of Oklahoma.—(AAA)
DRAFT DROP *Son of John Wathan, major leaguer (1976-85); major league manager (1987-92) • Brother of Dusty Wathan, major leaguer (2002)*
3. David Callahan, 1b, Palm Bay (Fla.) HS.—(High A)
4. Heath Honeycutt, 3b, Georgia Tech.—(AA)
5. Matt Padgett, of, Clemson University.—(AAA)
6. Phill Lowery, lhp, Arizona State University.
7. Ryan Harber, lhp, Butler University.
8. Marc Sauer, rhp, Bishop Eustace HS, Gloucester, N.J.
9. *Mike Trussell, rhp, Menchville HS, Newport News, Va.
10. *Chris Heck, lhp, St. Joseph's (Pa.) University.
11. Matt DeMarco, ss, Gloucester Catholic HS, Gloucester City, N.J.
12. David Noyce, lhp, Furman University.
13. Paul McCurtain, rhp, University of Oklahoma.
14. Eric Jupe, rhp, Schreiner (Texas) College.
15. Heath Kelly, 2b, Auburn University.
16. John Seaman, rhp, Northwestern University.
17. *Josh Hochgesang, 3b, Stanford University.
**18. *Adam LaRoche, lhp-1b, Fort Scott (Kan.) HS.—(2004-15)**
DRAFT DROP *Son of Dave LaRoche, major leaguer (1970-83) • Brother of Andy LaRoche, major leaguer (2007-13)*
19. *Wendell Anderson, of, East Hartford (Conn.) HS.
20. David Campos, lhp, Fresno (Calif.) CC.
21. Matt Frick, c, University of Alabama.
22. *Mike Wright, c, San Jose State University.
23. *Matt Krabbe, rhp, Larkin HS, Elgin, Ill.
24. Terrence Smalls, 2b-ss, The Citadel.
25. *Scott Murphy, rhp, Parkview HS, Lilburn, Ga.
**26. Kevin Olsen, rhp, University of Oklahoma.—(2001-03)**
27. Willy Hill, of, University of Oklahoma.
28. *Kevin Ryan, rhp, Morton (Ill.) JC.
29. Drew Niles, ss, Bowling Green State University.
30. *Vince Harrison, ss-2b, Princeton HS, Cincinnati.
31. *Jon Topolski, of, Baylor University.
32. Randy Rigsby, 3b, East Carolina University.
33. *John Kocur, rhp, Cooper City (Fla.) HS.
34. *Adam Bragg, of, Bishop Verot HS, Cape Coral, Fla.
35. *John Moylan, c, Sacred Heart HS, San Francisco.
36. *Chris Halgren, c, Mount Hood (Ore.) CC.
37. *Eric Bernhardt, rhp, Cowley County (Kan.) CC.
38. *Jorge Arceo, rhp, Lincoln HS, Stockton, Calif.
39. *Jeff Wagner, of, San Jacinto (Texas) JC.
40. Julio Rivas, c, Washington and Lee HS, Arlington, Va.
41. *Bryan Lee, of, El Camino HS, Sacramento, Calif.
42. *Daniel Pettit, rhp, North Stafford HS, Stafford, Va.
43. *Shawn Sabo, rhp, Oswego (Ill.) HS.
44. *Shawn Norris, ss, Alta HS, Draper, Utah.
45. *Peter Selden, rhp, Monroe (N.Y.) CC.
46. *Greg Mickles, of, Maple Shade (N.J.) HS.
47. +Aaron Alvarez, c, Chattahoochee HS, Duluth, Ga. / Middle Georgia CC.
48. *Rigo Orozco, c, Capuchino HS, San Bruno, Calif.
49. *Rudy Simpson, of, Etiwanda HS, Alta Loma, Calif.

## HOUSTON ASTROS (19)

**1. Brad Lidge, rhp, University of Notre Dame** (Choice from Rockies as compensation for Type A free agent Darryl Kile).**—(2002-12)**
1. (Choice to Giants as compensation for Type B free agent Doug Henry)
1. Mike Nannini, rhp, Green Valley HS, Henderson, Nev. (Supplemental choice—37th—as compensation for Kile).—(AAA)
2. (Choice to Cubs as compensation for Type B free agent Dave Clark)
3. *Brad Busbin, rhp, Dr. Phillips HS, Orlando, Fla.—(Short-season A)
DRAFT DROP *Attended Georgia Tech; re-drafted by Phillies, 2002 (27th round)*
4. *Jason Van Meetren, of, Bishop Gorman HS, Las Vegas, Nev.—(High A)
DRAFT DROP *Attended Stanford; re-drafted by Mariners, 2001 (13th round)*
5. Scott Barrett, lhp, San Jacinto (Texas) JC.—(Short-season A)
**6. David Matranga, ss, Pepperdine University.—(2003-05)**
**7. John Buck, c, Taylorsville HS, Salt Lake City.—(2004-14)**
8. Jesse Joyce, 3b, Cal State Los Angeles.
**9. Morgan Ensberg, 3b, University of Southern California.—(2000-08)**
**10. Keith Ginter, 2b, Texas Tech.—(2000-05)**
11. Kevin Jordan, 3b-of, Texas Tech.
12. Jeremy Ryan, rhp, Maple Woods (Mo.) CC.
13. Doug Sessions, rhp, Armstrong Atlantic State (Ga.) College.
14. *Jacob Baker, 3b, Rice University.
15. Charley Carter, 1b, Baylor University.
16. Derek Nicholson, of, University of Florida.
**17. Colin Porter, of, University of Arizona.—(2003-04)**
18. Rich Terwilliger, rhp, CC of the Finger Lakes (N.Y.).
19. Bryon Wilkerson, rhp, University of Mary Hardin-Baylor (Texas).
20. Anthony Ramirez, 3b, Carson (Calif.) HS.
21. *Brian Messer, rhp, University of New Mexico.
22. Garrett Zyskowski, lhp, West Virginia University.
23. Brandon Smith, rhp, Northeast Louisiana University.
24. Josh Dimmick, c, University of Kansas.
25. Jacob Whitney, lhp, Iowa State University.
26. Robert Carillo, 1b, Montgomery HS, San Diego.
27. *Bobby Burns, c, Bingham HS, South Jordan, Utah.
28. *Chris Sheffield, rhp, Stephen F. Austin HS, Richmond, Texas.
29. Brandon Buckley, c, Texas Tech.
30. *Jordan Hunt, rhp, Evergreen HS, Vancouver, Wash.
31. *Alex Dvorsky, c, Marion (Iowa) HS.
32. *Bernard Gonzalez, of, Brito Private HS, Miami.
33. +Gavin Wright, of, Blinn (Texas) JC.
34. *Ryan Humphrey, lhp, Indian River (Fla.) CC.
35. *Brett Kay, c, Mater Dei HS, Villa Park, Calif.
36. *Benson Barrera, rhp, Skyview HS, Nampa, Idaho.
37. *Jeremy Frost, c, Oviedo (Fla.) HS.
38. *Bryan Edwards, rhp, Northeast Texas CC.
39. *Roberto Zaldivar, rhp, Arroyo HS, San Lorenzo, Calif.
40. *Ray Leyba, lhp, Choctaw (Okla.) HS.
41. *Mike McHugh, rhp, Helix HS, La Mesa, Calif.

## KANSAS CITY ROYALS (4)

**1. Jeff Austin, rhp, Stanford University.—(2001-03)**
1. Matt Burch, rhp, Virginia Commonwealth University (Choice from Diamondbacks as compensation for Type A free agent Jay Bell).—(AA)
**1. Chris George, lhp, Klein HS, Spring, Texas** (Supplemental choice—31st—as compensation for Bell).**—(2001-04)**
2. Robbie Morrison, rhp, University of Miami.—(AA)
3. Ben Cordova, of, Marian Catholic HS, Chula Vista, Calif.—(Low A)
4. Monty Ward, rhp, Texas Tech.—(Low A)

**5. Scott Chiasson, rhp, Eastern Connecticut State University.—(2001-02)**
6. Mike Curry, of, University of South Carolina.
7. Jeremy Dodson, of, Baylor University.
**8. Norris Hopper, ss, Shelby (N.C.) HS.—(2006-08)**
**9. Paul Phillips, of, University of Alabama.—(2004-10)**
10. Jeremy Jackson, lhp, Mississippi State University.
11. Cary Ammons, lhp, Southeastern Oklahoma State University.
12. Manny Santana, c, Maestro Ladi HS, Vega Alta, P.R.
**13. Brian Shackelford, of, University of Oklahoma.—(2005-06)**
**14. Shawn Sedlacek, rhp, Iowa State University.—(2002)**
15. *Brock Griffin, c, Jesuit HS, Portland, Ore.
16. Craig Jones, rhp, University of Southern California.
17. Charles Hamilton, rhp, Hollandale Simmons HS, Delta, Miss.
18. Ryan Hill, rhp, Wabash Valley (Ill.) JC.
19. *Aaron Fausett, of, Beaverton (Ore.) HS.
20. Javier Pamus, rhp, San Jose State University.
21. James Shanks, of, Solomon HS, North Augusta, S.C.
22. Wayne Lee, rhp, University of Washington.
23. Corey Hart, 2b, University of Oklahoma.
24. Ryan Fry, of, University of Missouri.
25. Jeremy Freitas, of, University of Southern California.
26. *Jeff Trzos, lhp, North Farmington HS, Farmington Hills, Mich.
27. Yancy Ayres, c, Kansas State University.
28. Mike Russo, rhp, Queens (N.Y.) College.
29. Sean Bryan, 3b, Maple Woods (Mo.) JC.
30. *Trevor Mote, ss, Yavapai (Ariz.) JC.
31. *Michael Denard, ss, Oakland (Calif.) Tech HS.
32. Jim Essian Jr., c, Troy (Mich.) HS.
DRAFT DROP *Son of Jim Essian, major leaguer (1973-84); major league manager (1991)*
33. *Jason Bartz, rhp, Manatee HS, Bradenton, Fla.
34. *Damon Dombrowski, rhp, Truman HS, Independence, Mo.
35. *Gabe Boruff, c, Ephrata (Wash.) HS.
36. *Shane Scoville, c, Ridge HS, Basking Ridge, N.J.
37. *Jeffrey Jobe, rhp, Seward County (Kan.) CC.
38. *Lane Crews, rhp, Glades Day HS, Belle Glade, Fla.
39. *Shawn Barksdale, rhp, Wallace State (Ala.) CC.
40. *Nathan Price, rhp, Cleveland, Miss.
41. *Adam Lingenfelter, rhp, Buchholz HS, Gainesville, Fla.
42. Felipe Alou Jr., of, Canada (Calif.) JC.
DRAFT DROP *Son of Felipe Alou, major leaguer (1958-74); major league manager (1992-2006) • Brother of Moises Alou, major leaguer (1990-2008)*

## LOS ANGELES DODGERS (23)

**1. Bubba Crosby, of, Rice University.—(2003-06)**
2. Mike Fischer, rhp, University of South Alabama.—(AA)
3. *Alex Santos, rhp, University of Miami.—(AAA)
DRAFT DROP *Returned to Miami (Fla.); re-drafted by Devil Rays, 1999 (4th round)*
4. Eric Riggs, ss, University of Central Florida.—(AAA)
**5. Scott Proctor, rhp, Florida State University.—(2004-11)**
6. Ryan Moskau, lhp-1b, University of Arizona.
DRAFT DROP *Son of Paul Moskau, major leaguer (1977-83)*
**7. David Ross, c, University of Florida.—(2002-15)**
8. Thomari Story-Harden, 1b, El Cerrito HS, Richmond, Calif.
9. Joel Williams, rhp, Yoncalla (Ore.) HS.
10. Lance Caraccioli, lhp, Northeast Louisiana University.
11. Christian Bridenbaugh, lhp, Central HS, Martinsburg, Pa.
12. J.K. Taylor, rhp, Louisa (Va.) HS.
13. C.J. Thomas, of-rhp, McLane HS, Fresno, Calif.
14. Robb Gorr, 1b-of, University of Southern California.
15. Paul Avery, lhp, Pepperdine University.
16. Jim Goelz, ss, New York Tech.
17. Alex Piedra, rhp, Southridge HS, Miami.
18. Tony Richards, c, North Dakota State University.
19. Jeremy Meccage, rhp, University of Iowa.
20. Tim Harrell, rhp, Liberty University.
21. Jacob Sampson, ss, Curtis HS, Tacoma, Wash.
22. Anthony Gomes, rhp, San Joaquin Delta (Calif.) JC.
23. Jason Moody, lhp, Spartanburg Methodist (S.C.) JC.
24. Allen Davis, lhp, Northwestern State University.
25. Scott Barnsby, rhp, University of Massachusetts.
26. Matt Greer, c, Louisiana Tech.
27. Nick Theodorou, 2b, UCLA.
28. *Corry Parrott, of, Pasadena (Calif.) CC.
29. *David Baum, lhp, Martin County HS, Stuart, Fla.
30. *Lloyd Turner, ss, Hephzibah (Ga.) HS.
31. *Paul Brown, lhp, Citrus (Calif.) JC.
32. *Darren Heal, c, Indian River (Fla.) JC.
33. *Herman Dean, of, Monrovia (Calif.) HS.
34. *Carlos Claudio, ss, Wilma Chavez HS, Guaynabo, P.R.
35. *Rashad Parker, ss, Crossroads HS, Santa Monica, Calif.
36. *Curt Borland, rhp, Centaurus HS, Broomfield, Colo.
37. *Josh McMillen, of, West Virginia University.
38. *Josh Berndt, lhp, Oshkosh West HS, Oshkosh, Wis.
39. *Marc-Andre Lagace, lhp, Louis Riel HS, Blackburn Hamlet, Ontario.
40. +Clint Hosford, rhp, Carson Graham HS, North Vancouver, B.C. / Capilano (B.C.) JC.
41. *Doug Vandecaveye, 3b, Tilbury District HS, Tilbury, Ontario.
42. *Jahseam George, lhp, JC of the Sequoias (Calif.).
43. *Jorge Roman, rhp, Jose de Diego HS, Aguadilla, P.R.
44. *Joey Hart, c, Grayson County (Texas) CC.
45. *Brandon Smith, 1b, Cypress (Calif.) JC.
**46. *Steve Andrade, rhp, American River (Calif.) JC.—(2006)**
47. *Harry Arocho, of, Benito Cerezo HS, Aguadilla, P.R.
48. *Chad Marchand, rhp, Lethbridge (Alberta) CC.
49. *Wayne Stone, 3b, A.B. Miller HS, Rialto, Calif.
50. *Blake McGinley, lhp, Bakersfield (Calif.) JC.

## MILWAUKEE BREWERS (13)

1. J.M. Gold, rhp, Toms River North HS, Toms River, N.J.—(High A)
**2. Nick Neugebauer, rhp, Arlington HS, Riverside, Calif.—(2001-02)**
3. Derry Hammond, of, West Point (Miss.) HS.—(High A)
4. *Rhett Parrott, rhp, Northwest Whitfield HS, Dalton, Ga.—(AAA)
DRAFT DROP *Attended Georgia Tech; re-drafted by Cardinals, 2001 (9th round)*
5. Chris Pine, rhp, Oregon State University.—(AAA)
**6. Bill Hall, ss, Nettleton (Miss.) HS.—(2002-12)**
7. Jason Fox, of, Florida Southern College.
8. Mike Penney, rhp, University of Southern California.
9. Ryan Bordenick, c, University of South Carolina.
10. James Johnson, lhp, University of Arizona.
11. Jeff Pickler, 2b, University of Tennessee.
12. Chris Barton, rhp, University of Connecticut.
13. *Heath McMurray, rhp, San Jacinto (Texas) JC.
14. *Charles Kegley, rhp, Middleburg (Fla.) HS.
15. Jose Montenegro, 3b, University of Oklahoma.
16. *Hector Guadalupe, ss, Arundel HS, Gambrills, Md.
17. *Steve Correa, lhp, Elk Grove (Calif.) HS.
18. Rickey Lewis, rhp, Mississippi Valley State University.
19. Scott Geitz, rhp, Southwest Missouri State University.
20. *Jeff Becker, 3b, Duke University.
21. Ryan Poe, rhp, Saddleback (Calif.) CC.
22. *Erik Smallwood, of, Tate HS, Gonzalez, Fla.
23. Eric Ayala, 2b, Northeast Texas CC.
24. Fontella Jones, rhp, Mississippi Valley State University.
25. Jack Krawczyk, rhp, University of Southern California.
26. Dan Mathews, rhp, Indiana University-Purdue University.
27. Jon Harraid, rhp, Sam Houston State University.
28. Tyrone Wayne, rhp, St. John's University.
29. Eduardo Figueroa, 1b, University of Tennessee.
DRAFT DROP *Son of Ed Figueroa, major leaguer (1974-81)*
30. Casey Davis, of, Wichita State University.
DRAFT DROP *Son of Willie Davis, major leaguer (1960-79)*
31. Lee Jaramillo, c, University of Wisconsin-Milwaukee.
32. Roberto Maysonet, rhp, Vega Baja, P.R.
33. Mac Mackiewitz, 1b, University of North Florida.
34. *Curt Kautsch, rhp, University of Texas.
35. *Stephen York, of, Arizona Western JC.
36. Bill Eaton, of, University of South Florida.
37. *Al Corbeil, c, Manatee (Fla.) CC.
38. *Jonathon Kuelz, rhp, West Lutheran HS, Minnetonka, Minn.
39. *Dustin Wagoner, rhp, Corona (Calif.) HS.
40. *Ken Harold, c, Denham Springs (La.) HS.
41. *Brian Wojtkowski, of, Peoria (Ariz.) HS.
42. *Chris Vallette, rhp, Angelina (Texas) JC.
43. *Pedro Gavillan, 3b, John I. Leonard HS, Lake Worth, Fla.
44. *Jeff Eure, 3b, Upper Dauphin HS, Pillow, Pa.
45. *Devin Butler, 1b, Key West (Fla.) HS.
46. *Nicholas Murphy, rhp, Central Florida CC.
47. *Landon Jacobsen, rhp, Trinidad State (Colo.) JC.
48. *Chad Christianson, lhp, Seabreeze HS, Ormond Beach, Fla.
49. *Nick Wash, 3b, Picayune (Miss.) HS.
50. *Michael Wojtkowski, of, Peoria (Ariz.) HS.

## MINNESOTA TWINS (6)

1. Ryan Mills, lhp, Arizona State University.–(AAA)
DRAFT DROP *Son of Dick Mills, major leaguer (1970)*
2. Marcus (Sents) Moseley, rhp, Cookeville (Tenn.) HS.—(High A)
3. Brent Hoard, lhp, Stanford University.—(AAA)
4. Pete Fisher, rhp, University of Alabama.—(AA)
5. Mickey Blount, rhp, Kansas State University.—DNP
6. *Brad Pautz, rhp, University of Minnesota.
7. *Sam Taulli, lhp, Lafayette (La.) HS.
8. John Edwards, c, Triton (Ill.) JC.
**9. Saul Rivera, rhp, University of Mobile (Ala.).—(2006-10)**
10. *Ryan Lundquist, of, University of Arkansas.
11. Jon Pridie, rhp, Prescott (Ariz.) HS.
12. Kareem Johnson, of, J. Lloyd Crowe HS, Trail, B.C.
13. Kyle Hawthorne, ss, Pensacola (Fla.) JC.
**14. *Mike Gosling, lhp, East HS, Salt Lake City.—(2004-2009)**
15. *Brian Haskell, lhp, Canyon Springs HS, Moreno Valley, Calif.
16. Jose Espinal, rhp, Canovanas, P.R.
**17. *J.J. Putz, rhp, University of Michigan.—(2003-14)**
**18. *Kevin Thompson, ss, Western Hills HS, Fort Worth, Texas.—(2006-07)**
19. Kevin Hodge, ss-3b, Rice University.
20. Brad Frazier, rhp, University of Mobile (Ala.).
21. *Marc Bluma, rhp, Wichita State University.
DRAFT DROP *Brother of Jaime Bluma, major leaguer (1996)*
22. +Rhett Riviere, rhp, St. Michael's Academy, Austin, Texas / Northeast Texas JC.
23. Andy Butler, rhp, Bowling Green State University.
**24. Juan Padilla, rhp, Jacksonville University.—(2004-05)**
25. Eric Sandberg, 1b, Ferris HS, Spokane, Wash.
26. *Jason Scobie, rhp, McLennan (Texas) JC.
27. Craig Selander, of, University of Minnesota.
28. Dave Marciniak, 2b, Rutgers University.
29. Lestor Victoria, lhp, University of Central Florida.
30. *Jonathan Muller, 3b, Arapahoe HS, Littleton, Colo.
31. Brian McMillan, of, University of Evansville.
32. Todd Collura, c, Polk (Fla.) CC.
33. *Bryan Gidge, rhp, University of Nevada-Las Vegas.
**34. Kevin Frederick, rhp, Creighton University.—(2002-04)**
35. *Mack Lambert, rhp, Pearl River (La.) HS.
36. Richard Denholm, rhp, Edgewater HS, Orlando, Fla.
37. *Ben Smith, rhp, Brownwood (Texas) HS.
**38. Tommy Watkins, ss, Riverdale HS, Fort Myers, Fla.—(2007)**
39. *Nathan Kent, rhp, Motlow State (Tenn.) CC.
40. *Joe Maruffi, rhp, St. Pius X HS, Albuquerque, N.M.
41. *Kayzell Milton, of, Homestead HS, Fremont, Calif.
42. *Andy Neufeld, ss, Manatee (Fla.) CC.
43. *Taylor Grant, lhp, Newport HS, Bellevue, Wash.
44. *Bobby Wood, rhp, Cherry Creek HS, Englewood, Colo.
45. *Ernie Bascuas, rhp, Miami-Dade CC North.
46. *Mike Bradley, rhp, Dr. Phillips HS, Orlando, Fla.
47. *Wade Clark, rhp, Santa Ynez HS, Los Olivos, Calif.
48. *Daniel Olson, rhp, Loveland (Colo.) HS.
49. *Desmond Dailey, of, Eastern Arizona JC.

## MONTREAL EXPOS (11)

1. Josh McKinley, ss, Malvern Prep, Downingtown, Pa.—(AA)
**1. Brad Wilkerson, of-lhp, University of Florida** (Supplemental choice—33rd—as compensation for Type A free agent Darrin Fletcher).**—(2001-08)**
2. Eric Good, lhp, Mishawaka (Ind.) HS.—(High A)
3. Clyde Williams, 1b, Seminole HS, Sanford, Fla. (Choice from Blue Jays as compensation for Fletcher).—(High A)
3. *Kevin Kelly, 3b, Gloucester Catholic HS, Brooklawn, N.J.—(Low A)
DRAFT DROP *Attended Duke; re-drafted by Giants, 2002 (5th round)*
4. Rob Castelli, rhp, Eastern Illinois University.—(High A)
5. Ryan Lentz, 3b, University of Washington.—(High A)
DRAFT DROP *Son of Mike Lentz, first-round draft pick, Padres (1975)*
6. Wes Chisnall, rhp, Etiwanda HS, Alta Loma, Calif.
7. Brad Piercy, c, North Carolina State University.
8. Scott Sandusky, c, Texas A&M University.
9. Juan Ortiz, of, Eastern District HS, Brooklyn, N.Y.
10. Ryan Grantham, rhp, Aldershot HS, Burlington, Ontario.
11. *Jason Walker, lhp, Ontario (Calif.) HS.
12. Scott Dobson, rhp, North Carolina State University.
13. Jason Hendricks, of, University of Arizona.
14. Kevin Hook, ss, Loyola Marymount University.
15. *Steve Baker, of, Rome (N.Y.) Free Academy.
16. Derick Urquhart, of, University of South Carolina.
17. Kyle Sheldon, rhp, Florida Southern College.
**18. Jimmy Serrano, rhp, University of New Mexico.—(2004)**
19. Omar Rosado, 2b, Dr. Agustin Stahl HS, Toa Baja, P.R.
20. Brandon Agamennone, rhp, University of Maryland.
21. Jason Kanovich, lhp, Shippensburg (Pa.) University.
22. Trevor Wamback, rhp, Dalhousie (N.S.) University.
23. Jamie Hammond, ss, West Virginia University.
24. *Joe Clark, rhp, Chugiak HS, Eagle River, Alaska.
25. *Casey Fuller, lhp, Sacramento (Calif.) CC.
26. Brad Waldron, rhp, Iowa State University.
27. Steve Toriz, rhp, East Los Angeles JC.
28. +Rich Lane, of, Tustin (Calif.) HS / Santa Ana (Calif.) CC.
29. *Michael Castleberry, rhp, Batesville (Ark.) HS.
30. *Matt Romero, of, Spanish Fork (Utah) HS.
31. *Jeff Reboin, lhp, San Juan HS, Carmichael, Calif.
32. Andrew Frierson, lhp, JC of San Mateo (Calif.).
33. *Josh Merrigan, lhp, Butler County (Kan.) CC.
34. +Charles Dubuc, lhp, St. Jean College HS, Iberville, Quebec.
35. *Jeff Lincoln, rhp, American River (Calif.) JC.
36. *Nathan Kershaw, of, Hoke County HS, Raeford, N.C.
37. *Clint Dunbar, rhp, Norman (Okla.) HS.
38. *Chris Richards, of, Burlington (Vt.) HS.
39. *Anthony Watts, lhp, Lincoln HS, San Diego.
40. *Josh Laidlaw, of, Arizona Western JC.

41. *Alexandre Groleau, rhp, Edouard Montpetit HS, Longueuil, Quebec.
42. *Ross Bennett, of, Central HS, Cape Girardeau, Mo.
43. *Jace Brewer, ss, Washington (Okla.) HS.
44. Ron Chiavacci, rhp, Kutztown (Pa.) University.
45. *Tomas Perez, ss, John Burroughs HS, Burbank, Calif.

## NEW YORK METS (21)

**1. Jason Tyner, of, Texas A&M University.—(2000-08)**
**2. Pat Strange, rhp, Central HS, Springfield, Mass.—(2002-03)**
3. Jason Saenz, lhp, University of Southern California.—(AAA)
4. *Jason Moates, rhp, Meridian (Miss.) CC.–(High A)
DRAFT DROP *Attended Middle Tennessee State; re-drafted by Reds, 2000 (28th round)*
**5. Craig Brazell, c, Jefferson Davis HS, Montgomery, Ala.—(2004-07)**
6. Marvin Seale, of, Durango (Colo.) HS.
7. Ryan Smith, c, Mifflinburg (Pa.) Area HS.
8. *Vince Vazquez, rhp, Chaminade Madonna HS, Hollywood, Fla.
9. Todd Bellhorn, lhp, University of Central Florida.
DRAFT DROP *Brother of Mark Bellhorn, major leaguer (1997-2007)*
10. Larnell Hamn, of, Potomac HS, Triangle, Va.
11. Josh Perich, of, Northwestern Lehigh HS, Slatington, Pa.
**12. *Ryan Budde, c, Midwest City (Okla.) HS.—(2007-10)**
13. Andy Cook, rhp, College of William & Mary.
**14. Gil Velazquez, ss, Paramount (Calif.) HS.—(2008-13)**
15. David Hunter, 1b, Porterville (Calif.) JC.
16. *Scott Bikowski, of, Florida Southern College.
**17. Ty Wigginton, ss, University of North Carolina-Asheville.—(2002-13)**
18. Brian Cole, of, Navarro (Texas) JC.
DRAFT DROP *Died as active player (March 31, 2001)*
19. Frank Graham, rhp, Columbus State (Ohio) JC.
20. *Jason Clements, ss, Riverside (Calif.) CC.
21. Robert Lugo, 1b, Patria la Torres Ramirez HS, San Sebastian, P.R.
22. +Brian Shipp, ss, Meridian (Miss.) CC.
**23. +Jaime Cerda, lhp, Fresno (Calif.) CC.—(2002-05)**
24. Gene Gobbel, ss, Presbyterian (S.C.) College.
25. *John Wesley, rhp, W.T. Clarke HS, Westbury, N.Y.
26. Jason Osborn, c, Sehome HS, Bellingham, Wash.
27. *Justin Smith, lhp, University of Alabama.
28. Marc Ludvigsen, of, University of North Carolina-Asheville.
29. Alex Zardis, 2b, Edmonds (Wash.) CC.
30. Alex Stoffels, c, Indian Hills (Iowa) CC.
31. Rene Vega, lhp, Dominican (N.Y.) College.
32. Pedro Rodriguez, of, Rollins (Fla.) College.
33. Greg Halvorson, c-rhp, Arizona State University.
34. Billy Martin, 3b, University of Texas-Arlington.
35. *Edwin Franco, lhp, Florida International University.
**36. Earl Snyder, 1b, University of Hartford.—(2002-04)**
37. *Mike Wodnicki, rhp, Southington (Conn.) HS.
38. Gary Bohannon, rhp, Kennesaw State (Ga.) University.
39. Justin Kurtz, rhp, Brewton Parker (Ga.) College.
40. Mike Prokop, rhp, Kennesaw State (Ga.) University.
41. *Joseph Yarbrough, lhp, Hazel Green (Ala.) HS.
42. *Ben Leuthard, 1b, Mission Bay HS, San Diego.
43. Tom Paciorek Jr., of, Southern Tech (Ga.) Institute.
DRAFT DROP *Son of Tom Paciorek, major leaguer (1970-87)*
44. *Ruben Feliciano, rhp, Bushwick HS, Brooklyn, N.Y.
45. *Chris Nelson, of, Pasadena (Calif.) CC.
46. +Ken Chenard, rhp, Fullerton (Calif.) JC.
47. *Ben Vargas, rhp, El Monte HS, Azusa, Calif.
48. *Chris Taylor, of, Riverside (Calif.) CC.
49. *Newton Hausmann, lhp, Red Bank Catholic HS, Colts Neck, N.Y.
50. Aaron Hee, lhp, Taft (Calif.) JC.

## NEW YORK YANKEES (24)

1. Andy Brown, of, Richmond (Ind.) HS.—(AA)
**1. *Mark Prior, rhp, University HS, San Diego** (Supplemental choice—43rd—for failure to sign 1997 first-round draft pick Tyrell Godwin).**—(2002-06)**
DRAFT DROP *Attended Vanderbilt; re-drafted by Cubs, 2001 (1st round); first player from 2001 draft to reach majors (May 22, 2002)*
**2. Randy Keisler, lhp, Louisiana State University.—(2000-07)**
**3. Drew Henson, 3b-rhp, Brighton (Mich.) HS.—(2002-03)**
DRAFT DROP *Quarterback, National Football League (2004-08)*
4. +Ivan Reyes, ss, Liceo Hispano Americano HS, Bayamon, P.R. / Miami-Dade North CC.—(AA)
5. Brian Rogers, rhp, The Citadel.—(AAA)
**6. Brett Jodie, rhp, University of South Carolina.—(2001)**
7. Ryan Ridenour, lhp, Texas Christian University.
8. David Fowler, of, McCluer North HS, Florissant, Mo.
9. Allen Greene, of, University of Notre Dame.
10. *Damon Thames, ss, Rice University.
11. Casey DeGroote, 3b, West Vigo HS, West Terre Haute, Ind.
12. Jeff Sheffield, of, University HS, Spokane, Wash.
13. *Charlie Isaacson, rhp, Shawnee Mission West HS, Overland Park, Kan.
14. Brett Weber, rhp, University of Illinois.
15. Justin Reisinger, rhp, Adena HS, Clarksburg, Ohio.
16. *Gabe Crecion, rhp, UCLA.
17. Jeff Shaddix, rhp, Texas Christian University.
18. *Danny Delmas, rhp, Odessa (Texas) JC.
19. Brad Elwood, c, West Virginia University.
20. Dusty Rhodes, of, University of Illinois.
21. Neal Gregg, 1b, William Carey (Miss.) College.
22. Jeff Sziksai, 2b, Western Carolina University.
23. Mark Carek, ss, Ohio State University.
24. +Jason Willis, rhp, East Central (Miss.) JC.
25. +Mario Gardea, rhp, Odessa (Texas) HS / Odessa (Texas) JC.
26. *Javy Rodriguez, ss, Gulliver Prep, Miami.
27. Scott Massucco, c, St. Thomas Aquinas HS, Fort Lauderdale, Fla.
28. *Lee Gwaltney, rhp, Aledo HS, Willow Park, Texas.
29. *Adam Manley, of, JC of Southern Idaho.
30. *Brian Conley, lhp, Gladewater (Texas) HS.
31. +Elvis Corporan, ss, Espiritu Santo HS, Baja, P.R. / Lake City (Fla.) CC.
32. *Jay Signorelli, rhp, Manatee (Fla.) CC.
33. *Jeff Hunter, rhp, Meridian (Miss.) CC.
**34. +Brandon Claussen, lhp, Howard (Texas) JC.—(2003-06)**
35. *Michael Gosz, ss, Treasure Valley (Ore.) CC.
**36. *Eric Eckenstahler, lhp, Illinois State University.—(2002-03)**
37. *Jarrell McIntyre, ss, Laguna Creek HS, Elk Grove, Calif.
38. *Chad Christian, lhp, Northeast Jones HS, Laurel, Miss.
39. *Luke Miller, rhp, Rolla (Mo.) HS.
**40. *Nook Logan, ss, Natchez (Miss.) HS.—(2004-07)**
41. David Kloes, rhp, West Virginia University.
42. *Justin Nash, rhp, Calvert Hall HS, Hunt Valley, Md.
43. *Kris Ehmke, rhp, Hill (Texas) JC.
44. *Marc Love, of, Coldspring (Texas) HS.
45. *Jeff Moye, rhp, Hardin-Jefferson HS, Kountze, Texas.
46. Jeff Carlson, rhp, Quinnipiac College.
47. Jeff Nettles, 3b, Palomar (Calif.) JC.
DRAFT DROP *Son of Graig Nettles, major leaguer (1967-88)*
48. *Kyle Geswein, 1b, Carroll HS, Dayton, Ohio.
49. *Corey Lawson, rhp, Windsor (Mo.) HS.
50. *Joseph List, rhp, Beechwood HS, Fort Mitchell, Ky.

## OAKLAND ATHLETICS (2)

**1. Mark Mulder, lhp, Michigan State University.—(2000-08)**
**2. +Gerald Laird, c, La Quinta HS, Westminster, Calif. / Cypress (Calif.) CC.—(2003-15)**
3. Kevin Miller, ss, University of Washington.—(High A)
4. Jeff Schultz, rhp, Cypress (Calif.) CC.—(High A)
**5. Jason Hart, 1b, Southwest Missouri State University.—(2002)**
6. Gary Schneidmiller, ss, Don Lugo HS, Chino, Calif.
7. Donato Calandriello, lhp, College of Charleston.
**8. Eric Byrnes, of, UCLA.—(2000-10)**
**9. Jon Adkins, rhp, Oklahoma State University.—(2003-08)**
10. Bert Snow, rhp, Vanderbilt University.
11. Jay Pecci, ss, Stanford University.
12. Eric Thompson, rhp, Ohio State University.
**13. *Jeff Bajenaru, rhp, Riverside (Calif.) CC.—(2004-06)**
14. *Mike Lockwood, of, Ohio State University.
15. Rusty Keith, of, Portland State University.
16. Shane Bazzell, rhp, New Hope HS, Columbus, Miss.
17. +Elih Velazquez, lhp, Jose Campeche HS, San Lorenzo, P.R. / Indian Hills (Iowa) CC.
18. Justin Hall, ss, Long Beach State University.
19. Justin Nixon, of, Walla Walla (Wash.) CC.
20. DeWayne Betts, of, Lakewood (Calif.) HS.
21. *Casey Bookout, 1b, University of Oklahoma.
22. Aaron Nieckula, c, University of Illinois.
**23. Tyler Yates, rhp, University of Hawaii-Hilo.—(2004-09)**
DRAFT DROP *Brother of Kirby Yates, major leaguer (2014-15)*
24. *Bryan Williamson, of, University of Washington.
25. Jim Brink, rhp, University of Nevada-Reno.
26. J.P. Schmidt, ss, Highland HS, Palmdale, Calif.
27. Jason Dobis, rhp, University of Minnesota.
28. Matt Forbes, of, Muscatine (Iowa) CC.
29. Matt Howe, 3b, Texas Christian University.
DRAFT DROP *Son of Art Howe, major leaguer (1974-85); major league manager (1989-2004)*
30. Anthony Taylor, rhp, University of Southern Colorado.
31. *Michael Woods, 2b, Broadmoor HS, Baton Rouge, La.
DRAFT DROP *First-round draft pick (32nd overall), Tigers (2001)*
32. Kurt Nantkes, rhp, Hinkley HS, Aurora, Colo.
33. Alex Negron, rhp, Southeastern (Iowa) CC.
34. *Newt Parent, c, Phoenix (Ore.) HS.
35. Brad Moore, rhp, University of Northern Iowa.
36. *Alex Torres, lhp, Cochise County (Ariz.) CC.
37. *Marshall Rubens, rhp, American River (Calif.) JC.
38. *Billy Green, of, Spring (Texas) HS.
39. *Bryan Ball, rhp, Taylorsville HS, Salt Lake City.
40. *Zack Riera, c, Florida HS, Tallahassee, Fla.
41. *James Mears, rhp, Indian Hills (Iowa) CC.
42. *John Dean, of, Magnolia (Texas) HS.
**43. *Mike Cervenak, 3b, University of Michigan.—(2008)**

## PHILADELPHIA PHILLIES (1)

**1. Pat Burrell, 3b-1b, University of Miami.—(2000-11)**
**1. Eric Valent, of, UCLA** (Supplemental choice—42nd—for failure to sign 1997 first-round draft pick J.D. Drew).**—(2001-05)**
2. Brad Baisley, rhp, Land O'Lakes (Fla.) HS.—(AA)
**3. Jorge Padilla, of, Florida Air Academy, Melbourne, Fla.—(2009)**
**4. Jason Michaels, of, University of Miami.—(2001-11)**
5. Kennon McArthur, c, Sylacauga (Ala.) HS.
6. *Tommy Whiteman, ss, Midwest City (Okla.) HS.
7. Jarrod Lawson, rhp, Potosi (Mo.) HS.
8. Mike Wilson, rhp, Granite Hills HS, El Cajon, Calif.
**9. Ryan Madson, rhp, Valley View HS, Moreno Valley, Calif.—(2003-15)**
10. Ken Westmoreland, rhp, University of Alabama-Huntsville.
11. Ben Jewson, 3b, Waukesha North HS, Waukesha, Wis.
12. Ian Rauls, of, Old Dominion University.
**13. *Adam Peterson, rhp, Oconto Falls (Wis.) HS.—(2004)**
14. Greg Kubes, lhp, Sam Houston State University.
**15. Geoff Geary, rhp, University of Oklahoma.—(2003-09)**
16. Chris Pilato, rhp, Villanova University.
17. Chip DeNure, ss, Ripon (Wis.) College.
18. Nate Espy, 1b, Lurleen B. Wallace (Ala.) CC.
19. Jeremy Salazar, c, Florida State University.
20. Jeremy Wedel, rhp, Armstrong Atlantic State (Ga.) University.
**21. Nick Punto, ss, Saddleback (Calif.) JC.—(2001-14)**
22. Matt Bailie, rhp, Oregon State University.
23. Cary Hiles, rhp, University of Memphis.
24. Shayne Carnes, of, University of Alabama-Birmingham.
25. *Aric LeClair, lhp, Crowder (Mo.) JC.
26. Mike Zipser, rhp, University of Nevada-Reno.
27. Ron McGinnis, c, University of Texas-San Antonio.
28. Chris Maness, rhp, Elon College.
29. Andrew Wiedl, lhp, Winona State (Minn.) University.
30. Kurt Blackmon, rhp, North Carolina State University.
31. Buzz Hannahan, 2b, University of St. Thomas (Minn.).
32. *Abraham Ayala, 3b, Discipulos de Cristo HS, Bayamon, P.R.
33. Wes Rachels, 2b, University of Southern California.
34. David Ciesla, lhp, Arkansas Tech University.
35. *Pete Montrenes, rhp, Ocean View HS, Fountain Valley, Calif.
36. Roger Rodeheaver, 1b, Indiana University.
37. Ed Grammer, rhp, Union (Tenn.) University.
38. *Lance Cooley, ss, Killeen (Texas) HS.
39. Jeremy Deitrick, c, Penn State University.
40. *Todd Henry, rhp, Bakersfield (Calif.) JC.
41. T.J. Donovan, rhp, Elon College.
42. *Kirk Nordness, ss, Beaverton (Ore.) HS.
43. *Earnest Graham, of, Mariner HS, Fort Myers, Fla.
DRAFT DROP *Running back, National Football League (2004-11)*

## PITTSBURGH PIRATES (15)

1. Clint Johnston, lhp-of, Vanderbilt University.—(AA)
2. Jeremy Cotten, 3b-rhp, Fuquay-Varina (N.C.) HS.—(High A)
3. Jeremy Harts, of-lhp, Columbia HS, Decatur, Ga.—(AA)
4. Eddy Furniss, 1b, Louisiana State University.—(AA)
5. Raynier Cardona, c, Patria la Torres Ramirez HS, San Sebastian, P.R.—(Rookie)
6. Brice Pelfrey, ss, Tate HS, Gonzalez, Fla.
7. James White, rhp, Chico (Calif.) HS.
8. *Chuck Crowder, lhp, Georgia Tech.
9. Giovanni Gonzalez, rhp, Northwest Christian Academy, Miami.
10. David Diaz, c, Hialeah-Miami Lakes HS, Hialeah, Fla.
11. *Chris Smith, lhp-of, Wantagh (N.Y.) HS.
DRAFT DROP *First-round draft pick (7th overall), Orioles (2001)*
12. Willie Burton, of, Lake Wales (Fla.) HS.
13. Ben Levesque, rhp, Cary (N.C.) HS.
14. *John Breck, rhp, Bridgewater-Raritan HS, Bridgewater, N.J.
**15. *Craig House, rhp, University of Memphis.—(2000)**
16. *Russ Rohlicek, lhp, College Park HS, Pleasant Hill, Calif.
**17. Dave Williams, lhp, Delaware Tech & CC.—(2001-07)**
**18. Joe Beimel, lhp, Duquesne University.—(2001-15)**
**19. Jeff Bennett, rhp, Gordonsville (Tenn.) HS.—(2007-09)**
**20. Mike Johnston, lhp, Garrett (Md.) CC.—(2004-05)**
21. Mike Bumatay, lhp-of, Clovis (Calif.) HS.
22. Josh Miller, c, Silver Bluff HS, Aiken, S.C.
23. *Tyson Thompson, of, Inglemoor HS, Bothell, Wash.
24. David Hawk, lhp, Vista West HS, Bakersfield, Calif.

25. *Thom Ott, rhp, Greenbrier Christian Academy, Chesapeake, Va.
**26. *Jon Switzer, lhp, Clear Lake HS, Houston.—(2003-09)**
27. Casey Cloud, c, UCLA.
**28. Steve Sparks, rhp, University of South Alabama.—(2000)**
29. *Scott Gardner, lhp, Cardinal Gibbons HS, Coral Springs, Fla.
30. *Matt Vorwald, rhp, Freeport (Ill.) HS.
31. *Eric Tatum, lhp, Forest Hill HS, West Palm Beach, Fla.
32. *Wyatt Allen, rhp, Brentwood Academy, Nashville.
DRAFT DROP *First-round draft pick (39th overall), White Sox (2001)*
33. *Marcus Nettles, of, Whitney Young HS, Chicago.
34. *Traviss Hodge, 1b, Highland HS, Agua Dulce, Calif.
35. *Trevor Hutchinson, rhp, Torrey Pines HS, San Diego.
DRAFT DROP *Brother of Chad Hutchinson, first-round draft pick, Braves (1995); second-round draft pick, Cardinals (1998); major leaguer (2001); quarterback, National Football League (2002-04)*
36. *Mike Wombacher, 1b, Yavapai (Ariz.) JC.
37. *Justin Fry, rhp, Ohio State University.
38. Shaun Skrehot, ss, University of Houston.
39. Veon Harris, rhp, East Mississippi JC.
40. *Jeff Ellena, ss, Walnut HS, Diamond Bar, Calif.
41. *Christian Ortiz, of, Arcadia (Calif.) HS.
42. +Scott Glaser, lhp, University of South Florida.
43. Eric Stanton, 3b, University of South Carolina.
44. *Brian Walker, lhp, Westminster Christian HS, Miami.
45. Brian Cronk, 3b-of, Eastern New Mexico University.
46. *Jamie Shearin, c, East Wake HS, Knightdale, N.C.
47. *Josh Renick, 2b, Manatee (Fla.) JC.
DRAFT DROP *Son of Rick Renick, major leaguer (1968-72)*

## ST. LOUIS CARDINALS (5)

**1. J.D. Drew, of, St. Paul (Northern League).—(1998-2011)**
DRAFT DROP *First-round draft pick (2nd overall), Phillies (1997); first player from 1998 draft to reach majors (Sept. 8, 1998) • Brother of Tim Drew, first-round draft pick, Indians (1997); major leaguer (2000-04) • Brother of Stephen Drew, first-round draft pick, Diamondbacks (2004); major leaguer (2006-15)*
**1. *Ben Diggins, 1b-rhp, Bradshaw Mountain HS, Dewey Ariz.** (Supplemental choice—32nd—as compensation for Type A free agent Dennis Eckersley).**—(2002)**
DRAFT DROP *Attended Arizona; re-drafted by Dodgers, 2000 (1st round)*
**2. Chad Hutchinson, rhp, Stanford University.—(2001)**
DRAFT DROP *First-round draft pick (26th overall), Braves (1995); quarterback, National Football League (2002-04) • Brother of Trevor Hutchinson, 35th-round draft pick, Pirates (1998)*
2. Tim Lemon, of, La Mirada (Calif.) HS (Choice from Red Sox as compensation for Eckersley).—(High A)
3. Gabe Johnson, c, Atlantic HS, Delray Beach, Fla.—(AAA)
**4. Bud Smith, lhp, Los Angeles Harbor JC.—(2001-02)**
**5. Steve Stemle, rhp, Western Kentucky University.—(2005-06)**
6. Kris Rayborn, lhp, Purvis (Miss.) HS.
7. Brad Freeman, ss-of, Mississippi State University.
8. Greg Clark, c, University of Arizona.
**9. Jack Wilson, ss, Oxnard (Calif.) JC.—(2001-12)**
10. +Pedro Zazueta, rhp, Amphitheater HS, Tucson, Ariz. / Yavapai (Ariz.) JC.
11. *Joel Vega, lhp, Ohio Dominican College.
12. *Jeff Waldron, c, Boston College.
**13. Les Walrond, lhp, University of Kansas.—(2003-08)**
14. Jason Bowers, ss, Gulf Coast (Fla.) CC.
15. Johnny Hernandez, of, Xaverian HS, Brooklyn, N.Y.

**Tigers first-rounder Jeff Weaver went 14th overall, six years before his brother Jered went 12th**

16. Scott Prather, lhp, Georgia Tech.
17. Matt Gargano, rhp, Dixie (Utah) JC.
**18. Esix Snead, of, University of Central Florida.—(2002-04)**
19. Travis Held, rhp, University of Central Florida.
20. Chris Kelly, 3b, Catawba (N.C.) College.
21. Jim Molina, of, Florida International University.
22. *Mike Rerick, lhp, University of North Dakota.
23. Andy Shibilo, rhp, Pepperdine University.
24. Rick Gonzales, rhp, University of New Mexico.
25. Jon Hand, rhp, Virginia Tech.
26. *Steve Parker, rhp, Key West (Fla.) HS.
27. Ryan Christianson, rhp, University of Nebraska-Omaha.
28. Jason Marr, rhp, Long Beach State University.
29. Jeff Viles, rhp, Rockhurst (Mo.) College.
30. Eric Gutshall, rhp, Yale University.
31. Troy McNaughton, rhp, Brigham Young University.
32. Troy Farnsworth, 2b, Brigham Young University.
33. Tommy Kidwell, 2b, Yale University.
34. *Kyle Boyer, ss, Bonneville HS, Ogden, Utah.
35. *Dustin Hawkins, of, Bonneville HS, Ogden, Utah.
36. *Andrew Ecklund, c, San Luis Obispo (Calif.) HS.
37. *Brent Cordell, c, Incline HS, Incline Village, Nev.
38. *Seth Jerue, ss, Westfield (Mass.) HS.
39. *Vic Buttler, of, Westchester HS, Hawthorne, Calif.
40. *Scott Neal, of, North HS, Bakersfield, Calif.
**41. *Justin Knoedler, c, Springfield (Ill.) HS.—(2004-06)**
42. *Brandon Tisher, 1b, Durango (Colo.) HS.
43. *Scott Sorensen, rhp, Fruita Monument HS, Grand Junction, Colo.
44. *Matt Harvick, c, North HS, Bakersfield, Calif.
45. *Matt Van Alsburg, of, Fort Collins (Colo.) HS.

## SAN DIEGO PADRES (9)

**1. Sean Burroughs, 3b, Woodrow Wilson HS, Long Beach, Calif.—(2002-12)**
DRAFT DROP *Son of Jeff Burroughs, first overall draft pick, Senators (1969); major leaguer (1970-85)*
2. (Choice to Braves as compensation for loss of Type B free agent Greg Myers)
3. *Beau Craig, c, Grossmont HS, La Mesa, Calif.—(AAA)
DRAFT DROP *Attended Southern California; re-drafted by Athletics, 2000 (6th round)*
4. Travis Devine, rhp, Dacula (Ga.) HS.—(Low A)
DRAFT DROP *Son of Adrian Devine, major leaguer (1973-80)*
5. Kevin Eberwein, 3b-of, University of Nevada-Las Vegas.—(AAA)
6. *Dale Deveraux, rhp, American Fork (Utah) HS.
7. Brian Berryman, rhp, University of Michigan.
8. Jeremy Owens, of, Middle Tennessee State University.
9. Sean Campbell, c, University of Nevada-Las Vegas.
10. John Meyers, rhp, Grayson County (Texas) JC.
11. Josh Loggins, of, University of Kentucky.
12. Joe Dusan, 1b, Sacramento (Calif.) CC.
13. *Thom Dreier, rhp, Oklahoma State University.
14. Ryan Hawkins, rhp, Lurleen B. Wallace (Ala.) JC.
15. Casey Bell, rhp, Crowder (Mo.) JC.
**16. Steve Watkins, rhp, Lubbock, Texas.—(2004)**
**17. Brian Lawrence, rhp, Northwestern State University.—(2001-07)**
18. Aaron Kramer, rhp, Arizona State University.
**19. Jeremy Fikac, rhp, Southwest Texas State University.—(2001-04)**
20. *Eron Morrow, 1b, Woodrow Wilson HS, Tacoma, Wash.
21. Keith Forbes, rhp, Lurleen B. Wallace (Ala.) JC.
22. Jon Cook, of, San Francisco State University.
23. Jack Wickersham, 2b, Southwest Texas State University.
24. *Jerymane Beasley, of, Spokane Falls (Wash.) CC.
25. *Jonathan Segarra, lhp, Frank Phillips (Texas) JC.
26. Ryan Bauer, rhp, Fontbonne (Mo.) College.
27. *Ralph Roberts, of, Cherryville (N.C.) HS.
28. Jeremy Reed, c, Lookout Valley HS, Chattanooga, Tenn.
**29. Cliff Bartosh, lhp, Duncanville (Texas) HS.—(2004-05)**
**30. +Eric Cyr, lhp, Seminole (Okla.) JC.—(2002)**
31. Shawn Hazen, of, Princeton University.
32. +Geoff Jones, lhp, Montezuma-Cortez HS, Cortez, Colo. / Dixie (Utah) JC.
33. Bryan Schmidt, ss, University of Nebraska.
34. *Simon Mitchell, of, Bellevue (Wash.) CC.
35. +Josh Barbarossa, 1b, Chesterton HS, Valparaiso, Ind. / Triton (Ill.) JC.
36. *Nathan Sturdivant, rhp, Westmoore HS, Oklahoma City, Okla.
37. *Felix Castillo, rhp, Colegio Maria Auxiliadora HS, Rio Grande, P.R.
**38. *Trey Hodges, rhp, Blinn (Texas) JC.—(2002-03)**
39. +Jonathan Stone, c, Sacramento (Calif.) CC.
40. *Clint Kelley, rhp, Morton (Ill.) JC.
41. *Charis Britt, c, Gulf Coast (Fla.) CC.
**42. Alex Pelaez, 3b, San Diego State University.—(2002)**
**43. *Jason Jones, rhp, Kennesaw State (Ga.) University.—(2003)**
44. *Jesse Gutierrez, c, Texas Southmost JC.

## SAN FRANCISCO GIANTS (25)

**1. Tony Torcato, 3b, Woodland (Calif.) HS** (Choice from Astros as compensation for Type B free agent Doug Henry).**—(2002-05)**
**1. Nate Bump, rhp, Penn State University.—(2003-05)**
1. Arturo McDowell, of, Forest Hill HS, Jackson, Miss. (Choice from Devil Rays as compensation for Type A free agent Roberto Hernandez).—(AA)
1. Chris Jones, lhp, South Mecklenburg HS, Charlotte, N.C. (Supplemental choice—38th—as compensation for Hernandez).—(AA)
1. Jeff Urban, lhp, Ball State University (Supplemental choice—41st—as compensation for Type A free agent Wilson Alvarez).—(AAA)
2. Sammy Serrano, c, Stetson University.—(High A)
**2. Chris Magruder, of, University of Washington** (Choice from Devil Rays as compensation for Alvarez).**—(2001-05)**
3. Mike Dean, c, Oral Roberts University.—(High A)
4. Josh Santos, lhp, University of Connecticut.—(High A)
**5. Ryan Vogelsong, rhp, Kutztown (Pa.) University.—(2000-15)**
6. Jake Esteves, rhp, Louisiana State University.
**7. Doug Clark, of, University of Massachusetts.—(2005-06)**
8. Todd Ozias, rhp, University of Miami.
**9. Cody Ransom, ss, Grand Canyon University.—(2001-13)**
10. Chris Jackson, rhp, Wasson HS, Colorado Springs, Colo.
**11. Erasmo Ramirez, lhp, Cal State Fullerton.—(2003-07)**
12. Randy Goodrich, rhp, Fresno State University.
13. John Summers, 1b, University of Utah.
14. Mike Huller, lhp, George Mason University.
15. Jeff Allen, of, Illinois State University.
16. Erik Mattern, 2b-ss, University of Arizona.
17. Joseph Ojeda, rhp, St. Francis (N.Y.) College.
18. +David Brous, lhp, Del Norte HS, Crescent City, Calif. / JC of the Redwoods (Calif.).
19. *Ben Quick, rhp, Riverside (Calif.) CC.
20. *Santiago Narciandi, 3b, Miami (Fla.) Senior HS.
21. Benji Miller, rhp, Liberty University.
22. *Teddy Sutton, lhp, Colton (Calif.) HS.
23. Jake Mapes, c, Riverside (Calif.) CC.
24. *Ken Trapp, rhp, Alvin (Texas) CC.
25. *Oscar Vargas, ss, James Logan HS, Union City, Calif.
26. *Jason Barrow, of, Canby Union HS, Canby, Ore.
27. Steve Hill, ss, Oklahoma State University.

28. *Chad Ertel, rhp, Elmira District HS, St. Clements, Ontario.
29. *Kyle Middleton, rhp, Escambia HS, Pensacola, Fla.
30. *Grant Abrams, ss, Tarpon Springs HS, Palm Harbor, Fla.
31. *Cade Sanchez, rhp, University of Texas-Arlington.
32. *Jackson Markert, rhp, Connors State (Okla.) JC.
33. *Ryan Gonzales, rhp, Riverside (Calif.) CC.
34. *Travis McGreal, rhp, Heritage HS, Littleton, Colo.
35. *Matt Dryer, ss, McQuaid Jesuit HS, Rochester, N.Y.
36. *Josh Souza, rhp, Turlock (Calif.) HS.
37. *Dan Kelly, lhp, Okaloosa-Walton (Fla.) JC.
38. *Winston Woods, of, Coral Shores HS, Key Largo, Fla.
39. *Joel Vasquez, of, Booker HS, Sarasota, Fla.
40. *Bill Nahorodny Jr., of, Clearwater (Fla.) HS.

DRAFT DROP *Son of Bill Naharodny, major leaguer (1976-84)*

41. *Marcellus Presley, of, Sacramento (Calif.) CC.
42. Carlos Frazier, of, Smackover (Ark.) HS.
43. *Scott Goodman, of, Cuesta (Calif.) JC.
44. *Dorian Cameron, ss, Coastal Carolina University.
45. *Cody Sudbeck, rhp, Tyler (Texas) JC.

## SEATTLE MARINERS (22)

**1. Matt Thornton, lhp, Grand Valley State (Mich.) University.—(2004-15)**
2. *Jeff Verplancke, rhp, Cal State Los Angeles.—(AAA)

DRAFT DROP *Returned to Cal State Los Angeles; re-drafted by Giants, 1999 (11th round)*

**3. Andy Van Hekken, lhp, Holland (Mich.) HS.—(2002)**
4. Jerry Amador, of, Luis Felipe Crespo HS, Camuy, P.R.—(High A)
5. Corey Freeman, ss, King HS, Tampa.—(AAA)
6. Jake Weber, of, North Carolina State University.
7. Shawn McCorkle, 1b, Montclair State (N.J.) University.
8. Craig Kuzmic, c-3b, Texas A&M University.
9. Neil Longo, rhp, Manhattan College.
10. *Jason Pomar, rhp, University of South Carolina.
11. *Jarrett Shearin, of, University of North Carolina.
12. Justin Dunning, rhp, Stanford University.

DRAFT DROP *Son of Steve Dunning, first-round draft pick, Indians (1970); major leaguer (1970-77)*

13. Israel Cruz, ss, Dr. Jose M. Lazaro HS, Carolina, P.R.
14. Schuyler Doakes, ss, Jackson State University.
15. Wilfredo Quintana, of, Indian Hills (Iowa) CC.
16. Patrick Barnes, lhp, Englewood HS, Jacksonville, Fla.
17. Steve Wright, of, Liberty University.
18. Craig Willis, rhp, Pacific Lutheran (Wash.) University.
19. Rick Southall, 1b-of, Portland State University.
20. *Jon Nelson, ss, Timpanogos HS, Orem, Utah.
21. *Brandon DeJaynes, rhp, Quincy (Ill.) HS.
22. *Mike Myers, ss, Bishop Verot HS, Cape Coral, Fla.
23. *Brian Hartung, rhp, Sinton (Texas) HS
24. Matt Woodward, 1b, Florida State University.

DRAFT DROP *Son of Woody Woodward, major leaguer (1963-71); general manager, Yankees (1987); general manager, Phillies (1988); general manager, Mariners (1989-99)*

25. *Craig Helmandollar, lhp, North Stafford HS, Stafford, Va.
26. Caleb Balbuena, rhp, Long Beach State University.
27. Jason Crist, lhp, Southwest Missouri State University.
28. Bo Robinson, 3b, University of North Carolina-Charlotte.
29. *Derald Deason, of, Orange HS, Santa Ana, Calif.
**30. *John Rheinecker, lhp, Belleville Area (Ill.) CC.—(2006-07)**

DRAFT DROP *First-round draft pick (37th overall), Athletics (2001)*

31. Roy Wells, rhp, Volunteer State (Tenn.) CC.
32. *Clay Bried, of, Apache Junction HS, Mesa, Ariz.
33. *Brandon Pack, c, Cypress (Calif.) JC.
34. *Nick Padilla, rhp, Cerritos (Calif.) JC.
35. *Guarionez Rodriguez, 2b, Medardo Carazo HS, Trujillo Alto, P.R.
36. *Tim Dierkes, c, Mehlville HS, St. Louis.
37. *Michael Kashuba, rhp, Clarence Fulton HS, Vernon, B.C.
38. *Clint Patton, c, Sonora HS, Brea, Calif.
39. *Aaron Kirkland, rhp, Lurleen B. Wallace (Ala.) CC.
40. *Adam Thomas, rhp, North Miami HS, Miami.
41. *Nicholas Hobbs, of, Chaparral HS, Las Vegas, Nev.
42. *Geoff Comfort, of, Serra HS, Burlingame, Calif.
43. *James Farris, c, Hattiesburg (Miss.) HS.
44. *Israel Torres, lhp, Cerritos (Calif.) JC.
45. *Drew Parkin, rhp, Aliso Niguel HS, Laguna Niguel, Calif.
46. *Ernie Durazo, 3b, Pima (Ariz.) CC.
47. *Clayton McCullough, c, Rose HS, Greenville, N.C.
48. *Greg Pines, c, Saddleback (Calif.) CC.
**49. +Scott Achison, rhp, Texas Christian University.—(2004-15)**
50. *David Holliday, rhp, Anderson-Shiro HS, Navasota, Texas.

## TAMPA BAY DEVIL RAYS (29)

1. (Choice to Giants as compensation for Type A free agent Roberto Hernandez)
2. (Choice to Giants as compensation for Type A free agent Wilson Alvarez)
3. (Choice to White Sox as compensation for Type A free agent Dave Martinez)
4. Josh Pressley, 1b-rhp, Westminster Academy, Fort Lauderdale, Fla.—(AAA)
**5. Aubrey Huff, 3b, University of Miami.—(2000-12)**
**6. Ryan Rupe, rhp, Texas A&M University.—(1999-2003)**
7. John Jacobs, 3b, Marin Catholic HS, Kentfield, Calif.
**8. Joe Kennedy, lhp, Grossmont (Calif.) JC.—(2001-07)**

DRAFT DROP *Died as active major leaguer (Nov. 23, 2007)*

9. Brian Martin, c, Central Union HS, El Centro, Calif.
10. *Ben Keiter, rhp, Arvada West HS, Arvada, Colo.
11. Steven Goodson, of, Cowley County (Kan.) CC.
12. Adam Flohr, lhp, Portland State University.
13. Patrick Dickson, lhp, Dalton (Ga.) HS.
14. Pat Hertzel, rhp, Kansas State University.
15. Charles Armstrong, lhp, Contra Costa (Calif.) JC.
16. +Neal Frendling, rhp, Lake Central HS, Dyer, Ind. / Rend Lake (Ill.) JC.
17. *Mike Rodriguez, of, Cooper City (Fla.) HS.
**18. Brandon Backe, ss, Galveston (Texas) JC.—(2002-09)**
19. *Art Garland, of, Santa Ana (Calif.) JC.
20. *Preston Larrison, rhp, Aurora West HS, Aurora, Ill.
21. *Darin Moore, rhp, University of the Pacific.
22. Dan Grummit, 1b, Shawnee State (Ohio) University.
23. Frank Moore, 2b, Middle Georgia JC.
**24. *Ryan Jorgensen, c, San Jacinto (Texas) JC.—(2005-08)**
25. Talley Haines, rhp, Freed-Hardeman (Tenn.) University.
26. *George Moran, rhp, Red Bluff (Calif.) HS.
27. Jim Lira, rhp, Laredo (Texas) JC.
28. *Chad Cossette, c, Edmonds (Wash.) CC.
29. *Jeremy Manning, lhp, Pitt (N.C.) CC.
30. *Gary Welch, rhp, Howard (Texas) JC.
31. *Chris Wailand, rhp, Manatee HS, Bradenton, Fla.
32. Sean Mahoney, of, Florida International University.
33. *Rudolph Frolish, lhp, Ansonia (Conn.) HS.
34. Matt Schuldt, rhp, University of Nebraska.
35. Monte McGillivray, lhp, San Jacinto (Texas) JC.
**36. *Tim Olson, ss, Hutchinson (Kan.) JC.—(2004-05)**
**37. *Brandon Medders, rhp, Hillcrest HS, Duncanville, Ala.—(2005-10)**
38. *Andrew Cook, rhp, Antioch (Calif.) HS.
39. *Edwin Rodriguez, 1b, Ponce (P.R.) HS.
40. *Michael McCuan, rhp, Butler County (Kan.) CC.
41. *Jeff Bruksch, rhp, Beverly Hills (Calif.) HS.
42. *Dane Hutchens, rhp, McLennan (Texas) JC.
43. *Brandon Culp, rhp, Wallace State (Ala.) JC.
44. *Mark Carter, lhp, Hewitt-Trussville HS, Trussville, Ala.
45. *Harold Goodille, of, Modesto (Calif.) JC.
46. Cody Getz, lhp, JC of Eastern Utah.
47. *Brooks Stephens, 1b, Stetson University.
**48. *Mike Jacobs, c, Hilltop HS, Chula Vista, Calif.—(2005-12)**
49. *Justin Hancock, ss, Bloomingdale HS, Valrico, Fla.
50. Luis Candelaria, of, Hill (Texas) JC.

## TEXAS RANGERS (10)

**1. Carlos Pena, 1b, Northeastern University.—(2001-14)**
2. Cody Nowlin, of, Clovis (Calif.) HS.—(High A)
**3. *Barry Zito, lhp, Los Angeles Pierce JC.—(2000-15)**

DRAFT DROP *Attended Southern California; redrafted by Athletics, 1999 (1st round)*

4. Antwon Rollins, of, Encinal HS, Alameda, Calif.—(Low A)

DRAFT DROP *Brother of Jimmy Rollins, major leaguer (2001-15)*

5. Ryan Dittfurth, rhp, Union HS, Tulsa, Okla.—(AA)
6. Frankie McGill, rhp, Tate HS, Gonzalez, Fla.
7. John Stewart, lhp, Western Michigan University.
8. *Brad Ticehurst, of, University of Southern California.
**9. Andy Pratt, lhp, Chino Valley (Ariz.) HS.—(2002-04)**
10. Justin Backsmeyer, rhp, DeSmet Jesuit HS, St. Louis.
11. Cesar Castaneda, 3b, Dallas Baptist University.
12. Dan Boublis, rhp, Villanova University.
13. Jeremiah Bullock, lhp, Kuna (Idaho) HS.
14. Derek Ottevaere, 1b, Western Michigan University.
15. Ole Vigeland, rhp, Washington State University.
16. Domingo Valdez, rhp, Moody HS, Corpus Christi, Texas.
17. David Meliah, ss, University of San Francisco.
18. Mike Schaeffer, lhp, St. Louis University.
19. Michael Daniel, rhp, Lambuth (Tenn.) University.
20. *Ryan Knox, of, Illinois State University.
21. Matt Kosderka, rhp, Willamette (Ore.) University.
22. *Randall Shelley, 3b, Santa Margarita HS, Rancho Santa Margarita, Calif.
23. Frank Marciante, 1b, Palm Beach (Fla.) JC.
24. Jason Edgar, 2b, University of Connecticut.
25. *Brandon Moorhead, rhp, Franklin County HS, Gainesville, Ga.
26. Jimmie Romano, c, University of South Florida.

DRAFT DROP *Brother of Jason Romano, first-round draft pick, Rangers (1997); major leaguer (2002-05)*

27. Jeremy Jones, c, Arizona State University.
28. Rob LaMarsh, lhp, Southern Illinois University-Edwardsville.
29. *Ron Corona, rhp, Cypress (Calif.) JC.
**30. *Jaime Bubela, of, Blinn (Texas) JC.—(2005)**
31. Marcos Quinones, ss, Dallas Baptist University.
32. *Greg Summers, of, Port St. Joe (Fla.) HS.
33. +Ryan Cullen, lhp, Satellite HS, Satellite Beach, Fla.
34. *Josh Bolingbroke, c, Pleasant Grove (Utah) HS.
35. William Villamil, lhp, Academia Presbiteriana HS, Carolina, P.R.
36. Eric Moore, rhp, Lambuth (Tenn.) University.
37. *Jon Harris, rhp, Maple Woods (Mo.) JC.
38. *Trent Pratt, c, Tooele (Utah) HS.
39. Greg Ryan, lhp-1b, Eastern Michigan University.
40. *Craig Mosher, lhp, JC of Southern Idaho.
41. *Scott Nicholson, lhp, Lower Columbia (Wash.) JC.
42. *Ross Peeples, lhp, Crisp County Academy, Cordele, Ga.
43. *Derrick Foster, rhp, Pell City (Ala.) HS.
44. *Josh Hollingsworth, ss, Dunedin (Fla.) HS.
45. *Greg Bochy, rhp, Palomar (Calif.) JC.

DRAFT DROP *Son of Bruce Bochy, major leaguer (1978-87); major league manager (1995-2015) • Brother of Brett Bochy, major leaguer (2014-15)*

46. *Damon Sementilli, rhp, Norwalk (Conn.) CC.
47. *Roy York, of, Cowley County (Kan.) CC.
48. *Shaun Rudi, of, Baker HS, Baker City, Ore.

DRAFT DROP *Son of Shaun Rudi, major leaguer (1967-82)*

49. *Marcis Hassell, of, Sam Houston HS, Arlington, Texas.
50. *Albert Montes, rhp, Socorro HS, El Paso, Texas.

## TORONTO BLUE JAYS (8)

**1. Felipe Lopez, ss, Lake Brantley HS, Altamonte Springs, Fla.—(2001-11)**
2. (Choice to Orioles as compensation for Type A free agent Randy Myers)
3. (Choice to Expos as compensation for Type A free agent Darrin Fletcher)
4. Ryan Bundy, c, University of Washington.—(High A)
5. *Lee Delfino, ss, Pickering (Ontario) HS.–(High A)

DRAFT DROP *Attended East Carolina; re-drafted by Blue Jays, 2001 (6th round)*

6. Joe Orloski, rhp, Green Valley HS, Henderson, Nev.
7. Tyler Thompson, of, Indiana State University.
8. Mike Kremblas, c, Ohio State University.
9. Steve Murray, lhp, St. Peters HS, Peterborough, Ontario.
10. Jarrod Kingrey, rhp, University of Alabama.
11. *Ray Aguilar, lhp, El Monte HS, South El Monte, Calif.
12. Eric Place, lhp, Western Michigan University.
13. Adam Huxhold, lhp, Lewis-Clark State (Idaho) College.
**14. Jay Gibbons, 1b, Cal State Los Angeles.—(2001-11)**
15. Richard Lee, 1b, Mississippi State University.
16. Brandon Jackson, ss, Southwest Missouri State University.
17. Rueben St. Amand, rhp, Capital HS, Olympia, Wash.
18. Ryan Fleming, of, University of Dayton.
**19. Bob File, 3b, Philadelphia College of Textiles.—(2001-04)**
20. Auntawn Riggins, ss, Texas Southern University.
**21. Franklyn Gracesqui, lhp, George Washington HS, New York.—(2004)**
**22. *Adam Stern, of, St. Thomas Aquinas HS, London, Ontario.—(2005-10)**
23. Justin Davies, of, Queens (N.Y.) College.
24. *Maurice Murray, of, Hawkinsville (Ga.) HS.
25. *Nestor Rivera, ss, Josefa Pastrana HS, Aguas Buenase, P.R.
26. *Matt Sorensen, rhp, Cerritos (Calif.) JC.
27. *Stevie Daniel, ss, Northside HS, Jackson, Tenn.
28. *Shawn Lynn, rhp, George Henry Academy, North York, Ontario.
29. *Jason Shelley, ss, Northeast Louisiana University.
30. *Garris Gonce, c, Clay HS, Orange Park, Fla.
31. +Ryan Houston, rhp, Escambia HS, Pensacola, Fla. / Pensacola (Fla.) JC.
32. *Jason Lind, lhp, Moon Valley HS, Phoenix.
33. *Ryan Smith, rhp, South Hills HS, West Covina, Calif.
**34. *Bobby Cramer, lhp, Fullerton (Calif.) JC.—(2010-11)**
35. +Cameron Reimers, rhp, JC of Southern Idaho.
36. *Lee Southard, rhp, Seminole (Okla.) JC.
37. *Justin Williams, of, Columbia Basin (Wash.) JC.
38. +Aaron Dean, rhp, Canada (Calif.) JC.
39. *Joel Alvarado, c, Miguel Melendez HS, Cayey, P.R.
40. *Brian Hutchinson, lhp, Western Carolina University.
41. Mike Stafford, lhp, Ohio State University.

DRAFT DROP *Son of Bill Stafford, major leaguer (1960-67)*

42. *Justin Valente, of, Greenwich HS, Cos Cob, Conn.
43. *Travis Beckham, rhp, Port Dover (Ontario) Composite HS.
44. *Greg Palmer, lhp, Clackamas (Ore.) JC.
45. *Brian Ackerson, rhp, Fountain Valley (Calif.) HS.
46. *D.J. Loland, rhp, Northeast Louisiana University.
47. *Kenny Huff, of, Horizon HS, Scottsdale, Ariz.
48. *Isaac Iorg, ss, Karns HS, Knoxville, Tenn.

DRAFT DROP *Son of Garth Iorg, major leaguer (1978-87) • Brother of Eli Iorg, first-round draft pick, Astros (2005)*

49. *Troy Wilkins, rhp, Mountain Home (Idaho) HS.
50. *Jeff Wagner, c, University of Notre Dame.

# 1999

## AT A GLANCE

### This Date In History
June 2-3

### Best Draft
**ST. LOUIS CARDINALS. ALBERT PUJOLS** was far and away the best talent to come from the 1999 draft, despite being a 13th-round pick. The Cardinals also signed seven other future big leaguers, including **COCO CRISP** (7).

### Worst Draft
**CHICAGO CUBS.** The Cubs were criticized for drafting Wichita State's **BEN CHRISTENSEN** (1), who was suspended for the latter part of the 1999 college season for intentionally beaning a player, and his pro career was short-lived because of injuries, leaving **STEVE SMYTH** (4) as the only pick the Cubs signed who played for the team. He went 1-3, 9.35 in 2002.

### First-Round Bust
**CHANCE CAPLE, RHP, CARDINALS.** With a record 16 first-rounders who didn't reach the majors, there were plenty of candidates, but Caple did not advance past Class A in five minor league seasons. He went 11-20, 4.36.

### Second Best
**CARL CRAWFORD, OF, DEVIL RAYS.** Crawford was a four-time all-star with the Devil Rays, and hit .296-104-592 with 409 stolen bases in nine seasons with Tampa Bay. His production dipped with the Red Sox and Dodgers but he remained active in 2016.

### Late-Round Find
**ALBERT PUJOLS, 3B, CARDINALS (13TH ROUND).** Pujols became the best hitter of his era, despite being the 402nd player drafted. Pujols signed on Aug. 17 when the Cards bumped their bonus offer to $60,000, and it took him just 133 games to reach the majors.

### Never Too Late
**BRIAN BUSCHER, SS, RED SOX (50TH ROUND).** Only

# Draft lacks turbulence but more records fall

Unlike previous drafts of the decade, the 1999 event proved to be relatively tranquil. Players signed quickly, with little of the rancor that had characterized negotiations in previous years.

Part of that no doubt was because polarizing agent Scott Boras did not represent any first-round choices. Part of it also was that major league clubs had reluctantly come to accept the rapid escalation of first-round bonuses. Every first-rounder was under contract or had agreed to terms by Sept. 1.

So it hardly caused a ripple when North Carolina high school outfielder Josh Hamilton, Texas prep righthander Josh Beckett and University of Southern California catcher Eric Munson, the first three picks in 1999, signed for the largest bonuses to date, aside from those signed by the loophole free agents of 1996.

Hamilton, drafted first overall by the Tampa Bay Devil Rays, signed a standard minor league contract that provided a bonus of $3.96 million. Beckett and Munson signed major league deals. Beckett's contract with the Florida Marlins was worth $7 million overall, including a $3.625 million bonus. Munson was guaranteed $6.75 million by the Detroit Tigers, including a $3.5 million bonus.

The average first-round bonus was $1,809,767, a modest 10.4 percent increase over the 1998 average of $1,637,667, but a 10-fold increase over the 1989 average of $176,008. It topped the record first-round average of $1,794,383 set in 1996, when four loophole free agents received contracts worth a total of $29.275 million.

A total of 33 players drafted in 1999 received signing bonuses of more than $1 million, including all but one first-rounder. An additional 47 players got at least $500,000, including four drafted after the 10th round. In all, 136 players received at least $200,000, the equivalent of the 1999 major league minimum salary.

The Baltimore Orioles, who had seven of the first 50 selections in the draft, spent a record $8.92 million on signing bonuses. The Devil Rays paid big for Hamilton, then gave $1.245 million to outfielder Carl Crawford, the largest amount for a second-round pick. The Devil Rays committed $7.042 million in bonuses to their draft picks.

The San Diego Padres ($6,654,500), Chicago White Sox ($6,641,000) and Kansas City Royals ($6,572,000) also spent upward of $6 million. Those three teams and the Orioles had a combined 21 selections before the start of the second round.

Money flowed in the international market as well. Righthander Danys Baez, a Cuban defector, got a $4.5 million bonus from the Cleveland Indians as part of a $14.5 million package. The Arizona Diamondbacks signed righthander Byung-Hyun Kim for $2.25 million, a record for a South Korean. The Colorado Rockies paid $2.2 million

Josh Beckett was one of the most celebrated high school pitchers of the draft era, and he fulfilled his promise in the major leagues, punctuated by brilliance in the 2003 and '07 postseasons

for righthander Chin-Hui Tsao, a record for a player from Taiwan. And the Marlins spent $1.8 million for shortstop Miguel Cabrera, a record for a Venezuelan.

Many clubs selected players in the early rounds of the 1999 draft on the basis of signability or affordability rather than talent. So it didn't come as a surprise when just 14 of the 30 first-rounders made it to the major leagues, the only draft when fewer than half of the first-rounders didn't pan out. Three first-rounders didn't advance past Class A. The draft pool was considered top-heavy in pitching, but many of the better prospects were waylaid by elbow and shoulder problems.

The best player by far to come from the 1999 draft was then-third baseman Albert Pujols, a 13th-rounder selected by the St. Louis Cardinals from a Missouri junior college. His accumulated Wins Above Replacement through the 2015 season was 99.7; next best was righthander Jake Peavy at 40.9. Peavy, too, waited for his name to be called, going to the Padres as a 14th-round selection.

## CLEARLY DEFINED BIG THREE

Hamilton, Beckett and Munson were almost universally regarded as the top prospects in the 1999 draft crop, and they went off the board in that order. The 6-foot-4, 205-pound Hamilton,

## 1999: THE FIRST ROUNDERS

| CLUB: PLAYER, POS., SCHOOL | HOMETOWN | B-T | HT. | WT. | AGE | BONUS | FIRST YEAR | LAST YEAR | PEAK LEVEL (YEARS) |
|---|---|---|---|---|---|---|---|---|---|
| **1. Devil Rays: Josh Hamilton, of, Athens Drive HS** | **Raleigh, N.C.** | **L-L** | **6-4** | **200** | **18** | **$3,960,000** | **1999** | **Active** | **Majors (9)** |
| Freakish athlete with power, speed, mid-90s fastball; addiction issues continually affected career, kept him out of majors until 2007, yet he won AL MVP in 2010. | | | | | | | | | |
| **2. *Marlins: Josh Beckett, rhp, Spring HS** | **Spring, Texas** | **R-R** | **6-5** | **205** | **19** | **$3,625,000** | **2000** | **2014** | **Majors (14)** |
| Arguably top prep RHP in draft era with 97-99 FB, knee-buckling curve; signed $7M MLB contract, 138 career wins, defined by brilliance in 2003, 2007 postseasons. | | | | | | | | | |
| **3. *Tigers: Eric Munson, c, Southern California** | **San Diego** | **L-R** | **6-3** | **220** | **21** | **$3,500,000** | **1999** | **2010** | **Majors (9)** |
| Best college bat, showed classic LH swing, power; jury out on catching skills, moved to 1B/3B when hurt back in 2000, never hit as expected in majors. | | | | | | | | | |
| **4. Diamondbacks: Corey Myers, ss, Desert Vista HS** | **Phoenix** | **R-R** | **6-2** | **205** | **19** | **$2,000,000** | **1999** | **2007** | **Class AAA (3)** |
| Hit .500-22-77 as prep SR, smashed state records, then had big predraft workout for D-backs; one-tool player who never found defensive home, fell out of favor. | | | | | | | | | |
| **5. Twins: B.J. Garbe, of, Moses Lake HS** | **Moses Lake, Wash.** | **R-R** | **6-2** | **195** | **18** | **$2,750,000** | **1999** | **2006** | **Class AA (4)** |
| Talented two-way player on star-studded HS team; had trouble translating ability into baseball skills, never figured it out at plate, hit .235/37 HRs in eight seasons. | | | | | | | | | |
| **6. Expos: Josh Girdley, lhp, Jasper HS** | **Jasper, Texas** | **L-L** | **6-3** | **175** | **18** | **$1,700,000** | **1999** | **2004** | **Class A (5)** |
| Made strides as prep SR (9-2, 0.34), headlined by 29-SO game, but obvious signability pick; showed early promise before two motorcycle accidents doomed career. | | | | | | | | | |
| **7. Royals: Kyle Snyder, rhp, North Carolina** | **Sarasota, Fla.** | **R-R** | **6-8** | **215** | **21** | **$2,100,000** | **1999** | **2009** | **Majors (5)** |
| No. 1 prospect in Cape Cod in summer of '98 with 96 FB; all downhill thereafter as injuries compromised velocity, career in minors (14-24, 3.80), majors (8-17, 5.56). | | | | | | | | | |
| **8. Pirates: Bobby Bradley, rhp, Wellington HS** | **Wellington, Fla.** | **R-R** | **6-1** | **170** | **18** | **$2,225,000** | **1999** | **2005** | **Class AAA (1)** |
| Dominated prep ranks (21-1, 0.38, 161 IP, 21 BB/278 SO as JR/SR), lower minors with dynamite curve, but elbow gave out, endured five surgeries before release. | | | | | | | | | |
| **9. Athletics: Barry Zito, lhp, Southern California** | **La Mesa, Calif.** | **L-L** | **6-4** | **205** | **21** | **$1,590,000** | **1999** | **Active** | **Majors (15)** |
| Played for three colleges in three years, struck out 412 in 301 IP with big, looping curve; pick questioned due to soft-tossing style, but won 165 MLB games. | | | | | | | | | |
| **10. Brewers: Ben Sheets, rhp, Northeast Louisiana** | **St. Amant, La.** | **R-R** | **6-2** | **195** | **20** | **$2,450,000** | **1999** | **2012** | **Majors (10)** |
| Burst on scene as college JR with mid-90s FB, nasty curve; beat Cuba 4-0 for gold in 2000 Olympics, MLB career marked by occasional brilliance mixed with injury. | | | | | | | | | |
| **11. Mariners: Ryan Christianson, c, Arlington HS** | **Riverside, Calif.** | **R-R** | **6-2** | **210** | **18** | **$2,100,000** | **1999** | **2007** | **Class AAA (3)** |
| Hailed as one of best prep catching prospects in years with power, defensive skills; career derailed by elbow/shoulder injuries in minors, eroded bat speed. | | | | | | | | | |
| **12. Phillies: Brett Myers, rhp, Englewood HS** | **Jacksonville, Fla.** | **R-R** | **6-4** | **215** | **18** | **$2,050,000** | **1999** | **2013** | **Majors (12)** |
| Career as amateur boxer translated to aggressive approach on mound, fiery personality; strong/mature frame, 92-96 FB/big curve led to 97 wins in majors. | | | | | | | | | |
| **13. Orioles: Mike Paradis, rhp, Clemson** | **Auburn, Mass.** | **R-R** | **6-2** | **205** | **21** | **$1,700,000** | **1999** | **2004** | **Class AAA (1)** |
| Hard-throwing Northeast product had limited success in college due to command, was no better in pros (29-47, 5.24), rarely matched performance to potential. | | | | | | | | | |
| **14. Reds: Ty Howington, lhp, Hudson's Bay HS** | **Vancouver, Wash.** | **B-L** | **6-4** | **225** | **18** | **$1,750,000** | **2000** | **2005** | **Class AA (3)** |
| All the rage as prep sophomore with power stuff, big frame, feel for pitching, but mechanics slipped, contributed to injury-plagued pro career (22-35, 4.08). | | | | | | | | | |
| **15. White Sox: Jason Stumm, rhp, Centralia HS** | **Centralia, Wash.** | **R-R** | **6-2** | **215** | **18** | **$1,750,000** | **1999** | **2005** | **Class AA (1)** |
| Velocity spiked to 92-95 mph in draft year, 96-98 with mid-80s slider early in Sox career; never overcame elbow/shoulder surgeries, went 7-16, 4.10 in minors. | | | | | | | | | |
| **16. Rockies: Jason Jennings, rhp, Baylor** | **Mesquite, Texas** | **L-R** | **6-3** | **235** | **20** | **$1,675,000** | **1999** | **2010** | **Majors (9)** |
| BA College POY after going 13-2, 2.58 (147 IP/172 SO) on mound, .386-17-68 at plate; only MLB player to hit HR, pitch shutout in debut, went 62-74, 4.95 in career. | | | | | | | | | |
| **17. Red Sox: Rick Asadoorian, of, Northbridge HS** | **Whitinsville, Mass.** | **R-R** | **6-2** | **185** | **18** | **$1,725,000** | **2000** | **2008** | **Class AAA (2)** |
| Sox spent record bonus on local five-tool talent, gave up on him early; best known for big RF arm, became pitcher after he struggled to hit in minors (.249-44-285). | | | | | | | | | |
| **18. Orioles: Richard Stahl, lhp, Newton County HS** | **Covington, Ga.** | **R-L** | **6-7** | **200** | **18** | **$1,795,000** | **2000** | **2006** | **Class AAA (1)** |
| Projection galore with long/lean frame, loose/quick arm; signed day before classes started at Georgia Tech, but battled injuries throughout 27-39, 4.23 career. | | | | | | | | | |
| **19. Blue Jays: Alex Rios, 3b/of, San Pedro Martir HS** | **Guaynabo, P.R.** | **R-R** | **6-5** | **185** | **18** | **$845,000** | **1999** | **Active** | **Majors (12)** |
| Signability pick with only sub-$1M first-round bonus; career slow to evolve as he grew into lean frame, but MLB all-star at 25-26, settled in as solid big leaguer. | | | | | | | | | |
| **20. Padres: Vince Faison, of, Toombs County HS** | **Lyons, Ga.** | **L-R** | **5-11** | **185** | **18** | **$1,415,000** | **1999** | **2007** | **Class AAA (1)** |
| Elite Georgia football recruit had best speed/athleticism in draft, though tools eroded as he got stronger, added power; hit .245-61-329, 117 SBs, stalled in Triple-A. | | | | | | | | | |
| **21. Orioles: Larry Bigbie, of, Ball State** | **Hobart, Ind.** | **L-R** | **6-4** | **190** | **21** | **$1,200,000** | **1999** | **2007** | **Majors (6)** |
| Impressed scouts with LH swing, power; only one of four Orioles first-rounders to have meaningful MLB career (.267-31-137), though implicated in steroid use. | | | | | | | | | |
| **22. White Sox: Matt Ginter, rhp, Mississippi State** | **Winchester, Ky.** | **R-R** | **6-1** | **215** | **21** | **$1,275,000** | **1999** | **2009** | **Majors (7)** |
| Modest success in college (16-11, 5.30), minors (43-55, 3.49), majors (5-7, 5.43) as starter/reliever with mid-90s fastball, tight slider, never mastered command. | | | | | | | | | |
| **23. Orioles: Keith Reed, of, Providence College** | **Yarmouth Port, Mass.** | **R-R** | **6-4** | **215** | **20** | **$1,150,000** | **1999** | **2006** | **Majors (1)** |
| Raw but athletic player had breakout season (.398-17-79) in final year of Providence program; showed flashes in pro career, but plagued by inconsistency. | | | | | | | | | |
| **24. Giants: Kurt Ainsworth, rhp, Louisiana State** | **Baton Rouge, La.** | **R-R** | **6-3** | **185** | **20** | **$1,300,000** | **1999** | **2004** | **Majors (4)** |
| Limited to 8 IP in first two years at LSU by TJ surgery, went 13-6, 3.45 in '99, won both starts for 2000 Olympic gold medalists; shoulder issues impacted pro career. | | | | | | | | | |
| **25. Royals: Mike MacDougal, rhp, Wake Forest** | **Mesa, Ariz.** | **R-R** | **6-4** | **185** | **22** | **$1,150,000** | **1999** | **2014** | **Majors (12)** |
| Three-time draftee emerged as first-rounder with moving fastball that often hit triple digits; struggled to control pitch in checkered MLB career as reliever. | | | | | | | | | |
| **26. Cubs: Ben Christensen, rhp, Wichita State** | **Goddard, Kan.** | **R-R** | **6-4** | **205** | **21** | **$1,062,500** | **1999** | **2004** | **Class AA (2)** |
| Controversial pick after he intentionally beaned, injured player in college game; had ideal frame, command of four pitches, but felled by elbow/shoulder surgeries. | | | | | | | | | |
| **27. Yankees: David Walling, rhp, Arkansas** | **Lakeside, Calif.** | **R-R** | **6-5** | **215** | **20** | **$1,075,000** | **1999** | **2002** | **Class AAA (2)** |
| Fanned 283 in 224 IP at Arkansas with 88-93 mph fastball, on fast track before developed mental block throwing to plate with runners on base, never overcame it. | | | | | | | | | |
| **28. Padres: # Gerik Baxter, rhp, Edmonds-Woodway HS** | **Edmonds, Wash.** | **R-R** | **6-2** | **185** | **19** | **$1,100,000** | **1999** | **2000** | **Class A (1)** |
| Fourth Washington prep first-rounder, showed promise with 95-99 FB early in Padres career; killed in July 2001 car accident when his truck blew tire and crashed. | | | | | | | | | |
| **29. Padres: Omar Ortiz, rhp, Texas-Pan American** | **Brownsville, Texas** | **B-R** | **6-1** | **210** | **21** | **$1,050,000** | **1999** | **2003** | **Class AA (2)** |
| Obscure player at obscure school broke out with 95 mph FB, tenacious approach; struggled to throw strikes in pro ball with inconsistent mechanics. | | | | | | | | | |
| **30. Cardinals: Chance Caple, rhp, Texas A&M** | **Southlake, Texas** | **R-R** | **6-6** | **215** | **20** | **$1,200,000** | **1999** | **2004** | **Class A (5)** |
| Signed late, never developed momentum in five-year pro career plagued by injuries/ineffectiveness; had all the raw material, but went underachieving 11-20, 4.36. | | | | | | | | | |

**Signed to major league contract. # Deceased.*

## AT A GLANCE

three players were drafted later than Buscher, who did not sign out of a Florida high school. After he hit .393-15-66 in his senior season at South Carolina, the Giants took him in the third round of the 2003 draft. Buscher hit .266-8-69 in three big league seasons.

### Overlooked

**BOBBY KIELTY, OF, TWINS.** Kielty went undrafted in 1998 as a fourth-year junior at Mississippi, despite hitting .307-16 49. His status soared that summer in the Cape Cod League, where he won the MVP award. Kielty agreed to sign with the Twins in February 1999 for a $500,000 bonus, a record for an undrafted American player. He played seven years in the majors with four clubs, hitting .254-53-253.

### International Gem

**MIGUEL CABRERA, SS, MARLINS.** The Marlins signed Cabrera for a $1.8 million bonus, a record at the time for a player from Venezuela. He became a four-time batting champion for the Tigers, after the Marlins traded him following the 2007 season. Cabrera's contract was dwarfed later in 1999 by the four-year, $14.5 million deal the Indians gave righthander **DANYS BAEZ**, a Cuban defector who had a 40-57 record in 10 major league seasons.

### Minor League Take

**JOSH BECKETT, RHP, MARLINS.** Beckett spent one full season in the minors before a 14-year career in the majors. In 26 starts at Class A Brevard County and Double-A Portland in 2001, he went 14-1, 1.54 with 203 strikeouts in 140 innings, walked 34 and gave up 82 hits.

### One Who Got Away

**BOBBY HILL, SS, WHITE SOX (2ND ROUND).** Hill was projected as a first-rounder after hitting .391 with

CONTINUED ON PAGE 512

## AT A GLANCE

CONTINUED FROM PAGE 511

10 homers and 52 stolen bases as a junior at Miami. He slipped to 66th overall. Rather than return to college for his senior year, Hill signed with Newark of the independent Atlantic League, where he played the 2000 season. The Cubs drafted Hill in the second round that June, and he eventually signed for a $1,425,000 bonus.

### He Was Drafted?

**RICKY MANNING, OF, TWINS (22ND ROUND).** The Twins spent $275,000 to sign the speedy, athletic Manning, but allowed him to play football at UCLA, where he became one of the nation's top cornerbacks. Manning had little success in four seasons in the Twins system and quit after he was selected in the third round of the 2003 NFL draft by the Charlotte Panthers. He played six seasons in the NFL.

### Did You Know . . .

Moses Lake, Wash. (pop. 15,000) had a big impact on the 1999 draft, producing four picks in the first two rounds. Outfielder **B.J. GARBE** (Twins/1st), catcher **RYAN DOUMIT** (Pirates/2nd) and outfielder **JASON COOPER** (Phillies/2nd) were 1999 grads, and **JEFF HEAVERLO** (Mariners/1st supplemental) attended the school before moving on to the University of Washington.

### They Said It

Diamondbacks scouting director **DON MITCHELL**, on his club's surprise selection of local product **COREY MYERS** with the fourth overall selection: "Other teams don't know Myers like we do. We're talking about a player who is a plus hitter, with plus power and tremendous makeup and knowledge of the game. Why take the chance that someone else might pick him?"—*Myers did not advance past Triple-A, hitting .273 with 59 homers in nine minor league seasons.*

18, lit up radar guns at Athens Drive High in Raleigh, N.C., with a 95-97 mph fastball, usually enough by itself to land a high school lefthander in the first round. But Hamilton's athleticism, graceful actions and massive power potential kept scouts focused on him as an outfielder. He hit .529 with 13 home runs in his senior season, and had a 7-1, 2.50 record with 95 strikeouts in 55 innings.

The 19-year-old Beckett was one of the most acclaimed high school pitchers ever, even before his senior year at Spring (Texas) High, and a legitimate candidate to be the first prep righthander to be selected first overall. Working with a 94-96 mph fastball and a hard, biting curveball, he went 10-1, 0.46 with 155 strikeouts in 76 innings in his senior season, following up a 13-2, 0.39 record with 178 strikeouts in 89 innings for his junior year.

Munson, 21, missed two months of his junior season at USC because of a broken right hand. The injury healed in time for Munson, an unsigned second-rounder in 1996, to return for NCAA tournament play before the draft.

The Devil Rays and Marlins braintrusts debated the merits of Hamilton and Beckett, weighing every conceivable attribute, and ultimately decided they couldn't go wrong with either player.

"Both Joshes were just fantastic baseball players, as equal as you could find," Devil Rays scouting director Dan Jennings said. "Josh Hamilton was one of the two best high school position players I'd ever seen, and the other was Alex Rodriguez. Josh Beckett was an incredibly poised, polished pitcher who was destined for great things. You pick one, and the other is just as good."

By draft day, the Devil Rays had settled on Hamilton, and barely 48 hours later announced they had signed him.

"We got ourselves a real old-fashioned ballplayer," Jennings said. "Besides all the obvious tools, Josh has all the intangibles you'd want to see in a ballplayer. He has a great natural rhythm and pace to his game."

Hamilton remained a blue-chip prospect until injuries and a drug addiction derailed his career, beginning in 2001. He went into a deep spiral and was out of baseball for the better part of four years. He made several unsuccessful attempts at rehabilitation, and was suspended for the 2004 and '05 seasons by Major League Baseball after a series of failed drug tests. But just as his fading career had all but slipped away, he was claimed by the Cincinnati Reds in the 2006 Rule 5 draft (the Cubs took him on the Reds' behalf). He hit .292 with 19 home runs in 90 games in Cincinnati in 2007, but the Reds traded him to the Texas Rangers after the season.

Eric Munson

Hamilton had a breakout season in 2008, and two years later won the American League batting title and MVP award. Injuries, inconsistent performance, and substance-abuse relapses continued to take a toll, however, and while Hamilton was still an active player entering the 2016 season, a knee injury kept him out all year.

## How They Should Have Done It

Based on the career WAR (Wins Above Replacement, as calculated by Baseball-Reference.com) numbers achieved by all the players eligible for the 1999 draft through the 2015 season, here's how the first round should have unfolded. Numbers in parentheses indicate the round when the player was actually drafted.

| | Player, Pos. | Actual Draft | WAR | Bonus |
|---|---|---|---|---|
| 1. | Albert Pujols, 3b | Cardinals (13) | 99.7 | $60,000 |
| 2. | Jake Peavy, rhp | Padres (15) | 40.9 | $100,000 |
| 3. | Carl Crawford, of | Devil Rays (2) | 39.9 | $1,245,000 |
| 4. | Josh Beckett, rhp | Marlins (1) | 35.9 | $3,625,000 |
| 5. | John Lackey, rhp | Angels (2) | 34.0 | $470,000 |
| 6. | Mark Ellis, ss | Royals (9) | 33.4 | $1,000 |
| 7. | Barry Zito, lhp | Athletics (1) | 32.6 | $1,590,000 |
| 8. | Shane Victorino, of | Dodgers (6) | 31.2 | $115,000 |
| 9. | Brian Roberts, ss | Orioles (1-S) | 30.3 | $650,000 |
| 10. | Brandon Phillips, ss | Expos (2) | 29.2 | $607,000 |
| 11. | Coco Crisp, 2b | Cardinals (7) | 28.7 | $85,000 |
| 12. | Josh Hamilton, of | Devil Rays (1) | 28.1 | $3,960,000 |
| 13. | Alexis Rios, of | Blue Jays (1) | 27.6 | $845,000 |
| 14. | Justin Morneau, c | Twins (3) | 27.0 | $290,000 |
| 15. | Marlon Byrd, of | Phillies (10) | 25.2 | $38,000 |
| 16. | Ben Sheets, rhp | Brewers (1) | 23.4 | $2,450,000 |
| 17. | Aaron Harang, rhp | Rangers (6) | 19.7 | $110,000 |
| 18. | Eric Bedard, lhp | Orioles (6) | 17.5 | $80,000 |
| 19. | Lyle Overbay, 1b | Diamondbacks (18) | 16.9 | $1,000 |
| 20. | Angel Pagan, of | Mets (4) | 16.0 | $255,000 |
| 21. | Brett Myers, rhp | Phillies (1) | 14.4 | $2,050,000 |
| 22. | Hank Blalock, 3b | Rangers (3) | 13.5 | $288,000 |
| | J.J. Putz, rhp | Mariners (6) | 13.5 | $10,000 |
| 24. | Cody Ross, of | Tigers (4) | 13.3 | $340,000 |
| 25. | Jason Jennings, rhp | Rockies (1) | 11.4 | $1,675,000 |
| 26. | Ryan Ludwick, of | Athletics (2) | 10.5 | $567,500 |
| 27. | Reed Johnson, of | Blue Jays (17) | 10.3 | $12,500 |
| 28. | Jason Frasor, rhp | Tigers (33) | 9.6 | $1,000 |
| 29. | Ryan Doumit, c | Pirates (2) | 9.2 | $600,000 |
| 30. | Lew Ford, of | Red Sox (12) | 8.4 | $1,000 |

| | Top 3 Unsigned Players | | | Year Signed |
|---|---|---|---|---|
| 1. | Rich Harden, rhp | Mariners (38) | 17.6 | 2000 |
| 2. | Adam LaRoche, 1b | Marlins (42) | 14.1 | 2000 |
| 3. | Noah Lowry, lhp | Rangers (19) | 10.2 | 2001 |

After the Devils Rays drafted Hamilton, it was a question of whether Beckett and Munson's contract demands might drop them out of the top three spots. Both held firm on their demands for a major league contract. Munson got his from the Tigers in relatively short order, while Beckett waited the entire summer before the Marlins gave in.

Beckett and his adviser, Michael Moye, originally sought a deal in the $8 million-$10 million range. The Marlins offered roughly what Hamilton received. On Aug. 26, four days before Beckett was scheduled to enroll at Blinn (Texas) Junior College, the Marlins gave him a major league contract.

"You're talking about a 19-year-old pitcher, not a 17-year-old pitcher," Florida general manager Dave Dombrowski said. "You're talking about someone with a lot of talent. I think there are a lot of other organizations who would have given him a big league contract."

Beckett became the first high school player from the class of 1999 to reach the majors, and he quickly became one of the game's elite pitchers. He earned World Series rings with both the Marlins and the Red Sox, and won 138 games over a 14-year big league career.

Munson was expected to move quickly through the Tigers system and provide a potent lefthanded bat. "History has shown that it's easier for pitchers to move faster than it is for hitters," Tigers general manager Randy Smith said. "But I wouldn't bet against him. We expect him to be here quickly. He's a pretty polished guy right now. He swings the bat very well."

Munson clearly lacked the tools to be an everyday catcher in the big leagues, and the Tigers wasted little time in moving him to first base. He had a short, powerful swing, but the power he had shown in college and in the minors did not manifest in the majors. In parts of nine major league seasons, he hit .214 with 49 homers.

### SIGNABILITY DICTATES SURPRISES

The cost of signing players made assessing signability just as important as assessing talent, and it was never more apparent than when the Diamondbacks spent the fourth overall pick on Phoenix high school shortstop Corey Myers. Myers set Arizona high school records with 22 home runs and 77 RBIs as a senior, but he was far from a consensus first-round talent. He agreed before the draft on a $2 million signing bonus, $700,000 less than righthander Jeff Austin had received in the same draft slot a year earlier.

"Other teams don't know Myers like we do," said Diamondbacks scouting director Don Mitchell, who resigned shortly after the draft to become an agent. "We're talking about a player who is a plus hitter with plus power, and has tremendous makeup and knowledge of the game. Why take the chance that someone else might pick him?"

Myers didn't hit well in the minor leagues and moved to first base. His career peaked in Triple-A. Along with Hamilton, Myers was one of as many as nine first-rounders, including four among the first 10 picks, who agreed on terms before the draft and signed soon after being selected.

Lefthander Josh Girdley, selected sixth overall by the Montreal Expos, and righthander Kyle Snyder, picked seventh by the Royals, also agreed to predraft deals. The cash-strapped Expos signed Girdley for $1.7 million. He struck out 29 hitters in a 10-inning game as a senior at Jasper (Texas) High, while going 9-2, 0.34 with 178 strikeouts in 82 innings, but was not considered a first-round prospect by most teams. He did not get past Class A in a six-year career in the Expos system, battling arm and knee problems stemming from two motorcycle accidents in 2001.

### Fastest To The Majors

| | Player, Pos. | Drafted (Round) | Debut |
|---|---|---|---|
| 1. | Eric Munson, 1b | Tigers (1) | July 18, 2000 |
| 2. | Barry Zito, lhp | Athletics (1) | July 22, 2000 |
| 3. | Craig House, rhp | Rockies (12) | Aug. 6, 2000 |
| 4. | Matt Ginter, rhp | White Sox (1) | Sept. 1, 2000 |
| 5. | Albert Pujols, 3b | Cardinals (12) | April 2, 2001 |

**FIRST HIGH SCHOOL SELECTION:** Josh Beckett, rhp (Marlins/1, Sept. 4, 2001)

### DRAFT SPOTLIGHT: JOSH HAMILTON

RICK BATTLE

**Substance abuse sidetracked Josh Hamilton's career for years, but through it all his unmistakeable talent eventually won out**

Dan Jennings was Tampa Bay's scouting director in 1999, when the Devil Rays selected Josh Hamilton, a 6-foot-4, 200-pound outfielder from Raleigh, N.C., with the No. 1 pick in the draft. Jennings later watched with dismay as Hamilton fell into a battle with drug dependency.

Few people were more thrilled than Jennings when Hamilton resurrected his career in 2007 with the Cincinnati Reds. Jennings, by then with the Florida Marlins, said: "This isn't just a great baseball story. This is a great human interest story. I don't know of anyone in baseball that's not pulling for Josh."

Hamilton was on the fast track before his career was sidetracked by injuries and a drug addiction in 2002. Major League Baseball lifted his suspension for drug abuse in 2006, and Hamilton, after playing in just 15 games at the short-season level over four years, got the break of his career in December, when the Chicago Cubs selected him in the Rule 5 draft and sold his rights to the Reds.

Healthy and drug-free, Hamilton easily won a major league roster spot with the Reds and made his long-awaited major league debut on April 2, 2007, as a pinch-hitter, receiving a 22-second standing ovation from the Reds crowd. As he waited to bat, Cubs catcher Michael Barrett leaned in and said: "You deserve it, Josh. Take it all in, brother."

The Reds traded Hamilton to the Texas Rangers after the season and he developed into a superstar, winning the 2010 American League MVP award. He later signed a lucrative free-agent contract with the Los Angeles Angels, suffered a drug relapse after his second season with the team, and returned to the Rangers in a trade. Hamilton was still active entering the 2016 season, a career .290 hitter in the major leagues with 200 home runs.

Jennings said he had no doubt Hamilton would have a successful rookie season. "It's a tribute to his talent that he's been able to maintain his skills," he said. "He's still a plus runner, still has that 80 power, still has a big arm, and he has all the instincts to play either center field or right field. I'm impressed that he has been able to knock off four years of rust and jump right back in. I was hoping beyond hope that he'd be able to come back. But he needed to be drug free and get his life straight first for that to happen."

What Jennings remembered most about scouting Hamilton was the person, not the player. His makeup convinced Jennings that Hamilton would see his way through his struggles. "I remember him hitting about a 450-foot home run one day, and he immediately went over and gave his grandmother a kiss," Jennings said. "I was impressed with the way he interacted so well with his teammates. But I was particularly struck with the way he reached out to a young man who was obviously handicapped. He made him out to be his best buddy, not by lowering himself down to his level but by raising the boy up to his. He was the All-America kid if you ever saw one."

As a 19-year-old in 2001, Hamilton went to spring training with the Devil Rays with an outside chance of making the leap from Class A to the majors. But things turned after he was involved in an auto accident on March 3. He began experiencing back pain, which lingered into the first month of the 2001 season, after he had been assigned to Double-A Orlando, and Hamilton returned to the Rays training facility in Florida for rehabilitation.

He started using drugs and soon was an addict. MLB suspended Hamilton for 30 days in February 2004 for failing at least two drug tests and using a substance believed to be cocaine. After failing at least two more tests, he was suspended for a year on March 19. After subsequent violations, MLB extended the suspension through the 2005 season.

"Since I drafted Hamilton No. 1, I would get asked all the time if I'd still do it the same way," Jennings said, "and there's no question I would. Outside of Alex Rodriguez, Josh Hamilton is the best kid I have ever scouted."

## WORTH NOTING

■ Florida State infielder **MARSHALL MCDOUGALL** enjoyed perhaps the greatest single game in college baseball history. On May 9, 1999, he went 7-for-7 and set NCAA records with six home runs, 16 RBIs and 25 total bases in a 26-2 win over Maryland. It didn't help his draft stock; McDougall was selected in the 26th round by the Red Sox. He did not sign, was drafted in the ninth round by the A's a year later, and played in 18 major league games with the Rangers in 2005.

■ The Red Sox had the most difficulty signing their premium draft picks, even though they emphasized talent with New England ties. It took them a month to sign a player from the first 10 rounds, and they didn't reach agreement with their selections from the fourth-ninth rounds, although Northeastern lefthander **GREG MONTALBANO**, their fifth-round selection, signed the following spring as a fifth-year senior for $130,000. First-rounder **RICK ASADOORIAN**, a Massachusetts prep product, signed days before he was scheduled to enroll at the University of Florida. He got a club record $1,725,500 bonus. Mississippi State righthander **HANK THOMS**, a ninth-round pick, rejected Boston's $3,500 offer and signed with the independent Northern League.

■ A record 44 Canadians were drafted, topping the previous mark of 40 set in 1994. The first was New Westminster, B.C., catcher **JUSTIN MORNEAU**, selected in the third round by the Twins. Morneau moved to first base in his first pro season, and he played 13 years in the majors, earning American League MVP honors in 2006 while hitting .321 with 34 homers and 130 RBIs.

■ Three high school pitchers shared the highest grade (on the 20-80 scale) in the Major League Scouting Bureau's rankings. Texas righthander **JOSH BECKETT**, the No.

The 6-foot-7 Snyder, after a dominant summer in the Cape Cod League in 1998 and strong start to his junior season at the University of North Carolina, was in the running to be the first overall pick. But he developed elbow tendinitis, lost velocity on his fastball and dropped six of his last eight decisions. Snyder signed with the Royals for $2.1 million, but his career was diminished by elbow and shoulder injuries. In parts of five seasons in the majors from 2003-08, he went 8-17, 5.56.

Injuries also ruined the promising career of Florida high school righthander Bobby Bradley, selected eighth overall by the Pittsburgh Pirates. With a fastball that peaked at 94 mph and one of the best curveballs in the draft, Bradley went 12-1, 0.38 with 13 walks and 156 strikeouts in 92 innings at Wellington High, leading his team to the Florida 6-A title. He dominated hitters in his first two pro seasons before elbow and shoulder injuries took a toll, landing him on the disabled list in every season from 2000-05. After drawing his release, Bradley became a pro golfer.

Another noteworthy first-round selection who agreed to a predraft deal was Puerto Rican outfielder Alex Rios (19th overall), who signed with the Toronto Blue Jays for $845,000. Despite receiving the smallest bonus in the round, Rios had a highly productive major league career.

The Padres got commitments from each of their three first-round draft choices, yet none reached the major leagues. Washington high school righthander Gerik Baxter (28th overall), the second of San Diego's first-round picks, was killed in a car wreck on July 29, 2001.

The Reds struggled to find enough money to strike a deal with their first-round pick, Washington high school lefthander Ty Howington.

### Top 25 Bonuses

| | Player, Pos. | Drafted (Round) | Order | Bonus |
|---|---|---|---|---|
| **1.** | ***Josh Hamilton, of** | **Devil Rays (1)** | **1** | **$3,960,000** |
| **2.** | ***Josh Beckett, rhp** | **Marlins (1)** | **2** | **#$3,625,000** |
| **3.** | **Eric Munson, c** | **Tigers (1)** | **3** | **#$3,500,000** |
| 4. | *B.J. Garbe, of | Twins (1) | 5 | $2,750,000 |
| **5.** | **Ben Sheets, rhp** | **Brewers (1)** | **10** | **$2,450,000** |
| 6. | *Bobby Bradley, rhp | Pirates (1) | 8 | $2,250,000 |
| **7.** | **Kyle Snyder, rhp** | **Royals (1)** | **7** | **$2,100,000** |
| | ***Ryan Christianson, c** | **Mariners (1)** | **11** | **$2,100,000** |
| **9.** | ***Brett Myers, rhp** | **Phillies (1)** | **12** | **$2,050,000** |
| 10. | *Corey Myers, ss | Diamondbacks (1) | 4 | $2,000,000 |
| 11. | *Richard Stahl, lhp | Orioles (1) | 18 | $1,795,000 |
| 12. | *Ty Howington, lhp | Reds (1) | 14 | $1,750,000 |
| | *Jason Stumm, rhp | White Sox (1) | 15 | $1,750,000 |
| 14. | *Rick Asadoorian, of | Red Sox (1) | 17 | $1,725,500 |
| 15. | *Josh Girdley, lhp | Expos (1) | 6 | $1,700,000 |
| | Mark Paradis, rhp | Orioles (1) | 13 | $1,700,000 |
| **17.** | **Jason Jennings, rhp** | **Rockies (1)** | **16** | **$1,675,000** |
| **18.** | **Barry Zito, lhp** | **Athletics (1)** | **9** | **$1,590,000** |
| 19. | *Vince Faison, of | Padres (1) | 20 | $1,415,000 |
| 20. | Nick Stocks, rhp | Cardinals (1-S) | 36 | $1,410,000 |
| **21.** | **Kurt Ainsworth, rhp** | **Giants (1)** | **24** | **$1,300,000** |
| | ***Casey Daigle, rhp** | **D-backs (1-S)** | **31** | **$1,300,000** |
| **23.** | **Matt Ginter, rhp** | **White Sox (1)** | **22** | **$1,275,000** |
| **24.** | ***Carl Crawford, of** | **Devil Rays (2)** | **52** | **$1,245,000** |
| **25.** | **Larry Bigbie, of** | **Orioles (1)** | **21** | **$1,200,000** |
| | Chance Caple, rhp | Cardinals (1) | 30 | $1,200,000 |

*Major leaguers in bold. *High school selection. #Major league contract.*

### Largest Bonuses By Round

| | Player, Pos. | Club | Bonus |
|---|---|---|---|
| **1.** | *** Josh Hamilton, of** | **Devil Rays** | **$3,960,000** |
| 1-S. | Nick Stocks, rhp | Cardinals | $1,410,000 |
| **2.** | *** Carl Crawford, of** | **Devil Rays** | **$1,245,000** |
| 3. | * Neil Jenkins, 1b | Tigers | $900,000 |
| 4. | * Jeff Randazzo, lhp | Twins | $392,500 |
| 5. | Matt McClendon, rhp | Braves | $900,000 |
| 6. | * Charles Frazier, of | Marlins | $300,000 |
| 7. | * Brett Evert, rhp | Braves | $169,500 |
| **8.** | **Chris Capuano, lhp** | **Diamondbacks** | **$145,000** |
| 9. | * Brian Specht, ss | Angels | $600,000 |
| 10. | * Nathan Cromer, lhp | Devil Rays | $140,000 |
| 11. | Jeff Verplancke, rhp | Giants | $600,000 |
| 12. | * Jorge Maduro, c | Devil Rays | $125,000 |
| 13. | Keto Anderson, 2b | Cubs | $45,000 |
| **14.** | **# Brandon Lyon, rhp** | **Blue Jays** | **$125,000** |
| 15. | # Andrew Earley, rhp | Cubs | $180,000 |
| 16. | *# Matt Allegra, of | Athletics | $100,000 |
| 17. | * Brad Stiles, lhp | Royals | $100,000 |
| 18. | * Ryan Dorsey, ss | Pirates | $60,000 |
| 19. | Ging Aaron, 2b | Devil Rays | $40,000 |
| 20. | * Brandon Sing, ss | Cubs | $92,500 |
| **21.** | **# Jason Davis, rhp** | **Indians** | **$250,000** |
| 22. | * Ricky Manning, of | Twins | $275,000 |
| 23. | * Kyle Colton, rhp | Braves | $215,000 |
| 24. | *# Kevin Collins, of | Cubs | $68,000 |
| 25. | * Aaron Story, lhp | Pirates | $27,000 |
| Other | *# Jason Norderum, lhp | Expos (31) | $500,000 |

*Major leaguers in bold. *High school selection. #Signed as draft-and-follow.*

The organization spent much of its amateur signing budget in March by acquiring Dominican outfielder Alejandro Diaz, 20, from Japan's Hiroshima Carp, at a cost of $2.1 million in posting fees and a bonus to Diaz, who never fulfilled his potential.

So the Reds reached a contract agreement with Howington during the summer, although they didn't officially sign him until Nov. 1 for a bonus of $1.75 million—which allowed them to borrow from their 2000 budget. Howington spent five years in the Reds system and did not advance beyond Double-A because of arm injuries.

JIM MCLEAN

B.J. Garbe

Baxter and Howington were among four players from the state of Washington drafted in the first round, and among nine selected by the end of the second round. Moses Lake High outfielder B.J. Garbe, who signed with the Minnesota Twins for $2.75 million as the fifth pick overall, was considered the best high school athlete and hitter in the draft pool. He thrived as both a hitter and pitcher, and earned acclaim as the Washington 3-A football player of the year. Scouts gave him high marks for his bat speed and compact swing, as well as his center-field skills. Garbe, though, did not advance past Double-A in eight pro seasons. He struggled with pitch recognition, and eye examinations determined that Garbe was afflicted by night blindness. In 722 minor league games, he hit .235 with 37 homers.

## Highest Unsigned Picks

| Player, Pos., Team (Round) | College | Re-Drafted |
|---|---|---|
| Jason Cooper, of, Pirates (2) | Stanford | Indians '02 (3) |
| Bobby Hill, ss, White Sox (2) | None | Cubs '00 (2) |
| Alberto Concepcion, c, Padres (2) | Southern California | Red Sox '02 (21) |
| Drew Meyer, ss, Dodgers (2) | South Carolina | Rangers '02 (1) |
| Kiki Bengochea, rhp, Royals (3) | Miami (Fla.) | Rangers '02 (11) |
| Brandon Sloan, rhp, White Sox (4)* | Wichita State | Marlins '00 (7) |
| Jeff Baker, ss, Indians (4) | Clemson | Rockies '02 (4) |
| Rory Shortell, rhp, Red Sox (4) | San Diego State | Astros '02 (3) |
| Rob Corrado, rhp, Yankees (4) | Kentucky | Rangers '02 (30) |
| Joe Saunders, lhp, Phillies (5) | Virginia Tech | Angels '02 (1) |

**TOTAL UNSIGNED PICKS:** Top 5 Rounds (12), Top 10 Rounds (30)

**Returned to same school.*

Moses Lake High teammates Ryan Doumit (Pirates) and Jason Cooper (Phillies) were selected in the second round, marking the first time that a high school had produced three picks in the first two rounds in the same year. University of Washington righthander Jeff Heaverlo (Mariners), selected 33rd overall, was also a Moses Lake alum.

Doumit signed with the Pirates and forged a successful 10-year major league career. Cooper opted to attend college at Stanford, where he played both baseball and football. As the 63rd choice, he was the highest unsigned pick in the 1999 draft. Cooper later played 10 years in the minor leagues, peaking in Triple-A.

The fourth of Washington's crop of first-rounders was Centralia High righthander Jason Stumm, selected 15th overall by the White Sox. Like many other top pitching prospects in the 1999 class, Stumm stalled out because of arm problems. He endured two elbow and two shoulder surgeries in a seven-year career that peaked in Double-A. In 90 appearances he went 7-16, 4.10.

Baxter was on a fast track to the Padres rotation. At the time of his car accident, he was traveling from Phoenix to Lake Elsinore, Calif., to continue rehabbing an elbow injury. A tire on his pickup truck blew out and the truck rolled, killing Baxter and his former high school teammate, Mark Hilde, who was drafted by the Oakland A's in 2001.

### HEAVY EMPHASIS ON PITCHING

Pitching dominated the 1999 draft like few drafts in history. Eleven of the first 16 picks and 20 of the 30 first-rounders were pitchers. In one stretch, from Kurt Ainsworth at No. 24 to Nick Stocks at No. 36, pitchers were taken with 13 straight picks. The emphasis on arms came even though at least 10 high-profile pitchers had Tommy John surgery before the draft, and many others had it after they were selected.

The San Francisco Giants showed no misgivings in taking Ainsworth, even though he had pitched only eight innings the previous two years after Tommy John surgery. As an LSU junior, Ainsworth proved he was as good as new by going 13-6, 3.45 with 157 strikeouts in 130 innings. He went just 6-8, 5.17 in an abbreviated major league career curtailed by shoulder issues.

The Giants picked righthander Jeff Verplancke in the 11th round and signed him for $600,000, even as Verplancke, an unsigned second-rounder in 1998, missed the 1999 season while rehabbing from Tommy John surgery. Verplancke went 12-28, 4.90 in a three-year career in the minors.

With the 26th pick, the Chicago Cubs gave Wichita State righthander Ben Christensen a $1.0625 million bonus, and like many of his first-round peers, his pro career was plagued by arm problems. He endured surgeries to both his right elbow and right shoulder and went just 12-19, 4.64 in 74 appearances, none above Double-A.

Picking right after the Cubs, the New York Yankees selected 6-foot-5, 215-pound righthander David Walling, who set a school record at the University of Arkansas by striking out 155 in 121 innings during his junior season while going 10-7, 3.78. A year earlier, he began his NCAA Division I career by pitching 37 straight scoreless innings.

Walling was in Triple-A by 2001, but he developed an anxiety disorder so acute that he missed most of the season. He became so distracted by runners on base that he could not concentrate on throwing the ball to the plate. By 2002 his career was over. In 58 games over four seasons in the minors, he went 24-24, 4.10.

The Orioles, White Sox, Royals and Padres, who combined to make 21 picks before the second round started, invested in pitchers, taking 16 in all. The White Sox selected pitchers with 14 of their first 15 picks, including their top five, and the Royals drafted pitchers with their top seven picks.

The Orioles had four of the first 23 picks, and three more before they lost their next four choices for signing major league free agents Albert Belle, Will Clark, Delino DeShields and Mike Timlin. They didn't lose their first-rounder because it was protected as one of the top 15 picks, and gained six picks after losing Roberto Alomar, Eric Davis and Rafael Palmeiro as free agents.

"It's a crime what's happened with Baltimore this year," an American League scouting director

## One Team's Draft: Minnesota Twins

| Player, Pos. | Bonus | Player, Pos. | Bonus | Player, Pos. | Bonus |
|---|---|---|---|---|---|
| 1. *B.J. Garbe, of | $2,750,000 | 10. *Jim Caine, rhp | Did not sign | 19. Paul Poplin, rhp | $15,000 |
| **2. *Rob Bowen, c** | **$605,000** | 11. *Mike Prochaska, lhp | Did not sign | **20. *Travis Bowyer, rhp** | **$12,000** |
| **3. *Justin Morneau, c** | **$290,000** | 12. Kevin Johnson, rhp | Did not sign | 21. Chad Wandall, ss | $1,000 |
| 4. *Jeff Randazzo, lhp | $392,500 | 13. *Seth Morris, rhp/of | Did not sign | 22. *Ricky Manning, of | $275,000 |
| 5. Brent Schoening, rhp | $135,000 | **14. *Brian Slocum, rhp** | **Did not sign** | **23. Willie Eyre, rhp** | **$7,500** |
| **6. *Brian Wolfe, rhp** | **$125,000** | 15. John Wilson, c/of | Did not sign | 24. *Danny Matienzo, c | Did not sign |
| 7. *Darren Ciraco, of | Did not sign | 16. Kevin West, of | $15,000 | 25. Craig Patterson, c | Did not sign |
| 8. Matt Scanlon, 3b | $70,000 | 17. John Larson, rhp | Did not sign | **Other Terry Tiffee (26), 1b** | **$55,000** |
| 9. Grant Gregg, lhp | Did not sign | 18. *Barry Quickstad, 2b | $20,000 | | |

*Major leaguers in bold. *High school selection.*

### WORTH NOTING

2 pick overall; California righthander **RONEY JOHNSON**, a sixth-round pick of the Rockies; and Georgia lefthander **RICHARD STAHL**, a first-round selection of the Orioles each had a grade of 70. Johnson and Stahl did not reach the majors, their careers stalled by injuries.

■ Despite not having a first-round pick, the Braves spent $3.1 million on their first six selections. They gave $800,000 to second-rounder **MATT BUTLER**, $700,000 to third-rounder **PAT MANNING** and $950,000 to fifth-rounder **MATT MCCLENDON**. It was the richest bonus ever given to a fifth-round choice. McClendon, an unsigned supplemental first-round pick of the Reds in 1996, fell because of a chest injury that hampered his season at Florida. He was represented by **SCOTT BORAS**, who did not have a first-round client for the first time since 1985. Boras also struck a $1.3 million deal for righthander **CASEY DAIGLE** (Diamondbacks, 31st overall) and a $1.41 million agreement for righthander **NICK STOCKS** (Cardinals, 36th).

■ The Pirates drafted catcher **J.R. HOUSE** in the fifth round and signed him for a $250,000 bonus. House passed for more than 14,000 yards, a national record, in his career at Nitro (W.Va.) High, and set another national mark with 10 touchdown passes in a game. Because his father had residency in Florida and West Virginia, House spent his falls playing football at Nitro High and his spring semesters playing baseball in Florida. House showed early promise in the Pirates system, but illness, injuries and multiple surgeries stalled his development. He reached the major leagues with the Pirates briefly in 2003 and '04, and was released after six seasons. He enrolled at West Virginia in 2005 to resume his football career. But after a year as a third-string quarterback, House signed with the Astros and spent parts of three more seasons in the majors.

## IN FOCUS: BEN CHRISTENSEN

The usually conservative Chicago Cubs endured a firestorm of controversy when they used their first-round pick on Wichita State righthander Ben Christensen, who missed the final six weeks of the college season after being suspended for throwing at Evansville's Anthony Molina near the on-deck circle before a game on April 23.

Christensen claimed that he didn't mean to hit Molina and was just trying to prevent the batter from timing his pitches. The ball damaged Molina's left eye, leaving him with impaired vision. Christensen faced potential legal action, and eventually settled out of court for a reported $400,000.

Most clubs considered the 6-foot-4 Christensen a solid first-round talent. The Cubs organization stood behind the pitcher. "Obviously, we're very supportive of Ben," said Jim Hendry, Cubs director of scouting and player development. "We feel he's a quality young man. We would not have made the decision if we didn't feel he was a quality person off the field."

The Cubs gave Christensen a $1.0625 million bonus, and his pro career was plagued by arm problems. He endured surgeries to both his right elbow and right shoulder and went just 12-19, 4.64 in 74 appearances, none above Double-A.

said. "It's not right that a team already with a high payroll should profit like this. There's always been a flaw in the compensation system, but it has never been so acutely exposed as this year."

With the exception of future all-star second baseman Brian Roberts, the last of the seven early picks, the O's did not do well with their selections. Righthander Mike Paradis (13th overall) and lefthander Richard Stahl (18th) didn't reach the majors. Lefthander Scott Rice (44th) got to the big leagues in 2013, long after he had departed the Orioles. None produced as little as lefthander Josh Cenate, who spent one season in Rookie ball and never pitched again because of a shoulder injury.

Plenty of premium pitchers succeeded, though. Four of the first seven pitchers drafted won at least 94 games in the majors, led by lefthander Barry Zito (Athletics, ninth overall), who won 165 over a 14-year career. Beckett was next at 138, followed by righthanders Brett Myers (Phillies, 12th overall) and Ben Sheets (Brewers, 10th overall), who won 97 and 94, respectively. But no other pitcher matched the success of Peavy, an Alabama high school righthander who was the 249th pitcher drafted. He had a scholarship offer from Auburn, but instead accepted a $100,000 bonus from the Padres. In 14 seasons, Peavy went 147-117, 3.53 and twice led the National League in ERA.

### CARDS HIT JACKPOT IN PUJOLS

For sheer impact, no player in the class of 1999 came close to matching the achievements of Pujols, especially over the first 11 years of his career in a Cardinals uniform, when he hit .328 with 445 home runs and 1,329 RBIs. Yet Pujols was an afterthought in the draft, the 402nd player chosen.

Pujols' family emigrated to the United States from the Dominican Republic at age 16 and settled in Independence, Mo. He hit .593 with 35 homers and 124 RBIs in American Legion ball in the summer of 1998. After graduating from Fort Osage High in December and enrolling at Maple Woods (Mo.) CC in time for the 1999 spring season, Pujols continued to excel, hitting a grand slam off future big leaguer Mark Buehrle in his first game and batting .461 with 17 homers and 60 RBIs for the season.

Scouts acknowledged Pujols' bat was a lethal weapon but expressed concern about his thick body and subpar physical condition, as well as his somewhat stiff actions on defense. Some even claimed that he was older than his stated age of 19.

"They don't know what the hell they're doing here in the Midwest as far as drafting," Maple Woods coach Marty Kilgore said. "There are some idiots here that think they know the game. It is damn ridiculous—13th round.

"I had scouts come to me the next year after the draft and tell me they didn't turn him in. You got damn poor scouting, that is how you explain it. You have 100 guys who do their job and know what they're doing and another 200 scouting each other."

Pujols rejected the Cardinals initial $10,000 bonus offer and played that summer for Hays, Kan., in the semi-pro Jayhawk League. He continued to stand out as a hitter.

A. DELFACO

Albert Pujols lasted until the Cardinals took him in the 13th round, but he became the best player in the 1999 class by a wide margin

"The ball exploded off his bat, almost like it does now," Hays manager Frank Leo said after Pujols had established himself. "That was his first year using wood bats full-time, but his swing was already geared to contact. He hit doubles off the wall, not chinks over the infield. He always understood the game, things like baserunning and situations, even at a young age."

The Cardinals, realizing they had a potential star, increased their offer to $60,000, and Pujols signed in August. After spending the 2000 season in the minor leagues, he went to the big leagues to stay.

As usual, the days before the 1999 draft included frenzied negotiations with draft-and-follows from the 1998 draft. Cypress (Calif.) College catcher Gerald Laird (A's, second round, 1998) and Miami-Dade Community College North shortstop Ivan Reyes (Yankees, fourth round) both signed for $1 million. The stakes were lower for the 1999 draft-and-follows. Lefthander Jason Norderum of Sacramento City College, the 31st round pick of the Expos, signed for $500,000 in 2000. He was the only draft-and-follow to get more than $260,000.

### Largest Draft-And-Follow Bonuses

| Player, Pos. | Club (Round) | Bonus |
|---|---|---|
| 1. * Jason Norderum, lhp | Expos (31) | $500,000 |
| **2. * Angel Pagan, of** | **Mets (4)** | **$255,000** |
| **3. Jason Davis, rhp** | **Indians (21)** | **$250,000** |
| 4. Michael Tejada, c | Rockies (27) | $200,000 |
| 5. Andrew Earley, rhp | Cubs (15) | $180,000 |
| 6. Greg Montalbano, lhp | Red Sox (5) | $130,000 |
| **7. Brandon Lyon, rhp** | **Blue Jays (14)** | **$125,000** |
| **8. Kevin Thompson, ss** | **Yankees (31)** | **$115,000** |
| 9. Dustin Lansford, rhp | Brewers (5) | $100,000 |
| * Matt Allegra, of | Athletics (16) | $100,000 |

*Major leaguers in bold. *High school selection.*

# 1999 Draft List

**Did not sign. Major leaguers in bold, with first and last years noted. Order of selection indicated in parentheses. For the first five rounds, the peak level of each player is noted. + Signed as draft-and-follow (Second school noted if applicable).*

## ANAHEIM ANGELS (17)

1. (Choice to Red Sox as compensation for Type A free agent Mo Vaughn)
**2. John Lackey, rhp, Grayson County (Texas) CC.—(2002-15)**
3. Phil Wilson, rhp, Poway (Calif.) HS.—(AA)
4. Stan Bukowski, rhp, Dunedin (Fla.) HS.—(High A)
5. Vince LaCorte, rhp, San Jose State University.—(Low A)
DRAFT DROP *Son of Frank LaCorte, major leaguer (1975-84)*
**6. Dusty Bergman, lhp, University of Hawaii.—(2004)**
7. Alan Wawrzyniak, rhp, Philadelphia College of Textiles.
8. Aaron Franke, rhp, Owens (Ohio) CC.
9. Brian Specht, ss/2b, Doherty HS, Colorado Springs, Colo.
**10. Robb Quinlan, 1b, University of Minnesota.—(2003-10)**
DRAFT DROP *Brother of Tom Quinlan, major leaguer (1990-96)*
11. Chris Barski, c, New Mexico State University.
12. Mike O'Keefe, of, Providence College.
**13. Alfredo Amezaga, ss, St Petersburg (Fla.) JC.—(2002-11)**
14. Jon Palmieri, 1b, Wake Forest University.
15. Sean Brummett, lhp, Indiana State University.
16. Brandon Jackson, of, Savannah State (Ga.) University.
17. Scott Bikowski, of, Florida Southern College.
18. +Shayne Wright, rhp, Sacramento (Calif.) CC.
**19. Gary Johnson, of, Brigham Young University.—(2003)**
20. Brent Haworth, rhp, Rollins (Fla.) College.
21. Jeff Wagner, c, University of Notre Dame.
22. *Pat Osborn, ss, Bakersfield (Calif.) HS.
23. Alcides Duverge, c, Norwalk (Conn.) CC.
24. Ben Grezlovski, rhp, University of Florida.
25. Shayne Ferrier, rhp, Southwest Missouri State University.
26. Palmer Ebanks, rhp, Jacksonville University.
**27. Tom Gregorio, c, Troy State University.—(2003)**
28. Luke Sullivan, lhp, New Mexico State University.
29. Brett Schreyer, rhp, Florida Atlantic University.
30. Chip Gosewisch, 2b, Arizona State University.
31. *Kevin Tillman, 3b, Arizona State University.
DRAFT DROP *Brother of Pat Tillman, defensive back, National Football League (1998-2001)*
32. Chris Hills, of, Jackson State University.
33. Tim Boeth, 3b-ss, University of Central Florida.
34. Patrick Bowen, rhp, St. Leo (Fla.) College.
35. Craig Glysch, rhp, University of Wisconsin-Oshkosh.
36. Pete Orgill, c-1b, University of Washington.
37. *Jason Farren, rhp, Gulf Coast (Fla.) CC.
38. *Jermie Fitzgerald, lhp, Cowley County (Kan.) CC.
39. *Robert Ellis, lhp, Mission (Calif.) JC.
40. *Ryan Smith, rhp, Chipola (Fla.) JC.
41. Brandon Martin, of, Riverside (Calif.) CC.
42. +David Wolensky, rhp, Chipola (Fla.) JC.
43. *Jeremy Paul, c, Buffalo Grove (Ill.) HS.
44. *Moises Feliz, ss, Chipola (Fla.) JC.
45. Bill Curtis, of, Grand Canyon University.
DRAFT DROP *Brother of Chad Curtis, major leaguer (1992-2001)*
46. *George Malone, of, Victor Valley HS, Victorville, Calif.
47. +Adam Thomas, rhp, St Petersburg (Fla.) CC.
48. *Klent Corley, rhp, Greenway HS, Phoenix.
49. Garry Templeton Jr., ss, North Carolina A&T University.
DRAFT DROP *Son of Garry Templeton, major leaguer (1976-91)*
50. Jeff Nebel, rhp, Mercer University.

## ARIZONA DIAMONDBACKS (4)

1. Corey Myers, ss, Desert Vista HS, Phoenix.—(AAA)
**1. Casey Daigle, rhp, Sulphur (La.) HS** (Supplemental choice—31st—as compensation for Type A free agent Devon White).—**(2004-10)**
2. (Choice to Astros as compensation for Type A free agent Randy Johnson)
2. Jeremy Ward, rhp, Long Beach State University (Choice from Dodgers as compensation for White).—(AAA)
3. (Choice to Red Sox as compensation for Type A free agent Greg Swindell)
4. (Choice to Rangers as compensation for Type A free agent Todd Stottlemyre)
5. (Choice to Padres as compensation for Type A free agent Steve Finley)
6. *Justin Maureau, lhp, Highlands Ranch (Colo.) HS.
7. Ryan Owens, ss, Cal State Fullerton.
**8. Chris Capuano, lhp, Duke University.—(2003-15)**
**9. Matt Kata, ss, Vanderbilt University.—(2003-09)**
10. *Matt Abram, 3b, Chaparral HS, Scottsdale, Ariz.
11. *Ben King, lhp, Grapevine (Texas) HS.
**12. Doug Devore, of, Indiana University.—(2004)**
13. *Jesse Harper, rhp, Brazoswood HS, Clute, Texas.
14. *Todd Gelatka, rhp, Trabuco Hills HS, Lake Forest, Calif.
15. Todd Kasper, c, Yale University.
16. Greg Perkin, rhp, Kingwood (Texas) HS.
17. Shawn Lagana, ss, Lakewood HS, Cypress, Calif.
**18. Lyle Overbay, 1b-of, University of Nevada-Reno.—(2001-14)**
19. Jack Santora, ss, UCLA.
20. Justin Graham, of, West Virginia State College.
21. Tim Stanton, lhp, Florida Southern College.
22. Mike Davis, rhp, Lyon County HS, Eddyville, Ky.
23. Evan Fahrner, rhp, Bradley University.
24. Toby Harris, rhp, University of Nevada-Reno.
25. Travis Oglesby, c, Armstrong Atlantic State (Ga.) University.
26. Kevin Burns, of, Troy State University.
27. Dan Jackson, rhp, St Louis CC-Forest Park.
28. Dan Williford, 1b, University of Mobile (Ala.).
29. Dale Deveraux, rhp, JC of Southern Idaho.
30. *Hans Smith, lhp, Fresno State University.
31. Joe Kalczynski, c, Michigan State University.
32. *Jim Kavourias, 1b, Pensacola (Fla.) JC.
33. Joe Yakopich, ss, St. Thomas of Villanova HS, Amherstburg, Ontario.
34. Cody Sundbeck, rhp, Dallas Baptist University.
35. James Wollscheid, rhp, McMurry (Texas) University.
36. Steven Tomshack, c, University of Maryland.
37. Derek Forbes, rhp, South Mountain (Ariz.) CC.
38. *Erick Contreras, ss, Garden City (Kan.) CC.
39. *Carlton Wells, lhp, Hillsborough (Fla.) CC.
40. *Aaron Sobieraj, rhp, Dunedin (Fla.) HS.
41. Josh Goldfield, c, Moorpark (Calif.) JC.
42. Brian Matzenbacher, rhp, Southern Illinois University-Edwardsville.
43. Todd Myers, rhp, Lamar University.
44. *Aaron Pullin, rhp, Midland (Texas) HS.
45. *Jered Liebeck, rhp, Mountain Ridge HS, Glendale, Ariz.
46. *Scott Buffington, rhp, Lamar (Colo.) CC.
47. Chris Jorgenson, of, McCoy HS, New Brigden, Alberta.
48. *Keith Schuttler, of, Agua Fria HS, Litchfield Park, Ariz.
49. *Chris Churchill, c, Abilene (Texas) HS.
50. *Peter Hawley, of, Branford (Conn.) HS.

## ATLANTA BRAVES (30)

1. (Choice to Cardinals as compensation for Type A free agent Brian Jordan)
2. Matt Butler, rhp, Hattiesburg (Miss.) HS.—(High A)
3. Pat Manning, ss, Mater Dei HS, Anaheim Hills, Calif.—(High A)
4. Alec Zumwalt, of, East Forsyth HS, Kernersville, N.C.—(AAA)
5. Matt McClendon, rhp, University of Florida.—(AAA)
DRAFT DROP *First-round draft pick (33rd overall), Reds (1996)*
**6. Andrew Brown, rhp, Trinity Christian Academy, Deltona, Fla.—(2006-08)**
7. Brett Evert, rhp, North Salem HS, Salem, Ore.
8. *Chris Spencer, rhp, Humble (Texas) HS.
9. Angelo Burrows, of, Killian HS, Miami.
10. Bryan Cetani, lhp, Deep Valley Christian HS, Ukiah, Calif.
11. Chris Trevino, lhp, Andrews (Texas) HS.
**12. Ben Kozlowski, lhp, Santa Fe (Fla.) CC.—(2002)**
13. *Shaud Williams, ss, Andrews (Texas) HS.
**14. Garrett Jones, 1b, Andrew HS, Tinley Park, Ill.—(2007-15)**
15. *David Fiala, rhp, Orange Park (Fla.) HS.
16. Kevin Green, c, Georgia Perimeter JC.
17. *Efren Lira, rhp, Walnut (Calif.) HS.
18. Tom Curtiss, lhp, University of Maryland.
19. *Scott Wade, rhp, Sullivan South HS, Kingsport, Tenn.
20. Collin Remekie, of, Martin County HS, Stuart, Fla.
21. Wes Rasmussen, ss, Moorpark (Calif.) HS.
22. Bryce Terveen, c, University of the Pacific.
23. Kyle Colton, rhp, Bishop Moore HS, Longwood, Fla.
24. Alva Thompson, c, Southern University.
**25. John Foster, lhp, Lewis-Clark State (Idaho) College.—(2002-05)**
26. Shannin Veronie, rhp, Cal State Chico.
27. Chris Chavez, rhp, Florida State University.
28. *Ryan Hubbard, ss, Huntington Beach (Calif.) HS.
29. *Travis Suereth, 1b, Buchholz HS, Gainesville, Fla.
30. Jeff Rodriguez, c, Florida International University.
31. *Zachary Parker, lhp, Westwood HS, Austin, Texas.
32. Joseph Francisco, of, Wagner College.
33. +Tom Parrott, 3b, Merritt Island (Fla.) HS / Daytona (Fla.) CC.
34. Curt Fiore, 3b, Loyola Marymount University.
35. *Jeremy Barker, lhp, Willows (Calif.) HS.
36. Shaun Argento, c, New Mexico Highlands University.
37. *Jonathan Schuerholz, ss, Lovett School, Atlanta.
DRAFT DROP *Son of John Schuerholz, general manager, Royals (1981-90); general manager/president, Braves (1990-2015)*
38. Anthony Sclafani, rhp, St. Peters HS, Staten Island, N.Y.
39. Ryan Erwin, rhp, Monte Vista HS, Spring Valley, Calif.
40. *Joshua Parker, rhp, Thompson HS, Alabaster, Ala.
41. *Michael Gleason, rhp, Butler County (Kan.) CC.
42. *Klint Richardson, rhp, Lyons (N.Y.) HS.
43. *Michael Koppin, ss, Stephens County HS, Eastanollee, Ga.
44. +Toby Staveland, rhp, Mendocino (Calif.) CC.
45. +Grant Abrams, ss, St Petersburg (Fla.) CC.
46. *J.C. Barnett, rhp, Fort Meade (Fla.) HS.
47. *James Anderson, c, John W. North HS, Riverside, Calif.
48. *August Marsala, 3b, Buffalo (Mo.) HS.
49. Nathan Kent, rhp, University of Kentucky.
50. *Scott Leitz, lhp, Vanguard HS, Ocala, Fla.

## BALTIMORE ORIOLES (13)

1. Mike Paradis, rhp, Clemson University.—(AAA)
1. Richard Stahl, lhp, Newton County HS, Covington, Ga. (Choice from Cardinals as compensation for Type A free agent Eric Davis).—(AAA)
**1. Larry Bigbie, of, Ball State University** (Choice from Rangers as compensation for Type A free agent Rafael Palmeiro).—**(2001-06)**
**1. Keith Reed, of, Providence College** (Choice from Indians as compensation for Type A free agent Roberto Alomar).—**(2005)**
1. Josh Cenate, lhp, Jefferson HS, Shenandoah Junction, W.Va. (Supplemental choice—34th—as compensation for Alomar).—(Rookie)
**1. Scott Rice, lhp, Royal HS, Simi Valley, Calif.** (Supplemental choice—44th—as compensation for loss of Davis).—**(2013-14)**
**1. Brian Roberts, ss, University of South Carolina** (Supplemental choice—50th—as compensation for Palmeiro).—**(2001-14)**
2. (Choice to White Sox as compensation for Type A free agent Albert Belle)
3. (Choice to Mariners as compensation for Type A free agent Mike Timlin).
3. Jon Kessick, c, Ball State University (Choice from Dodgers as compensation for Type B free agent Alan Mills).—(High A)
4. (Choice to Cardinals as compensation for Type A free agent Delino DeShields)
5. (Choice to Rangers as compensation for Type A free agent Will Clark)
**6. Erik Bedard, lhp, Norwalk (Conn.) CC.—(2002-14)**
7. David Farren, rhp, Texas HS, Texarkana, Texas.
8. Matt Tate, rhp, Holmes County HS, Bonifay, Fla.
9. Pete Shier, ss, Hilliard Davidson HS, Columbus, Ohio.
10. Octavio Martinez, c, Bakersfield (Calif.) JC.
11. *Kraig Brinkman, rhp, Napa (Calif.) HS.
12. Brad Rogers, rhp, Wellington SS, Nanaimo, B.C.
13. +Drew Hassler, rhp, Arcadia HS, Phoenix / South Mountain (Ariz.) JC.
DRAFT DROP *Son of Andy Hassler, major leaguer (1971-85)*
14. Matt Riordan, of, Loyola Marymount University.
15. *Brock Ralph, of, University of Wyoming.
DRAFT DROP *Wide receiver, Canadian Football League (2003-11)*
16. Shaun Babula, lhp, Philadelphia College of Textiles.
17. *Jason Tourangeau, rhp, South Carroll HS, Mount Airy, Md.
18. Kyle Martin, c, Selah (Wash.) HS.
19. Nicolas Garcia, ss, Desert View HS, Tucson, Ariz.
20. Steve Salargo, of, East Carolina University.
21. *Shane Waroff, rhp, Fullerton (Calif.) JC.
22. *Beau Kemp, rhp, Nathan Hale HS, Tulsa, Okla.
**23. Aaron Rakers, rhp, Southern Illinois University-Edwardsville.—(2004-07)**
**24. Willie Harris, 2b-ss, Kennesaw State University.—(2001-12)**
**25. *Mitch Jones, 3b, Arizona State University.—(2009)**
26. Mike Seestedt, c, University of Michigan.
27. Rodney Ormond, rhp, North Carolina State University.
28. *Matt Larson, rhp, Corona Del Mar HS, Costa Mesa, Calif.
29. *Martin LaRocca, rhp, Archbishop Rummel, Metairie, La.
30. *Kyle Yudizky, of, Duncanville (Texas) HS.
31. *Kyle Roat, c, Coweta (Okla.) HS.
32. *Keven Virtue, of, A.B. Lucas HS, London, Ontario.
33. Chase Phillips, rhp, Maysville HS, Zanesville, Ohio.
**34. *Doug Slaten, lhp, Glendale (Calif.) JC.—(2006-12)**
35. Kelvin Pickering, c, King HS, Tampa.
DRAFT DROP *Brother of Calvin Pickering, major leaguer (1998-2005)*
36. *Andrew Corona, 1b, Moorpark (Calif.) CC.
37. *Ryan Rocheleau, lhp, Hemet (Calif.) HS.
38. Charlie Dees, of, Chipola (Fla.) JC.
39. Gary Cates, 2b, Brandon (Fla.) HS.
40. *Matt Roy, rhp, Johnstown-Monroe HS, Johnstown, Ohio.
**41. *Sean White, rhp, Mercer Island (Wash.) HS.—(2007-10)**
42. *Nicholas Vitielliss, rhp, Thomas Stone HS, Waldorf, Md.
43. Terry Plank, rhp, Methodist (N.C.) College.
44. Wil Sowers, 3b, West Virginia State College.
45. *Brad Guglielmelli, 3b, Cuesta (Calif.) JC.
46. *Pat Tobin, c, Dun Barton SS, Pickering, Ontario.
47. *Judd Richardson, rhp, Country Day SS, Terra Cotta, Ontario.
48. *Michael Roga, rhp, Pine Ridge SS, Pickering, Ontario.
49. *Mark Perkins, rhp, Claremont SS, Victoria, B.C.
50. *Kyle Baumgartner, ss, Olympic HS, Bremerton, Wash.

## BOSTON RED SOX (25)

1. Rick Asadoorian, of, Northbridge HS, Whitinsville, Mass. (Choice from Angels as compensation for Type A free agent Mo Vaughn).—(AAA)
1. (Choice to Royals as compensation for Type A free agent Jose Offerman)
1. Brad Baker, rhp, Pioneer Valley HS, Leyden,

Mass. (Supplemental choice—40th—as compensation for Vaughn).—(AAA)

**1. Casey Fossum, lhp, Texas A&M University** (Supplemental choice—48th—as compensation for Type A free agent Greg Swindell).—**(2001-09)**

2. Mat Thompson, rhp, Timberline HS, Boise, Idaho.—(High A)

**3. Rich Rundles, lhp, Jefferson County HS, New Market, Tenn.** (Choice from Diamondbacks as compensation for Swindell).—**(2008-09)**

3. Antron Seiber, of, Independence (La.) HS.—(High A)

4. *Rory Shortell, rhp, Madison HS, Portland, Ore.—(High A)

DRAFT DROP *Attended San Diego State; re-drafted by Astros, 2002 (3rd round)*

5. +Greg Montalbano, lhp, Northeastern University.—(AA)

6. *Jon Kail, of, Baldwin HS, Pittsburgh.

7. *Richard Carroll, 1b, Venice (Fla.) HS.

8. *Andy Heimbach, rhp, Mount Vernon Nazarene (Ohio) College.

9. *Hank Thoms, rhp, Mississippi State University.

10. Brian Wiese, of, Mississippi State University.

11. Kregg Jarvais, c, University of Maine.

**12. Lew Ford, of, Dallas Baptist University.—(2003-12)**

13. Mike Dwyer, 1b, University of Richmond.

14. B.J. Leach, rhp, Florida Southern College.

15. *Brian Wiley, rhp, The Citadel.

**16. *Charlie Manning, lhp, Polk (Fla.) CC.—(2008)**

17. *Trae Duncan, 3b, Mississippi Gulf Coast JC.

18. Jeff Waldron, c, Boston College.

19. Jason Bottenfield, rhp, University of Texas-Pan American.

20. Dan Generelli, rhp, Quinsigamond (Mass.) CC.

21. *Jason Henderson, rhp, Bishop Hendricken HS, Coventry, R.I.

22. *Ellis Debrow, 1b-of, Woodham HS, Pensacola, Fla.

23. *Nicolas Puckett, lhp, Timberline HS, Boise, Idaho.

24. *Rex Rundgren, ss, Mid Pacific Institute, Honolulu, Hawaii.

DRAFT DROP *Son of rock star Todd Rundgren*

25. *Tim McCabe, ss, North Catholic HS, Wexford, Pa.

**26. *Marshall McDougall, 2b, Florida State University.—(2005)**

**27. *Mark Kiger, 2b, Grossmont (Calif.) JC.—(2006)**

28. Jonathan Anderson, ss, University of Illinois.

29. +Bart Hollis, rhp, Lawrence County HS, Moulton, Ala. / Northwest Shoals (Ala.) CC.

30. *Charles Frasier, 3b, Santa Rosa (Calif.) JC.

**31. *Jaime Bubela, of, Baylor University.—(2005)**

32. *David Flournoy, of, Deer Valley HS, Antioch, Calif.

33. Perry Miley, of, William Carey (Miss.) College.

**34. Dan Giese, rhp, University of San Diego.—(2007-09)**

35. Ben Marbury, of, Rockford, Ala.

36. *Jon Brandon, of, Panola (Texas) JC.

**37. *Chris Mabeus, rhp, Eastern Arizona JC.—(2006)**

38. *Jesse Cooksey, rhp, Port Neches-Groves HS, Port Arthur, Texas.

39. *Matt Ames, 1b, Stanhope Elmore HS, Millbrook, Ala.

40. *Anthony Bass, of, Booker T. Washington HS, Tulsa, Okla.

41. *Justin Smetana, lhp, Cardinal HS, Huntsburg, Ohio.

42. *Brian Rinehart, 2b, Southington (Conn.) HS.

43. *Ryan Coffin, rhp, Desert Vista HS, Tempe, Ariz.

44. *Alan Lindsey, of, Lee-Davis HS, Mechanicsville, Va.

45. Brady Williams, 3b, Pasco Hernando (Fla.) CC.

DRAFT DROP *Son of Jimy Williams, major leaguer (1966-67); major league manager (1986-2004)*

46. Joe Kerrigan, ss, Temple University.

DRAFT DROP *Son of Joe Kerrigan, major leaguer (1976-80); major league manager (2001)*

47. *James Burgess, of, Durango HS, Las Vegas, Nev.

48. *Joseph Kjose, rhp, Cochise County (Ariz.) CC.

49. *Jordan Remy, 2b, Weston (Mass.) HS.

DRAFT DROP *Son of Gerry Remy, major leaguer (1975-84)*

**50. *Brian Buscher, ss, Terry Parker HS, Jacksonville, Fla.—(2007-09)**

## CHICAGO CUBS (26)

1. Ben Christensen, rhp, Wichita State University.—(AA)

2. Michael Mallory, of, Dinwiddie County HS, Dinwiddie, Va.—(AA)

3. Ryan Gripp, 3b, Creighton University.—(AA)

**4. Steve Smyth, lhp, University of Southern California.—(2002)**

5. *Todd Deininger, rhp, Joliet Township HS, Joliet, Ill.—(Low A)

DRAFT DROP *Attended Texas A&M; re-drafted by White Sox, 2002 (9th round)*

6. Ben Shaffar, rhp, University of Kentucky.

7. Mike Dzurilla, 2b, St. John's University.

8. Dustin Pate, rhp, Daniel HS, Clemson, S.C.

9. Chris Curry, c, Mississippi State University.

DRAFT DROP *Baseball coach, Arkansas-Little Rock (2015)*

10. Jim Deschaine, ss, Brandeis (Mass.) University.

11. Tim Lavery, lhp, University of Illinois.

12. Condor Cash, of, Stephens County School, Toccoa, Ga.

13. Keto Anderson, 2b, Chipola (Fla.) JC.

DRAFT DROP *Brother of Marlon Anderson, major leaguer (1998-2009)*

14. Jandin Thornton-Murray, ss, St. Louis HS, Honolulu, Hawaii.

15. +Andrew Earley, rhp, Okaloosa-Walton (Fla.) CC.

16. Tony Gsell, 2b, Old Dominion University.

17. Derrick Cohens, of, Lake City (Fla.) CC.

18. James Eppeneder, lhp, Diablo Valley (Calif.) CC.

**19. John Webb, rhp, Manatee (Fla.) CC.—(2004-05)**

20. Brandon Sing, ss-1b, Joliet Township HS, Joliet, Ill.

21. *Rylie Ogle, lhp, Long Beach (Calif.) CC.

22. *Martin Calderon, ss, El Modena HS, Orange, Calif.

**23. Pete Zoccolillo, 1b-of, Rutgers University.—(2003)**

24. +Kevin Collins, of, Land O'Lakes (Fla.) HS / Pasco Hernando (Fla.) CC.

25. Ryan Van Horn, c, University of Oklahoma.

26. Ben Johnstone, of, Yale University.

27. Casey Kopitzke, c, University of Wisconsin-Oshkosh.

28. *David Lemon, of, Eustis HS, Heathrow, Fla.

DRAFT DROP *Son of Chet Lemon, first-round draft pick, Athletics (1972); major leaguer (1975-90)*

29. *Ryan Jackson, c, McNeil HS, Austin, Texas.

**30. +Ray Sadler, of, Hill (Texas) JC.—(2005)**

31. *Blake Melstrom, c, South Hills HS, West Covina, Calif.

32. *Jorge Acevedo, of, Efrain Sanchez Hidalgo HS, Moca, P.R.

33. *Greg Hanoian, of, University of Southern California.

34. *Stephen Solwick, rhp, Rio Rancho (N.M.) HS.

35. Eduardo Marquez, of, Nicholls State University.

36. *Jason MacKintosh, lhp, Cerro Coso (Calif.) CC.

37. Jeff Ryan, ss, Wichita State University.

38. *Cody Willis, rhp, Deweyville (Texas) HS.

39. *Federico Baez, 3b, Jose S. Alegria HS, Dorado, P.R.

40. *Justin Valenti, of, Norwalk (Conn.) CC.

41. *Beau Benton, of, Central Florida CC.

42. *Donn Bair, lhp-of, Merced (Calif.) HS.

43. +Bryan Golden, c, Potomac State (W.Va.) JC.

44. *Jeremy Mannin, lhp, Wenatchee (Wash.) HS.

45. *Justin Sims, of, Karns HS, Knoxville, Tenn.

46. Chris Adams, rhp, McLennan (Texas) CC.

**47. *Dale Thayer, rhp, Edison HS, Huntington Beach, Calif.—(2009-15)**

48. *Charles Talanoa, rhp, El Segundo (Calif.) HS.

49. *Ryan Johnson, of, Laguna Hills (Calif.) HS.

50. *Thomas Syc, rhp, Carl Sandburg HS, Orland Park, Ill.

## CHICAGO WHITE SOX (15)

1. Jason Stumm, rhp, Centralia (Wash.) HS.—(AA)

**1. Matt Ginter, rhp, Mississippi State University** (Choice from Mets as compensation for Type A free agent Robin Ventura).—**(2000-08)**

1. Brian West, rhp, West Monroe HS, Monroe, La. (Supplemental choice—35th—as compensation for Type A free agent Albert Belle).—(AAA)

1. Rob Purvis, rhp, Bradley University (Supplemental choice—45th—as compensation for Ventura).—(AAA)

**2. Danny Wright, rhp, University of Arkansas** (Choice from Orioles as compensation for Belle).—**(2001-04)**

**2. *Bobby Hill, ss, University of Miami.—(2002-05)**

DRAFT DROP *Played for Newark (Atlantic); re-drafted by Cubs, 2000 (2nd round)*

**3. Jon Rauch, rhp, Morehead State University.—(2002-13)**

4. *Brandon Sloan, rhp, Wichita State University.—(AAA)

DRAFT DROP *Returned to Wichita State; re-drafted by Marlins, 2000 (7th round).*

**5. Josh Stewart, lhp, University of Memphis.—(2003-04)**

**6. David Sanders, lhp, Barton County (Kan.) CC.—(2003-05)**

7. Scott Patten, rhp, Tecumseh (Okla.) HS.

8. Dennis Ulacia, lhp, Monsignor Pace HS, Opa Locka, Fla.

9. Corwin Malone, lhp, Thomasville (Ala.) HS.

**10. Matt Guerrier, rhp, Kent State University.—(2004-14)**

11. Alex Hollifield, rhp, Stranahan HS, Fort Lauderdale, Fla.

12. Derek Stanley, of, North Florida JC.

13. Casey Rogowski, of, Catholic Central HS, Livonia, Mich.

14. Spencer Oborn, of, Cal State Fullerton.

15. Julio Reyes, 1b-of, Miami (Fla.) Senior HS.

16. *Ben Birk, of, University of Minnesota.

17. *Ryan Childs, 3b-rhp, Damascus HS, Gaithersburg, Md.

**18. *Scott Hairston, ss, Canyon del Oro HS, Tucson, Ariz.—(2004-14)**

DRAFT DROP *Grandson of Sam Hairston, major leaguer (1951) • Son of Jerry Hairston, major leaguer (1973-89) • Brother of Jerry Hairston Jr., major leaguer (1998-2013)*

19. Che Done, rhp, Monsignor Pace HS, Miami.

20. *David Brockman, rhp, Glendale (Ariz.) JC.

21. Daniel Martinez, lhp, Southwestern (Calif.) JC.

22. Kris McWhirter, rhp, Volunteer State (Tenn.) CC.

23. Joe Curreri, rhp, Long Island University.

24. Todd Holt, of, Louisburg (N.C.) JC.

25. Rocky Hughes, lhp, Pratt (Kan.) CC.

**26. Joe Valentine, rhp, Jefferson Davis (Ala.) JC.—(2003-05)**

**27. *Dan Ortmeier, of-1b, Lewisville HS, Highland Village, Texas.—(2005-08)**

28. +Wally Rosa, c, Brito Private HS, Miami / Palm Beach (Fla.) CC.

29. Jason Rummel, 2b, Towson State University.

30. +Jonathan Cavin, of, Connors State (Okla.) JC.

31. *Juan Gutierrez, of, Coral Park HS, Miami.

32. *Michel Valdez, of, Miami-Dade CC.

33. *Tony Neal, rhp, Faulkner State (Ala.) JC.

34. +Matt Salvesan, 3b, Kishwaukee (Ill.) JC.

35. *Greg Sandifer, rhp, Palomar (Calif.) JC.

**36. +Jeff Bajenaru, rhp, University of Oklahoma.—(2004-06)**

37. *Michael Eady, of, West Ouachita HS, Eros, La.

38. Trent Roehler, c, Fort Hays State (Kan.) University.

39. *Paul Beaudreau, c, El Modena HS, Orange, Calif.

40. *Jeremy Castillo, of, Southridge HS, Miami.

41. *Eric Johnson, rhp, Southridge HS, Miami.

42. *John Koonig, rhp, Jefferson (Mo.) JC.

43. *Kris Gross, rhp, Lee's Summit (Mo.) HS.

44. *Armando Perez, lhp, Montgomery HS, San Ysidro, Calif.

45. *James Hymon, ss, Kishwaukee (Ill.) JC.

46. *Dustin Scheffel, rhp, Oak Ridge HS, Cameron Park, Calif.

47. *C.J. Steele, ss, Connors State (Okla.) JC.

48. *Mike Cox, c, Riverview HS, Sarasota, Fla.

49. *Austin Rappe, of, Virginia Tech.

50. *Adam Heiden, rhp, Denison (Iowa) HS.

## CINCINNATI REDS (14)

1. Ty Howington, lhp, Hudson's Bay HS, Vancouver, Wash.—(AA)

**2. Ben Broussard, 1b, McNeese State University.—(2002-08)**

3. Brandon Love, rhp, Viola (Ark.) HS.—(Low A)

4. Kenny Lutz, rhp, Collinsville HS, Caseyville, Ill.—(Rookie)

**5. *Mike Esposito, rhp, Cimarron-Memorial HS, Las Vegas, Nev.—(2005)**

DRAFT DROP *Attended Arizona State; re-drafted by Rockies, 2002 (12th round)*

6. Alex LeFlore, of, Pinellas Park (Fla.) HS.

DRAFT DROP *Son of Ron LeFlore, major leaguer (1974-82)*

7. Corey Barrow, of, Clarke Central HS, Athens, Ga.

8. Ryan Lundquist, c, University of Arkansas.

9. Casey Bookout, 1b, University of Oklahoma.

**10. Scott Dunn, rhp, University of Texas.—(2004-06)**

11. Paul Darnell, lhp, Tarleton State (Texas) University.

12. Josh Spoerl, 3b, University of Texas.

13. *Travis Wong, 1b, Timberline HS, Boise, Idaho.

14. David Bradley, rhp, Marietta (Ohio) College.

15. Rafael Erazo, rhp, Oklahoma Christian University.

16. Paco Escamilla, rhp, Lubbock Christian (Texas) University.

17. Kyle Moncrief, 1b, West Monroe HS, Monroe, La.

18. Matt Dehner, ss, Oklahoma City University.

19. B.J. Hawes, ss, Augusta Christian School, Appling, Ga.

20. Mark Burnett, 2b, University of Arkansas.

**21. Brad Salmon, rhp, Jefferson Davis (Ala.) CC.—(2007)**

22. +Mike Fawcett, rhp, Central Michigan University.

23. Matt Nanninga, rhp, Bellevue (Neb.) University.

24. Carlos Hines, rhp, Smithfield-Selma HS, Selma, N.C.

25. Kevin Schnall, c, Coastal Carolina University.

26. Jason Huth, ss, Texas Tech.

27. Michael Landkammer, rhp, Mankato State (Minn.) University.

28. Thomas Pike, rhp, McMurry (Texas) University.

**29. Mike Neu, rhp, University of Miami.—(2003-04)**

DRAFT DROP *Baseball coach, Pacific (2015)*

30. *Jonathan Sheaffer, of, South Mountain (Ariz.) CC.

31. Corey Ward, of, Odessa (Texas) JC.

32. *Jack Arroyo, 2b, East Union HS, Prundale, Calif.

33. Jason Howard, c, East Carolina University.

34. +Stace Pape, rhp, University of Texas-San Antonio.

35. *Evan Conley, ss, Manatee HS, Bradenton, Fla.

**36. *Rich Hill, lhp, Milton (Mass.) HS.—(2005-15)**

37. Jerymane Beasley, of, Eastern Washington University.

38. *Blake Bodenmiller, lhp, West Orange HS, Orlando, Fla.

39. *Josh Andrade, rhp, Sandalwood HS, Jacksonville, Fla.

40. *Matt Allen, rhp, Vernon Regional (Texas) JC.

41. *Garrett Alwert, lhp, Bethel HS, Puyallup, Wash.

42. *Bryan Erstad, of, Jamestown (N.D.) HS.

DRAFT DROP *Brother of Darin Erstad, first overall draft pick, Angels (1995); major leaguer (1996-2009)*

43. Nate Rewers, 2b, University of Richmond.

44. *Marlyn Tisdale, rhp, University of Tennessee.

45. Paul Brown, lhp, Citrus (Calif.) JC.

46. *Matt Lynch, lhp, John Carroll HS, Fort Pierce, Fla.

47. Leon Smith, of, Greenbrier HS, Appling, Ga.

48. *Scott Hindman, lhp, Fremd HS, Inverness, Ill.

49. *Gerrit Simpson, rhp, Connors State (Okla.) CC.

50. *Cory Whitlock, ss, De Soto (Texas) HS.

## CLEVELAND INDIANS (23)

1. (Choice to Orioles as compensation for Type A free agent Roberto Alomar)

2. Will Hartley, c, Bradford HS, Starke, Fla.—(Rookie)

3. Eric Johnson, of, Western Carolina University.—(AA)

**4. *Jeff Baker, ss, Gar-Field HS, Woodbridge, Va.—(2005-15)**

DRAFT DROP *Attended Clemson; re-drafted by Rockies, 2002 (4th round)*

5. Curtis Gay, 1b, Oklahoma City University.—(Low

A)
6. Shane Wallace, lhp, Newman Smith HS, Carrollton, Texas.
7. *Daylon Monette, of, A.B. Miller HS, Fontana, Calif.
8. Devin Rogers, rhp, Nicholls State University.
9. Stephen Cowie, rhp, Duke University.
**10. Fernando Cabrera, rhp, Discipulos de Cristo HS, Bayamon, P.R.—(2004-10)**
11. *Monte Mansfield, rhp, Hesperia (Calif.) HS.
12. Francis Finnerty, c, Wellington (Fla.) Community HS.
13. Adam Barr, lhp, South Williamsport Area HS, Williamsport, Pa.
14. Josh Martin, lhp, Wyman King Academy, Columbia, S.C.
15. Brody Lynn, ss, Kapaun-Mount Carmel HS, Wichita, Kan.
16. Anthony Marini, lhp, Kennesaw State University.
17. Chris Kelley, rhp, College of William & Mary.
18. Kyle Moyer, 1b, Mohawk Local HS, Tiffin, Ohio.
19. Travis Santini, of, Lely HS, Naples, Fla.
20. *Louis Wieben, lhp, St. Mary HS, Secaucus, N.J.
**21. +Jason Davis, rhp, Cleveland State (Tenn.) CC.—(2002-08)**
22. *Jeffrey Reboin, lhp, Sacramento (Calif.) CC.
23. *Anthony Tomey, rhp, Catholic Central HS, Northville, Mich.
24. Phil Rosengren, rhp, Northwestern University.
25. Chris Lotterhos, 2b, Mississippi State University.
**26. Kyle Denney, rhp, University of Oklahoma.—(2004)**
27. *Jordan Olson, lhp, Crescenta Valley HS, La Crescenta, Calif.
28. *Matthew Spiess, rhp, Owosso (Mich.) HS.
29. *Roberto Vega, c, Adela Brenes Texidor HS, Guayama, P.R.
30. *William McKenzie, rhp, Sullivan South HS, Kingsport, Tenn.
31. Leyson Rivera, rhp, Luz A. Calderon HS, Carolina, P.R.
**32. *Ben Francisco, of, Servite HS, Fullerton, Calif.—(2007-13)**
33. *Scott Thomas, rhp, Watervliet (Mich.) HS.
34. *Kerry Hodges, of, New Mexico JC.
35. Mike Byrd, rhp, Vanderbilt University.
36. *Jerad Doty, of, Rio Vista (Texas) HS.
37. Teddy Sullivan, rhp, Duke University.
38. John Christ, rhp, Johns Hopkins (Md.) University.
39. Byron Ewing, 1b, Howard University.
40. *Neil Dudkowski, lhp, Lassen (Calif.) JC.
**41. *Royce Ring, lhp, Monte Vista HS, La Mesa, Calif.—(2005-10)**
DRAFT DROP *First-round draft pick (18th overall), White Sox (2002)*
42. *Anthony Lunetta, ss, Arlington HS, Riverside, Calif.
43. *Brad Harrison, of, Mandarin HS, Jacksonville, Fla.
44. *Michael Bishop, of-c, Kansas State University.
DRAFT DROP *Quarterback, National Football League (2000)*
45. *Doug Johnson, rhp, Pelham (N.H.) HS.
46. +Jeff Becker, 3b, Duke University.
47. Sammy Button, lhp, Jacksonville State University.
48. Simon Young, lhp, Georgia Tech.
49. *Neal Maybin, of, Brevard (Fla.) CC.
**50. *John Gall, 1b, Stanford University.—(2005-07)**

## COLORADO ROCKIES (16)

**1. Jason Jennings, rhp, Baylor University.—(2001-09)**
2. Ryan Kibler, rhp, King HS, Tampa.—(AA)
**3. Josh Bard, c, Texas Tech.—(2002-11)**
4. Chuck Crowder, lhp, Georgia Tech.—(AA)
5. Chris Testa, of, Palmdale (Calif.) HS.—(High A)
6. Roney Johnson, rhp, Woodcreek HS, Antelope, Calif.
7. Carlos Figueroa, ss, Gilberto Concepcion HS, Carolina, P.R.
8. Greg Catalanotte, of, University of Florida.
9. Colin Young, lhp, Fordham University.
10. Sean Daly, c, Golden West HS, Visalia, Calif.
11. Chris Moore, ss, Western Carolina University.
**12. Craig House, rhp, Memphis State University.—(2000)**
13. Rick Cercy, rhp, Morehead State University.
14. Eric McQueen, c, Georgia Tech.
15. Danny Phillips, 3b-of, Cal State Northridge.
16. Cam Esslinger, rhp, Seton Hall University.
17. Billy Gasparino, ss, Oklahoma State University.
18. *Brandon Caraway, 2b, University of Houston.
19. Dave Mulqueen, 3b, Marquette HS, Milwaukee.
20. Chris Warren, c, Howard University.
21. Matt Hoffman, rhp, Oral Roberts University.
22. *Darin Naatjes, of, West Lyon HS, Alvord, Iowa.
23. Javier Lorenzo, rhp, Miami-Dade CC.
24. Deryck Christensen, rhp, Eastside Catholic HS, Issaquah, Wash.
25. Ray Aguilar, lhp, Cypress (Calif.) JC.
26. *Bobby Brownlie, rhp, Edison (N.J.) HS.
DRAFT DROP *First-round draft pick (21st overall), Cubs (2002)*
27. +Michael Tejada, c, Brigham Young University.
**28. Justin Hampson, lhp, Belleville Area (Ill.) CC.—(2006-12)**
29. *Bryce Coppieters, of, Lethbridge (Alberta) CC.
30. *Rick Sander, rhp, Riverside (Calif.) CC.
31. *Andy Warren, rhp, Sam Houston State University.
32. *Casey Kelly, 1b, Westview HS, Portland, Ore.
**33. *Darren Clarke, rhp, H.B. Plant HS, Tampa.—(2007)**
34. *Joe Curran, lhp, Edmonds (Wash.) CC.
35. *Don Tolen, rhp, Orange Glen HS, Escondido, Calif.
36. *Tommy MacLane, lhp, St. Petersburg (Fla.) CC.
37. *Chad Liter, of, Madison Consolidated HS, Madison, Ind.
38. *Jason Kramer, lhp, Marcus HS, Flower Mound, Texas.
39. *Billy Dennis, of, Devine HS, Big Foot, Texas.
40. *Nicholas Gor, rhp, Esperanza HS, Yorba Linda, Calif.
41. *Eli Lapka, ss, Dodge City (Kan.) HS.
42. *Grant Mullen, 1b, St. Christopher's SS, Corunna, Ontario.
43. *Cortney Inman, rhp, Parkview HS, Springfield, Mo.
44. *Nick Loughren, rhp, Bishop Verot HS, Cape Coral, Fla.
45. *Nick McCurdy, rhp, Jefferson Davis (Ala.) JC.
46. +T.J. Bird, of, Mendocino (Calif.) CC.
47. *Kendall Jones, c, Broken Arrow (Okla.) HS.
48. *Manases Pabon, of, Indian Hills (Iowa) CC.
49. *Billy Wheeler, rhp, Crown Point (Ind.) HS.

## DETROIT TIGERS (3)

**1. Eric Munson, c, University of Southern California.—(2000-09)**
DRAFT DROP *First player from 1999 draft to reach majors (July 18, 2000)*
2. (Choice to Royals as compensation for Type A free agent Dean Palmer)
3. Neil Jenkins, 3b, William T. Dwyer HS, Jupiter, Fla.—(AA)
**4. Cody Ross, of, Carlsbad (N.M.) HS.—(2003-15)**
5. Dayle Campbell, of, Los Angeles Pierce JC.—(High A)
6. Brant Ust, 3b, University of Notre Dame.
7. Tim Kalita, lhp, University of Notre Dame.
8. Anthony Ware, 3b, Hamilton HS, Los Angeles.
9. Casey Rowe, rhp, Fresno State University.
10. Jerrod Fuell, rhp, Palo Verde HS, Tucson, Ariz.
11. Erick Burke, lhp, University of Houston.
12. Dan Davis, of, Osceola HS, Kissimmee, Fla.
13. Kevin Jackson, 3b, University of North Florida.
14. +Ross Garland, c, Walters State (Tenn.) CC.
15. Corey Richardson, of, New Mexico State University.
16. Stephen Bess, rhp, Rice University.
17. *Brad Steele, rhp, University of California.
18. Randy Leek, lhp, College of William & Mary.
19. Casey Williamson, of, Troy State University.
20. Dustin Beam, ss, Wright State University.
21. Corey McDonald, lhp, University of North Carolina-Greensboro.
22. Aaron Barnett, lhp, Middle Tennessee State University.
23. Jeremy Lewis, lhp, Central Cabarrus HS, Concord, N.C.
24. *Nathan Husser, 1b, Middletown HS, Newark, Del.
25. *Ed Romprey, ss, Fullerton (Calif.) JC.
26. Greg Watson, rhp, University of Tampa.
27. Johnny Gordon, of, Warner Southern (Fla.) College.
28. *Ryan Golem, rhp, Dearborn (Mich.) HS.
29. *Tim Leveque, rhp, Crespi HS, Northridge, Calif.
30. *Joe Urban, of, Santa Ana (Calif.) JC.
31. *Randy Thurman, lhp, Ringling (Okla.) HS.
**32. +Eric Eckenstahler, lhp, Illinois State University.—(2002-03)**
**33. Jason Frasor, rhp, Southern Illinois University.—(2004-15)**
34. Robert Hlousek, 3b, University of Missouri-St. Louis.
35. *Dennis Wyrick, ss, Bishop Amat HS, Azusa, Calif.
36. Jason Siegfried, c, University of Dayton.
37. +Miles Luuloa, ss, Laney (Calif.) CC.
38. *Corey Loomis, ss, Eastwood HS, Pemberville, Ohio.
39. *Kaulana Kuhaulua, ss, Los Angeles CC.
DRAFT DROP *Son of Fred Kuhaulua, major leaguer (1977-81)*
40. *Francisco Arteaga, rhp, Roosevelt HS, Los Angeles.
41. +John-Eric Hernandez, rhp, Cal State Chico.
42. *Peter Pirman, of, Triton (Ill.) JC.
43. *Phillip Mixter, rhp, Muskegon (Mich.) HS.
44. Jayson Drobiak, ss, University of Connecticut.

## FLORIDA MARLINS (2)

**1. Josh Beckett, rhp, Spring (Texas) HS.—(2001-14)**
DRAFT DROP *First 1999 high school draft pick to reach majors (Sept. 4, 2001)*
2. Terry Byron, rhp, Indian River (Fla.) JC.—(High A)
**3. Josh Wilson, ss, Mount Lebanon HS, Pittsburgh.—(2007-15)**
4. Dominic Woody, c, University of Washington.—(High A)
**5. Nate Robertson, lhp, Wichita State University.—(2002-10)**
6. Charlie Frazier, of, Toms River (N.J.) South HS.
DRAFT DROP *Brother of Todd Frazier, first-round draft pick, Reds (2007); major leaguer (2011-15)*
7. Jake Laidlaw, ss, Cheyenne HS, Las Vegas, Nev.
**8. Kevin Hooper, 2b, Wichita State University.—(2005-06)**
9. Ben Hickman, rhp, Louisiana Tech.
10. Scott Goodman, of, Arizona State University.
**11. Randy Messenger, rhp, Sparks (Nev.) HS.—(2005-09)**
12. Angel Sanchez, c, Vineland (N.J.) HS.
13. Bryan Moore, rhp, University of Houston.
14. Todd Moser, lhp, Florida Atlantic University.
15. Barry Schell, of, Palomar (Calif.) JC.
16. Jared Wykoff, rhp, Kinder (La.) HS.
17. Brad Haynes, rhp, Barren County HS, Glasgow, Ky.
18. David Johnston, rhp, Marshalltown (Iowa) HS.
19. Kevin Perkins, 2b, UC Riverside.
20. Shane Smuin, rhp, Utah Valley State JC.
21. Joe Sergent, lhp, Lamar University.
22. James Close, of, University of Nevada-Las Vegas.
23. *Jarrod Schmidt, 1b-rhp, Lassiter HS, Marietta, Ga.
24. Bryan Morse, lhp, Mount Olive (N.C.) College.
25. Dennis Anderson, c, University of Arizona.
26. Keith Herbert, ss, Boonsboro HS, Keedysvile, Md.
27. Thomas Bell, rhp, George Marshall HS, Vienna, Va.
28. Matt Ward, lhp, Texas A&M University.
29. Matt Postell, 1b, North Carolina State University.
30. Brandon Bowe, rhp, Louisiana State University.
31. *Kenny Riley, c, Reed HS, Sparks, Nev.
32. *Dustin Griffith, rhp, Dakota Ridge HS, Littleton, Colo.
33. +Mike Flannery, rhp, Gloucester County (N.J.) CC.
34. *John Moylan, c, Canada (Calif.) JC.
35. Enrique Mendieta, of, Norfolk State University.
36. *Kevin Snowden, of, Eleanor Roosevelt HS, Lanham, Md.
37. *Derek Caraway, rhp, Andalusia (Ala.) HS.
38. *Robert Glaser, of, San Joaquin Delta (Calif.) JC.
39. *Chance Scott, ss, Pleasant Grove (Utah) HS.
40. *Matt Krabbe, rhp, Triton (Ill.) JC.
41. *Jeff Nichols, rhp, Rice University.
**42. *Adam LaRoche, 1b, Fort Scott (Kan.) CC.—(2004-15)**
DRAFT DROP *Son of Dave LaRoche, major leaguer (1970-83) • Brother of Andy LaRoche, major leaguer (2007-13)*
43. *Darin Phalines, rhp, Gloucester County (N.J.) CC.
44. Alonso Gomez, 3b, JC of San Mateo (Calif.).
45. *John Anderson, rhp, Pine Bluff (Ark.) HS.
46. *Ben Vannatter, c, Amelia (Ohio) HS.
47. *Jacob Robertson, of, Twin Falls (Idaho) HS.
48. Quian Davis, of, Buena Regional HS, Minotola, N.J.
49. *John Zamora, rhp, Cabrillo (Calif.) JC.
50. *Anthony Aceves, of, Howard HS, Columbia, Md.

## HOUSTON ASTROS (29)

1. (Choice to Padres as compensation for Type A free agent Ken Caminiti)
1. Mike Rosamond, of, University of Mississippi (Supplemental choice—42nd—as compensation for Type A free agent Randy Johnson).—(AAA)
2. Jay Perez, c, Seymour (Conn.) HS (Choice from Diamondbacks as compensation for Johnson).—(Rookie)
2. Travis Anderson, rhp, University of Washington.—(AA)
3. Jimmy Barrett, rhp, Fort Hill HS, Cumberland, Md.—(High A)
4. Jon Topolski, of, Baylor University.—(AAA)
**5. Mike Gallo, lhp, Long Beach State University.—(2003-06)**
**6. Jason Lane, of, University of Southern California.—(2002-14)**
7. Nick Roberts, rhp, Southern Utah University.
**8. Chris Sampson, ss-rhp, Texas Tech.—(2006-10)**
9. Jon Helquist, ss, University Christian HS, Jacksonville, Fla.
**10. *Greg Dobbs, 3b, Long Beach State University.—(2004-14)**
11. Kris Kann, rhp, Mansfield (Pa.) University.
12. Royce Huffman, 3b, Texas Christian University.
13. Garett Gentry, c, Victor Valley (Calif.) CC.
14. Brian Schmitt, 1b, Blinn (Texas) JC.
15. *Bryan Edwards, rhp, Northeast Texas CC.
16. Daniel Parker, rhp, Diablo Valley (Calif.) JC.
17. Ryan Jamison, rhp, University of Missouri.
18. Mike Hill, of-2b, Oral Roberts University.
19. Jon Andrianoff, ss, Portville Central HS, Olean, N.Y.
20. Derrick Johnson, lhp, Wallace State (Ala.) CC.
21. *Russ Morgan, lhp, Purdue University.
22. *Stephen Ghutzman, c, Spring (Texas) HS.
23. Jason Maule, 2b, Central Connecticut State University.
24. Brian O'Connor, c, Valparaiso University.
25. Chris George, rhp, University of Missouri.
26. *Lance Ericksen, rhp, University of Utah.
27. *Shane Hall, rhp, Sierra Vista HS, Hereford, Ariz.
**28. *Marc Gwyn, rhp, Rice University.—(2007)**
29. *David Frame, rhp, Westfield HS, Houston.
30. *Steven Mortimer, 1b, Richland (Wash.) HS.
31. *Javier Andueza, rhp, West Valley (Calif.) JC.
32. *Billy Zbacnik, 1b, University HS, San Diego.
33. Steven Hoover, of, Cal State Stanislaus.
34. J.C. Ortiz, lhp, University of New Mexico.
35. *Justin Toone, rhp, Kingwood (Texas) HS.
36. +Jordan Hunt, rhp, Edmonds (Wash.) CC.
37. +Abraham Ayala, 3b, Miami-Dade CC.
38. *Deshain Beasley, of, Kamiakin HS, Kennewick, Wash.
39. Jeffrey Blitstein, rhp, Chapman (Calif.) College.
40. *Darrick Bingham, rhp, Canada (Calif.) JC.
41. *Ray Leyba, lhp, Cowley County (Kan.) CC.

## KANSAS CITY ROYALS (7)

**1. Kyle Snyder, rhp, University of North Carolina.—(2003-08)**
**1. Mike MacDougal, rhp, Wake Forest University** (Choice from Red Sox as compensation for Type A free agent Jose Offerman).—**(2001-12)**
1. Jay Gehrke, rhp, Pepperdine University (Supplemental choice—32nd—as compensation for Offerman).—(High A)
**1. Jimmy Gobble, lhp, John Battle HS,**

**Bristol, Va.** (Supplemental choice—43rd—as compensation for Type A free agent Dean Palmer).**—(2003-09)**
**2. Brian Sanches, rhp, Lamar University** (Choice from Tigers as compensation for Palmer).**—(2007-12)**
**2. Wes Obermueller, rhp, University of Iowa.—(2002-07)**
3. *Kiki Bengochea, rhp, Christopher Columbus HS, Miami.—(High A)
DRAFT DROP *Attended Miami (Fla.); re-drafted by Rangers, 2002 (11th round)*
4. Mackeel Rodgers, ss, Jackson HS, Miami.—(Low A)
**5. Ken Harvey, 1b, University of Nebraska.—(2001-05)**
6. Ryan Baerlocher, rhp, Lewis-Clark State (Idaho) College.
7. Jim McAuley, c, University of Louisville.
8. Eric Nelson, 2b, Baylor University.
**9. Mark Ellis, ss, University of Florida.—(2002-14)**
10. Jesse Kurtz-Nicholl, lhp, Rice University.
11. Edwin Franco, lhp, Florida International University.
**12. Tony Cogan, lhp, Stanford University.—(2001)**
13. G.J. Raymundo, 3b, Pepperdine University.
14. Jarrett Shearin, of, University of North Carolina.
15. Casey Dunn, c, Auburn University.
DRAFT DROP *Baseball coach, Samford (2005-15)*
16. *Sam Smith, rhp, Trinidad State (Colo.) JC.
17. Brad Stiles, lhp, Lamar (Colo.) HS.
**18. *Brandon Medders, rhp, Shelton State (Ala.) CC.—(2005-10)**
19. Jermaine Smiley, of, Bellevue (Wash.) CC.
20. *Juan Figueroa, rhp, Jose M. Lazaro HS, Carolina, P.R.
21. *Brian Nagore, c, James Logan HS, Hayward, Calif.
**22. Chad Santos, 1b, St. Louis HS, Kaneohe, Hawaii.—(2006)**
23. *Pat Magness, 1b, Wichita State University.
24. Brian Johnson, c, University of Nebraska.
25. Chris Cabaj, rhp, Ball State University.
26. Raul Garcia, rhp, Florida International University.
27. *Ben Carter, c, Bowie (Texas) HS.
28. *Brian Lockwood, rhp, Torrance (Calif.) HS.
29. *Lukas Guidroz, rhp, Enterprise State (Ala.) JC.
30. *Richard Frink, c, Mission Bay HS, San Diego.
31. *Jason Crear, of, King HS, Houston.
32. *Jason Arre, lhp, Toms River South HS, Beachwood, N.J.
33. Michael Clay, ss-c, Southeastern Oklahoma State University.
34. *William Austin, rhp, Salina (Okla.) HS.
35. *Marcus Wyatt, of, Fontana (Calif.) HS.
36. Julian Gonzalez, of, University of Virginia.
**37. *Bryan Bullington, rhp, Madison (Ind.) Consolidated HS.—(2005-10)**
DRAFT DROP *First overall draft pick, Pirates (2002)*
38. *Adam Lingenfelter, rhp, Florida CC.
39. Abel Garcia, lhp, Laredo (Texas) JC.
40. *Jason Fransz, of, Arlington HS, San Jacinto, Calif.
41. *Herman Wright, of, Odem (Texas) HS.
42. *Anthony Mercado, rhp, Veve Calzada HS, Fajardo, P.R.
43. Keronn Walker, c, Bluefield (Va.) College.
44. *Shane Menn, rhp, Calallen HS, Robstown, Texas.
45. Jacob Baker, 1b, Rice University.
46. *Jason Maloney, rhp, Stranahan HS, Fort Lauderdale, Fla.
47. *Greg Bauer, rhp, Wichita State University.
48. *Lee Peach, rhp, Memorial HS, Newburgh, Ind.
49. +Kyle Middleton, rhp, Jefferson Davis (Ala.) JC.
50. +Byron Russell, of, Pamlico County HS, Bayboro, N.C. / Southeastern (N.C.) CC.

## LOS ANGELES DODGERS (20)

1. (Choice to Padres as compensation for Type A free agent Kevin Brown)
**1. Jason Repko, ss-of, Hanford HS, West Richland, Wash.** (Supplemental choice—37th—as compensation for Type A free agent Scott Radinsky).**—(2005-12)**
2. Brennan King, ss, Oakland HS, Murfreesboro, Tenn. (Choice from Cardinals as compensation for Radinsky).—(AAA)
2. (Choice to Diamondbacks as compensation for Type A free agent Devon White)
**2. *Drew Meyer, ss-of, Bishop England HS, Charleston, S.C.** (Supplemental choice—83rd—as compensation for Type C free agent Brian Bohanon).**—(2006)**
DRAFT DROP *Attended South Carolina; re-drafted by Rangers, 2002 (1st round)*
3. (Choice to Orioles as compensation for Type B free agent Alan Mills)
**4. Joe Thurston, ss, Sacramento (Calif.) CC.—(2002-11)**
5. Phil Devey, lhp, University of Southwestern Louisiana.—(AAA)
**6. Shane Victorino, of, St. Anthony's HS, Wailuku, Hawaii.—(2003-15)**
7. Jose Escalera, of, Carlos Escobar Lopez HS, Loiza, P.R.
8. T.J. Nall, rhp, Schaumburg (Ill.) HS.
9. Jonathan Berry, rhp, Newberry (S.C.) College.
10. Lamont Matthews, of, Oklahoma State University.
**11. Eric Junge, rhp, Bucknell University.—(2002-03)**
12. Josh Dalton, ss, Louisiana State University.
13. Jon Hale, c, Southwest Missouri State University.
14. Randy Hadden, rhp, University of South Carolina.
15. Wade Parrish, lhp, Washington State University.
16. *Tymber Lee, rhp, Wichita State University.
17. Scott Martin, rhp, Central Connecticut State University.
18. John Rozich, c, Kutztown (Pa.) University.
19. Harold Eckert, rhp, Florida International University.
20. *Ryan Hamilton, rhp, University of San Diego.
21. Chris Snow, of, Desert Vista HS, Phoenix.
22. *Tim Cunningham, lhp, Rocklin (Calif.) HS.
**23. +Reggie Abercrombie, of, Columbus (Ga.) HS / Lake City (Fla.) CC.—(2006-08)**
**24. *Shane Nance, lhp, University of Houston.—(2002-04)**
25. *Clint Chauncey, c, Terry Parker HS, Jacksonville, Fla.
26. *Traviss Hodge, 1b, Los Angeles Pierce JC.
27. *Lucas Robertson, rhp, Butler County (Kan.) CC.
28. +Mike Keirstead, rhp, St. Malachy's HS, St. John, New Brunswick / Eastern Oklahoma State JC.
29. *Zach Cates, 1b, Mesa (Ariz.) CC.
30. *Ryan Brnardic, rhp, Sandwich SS, LaSalle, Ontario.
31. *Justin Glenn, of, Sheridan HS, Little Rock, Ark.
32. *Nolan McManus, rhp, Sierra (Calif.) JC.
33. Clif Wren, c, Mississippi State University.
34. *Nom Siriveaw, of, Eastern Oklahoma State JC.
35. *Kegan O'Toole, c, Jackson HS, Bothell, Wash.
36. *Ryan Harris, rhp, Woodstock (New Brunswick) HS.
37. *Miguel Heredia, rhp, Eastern Oklahoma State JC.
38. *Chris Hunter, rhp, Mountain View HS, Lindon, Utah.
39. *Chris Hanne, lhp, Duluth (Ga.) HS.
40. *Michael Pelsnik, rhp, Horizon HS, Phoenix.
41. Keith Godbolt, of, Hillsborough HS, Tampa.
42. *Rob Harrand, rhp, Regina, Sask.
43. *Kyle Bateman, rhp, Coconino HS, Flagstaff, Ariz.
44. *Robby Sumner, 1b, Pace (Fla.) HS.
45. *Erik Lohse, rhp, Butte (Calif.) JC.
DRAFT DROP *Brother of Kyle Lohse, major leaguer (2001-15)*
46. *Chris Bell, rhp, Christopher Columbus HS, Miami.
47. *Joey Black, rhp, Bonneville HS, Ogden, Utah.
48. *Scott Wilson, c, Ellensburg (Wash.) HS.
49. *Jayson Casiano, 1b, Monserrate Leon de Irriza HS, Cabo Rojo, P.R.
50. *Jonathan Morel, 1b, Colegio San Agustin HS, Cabo Rojo, P.R.

## MILWAUKEE BREWERS (10)

**1. Ben Sheets, rhp, Northeast Louisiana University.—(2001-12)**
DRAFT DROP *Cousin of Andy Sheets, major leaguer (1996-2002)*
2. Kade Johnson, c, Seminole State (Okla.) JC.—(AA)
**3. Ruddy Lugo, rhp, Xaverian HS, Brooklyn, N.Y.—(2006-07)**
DRAFT DROP *Brother of Julio Lugo, major leaguer (2000-11)*
4. Travis Horne, lhp, First Coast HS, Jacksonville, Fla.—(Rookie)
5. +Dustin Lansford, rhp, McLennan (Texas) CC.—(Low A)
6. Mark Ernster, 2b, Arizona State University.
7. Jeff Robinson, rhp, University of Southwestern Louisiana.
**8. David Pember, rhp, Western Carolina University.—(2002)**
9. Bryan Tindell, c, Avon Park (Fla.) HS.
**10. Ben Hendrickson, rhp, Jefferson HS, Bloomington, Minn.—(2004-06)**
11. Will Ford, of, Rice University.
12. Frank Wagner, lhp, University of Minnesota.
13. Terry Mayo, of, Eastern Guilford HS, Greensboro, N.C.
14. Steven Truitt, of, Texas A&M University.
15. Chris McGee, rhp, Mansfield (Pa.) University.
16. *Jason Tibesar, of, South Mountain (Ariz.) CC.
17. Chris Olean, rhp, University of St. Thomas (Minn.).
18. Steve Scarborough, ss, Texas A&M University.
19. *Will Hudson, ss, Fountain Valley (Calif.) HS.
20. Kevin Grater, rhp, University of Wisconsin-Oshkosh.
21. Ben Wallace, lhp, Quarbin HS, Hubbardston, Mass.
22. *Chad Clark, rhp, Glendora (Calif.) HS.
23. *Chad Sadowski, rhp, University of Wisconsin-Milwaukee.
24. Ryan Knox, of, Illinois State University.
25. Casey Trout, ss, University of Maryland.
26. Anthony Forelli, 1b, Old Dominion University.
27. Brad Ralston, rhp, Texas Tech.
28. Jeremy Durkee, lhp, Cuyahoga Falls (Ohio) HS.
29. Darrell Gaston, rhp, University of Mobile (Ala.).
30. Robert Pregnolato, of, Palm Beach Atlantic (Fla.) College.
31. Corey Artieta, lhp, Northeast Louisiana University.
32. Justin Gordon, lhp, Massasoit (Mass.) CC.
33. Chris Schilling, c, Daniel HS, Central, S.C.
34. Jason Kelley, rhp, Bowling Green State University.
35. Jeff Kenney, ss, University of Richmond.
36. Jeremy Krismer, rhp, Oklahoma State University.
37. *Devin Butler, 1b, Hillsborough (Fla.) JC.
38. *Matt Gieble, lhp, Woodland (Calif.) HS.
39. *Sean Sivers, lhp, Kearny HS, San Diego.
40. Jeff House, rhp, Stetson University.
41. J.J. January, ss, Callaway HS, Jackson, Miss.
42. Brian Foster, c, Western Alamance HS, Burlington, N.C.
43. Chris Simonson, rhp, University of Wisconsin.
44. *William Vazquez, rhp, Indian Hills (Iowa) CC.
45. *Jason France, lhp, Central Arizona JC.
46. +Josh Lake, c, Buena HS, Ventura, Calif. / Ventura (Calif.) JC.
47. *Ryan Warpinski, rhp, Denmark HS, Maribel, Wis.
48. *Amos Burgess, of, Lone Peak (Utah) HS.
49. *Blair Bourque, of, Taunton (Mass.) HS.

## MINNESOTA TWINS (5)

1. B.J. Garbe, of, Moses Lake (Wash.) HS.—(AA)
**2. Rob Bowen, c, Homestead HS, Fort Wayne, Ind.—(2003-08)**
**3. Justin Morneau, c, New Westminster (B.C.) SS.—(2003-15)**
4. Jeff Randazzo, lhp, Cardinal O'Hara HS, Broomall, Pa.—(AA)
5. Brent Schoening, rhp, Auburn University.—(AAA)
**6. Brian Wolfe, rhp, Servite HS, Anaheim, Calif.—(2007-09)**
7. *Darren Ciraco, of, Pelham Memorial HS, Pelham, N.Y.
8. Matt Scanlon, 3b, University of Minnesota.
9. *Grant Gregg, lhp, McLennan (Texas) CC.
10. *Jim Caine, rhp, St. Charles (Ill.) HS.
11. *Mike Prochaska, lhp, Leesville Road HS, Raleigh, N.C.
12. *Kevin Johnson, rhp, University of California.
13. *Seth Morris, rhp-of, Hamilton (Ohio) HS.
**14. *Brian Slocum, rhp, Iona Prep School, Eastchester, N.Y.—(2006-08)**
15. *John Wilson, c-of, University of Kentucky.
16. Kevin West, of, Mendocino (Fla.) CC.
17. *John Larson, rhp, Eastern Illinois University.
18. Barry Quickstad, 2b, Waseca (Minn.) HS.
19. Paul Poplin, rhp, University of North Carolina-Charlotte.
**20. Travis Bowyer, rhp, Liberty HS, Bedford, Va.—(2005)**
21. Chad Wandall, ss, Auburn University.
22. Ricky Manning, of, Edison HS, Fresno, Calif.
DRAFT DROP *Defensive back, National Football League (2003-08)*
**23. Willie Eyre, rhp, JC of Eastern Utah.—(2006-11)**
DRAFT DROP *Brother of Scott Eyre, major leaguer (1997-2009)*
24. *Danny Matienzo, c, Christopher Columbus HS, Miami.
25. *Craig Patterson, c, Cal State Fullerton.
**26. Terry Tiffee, 1b, Pratt (Kan.) CC.—(2004-08)**
27. Jess Turner, rhp, Centralia (Wash.) JC.
28. Brad Weis, lhp, Auburn University.
29. Sherwin Lockridge, ss, Florida A&M University.
30. Matt Reed, ss, Haines City (Fla.) HS.
31. *Ryan Miller, rhp, University of Evansville.
32. *Jeff Balser, rhp, Venice (Fla.) HS.
33. *Billy Keppinger, of, Lake City (Ga.) CC.
34. +John Thomman, of, Levelland (Texas) HS / Odessa (Texas) JC.
35. Jason Richardson, rhp, Polk (Fla.) CC.
36. *Joey Monahan, ss, Wheeler HS, Marietta, Ga.
DRAFT DROP *Great-grandson of Howie Morenz, hockey Hall of Famer (1923-37) • Grandson of Boom Boom Geoffrion, hockey Hall of Famer (1951-68) • Son of Hartland Monahan, NHL player (1973-81) • Brother of Shane Monahan, major leaguer (1998-99)*
37. Digno Torres, of, Lake City (Fla.) CC.
38. +Scott Blackwell, rhp, Lincoln Land (Ill.) CC.
39. *Beau Vaughan, rhp, Mountain Ridge HS, Glendale, Ariz.
40. +Richard Smart, lhp, Gulf Coast (Fla.) CC.
41. *Michael Stavey, 1b, Eustis (Fla.) HS.
42. Michael Wrenn, c, St. Leo (Fla.) College.
43. Bryan Williamson, of, University of Washington.
44. *Charles Campbell, rhp, Bay HS, Panama City, Fla.
**45. *Pat Neshek, rhp, Park Center HS, Brooklyn Park, Minn.—(2006-15)**
46. *Maurice Powell, rhp, Upland HS, Alta Loma, Calif.
47. *Luke Field, rhp, Barton County (Kan.) CC.
48. *Casey Rauschenberger, 3b, Oakland HS, Murfreesboro, Tenn.
49. *David Slevin, ss, John Carroll HS, Port St. Lucie, Fla.
50. *Joseph Ammirato, of, Marina HS, Long Beach, Calif.

## MONTREAL EXPOS (6)

1. Josh Girdley, lhp, Jasper (Texas) HS.—(High A)
**2. Brandon Phillips, ss, Redan HS, Stone Mountain, Ga.—(2002-15)**
3. Drew McMillan, c, El Dorado HS, Placentia, Calif.—(AA)
**4. Matt Cepicky, of, Southwest Missouri State University.—(2002-06)**
5. Pat Collins, rhp, St. John's University.—(AA)
6. Dom Ambrosini, of, Connetquot HS, Ronkonkoma, N.Y.
7. Bret Boyer, ss, Largo (Fla.) HS.
DRAFT DROP *Son of Cletis Boyer, major leaguer (1955-71)*
8. Luke Lockwood, lhp, Silverado HS, Victorville, Calif.
**9. Brandon Watson, 2b, Westchester HS, Los Angeles.—(2005-07)**
10. Grant Dorn, rhp, North Carolina State University.
11. David Lutz, of, Monte Vista HS, Spring Valley, Calif.
12. *Brian Stavisky, of, Port Allegany (Pa.) HS.
13. Chris Humrich, rhp, Armstrong Atlantic State (Ga.) University.
14. Brian Preston, c, Wichita State University.
**15. Val Pascucci, rhp, University of Oklahoma.—(2004-11)**

**16. Matt Watson, 3b-2b, Xavier University.—(2003-10)**
17. Josh Emmerick, c, Rancho Buena Vista HS, Oceanside, Calif.
18. *Pat Wyrick, rhp, Atoka (Okla.) HS.
19. *Pierre Blount, of, Colton (Calif.) HS.
20. *Leonard Landeros, lhp, Hanford (Calif.) HS.
21. Mark Thomas, 1b, Youngstown State University.
22. Matt Brown, 3b, Eastern Randolph HS, Randleman, N.C.
23. *Israel Torres, lhp, Cerritos (Calif.) JC.
24. Eric Charron, rhp, Marie-Anne HS, Montreal.
25. Chuck Crumpton, rhp, Arizona State University.
26. Lou Melucci, 2b, University of Pittsburgh.
27. *Manuel Diaz, rhp, John Glenn HS, Norwalk, Calif.
28. *Mike Natale, rhp, Santa Ana (Calif.) JC.
29. *Francisco Chavez, rhp, Socorro HS, El Paso, Texas.
30. *Alex Groleau, rhp, Edouard Montpetit HS, Montreal.
31. +Jason Norderum, lhp, Shasta HS, Redding, Calif. / Sacramento (Calif.) CC.
32. *Jason Stevenson, lhp, Foothill HS, Redding, Calif.
33. *Victor Rosario, of, Sandalwood HS, Jacksonville, Fla.
34. +Eric Langill, c, Des Moines Area (Iowa) CC.
35. Todd Johannes, c, University of Florida.
36. *Jerry Alexander, ss, Westchester HS, Hawthorne, Calif.
37. *Julio Acosta, c, Perkiomen School, Pennsburg, Pa.
38. *Joseph Clark, rhp, JC of Southern Idaho.
39. *Travis Edwards, of, Cerritos (Calif.) JC.
40. *Wes Cain, rhp, Marietta (Okla.) HS.
41. *Jonnie Mazzeo, rhp, LaSalle SS, Kingston, Ontario.
42. *Grant Oltjenbruns, of, Fresno (Calif.) CC.
43. *Chris Sieman, c, Blanchard (Okla.) HS.
44. *Charles Rohr, rhp, Citrus (Calif.) JC.
45. *Chris Richard, of, Norwalk (Conn.) CC.
46. *Matt Alexander, c, Trinidad State (Colo.) JC.
47. *Matt Romero, of, Utah Valley State JC.
48. Antonio Garris, 3b-of, Pitt (N.C.) CC.

## NEW YORK METS (22)

1. (Choice to White Sox as compensation for Type A free agent Robin Ventura)
**2. Neal Musser, lhp, Benton Central HS, Otterbein, Ind.—(2007-08)**
2. Jake Joseph, rhp, Cosumnes River (Calif.) JC (Supplemental choice—84th—as compensation for Type C free agent Armando Reynoso).—(AAA)
**3. Jeremy Griffiths, rhp, University of Toledo.—(2003-04)**
**4. +Angel Pagan, of, Republica De Colombia HS, Rio Piedras, P.R. / Indian River (Fla.) CC.—(2006-15)**
5. Nick James, rhp, Allan Hancock (Calif.) JC.—(Rookie)
6. *Tyler Parker, c, Lassiter HS, Marietta, Ga.
7. Rodney Nye, 3b, University of Arkansas.
DRAFT DROP *Brother of Ryan Nye, major leaguer (1997-98)*
8. Forrest Lawson, of, Rogers HS, Puyallup, Wash.
9. Wayne Lydon, of, Valley View HS, Jessup, Pa.
**10. Prentice Redman, of, Bevill State (Ala.) CC.—(2003)**
DRAFT DROP *Brother of Tike Redman, major leaguer (2000-07)*
11. Joey Cole, rhp, University of Texas-Pan American.
12. Paul Viole, rhp, Seton Hall University.
13. Robert McIntyre, ss, Hillsborough HS, Tampa.
14. John Hendricks, lhp, Wake Forest University.
15. Steven Elzy, c, University of New Mexico.
16. *Gene Desalme, lhp, St. Louis CC-Meramec.
17. Kevin Ciarrachi, c, University of Northern Iowa.
18. Matt Smith, rhp, Southwest Missouri State University.
19. *Jose Pabon, 2b, Potomac HS, Dumfries, Va.
20. *Rob Henkel, lhp, UCLA.
21. *Adam Manley, of, JC of Southern Idaho.
22. *Kyle Woods, of, University of Washington.
23. *Terry Jackson, ss, Westside HS, Augusta, Ga.
24. *Dustin Brisson, 1b, University of Central Florida.
25. Matt Dyer, c, Manchester (Ind.) College.
26. Brad Wright, of, UC Santa Barbara.
27. Sam Lopez, ss, Fresno (Calif.) CC.

Athletics first-rounder Barry Zito won 165 major league games with the A's and Giants

28. +Steve Bennett, rhp, Gonzaga University.
29. *Bryan Loeb, c, Baylor University.
30. Matt Mize, 2b, University of Texas-Arlington.
31. Orlando Roman, rhp, Indian Hills (Iowa) CC.
32. Brian Williamson, rhp, Cornell University.
33. Lionel Rogers, rhp, Fresno (Calif.) CC.
34. Pat O'Sullivan, of, Austin Peay State University.
35. *Jamie Gonzales, rhp, Porterville (Calif.) CC.
36. *Aaron Ledbetter, rhp, Cedarville HS, Fort Smith, Ark.
37. Graeme Brown, rhp, Brown University.
**38. Mike Jacobs, c, Grossmont (Calif.) JC.—(2005-12)**
39. *Carrington Fisk, rhp, Keene (N.H.) HS.
DRAFT DROP *Nephew of Carlton Fisk, major leaguer (1969-93)*
40. Cory Harris, of, Pensacola (Fla.) JC.
41. *Philip Perry, rhp, Walton HS, Marietta, Ga.
42. *Darius Shelby, of, Valley View HS, Moreno Valley, Calif.
43. *Ryan Hay, c, St. Paul SS, Niagara Falls, Ontario.
44. *Brian Kelly, rhp, Southaven HS, Olive Branch, Miss.
45. +Ross Peeples, lhp, Middle Georgia JC.
46. *Aaron Gureckis, of, Nashua (N.H.) HS.
47. *Andre DeCordova, ss, Monsignor Pace HS, Hialeah, Fla.
48. *Vincent White, of, John Abbott HS, Beaconsfield, Quebec.
49. *Eric Bernier, of, Edouard Montpetit HS, Montreal.
50. *John Hoyos, lhp, San Gabriel HS, Rosemead, Calif.

## NEW YORK YANKEES (27)

1. David Walling, rhp, University of Arkansas.—(AAA)
2. Tommy Winrow, of, Bishop Verot HS, Fort Myers, Fla.—(AA)
**3. Alex Graman, lhp, Indiana State University.—(2004-05)**
4. *Rob Corrado, rhp, Oakwood HS, Dayton, Ohio.—(Low A)
DRAFT DROP *Attended Kentucky; re-drafted by Rangers, 2002 (30th round)*
5. Seth Taylor, ss, University of South Alabama.—(AA)
6. Reggie Laplante, rhp, Ahuntsic College HS, Montreal.
**7. Andy Phillips, 3b, University of Alabama.—(2004-08)**
8. Scott Oliver, rhp, College of Charleston.
9. Jeff Leaumont, 1b, Louisiana State University.
10. Brad Ticehurst, of, University of Southern California.
11. *Jeffrey Moye, rhp, Seminole State (Okla.) JC.
12. Lou Witte, rhp, Xavier University.
13. Brian Peeples, lhp, First Coast HS, Jacksonville, Fla.
14. Todd Mitchell, ss, Illinois State University.
15. Casey Baker, ss, Towanda HS, Wysox, Pa.
16. Brian Grace, rhp, Louisiana State University.
17. Ricky Spears, rhp, Gore (Okla.) HS.
18. Dominic Correa, 2b, University of Southern California.
19. John Kremer, rhp, University of Evansville.
20. *Jesse Floyd, rhp, Nederland (Texas) HS.
21. Michael Aldridge, c, Eastern Michigan University.
22. *Chris Klosterman, 3b-of, Cypress (Calif.) JC.
23. Chad Sutter, c, Tulane University.
DRAFT DROP *Son of Bruce Sutter, major leaguer (1976-88)*
24. Joshua McCloud, rhp, Bowsher HS, Holland, Ohio.
25. *Brian Reed, rhp, Amory (Miss.) HS.
26. *Darin Davis, 2b, Palisades (Calif.) HS.
27. *John Dimercurio, c, Highlands Ranch (Colo.) HS.
28. *Chris Dobbins, rhp, Central Alabama CC.
29. *Sean Lichter, rhp, Deer Valley HS, Glendale, Ariz.
**30. *Sean Henn, lhp, Aledo (Texas) HS.—(2005-13)**
**31. +Kevin Thompson, ss, Grayson County (Texas) JC.—(2006-07)**
32. *Ryan Fry, 3b, Nazareth Area HS, Stockertown, Pa.
33. *Santiago Narciandi, c, Miami-Dade CC.
**34. *Chad Bentz, lhp, Douglas HS, Juneau, Alaska.—(2004-05)**
35. *Allen Buckley, rhp, East Central (Miss.) JC.
36. *Nathan Bowden, 3b, Northwest Mississippi CC.
37. *Michael Hurd, lhp, Arapahoe HS, Littleton, Colo.
38. *Michael Brown, of, Centreville HS, Dayton, Ohio.
39. *Jacob Pierce, rhp, Navarro (Texas) JC.
40. *Jonathan Habrack, lhp, Dallas Senior HS, Shavertown, Pa.
41. *Rob Garibaldi, of, Santa Rosa (Calif.) JC.
42. *Ben Hedgecock, rhp, Gaither HS, Tampa.
43. Jason Faigin, rhp, Rowan (N.J.) College.
44. *Jeremiah Porter, of, Columbia River HS, Vancouver, Wash.
45. *Ruben Mancilla, 3b, Costa Mesa (Calif.) HS.
46. *Beau Dannemiller, rhp, John A. Logan (Ill.) JC.
47. *John Perry, 1b, Arapahoe HS, Littleton, Colo.
48. *David Lower, c, Culver Military Academy, Alexandria, Ind.
49. *Henry Caban, rhp, Lehman HS, Bronx, N.Y.
50. *Mark Cooper, 1b, Texas City (Texas) HS.

## OAKLAND ATHLETICS (9)

**1. Barry Zito, lhp, University of Southern California.—(2000-15)**
**2. Ryan Ludwick, of, University of Nevada-Las Vegas.—(2002-14)**
DRAFT DROP *Brother of Eric Ludwick, major leaguer (1996-99)*
3. Jorge Soto, c-1b, Troy State University.—(High A)
4. Keith Surkont, rhp, Williams (Mass.) College.—(AA)
DRAFT DROP *Grandson of Max Surkont, major leaguer (1949-57)*
5. Darin Moore, rhp, University of the Pacific.—(AA)
**6. Mario Ramos, lhp, Rice University.—(2003)**
7. Josh Hochgesang, 3b, Stanford University.
**8. Justin Lehr, rhp-c, University of Southern California.—(2004-09)**
9. Kirk Asche, of, Jacksonville University.
10. Justin Sobchuk, rhp, Sehome HS, Bellingham, Wash.
DRAFT DROP *Son of Dennis Sobchuk, first overall draft pick, Cincinnati Stingers/World Hockey Association (1973); forward, National Hockey League (1979-83)*
11. Michael Wenner, of, Rider University.
12. *Jay Garthwaite, of, Kent Meridan HS, Kent, Wash.
13. Jason Pomar, rhp, University of South Carolina.
14. Alvyn Ellis, 1b, Clackamas (Ore.) CC.
15. *Anthony Cicero, c, Cleveland HS, Van Nuys, Calif.
16. +Matt Allegra, of, Lake Mary (Fla.) HS / Manatee (Fla.) CC.
17. Bryan Mazur, lhp, University of North Carolina-Wilmington.
18. G.W. Keller, of, University of Alabama.
19. Jason Clements, ss, Oral Roberts University.
20. Matt Gage, rhp, Eastern Illinois University.
21. Cade Sanchez, rhp, University of Texas-Arlington.
22. *Edmund Muth, of, Stanford University.
23. Mike Lockwood, of, Ohio State University.
24. Brad Henderson, 2b, University of Mississippi.
25. *Fernando De Aza, rhp, Colegio Universario, Carolina, P.R.
26. Jacob Beckman, rhp, Glen Oaks (Mich.) CC.
27. +Donaldo Atencio, rhp, Kirtland Central HS, Kirtland, N.M. / New Mexico JC.
28. Nate Hilton, rhp, Iowa State University.
29. *Andre Marshall, of, Walla Walla (Wash.) CC.
30. *Dwight Edge, of, University of Tampa.
31. *Kris Mancini, of, CC of Rhode Island.
32. Micah Dunphy, lhp, Sauk Valley (Ill.) CC.
33. *Alex Coleman, of, Poly HS, Long Beach, Calif.
34. *Geoff Comfort, of, JC of San Mateo (Calif.)
35. +Darvin Withers, rhp, Spartanburg Methodist (S.C.) JC.
36. *Jerry Knox, rhp, Oakland HS, Murfreesboro, Tenn.
37. Jorge Ortiz, 3b, Miguel Melendez Munoz HS, Cayey, P.R.
38. *Frank James, lhp, Navarro (Texas) JC.
39. *Brandon Bahr, rhp, Gulf Coast HS, Marco Island, Fla.
40. *Jared Joaquin, rhp, Lower Columbia (Wash.) CC.
41. *James Cole, lhp, Navarro (Texas) JC.
42. *Kellyn Shafer, rhp, Lane (Ore.) CC.
43. *Zach Gordon, ss, Moorpark (Calif.) JC.
44. *Eric Kitchen, 3b, Durango HS, Las Vegas, Nev.
45. *William Zeier, of, Laney (Calif.) JC.

## PHILADELPHIA PHILLIES (12)

1. **Brett Myers, rhp, Englewood HS, Jacksonville, Fla.—(2002-13)**
2. *Jason Cooper, of, Moses Lake (Wash.) HS.—(AAA)

DRAFT DROP *Attended Stanford; re-drafted by Indians, 2002 (3rd round)*

3. Russ Jacobson, c, University of Miami.—(AAA)
4. Brad Pautz, rhp, University of Minnesota.—(AA)
5. ***Joe Saunders, lhp, West Springfield HS, Springfield, Va.—(2005-14)**

DRAFT DROP *Attended Virginia Tech; re-drafted by Angels, 2002 (1st round)*

6. Daniel Tosca, c, Durant HS, Seffner, Fla.

DRAFT DROP *Nephew of Carlos Tosca, major league manager (2002-04)*

7. *David Gil, rhp, University of Miami.
8. Jesse Thrasher, rhp, Benton HS, St. Joseph, Mo.
9. Julio Collazo, ss, Mississippi Delta JC.
10. **Marlon Byrd, of, Georgia Perimeter JC.—(2002-15)**
11. Allen Legette, rhp, Stratford HS, Goose Creek, S.C.
12. Brian Bush, of, University of Michigan.
13. **Frank Brooks, lhp, St Peter's College.—(2004-05)**
14. *Jovanathan Clark, of, Vallejo (Calif.) HS.
15. Mark Outlaw, lhp, Baylor University.
16. Chris Keelin, rhp, Montclair State (N.J.) College.
17. Brad Tucker, rhp, Pepperdine University.
18. Robert Avila, c, The Master's (Calif.) College.
19. *Trey Saye, rhp, Newberry (S.C.) HS.
20. Hector Serrano, c, Juan Ponce de Leon HS, Arecibo, P.R.
21. Aaron Merhoff, of, Texas Lutheran College.
22. Justin Duarte, 1b, Azusa Pacific (Calif.) University.
23. Todd Eagle, c, Albany (Calif.) HS.
24. Joe Schley, of, Southern Illinois University.
25. Brian Hitchcox, ss, Samford University.
26. Justin Fry, rhp, Ohio State University.
27. Daniel O'Neill, c, University of Illinois.
28. Tom Batson, 3b, Northwestern State University.
29. *Randon Ho, lhp, University of Hawaii.
30. Chad Smith, rhp, Indiana University.
31. Wade Van Vark, of, Central (Iowa) College.
32. Jay Sitzman, of, Arizona State University.
33. Dean Muthig, 3b, Carthage (Wis.) College.
34. Ben Carey, lhp, Cuesta (Calif.) JC.
35. *Chris Herman, ss, Mount San Antonio (Calif.) CC.
36. *Todd Simo, rhp, New Providence (N.J.) HS.
37. Ryan Brookman, rhp, University of Wisconsin-Whitewater.
38. *Jon Uhl, rhp, Leto Comprehensive HS, Tampa.
39. ***Kameron Loe, rhp, Granada Hills HS, Chatsworth, Calif.—(2004-13)**
40. +Lawrence Alexander, of, Chandler (Okla.) HS / Cowley County (Kan.) CC.
41. Todd Oetting, c, Jefferson City (Mo.) HS.
42. Erick Rivera, of, Luis Munoz Rivera HS, Utuado, P.R.
43. *Nicholas White, rhp, Arapahoe HS, Littleton, Colo.
44. *Jordan Pickens, 3b, Atascadero (Calif.) HS.

## PITTSBURGH PIRATES (8)

1. Bobby Bradley, rhp, Wellington (Fla.) HS.—(AAA)
2. **Ryan Doumit, c, Moses Lake (Wash.) HS.—(2005-14)**
3. Aron Weston, of, Solon (Ohio) HS.—(AA)
4. Justin Reid, rhp, UC Davis.—(AAA)
5. **J.R. House, c, Seabreeze HS, Ormond Beach, Fla.—(2003-08)**
6. B.J. Barns, of, Duquesne University.
7. Matt Schneider, of, University of North Florida.
8. Jon Searles, rhp, Huntington (N.Y.) HS.
9. Shane Wright, rhp, Texas Tech.
10. Jeremy Sickles, c, Cal State Northridge.
11. *Craig Munroe, 1b, University of Maryland.
12. Jay Langston, 3b-of, Georgia State University.
13. Josh Hudnall, ss, Ouachita Christian HS, Monroe, La.
14. Daniel Hudson, of-rhp, Mississippi Gulf Coast JC.
15. Joe Burruezo, rhp-of, Jesuit HS, Tampa.
16. Justin Martin, 2b, University of Nevada-Reno.
17. Cliff Reik, 3b, Cary (N.C.) HS.
18. Ryan Dorsey, ss, Riverdale Baptist HS, Upper Marlboro, Md.
19. ***Brian Tallet, lhp, Louisiana State University.—(2002-11)**
20. Elliott Sarabia, ss, University of Nevada-Las Vegas.
21. *Derek Ver Helst, lhp, Spearfish (S.D.) HS.
22. *Jason Wilson, of-rhp, San Augustine (Texas) HS.
23. Michael Piercy, of, Kean (N.J.) University.
24. Josh Bonifay, ss/2b, University of North Carolina-Wilmington.

DRAFT DROP *Son of Cam Bonifay, general manager, Pirates (1993-2001)*

25. Aaron Story, lhp, Lawrence County HS, Lawrenceburg, Tenn.
26. *Ja'mar Clanton, ss, Proviso West HS, Bellwood, Ill.
27. +Kenny Henderson, lhp, New York Tech.
28. *Andrew Green, rhp, Ouachita Parish HS, Monroe, La.
29. Rodney Hancock, lhp, The Citadel.
30. Derek Hurley, lhp, Seton Hall University.
31. **Walter Young, 1b, Purvis (Miss.) HS.—(2005)**
32. Jason Biddlestone, rhp, Columbus State (Ohio) CC.
33. Michael Sabens, rhp, Berry (Ga.) College.
34. Kurt Bultmann, 2b, Clemson University.
35. Mo Douglas, 1b, University of Southwestern Louisiana.
36. *Ryan Fillingim, c-of, Fairhope (Ala.) HS.
37. Troy Satterfield, lhp, University of Central Florida.
38. *Ryan Stanek, c, New Providence (N.J.) HS.
39. Patrick O'Brien, rhp, Walsh Jesuit HS, Bath, Ohio.
40. *Seth Hill, lhp-1b, Sandwich (Ill.) HS.
41. Brian Messer, rhp, University of New Mexico.
42. *Frank Torre, lhp, Palm Beach Gardens, Fla.

DRAFT DROP *Son of Frank Torre, major leaguer (1956-63) • Nephew of Joe Torre, major leaguer (1960-77); major league manager (1977-2010)*

43. *Daniel Stringer, rhp, Brazoswood HS, Clute, Texas.
44. *Michael Oehlberg, lhp, Guilford HS, Rockford, Ill.
45. *Raul Nieves, ss, University of Mobile (Ala.).
46. Chris Batcheller, c, Washington & Lee (Va.) University.
47. *Bryce Morrison, of, Leander (Texas) HS.
48. *Jude Voltz, 1b, University of Mississippi.
49. Brian Pollard, of, University of Florida.
50. Landon Jacobsen, rhp, Trinidad State (Colo.) JC.

## ST. LOUIS CARDINALS (18)

1. (Choice to Orioles as compensation for Type A free agent Eric Davis)
1. Chance Caple, rhp, Texas A&M University (Choice from Braves as compensation for Type A free agent Brian Jordan).—(High A)
1. Nick Stocks, rhp, Florida State University (Supplemental choice—36th—as compensation for Jordan).—(AAA)
1. **Chris Duncan, 1b, Canyon del Oro HS, Tucson, Ariz.** (Supplemental choice—46th—as compensation for Type A free agent Delino DeShields).**—(2005-09)**

DRAFT DROP *Son of Dave Duncan, major leaguer (1964-76) • Brother of Shelley Duncan, major leaguer (2013)*

2. (Choice to Dodgers as compensation for Type A free agent Scott Radinsky)
2. **Josh Pearce, rhp, University of Arizona** (Supplemental choice—82nd—as compensation for Type C free agent Tom Lampkin).**—(2002-04)**
3. B.R. Cook, rhp, Oregon State University.—(AAA)
4. **Ben Johnson, of, Germantown (Tenn.) HS** (Choice from Orioles as compensation for DeShields).**—(2005-07)**
4. **Jimmy Journell, rhp, University of Illinois.—(2003-05)**
5. Charles Williams, of, Rice University.—(High A)
6. Josh Teekel, rhp, Belaire HS, Greenwell Springs, La.
7. **Coco Crisp, 2b, Los Angeles Pierce JC.—(2002-15)**
8. Shawn Schumacher, c-3b, Texas A&M University.
9. Damon Thames, ss, Rice University.
10. Kevin Sprague, lhp, McNeese State University.
11. *Aaron Davidson, 2b, Cuesta (Calif.) CC.
12. Brent Spooner, c, University of Central Florida.
13. **Albert Pujols, 3b, Maple Woods (Mo.) CC.—(2001-15)**
14. Matt Vincent, lhp, Lindsey Wilson (Ky.) College.
15. Travis Bailey, 3b, Florida Atlantic University.
16. Cheyenne Janke, rhp, Nicholls State University.
17. Mike Perkins, rhp, Manatee (Fla.) JC.
18. Paul Fahs, rhp, Briarcliffe (N.Y.) JC.
19. *Chris Beck, of, Cal State Fullerton.
20. Scott Layfield, rhp, Valdosta State (Ga.) University.
21. Jeremy Cummings, rhp, West Virginia University.
22. Mike Floyd, of, University of Florida.
23. Chris Fiora, rhp, Towson State University.
24. **Mike Crudale, rhp, Santa Clara University.—(2002-03)**
25. Mark Penberthy, c, The Master's (Calif.) College.
26. *Justin Berg, c, Rice University.
27. Donavan Graves, rhp, Booneville (Mo.) HS.
28. Brandon Peck, lhp, Kansas State University.
29. Justin Albertsen, of, El Camino (Calif.) JC.
30. Mark Butler, rhp, Bellevue (Neb.) University.
31. Matt Parker, rhp, Mercer University.
32. Trevor Sansom, rhp, West Virginia State College.
33. **Bo Hart, ss-2b, Gonzaga University.—(2003-04)**
34. *Jake Moon, rhp, Cypress (Calif.) JC.
35. Aaron Dinkel, rhp, JC of Eastern Utah.
36. *Jeff Cruz, lhp, Fullerton (Calif.) CC.
37. Chad Yates, rhp, University of Arkansas.
38. Chris Buckley, of, North Arkansas CC.
39. Monte Lee, of, College of Charleston.
40. *Ronnie Corona, rhp, Cypress (Calif.) JC.

## SAN DIEGO PADRES (28)

1. Vince Faison, of, Toombs County HS, Lyons, Ga. (Choice from Dodgers as compensation for Type A free agent Kevin Brown).—(AAA)
1. Gerik Baxter, rhp, Edmonds-Woodway HS, Edmonds, Wash.—(Low A)

DRAFT DROP *Died as active player (June 29, 2001)*

1. Omar Ortiz, rhp, University of Texas-Pan American (Choice from Astros as compensation for Type A free agent Ken Caminiti).—(AA)
1. Casey Burns, rhp, University of Richmond (Supplemental choice—41st—as compensation for Brown).—(Low A)
1. **Mike Bynum, lhp, University of North Carolina** (Supplemental choice—49th—as compensation for Caminiti).**—(2002-04)**
1. Nick Trzesniak, c, Andrew HS, Tinley Park, Ill. (Supplemental choice—51st—as compensation for Type A free agent Steve Finley).—(AAA)
2. *Alberto Concepcion, c, El Segundo (Calif.) HS.—(AAA)

DRAFT DROP *Attended Southern California; re-drafted by Red Sox, 2002 (21st round)*

3. Josh Vitek, rhp, Fayetteville (Texas) HS.—(Short-season A)
4. Jason Moore, ss, University of Texas.—(AA)
5. Chris Heck, lhp, Clemson University (Choice from Diamondbacks as compensation for Finley).—(Rookie)
5. **Mike Thompson, rhp, Lamar (Colo.) HS.—(2006-07)**
6. Blair DeHart, rhp, James Madison University.
7. John Scheschuk, 1b, Texas A&M University.
8. Todd Donovan, of, Siena College.
9. John Puccinelli, ss-3b, Notre Dame HS, Toluca Lake, Calif.
10. Todd Shiyuk, lhp, University of Alabama-Huntsville.
11. *Brian Adams, lhp, Clemson University.
12. Brian Ward, 2b, North Carolina State University.
13. *Tony Adler, rhp, Greenhill HS, Dallas.
14. **Bobby Scales, 2b, University of Michigan.—(2009-10)**
15. **Jacob Peavy, rhp, St. Paul's HS, Semmes, Ala.—(2002-15)**
16. Greg Ienni, of, Cal State Los Angeles.
17. ***Brandon Fahey, 3b, Duncanville (Texas) HS.—(2006-08)**

DRAFT DROP *Son of Bill Fahey, first overall draft pick, January 1970/secondary phase, Senators (1970); major leaguer (1971-83)*

18. Andres Pagan, c, Luis Munoz Marin HS, Yauco, P.R.
19. Jake Huff, c, Mesa State (Colo.) College.
20. *Matt Moran, rhp, Cosumnes River (Calif.) JC.
21. Troy Schader, ss, Oregon State University.
22. *Kevin Howard, 3b, Westlake HS, Thousand Oaks, Calif.
23. *Mike Mueller, rhp, West Bend East HS, West Bend, Wis.
24. *Jeremy Alford, 3b, Benton (La.) HS.
25. Anthony Vandemore, of, Truman State (Mo.) University.
26. *Shawn Lynn, rhp, Seminole State (Okla.) JC.
27. *Chris Adolph, of, University of Nevada-Las Vegas.
28. *Chad Dias, c, Bellevue (Wash.) CC.
29. *B.J. Long, of, Evans HS, Martinez, Ga.
30. *Jason Hammond, of, West Hills HS, Santee, Calif.
31. *Jarrett Roenicke, of, Yuba (Calif.) CC.

DRAFT DROP *Son of Gary Roenicke, first-round draft pick, Expos (1973); major leaguer (1976-88)*

32. Jeremy Webster, lhp, Salt Lake (Utah) CC.
33. ***Shawn Hill, rhp, Bishop Redding HS, Georgetown, Ontario.—(2004-12)**
34. *Michael Saunches, 1b, Argenta-Oreana HS, Decatur, Ill.
35. Jeff Rizzo, 3b, Stanford University.
36. *Anthony Bianucci, of, W.T. Woodson HS, Fairfax, Va.
37. *Kevin Okimoto, 1b, Santa Clara University.
38. *Marcellus Dawson, of, Wauwatosa East HS, Milwaukee.
39. *Chris Wilkins, rhp, The Dalles (Ore.) HS.
40. *Jared Vance, rhp, Connorsville (Ind.) HS.

## SAN FRANCISCO GIANTS (24)

1. **Kurt Ainsworth, rhp, Louisiana State University.—(2001-04)**
1. **Jerome Williams, rhp, Waipahu HS, Honolulu** (Supplemental choice—39th—as compensation for Type A free agent Jose Mesa).**—(2003-15)**
2. J.T. Thomas, lhp, Righetti HS, Orcutt, Calif. (Choice from Mariners as compensation for Mesa).—(AAA)
2. **Jack Taschner, lhp, University of Wisconsin-Oshkosh.—(2005-10)**
3. Sean McGowan, 1b, Boston College.—(AAA)
4. Jeremy Cunningham, rhp, Cal Poly San Luis Obispo.—(High A)
5. Ryan Cox, rhp, Southern Illinois University-Edwardsville.—(AAA)
6. Ryan Pini, of, Dixie (Utah) JC.
7. Joe Jester, ss, University of Arkansas.
8. Kevin Vent, rhp, University of Arkansas.
9. Josh Cook, ss, Yuba (Calif.) CC.
10. Anthony Yacco, rhp, Mahopac (N.Y.) HS.
11. Jeff Verplancke, rhp, Cal State Los Angeles.
12. *Ronnie Merrill, ss, University of Tampa.
13. Fletcher Lee, rhp, Lewis-Clark State (Idaho) College.
14. *Mike Meyer, rhp, University of Arizona.
15. Deron Featherstone, rhp, North Carolina A&T University.
16. Micah Holst, of, Southwest Missouri State University.
17. Vance Cozier, rhp, St. Bonaventure University.
18. Brian Meagher, lhp, JC of San Mateo (Calif.).
19. *Ryan Cheo, lhp, Saddleback (Calif.) CC.
20. +Anthony Turco, c, St. Petersburg (Fla.) JC.
21. Ryan Luther, ss, Lewis-Clark State (Idaho) College.
22. *Jason Barrow, of, Chemeketa (Ore.) CC.
23. Mike Zirelli, rhp, Cal Poly San Luis Obispo.
24. ***Bill Murphy, lhp, Arlington HS, Riverside, Calif.—(2007-09)**
25. *Andrew Edwards, rhp, Christ the King HS, Queens, N.Y.
26. +Kevin Alexander, ss, Modesto (Calif.) JC.
27. +Troy Gustafson, of, Blaine (Minn.) HS/Iowa Western JC.
28. Lars Hansen, c, University of Hawaii.
29. Troy Ransom, of, South Mountain (Ariz.) CC.

DRAFT DROP *Brother of Cody Ransom, major leaguer (2001-13)*

30. +Ryan Davis, of, Cosumnes River (Calif.) JC.
31. Scott Daeley, of, Wake Forest University.
32. *Tim Gilhooly, c, San Ramon Valley HS, Danville, Calif.

33. *Kavonski Chatman, lhp-of, Northeast Texas CC.
34. *Scott Shoemaker, rhp, Granite Hills HS, El Cajon, Calif.
35. *Robert Lorona, ss, Hayden HS, Winkelman, Ariz.
36. *Bryan Lang, of, Scottsdale (Ariz.) CC.
37. *Chris Norris, rhp, Central Arizona CC.
38. *Drew Endicott, rhp, Carthage (Mo.) HS.
39. Paul Turco, ss, Auburn University.
40. *Travis Veracka, lhp, University of Massachusetts.
41. *Winston Woods, of, Broward (Fla.) CC.
42. *Jason Hickman, lhp, Ball State University.
43. *Brett Cayton, c, Fountain Valley (Calif.) HS.
44. *Daniel August, rhp, St Petersburg (Fla.) JC.
45. *Chad Ashlock, rhp, University of Texas-Arlington.
46. +Wesley Faust, rhp, Oklahoma Baptist University.
47. *Oscar Vargas, ss, Chabot (Calif.) JC.
48. *Jamie Aloy, 1b, University of Hawaii.
49. *Joshua Sousa, rhp, Modesto (Calif.) JC.
50. Brian Grochol, of, Canada (Calif.) CC.

## SEATTLE MARINERS (11)

1. Ryan Christianson, c, Arlington HS, Riverside, Calif.—(AAA)
1. Jeff Heaverlo, rhp, University of Washington (Supplemental choice—33rd—as compensation for Type A free agent Mike Timlin).—(AAA)
DRAFT DROP *Son of Dave Heaverlo, major leaguer (1975-81)*
2. (Choice to Giants as compensation for Type A free agent Jose Mesa)
3. **Willie Bloomquist, ss, Arizona State University.—(2002-15)**
3. Sheldon Fulse, ss, George Jenkins HS, Bartow, Fla. (Choice from Orioles as compensation for Timlin).—(AA)
4. Vaughn Schill, ss, Duke University.—(High A)
5. **Clint Nageotte, rhp, Brooklyn (Ohio) HS.—(2004-06)**
6. **J.J. Putz, rhp, University of Michigan.—(2003-14)**
7. *Michael Davies, lhp, Westview HS, Beaverton, Ore.
8. **Termel Sledge, of, Long Beach State University.—(2004-07)**
9. **Steve Kent, lhp, Florida International University.—(2002)**
10. Justin Smith, lhp, University of Alabama.
11. Hawkeye Wayne, rhp, Columbia University.
DRAFT DROP *Brother of Justin Wayne, first-round draft pick, Expos (2000); major leaguer (2002-04)*
12. *Larry Brown, of, San Fernando (Calif.) HS.
13. **Justin Leone, ss, St. Martin's (Wash.) College.—(2004-06)**
14. Oscar Ramirez, ss, St. Petersburg (Fla.) JC.
15. O.J. Burton, rhp, Florida Atlantic University.
16. Sean Parnell, of, University of Wisconsin-Oshkosh.
17. Brian Hertel, 1b, University of Nevada-Las Vegas.
18. Kris Gundrum, of, Western Michigan University.
19. *Brandon Roberson, rhp, Texas Tech.
20. Kevin Olore, rhp, Marist College.
21. *Craig Helmandollar, lhp, Potomac State (W.Va.) College.
22. *Jason Edmonds, rhp-3b, De Anza HS, San Pablo, Calif.
23. *Zeph Zinsman, 1b, Mission (Calif.) JC.
24. *Ryan Simon, rhp, Chamberlain HS, Tampa.
25. ***Dan Davidson, lhp, Mosley HS, Lynn Haven, Fla.—(2009)**
26. *Matt Walter, rhp, Brandon (Fla.) HS.
27. *Andrew Rempel, of, W.J. Mouat HS, Abbotsford, B.C.
28. *Jonathan Kuelz, rhp, Odessa (Texas) JC.
29. *Lee Gwaltney, rhp, McLennan (Texas) CC.
30. *Michael Squibb, lhp, South HS, Hagerstown, Md.
31. *Travis Allen, rhp, Quartz Hill HS, Lancaster, Calif.
32. *Andrew Wells, rhp, Mounds HS, Bixby, Okla.
33. +Chuck Lopez, of, Long Beach State University.
34. *Chris Bono, c, Brevard (Fla.) CC.
35. *Brian McDevitt, rhp, Waubonsie Valley HS, Naperville, Ill.
36. *Eddie Menchaca, rhp, Westwood HS, Mesa, Ariz.
37. *Glenn Tucker, rhp, Coral Shores HS, Tavenier, Fla.
38. ***Rich Harden, rhp, Claremont SS, Victoria, B.C.—(2003-11)**
39. *Kellen Dedge, ss, Suwannee HS, Jasper, Fla.
40. *Jeff Thompson, 3b, Torrance HS, Lomita, Calif.
41. *Guarionez Rodriguez, 2b, Miami-Dade CC.
42. *Tyson Munn, of, Earl Marriott SS, Surrey, B.C.
43. ***Chris Snyder, c, Spring Woods HS, Houston.—(2004-13)**
44. *Steve Hassett, lhp, Sarasota (Fla.) HS.
45. *Jon Nelson, 3b, Dixie (Utah) JC.
46. *Ben Ashworth, rhp, Battle Ground Academy, Franklin, Tenn.
47. *Jared Cudd, rhp, Sentinel (Okla.) HS.
48. *Shawn Brooks, rhp, Lamar (Colo.) CC.
49. *Mark Leith, rhp, David Thompson SS, Vancouver, B.C.
50. *Nate Doorlag, 1b, Plainwell (Mich.) HS.

## TAMPA BAY DEVIL RAYS (1)

1. **Josh Hamilton, of, Athens Drive HS, Raleigh, N.C.—(2007-15)**
2. **Carl Crawford, of, Jefferson Davis HS, Houston.—(2002-15)**
3. **Doug Waechter, rhp, Northeast HS, St. Petersburg, Fla.—(2003-09)**
4. Alex Santos, rhp, University of Miami.—(AAA)
5. **Seth McClung, rhp, Greenbrier East HS, Lewisburg, W.Va.—(2003-09)**
6. *Eric Henderson, lhp, Santa Fe (Fla.) CC.
7. Andrew Beinbrink, 3b, Arizona State University.
8. *Ryan Gloger, lhp, Jesuit HS, Tampa.
9. Dan Ortiz, 1b, Hemet HS, Nuevo, Calif.
10. Nathan Cromer, rhp, Lincoln HS, Des Moines, Iowa.
DRAFT DROP *Twin brother of Jason Cromer, 11th-round draft pick, Devil Rays (1999)*
11. Jason Cromer, lhp, Lincoln HS, Des Moines, Iowa.
DRAFT DROP *Twin brother of Nathan Cromer, 10th-round draft pick, Devil Rays (1999)*
12. Jorge Maduro, c, Monsignor Pace HS, Miami.
13. Jason Pruett, lhp, Brookhaven (Texas) JC.
14. **Jeff Ridgway, lhp, Port Angeles (Wash.) HS.—(2007-08)**
15. Scott Vandermeer, rhp, McMain HS, New Orleans, La.
16. *Daniel Lopaze, rhp-ss, Potomac HS, Lakeridge, Va.
17. **Matt Diaz, of, Florida State University.—(2003-13)**
18. ***Ryan Raburn, ss, Durant HS, Dover, Fla.—(2004-15)**
19. Ging Aaron, 2b, Santa Ana (Calif.) JC.
20. Chris Crawford, rhp, University of Georgia.
21. ***Mike Fontenot, 2b, Salmen HS, Slidell, La.—(2005-12)**
DRAFT DROP *First-round draft pick (19th overall), Orioles (2001)*
22. *Cortney Jenkins, rhp, Lamar University.
23. Travis Minix, rhp, Ball State University.
24. *Mark Carter, lhp, Wallace State (Ala.) CC.
25. Matt Dailey, lhp, UC Santa Barbara.
26. *Aaron Sheffield, rhp, Pope HS, Marietta, Ga.
27. Justin Schuda, c, Murietta Valley HS, Murrieta, Calif.
28. *Scott Berney, rhp, University of Connecticut.
29. *Michael Hernandez, lhp, Central Union HS, Fresno, Calif.
30. *Jim Harrelson, rhp, Modesto (Calif.) JC.
31. *Curtis White, lhp, Lindsay (Okla.) HS.
32. *Josh Nichols, lhp, Bradford HS, Starke, Fla.
33. *Cortney Hill, 2b, Eastern Oklahoma State JC.
34. *Phil Klaiber, 3b, Schenectady County (N.Y.) CC.
35. +Kevin O'Brien, 1b, Tarpon Springs HS, Dunedin, Fla. / St. Petersburg (Fla.) CC.
36. *Ralph Roberts, of, Lenoir (N.C.) CC.
37. *Matt Lederhos, rhp, Westwood (Mass.) HS.
38. *Teryn Stanley, ss, Horizon Christian HS, San Diego.
39. *Kevin Beavers, lhp, Saddleback (Calif.) CC.
40. *Peter Bonifas, rhp, Marquette HS, Bellevue, Iowa.
41. Glenn Katz, of, University of Connecticut.
42. *Ben Himes, of, Westlake HS, Austin, Texas.
43. *Trevor Tacker, rhp, Carroll HS, Southlake, Texas.
44. *Josh Radke, ss, Bozeman (Mon.) HS.
45. *Chad Coder, of, East Lake HS, Redmond, Wash.
46. *Bo Ashabraner, rhp, Esperanza HS, Yorba Linda, Calif.
47. *Chadd Blasko, rhp, Mishawaka (Ind.) HS.
DRAFT DROP *First-round draft pick (36th overall), Cubs (2002)*
48. *Casey Blalock, rhp, Panola (Texas) JC.
49. *Randy Walter, of, Huntley Project HS, Ballantine, Mon.
50. *Allen Nevels, rhp, Taloga HS, Putnam, Okla.

## TEXAS RANGERS (21)

1. (Choice to Orioles as compensation for Type A free agent Rafael Palmeiro)
1. **Colby Lewis, rhp, Bakersfield (Calif.) JC** (Supplemental choice—38th—as compensation for Type A free agent Todd Stottlemyre).**—(2002-15)**
1. David Mead, rhp, Soddy Daisy HS, Chattanooga, Tenn. (Supplemental choice—47th—as compensation for Type A free agent Will Clark).—(High A)
2. **Nick Regilio, rhp, Jacksonville University.—(2004-05)**
3. **Hank Blalock, ss, Rancho Bernardo HS, San Diego.—(2002-10)**
4. **Kevin Mench, of, University of Delaware** (Choice from Diamondbacks as compensation for Stottlemyre).**—(2002-10)**
4. Chris Jaile, c, Christopher Columbus HS, Miami.—(High A)
5. **Andy Cavazos, rhp, Brazoswood HS, Clute, Texas** (Choice from Orioles as compensation for Clark).**—(2007)**
5. Victor Hillaert, rhp, Shippensburg (Pa.) University.—(Low A)
6. **Aaron Harang, rhp, San Diego State University.—(2002-15)**
7. *Luz Portobanco, rhp, Miami (Fla.) Senior HS.
8. John Rahrer, rhp, Emmett (Idaho) HS.
9. Brett Cadiente, of, Arizona State University.
10. Jason Bryan, of, New Utrecht HS, Brooklyn, N.Y.
11. Justin Echols, rhp, Greenway HS, Phoenix.
12. Mike Scuglik, lhp, Xavier University.
13. **Jason Jones, of, Kennesaw State University.—(2003)**
14. Ernest Villegas, of, Northeast Texas CC.
15. ***Dennis Sarfate, rhp, Gilbert HS, Chandler, Ariz.—(2006-09)**
16. *Joel Alvarado, c, Garden City (Kan.) CC.
17. Orlando Cruz, of, Jose Collazo Colon HS, Juncos, P.R.
18. *Raymond Knight, c, St. John's Prep, Jamaica, N.Y.
19. ***Noah Lowry, lhp, Ventura (Calif.) JC.—(2003-07)**
DRAFT DROP *First-round draft pick (30th overall), Giants (2001)*
20. *Kevin Marshall, of, Martin HS, Arlington, Texas.
21. *Michael Falco, of, Agoura HS, Westlake Village, Calif.
22. *Nick Devenney, rhp, Holmes (Miss.) JC.
23. *Denny Summerall, of, Armwood HS, Seffner, Fla.
24. *Dan Sauer, rhp, Modesto (Calif.) JC.
25. *Matt Trepkowski, lhp, Killeen HS, Fort Hood, Texas.
26. *Jason Reuss, 1b, Orange Coast (Calif.) JC.
DRAFT DROP *Son of Jerry Reuss, major leaguer (1969-90)*
27. *Ryan Mottl, rhp, Clemson University.
28. *Justin Sherman, rhp, Durango HS, Las Vegas, Nev.
29. *Erick Monzon, 2b, Nuestra Senor HS, Carolina, P.R.
30. *Dustin Smith, c, Girard (Kan.) HS.
31. *Bobby Bowman, rhp, Pell City (Ala.) HS.
32. *Josue Lopez, 1b, El Toro HS, Trabuco Canyon, Calif.
33. *Tony Piazza, c, Fairview HS, Cody, Wyo.
34. *Ignacio Suarez, ss, John Bowne HS, Corona, N.Y.
35. *Ed Erickson, 1b, University of Washington.
36. *J.R. Crider, rhp, Phoenix JC.
37. *Jared Hartness, rhp, Jonesboro (Ga.) HS.
38. +Rich Gilbert, lhp, JC of Eastern Utah / CC of Southern Nevada.
39. *Chad Williams, lhp, Tucson HS, Arivaca, Ariz.
40. *Josh Hollingsworth, 3b, St. Petersburg (Fla.) JC.
41. *Andrew Fryson, rhp, James A. Shank HS, Gretna, Fla.
42. Adam Poe, of, University of South Carolina.
43. *Michael Sills, lhp, Leon HS, Tallahassee, Fla.
44. *Russel Reeves, lhp, Imperial (Calif.) HS.
45. *Brad Hertel, of, Clovis West HS, Fresno, Calif.
46. **+Jason Botts, 1b, Glendale (Calif.) JC.—(2005-08)**
47. *Marty Hayes, rhp, University of San Diego.
48. *Nick Priest, 1b, El Capitan HS, El Cajon, Calif.
49. *Nathan Neibauer, of, Overland HS, Aurora, Colo.
50. *Clay Chesser, of, Golden West HS, Visalia, Calif.

## TORONTO BLUE JAYS (19)

1. **Alexis Rios, 3b, San Pedro Martir HS, Guaynabo, P.R.—(2004-15)**
2. Michael Snyder, 3b, Ayala HS, Chino Hills, Calif.—(AA)
3. **Matt Ford, lhp, Taravella HS, Tamarac, Fla.—(2003)**
4. Brian Cardwell, rhp, Sapulpa (Okla.) HS.–(High A)
5. Scott Porter, rhp, Jacksonville University.—(High A)
6. D.J. Hanson, rhp, Richland (Wash.) HS.
7. Derrick Nunley, rhp, Englewood HS, Jacksonville, Fla.
8. Ryan McCullem, lhp, Hickman HS, Columbia, Mo.
9. Josh Holliday, c/3b, Oklahoma State University.
DRAFT DROP *Brother of Matt Holliday, major leaguer (2004-15) • Baseball coach, Oklahoma State (2013-15)*
10. Rob Cosby, ss, Academie Bautista, San Juan, P.R.
11. Chuck Kegley, rhp, Okaloosa-Walton (Fla.) JC.
12. Chris Weekly, ss, New Mexico State University.
13. Marc Bluma, rhp, Wichita State University.
DRAFT DROP *Brother of Jaime Bluma, major leaguer (1996)*
14. **+Brandon Lyon, rhp, Dixie (Utah) JC.—(2001-13)**
15. Tim Newman, rhp, Walla Walla (Wash.) CC.
16. Jim Detwiler, lhp, Old Dominion University.
17. **Reed Johnson, of, Cal State Fullerton.—(2003-15)**
18. Peyton Lewis, rhp, Creighton University.
19. Ryan Spille, lhp, Southeast Missouri State University.
20. Thom Dreier, rhp, Oklahoma State University.
21. Robert Hamann, rhp, Wheaton (Ill.) College.
22. Justin Stine, lhp, University of Missouri.
23. *Andre Monroe, of, Santa Monica HS, Palmdale, Calif.
24. *Jeremy Cook, rhp, San Diego State University.
25. *Joshua Berry, lhp, Lake Stevens HS, Everett, Wash.
26. Doug Roper, rhp-ss, Clemson University.
27. *Angel Molina, of, Colegio Cristo Rey, Santa Isabel, P.R.
28. *Kirk Gosch, lhp, Coeur D'Alene (Idaho) HS.
29. Chris Baker, rhp, Oklahoma City University.
30. *Jerome McCoy, ss, Eastern Hills HS, Fort Worth, Texas.
31. *Charles Tasiaux, rhp, Ahuntsic College HS, Montreal.
32. Aaron Fera, of, Georgia College.
33. *Collin Perschon, rhp, Bellevue, Wash.
34. Lee Southard, rhp, Seminole State (Okla.) JC.
35. Matt Bimeal, rhp, Conemaugh Township HS, Davidsville, Pa.
36. Doug Dimma, lhp, Valdosta State (Ga.) University.
37. *Robbie Findlay, rhp, Michael Power HS, Etobicoke, Ontario.
38. *Mike Tisdale, rhp, St. Peters SS, Peterborough, Ontario.
39. *Wilton Reynolds, of, Cosumnes River (Calif.) JC.
40. Brian Mitchell, 2b, University of Iowa.
41. *Jeff Flegler, of, Gloucester, N.J.
42. *Judson Jones, lhp, Meridian (Miss.) CC.
43. *Chad Scarbery, rhp, Clovis HS, Fresno, Calif.
DRAFT DROP *Son of Randy Scarbery, first-round draft pick, Astros (1970); first-round draft pick, Athletics (1973); major leaguer (1979-80)*
44. *Jonathan Youngblood, ss, Arkansas HS, Texarkana, Ark.
45. *Brendon Stafford, rhp, St. Mathews HS, Gloucester, Ontario.
46. *Brooks McNiven, rhp, Kalamalka SS, Vernon, B.C.
47. *Garris Gonce, c, Florida CC.
48. *Jon Slack, of, Green Valley HS, Henderson, Nev.
49. *Phillip Banta, rhp, Bellevue (Wash.) CC.
50. *Derek Brehm, lhp, East Central HS, San Antonio, Texas.

# 2000

## AT A GLANCE

### This Date In History
June 8-10

### Best Draft
**MONTREAL EXPOS.** New ownership brought optimism in Montreal that stability might return to the downtrodden franchise. The Expos spent like never before in the 2000 draft, signing **JUSTIN WAYNE** (1) to a club-record $2.95 million bonus and giving $2 million to **GRADY SIZEMORE** (3). Wayne didn't pan out, but Sizemore, **CLIFF LEE** (4) and **JASON BAY** (22) all did. Imagine if they had signed local product **RUSSELL MARTIN** (35).

### Worst Draft
**BALTIMORE ORIOLES.** None of the first 31 players the Orioles drafted reached the big leagues, but each of their picks from rounds 32-36 did. Only one, **KURT BIRKINS** (33), signed with the Orioles. He went 6-4, 5.85 in three seasons in the majors.

### First-Round Busts
**MATT WHEATLAND, RHP, TIGERS; SCOTT HEARD, C, RANGERS.** They were batterymates for San Diego's Rancho Bernardo High. Neither advanced beyond Class A. Wheatland was burdened by shoulder problems and endured three surgeries in his first two years. In 34 appearances over three minor league seasons, he went 3-5, 4.07. Heard quit after four seasons in the Rangers system, batting .245-24-145.

### Second Best
**CHAD QUALLS, RHP, ASTROS.** Lots of premium talent fell to the second round because of high price tags. But Qualls, who received a modest $415,000 bonus, had the best career. He was still active in 2016, with a 48-46, 3.78 record and 74 saves in 775 big league games.

### Late-Round Find
**JOSE BAUTISTA, 3B, PIRATES (20TH ROUND).** Bautista, from the

# Muddled talent, bonus efforts scramble draft

Veteran scouts called the 2000 talent pool the most unpredictable they had ever encountered, and the draft unfolded accordingly.

With little to separate the top prospects, signability drove the early selections like never before. Not only did nine of the first 11 picks agree to deals in advance of the draft, but several high-priced, highly regarded players fell when they wouldn't commit to pre-draft offers.

Bonuses were all over the board in the first round, with both the highest and lowest outlays to that point in the draft's evolution.

"It's the most confusing top group in the 13 years I've been scouting," said Minnesota Twins scouting director Mike Radcliff, whose team had the second pick. "That's not to say there won't be a bounty of major leaguers down the line, but it's a rather chaotic, confused mix of talent."

The Florida Marlins took unheralded San Diego high school first baseman Adrian Gonzalez with the No. 1 pick, though he was regarded by some clubs as no more than a mid-first-round talent. Gonzalez and the Marlins agreed on a $3 million signing bonus four days before the draft.

Baseball rules prohibited predraft deals, but if anything, Major League Baseball congratulated the Marlins rather than admonished them. The commissioner's office held a negotiating seminar in Atlanta on May 15, three weeks prior to the draft, and the message to club officials was clear: Get a handle on bonuses by taking a hardline stance with agents. It was obvious the message hit home.

In many cases, teams passed over players who were either deemed unsignable or would not agree in advance to financial parameters. Several players projected as early first-round picks fell to the second round and further.

Gonzalez became the first No. 1 selection in eight years to receive less than his counterpart the year before: outfielder Josh Hamilton, who got a record $3.96 million bonus from the Tampa Bay Devil Rays in 1999. Asked if economics was a factor in his club's selection, Marlins scouting director Al Avila offered a succinct answer: "None."

"We felt he was the most complete player we could select in that No. 1 slot," Avila said. "He comes from a great family. He has the skills and the leadership qualities. We felt he was our guy."

Many scouts regarded California high school righthander Matt Harrington as the top prospect in the draft. His fastball was consistently clocked at 94-95 mph and topped out at 98. But he came with a high price tag, and the Marlins hardly considered him. The Twins showed significant interest but passed when he wouldn't commit to an agreement the night before the draft. He fell to the Colorado Rockies with the seventh pick overall.

Harrington didn't sign with the Rockies, delaying his professional career after agent Tommy

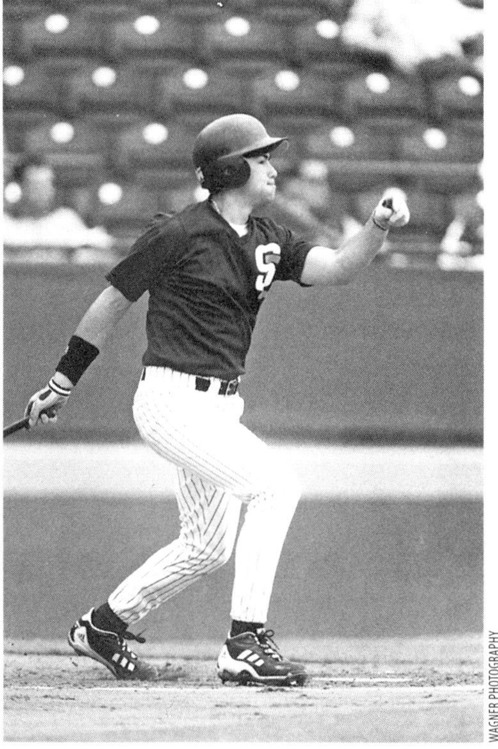

WAGNER PHOTOGRAPHY

Adrian Gonzalez became the No. 1 pick in a complicated 2000 draft because of his willingness to agree to predraft terms with the Marlins, but his talent carried him to a long major league career

Tanzer and the Rockies engaged in one of the most acrimonious negotiations in draft history. Harrington was drafted in each of the following four years, but he never played Organized Baseball, spending his pro career in independent leagues.

## DESPITE EFFORTS, BONUS RECORDS FALL

Major League Baseball made a concerted effort to curb signing bonuses, and for the better part of eight weeks, teams cooperated. Twenty-three of the 30 first-rounders, along with 76 of the top 100 picks, had agreed to terms, and most of the players signed promptly, avoiding drawn-out negotiations. With a few exceptions, players' signing bonuses slotted into the draft order, with Gonzalez's modest $3 million bonus setting the pace.

"I'm smiling because that's what negotiating training is all about," said Sandy Alderson, MLB's vice president of baseball operations. "There was a time when everybody was concerned about allowing draftees to have any professional representation. Now the professional representation in many cases exceeds the representation that clubs are getting."

The calm was shattered on July 27, when the Chicago White Sox signed Stanford outfielder Joe Borchard, their first-round pick, to a $5.3 million bonus, the richest ever for a player signing

## 2000: THE FIRST ROUNDERS

| CLUB: PLAYER, POS., SCHOOL | HOMETOWN | B-T | HT. | WT. | AGE | BONUS | FIRST YEAR | LAST YEAR | PEAK LEVEL (YEARS) |
|---|---|---|---|---|---|---|---|---|---|
| **1. Marlins: Adrian Gonzalez, 1b, Eastlake HS** | Chula Vista, Calif. | L-L | 6-2 | 190 | 18 | $3,000,000 | 2000 | Active | Majors (12) |
| Signability pick in mediocre class, but developed into productive big leaguer with sweet swing, evolving power, Gold Glove skills, though never with Marlins. | | | | | | | | | |
| **2. Twins: Adam Johnson, rhp, Cal State Fullerton** | San Diego | R-R | 6-2 | 210 | 20 | $2,500,000 | 2000 | 2006 | Majors (2) |
| Polished college arm led NCAA with 166 SO as JR, fanned 365 in 274 IP over three years; rushed to majors, had contentious career with Twins, flamed out quickly. | | | | | | | | | |
| **3. Cubs: Luis Montanez, ss, Coral Park HS** | Miami | R-R | 6-0 | 170 | 18 | $2,750,000 | 2000 | 2013 | Majors (4) |
| Smooth/easy actions at SS, playable hitting skills, but lacked speed/athleticism; languished for years in minors as outfielder, got late MLB shot with Orioles. | | | | | | | | | |
| **4. Royals: Mike Stodolka, lhp/1b, Centennial HS** | Corona, Calif. | L-L | 6-2 | 205 | 18 | $2,500,000 | 2000 | 2008 | Class AAA (1) |
| Near-equal ability as HS hitter (.593-16-45), pitcher (11-1, 1.13); Royals put him on mound initially (20-39, 6.10) until arm issues surfaced, switched roles in 2006. | | | | | | | | | |
| **5. Expos: Justin Wayne, rhp, Stanford** | Honolulu, Hawaii | R-R | 6-4 | 205 | 21 | $2,950,000 | 2000 | 2005 | Majors (3) |
| Signed club-record bonus but lacked go-to pitch; advanced college arm with command/savvy approach, but 5-8, 6.10 MLB career impacted by 2004 shoulder injury. | | | | | | | | | |
| **6. Devil Rays: Rocco Baldelli, of, Bishop Hendricken HS** | Warwick, R.I. | R-R | 6-4 | 180 | 18 | $2,250,000 | 2000 | 2010 | Majors (7) |
| Drew Joe DiMaggio comparisons with easy athleticism/tools, 2002 BA Minor League POY before blossoming career cut short by knee/elbow injuries, muscle disorder. | | | | | | | | | |
| **7. Rockies: Matt Harrington, rhp, Palmdale HS** | Palmdale, Calif. | R-R | 6-3 | 180 | 18 | Unsigned | Did Not Play Organized Baseball | | |
| Best raw arm in draft with 95-98 FB, but victim of most acrimonious negotiation ever; drafted five times, never signed, spent entire career in independent leagues. | | | | | | | | | |
| **8. Tigers: Matt Wheatland, rhp, Rancho Bernardo HS** | San Diego | R-R | 6-5 | 215 | 18 | $2,150,000 | 2000 | 2004 | Class A (3) |
| Went 11-1, 1.86 as prep SR, but scouts overlooked declining velocity; shoulder blew up, had three surgeries in first two pro years, went 3-5, 4.07 in brief career. | | | | | | | | | |
| **9. Padres: Mark Phillips, lhp, Hanover HS** | Hanover, Pa. | L-L | 6-3 | 190 | 18 | $2,200,000 | 2000 | 2003 | Class A (3) |
| Made early impression with effortless delivery, FB that topped at 97; fell out of favor with Padres with suspect work habits, hurt elbow in first spring with Yankees. | | | | | | | | | |
| **10. Angels: Joe Torres, lhp, Gateway HS** | Kissimmee, Fla. | L-L | 6-2 | 175 | 17 | $2,080,000 | 2000 | 2012 | Class AAA (2) |
| Low/mid-90s velocity dipped significantly after signing, still held his own in lower minors before TJ surgery in 2003; hung around minors in relief role until 2012. | | | | | | | | | |
| **11. Brewers: Dave Krynzel, of, Green Valley HS** | Henderson, Nev. | L-L | 6-1 | 180 | 18 | $1,950,000 | 2000 | 2009 | Majors (2) |
| With 80 grade speed, leadoff skills, CF ability, drew comparisons to Johnny Damon; moved quickly to Triple-A, but higher-level pitching proved too challenging. | | | | | | | | | |
| **12. White Sox: Joe Borchard, of, Stanford** | Camarillo, Calif. | B-R | 6-5 | 220 | 21 | $5,300,000 | 2000 | 2010 | Majors (6) |
| NFL potential as Stanford QB provided leverage for record bonus; had huge raw power/big RF arm, but struggled to make consistent contact in failed MLB career. | | | | | | | | | |
| **13. Cardinals: Shaun Boyd, of, Vista HS** | Oceanside, Calif. | R-R | 5-11 | 185 | 18 | $1,750,000 | 2000 | 2007 | Class AAA (2) |
| Impressed scouts with speed, line-drive stroke, breakout SR year (.580-13-25, 30 SB), but struggled to find defensive home, stunted offensive development. | | | | | | | | | |
| **14. Orioles: Beau Hale, rhp, Texas** | Mauriceville, Texas | R-R | 6-1 | 200 | 21 | $2,250,000 | 2001 | 2007 | Class AA (4) |
| Improved from 1-6, 6.39 in first two college seasons to 12-6, 3.10 with 95-97 mph FB; never got untracked in pros with string of elbow/shoulder injuries. | | | | | | | | | |
| **15. Phillies: Chase Utley, 2b, UCLA** | Long Beach, Calif. | L-R | 6-0 | 180 | 21 | $1,780,000 | 2000 | Active | Majors (13) |
| Initial concerns over slender frame, defense, but hit .382-22-69 for UCLA, became fixture at 2B for Phils, six-time all-star, best talent in draft because of potent bat. | | | | | | | | | |
| **16. Mets: Billy Traber, lhp, Loyola Marymount** | El Segundo, Calif. | L-L | 6-3 | 190 | 20 | $400,000 | 2001 | 2010 | Majors (5) |
| Agreed on $1.7 M bonus, forced to accept lower amount when physical revealed ligament damage in elbow; proved durable, though he won just 12 MLB games. | | | | | | | | | |
| **17. Dodgers: Ben Diggins, rhp, Arizona** | Phoenix | R-R | 6-6 | 230 | 20 | $2,200,000 | 2001 | 2005 | Majors (1) |
| Two-way talent with electric arm, big raw power; went to mound in pros, but velocity/command fluctuated, never developed secondary stuff or won MLB game. | | | | | | | | | |
| **18. Blue Jays: Miguel Negron, of, Manuela Toro HS** | Caguas, P.R. | L-L | 6-2 | 165 | 17 | $950,000 | 2000 | 2011 | Class AAA (2) |
| Second straight draft Jays took Puerto Rican OF with signability pick; pure CF skills, raw speed were best tools, poor plate approach doomed him to career in minors. | | | | | | | | | |
| **19. Pirates: Sean Burnett, lhp, Wellington HS** | Wellington, Fla. | L-L | 6-1 | 170 | 17 | $1,650,000 | 2000 | 2014 | Majors (8) |
| Second straight year Bucs took Wellington HS arm; finesse approach with excellent command, had success as MLB reliever before elbow issues resurfaced. | | | | | | | | | |
| **20. Angels: Chris Bootcheck, rhp, Auburn** | LaPorte, Ind. | R-R | 6-5 | 195 | 21 | $1,800,000 | 2001 | 2014 | Majors (7) |
| Had ingredients for success with frame, loose arm, raw stuff, bloodlines, but career never took off as projected in minors (76-66, 4.56), majors (3-7, 6.57). | | | | | | | | | |
| **21. Giants: Boof Bonser, rhp, Gibbs HS** | Pinellas Park, Fla. | R-R | 6-4 | 225 | 18 | $1,245,000 | 2000 | 2013 | Majors (4) |
| First-round reach had early success in minors when fastball touched 96 mph; legally changed name to Boof at 18, sent from Giants to Twins in one-sided '03 trade. | | | | | | | | | |
| **22. Red Sox: Phil Dumatrait, lhp, Bakersfield (Calif.) JC** | Bakersfield, Calif. | L-L | 6-2 | 175 | 18 | $1,275,000 | 2000 | 2011 | Majors (4) |
| Stock soared when he added 10-12 mph in velocity; career never took off with Sox, had TJ surgery after trade to Reds, but eventually found way to majors. | | | | | | | | | |
| **23. *Reds: David Espinosa, ss, Gulliver Prep** | Miami | B-R | 6-2 | 175 | 18 | None | 2001 | 2009 | Class AAA (3) |
| High-profile talent with speed/gap power/switch-hit skills, slid because of bonus demands; signed unique major league deal with Reds that included no bonus. | | | | | | | | | |
| **24. Cardinals: Blake Williams, rhp, SW Texas State** | San Marcos, Texas | R-R | 6-5 | 210 | 21 | $1,375,000 | 2000 | 2003 | Class A (4) |
| Made huge strides in weeks leading up to draft, early in pro career with mid-90s FB, dominant curve, but struck down by '01 TJ surgery, went just 2-11 after return. | | | | | | | | | |
| **25. Rangers: Scott Heard, c, Rancho Bernardo HS** | San Diego | L-R | 6-2 | 190 | 18 | $1,475,000 | 2000 | 2003 | Class A (4) |
| Considered for No. 1 overall because of elite catching skills, but hit sub-.300 as SR; played four uninspiring seasons in minors, saw writing on wall, abruptly retired. | | | | | | | | | |
| **26. Indians: Corey Smith, ss, Piscataway HS** | Piscataway, N.J. | R-R | 6-0 | 200 | 18 | $1,375,000 | 2000 | 2012 | Class AAA (3) |
| In Gary Sheffield mold with bat speed/HR potential, other tools; pro career never came together because of poor hitting approach, struggles on defense. | | | | | | | | | |
| **27. Astros: Robert Stiehl, rhp, El Camino (Calif.) JC** | Torrance, Calif. | R-R | 6-3 | 200 | 19 | $1,250,000 | 2000 | 2007 | Class AA (1) |
| Converted catcher with huge arm; almost never healthy after signing, had two shoulder surgeries in 2002, was inching back as a reliever before shattered leg/ankle. | | | | | | | | | |
| **28. Yankees: David Parrish, c, Michigan** | Yorba Linda, Calif. | R-R | 6-3 | 215 | 20 | $1,425,000 | 2000 | 2008 | Class AAA (4) |
| Big reach in first round because Steinbrenner feared losing Jorge Posada to free agency, mandated need for catcher; Lance's son bounced around minors nine years. | | | | | | | | | |
| **29. Braves: Adam Wainwright, rhp, Glynn Academy** | St. Simons Island, Ga. | R-R | 6-7 | 195 | 18 | $1,250,000 | 2000 | Active | Majors (10) |
| Classic Braves projection draft with local roots; team's top prospect in '03 when sent to Cards in J.D. Drew deal, became two-time NL wins leader, three-time all-star. | | | | | | | | | |
| **30. Braves: Scott Thorman, 3b, Preston HS** | Cambridge, Ontario | L-R | 6-3 | 210 | 18 | $1,225,000 | 2000 | 2011 | Majors (2) |
| Two-way player with raw power/arm strength; career slow to develop with '01 shoulder surgery, inconsistency at plate, never tapped into power in brief MLB look. | | | | | | | | | |

**Signed to major league contract.*

## AT A GLANCE

Dominican Republic, was drafted by the Pirates after an injury-plagued freshman year at Chipola (Fla.) JC. He had a breakout sophomore season and signed for $559,500 as a draft-and-follow. Bautista didn't emerge until he was traded to the Blue Jays in 2008. He hit 243 homers, including 54 in 2010, in his first eight seasons with Toronto and remained one of the game's best power hitters in 2016.

### Never Too Late

**BRIAN BUSCHER, 3B, DIAMONDBACKS (50TH ROUND).** Just like in 1999, Buscher went unsigned as a 50th-round pick. He subsequently was the latest choice in the 2000 draft to play in the big leagues.

### Overlooked

**COLTER BEAN, RHP, YANKEES; MIKE CERVENAK, 3B, YANKEES; JIM RUSHFORD, OF, BREWERS.** They were the only players to sign in 2000 as nondrafted free agents who reached the major leagues.

### International Gem

**ICHIRO SUZUKI, OF, MARINERS.** With seven straight batting titles in Japan, Ichiro was an accomplished player when the Mariners paid a $13 million posting fee to acquire his rights prior to the 2000 season and signed him to a three-year, $14 million contract. He spent 11 seasons in Seattle, winning two batting titles and setting a major league record for hits in a season, 262 in 2004. He remained active in 2016.

### Minor League Take

**DAVID ESPINOSA, SS, REDS.** The Reds had nearly exhausted their 2000 signing budget before signing Espinosa to an eight-year, $2.75 million major league contract with no signing bonus, in effect deferring the cost of his bonus. Espinosa did not play a day in the major leagues,

CONTINUED ON PAGE 526

## AT A GLANCE

CONTINUED FROM PAGE 525

hitting .251-62-325 in eight seasons in the minors and then playing nine seasons in independent leagues.

### One Who Got Away

**MATT HARRINGTON, RHP, ROCKIES (1ST ROUND).** Harrington didn't sign with the Rockies as the seventh pick overall, after talks between his agent, Tommy Tanzer, and the Rockies broke down into the nastiest negotiation in draft history. Tanzer sought a $4.95 million bonus, based on the $3.96 million bonus paid to 1999 No. 1 pick Josh Hamilton, plus 25 percent for inflation. The Rockies countered with an eight-year major league contract, which was rejected. Harrington was selected in each of the next four drafts—in each case in a descending round—and did not sign with any of the teams that picked him.

### He Was Drafted?

**MICHAEL VICK, OF, ROCKIES (30TH ROUND).** The Rockies took a flier on the athletic Vick after he finished third in Heisman Trophy balloting after the 1999 season as a freshman at Virginia Tech. A year later, he was the No. 1 pick overall in the NFL draft. Vick did not play baseball in college.

### Did You Know . . .

A record 16 first-round picks from the 2000 draft played independent baseball at some point in their careers, an indicator of the underwhelming and underachieving talent that permeated the first round.

### They Said It

Agent **TOMMY TANZER**, the representative for Rockies first-round draft pick **MATT HARRINGTON**, after a negotiating session with the Rockies: "The Rockies staff, when I was done with them, looked like highway pizza—they were all laying by the side of the road like they got hit by a Lincoln Continental going 100 miles an hour."

WAGNER PHOTOGRAPHY

**White Sox first-rounder Joe Borchard set a new draft standard with his $5.3 million bonus, but his major league career did not pan out**

with the team that drafted him. Borchard topped Hamilton's record mark by 34 percent.

Borchard, the 12th overall selection, was expected to get more than Gonzalez, given his negotiating leverage. He was slated to be Stanford's starting quarterback in the fall and was regarded as one of the top QB prospects for the 2001 NFL draft. Negotiations lagged all summer, and as football practice drew near, Borchard and his agent, Jim McDowell, raised the ante from $3.5 million to $4 million to $5.3 million. Due to Borchard's status as a two-sport athlete, the White Sox could have paid out his bonus over a five-year period, but agreed to give him all of his money by January 2003—provided Borchard gave up football.

"In my judgment, it isn't a good signing," Alderson said. "It's unfortunate when clubs that are usually at the forefront of industry criticism end up adopting the same practices themselves."

White Sox scouting director Duane Shaffer considered Borchard's bonus reasonable, given that he had football as leverage and also was the top-rated player on the Sox's draft board. Shaffer noted the contract was in line with the major league deals signed a year earlier by Josh Beckett and Eric Munson, the second and third picks overall.

"For people to criticize us, it's totally unfair," Shaffer said.

Once Borchard signed, other lucrative deals soon followed. Texas high school first baseman Jason Stokes and two college players, Stanford righthander Jason Young and California third baseman Xavier Nady, all were considered early first-round material but fell to the second round because of their bonus demands. They ended up getting paid as first-rounders: Young, $2.75 million from the Rockies; Stokes, $2.027 million from the Marlins; and Nady, $1.1 million from the San Diego Padres as part of a major league contract that guaranteed him another $1.75 million.

Two other developments that drew the ire of the commissioner's office were the signings of third-rounder Grady Sizemore by the Montreal Expos and fifth-rounder Jace Brewer by the Devil Rays. The Expos lured Sizemore, a Washington high school outfielder, away from a football career at the University of Washington with a $2 million bonus. Brewer, a sophomore-eligible shortstop at Baylor, signed a four-year, major league contract with a total value of $1.5 million, including a $450,000 bonus.

Several more first round-equivalent bonuses spilled into the later rounds. Princeton righthander Chris Young, a third-rounder, signed with the Pittsburgh Pirates for $1.65 million. The 6-foot-10 Young was a two-sport star in college with aspirations of playing in the NBA. Two fourth-rounders, righthander Zach Miner (Braves) and lefthander Sam Hays (Mariners), signed deals for $1.25 million and $1.2 million.

Lefthander Sean Henn, a 32nd-round pick of the New York Yankees, didn't sign until the following spring after his sophomore year at McLennan

## How They Should Have Done It

Based on career WAR (Wins Above Replacement, as calculated by Baseball-Reference.com) achieved by players eligible for the 2000 draft through the 2015 season, here's how the first round should have unfolded. Numbers in parentheses indicate the round when the player was drafted. Asterisks denote players who signed as draft-and-follows.

| | Player, Pos. | Actual Draft | WAR | Bonus |
|---|---|---|---|---|
| 1. | Chase Utley, 2b | Phillies (1) | 62.3 | $1,780,000 |
| 2. | Cliff Lee, lhp | Expos (4) | 44.3 | $275,000 |
| 3. | Adrian Gonzalez, 1b | Marlins (1) | 41.8 | $3,000,000 |
| 4. | Adam Wainwright, rhp | Braves (1) | 36.6 | $1,250,000 |
| 5. * | Jose Bautista, 3b | Pirates (20) | 33.8 | $559,500 |
| 6. | Brandon Webb, rhp | Diamondbacks (8) | 31.4 | $68,000 |
| 7. | Yadier Molina, c | Cardinals (4) | 30.4 | $325,000 |
| 8. | James Shields, rhp | Devil Rays (16) | 29.1 | $262,500 |
| 9. | Grady Sizemore, of | Expos (3) | 27.2 | $2,000,000 |
| 10. | Mike Napoli, c | Angels (17) | 26.6 | $105,000 |
| 11. | Jason Bay, of | Expos (22) | 24.3 | $1,000 |
| 12. | Edwin Encarnacion, 3b | Rangers (9) | 23.9 | $55,000 |
| 13. | David DeJesus, of | Royals (4) | 23.0 | $235,000 |
| 14. | Dontrelle Willis, lhp | Cubs (8) | 20.3 | $200,000 |
| 15. | Chris Young, rhp | Pirates (3) | 19.1 | $1,650,000 |
| 16. | Josh Willingham, ss | Marlins (17) | 18.4 | $16,000 |
| 17. * | Rich Harden, rhp | Athletics (17) | 17.6 | $60,000 |
| 18. | Kelly Johnson, ss | Braves (1-S) | 17.4 | $790,000 |
| 19. | Freddy Sanchez, ss | Red Sox (11) | 15.8 | $1,000 |
| 20. | Clint Barmes, ss | Rockies (10) | 15.4 | $45,000 |
| 21. | Corey Hart, of | Brewers (11) | 14.7 | $45,000 |
| 22. | Adam LaRoche, 1b | Braves (29) | 14.1 | $40,000 |
| 23. | Rocco Baldelli, of | Devil Rays (1) | 10.2 | $2,250,000 |
| 24. | Ryan Church, of | Indians (14) | 9.1 | $1,500 |
| 25. | Bobby Jenks, rhp | Angels (5) | 8.5 | $165,000 |
| 26. | Chad Qualls, rhp | Astros (2) | 6.5 | $415,000 |
| 27. | Nate McLouth, of | Pirates (25) | 6.3 | $400,000 |
| 28. | Sean Burnett, lhp | Pirates (1) | 6.0 | $1,650,000 |
| 29. | Joe Inglett, of | Indians (8) | 4.9 | $20,000 |
| 30. | Michael Morse, ss | White Sox (3) | 4.7 | $365,000 |

| | Top 3 Unsigned Players | | | Year Signed |
|---|---|---|---|---|
| 1. | Ian Kinsler, ss | Diamondbacks (29) | 46.7 | 2003 |
| 2. | Russell Martin, 3b | Expos (35) | 33.3 | 2002 |
| 3. | Aaron Hill, ss | Angels (7) | 23.4 | 2003 |

(Texas) JC. He got a $1.701 million signing bonus, a record for a draft-and-follow. Henn injured his elbow in his first season in the Yankees system, but eventually got to the major leagues, going 2-10, 7.42 in six seasons.

While other teams lavished rich bonuses on draft picks, the Cincinnati Reds signed both their first-round and second-round choices without paying them a signing bonus, the only time that has happened in draft history. The Reds drafted Florida high school shortstop David Espinosa and Pepperdine catcher Dane Sardinha, but the team didn't have the money in their budget to pay the going rate for either player. Reds general manager Jim Bowden struck a deal with Scott Boras, the agent for both players, to sign each to a major league contract, which enabled the Reds to defer financial compensation to future years.

Espinosa's deal was spread over eight years and guaranteed him $2.95 million, with the potential to earn as much as $5 million through incentives and roster bonuses. Sardinha's package, spread over six years, guaranteed him $1.95 million with incentives and roster bonuses providing for a maximum of $2.4 million. "We had to get creative to get these deals done," Boras said.

The 29 first-round picks who signed received an average bonus of $1,872,586, just a 3 percent increase over the 1999 average of $1,809,767. Considering that Espinosa did not get a bonus, New York Mets first-rounder Billy Traber (16th overall) signed for $400,000 due to ligament damage in his elbow, and Harrington did not sign, the average could have been considerably higher.

The average second-round bonus of $767,172 was substantially greater than the previous record of $585,408 set in 1999, and that figure did not reflect the full financial impact of the major league contracts signed by Nady and Sardinha. In all, 17 players received at least $2 million in 2000, compared with 10 a year earlier.

The Atlanta Braves, in the midst of 10 straight postseason appearances, spent $8.396 million on bonuses, more than any other team, but less than the record $8.92 million the Baltimore Orioles spent a year earlier. The Braves made eight draft choices before the Seattle Mariners made their first selection.

The Pirates and Expos, despite their small-market status, were among the most aggressive spenders. The Pirates spent $6,629,500, and the Expos doled out $5,905,500. They were the only clubs to spend more than $1 million on their third-round

## Fastest To The Majors

| Player, Pos. | Drafted (Round) | Debut |
|---|---|---|
| 1. # Xavier Nady, 1b | Padres (2) | Sept. 30, 2000 |
| 2. Adam Johnson, rhp | Twins (1) | July 16, 2001 |
| 3. Bobby Hill, 2b | Cubs (2) | May 10, 2002 |
| 4. Ryan Bukvich, rhp | Royals (11) | July 12, 2002 |
| 5. Joe Borchard, of | White Sox (1) | Sept. 2, 2002 |
| Ben Diggins, rhp | Dodgers (1) | Sept. 2, 2002 |

**FIRST HIGH SCHOOL SELECTION:** Rocco Baldelli, of (Devil Rays/1, March 31, 2003)

*#Debuted in major leagues.*

## DRAFT SPOTLIGHT: MATT HARRINGTON

LARRY GOREN

**Matt Harrington had ability that matched anyone in the 2000 class, but he never signed that year or ever played in the affiliated minor leagues**

Agent Tommy Tanzer said the Colorado Rockies agreed before the 2000 draft to meet Matt Harrington's demand of a $4.95 million signing bonus. The Rockies denied that, asserting they merely indicated money would not keep them from drafting Harrington, which they did with the seventh overall pick.

From there, Tanzer and the Rockies engaged in one of the most bitter negotiations in draft history, a fierce, yearlong war of words that ended with Harrington leaving millions of dollars on the table and starting down a path to baseball oblivion.

A 6-foot-5 righthander from Palmdale (Calif.) High with a fastball that peaked at 98 mph, Harrington was arguably the top prospect in the entire 2000 draft pool. But with teams on notice to hold the line on signing bonuses after years of rampant inflation, the first six teams determined that his bonus demands were out of line and passed on him.

The Rockies, though, were confident they could strike a deal and took him. Tanzer wanted a $4.95 million signing bonus for Harrington and contended the Rockies agreed to meet Harrington's figure, but reneged. Josh Byrnes, the Rockies assistant general manager, maintained no such offer was made. "I was trying to be as noncommittal as I could," Byrnes said, "but give him the one indisputable promise: 'He will not get past our pick.' There were no financial assurances. Tommy heard what he wanted to hear."

From an initial offer of $2.2 million, the Rockies increased their tender over the next several weeks to $3.2 million and then to $4 million after the Chicago White Sox signed their top pick, Joe Borchard, for a record bonus of $5.3 million. In harsher terms, Tanzer told the Rockies to shove it. A war of words ensued, first privately, then through the media. The Rockies grew increasingly frustrated that members of their front office were stymied in attempts to meet with the Harrington family without Tanzer present.

The Rockies increased their offer over the next eight months and eventually presented Harrington with a major league contract valued at $4.9 million. Tanzer rejected the offer out of hand. The Harrington family said later they were pressured by Tanzer not to take the deal. The offer was taken off the table, and the sides never came to an agreement.

Harrington had committed to pitching for Arizona State, but decided to forgo college and instead join the St. Paul Saints of the independent Northern League before the 2001 draft. Playing against older players with professional experience, Harrington was overmatched and began overthrowing to compensate. He steadily lost velocity on his fastball, and in 19 innings with the Saints went 0-2, 9.47.

Harrington slipped to the Padres with the 58th overall pick in the 2001 draft. The Harrington family fired Tanzer a few weeks into talks with the Padres and later sued him for mishandling negotiations. (The case was settled out of court.) Harrington hired Scott Boras, but he couldn't get a deal with the Padres, whose best offer was $1.2 million.

Harrington was drafted three more times, by the Devil Rays, Reds and Yankees, but did not sign. He continued to regress, enduring arm problems at times and appearing to lose confidence in himself after repeated shaky outings in independent ball.

The Harringtons blamed both Tanzer and Boras for their son's predicament.

"I felt very responsible because, as a father, I should have been able to take more control of it," said Bill Harrington. "But at the same time, we did trust another human being we hired to make sure that was taken care of properly. We didn't want to be taken advantage of by an organization, but we didn't want things to fall apart, either."

Harrington finally signed with the Chicago Cubs as a nondrafted free agent in 2006, receiving a $1,000 bonus. He was released during spring training the following year and returned to independent ball before calling it a career in 2007 at age 25.

"It hasn't been a perfect journey, but it's my journey," Harrington said. "I'm sure there are a lot of people out there who think I'm an idiot because I turned down a $4 million contract. But there were other things involved, and the advice I received wasn't great. I've had to live with that, and I'm just trying to make the best of a bad situation."

## WORTH NOTING

Louisiana State won its fifth College World Series title in 10 years in 2000, beating Stanford, 6-5, in the final. The Cardinal featured three of the five players who got the richest signing bonuses after being drafted that year: outfielder **JOE BORCHARD**, and righthanders **JUSTIN WAYNE** and **JASON YOUNG**. LSU was led by catcher **BRAD CRESSE**, a fifth-round pick of the Diamondbacks, who drove in the winning run in the bottom of the ninth of the championship game. Cresse led the NCAA ranks in homers (30), RBIs (106) and total bases (217) that year, and first baseman **BRAD HAWPE**, an 11th-round pick of the Rockies, set an NCAA single-season record with 36 doubles.

San Diego's Rancho Bernardo High produced two first-rounders in 2000: righthander **MATT WHEATLAND** (Tigers, eighth overall) and catcher **SCOTT HEARD** (Rangers, 25th). It was the third time high school teammates went in the first round of the same draft. It first happened in 1972 with Rancho Cordova (Calif.) High outfielder Mike Ondina (White Sox) and shortstop Jerry Manuel (Tigers), and again 25 years later with third baseman Michael Cuddyer (Twins) and lefthander John Curtice (Red Sox) of Great Bridge High in Chesapeake, Va.

Team USA won the gold medal at the 2000 Sydney Olympics, beating Cuba, 4-0, in the gold medal game on the three-hit pitching of righthander **BEN SHEETS**, a Brewers farmhand at the time and a 1999 first-round pick. It was the first time the tournament was open to professionals. Team USA featured minor leaguers and won seven of eight games in the eight-nation event.

The Pirates took a pitcher from Wellington (Fla.) Community High in the first round for the second straight year. After choosing righthander **BOBBY BRADLEY** at No. 8 in 1999, they

picks. The Expos also committed the third-highest bonus in the first round, to Stanford righthander Justin Wayne ($2.95 million). And the Pirates paid the largest bonus in the fifth (Jason Sharber, $500,000), seventh (Cole Burzynski, $175,000), 20th (Jose Bautista, $559,500) and 25th rounds (Nate McLouth, $400,000).

### MARLINS SET TONE WITH TOP PICK

With the first overall selection, the Marlins made it a priority to lock up a player before the draft and avoid spending as much as they did to sign Beckett in 1999. Beckett held out for most of the summer before securing a $7 million big league deal that included a $3.625 million bonus. The Marlins didn't view any players in the 2000 draft pool to be the equal of Hamilton and Beckett.

Some 12 to 15 players were considered as the potential first overall pick. The Marlins focused initially on Harrington, the hardest-throwing pitcher in the draft, but it was fleeting because of Harrington's financial demands. Two weeks before the draft, the Marlins narrowed their list to two San Diego high school players, Gonzalez and catcher Scott Heard, with Pennsylvania high school lefthander Mark Phillips an outside possibility.

Both Gonzalez and Heard had plenty of support from Florida's California-based scouts, but others in the organization had doubts that Gonzalez would develop enough power. However, he was willing to accept their bonus offer before the draft.

It took awhile, but Gonzalez developed into one of the best run producers in the major leagues, more than justifying his selection. Starting in 2006, he hit .292 with 283 homers and 1,032 RBIs over a 10-year span, and played Gold Glove defense. Gonzalez was long gone from Florida by that time, having been traded to the Texas Rangers, Padres, Boston Red Sox and finally the Los Angeles Dodgers. He was still active in 2016.

The Marlins got little direct benefit for making the right call on Gonzalez, but could take solace that they chose him instead of Harrington, Heard or Phillips, none of whom came close to reaching the big leagues. Phillips, the ninth overall selection, by the Padres, did not get past Double-A in a four-year career impacted by arm injuries. Heard, a defensive specialist with a suspect bat, was the 25th pick, by the Rangers. He quit after four seasons, none above Class A.

The Twins, too, considered Harrington before spending the second overall pick on Cal State Fullerton righthander Adam Johnson, the NCAA strikeout leader, who signed within a matter of days for $2.5 million. The Chicago Cubs took Miami high school shortstop Luis Montanez with the No. 3 selection and announced his signing for a $2.75 million bonus two days later. Both bonuses were substantially below the amounts for the corresponding picks a year earlier.

Holding the fourth overall pick, the Kansas City Royals took California high school lefthander Mike Stodolka, who signed the next day for $2.5 million. The Expos followed by taking Wayne, who was pitching in the College World Series. They believed they had a deal in place with the Stanford righthander, but it fell apart and Wayne didn't sign

### Top 25 Bonuses

| Player, Pos. | Drafted (Round) | Order | Bonus |
|---|---|---|---|
| **1. Joe Borchard, of** | **White Sox (1)** | **12** | **$5,300,000** |
| **2.* Adrian Gonzalez, 1b** | **Marlins (1)** | **1** | **$3,000,000** |
| **3. Justin Wayne, rhp** | **Expos (1)** | **5** | **$2,950,000** |
| **4.* Luis Montanez, ss** | **Cubs (1)** | **3** | **$2,750,000** |
| **Jason Young, rhp** | **Rockies (1)** | **47** | **$2,750,000** |
| **6. Adam Johnson, rhp** | **Twins (1)** | **2** | **$2,500,000** |
| * Mike Stodolka, lhp/1b | Royals (1) | 4 | $2,500,000 |
| **8.* Rocco Baldelli, of** | **Devil Rays (1)** | **6** | **$2,250,000** |
| Beau Hale, rhp | Orioles (1) | 14 | $2,250,000 |
| 10.* Mark Phillips, lhp | Padres (1) | 9 | $2,200,000 |
| **Ben Diggins, rhp** | **Dodgers (1)** | **17** | **$2,200,000** |
| 12.* Matt Wheatland, rhp | Tigers (1) | 8 | $2,150,000 |
| 13.* Joe Torres, lhp | Angels (1) | 10 | $2,080,000 |
| 14.* Jason Stokes, of | Marlins (1) | 41 | $2,027,000 |
| **15.* Grady Sizemore, of** | **Expos (3)** | **75** | **$2,000,000** |
| **16.* David Krynzel, of** | **Brewers (1)** | **11** | **$1,950,000** |
| **17. Chris Bootcheck, rhp** | **Angels (1)** | **20** | **$1,800,000** |
| **18. Chase Utley, 2b** | **Phillies (1)** | **15** | **$1,780,000** |
| 19.* Shaun Boyd, of | Cardinals (1) | 13 | $1,750,000 |
| **20.# Sean Henn, lhp** | **Yankees (26)** | **788** | **$1,701,000** |
| **21.* Sean Burnett, lhp** | **Pirates (1)** | **19** | **$1,650,000** |
| **Chris Young, rhp** | **Pirates (3)** | **89** | **$1,650,000** |
| 23.* Scott Heard, c | Rangers (1) | 25 | $1,475,000 |
| 24. David Parrish, c | Yankees (1) | 28 | $1,425,000 |
| **Bobby Hill, ss** | **Cubs (2)** | **43** | **$1,425,000** |

*Major leaguers in bold. *High school selection. #Signed as draft-and-follow.*

for almost two months, getting $2.95 million.

Of the top five picks, scouts said Montanez was the only one who likely would have gone that early based solely on talent. Johnson, Montanez and Wayne all had brief, unproductive careers in the major leagues, and Stodolka peaked in Triple-A.

### UNCONVENTIONAL FIRST-ROUNDERS

The emphasis in both the 1999 and 2000 drafts was on signability, which might help explain why just 16 of 30 first-round picks in 2000 and 14 in 1999 reached the major leagues, a 50 percent success rate that ranks as the poorest two-year stretch in draft history. In the same time period, only 17 of 31 supplemental first-rounders and 31 of 60 second-rounders got to the big leagues.

Among players drafted in the first round in 2000, only Gonzalez, second baseman Chase Utley (Phillies, 15th overall) and righthander Adam Wainwright (Braves, 29th) enjoyed superior careers. Outfielder Rocco Baldelli (Devil Rays, sixth) would have joined that group had his promising career not been compromised by injuries and illness. Among 17 pitchers taken in the first round, only nine made it to the majors, and Wainwright was the only one with a winning record.

Traber, a lefthander who went 10-4, 3.15 with 156 strikeouts in 123 innings as a junior at Loyola Marymount, was the Mets' first-round pick. He agreed to a $1.7 million bonus in mid-August, but the Mets retracted the offer after a physical revealed a partial ligament tear in Traber's left elbow. He later agreed to a devalued $400,000 signing bonus. Traber didn't pitch for the Mets during his five-year, major league career, but appeared in 215 games for other teams, posting a 12-14, 5.65 record.

## Largest Bonuses By Round

| | Player, Pos. | Club | Bonus |
|---|---|---|---|
| **1.** | **Joe Borchard, of** | **White Sox** | **$5,300,000** |
| 1-S. | * Tripper Johnson, 3b | Orioles | $1,050,000 |
| **2.** | **Jason Young, rhp** | **Rockies** | **$2,750,000** |
| **3.** | *** Grady Sizemore, of** | **Expos** | **$2,000,000** |
| **4.** | *** Zach Miner, rhp** | **Braves** | **$1,250,000** |
| 5. | * Jeff Sharber, rhp | Pirates | $500,000 |
| **6.** | *** Taylor Buchholz, rhp** | **Phillies** | **$375,000** |
| 7. | * Jerry Oakes, rhp | Brewers | $175,000 |
| | * Cole Burzynski, rhp | Pirates | $175,000 |
| | **Erick Threets, lhp** | **Giants** | **$175,000** |
| | * Brian Almeida, rhp | Braves | $175,000 |
| **8.** | ***# Nick Masset, rhp** | **Rangers** | **$225,000** |
| 9. | Tanner Eriksen, rhp | Diamondbacks | $190,000 |
| **10.** | ***# Heath Phillips, lhp** | **White Sox** | **$90,000** |
| 11. | * Kevin Cust, c | Braves | $200,000 |
| 12. | * Brad George, rhp | Reds | $450,000 |
| 13. | * Matt Yeatman, rhp | Brewers | $150,000 |
| 14. | * Mike Machen, rhp | Braves | $150,000 |
| 15. | * Eric Mosley, rhp | Yankees | $150,000 |
| 16. | # Anthony Pannone, rhp | Giants | $500,000 |
| **17.** | **Doug Slaten, lhp** | **Diamondbacks** | **$275,000** |
| 18. | Vince Perkins, rhp | Blue Jays | $40,000 |
| 19. | # Brian Lockwood, rhp | Devil Rays | $200,000 |
| **20.** | **# Jose Bautista, 3b** | **Pirates** | **$559,500** |
| 21. | # Zach Parker, lhp | Rockies | $625,000 |
| 22. | * Ron Davenport, ss | Blue Jays | $140,000 |
| 23. | * Rylan Reed, rhp | White Sox | $425,000 |
| **24.** | **# Shawn Riggans, c** | **Devil Rays** | **$200,000** |
| **25.** | *** Nate McLouth, of** | **Pirates** | **$400,000** |
| **Other** | **# Sean Henn, lhp** | **Yankees (26)** | **$1,701,000** |

*Major leaguers in bold. *High school selection. #Signed as draft-and-follow.*

Both the Reds and Devil Rays had to be creative in order to get their top picks signed, in most cases deferring their financial obligations to later years. The Devil Rays used their first pick on Baldelli, a multi-sport high school athlete from Rhode Island. They were able to spread his $2.25 million bonus over a five-year period by taking advantage of the draft rule as it applied to two-sport athletes.

In addition to a baseball scholarship offer from Wake Forest, Baldelli had a scholarship offer to UCLA for volleyball and an invitation to play basketball at Princeton. He also was a state champion sprinter. "He's a special athlete with all the quick-twitch muscles," Rays scouting director Dan Jennings said. "Even at 6-foot-4, he runs extremely well and is very graceful."

The Rays also were able to sign Brewer, their fifth-round pick, by giving him a major league contract, enabling them to pay most of his $1.5 million deal on an incremental basis.

Baldelli's career was cut short in its prime by a muscle disorder, and Brewer did not play above Triple-A in eight pro seasons. Per his contract, Brewer was promoted to the Devil Rays in September 2000, but did not appear in a game.

The Reds secured their first- and second-round picks, Espinosa and Sardinha, by signing them to major league contracts with no signing bonuses. They signed Arkansas high school righthander Dustin Moseley, a supplemental first-rounder, for $930,000, but only by waiting until Nov. 1, the start of a new fiscal year. Effectively, the team borrowed from its 2001 budget to pay Moseley.

Espinosa spent two years in the Reds farm system before being traded to the Detroit Tigers. He played through 2015, including eight seasons in independent ball, but never set foot in the majors. Moseley spent seven seasons in the majors (none with the Reds) and went 15-21, 4.67. Sardinha's big league career lasted six seasons, though he played in just two games for the Reds.

Had Stokes, Young and Nady, in particular, been more amenable to signing, they almost assuredly would have been selected among the first 10 picks and not slipped to the second round.

The 6-foot-4, 225-pound Stokes was considered the top high school power-hitting prospect in the draft, but when he asked for $2.5 million before the draft, he dropped to the first pick of the second round (Marlins, 41st overall). Florida signed Stokes two days before he was set to enroll at the University of Texas, and his bonus was larger than what 18 first-rounders received.

Given that the Marlins, one of the industry's most cost-conscious teams, had spent more than $5 million on two high school first basemen, it was inevitable that one would be expendable. The Marlins decided to part ways with Gonzalez, especially after Stokes hit .341 with 27 homers in low Class A in 2002. Stokes, however, did not advance past Triple-A, and Gonzalez developed into standout major league player.

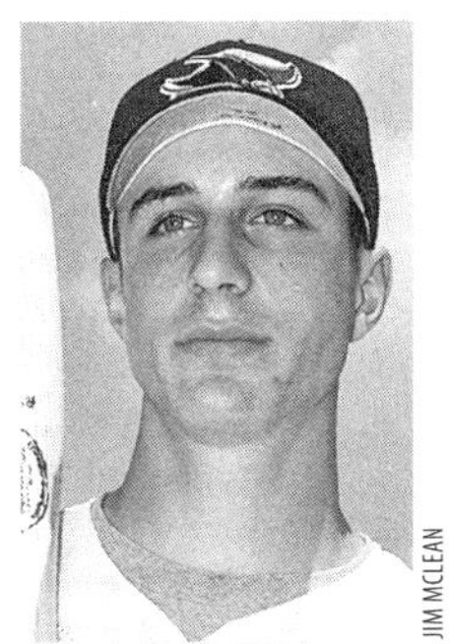

JIM MCLEAN

Rocco Baldelli

The Rockies considered selecting Young instead of Harrington with the seventh overall pick, and were excited when Young was still available at No. 47. Young would not agree to a predraft financial

## One Team's Draft: Pittsburgh Pirates

| Player, Pos. | Bonus | Player, Pos. | Bonus | Player, Pos. | Bonus |
|---|---|---|---|---|---|
| **1. *Sean Burnett, lhp** | **$1,650,000** | 10. Brandon Chaves, ss | $60,000 | 19. * Mike Connolly, lhp | $25,000 |
| 2. *David Beigh, rhp | $635,000 | 11. *Kyle Parcus, lhp | Did not sign | **20. Jose Bautista, 3b** | **$559,500** |
| **3. Chris Young, rhp** | **$1,635,000** | 12. *Jason Keyser, rhp | $50,000 | 21. John Larson, rhp | Did not sign |
| 4. Patrick Boyd, of | Did not sign | 13. Troy Veleber, of | $67,500 | 22. Shannon Cabell, lhp | $20,000 |
| 5. *Jason Sharber, rhp | $500,000 | 14. Victor Buttler, of | $60,000 | 23. Josh Higgins, rhp | $20,000 |
| 6. *Josh Shortslef, lhp | $200,000 | 15. *Sean Smith, 3b-of | $40,000 | 24. * Ryan Kanekeberg, rhp | Did not sign |
| 7. *Cole Burzynski, rhp | $175,000 | 16. David Baum, lhp | $61,000 | **25. *Nate McLouth, 2b** | **$400,000** |
| 8. *Kurt Shafer, rhp | $125,000 | 17. Daylon Monette, of | Did not sign | **Other*Ian Snell (26), rhp** | **$20,000** |
| 9. *Chris Bass, ss | $85,000 | 18. Jon Pagan, 1b | $30,000 | | |

*Major leaguers in bold. *High school selection.*

### WORTH NOTING

selected lefthander **SEAN BURNETT** at No. 19 in 2000.

Agent **SCOTT BORAS'** influence on the 2000 draft didn't end with the nine players he represented. He also was the guiding force behind North Carolina high school catcher **LANDON POWELL'S** effort to circumvent the draft. Powell, a junior at Apex High, was projected as a top prospect for the 2001 draft, but he procured a general equivalency diploma and petitioned Major League Baseball for inclusion in the 2000 draft. When no team drafted Powell—because no one realized he was eligible—Boras made a case that the player should be declared a free agent, according to draft rules in place, and eligible to sign with any club. The commissioner's office imposed a signing freeze on Powell while it investigated. On Aug. 9, MLB ruled that he was a free agent, but Powell had lost two months of negotiating time by then, and the response by clubs to his bold maneuver was lukewarm. Fewer than half of the major league clubs had representatives at two workouts designed to showcase Powell. He received generally positive reviews, but many scouts said they needed more time to evaluate him. "We had no interest," Phillies scouting director Mike Arbuckle said. "I get tired of Scott looking for loopholes to circumvent the draft. If Landon Powell was so special, then maybe. But I don't think he's a franchise-type player. We won't dive into that." The Powell case became much ado about nothing. He returned to Apex High in the fall and then enrolled at the University of South Carolina for the spring semester, which postponed his draft eligibility to 2003. He didn't sign with the Cubs that year after being selected in the 25th round, and returned to college for his senior year. Powell was chosen in the first round of the 2004 draft by the Athletics, and he played briefly in the major leagues.

**IN FOCUS: ADRIAN GONZALEZ**

STEVE MOORE

The Marlins' sentiment to select Adrian Gonzalez with the No. 1 pick in the 2000 draft wasn't universally shared, but this draft wasn't about trying to line up talent. It was more about teams taking the best player they could sign, and the Marlins achieved their goal—even as there were doubts that Gonzalez might ever develop top-of-the-line power required of a first baseman in an era of offensive fireworks.

"That was a big thing, getting everything done quickly," said Gonzalez, who hit .598-14-37 as a prep senior. "That takes a lot of pressure off your back. Now all I have to do is play ball."

As expected, Gonzalez struggled to hit for power in the minors, was quickly dispatched by the Marlins and never asserted himself as a big leaguer in his first seven pro seasons; he had just a .229 average and seven homers in 59 games with the Rangers to show for his career through the 2005 season.

But in 2006, after being traded for a second time, Gonzalez suddenly evolved into a legitimate power threat and over the next 10 years, first with the Padres, and then with the Red Sox and Dodgers, he hit an aggregate .292 with 283 homers and 1,032 RBIs. He established himself as one of the best all-around hitters in the game—and a player worthy of being the No. 1 pick.

## Highest Unsigned Picks

| Player, Pos., Team (Round) | College | Re-Drafted |
|---|---|---|
| Matt Harrington, rhp, Rockies (1) | None | Padres '01 (2) |
| Aaron Heilman, rhp, Twins (1) | * Notre Dame | Mets '01 (1) |
| Tyrell Godwin, of, Rangers (1) | * North Carolina | Blue Jays '01 (3) |
| Tagg Bozied, 1b, Twins (2) | * San Francisco | Padres '01 (3) |
| Jon Skaggs, rhp, Orioles (4) | * Rice | Yankees '01 (1) |
| Patrick Boyd, of, Pirates (4) | * Clemson | Rangers '01 (7) |
| Marc Kaiser, rhp, Reds (4) | Arizona | Rockies '03 (10) |
| Eric Keefner, 3b, Astros (4) | Arizona State | White Sox '02 (22) |
| Brian Montalbo, rhp, Braves (4) | California | Brewers '03 (7) |
| Tony Richie, c, White Sox (5) | Florida State | Cubs '03 (4) |

**TOTAL UNSIGNED PICKS:** Top 5 Rounds (12), Top 10 Rounds (24)

**Returned to same school.*

arrangement, slipped out of the first round, and held out most of the summer. He signed one day before he was scheduled to return to Stanford for his senior year. The Rockies gave Young a club-record bonus, which also was the richest bonus outside the first round in 2000. The 12th college pitcher selected, Young received a larger bonus than any other college pitcher except Wayne, the fifth overall pick. Young made no impact in the major leagues, going 0-3, 9.71 in 10 appearances in 2003-04.

Nady, the top-rated college prospect at the outset of the 2000 season, lasted until No. 49 because he sought a contract in line with what Munson had received a year earlier. Per the four-year, $2.85 million deal the Padres gave him on Sept. 17, Nady was promoted to the big leagues later that month, the first player from the 2000 draft to reach the majors. His big league career lasted 12 years, and he hit .268 with 105 homers.

### TEAMS CONSPIRE TO LIMIT BONUSES

MLB held a negotiating seminar prior to the 2000 draft intended to help clubs hold the line on signing bonuses. While it gave no official mandates, to avoid running afoul of the union and being accused of collusion, it became apparent that $3 million was the suggested benchmark for the first pick in the draft, and $1 million for the 30th and last pick in the first round. Teams were expected to slot bonuses accordingly, and they did for the most part.

By June 19, two weeks after the two-day draft began, 13 first-round picks had signed, and the bonuses, on average, were almost 10 percent less than for the corresponding picks a year earlier. That was in stark contrast to the previous few years, when bonuses often increased across the board at a rate of 30 to 40 percent.

"I've never seen negotiations occur before like they have this year," said agent David Sloane, who negotiated his first contract for a first-round pick in 1975. "There's no question teams are playing with other team's figures, both above and below them."

Sloane negotiated a $2.08 million deal with the Anaheim Angels for Florida high school lefthander Joe Torres, the 10th overall pick. Not only was Torres' bonus $370,000 less than the figure paid in that draft slot a year earlier, but the amount was slotted between the $2.15 million the Padres gave the eighth pick, righthander Matt Wheatland, and the $1.95 million bonus the Brewers gave outfielder David Krynzel, the 11th pick.

Tanzer, who represented Harrington and four other first-rounders, was convinced teams colluded. "There's no question that a collective strategy on the part of the clubs is at work here," he said. "Negotiations are more contrived, a little more centrally controlled than they've ever been."

Boras had nine clients in the draft, and all were selected later than their talent might indicate because of signability concerns. They included Espinosa and Auburn University righthander Chris Bootcheck, who were selected in the first round but went considerably lower than expected.

Nady, Sardinha and Young were rated as early first-round material, but not drafted until the second round, where they joined two other Boras clients, first baseman Tag Bozied (Twins) and infielder Bobby Hill (Cubs). All were initially offered substantially less than their talent warranted, but Boras held firm, even as his players remained unsigned entering September.

"Teams will do what's best for themselves," Boras said. "They always do. Everything so far is consistent with recent draft history. A lot of the best players this year were not drafted in the top round, that's obvious to everyone. And it's because they would not agree to pre-draft deals."

Espinosa and Sardinha signed their unique deals with the Reds on Sept. 1. Miner also signed that day with the Braves, getting a record bonus for a fourth-round choice. Bootcheck, the 20th overall pick, was still at an impasse with the Angels three weeks after classes began for his senior year at Auburn. He and the Angels finally agreed to a $1.8 million deal on Sept. 8. Later that month, Nady and Young finalized their deals with the Padres and Rockies for amounts that were in keeping with their status as two of the top talents in the draft.

That left Hill, Bozied and fourth-rounder Patrick Boyd unsigned. Boras negotiated a $1.425 million bonus for Hill on Dec. 19. Hill had been a second-rounder of the White Sox a year earlier out of the University of Miami, but did not sign and spent the 2000 season playing for Newark of the independent Atlantic League rather than return to college for his senior year. Hill was the third member of the Class of 2000 to reach the majors.

Bozied (San Francisco) and Boyd (Clemson) both returned to college for their senior season, and each went through another long and drawn out process a year later before signing.

## Largest Draft-And-Follow Bonuses

| | Player, Pos. | Club (Round) | Bonus |
|---|---|---|---|
| **1.** | **Sean Henn, lhp** | **Yankees (26)** | **$1,701,000** |
| 2. | Zach Parker, lhp | Rockies (21) | $625,000 |
| **3.** | **Jose Bautista, 3b** | **Pirates (20)** | **$559,500** |
| **4.** | *** Kason Gabbard, lhp** | **Red Sox (29)** | **$550,000** |
| 5. | Jon Asahina, rhp | Marlins (31) | $512,500 |
| 6. | Anthony Pannone, rhp | Giants (16) | $500,000 |
| **7.** | **Kurt Birkins, of/lhp** | **Orioles (33)** | **$395,000** |
| **8.** | *** Nick Masset, rhp** | **Rangers (8)** | **$225,000** |
| 9. | Brian Lockwood, rhp | Devil Rays (19) | $200,000 |
| | **Shawn Riggans, c** | **Devil Rays (24)** | **$200,000** |

*Major leaguers in bold. *High school selection.*

# 2000 Draft List

**Did not sign. Major leaguers in bold, with first and last years noted. Order of selection indicated in parentheses. For the first five rounds, the peak level of each player is noted. + Signed as draft-and-follow (Second school noted if applicable).*

## ANAHEIM ANGELS (10)

1. Joe Torres, lhp, Gateway HS, Kissimmee, Fla.—(AAA)
**1. Chris Bootcheck, rhp, Auburn University** (Choice from Athletics as compensation for Type B free agent Mike Magnante).**—(2003-13)**
2. Jared Abruzzo, c, El Capitan HS, La Mesa, Calif.—(AA)
**3. Tommy Murphy, ss, Florida Atlantic University.—(2006-07)**
4. Charlie Thames, rhp, University of Texas.—(AA)
**5. Bobby Jenks, rhp, Spirit Lake, Idaho.—(2005-11)**
6. Brandon O'Neal, rhp, University of Kansas.
**7. *Aaron Hill, ss, Redwood HS, Visalia, Calif.—(2005-15)**
DRAFT DROP *First-round draft pick (13th overall), Blue Jays (2003)*
8. Adam Pace, lhp, Dominican (N.Y.) College.
9. Jason Coulie, of, Bates (Maine) College.
**10. Matt Hensley, rhp, Grossmont (Calif.) JC.—(2004)**
11. *Garrett Patterson, lhp, McAlester (Okla.) HS.
12. Scott Schneider, rhp, Norfolk State University.
13. Josh Gray, of, Rock Creek HS, Durant, Okla.
14. Kevin Jenkins, of, Northwestern HS, Miami.
15. *Geoff Smart, lhp, Kalamalka SS, Vernon, B.C.
16. Johnny Raburn, ss, University of South Florida.
DRAFT DROP *Brother of Ryan Raburn, major leaguer (2004-15)*
**17. Mike Napoli, c, Flanagan HS, Cooper City, Fla.—(2006-15)**
18. Tony Socarras, c, University of Florida.
19. Brandon Rogers, c, San Diego State University.
20. Brett Cimorelli, rhp, Zephyrhills (Fla.) HS.
21. Rich Fischer, rhp, San Bernardino Valley (Calif.) JC.
22. Jeremy Ward, lhp, Florida Southern College.
23. *Brian Finch, rhp, Columbia HS, Brazoria, Texas.
24. Ryan Withey, of, Florida Atlantic University.
25. +Ransel Melgarejo, of, Miami (Fla.) Senior HS / Broward (Fla.) JC.
26. J.R. Warner, of, University of Missouri.
27. Zack Roper, of, Florida Atlantic University.
28. *Leo Calderon, rhp, Killian HS, Miami.
29. Kevin Kay, c, University of North Florida.
30. Larry Bowles, lhp, Virginia Tech.
31. Jeff Stockton, ss, University of North Florida.
32. *Clint Hart, lhp, Florida CC.
33. Adam Belicic, lhp, George Washington University.
34. *James Langham, of, Jones County HS, Gray, Ga.
35. Tymber Lee, rhp, Wichita State University.
36. *Jon Chretien, rhp, LaGrange HS, Lake Charles, La.
37. Gilbert Landestoy, rhp, Florida International University.
38. *Richard Brantley, lhp, Apopka (Fla.) HS.
39. *Casey Mutter, rhp, Rialto (Calif.) HS.
40. *David Marchbanks, lhp, Mauldin HS, Simpsonville, S.C.
41. *Kellen Dupree, rhp, Baker County HS, MacClenny, Fla.
42. *Adam Lesko, rhp, Cheyenne HS, Las Vegas, Nev.
43. +Jeff Balser, rhp, Polk (Fla.) CC.
44. *Ron Ennis, lhp, Polk (Fla.) CC.
45. *Brian Nagore, c, Okaloosa-Walton (Fla.) CC.
46. *Robert Bellazetin, 3b, Miami (Fla.) Senior HS.
47. *Dan Stillman, rhp, University of Central Florida.
48. *Andrew Daly, rhp, Indian River (Fla.) CC.
49. *Zack Matthews, of, Howard (Texas) JC.
**50. *David Murphy, 1b-of, Klein HS, Spring, Texas.—(2006-15)**
DRAFT DROP *First-round draft pick (17th overall), Red Sox (2003)*

**Braves first-rounder Adam Wainwright blossomed into an ace after a trade to the Cardinals**

## ARIZONA DIAMONDBACKS (29)

1. (Choice to Braves as compensation for Type A free agent Russ Springer)
**2. Mike Schultz, rhp, Loyola Marymount University.—(2007)**
**3. Bill White, lhp, Jacksonville State University.—(2007-08)**
**4. Josh Kroeger, of, Scripps Ranch HS, San Diego.—(2004)**
5. Brad Cresse, c, Louisiana State University.—(AAA)
6. Scott Barber, rhp, University of South Carolina
**7. Tim Olson, of, University of Florida.—(2004-05)**
**8. Brandon Webb, rhp, University of Kentucky.—(2003-09)**
9. Tanner Eriksen, rhp, University of Southern California.
10. Cedrick Harris, of, Louisiana State University.
11. +Rick Haydel, ss, University of Louisiana-Lafayette.
**12. Brian Bruney, rhp, Warrenton (Ore.) HS.—(2004-12)**
13. Pete Sikaras, rhp, University of St. Francis (Ill.).
14. +Jesus Cota, 1b, Pima (Ariz.) CC.
15. Julius Foreman, of, Augusta (Ga.) College.
16. Will Rosellini, rhp, University of Dallas.
**17. Doug Slaten, lhp, Los Angeles Pierce JC.—(2006-12)**
18. Vince Eppolito, rhp, Shippensburg (Pa.) University.
19. Aric LeClair, lhp, Indiana State University.
20. Chris Lesieur, rhp, University of New Haven.
21. Jason Williams, ss, University of California.
22. +Corby Medlin, rhp, Katy (Texas) HS / San Jacinto (Texas) JC.
23. *Brett Korth, rhp, Genoa-Kingston HS, Genoa, Ill.
**24. Andy Green, 2b, University of Kentucky.—(2004-09)**
25. James Gregg, rhp, George C. Wallace (Ala.) CC.
26. Greg Belson, rhp, Montclair State (N.J.) College.
27. John Sherlock, c, Hopkins HS, Minnetonka, Minn.
28. Matt Steele, rhp, University of Georgia.
**29. *Ian Kinsler, ss, Canyon del Oro HS, Tucson, Ariz.—(2006-15)**
30. *Ryan Costello, lhp, Gloucester County (N.J.) CC.
31. John Massey, c, University of Tennessee.
32. *Ralph Roberts, of-rhp, Lenoir (N.C.) CC.
33. *Khari Council, 1b, McClancy Memorial HS, Jamaica, N.Y.
34. Steve Woodward, of, Cal State Fullerton.
35. Joe Ricciardi, rhp, Saint Leo (Fla.) College.
36. Joey Cramblitt, rhp, University of Mississippi.
37. *Trey Rice, lhp, Galveston (Texas) JC.
38. *Oscar Mattox, lhp, Phoenix JC.
39. *Brandon Simon, of, West Hills (Calif.) CC.
40. *Josh Perrault, rhp, Red Mountain HS, Mesa, Ariz.
41. Orlando Delanuez, ss, Miami Springs (Fla.) HS.
42. *Charles Parkinson, of, Blue Ridge HS, Lakeside, Ariz.
43. Carlton Wells, lhp, Hillsborough (Fla.) CC.
44. Marques Chilsom, of, Brandon (Fla.) HS.
45. *Robert Ramsey, rhp, Bowie HS, Austin, Texas.
46. *Luis Trinidad, lhp, Long Beach (Calif.) CC.
47. *Andrew Wishy, of, Raytown South HS, Kansas City, Mo.
48. *Creighton Kahoalii, c, Newark Memorial HS, Fremont, Calif.
49. *Eric Anderson, lhp, Lake Dallas HS, Corinth, Texas.
**50. *Brian Buscher, 3b, Central Florida CC.—(2007-09)**

## ATLANTA BRAVES (30)

**1. Adam Wainwright, rhp, Glynn Academy, St. Simons, Ga.** (Choice from Diamondbacks as compensation for Type A free agent Russ Springer).**—(2005-15)**
**1. Scott Thorman, 3b, Preston HS, Cambridge, Ontario.—(2006-07)**
**1. Kelly Johnson, ss, Westwood HS, Austin, Texas** (Supplemental choice—38th—as compensation for Type A free agent Jose Hernandez).**—(2005-15)**
1. Aaron Herr, ss, Hempfield HS, Lancaster, Pa. (Supplemental choice—40th—as compensation for Springer).—(AAA)
DRAFT DROP *Son of Tommy Herr, major leaguer (1979-91)*
2. Bubba Nelson, rhp, Riverdale Baptist HS, Fort Washington, Md. (Choice from Brewers as compensation for Hernandez).—(AAA)
2. Bryan Digby, rhp, McIntosh HS, Peachtree City, Ga.—(AA)
**3. Blaine Boyer, rhp, Walton HS, Marietta, Ga.—(2005-15)**
**4. Zach Miner, rhp, Palm Beach Gardens (Fla.) HS** (Choice from Devil Rays as compensation for Type B free agent Gerald Williams).**—(2006-13)**
4. *Brian Montalbo, rhp, Dimond HS, Anchorage, Alaska.—(Low A)
DRAFT DROP *Attended California; re-drafted by Brewers, 2003 (7th round) • Son of Mel Montalbo, defensive back, National Football League (1962)*
**5. Chris Waters, rhp, South Florida CC.—(2008-09)**
6. Matt Merricks, lhp, Oxnard (Calif.) HS.
DRAFT DROP *Brother of Charles Merricks, 17th-round draft pick, Rockies (2000)*
7. Brian Almeida, rhp, Lemon Bay HS, Englewood, Fla.
8. Robert Perkins, c, Modesto (Calif.) JC.
9. Ahmad Woods, of, Redan HS, Stone Mountain, Ga.
10. Rod Douglas, rhp, Colmesneil (Texas) HS.
11. Kevin Cust, c, Immaculata HS, Flemington, N.J.
DRAFT DROP *Brother of Jack Cust, first-round draft pick, Diamondbacks (1997); major leaguer (2001-11)*
12. Keoni DeRenne, ss, University of Arizona.
13. Jonathan Rogers, rhp, Robert E. Lee HS, Midland, Texas.
14. Mike Machen, rhp, McGill-Toolen HS, Mobile, Ala.
15. Armando Tejero, 1b, Elvira M. Colon HS, Santa Isabel, P.R.
16. Andrew Bent, rhp, University of Nebraska.
**17. Trey Hodges, rhp, Louisiana State University.—(2002-03)**
18. *Mike Davern, rhp, Brea-Olinda HS, Brea, Calif.
**19. Charles Thomas, of, Western Carolina University.—(2004-05)**
20. +Kyle Roat, c, Connors State (Okla.) JC.
21. Matt Wright, rhp, Robinson HS, Lorena, Texas.
22. Josh Tillery, rhp, Dodge City (Kan.) CC.
23. Mike Smalley, lhp, University of Florida.
24. Robert Moose, 1b, Bridgewater (Va.) College.
25. *Tim McClendon, rhp, Dr. Phillips HS, Orlando, Fla.
DRAFT DROP *Brother of Matt McClendon, first-round draft pick, Braves (1996)*
26. Alph Coleman, of, Texas Southern University.
27. *Josh Wyrick, of, Centennial HS, Bakersfield, Calif.
28. Erick Contreras, ss, Culver-Stockton (Mo.) College.
**29. Adam LaRoche, 1b, Seminole State (Okla.) CC.—(2004-15)**
DRAFT DROP *Son of Dave LaRoche, major leaguer (1970-83) • Brother of Andy LaRoche, major leaguer (2007-13)*
30. Quentin Jones, rhp, Norfolk State University.
**31. *Delwyn Young, 2b, Little Rock HS, Lancaster, Calif.—(2006-10)**
**32. *Callix Crabbe, 2b, Stone Mountain HS, Lithonia, Ga.—(2008)**
**33. *Anthony Gwynn, of, Poway (Calif.) HS.—(2006-14)**
DRAFT DROP *Son of Tony Gwynn, major leaguer (1982-2001)*
34. *Adam Brandenburg, lhp, South Gwinnett HS, La Grange, Ga.
35. *William Hall, lhp, Evant HS, Hamilton, Texas.
36. *Efren Lira, rhp, Mount San Antonio (Calif.) JC.
37. *Joshua Parker, rhp, Wallace State (Ala.) CC.
38. +Francisco Arteaga, rhp, East Los Angeles JC.
39. *Jimmy Rhodes, rhp, Jefferson HS, Shepherdstown, W.Va.
40. *Adam Hilzendeger, rhp, Palmdale (Calif.) HS.
41. *Shane Hawk, lhp, Midwest City (Okla.) HS.
42. *Zach Watson, rhp, Columbus (Ga.) HS.

43. *Daniel Anderson, of, Temple (Texas) JC.
44. *Tanner Holecek, of, Temple (Texas) JC.
45. *Craig Bragg, of, Bellarmine Prep, San Jose, Calif.
46. *Brandon Green, ss, Adair (Okla.) HS.
47. *Justin Bergh, rhp, Oak Hall HS, Reddick, Fla.
48. *Jason Herman, rhp, Marshfield (Mo.) HS
49. *Bill Edwards, rhp, Evangelical Christian HS, Cordova, Tenn.
50. *Drew Jackson, of, University HS, Morgantown, W.Va.

## BALTIMORE ORIOLES (14)

1. Beau Hale, rhp, University of Texas.—(AA)
1. Tripper Johnson, 3b-rhp, Newport HS, Bellevue, Wash. (Supplemental choice—32nd—as compensation for Type A free agent Arthur Rhodes).—(AA)
2. (Choice to Twins as compensation for Type A free agent Mike Trombley)
3. Richard Bartlett, rhp, Kamiakin HS, Kennewick, Wash.—(AA)
3. Tommy Arko, c, Cooper HS, Abilene, Texas (Choice from Mariners as compensation for Rhodes).—(High A)
4. *Jon Skaggs, rhp, Rice University.—(AA)

DRAFT DROP *Returned to Rice; re-drafted by Yankees, 2001 (1st round)*

5. Doug Gredvig, 1b, Sacramento (Calif.) CC.—(AA)
6. Brandon Spillers, rhp, Tattnall Square Academy, Roberta, Ga.
7. B.J. Littleton, of, Lamar University.
8. Jayme Sperring, rhp, Rice University.

DRAFT DROP *Son of Rob Sperring, major leaguer (1974-77)*

9. Mike Russell, c, Bothell (Wash.) HS.
10. Casey Cahill, rhp, Immaculata HS, New Brunswick, N.J.
11. *Darren Heal, rhp, Oklahoma State University.
12. Kris Wilken, c-3b, University of Houston.
13. Ryan Keefer, rhp, Southern Columbia Area HS, Catawissa, Pa.
14. Brian Forystek, lhp, Illinois State University.
15. Thomas Joyce, of, First Presbyterian HS, Macon, Ga.
16. D.J. Jones, lhp, University of Texas.
17. Joel Crump, lhp, Yuma (Ariz.) HS.
18. *Kyle Sleeth, lhp, Northglenn HS, Westminster, Colo.

DRAFT DROP *First-round draft pick (3rd overall), Tigers (2003)*

19. Shayne Ridley, ss, Ball State University.

DRAFT DROP *Twin brother of Jeremy Ridley, 34th-round draft pick, Blue Jays (2000)*

20. *Ryan Mask, rhp, Garces Memorial HS, Bakersfield, Calif.
21. *Fraser Dizard, lhp, Meadowdale HS, Edmonds, Wash.
22. Aaron Bouie, rhp, St. Bonaventure University.
23. *Eric Walsh, rhp, El Toro HS, Mission Viejo, Calif.
24. Raul Rodriguez, ss, Iowa Western CC.
25. *Jeff Petersen, rhp, Kentwood HS, Covington, Wash.
26. Dan Marchetti, rhp, Ohio Wesleyan University.
27. *Scott Koffman, rhp, Olympus HS, Salt Lake City.
28. *Robert Cheatwood, lhp, Allan Hancock (Calif.) JC.
29. *Wes Morrow, rhp, Sherman (Texas) HS.
30. *Donnie Poles, of, Harding HS, Charlotte, N.C.
31. *Andy Hargrove, 1b, St. Ignatius HS, Cleveland.

DRAFT DROP *Son of Mike Hargrove, major leaguer (1974-85); major league manager (1991-2007)*

**32. *Brandon Fahey, 3b, Grayson County (Texas) CC.—(2006-08)**

DRAFT DROP *Son of Bill Fahey, first overall draft pick, Senators (1970); major leaguer (1971-83)*

**33. +Kurt Birkins, of-lhp, Los Angeles Pierce JC.—(2006-08)**
**34. *Josh Banks, rhp, Severna Park HS, Arnold, Md.—(2007-10)**
**35. *Jeff Salazar, of, Connors State (Okla.) JC.—(2006-09)**
**36. *Tim Stauffer, rhp, Saratoga Central Catholic HS, Saratoga Springs, N.Y.—(2005-15)**

DRAFT DROP *First-round draft pick (4th overall), Padres (2003)*

37. *Ryan Newman, ss, Scottsdale (Ariz.) CC.
38. *Chaz Macklin, c, East St. Louis (Ill.) HS.
39. *Matt Harter, c, Penns Valley Area HS, Springs Mill, Pa.
40. *Sean Patrick, c, John Logan (Ill.) CC.
41. *Justin Ruchti, c, San Jacinto (Texas) JC.
42. *Eric Fagan, lhp, Taft (Calif.) JC.

## BOSTON RED SOX (22)

**1. Phil Dumatrait, lhp, Bakersfield (Calif.) JC.—(2007-11)**
**2. Manny Delcarmen, rhp, West Roxbury HS, Hyde Park, Mass.—(2005-10)**
3. Matt Cooper, 1b, Ripley HS, Stillwater, Okla.—(High A)
4. Brandon Mims, lhp, Prattville (Ala.) HS.—(Short-season A)
**5. Brian Esposito, c, University of Connecticut.—(2007-10)**
6. Kenny Perez, ss, South Miami HS, Miami.
7. Tony Fontana, rhp, Bowling Green State University.
8. Brian Adams, lhp, Liberty University.
9. Patrick Johnson, of, William Carey (Miss.) College.
10. *Eric Doble, rhp, Arizona State University.
**11. Freddy Sanchez, ss, Oklahoma City University.—(2002-11)**
12. Shane Hall, rhp, Eastern Arizona JC.
13. *Mike Quintana, of, Florida International University.
14. Ian Perio, lhp, University of San Francisco.
15. Dustin Brisson, 3b, University of Central Florida.
16. Josh Thigpen, rhp, Rogers HS, Greenville, Ala.
17. Chris Elmore, lhp, University of North Carolina.
18. *Haas Pratt, 3b, Rancho Bernardo HS, San Diego.
19. Justin Sherrod, 3b, Rollins (Fla.) College.
20. Brian Bentley, rhp, University of Louisville.
21. *Ryan Carroll, rhp, Mississippi State University.
22. Felix Villegas, rhp, Muscatine (Iowa) CC.
23. Raul Nieves, ss, University of Mobile (Ala.).
24. Freddie Money, of, Wallace State (Ala.) CC.
25. *Jon Gutierrez, lhp, Central Arizona JC.
26. *Marcellus Dawson, of, Muscatine (Iowa) CC.
27. *James Morrison, rhp, Beulah HS, Valley, Ala.
28. *Travis Kaats, of, Desert Mountain HS, Scottsdale, Ariz.
**29. +Kason Gabbard, lhp, Royal Palm Beach (Fla.) HS / Indian River (Fla.) CC.—(2006-08)**
30. *Jeremy Terni, ss, Montville HS, Uncasville, Conn.
31. *Tom Major, rhp, New London (Conn.) HS.
32. *Eric Rollins, rhp, Latta (Okla.) HS.
33. *Barton Braun, lhp, Vallejo (Calif.) HS.
34. *John Carreon, rhp, Arizona Western JC.
**35. +Dusty Brown, c, Bradshaw Mountain HS, Prescott Valley, Ariz. / Yavapai (Ariz.) JC.—(2009-11)**
36. *Mike Guerrero, of, South Mountain (Ariz.) CC.
37. +Brett Bonvecho, 3b, Prospect HS, Saratoga, Calif. / West Valley (Calif.) JC.
38. *Daniel Coffee, of, St. Bernard's HS, Old Lyme, Conn.
39. *Gabriel Roberti, rhp, West Hills HS, Lakeside, Calif.
40. *Brad Bettcher, rhp, Palo Verde HS, Tucson, Ariz.
41. *Ferrari Miller, of, Castlemont HS, Oakland.
42. *Javi Herrera, c, Gulliver Prep, Miami.
**43. *Chris Duffy, of, South Mountain (Ariz.) CC.—(2005-09)**
44. *Kevin Brown, 1b, University of Miami (Fla).
45. *Nathan Goodrich, lhp, Mercyhurst (Pa.) College.
46. *Donald Benson, 3b, Mount San Jacinto (Calif.) JC.

## CHICAGO CUBS (3)

**1. Luis Montanez, ss, Coral Park HS, Miami.—(2008-11)**
**2. Bobby Hill, ss, Newark (Atlantic League).—(2002-05)**
3. Aaron Krawiec, lhp, Villanova University.—(AA)
3. Nic Jackson, of, University of Richmond (Choice from Devil Rays as compensation for Type B free agent Steve Trachsel).—(AAA)
**4. Todd Wellemeyer, rhp, Bellarmine (Ky.) College.—(2003-10)**
5. Gary Banks, ss, Southern Choctaw HS, Gilbertown, Ala.—(Short-season A)

DRAFT DROP *Wide receiver, National Football League (2008-10)*

6. J.J. Johnson, ss, Greenbrier HS, Appling, Ga.
**7. Ryan Jorgensen, c, Louisiana State University.—(2005-08)**
**8. Dontrelle Willis, lhp, Encinal HS, Alameda, Calif.—(2003-11)**
9. Mark Freed, lhp, Mississippi State University.
10. Blake Blasi, 2b, Wichita State University.
**11. Jon Leicester, rhp, University of Memphis.—(2004-07)**
12. Antoine Cameron, of, Riverside (Calif.) CC.
13. Jeremy Flanagan, rhp, San Lorenzo HS, Richmond, Calif.
**14. Jason Dubois, of, Virginia Commonwealth University.—(2004-05)**
15. *Matt Tribble, of, Wheaton Warrenville HS, Wheaton, Ill.
16. *Chad Corona, ss-3b, Santa Fe Christian HS, Carlsbad, Calif.
17. *David Jablonski, rhp, Lord Beaverbrook HS, Calgary, Alberta.
**18. Buck Coats, ss, Valdosta (Ga.) HS.—(2006-08)**
19. +Nick Williamson, of, Benedictine HS, Richmond, Va. / Louisburg (N.C.) JC.
**20. Carmen Pignatiello, lhp, Providence Catholic HS, Frankfurt, Ill.—(2007-08)**
21. Lukas McKnight, c, Triton (Ill.) JC.
22. Peter Graham, of, St. John's University.
23. John-Paul Glascock, rhp, Fullerton (Calif.) JC.
24. *Lance Dawkins, ss, Caledonia HS, Columbus, Miss.
25. Scott Fries, lhp, University of Nebraska.
26. *Jonathan Anderson, of, Grace Prep Academy, Cedar Hill, Texas.
**27. Jason Szuminski, rhp, Massachusetts Institute of Technology.—(2004)**
28. Ryan Burnau, rhp, Huntington North HS, Markle, Ind.
29. *Matt Samuels, rhp, South Vigo HS, Terre Haute, Ind.
30. *Pat Flynn, of, Providence Catholic HS, New Lenox, Ill.
31. +Wes O'Brien, rhp, Don Lugo HS, Chino Hills, Calif. / Fullerton (Calif.) JC.
32. *Orlando Diaz, ss-2b, Downers Grove North HS, Downers Grove, Ill.
33. *Larry Barnes, 3b, Pine Bluff (Ark.) HS.
34. Eric Albright, rhp-3b, Chapman (Calif.) University.
35. *Rocky Evans, rhp, Motlow State (Tenn.) CC.
36. *Brett Watkins, 1b, Petal (Miss.) HS.
37. *Donnie Bair, lhp-of, Merced (Calif.) JC.
38. *Jon Nourie, lhp, Munster (Ind.) HS.
39. *Joseph Catomer, rhp, Prospect HS, Mount Prospect, Ill.
40. *Jeremy Mannin, lhp, Wenatchee Valley (Wash.) CC.
41. *Brad Blackwell, rhp, Broken Arrow (Okla.) HS.
42. *Federico Baez, 3b, Laredo (Texas) CC.
43. *Thomas Olejniczak, rhp, Fayetteville (Ark.) HS.
44. *Stephen Solwick, rhp, Belleville Area (Ill.) CC.
45. Sammy Cooper, ss, University of New Orleans.
46. *Jason McIntire, rhp, Plainville (Conn.) HS.
47. *Jamil Knight, rhp, Selma (Ala.) HS.
48. *Lance Laury, of, Lower Richland HS, Hopkins, S.C.
49. *J.E. Cruz, ss, Bellaire (Texas) HS.

DRAFT DROP *Son of Jose Cruz, major leaguer (1970-88) • Brother of Jose Cruz Jr., major leaguer (1997-2008)*

50. *Nate Pendley, lhp, West Albany (Ore.) HS.

## CHICAGO WHITE SOX (12)

**1. Joe Borchard, of, Stanford University.—(2002-07)**
**2. Tim Hummel, ss, Old Dominion University.—(2003-04)**
**3. Michael Morse, ss, Nova HS, Plantation, Fla.—(2005-15)**
4. Alvin Jones, rhp, Seguin (Texas) HS.—(Rookie)
5. *Tony Richie, c, Bishop Kenny HS, Jacksonville, Fla.—(AAA)

DRAFT DROP *Attended Florida State; re-drafted by Cubs, 2003 (4th round)*

6. Bjorn Ivy, of, Shannon (Miss.) HS.
7. Eddie Young, of, Jones County HS, Macon, Ga.
8. Chris Amador, ss, Luis Felipe Crespo HS, Camuy, P.R.
9. Jason Aspito, of, Loyola Marymount University.
**10. +Heath Phillips, lhp-1b, Central HS, Evansville, Ind. / Lake City (Fla.) JC.—(2007)**
11. Tommy Nicholson, 2b, University of Texas.
12. Mike Spidale, ss, Nazareth Academy, Broadview, Ill.
13. Derek Wigginton, of, University of Alabama.
14. James Sweeney, lhp, Holy Cross College.
15. John Lackaff, 2b, Miami (Ohio) University.
16. Brian Graham, rhp, University of Portland.
17. *Ryan Liermann, 3b, Downers Grove South HS, Downers Grove, Ill.
18. Curtis Young, rhp, Lamar (Colo.) CC.
19. *Scott Perhla, lhp, Southridge HS, Miami.
20. *Etienne Ratte-Delorme, rhp, Edouard Montpetit HS, St. Hubert, Quebec
21. *Joe Solis, rhp, Christopher Columbus HS, Miami.
22. *Gerron McGary, lhp, Nashville (Ark.) HS.
23. Rylan Reed, rhp-1b, Crossett (Ark.) HS.
24. *Kyle Boyer, 3b, Temecula Valley HS, Temecula, Calif.
25. *Travis NeSmith, lhp, Gulliver Prep, Miami.
26. *Victor Martinez, of, Barbara Goleman HS, Hialeah, Fla.
27. Brad Murray, lhp, Embry-Riddle (Fla.) University.
28. Brad Bohannan, rhp, University of Arkansas.
29. Anthony Monegan, of, Kishwaukee (Ill.) JC.
30. *Brian Keating, rhp, Lewis & Clark (Ill.) CC.
31. Darren Ciraco, of, Briarcliffe (N.Y.) JC.
32. +Brandon Bounds, of, Mansfield (Texas) HS / Grayson County (Fla.) CC.
33. *Jeff Lundgren, c, Chaparral HS, Scottsdale, Ariz.
34. *Ricky Spivey, rhp, Glen Este HS, Cincinnati.
35. *Michael Oehlberg, lhp, Kishwaukee (Ill.) CC.
36. Armando Perez, lhp, Southwestern (Calif.) JC.
37. *Matt Maley, of, Killian HS, Miami.
**38. *Tom Gorzelanny, lhp, Marist HS, Orland Park, Ill.—(2005-15)**
39. +Tyrel Davis, 3b-of, Columbia Basin (Wash.) CC.
40. *Jarod Tate, lhp, Lumberton (Texas) HS.
41. *Brian Barr, rhp, Arkansas HS, Texarkana, Ark.
42. *Fernando Alvarez, of, Dodge City (Kan.) CC.
43. *Brian Schweiger, c, Fontana (Calif.) HS.
44. *Dustin Knight, c, North Little Rock (Ark.) HS.
45. *Danny Girardo, of, Coral Park HS, Miami.
46. *John Grose, c, Green Valley HS, Henderson, Nev.
47. *Corry Parrott, of, Long Beach State University.
48. *Jason Hutton, of, University of North Carolina-Charlotte.
49. *Tony Sterioti, rhp, Kishwaukee (Ill.) JC.
50. *Freddie Mitchell, of, UCLA.

DRAFT DROP *Wide receiver, National Football League (2001-04)*

## CINCINNATI REDS (23)

1. David Espinosa, ss, Gulliver Prep, Miami.—(AAA)
**1. Dustin Moseley, rhp, Arkansas HS, Texarkana, Ark.** (Supplemental choice—34th—as compensation for Type A free agent Juan Guzman).**—(2006-12)**
**2. Dane Sardinha, c, Pepperdine University** (Choice from Devil Rays as compensation for Guzman).**—(2003-11)**

DRAFT DROP *Brother of Bronson Sardinha, first-round draft pick, Yankees (2001); major leaguer (2007)*

**2. Ryan Snare, lhp, University of North Carolina.—(2004)**
3. David Gil, rhp, University of Miami.—(AAA)
4. *Marc Kaiser, rhp, Reno (Nev.) HS.—(AAA)

DRAFT DROP *Attended Arizona; re-drafted by Rockies, 2003 (10th round)*

5. *Roydell Williams, of, East St. John HS, LaPlace, La.—DNP

DRAFT DROP *Attended Tulane; never re-drafted; wide receiver, National Football League (2005-10)*

6. Ryan Mottl, rhp, Clemson University.
7. Dan Fletcher, rhp, Bridge City (Texas) HS.
8. *Dan Gooris, lhp, Creighton University.
9. Bryan Edwards, rhp, Newark (Atlantic League).
10. Noochie Varner, 3b, St. Catharine (Ky.) JC.
11. Chris Williamson, 1b, McNeese State University.
12. Brad George, rhp, Canyon HS, New Braunfels,

Texas.
13. Omar Lopez, rhp, Blanca Malaret HS, Sabana Grande, P.R.
14. *Eric Sultemeier, of-ss, New Braunfels (Texas) HS.
15. Brian Ross, lhp, Old Dominion University.
16. *Jason Arnold, rhp, University of Central Florida.
17. Adam Sheefel, lhp, Ball State University.
18. Jeff Schachleiter, rhp, Colerain HS, Cincinnati.
19. *Danny Eisentrager, rhp-ss, Sacramento (Calif.) CC.
20. Matt Bynum, rhp, Chipola (Fla.) JC.
21. *Matt Moyer, rhp, Shelton State (Ala.) CC.
22. Clint Collins, rhp, University of South Carolina.
**23. Steve Smitherman, of, University of Arkansas-Little Rock.—(2003)**
24. Todd Stone, c, Southeastern Oklahoma State University.
25. Josh Tomsu, rhp, Southwest Texas State University.
26. Brandon Culp, rhp, Jacksonville State University.
27. Ryan Smith, of, University of Texas-San Antonio.
28. *Jason Moates, rhp, Middle Tennessee State University.
29. Andy Boutwell, rhp, Valdosta State (Ga.) University.
30. *Ron Hayward, of, Bishop State (Ala.) JC.
31. *Danny Touchet, rhp, Palm Beach Lakes (Fla.) HS.
32. Nathan Culwell, c-of, Wayland Baptist (Texas) University.
33. *Gerrit Simpson, rhp, Connors State (Okla.) JC.
34. *Rod Allen, 3b, Desert Vista HS, Phoenix.
DRAFT DROP *Son of Rod Allen, major leaguer (1983-88)*
35. *Andrew Murray, ss, John Tyler HS, Tyler, Texas.
36. *Bo Dickerson, lhp, T.C. Roberson HS, Asheville, N.C.
37. Sean Patterson, 1b, Cascade HS, Everett, Wash.
38. *Jason John, rhp, Calallen HS, Corpus Christi, Texas.
39. *Brendon Davis, rhp, Richland (Texas) JC.
40. +Dwayne Wagnon, rhp, Calallen HS, Corpus Christi, Texas.
41. *Herman Rogers, rhp, Athens (Texas) HS.
42. *Eric Mitchell, c, George Washington University.
43. Mike Laesch, rhp, Iowa State University.
44. Bryan Anderson, ss, Southwest Texas State University.
45. Eric Spadt, 2b, Penn State University.
**46. *Chris Schroder, rhp, Oklahoma City University.—(2006-08)**
47. Eddie Sparks, c, East Tennessee State University.
48. *John Paul Garcia, rhp, Uvalde (Texas) HS.
49. *Brandon Pyles, rhp, Kennedale HS, Arlington, Texas.
50. *Jude Auzenne, rhp, Humble (Texas) HS.

## CLEVELAND INDIANS (26)

1. Corey Smith, ss, Piscataway (N.J.) HS.—(AAA)
**1. Derek Thompson, lhp, Land O'Lakes (Fla.) HS** (Supplemental choice—37th—as compensation for Type A free agent Mike Jackson).—**(2005)**
**2. Brian Tallet, lhp, Louisiana State University** (Choice from Phillies as compensation for Jackson).—**(2002-11)**
2. Mark Folsom, of, West Orange HS, Winter Garden, Fla.—(Low A)
3. Sean Swedlow, c, San Dimas (Calif.) HS.—(Low A)
4. Adam Cox, of, Darton (Ga.) College.—(High A)
5. Rashad Eldridge, of, First Presbyterian HS, Macon, Ga.—(AAA)
6. Kyle Evans, rhp, Baylor University.
7. Victor Kleine, lhp, John A. Logan (Ill.) JC.
**8. Joe Inglett, of, University of Nevada-Reno.—(2007-11)**
9. *Scott Tolbert, rhp, Madison County HS, Danielsville, Ga.
10. Tom Canale, rhp, California Lutheran University.
11. Scott Threinen, 3b, Kasson-Mantorville HS, Mantorville, Minn.
12. *Jason Colson, rhp, Winthrop University.
13. Jeff Haase, c, Cleveland State University.
**14. Ryan Church, of, University of Nevada-Reno.—(2004-10)**
15. Nate Janowicz, of, University of South Carolina.
16. Luke Field, rhp, Arizona State University.
17. Brandon Matheny, lhp, Emory & Henry (Va.) College.
18. *Jeremy Rogelstad, rhp, San Jose State University.
19. Chad Cislak, rhp, UCLA.
20. Ryan Larson, rhp, Sacramento (Calif.) CC.
21. Steve Fugarino, rhp, Iona University.
22. Vance Pietro, 3b, Creighton University.
23. *Brandon Harmsen, rhp, Jemison (Mich.) HS.
24. *Chris Houser, 3b, University of Texas.
25. Andy Helmer, rhp, Purdue University.
26. Rodney Choy Foo, ss, Kailua (Hawaii) HS.
27. Johri Litman, rhp, Yavapai (Ariz.) JC.
28. *Jeff Opalewski, rhp, Heritage HS, Saginaw, Mich.
**29. +Jon Van Every, of, Itawamba (Miss.) JC.—(2008-10)**
**30. *Brian Wilson, rhp, Londonderry (N.H.) HS.—(2006-14)**
**31. *Conor Jackson, 3b, El Camino Real HS, Woodland Hills, Calif.—(2005-11)**
DRAFT DROP *First-round draft pick (19th overall), Diamondbacks (2003)*
32. +Scott Thomas, rhp, Lake Michigan CC.
33. *Ashley Dunlap, lhp, Palomar (Calif.) JC.
34. Steve Fitch, rhp, Kutztown (Pa.) University.
35. *Will McKenzie, rhp, Walters State (Tenn.) CC.
36. *J.T. Schultz, lhp, East HS, Appleton, Wis.
37. Damon Katz, 2b, Pepperdine University.
38. Robert Sierer, rhp, Bluffton (Ohio) College.
39. *Curtis Ledbetter, c, Lawrence (Kan.) HS.
40. *Jon Hooker, rhp, University of Kentucky.
**41. Eric Crozier, 1b, Norfolk State University.—(2004)**
42. *Silas Ah Sui, 3b, JC of the Siskiyous (Calif.).
43. Ron Colvard, rhp, The Citadel.
44. *Joe Little, lhp, Arvada (Colo.) HS.
45. *Mark Carroll, ss, Arcadia (Calif.) HS.
46. *Chris Appuhn, rhp, Millard North HS, Omaha, Neb.

## COLORADO ROCKIES (7)

1. *Matt Harrington, rhp, Palmdale (Calif.) HS.—DNP
DRAFT DROP *Played for St. Paul (Northern); re-drafted by Padres, 2001 (2nd round)*
**2. Jason Young, rhp, Stanford University.—(2003-04)**
3. Chris Buglovsky, rhp, College of New Jersey.—(AAA)
**4. Cory Vance, lhp, Georgia Tech.—(2002-03)**
**5. Garrett Atkins, 1b-3b, UCLA.—(2003-10)**
**6. Scott Dohmann, rhp, University of Louisiana-Lafayette.—(2004-08)**
7. Edmund Muth, of, Stanford University.
8. Dan Conway, c, Wake Forest University.
9. Nick Webb, lhp, University of Louisiana-Lafayette.
**10. Clint Barmes, ss, Indiana State University.—(2003-15)**
**11. Brad Hawpe, 1b, Louisiana State University.—(2004-13)**
**12. Sean Green, rhp, University of Louisville.—(2006-11)**
13. William Vazquez, rhp, Indian Hills (Iowa) CC.
14. *Bob Zimmermann, rhp, DeSmet HS, St. Louis.
**15. Justin Huisman, rhp, University of Mississippi.—(2004)**
DRAFT DROP *Brother of Rick Huisman, major leaguer (1995-96)*
16. Jose Vasquez, of, Booker HS, Sarasota, Fla.
17. Charles Merricks, lhp, UCLA
DRAFT DROP *Brother of Matt Merricks, sixth-round draft pick, Braves (2000)*
18. Scott Berney, rhp, Clemson University.
19. Joe Abell, rhp, University of New Mexico.
20. Ross Pilkington, ss, Loveland HS, Fort Collins, Colo.
21. +Zach Parker, lhp, San Jacinto (Texas) JC.
22. Bryan Peck, 3b, Middle Tennessee State University.
23. Josh Pride, 3b, Middle Tennessee State University.
24. Eric Storey, 3b, Butler University.
25. Kevin Blocker, ss, Wofford College.
26. *Darin Davis, 2b, Cypress (Calif.) JC.
27. *Joe Curran, lhp, Edmonds (Wash.) CC.
28. *Steve Guthrie, 3b, Palomar (Calif.) JC.
29. *Marcus Townsend, of, Waller (Texas) HS.
30. *Michael Vick, of, Virginia Tech.
DRAFT DROP *First overall draft pick, Atlanta Falcons, National Football League (2001); quarterback, NFL (2001-15)*
31. *Adam Heether, ss, Ripon Christian HS, Ripon, Calif.
32. *Chris Netwall, c, Penn State University.
33. *Nick McCurdy, rhp, Jefferson Davis (Ala.) CC.
34. *Grant Mullen, 1b, Gordon (Mass.) College.
**35. +Darren Clarke, rhp, South Florida CC.—(2007)**
36. *Mike Perdomo, of, Barbara Goleman HS, Miami.
37. *Jason Frome, of, Indiana State University.
38. +Jentry Beckstead, rhp, Salt Lake (Utah) CC.
39. Michael Davies, lhp, Mount Hood (Ore.) CC.
40. *Josh Bryant, rhp, South Cobb HS, Austell, Ga.
41. *Sean Johnson, rhp-ss, Clinton (Iowa) HS.
42. *Chad Liter, of, Wabash Valley (Ill.) JC.
43. *Seth McCauley, c, Three Forks (Mon.) HS.
44. *Matt Farnum, rhp, Dakota Ridge HS, Littleton, Colo.
45. *Chad Reeves, of, Pomona HS, Arvada, Colo.
46. *Matt Barker, 2b, Niwot HS, Longmont, Colo.
47. *Don Rogers, 3b, DeSmet Jesuit HS, St. Louis.
48. *David Rose, of, El Cerrito HS, Richmond, Calif.
49. *Jason Kramer, lhp, Vernon Regional (Texas) JC.
50. *Daniel Bria, rhp, Lassen (Calif.) JC.

## DETROIT TIGERS (8)

1. Matt Wheatland, rhp, Rancho Bernardo HS, San Diego.—(Low A)
2. Chad Petty, lhp, Chalker HS, West Farmington, Ohio.—(High A)
**3. Nook Logan, ss, Copiah-Lincoln (Miss.) CC.—(2004-07)**
**4. Mark Woodyard, rhp, Bethune-Cookman College.—(2005)**
5. Miles Durham, of, Texas Tech.—(Low A)
6. Matt Parris, rhp, Highland HS, Palmdale, Calif.
7. Ronnie Merrill, ss, University of Tampa.
8. Andy Warren, rhp, Sam Houston State University.
9. *Mike Hofius, 1b, Lakewood (Calif.) HS.
10. Lee Rodney, rhp, Kennesaw State University.
11. Jeremy Johnson, rhp, Mooresville (N.C.) HS.
12. Nate Tekavec, rhp, Miami (Ohio) University.
13. Forrest Johnson, c, UCLA.
14. *Kevin Johnson, rhp, University of California.
15. *Cole Bruce, 3b, Brazoswood HS, Clute, Texas.
16. *Ryan Schroyer, rhp, Canyon del Oro HS, Tucson, Ariz.
17. Matthew Birkett, of, West Torrance HS, Torrance, Calif.
18. Emmanuel Valentin, rhp, Rafael Lopez Landron HS, Guayama, P.R.
19. Antoine Tellis, of, Harlan Community HS, Chicago.
20. Jeremy Swindell, lhp, University of Houston.
21. Jeff Leuenberger, rhp, Long Beach State University.
22. Ryan Neill, 1b-of, Oral Roberts University.
23. Tommy Muldoon, rhp, Eckerd (Fla.) College.
24. Tapley Holland, of, University of Dallas.
25. Hugh Quattlebaum, 3b, Amherst (Mass.) College.
26. Mark Moccia, 2b, Concordia (N.Y.) College.
27. Joe Gerber, 1b, Oregon State University.
28. *Scott Sturkie, rhp, Coastal Carolina University.
29. Mike Steele, rhp, Central Michigan University.
30. Shawn Lambert, 1b, Buchanan HS, Clovis, Calif.
31. +Demetrius Heath, 2b, Louisburg (N.C.) JC.
32. *Brian Eck, rhp, Blinn (Texas) JC.
33. Josh VanVessen, lhp, Point Loma Nazarene (Calif.) College.
34. Jim Pitney, rhp, North Carolina Wesleyan College.
35. *Ryan Cremeans, lhp, Adrian (Mich.) HS.
36. +Jerry Dunn, rhp, Spartanburg Methodist (S.C.) JC.
37. Matt Walker, of, George Washington University.
38. *Chris Langlois, rhp, River Ridge HS, New Port Richey, Fla.
39. *Luis Alicea, rhp, Osceola Senior HS, Kissimmee, Fla.
40. *Josh Bishop, rhp, Permian HS, Odessa, Texas.
41. Jordan Gerk, lhp, Oral Roberts University.
42. Shawn Hannah, rhp, Fresno State University.
43. *Rafael Mojica, rhp, Amalia Marin HS, San Juan, P.R.

## FLORIDA MARLINS (1)

1. Adrian Gonzalez, 1b, Eastlake HS, Chula Vista, Calif.—(2004-15)
DRAFT DROP *Brother of Edgar Gonzalez, 30th-round draft pick, Devils Rays (2000)*
2. Jason Stokes, 1b, Coppell (Texas) HS.—(AAA)
3. Rob Henkel, lhp, UCLA.—(AAA)
4. Anthony Brewer, of, Simeon HS, Chicago.—(Low A)
5. Jim Kavourias, of, University of Tampa.—(AA)
6. Will Smith, of, Palo Verde HS, Tucson, Ariz.
7. Brandon Sloan, rhp, Wichita State University.
8. Matt Massingale, rhp, University of Washington.
9. *Jesse Kozlowski, rhp, Westlake HS, Thousand Oaks, Calif.
10. *Bill Clayton, rhp, Glenwood HS, Chatham, Ill.
11. Steve Sawyer, rhp, Southeastern Louisiana University.
12. Pat Magness, 1b, Wichita State University.
13. Phillip Akens, rhp, Fallston HS, Belair, Md.
14. Robert Jones, lhp, College of William & Mary.
15. Tim Schilling, lhp, Elon College.
16. Daniel Hicks, 1b, Lake Sumter (Fla.) CC.
**17. Josh Willingham, ss, University of North Alabama.—(2004-14)**
18. Chris Key, lhp, San Jose State University.
19. Brian Rogers, c, College of William & Mary.
20. Adam Sterrett, rhp, Robert E. Lee HS, Staunton, Va.
21. Matt Easterday, 2b, Georgia Southern University.
22. *David Gresky, of, St. Ignatius HS, North Royalton, Ohio.
23. *Daniel Moore, lhp, North Rowan HS, Spencer, N.C.
24. +Ben Birk, lhp, University of Minnesota.
25. Mike McNutt, rhp, Mount St. Joseph (Ohio) College.
26. *Nate Staggs, rhp, University HS, San Diego.
27. *Josh Muecke, lhp, Scripps Ranch HS, San Diego.
28. *Patrick Green, ss, Milton HS, Alpharetta, Ga.
29. *Casey Hoorelbeke, of-rhp, North Idaho JC.
30. *Dustin Griffith, rhp, Seward County (Kan.) CC.
31. +Jon Asahina, rhp, Fresno (Calif.) CC.
32. *Derek Mills, rhp, Fresno (Calif.) CC.
33. *Jim Samolovitch, of, West Mifflin (Pa.) HS.
34. *Joey Sexton, lhp, Johnson HS, Savannah, Ga.
35. *J.T. Sherman, rhp, Dixie (Utah) JC.
36. *Erik Dean, ss, Wilcox HS, Santa Clara, Calif.
37. *Josh Barton, rhp, Millington (Tenn.) HS.
38. *Anthony Aceves, of, Dundalk (Md.) CC.
39. *Nathan Kopszywa, rhp, D'Iberville (Miss.) HS.
40. *Christian Larsen, ss, San Mateo HS, Foster City, Calif.
41. *Jared Brite, rhp, Centennial HS, Bakersfield, Calif.
42. *Justin Knapp, ss, Arlington Country Day HS, Jacksonville, Fla.
43. *Steve Ramsey, 1b, Eastlake HS, Redmond, Wash.
44. *Levi Webber, 1b, Glide (Ore.) HS.
45. Jeff Stevens, of, UC Riverside.

## HOUSTON ASTROS (27)

1. Robert Stiehl, rhp, El Camino (Calif.) JC.—(AA)
**2. Chad Qualls, rhp, University of Nevada-Reno.—(2004-15)**
3. Anthony Pluta, rhp, Las Vegas (Nev.) HS.—(High A)
4. *Eric Keefner, 3b, De la Salle HS, Bridgeview, Ill.—(Rookie)
DRAFT DROP *Attended Arizona State; re-drafted by White Sox, 2002 (22nd round)*
5. Jake Whitesides, of, Hickman HS, Columbia, Mo.—(Low A)
6. Tommy Whiteman, ss, University of Oklahoma.
7. Joe Lydic, 3b, University of Pittsburgh.
**8. Cory Doyne, rhp, Land O'Lakes HS, Lutz, Fla.—(2007)**
**9. Eric Bruntlett, ss, Stanford University.—(2003-09)**
10. Nate Nelson, 3b, University of Louisiana-Lafayette.
**11. *Bob McCrory, rhp, Columbus HS, Steens, Miss.—(2008-09)**
12. Ryan Hamilton, rhp, University of San Diego.
13. Anthony Acevedo, of, Fresno State University.

14. Tony Angel, 2b, Loyola Marymount University.
**15. Todd Self, of, University of Louisiana-Monroe.—(2005)**
16. Monte Mansfield, rhp, Riverside (Calif.) CC.
17. Ralph Hicks, lhp, Centanary College.
18. Eric Lee, of, University of Houston.
**19. *Michael Bourn, of-ss, Nimitz HS, Humble, Texas.—(2006-15)**
20. Jory Coughenour, rhp, University of Pittsburgh.
21. *Steven Mortimer, 1b, Yakima Valley (Wash.) CC.
22. *Jorge Ruiz, 2b, Notre Dame HS, Caguas, P.R.
23. Mark Hamilton, lhp, Texas Christian University.
24. Paul Lockhart, of, San Diego State University.
25. Craig Petulla, rhp, Slippery Rock (Pa.) University.
26. Jon Krysa, rhp, Rockhurst (Mo.) College.
27. *Andy Hutchings, rhp, Alfred State (N.Y.) JC.
28. Damon Yee, rhp, Vanderbilt University.
29. *Ben Johnson, c, Bellevue (Wash.) HS.
**30. Mike Burns, rhp, Cal State Los Angeles.—(2005-09)**
31. T.J. Soto, 2b, Louisiana Tech.
32. Mickey McKee, c-1b, Tulane University.
33. *Weston Burnette, rhp, Owen HS, Swannanoa, N.C.
34. *Jesse Floyd, rhp, San Jacinto (Texas) JC.
35. *David Frame, rhp, Blinn (Texas) JC.
36. *Chris Spencer, rhp, San Jacinto (Texas) JC.
37. *George Drusina, rhp, El Paso (Texas) CC.
38. *Chris Sawyers, rhp-ss, Evergreen HS, Ariel, Wash.
39. *Darryl Chever, of, Delaware Tech & CC.
40. *Deshain Beasley, of, Bellevue (Wash.) CC.
41. *Aaron Coiteux, 2b, Evergreen HS, Vancouver, Wash.
42. *Jason Godkin, lhp, Chabot (Calif.) JC.
**43. *Jason Windsor, rhp, Leigh HS, San Jose, Calif.—(2006)**

## KANSAS CITY ROYALS (4)

1. Mike Stodolka, lhp-1b, Centennial HS, Corona, Calif.—(AAA)
**2. Mike Tonis, c, University of California.—(2004)**
3. Scott Walter, c, Loyola Marymount University.—(AAA)
**4. David DeJesus, of, Rutgers University.—(2003-15)**
**5. Zach McClellan, rhp, Indiana University.—(2007)**
**6. Brian Bass, rhp, Robert E. Lee HS, Montgomery, Ala.—(2008-10)**
7. Kahi Kaanoi, rhp, Kamehameha HS, Kaneohe, Hawaii.
8. Luis Cotto, ss, Institutio Cumbre, Carolina, P.R.
9. Luis Escobar, c, Fernando Callejo HS, Manati, P.R.
10. Jason Fingers, rhp, Arizona State University.
DRAFT DROP *Son of Rollie Fingers, major leaguer (1968-85)*
**11. Ryan Bukvich, rhp, Brandon, Miss.—(2002-08)**
12. Darren Fenster, ss, Rutgers University.
13. Jon Metzger, lhp, University of Virginia.
14. Justin Gemoll, 3b, University of Southern California.
**15. *Adam Peterson, rhp, Wichita State University.—(2004)**
16. Joey Baker, rhp, San Jose State University.
17. Billy Keppinger, of, Cumberland (Tenn.) University.
18. Trey Saye, rhp, Newberry, S.C.
19. Aaron Melebeck, ss, University of Houston.
20. Justin Cowan, c, University of Nebraska.
21. Ian Ferguson, rhp, Regis (Colo.) University.
22. Mike Natale, rhp, Lewis-Clark State (Idaho) College.
23. *Bobby Mosby, rhp, East St Louis (Ill.) HS.
24. Michael Matthews, of, Columbia State (Tenn.) CC.
25. *Billy Brian, rhp, Louisiana State University.
26. Dusty Wrightsman, rhp, Faulkner State (Ala.) JC.
27. Marco Cunningham, of, Texas Tech.
28. *Louis Wieben, lhp, Pitt (N.C.) CC.
29. *Daniel McKinney, lhp, White Station HS, Memphis, Tenn.
30. Jeb Thomas, rhp, Montreat (N.C.) College.
**31. +Ruben Gotay, 2b-ss, Indian Hills (Iowa) CC.—(2004-08)**
32. *Rich Carroll, 1b, St. Petersburg (Fla.) JC.
33. *Jason Cierlik, lhp, Kirkwood (Iowa) CC.
34. *Luca Petrocelli, rhp, Hackensack (N.J.) HS.
35. *Brad Knox, rhp, Cypress Falls HS, Houston.
36. *Darnell Suber, of, Laurens (S.C.) HS.
37. *Marland Williams, of, Williston (Fla.) HS.
38. *John Caruso, c, Chaparral HS, Las Vegas, Nev.
39. *Bill Hooten, rhp, Evangel Christian HS, Waskor, Texas.
40. *Mike Abdalla, rhp, Youngstown State University.
41. *Dustin Timm, rhp, Yutan (Neb.) HS.
42. Odannys Ayala, of, Frank Phillips (Texas) JC.
43. *Britt Bearden, ss-2b, Lexington (S.C.) HS.
44. *Stephen Nielsen, rhp, Joliet Catholic HS, Joliet, Ill.
45. *Reinaldo Colon, rhp, Ramirez HS, San Sebastian, P.R.
46. *Seth Davidson, ss, University of Southern California.
47. *Brandon Bird, rhp, Northwest HS, Omaha, Neb.
48. *Reeves Smith, rhp, Cleveland (Miss.) HS.
49. *Clint Mokry, rhp, Taylor HS, Coupland, Texas.
50. Hector Rosado, lhp, Hill (Texas) JC.

## LOS ANGELES DODGERS (17)

**1. Ben Diggins, rhp, University of Arizona.—(2002)**
**2. Joel Hanrahan, rhp, Norwalk (Iowa) HS.—(2007-13)**
3. Jeff Tibbs, rhp, Davis HS, Farmington, Utah.—(Rookie)
**4. Koyie Hill, c-3b, Wichita State University.—(2003-14)**
5. Heath Totten, rhp, Lamar University.—(AAA)
6. Greg Withelder, lhp, Wilmington (Del.) College.
7. Jared Price, c, Minidoka County HS, Rupert, Idaho.
8. Jason Hickman, lhp, Ball State University.
**9. *Humberto Sanchez, rhp, South Bronx (N.Y.) HS.—(2008)**
10. *Drew Toussaint, c, Centennial HS, Los Angeles.
**11. Shane Nance, lhp, University of Houston.—(2002-04)**
12. Travis Ezi, of, Southwestern HS, Baltimore.
13. Ronte Langs, of, Oklahoma State University.
14. Jonathan Lorenzen, rhp, Katella HS, Anaheim, Calif.
15. Derek Michaelis, 1b, Rice University.
16. Adrian Mendoza, 1b, Cal State Northridge.
17. Jason Olson, rhp, Armstrong Atlantic State (Ga.) University.
18. Casey Kennedy, rhp, University of Central Florida.
19. *Kevin Poenitzsch, rhp, Galveston (Texas) CC.
20. *Aaron Rice, c, A.B. Miller HS, Fontana, Calif.
21. Steven Langone, rhp, Boston College.
22. Greg Bauer, rhp, Wichita State University.
23. Victor Martinez, 3b, Iver Ranum HS, Westminster, Colo.
24. Zach Lekse, ss, University of Oklahoma.
25. Nathan Lipowicz, of, Central Missouri State University.
26. Nick Alvarez, of, St. Thomas (Fla.) University.
27. Brian Steffek, rhp, Houston Baptist University.
28. Aaron Andrews, rhp, Auburn University-Montgomery.
**29. *Ryan Sadowski, rhp, Western HS, Davie, Fla.—(2009)**
30. Clifton Glidewell, lhp, Northwestern State University.
31. *Frank Esposito, lhp, Sierra (Calif.) JC.
32. +Ryan Johansen, rhp, South Florida CC / Indian River (Fla.) CC.
33. *Brad Jalbert, of, St. Joseph's HS, Saskatoon, Sask.
34. *Patrick Hicklen, rhp, Oakland HS, Murfreesboro, Tenn.
35. *Erik Lohse, rhp, Sacramento (Calif.) CC.
DRAFT DROP *Brother of Kyle Lohse, major leaguer (2001-15)*
36. *Dustin Schroer, of, Johnston Heights HS, Surrey, B.C.
**37. +Victor Diaz, 2b, Roberto Clemente HS, Chicago / Grayson County (Texas) CC.—(2004-07)**
**38. *Brian Barton, of, Westchester HS, Los Angeles.—(2008-09)**
39. *Demetrick Drumming, 2b, Spartanburg Methodist (S.C.) JC.
40. *Kyle Bateman, rhp, Central Arizona JC.
41. *Michael Lynch, c, Oak Forest (Ill.) HS.
42. *Timi Moni-Erigbali, of, Columbus (Ga.) HS.
43. *Danny Desclouds, rhp, Sir Robert Borden HS, Nepean, Ontario.
44. *Josh Mayo, ss, Sacramento (Calif.) CC.
45. *Justin Glenn, of, Cowley County (Kan.) CC.
46. *Marcus Davila, rhp, Key West (Fla.) HS.
47. *Jason Blejwas, rhp, Vernon Regional (Texas) JC.
48. *Jayson Berrios, rhp, Discipulos de Cristo HS, Bayamon, P.R.
49. *Shawn Kott, rhp, L.P. Miller Comprehensive HS, Nipawin, Sask.
50. *Brooks Bollinger, 3b, University of Wisconsin.
DRAFT DROP *Quarterback, National Football League (2003-08)*

## MILWAUKEE BREWERS (11)

**1. Dave Krynzel, of, Green Valley HS, Henderson, Nev.—(2004-05)**
2. (Choice to Braves as compensation for Type A free agent Jose Hernandez)
3. Dane Artman, lhp, Westminster Academy, Fort Lauderdale, Fla.—(Low A)
4. Eric Henderson, lhp, University of North Carolina.—(High A)
5. Jason Belcher, c, Walnut Ridge (Ark.) HS.—(AA)
6. Brian Hicks, of, Natchitoches Central HS, Natchitoches, La.
7. Jerry Oakes, rhp, Archbishop Carroll HS, Upper Darby, Pa.
8. Bill Scott, of, UCLA.
9. Ryan Miller, rhp, University of Evansville.
10. Brian Nielsen, lhp, Seminole HS, Sanford, Fla.
**11. Corey Hart, of, Greenwood HS, Bowling Green, Ky.—(2004-15)**
12. Heath McMurray, rhp, Louisiana State University.
13. Matt Yeatman, rhp, Tomball (Texas) HS.
14. Todd West, ss, University of Texas.
15. Daniel Hall, rhp, Campbell University.
16. *Scott Roehl, rhp, Shoreland Lutheran HS, Somers, Wis.
17. Daryl Clark, 3b, University of North Carolina-Charlotte.
18. Jonah McClanahan, of, Monterey (Calif.) HS.
19. Zach Thompson, of, Callaway HS, Jackson, Miss.
20. *Troy Pickford, rhp, Fresno (Calif.) CC.
21. Jeremy Shorey, rhp, Lisbon (Maine) HS.
22. Scott Candelaria, ss, University of New Mexico.
23. *Brent Lewis, 3b, Germantown (Tenn.) HS.
24. Jude Voltz, 1b, University of Mississippi.
25. *Luis Alvarado, lhp, Luis Pales Matos HS, Bayamon, P.R.
26. *Michael Reiss, rhp, Vaughan SS, Thornhill, Ontario.
DRAFT DROP *Twin brother of Steven Reiss, 27th-round draft pick, Twins (2000)*
27. Travis Hake, ss-2b, Carson-Newman (Tenn.) College.
28. +Todd Gelatka, rhp, Golden West (Calif.) JC.
29. *Andrew Friedberg, lhp, Arizona State University.
30. *Casey Myers, c, Arizona State University.
DRAFT DROP *Brother of Corey Myers, first-round draft pick, Diamondbacks (1999)*
31. *Mike Kabel, c, Denham Springs (La.) HS.
32. Kelly Werner, lhp, University of Minnesota.
**33. *Jon Coutlangus, of-lhp, Indian River (Fla.) CC.—(2007)**
34. *Wally Sevilla, ss-2b, Palm Beach (Fla.) JC.
35. *Michael Oiler, rhp, University of Wisconsin-Milwaukee.
36. *Barry Paulk, of, Florida International University.
37. Shaun Gragg, c, Central Michigan University.
38. *Markum King, 1b, Laney (Calif.) JC.
39. +Ryan Trytten, rhp, Ottumwa HS, Agency, Iowa / Marshalltown (Iowa) CC.
40. *Alan Abram, of, Valley HS, West Des Moines, Iowa.
41. *David Walczak, 1b, CC of Rhode Island.
42. Byron Batson, rhp, Campbell University.
43. Kevin Shrout, rhp, University of Virginia.
44. Mike Shwam, rhp, Cal Poly San Luis Obispo.
45. *Steve Bray, rhp, Norwalk (Conn.) CC.
46. *Steve Tracey, rhp, Columbus State (Ohio) CC.
47. *Jason Henderson, rhp, CC of Rhode Island.
48. *Matt Mahoney, rhp, University of North Dakota.
49. Ryan Nohr, of, Diablo Valley (Calif.) JC.
50. *Aaron Rowe, lhp, Novi (Mich.) HS.

## MINNESOTA TWINS (2)

**1. Adam Johnson, rhp, Cal State Fullerton.—(2001-03)**
**1. *Aaron Heilman, rhp, University of Notre Dame** (Supplemental choice—31st overall—as compensation for Type A free agent Mike Trombley).**—(2003-11)**
DRAFT DROP *Returned to Notre Dame; re-drafted by Mets, 2001 (1st round)*
2. *Tagg Bozied, 1b, University of San Francisco.—(AAA)
DRAFT DROP *Returned to San Francisco; re-drafted by Padres, 2001 (3rd round)*
**2. J.D. Durbin, rhp, Coronado HS, Scottsdale, Ariz.** (Choice from Orioles as compensation for Trombley).**—(2004-07)**
3. Colby Miller, rhp, Weatherford (Okla.) HS.—(AA)
**4. Jason Miller, lhp, Sarasota (Fla.) HS.—(2007)**
5. Edgardo LeBron, ss, Florencia Garcia HS, Las Piedras, P.R.—(Low A)
6. Ronnie Corona, rhp, Cal State Fullerton.
7. James Tomlin, of, St. Bernard HS, Los Angeles.
8. Henry Bonilla, rhp, Tulane University.
9. Ken Holubec, lhp, University of Louisiana-Monroe.
10. Kelley Gulledge, c, University of Alabama.
**11. Josh Rabe, of, Quincy (Ill.) University.—(2006-07)**
**12. Jason Kubel, of, Highland HS, Palmdale, Calif.—(2004-14)**
13. *Shane Boyd, rhp, Henry Clay HS, Lexington, Ky.
DRAFT DROP *Quarterback, National Football League (2006-08)*
14. Cory Agar, c, Dunedin (Fla.) HS.
15. Jeff Lincoln, rhp, Western Kentucky University.
16. Dan Decola, c, Slippery Rock (Pa.) University.
**17. *Paul Maholm, lhp, Germantown (Tenn.) HS.—(2005-14)**
DRAFT DROP *First-round draft pick (8th overall), Pirates (2003)*
18. Andy Persby, rhp, University of Minnesota.
19. Bruce Dohrman, of, Garrett (Ind.) HS.
20. *T.J. Prunty, rhp, St. Paul Academy HS, Inner Grove Heights, Minn.
21. *Mark Michael, 3b/rhp, Gloucester Catholic HS, Gloucester City, N.J.
22. *Brett Groves, ss, Florida State University.
23. *Jered Goodwin, rhp, Oviedo (Fla.) HS.
24. +J.R. Taylor, ss, Skyline HS, Oakland / Sacramento (Calif.) CC.
25. Joey Hamer, c, Newbury Park (Calif.) HS.
26. *Jeremy Fortner, rhp, Venice (Fla.) HS.
27. *Stephen Reiss, rhp, Vaughan SS, Thornhill, Ontario.
DRAFT DROP *Twin brother of Michael Reiss, 26th-round draft pick, Brewers (2000)*
**28. *Daniel Davidson, lhp, Gulf Coast (Fla.) CC.—(2009)**
29. Tom Sullivan, lhp, Slippery Rock (Pa.) University.
30. Shawn Cline, c, Baker County HS, MacClenny, Fla.
31. Beau Kemp, rhp, Saddleback (Calif.) CC.
32. Cody Kimball, rhp, MacArthur HS, Irving, Texas.
33. *David Nowak, of, Arcadia HS, Scottsdale, Ariz.
34. Luke Martin, lhp, Embry-Riddle (Fla.) University.
35. Greg Stokes, 3b, Slippery Rock (Pa.) University.
36. Pedro Sanchez, lhp, Adolfina Irizarry HS, Toa Baja, P.R.
37. +Chad Pylate, rhp, Vancleave (Miss.) HS / Faulkner State (Ala.) JC.
38. *John Lynch, lhp, Elk River HS, Rogers, Minn.
39. *Marco Gonzales, c, Eastlake HS, Chula Vista, Calif.
40. Scott Suraci, of, Hawaii Pacific University.
41. Terry Corn, rhp, Florida Southern College.
42. *Steve Garrabrants, 2b, Moon Valley HS, Phoenix.
43. *Jeff Marquez, rhp, Brito Private HS, Miami.
44. *Brian Poetschlag, rhp, Magnolia HS, Anaheim, Calif.
45. *Coy Polk, rhp, Coppell (Texas) HS.
46. +Brian Baron, 2b, UCLA.
47. *Peter Eberhardt, c, Whittier Christian HS, Whittier, Calif.
48. *Tanner Munsey, c, Oyster River HS, Durham, N.H.
49. *Ben Riley, lhp, Iowa Western CC.

50. *Brett Garrard, ss, Brownsbrug (Ind.) HS.

## MONTREAL EXPOS (5)

1. **Justin Wayne, rhp, Stanford University.—(2002-04)**
2. (Choice to Blue Jays as compensation for Type A free agent Graeme Lloyd)
3. **Grady Sizemore, of, Cascade HS, Mill Creek, Wash.—(2004-15)**
4. **Cliff Lee, lhp, University of Arkansas.—(2002-14)**
5. Thomas Mitchell, rhp, Bladenboro (N.C.) HS.—(Low A)
6. **Shawn Hill, rhp, Bishop Reding HS, Georgetown, Ontario.—(2004-12)**
7. ***Wes Littleton, rhp, Vista HS, Oceanside, Calif.—(2006-08)**
8. **Phil Seibel, lhp, University of Texas.—(2004)**
9. Benji DeQuin, lhp, Gavilan (Calif.) JC.
10. Darryl Jenkins, ss, Plainfield (Ill.) HS.
11. Seth Johnson, 3b, Kelso (Wash.) HS.
12. +Jason Stevenson, lhp, Sacramento (Calif.) CC.
13. Craig Kerner, of, SUNY Cortland.
14. Ben Washburn, rhp, UC Riverside.
15. Mike Rose, rhp, Oral Roberts University.
16. Phil Downing, of, Arizona State University.
17. Derrick DePriest, rhp, University of North Carolina.
18. Jordan Griswold, lhp, Shiloh HS, Lilburn, Ga.
19. Justin Estel, rhp, Mississippi State University.
20. ***Freddy Lewis, of, Mississippi Gulf Coast JC.—(2006-12)**
21. +Josh Vaughn, lhp, Cowley County (Kan.) CC.
22. **Jason Bay, of, Gonzaga University.—(2003-13)**
23. *Reid Santos, lhp, Castle HS, Kaneohe, Hawaii.
24. Eric Miller, ss, Florida International University.
25. Mike Bolson, rhp, University of Wisconsin-Whitewater.
26. Scott Russo, lhp, Penn State University.
27. *Leonard Landeros, lhp, JC of the Sequoias (Calif.).
28. Ryan Ellis, 2b, Point Park (Pa.) College.
29. *Jim Brauer, rhp, Carmel (Ind.) HS.
30. Dan Sauer, rhp, Modesto (Calif.) JC.
31. Nick Schnabel, 2b, East Carolina University.
32. Chris Bye, rhp, St. Mary's (Calif.) College.
33. *Justin Pouk, ss, Streator Township HS, Streator, Ill.
34. *Nick Currin, rhp-of, Rex Putnam HS, Milwaukie, Ore.
35. ***Russell Martin, 3b, Edouard Montpetit HS, Montreal.—(2006-15)**
36. *Chad Scarbery, rhp, Fresno (Calif.) CC.

DRAFT DROP *Son of Randy Scarbery, first-round draft pick, Astros (1970); first-round draft pick, Athletics (1973); major leaguer (1979-80)*

37. *Derek Adams, rhp, Sultana HS, Hesperia, Calif.
38. Luis Rosas, ss, Dr. Pila HS, Bayamon, P.R.
39. *Johnny King, of, Teutopolis (Ill.) HS.
40. *Ivan Naccarata, ss, Edouard Montpetit HS, Longueil, Quebec.
41. *Toby Barnett, c, JC of Southern Idaho.
42. *Zach Brooks, rhp, Columbia Basin (Wash.) CC.
43. *Alex Groleau, rhp, Seminole State (Okla.) JC.
44. **Anthony Ferrari, lhp, Lewis-Clark State (Idaho) College.—(2003)**
45. ***Jeff Karstens, c, Mount Miguel HS, San Diego.—(2006-12)**
46. *Scott Jensen, rhp, Clovis West HS, Fresno, Calif.
47. *Jim Gulden, rhp, Lewisburg (Pa.) HS.
48. *Pierre Blount, of, Riverside (Calif.) CC.
49. *Victor Rosario, of, Lake City (Fla.) CC.
50. *Bob Brethauer, lhp, Bishop O'Dowd HS, Oakland.

## NEW YORK METS (25)

1. **Billy Traber, lhp, Loyola Marymount University** (Choice from Mariners as compensation for Type A free agent John Olerud).—**(2003-09)**
1. (Choice to Rangers as compensation for Type A free agent Todd Zeile)
1. **Bobby Keppel, rhp, DeSmet HS, Chesterfield, Mo.** (Supplemental choice—36th—as compensation for Olerud).—**(2006-09)**
2. Matt Peterson, rhp, Rapides HS, Alexandria, La.—(AAA)
3. Josh Reynolds, rhp, Central Missouri State University.—(High A)
4. Brandon Wilson, c, Christian Life Academy, Baton Rouge, La.—(High A)
5. Quenten Patterson, rhp, Oklahoma State University.—(Low A)
6. **Chris Basak, ss, University of Illinois.—(2007)**
7. **Jeff Duncan, of, Arizona State University.—(2003-04)**

DRAFT DROP *Baseball coach, Kent State (2014-15)*

8. Chad Bowen, rhp, Gallatin HS, Hendersonville, Tenn.
9. Nick Mattioni, rhp, Florida Atlantic University.
10. *Travis Veracka, lhp, University of Massachusetts.
11. John Wilson, c, University of Kentucky.
12. *Todd Faulkner, 1b, Auburn University.
13. *Collin Perschon, rhp, Bellevue (Wash.) CC.
14. *Luis Robles, c, Rialto (Calif.) HS.
15. Wayne Ough, rhp, Trinidad State (Colo.) JC.
16. *B.J. Benik, rhp, Seton Hall University.
17. *Mike Nunez, rhp, Cal State Fullerton.
18. Mike Cox, lhp, University of Texas-Pan American.
19. *Travis Rios, rhp, Eustis HS, Leesburg, Fla.
20. Chad Elliott, lhp, Cal State Sacramento.
21. *Scott Shoemaker, rhp, Grossmont (Calif.) JC.
22. *Todd Nicholas, lhp, Fort Dale Academy, Greenville, Ala.
23. Tony Coyne, ss, Yale University.
24. *Jonathan Craig, rhp, Young Harris (Ga.) JC.
25. *Skyler Fulton, of, Capital HS, Olympia, Wash.

DRAFT DROP *Wide receiver, National Football League (2006)*

26. Bubba Castaneda, c, University of Texas-San Antonio.
27. John-Edward Raffo, 1b-of, Florida Atlantic University.
28. Justin Wendt, 3b, St. David Catholic HS, Waterloo, Ontario.
29. *Chris Davis, rhp, Reedley (Calif.) JC.
30. Tim Flannigan, 3b, Saint Xavier (Ill.) University.
31. *T.J. Hepworth, lhp, Carteret (N.J.) HS.
32. *Tim Lavigne, rhp, University of Virginia.
33. Freddy Jimenez, of, Monsignor Pace HS, Miami.
34. Tanner Osberg, rhp, River Glen HS, Red Deer, Alberta.
35. David Byard, rhp, Mount Vernon Nazarene (Ohio) College.
36. Luz Portobanco, rhp, Miami-Dade CC.
37. *Nathen Vicari, lhp, Yuba (Calif.) CC.
38. +Ryan Danly, lhp, Jefferson HS, Cedar Rapids, Iowa / Kirkwood (Iowa) JC.
39. *Brendan Winn, of, Merritt Island (Fla.) HS.
40. +Joe Jiannetti, 3b, St. Petersburg (Fla.) HS / Daytona Beach (Fla.) CC.
41. *Verissimo Pereira, c, Edouard Montpetit HS, Montreal.
42. ***Greg Burke, rhp, Gloucester Catholic HS, Gloucester City, N.J.—(2009-13)**
43. *Cristian Cajigas, ss, Dr. Carlos Gonzalez HS, Aguada, P.R.
44. *Justin Harris, ss, Manatee (Fla.) JC.
45. +Brett Harper, 3b, Desert Mountain HS, Scottsdale, Ariz. / Scottsdale (Ariz.) CC.

DRAFT DROP *Son of Brian Harper, major leaguer (1979-95)*

46. *Jody Roughton, 3b, Maple Woods (Mo.) CC.
47. +David Housel, 2b, West Morris HS, Chester, N.J. / Daytona Beach (Fla.) CC.
48. *Danny Rubino, rhp, Coconut Creek (Fla.) HS.
49. *Eddie Cannon, rhp, Sebring (Fla.) HS.
50. *Jamar Hill, 3b-of, Bartlett HS, Anchorage, Alaska.

## NEW YORK YANKEES (28)

1. David Parrish, c, University of Michigan.—(AAA)

DRAFT DROP *Son of Lance Parrish, first-round draft pick, Tigers (1974); major leaguer (1977-95)*

2. Danny Borrell, lhp, Wake Forest University.—(AAA)
3. Jason Grove, of, Washington State University.—(AA)
4. **Matt Smith, lhp, Oklahoma State University.—(2006-07)**
5. Andy Beal, lhp, Vanderbilt University.—(AAA)
6. Jeremy King, rhp, DeSoto HS, Nocatee, Fla.
7. **Mitch Jones, of, Arizona State University.—(2009)**
8. Sam Bozanich, 2b, University of Alabama.
9. Eric Reynolds, lhp, Itawamba (Miss.) JC.
10. **Jason Anderson, rhp, University of Illinois.—(2003-05)**

DRAFT DROP *Baseball coach, Eastern Illinois (2013-15)*

11. Jason Smith, rhp, Kamiakin HS, Kennewick, Wash.
12. Kyle Stanton, rhp, Ohio Wesleyan University.
13. Mike Wombacher, 1b, University of Louisiana-Monroe.
14. *Nic Touchstone, lhp, Sumter (S.C.) HS.
15. Eric Mosley, rhp, Bishop Kelly HS, Tulsa, Okla.
16. Clinton Chauncey, c, Florida CC.
17. Ryan Gill, rhp, University of Louisiana-Lafayette.
18. *Josh Smith, rhp, Crawford HS, McGregor, Texas.
19. ***Brad Halsey, lhp, Hill (Texas) JC.—(2004-06)**
20. *Darric Merrell, rhp, Temecula Valley HS, Temecula, Calif.
21. Anthony Calabrese, ss, Seton Hall University.
22. Eric Olson, 3b, Boston College.
23. Jeff Segar, 3b, University of Montevallo (Ala.).
24. *Scott Barber, rhp, Kishwaukee (Ill.) JC.
25. Eric Schmitt, rhp, Wake Forest University.
26. **+Sean Henn, lhp, McLennan (Texas) JC.—(2005-13)**
27. *Shaun O'Connor, rhp, Navarro (Texas) JC.
28. +Trevor Tacker, rhp, McLennan (Texas) JC.
29. *David Lindsay, rhp, Itawamba (Miss.) JC.
30. +Tommy Rojas, c, Silverado HS, Henderson, Nev. / CC of Southern Nevada.
31. *Bo Edmiston, lhp, Mississippi Delta JC.
32. ***Chris Dickerson, of, Notre Dame HS, Van Nuys, Calif.—(2008-14)**
33. *Dan Mead, lhp, Worthington (Ohio) HS.
34. *Luke Carroll, c, Northwest Mississippi CC.
35. +John Ramistella, of, Santa Barbara (Calif.) CC / Monterey (Calif.) JC.
36. Jeff Gates, c, Cal State Fullerton.
37. *Justin Whitlock, rhp, Ryan HS, Denton, Texas.
38. *Joe Bunton, 3b, Cerritos (Calif.) JC.
39. *Aaron Edwards, c, Marshall County HS, Benton, Ky.
40. +Jeff Kennard, rhp, Centerville (Ohio) HS/Rend Lake (Ill.) CC.
41. *Peter Stonard, ss, Clayton (Mo.) HS.
42. *David Ryan, ss, Coppell (Texas) HS.
43. *Andrew Ogelsby, c, Denham Springs (La.) HS.
44. *Jacob Willett, of, Latexo HS, Huntsville, Texas.
45. +Ryan Clark, lhp, Owens (Ohio) CC.
46. *Steven Pickerell, c, Norwood (Okla.) HS.
47. Tim Nettles, 3b, University of North Carolina-Asheville.

DRAFT DROP *Son of Graig Nettles, major leaguer (1967-88)*

48. *Brandon Chreene, of, Sibley HS, Minden, La.
49. *Angel Rios, c, Pablo Colon Berdecia HS, Barranquitas, P.R.
50. *Joe Powers, rhp, Wright State University.

## OAKLAND ATHLETICS (20)

1. (Choice to Angels as compensation for Type B free agent Mike Magnante)
2. **Freddie Bynum, ss, Pitt County (N.C.) CC.—(2005-08)**
3. Daylan Holt, of, Texas A&M University.—(AAA)
4. Kevin McGerry, rhp, St. John's University.—(High A)
5. *Kenny Baugh, rhp, Rice University.—(AAA)

DRAFT DROP *Returned to Rice; re-drafted by Tigers, 2001 (1st round)*

6. Beau Craig, c, University of Southern California.
7. **Marc Gwyn, rhp, Rice University.—(2007)**
8. Kyle Crowell, rhp, University of Houston.
9. **Marshall McDougall, 3b, Florida State University.—(2005)**
10. Derell McCall, rhp, Tate HS, Gonzalez, Fla.
11. Matt Bowser, of, University of Central Florida.
12. *Steve Ellis, rhp, Bradley University.
13. *Larry Grayson, of, Oviedo (Fla.) HS.
14. Mike Ziegler, rhp, Florida State University.
15. ***Kevin Barry, rhp, Rider University.—(2006-07)**
16. Chris Scarcella, rhp, Texas A&M University.
17. **+Rich Harden, rhp, Central Arizona JC.—(2003-11)**
18. Matt O'Brien, lhp, Washington State University.
19. Chris Tritle, of, Center Point-Urbana HS, Center Point, Iowa.
20. *John Hudgins, rhp, Mission Viejo (Calif.) HS.
21. *Kip Bouknight, rhp, University of South Carolina.
22. John Suomi, c, Caribou (B.C.) University-College.
23. Dan Jackson, rhp, Florida Atlantic University.
24. Steve Fischer, rhp, University of the Pacific.
25. T.J. Gilpatrick, rhp, Mesa State (Colo.) College.
26. Conor Brooks, rhp, Dartmouth College.
27. *Tripp Kelly, 1b, University of South Carolina.
28. *Sam Hewitt, rhp, Lenoir (N.C.) CC.
29. **Ron Flores, lhp, University of Southern California.—(2005-07)**

DRAFT DROP *Brother of Randy Flores, major leaguer (2002-10)*

30. Joe Cirone, of, Rutgers University.
31. *Dan Valentin, rhp, Liberty University.
32. *Bryan Moore, 1b, Indian River (Fla.) CC.
33. *Anthony Bennett, rhp, Blue Mountain (Ore.) CC.
34. *Robbie Findlay, rhp, Seminole State (Okla.) JC.
35. *Shannon Telles, of, Waianae (Hawaii) HS.
36. *Mike Serrata, of, Hueneme HS, Oxnard, Calif.
37. *Derek Wilson, rhp, Mount San Jacinto (Calif.) JC.
38. *Domanic Roses, rhp, Mount Hood (Ore.) CC.
39. *James Garvey, rhp, La Quinta HS, Westminster, Calif.
40. Richie Rodarmel, rhp-3b, Shippensburg (Pa.) University.
41. *Karl Jernigan, ss, Florida State University.
42. *Jeff Carlsen, rhp, University of Washington.
43. Jon Shirley, rhp, University of California.
44. *Jordan De Voir, 3b, Southridge HS, Kennewick, Wash.
45. *John Voita, c, Granada Hills HS, Northridge, Calif.
46. *Fernando De Aza, rhp, Wabash Valley (Ill.) JC.

## PHILADELPHIA PHILLIES (15)

1. **Chase Utley, 2b, UCLA.—(2003-15)**
2. (Choice to Indians as compensation for Type A free agent Mike Jackson)
3. Keith Bucktrot, rhp, Claremore (Okla.) HS.—(AA)
4. Danny Gonzalez, ss, Florida Air Academy, Melbourne, Fla.—(AA)
5. Matt Riethmaier, rhp, University of Arkansas.—(Low A)
6. **Taylor Buchholz, rhp, Springfield (Pa.) HS.—(2006-11)**
7. Tony Cancio, 1b, H.B. Plant HS, Tampa.
8. Ryan Carter, lhp, UCLA.
9. Felix Ortega, c, Medardo Carazo HS, Trujillo Alto, P.R.
10. Scott Youngbauer, ss, Georgia State University.
11. Brandon Mayfield, rhp, Auburn University.
12. Brandon Caraway, of, University of Houston.
13. Carlos Rivera, 1b, Santo Tomas de Aquina HS, Toa Baja, P.R.
14. Mark McRoberts, 3b-of, Granite Hills HS, San Diego.
15. Todd Meldahl, lhp, Washington State University.
16. *Jeremy Hudson, rhp, Jefferson State (Ala.) CC.
17. **Travis Chapman, 3b, Mississippi State University.—(2003)**
18. Reggie Griggs, 1b, Florida A&M University.
19. Dave Hoffman, lhp, Bradley University.
20. Anthony Hensley, of, Baylor University.
21. Julio Campos, ss, Missouri Baptist College.
22. Jamie Bennett, rhp, University of Tennessee.
23. Chad Sadowski, rhp-1b, University of Wisconsin-Milwaukee.
24. Melvin Anderson, ss, Southern University.
25. Doug Stasio, rhp, New York Tech.
26. Brad Steele, rhp, University of California.
27. Trevor Bullock, lhp, University of Nebraska.
28. Kevin Donovan, lhp, Mississippi State University.
29. *Ryan Myers, rhp, CC of Southern Nevada.
30. *Chad White, lhp-of, Prattville (Ala.) HS.
31. Preston Underdown, 2b-3b, Baylor University.
32. Kevin Sullivan, c, Carthage (Wis.) College.
33. Dan Adams, rhp, Kent State University.
34. *Mike Mueller, rhp, Triton (Ill.) JC.
35. *Jason Sugden, of, Central Dauphin HS, Harrisburg, Pa.

36. Andy Elskamp, rhp, University of Wisconsin-La Crosse.
37. *Kyle Bakker, lhp, Millard West HS, Omaha, Neb.
38. *Jason Fransz, of, Riverside (Calif.) CC.
39. *Jason Martinez, lhp, Central HS, Grand Junction, Colo.

DRAFT DROP *Son of Tippy Martinez, major leaguer (1974-88)*

## PITTSBURGH PIRATES (19)

1. **Sean Burnett, lhp, Wellington (Fla.) Community HS.—(2004-14)**
2. David Beigh, rhp, Harrison HS, Battle Ground, Ind.—(Low A)
3. **Chris Young, rhp, Princeton University.—(2004-15)**
4. *Patrick Boyd, of, Clemson University.—(AA)

DRAFT DROP *Returned to Clemson; re-drafted by Rangers, 2001 (7th round)*

5. Jason Sharber, rhp, Oakland HS, Murfreesboro, Tenn.—(High A)
6. Josh Shortslef, lhp, Hannibal Central HS, Sterling, N.Y.
7. Cole Burzynski, rhp, Navasota (Texas) HS.
8. Kurt Shafer, rhp, Land O'Lakes (Fla.) HS.
9. Chris Bass, ss, Madison (Ind.) HS.
10. Brandon Chaves, ss, University of Hawaii-Hilo.
11. *Kyle Parcus, lhp, Rosebud-Lott HS, Rosebud, Texas.
12. Jason Keyser, rhp, Boyd County HS, Ashland, Ky.
13. Troy Veleber, of, Jacksonville University.
14. Victor Buttler, of, El Camino (Calif.) JC.
15. Sean Smith, 3b-of, Joliet West HS, Joliet, Ill.
16. David Baum, lhp, Okaloosa-Walton (Fla.) CC.
17. *Daylon Monette, of, Cypress (Calif.) JC.
18. Jon Pagan, 1b, El Camino (Calif.) CC.
19. Mike Connolly, lhp, Oneonta (N.Y.) HS.
20. **+Jose Bautista, 3b, Chipola (Fla.) JC.—(2004-15)**
21. *John Larson, rhp, Eastern Illinois University.
22. Shannon Cabell, lhp, West Virginia State University.
23. Josh Higgins, rhp, The Master's (Calif.) College.
24. *Ryan Kanekeberg, rhp, Kamiak HS, Everett, Wash.
25. **Nate McLouth, 2b, Whitehall (Mich.) HS.—(2005-14)**
26. **Ian Snell, rhp, Caesar Rodney HS, Camden, Del.—(2004-10)**
27. Alex Cruz, ss, Pasco Comprehensive HS, Ridge Manor, Fla.
28. *Brian Hall, ss, Carlsbad (N.M.) HS.
29. *Denver Kitch, ss, Yukon (Okla.) HS.
30. *Chris Gale, rhp, Oyster River HS, Durham, N.H.

DRAFT DROP *Son of Rich Gale, major leaguer (1978-84)*

31. *Jeremy Blaylock, rhp, North Hall HS, Gainesville, Ga.
32. *Dan Mackey, rhp, McQuaid Jesuit HS, Rochester, N.Y.
33. +Mike Cockrell, ss, Los Angeles Harbor JC.
34. Mike Fortin, rhp, American International (Mass.) College.
35. Victor Ramos, c, Cayey, P.R.
36. ***Scott Baker, rhp, Captain Shreve HS, Shreveport, La.—(2005-15)**
37. *Joseph McBride, ss, El Cerrito (Calif.) HS.
38. Kevin Lee, rhp, Wheaton North HS, Wheaton, Ill.
39. Tristan Johnson, 1b, Woonsocket (R.I.) HS.
40. *Adam Blair, rhp, Okaloosa-Walton (Fla.) CC.
41. +Michael Collum, ss, Indian River (Fla.) CC.
42. *Jasha Balcom, 2b, Dublin (Ga.) HS.
43. *Jason Wilson, of-rhp, Eastern Oklahoma State JC.
44. *Landon Kersey, lhp, Caruthersville (Mo.) HS.
45. *Garrett Greer, c, Veterans Memorial HS, Peabody, Mass.
46. *Seth Hill, lhp-1b, Kishwaukee (Ill.) CC.
47. *Matt Lindenmeyer, c, Butler County (Kan.) CC.
48. *Andrew Kasperek, c, Weimar (Texas) HS.
49. Marc Love, of, Galveston (Texas) JC.
50. +Josh Shackleford, lhp, South Grand Prairie HS, Grand Prairie, Texas / Navarro (Texas) JC.

## ST. LOUIS CARDINALS (13)

1. Shaun Boyd, of, Vista HS, Oceanside, Calif.—(AAA)
1. Blake Williams, rhp, Southwest Texas State University (Choice from Rangers as compensation for Type B free agent Darren Oliver).—(High A)

First-round pick Chase Utley quickly made himself a fixture at second base for the Phillies

DAVID SCHOFIELD

2. **Chris Narveson, lhp, T.C. Roberson HS, Arden, N.C.—(2006-15)**
3. Chase Voshell, ss, Wake Forest University.—(High A)
4. **Yadier Molina, c, Maestro Ladi HS, Vega Alta, P.R.—(2004-15)**

DRAFT DROP *Brother of Bengie Molina, major leaguer (1998-2010) • Brother of Jose Molina, major leaguer (1999-2014)*

5. Josh Axelson, rhp, Michigan State University.—(AA)
6. Justin Woodrow, of, Knoch HS, Saxonburg, Pa.
7. Shaun Stokes, rhp, William Paterson (N.J.) University.
8. Dan Moylan, c, University of North Carolina.
9. John Novinsky, rhp, Iona (N.Y.) College.
10. **Carmen Cali, lhp, Florida Atlantic University.—(2004-07)**
11. **John Gall, 1b, Stanford University.—(2005-07)**
12. Roddy Friar, c, University of Southern Colorado.
13. Matt Galante, 2b, St. John's University.
14. Dee Haynes, of, Delta State (Miss.) University.
15. Chris Morris, of, The Citadel.
16. Jutt Hileman, ss, Palmyra Area (Pa.) HS.
17. *Kaulana Kuhaulua, ss, Los Angeles CC.

DRAFT DROP *Son of Fred Kuhaulua, major leaguer (1977-81)*

18. *Marc LaMacchia, rhp-ss, East Lake HS, Palm Harbor, Fla.
19. Chet Medlock, rhp, McNeese State University.
20. Landon Brandes, 3b, University of Missouri.
21. Bryan Schultz, rhp, University of Nevada-Reno.
22. Billy Schmitt, 3b, Green Valley HS, Henderson, Nev.
23. Mike Meyer, rhp, University of Arizona.
24. John Lockhart, rhp, Centenary College.
25. Ryan Hamill, c, UCLA.
26. Matt Dogero, c, Santa Barbara (Calif.) CC.
27. *Derek Roper, rhp, Hutchinson (Kan.) CC.
28. Bryan Grassing, rhp, St. Leo (Fla.) College.
29. Dave Lindsey, rhp, Loyola (La.) University.
30. *Mailon Kent, of, Auburn University.
31. Dan Firlit, ss, Southwest Missouri State University.
32. Dallas Pallaro, 2b, Dixie (Utah) JC.
33. Richie Burgess, rhp, San Bernardino Valley (Calif.) JC.
34. **+Tyler Johnson, lhp, Moorpark (Calif.) JC.—(2005-07)**
35. John Santor, 1b, Highland HS, Palmdale, Calif.
36. *Troy Grimmer, rhp, Rex Putnam HS, Milwaukie, Ore.
37. Matt Vriesenga, rhp, Western Michigan University.
38. *Bruce Nelson, c, Rockhurst (Mo.) College.
39. Preston Harriman, 3b, North Arkansas CC.
40. Nate Meza, rhp, Palomar (Calif.) JC.
41. Brian Fatur, of, Moorpark (Calif.) CC.
42. *Ty Soto, ss, Centennial HS, Bakersfield, Calif.
43. *Adam Pritchard, of, Griffin (Ga.) HS.
44. *Chad Cummings, rhp, Saddleback (Calif.) CC.
45. Kelly Johnson, rhp, Yavapai (Ariz.) CC.
46. *Matt Pender, rhp, Middle Georgia JC.
47. *Felipe Tetelboin, ss, Grant HS, Van Nuys, Calif.

## SAN DIEGO PADRES (9)

1. Mark Phillips, lhp, Hanover (Pa.) HS.—(High A)
2. **Xavier Nady, 3b, University of California.—(2000-14)**

DRAFT DROP *First player from 2000 draft to reach major leagues (Sept. 30, 2000)*

3. Omar Falcon, c, Southridge HS, Miami.—(AA)
4. Mewelde Moore, of, Belaire HS, Baton Rouge, La.—(Rookie)

DRAFT DROP *Running back, National Football League (2004-12)*

5. **Jon Huber, rhp, North Fort Myers (Fla.) HS.—(2006-07)**
6. Ryan Earey, rhp, University of North Carolina.
7. Lee McCool, ss, University of North Florida.
8. David Giorgis, of, Rancho Bernardo HS, San Diego.
9. J.K. Scott, rhp, Ramona (Calif.) HS.
10. Kevin Nulton, ss, El Capitan HS, Lakeside, Calif.
11. Joel Klatt, 3b, Pomona HS, Arvada, Colo.
12. *Juan Valle, lhp, Efrain Hidalgo HS, Moca, P.R.
13. **Justin Germano, rhp, Claremont (Calif.) HS.—(2004-14)**
14. J.P. Woodward, 1b, University of Houston.
15. +John DiBetta, ss, CC of Southern Nevada.
16. Charles Lawton, rhp, Palatka (Fla.) HS.
17. Jarrett Roenicke, of, Yuba (Calif.) JC.

DRAFT DROP *Son of Gary Roenicke, first-round draft pick, Expos (1973); major leaguer (1976-88)*

18. *Corey Alexander, of, Forest Brook HS, Houston.
19. *Drew Jenson, 1b, El Capitan HS, Lakeside, Calif.
20. Nick Day, of, Brigham Young University.
21. *Mike Adams, lhp, Cherokee HS, Canton, Ga.
22. **J.J. Furmaniak, 3b-ss, Lewis (Ill.) University.—(2005-07)**
23. Craig Thompson, 1b-of, Stanford University.
24. Edgardo Laureano, rhp, Lorenzo Vizcarrondo HS, Bayamon, P.R.
25. **Jack Cassel, rhp, Los Angeles Pierce JC.—(2007-08)**

DRAFT DROP *Brother of Matt Cassel, quarterback/National Football League (2005-14)*

26. ***Chad Cordero, rhp, Don Lugo HS, Chino, Calif.—(2003-10)**

DRAFT DROP *First-round draft pick (20th overall), Expos (2003)*

27. **Kevin Reese, of, University of San Diego.—(2005-06)**
28. John Herbert, rhp, University of San Francisco.
29. Denny Chapman, rhp, Towson University.
30. Jesse Bussard, rhp, Sonoma State (Calif.) University.
31. *Noah Grubenhoff, rhp, Selah (Wash.) HS.
32. *Jamie Franey, rhp, Ascension College HS, Bay Roberts, Newfoundland.
33. Jarrod Bitter, c, University of Houston.
34. Marc Dulkowski, rhp, Andrew HS, Tinley Park, Ill.
35. Claiborne Daniels, of, Stephen F. Austin HS, Richmond, Texas.
36. *Michael Brown, of, Chipola (Fla.) JC.
37. *Alshawn Rodgers, of, Jordan HS, Long Beach, Calif.
38. *Hunter Brown, ss, Galveston (Texas) JC.
39. Justin Williams, rhp, Seward County (Kan.) CC.
40. Andre Gomez, c, Cal Poly Pomona.
41. *Matt Pollard, rhp, Poteau (Okla.) HS.
42. *Jose Garcia, 2b, T. Alva Edison HS, Caguas, P.R.
43. *David Sanders, lhp, Jenks (Okla.) HS.
44. *Jason Hammond, of, Grossmont (Calif.) JC.
45. *Daniel Shanahan, rhp, UMS Wright HS, Mobile, Ala.

## SAN FRANCISCO GIANTS (21)

1. **Boof Bonser, rhp, Gibbs HS, Pinellas Park, Fla.—(2006-10)**
2. **Lance Niekro, 3b, Florida Southern College.—(2003-07)**

DRAFT DROP *Son of Joe Niekro, major leaguer (1967-88) • Nephew of Phil Niekro, major leaguer (1964-87)*

3. Brion Treadway, rhp, University of North Carolina-Charlotte.—(AA)
4. Ryan Hannaman, lhp, Murphy HS, Mobile, Ala.—(High A)
5. Kyle Gross, rhp, Cuesta (Calif.) JC.—(High A)

DRAFT DROP *Son of Wayne Gross, major leaguer (1976-86)*

6. Chad Ashlock, rhp, Southern Nazarene (Okla.) University.
7. **Erick Threets, lhp, Modesto (Calif.) JC.—(2010)**
8. Nick Wilfong, of, University of Missouri.
9. Edwin Maldonado, ss, Oklahoma Christian University.
10. **Adam Shabala, of, University of Nebraska.—(2005)**
11. Jackson Markert, rhp, Oral Roberts University.
12. Elliot Strankman, ss, Lewis-Clark State (Idaho) College.
13. ***Justin Knoedler, c, Lincoln Land (Ill.) CC.—(2004-06)**
14. Jason Farmer, rhp, Riverside (Calif.) CC.
15. Matt Faas, rhp, Florida Southern College.
16. +Anthony Pannone, rhp, Seward County (Kan.) CC.
17. Rafael Rigueiro, rhp, Southern Nazarene (Okla.) University.
18. Luke Anderson, rhp, University of Nevada-Las Vegas.
19. Dan Padgett, lhp, Northwestern University.
20. Jeff Clark, rhp, University of Connecticut.
21. *Steve Gendron, ss, Berkeley Prep, Tampa.
22. **Jason Ellison, of, Lewis-Clark State (Idaho) College.—(2003-08)**
23. +Robert King, rhp, Modesto (Calif.) JC.
24. Jim Harrelson, rhp, Modesto (Calif.) JC.
25. Danny Trumble, of, University of San Francisco.
26. *Matt Larson, rhp, Golden West (Calif.) JC.
27. *Jino Gonzalez, lhp, Cimarron-Memorial HS, Las Vegas, Nev.
28. ***Alex Hinshaw, lhp, Claremont (Calif.) HS.—(2008-12)**
29. *Denny Hernandez, lhp, Brito Private HS, Miami.
30. Jason Pekar, of, University of Houston.

**31. +Brian Burres, lhp, Mount Hood (Ore.) CC.—(2006-11)**
32. Todd Uzzell, rhp, New Mexico State University.
**33. Trey Lunsford, c, Texas Tech.—(2002-03)**
**34. *Jonathan Albaladejo, rhp, Colegio Janil, Vega Alta, P.R.—(2007-12)**
35. Matt Keating, 1b, Northeastern University.
36. *Matt Gibson, 1b, Sarasota (Fla.) HS.
37. *Jeremy Schmidt, rhp, Manatee (Fla.) CC.
38. Elgin Graham, lhp, Bethune-Cookman College.
39. *Greg Stone, ss, Connors State (Okla.) JC.
40. Mark Walker, of, University of Miami.
41. *Michael Cox, c, St. Petersburg (Fla.) JC.
42. Bryan Carter, of, Embry-Riddle (Fla.) University.
43. *Craig Molldrem, rhp, Boscobel (Wis.) HS.
44. *Jason Daily, rhp, San Luis Obispo (Calif.) HS.
45. *Calvin Fugett, 3b, Montebello HS, Aurora, Colo.
46. *Austin Allen, ss, Beaverton (Ore.) HS.
47. Bryan Gann, 2b, Oral Roberts University.
48. *Lou Colletti, ss, Timothy Christian HS, Wood Dale, Ill.
49. *Nick Conte, c, Serra HS, San Carlos, Calif.
50. *Bennett Elder, c, Lakeside HS, Martinez, Ga.

## SEATTLE MARINERS (16)

1. (Choice to Mets as compensation for Type A free agent John Olerud)
2. (Choice to Rangers as compensation for Type A free agent Aaron Sele)
3. (Choice to Orioles as compensation for Type A free agent Arthur Rhodes)
4. Sam Hays, lhp, Waco (Texas) HS.—(Short-season A)

DRAFT DROP *Grandson of Sid Hudson, major leaguer (1940-54)*

5. Derrick Van Dusen, lhp, Riverside (Calif.) CC.—(AA)
**6. Jamal Strong, of, University of Nebraska.—(2003-05)**
**7. Jaime Bubela, of, Baylor University.—(2005)**
8. Rett Johnson, rhp, Coastal Carolina University.
**9. *Charlie Manning, lhp, University of Tampa.—(2008)**
10. Ryan Ketchner, lhp, John I. Leonard HS, Lantana, Fla.
11. Blake Bone, 3b, University of Alabama-Huntsville.
12. Erick Swanson, lhp, Oakland University.
13. Skip Wiley, rhp, Chaminade-Madonna HS, Pembroke Pines, Fla.
14. Manny Crespo, of, University of Miami.
15. Jake Daubert, 3b, Rutgers University.
16. Jared Jones, of, Florida State University.
17. *Steven Moore, of, Dominguez HS, Culver City, Calif.
18. *Jonathan Doulliard, c, Harrison HS, Kennesaw, Ga.
19. Tanner Watson, rhp, Arnprior (Ontario) District HS.
20. *Miguel Martinez, lhp, Maria Auxiliadora HS, Carolina, P.R.
21. *Robbie Van, lhp, Silverado HS, Las Vegas, Nev.
22. Larry Brown, of, JC of the Canyons (Calif.).
**23. *Jason Hammel, rhp, South Kitsap HS, Port Orchard, Wash.—(2006-15)**
24. *William Corbin, c, Jefferson HS, Lafayette, Ind.
25. *Kyle Pawelczyk, lhp, Elkins (W.Va.) HS.
26. *Jose Cruz, of, Florida Air Academy, Melbourne, Fla.
27. Theo Heflin, lhp, Hutchinson (Kan.) CC.
28. *Thomas Williams, of, McCallum HS, Austin, Texas.
29. *Brandon Espinosa, rhp, Mater Dei HS, Santa Ana, Calif.
30. *Fred Ambres, rhp, Ranger (Texas) JC.

DRAFT DROP *Brother of Chip Ambres, first-round draft pick, Marlins (1998); major leaguer (2005-08)*

31. *Jason Looper, ss, Sentinel (Okla.) HS.
32. Phil Cullen, rhp, University of Utah.
33. *Ben Hudson, c, Truett McConnell (Ga.) JC.
34. *Chris E. Way, rhp, Groves HS, Sylvan Lake, Mich.
35. *Chris S. Way, rhp, Ridgewood HS, Spring Hill, Fla.
36. *Ben Williams, ss, Calloway HS, LaGrange, Ga.
**37. *Billy Sadler, rhp, Pensacola Catholic HS, Pensacola, Fla.—(2006-09)**
38. *Colby Summer, ss, Mountain View HS, Bend, Ore.
**39. *John Nelson, ss-rhp, University of Kansas.—(2006)**
40. *Justin Ottman, lhp, North Rockland HS, Garnersville, N.Y.
41. *Ryan Welborn, of, Yukon (Okla.) HS.
42. *Ronnie Brown, of, Cartersville (Ga.) HS.

DRAFT DROP *Running back, National Football League (2005-14)*

43. *Craig Moreland, of, Trousdale County HS, Hartsville, Tenn.
44. Dennis Cervenka, lhp, McLennan (Texas) CC.
45. Alex Cadena, c, Galveston (Texas) JC.
46. *Derrell Smith, ss, Palm Beach Lakes HS, West Palm Beach, Fla.
47. +Chris Collins, c, South Mountain (Ariz.) CC.
48. *Philip Perry, of, Lakewood (Calif.) HS.
49. *Isaac Johnson, of, Willcox HS, Thatcher, Ariz.
50. *Matt Armstrong, c-1b, Eustis (Fla.) HS.

## TAMPA BAY DEVIL RAYS (6)

**1. Rocco Baldelli, of, Bishop Hendricken HS, Warwick, R.I.—(2003-10)**

DRAFT DROP *First 2000 high school draft pick to reach majors (March 31, 2003)*

2. (Choice to Reds as compensation for Type A free agent Juan Guzman)
3. (Choice to Cubs as compensation for Type A free agent Steve Trachsel)
4. (Choice to Braves as compensation for Type A free agent Gerald Williams)
5. Jace Brewer, ss, Baylor University.—(AAA)
6. Danny Massiatte, c, University of Louisiana-Lafayette.
7. Mike Krga, ss, St. Ignatius HS, Chicago.
**8. Mark Malaska, lhp, Akron University.—(2003-04)**
9. John Dischiavo, rhp, Las Vegas (Nev.) HS.
10. John Benedetti, rhp, Augustana (Ill.) College.
11. Hans Smith, lhp, Fresno State University.
12. Kelly Eddlemon, 3b, Sam Houston State University.
13. Rich Dorman, rhp, Western Baptist (Ore.) College.
14. Tim Coward, rhp, Guilford (N.C.) College.
15. Nate Dion, of, Yukon (Okla.) HS.
**16. James Shields, rhp, Hart HS, Valencia, Calif.—(2006-15)**
17. Adam Bonner, of, Jefferson State (Ala.) CC.
18. Matthew Martunas, lhp, Presbyterian (S.C.) College.
19. +Brian Lockwood, rhp, Los Angeles Harbor JC.
20. *Nick Lyon, of, UCLA.
21. *Mark Weinmunson, lhp, De la Salle HS, New Orleans, La.
22. Daniel Marsh, c, University of North Carolina-Wilmington.
23. Julius Anderson, rhp, Bishop State (Ala.) JC.
**24. +Shawn Riggans, c, Indian River (Fla.) CC.—(2006-09)**
25. Elliott Shaw, rhp, San Jose (Calif.) CC.
26. *Ryan Mulhern, 1b, Trinidad State (Colo.) JC.
27. Alex Marconi, c, Kent State University.
28. Benito Gomez, lhp, Laredo (Texas) JC.
29. Chad Hill, of, University of Mississippi.
**30. Edgar Gonzalez, ss, San Diego State University.—(2008-09)**

DRAFT DROP *Brother of Adrian Gonzalez, first overall draft pick, Marlins (2000); major leaguer (2004-15)*

31. *Danny Muegge, rhp, McLennan (Texas) CC.
32. *Taylor George, rhp, Poly HS, Long Beach, Calif.
33. *Keeyon Sanders, of, Belaire HS, Baton Rouge, La.
**34. *Nick Blackburn, rhp, Del City HS, Norman, Okla.—(2007-12)**
35. *Brett Davis, 1b, Lovejoy HS, Hampton, Ga.
**36. *Colt Morton, c, Kings Academy, West Palm Beach, Fla.—(2007-08)**
**37. *Shane Costa, of, Golden West HS, Visalia, Calif.—(2005-07)**
**38. *Steven Jackson, rhp, Summerville (S.C.) HS.—(2009-10)**
39. *Griffin Zarbrough, lhp, Wallace State (Ala.) CC.
40. +Jason Habel, of, CC of Southern Nevada.
41. *Jon Dobyns, rhp, Desert Vista HS, Phoenix.
42. *Edwar Gonzalez, of, South Miami HS, Miami.
43. *Vince Davis, lhp, Harlan HS, Chicago.
**44. *Micah Hoffpauir, of, Lon Morris (Texas) JC.—(2008-10)**
**45. *Luke Scott, of, Oklahoma State University.—(2005-07)**
46. *Curtis White, lhp, Seward County (Kan.) CC.
47. Juan Renteria, rhp, Driscoll, Texas.
48. *Chad Christy, of, Trinidad State (Colo.) JC.
49. *Andrew Martin, lhp, University HS, San Diego.
50. *Corey Hicks, rhp, Lakewood (Calif.) HS.

## TEXAS RANGERS (24)

1. (Choice to Cardinals as compensation for Type B free agent Darren Oliver)
1. Scott Heard, c, Rancho Bernardo HS, San Diego (Choice from Mets as compensation for Type A free agent Todd Zeile).—(High A)
**1. *Tyrell Godwin, of, University of North Carolina** (Supplemental choice—35th—as compensation for Type A free agent Aaron Sele).**—(2005)**

DRAFT DROP *Returned to North Carolina; re-drafted by Blue Jays, 2001 (3rd round).*

1. Chad Hawkins, rhp, Baylor University (Supplemental choice—39th—as compensation for loss of Zeile).—(High A)
**2. Jason Bourgeois, ss, Forest Brook HS, Houston** (Choice from Mariners as compensation for Sele).**—(2008-15)**
2. Randy Truselo, rhp, Delcastle Tech, Wilmington, Del.—(Low A)
3. Chris Russ, lhp, Towson University.—(High A)
**4. Laynce Nix, of, Midland (Texas) HS.—(2003-13)**
5. Greg Runser, rhp, University of Houston.—(AA)
6. Matt Meisenheimer, rhp, Greenville (Texas) HS.
**7. *Virgil Vasquez, rhp, Santa Barbara (Calif.) HS.—(2007-09)**
**8. +Nick Masset, rhp, Pinellas Park HS, Largo, Fla. / St. Petersburg (Fla.) JC.—(2007-15)**
**9. Edwin Encarnacion, 3b, Manuela Toro HS, Caguas, P.R.—(2005-15)**
10. Billy Montgomery, of, San Diego State University.
11. *Mike Moat, rhp, Niwot HS, Longmont, Colo.
12. Branden Pack, c, University of South Carolina.
13. *Chris Wailand, rhp, Manatee (Fla.) CC.
14. *Myron Leslie, 3b, Brandon HS, Valrico, Fla.
15. *Scott Nicholson, lhp, Oregon State University.
16. Anthony Mongelluzzo, 3b, Florida Atlantic University.
17. *Andy Myette, rhp, Guildford Park HS, Surrey, B.C.

DRAFT DROP *Brother of Aaron Myette, first-round draft pick, Chicago White Sox (1997); major leaguer (1999-2004)*

18. Keith Stamler, rhp, St. John's University.
**19. +A.J. Murray, lhp, Uintah HS, Vernal, Utah / Salt Lake (Utah) CC.—(2007-08)**
20. Tyler Martin, 2b-ss, Mississippi State University.
21. Michael Gleason, rhp, Bountiful (Utah) HS.
22. *Caleb Crosby, rhp, Chipola (Fla.) JC.
23. Austin Evans, of, Pepperdine University.
24. Tim Riley, 2b-of, James Madison University.
25. Frank Sansonetti, of, College of Staten Island (N.Y.).
26. Jason Gray, of, Rice University.
27. *Sean Thompson, lhp, El Camino (Calif.) JC.
28. *Ryan Heath, rhp, Midvale HS, Mesa, Idaho.
29. *Justin Quaempts, rhp, Linn-Benton (Ore.) CC.
30. +Nick Devenney, rhp, Delgado (La.) CC.
31. *Joe Lane, rhp, Osbourn HS, Manassas, Va.
32. Casey Berry, rhp, Cowley County (Kan.) CC.
33. *Michael Vargo, rhp, Fountain Hills (Ariz.) HS.
34. *Garrett Bauer, lhp, Lafayette HS, St. Louis.
35. *Worth Scott, of-lhp, Hendersonville (Tenn.) HS.
36. *Scott Ellison, rhp, Houston HS, Woodland, Miss.
37. *Chris Pillsbury, rhp, Arlington Country Day HS, Jacksonville, Fla.
38. +Dustin Smith, c, Cowley County (Kan.) CC.
39. *Mike Steller, rhp, George Mason University.
40. *Brian Pecor, lhp, Overton HS, Memphis, Tenn.
41. *Ben Ashworth, rhp, St. Petersburg (Fla.) JC.
42. *Juan Serrato, rhp, Norte Vista HS, Riverside, Calif.
43. *Erik Thompson, rhp, Pine Forest HS, Pensacola, Fla.
44. *Julian Davis, 1b, Brandon HS, Valrico, Fla.
45. *James Radford, rhp, Bartow (Fla.) HS.
46. *Matt Kline, of, Arroyo Grande HS, Pismo Beach, Calif.
47. +Jason Guy, of, Charlotte HS, Fort Myers, Fla. / Polk (Fla.) CC.
48. *Ryan Lupul, lhp, North Idaho JC.
49. *Shane Reedy, rhp, Kearns (Utah) HS.
50. Ruben Feliciano, rhp, Kingsborough (N.Y.) CC.

## TORONTO BLUE JAYS (18)

1. Miguel Negron, of, Manuela Toro HS, Caguas, P.R.—(AAA)
**1. Dustin McGowan, rhp, Long County HS, Ludowici, Ga.** (Supplemental choice—33rd—as compensation for Type A free agent Graeme Lloyd).**—(2005-15)**
2. Peter Bauer, rhp, University of South Carolina (Choice from Expos as compensation for Lloyd).—(AAA)
2. Dominic Rich, 2b, Auburn University.—(AA)
3. Morrin Davis, of, Hillsborough HS, Tampa.—(Low A)
4. Raul Tablado, ss, Southridge HS, Miami.—(AA)
**5. Mike Smith, rhp, University of Richmond.—(2002-06)**
**6. Rich Thompson, of, James Madison University.—(2004-12)**
7. Aaron Sisk, 3b, University of New Mexico.
8. Dave Abbott, rhp, University of Arizona.
9. Nom Siriveaw, 3b-of, Eastern Oklahoma State JC.
10. Jerrod Payne, rhp, University of North Florida.
11. Tracey Thorpe, rhp, Melbourne (Fla.) HS.
**12. Vinnie Chulk, rhp, St. Thomas (Fla.) University.—(2003-12)**
13. Shawn Fagan, 3b, Penn State University.
14. +Charles Talanoa, rhp, Los Angeles Harbor JC.
15. Eric Stephenson, lhp, Triton HS, Benson, N.C.

DRAFT DROP *Son of Earl Stephenson, major leaguer (1971-78)*

16. Rich Brosseau, ss, University of Minnesota.

DRAFT DROP *Son of Frank Brosseau, major leaguer (1969-71)*

17. Josh McMillan, lhp, Riverside (Calif.) CC.
18. +Vince Perkins, rhp, Lake City (Fla.) CC.
19. Alex Blackburn, c, A.B. Lucas SS, London, Ontario.
20. Andy McCulloch, rhp, University of Nevada-Las Vegas.
21. Jesse Harper, rhp, Galveston (Texas) JC.
22. Ron Davenport, ss, Leesville Road HS, Raleigh, N.C.
23. Scott Cavey, rhp, University of Notre Dame.
24. Kurt Keene, 2b, University of Florida.
25. Willie Rivera, ss, Turabo (P.R.) University.
26. Jeremy Johnson, of, Southeast Missouri State University.
27. Brian Sellier, of, Grand Canyon University.
28. Chris Small, c, Princeton University.
29. *Chris Neuman, lhp, Western Hills HS, Fort Worth, Texas.
30. Lanny Patten, rhp, Allan Hancock (Calif.) JC.
31. Will Morris, rhp, Cal Poly Pomona.
32. Kris Kozlowski, lhp, Fordham University.
33. Tommy Callen, 2b, University of California.
34. Jeremy Ridley, 2b, Ball State University.

DRAFT DROP *Twin brother of Shayne Ridley, 19th-round draft pick, Orioles (2000)*

35. *Blake Gill, 2b, Manatee HS, Bradenton, Fla.
36. Steve Wood, 1b, Cal Poly San Luis Obispo.
37. Jeromie Spillman, lhp, Grand Canyon University.
38. Dan Huesgen, rhp, Southeast Missouri State University.
39. +Neesan Zieour, 2b, Sacramento (Calif.) CC.
40. *Tom McLane, lhp, St. Petersburg (Fla.) JC.
41. *Kirk Gosch, lhp, Spokane (Wash.) CC.
42. *Matt Sorensen, rhp, Cal State Fullerton.
43. *Matt Kniginyzky, rhp, Lorne Park SS, Mississauga, Ontario.
44. *Derek McNeil, 2b, Land O'Lakes (Fla.) HS.
45. *Dennis Robinson, rhp, Lakeland HS, Putnam Valley, N.Y.
46. *Pat Breen, of, Servite HS, Santa Ana, Calif.
47. Casey Martinez, c, Sacramento State University.

DRAFT DROP *Son of Buck Martinez, major leaguer (1969-86); major league manager (2001-02)*

**48. *Cody Clark, c, Fayetteville (Ark.) HS.—(2013)**
49. *Jacob Bailey, rhp, Indian River (Fla.) CC.
50. Stuart McFarland, lhp, University of Florida.

# 2001

## AT A GLANCE

### This Date In History
June 5-6

### Best Draft
**CHICAGO CUBS.** Even though shoulder issues struck down **MARK PRIOR** (1) in the prime of his career, the Cubs had a noteworthy draft, selecting 13 future big leaguers, more than any club. Prior was the most successful, and **RICKY NOLASCO** (4) and **GEOVANY SOTO** (11) were still active in 2016.

### Worst Draft
**KANSAS CITY ROYALS.** The Royals believed they scored a coup by securing the hardest thrower in the draft, **COLT GRIFFIN** (1), and the best athlete, **ROSCOE CROSBY** (2). Griffin was cut down by injury and Crosby never played in the Royals system, and they had little to show for their 50 picks.

### First-Round Bust
**CHRIS SMITH, LHP, ORIOLES.** Smith transferred from Florida State to an NAIA school in order to pitch, and emerged as a top prospect with a mid-90s fastball. His pro career was short-lived. He suffered a shoulder injury in his first spring training and made only 24 appearances in four seasons before being released, going 2-4, 7.47.

### Second Best
**DAN HAREN, RHP, CARDINALS.** Haren, the 72nd player selected, enjoyed a better major league career than all but three players drafted ahead of him (**JOE MAUER, MARK TEIXEIRA** and **DAVID WRIGHT**). He went 151-131, 3.77 with eight clubs over 13 years.

### Late-Round Find
**JASON BARTLETT, SS, PADRES (13TH ROUND).** Bartlett spent less than a year in the Padres system before being traded to the Twins. He played 10 seasons in the majors, the best in 2009, when he hit .320-14-66 with 30 stolen bases for Tampa Bay.

# Twins make tough call, hit paydirt with Mauer

The Minnesota Twins held the No. 1 overall pick in the 2001 draft, which could have been considered either a blessing or a curse. The previous time the Twins led off the draft, in 1983, they chose righthander Tim Belcher but couldn't sign him. And the team had a history of being unable to strike agreements with first-round picks, doing it a draft-record six times, including Jason Varitek in 1993 and Travis Lee in 1996.

In 2000, the Twins didn't sign supplemental first-rounder Aaron Heilman and second-rounder Tagg Bozied, two of their first three picks. They wanted to draft high school righthander Matt Harrington with the No. 2 overall pick, but concerns about his bonus demands led the club to strike a predraft deal with Cal State Fullerton righty Adam Johnson. On pure talent, Johnson deserved to go about 10 choices later, although he reached the majors in his first full pro season.

The talent pool in 2001 was considered stronger than ever, which added to the Twins' dilemma. University of Southern California righthander Mark Prior was the consensus top prospect and coming off a brilliant junior season. The budget-conscious Twins, though, were uncertain they would be able to meet Price's bonus demands.

Come draft day, they selected catcher Joe Mauer, a high school player from Cretin-Derham Hall in St. Paul, just eight miles from the Twins home park in Minneapolis. As a senior, he hit .605 with 15 home runs.

"It was something else," Mauer said of the draft-day phone call from the Twins. "I looked at my mom and dad, and we were all crying. It was just an unbelievable feeling."

The Twins were criticized for passing on the 6-foot-5, 215-pound Prior, who was snapped up by the Chicago Cubs with the No. 2 pick. But Minnesota officials did not view Mauer as a compromise choice. He was the top high school prospect in the nation, an athletically gifted catcher with five-tool potential. He also had been the 2000 national high school football player of the year, and was a quarterback recruit of Florida State.

"He's a legitimate No.1 pick," Twins scouting director Mike Radcliff said. "I know a number of teams thought he may be the best guy in the draft. We had four guys we thought were legitimate No. 1 picks. We were fortunate in that regard. But let's be honest. We've had trouble signing players in our recent history. We are who we are. We have limited resources and we have to deal with it. Joe was the best fit."

The Twins also considered Georgia Tech third baseman Mark Teixeira and Middle Tennessee State righthander Dewon Brazelton. The team contacted the families or representatives of all four players on the day of the draft to determine if an agreement might be reached. With no deal in place, the Twins moved on Mauer.

TONY FARLOW

Local boy Joe Mauer hit almost from the day the Twins signed him, earning three American League batting titles; he went on to long-term major league success as a catcher and then a first baseman

Radcliff said the team went to great lengths to determine if it could sign Prior, who reportedly was looking for money comparable to the $17 million deal the New York Yankees gave third baseman Drew Henson earlier that year. Henson had been in the Yankees farm system since 1998, and he also was a highly regarded quarterback at the University of Michigan. By accepting the deal, Henson had to give up football. Coincidentally, the Yankees had drafted Prior two rounds ahead of Henson in 1998, but were unable to sign him.

"We did everything we could," Radcliff said. "We had hours of conversation with them, and we watched every game he pitched all spring. I don't know what else we could have done. No one had really any idea where that one would end up."

Mauer didn't come cheap. He got a $5.15 million bonus, the largest ever for a high school player signing with the team that drafted him. The Twins also spent a total of $7.974 million, more than any other team. And history showed Minnesota made the right call. Mauer became a three-time batting champion and three-time Gold Glove winner. Prior's career, though impressive in the short term, blew up because of shoulder problems.

## 2001: THE FIRST ROUNDERS

| CLUB: PLAYER, POS., SCHOOL | HOMETOWN | B-T | HT. | WT. | AGE | BONUS | FIRST YEAR | LAST YEAR | PEAK LEVEL (YEARS) |
|---|---|---|---|---|---|---|---|---|---|
| 1. Twins: Joe Mauer, c, Cretin-Derham Hall HS | St. Paul, Minn. | L-R | 6-4 | 215 | 18 | $5,150,000 | 2001 | Active | Majors (12) |
| Seen as compromise choice, but history has justified Twins' selection of hometown product/two-sport star; won three AL batting titles, three Gold Gloves. | | | | | | | | | |
| 2. *Cubs: Mark Prior, rhp, Southern California | San Diego | R-R | 6-5 | 225 | 20 | $4,000,000 | 2002 | 2013 | Majors (5) |
| "Best college pitcher ever" subject of massive hype, seemed destined for greatness with easy delivery, devastating arsenal; career doomed by shoulder issues. | | | | | | | | | |
| 3. *Devil Rays: Dewon Brazelton, rhp, Middle Tenn. State | Tullahoma, Tenn. | R-R | 6-4 | 205 | 21 | $4,200,000 | 2002 | 2007 | Majors (5) |
| Set Team USA record with 0.61 ERA, dominant as college JR (13-2, 1.42, 127 IP/154 SO), plus control for power pitcher, but never hit stride in majors (8-25, 6.38). | | | | | | | | | |
| 4. Phillies: Gavin Floyd, rhp, Mount St. Joseph HS | Severna Park, Md. | R-R | 6-6 | 210 | 18 | $4,200,000 | 2002 | Active | Majors (12) |
| Long-established youth talent had No. 1 starter stuff with mid-90s FB, power curve; signed club-record bonus, pitched dozen years in majors; still active in 2016. | | | | | | | | | |
| 5. *Rangers: Mark Teixeira, 3b, Georgia Tech | Severna Park, Md. | B-R | 6-2 | 215 | 21 | $4,500,000 | 2002 | Active | Majors (13) |
| Best college bat led to four-year, $9.5 million major league deal, despite ankle fracture in draft year; racked up 394 HRs/1,254 RBIs, five Gold Gloves in majors. | | | | | | | | | |
| 6. Expos: Josh Karp, rhp, UCLA | Bothell, Wash. | R-R | 6-5 | 195 | 20 | $2,650,000 | 2002 | 2005 | Class AAA (2) |
| Elite-level stuff, but underachieved in college (23-7, 4.23), four minor league seasons (24-32, 4.74), never reached majors; shoulder surgery ended career. | | | | | | | | | |
| 7. Orioles: Chris Smith, lhp, Cumberland (Tenn.) | Wantagh, N.Y. | B-L | 5-11 | 190 | 21 | $2,175,000 | 2001 | 2005 | Class A (2) |
| Spent two years at Florida State as hitter before transfer to NAIA school to exploit 94 mph fastball; pro career (2-4, 7.47) limited by shoulder/elbow problems. | | | | | | | | | |
| 8. Pirates: John Van Benschoten, 1b/rhp, Kent State | Milford, Ohio | R-R | 6-4 | 215 | 21 | $2,400,000 | 2001 | 2011 | Majors (3) |
| Legit power bat/arm; hit .440-31-84, led NCAA in HRs, but Pirates preferred 95 mph FB, upside on mound; unfortunate result was 2-13, 9.20 MLB record. | | | | | | | | | |
| 9. Royals: Colt Griffin, rhp, Marshall HS | Marshall, Texas | R-R | 6-4 | 198 | 18 | $2,400,000 | 2001 | 2005 | Class AA (2) |
| Pop-up prospect celebrated as first documented prep arm to top 100 mph; never developed command/secondary pitches before shoulder problems ended career. | | | | | | | | | |
| 10. Astros: Chris Burke, ss, Tennessee | Louisville, Ky. | R-R | 5-11 | 190 | 21 | $2,125,000 | 2001 | 2010 | Majors (6) |
| SEC player of year (.435-20-60, 49 SBs), led NCAA in runs/hits/total bases; compared to Astros star Craig Biggio in all phases, but struggled to meet expectations. | | | | | | | | | |
| 11. Tigers: Kenny Baugh, rhp, Rice | Houston | R-R | 6-4 | 195 | 22 | $1,800,000 | 2001 | 2009 | Class AAA (3) |
| Went 41-8, 2.72 in four years at Rice, set school mark with 163 Ks as SR, but 205 IP in college/first pro year blamed for shoulder problems that plagued career. | | | | | | | | | |
| 12. Brewers: Mike Jones, rhp, Thunderbird HS | Phoenix | R-R | 6-5 | 210 | 18 | $2,075,000 | 2001 | 2010 | Class AAA (2) |
| Touched 98 mph in HS, was on fast track early in career before elblow/shoulder issues led to three surgeries; hung on with Brewers for 10 years before retiring. | | | | | | | | | |
| 13. Angels: Casey Kotchman, 1b, Seminole HS | Seminole, Fla. | L-L | 6-3 | 210 | 18 | $2,075,000 | 2001 | 2015 | Majors (10) |
| Son of noted scout/minor league skipper; fluid/advanced swing, Gold Glove skills propelled him to majors at 21 but lack of power made him complementary player. | | | | | | | | | |
| 14. Padres: Jake Gautreau, 3b, Tulane | McAllen, Texas | L-R | 5-11 | 185 | 21 | $1,875,000 | 2001 | 2007 | Class AAA (5) |
| Led nation in RBIs, sparked Tulane to first CWS appearance by hitting .355-21-96; holes in swing exposed in pros, and career compromised by ulcerative colitis. | | | | | | | | | |
| 15. Blue Jays: Gabe Gross, of, Auburn | Dothan, Ala. | L-R | 6-3 | 205 | 21 | $1,865,000 | 2001 | 2010 | Majors (7) |
| Fluid/graceful athlete spent freshman year in college as QB, three seasons as power-hitting RF (.375-35-218); spent most of MLB career as fourth OF, pinch-hitter. | | | | | | | | | |
| 16. White Sox: Kris Honel, rhp, Providence Catholic HS | New Lenox, Ill. | R-R | 6-5 | 190 | 18 | $1,500,000 | 2001 | 2008 | Class AA (5) |
| Local product with mid-90s FB, tantalizing knuckle-curve; made steady progress in first three years, then sharp decline with elbow issues, inconsistency. | | | | | | | | | |
| 17. Indians: Dan Denham, rhp, Deer Valley HS | Antioch, Calif. | R-R | 6-1 | 195 | 18 | $1,860,000 | 2001 | 2009 | Class AAA (3) |
| First of Indians four first-rounders dominated prep ranks (9-2, 1.42, 74 IP/134 SO) with 94-96 FB, but control issues led to unfulfilled nine-year pro career. | | | | | | | | | |
| 18. Mets: Aaron Heilman, rhp, Notre Dame | Logansport, Ind. | R-R | 6-5 | 225 | 22 | $1,508,705 | 2001 | 2012 | Majors (9) |
| Two-time first-rounder fashioned 43-7, 2.50 college record (15-0, 1.74 as SR); began pro career as starter, spent bulk of major league time (35-46, 4.40) in relief. | | | | | | | | | |
| 19. Orioles: Mike Fontenot, 2b, Louisiana State | Slidell, La. | L-R | 5-8 | 180 | 21 | $1,300,000 | 2002 | 2014 | Majors (7) |
| Teamed with SS Ryan Theriot to win 2000 CWS, later as DP combo for Cubs; offensive-oriented player with surprising pop for size, hit .265-27-163 in majors. | | | | | | | | | |
| 20. Reds: Jeremy Sowers, lhp, Ballard HS | Louisville, Ky. | L-L | 6-1 | 165 | 18 | Unsigned | 2005 | 2010 | Majors (4) |
| Controversial pick for budget-strapped Reds, who chose most unsignable player with no intention of signing him; later signed as Indians top choice in 2004. | | | | | | | | | |
| 21. Giants: Brad Hennessey, rhp, Youngstown State | Toledo, Ohio | R-R | 6-2 | 180 | 21 | $1,382,500 | 2001 | 2011 | Majors (5) |
| Split time as RHP/SS in 2000 with limited success; career took off as pitcher with velocity jump to mid-90s, addition of slider; spent five years for Giants as starter. | | | | | | | | | |
| 22. Diamondbacks: Jason Bulger, rhp, Valdosta State | Snellville, Ga. | R-R | 6-4 | 205 | 22 | $950,000 | 2002 | 2012 | Majors (7) |
| Late bloomer on mound became pitcher midway through 2000 season, went 7-2, 1.47 as SR closer while touching 97; elbow/shoulder problems impacted career. | | | | | | | | | |
| 23. Yankees: John-Ford Griffin, of, Florida State | Sarasota, Fla. | L-L | 6-2 | 195 | 21 | $1,200,000 | 2001 | 2009 | Majors (2) |
| Hitting machine in college hit school-record .427 over career, but skills regressed in pros as he went for power at expense of average, hit just .267 in minors. | | | | | | | | | |
| 24. Braves: Macay McBride, lhp, Screven County HS | Sylvania, Ga. | L-L | 5-11 | 185 | 18 | $1,340,000 | 2001 | 2008 | Majors (3) |
| Little lefty dominated Georgia preps (11-2, 1.32, 79 IP/160 SO) with 93-96 FB, feel for pitching; slowed by control issues, career ended by broken bone in elbow. | | | | | | | | | |
| 25. Athletics: Bobby Crosby, ss, Long Beach State | Cypress, Calif. | R-R | 6-3 | 195 | 21 | $1,350,000 | 2001 | 2010 | Majors (8) |
| Son of ex-big leaguer had advanced skills/instincts in field, decent bat; breakout rookie season for A's (.239-22-64) in 2004, but never duplicated that performance. | | | | | | | | | |
| 26. Athletics: Jeremy Bonderman, rhp, Pasco HS | Pasco, Wash. | R-R | 6-1 | 210 | 18 | $1,350,000 | 2002 | 2013 | Majors (9) |
| Only prep JR ever drafted in first round; traded to Tigers in 2002, called up from high-A year later, overmatched rookie (6-19, 5.56) on one of history's worst teams. | | | | | | | | | |
| 27. Indians: Alan Horne, rhp, Marianna HS | Marianna, Fla. | R-R | 6-3 | 170 | 18 | Unsigned | 2006 | 2011 | Class AAA (1) |
| Drafted six slots ahead of HS batterymate Jeff Mathis; attended three colleges in next four years, drafted by Yankees (2005/11th round), derailed by shoulder issues. | | | | | | | | | |
| 28. Cardinals: Justin Pope, rhp, Central Florida | Lake Worth, Fla. | B-R | 6-0 | 180 | 21 | $900,000 | 2001 | 2008 | Class AAA (2) |
| Dominant spring (15-1, 1.68, 123 IP, 27 BB/158 SO), set NCAA record with 38-IP scoreless streak; undersized arm/marginal stuff caught up to him in pros. | | | | | | | | | |
| 29. Braves: Josh Burrus, ss, Wheeler HS | Marietta, Ga. | R-R | 6-0 | 180 | 17 | $1,250,000 | 2001 | 2010 | Class AAA (1) |
| Second Georgia player taken by Braves in top round; overmatched in all phases in first three pro years, but speed/power/athleticism surfaced after switch to OF. | | | | | | | | | |
| 30. Giants: Noah Lowry, lhp, Pepperdine | Ojai, Calif. | L-L | 6-2 | 190 | 20 | $1,175,000 | 2001 | 2007 | Majors (5) |
| Didn't match career success of Pepperdine teammate Dan Haren (Cards/second round), but won 14 games in '07 for Giants before injuries proved his undoing. | | | | | | | | | |

**Signed to major league contract.*

## AT A GLANCE

### Never Too Late

**ZACH JACKSON, LHP, WHITE SOX (50TH ROUND).** Jackson did not sign with the White Sox out of a Pennsylvania high school. In three college seasons the 6-foot-5 lefthander improved his stock to a 2004 supplemental first-round selection of the Blue Jays (32nd overall). In three major league seasons with the Brewers and Indians, he went 4-5, 5.83.

### Overlooked

**MIKE ADAMS, RHP, BREWERS.** Undrafted out of Texas A&M-Kingsville, where he played baseball and basketball, Adams spent 10 years in the majors, including from 2008-12 when he was one of the game's elite set-up men. Adams went 21-20, 2.41 in 408 appearances, walking 126 and striking out 409 in 407 innings.

### International Gem

**ROBINSON CANO, 2B, YANKEES.** Cano, from the Dominican Republic, signed with the Yankees for $100,000. His emergence came in the midst of a decade-long stretch of draft futility by the Yankees, which left their farm system threadbare. Cano batted .309-204-822 as a five-time all-star for the Yankees before signing with the Mariners as a free agent.

### Minor League Take

**JOE MAUER, C, TWINS.** Mauer earned BA Minor League Player of the Year honors in 2003. Between Class A Fort Myers and Double-A New Britain, he hit .338-5-85, and earned praise for his superior skills behind the plate.

### One Who Got Away

**JEREMY SOWERS, LHP, REDS (1ST ROUND).** The Reds continued to have draft budget problems. Their solution was to spend their first-round pick on Sowers, who was asking for $3 million. The Reds offered

**CONTINUED ON PAGE 540**

## AT A GLANCE

CONTINUED FROM PAGE 539

$1.4 million, and Sowers was off to Vanderbilt. Three years later, he was the sixth overall pick in the draft.

### He Was Drafted?

**CEDRIC BENSON, OF, DODGERS (12TH ROUND).** Benson was the nation's top running back recruit, but that didn't stop the Dodgers from signing him for a $250,000 bonus. Benson played nine games in the Rookie-level Gulf Coast League club a year later, and that was it for his pro baseball career. Benson played football at Texas and was the fourth overall pick in the 2005 NFL draft. He was one of seven players in the 2001 baseball draft who played in the NFL.

### Did You Know . . .

Diamondbacks first-rounder **JASON BULGER** was one of a record three brothers selected in the same draft. Younger brothers **KEVIN** (43rd round) and **BRIAN** (49th round) were picked by the Giants. Brother acts were common in the 2001 draft. **STEPHEN DREW** (Pirates, 11th) was the younger brother of J.D. and Tim. **BRONSON** (Yankees, first) and **DUKE SARDINHA** (Rockies, 41st) were the younger brothers of Dane. **JOE MAUER** (Twins) was the younger brother of **JAKE** (Twins, 23rd) and Bill, who signed with the Twins in 2003 as a nondrafted free agent. **MICHAEL CUST** (Cardinals, 35th) was the third Cust brother to be drafted.

### They Said It

Royals senior adviser **ART STEWART**, a veteran of 48 years of scouting, on his club signing **ROSCOE CROSBY**: "The only player I can compare him to in the last 20 years is Junior Griffey. He has those kinds of tools Junior had in high school. The same ability: arm strength, running speed, raw power. All the ingredients."—*Crosby did not play a game of professional baseball.*

## ABILITY TRUMPS SIGNABILITY

For the first time in six years, the consensus top five prospects in the draft pool were the first five picks. That had not happened since 1995, when Darin Erstad, Ben Davis, Jose Cruz Jr., Kerry Wood and Ariel Prieto went off the board. Concerned about escalating bonuses, teams had placed a premium on players they could sign, even if they were not the top-rated talents.

In 2000, for instance, 10 of the first 11 picks were determined by the player's willingness to sign a predraft deal. A year later, only Cumberland (Tenn.) University lefthander Chris Smith and Rice University senior righthander Kenny Baugh agreed to deals in advance of the draft. Smith was drafted by the Baltimore Orioles with the seventh pick overall, and Baugh was taken by the Detroit Tigers with the 11th pick.

Some scouts considered Prior the best college pitcher of all time, and Teixeira was held in higher regard than any other recent power-hitting prospect. Maryland high school righthander Gavin Floyd, who came from the same Maryland high school that produced Teixeira, headlined an exceptional group of prep righthanders. Brazelton had two dominant pitches and wasn't expected to require much of an apprenticeship in the minors.

"The better guys, the upper echelon, are more high profile," said an official from a team with an early selection. "The top three or four guys have high ceilings. When you have a Mark Prior and a Mark Teixeira coming out of college in the same year, there was no one like that last year. Maybe Joe Borchard, but he's not up there with Teixeira."

Like the Twins, the Cubs were uncertain what Prior would cost, but they decided they couldn't pass on him. John Stockstill, running his first draft as the Cubs scouting director, said the club decided in March to take Prior if he was available. As Baseball America's 2001 College Player of the Year, Prior went 15-1, 1.69 with an NCAA-leading 202 strikeouts in 138 innings. He overmatched hitters with impeccable command of a 94-97 mph fastball and a sharp curve. His combination of size, control, mound presence and work ethic further set him apart from other recent pitching prospects.

JACK REINER

Mark Teixeira

"There are pitchers who had better stuff, maybe a better curveball, or threw 99 rather than 96-97," Stockstill said. "But Mark's a very good pitcher. He has the best college command I've seen in the last 10 years."

Prior was the first player from the class of 2001 to reach the majors, debuting on May 22, 2002. A year later, he went 18-6, 2.43 with 50 walks and 245 strikeouts in 211 innings, and was third in the National League Cy Young Award voting. Prior pitched two impressive postseason games for the Cubs, and had a 3-0 lead in the eighth inning of the sixth game of the National League Championship Series against the Florida Marlins until the infamous Steve Bartman incident. The Cubs collapsed, losing the final two games and falling short of the World Series again.

From his first start in September 2003 through his complete game against the Atlanta Braves in the Division Series, Prior racked up pitch counts of 131, 129, 109, 124, 131, 133, 133. He was never the same, enduring an assortment of injuries, including recurring shoulder problems.

After going 1-6, 7.21 in nine starts for the Cubs in 2006, Prior was done in the major leagues, although he hung on for another seven years in the minors and independent leagues. Prior went 42-29, 3.51 in his five-year major league career. His career ratio of 10.4 strikeouts per nine innings trailed only Hall of Famer Randy Johnson among major league pitchers with at least 500 innings.

The Tampa Bay Devil Rays, who had trouble meeting payroll in May, took Brazelton with the No. 3 selection. He emerged as a top prospect with Team USA in the summer of 2000, showcasing a superb fastball to go with the best changeup in the college ranks. Brazelton went 13-2, 1.42 with 24 walks and 154 strikeouts in 127 innings in his junior season at Middle Tennessee State.

## How They Should Have Done It

Based on the career WAR (Wins Above Replacement, as calculated by Baseball-Reference.com) numbers achieved by all the players eligible for the 2001 draft through the 2015 season, here's how the first round should have unfolded. Numbers in parentheses indicate the round when the player was actually drafted.

| | Player, Pos. | Actual Draft | WAR | Bonus |
|---|---|---|---|---|
| 1. | Mark Teixeira, 3b | Rangers (1) | 52.4 | $4,500,000 |
| 2. | David Wright, 3b | Mets (1-S) | 50.1 | $950,000 |
| 3. | Joe Mauer, c | Twins (1) | 47.8 | $5,150,000 |
| 4. | Dan Haren, rhp | Cardinals (2) | 35.4 | $530,000 |
| 5. | Kevin Youkilis, 3b | Red Sox (8) | 32.7 | $12,000 |
| 6. | J.J. Hardy, ss | Brewers (2) | 26.8 | $735,000 |
| 7. | Jason Bartlett, ss | Padres (13) | 18.4 | $1,000 |
| 8. | Dan Uggla, 2b | Diamondbacks (11) | 17.6 | $40,000 |
| 9. | C.J. Wilson, lhp | Rangers (5) | 16.6 | $188,000 |
| 10. | Mark Prior, rhp | Cubs (1) | 16.5 | $4,000,000 |
| 11. | Ryan Howard, 1b | Phillies (5) | 16.4 | $230,000 |
| | Chris Young, of | White Sox (16) | 16.4 | $90,000 |
| 13. | Gavin Floyd, rhp | Phillies (1) | 15.7 | $4,200,000 |
| 14. | Luke Scott, of | Indians (9) | 12.1 | $10,000 |
| 15. | Geovany Soto, c | Cubs (11) | 11.4 | $59,000 |
| 16. | Rajai Davis, of | Pirates (38) | 10.9 | $80,000 |
| 17. | Edwin Jackson, rhp | Dodgers (6) | 10.6 | $150,000 |
| 18. | Ricky Nolasco, rhp | Cubs (4) | 10.4 | $335,000 |
| 19. | Mike Adams, rhp | Brewers (NDFA) | 10.3 | $2,500 |
| 20. | Noah Lowry, lhp | Giants (1) | 10.2 | $1,175,000 |
| | Zach Duke, lhp | Pirates (20) | 10.2 | $260,000 |
| 22. | Jim Johnson, rhp | Orioles (5) | 8.7 | $400,000 |
| 23. | Kelly Shoppach, c | Red Sox (2) | 8.1 | $737,500 |
| 24. | Casey Kotchman, 1b | Angels (1) | 7.5 | $2,075,000 |
| 25. | Jack Hanahan, 3b | Tigers (3) | 6.7 | $435,000 |
| 26. | Scott Hairston, 2b | Diamondbacks (3) | 6.5 | $400,000 |
| 27. | Ryan Theriot, ss | Cubs (3) | 6.4 | $485,000 |
| 28. | Bobby Crosby, ss | Athletics (1) | 5.4 | $1,350,000 |
| | Chad Tracy, 3b | Diamondbacks (7) | 5.4 | $80,000 |
| 30. | Neal Cotts, lhp | Athletics (2) | 5.3 | $525,000 |

| | Top 3 Unsigned Players | | | Year Signed |
|---|---|---|---|---|
| 1. | Ian Kinsler, 2b | Diamondbacks (26) | 46.7 | 2003 |
| 2. | Nick Markakis, of/lhp | Reds (35) | 27.4 | 2003 |
| 3. | Andre Ethier, of | Athletics (37) | 22.0 | 2003 |

Choosing fourth, the Philadelphia Phillies opted for Floyd. Scott Boras, Teixeira's agent, had warned both the Rays and Phillies that his client wouldn't sign with either club. The Rangers had a major league-high 6.10 ERA on draft day, underscoring their dire need for pitching, but they couldn't resist Teixeira, even though he had missed most of his junior year at Georgia Tech because of a broken foot. As a sophomore, he batted .427 with 18 home runs and was Baseball America's College Player of the Year.

"We thought there was a chance he might get to us," Rangers scouting director Tim Hallgren said. "Everyone said, 'You've got to take a pitcher.' But when it got to us, the pitchers remaining didn't match up to him. We were always looking for the best available talent with the fifth pick."

Radcliff, whose Twins set the tone by taking Mauer, said it was nice to see the best players go to the teams picking at the top of the draft. "All of us agree that the way the draft is set up, it behooves everyone if the selections go the way they went this time," he said. "There was a pretty good consensus that the five or six top guys went first."

## SIGNINGS DRAG OUT ALL SUMMER

Unlike in 2000, when eight of the top 10 picks signed within two weeks of being drafted, the top selections in 2001 were much slower to reach agreements. Mauer, despite having the leverage of a football scholarship offer from Florida State—he could have followed fellow Cretin-Derham two-sport alum and 2000 Heisman Trophy winner Chris Weinke—was the quickest to agree to terms.

Mauer accepted a $5.15 million bonus on July 17. The only drafted player ever to receive more from the team that selected him was Borchard, who got $5.3 million from the Chicago White Sox as the No. 12 overall pick in 2000. The Twins used Mauer's football ability to their advantage, spreading his bonus over five years as permitted by rules applying to two-sport athletes. The Twins wanted to backload the contract to protect themselves in case Mauer decided to resume his football career, but the two sides agreed to split the bonus between the front and back ends of the deal.

Mauer's pro debut was a smashing success. He joined his brother Jake, Minnesota's 23rd-round pick in 2001, at Rookie-level Elizabethton and batted .400 in 32 games. He excelled at every level in the Twins system on his way to an all-star career in the majors.

None of the other top five picks signed in time to make their debut in 2001. All signed in late August, with Prior, Brazelton and Teixeira getting lucrative major league deals.

### Fastest To The Majors

| | Player, Pos. | Drafted (Round) | Debut |
|---|---|---|---|
| 1. | Mark Prior, rhp | Cubs (1) | May 22, 2002 |
| 2. | Kirk Saarloos, rhp | Astros (3) | June 18, 2002 |
| 3. | Dewon Brazelton, rhp | Devil Rays (1) | Sept. 13, 2002 |
| 4. | Mark Teixeira, 3b | Rangers (1) | April 1, 2003 |
| 5. | * Jeremy Bonderman, rhp | Athletics (1) | April 2, 2003 |

*High school selection.*

## DRAFT SPOTLIGHT: COLT GRIFFIN / ROSCOE CROSBY

The Kansas City Royals couldn't believe their good fortune in 2001 when they landed not one, but two highly regarded high school players: Texas righthander Colt Griffin in the first round and South Carolina two-sport star Roscoe Crosby in the second.

"We got the best high school arm in the country, and we got probably the best athlete in the draft," Royals general manager Allard Baird said. "If somebody would have told me before the draft we were going to get Griffin and Crosby, I would have said, 'You're nuts.' "

Baird thought Griffin could be the second coming of Nolan Ryan, and Crosby was another Ken Griffey Jr. Griffin had become the first prep pitcher to throw a documented 100 mph that spring. Crosby was the nation's second-ranked college football recruit, and scouts thought he was an even better baseball prospect. Both players, however, turned out to be empty promises. Griffin never came close to throwing in triple digits as a pro in a career that peaked in Double-A. Crosby's star-crossed career—a mix of personal tragedy and injuries—never even got off the ground.

DAN ARNOLD

Colt Griffin

The Royals drafted Griffin with the ninth overall pick and signed him for a $2.4 million bonus. Griffin's fastball had been clocked at 88-89 mph as a junior, and he was regarded as the third-best pitcher on the Marshall (Texas) High staff entering his senior year. By adding 20 pounds to his 6-foot-3 frame and adapting a high three-quarters arm angle that increased his velocity, Griffin suddenly became a top prospect.

On a 42-degree March night in Natchitoches, La., in his second game of the 2001 season, Griffin hit 97 mph with his fastball. Most of the scouts were there to see the opposing pitcher. "It was a circus from that night on," said Marshall coach Jackie Lloyd. Some 100 scouts were in Lufkin, Texas, on April 4, when Griffin threw several pitches that reached 100 mph and topped at 101. "I've never seen anyone throw harder," said Cincinnati Reds scout Gary Hughes, a 30-year veteran.

Griffin was so dominant, striking out 113 in 65 innings, that the Royals overlooked his chronic control problems, confident that professional instructors could help him. It didn't happen. In six years in the Royals organization, Griffin walked 278 and threw 82 wild pitches in 374 innings. He still reached the low to mid-90s, but Griffin never again hit 100 mph. If anything, he dialed down the velocity on his fastball in an effort to throw more strikes. His inability to develop a quality breaking pitch also plagued him.

Griffin suffered a shoulder injury and had surgery near the end of the 2005 season, and after reinjuring the shoulder the following spring, he decided to retire. Griffin went 19-25, 4.79 for his career, peaking at Double-A. "After surgery," he said, "it was to the point that I felt like I forgot how to throw a baseball. It wasn't fun anymore."

The 6-foot-3, 210-pound Crosby was available in the second round because of his commitment to play football at Clemson. Kansas City not only gave him a $1.75 million bonus, but also allowed him to continue playing football. "When I first saw him," said Royals scout Kevin Floyd, "I told my boss, 'Look, I've been doing this 25 years. I've never seen anything like this kid. He may be the perfect baseball player.' "

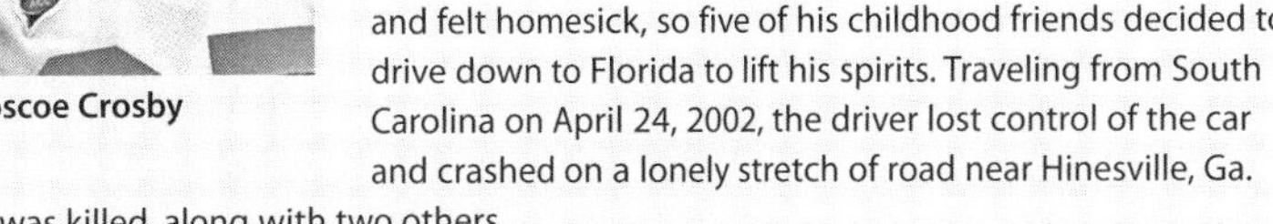

Roscoe Crosby

Crosby thrived immediately as a wide receiver, setting numerous school freshman records in 2001. He had money and growing fame, and he loved it all. "I won't lie. I wanted to live the good life," Crosby said. "The money, the fame, the jewelry and cars. I wanted all of it because to me, at that age, I thought those things meant I was successful."

Crosby reported to spring training with the Royals in 2002 and felt homesick, so five of his childhood friends decided to drive down to Florida to lift his spirits. Traveling from South Carolina on April 24, 2002, the driver lost control of the car and crashed on a lonely stretch of road near Hinesville, Ga. He was killed, along with two others.

While Crosby grieved, the Royals determined he needed Tommy John surgery on his right elbow, which had bothered him since high school. That cost him the baseball season and his sophomore season of football at Clemson. Crosby fell into depression. He then suffered another personal tragedy when a younger brother drowned.

Unable to cope and with his athletic career on hold, Crosby acknowledged that he contemplated suicide. He left pro baseball without playing in a game, and soon quit football, too. The Royals terminated his contract in 2003, placed him on the restricted list and successfully sued him for $750,000, the remaining portion of his $1.75 million bonus.

### WORTH NOTING

Three brothers from Georgia were drafted in 2001. Righthander **JASON BULGER** of Valdosta State was a first-round pick of the Diamondbacks (22nd overall) and his younger brothers were drafted by the Giants. **KEVIN**, a shortstop from Brookwood High, went in the 43rd round, and **BRIAN**, a righthander from South Georgia JC, was selected in the 49th round. Only Jason reached the majors.

**BRONSON SARDINHA**, a supplemental first-round pick of the Yankees, became the highest-drafted Hawaii high school player ever. His older brother **DUKE** was selected in the 41st round by the Rockies, and his oldest brother Dane was a second-round pick of the Reds in 2000. **STEPHEN DREW** (Pirates, 11th) followed in the footsteps of older brothers J.D. and Tim, both former first-rounders, and Stephen became a first-rounder in 2004 after spending three years at Florida State. **MICHAEL CUST** (Cardinals, 35th) was the third brother in his family to be drafted. Neither Drew nor Cust signed in 2001.

Three sets of twins were picked in 2001: **JASON** (Tigers, sixth round) and **JUSTIN KNOEDLER** (Giants, fifth); **MATT** (Brewers, 43rd) and **VINCE SERAFINI** (Twins, sixth); and **MARK** (Blue Jays, 29th) and **P.J. MCDONALD** (Blue Jays, 43rd).

Seminole (Fla.) High, ranked No. 1 wire-to-wire in Baseball America's national poll, became the first high school to have six players selected in one draft. First baseman **CASEY KOTCHMAN** was the 13th overall pick, going to the Angels, who employed his father Tom as a scout and minor league manager. With Tom serving as his agent, Casey received a $2.075 million bonus. College World Series champion Miami had the most picks (13) of four-year colleges, while Riverside CC, the California juco champion, had nine players drafted, most among two-year schools.

The Cubs didn't begin negotiating in earnest with Prior until Aug. 5. He got a five-year major league contract worth $10.5 million, the largest guaranteed payout ever to a drafted player. It included a $4 million bonus, incentives and player options in the final two years, giving Prior flexibility in the event he became eligible for major league arbitration before the contract expired, and protection in the case of a big-league work stoppage.

The Prior family was frustrated that it took so long to reach a deal. "We didn't want to hold out," said Jerry Prior, Mark's father. "We knew this would establish some new standards and that it could take time to negotiate, but the process leaves you twisting in the wind. The inaction was more frustrating than anything else. We wound up in the exact same position as the clients of some of the more volatile agents."

Boras got a rich deal for Teixeira, who signed on Aug. 22, the same day as Prior. The Rangers anted up a four-year major league contract worth a guaranteed $9.5 million, including a $4.5 million signing bonus and easily attainable roster bonuses.

On the same day that Prior and Teixeira reached agreements, Phillies scouting director Mike Arbuckle said his team would not sign Floyd, who was set to attend the University of South Carolina. The Floyd family initially asked for a $7 million bonus, then a major league contract, and then a bonus comparable with what Mauer received.

Floyd turned down the Phillies' $4 million offer, and that evening he and his older brother Mike, an outfielder at South Carolina whom the Phillies drafted in the 22nd round, began the drive to college. A day later, agent Ron Shapiro called Arbuckle to see if a deal still could be worked out. The Phillies increased their offer and signed Floyd shortly before midnight for a $4.2 million bonus. Mike Floyd signed for $65,000.

Dewon Brazelton

Meanwhile, cash-strapped Tampa Bay was trying to come up with a creative way to land Brazelton. The Devil Rays offered just $250,000 up front as part of a five-year contract, a proposal that Brazelton dismissed as "chump change." On Aug. 24 he accepted a five-year, $4.8 million major league contract that included a $4.2 million bonus spread over the length of the deal. He joined the Devil Rays in September, but didn't appear in a game after a summer-long layoff.

"It's something I wanted more than anything," Brazelton said of becoming an instant big leaguer. "I realized they were not going to give me all the money, but that's something you can't put a price tag on. If I get to play some, that would be fine, but you can't put a price tag on being able to live the life of a major league ballplayer. I feel like the next time won't be my first time, that I'll already have major league experience. I will probably seem like a little girl to them because I'm pretty sure the first time I step on that field I'll probably break down in tears or something."

### Top 25 Bonuses

| | Player, Pos. | Drafted (Round) | Order | Bonus |
|---|---|---|---|---|
| **1.** | ***Joe Mauer, c** | **Twins (1)** | **1** | **$5,150,000** |
| **2.** | **Mark Teixeira, 3b** | **Rangers (1)** | **5** | **#$4,500,000** |
| **3.** | **Dewon Brazelton, rhp** | **Devil Rays (1)** | **3** | **#$4,200,000** |
| | ***Gavin Floyd, rhp** | **Phillies (1)** | **4** | **$4,200,000** |
| **5.** | **Mark Prior, rhp** | **Cubs (1)** | **2** | **#$4,000,000** |
| **6.** | **Josh Karp, rhp** | **Expos (1)** | **6** | **$2,650,000** |
| **7.** | **John Van Benschoten, rhp** | **Royals (1)** | **8** | **$2,400,000** |
| | *Colt Griffin, rhp | Royals (1) | 9 | $2,400,000 |
| 9. | Chris Smith, lhp | Orioles (1) | 7 | $2,175,000 |
| **10.** | **Chris Burke, 2b** | **Astros (1)** | **10** | **$2,100,000** |
| 11. | *Mike Jones, rhp | Brewers (1) | 12 | $2,075,000 |
| | ***Casey Kotchman, 1b** | **Angels (1)** | **13** | **$2,075,000** |
| 13. | *Michael Garciaparra, ss | Mariners (1-S) | 36 | $2,000,000 |
| | **Mike Gosling, lhp** | **Diamondbacks (2)** | **66** | **$2,000,000** |
| 15. | Jake Gautreau, 1b | Padres (1) | 14 | $1,875,000 |
| **16.** | **Gabe Gross, of** | **Blue Jays (1)** | **15** | **$1,865,000** |
| 17. | *Dan Denham, rhp | Indians (1) | 17 | $1,860,000 |
| **18.** | **Kenny Baugh, rhp** | **Tigers (1)** | **11** | **$1,800,000** |
| 19. | *Roscoe Crosby, of | Royals (2) | 53 | $1,750,000 |
| **20.** | **Aaron Heilman, rhp** | **Mets (1)** | **18** | **$1,508,750** |
| 21. | *Kris Honel, rhp | White Sox (1) | 16 | $1,500,000 |
| **22.** | ***† Blake Hawksworth, rhp** | **Cardinals (28)** | **854** | **$1,475,000** |
| **23.** | **Brad Hennessey, rhp** | **Giants (1)** | **21** | **$1,382,500** |
| **24.** | **Bobby Crosby, ss** | **Athletics (1)** | **25** | **$1,350,000** |
| | ***Jeremy Bonderman, rhp** | **A's (1)** | **26** | **$1,350,000** |

*Major leaguers in bold. *High school selection. #Major league contract. †Signed as draft-and-follow.*

Teixeira was as successful as any player drafted in 2001, though the latter stages of his career were dented by injuries. With his superior raw power, bat skills and plate discipline, he homered 394 times and drove in 1,254 runs through his first 13 major league seasons and was still active in 2016.

Floyd enjoyed a solid 12-year major league career as a starting pitcher. Brazelton proved to be the biggest disappointment of the group, in large part because he was rushed to the majors. In 63 appearances from 2002-06, he went 8-25, 6.38, rarely demonstrating the command that had shot him up draft boards in 2001.

The success rate for the next 12 selections wasn't nearly as good. Only eight of the picks from No. 6 to No. 17 reached the highest level.

### BONUSES RISE TO RECORD LEVELS

Two first-rounders went unsigned in 2001, the first time that many didn't reach agreement since 1997. The 28 players who turned pro received an average bonus of $2,162,723, a 15 percent increase over 2000. The 2001 mark was not only a record, but it would represent the largest annual bonus average for another seven years. Fourteen players received bonuses of $2 million or more: 12 of the first 13 choices, Seattle Mariners supplemental first-rounder Michael Garciaparra and Arizona Diamondbacks second-rounder Mike Gosling.

UCLA righthander Ryan Karp, the No. 6 overall pick, was the last of the first-rounders to sign, agreeing to a $2.65 million bonus with the Montreal Expos on Sept. 28. The 6-foot-5 Karp had the raw stuff to be an elite pitcher, but didn't dominate in three years at UCLA (23-7, 4.23) and

## Largest Bonuses By Round

| | Player, Pos. | Club | Bonus |
|---|---|---|---|
| 1. | * **Joe Mauer, c** | **Twins** | **$5,150,000** |
| 1-S. | * Michael Garciaparra, ss | Mariners | $2,000,000 |
| 2. | **Mike Gosling, lhp** | **Diamondbacks** | **$2,000,000** |
| 3. | Tagg Bozied, 1b | Padres | $725,000 |
| 4. | * Terry Jones, ss | Phillies | $500,000 |
| 5. | * **Jim Johnson, rhp** | **Orioles** | **$400,000** |
| 6. | * Quan Cosby, of | Angels | $825,000 |
| 7. | * Tyler Adamczyk, rhp | Cardinals | $1,000,000 |
| 8. | Warren Hanna, c | Cubs | $170,000 |
| 9. | * Billy Simon, rhp | Red Sox | $325,000 |
| 10. | * Greg Moreira, rhp | Brewers | $135,000 |
| 11. | Marcus Nettles, of | Padres | $75,000 |
| 12. | * Cedric Benson, of | Dodgers | $250,000 |
| 13. | Brian Sager, rhp | White Sox | $325,000 |
| 14. | * Tommy Nichols, 1b | Devil Rays | $128,000 |
| 15. | *# Micah Posey, lhp | Angels | $180,000 |
| 16. | *# Sean Smith, rhp | Indians | $1,200,000 |
| 17. | * Chris Neylan, lhp | Blue Jays | $265,000 |
| 18. | # Dayton Buller, c | Giants | $400,000 |
| 19. | Isaac Iorg, ss | Blue Jays | $100,000 |
| 20. | * **Zach Duke, lhp** | **Pirates** | **$260,000** |
| | * Brian Miller, rhp | White Sox | $260,000 |
| 21. | * Matt Ware, of | Mariners | $200,000 |
| | * Cody Gunn, c | Cardinals | $200,000 |
| 22. | * Jimmy Schultz, rhp | Indians | $117,500 |
| 23. | Casey Shumake, rhp | Pirates | $200,000 |
| | * **Matt Albers, rhp** | **Astros** | **$200,000** |
| 24. | * Charlie Lisk, c | White Sox | $390,000 |
| 25. | Several tied at | | $15,000 |
| **Other#** | **Blake Hawksworth, rhp** | **Cardinals (28)** | **$1,475,000** |

*Major leaguers in bold. *High school selection. #Signed as draft-and-follow.*

underachieved in four minor league seasons (24-32, 4.74) before his career ended after the 2005 season because of shoulder surgery.

Chris Smith, selected seventh overall, and John Van Benschoten, taken eighth, established their worth in college primarily with their bats, but the Orioles and Pittsburgh Pirates developed both players as pitchers—with little success.

Smith spent his first two seasons at Florida State as an outfielder, hitting .375 with 14 homers as a sophomore while making four pitching appearances. After Florida State coach Mike Martin denied Smith's request to pitch more as a junior, Smith transferred to Cumberland, an NAIA power, where he went 9-2, 2.13 with 115 strikeouts in 84 innings, showing a 94 mph fastball. Smith also hit .414 with 17 homers and 67 RBIs, but most scouts liked him better as a pitcher. Smith hurt his shoulder after signing with the Orioles and later

GEORGE GOJKOVICH

**Mark Prior earned acclaim as the best college pitching prospect ever, but injuries cut him down after a promising start to his career**

had Tommy John surgery. He won two games in 24 minor league appearances.

Like Van Benschoten, first-rounders Chris Burke (Astros, 10th overall) and Jake Gautreau (Padres, 14th) were top college hitters. Burke led NCAA Division I in runs (105) and hits (118) and tied Van Benschoten in total bases (221), and Gautreau was the RBIs leader (96). Burke reached the majors, but Gautreau did not.

The Kansas City Royals, selecting ninth, took righthander Colt Griffin, the first high school pitcher documented to throw 100 mph. Barely on scouts' radar at the outset of the 2001 season, Griffin was throwing in the high 90s in his first few games for Marshall (Texas) High and reached triple digits on April 4. His pro career fell far short of expectations, however. He didn't approach 100 mph with his fastball, was plagued by control issues during his six-year minor league career and retired after undergoing shoulder surgery.

A high school junior was drafted in the first round for the first time. Pasco (Wash.) High righthander Jeremy Bonderman, Team USA's ace at the 2000 World Junior Championship, passed his GED test and petitioned Major League Baseball to enter the draft. The Oakland Athletics selected him 26th overall and signed him for $1.35 million. Bonderman became the first high school player from the class of 2001 to reach the majors, getting there after he was traded to the Tigers.

Kentucky high school lefthander Jeremy Sowers, the 20th overall selection, and Florida prep righty Alan Horne, chosen 27th, went unsigned. Sowers chose Vanderbilt over a modest offer from the Cincinnati Reds. Horne turned down the

## One Team's Draft: Anaheim Angels

| | Player, Pos. | Bonus |
|---|---|---|
| 1. | * **Casey Kotchman, 1b** | **$2,075,000** |
| 1. | * **Jeff Mathis, c** | **$850,000** |
| 2. | **Dallas McPherson, 3b** | **$660,000** |
| 3. | **Steven Shell, rhp** | **$460,000** |
| 3. | **Jacob Woods, lhp** | **$442,500** |
| 4. | Mike Nickoli, rhp | $275,000 |
| 5. | Brad Pinkerton, lhp | $175,000 |
| 6. | * Quan Cosby, of | $825,000 |
| 7. | **Rich Hill, lhp** | **Did not sign** |
| 8. | Justin Turner, 3b | $70,000 |
| 9. | * Devin Ivany, c | Did not sign |
| 10. | * **Matt Brown, 3b** | **$48,500** |
| 11. | * Johnathon Shull, rhp | $33,000 |
| 12. | **Ryan Budde, c** | **$150,000** |
| 13. | Tony Arthur, lhp | $5,000 |
| 14. | Jason Dennis, lhp | $22,500 |
| 15. | * Micah Posey, rhp | $180,000 |
| 16. | Al Corbeil, c | $2,500 |
| 17. | * Bruce Galloway, rhp | Did not sign |
| 18. | Ed Tolzien, 1b | $2,500 |
| 19. | **Nick Gorneault, of** | **$2,500** |
| 20. | * Justin Nelson, of | Did not sign |
| 21. | David Gates, of | $18,000 |
| 22. | * Brock Keffer, rhp | Did not sign |
| 23. | Mitch Arnold, rhp | $107,500 |
| 24. | * William Robbins, rhp | Did not sign |
| 25. | Mark O'Sullivan, rhp | $1,000 |
| Other | Kelly Sisco (27), lhp | $60,000 |

*Major leaguers in bold. *High school selection.*

## WORTH NOTING

■ Maryland prep righthander **GAVIN FLOYD**, drafted fourth overall by the Phillies, had the highest grade in the 2001 draft from the Major League Scouting Bureau. His grade on the 20-80 scale was 68.5. Next were USC righthander **MARK PRIOR** (67), California prep righthander **DAN DENHAM** (66) and Texas prep righthander **COLT GRIFFIN** (65.5).

■ No. 1 pick **JOE MAUER**, a Minnesota high school product drafted by the Twins, was one of four first-round picks selected by his home state club. The White Sox chose New Lenox, Ill., high school righthander **KRIS HONEL** (16th overall). The Braves had three of the top 40 picks and used them all on Georgia players: high school lefty **MACAY MCBRIDE** (24th overall), prep shortstop **JOSH BURRUS** (29th) and Georgia Tech second baseman **RICHARD LEWIS** (40th). "It doesn't matter what area of the country they were from," Braves scouting director Roy Clark said.

■ In addition to **ROSCOE CROSBY** (Royals, second round), who played football at Clemson, other significant two-sport talents who signed pro baseball contracts and also played college football were outfielder **CEDRIC BENSON**, who became a top running back at the University of Texas after being drafted in the 12th round by the Dodgers; and **MATT WARE**, a defensive back at UCLA and the 21st-round selection of the Mariners. Benson received a $250,000 bonus and played in nine games in Rookie ball in 2002 before deciding to devote his attention to football. He became a first-round pick of the NFL's Chicago Bears in 2005. Ware signed with the Mariners for $200,000 and played two seasons. Outfielder **QUAN COSBY** received an $825,000 bonus from the Angels, but Cosby quit baseball after four minor league seasons and became a standout wide receiver at Texas. Benson, Ware and Cosby played in the NFL.

## IN FOCUS: JOHN VAN BENSCHOTEN

John Van Benschoten burst into prominence in 2001 when he hit an NCAA-leading 31 homers at Kent State in his junior season. With his combination of power, speed and arm strength, most teams saw him as the best college athlete in the 2001 draft and projected him as a prototypical right fielder. He hit .441 with 23 stolen bases, and also posted a 2-2, 2.81 record with eight saves and 63 strikeouts in 48 innings.

"The Pirates were the only club that looked at me as a pitcher," he said. "So this does come as a little bit of a surprise. I fully expected to be drafted as a hitter. But I like to pitch, too. I'll do whatever the Pirates want."

The Pirates brought Van Benschoten to Pittsburgh for a workout a week prior to the draft. "I watched him take the mound and I watched him step into the batting cage," scouting director Mickey White said. "He seemed to have more of a presence on the mound. He is definitely a fine hitting prospect, but we really believe he has a chance to become an outstanding pitcher."

Van Benschoten threw a mid-90s fastball, but never developed into a consistent pitcher, his career often interrupted by shoulder problems. He went 2-13, 9.20 in three major league seasons with the Pirates. That is the highest ERA in MLB history for a pitcher with at least 75 innings.

## Highest Unsigned Picks

| Player, Pos., Team (Round) | College | Re-Drafted |
|---|---|---|
| Jeremy Sowers, lhp, Reds (1) | Vanderbilt | Indians '04 (1) |
| Alan Horne, rhp, Indians (1) | Mississippi | Angels '04 (30) |
| J.P. Howell, lhp, Braves (2) | USC | Royals '04 (1) |
| Matt Harrington, rhp, Padres (2) | None | Devil Rays '02 (13) |
| Matt Chico, lhp, Red Sox (2) | USC | D-backs '03 (3) |
| Trey Taylor, lhp, Rockies (2) | Baylor | Cubs '04 (20) |
| Jeremy Guthrie, rhp, Pirates (3) | * Stanford | Indians '02 (1) |
| Jon Zeringue, c, White Sox (3) | Louisiana State | D-backs '04 (2) |
| David Bush, rhp, Devil Rays (4) | * Wake Forest | Blue Jays '02 (2) |
| Josh Baker, rhp, Rangers (4) | Alabama | Brewers '04 (4) |

**TOTAL UNSIGNED PICKS:** Top 5 Rounds (12), Top 10 Rounds (29)

**Returned to same school.*

Cleveland Indians and went to the University of Mississippi.

Cincinnati club officials acknowledged that the Reds, who had serious budget issues, knew they had little chance to sign Sowers. He came from a well-to-do family that wanted him to attend college and set an asking price of about $3 million. The Reds offered $1.4 million, and were quite content to save the money and get a supplemental first-rounder in the 2002 draft in return.

"We didn't take him with the idea that we knew we couldn't sign him," a Reds official said, "because we've found a way to get this kind of player done in the past. But we knew it was a longshot."

Sowers was drafted in the first round in 2004 (sixth overall) by the Indians after three successful years at Vanderbilt. Horne began his college career at Mississippi and ended it at Florida, with a stop in between at Chipola (Fla.) JC after missing a season while recovering from Tommy John surgery. He signed after being drafted in the 11th round by the Yankees in 2005. Sowers reached the majors, but had a disappointing seven-year career, going 18-30, 5.18. Horne's pro career peaked in Triple-A.

Jeremy Sowers

The most noteworthy player to go unsigned was righthander Matt Harrington, a second-round pick of the San Diego Padres. He had turned down the Colorado Rockies a year earlier as the seventh overall pick after highly contentious negotiations led by his agent, Tommy Tanzer. He signed with the independent Northern League's St. Paul Saints to remain in competition and showcase himself for the 2002 draft. Harrington, though, fared poorly for the Saints, struggling to command his pitches and posting a 9.47 ERA in 18 innings.

When negotiations stalled with the Padres, Harrington replaced Tanzer with Boras, who recommended that Harrington reject a reported $1.2 million offer. He again went unsigned. The scenario repeated itself three more times, and Harrington never pitched in either the minor or major leagues.

## MAJOR DRAFT-AND-FOLLOW IMPACT

The draft-and-follow rule had a greater impact in 2001 than any other time, both in terms of players from the 2000 draft who signed and 2001 picks who agreed to terms the next spring.

McLennan (Texas) CC lefthander Sean Henn, a 26th-round pick of the Yankees in 2000, received the largest bonus to date by a draft-and-follow when he signed for $1.701 million. Henn elevated his stock by throwing as hard as 98 mph, and likely would have been picked in the first round in 2001 had the Yankees not signed him. Henn suffered an elbow injury soon after turning pro and had Tommy John surgery. He pitched in six seasons in the majors, going 2-10, 7.42.

Four junior college players received bonuses of at least $1 million before the 2002 draft, led by American River (Calif.) lefthander Manny Parra, who signed with the Milwaukee Brewers for $1.55 million, and Bellevue (Wash.) righthander Blake Hawksworth, who signed with the St. Louis Cardinals for $1.45 million. Both reached the majors.

Except for Mauer, no 2001 first-rounders were in position to leverage their signing bonus by being a two-sport athlete. But there were plenty of noteworthy football players in the draft, at least three of whom signed baseball contracts.

South Carolina high school outfielder Roscoe Crosby initially was projected as one of the top 10 picks in the draft, and he also showed great potential as a wide receiver. The Royals considered taking Crosby with the No. 9 overall pick, but his football scholarship offer from Clemson gave them pause, and they selected him instead in the second round. Crosby signed for a $1.75 million bonus spread over five years, and the Royals agreed that he could play football as well as baseball.

Crosby, though, did not play a game of professional baseball. He signed too late to play in 2001 before reporting to football practice and missed the 2002 season while rehabbing from Tommy John surgery. The Royals expected him to start his career in 2003, but Crosby, beset by personal problems as well as pressure from Clemson officials to return to school in order to maintain his football eligibility, left spring training and quit baseball. He did not play another down of college football, either.

The Royals placed Crosby on the restricted list and took him to arbitration in a successful effort to void his contract and recoup $750,000 of his signing bonus.

## Largest Draft-And-Follow Bonuses

| | Player, Pos. | Club (Round) | Bonus |
|---|---|---|---|
| **1.** | *** Blake Hawksworth, rhp** | **Cardinals (28)** | **$1,475,000** |
| **2.** | **Manny Parra, lhp** | **Brewers (26)** | **$1,250,000** |
| 3. | * Sean Smith, rhp | Indians (16) | $1,200,000 |
| **4.** | **Humberto Sanchez, rhp** | **Tigers (31)** | **$1,000,000** |
| 5. | Shane Reedy, rhp | Cardinals (44) | $500,000 |
| 6. | Dayton Buller, c | Giants (18) | $400,000 |
| 7. | Mike Rodriguez, rhp | Dodgers (45) | $275,000 |
| **8.** | *** Matt Albers, rhp** | **Astros (23)** | **$200,000** |
| 9. | * Micah Posey, rhp | Angels (15) | $180,000 |
| 10. | * Kyle Jackson, rhp | Red Sox (32) | $175,000 |

*Major leaguers in bold. *High school selection.*

# 2001 Draft List

**Did not sign. Major leaguers in bold, with first and last years noted. Order of selection indicated in parentheses. For the first five rounds, the peak level of each player is noted.*
*+ Signed as draft-and-follow (Second school noted if applicable).*

## ANAHEIM ANGELS (13)

**1. Casey Kotchman, 1b, Seminole (Fla.) HS.—(2004-13)**
**1. Jeff Mathis, c, Marianna (Fla.) HS** (Supplemental choice—33rd—as compensation for Type A free agent Mark Petkovsek).—**(2005-15)**
**2. Dallas McPherson, 3b, The Citadel.—(2004-11)**
**3. Steven Shell, rhp, El Reno (Okla.) HS** (Choice from Rangers as compensation for Petkovsek).**—2008-09)**
**3. Jake Woods, lhp, Bakerfield (Calif.) JC.—(2005-08)**
4. Mike Nickoli, rhp, Birmingham-Southern College.—(AA)
5. Brad Pinkerton, lhp, Elon College.—(Rookie)
6. Quan Cosby, of, Mart (Texas) HS.
DRAFT DROP *Wide receiver, National Football League (2009-12)*
**7. *Rich Hill, lhp, University of Michigan.—(2005-15)**
8. Justin Turner, 3b, Warner Southern (Fla.) College.
9. *Devin Ivany, c, Cardinal Gibbons HS, Fort Lauderdale, Fla.
**10. Matt Brown, 3b, Coeur d'Alene (Idaho) HS.—(2007-08)**
11. Johnathon Shull, rhp, Eastside HS, Butler, Ind.
**12. Ryan Budde, c, Oklahoma State University.—(2007-10)**
13. Tony Arthur, lhp, Arkansas State University.
14. Jason Dennis, lhp, University of California.
15. +Micah Posey, rhp, North Florida Christian HS, Tallahassee, Fla. / Tallahassee (Fla.) CC.
16. Al Corbiel, c, Florida Southern College.
17. *Bruce Galloway, lhp, Allen (Texas) HS.
18. Ed Tolzien, 1b, Illinois State University.
**19. Nick Gorneault, of, University of Massachusetts.—(2007)**
20. *Justin Nelson, of, Rancho Buena Vista HS, Vista, Calif.
21. David Gates, of, University of Alabama-Huntsville.
22. *Brock Keffer, rhp, LaSalle-Peru Township HS, Peru, Ill.
23. +Mitch Arnold, rhp, New Mexico JC / Modesto (Calif.) JC.
24. *William Robbins, rhp, Lockhart HS, Sharon, S.C.
25. Mark O'Sullivan, rhp, Rollins (Fla.) College.
26. *Jason Durbin, of, Atwater (Calif.) HS.
27. +Kelly Sisco, lhp, Connors State (Okla.) JC.
28. Ryan Nevins, ss, New York Tech.
**29. *Carlos Corporan, 1b, Francisco Oller HS, Catano, P.R.—(2009-15)**
30. Kris Sutton, rhp, University of Tampa.
31. Ryan Bailey, rhp, University of Utah.
**32. Steve Andrade, rhp, Cal State Stanislaus.—(2006)**
**33. *Scott Lewis, lhp, Washington HS, Washington Court House, Ohio.—(2008-09)**
34. Casey Smith, 2b, Troy State University.
35. Blake Allen, rhp, University of Alabama-Birmingham.
36. *Steven Trosclair, rhp, Southeastern Louisiana University.
37. *James Morris, lhp, Eldorado (Ill.) HS.
38. *Thomas Sgueglia, 2b, Mount Saint Michael HS, Bronx, N.Y.
39. Jaime Steward, lhp, LeMoyne College.
40. *Alan Crigger, rhp, Okaloosa-Walton (Fla.) CC.
41. Brent Del Chiaro, c, University of Kansas.
42. Ryan Webb, 3b, Cal State Chico.
43. *David Bartelt, rhp, Jesuit HS, Odessa, Fla.
44. Mike Eylward, 3b, University of South Florida.
45. Greg Porter, 3b, Texas A&M University.
46. *Alberto Marrero, c, Luis Pales Matos HS, Bayamon, P.R.
47. *Jorge Marrero, of, Jose Collazo Colon HS, Juncos, P.R.
48. *Collin Mahoney, c, Mount St. Michael HS, Bronx, N.Y.
49. *Stephen Nielsen, rhp, Triton (Ill.) JC.
50. *Kevin Letz, rhp, Hanks HS, El Paso, Texas.

## ARIZONA DIAMONDBACKS (22)

**1. Jason Bulger, rhp, Valdosta State (Ga.) University.—(2005-11)**
DRAFT DROP *Brother of Kevin Bulger, 43rd-round draft pick, Giants (2001) • Brother of Brian Bulger, 49th-round draft pick, Giants (2001)*
**2. Mike Gosling, lhp, Stanford University.—(2004-09)**
**3. Scott Hairston, 2b, Central Arizona JC.—(2004-14)**
DRAFT DROP *Grandson of Sam Hairston, major leaguer (1951) • Son Jerry Hairston, major leaguer (1973-89) • Brother of Jerry Hairston, major leaguer (1998-2013)*
4. Justin Wechsler, rhp, Ball State University.—(AA)
5. Richie Barrett, of, Ursinas (Pa.) College.—(Low A)
**6. *Matt Fox, rhp, Stoneman Douglas HS, Coral Springs, Fla.—(2010)**
DRAFT DROP *First-round draft pick (35th overall), Twins (2004) • Brother of Mike Fox, 50th-round draft pick, Cardinals (2001)*
**7. Chad Tracy, 3b, East Carolina University.—(2004-13)**
**8. Brandon Medders, rhp, Mississippi State University.—(2005-10)**
9. Jarred Ball, of, Tomball (Texas) HS.
10. *Matt Durkin, rhp, Willow Glen HS, San Jose, Calif.
**11. Dan Uggla, 2b, University of Memphis.—(2006-15)**
12. Erick Macha, 2b-ss, Texas Christian University.
13. Shane Waroff, rhp, Cal State Fullerton.
14. Josh Clark, rhp, Southern Illinois University-Edwardsville.
15. Sam Taulli, lhp, Chipola (Fla.) JC.
16. Michael DiRosa, c, University of Miami.
17. Jay Belflower, rhp, University of Florida.
18. Mike Garber, lhp, San Diego State University.
19. Dustin Vugtoveen, of, Grand Valley State (Mich.) University.
**20. *Eddie Bonine, rhp, Glendale (Ariz.) CC.—(2008-10)**
21. *Brett Smith, rhp, Sonora HS, La Habra, Calif.
22. Ryan Holsten, rhp, Fairfield University.
23. Scott Hilinski, ss, Warner Southern (Fla.) College.
24. Phil Avlas, c, Kennedy HS, North Hills, Calif.
25. *Chase Bassham, lhp, Western Hills HS, Benbrook, Texas.
**26. *Ian Kinsler, ss-2b, Central Arizona JC.—(2006-15)**
27. Cliff McMachen, lhp, CC of Southern Nevada.
28. Clark Mace, of, Miami (Ohio) University.
29. +Ryan Coffin, rhp, Chandler-Gilbert (Ariz.) CC.
30. +Alex Frazier, of, Lurleen B. Wallace State (Ala.) JC.
31. *Jason Bingham, lhp, Pima (Ariz.) CC.
32. Jeramy Janz, of, University of San Francisco.
33. *Daniel Morris, lhp, Mosley HS, Southport, Fla.
34. *Trent Pratt, c, Auburn University.
35. *Chad Halbert, lhp, Cypress HS, Buena Park, Calif.
36. +Marland Williams, of, North Florida CC.
37. *Brett Dowdy, 3b, Manatee (Fla.) JC.
38. *Quinn Stewart, of, Dallas Christian HS, Rowlett, Texas.
39. *Brian Cooper, ss, Bakersfield (Calif.) HS.
40. *Cary Nelson, of, Channelview (Texas) HS.
41. *Jesse Torborg, of, Connetquot HS, Ronkonkoma, N.Y.
42. Mike Thiessen, of, Air Force Academy.
43. *Matt Raguse, rhp, St. Louis CC-Forest Park.
44. *Jon Felfoldi, lhp, La Jolla, Calif.
45. Matt Wilkinson, rhp, Southern Illinois University-Edwardsville.
46. *Arlow Hanen, of, North HS, Phoenix.
47. *Matt Grooms, of, St. James HS, Montgomery, Ala.
**48. *Seth Smith, of, Hillcrest Christian HS, Jackson, Miss.—(2007-15)**
49. *Troy Pickford, rhp, Fresno (Calif.) CC.
50. *Scott Foresman, rhp, American Heritage HS, Miramar, Fla.

## ATLANTA BRAVES (29)

**1. Macay McBride, lhp, Screven County HS, Sylvania, Ga.** (Choice from Dodgers as compensation for Type A free agent Andy Ashby).—**(2005-07)**
1. Josh Burrus, ss, Wheeler HS, Marietta, Ga.—(AAA)
1. Richard Lewis, 2b, Georgia Tech (Supplemental choice—40th—as compensation for Ashby).—(AAA)
**2. *J.P. Howell, lhp, Jesuit HS, Sacramento, Calif.** (Choice from Pirates as compensation for Type B free agent Terry Mulholland).**—(2005-15)**
DRAFT DROP *Attended Southern California; re-drafted by Royals, 2004 (1st round)*
2. Cole Barthel, 3b, Decatur (Ala.) HS.—(Low A)
**3. Adam Stern, of, University of Nebraska.—(2005-10)**
**4. Kyle Davies, rhp, Stockbridge (Ga.) HS.—(2005-11)**
5. Matt Esquivel, of, McArthur HS, San Antonio, Texas.—(AAA)
6. Billy McCarthy, of, Rutgers University.
7. Roberto Nieves, rhp, Ileana de Gracia HS, Vega Alta, P.R.
8. Alonzo Ruelas, c, Grayson County (Texas) CC.
9. Donnie Furnald, rhp-3b, Cal Poly Pomona.
**10. Willie Collazo, lhp, Florida International University.—(2007)**
**11. Anthony Lerew, rhp, Northern Senior HS, Wellsville, Pa.—(2005-10)**
12. Mailon Kent, of, Auburn University.
13. Bryon Jeffcoat, 2b, University of South Carolina.
**14. Kevin Barry, rhp, Rider College.—(2006-07)**
15. Dexter Cooper, rhp, Etowah HS, Woodstock, Ga.
16. Roberto Santana, of, Jose Collazo Colon HS, Las Piedras, P.R.
17. *Anthony Mandel, rhp, Pensacola Catholic HS, Pensacola, Fla.
18. +Justin Parker, lhp, University of Tennessee.
19. Kevin Brown, 1b, University of Miami.
20. Greg Miller, of, James Madison University.
21. Adam Sokoll, rhp, Oakland University.
22. Dewayne Jones, c, Jackson State University.
23. Brian Strong, c, Ferrum (Va.) College.
24. Fred Wray, rhp, University of North Carolina-Wilmington.
25. Travis Anderson, c, Burney, Calif.
26. *Alex Trommelen, rhp, Pace (Fla.) HS.
27. *Cesar Montes de Oca, rhp, Bethune-Cookman College.
28. Dominique Partridge, of, Northgate HS, Newnan, Ga.
**29. *Delwyn Young, 2b, Riverside (Calif.) CC.—(2006-10)**
30. *Tyler Jones, rhp, Martin HS, Arlington, Texas.
31. *Justin Willis, of, Parkland (Ill.) JC.
32. *Jeff Howell, c, Merritt Island (Fla.) HS.
33. *Ken Livesley, rhp, Amos Alonzo Stagg HS, Stockton, Calif.
34. *Andrew Alvarado, rhp, James Logan HS, Union City, Calif.
35. *John Grose, c, Chandler-Gilbert (Ariz.) JC.
36. *Jesse Craig, rhp, Basic HS, Henderson, Nev.
37. Robert Mason, lhp, Walnut (Calif.) HS.
38. *Matt Mercurio, ss, Avon Park (Fla.) HS.
39. *Matt Campbell, lhp, Hillcrest HS, Simpsonville, S.C.
DRAFT DROP *First-round draft pick (29th overall), Royals (2004)*
40. *Brandon Williams, c, Coeur d'Alene (Idaho) HS.
41. *Ryan Morgan, 3b, Boston College HS, Weymouth, Mass.
42. *Paco Figueroa, ss, Gulliver Prep, Miami.
DRAFT DROP *Brother of Danny Figueroa, 48th-round draft pick, Braves (2001)*
43. *Tim McClendon, rhp, Valencia (Fla.) CC.
44. *Adam Horner, 3b, University HS, Irvine, Calif.
45. *Andrew Bowdish, rhp, St. Michaels Prep, San Jose, Calif.
**46. *Dallas Braden, lhp, Amos Alonzo Stagg HS, Stockton, Calif.—(2007-11)**
47. *Curtis White, lhp, Seward County (Kan.) CC.
48. *Danny Figueroa, of, Gulliver Prep, Miami.
DRAFT DROP *Brother of Paco Figueroa, 42nd-round draft pick, Braves (2001)*
49. *Adam Hilzendeger, rhp, Moorpark (Calif.) JC.
50. Vontrez Wilson, of, University of Southern Colorado.

## BALTIMORE ORIOLES (7)

1. Chris Smith, lhp, Cumberland (Tenn.) University.—(Low A)
**1. Mike Fontenot, 2b, Louisiana State University** (Choice from Yankees as compensation for Type A free agent Mike Mussina).—**(2005-12)**
1. Bryan Bass, ss, Seminole (Fla.) HS (Supplemental choice—31st—as compensation for Mussina).—(AA)
2. (Choice to Indians as compensation for Type A free agent David Segui)
3. Dave Crouthers, rhp, Southern Illinois University-Edwardsville.—(AA)
**4. Rommie Lewis, lhp, Newport HS, Bellevue, Wash.—(2010-11)**
**5. Jim Johnson, rhp, Endicott-Union HS, Endicott, N.Y.—(2006-15)**
**6. Eli Whiteside, c, Delta State (Miss.) University.—(2005-14)**
7. Joe Coppinger, rhp, Seminole State (Okla.) JC.
DRAFT DROP *Brother of Rocky Coppinger, major leaguer (1996-2001)*
**8. Chris Britton, rhp, Plantation (Fla.) HS.—(2006-08)**
9. Dustin Yount, 1b, Chaparral HS, Phoenix.
DRAFT DROP *Son of Robin Yount, major leaguer (1974-93)*
10. Woody Cliffords, of, Pepperdine University.
11. *John Hardy, ss, Centennial HS, Boise, Idaho.
DRAFT DROP *Cousin of J.J. Hardy, second-round draft pick, Brewers (2001); major leaguer (2005-15)*
12. T.W. Mincey, lhp, The Citadel.
13. Richard Salazar, lhp, Miami-Dade CC.
14. Cory Keylor, of, Ohio University.
15. Cory Morris, rhp, Dallas Baptist University.
16. Brad Edwards, lhp, Indiana University.
17. James Tiller, rhp, Elysian Fields (Texas) HS.
18. *Trevor Caughey, lhp, San Luis Obispo (Calif.) HS.
19. Adam Thomas, of, Abilene Christian (Texas) University.
20. *Andrew Perkins, lhp, Cal Poly Pomona.
21. *Dustin Hahn, of, Galena HS, Reno, Nev.
DRAFT DROP *Son of Don Hahn, major leaguer (1969-75)*
22. *Adam Larson, rhp, Mississippi State University.
23. Josh Potter, rhp, Philipsburg Osceola HS, Philipsburg, Pa.
24. Adam Manley, 1b, Missouri Valley (Mo.) College.
25. Richard Hackett, of, University of the Pacific.
26. *Brent Burger, rhp, Paso Robles (Calif.) HS.
**27. *Antoan Richardson, of, American Heritage HS, Delray Beach, Fla.—(2011-14)**
28. *Adam Dunavant, lhp, Prince George HS, Disputania, Va.
29. *Kyle Schmidt, rhp, Dunedin (Fla.) HS.
30. *Coby Mavroulis, of, Cooper HS, Abilene, Texas.
31. *Evan Seibly, lhp, Moorpark (Calif.) HS.
32. *Lorenzo Mack, of, Larue County HS, Hodgenville, Ky.
33. *Daniel Hanna, c, Eastern Arizona JC.
34. *Michael Coles, of, Hammond (Ind.) HS.
35. *Joshua Wilkening, rhp, Green River (Wash.) CC.
36. Jeff Montani, rhp, Binghamton University.
37. *Dwayne Carter, rhp, East Bakersfield (Calif.) HS.
38. *Sean Letsinger, rhp, Glen Oaks (Mich.) CC.
39. *Jesse Saunders, lhp, Eastside Catholic HS, Seattle.
40. +Michael Done, 3b, University of Washington.
41. *Eric Blevins, rhp, Sullivan East HS, Bluff City, Tenn.
42. *Josh Palm, rhp, Conneaut Lake (Pa.) HS.
**43. *Justin Maxwell, of, Sherwood HS, Olney, Md.—(2007-15)**
44. +Doug Brubaker, rhp, Hill (Texas) JC / New Mexico JC.
45. *Tabor Woolard, rhp, Antonian HS, San Antonio, Texas.
46. *Jonathon Fowler, lhp, Kirk Academy, Grenada, Miss.
47. *Anthony Cupps, rhp, University Christian HS, Madison, Miss.
48. *Bryan Johnson, lhp, Selah (Wash.) HS.
49. *Oscar Serrato, rhp, Riverside (Calif.) CC.

## BOSTON RED SOX (17)

1. (Choice to Indians as compensation for Type A free agent Manny Ramirez)
**2. Kelly Shoppach, c, Baylor University** (Choice from Phillies as compensation for Type B free agent Rheal Cormier).**—(2005-13)**
**2. *Matt Chico, lhp, Fallbrook (Calif.) HS.—(2007-10)**
DRAFT DROP *Attended Southern California; re-drafted by Diamondbacks, 2003 (3rd round)*
3. Jon DeVries, c, Irvine (Calif.) HS.—(High A)
4. Stefan Bailie, 1b, Washington State University.—(AA)
5. Eric West, ss, Southside HS, Gadsden, Ala.—(Low A)
**6. *Justin James, rhp, Yukon (Okla.) HS.—(2010)**
7. Rolando Viera, lhp, Havana, Cuba.
**8. Kevin Youkilis, 3b, University of Cincinnati.—(2004-14)**
9. Billy Simon, rhp, Wellington Community HS, Wellington, Fla.
10. *Ben Crockett, rhp, Harvard University.
11. Shane Rhodes, lhp, West Virginia University.
12. Ryan Brunner, of, University of Northern Iowa.
13. Alec Porzel, ss, University of Notre Dame.
14. Chris Farley, rhp, Mahar Regional HS, Orange, Mass.
15. *Ryan Carroll, rhp, Mississippi State University.
16. *Tony Gonzalez, of, Framingham (Mass.) HS.
17. Michael Grant, rhp, Danville Area (Ill.) JC.
18. Brian Lane, rhp, University of Richmond.
**19. *Jeremy Brown, c, University of Alabama.—(2006)**
DRAFT DROP *First-round draft pick (35th overall), Athletics (2002)*
20. +Devoris Williams, ss, Greensboro (Ala.) HS / Lurleen B. Wallace (Ala.) JC.
21. Charlie Weatherby, rhp, University of North Carolina-Wilmington.
22. Jed Rogers, rhp, Boston College.
23. Pedro Suarez, rhp, Mount Miguel HS, Spring Valley, Calif.
24. *Jason Ramos, ss, Braddock HS, Miami.
25. Kris Coffey, of, Dallas Baptist University.
26. Ken Trapp, rhp, Dallas Baptist University.
27. Bryan Kent, 2b, Southwest Texas State University.
28. *Steven Ponder, lhp, Texas A&M University.
29. Mario Campos, 3b, Trevecca Nazarene (Tenn.) University.
30. Rick Sander, rhp, Cal State San Bernardino.
31. Brett Rudrude, rhp, Cal State San Bernardino.
32. +Kyle Jackson, rhp, Alvirne HS, Litchfield, N.H. / St. Petersburg (Fla.) JC.
33. *Chris Honsa, rhp, Corona del Sol HS, Chandler, Ariz.
34. *Floyd Brown, 3b, Auburn (Ala.) HS.
35. *Koley Kolberg, rhp, Coppell (Texas) HS.
36. *Adam Sabari, 1b, Cardinal Mooney HS, Sarasota, Fla.
37. *Emmanuel Lopez, 1b, Globe (Ariz.) HS.
38. *Jacob Almestica, rhp, Medardo Carazo HS, Trujillo Alta, P.R.
39. *Ricky Bauer, rhp, Mid Pacific Institute, Kaneohe, Hawaii.
40. *J.B. Bolen, of, Illinois Central JC.
41. *Bart Braun, lhp, Napa Valley (Calif.) JC.
42. *Tommy Major, rhp, Briarcliffe (N.Y.) JC.
43. *Tanner Wootan, ss, Mountain View HS, Mesa, Ariz.
44. *Terrence Taylor, of, CC of Marin (Calif.).
45. Brent Tarbett, of, CC of Southern Nevada.
46. *Chris Keeran, of, Eastlake HS, Chula Vista, Calif.
47. Donald Benson, 3b, Mount San Jacinto (Calif.) JC.

## CHICAGO CUBS (2)

**1. Mark Prior, rhp, University of Southern California.—(2002-06)**
DRAFT DROP *First player from 2001 draft to reach majors (May 22, 2002)*
**2. Andy Sisco, lhp, Eastlake HS, Sammamish, Wash.—(2005-07)**
**3. Ryan Theriot, ss, Louisiana State University.—(2005-12)**
**4. Ricky Nolasco, rhp, Rialto (Calif.) HS.—(2006-15)**
DRAFT DROP *Brother of David Nolasco, 23rd-round draft pick, Brewers (2001)*
**5. Brendan Harris, ss, College of William & Mary.—(2004-13)**
6. Adam Wynegar, lhp, James Madison University.
**7. Sergio Mitre, rhp, San Diego CC.—(2003-11)**
8. Warren Hanna, c, University of South Alabama.
9. *Alan Bomer, rhp, Iowa State University.
10. Corey Slavik, 3b, Wake Forest University.
**11. Geovany Soto, c, American Military Academy, Rio Piedras, P.R.—(2007-15)**
12. Jason Blanton, rhp, North Carolina State University.
13. Tony Garcia, ss, Pepperdine University.
**14. *Khalil Greene, ss, Clemson University.—(2003-09)**
DRAFT DROP *First-round draft pick (13th overall), Padres (2002)*
15. Kevin Hairr, of, University of North Carolina-Wilmington.
16. Dwaine Bacon, of, Florida A&M University.
17. Nick Martin, lhp, Rice University.
18. Steve Ellis, rhp, Bradley University.
19. Mark Carter, lhp, University of Alabama.
20. Josh Arteaga, ss, Virginia Commonwealth University.
21. Brad Bouras, 1b, Columbus State (Ga.) University.
22. Jeff Carlsen, rhp, University of Washington.
23. B.J. Benik, rhp, Seton Hall University.
24. Luis Reyes, rhp, East Central (Miss.) JC.
25. Eric Servais, 3b, University of Wisconsin-Oshkosh.
26. *Jesse Krause, rhp, Columbia City (Ind.) HS.
27. *Chad Farr, lhp, Christian Brothers HS, Memphis, Tenn.
**28. *Tony Sipp, lhp, Moss Point (Miss.) HS.—(2009-15)**
29. Rick Devinney, c, Western HS, Fullerton, Calif.
30. *Kyle DuBois, rhp, Cox HS, Virginia Beach, Va.
DRAFT DROP *Brother of Jason DuBois, major leaguer (2004-05)*
31. Daniel Foli, rhp, Walters State (Tenn.) CC.
DRAFT DROP *Son of Tim Foli, first overall draft pick (1968); major leaguer (1970-85)*
**32. *Jeff Larish, ss, McClintock HS, Tempe, Ariz.—(2008-10)**
33. *Brian Stavisky, of, University of Notre Dame.
34. *Charlie Isaacson, rhp, University of Arkansas.
35. *Justin McCarty, of, Wichita State University.
36. *Aaron O'Dell, rhp, Bend (Ore.) HS.
37. *Edwar Gonzalez, of, Seminole State (Okla.) JC.
38. *Jeff Teasley, rhp, Grossmont HS, La Mesa, Calif.
**39. *Jesse Chavez, rhp, A.B. Miller HS, Fontana, Calif.—(2008-15)**
**40. *Matt Pagnozzi, c, Highland HS, Gilbert, Ariz.—(2009-14)**
DRAFT DROP *Nephew of Tom Pagnozzi, major leaguer (1987-98)*
**41. *Wes Whisler, lhp-1b, Noblesville (Ind.) HS.—(2009)**
42. *Mark Jecmen, rhp, Diamond Bar (Calif.) HS.
43. *Kevin Culpepper, lhp, Stephens County School, Toccoa, Ga.
44. *Jared Eichelberger, rhp, Marian Catholic HS, San Diego.
DRAFT DROP *Son of Juan Eichelberger, major leaguer (1978-88)*
45. *Jamil Knight, rhp, Shelton State (Ala.) CC.
46. *Chris Niesel, rhp, St. Thomas Aquinas HS, Fort Lauderdale, Fla.
47. *Taylor Gartz, lhp, Clear Lake HS, Seabrook, Texas.
48. *Kevin Randel, ss, Riverside (Calif.) CC.
49. *Mike Pete, lhp, Armwood HS, Brandon, Fla.
50. *Patrick McIntyre, c, Vallivue HS, Caldwell, Idaho.

## CHICAGO WHITE SOX (27)

1. Kris Honel, rhp, Providence Catholic HS, New Lenox, Ill. (Choice from Marlins as compensation for Type A free agent Charles Johnson).—(AA)
1. (Choice to Indians as compensation for Type A free agent Sandy Alomar)
1. Wyatt Allen, rhp, University of Tennessee (Supplemental choice—39th—as compensation for Johnson).—(AAA)
2. Ryan Wing, lhp, Riverside (Calif.) CC.—(AAA)
3. *Jon Zeringue, c, E.D. White HS, Thibodeaux, La.—(AA)
DRAFT DROP *Attended Louisiana State; re-drafted by Diamondbacks, 2004 (2nd round)*
4. *Jay Mattox, of, Conway (Ark.) HS.—DNP
DRAFT DROP *Attended Arkansas; re-drafted by Angels, 2003 (35th round)*
**5. Andy Gonzalez, ss, Florida Air Academy, Melbourne, Fla.—(2007-09)**
6. Stevie Daniel, 2b-ss, University of Tennessee.
7. *Brandon Camardese, lhp, Chaminade-Madonna HS, Cooper City, Fla.
8. Andrew Fryson, rhp, Wallace State (Ala.) JC.
9. Jim Bullard, lhp, UC Santa Barbara.
10. Tim Bittner, lhp, Marist University.
11. Tim Huson, 3b, Central Arizona JC.
**12. Chris Stewart, c, Riverside (Calif.) CC.—(2006-15)**
13. Brian Sager, rhp, Georgia Tech.
14. *Matt Mitchell, rhp, JC of Lake County (Ill.).
15. Anthony Webster, of, Riverside HS, Parsons, Tenn.
**16. Chris Young, of, Bellaire (Texas) HS.—(2006-15)**
17. +Jason McCurdy, lhp, South Dade HS, Miami / Broward (Fla.) CC.
18. Justin Dowdy, lhp, Rancho Bernardo HS, San Diego.
19. *Wes Swackhamer, of, Delbarton HS, Morristown, N.J.
20. Brian Miller, rhp, Charlotte (Mich.) HS.
21. *Lou Palmisano, c, St. Thomas Aquinas HS, Fort Lauderdale, Fla.
22. Andrew Salvo, 2b, University of Delaware.
23. Josh Fields, rhp, Mesa (Ariz.) CC.
24. Charlie Lisk, c, Fort Mill (S.C.) HS.
**25. Charlie Haeger, rhp, Catholic Central HS, Plymouth, Mich.—(2006-10)**
26. *Dustin Roddy, c, Searcy (Ark.) HS.
27. +Tom Collaro, of, Piper HS, Sunrise, Fla. / Palm Beach (Fla.) CC.
28. *Jonathan Forest, rhp, Edouard Montpetit HS, St. Hubert, Quebec.
29. *Matt Sibigtroth, ss, Hampshire (Ill.) HS.
30. Heath Dobyns, rhp, University of Northern Colorado.
31. Nik Lubisich, lhp, Willamette (Ore.) University.
32. *Heath Castle, lhp, St. Catharine (Ky.) JC.
33. *Sean Kramer, lhp, Cornwall HS, New Windsor, N.Y.
34. +Tim Tisch, lhp, San Diego Mesa JC.
35. *Mike Moljewski, lhp, De la Salle Collegiate HS, Shelby, Mich.
36. *Brent Speck, lhp, Broward (Fla.) JC.
37. *Juan Razzo, rhp, San Diego CC.
38. *Kenyatta Davis, of, Harlan Community Academy, Chicago.
39. +J.D. Johnson, rhp, Del Norte HS, Moriarty, N.M. / Trinidad State (Colo.) JC.
40. *Chris Roque, 3b, Monsignor Pace HS, Opa Locka, Fla.
41. *Chris Martinez, of, Florida Christian HS, Miami.
42. *Nick McMillan, rhp, El Dorado HS, Placentia, Calif.
43. Freddie LeBron, 2b, New Mexico JC.
44. *Ken Pridgeon, rhp, Cy Fair HS, Cypress, Texas.
45. +Gerron McGary, lhp-of, Texarkana (Texas) JC.
46. *Roy Irle, rhp, Madison Heights HS, Anderson, Ind.
47. *Adrian Casanova, c, Coral Park HS, Miami.
48. *Josh Crede, 3b, Fatima HS, Westphalia, Mo.
DRAFT DROP *Brother of Joe Crede, major leaguer (2000-09)*
49. *Richard Morman, of, Fayetteville (Ark.) HS.
**50. *Zach Jackson, lhp, Seneca Valley HS, Cranberry Township, Pa.—(2006-09)**
DRAFT DROP *First-round draft pick (32nd overall), Blue Jays (2004)*

## CINCINNATI REDS (20)

**1. *Jeremy Sowers, lhp, Ballard HS, Louisville, Ky.—(2006-09)**
DRAFT DROP *Attended Vanderbilt; re-drafted by Indians, 2004 (1st round)*
2. Justin Gillman, rhp, Mosley HS, Panama City, Fla.—(Low A)
3. Alan Moye, of, Pine Tree HS, Longview, Texas.—(High A)
4. Steve Kelly, rhp, Georgia Tech.—(AA)
5. Daylan Childress, rhp, McLennan (Texas) CC.—(AAA)
6. Scott Light, rhp, Elon College.
7. Bobby Basham, rhp, University of Richmond.
8. *Jose Rodriguez, c, Warren HS, Downey, Calif.
9. Junior Ruiz, of-2b, San Jose State University.
10. Bryan Prince, c, Georgia Tech.
11. *Keith Ramsey, lhp, University of Florida.
12. *Craig Bartosh, of, Duncanville (Texas) HS.
13. *Tanner Brock, rhp, Mississippi State University.
14. David Molidor, 3b, UC Santa Barbara.
15. Matt McWilliams, lhp, Cumberland (Tenn.) University.
16. Jason Vavao, 1b, Los Angeles Harbor CC.
17. Richard Bartel, rhp, Grapevine (Texas) HS.
DRAFT DROP *Quarterback, National Football League (2008-11)*
18. Jeff Bannon, ss, UC Santa Barbara.
19. Justin Davis, of, Cal Poly Pomona.
20. Jesse Gutierrez, c, St. Mary's (Texas) University.
21. *John Palmer, rhp, Georgia Perimeter JC.
DRAFT DROP *Son of David Palmer, major leaguer (1978-89)*
22. Ryan Fry, c, Young Harris (Ga.) JC.
23. Joe Powers, rhp, Wright State University.
24. Jay Adams, rhp, Pepperdine University.
25. Curtus Moak, lhp, University of Cincinnati.
26. *Will Crouch, 1b, Westlake HS, Austin, Texas.
27. Weston Burnette, rhp, Young Harris (Ga.) JC.
28. *Brian Martin, lhp, Texas City (Texas) HS.
29. *Seth Epstein, lhp, JC of the Canyons (Calif.).
DRAFT DROP *Son of Mike Epstein, major leaguer (1966-74)*
30. *Darin Blackburn, rhp, Fort Myers (Fla.) HS.
31. *Aaron Trolia, rhp, Edmonds (Wash.) CC.
32. +David Shafer, rhp, Central Arizona JC.
33. *David Asher, lhp, University HS, Orlando, Fla.
34. Domonique Lewis, 2b, Southwest Texas State University.
**35. *Nick Markakis, lhp-of, Woodstock (Ga.) HS.—(2006-15)**
DRAFT DROP draft pick (7th overall), Orioles (2003)
36. * Isaac Dillon, of, Nettleton HS, Jonesboro, Ark.
37. *Erik Meyer, rhp, La Mirada (Calif.) HS.
38. *Justin Myers, rhp, Symmes Valley HS, Scottown, Ohio.
39. +Miles Carpenter, rhp, Pickens HS, Jasper, Ga. / Young Harris (Ga.) JC.
40. *Ben Rulon, lhp, Columbus (Ga.) HS.
41. *Douglas Curley, c, Granite Bay HS, Roseville, Calif.
42. *Brandon Moorhead, rhp, University of Georgia.
43. *Kyle Broussard, ss, Carencro (La.) HS.
44. *Francis Poni, c, Carson (Calif.) HS.
45. *Mark Schramek, rhp-3b, University of Texas-San Antonio.
DRAFT DROP *First-round draft pick (40th overall), Reds (2002)*
46. *Bart Hunton, c, Dublin Coffman HS, Dublin, Ohio.
47. Raymond Gonzalez, of, Jose Campeche HS, San Lorenzo, P.R.
48. *Jeffrey Crinklaw, c, Ohlone (Calif.) JC.
49. *Trey Hearne, of, Lufkin (Texas) HS.
50. *Clay Alarcon, ss, Sequoia HS, Redwood City, Calif.

## CLEVELAND INDIANS (21)

1. Dan Denham, rhp, Deer Valley HS, Antioch, Calif. (Choice from Red Sox as compensation for Type A free agent Manny Ramirez).—(AAA)
1. (Choice to Giants as compensation for Type A free agent Ellis Burks)
1. *Alan Horne, rhp, Marianna (Fla.) HS (Choice from White Sox as compensation for Type A free agent Sandy Alomar).—(AAA)
DRAFT DROP *Attended Mississippi; re-drafted by Angels, 2004 (30th round)*
**1. J.D. Martin, rhp, Burroughs HS, Ridgecrest, Calif.** (Supplemental choice—35th—as compensation for Ramirez).**—(2009-10)**
1. Michael Conroy, of, Boston College HS, Dorchester, Mass. (Supplemental choice—

43rd—as compensation for Type A free agent David Segui).—(High A)
2. Jake Dittler, rhp, Green Valley HS, Henderson, Nev. (Choice from Orioles as compensation for Segui).—(AAA)
2. (Choice to Tigers as compensation for Type A free agent Juan Gonzalez)
3. Nick Moran, rhp, Fresno State University.—(High A)
4. Travis Foley, rhp, Butler HS, Louisville, Ky.—(AAA)
5. Marcos Mendoza, lhp, San Diego State University.—(AA)
6. Jim Ed Warden, rhp, Tennessee Tech.
7. Josh Noviskey, of, Newton (N.J.) HS.
8. Mike Quintana, of, Florida International University.
**9. Luke Scott, of, Oklahoma State University.—(2005-13)**
10. *Brian Harrison, rhp, Dalton (Ga.) HS.
11. Brad Guglielmelli, c, Allan Hancock (Calif.) JC.
12. Scott Sturkie, rhp, Coastal Carolina University.
13. Matt Knox, of, Millersville (Pa.) University.
14. Doug Lantz, rhp, University of Kansas.
15. *Martin Vergara, rhp, DePaul HS, Wayne, N.J.
16. +Sean Smith, rhp, College Park HS, Pleasant Hill, Calif. / Sacramento (Calif.) CC.
17. *David Jensen, 1b, Brigham Young University.
18. T.J. Burton, rhp, Notre Dame HS, Ottawa, Ontario.
19. Luis Alvarado, lhp, University of Puerto Rico.
20. +Michael Rogers, rhp, Oral Roberts University.
21. Richard Spaulding, lhp, Lexington (Ky.) CC.
22. Jimmy Schultz, rhp, Klein Forest HS, Houston.
23. Kent Myers, c, Mesa State (Colo.) College.
24. Matt Blethen, lhp, West Virginia University.
25. Rickie Morton, of, University of the Pacific.
26. Bryce Uegawachi, ss, Hawaii Pacific University.
27. *Josh Lex, c, Sacramento (Calif.) CC.
28. *Brandon Harmsen, rhp, Grand Rapids (Mich.) CC.
29. *Chris Hunter, rhp, Lindon, Utah.
30. Keith Lillash, 2b, Cleveland State University.
31. Brian Kirby, c, University of Arkansas.
32. Andy Baxter, 1b, East Tennessee State University.
33. Chad Peshke, 2b, UC Santa Barbara.
34. *Aaron Mardsen, lhp, Hutchinson (Kan.) CC.
35. Chris Cooper, lhp, University of New Mexico.
36. Jose Cruz, of, Metropolitan (P.R.) University.
37. Todd Culp, rhp, University of the Pacific.
38. *Neto Quiroz, lhp, Saddleback (Calif.) CC.
39. Brian Farman, rhp, Pacific Lutheran (Wash.) University.
40. *Aaron Russell, rhp, Cerro Coso (Calif.) CC.
41. *Ross Lewis, rhp-of, University Christian HS, Jacksonville, Fla.
42. *Kyle Allen, lhp, Trabuco Hills HS, Rancho Santa Margarita, Calif.
43. *Vince Davis, lhp, New Mexico JC.
**44. *Garrett Mock, rhp, North Shore HS, Houston.—(2008-10)**
45. *Brett Ashman, rhp, Modesto (Calif.) JC.
46. Todd Pennington, rhp, Southeast Missouri State University.
47. *Billy Brian, rhp, Louisiana State University.
48. *Douglas Brooks, rhp, Henry Ford (Mich.) CC.
49. *Jason Columbus, 1b, New Mexico JC.
50. *James Burok, rhp, Valley View HS, Archbald, Pa.

## COLORADO ROCKIES (18)

1. (Choice to Mets as compensation for Type A free agent Mike Hampton)
**1. Jayson Nix, ss, Midland (Texas) HS** (Supplemental choice—44th—for failure to sign 2000 first-round draft pick Matt Harrington).**—(2008-14)**
DRAFT DROP *Brother of Laynce Nix, major leaguer (2003-13)*
2. (Choice to Yankees as compensation for Type A free agent Denny Neagle)
2. *Trey Taylor, lhp, Mansfield (Texas) HS (Supplemental choice—75th—as compensation for Type C free agent Julian Tavarez).—(Rookie)
DRAFT DROP *Attended Baylor; re-drafted by Cubs, 2004 (20th round)*
3. Jason Frome, of, Indiana State University.—(High A)
4. Jay Mitchell, rhp, LaGrange (Ga.) HS.—(Low A)
5. Gerrit Simpson, rhp, University of Texas.—(AA)
6. Jamie Tricoglou, rhp, Kennesaw State University.
**7. Cory Sullivan, of, Wake Forest University.—(2005-10)**
8. Scott Nicholson, lhp, Oregon State University.
9. James Sweeney, c, Bellaire (Texas) HS.
10. Tony Miller, of, University of Toledo.
11. Jay Fardella, rhp, St. Francis (N.Y.) College.
12. Bryan Ingram, c, Oregon State University.
13. Kip Bouknight, rhp, University of South Carolina.
14. Levi Frary, rhp, University of Texas-Pan American.
15. David Burkholder, 1b, Grand View (Iowa) College.
16. Beau Dannemiller, rhp, Kent State University.
17. Judd Songster, rhp, University of Southern Colorado.
18. Buddy Gallagher, lhp, Rutgers University.
19. Ashley Freeman, 3b, Vanderbilt University.
**20. *Matt Palmer, rhp, Southwest Missouri State University.—(2008-12)**
21. *Roberto Martinez, rhp, Riverview HS, Brandon, Fla.
22. Trey George, of, Bellaire HS, Houston.
**23. *Eric Patterson, ss, Harrison HS, Kennesaw, Ga.—(2007-11)**
DRAFT DROP *Brother of Corey Patterson, first-round draft pick, Cubs (1998); major leaguer (2000-13)*
24. Casey Lambert, ss, University of Alabama.
25. *Mike Huggins, 1b, Baylor University.
26. *Jake Glanzmann, lhp, West Springfield HS, Springfield, Va.
27. Jeff Cruz, lhp, Long Beach State University.
28. *Adam Heether, 3b, Modesto (Calif.) JC.
29. Peter Greenbush, rhp, Massachusetts College.
30. +Jonathan Varcarcel, lhp, Margarita Janer HS, Guaynabo, P.R. / Daytona Beach (Fla.) CC.
31. *Jino Gonzalez, lhp, CC of Southern Nevada.
32. *Josh Merino, rhp, Kirkwood (Iowa) CC.
33. *Sean Hofferd, of, Bend (Ore.) HS.
**34. *Chris Gimenez, c, Gilroy (Calif.) HS.—(2009-15)**
35. *Jeff MacDonald, rhp, Lethbridge (Alberta) CC.
36. *Brandon Freese, rhp, Skyview HS, Vancouver, Wash.
37. *Chris Buechner, rhp, Little Cypress-Mauriceville HS, Orange, Texas.
38. *Vern Sterry, rhp, Cypress (Calif.) JC.
39. *Lucas Gaskamp, lhp, Northeast Texas CC.
40. +Pedro Diaz, rhp, Seminole State (Okla.) JC.
41. *Duke Sardinha, 3b, Pepperdine University.
DRAFT DROP *Brother of Dane Sardinha, major leaguer (2003-05) • Brother of Bronson Sardinha, first-round draft pick, Yankees (2001); major leaguer (2007)*
42. *Coby Hughes, of, Branson HS, Walnut Shade, Mo.
43. *Kelly Castles, rhp, McLaughlin HS, Milton Freewater, Ore.
44. *Josh Bryant, rhp, Wallace State (Ala.) CC.
45. *Brandon Young, of, Springfield North HS, Springfield, Ohio.
46. *Sergio Silva, rhp, JC of the Sequoias (Calif.)
47. *John Toffey, rhp, St. Sebastian's HS, Barnstable, Mass.
48. *Andrew York, c, JC of the Siskiyous (Calif.).
49. *J.R. Revere, of, Georgia Southern University.
50. *Mike Marksbury, rhp, Miami (Ohio) University.

## DETROIT TIGERS (11)

1. Kenny Baugh, rhp, Rice University.—(AAA)
1. Michael Woods, 2b, Southern University (Supplemental choice—32nd—as compensation for Type A free agent Juan Gonzalez).—(AA)
2. Preston Larrison, rhp, University of Evansville.—(AAA)
2. Matt Coenen, lhp, Charleston Southern University (Choice from Indians as compensation for Gonzalez).—(AA)
**3. Jack Hannahan, 3b, University of Minnesota.—(2006-14)**
**4. Mike Rabelo, c, University of Tampa.—(2006-08)**
**5. Ryan Raburn, 3b, South Florida CC.—(2004-15)**
6. Jason Knoedler, of, Miami (Ohio) University.
DRAFT DROP *Twin brother of Justin Knoedler, fifth-round draft pick, Giants (2001); major leaguer (2004-06)*
7. Tom Farmer, rhp, University of Miami.
**8. Don Kelly, ss, Point Park (Pa.) College.—(2007-15)**
9. David Mattle, of, Kent State University.
10. Vincent Blue, of, Lamar HS, Houston.
11. *Eric Thomas, rhp, Briarcliffe (N.Y.) JC.
12. Jamie Gonzales, rhp, UC Santa Barbara.
13. Landon Stockman, rhp, Kennesaw State University.
14. Matt Williams, of, Fontana (Calif.) HS.
15. Kevin McDowell, lhp, Bucknell University.
DRAFT DROP *Son of Sam McDowell, major leaguer (1961-75)*
16. *Joey Metropoulos, 3b, Monte Vista HS, Jamul, Calif.
17. Dan Smith, rhp, University of Miami.
18. Alex Trezza, c, Stony Brook University.
19. Billy Ryan, 3b, Briarcliffe (N.Y.) JC.
20. Jason Moates, rhp, Middle Tennessee State University.
21. *Tim Dorn, 1b, Monrovia (Calif.) HS.
22. Francisco Rosado, of, Antelope Valley (Calif.) JC.
23. Mike Scott, of, University of Connecticut.
24. *John Schneider, c, University of Delaware.
25. Chris Kolodzey, of, University of Delaware.
26. Herman Dean, of, Citrus (Calif.) JC.
27. Mike Kobow, rhp, University of Minnesota.
28. Jon Connolly, lhp, Oneonta (N.Y.) HS.
29. +Garth McKinney, of, Walters State (Tenn.) CC.
30. John Birtwell, rhp, Harvard University.
**31. +Humberto Sanchez, rhp, Rockland (N.Y.) CC / Connors State (Okla.) JC.—(2008)**
32. Trevor Leu, of, Oral Roberts University.
33. Michael Howell, rhp, SUNY Binghamton.
34. Ian Ostlund, lhp, Virginia Tech.
35. Chuck Lombardy, rhp, Ohio University.
36. Jed Stringham, of, UC Santa Barbara.
37. *Kevin Miller, lhp, Cuesta (Calif.) JC.
38. *Adam Harben, rhp, Central Arkansas Christian HS, Little Rock, Ark.
39. *Robert White, lhp, Spartanburg Methodist (S.C.) JC.
40. Tom Lyons, rhp, Downers Grove North HS, Downers Grove, Ill.
41. *Trey Holloway, lhp, Booneville (Ark.) HS.
42. *Coby Judd, lhp, Simi Valley (Calif.) HS.
43. *Sean Richardson, c, Vista (Calif.) HS.
44. (void) Phil Sobkow, rhp, Butte (Calif.) JC
45. *Brent Hale, rhp, Peninsula HS, Rancho Palos Verdes, Calif.
46. *Lonnie Patterson, rhp, Harlan HS, Chicago.

## FLORIDA MARLINS (16)

1. (Choice to White Sox as compensation for Type A free agent Charles Johnson)
2. Garrett Berger, rhp, Carmel (Ind.) HS.—(Rookie)
3. Allen Baxter, rhp, Varina HS, Sandston, Va.—(High A)
**4. Chris Resop, rhp-of, Barron Collier HS, Naples, Fla.—(2005-13)**
5. *Tyler Lumsden, lhp, Cave Spring HS, Roanoke, Va.—(AAA)
DRAFT DROP *Attended Clemson; re-drafted by White Sox, 2004 (1st round)*
6. Adam Bostick, lhp, Greensburg-Salem HS, Greensburg, Pa.
7. Lincoln Holdzkom, rhp, Arizona Western CC.
**8. Jeff Fulchino, rhp, University of Connecticut.—(2006-11)**
9. Dustin Kupper, rhp, Pima (Ariz.) CC.
10. Kody Naylor, rhp, Western Michigan University.
11. Rex Rundgren, ss, Sacramento (Calif.) CC.
DRAFT DROP *Son of rock star Todd Rundgren*
12. Nic Ungs, rhp, University of Northern Iowa.
13. Lance Davis, rhp, George County HS, Lucedale, Miss.
14. Michael Tucker, 3b, Florida Southern College.
15. *Doug Boone, c, Ball State University.
16. Hunter Wyant, ss, University of Virginia.
17. Kevin Cave, rhp, Xavier University.
18. Josh Coffey, c, Lee Davis HS, Mechanicsville, Va.
19. Louis Evans, lhp, San Jose (Calif.) CC.
20. Carl Lafferty, c, University of Mississippi.
21. *Dane Mason, rhp, Cherokee HS, Marlton, N.J.
22. Jason Helps, ss, Central Michigan University.
23. Wes McCrotty, lhp, University of Arkansas.
24. John Skinner, rhp, San Diego State University.
25. Philip Hartig, 1b, The Citadel.
**26. *Adam Russell, rhp, North Olmsted (Ohio) HS.—(2008-11)**
27. Franco Blackburn, of, Southern University.
28. *Jon Hunton, rhp, North Plainfield (N.J.) HS.
29. Gooby Gerlits, c-of, Stoneman Douglas HS, Parkland, Fla.
30. *Nick Pesco, rhp, Tokay HS, Lodi, Calif.
31. *Chris Johnston, rhp, Smoky Hills HS, Aurora, Colo.
32. *Sergio Roman, c, Bishop Carroll HS, Wichita, Kan.
33. Torik Harrison, rhp, Southern University.
34. Steve Thomas, rhp, Nova Southeastern (Fla.) University.
35. Marc Rittenhouse, 2b, University of Washington.
36. Kevin Halamicek, rhp, Cal State Dominguez Hills.
37. Kris Clute, 2b, University of Miami.
38. Ronnie Goodwin, rhp, University of Mississippi.
39. *Justin Ottman, lhp, Rockland (N.Y.) CC.
40. Tyson Graham, of, North Gaston HS, Dallas, N.C.
41. *Eric Otero, 2b, Monignor Pace HS, Miami.
42. *Josh Perrault, rhp, South Mountain (Ariz.) CC.
43. *Isaac Garza, rhp, Odem (Texas) HS.
44. *Cliff Dancy, of, Pine Forest HS, Pensacola, Fla.
45. *Nick Blasi, of, Butler County (Kan.) CC.
46. *Andrew Vansickle, of, Senatobia (Miss.) HS.
47. *Chas Taylor, rhp, Westlake HS, Austin, Texas.
48. *Derek Hutton, ss, Palm Beach Gardens (Fla.) HS.
DRAFT DROP *Son of Tommy Hutton, major leaguer (1966-81)*
**49. *Phil Coke, lhp, Sonora HS, Twain Harte, Calif.—(2008-15)**
50. *Steve Stanley, of, University of Notre Dame.

## HOUSTON ASTROS (10)

**1. Chris Burke, 2b-ss, University of Tennessee.—(2004-09)**
2. Mike Rodriguez, of, University of Miami.—(AAA)
**3. Kirk Saarloos, rhp, Cal State Fullerton.—(2002-08)**
**4. Phillip Barzilla, lhp, Rice University.—(2006)**
**5. Charlton Jimerson, of, University of Miami.—(2006-08)**
6. Russ Rohlicek, lhp, Long Beach State University.
7. Ryan Stegall, ss, University of Missouri.
**8. Brooks Conrad, 2b, Arizona State University.—(2008-14)**
9. Kerry Hodges, of, Texas Tech.
**10. *Lance Cormier, rhp, University of Alabama.—(2004-11)**
**11. D.J. Houlton, rhp, University of the Pacific.—(2005-07)**
12. Chris Little, lhp, St. Louis CC-Forest Park.
13. Kendall Jones, c, Texarkana (Texas) CC.
14. Clint Hoover, 1b, University of California.
15. Trevor Mote, 2b, Baylor University.
16. Brian Rodaway, lhp, University of Nebraska.
17. Thomas Bayrer, rhp, Campbell University.
18. Jose Deleon, rhp, Nixon-Smiley HS, Nixon, Texas.
19. Ryan Kochen, ss, Western Michigan University.
20. Mark Obradovich, c, Gadsden State (Ala.) CC.
21. *Jeff Derrickson, c, Bryan Station HS, Lexington, Ky.
22. Justin Humphries, c, Episcopal HS, Richmond, Texas.
**23. +Matt Albers, rhp, Clements HS, Sugar Land, Texas / San Jacinto (Texas) JC.—(2006-15)**
24. Cameron Likely, of, University of South Alabama.
25. Chad Durham, rhp, Texas Christian University.
26. Steven Checksfield, of, University of Albany.
27. *Henry Colbert, rhp, Columbia Basin (Wash.) CC.
28. Seth Bobbit, rhp, Birmingham-Southern College.
29. *Raymar Diaz, of, Luis Hernaiz Verone HS, Canovanas, P.R.
30. Jjallil Sandoval, ss, Cal State Los Angeles.
31. Brian Middleton, rhp, West Viginia State College.
32. Billy Jacobson, of, Rice University.
33. John Fagan, 1b, San Jose State University.
34. Brandon Macchi, of, San Jose State University.
35. *Travis Teeter, rhp, Rensselaer Polytechnic (N.Y.)

Institute.
36. Andrew Perry, rhp, Cal State Pomona.
37. *Jared Gothreaux, rhp, McNeese State University.
38. *Ryan McKeller, rhp, Pflugerville (Texas) HS.
39. *Paul Hazeres, rhp, Carolina Forest HS, Conway, S.C.
40. *Osvaldo Diaz, rhp, Havana, Cuba.
41. *Chris Saywers, rhp-ss, Edmonds (Wash.) CC.
42. *Pat Wells, lhp, West Jordan (Utah) HS.
43. Pat McNair, rhp, Virginia Commonwealth University.
44. *Lance Dawkins, ss, Meridian (Miss.) CC.
45. *Kyle Thompson, rhp, Valley Center HS, Escondido, Calif.
46. *Justin Ard, of, Clear Lake HS, Houston.
47. *Eric Turnbow, ss, Jordan HS, Sandy, Utah.
48. *Ben Leuthard, of, San Diego State University.
49. *Kevin House, of, Alabama Southern JC.

## KANSAS CITY ROYALS (9)

1. Colt Griffin, rhp, Marshall (Texas) HS.—(AA)
2. Roscoe Crosby, of, Union HS, Buffalo, S.C.—DNP
3. Matt Ferrara, 3b, Westminster Academy, Fort Lauderdale, Fla.—(Low A)
4. John Draper, c, Cal State Los Angeles.—(AA)
5. Chamar McDonald, 1b, Madison Central HS, Madison, Miss.—(Low A)
6. Clint Frost, rhp, Jordan HS, Columbus, Ga.
7. Chris Tierney, lhp, Lockport (Ill.) HS.
8. Ira Brown, rhp, Willis (Texas) HS.
9. Justin Nelson, lhp-of, Platte Valley HS, Kersey, Colo.
10. Danny Tamayo, rhp, University of Notre Dame.
**11. Angel Sanchez, of, Florencia Garcia HS, Las Piedras, P.R.—(2006-13)**
12. Victor Rosario, of, Lake City (Fla.) CC.
13. Cedric Watkins, of, Bassett (Va.) HS.
**14. Devon Lowery, rhp, South Point HS, Belmont, N.C.—(2008)**
15. *Danny Zell, lhp, Angelina (Texas) JC.
**16. Mel Stocker, of, Arizona State University.—(2007)**
17. Marcus Chandler, of, Southern University.
18. Alexis Alexander, of, Medical Lake (Wash.) HS.
19. Mervin Williams, of, East St. John HS, Garyville, La.
20. Peter Gunny, of, Los Angeles Pierce JC.
21. Brian Melnyk, lhp, Point Park (Pa.) College.
22. Chris Fallon, 1b, St. John's University.
23. *Jermaine Johnson, of, Glynn Academy, Brunswick, Ga.
24. J.D. Alleva, c, Duke University.
25. Rick Zary, rhp, Limestone (S.C.) College.
26. *Derek DeCarlo, rhp, Southridge HS, Miami.
27. +Derrik Lytle, of, Mesa (Ariz.) CC.
28. +Lucas Palmer, rhp, Baker HS, Baker City, Ore. / Columbia Basin (Wash.) CC.
29. *Bryan McCaulley, rhp, Barbe HS, Lake Charles, La.
30. *Zeke Parraz, ss, Green Valley HS, Henderson, Nev.
31. Jacob Guzman, c, Palomar (Calif.) JC.
32. *Julio Medina, rhp, Elk Grove (Ill.) HS.
33. John Barnett, rhp, Arizona Western JC.
34. Erik Dean, ss, West Valley (Calif.) JC.
35. *Barry Richardson, rhp, Lake City (Fla.) CC.
36. *Chris Washington, rhp, Port St. Lucie (Fla.) HS.
37. *Brad Knox, rhp, Blinn (Texas) JC.
38. *James Dayley, rhp, Utah Valley CC.
**39. *Taylor Tankersley, lhp, Warren Central HS, Vicksburg, Miss.—(2006-10)**
DRAFT DROP *First-round draft pick (27th overall), Marlins (2004)*
40. *Jason Snyder, rhp, Alta HS, Sandy, Utah.
41. *Rene Pablos, lhp, Cochise County (Ariz.) CC.
42. *Nick Cadena, c, Apollo HS, Glendale, Ariz.
43. *Stephen Green, of, Moahalua HS, Honolulu, Hawaii.
44. *Brady Everett, c, Federal Way HS, Kent, Wash.
45. Curtis Legendre, 3b-c, Angelina (Texas) JC.
46. *Bret Berglund, 3b, Kent Denver HS, Englewood, Colo.
47. *Caleb Irwin, rhp, Temple (Texas) JC.
48. *Ryan Coiner, rhp, Las Vegas HS.
49. *Ryan Patterson, of, Rowlett (Texas) HS.
50. Bo Baker, rhp, Eastern Arizona JC.

## LOS ANGELES DODGERS (24)

1. (Choice to Braves as compensation for Type A free agent Andy Ashby)
2. Brian Pilkington, rhp, Santiago HS, Garden Grove, Calif.—(AA)
3. David Taylor, rhp, Southlake HS, Clermont, Fla.—(Rookie)
4. Kole Strayhorn, rhp, Shawnee HS, Seminole, Okla.—(AA)
5. Steve Nelson, rhp, Cole Harbour District HS, Dartmouth, Nova Scotia.—(High A)
**6. Edwin Jackson, of, Shaw HS, Columbus, Ga.—(2003-15)**
7. David Cuen, lhp, Cibola HS, Somerton, Ariz.
8. David Cardona, of, San Jose de Calasanza HS, Trujillo Alta, P.R.
9. Sean Pierce, of, San Diego State University.
10. Thom Ott, rhp, University of Nebraska.
11. Luis Gonzalez, lhp, Florida Air Academy, Melbourne, Fla.
12. Cedric Benson, of, Robert E. Lee HS, Midland, Texas.
DRAFT DROP *First-round draft pick, Chicago Bears/ National Football League (2005); running back, NFL (2005-12)*
13. Matt Kauffman, lhp, San Jose State University.
14. Ryan Carter, of, Riverdale HS, Fort Myers, Fla.
15. Jimmy Stewart, rhp, Sabino HS, Tucson, Ariz.
16. Josh Canales, ss, UCLA.
17. Michael Johnson, of, University of Arkansas-Little Rock.
18. Vance McCracken, rhp, West Virginia University.
19. *John Urick, 1b, Cowley County (Kan.) CC.
20. Billy Malone, 2b, Robert Morris (Ill.) College.
21. +Jereme Milons, of, Starkville (Miss.) HS / Jefferson Davis (Ala.) JC.
22. Scott Gillitzer, 2b, University of Wisconsin-Milwaukee.
23. *Les Dykes, lhp, Parklane Academy, McComb, Miss.
24. *Ryan Lennerton, lhp, Brookswood SS, Langley, B.C.
25. *Garrett Murdy, rhp, Mission Viejo HS, Laguna Hills, Calif.
26. *Jay Sadlowe, rhp, Farragut HS, Knoxville, Tenn.
27. *Eric Hutcheson, lhp, Florala HS, Lockhart, Ala.
28. *Kyle Crist, rhp, Granite Bay HS, Grant, Calif.
29. *Dennis Bigley, 1b, Dallas Christian HS, Lancaster, Texas.
30. *Tom Wilson, lhp, Central Cabarrus HS, Concord, N.C.
31. *David Parker, rhp, Sisler HS, Winnipeg, Manitoba.
**32. *Michael Hollimon, ss, Jesuit Prep, Dallas.—(2008)**
33. Jason Stefani, lhp, Albertson (Idaho) College.
34. *Brian Devereaux, rhp, Hollywood Christian HS, Fort Lauderdale, Fla.
35. *Chris Casey, lhp, Hunstville (Texas) HS.
36. *Brian Cleveland, ss, San Jose (Calif.) CC.
37. *Dustin Schroer, of, Surrey, B.C.
38. *Ryan Hamilton, ss, Klein HS, Spring, Texas.
39. *William Johnson, 1b, North Springs HS, College Park, Ga.
40. *Cameron Feightner, rhp, Beaverton HS, Portland, Ore.
41. *Jim Gregory, lhp, Crockett (Texas) HS.
42. *Jordan Kissock, of, Delphi Academy, Surrey, B.C.
**43. *Clint Sammons, c, Parkview HS, Stone Mountain, Ga.—(2007-09)**
44. *Clay Wehner, c, Thomasville (Ga.) HS.
45. +Mike Rodriguez, rhp, Sierra (Calif.) JC.
46. +Mike Lynch, c, South Suburban (Ill.) JC.
47. *Devin Monds, rhp, Nepean HS, Ottawa, Ontario.
48. *Danny Desclouds, rhp, Connors State (Okla.) JC.
49. *Jason Schuler, c, Lake County (Ill.) JC.
50. *Brooks Bollinger, 3b, University of Wisconsin.
DRAFT DROP *Quarterback, National Football League (2003-08)*

## MILWAUKEE BREWERS (12)

1. Mike Jones, rhp, Thunderbird HS, Phoenix.—(AAA)
**2. J.J. Hardy, ss, Sabino HS, Tucson, Ariz.—(2005-15)**
DRAFT DROP *Cousin of John Hardy, 12th-round draft pick, Orioles (2001)*
3. Jon Steitz, rhp, Yale University.—(Low A)
**4. Brad Nelson, 1b, Bishop Garrigan HS, Algona, Iowa.—(2008-09)**
5. Judd Richardson, rhp, Miami (Ohio) University.—(Low A)
6. Calvin Carpenter, rhp, Natchitoches Central HS, Natchotoches, La.
7. Taylor McCormack, 3b, Dunedin (Fla.) HS.
DRAFT DROP *Don of Don McCormack, major leaguer (1980-81)*
8. Brandon Gemoll, 1b, Fresno State University.
**9. Dennis Sarfate, rhp, Chandler-Gilbert (Ariz.) CC.—(2006-09)**
10. Greg Moreira, rhp, Lake Brantley HS, Apopka, Fla.
11. *David Slevin, 2b, Indian River (Fla.) JC.
12. *Ray Liotta, rhp, Archbishop Rummel HS, Metairie, La.
13. Travis Hinton, 1b, Chandler-Gilbert (Ariz.) CC.
14. Aaron Sheffield, rhp, Young Harris (Ga.) JC.
**15. *Tim Dillard, c, Saltillo (Miss.) HS.—(2008-12)**
DRAFT DROP *Son of Steve Dillard, major leaguer (1985-82)*
16. Gene DeSalme, lhp, Northwestern State University.
17. *Justin Wilson, lhp, Chandler (Ariz.) HS.
18. Jeff Eure, c, Old Dominion University.
19. Joel Alvarado, c, University of Texas-Arlington.
20. *Josh Smith, rhp, Lake Havasu City HS, Lake Havasu, Ariz.
21. Orlando Viera, of, Dra Conchita Cuevas HS, Gurabo, P.R.
22. *Damarius Bilbo, of, Moss Point (Miss.) HS.
23. David Nolasco, rhp, Riverside (Calif.) CC.
DRAFT DROP *Brother of Ricky Nolasco, fourth-round draft pick, Cubs (2001); major leaguer (2006-15)*
24. Daniel J. Kolb, rhp, Manatee (Fla.) CC.
**25. Chris Barnwell, ss, Flagler (Fla.) College.—(2006)**
**26. +Manny Parra, lhp, American River (Calif.) JC.—(2007-15)**
27. Daniel Boyd, of, University of South Florida.
**28. Chris Saenz, rhp, Pima (Ariz.) CC.—(2004)**
29. *Jamie McAlister, rhp, Clearwater HS, Piedmont, Mo.
30. Chris Gittings, rhp, De Sales HS, Louisville, Ky.
31. *Andrew Sigerich, rhp, Downers Grove North HS, Downers Grove, Ill.
32. *Jon Calmes, rhp, Eastlake HS, Sammamish, Wash.
33. *Greg Esteves, ss, River Ridge HS, New Port Richey, Fla.
34. *Fuarieuir Miller, of, Laney (Calif.) JC.
35. +Stephen Hunt, of, Chandler-Gilbert (Ariz.) CC.
36. Rusty Huggins, lhp, Central Florida CC.
37. Tom Carrow, of, University of Tampa.
38. *Ross Hawley, rhp, Augustana (S.D.) College.
39. *Travis Johnson, of, Shannon (Miss.) HS.
40. *Jeremy Wilson, c, Catholic Central HS, Burlington, Wis.
41. Hubert Pruett, rhp, Kamehameha HS, Pearl City, Hawaii.
42. Ralph Santana, ss, Lake Sumter (Fla.) CC.
43. Matt Serafini, c, University of Evansville.
DRAFT DROP *Twin brother of Vince Serafini, sixth-round draft pick, Twins (2001)*
44. Corry Parrott, of, Long Beach State University.
45. *Jason Costello, lhp, Clearwater (Fla.) HS.
46. *Jordi Szabo, of, Carlsbad (Calif.) HS.
47. *Joseph Costentino, of, Bishop Gorman HS, Henderson, Nev.
48. *Brian Harper, lhp, North Little Rock (Ark.) HS.
49. *Nicholas Stillwagon, c, Biloxi (Miss.) HS.
50. Chris Haggard, c, University of Oklahoma.

## MINNESOTA TWINS (1)

**1. Joe Mauer, c, Cretin-Derham Hall, St. Paul, Minn.—(2004-15)**
DRAFT DROP *Brother of Jake Mauer, 23rd-round draft pick, Twins (2001)*
2. Scott Tyler, rhp, Downingtown (Pa.) HS.—(AA)
**3. Jose Morales, ss, Academie la Providencia HS, Rio Piedras, P.R.—(2007-11)**
4. Angel Garcia, rhp, Nicolas Sevilla HS, Dorado, P.R.—(AAA)
5. Jeremy Brown, rhp, University of Georgia.—(Rookie)
6. Vince Serafini, lhp, University of Evansville.
DRAFT DROP *Twin brother of Matt Serafini, 43rd-round draft pick, Brewers (2001)*
7. Matt Vorwald, rhp, University of Illinois.
8. Jared Hemus, lhp, Grossmont (Calif.) JC.
9. Dusty Gomon, 1b, Terry Parker HS, Jacksonville, Fla.
10. Garrett Guzman, of, Green Valley HS, Henderson, Nev.
11. Josh Renick, ss, Middle Tennessee State University.
DRAFT DROP *Son of Rick Renick, major leaguer (1968-72)*
12. Kaulana Kuhaulua, 2b, Long Beach State University.
DRAFT DROP *Son of Fred Kuhaulua, major leaguer (1977-81)*
**13. Kevin Cameron, rhp, Georgia Tech.—(2007-09)**
14. *Ryan Anderson, lhp, Gaither HS, Tampa.
15. Brett Lawson, rhp, Northwestern Oklahoma State University.
16. *Brian Stitt, rhp, Wellington Community HS, Wellington, Fla.
**17. *Matt Macri, ss, Dowling HS, Clive, Iowa.—(2008)**
18. Robert Guzman, of, Cal State Fullerton.
19. Scott Whitrock, of, Madison (Wis.) Area Tech CC.
20. *Anthony Albano, of, Brother Rice HS, Chicago.
21. Felix Molina, 2b, Eugenio Maria de Hostos HS, Trujillo Alto, P.R.
22. Ryan Smith, c, Citrus (Calif.) JC.
23. Jake Mauer, 2b, University of St. Thomas (Minn.).
DRAFT DROP *Brother of Joe Mauer, first overall draft pick, Twins (2001); major leaguer (2004-15)*
24. Bryan Kennedy, c, Long Beach State University.
DRAFT DROP *Brother of Adam Kennedy, first-round draft pick, Cardinals (1997); major leaguer (1999-2013)*
25. Josh Johnson, c, Ridgway (Pa.) HS.
26. *John Herrera, rhp, Redlands (Calif.) HS.
27. +Justin Elliott, c, Lake Gibson HS, Lakeland, Fla. / South Florida CC.
28. Brian Gates, rhp, University of Tennessee.
**29. +Nick Blackburn, rhp, Seminole State (Okla.) JC.—(2007-12)**
30. Josh Daws, rhp, Jacksonville University.
31. *Ben Thomas, 3b, Central HS, Rapid City, S.D.
32. *Jason Wilmes, lhp, Somerset (Wis.) HS.
33. *Ryan Gehring, lhp, Catholic Central HS, Burlington, Wis.
34. *Marshall Hendon, lhp, Christian Brothers HS, Sacramento, Calif.
35. *Bookie Gates, 2b, Washington State University.
36. Kenny Huff, of, University of Arizona.
37. Shawn Tarkington, rhp, Seton Hall University.
38. Matt Abram, 2b-of, University of Arizona.
39. Nick Niedbalski, lhp, East Central (Mo.) JC.
40. Erik Lohse, rhp, Sacramento (Calif.) CC.
DRAFT DROP *Brother of Kyle Lohse, major leaguer (2001-15)*
41. Ryan Spataro, of, St. Peters SS, Barrie, Ontario.
42. Pat Tingley, lhp, Indiana State University.
**43. *Jason Vargas, lhp, Apple Valley (Calif.) HS.—(2005-15)**
44. Jacob Hader, lhp, Belton (Mo.) HS.
45. *Josh Smith, of, Canyon Springs HS, Moreno Valley, Calif.
46. *Mitch Pruemer, rhp, Rend Lake (Ill.) CC.
47. *Daniel Smith, of, Eau Gallie HS, Melbourne, Fla.
48. *William Guzman, ss, Northwest Christian Academy, Miami.
49. *Jason Paul, rhp, Ball State University.
50. *Robert Strickland, 2b, Frostproof (Fla.) HS.

## MONTREAL EXPOS (6)

1. Josh Karp, rhp, UCLA.—(AAA)
2. Donald Levinski, rhp, Weimar (Texas) HS.—(High A)
**3. Mike Hinckley, lhp, Moore (Okla.) HS.—(2008-09)**
4. Nick Long, rhp, Shaw HS, Columbus, Ga.—(Low A)
5. Reggie Fitzpatrick, of, McNair HS, Atlanta.—

(AAA)
6. **Josh Labandeira, ss, Fresno State University.—(2004)**
7. **Chad Bentz, lhp, Long Beach State University.—(2004-05)**
8. Greg Thissen, 3b, Triton (Ill.) JC.
9. Shawn Norris, 3b, Cal State Fullerton.
10. Eddie Diaz, rhp, Colonial HS, Orlando Fla.
11. *Kyle Pawelczyk, lhp, Chipola (Fla.) JC.
12. Danny Kahr, c, Durango HS, Las Vegas, Nev.
13. Tyler Kirkman, rhp, Mount Carmel (Ill.) HS.
14. Jason Walker, lhp, University of the Pacific.
15. Tory Imotichy, lhp, Purcell (Okla.) HS.
16. Warmar Gomez, rhp, Casiano Cepeda HS, Rio Grande, P.R.
17. David Maust, lhp, West Virginia University.
18. Rob Caputo, rhp, University of Alabama-Birmingham.
19. **Chris Schroder, rhp, Oklahoma City University.—(2006-08)**
20. Jason Greene, ss, Minford (Ohio) HS.
21. ***Tim Wood, rhp, Sabino HS, Tucson, Ariz.—(2009-11)**
22. *Arlandus Brown, of, Copiah-Lincoln (Miss.) JC.
23. +Ja'mar Clanton, ss, Triton (Ill.) JC.
24. *Jimmy Treece, rhp, Poly HS, Riverside, Calif.
25. *Zach Lerch, rhp, Prairie HS, Cedar Rapids, Iowa.
26. *Jerrell Jackson, of, Altoona (Pa.) Area HS.
27. *Daniel Smith, rhp, Sacramento (Calif.) CC.
28. *Michael Richardson, rhp, Richland (Wash.) HS.
29. *Mark Rodrigues, rhp, Kauai HS, Koloa, Hawaii.
30. *Jared Brown, lhp, Notre Dame Catholic HS, Milford, Conn.
31. *Jamieson Boulanger, lhp, Concordia (Quebec) University.
32. *Jean-Sabastien Varney, rhp, Edouard Montpetit HS, St. Hubert, Quebec.
33. *Jeremey White, lhp, Victor Valley (Calif.) CC.
34. *Henry Gutierrez-Portalatin, c, Florida Air Academy, Melbourne, Fla.
35. *Michael Springsteen, rhp, Marshalltown (Iowa) CC.
36. *Cole Zumbro, rhp, Franklin (Miss.) HS.
37. *P.J. Connelly, lhp, Beloit Memorial HS, Beloit, Wis.
38. *David LeClerc, lhp, Laval, Quebec.
39. *Jecorey Matthews, of, Northwest Classen HS, Oklahoma City, Okla.
40. *Fred Perkins, of, Brookhaven (Miss.) HS.
41. *Travis Becktel, of, Capistrano Valley HS, Mission Viejo, Calif.
42. *John Taylor, lhp, Northside HS, Northport, Ala.
43. *Joseph Gullion, ss, Johnson County (Kan.) CC.
44. *Brian Hipps, of, San Diego Mesa CC.
45. *Franklin Jimenez, 2b, Muscatine (Iowa) CC.
46. *Josh Ranson, of, Chatfield HS, Littleton, Colo.
47. ***Ross Wolf, rhp, Newton HS, Wheeler, Ill.—(2007-13)**
48. *Chris Jones, c, Edison HS, Fresno, Calif.
49. *Matthew Hayes, lhp, Effingham (Ill.) HS.
50. *Chad Scarbery, rhp, Fresno (Calif.) CC.

DRAFT DROP *Son of Randy Scarbery, first-round draft pick, Astros (1970); first-round draft pick, Athletics (1973); major leaguer (1979-80)*

## NEW YORK METS (26)

1. **Aaron Heilman, rhp, University of Notre Dame** (Choice from Rockies as compensation for Type A free agent Mike Hampton).**—(2003-11)**
1. (Choice to Athletics as compensation for Type A free agent Kevin Appier)
1. **David Wright, 3b, Hickory HS, Chesapeake, Va.** (Supplemental choice—38th—as compensation for Hampton).**—(2004-15)**
2. Alhaji Turay, of, Auburn (Wash.) HS.—(AA)
2. Corey Ragsdale, ss, Nettleton HS, Jonesboro, Ark. (Supplemental choice—76th—as compensation for Type C free agent Bobby Jones).—(AAA)
3. **Lenny DiNardo, lhp, Stetson University.—(2004-09)**
4. Brian Walker, lhp, University of Miami.—(High A)
5. **Danny Garcia, 2b, Pepperdine University.—(2003-04)**
6. Jason Weintraub, rhp, Jefferson HS, Tampa.
7. Tyler Beuerlein, c, Grand Canyon University.
8. Brett Kay, c, Cal State Fullerton.
9. Jayson Weir, lhp, Boone HS, Orlando, Fla.
10. Ryan Olson, lhp, University of Nevada-Las Vegas.
11. D.J. Mattox, rhp, Anderson (S.C.) College.
12. Derran Watts, of, University of British Columbia.
13. Jay Caligiuri, 3b, Cal State Los Angeles.
14. *Kyle Larsen, 1b, Eastlake HS, Sammamish, Wash.
15. Jason Scobie, rhp, Louisiana State University.
16. **Joe Hietpas, c, Northwestern University.—(2004)**
17. Frank Corr, of, Stetson University.
18. *Justin Barnes, ss, Merritt Island (Fla.) HS.
19. *Josh Alliston, rhp, Long Beach State University.
20. *Trevor Hutchinson, rhp, University of California.

DRAFT DROP *Brother of Chad Hutchinson, first-round draft pick, Braves (1995); major leaguer (2001); quarterback, National Football League (2002-04)*

21. Blake McGinley, lhp, Texas Tech.
22. David Bacani, 2b, Cal State Fullerton.
23. John Toner, of, Western Michigan University.
24. *Josh Deel, rhp, Wolfson HS, Jacksonville, Fla.
25. *Nathaniel Craft, lhp, Palm Harbor University HS, Palm Beach, Fla.
26. Justin Sassanella, of, De Kalb HS, Auburn, Ind.
27. Eric Templet, rhp, University of Louisiana-Lafayette.
28. Rylie Ogle, lhp, UC Santa Barbara.
29. Domingo Acosta, rhp, Palm Beach (Fla.) JC.
30. Chris Sherman, rhp, San Jose State University.
31. *Buddy Hausmann, lhp, Seton Hall University.
32. *Cole Armstrong, c, Delphi Academy, Surrey, B.C.
33. +Taylor George, rhp, Cypress (Calif.) JC.
34. Sean Pittman, ss-2b, North Georgia College.
35. *Wayne Foltin, rhp, Centennial HS, Bakersfield, Calif.
36. *Phillip Tyson, rhp, Katella HS, Anaheim, Calif.
37. *Jose Torres, c, Centennial HS, Corona, Calif.
38. *Luis Roberts, lhp, Dartmouth (Nova Scotia) HS.
39. *Michael Almand, lhp, Stockbridge (Ga.) HS.
40. *Jay Sawatski, lhp, Westark (Ark.) CC.

DRAFT DROP *Grandson of Carl Sawatski, major leaguer (1948-63)*

41. Sean Farrell, lhp, Briarcliffe (N.Y.) JC.
42. *Chris Davis, rhp, Fresno (Calif.) CC.
43. *Michael Schaeffer, rhp, Wilson HS, Sinking Springs, Pa.
44. ***Randy Wells, c, Southwestern Illinois JC.—(2008-12)**
45. *Eddie Cannon, rhp, South Florida CC.
46. *Karnie Vertz, rhp, Porterville (Calif.) JC.
47. *Michael Hawkins, of, Eisenhower HS, Rialto, Calif.
48. +Jamar Hill, 3b, Santa Ana (Calif.) JC.
49. *Paul Labiche, rhp, Reserve Christian HS, La Place, La.
50. *DeWayne Carver, rhp, Santa Fe (Fla.) CC.

## NEW YORK YANKEES (19)

1. (Choice to Orioles as compensation for Type A free agent Mike Mussina)
1. **John-Ford Griffin, of, Florida State University** (Choice from Mariners as compensation for Type A free agent Jeff Nelson).**—(2005-07)**
1. **Bronson Sardinha, ss, Kamehameha HS, Honolulu, Hawaii** (Supplemental choice—34th—as compensation for Type A free agent Denny Neagle).**—(2007)**

DRAFT DROP *Brother of Dane Sardinha, major leaguer (2003-05) • Brother of Duke Sardinha, 41st-round draft pick, Rockies (2001).*

1. Jon Skaggs, rhp, Rice University (Supplemental choice—42nd—as compensation for Nelson).—(AA)
2. **Shelley Duncan, of, University of Arizona** (Choice from Rockies as compensation for Neagle).**—(2007-13)**

DRAFT DROP *Son of Dave Duncan, major leaguer (1964-76) • Brother of Chris Duncan, first-round draft pick, Cardinals (1999); major leaguer (2005-09)*

2. Jason Arnold, rhp, University of Central Florida.—(AAA)
3. **Chase Wright, lhp, Iowa Park (Texas) HS.—(2007)**
4. Aaron Rifkin, 1b, Cal State Fullerton.—(AAA)
5. Jeff Christensen, of, University of Tennessee.—(Low A)
6. Rik Currier, rhp, University of Southern California.
7. **Andy Cannizaro, ss, Tulane University.—(2006-08)**
8. ***Adam Peterson, rhp, Wichita State University.—(2004)**
9. **Charlie Manning, lhp, University of Tampa.—(2008)**
10. Jared Pitney, 1b, Pepperdine University.
11. Brian Strelitz, rhp, Texas A&M University.
12. Chris Russ, rhp, Texas A&M University.
13. Adam Wheeler, rhp, Campbell HS, Smyrna, Ga.
14. *Trent Henderson, rhp, Pratt (Kan.) CC.
15. John Picco, lhp, Villanova HS, LaSalle, Ontario.
16. *Nic Touchstone, lhp, Okaloosa-Walton (Fla.) JC.
17. *Quinton Robertson, rhp, Texarkana (Texas) JC.
18. *Josh Smith, rhp, Navarro (Texas) JC.
19. *Mike McGowan, rhp, Newman Smith HS, Carrollton, Texas.
20. *Jason McMillan, lhp, Dundee Crown HS, Carpentersville, Ill.
21. **Omir Santos, c, East Central (Mo.) JC.—(2008-13)**
22. Todd Faulkner, 1b, Auburn University.
23. Kaazim Summerville, of, St. Mary's (Calif.) College.
24. Bobby Wood, rhp, University of Michigan.
25. *Madison Edwards, c, Midland (Texas) HS.
26. *Andrew Marcus, rhp, Tyler (Texas) JC.
27. *Jeff Tuttle, of, Cypress (Calif.) JC.
28. *Brandon Jones, of, Liberty Eylau HS, Texarkana, Texas.

DRAFT DROP *Wide receiver, National Football League (2005-10)*

29. ***Philip Humber, rhp, Carthage (Texas) HS.—(2006-13)**

DRAFT DROP *First-round draft pick (3rd overall), Mets (2004)*

30. +Danny Schwab, 1b, Arvada West HS, Arvada, Colo. / Pima (Ariz.) CC.
31. *Ricky Stover, lhp, Navarro (Texas) JC.
32. *Aaron Edwards, c, John A. Logan (Ill.) JC.
33. *Chris Weakley, ss, Albany HS, El Cerrito, Calif.
34. +Chris Kemlo, rhp, McLaughlin HS, Oshawa, Ontario / Santa Fe (Fla.) JC.
35. Kevin Goodrum, lhp, Ohio State University.
36. *Fernando Fuentes, c, Weehawken (N.J.) HS.
37. +Josh Kerschen, rhp, CC of Southern Nevada.
38. *Brent Jackson, lhp, Henderson (Texas) HS.
39. *Tate Wallis, rhp, Ennis (Texas) HS.
40. *Hans Gleason, of, El Modena HS, Orange, Calif.
41. *Jonathan Mercer, of, Jefferson (Mo.) JC.
42. *Greg Taylor, ss, St. Louis CC-Forest Park.
43. *Michael Bass, rhp, Santana HS, Santee, Calif.
44. *Eric Hullinger, rhp, Oak Forest (Ill.) HS.
45. *Jose Robles, rhp, East Central (Mo.) JC.
46. *Domenic Ficco, lhp, Regis Jesuit HS, Aurora, Colo.
47. *Chad Borek, rhp, Northmont HS, Dayton, Ohio.
48. *Brian Carpenter, of, Fairfield (Ohio) HS.
49. *Aneury Pichardo, ss, Miramar (Fla.) HS.
50. ***Brandon Boggs, of, Pope HS, Marietta, Ga.—(2008-11)**

## OAKLAND ATHLETICS (25)

1. **Bobby Crosby, ss, Long Beach State University.—(2003-10)**

DRAFT DROP *Son of Ed Crosby, major leaguer (1970-76)*

1. **Jeremy Bonderman, rhp, Pasco (Wash.) HS** (Choice from Mets as compensation for Type A free agent Kevin Appier).**—(2003-13)**

DRAFT DROP *First 2001 high school draft pick to reach majors (April 2, 2003)*

1. **John Rheinecker, lhp, Southwest Missouri State University** (Supplemental choice—37th—as compensation for Appier).**—(2006-07)**
2. **Neal Cotts, lhp, Illinois State University.—(2003-15)**
3. J.T. Stotts, ss, Cal State Northridge.—(AAA)
4. **Marcus McBeth, of-rhp, University of South Carolina.—(2007)**
5. Jeff Bruksch, rhp, Stanford University.—(AAA)
6. Austin Nagle, of, Barbe HS, Lake Charles, La.
7. **Dan Johnson, 1b, University of Nebraska.—(2005-15)**
8. Mike Frick, rhp, Cal State Northridge.
9. Casey Myers, c, Arizona State University.

DRAFT DROP *Brother of Corey Myers, first-round draft pick, Diamondbacks (1999)*

10. **Mike Wood, rhp, University of North Florida.—(2003-07)**
11. J.R. Crider, rhp, Lewis-Clark State (Idaho) College.
12. Jeff Christy, of, Stetson University.
13. **Chris Mabeus, rhp, Lewis-Clark State (Idaho) College.—(2006)**
14. Brett Price, lhp, University of South Carolina.
15. Jason Basil, of, Georgia Tech.
16. *Steve Reba, rhp, Clemson University.
17. *Pete Montrenes, rhp, University of Mississippi.
18. *Jacob Dixon, rhp, Rowva HS, Oneida, Ill.
19. J.J. Pierce, of, Wayland Baptist (Texas) University.
20. Jeff Muessig, rhp, Briarcliffe (N.Y.) JC.
21. Jeff Coleman, rhp, University of Hawaii.
22. Harold Holbert, 2b, Locke HS, Los Angeles.
23. Kory Wayment, ss, Salt Lake (Utah) CC.
24. *Dylan Putnam, rhp, Michigan State University.
25. Andy Neufeld, 3b, University of Georgia.
26. Chris Gill, rhp-3b, Phoenix JC.
27. Bryan Simmering, rhp, Towson State University.
28. Matt Groff, of, Tulane University.
29. Leonard Landeros, lhp, JC of the Sequoias (Calif.).
30. *Thomas Braun, rhp, Kingwood (Texas) HS.
31. Brian Rooke, of, University of Hawaii-Hilo.
32. *Mark Hilde, 3b, Woodway HS, Edmonds, Wash.

DRAFT DROP *Died as active player (July 30, 2001)*

33. +Dan Fyvie, rhp, Fenton (Mich.) HS / Mott (Mich.) CC.
34. *Adolfo Garza, rhp, Walla Walla (Wash.) CC.
35. *Trenton Froehlich, lhp, Lompoc (Calif.) HS.
36. *Cooper Fouts, c, Bishop Gorman HS, Las Vegas, Nev.
37. ***Andre Ethier, of, Chandler-Gilbert (Ariz.) CC.—(2006-15)**
38. *Rob Lacheur, rhp, Prairie Baseball Academy, Lethbridge, Alberta.
39. *Nic Crosta, of, Highline HS, Seattle.

## PHILADELPHIA PHILLIES (4)

1. **Gavin Floyd, rhp, Mount St. Joseph HS, Severna Park, Md.—(2004-15)**

DRAFT DROP *Brother of Michael Floyd, 22nd-round draft pick, Phillies (2001)*

2. (Choice to Red Sox as compensation for Type B free agent Rheal Cormier)
3. (Choice to Mariners as compensation for Type B free agent Jose Mesa)
4. Terry Jones, ss, Upland (Calif.) HS.—(High A)
5. **Ryan Howard, 1b, Southwest Missouri State University.—(2004-15)**
6. Bryan Hansen, of, Longwood HS, Coram, N.Y.
7. Vinny DeChristofaro, lhp, Richmond Hill (Ga.) HS.
8. Taft Cable, rhp, University of North Carolina-Greensboro.
9. **Chris Roberson, of, Feather River (Calif.) JC.—(2006-07)**
10. ***Rocky Cherry, rhp, University of Oklahoma.—(2007-08)**
11. Matt Sweeney, rhp, Steinert HS, Yardville, N.J.
12. Rod Perry, of, Penn State University.

DRAFT DROP *Son of Rod Perry Sr., defensive back, National Football League (1975-84)*

13. Andre Marshall, of, University of Washington.
14. Mario Delgado, of, Oklahoma City University.
15. Tim Davis, lhp, University of South Alabama.
16. Ben Margalski, c, Southwest Missouri State University.
17. Ryan Hutchison, rhp, Western Kentucky University.
18. Ben Ally, rhp, Warner Southern (Fla.) College.
19. Matt Squires, lhp, Whitworth (Wash.) College.
20. Vince Vukovich, of, University of Delaware.

DRAFT DROP *Son of John Vukovich, major leaguer (1970-81)*

21. *Julian Williams, of, Upland (Calif.) HS.
22. Michael Floyd, of, University of South Carolina.

DRAFT DROP *Brother of Gavin Floyd, first-round draft pick, Phillies (2001); major leaguer (2004-15)*

23. Josh Cisneros, c, West Virginia University.
24. Kris Lammers, lhp, Middle Tennessee State University.
25. Josh Scott, lhp, Baylor University.
26. Layne Dawson, rhp, University of Memphis.
27. Jason Bernard, rhp, Troy State University.

28. Mike Nall, rhp, Northwestern University.
29. *Jeremy Kurella, ss, University of Central Florida.
30. Kris Bennett, 3b, University of Tennessee.
31. Ryan Johnston, c, Sonoma State (Calif.) University.
32. Josh Miller, rhp, North Carolina State University.
33. Dan McCall, lhp, Penn State University.
34. Brian Schriner, rhp, University of Louisiana-Monroe.
35. Nick Glaser, rhp, Clemson University.
36. Jeff Phelps, 3b, Arizona State University.
37. Wes Carroll, ss, University of Evansville.
DRAFT DROP *Brother of Jamey Carroll, major leaguer (2002-13) • Baseball coach, Evansville (2009-15)*
38. *Jaime Martinez, 1b, Hueneme HS, Oxnard, Calif.
**39. *Jason Jaramillo, c, Racine Case HS, Franksville, Wis.—(2009-11)**
40. *Arnold Hughey, lhp, Venice (Fla.) HS.
41. *Dustin Miller, rhp, Diamond Bar (Calif.) HS.
42. *Will Thompson, 1b, Loyola Sacred Heart HS, Missoula, Mon.
43. *Andy Lytle, rhp, Highlands Ranch (Colo.) HS.
44. *Humberto Gonzales, ss-2b, Rainier Beach HS, Seattle.
45. *Jared Birrenkott, c, Granite Hills HS, El Cajon, Calif.
46. *Allen Hicks, of, King HS, Tampa.
47. Sean Walsh, 3b-of, North Carolina State University.
48. Maximo Reyes, rhp, St. Petersburg (Fla.) JC.

## PITTSBURGH PIRATES (8)

**1. John VanBenschoten, rhp-1b, Kent State University.—(2004-08)**
2. (Choice to Braves as compensation for Type B free agent Terry Mulholland)
**3. *Jeremy Guthrie, rhp, Stanford University.—(2004-15)**
DRAFT DROP *Returned to Stanford; re-drafted by Indians, 2002 (1st round)*
**4. Jeff Keppinger, ss, University of Georgia.—(2004-13)**
5. Travis Chapman, 1b, Indian River (Fla.) CC.—(High A)
6. Drew Friedberg, lhp, Arizona State University.
7. Michael McCuistion, c, Yucaipa (Calif.) HS.
**8. Chris Duffy, of, Arizona State University.—(2005-09)**
9. *Jason Fellows, 1b, Berkmar HS, Lawrenceville, Ga.
10. *Aaron Bulkley, ss, Port Byron (N.Y.) HS.
**11. *Stephen Drew, ss, Lowndes HS, Valdosta, Ga.—(2006-15)**
DRAFT DROP *First-round draft pick (15th overall), Diamondbacks (2004) • Brother of J.D. Drew, first-round draft pick, Phillies (1997); first-round draft pick, Cardinals (1998); major leaguer (1998-2011) • Brother of Tim Drew, first-round draft pick, Indians (1997); major leaguer (2000-04)*
12. Tim Brown, 1b, Sheldon HS, Eugene, Ore.
13. Jeff Dutremble, lhp, Dartmouth University.
14. Jason Kiley, rhp, St. Charles East HS, St. Charles, Ill.
15. Jeff Miller, rhp, University of New Orleans.
16. *Jon Smith, lhp, Cal State Fullerton.
17. *Tim Morley, lhp, Stevenson HS, Buffalo Grove, Ill.
18. Lino Mariot, ss, Woodbridge (N.J.) HS.
**19. Jonathan Albaladejo, rhp, Miami-Dade CC.—(2007-12)**
**20. Zach Duke, lhp, Midway HS, Clifton, Texas.—(2005-15)**
21. *Tim Pahuta, c-1b, Hunterdon Central HS, Whitehouse Station, N.J.
22. *Jon Koch, rhp, Berrien Springs (Mich.) HS.
23. Casey Shumaker, rhp, Jacksonville University.
24. +Marcus Davila, rhp, Tallahassee (Fla.) CC.
25. *Robert Coomer, rhp, John A. Logan (Ill.) JC.
DRAFT DROP *Brother of Ron Coomer, major leaguer (1995-2003)*
26. Jhosandy Morel, lhp, Emerson HS, Union City, N.J.
27. Dan D'Amato, lhp, North Carolina State University.
28. Claudell Clark, lhp, Norfolk State University.
29. +Scott Tower, lhp, Temple (Texas) JC.
30. +Kody Kirkland, 3b, Pocatello (Idaho) HS / JC of Southern Idaho.
31. Brady Borner, lhp, Wayne State (Neb.) College.
32. *Chris Torres, c, Vero Beach (Fla.) HS.
**33. Chris Shelton, c, University of Utah.—(2004-09)**
34. *Brett Korth, rhp, Kishwaukee (Ill.) JC.
35. *Renardo Pitts, of, Jones County HS, Gray, Ga.
36. *Adam Riddle, of, New Mexico JC.
37. *Eddie Elias, rhp, Brito Private HS, Miami.
**38. Rajai Davis, 2b, University of Connecticut-Avery Point JC.—(2006-15)**
39. *Taylor Johnson, of, Skyview HS, Vancouver, Wash.
40. *Jase Turner, 1b, Skyline HS, Oakland.
41. *Scott Wearne, 2b, Chipola (Fla.) JC.
42. *Preston Simms, rhp, Bethany HS, Oklahoma City, Okla.
**43. Shane Youman, lhp, Louisiana State University.—(2006-07)**
**44. *Joe Martinez, rhp, Seton Hall Prep HS, West Orange, N.J.—(2009-13)**
45. *Brent Sportsman, rhp, Elgin (Ill.) CC.
46. *Matthew Davis, lhp-of, Terry Parker HS, Jacksonville, Fla.
47. *Joshua MacDonald, rhp, Notre Dame HS, Milford, Conn.
48. *Anthony Cekovsky, rhp, Southington (Conn.) HS.
49. *Jeb Gibbs, rhp, Pope HS, Villa Ricca, Ga.
50. Justin Rethwisch, of, Antelope Valley (Calif.) JC.

## ST. LOUIS CARDINALS (28)

1. Justin Pope, rhp, University of Central Florida.—(AAA)
**2. Dan Haren, rhp, Pepperdine University.—(2003-15)**
**3. Joe Mather, ss, Mountain Pointe HS, Phoenix.—(2008-12)**
4. Josh Brey, lhp, Liberty University.—(High A)
**5. Skip Schumaker, of, UC Santa Barbara.—(2005-15)**
6. John Killalea, lhp, Seminole (Fla.) HS.
7. Tyler Adamczyk, rhp, Westlake HS, Westlake Village, Calif.
**8. John Nelson, ss, University of Kansas.—(2006)**
9. Rhett Parrott, rhp, Georgia Tech.
10. Seth Davidson, ss, University of Southern California.
11. Jesse Roman, 1b, Rice University.
12. Ben Julianel, rhp, San Diego State University.
13. Chris Netwall, c, Penn State University.
14. Jordan Robison, of, Northwestern State University.
15. Matt Williams, 3b, Baylor University.
16. Mike Wodnicki, rhp, Stanford University.
17. Josh Merrigan, lhp, Oklahoma State University.
18. Neal Simoneaux, ss, University of Louisiana-Lafayette.
**19. *Shane Komine, rhp, University of Nebraska.—(2006-07)**
20. *Bryce Kartler, lhp, Arizona State University.
21. Cody Gunn, c, Brewster (Wash.) HS.
22. Bryan Moore, 1b, Louisiana State University.
**23. *Kevin Correia, rhp, Cal Poly San Luis Obispo.—(2003-15)**
DRAFT DROP *First player from 2002 draft to reach majors (July 10, 2003)*
24. Aaron Ledbetter, rhp, Westark (Ark.) CC.
25. Dan Kantrovitz, 2b, Brown University.
DRAFT DROP *Scouting director, Cardinals (2011-14)*
26. Aaron Russelburg, rhp, Murray State University.
27. *Lee Gwaltney, rhp, Louisiana Tech.
**28. +Blake Hawksworth, rhp, Eastlake HS, Sammamish, Wash. / Bellevue (Wash.) CC.—(2009-11)**
29. Pilar Amaya, ss, San Diego State University.
30. Jeff Jones, of, Long Beach State University.
31. *Marcus Markray, lhp, Springhill (La.) HS.
32. Andrew Davie, 1b, Central Arkansas Christian HS, Little Rock, Ark.
33. *Jacob Nowlen, rhp, University of Arkansas-Monticello.
34. Matt Pearl, of, UCLA.
35. *Michael Cust, of, Immaculata HS, Whitehouse Station, N.J.
DRAFT DROP *Brother of Jack Cust, first-round draft pick, Diamondbacks (1997); major leaguer (2001-11)*
36. *Billy Biggs, rhp, West Virginia University.
37. *Richard Quihuis-Bell, 1b, Central Arizona JC.
38. Jared Blasdell, rhp, Cal Poly San Luis Obispo.
39. Dan Shouse, lhp, St. Louis University.
40. Steve Green, of, University of Arkansas-Monticello.
41. Travis Palmer, rhp, University of Utah.
42. Anthony Rawson, lhp, University of Southern Mississippi.
43. *Jesse Kozlowski, rhp, Los Angeles Pierce JC.
44. +Shane Reedy, rhp, Utah Valley State JC.
45. *Billy Paganetti, of, Galena HS, Reno, Nev.
46. *Drew Davidson, of, Dowling HS, West Des Moines, Iowa.
**47. +Terry Evans, 3b, Middle Georgia JC.—(2007-10)**
48. Michael Levy, c, Dartmouth College.
49. *Sam Fisher, rhp, University of Dayton.
50. Mike Fox, ss, University of Central Florida.
DRAFT DROP *Brother of Matt Fox, sixth-round draft pick, Diamondbacks (2001); first-round draft pick (35th overall), Twins (2004); major leaguer (2004)*

## SAN DIEGO PADRES (14)

1. Jake Gautreau, 3b, Tulane University.—(AAA)
2. *Matt Harrington, rhp, St. Paul (Northern League).—DNP
DRAFT DROP *No school; re-drafted by Devil Rays, 2002 (13th round); first-round draft pick (7th overall), Rockies (2000)*
3. Tagg Bozied, 1b-3b, University of San Francisco.—(AAA)
**4. Josh Barfield, 2b, Klein HS, Spring, Texas.—(2006-09)**
DRAFT DROP *Son of Jesse Barfield, major leaguer (1981-92)*
5. Greg Sain, c-3b, University of San Diego.—(AAA)
6. Jason Weidmeyer, lhp, University of Memphis.
7. Doc Brooks, of, University of Georgia.
**8. David Pauley, rhp, Longmont (Colo.) HS.—(2006-12)**
9. Jon Benick, 1b, University of Virginia.
10. Ben Fox, lhp, Dixie State (Utah) JC.
11. Marcus Nettles, of, University of Miami.
12. Jordan Pickens, 1b, Cuesta (Calif.) JC.
**13. Jason Bartlett, ss, University of Oklahoma.—(2004-14)**
14. Josh Carter, of, Oregon State University.
**15. *Carlos Fisher, rhp-of, Duarte (Calif.) HS.—(2009-11)**
16. Jon Brandt, rhp, UCLA.
17. Trevor Brown, c, Lewis-Clark State (Idaho) College.
18. *Scott Shapiro, rhp, St. Augustine HS, Oceanside, Calif.
19. Jason Anderegg, rhp, Belmont University.
20. *Jeremy Slayden, of, Oakland HS, Murfreesboro, Tenn.
21. Rusty Tucker, lhp, University of Maine.
**22. *Drew Macias, of, Alta Loma HS, Rancho Cucamonga, Calif.—(2007-09)**
23. *Kyle Cullinan, 3b, Fullerton (Calif.) HS.
24. Joseph Hastings, 1b, East Carolina University.
25. Scott Kelly, lhp, Missouri Valley (Mo.) College.
26. Matt Hellman, of, Lewis-Clark State (Idaho) College.
27. *Elliot Singletary, 2b, North Fort Myers (Fla.) HS.
28. *Michael Watson, lhp, Midland (Texas) JC.
29. *Brendan Katin, c, Fort Myers (Fla.) HS.
30. *Matt Hobbs, lhp, University of Missouri.
31. *Hunter Brown, 3b, Rice University.
**32. *Irving Falu, 2b, Angel P. Millan HS, Carolina, P.R.—(2012-14)**
33. *Rashad Smith, of, Lambuth (Tenn.) University.
34. Zach Wykoff, rhp, Oxford, Ga.
35. *Chad Etheridge, of, Friendship Christian HS, Old Hickory, Tenn.
36. *Shawn LeBlanc, rhp, Bourgeois HS, Gray, La.
37. *John Coker, of, Muskogee (Okla.) HS.
38. +Anthony Lester, of, Hillsborough (Fla.) CC.
39. *Nick Walter, of, Hun School, Princeton, N.J.
40. *Josh Archer, c, Henry County HS, Paris, Tenn.
41. *Marcos Martinez, 1b, Chaffey (Calif.) JC.

## SAN FRANCISCO GIANTS (30)

**1. Brad Hennessey, rhp, Youngstown State University** (Choice from Indians as compensation for Type A free agent Ellis Burks).**—(2004-08)**
**1. Noah Lowry, lhp, Pepperdine University.—(2003-07)**
**1. Todd Linden, of, Louisiana State University** (Supplemental choice—41st—as compensation for Burks).**—(2003-07)**
**2. Jesse Foppert, rhp, University of San Francisco.—(2003-05)**
3. Julian Benavidez, 3b, Diablo Valley (Calif.) CC.—(AA)
4. Josh Cram, rhp, Clemson University.—(High A)
**5. Justin Knoedler, rhp-c, Miami (Ohio) University.—(2004-06)**
DRAFT DROP *Twin brother of Jason Knoedler, sixth-round draft pick, Tigers (2001)*
6. David Cash, rhp, University of California.
7. Jamie Athas, ss, Wake Forest University.
**8. Jason Waddell, lhp, Riverside (Calif.) CC.—(2009)**
9. *T.J. Large, rhp, Seminole (Fla.) HS.
10. Wes Hutchinson, rhp, Lewis-Clark State (Idaho) College.
11. Derin McMains, 2b, University of Arkansas-Little Rock.
12. Albert Montes, rhp, University of Texas.
13. Juan Serrato, rhp, Riverside (Calif.) CC.
14. *Jeff Timmons, c, Nova HS, Hollywood, Fla.
15. Tyler Von Schell, 1b, UC Santa Barbara.
16. Craig James, rhp, Killian HS, Miami.
**17. Steve Holm, ss-c, Oral Roberts University.—(2008-11)**
18. +Dayton Buller, c, Fresno (Calif.) CC.
19. Rob Meyer, of, University of California.
20. *Richard Giannotti, of, St. Thomas Aquinas HS, Fort Lauderdale, Fla.
21. Miguel Miranda, ss, University of Arkansas-Little Rock.
22. Karl Jernigan, of, Florida State University.
23. Petersen Benjamin, rhp, Florida Atlantic University.
24. *T.J. Healey, rhp, Cardinal Gibbons HS, Fort Lauderdale, Fla.
25. Ryan Meaux, lhp, Lamar (Colo.) CC.
**26. *Bobby Wilson, c, Seminole (Fla.) HS.—(2008-15)**
27. Keith Anderson, c-3b, Cal Poly San Luis Obispo.
28. David Hixson, rhp, Gonzaga University.
29. Matt Huntingford, of, Florida International University.
30. *Joe Mercer, c, American River (Calif.) JC.
31. Chris Ciesluk, ss, Taunton (Mass.) HS.
32. +Brian Stirm, rhp, West Valley (Calif.) JC.
33. R.D. Spiehs, rhp, University of Nebraska.
34. +Aaron Hornostaj, 2b, Saint Thomas of Villanova HS, Waterloo, Ontario / Connors State (Okla.) JC.
35. *Chris Hamblen, c, University of Cincinnati.
36. *Matt Hopper, rhp-1b, University of Nebraska.
37. *Todd Mittauer, rhp, Dade Christian HS, Cooper City, Fla.
38. *Lamont Jordan, 2b, Dinwiddie (Va.) HS.
39. *Matthew Somnis, rhp, Tumwater HS, Olympia, Wash.
40. Rudy Garcia, rhp, Lake Worth (Fla.) HS.
41. *Austin Allen, ss, Mount Hood (Ore.) CC.
42. *P.J. Hiser, rhp, Hagerstown (Md.) JC.
43. *Kevin Bulger, ss, Brookwood HS, Snellville, Ga.
DRAFT DROP *Brother of Jason Bulger, first-round draft pick, Diamondbacks (2001); major leaguer (2005-11) • Brother of Brian Bulger, 49th-round draft pick, Giants (2001)*
44. Jonny Williams, c, University of Missouri.
45. *Karl Amonite, 1b, Connors State (Okla.) JC.
46. *Brent Adcock, rhp, Lebanon HS, Watertown, Tenn.
**47. Scott Munter, rhp, Butler County (Kan.) CC.—(2005-07)**
48. *Paul O'Toole, c, University of Notre Dame.
49. *Brian Bulger, rhp, South Georgia JC.
DRAFT DROP *Brother of Jason Bulger, first-round draft pick, Diamondbacks (2001); major leaguer (2005-11) • Brother of Kevin Bulger, 43rd-round draft pick, Giants (2001)*
50. *P.J. McGinnis, rhp, Central Missouri State University.

## SEATTLE MARINERS (23)

1. (Choice to Yankees as compensation for Type A free agent Jeff Nelson)
1. Michael Garciaparra, ss, Don Bosco HS, La Habra

Heights, Calif. (Supplemental choice—36th—as compensation for Type A free agent Alex Rodriguez).—(AAA)

DRAFT DROP *Brother of Nomar Garciaparra, first-round draft pick, Red Sox (1994); major leaguer (1996-2009)*

2. **Rene Rivera, c, Papa Juan XXIII HS, Bayamon, P.R.** (Choice from Rangers as compensation for Rodriguez).—**(2004-15)**
2. **Michael Wilson, of, Booker T. Washington HS, Tulsa, Okla.—(2011)**
3. Lazaro Abreu, c, Southridge HS, Miami (Choice from Phillies as compensation for Type B free agent Jose Mesa).—(Rookie)
3. Tim Merritt, ss, University of South Alabama.—(AA)
4. **Bobby Livingston, lhp, Trinity Christian HS, Lubbock, Texas.—(2006-07)**
5. John Cole, 2b-of, University of Nebraska.—(Low A)
6. Justin Ockerman, rhp, Garden City (Mich.) HS.
7. ***John Axford, rhp, Assumption College SS, Brantford, Ontario.—(2009-15)**
8. Jeff Ellena, ss, Cal Poly Pomona.
9. Justin Blood, lhp, Franklin Pierce (N.H.) College.

DRAFT DROP *Baseball coach, Hartford (2012-15)*

10. Beau Hintz, lhp, Fresno State University.
11. Josh Ellison, of, Westminster Academy, Fort Lauderdale, Fla.
12. Mike Hrynio, 3b, Dover HS, Mine Hill, N.J.
13. Jason Van Meetren, of, Stanford University.
14. Blake Woods, ss, Grand Canyon University.
15. +Chris Colton, of, Newnan (Ga.) HS / Middle Georgia JC.
16. Sean Peless, 1b, Edmonds (Wash.) CC.
17. Ramon Royce, rhp, Lewis-Clark State (Idaho) College.
18. John Williamson, of, East Carolina University.
19. Brian Sabourin, rhp, Dakota Collegiate HS, Winnipeg, Manitoba.
20. ***David Purcey, lhp, Trinity Christian Academy, Dallas.—(2008-13)**

DRAFT DROP *First-round draft pick (16th overall), Blue Jays (2004)*

21. Matt Ware, of, Loyola HS, Malibu, Calif.

DRAFT DROP *Defensive back, National Football League (2004-10)*

22. *Ladd Hall, rhp, Buena HS, Hereford, Ariz.
23. *Aaron Braithwaite, of, Killian HS, Miami.
24. *Garry Bakker, rhp, Suffern HS, Sloatsburg, N.Y.
25. Eddie Olszta, c, Butler University.
26. Jonathan Nelson, 3b, Dixie State (Utah) JC.
27. Tim Bausher, rhp, Kutztown (Pa.) University.
28. +Wes Morrow, rhp, Grayson County (Texas) CC.
29. *Kyle Aselton, lhp, West HS, Chehalis, Wash.
30. ***Billy Sadler, rhp, Pensacola (Fla.) JC.—(2006-09)**
31. Jason Rainey, of, Texas Tech.
32. *Bryan Vickers, c, Perrysburg (Ohio) HS.
33. *Tom Keefer, rhp, Byng HS, Sasakwa, Okla.
34. *Trevor Heid, of, Dixie State (Utah) JC.
35. *Todd Holliday, lhp, South Charleston (W.Va.) HS.
36. Ben Hudson, c, Truett-McConnell (Ga.) JC.
37. +Miguel Martinez, lhp, Miami-Dade CC.
38. ***Bobby Cramer, lhp, Long Beach State University.—(2010-11)**
39. *Aaron Ruchti, c, Klein Forest HS, Houston.
40. *Marquis Pettis, of, Diablo Valley (Calif.) JC.
41. *Kevin Guyette, rhp, Chaparral HS, Paradise Valley, Ariz.
42. *Ryan Brincat, of, Mira Costa HS, Manhattan Beach, Calif.
43. *Bradley Pahs, c, Chesterton HS, Porter, Ind.
44. *William Keyes, rhp, St. James (Md.) HS.
45. *Brandon Fusilier, of, Navarro (Texas) JC.
46. *Alan Gannaway, rhp, Bessemer Academy, McCalla, Ala.
47. *Ethan Katz, rhp, University HS, Los Angeles.
48. *Luis DeJesus, ss, Teodoro Aguilar Mora HS, Yabucoa, P.R.
49. *Nick Hamilton, of, West Lowndes HS, Starkville, Miss.
50. *Brandon Espinosa, rhp, Santa Ana (Calif.) JC.

## TAMPA BAY DEVIL RAYS (3)

1. **Dewon Brazelton, rhp, Middle Tennessee State University.—(2002-06)**
2. **Jon Switzer, lhp, Arizona State University.—(2003-09)**
3. Chris Flynn, rhp, University at Stony Brook.—(AAA)
4. ***David Bush, rhp, Wake Forest University.—(2004-13)**

DRAFT DROP *Returned to Wake Forest; re-drafted by Blue Jays, 2002 (2nd round)*

5. **Chris Seddon, lhp, Canyon HS, Santa Clarita, Calif.—(2007-12)**
6. Matt Rico, of, Fresno (Calif.) CC.
7. Tim King, lhp, Deer Park (Texas) HS.
8. Aaron Clark, of, University of Alabama.
9. **Fernando Cortez, ss, Grossmont (Calif.) CC.—(2005-07)**
10. Jason St. Clair, ss, Desert Vista HS, Phoenix.
11. ***Mark Worrell, rhp, John I. Leonard HS, Boynton Beach, Fla.—(2008-11)**
12. Pierre Blount, of, Chaffey (Calif.) JC.
13. Vince Harrison, 2b, University of Kentucky.
14. Tommy Nichols, 1b, Armijo HS, Fairfield, Calif.
15. Eric Miller, lhp, Gulf Coast HS, Naples, Fla.
16. *Tim Layden, lhp, Deer Park (N.Y.) HS.
17. Mike Navaroli, rhp, Indian River (Fla.) CC.
18. **Jonny Gomes, of, Santa Rosa (Calif.) CC.—(2003-15)**
19. ***Jason Hammel, rhp, Treasure Valley (Ore.) CC.—(2006-15)**
20. Jake Carney, rhp, University of Dallas.
21. Jarod Matthews, rhp, Yelm HS, Olympia, Wash.
22. John Paul Davis, 1b, Arkansas Tech.
23. Brent Cordell, c, Cosumnes River (Calif.) JC.
24. Brian Wolotka, of, Valparaiso University.
25. *Daron Roberts, c, Westview HS, Portland, Ore.

DRAFT DROP *Son of Dave Roberts, first overall draft pick, Padres (1972); major leaguer (1972-82)*

26. *John Asanovich, 2b, Highland HS, Gold Canyon, Ariz.
27. Gabby Martinez, 1b, Blanca Malaret HS, Sabana Grande, P.R.
28. *Mumba Rivera, rhp, Marshalltown (Iowa) CC.
29. Joshua Parker, rhp, Wallace State (Ala.) CC.
30. *Matt Wilkerson, of, Santa Margarita HS, Trabuco Canyon, Calif.
31. *Diego Lopez, rhp, Calexico (Calif.) HS.
32. **Joey Gathright, of, Bonnabel HS, La Place, La.—(2004-11)**
33. Tyson Thompson, rhp, Washington State University.
34. **Chad Gaudin, rhp, Crescent City Baptist HS, Harahan, La.—(2003-13)**
35. *Bryan Banks, rhp, Dunedin (Fla.) HS.
36. *Michael White, lhp, Countryside (Fla.) HS.
37. *Michael Rider, rhp, Armijo HS, Fairfield, Calif.
38. ***Thomas Diamond, rhp, Archbishop Rummel HS, Metairie, La.—(2010)**

DRAFT DROP *First-round draft pick (10th overall), Rangers (2004)*

39. *Greg Dini, c, Bishop Moore HS, Longwood, Fla.
40. *Brett Davis, 1b, Southern Union State (Ala.) JC.
41. *Derek Acosta, rhp, Capistrano Valley HS, Mission Viejo, Calif.
42. *Kevin Bertrand, rhp, JC of the Sequoias (Calif.).
43. *Griffin Zarbrough, lhp, Wallace State (Ala.) CC.
44. +Dan Van Ruiten, 3b, St. John Bosco HS, LaMirada, Calif. / Cerritos (Calif.) JC.
45. *Matt Lukevics, 2b, Jesuit HS, Tampa.
46. *Chris Eickhorst, c, Kean (N.J.) University.
47. *Eric Beattie, rhp, Riverview HS, Valrico, Fla.
48. ***Brad Davis, c, Capistrano Valley HS, Mission Viejo, Calif.—(2010)**
49. *Darwin Pittman, 1b, East St. John HS, Garyville, La.
50. Nick Aiello, lhp, Oklahoma Christian University.

## TEXAS RANGERS (5)

1. **Mark Teixeira, 3b, Georgia Tech.—(2003-15)**
2. (Choice to Mariners as compensation for Type A free agent Alex Rodrgriguez)
3. (Choice to Angels as compensation for Type A free agent Mark Petkovsek)
4. *Josh Baker, rhp, Memorial HS, Houston.—(High A)

DRAFT DROP *Attended Alabama; re-drafted by Brewers, 2004 (4th round) • Son of Johnny Baker, linebacker, National Football League (1963-67)*

5. **C.J. Wilson, lhp, Loyola Marymount University.—(2005-15)**
6. Ben Keiter, rhp, Wichita State University.
7. Patrick Boyd, of, Clemson University.
8. Masjid Khairy, of, Los Angeles CC.
9. Gerald Smiley, rhp, Rainier Beach, Seattle.
10. Rob Moravek, rhp, University of Georgia.
11. Greg Buscher, 3b, Terry Parker HS, Jacksonville, Fla.
12. Paul Abraham, rhp, Shippensburg (Pa.) University.
13. Michael Paustian, rhp, Fresno (Calif.) CC.
14. Chris Bradshaw, rhp, Texas Christian University.
15. *Ryan Dixon, rhp, Seminole (Fla.) HS.
16. Royce Hampton, lhp, Lehi (Utah) HS.
17. Randall Shelley, 3b, UCLA.
18. Nathan Bright, rhp, University of Northern Colorado.
19. +Craig Frydendall, lhp, Cowley County (Kan.) CC.
20. Jason Patty, ss, Fort Hays State (Kan.) University.
21. *Chad Oliva, c, Jacksonville University.
22. Brad Stockton, of, Georgia Tech.
23. *Scott Beerer, rhp, Orange Coast (Calif.) CC.
24. *Richie Gardner, rhp, Santa Rosa (Calif.) JC.
25. *Ryan Rote, rhp, Kettle Moraine HS, Delafield, Wis.
26. +Dustin Scheffel, rhp, Sacramento (Calif.) CC.
27. *Tim Lloyd, of, Christian Brothers HS, Memphis, Tenn.
28. *Troy Roberson, rhp, University of Miami.
29. *Ryan Mask, rhp, Bakersfield (Calif.) JC.
30. Andrew Campbell, lhp, Linn-Benton (Ore.) CC.
31. *Brandon Alford, lhp, Marshall (Texas) HS.
32. *Brandon Cornwell, rhp, James Madison University.
33. +Jeff Moye, rhp, Cowley County (Kan.) CC.
34. ***Dane De la Rosa, rhp, Elsinore HS, Wildomar, Calif.—(2011-14)**
35. *Jarvis Hicks, rhp, Durant HS, Plant City, Fla.
36. *Tony Irvin, rhp, Chamberlain HS, Tampa.
37. *Jason Ward, rhp, Spanish Fork (Utah) HS.
38. *Drake Wade, of, George Jenkins HS, Lakeland, Fla.
39. *Jeremy Zick, rhp, Riverside (Calif.) CC.
40. *Jose Romo, lhp, Riverside HS, El Paso, Texas.
41. ***Clay Timpner, lhp-of, LaBelle HS, Alva, Fla.—(2008)**
42. *Reid Santos, lhp, Saddleback (Calif.) JC.
43. ***Jason Windsor, rhp, West Valley (Calif.) JC.—(2006)**
44. *Andy Myette, rhp, JC of Southern Idaho.

DRAFT DROP *Brother of Aaron Myette, first-round draft pick, White Sox (1997); major leaguer (1999-2004)*

45. *Luke Steidlmayer, rhp, UC Davis.
46. *Jarle Brooks, rhp, Puyallup (Wash.) HS.
47. +Joldy Watts, rhp, JC of Eastern Utah.
48. *Joseph Martinson, rhp, Payson (Utah) HS.
49. *Travis Kassebaum, of, Auburn (Wash.) HS.
50. *Clayne Garrett, 3b, Murray (Utah) HS.

## TORONTO BLUE JAYS (15)

1. **Gabe Gross, of, Auburn University.—(2004-10)**
2. **Brandon League, rhp, St. Louis HS, Honolulu, Hawaii.—(2004-15)**
3. **Tyreli Godwin, of, University of North Carolina.—(2005)**

DRAFT DROP *First-round draft pick (24th overall), Yankees (1997); first-round draft pick (35th overall), Rangers (2000)*

4. Chris Sheffield, rhp, University of Miami.—(Low A)
5. **Michael Rouse, ss, Cal State Fullerton.—(2006-07)**
6. Lee Delfino, ss, East Carolina University.
7. Jason Colson, rhp, Winthrop University.
8. Sean Grimes, lhp, Saunders SS, London, Ontario.
9. Luke Hetherington, of, Kentwood HS, Covington, Wash.
10. Ryan Costello, lhp, Montclair State (N.J.) University.
11. *Sean Gamble, of, Jefferson Davis HS, Montgomery, Ala.

DRAFT DROP *Son of Oscar Gamble, major leaguer (1969-85)*

12. Ernie Durazo, 1b, University of Arizona.

DRAFT DROP *Brother of Erubiel Durazo, major leaguer (1999-2005)*

13. Brendan Fuller, rhp, University of South Florida.
14. David Corrente, c, Chatham-Kent SS, Chatham, Ontario.
15. *Nick Thomas, rhp, Laguna Creek HS, Elk Grove, Calif.
16. *Rock Mills, c, Pepperdine University.
17. Chris Neylan, lhp, Steinert HS, Trenton, N.J.
18. Aaron McEachran, 3b, University of Northern Iowa.
19. Isaac Iorg, ss, Knoxville, Tenn.

DRAFT DROP *Son of Garth Iorg, major leaguer (1978-87) • Brother of Eli Iorg, first-round draft pick, Astros (2005)*

20. Jon Ashford, of, Covington (Tenn.) HS.

DRAFT DROP *Son of Tucker Ashford, major leaguer (1976-84)*

21. ***Jeff Fiorentino, of, Nova HS, Hollywood, Fla.—(2005-09)**
22. Darren Heal, rhp, Oklahoma State University.
23. *Garrick Evans, of, Lake Braddock HS, Burke, Va.
24. **Dave Gassner, lhp, Purdue University.—(2005)**
25. Mark Comolli, rhp, Delaware Tech & CC.
26. Nick Tempesta, ss, Eastern Connecticut State University.
27. *Adam Daniels, lhp, North Vancouver, B.C.
28. *Joel Kirsten, lhp, Los Angeles Pierce JC.
29. *Mark McDonald, rhp, Robinson HS, Burlington, Ontario.

DRAFT DROP *Twin brother of P.J. McDonald, 43rd-round draft pick, Blue Jays (2001)*

30. *Javier Lopez, of, Northwest Christian Academy, Hollywood, Fla.
31. *Robert Grana, c, Cimarron Memorial HS, Las Vegas, Nev.
32. *Adam Sanabria, lhp, Lake Mary HS, Longwood, Fla.
33. *Kellen Ludwig, rhp, Lee County HS, Leesburg, Ga.
34. *Brian Ennis, rhp, Harding University HS, Charlotte, N.C.
35. *Nicholas Gor, rhp, Saddleback (Calif.) CC.
36. *Brian McFadden, of, Lake City (S.C.) HS.
37. *Felix Peguero, of, Bladensburg (Md.) HS.
38. Tim Whittaker, c, University of South Carolina.
39. *Adam Rodgers, c, Grapevine (Texas) HS.
40. *Alex Castellvi, c, Plant HS, Tampa.
41. *Ryan Olivo, 2b, Grapevine (Texas) HS.
42. *Jared Sanders, rhp, Mount Hood (Ore.) CC.
43. *P.J. McDonald, rhp, Robinson HS, Burlington, Ontario.

DRAFT DROP *Twin brother of Mark McDonald, 29th-round draft pick, Blue Jays (2001)*

44. *Kevin Johnston, rhp, Matheson HS, Surrey, B.C.
45. *Lawrence Best-Berfet, 2b, CC of Morris County (N.J.).
46. ***Sean Barker, of, Louisiana State University.—(2007)**
47. *Chris Jones, 1b, Heritage HS, Colleyville, Texas.
48. *Scott Shoemaker, rhp, Grossmont (Calf.) CC.
49. *Kenny Holmberg, 2b, Dunedin (Fla.) HS.
50. *Floyd Albert, lhp, Kernohan Park HS, St. Catharines, Ontario.

# 2002

## AT A GLANCE

### This Date In History
June 4-5

### Best Draft
**LOS ANGELES DODGERS.** The Dodgers landed six productive big leaguers in the first 17 rounds. They developed **JAMES LONEY** (1) as a first baseman rather than a pitcher, converted **JAMES MCDONALD** (11) from first baseman to pitcher and moved **RUSSELL MARTIN** (17) from third base to catcher. All three thrived at new positions.

### Worst Draft
**SEATTLE MARINERS.** The Mariners failed to sign two of their first three picks. Among players they did sign, the combined yield in a Seattle uniform was four home runs by a pair of late-round picks. The Mariners made amends by signing future ace **FELIX HERNANDEZ** as an international free agent.

### First-Round Bust
**CHRIS GRULER, RHP, REDS.** Hall of Fame catcher Johnny Bench worked out Gruler before the draft and said Gruler, who featured a 94-96 mph fastball, had a better curve and changeup than Tom Seaver had in his playing days. Gruler had the first of three shoulder surgeries within a year of signing with the Reds and went 3-5, 5.08 in 27 appearances over five minor league seasons.

### Second Best
**JOEY VOTTO, C, REDS.** If the Reds got shortchanged with Gruler, they more than made up for it by selecting Votto, an unheralded high school catcher from Canada, in the second round. Votto became an offensive force after moving to first base. He earned National League MVP honors in 2010 and led the league in walks four times in nine seasons.

### Late-Round Find
**RUSSELL MARTIN, 3B, DODGERS (17TH ROUND).** Martin was converted

# Less-heralded efforts best 'Moneyball' draft

The 2002 draft became synonymous with the best-selling book and movie "Moneyball," which documented the quest of the Oakland Athletics to identify undervalued talent.

As a low-revenue club that needed to maximize its resources to remain competitive, the A's viewed the 2002 draft as a golden opportunity to acquire players who had been vetted by both traditional scouting methods and the team's pioneering advanced analytics. They held seven of the first 39 picks, and expected to get more than their share of top talent. Author Michael Lewis was embedded with the team to chronicle its every move.

The A's draft haul, however, did not live up to billing. They drafted more players who reached the majors than any club (14), but only first-rounders Nick Swisher and Joe Blanton delivered a meaningful return on Oakland's investment. Despite their limited resources, the A's spent $9,165,500 to sign their picks, a draft record.

Other teams fared better. A record number of players drafted in both the first (24 of 30) and second (19 of 30) rounds reached the majors. Fourteen first-rounders were among the 30 most productive big league players from the class, according to career Wins Above Replacement (WAR), another draft record.

For the first time in 16 years, the average first-round bonus decreased from the previous year. The 2002 average of $2,107,845 was 2.2 percent lower than the 2001 average. For the most part, bonuses slotted in order throughout the first round, and the 24 highest bonuses went to the first 24 players selected, though not in order. Those developments were evidence that Major League Baseball's effort to put a drag on signing bonuses was working.

Seven of the first eight players drafted came from the high school ranks, and many of the most successful players proved to be from that demographic. The A's, however, chose lower-risk college talent almost exclusively, signing only one prep player.

Ball State righthander Bryan Bullington, the No. 1 pick, ranks among the biggest underachievers ever for his draft slot. He gained his first and only victory in the major leagues more than eight years after he was selected by the Pittsburgh Pirates. Bullington had a 1-9, 5.60 record over parts of five seasons with four different teams. The Pirates signed the 6-foot-5, 210-pound Bullington for a $4 million bonus, considerably less than the $5.15 million deal that top pick Joe Mauer received from the Minnesota Twins a year earlier.

Other notable developments in 2002 included a fall from grace for Rutgers righthander Bobby Brownlie, the consensus top talent entering the season; the best collection of high-end talent ever to come from Canada; a home run chase in the high school ranks; and severe cases of social anxiety disorder and depression that afflicted the careers of three first-rounders, including righthander Zack Greinke, who overcame those issues to emerge as the best player in the class.

ROBERT GURGANUS

**Ball State righthander Bryan Bullington came on strong during the 2002 season and was taken by the Pirates with the No. 1 pick, but he earned just one major league win in his career**

## PIRATES SETTLE ON BULLINGTON

The Pirates held the first pick in the 1996 draft, viewed Clemson righthander Kris Benson as the best player, and took him. Six years later, they had much less conviction in their choice of Bullington.

"This is a good draft, depth-wise," said Tampa Bay Devil Rays scouting director Dan Jennings, whose team picked second. "I don't think there's a single person who has separated himself from the group at the top, but it has good depth, except for college position players, which is just bad."

Bullington pushed his velocity to 96 mph as a junior and was consistently in the 92-94 range. He went 11-3, 2.84 with 18 walks and 139 strikeouts in 105 innings, earning his second straight Mid-American Conference pitcher of the year award.

Five days before the draft, the Pirates whittled their candidates to Bullington, Virginia high school shortstop B.J. Upton and Canadian prep lefthander Adam Loewen.

Bullington had an impressive predraft workout in front of Pirates general manager Dave Littlefield and scouting director Ed Creech, but Creech still

## 2002: THE FIRST ROUNDERS

| CLUB: PLAYER, POS., SCHOOL | HOMETOWN | B-T | HT. | WT. | AGE | BONUS | FIRST YEAR | LAST YEAR | PEAK LEVEL (YEARS) |
|---|---|---|---|---|---|---|---|---|---|
| 1. Pirates: Bryan Bullington, rhp, Ball State | Madison, Ind. | R-R | 6-5 | 220 | 21 | $4,000,000 | 2003 | 2010 | Majors (5) |
| Emerged as surprise top pick with command of 92-96 FB, lethal slider; stuff flattened out in injury-riddled career in minors, went 1-9, 5.60 in parts of five seasons. | | | | | | | | | |
| 2. Devil Rays: B.J. Upton, ss, Greenbrier Christian Acad. | Chesapeake, Va. | R-R | 6-2 | 170 | 17 | $4,600,000 | 2003 | Active | Majors (11) |
| Superior athlete at premium position, projected power in wiry frame; flashed superior tools in majors but played way off SS, became too strikeout-prone. | | | | | | | | | |
| 3. Reds: Chris Gruler, rhp, Liberty Union HS | Brentwood, Calif. | R-R | 6-3 | 200 | 18 | $2,500,000 | 2002 | 2006 | Class A (2) |
| Poster child for risk in HS arms; deserving pick with mid-90s FB/power curve, hurt shoulder in 2003, pitched 48 more IP, endured three reconstruction surgeries. | | | | | | | | | |
| 4. *Orioles: Adam Loewen, lhp/of, Fraser Valley HS | Surrey, B.C. | L-L | 6-6 | 215 | 18 | $3,200,000 | 2003 | Active | Majors (5) |
| Highest Canadian-born pick ever, signed DFE record deal just before '03 draft; sandwiched MLB career as LHP from 2006-08/2015, around time as OF in 2011. | | | | | | | | | |
| 5. Expos: Clint Everts, rhp, Cypress Falls HS | Houston | B-R | 6-2 | 170 | 17 | $2,500,000 | 2003 | 2013 | Class AAA (4) |
| Less heralded prep teammate of Scott Kazmir, primarily SS before nasty curve elevated draft status; had TJ surgery in 2004, never same again, won 41 pro games. | | | | | | | | | |
| 6. Royals: Zack Greinke, rhp, Apopka HS | Orlando, Fla. | R-R | 6-2 | 185 | 18 | $2,475,000 | 2002 | Active | Majors (12) |
| Set most of school's offensive records, wanted to be pro hitter but stuff/athleticism made him obvious pitcher; MLB career almost derailed by social anxiety issues. | | | | | | | | | |
| 7. Brewers: Prince Fielder, 1b, Eau Gallie HS | Melbourne, Fla. | L-R | 5-11 | 285 | 18 | $2,400,000 | 2002 | Active | Majors (11) |
| Son of former AL HR king was polarizing prospect with oversized frame but peerless power; Brewers gambled, won with his superior plate skills/production. | | | | | | | | | |
| 8. Tigers: Scott Moore, ss, Cypress HS | Cypress, Calif. | L-R | 6-2 | 180 | 18 | $2,300,000 | 2002 | 2015 | Majors (5) |
| Compared to Eric Chavez at bat, Chipper Jones in field, but going nowhere before timely trade to Cubs in 2005; made adjustments, salvaged five MLB seasons. | | | | | | | | | |
| 9. Rockies: Jeff Francis, lhp, British Columbia | Vancouver, B.C. | L-L | 6-5 | 200 | 21 | $1,850,000 | 2002 | 2015 | Majors (11) |
| Joined Loewen as top Canadian 1-2 duo in draft history; put himself on map with 12 shutouts between summer/college ball in '01, had marginal stuff/MLB success. | | | | | | | | | |
| 10. Rangers: Drew Meyer, ss, South Carolina | Charleston, S.C. | L-R | 5-11 | 185 | 20 | $1,875,000 | 2002 | 2010 | Majors (1) |
| Best college athlete in draft with speed, arm strength, but other tools were short in pro ball; never hit enough with unorthodox approach to justify everyday role. | | | | | | | | | |
| 11. Marlins: Jeremy Hermida, of, Wheeler HS | Marietta, Ga. | L-R | 6-4 | 195 | 18 | $2,012,500 | 2002 | 2014 | Majors (8) |
| Best pure bat in prep ranks with advanced approach, consistent contact; hit grand slam in first MLB at-bat, but career (.257-65-250) never took off as expected. | | | | | | | | | |
| 12. Angels: Joe Saunders, lhp, Virginia Tech | Springfield, Va. | L-L | 6-4 | 200 | 20 | $1,825,000 | 2002 | 2015 | Majors (10) |
| Lacked overpowering stuff, but safe pick with feel, strike-throwing ability; injuries impacted career, still won 89 MLB games with fastball/change combo. | | | | | | | | | |
| 13. Padres: Khalil Greene, ss, Clemson | Key West, Fla. | R-R | 5-10 | 190 | 22 | $1,500,000 | 2002 | 2009 | Majors (7) |
| Surged into first round on strength of breakout .470-27-91 senior year; tormented by social-anxiety disorder, walked away from promising MLB career in 2009. | | | | | | | | | |
| 14. Blue Jays: Russ Adams, ss, North Carolina | Laurinburg, N.C. | L-R | 6-1 | 175 | 21 | $1,785,000 | 2002 | 2011 | Majors (5) |
| On fast track to majors with all tools except power, hit .370-7-55 with 45 SBs as college JR, but showed little staying power in majors; hit .247-17-113 in 286 games. | | | | | | | | | |
| 15. Mets: Scott Kazmir, lhp, Cypress Falls HS | Houston | L-L | 6-0 | 175 | 18 | $2,150,000 | 2002 | Active | Majors (11) |
| Most dominant/discussed arm in class, went 19-2, 0.40 (139 IP/301 SO) as prep JR/SR with explosive mid-90s FB; MLB career characterized by big peaks/valleys. | | | | | | | | | |
| 16. Athletics: Nick Swisher, 1b/of, Ohio State | Parkersburg, W.Va. | B-L | 6-0 | 200 | 21 | $1,780,000 | 2002 | Active | Majors (12) |
| Centerpiece of "Moneyball" draft with raw power, advanced on-base skills; had best career of seven first-rounders with nine straight 20-HR seasons, high walk rate. | | | | | | | | | |
| 17. Phillies: Cole Hamels, lhp, Rancho Bernardo HS | San Diego | L-L | 6-3 | 175 | 18 | $2,000,000 | 2003 | Active | Majors (10) |
| Broken left arm as prep JR scared away teams, but shot to majors with command of three plus pitches, poised approach; became one of game's dominant lefties. | | | | | | | | | |
| 18. White Sox: Royce Ring, lhp, San Diego State | San Diego | L-L | 6-0 | 220 | 21 | $1,600,000 | 2002 | 2012 | Majors (5) |
| Led nation with 17 SV on strength of 92-94 FB, knee-buckling curve; struggled with weight/suspect stuff in majors, relegated to set-up role, went 3-3, 5.29, 0 SV. | | | | | | | | | |
| 19. Dodgers: James Loney, 1b/lhp, Elkins HS | Missouri City, Texas | L-L | 6-3 | 205 | 18 | $1,500,000 | 2002 | Active | Majors (10) |
| 1B/LHP on nation's top HS team; generated greater interest on mound, but Dodgers saw more upside with swing, feel for stike zone, superior skills around bag. | | | | | | | | | |
| 20. Twins: Denard Span, of, Tampa Catholic HS | Tampa | L-L | 6-1 | 175 | 18 | $1,700,000 | 2003 | Active | Majors (8) |
| All-state WR compared to Kenny Lofton with elite speed, LH bat with gap power; struggled to reach majors, soon became effective leadoff man, quality defender. | | | | | | | | | |
| 21. Cubs: Bobby Brownlie, rhp, Rutgers | Edison, N.J. | R-R | 6-0 | 210 | 21 | $2,500,000 | 2003 | 2009 | Class AAA (4) |
| No. 1 prospect at outset of spring with 95-96 FB, hammer curve; biceps tendinitis led to velocity drop, shoulder issues blamed for 38-45 mark in minors. | | | | | | | | | |
| 22. *Indians: Jeremy Guthrie, rhp, Stanford | Ashland, Ore. | R-R | 6-1 | 195 | 23 | $3,000,000 | 2003 | Active | Majors (12) |
| Fifth-year college JR spent one year at BYU, two years on Mormon mission, signed $4 million major league contract; polished arm with command of four pitches. | | | | | | | | | |
| 23. Braves: Jeff Francoeur, of, Parkview HS | Lilburn, Ga. | R-R | 6-4 | 205 | 18 | $2,200,000 | 2002 | Active | Majors (11) |
| Best two-sport athlete in draft lured away from Clemson football offer; five-tool potential with strong makeup, but suspect hitting approach limited MLB career. | | | | | | | | | |
| 24. Athletics: Joe Blanton, rhp, Kentucky | Brownsville, Ky. | R-R | 6-3 | 225 | 21 | $1,400,000 | 2002 | Active | Majors (11) |
| Not heavily scouted until he outdueled Bullington in 16-SO effort; ability to throw strikes with average stuff made him consummate .500 pitcher over MLB career. | | | | | | | | | |
| 25. Giants: Matt Cain, rhp, Houston HS | Germantown, Tenn. | R-R | 6-3 | 185 | 17 | $1,375,000 | 2002 | Active | Majors (11) |
| Unheralded arm with FB at 88-94 MPH, got better with every start as prep SR (7-3, 1.02, 62 IP/83 SO); dominated at times in MLB career, spun 2012 perfect game. | | | | | | | | | |
| 26. Athletics: John McCurdy, ss, Maryland | Crofton, Md. | R-R | 6-2 | 200 | 21 | $1,375,000 | 2002 | 2006 | Class AA (1) |
| Breakout season (.443-19-77, 20 SB) proved aberration; struggled to hit with wood in five pro seasons (.254-33-228, 36 SB), never hit stride defensively. | | | | | | | | | |
| 27. Diamondbacks: Sergio Santos, ss/rhp, Mater Dei HS | Hacienda Heights, Calif. | R-R | 6-3 | 200 | 18 | $1,400,000 | 2002 | 2015 | Majors (6) |
| Had tools to excel as SS, but languished until 2009 when Sox converted him to closer; reached big leagues with 97 FB, but plagued by injuries/inconsistency. | | | | | | | | | |
| 28. Mariners: John Mayberry Jr., 1b, Rockhurst HS | Kansas City, Mo. | R-R | 6-5 | 200 | 18 | Unsigned | 2005 | 2015 | Majors (7) |
| Son of John ('66 first-rounder), became two-time first-rounder in 2005 (Rangers); athlete with strength to hit, but MLB career plagued by high SO totals. | | | | | | | | | |
| 29. Astros: Derick Grigsby, rhp, Northeast Texas CC | Marshall, Texas | R-R | 6-0 | 200 | 19 | $1,125,000 | 2003 | 2004 | Class A (2) |
| Texas transfer went 3-7, 3.68, but top juco arm with 95 mph FB, power slider; overcome by depression in short pro career, went 16-20, 4.79 in two Class A seasons. | | | | | | | | | |
| 30. Athletics: Ben Fritz, c/rhp, Fresno State | San Jose, Calif. | R-R | 6-4 | 220 | 21 | $1,200,000 | 2002 | 2008 | Class AAA (1) |
| Legit two-way talent in college with 10 HRs, 9 wins as JR; showed more upside on mound with lively 92-94 FB, but elbow/shoulder issues doomed pro career. | | | | | | | | | |

*Signed to major league contract.

## AT A GLANCE

to catcher after signing with the Dodgers for a $40,000 bonus, and went on to become a four-time all-star. His career far surpassed that of fellow Canadian **ADAM LOEWEN**, the fourth overall pick who followed Martin to Chipola (Fla.) JC before signing with the Orioles for $4.08 million.

### Never Too Late

**BROCK PETERSON, 3B, TWINS (49TH ROUND).** Peterson signed for $50,000 out of a Washington high school. After an 11-year journey through the minors and independent ball, he got a brief major league shot with the Cardinals in 2013, hitting .077 in 23 games.

### Overlooked

**RYAN HANIGAN, C, REDS.** Undrafted out of Division II Rollins (Fla.) College, Hanigan spent the summer playing in the Cape Cod League and improved his stock enough that he signed with the Reds as a free agent. Hanigan played in nine seasons in the majors, the first seven with the Reds.

### International Gem

**FELIX HERNANDEZ, RHP, MARINERS.** Hernandez, a 16-year-old Venezuelan, signed with the Mariners for $710,000. The major international signing that year was Japanese star **HIDEKI MATSUI'S** $21 million deal with the Yankees. Hernandez proved to be one of the greatest values ever on the international market. Through 11 major league seasons, he went 143-101, 3.12, and was still going strong in 2016.

### Minor League Take

**ADAM LOEWEN, LHP/OF, ORIOLES.** Loewen, the highest-drafted Canadian ever, had first-round potential as both a pitcher and hitter. He surfaced with the Orioles as a pitcher from 2006-08, but two

CONTINUED ON PAGE 554

## AT A GLANCE

CONTINUED FROM PAGE 553

stress fractures in his elbow short-circuited his career on the mound. Loewen returned to the minors as an outfielder, got back to the major leagues briefly in 2011, then resumed his pitching career and was back in the major leagues in 2015. He went 28-27, 3.35 in 137 appearances in the minors over a 13-year period, and hit .262 with 57 homers in 561 games in the same span.

### One Who Got Away

**JEFF CLEMENT, C, TWINS (12TH ROUND).** Clement set the high school career home run record with 75 for Marshalltown (Iowa) High. He decided to attend college at Southern California after slipping from a potential first-round pick to the 12th round. He hit 46 homers in three years at USC, and was the third overall pick in 2005.

### He Was Drafted?

**BRANDON WEEDEN, RHP/C, YANKEES (2ND ROUND).** Weeden accepted a $565,000 bonus from the Yankees to forgo college football. After going 19-26, 5.02 in five years in the minors for three organizations, Weeden quit baseball and enrolled at Oklahoma State to play quarterback. He passed for 4,328 yards as a senior and was the Cleveland Browns' first-round pick in the 2012 NFL draft. At 28, he was the oldest NFL first-round pick ever.

### Did You Know . . .

The 2002 draft set still-standing records for Canada, from highest player drafted (**ADAM LOEWEN**, fourth overall) to most Canadians selected overall (48).

### They Said It

Athletics general manager **BILLY BEANE** on his team's so-called "Moneyball" draft: "This is the best draft I've ever been a part of. We got everything we wanted, and more."

favored Upton, only to be overruled by the GM and Pirates owner Kevin McClatchy.

"As much as we could sit here and bemoan that there are no Mark Priors out there," Creech said, "we've still got to play the cards we are dealt. We'll take the best player who's out there. A predraft deal would be convenient, but that's not always the best way to go. Would we like it to happen? Yes. But are we going out of our way to make it happen? No."

The Pirates contacted Bullington's agents at the International Management Group to discuss bonus parameters prior to the draft. They threw out $4 million, and IMG countered at $6 million. The Pirates then made offers to Upton and Loewen, but both declined to counter. Pittsburgh also inquired about Texas high school lefthander Scott Kazmir, although it didn't regard him as highly as some other teams. The Bucs circled back to Bullington, who found out he was the No. 1 pick while listening to MLB's Internet broadcast of the draft.

"I heard it when everyone else did," Bullington said. "I had heard I was in their top three for the last couple of days, but that was it."

Signing the pitcher was a five-month ordeal that ended on Oct. 30 with Bullington accepting about what the Pirates offered the day they drafted him. The longest previous holdout by a No. 1 pick who eventually signed came in 1997, when Rice righthander Matt Anderson came to terms with the Detroit Tigers on Dec. 23.

"I think everyone is happy because everyone comes out a winner," Creech said. "We got the guy we wanted to bring into our organization, and he gets the chance to play professional baseball."

B.J. Upton

Bullington's career did not evolve as the Pirates expected. After three solid but unspectacular seasons in the minors, he was recalled by the Pirates in September 2005 and made one relief appearance before being shut down because of a sore shoulder that required surgery and kept him out of the 2006 season. His shoulder continued to bother him sporadically, and his career floundered. Bullington's only shining moment came on Aug. 15, 2010, with the Kansas City Royals, when he pitched eight scoreless innings and gave up two hits in a 1-0 win over the New York Yankees for his only major league victory.

Upton, selected second by the Devil Rays, and Stanford righthander Jeremy Guthrie, chosen 22nd by the Cleveland Indians, had received the largest signing packages until Bullington signed. Upton's $4.6 million deal was scheduled to be paid out over a five-year period, while Guthrie's contract, a major league deal valued at $4 million, was to be paid out over four years. Bullington's bonus was slated to be paid in full by 2003.

Negotiations between Upton, an athletic, 17-year-old shortstop who hit .641 with 11 home runs and 21 stolen bases as a senior at Greenbrier Christian Academy in Chesapeake, Va., and the Devil Rays stretched until Sept. 11. The cash-strapped club began negotiations with a $3.2 million bonus offer, but only $100,000 payable upon signing. The balance would be spread over five years, allowed by Major League Baseball rules because of Upton's status as a two-sport athlete, although the rule was liberally applied in this case. The 6-foot-3, 180-pound Upton had played football in high school, but never considered pursuing the sport in college. Upton's $4.6 million bonus included only $250,000 payable immediately.

"With his overall package of tools, his athleticism and age on his side, the sky's the limit," Rays general manager Chuck Lamar said. "There's no ceiling on how good he can be depending on how bad he wants it, and we think he has the makeup to use that ability."

Upton's younger brother, Justin, became the No. 1 overall pick in the 2005 draft, making the Uptons the highest-drafted brother combo in draft history. After eight seasons with the Rays, during which he hit .244 with 144 homers and stole 273 bases, B.J. played alongside his brother with the

### How They Should Have Done It

Based on the career WAR (Wins Above Replacement, as calculated by Baseball-Reference.com) numbers achieved by all the players eligible for the 2002 draft through the 2015 season, here's how the first round should have unfolded. Numbers in parentheses indicate the round when the player was actually drafted.

| | Player, Pos. | Actual Draft | WAR | Bonus |
|---|---|---|---|---|
| 1. | Zack Greinke, rhp | Royals (1) | 51.9 | $2,475,000 |
| 2. | Cole Hamels, lhp | Phillies (1) | 46.1 | $2,000,000 |
| 3. | Joey Votto, c | Reds (2) | 43.4 | $600,000 |
| 4. | Curtis Granderson, of | Tigers (3) | 41.8 | $469,000 |
| 5. | Jon Lester, lhp | Red Sox (2) | 34.8 | $1,000,000 |
| 6. | Russell Martin, 3b | Dodgers (17) | 33.3 | $40,000 |
| 7. | Matt Cain, rhp | Giants (1) | 31.7 | $1,375,000 |
| 8. | Howie Kendrick, 2b | Angels (10) | 28.6 | $100,000 |
| 9. | Brian McCann, c | Braves (2) | 27.9 | $750,000 |
| 10. | Prince Fielder, 1b | Brewers (1) | 25.1 | $2,400,000 |
| 11. | Denard Span, of | Twins (1) | 24.0 | $1,700,000 |
| 12. | Josh Johnson, rhp | Marlins (4) | 23.8 | $300,000 |
| 13. | Scott Kazmir, lhp | Mets (1) | 22.8 | $2,150,000 |
| 14. | Nick Swisher, 1b/of | Athletics (1) | 21.7 | $1,780,000 |
| 15. | Jeremy Guthrie, rhp | Indians (1) | 18.2 | $3,000,000 |
| 16. | B.J. Upton, ss | Devil Rays (1) | 14.9 | $4,600,000 |
| 17. | James Loney, 1b | Dodgers (1) | 11.9 | $1,500,000 |
| 18. | Jesse Crain, rhp | Twins (2) | 11.8 | $650,000 |
| 19. | Jason Hammel, rhp | Devil Rays (10) | 11.1 | $65,000 |
| 20. | Chris Denorfia, of | Reds (19) | 10.3 | $1,000 |
| 21. | Joe Blanton, rhp | Athletics (1) | 10.0 | $1,400,000 |
| 22. | Brandon McCarthy, rhp | White Sox (17) | 9.6 | $40,000 |
| 23. | Jeff Francis, lhp | Rockies (1) | 9.3 | $1,850,000 |
| 24. | Jonathan Broxton, rhp | Dodgers (2) | 9.0 | $685,000 |
| 25. | Joe Saunders, lhp | Angels (1) | 8.8 | $1,825,000 |
| | Ryan Hanigan, c | Reds (NDFA) | 8.8 | None |
| 27. | Khalil Greene, ss | Padres (1) | 8.4 | $1,500,000 |
| 28. | Randy Wells, c | Cubs (38) | 7.9 | $11,000 |
| 29. | Nyjer Morgan, of | Pirates (33) | 7.3 | $2,000 |
| 30. | Pat Neshek, rhp | Twins (6) | 6.9 | $132,500 |
| | Craig Breslow, lhp | Brewers (26) | 6.9 | $1,000 |

| | Top 3 Unsigned Players | | | Year Signed |
|---|---|---|---|---|
| 1. | Hunter Pence, of | Brewers (40) | 27.7 | 2004 |
| 2. | Jacoby Ellsbury, of | Devil Rays (23) | 26.3 | 2005 |
| 3. | Jonathan Papelbon, rhp | Athletics (40) | 23.9 | 2003 |

Atlanta Braves during the 2013-14 seasons. The brothers played together again with the San Diego Padres during the 2015 season.

### SIGNABILITY DICTATES SELECTIONS

One of the players notably absent among the top 14 selections was Kazmir. He had been mentioned as a candidate for Cincinnati's pick at No. 3, and Reds officials indicated they were split between Kazmir or California prep righthander Chris Gruler. Both had pitching sessions at Cincinnati's Cinergy Field the weekend prior to the draft, and word spread that Gruler's workout was lackluster and Kazmir's was spectacular.

Reds officials never talked money with Kazmir, who reportedly wanted a bonus in the $4 million range. Instead, they used Kazmir's presence at the workout to leverage Gruler into signing for a $2.5 million bonus—a club record, but little more than half the $4.8 million Dewon Brazelton received as the No. 3 pick in the 2001 draft. An agreement with Gruler was announced soon after he was selected. Kazmir, meanwhile, wasn't selected until the 15th pick, by the New York Mets.

Gruler's fastball was clocked as high as 97 mph during his first year in the Reds system. The following year at Class A Dayton, he gave up 19 runs in less than six innings in his first three starts. He subsequently had shoulder surgery, and his career was as good as over. He went 3-5, 5.08 in 27 career appearances, none above Class A.

With Gruler's bonus setting the tone, 12 of the first 14 players drafted agreed on bonuses less than what the corresponding picks received in 2001. Over the next 16 slots, all but one pick earned more than players in a similar slot in 2001. For the first time in draft history, every first-rounder who signed received a bonus of at least $1 million.

Some thought the Texas Rangers would draft Kazmir with the No. 10 pick, their only selection in the first five rounds after investing heavily in major league free agents the previous offseason. Instead, the Rangers took South Carolina shortstop Drew Meyer, the first college position player drafted. He signed quickly for $1.875 million. Meyer was considered the best college athlete in the draft, but few thought he would hit well enough to be an everyday player in the big leagues, and they were right. His major league career amounted to five games.

The next two college position players also were shortstops: Clemson's Khalil Greene, chosen by the Padres with the 13th selection; and North Carolina's Russ Adams, claimed a pick later by the Toronto Blue Jays. Greene enjoyed a spectacular senior season, hitting .470 with 27 home runs

### Fastest To The Majors

| | Player, Pos. | Drafted (Round) | Debut |
|---|---|---|---|
| 1. | Kevin Correia, rhp | Giants (4) | July 10, 2003 |
| 2. | Khalil Greene, ss | Padres (1) | Sept. 3, 2003 |
| 3. | * Zack Greinke, rhp | Royals (1) | May 22, 2004 |
| 4. | Lance Cormier, rhp | Diamondbacks (4) | June 19, 2004 |
| | Brad Halsey, lhp | Yankees (8) | June 19, 2004 |

**High school selection.*

### DRAFT SPOTLIGHT: ZACK GREINKE

LARRY SMITH

**Zack Greinke overcame depression and social anxiety disorder as he rose through the Royals system to become one of the best pitchers in baseball**

Zack Greinke, Khalil Greene and Derick Grigsby were all first-round selections in the 2002 draft, but more significantly all three were afflicted by mental illnesses that impacted their careers.

Greinke was able to overcome social anxiety disorder and achieve a long and successful major league career that was still going strong in 2016. Greene and Grigsby were not as fortunate. Greene also suffered from social anxiety disorder, while Grigsby dealt with depression.

The Kansas City Royals selected Greinke with the sixth overall pick and signed him for a $2.475 million bonus. He was in the major leagues two years later at age 20. By 2006, haunted by depression and anxiety, the introverted Greinke hated going to the ballpark. He walked out on the Royals during spring training with no plans of ever returning.

The Royals stepped back and gave Greinke the time he needed to work on his challenges. "We had no idea if he was going to come back," pitching coach Bob McClure said, "but we also knew this wasn't about baseball, it was about a young man and his life."

McClure, new to the Royals in 2006, experienced firsthand the anguish Greinke was experiencing. He called McClure aside during his first bullpen session that spring and said: "I have three things to tell you. No. 1, I'm not going to throw a two-seam fastball. No. 2, I'm not going to throw a changeup. No. 3, I don't like listening to pitching coaches."

With that, Greinke finished the session by defiantly throwing nothing but fastballs. He walked away the following day. The Royals had sensed that Greinke was unhappy, but didn't realize the extent of his distress. Upon returning home to Florida, Greinke saw a psychologist, who diagnosed his condition and prescribed antidepressants for him.

After several weeks away, a reinvigorated Greinke returned to baseball, spending the balance of 2006 at Double-A before being promoted to the Royals in September. By 2009, with the help of continued counseling and medication, he had blossomed into one of the best pitchers in baseball, winning the American League Cy Young Award for a 65-97 team.

Greinke grew tired of playing for a losing team and asked the Royals to trade him. They sent him to the Brewers, where he went 16-6 in 2011. Then he was off to the Dodgers, where he went 57-17 over a four-year period before signing one of the richest contracts in history with the Diamondbacks prior to the 2016 season.

Greene had one of the best seasons in college history as a senior at Clemson in 2002 and was the 13th player selected in 2002, going to the Padres. He was their everyday shortstop a year later and was Baseball America's Rookie of the Year in 2004. He had a breakout season in 2007, with 27 homers, 97 RBIs and just 11 errors.

After an injury-plagued 2008 season, he was traded to the Cardinals, and developed an intense fear of failure. Greene reached a point that he would try to inflict pain on himself as a form of punishment. He was treated for social anxiety disorder, but two stays on the disabled list in 2009 to regroup didn't seem to help. Greene was 29 when he quit baseball, frozen at 736 major league games, a .245 batting average and 90 home runs.

"One of the things that people don't really see is how he internalizes so much," Padres manager Bud Black said. "He doesn't let it out, but he's a player who cares a great deal about his performance to the point where it gets to him. I wish he could just let go, and enjoy how good he is. But for whatever reason, he can't do it."

Grigsby, a righthander, was the 29th pick in the first round, drafted by the Astros out of Northeast Texas CC. He played in just two minor league seasons before leaving baseball, unable to overcome depression. Grigsby's 38-year-old mother died unexpectedly in 2001 during bladder surgery, and his father was seriously injured in a motorcycle accident a year later. Grigsby had purchased the motorcycle with part of his bonus money.

Grigsby spent his freshman season at Texas, pitching in only 11 innings in the wake of mother's death. He transferred to Northeast Texas to be closer to home and developed into the top juco pitching prospect in the 2002 draft. He never developed as a pro. After going 14-18, 4.79 during the 2003-04 seasons at low-level leagues, he left the game.

## WORTH NOTING

■ For the second year in a row, a third baseman selected by the Athletics died within weeks after being drafted. Louisiana State third baseman **WALLY PONTIFF**, a 21st-round pick, died at his parents' home in Metairie, La., on July 24, of what was determined to be a heart abnormality. A year earlier, Washington high school third baseman **MARK HILDE**, a 32nd-round pick, was killed in a vehicle driven by Padres former first-rounder **GERIK BAXTER** that crashed near Indio, Calif.

■ Texas A&M didn't make the 64-team NCAA regional field, but had more players drafted that any other school (11). Texas, the College World Series champion, had eight. At the prep level, Durango High of Las Vegas and Xaverian High of Brooklyn each had five players drafted. Florida's St. Petersburg JC had more players drafted (9) than any junior college, but fell short of winning the Florida state tournament.

■ Rutgers righthander **BOBBY BROWNLIE** received the top grade from the Major League Scouting Bureau for players in the 2002 draft pool. Brownlie got a 61 on the 20-80 scouting scale. Two-way Canadian talent **ADAM LOEWEN**, the fourth overall pick, graded out at 60 as a pitcher and 52 as an outfielder, and reached the majors in both roles.

■ Teams held the line on signing bonuses in the first five rounds, paying players according to their draft slot. But those guidelines went out the window in later rounds. Five bonus records were set for different rounds, four by players who signed as draft-and-follows in 2003. Washington high school first baseman **TRAVIS ISHIKAWA**, a 21st round pick, received a $955,000 bonus from the Giants. "We obviously had him much higher on our draft board," Giants GM Brian Sabean said.

■ Loewen set the all-time bonus record for a draft-and-

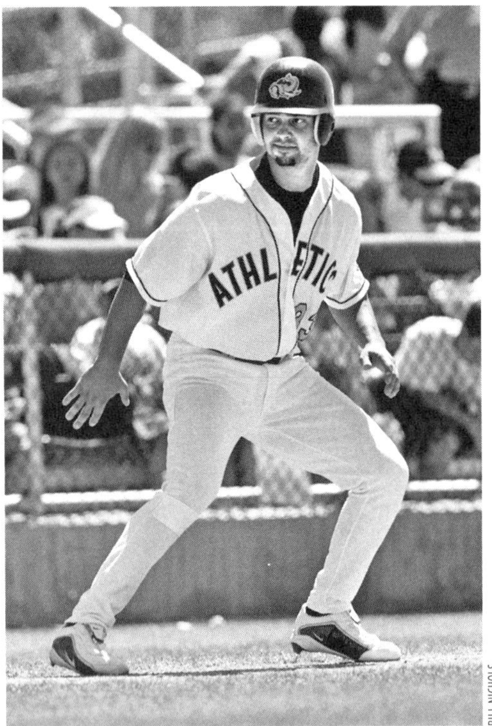


BILL NICHOLS

**Nick Swisher, the son of former big leaguer Steve, was the most successful big leaguer from the Athletics' Moneyball draft class**

and 91 RBIs, and leading the NCAA ranks in runs (93), hits (134), doubles (33) and total bases (250). He had the most successful major league career of the three college shortstops, although it was cut short after seven seasons when Greene developed a social anxiety disorder.

After Greene and Adams, it finally was Kazmir's turn. The 6-foot lefty had an explosive 95-96 mph fastball and two other above-average pitches. He drew comparisons with two other undersized lefthanders, Billy Wagner and Ron Guidry, and might have been a candidate to go No. 1 overall if he was taller. Kazmir went 11-2, 0.37 with 19 walks and 172 strikeouts in 75 innings as a senior at Houston's Cypress Falls High and was Baseball America's High School Player of the Year.

Kazmir agreed to a $2.15 million bonus on Aug. 2, and did not dwell on being drafted later than he expected. "There are a lot of rumors going around, like I wanted $100 million or whatever," he said. "I don't know what it is. I'm just happy I'm with the Mets."

Kazmir wasn't even the first player on his high school team to be drafted. That honor went to righthander/shortstop Clint Everts, drafted by the Montreal Expos with the fifth pick overall. Cy Falls became the fourth high school ever to produce two first-round picks in the same draft.

Everts had an excellent curveball to go with a 91-94 mph fastball, and at 6-foot-2, 170 pounds had a more projectable frame than Kazmir. Everts went 9-3, 1.30 with 28 walks and 157 strikeouts in 81 innings as a senior, and excelled as a shortstop with his switch-hitting skills and superior defense.

Everts signed on Aug. 24 for a $2.5 million bonus, $350,000 more than Kazmir received. Everts pitched 11 years in pro ball, but he did not reach the major leagues. He never was the same after Tommy John surgery in 2004. In 341 minor league appearances with three organizations, he went 41-46, 4.11.

Kazmir became a two-time all-star with the Rays before injuries short-circuited his career in his late 20s. He played independent ball and winter league ball in 2012, launching a comeback that got him back to the major leagues. He became an all-star with the A's in 2015, and signed a three-year, $48 million contract with the Los Angeles Dodgers prior to the 2016 season.

For all the attention paid to Kazmir and other high school pitchers in the 2002 class, Greinke proved to be the best of the bunch. Selected sixth overall by the Royals, Greinke primarily was a power-hitting shortstop at Apopka (Fla.) High, hitting 31 homers during his four years and never batting less than .444 in a season. Greinke pitched in relief as a sophomore and junior. Moved into the rotation as a senior, he went 9-2, 0.55 with 118 strikeouts, 8 walks and 22 hits in 63 innings. He had command of five pitches, including a fastball that touched 97 mph, and showed instincts for pitching well beyond his years.

"Zack is not only athletic, but a very advanced high school pitcher," Royals scouting director Deric Ladnier said. "When he does make a mistake with a pitch, he knows he makes a mistake and why he makes a mistake. He'll step back off the mound and make an adjustment. I saw him four times, and every time it was lights out. We feel like he's a guy who can move quickly through our minor league system and get to the major leagues in a hurry."

Greinke did in fact breeze through the minors, posting a 16-5, 2.05 record with 27 walks and 144 strikeouts in 180 innings. He was in the major leagues by age 20, but struggled until doctors were

### Top 25 Bonuses

| Player, Pos. | Drafted (Round) | Order | Bonus |
|---|---|---|---|
| **1. *B.J. Upton, ss** | **Devil Rays (1)** | **2** | **$4,600,000** |
| **2. Brian Bullington, rhp** | **Pirates (1)** | **1** | **$4,000,000** |
| **3.*#Adam Loewen, lhp/of** | **Orioles (1)** | **4** | **$3,200,000** |
| **4. Jeremy Guthrie, rhp** | **Indians (1)** | **22** | **$3,000,000** |
| 5. * Chris Gruler, rhp | Reds (1) | 3 | $2,500,000 |
| * Clint Everts, rhp | Expos (1) | 5 | $2,500,000 |
| Bobby Brownlie, rhp | Cubs (1) | 21 | $2,500,000 |
| **8. * Zack Greinke, rhp** | **Royals (1)** | **6** | **$2,475,000** |
| **9. * Prince Fielder, 1b** | **Brewers (1)** | **7** | **$2,375,000** |
| **10. * Scott Moore, ss** | **Tigers (1)** | **8** | **$2,300,000** |
| **11. * Jeff Francoeur, of** | **Braves (1)** | **23** | **$2,200,000** |
| **12. * Scott Kazmir, lhp** | **Mets (1)** | **15** | **$2,150,000** |
| **13. * Jeremy Hermida, of** | **Marlins (1)** | **11** | **$2,012,500** |
| **14. * Cole Hamels, lhp** | **Phillies (1)** | **17** | **$2,000,000** |
| **15. Drew Meyer, ss** | **Rangers (1)** | **10** | **$1,875,000** |
| **16. Jeff Francis, lhp** | **Rockies (1)** | **9** | **$1,850,000** |
| **17. Joe Saunders, lhp** | **Angels (1)** | **12** | **$1,825,000** |
| **18. Russ Adams, ss** | **Blue Jays (1)** | **14** | **$1,785,000** |
| **19. Nick Swisher, 1b/of** | **Athletics (1)** | **16** | **$1,775,000** |
| **20. * Denard Span, of** | **Twins (1)** | **20** | **$1,700,000** |
| **21. Royce Ring, lhp** | **White Sox (1)** | **18** | **$1,600,000** |
| **22. Khalil Greene, ss** | **Padres (1)** | **13** | **$1,500,000** |
| *** James Loney, 1b** | **Dodgers (1)** | **19** | **$1,500,000** |
| **24. Joe Blanton, rhp** | **Athletics (1)** | **24** | **$1,400,000** |
| **25. * Sergio Santos, ss** | **Diamondbacks (1)** | **27** | **$1,400,000** |

*Major leaguers in bold. *High school selection. #Signed as draft-and-follow.*

## Largest Bonuses By Round

| | Player, Pos. | Club | Bonus |
|---|---|---|---|
| **1.** | *** B.J. Upton, ss** | **Devil Rays** | **$4,600,000** |
| 1-S. | * Greg Miller, lhp | Dodgers | $1,200,000 |
| **2.** | *** Jon Lester, lhp** | **Red Sox** | **$1,000,000** |
| 3. | * Mike Nixon, c | Dodgers | $950,000 |
| 4. | *# Wardell Starling, rhp | Pirates | $500,000 |
| **5.** | *** Hayden Penn, rhp** | **Orioles** | **$300,000** |
| 6. | * Cody Haerther, 3b | Cardinals | $250,000 |
| **7.** | *** Tom Wilhelmsen, rhp** | **Brewers** | **$250,000** |
| 8. | James Holcomb, rhp | Angels | $185,000 |
| 9. | * Tyler Pelland, lhp | Red Sox | $240,000 |
| 10. | Brian Stitt, rhp | Mariners | $120,000 |
| 11. | Kiki Bengochea, rhp | Rangers | $550,000 |
| **12.** | **Mike Esposito, rhp** | **Rockies** | **$750,000** |
| 13. | # Reid Santos, lhp | Indians | $412,500 |
| 14. | Darin Naatjes, rhp | Phillies | $600,000 |
| **15.** | **Kila Kaaihue, 1b** | **Royals** | **$87,500** |
| **16.** | **# Dana Eveland, lhp** | **Brewers** | **$336,000** |
| 17. | * Randy Braun, of | Blue Jays | $250,000 |
| 18. | * Bryan Millikan, rhp | Giants | $750,000 |
| 19. | * Cole Smith, rhp | Devil Rays | $225,000 |
| **20.** | **# George Kottaras, c** | **Padres** | **$300,000** |
| **21.** | *** Travis Ishikawa, 1b** | **Giants** | **$955,000** |
| 22. | Scott Hindman, lhp | Angels | $122,500 |
| **23.** | *** Eric Hacker, rhp** | **Yankees** | **$150,000** |
| 24. | * Brett Martinez, c | Angels | $90,000 |
| 25. | # Nick Pesco, rhp | Indians | $465,000 |
| **Other** | **# Jared Wells, rhp** | **Padres (31)** | **$400,000** |

*Major leaguers in bold. *High school selection. #Signed as draft-and-follow.*

able to bring his anxiety condition under control with medication. Greinke soon became one of the game's best pitchers, and by the end of the 2015 season had a 140-93, 3.36 record.

### LOEWEN HEADLINES CANADIAN PICKS

The Baltimore Orioles had the No. 4 pick in the 2002 draft and made Loewen, a two-way player from Surrey, B.C., the highest-drafted Canadian ever. Five picks later, the Colorado Rockies selected another Canadian, University of British Columbia lefthander Jeff Francis. The pitchers grew up within five miles of each other in the suburbs of Vancouver. Neither of Canada's major league teams had a chance to draft Loewen, and the Expos showed only passing interest in Francis.

Francis agreed quickly on a $1.85 million bonus, while Loewen engaged in one of the longest negotiations ever for a first-rounder. Baltimore initially offered $2 million, while Loewen and agent Michael Moye sought $4.8 million. The Orioles moved to $2.5 million, and the Loewen camp came down to $3.9 million.

With negotiations at a stalemate, Loewen decided to head for college. He initially planned to attend Arizona State, but instead enrolled at Chipola (Fla.) JC, which allowed him to continue negotiations with the Orioles until just before the 2003 draft. Loewen was the first first-rounder to opt for a juco since the draft-and-follow era began in 1986, when the January draft was phased out.

The 6-foot-6, 210-pound Loewen went 6-1, 2.47 as a freshman, showing a fastball that consistently registered between 90-94 mph and a curveball rated as major league ready. Loewen had until midnight on May 26, 2003, to strike a deal with the Orioles, and it happened in the final hour, when they offered a major league contract worth $4.02 million—a $3.2 million signing bonus spread over four years and at least $820,000 in salary over five years. It was essentially the same package he had sought the previous summer.

Loewen reached the major leagues as a starting pitcher in 2006, but elbow injuries over a three-year period all but ended his career as a pitcher. He was released after the 2008 season and headed back to the minor leagues in an attempt to resurrect his career as an outfielder. He made it with the Blue Jays in that capacity briefly in 2011, then hung on for two more years in the minors. By that time, Loewen no longer had pain in his elbow and decided to try pitching again. He got a minor league deal with the Phillies in April 2014, and a year later was throwing 95 mph. Loewen made 20 relief appearances for the Phillies to close out the 2015 season, pitching in the big leagues for the first time in seven years.

Francis had a more conventional career as a big league pitcher, going 72-82, 4.98 in 252 appearances over 11 seasons.

Loewen and Francis were among a record 48 Canadians drafted in 2002. The best, by far, proved to be then-catcher Joey Votto, a second-round pick of the Reds out of a Toronto high school. Entering the 2016 season, he had hit .311 with 192 homers and 633 RBIs in nine seasons as the Reds first baseman, and was the National League MVP in 2010. Other Canadians drafted in 2002 who thrived in the major leagues included righthander Jesse Crain, a second-round pick of the Twins, and third baseman Russell Martin, a 17th-round pick of the Dodgers, who switched positions to catcher.

LARRY GOREN

Jeff Francis

### BORAS CLIENTS PASSED OVER

The common theme among players who fell in the draft was their association with agent Scott Boras. Two of the best college pitchers, Brownlie and Guthrie, slid from the top third of the first round to the bottom third because of signability concerns. Clemson infielder Jeff Baker and hard-throwing high school pitchers Mark McCormick and Jason Neighborgall were projected as first-rounders, but did not get drafted until later.

"It was interesting to see where some of the Boras guys fell," one scouting director said. "They really tumbled. The feeling I got from a lot of our scouts was that those guys didn't show the ability of a premium guy, and it's not worth going through the battle. His guys didn't separate themselves."

Boras' hardline approach was evident in the 2000 and '01 drafts, when several of his clients slipped out of the first round yet still were paid first-round money when teams relented rather than lose the player. By late August 2002, Boras had struck deals

### WORTH NOTING

follow player, getting $3.2 million as part of a $4.02 million major league contract on the eve of the 2003 draft. The next largest contracts for draft-and-follow players were given to Clemson first baseman **MICHAEL JOHNSON** (second round, Padres) and Texas junior college righthander **WARDELL STARLING** (fourth, Pirates), who each signed for $500,000. Johnson had returned to school as a fifth-year senior, which enabled the Padres to retain his rights until just before the 2003 draft.

■ Major League Baseball owners and the union agreed in principle to significant changes in the draft as part of a new Basic Agreement that was up for renewal on Aug. 30, 2002. But in the haste to get a deal in place and avoid a work stoppage, the draft changes were tabled. The focal point of the changes was compensation for draft choices. Teams that failed to sign a first-round pick would be entitled to a bonus choice in the next year's draft. For instance, if a team did not sign the No. 3 overall pick, it would receive a choice after the third selection a year later. Under existing rules, teams received a pick between the first and second rounds, which often fell between the 35th and 40th choice overall. Sandy Alderson, Major League Baseball's executive vice president of baseball operations, said the intent of the new rule was to give teams greater leverage. There also was talk of a worldwide draft, the possible trading of draft picks and a potential reduction in the number of rounds from 50 to 20-38. The proposed changes never were enacted, largely because the owners and the union in subsequent meetings couldn't agree on the specific terms when the Basic Agreement was being finalized. Both sides agreed to revert to the old rules and revisit the proposals at a later date. More than a decade later, the draft remained largely unchanged.

CONTINUED ON PAGE 558

**WORTH NOTING**

CONTINUED FROM PAGE 557

Beyond "Moneyball," a compelling storyline in 2002 was a chase by four players to become the all-time high school home run leader. Entering the season, 6-foot-1, 205-pound **JEFF CLEMENT**, a senior at Marshalltown (Iowa) High and one of the nation's top catching prospects, had 59 homers, 11 shy of the career mark set in 1998 by Drew Henson. Clement pushed the record to 75 homers. Another Iowa player, **JAMES PETERSON** of Winterset High, finished his career with 73 homers, although his official number is 68. Peterson hit five homers as an eighth grader, and the National Federation of State High School Associations recognizes statistics only from grades 9-12. Four of the top five home run hitters in prep history completed their careers in 2002. **MICAH OWINGS** of Gainesville (Ga.) High finished with 69, and **KEVIN BOOKOUT** of Stroud (Okla.) High had 65. Clement slipped to the 12th round, picked by the Twins. He did not sign, and instead attended college at Southern California and was the No. 3 overall pick in the 2005 draft. Owings, an unsigned second-round pick of the Rockies, attended Georgia Tech and later got to the major leagues as a pitcher. Peterson wasn't drafted in 2002, but he signed with the Dodgers as a 16th-round pick in 2003 after a year in junior college. Bookout, an exceptional athlete, was never drafted in baseball. He set national high school records in the discus and shot put, excelled in basketball at the University of Oklahoma, and tried out for the NFL. He wasn't Oklahoma's only all-around star. **BRANDON WEEDEN** of Edmond Santa Fe High was a highly recruited quarterback and an all-state baseball player. Drafted in the second round by the Yankees as a pitcher, Weeden signed for a $565,000 bonus. After going 19-26, 5.02 in five minor league seasons, he went to Oklahoma State to play football.

for righthander Blake Hawksworth, a 28th-round draft-and-follow player from 2001 who signed with the St. Louis Cardinals on the eve of the 2002 draft for $1.475 million; and righthander Kiki Bengochea, an 11th-round pick of the Rangers who received a $550,000 deal, which was comparable to late second-round money. The agent, though, had other clients who had yet to sign.

Boras long maintained that players should be paid what their talent warranted, regardless of where they were drafted. In the case of Brownlie (Cubs, 21st overall) and Guthrie, Boras said both deserved more than slot money (roughly $1.5 million) and were willing to wait for what he deemed to be fair deals.

Brownlie complemented a 94-96 mph fastball with a hammer curve, and initially was considered the top overall prospect in the 2002 draft pool. But he developed a sore arm during his junior season at Rutgers and went just 6-6, 3.53 with 66 strikeouts in 79 innings. An MRI exam prior to the draft showed no serious issues with Brownlie's arm. Doctors diagnosed the soreness as biceps tendinitis and a bruise near the humerus bone.

Bobby Brownlie

Brownlie's arm issues, as well as his reported $4 million asking price and association with Boras, scared off many clubs, but the Cubs were not among them. "I wasn't shocked, but I was somewhat surprised he was still there," Cubs scouting director John Stockstill said. "Bobby was at the top of our list, and we knew we might get somewhere close. But you never know."

Brownlie and the Cubs didn't agree on a deal until the following May. He received a $2.5 million bonus, equivalent to what Gruler and Everts had received as the third and fifth overall picks. In four seasons in the Cubs organization, Brownlie never showed the same electric stuff he had shown in college. After going 3-14, 6.33 in Double-A and Triple-A in 2006, he was released. Brownlie kicked around with three other organizations and in independent ball before giving up in 2009.

Guthrie was a polished college pitcher, and the Indians thought he might be the first player from the 2002 class to reach the major leagues. That timetable was delayed because Guthrie didn't sign until Oct. 3, getting a four-year, $4 million deal that included a club-record $3 million bonus. He started his college career in 1998 at Brigham Young, then spent two years on a Mormon mission, and upon his return enrolled at Stanford, where he went 13-2, 2.51 in 2002. Guthrie didn't win a game for the Indians from 2004-06, but settled into a respectable career with other clubs, going 91-108, 4.37 in 12 major league seasons.

One of Boras' biggest challenges was getting a deal for Baker, who at one point was considered the top college position prospect in the draft. Once teams heard Baker wanted at least $2 million, he fell to the fourth round. Baker, who hit .325 with 25 homers and 87 RBIs during his junior season at Clemson, didn't sign until October, when the Rockies gave him what Boras wanted: a four-year major league deal that guaranteed $2 million and included a $200,000 signing bonus. Baker hung around the major leagues in a journeyman capacity for 11 seasons, hitting .264 with 54 homers.

Neighborgall (Red Sox, seventh round) and McCormick (Orioles, 11th round) fell further than most of Boras' clients. Neighborgall attended Georgia Tech rather than sign, and McCormick enrolled at Baylor. A third high school player represented by Boras, righthander Mike Pelfrey (Devil Rays, 15th), ended up at Wichita State and was a first-round pick three years later.

Other Boras clients were Purdue righthander Chadd Blasko, a supplemental first-round pick of the Cubs, and University of California righthander Trevor Hutchinson, a third-round choice of the Florida Marlins. Blasko signed for $1.05 million,

## Highest Unsigned Picks

| Player, Pos., Team (Round) | College | Re-Drafted |
|---|---|---|
| John Mayberry Jr., 1b, Mariners (1) | Stanford | Rangers '05 (1) |
| Micah Owings, rhp, Rockies (2) | Georgia Tech | Cubs '04 (19) |
| Tyler Greene, ss, Braves (2) | Georgia Tech | Cardinals '05 (1) |
| Mark Sauls, rhp, Twins (3) | Florida State | Never |
| Eddy Martinez-Esteve, of, Mariners (3) | Florida State | Giants '04 (2) |
| Mark Romanczuk, lhp, Devil Rays (4) | Stanford | D-backs '05 (4) |
| Jarrad Page, of, Brewers (5) | UCLA | Brewers '05 (32) |
| Nick Hundley, c, Marlins (5) | Arizona | Padres '05 (2) |
| Clete Thomas, of, Twins (5) | Auburn | Tigers '05 (6) |
| Shawn Scobee, of, Cubs (5) | CS Fullerton | Blue Jays '06 (14) |

**TOTAL UNSIGNED PICKS:** Top 5 Rounds (13), Top 10 Rounds (33)

## One Team's Draft: Oakland Athletics

| | Player, Pos. | Bonus |
|---|---|---|
| **1.** | **Nick Swisher, 1b** | **$1,775,000** |
| **1.** | **Joe Blanton, rhp** | **$1,400,000** |
| 1. | John McCurdy, ss | $1,375,000 |
| 1. | Ben Fritz, rhp | $1,200,000 |
| **1.** | **Jeremy Brown, c** | **$350,000** |
| 1. | Steve Obenchain, rhp | $750,000 |
| **1.** | **Mark Teahen, 3b** | **$725,000** |
| 2. | Steve Stanley, of | $200,000 |
| **3.** | **Bill Murphy, lhp** | **$400,000** |
| **4.** | **John Baker, c** | **$268,000** |
| **5.** | **Mark Kiger, ss** | **$70,000** |
| 6. | Brian Stavisky, of | $170,000 |
| 7. | Brant Colamarino, 1b | $92,500 |
| **8.** | **Jared Burton, rhp** | **$75,000** |
| **9.** | **Shane Komine, rhp** | **$17,500** |
| 10. | J.R. Pickens, rhp | $55,000 |
| 11. | Justin Crowder, lhp | $5,000 |
| 12. | Kirk Nordness, of | $4,000 |
| 13. | Tyler Klippenstein, 3b | $32,500 |
| 14. | Brad Knox, rhp | $22,500 |
| 15. | Chris Dunwell, rhp | $22,500 |
| 16. | Lloyd Turner, 2b | $2,500 |
| 17. | Dave Harriman, c | $2,500 |
| 18. | *Jose Corchado, rhp | $15,000 |
| 19. | *Dusty Barnard, rhp | Did not sign |
| **20.** | ***Trevor Crowe, ss** | **Did not sign** |
| 21. | Wally Pontiff, 3b | Did not sign |
| 22. | Shawn Kohn, rhp | $2,000 |
| 23. | Chris Shank, rhp | $10,000 |
| 24. | Danny Gibbons, of | $7,500 |
| 25. | Steve Schlisky, rhp | $35,000 |
| **Other** | ***Jonathan Papelbon (40), rhp** | **Did not sign** |

*Major leaguers in bold. *High school selection.*

and Hutchinson for $375,000. Neither reached the major leagues.

## SIGNABILITY INFLUENCES SELECTIONS

Aside from the players represented by Boras, the first-rounders most affected by signability concerns were three high school players: California lefthander Cole Hamels (Phillies, 17th overall), Georgia outfielder Jeff Francoeur (Braves, 23rd) and Missouri outfielder John Mayberry Jr. (Mariners, 28th). Francoeur agreed to terms on July 8, while Hamels stretched out negotiations before signing on Aug. 28. Mayberry didn't sign and enrolled at Stanford; he was the only unsigned first-rounder.

Francoeur, a prep All-America defensive back at Parkview High in Lilburn, Ga., and a Clemson football recruit, was the only first-rounder with legitimate two-sport potential. He sent a fax to MLB teams two days before the draft indicating that he wanted a $4 million bonus. The Braves made a predraft offer less than that figure and were told that another team, believed to be the Boston Red Sox, had agreed to the amount. The Braves drafted Francoeur anyway and signed him for a club-record $2.2 million bonus.

Francoeur was one of the most athletic players in the draft and a legitimate five-tool prospect. He hit 29 homers in his first full season with the Braves, and a year later batted .293 with 105 RBIs and won a Gold Glove. Francoeur's ultimate success was undone by a lack of plate discipline, though he carved out a long major league career with seven different teams.

Hamels, a product of San Diego prep baseball power Rancho Bernardo High, missed his junior season after breaking the humerus bone in his left arm. A year later, showing command of three quality pitches, he went 10-0, 0.39 with 130 strikeouts in 71 innings, prompting at least one club to rate him as the top pitcher available. The Phillies signed Hamels for $2 million, and he soon launched a highly successful career. By the end of the 2015 season, he had won 117 big league games and trailed only Greinke among 2002 draftees.

MIKE JANES

Cole Hamels

Mayberry, a son of former all-star first baseman John Mayberry, was under consideration by at least two clubs picking in the top 10, but he fell to the end of the first round after telling clubs that he wanted $3 million. The Mariners didn't come close, and Mayberry was off to Stanford. He was a 2005 first-round pick of the Rangers.

Mayberry was one of three first-round picks whose fathers were former major league all-stars. The others were Prince Fielder and Swisher.

Fielder, a Florida high school first baseman, was chosen seventh overall by the Milwaukee Brewers. His father, Cecil, led the American League in homers twice and in RBIs on three occasions during the 1990s. The 5-foot-11, 275-pound Fielder was perhaps the best power-hitting prospect in the draft. In a predraft workout at Milwaukee's Miller Park, he launched two balls into the upper deck.

Brewers special-assignment scout Bill Lajoie was the general manager of the Tigers when Cecil Fielder played for the team. Lajoie remembered 12-year-old Prince taking batting practice at Tiger Stadium and driving balls into the upper deck.

Fielder lived up to his draft slot. In seven seasons with the Brewers before leaving as a free agent after the 2011 season, he hit .282 with 230 homers.

Swisher's father, Steve, was a catcher who played in nine major league seasons after being a 1973 first-round draft choice of the White Sox. The younger Swisher, the first of Oakland's four first-round selections, hit .348 with 10 home runs and 52 RBIs in his junior season at Ohio State.

## MONEYBALL OFFERS UNIQUE TWIST

Oakland's draft room erupted when the team called Swisher's name with its first pick, No. 16 in the first round. "Swisher was a guy we liked from the beginning," A's scouting director Eric Kubota said. "We felt very confident with his ability and instincts. As it got closer to our pick, when somebody else's name got called, a cheer went up. When we finally got him, everybody was cheering and yelling."

Swisher was the rallying point of Oakland's "Moneyball" draft, in which the A's made a concerted attempt to identify undervalued assets (notably, the ability to reach base), much like financial traders on Wall Street took advantage of derivative securities in the 1980s and made fortunes. A's general manager Billy Beane believed his small-market club could compete for a fraction of what other clubs were spending on talent. His aim was to implement quantitative analysis to maximize profits and minimize inefficiency.

Swisher hit .250 with 244 homers and 801 RBIs in 12 major league seasons and was still active in 2016. Blanton, too, had success in the big leagues, going 90-91, 4.45 over 11 years, including five with the A's, after being chosen with the 24th pick overall. Shortstop John McCurdy (26th overall) and righthander Ben Fritz (30th) did not reach the majors.

"Moneyball" fueled considerable debate in the scouting community, pitting old-school methods against advanced analytical metrics. If nothing else, it shone light on the pitfalls of player procurement at the amateur level.

### Largest Draft-And-Follow Bonuses

| | Player, Pos. | Club (Round) | Bonus |
|---|---|---|---|
| **1.** | ***Adam Loewen, lhp/of** | **Orioles (1)** | **$3,200,000** |
| 2. | Michael Johnson, 1b | Padres (2) | $500,000 |
| | *Wardell Starling, rhp | Pirates (4) | $500,000 |
| 4. | Nick Pesco, rhp | Indians (25) | $465,000 |
| 5. | Reid Santos, lhp | Indians (13) | $412,500 |
| 6. | Jared Wells, rhp | Padres (31) | $400,000 |
| **7.** | **Dana Eveland, lhp** | **Brewers (16)** | **$336,000** |
| **8.** | **Tim Dillard, c** | **Brewers (34)** | **$300,000** |
| | **George Kottaras, c** | **Padres (20)** | **$300,000** |
| **10.** | ***Boone Logan, lhp** | **White Sox (20)** | **$250,000** |

*Major leaguers in bold. *High school selection.*

### IN FOCUS: JEREMY BROWN

BRIAN WESTERHOLT

With their celebrated "Moneyball" draft, the Oakland A's applied progressive thinking over conventional baseball wisdom and made a concerted attempt to take advantage of undervalued assets in the draft. The A's targeted players such as University of Alabama senior Jeremy Brown in the early rounds. He was representative of college players who had premium on-base ability, which the A's regarded as the most undervalued asset in the game.

Brown, a 5-foot-10, 225-pound catcher, was appealing to the A's because he hit well (.320-11-64) and had a discerning eye (NCAA-leading 69 walks), while other clubs rated him as a marginal athlete lacking the skills to become a major league catcher. Some projected Brown as a late-round choice worth no more than a $5,000 signing bonus. The A's chose him with a supplemental first-round pick and gave him a $350,000 bonus.

He came to symbolize Oakland's unique approach to roster building. Brown reached the majors briefly in 2006 and garnered three hits in 10 at-bats for the A's, but had an unfulfilled six-year career overall and had to live with the burden of his unfavorable portrayal in "Moneyball" throughout his professional odyssey before retiring in 2008 for what were described as "personal, off-the-field issues."

# 2002 Draft List

**Did not sign. Major leaguers in bold, with first and last years noted. Order of selection indicated in parentheses. For the first five rounds, the peak level of each player is noted. + Signed as draft-and-follow (Second school noted if applicable).*

## ANAHEIM ANGELS (12)

**1. Joe Saunders, lhp, Virginia Tech.—(2005-14)**
**2. Kevin Jepsen, rhp, Bishop Manogue HS, Sparks, Nev.—(2008-15)**
3. Kyle Pawelczyk, lhp, Chipola (Fla.) JC.—(Low A)
4. Jordan Renz, of, Tulsa Union HS, Broken Arrow, Okla.—(AA)
5. Javy Rodriguez, ss, University of Miami.—(AAA)
6. Chris Walston, 1b, El Capitan HS, Lakeside, Calif.
7. *Jeff Leise, of, University of Nebraska.
8. James Holcomb, rhp, University of Nevada-Reno.
9. Caleb Maher, of, Ceres (Calif.) HS.
**10. Howie Kendrick, 2b, St John's River (Fla.) CC.—(2006-15)**
11. Aaron Peel, of, Seminole (Texas) HS.
12. Ryan Kenning, of, New Mexico State University.
13. Ozzie Lugo, rhp, Florida International University.
14. Ronnie Ray, rhp, Pacific (Mo.) HS.
15. Justin Hancock, 3b, Florida Southern College.
16. Tommy Duenas, c, Florida International University.
17. *Tony Mandel, rhp, Chipola (Fla.) JC.
18. Nic Touchstone, lhp, Okaloosa-Walton (Fla.) JC.
19. Mike Perdomo, of, Broward (Fla.) CC.
20. *Ryan Broderick, of, Palm Desert HS, Rancho Mirage, Calif.
21. Max McCarthy, lhp, Yale University.
22. Scott Hindman, lhp, Princeton University.
23. *Andrew Slorp, rhp, Bellarmine Prep, Morgan Hill, Calif.
24. +Brett Martinez, c, Redlands East Valley HS, Redlands, Calif. / Riverside (Calif.) CC.
25. +Michel Simard, rhp, St. Petersburg (Fla.) JC.
26. Alex Dvorsky, c, University of Northern Iowa.
27. Bryan Williams, rhp, Jacksonville University.
28. Jake Mathis, 3b, University of Alabama-Huntsville.
DRAFT DROP *Brother of Jeff Mathis, first-round draft pick, Angels (2001); major leaguer (2005-15)*
29. *Ryan Rote, rhp, Kishwaukee (Ill.) JC.
30. Jeffrey Marquez, rhp, Broward (Fla.) CC.
31. +Ross Lewis, rhp-of, Central Florida CC.
32. *Chris Hunter, rhp, Utah Valley State JC.
33. +Chris Roque, rhp, Broward (Fla.) CC.
34. *Jeremy King, lhp, Itawamba (Miss.) JC.
35. Jason Sugden, of, Harrisburg, Pa.
36. *Matt Byrd, c, James Hunt HS, Kenly, N.C.
37. *Trevor Wheedon, c, Nordhoff HS, Ojai, Calif.
38. *Buck Shaw, rhp, Wagoner (Okla.) HS.
39. *Taylor McIntyre, lhp, Edmond Santa Fe HS, Oklahoma City, Okla.
40. *Adam Rodgers, c, Grayson County (Texas) CC.
41. +Jason Cox, 1b, Lamar (Colo.) CC.
42. *Brad Beaman, of, Northglenn HS, Thornton, Colo.
**43. *Steven Delabar, rhp, Volunteer State (Tenn.) CC.—(2011-15)**
44. +Wayne Hedden, rhp, Hillsborough (Fla.) CC.
45. *Shawn McGill, c, South Kingstown HS, Wakefield, R.I.
46. *Brock Keffer, rhp, Illinois Valley CC.
47. +Karl Gelinas, rhp, Edouard Montpetit HS, Montreal / Northeastern Oklahoma A&M JC.
**48. +Bobby Wilson, c, St. Petersburg (Fla.) CC.—(2008-15)**
49. +Jason Corbett, rhp, Palm Harbor University HS, Palm Harbor, Fla. / Hillsborough (Fla.) CC.
50. *Cody Dickens, rhp, Forbush HS, East Bend, N.C.

## ARIZONA DIAMONDBACKS (27)

**1. Sergio Santos, ss-rhp, Mater Dei HS, Hacienda Heights, Calif.—(2010-15)**
**2. Chris Snyder, c, University of Houston.—(2004-13)**
3. Jared Doyle, lhp, James Madison University.—(AA)
**4. Lance Cormier, rhp, University of Alabama.—(2004-11)**
5. Mark Rosen, lhp, Salisbury (Conn.) Prep.—(AA)
**6. Brian Barden, 3b, Oregon State University.—(2007-10)**
7. Matt Henrie, rhp, Clemson University.
8. *Ryan Mahoney, c, Carmel HS, Patterson, N.Y.
9. Klent Corley, rhp, Grand Canyon University.
10. *Mike Pierce, c, Clovis (Calif.) HS.
11. Neb Brown, 2b, Oklahoma State University.
12. Mitch Douglas, lhp, Augusta State (Ga.) University.
13. Adam Haley, ss, University of Louisville.
14. Jay Garthwaite, of, University of Washington.
**15. Dustin Nippert, rhp, West Virginia University.—(2005-10)**
16. Bryan Johnson, 1b, University of Washington.
17. Donnie Saba, of, University of Utah.
18. Matt Morgan, ss, Lewis-Clark State (Idaho) College.
19. Sam Smith, rhp, University of South Alabama.
DRAFT DROP *Grandson of Bob Smith, major leaguer (1955-59)*
20. Jeff Stanek, 1b, Southern Illinois University.
21. Dan Callahan, of, Tufts (Mass.) University.
22. *Kenneth Parker, 1b, Henry Foss HS, Tacoma, Wash.
23. Jared Bonnell, rhp, University of Nevada-Las Vegas.
24. Matt Incinelli, rhp, University of North Florida.
25. Bookie Gates, 2b, Washington State University.
26. Wes Gilliam, lhp, University of Illinois-Chicago.
27. Josh Kranawetter, rhp, Polk (Fla.) CC.
28. Sean Luellwitz, 1b-c, Vanderbilt University.
29. *Mike Buss, rhp, Wellington (Fla.) Community HS.
30. *Anthony Isabella, of, Chemeketa (Ore.) CC.
31. +Clint Goocher, lhp, San Jacinto (Texas) JC.
32. *T.J. Large, rhp, Chipola (Fla.) JC.
33. *Donta Warfield, ss, Riverview HS, Sarasota, Fla.
34. *Jesus Albino, rhp, Northwest Mississippi CC.
35. *Jake Hanen, of, Scottsdale (Ariz.) CC.
36. *Nicholas Richardson, c, Elgin (Ill.) CC.
37. *Kirk Gross, rhp, San Ramon Valley HS, Danville, Calif.
38. *Matt Falk, rhp, Dana Hills HS, San Juan Capistrano, Calif.
39. Grady Symonds, c, University of Hawaii.
40. Billy Biggs, rhp, West Virginia University.
41. Keith Whatley, lhp, University of Houston.
42. *Mike Ridgway, lhp, Tacoma (Wash.) CC.
43. *Kris Krise, rhp, Crescenta Valley HS, La Crescenta, Calif.
44. *Conor Lalor, rhp, Houston HS, Germantown, Tenn.
45. *Jon Crosby, rhp, Christian Brothers HS, Germantown, Tenn.
46. *Ryan Gloger, lhp, University of South Florida.
47. Robert Ferns, rhp, Darton (Ga.) CC.
48. *Ronald Lowe, lhp, Ridgewood HS, New Port Richey, Fla.
49. *Matthew Raguse, rhp, St. Louis CC-Forest Park.
50. *Kyle Reynolds, ss, Second Baptist HS, Houston.
DRAFT DROP *Son of Craig Reynolds, first-round draft pick, Pirates (1971); major leaguer (1975-89)*

## ATLANTA BRAVES (23)

**1. Jeff Francoeur, of, Parkview HS, Lilburn, Ga.—(2005-15)**
**1. Dan Meyer, lhp, James Madison University** (Supplemental choice—34th—as compensation for Type A free agent Steve Karsay).—**(2004-10)**
**2. Brian McCann, c, Duluth (Ga.) HS.—(2005-15)**
**2. *Tyler Greene, ss, St. Thomas Aquinas HS, Plantation, Fla.** (Choice from Yankees as compensation for Karsay).—**(2009-13)**
DRAFT DROP *Attended Georgia Tech; re-drafted by Cardinals, 2005 (1st round)*
**3. Charlie Morton, rhp, Joel Barlow HS, Redding, Conn.—(2008-15)**
4. Steve Russell, rhp, Cimarron Memorial HS, Las Vegas, Nev.—(High A)
5. *Kris Harvey, c, Bandys HS, Catawba, N.C.—(AA)
DRAFT DROP *Attended Clemson; re-drafted by Marlins, 2005 (2nd round) • Son of Brian Harvey, major leaguer (1987-95) • Brother of Hunter Harvey, first-round draft pick, Orioles (2013)*
6. James Jurries, 1b, Tulane University.
7. *Patrick Clayton, rhp, Walton HS, Marietta, Ga.
8. Jon Schuerholz, ss, Auburn University.
DRAFT DROP *Son of John Schuerholz, general manager, Royals (1981-91); general manager/president, Braves (1991-2015)*
9. *Nick Starnes, rhp, Graham HS, Haw River, N.C.
10. Yaron Peters, 1b, University of South Carolina.
11. Mike Grasso, 2b, University of Albany.
12. Wes Timmons, ss, Bethune-Cookman College.
13. Dan Mead, lhp, Manatee (Fla.) JC.
14. Michael Reiss, rhp, Seminole (Fla.) CC.
DRAFT DROP *Twin brother of Steven Reiss, 25th-round draft pick, Braves (2002)*
15. *J.P. Lowen, c, Lassiter HS, Marietta, Ga.
16. Mike Mueller, rhp, Auburn University.
17. Brad David, lhp, Louisiana State University.
18. Josh Adams, lhp, Franklin (Ind.) College.
19. Fernando Tadefa, lhp, St. Mary's (Texas) University.
**20. Chuck James, lhp, Chattahoochee Valley (Ala.) CC.—(2005-11)**
21. Aaron Parker, rhp, Sonoma State (Calif.) University.
22. *Trey Shields, rhp, Bay HS, Panama City, Fla.
23. *Tim Cunningham, lhp, Stanford University.
24. Paul Bush, rhp, Georgia Southwestern College.
25. Steven Reiss, rhp, Seminole (Fla.) CC.
DRAFT DROP *Twin brother of Michael Reiss, 14th-round draft pick, Braves (2002)*
26. *Chris Maher, rhp, Pensacola (Fla.) JC.
27. *T.J. Stanton, rhp, Lake City (Fla.) CC.
28. +Devin Anderson, lhp, West Orange HS, Ocoee, Fla. / Pensacola (Fla.) CC.
29. *Mark Wagner, c, Mayfair HS, Lakewood, Calif.
30. *Cooper Osteen, ss, Indian River (Fla.) CC.
31. *Brandon Nall, rhp, George C. Wallace (Ala.) CC.
32. *Darrell Qualls, ss, Middleburg (Fla.) HS.
33. *Jacob Eckley, lhp, Burke HS, Omaha, Neb.
34. *Ryan Patterson, of, Texarkana (Texas) CC.
35. *Ken Brock, lhp, Lane (Ore.) CC.
36. *Abraham Vargas, rhp, Bay City (Texas) HS.
37. *Matt Dale, lhp, Walton HS, Marietta, Ga.
38. *Jeff Timmons, c, Manatee (Fla.) CC.
39. *Brett Young, 1b, Gloucester County (N.J.) CC.
40. *Kevin Kotch, c, Middlesex (N.J.) HS.
41. *David Hayes, rhp, American Heritage HS, Sunrise, Fla.
42. *Ryan Paul, lhp, Moorpark (Calif.) HS.
43. *Ken Livesley, rhp, Cosumnes River (Calif.) CC.
44. *Chris Tyndall, rhp, Armstrong (Ill.) HS.
45. +Danny Collins, lhp, Indian River (Fla.) CC / Daytona Beach (Fla.) CC.
46. *Brandon Judge, rhp, Santa Margarita HS, Rancho Santa Margarita, Calif.
47. Rick Aguilar, lhp, Cypress (Calif.) JC.
48. *Christopher Widing, lhp, East Paulding HS, Dallas, Ga.
49. *Christopher Dunbar, of, La Conner HS, Camano Island, Wash.
50. *Matt Handley, lhp, Greater Atlanta Christian HS, Duluth, Ga.

## BALTIMORE ORIOLES (4)

**1. +Adam Loewen, lhp, Fraser Valley Christian HS, Surrey, B.C. / Chipola (Fla.) JC—(2006-15)**
2. Corey Shafer, of, Choctaw (Okla.) HS.—(Low A)
**3. Val Majewski, of, Rutgers University.—(2004)**
4. Tim Gilhooly, of, University of the Pacific.—(Short-season A)
**5. Hayden Penn, rhp, Santana HS, Santee, Calif.—(2005-10)**
**6. John Maine, rhp, University of North Carolina-Charlotte.—(2004-13)**
7. Paul Henry, rhp, Ball State University.
8. Ryan Hubele, c, University of Texas.
9. Trevor Caughey, lhp, Cuesta (Calif.) JC.
10. Matt Bolander, rhp, Pendleton Heights HS, Anderson, Ind.
11. *Mark McCormick, rhp, Clear Creek HS, Clear Lake Shores, Texas.
DRAFT DROP *First-round draft pick (43rd overall), Cardinals (2005)*
**12. Brandon Fahey, 3b, University of Texas.—(2006-08)**
DRAFT DROP *Son of Bill Fahey, first overall draft pick, January 1970/regular phase, Senators; major leaguer (1971-83)*
13. Mike Huggins, 1b, Baylor University.
14. Matthew Rohr, lhp, Cal State San Bernardino.
15. Matt Howerton, of, Riverdale HS, Fort Myers, Fla.
16. Gera Alvarez, ss, Texas Tech.
17. Neal Stephenson, of, Texas A&M University.
18. Carl Makowsky, rhp, Northwestern State University.
19. Mike Patitucci, lhp, Oklahoma State University.
20. George Cox, c, University of Central Florida.
21. Gregg Davies, of, Towson University.
22. Zach Sutton, rhp, University of Central Florida.
23. Jason Cierlik, lhp, Minnesota State University-Mankato.
24. *Ryan Soehlig, 3b, University of North Florida.
25. Tim Thurman, 1b, Cal Poly Pomona.
26. Erik Smallwood, of, University of South Alabama.
**27. *Antoan Richardson, of, Palm Beach (Fla.) JC.—(2011-14)**
28. Zach Davis, of, J.A. Fair HS, Little Rock, Ark.
29. Eddie Colbert, of, Catonsville (Md.) CC.
30. Melvin Spivey, rhp, University of South Alabama.
31. Justin Nash, rhp, Penn State University.
32. Whitney Robinson-Pierce, c, Cuesta (Calif.) JC.
33. Ryan Childs, rhp, Clemson University.
34. Levi Robinson, ss, Texas Christian University.
35. Nick McCurdy, rhp, Oklahoma State University.
36. *Jordan Compton, lhp, Haysi (Va.) HS.
37. +Russell Petrick, lhp, Bellevue (Wash.) CC.
38. *Alex Muszynski, 1b, Alpena (Mich.) HS.
39. +Henry Lozado, rhp, Adolfina Irizarry de Puig HS, Toa Baja, P.R. / Palm Beach (Fla.) CC.
40. *Steven Guerra, rhp, Paso Robles (Calif.) HS.
41. *Chuck White, c, Overlea HS, Baltimore.
42. *Barry Roe, rhp, Heath (Okla.) HS.
43. *Randy Youtsey, 2b, Coolidge (Ariz.) HS.
44. *Bradford Wiggins, of, Arlington Heights HS, Fort Worth, Texas.
45. Jim Cooney, lhp, Florida Atlantic University.
46. *David Mittelberger, lhp, Righetti HS, Santa Maria, Calif.
47. *Andre Psaradelis, of, Bellevue (Wash.) CC.
48. Mark Wahl, c, University of Dayton.
49. *Gabe Somarriba, of, Florida Atlantic University.
50. *Allen Ponder, rhp, Lee-Scott Academy, Auburn, Ala.

## BOSTON RED SOX (16)

1. (Choice to Athletics as compensation for Type A free agent Johnny Damon)
**2. Jon Lester, lhp, Bellarmine Prep, Puyallup, Wash.—(2006-15)**
3. Scott White, 3b, Walton HS, Marietta, Ga.—(High A)
**4. Chris Smith, rhp, UC Riverside.—(2008-10)**
5. Chad Spann, ss, Southland Academy, Buena Vista, Ga.—(AAA)
**6. *Barret Browning, lhp, Wayne County HS, Jesup, Ga.—(2012)**
7. *Jason Neighborgall, rhp, Riverside HS, Durham, N.C.
**8. Brandon Moss, ss, Loganville HS, Monroe, Ga.—(2007-15)**
9. Tyler Pelland, lhp, Mount Abraham HS, Bristol, Vt.
10. Greg Stone, ss, Bacone (Okla.) JC.
11. Mike Goss, of, Jackson State University.
12. *Dustin Majewski, of, University of Texas.
13. *Stoney Stone, rhp, Ruston (La.) HS.
14. Andy Priola, rhp, Faulkner (Ala.) University.
15. Ian Cronkhite, of, Westmoore HS, Oklahoma City, Okla.
16. Peter Ciofrone, ss, Smithtown HS, Nesconset, N.Y.
17. Arian Alcala, 3b, St. Thomas (Fla.) University.
18. Brandon Smith, rhp, Southeast Missouri State University.
19. Tom MacLane, lhp, Florida Atlantic University.
20. Luis Villarreal, lhp, Northwood (Texas) University.
21. Alberto Concepcion, c, University of Southern California.
22. *John Anderson, rhp, Arkansas State University.
23. David Pahucki, rhp, Siena College.
24. Pat Boran, ss, Princeton University.
25. Jim Buckley, c, Siena College.
26. *Adam Davis, rhp, Metter HS, Pulaski, Ga.
27. *Michael Armstrong, of, Chabot (Calif.) JC.

28. Mike Barclay, of, University of South Florida.
29. *Matt Clarkson, c, Broken Arrow (Okla.) HS.
30. *Jonathan Williams, rhp, Opelika (Ala.) HS.
31. *Steve Boggs, of, San Diego HS.
32. *Brock Hunton, rhp, Dublin Coffman HS, Dublin, Ohio.
33. *Luke Taylor, rhp, Lowndes HS, Valdosta, Ga.
34. *Mitchell Woolf, rhp, Madison HS, Rexburg, Idaho.
35. Jose Vaquedano, rhp, Vernon Regional (Texas) JC.
36. *Don Powers, rhp, Shawnee (Okla.) HS.
**37. *Ricky Romero, lhp, Theodore Roosevelt HS, Los Angeles.—(2009-13)**
DRAFT DROP *First-round draft pick (6th overall), Blue Jays (2005)*
38. *Koley Kolberg, rhp, Navarro (Texas) JC.
39. *Tyler Jacobson, rhp, Auburn Riverside HS, Sumner, Wash.
40. *Dustin Roddy, c, Northeast Texas JC.
41. *Matt Inouye, c, Mid-Pacific Institute, Honolulu, Hawaii.
42. *Rosalino Valenzuela, rhp, Marcos de Niza HS, Guadalupe, Ariz.
43. *Lance Schartz, c, Garden City (Kan.) CC.
44. *David Baker, c, Rogers HS, Puyallup, Wash.
**45. *Brian Bannister, rhp, University of Southern California.—(2006-10)**
DRAFT DROP *Son of Floyd Bannister, first overall draft pick (1976); major leaguer (1977-92)*
46. *West Harris, lhp, Lone Oak HS, Paducah, Ky.
47. Anthony Bianucci, of, Daytona Beach (Fla.) CC.
48. *Sergio Roman, c, Allen County (Kan.) CC.
49. *Robert Caruso, 1b, Chaminade-Madonna Prep, Pembroke Pines, Fla.
50. *Seth Dhaenens, ss, Mountain Pointe HS, Chandler, Ariz.

## CHICAGO CUBS (21)

1. Bobby Brownlie, rhp, Rutgers University.—(AAA)
1. Luke Hagerty, lhp, Ball State University (Supplemental choice—32nd—as compensation for Type A free agent David Weathers).—(High A)
1. Chadd Blasko, rhp, Purdue University (Supplemental choice—36th—as compensation for Type A free agent Rondell White).—(AA)
1. Matt Clanton, rhp, Orange Coast (Calif.) JC (Supplemental choice—38th—as compensation for Type A free agent Todd Van Poppel).—(Short-season A)
2. Brian Dopirak, 1b, Dunedin (Fla.) HS (Choice from Mets as compensation for Weathers).—(AAA)
2. Justin Jones, lhp, Kellam HS, Virginia Beach, Va.—(AA)
**3. Billy Petrick, rhp, Morris (Ill.) HS.—(2007)**
3. Matt Craig, ss, University of Richmond (Choice from Yankees as compensation for White).—(AAA)
**4. Rich Hill, lhp, University of Michigan** (Choice from Rangers as compensation for Van Poppel).**—(2005-15)**
4. Alan Rick, c, Palatka (Fla.) HS.—(AA)
5. *Shawn Scobee, of, Rio Linda (Calif.) HS.—(Short-season A)
DRAFT DROP *Attended Cal State Fullerton; re-drafted by Blue Jays, 2006 (14th round)*
6. Chris Walker, of, Georgia Southern University.
7. Joey Monahan, ss, Liberty University.
DRAFT DROP *Great grandson of Howie Morenz, hockey Hall of Famer (1923-37) • Grandson of Boom Boom Geoffrion, hockey Hall of Famer (1950-68) • Son of Hartland Monahan, NHL player (1973-81) • Brother of Shane Monahan, major leaguer (1998-99)*
8. Jason Fransz, of, University of Oklahoma.
**9. Adam Greenberg, of, University of North Carolina.—(2005-12)**
10. Keith Butler, of, Liberty University.
11. Chris Miller, c, UC Irvine.
12. Jason Wylie, rhp, University of Utah.
**13. Micah Hoffpauir, of, Lamar University.—(2008-10)**
**14. Rocky Cherry, rhp, University of Oklahoma.—(2007-08)**
15. C.J. Medlin, c, Seminole State (Okla.) JC.
16. Jemel Spearman, ss, Georgia Southern University.
17. *Forrest Beverly, lhp, Conway (S.C.) HS.
18. Donnie Hood, ss, Kennesaw State (Ga.) University.
19. Rick Atlee, rhp, Lamar University.
20. Matthew Hines, rhp, Olivet Nazarene (Ill.) University.
21. Paul O'Toole, c, University of Notre Dame.
**22. *Taylor Teagarden, c, Creekview HS, Carrollton, Texas.—(2008-15)**
23. Steve O'Sullivan, ss, Marist College.
24. *Ben Thurmond, rhp, Winthrop University.
25. +Bear Bay, rhp, Angelina (Texas) JC.
26. *Jeff Jacobsen, rhp, Durango HS, Las Vegas, Nev.
27. Travis Welsch, ss-2b, University of Northern Iowa.
28. *Evan Seibly, lhp, Los Angeles Pierce JC.
29. Brett Lewis, rhp, Georgia Southern University.
30. *Kyle Emmons, ss, Chaparral HS, Scottsdale, Ariz.
31. *Kurt Steele, rhp-ss, Crescent Valley HS, Corvallis, Ore.
32. *Jose Rios, ss, Pablo Gonzalez Bendecia HS, Barranquitas, P.R.
33. *Adam Harvey, c, Celina (Texas) HS.
34. *Grant Staniszewski, c, Marquette HS, Chesterfield, Mo.
35. *Anthony McLin, c, McLaurin HS, Florence, Miss.
36. *Kalen Gibson, rhp, Webster HS, Slaughters, Ky.
37. *Kyle DuBois, rhp, Manatee (Fla.) JC.
DRAFT DROP *Brother of Jason DuBois, major leaguer (2004-05)*
**38. Randy Wells, c, Southwestern Illinois JC.—(2008-12)**
39. *Daniel DeSouza, of, Xaverian HS, Brooklyn, N.Y.
40. *Collin Walker, rhp, Minooka HS, Channahon, Ill.
41. *Mark Holliman, rhp, Germantown (Tenn.) HS.
42. *Geoff Orr, ss, Carl Sandburg HS, Orland Park, Ill.
43. *Cory Anderson, rhp, Chaparral HS, Scottsdale, Ariz.
44. *Jose Cortez, c, Pomona-Pitzer (Calif.) College.
45. *Chris Ericksen, lhp, Joliet Catholic Academy, Joliet, Ill.
46. +Patrick McIntyre, c, Walla Walla (Wash.) JC.
47. *Josh Morgan, c, Thomasville (Ala.) HS.
48. *Clemon Bailey, of, Southern HS, Durham, N.C.
49. *Gary Kerschke, rhp, Bartlett HS, Hanover Park, Ill.
50. *Brian Kayser, 1b, Bartlesville (Okla.) HS.

## CHICAGO WHITE SOX (18)

**1. Royce Ring, lhp, San Diego State University.—(2005-10)**
**2. Jeremy Reed, of, Long Beach State University.—(2004-11)**
**3. Josh Rupe, rhp, Louisburg (N.C.) JC.—(2005-11)**
4. Ryan Rodriguez, lhp, Keller (Texas) HS.—(AAA)
5. B.J. LaMura, rhp, Clemson University.—(AAA)
**6. *Chris Getz, ss, Grosse Pointe South HS, Grosse Pointe Farms, Mich.—(2008-14)**
7. Micah Schnurstein, 3b, Basic HS, Henderson, Nev.
**8. Sean Tracey, rhp, UC Irvine.—(2006)**
9. Todd Deininger, rhp, Texas A&M University.
10. Orionny Lopez, rhp, Forest Hill HS, West Palm Beach, Fla.
11. Matt Herring, 1b-of, Georgia Southern University.
12. *Jayson Ruhlman, lhp, L'Anse Creuse North HS, Macomb, Mich.
13. Demetrius Banks, lhp, Chattahoochee Valley (Ala.) CC.
14. *Christian Madson, rhp, Bloomingdale HS, Valrico, Fla.
15. Adam Larson, rhp, Middle Tennessee State University.
16. Daniel Haigwood, lhp, Midland HS, Batesville, Ark.
**17. Brandon McCarthy, rhp, Lamar (Colo.) CC.—(2005-15)**
18. Shane Scoville, c, University of South Alabama.
19. *Paul Keck, c, Granada HS, Pleasanton, Calif.
**20. +Boone Logan, lhp, Sandra Day O'Connor HS, Helotes, Texas / Temple (Texas) JC.—(2006-15)**
21. Seth Morris, of, University of Kentucky.
22. Eric Keefner, 1b, Mesa (Ariz.) CC.
23. *David Beasley, lhp, Cooper City (Fla.) HS
24. Thomas Brice, 1b-of, Faulkner State (Ala.) JC.
**25. +Jay Marshall, lhp, Jefferson (Mo.) JC.—(2007-09)**
26. *Kris Dufner, ss, University of Delaware.
27. Michael Bohlander, 1b, Pace (N.Y.) University.
**28. *Hector Ambriz, rhp, Valencia HS, Placentia, Calif.—(2010-14)**
29. *Neil Giesler, 3b, Jasper (Ind.) HS.
30. Jacob Nowlen, rhp, University of Arkansas-Monticello.
31. Edgar Varela, 3b, Long Beach State University.
32. Rick Hummel, rhp, University of Indianapolis.
**33. *Tony Sipp, lhp, Okaloosa-Walton (Fla.) CC.—(2009-15)**
34. *Brandon Durden, lhp, Cook (Ga.) HS.
35. *Eric Everly, lhp, Seagoville (Texas) HS.
36. *Jason Pilkington, lhp, Central Arizona JC.
37. Jamin Hutchingson, rhp, Fayetteville (Ark.) HS.
38. *D.J. Wabick, of, Amos Alonzo Stagg HS, Palos Park, Ill.
39. *Gabriel Casanova, 2b, Coral Park HS, Miami.
40. *Dennis Pawelek, rhp, Snow (Utah) JC.
DRAFT DROP *Brother of Mark Pawelek, first-round draft pick, Cubs (2005)*
**41. *Daniel Barone, rhp, Monterey Peninsula (Calif.) JC.—(2007)**
42. Ian Ganzer, rhp, Monterey Peninsula (Calif.) JC.
43. *Matthew Sibigtroth, ss, Kishwaukee (Ill.) JC.
44. *Ramon Castro, 2b-ss, George Washington HS, New York.
45. *Jorge Mico, c, Hialeah (Fla.) HS.
46. *Jeremy Paul, c, Trinity International (Ill.) University.
DRAFT DROP *Brother of Josh Paul, major leaguer (1999-2007)*
47. *Tim Grogan, ss, Covington Catholic HS, Fort Wright, Ky.
48. *Anthony Manuel, 2b, Kishwaukee (Ill.) JC.
DRAFT DROP *Son of Jerry Manuel, first-round draft pick, Tigers (1972); major leaguer (1975-82); major league manager (1998-2010)*
**49. +Fernando Hernandez, rhp, Southwest HS, Miami / Broward (Fla.) CC.—(2008)**
50. Matt Payne, rhp, University of California.

## CINCINNATI REDS (3)

1. Chris Gruler, rhp, Liberty Union HS, Brentwood, Calif.—(Low A)
1. Mark Schramek, 3b, University of Texas-San Antonio (Supplemental choice—40th—for failure to sign 2001 first-round pick Jeremy Sowers).—(AA)
**2. Joey Votto, c, Richview Collegiate Institute, Toronto.—(2007-15)**
3. Kyle Edens, rhp, Baylor University.—(AA)
4. Camilo Vazquez, lhp, Hialeah (Fla.) HS.—(AAA)
5. Kevin Howard, 3b, University of Miami.—(AAA)
6. Walter Olmstead, 1b, Texas Christian University.
7. Corey Wachman, rhp, Valdosta State (Ga.) University.
8. O.J. King, rhp, Northwestern State University.
9. Steve Booth, c, University of San Francisco.
10. Frankie Keller, lhp, Abilene Christian (Texas) University.
11. Mike Bassett, of, George Washington University.
12. Don Gemmell, rhp, San Jose State University.
13. *Jose Enrique Cruz, ss, Rice University.
DRAFT DROP *Son of Jose Cruz, major leaguer (1970-88) • Brother of Jose Cruz Jr., major leaguer (1997-2008)*
14. Joe Curran, lhp, Fort Hays State (Kan.) University.
15. *Glenn Kamis, rhp, Elgin (Ill.) CC.
16. Jonathan George, rhp, Camden Catholic HS, Pennsauken, N.J.
17. *Ben Lavender, c, Pelham (Ala.) HS.
18. *Zach McCormack, lhp, Sacramento CC.
**19. Chris Denorfia, of, Wheaton (Mass.) College.—(2005-15)**
20. *Tyler Coon, lhp, Silverado HS, Las Vegas, Nev.
21. *Jon Causey, rhp, Moorpark (Calif.) JC.
22. *Matt Luca, rhp, Ball HS, Galveston, Texas.
**23. *Nick Markakis, lhp-of, Young Harris (Ga.) JC.—(2006-15)**
DRAFT DROP *First-round draft pick (7th overall), Orioles (2003)*
24. Jarrod Schmidt, c-rhp, Clemson University.
25. Bobby Mosby, 1b, Northeastern Oklahoma A&M JC.
26. *Chris Dunn, ss, Chaparral HS, Parker, Colo.
27. *Juan Velazquez, rhp, Montgomery HS, San Diego.
28. *Jay Tust, 2b, Stadium HS, Tacoma, Wash.
29. Brad Correll, ss, Limestone (S.C.) College.
30. Justin Knoff, rhp, Siena College.
31. Mayque Quintero, rhp, Sonoma County/Western League.
32. *Gerald Smith, of, Thomas Jefferson HS, Tampa.
33. *Bart Braun, lhp, Diablo Valley (Calif.) JC.
34. *Cody McAllister, rhp, Snohomish (Wash.) HS.
35. *Stantrel Smith, of, Towers HS, Decatur, Ga.
36. Matt Krimmel, 3b, George Washington University.
37. Shawn Aichele, rhp, Western Hills HS, Cincinnati.
38. *Hardy Hutto, rhp, Garden City (Kan.) CC.
39. +Calvin Medlock, rhp, Westbury HS, Houston / North Central Texas CC.
40. Chris Bell, rhp, Miami-Dade North CC.
41. *Marcus Townsend, of, University of Texas-Brownsville.
42. *Danny Kelly, ss, Durango HS, Las Vegas, Nev.
43. +Derek Hawk, rhp, Mendocino (Calif.) CC.
44. *Jason Baca, rhp, Sweeny (Texas) HS.
45. *Dennis Leduc, rhp, Cuesta (Calif.) JC.
46. Troy Cairns, ss, University of New Mexico.
47. +Michael Bryant, rhp, Sam Rayburn HS, Pasadena, Texas / Hill (Texas) JC.
48. Travis Wong, 1b, Texas A&M University.
49. Billy Dennis, of, Incarnate Word (Texas) University.
50. *Ben Himes, of, Texas A&M University.

## CLEVELAND INDIANS (22)

**1. Jeremy Guthrie, rhp, Stanford University.—(2004-15)**
1. Matt Whitney, 3b, Palm Beach Gardens (Fla.) HS (Supplemental choice—33rd—as compensation for Type A free agent Juan Gonzalez).—(AAA)
1. Micah Schilling, 2b, Silliman Institute, Clinton, La. (Supplemental choice—41st—for failure to sign 2001 first-round pick Alan Horne).—(High A)
**2. Brian Slocum, rhp, Villanova University.—(2006-08)**
2. Pat Osborn, 3b, University of Florida (Supplemental choice—72nd—as compensation for Type C free agent Marty Cordova).—(AA)
3. Jason Cooper, of, Stanford University (Choice from Rangers as compensation for Gonzalez).—(AAA)
3. Dan Cevette, lhp, Elkland (Pa.) HS.—(AAA)
4. Fernando Pacheco, 1b, Montgomery HS, San Ysidro, Calif.—(Low A)
**5. Ben Francisco, of, UCLA.—(2007-13)**
6. Michael Hernandez, lhp, Fresno State University.
7. Brian Wright, of, North Carolina State University.
8. Blake Allen, lhp, Union (Tenn.) University.
9. Shaun Larkin, 2b, Cal State Northridge.
10. Keith Ramsey, lhp, University of Florida.
11. Bill Peavey, 1b, University of Southern California.
DRAFT DROP *Brother of Pat Peavey, 33rd-round draft pick, Astros (2002)*
12. Chad Longworth, of, J.J. Kelly HS, Wise, Va.
13. +Reid Santos, lhp, Saddleback (Calif.) CC.
14. *Mike Mitchell, rhp, St. Charles (Mo.) JC.
15. Nathan Panther, of, Muscatine (Iowa) CC.
16. Omar Casillas, c, Ana J. Candelas HS, Cidra, P.R.
17. *Jeff Ostrander, lhp, Patrick Henry HS, Montpelier, Va.
18. Jahseam George, lhp, San Jose State University.
19. *Curt Mendoza, of, Redlands (Calif.) HS.
20. Chris White, lhp, Kent State University.
21. *Zeke Parraz, ss, CC of Southern Nevada.
22. Clayton McCullough, c, East Carolina University.
23. *Aaron Tennyson, lhp, Milan (Mich.) HS.
24. *Dan Donaldson, lhp, Memorial HS, Houston.
25. +Nick Pesco, rhp, Cosumnes River (Calif.) JC.
26. *Jose Cardona, lhp, American Military Academy, Guaynabo, P.R.

27. *Derek Dunne, rhp, Sullivan (Mo.) HS.
28. *Tim Sabo, rhp, Don Bosco Prep, Suffern, N.Y.
29. *Ruben Flores, rhp, Riverside HS, El Paso, Texas.
30. Daniel Eisentrager, rhp, Long Beach State University.
31. Jeff Davis, rhp, University of Kansas.
32. Shea Douglas, lhp, University of Southern Mississippi.
**33. *Jensen Lewis, rhp, Anderson HS, Cincinnati.—(2007-10)**
34. *Chris Williams, c, Marcus HS, Flower Mound, Texas.
35. *Kevin Hawkins, rhp, Embry-Riddle Aeronautical (Fla.) College.
36. *Aaron Braithwaite, of, Indian River (Fla.) CC.
37. *Luis DeJesus, ss, New Mexico JC.
38. *John Moran, ss, Southaven (Miss.) HS.
39. Blake Taylor, rhp, University of South Carolina.
40. *Shea McFeely, ss, Federal Way (Wash.) HS.
41. *Andrew Knight, lhp, Maize HS, Wichita, Kan.
42. *Chris Rosario, of, Pine Ridge HS, Deltona, Fla.
43. *Matt Paz, rhp, Long Beach State University.
44. *Richard Wells, 3b, Glendale (Calif.) JC.
45. *Truan Mehl, of, Hutchinson (Kan.) CC.
46. Aaron Davidson, 2b, University of Florida.
47. *Jimmy Mayer, ss, Somerset (Pa.) HS.
48. *Bryce Kartler, lhp, Arizona State University.
49. *Daniel Lindner, rhp, Potomac State (W.Va.) JC.
50. *Ricardo Concepcion, of, Petra Corretjer HS, Manati, P.R.

## COLORADO ROCKIES (9)

**1. Jeff Francis, lhp, University of British Columbia.—(2004-15)**
**2. *Micah Owings, rhp, Gainesville (Ga.) HS.—(2007-12)**
DRAFT DROP *Attended Georgia Tech; re-drafted by Cubs, 2004 (19th round)*
3. Ben Crockett, rhp, Harvard University.—(AAA)
**4. Jeff Baker, 3b, Clemson University.—(2005-15)**
5. Neil Wilson, c, Vero Beach (Fla.) HS.—(AAA)
5. Doug Johnson, rhp, Bryant (R.I.) College (Choice from Rangers as compensation for Type B free agent Jay Powell).—(High A)
**6. Sean Barker, of, Louisiana State University.—(2007)**
**7. Ryan Spilborghs, of, UC Santa Barbara.—(2005-11)**
**8. Jeff Salazar, of, Oklahoma State University.—(2006-09)**
9. John Tetuan, rhp, Wichita State University.
10. Isaac Pavlik, lhp, Seton Hall University.
**11. Ryan Shealy, 1b, University of Florida.—(2005-10)**
**12. Mike Esposito, rhp, Arizona State University.—(2005)**
13. Brian Barre, of, University of Southern California.
14. Bernie Gonzalez, of, Florida International University.
15. Andy Bushey, c-3b, University of Notre Dame.
16. *Brad Corley, of, Pleasure Ridge Park HS, Louisville, Ky.
17. Steven Ponder, rhp, Texas A&M University.
18. Chris Young, rhp, Mississippi State University.
19. Duke Sardinha, 3b, Pepperdine University.
DRAFT DROP *Brother of Dane Sardinha, major leaguer (2003-05) • Brother of Bronson Sardinha, first-round draft pick, Yankees (2001); major leaguer (2007)*
20. Dan Street, 3b, University of Virginia.
21. Steve Reba, rhp, Clemson University.
22. *Pete Montrenes, rhp, University of Mississippi.
23. Carson White, 2b, University of California.
24. Mitsuru Sakamoto, of, Arizona Western JC.
25. Rock Mills, c, Pepperdine University.
26. K.J. Hendricks, ss, University of Texas-Arlington.
27. *Lance Beus, lhp, Cochise County (Ariz.) CC.
28. *Jose Lado, lhp, Delgado (La.) JC.
29. Rich Cartier, rhp, Cuesta (Calif.) JC.
30. *Aaron Gamboa, lhp, Bakersfield (Calif.) JC.
31. *Daniel Lonsberry, rhp, Northeast Texas CC.
32. *Derek Patterson, lhp, Evangel Christian Academy, Keithville, La.
33. Mike Watson, rhp, Penn State University.
**34. *Ryan Mattheus, rhp, Galt Union HS, Galt, Calif.—(2011-15)**
35. *Robert Madsen, rhp, McLennan (Texas) CC.
36. *Clayton Trenary, of, Crystal River (Fla.) HS.
37. *Victor Alvarez, ss, Chipola (Fla.) JC.
**38. *Drew Sutton, ss, Texarkana (Texas) CC.—(2009-12)**
39. Tomas Santiago, rhp, Pikeville (Ky.) College.
**40. *Matt Garza, rhp, Washington Union HS, Fresno, Calif.—(2006-15)**
DRAFT DROP *First-round draft pick (25th overall), Twins (2005)*
41. *Johnny Defendis, of, Xaverian HS, Brooklyn, N.Y.
42. Jason Dooley, rhp, Bethune-Cookman College.
43. *Justin Hoyman, rhp, Brevard (Fla.) CC.
44. *Ryan Earnest, rhp, Hardaway HS, Columbus, Ga.
45. *Tyler Littlehales, of, Boulder (Colo.) HS.
46. +Joshua Merino, rhp, Kirkwood (Mo.) CC.
47. *John Brownell, rhp, Butler County (Kan.) CC.
48. *Jim Popp, rhp, Duquesne University.
49. *Jared Theodorakos, lhp, Baylor University.
50. *Andrew York, c, JC of the Siskiyous (Calif.).

## DETROIT TIGERS (8)

**1. Scott Moore, ss, Cypress HS, Long Beach, Calif.—(2006-12)**
**2. Brent Clevlen, of, Westwood HS, Cedar Park, Texas.—(2006-10)**
**3. Curtis Granderson, of, University of Illinois-Chicago.—(2004-15)**
3. Matt Pender, rhp, Kennesaw State University (Choice from Mets as compensation for Type B free agent Roger Cedeno).—(High A)
4. Robbie Sovie, of, Stratford Academy, Macon, Ga.—(Short-season A)
5. Bo Flowers, of, Walter Lutheran HS, Maywood, Ill.—(Low A)
6. Chris Maples, rhp-3b, University of North Carolina.
7. Wilton Reynolds, of, Oral Roberts University.
8. Troy Pickford, rhp, Oral Roberts University.
9. Marcos Hernandez, rhp, Juan Ponce de Leon HS, San Juan, P.R.
**10. Luke Carlin, c, Northeastern University.—(2008-12)**
**11. Joel Zumaya, rhp, Bonita Vista HS, Chula Vista, Calif.—(2006-10)**
12. Corey Hamman, lhp, Montclair State (N.J.) University.
**13. *Anthony Reyes, rhp, University of Southern California.—(2005-09)**
14. Jason Graham, rhp, University of Central Florida.
**15. Jesse Carlson, lhp, University of Connecticut.—(2008-10)**
16. Michael Smith, lhp, Valdosta State (Ga.) University.
17. Rob Watson, ss, Oklahoma State University.
18. *Jacob Coash, lhp, Canyon HS, Saugus, Calif.
19. Rafael Mendez, c, Notre Dame HS, Caguas, P.R.
20. Jason Kennedy, of, University of Minnesota.
21. Corey Loomis, 2b, Bowling Green University.
22. *Cameron McGuire, c, South Grand Prairie (Texas) HS.
23. Drew Caravella, 1b, Ohio Wesleyan University.
24. Jody Roughton, 3b, University of Missouri.
25. *Daniel Nelson, ss, Crenshaw HS, Los Angeles.
26. Billy Kieninger, rhp, Miami (Ohio) University.
27. Damian Myers, lhp, Concordia (N.Y.) College.
28. Everett Hancock, lhp, University of North Carolina-Greensboro.
29. *Miguel Donate, 1b, Morell HS, Vega Alta, P.R.
30. David Garcia, ss, Santa Ana (Calif.) JC.
31. *Chris McCuiston, of, Michigan State University.
32. *Douglas Webb, rhp, Newbury Park (Calif.) HS.
33. *Jose Rodriguez, c, Cypress (Calif.) JC.
34. Jason Allec, c, Cal State Northridge.
35. *Brandon McCormick, rhp, W.W. King Academy, Batesburg, S.C.
36. Chris Steinborn, lhp, Lakeland (Ohio) CC.
37. *Ronnie Baron, rhp, Blinn (Texas) JC.
38. Ed Romprey, ss, Bellevue (Neb.) College.
39. Kevin McDonald, c, University of Maryland.
40. *Matt Taylor, lhp, Antioch (Tenn.) HS.
41. Edgar Ortiz, 1b, Compton (Calif.) CC.
42. *Travis Simmons, 3b, Cleveland (Tenn.) HS.
43. *Corey McCoy, of, Pine Bluff (Ark.) HS.
44. *Sean Richardson, c, Palomar (Calif.) JC.

## FLORIDA MARLINS (11)

**1. Jeremy Hermida, of, Wheeler HS, Marietta, Ga.—(2005-12)**
**2. Robert Andino, ss, Southridge HS, Miami.—(2005-13)**
3. Trevor Hutchinson, rhp, University of California.—(AA)
DRAFT DROP *Brother of Chad Hutchinson, first-round draft pick, Braves (1995); major leaguer (2001); quarterback, National Football League (2002-04)*
**4. Josh Johnson, rhp, Jenks HS, Tulsa, Okla.—(2005-13)**
**5. *Nick Hundley, c, Lake Washington HS, Redmond, Wash.—(2008-15)**
DRAFT DROP *Attended Arizona; re-drafted by Padres, 2005 (2nd round)*
**6. Scott Olsen, lhp, Crystal Lake South HS, Crystal Lake, Ill.—(2005-10)**
7. Xavier Arroyo, of, Antilles HS, Fort Buchanan, P.R.
8. Ryan Warpinski, rhp, Texas A&M University.
**9. Eric Reed, of, Texas A&M University.—(2006-07)**
10. Robert Word, 1b, University of Virginia.
11. Patrick Arlis, c, University of Illinois.
12. Jimmy deMontel, rhp, Bellevue (Neb.) College.
13. Kevin Randel, ss, Long Beach State University.
**14. Travis Chick, rhp, Whitehouse (Texas) HS.—(2006)**
15. Tom Merkle, 3b, New York Tech.
16. *Chris Goodman, rhp, Georgia Tech.
17. Evan Greusel, rhp, University of Oklahoma.
**18. Ross Wolf, rhp, Wabash Valley (Ill.) CC.—(2007-13)**
19. Jordan Baker, of, Zane Trace HS, Chillicothe, Ohio.
20. Jason Iehl, rhp, Downers Grove North HS, Woodridge, Ill.
21. Waylon Byers, lhp, University of Nebraska.
22. Shaun O'Connor, rhp, Pasco Hernando (Fla.) CC.
23. Carl Primus, rhp, Southern University.
24. Andy Rohleder, of, University of Evansville
25. Eric Ordorica, 2b, Azusa Pacific (Calif.) University.
26. *Brae Wright, lhp, Southaven (Miss.) HS.
27. Casey Blalock, rhp, Louisiana Tech.
28. *Aaron Gabriel, rhp, Lake City HS, Coeur d'Alene, Idaho.
29. Chris Gabriel, rhp, Chaffey (Calif.) JC.
30. *Kurt Koehler, rhp, Pinole Valley HS, Pinole, Calif.
31. Kyle Eazor, lhp, Chandler-Gilbert (Ariz.) CC.
32. Dan Olson, rhp, University of Kansas.
33. Joe Apotheker, of, Barry (Fla.) University.
34. *Kyle Dickson, rhp, Granada HS, Livermore, Calif.
35. *Greg Goetz, lhp, Newport HS, Bellevue, Wash.
36. *Neil Warchol, rhp, St. Laurence HS, Burbank, Ill.
37. *Ryan Anderson, lhp, St. Petersburg (Fla.) JC.
38. *P.J. Connelly, lhp, Cowley County (Kan.) CC.
39. *Matthew Miller, of, Modesto (Calif.) JC.
40. *Bradley Pahs, c, Triton (Ill.) JC.
**41. *Rob Johnson, c, Saddleback (Calif.) CC.—(2007-13)**
42. +Zach Lerch, rhp, Muscatine (Iowa) CC.
43. *Tyler Williams, c, North Delta SS, Delta, B.C.
**44. +Tim Wood, rhp, Pima (Ariz.) CC.—(2009-11)**
45. *Shany Carle, rhp, University of Quebec.
46. +Nick Ewen, of, Triton (Ill.) JC.
47. *Jacob Manning, of, Mineral Area (Mo.) JC.
48. *Matthew Hayes, lhp, Parkland (Ill.) JC.
49. *Michael Gaffney, ss, New York Tech.
50. *Dustin Hughes, c, Northgate HS, Walnut Creek, Calif.

## HOUSTON ASTROS (29)

1. Derick Grisby, rhp, Northeast Texas CC.—(Low A)
**2. Mitch Talbot, rhp, Canyon View HS, Cedar City, Utah.—(2008-11)**
3. Rory Shortell, rhp, San Diego State University.—(High A)
**4. Mark McLemore, lhp, Oregon State University.—(2007)**
**5. *Pat Misch, lhp, Western Michigan University.—(2006-11)**
DRAFT DROP *Returned to Western Michigan; re-drafted by Giants, 2003 (7th round)*
6. J.P. Duran, rhp, St. Mary's (Texas) University.
7. +Scott Robinson, 1b-of, Rancho Bernardo HS, San Diego / Palomar (Calif.) JC.
DRAFT DROP *Son of Bruce Robinson, first-round draft pick, Athletics (1975); major leaguer (1978-80)*
8. Bill Westhoff, rhp, University of Dallas.
9. Drew Topham, ss, Stanford University.
10. *Brad Chedister, rhp, Panola (Texas) JC.
11. Jason Reuss, of, University of Nevada-Las Vegas.
DRAFT DROP *Son of Jerry Reuss, major leaguer (1969-90)*
12. Chance Douglass, rhp, Canyon Randall HS, Amarillo, Texas.
13. Nic Covarrubias, of, Long Beach State University.
14. *B.J. Boening, rhp, Yoakum HS, Portland, Texas.
15. Jeff Mackor, c, Boston College.
16. Jared Gothreaux, rhp, McNeese State University.
17. Daniel Freeman, rhp, Texarkana (Texas) CC.
18. Brent Long, rhp, Brevard (N.C.) College.
19. Aaron Heitzman, lhp, Minnesota State University-Mankato.
20. *Justin Glover, of, Grant HS, Portland, Ore.
21. *Ivan Naccarata, 2b, Chipola (Fla.) JC.
22. Sam Fischer, rhp, University of Dayton.
23. Jesse Harrington, ss, Concordia (Ore.) University.
24. *Nick Tisone, rhp, Mandeville HS, Covington, La.
25. *Ethien Santana, of, Colegio Bautista HS, Carolina, P.R.
26. Randy McGarvey, c, Coastal Carolina University.
27. *Shawn Burris, lhp, Poteet HS, Mesquite, Texas.
28. Kevin Davidson, c, Rollins (Fla.) College.
29. Sean Kramer, rhp, Hill (Texas) JC.
30. *Ladd Hall, rhp, Eastern Arizona JC.
31. Andrew Salmela, 1b, Augustana (S.D.) College.
32. *Tyson Olson, of, Dixie State (Utah) JC.
33. Pat Peavey, 3b, University of Santa Clara.
DRAFT DROP *Brother of Bill Peavey, 11th-round draft pick, Indians (2002)*
34. Mike Lorsbach, of, Rice University.
35. *Shawn Williams, of, Clearwater Central Catholic HS, Palm Harbor, Fla.
DRAFT DROP *Son of Jimy Williams, major leaguer (1966-67); major league manager (1986-2004)*
36. Adam Seuss, of, UC Riverside.
37. Dustin Hawkins, of, Wichita State University.
38. Ryan Larson, 3b, UC San Diego.
**39. *Nick Stavinoha, of, San Jacinto (Texas) JC.—(2008-10)**
40. *Adam Yesalusky, lhp, Minersville (Pa.) HS.
**41. *Scott Feldman, rhp, JC of San Mateo (Calif.).—(2005-15)**
42. *Chase Medford, lhp-of, Richland (Texas) HS.
43. *Freddie Thon, 1b, Baldwin HS, Guaynabo, P.R.
DRAFT DROP *Nephew of Dickie Thon, major leaguer (1979-93)*
44. *William Mac-Holmes, rhp, Northwest HS, Omaha, Neb.
45. +Ryan McKeller, rhp, McLennan (Texas) CC / New Mexico JC.
46. *Eric Brock, rhp, Santa Margarita HS, Laguna Niguel, Calif.
47. +Raymar Diaz, of, Laredo (Texas) CC.
48. *Kyle Thompson, rhp, Palomar (Calif.) CC.

## KANSAS CITY ROYALS (6)

**1. Zack Greinke, rhp, Apopka HS, Orlando, Fla.—(2004-15)**
DRAFT DROP *First 2002 high school draft pick to reach majors (May 22, 2004)*
2. Adam Donachie, c, Timber Creek HS, Orlando, Fla.—(AAA)
3. David Jensen, 1b, Brigham Young University.—(High A)
4. Danny Christensen, lhp, Xaverian HS, Brooklyn, N.Y.—(AA)
**5. Donnie Murphy, ss, Orange Coast (Calif.) JC.—(2004-14)**
**6. *Brandon Jones, ss, Wewahitchka (Fla.) HS.—(2007-09)**
**7. Jonah Bayliss, rhp, Trinity (Conn.) College.—(2005-07)**
8. Kenard Springer, 3b, Nettleton (Miss.) HS.
**9. Matt Tupman, c, University of Massachusetts-Lowell.—(2008)**

10. Greg Atencio, rhp, Lamar (Colo.) CC.
11. *Kainoa Obrey, 3b, Brigham Young University.
12. Adam Keim, ss, Coastal Carolina University.
13. Rusty Meyer, c, Texas A&M University.
14. Steven Chamberlain, rhp, University of Portland.
**15. Kila Kaaihue, 1b, Iolani HS, Honolulu, Hawaii.—(2008-12)**
16. Eric Ackerman, lhp, University of Pittsburgh.
17. Jason Bartz, rhp, University of South Florida.
18. Donnie Poles, of, Pitt (N.C.) CC.
19. *Alex Crooks, 1b, Sierra Vista HS, Azusa, Calif.
20. Nate Zettler, rhp, Union (Ky.) College.
21. *Steve Mena, 3b, South Miami HS, Miami.
22. *Nick Bates, rhp, Michigan State University.
23. Tim Frend, of, Davidson College.
24. Michael Aguilar, rhp, Franklin HS, Portland, Ore.
25. Carlos Caballero, of, Ines Maria Mendoza HS, Cabo Rojo, P.R.
26. *J.J. Brown, of, Vicksburg (Miss.) HS.
27. *Michael Hernandez, of, Xaverian HS, Brooklyn, N.Y.
28. +Robert Grana, c, CC of Southern Nevada / Dixie State (Utah) JC.
29. *Michael Honce, rhp, Bridgeport (W.Va.) HS.
30. *Clinton Johnson, rhp, Murrah HS, Jackson, Miss.
31. *Matt Castillo, of, Mesa (Ariz.) CC.
32. Bernard Stephens, of, Virginia State University.
**33. *Cesar Carrillo, rhp, Mount Carmel (Ill.) HS.—(2009)**
DRAFT DROP *First-round draft pick (18th overall), Padres (2005)*
34. Eric Lonnquist, ss, Minnesota State University-Mankato.
35. *Tyler Kimmons, rhp, Mandeville (La.) HS.
36. *Chris Turner, c, El Dorado (Ark.) HS.
37. *Jason Ward, rhp, Utah Valley State JC.
38. Justin Taylor, rhp, Baylor University.
39. *Eric Hullinger, rhp, Kishwaukee (Ill.) JC.
40. *Vince Berry, of, Triton (Ill.) JC.
41. Drew Endicott, rhp, University of Missouri.
42. *Odell Cosby, of, Paris (Ky.) HS.
43. David Nelson, lhp, North Carolina A&T University.
44. *Bryan McCaulley, rhp, San Jacinto (Calif.) JC.
45. *Andrew Scholl, of-1b, Lamar (Colo.) CC.
46. *Devan Ewell, of, Osborne HS, Manassas, Va.
47. *Ty Wallace, c, Newman Smith HS, Carrollton, Texas.
48. Lenny Bays, rhp, Northern Kentucky University.
49. *Luis Rivera, ss, Carvin School, Carolina, P.R.
50. *Matt Hobbs, lhp, University of. Missouri.

## LOS ANGELES DODGERS (19)

**1. James Loney, 1b-lhp, Elkins HS, Missouri City, Texas.—(2006-15)**
1. Greg Miller, lhp, Esperanza HS, Yorba Linda, Calif. (Supplemental choice—31st—as compensation for Type A free agent Chan Ho Park).—(AAA)
2. Zach Hammes, rhp, Iowa City (Iowa) HS (Choice from Rangers as compensation for Park).—(AAA)
**2. Jonathan Broxton, rhp, Burke County HS, Waynesboro, Ga.—(2005-15)**
3. Mike Nixon, c, Sunnyslope HS, Phoenix.—(AAA)
**4. Delwyn Young, 2b, Santa Barbara (Calif.) CC.—(2006-10)**
5. Mike Megrew, lhp, Chariho Regional HS, Hope Valley, R.I.—(AAA)
6. Marshall Looney, lhp, La Pine (Ore.) HS.
7. David Bagley, 3b, University of San Diego.
8. Jamaal Hamilton, lhp, Monterey HS, Lubbock, Texas.
9. *Denver Kitch, ss, University of Oklahoma.
10. Ryan Williams, rhp, Old Dominion University.
**11. +James McDonald, 1b-rhp, Poly HS, Long Beach, Calif. / Golden West (Calif.) JC.—(2008-13)**
DRAFT DROP *Son of James McDonald, tight end, National Football League (1983-87)*
12. Ryan Owen, c, Wichita State University.
13. Julio LaSalle, rhp, Palm Beach Atlantic (Fla.) College.
14. *Karl Mejlholm, rhp, Dover Bay HS, Nanaimo, B.C.
**15. Eric Stults, lhp, Bethel (Ind.) College.—(2006-15)**
16. Sambu Ndungidi, of, St. Georges HS, Montreal.

**The Brewers drafted Prince Fielder, son of AL home run champ Cecil, with the seventh pick**

DRAFT DROP *Brother of Ntema Ndungidi, first-round draft pick, Orioles (1997)*
**17. Russell Martin, 3b, Chipola (Fla.) JC.—(2006-15)**
18. *Curtis Hudson, c, Yuba City (Calif.) HS.
19. Michael White, lhp, St. Petersburg (Fla.) JC.
20. *Andrew Walker, rhp, Cowley County (Kan.) CC.
21. *Brian Tracy, rhp, Claremont (Calif.) HS.
DRAFT DROP *Son of Jim Tracy, major leaguer (1980-81); major league manager (2001-12)*
22. Brett Wayne, ss, St. Mary's (Calif.) College.
23. *Josh Bartusick, 1b, Fountain Valley (Calif.) HS.
24. +D.J. Jackson, of, Jesuit HS, Portland, Ore. / Chandler-Gilbert (Ariz.) JC.
25. +Alvin Hayes, rhp, Alabama Southern CC.
26. Jarod Plummer, rhp, South Garland HS, Garland, Texas.
27. Mike Potoczny, rhp, North Marion HS, Farmington, W. Va.
**28. *Robert Ray, rhp, Lufkin (Texas) HS.—(2009-10)**
29. +Dom Laurin, ss-2b, Eastern Oklahoma State JC.
30. *Edward Roberts, rhp, Key West (Fla.) HS.
31. Ross Hawley, rhp, Kansas State University.
32. *Richie Robnett, of, Santa Barbara (Calif.) CC.
DRAFT DROP *First-round draft pick (26th overall), Athletics (2004)*
33. *Eddie Baeza, rhp, Poly HS, Sun Valley, Calif.
**34. *Doug Mathis, rhp, Show Low (Ariz.) HS.—(2008-10)**
35. *Matt Long, rhp, Granville (Ohio) HS.
36. Bryan Goelz, of, New York Tech.
37. *Jon Riggleman, 3b, Hillsborough (Fla.) CC.
DRAFT DROP *Son of Jim Riggleman, major league manager (1992-2011)*
38. *Danny Forrer, lhp, Jefferson Davis HS, Montgomery, Ala.
**39. *Luke Hochevar, rhp, Fowler (Col.) HS.—(2007-15)**
DRAFT DROP *First-round draft pick (40th overall), Dodgers (2005); first overall draft pick, Royals (2006)*
40. *Eric Wolfe, 1b, York Mills HS, Willowdale, Ontario.
41. *Ryan Lennerton, Eastern Oklahoma State JC.
42. *Nathan Warrick, of, Belton (Texas) HS.
43. David Parker, rhp, Eastern Oklahoma State CC.
44. *James Bailie, c, Kodiak (Alaska) HS.
45. *Justin Estrada, ss, Tampa Jesuit HS, Tampa.
46. Mickey Jordan, of, Armstrong Atlantic State (Ga.) University.
47. +Chad Bailey, lhp, North Idaho JC / Seminole State (Okla.) JC.
48. *Andre Trahan, of, Yuba (Calif.) CC.
49. *Jeff Cristy, c, Southeast HS, Lincoln, Neb.
50. *Jason Farrand, c, Conway (S.C.) HS.

## MILWAUKEE BREWERS (7)

**1. Prince Fielder, 1b, Eau Gallie HS, Melbourne, Fla.—(2005-15)**
2. Josh Murray, ss, Tampa Jesuit HS, Tampa.—(High A)
3. Eric M. Thomas, rhp, University of South Alabama.—(High A)
4. Nic Carter, of, Campbell University.—(Low A)
5. *Jarrad Page, ss, San Leandro (Calif.) HS.—(AAA)
DRAFT DROP *Attended UCLA; re-drafted by Brewers, 2005 (32nd round); defensive back, National Football League (2006-11)*
6. Khalid Ballouli, rhp, Texas A&M University.
DRAFT DROP *Grandson of Dick Fowler, major leaguer (1941-52)*
**7. Tom Wilhelmsen, rhp, Tucson Magnet HS, Tucson, Ariz.—(2011-15)**
8. *Steve Kahn, rhp, Servite HS, Anaheim, Calif.
9. Edwin Walker, lhp, Highland HS, San Antonio, Texas.
10. Jeremy Frost, c, University of Central Florida.
11. *Brian Hernandez, c, John I. Leonard HS, Boynton Beach, Fla.
**12. Callix Crabbe, 2b, Manatee (Fla.) CC.—(2008)**
13. *Tila Reynolds, ss, University of Washington.
14. Kennard Bibbs, of, Oklahoma City University.
15. +Justin Barnes, rhp, Manatee (Fla.) CC.
**16. +Dana Eveland, lhp, Hill (Texas) JC / JC of the Canyons (Calif.).—(2005-15)**
17. +Adam Mannon, of, Hamilton HS, Chandler, Ariz. / Chandler-Gilbert (Ariz.) JC.
18. *Steven White, rhp, Baylor University.
19. Jeremy Hall, rhp, University of Central Florida.
20. Tyler Shepple, rhp, University of Washington.
21. Josh Alliston, rhp, Long Beach State University.
22. Lendon Willis, 3b, Motlow State (Tenn.) CC.
23. Keith Bohanan, 3b, Oklahoma City University.
24. Arturo Bravo, c, Montgomery HS, San Ysidro, Calif.
25. John Vanden Berg, c, University of Wisconsin-Milwaukee.
**26. Craig Breslow, lhp, Yale University.—(2005-15)**
27. Dallas Bates, of, Chandler (Ariz.) HS.
28. Eric A. Thomas, rhp, Southern University.
29. Steve Moss, of, Notre Dame HS, Sherman Oaks, Calif.
30. Justin Gabriel, lhp, University of Louisiana-Lafayette.
31. Jason Baker, rhp, George Washington University.
32. +Simon Beresford, rhp, Tyler (Texas) JC / Texarkana (Texas) JC.
33. Jeff Housman, lhp, Cal State Fullerton.
**34. +Tim Dillard, c, Itawamba (Miss.) CC.—(2008-12)**
DRAFT DROP *Son of Steve Dillard, major leaguer (1975-82)*
35. *Emmanuel Cividanes, of, Colegio San Antonio HS, San Juan, P.R.
36. *Daniel Carter, rhp, Tallahassee (Fla.) CC.
37. *Stephen Bryant, c, Warren Central HS, Indianapolis, Ind.
38. *David Hancox, rhp, Pasco Hernando (Fla.) CC.
39. *Juan Herrera, lhp, Arizona Western JC.
**40. *Hunter Pence, of, Texarkana (Texas) CC.—(2007-15)**
41. *Jonathan Shapland, of, St. Petersburg (Fla.) JC.
42. *Neil Avery, lhp-of, Dartmouth HS, North Dartmouth, Mass.

## MINNESOTA TWINS (20)

**1. Denard Span, of, Tampa Catholic HS, Tampa.—(2008-15)**
**2. Jesse Crain, rhp, University of Houston.—(2004-13)**
3. *Mark Sauls, rhp, Bay HS, Panama City, Fla.—(Rookie)
DRAFT DROP *Attended Florida State; never re-drafted*
4. Alex Merricks, lhp, Oxnard (Calif.) HS.—(Rookie)
**5. *Clete Thomas, of, Mosley HS, Lynn Haven, Fla.—(2008-13)**
DRAFT DROP *Attended Auburn; re-drafted by Tigers, 2005 (6th round)*
**6. Pat Neshek, rhp, Butler University.—(2006-15)**
7. Ricky Barrett, lhp, University of San Diego.
**8. *Adam Lind, 1b, Highland HS, Anderson, Ind.—(2006-15)**
9. Doug Deeds, of, Ohio State University.
**10. Kyle Phillips, c, El Capitan HS, Lakeside, Calif.—(2009-11)**
**11. +Evan Meek, rhp, Inglemoor HS, Bothell, Wash. / Bellevue (Wash.) CC.—(2008-14)**
**12. *Jeff Clement, c, Marshalltown (Iowa) HS.—(2007-12)**
DRAFT DROP *First-round draft pick (3rd overall), Mariners (2005)*
13. *Bo Pettit, rhp, Louisiana State University.
**14. *Garrett Mock, rhp, Grayson County (Texas) CC.—(2008-10)**
15. Adam Harben, rhp, Westark (Ark.) CC.
16. KC Jones, rhp, Eatonville (Wash.) HS.
17. *Adam Hawes, rhp, St. Theresa's Catholic HS, Victoria Harbour, Ontario.
18. Javier Lopez, of, Galveston (Texas) JC.
19. *Adam Daniels, lhp, North Vancouver, B.C.

20. *Ryan Schreppel, lhp, Lincoln HS, Stockton, Calif.
21. T.J. Prunty, rhp, University of Miami.
22. Justin Sims, of, Middle Tennessee State University.
23. Danny Matienzo, c, University of Miami.
24. *Josh Petersen, 1b, Jupiter (Fla.) HS.
25. Justin Keeling, lhp, California Lutheran University.
26. *Jared Johnson, rhp, Cimarron Memorial HS, Las Vegas, Nev.
27. Ronnie Perodin, of, El Camino (Calif.) CC.
28. *Hasan Rasheed, of, Whites Creek HS, Nashville, Tenn.
29. *James Avery, rhp, Central Collegiate HS, Moose Jaw, Sask.
30. *Roberto Martinez, rhp, St. Petersburg (Fla.) CC.
31. +Terry Killion, rhp, Bowie HS, Austin, Texas / Temple (Texas) JC.
32. +Jon Koch, rhp, Lake City (Fla.) CC.
33. *Tom Ferrara, rhp, Brevard (Fla.) CC.
34. *Christian Castorri, rhp, Thomas County Central HS, Thomasville, Ga.
35. Tarrence Patterson, of, Bartow HS, Lakeland, Fla.
36. John Cahill, rhp, Lakewood (Calif.) HS.
37. *Mike Costantino, 3b, Somerset (Mass.) HS.
38. *Toby Gardenhire, ss, Westark (Ark.) CC.

DRAFT DROP *Son of Ron Gardenhire, major league manager (2002-14)*

39. *Brandon Doddo, c, Cooper City (Fla.) HS.
40. *Rodney Story, lhp, Gulf Coast (Fla.) CC.
41. *Chris Brown, 2b, Cooper City (Fla.) HS.
42. +Kyle Geiger, c, Rend Lake (Ill.) JC.
43. *Jacob Jean, lhp, Cosumnes River (Calif.) CC.
44. *Chris Beatty, ss, Kokomo (Ind.) HS.
45. *John Stocco, rhp, Academy of Holy Angels HS, Richfield, Minn.
46. *Wayne Renfrow, rhp, Kellam HS, Virginia Beach, Va.
47. *Brandon Carlton, lhp, Bay HS, Panama City, Fla.
48. *Brandon Cohen, of, River Dell HS, Oradell, N.J.
49. **Brock Peterson, 3b, W.F. West HS, Chehalis, Wash.—(2013)**
50. *Mike Ballard, lhp, Ocean Lakes HS, Virginia Beach, Va.

## MONTREAL EXPOS (5)

1. Clint Everts, rhp, Cypress Falls HS, Houston.—(AAA)
2. **Darrell Rasner, rhp, University of Nevada.—(2005-08)**
3. Larry Broadway, 1b, Duke University.—(AAA)
4. Jon Felfoldi, lhp, Glendale (Calif.) CC.—(AA)
5. Anthony Pearson, rhp, Jackson State University.—(High A)
6. Chad Chop, 1b, Vanguard (Calif.) University.
7. **Mike O'Connor, lhp, George Washington University.—(2006-11)**
8. *Friedel Pinkston, rhp, Hart County HS, Hartwell, Ga.
9. Chris Barlow, rhp, Le Moyne College.

DRAFT DROP *Son of Mike Barlow, major leaguer (1975-81)*

10. *Justin Azze, lhp, Orange Coast (Calif.) JC.
11. **Jason Bergmann, rhp, Rutgers University.—(2005-10)**
12. Danny Rueckel, rhp, Furman University.
13. Brett Nyquist, lhp, College of St. Scholastica (Minn.).
14. Erik Fiedler, rhp, San Diego State University.
15. Isaiah Wright, rhp, Dover (Del.) HS.
16. Brian Ellerson, ss, Montclair State (N.J.) University.
17. Jason Conlisk, ss, Fordham University.
18. Anthony Brown, of, George Washington University.
19. Franklyn Jimenez, 2b, Muscatine (Iowa) CC.
20. Tim Sweeney, ss, Rutgers University.
21. Stockton Davis, rhp, Oral Roberts University.
22. *Marcus Davis, rhp, Luray (Va.) HS.
23. Nathan Weese, of, University of Utah.
24. Matt Swope, of, University of Maryland.
25. Adrian Urquhart, of, Alabama State University.
26. Maurice Cobb, of, Rocky Mount (N.C.) HS.
27. *Matt Bonovich, c, University of Southern California.
28. *Tony Irvin, rhp, Hillsborough (Fla.) CC.
29. *Tim Hudnall, 1b, Lake Michigan JC.
30. *Robert Rohrbaugh, lhp, Littlestown (Pa.) Area HS.
31. *Ruben Kerbs, lhp, Wichita State University.
32. *Cam O'Donnell, rhp, Middle Georgia JC.
33. *Andrew Wells, lhp, St. Stephens-St. Agnes HS, Alexandria, Va.
34. *Jack Lyons, lhp, Maret HS, Washington, D.C.
35. ***Sean White, rhp, University of Washington.—(2007-10)**
36. *Jeff Miller, 1b, Pine Grove (Pa.) Area HS.
37. *Jarvis Hicks, rhp, South Florida CC.
38. *Nick Ponomarenko, rhp, Cuesta (Calif.) JC.
39. *Jon Hunton, rhp, Miami-Dade CC North.
40. *Bryan Coffey, rhp, Culpepper HS, Rixeyville, Va.
41. *Michael Romeo, 3b, Lindenhurst (N.Y.) HS.
42. *Randy Dicken, rhp, Allegany (Md.) CC.
43. *Brody Taylor, lhp, Louisburg (N.C.) CC.
44. *Michael Gibbs, rhp, Roxborough HS, Philadelphia.
45. ***Jon Link, rhp, Chantilly (Va.) HS.—(2010)**
46. *Marc Nunez, rhp, Countryside HS, St. Petersburg, Fla.
47. *Ronald Ball, rhp, John F. Kennedy HS, Buena Park, Calif.
48. Ken Beck, rhp, University of Maryland.
49. *James Treece, rhp, Orange Coast (Calif.) CC.
50. *Joe Gregory, rhp, Western HS, Davie, Fla.

## NEW YORK METS (15)

1. **Scott Kazmir, lhp, Cypress Falls HS, Houston.—(2004-15)**
2. (Choice to Cubs as compensation for Type A free agent David Weathers)
3. (Choice to Tigers as compensation for Type B free agent Roger Cedeno)
4. Bobby Malek, of, Michigan State University.—(AAA)
5. Jon Slack, of, Texas Tech.—(AAA)
6. Adam Elliott, rhp, Clayton Valley HS, Concord, Calif.
7. Jim Anderson, c, UC Riverside.
8. Tyler Davidson, of, University of Washington.
9. *Christian Colonel, ss, JC of Southern Idaho.
10. **Matt Lindstrom, rhp, Ricks (Idaho) JC.—(2007-14)**
11. Kelvin Garay, lhp, Colegio Santa Cruz HS, Trujillo Alta, P.R.
12. Shawn Bowman, 3b, Dr. Charles Best SS, Coquitlam, B.C.
13. Blake Whealy, 2b, University of Evansville.
14. Jeff Brewer, rhp, University of British Columbia.
15. *Elvys Quezada, rhp, Seton Hall University.
16. Zac Clements, c, Christian Brothers (Tenn.) University.
17. Laron Wilson, of, Longwood (Va.) College.
18. Ivan Maldonado, rhp, Indian Hills (Iowa) CC.
19. Bryan King, rhp, Mesa State (Colo.) College.
20. Will Hudson, ss, Oregon State University.
21. *Brendan Winn, of, Brevard (Fla.) CC.
22. Tim McNab, rhp, Florida Atlantic University.
23. Rashad Parker, of, UCLA.
24. Robert Paulk, rhp, North Florida JC.
25. *Nathan Kiser, 1b, Lebanon (Va.) HS.
26. *Kyle Cullinan, 3b, Fullerton (Calif.) JC.
27. *Ricky Steik, rhp, John F. Kennedy HS, La Palma, Calif.
28. *Chris Munn, rhp, St. Thomas Aquinas HS, Fort Lauderdale, Fla.
29. *Timothy Didjurgis, rhp, Pima (Ariz.) JC.
30. ***Chris Robinson, c, Lord Dorchester SS, Dorchester, Ontario.—(2013)**
31. +Marcos Cabral, ss-2b, Southwest HS, Miami / Broward (Fla.) CC.
32. +Todd Dulaney, 2b, Wabash Valley (Ill.) JC.
33. *Tim Jones, of, Morristown (N.J.) HS.
34. Chase Lambin, ss, University of Louisiana-Lafayette.
35. *John Findley, rhp, Nettleton HS, Jonesboro, Ark.
36. *Joey Huskins, c, Fountain Valley (Calif.) HS.
37. +Billy Weitzman, rhp, Briarcliffe (N.Y.) JC.
38. *Derek Antelo, rhp, Broward (Fla.) JC.
39. *Dewayne Carver, rhp, Daytona Beach (Fla.) CC.
40. *Jonathan Malo, ss, Montmorency (Quebec) College.
41. *Steven Romero, rhp, South Hills HS, Walnut, Calif.
42. *Ryan DiPietro, lhp, Berlin HS, Kensington, Conn.
43. *Jeremy Brown, of, Sylvan Hills HS, Sherwood, Ark.
44. +Ian Bladergroen, 1b, Lamar (Colo.) CC.
45. *Brian Rabbitt, rhp, Brookdale (N.J.) CC.
46. *Doug Fink, rhp, Southington (Conn.) HS.
47. *Troy Roberson, rhp, University of Miami.
48. *Alfred Profeet, c, Delaware Tech & CC.
49. *Esteban Lopez, c, Chandler (Ariz.) HS.
50. *Jack Spradlin, lhp, Eastlake HS, Chula Vista, Calif.

## NEW YORK YANKEES (24)

1. (Choice to Athletics as compensation for Type A free agent Jason Giambi)
2. (Choice to Braves as compensation for Type A free agent Steve Karsay)
2. Brandon Weeden, rhp-ss, Santa Fe HS, Edmond, Okla. (Choice from Cardinals as compensation for Type B free agent Tino Martinez).—(High A)

DRAFT DROP *First-round draft pick, Cleveland Browns/ National Football League (2012); quarterback, NFL (2012-15)*

3. (Choice to Cubs as compensation for Type A free agent Rondell White)
4. Alan Bomer, rhp, University of Texas.—(Short-season A)
5. **Matt Carson, of, Brigham Young University.—(2009-13)**
6. Brandon Harmsen, rhp, Grand Rapids (Mich.) JC.
7. Ross Michelsen, 1b, Lamar (Texas) HS.
8. **Brad Halsey, lhp, University of Texas.—(2004-06)**
9. Eric Verbryke, of, Cal State Northridge.
10. Gary Bell, lhp, University of South Carolina.
11. Scott McClanahan, of, University of Alabama.
12. Matt Mamula, 1b, Point Loma Nazarene (Calif.) College.
13. Blake Blase, 1b, Jefferson (Mo.) JC.
14. Ray Clark, rhp, University of Texas.
15. Philip Tribe, rhp, Rice University.
16. Jared Koutnik, ss, Michigan State University.
17. Gabe Lopez, 2b, San Jose State University.
18. Luis Robles, c, Riverside (Calif.) CC.
19. Jon Sheaffer, of, Arizona State University.
20. Ben King, lhp, University of Texas.
21. Hector Zamora, 3b, San Jose State University.
22. *Skyler Fulton, of, Skagit Valley (Wash.) JC.

DRAFT DROP *Wide receiver, National Football League (2006)*

23. **Eric Hacker, rhp, Duncanville (Texas) HS.—(2009-12)**
24. **+Dane de la Rosa, rhp, Riverside (Calif.) CC.—(2011-14)**
25. Josh Neitz, rhp, Saint Leo (Fla.) College.
26. **+Phil Coke, lhp, San Joaquin Delta (Calif.) JC.—(2008-15)**
27. +Mike Knox, rhp, Jesuit College Prep, Dallas/ Navarro (Texas) JC.
28. Nathan Kopp, lhp, Wright State University.
29. Charlie Isaacson, rhp, University of Arkansas.
30. *Kyle Marlatt, rhp, San Jacinto (Texas) JC.
31. Paul Thorp, rhp, Baylor University.
32. Justin Meccage, rhp, Oklahoma State University.
33. *David Smith, lhp, Parkland (Ill.) JC.
34. Nathan Bowden, ss, University of North Alabama.
35. *Michael Brown, rhp, Owasso (Okla.) HS.
36. Doug Boone, c, Ball State University.
37. +Richard Cowan, rhp, Navarro (Texas) JC.
38. *Justin Keadle, rhp, Cypress (Calif.) JC.
39. *Randy Gattis, rhp, Mesquite HS, Dallas.
40. Joseph DiFranco, rhp, St. Thomas (Fla.) University.
41. Mike Miehls, c, Tennessee Tech.
42. *Matt Goodson, rhp, Galveston (Texas) JC.
43. *Jason Maes, lhp, Folsom HS, Elk Grove, Calif.
44. Matt Brumit, rhp, Youngstown State University.
45. *Matt Yost, 1b, Elk City (Okla.) HS.
46. Jared Treadway, of, College of Wooster (Ohio).
47. *Ryan Jennings, rhp, James Monroe HS, Lindside, W.Va.
48. *Billy Carnline, rhp, New Caney (Texas) HS.
49. *Levi Dartt, lhp, Denton (Texas) HS.
50. *Arthur Christal, of, Ennis (Texas) HS.

## OAKLAND ATHLETICS (26)

1. **Nick Swisher, 1b-of, Ohio State University** (Choice from Red Sox as compensation for Type A free agent Johnny Damon).**—(2004-15)**
1. **Joe Blanton, rhp, University of Kentucky** (Choice from Yankees as compensation for Type A free agent Jason Giambi).**—(2004-13)**
1. John McCurdy, ss, University of Maryland.—(AA)
1. Ben Fritz, c/rhp, Fresno State University (Choice from Cardinals as compensation for Type A free agent Jason Isringhausen).—(AAA)
1. **Jeremy Brown, c, University of Alabama** (Supplemental choice—35th—as compensation for Giambi).**—(2006)**
1. Steve Obenchain, rhp, University of Evansville (Supplemental choice—37th—as compensation for Isringhausen).—(AA)
1. **Mark Teahen, 3b, St. Mary's (Calif.) College** (Supplemental choice—39th—as compensation for Damon).**—(2005-11)**
2. Steve Stanley, of, University of Notre Dame.—(AAA)
3. **Bill Murphy, lhp, Cal State Northridge.—(2007-09)**
4. **John Baker, c, University of California.—(2008-14)**
5. **Mark Kiger, ss, University of Florida.—(2006)**
6. Brian Stavisky, of, University of Notre Dame.
7. Brant Colamarino, 1b, University of Pittsburgh.
8. **Jared Burton, rhp, Western Carolina University.—(2007-14)**
9. **Shane Komine, rhp, University of Nebraska.—(2006-07)**
10. J.R. Pickens, rhp, University of Mississippi.
11. Justin Crowder, lhp, Rice University.
12. Kirk Nordness, of, Armstrong Atlantic State (Ga.) University.
13. Tyler Klippenstein, 3b, University of Lethbridge (Alberta).
14. Brad Knox, rhp, Central Arizona JC.
15. Chris Dunwell, rhp, San Diego State University.
16. Lloyd Turner, 2b, Kennesaw State University.
17. David Harriman, c, Armstrong Atlantic State (Ga.) University.
18. Jose Corchado, rhp, Hilberto Domenech HS, Isabela, P.R.
19. *Dusty Barnard, rhp, Moore (Okla.) HS.
20. ***Trevor Crowe, ss, Westview HS, Portland, Ore.—(2009-13)**

DRAFT DROP *First-round draft pick (14th overall), Indians (2005)*

21. *Wally Pontiff, 3b, Louisiana State University.
22. Shawn Kohn, rhp, University of Washington.
23. Chris Shank, rhp, Franklin Pierce (N.H.) College.
24. Danny Gibbons, of, Central Michigan University.
25. Steve Schilsky, rhp, Illinois Wesleyan University.
26. Ty Bubalo, c, Beaverton (Ore.) HS.
27. *Greg Dupas, rhp, Arlington HS, Riverside, Calif.
28. Andy Dickinson, lhp, University of Illinois.
29. Danny Barnett, rhp, Salt Lake (Utah) CC.
30. *Brian Rodgers, of, Berkmar HS, Lilburn, Ga.
31. ***Brad Ziegler, rhp, Southwest Missouri State University.—(2008-15)**
32. ***J.R. Towles, c, Crosby (Texas) HS.—(2007-11)**
33. *Nate Nelson, 1b, Holy Name Central Catholic HS, Worcester, Mass.
34. *Rene Quintana, ss, Patria la Torres HS, San Sebastien, P.R.
35. *Robby Jacobson, c, Durango HS, Las Vegas, Nev.
36. Jed Morris, c, University of Nebraska.
37. *Mark Rodrigues, rhp, Los Medanos (Calif.) JC.
38. *Jason Williams, rhp, Cactus Shadows HS, Cave Creek, Ariz.
39. *Joel Evans, rhp, Columbia Basin (Wash.) CC.
40. ***Jonathan Papelbon, rhp, Mississippi State University.—(2005-15)**
41. +Don Sutton, 1b, Durango HS, Las Vegas, Nev. / CC of Southern Nevada.
42. *Joe Ryan, rhp, Assumption HS, Davenport, Iowa.
43. *Curtis White, lhp, University of Oklahoma.
44. ***Ty Taubenheim, rhp, Edmonds (Wash.) CC.—(2006-08)**
45. *Matthew Elfeldt, rhp, Boston College.

## PHILADELPHIA PHILLIES (17)

1. **Cole Hamels, lhp, Rancho Bernardo HS, San Diego.—(2006-15)**
2. **Zach Segovia, rhp, Forney (Texas) HS.—**

**(2007-09)**
3. Kiel Fisher, 3b-of, Poly HS, Riverside, Calif.—(Low A)
4. Nick Bourgeois, lhp, Tulane University.—(AA)
5. Jake Blalock, 3b, Rancho Bernardo HS, San Diego.—(AA)

DRAFT DROP *Brother of Hank Blalock, major leaguer (2002-10)*

6. Lee Gwaltney, rhp, Louisiana Tech.
7. Robby Read, rhp, Florida State University.
8. *Steven Doetsch, of, Dunedin (Fla.) HS.
9. Rob Harrand, rhp, San Diego State University.
10. Ryan Barthelemy, 1b, Florida State University.
11. ***T.J. Beam, rhp, University of Mississippi.—(2006-08)**
12. Trent Pratt, c, Auburn University.
13. Brian Manfred, c, San Diego State University.
14. Darin Naatjes, rhp, Stanford University.
15. Victor Menocal, ss, Georgia Tech.
16. Omar Bramasco, ss, Long Beach (Calif.) CC.
17. **Scott Mathieson, rhp, Aldergrove (B.C.) SS.—(2006-11)**
18. Chad Oliva, c, Jacksonville University.
19. **Bobby Korecky, rhp, University of Michigan.—(2008-14)**
20. Karl Nonemaker, of, Vanderbilt University.
21. *Brett McMillan, 3b, Ponderosa HS, Shingle Springs, Calif.
22. *Brad McCann, 3b, Gulf Coast (Fla.) CC.

DRAFT DROP *Brother of Brian McCann, major leaguer (2005-15)*

23. *Jason Fletcher, rhp, Indian River (Fla.) CC.
24. Whit Bryant, lhp, Elon College.
25. Zach Minor, rhp, Fresno State University.
26. Erik Winegarden, c, New Mexico State University.
27. Brad Busbin, rhp, University of Central Florida.
28. Derek Brewster, rhp, Louisiana Tech.
29. Adam Steen, rhp, Minnesota State University-Mankato.
30. Ryan Wardinsky, ss, Texas A&M University.
31. Jeremy Isenhower, 2b, Southwest Missouri State University.
32. Rob Cafiero, 1b, Villanova University.
33. Jeremy Rogelstad, rhp, San Jose State University.
34. Beau Richardson, lhp, Tulane University.
35. Josh Paddock, rhp, Aurora (Ill.) University.
36. *Keahi Rawlins, rhp, Molokai HS, Kaunakakai, Hawaii.
37. Tim Gradoville, c, Creighton University.
38. *Corey Carter, of, West Point (Miss.) HS.
39. *Daniel Lewis, rhp, Folsom (Calif.) HS.
40. *Brandon Joseph, of, A.J. Dimond HS, Anchorage, Alaska.
41. *McCay Green, rhp, Edgewater HS, Orlando, Fla.
42. *Clay Dirks, lhp, Hernando (Miss.) HS.
43. *Byron Cragg, rhp, Galena HS, Reno, Nev.
44. *Jacob Habsieger, lhp, Festus (Mo.) HS.
45. ***Sam Lecure, rhp, Helias HS, Centertown, Mo.—(2010-15)**
46. ***Dusty Ryan, c, Golden Valley HS, Merced, Calif.—(2008-09)**
47. *Ryan Greives, rhp, Benton Central HS, Otterbein, Ind.
48. *Dennis Winn, ss, Bowling Green, Ky.

## PITTSBURGH PIRATES (1)

1. **Bryan Bullington, rhp, Ball State University.—(2005-10)**
2. Blair Johnson, rhp, Washburn HS, Topeka, Kan.—(AA)
3. Taber Lee, ss, San Diego State University.—(AAA)

DRAFT DROP *Brother of Travis Lee, first-round draft pick, Twins (1996); major leaguer (1998-2006)*

4. +Wardell Starling, rhp, Elkins HS, Missouri City, Texas / Odessa (Texas) JC.—(AA)
5. Alex Hart, rhp, University of Florida.—(High A)
6. **Brad Eldred, 1b, Florida International University.—(2005-12)**
7. **Matt Capps, rhp, Alexander HS, Douglasville, Ga.—(2005-12)**
8. Bobby Kingsbury, of, Fordham University.
9. Joe Hicks, of, Forest Brook HS, Houston.
10. **Dave Davidson, lhp, Denis Morris HS, Thorold, Ontario.—(2007-09)**
11. Anthony Bocchino, of, Marist College.
12. Brian Holliday, rhp, Moon Area HS, Moon Township, Pa.
13. *Chris Cunningham, c, University of Arizona.
14. John Smith, 2b, Middle Georgia JC.
15. Jon Schneider, rhp, Liberty University.
16. John Hummel, lhp, Schaumburg (Ill.) HS.
17. **Chris DeMaria, rhp, Long Beach State University.—(2005-06)**
18. *Jeff Watchko, rhp, Georgia Tech.
19. *Herbert Andres, rhp, W.J. Mouat HS, Abbotsford, B.C.
20. Russ Bayer, lhp, Miami (Ohio) University.
21. Chris Holt, rhp, Flagler (Fla.) College.
22. *Paul Harp, rhp, Middle Georgia JC.
23. Dean Devine, 3b-2b, University of South Dakota.
24. Sam Christensen, 1b, University of Southern Colorado.
25. *Matt Cundiff, rhp, Cooper City (Fla.) HS.
26. *Calvin Beamon, of, Smoky Hill HS, Aurora, Colo.
27. *Gene Filyaw, ss, Jasper (Texas) HS.
28. +Anthony Stevens, ss, South Doyle HS, Knoxville, Tenn. / Volunteer State (Tenn.) JC.
29. +Francis Poni, c, Los Angeles Harbor JC.
30. *Chris Toneguzzi, rhp, Markville SS, Thunder Bay, Ontario.
31. *William Webster, c, Moon Valley HS, Phoenix.
32. *Angel Colon, of, San Vicente de Paul HS, Toa Baja, P.R.
33. **Nyjer Morgan, of, Walla Walla (Wash.) CC.—(2007-14)**
34. *Adam Howard, rhp, Ooltewah (Tenn.) HS.
35. *Eric King, 2b, Los Medanos (Calif.) JC.
36. *Ryan Aldridge, rhp, Wayne County HS, Jesup, Ga.
37. *Tony Snow, rhp, Cascade HS, Everett, Wash.
38. *Phillip Stillwell, rhp, North Florida JC.
39. *Chase Moore, of, St. Mary's College HS, Albany, Calif.
40. *Matt Maropis, ss, Franklin Regional HS, Murrysville, Pa.
41. *Rollie Gibson, lhp, Buchanan HS, Fresno, Calif.
42. Chaz Lytle, of, University of Georgia.
43. *Michael Hicks, lhp, St. Stephens HS, Hickory, N.C.

## ST. LOUIS CARDINALS (30)

1. (Choice to Athletics as compensation for Type A free agent Jason Isringhausen)
2. (Choice to Yankees as compensation for Type B free agent Tino Martinez)
3. Calvin Hayes, ss, East Rowan HS, Salisbury, N.C.—(High A)
4. Kyle Boyer, ss, Dixie State (Utah) JC.—(Low A)
5. *Josh Bell, c, North Side HS, Jackson, Tenn.—(Low A)

DRAFT DROP *Attended Auburn; re-drafted by Dodgers, 2005 (4th round)*

6. Cody Haerther, 3b, Chaminade Prep, Chatsworth, Calif.
7. David Williamson, lhp, University of Massachusetts-Lowell.
8. Tyler Parker, c, Georgia Tech.
9. Travis Hanson, ss, University of Portland.
10. Matt Lemanczyk, of, Sacred Heart University.

DRAFT DROP *Son of Dave Lemanczyk, major leaguer (1973-80)*

11. David Brockman, rhp, Grand Canyon University.
12. Bob Runyon, rhp, Fresno State University.
13. **Reid Gorecki, of, University of Delaware.—(2009)**
14. Joe Van Gorder, lhp, West Virginia University.
15. Daylon Monette, of, Oklahoma State University.
16. **Brad Thompson, rhp, Dixie State (Utah) JC.—(2005-10)**
17. *Chad Clark, rhp, University of Southern California.
18. Scott Schweitzer, lhp, Kentucky Wesleyan College.
19. *Ryan Mulhern, of, University of South Alabama.
20. Hal Chafey, lhp, Francis Marion (S.C.) University.
21. Gabe Veloz, 2b, New Mexico State University.
22. Andy Davidson, lhp, Cal State Northridge.
23. Rich Scalamandre, rhp, Dominican (N.Y.) College.
24. Kevin Coleman, rhp, University of Florida.
25. **Kyle McClellan, rhp, Hazelwood West HS, Hazelwood, Mo.—(2008-13)**
26. Mitch Maio, rhp, University of Utah.
27. *Matt Elliott, rhp, Basic HS, Henderson, Nev.
28. Melvin Falu, 2b, Southern Arkansas University.
29. Wes Jaillet, rhp, St. Louis University.
30. Zach Cates, 1b, Oklahoma State University.
31. Garris Gonce, of, University of South Carolina.
32. *Sean Kasmar, ss, Las Vegas (Nev.) HS.
33. Josh Bridges, c, Martin Methodist (Tenn.) College.
34. **Mike McCoy, 2b, University of San Diego.—(2009-12)**
35. *Julian Williams, of, Long Beach (Calif.) CC.
36. James Mondesir, rhp, Dominican (N.Y.) College.
37. Tyler Durham, 2b, Northwestern State University.
38. *Matt Varner, rhp, Angelina (Texas) JC.
39. Jeff Tolotti, of, University of Nevada.
40. Brian Flynn, rhp, St. Thomas Aquinas (N.Y.) College.
41. Jonathan Estes, rhp, Freed-Hardeman (Tenn.) College.
42. +Kevin Estrada, ss, Pepperdine University.
43. Joey Vandever, of, University of Evansville.
44. *Brock Jacobsen, of, Dixie State (Utah) JC.
45. *Sean Clark, rhp, Chaminade Prep, Chatsworth, Calif.
46. Jason Galbraith, lhp, Concordia (N.Y.) College.
47. *Chris Gibson, 1b-of, Bellevue East HS, Bellevue, Neb.

DRAFT DROP *Son of Bob Gibson, major league (1959-75)*

48. *Philip Perry, rhp, Georgia Tech.
49. *David Dennis, lhp, Valhalla HS, El Cajon, Calif.
50. *John Powell, rhp, McGehee HS, Tillar, Ark.

## SAN DIEGO PADRES (13)

1. **Khalil Greene, ss, Clemson University.—(2003-09)**
2. +Michael Johnson, 1b, Clemson University.—(AAA)
3. Kennard Jones, of, University of Indiana.—(AAA)
4. Aaron Coonrod, rhp, John A. Logan (Ill.) JC.—(High A)
5. Sean Thompson, lhp, Thunder Ridge HS, Denver.—(AAA)
6. Adam Shorsher, c, San Jose State University.
7. *Matt Lynch, lhp, Florida State University.
8. Luke Steidlmayer, rhp, UC Davis.
9. Brian Burgamy, 2b, Wichita State University.
10. L.J. Biernbaum, of, Florida Atlantic University.
11. Brandon Wilson, rhp, Okaloosa-Walton (Fla.) JC.
12. **Paul McAnulty, 1b, Long Beach State University.—(2005-10)**
13. ***Lance Pendleton, rhp, Kingwood (Texas) HS.—(2011)**
14. Gabe Ribas, rhp, Northwestern University.
15. Rolando Agosto, ss, Union (Tenn.) University.
16. Kevin Beavers, lhp, Pepperdine University.
17. Rashad Smith, of, Lambuth (Tenn.) University.
18. *Bruce Gallaway, lhp, Grayson County (Texas) CC.
19. *Spencer Grogan, lhp, Okaloosa-Walton (Fla.) CC.
20. **+George Kottaras, c, Connors State (Okla.) JC.—(2008-14)**
21. ***Andy LaRoche, ss, Grayson County (Texas) CC.—(2007-13)**

DRAFT DROP *Son of Dave LaRoche, major leaguer (1970-83) • Brother of Adam LaRoche, major leaguer (2004-15)*

22. David Krisch, lhp, Cal Poly Pomona.
23. Rusty Moore, of, Bethune-Cookman College.
24. Adam Montarbo, rhp-3b, Cal State Chico.
25. *Chuck Bechtel, rhp, Marist University.
26. E.J. Laratta, rhp, Ohio State University.
27. Brian Whitaker, rhp, University of North Carolina-Wilmington.
28. Mike Richardson, of-c, Sonoma State (Calif.) University.
29. Steve Baker, of, Liberty University.
30. +Danny Delao, lhp, Fresno (Calif.) CC.
31. **+Jared Wells, rhp, Tyler (Texas) JC / San Jacinto (Texas) JC.—(2008)**
32. *Jesse Estrada, rhp, Socorro HS, El Paso, Texas.
33. *Bo Banach, 3b, Lakewood (Calif.) HS.
34. *Bill Silvestri, rhp, Dixie State (Utah) JC.
35. **+Drew Macias, of, Chaffey (Calif.) JC / Dixie State (Utah) JC.—(2007-09)**
36. Greg Bochy, rhp, Cal Poly San Luis Obispo.

DRAFT DROP *Son of Bruce Bochy, major leaguer (1978-87); major league manager (1995-2015) • Brother of Brett Bochy, major leaguer (2014-15)*

37. *Corey Hall, rhp, Seminole State (Okla.) JC.
38. *Brendan Katin, c, Okaloosa-Walton (Fla.) JC.
39. *Scott Lonergan, rhp, Poway (Calif.) HS.
40. *Daniel Fitch, c, Mount Carmel HS, San Diego.
41. *Ryan Werner, c, San Diego CC.
42. +Brian Wahlbrink, of, UC Riverside.
43. *Jason Catala, of, Margarita Janer HS, Guaynabo, P.R.
44. *Marcus Barriger, rhp, Kaskaskia (Ill.) CC.
45. +Chad Etheridge, of, Columbia State (Tenn.) CC/ Volunteer State (Tenn.) JC.
46. *Craig Bartosh, of, Grayson County (Texas) CC.
47. *Stephen Nam, 1b-2b, Iona College HS, Mississauga, Ontario.
48. *Matthew Morizio, rhp-ss, Waltham (Mass.) HS.
49. *John Parscal, lhp, Northglenn HS, Denver.
50. *Chris Regan, 1b-of, Earl Wooster HS, Reno, Nev.

## SAN FRANCISCO GIANTS (25)

1. **Matt Cain, rhp, Houston HS, Germantown, Tenn.—(2005-15)**
2. **Freddie Lewis, of, Southern University.—(2006-12)**
3. **Dan Ortmeier, of, University of Texas-Arlington.—(2005-08)**
4. **Kevin Correia, rhp, Cal Poly San Luis Obispo.—(2003-15)**

DRAFT DROP *First player from 2002 draft to reach majors (July 10, 2003)*

5. Kevin Kelly, ss, Duke University.—(Low A)
6. **Jesse English, lhp, Rancho Buena Vista, Vista, Calif.—(2010)**
7. +Michael Musgrave, rhp, Forest HS, Ocala, Fla. / Central Florida CC.
8. **Clay Hensley, rhp, Lamar University.—(2005-12)**
9. Randy Walter, of, Wichita State University.
10. Glenn Woolard, rhp, Kutztown (Pa.) University.
11. Jake Wald, ss, George Washington University.
12. *Kellen Ludwig, rhp, Chipola (Fla.) JC.
13. Aaron Soberiaj, 3b, University of Florida.
14. Josh Habel, lhp, University of Northern Iowa.
15. Matt Dryer, 1b, University of Miami.
16. Greg Bruso, rhp, UC Davis.
17. Luke Nelson, rhp, Southern Illinois University.
18. Bryan Millikan, rhp, Black Hills HS, Olympia, Wash.
19. *David Timm, lhp, Seminole (Fla.) CC.
20. Ben Mitchell, rhp, Grand Canyon University.
21. **Travis Ishikawa, 1b-of, Federal Way (Wash.) HS.—(2006-15)**
22. Nelson Lopez, rhp, Florida Atlantic University.
23. *Neil Walton, ss, Santa Cruz (Calif.) HS.
24. +Jay Knowlton, ss, Lewis-Clark State (Idaho) College.
25. *Justin Gee, rhp, Sarasota (Fla.) HS.
26. *Sean Rierson, rhp, University of Arizona.
27. +Ryan McGovern, lhp, W.J. Mouat HS, Abbotsford, B.C. / Collin County (Texas) JC.
28. *Philip Tapley, rhp, Greenbrier HS, Evans, Ga.
29. ***Alex Hinshaw, lhp, Chaffey (Calif.) JC.—(2008-12)**
30. *Matt Somnis, rhp, Lassen (Calif.) JC.
31. **Matt Palmer, rhp, Southwest Missouri State University.—(2008-12)**
32. Jamie Bateman, rhp, Massachusetts College of Liberal Arts.
33. *Brett Cooley, 1b-of, University of Houston.
34. *Phil Monte, lhp, Cosumnes River (Calif.) JC.
35. *Ryan Stevenson, of, Chabot (Calif.) JC.
36. David Stone, of, University of Virginia.
37. *Chris Sweet, rhp, University of Virginia.
38. *Randal Hodge, lhp, Pearl-Cohn HS, Nashville, Tenn.
39. Anthony Moreno, rhp, South Mountain (Ariz.) CC.
40. *Mike Redford, rhp, Woodland HS, Sacramento, Calif.
41. *Danny Muegge, rhp, University of Texas.
42. Andrew Jefferson, lhp, Southwest Missouri State University.
43. *Jason Chavez, rhp, Mineral Area (Mo.) JC.
44. *Tim Torres, ss, Diablo Valley (Calif.) JC.
45. *Matt Berezay, of, Sierra HS, Manteca, Calif.
46. *Matt Ircandia, lhp, Semiahmoo HS, Surrey, B.C.
47. *Scott Dodge, of, Cuesta (Calif.) JC.
48. *Dante Brinkley, of, Southwest Missouri State

University.
49. *Zach Borowiak, ss, Southeast Missouri State University.
50. *Robert Davis, c, Greenbrier HS, Evans, Ga.

## SEATTLE MARINERS (28)

**1. *John Mayberry Jr., of, Rockhurst HS, Kansas City, Mo.—(2009-15)**
DRAFT DROP *Attended Stanford; re-drafted by Rangers, 2005 (1st round) • Son of John Mayberry, first-round draft pick, Astros (1967); major leaguer (1968-82)*
2. Josh Womack, of, Crawford HS, San Diego.—(AAA)
3. *Eddy Martinez-Esteve, of, Westminster Christian HS, Miami.—(AAA)
DRAFT DROP *Attended Florida State; re-drafted by Giants, 2004 (2nd round)*
4. Randy Frye, rhp, Lake Orion (Mich.) HS.—(Low A)
5. Kendall Bergdall, lhp, Cimarron HS, Lahoma, Okla.—(Low A)
**6. Troy Cate, lhp, Ricks (Idaho) JC.—(2007)**
7. Evel Bastida-Martinez, 2b, Hialeah, Fla.
8. Brandon Perry, lhp, Graham (N.C.) HS.
9. Terry Forbes, rhp, Auburn Drive HS, Halifax, N.S.
10. Brian Stitt, rhp, Indian River (Fla.) CC.
11. Jared Thomas, lhp, Oakland University.
12. Matt Hagen, 3b, Liberty University.
13. T.A. Fulmer, rhp, The Citadel.
14. Theiborh Almanzar, c, Bronx (N.Y.) CC.
**15. *Gaby Sanchez, 3b, Brito Private HS, Miami.—(2008-14)**
16. Ryan Leaist, rhp, Montreat (N.C.) College.
17. Corey Harrington, ss, New Mexico State University.
18. Gary Harris, of, Georgia College.
19. Chris Kroski, c, St. Petersburg (Fla.) CC.
20. David Viane, rhp, Oakland University.
21. Eric Blakeley, 2b, Indiana University.
22. Hunter Brown, 3b, Rice University.
**23. *Travis Buck, ss, Richland (Wash.) HS.—(2007-12)**
DRAFT DROP *First-round draft pick (36th overall), Athletics (2005)*
24. *Johnnie Bassham, lhp, Grayson County (Texas) CC.
25. *Cory Vanderhook, c, Edison HS, Fountain Valley, Calif.
26. David Bernat, rhp, South Miami HS, Miami.
27. *Royce Dickerson, of, Central HS, Kalamazoo, Mich.
28. Vance Hall, lhp, Allderdice HS, Pittsburgh.
29. +Michael Nesbitt, of, Los Angeles Pierce JC.
**30. T.J. Bohn, of, Bellevue (Neb.) College.—(2006-08)**
31. *Clayton Stewart, rhp, San Jacinto (Texas) JC.
32. *Dane Awana, lhp, Waianae (Hawaii) HS.
33. *Kile Patrick, rhp, Apopka (Fla.) HS.
34. *Brady Burrill, c, Michigan State University.
35. *Patrick Pfeiffer, rhp, Brentwood School, Los Angeles.
36. *Jermaine Smith, ss, King HS, Tampa.
37. +Brad Rose, rhp, Walters State (Tenn.) CC.
38. *Deandre Green, of, Encinal HS, Alameda, Calif.
**39. +Bryan LaHair, of, St. Petersburg (Fla.) JC.—(2008-12)**
40. *Josh Cooper, rhp, Pueblo South HS, Pueblo, Colo.
41. *Andrew Edwards, rhp, Florida International University.
42. *Brandon Jones, 1b, Grayson County (Texas) CC.
43. *Adam Pernasilici, of-1b, St. Anne HS, Tecumseh, Ontario.
44. *Omar Borges, of, Brito Private HS, Miami.
45. *Ray Lockhart, of, Compton (Calif.) HS.
46. *Roberto Mena, 2b, Pedro Falu Orellano HS, Rio Grande, P.R.
47. *Jason Godin, rhp, North Stafford HS, Stafford, Va.
48. +Cardoza Tucker, rhp, Bullard HS, Fresno, Calif. / Fresno (Calif.) CC.
49. *Aaron Ruchti, c, San Jacinto (Texas) JC.
50. Oliver Arias, rhp, CC of Rhode Island.

## TAMPA BAY DEVIL RAYS (2)

**1. B.J. Upton, ss, Greenbrier Christian Academy, Chesapeake, Va.—(2004-15)**
DRAFT DROP *Brother of Justin Upton, first overall draft pick, Diamondbacks (2005); major leaguer (2007-15)*
**2. Jason Pridie, of, Prescott (Ariz.) HS.—(2008-15)**
**3. Elijah Dukes, of, Hillsborough HS, Tampa.—(2007-09)**
**4. Wes Bankston, of, Plano East HS, Plano, Texas.—(2008)**
5. *Mark Romanczuk, lhp, St. Mark's HS, Newark, Del.—(Low A)
DRAFT DROP *Attended Stanford; re-drafted by Diamondbacks, 2005 (4th round)*
**6. *Cesar Ramos, lhp, El Rancho HS, Pico Rivera, Calif.—(2009-15)**
DRAFT DROP *First-round draft pick (35th overall), Padres (2005)*
7. Scott Autrey, rhp, University of North Carolina.
8. Joey Gomes, of, Santa Clara University.
DRAFT DROP *Brother of Jonny Gomes, major leaguer (2003-15)*
**9. *Chris Leroux, c-rhp, St. Joseph's SS, Mississauga, Ontario.—(2009-14)**
10. Jason Hammel, rhp, Treasure Valley (Ore.) JC.—(2006-15)
11. Adam Moreno, rhp, Fresno (Calif.) HS.
12. Blair Irvin, of, Patterson (La.) HS.
13. *Matt Harrington, rhp, Long Beach/Western League.
DRAFT DROP *First-round draft pick (7th overall), Rockies (2000)*
14. Nicholas DeBarr, rhp, Lassen (Calif.) JC.
**15. *Mike Pelfrey, rhp, Wichita Heights HS, Wichita, Kan.—(2006-15)**
DRAFT DROP *First-round draft pick (9th overall), Mets (2005)*
16. Mike Prochaska, lhp, North Carolina State University.
17. Ernest Woodruff, c, Gulf Coast (Fla.) CC.
18. Romelio Lopez, rhp, Conroe (Texas) HS.
19. Cole Smith, rhp, Rockwall (Texas) HS.
20. Jarred Farrell, rhp, Hahnville HS, Boutte, La.
21. *Chris Garcia, rhp, Xaverian HS, Brooklyn, N.Y.
22. *Travis Ingle, rhp, Cal State Fullerton.
**23. *Jacoby Ellsbury, of, Madras (Ore.) HS.—(2007-15)**
DRAFT DROP *First-round draft pick (23rd overall), Red Sox (2005)*
24. Adam Nikolic, of, Cal State Northridge.
25. Brian Bulger, rhp, Georgia College.
DRAFT DROP *Brother of Jason Bulger, first-round draft pick, Diamondbacks (2001); major leaguer (2005-11)*
26. Jarrad LaVergne, lhp, Westgate HS, New Iberia, La.
27. Brandon Mann, lhp, Mount Rainier HS, Des Moines, Wash.
28. *Adam Olerio, rhp, North Kingston (R.I.) HS.
29. *Mike McGowan, rhp, Navarro (Texas) JC.
30. *Mike Geddes, rhp, Jenison (Mich.) HS.
31. Isiah Garner, lhp, University of Arkansas-Pine Bluff.
32. *Rodney Keener, lhp, Minden (La.) HS.
33. Colt Simmons, c, Durango HS, Las Vegas, Nev.
34. *John-Austin Emmons, of, Wharton County (Texas) JC.
35. *Luke Cosmos, rhp, McAteer HS, San Francisco.
36. *Jake Muyco, c, Richland (Wash.) HS.
37. Shane Shelley, ss, Belle Chasse (La.) HS.
38. +Matt Cobb, lhp, Shelton State (Ala.) CC.
39. *Brandon Rousseve, ss, Holy Cross HS, New Orleans, La.
40. *Justin Hopes, rhp, Jeanerette (La.) HS.
41. *Daron Roberts, c, Cosumnes River (Calif.) JC.
DRAFT DROP *Son of Dave Roberts, first overall draft pick, Padres (1972); major leaguer (1972-82)*
42. *Brandon Federici, lhp, Riverview HS, Oakmont, Pa.
43. Steve Skinner, 2b, Santa Rosa (Calif.) JC.
44. *Rolando Quinonez, c, San Juan, P.R.
45. *Justin Standridge, rhp, Clay-Chalkville HS, Pinson, Ala.
DRAFT DROP *Brother of Jason Standridge, first-round draft pick, Devil Rays (1997); major leaguer (2001-07)*
46. +Jino Gonzalez, lhp, CC of Southern Nevada.
47. *Adam Dalby, c, Daingerfield HS, Hughes Spring, Texas.
48. *Jason Urquidez, rhp, Central Arizona JC.
49. Shane Sanders, rhp, University of Alabama.
50. *Bryan Banks, rhp, St. Petersburg (Fla.) JC.

## TEXAS RANGERS (10)

**1. Drew Meyer, ss, University of South Carolina.—(2006)**
2. (Choice to Dodgers as compensation for Type A free agent Chan Ho Park)
3. (Choice to Indians as compensation for Type A free agent Juan Gonzalez)
4. (Choice to Cubs as compensation for Type A free agent Todd Van Poppel)
5. (Choice to Rockies as compensation for Type B free agent Jay Powell)
6. John Barnett, rhp, Florida Southern College.
7. Andrew Tisdale, rhp, Chapman (Calif.) College.
8. Chris O'Riordan, 2b, Stanford University.
9. *Steven Herce, rhp, Rice University.
10. Nate Gold, 1b, Gonzaga University.
11. Kiki Bengochea, rhp, University of Miami.
12. Erik Thompson, rhp, Pensacola (Fla.) JC.
13. Chris Hamblen, c, University of Cincinnati.
14. Charlie Bilezikjian, of, St. John's University.
**15. Sam Narron, lhp, East Carolina University.—(2004)**
DRAFT DROP *Grandson of Sam Narron, major leaguer (1935-43)*
16. Josh Kreuzer, 1b, West Valley (Calif.) JC.
17. *Chris Wilson, 3b, Redlands (Calif.) HS.
18. Cameron Coughlan, 2b, Brigham Young University.
19. *Jesus Maldonado, rhp, Manuel Mediavilla Negron HS, Humacao, P.R.
**20. Kameron Loe, rhp, Cal State Northridge.—(2004-13)**
21. Jason Mann, c, Central Alabama CC.
22. *Rob Andrews, of, Rancho Buena Vista HS, Vista, Calif.
23. Craig Ringe, ss, Central Missouri State University.
24. *Chad Decker, lhp, Valley View HS, Moreno Valley, Calif.
25. Joel Kirsten, lhp, Los Angeles Pierce JC.
26. Julius Smith, lhp, Lewiston (Idaho) HS.
27. *John McCarthy, of, St. Rita HS, Palos Park, Ill.
28. *Jake Tompkins, rhp, Louisiana State University.
29. Nick Shields, c, Wright State University.
30. Rob Corrado, rhp, University of Kentucky.
31. *Michael Tamulionis, rhp, St. John's University.
32. Gary Hogan, rhp, University of Arkansas.
33. Luke Grayson, of, Manatee (Fla.) CC.
34. *Charles Fletcher, of, North Springs HS, Atlanta.
35. *Ken Pokryfke, lhp, Wilmot Union HS, Wilmot, Wis.
36. *Frans Meyer, 3b, Northridge HS, Layton, Utah.
37. *Dion McDaniel, of, Hales Franciscan HS, Chicago.
38. *Robbie Wachman, rhp, Middle Georgia JC.
39. *Paul Sandoval, rhp-3b, Trabuco Hills HS, Mission Viejo, Calif.
40. *Jared Gaston, ss-of, Cleveland (Tenn.) HS.
41. *Andy Myette, rhp, Kwantlen (B.C.) JC.
DRAFT DROP *Brother of Aaron Myette, first-round draft pick, White Sox (1997); major leaguer (1999-2004)*
**42. +Jesse Chavez, rhp, Riverside (Calif.) CC.—(2008-15)**
43. *Ronald Harris, c, George Washington HS, Denver.
44. *Ryan Mieszala, of, Greenway HS, Glendale, Ariz.
45. *Tom Zimmerman, rhp, Whitnall HS, Milwaukee.
46. *Josh Hernandez, c-3b, Los Lunas (N.M.) HS.
47. *Paul Oseguera, lhp, La Costa Canyon HS, Carlsbad, Calif.
48. *Steven Friend, ss-of, Kishwaukee (Ill.) JC.
49. *Brad Burkhead, of, Northwest Mississippi CC.
50. *Will Peterson, of, Valdosta (Ga.) HS.

## TORONTO BLUE JAYS (14)

**1. Russ Adams, ss, University of North Carolina.—(2004-09)**
**2. David Bush, rhp, Wake Forest University.—(2004-13)**
3. Justin Maureau, lhp, Wichita State University.—(High A)
**4. Adam Peterson, rhp, Wichita State University.—(2004)**
5. Chad Pleiness, rhp, Central Michigan University.—(High A)
**6. Jason Perry, of, Georgia Tech.—(2008)**
7. Brian Grant, rhp, C.B. Aycock HS, Goldsboro, N.C.
8. Chris Leonard, lhp, Miami (Ohio) University.
9. Russell Savickas, rhp, Johnston (R.I.) HS.
10. Eric Arnold, 2b, Rice University.
11. Jason Waugh, of, St. Mary's (Calif.) College.
12. Michael Roga, rhp, Armstrong Atlantic State (Ga.) University.
13. John Schneider, c, University of Delaware.
14. Mike Galloway, 1b-of, Miami (Ohio) University.
15. David Smith, of, West Virginia State College.
16. *Aric Van Gaalen, lhp, Harry Ainlay HS, Edmonton, Alberta.
17. Randy Braun, of, Belton (Mo.) HS.
**18. Jordan DeJong, rhp, Cal State Fullerton.—(2007)**
19. Brad Hassey, ss, University of Arizona.
DRAFT DROP *Son of Ron Hassey, major leaguer (1978-91)*
20. *Jesus Carnevale, lhp, Fernando Suria Chavez HS, Arecibo, P.R.
21. *Melvin Burkhalter, 1b, Seminole (Fla.) CC.
22. Erik Rico, of, Cornell University.
23. Bubbie Buzachero, rhp, Tennessee Tech.
24. *Matt Farnum, rhp, Texas A&M University.
25. Zeph Zinsman, 1b, Lewis-Clark State (Idaho) College.
**26. +Dewon Day, rhp, Southern University.—(2007)**
27. *Jared Odom, rhp, Vero Beach (Fla.) HS.
28. Paul Richmond, c, Baylor University.
**29. Erik Kratz, c, Eastern Mennonite (Va.) University.—(2010-15)**
30. A.J. Porfirio, of, Rice University.
31. Jeff Terrell, lhp, University of Tennessee.
32. Michael Seifert, lhp, Rend Lake (Ill.) JC.
33. Carlo Cota, 2b, San Diego State University.
34. Justin Owens, of, Coastal Carolina University.
35. Andy Torres, rhp, Lewis-Clark State (Idaho) College.
36. Scott Dragicevich, ss, Stanford University.
37. *Ross Swisher, lhp, Hudson's Bay HS, Vancouver, Wash.
38. *Bryan Hansen, lhp, Fontana (Calif.) HS.
39. +Nick Thomas, rhp, Sacramento (Calif.) CC.
40. *Danny Anderson, of, San Joaquin Delta (Calif.) JC.
41. *Adam Carr, rhp, San Lorenzo (Calif.) HS.
42. *Dirk Kleinmann, lhp, King (Tenn.) College.
43. *Chris Nicoll, rhp, Righetti HS, Santa Maria, Calif.
44. +Ben Harrison, lhp, Colleyville Heritage HS, Colleyville, Texas / North Central Texas JC.
45. *Brandon Bailey, c-of, Sacramento (Calif.) CC.
46. *Justin Tordi, ss, Dr. Phillips HS, Orlando, Fla.
47. *Tim Maloney, of, Kansas State University.
**48. *Drew Butera, c, Bishop Moore HS, Orlando, Fla.—(2010-15)**
DRAFT DROP *Son of Sal Butera, major leaguer (1980-88)*
49. *James Jewell, of, Theodore Roosevelt HS, Gary, Ind.
50. *J. Brent Cox, rhp, Bay City (Texas) HS.

# 2003

# MLB effort to squelch bonuses bears fruit

LARRY GOREN

**Dmitri Young, the No. 4 pick in the 1991 draft and a member of the Detroit Tigers in 2003, was on hand to interview his younger brother Delmon after the Devil Rays took him with the No. 1 overall pick, and Dmitri surprised him by arriving in a limousine for the draft day celebration**

After a decade of rampant bonus inflation, Major League Baseball intervened in 2000 with measures aimed at slowing the growth. Bonuses for players in two of the next three drafts decreased to rates not seen since the 1980s, but that was nothing compared with 2003, when the average first-round bonus dropped by 16.2 percent, easily the largest year-to-year decrease in the draft's history. No player received a $4 million bonus; in the previous three drafts, eight players got bonuses of $4 million or more.

Baseball's labor agreement did not allow formal slotting of signing bonuses, but MLB began holding seminars with club officials in 2000 aimed at giving them monetary guidelines for the early rounds. MLB's efforts showed success in 2002, when bonuses for first-rounders decreased for the first time since 1986. A year later, the first-round average was $1,766,667, the lowest since 1998 and almost $90,000 less than MLB had set as a goal.

"If you're not willing to sign for slot money," one agent said, "you're going to start sliding through the draft."

MLB recommended a specific bonus for each slot in the first round, and just six players got more than those amounts: the top three picks and three other players who might have been top 10 selections if not for signability. They were Tulane first baseman Michael Aubrey (Indians, 11th overall), Florida high school outfielder Lastings Milledge (Mets, 12th) and Massachusetts prep righthander Jeff Allison (Marlins, 16th).

No. 1 overall pick Delmon Young got a $3.7 million bonus from the Tampa Bay Devil Rays as part of a five-year major league contract worth a guaranteed $5.8 million. That was the richest bonus in 2003, but the lowest top bonus since 1998, when Corey Patterson signed with the Chicago Cubs for the same amount.

The Milwaukee Brewers handed out the only other major league contract, giving second baseman Rickie Weeks, the second player picked, a $4.8 million deal that included a $3.6 million bonus. The Brewers spent more money than any other team, though their total of $6,514,600 was a six-year low mark for the biggest spender, and 29 percent lower than the 2002 leader, the Oakland A's ($9,165,500).

Teams also found it easier to sign players than ever before. Eighteen first-rounders were signed by the end of June, and all but five—including the first four picks—were under contact by the end of July. For the first time, every player selected in the first two rounds came to terms.

Florida high school pitcher Andrew Miller, the first pick in the third round (Devil Rays, No. 68 overall), turned down a major league contract worth more than $2 million and enrolled at North Carolina. Just 14 of the 307 players in the first 10 rounds went unsigned, which also was unprecedented. The previous low was 24 in 2000.

### RAYS TAKE YOUNG OVER WEEKS

Tampa Bay, picking first overall for the second

## AT A GLANCE

### This Date In History
June 3-4

### Best Draft
**LOS ANGELES DODGERS.** The Dodgers selected a draft-high 12 future big leaguers, including **CHAD BILLINGSLEY** (1), Matt **KEMP** (5) and **A.J. ELLIS** (18). Four other picks each played at least five seasons in the majors.

### Worst Draft
**DETROIT TIGERS. KYLE SLEETH** (1), the third pick overall, fell far short of the majors in a brief, injury-plagued career. The Tigers signed six future big leaguers, but only **DUSTY RYAN**, a 48th-round draft-and-follow, did anything in a Detroit uniform, hitting .257 in 27 games.

### First-Round Bust
**BRAD SULLIVAN, RHP, ATHLETICS.** Sullivan might have been the nation's most dominant pitcher as a sophomore at Houston, posting a 13-1, 1.83 record with an NCAA-leading 157 strikeouts in 128 innings. He also went 7-0, 0.72 for USA Baseball's college national team. Sullivan's performance slipped as a junior, and continued to decline in five seasons in the A's system, none above Class A. He went 10-14, 5.94.

### On Second Thought
**ANDRE ETHIER, OF, ATHLETICS.** The A's got no direct benefit from the three players they drafted ahead of Ethier, and they traded the Arizona State product to the Dodgers prior to the 2006 season before he appeared in a game for the A's. He hit .286 with 158 home runs in 10 seasons with the Dodgers, and was still active in 2016.

### Late-Round Find
**IAN KINSLER, 2B, RANGERS (17TH ROUND).** According to WAR, Kinsler is the most productive player from the 2003 draft. In 10 major league seasons (eight with

CONTINUED ON PAGE 568

## AT A GLANCE

CONTINUED FROM PAGE 567

the Rangers, two with the Tigers), he hit .276 with 184 home runs, 702 RBIs and 197 stolen bases, and made four all-star teams. Kinsler was still active in 2016.

### Never Too Late

**JEFF MANSHIP, RHP, DIAMONDBACKS (50TH ROUND).** The last of the four players drafted in the 50th round who reached the big leagues, Manship opted for Notre Dame rather than sign with the Diamondbacks. He was drafted in the 14th round by the Twins in 2006, and had a 5-9, 5.40 record in seven big league seasons.

### Overlooked

**GEORGE SHERRILL, LHP, MARINERS.** Undrafted in 1999 out of Austin Peay, Sherrill spent five years pitching in independent leagues before signing with the Mariners. A year later, he was in the big leagues and remained there for nine seasons, pitching in 442 games (all in relief) for four clubs and going 19-17, 3.77 with 56 saves.

### International Gem

**PABLO SANDOVAL, C, GIANTS.** Sandoval, a catcher from Venezuela, wasn't regarded as one of the Giants' top prospects when he made his big league debut in 2008 as a 5-foot-11, 265-pound third baseman. He hit .294 with 106 home runs and 462 RBIs in seven seasons with the Giants, and was instrumental in their three World Series titles. The Mets signed Japanese star **KAZ MATSUI** to a $20 million contract in 2003, but his seven-year career paled in comparison to what Sandoval achieved.

### Minor League Take

**BRANDON WOOD, SS, ANGELS.** Wood produced one of the best seasons in modern minor league history in 2005, hitting .321 with 43 home runs and 115 RBIs for Class A Rancho Cucamonga. Including six

## 2003: THE FIRST ROUNDERS

| CLUB: PLAYER, POS., SCHOOL | HOMETOWN | B-T | HT. | WT. | AGE | BONUS | FIRST YEAR | LAST YEAR | PEAK LEVEL (YEARS) |
|---|---|---|---|---|---|---|---|---|---|
| 1. *Devil Rays: Delmon Young, of, Camarillo HS | Camarillo, Calif. | R-R | 6-2 | 200 | 17 | $3,700,000 | 2004 | 2015 | Majors (10) |
| Advanced tools at young age, especially huge raw power/arm strength; became one-dimensional talent in hot/cold MLB career; free swinger, poor on-base skills. | | | | | | | | | |
| 2. *Brewers: Rickie Weeks, 2b, Southern | Altamonte Springs, Fla. | R-R | 6-0 | 195 | 20 | $3,600,000 | 2003 | Active | Majors (12) |
| Lightly recruited prep player led NCAA in hitting twice, set career mark at .473; lightning-quick hands at plate evident early in MLB marked by steep decline at end. | | | | | | | | | |
| 3. Tigers: Kyle Sleeth, rhp, Wake Forest | Westminster, Colo. | R-R | 6-5 | 205 | 21 | $3,350,000 | 2004 | 2007 | Class AA (2) |
| Won 31 G in three years at Wake, tied NCAA record with 26-game win streak; Tigers tried to fix crossfire delivery, led to '05 TJ surgery, never regained electric stuff. | | | | | | | | | |
| 4. Padres: Tim Stauffer, rhp, Richmond | Saratoga Springs, N.Y. | R-R | 6-2 | 205 | 21 | $750,000 | 2004 | Active | Majors (10) |
| Had big SO (15-3, 1.54), JR years (114 IP, 19 BB/146), but MRI revealed shoulder issue, cost him $2.6M bonus; pro career started slowly before long run as reliever. | | | | | | | | | |
| 5. Royals: Chris Lubanski, of, Kennedy-Kendrick HS | Schwenksville, Pa. | L-L | 6-3 | 180 | 18 | $2,100,000 | 2003 | 2011 | Class AAA (4) |
| Flashed raw tools (except arm) in impressive prep career, but speed/defense regressed as pro when he bulked up in attempt to add more power to game. | | | | | | | | | |
| 6. Cubs: Ryan Harvey, of, Dunedin HS | Palm Harbor, Fla. | R-R | 6-5 | 192 | 18 | $2,400,000 | 2003 | 2010 | Class AA (3) |
| Prototype RF in Dale Murphy mold with size, raw power, speed, Gold-Glove skills, but struggled in minors to refine long swing, make consistent contact. | | | | | | | | | |
| 7. Orioles: Nick Markakis, lhp/of, Young Harris (Ga.) JC | Woodstock, Ga. | L-L | 6-2 | 185 | 19 | $1,850,000 | 2003 | Active | Majors (10) |
| Two-time juco player of year led nation in wins (12), SOs (160) on mound, RBIs (92) as hitter; O's chose to develop bat, evolved into complete player. | | | | | | | | | |
| 8. Pirates: Paul Maholm, lhp, Mississippi State | Holly Springs, Miss. | L-L | 6-2 | 215 | 20 | $2,200,000 | 2003 | 2014 | Majors (10) |
| College lefty with command of four pitches/mound presence; not overpowering, but mixed pitches well, had serviceable 10-year MLB career (77-100, 4.30). | | | | | | | | | |
| 9. Rangers: John Danks, lhp, Round Rock HS | Round Rock, Texas | L-L | 6-2 | 190 | 18 | $2,100,000 | 2003 | Active | Majors (9) |
| Drafted by Rangers, spent major league career with White Sox (which drafted brother Jordan in 2008); thrived with live arm (92-94 FB, power curve), clean delivery. | | | | | | | | | |
| 10. Rockies: Ian Stewart, 3b, La Quinta HS | Garden Grove, Calif. | L-R | 6-3 | 200 | 18 | $1,950,000 | 2003 | 2015 | Majors (7) |
| Starred alongside Ian Kennedy (USC first-rounder in 2006) on SoCal prep power; long swing/pull-conscious approach limited his major league contributions. | | | | | | | | | |
| 11. Indians: Michael Aubrey, 1b, Tulane | Shreveport, La. | L-L | 6-1 | 195 | 21 | $2,010,000 | 2003 | 2011 | Majors (2) |
| When healthy, best natural hitter in Indians system; hit .420-18-79 as Tulane JR, but chronic back problems began in college, impacted pro career at every step. | | | | | | | | | |
| 12. Mets: Lastings Milledge, of, Lakewood Ranch HS | Palmetto, Fla. | R-R | 6-1 | 180 | 18 | $2,075,000 | 2003 | 2011 | Majors (6) |
| Dynamic five-tool talent in small package; slid to 12th over mixed success with wood, high price tag, off-field issues; limited bat short-circuited big league career. | | | | | | | | | |
| 13. Blue Jays: Aaron Hill, ss, Louisiana State | Visalia, Calif. | R-R | 5-11 | 195 | 21 | $1,675,000 | 2003 | Active | Majors (11) |
| SEC player of year (.358-9-67), not flashy but in demand with easy/compact swing, plus tools across board; lacked footwork/quickness at SS, became 2B in pros. | | | | | | | | | |
| 14. Reds: Ryan Wagner, rhp, Houston | Yoakum, Texas | R-R | 6-4 | 210 | 20 | $1,400,000 | 2003 | 2009 | Majors (5) |
| Reached majors in five weeks on strength of eye-popping resume (15 SV, .147 OBA, 79 IP/148 SO), raw stuff (91-94 sinker/unhittable slider) as draft-eligible soph. | | | | | | | | | |
| 15. White Sox: Brian Anderson, of, Arizona | Tucson, Ariz. | R-R | 6-2 | 205 | 21 | $1,600,000 | 2003 | 2011 | Majors (5) |
| Burst on draft scene as college JR with revamped swing/hitting approach (.366-14-62 vs. .275-5-30 in 2002), five-tool ability, but bat never clicked in majors. | | | | | | | | | |
| 16. Marlins: Jeff Allison, rhp, Veterans Memorial HS | Peabody, Mass. | R-R | 6-2 | 195 | 18 | $1,850,000 | 2003 | 2011 | Class AA (3) |
| Similar storyline as Josh Hamilton; immense talent (9-0, 0.00, 64 IP, 9 BB/142 SO as prep SR) who struggled with addiction, but his comeback fell short. | | | | | | | | | |
| 17. Red Sox: David Murphy, of, Baylor | Spring, Texas | L-L | 6-3 | 185 | 21 | $1,525,000 | 2003 | Active | Majors (10) |
| Red Sox sold on big '02 summer on Cape, JR season (.413-11-67), sweet stroke/advanced plate discipline, skills in field, but never fully tapped into raw power. | | | | | | | | | |
| 18. Indians: Brad Snyder, of, Ball State | Bellevue, Ohio | L-R | 6-3 | 210 | 21 | $1,525,000 | 2003 | 2014 | Majors (3) |
| Struggle with plate discipline/two-strike approach in brief, unproductive MLB career (.167-2-8) masked his superior raw power, arm strength, speed for size. | | | | | | | | | |
| 19. Diamondbacks: Conor Jackson, 1b, California | Woodland Hills, Calif. | R-R | 6-3 | 210 | 21 | $1,500,000 | 2003 | 2013 | Majors (7) |
| Son of actor John Jackson; perennial .300 hitter in college/minors with keen batting eye, intriguing raw power, but never replicated success in majors. | | | | | | | | | |
| 20. Expos: Chad Cordero, rhp, Cal State Fullerton | Chino, Calif. | R-R | 6-0 | 195 | 21 | $1,350,000 | 2003 | 2013 | Majors (7) |
| Proven college closer with 91-94 mph FB, command of three pitches, but surprise first-rounder because of small frame; moved quickly to majors, 47 SV in '05. | | | | | | | | | |
| 21. Twins: Matt Moses, 3b, Mills Godwin HS | Richmond, Va. | L-R | 6-0 | 210 | 18 | $1,450,000 | 2003 | 2009 | Class AAA (1) |
| Elite HS bat with line-drive stroke; thrived at plate in low minors, hit wall in Double-A (.238), Triple-A (.224); other tools subpar, so doomed when stopped hitting. | | | | | | | | | |
| 22. Giants: David Aardsma, rhp, Rice | The Woodlands, Texas | R-R | 6-5 | 200 | 21 | $1,425,000 | 2003 | Active | Majors (9) |
| Cemented draft status as dominant closer for CWS champions; had explosive life on 95-98 FB, spun wheels in pros before 38-SV season for Mariners in '09. | | | | | | | | | |
| 23. Angels: Brandon Wood, ss, Horizon HS | Scottsdale, Ariz. | R-R | 6-2 | 180 | 18 | $1,300,000 | 2003 | 2013 | Majors (5) |
| Headed for greatness after 57-HR season in 2005 between A-ball, Arizona Fall League, surehanded skills at SS; holes in swing exposed in majors (.186-18-64). | | | | | | | | | |
| 24. Dodgers: Chad Billingsley, rhp, Defiance HS | Defiance, Ohio | R-R | 6-2 | 195 | 18 | $1,375,000 | 2003 | 2015 | Majors (9) |
| Undersized, but prototype power arm with 92-95 FB, 85-86 slider; fanned 138 in 69 IP as prep SR, had success in minors, early in MLB career before TJ surgery in '09. | | | | | | | | | |
| 25. Athletics: Brad Sullivan, rhp, Houston | Nederland, Texas | R-R | 6-1 | 190 | 21 | $1,360,000 | 2003 | 2007 | Class A (4) |
| Candidate for No. 1 pick after dominant 2002 (13-1, 1.83, national-high 157 SO; 7-0, 0.72 with Team USA); inconsistent in 2003, nasty stuff disappeared as pro. | | | | | | | | | |
| 26. Athletics: Brian Snyder, 3b, Stetson | Wellington, Fla. | R-R | 5-11 | 195 | 21 | $1,325,000 | 2003 | 2008 | Class AA (3) |
| A's Moneyball approach continued; went for player with wood-bat skills/plate discipline, marginal defense; power never evolved, career peaked in Double-A. | | | | | | | | | |
| 27. Yankees: Eric Duncan, 3b, Seton Hall Prep | Florham Park, N.Y. | L-R | 6-1 | 205 | 18 | $1,250,000 | 2003 | 2012 | Class AAA (4) |
| New Jersey kid with LH power tailor-made for Yankee Stadium; early promise with quick, polished stroke, but never panned out as game faltered in Triple-A. | | | | | | | | | |
| 28. Cardinals: Daric Barton, c, Marina HS | Huntington Beach, Calif. | L-R | 5-11 | 195 | 17 | $975,000 | 2003 | Active | Majors (8) |
| Looked like A's type with advanced hitting ability/plate discipline, and sure enough team traded for him in '04; limited by lack of athleticism/power/defensive skills. | | | | | | | | | |
| 29. Diamondbacks: Carlos Quentin, of, Stanford | Chula Vista, Calif. | R-R | 6-2 | 215 | 20 | $1,100,000 | 2004 | 2015 | Majors (9) |
| Spent eight years in majors on strength of power/plate discipline, classic RF skills; earned two all-star nods with White Sox, but string of injuries took major toll. | | | | | | | | | |
| 30. Royals: Mitch Maier, c, Toledo | Novi, Mich. | L-R | 6-2 | 195 | 20 | $900,000 | 2003 | 2014 | Majors (6) |
| Led MAC in hitting as FR (.444), JR (.448), intrigued scouts as LH hitting-catcher with speed; moved to OF in pros, never hit enough to justify everyday MLB role. | | | | | | | | | |

**Signed to major league contract.*

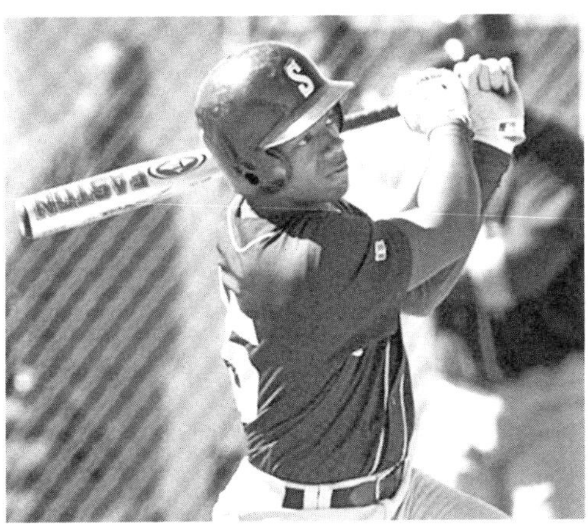

One of the best hitters in NCAA history, Rickie Weeks was the No. 2 pick and had a long, if not overly successful, major league career

time in four years, settled on Young, a hard-hitting, high school outfielder from Camarillo (Calif.) High, the night before the June 3 draft. That made the Brewers' selection of Weeks, a record-setting slugger from Southern University, almost a formality, considering the two were considered the best prospects in a largely uninspiring draft crop.

Young didn't find out he was the first pick until hearing it on MLB's Internet draft broadcast. His father, Larry, knew beforehand that the Devil Rays would choose his son, but kept it a secret. His son had the requisite Tampa Bay cap and T-shirt on hand for photo opportunities, but conceded he thought the Devil Rays were going with Weeks.

The Rays had lengthy discussions about Young, Weeks and, to a lesser extent, Florida high school outfielder Ryan Harvey, and kept coming back to Young, general manager Chuck LaMar said.

The 6-foot-3, 205-pound Young, the most accomplished high school hitter in the draft pool, projected as a slugging right fielder with a powerful arm. He was on the radar of most clubs by age 13, and set a U.S. junior national team record with 16 homers in 2002. In 65 at-bats in an injury-plagued senior season in high school, Young hit .523 with 7 home runs and 28 RBIs.

"He is one of the finest power hitters our scouts have evaluated, not only this year but over the years," Devil Rays scouting director Cam Bonifay said. "He's the kind of guy that you don't get out of your seat and go buy a hot dog when you know he's coming to the plate. You want to stay there and watch him hit. He lights up your eyes."

Young sounded relaxed and confident after being drafted, saying he wasn't going to put pressure on himself. He said he hoped to be in the major leagues by 2005. "That gives me two years. I want to be there as quick as possible, like Andruw Jones, Ken Griffey Jr., and A-Rod. I'm trying to be just like them, to get to the big leagues as quick as possible and be dominant like they are."

Young's older brother, Dmitri, was the fourth overall pick in the 1991 draft, distinguishing them as the highest-drafted siblings in history for two years until upstaged by the Upton brothers: Justin, the top pick in the 2005 draft who joined B.J., the second overall selection in 2002.

Dmitri also had coincidentally been drafted by the Devil Rays—in the November 1997 expansion draft, though never played a game in Tampa Bay as he was promptly traded to the Cincinnati Reds in a prearranged deal. In 2003, he was a member of the Detroit Tigers, and because the Tigers were in San Diego on June 3 to play the Padres, Dmitri was able to surprise his brother by arriving via limousine for the draft-day celebration.

Young was the last of the 30 first-round picks in 2003 to sign, agreeing to terms on Sept. 9. He made it to the Devil Rays in September 2006, after hitting .317 with 85 home runs and 402 RBIs in 489 games in three minor league seasons. He might have gotten to the big leagues earlier if not for an incident early in the 2006 season at Triple-A Durham. On April 26, Young was ejected for arguing a disputed third strike call. On his return to the dugout, he flung his bat underhanded, end-over-end in the direction of the umpire. It hit the umpire on the chest and arm, and the International League suspended Young for 50 games without pay. The altercation was not the first he had with an umpire. In 2005, playing for Double-A Montgomery, Young received a three-game suspension for bumping an umpire.

Young's major league career lasted 10 seasons, but he fell far short of expectations. Projected as

## How They Should Have Done It

Based on the career WAR (Wins Above Replacement, as calculated by Baseball-Reference.com) numbers achieved by all the players eligible for the 2003 draft through the 2015 season, here's how the first round should have unfolded. Numbers in parentheses indicate the round when the player was actually drafted.

| | Player, Pos. | Actual Draft | WAR | Bonus |
|---|---|---|---|---|
| 1. | Ian Kinsler, ss | Rangers (17) | 46.7 | $30,000 |
| 2. | Adam Jones, ss | Mariners (1-S) | 27.5 | $925,000 |
| 3. | Nick Markakis, of | Orioles (1) | 27.4 | $1,850,000 |
| 4. | Jonathan Papelbon, rhp | Red Sox (4) | 23.9 | $264,500 |
| 5. | Aaron Hill, ss | Blue Jays (1) | 23.4 | $1,675,000 |
| 6. | Michael Bourn, of | Phillies (4) | 23.1 | $299,000 |
| 7. | Andre Ethier, of | Athletics (2) | 22.0 | $580,000 |
| 8. | Matt Kemp, of | Dodgers (6) | 21.8 | $130,000 |
| 9. | John Danks, lhp | Rangers (1) | 21.5 | $2,100,000 |
| 10. | Chad Billingsley, rhp | Dodgers (1) | 16.9 | $1,375,000 |
| 11. | Scott Baker, rhp | Twins (2) | 15.7 | $600,000 |
| 12. | Brendan Ryan, ss | Cardinals (7) | 15.1 | $100,000 |
| 13. | Shaun Marcum, rhp | Blue Jays (3) | 13.4 | $449,000 |
| 14. | Brad Ziegler, rhp | Phillies (20) | 12.2 | $1,000 |
| 15. | Paul Maholm, lhp | Pirates (1) | 12.1 | $2,200,000 |
| 16. | Rickie Weeks, 2b | Brewers (1) | 11.6 | $3,600,000 |
| | Tyler Clippard, rhp | Yankees (9) | 11.6 | $75,000 |
| 18. | Carlos Quentin, of | Diamondbacks (1) | 10.4 | $1,000,000 |
| 19. | David Murphy, of | Red Sox (1) | 10.2 | $1,625,000 |
| 20. | John Jaso, c | Devil Rays (12) | 9.9 | $60,000 |
| 21. | Sean Marshall, lhp | Cubs (6) | 9.8 | $143,000 |
| 22. | Daric Barton, c | Cardinals (1) | 9.1 | $975,000 |
| 23. | Matt Harrison, lhp | Braves (3) | 9.0 | $395,000 |
| 24. | Scott Feldman, rhp | Rangers (30) | 8.8 | $100,000 |
| 25. | Sean Rodriguez, ss | Angels (3) | 7.7 | $400,000 |
| | Kevin Kouzmanoff, 3b | Indians (6) | 7.7 | $45,000 |
| 27. | A.J. Ellis, c | Dodgers (18) | 7.6 | $2,500 |
| 28. | Chad Cordero, rhp | Expos (1) | 7.5 | $1,350,000 |
| | Mike Aviles, ss | Royals (7) | 7.5 | $1,000 |
| 30. | Jarrod Saltalamacchia, c | Braves (1-S) | 6.9 | $950,000 |

| Top 3 Unsigned Players | | | | Year Signed |
|---|---|---|---|---|
| 1. | Max Scherzer, rhp | Cardinals (43) | 31.6 | 2006 |
| 2. | Tim Lincecum, rhp | Cubs (48) | 22.7 | 2006 |
| 3. | Doug Fister, rhp | Giants (49) | 19.4 | 2006 |

## AT A GLANCE

late-season games with Triple-A Salt Lake City, he eclipsed 100 extra-base hits. Wood hit .278 with 175 home runs and 636 RBIs in 10 seasons in the minors, but had little success in the major leagues, hitting .186 with 18 home runs and 64 RBIs in 700 at-bats over parts of five seasons.

### One Who Got Away

**ANDREW MILLER, LHP, DEVIL RAYS (3RD ROUND).** Miller was the 68th overall selection, and the first in the 2003 draft who did not sign. He enhanced his draft position after three years in college at North Carolina, becoming the sixth pick overall in 2006, and developed into an elite relief pitcher in the major leagues.

### He Was Drafted?

**DENNIS DIXON, OF, REDS (20TH ROUND).** Dixon had an NFL career as a backup quarterback, playing for two Super Bowl champions. One of the nation's top two-sport athletes in 2003, he didn't sign with the Reds out of high school, opting to play football at Oregon. As a junior, Dixon was a fifth-round draft choice of the Braves in 2007, and hit .176 in 74 at-bats after signing. He gave up baseball after the Pittsburgh Steelers selected in the fifth round of the 2008 NFL draft.

### Did You Know . . .

Miami's Brito Private High, a school with an enrollment of little more than 100, had six players drafted, tying the record for most players selected from one high school in a single draft.

### They Said It

Marlins owner **JEFFREY LORIA** on first-round pick **JEFF ALLISON**, whose career was ruined because of a drug addiction: "I feel sad for the kid, but he's going to have to get himself together. I hope he does because he's got a great talent and great ability. He has a gift and it would be a shame to waste that gift."

## DRAFT SPOTLIGHT: JEFF ALLISON

Jeff Allison slipped to the 16th overall pick in the 2003 draft because many clubs feared that his bonus demands would be excessive. But if anyone had known about his dirty little secret, he undoubtedly would have fallen much further.

In terms of natural pitching ability, there might not have been a better prospect in the 2003 draft pool than Allison. Not after he assembled a masterful 9-0, 0.00 record and struck out 142 while walking just nine in 64 innings as a senior at Veterans Memorial High in Peabody, Mass. Not after he blew hitters away with a lethal combination of a fastball up to 97 mph and knee-buckling curve, along with exquisite command of every pitch in his arsenal.

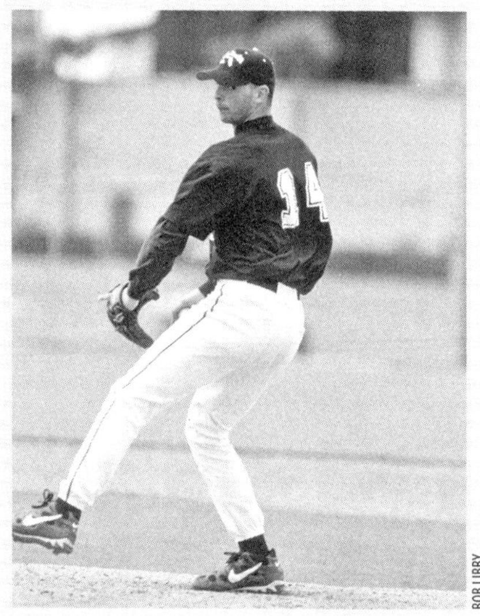
BOB LIBBY

Jeff Allison was one of the top prep pitchers in the 2003 class, but his career was undone by drug abuse

The Florida Marlins could hardly contain their excitement when Allison fell into their laps after 15 other clubs chose to abide by the wishes of the commissioner's office and toe the line on signing bonuses. The Marlins believed they had just landed the second coming of Josh Beckett, whom they had drafted with their top draft pick four years earlier and was in the process of leading them to their second World Series conquest in six years.

"He looked outstanding," Marlins manager Jack McKeon said after Allison showcased his raw stuff in a workout shortly after signing. "He had outstanding stuff, and you could envision this guy being in the big leagues in a couple of years. His stuff was that good."

Unbeknownst to the Marlins, or anyone else, Allison was in the midst of becoming addicted to the prescription painkiller OxyContin on the day he was drafted. By the time he agreed to a $1.85 million bonus six weeks after the draft, Allison was hooked.

Less than a year later, with his drug addiction out of control, Allison nearly died of a heroin overdose. He had thrown just nine professional innings when his promising baseball career came crashing down. "I was so young and I was so stupid that I didn't understand a lot of things, including life itself," Allison said years later. "I just didn't get it."

Though he managed to curb his addiction enough to make 17 starts at low Class A Greensboro in 2005, Allison soon relapsed and his addiction over the next two years led him down unimaginable paths—much like it did over a corresponding period for Josh Hamilton. In addition to the 2004 season, which he spent on baseball's restricted list, Allison missed all of 2006 and '07 while enduring a second near-fatal heroin overdose and being arrested on multiple occasions for felony and misdemeanor charges related to his drug habit.

At the depths of his despair in late 2006, while in the throes of his addiction and dodging a warrant for his arrest, he found himself alone and penniless, shivering in the rain as he walked 33 miles along a remote and lonesome road in North Carolina.

"My absolute bottom," he said.

Allison ultimately spent 75 days in jail for skipping out on a court-ordered drug treatment program, and much of his lucrative signing bonus was either squandered on his drug habit or withheld by the Marlins, through fines and suspensions.

"I feel sad for the kid, but he's going to have to get himself together," said Marlins owner Jeffrey Loria, after Allison left the team's spring-training complex unexcused in 2006 for the second time in two years. "I hope he does because he's got a great talent and a great ability. He has a gift and it would be a shame to waste that gift."

Even after losing nearly four years to drugs, the Marlins stood by Allison's side and welcomed him back in 2008 when he put all his transgressions behind him, and came clean. He pitched for four seasons in the Marlins organization—two each in high Class A and Double-A—and even made the Florida State League all-star team in 2008.

But hopes of a Hamilton-like redemption story were dashed in 2011 when he hurt his elbow and the zip on his fastball disappeared. His career, which almost ended before it started, finally came to a close after that season when he was released by the Marlins. For the considerable promise that he displayed as a prep pitching sensation, all Allison had to show for it was a 31-38, 4.65 record in an unfulfilled six-year minor league career.

a player with 40-home-run potential, he did not hit more than 21 in a season, hitting 105 overall and batting .284. Young played for six clubs before being released by the Baltimore Orioles during the 2015 season.

Weeks, too, had a disappointing career. He was a .249 hitter in 11 seasons with the Brewers and played sparingly for one season with the Seattle Mariners before being released. Weeks managed to land a position as a reserve with the Arizona Diamondbacks during spring training in 2016.

### TRIO OF PICKS REACH MAJORS

Weeks held out for more than two months before accepting a five-year major league deal from the Brewers that set the stage for Young's similar contract with the Rays, signed a month later.

Weeks was Baseball America's 2003 College Player of the Year, won NCAA Division I batting titles in 2002 and 2003, led the nation in on-base percentage (.609) as a junior, and left Southern as the all-time NCAA leader in batting (.473) and slugging percentage (.927). He hit .358 in 21 minor league games before the Brewers promoted him in September 2003.

Weeks was the third 2003 draftee to reach the big leagues. The first two were college closers, Houston righthander Ryan Wagner, chosen 14th overall by the Reds, and Cal State Fullerton righthander Chad Cordero, picked 20th by the Montreal Expos. It was the most draft choices to reach the big leagues in their draft year since 1978, when five players made the jump, including No. 1 overall pick Bob Horner (Braves).

Wagner, who broke a 39-year-old NCAA Division I record by averaging 16.8 strikeouts per nine innings as a junior, was considered the most big league-ready prospect in the draft. He retired all five batters he faced in his debut against the Houston Astros on July 19, which came 46 days after the draft. It was the swiftest trip to the majors since Ariel Prieto went from the No. 5 overall pick to the A's in 28 days in 1995.

Wagner's best pitch was a hard slider, and initially it proved to be as effective in the majors as it had been in college. He went 2-0, 1.66 in 17 appearances with the Reds in 2003, and was a candidate to be the team's closer the following season. But Wagner never again came close to his early success. He was plagued by mechanical issues throughout his five major league seasons, suffered a torn labrum in 2007, and retired two years later.

Some teams thought the Expos drafted Cordero too high, but he fit two important criteria for a team with an uncertain future: He signed quickly

### Fastest To The Majors

| | Player, Pos. | Drafted (Round) | Debut |
|---|---|---|---|
| 1. | Ryan Wagner, rhp | Reds (1) | July 19, 2003 |
| 2. | Chad Cordero, rhp | Expos (1) | Aug. 30, 2003 |
| 3. | Rickie Weeks, 2b | Brewers (1) | Sept. 15, 2003 |
| 4. | David Aardsma, rhp | Giants (1) | April 6, 2004 |
| 5. | Abe Alvarez, lhp | Red Sox (2) | July 22, 2004 |

**FIRST HIGH SCHOOL SELECTION:** Matt Kemp, of (Dodgers/5, May 28, 2006)

## Top 25 Bonuses

| | Player, Pos. | Drafted (Round)Order | | Bonus |
|---|---|---|---|---|
| 1. | * **Delmon Young, of** | **Devil Rays (1)** | **1** | **#$3,700,000** |
| 2. | **Rickie Weeks, 2b** | **Brewers (1)** | **2** | **#$3,600,000** |
| 3. | Kyle Sleeth, rhp | Tigers (1) | 3 | $3,350,000 |
| 4. | * Ryan Harvey, of | Cubs (1) | 6 | $2,400,000 |
| 5. | **Paul Maholm, lhp** | **Pirates (1)** | **8** | **$2,200,000** |
| 6. | * Chris Lubanski, of | Royals (1) | 5 | $2,100,000 |
| | * **John Danks, lhp** | **Rangers (1)** | **9** | **$2,100,000** |
| 8. | * **Lastings Milledge, of** | **Mets (1)** | **12** | **$2,075,000** |
| 9. | Vince Sinisi, of | Rangers (2) | 46 | $2,070,000 |
| 10. | **Michael Aubrey, 1b** | **Indians (1)** | **11** | **$2,010,000** |
| 11. | * **Ian Stewart, 3b** | **Rockies (1)** | **10** | **$1,950,000** |
| 12. | **Nick Markakis, of** | **Orioles (1)** | **7** | **$1,850,000** |
| | * Jeff Allison rhp | Marlins (1) | 16 | $1,850,000 |
| 14. | **Aaron Hill, ss** | **Blue Jays (1)** | **13** | **$1,675,000** |
| 15. | **Brian Anderson, of** | **White Sox (1)** | **15** | **$1,600,000** |
| 16. | **David Murphy, of** | **Red Sox (1)** | **17** | **$1,525,000** |
| | **Brad Snyder, of** | **Indians (1)** | **18** | **$1,525,000** |
| 18. | **Conor Jackson, 3b** | **Diamondbacks (1)** | **19** | **$1,500,000** |
| 19. | * Matt Moses, 3b | Twins (1) | 21 | $1,450,000 |
| 20. | **David Aardsma, rhp** | **Giants (1)** | **22** | **$1,425,000** |
| 21. | **Ryan Wagner, rhp** | **Reds (1)** | **14** | **$1,400,000** |
| 22. | * **Chad Billingsley, rhp** | **Dodgers (1)** | **24** | **$1,375,000** |
| 23. | Brad Sullivan, rhp | Athletics (1) | 25 | $1,360,000 |
| 24. | **Chad Cordero, rhp** | **Expos (1)** | **20** | **$1,350,000** |
| 25. | **Brian Snyder, 3b** | **Athletics (1)** | **26** | **$1,325,000** |

*Major leaguers in bold. *High school selection. #Major league contract.*

for below-slot money ($1.35 million) and was close to the big leagues. The 6-foot, 195-pound Cordero worked in 12 games after being promoted on Aug. 30, going 1-0, 1.64 with a save.

Unlike Wagner, Cordero excelled as a closer, becoming the second-fastest in major league history to achieve 100 saves. He won the last game in Expos history in 2004, and led the majors with 47 saves in the franchise's first season as the Washington Nationals. Cordero enjoyed two more successful seasons before his career tailed off.

A total of 220 players from the class of 2003 reached the majors, most since the 1990 group (237). However, there was more quantity than quality. Only Ian Kinsler, a 17th-round draft pick of the Rangers, had a career WAR (Wins Above Replacement) above 30.0, the only time in the first 40 years of the draft that only one player in a class reached that level.

### LOEWEN SHATTERS DRAFT RECORD

Chipola (Fla.) JC lefthander Adam Loewen was part of the prior year's draft class, but he exerted plenty of influence on the 2003 process by waiting until minutes before the midnight deadline on May 26 to sign a major league contract with the Orioles. It provided for a $3.2 million bonus and a $4.02 million guarantee over five years.

Had he not signed, Loewen likely would have been the first or second pick. His bonus obliterated the previous record for a draft-and-follow, which was the $1.701 million that Sean Henn got from the New York Yankees in 2001.

The Orioles wound up with both of the top draft-and-follows from the 2002 draft after the Reds were unable to sign Markakis, a Young Harris (Ga.) JC lefthander/outfielder whom they had selected in the 23rd round. Markakis, Baseball America's Junior College Player of the Year in both 2002 and '03, led all juco players in wins and strikeouts as a pitcher in his sophomore year, and in RBIs. He turned down a $1.5 million offer from the Reds and entered the 2003 draft. Trying to conserve money after signing Loewen, the Orioles initially attempted to get Aubrey to accept a below-slot bonus for their No. 7 pick. When he declined, they took Markakis and signed him for $1.85 million, $450,000 less than MLB's recommendation.

Markakis threw a 92-94 mph fastball, and most teams preferred him as a pitcher. However, the Orioles liked him better as a hitter and trained him as an outfielder. He impressed the Orioles during a workout the day before the draft.

Loewen's career fell short of expectations because of elbow problems, while Markakis proved his worth by hitting .291 with 143 home runs and 707 RBIs in his first 10 seasons in the major leagues and winning two Gold Gloves as a strong-armed right fielder. He was still active in 2016.

A record 78 players drafted in 2002 signed as draft-and-follows prior to the 2003 draft. Among players drafted in 2003 who didn't sign until the following spring, the only one who received a seven-figure bonus was righthander Luis Cota, a 10th-round pick of the Kansas City Royals, who got $1.05 million after substantially improving his worth during his freshman season at South Mountain (Ariz.) JC.

BILL NICHOLS

Nick Markakis

The five players drafted by the financially strapped Royals before they selected Cota each received a bonus of just $1,000, with the exception of eighth-rounder Mike Aviles, a senior shortstop from Concordia (N.Y.) College, who got $1,500. Aviles played eight seasons in the majors and easily was the most successful player the Royals drafted in 2003. Cota fell short of expectations by winning just 15 games in an injury-plagued minor league career. The team's first-round pick, Pennsylvania prep outfielder Chris Lubanski (fifth overall), did not advance beyond Triple-A in nine seasons.

### SHOULDER WEAKNESS COSTS STAUFFER

Scouts determined early in the spring of 2003 that Wake Forest's Kyle Sleeth and Richmond's Tim Stauffer were the top college pitchers available. The Tigers took Sleeth third overall, and the San Diego Padres followed by selecting Stauffer.

Padres scouting director Bill Gayton said Stauffer's makeup was one of the deciding factors in the decision. Stauffer's character became evident when he and his agent, Ron Shapiro, told the team that he had weakness in his right shoulder. MLB recommended $2.8 million for the fourth slot, and the Padres initially offered $2.6 million. After Stauffer's revelation, he signed for $750,000, the smallest bonus in the first round. Sleeth received $3.35 million from the Tigers.

### WORTH NOTING

A total of 1,480 players were drafted in 2003. Arizona State led all colleges with 12 draftees, starting with outfielder **ANDRE ETHIER** (Athletics, second round). Cal State Fullerton had 11, including righthander **CHAD CORDERO** in the first round. Texas A&M had eight pitchers selected, including three in the second round.

Miami's Brito Private High, with an enrollment of just over 100, tied a prep record set in 2001 by Seminole (Fla.) High when it had six players drafted, although none higher than 23rd-round catcher **DANNY SANTIN** (Mariners). Round Rock (Texas) High had three picks in the first five rounds: lefthander **JOHN DANKS** (Rangers, first round), third baseman **TRAVIS SCHLICTING** (Rangers, fourth round) and righthander **MATT NACHREINER** (White Sox, fifth).

Florida high school lefthander **ANDREW MILLER** earned the highest grade from the Major League Scouting Bureau among players in the 2003 draft pool, a 71 on the 20-80 scouting scale. After Miller were Massachusetts prep righthander **JEFF ALLISON** (68.5), California prep righthander **JARED HUGHES** (65), a 16th-round pick of the Devil Rays who attended Long Beach State and was drafted in the fourth round in 2006; and Virginia prep righthander **JAY SBORZ** (65), a second-round pick of the Tigers.

Rice won its first College World Series in 2003 on the strength of a pitching staff that featured junior righthander **DAVID AARDSMA** (7-3, 2.97, 12 saves) and sophomore righthanders **JEFF NIEMANN** (17-0, 1.70), **WADE TOWNSEND** (11-2, 2.20) and **PHIL HUMBER** (11-3, 3.30). Niemann led the nation in wins, and Townsend was the strikeout leader with 164. Aardsma was a first-round pick of the Giants in 2003, and the other three were among the first eight picks in 2004.

## WORTH NOTING

Five bonus records were set in different rounds in 2003: by righthander **LUIS COTA** (Royals), $1.05 million for a 10th-rounder; by **JIMMY BARTHMAIER** (Astros), $750,000 bonus for a 13th-rounder; by righthander **RYAN MATTHEUS** (Rockies), $750,000 for a 17th rounder; by **ADAM LAROCHE** (Dodgers), $1 million for a 39th rounder; and righthander **JASON SMITH** (Red Sox), $125,000 for a 49th rounder.

Home runs at the college level were down 25 percent from 1998, and batting averages were down 15 percentage points, after NCAA legislation that mandated less potent aluminum bats. Pitching dominated as it hadn't in nearly a decade. First-rounder **KYLE SLEETH** set a record for most consecutive wins over a three-year period (26), and first-rounder **RYAN WAGNER** for most strikeouts per nine innings (16.9). **MATT DESALVO**, a fifth-year righthander with Division III Marietta (Ohio) College, set NCAA records for career wins (53) and strikeouts (603). As a fifth-year senior, he was not subject to the draft and signed with the Yankees as a free agent.

The Red Sox spent more than they ever had on draft picks and sent out a release detailing how they were one of just four teams to sign 19 of their top 20 picks, and spent a club record $5.5 million to sign 32 players. The Red Sox had invested $3.1 million in bonuses in 2002, $2.9 million in 2001 and $3.4 million in 2000. The Red Sox signed first-rounder **DAVID MURPHY** for $1.525 million, supplemental first-rounder **MATT MURTON** for $1.01 million, and second-rounders **ABE ALVAREZ** and **MICKEY HALL** for $700,000 and $800,000, respectively. Only four of their 52 picks reached the majors, among them fourth-rounder **JONATHAN PAPELBON**, who signed for $264,500 and developed into an elite major league closer.

Stauffer, who went 31-13, 2.16 with 362 strikeouts in 346 innings in his career at Richmond, said his shoulder felt sore for longer than normal after his final college start, a 10-8 loss to UC Riverside in NCAA regionals, four days before the draft. An MRI in July didn't reveal any damage, but Stauffer's shoulder was weak from wear on his labrum and rotator cuff. He worked with Padres trainers and planned to pitch in instructional league with a goal of being 100 percent by spring training.

Stauffer said he had no reservations about telling the Padres about his shoulder. "It was going to be found out eventually," he said. "I wanted to tell them personally. They were pretty shocked, as shocked as we were. They had no idea."

Stauffer got to the major leagues in 2005, had shoulder surgery in 2007, and missed almost two seasons. He came back and pitched until 2015, going 33-34, 3.97 for his career.

Sleeth went 31-6, 3.48 at Wake Forest, including an NCAA record-tying 26-game winning streak that extended from his freshman to junior seasons. The Tigers attempted to change Sleeth's crossfire delivery, concerned it would lead to arm problems, but he had trouble adapting to new mechanics and developed a sore elbow. He missed the 2005 season and most of '06 while recovering from Tommy John surgery. Sleeth went 12-21, 6.30 in three minor league seasons before retiring in 2008.

## Largest Bonuses By Round

| | Player, Pos. | Club | Bonus |
|---|---|---|---|
| **1.** | ***Delmon Young, of** | **Devil Rays** | **$3,700,000** |
| 1-S. | *Adam Miller, rhp | Indians | $1,025,000 |
| 2. | Vince Sinisi, of | Rangers | $2,070,000 |
| **3.** | ***Steve Lerud, c** | **Pirates** | **$512,500** |
| **4.** | ***Travis Schlichting, 3b** | **Devil Rays** | **$400,000** |
| 5. | Jon Barratt, lhp | Devil Rays | $300,000 |
| 6. | *Jason Stephens, rhp | Yankees | $500,000 |
| 7. | Jose Perez, of | Yankees | $210,000 |
| 8. | *Josh Cowles, of | Angels | $150,000 |
| | Josh Smith, rhp | Yankees | $150,000 |
| 9. | Kellen Ludwig, rhp | Giants | $90,000 |
| 10. | *#Luis Cota, rhp | Royals | $1,050,000 |
| 11. | Adam Pavkovich, ss | Angels | $140,000 |
| 12. | Ruben Flores, rhp | Mariners | $70,000 |
| **13.** | ***Jimmy Barthmaier, rhp** | **Astros** | **$750,000** |
| 14. | *Kelly Shearer, lhp | Angels | $210,000 |
| 15. | Chris Turner, of | Red Sox | $140,000 |
| **16.** | ***Aaron Laffey, lhp** | **Indians** | **$363,000** |
| 17. | #Kurt Koehler, rhp | Marlins | $275,000 |
| 18. | *Michael Wagner, lhp | Yankees | $95,000 |
| **19.** | **#Ryan Mattheus, rhp** | **Rockies** | **$700,000** |
| 20. | Kyle Bakker, lhp | Braves | $165,000 |
| 21. | Marc LaMacchia, rhp | Rangers | $235,000 |
| 22. | John Urick, 1b | Yankees | $75,000 |
| 23. | Robert Ransom, rhp | Cubs | $175,000 |
| **24.** | **#Brandon Jones, of** | **Braves** | **$215,000** |
| 25. | Richard Hummel, of | Orioles | $13,000 |
| **Other** | **Andy LaRoche, ss** | **Dodgers (39)** | **$1,000,000** |

*Major leaguers in bold. *High school selection. #Signed as draft-and-follow.*

### CONTROVERSY INVOLVES MILLEDGE

The strength of the 2003 draft supposedly was an impressive crop of high school outfielders. Led by Young, four of the first 12 selections came from that demographic. None panned out as expected.

Lubanski, taken by the Royals with the fifth pick and signed for a below-slot $2.1 million bonus, hit nearly .500 over his four-year prep career. His superior speed was an asset both on the bases and in center field, and it was anticipated that his power would evolve once he matured into his 6-foot-3, 185-pound frame. But as Lubanski got bigger and stronger, he lost speed, which pushed him to left field and curtailed his basestealing ability. He never developed as a hitter, either, batting .252 in four seasons at Triple-A before leaving pro ball.

The 6-foot-5, 215-pound Harvey, who drew comparisons to Dale Murphy for his raw power, superior speed and defense in right field, was under consideration to go No. 1 overall until he injured his knee the previous fall. He missed the first 17 games of his 2003 high school season, and slipped to the Cubs at No. 6.

Harvey, who received a $2.4 million bonus, did not hit with any regularity in eight seasons in the minors. A free swinger with a long stroke, he hit .244 with 117 homers and struck out 711 times in 642 games, none above Double-A.

Milledge, selected by the Mets with the 12th pick overall, had five-tool ability, but his off-field issues scared some clubs. He was a 16-year-old junior at Northside Christian School in St. Petersburg, Fla., in the fall of 2001 when police invesigated him for having sexual relations with girls as young as 12 and 13. No charges were brought, though Milledge admitted to having consensual sex with his 15-year-old girlfriend.

Northside Christian officials expelled Milledge on May 17, 2002, three days after the school's baseball team lost in the Florida state 1-A finals, then rescinded the expulsion three weeks later. But he transferred to Lakewood Ranch High in nearby Bradenton for his senior year, and led the baseball team to the 2003 state 5-A championship.

## One Team's Draft: Los Angeles Dodgers

| | Player, Pos. | Bonus |
|---|---|---|
| **1.** | ***Chad Billingsley, rhp** | **$1,375,000** |
| 2. | *Chuck Tiffany, lhp | $1,100,000 |
| 3. | *Cory Van Allen, lhp | Did not sign |
| **4.** | ***Xavier Paul, of** | **$270,000** |
| 5. | *Jordan Pratt, rhp | $175,000 |
| **6.** | ***Matt Kemp, of** | **$130,000** |
| **7.** | ***Wesley Wright, lhp** | **$120,000** |
| **8.** | ***Lucas May, 3b** | **$100,000** |
| 9. | Brett Dowdy, 2b | $75,000 |
| 10. | Phil Sobkow, rhp | $45,000 |
| 11. | *Tony Harper, c | $33,000 |
| 12. | *Cody White, lhp | $46,500 |
| 13. | *Derik Olvey, rhp | Did not sign |
| 14. | *David Pfeiffer, lhp | $75,000 |
| **15.** | ***Russ Mitchell, ss** | **$45,000** |
| 16. | James Peterson, 1b | $112,500 |
| 17. | *Steven Sapp, of | $30,000 |
| **18.** | **A.J. Ellis, c** | **$2,500** |
| **19.** | ***Matt Antonelli, ss** | **Did not sign** |
| 20. | *Chad Barben, 3b | Did not sign |
| **21.** | ***Travis Denker, 2b** | **$100,000** |
| 22. | *Doug Frame, lhp | Did not sign |
| 23. | Taylor Slimak, c | $2,500 |
| 24. | *Ben Snyder, of | Did not sign |
| 25. | *Kevin Skogley, lhp | Did not sign |
| **Other** | **Andy LaRoche (39), ss** | **$1,000,000** |

*Major leaguers in bold. *High school selection.*

## Highest Unsigned Picks

| Player, Pos., Team (Round) | College | Re-Drafted |
|---|---|---|
| Andrew Miller, lhp, Devil Rays (3) | North Carolina | Tigers '06 (1) |
| Drew Stubbs, of, Astros (3) | Texas | Reds '06 (1) |
| Cory Van Allen, lhp, Dodgers (3) | Baylor | Nationas '06 (5) |
| Ben Harrison, of, Indians (4) | * Florida | Rangers '04 (7) |
| Marc Cornell, rhp, Reds (5) | * Ohio | Rangers '04 (19) |
| Brandon McArthur, ss, Twins (5) | Florida | Never |
| Cory Patton, of, Padres (6) | * Texas A&M | Blue Jays '04 (6) |
| C.J. Smith, 1b, Pirates (6) | * Florida | Orioles '04 (5) |
| Jordan Parraz, rhp, Phillies (6) | JC So. Nevada | Astros '04 (3) |
| Adam Trent, rhp, Tigers (8) | Young Harris (Ga.) | Royals '04 (17) |

**TOTAL UNSIGNED PICKS:** Top 5 Rounds (6), Top 10 Rounds (14)

**Returned to same school.*

The Mets had followed Milledge throughout high school and said they trusted his character enough to draft him. The two sides appeared to be close to a contract when new allegations surfaced that Milledge had engaged in improper behavior. The Mets had a private investigator look into the charges and were comfortable with the findings. They signed Milledge on Aug. 19 for a $2.075 million bonus, to be spread over five years, per draft rules governing two-sport athletes. Milledge hadn't played football since emerging as a top baseball prospect in 2001, but Mississippi Gulf Coast CC offered him the chance to play both sports.

The 6-foot-1, 180-pound Milledge showed superior bat speed, foot speed and arm strength. He was in the major leagues by age 21. But his brash personality rubbed many Mets players the wrong way. When he failed to establish himself as an everyday player, the Mets traded him, and he bounced from one club to another over an undistinguished six-year major league career, batting .269 with 33 home runs in 433 games.

TONY FARLOW

Lastings Milledge

Milledge wasn't the only first-rounder whose career was marred by off-field issues. Righthander Jeff Allison, who didn't give up an earned run in his senior year at Veterans Memorial High in Peabody, Mass., and was selected with the 16th overall pick by the Florida Marlins, suffered from drug addiction. He didn't get past Double-A, going 31-38, 4.65 in the minor leagues.

Minnesota Twins first-rounder Matt Moses (21st overall), a third baseman from Mills Godwin High in Richmond, Va., had to deal with a health scare. After agreeing to a $1.45 million bonus, Moses was set to make his debut in the Rookie-level Gulf Coast League, until a physical examination revealed a heart abnormality.

Fortunately for Moses, doctors determined that neither his life nor his career was in jeopardy. He had a tiny hole in his heart, which was repaired at Miami Children's Hospital, and he was working out three days later. He started playing on July 31, and batted .385 in 16 games over the remainder of the season. He struggled to build on that, though. In 596 minor league games over seven seasons, including one in Triple-A, he batted .249 with 47 homers.

### SECOND-ROUNDER SINISI CASHES IN

While most clubs toed the line on bonus payments, several players received amounts significantly greater than their recommended slot value. They included Rangers second-rounder Vince Sinisi, Astros 13th-rounder Jimmy Barthmaier and Dodgers 39th-rounder Andy LaRoche.

Sinisi was considered the third-best college hitting prospect, behind Weeks and Aubrey, but he had three signability strikes: He was a sophomore-eligible player with extra leverage; he was at Rice, a school where players didn't often leave early; and his agent was Scott Boras. A first baseman/outfielder who might have been a top 10 pick based on ability, he signed for $2.07 million. Boras' only client in 2003 besides Sinisi in the top five rounds was Baylor righthander Steven White, a fourth-round pick of the Yankees who held out for several months before signing for $250,000.

Barthmaier, a Georgia high school righthander, made a late push for the first round after improving his fastball into the 91-95 mph range. He also was a quarterback recruited by several Southeastern Conference colleges and was vague about his willingness to give up football. A $750,000 bonus got Barthmaier to commit to baseball.

It was the largest bonus paid out that year by the Astros, who adhered to the slot recommendations of MLB in the early rounds. They did not have a first-round pick, but refused to budge in negotiations with outfielder Drew Stubbs, a local product with first-round ability whom they drafted in the third round. When the Astros lost Stubbs to the University of Texas, they allocated the bonus money earmarked for him to Barthmaier.

The Padres were unable to sign LaRoche, a 21st-round draft-and-follow player from 2002. The Dodgers drafted the shortstop the following year in the 39th round, and that summer LaRoche developed into the best position player prospect in the Cape Cod League. He likely would have been a first-rounder in 2004 if the Dodgers had not signed him for $1 million, the highest bonus in the 2003 draft after the second round. LaRoche came from a baseball family; his father, Dave, and brother, Adam, played in the big leagues.

## Largest Draft-And-Follow Bonuses

| Player, Pos. | Club (Round) | Bonus |
|---|---|---|
| 1. * Luis Cota, rhp | Royals (10) | $1,050,000 |
| **2. Ryan Mattheus, rhp** | **Rockies (19)** | **$700,000** |
| 3. Kurt Koehler, rhp | Marlins (17) | $275,000 |
| 4. Chris Rayborn, rhp | Padres (34) | $250,000 |
| **5. * Johnny Venters, lhp** | **Braves (30)** | **$240,000** |
| **6. Brandon Jones, of** | **Braves (24)** | **$215,000** |
| 7. Stuart Alexander, rhp | Marlins (29) | $200,000 |
| 8. Jason Snyder, rhp | Mariners (17) | $160,000 |
| 9. * Marcus Sanders, ss | Giants (17) | $150,000 |
| 10. Stantrel Smith, of | Angels (16) | $132,000 |

*Major leaguers in bold. *High school selection.*

### IN FOCUS: BRANDON WOOD

ANDREW WOOLLEY

No high school hitter in the 2003 draft may have generated greater hype only to fall short more than Brandon Wood, a shortstop turned third baseman. He became a dynamic hitter in the minors but never swung the bat the same way in the majors.

Selected by the Angels with the 23rd pick overall, Wood dramatically raised his profile for the draft as a senior after hitting .500 with 20 homers at Horizon High in Scottsdale, Ariz. Two years later, he hit .321 with 51 doubles and 43 homers at Class A Rancho Cucamonga, and reached rare air by accumulating 100 extra-base hits on the season after finishing the 2005 campaign in Triple-A. That fall, he went about validating his status as one of the game's elite prospects by setting an Arizona Fall League record by drilling 14 more homers.

He was compared to a young Cal Ripken Jr., a shortstop with deceptively smooth actions in the field and a middle-of-the-order bat. But for all of Wood's prowess in the minors, the holes in his swing were exposed in the majors. He lacked plate discipline and had poor pitch selection, and his unwillingness to shorten his swing hurt his two-strike approach.

In 700 major league at-bats over five seasons, Wood hit an anemic .186 with 18 home runs and 218 strikeouts.

# 2003 Draft List

**Did not sign. Major leaguers in bold, with first and last years noted. Order of selection indicated in parentheses. For the first five rounds, the peak level of each player is noted.*
*+ Signed as draft-and-follow (Second school noted if applicable).*

## ANAHEIM ANGELS (23)

1. **Brandon Wood, ss, Horizon HS, Scottsdale, Ariz.—(2007-11)**
2. Anthony Whittington, lhp, Buffalo HS, Putnam, W.Va.—(Rookie)
3. **Sean Rodriguez, ss, Braddock HS, Miami.—(2008-15)**
4. Bob Zimmerman, rhp, Southwest Missouri State University.—(AA)
5. Blake Balkcom, of, Florida State University.—(High A)
6. Jesse Smith, rhp, Illinois Valley CC.
7. **Reggie Willits, of, University of Oklahoma.—(2006-11)**
8. Josh Cowles, of, Redlands East Valley HS, Redlands, Calif.
9. Von Stertzbach, rhp, University of Central Florida.
10. Patrice Lepage, c, Edouard Montpetit College HS, Montreal.
11. Adam Pavkovich, ss, University of Alabama.
12. Andy Hill, rhp, Brewster (Wash.) HS.
13. **Daniel Davidson, lhp, Florida State University.—(2009)**
14. Kelly Shearer, lhp, Lawrence E. Elkins HS, Missouri City, Texas.
15. David Austen, rhp, University of South Florida.
16. +Stantrel Smith, of, North Florida CC.
17. Matt Pali, of, Florida Atlantic University.
18. **Fernando Rodriguez, rhp, El Paso (Texas) CC.—(2009-15)**
19. Billy Boyer, 2b, Enumclaw (Wash.) HS.
20. ***Jason Donald, ss, Buchanan HS, Clovis, Calif.—(2010-12)**
21. *Josh Land, of, Milton (Fla.) HS.
22. B.J. Brown, lhp, Oakland University.
23. *Brett Douglas, rhp, Westminster (Calif.) HS.
24. Chad Hauseman, of, Jacksonville University.
25. *Justin Brashear, c, Barbe HS, Lake Charles, La.
26. +Joe Rowe, rhp, Central Alabama CC.
27. *Jimmy Durette, lhp, Ahuntsic College HS, Martine, Quebec.
28. *Nick Roxby, 2b, North Florida JC.
29. *Drew Fiorenza, rhp, Okaloosa-Walton (Fla.) CC.
30. *Adam Frank, c, Lamar (Colo.) CC.
31. ***David Huff, lhp, Edison HS, Huntington Beach, Calif.—(2009-15)**

DRAFT DROP *First-round draft pick (39th overall), Indians (2006)*

32. *Keith Williams, of, Gulf Coast (Fla.) CC.
33. *Ricky Bambino, c, Foothill HS, Redding, Calif.
34. *Jason Blackey, rhp, Malaspina (B.C.) CC.
35. *Jay Mattox, of, Chipola (Fla.) JC.
36. +Brandon Doddo, 3b, Broward (Fla.) CC.
37. *Tommy Baumgardner, lhp, Indian River (Fla.) CC.
38. *Ron Lowe, lhp, Pasco-Hernando (Fla.) CC.
39. *Nate Boman, lhp, Patrick Henry HS, San Diego.
40. ***Brandon Morrow, rhp, Rancho Cotate HS, Rohnert Park, Calif.—(2007-15)**

DRAFT DROP *First-round draft pick (5th overall), Mariners (2006)*

41. Chris Hunter, rhp, Utah Valley State JC.
42. *Cody Nelson, ss, Chabot (Calif.) JC.
43. *Caleb Hatfield, rhp, Red Bluff (Calif.) HS.
44. *John Mariotti, rhp, Chaminade College HS, Toronto.
45. *Chris Noonan, lhp, Seton Hall University.
46. *Hank Lanto, c, Modesto (Calif.) HS.
47. *Ryan Anderson, lhp, St. Petersburg (Fla.) CC.
48. *Jeremy Labigano, lhp, Westwood HS, Fort Pierce, Fla.
49. *Evan Bailey, rhp, Westsyde SS, Kamloops, B.C.
50. ***Kris Johnson, lhp, Blue Springs (Mo.) HS.—(2013-14)**

DRAFT DROP *First-round draft pick (40th overall), Red Sox (2006)*

## ARIZONA DIAMONDBACKS (29)

1. **Conor Jackson, 1b, University of California** (Choice from Mariners as compensation for Type B free agent Greg Colbrunn).**—(2005-11)**

DRAFT DROP *Son of actor John Jackson*

1. **Carlos Quentin, of, Stanford University.—(2006-14)**
2. **Jamie D'Antona, 3b, Wake Forest University.—(2008)**
3. **Matt Chico, lhp, Palomar (Calif.) JC.—(2007-10)**
4. Chris Kinsey, rhp, Cal State Sacramento.—(AAA)
5. Jeff Cook, of, University of Southern Mississippi.—(High A)
6. Orlando Mercado, c, Antonio Luchetti HS, Arecibo, P.R.

DRAFT DROP *Son of Orlando Mercado, major leaguer (1982-90)*

7. Dustin Glant, rhp, Purdue University.
8. Robbie Van, lhp, University of Nevada-Las Vegas.
9. Steve Garrabrants, 2b, Arizona State University.
10. Adam Bass, rhp, University of Alabama-Huntsville.
11. Tila Reynolds, ss, University of Washington.
12. Jon Kaplan, of, Tulane University.
13. Todd Buchanan, 1b, Western Carolina University.
14. Brian Rose, c, University of Florida.
15. Ben Krantz, rhp, University of Pennsylvania.
16. Ruben Kerbs, lhp, Wichita State University.
17. Jayson Santiago, of, Maestro Ladi HS, Vega Alta, P.R.
18. ***Chris Coghlan, c, East Lake HS, Tarpon Springs, Fla.—(2009-15)**

DRAFT DROP *First-round draft pick (36th overall), Marlins (2006)*

19. Danny Muegge, rhp, University of Texas.
20. Joe Carque, rhp, San Diego State University.
21. Chad Clark, rhp, Azusa Pacific (Calif.) University.
22. Walt Novosel, lhp, Ohio University.
23. Travis McAndrews, of, University of Southern California.
24. Allen Mottram, c, University of Massachusetts-Lowell.
25. Kellen Raab, lhp, University of Wisconsin-Parkside.
26. Travis Van Zile, of, University of Wisconsin-Whitewater.
27. Jason McStoots, ss, Missouri Baptist College.
28. Brian Viafore, 1b, Central Washington University.
29. *Tony Festa, 3b, UC Riverside.
30. Greg Mathis, of, Southwest Missouri State University.
31. Tim Vaillancourt, rhp, Delaware State University.
32. Andrew McCreery, 3b, University of Pennsylvania.
33. *Brandon Belcher, lhp, Ruston (La.) HS.
34. Gabe Rio, lhp, Florida Southern College.
35. Alex Cremidan, rhp, UC San Diego.
36. Derik Nippert, rhp, Ohio Valley (W.Va.) College.

DRAFT DROP *Twin brother of Dustin Nippert, major leaguer (2005-10)*

37. *Ryan LaCross, lhp, Lakewood Ranch HS, Bradenton, Fla.
38. Shane Dove, lhp, Spartanburg Methodist (S.C.) JC.
39. Cristobal Melendez, of, Missouri Baptist College.
40. *Connor Rapkoch, c, Bellarmine Prep, Tacoma, Wash.
41. *Kevin Stiehl, lhp, West Torrance HS, Torrance, Calif.
42. Mike Guerrero, of, Arizona State University.
43. *Matt Mammen, lhp, St. Charles (Mo.) CC.
44. *Jacob Coash, lhp, JC of the Canyons (Calif.).
45. *Josh Terrell, 1b, Lurleen B. Wallace State (Ala.) JC.
46. *Lester Contreras, ss, Champagnat Catholic HS, Hialeah, Fla.
47. *Brody Taylor, lhp, Louisburg (N.C.) JC.
48. *Ben Colton, rhp, Reno (Nev.) HS.
49. *Juan Velazquez, rhp, Grossmont (Calif.) CC.
50. ***Jeff Manship, rhp, Ronald Reagan HS, San Antonio, Texas.—(2009-15)**

## ATLANTA BRAVES (30)

1. (Choice to Royals as compensation for Type B free agent Paul Byrd)
1. **Luis Atilano, rhp, Gabriela Mistral HS, San Juan, P.R.** (Supplemental choice—35th—as compensation for Type A free agent Tom Glavine).**—(2010)**
1. **Jarrod Saltalamacchia, c, Royal Palm Beach HS, West Palm Beach, Fla.** (Supplemental choice—36th—as compensation for Type A free agent Mike Remlinger).**—(2007-15)**
2. **Jo Jo Reyes, lhp, Poly HS, Riverside, Calif.** (Choice from Cubs as compensation for Remlinger).**—(2007-11)**
2. Paul Bacot, rhp, Lakeside HS, Atlanta.—(Low A)
3. Jacob Stevens, lhp, Cape Coral (Fla.) HS (Choice from Mets as compensation for Glavine).—(AAA)
3. **Matt Harrison, lhp, South Granville HS, Stem, N.C.—(2008-15)**
4. **Jamie Romak, 3b, A.B. Lucas SS, London, Ontario.—(2014-15)**
5. Chris Vines, rhp, Pelham (Ala.) HS.—(High A)
6. Asher Demme, rhp, South Lakes HS, Reston, Va.
7. Ryan Basner, rhp, Western Carolina University.
8. **Sean White, rhp, University of Washington.—(2007-10)**
9. Adam Stanley, lhp, Garner (N.C.) HS.
10. Brad Nelson, rhp, Lenoir (N.C.) CC.
11. Glenn Tucker, rhp, East Carolina University.
12. *Casey Spanish, of, University of Kansas.
13. +Mark Jurich, of, University of Louisville.
14. Steven Doetsch, of, Indian River (Fla.) CC.
15. Ben Thomas, 3b, Midland (Texas) JC.
16. Cole Armstrong, c, Chipola (Fla.) JC.
17. Keith Eichas, 1b, Temple (Texas) JC.
18. *Keith Weiser, lhp, Talawanda HS, Hamilton, Ohio.
19. Andy Barden, c, Virginia Military Institute.
20. Kyle Bakker, lhp, Georgia Tech.
21. ***Brooks Brown, rhp, Portal (Ga.) HS.—(2014-15)**

DRAFT DROP *First-round draft pick (34th overall), Diamondbacks (2006)*

22. Jacob Blakeney, rhp, Mississippi State University.
23. Jamie Hemingway, of, University of North Carolina-Wilmington.
24. **+Brandon Jones, of, Tallahassee (Fla.) CC.—(2007-09)**
25. ***Quintin Berry, of, Morse HS, San Diego.—(2012-15)**
26. C.J. Bressoud, c, North Cobb HS, Kennesaw, Ga.
27. *Brandon Berdoll, lhp, Temple (Texas) JC.
28. *Kyle Perry, rhp, Ball HS, Galveston, Texas.
29. *Drew Shetrone, rhp, Apopka (Fla.) HS.
30. **+Jonny Venters, lhp, Lake Brantley HS, Altamonte Springs, Fla. / Indian River (Fla.) CC.—(2010-12)**
31. +Jon Schaus, rhp, East Lake HS, Palm Harbor, Fla. / Central Florida CC.
32. +Larry Williams, 1b, Hawthorne HS, Lawndale, Calif. / Los Angeles Harbor JC.
33. ***Daniel Stange, rhp, Elsinore HS, Wildomar, Calif.—(2010-13)**
34. *Michael Gibbs, rhp, Chipola (Fla.) JC.
35. *Daniel Rios, 1b, Mount Whitney HS, Visalia, Calif.
36. *Justin Phillips, ss, Louisburg (N.C.) JC.
37. *Cody Pyle, 3b, Smithson Valley HS, Spring Branch, Texas.
38. *Eric Chown, rhp, University of Massachusetts.
39. *Eugene Edwards, 1b, Mayfair HS, Bellflower, Calif.
40. *Joey Doan, rhp, Baker HS, Mobile, Ala.
41. *John Ray, c, Monarch HS, Louisville, Colo.
42. *Marcus Covington, rhp, East Rutherford HS, Forest City, N.C.
43. *Zech Zinicola, rhp, Arlington HS, San Bernardino, Calif.
44. *Tony Portugal, rhp, Northeast HS, Fort Lauderdale, Fla.
45. *David Crook, lhp, Monte Vista HS, Spring Valley, Calif.
46. *Lyall Foran, c, Delta SS, Ladner, B.C.
47. *Joe Northrup, rhp, West Covina (Calif.) HS.
48. +Tony Harris, lhp, Surry (N.C.) CC.
49. *Kyle Price, 2b, Green Valley HS, Henderson, Nev.
50. *John Scaglione, rhp, Palm Beach Gardens HS, Lake Park, Fla.

## BALTIMORE ORIOLES (7)

1. **Nick Markakis, of-lhp, Young Harris (Ga.) JC.—(2006-15)**
2. Brian Finch, rhp, Texas A&M University.—(AA)
3. **Chris Ray, rhp, College of William & Mary.—(2005-11)**
4. **Bob McCrory, rhp, University of Southern Mississippi.—(2008-09)**
5. **Nate Spears, ss, Charlotte HS, Port Charlotte, Fla.—(2011-12)**
6. Eric Sultemeier, of, University of Texas.
7. Justin Azze, lhp, University of Hawaii.
8. *Nathan Nery, lhp, Moon Area HS, Moon Township, Pa.
9. Jarod Rine, of, West Virginia University.
10. Jacob Duncan, of, Texas Christian University.
11. Matt Houston, c, Oklahoma City University.
12. Matt Pulley, 3b, Woodland (Calif.) HS.
13. **James Hoey, rhp, Rider University.—(2006-11)**
14. Brian Bock, c, University of Hawaii.
15. *Jordan Timm, lhp, University of Wisconsin-Oshkosh.
16. Alan Beck, of, Western Carolina University.
17. Lorenzo Scott, of, Ball State University.
18. Jason Furrow, lhp, Judson (Texas) HS.
19. ***Matt Tolbert, 2b, University of Mississippi.—(2008-11)**
20. Tony Neal, rhp, University of South Alabama.
21. *David Cash, ss, Northside Christian HS, St. Petersburg, Fla.

DRAFT DROP *Son of Dave Cash, major leaguer (1969-80)*

22. Zach Dixon, lhp, Texas A&M University.
23. Dennis Wyrick, 3b, Arizona State University.
24. Josh McCurdy, of, Niagara University.
25. Richard Hummel, of, Tombstone HS, Sierra Vista, Ariz.
26. *Brian LeClerc, of, Northside Christian HS, Clearwater, Fla.
27. Travis Brown, ss, Western Kentucky University.
28. Russ Brocato, rhp, University of Pennsylvania.
29. *Jason Ward, rhp, Utah Valley State JC.
30. Chris Osentowski, rhp, Texas Christian University.
31. Ryan Brnardic, rhp, Southeastern Oklahoma State University.
32. Landon Wareham, 2b, Mesa State (Colo.) College.
33. *Jake Muyco, c, Columbia Basin (Wash.) CC.
34. Brad Wiggins, of, Howard (Texas) CC.
35. *Richard Orange, of, Greenville (Texas) HS.
36. *Danny Martin, of, Dunedin (Fla.) HS.
37. *David Smith, rhp, Chrysler HS, New Castle, Ind.
38. *Matthew Garnett, lhp, Stockdale HS, Bakersfield, Calif.
39. *Shaun Corning, lhp, Madison (Wis.) Area Tech JC.
40. *Joe Welsh, lhp, Grand Rapids (Mich.) CC.
41. *Aaron Feterl, rhp, Crescenta Valley HS, La Crescenta, Calif.
42. Chad Boudon, of, University of Washington.
43. Kyle George, ss, University of Maryland.
44. *Scott Houin, of, Rampart HS, Colorado Springs, Colo.
45. *Brett Jensen, rhp, Iowa Central CC.
46. *Gregory Young, of, Old Mill HS, Millersville, Md.
47. *Roy Irle, rhp, Rend Lake (Ill.) JC.
48. *Cameron McGuire, c, McLennan (Texas) JC.
49. ***Casey Janssen, rhp, UCLA.—(2006-15)**
50. *Adam Ricciardulli, of, Mission Bay HS, San Diego.

## BOSTON RED SOX (17)

1. **David Murphy, of, Baylor University.—(2006-15)**
1. **Matt Murton, of, Georgia Tech** (Supplemental choice—32nd—as compensation for Type A free agent Cliff Floyd).**—(2005-09)**
2. **Abe Alvarez, lhp, Long Beach State University** (Choice from Mets as compensation for Floyd).**—(2004-06)**
2. Mickey Hall, of, Walton HS, Marietta, Ga.—(AAA)
3. Beau Vaughan, rhp, Arizona State University.—(AAA)
4. **Jonathan Papelbon, rhp, Mississippi State University.—(2005-15)**
5. Brian Marshall, lhp, Virginia Commonwealth University.—(Low A)

DRAFT DROP *Twin brother of Sean Marshall, sixth-round draft pick, Cubs (2003); major leaguer (2006-14)*

6. Jessie Corn, rhp, Jacksonville State University.
7. Jeremy West, c, Arizona State University.
8. Lee Curtis, 2b, College of Charleston.
9. John Wilson, rhp, Northeastern (Colo.) JC.
10. Chris Durbin, of, Baylor University.
11. Barry Hertzler, rhp, Central Connecticut State

University.
12. Justin Sturge, lhp, Coastal Carolina University.
13. Zak Basch, rhp, University of Nevada.
14. Zach Borowiak, ss, Southeast Missouri State University.
15. Chris Turner, of, Texarkana (Texas) JC.
16. Kevin Ool, lhp, Marist College.
17. +Willie Newton, lhp, Mountain View HS, Orem, Utah / Salt Lake (Utah) CC.
18. Tom Cochran, lhp, Middle Georgia JC.
19. Jarrett Gardner, rhp, University of Arkansas.
20. *Josh Morris, of, Cartersville (Ga.) HS.
21. Mike Dennison, rhp, Wichita State University.
22. Kala Kaaihue, c, Iolani HS, Kailua, Hawaii.
23. David Coffey, of, University of Georgia.
24. Ignacio Suarez, ss, Southwest Texas State University.
25. *Drew Moffitt, of, Wichita State University.
26. Jason Ramos, ss, St. Petersburg (Fla.) JC.
27. *Drew Sharpe, ss, Los Angeles Pierce JC.
28. Davey Penny, rhp, East Carolina University.
29. Doug Fink, rhp, Manatee (Fla.) JC.
30. David Sanders, lhp, Wichita State University.
31. *Greg Schilling, lhp, Taravella HS, Coral Springs, Fla.
32. *Matt Pike, rhp, Centennial HS, Pueblo, Colo.
33. Scooter Jordan, of, Texas Tech.
34. Arthur Santos, rhp, Florida International University.
35. Erich Cloninger, c, Liberty University.
DRAFT DROP *Grandson of Tony Cloninger, major leaguer (1961-72)*
36. *Ben Sosebee, rhp, Truett-McConnell (Ga.) JC.
**37. *Chris Johnson, ss, Bishop Verot HS, Fort Myers, Fla.—(2009-15)**
DRAFT DROP *Son of Ron Johnson, major leaguer (1982-84)*
38. *Michael McBryde, of, Palm Beach Gardens HS, North Palm Beach, Fla.
39. *Jeffrey Culpepper, of, Gonzaga University.
40. *Michael Rutledge, ss, Cullman (Ala.) HS.
41. Lance Shartz, c, Garden City (Kan.) CC.
42. *Dallas Williams, of, Pike HS, Indianapolis, Ind.
DRAFT DROP *Son of Dallas Williams, first-round draft pick, Orioles (1976); major leaguer (1981-83)*
43. *Scott Thomas, c, Chaminade College Prep, St. Louis.
DRAFT DROP *Son of Lee Thomas, major leaguer (1961-68); general manager, Phillies (1988-97)*
44. *Tom Caple, of, University of San Diego.
45. *Terrence Cramer, rhp, Palm Beach (Fla.) JC.
46. *Victor Rodriguez, c, Cape Coral (Fla.) HS.
47. *A.J. Loyd, of, Bishop Carroll HS, Wichita, Kan.
48. *Adam Davis, rhp, Middle Georgia JC.
49. Jason Smith, rhp, Bourne (Mass.) HS.
50. +Mitch Stachowsky, c, JC of Southern Idaho.

## CHICAGO CUBS (6)

1. Ryan Harvey, of, Dunedin (Fla.) HS.—(AA)
2. (Choice to Braves as compensation for Type A free agent Mike Remlinger)
**3. Jake Fox, c, University of Michigan.—(2007-11)**
4. Tony Richie, c, Florida State University.—(AAA)
**5. Darin Downs, lhp, Santaluces HS, Boynton Beach, Fla.—(2012-14)**
**6. Sean Marshall, lhp, Virginia Commonwealth University.—(2006-14)**
DRAFT DROP *Twin brother of Brian Marshall, fifth-round draft pick, Red Sox (2003)*
7. Kyle Boyer, of, Cal State Fullerton.
8. (void) Matt Lincoln, lhp, Santa Ana (Calif.) JC.
9. Drew Larsen, ss, Salt Lake (Utah) CC.
**10. Casey McGehee, 3b, Fresno State University.—(2008-15)**
11. Nick Jones, 2b, Virginia Commonwealth University.
12. Chuck Hickman, ss, Nicholls State University.
13. *Ryan Coultas, ss, UC Davis.
**14. *Matt LaPorta, c, Charlotte HS, Port Charlotte, Fla.—(2009-12)**
DRAFT DROP *First-round draft pick (7th overall), Brewers (2007)*
15. Tony McQuade, of, Florida State University.
16. Matt Weber, rhp, Boylan Catholic HS, Rockford, Ill.
17. Tim Kalita, rhp, University of Notre Dame.
18. Trey Johnston, 3b, Schaumburg (Ill.) HS.
19. Brian Carter, lhp, University of Washington.
20. Lance Dawkins, ss, McNeese State University.
21. Reid Willett, rhp, University of Rhode Island.
22. Craig Green, rhp, Bakersfield (Calif.) JC.
23. Robert Ransom, rhp, Vanderbilt University.
**24. *Sam Fuld, of, Stanford University.—(2007-15)**
**25. *Landon Powell, c, University of South Carolina.—(2009-11)**
DRAFT DROP *First-round draft pick (24th overall), Athletics (2004)*
**26. *Barret Browning, lhp, Middle Georgia JC.—(2012)**
27. Jose Rios, ss, Pablo Gonzalez Benedicia HS, Barranquitas, P.R.
28. Adam Tidball, c, University of Richmond.
29. *Matt Brown, rhp, University of California.
30. *Corteze Armstrong, of, Hiwassee (Tenn.) JC.
31. *Chris Ortmeier, rhp, Marcus HS, Flower Mound, Texas.
DRAFT DROP *Brother of Dan Ortmeier, major leaguer (2005-08)*
32. *Adam Tobler, rhp, Rochelle (Ill.) HS.
33. Jasha Balcom, of, University of Georgia.
34. *Adam Harvey, c, Grayson County (Texas) CC.
35. Sean Overholt, rhp, University of Utah.
36. *Jason Fellows, 1b, Georgia Perimeter JC.
37. *Chris Ericksen, lhp, South Suburban (Ill.) CC.
38. *Skyler Southwick, rhp, Dixie State (Utah) JC.
39. David Gresky, of, Northwestern University.
40. Danny Lopaze, 1b, Virginia Commonwealth University.
41. *Doug Low, c, Foothill HS, Henderson, Nev.
42. *Danny Calvert, rhp, Grain Valley HS, Blue Springs, Mo.
43. *Brandon Harmon, rhp, Shadle Park HS, Spokane, Wash.
44. *Cyle Hankerd, 1b-of, South Hills HS, Covina, Calif.
45. Jose Sanchez, c, West Covina (Calif.) HS.
46. *Jefferies Tatford, 3b, St. Thomas Moore HS, Lafayette, La.
47. *Justin Simmons, lhp, University of Texas.
**48. *Tim Lincecum, rhp, Liberty HS, Renton, Wash.—(2007-15)**
DRAFT DROP *First-round draft pick (10th overall), Giants (2006)*
49. *Brian Cleveland, ss, University of Tennessee.
50. *Kris Rochelle, c, Mills Godwin HS, Richmond, Va.

## CHICAGO WHITE SOX (15)

**1. Brian Anderson, of, University of Arizona.—(2005-09)**
**2. Ryan Sweeney, of, Xavier HS, Cedar Rapids, Iowa.—(2006-14)**
3. Clint King, of, University of Southern Mississippi.—(Low A)
4. Robert Valido, ss, Coral Park HS, Miami.—(AAA)
5. Matt Nachreiner, rhp, Round Rock (Texas) HS.—(Rookie)
6. Chris Kelly, of, Pepperdine University.
7. Jim Casey, rhp, Azle (Texas) HS.
8. John Russ, rhp, Frank Phillips (Texas) JC.
9. David Cook, of, Miami (Ohio) University.
10. Fraser Dizard, lhp, University of Southern California.
11. *Ricky Brooks, rhp, North Tonawanda (N.Y.) HS.
**12. *Donnie Veal, lhp, Buena HS, Hereford, Ariz.—(2009-15)**
13. *Wes Hodges, ss, The Baylor School, Ooltewah, Tenn.
14. Ricardo Nanita, of, Florida International University.
15. *Greg Moviel, lhp, St. Ignatius HS, Cleveland.
DRAFT DROP *Brother of Paul Moviel, 36th-round draft pick, White Sox (2003)*
16. *Cody Dickens, rhp, Surry (N.C.) CC.
17. *Guillermo Martinez, ss, Coral Park HS, Miami.
18. Cory Haggerty, 2b, Cortland State (N.Y.) University.
19. Mike Moat, rhp, San Diego State University.
20. J.J. Schmidt, ss, Mira Mesa HS, San Diego.
21. Matt Lenderman, c, Plano East HS, Plano, Texas.
22. +Travis Doyle, lhp, Grand Rapids (Mich.) CC.
23. John Hurd, rhp, JC of Southern Idaho.
24. *Burke Baldwin, lhp, Neuqua Valley HS, Naperville, Ill.
25. Antoin Gray, 3b, Southern University.
26. *Logan Williamson, lhp, Pensacola Catholic HS, Pensacola, Fla.
27. Dwayne Pollok, rhp, Texas A&M University.
28. *Van Pope, 3b, Meridian (Miss.) CC.
29. *Gerardo Cabrera, of, Miami-Dade CC South.
30. *Brandon Lowe, 1b, Vidalia HS, Mount Vernon, Ga.
31. *Robbie Grinestaff, c, Jeffersonville (Ind.) HS.
32. *Josh Morgan, of, Meridian (Miss.) CC.
33. *Alex Acevedo, ss, Dr. Carlos Gonzales HS, Aguada, P.R.
34. Scott Martin, of, Delaware State University.
35. Sean Thompson, lhp, UC Santa Barbara.
36. Paul Moviel, rhp, Kishwaukee (Ill.) JC.
DRAFT DROP *Brother of Greg Moviel, 15th-round draft pick, White Sox (2003)*
37. *Neil Giesler, 1b, Okaloosa-Walton (Fla.) JC.
38. *Michael Mendrin, lhp, Central HS, Fresno, Calif.
39. *Jason Sullivan, rhp, Joplin (Mo.) HS.
40. +Matt Deuchler, c, James Madison University.
41. +Rolando Acosta, ss, Pima (Ariz.) CC.
42. +Eric Everly, lhp, Olney Central (Ill.) JC.
43. +Dustin Shafer, ss, Russell HS, Flatwoods, Ky. / St. Catharine (Ky.) JC.
44. *Brandon Johnson, 2b, Crowder (Mo.) JC.
45. *Mitchell Woolf, rhp, JC of Southern Idaho.
46. *Greg Del George, ss, Monsignor Farrell HS, Staten Island, N.Y.
47. *Richard O'Brien, c, Catholic HS, Little Rock, Ark.
48. *Mike Alvarez, rhp, Monsignor Pace HS, Opelika, Fla.
49. *Tim Edmeades, 3b, Buena Regional HS, Weymouth, N.J.
50. *Sean Gaston, c, Brownsburg (Ind.) HS.

## CINCINNATI REDS (14)

**1. Ryan Wagner, rhp, University of Houston.—(2003-07)**
DRAFT DROP *First player from 2003 draft to reach majors (July 19, 2003)*
2. Thomas Pauly, rhp, Princeton University.—(High A)
3. Willy Jo Ronda, ss, Gabriela Mistral HS, San Juan, P.R.—(Rookie)
4. Kenny Lewis, of, George Washington HS, Danville, Va.—(Low A)
DRAFT DROP *Son of Kenny Lewis, running back, National Football League (1980-83)*
5. *Marc Cornell, rhp, Ohio University.—DNP
DRAFT DROP *Returned to Ohio; re-drafted by Rangers, 2004 (19th round)*
6. Richie Gardner, rhp, University of Arizona.
**7. Carlos Guevara, rhp, St. Mary's (Texas) University.—(2008)**
8. Damian Ursin, rhp, Southern University.
9. Ben Himes, of, Oklahoma City University.
10. *Andy D'Alessio, 1b, Barron Collier HS, Naples, Fla.
11. Blake Hendley, rhp, Oklahoma City University.
12. James Paduch, rhp, Concordia (Ill.) University.
13. Matt Gray, of, Butler County (Kan.) CC.
14. *Marcus Townsend, of, Southern University.
15. *Jo Jo Batten, of, Telfair County HS, McRae, Ga.
**16. Chris Dickerson, of, University of Nevada.—(2008-14)**
17. Brock Till, rhp, Bradley University.
18. Kyle Smith, of, Houston Baptist University.
19. *Charles Benoit, lhp, Carroll HS, Southlake, Texas.
20. *Dennis Dixon, of, San Leandro (Calif.) HS.
DRAFT DROP *Quarterback, National Football League (2008-11)*
21. *Todd Nicholas, lhp, Mississippi State University.
22. *Brian Barr, rhp, Southern Arkansas University.
23. Chad Ziemendorf, c, UC Santa Barbara.
24. *Matt Harrington, rhp, Fort Worth/Central League.
DRAFT DROP *First-round draft pick (7th overall), Rockies (2000) • Brother of Troy Harrington, 44th-round draft pick, Pirates (2003)*
25. *Jack Harris, 3b, Ronald Reagan HS, San Antonio, Texas.
26. Jeff Urgelles, c, Savannah State (Ga.) University.
27. +Zac Stott, rhp, Dixie State (Utah) JC.
28. *Dustin Evans, rhp, Adairsville HS, Taylorsville, Ga.
29. Philip Gentry, of, University of Texas-San Antonio.
30. *Michael Brown, rhp, Grayson County (Texas) JC.
**31. *Josh Newman, lhp, Ohio State University.—(2007-08)**
**32. *German Duran, ss, Paschal HS, Fort Worth, Texas.—(2008)**
33. David Talamantez, rhp, Lamar University.
34. Evan Conley, c, Jacksonville State University.
35. Matt Trepkowski, lhp, Incarnate Word (Texas) College.
36. *Nick Vaughn, rhp, Oak Ridge HS, Dorado Hills, Calif.
37. *Bart Braun, lhp, Southeastern Louisiana University.
38. *Adam Hicks, 3b, Scottsdale (Ariz.) CC.
39. Clay Cleveland, 1b, Savannah State (Ga.) University.
40. *Jake McCarter, rhp, Tivy HS, Kerrville, Texas.
41. Jordan Belcher, of, Augusta Christian HS, Augusta, Ga.
42. *David Scott, c, Northside Christian HS, Pinellas Park, Fla.
DRAFT DROP *Son of Donnie Scott, major leaguer (1983-91)*
43. *Nick Devito, 1b, Hingham (Mass.) HS.
44. *Carlyle Holliday, of, University of Notre Dame.
DRAFT DROP *Quarterback, National Football League (2005-08)*
45. *Rusty Beale, ss, Stetson University.
46. Brian Wyatt, rhp, Vernon Regional (Texas) JC.
47. *Dane Mason, rhp, Gloucester County (N.J.) JC.
48. +Johntavis Character, of, McNair HS, Decatur, Ga. / Middle Georgia JC.
49. *Jordan Mayer, 1b, Alexandria (La.) HS.
**50. *Colin Curtis, of, Issaquah (Wash.) HS.—(2010)**

## CLEVELAND INDIANS (11)

**1. Michael Aubrey, 1b, Tulane University.—(2008-09)**
**1. Brad Snyder, of, Ball State University** (Choice from Phillies as compensation for Type A free agent Jim Thome).**—(2010-14)**
DRAFT DROP *Brother of Ben Snyder, 24th-round draft pick, Dodgers (2003)*
1. Adam Miller, rhp, McKinney (Texas) HS (Supplemental choice—31st—as compensation for Thome).—(AAA)
2. Javi Herrera, c, University of Tennessee.—(AAA)
**3. Ryan Garko, c, Stanford University.—(2005-10)**
4. *Ben Harrison, of, University of Florida.—(AAA)
DRAFT DROP *Returned to Florida; re-drafted by Rangers, 2004 (7th round)*
5. Juan Valdes, of, Fernando Callejo HS, Manati, P.R.—(AA)
**6. Kevin Kouzmanoff, 3b, University of Nevada.—(2006-14)**
7. Matt Davis, rhp, Ohio State University.
8. Bo Ashabraner, rhp, Long Beach State University.
9. Anthony Lunetta, ss, University of Southern California.
10. Scott Roehl, rhp, University of Arkansas.
11. Ryan Mulhern, of, University of South Alabama.
12. Brandon Pinckney, ss, Sacramento (Calif.) CC.
13. *Steven Reinhold, 2b, Tuscola HS, Waynesville, N.C.
14. *Denton Williams, of, A&M Consolidated HS, College Station, Texas.
15. Ryan Spilman, c, Mount Vernon (Ind.) HS.
DRAFT DROP *Son of Harry Spilman, major leaguer (1978-89)*
**16. Aaron Laffey, lhp, Allegany HS, Cumberland, Md.—(2007-15)**
17. Jeff Pry, rhp, Franklin HS, Portland, Ore.
18. *Dusty Barnard, rhp, Connors State (Okla.) JC.
19. *Joey Huskins, c, Cypress (Calif.) JC.
20. *Shane Mathews, rhp, St. Stephens HS, Conover, N.C.
21. Adam Brandenburg, lhp, Kennesaw State University.
22. *Matt Elliot, rhp, Dixie State (Utah) JC.
23. Tim Montgomery, of, University of Hawaii.
24. Ryan Goleski, 1b-of, Eastern Michigan University.
25. *Travis DeBondt, lhp, Bakersfield (Calif.) JC.
26. *Andrew Johnston, rhp, Jefferson (Mo.) JC.

27. *Mike Felix, rhp, Rutherford HS, Panama City, Fla.
28. *Jason James, of, Kishwaukee (Ill.) JC.
29. Brett Parker, ss, University of South Alabama.
30. *James Smith, rhp, Merced (Calif.) JC.
31. Mark Harris, rhp, College of William & Mary.
**32. *Steven Jackson, rhp, Clemson University.—(2009-10)**
33. *Joe Reid, rhp, St. John's University.
34. Roger Lincoln, lhp, Stetson University.
35. *Bart Babineaux, of, El Camino (Calif.) JC.
36. *Jared Goedert, 3b, Concordia (Kan.) HS.
37. *Zach Wallis, lhp, Enid (Okla.) HS.
38. *Neall French, c, Grand Rapids (Mich.) CC.
39. *Jim Rapoport, of, Chaminade Prep, Westlake Village, Calif.
40. *Adrian Schau, rhp, Villanova University.
41. *Jake Leonhardt, rhp, Cypress Fairbanks HS, Cypress, Texas.
42. Adam Hanson, rhp, Wake Forest University.
43. Joe Weaver, rhp, Oklahoma State University.
44. *Kyle Muschara, rhp, Lassiter HS, Marietta, Ga.
45. *Rafael Cotto, of, Miguel Such HS, Rio Piedras, P.R.
46. *James O'Neill, lhp, Milford HS, Highland, Mich.
47. *Chad Corona, 3b, San Diego State University.
48. *Jordan Karnofsky, of, Christian Brothers HS, Sacramento, Calif.
49. *David Horlacher, rhp, Dixie State (Utah) JC.
50. *Seth Button, of, Elk Lake HS, Meshoppen, Pa.

## COLORADO ROCKIES (10)

**1. Ian Stewart, 3b, La Quinta HS, Garden Grove, Calif.—(2007-14)**
2. Scott Beerer, rhp, Texas A&M University.—(AAA)
3. Aaron Marsden, lhp, University of Nebraska.—(High A)
4. Rick Guarno, c, University of Arkansas-Little Rock.—(AAA)
5. Christian Colonel, ss, Texas Tech.—(AAA)
6. Randy Blood, 2b, UC Riverside.
7. Larry Robles, rhp, Cal State Dominguez Hills.
8. Darric Merrell, rhp, Cal State Fullerton.
9. Gene Reynolds, ss, University of Tampa.
10. Marc Kaiser, rhp, Lewis-Clark State (Idaho) College.
11. John Restrepo, of, Santa Ana (Calif.) JC.
12. Joe Gaetti, of, North Carolina State University.
DRAFT DROP *Son of Gary Gaetti, major leaguer (1981-2000)*
13. Matt Brinson, 1b, Mississippi State University.
14. J.P. Gagne, rhp, University of Notre Dame.
15. Mark Ion, rhp, Lamar University.
16. Mike Wiley, lhp, Stetson University.
17. *Jim Brauer, rhp, University of Michigan.
18. *Friedel Pinkston, rhp, Chipola (Fla.) JC.
**19. +Ryan Mattheus, rhp, Sacramento (Calif.) CC.—(2011-15)**
20. Scott Anderson, ss, Cal Poly San Luis Obispo.
21. Ryan Fox, of, University of Arkansas.
22. *Adam Daniels, lhp, Eastern Oklahoma State JC.
23. Brian Lynch, rhp, Ball State University.
24. Jeff Watchko, rhp, Georgia Tech.
25. Jordan Czarniecki, of, University of Tennessee.
**26. Cole Garner, of, La Quinta HS, Westminster, Calif.—(2011)**
27. Jason DiAngelo, rhp, West Virginia University.
28. *Ricardo Rivas, rhp, El Paso (Texas) CC.
**29. *David Hernandez, rhp, Elk Grove (Calif.) HS.—(2009-13)**
**30. +Eric Young Jr., 2b, Piscataway (N.J.) HS / Chandler-Gilbert (Ariz.) CC.—(2009-15)**
DRAFT DROP *Son of Eric Young, major leaguer (1992-2006)*
31. *Aaron George, rhp, Scottsdale (Ariz.) CC.
32. *Kyle Allen, lhp, Orange Coast (Calif.) JC.
33. *Garret Baker, 3b, Modesto (Texas) JC.
34. *Stoney Stone, rhp, Texarkana (Texas) JC.
35. *Kyle Wright, rhp, Columbia Basin (Wash.) CC.
36. *Derek Patterson, lhp, Northeast Texas JC.
**37. *Jesse Litsch, rhp, Dixie Hollins HS, St. Petersburg, Fla.—(2007-11)**
38. *Ryan Snell, rhp, Skyline HS, Sammamish, Wash.
39. *Don Powers, rhp, Seminole State (Okla.) JC.
40. *David Hurst, lhp, Florida CC.
41. *Brandon Anderson, of, Wayland (Mass.) HS.
42. *Carlos Moreno, rhp, Odessa (Tex.) CC.
43. *Justin Jameson, of, Creekside HS, Fairburn, Ga.
44. *Robert Rose, rhp, Cleveland State (Tenn.) CC.
45. *Joshua Banda, c, Artesia HS, Lakewood, Calif.
46. +Jason Van Kooten, ss, Regis Jesuit HS, Aurora, Colo. / Seward County (Kan.) CC.
47. *Jose Cardona, lhp, San Juan, P.R.
48. *Ryan Flavell, c, Clarendon (Texas) JC.
49. *Jason Martinez, lhp, Mesa State (Colo.) College.
50. *Michael Jenkins, 3b, Hiwassee (Tenn.) CC.

## DETROIT TIGERS (3)

1. Kyle Sleeth, rhp, Wake Forest University.—(AA)
**2. Jay Sborz, rhp, Langley HS, Great Falls, Va.—(2010)**
**3. Tony Giarratano, ss, Tulane University.—(2005)**
4. Josh Rainwater, rhp, DeRidder (La.) HS.—(AAA)
5. Danny Zell, lhp, University of Houston.—(AA)
6. Cody Collet, c, Newbury Park (Calif.) HS.
**7. Virgil Vasquez, rhp, UC Santa Barbara.—(2007-09)**
8. *Adam Trent, rhp, Ooltewah (Tenn.) HS.
9. Eric Rodland, 2b, Gonzaga University.
10. *Sean Henry, of, Armijo HS, Suisun City, Calif.
**11. Brian Rogers, rhp, Georgia Southern University.—(2006-07)**
12. Jeremy Laster, of, Hunters Lane HS, Nashville, Tenn.
13. Michael Brown, of, College of William & Mary.
14. Luis Sabino, of, Wabash Valley (Ill.) JC.
15. Andy Baldwin, rhp, Western Kentucky University.
**16. Jordan Tata, rhp, Sam Houston State University.—(2006-07)**
17. *Ronnie Martin, lhp, St. Mary's HS, St. Louis, Mo.
18. *Josh Wahpepah, rhp, Cowley County (Kan.) CC.
19. Andrew Graham, c, Armstrong Atlantic State (Ga.) College.
20. Nick McIntyre, 2b, Purdue University.
21. Jacob Ford, 3b, Spalding (Ky.) University.
22. Richie Burgos, 1b, Cal State Fullerton.
23. Bobby Huddleston, c, Auburn University.
24. Chris Homer, rhp, Marist College.
25. Nathan Doyle, ss, James Madison University.
26. Lavon Lewis, rhp, Northeastern Oklahoma A&M JC.
27. Aaron McRae, c, LSU-Shreveport.
28. *Steven Alexander, 1b, Rocklin (Calif.) HS.
29. Kelly Hunt, 1b, Bowling Green State University.
30. Anthony Tomey, rhp, Eastern Michigan University.
31. +Justin Justice, of, Tavares HS, Leesburg, Fla. / Lake Sumter (Fla.) CC.
32. Justin Barnes, c, University of Alabama-Huntsville.
33. Kenon Ronz, lhp, Harvard University.
34. *Chaz Schilens, of, Highland HS, Mesa, Ariz.
DRAFT DROP *Wide receiver, National Football League (2008-12)*
35. *Ryan Muller, rhp, Live Oak HS, Morgan Hill, Calif.
36. John McGorty, 1b, Marist College.
37. *Alberto Cruz, 3b, Chandler (Ariz.) HS.
38. *John Juergens, c, Bradley Bourbonnais HS, Bourbonnais, Ill.
**39. *Dustin Richardson, lhp, Cowley County (Kan.) CC.—(2009-10)**
40. *Emmanuel Vasquez, rhp, Nicholas Rodriguez HS, Corozal, P.R.
41. Ezequiel Perez, rhp, Missouri Baptist College.
42. Daniel Spring, rhp, Brown University.
43. Brian Santo, rhp, Mount St. Mary's (Md.) College.
44. Kurt Piantek, 1b, Trinity (Conn.) College.
45. *Joshua Tarnow, c, Corona del Sol HS, Chandler, Ariz.
46. *Clay Britton, of, Canyon HS, Canyon Country, Calif.
47. *Travis Simmons, 3b, Cleveland State (Tenn.) CC.
**48. +Dusty Ryan, c, Merced (Calif.) JC.—(2008-09)**
49. Reese Baez, rhp, Northwood (Texas) University.
50. *Brandon McCormick, rhp, Spartanburg Methodist (S.C.) JC.

## FLORIDA MARLINS (16)

1. Jeff Allison, rhp, Veterans Memorial HS, Peabody, Mass.—(AA)
**2. Logan Kensing, rhp, Texas A&M University.—(2004-15)**
3. Jonathan Fulton, ss, George Washington HS, Danville, Va.—(AA)
**4. Jai Miller, of, Selma (Ala.) HS.—(2008-11)**
5. Cole Seifrig, 3b, Heritage Hills HS, Lincoln City, Ind.—(Low A)
6. Lee Mitchell, 3b, University of Georgia.
DRAFT DROP *Brother of Russ Mitchell, 15th-round draft pick, Dodgers (2003)*
7. David Marchbanks, lhp, University of South Carolina.
8. Tanner Rogers, c, Columbine HS, Littleton, Colo.
9. David Humen, rhp, Bethel (Ind.) College.
10. J.T. Restko, 3b, Marist HS, Tinley Park, Ill.
11. Zach McCormack, lhp, Sacramento (Calif.) CC.
12. Joe Mazzuca, ss, Northern Illinois University.
13. Chris Pillsbury, rhp, Florida Atlantic University.
14. Scott Nestor, rhp, Chaffey (Calif.) JC.
15. Mikela Olsen, of, Cal State Sacramento.
16. Jon-Michael Nickerson, lhp, Stanhope Elmore HS, Millbrook, Ala.
17. +Kurt Koehler, rhp, Sacramento (Calif.) CC.
18. Craig Lybarger, lhp, Jefferson State (Ala.) CC.
19. Nathan Nowicki, rhp, Colorado State University.
20. Seferino Encarnacion, of, Orange Park, Fla.
21. *Brandon Tripp, of, Los Alamitos (Calif.) HS.
22. Ryan Blake, c, University of North Carolina.
**23. *Tony Watson, lhp, Dallas Center-Grimes HS, Grimes, Iowa.—(2011-15)**
24. Scott Dierks, of, Santa Clara University.
**25. *Alex Hinshaw, lhp, Chaffey (Calif.) JC.—(2008-12)**
26. Ben Schroeder, of, Ball State University.
27. *Todd Johnson, of, Provine HS, Jackson, Miss.
28. Greg Bartlett, lhp, Phoenix JC.
29. +Stu Alexander, rhp, Windsor (Calif.) HS / Santa Rosa (Calif.) JC.
30. Ryan Bear, of, University of Central Florida.
31. Spencer Wyman, c, University of Oklahoma.
32. Kris Thedorf, of, Elgin (Ill.) CC.
33. Roy Friesen, rhp, Columbia Basin (Wash.) CC.
34. Antonio Orozco, rhp, California Baptist College.
35. Justin Mattison, of, Virginia Commonwealth University.
36. *Rodney Rutherford, of, Shaw HS, Columbus, Ga.
37. Nick Lovato, lhp, Cal State Fullerton.
38. *Chris Bodishbaugh, rhp, Freedom HS, Oakley, Calif.
39. *Neal Warchol, rhp, Triton (Ill.) JC.
40. *Geoff Rottmayer, of, Countryside HS, Clearwater, Fla.
41. *Randall Clay, ss, Rattan (Okla.) HS.
**42. Jim Aducci, of, Evergreen Park (Ill.) HS.—(2013-14)**
DRAFT DROP *Son of Jim Adduci, major leaguer (1983-89)*
43. *Jared Johnson, rhp, Kelowna, B.C.
44. *Ben Hodges, ss, Allan Hancock (Calif.) JC.
45. *Chris Allen, c, South Williamsport Area HS, Duboistown, Pa.
46. *Angel Flores, c, Petra Corret O'Neill HS, Manati, P.R.
47. *Chilion Stapleton, rhp, Mississippi Delta JC.
DRAFT DROP *Twin brother of Ashkelon Stapleton, 48th-round draft pick, Marlins (2003)*
48. *Ashkelon Stapleton, rhp, Mississippi Delta JC.
DRAFT DROP *Twin brother of Chilion Stapleton, 47th-round draft pick, Marlins (2003)*
49. *Kyle Dickson, rhp, Sacramento (Calif.) CC.
50. *George Otero, ss, Hialeah (Fla.) HS.

## HOUSTON ASTROS (22)

1. (Choice to Giants as compensation for Type A free agent Jeff Kent)
**2. Jason Hirsh, rhp, California Lutheran University.—(2006-08)**
**3. *Drew Stubbs, of, Atlanta (Texas) HS.—(2009-15)**
DRAFT DROP *Attended Texas; re-drafted by Reds, 2006 (1st round)*
**4. Josh Anderson, of, Eastern Kentucky University.—(2007-09)**
5. Josh Muecke, lhp, Loyola Marymount University.—(AAA)
6. Cliff Davis, rhp, Eupora (Miss.) HS.
7. Jeff Jorgensen, of, Rice University.
8. Mike Collar, rhp, University of Maine.
9. Brock Koman, 3b, University of Michigan.
10. Beau Hearod, of, University of Alabama.
11. *Nick Green, rhp, Darton (Ga.) JC.
12. Wade Robinson, ss, Louisiana Tech.
**13. Jimmy Barthmaier, rhp, Roswell (Ga.) HS.—(2008)**
**14. *Mike Dunn, of, Cimarron Memorial HS, Las Vegas, Nev.—(2009-15)**
15. Bo Edmiston, rhp, Mississippi College.
16. Jamie Merchant, rhp, University of Vermont.
17. Pat O'Brien, c, Kent State University.
18. Kevin Vital, 1b, Southern University.
**19. Edwin Maysonet, 2b, Delta State (Miss.) University.—(2008-12)**
20. Brian Skaug, 2b, California Lutheran University.
21. Kerri Fair, of, Jacksonville State University.
22. Lance Koenig, 2b, Monmouth University.
**23. Mark Saccomanno, 3b, Baylor University.—(2008)**
24. Ryan Yurek, rhp, Loyola Marymount University.
25. Mario Garza, c, University of Florida.
26. Robert Ramsey, rhp, Texas A&M University.
27. *Omar Arif, lhp, Poteet HS, Mesquite, Texas.
28. Chad Prosser, ss, University of North Carolina.
29. Jason Corapci, 2b, Cal State Fullerton.
30. *Scott Bradley, 2b, Chabot (Calif.) JC.
31. *Brandon McDougall, ss, Diablo Valley (Calif.) CC.
32. *Justin O'Bannon, rhp, Kingwood (Texas) HS.
33. Michael Walls, 3b, St. Joseph's University.
34. *Shawn Burris, lhp, North Central Texas JC.
35. *John Slusarz, rhp, University of Connecticut-Avery Point JC.
**36. *Logan Ondrusek, rhp, St. Paul HS, Shriner, Texas.—(2010-14)**
37. *Ethien Santana, of, Laredo (Texas) JC.
38. *Victor Ferrante, rhp, Benicia HS, Vallejo, Calif.
39. *Josh Smith, rhp, Riverside (Calif.) CC.
40. *David Roberts, of, The Woodlands (Texas) HS.
41. *Ray Stokes, 2b, San Leandro (Calif.) HS.
42. *Shane Buschini, 1b, California HS, San Ramon, Calif.

## KANSAS CITY ROYALS (5)

1. Chris Lubanski, of, Kennedy-Kenrick HS, Schwenksville, Pa.—AAA)
**1. Mitch Maier, c, University of Toledo** (Choice from Braves—30th—as compensation for Type B free agent Paul Byrd).**—(2006-12)**
**2. Shane Costa, of, Cal State Fullerton.—(2005-07)**
3. Brian McFall, 1b, Chandler-Gilbert (Ariz.) JC.—(AA)
4. Miguel Vega, 3b, Carmen B. Huyke HS, Arroyo, P.R.—(High A)
5. Chris Goodman, rhp, Georgia Tech.—(Low A)
**6. Ryan Braun, rhp, University of Nevada-Las Vegas.—(2006-07)**
**7. Mike Aviles, ss, Concordia (N.Y.) College.—(2008-15)**
8. Brandon Powell, 2b, Coastal Carolina University.
9. John Gragg, lhp, Bethune-Cookman College.
10. +Luis Cota, rhp, Sunnyside HS, Tucson, Ariz. / South Mountain (Ariz.) CC.
**11. Dusty Hughes, lhp, Delta State (Miss.) University.—(2009-11)**
12. Robbie McClellan, rhp, Arizona State University.
13. Mike Gaffney, ss, New York Tech.
14. Steve Bray, rhp, University of New Haven.
15. Jake Mullis, rhp, University of North Carolina-Wilmington.
16. Bryan Graham, of, William Paterson (N.J.) University.
17. *Keoni Ruth, ss, Kamehameha HS, Honolulu, Hawaii.
18. Jeff Barry, of, University of Vermont.
19. *Nick Tisone, rhp, Pearl River (Miss.) CC.
20. *Michael Hernandez, of, Daytona Beach (Fla.) CC.
**21. Irving Falu, 2b, Indian Hills (Iowa) CC.—(2012-14)**
22. *Phillip Andersen, rhp, Chandler-Gilbert (Ariz.) CC.
23. *Pat Bresnehan, rhp, Dover Sherborn HS, Dover, Mass.
24. *Wayne Daman, rhp, Forks (Wash.) HS.
25. *Jim West, rhp, River Valley HS, Fort Mohave, Ariz.
26. +Mitch Goins, rhp, New Mexico JC.
27. *Kendall Thurman, rhp, Angelina (Texas) JC.

28. *Derrick Thomas, rhp, Captain Shreve HS, Shreveport, La.
29. *Derrick Arnold, ss, Tallahassee (Fla.) CC.
30. *Austin Pride, c, Lake Mary (Fla.) HS.
31. *D'Antonio Warren, rhp, Woodham HS, Pensacola, Fla.
32. +Darrell Qualls, 3b, Lake City (Fla.) CC.
33. *Adam Miller, rhp, Knoxville (Iowa) HS.
34. Walter Sevilla, 2b, University of Tennessee.
35. +John Sokoll, lhp, Solon (Iowa) HS / Kirkwood (Iowa) CC.
36. *Chris Malone, rhp, San Joaquin Delta (Calif.) CC.
37. *Clay Young, lhp, St. Francis HS, La Canada, Calif.
DRAFT DROP *Son of Matt Young, major leaguer (1983-93)*
38. *Jeff Ostrander, lhp, Louisburg (N.C.) JC.
39. Eddie Solis, 3b, Eastlake HS, San Diego.
**40. *Todd Redmond, rhp, Northside Christian HS, St. Petersburg, Fla.—(2012-15)**
41. *Andy Underwood, rhp, Madera (Calif.) HS.
42. *Josh Hernandez, 2b, El Paso (Texas) CC.
43. *Matt Mallory, rhp, Central HS, Grand Junction, Colo.
44. *Vince Berry, of, Triton (Ill.) JC.
45. *Andy Groves, rhp, John Glenn HS, Walkerton, Ind.
**46. *Robert Coello, c, Lake Region HS, Winter Haven, Fla.—(2010-13)**
47. *Jimmy Wallace, rhp, Bossier Parish (La.) CC.
48. *Zach Weidenaar, of, Bozeman (Mon.) HS.
49. *Gered Mochizuki, ss, Baldwin HS, Wailuku, Hawaii.
50. *Keven Whalen, 3b, Mid-Pacific Institute, Kanoehe, Hawaii.

## LOS ANGELES DODGERS (24)

**1. Chad Billingsley, rhp, Defiance (Ohio) HS.—(2006-15)**
2. Chuck Tiffany, lhp, Charter Oak HS, Covina, Calif.—(AA)
3. *Cory Van Allen, lhp, Clements HS, Sugar Land, Texas.—(AAA)
DRAFT DROP *Attended Baylor; re-drafted by Nationals, 2006 (5th round)*
**4. Xavier Paul, of, Slidell (La.) HS.—(2009-14)**
5. Jordan Pratt, rhp, Central HS, Independence, Ore.—(AAA)
**6. Matt Kemp, of, Midwest City (Okla.) HS.—(2006-15)**
DRAFT DROP *First 2003 high school draft pick to reach majors (May 28, 2006)*
**7. Wesley Wright, lhp, Goshen (Ala.) HS.—(2008-15)**
**8. Lucas May, 3b, Parkway West HS, Chesterfield, Mo.—(2010)**
9. Brett Dowdy, 2b, University of Florida.
10. Phil Sobkow, rhp, Central Missouri State University.
11. +Tony Harper, c, Oak Creek HS, South Milwaukee / Frank Phillips (Texas) CC.
12. +Cody White, lhp, Pleasant Grove HS, Texarkana, Texas / Texarkana (Texas) CC.
13. Derik Olvey, rhp, Pelham (Ala.) HS.
14. +David Pfeiffer, lhp, Lincoln Park Academy, St. Lucie, Fla. / Indian River (Fla.) CC.
**15. Russ Mitchell, ss, Cartersville (Ga.) HS.—(2010-11)**
DRAFT DROP *Brother of Lee Mitchell, 6th-round draft pick, Marlins (2003)*
16. James Peterson, 1b, Indian Hills (Iowa) CC.
17. Steven Sapp, of, West Torrance HS, Los Angeles.
**18. A.J. Ellis, c, Austin Peay State University.—(2008-15)**
**19. *Matt Antonelli, ss, St. John's Prep, Danvers, Mass.—(2008)**
DRAFT DROP *First-round draft pick (17th overall), Padres (2006)*
20. *Chad Barben, 3b, Taylorsville (Utah) HS.
**21. Travis Denker, 2b, Brea-Olinda HS, Brea, Calif.—(2008)**
22. *Doug Frame, lhp, Tomball (Texas) HS.
23. Taylor Slimak, c, California Lutheran University.
24. *Ben Snyder, lhp, Bellevue (Ohio) HS.
DRAFT DROP *Brother of Brad Snyder, first-round draft pick, Indians (2003); major leaguer (2010-14)*
25. *Kevin Skogley, lhp, Hermiston (Ore.) HS.
26. Thomas Piazza, c, Palm Beach Atlantic (Fla.) College.
DRAFT DROP *Brother of Mike Piazza, major leaguer (1992-2007)*
27. +Jesus Castillo, rhp, Tucson (Ariz.) HS / Pima (Ariz.) CC.
**28. *Adam Moore, c, Northeast Texas CC.—(2009-14)**
29. *Adam Parliament, of, Penticton (B.C.) SS.
**30. *Mark Melancon, rhp, Golden HS, Arvada, Colo.—(2009-15)**
31. *Garrett Kohler, rhp, Cimarron-Memorial HS, Las Vegas, Nev.
32. *Kyle Reichert, rhp, Porterville (Calif.) JC.
33. *Ryan Zaft, rhp, Yuba (Calif.) CC.
34. *Brett Lawler, 1b, A&M Consolidated HS, College Station, Texas.
35. *Antonio Anderson, of, Greene County HS, Leakesville, Miss.
36. *Drew Jeffcoat, lhp, Martin HS, Arlington, Texas.
37. Michael Ludwig, 1b, St. Olaf (Minn.) College.
38. *Justin Ferreira, of, Stoneman Douglas HS, Parkland, Fla.
**39. Andy LaRoche, ss, Grayson County (Texas) CC.—(2007-13)**
DRAFT DROP *Son of Dave LaRoche, major leaguer (1970-83) • Brother of Adam LaRoche, major leaguer (2004-15)*
40. *D.J. Lewis, 1b, San Fernando (Calif.) HS.
41. *Matt Votaw, 3b, Brea-Olinda HS, Brea, Calif.
42. *Cory Vanderhook, c, Golden West (Calif.) JC.
43. *Clay Van Hook, ss, Brenham (Texas) HS.
44. *Travis Check, c, Logan HS, La Crosse, Wis.
45. *Cass Rhynes, c, Bluefield HS, Cornwall, P.E.I.
46. *Steven Paddock, of, Milford (Mass.) HS.
47. *Matt Chase, rhp, Naaman Forest HS, Garland, Texas.
48. *Kyle Rapp, of, Milford HS, Cincinnati.
49. *Clarence Farmer, of, University of Arizona.
50. *Curtis Hudson, c, Yuba (Calif.) JC.

## MILWAUKEE BREWERS (2)

**1. Rickie Weeks, 2b, Southern University.—(2003-15)**
**2. Anthony Gwynn, of, San Diego State University.—(2006-14)**
DRAFT DROP *Son of Tony Gwynn, major leaguer (1982-2001)*
3. Lou Palmisano, c, Broward (Fla.) CC.—(AA)
DRAFT DROP *Brother of Nic Palmisano, 33rd-round draft pick, Pirates (2003)*
4. Charlie Fermaint, of, Jose S. Alegria HS, Dorado, P.R.—(AA)
5. Bryan Opdyke, c, Catalina Foothills HS, Tucson, Ariz.—(Rookie)
6. Robbie Wooley, rhp, Taylor HS, Kokomo, Ind.
7. Brian Montalbo, rhp, University of California.
DRAFT DROP *Son of Mel Montalbo, defensive back, National Football League (1962)*
8. Ryan Marion, rhp, Glenn HS, Kernersville, N.C.
9. Greg Kloosterman, lhp, Bethel (Ind.) College.
10. Tyler Morrison, rhp, Glendora (Calif.) HS.
11. Adam Heether, 3b, Long Beach State University.
**12. Carlos Corporan, 1b-c, Lake City (Fla.) CC.—(2009-15)**
13. *Luke Cannon, of, North Central Texas CC.
14. *Garrett Bussiere, c, Northglenn HS, Thornton, Colo.
15. +Joel Rivera, of, Hoboken (N.J.) HS / Brookdale (N.J.) JC.
**16. Mitch Stetter, lhp, Indiana State University.—(2007-11)**
17. Tommy Hawk, rhp, Cabrillo HS, Lompoc, Calif.
18. Oscar Montes, rhp, Flanagan HS, Cooper City, Fla.
**19. Ty Taubenheim, rhp, Edmonds (Wash.) CC.—(2006-08)**
20. Nick Slack, rhp, Lake City (Fla.) CC.
21. *Taylor Meier, rhp, Orangewood Christian HS, Maitland, Fla.
22. Terry Trofholz, of, Texas Christian University.
23. *Jon Mungle, of, Mississippi State University.
**24. Drew Anderson, of, University of Nebraska.—(2006)**
25. +Jared Theodorakos, lhp, Baylor University.
26. +Hasan Rasheed, of, Lake City (Fla.) CC.
27. Daniel McKenna, rhp, Rutgers-Camden University.
28. Kenny Durost, rhp, Lubbock Christian (Texas) University.
29. Ricky Stover, lhp, University of Texas-Arlington.
30. Robby Deevers, of, University of Texas-Arlington.
31. *Sheldon Catchot, lhp, North Shore HS, Slidell, La.
32. Will Lewis, 2b, Texas Christian University.
33. *Chad Miller, 1b, Mesquite HS, Gilbert, Ariz.
34. Dan Grybash, rhp, Carthage (Wis.) College.
35. Phil Hendrix, rhp, Virginia Military Institute.
36. *Joe Ayers, ss, Juneau (Alaska) HS.
37. +Justin Wilson, lhp, Chandler-Gilbert (Ariz.) CC.
38. *Brent Weaver, rhp, Midwest City (Okla.) HS.
39. *Wes Yeary, rhp, Leon HS, Tallahassee, Fla.
40. +Robert Hinton, rhp, Riverview HS, Sarasota, Fla. / Manatee (Fla.) CC.
DRAFT DROP *Son of Rich Hinton, major leaguer (1971-79)*
41. *Evan Baubles, c, Wall HS, Wall Township, N.J.
42. *Zach Kohan, ss, Juneau-Douglas HS, Juneau, Alaska.
43. *Daryl Maday, rhp, Westocha Central HS, Bristol, Wis.
44. *Raynel Robles-Encarnacion, 2b, Florida Air Academy, Melbourne, Fla.
45. *Tim Grubbs, rhp, Lake City (Fla.) CC.
46. +Clay Blevins, c, Cowley County (Kan.) CC.
47. *Ryan Zink, rhp, La Follette HS, Madison, Wis.
48. *Calvin Thompson, of, Shaw HS, East Cleveland, Ohio.
49. *Justin Sarka, rhp, Englewood HS, Jacksonville, Fla.
50. *Luis Pardo, rhp, Westminster Christian HS, Miami.

## MINNESOTA TWINS (21)

1. Matt Moses, 3b, Mills Godwin HS, Richmond, Va.—(AAA)
**2. Scott Baker, rhp, Oklahoma State University.—(2005-15)**
3. Johnny Woodard, 1b, Cosumnes River (Calif.) JC.—(High A)
4. David Shinskie, rhp, Mount Carmel Area HS, Kulpmont, Pa.—(AA)
5. *Brandon McArthur, ss, Armwood HS, Seffner, Fla.—DNP
DRAFT DROP *Attended Florida; never re-drafted*
6. Errol Simonitsch, lhp, Gonzaga University.
7. Chris Schutt, rhp, Cornell University.
8. Brandon McConnell, rhp, Foothill HS, Red Bluff, Calif.
9. Kevin Culpepper, lhp, Georgia Southern University.
10. Chris Marini, lhp, Glendale (Ariz.) CC.
11. *Ryan Schroyer, rhp, Arizona State University.
12. Steven Duguay, rhp, Gulf Coast (Fla.) CC.
13. David Winfree, 1b, First Colonial HS, Virginia Beach, Va.
**14. Levale Speigner, rhp, Auburn University.—(2007-08)**
DRAFT DROP *Brother of Brent Speigner, 50th-round draft pick, Devils Rays (2003)*
15. *Trey Shields, rhp, Gulf Coast (Fla.) CC.
16. Michael Rogers, lhp, Del City (Okla.) HS.
17. +Danny Vais, rhp, Seward County (Kan.) CC.
18. Eli Tintor, c, Hibbing (Minn.) HS.
19. Jon Uhl, rhp, University of South Florida.
20. Gregory Najac, c, Mons, Belgium.
21. *Scott Leffler, c, Dunedin (Fla.) HS.
22. Joe Gault, rhp, Canyon HS, Canyon Country, Calif.
23. *Charles Smith, rhp, Casa Roble HS, Orangevale, Calif.
24. Patrick Ortiz, ss, Alfonso Casta Martinez HS, Maunabo, P.R.
**25. *John Gaub, lhp, South St. Paul (Minn.) HS.—(2011)**
26. Jason Bowlin, rhp, Volunteer State (Tenn.) CC.
27. *Peter Taraskevich, rhp, American Heritage HS, Sunrise, Fla.
28. *Josh Oslin, rhp, Mora (Minn.) HS.
29. Bo Pettit, rhp, Louisiana State University.
30. Josh Gray, lhp, Lamar University.
31. Kris Lankford, rhp, Western Oklahoma State JC.
32. *Nicholas Bleau, lhp, St. Elizabeth-Anne HS, Mercier, Quebec.
33. *Yvenson Bernard, of, Boca Raton (Fla.) Community HS.
34. *Quentin Andes, rhp, Cibola HS, Albuquerque, N.M.
35. *Phillip Utley, rhp, Central Merry HS, Jackson, Tenn.
36. *Marquez Smith, 3b, Forest HS, Ocala, Fla.
37. Heath Anderson, c, Pensacola (Fla.) JC.
**38. *Travis Metcalf, 3b, University of Kansas.—(2007-08)**
39. Jesse Collins, c, University of North Florida.
40. +Adam Hawes, rhp, Connors State (Okla.) JC.
41. John Rumsey, of, San Diego Mesa JC.
42. Mitchell Zamojc, of, University of British Columbia.
43. Travis Kalin, ss, Bishop Moore HS, Orlando, Fla.
44. Larry Jones, of, Baldwin County HS, Minette, Ala.
**45. *Steve Pearce, ss, Indian River (Fla.) CC.—(2007-15)**
46. *Brant Rustich, rhp, Grossmont HS, San Diego.
47. *Clayton Trenary, of, Central Florida CC.
48. *Jared Swart, rhp, Cimarron HS, Ames, Okla.
**49. *Michael Hollimon, ss, University of Texas.—(2008)**
50. *Andrew De la Garza, lhp, Norwell HS, Ossian, Ind.

## MONTREAL EXPOS (20)

**1. Chad Cordero, rhp, Cal State Fullerton.—(2003-10)**
**2. Jerry Owens, of, The Master's (Calif.) College.—(2006-09)**
**3. Kory Casto, of, University of Portland.—(2007-08)**
4. Edgardo Baez, of, Jose S. Alegria HS, Dorado, P.R.—(AAA)
5. Trey Webb, ss, Baylor University.—(AA)
**6. Josh Whitesell, 1b, Loyola Marymount University.—(2008-09)**
7. Devin Perrin, rhp, Grand Canyon University.
**8. Daryl Thompson, rhp, La Plata HS, Mechanicsville, Md.—(2008-11)**
9. Gabriel Sosa, lhp, Lino Padron Rivera HS, Vega Baja, P.R.
10. Victor Hamisevicz, 1b, Gonzaga College HS, Dunn Loring, Va.
11. A.J. Wideman, lhp, Streetsville HS, Mississauga, Ontario.
12. Mike St. Martine, c, Monmouth University.
13. Brad Ditter, 2b, New Mexico State University.
14. Larry York, 2b, Liberty University.
15. Brett Reid, rhp, Avila (Mo.) College.
16. Ricky Jenkins, rhp, University of South Carolina-Aiken.
**17. Luke Montz, c, Hill (Texas) JC.—(2008-13)**
18. Eduardo Nunez, ss, American Military Academy, Guaynabo, P.R.
19. Jeremy Plexico, lhp, Winthrop University.
20. +Terry Engles, rhp, St. Peters Boys HS, Staten Island, N.Y. / Seminole (Fla.) CC.
**21. *Joe Bisenius, rhp, Iowa Western CC.—(2007-10)**
22. Gus Hlebovy, rhp, Kent State University.
23. *Brett Cooley, 1b, University of Houston.
24. *Jonathan Hunton, rhp, Hutchinson (Kan.) JC
25. James Russell, rhp, Villanova University.
**26. Jim Henderson, rhp, Tennessee Wesleyan College.—(2012-14)**
27. Bret Pignatiello, c, Eastern Illinois University.
DRAFT DROP *Brother of Carmen Pignatiello, major leaguer (2007-08)*
28. Oscar Bernazard, 2b, Lindenwood (Mo.) University.
29. James Lehman, rhp, Notre Dame HS, Brampton, Ontario.
30. *Matt Buck, lhp, Cactus Shadows HS, Cave Creek, Ariz.
31. *Chris Hufft, rhp, West Hills HS, Santee, Calif.
32. *B.J. Weidenbach, of, Fresno (Calif.) CC.
33. *Gabe Suarez, ss, Arcadia HS, Scottsdale, Ariz.
34. *Matt Montgomery, rhp, Watkins Mill HS, Gaithersburg, Md.
35. Doug Vroman, of, University of New Haven.
36. *Konrad Thieme, rhp, Westlake HS, Westlake Village, Calif.
37. *Brendan Murphy, 1b, Grace Baptist Academy, Chattanooga, Tenn.
38. +Seth Bynum, ss, Indiana University.
39. *Trent Kline, c, West York Area HS, York, Pa.
40. *Jacob Cook, lhp, Lee Davis HS, Mechanicsville,

Va.
41. *Jonathan Kalkau, rhp, Holy Trinity HS, Hicksville, N.Y.
42. *Scott Rogowski, rhp, White County HS, Doyle, Tenn.
43. *Anthony Savio, rhp, American River (Calif.) JC.
44. *Michael Ambort, c, South Side HS, Rockville Centre, N.Y.
45. *Sean O'Brien, 1b, Horace Greeley HS, Chappaqua, N.Y.
46. Alexis Morales, rhp, Oakton (Ill.) CC.
47. *Steven Romero, rhp, Mount San Antonio (Calif.) JC.
**48. *Lance Zawadzki, ss, St. John's HS, Ashland, Mass.—(2010)**
49. *Kyle Nicholson, rhp, A&M Consolidated HS, College Station, Texas.
50. *Michael James, rhp, University of Connecticut.

## NEW YORK METS (12)

**1. Lastings Milledge, of, Lakewood Ranch HS, Palmetto, Fla.—(2006-11)**
2. (Choice to Red Sox as compensation for Type A free agent Cliff Floyd)
3. (Choice to Braves as compensation for Type A free agent Tom Glavine)
4. Shane Hawk, lhp, Oklahoma State University.—(High A)
5. Corey Coles, of, University of Louisiana-Lafayette.—(AAA)
6. Mateo Miramontes, rhp, University of Nevada-Reno.
**7. Brian Bannister, rhp, University of Southern California.—(2006-10)**
DRAFT DROP *Son of Floyd Bannister, first overall draft pick, Astros (1976); major leaguer (1977-92)*
8. Seth Pietsch, of, Oregon State University.
9. Vince Cordova, rhp, Loyola Marymount University.
10. David Reaver, ss, University of Richmond.
11. Andy Sides, rhp, De Soto (Mo.) HS.
12. Anthony Piazza, c, Southwest Missouri State University.
**13. Carlos Muniz, rhp, Long Beach State University.—(2007-08)**
14. Stacy Bennett, 3b, Armstrong Atlantic State (Ga.) University.
15. *Harold Mozingo, rhp, Essex HS, Tappahannock, Va.
16. David Smith, lhp, Pfeiffer (N.C.) University.
17. Ryan Meyers, rhp, Round Valley HS, Springerville, Ariz.
18. *Kyle McCulloch, rhp, Bellaire HS, Houston.
DRAFT DROP *First-round draft pick (29th overall), White Sox (2006)*
19. Ryan Harvey, of, UC Riverside.
20. *Trip Mealor, rhp, Oconee County HS, Bishop, Ga.
21. Travis Garcia, ss, Iona College.
22. Greg Ramirez, rhp, Pepperdine University.
23. Dante Brinkley, of, Southwest Missouri State University.
24. Troy Fry, rhp, Berry (Ga.) College.
**25. Evan MacLane, lhp, Feather River (Calif.) CC.—(2010)**
26. Kevin Rios, ss, Concordia (Calif.) University.
**27. *Deunte Heath, rhp, Newton County HS, Decatur, Ga.—(2012-13)**
28. Cory Wells, of, Plant City (Fla.) HS.
29. *Justin Valdes, rhp, Dunedin (Fla.) HS.
30. *Adam Carr, rhp, West Valley (Calif.) JC.
31. *Jordan Newton, c, Larue County HS, Hodgenville, Ky.
32. Humberto Gonzalez, ss, Feather River (Calif.) JC.
33. *Abel Newton, rhp, University of Arkansas-Fort Smith JC.
34. *Drew Johnson, rhp, Wylie (Texas) HS.
35. *Patrick Howe, lhp, Faith Baptist HS, Longmont, Colo.
36. Jim Wallace, c, Santa Clara University.
37. *Alex Turner, of, Catonsville (Md.) CC.
38. *Simon Gagnon, lhp, Montmorency (Quebec) College.
39. *Garrett Young, 3b, Edison HS, Fountain Valley, Calif.
40. *Dan Fischer, rhp, Los Angeles Pierce JC.
41. *Mike Bartley, rhp, Alleghany HS, Covington, Va.
42. *Brian Baugher, rhp, Brunswick HS, Frederick, Md.
43. *Mike Chambless, c, Round Rock (Texas) HS.
44. +Tom Sgueglia, 3b, Rockland (N.Y.) CC.
45. *Jean-Michael Rochon-Salvas, rhp, Edouard Montpetit HS, Longeuil, Quebec.
46. *Joel Thorney, rhp, Leaside HS, Toronto.
47. David Torres, rhp, University of Central Florida.
48. +Jon Malo, ss, Miami-Dade CC.
49. *Grover Benton, of, Webber (Fla.) College.
50. *Lester Aragon, c, Brito Private HS, Miami.

## NEW YORK YANKEES (27)

1. Eric Duncan, 3b, Seton Hall Prep, Florham Park, N.J.—(AAA)
2. Estee Harris, of, Islip HS, Central Islip, N.Y.—(High A)
3. Tim Battle, of, McIntosh HS, Peachtree City, Ga.—(High A)
4. Steven White, rhp, Baylor University.—(AAA)
5. Cory Stuart, rhp, University of British Columbia.—(Low A)
6. Jason Stephens, rhp, Tallmadge (Ohio) HS.
7. Jose Perez, of, Oceanside (Calif.) HS.
8. Josh Smith, rhp, University of Texas.
**9. Tyler Clippard, rhp, J.W. Mitchell HS, Trinity, Fla.—(2007-15)**
**10. T.J. Beam, rhp, University of Mississippi.—(2006-08)**
11. Bryce Kartler, lhp, Arizona State University.
12. Brad Blackwell, rhp, North Carolina State University.
13. Michael Gardner, rhp, Miami (Ohio) University.
14. Jose Enrique Cruz, 2b, Rice University.
DRAFT DROP *Son of Jose Cruz, major leaguer (1970-88) • Brother of Jose Cruz Jr., first-round draft pick, Mariners (1995); major leaguer (1997-2008)*
15. Elvys Quezada, rhp, Seton Hall University.
16. Heath Castle, lhp, University of Kentucky.
**17. *David Purcey, lhp, University of Oklahoma.—(2008-13)**
DRAFT DROP *First-round draft pick (16th overall), Blue Jays (2004)*
18. +Michael Wagner, lhp, Lincoln Park Academy, Fort Pierce, Fla. / Indian River (Fla.) JC.
**19. Jeff Karstens, rhp, Texas Tech.—(2006-07)**
**20. *Daniel Bard, rhp, Charlotte Christian HS, Charlotte, N.C.—(2009-13)**
DRAFT DROP *First-round draft pick (28th overall), Red Sox (2006) • Brother of Luke Bard, first-round draft pick, Twins (2012)*
21. *Richard Brindle, rhp, Peru (Ind.) HS.
22. John Urick, 1b, Oklahoma State University.
DRAFT DROP *Grandson of Whitey Herzog, major leaguer (1956-63); major league manager (1973-90)*
23. *Josh Smith, rhp, Central Arizona JC.
24. *Jeremiah Shepherd, rhp, Kilgore (Texas) HS.
25. *Kevin Smith, 3b, Cypress (Calif.) JC.
26. *Ryan Aldridge, rhp, Middle Georgia JC.
27. +Andrew Edwards, rhp, Florida International University.
28. *Scott Kelly, rhp, St. Louis CC-Forest Park.
29. Adam Unger, 2b, Great Neck South HS, Great Neck, N.Y.
30. *Grant Duff, rhp, JC of the Sequoias (Calif.).
31. *Joe Larman, c, Purcell (Okla.) HS.
32. *Jeff Jacobsen, rhp, CC of Southern Nevada.
33. *Gary Keithley, rhp, Cleburne (Texas) HS.
34. *Robbie Widlansky, 3b, Taravella HS, Coral Springs, Fla.
35. Hector Gonzalez, 2b, Brito Private HS, Miami.
36. *Jose Hernandez, rhp, Oceanside (Calif.) HS.
37. *Blake Murphy, c, Tuscola HS, Waynesville, N.C.
38. *David Welch, lhp, Texarkana (Texas) CC.
39. *Mikel McIntyre, of, Antioch (Calif.) HS.
**40. *Brandon Kintzler, rhp, Pasadena (Calif.) CC.—(2012-15)**
41. *Carleton Hargrove, lhp, San Diego CC.
42. Taylor Mattingly, 1b, Evansville (Ind.) Central HS.
DRAFT DROP *Son of Don Mattingly, major leaguer (1982-95), major league manager (2011-15) • Brother of Preston Mattingly, first-round draft pick, Dodgers (2006)*
**43. +Justin Berg, rhp, Indian Hills (Iowa) CC.—(2009-11)**
44. *Mike Martinez, rhp, Cal State Fullerton.
45. Andre Randolph, 2b, Felecian (N.J.) College.
DRAFT DROP *Son of Willie Randolph, major leaguer (1975-92); major league manager (2005-08)*
46. *Jonathan Bertschinger, of, Fossil Ridge HS, Keller, Texas.
**47. *Dan McCutchen, rhp, Grayson County (Texas) JC.—(2009-14)**
48. *Eric Schaler, rhp, Cherry Creek HS, Englewood, Colo.
49. *David Ferazza, c, American River (Calif.) JC.
50. *Mike Muscato, c, Glendale (Ariz.) CC.

## OAKLAND ATHLETICS (25)

1. Brad Sullivan, rhp, University of Houston.—(High A)
1. Brian Snyder, 3b, Stetson University (Choice from Giants as compensation for Type A free agent Ray Durham).—(AA)
**1. Omar Quintanilla, ss, University of Texas** (Supplemental choice—33rd—as compensation for Durham).**—(2005-14)**
**2. Andre Ethier, of, Arizona State University.—(2007-15)**
3. Dustin Majewski, of, University of Texas.—(AAA)
4. Eddie Kim, 1b, James Madison University.—(Low A)
5. Trent Peterson, lhp, Florida State University.—(AAA)
6. Luke Appert, 2b, University of Minnesota.
7. David Castillo, c, Oral Roberts University.
8. Mike McGirr, rhp, University of Richmond.
9. Grant Reynolds, rhp, Kennesaw State University.
10. Matt Lynch, lhp, Florida State University.
11. Vasili Spanos, 3b, Indiana University.
12. Brian Ingram, ss, Elon University.
13. Eddie Cornejo, ss, University of Oklahoma.
14. Anthony Zambotti, rhp, Indiana (Pa.) University.
15. Steve Bondurant, lhp, University of South Carolina.
16. *Vern Sterry, rhp, North Carolina State University.
17. Ryan France, rhp, Chapman (Calif.) University.
18. *Billy Becher, 1b, New Mexico State University.
19. *Graham Harrison, c, Tulare Union HS, Tulare, Calif.
20. Gordon Corder, 1b, Gonzaga University.
21. *Braedyn Pruitt, ss, King's Academy, West Palm Beach, Fla.
22. *Brian Peacock, c, Palmetto (Fla.) HS.
**23. *J.R. Towles, c, Collin County (Texas) CC.—(2007-11)**
24. *Cory Hahn, rhp, Tulane University.
25. Sean Farrell, of, University of North Carolina.
**26. *Brian Horwitz, of, University of California.—(2008)**
27. Jim Heuser, lhp, Illinois Valley CC.
28. Jared Trout, rhp, University of Rhode Island.
29. *Alex Woodson, lhp, Stella Marquez HS, Salinas, P.R.
30. *Justin Cassel, rhp, Chatsworth (Calif.) HS.
DRAFT DROP *Brother of Jack Cassel, major leaguer (2007-08) • Brother of Matt Cassel, quarterback, National Football League (2005-15)*
31. *Joel Fountain, rhp, Feather River (Calif.) CC.
32. *Steve Sollmann, 2b, University of Notre Dame.
33. Eric Macha, 3b, Case Western Reserve (Ohio) University.
DRAFT DROP *Son of Ken Macha, major leaguer (1974-81); major league manager (2003-10)*
34. *Broc Coffman, lhp, Rainier (Ore.) HS.
35. Mike Mitchell, rhp, St. Charles (Mo.) CC.
36. *Matt Ryals, rhp, Wilson HS, Hacienda Heights, Calif.
**37. *Sean Kazmar, ss, CC of Southern Nevada.—(2008)**
38. *Zach Simons, rhp, Glenns Ferry (Idaho) HS.
**39. *Josh Rodriguez, 2b, South Houston HS, Houston.—(2011)**
40. *Chris Westervelt, c, Stetson University.

## PHILADELPHIA PHILLIES (18)

1. (Choice to Indians as compensation for Type A free agent Jim Thome)
2. (Choice to Giants as compensation for Type B free agent David Bell)
3. Tim Moss, 2b, University of Texas.—(AA)
**4. Michael Bourn, of, University of Houston.—(2006-15)**
5. Javon Moran, of, Auburn University.—(AAA)
6. *Jordan Parraz, rhp, Green Valley HS, Henderson, Nev.
**7. Kyle Kendrick, rhp, Mount Vernon (Wash.) HS.—(2007-15)**
8. Matt Linder, rhp, Winston Churchill HS, Thunder Bay, Ontario.
9. Jason Crosland, 3b, Lamar (Colo.) CC.
10. Matt Hopper, 1b, University of Nebraska.
11. *Myron Leslie, 3b, University of South Florida.
12. Kyle Parcus, lhp, Texas A&M University.
13. Joe Wilson, lhp, University of Maryland-Baltimore County.
14. Jose Cortez, c, Pomona-Pitzer (Calif.) College.
15. Joe Brunink, 1b, Grand Valley State (Mich.) University.
16. Nate Cabrera, rhp, Trinidad State (Colo.) JC.
17. Derek Griffith, lhp, Birmingham-Southern College.
**18. *Rob Johnson, c, Saddleback (Calif.) JC.—(2007-13)**
19. Joe Diefenderfer, lhp, Santa Clara University.
**20. Brad Ziegler, rhp, Southwest Missouri State University.—(2008-15)**
21. Caleb McConnell, rhp, University of Louisiana-Monroe.
22. Marc Tugwell, 2b, Virginia Tech.
23. Charlie Waite, c, University of Mississippi.
24. J.D. Foust, of, University of Toledo.
25. C.J. Woodrow, rhp, University of Minnesota.
26. Dan Hodges, lhp, Florida State University.
27. Brad Overton, rhp, University of North Carolina-Wilmington.
28. *Blair Erickson, rhp, Jesuit HS, Fair Oaks, Calif.
29. Justin Cerrato, rhp, University of North Florida.
30. Ryan Harris, ss, Eisenhower HS, Rialto, Calif.
31. Matt Padilla, rhp, American River (Calif.) CC.
32. Jake Tompkins, rhp, Louisiana State University.
33. Justin Libey, rhp, Manchester (Ind.) College.
34. Justin Riley, c, North Carolina State University.
35. Jason Pritchard, rhp, Baylor University.
36. *Brett Amyx, 3b, Coppell (Texas) HS.
37. Jesse Torborg, of, Suffolk County (N.Y.) CC.
38. *Edgar Mercado, ss, Stoneman Douglas HS, Parkland, Fla.
39. *Eddie Romero, lhp, Central Union HS, Fresno, Calif.
40. +Andy Barb, c, Juanita HS, Kirkland, Wash. / Kirkwood (Iowa) CC.
**41. *Greg Reynolds, rhp, Terra Nova HS, Pacifica, Calif.—(2008-13)**
DRAFT DROP *First-round draft pick (2nd overall), Rockies (2006)*
42. *Matt Lambeth, of, Mesa (Ariz.) CC.
43. *Cole Buchanan, lhp, Santiago HS, Corona, Calif.
44. *Cal Stanke, rhp, St. Mary Central HS, Neenah, Wis.
45. *Jerod Estey, of, Moffat County HS, Craig, Colo.
46. *Ryan Tabor, lhp, Green Valley HS, Henderson, Nev.
**47. *Michael Crotta, rhp, Martin County HS, Stuart, Fla.—(2011)**
48. *Kyle Nash, rhp, Mater Dei HS, Huntington Beach, Calif.
49. *Adam Sorgi, ss, Capistrano Valley HS, Mission Viejo, Calif.
50. *Tad Reida, ss, Western HS, Kokomo, Ind.

## PITTSBURGH PIRATES (8)

**1. Paul Maholm, lhp, Mississippi State University.—(2005-14)**
**2. Tom Gorzelanny, lhp, Triton (Ill.) JC.—(2005-15)**
**3. Steve Lerud, c, Galena HS, Reno, Nev.—(2012-13)**
4. Kyle Pearson, rhp, Mosley HS, Panama City, Fla.—(AA)
**5. Craig Stansberry, 3b, Rice University.—(2007-09)**
6. *C.J. Smith, 1b, University of Florida.
7. Russell Johnson, rhp, Benjamin Russell HS, Alexander City, Ala.
8. Sergio Silva, rhp, University of the Pacific.
9. Kent Wulf, 2b, Quartz Hill HS, Lancaster, Calif.
10. John Peabody, of, Rancho Bernardo HS, San Diego.
11. John Santiago, 3b, Nuestra Senora Del Carmen

HS, Trujillo Alta, P.R.
12. Adam Boeve, of, University of Northern Iowa.
13. *Lee Land, rhp, Riverside HS, Durham, N.C.
14. Jake Cuffman, rhp, Butler Area HS, Butler, Pa.
15. Dustin Molleken, rhp, Lethbridge (Alberta) CC.
DRAFT DROP *Son of Lorne Molleken, coach, Chicago Blackhawks, National Hockey League (1999-2000)*
16. Justin Harris, ss, University of South Carolina.
17. Steven Herce, rhp, Rice University.
18. Pedro Powell, of, Middle Georgia JC.
19. *Dallas Buck, rhp, Newberg (Ore.) HS.
20. Brett Holmes, of, Auburn University-Montgomery.
DRAFT DROP *Grandson of Bill Virdon, major leaguer (1955-68); major league manager (1972-84)*
21. *Clay Hamilton, rhp, Penn State University.
22. Chris Hernandez, rhp, University of South Carolina.
23. +Gregory Picart, ss, Adela Brenes Texidor HS, Guayama, P.R. / Miami-Dade North CC.
24. **Josh Sharpless, rhp, Allegheny (Pa.) College.—(2006-07)**
25. ***Matt Downs, rhp, Shelton State (Ala.) CC.—(2009-12)**
26. *Owen Williams, lhp, Edmonds (Wash.) CC.
27. *Clegg Snipes, rhp, Lincoln HS, Tallahassee, Fla.
28. *Matthew Creighton, lhp, Meridian (Miss.) CC.
29. *Jimmy Van Ostrand, of, Allan Hancock (Calif.) JC.
30. *Joey Friddle, ss, Young Harris (Ga.) JC.
31. *Cody Doonan, rhp, Kirkwood (Iowa) CC.
32. *Sean Coughlin, c, Golden (Colo.) HS.
33. *Nic Palmisano, 1b, Broward (Fla.) CC.
DRAFT DROP *Brother of Lou Palmisano, third-round draft pick, Brewers (2003)*
34. ***Jeremy Horst, lhp, Des Lacs-Burlington HS, Des Lacs, N.D.—(2011-13)**
35. *Nick Colborn, rhp, Blue Mountain (Ore.) CC.
36. *Andy Mudd, of, Scotland HS, Laurinburg, N.C.
37. *Daniel Brown, lhp, Bakersfield (Calif.) CC.
38. *Robert Felmy, of, Georgia Perimeter JC.
39. *Peter Wiggins, rhp, Patterson HS, Morgan City, La.
40. *Christian Romple, c, West Valley HS, Yakima, Wash.
41. *Chandler Miller, rhp, Young Harris (Ga.) JC.
42. *Tony Snow, rhp, Edmonds (Wash.) CC.
43. *Lance Scoggins, lhp, Bolton HS, Memphis, Tenn.
44. *Troy Harrington, rhp, Palmdale (Calif.) HS.
DRAFT DROP *Brother of Matt Harrington, 24th-round draft pick, Reds (2003); first-round draft pick, Rockies (2000)*
45. *Domingo Reyes, lhp, Brito Private HS, Miami.
46. *Cody Lovejoy, c, Cypress (Calif.) HS.
47. *Bryan Henry, rhp, Florida HS, Tallahassee, Fla.
48. +Antonio Westfield, of, Cleveland (Tenn.) HS / Walters State (Tenn.) CC.
49. *Raul Torres, rhp, Puerto Rico Advance College HS, Bayamon, P.R.
50. ***Rhyne Hughes, 1b, Pearl River (Miss.) CC.—(2010)**

## ST. LOUIS CARDINALS (28)

1. **Daric Barton, c, Marina HS, Huntington Beach, Calif.—(2007-14)**
2. **Stuart Pomeranz, rhp, Houston HS, Collierville, Tenn.—(2012)**
DRAFT DROP *Brother of Drew Pomeranz, first-round draft pick, Indians (2010); major leaguer (2011-15)*
3. **Dennis Dove, rhp, Georgia Southern University.—(2007)**
4. Mark Michael, rhp, University of Delaware.—(High A)
5. Brandon Yarbrough, c, Richmond HS, Ellerbe, N.C.—(AAA)
6. Matt Weagle, rhp, Franklin Pierce (N.H.) College.
7. **Brendan Ryan, ss, Lewis-Clark State (Idaho) College.—(2007-15)**
8. **Matt Pagnozzi, c, Central Arizona JC.—(2009-14)**
DRAFT DROP *Son of Tom Pagnozzi, major leaguer (1987-98)*
9. Justin Garza, rhp, Seminole State (Okla.) JC.
10. Buddy Blair, lhp, University of Oklahoma.
11. Nathan Kopszywa, rhp, Crichton (Tenn.) College.
12. *Calvin Beamon, of, CC of Southern Nevada.
13. Kainoa Obrey, 3b, Brigham Young University.
14. ***Ian Kennedy, rhp, La Quinta HS, Huntington Beach, Calif.—(2007-15)**
DRAFT DROP *First-round draft pick (21st overall), Yankees (2006)*
15. **Anthony Reyes, rhp, University of Southern California.—(2005-09)**
16. Omar Pena, ss, Northeastern University.
DRAFT DROP *Brother of Carlos Pena, major leaguer (2001-14)*
17. Kevin House, of, University of Memphis.
18. Jose Virgil, of, Oklahoma State University.
DRAFT DROP *Grandson of Ozzie Virgil, major leaguer (1956-69) • Son of Ozzie Virgil, major leaguer (1980-90)*
19. **Jason Motte, c, Iona College.—(2008-15)**
20. Jordan Pals, rhp, Eastern Illinois University.
21. Jason Burch, rhp, University of Nebraska.
22. *Derik Drewett, rhp, Watson Chapel HS, Sherrill, Ark.
23. Matt Blanton, lhp, Hendrix (Ark.) College.
24. Tee Thomas, 2b, Mississippi Valley State University.
25. Tavaris Gary, of, Cumberland (Tenn.) University.
26. Levi Webber, of, Oregon State University.
27. Jason John, rhp, Grayson County (Texas) JC.
28. Tanner Wootan, 2b, Chandler-Gilbert (Ariz.) JC.
29. Brantley Jordan, lhp, University of Texas.
30. *Matt Lane, rhp, Iowa Western CC.
31. Mike Tamulionis, rhp, St. John's University.
32. Derek Roper, rhp, University of Missouri.
33. Casey Grimm, of, Seton Hall University.
34. ***Kevin Mulvey, rhp, Bishop Ahr HS, Edison, N.J.—(2009-10)**
35. *Peter Eberhardt, rhp, Cerritos (Calif.) JC.
36. *John Powell, rhp, Carl Albert State (Okla.) JC.
37. Sal Frisella, of, Southern Illinois University.
38. ***Brent Sinkbeil, rhp, Charles Page HS, Sand Springs, Okla.—(2010)**
DRAFT DROP *First-round draft pick (19th overall), Marlins (2006)*
39. *T.J. Brewer, rhp, Bloomington South HS, Bloomington, Ind.
40. Peter Soteropoulos, lhp, University of Connecticut.
41. *Ryan Castellanos, 3b, Silverado HS, Las Vegas, Nev.
42. *Roy Merritt, of, Nimitz HS, Houston.
43. ***Max Scherzer, rhp, Parkway Central HS, St. Louis.—(2008-15)**
DRAFT DROP *First-round draft pick (11th overall), Diamondbacks (2006)*
44. *Ryan Reichelderfer, 1b, University of Arkansas-Fort Smith JC.
45. Josh Markham, lhp, Riverdale HS, Murfreesboro, Tenn.
46. ***Kam Micholio, rhp, JC of Eastern Utah.—(2008-11)**
47. *Tobirus Bell, of, John Wood (Ill.) CC.

## SAN DIEGO PADRES (4)

1. **Tim Stauffer, rhp, University of Richmond.—(2005-15)**
2. Daniel Moore, lhp, University of North Carolina.—(Low A)
3. **Colt Morton, c, North Carolina State University.—(2007-08)**
4. Peter Stonard, ss, San Diego State University.—(High A)
5. Billy Hogan, ss, Chandler-Gilbert (Ariz.) JC.—(Low A)
6. *Cory Patton, of, Texas A & M University.
7. Clark Girardeau, rhp, University of South Alabama.
8. **Dirk Hayhurst, rhp, Kent State University.—(2008-09)**
9. Matt Lauderdale, c, College of Charleston.
10. Fernando Valenzuela Jr., 1b, University of Nevada-Las Vegas.
DRAFT DROP *Son of Fernando Valenzuela, major leaguer (1980-97)*
11. Justin Smyres, ss, Cal State Fullerton.
DRAFT DROP *Grandson of Clancy Smyres, major leaguer (1944)*
12. Jeff Leise, of, University of Nebraska.
13. Ryan Johnson, of, Wake Forest University.
14. *Steve Gendron, ss, Mississippi State University.
15. Chuck Bechtel, rhp, Marist College.
16. *Zane Carlson, rhp, Baylor University.
17. *Justin Sokol, rhp, Iowa Central CC.
18. Greg Conden, rhp, George Washington University.
19. *Jesse Estrada, rhp, Grayson County (Texas) CC.
20. **Leo Rosales, rhp, Cal. State Northridge.—(2008-10)**
21. Brett Burnham, ss, University of Connecticut.
22. Brandon Kaye, 1b, Oklahoma City University.
23. **Eddie Bonine, rhp, University of Nevada.—(2008-10)**
24. Ronnie Robinson, rhp, Georgia State University.
25. *Chuckie Caufield, of, Seminole State (Okla.) JC.
26. ***Steven Wright, rhp, Valley View HS, Moreno Valley, Calif.—(2013-15)**
27. *John Banach, 3b, Los Angeles Harbor (Calif.) JC.
28. *Corey McCoy, of, University of Arkansas-Fort Smith JC.
29. **+Steven Delabar, rhp, Volunteer State (Tenn.) CC.—(2011-15)**
30. *Ben Cox, rhp, San Jacinto (Texas) JC.
31. *Alan Tungate, rhp, St. Catharine (Ky.) JC.
32. *Chad Catalano, rhp, Pearl River (Miss.) CC.
33. *Colin Carter, lhp, Liberty Christian HS, Frisco, Texas.
34. +Chris Rayborn, rhp, Meridian (Miss.) CC.
35. *Dean Turner, rhp, Bellevue (Wash.) CC.
36. *Josh Sawatzky, rhp, W.C. Miller Collegiate HS, Altona, Manitoba.
37. *Thomas Skipper, of, Sandy Union HS, Sandy, Ore.
38. Ryan Klatt, rhp, Biola (Calif.) University.
39. *Ryan McGraw, of, Coastal Carolina University.
40. *Zach Shadle, rhp, Bethel HS, Spanaway, Wash.
41. *Pat Warfle, of, Eau Gallie HS, Melbourne, Fla.
42. *Nigel Goodwin, rhp, Spokane Falls (Wash.) CC.
43. Nathan Rogers, lhp, Connors State (Okla.) JC.
44. *Justin Wichert, rhp, Cowley County (Kan.) CC.
45. *Clay Collier, c, Edmond North HS, Edmond, Okla.
46. Brian Edwards, of, Metro State (Colo.) College.
47. *Bryan Eubanks, rhp, Meridian (Miss.) CC.
48. Tom Vincent, of, McKellar, Australia.
49. *Nate Simms, c, Central HS, Grand Junction, Colo.
50. *Sean Rierson, rhp, University of Arizona.

## SAN FRANCISCO GIANTS (26)

1. **David Aardsma, rhp, Rice University** (Choice from Astros as compensation for Type A free agent Jeff Kent).**—(2004-15)**
1. (Choice to Athletics as compensation for Type A free agent Ray Durham)
1. Craig Whitaker, rhp, Lufkin (Texas) HS (Supplemental choice—34th—as compensation for Kent).—(AAA)
2. Todd Jennings, c, Long Beach State University (Choice from Phillies as compensation for Type B free agent Dave Bell).—(AAA)
2. **Nate Schierholtz, 3b, Chabot (Calif.) JC.—(2007-14)**
3. **Brian Buscher, 3b, University of South Carolina.—(2007-09)**
4. Brooks McNiven, rhp, University of British Columbia.—(AAA)
5. Mike Wagner, of, University of Washington.—(AA)
6. **Billy Sadler, rhp, Louisiana State University.—(2006-09)**
7. **Pat Misch, lhp, Western Michigan University.—(2006-11)**
8. Tim Hutting, ss, Long Beach State University.
9. Kellen Ludwig, rhp, Chipola (Fla.) JC.
10. Jesse Schmidt, of, Cal State Sacramento.
11. Jeff Petersen, rhp, University of Washington.
12. **Ryan Sadowski, rhp, University of Florida.—(2009)**
13. Nick Conte, c, St. Mary's (Calif.) University.
14. Sean Martin, rhp, Cal State Fullerton.
15. Ben Thurmond, rhp, Arizona State University.
16. Mike Mooney, of, JC of San Mateo (Calif.).
17. +Marcus Sanders, ss, Sarasota (Fla.) HS / South Florida CC.
18. Patrick Dobson, of, University of Nevada-Las Vegas.
DRAFT DROP *Son of actor Kevin Dobson*
19. **Jon Coutlangus, of-lhp, University of South Carolina.—(2007)**
20. *Raul Rodriguez, c, Florida Christian HS, Miami.
21. *Sean Watson, rhp, Florida Christian HS, Miami.
22. *Nathan Fogle, rhp, Mount Hood (Ore.) CC.
23. Mike Kunes, lhp, UCLA.
24. **Brian Wilson, rhp, Louisiana State University.—(2006-14)**
25. *Nolan Mulligan, rhp, Chaminade-Madonna Prep, Hollywood, Fla.
26. *Tyler Coon, lhp, CC of Southern Nevada.
27. *Omar Aguilar, rhp, Livingston (Calif.) HS.
28. *Roberto Gonzalez, of, Sunny Hills HS, Fullerton, Calif.
29. +Danny DeSouza, of, Connors State (Okla.) JC.
30. Derek Barrow, 3b, Campbell University.
31. *Eddy Baez, rhp, Mission (Calif.) JC.
32. *O.D. Gonzalez, of, American HS, Miami.
33. Travis NeSmith, lhp, Florida Atlantic University.
34. *Cody McAllister, rhp, Edmonds (Wash.) CC.
35. ***Tyson Brummett, rhp, Spanish Fork (Utah) HS.—(2012)**
36. Tim Alvarez, lhp, Southeast Missouri State University.
37. *Shannon Wirth, lhp, Mount Hood (Ore.) CC.
38. *Jordan Hafer, 1b, Deerfield Beach (Fla.) HS.
39. *Mike Pierce, c, Fresno CC.
40. *Dylan Gonzalez, rhp, American Heritage HS, Plantation, Fla.
41. *Mike Johnston, lhp, Ball State University.
42. ***Luis Martinez, c, Coral Park HS, Miami.—(2011-12)**
43. *Mike Bell, c, Red Bluff (Calif.) HS.
44. +John Odom, rhp, Tallahassee (Fla.) CC.
45. *James Braden, rhp, Manatee (Fla.) JC.
46. *Brandon Federici, lhp, Polk (Fla.) CC.
47. *Thomas Correa, ss, Florin HS, Sacramento, Calif.
48. *Matt Berezay, of, Modesto (Calif.) JC.
49. ***Doug Fister, rhp, Merced (Calif.) JC.—(2009-15)**
50. *Jim Popp, rhp, Duquesne University.

## SEATTLE MARINERS (19)

1. (Choice to Diamondbacks as compensation for Type B free agent Greg Colbrunn)
1. **Adam Jones, ss-rhp, Morse HS, San Diego** (Supplemental choice—37th—for failure to sign 2002 first-round pick John Mayberry Jr.).**—(2006-15)**
2. Jeff Flaig, 3b, El Dorado HS, Placentia, Calif.—(High A)
3. **Ryan Feierabend, lhp, Midview HS, Grafton, Ohio.—(2006-14)**
4. Paul Fagan, lhp, Bartram Trail HS, Jacksonville, Fla.—(High A)
5. Casey Abrams, lhp, Wright State University.—(Low A)
6. **Eric O'Flaherty, lhp, Walla Walla (Wash.) HS.—(2006-15)**
7. Jeremy Dutton, 3b, North Carolina State University.
8. Tom Oldham, lhp, Creighton University.
9. Justin Ruchti, c, Rice University.
10. Mike Cox, 3b, Florida Atlantic University.
11. Joe Woerman, rhp, San Diego CC.
12. Ruben Flores, rhp, El Paso (Texas) CC.
13. Shawn Nottingham, lhp, Jackson HS, Canton, Ohio.
14. Tim Dorn, rhp, East Los Angeles JC.
15. ***Scott Maine, lhp, Dwyer HS, Palm Beach Gardens, Fla.—(2010-12)**
16. Brian Schweiger, c, Cal State San Bernardino.
17. +Jason Snyder, rhp, Dixie State (Utah) JC.
18. James Hymon, ss, Rust (Miss.) College.
19. Aaron Jensen, rhp, Springville (Utah) HS.
20. *C.J. Gaddis, of, Hoke County HS, Raeford, N.C.
DRAFT DROP *Fifth-round draft pick, Philadelphia Eagles, National Football League (2007)*
21. Casey Craig, of, Granite Hills HS, La Mesa, Calif.
22. Sam Bradford, of, Gardner-Webb University.
23. +Danny Santin, c, Brito Private HS, Miami / Miami-Dade CC.
24. Kenny Falconer, rhp, University of Kansas.
25. *Jason Cable, lhp, Palmdale (Calif.) HS.
26. *Dwayne Lynah, of, Spartanburg Methodist (S.C.) JC.
27. *Richard Breshears, rhp, Hutchinson (Kan.) CC.
28. *Daniel McDonald, lhp, Theodore (Ala.) HS.
29. *Chris Garcia, rhp, Brooklyn, N.Y.
30. *Steve Santos, rhp, Los Medanos (Calif.) JC.
31. ***Doug Mathis, rhp, Central Arizona JC.—**

(2008-10)
32. *Adam Poole, lhp, Lincoln Trail (Ill.) JC.
33. *Blake Rampy, rhp, Tomball (Texas) HS.
34. *Paul Keck, c, Sacramento (Calif.) CC.
35. *Andy Reichard, rhp, State College (Pa.) HS.
36. *Alex Baboulas, lhp, Birchmount Park Collegiate Institute, Toronto.
37. *Joel Allin, lhp, Stockbridge (Ga.) HS.
38. *Yusuf Carter, c, Canarsie HS, Brooklyn, N.Y.
39. +Trevor Heid, of, Dixie State (Utah) JC.
40. *Mark Tournangeau, rhp, Queen Elizabeth Park HS, Scarborough, Ontario.
41. *Dane Awana, lhp, Saddleback (Calif.) CC.
42. *Danny Santiesteban, of, Brito Private HS, Miami.
43. *Harold Williams, rhp, Cerritos (Calif.) CC.
44. *Edwin Totesault, ss, Brito Private HS, Miami.
45. *McCay Green, rhp, Lake Sumter (Fla.) CC.
46. *Mike Hofius, 1b, Long Beach State University.
47. *Dan Kapala, rhp, Shrine HS, Royal Oak, Mich.
48. *Markus Roberts, ss, Deer Valley HS, Antioch, Calif.

DRAFT DROP *Son of Bip Roberts, major leaguer (1986-98)*

49. *Jose Laffitte, of, Miami (Fla.) Senior HS.
50. *Tim Turner, of, East Tennessee State University.

## TAMPA BAY DEVIL RAYS (1)

1. **Delmon Young, of, Camarillo (Calif.) HS.—(2006-15)**

DRAFT DROP *Brother of Dmitri Young, first-round draft pick, Cardinals (1991); major leaguer (1996-2008)*

2. **James Houser, lhp, Sarasota (Fla.) HS.—(2010)**
3. ***Andrew Miller, lhp, Buchholz HS, Gainesville, Fla.—(2006-15)**

DRAFT DROP *Attended North Carolina; re-drafted by Tigers, first round (2006); first player from 2006 draft to reach majors (Aug. 30, 2006)*

4. **Travis Schlichting, 3b, Round Rock (Texas) HS.—(2009-10)**
5. Jon Barratt, lhp, Hillcrest HS, Springfield, Mo.—(AA)
6. Christian Lopez, c, Hialeah HS, Miami Lakes, Fla.
7. Brian Henderson, lhp, University of Houston.
8. Matthew Maniscalco, ss, Mississippi State University.
9. ***Billy Buckner, rhp, Young Harris (Ga.) JC.—(2007-14)**
10. Shaun Cumberland, of, Pace (Fla.) HS.
11. Chad Cooper, 2b, Middle Tennessee State University.
12. **John Jaso, c, Southwestern (Calif.) JC.—(2008-15)**
13. **Chad Orvella, rhp, North Carolina State University.—(2005-07)**
14. Aaron Gangi, lhp, University of Akron.
15. Andy Weimar, rhp, LeMoyne College.
16. ***Jared Hughes, rhp, Santa Margarita HS, Laguna Niguel, Calif.—(2011-15)**
17. Chris Gustafson, of, Kamiak HS, Granite Falls, Wash.
18. +Jason Cayton, rhp, Cerritos (Calif.) JC.
19. ***Josh Geer, rhp, Navarro (Texas) JC.—(2008-09)**
20. Mark Schleicher, 2b, Pfeiffer (N.C.) University.
21. *Casey Hudspeth, rhp, Sarasota (Fla.) HS.
22. *Rod Allen, of, Arizona State University.

DRAFT DROP *Son of Rod Allen, major leaguer (1983-88)*

23. Ryan McCally, rhp, Stanford University.
24. *Chris Shaver, lhp, College of William & Mary.
25. Stephen Jones, of, University of Alabama-Birmingham.
26. Joe Little, lhp, University of Arizona.
27. *Adam Roos, 3b, Hamarskjeld HS, Thunder Bay, Ontario.
28. *Andrew Swanson, rhp, Galesburg (Ill.) HS.
29. Fernando Puebla, ss, Southern University.
30. ***Adam Ottavino, rhp, Berkeley Carroll HS, Brooklyn, N.Y.—(2010-15)**

DRAFT DROP *First-round draft pick (30th overall), Cardinals (2006)*

31. Tom Lagreid, c, Everett (Wash.) CC.
32. Matt Travis, lhp, Santa Clara University.
33. Jordan Olson, lhp, University of Southern California.
34. *Travis Fuller, lhp, Hayesville (N.C.) HS.
35. *Gus Jacobson, rhp, Cactus Shadows HS, Cave Creek, Ariz.
36. ***Wade Leblanc, lhp, Barbe HS, Lake Charles, La.—(2008-14)**
37. ***Kris Medlen, ss-rhp, Gahr HS, Cerritos, Calif.—(2009-15)**
38. Kris Dufner, ss, University of Delaware.
39. *Kevin Allen, of, West Henderson HS, Hendersonville, N.C.
40. *Graham Baxter, rhp, McQueen HS, Reno, Nev.
41. *Leon Johnson, of, Thatcher (Ariz.) HS.
42. Travis Beech, 2b, Austin Peay State University.
43. *Grant Theophilus, lhp, Ocean View HS, Huntington Beach, Calif.
44. Josh Kendrick, 1b, University of Mobile (Ala.).
45. Brandon Rousseve, ss, Meridian (Miss.) CC.
46. J.B. Bolen, of, University of Louisville.
47. *Brad Matthews, 2b, Surry (N.C.) CC.
48. *Derrick Shaw, ss, Benton HS, Bossier City, La.
49. *Lars Davis, c, Grand Prairie Composite HS, Grande Prairie, Alberta.
50. Brent Spiegner, rhp, Vestavia Hills, Ala.

DRAFT DROP *Brother of Levale Speigner, 14th-round draft pick, Twins (2003); major leaguer (2007-08)*

## TEXAS RANGERS (9)

1. **John Danks, lhp, Round Rock (Texas) HS.—(2007-15)**

DRAFT DROP *Brother of Jordan Danks, major leaguer (2012-15)*

2. Vince Sinisi, 1b, Rice University.—(AAA)
3. John Hudgins, rhp, Stanford University.—(AAA)
4. **Wes Littleton, rhp, Cal State Fullerton.—(2006-08)**
5. Matt Lorenzo, rhp, Kent State University.—(AA)
6. Adam Bourassa, of, Wake Forest University.
7. Matt Farnum, rhp, Texas A&M University.
8. Jeremy Cleveland, of, University of North Carolina.
9. Tim Cunningham, lhp, Stanford University.
10. Adam Fox, 3b, Ohio University.
11. **Cody Clark, c, Wichita State University.—(2013)**
12. Andrew Wishy, of, University of Arkansas.
13. Emerson Frostad, 3b, Lewis-Clark State (Idaho) College.
14. Brian Mattoon, lhp, LeMoyne College.
15. Chris Alexander, 1b, University of New Mexico.
16. Kevin Altman, rhp, Rubidoux HS, Riverside, Calif.
17. **Ian Kinsler, ss, University of Missouri.—(2006-15)**
18. +Cain Byrd, rhp, Southwood HS, Shreveport, La. / San Jacinto (Texas) JC.
19. Bobby Bowman, rhp, Jacksonville University.
20. Micah Furtado, 2b, Lewis-Clark State (Idaho) College.
21. Marc LaMacchia, rhp, Florida State University.
22. Dane Bubela, of, Rice University.

DRAFT DROP *Brother of Jaime Bubela, major leaguer (2005)*

23. Jonathan Ramos, rhp, Tomas C. Ongay HS, Bayamon, P.R.
24. *Ben Rowe, rhp, Oregon State University.
25. Justin Hatcher, c, Texas Christian University.
26. Ian Gac, 1b, Edmonds-Woodway HS, Seattle.
27. Johnny Washington, ss, Mount San Jacinto (Calif.) JC.
28. ***Brad Lincoln, rhp, Brazoswood HS, Clute, Texas.—(2010-14)**

DRAFT DROP *First-round draft pick (4th overall), Pirates (2006)*

29. Chris Cordeiro, rhp, UCLA.
30. **Scott Feldman, rhp, JC of San Mateo (Calif.).—(2005-15)**
31. *Rosalino Valenzuela, rhp, Central Arizona JC.
32. *Colby Paxton, rhp, Auburn University.
33. Scott Welch, ss, University of Minnesota.
34. *Sammy Hewitt, 3b, University of North Carolina.
35. *Austin Faught, lhp, University of Louisiana-Lafayette.
36. *Dwayne White, of, Cowley County (Kan.) CC.
37. *Loren Deans, of, Capistrano Valley HS, Mission Viejo, Calif.
38. *Paul Sandoval, rhp, Saddleback (Calif.) JC.
39. *Josh Lansford, 3b, St. Francis HS, Santa Clara, Calif.

DRAFT DROP *Son of Carney Lansford, major leaguer (1978-92)*

40. *Matt Vogel, 2b, East Los Angeles JC.
41. *Francisco Mora, rhp, Eastlake HS, Chula Vista, Calif.
42. *Charles Hesseltine, lhp, Maloney HS, Meriden, Conn.
43. *Hunter Harrigan, c, Cowley County (Kan.) CC.
44. *Curtis White, lhp, University of Oklahoma.

## TORONTO BLUE JAYS (13)

1. **Aaron Hill, ss, Louisiana State University.—(2005-15)**
2. **Josh Banks, rhp, Florida International University.—(2007-10)**
3. **Shaun Marcum, rhp, Southwest Missouri State University.—(2005-15)**
4. Kurt Isenberg, lhp, James Madison University.—(AA)
5. **Justin James, rhp, University of Missouri.—(2010)**
6. Christian Snavely, of, Ohio State University.
7. Danny Core, rhp, Florida Atlantic University.
8. Chad Mulholland, rhp, Southwest Missouri State University.
9. **Jamie Vermilyea, rhp, University of New Mexico.—(2007)**
10. Jayce Tingler, of, University of Missouri.
11. **Tom Mastny, rhp, Furman University.—(2006-08)**
12. Jayson Rodriguez, rhp, Indian River (Fla.) CC.
13. Matt Foster, lhp, U.S. Naval Academy.
14. Jeremy Harper, rhp, Virginia Military Institute.
15. Vito Chiaravalloti, 1b, University of Richmond.
16. Joey Reiman, c, Grand Canyon University.
17. Jordy Templet, rhp, University of Louisiana-Lafayette.
18. **Ryan Roberts, 3b, University of Texas-Arlington.—(2006-14)**
19. +Adrian Martin, rhp, South Fork HS, Stuart, Fla. / Indian River (Fla.) CC.
20. *Brad Depoy, rhp, The Woodlands (Texas) HS.
21. Mark Sopko, rhp, Arizona State University.
22. Vinny Esposito, 3b, Rutgers University.
23. Jeremy Acey, 2b, Skyline (Calif.) JC.
24. *Nick Evangelista, rhp, University of Pittsburgh.
25. Brian Patrick, 2b, Duke University.
26. Kyle Thousand, of, University of Iowa.
27. Brian Reed, rhp, University of Alabama.
28. *Patrick Breen, of, Cal Poly San Luis Obispo.
29. *Ben Nieto, lhp, Riverside (Calif.) CC.
30. Billy Wheeler, rhp, South Suburban (Ill.) JC.
31. Kiki Canizal, rhp, Union (N.Y.) College.
32. Brad Mumma, lhp, Western Michigan University.
33. Joey Wolfe, c, University of Louisiana-Monroe.
34. Jeremy Noegel, rhp, University of West Florida.
35. *Jim Burt, 1b, University of Miami.

DRAFT DROP *Son of Jim Burt, nose tackle, National Football League (1981-91)*

36. *Matt Trink, rhp, Horizon HS, Scottsdale, Ariz.
37. *Aric Van Gaalen, lhp, St. Petersburg (Fla.) JC.
38. *Jack Ryser, of, Santa Ana (Calif.) JC.
39. *William Blackmon, lhp, Arlington Heights HS, Fort Worth, Texas.
40. *Jimmy Coker, lhp, Spartanburg (Methodist (S.C.) JC.
41. Scott Tolbert, rhp, Georgia Southern University.
42. Jeremy Knicely, c, Longwood (Va.) College.

DRAFT DROP *Son of Alan Knicely, major leaguer (1979-86)*

43. *Ryan Gordon, lhp, University of North Carolina-Greensboro.
44. *Brent Johnson, of, University of Nevada-Las Vegas.
45. *Paul Franko, 1b, Horizon, HS, Scottsdale, Ariz.
46. *Paul Marlow, rhp, Elgin Park HS, White Rock, B.C.
47. *Jeff Walker, lhp, Vernon Regional (Texas) JC.
48. *Bryan Hansen, lhp, Kishwaukee (Ill.) JC.
49. Michael Rider, rhp, Cosumnes River (Calif.) JC.
50. *Angel Hernandez, of, Champagnat Catholic HS, Hialeah, Fla.

# Padres' late shift leads to bad decision at No. 1

A month before the 2004 draft, the San Diego Padres narrowed their short list of candidates for the No. 1 overall pick to three collegians: shortstop Stephen Drew of Florida State, righthander Jeff Niemann of Rice and righthander Jered Weaver of Long Beach State.

Weaver was the front-runner for most of the spring. But with a week to go before the draft, Padres general manager Kevin Towers conceded that his club was leaning toward Drew. As late as June 4, three days before the draft, Drew appeared to be San Diego's choice, and the teams picking immediately behind the Padres began to plan accordingly.

All that changed after Towers met with Padres owner John Moores. They determined that Drew and Weaver were not worth the bonuses they wanted, and ruled out Niemann because injuries had compromised his 2004 season. That left scouting director Bill Gayton and his staff scrambling for a prospect worthy of the No. 1 selection.

Shortstop Matt Bush, from San Diego's Mission Bay High, learned of the Padres' quandary and took matters into his own hands, calling area scout Tim McWilliam.

"I knew the Padres had never made a final decision," Bush said. "They were looking at Stephen Drew at the time, but I was still in the mix. I've always been a Padres fan, and I really wanted to be a Padre. I called Tim and told him I wanted to be a Padre."

McWilliam went to Gayton, and the Padres began to seriously consider Bush. A large Padres contingent went to San Diego State to watch him play in the California Interscholastic Federation Division III championship game. Bush went 4-for-5, setting a state record with 214 career hits, and pitched a four-hitter in Mission Bay's 13-4 victory.

"We had been in the draft room for over a week when we went out to SDSU to see that game," Gayton said. "That night was the first night in a while that I slept well."

The Padres and Bush's agents agreed on the parameters of a $3.15 million signing bonus on the eve of the draft. A day later he was the first player selected, and shortly after the three-day draft ended, the Padres announced that Bush was under contract.

"I've been in the business for a long time, and this is the first time this has happened in the first round," Gayton said. "It's unique, but this is what you hope for. You want players who want to be a part of your organization."

Bush's bonus represented the lowest value for a No. 1 overall pick since 2000, when another San Diego area high school player, Adrian Gonzalez, signed for $3 million with the Florida Marlins. The Padres, while acknowledging that money always enters into decisions at the top of the draft, said they viewed Bush as the best high school prospect available, and a better value at $3.15 million than anyone else they had near the top of their draft board.

MIRO

With the first pick, the Padres took shortstop Matt Bush, a local high school product, but to their regret, Bush never came close to living up to expectations, mixing poor performance with off-field woes

Bush showed exemplary defensive skills at shortstop, and he had the best arm strength of any position player available, having been clocked at 96 mph when he pitched. He had the smallest stature of any No. 1 pick ever at 5-foot-10, 170 pounds, but his athleticism stood out, and the Padres liked his offensive potential. Bush hit .447 with 11 homers in his senior high school season, and went 9-1, 0.53 on the mound.

Had San Diego not chosen Bush, he likely would have slipped to the sixth or seventh pick overall in a draft unusually rich in pitching. He became the third No. 1 overall choice selected by his hometown team, and the first since the Minnesota Twins picked catcher Joe Mauer in 2001.

For the Padres and Bush, however, any chance of a local-kid-makes-good angle quickly turned sour. Bush almost immediately encountered off-field problems, often sparked by alcohol consumption. The Padres reprimanded him, suspended him and even questioned their decision to draft him. That hardly proved to be a wake-up call for their young protégé.

## AT A GLANCE

### This Date In History
June 7-8

### Best Draft
**COLORADO ROCKIES.** The Rockies didn't get what they expected from **CHRIS NELSON** (1), but eight of their first 10 selections reached the majors, and a draft-high 13 overall. The most successful were **SETH SMITH** (2), **CHRIS IANNETTA** (4) and **DEXTER FOWLER** (14), who were all still active in 2016

### Worst Draft
**SAN DIEGO PADRES.** The Padres made a colossal gaffe by taking **MATT BUSH** with the first overall pick, and the choices after that didn't make up for it. They equaled two other clubs by selecting a draft-low four players who went on to play in the majors.

### First-Round Bust
**MATT BUSH, SS, PADRES.** Bush, a San Diego high school product, wore out his welcome before he ever played a game. He was arrested for his involvement in a fight outside an Arizona bar and suspended by the team. Bush's career was all downhill from there. Injuries, poor performance as both a pitcher and position player and repeated legal run-ins made him one of the biggest busts in draft history. He did at least reach the big leagues with the Rangers in 2016 as a relief pitcher.

### On Second Thought
**DUSTIN PEDROIA, SS, RED SOX.** Pedroia, the 65th player drafted, didn't measure up as a first-rounder on the basis of his raw tools, but he more than compensated with his scrappy, spirited style of play and performance. A classic overachiever, Pedroia starred for three years at shortstop for Arizona State and 10 at second base for the Red Sox, earning the 2008 American League MVP and four Gold Glove Awards.

CONTINUED ON PAGE 582

## AT A GLANCE

CONTINUED FROM PAGE 581

### Late-Round Find

**LORENZO CAIN, OF, BREWERS (17TH ROUND).** Cain played baseball for the first time as an 11th-grader at a Florida high school, after being cut from the basketball team. The Brewers signed him for $95,000 in the spring of 2005 as a draft-and-follow. He spent the better part of the next eight years in the minors before blooming into a standout major league player with the Royals, joining them in a trade that sent Zack Greinke to the Brewers. As a 2015 all-star, Cain set career highs in batting (.307), homers (16), RBIs (69) and steals (28).

### Never Too Late

**CHRIS DAVIS, 3B/RHP, YANKEES (50TH ROUND).** Davis improved from a 50th-rounder out of a Texas high school, opting for Navarro (Texas) JC, where he was a 35th-rounder in 2005, to a fifth-rounder in 2006. After eight major league seasons, he had 199 homers.

### Overlooked

**MATT DALEY, RHP, ROCKIES.** Undrafted in 2004 as a senior at Bucknell, Daley signed with the Rockies. He made 112 major league pitching appearances, going 2-3, 4.47.

### International Gem

**JOHNNY CUETO, RHP, REDS.** Cueto, from the Dominican Republic, signed with the Reds for $35,000. He reached the majors in 2008 and went 92-63, 3.21 over eight seasons with the Reds. Cueto was traded to the Royals in 2015, and signed a lucrative contract after the season with the Giants.

### Minor League Take

**BILLY BUTLER, 3B, ROYALS.** Butler left little doubt that he would evolve into an effective major league hitter by blistering the ball at a .336 clip, with a .561 slug-

## 2004: THE FIRST ROUNDERS

| CLUB: PLAYER, POS., SCHOOL | HOMETOWN | B-T | HT. | WT. | AGE | BONUS | FIRST YEAR | LAST YEAR | PEAK LEVEL (YEARS) |
|---|---|---|---|---|---|---|---|---|---|
| 1. Padres: Matt Bush, ss/rhp, Mission Bay HS | San Diego | R-R | 5-10 | 170 | 18 | $3,150,000 | 2004 | Active | Class AA (1) |
| Biggest first-pick fiasco ever; Padres went for local story, got burned by off-field troubles, poor performance, injuries; served jail time for 2012 hit-and-run wreck. | | | | | | | | | |
| 2. *Tigers: Justin Verlander, rhp, Old Dominion | Manakin-Sabot, Va. | R-R | 6-5 | 200 | 21 | $3,150,000 | 2005 | Active | Majors (11) |
| Tigers hit paydirt with best college arm in draft; overcame command issues with mechanical adjustments, dominated in majors (155-97, 3.52) with electric stuff. | | | | | | | | | |
| 3. *Mets: Philip Humber, rhp, Rice | Carthage, Texas | R-R | 6-4 | 220 | 21 | $3,000,000 | 2005 | 2014 | Majors (8) |
| Seen as safest pick among Rice trio of arms, had 2007 TJ surgery; struggled to regain college form in 16-23, 5.31 MLB career highlighted by unlikely perfect game. | | | | | | | | | |
| 4. *Devil Rays: Jeff Niemann, rhp, Rice | Houston | R-R | 6-9 | 260 | 21 | $3,200,000 | 2005 | 2012 | Majors (5) |
| Struggled to repeat 2003 success (17-0, 1.70) as JR (6-3, 3.02); intimidating presence with size/stuff, promising career took major hit with 2013 shoulder surgery. | | | | | | | | | |
| 5. Brewers: Mark Rogers, rhp, Mount Ararat HS | Topsham, Me. | R-R | 6-2 | 205 | 18 | $2,200,000 | 2004 | 2014 | Majors (2) |
| Second-highest Maine draft topped out at 98 mph in HS; battled command early, tore labrum in 2006, battled back to go 3-1, 3.49 in brief look with Brewers. | | | | | | | | | |
| 6. Indians: Jeremy Sowers, lhp, Vanderbilt | Louisville, Ky. | L-L | 6-1 | 165 | 21 | $2,475,000 | 2005 | 2010 | Majors (4) |
| Two-time first-rounder; Vandy's No. 1 starter for three years, pounded zone with four pitches but not overpowering; promising start before shoulder issues took toll. | | | | | | | | | |
| 7. Reds: Homer Bailey, rhp, La Grange HS | La Grange, Texas | R-R | 6-4 | 185 | 18 | $2,300,000 | 2004 | Active | Majors (9) |
| Dominant prep arm (15-0, 0.68, 93 IP/201 SO) with 92-96 mph FB, hammer curve; struggled to secure regular job before spinning pair of no-hitters in 2012-13. | | | | | | | | | |
| 8. Orioles: Wade Townsend, rhp, Rice | Dripping Springs, Texas | R-R | 6-4 | 225 | 21 | Unsigned | 2005 | 2009 | Class AA (1) |
| Best command/curve of Rice trio, went 12-0, 1.80 (120 IP/148 SO) as JR; victim of last-second switch by penny-pinching O's, re-drafted in same spot in 2005. | | | | | | | | | |
| 9. Rockies: Chris Nelson, ss, Redan HS | Stone Mountain, Ga. | R-R | 5-11 | 175 | 18 | $2,150,000 | 2004 | Active | Majors (5) |
| One of top HS athletes in draft with superior speed/arm strength, polished bat, fluid actions in field; never fulfilled potential in any area in injury-plagued career. | | | | | | | | | |
| 10. Rangers: Thomas Diamond, rhp, New Orleans | Metairie, La. | R-R | 6-3 | 230 | 21 | $2,025,000 | 2004 | 2011 | Majors (1) |
| Priced himself out of draft as prep SR, but hot commodity three years later with 96 mph FB; never developed secondary pitches to dominate in majors, high minors. | | | | | | | | | |
| 11. Pirates: Neil Walker, c, Pine Richland HS | Gibsonia, Pa. | B-R | 6-3 | 205 | 18 | $1,950,000 | 2004 | Active | Majors (7) |
| Dad (Tom), uncle (Chip Lang) pitched in majors; hometown pick had athleticism, hit .656-12-41 as prep SR, career took off after switch to 3B in 2007, later to 2B. | | | | | | | | | |
| 12. Angels: Jered Weaver, rhp, Long Beach State | Simi Valley, Calif. | R-R | 6-7 | 205 | 21 | $4,000,000 | 2005 | Active | Majors (10) |
| Talk of college game with 15-1, 1.62 record (144 IP, 21 BB/213 SO), excellent command/deception with modest stuff; held out for nearly a year but paid dividends. | | | | | | | | | |
| 13. Expos: Bill Bray, lhp, William & Mary | Virginia Beach, Va. | L-L | 6-3 | 215 | 21 | $1,750,000 | 2004 | 2013 | Majors (6) |
| Transplanted Expos went for first-round college closer second year in row; had 92-94 FB, plus slider but best MLB years with Reds in 2008-11 as lefty specialist. | | | | | | | | | |
| 14. Royals: Billy Butler, 3b, Wolfson HS | Jacksonville, Fla. | R-R | 6-2 | 225 | 18 | $1,400,000 | 2004 | Active | Majors (9) |
| Signability pick as mature hitter who lacked athleticism/speed/footwork for regular position; Royals bet on bat and won, hit .336 in minors. .290 in MLB as DH. | | | | | | | | | |
| 15. *Diamondbacks: Stephen Drew, ss, Florida State | Valdosta, Ga. | R-R | 6-2 | 225 | 21 | $4,000,000 | 2005 | Active | Majors (10) |
| Candidate for No. 1 pick as five-tool SS, best bat in college ranks; slipped because teams wary of Boras connection, injury history, same stoic approach as brother J.D. | | | | | | | | | |
| 16. Blue Jays: David Purcey, lhp, Oklahoma | Addison, Texas | L-L | 6-5 | 240 | 22 | $1,600,000 | 2004 | 2014 | Majors (5) |
| Three-time draft made strides as college JR with curve/command, mental toughness; career in minors impacted by injuries, in majors by control/faulty mechanics. | | | | | | | | | |
| 17. Dodgers: Scott Elbert, lhp, Seneca HS | Seneca, Mo. | L-L | 6-2 | 190 | 19 | $1,575,000 | 2004 | 2015 | Majors (6) |
| Top running back recruit chose Dodgers; live arm with 92-95 mph FB, mid-80s slider, but plagued by injuries, never gained command in 4-3, 3.53 MLB career. | | | | | | | | | |
| 18. White Sox: Josh Fields, 3b, Oklahoma State | Ada, Okla. | R-R | 6-2 | 210 | 21 | $1,550,000 | 2004 | 2013 | Majors (5) |
| Two-sport college star set Cowboys record with 55 career TD passes, hit .364-25-131; had plus arm/raw power, but poor plate discipline proved undoing. | | | | | | | | | |
| 19. Cardinals: Chris Lambert, rhp, Boston College | Manchester, N.H. | R-R | 6-1 | 205 | 21 | $1,525,000 | 2004 | 2009 | Majors (2) |
| Shortstop/hockey player in HS didn't develop pitching skills until college, FB soon peaked at 96-97 mph; never saw same power stuff in pros; 1-3, 7.36 MLB record. | | | | | | | | | |
| 20. Twins: Trevor Plouffe, ss, Crespi Carmelite HS | Encino, Calif. | R-R | 6-1 | 175 | 18 | $1,500,000 | 2004 | Active | Majors (6) |
| Was 33-6 as prep pitcher, didn't focus on everyday role until SR year; moved methodically through Twins system, grabbed 3B job when power emerged in 2012. | | | | | | | | | |
| 21. Phillies: Greg Golson, of, John Connally HS | Austin, Texas | R-R | 6-0 | 190 | 18 | $1,475,000 | 2004 | 2013 | Majors (4) |
| Best prep athlete/fastest runner in draft projected as complete package with CF skills, arm, raw power, but never became finished product, struggled to hit. | | | | | | | | | |
| 22. Twins: Glen Perkins, lhp, Minnesota | Stillwater, Minn. | L-L | 6-0 | 200 | 21 | $1,425,000 | 2004 | Active | Majors (10) |
| Local product had stuff, three-pitch mix to start, but never thrived until moved to closer in 2011; became dominant for Twins in role with 95-97 mph FB, slider. | | | | | | | | | |
| 23. Yankees: Phil Hughes, rhp, Foothill HS | Santa Ana, Calif. | R-R | 6-5 | 220 | 18 | $1,400,000 | 2004 | Active | Majors (9) |
| Went 21-1, 0.74 in last two HS years, became best arm developed by Yankees in years; career in New York marked by oversized expectations, inconsistency. | | | | | | | | | |
| 24. Athletics: Landon Powell, c, South Carolina | Apex, N.C. | B-R | 6-3 | 225 | 22 | $1,000,000 | 2004 | 2013 | Majors (3) |
| Tested legality of draft as prep junior, finally joined pro ranks after hitting .332-19-65 as Gamecocks SR; conditioning/injuries clouded brief major league career. | | | | | | | | | |
| 25. Twins: Kyle Waldrop, rhp, Farragut HS | Knoxville, Tenn. | R-R | 6-4 | 190 | 18 | $1,000,000 | 2004 | 2013 | Majors (2) |
| Headed to Vanderbilt after dominant two-way prep season (14-0, 0.15; .474-12-54); ground-ball pitcher with modest stuff, emerged as reliever after injuring shoulder. | | | | | | | | | |
| 26. Athletics: Richie Robnett, of, Fresno State | Visalia, Calif. | L-L | 5-10 | 195 | 20 | $1,325,000 | 2004 | 2009 | Class AAA (4) |
| Stock soared after he hit .381-13-51, handled Rice arms in conference series as draft-eligible soph; had legit raw power, but swung/missed too much in minors. | | | | | | | | | |
| 27. Marlins: Taylor Tankersley, lhp, Alabama | Vicksburg, Miss. | L-L | 6-1 | 220 | 21 | $1,300,000 | 2004 | 2011 | Majors (4) |
| Used as starter/reliever in Alabama career, went 2-5, 2.00 with 4 SV as JR with 88-94 mph FB, power slider; lefthanded specialist in undistinguished pro career. | | | | | | | | | |
| 28. Dodgers: Blake DeWitt, 2b, Sikeston HS | Sikeston, Mo. | L-R | 5-11 | 175 | 18 | $1,200,000 | 2004 | 2013 | Majors (6) |
| Dodgers tapped second Missouri product in first round; bat/power were best tools, but never showed sustained power for 3B, speed/range to settle at second. | | | | | | | | | |
| 29. Royals: Matt Campbell, lhp, South Carolina | Simpsonville, S.C. | L-L | 6-2 | 170 | 21 | $1,100,000 | 2004 | 2007 | Class A (2) |
| Went 10-4, 2.88 (112 IP/135 SO) as JR, led Gamecocks to three straight CWS trips; polished lefty with below-average stuff, never recovered from '05 labrum surgery. | | | | | | | | | |
| 30. Rangers: Eric Hurley, rhp, Wolfson HS | Jacksonville, Fla. | R-R | 6-4 | 195 | 18 | $1,050,000 | 2004 | 2012 | Majors (1) |
| Along with Butler, fifth set of HS first-round teammates; went 15-1, 0.73 as SR, on fast track with 92-95 mph FB, plus slider before rotator-cuff surgery in 2009. | | | | | | | | | |

*Signed to major league contract.

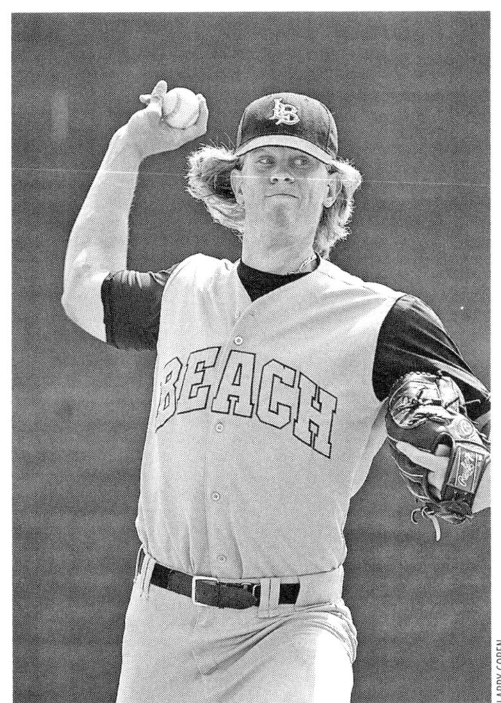


LARRY GOREN

**Jered Weaver's performance at Long Beach State matched USC's Mark Prior three years earlier, but scouts did not consider him Prior's equal**

Bush's career unraveled as he repeatedly ran afoul of the law and endured a series of injuries. He wasn't close to reaching the major leagues when the Padres sold him to the Toronto Blue Jays in February 2009. The Jays released him before the season started, and the Tampa Bay Rays signed him for the 2010 season.

Bush was arrested in a drunken-driving incident in March 2012 and ended up serving more than three years in jail on DUI and hit-and-run charges. After being released from jail in October 2015, Bush signed a minor league contract with the Texas Rangers. He unexpectedly earned a spot in the major league bullpen in 2016, making his first big league appearance nearly 12 years after he was drafted.

## DREW, WEAVER DRIVE FIRST ROUND

Bush's selection by San Diego with the No. 1 pick set the tone for one the most confusing, mixed-up drafts in history. Consider:

- The Padres signed Bush quickly, but an unprecedented five other first-rounders had yet to agree to terms by the end of the 2004 major league season. Drew and Weaver held out until a week before the 2005 draft.
- Bush didn't come close to reaching the big leagues for years, but a then-record 26 of 30 first-round picks did, including Old Dominion righthander Justin Verlander, who was selected second overall by the Detroit Tigers. The Padres showed only a passing interest in Verlander, and that glaring oversight trumped the 1966 Steve Chilcott-instead-of-Reggie-Jackson debacle as the biggest gaffe in draft history involving the No. 1 pick.
- The willingness of clubs, notably the Padres, to consider the undersized Bush with a premium pick only underscored their reluctance to embrace

## How They Should Have Done It

Based on career WAR (Wins Above Replacement, as calculated by Baseball-Reference.com) achieved by players eligible for the 2004 draft through the 2015 season, here's how the first round should have unfolded. Numbers in parentheses indicate the round when the player was drafted. Asterisk denotes player who signed as a draft-and-follow.

| | Player, Pos. | Actual Draft | WAR | Bonus |
|---|---|---|---|---|
| 1. | Dustin Pedroia, ss | Red Sox (2) | 45.1 | $575,000 |
| 2. | Justin Verlander, rhp | Tigers (1) | 43.6 | $3,150,000 |
| 3. | Ben Zobrist, ss | Astros (6) | 38.5 | $55,000 |
| 4. | Jered Weaver, rhp | Angels (1) | 36.8 | $4,000,000 |
| 5. | Hunter Pence, of | Astros (2) | 27.7 | $575,000 |
| 6. | Yovani Gallardo, rhp | Brewers (2) | 23.0 | $725,000 |
| 7. * | Lorenzo Cain, of | Brewers (17) | 19.6 | $95,000 |
| 8. | Gio Gonzalez, lhp | White Sox (1-S) | 19.0 | $850,000 |
| 9. | Neil Walker, 2b | Pirates (1) | 16.3 | $1,950,000 |
| 10. | Stephen Drew, ss | Diamondbacks (1) | 16.2 | $4,000,000 |
| 11. | Ian Desmond, ss | Expos (3) | 15.5 | $430,000 |
| 12. | Huston Street, rhp | Athletics (1-S) | 14.9 | $800,000 |
| 13. | Kurt Suzuki, c | Athletics (2) | 14.5 | $550,000 |
| 14. | Chris Iannetta, c | Rockies (4) | 14.3 | $305,000 |
| 15. | Dexter Fowler, of | Rockies (14) | 14.0 | $925,000 |
| 16. | Phil Hughes, rhp | Yankees (1) | 12.3 | $1,400,000 |
| 17. | Billy Butler, 3b | Royals (1) | 11.5 | $1,400,000 |
| | Jason Vargas, lhp | Marlins (2) | 11.5 | $525,000 |
| 19. | Adam Lind, 1b | Blue Jays (3) | 11.3 | $445,000 |
| 20. | Seth Smith, of | Rockies (2) | 11.2 | $690,000 |
| 21. | J.A. Happ, lhp | Phillies (3) | 9.0 | $420,000 |
| 22. | Glen Perkins, lhp | Twins (1) | 8.9 | $1,425,000 |
| 23. | Wade Davis, rhp | Devil Rays (3) | 8.0 | $475,000 |
| 24. | J.P. Howell, lhp | Royals (1-S) | 7.9 | $1,000,000 |
| | Mark Trumbo, rhp/3b | Angels (18) | 7.9 | $1,425,000 |
| 26. | Trevor Plouffe, ss | Twins (1) | 7.7 | $1,500,000 |
| 27. | Casey Janssen, rhp | Blue Jays (4) | 7.6 | $150,000 |
| 28. | Homer Bailey, rhp | Reds (1) | 7.3 | $2,300,000 |
| 29. | Mark Reynolds, 3b | Diamondbacks (16) | 6.1 | $50,000 |
| 30. | Jake McGee, lhp | Devil Rays (5) | 6.0 | $215,000 |

| | Top 3 Unsigned Players | | | Year Signed |
|---|---|---|---|---|
| 1. | David Price, lhp | Dodgers (19) | 29.0 | 2007 |
| 2. | Jake Arrieta, rhp | Reds (31) | 15.5 | 2007 |
| 3. | Todd Frazier, 3b | Rockies (37) | 15.3 | 2007 |

Arizona State's shortstop, 5-foot-9 Dustin Pedroia. He lasted until the second round (65th overall), drafted by the Boston Red Sox. Pedroia became the most productive big leaguer to emerge from the class of 2004, according to WAR (Wins Above Replacement). He helped the Red Sox to World Series titles in 2007 and 2013, and was selected the American League MVP in 2008.

Much of the confusion in the first round was a byproduct of the ongoing pressure by Major League Baseball to hold the line on signing bonuses, particularly after the efforts yielded significant results in 2003, when bonuses showed a 16.2 percent decrease from 2002.

Most clubs signed their early-round picks according to the unofficial, predetermined slots established by the commissioner's office. But the uncertainty surrounding Drew and Weaver, the consensus best player and pitcher in the draft, upset the flow of the first round. Both were represented by Scott Boras, and most clubs, including the Padres, preferred to steer clear of the polarizing agent.

From the start, there was no clear destination for Weaver or Drew. Weaver reportedly wanted an eight-figure deal similar to the record $10.5 mil-

## AT A GLANCE

ging average, in 397 games over five minor league seasons in the Royals system.

### One Who Got Away

**WADE TOWNSEND, RHP, ORIOLES (1ST ROUND).** Townsend, one of three first-round arms from Rice, was the only player from the first three rounds in 2004 who did not sign. He was taken by the Orioles with the eighth pick overall and drafted in the same slot a year later by the Devil Rays—even as he chose not to play that spring for Rice, or any team..

### He Was Drafted?

**MATT MOORE, 3B, ANGELS (22ND ROUND).** Moore spent four years as a college quarterback (two at UCLA, two at Oregon State) and nine more in the NFL (four with the Dallas Cowboys, five with the Miami Dolphins), yet he was drafted in baseball, not football. The Angels drafted Moore in 2004 after he dropped out of UCLA, was attending JC of the Canyons and playing baseball in a Southern California semi-pro league. His raw ability impressed scouts, but Moore did not sign.

### Did You Know . . .

Mets first-rounder **PHIL HUMBER** had an undistinguished major league career, going 16-23, 5.31 over eight seasons with four clubs. But he enjoyed a brief encounter with greatness on April 21, 2012, when he pitched the 22nd perfect game in major league history while with the White Sox.

### They Said It

First overall pick **MATT BUSH**, whose call to Padres scout **TIM MCWILLIAM** helped prompt the team to make one of the worst choices in draft history: "I knew the Padres had never made a final decision. I was still in the mix. I've always been a Padres fan, and I really wanted to be a Padre. I called Tim and told him I wanted to be a Padre."

## DRAFT SPOTLIGHT: MATT BUSH

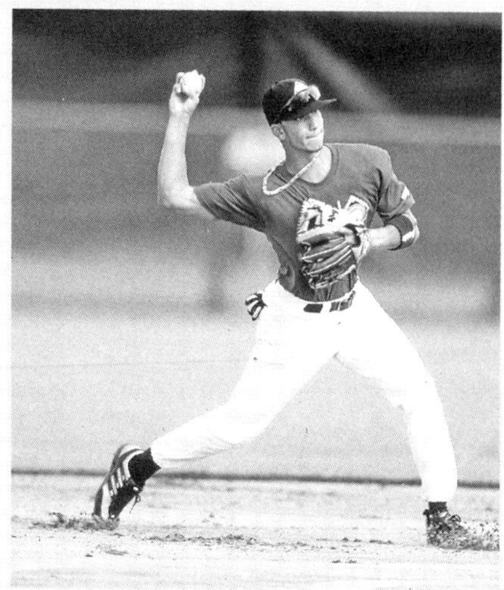

Matt Bush was a major disappointment for the Padres, but he reached the majors as a pitcher in 2016

As a dynamic high school shortstop and pitcher at San Diego's Mission Bay High, Matt Bush was well known to the Padres organization. The team had the first overall pick in the 2004 draft and found itself in a quandary on the eve of the draft, leading Padres officials to make a snap decision to select Bush. To their regret, the Padres quickly learned just how little they knew about the local kid.

Padres scouts preferred shortstop Stephen Drew or righthander Jered Weaver as the first pick in the draft, but team ownership was wary those players would be too expensive. Bush agreed to a $3.15 million bonus, and the ink was barely dry on the deal when the Padres started second-guessing their decision.

On the night his signing was announced, Bush and some of his friends were invited to watch the Padres game from a suite at brand new Petco Park. They trashed the place. On June 20, at Padres camp in Peoria, Ariz., a day before his scheduled professional debut, the 18-year-old Bush and his 23-year-old brother, Jeremy, were arrested at 1 a.m. and jailed after they were denied entrance to a bar and fought with bouncers.

The Padres suspended Bush for six weeks while the team contemplated how to deal with him, ranging from hiring a private investigator to conducting an extensive background check on Bush to incorporating personal-conduct clauses in a restructured contract to voiding the contract altogether. "I believe in the theory of redemption," Padres owner John Moores said. "I've had multiple second chances, and I think we ought to give this kid at least one, too. But we expect him to toe the line and be the best baseball player he can be."

After the Padres reinstated Bush, he hit .192 in 28 games at two low-level leagues in 2004 and committed 17 errors. Over the next two years in the low Class A Midwest League, Bush continued to struggle at the plate and in the field, though he appeared to be maturing.

"A lot of people have thrown him under the bus," Padres farm director Tye Waller said after Bush hit .232 with two home runs and committed 38 errors in 2005. "A lot of people have given up on him already and that's not fair. Plenty of 19-year-olds struggle in their first full season. He's learned a lot and he's come a long way personally to get to the level he's at."

The 2006 season brought more adversity. Bush broke his ankle during spring training and later pulled both hamstrings. He played in just 21 games and failed to distinguish himself at the plate or in the field. After he struggled again at the outset of the 2007 season, the Padres decided his future was as a pitcher. He soon was throwing his fastball up to 98 mph and displaying surprising polish for someone who had not pitched in three years. Bush blew hitters away with his overpowering stuff, and Padres officials were more optimistic about his future than at any point since he signed three years earlier.

It wasn't long, however, before Bush's career—and life—spiraled out of control. In August 2007 in the Midwest League, he tore a ligament in his right elbow. He had Tommy John surgery and missed the 2008 season. While rehabbing, he was involved in another altercation outside a bar near the Padres complex in Arizona. In February 2009, the Padres were informed that Bush was under investigation for assault and public drunkenness at a San Diego high school. Two days later, the Padres sold Bush to the Toronto Blue Jays. The Blue Jays released him after he was accused of assaulting a woman at a party in Dunedin, Fla., on March 30.

He sat out the 2009 season, and was signed in January 2010 by the Tampa Bay Rays. Bush was plagued by injuries that season, but in 2011 he showed promise in Double-A as a relief pitcher, striking out 77 in 50 innings with a fastball that reached 100 mph. However, he would not pitch again for the Rays.

On March 22, 2012, Bush was arrested on charges that included driving under the influence and leaving the scene of accident, related to a hit-and-run crash in Port Charlotte, Fla., that seriously injured a 72-year-old motorcyclist. Bush spent more than three years in a Florida state prison before being released in October 2015.

Still not done with baseball, Bush signed a minor league contract with the Texas Rangers for the 2016 season. At age 30, he finally reached the big leagues on May 13, 2016, finding a home in the Rangers bullpen.

lion guarantee Mark Prior got from the Chicago Cubs as the No. 2 choice in 2001, and Drew was believed to be seeking a deal similar to the $9.5 million that Mark Teixeira got from the Rangers as the No. 5 pick in 2001.

"When you're dealing with Boras, if his player is head and shoulders above everyone else, you have no problem dealing with him," a National League scouting director said. "But Jered Weaver is not Mark Prior. He's a good competitor and he has great command, but he's not a No. 1 starter in the big leagues right now. You'd rather spend that money elsewhere."

Weaver slid to the 12th overall pick, going to the Los Angeles Angels, whose new owner, Arte Moreno, had no qualms about spending big on talent. The Angels had committed $145.75 million to sign free agents Vladimir Guerrero, Bartolo Colon and Kelvim Escobar during the previous offseason.

New Angels scouting director Eddie Bane said he didn't know until two minutes before the draft that he could choose Weaver. But Bane was ready. "We did our homework," he said. "We started when Jered first got to Long Beach. I watched him in intrasquad games back in January. All our guys had seen him. We didn't back off because of reports in the paper. We do our stuff privately. We were prepared if he was there at 12 to take him."

Weaver, a younger brother of Jeff Weaver, a 1998 first-round pick of the Tigers, was brilliant both with Team USA's college national team in the summer of 2003, when he pitched 46 consecutive scoreless innings, and as a junior at Long Beach State, where he went 15-1, 1.62 with 21 walks, 213 strikeouts and 81 hits allowed in 144 innings. Weaver's stats were in line with those of Prior three years earlier at Southern California, in what was then hailed as one of the greatest seasons by a college pitcher in the draft era.

However, few scouts rated Weaver's raw stuff on a par with Prior's, even as Weaver dominated with a 91-95 mph fastball, two variations of a nearly unhittable slider, an advanced feel for pitching, excellent command and deception in his unconventional delivery.

The Arizona Diamondbacks were considering college lefthanded pitchers until Drew unexpectedly fell to them with the 15th pick. He ranked second on their draft board, trailing only Weaver.

Drew's older brothers, J.D. and Tim, were first-round picks and played in the major leagues. J.D. and Stephen both played at Florida State, and each was considered the best hitter in the college ranks in his junior season. Stephen hit .344 with 17

### Fastest To The Majors

| | Player, Pos. | Drafted (Round) | Debut |
|---|---|---|---|
| 1. | Huston Street, rhp | Athletics (1-S) | April 6, 2005 |
| 2. | Cla Meredith, rhp | Red Sox (6) | May 8, 2005 |
| 3. | Jeff Fiorentino, of | Orioles (3) | May 12, 2005 |
| 4. | J.P. Howell, lhp | Royals (1-S) | June 11, 2005 |
| 5. | Justin Verlander, rhp | Tigers (1) | July 4, 2005 |

**FIRST HIGH SCHOOL SELECTION:** Phil Hughes, rhp (Yankees/1, April 26, 2007)

## Top 25 Bonuses

| | Player, Pos. | Drafted (Round) | Order | Bonus |
|---|---|---|---|---|
| 1. | **Jered Weaver, rhp** | Angels (1) | 12 | $4,000,000 |
| | **Stephen Drew, ss** | Diamondbacks (1) | 15 | #$4,000,000 |
| 3. | **Jeff Niemann, rhp** | Rays (1) | 4 | #$3,200,000 |
| 4. | * Matt Bush, ss | Padres (1) | 1 | $3,150,000 |
| | **Justin Verlander, rhp** | Tigers (1) | 2 | #$3,150,000 |
| 6. | **Philip Humber, rhp** | Mets (1) | 3 | #$3,000,000 |
| 7. | **Jeremy Sowers, lhp** | Indians (1) | 6 | $2,475,000 |
| 8. | * **Homer Bailey, rhp** | Reds (1) | 7 | $2,300,000 |
| 9. | * **Matt Tuiasosopo, ss** | Mariners (3) | 93 | $2,290,000 |
| 10. | * **Mark Rogers, rhp** | Brewers (1) | 5 | $2,200,000 |
| 11. | * **Chris Nelson, ss** | Rockies (1) | 8 | $2,150,000 |
| 12. | **Thomas Diamond, rhp** | Rangers (1) | 10 | $2,025,000 |
| 13. | * **Neil Walker, c** | Pirates (1) | 11 | $1,950,000 |
| 14. | **Bill Bray, lhp** | Expos (1) | 13 | $1,750,000 |
| 15. | **David Purcey, lhp** | Blue Jays (1) | 16 | $1,600,000 |
| 16. | * **Scott Elbert, lhp** | Dodgers (1) | 17 | $1,575,000 |
| | * Mike Rozier, lhp | Red Sox (12) | 365 | $1,575,000 |
| 18. | **Josh Fields, 3b** | White Sox (1) | 18 | $1,550,000 |
| 19. | **Chris Lambert, rhp** | Cardinals (1) | 19 | $1,525,000 |
| 20. | * **Trevor Plouffe, ss** | Twins (1) | 20 | $1,500,000 |
| 21. | * **Greg Golson, of** | Phillies (1) | 21 | $1,475,000 |
| 22. | **Glen Perkins, lhp** | Twins (1) | 22 | $1,425,000 |
| | **Mark Trumbo, rhp/3b** | Angels (18) | 533 | $1,425,000 |
| 24. | * **Billy Butler, 3b** | Royals (1) | 14 | $1,400,000 |
| | * **Philip Hughes, rhp** | Yankees (1) | 23 | $1,400,000 |

*Major leaguers in bold. *High school selection. #Major league contract.*

home runs, 56 RBIs and 12 stolen bases. J.D. was even better seven years earlier, hitting .455 with 31 home runs, 100 RBIs and 32 stolen bases.

### NEGOTIATIONS DRAG ON INTO 2005

Both the Angels and Diamondbacks realized quickly that neither Weaver nor Drew would sign quickly. The Angels hadn't moved beyond the preliminary stages of negotiations with Weaver as of late October. Talks between the Diamondbacks and Drew briefly heated up in late August.

Drew enrolled for his senior year at Florida State and was set to attend his first class on Aug. 31 before changing his mind and withdrawing. The Diamondbacks offered him a four-year big league contract, including a bonus of more than $3 million and the potential to make more than $7 million. But the Drew camp claimed the Diamondbacks had agreed when they drafted him that he was worth $8 million-$10 million, which the team denied.

Further complicating matters was Arizona's front-office shakeup, with former agent Jeff Moorad replacing Jerry Colangelo as the club's chief executive. Baseball sources said the Diamondbacks were wary of exceeding MLB's recommendation for Drew's bonus because they feared drawing the wrath of other owners, who had to approve Moorad's appointment. Approval already was less than certain because owners were leery of a former agent taking over a club, especially one who had angered some teams and had conflicts with other agents, including a bitter rivalry with Boras.

With negotiations still at a stalemate in the weeks before the 2005 draft, both Drew and Weaver joined the Camden Riversharks of the independent Atlantic League. Drew was leading the league in batting (.427), on-base percentage (.484) and slugging percentage (.744) when he agreed to terms with the Diamondbacks. Weaver never appeared in a game with the Riversharks.

Both players signed minutes before the May 31 midnight deadline, ending the longest holdouts in draft history. Weaver accepted a $4 million bonus from the Angels instead of the club's offer of a major league contract with an overall value of $5.25 million. Drew signed a five-year major league contract that included a $4 million bonus and guaranteed him $5.5 million. He also stood to make another $2 million in easily attainable incentives. The $4 million bonuses were the largest for players in the 2004 draft.

Weaver proved to be a solid, dependable starter over 10 seasons with the Angels, twice leading the American League in wins. He had 138 career victories entering the 2016 season. Only Verlander had a better career among pitchers drafted in 2004.

Drew's 10-year major league odyssey got on solid footing in his first five years, but his production tailed off over the next five as he bounced among clubs and morphed into a utility role. Overall, he had a .251 average and 114 homers entering the 2016 season.

Drew and Weaver were not the only high-profile players in the 2004 draft who were in no hurry to sign. Joining them were Verlander and three pitchers from Rice: Niemann, Philip Humber and Wade Townsend.

CLIFF WELCH

Stephen Drew

Humber was selected with the third overall pick by the New York Mets. Niemann went fourth to the Tampa Bay Devil Rays, and Townsend went eighth to the Baltimore Orioles. They went a combined 31-7, 2.28 with 396 strikeouts in 315 innings for a Rice team that faltered down the stretch and failed to reach the College World Series after going 39-5, 2.39 with 458 strikeouts in 384 innings a year earlier for a team that won the CWS.

With the exception of Townsend, who broke off talks with the Orioles in late August and returned to Rice for his senior year, every other unsigned first-rounder kept his options open by not returning to college.

Unlike Drew and Weaver, who wanted deals in line with some of the biggest contracts ever signed by draft choices and were destined to be the last to reach agreements, Verlander, Humber and Niemann seemed to be waiting for others to sign first and establish a market value.

### MAJOR LEAGUE DEALS MULTIPLY

The dominoes began to fall on the largest group of holdouts in draft history when the Tigers signed Verlander on Oct. 25 for a bonus of $3.15 million, the same figure Bush had agreed to with the Padres almost five months earlier. The Tigers agreed to sweeten the pot to a guaranteed $4.5 million by incorporating Verlander's bonus into a five-year

### WORTH NOTING

■ Rice University righthanders **PHILIP HUMBER**, **JEFF NIEMANN** and **WADE TOWNSEND** were among the first eight picks in the draft, making them the highest-drafted trio of teammates ever. The University of Michigan (Rick Leach, Steve Howe and Steve Perry in 1979) and Fresno State (Steve Hosey, Eddie Zosky and Tom Goodwin in 1989) had been the only other schools to produce three first-rounders in the same draft. The University of Miami did it in 2008 and Vanderbilt in 2015. None of the Rice pitchers found sustained success in the major leagues, though Humber did pitch a perfect game in 2012. Townsend actually might have gone on to the most notable career, as a professional poker player.

■ Third baseman **BILLY BUTLER** (No. 14, Royals) and righthander **ERIC HURLEY** (No. 30, Rangers) of Wolfson High in Jacksonville, Fla., became the fifth pair of high school teammates to go in the first round of the same draft. Mike Ondina and Jerry Manuel of Cordova High in Rancho Cordova, Calif., were first-rounders in 1972. Next came Michael Cuddyer and John Curtice from Great Bridge High of Chesapeake, Va., in 1997, followed by Matt Wheatland and Scott Heard from San Diego's Rancho Bernardo High in 2000, and Clint Everts and Scott Kazmir from Houston's Cypress Falls High in 2002.

■ With 12 selections, the Puerto Rico Baseball Academy established a draft record for most players picked from one high school team. The school tied its record in 2007.

■ With approval from the union, baseball's owners moved to revamp the order of selection in the draft rotation, beginning in 2005. American and National League clubs no longer would alternate taking the first pick and each subse-

CONTINUED ON PAGE 586

## WORTH NOTING

CONTINUED FROM PAGE 585

quent pick, as had been the custom since the draft's outset. The draft order would be determined by the reverse order of each team's won-lost record the previous season, regardless of leaguee.

■ The Major League Scouting Bureau gave its two highest predraft grades, both 70 (on the 20-80 scouting scale), to Old Dominion righthander **JUSTIN VERLANDER**, who went second overall to the Tigers, and Texas prep righthander **HOMER BAILEY**, who went seventh overall to the Reds. Next was Maine high school righthander **MARK ROGERS** with a 65. Rogers was the fifth overall pick to the Brewers.

■ Righthander **MATT HARRINGTON** was drafted for a fifth and final time in 2004, by the Yankees in the 36th round. The top talent of the 2000 draft who turned down a seven-figure offer from the Rockies, Harrington was drafted in each successive year but never pitched in Organized Baseball. He was pitching for Fort Worth of the independent Central League in 2004, but after he suffered a rotator cuff injury and underwent surgery, the Yankees made no attempt to sign him.

■ The antithesis to Moneyball in the 2004 draft might have been Princeton University outfielder **B.J. SZYMANSKI**, drafted in the second round by the Reds. The 6-foot-5, 205-pound Szymanski focused on football as a college freshman. He didn't play baseball until his sophomore year, and emerged as a top prospect in 2004 for his combination of power and speed. "He's as good an athlete as there is in college baseball," said an American League cross-checker. "He's a potential five-tool guy, a switch-hitter with power from both sides." Szymanski signed with the Reds for a $725,000 bonus and played in their farm system for five seasons, hitting .240 with 53 homers.

major league contract, the first of four given to 2004 draft picks. Humber, Niemann and Drew also signed big league deals.

Negotiations between Verlander and the Tigers appeared to end in mid-October, when the Tigers notified Verlander's agent, Mike Milchin of SFX, that they were withdrawing their offer. But Verlander's father, Richard, a former union representative with the Communications Workers of America, played a key role in getting talks restarted that led to a contract resolution. He called Tigers scouting director Greg Smith, and they reached an agreement.

The 6-foot-4, 190-pound Verlander, undrafted out of a Virginia high school three years earlier, became Old Dominion's No. 1 starter as a freshman and went 7-6 in each of his three seasons with the Monarchs. By his junior year, Verlander had developed the best fastball in the draft, a pitch that peaked at 99 mph with hard sinking and running action, and his secondary pitches also were of first-round quality. He struck out 151 and walked 43 in 106 innings during his junior season.

"As we narrowed our focus, we kept coming back to Justin and what he brings to the mound and his makeup," Smith said. "He'll pitch anywhere from 92 to 98 mph with good life on his fastball. His breaking ball is a strikeout pitch and he has a good changeup. Some of the criticism he received for a lack of consistency was overblown."

Verlander dominated as a first-year pro, going 11-2, 1.29 with 26 walks and 136 strikeouts in 119 innings in high Class A and Double-A. He was in Detroit by the end of the 2005 season, and over the next 10 seasons dominated like few other big league pitchers, going 155-97, 3.52 with 1,921 strikeouts in 2,092 innings.

The Mets struck a deal with Humber on Jan. 11, 2005, a five-year, major league contract that included a $3 million bonus and guaranteed him $4.2 million. Humber's agent, Michael Moye, was motivated to sign because of a change in the federal tax law that made signing bonuses subject to Medicare and Social Security taxes, effective Jan. 12.

ANDREW WOOLLEY

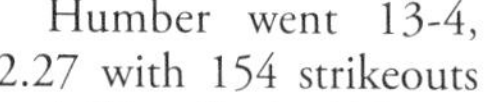

Philip Humber

Humber went 13-4, 2.27 with 154 strikeouts and 37 walks in 115 innings in his junior season at Rice. He began his pro career in the high Class A Florida State League in 2005, and had Tommy John surgery later that year. With the exception of the perfect game he pitched for the Chicago White Sox in 2012, Humber had an undistinguished big-league career, going 16-23, 5.31 in eight seasons.

The Devil Rays signed Niemann on Jan. 20, giving him a $3.2 million bonus and $5.2 million in guarantees. The 6-foot-9, 290-pound Niemann had been pegged as a top prospect for the 2004 draft after coming off a dominant sophomore season at Rice, when he went 17-0, 1.70, throwing a fastball that routinely touched 97-98 mph and

### Largest Bonuses By Round

| | Player, Pos. | Club | Bonus |
|---|---|---|---|
| **1.** | **Jered Weaver, rhp** | **Angels** | **$4,000,000** |
| | **Stephen Drew, ss** | **Diamondbacks** | **$4,000,000** |
| **1-S.** | **Zach Jackson, lhp** | **Blue Jays** | **$1,017,500** |
| 2. | Grant Johnson, rhp | Cubs | $1,260,000 |
| **3.** | ***Matt Tuiasosopo, ss** | **Mariners** | **$2,290,000** |
| 4. | *Chuck Lofgren, lhp | Indians | $650,000 |
| 5. | Andrew Kown, rhp | Tigers | $224,500 |
| 6. | Several tied at | | $160,000 |
| 7. | *Phillippe Valliquette, lhp | Reds | $300,000 |
| 8. | Kyle Bono, rhp | Red Sox | $432,000 |
| **9.** | ***Troy Patton, lhp** | **Astros** | **$550,000** |
| 10. | *Matt Walker, rhp | Devil Rays | $500,000 |
| **11.** | ***#Michael Saunders, 3b** | **Mariners** | **$237,500** |
| 12. | *Mike Rozier, lhp | Red Sox | $1,575,000 |
| 13. | *Kyle Rogers, rhp | Rangers | $210,000 |
| **14.** | ***Dexter Fowler, of** | **Rockies** | **$925,000** |
| 15. | *Brandon Verley, of | Marlins | $200,000 |
| 16. | *Alexandre Periard, rhp | Brewers | $243,000 |
| 17. | *Jon Mark Owings, of | Braves | $160,000 |
| **18.** | ***Mark Trumbo, rhp/3b** | **Angels** | **$1,425,000** |
| 19. | *#Brad Clapp, rhp | Pirates | $350,000 |
| 20. | *Edwin Roman, of | Diamondbacks | $100,000 |
| | **J.R. Towles, c** | **Astros** | **$100,000** |
| 21. | *#Carlton Smith, rhp | Indians | $375,000 |
| 22. | Joe Wice, lhp | Blue Jays | $100,000 |
| **23.** | ***#Zach Phillips, lhp** | **Rangers** | **$160,000** |
| **24.** | **#Jesse Litsch, rhp** | **Blue Jays** | **$138,000** |
| 25. | Michael Jones, of | Red Sox | $30,000 |
| Other | #Stephen Marek, rhp | Angels (40) | $800,000 |

*Major leaguers in bold. *High school selection. #Signed as draft-and-follow.*

an 87 mph slider that was rated the best breaking pitch in the college ranks. Niemann had minor elbow surgery prior to his junior season and sustained a groin injury in April that sidelined him for almost a month. As a result, his velocity fell off and cost him on some teams' draft boards, but the Rays believed he was healthy when they drafted him with the fourth pick.

ANDREW WOOLLEY

Jeff Niemann

Niemann's first two pro seasons were interrupted by shoulder injuries, delaying his major league debut until 2008. He pitched injury-free seasons for Tampa Bay in 2009 and 2010, winning 27 games, but later had a recurrence of his shoulder problems. His career ended in 2013.

Though Niemann won just 40 games as a big leaguer, he proved to be the most successful of Rice's vaunted trio of starting pitchers. Townsend's career was a major disappointment.

Orioles scouting director Tony DeMacio wanted to draft Georgia high school shortstop Chris Nelson instead of Townsend with the eighth pick. But Orioles owner Peter Angelos intervened, insisting on a college pitcher who would sign for an amount below MLB's recommended bonus for the No. 8 slot, about $2.2 million.

The Orioles offered Townsend $1.85 million and never moved off that number. Townsend not only declined the offer, but also ranted against Orioles executive vice president Jim Beattie. Unlike his fellow draft holdouts, Townsend returned to college. He no longer was eligible to sign with the Orioles and would go into the 2005 draft pool, per major league rules, but Townsend attempted to buck the system, denouncing his final season of eligibility by declaring that he had an agent.

Townsend and his agent, Casey Close, argued that he should be able to continue negotiating with the Orioles because he no longer had college eligibility. MLB, however, didn't agree, leaving Townsend on the sideline until the 2005 draft. He was drafted eighth overall again, by the Devil Rays, and signed quickly for a bonus of $1.5 million, $350,000 less than what he turned down from the Orioles a year earlier.

Townsend struggled to regain the above-average stuff he flashed during his sophomore and junior seasons at Rice, when he went 23-2, 2.00 with 312 strikeouts in 239 innings. He went 0-4, 5.49 in short-season Class A before having Tommy John surgery that caused him to miss the 2006 season. Townsend had a career 7-21, 5.59 record when the Rays released him in 2009. He pitched briefly in Mexico and moved there permanently. Townsend didn't make it to the baseball big leagues, but he did become a world-class poker player, competing annually in the World Series of Poker.

### BONUSES TAKE SHARP UPTURN

Major League Baseball's efforts to keep signing bonuses in check worked well in 2003, when first-rounders averaged $1,765,667, the lowest figure since 1998 and a significant drop from the previous year. MLB anticipated maintaining the status quo in 2004, and the first 24 first-rounders that signed received an average of $1.645 million. But once Weaver, Drew and three others signed, the first-round average was $1,958,448, a 10.9 percent spike from the previous year.

The Angels spent $8,116,500, a significant uptick from the highest total in 2003, when the Milwaukee Brewers committed $6,514,600. The Angels' outlay fell short of the mark of $9,165,500 that the Oakland A's spent in 2002. The Twins, with five selections before the start of the second round, spent $6.863 million, followed by the Rangers ($6.788 million), Diamondbacks ($6.563 million) and Athletics ($6.359 million).

It was no secret that Moreno, the new Angels owner, had deep pockets and was willing to dig deep in order to upgrade his club. Weaver's $4 million bonus ate up a big chunk of the Angels' allotment. The team didn't have second- and third-round picks, and failed to sign fourth-rounder Patrick White, a two-sport star from the Alabama high school ranks, who opted for college football at West Virginia.

With money in their budget, the Angels made several late-round gambles, signing 18th-rounder Mark Trumbo for $1.425 million, 40th-rounder Stephen Marek for $800,000 and 14th-rounder Nick Adenhart for $710,000.

It was widely known that Trumbo, a Villa Park (Calif.) infielder/pitcher with first-round credentials, wanted a seven-figure bonus to give up a baseball scholarship from USC. Adenhart, a righthanded pitcher, was regarded as first-round material until he suffered an elbow injury during an early season game at Williamsport (Md.) High. Marek, also a righthanded pitcher, was a draft-and-follow who improved significantly during his 2005 sophomore season at San Jacinto (Texas) JC.

LARRY GOREN

Mark Trumbo

Trumbo was highly rated as a pitcher, but the Angels saw a potential power hitter in the 6-foot-5, 225-pound player, and trained him initially as a third baseman.

Taking batting practice on Aug. 13, with Anaheim general manager Bill Stoneman, manager Mike Scioscia and batting coach Mickey Hatcher watching, Trumbo hit two balls off the rocks in deep left-center field at Angel Stadium. He signed a day later, and soon the Angels had a power hitter. He hit 95 homers for them from 2011-2013 before being traded to the Diamondbacks.

Marek was selected the most outstanding pitcher at the 2004 Junior College World Series as a freshman at San Jacinto. His velocity reached 94-96 mph and topped out at 98 the following spring. He likely would have been a second- or third-round pick in 2005 had the Angels not signed him for a bonus that was more than double the amount paid to the next highest 2004 draft-and-follow. Marek pitched for eight seasons without getting to the major leagues.

At least seven bonus records were set in individual rounds in 2004, including the amounts the Angels gave to Trumbo and Marek in the 18th and 40th rounds, respectively. Mike Rozier also got a

## One Team's Draft: Colorado Rockies

| Player, Pos. | Bonus | Player, Pos. | Bonus | Player, Pos. | Bonus |
|---|---|---|---|---|---|
| **1. *Chris Nelson, ss** | **$2,150,000** | **10. Jarrett Grube, rhp** | **$7,500** | **19. Josh Newman, lhp** | **$1,000** |
| **2. Seth Smith, of** | **$690,000** | 11. Chris Buechner, rhp | $50,000 | 20. *Rene Garcia, rhp | Did not sign |
| **3. Steven Register, rhp** | **$450,000** | **12. David Patton, rhp** | **$30,000** | 21. Matt Prendergast, rhp | $1,000 |
| **4. Chris Iannetta, c** | **$305,000** | 13. Matt Miller, of | $30,000 | 22. Stephen Edsall, rhp | $1,000 |
| **5. Matt Macri, 3b** | **$205,000** | **14. *Dexter Fowler, of** | **$925,000** | 23. Jason Metzger, lhp | $1,000 |
| **6. Joe Koshansky, 1b** | **$40,000** | 15. Justin Nelson, of | $35,000 | 24. Rob Hosgood, of | $1,000 |
| 7. Jake Postlewait, lhp | $30,000 | 16. Pat Stanley, rhp | $15,000 | 25. *Aaron Lovett, rhp | Did not sign |
| **8. Jim Miller, rhp** | **$12,000** | 17. *Dominick Foster, rhp | Did not sign | **Other *Xavier Cedeno (31), lhp** | **$245,000** |
| 9. Dustin Hahn, 3b | $70,000 | 18. Jeff Dragicevich, ss | $1,000 | | |

*Major leaguers in bold. *High school selection.*

## WORTH NOTING

The most noteworthy two-sport athlete in the 2004 draft was Oklahoma State third baseman **JOSH FIELDS**, who was selected 18th overall by the White Sox after hitting .364 with 25 homers in three college seasons. Over the same period, the 6-foot-2, 210-pound Fields passed for a school record 55 touchdowns. He gave up football as part of his $1.55 million deal with the White Sox. Fields homered in his first major league at-bat in 2007, but never established himself as a consistent hitter, batting .234 with 34 home runs and 107 RBIs in five seasons.

A record-low three players went unsigned in the first five rounds of the 2004 draft, and only 14 of the 311 players in the first 10 rounds didn't agree to terms, tying a mark set in 2003. Every high school player in the first three rounds signed, which never had happened.

San Diego had the top pick in the draft for a fifth time, tying the Mets for the most in draft history. The Padres also selected first in 1970 (Mike Ivie), 1972 (Dave Roberts), 1974 (Bill Almon) and 1988 (Andy Benes).

Cuba won the 2004 Olympic baseball competition, beating upstart Australia, 6-2, in the gold-medal game at Athens, Greece, for its third gold medal in four Olympics. The United States failed to qualify for the eight-nation tournament after getting upset by Mexico, 2-1, in the quarterfinals of the Americas qualifying tournament in November 2003.

Georgia prep outfielder **DEXTER FOWLER** probably would not have been signed by the Rockies had they not traded major leaguer Larry Walker to the Cardinals on Aug. 6. Colorado saved $9.25 million by trading him, and signed Fowler 11 days later for $925,000. Fowler was a premium talent, but a Miami commitment clouded his signability, and he fell to the 14th round.

**IN FOCUS: NICK ADENHART**

MORRIS FOSTOFF

Nick Adenhart opened the 2004 season as one of the nation's top high school pitching prospects. He did nothing to hurt his stock by tossing a perfect game with 15 strikeouts in his first outing, but then injured his elbow and required Tommy John surgery. Undeterred, the Angels took a 14th-round flier on the 6-foot-3, 185-pound righthander in the hopes that he still might sign rather than attend college at North Carolina.

"It's a gamble, but he would have gone in the top eight in the country," Angels scouting director Eddie Bane said. "One of the things we were able to sell him on is that we do a better job rehabbing guys than any college does. We're just really excited. We preach thinking outside the box, and it doesn't get much further outside the box than this."

Adenhart signed with the Angels on July 28 and rehabbed for the next year. He made his first appearance as a pro late in the 2005 season. He quickly regained his old form and progressed to the big leagues, making his debut in 2008. Within hours of making his first 2009 start with the Angels, and pitching six scoreless innings in just his fourth major league game on April 8, Adenhart, 22, was killed in a hit-and-run accident in Fullerton, Calif. The car he was riding in was broadsided by a vehicle that ran a red light. Two other passengers were also killed.

## Highest Unsigned Picks

| Player, Pos., Team (Round) | College | Re-Drafted |
|---|---|---|
| Wade Townsend, rhp, Orioles (1) | None | Devil Rays '05 (1) |
| Patrick White, of, Angels (4) | West Virginia | Angels '07 (27) |
| Adrian Ortiz, of, Cubs (5) | Pepperdine | Royals '07 (5) |
| Chris Carpenter, rhp, Tigers (7) | Kent State | Yankees '07 (18) |
| Seth Johnston, 2b, Orioles (7) | * Texas | Padres '05 (5) |
| Buck Cody, lhp, Cardinals (7) | * Texas | Giants '05 (16) |
| Alex Garabedian, c, Yankees (7) | Miami | Dodgers '07 (8) |
| Neil Jamison, rhp, Mets (8) | * Long Beach State | Padres '05 (6) |
| Jimmy Shull, rhp, D-backs (8) | * Cal Poly | Athletics '05 (4) |
| Omar Aguilar, rhp, Giants (8) | Merced (Calif.) JC | Brewers '05 (30) |

**TOTAL UNSIGNED PICKS:** Top 5 Rounds (3), Top 10 Rounds (14)

**Returned to same school.*

record deal, signing with the Red Sox as a 12th rounder for a $1.575 million bonus.

For the third time in four years, the Red Sox had forfeited their first-round pick for signing a major league free agent, but they valued Rozier, a lefthander from Henry County High in Stockbridge, Ga., as first-round material. He threw an 88-92 mph fastball that touched 94 and a curveball that showed flashes of becoming a well above-average pitch.

Rozier might not have lasted past the third round had he not accepted a football scholarship from North Carolina. He agreed to give up football as part of his contract, and had a disappointing baseball career, going 16-24, 5.23 in four years in the Red Sox organization. He pitched in just one game above the Class A level.

Other records were set by Woodinville (Wash.) High shortstop Matt Tuiasosopo, who signed with the Seattle Mariners as a third-round pick for $2.29 million; University of Central Florida righthander Kyle Bono, an eighth-rounder who got $432,000 from the Red Sox; outfielder Dexter Fowler of Milton High in Alpharetta, Ga., who received $925,000 from the Rockies as a 14th-rounder; and University of Massachusetts catcher Frank Curreri, a 41st-round pick of the Diamondbacks, who signed for $200,000. Only Tuiasosopo and Fowler made it to the major leagues.

### EMPHASIS ON PITCHING

In contrast to 2003, when a record-tying 20 hitters were selected in the first round, the emphasis in 2004 was on pitching.

Nineteen pitchers went in the first round, one short of the record set in 1999 and equaled in 2001, including seven of the first eight selections. The emphasis on pitching followed a trend in which pitchers had accounted for 55.5 percent of the first-round picks since 1994, up from 38.9 percent for the first 25 years of the draft.

There also was an increased emphasis on older talent. More college players were selected (996) than in any other draft up to that point, and the 70 percent rate in the first 10 rounds was the highest ever. Not surprisingly, more college players than ever before (732) signed contracts.

The emphasis on more experienced players was an outgrowth of "Moneyball," the performance-based approach to scouting and development popularized by the Athletics. The Cardinals became the biggest practitioners of the approach in 2004, taking college or junior college players with their first 26 picks and 43 of their 47 selections. The A's and Blue Jays each drafted just five high school players.

No player seemed to embody "Moneyball" more than Pedroia, who had a superb three-year career at Arizona State, ranking among the school's all-time leaders in batting average (.384), hits (298), doubles (71) and on-base percentage (.466) when he left. Pedroia won over a legion of doubters who didn't believe he had the size or the tools to be an early-round pick, much less a successful big leaguer.

A classic overachiever in his unassuming 5-foot-8, 165-pound frame, Pedroia won over a legion of doubters at ASU, including coach Pat Murphy. "We learned that if we told this kid he couldn't do it, he was going to go ahead and show us that he could."

Dustin Pedroia

Without a first-round pick, the Red Sox were elated that Pedroia was still available when they drafted in the second round.

"When you've accomplished what he has and can do what he can do, you're not a performance player or a tools player—you're a special player," Red Sox general manager Theo Epstein said. "That's why we drafted him."

The A's didn't drift far from their usual approach, drafting South Carolina senior catcher Landon Powell with the first of their two first-round picks (24th overall) and Texas junior closer Huston Street with the second of their two supplemental first-round selections (40th overall).

Powell had tried unsuccessfully to circumvent the draft while a junior in high school by getting a GED and being declared a free agent after no team drafted him. He negated the decision, though, by going to college, when few teams showed interest. He signed quickly with the A's four years later for a $1 million bonus, and reached the major leagues for a brief period. Street became the first player from the class of 2004 to reach the majors. He had 315 saves entering the 2016 season.

## Largest Draft-And-Follow Bonuses

| | Player, Pos. | Club (Round) | Bonus |
|---|---|---|---|
| 1. | Stephen Marek, rhp | Angels (40) | $800,000 |
| 2. | *Carlton Smith, rhp | Indians (21) | $375,000 |
| 3. | *Brad Clapp, rhp | Pirates (19) | $350,000 |
| **4.** | ***Xavier Cedeno, lhp** | **Rockies (31)** | **$245,000** |
| **5.** | ***Michael Saunders, 3b** | **Mariners (11)** | **$237,500** |
| 6. | Brett Zamzow, rhp | Rangers (28) | $200,000 |
| | Eddy Baeza, rhp | Diamondbacks (47) | $200,000 |
| **8.** | ***Darren Ford, of** | **Brewers (18)** | **$160,000** |
| | ***Zach Phillips, lhp** | **Rangers (23)** | **$160,000** |
| **10.** | **Todd Redmond, rhp** | **Pirates (39)** | **$145,000** |

*Major leaguers in bold. *High school selection.*

# 2004 Draft List

**Did not sign. Major leaguers in bold, with first and last years noted. Order of selection indicated in parentheses. For the first five rounds, the peak level of each player is noted. + Signed as draft-and-follow (Second school noted if applicable).*

## ARIZONA DIAMONDBACKS (15)

1. **Stephen Drew, ss, Florida State University.—(2006-15)**
DRAFT DROP *Brother of J.D. Drew, first-round draft pick, Phillies (1997); first-round draft pick, Cardinals (1998); major leaguer (1998-2006) • Brother of Tim Drew, first-round draft pick, Indians (1997); major leaguer (2000-04)*
2. Jon Zeringue, of, Louisiana State University.—(AA)
3. **Garrett Mock, rhp, University of Houston.—(2008-10)**
4. **Ross Ohlendorf, rhp, Princeton University.—(2007-15)**
5. Cesar Nicolas, 1b, Vanderbilt University.—(AAA)
6. Brandon Burgess, of, Sonoma State (Calif.) University.
7. Koley Kolberg, rhp, University of Arizona.
8. *Jimmy Shull, rhp, Cal Poly San Luis Obispo.
9. A.J. Shappi, rhp, UC Riverside.
10. **Steven Jackson, rhp, Clemson University.—(2009-10)**
11. Darryl Lawhorn, of, East Carolina University.
DRAFT DROP *Twin brother of Trevor Lawhorn, ninth-round draft pick, Reds (2004)*
12. Richard Mercado, c, University of Arizona.
13. ***Antoan Richardson, of, Vanderbilt University.—(2011-14)**
14. Lester Contreras, ss, St. Petersburg (Fla.) JC.
15. Dan Pohlman, c, Northwestern University.
16. **Mark Reynolds, ss, University of Virginia.—(2007-15)**
17. **Chris Carter, 1b, Stanford University.—(2008-10)**
18. Vince Davis, lhp, Southern University.
19. Derek Bruce, ss, Lewis-Clark State (Idaho) College.
20. Edwin Roman, of, Princeton (Ind.) Community HS.
21. Chris Thompson, rhp, University of Mississippi.
22. Luis Lajara, of, Santo Domingo, D.R.
23. Travis Gulick, of, Michigan State University.
24. Trey Hendricks, 1b, Harvard University.
25. Todd Stein, lhp, Illinois State University.
26. Eric Schindewolf, 2b, Texas A&M University.
27. Garrett Bauer, lhp, Missouri Baptist College.
28. Ramon Downing, 2b, Wabash Valley (Ill.) CC.
29. *Chris Bowen, lhp, University of Maryland.
30. Kevin Williams, of, University of South Alabama.
31. Marcus Townsend, of, Southern University.
32. Josh Buhagier, of, Long Beach State University.
33. *Joseph Campbell, 3b, Fremd HS, Palatine, Ill.
34. ***David Hernandez, rhp, Cosumnes River (Calif.) JC.—(2009-15)**
35. +Jo Jo Batten, 2b, Middle Georgia JC.
36. *Craig Heyer, rhp, Coronado HS, Scottsdale, Ariz.
37. Billy Lockin, ss, Loyola Marymount University.
38. +Lorenzo Church, rhp, Misison Bay HS, San Diego / Central Arizona JC.
39. *Michael Jarman, lhp, Edmond North HS, Edmond, Okla.
40. *Ulrich Snijders, c, Trinity Christian Academy, West Palm Beach, Fla.
41. Frank Curreri, c, University of Massachusetts.
42. *Brandon Pullen, lhp, Idaho Falls (Idaho) HS.
43. *Brandon White, 3b, Surry (N.C.) CC.
44. Adam Howard, rhp, Walters State (Tenn.) CC.
45. *Ryan McKibben, rhp, Aliso Niguel HS, Aliso Viejo, Calif.
46. *Ryan Castellanos, 3b, CC of Southern Nevada.
47. +Eddy Baeza, rhp, Mission (Calif.) JC / Los Angeles Valley JC.
48. *Ryan Mooradian, lhp, Essex (Md.) CC.
49. *Carlos Soto, of, Wabash Valley (Ill.) JC.
50. +Kyler Newby, rhp, Mesa (Ariz.) CC.

## ATLANTA BRAVES (30)

1. (Choice to Rangers as compensation for Type B free agent John Thomson)
2. Eric Campbell, 3b, Gibson Southern HS, Owensville, Ind.—(AA)
3. J.C. Holt, 2b, Louisiana State University.—(AAA)
4. **James Parr, rhp, La Cueva HS, Albuquerque, N.M.—(2008-09)**
5. Van Pope, 3b, Meridian (Miss.) CC.—(AAA)
6. **Clint Sammons, c, University of Georgia.—(2007-09)**
7. Trae Wiggins, lhp, Brewton Parker (Ga.) College.
8. Derrick Arnold, ss, Tallahassee (Fla.) CC.
9. Jeff Katz, rhp, Cheshire (Conn.) HS.
10. Brady Endl, lhp, University of Wisconsin-Whitewater.
11. Wes Letson, lhp, Birmingham-Southern College.
12. Jeff Long, rhp, Gardner-Webb University.
13. Todd Blackford, rhp, Triton HS, Bourbon, Ind.
14. Mike Rozema, ss, St. John's University.
15. Jason Paul, rhp, Southern New Hampshire University.
16. Zach Schreiber, rhp, Duke University.
17. Jon Mark Owings, of, Gainesville (Ga.) HS.
DRAFT DROP *Brother of Micah Owings, 19th-round draft pick, Cubs (2004); major leaguer (2007-12)*
18. ***Brad Emaus, ss, East Coweta HS, Sharpsburg, Ga.—(2011)**
19. Scott Brazeale, ss, Berkeley HS, Moncks Corner, S.C.
20. *Christian Marrero, of, Monsignor Pace HS, Miami.
21. Tyler Wilson, lhp, Andalusia (Ala.) HS.
22. Troy Harp, c, Middle Tennessee State University.
23. *Austin Hyatt, rhp, Marietta (Ga.) HS.
24. *Josh Flores, of, Lincoln-Way Central HS, New Lenox, Ill.
25. *Judson Norton, rhp, Manatee (Fla.) CC.
26. Adam Parliament, of, El Paso (Texas) CC.
27. ***Tyler Flowers, c-1b, Blessed Trinity HS, Marietta, Ga.—(2009-15)**
28. *Joey Lieberman, 1b, Meridian (Miss.) CC.
29. +Trevion Griffin, of, Lurleen B. Wallace (Ala.) JC.
30. *Kurt Houck, rhp, Boyertown (Pa.) HS.
31. +Jamie Richmond, rhp, Cawthraw SS, Mississauga, Ontario / Texarkana (Texas) JC.
32. *Clay Caulfield, rhp, Lawrence Park Collegiate HS, Toronto.
33. *Brian Murphy, rhp, Torrey Pines HS, San Diego.
34. *Luis Sanchez, ss, Puerto Rico Baseball Academy, Caguas, P.R.
35. *Shawn Lee, c, Gosnell (Ark.) HS.
36. +Phillip Britton, c, Olney Central (Ill.) JC.
37. +Joshua Ward, rhp, Seminole HS, Donalsonville, Ga. / Chipola (Fla.) JC.
38. *Ryan Horton, lhp, Bishop Moore HS, Orlando, Fla.
39. ***Sean Doolittle, lhp-1b, Shawnee HS, Medford, N.J.—(2012-15)**
DRAFT DROP *First-round draft pick (41st overall), Athletics (2007)*
40. *Jared Shaffer, ss, Kiski Area HS, Vandergrift, Pa.
41. *Steven Creswell, lhp, Rim of the World HS, Crestline, Calif.
42. ***Eric Farris, ss, Hamilton HS, Chandler, Ariz.—(2011-12)**
43. *Adam Myers, rhp, Herbert Hoover HS, Clendenin, W.Va.
44. *Daniel Rios, 1b, JC of the Sequoias (Calif.).
45. +Jesse Warren, lhp, Western Alamance HS, Elon College, N.C. / Rockingham (N.C.) CC.
46. +Marcus Covington, rhp, Louisburg (N.C.) JC.
47. *Kevin Camacho, rhp, Santa Fe Springs (Calif.) HS.
48. *Eric Evans, lhp, UMS Wright HS, Mobile, Ala.
49. *William Tanner, rhp, White Knoll HS, Lexington, S.C.
50. *Eric Gonzalez, rhp, Cochise County (Ariz.) CC.

## BALTIMORE ORIOLES (8)

1. *Wade Townsend, rhp, Rice University.—(AA)
DRAFT DROP *No school; re-drafted by Devil Rays, 2005 (1st round)*
2. (Choice to Athletics as compensation for Type A free agent Miguel Tejada)
3. **Jeff Fiorentino, 1b-of, Florida Atlantic University.—(2005-09)**
4. **Brad Bergesen, rhp, Foothill HS, Pleasanton, Calif.—(2009-12)**
5. C.J. Smith, of, University of Florida.—(Low A)
6. Bryce Chamberlin, rhp, Washington State University.
7. *Seth Johnston, 2b, University of Texas.
8. David Haehnel, lhp, University of Illinois-Chicago.
9. Joey Howell, of, Santaluces HS, West Palm Beach, Fla.
10. Drew Moffitt, of, Wichita State University.
11. **Kevin Hart, rhp-1b, University of Maryland.—(2007-09)**
12. Dan Puente, c, Bradley University.
13. Denver Kitch, ss, Oklahoma City University.
14. Kyle Schmidt, rhp, University of South Florida.
15. ***Will Venable, of, Princeton University.—(2008-15)**
DRAFT DROP *Son of Max Venable, major leaguer (1979-91)*
16. Andy Schindling, rhp, St. John's Collegiate HS, Bowie, Md.
17. Kyle Boehm, rhp, Oakland University.
18. Trent Baysinger, lhp, University of Washington.
19. *Matt McGuirk, of, Arlington Heights HS, Fort Worth, Texas.
20. Jonathan Tucker, 2b, University of Florida.
21. Ryan Finan, 1b, Lamar University.
22. Rob Marconi, 3b, Northern Illinois University.
23. Ryan Schwabe, lhp, University of Louisiana-Monroe.
24. *Dale Mollenhauer, ss, Pine Richland HS, Gibsonia, Pa.
25. Zach Minor, lhp, Northern Illinois University.
26. Kevin Kotch, c, Cecil (Md.) CC.
27. Cody Wargo, c, Indiana University.
28. *Alex Graham, rhp, University of the Pacific.
29. *Marc Young, lhp, Riverside HS, Greer, S.C.
30. ***Jaime Garcia, lhp, Sharyland (Texas) HS.—(2008-15)**
31. *Matthew Garnett, lhp, Bakersfield (Calif.) JC.
32. *Jeff Jeffords, rhp, Spartanburg Methodist (S.C.) JC.
33. *Jared Elmore, rhp, Raymond (Miss.) HS.
34. *Nick Burns, c, Palomar (Calif.) CC.
35. *Andrew Crisp, ss, Riverside HS, Greer, S.C.
DRAFT DROP *Twin brother of Adam Crisp, 38th-round draft pick, Orioles (2004)*
36. *Derik Drewett, rhp, University of Arkansas-Fort Smith JC.
37. *Ian Harrington, lhp, Bellevue (Wash.) CC.
38. *Adam Crisp, of, Riverside HS, Greer, S.C.
DRAFT DROP *Twin brother of Andrew Crisp, 35th-round draft pick, Orioles (2004)*
39. *Larry Hill, lhp, Smithson Valley HS, Spring Branch, Texas.
40. *Jason Roach, lhp, Sacramento (Calif.) CC.
41. *Demetrios Marinos, c, Steinert HS, Hamilton, N.J.
42. *Brian Blackburn, c, Kellogg (Mich.) CC.
43. *Bryan Casey, c, Kofa HS, Yuma, Ariz.
44. *Leonardo Calderon, lhp, Puerto Rico Baseball Academy, Loiza, P.R.
45. Samuel Basta, lhp, Marquette University HS, Milwaukee.
46. *Casey Larson, of, Paso Robles (Calif.) HS.
47. *Bailey Daniels, rhp, Manteo (N.C.) HS.
48. *Matt Lane, rhp, Iowa Western CC.
49. Clifton Turner, of, CC of Baltimore-Catonsville.
50. *Michael Banks, rhp, Lake Michigan JC.

## BOSTON RED SOX (24)

1. (Choice to Athletics as compensation for Type A free agent Keith Foulke)
2. **Dustin Pedroia, ss, Arizona State University.—(2006-15)**
3. Andrew Dobies, lhp, University of Virginia.—(AAA)
4. **Tommy Hottovy, lhp, Wichita State University.—(2011-12)**
5. Ryan Schroyer, rhp, San Diego State University.—(AAA)
6. **Cla Meredith, rhp, Virginia Commonwealth University.—(2005-10)**
DRAFT DROP *First player from 2004 draft to reach majors (May 8, 2005)*
7. Pat Perry, c, University of Northern Colorado.
8. Kyle Bono, rhp, University of Central Florida.
9. Matt Vanderbosch, of, Oral Roberts University.
10. ***Steve Pearce, 1b, University of South Carolina.—(2007-15)**
11. Ryan Phillips, lhp, Barton County (Kan.) CC.
12. Mike Rozier, lhp, Henry County HS, Stockbridge, Ga.
13. Matt Ciaramella, of, University of Utah.
14. **R.J. Swindle, rhp, Charleston Southern University.—(2008-09)**
15. Dustin Kelly, ss, Cuesta (Calif.) JC.
16. *Matt Clarkson, c, University of Arkansas-Fort Smith JC.
17. *Jeremy Haynes, of, Madison County HS, Madison, Fla.
18. Randy Beam, lhp, Florida Atlantic University.
19. Logan Sorensen, 1b, Wichita State University.
20. *Brian Van Kirk, c, Westminster Academy, Fort Lauderdale, Fla.
21. Chuck Jeroloman, ss, Auburn University.
22. Tim Burgess, 1b, Georgia State University.
23. Matt Goodson, rhp, University of Texas.
24. *Matt Spencer, 1b, Morristown West HS, Morristown, Tenn.
25. +Michael Jones, of, Arizona Western JC.
26. *Jake Renshaw, rhp, Ventura (Calif.) CC.
27. *Justin Phillabaum, rhp, Royal Palm Beach HS, West Palm Beach, Fla.
28. Michael James, rhp, University of Connecticut.
29. David Seccombe, rhp, University of Nevada-Las Vegas.
30. Drew Ehrlich, rhp, Stanford University.
31. *Brendan Winn, of, University of South Carolina.
32. *Brad Hertzler, lhp, East Providence (R.I.) HS.
33. John Wells, lhp, Timber Creek HS, Orlando, Fla.
34. Andrew Pinckney, 3b, Emory (Ga.) University.
35. *Bo Lanier, rhp, University of Georgia.
36. Cooper Eddy, rhp, University of New Mexico.
37. *Glenn Swanson, lhp, UC Irvine.
38. *Colby Summer, rhp, University of Hawaii.
39. *Zak Farkes, ss, Harvard University.
40. *Nick Francona, lhp, Lawrenceville HS, Yardley, Pa.
DRAFT DROP *Grandson of Tito Francona, major leaguer (1956-70) • Son of Terry Francona, first-round draft pick, Expos (1980); major leaguer (1981-90); major league manager (1997-2015)*
41. ***Steve Edlefsen, ss, Barton County (Kan.) CC.—(2011-12)**
42. *Kyle Peter, of, Archbishop O'Hara HS, Kansas City, Mo.
43. *Tyler Latham, rhp, Hewitt-Trussville HS, Trussville, Ala.
44. *Beau Mills, 3b, Golden West HS, Visalia, Calif.
DRAFT DROP *First-round draft pick (13th overall), Indians (2007) • Son of Brad Mills, major leaguer (1980-83); major league manager (2010-12)*
45. *Adam Campbell, 3b, University of British Columbia.
46. Tom Caple, of, University of San Diego.
47. Austin Easley, 1b, University of Florida.
48. *Felipe Garcia, c-1b, Cal State Fullerton.
49. *Blake Tillett, lhp, Brandon (Fla.) HS.
50. *Raudel Alfonso, rhp, Hialeah (Fla.) HS.

## CHICAGO CUBS (25)

1. (Choice to Twins as compensation for Type A free agent LaTroy Hawkins)
2. Grant Johnson, rhp, University of Notre Dame.—(AA)
3. Mark Reed, c, Bonita HS, La Verne, Calif.—(AAA)
DRAFT DROP *Brother of Jeremy Reed, major leaguer (2004-11)*
4. Chris Shaver, lhp, College of William & Mary.—(AAA)
5. *Adrian Ortiz, of, Puerto Rico Baseball Academy, Caguas, P.R.—(High A)
DRAFT DROP *Attended Pepperdine; re-drafted by Royals, 2007 (5th round)*
6. Tim Layden, lhp, Duke University.
7. **Mitch Atkins, rhp, Northeast Guilford HS, Browns Summit, N.C.—(2009-11)**
8. **Eric Patterson, 2b, Georgia Tech.—(2007-11)**
DRAFT DROP *Brother of Corey Patterson, first-round draft pick, Cubs (1998); major leaguer (2000-11)*
9. Ryan Norwood, 1b, East Carolina University.
10. **Sam Fuld, of, Stanford University.—(2007-15)**
11. Jonathan Hunton, rhp, Lamar University.
12. **Sean Gallagher, rhp, St. Thomas Aquinas HS, Fort Lauderdale, Fla.—(2007-10)**
13. *Ryan Moorer, rhp, Veterans Memorial HS, Peabody, Mass.

14. *Eli Iorg, of, University of Tennessee.
DRAFT DROP *First-round draft pick (38th overall), Astros (2005) • Son of Garth Iorg, major leaguer (1978-87) • Brother of Cale Iorg, 16th-round draft pick, Devil Rays (2004)*
15. Alfred Joseph, of, Moody HS, Corpus Christi, Texas.
16. J.R. Mathes, lhp, Western Michigan University.
**17. Jeremy Blevins, lhp, University of Dayton.—(2007-15)**
18. Jake Marsello, rhp, Boston College.
**19. *Micah Owings, rhp, Georgia Tech.—(2007-12)**
DRAFT DROP *Brother of Jon Mark Owings, 17th-round draft pick, Braves (2004)*
20. *Trey Taylor, lhp, Baylor University.
21. Will Fenton, rhp, University of Washington.
22. *Walter Diaz, ss, Braddock HS, Miami.
23. Chris Gaskin, 1b, Manhattan College.
24. +Jeff Culpepper, of, Gonzaga University.
25. *Casey Erickson, rhp, Glenwood HS, Chatham, Ill.
26. *Paul Cinder, rhp, Lake Mary HS, Longwood Fla.
27. Jason Kosow, rhp, Babson (N.H.) College.
28. Jon Douillard, c, Vanderbilt University.
29. Mike Svetlic, 2b, UCLA.
**30. Russ Canzler, 3b, Hazleton Area HS, Conyngham, Pa.—(2011-12)**
31. Jesse Estrada, rhp, Grayson County (Texas) JC.
32. *Cody Gilbert, 3b, Lincoln HS, Vincennes, Ind.
33. +Randy Brown, of, Jonesboro (Ga.) HS / North Florida CC.
34. *Dustin Bamberg, c, Winter Haven (Fla.) HS.
35. *Drew O'Connell, rhp, Barrington HS, South Barrington, Ill.
36. *Colby Wark, rhp, Redmond HS, Terrebonne, Ore.
37. *Michael Hyle, rhp, University of Georgia.
38. *Kurt Eichorn, of, Kent State University.
39. *Trent Luyster, lhp, Ohio State University.
40. *Marcus Crockett, of, St. Bernard HS, Inglewood, Calif.
41. *Kenn Kasparek, rhp, Weimar (Texas) HS.
42. Ryan Morgan, 3b, Boston College.
43. *Adam Daniels, lhp, Eastern Oklahoma State JC.
44. Zane Green, of, Clemson University.
45. *Christopher Dunkin, c, La Porte (Texas) HS.
46. *Greg Fudacz, lhp, Cle Elum-Roslyn HS, Cle Elum, Wash.
47. *Andrew Liebel, rhp, Damien HS, Pomona, Calif.
48. Olin Wick, c, University of Puget Sound.
49. *Brandon Harmon, rhp, Columbia Basin (Wash.) JC.
50. Gerald Miller, of, Prarie View A&M University.

## CHICAGO WHITE SOX (18)

**1. Josh Fields, 3b, Oklahoma State University.—(2006-10)**
1. Tyler Lumsden, lhp, Clemson University (Supplemental choice—34th—as compensation for Type A free agent Bartolo Colon).—(AAA)
**1. Gio Gonzalez, lhp, Monsignor Pace HS, Miami** (Supplemental choice—38th—as compensation for Type A free agent Tom Gordon).**—(2008-15)**
**2. Wes Whisler, lhp-1b, UCLA** (Choice from Angels as compensation for Colon).**—(2009)**
**2. Donny Lucy, c, Stanford University.—(2007-11)**
2. Ray Liotta, lhp, Gulf Coast (Fla.) CC (Choice from Yankees as compensation for Gordon).—(AAA)
3. Grant Hansen, rhp, Oklahoma City University.—(Low A)
**4. Lucas Harrell, rhp, Ozark (Mo.) HS.—(2010-14)**
**5. Brandon Allen, of, Montgomery (Texas) HS.—(2009-12)**
**6. Adam Russell, rhp, Ohio University.—(2008-11)**
7. Tim Murphey, lhp, Glascock County HS, Gibson, Ga.
8. Nick Lemon, rhp, Brigham Young University.
9. Ryan McCarthy, 3b, UCLA.
10. Adam Ricks, 2b, University of Miami.
11. Garry Bakker, rhp, University of North Carolina.
12. Daron Roberts, of, Cal State San Bernardino.
DRAFT DROP *Son of Dave Roberts, first overall draft pick, Padres (1972); major leaguer (1982-82)*
**13. Jack Egbert, rhp, Rutgers University.—(2009-12)**
14. Michael Swain, 3b, Wabash Valley (Ill.) JC.
**15. Carlos Torres, rhp, Kansas State University.—(2009-15)**
16. Fernando Alvarez, of, Florida International University.
17. *Jacob Wild, rhp, Bakersfield (Calif.) JC.
18. *Brett Scarpetta, rhp, Hononegah HS, Rockton, Ill.
19. Caleb Cooper, 3b, Cal State Hayward.
20. *Michael Dubee, rhp, Riverview HS, Sarasota, Fla.
21. *Brian Flores, lhp, Carlsbad (N.M.) HS.
22. *Matt Mansilla, ss, American Heritage HS, Pembroke, Fla.
23. Derek McNeil, ss, St. Leo (Fla.) College.
24. Josh Hansen, c, University of San Diego.
25. *Justin Sincock, rhp, Millikan HS, Long Beach, Calif.
26. *Danny Jordan, 3b, Gulliver Prep, Miami.
27. +Logan Williamson, lhp, Pensacola (Fla.) JC.
28. *Greg Young, of, Delaware Tech JC.
29. Frank Viola, rhp, Florida CC.
DRAFT DROP *Son of Frank Viola, major leaguer (1982-96)*
30. Mike Zaleski, rhp, Indiana State University.
31. +Nick Walters, lhp, Mountain Ridge HS, Glendale, Ariz. / Dixie State (Utah) JC.
32. *Eric Sheridan, rhp, Saddleback (Calif.) JC.
33. *Brandon Cooney, rhp, Broward (Fla.) CC.
34. Mario Suarez, 3b, Florida International University.
35. Evan Tartaglia, of, Elon University.
36. *Kenny Williams, of, Plainfield (Ill.) HS.
DRAFT DROP *Son of Kenny Williams, major leaguer (1986-91); general manager, White Sox (2000-12)*
37. *Robbie Grinestaff, c, Okaloosa-Walton (Fla.) CC.
38. *Shaun Spearman, ss, St. Pius X HS, Atlanta.
39. *James Leigh, lhp, Bryant (Ark.) HS.
40. Justin Roelle, lhp, Iowa Western CC.
41. *Matthew Rozier, rhp, Meridian (Miss.) CC.
42. *Michael Schower, lhp, Riverview HS, Sarasota, Fla.
43. *Ian Murray, rhp, Jefferson (Mo.) JC.
44. *Steven Muck, rhp, Covington Catholic HS, Park Hills, Ky.
45. *Jason Sullivan, rhp, Crowder (Mo.) JC.
46. *Jason Rodriquez, ss, Alta Loma HS, Rancho Cucamonga, Calif.
47. *Richard O'Brien, c, Little Rock, Ark.
48. Peter Vuckovich, c, Clarion (Pa.) University.
DRAFT DROP *Son of Pete Vuckovich, major leaguer (1975-86)*
49. Garrett Guest, 2b, St. Joseph's (Ind.) College.
50. *Bryan Wagner, rhp, Thunderbird HS, Phoenix.

## CINCINNATI REDS (7)

**1. Homer Bailey, rhp, La Grange (Texas) HS.—(2007-15)**
2. B.J. Szymanski, of, Princeton University.—(AAA)
**3. Craig Tatum, c, Mississippi State University.—(2009-11)**
4. Rafael Gonzalez, rhp, George Washington HS, Bronx, N.Y.—(High A)
**5. Paul Janish, ss, Rice University.—(2008-15)**
6. Lonny Roa, c, Puerto Rico Baseball Academy, San Juan, P.R.
7. Philippe Valiquette, lhp, Edouard Montpetit HS, St. Laurent, Quebec.
8. Greg Goetz, lhp, Bellevue (Wash.) CC.
9. Trevor Lawhorn, 2b, East Carolina University.
DRAFT DROP *Twin brother of Darryl Lawhorn, 11th-round draft pick, Diamondbacks (2004)*
10. Terrell Young, rhp, Grenada (Miss.) HS.
11. *Jason Urquidez, rhp, Arizona State University.
12. Cody Strait, of, University of Evansville.
13. Drew Anderson, 2b, Ohio State University.
14. Jared Sanders, rhp, Oregon State University.
15. J.D. Reininger, 3b, University of Texas.
16. Travis Kaats, of, Grand Canyon University.
17. *Milton Loo, ss, Molokai HS, Hoolehua, Hawaii.
18. Charles O'Neal, lhp, Chipola (Fla.) JC.
19. Drew Jenson, lhp, San Diego State University.
**20. Robert Coello, c, Okaloosa-Walton (Fla.) CC.—(2010-13)**
21. Blake Honey, ss, Lafayette County HS, Lewisville, Ark.
22. Matt Levering, 3b, Regis (Colo.) University.
23. Pedro Hawkins, of, Green River (Wash.) CC.
24. Adam Gillihan, rhp, Crowder (Mo.) JC.
25. *Robbie Nickols, lhp, Sabino HS, Tucson, Ariz.
26. Johnny Dillard, rhp, Southwestern Oklahoma State University.
27. James Langham, of, Georgia College & State University.
28. *Donnie Ecker, of, Los Altos (Calif.) HS.
29. Terrance Sparks, lhp, Prairie View A&M University.
30. David Griffin, lhp, Fresno State University.
**31. *Jacob Arrieta, rhp, Plano East HS, Plano, Texas.—(2010-15)**
32. Robbie Wachman, rhp, Valdosta State (Ga.) University.
33. *Dylan Moseley, rhp, Arkansas HS, Texarkana, Ark.
DRAFT DROP *Brother of Dustin Moseley, first-round draft pick, Reds (2000); major leaguer (2006-12)*
34. Drew Phillips, ss, Northwestern Oklahoma State University.
35. *Robert Palencia, rhp, Monsignor Pace HS, Opa Locka, Fla.
36. T.J. Johnson, lhp, Central Michigan University.
37. *Andrew Wells, of, Union HS, Tulsa, Okla.
38. *Robert Orton, c, Florida Atlantic University.
DRAFT DROP *Son of John Orton, first-round draft pick, Angels (1987); major leaguer (1989-93)*
39. *Mario Colletto, 1b, Simi Valley (Calif.) HS.
40. Brad Morenko, rhp, Oakland University.
41. *Scott Mueller, rhp, Greenway HS, Phoenix.
42. *Ben Price, ss, Terra Linda HS, San Rafael, Calif.
43. Ben Parker, rhp, Huston-Tillotson (Texas) College.
44. *Jacob Long, c, Johansen HS, Modesto, Calif.
45. J.D. Roberts, of, University of Michigan.
DRAFT DROP *Son of Leon Roberts, major leaguer (1974-84)*
46. *Justin Glover, 1b-of, Westside HS, Houston.
47. *Bradley Jarrell, 1b, Denham Springs (La.) HS.
48. Brad Key, 3b, University of South Carolina-Aiken.
49. *Tyler Cales, rhp, James Madison HS, San Antonio, Texas.
50. +Juan Buck, of, East HS, Anchorage, Alaska / South Mountain (Ariz.) CC.

## CLEVELAND INDIANS (6)

**1. Jeremy Sowers, lhp, Vanderbilt University.—(2006-09)**
DRAFT DROP *First-round draft pick (20th overall), Reds (2001)*
2. Justin Hoyman, rhp, University of Florida.—(Low A)
**3. Scott Lewis, lhp, Ohio State University.—(2008-09)**
4. Chuck Lofgren, lhp-of, Serra HS, Burlingame, Calif.—(AAA)
5. Mike Butia, of, James Madison University.—(High A)
6. Cody Bunkelman, rhp, Itasca (Minn.) CC.
7. Mark Jecmen, rhp, Stanford University.
8. Justin Pekarek, lhp, University of Nebraska.
9. Chris Niesel, rhp, Notre Dame University.
10. *Reinaldo Alicano, of, Josefina Barcelo HS, Guaynabo, P.R.
11. *Brian Logan, lhp, Varina HS, Richmond, Va.
12. *Jordan Chambless, rhp, Calallen HS, Corpus Christi, Texas.
13. Jason Denham, of, Deer Valley HS, Antioch, Calif.
DRAFT DROP *Brother of Dan Denham, first-round draft pick, Indians (2001)*
14. *Jeff Sues, rhp, Vanderbilt University.
15. Brian Finegan, ss, University of Hawaii.
16. *Josh Williamson, rhp, Columbia Basin (Wash.) CC.
17. Marshall Szabo, 2b, University of Georgia.
18. *Danny Calvert, rhp, Hutchinson (Kan.) CC.
**19. Chris Gimenez, c-of, University of Nevada.—(2009-15)**
20. Derrick Peterson, 3b, Eastern Michigan University.
21. +Carlton Smith, rhp, Piscataway (N.J.) HS / Okaloosa-Walton (Fla.) CC.
DRAFT DROP *Brother of Corey Smith, first-round draft pick, Indians (2000)*
22. *Jeff Corsaletti, of, University of Florida.
23. Michael Storey, lhp, Bellevue West HS, Bellevue, Neb.
**24. Wyatt Toregas, c, Virginia Tech.—(2009-11)**
25. *David Newman, lhp, San Jacinto (Texas) JC.
26. Justin Holmes, ss, University of Georgia.
27. Adrian Schau, rhp, Villanova University.
28. +Doodle Hicks, lhp, Virginia HS, Bristol, Va. / Walters State (Tenn.) CC.
29. P.J. Hiser, of, University of Pittsburgh.
30. Alfred Ard, of, Southern University.
31. *Doug Pickens, c, Brother Rice HS, West Bloomfield, Mich.
32. Kyle Collins, rhp, University of San Diego.
33. Paul Lubrano, lhp, University of Georgia.
34. *Ashton Shewey, lhp, Payson (Ariz.) HS.
35. Ryan Knippschild, lhp, University of Kansas.
36. *Jeff Kamrath, rhp, University of Virginia.
37. *Blake Gill, 2b, Louisiana State University.
38. Jose Amaya, rhp, San Jose State University.
39. *Preston Clark, c, Rockwall (Texas) HS.
40. Dustin Roddy, rhp, Nicholls State University.
41. *David Coulon, lhp, Hanford (Calif.) HS.
42. Josh Harris, rhp, Lamar University.
43. *Trevor Mortensen, of, Santa Ana (Calif.) JC.
44. *Phil Shirek, rhp, University of Nebraska.
**45. Tony Sipp, lhp, Clemson University.—(2009-15)**
46. *Chris Sosa, of, West Hills (Calif.) JC.
47. *Tyler Beranek, 1b, Waukesha South HS, Waukesha, Wis.
48. *Brian Winings, rhp, University of Pennsylvania.
49. +Jose Chavez, ss, Santa Ana (Calif.) JC.
50. *Tim Battaglia, rhp, University of Minnesota-Duluth.

## COLORADO ROCKIES (9)

**1. Chris Nelson, ss, Redan HS, Decatur, Ga.—(2010-14)**
**2. Seth Smith, of, University of Mississippi.—(2007-15)**
**3. Steven Register, rhp, Auburn University.—(2008-09)**
**4. Chris Iannetta, c, University of North Carolina.—(2006-15)**
**5. Matt Macri, 3b, Notre Dame University.—(2008)**
**6. Joe Koshansky, 1b, University of Virginia.—(2007-08)**
7. Jake Postlewait, lhp, Oregon State University.
**8. Jim Miller, rhp, University of Lousiana-Monroe.—(2008-14)**
9. Dustin Hahn, 3b, Sacramento (Calif.) CC.
DRAFT DROP *Son of Don Hahn, major leaguer (1969-75)*
**10. Jarrett Grube, rhp, University of Memphis.—(2014)**
11. Chris Buechner, rhp, Lamar University.
**12. David Patton, rhp, Green River (Wash.) CC.—(2009)**
13. Matt Miller, of, Texas State University.
**14. Dexter Fowler, of, Milton HS, Alpharetta, Ga.—(2008-15)**
15. Justin Nelson, of, University of California.
16. Pat Stanley, rhp, Pace (N.Y.) University.
17. *Dominick Foster, rhp, Buchanan HS, Clovis, Calif.
18. Jeff Dragicevich, ss, University of California.
**19. Josh Newman, lhp, Ohio State University.—(2007-08)**
20. *Rene Garcia, rhp, Sunnyside HS, Tuscon, Ariz.
21. Matt Prendergast, rhp, Virginia Commonwealth University.
22. Stephen Edsall, rhp, Rollins (Fla.) College.
23. Jason Metzger, lhp, University of North Carolina-Greensboro.
24. Rob Hosgood, of, Central Connecticut State University.
25. *Aaron Lovett, rhp, Brownstown (Ill.) HS.
26. Kyle Wilson, c, Fresno State University.
27. *Andrew Koubek, lhp, Eau Gallie HS, Melbourne, Fla.
28. Steven Thomas, rhp, Texas Tech.
29. *Kyle Foster, lhp, Castle Rock (Wash.) HS.
30. *Michael Criswell, lhp, Lincoln HS, Tallahassee, Fla.
**31. +Xavier Cedeno, lhp, Asuncioan Rodriguez**

HS, Desal, P.R. / Miami-Dade CC.—(2011-15)**

32. *Jackie Davidson, rhp, Richland (Texas) CC.

DRAFT DROP *Son of Jackie Davidson, first-round draft pick, Cubs (1983)*

33. *Justin Jameson, of, Southern Union (Ala.) JC.
34. *Kurt Crowell, of, East Los Angeles JC.
35. *Josiah Cowden, rhp, Cypress Community Christian HS, Kingwood, Texas
36. Jeremey White, lhp, Caly Poly Ponoma.
37. ***Todd Frazier, of, Toms River (N.J.) South HS.—(2011-15)**

DRAFT DROP *First-round draft pick (34th overall), Reds (2007) • Brother of Jeff Frazier, third-round draft pick, Tigers (2004); major leaguer (2010)*

38. *Rey Gonzalez, rhp, St. Petersburg (Fla.) JC.
39. *Jonathan Santos, ss, Puerto Rico Baseball Academy, Caguas, P.R.
40. *Gary McKissick, lhp, Itawamba (Miss.) JC.
41. *Chris Henry, lhp, San Joaquin Delta (Calif.) JC.
42. *Colt Sedbrook, 2b, Broomfield (Colo.) HS.
43. *Tony Snow, rhp, Edmonds (Wash.) CC.
44. *Justin Keadle, rhp, Wake Forest University.
45. *Colby Lehman, lhp, Bishop (Calif.) HS.
46. *Kody Keroher, rhp, Solano (Calif.) JC.
47. *Josh Banda, of, Cypress (Calif.) JC.
48. *J.T. LaFountain, c, University of Louisville.
49. *Brian Brohm, of, Trinity HS, Louisville, Ky.

DRAFT DROP *Quarterback, National Football League (2008-10)*

50. *Andy Goff, 2b, Mount Lebanon HS, Pittsburgh.

## DETROIT TIGERS (2)

1. **Justin Verlander, rhp, Old Dominion University.—(2005-15)**
2. Eric Beattie, rhp, University of Tampa.—(Low A)
3. **Jeff Frazier, of, Rutgers University.—(2010)**

DRAFT DROP *Brother of Todd Frazier, 37th-round draft pick, Rockies (2004); major leaguer (2011-15)*

4. Collin Mahoney, rhp, Clemson University.—(Low A)
5. Andrew Kown, rhp, Georgia Tech.—(AAA)
6. **Brent Dlugach, ss, University of Memphis.—(2009)**
7. ***Chris Carpenter, rhp, Bryan (Ohio) HS.—(2011-12)**
8. **Luke French, lhp, Heritage HS, Littleton, Colo.—(2009-10)**
9. Brandon Timm, of, Broken Arrow (Okla.) HS.
10. Cory Middleton, ss, Escambia HS, Pensacola, Fla.
11. Josh Kauten, rhp, Illinois State University.
12. Cole Miller, c, JC of the Siskiyous (Calif.).
13. Brooks Colvin, ss, Southwest Missouri State University.
14. James Skelton, c, West Covina (Calif.) HS.
15. Matt O'Brien, rhp, Florida Atlantic University.
16. Steve Young, 2b, Princeton University.
17. Dan Konecny, rhp, Northwestern University.
18. ***Chris Martin, rhp, Arlington (Texas) HS.—(2014-15)**
19. Tyler Jacobson, rhp, Central Arizona JC.
20. Ed Clelland, lhp, Gonzaga University.
21. Matthew Righter, rhp, Johns Hopkins (Md.) University.
22. Thomas Royals, rhp, Pearl River (Miss.) CC.
23. Vince Berry, of, Triton (Ill) JC.
24. Jordan Foster, of, Lamar University.
25. Robbie Tulk, rhp, UC Davis.
26. *Thad McBurrows, lhp, Lake Wales (Fla.) HS.
27. Dominic Carmosino, lhp, Oakland University.
28. Brian Hensen, lhp, Elon University.
29. Octavio Amezquita, ss, University of the Pacific.
30. Josh Lee, 1b, McMurray (Texas) University.
31. Leonardo Grullon, of, University of South Florida.
32. Nate Bumstead, rhp, Louisiana State University.
33. Kevin Brower, rhp, University of North Carolina.
34. Dallas Trahern, rhp, Owasso (Okla.) HS.
35. *Clay Britton, of, Weatherford (Texas) JC.
36. *Travis DeBondt, of, Bakersfield (Calif.) CC.
37. *Ramon Navarro, ss, Triton (Ill.) JC.
38. Jamaal Peoples, of, Philadelphia (Miss.) HS.
39. *Adrian Bowens, ss, Lumberton (Miss.) HS.
40. *Kevin McAtee, 1b, Regis Jesuit HS, Littleton, Colo.
41. *Bryan Sheffield, of, Williston (Fla.) HS.
42. *Trenton Lare, lhp, Coffeeville (Kan.) CC.
43. ***Chris Schwinden, rhp, Golden West HS, Visalia, Calif.—(2011-12)**
44. *Tyler Fockler, rhp, Scotts Valley (Calif.) HS.
45. Lionel Roberts, 1b, John McDonogh HS, New Orleans, La.
46. *Alec Sheppard, rhp, Colorado Springs Christian School, Colorado Springs, Colo.
47. *Rene Recio, rhp, Oral Roberts University.
48. *Bernard Williams, of, East Marion HS, Columbia, Miss.
49. *Dominic De la Osa, ss, Archbishop Carroll HS, Coral Gables, Fla.
50. +Maxwell Leon, 2b, South Mountain (Ariz.) JC.

## FLORIDA MARLINS (27)

1. **Taylor Tankersley, lhp, University of Alabama.—(2006-10)**
2. **Jason Vargas, lhp, Long Beach State University.—(2005-15)**
3. Greg Burns, of, Walnut HS, West Covina, Calif.—(AAA)
4. Jamar Walton, of, Greensville County HS, Emporia, Va.—(High A)
5. **Brad Davis, c, Long Beach State University.—(2010)**
6. Brad McCann, 3b, Clemson University.

DRAFT DROP *Brother of Brian McCann, major leaguer (2005-15)*

7. Jared Gaston, of, Walters State (Tenn.) JC.
8. Craig Molldrem, rhp, University of Minnesota.
9. Joe Pietro, of, University of New Orleans.
10. **Brett Carroll, 3b, Middle Tennessee State University.—(2007-12)**
11. **Daniel Barone, rhp, Sonoma State (Calif.) University.—(2007)**
12. Jeff Gogal, lhp, Montclair State (N.J.) University.
13. Steve Gendron, ss-3b, Mississippi State University.
14. Patrick Hogan, rhp, Clemson University.
15. Brandon Verley, of, Columbia HS, White Salmon, Wash.
16. Brian Cleveland, ss, University of Tennessee.
17. *Barry Gunther, c, University of Mississippi.
18. Nathan Messner, 3b, Muncy (Pa.) HS.
19. *John Parker Wilson, c, Hoover (Ala.) HS.

DRAFT DROP *Quarterback, National Football League (2009-12)*

20. Rhett James, rhp, Florida State University.
21. *Marcus Davis, of, East Central (Miss.) JC.
22. Chris Mobley, rhp, Middle Tennessee State University.
23. Ted Ledbetter, of, Oklahoma City University.
24. Jeff Lacher, rhp, Mississippi State University.
25. *Agustin Montanez, ss, Ramon Vila Mayo HS, Rio Piedras, P.R.
26. *Kevin Turmail, rhp, St. Louis CC-Forest Park.
27. Brian Hoff, rhp, UC Riverside.
28. ***Charlie Blackmon, lhp, North Gwinnett HS, Suwanee, Ga.—(2011-15)**
29. Aaron Easton, rhp, University of Massachusetts-Lowell.
30. *Joseph Munn, lhp, Foothill HS, Pleasanton, Calif.
31. Parrish Castor, lhp, St. Anselm (N.H.) College.
32. *Jared Petrovich, lhp, Shamokin Area HS, Coal Township. Pa.
33. Clay Westmoreland, rhp, University of Utah.
34. Jarrett Santos, rhp, University of North Carolina-Greensboro.
35. *Drew Shetrone, rhp, Seminole (Fla.) CC.
36. *Sebastien Vendette, rhp, Ahuntsic College HS, Laval, Quebec.
37. Juan Figueroa, 1b, Bethune-Cookman College.
38. *Zach Barrett, of, Reitz Memorial HS, Evansville, Ind.
39. Beau McMillan, 2b, Lynn (Fla.) University.
40. *Gerald Watson, 2b, Central Catholic HS, Morgan City, La.
41. *Zach Taylor, 3b, Canyon Springs HS, Moreno Valley, Calif.
42. *Steve Santos, rhp, Diablo Valley (Calif.) CC.
43. *Reyes Dorado, rhp, A.B. Miller HS, Fontana, Calif.
44. *Charles Jestice, rhp, Memorial HS, Tulsa, Okla.
45. *Matt Bates, rhp, Illinois Valley CC.
46. *Jared Johnson, rhp, Central Arizona JC.
47. *Michael Mulholland, lhp, Lincoln Trail (Ill.) JC.
48. *Brady Decker, rhp, Red Hill HS, Bridgeport, Ill.
49. *Chris Kirkland, c, South Doyle HS, Knoxville, Tenn.
50. *Saunders Ramsey, rhp, Mississippi State University.

## HOUSTON ASTROS (23)

1. (Choice to Yankees as compensation for Type A free agent Andy Pettitte)
2. **Hunter Pence, of, University of Texas-Arlington.—(2007-15)**
3. Jordan Parraz, of, CC of Southern Nevada.—(AAA)
4. Lou Santangelo, c, Clemson University.—(AAA)
5. Mitch Einertson, 2b, Rancho Buena Vista HS, Oceanside, Calif.—(AA)
6. **Ben Zobrist, ss, Dallas Baptist University.—(2006-15)**
7. Andy Alvarado, rhp, Chabot (Calif.) JC.
8. Evan Englebrook, rhp, Shippensburg (Pa.) University.
9. **Troy Patton, lhp, Tomball HS, Magnolia, Texas.—(2007-14)**
10. Eric Cavers, c, Franklin Pierce (N.H.) College.
11. Jonny Ash, 2b, Stanford University.
12. Bryan Triplett, ss, University of South Carolina.
13. **Chad Reineke, rhp, Miami (Ohio) University.—(2008-11)**
14. Ole Sheldon, 1b, University of Oklahoma.
15. **Drew Sutton, ss, Baylor University.—(2009-12)**
16. Garrett Murdy, rhp, Texas A&M University-Kingsville.
17. Beau Torbert, of, Faulkner (Ala.) University.
18. Chris Clark, c, Eastern Kentucky University.
19. *Jared Clark, rhp-of, Valencia (Calif.) HS.
20. **J.R. Towles, c, North Central Texas JC.—(2007-11)**
21. Ryan Reed, of, Louisiana State University-Eunice JC.
22. Matt Brown, rhp, University of California.
23. Jeff Wigdahl, lhp, St. Mary's (Texas) University.
24. Brandon Averill, 3b, UCLA.
25. *Andrew Darnell, of, Castro Valley (Calif.) HS.
26. Jared Brite, rhp, Kansas State University.
27. Casey Brown, rhp, University of Oklahoma.
28. Chris Sotro, rhp, Cal Poly Pomona.
29. Brad James, rhp, North Central Texas JC.
30. Brandon Barganier, of, Temple (Texas) JC.
31. Chris Uhle, ss, Eastern Illinois University.
32. Neil Sellers, 3b, Eastern Kentucky University.
33. James Cooper, of, Grambling State University.
34. *Nick Cobler, lhp, Strake Jesuit College Prep, Houston.
35. *Kyle Woodruff, rhp, Leland HS, San Jose, Calif.
36. Anthony DeWitt, rhp, University of Southern Mississippi.
37. Brad Chedister, rhp, Louisiana Tech.
38. *Brandon Todd, rhp, Central Florida CC.
39. *Zachary Williams, rhp, Lindsay (Okla.) HS.
40. *Dane Ponciano, c, Mount Miguel HS, Grossmont, Calif.
41. *Casey McCleskey, of, Burkburnett (Texas) HS.
42. *Josh Smith, rhp, Riverside (Calif.) CC.
43. *Tom Rafferty, of, Temple (Texas) JC.
44. *Vladimir Frias, ss, Chipola (Fla.) JC.
45. *Chris Siewert, ss, CC of Southern Nevada.
46. Anthony Adler, rhp, University of Texas-Dallas.
47. +Corey Bass, rhp, Pearl River (Miss.) CC.
48. *Eric Epperson, of, Arlington Heights HS, Fort Worth, Texas.
49. *Matthew Gardner, c, Andrews (Texas) HS.
50. *Victor Ferrante, rhp, Solano (Calif.) JC.

## KANSAS CITY ROYALS (14)

1. **Billy Butler, 1b-3b, Wolfson HS, Jacksonville, Fla.—(2007-15)**
1. Matt Campbell, lhp, University of South Carolina (Choice from Giants as compensation for Type B free agent Michael Tucker).—(High A)
1. **J.P. Howell, lhp, University of Texas** (Supplemental choice—31st—as compensation for Type A free agent Raul Ibanez).—**(2005-15)**
2. **Billy Buckner, rhp, University of South Carolina.—(2007-14)**
2. **Erik Cordier, rhp, Southern Door HS, Sturgeon Bay, Wis.** (Choice from Mariners as compensation for Ibanez).**—(2014-15)**
3. Josh Johnson, ss, Middleton HS, Tampa.—(AAA)

DRAFT DROP *Son of Larry Doby Johnson, major leaguer (1972-78)*

4. Nate Moore, rhp, Troy State University.—(High A)
5. Henry Barrera, rhp, Rosemead (Calif.) HS.—(AA)
6. Brad Blackwell, rhp, University of South Carolina.
7. Patrick Green, rhp, University of Louisiana-Monroe.
8. **Ed Lucas, ss, Dartmouth University.—(2013-14)**
9. Chris McConnell, ss, Delsea HS, Franklinville, N.J.
10. Bobby Beeson, lhp, Southern Arkansas University.
11. Josh Haney, 2b, Texas Tech.
12. Brad Hayes, 3b, Arkansas State University.
13. Travis Trammell, rhp, University of Arkansas-Little Rock.
14. *Kyle Howe, rhp, North Kitsap HS, Poulsbo, Wash.
15. +Gilbert De La Vara, lhp, Pima (Ariz.) CC.
16. Patrick Hicklen, rhp, University of Tennessee.
17. *Adam Trent, rhp, Ooltewah, Tenn.
18. Drew Coffey, lhp, Mingus Union HS, Cottonwood, Ariz.
19. *Kade Keowen, 1b, Central HS, Baton Rouge, La.
20. Adam Rowe, lhp, Mount Vernon Nazarene (Ohio) College.
21. *Andrew Underwood, rhp, Fresno CC.
22. Ethien Santana, of, Laredo (Texas) CC.
23. +O.D. Gonzalez, of, Broward (Fla.) CC.
24. *Myles Ioane, lhp, Waiakea HS, Hilo, Hawaii.
25. *Garrick Evans, of, Clemson University.
26. Nick Cerulo, of, Rutgers University.
27. Zane Carlson, rhp, Baylor University.
28. *Martin Beno, rhp, Horn Lake HS, Lake Cormorant, Miss.
29. *Riley Hollingsworth, rhp, Minden (La.) HS.
30. *Kris Krise, rhp, JC of the Canyons (Calif.).
31. *Kevin Clark, of, Armwood HS, Seffner, Fla.
32. *Tyler Hogan, of, Servite HS, Anaheim, Calif.
33. *Jimmy Wallace, rhp, Pratt (Kan.) CC.
34. Kyle Crist, rhp, University of California.
35. *Vinny Biancamano, ss, Cactus HS, Glendale Ariz.
36. *Eric Krebs, rhp, Alvin (Texas) CC.
37. *Kyle Hartz, of, De Anza (Calif.) JC.
38. ***David Herndon, rhp, Mosley HS, Lynn Haven, Fla.—(2010-12)**
39. *Will Jostock, rhp, Lapeer West HS, Lapeer, Mich.
40. *Johnnie Santangelo, rhp, Bossier Parish (La.) CC.
41. *Kendall Thurman, rhp, Angelina (Texas) JC.
42. *Anthony Marbry, rhp, Jackson State (Tenn.) CC.
43. *Tyler Brown, rhp, Lane (Ore.) CC.
44. *Ty Sarchet, rhp, Kalani HS, Honolulu, Hawaii.
45. *Jacob Myking, c, Kalaheo HS, Kailua, Hawaii.
46. *Randy Rundgren, ss, Mid-Pacific Institute, Honolulu, Hawaii.
47. *Mark Serrano, rhp, Downey (Calif.) HS.
48. *Ernie Medina, rhp, San Jacinto (Calif.) HS.
49. *Tyler Jennings, of, Daphne (Ala.) HS.
50. Jefferson Infante, c, Ramapo (N.J.) College.

## LOS ANGELES ANGELS (12)

1. **Jered Weaver, rhp, Long Beach State University.—(2006-15)**

DRAFT DROP *Brother of Jeff Weaver, first-round draft pick, Tigers (1998); major leaguer (1999-2010)*

2. (Choice to White Sox as compensation for Type A free agent Bartolo Colon)
3. (Choice to Blue Jays as compensation for Type A free agent Kelvim Escobar)
4. *Pat White, of, Daphne (Ala.) HS.—DNP

DRAFT DROP *Attended West Virginia; re-drafted by Angels, 2007 (27th round); quarterback, National Football League (2009)*

5. Luis Rivera, of, Ramon Vila Mayo HS, Rio Piedras, P.R.—(Low A)
6. Josh LeBlanc, 2b, Southern University.
7. Bill Layman, rhp, University of North Florida.
8. **Freddy Sandoval, 3b, University of San Diego.—(2008-09)**
9. Hainley Statia, ss, Trinity Christian Academy, Boynton Beach, Fla.
10. Doug Reinhardt, 3b, Santa Margarita Catholic HS, Laguna Beach, Calif.

11. Clifton Remole, 1b, Georgia Tech.
12. Tyler Johnson, of, Haskell (Okla.) HS.
13. Andrew Toussaint, 3b, Southern University.
**14. Nick Adenhart, rhp, Williamsport (Md.) HS.—(2008-09)**
DRAFT DROP *Died as active major leaguer (April 9, 2009)*
15. *Adam Crabtree, rhp, Phillips Academy, Andover, Mass.
16. Chris Waters, rhp, University of North Florida.
17. Ryan Aldridge, rhp, Middle Georgia JC.
**18. Mark Trumbo, rhp-3b, Villa Park HS, Orange, Calif.—(2010-15)**
19. David Hernandez, rhp, Miami-Dade CC South.
20. D.T. McDowell, of, Tucker HS, Atlanta.
21. *Stan Posluszny, of, West Virginia University.
22. *Matt Moore, 3b, Newhall, Calif.
DRAFT DROP *Quarterback, National Football League (2007-15)*
23. Ben Johnson, c, University of Washington.
24. Nate Sutton, 2b, UC Santa Barbara.
25. Casey Mutter, rhp, Cal State San Bernardino.
26. Jaime Douglas, lhp, University of Central Florida.
**27. Martin Maldonado, c, Dr. Juan J. Maunez Pimentel HS, Naguabo, P.R.—(2011-15)**
28. *Cristen Tapia, 1b, Tucson Magnet HS, Tucson, Ariz.
29. Billy Edwards, rhp, University of Memphis.
30. *Alan Horne, rhp, Chipola (Fla.) JC.
DRAFT DROP *First-round draft pick (27th overall), Indians (2001)*
31. *Ricky Bambino, c, Sierra (Calif.) JC.
32. Brooks Shankle, 3b, University of Texas-San Antonio.
33. Frederic Carney, rhp, Regis (Colo.) University.
**34. Bobby Cassevah, rhp, Pace (Fla.) HS.—(2010-12)**
35. Nick Green, rhp, Darton (Ga.) JC.
36. *John Mariotti, rhp, Gulf Coast (Fla.) JC.
37. *Clayton Trenary, of, Central Florida CC.
38. Rich Giannotti, of, University of Miami.
39. Mike Sweeney, lhp, St. Petersburg (Fla.) CC.
40. +Stephen Marek, rhp, San Jacinto (Texas) JC.
41. *William Cooper, rhp, Shelton State (Ala.) JC.
42. *Patrick Warfle, of, Daytona Beach (Fla.) CC.
43. *Chris Lombardo, rhp, Etiwanda (Calif.) HS.
44. +Grant Harper, of, San Pedro (Calif.) HS / Los Angeles Harbor JC.
45. *Andrew Colon, rhp, Choctawhatchee HS, Fort Walton Beach, Fla.
46. *Marquez Smith, 3b, Daytona Beach (Fla.) JC.
**47. *Erik Davis, rhp, Mountain View (Calif.) HS.—(2013)**
48. *Julian Laurean, 2b, Chandler-Gilbert (Ariz.) CC.
49. *Nick Dashnaw, rhp, Santa Clarita Christian HS, Santa Clarita, Calif.
50. +Abel Nieves, 2b, Middle Georgia JC.

## LOS ANGELES DODGERS (17)

**1. Scott Elbert, lhp, Seneca (Mo.) HS.—(2008-14)**
**1. Blake DeWitt, ss, Sikeston (Mo.) HS** (Choice from Yankees as compensation for Type A free agent Paul Quantrill).**—(2008-13)**
1. Justin Orenduff, rhp, Virginia Commonwealth University (Supplemental choice—33rd—as compensation for Quantrill).—(AAA)
2. Blake Johnson, rhp, Parkview Baptist HS, Baton Rouge, La.—(AAA)
3. Cory Dunlap, 1b, Contra Costa (Calif) JC.—(AAA)
**4. Javy Guerra, rhp, Denton Ryan HS, Denton, Texas.—(2011-15)**
5. Anthony Raglani, of, George Washington University.—(AA)
6. Daniel Batz, 1b, University of Rhode Island.
7. B.J. Richmond, of, Spartanburg Methodist (S.C.) JC.
8. Carlos Medero-Stullz, c, Barbara Goleman HS, Hialeah, Fla.
9. David Nicholson, 3b, University of California.
**10. Cory Wade, rhp, Kentucky Wesleyan College.—(2008-12)**
11. Chris Westervelt, c, Stetson University.
12. Sam Steidl, of, University of Minnesota.
**13. *Jeff Larish, of, Arizona State University.—(2008-10)**
14. Brian Akin, rhp, Davidson College.
**15. *Joe Savery, lhp-1b, Lamar HS, Bellaire, Texas.—(2011-14)**
DRAFT DROP *First-round draft pick (19th overall), Phillies (2007)*
16. *Chase Dardar, rhp, Delgado (La.) CC.
17. *Danny Forrer, lhp, Chipola (Fla.) JC.
18. Matt Paul, 2b, Southern University.
DRAFT DROP *Brother of Xavier Paul, major leaguer (2009-14)*
**19. *David Price, lhp, Blackman HS, Murfreesboro, Tenn.—(2008-15)**
DRAFT DROP *First overall draft pick, Devil Rays (2007)*
20. Mark Alexander, rhp, University of Missouri.
21. Justin Simmons, lhp, University of Texas.
22. Kyle Wilson, rhp, UCLA.
23. Kenny Plaisance, rhp, Louisiana State University-Eunice JC.
24. *Kody Kaiser, ss, Santa Fe HS, Edmond, Okla.
**25. Justin Ruggiano, of, Texas A&M University.—(2007-15)**
26. *Ben Petralli, c, Weatherford (Texas) HS.
DRAFT DROP *Son of Geno Petralli, major leaguer (1982-93)*
27. *Keon Graves, c, Dillon (S.C.) HS.
28. *Brett Lawler, 1b, San Jacinto (Texas) JC.
29. *Ryan Strieby, 1b, Edmonds (Wash.) CC.
30. *Paul Gran, ss, Bothell (Wash.) HS.
31. *Ryan Koch, rhp, Osceola HS, Pinellas Park, Fla.
**32. *Mike Stutes, rhp, Lake Oswego (Ore.) HS.—(2011-13)**
33. +James Gilbert, rhp, Chabot (Calif.) JC.
34. *Chris LeMay, lhp, Kwantlen (B.C.) College.
35. *Lynn Henry, of, Buras (La.) HS.
36. *Mike Burgher, of, Shorecrest HS, Seattle.
37. +Jeremy Brown, of, Pratt (Kan.) CC.
38. Justin Crist, 2b, Chandler-Gilbert (Ariz.) CC.
39. *Michael Branham, rhp, Jesuit HS, Tampa.
40. Brandon Carter, ss, Old Dominion University.
41. *Troy Grundy, rhp, Carbon HS, North Price, Utah.
42. *Chris Johnson, rhp, Cabell-Midland HS, Huntington, W.Va.
43. *Davis Bilardello, lhp, Vero Beach (Fla.) HS.
DRAFT DROP *Son of Dann Bilardello, major leaguer (1983-92)*
44. *Kyle Rapp, lhp, Wabash Valley (Ill.) CC.
45. *Michael Hernandez, of, Connors State (Okla.) CC.
46. *Andrew Brewer, rhp, Metro Christian Academy, Tulsa, Okla.
47. *Bobby Bratton, ss, Columbia Central HS, Columbia, Tenn.
48. Joe Norrito, rhp, Nova Southeastern University.
49. *Scott Bates, c, Salado HS, Belton, Texas.
50. *Ross Hoffman, 1b, Bakersfield (Calif.) CC.

## MILWAUKEE BREWERS (5)

**1. Mark Rogers, rhp, Mount Ararat HS, Orr's Island, Maine.—(2010-12)**
**2. Yovani Gallardo, rhp, Trimble Tech, Fort Worth, Texas.—(2007-15)**
3. Josh Wahpepah, rhp, Cowley County (Kan.) CC.—(AA)
4. Josh Baker, rhp, Rice University.—(High A)
DRAFT DROP *Son of Johnny Baker, linebacker, American Football League (1963-67)*
**5. Angel Salome, c, George Washington HS, Bronx, N.Y.—(2008)**
6. Stephen Chapman, of, Marianna (Fla.) HS.
7. Greg Langille, rhp, Charles Allen HS, New Bedford, Nova Scotia.
8. Brandon Parillo, lhp, Marina HS, Huntington Beach, Calif.
9. Derek DeCarlo, rhp, Florida International University.
10. Steve Sollmann, 2b, Notre Dame University.
11. Lenny Leclercq, ss, West Vigo HS, Terre Haute, Ind.
**12. *Andrew Albers, lhp, John Paul II HS, North Battleford, Sask.—(2013-15)**
13. Angel Ayala, 1b, Lino Padron Rivera HS, Vega Baja, P.R.
14. Grant Richardson, 1b, Washington State University.
15. David Johnson, rhp, UCLA.
16. Alexandre Periard, rhp, Poly Deux-Montagnes HS, St. Eustache, Quebec.
**17. +Lorenzo Cain, of, Madison County HS, Madison, Fla. / Tallahassee (Fla.) CC.—(2010-15)**
**18. +Darren Ford, of, Vineland (N.J.) HS / Chipola (Fla.) CC.—(2010-11)**
19. Josh Brady, of, Texas Tech.
20. *Jose Garcia, rhp, Indians Hills (Iowa) CC.
21. *Drew Bowman, lhp, Dakota Ridge HS, Morrison, Colo.
22. +Matt Kretzschmar, rhp, San Pedro (Calif.) HS / Rio Hondo (Calif.) JC.
23. Tony Festa, 3b, UC Riverside.
24. *Jose Delgado, rhp, Puerto Rico Baseball Academy, Caguas, P.R.
25. *Sean Morgan, rhp, Clements HS, Sugar Land, Texas.
26. *Dustin Timm, rhp, University of Nebraska.
27. *Ty Prior, rhp, Olympia HS, Orlando, Fla.
28. *Ronnie Prettyman, 3b, Cal State Fullerton.
29. *Ryan Paterson, rhp, Lake Cowichan HS, Duncan, B.C.
30. *Brian Johnson, rhp, East Islip (N.Y.) HS.
**31. *Kanekoa Texeira, rhp, Kamehameha HS, Kula, Hawaii.—(2010-11)**
32. Joel Needham, rhp, UC Davis.
33. Luis Bernal, rhp, Pima (Ariz.) CC.
34. *Kris Dabrowiecki, rhp, Ursula Franklin Academy, Toronto.
35. *Chris Copot, c, John Diefenbaker HS, Prince Albert, Sask.
36. *Stephen Barnes, rhp, First Coast HS, Jacksonville, Fla.
37. *Sean McCraw, c, Alvin (Texas) HS.
38. *Donald Jordat, rhp, Summit Christian HS, Lake Worth, Fla.
39. *Jeremy Bloor, lhp, Grand Rapids (Mich.) CC.
40. *Chris Rickey, lhp, Reno (Nev.) HS.
41. *James Coker, lhp, Spartanburg Methodist (S.C.) JC.
42. +Josh Louis, rhp, Temple (Texas) JC.
43. *Brandon Jasper, 1b, Newport Harbor HS, Cerritos, Calif.
44. *Jon Mungle, of, Mississippi State University.
45. *Deik Scram, of, Cowley County (Kan.) CC.
46. *Louis Metzner, rhp, Langley, B.C.
47. +Derek Miller, lhp, University of Vermont / University of Nebraska.
48. *Brandon Glover, of, McKinney (Texas) HS.
49. *Shane Buriff, lhp, Sickles HS, Tampa.
50. *Chad Miller, 1b, Chandler-Gilbert (Ariz.) CC.

## MINNESOTA TWINS (20)

**1. Trevor Plouffe, ss, Crespi HS, Northridge, Calif.—(2010-15)**
**1. Glen Perkins, lhp, University of Minnesota** (Choice from Mariners as compensation for Type A free agent Eddie Guardado).**—(2006-15)**
**1. Kyle Waldrop, rhp, Farragut HS, Knoxville, Tenn.** (Choice from Cubs as compensation for Type A free agent LaTroy Hawkins).**—(2011-12)**
**1. Matt Fox, rhp, University of Central Florida** (Supplemental choice—35th—as compensation for Guardado).**—(2010)**
1. Jay Rainville, rhp, Bishop Hendricken HS, Pawtucket, R.I. (Supplemental choice—39th—as compensation for Hawkins).—(AA)
**2. Anthony Swarzak, rhp, Nova HS, Fort Lauderdale, Fla.—(2009-15)**
3. Eddie Morlan, rhp, Coral Park HS, Miami.—(AA)
4. Mark Robinson, of, Mountain View HS, El Monte, Calif.—(Low A)
5. Jeff Schoenbachler, lhp, Reno (Nev.) HS.—(Rookie)
6. Patrick Bryant, rhp, Pensacola Catholic HS, Gulf Breeze, Fla.
7. John Williams, lhp, Middle Tennessee State University.
8. Jay Sawatski, lhp, University of Arkansas.
DRAFT DROP *Grandson of Carl Sawatski, major leaguer (1948-63)*
9. J.P. Martinez, rhp, University of New Orleans.
10. Jeremy Pickrel, of, Illinois State University.
11. Kyle Aselton, lhp, Oregon State University.
12. *Shane Boyd, rhp, University of Kentucky.
DRAFT DROP *Quarterback, National Football League (2006-07)*
13. +Walter Patton, rhp, Lincoln Land (Ill.) CC.
14. Javi Sanchez, c, University of Notre Dame.
15. Juan Portes, ss, Malden, Mass.
**16. Matt Tolbert, ss, University of Mississippi.—(2008-11)**
17. *Eammon Portice, rhp, Fort Lauderdale HS, Oakland Park, Fla.
18. *Josh Rose, rhp, Mariner HS, Cape Coral, Fla.
19. *Tate Casey, rhp, Longview (Texas) HS.
20. Tim Lahey, c, Princeton University.
21. Joe Abellera, 3b, Hopkins HS, Minnetonka, Minn.
22. *Vinnie Scarduzio, lhp, Jupiter Community HS, Jupiter, Fla.
23. *Tim Arnold, lhp, Fallbrook (Calif.) HS.
24. *Garrett White, lhp, San Jacinto (Texas) JC.
25. *Joe Welsh, lhp, Grand Rapids (Mich.) CC.
26. Deacon Burns, of, Northern State (S.D.) University.
27. Landon Burt, of, San Diego State University.
28. +Aaron Craig, rhp, Century HS, Rochester, Minn. / Grayson County (Texas) CC.
29. Ricky Prady, of, Sebastian River HS, Sebastian, Fla.
30. +Daniel Berg, 3b, Texarkana (Texas) JC.
31. *Jason Laird, rhp, Henry County HS, Hampton, Ga.
32. *Nolan Mulligan, rhp, Broward (Fla.) CC.
33. *Sean Kalmen, rhp, Katella HS, Anaheim, Calif.
**34. *Rene Tosoni, of, Terry Fox SS, Port Coquitlam, B.C.—(2011)**
35. Jeff Mousser, rhp, Arizona State University.
36. *John Thies, lhp, Meramec (Mo.) CC.
37. *Gregory D'Oleo, c, Ramon Vila Mayo HS, Toa Baja, P.R.
38. +Josh Land, of, Okaloosa-Walton (Fla.) CC.
39. +Danny Santiesteban, of, Palm Beach (Fla.) CC.
40. *Justin Otto, rhp, Chandler (Okla.) HS.
41. *Eric Sweeney, rhp, Mount Carmel HS, San Diego.
42. *Greg Schilling, lhp, Broward (Fla.) CC.
43. Robbie Hebert, rhp, Nicholls State University.
44. *Tony Joiner, of, Haines City (Fla.) HS.
45. *Lance Lofton, 3b, Connally HS, Waco, Texas.
46. *Matt Rizzotti, 1b, Archbishop Molloy HS, Jamaica, N.Y.
47. *Chris Petrie, of, Lake City (Fla.) CC.
48. *Ryne Nelson, rhp, Dickinson (Texas) HS.
49. *Nicholas Bleau, lhp, Gulf Coast (Fla.) CC.
50. *Taylor Cameron, rhp, Cypress (Calif.) JC.

## MONTREAL EXPOS (13)

**1. Bill Bray, lhp, College of William & Mary.—(2006-12)**
2. Erick San Pedro, c, University of Miami.—(AAA)
**3. Ian Desmond, ss, Sarasota (Fla.) HS.—(2009-15)**
**4. Collin Balester, rhp, Huntington Beach (Calif.) HS.—(2008-15)**
5. Greg Bunn, rhp, East Carolina University.—(High A)
6. Devin Ivany, c, University of South Florida.
7. Marvin Lowrance, of, Golden West (Calif.) JC.
8. Leonard Davis, 3b, Fresno (Calif.) CC.
9. Brandon Conway, ss, Frederick (Md.) CC.
10. Duron Legrande, of, North Carolina A&T University.
11. David Trahan, rhp, Alvin (Texas) JC.
**12. *Robert Mosebach, of, Hillsborough (Fla.) CC.—(2009)**
13. David Travis, 2b, Southern Wesleyan (S.C.) University.
14. Lyndsey Simmons, c, New York Tech.
15. *Michael Wlodarczyk, lhp, Boston College.
16. Thomas Wilson, lhp, Catawba (N.C.) College.
17. John Poppert, c, East Carolina University.
18. Matt Perks, rhp, Mercer County (N.J.) CC.
19. Ben Cox, rhp, Lamar University.
20. Gene Yost, lhp, Averett (Va.) University.
21. *Ibrahim Lopez, of, Puerto Rico Baseball Academy, Carolina, P.R.
22. Aaron Jackson, rhp, St. Augustine (Fla.) HS.
23. Ryan Harrison, rhp, South Carroll HS, Woodbine, Md.
24. *Steven Hornostaj, ss, St. David Catholic HS, Waterloo, Ont.
25. Steven Cook, rhp, University of North Carolina-Asheville.
26. Gabe Suarez, ss, South Mountain (Ariz.) CC.
27. *Ladd Hall, rhp, Arizona State University.
28. Chris Lugo, rhp, Hudson Catholic HS, Hoboken,

N.J.
29. *Steven Hirschfeld, rhp, Grand County HS, Moab, Utah.
30. *Brendan Murphy, 1b, Garden City (Kan.) CC.
31. *P.J. Treadaway, rhp, Archbishop Hannan HS, Carrier, Miss.
32. *Matt Averitt, rhp, New Mexico JC.
33. *Chris Whisenhunt, lhp, Fort Worth Christian HS, North Richland Hills, Tex
**34. Brett Campbell, rhp, Kennesaw State University.—(2006)**
35. Rudy Garza, rhp, Hill (Texas) JC.
36. *Todd Nicholas, lhp, Troy State University.
37. *Jamie Gant, rhp, Mississippi State University.
38. *Daniel Cooper, rhp, Costa Mesa (Calif.) HS.
39. +Brian Peacock, c, Manatee (Fla.) JC.
40. Melvin Perez, 3b, George Washington HS, Bronx, N.Y.
41. *Joe Dunigan, of, St. Ignatius Prep, Chicago.
42. *Brent Gaphardt, lhp, Dundalk (Md.) CC.
43. *Andy Gale, rhp, Philips Exeter Academy, Durham, N.H.
DRAFT DROP *Son of Rich Gale, major leaguer (1978-84)*
44. *Phillip Valle, ss, Bellevue Christian HS, Clyde Hill, Wash.
45. *Austin Reilly, ss, Fort Worth Country Day HS, Fort Worth, Texas.
46. *Robert Molinaro, ss, American Heritage HS, Boca Raton, Fla.
DRAFT DROP *Son of Bobby Molinaro, major leaguer (1975-83)*
47. *Jonathan Del Franco, rhp, Bridgewater-Raritan HS, Bridgewater, N.J.
48. *Carlos Ceron, rhp, Miami-Dade CC North.
49. *Patrick Kanakevich, rhp, Georgetown Prep, Rockville, Md.
50. *Joel Collins, c, Cardinal Carter SS, Richmond Hill, Ontario.

## NEW YORK METS (3)

**1. Philip Humber, rhp, Rice University.—(2006-13)**
2. Matt Durkin, rhp, San Jose State University.—(Low A)
3. Gaby Hernandez, rhp, Belen Jesuit HS, Miami.—(AAA)
4. Aaron Hathaway, c, University of Washington.—(High A)
**5. Nick Evans, 3b, St. Mary's HS, Phoenix.—(2008-14)**
6. Ryan Coultas, ss, UC Davis.
7. Scott Hyde, rhp, George Fox (Ore.) College.
8. *Neil Jamison, rhp, Long Beach State University.
**9. Mike Carp, 1b, Lakewood (Calif.) HS.—(2009-14)**
10. Brahiam Maldonado, of, St. Francis HS, Loiza, P.R.
11. Josh Wyrick, of, Porterville (Calif.) CC.
12. Jeff Landing, rhp, Virginia Tech.
13. *Martinez Allen, of, Dunnellon (Fla.) HS.
14. *Brad Meyers, rhp, Servite HS, Yorba Linda, Calif.
15. Grant Psomas, ss, West Virginia University.
16. Parris Austin, of, Douglas County HS, Douglasville, Ga.
17. Joe Williams, lhp, St. Xavier (Ill.) University.
18. Kyle Brown, of, LeMoyne College.
19. Jim Burt, 1b, University of Miami.
DRAFT DROP *Son of Jim Burt, nose tackle, National Football League (1981-91)*
20. Sean Henry, ss, Diablo Valley (Calif.) JC.
21. *Tim Smith, of, Birchmount Park HS, Scarborough, Ontario.
22. Caleb Stewart, of, University of Kentucky.
23. Michael Devaney, rhp, Concordia (Ore.) University.
24. Bryan Zech, 2b, Florida State University.
25. Jonathan Castillo, rhp, Miami-Dade CC South.
26. Rafael Arroyo, c, Cal State Los Angeles.
27. Bryant Suggs, of, Hillsborough (Fla.) CC.
28. Armand Gaerlan, ss, University of San Francisco.
29. Mike Swindell, rhp, University of Oklahoma.
30. Blake Eager, rhp, Metropolitan State (Colo.) University.
31. *Erin Jones, rhp, Francis Marion (S.C.) University.
32. *Jason James, of, Kishwaukee (Ill.) JC.
33. Matt Fisher, 2b, UC Irvine.
34. *Jeremiah Lokken, of, Eagle View Academy, Jacksonville, Fla.
35. *Garret Halleran, rhp, Central Arizona JC.
36. +Jake Harrington, rhp, Northeastern (Colo.) JC.
37. *Brad Burns, rhp, Lookeba Sickles HS, Gracemont, Okla.
38. *Zack Sterner, rhp, Franklin (Pa.) Regional HS.
39. *Bryan Lee, rhp, Cuesta (Calif.) JC.
40. *Julio Rodriguez, of, Manuel Mendez Liceaga HS, San Sebastian, P.R.
41. +Jacob Ruckle, rhp, Mohave HS, Bullhead City, Ariz. / Chandler-Gilbert (Ariz.) JC.
42. *Jim Brauer, rhp, University of Michigan.
43. *Ian Thurman-Kelly, lhp, Eastern New Mexico University.
44. *Lance Scoggins, lhp, Okaloosa-Walton (Fla.) CC.
45. *Daniel McDonald, rhp, Morris Hills HS, Rockaway, N.J.
**46. *Jeremy Hefner, rhp, Perkins Tryon HS, Perkins, Okla.—(2012-13)**
47. *Ryan Paul, lhp, Los Angeles Pierce JC.
48. *Morgan Carlile, lhp, Three Oaks HS, Summerside, Prince Edward Island.
49. *Daniel Buller, lhp, Fresno (Calif.) CC.
50. *Sean Cunningham, lhp, Bullard HS, Fresno, Calif.

## NEW YORK YANKEES (28)

1. **Philip Hughes, rhp, Foothill HS, Santa Ana, Calif.** (Choice from Astros as compensation for Type A free agent Andy Pettitte).**—(2007-15)**
DRAFT DROP *First 2004 high school draft pick to reach majors (April 26, 2007)*
1. (Choice to Dodgers as compensation for Type A free agent Paul Quantrill)
1. Jon Poterson, c, Chandler (Ariz.) HS (Supplemental choice—37th—as compensation for Pettitte).—(Low A)
1. **Jeff Marquez, rhp, Sacramento (Calif.) CC** (Supplemental choice—41st—as compensation for Type A free agent David Wells).**—(2010-11)**
2. Brett Smith, rhp, UC Irvine (Choice from Padres as compensation for Wells).—(AA)
2. (Choice to White Sox as compensation for Type A free agent Tom Gordon)
**3. Christian Garcia, rhp, Gulliver Prep, Miami.—(2012)**
4. Jason Jones, rhp, Liberty University.—(AAA)
5. Jesse Hoover, rhp, Indiana Tech.—(High A)
6. Nate Phillips, ss, Grace Prep Academy, Roanoke, Texas.
7. *Alex Garabedian, c, Christopher Columbus HS, Miami.
8. Mike Martinez, rhp, Cal State Fullerton.
9. Grant Plumley, ss, Oral Roberts University.
10. Ben Scheinbaum, lhp, University of Nevada-Las Vegas.
11. Cody Ehlers, 1b, University of Missouri.
12. Rod Allen, of, Oklahoma State University.
DRAFT DROP *Son of Rod Allen, major leaguer (1983-88)*
13. P.J. Pilittere, c, Cal State Fullerton.
14. Ben Jones, 1b, University of Louisiana-Monroe.
15. Robert Villanova, of, Iona College.
16. Ryan Haag, 2b, Fresno State University.
17. Even Tierce, of, Texas State University.
18. Yosvany Almario-Cabrera, 3b, Miami-Dade CC South.
19. Jordan DeVoir, ss, University of Illinois-Chicago.
20. Jose Tadeo, rhp, Culver-Stockton (Mo.) College.
21. Scott Rich, of, Rider University.
22. *Patrick Caldwell, lhp, Yavapai (Ariz.) JC.
23. *Jamarkus James, of, Grand Prairie (Texas) HS.
24. *Ryan Tabor, lhp, CC of Southern Nevada.
25. *Garrison Campfield, rhp, Navarro (Texas) JC.
26. Sean Kramer, lhp, Iona College.
27. *Jeremiah Shepherd, rhp, Texarkana (Texas) JC.
DRAFT DROP *Son of Ron Shepherd, major leaguer (1984-86)*
28. *Jake McCarter, rhp, Navarro (Texas) JC.
29. *Kyle Ginley, rhp, Dunnellon (Fla.) HS.
30. *Jonathan Lindenberger, rhp, San Jacinto (Texas) JC.
31. +Grant Duff, rhp, JC of the Sequoias (Calif.).
32. *Clint Preisendorfer, lhp, La Jolla Country Day HS, La Jolla, Calif.
**33. +Mike Dunn, 1b-lhp, CC of Southern Nevada.—(2009-15)**
34. *Jonathan Bertschinger, of, Navarro (Texas) JC.
35. *Michael Hale, lhp, Ball State University.
36. *Matt Harrington, rhp, Fort Worth Cats / Central League.
DRAFT DROP *First-round draft pick (7th overall), Rockies (2000)*
37. *Ryan Rote, rhp, Vanderbilt University.
DRAFT DROP *Grandson of Tobin Rote, quarterback, National Football league/American Football League (1950-66)*
38. *Joseph Krebs, lhp, Navarro (Texas) JC.
39. *Tim LeMaster, of, Perry Meridian HS, Indianapolis, Ind.
40. Nathan Griffin, c, Oral Roberts University.
41. *Mike Lomba, lhp, Sacramento (Calif.) CC.
42. *Ronald Ball, rhp, Cypress (Calif.) JC.
43. *Keaton Hougen, rhp, Wylie (Texas) HS.
44. *Harrison Ashmore, rhp, Mansfield (Texas) HS.
45. *Drew Fiorenza, rhp, Middle Georgia JC.
46. +Juan Velazquez, rhp, Grossmont (Calif.) CC.
47. *Justin O'Bannon, rhp, San Jacinto (Texas) JC.
48. *Erik Morrison, ss, Arroyo Grande (Calif.) HS.
49. *Andrew Spaulding, of, Purcell Marian HS, Cincinnati.
**50. *Chris Davis, 3b, Longview (Texas) HS.—(2008-15)**

## OAKLAND ATHLETICS (26)

1. **Landon Powell, c, University of South Carolina** (Choice from Red Sox as compensation for Type A free agent Keith Foulke).**—(2009-11)**
1. Richie Robnett, of, Fresno State University.—(AAA)
1. **Danny Putnam, of, Stanford University** (Supplemental choice—36th—as compensation for Foulke).**—(2007)**
1. **Huston Street, rhp, University of Texas** (Supplemental choice—40th—as compensation for Type A free agent Miguel Tejada).**—(2005-15)**
DRAFT DROP *First player from 2004 draft to reach majors (April 6, 2005)*
2. Michael Rogers, rhp, North Carolina State University (Choice from Orioles as compensation for Tejada).—(AA)
**2. Kurt Suzuki, c, Cal State Fullerton.—(2007-15)**
**3. Jason Windsor, rhp, Cal State Fullerton.—(2006)**
**4. Ryan Webb, rhp, Clearwater Central Catholic HS, Palm Harbor, Fla.—(2009-15)**
DRAFT DROP *Son of Hank Webb, major leaguer (1972-77)*
**5. Kevin Melillo, 2b, University of South Carolina.—(2007)**
6. Derek Tharpe, lhp, University of Tennessee.
7. Jarod McAuliff, rhp, University of Oklahoma.
8. Myron Leslie, 3b, University of South Florida.
9. Chad Boyd, of, El Camino Real HS, West Hills, Calif.
**10. Tommy Everidge, 1b, Sonoma State (Calif.) University.—(2009)**
11. Steve Sharpe, rhp, Central Missouri State University.
12. Nick Blasi, of, Wichita State University.
13. Scott Drucker, rhp, University of Tennessee.
14. *Jorge Charry, rhp, Puerto Rico Baseball Academy, Fajardo, P.R.
15. Ryan Ford, lhp, Eastern Michigan University.
16. Tyler Best, c, Lewis-Clark State (Idaho) College.
17. Clay Tichota, rhp, Regis (Colo.) University.
18. *Jeremy Slayden, of, Georgia Tech.
19. Ryan Ruiz, 2b, University of Nevada-Las Vegas.
20. Robert Semerano, rhp, Fordham University.
21. Chalon Tietje, of, Cal Poly San Luis Obispo.
22. Ryan Jones, of, East Carolina University.
23. Shawn Martinez, rhp, Colorado State University-Pueblo.
**24. Dallas Braden, lhp, Texas Tech.—(2007-11)**
25. *Jim Conroy, rhp, University of Illinois.
26. Steven Carter, rhp, Coastal Carolina University.
27. *Clayton Turner, rhp, Northwestern State University.
28. Andre Piper-Jordan, of, Everett (Wash.) CC.
29. Wesley Long, ss, University of Alabama-Huntsville.
30. Haas Pratt, 1b, University of Arkansas.
**31. Connor Robertson, rhp, Birmingham-Southern College.—(2007-08)**
**32. Jeff Gray, rhp, Southwest Missouri State University.—(2008-12)**
33. Scott Fairbanks, rhp, Lewis-Clark State (Idaho) College.
34. *Yusuf Carter, of, El Paso (Texas) CC.
35. *Broc Coffman, lhp, Lower Columbia (Wash.) JC.
36. *Matt Cassel, rhp, University of Southern California.
DRAFT DROP *Quarterback, National Football League (2005-14) • Brother of Jack Cassel, major leaguer (2007-08)*
37. *Beau Seabury, c, Skajit Valley (Wash.) CC.
38. *Drew Saberhagen, 1b-lhp, Calabasas (Calif.) HS.
DRAFT DROP *Son of Bret Saberhagen, major leaguer (1984-2001)*
39. *Joseph Florio, 2b, Blair Academy, Blairstown, N.J.
40. *Danny Figueroa, of, University of Miami.

## PHILADELPHIA PHILLIES (21)

**1. Greg Golson, of, John Connally HS, Austin, Texas.—(2008-11)**
**2. Jason Jaramillo, c, Oklahoma State University.—(2009-11)**
**3. J.A. Happ, lhp, Northwestern University.—(2007-15)**
**4. Lou Marson, c, Coronado HS, Scottsdale, Ariz.—(2008-13)**
5. Andy Baldwin, lhp, Oregon State University.—(AAA)
6. Sean Gamble, of, Auburn University.
DRAFT DROP *Son of Oscar Gamble, major leaguer (1969-85)*
7. John Hardy, 2b, University of Arizona.
DRAFT DROP *Cousin of J.J. Hardy, major leaguer (2005-15)*
8. Sam Orr, ss, Biola (Calif.) University.
9. Andy Macfarlane, of, Treasure Valley (Ore.) CC.
10. Reece Cresswell, c, Perryton (Texas) HS.
11. Carl Galloway, 1b, Biola (Calif.) University.
**12. Joe Bisenius, rhp, Oklahoma City University.—(2007-10)**
13. *James Adkins, lhp, Wilson Central HS, Mount Juliet, Tenn.
DRAFT DROP *First-round draft pick (39th overall), Dodgers (2007)*
14. Jason Martinez, lhp, Mesa State (Colo.) College.
DRAFT DROP *Son of Tippy Marinez, major leaguer (1974-88)*
15. Zac Cline, lhp, West Virginia University.
16. Kyle Allen, lhp, Lewis-Clark State (Idaho) College.
17. Ryan Frith, of, University of Southern Mississippi.
18. Greg Isaacson, 2b, University of Washington.
19. Jacob Barrack, rhp, Pepperdine University.
20. Nathan Johnson, rhp, University of Iowa.
21. Buck Shaw, 1b, Connors State (Okla.) JC.
22. Anthony Buffone, 3b, University of Maryland.
23. Kevin Rose, rhp, University of San Francisco.
24. Aaron Wilson, rhp, University of San Diego.
25. Joe Dirnberger, 3b, Mesa State (Colo.) College.
26. Nick Evangelista, rhp, University of Pittsburgh.
27. *Jason Appel, of, John F. Kennedy HS, Plainview, N.Y.
28. +Chris Raulinaitis, rhp, Sacramento (Calif.) CC.
29. Josh Mader, ss, University of New Mexico.
30. Kevin Shepard, lhp, Boston College.
31. *Jesse Kovacs, ss, University of the Pacific.
32. Nick Shimer, 3b, George Mason University.
33. Clary Carlsen, rhp, University of Hawaii.
34. +Alex McEnaney, rhp, Royal Palm Beach HS, West Palm Beach, Fla. / Palm Beach (Fla.) CC.
DRAFT DROP *Son of Will McEnaney, major leaguer (1974-79)*
35. Derek Brant, c, Grand View (Iowa) College.
**36. *Andrew Romine, ss, Trabuco Hills HS, Mission Viejo, Calif.—(2010-15)**
DRAFT DROP *Son of Kevin Romine, major leaguer (1985-91) • Brother of Austin Romine, major leaguer (2011-15)*
37. *Steven Marquardt, 3b, Kennewick (Wash.) HS.
38. *James Brown, rhp, Brunswick (Ga.) HS.
39. *Dusty Brabender, rhp, Oregon (Wis.) HS.
40. Michael Mihalik, rhp, University of Delaware.

41. *Bryce Massanari, c, Centennial HS, Las Vegas, Nev.
42. Curt Miaso, of, Chaparral HS, Scottsdale, Ariz.
43. *Jerome Wooley, of, Columbia HS, Decatur, Ga.
44. *Erik Morris, c, Michigan State University.

DRAFT DROP *Son of Jack Morris, major leaguer (1977-94)*

45. *Lucas Miranda, 3b, Ferndale (Calif.) HS.
46. *Aaron Brown, rhp, Clear Creek HS, League City, Texas.
47. *Brendan Lafferty, lhp, Poly HS, Riverside, Calif.
48. *Esteban Lopez, c, Yavapai (Ariz.) JC.
49. *Willie Mays, of, Bryan Station HS, Lexington, Ky.
50. *Matt Johnson, 1b, Bryan HS, Omaha, Neb.

## PITTSBURGH PIRATES (11)

1. **Neil Walker, c, Pine Richland HS, Gibsonia, Pa.—(2009-15)**

DRAFT DROP *Son of Tom Walker, major leaguer (1972-77)*

2. **Brian Bixler, ss, Eastern Michigan University.—(2008-12)**
3. Eddie Prasch, 3b, Milton HS, Alpharetta, Ga.—(AA)
4. Joe Bauserman, rhp, Lincoln HS, Tallahassee, Fla.—(Low A)
5. Kyle Bloom, lhp, Illinois State University.—(AA)
6. A.J. Johnson, of, Tallahassee (Fla.) CC.
7. Jason Quarles, rhp, Southern University.
8. Eric Ridener, rhp, Taravella HS, Coral Springs, Fla.
9. Chris Covington, of, Brookwood HS, Snellville, Ga.
10. Derek Hankins, rhp, University of Memphis.
11. Matt Guillory, rhp, University of Louisiana-Monroe.
12. *J.P. Padron, 3b, Clear Creek HS, League City, Texas.
13. Brett Grandstrand, 2b, Coastal Carolina University.
14. Jermel Lomack, 2b, Prairie View A&M University.
15. *John Slone, c, Miami (Ohio) University.
16. Ryan Herbort, rhp, Northwest Whitfield HS, Dalton, Ga.
17. Matt Bishop, rhp, East Carolina University.
18. ***Cory Luebke, lhp, Marion HS, Maria Stein, Ohio.—(2010-12)**

DRAFT DROP *First-round draft pick (63rd overall), Padres (2007)*

19. +Brad Clapp, rhp, Juanita HS, Kirkland, Wash. / Bellevue (Wash.) CC.
20. Brandon Reddinger, c, Washington State University.
21. Derek Drage, rhp, Southwest Missouri State University.
22. Mike Hofius, 1b, Long Beach State University.
23. Dustin Craig, rhp, Sam Houston State University.
24. Joe Salas, lhp, University of New Mexico.
25. Kevin Miller, rhp, Bucknell University.
26. *Jason Tweedy, ss, Newark Memorial HS, Newark, Calif.
27. *Scott Leffler, c, Lake City (Fla.) CC.
28. *Pat McAnaney, lhp, Westhill HS, Syracuse, N.Y.
29. *Christian Romple, c, Big Bend (Wash.) CC.
30. Issael Gonzalez, 2b, Edouard Montpetit HS, Montreal.
31. *Oliver Marmol, ss, Dr. Phillips HS, Orlando, Fla.
32. *Chris Palma, rhp, JC of the Canyons (Calif.).
33. *Justin Byler, c, Warren G. Harding HS, Warren, Ohio.
34. *Nick Beghtol, c, Mountainview HS, Fort Collins, Colo.
35. *Jeff Robinson, rhp, Roswell (Ga.) HS.
36. *Jose Nunez, ss, Puerto Rico Baseball Academy, Caguas, P.R.
37. *Tim Rice, lhp, University of Richmond.
38. *Keith Pedersen, lhp, Glide (Ore.) HS.
39. **+Todd Redmond, rhp, St. Petersburg (Fla.) CC.—(2012-15)**
40. ***Jeremy Horst, lhp, Iowa Western CC.—(2011-13)**
41. Dan Schwartzbauer, ss, Duquesne University.
42. *Mikel McIntyre, of, Diablo Valley (Calif.) JC.
43. *Stephen Ashcraft, of, Brentwood (Tenn.) HS.
44. *Sean Setzer, 1b, Woodrow Wilson HS, Portland, Ore.
45. *Corey Kemp, c, Centennial HS, Franklin, Tenn.
46. *Josh Scofield, lhp, Newport HS, Bellevue, Wash.
47. *Zach Phillips, rhp, Lee County HS, Sanford, N.C.
48. *Ricardo Rivas, rhp, El Paso (Texas) CC.
49. *Patrick Wandtke, lhp, West Orange HS, Winter Garden, Fla.
50. *Brock Lindeke, c, Soquel (Calif.) HS.

## ST. LOUIS CARDINALS (19)

1. **Chris Lambert, rhp, Boston College.—(2008-09)**
2. Mike Ferris, 1b, Miami (Ohio) University.—(AAA)
3. Eric Haberer, lhp, Southern Illinois University.—(AA)
4. Donnie Smith, rhp, Old Dominion University.—(High A)
5. Wes Swackhamer, of, Tulane University.—(High A)
6. **Jarrett Hoffpauir, 2b, University of Southern Mississippi.—(2009-10)**
7. *Buck Cody, lhp, University of Texas.
8. Matt Shepherd, ss, University of Southern Mississippi.
9. **Mike Parisi, rhp, Manhattan College.—(2008)**
10. Brady Toops, c, University of Arkansas.
11. Simon Williams, of, University of Maine.
12. **Mark Worrell, rhp, Florida International University.—(2008-11)**
13. Daniel Nelson, ss, Los Angeles Pierce JC.
14. Jake Mullinax, 2b, University of Nebraska.
15. Jeremy Zick, rhp, University of Mississippi.
16. Matt Scherer, lhp, LeMoyne College.
17. Chris Noonan, lhp, Seton Hall University.
18. *Cameron Blair, ss, Texas Tech.
19. Das Jesson, 3b, Cal State Los Angeles.
20. Chad Gabriel, of, Santa Ana (Calif.) JC.
21. Mike Sillman, rhp, University of Nebraska.
22. Billy Becher, 1b, New Mexico State University.
23. Phillip Andersen, rhp, Chandler-Gilbert (Ariz.) CC.
24. Jose Delgado, 2b, Texas Tech.
25. Mike Miller, of, Cal State Los Angeles.
26. Steven Sherman, of, University of North Carolina-Asheville.
27. *Christian Reyes, c, Jose M. Pestrana HS, Aguas Buenas, P.R.
28. Chris Della Rocco, rhp, Monmouth University.
29. Cory Taillon, c, Cal Poly San Luis Obispo.
30. Brandon Marcelli, c, Fresno State University.
31. Daniel Baysinger, rhp, Cornell University.
32. Austin Tubb, rhp, University of Southern Mississippi.
33. Micheal Gross, rhp, University of North Carolina.
34. Brett Cooley, 1b, University of Houston.
35. Brian Parish, rhp, Iona College.
36. Chris Bova, rhp, Ohio University.
37. Chris Patrick, ss, Fresno State University.
38. Adam Burton, c, University of Arkansas-Monticello.
39. Sam Herbert, of, Cal Poly San Luis Obispo.
40. Sean Dobson, of, University of Toledo.
41. Mark Broome, 3b, Delta State (Miss.) University.
42. Matt Rigoli, 1b, Parsippany (N.J.) HS.
43. Jessen Grant, rhp, Columbia University.
44. Quinton Robertson, rhp, University of Nebraska.
45. Gregg Pleeter, rhp, Fairleigh Dickinson University.
46. *Matt Johnson, rhp, Eupora (Miss.) HS.
47. *Nick Dinapoli, of, Buena HS, Ventura, Calif.

## SAN DIEGO PADRES (1)

1. Matt Bush, ss-rhp, Mission Bay HS, San Diego.—(AA)
2. (Choice to Yankees as compensation for Type A free agent David Wells)
3. Billy Killian, c, Chippewa Hills HS, Stanwood, Mich.—(AAA)
4. Daryl Jones, 1b, Westchester HS, Gardena, Calif.—(Low A)
5. **Sean Kazmar, ss, CC of Southern Nevada.—(2008)**
6. Jonathon Ellis, rhp, The Citadel.
7. Ricky Steik, rhp, Golden West (Calif.) JC.
8. Vern Sterry, rhp, North Carolina State University.
9. David O'Hagan, rhp, Stanford University.
10. Chris Kolkhorst, of, Rice University.
11. Matt Varner, rhp, University of Houston.
12. **Mike Ekstrom, rhp, Pt. Loma Nazarene (Calif.) University.—(2008-12)**
13. Jake Vose, rhp, University of Nevada-Las Vegas.
14. *Matt Montgomery, rhp, Okaloosa-Walton (Fla.) JC.
15. *Brandon Thomson, lhp, Gilbert (Ariz.) HS.
16. Ben Krosschell, rhp, Highlands Ranch (Colo.) HS.
17. Clayton Hamilton, rhp, Penn State University.
18. *Michael Moon, 3b, University of Southern California.
19. Craig Johnson, of, Cal State Sacramento.
20. Brian Fryer, of, New Mexico Highlands University.
21. Gary Gallegos, lhp, Biola (Calif.) University.
22. Kyle Stutes, lhp, Lamar University.
23. Rielly Embrey, 1b, San Diego State University.
24. Jodam Rivera, ss, Puerto Rico Baseball Academy, Hatillo, P.R.
25. Brian Burks, rhp, Georgia Tech.
26. Kelvin Vazquez, ss, Indians Hills (Iowa) CC.
27. Orlando Diaz, 3b, Jacksonville University.
28. B.J. Jenkins, rhp, Trevecca Nazarene (Tenn.) University.
29. E.J. Shanks, rhp, Oklahoma City University.
30. Adam Kroft, rhp, University of Albany.
31. Matt Thayer, of, UCLA.
32. *Todd Johnson, of, Meridian (Miss.) JC.
33. *Adam Miller, rhp, Indian Hills (Iowa) CC.
34. *Gary Moran, rhp, Fresno (Calif.) CC.
35. *Josh Bartusick, 1b, Golden West (Calif.) JC.
36. *Chorye Spoone, rhp, CC of Baltimore-Catonsville.
37. *Erik Lovett, of, Louisburg (N.C.) JC.
38. *Michael Lorentson, lhp, Malvern Prep, Springfield, Pa.
39. *Bobby Spain, 3b, Norman (Okla.) HS.
40. **Brandon Kintzler, rhp, Dixie State (Utah) JC.—(2010-15)**
41. *Taylor Bennett, rhp, Okaloosa-Walton (Fla.) CC.
42. **+Kyle Blanks, 1b, Moriarty HS, Edgewood, N.M. / Yavapai (Ariz.) CC.—(2009-15)**
43. *Zach Shadle, rhp, Tacoma (Wash.) JC.
44. *Omar Kadir, rhp, Lethbridge (Alberta) CC.
45. *Cameron Nickell, of, Columbia State (Tenn.) CC.
46. *Aaron Breit, rhp, Thomas More Prep HS, Hays, Kan.
47. *Sean Cunningham, 3b, Sinclair SS, Whitby, Ontario.
48. *David Minor, of, South Hagerstown (Md.) HS.
49. *Brandon Tuten, rhp, Mount Pleasant (Tenn.) HS.
50. *Brian Joynt, 1b, Indian Hills (Iowa) CC.

## SAN FRANCISCO GIANTS (29)

1. (Choice to Royals as compensation for Type B free agent Michael Tucker)
2. Eddy Martinez-Esteve, of, Florida State University.—(AAA)
3. **John Bowker, of, Long Beach State University.—(2008-11)**
4. **Clay Timpner, of, University of Central Florida.—(2008)**
5. Garrett Broshius, rhp, University of Missouri.—(AAA)
6. Justin Hedrick, rhp, Northeastern University.
7. Will Thompson, 1b, Santa Clara University.
8. *Omar Aguilar, rhp, Merced (Calif.) JC.
9. *Jamie Arnesen, lhp, Liberty HS, Bakersfield, Calif.
10. Spencer Grogan, lhp, Oklahoma State University.
11. Darrin Sack, rhp, Sonoma State (Calif.) University.
12. **Kevin Frandsen, 2b, San Jose State University.—(2006-14)**
13. *Thomas Martin, lhp, University of Richmond.
14. **Eugene Espinelli, lhp, Texas Christian University.—(2008)**
15. Jeff Palumbo, ss, George Mason University.
16. Emmanuel Cividanes, of, Broward (Fla.) CC.
17. Jordan Thomson, rhp, Northeastern University.
18. Jeremiah Luster, ss, Oceanside (Calif.) HS.
19. Nathan Pendley, lhp, Oregon State University.
20. Rickey Putman, rhp, University of Houston.
21. Simon Klink, 3b, Purdue University.
22. Doug MacKay, rhp, University of Utah.
23. Brad Groth, ss, Elmhurst (Ill.) College.
24. Matt Raguse, rhp, Miami (Ohio) University.
25. John Acha, 3b, Cal State Sacramento.
26. Trevor Wohlgemuth, rhp, Northern Illinois University.
27. **Jonathan Sanchez, lhp, Ohio Dominican College.—(2006-13)**
28. Charlie Babineaux, of, University of Mississippi.
29. +Ryan Shaver, rhp, Lower Columbia (Wash.) JC.
30. Kevin Jenson, rhp, Loyola Marymount University.
31. Kyle Haines, ss, Eastern Illinois University.
32. +Morgan Brinson, rhp, Walnut Grove SS, Langley, B.C. / Kwantlen (B.C.) JC.
33. Judson Richards, 1b, Pt. Loma Nazarene (Calif.) University.
34. *Jacob Coash, lhp, JC of the Canyons (Calif.)
35. Tim Grant, rhp, Dartmouth College.
36. Buster Lussier, rhp, Diman Vocational HS, Fall River, Mass.
37. *Erik Meyer, rhp, Eastern Washington University.
38. ***Tyson Brummett, rhp, Central Arizona JC.—(2012)**
39. *Brad Schwarzenbach, rhp, St. John Bosco HS, Bellflower, Calif.
40. *Mac Nelson, c, Timpanogas HS, Cedar Hills, Utah.
41. Chase Smith, rhp, University of Central Oklahoma.
42. *Ryan Addition, rhp, Western HS, Davie, Fla.
43. *Jack Spradlin, lhp, Southwestern (Calif.) JC.
44. T.J. Gornati, rhp, University of Pittsburgh.
45. *Kris Gibson, 1b, San Francisco State University.
46. +David Quinowski, lhp, Redlands (Calif.) HS / Riverside (Calif.) CC.
47. Matt Minor, rhp, University of Nevada-Las Vegas.
48. Benny Cepeda, rhp, Ohio Dominican College.
49. +Michael Santoro, of, Northern Illinois University.
50. *Garrett Lingle, 2b, Mission Bay HS, San Diego.

## SEATTLE MARINERS (22)

1. (Choice to Twins as compensation for Type A free agent Eddie Guardado)
2. (Choice to Royals as compensation for Type A free agent Raul Ibanez)
3. **Matt Tuiasosopo, ss, Woodinville (Wash.) HS.—(2008-13)**

DRAFT DROP *Son of Manu Tuiasosopo, defensive end/National Football League (1979-86) • Brother of Marques Tuiasosopo, quarterback/National Football League (2001-08)*

4. **Rob Johnson, c, University of Houston.—(2007-13)**
5. **Mark Lowe, rhp, University of Texas-Arlington.—(2006-15)**
6. Jermaine Brock, of, Ottawa Hills HS, Grand Rapids, Mich.
7. Sebastien Boucher, of, Bethune-Cookman College.
8. Marshall Hubbard, of, University of North Carolina.
9. Jeff Dominguez, ss, Puerto Rico Baseball Academy, Carolina, P.R.
10. Eric Carter, rhp, Delaware State University.
11. **+Michael Saunders, 3b, Lambrick Park SS, Victoria, B.C. / Tallahassee (Fla.) CC.—(2009-15)**
12. Steve Uhlmansiek, lhp, Wichita State University.
13. *Kris Kasarjian, of, Los Angeles Pierce JC.
14. Brent Johnson, of, University of Nevada-Las Vegas.
15. *Brent Thomas, of, Bellevue (Wash.) CC.
16. Chad Fillinger, rhp, Santa Clara University.
17. ***J.P. Arencibia, c, Westminster Christian HS, Miami.—(2010-15)**

DRAFT DROP *First-round draft pick (21st overall), Blue Jays (2007)*

18. Jack Arroyo, 2b, Cal State Sacramento.

DRAFT DROP *Son of Rudy Arroyo, major leaguer (1971)*

19. Brandon Green, ss, Wichita State University.
20. *Brian Chavez, ss, Quartz Hill HS, Palmdale, Calif.
21. Mumba Rivera, rhp, Bethune-Cookman College.
22. David Hall, of, San Diego State University.
23. *Ben Summerhays, 1b, Stanford University.
24. Greg Slee, c, Huntington (Ind.) College.
25. Joe Jacobitz, c, University of San Francisco.
26. *Zach Ashwood, lhp, The Colony (Texas) HS.
27. Aaron Trolia, rhp, Washington State University.
28. Adam Brandt, lhp, Otterbrien (Ohio) College.
29. Mike Ciccotelli, lhp, Villanova University.
30. +Rollie Gibson, lhp, Fresno (Calif.) CC.
31. *Chad Rothford, 1b, Fresno (Calif.) CC.

32. Don Clement, rhp, Colorado State University-Pueblo.
33. Marquise Liverpool, of, Don Bosco Prep, Ramsey, N.J.
**34. *Duke Welker, rhp, Woodinville (Wash.) HS.—(2013)**
35. *Brandon Javis, ss, Cross Creek HS, Augusta, Ga.
**36. *Nick Hagadone, lhp, Sumner (Wash.) HS.—(2011-15)**
DRAFT DROP *First-round draft pick (55th overall), Red Sox (2007)*
**37. *James Russell, lhp, Heritage HS, Colleyville, Texas.—(2010-15)**
DRAFT DROP *Son of Jeff Russell, major leaguer (1983-96)*
38. Harold Williams, lhp, Mount San Jacinto (Calif.) JC.
39. *Jake Opitz, ss, Heritage HS, Littleton, Colo.
40. +Michael Schilling, rhp, Fresno (Calif.) CC.
41. *Garrett Parcell, rhp, Norco (Calif.) HS.
42. +Erwin Jacobo, 3b, Braddock HS, Miami / Palm Beach (Fla.) CC.
43. *Luis Coste, of, Puerto Rico Baseball Academy, San Juan, P.R.
44. *Felix Martinez, of, Broward (Fla.) CC.
45. *Dwayne Lynah, of, Spartanburg Methodist (S.C.) JC.
46. *Daniel Martin, of, Indian River (Fla.) CC.
47. *Andrew McDonald, c, Sahuaro HS, Tucson, Ariz.
48. *Zachary Walden, c, Stockbridge HS, McDonough, Ga.
49. *Andrew Reichard, rhp, Seminole (Fla.) JC.
50. *Leighton Autrey, of, Navarro (Texas) JC.

## TAMPA BAY DEVIL RAYS (4)

**1. Jeff Niemann, rhp, Rice University.—(2008-12)**
**2. Reid Brignac, ss, St. Amant (La.) HS.—(2008-15)**
**3. Wade Davis, rhp, Lake Wales (Fla.) HS.—(2009-15)**
4. Matt Spring, c, Dixie State (Utah) JC.—(AAA)
**5. Jacob McGee, lhp, Edward Reed HS, Sparks, Nev.—(2010-15)**
6. Ryan Royster, of, Churchill HS, Eugene, Ore.
**7. Fernando Perez, of, Columbia University.—(2008-09)**
**8. Rhyne Hughes, 1b, Pearl River (Miss.) CC.—(2010)**
9. Joseph Muro, rhp, Mount San Antonio (Calif.) JC.
10. Matt Walker, rhp, Central HS, Baton Rouge, La.
11. Josh Asanovich, 2b, Arizona State University.
12. Chris Cunningham, of, South Suburban (Ill.) JC.
**13. Andy Sonnanstine, rhp, Kent State University.—(2007-11)**
14. +Woods Fines, rhp, Northwood HS, Pittsboro, N.C. / Louisburg (N.C.) JC.
15. Ken Brock, lhp, Lane (Ore.) CC.
16. *Cale Iorg, ss, Karns HS, Knoxville, Tenn.
DRAFT DROP *Son of Garth Iorg, major leaguer (1978-87) • Brother of Eli Iorg, 14th-round draft pick, Cubs (2004); first-round draft pick, Astros (2005)*
17. Marcus Barriger, rhp, Armstrong Atlantic State (Ga.) University.
18. +Jim Scholzen, ss, Hurricane (Utah) HS / Dixie State (Utah) JC.
19. Chris Nowak, 3b, University of South Carolina-Spartanburg.
20. *Matt Duryea, lhp, Marshfield HS, North Bend, Ore.
21. Pat Breen, of, University of Houston.
22. Ryan Bitter, rhp, Siena College.
23. Logan Wiens, 1b, Merced (Calif.) HS.
24. Francisco Leandro, of, Central Missouri State University.
**25. *Deunte Heath, rhp, Lake City (Fla.) CC.—(2012-13)**
26. Alex Crooks, 1b, East Los Angeles CC.
27. *Matt Goyen, lhp, Georgia College & State University.
28. Nick Wagner, rhp, Georgia Tech.
**29. *Daniel McCutchen, rhp, University of Oklahoma.—(2009-14)**
30. Aaron Walker, lhp, Georgia Tech.
31. *Craig Rodriguez, lhp, Pearl River (Miss.) CC.
32. *Matt Rainey, rhp, Odessa (Texas) JC.
33. Patrick Cottrell, ss, University of West Florida.
34. *Grant Theophilus, lhp, Cypress (Calif.) JC.
35. Billy Evers, rhp, Eckerd (Fla.) College.
36. *Ryan Davis, 3b, Chaparral HS, Scottsdale, Ariz.
37. *Brian McCormick, c, Arundel HS, Gambrills, Md.
38. *Ryan Conan, ss, Archbishop Mitty HS, San Jose, Calif.
39. Drew Bigda, lhp, College of Holy Cross.
40. *Jason Dean, of, Sacramento (Calif.) CC.
41. J.T. Hall, of, Southwest Mississippi JC.
42. *Matt Ware, lhp, Quartz Hill HS, Lancaster, Calif.
43. John Price, lhp, University of Mobile (Ala.).
44. +Matt Fields, 1b, Rainier Beach HS, Seattle / Green River (Wash.) CC.
45. Robbie Bouman, ss, Tusculum (Tenn.) College.
46. Chris Kelly, rhp, Jacksonville University.
47. *Ben Lanier, ss, Kinston (N.C.) HS.
48. *Andrew Gray, 1b, Holy Spirit HS, Tuscaloosa, Ala.
49. *Patrick Mahoney, c, Lincoln HS, Des Moines, Iowa.
50. *Jerrylee Scott, ss, Livonia (La.) HS.

## TEXAS RANGERS (10)

**1. Thomas Diamond, rhp, University of New Orleans.—(2010)**
**1. Eric Hurley, rhp, Wolfson HS, Jacksonville, Fla.** (Choice from Braves as compensation for Type B free agent John Thomson).**—(2008)**
2. K.C. Herren, of, Auburn (Wash.) HS.—(High A)
3. Micheal Schlact, rhp, Wheeler HS, Marietta, Ga.—(AA)
**4. Brandon Boggs, of, Georgia Tech.—(2008-11)**
**5. Mike Nickeas, c, Georgia Tech.—(2010-13)**
6. Billy Susdorf, of, UCLA.
7. Ben Harrison, of, University of Florida.
8. Mark Roberts, rhp, University of Oklahoma.
9. Jim Fasano, 1b, University of Richmond.
**10. *Justin Maxwell, of, University of Maryland.—(2007-15)**
**11. Travis Metcalf, 3b, University of Kansas.—(2007-08)**
12. *Kevin Ardoin, rhp, University of Louisiana-Lafayette.
13. Kyle Rogers, rhp, Ball HS, Galveston, Texas.
**14. Tug Hulett, 2b, Auburn University.—(2008-09)**
DRAFT DROP *Son of Tim Hulett, major leaguer (1983-96)*
15. John Lujan, rhp, New Mexico JC.
16. Jarrad Burcie, rhp, Tarleton State (Texas) University.
17. *Nic Crosta, of, Santa Clara University.
18. Freddie Thon, 1b, Brevard (Fla.) CC.
DRAFT DROP *Nephew of Dickie Thon, major leaguer (1979-93)*
19. Marc Cornell, rhp, Ohio University.
20. Shawn Phillips, rhp, Delaware State University.
21. Bobby Lenoir, ss, University of Richmond.
22. Ryan Griffith, c, Birmingham-Southern College.
**23. +Zach Phillips, lhp, Galt Union HS, Galt, Calif. / Sacramento (Calif.) CC.—(2001-13)**
24. Charles Isbell, rhp, Temescal Canyon HS, Lake Elsinore, Calif.
25. Ben Foster, lhp, Tennessee Temple University.
26. J.D. Cockroft, lhp, University of Miami.
27. Marlon Melendez, rhp, Chemeketa (Ore.) CC.
28. +Brett Zamzow, rhp, Navarro (Texas) JC.
29. *Justin Klipp, rhp, Cuesta (Calif.) JC.
30. Wally Backman, ss, Crook County HS, Prineville, Ore.
DRAFT DROP *Son of Wally Backman, first-round draft pick (1977); major leaguer (1980-93)*
31. Nicholas Casanova, rhp, Canyon HS, Corona, Calif.
32. Michael Mask, of, Texas Tech.
33. Luis Rodriguez, ss, New Mexico JC.
34. Clint Brannon, lhp, University of Arkansas.
**35. *Sam Demel, rhp, Spring (Texas) HS.—(2010-12)**
36. Jesse Ingram, rhp, University of California.
37. Justin Lensch, lhp, University of Louisiana-Monroe.
38. Craig Hurba, c, Mount Olive (N.C.) College.
39. Jose Torres, of, East Los Angeles JC.
40. Tony Irvin, rhp, Hillsborough (Fla.) JC.
41. Clayton Jerome, rhp, Texas Christian University.
42. +Joe Kemp, of, Indiana University.
43. *Austin Faught, lhp, University of Louisiana-Lafayette.
44. *Joe Franklin, 3b, Dawson (Mon.) CC.
45. *Jeffrey Hoffner, rhp, Yavapai (Ariz.) JC.
46. *Arthur Hill, rhp, Mount San Jacinto (Calif.) JC.
47. +Kellan McConnell, rhp, Santa Clara University.
48. *Brian Capon, c, Saddleback (Calif.) JC.
49. *Adam Resendez, of, Boswell HS, Fort Worth, Texas.
50. Ivan Ramirez, lhp, UC Santa Barbara.

## TORONTO BLUE JAYS (16)

**1. David Purcey, lhp, University of Oklahoma.—(2008-13)**
**1. Zach Jackson, lhp, Texas A&M University** (Supplemental choice—32nd—as compensation for Type A free agent Kelvim Escobar).**—(2006-09)**
**2. Curtis Thigpen, c, University of Texas.—(2007-08)**
**3. Adam Lind, 1b, University of South Alabama** (Choice from Angels as compensation for Escobar).**—(2006-15)**
3. Danny Hill, rhp, University of Missouri.—(AA)
**4. Casey Janssen, rhp, UCLA.—(2006-15)**
5. Ryan Klosterman, ss, Vanderbilt University.—(AAA)
6. Cory Patton, of, Texas A&M University.
7. Randy Dicken, rhp, Shippensburg (Pa.) University.
8. Chip Cannon, 1b, The Citadel.
9. Joey Metropoulos, 1b, University of Southern California.
10. Brian Hall, 2b, Stanford University.
11. Kristian Bell, rhp, Blinn (Texas) CC.
12. Eric Nielsen, of, University of Nevada-Las Vegas.
13. Kyle Yates, rhp, University of Texas.
14. Jordan Timm, lhp, University of Wisconsin-Oshkosh.
15. Mike MacDonald, rhp, University of Maine.
16. *Jose Castro, ss, Puerto Rico Baseball Academy, Caguas, P.R.
17. *Michael Cooper, rhp, Santa Ana (Calif.) JC.
18. Joey McLaughlin, rhp, Oklahoma City University.
DRAFT DROP *Son of Joey McLaughlin, major leaguer (1977-84)*
19. Aaron Mathews, of, Oregon State University.
20. *Bobby Scott, rhp, Stelly's SS, Saanich, B.C.
21. Scott Roy, rhp, University of Hartford.
22. Joe Wice, lhp, Dixie State (Utah) CC.
23. Daryl Harang, lhp, San Diego State University.
DRAFT DROP *Brother of Aaron Harang, major leaguer (2002-15)*
**24. +Jesse Litsch, rhp, South Florida CC.—(2007-11)**
25. Jason Armstrong, ss, Trinity (Texas) University.
26. Brian Bormaster, c, Tulane University.
27. Casey McKenzie, rhp, University of Tampa.
28. Josh Lex, c, Oral Roberts University.
29. Michael Macaluso, ss, University of South Florida.
30. Cory Hahn, rhp, Tulane University.
31. *Paul Franko, 3b, Scottsdale (Ariz.) CC.
32. Aaron Tressler, rhp, Penn State University.
33. Greg Powers, 3b, UC Santa Barbara.
34. Derek Tate, lhp, University of San Francisco.
35. Charles Anderson, of, University of Detroit.
36. David Hicks, 1b, North Carolina State University.
37. Anthony Garibaldi, 3b, Southeastern Louisiana University.
38. *Ben Humphrey, 1b, Olney Central (Ill.) JC.
39. *Matthew Trink, rhp, Yavapai (Ariz.) JC.
40. *Jacob Vasquez, 1b, Santa Ana (Calif.) JC.
41. *Derek Feldkamp, rhp, University of Michigan.
42. *Jon Hesketh, lhp, Brookswood SS, Langley, B.C.
**43. *Chad Beck, rhp, Panola (Texas) JC.—(2011-12)**
44. Eddie Cannon, rhp, Florida State University.
45. *Rodrick Ratliff, rhp, Labette (Kan.) CC.
46. *Brok Butcher, rhp, Santa Barbara (Calif.) CC.
47. *Colin Quarles, rhp, Melbourne (Fla.) HS.
48. *Ryan Harris, ss, San Bernardino Valley (Calif.) CC.
49. *Brad Miller, 1b, Ball State University.
50. *Jordan Lennerton, 1b, Brookswood SS, Langley, B.C.

2005

AT A GLANCE

### This Date In History
June 7-8

### Best Draft
**BOSTON RED SOX.** In a case of the rich getting richer, the defending World Series champions had five first-round picks. All five reached the majors, including **JACOBY ELLSBURY** and **CLAY BUCHHOLZ**.

### Worst Draft
**CHICAGO CUBS.** The Cubs struck out on **MARK PAWELEK** (1), who went 6-14 in a five-year minor league career. They selected just two players who reached the majors, neither of whom played for them.

### First-Round Bust
**WADE TOWNSEND, RHP, DEVIL RAYS.** Unsigned as the eighth overall pick in the 2004 draft, Townsend was drafted again a year later with the eighth selection. He signed for $1.5 million, less than the reported $1.85 million he rejected from the Orioles a year earlier. Townsend went 25-3, 2.05 at Rice from 2002-04, but his professional career went nowhere. After going 7-21, 5.59 in four years in the Rays system, he was released in 2009.

### Second Best
**YUNEL ESCOBAR, SS, BRAVES.** Escobar was among the few Cuban defectors who was subject to the draft because he assumed U.S. residency after arriving in the fall of 2004. The Braves signed him for a $475,000 bonus. Escobar repaid the investment over a nine-year major league career in which he hit .281 with 78 home runs and 440 RBIs for four clubs.

### Late-Round Find
**MATT JOYCE, OF, TIGERS (12TH ROUND).** Joyce led Florida Southern to the NCAA Division II title in 2005 before the Tigers drafted him. He spent most of an eight-year major league career with the Rays, hitting .242 with 93 home runs and 334 RBIs.

# Upton joins brother as elite first-rounder

Every year, the baseball draft involves different storylines, and a different chain of events invariably unfolds. The talent yield can vary greatly from one draft to the next, especially in the first round. Some drafts are blessed with more than their share of talent, while others are seen as relative duds. Count 2005 as one of the most bountiful drafts in history, especially for star power at the top.

With headliners like Justin Upton, Alex Gordon, Ryan Zimmerman, Ryan Braun, Troy Tulowitzki and Andrew McCutchen, all claimed among the first dozen picks, the 2005 crop featured more than its quota of future all-stars. No less than six of the first seven and eight of the initial 12 selections have played in at least one All-Star Game.

Whether 2005 ranks as the greatest draft ever remains to be seen, considering that numerous players remained active a decade later, but it was trending in that direction. Still, it had its work cut out to surpass some of the other noteworthy drafts in the event's 50-year history, such as the 1985 class, whose accumulated WAR (Wins Above Replacement) score of 495.6 among first-round picks sets it apart from every other draft. The 2005 first-rounders had a WAR score of 320.0 through the 2015 season, placing them fourth overall.

While 26 of 30 first-rounders in 2005 had reached the majors by 2015, that mark had already been surpassed by the 2008 first-round group, which had produced 27 big leaguers, including the first 21 selections, a draft record. The 1971 and '73 drafts each produced three Hall of Famers, as did 1985 (with the possibility of more to come). A case could be made for other draft classes on any number of criteria, though it's safe to say 2005 is on the short list of the best ever, even as the lack of high-end pitching might prove to be its downfall.

Only 1990 (237) and 2008 (247) had produced more future big leaguers than 2005's total of 227. And only the 2006 (118) and 2008 drafts (130) yielded more players from the first 10 rounds (116) that reached the big leagues.

The 2005 draft is most like the celebrated 1985 class for its preponderance of college players at the top of the board. In 1985, 11 of the first 12 selections were from the college ranks; two decades later, eight of the first nine were collegians.

The lone exception was Virginia high school shortstop Justin Upton, who was regarded by most clubs as a generational talent and all but established his credentials to be the first player drafted when he was just 14. Upton was drafted first overall by the Arizona Diamondbacks and signed for $6.1 million, a record bonus for a player signing with the team that drafted him. "The industry has a level of comfort with him that you don't often find with high school players," Diamondbacks scouting director Mike Rizzo said.

DAVID STONER

**Three years after his older brother B.J. (later Melvin Jr.) was the second overall pick in 2002, Justin Upton one-upped him and became the No. 1 overall pick of the Diamondbacks in a loaded 2005 draft**

"He's got a major league track record," said another scouting director. "He's going to hit. We've all seen him for a while with all the teams he's played on, from Team USA on down. Everyone has seen him against very good competition, and you've seen him in enough events that your scouts in different parts of the country all have seen him. His track record is as long or longer than most college players."

Upton's bonus trumped the mark set five years earlier by Stanford outfielder Joe Borchard, who signed with the Chicago White Sox for $5.3 million. It took Upton and the Diamondbacks until Jan. 26, 2006, to strike an agreement.

The Diamondbacks earned the first pick because of their 51-111 record in 2004, worst in the major leagues. In past years the Kansas City Royals would have been in line to make the initial selection because of their 58-104 mark, poorest in the American League, but a rule change, effective with the 2005 draft, abolished the practice of awarding the No. 1 choice on an alternating basis between leagues.

The Diamondbacks landed two premier shortstop prospects within the course of a week. They signed Stephen Drew, their 2004 first-round pick, seven days before the 2005 draft. Drew and a second unsigned first-rounder, righthander Jered Weaver, agreed to terms minutes before the May 31 midnight signing deadline for the prior year's draft.

Starting with Upton's lucrative deal, the

## 2005: THE FIRST ROUNDERS

| CLUB: PLAYER, POS., SCHOOL | HOMETOWN | B-T | HT. | WT. | AGE | BONUS | FIRST YEAR | LAST YEAR | PEAK LEVEL (YEARS) |
|---|---|---|---|---|---|---|---|---|---|
| 1. Diamondbacks: Justin Upton, ss, Great Bridge HS | Chesapeake, Va. | R-R | 6-1 | 195 | 17 | $6,100,000 | 2006 | Active | Majors (9) |
| One of most acclaimed athletes of draft era with superior bat/speed/arm; $6.1M bonus dwarfed other picks, reached MLB at 19, three all-star appearances by 27. | | | | | | | | | |
| 2. Royals: Alex Gordon, 3b, Nebraska | Lincoln, Neb. | L-R | 6-1 | 210 | 21 | $4,000,000 | 2006 | Active | Majors (9) |
| Five-tool talent, KC fan growing up, made MLB debut after 62 pro ABs, career floundered until converted to LF in 2010, became perennial all-star, Gold Glover. | | | | | | | | | |
| 3. Mariners: Jeff Clement, c, Southern California | Marshalltown, Iowa | L-R | 6-1 | 210 | 21 | $3,400,000 | 2005 | 2013 | Majors (4) |
| All-time prep career HR leader (75) hit 46 more in college, flashed LH power in minors before knees deteriorated, forced move to 1B, compromised MLB career. | | | | | | | | | |
| 4. Nationals: Ryan Zimmerman, 3b, Virginia | Virginia Beach, Va. | R-R | 6-2 | 210 | 20 | $2,975,000 | 2005 | Active | Majors (11) |
| Played youth ball with David Wright/Upton brothers; standout defender cemented draft stock at Virginia (.393-6-59) when power evolved; rapid rise to majors. | | | | | | | | | |
| 5. Brewers: Ryan Braun, 3b, Miami | Granada Hills, Calif. | R-R | 6-2 | 195 | 21 | $2,450,000 | 2005 | Active | Majors (9) |
| Excellent track record with bat (.388-18-76 as JR), moved from SS to 3B in college, to OF in majors; won 2011 NL MVP, but career tainted by injuries/PED issues. | | | | | | | | | |
| 6. Blue Jays: Ricky Romero, lhp, Cal State Fullerton | Los Angeles | R-L | 6-1 | 205 | 20 | $2,400,000 | 2005 | Active | Majors (5) |
| Went 30-9, 3.16 in college, led 2004 team to CWS title; in perplexing MLB career, went 50-32 in first three-plus seasons, then 1-13, 7.35 as mechanics deserted him. | | | | | | | | | |
| 7. Rockies: Troy Tulowitzki, ss, Long Beach State | Sunnyvale, Calif. | R-R | 6-3 | 225 | 20 | $2,300,000 | 2005 | Active | Majors (10) |
| Unknown prep player became best of long line of standout Dirtbags shortstops with five-tool ability; became five-time MLB all-star, two-time Gold Glover. | | | | | | | | | |
| 8. Devil Rays: Wade Townsend, rhp, Rice | Dripping Springs, Texas | R-R | 6-4 | 210 | 22 | $1,500,000 | 2005 | 2009 | Class AA (1) |
| Picked eighth for second straight draft despite sitting out year; TJ surgery in '08, labrum surgery in '09, went 7-21, 5.68 in minors; became professional poker player. | | | | | | | | | |
| 9. *Mets: Mike Pelfrey, rhp, Wichita State | Augusta, Kan. | R-R | 6-7 | 200 | 21 | $3,550,000 | 2006 | Active | Majors (10) |
| Dominant college arm (33-7, 2.18 at Wichita); signability concerns led to seven-month holdout, then signed $5.3M major league deal; up and down MLB career. | | | | | | | | | |
| 10. Tigers: Cameron Maybin, of, T.C. Roberson HS | Arden, N.C. | R-R | 6-3 | 200 | 18 | $2,650,000 | 2006 | Active | Majors (9) |
| Impressive physical tools with power, 6.4 speed in 60; hit .662 with 15 HRs, 32 SBs as HS senior; has struggled to hit consistently in majors (.251 AVG through '15). | | | | | | | | | |
| 11. Pirates: Andrew McCutchen, of, Fort Meade HS | Fort Meade, Fla. | R-R | 5-11 | 175 | 18 | $1,900,000 | 2005 | Active | Majors (7) |
| Overwhelmed HS competition with .709-16-42 SR year, .474 career mark; sprinter speed, surprising pop for size, won MVP/all-star honors, led Pirates resurgence. | | | | | | | | | |
| 12. Reds: Jay Bruce, of, West Brook HS | Beaumont, Texas | L-L | 6-3 | 195 | 18 | $1,800,000 | 2005 | Active | Majors (8) |
| Became legit talent as prep SR (.500-8-28, 18 SB), compared to Larry Walker, Jim Edmonds; blitzed through minors, but power negated by high strikeout rate. | | | | | | | | | |
| 13. Orioles: Brandon Snyder, c, Westfield HS | Chantilly, Va. | R-R | 6-2 | 210 | 18 | $1,700,000 | 2005 | Active | Majors (4) |
| Father Brian pitched in majors; versatile player, shifted between C-SS in HS, but bat was inadequate when shoulder injury forced shift to corner position. | | | | | | | | | |
| 14. Indians: Trevor Crowe, of, Arizona | Beaverton, Ore. | B-R | 6-0 | 190 | 21 | $1,695,000 | 2005 | 2014 | Majors (4) |
| Scrappy/high-performance college player hit .403-9-54 with 25 2Bs/15 3Bs/27 steals as JR; extra-base pop disappeared with wood, lacked CF instincts to be regular. | | | | | | | | | |
| 15. White Sox: Lance Broadway, rhp, Texas Christian | Mansfield, Texas | R-R | 6-4 | 190 | 21 | $1,570,000 | 2005 | 2010 | Majors (3) |
| Led Dallas Baptist to two Christian college national titles, transferred to TCU, went 15-1, 1.62 (117 IP/151 SO); polished arm, lacked raw stuff to excel in majors. | | | | | | | | | |
| 16. Marlins: Chris Volstad, rhp, Palm Beach Gardens HS | Palm Beach Gardens, Fla. | R-R | 6-7 | 190 | 18 | $1,600,000 | 2005 | Active | Majors (7) |
| Polished/projectable HS arm went 16-4, 0.75 (149 IP, 19 BB/189 SO) as JR/SR in HS with plus command; first prep arm drafted, stuff improved marginally in pros. | | | | | | | | | |
| 17. Yankees: C.J. Henry, ss, Putnam City HS | Oklahoma City, Okla. | R-R | 6-3 | 205 | 19 | $1,575,000 | 2005 | 2008 | Class A (3) |
| Impressive athlete with power/speed package, prime basketball recruit but huge overreach by Yankees; lot of errors/strikeouts, quit to reignite Kansas hoops career. | | | | | | | | | |
| 18. Padres: Cesar Carrillo, rhp, Miami | Hammond, Ind. | R-R | 6-3 | 175 | 21 | $1,550,000 | 2005 | 2012 | Majors (1) |
| Began Miami career with 24 straight wins, FB that peaked at 97; pro career stalled by elbow issues, loss of velocity, went 1-2, 13.50 in three big league starts. | | | | | | | | | |
| 19. Rangers: John Mayberry Jr., of, Stanford | Overland Park, Kan. | R-R | 6-6 | 230 | 21 | $1,525,000 | 2005 | Active | Majors (7) |
| Unsigned first-rounder in 2002, draft stock hurt by mediocre JR year (.303-9-53) after 16 HRs as SO; pro career mirrored college, flashed power, not enough contact. | | | | | | | | | |
| 20. Cubs: Mark Pawelek, lhp, Springville HS | Springville, Utah | L-L | 6-3 | 190 | 18 | $1,750,000 | 2005 | 2009 | Class A (5) |
| Most dominant Utah prep arm ever; went 10-0, 0.00 (63 IP/132 SO) as SR with 96 mph fastball; brief pro career (6-14, 3.94) sacked by immaturity, command issues. | | | | | | | | | |
| 21. Athletics: Cliff Pennington, ss, Texas A&M | Corpus Christi, Texas | B-R | 5-11 | 180 | 21 | $1,475,000 | 2005 | Active | Majors (8) |
| Gritty, high-energy player; college standout (.363-7-39, 29 SBs) whose modest tools never fully translated to pro ball; evolved into utility infielder in majors. | | | | | | | | | |
| 22. Marlins: Aaron Thompson, lhp, Second Baptist HS | Houston | L-L | 6-3 | 195 | 18 | $1,225,000 | 2005 | 2015 | Majors (3) |
| Two-way standout, considered most polished HS arm in draft, though raw stuff only average; never really blossomed professionally, carved out lefty bullpen niche. | | | | | | | | | |
| 23. Red Sox: Jacoby Ellsbury, of, Oregon State | Madras, Ore. | L-L | 6-1 | 185 | 21 | $1,400,000 | 2005 | Active | Majors (9) |
| Johnny Damon clone with speed, igniter skills in leadoff role, deceptive HR capacity; sparked 2011 World Series champs with .321-32-105/39 SB season. | | | | | | | | | |
| 24. Astros: Brian Bogusevic, lhp/of, Tulane | Palos Heights, Ill. | L-L | 6-3 | 215 | 21 | $1,375,000 | 2005 | 2015 | Majors (5) |
| Two-way college standout, pursued first as polished southpaw; went 14-21, 5.05 in four seasons before moving to OF in 2008, reached majors, hit .238-18-65. | | | | | | | | | |
| 25. Twins: Matt Garza, rhp, Fresno State | Easton, Calif. | R-R | 6-4 | 185 | 21 | $1,350,000 | 2005 | Active | Majors (10) |
| From 1-6, 9.55 as college FR, became first-rounder with 90-95 mph FB, plus breaking stuff; flashed dominance, but inconsistent with 81-89, 3.99 MLB career mark. | | | | | | | | | |
| 26. *Red Sox: Craig Hansen, rhp, St. John's | Glen Cove, N.Y. | R-R | 6-6 | 210 | 21 | $1,325,000 | 2005 | 2012 | Majors (4) |
| Showcased electric stuff (97-98 mph FB, slider) as dominant closer on Cape Cod, as college JR, but rushed to majors, never came close to fulfilling expectations. | | | | | | | | | |
| 27. Braves: Joey Devine, rhp, North Carolina State | Junction City, Kan. | R-R | 5-11 | 195 | 21 | $1,300,000 | 2005 | 2011 | Majors (5) |
| Braves uncharacteristically chose quick-fix reliever with top pick; gave up grand slams in first two MLB games; had one career SV, TJ surgery ended career. | | | | | | | | | |
| 28. Cardinals: Colby Rasmus, of, Russell County HS | Seale, Ala. | L-L | 6-1 | 175 | 18 | $1,000,000 | 2005 | Active | Majors (7) |
| Broke Bo Jackson state HR record in .484-24-66 senior year, led team to No. 1 national ranking; flashed power, CF skills in majors but also hit .244, strikeout prone. | | | | | | | | | |
| 29. Marlins: Jacob Marceaux, rhp, McNeese State | Jennings, La. | R-R | 6-1 | 195 | 21 | $1,000,000 | 2005 | 2009 | Class AA (2) |
| Exploded on college scene with 93-95 FB, improved secondary stuff; enigma as pro with wildly inconsistent delivery/stuff, went 14-26, 5.23 in five seasons. | | | | | | | | | |
| 30. Cardinals: Tyler Greene, ss, Georgia Tech | Plantation, Fla. | R-R | 6-2 | 185 | 21 | $1,100,000 | 2005 | 2014 | Majors (5) |
| Roller coaster college career, but breakout JR year (.372-12-72, 31 SB); athletic SS with speed/power, though all-or-nothing bat relegated him to utility role. | | | | | | | | | |

*Signed to major league contract.

## AT A GLANCE

### Never Too Late

**BUSTER POSEY, RHP/SS, ANGELS (50TH ROUND).** Posey, the 2012 National League MVP, wasn't the sixth-to-last player picked based on talent. It was all about his commitment to Florida State, where he became a catcher. Three years later, Posey was the fifth overall selection, going to the Giants.

### Overlooked

**JOE THATCHER, LHP, BREWERS.** Undrafted in 2004 after four seasons at Indiana State, Thatcher joined the independent Frontier League. A year later, he was signed by the Brewers, and two years after that he was in the big leagues with the Padres. Thatcher was still active as a situational reliever. In 403 relief appearances, he was 11-16, 3.40.

### International Gem

**ELVIS ANDRUS, SS, BRAVES.** Dominican Republic outfielder **FERNANDO MARTINEZ** signed with the Mets for $1.4 million, but Andrus, a Venezuela native, enjoyed a better career. After signing Andrus at age 16 for $500,000, the Braves parted with him in a 2007 trade with the Rangers for Mark Teixeira. He was the Opening Day shortstop in Texas at 20, and over the next seven seasons hit .270 with 27 home runs, 364 RBIs and 213 stolen bases.

### Minor League Take

**JAY BRUCE, OF, REDS.** Bruce was among six 2005 first-rounders that hit .300 or better as minor leaguers. Bruce separated himself from the pack in 2007, when he batted .331 with 26 homers, 46 doubles and 89 RBIs at three levels in the Reds system.

### One Who Got Away

**LUKE HOCHEVAR, RHP, DODGERS (1ST ROUND SUPPLEMENTAL).** Hochevar was considered one of the

CONTINUED ON PAGE 598

## AT A GLANCE

CONTINUED FROM PAGE 597

top college pitchers in the 2005 draft, but he slid to 40th overall because of concerns about his bonus demands. Hochevar, after negotiations that included an agent double-switch, did not sign with the Dodgers and went back into the 2006 draft, where the Royals selected him with the first overall pick.

### He Was Drafted?

**JARRAD PAGE, OF, ROCKIES (32ND ROUND).** Page, a two-sport athlete at UCLA, was drafted three times in baseball, including 2005. He cast his lot with football after being selected in the 2006 NFL draft by the Kansas City Chiefs. After ending his NFL career in 2012, Page played in 40 minor league games before washing out of baseball.

### Did You Know . . .

Righthander **JASON NEIGHBORGALL**, a third-round pick of the Diamondbacks, received a grade of 70 (on the 20-80 scale) from the Major League Scouting Bureau, the highest in the 2005 draft pool. The grade was based on his 6-foot-5 frame, along with a fastball that peaked in triple digits. But Neighborgall never showed an ability to throw strikes at Georgia Tech (113 walks in 101 innings) or in three years of pro ball (1-4, 17.36, 128 walks, 48 strikeouts in 42 innings).

### They Said It

Dodgers scouting director **LOGAN WHITE**, on negotiations with supplemental first-rounder **LUKE HOCHEVAR**, who was represented by Scott Boras: "He is banking on Scott saying he'll be able to duplicate what he did last season, get bigger and stronger, and get more money next year. For that to work, he'd have to be the first pick in the country."—*Sure enough, Hochevar was the No. 1 pick in the 2006 draft.*

Diamondbacks spent $9.776 million to sign their 2005 draft picks, the most spent by a team since the Diamondbacks, then an expansion team, committed upward of $18 million in 1996. That amount included high-priced deals for Travis Lee and John Patterson, two first-rounders who had been granted free agency because of improper contract-tendering procedures. The 2002 Oakland A's of "Moneyball" fame paid $9,165,500 in bonuses, the largest previous amount for a team signing its own draft choices.

## UPTON DESTINED TO BE TOP PICK

As a 14-year-old coming off his freshman year at Great Bridge High in Chesapeake, Va., Upton wasn't invited to participate in the California-based Area Code Games, a staple on the summer showcase circuit. He showed up anyway and dazzled scouts with his athletic ability and tools.

Upton, a younger brother of B.J. Upton, the second overall pick in the 2002 draft, quickly gained momentum as the potential No. 1 overall pick in the 2005 draft. That was a tough standard to live up to, and many young players have wilted under similar expectations, but Upton never did, continually excelling at showcases, on U.S. national teams and in high school. As a senior, he hit .519 with 12 homers.

"I heard that talk," Upton said. "The way I dealt with it was by playing the way I had been playing, trying to keep the pressure off my back."

The pressure relented on June 7, 2005, when the Diamondbacks selected Upton with the first choice. He and his brother became the highest-drafted siblings in draft history, surpassing the Young brothers, Dmitri (Cardinals, No. 4 in 1991) and Delmon (Devil Rays, No. 1 in 2003).

B.J. Upton, playing at the time for Triple-A Durham in the Tampa Bay Devil Rays system, was on a road trip in nearby Norfolk, Va., and at home with Justin on draft day. The brothers, family members and friends gathered in the library at Great Bridge High to follow the draft on the Internet. "It's good to see him succeed," B.J. said. "Going from playing baseball in the front yard and us fighting over it, and then he ended up being the No. 1 pick . . . I'm just real happy for him."

Rizzo said Upton had been his choice for months among a group of players that included college righthanders Mike Pelfrey of Wichita State, Luke Hochevar of Tennessee and Craig Hansen of St. John's. The Diamondbacks finalized their decision to take Upton the night before the draft.

"He is a tremendously gifted player, both in terms of his athletic ability and his baseball ability," Diamondbacks general manager Joe Garagiola Jr. said. "He has a maturity about him that is unbelievable for a player who is 17."

Few high school players in draft history compared with Upton. He was considered slightly better than B.J. when both players were at the same stages of their high school careers—the 6-foot-2, 185-pound Justin was stronger, faster and more advanced as a hitter. The only knock on Justin, as with B.J., was his erratic throwing at shortstop. While some scouts said they would move Upton to center field and envisioned him becoming the next Ken Griffey Jr., Rizzo said the Diamondbacks planned to develop Justin as a shortstop.

Upton had committed to attending college at North Carolina State, but he did not enroll in order to continue negotiating, even though the two sides were far apart in late August. The Diamondbacks offered Upton a $4.675 million bonus in the fall of 2005. Upton was seeking $6.25 million, and the sides compromised four months later at $6.1 million.

The only other first-round picks who remained unsigned entering August were Gordon, Pelfrey and North Carolina high school outfielder Cameron Maybin, drafted 10th overall by the Detroit Tigers. Maybin agreed on a $2.65 million bonus on Sept. 23. Gordon, the second overall pick, signed with the Royals for a $4 million bonus on Sept. 29.

That left Upton and Pelfrey, the top pitching prospect in the draft. Because of concerns about his signability, Pelfrey lasted until the New York Mets took him with the ninth pick. Represented by agent Scott Boras, he sought a big league contract similar to those given the top three college pitchers in the 2004 draft, deals that ranged from $4.2 million-$5.2 million in guaranteed money. Pelfrey held out until Jan. 10, 2006, agreeing with

## How They Should Have Done It

Based on the career WAR (Wins Above Replacement, as calculated by Baseball-Reference.com) numbers achieved by all the players eligible for the 2005 draft through the 2015 season, here's how the first round should have unfolded. Numbers in parentheses indicate the round when the player was actually drafted.

| | Player, Pos. | Actual Draft | WAR | Bonus |
|---|---|---|---|---|
| 1. | Troy Tulowitzki, ss | Rockies (1) | 40.4 | $2,300,000 |
| 2. | Ryan Braun, 3b | Brewers (1) | 40.0 | $2,450,000 |
| 3. | Andrew McCutchen, of | Pirates (1) | 38.1 | $1,900,000 |
| 4. | Ryan Zimmerman, 3b | Nationas (1) | 34.9 | $2,975,000 |
| 5. | Alex Gordon, 3b | Royals (1) | 31.8 | $4,000,000 |
| 6. | Brett Gardner, of | Yankees (3) | 26.9 | $210,000 |
| 7. | Jacoby Ellsbury, of | Red Sox (1) | 26.3 | $1,400,000 |
| 8. | Yunel Escobar, ss | Braves (2) | 24.8 | $475,000 |
| 9. | Justin Upton, ss | Diamondbacks (1) | 24.7 | $6,100,000 |
| 10. | Chase Headley, 3b | Padres (2) | 22.3 | $660,000 |
| 11. | Austin Jackson, of | Yankees (8) | 22.2 | $800,000 |
| 12. | Michael Brantley, of | Brewers (7) | 16.6 | $150,000 |
| 13. | Colby Rasmus, of | Cardinals (1) | 16.1 | $1,000,000 |
| 14. | Clay Buchholz, rhp | Red Sox (1-S) | 15.7 | $800,000 |
| 15. | Jay Bruce, of | Reds (1) | 15.5 | $1,800,000 |
| 16. | Matt Garza, rhp | Twins (1) | 13.2 | $1,350,000 |
| 17. | Will Venable, of | Padres (7) | 13.1 | $120,000 |
| 18. | Cliff Pennington, ss | Athletics (1) | 10.4 | $1,475,000 |
| 19. | Ricky Romero, lhp | Blue Jays (1) | 9.7 | $2,400,000 |
| | Matt Joyce, of | Tigers (12) | 9.7 | $60,000 |
| 21. | Cameron Maybin, of | Tigers (1) | 9.4 | $2,650,000 |
| 22. | Jed Lowrie, ss | Red Sox (1-S) | 9.1 | $762,500 |
| | Peter Bourjos, of | Angels (10) | 9.1 | $325,000 |
| 24. | Jaime Garcia, lhp | Cardinals (22) | 9.0 | $25,000 |
| 25. | Sergio Romo, rhp | Giants (28) | 8.8 | $2,500 |
| 26. | Jonathan Niece, lhp | Mets (7) | 8.2 | $175,000 |
| 27. | Travis Wood, lhp | Reds (2) | 7.9 | $600,000 |
| 28. | Jeremy Hellickson, rhp | Devil Rays (4) | 7.2 | $500,000 |
| 29. | Nick Hundley, c | Padres (2) | 7.0 | $465,000 |
| 30. | Marco Estrada, rhp | Nationals (6) | 6.8 | $152,000 |

| | Top 3 Unsigned Players | | | Year Signed |
|---|---|---|---|---|
| 1. | Buster Posey, rhp | Angels (50) | 28.2 | 2008 |
| 2. | Tim Lincecum, rhp | Indians (42) | 22.7 | 2006 |
| 3. | Doug Fister, rhp | Yankees (6) | 19.4 | 2006 |

the Mets on a major league deal that included a $3.55 million bonus and a total guarantee of $5.25 million.

Hansen, another Boras client, was the only other player from the 2005 draft to receive a major league contract. After falling to the Boston Red Sox at No. 26 because of signability concerns, Hansen signed on July 23 for four years and $4 million, including a $1.325 million bonus.

Boras also had been front and center in the longest-running negotiations in the 2004 draft, involving Drew and Weaver. Both reached agreements just minutes before the deadline, ending the longest holdouts in draft history. Weaver, a righthander from Long Beach State, accepted a $4 million bonus from the Los Angeles Angels. Drew, a shortstop from Florida State, signed a five-year major league contract with the Diamondbacks that provided a $4 million bonus and a total guarantee of $5.5 million.

## HOCHEVAR SAGA DRAGS ON

Major League Baseball's practice of making bonus recommendations for every pick in the first 10 rounds and compelling teams to make a case for exceeding those amounts continued to slow the growth of bonuses in 2005, especially in the first round. With few exceptions, bonuses lined up in lockstep, and 20 of the 30 first-round picks had signed by the end of June.

Before Pelfrey and Upton agreed to deals, the first-round average for the other 28 first-rounders was 7.2 percent lower than for the corresponding slots a year earlier. Pelfrey and Upton drove the average to $2.018 million, a 3.0 percent rise from 2004, when the average was $1,958,448.

The most significant deviations in the first round occurred with the eighth and ninth picks. The Devil Rays signed Rice University dropout Wade Townsend for $1.5 million after picking him eighth, and the Mets paid Pelfrey a $3.55 million bonus.

Bonuses continued to line up according to slots through the later rounds, with the exception being an $800,000 bonus paid by the New York Yankees to Texas high school outfielder Austin Jackson, an eighth-round choice. It took that kind of financial inducement to draw Jackson, a two-sport athlete who became an accomplished big leaguer, away from a basketball scholarship from Georgia Tech.

Bonuses beyond the 10th round were not as strictly regulated by MLB, and in two instances teams paid $500,000 to reel in a late pick: the Minnesota Twins in the 11th round to California prep righthander Brian Kirwan, and the

### Fastest To The Majors

| | Player, Pos. | Drafted (Round) | Debut |
|---|---|---|---|
| 1. | Joey Devine, rhp | Braves (1) | Aug. 20, 2005 |
| 2. | Ryan Zimmerman, 3b | Nationals (1) | Sept. 1, 2005 |
| 3. | Craig Hansen, rhp | Red Sox (1) | Sept. 19, 2005 |
| 4. | Mike Pelfrey, rhp | Mets (1) | July 8, 2006 |
| 5. | Matt Garza, rhp | Twins (1) | Aug. 11, 2006 |

**FIRST HIGH SCHOOL SELECTION:** Justin Upton, ss (Diamondbacks/1, Aug. 2, 2007)

## DRAFT SPOTLIGHT: ANDREW MCCUTCHEN

CLIFF WELCH

**Pirates fans found the cornerstone for their team's turnaround in Florida high school outfielder Andrew McCutchen**

The Pittsburgh Pirates ended a 20-year losing streak and made the National League playoffs in 2013. In the process, Andrew McCutchen was the NL MVP and became the face of the franchise. The last time the Pirates had topped .500 and made the playoffs was in 1992. Barry Bonds was the NL MVP that year and the acknowledged face of the franchise.

During his early years with the Pirates, McCutchen never dwelled on the persistent losing in Pittsburgh in the wake of Bonds' departure. "If people want to put that on us, let them put it on us," McCutchen said. "We don't put it on ourselves. We don't dwell on what happened in the past, because the past is the past and you can't change that."

Almost from the beginning, Pirates fans knew there was something special about McCutchen. The team selected him with its first choice in 2005, and it quickly became apparent that he was the best prospect the team had drafted since Bonds 20 years earlier. Expectations were heaped upon McCutchen, much as they had been on Bonds.

The son of a minister, McCutchen was taught the importance of maintaining a positive attitude during his formative years, and he embraced the role from the day he was drafted with the 11th pick overall out of Fort Meade (Fla.) High, after hitting .709 with 16 homers as a senior. "The Pirates showed the most interest in me out of all the teams and they made the best impression," McCutchen said. "They really stood out in my mind. They made me feel like they were the right organization for me."

The Pirates warmed to the 5-foot-11, 175-pound McCutchen for reasons beyond his impressive track record, which extended back to his days as an eighth grader, when he led high school hitters in Polk County with a .507 average. "Andrew has great athletic ability and speed," Pirates scouting director Ed Creech said. "Beyond that, he has a big league bat. He is one of the guys we definitely zeroed in on this spring."

Creech compared McCutchen with Marquis Grissom, whom he once managed in the Montreal Expos system. "Andrew has the same outstanding speed and ability to cover a lot of ground in center field like Grissom," Creech said. "And like Marquis, he has good power. He also has great makeup and comes from a very good family background like Marquis did."

The Pirates traded center fielder Nate McLouth, the team's most popular player, on June 4, 2009, to clear the position for the 22-year-old McCutchen. He was an immediate hit, giving long-suffering Pirates fans reason for hope with his inspired play at the plate, on the bases and in the field.

"There has been so much talk about Andrew, so much hype the last few years," Pirates manager John Russell said after McCutchen hit .286 with 12 homers, 54 RBIs and 22 stolen bases in 108 games as a rookie. "He had a lot of expectations to live up to, and he did. He got to the major leagues and was comfortable. You don't see that in every player who comes from the minor leagues. That's what separates the really good players."

McCutchen was so confident in his ability that he took his rookie success in stride. "I expected to do well," he said. "I would have been disappointed if I didn't."

McCutchen long had believed it was his destiny to not only become a major league player, but a star. "I was probably 5 years old when I first started playing tee-ball and I knew then that playing in the big leagues was what I wanted to do," he said.

Much like Bonds a generation earlier, McCutchen became a symbol of hope in Pittsburgh, and both had similar tenures in a Pirates uniform. McCutchen hit .298 with 150 homers, 557 RBIs and 153 stolen bases in his first seven seasons with the Pirates, and led the team to three straight playoff appearances from 2013-15. Bonds hit .275 with 176 home runs, 556 RBIs and 251 stolen bases in his seven-year tenure in Pittsburgh, and led the Pirates to postseason appearances in each of his final three years with the club.

Unlike Bonds, who bolted Pittsburgh for the riches of free agency, McCutchen signed a $51 million contract extension in 2012 that delayed his free agency and proved to be a bargain for the Pirates. He said loyalty was more important than money.

## WORTH NOTING

■ In contrast to the millions of dollars other teams shelled out on their 2005 draft picks, the Giants spent just $985,000, the lowest team total in more than a decade. The Giants didn't have a pick until the fourth round after signing major league free agents **ARMANDO BENITEZ**, **MIKE MATHENY** and **OMAR VIZQUEL** during the previous offseason. **BEN COPELAND**, the team's fourth-round pick, received the largest bonus, $227,000. The Giants signed **THOMAS NEAL**, a 36th-rounder, the following spring for $220,000.

■ After being drafted in a progressively lower round in each of the previous five drafts, including in the first round in 2000, righthander **MATT HARRINGTON** went undrafted in 2005, which meant he was free to sign with any team. He found no takers, after spending the previous three years with Fort Worth of the independent Central League.

■ Texas won the 2005 College World Series, never trailing in winning five straight games on its way to a sixth national title. Righthander **J. BRENT COX**, the team's highest draft pick (Yankees, second round), finished all five games, pitched 10 scoreless innings, earned a win and had two saves. Cox, who led the nation with 19 saves, signed with the Yankees for a $550,000 bonus. Cox once was targeted as a potential successor to **MARIANO RIVERA**, but his career stalled after he broke his right hand in a bar fight in December 2006. Cox then missed the 2007 season recovering from elbow surgery.

■ Cal State Fullerton, the 2004 College World Series champion, made a big impact on the 2005 draft with a record-tying 14 selections, even as the team failed to qualify for the CWS. The Titans equaled the record set in 1982 by Arizona State. Lefthander **RICKY ROMERO**, Fullerton's ace, was the sixth pick in the first round, and

Seattle Mariners in the 12th round to St. John's righthander Anthony Varvaro.

All other negotiations seemed like a cakewalk in comparison with the dealings between the Los Angeles Dodgers and Hochevar, a supplemental first-rounder. A righthander from the University of Tennessee, he tied for the NCAA lead in wins (15) and was second in strikeouts (154) during his junior season, and was considered second only to Pelfrey among pitchers available in the draft.

Like Pelfrey, Hochevar was advised by Boras, and he dropped out of the first round because of signability concerns. Before the draft, the Colorado Rockies asked Hochevar, a Colorado native, if he would sign for the MLB-recommended $2.3 million bonus as the No. 7 pick. Hochevar declined, indicating he wanted to be treated like the top college pitchers in the 2004 draft, four of whom signed for bonuses upward of $3 million. Hochevar slipped to 40th overall, the Dodgers' first pick in the draft.

Negotiations proceeded slowly, as they often did with Boras clients. By the end of August, the Dodgers had upped their offer from $850,000, MLB's recommendation for the No. 40 slot, to $2.3 million, matching what the Rockies had offered. Boras didn't counter, and Hochevar considered enrolling for his senior year at Tennessee, which would have sent him back into the draft pool. He eventually decided not to attend classes for the fall semester. On Sept. 2, Hochevar attended a birthday party for the mother of his close friend, Eli Iorg, a Tennessee teammate and the Astros' supplemental first-round pick. At Iorg's suggestion, Hochevar agreed to talk to Iorg's agent, Matt Sosnick.

Luke Hochevar

Accounts differed on who approached whom and what was said, but Hochevar signed a document stipulating that Sosnick, not Boras, was his adviser. Sosnick quickly negotiated a $2.98 million bonus with Dodgers scouting director Logan White, and Hochevar orally agreed to the terms. But after speaking to Boras, Hochevar reneged on the deal and rehired Boras.

Negotiations went nowhere, and by the following spring it was apparent a deal would not be forthcoming. Hochevar joined the Fort Worth Cats of the independent American Association, and in four starts he sufficiently impressed the Royals that they selected him with the first overall pick in the 2006 draft. He signed a four-year major league contract with the Royals that included a $3.5 million bonus and a total guarantee of $5.3 million. Hochevar became the highest unsigned pick in 2005.

With his representation of Pelfrey and Hochevar, not to mention Drew and Weaver, Boras cast a formidable shadow over the 2005 draft. And his influence didn't stop there, considering that he also advised three other first-rounders: Hansen, Utah prep lefthander Mark Pawelek (Cubs, 21st overall) and Georgia Tech shortstop Tyler Greene (Cardinals, 30th). Boras also had several other high-profile clients who slipped past the first round. Pawelek, the only high school player represented by Boras, signed in quick order for a bonus of $1.75 million, $250,000 over slot.

The Boras Corp., for all its impact on the 2005 draft, was upstaged in representation of top talent by another agency, IMG, whose client list included six first-rounders, including four players that were drafted before any of Boras' clients were selected.

### Top 25 Bonuses

| | Player, Pos. | Drafted (Round) | Order | Bonus |
|---|---|---|---|---|
| 1. | ***Justin Upton, ss** | **Diamondbacks (1)** | **1** | **$6,100,000** |
| 2. | **Alex Gordon, 3b** | **Royals (1)** | **2** | **$4,000,000** |
| 3. | **Mike Pelfrey, rhp** | **Mets (1)** | **9** | **#$3,500,000** |
| 4. | **Jeff Clement, c** | **Mariners (1)** | **3** | **$3,400,000** |
| 5. | **Ryan Zimmerman, 3b** | **Nationals (1)** | **4** | **$2,975,000** |
| 6. | ***Cameron Maybin, of** | **Tigers (1)** | **10** | **$2,650,000** |
| 7. | **Ryan Braun, 3b** | **Brewers (1)** | **5** | **$2,450,000** |
| 8. | **Ricky Romero, lhp** | **Blue Jays (1)** | **6** | **$2,400,000** |
| 9. | **Troy Tulowitzki, ss** | **Rockies (1)** | **7** | **$2,300,000** |
| 10. | ***Andrew McCutchen, of** | **Pirates (1)** | **11** | **$1,900,000** |
| 11. | ***Jay Bruce, of** | **Reds (1)** | **12** | **$1,800,000** |
| 12. | *Mark Pawelek, lhp | Cubs (1) | 20 | $1,750,000 |
| 13. | ***Brandon Snyder, c** | **Orioles (1)** | **13** | **$1,700,000** |
| 14. | **Trevor Crowe, of** | **Indians (1)** | **14** | **$1,695,000** |
| 15. | ***Chris Volstad, rhp** | **Marlins (1)** | **16** | **$1,600,000** |
| 16. | *C.J. Henry, ss | Yankees (1) | 17 | $1,575,000 |
| 17. | **Lance Broadway, rhp** | **White Sox (1)** | **15** | **$1,570,000** |
| 18. | ***Cesar Carrillo, rhp** | **Padres (1)** | **18** | **$1,550,000** |
| 19. | **John Mayberry Jr., of** | **Rangers (1)** | **19** | **$1,525,000** |
| 20. | Wade Townsend, rhp | Devil Rays (1) | 8 | $1,500,000 |
| 21. | **Cliff Pennington, ss** | **Athletics (1)** | **21** | **$1,475,000** |
| 22. | **Jacoby Ellsbury, of** | **Red Sox (1)** | **23** | **$1,400,000** |
| 23. | **Brian Bogusevic, lhp** | **Astros (1)** | **24** | **$1,375,000** |
| 24. | **Matt Garza, rhp** | **Twins (1)** | **25** | **$1,350,000** |
| 25. | **Craig Hansen, rhp** | **Red Sox (1)** | **26** | **#$1,325,000** |

*Major leaguers in bold. *High school selection. #Major league contract.*

### STAR QUALITY COLLEGE CROP

Scouts considered Upton in a class of his own in the 2005 draft, and the top college prospects also were highly regarded. In rapid order after Upton, the Royals took Gordon, a Nebraska third baseman and Baseball America's College Player of the Year; the Mariners chose Southern California power-hitting catcher Jeff Clement; the Washington Nationals selected Zimmerman, a slick-fielding third baseman from Virginia; and the Milwaukee Brewers took Braun, a hard-hitting third baseman from the University of Miami.

Only Clement, the nation's high school career home run leader, had been drafted previously. The emergence of Gordon, Zimmerman and Braun made third base a position of true strength in the college ranks. As juniors, Gordon hit .372 with 19 homers and 66 RBIs; Zimmerman went .393-6-59; and Braun went .388-18-76.

"There is no doubt this is a good year for third basemen," an American League scouting director said on the eve of the draft. "I think Gordon and Zimmerman are clearly at the head of the pack. Gordon is the total package: a profile guy with a history of production. With Zimmerman, you have

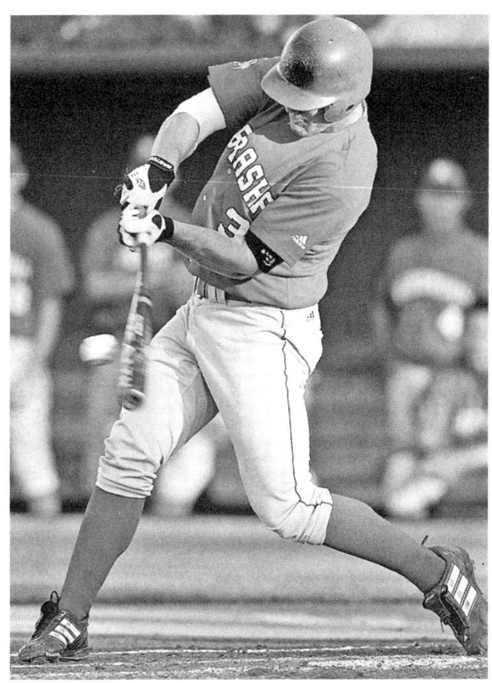

Second overall pick Alex Gordon enjoyed a standout career as a third baseman at Nebraska, then made a smooth transition to left field

to do some projection. He hasn't hit with a lot of power up to this point. Zimmerman also is arguably the best defender in the country at any position."

As teammates the previous summer on USA Baseball's college national team, Zimmerman played third base and Gordon spent most of his time at first base. While leading Team USA to the gold medal at the World University Games, Gordon was the tournament's offensive MVP, and Zimmerman led Team USA over the course of the summer in batting, home runs and RBIs. Braun's emergence occurred in the months leading up to the draft.

A decade later, none of the three was a third baseman in the major leagues, although each had enjoyed exemplary major league careers and remained with the teams that drafted them. Gordon and Braun moved to the outfield early in their careers. Zimmerman became a Gold Glove defender at third base, but eventually went to first base because of a shoulder injury that impeded his arm strength.

Clement and Upton, the other two members of the top five, also changed positions. Upton went to the outfield after the Diamondbacks determined he lacked the mechanics and throwing accuracy to become an everyday shortstop. Clement's career behind the plate was compromised by knee problems that necessitated a move to first base.

Though never the superstar the Diamondbacks projected him to be, Upton became a significant offensive talent with excellent raw power and speed. He had hit more than 25 homers in a season on five occasions, including a high of 31 in 2011, but had troubles on defense, leading National League outfielders in errors on three occasions. He played for three different teams through the 2015 season before signing a six-year, $132.75 million contract with the Tigers before the 2016 season.

Gordon, who grew up as a Royals fan in Lincoln, Neb., became the cornerstone of the team's rebuilding, which culminated in trips to the World Series in 2014 and '15. A productive hitter and three-time all-star, he became so proficient in left field that he won four straight Gold Gloves.

As the first draft pick in Nationals history, Zimmerman became the face of the franchise over the next decade. While his power was slow to evolve in college—he homered just once in his first two seasons at Virginia—he developed into a legitimate deep threat in an all-star career with the Nationals, homering 200 times in 11 years, with a best of 33 in 2009.

Braun emerged as the biggest star among the players taken with the first five picks in 2005. He was voted the National League MVP in 2011 and selected to six all-star teams. But Braun's achievements didn't come without controversy. He was suspended for the final 65 games of the 2013 season because of his involvement with performance-enhancing drugs.

The success stories that came out of the first round of the 2005 draft didn't stop with the top few picks. Tulowitzki, the latest in a line of talented shortstops from Long Beach State, was taken seventh by the Rockies, and McCutchen, a high school outfielder from Florida, went 11th to the Pittsburgh Pirates. In addition, three more outfielders drafted later in the round became successful big leaguers: Oregon State's Jacoby Ellsbury (Red Sox, 22nd overall), and high school players Jay Bruce from Texas (Reds, 12th) and Colby

## Largest Bonuses By Round

| | Player, Pos. | Club | Bonus |
|---|---|---|---|
| **1.** | ***Justin Upton, ss** | **Diamondbacks** | **$6,100,000** |
| 1-S. | Matt Torra, rhp | Diamondbacks | $1,025,000 |
| | ***Chaz Roe, rhp** | **Rockies** | **$1,025,000** |
| 2. | *Craig Italiano, rhp | Athletics | $725,500 |
| **3.** | **Taylor Teagarden, c** | **Rangers** | **$725,000** |
| **4.** | ***Jeremy Hellickson, rhp** | **Devil Rays** | **$500,000** |
| **5.** | **Jeff Larish, 1b** | **Tigers** | **$220,000** |
| **6.** | **Clete Thomas, of** | **Tigers** | **$152,500** |
| 7. | Jacob Rasner, rhp | Rangers | $250,000 |
| **8.** | ***Austin Jackson, of** | **Yankees** | **$800,000** |
| 9. | *R.J. Anderson, of | Rangers | $235,000 |
| **10.** | ***Peter Bourjos, of** | **Angels** | **$325,000** |
| 11. | *Brian Kirwan, rhp | Twins | $500,000 |
| **12.** | **Anthony Varvaro, rhp** | **Mariners** | **$500,000** |
| **13.** | ***Steve Johnson, rhp** | **Dodgers** | **$150,000** |
| 14. | Henry Wrigley, 1b | Devil Rays | $150,000 |
| | ***Scott Van Slyke, of** | **Dodgers** | **$150,000** |
| | #Willie Cabrera, of | Braves | $150,000 |
| 15. | Michael Bell, 2b | Brewers | $140,000 |
| 16. | Eric Krebs, rhp | Pirates | $250,000 |
| 17. | *Jared Edwards, c | Devil Rays | $260,000 |
| 18. | *Kevyn Feiner, ss | Reds | $150,000 |
| 19. | *Bradley Clark, rhp | Nationals | $60,000 |
| | *#Cole Miles, ss | Braves | $60,000 |
| 20. | #Bryan Casey, rhp | Royals | $235,000 |
| 21. | *Brandon James, rhp | Rangers | $41,000 |
| **22.** | **#Tommy Hanson, rhp** | **Braves** | **$325,000** |
| 23. | Jayson Ruhlman, lhp | Cubs | $175,000 |
| 24. | #James Simmons, of | Giants | $70,000 |
| 25. | Brok Butcher, rhp | Angels | $100,000 |
| Other | #Drew Miller, rhp | Padres (37) | $300,000 |

*Major leaguers in bold. *High school selection. #Signed as draft-and-follow.*

**WORTH NOTING**

every regular position player was drafted.

■ Alabama's Russell County High was recognized as the top high school team in the country, going 38-1 and winning the state 5-A title. Senior outfielder **COLBY RASMUS**, who hit .484 with 24 homers and 66 RBIs, was drafted in the first round by the Cardinals (28th overall). Junior pitchers **KASEY KIKER** and **CORY RASMUS**, Colby's brother, were drafted a year later. Kiker was selected by the Rangers with the 12th pick in 2006, and the younger Rasmus was a supplemental first-round selection of the Braves.

■ San Diego's Rancho Bernardo High and Flower Mound (Texas) High each had four players drafted, including three of the first 54 selections. Rancho Bernardo outfielder **JOHN DRENNEN** was taken with the 33rd overall pick, and Flower Mound's **CRAIG ITALIANO** and **PAUL KELLY** were selected with back-to-back picks in the second round.

■ The national high school record for consecutive wins by a team was set twice in 2005. The previous mark had stood since 1966, when New York's Archbishop Molloy High won 68 straight games. Albuquerque's La Cueva High stretched the record to 70 consecutive wins. Homer (Mich.) High won 75 straight before losing in the Michigan Division III championship game. Neither La Cueva nor Homer had a player drafted.

■ General managers voted in August by a 23-7 margin to pursue changes to the draft, among them moving it from the beginning to the end of June and instituting an August signing deadline. The proposals didn't gain additional traction beyond that and were tabled. In the previous 15 years, proposed changes to the draft resulted in just one significant change: capping the process at 50 rounds in 1998.

CONTINUED ON PAGE 602

## WORTH NOTING

CONTINUED FROM PAGE 601

The 2005 draft represented a low point for Puerto Rico baseball in terms of draft choices. Only seven players were selected, none before the 31st round. The lowest previous total since Puerto Ricans became eligible for the draft in 1989 was 19 in 2003. The number dipped to 14 in 2010 and 15 in 2013. At least one Puerto Rican was drafted in the first 10 rounds every year except 2005.

The Rockies struggled to corral their third-rounder, Rowlett (Texas) High righthander **KYLE HANCOCK**, who went 12-1, 0.90 and signed for $475,000. Before Hancock ever threw a pitch for the Rockies' Rookie-level Casper club, he developed second thoughts about his decision to play pro ball and walked away, forfeiting his signing bonus. By not accepting money from the Rockies, Hancock hoped he would maintain his amateur status and be allowed to fulfill his commitment to Arkansas, but his appeal was denied by the NCAA. Even with college no longer an option, Hancock still did not want to join the Rockies organization and was placed on baseball's restricted list. For the next three years, he attended classes at North Texas while pitching on the side in the Dallas Amateur Baseball Association. "There wasn't a day that went by where I thought, 'What if I had stuck it out?' or 'What if I went to school,'" Hancock said. "That's what I went to bed with each night. That definitely weighed on my mind. I never thought it would take me this long to get back into baseball." Hancock finally decided to resume his abandoned pro career in October 2008. He contacted the Rockies, who agreed to bring him back, and they sent him back to Casper, the team he walked away from three years earlier. Hancock's comeback didn't end on a positive note after he tore the labrum in his right shoulder in 2010 and never pitched again. He had a 4-6, 4.97 record in 19 appearances in Rookie ball.

Rasmus from Alabama (Cardinals, 28th).

Like the college players drafted ahead of him (except Clement), Tulowitzki was passed over in the draft out of high school only to blossom in college. His combination of power to all fields, along with advanced actions at a premium defensive position, made him one of the game's elite shortstops over a 10-year period. Tulowitzki hit better than .300 in four seasons, topped 30 homers twice and won two Gold Glove Awards.

For all the hype about Upton, McCutchen proved to be the best major league player among the high school players drafted in 2005. Entering the 2016 season, he was a five-time all-star and the 2013 National League MVP. His blend of speed, power, hitting ability and center-field skills not only made him one of the majors' most accomplished players, but also a catalyst in turning around the fortunes of the Pirates.

McCutchen headlined a crop of outfielders from the 2005 draft that was considered a superior group by almost any standard, and got even more impressive when Upton, Gordon and Braun were moved to outfield positions. No fewer than 12 first-rounders, 11 of whom reached the majors, were primarily outfielders at the zenith of their careers. And that doesn't begin to address later-round picks such as Jackson, Brett Gardner (Yankees, third round), Michael Brantley (Brewers, seventh), Will Venable (Padres, seventh) and Matt Joyce (Tigers, 12th), other outfielders who had noteworthy careers.

CARL KLINE

Ryan Braun

### SEVERAL FIRST-ROUNDERS FALL SHORT

Not every first-rounder or highly regarded prospect in the class of 2005 panned out, though. Lefthander Ricky Romero, drafted sixth overall by the Toronto Blue Jays and the first of a draft record-tying 14 selections from Cal State Fullerton, showed considerable promise by winning 42 games in his first three seasons in the majors, including an all-star season in 2011. The Jays signed him to a five-year, $30 million contract, and Romero's career started to fade a year later.

After winning eight of his first nine decisions in the 2012 season and improving his career record to 50-30, Romero endured a sudden, inexplicable meltdown and went just 1-13, 7.35 over the balance of the season, while leading the American League in walks. He didn't win another game for the Blue Jays after 2012 and was released in 2015 after fruitless attempts to retool his mechanics. As it was, his big league performance ranked third overall among all pitchers drafted in 2005, according to WAR.

Just as he had been in 2004, Townsend was selected with the eighth pick overall. He became the 13th player in draft history to be selected in the first round of two drafts, and Stanford outfielder John Mayberry Jr., selected 19th by the Texas Rangers, soon became the 14th.

The financially strapped Devil Rays were reluctant to pay the slot money allocated for the eighth pick ($2.2 million), and viewed Townsend as a player with first-round credentials that might sign at a discounted rate. The former Rice star had rejected a $1.85 million bonus offer from the Orioles in 2004 and chose to sit on the sideline for a year after relinquishing his college eligibility. But this time, Townsend quickly accepted a $1.5 million bonus from the Rays.

After a year away from the game, Townsend struggled to regain the form that had led to his 23-2, 2.00 record with 312 strikeouts in 239 innings over his final two years at Rice, pitching alongside fellow first-rounders Philip Humber and Jeff Niemann in what might have been the greatest pitching trio in college history. Townsend went 0-4, 5.49 in short-season ball before undergoing Tommy John surgery that caused him to miss the 2006 season. His career continued to be a mix of nagging injuries and poor performance, and in four minor league seasons he went 7-21, 5.59.

Townsend was the only player among the first 16 drafted in 2005 who did not reach the majors. The other first-rounders who did not reach the top level were Pawelek, Oklahoma two-sport star C.J. Henry (Yankees, 17th overall) and McNeese State righthander Jacob Marceaux (Marlins, 29th).

After years of poor drafts, the Yankees made a concerted effort to incorporate athletes into their barren farm system, and selected Henry, the Oklahoma high school basketball player of the year and one of the nation's top basketball recruits. Henry offered an intriguing power/speed package, but he barely had scratched the surface of his five-tool potential. The Yankees were retooling Henry's swing and converting him from shortstop to center

## One Team's Draft: Florida Marlins

| Player, Pos. | Bonus | Player, Pos. | Bonus | Player, Pos. | Bonus |
|---|---|---|---|---|---|
| **1. *Chris Volstad, rhp** | **$1,600,000** | **7. Chris Leroux, rhp** | **$152,000** | 18. Kyle Padgett, ss | $1,000 |
| **1. *Aaron Thompson, lhp** | **$1,225,000** | **8. Aaron Bates, 1b** | **Did not sign** | 19. Adam Wood, lhp | $1,000 |
| 1. Jacob Marceaux, rhp | $1,000,000 | 9. Jim Brauer, rhp | $10,000 | 20. Rafael Galbizo, rhp | $5,000 |
| **1. *Ryan Tucker, rhp** | **$975,000** | 10. *Cody Allen, 3b | $75,000 | 21. Colin Roberson, of | $1,000 |
| **1. *Sean West, lhp** | **$775,000** | 11. Andy Jenkins, c | $1,000 | **22. *Logan Morrison, 1b** | **$225,000** |
| 2. Kris Harvey, of | $575,000 | 12. Kyle Marlatt, rhp | Did not sign | 23. Justin Webb, c | $1,000 |
| **2. Brett Hayes, c** | **$450,000** | 13. Jeff Van Houten, of | $1,000 | 24. Matt Kutler, of | $1,000 |
| 3. Matt Goyen, lhp | $340,000 | 14. Travis Talbott, lhp | $1,000 | 25. Blake Jones, rhp | $1,000 |
| **4. Gaby Sanchez, c** | **$250,000** | 15. Paul Witt, ss | $1,000 | Other* Dustin Kaats (47), 2b | $122,000 |
| 5. *Kyle Winters, rhp | $166,000 | 16. Jon Lewis, rhp | $1,000 | | |
| 6. James Guerrero, 2b | $140,000 | 17. Zac McCamie, rhp | $1,000 | | |

*Major leaguers in bold. *High school selection.*

## Highest Unsigned Picks

| Player, Pos., Team (Round) | College | Re-Drafted |
|---|---|---|
| Luke Hochevar, rhp, Dodgers (1-S) | None | Royals '06 (1) |
| Bryan Morris, rhp, Devil Rays (3) | Motlow (Tenn.) JC | Dodgers '06 (1) |
| Josh Lindblom, rhp, Astros (3) | Tennessee | Dodgers '08 (2) |
| Brian Matusz, lhp, Angels (4) | San Diego | Orioles '08 (1) |
| Lance Lynn, rhp, Mariners (6) | Mississippi | Cardinals '08 (1) |
| Brad Cuthbertson, rhp, Giants (6) | Midland (Texas) JC | Blue Jays '06 (49) |
| Doug Fister, rhp, Yankees (6) | Fresno State | Mariners '06 (7) |
| Jemile Weeks, ss, Brewers (8) | Miami | Athletics '08 (1) |
| Aaron Bates, 1b, Marlins (8) | * N.C. State | Red Sox '06 (3) |
| Brad Barragar, rhp, Rangers (8) | Golden West (Calif.) JC | Never |

**TOTAL UNSIGNED PICKS:** Top 5 Rounds (4), Top 10 Rounds (16)

**Returned to same school.*

field when they traded him to the Philadelphia Phillies a little more than a year after he was drafted. After making limited strides with the Phillies, he was released after the 2007 season and re-signed by the Yankees.

After an injury-plagued season in 2008, Henry decided to quit baseball and pursue a basketball career. He spent a year each at Memphis and Kansas before finishing his college career at an NAIA school. Both his father, Carl, and his younger brother, Xavier, played in the NBA.

Pawelek set the Utah state career strikeout record while still a junior at Springville High, and completed his career with 476 strikeouts and a 36-2 record. As a senior, he went 10-0, 0.00 with 16 walks and 132 strikeouts in 63 innings. Pawelek threw his fastball in the mid-90s with an effortless delivery, yet struggled in his pro career.

He repeatedly angered Cubs officials with displays of immaturity and was sent home on one occasion for a violation of team rules. He broke his arm in 2007 when he tripped over a PlayStation while walking to the bathroom in the middle of the night. Pawelek remained in extended spring training to begin each full season he was with the Cubs before the team released him. He went 6-14, 3.94 in five minor league seasons, none above Class A.

### THREE MOVE QUICKLY TO MAJORS

For the second time in three years, three players went from the draft to the big leagues in the same season. The first was North Carolina State righthander Joey Devine, picked 27th overall by the Atlanta Braves. The Nationals promoted Zimmerman when major league rosters expanded on Sept. 1, and Hansen was promoted on Sept. 19.

Braves scouting director Roy Clark said Devine, who saved a school-record 36 games during his tenure at N.C. State, was nearly ready for the big leagues the day he was drafted.

Atlanta summoned the 6-foot Devine on Aug. 20 after he made 22 relief appearances in the minors. He took the loss in his debut, surrendering a 10th-inning grand slam. Devine also gave up a grand slam in his second outing, becoming the first pitcher in major league history to allow bases-loaded home runs in each of his first two games. Devine was added to the Braves' postseason roster and gave up a game-winning homer to Houston's Craig Biggio in the 18th inning of the decisive Game Four that ended the National League Division Series. He saved just one major league game over five years in 93 relief appearances.

The 6-foot-7 Hansen, who was picked by the Red Sox one spot ahead of Devine, saved 14 games and had a 1.68 ERA and 85 strikeouts in 64 innings in his junior year at St. John's. He had even better numbers the previous summer in the Cape Cod League, posting a 0.00 ERA with 10 saves, 2 walks and 41 strikeouts in 22 innings.

Hansen developed a tired arm late in the season, but recovered sufficiently and made his major league debut with the Red Sox in mid-September, appearing in four games. Hansen's fastball reached 97 mph and his slider peaked at 90 mph at St. John's, but he rarely showed that kind of stuff as a pro. In 95 appearances over four major league seasons, he went 4-9, 6.32 with three saves.

The Athletics, who got attention earlier in the decade by drafting almost exclusively college players, reversed course in 2005 and took high school players with six of their first nine selections. From 2000-04, the A's selected only five high school players in the first 10 rounds.

The Red Sox and St. Louis Cardinals were two of the staunchest supporters of the "Moneyball" approach to scouting and player development, but neither team followed that formula in 2005. St. Louis took six high school players in the first six rounds, and Boston four in the first five. A year earlier, the Cardinals drafted four high school players, and didn't sign any. The Red Sox drafted just one high school player in the first 16 rounds in both 2003 and '04.

The San Diego Padres made a pronounced shift in the other direction, taking only one domestic high school player in the first 29 rounds. In 2004, the Padres took players from the prep ranks with their first three picks, including shortstop Matt Bush with the No. 1 overall selection.

Fernando Martinez, a 16-year-old outfielder from the Dominican Republic, signed the richest contract among international players in 2005, agreeing to a $1.4 million bonus with the Mets. He played five seasons in the majors in an injury-riddled career, hitting .206 with nine homers.

Also on the international front, the Rockies drafted Tim Brewer from Ivanna Kean High in the U.S. Virgin Islands, unaware that the 17-year-old lefthander was an 11th-grader and ineligible for the draft.

## Largest Draft-And-Follow Bonuses

| Player, Pos. | Club (Round) | Bonus |
|---|---|---|
| **1. * Sean O'Sullivan, rhp** | **Angels (3)** | **$500,000** |
| **2. Tommy Hanson, rhp** | **Braves (22)** | **$325,000** |
| 3. Drew Miller, rhp | Padres (37) | $300,000 |
| 4. Bryan Casey, rhp | Royals (20) | $235,000 |
| **5. * Logan Morrison, 1b** | **Marlins (22)** | **$225,000** |
| 6. Milton Loo, 3b | Reds (9) | $220,000 |
| *** Thomas Neal, of** | **Giants (36)** | **$220,000** |
| 8. * Danny Gutierrez, rhp | Royals (33) | $195,000 |
| 9. * Blake King, rhp | Cardinals (44) | $180,000 |
| 10. Steve Marquardt, 3b | Rangers (23) | $170,000 |

*Major leaguers in bold. *High school selection.*

## IN FOCUS: JEFF CLEMENT

LARRY GOREN

The 2005 draft has been hailed as one of the strongest ever. The most obvious player to fall short of expectations was catcher Jeff Clement, selected third overall by the Mariners out of the University of Southern California.

Clement had a legendary career at an Iowa high school and still holds the national prep mark for most home runs (75). He continued to hit with power at USC, hitting 21 homers as a freshman and 46 over three years, marking him as the best power-hitting prospect in the 2005 class from the collegiate ranks.

Clement's pro career was compromised by knee problems that forced him to move from catcher to first base. He had three knee surgeries, which robbed his ability to hit for power. Over four years in the major leagues, he hit .218 with 14 homers.

"My (left) knee just couldn't do it anymore," Clement said. "I felt like I was improving as a player every year, but it all got washed out by the knee surgeries. And catching was the main reason I got hurt."

Clement's pro career mirrored that of Eric Munson, a lefthanded-hitting catcher from USC and the third overall pick in the 1999 draft. Scouts judged Munson's power as the best in his draft class, but his promising career also was compromised by injuries.

# 2005 Draft List

**Did not sign. Major leaguers in bold, with first and last years noted. Order of selection indicated in parentheses. For the first five rounds, the peak level of each player is noted. + Signed as draft-and-follow (Second school noted if applicable).*

## ARIZONA DIAMONDBACKS (1)

1. **Justin Upton, ss, Great Bridge HS, Chesapeake, Va.—(2007-15)**

DRAFT DROP *Brother of B.J. Upton, first-round draft pick, Devil Rays (2002); major leaguer (2004-14) • First 2005 high school draft pick to reach majors (Aug. 2, 2007)*

1. Matt Torra, rhp, University of Massachusetts (Supplemental choice—31st—as compensation for Type A free agent Richie Sexson).—(AAA)
2. Matt Green, rhp, University of Louisiana-Monroe.—(AAA)
3. Jason Neighborgall, rhp, Georgia Tech.—(Low A)
3. **Micah Owings, rhp, Tulane University** (Choice from Mariners as compensation for Sexson).**—(2007-12)**
4. Mark Romanczuk, lhp, Stanford University.—(Low A)
5. Chris Rahl, of, College of William & Mary.—(AAA)
6. **Greg Smith, lhp, Louisiana State University.—(2008-10)**
7. Anthony Cupps, rhp, University of Mississippi.
8. Ryan Schreppel, lhp, Cal State Fullerton.
9. Josh Ford, c, Baylor University.
10. Cody Evans, rhp, Long Beach State University.
11. *Brett Jacobson, rhp, Cactus Shadows HS, Carefree, Ariz.
12. Bryan Byrne, 1b, St. Mary's (Calif.) College.
13. *Daniel Roberts, lhp, Chipola (Fla.) JC.
14. **Rusty Ryal, 3b, Oklahoma State University.—(2009-10)**
15. Greg Thomson, of, St. John's University.
16. Craig Pfautz, lhp, Darton (Ga.) JC.
17. Jason Urquidez, rhp, Arizona State University.
18. Jake Elder, c, University of Minnesota.
19. Kyle Wright, rhp, Lewis-Clark State (Idaho) College.
20. Peter Duda, rhp, Stanford University.
21. Matt Krohe, lhp, Webber International (Fla.) University.
22. Maels Rodriguez, rhp, Hialeah, Fla.
23. Travis Tully, of, University of Houston.
24. Vince Bongiovanni, rhp, University of Miami.
25. *David Williams, of, Rutgers University.
26. *Brian Chavez, ss, JC of the Canyons (Calif.).
27. Matt Fowles, rhp, Illinois State University.
28. Joel Melendez, of, Southeastern (Iowa) CC.
29. *Trevor Pippin, 1b, McIntosh HS, Peachtree City, Ga.
30. *Reinaldo Alicano, of, Seminole (Fla.) CC.
31. *Craig Heyer, rhp, CC of Southern Nevada.
32. *Rene Garcia, rhp, South Mountain (Ariz.) CC.
33. *J.B. Paxson, c, Center Grove HS, Greenwood, Ind.
34. *Kevin Hammons, lhp, Cleveland State (Tenn.) CC.
35. *Ray Kruml, of, Indian Hills (Iowa) JC.
36. *Jonathan Runnels, lhp, San Jacinto (Texas) JC.
37. *Scott Mueller, rhp, South Mountain (Ariz.) CC.
38. *Tom Calahan, lhp, Saddleback (Calif.) CC.
39. *Dustin Renfrow, rhp, Jefferson (Mo.) JC.
40. *Eric Lawrence, rhp, Grand Rapids (Mich.) CC.
41. *Cheyne Hann, rhp, San Jose (Calif.) CC.
42. *Forrest Beverly, lhp, University of South Carolina.
43. Eric Butler, rhp, Tusculum (Tenn.) College.
44. *T.J. Peabody, rhp, Rancho Bernardo HS, San Diego.
45. *Drew Thomas, c, Neville HS, Monroe, La.
46. *Brandon Thomson, lhp, Chandler-Gilbert (Ariz.) CC.
47. Houston Summers, c, Northeast Guilford HS, Summerfield, N.C.
48. Aaron Gamboa, lhp, Mill Valley, Calif.
49. *Joseph Campbell, rhp, Wabash Valley (Ill.) JC.
50. *Ritchie Franklin, ss, Thompson HS, Alabaster, Ala.

## ATLANTA BRAVES (27)

1. **Joey Devine, rhp, North Carolina State University.—(2005-11)**

DRAFT DROP *First player from 2005 draft to reach majors (Aug. 20, 2005)*

1. Beau Jones, lhp, Destrehan (La.) HS (Supplemental choice—41st—as compensation for Type A free agent Jaret Wright).—(AAA)
2. **Yunel Escobar, ss, Miami.—(2007-15)**
2. Jeff Lyman, rhp, Monte Vista HS, Alamo, Calif. (Choice from Yankees as compensation for Wright).—(AAA)
3. **Jordan Schafer, of, Winter Haven (Fla.) HS.—(2009-15)**
4. **Mike Broadway, rhp, Pope County HS, Golconda, Ill.—(2015)**
5. Will Startup, lhp, University of Georgia.—(AAA)
6. Tyler Bullock, rhp, Baylor University.
7. Brandon Monk, 2b, La Grange (Ga.) HS.
8. Kyle Cofield, rhp, Southside HS, Rainbow City, Ala.
9. Steven Garcia, c, Temecula Valley HS, Temecula, Calif.
10. *Colin Carter, lhp, Grayson County (Texas) CC.
11. Michael Nix, rhp, Auburn University.
12. Rudy Quinonez, rhp, Fresno State University.
13. Quentin Davis, of, Francis Marion (S.C.) University.
14. +Willie Cabrera, of, Los Angeles Pierce JC.
15. ***Mason Tobin, rhp, Kentridge HS, Renton, Wash.—(2011)**
16. **+Jaye Chapman, rhp, Mosley HS, Lynn Haven, Fla. / Chipola (Fla.) JC.—(2012)**
17. *Clay Caulfield, rhp, Pensacola (Fla.) JC.
18. *Zac Oliver, lhp, Midway HS, Waco, Texas.
19. +Cole Miles, ss, Viewmont HS, Bountiful, Utah / CC of Southern Nevada.
20. ***Andrew Cashner, rhp, Conroe HS, Montgomery, Texas.—(2010-15)**

DRAFT DROP *First-round draft pick (19th overall), Cubs (2008)*

21. *Kris Cichoski, rhp, Durango HS, Las Vegas, Nev.
22. **+Tommie Hanson, rhp, Riverside (Calif.) CC.—(2009-13)**
23. *Bo O'Dell, rhp, Osceola Senior HS, Kissimmee, Fla.
24. *Justin Reynolds, of, Central HS, Independence, Ore.
25. *Matt Miller, of, Redmond (Wash.) HS.
26. *Michael Ryan, rhp, Lake City (Fla.) CC.
27. *Kyle Miller, 3b, Terry Parker HS, Jacksonville, Fla.
28. ***Louis Coleman, rhp, Pillow Academy HS, Greenwood, Miss.—(2011-15)**
29. *Tyler Musselwhite, rhp, Gainesville (Ga.) HS.
30. *Brett Wiggins, lhp, Cross Creek HS, Augusta, Ga.
31. *Cole McCurry, lhp, Surry (N.C.) CC.
32. *Brad Schwarzenbach, rhp, Cerritos (Calif.) JC.
33. **+Tyler Flowers, 1b, Chipola (Fla.) JC.—(2009-15)**
34. *Blake Holt, of, Belton HS, Salado, Texas.
35. *Blake Guthrie, c, Dan River HS, Ringgold, Va.
36. *Lou Green, rhp, Logan HS, Madison, W.Va.
37. David Williams, rhp, Surry (N.C.) CC.
38. *Brett Scarpetta, lhp, Madison (Wis.) Area Tech CC.
39. *Austin Fleet, rhp, Edmond Santa Fe HS, Edmond, Okla.
40. +James Curtis, rhp, Manatee (Fla.) JC.
41. *Michael Robbins, lhp, Meridian (Miss.) CC.
42. *Tommy Alexander, c, Santa Barbara (Calif.) CC.
43. *Ryan Littlejohn, of, Verdigris HS, Broken Arrow, Okla.
44. *Ben Jeffers, rhp, Madison County HS, Danielsville, Ga.
45. *Mike Griffith, rhp, Issaquah (Wash.) HS.
46. *Luis Sanchez, ss, Lake City (Fla.) CC.
47. *Aaron Brady, rhp, CC of Southern Nevada.
48. Nate Weidenaar, of, Bozeman (Mon.) HS.
49. *Jesse Simpson, rhp, Zachary (La.) HS.
50. +Derick Himpsl, lhp, Johnstown (N.Y.) HS / Lake City (Fla.) CC.

## BALTIMORE ORIOLES (13)

1. **Brandon Snyder, c, Westfield HS, Centreville, Va.—(2010-13)**

DRAFT DROP *Son of Brian Snyder, major leaguer (1985-89)*

1. **Garrett Olson, lhp, Cal Poly San Luis Obispo** (Supplemental choice—48th—for failure to sign 2004 first-round draft pick Wade Townsend).**—(2007-12)**
2. **Nolan Reimold, of, Bowling Green State University.—(2009-15)**
3. Brandon Erbe, rhp, McDonough School, Baltimore.—(AAA)
4. Kieron Pope, of, East Coweta HS, Gay, Ga.—(Low A)
5. Reid Hamblet, rhp, Biola (Calif.) University.—(Low A)
6. Blake Owen, rhp, Belmont University.
7. Bobby Andrews, of, Cal State Fullerton.
8. Chorye Spoone, rhp, Catonsville (Md.) JC.
9. Paco Figueroa, 2b, University of Miami.

DRAFT DROP *Brother of Danny Figueroa, 43rd-round draft pick, Orioles (2005)*

10. Ryan Stadanlick, rhp, St. Joseph's University.
11. Bruce Gallaway, lhp, Missouri Valley (Mo.) College.
12. ***John Raynor, of, University of North Carolina-Wilmington.—(2010)**
13. Kyle Dahlberg, c, Texas Christian University.
14. Mark Fleisher, 1b, Radford University.
15. *Brandon Kendricks, of, DeSoto HS, Ovilla, Texas.
16. **David Hernandez, rhp, Cosumnes River (Calif.) JC.—(2009-15)**
17. Jeff Moore, rhp, University of North Carolina-Wilmington.
18. *Michael Whitney, rhp, Cypress-Fairbanks HS, Houston.
19. *D.J. Lidyard, rhp, Lower Columbia (Wash.) JC.
20. Ryan Steinbach, ss, Indiana-Purdue University-Fort Wayne.
21. *Brian Logan, lhp, Louisburg (N.C.) CC.
22. Paul Chmiel, 1b, Pittston Area HS, Pittston, Pa.
23. *Elvin Vargas, of, Connors State (Okla.) JC.
24. Stuart Musslewhite, ss, Texas Christian University.
25. Daniel Lonsberry, rhp, Northwestern State University.
26. *Carlos Hernandez, lhp, Santa Clara (Calif.) HS.
27. +Chad Thall, lhp, Jefferson (Mo.) JC.
28. Miguel Abreu, 2b, East Central (Okla.) University.
29. ***Tanner Scheppers, rhp, Dana Hills HS, Laguna Niguel, Calif.—(2012-15)**

DRAFT DROP *First-round draft pick (44th overall), Rangers (2009)*

30. *Greg Young, of, Anne Arundel (Md.) CC.
31. *Arik Hempy, lhp, University of South Carolina.
32. *Josh Faiola, rhp, Dartmouth College.
33. *Tyrone Anu, of, Colonial HS, Orlando, Fla.
34. *Matt Sopic, rhp, Seward County (Kan.) CC.
35. *Patrick Egan, rhp, Quinnipiac University.
36. *Shawn Ferguson, rhp, Texas Christian University.
37. *Stephen Foster, lhp, Auburn (Wash.) HS.
38. +Chris Vinyard, c, Chandler-Gilbert (Ariz.) CC.
39. *Caleb Annesley, c, Blanchard (Okla.) HS.
40. *Harrison Bishop, rhp, Edmonds (Wash.) CC.
41. Mark Horner, lhp, Oklahoma City University.
42. +Bryan Lee, rhp, Cuesta (Calif.) JC.
43. Danny Figueroa, of, University of Miami.

DRAFT DROP *Brother of Paco Figueroa, 9th-round draft pick, Orioles (2005)*

44. Brian Bent, c, Catonsville (Md.) CC.
45. *Brad Rifkin, 1b, Park School, Columbia, Md.
46. *Benjamin Brian, of, Wayne HS, Waynesville, Ohio.
47. *Craig Johnson, rhp, Bellevue (Wash.) CC.
48. *Brent Davis, rhp, Clear Lake HS, Houston.
49. *Ryan Saldivar, c, Ryan HS, Denton, Texas.
50. *Jeremy Bloor, lhp, Grand Rapids (Mich.) CC.

## BOSTON RED SOX (28)

1. **Jacoby Ellsbury, of, Oregon State University** (Choice from Angels as compensation for Type A free agent Orlando Cabrera).**—(2007-15)**
1. **Craig Hansen, rhp, St. John's University** (Choice from Dodgers as compensation for Type A free agent Derek Lowe).**—(2005-09)**
1. (Choice to Cardinals as compensation for Type A free agent Edgar Renteria).
1. **Clay Buchholz, rhp, Angelina (Texas) JC** (Supplemental choice—42nd—as compensation for Type A free agent Pedro Martinez).**—(2007-15)**
1. **Jed Lowrie, 2b, Stanford University** (Supplemental choice—45th—as compensation for Cabrera).**—(2008-15)**
1. **Michael Bowden, rhp, Waubonsie Valley HS, Aurora, Ill.** (Supplemental choice—47th—as compensation for Lowe).**—(2008-13)**
2. Jon Egan, c, Cross Creek HS, Hephzibah, Ga. (Choice from Mets as compensation for Martinez).—(Low A)
2. (Choice to Padres as compensation for Type A free agent David Wells)
3. (Choice to Cubs as compensation for Type B free agent Matt Clement)
4. Scott Blue, rhp, Morro Bay (Calif.) HS.—(Rookie)
5. Reid Engel, of, Lewis-Palmer HS, Monument, Colo.—(AA)
6. Jeff Corsaletti, of, University of Florida.
7. Yahmed Yema, of, Florida International University.
8. J.T. Zink, rhp, Everett (Wash.) CC.
9. Mark Wagner, c, UC Irvine.
10. Kevin Guyette, rhp, University of Arizona.
11. Ismael Casillas, rhp, Benedictine (Kan.) College.
12. Kyle Fernandes, lhp, Massasoit (Mass.) CC.
13. Jay Johnson, of, Xavier University.
14. ***Pedro Alvarez, 3b, Horace Mann HS, Bronx, N.Y.—(2010-15)**

DRAFT DROP *First-round draft pick (2nd overall), Pirates (2008)*

15. *P.J. Thomas, rhp, Jeffersonville (Ind.) HS.
16. Matt Mercurio, 3b, Florida Southern College.
17. Dominic Ramos, ss, Texas State University.
18. *Nick Criaris, c, St. Peter's Prep, Jersey City, N.J.
19. Jim Baxter, lhp, Villanova University.
20. ***Charlie Blackmon, lhp, Young Harris (Ga.) JC.—(2011-15)**
21. *Drew Johnson, rhp, Navarro (Texas) JC.
22. *Orvil Aviles, lhp, Fernando Callejo HS, Manati, P.R.
23. Carl Lipsey, 2b, Jackson State University.
24. Jason Twomley, of, University of Massachusetts.
25. Ricardo Sanchez, c, Barry (Fla.) University.
26. ***Kirby Yates, rhp, Kauai HS, Koloa, Hawaii.—(2014-15)**

DRAFT DROP *Brother of Tyler Yates, major leaguer (2004-09)*

27. Matt Hancock, lhp, Oral Roberts University.
28. *Ryan Hinson, lhp, Northwestern HS, Rock Hill, S.C.
29. Chris Jones. rhp, Indiana State University.
30. +Ryan Colvin, rhp, Carroll HS, Southlake, Texas / Grayson County (Texas) CC.
31. **+Luis Exposito, c, Champagnat Catholic HS, Hialeah, Fla. / St. Petersburg (Fla.) CC.—(2012)**
32. Jeff Natale, 2b, Trinity (Conn.) College.
33. ***John Hester, c, Stanford University.—(2009-13)**
34. ***Allan Dykstra, 1b, Rancho Bernardo HS, Poway, Calif.—(2015)**

DRAFT DROP *First-round draft pick (23rd overall), Padres (2008)*

35. *Jason Determann, lhp, Louisiana State University.
36. *Mark McClure, rhp, Hillsborough HS, Tampa.
37. *Jason Schnitzer, rhp, Los Alamitos (Calif.) HS.
38. +Levi Tapia, c, Ralston Valley HS, Arvada, Colo. / Lamar (Colo.) CC.
39. Bubba Bell, of, Nicholls State University.
40. Blake Maxwell, rhp, Methodist (N.C.) College.
41. *Eddie Degerman, rhp, Rice University.
42. *Miguel Alicea, of, Manuela Toro HS, Caguas, P.R.
43. ***Jason Castro, c, Castro Valley (Calif.) HS.—(2010-15)**

DRAFT DROP *First-round draft pick (10th overall), Astros (2008)*

44. *Chris Garcia, 1b, Xaverian HS, Brooklyn, N.Y.
45. *Dustin Bamberg, c, Tallahassee (Fla.) CC.
46. T.J. Large, rhp, University of Alabama.
47. *Alex Wolfe, c, Timpanogos HS, Payson, Utah.
48. +Matt Sheely, of, Palm Beach Gardens (Fla.) HS / Seminole (Fla.) CC.
49. *Erik Turgeon, rhp, Dunedin (Fla.) HS.
50. *Colin Arnold, of, King's Academy, Palm Beach Gardens, Fla.

## CHICAGO CUBS (20)

1. Mark Pawelek, lhp, Springville (Utah) HS.—(High A)

2. **Donnie Veal, lhp, Pima (Ariz.) CC.—(2009-15)**
3. Mark Holliman, rhp, University of Mississippi.—(AAA)
3. Mike Billek, rhp, University of Central Florida (Choice from Red Sox as compensation for Type B free agent Matt Clement).—(High A)
4. Dylan Johnston, ss, Hamilton HS, Chandler, Ariz.—(High A)
5. Scott Taylor, rhp, Hermitage HS, Richmond, Va.—(High A)
6. Kyle Reynolds, ss, Baylor University.

DRAFT DROP *Son of Craig Reynolds, first-round draft pick, Pirates (1971); major leaguer (1975-89)*

7. Trey Taylor, lhp, Baylor University.
8. Jake Muyco, c, North Carolina State University.
9. Matt Avery, rhp, University of Virginia.
10. Joe Simokaitis, ss, University of Nebraska.
11. Michael Phelps, rhp, Central Missouri State University.
12. Yusuf Carter, c, El Paso (Texas) CC.

DRAFT DROP *Nephew of Joe Carter, first-round draft pick, Cubs (1981); major leaguer (1983-98)*

13. Brett Jackson, rhp, Modesto (Calif.) JC.
14. ***Tyler Graham, of, Oregon State University.—(2012)**
15. Roger Evenson, rhp, Northwest Nazarene (Idaho) College.
16. Jon Mueller, rhp, University of Minnesota.
17. Brandon Taylor, 3b, Brigham Young University.
18. Victor Liriano, of, El Paso (Texas) CC.
19. Kyle Holden, rhp, Cal State San Bernardino.
20. *L.V. Ware, of, North Atlanta HS, Atlanta.
21. Peter Farina, c, Virginia Commonwealth University.
22. Michael Hyle, rhp, University of Georgia.
23. Jayson Ruhlman, lhp, Central Michigan University.
24. Scott Hode, ss, University of Arkansas.
25. D.J. Lewis, of, Los Angeles Valley CC.
26. Nik Crouch, 1b, Vanguard (Calif.) University.
27. Davy Gregg, of, University of South Carolina.
28. Michael Greenhouse, lhp, University of Evansville.
29. Johnny Defendis, of, Rutgers University.
30. *Matt Liuzza, c, Louisiana State University.
31. *Brad DePoy, rhp, San Jacinto (Texas) JC.
32. *Colby Wark, rhp, Lower Columbia (Wash.) JC.
33. *B.J. Ferguson, rhp, Cottonwood HS, Salt Lake City.
34. +Cody Gilbert, 3b, Lincoln Trail (Ill.) JC.
35. *Drew O'Connell, rhp, John A. Logan (Ill.) JC.
36. *Needham Jones, lhp, Old Dominion University.
37. *Kyle Keen, of, University of Georgia.
38. Ryan Episcopo, of, Andrew (Ga.) JC.
39. Justin Morgan, c, University of Louisiana-Lafayette.
40. Ryan Chambers, lhp, Brigham Young University.
41. *Chris Rollins, rhp, Winslow Township HS, Blue Anchor, N.J.
42. *Noah Garza, rhp, Nolan HS, Fort Worth, Texas.
43. *Michael Brenly, c, Notre Dame HS, Scottsdale, Ariz.

DRAFT DROP *Son of Bob Brenly, major leaguer (1981-89); major league manager (2001-04)*

44. *Eddie Rush, of, Westlake HS, McDonough, Ga.
45. *Corey Madden, rhp, St. Mary's (Calif.) College.
46. +Luther Murphy, 1b, Hialeah Miami Lakes HS, Hialeah, Fla. / Palm Beach (Fla.) CC.
47. *Mario Williams, c, Hillsborough HS, Tampa.
48. *Andy Hawranick, c, Georgia Tech.
49. *Kyle Mura, 3b, Loyola Marymount University.
50. *Steven Morlock, rhp, UC Santa Barbara.

## CHICAGO WHITE SOX (15)

1. **Lance Broadway, rhp, Texas Christian University.—(2007-09)**
2. (Choice to Yankees as compensation for Type B free agent Orlando Hernandez)
3. Ricky Brooks, rhp, East Carolina University.—(AAA)
4. **Chris Getz, 2b, University of Michigan.—(2008-14)**
5. Ryan Rote, rhp, Vanderbilt University.—(AAA)
6. **Aaron Cunningham, of, Everett (Wash.) CC.—(2008-12)**
7. **Dan Cortes, rhp, Garey HS, Pomona, Calif.—(2010-11)**
8. **Clayton Richard, lhp, University of Michigan.—(2008-15)**
9. Joe Winn, rhp, Delgado (La.) JC.
10. Israel Chirino, lhp, University of Miami.
11. Jason Rice, rhp, Chaffey (Calif.) JC.
12. Sheldon Catchot, lhp, Delgado (La.) JC.
13. *Joey Fernandez, 1b, Braddock HS, Miami.
14. Derek Rodriguez, rhp, University of Nevada-Las Vegas.
15. **Chris Carter, 3b, Sierra Vista HS, Las Vegas, Nev.—(2010-15)**
16. Alex Woodson, lhp, Porterville (Calif.) CC.
17. *Enrique Garcia, rhp, Potomac State (W.Va.) JC.
18. Tim Sabo, rhp, Seton Hall University.
19. ***Jordan Danks, of, Round Rock (Texas) HS.—(2012-15)**

DRAFT DROP *Brother of John Danks, first-round draft pick, Rangers (2003); major leaguer (2007-15)*

20. Josh Morgan, of, University of South Alabama.
21. Raleigh Evans, lhp, Lake City (Fla.) CC.
22. +Christian Marrero, of, Broward (Fla.) JC.
23. ***Bobby LaFromboise, lhp, Rio Hondo (Calif.) JC.—(2013-15)**
24. *Tyler Wright, of, Charlotte HS, Punta Gorda, Fla.
25. *Andrew Beatty, lhp, West High, Aurora, Ill.
26. Anthony Carter, rhp, Georgia Perimeter JC.
27. +Danny Jordan, c, Broward (Fla.) CC.
28. *Justin Sincock, rhp, Golden West (Calif.) JC.
29. *Aljay Davis, 2b, Northeast Oklahoma A&M JC.
30. *Brandon Langston, rhp, Cleveland State (Tenn.) CC.
31. ***Lucas Luetge, lhp, Bellville HS, Industry, Texas.—(2012-15)**
32. *Matt Headley, lhp, San Jacinto (Texas) JC.
33. *Scott Savastano, ss, Plymouth North HS, Plymouth, Mass.
34. Tim Day, rhp, Michigan State University.
35. Marcos Causey, of, South Florida CC.
36. *Nate Templeton, rhp, Valley HS, Des Monies, Iowa.
37. *Brian Flores, lhp, New Mexico JC.
38. Enrique Escolano, rhp, Kell HS, Kennesaw, Ga.
39. *Jovan Rosa, ss, East Hartford (Conn.) HS.
40. *Rafael Vera, 2b, Sarasota (Fla.) HS.
41. Kris Welker, c, University of Iowa.
42. *Michael Kelly, lhp, Lafayette HS, Mayo, Fla.
43. *Brooks Dunn, lhp, Mississippi State University.
44. *Drew George, ss, Lower Columbia (Wash.) CC.
45. *Cody Wright, lhp, Bountiful, Utah.
46. *Brendan O'Donnell, of, Santa Barbara (Calif.) CC.
47. John Wolff, 2b, Harvard University.
48. *Chris Cassidy, lhp, Claremont (Calif.) HS.
49. Steven Squires, rhp, Wayne State (Mich.) University.

DRAFT DROP *Son of Mike Squires, major leaguer (1975-85)*

50. *Kyle Landers, lhp, Noblesville (Ind.) HS.

## CINCINNATI REDS (12)

1. **Jay Bruce, of, West Brook HS, Beaumont, Texas.—(2008-15)**
2. **Travis Wood, lhp, Bryant HS, Alexander, Ark.—(2010-15)**
3. Zach Ward, rhp, Gardner-Webb University.—(AA)
4. **Sam LeCure, rhp, University of Texas.—(2010-15)**
5. James Avery, rhp, Niagara University.—(AAA)
6. **Jeff Stevens, rhp, Loyola Marymount University.—(2009-11)**
7. Brandon Roberts, of, Cal Poly San Luis Obispo.
8. Michael Jones, ss, Wayne County HS, Jesup, Ga.
9. +Milton Loo, 3b, Yavapai (Ariz.) CC.
10. Bo Lanier, rhp, University of Georgia.
11. **Carlos Fisher, rhp, Lewis-Clark State (Idaho) College.—(2009-11)**
12. **Adam Rosales, ss, Western Michigan University.—(2008-15)**
13. **Logan Ondrusek, rhp, McLennan (Texas) CC.—(2010-14)**
14. Michael Griffin, 2b, Baylor University.
15. Michael DeJesus, 2b, Coastal Carolina University.

DRAFT DROP *Brother of David DeJesus, major leaguer (2003-15)*

16. Jason Vecchio, rhp, University of Texas-San Antonio.
17. David Wilson, lhp, Lander (S.C.) University.
18. Kevyn Feiner, ss, Sun Prairie (Wis.) HS.
19. Eric Eymann, ss, Kansas State University.
20. Ben Mummy, 1b, University of Nevada-Reno.
21. Ben Blumenthal, c, Erskine (S.C.) College.
22. +Robbie Nickols, lhp, Pima (Ariz.) CC.
23. James Morris, lhp, University of Illinois.
24. *Kyle Ginley, rhp, St. Petersburg (Fla.) JC.
25. Taylor Johnson, of, University of Washington.
26. *Matthew Salmon, of, South Aiken HS, Aiken S.C.
27. *Kenny Smalley, rhp, St. Charles (Ill.) HS.
28. *Judson Smith, rhp, Phoenix JC.
29. Russ Haltiwanger, rhp, Newberry (S.C.) College.
30. Mark Rodriguez, c, University of Texas-Pan American.
31. Abe Woody, rhp, Baylor University.
32. Chris Denove, c, UCLA.
33. *Leroy Hunt, of, Linden HS, Stockton, Calif.
34. Brandon Camardese, lhp, University of Miami.
35. Angel Colon, 3b, Iowa Wesleyan College.
36. *Lorenzo Douglas, rhp, Sachse HS, Garland, Texas.
37. +Jacob Long, c, Modesto (Calif.) JC.
38. *Kuyaunnis Miles, of, Russell County HS, Phenix City, Ala.
39. *Edwin Quirarte, rhp, Oxnard (Calif.) HS.
40. +Angel Cabrera, ss, Connors State (Okla.) JC.
41. Justin Tordi, ss, University of Florida.
42. ***John Axford, rhp, University of Notre Dame.—(2009-15)**
43. *Clay Long, rhp, Chipola (Fla.) JC.
44. *Jason Erickson, rhp, White River HS, Buckley, Wash.
45. *Andre Lamontagne, rhp, Ernest Righetti HS, Santa Maria, Calif.
46. *J.W. Brown, 1b, Howard (Texas) JC.
47. Matt Garrett, of, Grand Rapids (Mich.) CC.
48. *Gary Poynter, rhp, Marcus HS, Flower Mound, Texas
49. *Cody Allen, of, Coleman (Mich.) HS.
50. *Jake Christensen, of, Lockport Township HS, Lockport, Ill.

DRAFT DROP *Son of Jeff Christensen, quarterback, National Football League (1983-87)*

## CLEVELAND INDIANS (14)

1. **Trevor Crowe, of, University of Arizona.—(2009-13)**
1. Johnny Drennen, of, Rancho Bernardo HS, San Diego (Supplemental choice—33rd—as compensation for Type A free agent Omar Vizquel).—(AA)
2. Stephen Head, 1b, University of Mississippi.—(AAA)
3. Nick Weglarz, 1b, Lakeshore Catholic HS, Stevensville, Ontario.—(AAA)
3. Jensen Lewis, rhp, Vanderbilt University (Choice from Giants as compensation for Vizquel).—(2007-10)
4. **Jordan Brown, 1b, University of Arizona.—(2010-13)**
5. Kevin Dixon, rhp, Minnesota State University-Mankato.—(AA)
6. Joe Ness, rhp, Ball State University.
7. James Deters, rhp, Calvin (Mich.) College.
8. Ryan Edell, rhp, College of Charleston.
9. Roman Pena, of, Montgomery HS, San Diego.
10. Jason Schutt, rhp, Central Missouri State University.
11. Nick Petrucci, 3b, JC of the Canyons (Calif.).
12. Matt Fornasiere, ss, University of Minnesota.
13. *Barry Laird, rhp, Lee HS, Baytown, Texas.
14. Mike Finocchi, rhp, Louisburg (N.C.) JC.
15. *Chase Phillips, rhp, Monterey HS, Lubbock, Texas.
16. *Aaron Shafer, rhp, Troy Buchanan HS, Moscow Mills, Mo.
17. *Eric Barrett, lhp, Marion (Ill.) HS.
18. ***Desmond Jennings, of, Pinson Valley HS, Pinson, Ala.—(2010-15)**
19. *Tim Dennehy, lhp, Oak Park-River Forest HS, Oak Park, Ill.
20. +Scott Sumner, rhp, Louisiana College.
21. **Neil Wagner, rhp, North Dakota State University.—(2011-14)**
22. *Clint Storr, of, Key West (Fla.) HS.
23. *Dexter English, of, Encinal HS, Suisun City, Calif.
24. *Jake Hale, rhp, Alexander HS, Albany, Ohio.
25. Andy Lytle, ss, University of Iowa.
26. Thomas Cowley, lhp, Oklahoma State University.
27. ***Brandon Laird, 1b, La Quinta HS, Garden Grove, Calif.—(2011-13)**

DRAFT DROP *Brother of Gerald Laird, major leaguer (2003-15)*

28. Angel Claudio, rhp, Puerto Rico Baseball Academy, Caguas, P.R.
29. *John Curtis, c, Cal State Fullerton.
30. *Joel Martin, lhp, Marion Center HS, Homer, Pa.
31. Matt Loberg, rhp, University of Minnesota.
32. Brent Thomas, of, Texas Tech.
33. Trevor Mortensen, of, Cal State Fullerton.
34. *Arshwin Asjes, rhp, Gloucester County (N.J.) CC.
35. *Levi Laughlin, rhp, Connors State (Okla.) JC.
36. *Matt Yokley, rhp, Collierville (Tenn.) HS.
37. *Cody Satterwhite, rhp, Hillcrest Christian HS, Jackson, Miss.
38. *Daniel Lima, ss, Florida Christian HS, Miami.
39. *Jessie Mier, c, Irvine Valley (Calif.) JC.

DRAFT DROP *Brother of Jio Mier, first-round draft pick, Astros (2009)*

40. *DeWayne Carver, rhp, Oklahoma State University.
41. *Ashton Shewey, lhp, Chandler-Gilbert (Ariz.) CC.
42. ***Tim Lincecum, rhp, University of Washington.—(2007-15)**

DRAFT DROP *First-round draft pick (10th overall), Giants (2006)*

43. *Chadd Hartman, of, Olympia HS, Windermere, Fla.
44. *Travis Turek, rhp, Westlake HS, Westlake Village, Calif.
45. *Drew Fiorenza, rhp, Clemson University.
46. ***Blake Davis, ss, Cal State Fullerton.—(2011)**
47. *Gus Milner, of, University of Kansas.
48. *Joe Hunter, of, Mississippi State University.
49. *Ryan Wood, ss, Hylton HS, Woodbridge, Va.
50. *Cameron Satterwhite, of, Moeller HS, Cincinnati.

## COLORADO ROCKIES (7)

1. **Troy Tulowitzki, ss, Long Beach State University.—(2006-15)**
1. **Chaz Roe, rhp, Lafayette HS, Lexington, Ky.** (Supplemental choice—32nd—as compensation for Type A free agent Vinny Castilla).—**(2013-15)**
2. Daniel Carte, of, Winthrop University (Choice from Nationals as compensation for Castilla).—(AA)
2. Zach Simons, rhp, Everett (Wash.) CC.—(AAA)
3. Kyle Hancock, rhp, Rowlett (Texas) HS.—(Rookie)
4. Brandon Durden, lhp, Georgia College.—(AAA)
5. Josh Sullivan, rhp, Auburn University.—(AAA)
6. Corey Wimberly, 2b, Alcorn State University.
7. Geoff Strickland, ss, Florida Southern College.
8. James Burok, rhp, Old Dominion University.
9. Andrew Johnston, rhp, University of Missouri.
10. (void) *Garner Wetzel, ss, Millsaps (Miss.) College.
11. Chris Frey, of, University of Arizona.
12. *Dominick Foster, rhp, Fresno (Calif.) CC.
13. Mike Paulk, of, Cal State Northridge.
14. Kyle Blumenthal, c, Cal Poly San Luis Obispo.
15. Travis Becktel, of, San Jose State University.
16. Bret Berglund, of, Cal Poly San Luis Obispo.
17. Jimmy Freeman, lhp, Washington State University.
18. Brett Strickland, rhp, Georgia State University.
19. Byron Binda, rhp, Coastal Carolina University.
20. Andy Kreidermacher, rhp, Minnesota State University-Mankato.
21. ***Chris Martin, rhp, McLennan (Texas) CC.—(2014-15)**
22. Radames Nazario, ss, Pimentel HS, Naguabo, P.R.
23. Phil Cuadrado, 3b, Cumberland (Tenn.) University.
24. *Sean Toler, rhp, Parkway South HS, Manchester, Mo.
25. *Steven Hirschfeld, rhp, CC of Southern Nevada.
26. Ethan Katz, rhp, Cal State Sacramento.
27. Sean Ruthven, rhp, University of Georgia.

DRAFT DROP *Son of Dick Ruthven, first overall draft pick, January 1973/secondary phase, Phillies; major leaguer (1973-86)*

28. David Bechtold, lhp, Liberty University.
29. *Reese Havens, ss, Bishop England HS, Charleston, S.C.
DRAFT DROP *First-round draft pick (22nd overall), Mets (2008)*
30. Michael Milliron, ss, Penn State University.
**31. *Sean Halton, 1b, Fresno (Calif.) HS.—(2013)**
32. *Jarrad Page, of, UCLA.
DRAFT DROP *Defensive back, National Football League (2006-11)*
33. *Jordan Jarvis, rhp, Arcadia HS, Phoenix.
34. *Kyle Beitey, lhp, Lower Columbia (Wash.) JC.
35. (void) *Tim Brewer, rhp, Ivanna Eudora Kean HS, St. Thomas, V.I.
36. Chris Cook, 1b, Grand Canyon University.
37. *C.J. Belanger, of, Cypress HS, Stanton, Calif.
**38. *Barret Browning, lhp, Florida State University.—(2012)**
39. *Rod Scurry, rhp, Sierra (Calif.) JC.
DRAFT DROP *Son of Rod Scurry, first-round draft pick, Pirates (1974); major leaguer (1980-88)*
40. *Joseph Servais, c, Garden City (Kan.) CC.
41. *Jeremy Farrell, 3b, St. Ignatius HS, Cleveland.
DRAFT DROP *Son of John Farrell, major leaguer (1987-96); major league manager (2011-15)*
42. *Maikol Gonzales, ss, Louisburg (N.C.) JC.
43. *Jordan Rogers, rhp, Dayton (Texas) HS.
44. *Philip Myers, lhp, Ballard HS, Louisville, Ky.
45. *Chris Bell, of, Johnson HS, Gainesville, Ga.
46. *Garrett Vaughan, c, Sibley (La.) HS.
47. *Brent Weiss, 2b, St. Joseph Regional HS, Suffern, N.Y.
48. *Spencer Schuh, rhp, Harrison (Ark.) HS.
49. *Jordan Moore, lhp, Spokane Falls (Wash.) CC.
50. *James Pollack, c, North Broward Prep, Parkland, Fla.

## DETROIT TIGERS (10)

**1. Cameron Maybin, of, T.C. Roberson HS, Arden, N.C.—(2007-15)**
2. (Choice to Angels as compensation for Type A free agent Troy Percival)
**3. Chris Robinson, c, University of Illinois.—(2013)**
**4. Kevin Whelan, rhp, Texas A&M University.—(2011-14)**
**5. Jeff Larish, 1b, Arizona State University.—(2008-10)**
**6. Clete Thomas, of, Auburn University.—(2008-13)**
7. P.J. Finigan, rhp, Southern Illinois University.
8. Brendan Wise, rhp, Pratt (Kan.) JC.
9. *Paul Coleman, lhp, Pepperdine University.
10. Kevin Ardoin, rhp, University of Louisiana-Lafayette
**11. Anthony Claggett, rhp, UC Riverside.—(2009)**
**12. Matt Joyce, of, Florida Southern College.—(2008-15)**
13. Louis Ott, ss, Sacramento (Calif.) CC.
**14. Casper Wells, of, Towson University.—(2010-13)**
15. *Ben Petralli, c, Sacramento (Calif.) CC.
DRAFT DROP *Son of Geno Petralli, major leaguer (1982-93)*
**16. Michael Hollimon, ss, Oral Roberts University.—(2008)**
17. *Warner Jones, 2b, Vanderbilt University.
18. Agustin Guzman, 2b, Baton Rouge (La.) CC.
**19. Burke Badenhop, rhp, Bowling Green State University.—(2008-15)**
20. Erik Averill, lhp, Arizona State University.
**21. *David Adams, ss, Grandview Prep, Boca Raton, Fla.—(2013)**
22. Matt Norfleet, rhp, Tennessee Wesleyan College.
23. Mark Haske, ss, University of Cincinnati.
24. *Brett Bordes, lhp, Arizona State University.
25. Jacob Baxter, rhp, University of Texas-Arlington.
26. Schuyler Williamson, c, U.S. Military Academy.
**27. Will Rhymes, 2b, College of William & Mary.—(2010-12)**
28. *Ryan Paul, lhp, Los Angeles Pierce JC.
29. *Eric Fry, of, Barbe HS, Lake Charles, La.
30. Ryan Roberson, 1b, George Washington University.
31. Tim Robertson, rhp, Oral Roberts University.
32. Chris Torres, c, Cumberland (Tenn.) University.
33. Loren Fraser, rhp, UC Santa Barbara.
**34. *Alex Avila, 3b, Archbishop McCarthy HS, Pembroke Pines, Fla.—(2009-15)**
35. Jeff Hahn, rhp, Clemson University.
36. Gibbs Wilson, rhp, Weatherford (Texas) JC.
37. *Jeff Kunkel, c, University of Michigan.
**38. *Zach Putnam, rhp, Pioneer HS, Ann Arbor, Mich.—(2011-15)**
39. *Kiel Renfro, rhp, Texarkana (Texas) CC.
40. *Kyle Peter, of, Cloud County (Kan.) CC.
41. *Tony Pechek, c, South HS, Pueblo, Colo.
42. *Ben Rodewald, rhp, East Kenwood (Mich.) HS.
43. *Ryan Perry, ss, Rocklin (Calif.) HS.
44. *Adrian Casanova, c, Clemson University.
45. *Tyson Jaquez, 3b, Loyalton (Calif.) HS.
46. *David Mattox, rhp, North Arkansas CC.
47. *Albert Gonzalez, 2b, American HS, Hialeah, Fla.
48. *Kevin Hammons, rhp, Sierra (Calif.) JC.
49. *Anthony Capra, lhp, Arvada West High, Arvada, Colo.
50. *Jeff Whitlow, of, Detroit Country Day HS, Southfield, Mich.

## FLORIDA MARLINS (16)

**1. Chris Volstad, rhp, Palm Beach Gardens (Fla.) HS.—(2008-15)**
**1. Aaron Thompson, lhp, Second Baptist HS, Houston** (Choice from Giants as compensation for Type A free agent Armando Benitez).—**(2011-15)**
1. Jacob Marceaux, rhp, McNeese State University (Choice from Yankees as compensation for Type A free agent Carl Pavano).—(AA)
**1. Ryan Tucker, rhp, Temple City (Calif.) HS** (Supplemental choice—34th—as compensation for Benitez).**—(2008-11)**
**1. Sean West, lhp, Captain Shreve HS, Shreveport, La.** (Supplemental choice—44th—as compensation for Pavano).**—(2009-10)**
2. Kris Harvey, of, Clemson University.—(AA)
DRAFT DROP *Son of Bryan Harvey, major leaguer (1987-95) • Brother of Hunter Harvey, first-round draft pick, Baltimore Orioles (2013)*
**2. Brett Hayes, c, University of Nevada** (Supplemental choice—79th—as compensation for Type C free agent Mike Redmond).—**(2009-15)**
3. Matt Goyen, lhp, Georgia College.—(High A)
**4. Gaby Sanchez, c, University of Miami.—(2008-14)**
5. Kyle Winters, rhp, Pomona HS, Arvada, Colo.—(AA)
6. James Guerrero, 2b, San Diego State University.
**7. Chris Leroux, rhp, Winthrop University.—(2009-14)**
**8. *Aaron Bates, 1b, North Carolina State University.—(2009)**
9. Jim Brauer, rhp, University of Michigan.
10. Cody Allen, 3b, Elk Grove (Calif.) HS.
11. Andy Jenkins, c, Oregon State University.
12. *Kyle Marlatt, rhp, Texas A&M University.
13. Jeff Van Houten, of, University of Arizona.
14. Travis Talbott, lhp, University of California.
15. Paul Witt, ss, Baylor University.
16. Jon Lewis, rhp, University of Stony Brook.
17. Zac McCamie, rhp, University of South Carolina.
18. Kyle Padgett, ss, College of William & Mary.
19. Adam Wood, lhp, University of South Alabama.
20. Rafael Galbizo, rhp, Miami.
21. Colin Roberson, of, Virginia Wesleyan College.
**22. +Logan Morrison, 1b, Northshore HS, Slidell, La. / Maple Woods (Mo.) JC.—(2010-15)**
23. Justin Webb, c, University of North Carolina.
24. Matt Kutler, of, Brown University.
25. Blake Jones, rhp, Northwestern State University.
26. Scott Lindeen, rhp, University of La Verne (Calif.).
27. Jason Jarrett, rhp, Virginia Wesleyan College.
28. *Michael Thomasson, of, Laney (Calif.) JC.
29. *Jared Wesson, lhp, Itawamba (Miss.) CC.
30. Chris Haupt, c, Central Columbia HS, Bloomsburg, Pa.
31. *Matt Jones, lhp, Guildford Park SS, Surrey, B.C.
32. Adalberto Flores, rhp, Gurabo, P.R.
33. +Adam Howard, c, St. Louis CC-Meramec.
34. *Adam Abraham, 3b, Grosse Point South HS, Grosse Point, Mich.
35. *Jacob Taylor, c, Chaffey (Calif.) JC.
36. *Sean Boatright, of, Long Beach State University.
37. +Josh Short, of, Marysville-Pilchuck HS, Marysville, Wash. / Mount Hood (Ore.) CC.
38. *Steven Pujol, lhp, San Fernando (Calif.) HS.
39. *Jonathan Prevost, of, Ahunstic (Quebec) College.
40. *Eric Basurto, rhp, Chabot (Calif.) JC.
41. Luis Ramos, of, Jose de Diego HS, Mayaguez, P.R.
42. *David Woods, c, West Lauderdale HS, Bailey, Miss.
43. *Zach Barrett, 3b, Olney Central (Ill.) JC.
44. *Ryan Pollard, lhp, Illinois Central CC.
45. *Brady Decker, rhp, Olney Central (Ill.) CC.
46. *Stephen Schneider, 1b, Orange Coast (Calif.) CC.
47. +Dustin Kaats, 2b, Desert Mountain HS, Scottsdale, Ariz. / Yavapai (Ariz.) CC.
48. *Chris Bodishbaugh, rhp, Los Medanos (Calif.) JC.
49. *James Wallace, rhp, Benicia (Calif.) HS.
50. *Jared Banks, rhp, Los Medanos (Calif.) JC.

## HOUSTON ASTROS (24)

**1. Brian Bogusevic, lhp, Tulane University.—(2010-15)**
1. Eli Iorg, of, University of Tennessee (Supplemental choice—38th—as compensation for Type A free agent Carlos Beltran).—(AAA)
DRAFT DROP *Son of Garth Iorg, major leaguer (1978-87)*
2. Ralph Henriquez, c, Key West (Fla.) HS.—(AAA)
**3. Tommy Manzella, ss, Tulane University** (Choice from Mets as compensation for Beltran).**—(2009-10)**
**3. *Josh Lindblom, rhp, Harrison HS, West Lafayette, Ind.—(2011-14)**
DRAFT DROP *Attended Tennessee; re-drafted by Dodgers, 2008 (2nd round)*
4. Josh Flores, of, Triton (Ill.) JC.—(AA)
5. Billy Hart, 3b, University of Southern California.—(AA)
**6. Brandon Barnes, of, Cypress (Calif) JC.—(2012-15)**
7. Timothy Johnson, ss, Wissahickon HS, Penllyn, Pa.
8. Koby Clemens, 3b, Memorial HS, Houston.
DRAFT DROP *Son of Roger Clemens, first-round draft pick, Red Sox (1983); major leaguer (1984-2007)*
9. *Jordan Meaker, rhp, Flower Mound (Texas) HS.
10. Allen Langdon, of, Eagle HS, Boise, Idaho.
11. Cory Lapinski, lhp, Illinois Wesleyan University.
12. Tip Fairchild, rhp, University of Southern Maine.
13. Eric King, ss, University of Tennessee.
14. Mark Ori, 1b, Northwestern University.
15. Eric Sheridan, rhp, Saddleback (Calif.) CC.
16. Aaron Bulkley, of, Le Moyne University.
17. Andy Kroeker, c, Biola (Calif.) University.
18. *Brian Needham, rhp, John Foster Dulles HS, Sugar Land, Texas.
19. Drew Himes, rhp, Illinois Wesleyan University.
20. Ryan Mitchell, rhp, Magnolia (Texas) HS.
21. Scott Sarver, lhp, Cal State Fullerton.
22. *T.J. Steele, of, Canyon del Oro HS, Oro Valley, Ariz.
23. Chris Blazek, lhp, University of Vermont.
24. Sean Walker, rhp, Baylor University.
25. Jacob Hurry, lhp, Coastal Carolina University.
26. Michael Thompson, 3b, Santa Clara University.
27. *Matt Luca, rhp, University of Nevada-Las Vegas.
28. *Eric Baker, 2b, Mansfield (Pa.) University.
29. Jamie Gant, rhp, Mississippi State University.
30. Matt Hirsh, rhp, California Lutheran University.
DRAFT DROP *Brother of Jason Hirsh, major leaguer (2006-08)*
31. *Brad Stone, rhp, Quincy (Ill.) University.
32. Cole Graham, 1b, Triton (Ill.) JC.
33. +Reid Kelly, rhp, Desert Mountain HS, Scottsdale, Ariz. / Chandler-Gilbert (Ariz.) JC.
34. Nathan Warrick, of, University of Texas-Arlington.
35. +Andrew Darnell, of, Chabot (Calif.) JC.
36. Matt Cunningham, of, UC Riverside.
37. *Matt Bishop, rhp, Endicott (Mass.) College.
38. *Mike Colla, rhp, Clovis West HS, Fresno, Calif.
39. *Zachary Williams, rhp, Seminole State (Okla.) CC.
40. *Collin Fanning, of, Clarendon (Texas) JC.
41. *Casey McCleskey, of, Temple (Texas) JC.
42. Brandon Stricklen, rhp, Texas Southern University.
43. *Jacob Hower, rhp, American River (Calif.) JC.
44. *Nick Cobler, lhp, Northeast Texas CC.
45. *Craig Herrforth, rhp, Arrowhead Union HS, Hartland, Wis.
46. *Wes Musick, lhp, Hudson HS, Lufkin, Texas.

## KANSAS CITY ROYALS (2)

**1. Alex Gordon, 3b, University of Nebraska.—(2007-15)**
**2. Jeff Bianchi, ss, Lampeter-Strasburg HS, Lancaster, Pa.—(2012-15)**
3. Chris Nicoll, rhp, UC Irvine.—(AAA)
4. Joe Dickerson, of, Esperanza HS, Yorba Linda, Calif.—(AA)
5. Shawn Hayes, ss, Franklin Pierce (N.H.) College.—(Low A)
6. Ryan DiPietro, lhp, Eastern Connecticut State University.
7. Brent Fisher, lhp, Tolleson Union HS, Goodyear, Ariz.
8. Nick Doscher, c, Moore Catholic HS, Staten Island, N.Y.
9. Kiel Thibault, c, Gonzaga University.
10. Jeff Howell, c, Florida Southern College.
11. Michael Penn, rhp, University of Michigan.
12. Cody Harkcom, rhp, New Mexico JC.
13. Andrew Larsen, of, University of Stony Brook.
14. Antonio Sabatini, of, Erskine (S.C.) College.
15. Brady Everett, c, Washington State University.
16. Mario Santiago, rhp, Baton Rouge (La.) CC.
17. *Miguel Vasquez, ss, Dewitt Clinton HS, Bronx, N.Y.
18. Paul Raglione, rhp, Grant HS, Portland, Ore.
19. *Zane Chavez, c, Fallbrook (Calif.) HS.
20. +Bryan Casey, rhp, Arizona Western JC.
21. David Henninger, rhp, Messiah (Pa.) College.
22. *Justin Bristow, ss, Mills Godwin HS, Richmond, Va.
23. Matt Kniginyzky, rhp, High Point University.
24. Josh Colafemina, ss, College of St. Rose (N.Y.).
25. Kevin Bulger, rhp, College of Charleston.
DRAFT DROP *Brother of Jason Bulger, first-round draft pick, Diamondbacks (2001); major leaguer (2005-11)*
26. Jake McLintock, rhp, San Diego State University.
27. Jase Turner, 1b, Pomona-Pitzer (Calif.) College.
DRAFT DROP *Grandson of Jesse Gonder, major leaguer (1960-67)*
28. Felix Peguero, of, Oklahoma Baptist University.
29. Brandon Brantley, rhp, University of Science and Arts (Okla.).
30. Jeremy Jirschele, 2b, University of Wisconsin-Oshkosh.
31. Pedro Lopez, ss, Universidad del Turabo HS, Toa Baja, P.R.
32. *Michael Dubee, rhp, Okaloosa-Walton (Fla.) CC.
33. +Daniel Gutierrez, rhp, Rubidoux HS, Riverside, Calif. / Riverside (Calif.) CC.
34. Oscar Marrero, c, Juan Antonio Corretjer HS, Ciales, P.R.
35. *Luke Burnett, rhp, Carthage (Texas) HS.
36. *Matt Klimas, c, Broken Arrow (Okla.) HS.
37. *Nickolas Love, of, Enterprise (Ala.) HS.
38. *Jacob Myking, c, San Joaquin Delta (Calif.) JC.
39. *Steve Teno, lhp, St. Thomas of Villanova HS, La Salle, Ontario.
40. *Nick Romero, ss, Eastlake HS, Chula Vista, Calif.
41. *Anthony Rodriguez, ss, Puerto Rico Baseball Academy, Vega Baja, P.R.
42. *David McClain, rhp, North Shore HS, Houston.
43. *Tyler Backus, rhp, Mingus Union HS, Cottonwood, Ariz.
44. *Mark Serrano, rhp, Cypress (Calif.) CC.
45. *Eric Martinez, rhp, Eastlake HS, Chula Vista, Calif.
46. *Brian Paukovits, rhp, El Capitan HS, Lakeside, Calif.
47. *Kip Masuda, c, Mid-Pacific Institute, Kaneohe, Hawaii.
48. *Chester Wilson, 1b, St. Louis HS, Honolulu, Hawaii.
49. *Matt Gibbs, rhp, Modesto (Calif.) JC.
50. *Juan Perez, rhp, Jose Rojas Cortez HS, Orocovis, P.R.

## LOS ANGELES ANGELS (23)

1. (Choice to Red Sox as compensation for Type A free agent Orlando Cabrera)
**1. Trevor Bell, rhp, Crescenta Valley HS, La Crescenta, Calif.** (Supplemental choice—37th—as compensation for Type A free agent Troy Percival).**—(2009-14)**
2. Ryan Mount, ss, Ayala HS, Chino Hills, Calif. (Choice from Tigers as compensation for Percival).—(AA)
2. P.J. Phillips, ss, Redan HS, Stone Mountain, Ga.—(AAA)
DRAFT DROP *Brother of Brandon Phillips, major leaguer (2002-15)*
**3. +Sean O'Sullivan, rhp, Valhalla HS, El Cajon, Calif. / Grossmont (Calif.) JC.—(2009-15)**
**4. *Brian Matusz, lhp, St. Mary's HS, Cave Creek, Ariz.—(2009-15)**
DRAFT DROP *Attended San Diego; re-drafted by Orioles, 2008 (1st round)*
5. Tommy Mendoza, rhp, Monsignor Pace HS, Miami.—(AAA)
**6. Jeremy Moore, of, North Caddo HS, Vivian, La.—(2011)**
7. Robert Romero, rhp, Grayson County (Texas) CC.
8. *Matt Hall, ss, Horizon HS, Scottsdale, Ariz.
**9. Bobby Mosebach, rhp, Hillsborough (Fla.) CC.—(2009)**
**10. Peter Bourjos, of, Notre Dame HS, Scottsdale, Ariz.—(2010-15)**
DRAFT DROP *Son of Chris Bourjos, major leaguer (1980)*
11. *Tim Murphy, of, Rancho Buena Vista HS, Vista, Calif.
12. Greg Dini, c, Tulane University.
13. *Bryce Cox, rhp, Rice University.
14. *Stephen Brock, rhp, Chipola (Fla.) JC.
15. Brad Coon, of, Trevecca Nazarene (Tenn.) University.
16. Darrell Sales, 1b, West Valley (Calif.) CC.
17. Ryan Pressley, 1b, Evans HS, Martinez, Ga.
18. Jim West, rhp, Chandler-Gilbert (Ariz.) CC.
19. Anthony Sullivan, rhp, St. John's University.
20. *Martinez Allen, of, North Florida JC.
21. *Brad Suttle, 3b, Boerne (Texas) HS.
22. *Chris Nash, 1b, Marquette HS, Chesterfield, Mo.
**23. *Deunte Heath, rhp, Lake City (Fla.) CC.—(2012-13)**
24. Dallas Morris, 3b, University of Louisiana-Lafayette.
25. Brok Butcher, rhp, Oxnard (Calif.) JC.
26. Kevin Lynch, rhp, Florida State University.
27. Colby Overstreet, 1b, Oklahoma City University.
28. *Blair Brejtfus, rhp, Arcadia HS, Phoenix.
29. *Vinnie Scarduzio, 1b, Broward (Fla.) CC.
30. *Neil Medchill, c, Lake Orion HS, Oxford, Mich.
31. Tim Didjurgis, rhp, Regis (Colo.) University.
32. *Braden Wells, of, Dixie State (Utah) JC.
33. Marco Albano, ss, Boston College.
**34. *Brian Schlitter, rhp, Lake City (Fla.) CC.—(2010-15)**
**35. *Chris Davis, 3b, Navarro (Texas) JC.—(2008-15)**
36. +Jacob Dixon, rhp, University of North Florida.
37. +Jeremy Haynes, rhp, Tallahassee (Fla.) CC.
38. Flint Wipke, c, Georgia Southern University.
39. *Brent Milleville, c, Maize HS, Wichita, Kan.
40. *Rian Kiniry, of, Chaminade-Madonna Prep, Hollywood, Fla.
41. *Joe Klein, rhp, Patuxent HS, Lusby, Md.
42. *Carlos Del Rosario, of, George Washington HS, New York.
43. *Brent Solich, lhp, Manatee (Fla.) JC.
44. *Michael Bunton, lhp, Tallahassee (Fla.) CC.
45. *Shay Conder, c, American Fork (Utah) HS.
46. *Julian Laurean, 2b, Chandler-Gilbert (Ariz.) CC.
47. +Seth Loman, 1b, Lamar (Colo.) CC.
48. Cody Fuller, of, Texas Tech.
**49. *Anthony Vasquez, of, Ronald Reagan HS, San Antonio, Texas.—(2011)**
**50. *Buster Posey, rhp-ss, Lee County HS, Leesburg, Ga.—(2009-15)**
DRAFT DROP *First-round draft pick (5th overall), Giants (2008)*

## LOS ANGELES DODGERS (26)

1. (Choice to Red Sox as compensation for Type A free agent Derek Lowe)
**1. *Luke Hochevar, rhp, University of Tennessee** (Supplemental choice—40th—as compensation for Type A free agent Adrian Beltre).**—(2007-15)**
DRAFT DROP *Played for Fort Worth (American Association); re-drafted by Royals, 2006 (1st round, 1st pick)*
**2. Ivan De Jesus, ss, Puerto Rico Baseball Academy, Guaynabo, P.R.** (Choice from Mariners as compensation for Beltre).**—(2011-12)**
DRAFT DROP *Son of Ivan De Jesus, major leaguer (1974-88)*
**2. Josh Wall, rhp, Central Private HS, Walker, La.—(2012-14)**
3. Sergio Pedroza, of, Cal State Fullerton.—(AAA)
**4. Josh Bell, 3b, Santaluces HS, Lantana, Fla.—(2010-12)**
**5. Jonathan Meloan, rhp, University of Arizona.—(2007-09)**
**6. Brent Leach, lhp, Delta State (Miss.) University.—(2009)**
7. Chris Hobdy, rhp, Monterey HS, Lubbock, Texas.
8. David Horlacher, rhp, Brigham Young University.
9. *Michael Davitt, rhp, Davidson HS, Mobile, Ala.
**10. Trayvon Robinson, of, Crenshaw HS, Los Angeles.—(2011-12)**
11. Adam Godwin, of, Troy University.
12. Kris Krise, rhp, Cal State Chico.
**13. Steve Johnson, rhp, St. Paul's HS, Brooklandville, Md.—(2012-15)**
DRAFT DROP *Son of Dave Johnson, major leaguer (1987-93)*
**14. Scott Van Slyke, of, John Burroughs HS, Ladue, Mo.—(2012-15)**
DRAFT DROP *Son of Andy Van Slyke, first-round draft pick, Cardinals (1979); major leaguer (1983-95) • Brother of A.J. Van Slyke, 23rd-round draft pick, Cardinals (2005)*
15. Wilfredo Diaz, lhp, Puerto Rico Baseball Academy, Caguas, P.R.
16. *George McDonald, c, Westchester HS, Playa Del Rey, Calif.
17. *Kyle Henson, c, Oak Ridge HS, Conroe, Texas
18. *Kevin Carby, ss, Booker T. Washington HS, Tulsa, Okla.
19. Drew Locke, of, Boston College.
20. +Schuyler Tripp, lhp, Davis County HS, Drakesville, Iowa / Indian Hills (Iowa) JC.
21. Shane Justis, ss, Towson University.
22. *Travis DeBondt, of, Oral Roberts University.
23. *Jayson Whitehouse, of, Spartanburg Methodist (S.C.) JC.
24. Jon Dutton, lhp, Rancho Bernardo HS, San Diego.
25. *Kyle Foster, lhp, Lower Columbia (Wash.) JC.
**26. *Jordy Mercer, ss, Taloga (Okla.) HS.—(2012-15)**
27. *Matt Coburn, rhp, Humble (Texas) HS.
28. *Tim Segelke, lhp, Green River (Wash.) CC.
29. *Kent Williamson, rhp, Hayden HS, Topeka, Kan.
30. *Kyle Morgan, of, Bakersfield (Calif.) JC.
31. *Jonathan Forest, rhp, University of British Columbia.
32. *Nate Hammons, lhp, Broxton HS, Fort Cobb, Okla.
33. *Chris Lemay, lhp, Kwantlen (B.C.) JC.
34. *Shawn Loglisci, rhp, JC of Southern Idaho.
35. Rick Taloa, 1b, Santa Ana (Calif.) JC.
36. *Andrew Marquardt, rhp, St. Francis HS, Sierra Madre, Calif.
**37. *Justin Wilson, lhp, Buchanan HS, Clovis, Calif.—(2012-15)**
38. *Stephen Hermann, c, Penn Trafford HS, Harrison City, Pa.
39. *Jake Debus, lhp, Victor J. Andrew HS, Tinley Park, Ill.
40. Jason Mooneyham, 1b, Chapman (Calif.) University.
41. *Chris Johnson, rhp, John A. Logan (Ill.) JC.
**42. *Tony Cruz, c, Okaloosa-Walton (Fla.) CC.—(2011-15)**
43. *Brandon Rocha, c, Los Alamitos (Calif.) HS.
**44. *Chase D'Arnaud, ss, Los Alamitos (Calif.) HS.—(2011-15)**
DRAFT DROP *Brother of Travis D'Arnaud, first-round draft pick, Phillies (2007); major leaguer (2013-15)*
45. +Brian Mathews, 3b, Newton County HS, Covington, Ga. / Middle Georgia JC.
46. *Anthony Benner, 3b, Eastlake HS, Chula Vista, Calif.
47. *Mark Sunga, 3b, Notre Dame HS, Van Nuys, Calif.
48. *Paul Wourms, c, Thompson River (B.C.) University.
49. *Garet Hill, rhp, Biola (Calif.) University.
50. *Mitchell Houck, lhp, Cypress Bay HS, Weston, Fla.

## MILWAUKEE BREWERS (5)

**1. Ryan Braun, 3b, University of Miami.—(2007-15)**
2. (Choice to Athletics as compensation for Type A free agent Damian Miller)
3. Will Inman, rhp, Tunstall HS, Dry Fork, Va.—(AAA)
**4. Mat Gamel, 3b, Chipola (Fla.) JC.—(2008-12)**
5. Kevin Roberts, rhp, University of Houston.—(AA)
6. Steve Hammond, lhp, Long Beach State University.
**7. Michael Brantley, of, Fort Pierce Central HS, Port St. Lucie, Fla.—(2009-15)**
DRAFT DROP *Son of Mickey Brantley, major leaguer (1986-89)*
**8. *Jemile Weeks, ss, Lake Brantley HS, Altamonte Springs, Fla.—(2011-15)**
DRAFT DROP *First-round draft pick (12th overall), Athletics (2008) • Brother of Rickie Weeks, first-round draft pick, Brewers (2003); major leaguer (2003-14)*
9. Carlos Hereaud, 3b, Elkins HS, Missouri City, Texas.
**10. Steve Garrison, lhp, The Hun School, Ewing, N.J.—(2011)**
11. *Brent Allar, rhp, Weatherford (Texas) JC.
12. John Alonso, 1b, Polk (Fla.) CC.
13. *Ryan Babineau, c, Etiwanda HS, Alta Loma, Calif.
14. Mark James, rhp, Sinclair SS, Whitby, Ontario.
15. Michael Bell, 3b, Grayson County (Texas) CC.
**16. *Andrew Bailey, rhp, Wagner College.—(2009-15)**
17. *Tim Smith, of, Midland (Texas) CC.
**18. +Zach Braddock, lhp, Gloucester Catholic HS, Southampton, N.J. / Chipola (Fla.) JC.—(2010-11)**
19. Patrick Ryan, rhp, Embry-Riddle (Fla.) University.
20. David Welch, lhp, Texarkana (Texas) CC.
21. Justin Stires, rhp, Saddleback (Calif.) CC.
22. Kenny Holmberg, 2b, Embry-Riddle (Fla.) University.
23. Brendan Katin, of, University of Miami.
24. +Michael Ramlow, lhp, Owens (Ohio) CC.
**25. +Taylor Green, 2b, Cypress (Calif.) JC.—(2011-12)**
**26. *Jake Arrieta, rhp, Weatherford (Texas) JC.—(2010-15)**
27. Brad Willcutt, c, University of Southern Mississippi.
28. Scott McKnight, ss, Saddleback (Calif.) CC.
29. Dane Renkert, rhp, Washington State University.
30. Omar Aguilar, rhp, Merced (Calif.) JC.
31. *Patrick Murray, 1b, Marina HS, Huntington Beach, Calif.
32. *Spencer Pennington, of, University of Alabama.
33. *Jorge Core, rhp, Puerto Rico Baseball Academy, Bayamon, P.R.
34. +Brock Kjeldgaard, rhp, Indian Hills (Iowa) CC.
35. *Sebastien Vendette, rhp, Northeastern Oklahoma A&M JC.
36. *Stephen Barnes, rhp, Lake City (Fla.) CC.
37. *Chris Hopkins, of, Sierra (Calif.) JC.
38. Chris Jean, rhp, Texas State University.
39. +Brad Miller, ss, Cowley County (Kan.) CC.
40. Ryan Crew, ss, University of Texas-San Antonio.
41. *Jordan Lennerton, 1b, El Paso (Texas) CC.
42. *Chris Copot, c, Lethbridge (Alberta) CC.
43. *Kyle Eveland, 2b, Palmdale (Calif.) HS.
DRAFT DROP *Brother of Dana Eveland, major leaguer (2005-15)*
44. *George Washington, of, Demopolis HS, Boligee, Ala.
45. +Ulrich Snijders, c, St. Petersburg (Fla.) JC.
46. *Alex Lowrey, of, Monsignor Pace HS, Opa-Locka, Fla.
47. *Jay Broughton, rhp, Triton Central HS, Indianapolis, Ind.
48. *Fred Lewis, lhp, Buchholz HS, Gainesville, Fla.
49. *Cory Large, lhp, Bell HS, Bedford, Texas.
50. *Garret Regan, of, Sir Winston Churchill HS, Calgary, Alberta.

## MINNESOTA TWINS (25)

**1. Matt Garza, rhp, Fresno State University.—(2006-15)**
1. Henry Sanchez, 1b, Mission Bay HS, San Diego (Supplemental choice—39th—as compensation for Type A free agent Corey Koskie).—(Low A)
2. Paul Kelly, ss, Flower Mound (Texas) HS (Choice from Blue Jays as compensation for Koskie).—(High A)
**2. Kevin Slowey, rhp, Winthrop University.—(2007-14)**
2. Drew Thompson, ss, Jupiter Community HS, Tequesta, Fla. (Supplemental choice—80th—as compensation for Type C free agent Henry Blanco).—(High A)
DRAFT DROP *Son of Robby Thompson, major leaguer (1986-96)*
**3. Brian Duensing, lhp, University of Nebraska** (Choice from Nationals as compensation for Type B free agent Cristian Guzman).**—(2009-15)**
3. Ryan Mullins, lhp, Vanderbilt University.—(AAA)
4. Caleb Moore, c, East Tennessee State University.—(High A)
**5. Steven Tolleson, ss, University of South Carolina.—(2010-15)**
DRAFT DROP *Son of Wayne Tolleson, major leaguer (1981-90)*
6. J.W. Wilson, of, Midland (Texas) HS.
7. Greg Yersich, c, Andrean HS, Merrillville, Ind.
8. Danny Powers, rhp, Central Missouri State University.
9. Erik Lis, 1b, Evansville University.
10. Matt Betsill, 3b, Furman University.
11. Brian Kirwan, rhp, Santa Fe Christian HS, Del Mar, Calif.
**12. Alex Burnett, rhp, Ocean View HS, Huntington Beach, Calif.—(2010-13)**
13. Michael Allen, rhp, Arlington Country Day HS, Jacksonville, Fla.
14. *David Duncan, lhp, New Richmond (Ohio) HS.
15. *Michael Hacker, lhp, Cosumnes River (Calif.) JC.
**16. *Yonder Alonso, c, Coral Gables HS, Miami.—(2010-15)**
DRAFT DROP *First-round draft pick (7th overall), Reds (2008)*
17. *Robert Lara, c, Nova HS, Davie, Fla.
18. *Matt Morgal, rhp, Edmond Santa Fe HS, Edmond, Okla.
19. Sean Richardson, c, University of Kansas.
20. *Eric Santiago, ss, Natividad Rodriguez Gonza HS, Arroyo, P.R.
21. *Chris Kelley, rhp, San Jacinto (Texas) JC.
22. +Curtis Leavitt, lhp, Vasquez HS, Acton, Calif. / Oxnard (Calif.) JC.
**23. *David Herndon, rhp, Gulf Coast (Fla.) CC.—(2010-12)**
24. *Gustavo Duran, rhp, George Washington HS, Bronx, N.Y.
25. *Aaron Lovett, rhp, Kaskaskia (Ill.) JC.
26. *Michael Mopas, lhp, Iolani HS, Mililani, Hawaii.
27. *Evan Frederickson, lhp, Oakton HS, Oak Hill, Va.
DRAFT DROP *First-round draft pick (35th overall), Brewers (2008)*
28. *Josh Brink, rhp, Mennonite Educational Institute, Abbotsford, B.C.
29. *Steve Hernandez, rhp, Redwood HS, Visalia, Calif.
30. *Kiko Vazquez, 1b, Sebring (Fla.) HS.
31. *Kyle Carr, lhp, Linton (N.D.) HS.
32. +David Bromberg, rhp, Palisades HS, Los Angeles / Santa Ana (Calif.) JC.
33. *Brandon Trodick, of, Cimarron-Memorial HS, Las Vegas, Nev.
34. *Danny Cox, ss, W.F. West HS, Chehalis, Wash.
35. *Lukas Thomason, rhp, Brook Hill HS, Jacksonville, Texas.
**36. +Rene Tosoni, of, Chipola (Fla.) JC.—(2011)**

37. *James Leigh, lhp, Texarkana (Texas) CC.
38. *Carlos Rodriguez, c, Puerto Rico Baseball Academy, Vega Baja, P.R.
39. *Charles Duffey, rhp, Westminster (Calif.) HS.
**40. *Charlie Leesman, lhp, Elder HS, Cincinnati.—(2013-14)**
41. Toby Gardenhire, ss, University of Illinois.
DRAFT DROP *Son of Ron Gardenhire, major leaguer (1981-85); major league manager (2002-14)*
42. *Jacob Cox, c, Lakeland (Fla.) HS.
43. *Justin Parker, rhp, Fort Wayne (Ind.) HS.
44. Jose Cordero, rhp, Miami.
45. *Michael Kinsel, ss, Cretin-Derham Hall, St. Paul, Minn.
46. *Denver Wynn, rhp, Valleyview SS, Kamloops B.C.
47. *Mike Ballard, lhp, University of Virginia.
48. *Juan Rodriguez, c, Bayamon (P.R.) Military Academy.
49. *Dane Ponciano, c, CC of Southern Nevada.
50. *Justin Otto, rhp, Cowley County (Kan.) CC.

## NEW YORK METS (9)

**1. Mike Pelfrey, rhp, Wichita State University.—(2006-15)**
2. (Choice to Red Sox as compensation for Type A free agent Pedro Martinez)
3. (Choice to Astros as compensation for Type A free agent Carlos Beltran)
4. Hector Pellot, 2b, Puerto Rico Baseball Academy, Cidra, P.R.—(AA)
**5. Drew Butera, c, University of Central Florida.—(2010-15)**
DRAFT DROP *Son of Sal Butera, major leaguer (1980-88)*
6. Greg Cain, of, Gahr HS, Cerritos, Calif.
**7. Jon Niese, lhp, Defiance (Ohio) HS.—(2008-15)**
8. Sean McCraw, c, San Jacinto (Texas) JC.
**9. Bobby Parnell, rhp, Charleston Southern University.—(2008-15)**
10. Courtney Billingslea, of, Sinclair (Ohio) CC.
**11. *Luis Martinez, c, Jackson State (Tenn.) CC.—(2011-12)**
12. Matt Spath, of, Flagler Palm Coast HS, Bunnell, Fla.
**13. Josh Thole, c, Mater Dei HS, Breese, Ill.—(2009-15)**
14. *Ian Marshall, rhp, Gaithersburg (Md.) HS.
15. *Daniel Martin, rhp, Harleton HS, Marshall, Texas.
16. Eric Domangue, lhp, Alvin (Texas) JC.
**17. *Pedro Beato, rhp, Xaverian HS, Queens, N.Y.—(2011-14)**
DRAFT DROP *First-round draft pick (32nd overall), Orioles (2006)*
18. Eric Brown, rhp, Wingate (N.C.) University.
19. Tim Grogan, 3b, Western Kentucky University.
20. *Cody Railsback, rhp, Ryan HS, Denton, Texas.
21. Joe Holden, of, Molloy (N.Y.) College.
22. *Preston Paramore, c, Allen (Texas) HS.
23. Joe D'Alessandro, rhp, College of New Jersey.
24. Kyle Risinger, rhp, Galveston (Texas) CC.
25. D.J. Wabick, 1b, College of Charleston.
26. Kevin Tomasiewicz, lhp, University of Wisconsin-Whitewater.
27. David Koons, rhp, St. Leo (Fla.) College.
28. Greg Gonzalez, of, Cal State Chico.
29. Sal Aguilar, rhp, Lewis-Clark State (Idaho) College.
30. Steven Holquin, rhp, Porterville (Calif.) JC.
31. Matt Anderson, 3b, UC Irvine.
32. Jose Castro, ss, Miami-Dade CC North.
33. Daniel Arizmendi, lhp, Santa Ana (Calif.) JC.
34. Joseph Mihalics, 2b, University of Buffalo.
35. Mike Sharpe, of, St. Thomas Aquinas (N.Y.) College.
36. Jeramy Simmons, rhp, University of South Alabama.
37. Alex Beras, rhp, University of Scranton (Pa.).
38. *Pierre Miville-Deschenes, rhp, Edouard Montpetit HS, Montreal.
39. *Colin Thomson, rhp, Mountain View HS, Tucson, Ariz.
40. *Jacob Blackwood, 2b, Maple Woods (Mo.) CC.
41. +Nick Carr, rhp, Twin Falls (Idaho) HS / JC of Southern Idaho.
42. *Jared Barkdoll, c, Greencastle-Antrim HS, Greencastle, Pa.
43. *Javier Brown, ss, Valhalla HS, El Cajon, Calif.
44. *Phillip Pursino, c, St. Dominic HS, Stewart Manor, N.Y.
45. Anthony Manuel, 2b, Biola (Calif.) University.
DRAFT DROP *Son of Jerry Manuel, first-round draft pick, Tigers (1972); major leaguer (1975-82); major league manager (1998-2010)*
46. *Peter Tountas, ss, Maine South HS, Park Ridge, Ill.
47. *Samuel Lane, rhp, Pedro Menendez HS, Elkton, Fla.
**48. *Jeremy Hefner, rhp, Seminole State (Okla.) JC.—(2012-13)**
49. Will Jostock, rhp, Pensacola (Fla.) JC.
50. *Julio Rodriguez, of, Wabash Valley (Ill.) JC.

## NEW YORK YANKEES (29)

1. C.J. Henry, ss, Putnam City HS, Oklahoma City, Okla. (Choice from Phillies as compensation for Type B free agent Jon Lieber).—(High A)
DRAFT DROP *Son of Carl Henry, guard, National Basketball Association (1985-86) • Brother of Xavier Henry, first-round draft pick, Memphis Grizzlies/National Basketball Association (2010); guard, NBA (2010-14)*
1. (Choice to Marlins as compensation for Type A free agent Carl Pavano)
2. J. Brent Cox, rhp, University of Texas (Choice from White Sox as compensation for Type B free agent Orlando Hernandez).—(AAA)
2. (Choice to Braves as compensation for Type A free agent Jaret Wright)
**3. Brett Gardner, of, College of Charleston.—(2008-15)**
**4. Lance Pendleton, rhp, Rice University.—(2011)**
**5. Zach Kroenke, lhp, University of Nebraska.—(2010-11)**
**6. *Doug Fister, rhp, Fresno State University.—(2009-15)**
7. Garrett Patterson, lhp, University of Oklahoma.
**8. Austin Jackson, of, Ryan HS, Denton, Texas.—(2010-15)**
9. James Cooper, of, Loyola Marymount University.
10. Kyle Anson, 3b, Texas State University.
11. Alan Horne, rhp, University of Florida.
DRAFT DROP *First-round draft pick (27th overall), Indians (2001)*
12. Joe Muich, c, Wichita State University.
13. *Karl Amonite, 1b, Auburn University.
14. Joel Perez, of, Miami.
15. Josh Schmidt, rhp, University of the Pacific.
16. Chris Malec, 2b, UC Santa Barbara.
17. Keaton Everitt, rhp, University of Washington.
18. Joe Burke, c, St. John's University.
19. Jim Conroy, rhp, University of Illinois.
20. Bryan Rueger, lhp, Southern Illinois University.
21. *Hanseld Diaz, c, Miami-Dade CC.
22. *Michael Lee, rhp, Skyline HS, Issaquah, Wash.
23. *Matt Wallach, c, Cypress (Calif.) JC.
DRAFT DROP *Son of Tim Wallach, first-round draft pick, Expos (1979); major leaguer (1980-96)*
24. *Justin Phillabaum, 1b, Indian River (Fla.) CC.
25. Brad Canada, c, Bradley University.
26. *Patrick Caldwell, lhp, Yavapai (Ariz.) JC.
27. *Josh Morgan, rhp, University of Missouri-St. Louis.
28. *Derek Duclos, rhp, University of Richmond.
**29. *Justin Turner, 2b, Cal State Fullerton.—(2009-15)**
30. *Cameron Johnson, of, CC of Southern Nevada.
31. *Clint Preisendorfer, lhp, Palomar (Calif.) JC.
32. *Jared Souza, lhp, Navarro (Texas) JC.
33. Michael Mlotkowski, rhp, Oklahoma City University.
34. Felipe Garcia, 1b, Cal State Fullerton.
35. Andy Carter, rhp, Davidson College.
36. *Brett Summers, rhp, Lake Central HS, Dyer, Ind.
37. Jesse Bahr, lhp, Missouri Baptist College.
38. *Clay Young, lhp, Glendale (Calif.) JC.
39. *Miguel Ruiz, rhp, South Hills HS, Fort Worth, Texas.
40. *Mike Roskopf, 1b, CC of Southern Nevada.
41. *Chris Valencia, of, Westchester HS, Los Angeles.
42. *Josh Styes, rhp, Clay-Chalkville HS, Birmingham.
43. +Brady Salter, rhp, Aurora (Ill.) University.
44. *Justin Keadle, rhp, Wake Forest University.
**45. *Brett Pill, 1b, Cal State Fullerton.—(2011-13)**
46. Eric Wordekemper, rhp, Creighton University.
47. *Eric Hanlon, of, James Martin HS, Arlington, Texas.
48. *Andrew Rice, of, Itawamba (Miss.) CC.
49. *Diallo Fon, of, Las Lomas High, Walnut Creek, Calif.
50. *Blake Heym, c, Grayson County (Texas) CC.

## OAKLAND ATHLETICS (21)

**1. Cliff Pennington, ss, Texas A&M University.—(2008-15)**
**1. Travis Buck, of, Arizona State University** (Supplemental choice—36th—as compensation for Type A free agent Damian Miller).—**(2007-12)**
2. Craig Italiano, rhp, Flower Mound (Texas) HS (Choice from Brewers as compensation for Miller).—(AAA)
2. Jared Lansford, rhp, St. Francis HS, Santa Clara, Calif.—(AAA)
DRAFT DROP *Son of Carney Lansford, major leaguer (1978-92)*
**3. Vin Mazzaro, rhp, Rutherford (N.J.) HS.—(2009-15)**
4. Jimmy Shull, rhp, Cal Poly San Luis Obispo.—(High A)
5. Scott Deal, rhp, Curtis HS, University. Place, Wash.—(High A)
**6. Justin Sellers, ss, Marina HS, Huntington Beach, Calif.—(2011-14)**
DRAFT DROP *Son of Jeff Sellers, major leaguer (1985-88)*
7. Kevin Bunch, rhp, Serrano HS, Victorville, Calif.
8. Jason Ray, rhp, Azusa Pacific (Calif.) University.
9. Trey Shields, rhp, University of Alabama.
10. John Herrera, rhp, Lubbock Christian (Texas) University.
11. Steve Kleen, rhp, Pepperdine University.
**12. Jeff Baisley, 3b, University of South Florida.—(2008)**
13. Mike Massaro, of-lhp, Colorado State University-Pueblo.
14. Brad Davis, lhp, Lewis-Clark State (Idaho) College.
15. Jeff Bieker, of, Fort Hays State (Kan.) University.
**16. *Justin Smoak, 1b, Stratford HS, Goose Creek, S.C.—(2010-15)**
DRAFT DROP *First-round draft pick (11th overall), Rangers (2008)*
17. Isaac Omura, 2b, University of Hawaii.
**18. Anthony Recker, c, Alvernia (Pa.) College.—(2011-15)**
19. Julio Rivera, c, Puerto Rico Baseball Academy, Toa Alta, P.R.
20. Stephen Bryant, rhp, University of Hawaii.
21. Michael Madsen, rhp, Ohio State University.
22. Shawn Callahan, c, Central Missouri State University.
23. *James Bennett, of, University of Louisiana-Monroe.
24. Ben Ingold, ss, Wake Forest University.
25. Zeke Parraz, ss, University of Nevada-Las Vegas.
26. Ron Madej, lhp, Bellevue (Neb.) University.
27. Jess Lacasse, rhp, Bellevue (Neb.) University.
28. Mike Klug, 2b, University of North Alabama.
**29. Brad Kilby, lhp, San Jose State University.—(2009-10)**
30. T.J. Franco, rhp, University of San Francisco.
31. Josh Kay, rhp, University of Cincinnati.
32. *Jake Hammons, c, Snohomish (Wash.) HS.
33. *Matt Singleton, c, Ball State University.
34. *Edwin Mieles, rhp, Patria La Torres Ramirez HS, San Sebastian, P.R.
35. *Steven Braun, ss, Los Angeles Pierce JC.
36. +Shane Keough, ss, Northwood HS, San Jose, Calif. / Yavapai (Ariz.) JC.
DRAFT DROP *Grandson of Marty Keough, major leaguer (1956-66) • Son of Matt Keough, major leaguer (1977-86)*
37. *A.J. Huttenlocker, lhp, Edmonds (Wash.) CC.
38. *Nick Pulos, c, University of Pennsylvania.

## PHILADELPHIA PHILLIES (17)

1. (Choice to Yankees as compensation for Type B free agent Jon Lieber)
**2. Mike Costanzo, 3b, Coastal Carolina University.—(2012)**
**3. Matt Maloney, lhp, University of Mississippi.—(2009-12)**
4. Mike Durant, 3b, Berkeley (Calif.) HS.—(High A)
5. Brett Harker, rhp, College of Charleston.—(AAA)
6. Justin Blaine, lhp, University of San Diego.
7. Jermaine Williams, of, Los Angeles HS.
8. Jeremy Slayden, of, Georgia Tech.
9. Clay Harris, 2b, Louisiana State University.
**10. Josh Outman, lhp, Central Missouri State University.—(2008-14)**
**11. Tuffy Gosewisch, c, Arizona State University.—(2013-15)**
**12. Michael Zagurski, lhp, University of Kansas.—(2007-13)**
13. Matt Olson, rhp, Western Branch HS, Chesapeake, Va.
14. *Aja Barto, of, Stratford HS, Spring Branch, Texas.
15. P.J. Antoniato, ss, St. John's University.
16. Matt Edwards, 1b, University of Notre Dame.
17. Ronald Hill, rhp, University of North Carolina-Wilmington.
18. Darren Byrd, rhp, Pine Forest HS, Cantonment Fla.
**19. *David Huff, lhp, Cypress (Calif.) JC.—(2009-15)**
DRAFT DROP *First-round draft pick (39th overall), Indians (2006)*
**20. *Vance Worley, rhp, McClatchy HS, Sacramento, Calif.—(2010-15)**
21. Aaron Rawl, rhp, University of South Carolina.
22. Pat Overholt, rhp, Santa Clara University.
23. Derrick Mitchell, ss, Paw Paw (Mich.) HS.
24. Dennis Diaz, 2b, Florida International University.
25. Joe Frazee, of, Loyola Marymount University.
26. Brett Dalton, 2b, UC Irvine.
27. Steven Alexander, of, Sacramento (Calif.) CC.
28. Clayton Stewart, rhp, University of Texas.
29. Aaron Cheesman, c, Florida State University.
30. *Charles Benoit, lhp, Grayson County (Texas) CC.
31. Cooper Osteen, 2b, University of Mississippi.
32. *Tim Sherlock, of, Chaparral HS, Scottsdale, Ariz.
33. *Andrez Ibarz, rhp, Champagnat Catholic HS, Hialeah, Fla.
34. *Osvaldo Torres, 1b, Wabash Valley (Ill.) JC.
35. *Adam Greer, c, North Eugene (Ore.) HS.
36. *Nick Monett, c, Granite Hills HS, El Cajon, Calif.
37. *Kyle Bredenkamp, rhp, Millikan HS, Long Beach, Calif.
38. *Micah Sales, rhp, Madison County HS, Danielsville, Ga.
39. *Bobby Kennedy, lhp, Trinity Catholic HS, Ocala, Fla.
40. *Travis Jones, 2b, Lake City (Fla.) CC.
41. *Ryan Selden, ss, Canyon Springs HS, Moreno Valley, Calif.
42. *John Dischert, lhp, St. Mark's HS, Wilmington, Del.
**43. *Ryan Verdugo, lhp, Lake Stevens (Wash.) HS.—(2012)**
44. *Luis Alvarez, of, Pedro Falu Orellano HS, Rio Grande, P.R.
DRAFT DROP *Son of Orlando Alvarez, major leaguer (1973-76)*
45. *Mike Modica, lhp, Washington Township HS, Sewell, N.J.
46. *Jason Stacy, rhp, Westview HS, Phoenix.
47. Ben Blanton, ss, William Jewell (Mo.) College.
48. *Ben Hornbeck, lhp, Sunnyslope HS, Phoenix.
49. *Shane Erb, rhp, Father Judge High, Lewes, Del.
50. Tyler Gooch, rhp, University of Oklahoma.

## PITTSBURGH PIRATES (11)

**1. Andrew McCutchen, of, Fort Meade (Fla.) HS.—(2009-15)**
2. Brad Corley, of, Mississippi State University.—(AA)
3. James Boone, of, University of Missouri.—(AA)
**4. Brent Lillibridge, ss, University of Washington.—(2008-13)**
5. Jeff Sues, rhp, Vanderbilt University.—(AAA)
6. Cameron Blair, 2b, Texas Tech.
7. Justin Vaclavik, rhp, University of Houston.
**8. Steve Pearce, 1b, University of South Carolina.—(2007-15)**
9. Derrik Moeves, rhp, Northern Kentucky University.

10. Derek Antelo, rhp, Nova Southeastern (Fla.) University.
11. Chris Jones, c, Long Beach State University.
12. Jason Delaney, of, Boston College.
13. Matt Swanson, rhp, University of California.
14. Albert Laboy, of, John I. Leonard HS, West Palm Beach, Fla.
15. *Jarred Bogany, of, George Bush HS, Houston.
16. Eric Krebs, rhp, Alvin (Texas) JC.
17. Darren Newlin, rhp, University of Central Florida.
18. Ryan Searage, of, Eckerd (Fla.) College.

DRAFT DROP *Son of Ray Searage, major leaguer (1981-90)*

19. Daniel Rios, 1b, JC of the Sequoias (Calif.).
**20. *Ryan Lollis, of-lhp, Houston Christian HS, Houston.—(2015)**
21. *Elias Otero, ss, Puerto Rico Baseball Academy, Toa Alta, P.R.
22. *David DiNatale, of, Stoneman Douglas HS, Parkland, Fla.
23. Juan Mesa, of, Miami.

DRAFT DROP *Son of Jose Mesa, major leaguer (1987-2006)*

24. Jared Brown, lhp, Cumberland (Tenn.) University.
25. *Michael Wanamaker, rhp, Nyack HS, Valley Cottage, N.Y.
26. Tony Mansolino, 3b, Vanderbilt University.
27. Nash Robertson, rhp, UC Irvine.
28. *Clayton McMillan, lhp, Carthage (Texas) HS.
29. *Iain Sebastian, rhp, Columbus (Ga.) HS.
30. *Chad Povich, rhp, Dixie State (Utah) JC.
31. Jason Herman, rhp, University of West Alabama.
32. Duke Acors, rhp, Virginia Military Institute.
33. *Michael Klindt, of, Centennial HS, Roswell, Ga.
34. *Gary Bucuren, 3b, Ambridge Area HS, Sewickley, Pa.
35. *Lyndon Estill, of, Sammamish HS, Bellevue, Wash.
36. +Justin Byler, c, Gulf Coast (Fla.) CC.
37. *Eric Marshall, rhp, Barrington (Ill.) HS.
38. *Carl Uhl, of, Serrano HS, Phelan, Calif.
39. *Jason Brock, lhp, David Lipscomb HS, Nolensville, Tenn.
40. *Kenneth Wieda, rhp, John Hersey HS, Arlington Heights, Ill.
41. *Nick Beghtol, c, Dixie State (Utah) JC.
42. *Kyle Sweat, rhp, Apopka (Fla.) HS.
43. *Scott Kuhns, rhp, John Hersey HS, Arlington Heights, Ill.
44. *Jordan Latham, rhp, Centennial HS, Boise, Idaho.
45. *Philip Riley, rhp, Jackson State (Tenn.) CC.
46. *Kody Hinze, 1b, Nimitz HS, Houston.
47. *Ryan Lormand, ss, McLennan (Texas) CC.
48. *Paul Dickey, rhp, Lake Washington HS, Redmond, Wash.
49. *Francisco Ortiz, rhp, Puerto Rico Baseball Academy, Toa Alta, P.R.
50. *Stephen Merino, 3b, American Senior HS, Miami.

## ST. LOUIS CARDINALS (30)

**1. Colby Rasmus, of, Russell County HS, Phenix City, Ala.** (Choice from Red Sox as compensation for Type A free agent Edgar Renteria).**—(2009-15)**

DRAFT DROP *Brother of Cory Rasmus, first-round draft pick, Braves (2006); major leaguer (2013-15)*

**1. Tyler Greene, ss, Georgia Tech.—(2009-13)**
1. Mark McCormick, rhp, Baylor University (Supplemental choice—43rd—as compensation for Renteria).—(AA)
1. Tyler Herron, rhp, Wellington (Fla.) Community HS (Supplemental choice—46th—as compensation for Type A free agent Mike Matheny).—(AAA)
2. Josh Wilson, rhp, Whitehouse HS, Tyler, Texas (Choice from Giants as compensation for Matheny).—(Low A)
2. Nick Webber, rhp, Central Missouri State University.—(AAA)
3. Daryl Jones, of, Spring (Texas) HS.—(AAA)
**4. Bryan Anderson, c, Simi Valley (Calif.) HS.—(2010-15)**
**5. Mitchell Boggs, rhp, University of Georgia.—(2008-13)**
6. Wilfrido Pujols, of, Fort Osage HS, Independence, Mo.

DRAFT DROP *Cousin of Albert Pujols, major leaguer (2001-15)*

**7. Nick Stavinoha, of, Louisiana State University.—(2008-10)**
8. Jason Cairns, rhp, Central Michigan University.
9. Zach Zuercher, lhp, University of Rhode Island.
10. Randy Roth, c, Southeastern Louisiana University.
11. Steve Gonzalez, c, Programa Alcase HS, San Juan, P.R.
**12. *Daniel McCutchen, rhp, University of Oklahoma.—(2009-14)**
13. Malcolm Owens, of, San Bernardino Valley (Calif.) JC.
14. Michael Repole, rhp, Birmingham-Southern College.
15. Adam Daniels, lhp, Oklahoma State University.
16. Matt Lane, rhp, University of Louisiana-Monroe.
17. Michael Cooper, rhp, Fresno State University.
18. Brandon Garner, ss, Yale HS, Melvin, Mich.
19. *Miers Quigley, lhp, Roswell (Ga.) HS.
20. Shaun Garceau, rhp, Royal Palm Beach (Fla.) HS.
**21. Ryan Rohlinger, ss, University of Oklahoma.—(2088-11)**
**22. Jaime Garcia, lhp, Mission, Texas.—(2008-15)**
23. A.J. Van Slyke, 1b, University of Kansas.

DRAFT DROP *Son of Andy Van Slyke, first-round draft pick, Cardinals (1979); major leaguer (1983-95) • Brother of Scott Van Slyke, 14th-round draft pick, Dodgers (2005); major leaguer (2012-15)*

24. David Phillips, rhp, El Paso (Texas) CC.
25. Adam Rodgers, 1b, Rice University.
26. *Steven Blackwood, of, Georgia Tech.
27. Chuck Carter, of, Texas A&M University-Corpus Christi.
28. Trey Hearne, rhp, Texas A&M University-Corpus Christi.
29. Reid Price, lhp, College of Charleston.
30. Matt Trent, rhp, Wingate (N.C.) College.
31. Christian Lopez, ss, Juana Colon HS, Comerio, P.R.
32. Casey Rowlett, of, University of Arkansas.
33. Scott Vander Weg, rhp, Lamar University.
34. Kyle Sadlowski, rhp, Kutztown (Pa.) University.
35. Cory Meacham, rhp, Alabama Southern CC.
36. +Armando Carrasco, rhp, Saddleback (Calif.) CC.
37. Kenny Maiques, rhp, Rio Hondo (Calif.) CC.
38. *Steve Junker, lhp, Valley Forge HS, Parma Heights, Ohio.
39. Tyler Leach, rhp, Kings Mountain (N.C.) HS.
40. *Jesse Schoendienst, 2b, Old Dominion University.

DRAFT DROP *Grandson of Red Schoendienst, major leaguer (1945-63)*

41. *David Fonseca, ss, Thousand Oaks (Calif.) HS.
42. Josh Schwartz, lhp, Rowan (N.J.) University.
43. Michael Meagher, lhp, University of Maryland.
44. +Blake King, rhp, Bishop Kelley HS, Tulsa, Okla. / Eastern Oklahoma JC.
45. Kevin Fitzgerald, rhp, University of Stony Brook.
46. *Danny Feldman, rhp, Gloucester Catholic HS, West Deptford, N.J.
47. Adam Morris, 3b, Rice University.

## SAN DIEGO PADRES (18)

**1. Cesar Carrillo, rhp, University of Miami.—(2009)**
**1. Cesar Ramos, lhp, Long Beach State University** (Supplemental choice—35th—as compensation for Type A free agent David Wells).**—(2009-15)**
**2. Chase Headley, 3b, University of Tennessee.—(2007-15)**
**2. Nick Hundley, c, University of Arizona** (Choice from Red Sox as compensation for Wells).**—(2008-15)**
**3. Josh Geer, rhp, Rice University.—(2008-09)**
**4. Mike Baxter, of, Vanderbilt University.—(2010-15)**
5. Seth Johnston, ss, University of Texas.—(AAA)
6. Neil Jamison, rhp, Long Beach State University.
**7. Will Venable, of, Princeton University.—(2008-15)**

DRAFT DROP *Son of Max Venable, major leaguer (1979-91)*

8. John Madden, rhp, Auburn University.
9. Casey Smith, 1b, Erskine (S.C.) College.
10. Josh Alley, of, University of Tennessee.
**11. *Josh Tomlin, rhp, Angelina (Texas) JC.—(2010-15)**
12. +Aaron Breit, rhp, Garden City (Kan.) CC.
13. Arnold Hughey, lhp, Auburn University.
14. Billy Richardson, ss, East Carolina University.
15. *Josh Romanski, lhp-of, Norco HS, Corona, Calif.
16. Brent Carter, lhp, University of Alabama.
17. Chad Decker, lhp, UC Riverside.
18. Mike Sansoe, of, St. Mary's (Calif.) College.
19. *Gabriel Fargas, rhp, Puerto Rico Baseball Academy, Caguas, P.R.
20. Chad Steiner, 3b, Lamar (Colo.) CC.
21. Brian Cavanaugh, of, East Carolina University.
22. Drew Davidson, of, University of Illinois.
23. *Josh Conover, rhp, University of Washington.
24. John Slone, c, Miami (Ohio) University.
25. Grant Varnell, rhp, University of Texas-Arlington.
**26. Jon Link, rhp, Bluefield (Va.) College.—(2010)**
27. Ray Gill, 1b, Brevard (N.C.) College.
28. Brandon Higelin, lhp, Cal State Los Angeles.
29. +Rey Garramone, rhp, Denver North HS, Denver / Central Arizona JC.
30. *Todd Conerly, rhp, Angelina (Texas) JC.
31. *Tae Kwon, rhp, Hoover HS, Glendale, Calif.
32. *Tyson Ford, rhp, Timpanogos HS, Orem, Utah.
33. Adam Gold, rhp, University of California.
34. Geoff Vandel, lhp, Shaw HS, Columbus, Ga.
35. *Andrew Morgan, c, Norcross HS, Atlanta.
36. *Gary Moran, rhp, Fresno (Fla.) CC.
37. +Drew Miller, rhp, Seminole State (Okla.) JC.
38. *Jeremy McBryde, rhp, Midwest City (Okla.) HS.
39. *Patrick Norris, of, Butler County (Kan.) CC.
40. *Donnie Snow, lhp, Grossmont (Calif.) HS.
41. *Bret Bochsler, lhp, Inglemoor HS, Redmond, Wash.
42. *Terrence Dayleg, ss, North Surrey SS, Surrey, B.C.
43. *Justin Worby, c, Georgetown District HS, Acton, Ontario.
44. *Troy Dawe, rhp, Cardinal Newman Catholic SS, Toronto.
45. *Daniel Towe, c, Charlotte (Mich.) HS.
46. *Jeremy Shelby, of, Tates Creek HS, Lexington, Ky.

DRAFT DROP *Son of John Shelby, major leaguer (1981-91)*

47. *Mark Letchworth, of, Louisburg (N.C.) JC.
48. *Carson Bryant, rhp, JC of Southern Idaho.
49. Josh Thomas-Dotson, of, University of Oregon.
50. *Jason Ogata, ss, Westview HS, Portland, Ore.

## SAN FRANCISCO GIANTS (22)

1. (Choice to Marlins as compensation for Type A free agent Armando Benitez)
2. (Choice to Cardinals as compensation for Type A free agent Mike Matheny)
3. (Choice to Indians as compensation for Type A free agent Omar Vizquel)
4. Ben Copeland, of, University of Pittsburgh.—(AAA)
5. Daniel Griffin, rhp, Niagara University.—(AAA)
6. *Brad Cuthbertson, rhp, Lethbridge (Alberta) CC.
7. Joey Dyche, of, Lewis-Clark State (Idaho) College.
8. *Scotty Bridges, 2b, University of Arkansas.
9. Anthony Contreras, ss, San Jose State University.
10. Nick Pereira, rhp, University of San Francisco.
11. Henry Gutierrez, c, Troy University.
**12. Joe Martinez, rhp, Boston College.—(2009-13)**
13. Taylor Wilding, rhp, Cal Poly Pomona.
14. Brian Anderson, rhp, Long Beach State University.
**15. Alex Hinshaw, lhp, San Diego State University.—(2008-12)**
16. Buck Cody, lhp, University of Texas.
17. Mark Minicozzi, 3b, East Carolina University.
18. *Chad Wagler, rhp, Kent State University.
19. *Brandon Grabham, rhp, Grayson County (Texas) JC.
20. *Jon Gaston, of, Borah HS, Boise, Idaho.
21. Robert Grace, rhp, JC of the Desert (Calif.).
22. Taylor Creswell, of, Deer Valley HS, Antioch, Calif.
23. David Maroul, 3b, University of Texas.
24. +James Simmons, of, Vernon Regional (Texas) JC.
25. Barry Gunther, c, University of Mississippi.
26. Ivan Rusova, rhp, Oasis Alternative HS, Toronto.
**27. *Johnny Monell, c, Christopher Columbus HS, Bronx, N.Y.—(2013-15)**
**28. Sergio Romo, rhp, Mesa State (Colo.) College.—(2008-15)**
29. *Angel Nicolas, ss, Killian HS, Miami.
30. *Erik Meyer, rhp, Eastern Washington University.
31. Wayne Foltin, rhp, University of Nevada-Las Vegas.
32. *Damon Brewer, lhp, Lake City (Fla.) CC.
33. Chris Todd, 2b, Coastal Carolina University.
34. *Matt Long, rhp, Miami (Ohio) University.
**35. Antoan Richardson, of, Vanderbilt University.—(2011-14)**
**36. +Thomas Neal, of, Poway (Calif.) HS / Grossmont (Calif.) JC.—(2012-13)**
37. +David Newton, rhp, West Valley (Calif.) CC.
38. Ben Nieto, lhp, Riverside (Calif.) CC.
39. *Melvin Blackmon, lhp, Temecula Valley HS, Temecula, Calif.
40. *Kurt Lipton, of, Pine Crest HS, Boca Raton, Fla.
41. *Bo Merrell, ss, Perryton (Texas) HS.
42. *Tony Snow, rhp, Edmonds (Wash.) CC.
43. Chris Stanton, 1b, Virginia Tech.
44. *Reggie Fuller, lhp, Diablo Valley (Calif.) JC.
45. *Eric Dworkis, rhp, University of California.
46. *Jared Cranston, lhp, Seward County (Kan.) CC.
47. *George Snyder, rhp, Chaffey (Calif.) JC.
48. Adam Ortiz-Jusino, rhp, Brookdale (N.J.) CC.
**49. *Curtis Partch, rhp, Merced (Calif.) HS.—(2013-14)**
50. *Justin Robertson, rhp, Nipomo (Calif.) HS.

## SEATTLE MARINERS (3)

**1. Jeff Clement, c, University of Southern California.—(2007-12)**
2. (Choice to Dodgers as compensation for Type A free agent Adrian Beltre)
3. (Choice to Diamondbacks as compensation for Type A free agent Richie Sexson)
**4. Justin Thomas, lhp, Youngstown State University.—(2008-12)**
5. Stephen Kahn, rhp, Loyola Marymount University.—(AA)
**6. *Lance Lynn, rhp, Brownsburg (Ind.) HS.—(2011-15)**

DRAFT DROP *First round draft pick (39th overall), Cardinals (2008)*

7. Robert Rohrbaugh, lhp, Clemson University.
8. David Asher, lhp, Florida International University.
9. Bryan Sabatella, 3b, Quinnipiac University.
10. Ronnie Prettyman, 3b, Cal State Fullerton.
11. *Brian Contreras, of, Puerto Rico Baseball Academy, Caguas, P.R.
**12. Anthony Varvaro, rhp, St. John's University.—(2010-15)**
13. Reed Eastley, ss, Niagara University.
14. *Brad Boyer, 2b, University of Arizona.
**15. *John Holdzkom, rhp, Rancho Cucamonga (Calif.) HS.—(2014)**
16. *Grant Gerrard, of, Southern Illinois University.
**17. *James Russell, lhp, Navarro (Texas) JC.—(2010-15)**

DRAFT DROP *Son of Jeff Russell, major leaguer (1983-96)*

18. Curtis Ledbetter, 1b, University of Nebraska.
19. Brett Bannister, rhp, University of Southern California.

DRAFT DROP *Son of Floyd Bannister, first overall draft pick, Astros (1976); major leaguer (1977-92) • Brother of Brian Bannister, major leaguer (2006-10)*

20. +Travis Scott, c, Lincoln Land (Ill.) CC.
21. Nick Allen, rhp, Villanova University.
22. Alex Gary, of, Virginia Commonwealth University.
23. *Ryan Lindgren, rhp, Stillwater Area (Minn.) HS.
24. Kevin Gergel, c, Kennesaw State (Ga.) University.
25. +Will Brown, lhp, Downey HS, Modesto, Calif. / Modesto (Calif.) JC.
26. Ari Kafka, rhp, Quinnipiac University.
27. *Jeremy Hill, rhp, Ohlone (Calif.) JC.
28. Lance Beus, lhp, Brigham Young University.
29. *Eric Thomas, of, Buchholz HS, Gainesville, Fla.
30. Aric Van Gaalen, lhp, Lethbridge (Alberta) JC.
31. Jeff Gilmore, rhp, Stanford University.
32. Corby Heckman, 2b, Indiana University.

33. Julian Henson, c, Cordova (Tenn.) HS.
34. *Andrew Schneider, rhp, Franklin (Texas) HS.
35. *Blake Amador, of, Modesto (Calif.) JC.
36. *Max Kwan, c, Seattle Prep, Bellevue, Wash.
37. *Jesse Costa, rhp, Magnolia HS, Anaheim, Calif.
38. *Joe Agreste, 1b, Greenbrier Christian Academy, Chesapeake, Va.
**39. *Duke Welker, rhp, Seminole State (Okla.) JC.—(2013)**
40. *Eugene Edwards, of, Long Beach (Calif.) CC.
41. +Joe White, 1b, Georgia Perimeter JC.
42. Kevin Reynolds, of, Quincy (Ill.) University.
43. *Philip Roy, rhp, Southridge HS, Miami.
44. *Paul David Patterson, rhp, Northern Kentucky University.
45. *Luis Coste, of, Cochise County (Ariz.) CC.
46. Worth Lumry, lhp, Princeton University.
47. Andy Hargrove, 1b, Kent State University.
DRAFT DROP *Son of Mike Hargrove, major leaguer (1974-85); major league manager (1991-2007)*
48. *Matt Gardner, rhp, Grayson County (Texas) CC.
49. *Dennis Raben, 1b, St. Thomas Aquinas HS, Fort Lauderdale, Fla.
**50. *Xavier Scruggs, 1b, Poway (Calif.) HS.—(2014-15)**

## TAMPA BAY DEVIL RAYS (8)

1. Wade Townsend, rhp, Dripping Springs, Texas.—(AA)
DRAFT DROP *First-round draft pick (8th overall), Orioles (2004)*
2. Chris Mason, rhp, University of North Carolina-Greensboro.—(AAA)
**3. *Bryan Morris, rhp, Tullahoma (Tenn.) HS.—(2012-15)**
DRAFT DROP *Attended Motlow State (Tenn.) JC; re-drafted by Dodgers, 2006 (1st round)*
**4. Jeremy Hellickson, rhp, Hoover HS, Des Moines, Iowa.—(2010-15)**
5. Mike McCormick, 3b, Marist HS, Eugene, Ore.—(High A)
6. Greg Reinhard, rhp, University of Wisconsin-Whitewater.
7. Mike Wlodarczyk, lhp, Boston College.
8. Andrew Lopez, of, Elk Grove (Calif.) HS.
9. Derek Feldkamp, rhp, University of Michigan.
10. John Matulia, of, Eustis (Fla.) HS.
11. Jeff Kamrath, rhp, University of Virginia.
12. Ryan Zimmerman, rhp, Salt Lake (Utah) CC.
13. Ryan Morse, lhp, Southwest Minnesota State University.
14. Henry Wrigley, 1b, JC of San Mateo (Calif.).
15. Matt Fisher, rhp, Franklin Pierce (N.H.) College.
16. Neil Walton, ss, Cal State Fullerton.
17. Jared Edwards, c, Archbishop Rummel HS, New Orleans, La.
**18. *Tommy Hunter, rhp, Cathedral HS, Indianapolis, Ind.—(2008-15)**
DRAFT DROP *First-round draft pick (54th overall), Rangers (2007)*
**19. *Ike Davis, 1b/lhp, Chaparral HS, Scottsdale, Ariz.—(2010-15)**
DRAFT DROP *First round draft pick (18th overall), Mets (2008) • Son of Ron Davis, major leaguer (1978-88)*
**20. *Wade Miley, lhp, Loranger (La.) HS.—(2011-15)**
DRAFT DROP *First-round draft pick (43rd overall), Diamondbacks (2008)*
21. *Jared Bradford, rhp, Shelton State (Ala.) CC.
22. *Adam Hall, rhp, Pacific HS, Gray Summit, Mo.
**23. *Danny Dorn, of, Cal State Fullerton.—(2015)**
24. Neal Frontz, rhp, Jacksonville University.
**25. *Clay Mortensen, rhp, Treasure Valley (Ore.) CC.—(2009-13)**
DRAFT DROP *First-round draft pick (36th overall), Cardinals (2007)*
26. *Jeff Urlaub, lhp, Horizon HS, Scottsdale, Ariz.
27. *Rylan Ostrosky, rhp, Salisbury Composite HS, Edmonton, Alberta.
28. Matt Falk, rhp, University of San Diego.
29. Chad Pendarvis, lhp, Southeastern Louisiana University.
30. Chris Fessler, rhp, Yavapai (Ariz.) JC.
31. *Jordan Brown, ss-rhp, Hahnville HS, Luling, La.
32. Ryan Bethel, ss, Grand Canyon University.
33. *Tyler Reves, c, Wharton County (Texas) JC.
34. Matt Devins, ss, University of Stony Brook.
35. *Damien Mazzetti, 1b, North Mecklenburg HS, Huntersville, N.C.
36. *John Maschino, rhp, Edmond North HS, Edmond, Okla.
37. Carnell Parker, of, University of Mobile (Ala.).
38. Ben Rulon, lhp, Georgia State University.
39. *Michael McClaren, rhp, Durango HS, Las Vegas, Nev.
40. *Matt Gaudet, 1b, Archbishop Rummel HS, Metairie, La.
41. Garrett Groce, of, Columbus State (Ga.) University.
42. *Taylor Cobb, rhp, University of Central Florida.
43. *Josh Stewart, c, Bowling Green State University.
44. *Rashad Taylor, of, Riordan HS, San Francisco.
45. *Leon Johnson, of, Thatcher, Ariz.
DRAFT DROP *Brother of Elliot Johnson, major leaguer (2008-14)*
46. *Will Oliver, rhp, San Pasqual HS, Escondido, Calif.
47. *Eli Diaz, rhp, Baton Rouge (La.) CC.
48. Brad Matthews, 2b, Wallace State (Ala.) CC.
**49. *Casey Coleman, rhp, Mariner HS, Cape Coral, Fla.—(2010-14)**
DRAFT DROP *Grandson of Joe Coleman, major leaguer (1942-55) • Son of Joe Coleman, first-round draft pick, Senators (1965); major leaguer (1965-79)*
50. *Matt Duryea, lhp, Edmonds (Wash.) CC.

## TEXAS RANGERS (19)

**1. John Mayberry Jr., of, Stanford University.—(2009-14)**
DRAFT DROP *First-round draft pick (28th overall), Mariners (2002) • Son of John Mayberry, first-round draft pick, Astros (1967); major leaguer (1968-82)*
2. Johnny Whittleman, 3b, Kingwood (Texas) HS.—(AAA)
**3. Taylor Teagarden, c, University of Texas.—(2008-15)**
4. Shane Funk, rhp, Arnold HS, Panama City Beach, Fla.—(Rookie)
**5. Michael Kirkman, lhp, Columbia HS, Lake City, Fla.—(2010-14)**
**6. German Duran, 2b, Weatherford (Texas) JC.—(2008)**
7. Jake Rasner, rhp, Earl Wooster HS, Reno, Nev.
DRAFT DROP *Brother of Darrell Rasner, major leaguer (2005-08)*
8. *Brad Barragar, rhp, Golden West (Calif.) JC.
9. R.J. Anderson, of, Armwood HS, Seffner, Fla.
10. Matt Nevarez, rhp, San Fernando (Calif.) HS.
11. Nate Fogle, rhp, Oregon State University.
12. *Dexter Carter, rhp, Greenbrier Christian Academy, Chesapeake, Va.
**13. Doug Mathis, rhp, University of Missouri.—(2008-10)**
14. Steve Murphy, of, Kansas State University.
15. Kea Kometani, rhp, Pepperdine University.
16. Jesse Hall, lhp, Yavapai (Ariz.) JC.
**17. *Chris Dominguez, 3b, Gulliver Prep, Miami.—(2014-15)**
18. *Chase Fontaine, ss, Daytona Beach (Fla.) CC.
19. Brian Valichka, c, University of Delaware.
20. Joey Hooft, 2b, Arizona State University.
21. Brandon James, rhp, Carlisle (Pa.) HS.
22. *Jarrod Dumont, lhp, Riverside (Calif.) CC.
23. +Steve Marquardt, 3b, Columbia Basin (Wash.) CC.
24. *Zach Borba, of, Columbia Basin (Wash.) CC.
25. (void) *Brian Spielmann, rhp, Bradley University.
26. Ben Crabtree, c, Ohio University.
27. Jon Wilson, rhp, Winthrop University.
28. *Sergio Morales, of, Hollywood Hills HS, Hollywood, Fla.
29. Phil Hawke, 1b, University of Louisiana-Lafayette.
30. Truan Mehl, of, University of Maryland.
31. Austin Faught, lhp, University of Louisiana-Lafayette.
32. Renny Osuna, ss, New Mexico JC.
33. +Kevin Gossage, c, Coronado HS, Colorado Springs, Colo. / Yavapai (Ariz.) JC.
DRAFT DROP *Nephew of Goose Gossage, major leaguer (1972-94)*
34. *Shooter Hunt, rhp, Ramapo HS, Wyckoff, N.J.
DRAFT DROP *First-round draft pick (31st overall), Twins (2008)*
35. *Chris Hicks, rhp, Milton HS, Alpharetta, Ga.
36. *Steven Farris, rhp, Langham Creek HS, Houston.
37. +Tim Rodriguez, of, Centennial HS, Gresham, Ore./Mount Hood (Ore.) CC.
38. *Jeffrey Murphy, rhp, Yavapai (Ariz.) JC.
39. *David Makim, rhp, Monte Vista HS, Spring Valley, Calif.
40. Thomas Van Buskirk, rhp, Santa Clara University.
41. Warren Rosebrock, rhp, Cal State Sacramento.
42. *Travis Hill, rhp, Seminole State (Okla.) JC.
43. *Shawn Keil, of, Seminole (Fla.) HS.
44. Roberto Valiente, of, University of Tampa.
45. *Frank Lonigro, c, Fullerton (Calif.) JC.
46. +Thomas Berkery, c, Mississippi State University.
47. *Marc Nobriga, rhp, Hartnell (Calif.) JC.
48. Broc Coffman, lhp, Lower Columbia (Wash.) JC.
49. *Glenn Swanson, lhp, UC Irvine.
50. Joe Napoli, of, Bradley University.

## TORONTO BLUE JAYS (6)

**1. Ricky Romero, lhp, Cal State Fullerton.—(2009-13)**
2. (Choice to Twins as compensation for Type A free agent Corey Koskie)
3. Brian Pettway, of, University of Mississippi.—(AA)
4. Ryan Patterson, of, Louisiana State University.—(AA)
5. Eric Fowler, lhp, University of Mississippi.—(AA)
6. Josh Bell, c, Auburn University.
**7. Robert Ray, rhp, Texas A&M University.—(2009-10)**
8. Jacob Butler, of, University of Nevada-Reno.
9. Paul Phillips, rhp, Oakland University.
10. Josh Sowers, rhp, Yale University.
DRAFT DROP *Brother of Jeremy Sowers, first-round draft pick, Reds (2001); first-round draft pick, Indians (2004); major leaguer (2006-09)*
11. Wesley Stone, ss, A.B. Miller HS, Rialto, Calif.
12. Billy Carnline, rhp, Texas Tech.
13. Anthony Hatch, 3b, Nicholls State University.
14. Sean Stidfole, rhp, Penn State University.
15. Sean Shoffit, 2b, Cosumnes River (Calif.) JC.
16. Kyle Bohm, c, University of Michigan.
17. *Tyler Norrick, lhp, Southern Illinois University.
18. *Rob Hogue, lhp, St. Joseph HS, Edmonton, Alberta.
19. Rey Gonzalez, rhp, St. Petersburg (Fla.) JC.
20. Zach Kalter, of, University of Southern California.
21. Chris Martinez, c, St. Thomas (Fla.) University.
22. Dennis Bigley, rhp, Oral Roberts University.
23. *Manuel Garcia, rhp, Puerto Rico Baseball Academy, Toa Baja, P.R.
24. Alex McRobbie, rhp, UC Santa Barbara.
25. *Philip Carey, ss, A.B. Lucas HS, London, Ontario.
26. Marshall Bernhard, ss, University of Central Florida.
27. *Bobby Nicoll, rhp, University of Connecticut-Avery Point JC.
28. Scott Byrnes, rhp, Purdue University.
29. *John Roberts, of, Pryor (Okla.) HS.
30. Trent Luyster, lhp, Ohio State University.
31. *Jason Riley, c, North HS, Riverside, Calif.
32. Matt Cooksey, of, George Mason University.
33. *Jeff Tobin, lhp, University of British Columbia.
34. *Mace Thurman, lhp, Westlake HS, Austin, Texas.
35. *Derek Tarapacki, rhp, Yavapai (Ariz.) JC.
36. Hector Delgadillo, rhp, University of the Incarnate Word (Texas).
37. Chris Looze, 1b, George Mason University.
38. *Adam DiMichele, rhp, Okaloosa-Walton (Fla.) CC.
DRAFT DROP *Quarterback, Canadian Football League (2009-10)*
39. Josh Celigoy, 1b, Lewis-Clark State (Idaho) College.
40. Al Quintana, c, Cal State Northridge.
41. *Eric Oxio, of, Puerto Rico Baseball Academy, Ponce, P.R.
**42. *Brett Wallace, 1b, Justin-Siena HS, Sonoma, Calif.—(2010-15)**
DRAFT DROP *First-round draft pick (13th overall), Cardinals (2008)*
43. Connor Falkenbach, rhp, University of Florida.
44. *Eric Larson, of, Brown University.
45. +Michael Barbara, rhp, St. Petersburg (Fla.) JC.
46. *Corey Weglin, rhp, Sacramento (Calif.) CC.
47. *Kyle Thornton, rhp, Odessa (Texas) JC.
48. *Kevin Denis-Fortier, 1b, Edouard Montpetit HS, Quebec City, Quebec.
49. *Nick Nordgren, of, Jefferson HS, Cedar Rapids, Iowa.
50. *Brian Mooney, lhp, Walt Whitman HS, Huntington Station, N.Y.

## WASHINGTON NATIONALS (4)

**1. Ryan Zimmerman, 3b, University of Virginia.—(2005-15)**
2. (Choice to Rockies as compensation for Type A free agent Vinny Castilla)
3. (Choice to Twins as compensation for Type B free agent Cristian Guzman)
**4. Justin Maxwell, of, University of Maryland.—(2007-15)**
5. Ryan Delaughter, of, Ryan HS, Denton, Texas.—(Low A)
**6. Marco Estrada, rhp, Long Beach State University.—(2008-15)**
7. Mike Daniel, of, University of North Carolina.
8. Jack Spradlin, lhp, University of Southern California.
9. John Michael Howell, of, University of Central Florida.
10. Dee Brown, of, University of Central Florida.
DRAFT DROP *Son of Jerome Brown, defensive lineman, National Football League (1987-91)*
**11. John Lannan, lhp, Siena College.—(2007-14)**
**12. Craig Stammen, rhp, University of Dayton.—(2009-15)**
13. Andre Enriquez, rhp, Le Moyne College.
14. Deryck Johnson, of, Cypress Creek HS, Orlando, Fla.
15. Michael Wadkins, rhp, William E. Tolman HS, Pawtucket, R.I.
16. Josh Palm, rhp, Penn State University.
17. Eduardo Pichardo, rhp, Southridge HS, Miami.
18. Tim Pahuta, 1b, Seton Hall University.
19. Bradley Clark, rhp, Sickles HS, Tampa.
20. Ricky Shefka, rhp, Coastal Carolina University.
21. Coby Mavroulis, lhp, Texas A&M University.
22. Antonio Evangelista, rhp, Seminole State (Okla.) JC.
23. *Brett Jensen, rhp, University of Nebraska.
24. Jeff Taylor, rhp, Missouri Southern State College.
25. *Jose Peley, ss, Edouard Montpetit HS, Montreal.
26. *Doug Thennis, 3b, American River (Calif.) JC.
27. Andy Lane, 2b, Grand Canyon University.
28. *Hunter Pace, of, Hamilton HS, Chandler, Ariz.
29. *Pat Barnes, of, Southwest Mississippi JC.
30. *Brian Pruitt, 3b, Florida Christian HS, Miami.
31. *Clayton Conner, 3b, Pensacola Catholic HS, Pensacola, Fla.
32. *Daniel Schuh, of, Bishop Kenny HS, Jacksonville, Fla.
**33. +Ryan Buchter, lhp, Highland Regional HS, Blackwood, N.J. / Gloucester (N.J.) CC.—(2014)**
34. *Jordan Thibodeaux, lhp, San Jacinto (Texas) JC.
35. *Matt Averitt, rhp, New Mexico JC.
36. *Brett McMillan, 1b, UCLA.
37. *Brandon Hamilton, of, Woodlawn HS, Shreveport, La.
38. *Marcus Jones, of, Landon School, Washington, D.C.
39. *Jake McCarter, rhp, Navarro (Texas) JC.
40. *Anthony Williams, of, Mission Bay HS, San Diego.
**41. *Tyler Moore, 1b, Northwest Rankin HS, Brandon, Miss.—(2012-15)**
42. *P.J. Treadaway, rhp, Pearl River (Miss.) CC.
**43. *Scott Barnes, lhp, Cathedral HS, Springfield, Mass.—(2012-13)**
44. *Steven Hensley, rhp, Owen HS, Black Mountain, N.C.
45. *Anthony Shawler, rhp, Oscar Smith HS, Chesapeake, Va.
46. *Ibrahim Lopez, of, Lake City (Fla.) CC.
47. *Luis Feliz, of, New Brunswick (N.J.) HS.
48. *Will Cherry, of, George Jenkins HS, Lakeland, Fla.
49. *Terrance Brown, rhp, Bullard HS, Fresno, Calif.
50. *Jake Leonhardt, rhp, Angelina (Texas) JC.

# Royals get bailed out with Hochevar holdout

The Kansas City Royals, coming off a club-record 106-loss season, had the No. 1 selection in the 2006 draft, and they couldn't have picked a worse year to pick first. The talent didn't measure up to previous years in scouts' eyes, and the price tag of the consensus best prospect, University of North Carolina lefthander Andrew Miller, appeared to be too high for the Royals.

"This is not a great year to have the top pick," said Royals crosschecker Brian Murphy, who had seen all the candidates his team was considering. "I can think of at least eight players last year who were more attractive than any of the players in this year's draft."

The talent from the 2006 draft pool didn't prove to be as weak as initially perceived, but the Royals weren't relishing the task in front of them. The consensus top five prospects were college players: Miller, Washington righthander Tim Lincecum, Houston righthander Brad Lincoln, Long Beach State third baseman Evan Longoria and California righthander Brandon Morrow.

The Royals wanted a pitcher, and focused on the 6-foot-7, 210-pound Miller, the highest unsigned pick from the 2003 draft. They also looked closely at Lincecum and Lincoln, smallish righthanders who didn't fit the profile of a No. 1 overall pick.

While it seemed like everyone else had the Royals taking Miller, the club never fully embraced the big lefthander. Miller had privately acknowledged that he didn't want to become a part of one of baseball's worst teams, and he set a price tag that the budget-conscious Royals likely would not meet. The Royals were hesitant to get involved in a protracted holdout, as they had with Alex Gordon, the second overall selection a year earlier. And Kansas City didn't think Miller had the talent to warrant a possible record signing bonus.

It left the Royals in a quandary, lamenting a golden opportunity to rebuild their sagging fortunes. But in the weeks leading up to the draft, the Royals found a possible solution to their situation. Righthander Luke Hochevar, the highest unsigned pick from the 2005 draft, was making little headway in his negotiations with the Los Angeles Dodgers and would go into the 2006 draft pool if he failed to strike a deal a week before the draft. It gave the Royals the opening they needed.

The Royals had history with Hochevar. They had heavily scouted him a year earlier, when he led the NCAA ranks with 15 wins in his junior season at Tennessee, and considered him for their first selection before his late-season fade persuaded them to take Gordon.

With a second shot at Hochevar looking more likely, the Royals scouted all four of his starts in May for the Fort Worth Cats of the independent American Association. Hochevar, who had passed up his senior season in college, flashed a 92-95 mph fastball, along with an above-average slider and curveball, for general manager Allard Baird and a delegation of Royals officials in his final outing with Fort Worth.

Kansas City couldn't decide what to do with the No. 1 overall pick until righthander Luke Hochevar did not sign with the Dodgers out of the 2005 draft and thrust himself into the 2006 process

Once the closed period came and the Dodgers had not signed Hochevar, it was clear that he was squarely in the Royals' plans. But it wasn't a done deal, especially when Baird was fired a day after that scouting trip.

New general manager Dayton Moore worked behind the scenes with scouting director Deric Ladnier and other Royals officials to maneuver Hochevar into position. Scott Boras, Hochevar's agent, did his part, making it known that his client was anxious to sign for what the Royals were prepared to pay, essentially the amount that righthander Mike Pelfrey, the ninth overall pick in 2005 and a Boras client, received from the New York Mets. Pelfrey signed a major league contract that included a $3.55 million bonus and a total guarantee of $5.25 million.

It represented a win-win situation for both parties. It meant a substantial raise for Hochevar from what the Dodgers offered, and it gave the Royals an alternative to Miller or a compromise choice.

For Boras, it was the chance to return to the limelight at the top of the draft. He had been a driving force in the draft for 25 years, but not since Alex Rodriguez in 1993, following Ben McDonald in '89 and Brien Taylor in '91, had a Boras client been the first overall selection.

### WILD RIDE IN FIRST ROUND?

Major League Baseball had been setting bonus parameters for every slot in the first round and beyond for several years, based on economics rather than the quality of talent.

In both 2004 and 2005, each of the first 33 selections signed for a bonus of at least $1 million, and the top pick in 2005, Justin Upton, signed

## AT A GLANCE

### This Date In History
June 6-7

### Best Draft
**TAMPA BAY RAYS.** The Rays thought the Rockies, picking one spot ahead of them at No. 2, would take **EVAN LONGORIA** (1), after whom they would have taken **TIM LINCECUM.** The Rockies crossed up everyone by going for **GREG REYNOLDS,** enabling the Rays to get Longoria, who became the best position player in the 2006 draft. They added to their haul by landing **ALEX COBB** (4) and **DESMOND JENNINGS** (10).

### Worst Draft
**WASHINGTON NATIONALS.** The Nationals got no homers in 39 big league games from **CHRIS MARRERO** (1), supposedly one of the top power prospects in the draft, and didn't sign another future big leaguer among their first 34 picks.

### First-Round Bust
**BILLY ROWELL, 3B, ORIOLES.** Rowell, a New Jersey high school product, was a "can't-miss" power-hitting prospect, but his six-year career was marked by a lack of consistent power, a high strikeout rate, failure to find a defensive home and multiple suspensions for drug abuse. He briefly reached Double-A in his final season.

### Second Best
**JON JAY, OF, CARDINALS.** Jay hit .378 in three seasons at the University of Miami, and continued to swing a hot bat in seven minor league seasons (.300). He hit .294 through his first five big league seasons before an injury-plagued 2015 campaign dragged down the mark to .288.

### Late-Round Find
**JOSH REDDICK, OF, RED SOX (17TH ROUND).** The Red Sox gave Reddick a $140,000 signing bonus as a draft-and-follow after he hit .461 at Middle Georgia

CONTINUED ON PAGE 612

## AT A GLANCE

CONTINUED FROM PAGE 611

JC. He proved his worth in 2012, after being traded to the Athletics, when he hit 32 homers and earned a Gold Glove for his play in right field. Reddick had a .251 average with 86 homers through his first seven seasons in the majors.

### Never Too Late

**TRAVIS TARTAMELLA, C, DEVIL RAYS (50TH ROUND).** He didn't sign out of a California high school, and after playing at an NCAA Division II school received a $25,000 bonus to sign with the Cardinals in 2009 as a 19th-rounder. He batted .197 while persevering through seven minor league seasons, then made his major league debut on Sept. 23, 2015, hitting a single in his first at-bat.

### Overlooked

**DARREN O'DAY, RHP, ANGELS.** No one took the sidearmer after he posted a 23-9, 3.13 record with 20 saves, 41 walks and 190 strikeouts in 224 innings in four seasons at the University of Florida. He signed with the Angels as a 23-year-old free agent for $20,000 and distinguished himself over eight major league seasons with four different clubs, going 31-13, 2.33 in 457 relief appearances; in 441 innings, he walked 111 and struck out 428.

### International Gem

**SALVADOR PEREZ, C, ROYALS.** Infielder **ANGEL VILLALONA**, from the Dominican Republic, signed with the Giants for $2.1 million, and catcher **JESUS MONTERO**, a Venezuelan, signed with the Yankees for $1.65 million. Neither has come close to matching Perez, a Venezuelan who signed with the Royals for $65,000. Perez had a career .279 average with 64 home runs and had already won two Gold Glove Awards.

### Minor League Take

**TIM LINCECUM, RHP, GIANTS.** Lincecum was

## 2006: THE FIRST ROUNDERS

| CLUB: PLAYER, POS., SCHOOL | HOMETOWN | B-T | HT. | WT. | AGE | BONUS | FIRST YEAR | LAST YEAR | PEAK LEVEL (YEARS) |
|---|---|---|---|---|---|---|---|---|---|
| 1. *Royals: Luke Hochevar, rhp, Fort Worth (Ind.) | Fowler, Colo. | R-R | 6-5 | 205 | 22 | $3,500,000 | 2006 | Active | Majors (8) |
| Controversial 2005 holdout, forfeited SR year at Tennessee, hooked on with indy club; FB at 92-95 mph, but never hit stride with Royals until moved to set-up role. | | | | | | | | | |
| 2. Rockies: Greg Reynolds, rhp, Stanford | Pacifica, Calif. | R-R | 6-7 | 220 | 20 | $3,250,000 | 2006 | 2013 | Majors (3) |
| Rockies whiffed on athletic, former QB prospect; had mid-90s FB, but stuff flattened out after signing, couldn't get MLB hitters out (6-11, 7.02 in 123 innings). | | | | | | | | | |
| 3. Devil Rays: Evan Longoria, 3b, Long Beach State | Bellflower, Calif. | R-R | 6-2 | 213 | 20 | $3,000,000 | 2006 | Active | Majors (8) |
| Late developer, undrafted out of HS/JC as freshman; emerged at Long Beach State (.353-11-43), became '08 Rookie of Year, future all-star, two-time Gold Glover. | | | | | | | | | |
| 4. Pirates: Brad Lincoln, rhp, Houston | Clute, Texas | L-R | 6-0 | 200 | 21 | $2,750,000 | 2006 | Active | Majors (5) |
| Polished college arm (12-2, 1.69 as JR), also hit .295-14-53; fast-tracked as starter initially before 2007 TJ surgery/other arm issues, had more success in short role. | | | | | | | | | |
| 5. Mariners: Brandon Morrow, rhp, California | Rohnert Park, Calif. | R-R | 6-3 | 190 | 21 | $2,450,000 | 2006 | Active | Majors (9) |
| Unpopular pick by M's with hometown boy Lincecum on board; broke out with upper-90s FB, flashed impressive stuff but career marked by injury/inconsistency. | | | | | | | | | |
| 6. *Tigers: Andrew Miller, lhp, North Carolina | Gainesville, Fla. | L-L | 6-6 | 195 | 21 | $3,550,000 | 2006 | Active | Majors (10) |
| Third-round HS pick by Rays, rode dominant UNC career (27-9, 2.44, 309 IP/325 Ks) to biggest bonus in '06 class; evolved into legit MLB arm as reliever in late 20s. | | | | | | | | | |
| 7. Dodgers: Clayton Kershaw, lhp, Highland Park HS | Dallas | L-L | 6-3 | 220 | 18 | $2,300,000 | 2006 | Active | Majors (8) |
| First HS pick in college-heavy class, went 13-0, 0.77 (64 IP/139 SO) as SR; not even consensus best prep talent at time, but evolved into generational pitcher. | | | | | | | | | |
| 8. Reds: Drew Stubbs, of, Texas | Atlanta, Texas | R-R | 6-4 | 200 | 21 | $2,000,000 | 2006 | Active | Majors (7) |
| Gold Glove potential for rangy/athletic CF, but serious concerns over ability to make contact; has .244 BA, 924 Ks in 836 MLB games, also flashed power/speed. | | | | | | | | | |
| 9. Orioles: Billy Rowell, 3b, Bishop Eustace HS | Pennsauken, N.J. | L-R | 6-5 | 215 | 17 | $2,100,000 | 2006 | 2011 | Class AA (1) |
| First prep position player picked had raw power; briefly reached Double-A, dogged by makeup issues, drug suspension, lack of position, infrequent power. | | | | | | | | | |
| 10. Giants: Tim Lincecum, rhp, Washington | Renton, Wash. | L-R | 5-11 | 170 | 21 | $2,025,000 | 2006 | Active | Majors (9) |
| Polarizing player due to slender build, unorthodox mechanics, heavy college usage (342 IP, 491 Ks); Giants took gamble, rewarded with back-to-back Cy Youngs. | | | | | | | | | |
| 11. *Diamondbacks: Max Scherzer, rhp, Missouri | Chesterfield, Mo. | R-R | 6-2 | 210 | 21 | $3,000,000 | 2007 | Active | Majors (8) |
| Difficult college sign held out for year before agreeing on $4.3 million major league deal; blossomed after trade to Tigers, won 2013 AL Cy Young Award. | | | | | | | | | |
| 12. Rangers: Kasey Kiker, lhp, Russell County HS | Seale, Ala. | L-L | 5-11 | 185 | 18 | $1,600,000 | 2006 | 2011 | Class AA (2) |
| Played on powerful Alabama HS team with Rasmus brothers; undersized lefty with 94-96 mph FB, on track before command evaporated (91 IP/115 BB) in 2010-11. | | | | | | | | | |
| 13. Cubs: Tyler Colvin, of, Clemson | North Augusta, S.C. | L-L | 6-3 | 190 | 20 | $1,475,000 | 2006 | 2015 | Majors (6) |
| Hit .356-13-70 in breakout year at Clemson, but surprise first-rounder; had size, bat speed, loft swing for power, but hit just .239-49-178 in 441 MLB games. | | | | | | | | | |
| 14. Blue Jays: Travis Snider, of, Henry Jackson HS | Mill Creek, Wash. | L-L | 5-11 | 230 | 18 | $1,700,000 | 2006 | Active | Majors (8) |
| Most advanced prep bat in draft, surprising athleticism, was youngest big leaguer in 2008 debut; free swinger/vulnerable to LHP, limited impact in MLB. | | | | | | | | | |
| 15. Nationals: Chris Marrero, of, Monsignor Pace HS | Opa Locka, Fla. | R-R | 6-3 | 210 | 17 | $1,625,000 | 2006 | Active | Majors (2) |
| Came from baseball family (uncle, brother, cousin played pro ball); best tool always raw power, was slow to tap into it, also slow afoot, became defensive liability. | | | | | | | | | |
| 16. Brewers: Jeremy Jeffress, rhp, Halifax County HS | South Boston, Va. | R-R | 6-0 | 175 | 18 | $1,550,000 | 2006 | Active | Majors (6) |
| Hardest prep thrower in class regularly touched 100 mph; early pro career defined by drug suspensions, command issues, found MLB success in set-up role. | | | | | | | | | |
| 17. Padres: Matt Antonelli, 3b, Wake Forest | Danvers, Mass. | R-R | 6-1 | 195 | 21 | $1,575,000 | 2006 | 2013 | Majors (1) |
| State MVP in football/hockey, runner-up in baseball as prep SR; athleticism never played in pro ball, showed flashes with bat in low minors, hit wall at higher levels. | | | | | | | | | |
| 18. Phillies: Kyle Drabek, rhp, The Woodlands HS | The Woodlands, Texas | R-R | 6-1 | 190 | 18 | $1,550,000 | 2006 | Active | Majors (6) |
| Son of ex-Cy Young winner had high-end talent as SS/RHP, draft position compromised by off-field issues; pure stuff, but career limited by injuries, command issues. | | | | | | | | | |
| 19. Marlins: Brett Sinkbeil, rhp, Missouri State | Sand Springs, Okla. | R-R | 6-3 | 195 | 21 | $1,525,000 | 2006 | 2011 | Majors (1) |
| Lightly recruited, became first-rounder by adding 30 pounds/10 mph in velocity; pro career (21-32, 4.83; 2 IP in MLB) never took off, impacted by nagging injuries. | | | | | | | | | |
| 20. Twins: Chris Parmelee, of, Chino Hills HS | Chino Hills, Calif. | L-L | 6-2 | 205 | 18 | $1,500,000 | 2006 | Active | Majors (5) |
| Justified first-round selection with raw power/plus plate discipline; became too pull-conscious in pro ball, struggled vs LHP, limited to 1B by lack of speed. | | | | | | | | | |
| 21. Yankees: Ian Kennedy, rhp, Southern California | Westminster, Calif. | R-R | 6-0 | 195 | 21 | $2,250,000 | 2006 | Active | Majors (9) |
| Appealed to Yanks because of similarities to Mike Mussina in mound presence, moxie, command; stuff a little short, but won 20 in 2011, fanned 207 in 2014. | | | | | | | | | |
| 22. Nationals: Colton Willems, rhp, Carroll HS | Fort Pierce, Fla. | R-R | 6-4 | 175 | 17 | $1,425,000 | 2006 | 2010 | Class A (4) |
| First-rounder on strength of 93-97 mph FB, power slider; flourished early but never adapted to changes Nats made to stuff/mechanics in pros. | | | | | | | | | |
| 23. Astros: Max Sapp, c, Bishop Moore HS | Orlando, Fla. | L-R | 6-2 | 220 | 18 | $1,400,000 | 2006 | 2008 | Class A (3) |
| Had big power potential, limited experience as catcher, didn't do much at plate in three seasons (.224-7-81) before contracting viral meningitis, never played again. | | | | | | | | | |
| 24. Braves: Cody Johnson, of, Mosley HS | Lynn Haven, Fla. | L-R | 6-4 | 195 | 17 | $1,375,000 | 2006 | 2013 | Class AAA (1) |
| High-risk, high-reward player with huge LH power/swing-and-miss issues; hammered 132 HRs in minors, also averaged 174 Ks per year in first four full seasons. | | | | | | | | | |
| 25. Angels: Hank Conger, c, Huntington Beach HS | Huntington Beach, Calif. | B-R | 6-0 | 205 | 18 | $1,350,000 | 2006 | Active | Majors (6) |
| Son of Korean immigrants, named after Aaron; storied youth/prep baseball talent with slugging exploits, became coveted defender at MLB level with framing skills. | | | | | | | | | |
| 26. Dodgers: Bryan Morris, rhp, Motlow State (Tenn.) CC | Tullahoma, Tenn. | L-R | 6-3 | 175 | 19 | $1,325,000 | 2006 | Active | Majors (4) |
| Unsigned 2005 second-rounder moved up after year in JC; dealt to Pirates in Manny Ramirez three-way trade, raw stuff (90-95 FB/SL) evolved with move to pen. | | | | | | | | | |
| 27. Red Sox: Jason Place, of, Wren HS | Piedmont, S.C. | R-R | 6-3 | 205 | 18 | $1,300,000 | 2006 | 2011 | Class AA (3) |
| Two-sport prep star with five-tool potential, routinely put on mammoth BP displays with raw power; never ironed out hitch in swing, struggled to hit breaking stuff. | | | | | | | | | |
| 28. Red Sox: Daniel Bard, rhp, North Carolina | Charlotte, N.C. | R-R | 6-4 | 200 | 21 | $1,550,000 | 2007 | 2014 | Majors (5) |
| Teamed with Andrew Miller to lead UNC to CWS finals; flashed overpowering stuff with FB that peaked at 100, but promising career sabotaged by control issues. | | | | | | | | | |
| 29. White Sox: Kyle McCulloch, rhp, Texas | Houston | R-R | 6-3 | 185 | 21 | $1,050,000 | 2006 | 2011 | Class AAA (2) |
| Pitched Texas to CWS title in 2005, winning 12 games/championship game; modest stuff (88-91 mph FB) proved undoing in minors, went 39-48, 4.65 overall. | | | | | | | | | |
| 30. Cardinals: Adam Ottavino, rhp, Northeastern | Brooklyn, N.Y. | R-R | 6-5 | 215 | 20 | $950,000 | 2006 | 2015 | Majors (5) |
| Snuck into first round with 13-13 college record; struggled to make headway as starter, but hit stride in relief for Rockies before 2015 TJ surgery. | | | | | | | | | |

**Signed to major league contract.*

## How They Should Have Done It

Based on career WAR (Wins Above Replacement, as calculated by Baseball-Reference.com) achieved by players eligible for the 2006 draft through the 2015 season, here's how the first round should have unfolded. Numbers in parentheses indicate the round when the player was drafted. Asterisks denote players who signed as draft-and-follows.

| | Player, Pos. | Actual Draft | WAR | Bonus |
|---|---|---|---|---|
| 1. | Clayton Kershaw, lhp | Dodgers (1) | 48.5 | $2,300,000 |
| 2. | Evan Longoria, 3b | Devil Rays (1) | 42.7 | $3,000,000 |
| 3. | Max Scherzer, rhp | Diamondbacks (1) | 31.6 | $3,000,000 |
| 4. | Tim Lincecum, rhp | Giants (1) | 22.7 | $2,025,000 |
| 5. | Doug Fister, rhp | Mariners (7) | 19.4 | $50,000 |
| 6. | Josh Reddick, of | Red Sox (17) | 15.9 | $140,000 |
| 7. | Chris Davis, 1b | Rangers (5) | 14.9 | $172,500 |
| 8. | Darren O'Day, rhp | Angels (NDFA) | 14.4 | $20,000 |
| 9. | * Mat Latos, rhp | Padres (11) | 13.4 | $1,250,000 |
| 10. | Daniel Murphy, 3b | Mets (13) | 12.5 | $50,000 |
| 11. | Desmond Jennings, of | Devil Rays (10) | 12.2 | $150,000 |
| 12. | David Robertson, rhp | Yankees (17) | 11.5 | $200,000 |
| 13. | Jon Jay, of | Cardinals (2) | 11.0 | $480,000 |
| 14. | Ian Kennedy, rhp | Yankees (1) | 10.5 | $2,250,000 |
| 15. | Joe Smith, rhp | Mets (3) | 10.4 | $410,000 |
| 16. | Kris Medlen, rhp | Braves (10) | 10.3 | $85,000 |
| 17. | Jarrod Dyson, of | Royals (50) | 9.7 | $5,000 |
| 18. | Drew Stubbs, of | Reds (1) | 9.5 | $2,000,000 |
| | Chris Tillman, rhp | Mariners (2) | 9.5 | $680,000 |
| | David Freese, 3b | Padres (9) | 9.5 | $6,000 |
| | * Derek Holland, lhp | Rangers (25) | 9.5 | $200,000 |
| 22. | Justin Masterson, rhp | Red Sox (2) | 9.3 | $510,000 |
| | Alex Cobb, rhp | Devil Rays (4) | 9.3 | $400,000 |
| 24. | Craig Gentry, of | Rangers (10) | 9.2 | $10,000 |
| | Trevor Cahill, rhp | Athletics (2) | 9.2 | $560,000 |
| 26. | Justin Turner, 2b | Reds (7) | 8.9 | $50,000 |
| 27. | Chris Archer, rhp | Indians (5) | 8.8 | $161,000 |
| 28. | Brandon Morrow, rhp | Mariners (1) | 8.1 | $2,450,000 |
| 29. | Brett Anderson, lhp | Diamondbacks (2) | 8.0 | $950,000 |
| 30. | Joba Chamberlain, rhp | Yankees (1-S) | 7.5 | $1,100,000 |

| | Top 3 Unsigned Players | | | Year Signed |
|---|---|---|---|---|
| 1. | Paul Goldschmidt, 1b | Dodgers (49) | 24.1 | 2009 |
| 2. | Brandon Belt, of | Red Sox (11) | 12.6 | 2009 |
| 3. | Mike Leake, rhp | Athletics (7) | 12.5 | 2009 |

for a record $6.1 million bonus. Like the Royals, most teams were so unimpressed with the high-end talent in the 2006 draft that some advanced the notion that they might refuse to pay slot money and instead settle for players willing to accept signing bonuses more in line with their worth.

"It's not a signability thing," Cleveland Indians scouting director John Mirabelli said. "It's just the smart thing to do this year. I think you'll see teams that won't give market money, possibly all the way through the first round."

A number of clubs achieved cost certainty by striking predraft deals. The Colorado Rockies had an agreement in place with Stanford righthander Greg Reynolds, the second pick, for $3.25 million; the Tampa Bay Devil Rays with Longoria, the third pick, for $3 million; and the Pittsburgh Pirates with Lincoln, the fourth pick, for $2.75 million. All three agreements were for amounts significantly lower than the corresponding selections a year earlier. Reynolds signed for $750,000 less than Gordon, while Longoria took a $400,000 cut and Lincoln received $200,000 less. Morrow, the fifth selection, signed with the Seattle Mariners for $2.45 million, the same bonus for that slot a year earlier.

Miller was picked sixth by the Detroit Tigers, who were not scared off by word that his asking price was upward of $6 million. They had drafted righthander Justin Verlander and outfielder Cameron Maybin in the previous two years, each perceived to have a high price tag. After lengthy negotiations, the Tigers managed to sign both players, and they were confident they could strike a deal with Miller. His selection marked the first time in draft history that the first six picks came from college, although Hochevar technically was from the independent ranks.

"We were going to take the best player on our board, and that was Andrew Miller," Tigers scouting director David Chadd said after the draft. "The reason he slid to us, you could argue, is signability. I was stunned."

Miller went 13-2, 2.48 with 133 strikeouts in 123 innings during his junior season at North Carolina. He was the school's all-time strikeout leader (325), and had a 27-9, 2.85 record for his three-year career.

Signing bonuses for first-round picks peaked at an average of $2,154,280 million in 2001, and since had been steadily rolled back at MLB's urging to a point that the average bonus for the 22 first-rounders from the 2006 draft who signed by July 1 was just $1.708 million. That represented a drop of 26.1 percent in the past five years and a dip of 6.2 percent from the corresponding 22 picks from 2005.

Evan Longoria

Not only were players signing for less, but they were signing faster. "It's apparent the pressure the commissioner's office is putting on clubs to get this thing under control is having results," a scouting director said. "It's not perfect yet, but at least they're headed in the right direction."

By the time all 30 first-round picks had signed, the first-round average had swelled to $1,933,333, but that represented a dip from 2005 of 4.2 percent, the second-largest decrease in 30 years. Eleven first-rounders signed for smaller bonuses than the corresponding draft slot a year earlier, and 10 signed for identical bonuses.

### SIMILAR DEALS FOR HOCHEVAR, MILLER

Hochevar was one of five first-rounders who remained unsigned entering August, but he had agreed to terms without contentious negotiations, unlike other first-rounders in recent years. A year earlier, Upton signed almost eight months after being selected by the Arizona Diamondbacks.

"Recent history suggests the handful of top picks in the first round won't get signed until the end of the process," an agent said. "The commissioner's office doesn't want them to set the bar until the rest of the players are locked up, so you can expect Hochevar and Miller to be the last ones to sign."

The Royals announced the signing of Hochevar

### AT A GLANCE

probably ready for the majors while he was at the University of Washington, where he went 12-4, 1.94 with 199 strikeouts in 125 innings. He went 6-0, 1.00 with 26 hits allowed and 104 strikeouts in 13 starts from Class A to Triple-A before being promoted to the majors on May 6, 2007.

#### One Who Got Away

**PAUL GOLDSCHMIDT, 1B, DODGERS (49TH ROUND).** Goldschmidt was a late-round afterthought from a Houston-area high school who went on to play at Texas State. Less than a decade later, he was one of the game's top offensive performers.

#### He Was Drafted?

**JAKE LOCKER, RHP, ANGELS (40TH ROUND).** Locker was a multi-sport star at a Washington high school when the Angels drafted him in 2006. He didn't sign, and became an NFL-caliber quarterback at the University of Washington. The Angels drafted Locker again in 2009 as their 10th-round pick and gave him a $250,000 signing bonus. He had not played baseball in college, nor would he ever play in the Angels system. Locker went to the NFL in 2011 as the eighth overall pick in the draft.

#### Did You Know . . .

Between them, **CLAYTON KERSHAW** (the seventh pick in 2006) and **TIM LINCECUM** (the 10th pick) won five of the seven National League Cy Young Awards from 2008-14. **MAX SCHERZER** (11th pick) won the 2013 American League Cy Young.

#### They Said It

Agent **SCOTT BORAS**, on the emergence of righthander **LUKE HOCHEVAR**, the 40th pick in 2005, as the top selection in 2006: "His value has risen to where he was really the best pitcher in the draft. Last year coming out I'm not sure you could say that."

## DRAFT SPOTLIGHT: TIM LINCECUM

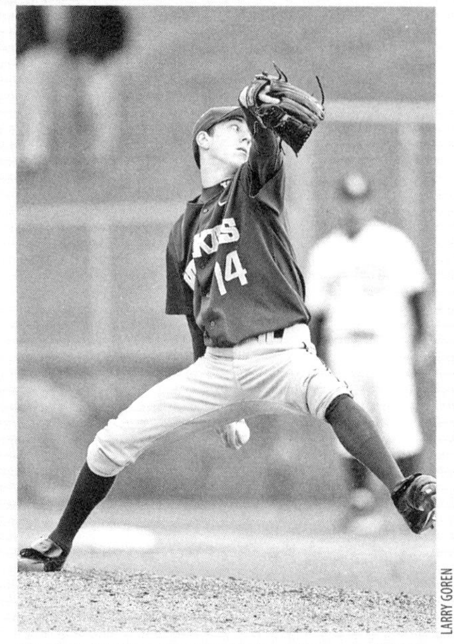
Tim Lincecum was a scouting challenge because of his size and mechanics, but he quickly found big league success

LARRY GOREN

Righthander Tim Lincecum was the most dazzling pitcher in college baseball during his junior season at the University of Washington. He struck out an NCAA-leading 199 hitters in 125 innings with a fastball that touched 100 mph and a curveball that was virtually unhittable. Scouts marveled at his velocity and diversity of pitches, and his tenaciousness on the mound.

So why did Lincecum last until the 10th pick overall in the 2006 draft? It all had to do with his slight, 5-foot-10, 170-pound physique, and his unconventional, contorted, pinwheel delivery.

"There aren't too many comparables at his size, especially as starting pitchers," said Cleveland Indians general manager Mark Shapiro, whose club drafted Lincecum in the 42nd round in 2005. "It looks like his head is going to snap off and his arm is going to fly off. Body type has something to do with it, but the way he throws does, too."

Lincecum's uneven performance (8-6, 3.11), sophomore standing and lofty bonus demands scared teams off, but the Indians were baffled in knowing exactly what they had—a potential ace or a medical disaster waiting to happen. It made them squeamish to take a leap of faith and commit the funds needed to sign their low-round draft pick, even as his dominant summer performance in the Cape Cod League provided a preview of the success he would enjoy as a UW junior in 2006.

By repeating his complicated delivery more consistently, enabling him to not only refine his command and pitchability but enhance the crispness of his overpowering raw stuff, Lincecum went 12-4, 1.94. He dominated his college competition like no other, and yet his arm proved so resilient that he often pitched in relief and made a start on the same weekend in Pacific-10 Conference play, with no loss in effectiveness.

His stock improved to the point that the Kansas City Royals considered taking him with the first overall pick in the 2006 draft. The Royals were fascinated with his almost-freakish ability to routinely throw fastballs in the high-90s, despite his limited physical stature. At the same time, they were resistant to taking a chance on a pitcher whose delivery defied conventional baseball norms.

"There was a feeling he was short, not a real physical kid, and mechanically he was going to break down because of the stress on his elbow and shoulder," said Orioles general manager Jim Duquette. "Our scouting department kind of pushed him down because of the medical aspect."

The Giants, drafting one spot after the Orioles, were looking for a power pitcher, and didn't hesitate to select Lincecum. "He was supposed to go at two or three. We're kind of shocked he got to us," Giants vice president of player personnel Dick Tidrow said. "We like Tim's arm, stuff and athleticism. He's got a power arm with good breaking stuff. He's a fast mover who can pitch in either a starting or relief role."

Lincecum's career began with lofty expectations, and he managed to exceed them. By age 26, he had won the National League Cy Young Award twice, been selected to play in the All-Star Game three times, and led the NL in strikeouts on three occasions. Lincecum played a key role in the Giants winning three World Series titles

Meanwhile, all of the college pitchers drafted ahead of him—Luke Hochevar, Greg Reynolds, Brad Lincoln, Brandon Morrow and Andrew Miller—accomplished only a fraction of what Lincecum achieved.

More than any pitcher in the big leagues, he was self-made, an engineering marvel and a product of both hard work and ingenuity.

Through the direction of his father Chris, Lincecum crafted a delivery while growing up in Washington that was specifically designed to accommodate and compensate for his undersized, though unusually athletic frame, and enabled him to dominate at every level he played.

to a four-year major league deal on Aug. 4, and as expected it was similar in size and structure to the contract Pelfrey signed a year earlier. The deal guaranteed Hochevar $5.2 million and included a bonus of $3.5 million. Other incentives, including roster bonuses, could inflate the amount to $6.95 million.

A day after the Royals signed Hochevar, Miller struck a similar contract with the Tigers. His deal included a bonus of $3.55 million, the largest in 2006, with a guaranteed value of $5.45 million. It also included incentives that could inflate his deal to $7.277 million if he pitched in the major leagues for the full life of the contract.

The most significant difference between the contracts was a guaranteed major league callup on Sept. 1 for Miller. While Hochevar was slated to report to the Arizona Fall League after making a handful of minor league starts, Miller became the first player from the 2006 class to reach the majors. He made his debut on Aug. 30 and appeared in eight games in relief the rest of the season.

A decade later, neither Hochevar nor Miller ranked among the 30 best players from the 2006 draft, according to career WAR (Wins Above Replacement), through the 2015 season.

Hochevar remained with the Royals and watched the club reach the World Series in both 2014 and '15, but he played an incidental role in the team's success. He missed the 2014 season recovering from Tommy John surgery, and went 1-1, 3.38 in 46 relief appearances a year later. Over the course of eight major league seasons, he had a 44-62, 5.01 record. The most productive player the Royals drafted in 2006 proved to be Jarrod Dyson, a junior college outfielder from Mississippi taken with the team's 50th and final pick.

Miller bounced around the majors for nine seasons, playing for four different clubs, before signing a four-year contract for $36 million with the New York Yankees prior to the 2015 season. He had only one save on his resume at that point, but quickly settled in as the Yankees' closer and had his best season, saving 38 games, posting a 1.97 ERA and striking out 97 in 59 innings.

Little did anyone realize when the 2006 draft unfolded that it would produce three pitchers—none named Hochevar or Miller—who would combine to win six Cy Young Awards, or that a first-rounder would engage in a lengthy holdout that superseded anything Hochevar or Miller went through.

The signings of Hochevar and Miller reduced the number of unsigned first-round picks to righthander Max Scherzer (Diamondbacks,

### Fastest To The Majors

| | Player, Pos. | Drafted (Round) | Debut |
|---|---|---|---|
| 1. | Andrew Miller, lhp | Tigers (1) | Aug. 30, 2006 |
| 2. | Joe Smith, rhp | Mets (3) | April 1, 2007 |
| 3. | Brandon Morrow, rhp | Mariners (1) | April 3, 2007 |
| 4. | Tim Lincecum, rhp | Giants (1) | May 6, 2007 |
| 5. | Joba Chamberlain, rhp | Yankees (1-S) | Aug. 7, 2007 |

**FIRST HIGH SCHOOL SELECTION:** Clayton Kershaw, lhp (Dodgers/1, May 25, 2008)

## Top 25 Bonuses

| | Player, Pos. | Drafted (Round) | Order | Bonus |
|---|---|---|---|---|
| 1. | **Andrew Miller, lhp** | **Tigers (1)** | **6** | **#$3,550,000** |
| 2. | **Luke Hochevar, rhp** | **Royals (1)** | **1** | **#$3,500,000** |
| 3. | **Greg Reynolds, rhp** | **Rockies (1)** | **2** | **$3,250,000** |
| 4. | **Evan Longoria, 3b** | **Rays (1)** | **3** | **$3,000,000** |
| | **Max Scherzer, rhp** | **Diamondbacks (1)** | **11** | **#$3,000,000** |
| 6. | **Brad Lincoln, rhp** | **Pirates (1)** | **4** | **$2,750,000** |
| 7. | **Brandon Morrow, rhp** | **Mariners (1)** | **5** | **$2,450,000** |
| 8. | ***Clayton Kershaw, lhp** | **Dodgers (1)** | **7** | **$2,300,000** |
| 9. | **Ian Kennedy, rhp** | **Yankees (1)** | **21** | **$2,250,000** |
| 10. | * Billy Rowell, ss | Orioles (1) | 9 | $2,100,000 |
| 11. | **Tim Lincecum, rhp** | **Giants (1)** | **10** | **$2,025,000** |
| 12. | **Drew Stubbs, of** | **Reds (1)** | **8** | **$2,000,000** |
| 13. | ***Travis Snider, of** | **Blue Jays (1)** | **14** | **$1,700,000** |
| 14. | ***Chris Marrero, 3b** | **Nationals (1)** | **15** | **$1,625,000** |
| 15. | * Kasey Kiker, lhp | Rangers (1) | 12 | $1,600,000 |
| 16. | **Matt Antonelli, 3b** | **Padres (1)** | **17** | **$1,575,000** |
| 17. | ***Jeremy Jeffress, rhp** | **Brewers (1)** | **16** | **$1,550,000** |
| | ***Kyle Drabek, rhp** | **Phillies (1)** | **18** | **$1,550,000** |
| | **Daniel Bard, rhp** | **Red Sox (1)** | **28** | **$1,550,000** |
| 20. | **Brett Sinkbeil, rhp** | **Marlins (1)** | **19** | **$1,525,000** |
| 21. | ***Chris Parmelee, of** | **Twins (1)** | **20** | **$1,500,000** |
| 22. | **Tyler Colvin, of** | **Cubs (1)** | **13** | **$1,475,000** |
| 23. | * Colton Willems, rhp | Nationals (1) | 22 | $1,425,000 |
| 24. | * Max Sapp, c | Astros (1) | 23 | $1,400,000 |
| 25. | * Cody Johnson, of | Braves (1) | 24 | $1,375,000 |

*Major leaguers in bold. *High school selection. #Major league contract.*

11th overall), like Hochevar a Boras client; and righthander Daniel Bard (Red Sox, 28th), Miller's college teammate. Technically a third first-rounder, Southern California righthander Ian Kennedy (Yankees, 21st), also had not signed, but he had agreed to terms on a $2.25 million bonus, considerably more than the amount allocated for his slot. The announcement of that deal, like Hochevar's and Miller's, was held up because of sensitivity that it might influence the Red Sox's negotiations with Bard and the Yankees' dealings with their supplemental first-round pick, University of Nebraska righthander Joba Chamberlain.

Kennedy's deal, which was larger than all but eight other first-rounders, was announced on Aug. 17. Bard and Chamberlain signed in short order for above-slot bonuses of $1.55 million and $1.1 million, respectively.

Scherzer, Bard and Chamberlain all had aspirations of being selected among the first 10 picks, but were knocked back by injuries or uneven performance in the spring. Scherzer had tendinitis in his pitching arm, and he missed a few starts after slamming a car door on his pitching hand. He became the latest Boras client to stretch out his signing until the following calendar year, much as Jered Weaver and Stephen Drew did in 2004.

After holding out for 11 months, Scherzer followed Hochevar's lead by joining independent Fort Worth prior to the 2007 draft. He went 1-0, 0.56 with 25 strikeouts in 16 innings over three starts, and finally signed with the Diamondbacks on May 31, 2007, a few hours before he would have gone into the 2007 draft pool. Like Hochevar and Miller, Scherzer signed a major league agreement. He received a $3 million bonus and a total guarantee of $4.3 million.

### RED SOX DEFY MLB'S WISHES

The over-slot bonuses paid by the Diamondbacks, Yankees and Boston Red Sox to first-round and supplemental first-round selections were in keeping with bonuses those clubs paid in later rounds that were often substantially greater than those being paid by the rank and file. As a result, the Red Sox spent more on bonuses than any club, $8.642 million. The Yankees ($6.68 million) and Diamondbacks ($6.6335 million) weren't far behind.

The Red Sox not only had four of the first 44 picks, but also made a point of pursuing players in the later rounds that slipped because of their bonus demands. They spent nearly $2 million on three high school players they drafted in the middle rounds. They gave $600,000 to ninth-round pick Ryan Kalish, an outfielder who was headed to college at Virginia; $425,000 on 16th-round pick Tyler Weeden, a catcher who was bound for Arkansas; and $825,000 on 18th-rounder Lars Anderson, a first baseman headed for California.

The biggest coup was Anderson, who projected as a possible supplemental first-round pick after hitting 15 home runs during his senior season at a northern California high school. Anderson's $1 million price tag and college commitment scared teams off. The Red Sox's draft included 13 future big leaguers, more than any other club.

In addition to Kennedy and Chamberlain, the Yankees went off the board to sign Dellin Betances, a local high school pitcher, for $1 million, a record for an eighth-round pick that broke the mark the Yankees set a year earlier by signing Texas prep outfielder Austin Jackson for $800,000. They also landed ninth-rounder Mark Melancon, a University of Arizona pitcher, for $600,000. Like Chamberlain, Melancon fell significantly from his

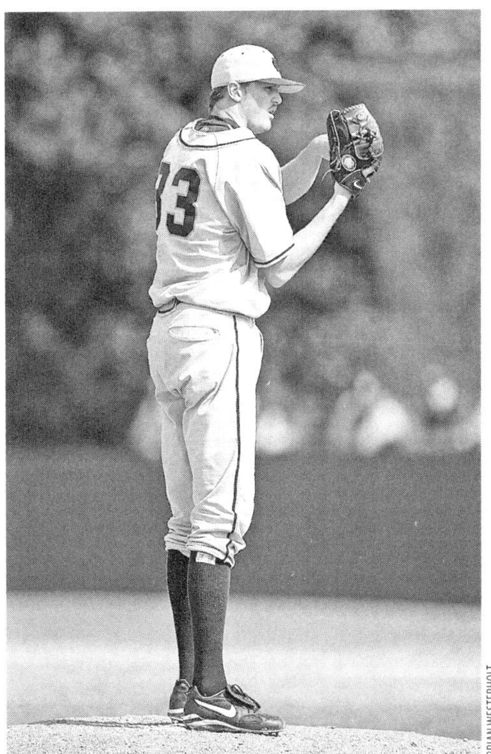

BRIAN WESTERHOLT

**North Carolina's Andrew Miller was the consensus top talent in the 2006 draft, but he didn't find success until he moved into a relief role**

### WORTH NOTING

According to the Major League Scouting Bureau, 15 of the top 16 players in the 2006 draft pool were pitchers. University of California righthander **BRANDON MORROW**, drafted fifth overall by the Mariners, had the highest mark, 70 (on the 20-80 scouting scale). University of Nebraska righthander **JOBA CHAMBERLAIN** (Yankees, 41st overall) and North Carolina lefthander **ANDREW MILLER** (Tigers, sixth) each had a 65 grade. The only non-pitcher among the top 16 was Washington state high school outfielder **JAKE LOCKER** (60), who also pitched in high school. Locker, better known as one of the nation's top quarterback recruits, was selected in the 40th round by the Angels.

Some of the biggest draft news of 2006 came during the World Series, when several changes were announced as part of a new Collective Bargaining Agreement. The changes included an Aug. 15 signing deadline, and draft-pick compensation for teams that failed to sign high-round picks as well as those that lost major league free agents. The 2006 draft also marked the end of the draft-and-follow rule. Beginning in 2007, teams that failed to sign a first-round pick no longer would receive an extra pick after the first round as compensation, but instead a pick in a corresponding slot the following year. The same criteria applied to unsigned second-rounders. A team that failed to sign a third-round pick would receive a pick between the third and fourth rounds. The new rule was aimed at curbing the growth of bonus payments, as teams theoretically could now walk away from negotiations with the reassurance of having a similar pick in the following draft. Clubs also wanted a system of prescribed, slotted bonuses for every high-round pick, but they learned early in the negotiations that the union would not accept that

CONTINUED ON PAGE 616

**WORTH NOTING**

CONTINUED FROM PAGE 615

proposal and instead focused on stronger compensation rules.

■ UCLA did not make it to the College World Series, but had 12 players drafted, more than any other school. Oregon State, the first Northern school to win the College World Series since Minnesota in 1964 (the year before the first draft), had nine players selected, the first being righthander **DALLAS BUCK** in the third round.

■ Tampa won the NCAA Division II national title, its fourth overall, and shared the D-II lead for most players drafted, five. Righthander **SERGIO PEREZ**, who earned a save in Tampa's 3-2, 10-inning, national championship game victory over Chico State, was the first D-II player drafted, going in the second round to the Astros. Ohio's Marietta College won its fourth NCAA Division III title behind the pitching of 6-foot-7 righthander **MIKE EISENREICH**, who struck out 12 in a 7-2 win in the championship game over Wheaton (Mass.) College. Eisenreich was the first D-III player drafted, going to the Indians in the eighth round. Idaho's Lewis-Clark State won its 14th NAIA World Series title with an NAIA-high four players drafted, the highest being **JUSTIN FULLER** in the 11th round. NAIA player of the year **BRIAN DINKELMAN** of McKendree (Ill.) University was the first NAIA player selected, in the eighth round. Tennessee's Walters State JC won the Junior College World Series on the strength of six drafted players, more than any other junior college. The Braves drafted three Walters State players in the rounds from 15-18.

■ The Dodgers signed their fourth-round pick, first baseman **KYLE ORR**, for $450,000. He was the first Canadian player drafted. The Dodgers were in no hurry to announce the deal as they had no open visa slots for foreign players, meaning that Orr wouldn't be able to begin

predraft ranking after missing the final few weeks of the college season because of a sore elbow.

The Yankees signed all of their picks through the first 13 rounds, spending almost $3 million more than MLB recommended. They also were big spenders on the international market, signing Venezuelan catcher Jesus Montero for $1.65 million, the second-largest bonus paid to a foreign player. That large-market teams like the Red Sox and Yankees were spending large amounts on amateur talent did not go unnoticed.

"The draft is the only chance we have to compete for talent with big-revenue clubs, and we'll do what we have to do this year, especially if those clubs are doing it," a scouting director said. "We're not going to toe the line any more, if those clubs can keep getting away with it. It shows how flawed the system is that we're working under, that they can do that and not be punished. It's not a true system where Major League Baseball can influence where the talent goes like it did this year."

Holding the line on bonuses also was of little consequence to the Atlanta Braves, who spent $8,057,200, some of it the following spring on late-round choices they had targeted as draft-and-follow players. The Braves signed six of their 2005 draft-and-follows prior to the 2006 draft, more than any other club. Atlanta signed 11 of their 2006 draft picks for bonuses of $200,000 or more, and another nine for at least $100,000.

## Largest Bonuses By Round

| | Player, Pos. | Club | Bonus |
|---|---|---|---|
| **1.** | **Andrew Miller, lhp** | **Tigers** | **$3,550,000** |
| **1-S.** | **Joba Chamberlain, rhp** | **Yankees** | **$1,100,000** |
| 2. | Wes Hodges, 3b | Indians | $1,000,000 |
| 3. | * Stephen King, ss | Nationals | $750,000 |
| 4. | * Marcus Lemon, ss | Rangers | $1,000,000 |
| **5.** | **Jeff Samadzija, rhp** | **Cubs** | **$250,000** |
| **6.** | *** Jacob Brigham, rhp** | **Rangers** | **$200,000** |
| 7. | * Robbie Alcombrack, c | Indians | $160,000 |
| **8.** | *** Dellin Betances, rhp** | **Yankees** | **$1,000,000** |
| **9.** | *** Ryan Kalish, of** | **Red Sox** | **$600,000** |
| | **Mark Melancon, rhp** | **Yankees** | **$600,000** |
| 10. | * Paolo Espino, rhp | Indians | $150,000 |
| | **Desmond Jennings, of** | **Devil Rays** | **$150,000** |
| 11. | * Chris Huseby, rhp | Cubs | $1,300,000 |
| **12.** | ***# Jordan Walden, rhp** | **Angels** | **$1,000,000** |
| 13. | * Brandon Holden, rhp | Pirates | $155,000 |
| 14. | * Drew Rundle of | Cubs | $500,000 |
| 15. | # Stephen Shults, 3b | Braves | $100,000 |
| 16. | Tyler Weeden, c | Red Sox | $420,000 |
| **17.** | **David Robertson, rhp** | **Yankees** | **$200,000** |
| **18.** | *** Lars Anderson, 1b** | **Red Sox** | **$825,000** |
| 19. | *# Lee Haydel, of | Brewers | $624,000 |
| **20.** | **Domonic Brown, of** | **Phillies** | **$200,000** |
| **21.** | **John Gaub, lhp** | **Indians** | **$155,000** |
| 22. | # Cole Rohrbaugh, lhp | Braves | $675,000 |
| 23. | # Tony Brown, of | Reds | $130,000 |
| 24. | Nick Parasan, ss | Twins | $115,000 |
| **25.** | **# Derek Holland, lhp** | **Rangers** | **$200,000** |
| Other | # Ryan Miller, lhp | Indians (36) | $450,000 |

*Major leaguers in bold. *High school selection. #Signed as draft-and-follow.*

### CUBS SNAG SAMARDZIJA

The Chicago Cubs lost their second-, third- and fourth-round picks for signing major league free agents, and then gambled their fifth-round selection on Notre Dame righthander Jeff Samardzija, a record-breaking wide receiver for the Fighting Irish with aspirations of being selected in the first round of the 2007 NFL draft. The 6-foot-5, 215-pound Samardzija was far from a complete pitcher, but the Cubs loved his power arm, athleticism and makeup. He went 21-6, 3.83 in three college seasons.

Jeff Samardzija

Samardzija was due to report for football practice at Notre Dame on Aug. 1 when the Cubs made a startling announcement: They had an agreement with the pitcher that would allow him to play his senior season of football and then start his pro baseball career. Word leaked that the value of the contract was $7.25 million, which drew the ire of commissioner Bud Selig.

"The whole industry is baffled by it," one scouting director said. "There was debate, to begin with, whether he was even a consensus first-round baseball talent. He's got the body and throws hard, but that's it. He has a long way to go with his secondary stuff and his ability to pitch."

The Cubs contended that Samardzija's contract was conditional on him making baseball his primary sport. Furthermore, they had five years to pay him under baseball's rules for distributing signing bonuses to two-sport players, and the deal was heavily backloaded, with Samardzija receiving just $250,000 up front.

The commissioner's office refused to approve the contract—which included a series of options that would allow Samardzija to earn the full value of $7.25 million if the team picked up each of the annual options—on the grounds that it was a minor league contract in scope. The Cubs didn't want to give him a major league deal, but after his first year in the Cubs system, Samardzija secured his future in baseball by signing a revamped five-year major league contract worth a guaranteed $10 million, with club options for a sixth and seventh years. He also received a full no-trade clause, unprecedented for a player of his experience.

Samardzija remained with the Cubs for seven seasons, going 31-42, 3.97, often alternating electrifying performances with subpar efforts. He then pitched for the Oakland A's and Chicago White Sox for two seasons before signing a five-year, $98 million contract with the San Francisco Giants prior to the 2016 season.

Samardzija wasn't the only surprise in the Cubs' draft. With their 11th-round pick, they drafted Florida high school righthander Chris Huseby, who had pitched fewer than nine innings over his junior and senior seasons while recovering from Tommy John surgery. He got a $1.3 million signing bonus, a record for an 11th-round selection, but didn't come close to justifying the investment. Huseby never fully regained the velocity on his fastball and went 7-13, 3.56 in six seasons in the minors. As a last resort, the Cubs tried him as an outfielder.

Several other teams also made high-risk high school selections in the 11th-round. The Red Sox picked Texas righthander Brandon Belt, the Rockies chose Texas lefthander Aaron Miller, the Pirates drafted North Carolina infielder Lonnie Chisenhall, and the San Diego Padres selected Florida righthander Mat Latos. All were considered first- or second-round material, but slipped because of their bonus demands.

The 11th round was significant because signing bonuses were closely monitored by Major League Baseball only through the first 10 rounds. Clubs felt they were less likely to incur the wrath of the commissioner's office if they paid bonuses that were substantially above slot in later rounds.

"It's not a coincidence," a scouting director said. "The 11th round is off the radar and teams are not as inclined to get the backlash that you get in the first 10 rounds, at least not initially."

The 6-foot-5, 225-pound Latos wanted a $3 million signing bonus. The Padres rejected the demand, and Latos enrolled at Broward (Fla.) JC, enabling him to continue negotiating with San Diego until just before the 2007 draft.

"Outside of (Kyle) Drabek, he had the best high school arm in the draft," one scouting director said. "As an industry, we gave him a number of chances to clean up his act, but he didn't. Between his makeup and some outrageous bonus demands, it cost him."

Latos went 10-3, 2.03 at Broward, showing a mid- to high-90s fastball. Feeling he was worth the gamble, the Padres gave Latos a $1.25 million signing bonus a few days before he would have entered the 2007 draft. It was the largest bonus for a 2006 draft-and-follow player.

Latos irritated his veteran Padres teammates with his abrasive personality when he was first called to the major leagues in 2009, but gained respect as he matured and his pitching ability emerged. He won 14 games on three occasions during his first five seasons. After seven seasons, Latos had a 64-55, 3.51 record, pitching for five different teams.

Righthander Jordan Walden, a 12th-round pick of the Los Angeles Angels, also was a draft-and-follow who signed a seven-figure deal. The hard-throwing Walden was the nation's top high school pitching prospect entering the 2006 season, but rarely flashed the 97-98 mph fastball he had shown previously at Mansfield (Texas) High, and his stock slipped accordingly. Walden enrolled at Grayson County (Texas) CC. The Angels maintained his rights and signed him the following spring for a $1 million bonus.

Walden worked exclusively as a reliever over six major league seasons, posting a 12-14, 3.00 record with 39 saves for three clubs. Both Latos and Walden were still active in 2016.

### KERSHAW EMERGES AS TOP TALENT

While the talent in the 2006 draft was generally panned, particularly at the top of the first round, three of the first 11 selections had combined to win six Cy Young Awards a decade later. Lefthander Clayton Kershaw, drafted seventh overall by the Dodgers and the first high school player selected, won National League Cy Young awards in 2011, '13 and '14. Lincecum won in 2008 and '09, and Scherzer was the American League winner in 2013.

Kershaw posted a 13-0, 0.77 record with 139 strikeouts in 64 innings for Highland Park High in Dallas, but lagged in acclaim behind righthander Kyle Drabek, a son of former Cy Young Award winner Doug Drabek. The younger Drabek helped lead The Woodlands High in suburban Houston to the 5-A state championship and No. 1 ranking nationally, going 14-0, 1.00 with 155 strikeouts in 91 innings. He hit .427 with 12 home runs and 41 RBIs in a lineup that also included future all-star Paul Goldschmidt. Drabek was drafted 18th overall by the Philadelphia Phillies.

After the Dodgers drafted Kershaw, the next pitcher selected was Lincecum, who went to the Giants with the 10th selection. The quick payoff among those two clubs went to the Giants. Lincecum developed into a two-time Cy Young winner while Kershaw, four years younger, was adjusting to the majors.

Kershaw soon blossomed into not just the best pitcher from the 2006 draft, but one of the best starting pitchers in baseball history. He had a 2.70 ERA when he reached 1,000 innings in 2013, the lowest for a starting pitcher at that milestone in baseball's modern era. By the end of the 2015 season, Kershaw had pitched 1,598 innings, and his ERA had dipped to 2.45 (easily the best of any starter of the draft era), along with a 113-56 record and 1,726 strikeouts.

The 5-foot-11, 170-pound Lincecum went 12-4, 1.94 as a junior at Washington and led NCAA pitchers with 199 strikeouts in 125 innings. He lasted until the 10th pick because of concerns about his slight build and unorthodox delivery.

## One Team's Draft: Boston Red Sox

| | Player, Pos. | Bonus |
|---|---|---|
| 1. | * Jason Place, of | $1,300,000 |
| **1.** | **Daniel Bard, rhp** | **$1,550,000** |
| **1.** | **Kris Johnson, lhp** | **$850,000** |
| 1. | * Caleb Clay, rhp | $775,000 |
| **2.** | **Justin Masterson, rhp** | **$510,000** |
| **3.** | **Aaron Bates, 1b** | **$440,000** |
| 3. | Bryce Cox, rhp | $250,000 |
| 4. | Jon Still, c | $225,000 |
| **5.** | **Dustin Richardson, lhp** | **$107,000** |
| 6. | Zach Daeges, 3b | $30,000 |
| **7.** | **Kris Negron, ss** | **$105,000** |
| 8. | * Rafael Cabreja, of | $65,000 |
| **9.** | *** Ryan Kalish, of** | **$600,000** |
| 10. | * Kyle Snyder, rhp | Did not sign |
| **11.** | *** Brandon Belt, of/lhp** | **Did not sign** |
| 12. | Ryan Khoury, ss | $5,000 |
| 13. | Jordan Craft, rhp | $50,000 |
| **14.** | **Matt LaPorta, 1b** | **Did not sign** |
| 15. | Jorge Jiminez, 3b | $15,000 |
| 16. | * Tyler Weeden, c | $420,000 |
| **17.** | **Josh Reddick, of** | **$140,000** |
| **18.** | *** Lars Anderson, 1b** | **$825,000** |
| 19. | Richie Lentz, rhp | $150,000 |
| 20. | * Kyle Gilligan, ss | Did not sign |
| 21. | Brian Steinocher, rhp | $50,000 |
| 22. | Mike Christl, rhp | Did not sign |
| 23. | Paul Smyth, of | $1,000 |
| 24. | Robert Phares, rhp | Did not sign |
| 25. | Sean Gleason, rhp | Did not sign |
| Other | Darren Blocker (36), 3b | $100,000 |

*Major leaguers in bold. *High school selection.*

### WORTH NOTING

playing professionally until instructional league in the fall. He spent four years in the organization, beginning in 2007, and did not advance beyond Rookie ball.

■ The Giants signed third baseman **ANGEL VILLALONA** for a $2.1 million bonus, a record for a player from the Dominican Republic, and the largest bonus for an international player in 2006. By comparison, the Athletics spent a total of $1,982,500 in signing bonuses. Villalona was one of five international players who received a bonus of at least $1 million.

■ Teams emphasized pitching early in the first round of the 2006 draft, and hitters were selected in increasing numbers as the round progressed. The Astros took Florida high school catcher **MAX SAPP** with the 23rd overall pick. The 6-foot-2, 220-pound Sapp was drafted for his considerable offensive potential, after hitting .591 with 10 homers and 48 RBIs as a senior at Orlando's Bishop Moore High. He had begun catching only a year earlier, and though he was not overly agile, Sapp had impressive arm strength and improving receiving skills. After struggling to hit in his first two seasons of pro ball (.237-3-52 in 136 games), Sapp was limited to 74 games in 2008 at Class A Lexington because of a series of afflictions, including a chronic sinus condition that soon threatened his life. In December 2008, Sapp contracted viral meningitis. He endured as many as 20 seizures when the membranes surrounding his brain and spinal cord swelled, and some were so violent that he had to be strapped into his bed for his safety. Sapp stopped breathing three times during a monthlong stay at a Florida hospital, and when he awoke from a medically induced coma, he had forgotten parts of the past two years. Sapp recovered, but his baseball career was finished. He was one of seven first-rounders who failed to reach the majors.

**IN FOCUS: CLAYTON KERSHAW**

After Clayton Kershaw posted a 13-0, 0.77 record with 139 strikeouts in 64 innings as a senior for Dallas' Highland Park High, Dodgers scouting director Logan White realized his chances of landing the lefthander in the 2006 draft were slim. The Dodgers had the seventh pick overall, and the two players at the top of their board were Kershaw and Long Beach State third baseman Evan Longoria.

On the eve of the draft, White went to Texas for one last look at Kershaw. He also scouted University of Houston righthander Brad Lincoln. Lincoln dominated in his start. The next day, Kershaw had his worst game of the season.

"He threw really poor," White said. "The leadoff hitter hit a home run. He was wild. His breaking ball was all over the place. He battled and won the game, 8-2 or 8-3. I was really excited. The teams picking in front of us were there. That was a big help. Lincoln threw really well. Kershaw didn't."

The Tigers, picking sixth, were the only team ahead of the Dodgers in the drafting order that seriously considered taking Kershaw. Instead, they chose University of North Carolina lefthander Andrew Miller, the consensus best prospect. The Dodgers happily took Kershaw with the next pick. "We were hoping and praying Clayton would get to us," White said.

## Highest Unsigned Picks

| Player, Pos., Team (Round) | College | Re-Drafted |
|---|---|---|
| Sean Black, rhp, Nationals (2) | Seton Hall | Yankees '09 (7) |
| Nick Fuller, rhp, Devil Rays (3) | South Carolina | Braves '08 (25) |
| Russ Moldenhauer, of, Angels (3) | Texas | Nationals '10 (24) |
| Devin Shepherd, of, Twins (5) | Oklahoma | Cardinals '08 (11) |
| Tim Bascom, rhp, Padres (6) | * Central Florida | Orioles '07 (4) |
| Sam Brown, rhp, Nationals (7) | N.C. State | D-backs '08 (18) |
| Mike Leake, rhp, Athletics (7) | Arizona State | Reds '09 (1) |
| Jarrad Page, of, Angels (7) | None | Never |
| Cole Figueroa, ss, Blue Jays (9) | Florida | Padres '08 (6) |
| Jeremy Barfield, of, Mets (9) | San Jacinto (Texas) JC | Athletics '08 (8) |

**TOTAL UNSIGNED PICKS:** Top 5 Rounds (3), Top 10 Rounds (16)

**Returned to same school.*

Even the hometown Mariners, with the fifth pick, passed on Lincecum in favor of Morrow, another college righthander.

Lincecum blew through the minors, going 6-0, 1.00 with 104 strikeouts in 63 innings in 13 starts. He earned the first of his two Cy Young Awards in his second year after being drafted, and was part of three World Series champions with the Giants.

Scherzer, despite his lengthy holdout, made a quick ascent to the majors after striking out 185 in 144 innings in 30 minor league appearances. His tenure with the Diamondbacks lasted only two years, amid concern by some in the organization that his violent delivery would lead to arm problems or limit him to a relief role. Arizona traded Scherzer to the Tigers after the 2009 season, and he emerged as one of the top pitchers in the majors. He went 21-3, 2.90 with 240 strikeouts in 214 innings in 2013, his Cy Young-winning season.

Max Scherzer

Longoria, the 2005 Cape Cod League MVP and the successor to Troy Tulowitzki as the shortstop at Long Beach State, became the most productive position player drafted in 2006. He impressed scouts with his advanced skills, both offensively and defensively, and made an immediate impact in Tampa Bay after reaching the majors in 2008. He became a three-time all-star, two-time Gold Glove winner, and the franchise leader in homers and RBIs.

### FIRST-ROUND FAILURES

The talent in the first round thinned out considerably after Kershaw, Lincecum, Longoria and Scherzer. Several highly ranked players fell far short of expectations, including Hochevar, who at least developed into a reliable relief pitcher. Reynolds and Lincoln also didn't fare as well as expected.

The 6-foot-7 Reynolds was best known in high school for his football skills as a quarterback, and he had a modest 13-10, 4.11 record in three years on the Stanford baseball team. Reynolds' fastball reached the mid-90s but lacked movement, and he was far from a polished pitcher when he was drafted.

Reynolds missed most of the 2007 season because of a shoulder injury. The Rockies, determined to get a return on their investment, promoted him to the majors after just 32 starts in the minors. Reynolds went 2-8, 8.13 in 2008, and his career never materialized after nagging arm issues. He went 6-11, 7.02 in three seasons in the majors.

Lincoln went 4-7, 4.76 as a sophomore at Houston, then improved dramatically a year later, going 12-2, 1.69 with 152 strikeouts in 127 innings. He also hit .295 with 14 homers as a DH.

Despite his 5-foot-11, 180-pound frame, Lincoln won over scouts with his lively mid-90s fastball, late-breaking curve and fierce competitive spirit. However, Lincoln's career was derailed by injuries, including Tommy John surgery that cost him the 2007 season and much of 2008. He reached Pittsburgh in 2010, but never made his mark, going 7-9, 4.61 in parts of three seasons.

Billy Rowell, selected ninth by the Baltimore Orioles, was the first high school position player drafted, and the highest-chosen first-rounder who did not reach the majors. Rowell was tagged as a "can't-miss" prospect after hitting .541 as a senior at a New Jersey high school and then debuting in the Orioles system by hitting .328 in 2006 while transitioning from shortstop to third base.

The wheels started coming off Rowell's promising career when he was reluctant to listen to Orioles instructors who wanted to modify his batting stance and swing path, and his power never emerged. He also had problems on defense, prompting two more position switches, and was suspended twice for drug-related issues. Rowell spent seven seasons in the Orioles system, but played in only 41 games above Class A.

Eighteen of the 30 first-round selections were pitchers, just short of the draft record of 20, set in 2001.

Drabek was among the most celebrated pitchers in the class. Some scouts said he had the best pure stuff among prep pitchers. His fastball reached 96 mph, and he threw a hard-to-hit, low-80s curveball. He slid to the Phillies with the 18th pick overall because of concerns about his fiery temper and maturity. Drabek's climb through the Phillies system was interrupted in 2007 by Tommy John surgery, and he later was traded to the Toronto Blue Jays in a deal that sent all-star pitcher Roy Halladay to the Phillies. Drabek's career stalled again in 2012 when he had a second Tommy John surgery.

## Largest Draft-And-Follow Bonuses

| | Player, Pos. | Club (Round) | Bonus |
|---|---|---|---|
| **1.** | *** Mat Latos, rhp** | **Padres (11)** | **$1,250,000** |
| **2.** | *** Jordan Walden, rhp** | **Angels (12)** | **$1,000,000** |
| 3. | Cole Rohrbaugh, lhp | Braves (22) | $675,000 |
| 4. | * Lee Haydel, of | Brewers (19) | $624,000 |
| 5. | * Chad Robinson, rhp | Brewers (12) | $500,000 |
| 6. | Ryan Miller, lhp | Indians (36) | $450,000 |
| **7.** | *** Rudy Owens, lhp** | **Pirates (28)** | **$390,000** |
| 8. | * Rob Bryson, rhp | Brewers (31) | $300,000 |
| **9.** | **Derek Holland, lhp** | **Rangers (25)** | **$200,000** |
| 10. | Sergio Morales, of | White Sox (12) | $180,000 |
| | Jovan Rosa, 3b | Cubs (22) | $180,000 |

*Major leaguers in bold. *High school selection.*

# 2006 Draft List

**Did not sign. Major leaguers in bold, with first and last years noted. Order of selection indicated in parentheses. For the first five rounds, the peak level of each player is noted. + Signed as draft-and-follow (Second school noted if applicable).*

## ARIZONA DIAMONDBACKS (11)

1. **Max Scherzer, rhp, University of Missouri.—(2008-15)**
1. **Brooks Brown, rhp, University of Georgia** (Supplemental choice—34th—as compensation for Type A free agent Tim Worrell).—**(2014-15)**
2. **Brett Anderson, lhp, Stillwater (Okla.) HS.—(2009-15)**
3. Dallas Buck, rhp, Oregon State University (Choice from Giants as compensation for Worrell).—(AA)
3. Cyle Hankerd, of, University of Southern California.—(AAA)
4. Bryant Thompson, rhp, Pensacola (Fla.) JC.—(Short-season A)
5. **Hector Ambriz, rhp, UCLA.—(2010-14)**
6. Joey Side, of, University of Georgia.
7. **Daniel Stange, rhp, UC Riverside.—(2010-13)**
8. Chase Christianson, rhp, University of South Alabama.
9. Eddie Romero, lhp, Fresno State University.
10. Tony Barnette, rhp, Arizona State University.
11. Daniel Fournier, rhp, Franklin Pierce (N.H.) College.
12. Andrew Fie, 3b, Trinity Christian Academy, Jacksonville, Fla.
13. **John Hester, c, Stanford University.—(2009-13)**
14. **Chad Beck, rhp, University of Louisiana-Lafayette.—(2011-12)**

**DRAFT DROP** *Brother of Casey Beck, eighth-round draft pick, Braves (2006)*

15. Matt Oxendine, ss, University of North Florida.
16. Blake Sharpe, 2b, University of Southern California.
17. Bret Reynolds, rhp, University of Missouri.
18. Brad Miller, 1b, Ball State University.
19. Tyler Jones, of, University of South Alabama.
20. *Enrique Garcia, rhp, Potomac State (W.Va.) JC.
21. Sean Smith, 2b, UCLA.
22. Danny Perales, of, University of Southern California.
23. Derrick Walker, of, Wabash Valley (Ill.) JC.
24. Andrew Beshenich, of, Norristown (Pa.) HS.
25. Shane Byrne, of, East Tennessee State University.
26. *Frank Corolla, rhp, Magnolia HS, Pinehurst, Texas.
27. Connor Janes, of, University of British Columbia.
28. Shea McFeely, 3b, Oregon State University.
29. *Drew Hayes, ss-rhp, McKenzie (Tenn.) HS.
30. **Clay Zavada, lhp, Southern Illinois University-Edwardsville.—(2009)**
31. *Kiel Roling, c, Central Arizona JC.
32. *Osmany Masso, ss, Miami Beach, Fla.
33. Osbek Castillo, rhp, Encino, Calif.
34. Tito Cruz, c, Long Beach State University.
35. *Casey Whitmer, rhp, Kilgore (Texas) HS.
36. *Jason Durst, rhp, Lake Sumter (Fla.) CC.
37. *Tyler Kmetko, 2b, University of Utah.
38. *Michael Guerrero, of, Meridian (Miss.) CC.
39. *Riley Etchebarren, of, Paradise Valley HS, Phoenix.

**DRAFT DROP** *Nephew of Andy Etchebarren, major leaguer (1962-78)*

40. *Nick Cejka, c, Columbia Basin (Wash.) CC.
41. *Quinton Marsh, lhp, Wickenburg (Ariz.) HS.
42. *Sean Coughlin, c, University of Kentucky.
43. *Jason Stidham, ss, Melbourne HS, Palm Bay, Fla.
44. Justin Brashear, c, University of Mississippi.
45. +Clay Conner, 3b, Okaloosa-Walton (Fla.) CC / Lurleen B. Wallace (Ala.) CC.
46. *Rene Garcia, rhp, Pima (Ariz.) CC.
47. *David Mixon, rhp, University of Louisiana-Monroe.
48. *Mike Solbach, rhp, Liberty University.
49. *Dominic Piazza, c, Notre Dame HS, Scottsdale, Ariz.
50. *Kendal Volz, rhp, Smithson Valley HS, Bulverde, Texas.

## ATLANTA BRAVES (24)

1. Cody Johnson, of, Mosley HS, Panama City, Fla.—(AAA)
1. **Cory Rasmus, rhp, Russell County HS, Phenix City, Ala.** (Supplemental choice—38th—as compensation for Type A free agent Kyle Farnsworth).—**(2013-15)**

**DRAFT DROP** *Brother of Colby Rasmus, first-round draft pick, Cardinals (2005); major leaguer (2009-15)*

1. Steve Evarts, lhp, Robinson HS, Tampa (Supplemental choice—43rd—as compensation for Type A free agent Rafael Furcal).—(Low AA)
2. **Jeff Locke, lhp, Kennett HS, Center Conway, N.H.** (Choice from Dodgers as compensation for Furcal).—**(2011-15)**
2. Dustin Evans, rhp, Georgia Southern University.—(AA)
2. Chase Fontaine, ss, Daytona Beach (Fla.) CC (Choice from Yankees as compensation for Farnsworth).—(High A)
3. Chad Rodgers, lhp, Walsh Jesuit HS, Stow, Ohio.—(High A)
4. Lee Hyde, lhp, Georgia Tech.—(AAA)
5. Kevin Gunderson, lhp, Oregon State University.—(AAA)

**DRAFT DROP** *Nephew of Eric Gunderson, major leaguer (1990-2000).*

6. Steve Figueroa, rhp, Edgewater HS, Orlando, Fla.
7. Adam Coe, 3b, Russell County HS, Phenix City, Ala.
8. Casey Beck, rhp, San Jacinto (Texas) JC.

**DRAFT DROP** *Brother of Chad Beck, 14th-round draft pick, Diamondbacks (2006)*

9. Tim Gustafson, rhp, Georgia Tech.
10. **Kris Medlen, rhp, Santa Ana (Calif.) JC.—(2009-15)**
11. Mikey Mehlich, rhp, Bishop Moore HS, Casselberry, Fla.
12. Josh Morris, 1b, University of Georgia.
13. Joe Johnson, rhp, Louisburg (N.C.) JC.
14. +Matt Small, rhp, Ipswich (Mass.) HS / Lake City (Fla.) CC.
15. +Stephen Shults, 3b, Walters State (Tenn.) JC.
16. *Jack Tilghman, rhp, Walters State (Tenn.) JC.
17. +Clay McMillan, lhp, Texarkana (Texas) CC / Panola (Texas) JC.
18. *J.B. Paxson, c, Walters State (Tenn.) CC.
19. **Deunte Heath, rhp, University of Tennessee.—(2012-13)**
20. *Jonathan Cluff, of, Bingham HS, South Jordan, Utah.
21. *Jordan Brown, rhp, Meridian (Miss.) CC.
22. +Cole Rohrbough, lhp, Western Nevada CC.
23. *Blake Guthrie, c, Louisburg (N.C.) CC.
24. *Zac Oliver, lhp, Paris (Texas) JC.
25. *Kyle Witten, rhp, Liberty HS, Bakersfield, Calif.
26. Ryne Reynoso, rhp, Boston College.
27. *Jacob Rodriguez, rhp, Whittier (Calif.) HS.
28. *Adam Milligan, of, Hardin County HS, Savannah, Tenn.
29. *Andy Dunn, rhp, John A. Logan (Ill.) JC.
30. +David Berres, of, South Suburban (Ill.) JC.
31. +Eric Barrett, lhp, John A. Logan (Ill.) JC.
32. *Brendon Porch, rhp, East Union HS, Blue Springs, Miss.
33. *Jordan Poirrier, ss, Riverside Academy, Reserve, La.
34. *Matt Morgal, rhp, Seminole State (Okla.) CC.
35. *Areyo Fleming, rhp, Central HS, Baton Rouge, La.
36. *Sampson Williams, of, Laney HS, Wilmington, N.C.
37. *Eric Broberg, 1b, Bishop Moore HS, Sanford, Fla.
38. *Josh Ashton, of, Rose HS, Greenville, N.C.
39. *Danny Davidson, rhp, Southern Union State (Ala.) JC.
40. *Tyreace House, of, Palmdale (Calif.) HS.
41. *Keegan Dennis, rhp, White County HS, Carmi, Ill.
42. *Ralph West, lhp, Gar-Field HS, Stafford, Va.
43. +L.V. Ware, of, Okaloosa-Walton (Fla.) JC.
44. *Kris Cichoski, rhp, CC of Southern Nevada.
45. ***Mason Tobin, rhp, Western Nevada CC.—(2011)**
46. *Tyler Musselwhite, rhp, Chipola (Fla.) JC.
47. *John Kessick, rhp, Lake Michigan JC.
48. *Travis Tucker, 2b, McLennan (Texas) JC.
49. *Blake Holt, of, Temple (Texas) JC.
50. *Matt Jordan, lhp, Hinds (Miss.) CC.

## BALTIMORE ORIOLES (9)

1. Billy Rowell, ss, Bishop Eustace Prep, Sewell, N.J.—(AA)
1. **Pedro Beato, rhp, St. Petersburg (Fla.) CC** (Supplemental choice—32nd—as compensation for Type A free agent B.J. Ryan).—**(2011-14)**
2. (Choice to Padres as compensation for Type A free agent Ramon Hernandez)
2. **Ryan Adams, ss, Jesuit HS, Mandeville, La.** (Choice from Blue Jays as compensation for Ryan).—**(2011)**
3. **Zach Britton, lhp, Weatherford (Texas) HS.—(2011-15)**
4. **Blake Davis, ss, Cal State Fullerton.—(2011)**
5. Tyler Henson, ss, Tuttle (Okla.) HS.—(AAA)
6. **Jason Berken, rhp, Clemson University.—(2009-12)**
7. Josh Tamba, rhp, Cypress (Calif.) JC.
8. Jedidiah Stephen, ss, Ohio State University.
9. Brett Bordes, lhp, Arizona State University.
10. *Emeel Salem, of, University of Alabama.
11. Anthony Martinez, 1b, Louisburg (N.C.) JC.
12. Brandon Tripp, of, Cal State Fullerton.
13. Ryan Ouellette, rhp, Indian River (Fla.) CC.
14. Brent Allar, rhp, Texas Christian University.
15. +Dustin Black, c, Cleveland State (Tenn.) CC.
16. Justin Johnson, c, University of Illinois-Chicago.
17. ***Tony Watson, lhp, University of Nebraska.—(2011-15)**
18. Nathan Nery, lhp, Stetson University.
19. Todd Davison, ss, University of Delaware.
20. Zach Dillon, c, Baylor University.
21. Luis Lopez, of, Cadilla de Martinez HS, Arecibo, P.R.
22. +Chris Salberg, lhp, Florida Atlantic University.
23. Aubrey Miller, rhp, Arkansas Tech.
24. Josh Faiola, rhp, Dartmouth University.
25. *Donald Anderson, rhp, Southwestern (Calif.) CC.
26. *Kipp Schutz, of, Harrison HS, Evansville, Ind.
27. Zach Jevne, rhp, University of Northern Iowa.
28. Michael Pierce, c, Fresno Pacific (Calif.) University.
29. *Brandon Kimbrel, rhp, Cameron-Yoe HS, Cameron, Texas.
30. *Chris Cassidy, lhp, Riverside (Calif.) CC.
31. *Zach Gerler, ss, Francis Howell Central HS, St. Charles, Mo.
32. *B.J. Dail, rhp, Millbrook HS, Raleigh, N.C.
33. +Drew Conklin, rhp, South Mountain (Ariz.) CC.
34. *Tyler Blandford, rhp, Daviess County HS, Owensboro, Ky.
35. *Matt Drummond, lhp, Paso Robles (Calif.) HS.
36. +Patrick Egan, rhp, Quinnipiac University.
37. *Michael Lane, of, Daviess County HS, Owensboro, Ky.
38. *Adam Urnberg, rhp, JC of Southern Idaho.
39. *Neal Davis, lhp, Catonsville HS, Baltimore.
40. Dave Cash, 2b, University of Florida.

**DRAFT DROP** *Son of Dave Cash, major leaguer (1969-80)*

41. *Scott Migl, rhp, St. Pius X HS, Houston.
42. *Jordan Durrance, lhp, Sierra HS, Manteca, Calif.
43. +Jose Kianes, of, Martin County HS, Stuart, Fla. / Palm Beach (Fla.) CC.
44. *Travis Lamar, rhp, Harrison HS, Evansville, Ind.
45. *Isaiah Stanback, of, University of Washington.

**DRAFT DROP** *Tight end, National Football League (2007-12)*

46. *Vinny DiFazio, c, Indian River (Fla.) CC.
47. *Troy Burki, lhp, Gig Harbor (Wash.) HS.
48. +Jason Mills, rhp, George Mason University / Kutztown (Pa.) University.
49. *Dan Watson, rhp, Manatee HS, Bradenton, Fla.
50. *Orlando Rodriguez, c, Heriberto Domenech HS, Isabela, P.R.

## BOSTON RED SOX (27)

1. Jason Place, of, Wren HS, Easley, S.C.—(AA)
1. **Daniel Bard, rhp, University of North Carolina** (Choice from Yankees as compensation for Type A free agent Johnny Damon).—**(2009-13)**
1. **Kris Johnson, lhp, Wichita State University** (Supplemental choice—40th—as compensation for Damon).—**(2013-14)**
1. Caleb Clay, rhp, Cullman (Ala.) HS (Supplemental choice—44th—as compensation for Type A free agent Bill Mueller).—(AAA)
2. **Justin Masterson, rhp, San Diego State University.—(2008-15)**
3. **Aaron Bates, 1b, North Carolina State University** (Choice from Dodgers as compensation for Mueller).—**(2009)**
3. Bryce Cox, rhp, Rice University.—(AA)
4. Jon Still, c, North Carolina State University.—(AA)
5. **Dustin Richardson, lhp, Texas Tech.—(2009-10)**
6. Zach Daeges, 3b, Creighton University.
7. **Kris Negron, ss, Cosumnes River (Calif.) JC.—(2012-15)**
8. Rafael Cabreja, of, James Monroe HS, New York.
9. **Ryan Kalish, of, Red Bank Catholic HS, Shrewsbury, N.J.—(2010-14)**
10. *Kyle Snyder, rhp, Wellington (Fla.) Community HS.
11. ***Brandon Belt, of-lhp, Hudson HS, Lufkin, Texas.—(2011-15)**
12. Ryan Khoury, ss, University of Utah.
13. Jordan Craft, rhp, Dallas Baptist University.
14. ***Matt LaPorta, 1b, University of Florida.—(2009-12)**

**DRAFT DROP** *First-round draft pick (7th overall), Brewers (2007)*

15. Jorge Jimenez, 3b, Porterville (Calif.) JC.
16. Tyler Weeden, c, Edmond Santa Fe HS, Edmond, Okla.
17. **Josh Reddick, of, Middle Georgia JC.—(2009-15)**
18. **Lars Anderson, 1b, Jesuit HS, Fair Oaks, Calif.—(2010-12)**
19. Richie Lentz, rhp, University of Washington.

**DRAFT DROP** *Son of Mike Lentz, first-round draft pick, Padres (1975)*

20. *Kyle Gilligan, ss, Etobicoke Collegiate Institute, Toronto.
21. Brian Steinocher, rhp, Stephen F. Austin University.
22. *Mike Christl, rhp, Bradley University.
23. Paul Smyth, of, San Diego State University.
24. *Robert Phares, rhp, Shelton State (Ala.) CC.
25. *Sean Gleason, rhp, Lamar (Colo.) CC.
26. *Chad Gross, 1b, Claremont (Calif.) HS.

**DRAFT DROP** *Son of Kevin Gross, major leaguer (1983-97)*

27. +Brantley New, rhp, Mercer University.
28. *Carmine Giardina, lhp, Durant HS, Valrico, Fla.
29. *Devin Foreman, 1b, Hales Franciscan HS, Chicago.
30. Ryne Lawson, rhp, University of West Alabama.
31. ***Logan Shafer, of, Cuesta (Calif.) JC.—(2011-15)**
32. Michael Chambers, 2b, Franklin Pierce (N.H.) College.
33. *Jeff Rea, 2b, Mississippi State University.
34. *Bryan Morgado, lhp, Florida Christian HS, Miami.
35. *Jeremy Rahman, of, Hazelwood Central HS, Florissant, Mo.
36. +Darren Blocker, 3b, Connors State (Okla.) JC.
37. ***Justin Marks, lhp, Owensboro Catholic HS, Owensboro, Ky.—(2014)**
38. Travis Beazley, rhp, Randolph-Macon (Va.) College.
39. *Jordan Abruzzo, c, University of San Diego.
40. *Corey Davisson, c, West HS, Bakersfield, Calif.
41. *Peter Tountas, ss, Jefferson (Mo.) JC.
42. *Troy Graybill, lhp, Sarasota (Fla.) HS.
43. Jeff Vincent, of, Niagara University.
44. *Andrew Leary, rhp, Sierra Vista HS, Las Vegas, Nev.
45. *Jake McCarter, rhp, University of Alabama.
46. *Junior Rodriguez, 3b, Coral Gables HS, Miami.
47. *Nick Hill, lhp, U.S. Military Academy.
48. Josh Papelbon, rhp, University of North Florida.

**DRAFT DROP** *Brother of Jonathan Papelbon, major leaguer (2005-14) • Brother of Jeremy Papelbon, 19th-round draft pick, Cubs (2006)*

49. *P.J. Thomas, rhp, Wabash Valley (Ill.) JC.
50. Darrell Fisherbaugh, rhp, University of Hawaii.

## CHICAGO CUBS (13)

1. **Tyler Colvin, of, Clemson University.—(2009-14)**
2. (Choice to Indians as compensation for Type A

free agent Bobby Howry)
3. (Choice to Giants as compensation for Type A free agent Scott Eyre)
4. (Choice to Twins as compensation for Type B free agent Jacque Jones)
**5. Jeff Samardzija, rhp, University of Notre Dame.—(2008-15)**
6. Josh Lansford, 3b, Cal Poly San Luis Obispo.
DRAFT DROP *Son of Carney Lansford, major leaguer (1978-92)*
**7. Steve Clevenger, ss, Chipola (Fla.) JC.—(2011-15)**
8. Billy Muldowney, rhp, University of Pittsburgh.
9. Cliff Anderson, of, Cottonwood HS, Sandy, Utah.
10. Jake Renshaw, rhp, Ventura (Calif.) JC.
11. Chris Huseby, rhp, Martin County HS, Palm City, Fla.
12. Kitt Kopach, rhp, Illinois State University.
13. Matt Camp, of, North Carolina State University.
14. Drew Rundle, of, Bend (Ore.) HS.
15. Matt Canepa, c, Cal Poly San Luis Obispo.
**16. Blake Parker, c-3b, University of Arkansas.—(2012-14)**
17. *Keoni Ruth, 2b, University of San Diego.
18. *Jose Hernandez, rhp, Edgewater HS, Orlando, Fla.
19. Jeremy Papelbon, lhp, University of North Florida.
DRAFT DROP *Brother of Jonathan Papelbon, major leaguer (2005-14) • Brother of Josh Papelbon, 48th-round draft pick, Red Sox (2006)*
20. Kevin Kreier, rhp, Foothill HS, Henderson, Nev.
21. Taylor Parker, lhp, University of Missouri.
22. +Jovan Rosa, 3b, Lake City (Fla.) CC.
23. Chuckie Platt, rhp, Lamar University.
24. Matt Matulia, ss, The Citadel.
25. *Jamie Bagley, rhp, Hargrave HS, Humble, Texas.
26. Michael Cooper, rhp, University of California.
27. +Cedric Redmond, rhp, Joliet Township HS, Joliet, Ill. / Oakton (Ill.) CC.
28. +Brett Summers, rhp, South Suburban (Ill.) JC.
29. +Jordan Latham, rhp, JC of Southern Idaho.
30. Donny Walters, rhp, Richland (Texas) JC.
31. *Bryan Collins, rhp, Alvin (Texas) CC.
32. Cesar Valentin, ss, Catalina Morales HS, Moca, P.R.
33. Brad Clipp, rhp, Point Loma Nazarene (Calif.) University.
34. Nate Samson, ss, Ocala Forest HS, Ocala, Fla.
35. *Marquez Smith, 3b, Clemson University.
36. Miguel Cuevas-Novas, rhp, Los Angeles Pierce JC.
37. *David Francis, rhp, St. Joseph SS, Mississauga, Ontario.
38. *Ben Feltner, of, Temple (Texas) JC.
**39. +Marcus Hatley, of, Mission Hills HS, San Marcos, Calif. / Palomar (Calif.) CC.—(2015)**
40. Eli Diaz, rhp, Texarkana (Texas) JC.
41. *Jonathan Negron, rhp, Puerto Rico Baseball Academy, Guaynabo, P.R.
42. *Ben Ornelas, of, Cypress (Calif.) JC.
43. *Anthony Morel, ss, Riverside (Calif.) CC.
44. *Daniel Berlind, rhp, Calabasas (Calif.) HS.
45. *Elliot Shea, of, Franklin Pierce (N.H.) College.
46. *Ryan Shook, lhp, Valley Christian Academy, Antelope, Calif.
47. Andrew McCormick, rhp, Pikeville (Ky.) College.
48. *Kenneth Goodline, rhp, North Monterey County HS, Castroville, Calif.
49. Ryne Malone, 3b, Florida State University.
50. *Ryan Davis, lhp, Eastlake HS, Sammamish, Wash.

## CHICAGO WHITE SOX (29)

1. Kyle McCulloch, rhp, University of Texas.—(AAA)
2. Matt Long, rhp, Miami (Ohio) University.—(AAA)
3. Justin Edwards, lhp, Olympia HS, Orlando, Fla.—(AA)
4. Tyler Reves, c, Texas Tech.—(High A)
5. John Shelby, 2b-of, University of Kentucky.—(AAA)
DRAFT DROP *Son of Johnny Shelby, major leaguer (1981-91)*
**6. Brian Omogrosso, rhp, Indiana State University.—(2012-13)**
7. Justin Cassel, rhp, UC Irvine.
DRAFT DROP *Brother of Jack Cassel, major leaguer (2007-08) • Brother of Matt Cassel, quarterback, National Football League (2005-15)*
8. Kent Gerst, of, Fort Zumwalt West HS, O'Fallon, Mo.
9. *Chris Duffy, 3b, Cypress Creek HS, Orlando, Fla.
10. Lee Cruz, of, University of Tampa.
11. Andrew Urena, rhp, Mercer University.
12. +Sergio Morales, of, Broward (Fla.) CC.
13. Tyson Corley, rhp, South Mountain (Ariz.) CC.
14. Mike Grace, 1b, Florida Southern College.
15. *Yasser Clor, rhp, Wilcox HS, Cupertino, Calif.
16. *Jose Jimenez, 3b, Monsignor Pace HS, Hialeah Gardens, Fla.
17. Kylee Hash, c, Basic HS, Henderson, Nev.
**18. *Lucas Luetge, lhp, San Jacinto (Texas) CC.—(2012-15)**
19. *Jeff Dunbar, c, UC Riverside.
20. *Wade Kapteyn, rhp, Illiana Christian HS, Lansing, Ill.
21. Matt Inouye, c, University of Hawaii.
**22. Kanekoa Texeira, rhp, Saddleback (Calif.) CC.—(2010-11)**
23. *Brandon Villalobos, lhp, Chaffey (Calif.) JC.
24. Michael Rocco, rhp, Cal State San Bernardino.
25. Joe Hunter, of, Mississippi State University.
26. David Wasylak, rhp, Lubbock Christian (Texas) University.
27. *Tyler Herriage, lhp, Marcus HS, Lewisville, Texas.
28. +Jedon Matthews, 3b, Horizon Christian HS, San Diego / San Diego CC.
29. Garrett Johnson, lhp, Orme School, Mayer, Ariz.
**30. +Hector Santiago, lhp, Bloomfield Vocational Tech, Newark, N.J. / Okaloosa-Walton (Fla.) CC.—(2011-15)**
31. Stefan Gartrell, of, University of San Francisco.
32. *Alex Curry, rhp, Canyon HS, Anaheim Hills, Calif.
33. *Chris Ulrey, of, New Palestine HS, Greenfield, Ind.
34. *Tyler Wright, of, South Florida CC.
35. *Adam Heisler, of, Baker HS, Mobile, Ala.
36. Matt Enuco, 2b, Rowan (N.J.) University.
37. *Adan Severino, of, Broward (Fla.) CC.
**38. *Jacob Petricka, rhp, Faribault (Minn.) HS.—(2013-15)**
39. *Clint Cisper, rhp, Northeastern State (Okla.) University.
40. Andrew Mead, of, SUNY Cortland.
41. *Mike Bolsenbroek, rhp, Santa Ana (Calif.) JC.
42. *Jose Jackson, 2b, South Florida CC.
43. +Jordan Cheatham, of, Pike HS, Indianapolis, Ind. / Wabash Valley (Ill.) CC.
44. *Andy Fernandez, rhp, Hialeah (Fla.) HS.
45. *Raul Duran, of, Saddleback HS, Santa Ana, Calif.
46. *Michael Cerda, 3b, Beyer HS, Modesto, Calif.
47. *Kyle Williams, 2b, Chaparral HS, Paradise Valley, Ariz.
DRAFT DROP *Son of Kenny Williams, major leaguer (1986-91); general manager, White Sox (2000-12) • Sixth-round draft pick, San Francisco 49ers/ National Football League (2010); wide receiver, NFL (2010-13)*
48. *Rafael Reyes, c, Palmer Trinity HS, Miami.
49. *Rafael Vera, 2b, Manatee (Fla.) JC.
50. Brendon O'Donnell, of, University of Texas-Permian Basin.

## CINCINNATI REDS (8)

**1. Drew Stubbs, of, University of Texas.—(2009-15)**
DRAFT DROP *Brother of Clint Stubbs, 49th-round draft pick, Rangers (2006)*
2. Sean Watson, rhp, University of Tennessee.—(AAA)
**3. Chris Valaika, ss, UC Santa Barbara.—(2010-14)**
4. Justin Reed, of, Hillcrest Christian HS, Jackson, Miss.—(High A)
**5. Josh Ravin, rhp, Chatsworth HS, Tarzana, Calif.—(2015)**
**6. Jordan Smith, rhp, CC of Southern Nevada.—(2010-11)**
**7. Justin Turner, 2b, Cal State Fullerton.—(2009-15)**
8. Travis Webb, lhp, Washington State University.
9. Jeremy Burchett, rhp, University of California.
**10. Josh Roenicke, rhp, UCLA.—(2008-13)**
DRAFT DROP *Son of Gary Roenicke, first-round draft pick, Expos (1973); major leaguer (1976-88) • Nephew of Ron Roenicke, major leaguer (1981-88); major league manager (2011-15)*
11. Brandon Rice, rhp, Spalding HS, Griffin, Ga.
12. Logan Parker, 1b, University of Cincinnati.
13. Kevin Gunter, rhp, Old Dominion University.
14. Carson Kainer, of, University of Texas.
15. Rafael Sanchez, 3b, Queensborough (N.Y.) CC.
16. Jamie Arneson, lhp, Bakersfield (Calif.) JC.
**17. Chris Heisey, of, Messiah (Pa.) College.—(2010-15)**
18. *Ryan Wehrle, ss, University of Nebraska.
19. Derrik Lutz, rhp, George Washington University.
**20. Eddy Rodriguez, c, University of Miami.—(2012)**
21. Chris White, rhp, Texas A&M University-Kingsville.
22. Adam Pointer, rhp, Alvin (Texas) CC.
23. +Tony Brown, of, Crestview (Fla.) HS / Okaloosa-Walton (Fla.) CC.
24. Anthony Esquer, c, Cal Poly Pomona.
25. Michael McKennon, of, University of Texas-San Antonio.
26. Anthony Gressick, rhp, Ohio University.
27. Kel Jones, of, Darton (Ga.) JC.
28. Tyler Hauschild, c, Edmonds (Wash.) JC.
29. Jason Louwsma, 3b, Florida Gulf Coast University.
30. Lee Tabor, lhp, Francis Marion (S.C.) University.
31. Eric Schaler, rhp, Dallas Baptist University.
**32. Danny Dorn, of, Cal State Fullerton.—(2015)**
33. *Justin Curry, rhp, Buford (Ga.) HS.
34. *Ben Ihde, 1b, Neenah (Wis.) HS.
35. *John Touchton, rhp, Kingwood (Texas) HS.
36. Nick Wandless, rhp, University of South Carolina-Aiken.
37. *Jarrod Gaskey, of, Azle (Texas) HS.
38. *Trevor Coleman, c, Dripping Springs (Texas) HS.
39. +Todd Waller, 3b, Cape Coral (Fla.) HS / Santa Fe (Fla.) CC.
40. *Tyler Dewitt, of, Ponderosa HS, Cameron Park, Calif.
41. *Jeremy Erben, rhp, New Braunfels (Texas) HS.
42. *John Housey, rhp, Nova HS, Hollywood, Fla.
43. *Geraldo Leal, rhp, Mission (Texas) HS.
44. *Jason Chapman, of, Truckee HS, Redwood City, Calif.
DRAFT DROP *Son of Kelvin Chapman, major leaguer (1979-85)*
45. *Michael Lachapelle, lhp, Sahuaro HS, Tucson, Ariz.
46. *Jordan Tiegs, rhp, Sauk Valley (Ill.) CC.
47. *Freuny Parra, c, Connors State (Okla.) CC.
48. *Jordan Shadle, ss, Green River (Wash.) CC.
49. *Cameron Bayne, of, St. Louis School, Honolulu, Hawaii.
50. *Blake Benveniste, 3b, Chaminade Prep, Woodland Hills, Calif.

## CLEVELAND INDIANS (25)

1. (Choice to Angels as compensation for Type B free agent Paul Byrd)
**1. David Huff, lhp, UCLA** (Supplemental choice—39th—as compensation for Type A free agent Bobby Howry).**—(2009-15)**
**2. Steven Wright, rhp, University of Hawaii** (Choice from Rangers as compensation for Type B free agent Kevin Millwood).**—(2013-15)**
**2. Josh Rodriguez, 2b, Rice University** (Choice from Cubs as compensation for Type A free agent Bobby Howry).**—(2001)**
2. Wes Hodges, 3b, Georgia Tech.—(AAA)
**2. Matt McBride, c, Lehigh University** (Supplemental choice—75th—as compensation for Type C free agent Scott Elarton).**—(2012-15)**
3. Adam Davis, ss, University of Florida.—(AA)
4. Ryan Morris, lhp, South Mecklenburg HS, Charlotte, N.C.—(High A)
**5. Chris Archer, rhp, Clayton (N.C.) HS.—(2012-15)**
6. Austin Creps, rhp, Texas A&M University.
7. Robbie Alcombrack, c, Bear River HS, Grass Valley, Calif.
8. Mike Eisenberg, rhp, Marietta (Ohio) College.
9. Jared Goedert, 3b, Kansas State University.
10. Paolo Espino, rhp, The Pendleton School, Bradenton, Fla.
11. Kelly Edmundson, c, University of Tennessee.
12. Dan Frega, rhp, Illinois State University.
13. *Brant Rustich, rhp, UCLA.
14. William Delage, lhp, Lamar University.
15. Matt Meyer, lhp, Boston College.
16. Stephen Douglas, of, East Tennessee State University.
17. Kyle Harper, rhp, Orange Coast (Calif.) JC.
18. Daryl King, of, Benicia (Calif.) HS.
**19. Josh Tomlin, rhp, Texas Tech.—(2010-15)**
**20. Vinnie Pestano, rhp, Cal State Fullerton.—(2010-15)**
**21. John Gaub, lhp, University of Minnesota.—(2011)**
22. Chuck Hargis, ss, East Tennessee State University.
23. Derrick Loop, lhp, Cal State Los Angeles.
24. Chris Nash, 1b, Johnson County (Kan.) CC.
25. *Alex Jordan, rhp, Cypress (Calif.) JC.
26. *Ty Pryor, rhp, University of Tennessee.
DRAFT DROP *Son of Greg Pryor, major leaguer (1976-86)*
27. *Chris Roberts, of, Oshkosh West HS, Oshkosh, Wis.
28. Dustin Realini, 3b, Santa Clara University.
29. *Thomas Benton, rhp, University of North Carolina-Wilmington.
30. Brett Carlin, lhp, Fullerton (Calif.) JC.
31. *Easton Gust, 2b, Cottonwood HS, Riverton, Utah.
32. David Uribes, 2b, Pepperdine University.
33. *Jarett Jackson, of, Thomas Jefferson HS, Kent, Wash.
**34. *Mike Bolsinger, rhp, McKinney North HS, McKinney, Texas.—(2014-15)**
35. Alan Brech, lhp, Bowling Green State University.
36. +Ryan Miller, lhp, Blinn (Texas) JC.
37. Brett Kinning, 2b, Arkansas State University.
38. Nathan Bunton, Midland Lutheran (Neb.) College.
39. Jimmy Brettl, lhp, Cal State Northridge.
40. *Josh Yates, c, Arkansas State University.
41. *Kyle Paul, c, Vernon Regional (Texas) JC.
42. *Roderick Barcelo, of, Lino Padron Rivera HS, Vega Baja, P.R.
43. Mike Pontius, rhp, Wentzville Holt HS, Wentzville, Mo.
44. *Brad Reid, rhp, Decatur HS, Federal Way, Wash.
45. *Zach Barger, of, Grossmont (Calif.) JC.
46. Dan Miltenberger, rhp, UCLA.
47. *Eric McKinney, of, Spiro (Okla.) HS.
48. +Travis Turek, rhp, Santa Barbara (Calif.) CC / Los Angeles Pierce JC.
49. *Ryan Mottern, rhp, University of Oklahoma.
50. *Vince Catricala, 3b, Jesuit HS, Sacramento, Calif.

## COLORADO ROCKIES (2)

**1. Greg Reynolds, rhp, Stanford University.—(2008-13)**
2. David Christensen, of, Stoneman Douglas HS, Parkland, Fla.—(High A)
3. Keith Weiser, lhp, Miami (Ohio) University.—(AAA)
4. Craig Baker, rhp, Cal State Northridge.—(AA)
5. Helder Velazquez, ss, Puerto Rico Baseball Academy, Aguas Buenas, P.R.—(High A)
6. Kevin Clark, of, Manatee (Fla.) CC.
**7. Michael McKenry, c, Middle Tennessee State University.—(2010-15)**
8. Brandon Hynick, rhp, Birmingham-Southern University.
**9. Will Harris, rhp, Louisiana State University.—(2012-15)**
10. David Arnold, rhp, Lincoln Trail (Ill.) JC.
11. *Aaron Miller, of, Channelview (Texas) HS.
DRAFT DROP *First-round draft pick (36th overall), Dodgers (2009)*
12. Austin Rauch, c, El Capitan HS, El Cajon, Calif.
13. Spencer Nagy, ss, Tallahassee (Fla.) CC.
14. Jeff Kindel, of, Georgia Tech.
15. Vic Ferrante, of, Solano (Calif.) JC.
16. Anthony Jackson, of, University of the Pacific.
17. Michael Gibbs, rhp, Virginia Commonwealth University.
**18. *Andrew Cashner, rhp, Angelina (Texas) JC.—(2010-15)**
DRAFT DROP *First-round draft pick (19th overall), Cubs*

(2008)
19. +Zack Murry, ss, Chanute (Kan.) HS / Neosho County (Kan.) CC.
20. Sean Jarrett, rhp, Oral Roberts University.
21. Andy Graham, rhp, UC Santa Barbara.
22. Jay Cox, of, University of North Carolina.
**23. *Scott Maine, lhp, University of Miami.—(2010-12)**
24. *Shane Dyer, rhp, Eaton (Colo.) HS.
25. *Jeremy Jones, of, North Carolina A&T University.
26. Devin Collis, lhp, University of Arkansas.
27. Matt Repec, ss, Winthrop University.
28. Tommy Baumgardner, lhp, University of Mississippi.
29. Shane Lowe, ss, New Bloomfield (Mo.) HS.
30. +Scott Robinson, of, Henry County HS, McDonough, Ga. / Okaloosa-Walton (Fla.) JC.
31. *Curtis Dupart, of, Woodinville (Wash.) HS.
32. *Miguel Valcarcel, rhp, Perkiomen School, Pennsburg, Pa.
33. Drew Shetrone, rhp, Cumberland (Tenn.) University.
34. *Jamie Niley, lhp, Elk Grove (Calif.) HS.
35. Josh Banda, 1b, California Baptist University.
36. *Michael Diaz, c, Luis Munoz Marin HS, Barranquitas, P.R.
37. *Zach Helton, 2b, Central HS, Knoxville, Tenn.
DRAFT DROP *Cousin of Todd Helton, first-round draft pick, Rockies (1995); major leaguer (1997-2013)*
38. *Jon Hesketh, lhp, Vernon Regional (Texas) JC.
39. *Jason Fuqua, lhp, Sterling HS, Baytown, Texas.
40. *David Luna, c, Piedmont HS, San Jose, Calif.
41. *Jay Taylor, rhp, West Seattle HS, Seattle.
**42. *Sean Halton, 1b, Fresno (Calif.) CC.—(2013)**
43. *Bryan Jaeger, of, LSU-Eunice JC.
44. *Scott Bachman, lhp, Rocky Mountain HS, Fort Collins, Colo.
45. *James Manning, rhp, Wallace State (Ala.) CC.
46. *Damion Carter, of, University of Southern Mississippi.
**47. *Justin Miller, rhp, Bakersfield (Calif.) JC.—(2014-15)**
48. *Jesus Cebollero, rhp, Puerto Rico Baseball Academy, San Sebastian, P.R.
49. *Paul Dickey, rhp, Lower Columbia (Wash.) JC.
50. *Jamie Johnson, of, West Ouachita HS, Calhoun, La.

## DETROIT TIGERS (6)

**1. Andrew Miller, lhp, University of North Carolina.—(2006-15)**
DRAFT DROP *First player from 2006 draft to reach majors (Aug. 30, 2006)*
2. Ronnie Bourquin, 3b, Ohio State University.—(AA)
**3. Brennan Boesch, of, University of California.—(2010-15)**
4. Ryan Strieby, 1b, University of Kentucky.—(AAA)
**5. Scott Sizemore, 2b, Virginia Commonwealth University.—(2010-14)**
6. Jordan Newton, c, Western Kentucky University.
7. Jonah Nickerson, rhp, Oregon State University.
8. Chris Cody, lhp, Manhattan University.
9. Zach Piccola, lhp, University of South Alabama.
10. L.J. Gagnier, rhp, Cal State Fullerton.
11. Hayden Parrott, 2b, Desert Mountain HS, Scottsdale, Ariz.
12. Joe Bowen, c, Vanguard HS, Ocala, Fla.
**13. Angel Castro, rhp, Western Oklahoma State JC.—(2015)**
14. Brett Jensen, rhp, University of Nebraska.
15. *Franco Valdes, c, Monsignor Pace HS, Miami.
16. Jeff Gerbe, rhp, Michigan State University.
17. *Ben Petralli, c, Sacramento CC.
DRAFT DROP *Son of Geno Petralli, major leaguer (1982-93)*
18. Deik Scram, of, Oklahoma State University.
**19. Duane Below, lhp, Lake Michigan JC.—(2011-13)**
**20. Casey Fien, rhp, Cal Poly San Luis Obispo.—(2009-15)**
21. Tom Thornton, lhp, University of Notre Dame.
22. Chris Krawczyk, rhp, Missouri State University.
23. Aaron Fuhrman, lhp, Pleasant Valley HS, Saylorsburg, Pa.
24. Joe Tucker, of, Kent State University.
25. *Casey Weathers, rhp, Vanderbilt University.
DRAFT DROP *First-round draft pick (8th overall), Rockies (2007)*
26. *Daniel Renfroe, of, Tattnall Square Academy, Lizella, Ga.
27. *Ryan Lindgren, rhp, Seminole State (Okla.) CC.
28. Derek Witt, rhp, Ohio University.
29. Chris Carlson, 1b, University of New Mexico.
30. *Philip Ortez, of, Scottsdale (Ariz.) CC.
31. Mike Sullivan, of, Ball State University.
32. Rudy Darrow, rhp, Nicholls State University.
33. *Kodiak Quick, rhp, University of Kansas.
34. +Brandon Johnson, rhp, Butler County (Kan.) CC.
35. Paul Hammond, lhp, University of Michigan.
36. *Chad Nading, rhp, East HS, Anchorage, Alaska.
37. *Ryan LaMotta, rhp, Baylor University.
38. Dana Arrowood, rhp, Old Dominion University.
39. Michael Bertram, 3b, University of Kentucky.
40. Adrian Casanova, c, Clemson University.
41. *Taylor Freeman, c, Carney (Okla.) HS.
**42. *Kevin Chapman, lhp, Westminster Academy, Margate, Fla.—(2013-15)**
43. *David Mattox, rhp, Connors State (Okla.) JC.
44. *Ryan Kilmer, of, Midwest City (Okla.) HS.
45. *Lance Durham, of, Roger Bacon HS, Cincinnati.
DRAFT DROP *Son of Leon Durham, first-round draft pick, Cardinals (1976); major leaguer (1980-89)*
46. *Kent Williamson, rhp, Cowley County (Kan.) CC.
47. Alec Shepherd, rhp, South Mountain (Ariz.) CC.
48. *Matt McDonald, rhp, Ulster County (N.Y.) CC.
49. *Kyle Peter, of, Cloud County (Kan.) CC.
50. *Alan Oaks, of, Divine Child HS, White Lake, Mich.

## FLORIDA MARLINS (19)

**1. Brett Sinkbeil, rhp, Missouri State University.—(2010)**
**1. Chris Coghlan, 3b, University of Mississippi** (Supplemental choice—36th—as compensation for Type A free agent A.J. Burnett).**—2009-15)**
2. Thomas Hickman, of-lhp, Pepperell HS, Rome, Ga.—(High A)
3. Torre Langley, lhp, Alexander HS, Winston, Ga. (Choice from Blue Jays as compensation for Burnett).—(AA)
**3. Scott Cousins, of-lhp, University of San Francisco.—(2010-13)**
4. Hector Correa, rhp, Lorenzo Coballes HS, Hatillo, P.R.—(AA)
**5. Chris Hatcher, c-rhp, University of North Carolina-Wilmington.—(2010-15)**
6. Justin Jacobs, ss, Chino HS, Pomona, Calif.
7. Don Czyz, rhp, University of Kansas
8. Daniel Garcia, ss, Nogales HS, La Puente, Calif.
**9. John Raynor, of, University of North Carolina-Wilmington.—(2010)**
**10. Graham Taylor, lhp, Miami (Ohio) University.—(2009)**
**11. Osvaldo Martinez, ss, Porterville (Calif.) JC.—(2010-2011)**
12. Brad Stone, rhp, Quincy (Ill.) University.
13. Drew Saylor, 2b, Kent State University.
**14. Jay Buente, rhp, Purdue University.—(2010-11)**
15. Guillermo Martinez, ss, University of South Alabama.
16. Jake Blackwood, 3b, Maple Woods (Mo.) CC.
17. Hunter Mense, of, University of Missouri.
18. Ross Liersemann, rhp, University of Akron.
19. Jordan Davis, rhp, University of Alabama.
20. *Steve Sultzbaugh, of, Westwood HS, Austin, Texas.
21. Corey Madden, rhp, St. Mary's (Calif.) College.
22. Kevan Kelley, lhp, Cal State San Bernardino.
23. (void) *Rylan Hanks, lhp, Cal State San Bernardino.
24. *Ernesto Rivera, of, Puerto Rico Baseball Academy, Canovanas, P.R.
25. Joel Fountain, rhp, St. Mary's (Calif.) College.
26. Andy Jackson, lhp, University of Central Arkansas.
27. (void) *Jeremy Hall, rhp, East Tennessee State University.
28. +Kedrick Martin, lhp, Meridian (Miss.) CC.
29. +Jonathan Van Looy, lhp, John Swett HS, Hercules, Calif. / Diablo Valley (Calif.) CC.
30. *Quinn Harris, ss, Elizabethtown (Ky.) HS.
31. *Willie Mays, of, Sinclair (Ohio) CC.
**32. Alex Sanabia, rhp, Castle Park HS, Chula Vista, Calif.—(2010-13)**
33. +Eric Basurto, rhp, Chabot (Calif.) JC.
34. *T.J. Kelly, rhp, Bakersfield (Calif.) JC.
35. *Chris Evans, c, Serrano HS, Pinon Hills, Calif.
36. *David Williams, of, Rutgers University.
37. *James Wallace, rhp, JC of Southern Idaho.
38. *Jeremie Tice, 3b, Tallahassee (Fla.) CC.
39. Spike McDougall, of, UC Irvine.
40. Tony Suarez, rhp, Southeastern Louisiana University.
41. *Kyle Barry, rhp, Madison (Wis.) Area Tech JC.
42. *Ryan Kussmaul, rhp, Madison (Wis.) Area Tech JC.
43. +William Jackel, rhp, Tallahassee (Fla.) CC.
44. *T.J. Forrest, rhp, Haughton HS, Benton, La.
45. *Kyle Price, 2b, Eastern Oklahoma State JC.
46. +Mitch MacDonald, 3b, Monterey Peninsula (Calif.) JC.
47. *Brooks Martin, rhp, Streator Township HS, Streator, Ill.
48. *Lance Hanmer, ss, Greensburg (Ind.) HS.
49. *Michael Hubbard, of, University of Arkansas-Fort Smith JC.
50. *Andrew Raponi, 1b, Monte Vista HS, Danville, Calif.

## HOUSTON ASTROS (23)

1. Max Sapp, c, Bishop Moore HS, Orlando, Fla.—(Low A)
2. Sergio Perez, rhp, University of Tampa.—(AAA)
3. Nick Moresi, of, Fresno State University.—(AA)
**4. Chris Johnson, ss, Stetson University.—(2009-15)**
5. Casey Hudspeth, rhp, University of South Florida.—(AA)
**6. Bud Norris, rhp, Cal Poly San Luis Obispo.—(2009-15)**
7. David Qualben, lhp, Pace (N.Y.) University.
8. Jimmy Van Ostrand, of, Cal Poly San Luis Obispo.
DRAFT DROP *Brother of David Van Ostrand, 35th-round draft pick, Yankees (2006)*
9. Greg Buchanan, 2b, Rice University.
**10. *Nate Karns, rhp, Martin HS, Arlington, Texas.—(2013-15)**
11. Tom Vessella, lhp, Whittier (Calif.) College.
12. Bryan Hallberg, rhp, Pace (N.Y.) University.
13. Chris Salamida, lhp, SUNY Oneonta.
14. Justin Tellam, c, Pepperdine University.
15. Kevin Fox, lhp, Biola (Calif.) University.
16. Drew Holder, of, Dallas Baptist University.
17. Justin Stiver, rhp, Florida Gulf Coast University.
18. Colt Adams, rhp, Dixie State (Utah) JC.
19. Orlando Rosales, of, University of Tampa.
20. *Mark Sobolewski, ss, Sarasota (Fla.) HS.
21. Anthony Bello, lhp, Nova Southeastern (Fla.) University.
22. Chad Wagler, rhp, Kent State University.
23. Tim Torres, ss, Oral Roberts University.
24. *Jonathan Wiedenbauer, lhp, Seabreeze HS, Ormond Beach, Fla.
DRAFT DROP *Son of Tom Wiedenbauer, major leaguer (1979)*
25. *Jamaal Hollis, rhp, Whitney Young HS, Chicago.
26. *Lenell McGee, 3b, Mount Carmel HS, South Holland, Ill.
27. Alberto Cruz, 1b, Cumberland (Tenn.) University.
DRAFT DROP *Son of Tommy Cruz, major leaguer (1973-77) • Nephew of Jose Cruz, major leaguer (1970-88) • Nephew of Hector Cruz, major leaguer (1973-82)*
28. Brandon Caipen, 3b, Youngstown State University.
29. +Rafael Parks, of, Greenbrier HS, Appling, Ga. / Georgia Military JC.
30. Eric Taylor, 3b, UCLA.
31. Kyle DeYoung, rhp, Florida Southern College.
32. Adam Hale, rhp, Texas A&M University.
33. *Codi Harshman, of, Sabino HS, Tucson, Ariz.
34. *John Anderson, rhp, Captain Shreve HS, Shreveport, La.
35. *Patrick Allen, of, Everett (Wash.) CC.
36. *Johnathan Moore, c, Lamar HS, Arlington, Texas.
DRAFT DROP *Son of Jackie Moore, major leaguer (1965); major league manager (1984-86)*
37. *Trent Henderson, ss, Newport HS, Bellevue, Wash.
DRAFT DROP *Son of Dave Henderson, first-round draft pick, Mariners (1977); major leaguer (1981-94)*
38. *Casey Anderson, c, West Ouachita HS, Calhoun, La.
39. *Will Kline, rhp, University of Mississippi.
40. *Steven Detwiler, ss, San Rafael HS, Forest Knolls, Calif.
41. +Axel Gonzalez, of, Rosalina Martinez HS, Palo Seco, P.R. / Wabash Valley (Ill.) CC.
42. *Kevin Sullivan, c, York Community HS, Elmhurst, Ill.
43. *Greg Joseph, of, Mount San Jacinto (Calif.) JC.
44. *Adam Pilate, of, Sylacauga (Ala.) HS.
45. *Cody Madison, of, Vista del Lago HS, Moreno Valley, Calif.
46. *Joey Wong, ss, Sprague HS, Salem, Ore.
47. *Michael Pericht, c, Providence Catholic HS, Orland Park, Ill.
48. *Jerry Quinones, lhp, Compton (Calif.) CC.
49. +Andy Launier, 1b, Sierra (Calif.) JC.
50. *Tyler Henley, of, Rice University.

## KANSAS CITY ROYALS (1)

**1. Luke Hochevar, rhp, Fort Worth / American Association.—(2007-15)**
DRAFT DROP *First-round draft pick (40th overall), Dodgers (2005)*
2. Jason Taylor, ss, Kellam HS, Virginia Beach, Va.—(High A)
**3. Blake Wood, rhp, Georgia Tech.—(2010-14)**
**4. Derrick Robinson, of, P.K. Yonge HS, Archer, Fla.—(2013)**
5. Jason Godin, rhp, Old Dominion University.—(AAA)
6. Harold Mozingo, rhp, Virginia Commonwealth University.
7. Brett Bigler, of, UC Riverside.
8. Josh Cribb, rhp, Clemson University.
9. Marc Maddox, 1b, University of Southern Mississippi.
10. Nick Van Stratten, of, St. Louis CC-Meramec.
11. Tyler Chambliss, rhp, Florida State University.
**12. Everett Teaford, lhp, Georgia Southern University.—(2011-15)**
13. Kurt Mertins, 2b, JC of the Desert (Calif.).
14. Daniel Best, rhp, University of Southern Mississippi.
15. Nick Francis, of, Pensacola (Fla.) JC.
16. T.J. Wilson, ss, Southern HS, Durham, N.C.
17. Matt Morizio, c-rhp, Northeastern University.
18. *Chase Larsson, of, Kitsilano SS, Vancouver, B.C.
19. *Jeff Inman, rhp, Garces Memorial HS, Bakersfield, Calif.
**20. *Brad Boxberger, rhp, Foothill HS, Santa Ana, Calif.—(2012-15)**
DRAFT DROP *Son of Rod Boxberger, first-round draft pick, Astros (1978)*
21. Burke Baldwin, lhp, Elgin (Ill.) CC.
22. Romas Hicks, rhp, Georgia State University.
23. Aaron Hartsock, rhp, California Baptist University.
24. *Tyler Moyneur, c, Arizona Western JC.
25. *Rafael Valenzuela, ss, Nogales (Ariz.) HS.
26. *Darrell Lockett, of, Weatherford (Texas) HS.
27. *Colby Killian, rhp, Warren County HS, McMinnville, Tenn.
28. *Michael Wheeler, of, Walters State (Tenn.) CC.
29. *Steve Rinaudo, ss, American River (Calif.) JC.
30. *Tyler Pearson, rhp, University of Northern Colorado.
31. Brandon Lance, c, New Mexico State University.
32. *Fernando Garcia, 2b, Immaculada Concepcion HS, Arecibo, P.R.
33. *Harold Smith, of, Palmetto (Fla.) HS.
34. *Jarrod Grace, 1b, Pensacola (Fla.) JC.
35. *Anthony Stovall. rhp, Kailua (Hawaii) HS.
36. *Manuel Garcia, rhp, Cochise County (Ariz.) CC.
37. *Kaleb Harst, c, St. Thomas Moore HS, Lafayette, La.
38. *Michael Dabbs, of, Cowley County (Kan.) CC.
39. *Tanner Moore, rhp, Thomasville (Ga.) HS.
40. *Chris Snipes, lhp, Warner Robins HS, Kathleen, Ga.
41. *Jeremy Toole, rhp, Huntsville (Texas) HS.

42. *Todd McBride, of, The Dalles (Ore.) HS.
43. *Brennan Thorpe, rhp, Saddleback (Calif.) JC.
44. +Bryan Paukovits, rhp, Southwestern (Calif.) CC / San Diego Mesa JC.
45. *Eric Martinez, rhp, Southwestern (Calif.) CC.
46. *Chase Lehr, rhp, Centennial HS, Phoenix.
47. *Ryan Cisterna, c, Chandler-Gilbert (Ariz.) JC.
48. *Colby Ho, 3b, Kaiser HS, Honolulu, Hawaii.
**49. *Rocky Gale, c, North Salem HS, Keizer, Ore.—(2015)**
**50. Jarrod Dyson, of, Southwest Mississippi CC.—(2010-15)**

## LOS ANGELES ANGELS (26)

**1. Hank Conger, c, Huntington Beach (Calif.) HS** (Choice from Indians as compensation for Type B free agent Paul Byrd).**—(2010-15)**
1. (Choice to Dodgers as compensation for Type A free agent Jeff Weaver)
2. (Choice to Nationals as compensation for Type B free agent Hector Carrasco)
3. *Russ Moldenhauer, of, Boerne (Texas) HS.—(Low A)
DRAFT DROP *Attended Texas; re-drafted by Nationals, 2010 (24th round)*
4. Clay Fuller, of, Smithson Valley HS, Bulverde, Texas.—(AA)
**5. David Herndon, rhp, Gulf Coast (Fla.) CC.—(2010-12)**
6. Robert Fish, lhp, A.B. Miller HS, San Bernardino, Calif.
7. *Jarrad Page, of, UCLA.
DRAFT DROP *Defensive back, National Football League (2006-11)*
8. Matt Sweeney, c, Magruder HS, Rockville, Md.
9. Nate Boman, lhp, University of San Diego.
10. Leo Calderon, lhp, Lake City (Fla.) CC.
11. David Pellegrine, rhp, Northeastern University.
**12. +Jordan Walden, rhp, Mansfield (Texas) HS / Grayson County (Texas) CC.—(2010-15)**
13. Blake Holler, lhp, Stanford University.
14. Chris Armstrong, lhp, Owasso (Okla.) HS.
15. Scott Knazek, c, Rider University.
**16. *Scott Carroll, rhp, Missouri State University.—(2014-15)**
17. Tadd Brewer, 2b, Lipscomb (Tenn.) University.
**18. *Charles Brewer, rhp, Chaparral HS, Paradise Valley, Ariz.—(2013)**
**19. Chris Pettit, of, Loyola Marymount University.—(2009-11)**
20. *J.D. Reichenbach, lhp, Central Bucks East HS, Doylestown, Pa.
21. *John Vincent, of, New Mexico State University.
22. *Michael Thomas, c, Thurgood Marshall HS, Missouri City, Texas.
23. Tim Schoeninger, rhp, University of Nevada-Reno.
24. *John Curtis, c, Cal State Fullerton.
25. *Jason Jarvis, rhp, Chaparral HS, Scottsdale, Ariz.
26. *Ryan Kelley, lhp, Indian River (Fla.) CC.
27. Matt Reilly, rhp, Pace (N.Y.) University.
**28. Barret Browning, lhp, Florida State University.—(2012)**
29. +Michael Davitt, rhp, Okaloosa-Walton (Fla.) CC.
30. *Kevin Skogley, lhp, University of Nevada-Las Vegas.
31. +Dylan Lindsey, rhp, Broward (Fla.) CC.
32. Chris Lewis, 2b, Stanford University.
33. Wilberto Ortiz, ss, Dowling (N.Y.) College.
34. *Bobby Wagner, of, Douglas (B.C.) JC.
35. Aaron Cook, rhp, University of Tampa.
36. Alex Fonseca, ss, Florida Atlantic University.
37. *Ronnie Welty, of, Mesquite HS, Gilbert, Ariz.
38. Eduardo Chile, rhp, Rollins (Fla.) College.
39. +Rian Kiniry, of, Broward (Fla.) CC.
40. *Jake Locker, rhp-of, Ferndale (Wash.) HS.
DRAFT DROP *First-round draft pick, Tennessee Titans/ National Football League (2011); quarterback, NFL (2011-14)*
41. *Brian Hobbs, of, Chipola (Fla.) CC.
42. *Derrick Conaster, rhp, Tallahassee (Fla.) CC.
43. Doug Brandt, lhp, Cal State San Bernardino.
44. +Lou Green, rhp, Chipola (Fla.) CC.
45. *Matt McCracken, lhp, Florida CC.
46. *Ryan Lipkin, c, Solano (Calif.) JC.
47. *Jonathan Plefka, rhp, Texas Tech.
48. *Abraham Gonzalez, rhp, Coachella Valley HS, Thermal, Calif.
49. Gordie Gronkowski, 1b, Jacksonville University.
50. +Tim Brewer, lhp, Ivanna Eudora Kean HS, Charlotte Amalie, V.I. / Connors State (Okla.) JC.

## LOS ANGELES DODGERS (7)

**1. Clayton Kershaw, lhp, Highland Park HS, Dallas.—(2008-15)**
DRAFT DROP *First 2006 high school draft pick to reach majors (May 25, 2008)*
**1. Bryan Morris, rhp, Motlow State (Tenn.) CC** (Choice from Angels as compensation for Type A free agent Jeff Weaver).**—(2012-15)**
1. Preston Mattingly, ss, Evansville Central HS, Evansville, Ind. (Supplemental choice—31st—as compensation for Weaver).—(High A)
DRAFT DROP *Son of Don Mattingly, major leaguer (1982-95); major league manager (2011-15)*
2. (Choice to Braves as compensation for Type A free agent Rafael Furcal)
3. (Choice to Red Sox as compensation for Type A free agent Bill Mueller)
4. Kyle Orr, 1b, Lambrick Park HS, Victoria, B.C.—(Rookie)
5. Kyle Smit, rhp, Spanish Springs HS, Sparks, Nev.—(AAA)
6. Garrett White, lhp, University of Mississippi.
7. Jaime Ortiz, 1b, San Alfonso de Ligorio HS, Guayama, P.R.
8. Tommy Giles, of, University of Miami.
9. Bridger Hunt, 3b, Central Missouri State University.
10. *Andy D'Alessio, 1b, Clemson University.
11. Justin Fuller, ss, Lewis-Clark State (Idaho) College.
12. Paul Coleman, lhp, Pepperdine University.
13. *Nick Akins, ss, Los Angeles (Calif.) HS.
**14. *Alex White, rhp, D.H. Conley HS, Greenville, N.C.—(2011-12)**
DRAFT DROP *First-round draft pick (15th overall), Indians (2009)*
15. +Griff Erickson, c, Westview HS, San Diego / San Diego Mesa JC.
16. *Justin Coats, ss, Texas HS, Texarkana, Texas.
17. Michael Rivera, 2b, University of Tennessee.
18. Joe Jones, rhp, University of Portland.
19. *Martin Beno, rhp, Mississippi Gulf Coast JC.
20. *Billy Bullock, rhp, Riverview HS, Valrico, Fla.
21. Matt Berezay, of, University of the Pacific.
22. Chris Jensen, of, UCLA.
23. Eric Thompson, rhp, Roseburg (Ore.) HS.
24. John Martin, c, Emporia State (Kan.) University.
25. Esteban Lopez, c, University of Hawaii.
26. *Kody Kaiser, 2b, University of Oklahoma.
27. *Anthony Casario, c, Overbrook HS, Pine Hill, N.J.
28. *Taylor Lewis, rhp, Canyon del Oro HS, Tucson, Ariz.
**29. *Roberto Perez, c, Eugenio Maria de Hostos HS, Mayaguez, P.R.—(2014-15)**
30. *Alex Burkard, lhp, Milton HS, Alpharetta, Ga.
31. *Jonathan Wilson, 3b, St. Charles (Mo.) HS.
32. *Jordan Kopycinski, c, St. Thomas HS, Houston.
33. *Kurt Bradley, 2b, University of Northern Iowa.
DRAFT DROP *Son of Phil Bradley, major leaguer (1983-90)*
34. *Luke Yoder, of, Liberty HS, Bakersfield, Calif.
**35. *Nick Buss, of, San Diego Mesa CC.—(2013)**
36. *Robert Taylor, c, Laredo (Texas) CC.
37. *Anthony Benner, 3b, Southwestern (Calif.) CC.
38. *Kameron Forte, c, Texas HS, Texarkana, Texas.
39. *Jake Debus, lhp, Moraine Valley (Ill.) CC.
40. *Chris Jones, ss, Redan HS, Lithonia, Ga.
41. *Todd McCraw, c, St, James HS, Myrtle Beach, S.C.
42. *Joe Dispensa, of, St. Rita HS, Chicago.
43. *Jordan Chambless, rhp, Texas A&M University.
**44. *Aaron Barrett, rhp, Evansville Central HS, Evansville, Ind.—(2014-15)**
45. *Greg Hendrix, lhp, North Atlanta HS, Atlanta.
46. *Ryan Aguayo, 2b, Servite HS, Pico Rivera, Calif.
47. *Brett Sowers, 3b, Cherry Creek HS, Englewood, Colo.
48. *Tanner Biagini, 3b, D.H. Conley HS, Greenville, N.C.
**49. *Paul Goldschmidt, 1b, The Woodlands (Texas) HS.—(2011-15)**
50. *Kurt Benton, rhp, West Stanly HS, Stansfield, N.C.

## MILWAUKEE BREWERS (16)

**1. Jeremy Jeffress, rhp, Halifax County HS, South Boston, Va.—(2010-15)**
2. Brent Brewer, ss-of, Sandy Creek HS, Tyrone, Ga.—(AA)
**3. Cole Gillespie, of, Oregon State University.—(2010-15)**
4. Evan Anundsen, rhp, Columbine HS, Littleton, Colo.—(AA)
5. Chris Errecart, of, University of California.—(AA)
6. Brae Wright, lhp, Oklahoma State University.
7. Andy Bouchie, c, Oral Roberts University.
8. Shane Hill, rhp, Florida Christian HS, Miami Springs, Fla.
9. Shawn Ferguson, rhp, Texas Christian University.
**10. Mike McClendon, rhp, Seminole (Fla.) CC.—(2010-12)**
11. Zach Clem, of, University of Washington.
12. +Chad Robinson, rhp, Silverado HS, Las Vegas, Nev. / CC of Southern Nevada.
13. Chris Toneguzzi, rhp, Purdue University.
14. Hector Bernal, ss, El Paso (Texas) CC.
15. Brett Whiteside, c, Mesquite HS, Chandler, Ariz.
16. R.J. Seidel, rhp, Central HS, La Crosse, Wis.
17. *Aaron Tullo, rhp, St. Petersburg (Fla.) HS.
18. *Andrew Clark, 1b, New Palestine (Ind.) HS.
19. +Lee Haydel, of, Riverside Academy, Reserve, La. / Delgado (La.) CC.
20. *Mehdi Djebbar, lhp, Ahuntsic College HS, Montreal.
21. Jesse D'Amico, c, Mohawk HS, Wampum, Pa.
22. J.T. King, rhp, Northeastern Oklahoma A&M JC.
23. *Scott Shuman, rhp, Tift County HS, Tifton, Ga.
24. Travis Wendte, rhp, University of Missouri.
25. Mike Goetz, of, University of Wisconsin-Milwaukee.
26. *Marc Lewis, lhp, Creighton University.
27. *T.J. Macy, rhp, Scottsdale (Ariz.) CC.
28. *Terrell Alliman, of, Bluevale Collegiate Institute, Waterloo, Ontario.
29. *David Newmann, lhp, Texas A&M University.
30. Jordan Swaydan, c, San Diego State University.
31. +Rob Bryson, rhp, William Penn HS, New Castle, Del. / Seminole (Fla.) CC.
32. +Nick Tyson, rhp, Timber Creek Regional HS, Blackwood, N.J. / Lake City (Fla.) CC.
33. Eric Newton, 2b, Santa Clara University.
34. Stuart Sutherland, rhp, Dallas Baptist University.
35. *Sanduan Dubose, 3b, Stillman (Ala.) College.
36. *Clay Jones, c, Bibb County HS, Brent, Ala.
37. *Wes Munson, ss, Fond du Lac (Wis.) HS.
38. *Todd Fitzgerald, lhp, San Jose (Calif.) CC.
39. Chuckie Caufield, of, University of Oklahoma.
40. *Alex Koronis, rhp, Monsignor Pace HS, Miami.
41. *Matt Poulk, 3b, University of North Carolina-Wilmington.
42. *Matt Peck, rhp, Cowley County (Kan.) CC.
43. D.J. Lidyard, rhp, Lower Columbia (Wash.) JC.
44. +Bryan Crosby, 3b, William Blount HS, Maryville, Tenn. / Cleveland State (Tenn.) CC.
45. *Matt Thompson, ss, Aztec (N.M.) HS.
46. *Aaron Johnson, c, Lethbridge (Alberta) CC.
47. *Matt Coburn, rhp, San Jacinto (Texas) CC.
48. *Brandon Owens, rhp, Heritage HS, Covington, Ga.
49. *Nicholas Spears, ss, Poway (Calif.) HS.
50. *Ricky Alvernaz, 3b, Tamanawis HS, White Rock, B.C.

## MINNESOTA TWINS (20)

**1. Chris Parmelee, of, Chino Hills (Calif.) HS.—(2011-15)**
**2. Joe Benson, c-of, Joliet Catholic Academy, Plainfield, Ill.—(2011)**
**3. Tyler Robertson, lhp, Bella Vista HS, Citrus Heights, Calif.—(2012-13)**
4. Whit Robbins, 1b, Georgia Tech (Choice from Cubs as compensation for Type B free agent Jacque Jones).—(AA)
4. Garrett Olson, 3b, Franklin Pierce (N.H.) College.—(High A)
5. *Devin Shepherd, of, Oxnard (Calif.) HS.–(High A)
DRAFT DROP *Attended Oklahoma; re-drafted by Cardinals, 2008 (11th round)*
6. Jeff Christy, c, University of Nebraska.
7. Jonathan Waltenbury, 1b, Henry Street HS, Whitby, Ontario.
**8. Brian Dinkelman, 2b, McKendree (Ill.) College.—(2011)**
9. Sean Land, lhp, University of Kansas.
10. *Jared Mitchell, of, Westgate HS, New Iberia, La.
DRAFT DROP *First-round draft pick (23rd overall), White Sox (2009)*
11. Steve Singleton, ss, University of San Diego.
12. Kevin Harrington, of, Royal HS, Simi Valley, Calif.
13. *Aaron Senne, of, Mayo HS, Rochester, Minn.
**14. Jeff Manship, rhp, University of Notre Dame.—(2009-15)**
DRAFT DROP *Brother of Matt Manship, 29th-round draft pick, Athletics (2006)*
15. Mark Dolenc, of, University of Minnesota-Mankato.
16. *Shayne Willson, of, Earl Marriott SS, Surrey, B.C.
**17. *Andy Oliver, lhp, Vermillion (Ohio) HS.—(2010-11)**
18. +Chris Anderson, lhp, Northern Essex (Mass.) CC.
**19. Danny Valencia, 3b, University of Miami.—(2010-15)**
20. Gilbert Buenrostro, c, Cuesta (Calif.) JC.
21. Eric Santiago, ss, Miami-Dade CC.
22. *Aaron Tennyson, lhp, University of Kentucky.
23. Thomas Wright, rhp, McGavock HS, Hermitage, Tenn.
24. Nick Papasan, ss, Granbury (Texas) HS.
25. *Dillon Baird, 3b, Prescott (Ariz.) HS.
26. *Kyle Mitchell, rhp, Mosley HS, Panama City, Fla.
27. *Joseph Thibou, c, Northeast HS, St. Petersburg, Fla.
28. *Dustin Williams, c, Woodlawn HS, Rison, Ark.
29. *Braxton Chisholm, c, St. Cloud (Fla.) HS.
30. +Michael Mopas, lhp, Golden West (Calif.) JC / Cuesta (Calif.) JC.
31. *Kyle Thornton, rhp, Cowley County (Kan.) CC.
32. *Andres Diaz, c, Santaluces HS, Boynton Beach, Fla.
33. *Alberto Espinosa, c, Brito Private HS, Miami.
34. *Marcel Champagnie, ss, Kaskaskia (Ill.) CC.
35. *Robby Donovan, rhp, Royal Palm Beach (Fla.) HS.
**36. *J.D. Martinez, of, Charles Flanagan HS, Miramar, Fla.—(2011-15)**
37. *Aaron Baker, c, Denton (Texas) HS.
38. *Randy Boone, rhp, University of Texas.
**39. +Anthony Slama, rhp, University of San Diego.—(2010-11)**
40. Michael Cowgill, 2b, James Madison University.
41. *Joan Ortiz, rhp, Juan Ponce de Leon HS, San Juan, P.R.
**42. *Chase Anderson, rhp, Rider HS, Wichita Falls, Texas.—(2014-15)**
43. *Frank Berry, rhp, First Colonial HS, Virginia Beach, Va.
44. *Isaac Castillo, 2b, Waimea HS, Kehena, Hawaii.
45. *Brandon Trodick, rhp, CC of Southern Nevada.
46. *Richard Breton, of, Keystone HS, Keystone Heights, Fla.
47. *Josh Chester, of, Cypress Bay HS, Weston, Fla.
48. *Stephen Vento, rhp, Palm Beach (Fla.) CC.
49. *Calvin Culver, of, Quartz Hill HS, Lancaster, Calif.
50. *Derek McCallum, ss, Hill-Murray HS, Shoreview, Minn.

## NEW YORK METS (18)

1. (Choice to Phillies as compensation for Type A free agent Billy Wagner)
**2. Kevin Mulvey, rhp, Villanova University.—(2009-10)**
**3. Joe Smith, rhp, Wright State University.—(2007-15)**
**4. John Holdzkom, rhp, Salt Lake (Utah) CC.—(2014)**
5. Steve Holmes, rhp, University of Rhode Island.—DNP
6. Scott Schafer, rhp, Pasadena Memorial HS, Pasadena, Texas.
7. Daniel Stegall, of, Greenwood (Ark.) HS.
8. Nathan Hedrick, rhp, Barton County (Kan.) CC.
9. *Jeremy Barfield, of, Klein HS, Spring, Texas.
DRAFT DROP *Son of Jesse Barfield, major leaguer (1981-92) • Brother of Josh Barfield, major leaguer (2006-09)*
10. +Phillips Orta, rhp, Western Nebraska CC.
11. *Andy Moye, rhp, Alpharetta (Ga.) HS.

12. Nick Giarraputo, 3b, Simi Valley (Calif.) HS.
**13. Daniel Murphy, 3b, Jacksonville University.—(2008-15)**
14. Todd Privett, lhp, JC of Southern Idaho.
15. *Justin Dalles, c, Park Vista Community HS, Lake Worth, Fla.
**16. Tobi Stoner, rhp, Davis & Elkins (W.Va.) College.—(2009-10)**
17. Stephen Puhl, c, St. Edward's (Texas) University.
DRAFT DROP *Son of Terry Puhl, major leaguer (1977-91)*
18. Ritchie Price, ss, University of Kansas.
DRAFT DROP *Baseball coach, South Dakota State (2008-11)*
19. *Justin Woodall, lhp-of, Lafayette County HS, Oxford, Miss.
20. Jason Jacobs, c, University of Georgia.
21. *Joel Wells, 1b, Abilene Christian (Texas) University.
22. Tim Stronach, rhp, Worcester State (Mass.) College.
23. Nick Waechter, rhp, Western Oregon State College.
24. Valentin Ramos, 1b, Sallisaw (Okla.) HS.
25. Steven Cheney, rhp, Gulf Coast (Fla.) CC.
26. Dustin Martin, of, Sam Houston State University.
27. Tim Haines, rhp, University of Texas-Pan American.
28. Will Bashelor, of, Dartmouth College.
29. Jake Eigsti, ss, Indiana State University.
30. Ricky Sparks, rhp, Dallas Baptist University.
31. Jeremy Hambrice, of, Southern Arkansas University.
32. Brad Roper-Hubbert, c, Alcorn State University.
33. Teddy Dziuba, c, Babson (Mass.) College.
34. J.R. Voyles, 2b, University of Texas-San Antonio.
35. James Newman, 2b, Erskine (S.C.) College.
36. Edgar Ramirez, rhp, Louisiana State University.
**37. Josh Stinson, rhp, Northwood HS, Shreveport, La.—(2011-14)**
38. J.J. Leaper, rhp, Sentinel (Okla.) HS.
39. Donald Green, of, Texas Southern University.
40. *Tyler Binkley, rhp, St. Mary's College HS, Sault Ste. Marie, Ontario.
**41. *Victor Black, rhp, Amarillo (Texas) HS.—(2013-14)**
DRAFT DROP *First-round draft pick (49th overall), Pirates (2009)*
42. *Terrell Stringer, rhp, Smith Station HS, Phenix City, Ala.
43. *Albert Cartwright, 2b, American Heritage HS, Plantation, Fla.
44. *Brad Schwarzenbach, rhp, Cerritos (Calif.) JC.
45. *Beau Pender, rhp, Gulf Coast (Fla.) CC.
46. Kyle Johnson, rhp, Chapman (Calif.) University.
47. *Shay Conder, c, CC of Southern Nevada.
48. Jon Koller, rhp, Oregon State University.
**49. *Johnny Monell, c, Seminole (Fla.) CC.—(2013-15)**
50. *Ryan Wolfe, lhp, Winter Park (Fla.) HS.

## NEW YORK YANKEES (28)

**1. Ian Kennedy, rhp, University of Southern California** (Choice from Phillies as compensation for Type A free agent Tom Gordon).—**(2007-15)**
1. (Choice to Red Sox as compensation for Type A free agent Johnny Damon)
**1. Joba Chamberlain, rhp, University of Nebraska** (Supplemental choice—41st—as compensation for Gordon).—**(2007-15)**
2. (Choice to Braves as compensation for Type A free agent Kyle Farnsworth)
**3. Zach McAllister, rhp, Illinois Valley Central HS, Chillicothe, Ill.—(2011-15)**
**4. Colin Curtis, of, Arizona State University.—(2010)**
**5. George Kontos, rhp, Northwestern University.—(2011-15)**
6. Mitch Hilligoss, ss, Purdue University.
7. Tim Norton, rhp, University of Connecticut.
**8. Dellin Betances, rhp, Grand Street Campus HS, New York.—(2011-15)**
**9. Mark Melancon, rhp, University of Arizona.—(2009-15)**
10. Casey Erickson, rhp, Springfield (Ill.) JC.
11. Seth Fortenberry, of, Baylor University.
12. Nick Peterson, rhp, University of Tampa.
**13. Daniel McCutchen, rhp, University of Oklahoma.—(2009-14)**
14. D.J. Hollingsworth, of, UC Riverside.
15. Gabe Medina, rhp, Emporia State (Kan.) University.
16. Paul David Patterson, rhp, Northern Kentucky University.
**17. David Robertson, rhp, University of Alabama.—(2008-15)**
18. *Del Howell, lhp, American Christian Academy, Northport, Ala.
19. Chris Kunda, 2b, Oregon State University.
**20. Kevin Russo, 2b, Baylor University.—(2010)**
21. Russell Raley, 2b, University of Oklahoma.
22. Brian Aragon, of, North Carolina State University.
23. Brandon Thomson, lhp, Chandler-Gilbert (Ariz.) CC.
24. Brian Baisley, c, University of South Florida.
DRAFT DROP *Brother of Jeff Baisley, major leaguer (2008)*
25. *Kevin Carby, ss, Texarkana (Texas) CC.
26. +Tim Dennehy, lhp, Chandler-Gilbert (Ariz.) CC.
27. *Michael Lee, rhp, Bellevue (Wash.) CC.
28. *Barrett Bruce, rhp, Flower Mound (Texas) HS.
29. *Orlando Torres, c, Puerto Rico Baseball Academy, Santa Isabel, P.R.
30. Brock Ungricht, c, San Diego State University.
31. *Zak Presley, of, Carroll HS, Keller, Texas.
32. *Tommy Palica, lhp, Golden West (Calif.) CC.
33. Luke Trubee, rhp, University of Dayton.
**34. *Tyler Ladendorf, ss, Maine West HS, Des Plaines, Ill.—(2015)**
35. *David Van Ostrand, 3b, Allan Hancock (Calif.) JC.
DRAFT DROP *Brother of Jimmy Van Ostrand, eighth-round draft pick, Astros (2006)*
36. *Jared Rogers, rhp, Duncanville HS, DeSoto, Texas.
37. Tim O'Brien, 3b, San Diego State University.
38. Nick Diyorio, of, Florida Southern College.
39. Kevin Smith, 1b, University of Oklahoma.
40. *Tanner Chitwood, lhp, Sulphur (Okla.) HS.
41. *Ohmed Danesh, of, Dr. Phillips HS, Orlando, Fla.
42. *Dan Duffy, ss, Mountain Ridge HS, Glendale, Ariz.
43. *Eric Erickson, lhp, Sarasota (Fla.) HS.
44. James LaSala, c, Iona College.
45. *Nathan Albert, rhp, Bakersfield (Calif.) JC.
46. *Jeff Ludlow, rhp, Palm Harbor University (Fla.) HS.
47. *Charles Smith, c, Second Baptist HS, Montgomery, Texas.
48. *Jeff Loveys, rhp, Ball State University.
49. Chase Odenreider, of, Creighton University.
50. *Sam Honeck, 1b, Grayson County (Texas) CC.

## OAKLAND ATHLETICS (22)

1. (Choice to Nationals as compensation for Type B free agent Esteban Loaiza)
**2. Trevor Cahill, rhp, Vista HS, Oceanside, Calif.—(2009-15)**
3. Matt Sulentic, of, Hillcrest HS, Dallas.—(AA)
4. Chad Lee, rhp, Barton County (Kan.) CC.—(Low A)
5. Jermaine Mitchell, of, University of North Carolina-Greensboro.—(AAA)
**6. Andrew Bailey, rhp, Wagner College.—(2009-15)**
**7. *Mike Leake, rhp, Fallbrook (Calif.) HS.—(2010-15)**
DRAFT DROP *First-round draft pick (8th overall), Reds (2009)*
8. Angel Sierra, of, Puerto Rico Baseball Academy, Cayey, P.R.
9. *Danny Hamblin, 1b, University of Arkansas.
10. Christian Vitters, ss, Fresno State University.
DRAFT DROP *Brother of Josh Vitters, first-round draft pick, Cubs (2007); major leaguer (2012)*
11. Jason Fernandez, rhp, University of Louisiana-Lafayette.
12. Shane Presutti, rhp, Franklin Pierce (N.H.) College.
13. Ben Jukich, lhp, Dakota Wesleyan (S.D.) College.
14. Todd Johnson, of, University of Southern Mississippi.
15. Kyle Christensen, rhp, Millikan HS, Long Beach, Calif.
16. Brandon Dewing, lhp, San Jose State University.
17. Michael Affronti, ss, LeMoyne College.
18. *Michael Ambort, c, Lamar University.
19. Greg Dowling, 1b, Georgia Southern University.
20. Josh McLaughlin, rhp, College of Charleston.
21. Jake Smith, c, East Carolina University.
22. Pat Currin, rhp, University of North Carolina-Greensboro.
23. Scott Moore, rhp, Texas State University.
24. Earl Oakes, rhp, Pace (N.Y.) University.
25. *Aaron Odom, lhp, Texas Tech.
26. Derrick Gordon, lhp, Lamar University.
27. Larry Cobb, of, College of Charleston.
28. Lorenzo Macias, of, Mount San Antonio (Calif.) JC.
29. Matt Manship, rhp, Stanford University.
DRAFT DROP *Brother of Jeff Manship, 14th-round draft pick, Twins (2006); major leaguer (2009-15)*
30. Josh Morgan, rhp, University of Missouri-St. Louis.
31. *Jonathan Pigott, of, Seabreeze HS, Ormond Beach, Fla.
32. *Nick Hernandez, lhp, Hialeah (Fla.) HS.
33. *Burke Lieppman, 1b, Prescott (Ariz.) HS.
34. *Steve Cochrane, c, Mission Viejo HS, Dove Canyon, Calif.
DRAFT DROP *Son of Dave Cochrane, major leaguer (1986-92)*
35. +Carlos Hernandez, lhp, West Valley (Calif.) JC.
36. *Jean Carlos Diaz, 3b, Academia Perpetuo Socorro, San Juan, P.R.
37. *David Fry, of, Bishop Gorman HS, Las Vegas, Nev.
38. *Rylan Sandoval, 2b, Chabot (Calif.) JC.
39. +Dante Love, c, San Diego CC.
40. *Goldy Simmons, rhp, Monte Vista HS, Spring Valley, Calif.
DRAFT DROP *Son of Nelson Simmons, major leaguer (1984-87)*
41. *Jeremy Weih, c, Wilton (Iowa) HS.

## PHILADELPHIA PHILLIES (21)

**1. Kyle Drabek, rhp, The Woodlands (Texas) HS** (Choice from Mets as compensation for Type A free agent Billy Wagner).—**(2010-15)**
DRAFT DROP *Son of Doug Drabek, major leaguer (1986-98)*
1. (Choice to Yankees as compensation for Type A free agent Tom Gordon)
**1. Adrian Cardenas, ss, Monsignor Pace HS, Miami Lakes, Fla.** (Supplemental choice—37th—as compensation for Wagner).—**(2012)**
**2. Drew Carpenter, rhp, Long Beach State University.—(2008-12)**
**3. Jason Donald, ss, University of Arizona.—(2010-12)**
4. D'Arby Myers, of, Westchester HS, Los Angeles.—(AAA)
**5. Quintin Berry, of, San Diego State University.—(2012-15)**
6. Dan Brauer, lhp, Northwestern University.
7. Charlie Yarbrough, 1b, Eastern Kentucky University.
8. T.J. Warren, of, Bethel HS, Vallejo, Calif.
9. Andrew Cruse, rhp, University of South Carolina.
10. Sam Walls, rhp, North Carolina State University.
11. Jarrod Freeman, rhp, Alta HS, Sandy, Utah.
12. Darin McDonald, of, Cherry Creek HS, Englewood, Colo.
DRAFT DROP *Brother of Donzell McDonald, major leaguer (2001-02) • Brother of Darnell McDonald, first-round draft pick, Orioles (1977); major leaguer (2004-13)*
13. Zach Penprase, ss, Mississippi Valley State University.
14. Gus Milner, of, University of Kansas.
15. *Riley Cooper, of, Clearwater Central Catholic HS, Clearwater, Fla.
DRAFT DROP *Wide receiver, National Football League (2010-14)*
16. Cody Montgomery, 3b, Dallas Baptist University.
17. Jay Miller, of, Washington State University.
18. Michael Dubee, rhp, Okaloosa-Walton (Fla.) JC.
19. Rob Roth, rhp, Lewiston (Idaho) HS.
**20. Domonic Brown, of, Redan HS, Lithonia, Ga.—(2010-15)**
21. Jacob Dempsey, of, Winthrop University.
22. Ben Pfinsgraff, rhp, University of Maryland.
23. Shawn McGill, c, Boston College.
24. Garet Hill, rhp, Biola (Calif.) University.
25. *Billy Mohl, rhp, Tulane University.
26. Will Savage, rhp, University of Oklahoma.
27. John Brownell, rhp, University of Oklahoma.
28. Herman Demmink, 3b, Clemson University.
29. Mike Fuentes, c, Coastal Carolina University.
30. Brian Capps, of, Texas Tech.
**31. *Bruce Billings, rhp, San Diego State University.—(2011-14)**
32. Alan Robbins, c, Winthrop University.
33. Mike DeVeaux, ss, Georgia College.
34. *Josh Thrailkill, rhp, T.C. Roberson HS, Arden, N.C.
35. *Rashad Taylor, of, Skyline (Calif.) JC.
**36. *Kyle Gibson, rhp, Greenfield Central HS, Greenfield, Ind.—(2013-15)**
DRAFT DROP *First-round draft pick (22nd overall), Twins (2009)*
37. *Shawn Epps, rhp, Northern Oklahoma CC.
38. *Bobby Haney, ss, Kings Park HS, Smithtown, N.Y.
39. *Gerard Mohrmann, rhp, Manitou Springs (Colo.) HS.
40. *Nathan Solow, lhp, La Cueva HS, Albuquerque, N.M.
41. *Michael Antonini, lhp, Georgia College.
42. *Daniel Faulkner, rhp, Bishop Noll Institute, Hammond, Ind.
43. *Yazy Arbelo, 1b, John Carroll HS, Port St. Lucie, Fla.
44. *Mike Petello, of, Saguaro HS, Scottsdale, Ariz.
45. *Patrick Murray, 1b, Santa Ana (Calif.) JC.
46. *Trayvone Johnson, c, Community Harvest Charter HS, Los Angeles.
47. *Tylien Manumaleuna, 3b, Dixie HS, St. George, Utah.
48. *Nick Morreale, c, Vernon Hills (Ill.) HS.
49. *Olivier Routhier-Pare, lhp, Ahuntsic College HS, Montreal.
50. *Matt Adams, 2b, King's Academy, Palm Beach Gardens, Fla.

## PITTSBURGH PIRATES (4)

**1. Brad Lincoln, rhp, University of Houston.—(2010-14)**
2. Mike Felix, lhp, Troy University.—(High A)
3. Shelby Ford, 2b, Oklahoma State University.—(AAA)
**4. Jared Hughes, rhp, Long Beach State University.—(2011-15)**
5. Pat Bresnehan, rhp, Arizona State University.—(AA)
6. Jim Negrych, 2b, University of Pittsburgh
7. Austin McClune, of, Edmond Santa Fe HS, Edmond, Okla.
**8. Alex Presley, of, University of Mississippi.—(2010-15)**
9. Steve McFarland, rhp, Lamar University.
10. Charles Benoit, lhp, Oklahoma State University.
**11. *Lonnie Chisenhall, ss-rhp, West Carteret HS, Newport, N.C.—(2011-15)**
DRAFT DROP *First-round draft pick (29th overall), Indians (2008)*
12. Kent Sakamoto, 1b, Fresno State University.
13. Brandon Holden, rhp, Stoneman Douglas HS, Coral Springs, Fla.
14. Greg Smith, 1b, Fordham University.
15. James Barksdale, of, University of North Alabama.
16. Kris Watts, c, Santa Clara University.
**17. Michael Crotta, rhp, Florida Atlantic University.—(2011)**
18. Francisco Ortiz, rhp, Toa Alta, P.R.
19. *Jason Moseby, of, Newport HS, Bellevue, Wash.
20. Matt Clarkson, c, Oklahoma State University.
21. *Kody Paul, rhp, Glynn Academy, Brunswick, Ga.
22. Miles Durham, of, Northwestern State University.
**23. *Preston Claiborne, 3b, Newman Smith HS, Carrolton, Texas.—(2013-14)**
24. Scott Massey, rhp, University of Southern Mississippi.
25. Adam Simon, rhp, San Diego State University.
**26. +Ryan Kelly, rhp, Hilton Head (S.C.) HS / Walters State (Tenn.) CC.—(2015)**
27. *Cache Breedlove, 3b, Edmond Santa Fe HS, Edmond, Okla.
**28. +Rudy Owens, lhp, Mesa (Ariz.) HS / Chandler-Gilbert (Ariz.) CC.—(2014)**

29. Brandon Williams, rhp, University of South Carolina-Upstate.
30. *Alphonso Owens, of, Dillon HS, Little Rock, S.C.
31. Jared Keel, 3b, Troy University.
32. Jorge Charry, rhp, Lake City (Fla.) JC.
33. Victor Alvarez, ss, Cumberland (Tenn.) University.
34. *Pernell Halliman, rhp, West Hills (Calif.) JC.
35. +Josue Peley, ss, Seminole State (Okla.) JC.
36. *Chad Arnold, rhp, Southridge HS, Kennewick, Wash.
37. Damian Walcott, of, Brookdale (N.J.) CC.
38. Brian McCullen, rhp, Western Carolina University.
39. Tom Hagan, of, University of Virginia.
40. *Philip Brannon, rhp, Broome HS, Spartanburg, S.C.
41. *Scott Kuhns, rhp, Parkland (Ill.) JC.
42. *Jonathan Harmston, lhp, Bullard HS, Fresno, Calif.
43. +Devin Copley, rhp, Gulf Coast (Fla.) CC.
44. *Tanner Hines, ss, Hudson HS, Lufkin, Texas.
45. *Paul-Michael Klingsberg, 1b, Notre Dame HS, Studio City, Calif.
46. *Ryan Groth, of, Indian River (Fla.) CC.
47. *Brandon Wilkerson, ss, Lamar HS, Arlington, Texas.
DRAFT DROP *Son of Curtis Wilkerson, major leaguer (1983-93)*
48. *Ken Wieda, rhp, Vernon Regional (Texas) JC.
49. *Carson Middleton, rhp, Lindale (Texas) HS.
50. *Marquis Zachary, of, Lake City (Fla.) CC.

## ST. LOUIS CARDINALS (30)

**1. Adam Ottavino, rhp, Northeastern University.—(2010-15)**
**1. Chris Perez, rhp, University of Miami** (Supplemental choice—42nd—as compensation for Type A free agent Matt Morris).**—(2008-14)**
2. Brad Furnish, lhp, Texas Christian University (Choice from Giants as compensation for Morris).—(AA)
**2. Jon Jay, of, University of Miami.—(2010-15)**
**2. Mark Hamilton, 1b, Tulane University** (Supplemental choice—76th—as compensation for Type C free agent Abraham Nunez).**—(2010-11)**
3. Gary Daley, rhp, Cal Poly San Luis Obispo.—(AAA)
4. Eddie Degerman, rhp, Rice University.—(AA)
**5. Shane Robinson, of, Florida State University.—(2009-15)**
6. Tyler Norrick, lhp, Southern Illinois University.
7. Luke Gorsett, of, University of Nebraska.
**8. Allen Craig, ss, University of California.—(2010-15)**
9. Matt North, rhp, Deer Valley HS, Vacaville, Calif.
10. *Blair Erickson, rhp, UC Irvine.
**11. P.J. Walters, rhp, University of South Alabama.—(2009-13)**
**12. David Carpenter, c, University of West Virginia.—(2011-15)**
13. Travis Mitchell, of, Parkway Central HS, Chesterfield, Mo.
**14. Jon Edwards, of, Keller (Texas) HS.—(2014-15)**
**15. *Lance Zawadzki, ss, San Diego State University.—(2010)**
**16. Tommy Pham, ss, Durango HS, Las Vegas, Nev.—(2014-15)**
17. Nathan Southard, of, Tulane University.
18. Amaury Cazana Marti, of, Miami.
19. Brandon Buckman, 1b, University of Nebraska.
20. *Brandon Cooney, rhp, Florida Atlantic University.
21. +Mark Diapoules, rhp, Martin County HS, Palm City, Fla. / Palm Beach (Fla.) CC.
22. Casey Mulligan, c, Valencia HS, Castaic, Calif.
23. +LaCurtis Mayes, rhp, Poly HS, Riverside, Calif. / Riverside (Calif.) CC.
24. *Bobby Gomez, lhp, University of Texas-Pan American.
25. +Demarcus Ingram, of, North Little Rock (Ark.) HS / Pensacola (Fla.) CC.
26. Garrett Bussiere, c, University of California.
27. Christian Reyes, c, Porterville (Calif.) JC.
**28. Luke Gregerson, rhp, St. Xavier (Ill.) University.—(2009-15)**
29. Will Groff, 2b, SUNY Cortland.
30. Jared Schweitzer, 3b, University of Kansas.
31. Mark Shorey, of, High Point University.
32. *Ross Smith, of, Dodge County HS, Eastman, Ga.
33. Brian Schroeder, lhp, UCLA.
DRAFT DROP *Son of Jay Schroeder, first-round draft pick, Blue Jays (1979); quarterback, National Football League (1985-94)*
34. Isa Garcia, 2b, University of Houston.
35. Jim Rapoport, of, Stanford University.
36. *Adrian Alaniz, rhp, University of Texas.
37. Logan Collier, rhp, Guilford (N.C.) College.
38. Scott Thomas, c, Missouri Baptist College.
DRAFT DROP *Son of Lee Thomas, major leaguer (1961-68); general manager, Phillies (1988-97)*
39. Matt Michael, lhp, Grand Canyon University.
40. *Tyler Mach, 3b, Oklahoma State University.
41. *Mitch Canham, c, Oregon State University.
DRAFT DROP *First-round draft pick (57th overall), Padres (2007)*
42. Kyle Mura, rhp-3b, Loyola Marymount University.
DRAFT DROP *Son of Steve Mura, major leaguer (1978-85)*
43. *Gabe Torres, ss, St. Peters Prep, East Orange, N.J.
44. *Cameron Grant, of, Hermitage HS, Lynchburg, Va.
45. *John Goodman, rhp, Georgia Tech.
46. *Robert Woodard, rhp, University of North Carolina.
47. +Nick Additon, lhp, Western HS, Davie, Fla. / Indian River (Fla.) JC.
48. *Garry Thomas, lhp, Pine Bluff (Ark.) HS.
49. *Gary Taylor, of, Holmes (Miss.) JC.
50. *Charles Matthews, rhp, Athens (Ga.) Academy.

## SAN DIEGO PADRES (17)

**1. Matt Antonelli, 3b, Wake Forest University.—(2008)**
1. Kyler Burke, of, Ooltewah HS, Chattanooga, Tenn. (Supplemental choice—35th—for loss of Type A free agent Ramon Hernandez).—(High A)
**2. Chad Huffman, 2b, Texas Christian University** (Choice from Orioles as compensation for Hernandez).**—(2010)**
**2. Wade LeBlanc, lhp, University of Alabama.—(2008-14)**
**3. Cedric Hunter, of, Martin Luther King HS, Decatur, Ga.—(2011)**
4. Nate Culp, lhp, University of Missouri.—(AAA)
5. Andy Underwood, rhp, Fresno State University.—(Low A)
6. *Tim Bascom, rhp, University of Central Florida.
7. Craig Cooper, 1b, University of Notre Dame.
8. Tom King, ss, Troy University.
**9. David Freese, 3b, University of South Alabama.—(2009-15)**
10. Kody Valverde, c, University of Alabama.
**11. +Mat Latos, rhp, Coconut Creek HS, Margate, Fla. / Broward (Fla.) CC.—(2009-15)**
12. Stephen Faris, rhp, Clemson University.
13. Mike Epping, of, University of New Orleans.
**14. *Grant Green, ss, Canyon HS, Anaheim, Calif.—(2013-15)**
DRAFT DROP *First-round draft pick (13th overall), Athletics (2009)*
15. Matt Buschmann, rhp, Vanderbilt University.
16. Ray Stokes, 2b, Cal State East Bay.
17. Tyler Mead, rhp, Skyview HS, Vancouver, Wash.
18. Garner Wetzel, ss, Millsaps (Miss.) College.
19. Brian Hernandez, c, Vanderbilt University.
20. Michael Campbell, of, University of South Carolina.
21. Luke Cannon, of, Texas State University.
22. Justin Pickett, 1b, Walters State (Tenn.) JC.
23. Brooks Dunn, lhp, Mississippi State University.
24. Nick Tucci, rhp, University of Connecticut.
25. Nick Kliebert, 2b, Pepperdine University.
26. +Jeremy McBride, rhp, Rose State (Okla.) JC.
27. Matt Huff, rhp, Regis (Colo.) College.
28. Jeremy Hunt, 1b, Villanova University.
29. A.J. Davidiuk, 3b, Furman University.
30. *Joseph Cates, rhp, Palomar (Calif.) JC.
31. Jon Kirby, rhp, Lee (Tenn.) University.
32. *Jordan Rogers, rhp, San Jacinto (Texas) JC.
33. *Sean Finefrock, rhp, Blanchard HS, Yukon, Okla.
34. *Casey Haerther, 1b, Chaminade Prep, Chatsworth, Calif.
35. *Joseph Cruz, rhp, South Hills HS, Baldwin Park, Calif.
36. *Daniel Johansen, rhp, Woodinville (Wash.) HS.
37. *Miguel Flores, rhp, St. John Bosco HS, Lynwood, Calif.
38. *Ben Francis, rhp, Mosley HS, Panama City, Fla.
39. *Chance Deason, lhp, Piedmont (Okla.) HS.
40. *Josh Casas, lhp, South El Monte (Calif.) HS.
41. *Mike Freeman, ss, Edgewater HS, Orlando, Fla.
42. *Luke Stewart, 3b, Normal West HS, Normal, Ill.
43. *Jeff Ramirez, ss, El Camino HS, South San Francisco.
44. *Jett Hart, ss, Puyallup (Wash.) HS.
45. *Bryce Lefebvre, 3b, Scottsdale (Ariz.) CC.
DRAFT DROP *Son of Jim Lefebvre, major leaguer (1965-72); major league manager (1989-99)*

## SAN FRANCISCO GIANTS (10)

**1. Tim Lincecum, rhp, University of Washington.—(2007-15)**
**1. Emmanuel Burriss, ss, Kent State University** (Supplemental choice—33rd—as compensation for Type A free agent Scott Eyre).**—(2008-15)**
2. (Choice to Cardinals as compensation for Type A free agent Matt Morris)
3. (Choice to Diamondbacks as compensation for Type A free agent Tim Worrell)
3. Clayton Tanner, lhp, De la Salle HS, Concord, Calif. (Choice from Cubs as compensation for Eyre).—(AAA)
4. Ben Snyder, lhp, Ball State University.—(AAA)
DRAFT DROP *Brother of Brad Snyder, first-round draft pick, Indians (2003); major leaguer (2010-14)*
5. Michael McBryde, of, Florida Atlantic University.—(AAA)
**6. Ryan Rohlinger, 3b, University of Oklahoma.—(2008-11)**
**7. Brett Pill, 1b, Cal State Fullerton.—(2011-13)**
8. Matt Klimas, c, Texarkana (Texas) CC.
**9. Brian Bocock, ss, Stetson University.—(2008-10)**
10. Ryan Paul, lhp, Cal State Fullerton.
11. Gib Hobson, rhp, North Carolina State University.
12. Matt Weston, of, University of Houston.
13. Brad Boyer, 2b, University of San Francisco.
14. Eric Stolp, rhp, University of the Pacific.
15. *Andrew Barbosa, lhp, Riverview HS, Sarasota, Fla.
16. Paul Oseguera, lhp, UCLA.
17. Kevin Pucetas, rhp, Limestone (S.C.) College.
18. *Jeff Stallings, rhp, North Carolina State University.
**19. Tyler Graham, of, Oregon State University.—(2012)**
20. Adam Paul, rhp, University of North Carolina-Wilmington.
21. Steven Calicutt, lhp, East Tennessee State University.
22. Bobby Felmy, of, University of Georgia.
23. *E.B. Crow, rhp, Sitka (Alaska) HS.
24. *Jeff Walters, rhp, Olympia HS, Orlando, Fla.
25. *Joseph Moos, ss, Williston HS, Bronson, Fla.
26. *Shane Mathews, rhp, East Carolina University.
27. Sean Van Elderen, of, Mesa State (Colo.) College.
28. *Dusty Harvard, of, Natrona County HS, Casper, Wyo.
29. *Nick Liles, 2b, Scotland County HS, Laurinburg, N.C.
30. Daryl Maday, rhp, University of Arkansas.
31. *Matt McMurtry, lhp, University of Minnesota-Mankato.
32. *Matt Fairel, lhp, Winter Haven (Fla.) HS.
33. *Chris Siewert, c, University of Tennessee.
34. Jared Cranston, lhp, University of Nebraska.
35. Adam Cowart, rhp, Kansas State University.
**36. Matt Downs, 3b, University of Alabama.—(2009-12)**
37. Lance Salsgiver, of, Harvard University.
38. *Ryan Butner, rhp, Hialeah (Fla.) HS.
39. *Lee Darracott, 3b, Vernon Regional (Texas) JC.
40. *Jonathon Amaya, of, Diamond Bar (Calif.) HS.
41. *Bo Merrell, 2b, Seward County (Kan.) CC.
42. *Brandon Grabham, rhp, Grayson County (Texas) CC.
43. *Kevin Boggan, rhp, Boston College.
44. *Kyle Lafrenz, c, Marshalltown (Iowa) CC.
45. *Matt Speake, rhp, New Mexico JC.
46. *Taylor Hammack, lhp, Angleton (Texas) HS.
47. *Ryan Bradley, lhp, Mattoon (Ill.) HS.
48. Evan Bush, 2b, University of Alabama.
49. *Jonathan Batts, c, University of North Carolina-Wilmington.
50. Robert Davis, c, University of South Carolina-Aiken.

## SEATTLE MARINERS (5)

**1. Brandon Morrow, rhp, University of California.—(2007-15)**
**2. Chris Tillman, rhp, Fountain Valley (Calif.) HS.—(2009-15)**
3. Tony Butler, lhp, Oak Creek (Wis.) HS.—(Low A)
4. Ricky Orta, rhp, University of Miami.—(AA)
**5. Nathan Adcock, rhp, North Hardin HS, Vince Grove, Ky.—(2011-15)**
**6. Adam Moore, c, University of Texas-Arlington.—(2009-14)**
**7. Doug Fister, rhp, Fresno State University.—(2009-15)**
8. Steve Richard, rhp, Clemson University.
9. Justin Souza, rhp, Sacramento (Calif.) CC.
10. Chris Minaker, ss, Stanford University.
11. Aaron Solomon, rhp, Cumberland (Tenn.) University.
12. Gavin Dickey, of, University of Florida.
13. Joe Kantakevich, rhp, College of William & Mary.
14. *Jared Baehl, 3b, North Posey HS, Poseyville, Ind.
15. Drew Fiorenza, rhp, Clemson University.
16. Austin Dirkx, rhp, University of Portland.
**17. *Dan Runzler, lhp, UC Riverside.—(2009-12)**
**18. Kam Mickolio, rhp, Utah Valley State College.—(2008-11)**
19. *Cam Nobles, rhp, Jackson HS, Mill Creek, Wash.
20. Johan Limonta, 1b, Miami-Dade CC.
21. +Brent Gaphardt, lhp, University of Delaware.
22. Fabian Williamson, lhp, Kennedy HS, Granada Hills, Calif.
23. Marcos Villezcas, ss, Brigham Young University.
24. Kyle Parker, rhp, University of Washington.
25. +Tyson Gillies, of, R.E. Mountain HS, Langley, B.C. / Iowa Western CC.
26. Greg Moviel, lhp, Vanderbilt University.
27. Bryan Ball, rhp, University of Florida.
28. Rocky Collis, rhp, Cornell University.
29. Greg Nesbitt, lhp, James Madison University.
30. Matt Vogel, ss, Lewis-Clark State (Idaho) College.
31. *David McClain, rhp, San Jacinto (Texas) JC.
32. *Joe Agreste, 1b, Potomac State (W.Va.) JC.
33. Rob Harmon, rhp, University of Arkansas-Little Rock.
34. Stan Posluszny, of, West Virginia University.
DRAFT DROP *Brother of Paul Posluszny, linebacker, National Football League (2007-14)*
35. Alex Meneses, ss, Barry (Fla.) University.
36. *Kyle Haas, rhp, Douglas (B.C.) JC.
37. *Chris Walden, rhp, Bellefontaine (Ohio) HS.
38. *Michael Drake, of, Cosumnes River (Calif.) JC.
39. +Philip Roy, rhp, Miami-Dade CC.
40. Haley Winter, rhp, UC Riverside.
41. Brandon Fromm, 1b, San Jose State University.
42. *Shane Cox, rhp, Alvin (Texas) CC.
43. *Clint Straka, rhp, Northern Oklahoma CC.
44. *Bryan Earley, rhp, Elder HS, Cincinnati.
DRAFT DROP *Son of Bill Earley, major leaguer (1986)*
45. *Jeremy Camacho, ss, Eagle Rock HS, Los Angeles.
46. +Robbie Dominguez, rhp, Cerritos (Calif.) JC.
47. *Sean Ward, of, Evans HS, Martinez, Ga.
48. *Jeremy Beeching, lhp, Volunteer State (Tenn.) CC.
49. *Ryne Tacker, rhp, Rice University.
50. *Tyler Sanford, c, Saguaro HS, Scottsdale, Ariz.

## TAMPA BAY DEVIL RAYS (3)

**1. Evan Longoria, 3b, Long Beach State University.—(2008-15)**
**2. Josh Butler, rhp, University of San**

**Diego.—(2009)**

3. *Nick Fuller, rhp, Kell HS, Marietta, Ga.—DNP

DRAFT DROP *Attended South Carolina; re-drafted by Braves, 2008 (25th round)*

**4. Alex Cobb, rhp, Vero Beach (Fla.) HS.—(2011-14)**

**5. Shawn O'Malley, ss, Southridge HS, Kennewick, Wash.—(2014-15)**

**6. Nevin Ashley, c, Indiana State University.—(2015)**

**7. Ryan Reid, rhp, James Madison University.—(2013)**

8. Tyree Hayes, rhp, Tomball (Texas) HS.

DRAFT DROP *Son of Charlie Hayes, major leaguer (1988-2001)*

9. Eligio Sonoqui, 1b, Cesar Chavez HS, Phoenix.

**10. Desmond Jennings, of, Itawamba (Miss.) JC.—(2010-15)**

11. Heath Rollins, rhp, Winthrop University.

12. *Teddy Hubbard, rhp, Hooks (Texas) HS.

**13. *Mike Minor, lhp, Forrest HS, Lewisburg, Tenn.—(2010-14)**

DRAFT DROP *First-round draft pick (7th overall), Braves (2009)*

14. Travis Barnett, rhp, Salt Lake (Utah) CC.

15. +K.D. Kang, of, Parkview HS, Lilburn, Ga. / Chattahoochee Valley (Ala.) JC.

16. Ryan Owen, lhp, Cal State Dominguez Hills.

17. *Ryan Thornton, of, American River (Calif.) JC.

18. *Jay Brown, rhp, Young Harris (Ga.) JC.

19. +Robi Estrada, ss, El Segundo (Calif.) HS / El Camino (Calif.) JC.

20. Erik Walker, rhp, University of North Carolina-Charlotte.

21. Joey Callender, 2b, Texas Tech.

22. +Mark Thomas, c, Alpharetta (Ga.) HS / Young Harris (Ga.) JC.

23. *Matt McCarney, of, Holy Trinity Catholic HS, Kanata, Ontario.

24. +Angel Chapa, rhp, Treasure Valley (Ore.) CC / JC of Southern Idaho.

25. *Blaine Howell, lhp, A.C. Reynolds HS, Asheville, N.C.

26. *Drew Parker, rhp, Lord Tweedsmuir HS, Surrey, B.C.

27. *Luis Lopez, of, St. Francis School, Carolina, P.R.

28. *Andrew Hagins, of, Oak Park-River Forest HS, Oak Park, Ill.

29. *Leon Johnson, of, Thatcher, Ariz.

DRAFT DROP *Brother of Elliot Johnson, major leaguer (2011-14)*

30. Jimmy Mayer, ss, University of Pittsburgh.

31. +Justin Reynolds, of, Mount Hood (Ore.) CC.

32. *Emmanuel Morales, of, Puerto Rico Baseball Academy, Aguas Buenas, P.R.

33. *Brooks Lindsley, 2b, Mount Hood (Ore.) CC.

34. *Stephen McCray, rhp, Parkview HS, Lilburn, Ga.

35. +Michael Ross, 2b, Northwest Mississippi CC.

36. *Wally Marciel, lhp, Iolani HS, Kailua, Hawaii.

37. *Kalvin Johnson, 1b, Iowa Western CC.

38. *Chris Dennis, 1b, St. Thomas of Villanova HS, Windsor, Ontario.

39. *Matt Miraldi, of, Bear River HS, Grass Valley, Calif.

40. *Brando Casalicchio, rhp, Cold Spring Harbor HS, Huntington, N.Y.

41. *Michael Dufek, of, Desert Mountain HS, Scottsdale, Ariz.

42. *Brandon Vernon, c, Overton HS, Nashville, Tenn.

43. *Victor Ramos, of, Miami (Fla.) Senior HS.

44. *Neil Hardon, of, Saguaro HS, Phoenix.

45. *Chris Wilson, rhp, Trinidad State (Colo.) JC.

46. *Candy Maldonado, of, Porterville (Calif.) JC.

DRAFT DROP *Son of Candy Maldonado, major leaguer (1981-95)*

47. *Brandon Brown, 3b, Tate HS, Cantonment, Fla.

48. *Alex McRee, lhp, Chestatee HS, Gainesville, Ga.

49. *Ryan Fraser, rhp, Walker Valley HS, Cleveland, Tenn.

**50. *Travis Tartamella, c, Los Osos HS, Alta Loma, Calif.—(2015)**

## TEXAS RANGERS (12)

1. Kasey Kiker, lhp, Russell County HS, Phenix City, Ala.—(AA)

2. (Choice to Indians as compensation for Type B free agent Kevin Millwood)

3. Chad Tracy, c, Pepperdine University.—(AAA)

DRAFT DROP *Son of Jim Tracy, major leaguer (1980-81); major league manager (2001-12)*

4. Marcus Lemon, ss, Eustis HS, Umatilla, Fla.—(AAA)

DRAFT DROP *Son of Chet Lemon, first-round draft pick, Athletics (1972); major leaguer (1975-90)*

**5. Chris Davis, 1b, Navarro (Texas) JC.—(2008-15)**

**6. Jacob Brigham, rhp, Central Florida Christian HS, Orlando, Fla.—(2015)**

7. Grant Gerrard, of, Southern Illinois University.

8. Josh Bradbury, of, Orange Coast (Calif.) JC.

9. Brennan Garr, rhp, University of Northern Colorado.

**10. Craig Gentry, of, University of Arkansas.—(2009-15)**

11. Craig Crow, rhp, Rice University.

12. Matt Jaimes, 3b, Chino HS, Ontario, Calif.

13. *Kevin Angelle, lhp, Bridge City HS, Orange, Texas.

14. Mike Ballard, lhp, University of Virginia.

15. Cody Himes, ss, JC of San Mateo (Calif.).

16. Cody Podraza, of, Tomball (Texas) HS.

17. +John Maschino, rhp, Seminole State (Okla.) JC.

18. Mike Wagner, rhp, Washington State University.

19. *Miguel Velazquez, of, Gabriela Mistral HS, San Juan, P.R.

20. *Tyler Fleming, rhp, Cowley County (Kan.) CC.

21. *Brandt Walker, rhp, St. Stephens Episcopal HS, Austin, Texas.

**22. *Cory Luebke, lhp, Ohio State University.—(2010-12)**

DRAFT DROP *First-round draft pick (63rd overall), Padres (2009)*

23. Jay Heafner, ss, Davidson College.

24. *Lance McClain, lhp, Walters State (Tenn.) CC.

**25. +Derek Holland, lhp, Wallace State (Ala.) CC.—(2009-15)**

26. *Kenny Gregory, 1b, Immaculata HS, Pittstown, N.J.

27. *Jared Olson, 3b, Frederick (Md.) CC.

28. *Schaeffer Hall, lhp, Lee's Summit (Mo.) HS.

29. Daniel Hoben, lhp, Chandler-Gilbert (Ariz.) CC.

30. Nick Cadena, 3b, Florida International University.

31. Adam Schaecher, rhp, Creighton University.

32. Shannon Wirth, rhp, Lewis-Clark State (Idaho) College.

33. +Eric Fry, of, San Jacinto (Texas) JC.

34. Austin Weilep, rhp, Lewis-Clark State (Idaho) College.

35. Brian Nelson, of, Corban (Ore.) College.

36. John Slusarz, rhp, University of Connecticut.

37. *John Lambert, lhp, Chesterton (Ind.) HS.

38. Jon Hollis, rhp, Yale University.

39. *Gary Poynter, rhp, Weatherford (Texas) JC.

40. +Chris Dennis, rhp, Auburn University.

41. *Brandon Gribbin, rhp, Golden West (Calif.) JC.

42. *Lance West, of, Captain Shreve HS, Shreveport, La.

43. *Shawn Sanford, rhp, Cinnaminson (N.J.) HS.

44. +Dan Sattler, rhp, Purdue University.

**45. Danny Herrera, lhp, University of New Mexico.—(2008-11)**

46. *Clifton Thomas, of, El Cajon Valley HS, El Cajon, Calif.

47. *Joseph Norwood, 3b, Modesto (Calif.) JC.

48. *Rylan Ostrosky, rhp, Lethbridge (Alberta) CC.

49. *Clint Stubbs, of, Atlanta (Texas) HS.

DRAFT DROP *Brother of Drew Stubbs, first-round draft pick, Reds (2006); major leaguer (2009-15)*

50. Patrick Donovan, lhp, Gonzaga University.

## TORONTO BLUE JAYS (14)

**1. Travis Snider, of, Jackson HS, Mill Creek, Wash.—(2008-15)**

2. (Choice to Orioles as compensation for Type A free agent B.J. Ryan)

3. (Choice to Marlins as compensation for Type A free agent A.J. Burnett)

4. Brandon Magee, rhp, Bradley University.—(AA)

5. Luke Hopkins, 1b, New Mexico State University.—(Short-season A)

6. Brian Jeroloman, c, University of Florida.

7. Jon Baksh, of, Florida Tech.

8. Danny O'Brien, lhp, Western Michigan University.

**9. *Cole Figueroa, ss, Lincoln HS, Tallahassee, Fla.—(2014-15)**

DRAFT DROP *Son of Bien Figueroa, major leaguer (1992) • Twin brother of Corey Figueroa, 42nd-round draft pick, Blue Jays (2006)*

10. Scott Campbell, 2b, Gonzaga University.

11. Matt Lane, c, University of Washington.

**12. Jonathan Diaz, ss, North Carolina State University.—(2013-15)**

13. Mikal Garbarino, of, San Dimas (Calif.) HS.

14. Shawn Scobee, of, University of Nevada-Reno.

15. Seth Overbey, rhp, University of Maryland.

16. Chase Lirette, rhp, University of South Florida.

17. Kyle Ginley, rhp, St. Petersburg (Fla.) CC.

18. Kyle Walter, lhp, Bucknell University.

19. Matt Liuzza, c, Louisiana State University.

20. Jonathan Del Campo, ss, Cibola HS, Yuma, Ariz.

21. Ron Lowe, lhp, St. Leo (Fla.) College.

**22. *Brad Mills, lhp, University of Arizona.—(2009-15)**

23. Adam Calderone, of, Florida Southern College.

24. *Keith Demorgandie, rhp, Orange Coast (Calif.) JC.

25. Luis Fernandez, ss, Miguel de Cervantes HS, Bayamon, P.R.

26. Chris Emmanuele, of, Northeastern University.

27. Patrick McGuigan, rhp, University of San Francisco.

28. Zach Dials, rhp, University of Kentucky.

29. *Ryan Basham, of, Michigan State University.

30. Raul Barron, ss, Pasadena (Calif.) CC.

31. Adam Rogers, rhp, University of Evansville.

32. John Tritz, rhp, University of Texas-San Antonio.

33. *Greg Lopez, ss, University of Notre Dame.

**34. Graham Godfrey, rhp, College of Charleston.—(2011-12)**

35. John Zinnicker, lhp, St. Bonaventure University.

36. *Dominique Rodgers, of, Sacramento (Calif.) CC.

37. Ben Zeskind, of, University of Richmond.

38. +Kevin Denis-Fortier, 1b, Crowder (Mo.) CC.

39. *Luke Tucker, rhp, Florida State University.

40. Ted Serro, rhp, Franklin & Marshall (Pa.) College.

41. C.J. Ebarb, c, Lamar University.

42. *Corey Figueroa, 2b, Lincoln HS, Tallahassee, Fla.

DRAFT DROP *Son of Bien Figueroa, major leaguer (1992) • Twin brother of Cole Figueroa, ninth-round draft pick, Blue Jays (2006); major leaguer (2014-15)*

43. Nathan Melek, rhp, University of New Mexico.

44. Kelly Sweppenhiser, 3b, Virginia Military Institute.

45. *Lee Vermeel, lhp, Malvern Collegiate Institute, Toronto.

46. *Mace Thurman, lhp, McLennan (Texas) CC.

47. *Wilberto Morales, 1b, Arizona Western JC.

48. *Jonathan Fernandez, ss, American Heritage HS, Westin, Fla.

DRAFT DROP *Son of Tony Fernandez, major leaguer (1983-2001)*

49. Brad Cuthbertson, rhp, Midland (Texas) JC.

50. Baron Frost, of, University of Southern California.

## WASHINGTON NATIONALS (15)

**1. Chris Marrero, 3b, Monsignor Pace HS, Hialeah Gardens, Fla.—(2011-13)**

1. Colton Willems, rhp, John Carroll HS, Fort Pierce, Fla. (Choice from Athletics as compensation for Type B free agent Esteban Loaiza).—(High A)

2. *Sean Black, rhp, Lenape HS, Mount Laurel, N.J.—(AA)

DRAFT DROP *Attended Seton Hall; re-drafted by Yankees, 2009 (7th round)*

2. Stephen Englund, ss-of, Bellevue (Wash.) HS (Choice from Angels as compensation for Type B free agent Hector Carrasco).—(Low A)

3. Stephen King, ss, Winter Park HS, Orlando, Fla.—(AA)

4. Glenn Gibson, lhp, Center Moriches (N.Y.) HS.—(High A)

DRAFT DROP *Son of Paul Gibson, major leaguer (1988-96)*

5. Cory VanAllen, lhp, Baylor University.—(AAA)

6. Zech Zinicola, rhp, Arizona State University.

7. *Sam Brown, rhp, Millbrook HS, Raleigh, N.C.

8. Sean Rooney, c, Saddleback (Calif.) CC.

9. *Joey Rosas, lhp, Yavapai (Ariz.) CC.

10. *Rico Salmon, c, Miami Sunset HS, Miami.

11. Desmond Jones, rhp, Middle Georgia JC.

**12. Cole Kimball, rhp, Centenary (N.J.) College.—(2011)**

13. Hassan Pena, rhp, Palm Beach (Fla.) CC.

14. Brett McMillan, 1b, UCLA.

15. *Dustin Dickerson, 3b, Midway HS, McGregor, Texas.

16. Pat Nichols, c, Old Dominion University.

17. Erik Arnesen, rhp, Grove City (Pa.) College.

18. Adam Carr, 1b, Oklahoma State University.

**19. *Sam Dyson, rhp, Jesuit HS, Tampa.—(2012-15)**

20. Alberto Tavarez, rhp, Western Oklahoma State JC.

21. Chris French, of, New Mexico JC.

22. Robby Jacobsen, c, George Mason University.

23. *Forrest Beverly, lhp, University of South Carolina.

24. Ricky Caputo, 3b, Hofstra University.

25. *Jim Birmingham, lhp, Overbrook HS, Pine Hill, N.J.

26. Brett Logan, c, University of Houston.

27. Dan Pfau, lhp, George Washington University.

28. *Michael Robbins, lhp, Meridian (Miss.) CC.

**29. *Khris Davis, of, Deer Valley HS, Glendale, Ariz.—(2013-15)**

30. *Burt Reynolds, ss, Bloomfield Vocational Tech, Newark, N.J.

31. Zach Baldwin, lhp, West Virginia State University.

32. Joe Welsh, lhp, University of Toledo.

**33. *Tyler Moore, 1b, Meridian (Miss.) CC.—(2012-15)**

34. *Taylor Kinzer, of, Homestead HS, Fort Wayne, Ind.

35. *D'Vontrey Richardson, of, Lee County HS, Albany, Ga.

36. Jeremy Goldschmeding, ss, Dallas Baptist University.

37. *Austin Hudson, rhp, Boone HS, Orlando, Fla.

38. *Zach Von Tersch, rhp, Cedar Falls (Iowa) HS.

39. *Andrew Doyle, rhp, Alleman HS, Rock Island, Ill.

40. *Nick Pearce, rhp, DeMatha Catholic HS, Silver Spring, Md.

**41. +Brad Peacock, rhp, Palm Beach Central HS, Wellington, Fla. / Palm Beach (Fla.) CC.—(2011-15)**

42. *Javier Martinez, rhp, Fordham University.

43. Cory Anderson, rhp, U.S. Coast Guard Academy.

44. *Chad Jenkins, lhp, Caravel Academy, Newark, Del.

45. *Adam Kramer, rhp, New Mexico JC.

46. *Jayson Brugman, ss, South Mountain (Ariz.) CC.

47. *Josh Rodriguez, c, Red Mountain HS, Mesa, Ariz.

48. *Kyle Page, of, Brevard (Fla.) CC.

DRAFT DROP *Son of Mitchell Page, major leaguer (1977-84)*

49. *Jarred Holloway, lhp, Russellville (Ark.) HS.

50. *J.J. Pannell, rhp, George Mason University.

# 2007

## AT A GLANCE

### This Date In History
June 7-8

### Best Draft
**ATLANTA BRAVES.** The Braves struck it rich by drafting **JASON HEYWARD** (1) and **FREDDIE FREEMAN** (2), two of the nation's best high school hitters. Their quest to land two of the best closers was thwarted when Georgia righthander **JOSH FIELDS** (2) and Alabama juco righthander **CRAIG KIMBREL** (33) did not sign. The Braves drafted Kimbrel again a year later and signed him.

### Worst Draft
**HOUSTON ASTROS.** No draft was more responsible than this one for the Astros pending collapse, which culminated in three 100-loss seasons from 2011-13. The Astros did not have first- or second-round picks and failed to sign their third- and fourth-rounders.

### First-Round Bust
**BEAU MILLS, 3B, INDIANS.** Mills had a big 2007 college season at Idaho's Lewis-Clark State, setting an NAIA record with 38 homers and leading the school to a 58-5 record and its 15th NAIA World Series title. But Mills struggled to tap into his raw power in six minor league seasons, routinely chasing pitches out of the strike zone. He hit .267 with 86 home runs and 406 RBIs in 629 games.

### On Second Thought
**GIANCARLO STANTON, OF, MARLINS.** Stanton drew comparisons with Hall of Famer Dave Winfield in high school for his prowess in baseball, football and basketball. He might have been the least proficient in baseball, but the Marlins were happy to get him in the second round. Stanton, who went by the first name of Mike early in his pro career, quickly became a premier power hitter in the major leagues, hitting 181 home runs in his first 708 games through the 2015 season.

# New draft tactics fail to curb bonus inflation

As the Tampa Bay Devil Rays new scouting director, R.J. Harrison presided over his first draft in 2007. The team had the dubious distinction of making the No. 1 selection, and Harrison had experience with the process.

In a playing, coaching and scouting career that spanned more than 30 years, Harrison had an association with the first overall pick on six previous occasions. He'd seen enough to know that for all the obvious ability inherent in a No. 1 choice, few measured up to the hype. He also knew that it was prudent to keep an open mind and not jump to any conclusions when deciding which player to take.

"Our goal, as an organization, is to take the best player available," Harrison said as the 2007 crop began taking shape. "We had a fair idea coming into the year who the top guys would be, and there have been no surprises yet. But I challenged our scouts every day to keep an open mind, to make sure they didn't close out guys that might become a Mike Mussina, or someone of that order. Every year there are some great major leaguers signed that are mid- to late-first rounders. You also have some clunkers at the top.

"I would rather have more candidates early on and do a diligent job scouting them than realize at the end of the process that we haven't done our homework on a couple of guys."

Vanderbilt lefthander David Price was the consensus top prospect from the outset and seemed to be a perfect fit for the Devil Rays, as he would address a pressing need for pitching in short order. Harrison acknowledged that Price was on his short list of four, and that at least one Rays scout had seen each of his starts.

"He's the standard by which we're measuring everyone at this point," Harrison said. "He's performed every time out. But there are such high expectations of the first pick, it is very tough living up to them."

Harrison's first exposure to a No. 1 overall pick was his college roommate at Arizona State, lefthander Floyd Bannister, who was the top pick of the Houston Astros in 1976.

"He was a tremendous talent, one of the best college pitchers I've ever seen," Harrison said. "But did he live up to being a 1-1? Probably not. He pitched 15 seasons in the big leagues, led the American League in strikeouts one year and had a good career by almost any standard, but the expectations are so high for No. 1 picks to live up to."

Harrison also played five years of pro ball, and was a Double-A teammate of outfielder Al Chambers, the top pick in the 1979 draft. Chambers never came close to living up his draft slot, hitting .208 in 57 major league games for the Seattle Mariners.

In 1981, Harrison was a player/pitching coach

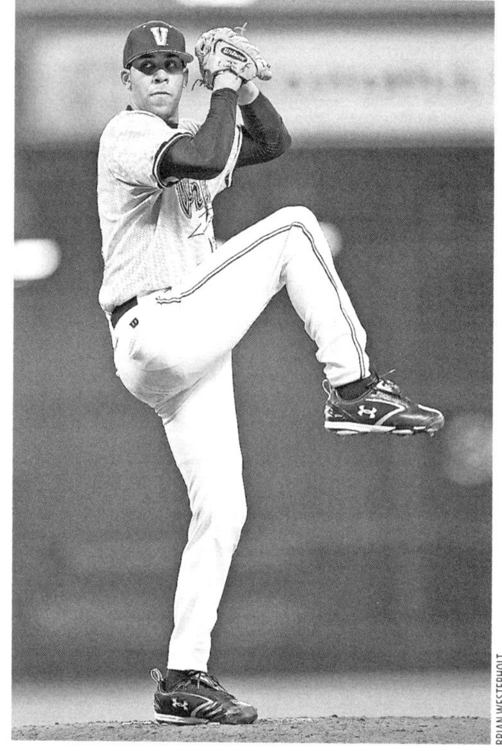

BRIAN WESTERHOLT

**David Price was a relatively easy choice for the Devil Rays as the No. 1 pick, and he went on to fulfill his promise and find stardom with Tampa Bay before leaving to seek greater fortune elsewhere**

for Seattle's Double-A club in Lynn, Mass., the initial destination for that year's No. 1 pick, Oral Roberts righthander Mike Moore. "He had a solid big league career," Harrison said, "but he never fulfilled the expectations inherent with being a 1-1 pick."

Harrison was an area scout for the New York Mets in 1994 when the team selected Florida State righthander Paul Wilson with the top pick. He was a national crosschecker for the Devil Rays in 1999 and 2003 when they selected high school outfielders Josh Hamilton and Delmon Young with the No. 1 overall picks.

For added measure, Harrison's father Bob was a longtime and highly respected scout who had a major role in four No. 1 selections: Chambers, Moore and Ken Griffey Jr. with the Mariners, and Darin Erstad with the California Angels.

"It's going to be a challenge to try and find the best prospect in this year's draft," Harrison said. "We hope to find the very best player we can, someone with great ability and great character, someone that will lift our club a long way."

The Devil Rays made the right choice. By taking Price with the No. 1 selection, the team got a player who was a cut above the rest of the field and lived up to his predraft hype like few other No. 1 overall picks in history. Two years after being draft-

## 2007: THE FIRST ROUNDERS

| CLUB: PLAYER, POS., SCHOOL | HOMETOWN | B-T | HT. | WT. | AGE | BONUS | FIRST YEAR | LAST YEAR | PEAK LEVEL (YEARS) |
|---|---|---|---|---|---|---|---|---|---|
| 1. *Devil Rays: David Price, lhp, Vanderbilt | Murfreesboro, Tenn. | L-L | 6-6 | 215 | 21 | $5,600,000 | 2008 | Active | Majors (8) |
| Golden Spikes winner went 11-1, 2.63 with national-best 194 Ks on strength of deft four-pitch mix, was lock to be first pick, with predictable MLB success. | | | | | | | | | |
| 2. Royals: Mike Moustakas, ss, Chatsworth HS | Chatsworth, Calif. | L-R | 6-0 | 185 | 18 | $4,000,000 | 2007 | Active | Majors (5) |
| Compromise choice by Royals; set California prep HR record, had long-ball success in minors, but took a few years in majors until things clicked late in 2014. | | | | | | | | | |
| 3. Cubs: Josh Vitters, 3b, Cypress HS | Cypress, Calif. | R-R | 6-3 | 195 | 17 | $3,200,000 | 2007 | 2014 | Majors (1) |
| Showed flashes of success in minors from 2007-11 before looking completely overmatched in 99-AB audition in majors, never seized Cubs 3B job. | | | | | | | | | |
| 4. Pirates: Daniel Moskos, lhp, Clemson | Greenville, S.C. | R-L | 6-1 | 210 | 21 | $2,475,000 | 2007 | Active | Majors (1) |
| Unpopular pick among frustrated Pirates fans with Wieters still on board; primarily closer in college with max-effort delivery, rarely showed same stuff in pros. | | | | | | | | | |
| 5. Orioles: Matt Wieters, c, Georgia Tech | Goose Creek, S.C. | B-R | 6-4 | 225 | 21 | $6,000,000 | 2008 | Active | Majors (7) |
| High-profille college career as power-hitting catcher (.359-35-198), closer (16 SV), excelled in minors, but promising start to MLB career slowed by 2014 TJ surgery. | | | | | | | | | |
| 6. Nationals: Ross Detwiler, lhp, Missouri State | Wentzville, Mo. | R-L | 6-5 | 185 | 21 | $2,150,000 | 2007 | Active | Majors (8) |
| First player from class to debut in majors, impressed with 90-94 sinker but never had staying power in majors as he struggled with inconsistent mechanics/injuries. | | | | | | | | | |
| 7. Brewers: Matt LaPorta, 1b, Florida | Port Charlotte, Fla. | R-R | 6-1 | 215 | 22 | $2,000,000 | 2007 | 2013 | Majors (4) |
| Sandwiched SEC player-of-year seasons as SO/SR around poor JR year; similar path in pros, flashed power potential but underperformed when moment at hand. | | | | | | | | | |
| 8. Rockies: Casey Weathers, rhp, Vanderbilt | Elk Grove, Calif. | R-R | 6-1 | 200 | 21 | $1,800,000 | 2007 | 2015 | Class AA (4) |
| Unheralded former JC outfielder had breakout year as closer (12-2, 49 IP/75 SO) with FB/SL combo; topped 100 in minors before being derailed by '08 TJ surgery. | | | | | | | | | |
| 9. Diamondbacks: Jarrod Parker, rhp, Norwell HS | Ossian, Ind. | R-R | 6-1 | 180 | 18 | $2,100,000 | 2008 | Active | Majors (4) |
| Smaller frame, but dominated as prep SR (12-0, 0.10), in minors before 2010 TJ surgery; successful major league career interrupted by second TJ/fractured elbow. | | | | | | | | | |
| 10. Giants: Madison Bumgarner, lhp, South Caldwell HS | Hudson, N.C. | R-L | 6-5 | 220 | 17 | $2,000,000 | 2008 | Active | Majors (7) |
| Success has followed every step of way: in HS (11-2, 1.05; .424-11-38), in minors (34-6, 2.00), in majors (85-58, 3.04), all trumped by magical 4-0, 0.25 W/S mark. | | | | | | | | | |
| 11. Mariners: Phillippe Aumont, rhp, Ecole Du Versant HS | Gatineau, Quebec | R-R | 6-7 | 225 | 18 | $1,900,000 | 2008 | Active | Majors (4) |
| Third-highest Canadian pick on record; had big frame, nasty stuff to become legit power arm, but struggled with mechanics/command/emotions in erratic career. | | | | | | | | | |
| 12. Marlins: Matt Dominguez, 3b, Chatsworth HS | Chatsworth, Calif. | R-R | 6-2 | 185 | 17 | $1,800,000 | 2007 | Active | Majors (4) |
| Second Chatsworth HS first-rounder; elite defender in all phases at 3B, but other tools suspect; flashed power in majors, but poor BB/SO ratio doomed career. | | | | | | | | | |
| 13. Indians: Beau Mills, 3b/1b, Lewis-Clark State (Idaho) | Visalia, Calif. | L-R | 6-3 | 220 | 20 | $1,575,000 | 2007 | 2012 | Class AAA (2) |
| Ex-Fresno State 3B had record-breaking NAIA season (38 HRs) in one year at Lewis-Clark; struggled to tap into power in pros, sore shoulder prompted move to 1B. | | | | | | | | | |
| 14. Braves: Jason Heyward, 1b/of, Henry County HS | McDonough, Ga. | L-L | 6-4 | 220 | 17 | $1,700,000 | 2007 | Active | Majors (6) |
| Braves had local product No. 2 on follow list, agonized as 13 teams passed; athletic talent with raw power, played 1B/LHP in HS, became Gold Glove OF in majors. | | | | | | | | | |
| 15. Reds: Devin Mesoraco, c, Punxsutawney HS | Punxsutawney, Pa. | R-R | 6-1 | 195 | 18 | $1,400,000 | 2007 | Active | Majors (5) |
| Power-hitting catcher struggled in minors before breakout .302-26-75 season in 2010; struggled to secure MLB job before .273-25-80 in 2014 got career on track. | | | | | | | | | |
| 16. Blue Jays: Kevin Ahrens, ss, Memorial HS | Houston | B-R | 6-2 | 180 | 18 | $1,440,000 | 2007 | 2015 | Class AA (2) |
| Showed athleticism, range, arm as prep SS; Jays moved him to 3B, likened him to Chipper Jones, but never hit for average or power during career in minors. | | | | | | | | | |
| 17. Rangers: Blake Beavan, rhp, Irving HS | Irving, Texas | R-R | 6-7 | 210 | 18 | $1,500,000 | 2008 | 2015 | Majors (4) |
| Had impeccable track record as amateur with shutout of Cuba at '06 world juniors, 9-2, 0.19 record as prep SR, but rarely flashed same 94-98 mph stuff in pro ranks. | | | | | | | | | |
| 18. Cardinals: Pete Kozma, ss, Owasso HS | Owasso, Okla. | R-R | 6-1 | 180 | 19 | $1,395,000 | 2007 | Active | Majors (5) |
| Excellent defender with superior range, arm, instincts; hit .522-11-55 as prep senior, but scouts never sold on bat, predictably struggled at plate in minors, majors. | | | | | | | | | |
| 19. Phillies: Joe Savery, lhp/1b, Rice | Houston | L-L | 6-3 | 215 | 21 | $1,372,500 | 2007 | 2014 | Majors (4) |
| Legit two-way college talent began pro career on mound, went 1-12 in '10 when stuff/command regressed, made switch to hitter before resumed career as reliever. | | | | | | | | | |
| 20. Dodgers: Chris Withrow, rhp, Midland Christian HS | Midland, Texas | R-R | 6-3 | 195 | 18 | $1,350,000 | 2007 | Active | Majors (3) |
| Trumped accomplishments of father Mike, ex-White Sox minor leaguer, by switching to reliever, reaching majors in 2013; strikeout artist with high-90s fastball. | | | | | | | | | |
| 21. Blue Jays: J.P. Arencibia, c, Tennessee | Miami | R-R | 6-1 | 210 | 21 | $1,327,500 | 2007 | Active | Majors (6) |
| Prolific power-hitting skills propelled him to major leagues, hit 119 HRs in minors/80 in majors, enabled him to overcome subpar defensive skills, high SO rate. | | | | | | | | | |
| 22. Giants: Tim Alderson, rhp, Horizon HS | Scottsdale, Ariz. | R-R | 6-7 | 210 | 18 | $1,290,000 | 2007 | 2015 | Class AAA (3) |
| Polished righty was in lock step with Bumgarner for Giants in minors (23-7 in 2008-09) before trade to Pirates, command deserted him, velocity dipped to mid-80s. | | | | | | | | | |
| 23. Padres: Nick Schmidt, lhp, Arkansas | Kirkwood, Mo. | B-L | 6-5 | 220 | 21 | $1,260,000 | 2007 | 2014 | Class AAA (3) |
| Polished/durable lefty never missed a start in 28-8, 2.83 college career, lasted seven pro IP before TJ surgery; lacked an out pitch, went 33-34, 4.64 in minos. | | | | | | | | | |
| 24. Rangers: Michael Main, rhp/of, DeLand HS | DeLand, Fla. | R-R | 6-2 | 170 | 18 | $1,237,500 | 2007 | 2013 | Class AA (2) |
| One of hardest HS throwers ever, regularly in upper 90s, but pro career dented by violent delivery/control issues; tried late switch to hitting, spent 2012-13 in CF. | | | | | | | | | |
| 25. White Sox: Aaron Poreda, lhp, San Francisco | San Francisco | L-L | 6-6 | 240 | 20 | $1,200,000 | 2007 | 2014 | Majors (2) |
| Oversized lefty always had velo, while command/secondary stuff lagged; reached majors in 2009, returned five years later after mixed success, 2013 TJ surgery. | | | | | | | | | |
| 26. Athletics: James Simmons, rhp, UC Riverside | Yorba Linda, Calif. | R-R | 6-4 | 215 | 20 | $1,192,500 | 2007 | 2015 | Class AAA (5) |
| Polished college arm with 93-94 mph FB, began pro career in Double-A, was on verge of majors in 2009 when he injured his shoulder, never regained velocity. | | | | | | | | | |
| 27. *Tigers: Rick Porcello, rhp, Seton Hall Prep | West Orange, N.J. | R-R | 6-5 | 190 | 18 | $3,580,000 | 2008 | Active | Majors (7) |
| Consensus top prep arm fell because of bonus demands, signed $7.2 million major league deal; fireballer reached MLB at 20 with change to sinker/slider style. | | | | | | | | | |
| 28. Twins: Ben Revere, of, Lexington Catholic HS | Lexington, Ky. | L-R | 5-9 | 165 | 19 | $750,000 | 2007 | Active | Majors (6) |
| Big surprise, signed smallest bonus for healthy first-rounder in 10 years; became successful big leaguer with contact approach, speed/quickness on bases/in CF. | | | | | | | | | |
| 29. Giants: Wendell Fairley, of, George County HS | Lucedale, Miss. | L-R | 6-2 | 190 | 19 | $1,000,000 | 2008 | 2012 | Class AA (2) |
| Third Giants first-rounder touted as five-tool player with limited baseball experience; speed (26 SBs)/power (8 HRs) never played in minors, released after 2012. | | | | | | | | | |
| 30. *Yankees: Andrew Brackman, rhp, N.C. State | Cincinnati | R-R | 6-10 | 240 | 21 | $3,350,000 | 2009 | 2013 | Majors (1) |
| Earned acclaim at N.C. State in basketball before focusing on pitching; fastball touched 99 mph; hurt elbow, slipped in draft, never recovered from TJ surgery. | | | | | | | | | |

**Signed to major league contract.*

## AT A GLANCE

### Late Round Find

**JOSH COLLMENTER, RHP, DIAMONDBACKS (15TH ROUND).** The Diamondbacks were among those clubs skeptical of Collmenter's unconventional, over-the-top delivery, even as he posted a 1.93 ERA with 117 strikeouts in 116 innings as a junior at Central Michigan. He had a 35-33, 3.50 record in his first five seasons with the Diamondbacks.

### Never Too Late

**EFREN NAVARRO, 1B/OF, ANGELS (50TH ROUND).** The Angels thought enough of Navarro to give him a $15,000 bonus as their final pick in the 2007 draft. He played in 129 games for the Angels over four big league seasons, hitting .246 with one home run and 20 RBIs.

### Overlooked

**TIM COLLINS, LHP, BLUE JAYS.** The Jays signed the 5-foot-6 Collins, a 17-year-old Massachusetts high school product, after he went undrafted in 2007. Despite his small frame, Collins had above-average stuff, including a fastball that peaked at 95-96 mph. In 265 minor league innings, he fanned 385 hitters. In four seasons with the Royals, his third major league organization, Collins struck out 220 in 211 innings while going 12-17, 3.54.

### International Gem

**STARLING MARTE, OF, PIRATES.** The Red Sox signed third baseman **MICHAEL ALMANZAR**, from the Dominican Republic, for $1.5 million, the largest bonus for an international player in 2007, but got no major league production for their investment. The Pirates spent $85,000 on Marte, also from the Dominican Republic, and he had a .283 average, 49 homers and 113 stolen bases in four major league seasons through 2015.

CONTINUED ON PAGE 628

## AT A GLANCE

CONTINUED FROM PAGE 627

### Minor League Take

**MATT WIETERS, C, ORIOLES.** Expectations for Wieters were high when he received a $6 million bonus from the Orioles after a celebrated career at Georgia Tech. He only added to the hype with a stellar minor league career, hitting .342 with 33 home runs and 124 RBIs in 174 games.

### One Who Got Away

**JOSH FIELDS, RHP, BRAVES (2ND ROUND).** At No. 69, Fields was the latest pick to become the highest unsigned selection in draft history, a curious development considering that he was a Braves fan and a closer at Georgia. Fields was drafted a year later with the 20th overall pick, by the Mariners, and signed the following February for a $1.5 million bonus. He reached the majors in 2013 with the Astros.

### They Were Drafted?

**RUSSELL WILSON, SS, ORIOLES (41ST ROUND); GOLDEN TATE, OF, DIAMONDBACKS (42ND ROUND).** Wilson, a quarterback, and Tate, a wide receiver, both opted for NFL careers. They played prominent roles when the Seattle Seahawks won the 2014 Super Bowl.

### Did You Know . . .

The only big leaguers since 1960 to hail from Punxsatawney, Pa., home of the famed groundhog, are **DEVIN MESORACO** (2007) and John Mizerock (1979), both catchers drafted in the first round.

### They Said It

Baseball commissioner **BUD SELIG**, on the draft being televised for the first time: "It's a great day for us, and this is such an important day. This is a special event and we want to communicate that to all of our fans. This is really a dramatic manifestation of how the sport has improved. This will get bigger and bigger."

ed, Price was part of a revitalized Devil Rays team that reached the 2008 World Series.

## DRAFT UNFOLDS AS EXPECTED

Price was one of a record-tying seven lefthanders selected in the first round of the 2007 draft. The draft also featured the strongest high school class in years. More prep players (17) were picked in the first round than collegians (13), reversing a recent tread. And for the first time, the draft was telecast live, with ESPN providing coverage of the first round and most of the supplemental first round.

The TV exposure was a significant step in the draft's evolution. Previous drafts had been held with little or no fanfare, conducted by teams on a conference call. The 2007 draft was held in an auditorium at Walt Disney World in Florida, with a full complement of ESPN baseball personalities on hand, as well as some of the players who were considered likely first-round picks.

"This is a special event, and we want to communicate that as best as possible to all of our fans," commissioner Bud Selig said. "This is really a dramatic manifestation of how the sport has improved. This will get bigger and bigger."

TOMASSO DEROSA

Bud Selig

In addition to TV exposure, the 2007 draft featured several rule changes, as part of a new Collective Bargaining Agreement between Major League Baseball and the Players Association. Among the changes were an Aug. 15 signing deadline, abolishment of the draft-and-follow rule, and more meaningful compensation for clubs unable to sign their premium picks.

Previously, a club's negotiating rights with a player attending a four-year college were lost as soon as the player entered his first class. For a player attending junior college, the club retained negotiating rights until one week before the following year's draft, a procedure commonly referred to as the draft-and-follow process.

The new rules established a deadline for all players. If a team did not sign a player by Aug. 15 (excluding college seniors whose eligibility had been exhausted), its rights were lost, regardless whether the player attended a four-year school or two-year school, or chose not to attend or return to college. An unsigned player no longer had any recourse but to wait until the following year's draft.

The signing deadline was designed to discourage extensive holdouts, which had become commonplace in recent drafts, among them Max Scherzer's 51-week holdout after the Arizona Diamondbacks drafted him in the first round in 2006.

The new rules also awarded clubs supplementary picks for the loss of major league free agents or their failure to sign second- and third-round selections from the previous year's draft.

Most of the measures were aimed at curbing signing bonuses, especially for first-rounders. But without a collectively bargained slotting system for bonuses, the commissioner's office continued to pressure clubs to put a drag on bonuses.

## How They Should Have Done It

Based on the career WAR (Wins Above Replacement, as calculated by Baseball-Reference.com) numbers achieved by all the players eligible for the 2007 draft through the 2015 season, here's how the first round should have unfolded. Numbers in parentheses indicate the round when the player was actually drafted.

| | Player, Pos. | Actual Draft | WAR | Bonus |
|---|---|---|---|---|
| 1. | Jason Heyward, of | Braves (1) | 31.2 | $1,700,000 |
| 2. | David Price, lhp | Rays (1) | 29.0 | $5,600,000 |
| 3. | Josh Donaldson, c | Cubs (1-S) | 25.1 | $652,500 |
| 4. | Giancarlo Stanton, of | Marlins (2) | 25.0 | $475,000 |
| 5. | Madison Bumgarner, lhp | Giants (1) | 23.3 | $2,000,000 |
| 6. | Jordan Zimmermann, rhp | Nationals (2) | 20.9 | $495,000 |
| 7. | Anthony Rizzo, 1b | Red Sox (6) | 16.0 | $325,000 |
| 8. | Jonathan Lucroy, c | Brewers (3) | 15.8 | $340,000 |
| 9. | Freddie Freeman, 1b | Braves (2) | 15.7 | $409,500 |
| 10. | Jake Arrieta, rhp | Orioles (5) | 15.5 | $1,100,000 |
| 11. | Todd Frazier, ss | Reds (1-S) | 15.3 | $825,000 |
| 12. | Matt Wieters, c | Orioles (1) | 14.6 | $6,000,000 |
| 13. | Corey Kluber, rhp | Padres (4) | 12.4 | $200,000 |
| 14. | Rick Porcello, rhp | Tigers (1) | 11.2 | $3,580,000 |
| 15. | Greg Holland, rhp | Royals (10) | 10.0 | $50,000 |
| 16. | Zack Cosart, ss | Reds (2) | 9.6 | $407,250 |
| 17. | Mike Moustakas, ss | Royals (1) | 8.9 | $4,000,000 |
| 18. | Darwin Barney, ss | Cubs (4) | 8.3 | $222,750 |
| 19. | Derek Norris, c | Nationals (4) | 7.9 | $210,000 |
| 20. | Josh Collmenter, rhp | Diamondacks (15) | 7.6 | $80,000 |
| 21. | Tony Watson, lhp | Pirates (9) | 7.5 | $85,000 |
| 22. | Ben Revere, of | Twins (1) | 7.3 | $750,000 |
| 23. | Brett Cecil, lhp | Blue Jays (1-S) | 6.6 | $810,000 |
| | Tommy Hunter, rhp | Rangers (1-S) | 6.6 | $585,000 |
| 25. | Jarrod Parker, rhp | Diamondbacks (1) | 6.1 | $2,100,000 |
| | Danny Duffy, lhp | Royals (3) | 6.1 | $365,000 |
| 27. | Lucas Duda, 1b | Mets (7) | 5.8 | $85,000 |
| 28. | Steve Cishek, rhp | Marlins (5) | 5.4 | $139,500 |
| 29. | Stephen Vogt, c | Devil Rays (12) | 4.6 | $6,000 |
| 30. | Dillon Gee, rhp | Mets (21) | 4.3 | $20,000 |
| | David Lough, of | Royals (11) | 4.3 | $49,500 |
| | Mitch Moreland, 1b | Rangers (17) | 4.3 | $60,000 |

| | Top 3 Unsigned Players | | | Year Signed |
|---|---|---|---|---|
| 1. | Chris Sale, lhp | Rockies (21) | 27.2 | 2010 |
| 2. | Craig Kimbrel, rhp | Braves (33) | 13.6 | 2008 |
| 3. | Brandon Belt, lhp | Braves (11) | 12.6 | 2009 |

## NEW DEADLINE HAS LIMITED IMPACT

The commissioner's office sent a directive to the 30 clubs prior to the 2007 draft, instructing them to roll back signing bonuses in the early rounds by 10 percent from what they had spent in 2006. Through July 10, the average bonus for the 13 first-rounders who had signed was $1.437 million, a dip of 26 percent from 2006. Among the top 100 selections, 65 had signed, and 31 had received bonuses that were 10 percent less than the corresponding slots a year earlier. Just two of the 65 bonuses were equal to the 2006 slots.

The reality, though, was that 17 of the best first-rounders remained unsigned. A signing frenzy near the deadline seemed inevitable, not only for first-round picks, but also for later selections that had slipped because of bonus demands.

"It's apparent with the large number of unsigned first-round picks that agents are not buying into the 10 percent rollback," an American League scouting director said. "I don't think there's any question that a number of premium players will be signed above slot in the next two or three weeks, but no team wants to be the first to make the move. I think you'll see a lot of deals getting done after Aug. 1, right after the major league trading deadline, when the general managers have a chance to get more involved."

Scott Boras represented 12 premium prospects, and only one, Matt LaPorta, the seventh overall pick, had signed as the deadline approached. Boras had counted on clubs relenting at the 11th hour in the past, and he expected that to be the case again. Among his unsigned clients were shortstop Mike Moustakas (Royals, second overall), catcher Matt Wieters (Orioles, fifth), righthanders Rick Porcello (Tigers, 27th) and Andrew Brackman (Yankees, 30th), and outfielder Julio Borbon (Rangers, 35th).

Boras' clients and upward of 60 other premium selections remained unsigned less than 48 hours before the deadline, setting the stage for the most frenzied signing period in the history of the draft.

### FEEDING FRENZY AT SIGNING DEADLINE

Price agreed to terms about six hours before the deadline, signing a six-year major league contract that included a $5.6 million bonus and $8.25 million in guaranteed money, with incentives that could drive the total value to $11.25 million. His bonus was some $2 million more than was recommended for the No. 1 pick.

Moustakas, from Chatsworth (Calif.) High, wanted a reported $7 million, but agreed to a $4 million bonus about 10 minutes before the 11:59 p.m. deadline. The Kansas City Royals were reluctant to go higher than $3.15 million, slot money for the second pick and what they believed Moustakas had agreed to on draft day. But Royals general manager Dayton Moore relented and agreed to pay California's all-time high school home run leader the same amount the team paid Alex Gordon as the second overall pick in 2005.

Third baseman Josh Vitters, from Cypress (Calif.) High, signed with the Chicago Cubs for $3.2 million, $500,000 over the slot for the No. 3 pick.

Those deals paled in comparison with what Wieters, a junior at Georgia Tech, received from the Baltimore Orioles. He signed for $6 million, nearly triple the recommended slot amount of $2.25 million, just three minutes before the deadline. At face value, it was the second-largest bonus in draft history for a player signing with the team that drafted him, trailing only the $6.1 million bonus Justin Upton received from the Diamondbacks as the No. 1 pick in 2005. But Upton's deal was payable over five years under

### Fastest To The Majors

| Player, Pos. | Drafted (Round) | Debut |
|---|---|---|
| 1. Ross Detwiler, lhp | Nationals (1) | Sept. 7, 2007 |
| 2. Tommy Hunter, rhp | Rangers (1-S) | Aug. 1, 2008 |
| 3. Eddie Kunz, rhp | Mets (1-S) | Aug. 3, 2008 |
| 4. David Price, lhp | Rays (1) | Sept. 14, 2008 |
| 5. * Rick Porcello, rhp | Tigers (1) | April 9, 2009 |

**High school selection.*

## DRAFT SPOTLIGHT: GIANCARLO STANTON

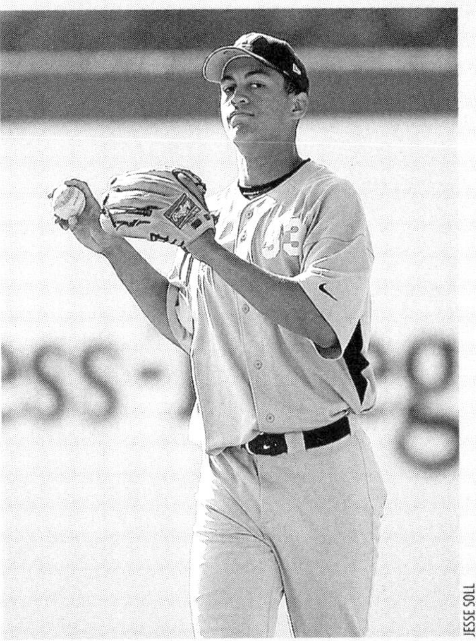

JESSE SOLL

Better known as Mike in high school, Stanton emerged when he put on a batting practice show at the Area Code Games

He was known as Mike Stanton when he began his professional career with the Florida Marlins in 2007, and Giancarlo Stanton when he signed the richest contract in North American sports history with the Miami Marlins seven years later. By any name, Stanton carved out a reputation as one of the most prodigious sluggers of his era.

When Stanton participated in the 2006 Area Code Games in Long Beach, Calif., he was a virtual unknown to hundreds of scouts who gathered to observe the top high school prospects for the 2007 draft. Most were there to see California prep hotshots Mike Moustakas, Josh Vitters and Matt Dominguez, not someone who batted barely .200 in his junior season at Notre Dame Academy in nearby Sherman Oaks. Yet the 6-foot-5, 210-pound Stanton stole the show, launching tape-measure home runs in one of the most impressive batting practice displays ever witnessed at the annual showcase.

Even as he spent hours refining his pull-oriented swing and had a breakout senior season, batting .393 with 12 homers, Stanton was more proficient as a wide receiver and defensive back in football, and a small forward in basketball. He was recruited by Division I colleges in all three sports, including Southern California and UCLA for football.

Most clubs thought Stanton was likely to pursue football. He struggled to hit a curveball and make consistent contact, so he was lightly scouted during his senior season of baseball. The Marlins, however, through the stellar work of area scout Tim McDonnell, got to know Stanton better than other clubs. They learned that baseball was his favorite sport, and he wanted to play professionally if the right opportunity presented itself.

"He was a big, athletic guy with bat speed, strength, a good body and very good athleticism," Marlins scouting director Stan Meek said. "He had some swing-and-miss when we saw him, but he also looked like a guy who had good body coordination, good body control. I saw him take BP, and saw him show big raw power. It seemed like the more he played, the more we saw him not chasing pitches. We saw more contact."

The Marlins drafted Dominguez with their first pick, and could not resist Stanton when their second turn came. "We thought we had a guy who had a chance to be a power/speed player and be an impact bat in the middle of the lineup," Meek said. "Was there risk involved? Sure. The risk is what had other people concerned to take him that high."

After signing for $475,000, Stanton quickly justified his worth. As an 18-year-old at Class A Greensboro, in his first full season, he slammed 39 homers. They weren't ordinary home runs, either. Stanton routinely hit balls that traveled 450 feet and beyond.

"No. 1, he's got bat speed," Marlins hitting coordinator John Mallee said. "No. 2, he's got some serious leverage. And No. 3, he's mechanically in sequence. He's got so much torque that he creates so much bat speed and leverage that it just equates to power."

After slamming 49 more homers over his next 182 minor league games, Stanton skipped Triple-A and was promoted to the big leagues on June 8, 2010, a manchild at age 20. He hit 22 homers in 100 games as a rookie and 34 a year later, a pace topped for a player his age only by Ken Griffey Jr. and Alex Rodriguez in the draft era. "The kid has potential that's unbelievable," raved then-Marlins manager Ozzie Guillen.

Before the 2012 season, Stanton announced he wanted to be called Giancarlo, as he had been until about fifth grade, when he made a change to Mike for simplicity sake. "I went by Mike because some people had difficulty pronouncing Giancarlo, especially when I was a kid. Giancarlo and Mike are both my names, I just prefer Giancarlo," he said.

Stanton hit a career-high 37 homers in 2012, and 37 again two years later. The Marlins made sure that the player they outmaneuvered everyone else on seven years earlier was going nowhere, signing him after the 2014 season to a 13-year, $325 million contract, a staggering figure matched only by the distance of some of his mighty home runs.

## WORTH NOTING

■ Vanderbilt lefthander **DAVID PRICE** was the top pick in the 2007 draft and also received the highest grade—a 69 on the 20-80 scouting scale—from the Major League Scouting Bureau. The next-highest grades went to players who were drafted all over the board. University of Georgia righthander **JOSH FIELDS** (68 grade) went 69th overall; North Carolina State righthander **ANDREW BRACKMAN** (66) went 30th; and Puerto Rican high school outfielder **ANGEL MORALES** (66) went 122nd. Seventeen players earned grades of 60 or higher, including 10 first-rounders.

■ Rice had 14 players drafted, the most from any school. That matched the record set by Arizona State in 1982 and equaled by Cal State Fullerton in 2005. The Puerto Rico Baseball Academy tied the high school mark it set in 2004 with 12 players selected.

■ Two college seniors were drafted with consecutive picks in the first round: Florida first baseman **MATT LAPORTA** at No. 7 and Vanderbilt closer **CASEY WEATHERS** at No. 8. In the first round of the previous five drafts, Khalil Greene in 2002 and Landon Powell in '04 were the only seniors picked. Roughly the same dynamic applied to college catchers. Georgia Tech's **MATT WIETERS** (fifth overall) and Tennessee's **J.P. ARENCIBIA** (21st) were first-rounders in '07. Only Jeff Clement in '05 and Powell were first-round catchers in the previous five drafts.

■ The Padres had the busiest draft, selecting 12 players in the first five rounds. They had five picks in the supplemental first-round. The Astros didn't make their first selection until pick No. 111, by which time the Padres had made eight selections.

■ The Braves drafted 6-foot-4, 200-pound University of Oregon quarterback **DENNIS DIXON** in the fifth round.

MATT STONER

**Matt Wieters accepted a $6 million bonus from the Orioles out of Georgia Tech, the second-largest straight bonus in draft history**

MLB's two-sport provision, and Wieters' bonus was payable in full by the end of the 2008 calendar year.

Despite MLB's determined efforts, signing bonuses for the 30 first-round picks increased by 8.5 percent to an average of $2,098,083, and more premium picks maximized their leverage by holding out until the deadline before signing. The 2007 first-round average was the third highest ever, trailing 2001 ($2,154,280) and 2002 ($2,106,793).

Among 184 players picked in the first five rounds, 171 signed and received an average bonus of $685,328. In 2006, 179 of the first 184 picks agreed to terms, getting an average bonus of $662,531. Despite MLB's directive for a 10 percent reduction, bonuses in the first five rounds rose 3 percent.

### PORCELLO, BRACKMAN SIGN MLB DEALS

Porcello, generally considered the top high school pitching prospect in the draft, became a prime target of Kansas City with the No. 2 pick overall. But in the days leading up to the draft, it became apparent that Porcello's price tag was too excessive for the budget-conscious Royals. Many expected the Royals to select Vitters, who was not represented by Boras, but instead Kansas City chose Moustakas, who was a Boras client.

Porcello, from New Jersey's Seton Hall Prep, slipped to No. 27 overall because of his bonus demands and commitment to North Carolina.

Brackman, a 6-foot-11 righthander from North Carolina State, slid to the New York Yankees at No. 30. Brackman, who threw a mid-90s fastball that peaked at 99 mph, was considered the second-best college pitching prospect early in 2007, behind Price, but he missed the latter portion of the season because of a sore elbow.

Two days before the signing deadline, almost half of the 30 first-rounders had not signed. Activity began to stir when the Atlanta Braves signed Georgia high school outfielder Jason Heyward, the 14th pick overall, for $1.7 million, $170,000 above slot. That was the first above-slot bonus for a 2007 first rounder, and Heyward more than justified it. Eight years later, his career WAR (Wins Above Replacement) grade was higher than any other player in the 2007 draft, Price included.

The following day, the Detroit Tigers signed Porcello to a $7.285 million major league deal that included a $3.85 million bonus. Porcello's contract matched the biggest guarantee ever given a high school draftee, set by righthander Josh Beckett in 1999.

Once Porcello signed, the rush was on. In the 36 hours before the deadline, every remaining first-rounder and supplemental first-rounder agreed to terms, none at the 10 percent cutback rate. More than 60 players signed during the final two days, many for amounts significantly above slot. Records for largest bonus were set in the fourth, fifth and sixth rounds.

The Yankees gave Brackman a major league deal that provided a $3.35 million bonus and guaranteed him $4.55 million, and could have been worth a draft record $13 million if he met all escalator clauses and team options. The contract stunned industry insiders, particularly since it was known that Brackman needed Tommy John surgery and would miss the 2008 season. Plagued by injuries throughout his career, Brackman pitched just two innings in the major leagues and went 17-35, 5.38 in five years in the minors.

The Yankees spent $8,035,500 in signing bonuses, the top figure in 2007. Next were the Devil Rays ($8.023 million), Orioles ($7.981 million), Tigers

### Top 25 Bonuses

| | Player, Pos. | Drafted (Round) | Order | Bonus |
|---|---|---|---|---|
| 1. | **Matt Wieters, c** | Orioles (1) | 5 | $6,000,000 |
| 2. | **David Price, lhp** | Rays (1) | 1 | #$5,600,000 |
| 3. | * **Mike Moustakas, ss** | Royals (1) | 2 | $4,000,000 |
| 4. | * **Rick Porcello, rhp** | Tigers (1) | 27 | #$3,580,000 |
| 5. | **Andrew Brackman, rhp** | Yankees (1) | 30 | #$3,350,000 |
| 6. | * **Josh Vitters, 3b** | Cubs (1) | 3 | $3,200,000 |
| 7. | **Daniel Moskos, lhp** | Pirates (1) | 4 | $2,475,000 |
| 8. | **Ross Detwiler, lhp** | Nationals (1) | 6 | $2,150,000 |
| 9. | * **Jarrod Parker, rhp** | Diamondbacks (1) | 9 | $2,100,000 |
| 10. | **Matt LaPorta, 1b** | Brewers (1) | 7 | $2,000,000 |
| | * **Madison Bumgarner, lhp** | Giants (1) | 10 | $2,000,000 |
| 12. | * **Phillippe Aumont, rhp** | Mariners (1) | 11 | $1,900,000 |
| 13. | Casey Weathers, rhp | Rockies (1) | 8 | $1,800,000 |
| | * **Matt Dominguez, 3b** | Marlins (1) | 12 | $1,800,000 |
| | * Jack McGeary, lhp | Nationals (6) | 190 | $1,800,000 |
| 16. | * **Jason Heyward, of** | Braves (1) | 14 | $1,700,000 |
| 17. | **Beau Mills, 3b** | Indians (1) | 13 | $1,575,000 |
| 18. | * **Blake Beavan, rhp** | Rangers (1) | 17 | $1,497,500 |
| | Cale Iorg, ss | Tigers (6) | 211 | $1,497,500 |
| 20. | * Kevin Ahrens, ss | Blue Jays (1) | 16 | $1,440,000 |
| 21. | * **Devin Mesoraco, c** | Reds (1) | 15 | $1,400,000 |
| 22. | * **Pete Kozma, ss** | Cardinals (1) | 18 | $1,395,000 |
| 23. | **Joe Savery, lhp** | Phillies (1) | 19 | $1,372,500 |
| 24. | * **Chris Withrow, rhp** | Dodgers (1) | 20 | $1,350,000 |
| 25. | **J.P. Arencibia, c** | Blue Jays (1) | 21 | $1,327,500 |

*Major leaguers in bold. *High school selection. #Major league contract.*

## Largest Bonuses By Round

| | Player, Pos. | Club | Bonus |
|---|---|---|---|
| 1. | **Matt Wieters, c** | **Orioles** | **$6,000,000** |
| 1-S. | * Josh Smoker, lhp | Nationals | $1,000,000 |
| | ***Neil Ramirez, rhp** | **Rangers** | **$1,000,000** |
| 2. | Will Kline, rhp | Devil Rays | $513,000 |
| 3. | * Nick Barnese, rhp | Devil Rays | $366,000 |
| 4. | Bradley Suttle, 3b | Yankees | $1,300,000 |
| 5. | **Jake Arrieta, rhp** | **Orioles** | **$1,100,000** |
| 6. | * Jack McGeary, lhp | Nationals | $1,800,000 |
| 7. | * David Mailman, 1b | Red Sox | $550,000 |
| 8. | * Taylor Grote, of | Yankees | $250,000 |
| 9. | Wynn Pelzer, rhp | Padres | $190,000 |
| 10. | * Carmen Angelini, ss | Yankees | $1,000,000 |
| 11. | * D.J. Jones, of | Devil Rays | $335,000 |
| 12. | * Julian Sampson, rhp | Phillies | $390,000 |
| 13. | * Kyle Ocampo, rhp | Rangers | $250,000 |
| 14. | **James Russell, lhp** | **Cubs** | **$350,000** |
| 15. | * Chris Jones, lhp | Indians | $350,000 |
| 16. | * Austin Bailey, rhp | Red Sox | $285,000 |
| 17. | Ryan Zink, rhp | Yankees | $123,000 |
| 18. | ***Hunter Strickland, rhp** | **Red Sox** | **$123,250** |
| 19. | Brett Butts, rhp | Braves | $75,000 |
| 20. | * Mike Lehmann, rhp | Royals | $123,000 |
| 21. | **Brian Broderick, rhp** | **Cardinals** | **$60,000** |
| 22. | * Jiwan James, rhp/of | Phillies | $150,000 |
| 23. | ***Drake Britton, lhp** | **Red Sox** | **$700,000** |
| 24. | Several tied at | | $25,000 |
| 25. | Tim Sexton, rhp | Dodgers | $123,000 |
| Other | * Keaton Hayenga, rhp | Royals (31) | $300,000 |

*Major leaguers in bold. *High school selection.*

($7.952 million) and Nationals ($7.8823 million).

In addition to Brackman, the Yankees paid heavily for fourth-rounder Bradley Suttle, a third baseman from the University of Texas, who signed for $1.3 million, and 10th-rounder Carmen Angelini, a Louisiana high school shortstop committed to Rice, who signed for $1 million. Both were records for those rounds. The Yankees paid out five of the top 14 bonuses beyond the first round.

There was considerable speculation in the days leading up to the signing deadline that big-revenue teams such as the Yankees and Boston Red Sox would announce a wave of over-slot signings. They were among a handful of clubs that resisted the recommendations of the commissioner's office to scale back bonus money, ostensibly because they contributed more money than other teams to baseball's central fund for revenue sharing and didn't want to be told how to allocate their resources.

No club took more speculative picks than the Red Sox, who had officially signed just three of their first eight selections, and eight of their top 17 as the deadline drew near. It came as no surprise when they announced the signings of numerous players to bonuses significantly above the recommended slot amounts.

The Red Sox forfeited their first-round pick, but among the players they targeted for above-slot bonuses were fifth-rounder Will Middlebrooks ($925,000), seventh-rounder David Mailman ($550,000) and 23rd-rounder Drake Britton ($700,000, a record for a 23rd rounder).

New York and Boston were also responsible for paying out the two largest bonuses on the international front as the Red Sox signed Dominican third baseman Michael Almanazar for $1.5 million while the Yankees spent $1.1 million on Dominican outfielder Kevin Deleon.

### ARRIETA, MCGEARY SET RECORDS

Among the recipients of other noteworthy bonuses at the deadline were Texas Christian righthander Jake Arrieta, who got a $1.1 million bonus from the Orioles, a record for a fifth-round pick; University of Alabama shortstop Cale Iorg, who signed with the Tigers for $1.4975 million as a sixth-round pick; and Massachusetts prep lefthander Jack McGeary, one of the top high school pitching prospects in the country, who was paid $1.8 million by the Nationals, a record for a sixth-rounder.

McGeary was considered first-round material entering his senior year at Roxbury Latin High, but he pitched inconsistently, and teams grew wary of his bonus demands. Even as the Nationals selected McGeary with the 190th pick and signed him for a record bonus, they agreed he could complete most of his academic requirements at Stanford before committing full-time to the Nationals.

When the Tigers drafted Iorg, he was completing a Mormon mission to Portugal and hadn't played baseball in two years, since his freshman season at Alabama. He was paid a substantial bonus for his slot because the Tigers believed it reflected his status as a likely first-rounder in 2008. Iorg was the second son of former big leaguer Garth Iorg, and his older brother, Eli, was a supplemental first-round pick of the Astros in 2005.

ROBERT GURGANUS

Jake Arrieta

Arrieta went 14-4, 2.35 as a sophomore at TCU, and ranked behind only Brackman among college righthanders entering the 2007 season. But he unexpectedly struggled with his velocity and command as a junior, and slipped in the draft. His major league career followed the same inconsistent path until 2015, when Arrieta went 22-6, 1.77 for the Cubs and won the National League Cy Young Award.

The Orioles went substantially over slot to sign both Arrieta and Wieters. Both were represented by Boras, and Baltimore owner Peter Angelos disliked dealing with the polarizing agent. Less than a half-hour before the signing deadline, the Orioles reportedly held firm on a $5.2 million offer to Wieters, but the catcher encouraged Boras to make a final counteroffer of a $6 million bonus, half to be paid upon approval of the contract and the remainder early the following year. The Orioles agreed to the $6 million for Wieters, and they paid Arrieta what he was seeking all along.

Unlike the Orioles, the Astros did not buck the commissioner's office and spent a draft-low $1.584 million on their selections. Unfortunately for them, it might have been the worst draft of the decade, contributing to the Astros enduring three straight 100-loss seasons from 2011-13.

The Astros didn't have a first- or second-round pick as the cost for signing major league free agents Carlos Lee and Woody Williams following the

### WORTH NOTING

He was a highly regarded baseball player at a northern California high school before signing to play football at Oregon. Dixon threw 12 touchdown passes for the Ducks in 2006 before losing his starting job, which made him more amenable to a potential baseball career. Dixon received a $137,700 bonus from the Braves, but played in their farm system for just one summer before returning to Oregon for his senior year of football. He was a fifth-round pick in the 2008 NFL draft and spent six years in the NFL.

■ The Yankees selected California high school catcher **AUSTIN ROMINE** in the second round, and the Angels took his older brother, **ANDREW**, a shortstop from Arizona State, in the fifth. Both succeeded in joining their father, **KEVIN**, in the majors. The elder Romine was a second-round pick in 1981 and played seven seasons in the big leagues.

■ Rangers second-round pick **MATT WEST**, who signed for $405,000, was suspended in August for 50 games for violating Major League Baseball's policy on performance-enhancing drugs. West, who hit .301 in 103 at-bats in the Rookie-level Arizona League, was the highest-drafted player ever suspended for PEDs in his debut season. A surprising power surge during his senior season at Bellaire (Texas) High in 2007 helped him climb draft boards.

■ One of the new rules for the 2007 draft awarded teams a compensatory selection in the first three rounds for unsigned draft picks, giving teams more leverage to sign players. The Braves were granted pick 69A (between picks 69 and 70) in the 2008 draft after failing to sign **JOSH FIELDS** with the 69th overall selection. The Red Sox got pick 84A for failing to sign Alabama prep first baseman **HUNTER MORRIS**, who attended Auburn.

CONTINUED ON PAGE 632

## WORTH NOTING

CONTINUED FROM PAGE 631

■ Reds supplemental first-rounder **TODD FRAZIER**, the 34th overall pick out of Rutgers, was the third Frazier brother to be drafted, joining Charles (1999, Marlins) and Jeff (2004, Tigers). Mets second-rounder **SCOTT MOVIEL** was the third Moviel brother drafted, joining Paul (2003, White Sox) and Greg (2006, Mariners).

■ The three U.S. military academies unexpectedly had prospects for the 2007 draft. Army and Navy each had two players drafted, and Air Force one. The academies previously had a total of four players selected in draft history. Army senior lefthander **NICK HILL** went in the seventh round to the Mariners and signed for $70,000, and righthander **MILAN DINGA** went in the 10th round to the Angels and signed for $20,000. Hill, the most decorated player in Army history, went 7-3, 1.91 with 100 strikeouts and 18 walks in 85 innings in his senior season. Dinga set Army's career record for saves with 27. Except for Army righthander Craig Jones, who was selected in the third round by the Mets in 1979 with a pick that was disallowed because Jones was too young, Hill and Dinga were the highest draft choices ever from the military academies. Army regulations allowed the pitchers to play professional baseball for up to two years before serving a three-year tour of military duty. Naval Academy student **MITCH HARRIS**, a junior righthander with a mid-90s fastball, was drafted by the Braves in the 24th round. Harris might have gone as early as the third round had he not been obligated to five years of active military duty before he could play baseball. Harris did not sign and was drafted in the 13th round a year later by the Cardinals. He signed the following March, put in his Navy service time, began playing in the minors in 2013 and reached the major leagues two years later. Harris was the first graduate of the Naval Academy to pitch in the majors in nearly 100 years.

2006 season. And with owner Drayton McLane firm on offering slot money to draft choices, the Astros didn't sign third-rounder Derek Dietrich, an Ohio prep infielder, and fourth-rounder Brett Eibner, a pitcher/outfielder from a Texas high school. The Astros did not pay a bonus of more than $135,000. The previous time a team did not sign any picks through the first four rounds was in 1980, when it happened to the Yankees.

To compound their problems, the Astros didn't offer arbitration to three departing free agents, pitchers Andy Pettitte and Russ Springer, and infielder Aubrey Huff, which may have brought them two first-round and two sandwich picks.

While seven Boras clients signed on the eve of the deadline, four of his players did not sign. The two most significant were University of Georgia righthander Josh Fields, a second-round pick of the Braves and Connecticut prep righthander Matt Harvey, a third-rounder of the Los Angeles Angels.

Fields, the 69th player drafted overall, was the latest selection in draft history to become the first not to sign. He was in the running to be a top pick at the outset of the 2007 season, but suffered a disappointing junior year for the Bulldogs. The Braves never offered him more than slot money (approximately $472,500), claiming that was the amount that Fields agreed to accept prior to the draft. As compensation, the Braves received a corresponding pick in the 2008 draft as compensation—one of six such selections that were awarded under terms of the new CBA deal.

Harvey was also a projected early first-round pick but didn't pitch up to par, and his price tag came into question. The Angels refused to offer Harvey more than $1 million—significantly short of his reported asking price of $2.5 million.

The St. Louis Cardinals also took a run at Texas outfielder Kyle Russell, who led the NCAA ranks with 28 homers as a draft-eligible sophomore, but were not willing to meet his $1.5 million price.

### THE PRICE IS RIGHT

Lefthanders were a popular demographic in 2007. Seven were selected in the first round, tying a record set in 2004. That included four of the top 10 picks, including Ross Detwiler, the first player from the class of 2007 to reach the majors. He was selected by the Nationals with the sixth pick overall and debuted on Sept. 7, 2007, almost 11 months before anyone else.

No lefties in the 2007 draft succeeded as well as Price, a five-time all-star and the 2012 Cy Young Award winner, or Madison Bumgarner, the only high school pitcher selected in the first round, who was the MVP of the 2014 World Series.

Angels scouting director Eddie Bane said the crop of lefties was the best he had seen. "It's far better than normal," he said. "It's as good as I've seen in 25 years."

The 6-foot-6, 215-pound Price was only the second lefthander in 30 years to be the first overall draft choice. He was routinely compared with Andrew Miller, the consensus top prospect in the 2006 draft. "You compare the two, and Price has more ability, more uniqueness to him," an AL scouting director said. "He's got more athletic ability, three solid pitches and better strike-zone ability. His command is inconsistent, but it's still worthy of being the No. 1 pick."

JOHN SPEAR

Mike Moustakas

The 6-foot-5, 220-pound Bumgarner rated as the best of a group of high school lefthanders that also included McGeary and Josh Smoker of Calhoun (Ga.) High, who also received six-figure bonuses. Bumgarner had the best arm strength of the trio, routinely touching 94-95 mph with easy arm action. His lack of a true breaking pitch and a somewhat unorthodox, high three-quarters delivery were of mild concern to scouts.

College closers were also prevalent in the 2007 class, notably Clemson lefthander Daniel Moskos (Pirates, fourth overall) and Vanderbilt senior righthander Casey Weathers (Rockies, eighth overall). Both were primarily outfielders early in their college careers before being converted into pitchers. Weathers was clocked in the high 90s, and posted a 12-2, 2.37 record with seven saves and 75 strikeouts in 49 innings in his senior season. He had been a 25th-round draft choice a year earlier.

It's rare for a high school player from the Northeast to be a first-round pick, but this was no ordinary draft class by that standard. The 2007 crop featured four high school arms that caused scouting directors and crosscheckers to spend much of April and May in that neck of the woods.

The 6-foot-6 Porcello and 6-foot-8 righthander Phillippe Aumont from Gatineau, Quebec (Mariners, 11th overall) went in the first round, while Harvey lasted until the third round and

### One Team's Draft: Philadelphia Phillies

| Player, Pos. | Bonus | Player, Pos. | Bonus | Player, Pos. | Bonus |
|---|---|---|---|---|---|
| **1. Joe Savery, lhp** | **$1,372,500** | 9. Chris Kissock, rhp | $50,000 | 19. *Cedric Johnson, of | Did not sign |
| **1. *Travis d'Arnaud, c** | **$832,500** | 10. Joe Rocchio, rhp | $10,000 | 20. *Carlos Moncrief, rhp | Did not sign |
| 2. *Travis Mattair, 3b | $395,000 | **11. Justin De Fratus, rhp** | **$50,000** | 21. Adam Sorgi, 2b | $5,000 |
| **3. *Brandon Workman, rhp** | **Did not sign** | 12. *Julian Sampson, rhp | $390,000 | 22. *Jiwan James, rhp/of | $150,000 |
| 3. Matt Spencer, of/lhp | $261,000 | 13. Luke Wertz, rhp | $60,000 | 23. Gerard Breslin, rhp | $1,000 |
| 4. Tyler Mach, 2b | $95,000 | 14. Jesus Villegas, ss | $16,000 | 24. Caleb Mangum, c | $1,000 |
| **5. Michael Taylor, of** | **$131,000** | 15. Karl Bolt, 1b | $5,000 | 25. Billy Harris, lhp | Did not sign |
| 6. Matt Rizzotti, 1b | $120,000 | **16. Brian Schlitter, rhp** | **$35,000** | **Other Jacob Diekman (30), lhp** | **$85,000** |
| 7. Tyson Brummett, rhp | $25,000 | 17. Zack Sterner, rhp | $20,000 | | |
| 8. Chance Chapman, rhp | $20,000 | 18. *Mark Adzick, lhp | Did not sign | | |

*Major leaguers in bold. *High school selection.*

## Highest Unsigned Picks

| Player, Pos., Team (Round) | College | Re-Drafted |
|---|---|---|
| Josh Fields, rhp, Braves (2) | *Georgia | Mariners '08 (1) |
| Hunter Morris, 1b, Red Sox (2) | Auburn | Brewers '10 (4) |
| Brandon Workman, rhp, Phillies (3) | Texas | Red Sox '10 (2) |
| Derek Dietrich, ss, Astros (3) | Georgia Tech | Devil Rays '10 (2) |
| Tommy Toledo, rhp, Padres (3) | Florida | Twins '10 (32) |
| Matt Harvey, rhp, Angels (3) | North Carolina | Mets 10 (1) |
| Blake Stouffer, 1b, Reds (4) | *Texas A&M | Nationals '08 (13) |
| Garrett Nash, ss, Rangers (4) | Oregon State | D-backs '10 (39) |
| Brett Eibner, of/rhp, Astros (4) | Arkansas | Royals '10 (2) |
| Kyle Russell, of, Cardinals (4) | *Texas | Dodgers '08 (3) |

**TOTAL UNSIGNED PICKS:** Top 5 Rounds (13), Top 10 Rounds (26)

**Returned to same school.*

McGeary slid to the sixth amidst signability concerns. Like Porcello, Harvey was a North Carolina recruit and landed in the first round himself three years later after fulfilling his college commitment.

Aumont became the third-highest Canadian ever selected, following two British Columbia lefthanders, Adam Loewen and Jeff Francis, who were selected with the fourth and ninth picks, respectively, in the 2002 draft.

The strength of the draft might have been high school position players, starting with three infielders from California: Moustakas, Vitters and Moustakas' teammate, Matt Dominguez, who was selected 12th overall by the Florida Marlins. Moustakas and Dominguez became the sixth set of prep teammates drafted in the same first round. Moustakas hit .577 with 24 homers as a senior. Dominguez was regarded as the more accomplished defender of the two, and he hit .443 with 13 homers.

Two of the biggest surprises of the first round were LaPorta, whom the Milwaukee Brewers took seventh overall, and Kentucky high school outfielder Ben Revere, selected 28th by the Minnesota Twins. With predraft agreements in place, they were among the first players to sign.

LaPorta, the 2005 NCAA Division I home run champion, was projected as a first-round pick in 2006, but he slumped badly, landed in the 14th round and returned to school. His power re-emerged as a senior, when he hit .402 with 20 homers. But with little bargaining power, LaPorta signed for a $2 million bonus, $70,000 below slot value. He got off to a roaring start in the minor leagues, hitting 13 home runs in 138 at-bats, but his major league career never panned out.

The 5-foot-9, 150-pound Revere was not widely considered first-round material, but he slipped in by agreeing to sign for $750,000, the only first-rounder who got a bonus of less than $1 million. Revere was among the draft's fastest players, with a time of 6.28 seconds over 60 yards. He had a fine pro debut, hitting .325 with 10 triples and 21 stolen bases in the Rookie-level Gulf Coast League, and emerged as a solid major league player.

According to career WAR scores through the 2015 season, Price was the most successful major league pitcher from the class of 2007, and Heyward was the best position player. Only 22 of 30 first-rounders reached the majors, and just eight had career WAR scores among the top 30 players in the class. Players drafted after the first round who became significant big leaguers included Josh Donaldson (Cubs, supplemental first round), Giancarlo Stanton (Marlins, second round), Corey Kluber (Padres, fourth round) and Arrieta.

### SANDWICH PICKS ABOUND

It wasn't clear until a week before the 2007 draft whether there would be 34 or 35 supplemental picks between the first and second rounds, but either way it represented a record. The final tally was in doubt until Scherzer, the Diamondbacks' top pick in 2006, signed minutes before he would have gone into the 2007 draft. Had Scherzer gone unsigned, the Diamondbacks would have received a supplemental pick as compensation.

Under terms of the new CBA, teams that lost a Type B major league free agent during the offseason were awarded a supplemental first-round pick, but only after compensation was awarded to teams losing Type A free agents. There were 17 Type A free agents, and 17 Type B free agents.

Teams that failed to sign their third-round picks from the previous year were entitled to a compensation selection at the end of the third round. There were four such selections, meaning the third round contained 34 picks.

Before 2007, a fifth-year college senior was eligible to sign as soon as he finished his last college class, provided the player had completed eight semesters in college prior to the start of his senior year and the player's college season was completed before the draft. The fifth-year senior rule was abandoned, effective with the 2007 draft.

The dissolution of the draft-and-follow rule was another key change in the 2007 draft. In effect, teams no longer could draft players destined for junior college and control their rights and track their progress for almost a year before deciding whether to sign them. Under the new rules, clubs had about two months to sign all their draft picks.

The most attractive draft-and-follows from the 2006 draft, the last year of the process, were Broward (Fla.) JC's Mat Latos and Grayson County (Texas) JC's Jordan Walden, both righthanded pitchers. The 6-foot-5, 210-pound Latos was under control to the San Diego Padres, who drafted him in the 11th round, and the 6-foot-5, 220-pound Walden remained property of the Angels, who selected him in the 12th round. Both players had until May 31 to sign, or go into the 2007 draft pool.

Latos and Walden were both considered potential first-rounders as high school seniors, but their stock waned in the weeks leading up to the 2006 draft—Latos mainly over concerns about his makeup, Walden over concerns that his velocity had decreased from the previous summer, when he was clocked at 99 mph. Both pitchers regained much of their worth in junior college. The Padres signed Latos for $1.25 million, and the Angels struck a deal with Walden for $1 million—roughly the going rate for late first-round picks in the previous few years.

A total of 176 junior college players were drafted in 2007, a drop from 383 a year earlier. The first juco player selected was Fresno (Calif.) Community College catcher Jameson Smith, a third-round pick of the Marlins.

### IN FOCUS: DAVID PRICE

David Price established himself as the top prospect for the 2007 draft by going 9-5, 4.16 with a school-record 153 strikeouts as a sophomore at Vanderbilt in 2006, and following that up with a dominant performance with Team USA, going 5-0, 0.21 with seven walks and 61 strikeouts in 44 innings. The gap only widened during his junior season.

"On ability, he's the guy," an American League scouting director said. "I can't see it any other way. He has clearly separated himself from the rest."

As Baseball America's College Player of the Year in 2007, the 6-foot-5 Price led the nation with 194 strikeouts in 133 innings, walked 31, and went 11-1, 2.63. His only loss came in a relief appearance in the 10th inning of an NCAA regional elimination game, when he served up a home run to the first batter he faced and No. 1-ranked Vanderbilt was bounced from the tournament. It didn't matter to the Devil Rays, who had long since locked in on Price as the top pick.

"It's really a testament to David," Rays general manager Andrew Friedman said. "It's a testament to who he is as a player and a person because you don't see that very often where a player in October that you have first on your draft board is able to maintain that rank. It is a great accomplishment, and it really speaks volumes about him."

# 2007 Draft List

**Did not sign. Major leaguers in bold, with first and last years noted. Order of selection indicated in parentheses. For the first five rounds, the peak level of each player is noted.*

## ARIZONA DIAMONDBACKS (9)

1. **Jarrod Parker, rhp, Norwell HS, Bluffton, Ind.—(2011-13)**
1. Wes Roemer, rhp, Cal State Fullerton (Supplemental choice—50th—as compensation for Type B free agent Craig Counsell).—(AAA)
1. **Ed Easley, c, Mississippi State University** (Supplemental choice—61st—as compensation for Type B free agent Miguel Batista).**—(2015)**
2. **Barry Enright, rhp, Pepperdine University.—(2010-13)**
3. **Rey Navarro, ss, Puerto Rico Baseball Academy, Caguas, P.R.—(2015)**
4. Sean Morgan, rhp, Tulane University.—(Low A)
5. Tyrell Worthington, of, South Central HS, Winterville, N.C.—(Short-season A)
6. **Scott Maine, lhp, University of Miami.—(2010-12)**
7. **Bryan Augenstein, rhp, University of Florida.—(2009-11)**
8. Taylor Harbin, 2b, Clemson University.
9. Mark Hallberg, ss, Florida State University.
10. Evan Frey, of, University of Missouri.
11. Josh Ellis, rhp, Wake Forest University.
12. Bryan Henry, rhp, Florida State University.
13. Sean Coughlin, c, University of Kentucky.
14. ***Bobby LaFromboise, lhp, University of New Mexico.—(2013-15)**
15. **Josh Collmenter, rhp, Central Michigan University.—(2011-15)**
16. Michael Mee, of, University of Minnesota.
17. Chance Wheeless, 1b, University of Texas
18. ***Sammy Solis, lhp, Agua Fria HS, Litchfield Park, Ariz.—(2015)**
19. Michael Solbach, rhp, Liberty University.
20. Pete Clifford, of, Jacksonville University.
21. Anthony Smith, of, St. John's University.
22. Ty Davis, rhp, Vanderbilt University.
23. Ian Harrington, lhp, University of Hawaii.
24. Luke Prihoda, rhp, Sam Houston State University.
25. Billy Spottiswood, rhp, Chico State (Calif.) University.
26. **Tommy Layne, lhp, Mount Olive (N.C.) College.—(2012-15)**
27. *Austin Garrett, lhp, Pensacola (Fla.) JC.
28. **Evan Scribner, rhp, Central Connecticut State University.—(2011-15)**
29. Omar Arif, lhp, Long Beach State University.
30. Bill Musselman, c, St. Louis University.
31. *Gary Bulman, rhp, Greenbrier Christian Academy, Virginia Beach, Va.
32. *Joey Stevens, c, Pensacola (Fla.) JC.
33. *Chuck Huggins, lhp, UC Santa Barbara.
34. *Chris Kelley, rhp, Rice University.
35. Josh Blake, lhp, Auburn University.
36. *Tyler Conn, lhp, University of Southern Mississippi.
37. Jimmy Principe, of, Brookdale (N.J.) CC.
38. Aaron Hanke, of, UC Davis.
39. Eli Rumler, ss, Kansas State University.
40. *Torrey Jacoby, ss, Notre Dame HS, Scottsdale, Ariz.

DRAFT DROP *Son of Brook Jacoby, major leaguer (1981-92)*

41. Danny Rosen, rhp, Florida State University.
42. *Golden Tate, of, Pope John Paul II HS, Hendersonville, Tenn.

DRAFT DROP *Wide receiver, National Football League (2010-15)*

43. *Andrew Allen, 1b, Desert Vista HS, Phoenix.

DRAFT DROP *Son of Rod Allen, major leaguer (1983-88)*

44. *Nick Ewing, rhp, Oakmont HS, Roseville, Calif.
45. *Garrett Bullock, lhp, Wake Forest University.
46. *Josh Garcia, 1b, Brophy Jesuit Prep, Phoenix.
47. *Mike Greco, 3b, Notre Dame HS, Scottsdale, Ariz.
48. Joe Ayers, ss, Boston College.
49. *Matt Newman, of, Brophy Jesuit Prep, Phoenix.
50. *Dylan Moseley, rhp, Louisiana Tech.

DRAFT DROP *Brother of Dustin Moseley, first-round draft pick, Reds (2000); major leaguer (2006-12)*

## ATLANTA BRAVES (14)

1. **Jason Heyward, of, Henry County HS, McDonough, Ga.—(2010-15)**
1. Jon Gilmore, 3b, Iowa City (Iowa) HS (Supplemental choice—33rd—as compensation for Type A free agent Danys Baez).—(AA)
2. ***Josh Fields, rhp, University of Georgia** (Choice from Orioles as compensation for Baez).**—(2013-15)**

DRAFT DROP *Returned to Georgia; re-drafted by Mariners, 2008 (1st round)*

2. **Freddie Freeman, 1b, El Modena HS, Villa Park, Calif.—(2010-15)**
3. **Brandon Hicks, ss, Texas A&M University.—(2010-14)**
4. **Cory Gearrin, rhp, Mercer University.—(2011-15)**
5. Dennis Dixon, of, University of Oregon.—(Rookie)

DRAFT DROP *Quarterback, National Football League (2008-11)*

6. Michael Fisher, ss, Georgia Tech.
7. Travis Jones, 2b, University of South Carolina.
8. *Colby Shreve, rhp, CC of Southern Nevada.
9. Tim Ladd, lhp, Georgia Tech.
10. Tommy Palica, lhp, Golden West (Calif.) JC.
11. ***Brandon Belt, lhp, San Jacinto (Texas) JC.—(2011-15)**
12. Nick Fellman, rhp, Minnesota State University.-Mankato.
13. Chad Maddox, of, University of Tennessee.
14. Caleb Brewer, rhp, Harris County HS, Fortson, Ga.
15. *Paul Demny, rhp, East Bernard (Texas) HS.
16. *Eddie Burns, rhp, Georgia Tech.
17. Benji Johnson, c, University of North Carolina.
18. Randy Gress, ss, Quinnipiac College.
19. Brett Butts, rhp, Auburn University.
20. C.J. Lee, of, East Tennessee State University.
21. Kuyaunnis Miles, of, Chattahoochee Valley (Ala.) JC.
22. *Lyle Allen, 1b, Cartersville (Ga.) HS.
23. *Edmond Sparks, c, Lovejoy (Ga.) HS.
24. ***Mitch Harris, rhp, U.S. Naval Academy.—(2015)**
25. Rico Reid, rhp, East Coweta HS, Newnan, Ga.
26. Daniel Elorriaga-Matra, c, Stoneman Douglas HS, Coral Springs, Fla.
27. *Adam Milligan, of, Walters State (Tenn.) JC.
28. Rashod Henry, of, Lumberton (Miss.) HS.
29. *Gary Gilheeney, rhp, Bishop Hendricken HS, Johnston, R.I.
30. *Rene Escobar, 1b, Riverside (Calif.) CC.
31. Benino Pruneda, rhp, San Jacinto (Texas) CC.
32. T.J. Wohlever, lhp, Western Nevada CC.
33. ***Craig Kimbrel, rhp, Wallace State-Hanceville (Ala.) CC.—(2010-15)**
34. *Robert Maddox, 1b, Villa-Angela St. Joseph HS, Euclid, Ohio.
35. *Chris Moon, of, Tucson Magnet HS, Tucson, Ariz.
36. *Vernell Warren, 2b, Grant HS, Portland, Ore.
37. *Randy Yard, rhp, Palm Desert (Calif.) HS.
38. *Will Casey, lhp, Kennesaw Mountain HS, Kennesaw, Ga.
39. *Elliott Armstrong, of, Harlan HS, Chicago.
40. *Taylor Whitenton, rhp, Heritage HS, Conyers, Ga.
41. *Sheldon Johnson, rhp, Deptford HS, Woodbury, N.J.
42. *Bryson Rahier, c, Cajon HS, San Bernardino, Calif.
43. *Ryan Chaffee, rhp, Chipola (Fla.) JC.
44. *Dock Doyle, c, Coastal Carolina University.
45. *T.J. Thomas, of, St. Dominic HS, Hicksville, N.Y.
46. *Brett Krill, of, Aliso Niguel HS, Laguna Niguel, Calif.
47. *Goldy Simmons, rhp, San Diego CC.

DRAFT DROP *Son of Nelson Simmons, major leaguer (1984-87)*

48. *Joe Lincoln, c, Tipton HS, Clarksburg, Mo.
49. *Tyrease House, of, JC of the Canyons (Calif.)
50. *Andrew Armstrong, lhp, Turner Ashby HS, Harrisonburg, Va.

## BALTIMORE ORIOLES (5)

1. **Matt Wieters, c, Georgia Tech.—(2009-15)**
2. (Choice to Braves as compensation for Type A free agent Danys Baez)
3. (Choice to Mets as compensation for Type A free agent Chad Bradford)
4. Tim Bascom, rhp, University of Central Florida.—(AAA)
5. **Jake Arrieta, rhp, Texas Christian University.—(2010-15)**
6. **Joe Mahoney, 1b, University of Richmond.—(2012-13)**
7. **Matt Angle, of, Ohio State University.—(2011)**
8. Shane Mathews, rhp, East Carolina University.
9. Malcolm Crowley, ss, Galveston (Texas) JC.
10. *Eryk McConnell, rhp, North Carolina State University.
11. Robbie Widlansky, of, Florida Atlantic University.
12. Wally Crancer, of, Georgia Tech.
13. Jordan Wolf, c, Xavier University.
14. Hank Williamson, rhp, San Jacinto (Texas) JC.
15. *Tyrone Hambly, 3b, Grayson County (Texas) CC.
16. Tyler Kolodny, 3b, El Camino Real HS, Woodland Hills, Calif.
17. Jason White, ss, University of Iowa.
18. John Mariotti, rhp, Coastal Carolina University.
19. Brian Parker, rhp, Lewis-Clark State (Idaho) College.
20. Sean Gleason, rhp, St. Mary's (Calif.) College.
21. Scott Mueller, rhp, Arizona State University.
22. Colin Allen, rhp, Lamar (Colo.) CC.
23. Tony Kirbis, rhp, Point Loma Nazarene (Calif.) University.
24. *Dan Klein, rhp, Servite HS, Los Alamitos, Calif.
25. Cliff Flagello, rhp, Shorter (Ga.) College.
26. Justin Moore, rhp, Chancellor HS, Fredericksburg, Va.
27. Kraig Binick, of, New York Tech.
28. Stephen Procner, lhp, Cleveland State University.
29. Danny Heller, of, Los Angeles Pierce JC.
30. Brandon Cooney, rhp, Florida Atlantic University.
31. Matt Tucker, 3b, Dallas Baptist University.
32. *Pete Andrelczyk, rhp, Coastal Carolina University.
33. Jacob Julius, of, University of Arkansas.
34. Kyle Touchatt, rhp, Wichita State University.
35. Eric Perlozzo, 2b, Shippensburg (Pa.) University.

DRAFT DROP *Son of Sam Perlozzo, major league manager, (2005-07)*

36. Calvin Lester, of, Prairie View A&M University.
37. *Merrill Kelly, rhp, Desert Mountain HS, Scottsdale, Ariz.
38. *Michael Harrington, of, College of Charleston.
39. *Joe Yermal, rhp, McDonogh School, Bel Air, Md.
40. Aaron Odom, lhp, Texas Tech.
41. *Russell Wilson, ss, The Collegiate School, Richmond, Va.

DRAFT DROP *Quarterback, National Football League (2012-15)*

42. Joe DiGeronimo, ss, Wagner College.
43. Cole McCurry, lhp, Tennessee Wesleyan College.
44. *Travis Dirk, rhp, Navarro (Texas) JC.
45. Jacob Smith, lhp, Brescia (Ky.) University.
46. Lee Ellis, of, California Lutheran University.
47. Preston Pehrson, c, Towson University.
48. Nick Ray, of, Northwest Nazarene (Idaho) College.
49. *Tyler Newsome, of, Marist HS, Palos Heights, Ill.
50. Mike Gioioso, ss, Mount St. Mary's College.

## BOSTON RED SOX (20)

1. (Choice to Dodgers as compensation for Type A free agent Julio Lugo)
1. **Nick Hagadone, lhp, University of Washington** (Supplemental choice—55th—as compensation for Type B free agent Alex Gonzalez).**—(2011-15)**
1. Ryan Dent, ss, Woodrow Wilson HS, Long Beach, Calif. (Supplemental choice—62nd—as compensation for Type B free agent Keith Foulke).—(AAA)
2. *Hunter Morris, 3b, Grissom HS, Huntsville, Ala.—(AAA)

DRAFT DROP *Attended Auburn; re-drafted by Brewers, 2010 (4th round)*

3. Brock Huntzinger, rhp, Pendleton Heights HS, Pendleton, Ind.—(AAA)
4. Chris Province, rhp, Southeastern Louisiana University.—(AAA)
5. **Will Middlebrooks, rhp-ss, Liberty Eylau HS, Texarkana, Texas.—(2012-15)**
6. **Anthony Rizzo, 1b, Stoneman Douglas HS, Parkland, Fla.—(2011-15)**
7. David Mailman, 1b, Providence HS, Charlotte, N.C.
8. Adam Mills, rhp, University of North Carolina-Charlotte.
9. Kade Keowen, of, LSU-Eunice JC.
10. Kenneth Roque, ss, Puerto Rico Baseball Academy, Cidra, P.R.
11. **Ryan Pressly, rhp, Marcus HS, Highland Village, Texas.—(2013-15)**
12. Eammon Portice, rhp, High Point University.
13. ***Justin Grimm, rhp, Virginia HS, Bristol, Va.—(2012-15)**
14. *Jacob Cowan, rhp, Roswell (Ga.) HS.
15. *Scott Green, rhp, University of Kentucky.
16. Austin Bailey, rhp, Prattville (Ala.) HS.
17. *Jaren Matthews, 1b, Don Bosco Prep HS, Teaneck, N.J.
18. **Hunter Strickland, rhp, Pike County HS, Griffin, Ga.—(2014-15)**
19. David Marks, of, Edmonds (Wash.) CC.
20. Dan Milano, c, Northeastern University.
21. Aaron Reza, ss, University of Oklahoma.
22. Will Latimer, lhp, Trinidad State (Colo.) JC.
23. **Drake Britton, lhp, Tomball HS, Magnolia, Texas.—(2013-14)**
24. *Matt Presley, of, Cheyenne Mountain HS, Colorado Springs, Colo.
25. *Seth Garrison, rhp, Texas Christian University.
26. Deshaun Brooks, 3b, Benedict (S.C.) College.
27. ***Yasmani Grandal, c, Miami Springs HS, Hialeah, Fla.—(2012-15)**

DRAFT DROP *First-round draft pick (12th overall), Reds (2010)*

28. ***Nick Tepesch, rhp, Blue Springs (Mo.) HS.—(2013-14)**
29. *Juan Carlin, lhp, Riverview HS, Sarasota, Fla.
30. Will Vazquez, c, Kent State University.
31. Daniel Buller, lhp, Fresno (Calif.) CC.
32. *Ridge Carpenter, of, Kalani HS, Mililani, Hawaii.
33. *Garrett Larsen, rhp, Texarkana (Texas) CC.
34. Tony Bajoczky, rhp, Duke University.
35. *Sean Tierney, lhp, Clover Hill HS, Mosely, Va.
36. *Scott Lyons, ss, Mount San Antonio (Calif.) JC.
37. Scott Lonergan, rhp, Rice University.
38. *Derrick Stultz, rhp, Wharton HS, Tampa.
39. *Jonathan Roof, ss, St. Mary HS, Paducah, Ky.

DRAFT DROP *Son of Gene Roof, major leaguer (1981-83) • Brother of Shawn Roof, 33rd-round draft pick, Tigers (2007)*

40. *Ryan Fischer, rhp, Lodi HS, Acampo, Calif.
41. *Mike Bourdon, c, Northwest Catholic HS, Simsbury, Conn.
42. Chad Povich, rhp, Dixie State (Utah) College.
43. *Scott Cure, lhp, Idalia (Colo.) HS.
44. Emmanuel Solano, ss, Miami-Dade CC.
45. Peter Gilardo, c-rhp, Dominican (N.Y.) College.
46. *Garrett Young, of, Liberty University.

## CHICAGO CUBS (3)

1. **Josh Vitters, 3b, Cypress HS, Anaheim, Calif.—(2012)**
1. **Josh Donaldson, c, Auburn University** (Supplemental choice—48th—as compensation for Type B free agent Juan Pierre).**—(2010-15)**
2. (Choice to Nationals as compensation for Type A free agent Alfonso Soriano)
3. Tony Thomas, 2b, Florida State University.—(AAA)
4. **Darwin Barney, ss, Oregon State University.—(2010-15)**
5. **Brandon Guyer, of, University of Virginia.—(2011-15)**
6. Casey Lambert, lhp, University of Virginia.
7. Ty Wright, of, Oklahoma State University.
8. Marquez Smith, 3b, Clemson University.
9. Clark Hardman, of, Cal State Fullerton.
10. Leon Johnson, of, Brigham Young University.

DRAFT DROP *Brother of Elliot Johnson, major leaguer (2008-14) • Brother of Cedric Johnson, 19th-round draft pick, Phillies (2007)*

11. Chris Siegfried, lhp, University of Portland.
12. Ryan Acosta, rhp, Clearwater Central Catholic HS, Clearwater, Fla.
13. Jonathan Wyatt, of, University of Georgia.
14. **James Russell, lhp, University of Texas.—(2010-15)**

DRAFT DROP *Son of Jeff Russell, major leaguer (1983-96)*
15. Marc Sawyer, 1b, Yale University.
16. Zach Ashwood, lhp, University of Kansas.
17. Arik Hempy, lhp, University of South Carolina.
18. Jeff Rea, 2b-of, Mississippi State University.
19. *Kyle Day, c, Michigan State University.
20. Jose Made, ss, Dominican (N.Y.) College.
21. Dustin Sasser, lhp, East Carolina University.
22. Craig Muschko, rhp, La Salle University.
23. Stephen Vento, rhp, Palm Beach (Fla.) CC.
24. Scott Meyer, rhp, Lamar University.
25. *Victor Sanchez, 3b, Gahr HS, Norwalk, Calif.
26. Michael Bunton, lhp, College of Charleston.
27. *Clayton Suss, rhp, Cooper City (Fla.) HS.
28. Bill Moss, 2b, University of Memphis.
**29. *Andrew Cashner, rhp, Angelina (Texas) JC.—(2010-15)**
DRAFT DROP *First-round draft pick (19th overall), Cubs (2008)*
30. Luke Sommer, of, University of San Francisco.
31. Brian Leclerc, of, University of Florida.
32. Luis Bautista, c, Florida International University.
33. *Preston Clark, c, University of Texas.
34. *Enrique Garcia, rhp, University of Miami.
35. *J.C. Casey, rhp, Kickapoo HS, Springfield, Mo.
36. Billy Mottran, 3b, Dowling (N.Y.) College.
37. *Mike McGee, rhp, Port St. Lucie (Fla.) HS.
38. Yuri Higgins, rhp, University of South Florida.
39. Roberto Sabates, c, Pompano Beach, Fla.
40. Corey Bachman, rhp, Virginia Military Institute.
41. *Jordan Herr, of, University of Pittsburgh.
DRAFT DROP *Son of Tommy Herr, major leaguer (1979-91) • Brother of Aaron Herr, first-round draft pick, Braves (2000)*
42. *Colt Sedbrook, 2b, University of Arizona.
43. *Garrett Clyde, rhp, San Jacinto (Texas) JC.
44. Bryan Jost, 1b, University of Minnesota.
45. *Ryan Lewis, of, Yakima Valley (Wash.) JC.
46. *Tyler Clark, rhp, Springfield Catholic HS, Springfield, Mo.
47. *Josh Walter, rhp, Texas State University.
48. *Carlos Rivera, of, Aurora East HS, Aurora, Ill.
49. *Jordan Rogers, rhp, San Jacinto (Texas) JC.
50. *Blake Murphy, c, Western Carolina University.

## CHICAGO WHITE SOX (25)

**1. Aaron Poreda, lhp, University of San Francisco.—(2009-14)**
2. Nevin Griffith, rhp, Middleton HS, Brandon, Fla.—(AA)
**3. John Ely, rhp, Miami (Ohio) University.—(2011-12)**
4. Leroy Hunt, rhp, Sacramento (Calif.) CC.—(AA)
**5. Nate Jones, rhp, Northern Kentucky University.—(2012-15)**
6. Johnnie Lowe, rhp, Point Loma Nazarene (Calif.) University.
7. Jimmy Gallagher, of, Duke University.
8. Lyndon Estill, of, Lower Columbia (Wash.) CC.
9. Kenny Gilbert, of, DeSoto (Texas) HS.
10. *B.J. Guinn, ss, Berkeley (Calif.) HS.
11. Jordan Kendall, of, Contra Costa (Calif.) CC.
12. Kevin Skogley, lhp, University of Nevada-Las Vegas.
13. Sergio Miranda, ss, Virginia Commonwealth University.
14. John Curtis, c, Cal State Fullerton.
15. Greg Paiml, ss, University of Alabama.
16. Nick Mahin, of, Cal State Fullerton.
17. Dale Mollenhauer, ss, East Carolina University.
18. Levi Maxwell, rhp, West Virginia University.
19. Henry Mabee, rhp, Morehead State University.
20. Logan Johnson, 2b, University of Louisville.
21. *Mitch Delaney, 1b, St. Thomas of Villanova HS, La Salle, Ontario.
22. Justin Klipp, rhp, Cal State Fullerton.
23. Charlie Shirek, rhp, University of Nebraska.
24. *Kevin Patterson, 1b, Oak Mountain HS, Birmingham, Ala.
25. Dan Albritton, rhp, Florida Southern College.
26. *Mike Bolsenbroek, rhp, Santa Ana (Calif.) JC.
27. *Caleb Hurst, rhp, Fred Beyer HS, Modesto, Calif.
28. *Christopher Epps, of, Dunwoody HS, Stone Mountain, Ga.
29. *Jabari Blash, of, Charlotte Amalie HS, St. Thomas, V.I.
30. *John Flanagan, lhp, Belleville Township West HS, Belleville, Ill.
31. *Eddie Orozco, rhp, Rubidoux HS, Riverside, Calif.
32. *Andre Lamontagne, rhp, Long Beach State University.
33. *Mitchell LeVier, of, Fullerton (Calif.) JC.
34. *Ryan Sharpley, rhp, Marshall (Mich.) HS.
35. *Zach Babitt, 2b, Albany HS, Richmond, Calif.
DRAFT DROP *Son of Shooty Babitt, major leaguer (1981)*
36. Oney Guillen, 2b, North Park (Ill.) University.
DRAFT DROP *Son of Ozzie Guillen, major leaguer (1985-2000); major league manager (2004-12)*
37. *Alex Rodriguez, 3b, La Salle HS, Miami Springs, Fla.
38. *Grant Monroe, rhp, Schaumburg (Ill.) HS.
DRAFT DROP *Son of Larry Monroe, first-round draft pick, White Sox (1974); major leaguer (1976)*
39. *Roderick Jones, of, Chamblee HS, Stone Mountain, Ga.
40. *Austin King, 2b, Gallia Academy, Gallipolis, Ohio.
41. *Devin Shines, 1b, Westwood HS, Austin, Texas.
DRAFT DROP *Son of Razor Shines, major leaguer (1983-87)*
42. *Mike Jones, of, Arizona State University.
43. *Baldwin Vargas, rhp, New Jersey City University.
44. *John Grim, 1b, John Hersey HS, Arlington Heights, Ill.
45. Ronnie Morales, lhp, Wichita State University.

## CINCINNATI REDS (15)

**1. Devin Mesoraco, c, Punxsutawney Area (Pa.) HS.—(2011-15)**
**1. Todd Frazier, ss, Rutgers University** (Supplemental choice—34th—as compensation for Type A free agent Rich Aurilia).—**(2011-15)**
DRAFT DROP *Brother of Jeff Frazier, major leaguer (2010)*
1. Kyle Lotzkar, rhp, South Delta SS, Delta, B.C. (Supplemental choice—53rd—as compensation for Type B free agent Scott Schoeneweis).—(AA)
**2. Zack Cozart, ss, University of Mississippi.—(2011-15)**
**3. Scott Carroll, rhp, Missouri State University** (Choice from Giants as compensation for Aurilia).—**(2014-15)**
**3. Neftali Soto, ss, Colegio Marista HS, Florida, P.R.—(2013-14)**
4. *Blake Stouffer, 1b, Texas A&M University.—(Low A)
DRAFT DROP *Returned to Texas A&M; re-drafted by Nationals, 2008 (13th round)*
5. Drew Bowman, lhp, University of Nebraska.—(AA)
6. Evan Hildenbrandt, rhp, Mennonite Educational Institute, Abbotsford, B.C.
7. Brandon Waring, 3b, Wofford College.
8. *Drew O'Neil, rhp, Penn State University.
9. Alex Oliveras, of, Puerto Rico Baseball Academy, Caguas, P.R.
10. Harris Honeycutt, rhp, University of South Carolina.
11. Jordan Wideman, c-of, Streetsville SS, Mississauga, Ontario.
12. Scott Gaffney, rhp-ss, Penn State University.
13. Brandon Menchaca, of, University of Delaware.
14. Joe Krebs, lhp, University of Texas.
15. Matt Klinker, rhp, Furman University.
16. Shea Snowden, lhp, Brandon (Miss.) HS.
17. *Jesse Craig, rhp, Brigham Young University.
**18. *Taylor Jordan, rhp, Merritt Island (Fla.) HS.—(2013-15)**
19. Jeff Jeffords, rhp, University of South Carolina.
20. Jake Kahaulelio, ss, Oral Roberts University.
**21. Jeremy Horst, lhp, Armstrong Atlantic State (Ga.) University.—(2011-13)**
22. Tyler Rhoden, rhp, Vanderbilt University.
23. Jason Bour, c, George Mason University.
24. Frank Meade, c, Rutgers University.
25. Eli Rimes, 1b, Sonoma State (Calif.) University.
**26. Curtis Partch, rhp, Merced (Calif.) JC.—(2013-14)**
27. *Jason Roenicke, rhp, Cuesta (Calif.) JC.
DRAFT DROP *Son of Gary Roenicke, first-round draft pick, Expos (1973); major leaguer (1976-88) • Brother of Josh Roenicke, major leaguer (2008-13) • Nephew of Ron Roenicke, major leaguer (1981-88); major league manager (2011-15)*
28. Derrick Conaster, rhp, Tallahassee (Fla.) CC.
29. Steve Otterness, lhp, Embry-Riddle (Fla.) University.
30. Brett Bartles, 3b, Duke University.
31. Jordan Hotchkiss, rhp, Brevard (N.C.) College.
32. *Brandon Douglas, ss, University of Northern Iowa.
33. Brodie Pullen, 3b, Calhoun (Ga.) HS.
34. Jeremy Vinyard, rhp, Boaz HS, Albertville, Ala.
**35. *Thad Weber, rhp, University of Nebraska.—(2012-13)**
36. *Leon Landry, 3b, Baker HS, Baton Rouge, La.
**37. *Scott Alexander, lhp, Cardinal Newman HS, Windsor, Calif.—(2015)**
38. *Ari Ronick, lhp, University of Portland.
**39. *Jimmy Nelson, rhp, Niceville (Fla.) HS.—(2013-15)**
40. *Ross Hopkins, c, Tyee HS, Seattle.
41. Kevin Hickey, of, Concordia (N.Y.) College.
42. *Sean Bierman, lhp, Kinnelon (N.J.) HS.
43. *Austin Taylor, 3b, Thomas County Central HS, Thomasville, Ga.
44. Josh Beal, rhp, Independence (Kan.) CC.
45. *Jordan Brown, rhp, Meridian (Miss.) CC.
46. *Mike McGuire, rhp, University of Delaware.
47. *Drew Benes, 3b, Westminster Christian Academy, St. Louis.
DRAFT DROP *Son of Andy Benes, first overall draft pick, Padres (1988); major leaguer (1989-2002)*
48. Michael Henry, rhp, St. Patricks HS, Sarnia, Ontario.
49. *Cameron Gray, rhp, Silverthorn Collegiate Institute, Toronto.
50. *Jordan Chambless, rhp, Texas A&M University.

## CLEVELAND INDIANS (13)

1. Beau Mills, 3b-1b, Lewis-Clark State (Idaho) College.—(AAA)
DRAFT DROP *Son of Brad Mills, major leaguer (1980-83); major league manager (2010-12)*
2. (Choice to Mets as compensation for Type A free agent Roberto Hernandez)
3. (Choice to Phillies as compensation for Type A free agent David Dellucci)
**4. T.J. McFarland, lhp, Amos Alonzo Stagg HS, Orland Park, Ill.—(2013-15)**
5. Jonathan Holt, rhp, University of Tampa.—(High A)
6. Bo Greenwell, of, Riverdale HS, Alva, Fla.
DRAFT DROP *Son of Mike Greenwell, major leaguer (1985-97)*
7. *Cole St. Clair, lhp, Rice University.
8. Mark Thompson, ss, Lewis-Clark State (Idaho) College.
9. Adam White, of, West Virginia University.
10. Heath Taylor, lhp, University of Oklahoma.
**11. *Matt Hague, 3b, University of Washington.—(2012-15)**
12. Gary Campfield, rhp, Texas A&M University.
13. Matt Brown, of, Wichita State University.
14. Daniel Morales, rhp, University of San Francisco.
15. Chris Jones, lhp, Gaither HS, Tampa.
16. *Doug Hogan, c, Clemson University.
17. *Miles Morgan, rhp, Texas Tech.
18. Kyle Landis, rhp, University of Pittsburgh.
19. *Bobby Coyle, of, Chatsworth (Calif.) HS.
20. Jeff Hehr, ss, Eastern Michigan University.
21. *Jared Clark, of, Cal State Fullerton.
22. *Sthil Sowers, rhp, North Lenoir HS, Grifton, N.C.
23. *Shaeffer Hall, lhp, Jefferson (Mo.) CC.
24. *Adam Zornes, c, Rice University.
25. *Kyle Leiendecker, lhp, Homestead HS, Fort Wayne, Ind.
26. Michael Valadez, c, Lee (Tenn.) University.
27. *Daniel Edwards, rhp, Kansas State University.
28. *Scott Savastano, ss, Franklin Pierce (N.H.) College.
29. Garrett Rieck, lhp, Chico State (Calif.) University.
**30. *Bryce Brentz, rhp, South Doyle HS, Knoxville, Tenn.—(2014)**
DRAFT DROP *First-round draft pick (36th overall), Red Sox (2010)*
31. *Jason Hessler, rhp, St. Joseph's (Pa.) University.
32. Joe Mahalic, rhp, Woodrow Wilson HS, Portland, Ore.
DRAFT DROP *Son of Drew Mahalic, linebacker, National Football League (1975-78)*
33. *Tyler Kuhn, 2b, West Virginia University.
**34. Josh Judy, rhp, Indiana Tech.—(2011)**
35. Brian Juhl, c, Stanford University.
36. P.J. Zocchi, rhp, Clemson University.
37. *Dean Kiekhefer, lhp, Oldham County HS, Crestwood, Ky.
38. Johnny Williams, rhp, University of Tampa.
**39. *Erik Jokisch, lhp, Virginia (Ill.) HS.—(2014)**
40. Dallas Cawiezell, rhp, Valparaiso University.
41. *Thomas Luce, rhp, Seminole State (Okla.) CC.
42. *Bryce Tafelski, c, Santa Ynez-Valley Union HS, Los Olivos, Calif.
43. *Travis Howell, c, Long Beach State University.
44. *Ryan Royster, of, UC Davis.
45. *Daniel Evatt, of, Grapevine HS, Colleyville, Texas.
46. Brock Simpson, of, University of Kansas.
47. Kevin Rucker, of, Pioneer Valley HS, Santa Maria, Calif.
48. Walter Diaz, ss, University of South Florida.
49. Matt Willard, ss, University of Arkansas.
50. Doug Pickens, c, University of Michigan.

## COLORADO ROCKIES (8)

1. Casey Weathers, rhp, Vanderbilt University.—(AA)
2. Brian Rike, of, Louisiana Tech.—(AA)
3. Lars Davis, c, University of Illinois.—(AAA)
4. Isaiah Froneberger, lhp, Forest Park HS, Atlanta.—(AA)
5. Connor Graham, rhp, Miami (Ohio) University.—(AA)
6. Cory Riordan, rhp, Fordham University.
7. Jeff Cunningham, 1b, University of South Alabama.
8. Parker Frazier, rhp, Bishop Kelley HS, Tulsa, Okla.
DRAFT DROP *Son of George Frazier, major leaguer (1978-87)*
**9. Jordan Pacheco, 2b, University of New Mexico.—(2011-15)**
10. Jeff Fischer, rhp, Eastern Michigan University.
11. Andy Groves, rhp, Purdue University.
12. Darin Holcomb, 3b, Gonzaga University.
13. Beau Seabury, c, University of Virginia.
14. *Kentrail Davis, of, Theodore (Ala.) HS.
DRAFT DROP *First-round draft pick (39th overall), Brewers (2009)*
15. Kenny Durst, lhp, West Virginia University.
16. Mitch Lively, rhp, Cal State Sacramento.
17. Austin Chambliss, rhp, Middle Georgia JC.
18. Brian Lapin, of, Fresno State University.
19. *Evan Chambers, of, Lakeland (Fla.) HS.
**20. Matt Reynolds, lhp, Austin Peay State University.—(2010-15)**
**21. *Chris Sale, lhp, Lakeland (Fla.) HS.—(2010-15)**
DRAFT DROP *First-round draft pick (13th overall), White Sox (2010)*
22. Bo Bowman, 1b, University of Louisiana-Monroe.
23. Randall Taylor, rhp, Dallas Baptist University.
24. Brandon Miller, lhp, Fresno State University.
25. Mike Mitchell, of, University of Virginia.
26. Stephen Shao, lhp, Vanderbilt University.
27. James Sims, of, Jackson State University.
28. Craig Rodriguez, lhp, University of Mississippi.
29. Andres Marrero, rhp, Puerto Rico Baseball Academy, Caguas, P.R.
**30. Bruce Billings, rhp, San Diego State University.—(2011-14)**
31. *Israel Troupe, of, Tift County HS, Tifton, Ga.
32. *Kenny Williams, of, Wichita State University.
DRAFT DROP *Son of Kenny Williams, major leaguer (1986-91); general manager, White Sox (2000-12)*
33. *Wayman Gooch, rhp, Ohlone (Calif.) JC.
34. *Travis Lawler, rhp, A&M Consolidated HS, College Station, Texas.
35. *Daniel Renken, rhp, Orange Lutheran HS, Cypress, Calif.
36. Joey Williamson, rhp, University of Notre Dame.
37. *Nick Gallego, 2b, Esperanza HS, Yorba Linda, Calif.
DRAFT DROP *Son of Mike Gallego, major leaguer (1985-97)*
38. Warren Schaeffer, ss, Virginia Tech.
39. Chris Vasami, 1b, Elon University.

40. *Richie Rowland, c, Cloverdale (Calif.) HS.
DRAFT DROP *Son of Rich Rowland, major leaguer (1990-95)*
41. Johnny Bowden, c, University of Southern California.
42. *David Coulon, lhp, University of Arizona.
43. *Devin Lohman, ss, Righetti HS, Santa Maria, Calif.
44. Chad Lembeck, of, Rice University.
45. *Zach Jones, c, Jordan HS, Draper, Utah.
46. *Kyle Saukko, rhp, Granite Bay HS, Roseville, Calif.
**47. *Logan Shafer, of, Cal Poly.—(2011-15)**
48. *Chris Morton, 3b, Bellevue (Wash.) HS.
49. Brandon Reichert, 1b, Florida State University.
50. *Billy McHenry, 2b, Cheyenne East HS, Cheyenne, Wyo.

## DETROIT TIGERS (27)

**1. Rick Porcello, rhp, Seton Hall Prep, Chester, N.J.—(2009-15)**
DRAFT DROP *First 2007 high school draft pick to reach majors (April 9, 2009); grandson of Sam Dente, major leaguer (1947-55)*
1. Brandon Hamilton, rhp, Stanhope Elmore HS, Deatsville, Ala. (Supplemental choice—60th—as compensation for Type B free agent Jamie Walker).—(Low A)
**2. Danny Worth, ss, Pepperdine University.—(2010-14)**
**3. Luke Putkonen, rhp, University of North Carolina.—(2012-14)**
**4. Charlie Furbush, lhp, Louisiana State University.—(2011-15)**
**5. Casey Crosby, lhp, Kaneland HS, Elburn, Ill.—(2012)**
6. Cale Iorg, ss, University of Alabama.
DRAFT DROP *Son of Garth Iorg, major leaguer (1978-87) • Nephew of Dane Iorg, major leaguer (1977-86)*
7. Devin Thomas, c, University of Rhode Island.
8. Manny Migueles, lhp, University of Miami.
9. Justin Henry, 2b-of, University of Mississippi.
10. *Dominic de la Osa, ss-of, Vanderbilt University.
11. Gary Perinar, rhp, University of Minnesota.
12. Chris White, of, Sacramento (Calif.) CC.
13. Londell Taylor, of, Vian (Okla.) HS.
14. *Chris Hernandez, of, Monsignor Pace HS, Pembroke Pines, Fla.
15. Kody Kaiser, of, Oklahoma City University.
16. Mark Brackman, rhp, William Jewell (Mo.) College.
17. Noah Krol, rhp, Wichita State University.
18. *Kevin Rhoderick, rhp, Horizon HS, Scottsdale, Ariz.
19. Andrew Hess, rhp, University of Michigan.
20. Erik Crichton, rhp, Oral Roberts University.
21. *Kyle Brule, rhp, Marcos de Niza HS, Chandler, Ariz.
22. Kris Rochelle, c, University of North Carolina-Charlotte.
23. Brandon Harrigan, c, Oklahoma City University.
24. *Barret Loux, rhp, Stratford HS, Houston.
DRAFT DROP *First-round draft pick (6th overall), Diamondbacks (2010)*
25. *Colin Kaline, 2b, Groves HS, Beverly Hills, Mich.
DRAFT DROP *Grandson of Al Kaline, major leaguer (1953-74)*
26. Matt Hoffman, lhp, Owasso (Okla.) HS.
**27. *Steve Susdorf, of, Fresno State University.—(2013)**
28. *Warren McFadden, of, Tulane University.
29. Wade Lamont, 1b, Flagler (Fla.) College.
DRAFT DROP *Son of Gene Lamont, first-round draft pick, Tigers (1965); major leaguer (1970-75); major league manager (1992-2000)*
30. Jon Kibler, lhp, Michigan State University.
31. Paul Nardozzi, rhp, University of Pittsburgh.
32. *Forrest Moore, lhp, Parkview Baptist HS, Baton Rouge, La.
33. Shawn Roof, ss, University of Illinois.
DRAFT DROP *Son of Gene Roof, major leaguer (1981-83) • Brother of Jonathan Roof, 39th-round draft pick, Red Sox (2007)*
34. Kyle Peter, of, Washburn (Kan.) University.
35. Sean Finefrock, rhp, Butler (Kan.) CC.
36. *Tanner Rindels, of, Seward County (Kan.) CC.
37. *Toby Matchulat, rhp, Redford Union HS, Redford, Mich.
38. *Austin Woodard, lhp, Bishop Carroll Catholic HS, Wichita, Kan.
39. *Jake Oberlechner, ss, Arkansas City (Kan.) HS.
40. D'Andre Vaughn, of, Tavares (Fla.) HS.
**41. *D.J. LeMahieu, ss, Brother Rice HS, Bloomfield Hills, Mich.—(2011-15)**
42. *Matt Robertson, rhp, Valley Center (Kan.) HS.
DRAFT DROP *Brother of Nate Robertson, major leaguer (2002-07)*
43. Richard Zumaya, rhp, Bonita Vista HS, Chula Vista, Calif.
DRAFT DROP *Brother of Joel Zumaya, major leaguer (2006-10)*
44. *Kolby Wood, rhp, Berrien Springs HS, Eau Claire, Mich.

## FLORIDA MARLINS (12)

**1. Matt Dominguez, 3b, Chatsworth HS, Lake Balboa, Calif.—(2011-14)**
DRAFT DROP *Brother of Jason Dominguez, 31st-round draft pick, Astros (2007)*
**2. Giancarlo Stanton, of, Notre Dame HS, Sunland, Calif.—(2010-15)**
3. Jameson Smith, c, Fresno (Calif.) CC.—(High A)
**4. Bryan Petersen, of, UC Irvine.—(2010-12)**
**5. Steve Cishek, rhp, Carson-Newman (Tenn.) College.—(2010-15)**
6. *Taiwan Easterling, of, Oak Grove HS, Hattiesburg, Miss.
7. Andrew Paulauskas, rhp, Tremper HS, Kenosha, Wis.
8. Jay Voss, lhp, Kaskaskia (Ill.) CC.
9. Marcus Crockett, of, Compton (Calif.) CC.
10. Brandon Barrow, lhp, Zachary (La.) HS.
11. Brett Durand, rhp, Delta State (Miss.) University.
12. Garrett Parcell, rhp, San Diego State University.
13. Chris Shafer, rhp, Cajon HS, San Bernardino, Calif.
14. Lucas Waters, 3b, Eastern Kentucky University.
15. Ryan Anetsberger, 3b, Illinois State University.
16. Adam Campbell, rhp, University of New Orleans.
17. Michael Pasek, ss, Apple Valley (Calif.) HS.
18. Chris Ingoglia, lhp, Stetson University.
19. *Charley Williams, of, Itawamba (Miss.) JC.
20. Marc Lewis, lhp, Creighton University.
21. Ryan Curry, 2b, Bradley University.
22. Chaz Gilliam, rhp, Cyril (Okla.) HS.
23. Daniel Prieto, lhp-of, Long Beach (Calif.) CC.
24. Kevin Hammons, lhp, Tusculum (Tenn.) College.
25. Kyle Kaminska, rhp, Naperville Central HS, Naperville, Ill.
26. Bryan Hagerich, of, University of Delaware.
27. Ray White, ss, Compton (Calif.) CC.
28. *Virgil Hill, ss, Valencia HS, Canyon Country, Calif.
29. Ben Lasater, 3b, College of Charleston.
30. A.J. Battisto, rhp, Georgia Southern University.
31. *Justin Harper, rhp, Yavapai (Ariz.) CC.
32. *Josh Thompson, c, Mercer University.
33. Derek Blackshear, rhp, McNeese State University.
34. Stephen Flake, rhp, Southern Tech (Ga.) Institute.
35. Josh Roberts, rhp, University of Portland.
36. Matt Mallory, rhp, University of Science & Arts (Okla.).
37. *Kellen St. Luce, lhp, All Saints Cathedral HS, St. Thomas, V.I.
38. *Tyler Waldron, rhp, Golden Sierra HS, Pilot Hill, Calif.
39. *Ricky Rossman, 1b, Claremont HS, La Verne, Calif.
40. *Mike McCravey, lhp, JC of the Canyons (Calif.).
41. *Skylar Crawford, rhp, Hartnell (Calif.) JC.
42. Brett Lawler, c, University of Arkansas-Little Rock.
43. *Stephen Kohlscheen, rhp, Norman North HS, Norman, Okla.
44. Ernie Banks, 1b, Norfolk State University.
45. *Kevin Stanley, c, Las Lomas HS, Walnut Creek, Calif.
**46. *John Hellweg, rhp, St. Dominic HS, St. Charles, Mo.—(2013)**
47. *Mitch Rider, c, North Gwinnett HS, Suwanee, Ga.
**48. *Jake Elmore, 2b, Wallace State-Hanceville (Ala.) CC.—(2012-15)**
49. *Kyle Rose, of, Robert E. Lee HS, Huntsville, Ala.
50. *Rafael Carlot, 3b, Southeastern (Iowa) CC.

## HOUSTON ASTROS (17)

1. (Choice to Rangers as compensation for Type A free agent Carlos Lee)
2. (Choice to Padres as compensation for Type A free agent Woody Williams)
**3. *Derek Dietrich, 3b, St. Ignatius HS, Parma, Ohio.—(2013-15)**
DRAFT DROP *Attended Georgia Tech; re-drafted by Rays, 2010 (2nd round) • Grandson of Steve Demeter, major leaguer (1959-60)*
4. *Brett Eibner, rhp-of, The Woodlands (Texas) HS.—(AAA)
DRAFT DROP *Attended Arkansas; re-drafted by Royals, 2010 (2nd round)*
5. Collin Delome, of, Lamar University.—(AAA)
6. David Dinelli, rhp, Sierra (Calif.) JC.
7. Russell Dixon, 2b, Auburn University.
**8. *Chad Bettis, rhp, Monterey HS, Lubbock, Texas.—(2013-15)**
9. Luis Pardo, rhp, Florida Gulf Coast University.
10. Matt Cusick, 2b, University of Southern California.
11. Rob Bono, rhp, Waterford (Conn.) HS.
12. Brian Pellegrini, 3b. St. Bonaventure University.
13. *Chad Jones, of, Southern University Lab School, Baton Rouge, La.
DRAFT DROP *Defensive back, National Football League (2010-11)*
14. Craig Corrado, of, University of Tampa.
15. *Matt Fitts, rhp, Lewis-Clark State (Idaho) College.
16. Devon Torrence, of, Canton South HS, East Sparta, Ohio.
DRAFT DROP *Defensive back, National Football League (2011)*
17. Mason Roberts, rhp, Cisco (Texas) JC.
18. Brian Esperson, rhp, Mercyhurst (Pa.) College.
19. Jon Fixler, c, Indiana University.
20. Kyle Greenwalt, rhp, Souderton Area HS, Harleysville, Pa.
21. Kyle Miller, c-3b, Central Florida CC.
22. Drew Anderson, of, University of New Orleans.
23. Charlie Gamble, 1b, North Carolina A&T University.
24. Philip Stringer, ss, Auburn University.
25. Kevin Carkeek, c, Oakland University.
26. Sal Iocono, c, Princeton University.
27. Brett Robinson, rhp, Florida Southern College.
28. Jared Pitts, of, Stephen F. Austin University.
29. Travis Sweet, of, University of Iowa.
30. Danny Gil, rhp, University of Miami.
31. Jason Dominguez, rhp, Pepperdine University.
DRAFT DROP *Brother of Matt Dominguez, first-round draft pick, Astros (2007); major leaguer (2011-14)*
32. David Miller, rhp, Stephen F. Austin University.
33. Cody Phipps, of, Vauxhall HS, Round Hill, Alta.
34. Brian Wabick, rhp, Oakton (Ill.) CC.
35. Jordan Powell, rhp, Southern Illinois University.
36. Albert Cartwright, of, Polk (Fla.) CC.
37. Jake Leonhardt, rhp, Stephen F. Austin University.
**38. *Robbie Weinhardt, rhp, Oklahoma State University.—(2010-11)**
39. *Brian Fletcher, ss, Starrs Mill HS, Fayetteville, Ga.
DRAFT DROP *Son of Scott Fletcher, major leaguer (1981-95)*
40. *Kyle Erdman, lhp, Oakton (Ill.) CC.
41. Colton Pitkin, lhp, Sterling HS, Baytown, Texas.
42. Chris Turner, of, Brandon (Fla.) HS.
43. Marques Williams, of, Compton (Calif.) CC.
44. Cat Everett, ss, Tulane University.

## KANSAS CITY ROYALS (2)

**1. Mike Moustakas, ss, Chatsworth HS, Northridge, Calif.—(2011-15)**
DRAFT DROP *Nephew of Tom Robson, major leaguer (1974-75)*
2. Sam Runion, rhp, A.C. Reynolds HS, Asheville, N.C.—(AAA)
**3. Danny Duffy, lhp, Cabrillo HS, Lompoc, Calif.—(2011-15)**
4. Mitch Hodge, rhp, Prince of Wales SS, Vancouver, B.C.—(Low A)
5. Adrian Ortiz, of, Pepperdine University.—(High A)
6. Fernando Cruz, ss, Puerto Rico Advancement College HS, Dorado, P.R.
7. Hilton Richardson, of, Lake Washington HS, Kirkland, Wash.
8. Casey Feickert, rhp, Antelope Valley (Calif.) JC.
9. *Zach Kenyon, rhp, Central HS, Davenport, Iowa.
**10. Greg Holland, rhp, Western Carolina University.—(2010-15)**
**11. David Lough, of, Mercyhurst (Pa.) College.—(2012-15)**
12. Sean McCauley, c, Osbourn HS, Manassas, Va.
13. Alex Caldera, rhp, Chaffey (Calif.) JC.
14. Matt Mitchell, rhp, Barstow (Calif.) HS.
15. Ryan Eigsti, c, Bradley University.
16. Patrick Norris, of, Oklahoma City University.
17. Ivor Hodgson, lhp, Mount St. Mary's College.
18. *Stephen Dodson, rhp, University of Georgia.
19. Joe Billick, c, Southern Tech (Ga.) Institute.
20. Mike Lehmann, rhp, Pearl River (Miss.) HS.
21. *Josh Billeaud, rhp, LSU-Eunice JC.
22. Jacob Rodriguez, rhp, East Los Angeles JC.
23. *Geoff Brown, lhp, Jackson HS, Mill Creek, Wash.
24. Ben Norton, rhp, University of Evansville.
**25. Clint Robinson, 1b, Troy University.—(2012-15)**
26. Nat Lovell, rhp, Fresno (Calif.) CC.
27. Dane Secott, rhp, Minnesota State University-Mankato.
28. Fernando Garcia, 2b, Manatee (Fla.) JC.
29. Kyle Martin, ss, Texas Tech.
30. Brett Amyx, 1b, University of Texas-Tyler.
31. Keaton Hayenga, rhp, Eastlake HS, Redmond, Wash.
32. Jake Lane, 1b, Austin Peay State University.
33. Wilson Tucker, of, Belmont University.
34. Thomas Hill, c, University of Albany.
35. *Garrett Weber, ss, Clovis HS, Fresno, Calif.
36. Mike Bionde, 2b, Rutgers University.
37. Derek Rodriguez, of, Ignacio (Colo.) HS.
38. *Brian Leach, rhp, Northwest Mississippi CC.
39. *Trevor Feeney, rhp, Northern Illinois University.
40. Clegg Snipes, rhp, Troy University.
41. *Tyler Topp, rhp, Riverside (Calif.) CC.
42. *Doug Antilla, rhp, MidAmerica Nazarene (Kan.) College.
43. *Chris Snipes, lhp, Middle Georgia JC.
44. *Chris Hopkins, of, Oregon State University.
45. Brandon Fowler, c, Westview HS, San Diego.
46. *Scott Boley, 3b, University of Toledo.
47. *John Anderson, rhp, Bossier Parrish (La.) CC.
48. Devery Van De Keere, 2b, University of Louisiana-Lafayette.
49. *Joe Vierra, 3b, Quartz Hill (Calif.) HS.
50. *Brandon Van Riper, c, Farmington (N.M.) HS.

## LOS ANGELES ANGELS (24)

1. (Choice to Rangers as compensation for Type A free agent Gary Matthews)
1. Jon Bachanov, rhp, University HS, Orlando, Fla. (Supplemental pick—58th—as compensation for Type B free agent Adam Kennedy).—(AA)
2. (Choice to Blue Jays as compensation for Type A free agent Justin Speier)
**3. *Matt Harvey, rhp, Fitch HS, Mystic, Conn.—(2012-15)**
DRAFT DROP *Attended North Carolina; re-drafted by Mets, 2010 (1st round)*
4. Trevor Pippin, of, Middle Georgia JC.—(Rookie)
**5. Andrew Romine, ss, Arizona State University.—(2010-15)**
DRAFT DROP *Son of Kevin Romine, major leaguer (1985-91) • Brother of Austin Romine, second-round draft pick, Yankees (2007); major leaguer (2011-14)*
**6. Ryan Brasier, rhp, Weatherford (Texas) JC.—(2013)**
7. Baron Short, rhp, Southern University.
8. Trevor Reckling, lhp, St. Benedicts HS, Newark, N.J.
9. Tyler Mann, of, Princess Anne HS, Virginia Beach, Va.
10. Milan Dinga, rhp, U.S. Military Academy.
11. *Martin Viramontes, rhp, Bullard HS, Fresno, Calif.
12. Michael Anton, lhp, Vail, Ariz.
13. *David Clark, rhp, University of Southern Mississippi.
14. *Tanner Robles, lhp, Cottonwood HS, Murray,

Utah.
15. Chris Garcia, 1b-3b, St. Petersburg (Fla.) JC.
**16. Mason Tobin, rhp, Everett (Wash.) JC.—(2011)**
17. Eddie McKiernan, rhp, Monrovia HS, Temple City, Calif.
18. *Zack Martin, 3b, Andrew (Ga.) JC.
19. Ryan Kennedy, 2b, University of Tampa.
20. Tremayne Holland, rhp, Brewton Parker (Ga.) College.
21. Justin Bass, 2b, Clements School, Sugar Land, Texas.
DRAFT DROP *Son of Kevin Bass, major leaguer (1982-95) • Brother of Garrett Bass, 42nd-round draft pick, Nationals (2007)*
22. *Steve Salas, rhp, Chandler-Gilbert (Ariz.) JC.
23. *Mike Bianucci, of, Auburn University.
24. DeAndre Miller, of, Loyola Marymount University.
25. Jordan Towns, rhp, University of West Georgia.
26. Michael Wing, ss, Upland HS, Rancho Cucamonga, Calif.
27. *Patrick White, of, West Virginia University.
DRAFT DROP *Quarterback, National Football League (2009-13)*
28. *Ty Pryor, rhp, University of North Florida.
DRAFT DROP *Nephew of Greg Pryor, major leaguer (1976-86)*
29. Brian Walker, c, University of Arkansas.
30. *Matt Davis, rhp, Jacksonville University.
31. Derek Schlecker, rhp, Western Michigan University.
32. Richard Bohlken, 2b, La Cueva HS, Albuquerque, N.M.
33. Donato Giovanatto, of, San Jose State University.
34. *Carlos Ramirez, c, Chandler-Gilbert (Ariz.) CC.
35. Luke Gordon, of, Georgia State University.
36. Jay Brossman, 3b, University of Utah.
37. Cephas Howard, rhp, University of South Carolina-Aiken.
38. Cory Page, rhp, Huntingtown (Md.) HS.
39. *Jayson Brown, rhp, Barry (Fla.) University.
40. Hector Estrella, 2b, University of Southern California.
41. *Matt Scioscia, 1b, Crespi Carmelite HS, Westlake Village, Calif.
DRAFT DROP *Son of Matt Scioscia, first-round draft pick, Dodgers (1976); major leaguer (1980-92); major league manager (2000-15)*
42. *Jeremy Thorne, rhp, Florida Southern College.
43. Terrell Alliman, of, Bluevale Collegiate Institute, Waterloo, Ontario.
44. *Alex Hale, rhp, University of Richmond.
45. *Chris Bullard, of, Harris County HS, Cataula, Ga.
46. *Brandon Lodge, ss, Tesoro HS, Coto de Caza, Calif.
47. *Billy Falasco, rhp, Seminole (Fla.) HS.
48. *Sean Loggins, c, McCluer North HS, St. Louis.
49. *Chris Vitus, rhp, Sheldon HS, Eugene, Ore.
**50. Efren Navarro, 1b, University of Nevada-Las Vegas.—(2011-15)**

## LOS ANGELES DODGERS (22)

1. **Chris Withrow, rhp, Midland Christian HS, Odessa, Texas** (Choice from Red Sox as compensation for Type A free agent Julio Lugo).—**(2013-14)**
1. (Choice to Giants as compensation for Type A free agent Jason Schmidt)
1. James Adkins, lhp, University of Tennessee (Supplemental choice—39th—as compensation for Lugo).—(AAA)
2. Michael Watt, lhp, Capistrano Valley HS, San Juan Capistrano, Calif.—(AAA)
3. Austin Gallagher, 3b, Manheim Township HS, Lancaster, Pa.—(High A)
**4. Andrew Lambo, of, Newbury Park (Calif.) HS.—(2013-15)**
5. *Kyle Blair, rhp, Los Gatos HS, Monte Sereno, Calif.—(AA)
DRAFT DROP *Attended San Diego; re-drafted by Indians, 2010 (4th round)*
6. Justin Miller, rhp, Johnson County (Kan.) CC.
7. Danny Danielson, rhp, Russell County HS, Phenix City, Ala.
8. Alex Garabedian, c, College of Charleston.
9. Jaime Pedroza, ss, UC Riverside.
10. Erik Kanaby, of, Lamar University.
11. Paul Koss, rhp, University of Southern California.
12. Jessie Mier, c, Lewis-Clark State (Idaho) College.
DRAFT DROP *Brother of Jiovanni Mier, first-round draft pick, Astros (2009)*
13. Bobby Blevins, rhp, LeMoyne College.
14. *Devin Fuller, rhp, Gilbert (Ariz.) HS.
15. Cal Stanke, rhp, University of Wisconsin-Oshkosh.
16. Andres Santiago, rhp, Colegio Carmen Sol HS, Toa Baja, P.R.
17. Chris Jacobs, 1b, Glenn HS, Winston-Salem, N.C.
18. Given Kutz, rhp, University of Portland.
19. Joris Bert, of, Frank Phillips (Texas) JC.
20. *Sean Koecheler, rhp, Palm Beach Gardens (Fla.) HS.
21. *Terry Doyle, rhp, Boston College.
22. Matt Wallach, c-1b, Cal State Fullerton.
DRAFT DROP *Son of Tim Wallach, first-round draft pick, Expos (1979); major leaguer (1980-96)*
23. *Nathan Carter, of, De la Salle HS, Concord, Calif.
24. Parker Dalton, ss, Texas A&M University.
25. Tim Sexton, rhp, Miami-Dade CC.
26. *Taylor Cole, rhp, Bishop Gorman HS, Las Vegas, Nev.
**27. *Rob Rasmussen, lhp, Poly HS, Arcadia, Calif.—(2014-15)**
28. *Nathan Woods, of, Xavier HS, Cedar Rapids, Iowa.
29. *Chad Keefer, 1b, North Central Texas JC.
30. *Justin Coats, ss, Seminole State (Okla.) CC.
31. *Rafael Thomas, of, Lufkin (Texas) HS.
32. *Matt Gardner, rhp, Oklahoma State University.
33. *Jonathan Gonzalez, rhp, Cardinal Hayes HS, New York.
34. *Garrett Poe, 1b, Silver City (N.M.) HS.
35. *Ryan Christenson, lhp, Arnett (Okla.) HS.
36. *Tim Jones, rhp, Redan HS, Stone Mountain, Ga.
37. Gabriel Casanova, 2b, Barry (Fla.) University.
**38. *Matt Szczur, c, Lower Cape May Regional HS, Cape May, N.J.—(2014-15)**
39. *John Hay, of, JC of the Canyons (Calif.).

## MILWAUKEE BREWERS (7)

**1. Matt LaPorta, 1b, University of Florida.—(2009-12)**
2. (Choice to Cardinals as compensation for Type A free agent Jeff Suppan)
**3. Jonathan Lucroy, c, University of Louisiana-Lafayette.—(2010-15)**
**4. Eric Farris, 2b, Loyola Marymount University.—(2011-12)**
**5. Caleb Gindl, of, Pace (Fla.) HS.—(2013-14)**
6. Dan Merklinger, lhp, Seton Hall University.
7. Efrain Nieves, lhp, Puerto Rico Baseball Academy, Toa Alta, P.R.
8. David Fonseca, ss, Los Angeles Pierce JC.
9. Kristian Bueno, lhp, Calallen HS, Corpus Christi, Texas.
**10. Eric Fryer, c, Ohio State University.—(2011-15)**
11. Cody Scarpetta, rhp, Guilford HS, Rockford, Ill.
12. Wes Etheridge, rhp, UC Irvine.
13. Chris Dennis, of, St. Thomas of Villanova SS, Amherstburg, Ontario.
**14. Donovan Hand, rhp, Jacksonville State University.—(2013-15)**
15. Joey Paciorek, 3b, Blaine (Wash.) HS.
DRAFT DROP *Son of Jim Paciorek, major leaguer (1987)*
16. Joel Morales, rhp, Puerto Rico Baseball Academy, Caguas, P.R.
17. Erik Miller, of, Scottsdale (Ariz.) CC.
18. Bobby Bramhall, lhp, Rice University.
**19. Zealous Wheeler, 3b, Wallace State-Hanceville (Ala.) CC.—(2014)**
20. Cameron Robulack, 1b, Silverthorn Collegiate Institute, Toronto.
21. *Connor Hoehn, rhp, St. John's College HS, Damascus, Md.
22. Matt Cline, ss, Long Beach State University.
23. *Cody Hawn, 1b, South Doyle HS, Knoxville, Tenn.
24. *Jonathan White, of, Vanderbilt University.
25. *Chad Bell, lhp, South Doyle HS, Knoxville, Tenn.
26. *Ben Feltner, of, Texas A&M University.
27. Josh Trejo, lhp, James Logan HS, Union City, Calif.
28. Steffan Wilson, 3b, Harvard University.
29. Travis Nevakshonoff, rhp, D.W. Poppy HS, Langley, B.C.
30. Corey Frerichs, rhp, Temple (Texas) JC.
31. *Jon Clarence, lhp, Columbus North HS, Columbus, Ind.
32. Miguel Vasquez, ss, Seminole (Fla.) CC.
33. Ryan Jensen, of, Langley, B.C.
34. Casey Baron, lhp, University of Maryland.
35. Curtis Rindal, 1b, University of Washington.
36. Curtis Pasma, lhp, University of the Pacific.
37. *Rick Hague, ss, Klein Collins HS, Spring, Texas.
38. Kurt Crowell, of, Cal State Los Angeles.
39. *Joe Scott, ss, Cal State Fullerton.
40. *Jordan Tanner, rhp, Neshannock HS, New Castle, Pa.
DRAFT DROP *Grandson of Chuck Tanner, major leaguer (1955-62); major league manager (1970-88)*
41. Adam Arnold, rhp, Thompson River (B.C.) University.
42. *Chase Reid, rhp, Carroll HS, Southlake, Texas.
43. *Cullen Sexton, rhp, Stevens Point (Wis.) HS.
44. Shawn Zarraga, c, Trinity Christian Academy, Boynton Beach, Fla.
45. *Matt Sergey, rhp, South Plantation HS, Plantation, Fla.
46. *Stewart Ijames, of, Owensboro Catholic HS, Owensboro, Ky.
47. *Aaron Tullo, rhp, St. Petersburg (Fla.) JC.

## MINNESOTA TWINS (28)

**1. Ben Revere, of, Lexington Catholic HS, Lexington, Ky.—(2010-15)**
2. Danny Rams, c-1b, Gulliver Prep, Miami.—(AA)
3. Angel Morales, of, Puerto Rico Baseball Academy, Arroyo, P.R.—(AA)
4. Reggie Williams, ss, Bellflower (Calif.) HS.—(High A)
5. *Nathan Striz, rhp, Santa Fe Catholic HS, Lakeland, Fla.—(AA)
DRAFT DROP *Attended North Carolina; re-drafted by Indians, 2010 (22nd round)*
6. Mike McCardell, rhp, Kutztown (Pa.) University.
7. Daniel Berlind, rhp, Los Angeles Pierce JC.
8. Danny Lehmann, c, Rice University.
9. Steve Hirschfield, rhp, San Diego State University.
10. Blair Erickson, rhp, UC Irvine.
11. Andrew Schmiesing, of, St. Olaf (Minn.) College.
12. Mike Tarsi, lhp, University of Connecticut.
13. *Elliott Soto, ss, Dundee-Crown HS, Algonquin, Ill.
14. Daniel Rohlfing, c, Oakville HS, St. Louis.
15. Daniel Latham, rhp, Tulane University.
16. Nelvin Fuentes, lhp, Puerto Rico Baseball Academy, Loiza, P.R.
17. *Jose Rodriguez, of, Hialeah (Fla.) HS.
18. Lee Martin, rhp, Southern Arkansas University.
19. Ben Petsch, c, Belmont University.
20. *Tom Farmer, rhp, University of Akron.
21. Ozzie Lewis, of, Fresno State University.
**22. *Mickey Storey, rhp, Florida Atlantic University.—(2012-13)**
23. *Josh Workman, 2b, Wichita State University.
24. Charles Nolte, rhp, San Diego State University.
25. Spencer Steedley, 1b, UNC Charlotte.
26. *Kyle Witten, rhp, Bakersfield (Calif.) JC.
27. *Kyle Heyne, rhp, Ball State University.
**28. *Seth Rosin, rhp, Mounds View HS, Shoreview, Minn.—(2014-15)**
29. *Fred Atkins, of, CC of Marin (Calif.).
30. *Josh Adams, ss, Eagle's View Academy, Jacksonville, Fla.
31. *Mike Kvasnicka, c, Lakeville North HS, Lakeville, Minn.
DRAFT DROP *First-round draft pick (33rd overall), Astros (2010)*
32. *J.R. Bromberg, rhp, Palisades HS, Los Angeles.
33. *Evan Danieli, rhp, Seton Hall Prep, East Hanover, N.J.
34. *Stephen Branca, ss, Newsome HS, Valrico, Fla.
35. *Ryan Strauss, rhp, Florida State University.
36. Domonique Rodgers, rhp, Kent State University.
37. *Julien Pollard, 2b, Washington HS, Tacoma, Wash.
38. Chris Cates, ss, University of Louisville.
39. *Joey Leftridge, of, Duncanville HS, Dallas.
**40. *Chase Anderson, rhp, North Central Texas JC.—(2014-15)**
41. *Jonathan Griffin, rhp, Lakewood Ranch HS, Bradenton, Fla.
42. *Troy Scott, 1b, Auburn (Wash.) HS.
43. Andres Diaz, c, Palm Beach (Fla.) JC.
44. *Zach Barger, of, Long Beach State University.
45. *Kevin Arico, rhp, North Hunterdon Regional HS, Flemington, N.J.
46. *Johnathan Williams, 3b, Niles North HS, Morton Grove, Ill.
**47. *Chris Heston, rhp, Seminole (Fla.) CC.—(2014-15)**
48. *Ken Smalley, rhp, John A. Logan (Ill.) JC.
49. *Nick Cobler, lhp, Butler (Kan.) CC.
50. *Chris Freshcorn, c, Alonso HS, Tampa.

## NEW YORK METS (29)

1. (Choice to Giants as compensation for Type A free agent Moises Alou)
1. **Eddie Kunz, rhp, Oregon State University** (Supplemental choice—42nd—as compensation for Type A free agent Roberto Hernandez).—**(2008)**
1. Nathan Vineyard, lhp, Woodland HS, Emerson, Ga. (Supplemental choice—47th—as compensation for Type A free agent Chad Bradford).—(Low A)
2. Scott Moviel, rhp, St. Edward HS, Berea, Ohio (Choice from Indians as compensation for Hernandez).—(High A)
2. Brant Rustich, rhp, UCLA.—(High A)
3. Eric Niesen, lhp, Wake Forest University (Choice from Orioles as compensation for Bradford).—(AAA)
3. Stephen Clyne, rhp, Clemson University.—(AA)
4. Richie Lucas, 3b, Wolfson HS, Jacksonville, Fla.—(AA)
**5. Zach Lutz, 3b, Alvernia (Pa.) College.—(2012-13)**
6. Guillaume Leduc, rhp, Edouard Montpetit (Quebec) JC.
**7. Lucas Duda, 1b, University of Southern California.—(2010-15)**
8. Dan McDonald, rhp, Seton Hall University.
9. Mike Olmstead, rhp, Cypress (Calif.) JC.
10. Brandon Richey, ss, Northwestern State University.
11. Matt Bouchard, ss, Georgetown University.
12. Will Morgan, rhp, Lewis-Clark State (Idaho) College.
13. Jordan Abruzzo, c, University of San Diego.
**14. Robert Carson, lhp, Hattiesburg (Miss.) HS.—(2012-13)**
15. Jefferies Tatford, c-of, University of Louisiana-Lafayette.
16. Chris Fournier, of-2b, George Mason University.
17. *Brandon Efferson, rhp, Zachary (La.) HS.
18. Mike Antonini, lhp, Georgia College.
19. Ernesto Gonzalez, ss, Wallace State-Dothan (Ala.) CC.
20. Dylan Owen, rhp, Francis Marion (S.C.) University.
**21. Dillon Gee, rhp, University of Texas-Arlington.—(2010-15)**
22. Tyler Vaughn, 3b, UC Irvine.
23. Norberto Navarro, c, Pasco Hernando (Fla.) JC.
24. Michael Parker, 2b, George Washington University.
25. Cole Abbott, rhp, Weber HS, Pleasant View, Utah.
26. Brad Burns, rhp, University of Oklahoma.
27. Kyle Catto, rhp, Southern Illinois University.
28. *Kyle Maxie, c, Pearl River (Miss.) CC.
29. Roy Merritt, lhp, Southern University.
30. *Rylan Sandoval, 2b, Chabot (Calif.) JC.
31. *Antonio Peraza, lhp, La Mirada HS, Norwalk, Calif.
**32. Juan Centeno, c, Antonio Luchetti HS, Arecibo, P.R.—(2013-15)**
33. *Nick Abshire, ss, Iowa (La.) HS.
34. Terry Johnson, ss, William Carey (Miss.) College.
35. Jason Lavorgna, rhp, Eastern Connecticut State University.
36. *Glen Johnson, ss, South Fork HS, Hobe Sound, Fla.
DRAFT DROP *Son of Howard Johnson, major leaguer (1982-95)*

37. Ricky Alvarez, 3b, Otay Ranch HS, Chula Vista (Calif.) HS.
38. Brandon Kawal, of, Concordia (Calif.) University.
39. Alonzo Harris, ss, McComb (Miss.) HS.

## NEW YORK YANKEES (30)

1. **Andrew Brackman, rhp, North Carolina State University.—(2011)**
2. **Austin Romine, c, El Toro HS, Lake Forest, Calif.—(2011-14)**

DRAFT DROP *Son of Kevin Romine, major leaguer (1985-91) • Brother of Andrew Romine, fifth-round draft pick, Angels (2007); major leaguer (2010-15)*

3. Ryan Pope, rhp, Savannah College of Art & Design (Ga.).—(AAA)
4. Bradley Suttle, 3b, University of Texas.—(AA)
5. Adam Olbrychowski, rhp, Pepperdine University.—(AA)
6. Chase Weems, c, Columbus (Ga.) HS.
7. Damon Sublett, 2b-rhp, Wichita State University.
8. Taylor Grote, of, The Woodlands (Texas) HS.
9. Austin Krum, of, Dallas Baptist University.
10. Carmen Angelini, ss, Alfred M. Barbe HS, Lake Charles, La.
11. Isaiah Howes, of, University of Louisville.
12. Manuel Barreda, rhp, Sahuarita HS, Amado, Ariz.
13. Nick Chigges, rhp, College of Charleston.
14. Braedyn Pruitt, 3b, Stetson University.
15. David Williams, of, Rutgers University.
16. *Dan Mahoney, rhp, Cushing Academy, Brighton, Mass.
17. Ryan Zink, rhp, University of Illinois-Chicago.
18. ***Chris Carpenter, rhp, Kent State University.—(2011-12)**
19. Taylor Holiday, of, UC Irvine.
20. Ryan Wehrle, ss, University of Nebraska.
21. Justin Snyder, 2b, University of San Diego.
22. Craig Heyer, rhp, University of Nevada-Las Vegas.
23. Matt Morris, of, UC Irvine.
24. *Greg Peavey, rhp, Hudson's Bay HS, Vancouver, Wash.
25. Jason Kiley, rhp, Florida Gulf Coast University.
26. Gary Gattis, of, Yavapai (Ariz.) CC.
27. **Brandon Laird, 3b, Cypress (Calif.) CC.—(2011-13)**

DRAFT DROP *Brother of Gerald Laird, major leaguer (2003-15)*

28. Jeff Livek, rhp, Carthage (Wis.) College.
29. *Matt Pilgreen, rhp, University of Louisiana-Lafayette.
30. Chris Carrara, 2b, Winthrop University.
31. *Chad Dawson, rhp, Indiana State University.
32. Brian Chavez, ss, University of San Francisco.
33. Fred Jones, rhp, University of Evansville.
34. ***Drew Storen, rhp, Brownsburg (Ind.) HS.—(2010-15)**

DRAFT DROP *First-round draft pick (10th overall), Nationals (2009)*

35. *Greg Holle, rhp, Christian Brothers Academy, Loudonville, N.Y.

DRAFT DROP *Son of Gary Holle, major leaguer (1979)*

36. Danny Cox, ss, University of Washington.
37. Steve Strausbaugh, of, Western Carolina University.
38. ***Erik Komatsu, of, Oxnard (Calif.) JC.—(2012)**
39. ***Eric Thames, of, Pepperdine University.—(2011-12)**
40. *Luke Murton, 1b, Georgia Tech.

DRAFT DROP *Brother of Matt Murton, major leaguer (2005-09)*

41. Jake Shafer, rhp, Missouri State University.
42. Chris Raber, 1b, Coastal Carolina University.
43. *Jason Chowning, rhp, Texarkana (Texas) CC.
44. *Tyler Herriage, lhp, Weatherford (Texas) CC.
45. ***Pat Venditte, rhp-lhp, Creighton University.—(2015)**
46. Daniel Kapala, rhp, University of Notre Dame.
47. *Colin Arnold, of, Daytona Beach (Fla.) CC.
48. *Scott Bittle, rhp, University of Mississippi.
49. *Kenny Toves, lhp, Carlsbad (N.M.) HS.
50. Larry Day, c, University of Connecticut.

## OAKLAND ATHLETICS (26)

1. James Simmons, rhp, UC Riverside.—(AAA)
1. **Sean Doolittle, 1b-lhp, University of Virginia** (Supplemental choice—41st—as compensation for Type A free agent Barry Zito).**—(2012-15)**
1. **Corey Brown, of, Oklahoma State University** (Supplemental choice—59th—as compensation for Type B free agent Frank Thomas).**—(2011-14)**
2. Grant Desme, of, Cal Poly (Choice from Giants as compensation for Zito).—(High A)
2. Josh Horton, ss, University of North Carolina.—(AAA)
3. **Sam Demel, rhp, Texas Christian University.—(2010-12)**
4. Travis Banwart, rhp, Wichita State University.—(AAA)
5. **Andrew Carignan, rhp, University of North Carolina.—(2011-12)**
6. Scott Hodsdon, rhp, Azusa Pacific (Calif.) University.
7. Lance Sewell, lhp, San Diego State University.
8. ***Daniel Schlereth, lhp, University of Arizona.—(2009-12)**

DRAFT DROP *First-round draft pick (26th overall), Diamondbacks (2008) • Son of Mark Schlereth, guard, National Football League (1989-2000)*

9. *Eric Berger, lhp, University of Arizona.
10. Danny Hamblin, 1b, University of Arkansas.
11. Mike Richard, ss, Prairie View A&M University.
12. ***Gary Brown, of, Diamond Bar (Calif.) HS.—(2014)**

DRAFT DROP *First-round draft pick (24th overall), Giants (2010)*

13. Justin Friend, rhp, Oklahoma State University.
14. Matt Smith, c, Texas Tech.
15. Brad Hertzler, lhp, University of Maine.
16. Brent Lysander, rhp, Sonoma State (Calif.) University.

DRAFT DROP *Son of Rick Lysander, major leaguer (1980-85)*

17. *Stephen Hunt, lhp, Tampa Jesuit HS, Brandon, Fla.
18. Matt Ray, ss, Middle Tennessee State University.
19. Dusty Napoleon, c, University of Iowa.
20. Dan Wentzell, of, George Fox (Ore.) University.
21. *Stephen Porlier, rhp, University of Oklahoma.
22. Aaron Jenkins, lhp, University of Northern Iowa.
23. J.D. Pruitt, of, University of Montevallo (Ala.).
24. Ray Rodriguez, of, Puerto Rico Baseball Academy, Caguas, P.R.
25. Jareck West, of, Delta State (Miss.) University.
26. *Tobias Streich, c, Johnsonburg HS, Ridgway, Pa.
27. Justin Frash, 3b, University of Hawaii.
28. Lee Land, rhp, University of North Carolina-Greensboro.
29. ***Collin Cowgill, of, University of Kentucky.—(2011-15)**
30. Chad Kerfoot, rhp, University of Delaware.
31. Fabian Gomez, lhp, Rockford (Ill.) College.
32. Bryan Collins, rhp, Central Missouri State University.
33. John Quine, rhp, University of San Francisco.
34. *Ryne Tacker, rhp, Rice University.
35. Herb Hudson, of, Mount San Jacinto (Calif.) JC.
36. *Trent Abbott, rhp, Fullerton (Calif.) JC.

DRAFT DROP *Son of Paul Abbott, major league (1990-2004)*

37. *Nick Longmire, of, Grossmont HS, La Mesa, Calif.
38. *Kevin Rath, lhp, Silverado HS, Las Vegas, Nev.
39. *Stan Widmann, ss, Clemson University.
40. *Dan Magnante, c, Campbell Hall HS, Van Nuys, Calif.
41. *James Wernke, lhp, Troy HS, Fullerton, Calif.
42. *Jonathan Johnston, c, Hamilton Township, N.J.
43. *Steve Cochrane, c, Yavapai (Ariz.) CC.

DRAFT DROP *Son of Dave Cochrane, major leaguer (1986-92)*

44. Ben Barrone, c, Winona State (Minn.) University.
45. *J.T. Wise, 3b, Louisiana State University.
46. *Conner Bernatz, of, Mater Dei HS, Newport Beach, Calif.
47. *Seth Blair, rhp, Rock Falls (Ill.) HS.

DRAFT DROP *First-round draft pick (46th overall), Cardinals (2010)*

48. Adam Klein, of, Cal State Los Angeles.
49. *Josh Bowman, rhp, Northeast HS, St. Petersburg, Fla.
50. *Stephen Hagen, 3b, Peninsula HS, Lakebay, Wash.

## PHILADELPHIA PHILLIES (19)

1. **Joe Savery, lhp, Rice University.—(2011-14)**
1. **Travis d'Arnaud, c, Lakewood HS, Long Beach, Calif.** (Supplemental choice—37th—as compensation for Type A free agent David Dellucci).**—(2013-15)**

DRAFT DROP *Brother of Chase d'Arnaud, major leaguer (2011-15)*

2. Travis Mattair, 3b, Southridge HS, Kennewick, Wash.—(AA)
3. ***Brandon Workman, rhp, Bowie (Texas) HS** (Choice from Indians as compensation for Dellucci).**—(2013-14)**

DRAFT DROP *Attended Texas; re-drafted by Red Sox, 2010 (2nd round)*

3. Matt Spencer, of-lhp, Arizona State University.—(AAA)
4. Tyler Mach, 2b, Oklahoma State University.—(Short-season A)
5. **Michael Taylor, of, Stanford University.—(2011-14)**
6. Matt Rizzotti, 1b, Manhattan College.
7. **Tyson Brummett, rhp, UCLA.—(2012)**
8. Chance Chapman, rhp, Oral Roberts University.
9. Chris Kissock, rhp, Lewis-Clark State (Idaho) College.
10. Joe Rocchio, rhp, Cal State Northridge.
11. **Justin De Fratus, rhp, Ventura (Calif.) JC.—(2011-15)**
12. Julian Sampson, rhp, Skyline HS, Sammamish, Wash.
13. Luke Wertz, rhp, University of Nebraska.
14. Jesus Villegas, ss, Porterville (Calif.) JC.
15. Karl Bolt, 1b, Air Force Academy.
16. **Brian Schlitter, rhp, College of Charleston.—(2010-15)**
17. Zack Sterner, rhp, Tennessee Wesleyan College.
18. *Mark Adzick, lhp, William Penn Charter HS, Haverford, Pa.
19. *Cedric Johnson, of, Thatcher (Ariz.) HS.

DRAFT DROP *Brother of Elliot Johnson, major leaguer (2008-14) • Brother of Leon Johnson, 10th-round draft pick, Cubs (2007)*

20. *Carlos Moncrief, rhp, Hillcrest Christian HS, Jackson, Miss.
21. Adam Sorgi, 2b, Stanford University.
22. Jiwan James, rhp-of, Williston (Fla.) HS.
23. Gerard Breslin, rhp, La Salle University.
24. Caleb Mangum, c, North Carolina State University.
25. *Billy Harris, lhp, University of Delaware.
26. Nolan Mulligan, rhp, Lynn (Fla.) University.
27. Richard Austin, rhp, Seton Hill (Pa.) University.
28. Chris Rhoads, rhp, University of Arkansas.
29. *Derek Hall, c, El Dorado HS, Orange, Calif.
30. **Jacob Diekman, lhp, Cloud County (Kan.) CC.—(2012-15)**
31. *Jeff Richard, rhp, Central Michigan University.
32. Kirk Bacsu, c, University of Evansville.
33. Rich Prall, c, La Salle University.
34. *Brett Hambright, c, Temescal Canyon HS, Lake Elsinore, Calif.
35. *Zach Cleveland, rhp, Golden (Colo.) HS.
36. *Kyle Benoit, rhp, Cardinal Leger SS, Brampton, Ontario.
37. Kyle Slate, rhp, Christian Brothers Academy, Sea Bright, N.J.
38. *Joe Paylor, of, Hillcrest HS, Dallas.
39. *Michael Branham, rhp, University of Florida.
40. *John Hinson, ss, A.C. Reynolds HS, Asheville, N.C.
41. *Tyler Gilder, rhp, Butte (Mon.) HS.

DRAFT DROP *Grandson of Dick Nen, major leaguer (1963-70) • Son of Robb Nen, major leaguer (1993-2002)*

42. *James Mahler, rhp, Jordan HS, Sandy, Utah.

DRAFT DROP *Son of Mickey Mahler, major leaguer (1977-86) • Nephew of Rick Mahler, major leaguer (1979-91)*

43. *Cory Vaughn, of, Jesuit HS, Elk Grove, Calif.

DRAFT DROP *Son of Greg Vaughn, major leaguer (1989-2003)*

44. *Brandon Bonner, rhp, Lakewood HS, St. Petersburg Beach, Fla.
45. *Mike Morrison, 1b, Bishop Luers HS, Fort Wayne, Ind.
46. *Damian Seguen, rhp, North Bergen HS, Williamston, N.J.
47. *Joey Manning, of, Bartow (Fla.) HS.
48. *Cody Winiarski, rhp, Union Grove HS, Franksville, Wis.
49. *Navarro Hall, of, Kennesaw Mountain HS, Kennesaw, Ga.
50. *Jeremy Penn, rhp, All Saints Cathedral HS, St. Thomas, V.I.

## PITTSBURGH PIRATES (4)

1. **Daniel Moskos, lhp, Clemson University.—(2011)**
2. **Duke Welker, rhp, University of Arkansas.—(2013)**
3. Brian Friday, ss, Rice University.—(AAA)
4. Quincy Latimore, of, Middle Creek HS, Apex, N.C.—(AA)
5. Andrew Walker, c, Texas Christian University.—(High A)
6. Matt Foust, rhp, University of Nebraska.
7. Juan Garcia, c, Puerto Rico Baseball Academy, Caguas, P.R.
8. Maurice Bankston, rhp, Texarkana (Texas) CC.
9. **Tony Watson, lhp, University of Nebraska.—(2011-15)**
10. Sean Giblin, rhp, Pearl River (N.Y.) HS.
11. *Runey Davis, of, Georgetown (Texas) HS.
12. Erik Huber, of, Eastern Illinois University.
13. Andrew Biela, c, Palatine HS, Algonquin, Ill.
14. **Kyle McPherson, rhp, University of Mobile (Ala.).—(2012)**
15. *Rey Cotilla, rhp, Miami Springs (Fla.) HS.
16. Zac Oliver, lhp, Paris (Texas) JC.
17. Harrison Bishop, rhp, University of Washington.
18. Marcus Davis, of, Alcorn State University.
19. Bobby Spain, ss, Oklahoma City University.
20. Brian Tracy, rhp, UC Santa Barbara.

DRAFT DROP *Son of Jim Tracy, major leaguer (1980-81); major league manager (2001-12)*

21. Matt Cavagnaro, 2b, Penn State University.
22. *Nico Navarro, c, Flanagan HS, Pembroke Pines, Fla.
23. *Luis Penate, ss, Flanagan HS, Pembroke Pines, Fla.
24. Chad Rice, ss, Virginia Military Institute.
25. Keanon Simon, of, Oklahoma State University.
26. *Steve Neff, lhp, Lancaster (S.C.) HS.
27. *Bob Revesz, lhp, Grove City Area HS, Grove City, Pa.
28. ***Matt Clark, 3b, Riverside (Calif.) CC.—(2014)**

DRAFT DROP *Son of Terry Clark, major leaguer (1988-97)*

29. *Brian Harrison, ss, Hilton Head (S.C.) HS.
30. *Josh Hula, c, Miami (Ohio) University.
31. Taylor Cameron, rhp, Point Loma Nazarene (Calif.) University.
32. Danny Forrer, lhp, Auburn University.-Montgomery.
33. Caleb Fields, 2b, Northwestern University.
34. *Cedric Pomerlee, lhp, Gentry HS, Indianola, Miss.
35. Tom Boleska, rhp, High Point University.
36. *Andrew Crisp, ss, University of South Carolina.
37. *Cody Springer, rhp, Montgomery (Texas) HS.
38. *Pat McAnaney, lhp, University of Virginia.
39. *J.C. Menna, rhp, Red Bank Catholic HS, Tinton Falls, N.J.
40. *Chad Poe, rhp, Bossier Parish (La.) CC.
41. *Demetrius Washington, 2b, Silver Bluff HS, New Ellenton, S.C.
42. Danny Bomback, 2b, Florida Atlantic University.
43. ***Cameron Rupp, c, Prestonwood Christian Academy, Plano, Texas.—(2013-15)**
44. *Dustin Emmons, rhp, Crescenta Valley HS, La Crescenta, Calif.
45. *Pernell Halliman, rhp, West Hills (Calif.) JC.
46. *Reyes Dorado, rhp, Riverside (Calif.) CC.
47. *Robby Broach, rhp, Archbishop Rummel HS, Luling, La.
48. Gary Amato, rhp, Penn State University.
49. *Erik Morrison, ss, University of Kansas.

DRAFT DROP *Nephew of Joe Amalfitano, major leaguer (1954-67)*

50. *Brandon Glover, of, San Diego State University.

## ST. LOUIS CARDINALS (18)

1. **Pete Kozma, ss, Owasso (Okla.) HS.—(2011-15)**

1. **Clay Mortensen, rhp, Gonzaga University** (Supplemental choice—36th—as compensation for Type A free agent Jeff Suppan).—**(2009-13)**
2. David Kopp, rhp, Clemson University (Choice from Brewers as compensation for Suppan).—(AAA)
2. **Jess Todd, rhp, University of Arkansas.—(2009-10)**
3. **Daniel Descalso, 3b, UC Davis.—(2010-15)**
4. *Kyle Russell, of, University of Texas.—(AAA)

DRAFT DROP *Returned to Texas; re-drafted by Dodgers, 2008 (3rd round)*

5. Thomas Eager, rhp, Cal Poly.—(AA)
6. Oliver Marmol, ss, College of Charleston.
7. Deryk Hooker, rhp, Mira Mesa HS, San Diego.
8. Tyler Henley, of, Rice University.
9. ***Mike Stutes, rhp, Oregon State University.—(2011-13)**
10. Beau Riportella, of, JC of the Sequoias (Calif.).
11. Adam Reifer, rhp, UC Riverside.
12. Brett Zawacki, rhp, LaSalle-Peru Township HS, LaSalle, Ill.
13. **Steven Hill, 1b, Stephen F. Austin University.—(2010-12)**
14. Josh Dew, rhp, Troy University.
15. **C.J. Fick, rhp, Cal State Northridge.—(2012)**
16. Antone DeJesus, of, University of Kentucky.
17. Matt Arburr, 3b, Pace (N.Y.) University.
18. **Andrew Brown, of, University of Nebraska.—(2011-14)**
19. Nick Peoples, of, University of Texas.
20. Brian Cartie, 3b, McNeese State University.
21. **Brian Broderick, rhp, Grand Canyon University.—(2011)**
22. Charlie Kingrey, of, McNeese State University.
23. Joey Hage, of, Stoneman Douglas HS, Coral Springs, Fla.
24. ***Sam Freeman, lhp, North Central Texas JC.—(2012-15)**
25. J.D. Stambaugh, lhp, Brigham Young University.
26. **Tony Cruz, 3b, Palm Beach (Fla.) CC.—(2011-15)**
27. Brian Buck, of, Santa Barbara (Calif.) CC.
28. Ross Oeder, 2b, Wright State University.
29. Charlie Pelt, 1b, Georgia State University.
30. Nick Derba, c, Manhattan College.
31. Dylan Gonzalez, rhp, Pepperdine University.
32. Nick Vera, 3b, Trinity (Texas) University.
33. Josh Fritsche, lhp, Oklahoma State University.
34. Steve Hill, rhp, Southeastern (Fla.) University.
35. **Michael Blazek, rhp, Arbor View HS, Las Vegas, Nev.—(2013-15)**
36. Collin Fanning, of, Brigham Young University.
37. *C.J. Ziegler, 1b, University of Arizona.
38. **Adron Chambers, of, Pensacola (Fla.) JC.—(2011-13)**
39. Rigoberto Lugo, rhp, Puerto Rico Baseball Academy, Barceloneta, P.R.
40. *Justin Dalles, c. St. Petersburg (Fla.) JC.
41. Chapo Delgado, rhp, Pima (Ariz.) CC.
42. Mike Folli, 2b, University of Buffalo.
43. Davis Bilardello, lhp, University of South Florida.

DRAFT DROP *Son of Dann Bilardello, major leaguer (1983-92)*

44. *Daniel Thomas, rhp, University of South Florida.
45. Jameson Maj, rhp, Abilene Christian (Texas) University.
46. Rob Sanzillo, c, Johns Hopkins (Md.) University.
47. Mateo Marquez, of, Cal State Dominguez Hills.
48. *Jason King, of, Dublin Jerome HS, Dublin, Ohio.
49. Zach Russell, rhp, Harmony Grove HS, Bearden, Ark.
50. *Stephen McCray, rhp, Young Harris (Ga.) JC.

## SAN DIEGO PADRES (23)

1. Nick Schmidt, lhp, University of Arkansas.—(AAA)
1. Kellen Kulbacki, of, James Madison University (Supplemental choice—40th—as compensation for Type A free agent Woody Williams).—(AA)
1. Drew Cumberland, ss, Pace (Fla.) HS (Supplemental choice—46th—as compensation for Type A free agent Dave Roberts).—(AA)
1. Mitch Canham, c, Oregon State University (Supplemental choice—57th—as compensation for Type B free agent Chan Ho Park).—(AAA)
1. **Cory Luebke, lhp, Ohio State University** (Supplemental choice—63rd—as compensation for Type B free agent Alan Embree).—**(2010-12)**
1. Danny Payne, of, Georgia Tech (Supplemental choice—64th—as compensation for Type B free agent Ryan Klesko).—(AAA)
2. **Eric Sogard, 2b, Arizona State University** (Choice from Astros as compensation for Williams).**—(2010-15)**
2. Brad Chalk, of, Clemson University.—(AAA)
3. *Tommy Toledo, rhp, Alonso HS, Tampa.—(AA)

DRAFT DROP *Attended Florida; re-drafted by Twins, 2010 (32nd round)*

4. **Corey Kluber, rhp, Stetson University** (Choice from Giants as compensation for Roberts).**—(2011-15)**
4. **Lance Zawadzki, ss, Lee (Tenn.) University.—(2010)**
5. **Jeremy Hefner, rhp, Oral Roberts University.—(2012-13)**
6. Emmanuel Quiles, c, Jesus Silverio Delgado HS, Sabana Hoyo, P.R.
7. Justin Baum, 3b, University of the Pacific.
8. Matt Teague, lhp, Carson-Newman (Tenn.) College.
9. Wynn Pelzer, rhp, University of South Carolina.
10. ***Christian Colon, ss, Canyon HS, Anaheim, Calif.—(2014-15)**

DRAFT DROP *First-round draft pick (4th overall), Royals (2010)*

11. Shane Buschini, of, University of San Diego.
12. **Luis Martinez, c, Cumberland (Tenn.) University.—(2011-12)**
13. Allen Harrington, lhp, Lamar University.
14. Keith Conlon, of, Texas Christian University.
15. Ryan Hill, of, Rutgers University.
16. Robert Perry, of, Long Beach State University.
17. **Brandon Gomes, rhp, Tulane University.—(2011-15)**
18. Robbie Blauer, 1b, UC Santa Barbara.
19. Adam McDaniel, rhp, University of Georgia.
20. Robert Woodard, rhp, University of North Carolina.
21. Tyler Davis, rhp, University of Hawaii.
22. Keoni Ruth, 2b, Concordia (Calif.) University.
23. Angel Mercado, of, Bethune-Cookman College.
24. Bryan Oland, rhp, Sonoma State (Calif.) University.
25. *Hunter Ovens, of, Cardinal Mooney HS, Bradenton, Fla.
26. **Andy Parrino, 2b, LeMoyne College.—(2011-15)**
27. Zach Brown, 1b, The Citadel.
28. Shawn Olsen, rhp, University of Southern California.
29. Brian Joynt, 3b, Oklahoma City University.
30. **Dylan Axelrod, rhp, UC Irvine.—(2011-15)**
31. **Colt Hynes, lhp, Texas Tech.—(2013-15)**
32. *Anthony Renteria, of, Great Oak HS, Temecula, Calif.

DRAFT DROP *Son of Rick Renteria, first-round draft pick, Pirates (1980); major leaguer (1986-94); major league manager (2014)*

33. ***A.J. Schugel, 3b, Mountain Vista HS, Highlands Ranch, Colo.—(2015)**
34. *Joseph Pagan, 1b, Archbishop Curley Notre Dame HS, Miami.
35. *Ross Wilson, ss, Hoover (Ala.) HS.

## SAN FRANCISCO GIANTS (10)

1. **Madison Bumgarner, lhp, South Caldwell HS, Lenoir, N.C.—(2009-15)**
1. Tim Alderson, rhp, Horizon HS, Phoenix (Choice from Dodgers as compensation for Type A free agent Jason Schmidt).—(AAA)
1. Wendell Fairley, of, George County HS, Lucedale, Miss. (Choice from Mets as compensation for Type A free agent Moises Alou).—(AA)
1. **Nick Noonan, ss, Francis Parker HS, San Diego** (Supplemental choice—32nd—as compensation for Alou).**—(2013-15)**
1. **Jackson Williams, c, University of Oklahoma** (Supplemental choice—43rd—as compensation for Schmidt).**—(2014-15)**
1. **Charlie Culberson, ss, Calhoun HS, Plainville, Ga.** (Supplemental choice—51st—as compensation for Type B free agent Mike Stanton).**—(2012-14)**

DRAFT DROP *Grandson of Leon Culberson, major leaguer (1943-48)*

2. (Choice to Athletics as compensation for Type A free agent Barry Zito)
3. (Choice to Reds as compensation for Type A free agent Rich Aurilia)
4. (Choice to Padres as compensation for Type A free agent Dave Roberts)
5. Chance Corgan, rhp, Texas Christian University.—(Low A)
6. Michael Ambort, c, Lamar University.
7. Kyle Nicholson, rhp, Texas A&M University.
8. Daniel Turpen, rhp, Oregon State University.
9. **Dan Runzler, lhp, UC Riverside.—(2009-12)**
10. **Joe Paterson, lhp, Oregon State University.—(2011-14)**
11. Evan McArthur, 3b, Cal State Fullerton.
12. Andrew Davis, 3b, Kent State University.
13. Andy Reichard, rhp, Georgia College.
14. Craig Clark, lhp, Penn State University.
15. Bruce Edwards, of, Auburn University.
16. **Steven Edlefsen, rhp, University of Nebraska.—(2011-12)**
17. John King, rhp, Lipscomb University.
18. Andy de la Garza, lhp, Coastal Carolina University.
19. Andy D'Alessio, 1b, Clemson University.
20. David Mixon, rhp, University of Louisiana-Monroe.
21. **Danny Otero, rhp, University of South Florida.—(2012-15)**
22. Oliver Odle, rhp, Oklahoma State University.
23. Drew Bowlin, rhp, Chattanooga State (Tenn.) JC.
24. Brock Bond, 2b, University of Missouri.
25. Casey Bond, of, Lipscomb University.
26. Ramon Corona, 2b, North Carolina State University.
27. Myles Schroder, of, Diablo Valley (Calif.) JC.
28. *Dan McDaniel, rhp, Chabot (Calif.) JC.
29. Lars Knepper, rhp, University of Hawaii-Hilo.
30. **Johnny Monell, c, Seminole (Fla.) CC.—(2013-15)**
31. Josh Lopez, ss, Lehigh HS, Fort Myers, Fla.
32. Dom Duggan, of, Coastal Carolina University.
33. Mike Loberg, of, Augustana (S.D.) College.
34. ***Tyler Ladendorf, ss, Howard (Texas) JC.—(2015)**
35. T.J. Brewer, rhp, Arkansas State University.
36. ***Paul Clemens, rhp, Louisburg (N.C.) JC.—(2013-14)**
37. Jason Neitz, lhp, East Carolina University.
38. J.J. Pannell, rhp, George Mason University.
39. Tim Egart, rhp, Arkansas State University.
40. Ben Wilshire, rhp, Austin Peay State University.
41. Brandon Grabham, rhp, Collin County (Texas) CC.
42. Chad Rothford, 1b, Oral Roberts University.
43. Shane Jordan, of, Stetson University.
44. Joe Edens, rhp, Samford University.
45. *Phil Disher, c, University of South Carolina.
46. *Jack Rye, of, Florida State University.
47. ***Ryan Verdugo, lhp, Skagit Valley (Wash.) CC.—(2012)**
48. *Andrew Barbosa, lhp, South Florida CC.
49. Trent Kline, c, University of South Carolina.
50. Mike Loree, rhp, Villanova University.

## SEATTLE MARINERS (11)

1. **Phillippe Aumont, rhp, Ecole Du Versant HS, Gatineau, Quebec.—(2002-15)**
1. **Matt Mangini, 3b, Oklahoma State University** (Supplemental choice—52nd—as compensation for Type B free agent Gil Meche).**—(2010)**
2. Denny Almonte, of, Florida Christian HS, Miami.—(AAA)
3. Danny Carroll, of, Valley View HS, Moreno Valley, Calif.—(AA)
4. Nolan Gallagher, rhp, Stanford University.—(Low A)
5. Joe Dunigan, of, University of Oklahoma.—(AAA)
6. James McOwen, of, Florida International University.
7. Nick Hill, lhp, U.S. Military Academy.
8. Donnie Hume, lhp, San Diego State University.
9. Aaron Brown, rhp, University of Houston.
10. Keith Renaud, rhp, Franklin Pierce (N.H.) College.
11. Jeff Dunbar, c, UC Riverside.
12. Ryan Moorer, rhp, University of Maryland.
13. **Shawn Kelley, rhp, Austin Peay State University.—(2009-15)**
14. Brandon McKerney, rhp, University of Washington.
15. Keith Meyer, rhp, Duquesne University.
16. Colin Buckborough, rhp, Stamford Collegiate HS, Niagara Falls, Ontario.
17. Ryan Rodriguez, rhp, University of Nevada.
18. Guy Welsh, 3b, University of North Carolina-Greensboro.
19. Roberto Mena, ss, University of Tampa.
20. *Stephen Penney, rhp, UC Riverside.
21. Travis Mortimore, lhp, Wayne State (Neb.) College.
22. Bryan Harris, rhp, Cal State Fullerton.
23. Broadie Downs, rhp, Modesto (Calif.) JC.
24. Matt Renfree, rhp, University of Nevada.
25. *Conrad Flynn, rhp, Robert E. Lee HS, Midland, Texas.
26. Jacob Wild, rhp, University of the Pacific.
27. Brooks Mohr, rhp, Elida (Ohio) HS.
28. *Josh Satow, lhp, Arizona State University.
29. Javier Martinez, rhp, Fordham University.
30. *Jason Nantz, 1b, Blackford HS, Hartford, Ind.
31. *Rod Scurry, rhp, University of Nevada.

DRAFT DROP *Son of Rod Scurry, first-round draft pick, Pirates (1974); major leaguer (1980-88)*

32. Blake Trinkler, 2b, Modesto (Calif.) JC.
33. *Chris Pecora, of, North Carolina Wesleyan College.
34. John DuRocher, rhp, University of Washington.
35. *Trent Rothlin, rhp, Fred T. Foard HS, Hickory, N.C.
36. *Cole Cook, rhp, Palisades Charter HS, Los Angeles.
37. *Donald Brown, of, Pepperdine University.
38. *Chris Kupillas, rhp, Central Michigan University.
39. *Michael Beltran, ss, St. John Bosco HS, Lakewood, Calif.
40. *Josh Liles, of, University School of Jackson, Jackson, Tenn.
41. *Matt Thomas, rhp, Chino Hills (Calif.) HS.
42. *Jack Peterson, 2b, La Jolla (Calif.) HS.
43. *Jason Buursma, rhp, Bucknell University.
44. *Forrest Snow, rhp, Lakeside HS, Nine Mile Falls, Wash.
45. *Clay Van Hook, 2b, University of Texas.
46. Kyle Haas, rhp, Northeastern Oklahoma A&M JC.
47. ***Brett Oberholtzer, lhp, William Penn HS, St. Georges, Del.—(2013-15)**
48. *Eric Maupin, rhp, Galena HS, Reno, Nev.
49. ***David Carpenter, rhp, New Mexico JC.—(2012-15)**
50. *Nick Purdy, of, St. Marys SS, Grafton, Ontario.

## TAMPA BAY DEVIL RAYS (1)

1. **David Price, lhp, Vanderbilt University.—(2008-15)**
2. Will Kline, rhp, University of Mississippi.—(Low A)
3. Nick Barnese, rhp, Simi Valley (Calif.) HS.—(AA)
4. David Newmann, lhp, Texas A&M University.—(AA)
5. Dustin Biell, of, Inglemoor HS, Kenmore, Wash.—(High A)
6. Emeel Salem, of, University of Alabama.
7. Reid Fronk, of, University of North Carolina.
8. **Matt Moore, lhp, Moriarty HS, Edgewood, N.M.—(2011-15)**
9. Cody Cipriano, 2b, UC Irvine.
10. Greg Sexton, 3b, College of William & Mary.
11. D.J. Jones, of, Gulf Shores (Ala.) HS.
12. **Stephen Vogt, c, Azusa Pacific (Calif.) University.—(2012-15)**
13. Brian Flores, lhp, Arizona State University.
14. Kyle Ayers, rhp, Oswego (Ill.) HS.
15. Michael Southern, rhp, West Hills (Calif.) JC.
16. Josh Johnson, rhp, Mississippi State University.
17. *Will Harvil, rhp, Young Harris (Ga.) JC.

18. Julius Dettrich, lhp, Arlington (Wash.) HS.
19. Kevin Boggan, rhp, Boston College.
20. Chris Luck, rhp, South Granville HS, Creedmoor, N.C.
21. Kevin Brophy, rhp, UCLA.
22. *Ryan Turner, rhp, Richland HS, North Richland Hills, Texas.
23. *Joel Carranza, c, Flanagan HS, Pembroke Pines, Fla.
24. John Baird, rhp, University of Cincinnati.
25. Justin Garcia, rhp, Western Nevada CC.
26. *Grimes Medlin, lhp, Young Harris (Ga.) JC.
27. John Mollicone, c, Fordham University.
28. Ben Humphrey, 1b, Central Michigan University.
29. *Robert Morey, rhp, Cape Henry Collegiate HS, Virginia Beach, Va.
30. Joseph Cruz, rhp, East Los Angeles JC.
31. *Stephen Sauer, rhp, Western Nevada CC.
32. *Thad Griffen, c, Barbe HS, Lake Charles, La.
33. *R.J. Preach, rhp, Brophy Jesuit Prep, Phoenix.
34. Kevin Chavez, rhp, St. Michaels HS, Santa Fe, N.M.
**35. *Joey Terdoslavich, c, Sarasota (Fla.) HS.—(2013-15)**
36. *Travis Stortz, lhp, Countryside HS, Safety Harbor, Fla.
37. Robert Della Grotta, rhp, Pepperdine University.
38. Jesse Darcy, rhp, Manhattan College.
39. *Joe Staley, c, Decatur (Texas) HS.
**40. *Will Smith, lhp, Northgate HS, Newnan, Ga.—(2012-15)**
41. Austin Hinkle, rhp, Coastal Carolina University.
42. *Sean Green, rhp, Chesterton (Ind.) HS.
43. *Brad Buehler, rhp, St. Pius X HS, Barnhart, Kan.
44. *Braden Degamo, c, Mariner HS, Lynnwood, Wash.
45. *Brett Miller, rhp, Montgomery HS, San Diego.
46. *Elliot Glynn, lhp, Woodrow Wilson HS, Los Alamitos, Calif.
47. *Kyle Decater, of, Bellevue (Wash.) CC.
48. *Matt Evers, lhp, Stratford HS, Houston.
49. *Kenny Burdi, of, Kishwaukee (Ill.) JC.
50. *Mark Peterson, lhp, Lincoln Park Academy, Fort Pierce, Fla.

## TEXAS RANGERS (16)

1. (Choice to Blue Jays as compensation for Type A free agent Frank Catalanotto)
**1. Blake Beavan, rhp, Irving (Texas) HS** (Choice from Astros as compensation for Type A free agent Carlos Lee).**—(2011-14)**
1. Michael Main, rhp-of, Deland HS, Deltona, Fla. (Choice from Angels as compensation for Type A free agent Gary Matthews).—(AA)
**1. Julio Borbon, of, University of Tennessee** (Supplemental choice—35th—as compensation for Lee).**—(2009-13)**
**1. Neil Ramirez, rhp, Kempsville HS, Virginia Beach, Va.** (Supplemental choice—44th—as compensation for Matthews).**—(2014-15)**
**1. Tommy Hunter, rhp, University of Alabama** (Supplemental choice—54th—as compensation for Type B free agent Mark DeRosa).**—(2008-15)**
**2. Matt West, ss, Bellaire HS, Houston.—(2014-15)**
**3. Evan Reed, rhp, Cal Poly San Luis Obispo.—(2013-14)**
4. *Garrett Nash, of, Jordan HS, Draper, Utah.—DNP

DRAFT DROP *Attended Oregon State; re-drafted by Diamondbacks, 2010 (39th round)*
**5. *John Gast, lhp, Lake Brantley HS, Longwood, Fla.—(2013)**
DRAFT DROP *Attended Florida State; re-drafted by Cardinals, 2010 (6th round)*
6. Bobby Wilkins, rhp, Valhalla HS, El Cajon, Calif.
7. Tim Smith, of, Arizona State University.
8. Jonathan Greene, c, Western Carolina University.
9. Davis Stoneburner, ss, James Madison University.
10. Andrew Laughter, rhp, University of Louisiana-Lafayette.
**11. *Anthony Ranaudo, rhp, St. Rose HS, Jackson, N.J.—(2014-15)**
DRAFT DROP *First-round draft pick (39th overall), Red Sox (2010)*
**12. *Drew Pomeranz, lhp, Collierville (Tenn.) HS.—(2011-15)**
DRAFT DROP *First-round draft pick (5th overall), Indians (2010)*
13. Kyle Ocampo, rhp, Poly HS, Riverside, Calif.
14. Matt Lawson, 2b, Missouri State University.
15. Hector Nelo, rhp, St. Thomas (Fla.) University.
**16. Josh Lueke, rhp, Northern Kentucky University.—(2011-14)**
**17. Mitch Moreland, lhp-1b, Mississippi State University.—(2010-15)**
18. Ryan Tatusko, rhp, Indiana State University.
19. Kyle Murphy, of, University of Kansas.
20. Kenny Smith, 2b, Western Carolina University.
**21. *Erik Davis, rhp, Stanford University.—(2013)**
22. Donnie Ecker, of, Lewis-Clark State (Idaho) College.
23. Jacob Kaase, ss, Texas Lutheran University.
24. Chris Gradoville, c, Creighton University.
**25. *Andy Wilkins, 3b, Broken Arrow (Okla.) HS.—(2014)**
26. *Kevin Keyes, of, Connally HS, Austin, Texas.
27. *Drew Gray, c, Longview (Mo.) JC.
28. Michael Ortiz, 1b, Palmetto HS, Miami.
29. Ryan Falcon, lhp, University of North Carolina-Greensboro.
30. Ben Henry, rhp, Loris (S.C.) HS.
31. Anton Maxwell, lhp, Oregon State University.
32. *Gaspar Santiago, lhp, Puerto Rico Baseball Academy, Vega Baja, P.R.
33. Jared Hyatt, rhp, Georgia Tech.
34. *Chase Huchingson, lhp, Fayetteville (Ark.) HS.
35. *Jeff Schaus, of, Barron Collier HS, Naples, Fla.
36. *Brian Dupra, rhp, Greece Athena HS, Rochester, N.Y.
37. *B.J. Salsbury, rhp, San Jacinto (Calif.) HS.
38. *Hunter Hill, rhp, Prestonwood Christian Academy, Dallas.
39. *Tyler Fleming, rhp, Cowley County (Kan.) CC.
40. *Sean Meehan, rhp, Centralia (Wash.) HS.
41. *Tom Edwards, 1b, Rutgers University.
42. Jason Sowers, 1b, Cowley County (Kan.) CC.
43. *Joey Rosas, lhp, Yavapai (Ariz.) CC.
44. *Kris Jiggitts, rhp, Colby (Kan.) CC.
45. Ryan Turner, lhp, Georgia Tech.
46. *Yoandy Barroso, of, Miami Springs HS, Miami.
47. *Ben Petralli, c, Sacramento (Calif.) CC.
DRAFT DROP *Son of Geno Petralli, major leaguer (1982-93)*
48. *Dillon Baird, 3b, Yavapai (Ariz.) JC.
49. *Brandon Hayes, of, Sheldon HS, Eugene, Ore.
DRAFT DROP *Nephew of Von Hayes, major leaguer (1981-92)*
50. *Paul Zarlengo, 1b, Marian Catholic HS, Homewood, Ill.

## TORONTO BLUE JAYS (21)

1. Kevin Ahrens, ss, Memorial HS, Houston (Choice from Rangers as compensation for Type A free agent Frank Catalanotto).—(AA)
**1. J.P. Arencibia, c, University of Tennessee.—(2010-15)**
**1. Brett Cecil, lhp, University of Maryland** (Supplemental choice—38th—as compensation for Type A free agent Justin Speier).**—(2009-15)**
1. Justin Jackson, ss, T.C. Roberson, Asheville, N.C. (Supplemental choice—45th—as compensation for Catalanotto).—(AA)
DRAFT DROP *Son of Chuck Jackson, major leaguer (1987-94)*
**1. Trystan Magnuson, rhp, University of Louisville** (Supplemental choice—56th—as compensation for Type B free agent Ted Lilly).**—(2011)**
2. John Tolisano, ss, Estero HS, Sanibel, Fla.—(AA)
2. Eric Eiland, of, Lamar HS, Houston (Choice from Angels as compensation for Speier).—(Low A)
3. Alan Farina, 3b, Clemson University.—(AA)
**4. Brad Mills, lhp, University of Arizona.—(2009-15)**
**5. Marc Rzepczynski, lhp, UC Riverside.—(2009-15)**
6. Michael McDade, 1b, Silverado HS, Las Vegas, Nev.
7. Randy Boone, rhp, University of Texas.
8. Scott Leffler, rhp, University of Tampa.
9. Marcus Walden, rhp, Fresno (Calif.) CC.
10. Joel Collins, c, University of South Alabama.
**11. Brad Emaus, 2b, Tulane University.—(2011)**
12. Steven Condotta, ss, Florida Tech.
13. Jonny Talley, c, Carlsbad HS, Oceanside, Calif.
14. Cody Crowell, lhp, Vanderbilt University.
15. Nathan Jennings, rhp, University of Texas-Tyler.
**16. Darin Mastroianni, 2b, University of Southern Indiana.—(2011-14)**
17. *Adalberto Santos, 2b, New Mexico JC.
18. *Chris Corrigan, rhp, San Jacinto (Texas) JC.
19. Brian Letko, lhp, Embry-Riddle (Fla.) University.
20. *Jake Hale, rhp, Ohio State University.
21. *Cody Dunbar, rhp, Texas Christian University.
22. *Matt Thomson, rhp, Santa Rosa (Calif.) JC.
23. Frank Gailey, lhp, West Chester (Pa.) University.
24. Jimmy Dougher, rhp, Cortland State (N.Y.) University.
25. Jay Monti, rhp, Sacred Heart University.-
27. Kyle Gilligan, ss, Connors State (Okla.) JC.
28. *Xorge Carrillo, c, McClintock HS, Tempe, Ariz.
29. *Jonathan Runnells, lhp, Rice University.
DRAFT DROP *Grandson of Pete Runnels, major leaguer (1951-64); major league manager (1966)*
30. *David Kaye, rhp, Riverview HS, Oakmont, Pa.

## WASHINGTON NATIONALS (6)

**1. Ross Detwiler, lhp, Missouri State University.—(2007-15)**
DRAFT DROP *First player from 2007 draft to reach majors (Sept. 7, 2007)*
1. Josh Smoker, lhp, Calhoun HS, Sugar Valley, Ga. (Supplemental choice—31st—as compensation for Type A free agent Alfonso Soriano).—(High A)
1. Michael Burgess, of, Hillsborough HS, Tampa (Supplemental choice—49th—as compensation for Type B free agent Jose Guillen).—(AA)
**2. Jordan Zimmermann, rhp, University of Wisconsin-Oshkosh** (Choice from Cubs as compensation for Soriano).**—(2009-15)**
**2. Jake Smolinski, ss, Boylan Catholic HS, Rockford, Ill.—(2014-15)**
**3. Steven Souza, ss, Cascade HS, Everett, Wash.—(2014-15)**
**4. Derek Norris, c, Goddard (Kan.) HS.—(2012-15)**
5. Brad Meyers, rhp, Loyola Marymount University.—(AAA)
6. Jack McGeary, lhp, Roxbury Latin HS, Newton, Mass.
7. P.J. Dean, rhp, New Caney (Texas) HS.
8. Adrian Alaniz, rhp, University of Texas.
9. Mark Gildea, of, Florida State University.
**10. Patrick McCoy, lhp, Sahuaro HS, Tucson.—(2014)**
11. Bill Rhinehart, 1b, University of Arizona.
12. Craig Stinson, c, Texas A&M University.
13. Steve Shepard, rhp, Franklin Pierce (Fla.) College.
14. Dan Lyons, ss, University of Minnesota.
15. Patrick Arnold, rhp, Huntington (W.Va.) HS.
16. Chris Blackwood, of, Gloucester County (N.J.) JC.
17. Luke Pisker, rhp, Virginia Commonwealth University.
18. *Sawyer Carroll, 1b, University of Kentucky.
19. Jeff Mandel, rhp, Baylor University.
20. *Daniel Cook, of, Florida Atlantic University.
21. Anthony Benner, 3b, Southwestern (Calif.) JC.
22. Jake Rogers, ss, South Dakota State University.
23. *David Duncan, lhp, Georgia Tech.
24. Rick Nolan, c, St. Leo (Fla.) College.
25. *Chris Berroa, of, Pennsauken (N.J.) HS.
26. *Kelvin Clark, of, Redan HS, Ellenwood, Ga.
27. Aaron Seuss, of, California Baptist University.
28. Boomer Whiting, of, University of Louisville.
29. Justin Phillabaum, rhp, Florida Atlantic University.
30. *Zach Pitts, rhp, University of Louisville.
31. *David Stewart, of, St. John Vianney HS, St. Louis.
32. *Daniel Killian, c, Chippewa Hills HS, Stanwood, Mich.
33. Jeffrey McCollum, rhp, Southern University.
34. *Kenn Kasparek, rhp, University of Texas.
35. *Alex Floyd, of, Hillsborough (Fla.) CC.
36. Martin Beno, rhp, Oklahoma State University.
37. Devin Drag, rhp, Chapman (Calif.) University.
38. Shane Erb, rhp, Hillsborough (Fla.) CC.
39. Caleb Staudt, rhp, St. Mary's (Texas) University.
40. Kai Tuomi, lhp, University of Evansville.
41. *Iden Nazario, lhp, Southridge HS, Miami.
42. Garrett Bass, of, Jacksonville State University.
DRAFT DROP *Son of Kevin Bass, major leaguer (1982-95) • Brother of Justin Bass, 21st-round draft pick, Angels (2007)*
43. *Mike Martinez, lhp, Christopher Columbus HS, Miami.
44. Clint Pridmore, 3b, Santa Rosa (Calif.) JC.
45. Travis Reagan, c, Rice University.
46. *Ryan Cisterna, c, Chandler-Gilbert (Ariz.) JC.
47. *Jeff Walters, rhp, St. Petersburg (Fla.) JC.
48. Kyle Gunderson, rhp, Rice University.
49. Jake Dugger, of, University of Arkansas.
50. Lindon Bond, of, Texas Southern University.

# 2008

# Posey proves big prize as teams open wallets

The 2008 draft was the most expensive ever, but on many counts the cost was justified. No other draft in history has produced as many future major leaguers in the first round, in the first 10 rounds and overall.

Among 30 players selected in the first round, 27 reached the majors, an unprecedented 90 percent success rate. The first 10 rounds included a record 130 players who reached the big leagues, and the overall count of 247 was another record. Prior to the 2008 draft, the records were 26 first-rounders (in 2004 and 2005), 118 in the initial 10 rounds (2006) and 227 overall (2005). The San Diego Padres drafted 16 future big leaguers, tying the most ever for one team since the draft was consolidated into one phase in 1987.

It all came at a significant cost. Major league teams spent a record $188,297,598 to sign their draft picks, a significant uptick from $151,830,550 a year earlier. Almost every bonus record fell by the wayside. Major League Baseball could afford it: The industry was in the midst of setting an attendance record for the fifth straight season, and revenue from other sources had reached unprecedented levels.

The Kansas City Royals spent $11.148 million to sign their draft picks, topping the previous record of $9.776 million (Diamondbacks, 2005), and three other clubs also eclipsed the old mark. The average first-round bonus of $2,449,785 was the largest ever, topping the previous high of $2,154,280, set it 2001, and was 16.8 percent higher than a year earlier.

The record bonus for a player was set twice in 2008. Georgia high school shortstop Tim Beckham, the first overall pick, signed with the Tampa Bay Rays for $6.15 million, topping the $6.1 million that Justin Upton received from the Arizona Diamondbacks in 2005. Just before the signing deadline, Florida State catcher Buster Posey, the fifth overall pick, agreed to a $6.2 million deal with the San Francisco Giants.

The records set in 2008 for draft choices reaching the big leagues have stood the test of time, but the bonus marks lasted only until the following year.

The Rays picked first in the draft for the second consecutive year, the first time the No. 1 choice was held by the same team in back-to-back years. It was the fourth time in the franchise's decade-long existence that it had the first pick.

Of greater significance to the organization and its fans, however, the Rays became the first team to own the top pick in the draft and appear in the World Series in the same season.

The top pick in 2007 was Vanderbilt lefthander David Price, who played a key role a year later in the Rays' resurgence and advance into postseason play. Tampa Bay narrowed its choice in 2008 to Beckham, who had the best combination of five-tool ability and baseball aptitude in the draft, and Posey, a proven, athletic catcher who could fill the team's biggest need.

BRIAN WESTERHOLT

**Buster Posey looked like the odds-on favorite to be the No. 1 pick, but when an outlandish $10 million price tag came out just before the draft, the Devil Rays shifted gears, to their eternal regret**

The Rays stayed true to their usual development approach, opting for upside and raw talent over polish and experience, and took Beckham. It was a mistake they would long regret. Posey became the unquestioned star of the 2008 draft class, and Beckham became one of the bigger No. 1 busts in draft annals.

## SIGNABILITY PLAYS SECONDARY ROLE

After the Rays started the process by taking Beckham instead of Posey, the 2008 draft went pretty much according to form. Teams drafted players on the basis of ability, giving little consideration to signability.

There were few, if any of the scenarios comparable with what transpired in the previous two drafts, when righthander Rick Porcello and lefthander Andrew Miller slid down the first round and into the grasp of the Detroit Tigers, who didn't hesitate to meet their financial demands.

By contrast, there wasn't a single team in 2008 that showed a reluctance to draft a player who might have slipped in past years for signability reasons. Even the Pittsburgh Pirates, with the No.

## AT A GLANCE

### This Date In History
June 5-6

### Best Draft
**SAN FRANCISCO GIANTS.** The Giants took **BUSTER POSEY** (1) and **BRANDON CRAWFORD** (4), no small reason why they won World Series titles in 2010, 2012 and 2014.

### Worst Draft
**TAMPA BAY RAYS.** The Rays went from last in the American League East in 2007 to the 2008 World Series. They had the No. 1 overall pick each year, and could have scored a major coup had they followed up the selection of David Price in 2007 by taking **BUSTER POSEY**, the unquestioned star of the 2008 class. Instead, the Rays went for underachieving **TIM BECKHAM** with the top pick and drafted only one other future big leaguer, **KYLE LOBSTEIN** (2).

### First-Round Bust
**ANTHONY HEWITT, 3B, PHILLIES.** Hewitt, one of just three first-rounders who didn't reach the big leagues, was floundering at Double-A in 2014 when the Phillies released him. In seven minor league seasons, he hit .223 and had a 94-763 walk-strikeout ratio in 595 games.

### Second Guessing
**TYSON ROSS, RHP, ATHLETICS.** Ross emerged as a quality starter after being traded to San Diego. The Padres also drafted Ross' younger brother, Joe, in the first round in 2011, and traded him to the Nationals prior to the 2015 season. Like Tyson, Joe blossomed into a solid major league starter.

### Late-Round Find
**TANNER ROARK, RHP, RANGERS (25TH ROUND).** Roark was an unlikely candidate to be drafted, much less surface in the big leagues five years later and post a 26-18, 3.12 record

**CONTINUED ON PAGE 642**

## AT A GLANCE

CONTINUED FROM PAGE 641

in three seasons with the Nationals. A University of Illinois dropout with an underwhelming fastball, Roark went 0-2, 21.41 in three appearances in the independent Frontier League in 2008.

### Never Too Late

**SEAN NOLIN, LHP, BREWERS (50TH ROUND).** The Brewers didn't sign Nolin, but recognized potential in the Delaware high school product. Two years later, he was drafted in the sixth round by the Blue Jays out of San Jacinto (Texas) JC. He reached the big leagues in 2014 before being traded to Oakland in a deal that sent Josh Donaldson to Toronto.

### Overlooked

**DANIEL NAVA, OF, RED SOX.** On June 12, 2010, Nava hit a grand slam on the first pitch he saw as a big leaguer, the first time that had happened since 1898. Nava, who stood 5-foot-5 as a high school senior, fought long odds to play baseball even in college. It took a breakout season in the independent Golden League for him to be noticed by a big league club. The Red Sox bought his contract for $1.

### International Gem

**ENDER INCIARTE, OF, DIAMONDBACKS.** Inciarte, from Venezuela, received a modest signing bonus from the Diamondbacks and developed into a solid major league outfielder, batting .292 in the 2014-15 seasons and excelling defensively. Meanwhile, righthander **MICHAEL YNOA**, a 16-year-old from the Dominican Republic, signed with the Athletics for $4.25 million, the most ever for a Latin American player. Beset by arm injuries, Ynoa did not advance beyond Class A.

### Minor League Take

**BUSTER POSEY, C, GIANTS.** Posey got the richest bonus in 2008, a then-draft record

## 2008: THE FIRST ROUNDERS

| CLUB: PLAYER, POS., SCHOOL | HOMETOWN | B-T | HT. | WT. | AGE | BONUS | FIRST YEAR | LAST YEAR | PEAK LEVEL (YEARS) |
|---|---|---|---|---|---|---|---|---|---|
| 1. Rays: Tim Beckham, ss, Griffin HS | Griffin, Ga. | R-R | 6-1 | 180 | 18 | $6,150,000 | 2008 | Active | Majors (2) |
| Rays rolled dice on shortstop with five-tool upside; drug suspension, torn ACL hampered slow-developing career, finally established himself as big leaguer in 2015. | | | | | | | | | |
| 2. *Pirates: Pedro Alvarez, 3b, Vanderbilt | New York | L-R | 6-2 | 225 | 21 | $6,355,000 | 2009 | Active | Majors (6) |
| Hit .349-49-162 in three years at Vandy, hailed as best bat in hitter-rich draft; has flashed power in major league career marked by high-strikeout, high-error totals. | | | | | | | | | |
| 3. Royals: Eric Hosmer, 1b, American Heritage HS | Cooper City, Fla. | L-L | 6-4 | 215 | 18 | $6,000,000 | 2008 | Active | Majors (5) |
| One of most polished/accomplished HS hitters in a decade, also threw mid-90s off mound, flashed Gold Glove potential on defense; key piece in Royals resurgence. | | | | | | | | | |
| 4. *Orioles: Brian Matusz, lhp, San Diego | Phoenix | L-L | 6-4 | 200 | 21 | $3,200,000 | 2009 | Active | Majors (7) |
| Projected as future ace after 12-2, 1.71 record, NCAA-leading 141 Ks at USD, brief/impressive career in minors; flopped as starter, trying to salvage career in relief. | | | | | | | | | |
| 5. Giants: Buster Posey, c, Florida State | Leesburg, Ga. | R-R | 6-1 | 205 | 21 | $6,200,000 | 2008 | Active | Majors (7) |
| In retrospect, obvious No. 1 pick; began college as SS/RHP, ended it by hitting .463-26-93 as standout catcher, Golden Spikes winner; keyed Giants to 3 W/S titles. | | | | | | | | | |
| 6. Marlins: Kyle Skipworth, c, Patriot HS | Riverside, Calif. | L-R | 6-3 | 195 | 18 | $2,300,000 | 2008 | 2015 | Majors (1) |
| LH-hitting catcher with power, SoCal background, all tools to excel; with .214 average, 831 Ks in 665 games, never hit in minors, though flashed power (93 HRs). | | | | | | | | | |
| 7. *Reds: Yonder Alonso, 1b, Miami | Coral Gables, Fla. | L-R | 6-2 | 215 | 21 | $2,000,000 | 2008 | Active | Majors (6) |
| Hit .370-24-72 as one of three Miami first-rounders; with 32 HRs in 508 MLB games, concern by scouts that power wouldn't translate to wood proved warranted. | | | | | | | | | |
| 8. White Sox: Gordon Beckham, ss, Georgia | Atlanta | R-R | 6-0 | 185 | 21 | $2,600,000 | 2008 | Active | Majors (7) |
| No relation to No. 1 pick Tim; hit .411-28-77 in aluminum-bat fueled JR year, made big splash as 2009 MLB rookie (.270-13-64) but bat has gone backward since. | | | | | | | | | |
| 9. Nationals: Aaron Crow, rhp, Missouri | Topeka, Kan. | R-R | 6-2 | 205 | 21 | Unsigned | 2009 | Active | Majors (4) |
| Went 13-0, 2.35 (107 IP/127 SO) with mid-90s fastball, nasty slider; turned down $3.5M bonus during acrimonious negotiations, resurfaced in '09 first round. | | | | | | | | | |
| 10. Astros: Jason Castro, c, Stanford | Castro Valley, Calif. | L-R | 6-3 | 215 | 20 | $2,070,000 | 2008 | Active | Majors (5) |
| From .167-1-14 backup Stanford soph 1B, exploded to .370-14-73 season as athletic junior C; defense-first approach, one of early building blocks in Astros revival. | | | | | | | | | |
| 11. Rangers: Justin Smoak, 1b, South Carolina | Goose Creek, S.C. | B-L | 6-4 | 215 | 21 | $3,500,000 | 2008 | Active | Majors (6) |
| Prep teammate of Matt Wieters (2007 first-rounder); highly decorated amateur player, set multiple USC offensive records but MLB career stunted by limited contact. | | | | | | | | | |
| 12. Athletics: Jemile Weeks, 2b, Miami | Altamonte Springs, Fla. | B-R | 5-10 | 175 | 21 | $1,910,000 | 2008 | Active | Majors (5) |
| Younger brother of Rickie (second overall, 2003), though less strength in bat; hit .363-13-62 with 22 SBs as Miami junior but bat too light for a regular MLB role. | | | | | | | | | |
| 13. Cardinals: Brett Wallace, 3b/1b, Arizona State | Napa, Calif. | L-R | 6-2 | 235 | 21 | $1,840,000 | 2008 | Active | Majors (5) |
| Polarizing prospect with switch-hit skills, surprising athleticism in less-than-ideal frame; hit .410-22-83 for ASU, but power has often abandoned him in pro ball. | | | | | | | | | |
| 14. Twins: Aaron Hicks, of/rhp, Wilson HS | Long Beach, Calif. | B-R | 6-2 | 175 | 18 | $1,780,000 | 2008 | Active | Majors (3) |
| Gifted athlete with two-way potential; threw mid-90s off mound, but Twins preferred speed, switch-hit ability, true CF skills, finally started to hit in majors in 2015. | | | | | | | | | |
| 15. Dodgers: Ethan Martin, rhp/3b, Stephens County HS | Toccoa, Ga. | R-R | 6-2 | 195 | 18 | $1,730,000 | 2009 | 2015 | Majors (2) |
| Projected first-rounder as power-hitting 3B until clocked in mid-90s; Dodgers gambled on higher upside on mound, has shown flashes but success sporadic. | | | | | | | | | |
| 16. Brewers: Brett Lawrie, c, Brookswood HS | Langley, B.C. | R-R | 5-11 | 200 | 18 | $1,700,000 | 2009 | Active | Majors (4) |
| Highest Canadian position player ever drafted; versatile player coveted mainly for bat, ended up with Blue Jays but has not lived up to promising 2011 MLB debut. | | | | | | | | | |
| 17. Blue Jays: David Cooper, 1b, California | Lodi, Calif. | L-L | 6-1 | 210 | 21 | $1,500,000 | 2008 | 2015 | Majors (2) |
| Teased scouts with power as Cal JR (.359-19-55), but HRs hard to come by as a pro; value evaporated with contact-oriented approach, below-average athleticism. | | | | | | | | | |
| 18. Mets: Ike Davis, 1b/of, Arizona State | Scottsdale, Ariz. | L-L | 6-4 | 215 | 21 | $1,575,000 | 2008 | Active | Majors (6) |
| Son of ex-MLB hurler Ron; showed raw power (.385-16-76, 26 2B), arm strength as RF/LHP (4-1, 2.25, 4 SV) in college, but MLB platoon role with spotty production. | | | | | | | | | |
| 19. Cubs: Andrew Cashner, rhp, Texas Christian | Lufkin, Texas | R-R | 6-5 | 185 | 21 | $1,540,000 | 2008 | Active | Majors (6) |
| Three-time draft pick blossomed as TCU closer (9-1, 9 SV, 54 IP/21 H) with upper 90s fastball; fought injuries but finally made MLB mark as Padres starter. | | | | | | | | | |
| 20. Mariners: Josh Fields, rhp, Georgia | Hull, Ga. | R-R | 6-0 | 180 | 22 | $1,750,000 | 2009 | Active | Majors (3) |
| Unsigned Braves '07 second-rounder, eased into top round as SR with dominant year (18 SV, 37 IP/63 SO); floundered in minors until Astros Rule 5 pick-up. | | | | | | | | | |
| 21. Tigers: Ryan Perry, rhp, Arizona | Marana, Ariz. | R-R | 6-4 | 200 | 21 | $1,480,000 | 2008 | 2015 | Majors (4) |
| Had 6.85 ERA in first two years, blossomed as JR with mid-90s fastball; big velo propelled him to Tigers, but command/secondary pitches not up to MLB standards. | | | | | | | | | |
| 22. Mets: Reese Havens, ss, South Carolina | Charleston, S.C. | L-R | 6-1 | 195 | 21 | $1,419,000 | 2008 | 2013 | Class AAA (1) |
| Polished college performer hit .359-18-57, profiled as offensive 2B in pros with modest speed/range, but career hampered by string of elbow/groin injuries. | | | | | | | | | |
| 23. Padres: Allan Dykstra, 1b, Wake Forest | San Diego | L-R | 6-4 | 230 | 21 | $1,150,000 | 2008 | 2015 | Majors (1) |
| Seventh 1B picked in historically rich draft at position; featured power, on-base skills, hit 49 HRs at Wake, 94 more in minors before earned first MLB shot at age 28. | | | | | | | | | |
| 24. Phillies: Anthony Hewitt, ss, Salisbury (Conn.) School | New York | R-R | 6-1 | 195 | 19 | $1,380,000 | 2008 | 2015 | Class AA (2) |
| Prototypical Phils pick from era; high-risk/high-return player with impressive tools, limited baseball skills; spent bulk of career in Class A (.223, 96 BB/779 SO). | | | | | | | | | |
| 25. Rockies: Christian Friedrich, lhp, Eastern Kentucky | Wilmette, Ill. | R-L | 6-3 | 210 | 20 | $1,350,000 | 2008 | Active | Majors (3) |
| Dominated in college for three seasons (20-7, 1.84, 245 IP, 327 SO), early pro years with 89-95 mph FB, big curve, but struggled since with command/injury issues. | | | | | | | | | |
| 26. Diamondbacks: Daniel Schlereth, lhp, Arizona | Highlands Ranch, Colo. | L-L | 6-1 | 210 | 22 | $1,330,000 | 2008 | Active | Majors (4) |
| Son of longtime NFL lineman/ESPN analyst Mark Schlereth; fast-tracked to MLB as reliever with 95-97 mph FB, had solid debut but battled shoulder problems since. | | | | | | | | | |
| 27. Twins: Carlos Gutierrez, rhp, Miami | Miami | R-R | 6-3 | 205 | 21 | $1,226,000 | 2008 | 2013 | Class AAA (3) |
| Dominated as UM closer (13 SV, 50 IP/72 SO) with sinker; Twins developed him as starter until 2011 shoulder injury, game never rebounded after surgery. | | | | | | | | | |
| 28. Yankees: Gerrit Cole, rhp, Orange Lutheran HS | Orange, Calif. | R-R | 6-3 | 200 | 17 | Unsigned | 2012 | Active | Majors (2) |
| Consensus top prep arm in otherwise barren class; considered unsignable due to UCLA commitment, Yankees gambled and lost; became top pick in 2011. | | | | | | | | | |
| 29. Indians: Lonnie Chisenhall, ss, Pitt CC | Morehead City, N.C. | L-R | 6-1 | 200 | 19 | $1,000,000 | 2008 | Active | Majors (4) |
| Kicked off South Carolina team as freshman for his part in theft; rehabbed reputation in JC with help of polished bat, reached big leagues quickly by age 22. | | | | | | | | | |
| 30. Red Sox: Casey Kelly, rhp/ss, Sarasota HS | Sarasota, Fla. | R-R | 6-3 | 195 | 18 | $3,000,000 | 2008 | Active | Majors (1) |
| Red Sox targeted Tennessee QB recruit as pitcher with 93-95 mph FB, allowed him to play SS initially to close deal; career compromised by shoulder surgery. | | | | | | | | | |

**Signed to major league contract.*

## How They Should Have Done It

Based on the career WAR (Wins Above Replacement, as calculated by Baseball-Reference.com) numbers achieved by all the players eligible for the 2008 draft through the 2015 season, here's how the first round should have unfolded. Numbers in parentheses indicate the round when the player was actually drafted.

| | Player, Pos. | Actual Draft | WAR | Bonus |
|---|---|---|---|---|
| 1. | Buster Posey, c | Giants (1) | 28.8 | $6,200,000 |
| 2. | Brett Lawrie, 3b | Brewers (1) | 14.0 | $1,700,000 |
| 3. | Brandon Crawford, ss | Giants (4) | 13.9 | $375,000 |
| 4. | Craig Kimbrel, rhp | Braves (3) | 13.6 | $391,000 |
| 5. | Lance Lynn, rhp | Cardinals (1-S) | 11.2 | $938,000 |
| 6. | Alex Avila, c | Tigers (5) | 11.0 | $169,000 |
| 7. | Eric Hosmer, 1b | Royals (1) | 9.0 | $6,000,000 |
| 8. | Jason Castro, c | Astros (1) | 8.6 | $2,070,000 |
| | Josh Harrison, 3b | Cubs (6) | 8.6 | $144,500 |
| 10. | Wade Miley, lhp | Diamondbacks (1-S) | 8.4 | $877,000 |
| 11. | Daniel Nava, of | Red Sox (NDFA) | 7.9 | None |
| 12. | Tanner Roark, rhp | Rangers (25) | 7.7 | $1,000 |
| 13. | Logan Forsythe, 3b | Padres (1-S) | 7.4 | $835,000 |
| 14. | Tyson Ross, rhp | Padres (2) | 7.3 | $694,000 |
| 15. | Danny Espinosa, ss | Nationals (3) | 7.2 | $525,000 |
| 16. | Gordon Beckham, ss | White Sox (1) | 7.1 | $2,600,000 |
| 17. | Dee Gordon, ss | Dodgers (4) | 6.6 | $250,000 |
| 18. | Lonnie Chisenhall, 3b | Indians (1) | 6.2 | $1,000,000 |
| 19. | Nathan Eovaldi, rhp | Dodgers (11) | 6.1 | $250,000 |
| 20. | Yonder Alonso, 1b | Reds (1) | 6.0 | $2,000,000 |
| 21. | Collin McHugh, rhp | Mets (18) | 5.4 | $80,000 |
| | Jarred Cosart, rhp | Phillies (38) | 5.4 | $550,000 |
| 23. | Jordy Mercer, ss | Pirates (3) | 5.2 | $508,000 |
| | Daniel Hudson, rhp | White Sox (5) | 5.2 | $180,000 |
| 25. | Pedro Alvarez, 3b | Pirates (1) | 5.1 | $6,355,000 |
| | Ike Davis, 1b | Mets (1) | 5.1 | $1,575,000 |
| | Vance Worley, rhp | Phillies (3) | 5.1 | $355,000 |
| 28. | Jake Odorizzi, rhp | Brewers (1-S) | 5.0 | $1,060,000 |
| 29. | Andrew Cashner, rhp | Cubs (1) | 4.7 | $1,540,000 |
| | Charlie Blackmon, of | Rockies (2) | 4.7 | $563,000 |
| | Tommy Milone, lhp | Nationals (10) | 4.7 | $65,000 |

| | Top 3 Unsigned Players | | | Year Signed |
|---|---|---|---|---|
| 1. | Jason Kipnis, of | Padres (4) | 16.1 | 2009 |
| 2. | Sonny Gray, rhp | Cubs (27) | 10.2 | 2011 |
| 3. | Yan Gomes, c | Red Sox (39) | 8.7 | 2009 |

2 pick, didn't hesitate to draft Vanderbilt third baseman Pedro Alvarez, the top prospect on some draft boards. In recent years, the Pirates had been reluctant to draft almost any player with a high price tag, but that mindset appeared to change with a new front office in place.

In addition to Beckham and Posey, the Rays considered Alvarez, University of San Diego lefthander Brian Matusz and Florida high school first baseman Eric Hosmer—and they wound up being the first five players drafted.

After a breakout junior season at Florida State, Posey appeared to have the edge over Beckham as the No. 1 pick in the weeks leading up to the draft. There were reports on the night before the draft that Posey's asking price had jumped to more than $10 million. Few teams took the report seriously, but it seemed to strengthen the Rays' resolve that Beckham was their man.

Beckham's signing bonus was $2.1 million more than the MLB-recommended amount for the No. 1 pick. The Rays quickly signed him for the record amount, and they didn't have to bear the full brunt of the deal in the short term, spreading the payments over five years because of Beckham's status as a two-sport athlete.

"We could have waited until Aug. 15 (the signing deadline) and seen how it played out, but for both sides it was very valuable to get him out playing," Rays executive vice president Andrew Friedman said. "So we were very aggressive in terms of how we negotiated. We think those first two months of professional baseball experience are worth a lot, so it was incredibly important to us to get him signed."

The 6-foot, 190-pound Beckham failed to develop as anticipated. It wasn't until his eighth season as a pro that he saw any meaningful time in the major leagues. In 87 games as a utility infielder with the Rays over parts of the 2014 and '15 seasons, he hit .229 with nine homers.

Posey signed for $50,000 more than Beckham and was playing for the Giants by 2009. He was the 2012 National League MVP, had already been a multiple time all-star and helped the Giants win three World Series titles. Entering the 2016 season, Posey was a career .310 hitter with 102 homers and 446 RBIs.

### CONTROVERSY OVER ALVAREZ SIGNING

Starting with the record bonuses received by Beckham and Posey, four of the six largest bonuses in draft history were paid in 2008. Alvarez, selected second by the Pirates, and Hosmer, who went third to the Royals, each signed for $6 million. All four players signed for bonuses significantly over slot.

From the Pittsburgh perspective, the irony was that new Pirates club president Frank Coonelly had previously worked in the commissioner's office and was the person responsible for encouraging clubs to toe the line on MLB's de facto slotting system that was instituted earlier in the decade to curb signing bonuses. Most teams had abided by Coonelly's recommendations in recent years, and the first-round average for bonuses steadily declined.

BILL MITCHELL

Pedro Alvarez

But a number of clubs paid little heed to baseball's unenforceable slotting system—different from slotting systems in place in the NFL and NBA, which were collectively bargained—and in 2007 the first-round bonus average climbed significantly to its third-highest figure ever. As more teams realized they were at a competitive disadvantage by following the rules, more teams started spending whatever they deemed appropriate.

The recommended slot for Alvarez was $3.5 million, but it was apparent that he would exceed that figure by a wide margin, especially because his agent was Scott Boras, who had negotiated most of the biggest contracts in recent draft history. As the signing deadline neared, one of the intriguing storylines was how Coonelly might handle negotiations with Boras. Ten first-round picks had yet to sign as the final day dawned, and many of the top picks, including Hosmer and Posey, went down to

### AT A GLANCE

$6.2 million. He hit .333 with 25 home runs and 118 RBIs in 172 minor league games before launching an exceptional major league career.

### Ones Who Got Away

**AARON CROW, RHP, NATIONALS (1ST ROUND); TANNER SCHEPPERS, RHP, PIRATES (2ND ROUND).** **GERRIT COLE**, an unsigned 2008 first-round pick of the Yankees who became the No. 1 pick in 2011, eventually gained more notoriety than Crow (Missouri) and Scheppers (Fresno State), who both elected to forgo returning to college in favor of pitching for independent league teams. Crow was drafted in the first round in 2009, and Scheppers was a supplemental first-rounder.

### He Was Drafted?

**ERIC DECKER, OF, BREWERS (39TH ROUND).** Decker was a baseball and football standout at the University of Minnesota. He was drafted twice in baseball as a speedy outfielder with offensive upside, but chose football after being selected in the third round of the 2010 NFL draft by the Denver Broncos. Decker became one of the NFL's top wide receivers.

### Did You Know . . .

The first round of the 2008 draft was the most successful ever on two counts: most consecutive picks who reached the big leagues (21), and most picks overall who reached the majors (27 of 30).

### They Said It

Nationals general manager **JIM BOWDEN**, after his club failed to sign **AARON CROW**: "The system doesn't work. To sit there and have the negotiations between 11:30 and 12, where you're talking about huge movements with lots of players . . . and deals got done at 11:59 with literally no conversations for long periods of time . . . I'm not sure that's the best way to do business for a sport."

## DRAFT SPOTLIGHT: BUSTER POSEY

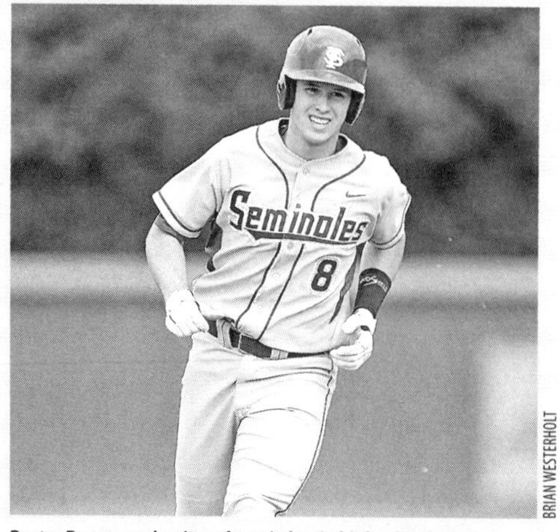

BRIAN WESTERHOLT

Buster Posey, predominantly a pitcher in high school, made a successful transition from shortstop to catcher in college

Buster Posey was a star pitcher in high school, and a Freshman All-America shortstop at Florida State. With his ability to excel at either position, his blossoming baseball career appeared to be nicely carved out for him.

But after fall practice during his sophomore year, when Posey played most of the time at third base, the Florida State coaching staff approached him with still another option. They wanted to convert him into a catcher, the only position he had never played. Posey quickly embraced the position change.

"He didn't go, 'You've got to be kidding me, I'm a freshman All-American as a shortstop, and you want me to catch?' It was none of that," Seminoles coach Mike Martin said. "It was, 'What can I do to help the team get better?' "

Martin, who was completing his third decade in coaching at the time, was reluctant to make the change. He did it at the urging of his son, Mike Martin Jr., a Florida State assistant who once made the transition himself in junior college and became a standout catcher for the Seminoles. Like an astute scout, Martin Jr. saw not what Posey was but what he had the potential to become. "I said to him, look, you've got the arm strength, the bat, the hands, the leadership skills," he said. "You don't run, which will hold you down (as a pro prospect) if you're a third baseman.' "

Posey took to catching like a duck to water, quickly showing the subtle actions and advanced skills that catchers often take years to cultivate. "The first two days, I had to teach him to put his gear on," Martin Jr. said. "A week later, it was, 'OK, this is going to work.' And three weeks later, it was, 'Holy cow, this guy's going to be really good.' "

By his junior year, Posey was the best defensive catcher in the college ranks, and the best all-around player. He was a polished hitter with a clean swing path and excellent strike-zone awareness. After hitting .382 with three home runs and 65 RBIs as a sophomore, he had a breakout junior season, leading the NCAA Division I ranks in hitting (.463), on-base percentage (.566), slugging (.879), hits (119), total bases (226) and RBIs (93). With 26 homers, he fell just two short of a national triple crown.

Posey not only excelled at the plate and behind it, but he also was Florida State's primary closer, posting six saves and a 1.17 ERA. He ditched his catching gear and closed out games with his 93-94 mph fastball, along with excellent command of a slider and changeup. In one game, he played all nine defensive positions and hit a grand slam.

While acknowledging Posey's superior ability, the elder Martin was equally impressed with his makeup and leadership skills. "The most remarkable thing about Buster's year was his desire to have the ball in his hand in the last-inning of a one-run game," Martin said. "You'll see guys back off in that situation when they haven't pitched in three weeks, but Buster would look you in the eye and say, 'I'm ready.' He was one of a kind."

The Tampa Bay Rays had the No. 1 pick in the 2008 draft and narrowed the choice to Georgia high school shortstop Tim Beckham and Posey, who also had been a high school shortstop in Georgia before heading off to Florida State. They chose Beckham.

John Barr scouted Posey frequently in his role as East Coast scouting coordinator for the Los Angeles Dodgers, and it surprised Posey when Barr told him the Dodgers would not draft him. "We're picking too low," Barr said, noting they had the 15th overall pick.

Early in 2008, Barr became scouting director for the San Francisco Giants, who had the fifth pick. "If he was there when we picked, we were going to take him," Barr said.

Posey did fall to the Giants. He received a $6.2 million bonus, the largest ever paid to a draft pick signing with the team that drafted him. Posey justified the investment many times over in a sterling career for the Giants and became the face of the franchise. In 2013, the Giants extended Posey an eight-year contract extension worth $167 million, a record in sum and length for a player with his level of experience.

By then, Posey had a Rookie of the Year award, National League MVP and batting title on his resume, along with two World Series titles (and a third yet to come). Few other players in major league history had achieved as much at a comparable age.

the last minute. Alvarez also was among the last players who agreed to terms.

More than a week later, however, Alvarez had not signed his deal, nor had he gone to Pittsburgh for a physical examination and an introductory news conference. On Aug. 27, the Pirates acknowledged they had requested that Alvarez be placed on baseball's restricted list, in response to an action taken by Boras to have Alvarez's contract nullified. The agent contended that the contract was filed after the midnight Aug. 15 deadline.

"The Pirates are confident that the contract reached with Pedro Alvarez was agreed to and submitted to Major League Baseball in a timely fashion and properly accepted by Major League Baseball," Coonelly said in a statement that was highly critical of Boras. "In fact, the contract between the Kansas City Royals and Eric Hosmer, another Boras client, was submitted to the office of the commissioner after our contract with Pedro was submitted. Mr. Boras has been informed that if he pursues a claim that our contract with Pedro was not timely, he puts Eric Hosmer's contract with Kansas City in jeopardy.

"Regrettably, we are not surprised that Mr. Boras would attempt to raise a meritless legal claim in an effort to compel us to renegotiate Pedro's contract to one more to his liking. We are, however, disappointed that Pedro would allow his agent to pursue this claim on his behalf. Pedro showed tremendous fortitude and independent thinking when he agreed to his contract on Aug. 15."

The Players Association filed a grievance against the Pirates and argued that Major League Baseball was complicit in extending the deadline. Union general counsel Michael Weiner said in a statement, "The Players Association learned from several sources that the commissioner's office had extended the deadline for negotiating and reporting signings with drafted players."

The grievance extended to Hosmer, who had played three games in the Royals system by that time. He was benched, pending a ruling.

It soon became clear that Boras had ample evidence that Alvarez's contract indeed was agreed to after the midnight deadline, even if it was just by two minutes. Once the grievance was resolved on Sept. 24, MLB pressured the Pirates into reopening negotiations with Alvarez and Boras. A day later, Alvarez signed a revised deal that included a four-year, major league contract with the same $6 million bonus. But the contract now was worth $6.355 million overall, with guaranteed minor league salaries accounting for the difference.

Coonelly subsequently acknowledged that the

### Fastest To The Majors

| | Player, Pos. | Drafted (Round) | Debut |
|---|---|---|---|
| 1. | Conor Gillaspie, 3b | Giants (1-S) | Sept. 9, 2008 |
| 2. | Ryan Perry, rhp | Tigers (1) | April 8, 2009 |
| 3. | Daniel Schlereth, lhp | Diamondbacks (1) | May 29, 2009 |
| 4. | Gordon Beckham, ss | White Sox (1) | June 4, 2009 |
| 5. | Brian Matusz, lhp | Orioles (1) | Aug. 4, 2009 |

**FIRST HIGH SCHOOL SELECTION:** Tyler Chatwood, rhp (Angels/2, April 11, 2011)

## Top 25 Bonuses

| | Player, Pos. | Drafted (Round) | Order | Bonus |
|---|---|---|---|---|
| 1. | **Buster Posey, c** | Giants (1) | 5 | $6,200,000 |
| 2. | ***Tim Beckham, ss** | Rays (1) | 1 | $6,150,000 |
| 3. | **Pedro Alvarez, 3b** | Pirates (1) | 2 | #$6,000,000 |
| | ***Eric Hosmer, 1b** | Royals (1) | 3 | $6,000,000 |
| 5. | **Justin Smoak, 1b** | Rangers (1) | 11 | $3,500,000 |
| 6. | **Brian Matusz, lhp** | Orioles (1) | 4 | #$3,200,000 |
| 7. | ***Casey Kelly, ss/rhp** | Red Sox (1) | 30 | $3,000,000 |
| 8. | **Gordon Beckham, ss** | White Sox (1) | 8 | $2,600,000 |
| 9. | ***Kyle Skipworth, c** | Marlins (1) | 6 | $2,300,000 |
| 10. | **Jason Castro, c** | Astros (1) | 10 | $2,070,000 |
| 11. | **Yonder Alonso, 1b** | Reds (1) | 7 | #$2,000,000 |
| | *Ryan Westmoreland, of | Red Sox (5) | 172 | $2,000,000 |
| 13. | **Jemile Weeks, 2b** | Athletics (1) | 12 | $1,910,000 |
| 14. | **Brett Wallace, 3b** | Cardinals (1) | 13 | $1,840,000 |
| 15. | ***Aaron Hicks, of/rhp** | Twins (1) | 14 | $1,780,000 |
| 16. | ***Ethan Martin, rhp/3b** | Dodgers (1) | 15 | $1,730,000 |
| 17. | ***Brett Lawrie, 3b** | Brewers (1) | 16 | $1,700,000 |
| 18. | **Ike Davis, 1b** | Mets (1) | 18 | $1,575,000 |
| | ***Robbie Ross, lhp** | Rangers (2) | 57 | $1,575,000 |
| 20. | **Andrew Cashner, rhp** | Cubs (1) | 19 | $1,540,000 |
| 21. | **David Cooper, 1b** | Blue Jays (1) | 17 | $1,500,000 |
| | ***Kyle Lobstein, lhp** | Rays (2) | 47 | $1,500,000 |
| 23. | **Ryan Perry, rhp** | Tigers (1) | 21 | $1,480,000 |
| 24. | Reese Havens, ss | Mets (1) | 22 | $1,419,000 |
| 25. | *Anthony Hewitt, ss | Phillies (1) | 24 | $1,380,000 |

*Major leaguers in bold. *High school selection. #Major league contract.*

original deal wasn't consummated until 12:02 a.m. on Aug. 16, but he was adamant that he had no prearranged deal for an extension with MLB. Boras did not challenge the validity of Hosmer's contract.

The grievance did not paint Alvarez in a positive light with Pirates fans, but he tried to make amends after the signing was announced.

"I just hope they judge me by what I do as a professional player because I'm going to work as hard as I possibly can to be the best player for the Pittsburgh Pirates and the fans of Pittsburgh," Alvarez said. "More than just being a good player, I want to be a leader, on the field and in the community once I get there."

The 6-foot-2, 225-pound Alvarez was regarded as the best power hitter in a hitter-rich draft, even as his junior year at Vanderbilt paled in comparison with his first two seasons. After hitting .359 with 40 homers as a freshman and sophomore, he hit .317 with nine homers as a junior, although his season was significantly compromised when he suffered a broken hamate bone in his right hand in his team's first game.

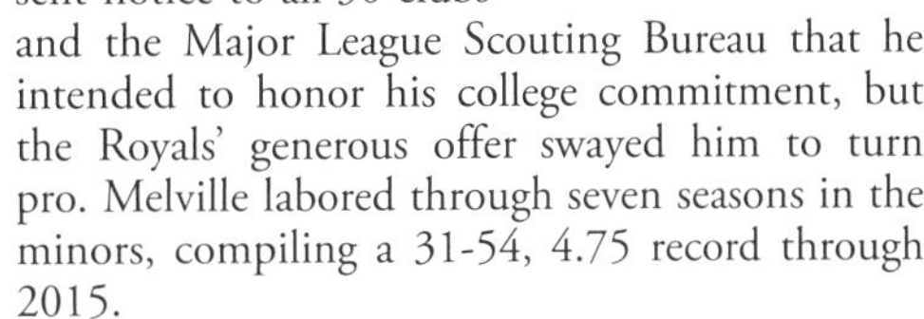

With Alvarez's lefthanded power, the Pirates had expectations that he would become a consistent 40-home run threat. But he peaked at 36 homers in 2013 in a six-year career with the Pirates that fell short of expectations. While Alvarez did hit 130 home runs, his power came at the expense of shortcomings in other phases of his game. He hit just .236 overall, with 808 strikeouts in 741 games through the 2015 season, his last with the Pirates.

Hosmer largely fulfilled his potential as the third pick in the draft. After a distinguished career as both a pitcher and first baseman at American Heritage School in Plantation, Fla., Hosmer transitioned seamlessly into pro ball. He was with the Royals by 2011, playing a key role in the team's resurgence that culminated in World Series appearances in 2014 and 2015. Hosmer hit .280 with 77 homers in his first five major league seasons through 2015.

### SEVERAL CLUBS SPEND BIG MONEY

Once the financial figures were in on the 2008 draft, teams realized they had spent money on signing bonuses like never before. In addition to the record amounts spent overall, by one team and first-round average, standards were set for average bonuses in the second, fourth, fifth, seventh, eighth and 10th rounds. A total of 43 bonuses of $1 million or more were paid, including still-standing individual records for the fifth round, by outfielder Ryan Westmoreland, who received $2 million from the Boston Red Sox; the seventh round, by righthander Brett Hunter (Athletics, $1.1 million); and the 15th round, by outfielder J.P. Martinez (Nationals, $1 million). In all, eight individual round records were set.

Besides the Royals, who set the pace by spending $11.148 million in bonuses to sign their picks, the Red Sox ($10.515 million), Devil Rays ($9.921 million) and Pirates ($9.7805 million) also eclipsed the previous record. Twenty clubs spent more than $5 million on bonuses.

In addition to signing Hosmer for $6 million, the Royals took a fourth-round gamble on supposedly unsignable Missouri righthander Tim Melville, who was among the nation's elite high school pitching prospects. The Royals signed the North Carolina recruit at the deadline for $1.25 million.

MIKE JANES

Casey Kelly

Melville's family had sent notice to all 30 clubs and the Major League Scouting Bureau that he intended to honor his college commitment, but the Royals' generous offer swayed him to turn pro. Melville labored through seven seasons in the minors, compiling a 31-54, 4.75 record through 2015.

The North Carolina baseball team lost another recruit when the Pirates drafted New Jersey high school righthander Quentin Miller in the 20th round and signed him for $900,000. He fell short of reaching the majors.

Despite having the 30th and last pick in the draft rotation, the reigning World Series champion Red Sox made a statement with some of their selections. In the first round, they went for Casey Kelly, a two-sport and two-way talent from Sarasota (Fla.) High. The Sox bought him away from a college football scholarship as a quarterback at Tennessee with a club-record bonus of $3 million, which they were able to pay over five years because of his dual-sport status.

The Red Sox drafted Kelly as a pitcher, but he wanted to play every day. The sides agreed that he could play his first season in the minors as a shortstop before gradually transitioning into a

### WORTH NOTING

■ The Cardinals tied a draft record, set by the Blue Jays in 2000, by signing their first 30 picks. The record was set nine months after the draft, when the Cards signed their 13th-rounder, Naval Academy righthander **MITCH HARRIS**, on March 2, 2009. Harris was committed to serving five years of active duty in the Navy before pursuing a professional baseball career. He had petitioned the Navy to alter his military obligation, but the request was denied. As a result, Harris didn't appear in a minor league game for the Cardinals for four years. He got to the major leagues in 2015.

■ American Heritage High of Plantation, Fla., went 31-2, won the Florida 3-A state title and finished the season as the nation's No. 1-ranked high school team. The Patriots had four players drafted, more than any other high school, including first baseman **ERIC HOSMER**, the No. 3 pick overall, who hit .470 with 11 homers, and was the team's closer. Hosmer had three hits and struck out the side in the final inning in Heritage's win in the state final.

■ Giants third baseman **CONOR GILLASPIE**, a supplemental first-round pick out of Wichita State, became the first member of the 2008 draft class to reach the majors, debuting on Sept. 9, little more than a month after signing for $970,000. He hit .419 with 11 homers and 82 RBIs as a college junior for the Shockers. Gillaspie's promotion to the Giants was a condition of his contract. He hit .272 in 92 at-bats in short-season Class A and Rookie ball before going to the major leagues, where he had one hit and two walks in seven plate appearances in 2008.

■ The Major League Scouting Bureau gave the highest predraft grades to two closers whose fastballs were clocked at 100 mph: Arizona's **RYAN PERRY**

CONTINUED ON PAGE 646

**WORTH NOTING**

CONTINUED FROM PAGE 645

and Pepperdine's **BRETT HUNTER**. Both had scores of 63, on the 20-80 scouting scale, and were among 14 players with grades of 60 or higher. Perry was a first-round pick of the Tigers, and Hunter was drafted in the seventh round by the A's. Hunter's stock fell after he injured his elbow in his second game of the college season. He was back to good health while pitching for USA Baseball's college national team during the summer, and the A's signed him for a $1.1 million bonus. Hunter was the only 2008 draft pick on the national team, which went 24-0 for the season and beat Japan, 1-0, in 12 innings in the gold medal game of the World University Championship.

■ With the emphasis on college talent in the 2008 draft, just two high school pitchers were taken in the first round, tying a record-low set in 1984 and equaled in 1988. The Dodgers were the first team to draft a prep pitcher, taking righthander **ETHAN MARTIN** with the 15th pick. He was primarily a third baseman until his senior year at Stephens County High in Georgia, and some clubs liked him best as a hitter. Martin hit .539 with 18 homers as a senior, and went 10-2, 1.52 with 162 strikeouts in 89 innings. He went just 2-9, 5.93 in 17 appearances over two seasons in the majors. The other high school pitcher drafted in the first round was righthander **GERRIT COLE**, picked 28th by the Yankees. He didn't sign, pitched three years at UCLA, and was the No. 1 pick in the 2011 draft.

■ Beginning in 2008, the Major League Scouting Bureau took on a new responsibility, drug testing the top 200 prospects prior to the draft, per an agreement between Major League Baseball and the Players Association. Players who tested positive did not face discipline because they were not under contract, but MLB notified every club of the

pitcher. Kelly hit .219 with two homers over parts of two minor league seasons, then continued on as a pitcher only. He got to the major leagues with the Padres in 2012, missed the following season after Tommy John surgery, and never won a game from 2013-15.

Boston also struck seven-figure deals with two high school outfielders: fourth-rounder Peter Hissey, from Unionville (Pa.) High, for $1 million; and Westmoreland, a fifth-round pick from Portsmouth (R.I.) High, for $2 million.

Hissey spent seven seasons in the Red Sox organization, peaking in Triple-A. Westmoreland's promising career was derailed in 2010, when doctors discovered a cavernous malformation in his brain, a potential life-threatening situation. By the time Westmoreland had the first of two brain surgeries in March 2010, his situation had become so dire that he was unable to walk, see or hear. The surgery and rehab disabled him for the better part of two years. Westmoreland was in the process of returning to baseball and making a comeback when he needed a second surgery in 2012, forcing him to retire.

Teams also spent big on the international market. The Oakland A's gave a record $4.25 million bonus to 16-year-old Dominican Republic righthander Michael Ynoa, and four other players from the same country received bonuses of $2 million or more.

Major League Baseball a year earlier had set the stage for much of what happened by miscalculating the effect that two draft rule changes—the Aug. 15 signing deadline and increased compensation for unsigned picks in the first three rounds—would have in giving clubs added leverage in negotiations with players and agents. And MLB compounded the issue with its recommendation in 2007 to slash bonus payments by 10 percent across the board. Those moves backfired, leading to an 8.5 percent hike in bonuses in the first round and a significant increase in the number of holdouts.

Eric Hosmer got a $6 million bonus from the Royals and was part of the organization's resurgence, becoming a cornerstone at first base

JESSE SOLL

## Largest Bonuses By Round

| | Player, Pos. | Club | Bonus |
|---|---|---|---|
| **1.** | **Buster Posey, c** | **Giants** | **$6,200,000** |
| 1-S. | Shooter Hunt, rhp | Twins | $1,080,000 |
| **2.** | ***Robbie Ross, lhp** | **Rangers** | **$1,575,000** |
| 3. | *Ross Seaton, rhp | Astros | $700,000 |
| 4. | *Tim Melville, rhp | Royals | $1,250,000 |
| 5. | *Ryan Westmoreland, of | Red Sox | $2,000,000 |
| **6.** | ***Robbie Grossman, of** | **Pirates** | **$1,000,000** |
| 7. | Brett Hunter, rhp | Athletics | $1,100,000 |
| 8. | *Bobby Bundy, rhp | Orioles | $600,000 |
| 9. | Steven Caseres, 1b | Dodgers | $250,000 |
| 10. | *Rashun Dixon, c | Athletics | $600,000 |
| 11. | *Rolando Gomez, ss | Angels | $450,000 |
| **12.** | **Matt Clark, 1b** | **Padres** | **$150,000** |
| 13. | *Tyler Wilson, rhp | Red Sox | $300,000 |
| 14. | *Tyler Massey, 1b | Rockies | $525,000 |
| 15. | *J.P. Ramirez, of | Nationals | $1,000,000 |
| **16.** | ***T.J. House, lhp** | **Indians** | **$750,000** |
| 17. | *Jake Kuebler, rhp | Royals | $150,000 |
| 18. | *Bobby Hansen, lhp | Nationals | $142,500 |
| 19. | *Blake Billings, rhp | Brewers | $200,000 |
| 20. | *Quinton Miller, rhp | Pirates | $900,000 |
| **21.** | ***Logan Watkins, ss** | **Cubs** | **$500,000** |
| 22. | Bryce Stowell, rhp | Indians | $725,000 |
| **23.** | ***Brandon Maurer, rhp** | **Mariners** | **$150,000** |
| 24. | *Kyle Allen, rhp | Mets | $150,000 |
| 25. | Erik Turgeon, rhp | Mets | $25,000 |
| Other* | Garrison Lassiter, ss | Yankees (27) | $675,000 |
| | **Dusty Coleman, ss** | **Athletics (28)** | **$675,000** |

*Major leaguers in bold. *High school selection.*

Clubs that adhered to the slotting system were losing out on talent to teams that were ignoring the recommendations of the commissioner's office. MLB's response was to relax the enforcement of the slotting system in 2008. The commissioner's office effectively told clubs in a predraft memo to select players based on ability, not signability.

Ten teams didn't abide by slot-money recommendations in the first round, including the first five. Teams collectively paid out first-round bonuses that were some $300,000 higher than in 2007. That figure didn't take into account the full value of major league contracts signed by three first-rounders. In addition to Alvarez, Matusz (fourth overall) earned a $3.4725 million package from the Baltimore Orioles, including a $3.2 million bonus, and first baseman Yonder Alonso (seventh overall) received a $4.55 million deal from the Cincinnati Reds, including a $2 million bonus.

### PREMIUM PICKS GO UNSIGNED

Two first-round picks went unsigned for the first time since 2001. The Washington Nationals and New York Yankees, big spenders in 2007, were unable to work out deals with University of Missouri righthander Aaron Crow (ninth overall) and California high school righthander Gerrit Cole (28th), respectively.

Crow attempted to leverage his position by

joining the independent Fort Worth Cats just prior to the signing deadline, which made him ineligible to return to college for his senior year. Crow, advised by Randy and Alan Hendricks, wanted a deal in the $9 million range, and the Nationals offered $2.1 million.

The disparity in the two positions was one thing, but the contract Matusz received from the Orioles as the No. 4 pick was another. Matusz, who led Division I pitchers with 141 strikeouts as a junior, generally was regarded as the top pitcher in the class, followed by Crow. When Matusz signed his $3,472,500 bonus just hours before deadline, the Nationals made what general manager Jim Bowden termed a "take-it-or-leave-it" offer to Crow of $3 million. Over the final hour of negotiations, the Nats went to $3.5 million, and Crow's camp countered at $4 million. The last-minute compromises weren't enough to bridge the gap, and Crow went unsigned.

"The system doesn't work," Bowden said. "To sit there and have the negotiations that took place with several clubs between 11:30 and 12, where you're talking about huge movements with lots of players . . . and deals got done at 11:59 with literally, I understand, no conversations for long periods of time . . . I'm not sure that's the best way to do business for a sport."

After failing to sign Crow, the Nationals used $1 million of the money allocated to sign him to bring in Ramirez, their 15th-round pick. Crow spent the 2008 season with Fort Worth and returned to the team the following spring in advance of the 2009 draft. He was drafted by the Royals with the 11th pick overall and signed for $1.5 million.

Cole, considered the hardest thrower in the high school ranks, had given the Yankees indications he was amenable to signing. But he seemed to have a change of heart before negotiations began in earnest, warming to the idea of attending college. Cole enrolled at UCLA, and three years later, as the first overall pick in the 2011 draft, set the all-time bonus record for a player signing with the team that drafted him by agreeing with the Pirates on $8 million.

Along with Cole, the Yankees failed to sign second-rounder Scott Bittle, who had led the NCAA ranks in strikeouts per nine innings (16.55) and was second in fewest hits per nine innings (4.46) as a dominant reliever at the University of Mississippi. The Yankees determined in a post-draft physical that Bittle had a damaged shoulder.

Despite not signing their first- and second-round picks, the Yankees spent $5.122 million on bonuses. They went significantly over slot to sign four later-round picks, including sixth-rounder Brett Marshall for $850,000 and 27th-rounder Garrison Lassiter for $675,000.

The Seattle Mariners had not signed their first-round selection, University of Georgia righthander Josh Fields (20th overall) by Aug. 15, but as a college senior he was not bound by the deadline. A Boras client, Fields signed on Feb. 9, 2009, for a $1.75 million bonus, an amount that not only was $250,000 above slot, but significant for a player with little bargaining leverage.

After Crow and Cole, Fresno State righthander Tanner Scheppers was the third-highest pick from the 2008 draft to go unsigned. Prior to suffering a shoulder injury late in the college season, Scheppers had pitched himself into the upper half of the first round with a fastball that peaked at 99 mph. He slipped to the Pirates in the second round when it was revealed he had a slight tear in his rotator cuff and a frayed labrum. Scheppers, who wasn't at full health by the signing deadline, sought a $1.2 million bonus, and the Pirates countered at $800,000.

BILL MITCHELL
Tanner Scheppers

Scheppers was ineligible academically to return to Fresno State. A year later, he was a supplemental first-round pick of the Rangers after pitching for independent St. Paul.

Fourteen first-rounders signed for slot money, and three others accepted below-slot offers. The Tigers, Toronto Blue Jays, St. Louis Cardinals and New York Mets adhered to the bonus slots provided by the commissioner's office.

The Blue Jays targeted hard-hitting Canadian catcher Brett Lawrie with the 17th pick, and were disappointed when the Milwaukee Brewers selected him with the 16th pick. The Jays instead drafted University of California first baseman David Cooper and signed him for $1.5 million, $130,000 less than the amount allocated for the slot. Little more than a year later, the Blue Jays acquired Lawrie in a trade with the Brewers.

The Padres selected Wake Forest first baseman Allan Dykstra with the 23rd overall pick, only to learn after the fact that he had avascular necrosis in

## One Team's Draft: San Francisco Giants

| | Player, Pos. | Bonus |
|---|---|---|
| 1. | **Buster Posey, c** | **$6,200,000** |
| 1. | **Conor Gillaspie, 3b** | **$970,000** |
| 2. | Selection to Phillies | |
| 3. | **Roger Kieschnick, of** | **$525,000** |
| 4. | **Brandon Crawford, ss** | **$375,000** |
| 5. | Edwin Quirate, rhp | $193,000 |
| 6. | **Eric Surkamp, lhp** | **$135,000** |
| 7. | Aaron King, lhp | $110,000 |
| 8. | **Scott Barnes, lhp** | **$100,000** |
| 9. | **Ryan Verdugo, lhp** | **$95,000** |
| 10. | *Ryan O'Sullivan, rhp | Did not sign |
| 11. | Justin Fitzgerald, rhp | $75,000 |
| 12. | Ari Ronick, lhp | $2,500 |
| 13. | **Juan Carlos Perez, of** | **$50,000** |
| 14. | Caleb Curry, of | $2,500 |
| 15. | Daniel Cook, 3b | $2,500 |
| 16. | C.J. Ziegler, 1b | $2,500 |
| 17. | Brian Irving, rhp | $2,500 |
| 18. | Brooks Lindsley, ss | $24,000 |
| 19. | Ryan Mantle, of | $24,000 |
| 20. | Trey Sutton, 2b | Did not sign |
| 21. | Mike Eifel, rhp | $2,500 |
| 22. | *Carter Bell, ss | Did not sign |
| 23. | Jason Jarvis, rhp | $100,000 |
| 24. | Wes Musick, lhp | Did not sign |
| 25. | Damon Wright, of | $2,500 |

*Major leaguers in bold. *High school selection.*

## WORTH NOTING

results. Players who refused the test were not eligible to be drafted.

■ The 2008 draft was a testament to college players. A record 1,068 collegians were drafted, topping the mark of 971 set a year earlier. That group included 21 in the first round, tying a record set in 1992. Longtime college powers Arizona State and Miami were big contributors. The Sun Devils had 15 players drafted, the most ever from one school, and Miami equaled the record for first-rounders with three. Not only did Arizona State's roster play a significant role in the draft, but so did a vintage crop of Sun Devils recruits. Five high school players with commitments to Arizona State were among the top 52 draft picks, including first-rounders **ERIC HOSMER**, **BRETT LAWRIE** and **KYLE SKIPWORTH**. Miami's first-rounders were **YONDER ALONSO**, **JEMILE WEEKS** and **CARLOS GUTIERREZ**. The only other schools in draft history to have three players drafted in the first round were Michigan in 1979, Fresno State in 1989, Rice in 2004 and Vanderbilt in 2015. Arizona State (49-13) finished atop the Pacific-10 Conference standings, but was stunned in NCAA super-regional play by upstart Fresno State, which then won its first College World Series championship. The Bulldogs did it without **TANNER SCHEPPERS** (8-2, 2.93), the team's best prospect, who was on the sideline throughout postseason play because of a sore shoulder. Fresno State (47-31) lost 12 of its first 20 games and ranked 89th nationally, according to the NCAA's RPI index. But the team rallied behind the pitching of **JUSTIN WILSON** (8-5, 4.34) and one of the greatest power displays in CWS history, beating Georgia in the best-of-three final, two games to one. Scheppers and Wilson (Pirates, fifth round) were the only Fresno State players drafted in the top 10 rounds.

**IN FOCUS: TIM BECKHAM**

DAVID STONER

Shortstop Tim Beckham, the No. 1 overall pick in the 2008 draft, stood out at Griffin (Ga.) High for his smooth tools, power potential and middle-of-the-diamond presence.

"You look at this ballplayer, and all of a sudden there's about five players that come to mind," Rays scouting director R.J. Harrison said. "It was kind of a combination of the Uptons (B.J. and Justin), Gary Sheffield, Orlando Hudson and Brandon Phillips. There are two things that separate this kid, why I think he has a chance to play shortstop. I think he has the physical ability to do it, and I think he has the personality."

Beckham signed quickly and joined his brother, Jeremy, a second baseman from Georgia Southern who had been drafted in the 17th round by the Rays, in the Rookie-level Appalachian League. The younger Beckham earned a promotion to the New York-Penn League before the season was over.

The 6-foot, 190-pound Beckham bogged down after that. He served a 50-game suspension for twice failing drug tests, and languished in Triple-A. It wasn't until his eighth season that he saw any meaningful time in the major leagues, and that was as a reserve middle infielder. In 87 games over parts of the 2014 and '15 seasons, he hit .229 with nine homers.

a hip, a condition that causes bone tissue deterioration. Dykstra had been cleared to play by doctors, but the Padres were concerned about his long-term health. The sides agreed to a bonus of $1.15 million, $250,000 under the slot value.

The Padres had a noteworthy draft, selecting 16 players who eventually played in the majors, including fourth-rounder Jason Kipnis, whom they failed to sign. That was one short of the record—the Mets' class of 1982 included 17 future major leaguers, and the Yankees' class of 1990 had 16.

With the 29th pick, the Indians took Pitt (N.C.) Community College third baseman Lonnie Chisenhall because he agreed to a predraft deal for $1.1 million, $130,000 under slot. That was $150,000 less than they paid their second-round pick, Texas prep righthander Trey Haley.

Lonnie Chisenhall

Chisenhall was a highly regarded freshman at the University of South Carolina in 2007 when he was arrested and charged with burglary and larceny for stealing items belonging to an assistant coach. He was dismissed from the baseball team, pleaded guilty to the charges, and received six months of probation. Chisenhall regrouped the following year in junior college, hitting .408 and pushing himself into the first round.

## FIRST BASEMEN IN FIRST ROUND

There was a run on first basemen in the first round of historic proportions. Six were selected among the first 23 picks, and a case could be made that it was eight, considering that Arizona State third baseman Brett Wallace (Cardinals, 13th overall) spent his first two years with the Sun Devils at first base and almost his entire pro career at the position; and Alvarez, the second pick overall, fell out of favor as a third baseman early in his major league career and became a first baseman. Wallace moved to third as a junior at Arizona State to accommodate teammate Ike Davis, who was selected by the Mets with the 18th pick.

Hosmer was the only high school player among the first-round first basemen. He was the third overall pick, followed by Alonso (Reds, seventh), Justin Smoak (Rangers, 11th), Cooper (Blue Jays, 17th), Davis (Mets) and Dykstra (Padres, 23rd).

A year earlier, the college first-base crop was so thin that just two were taken in the first five rounds. One, Matt LaPorta, moved to the outfield in pro ball; the other, Sean Doolittle, was a two-way player that most clubs liked best as a pitcher.

None of the college first basemen had been drafted in the top 15 rounds in 2005 out of high school. But their talent was apparent as soon as they started playing in college. Alonso was an immediate hit at the University of Miami, leading the Hurricanes in home runs and RBIs as a freshman, only the second freshman in school history to achieve that feat, along with Ryan Braun. Smoak hit 17 homers as a freshman at the University of South Carolina and led the Cape Cod League in homers that summer.

### Highest Unsigned Picks

| Player, Pos., Team (Round) | College | Re-Drafted |
|---|---|---|
| Aaron Crow, rhp, Nationals (1) | None | Royals '09 (1) |
| Gerrit Cole, rhp, Yankees (1) | UCLA | Pirates '11 (1) |
| Tanner Scheppers, rhp, Pirates (2) | None | Rangers '09 (1) |
| Scott Bittle, rhp, Yankees (2) | * Mississippi | Cardinals '09 (4) |
| Chase Davidson, 1b, Astros (3) | Georgia | Astros '11 (41) |
| Zach Cone, of, Angels (3) | Georgia | Rangers '11 (1) |
| Jason Kipnis, of, Padres (4) | * Arizona State | Indians '09 (2) |
| Chris Dominguez, 3b, Rockies (5) | * Louisville | Giants '09 (3) |
| Khiry Cooper, of, Angels (5) | Nebraska | Red Sox '12 (25) |
| Jason Esposito, 3b, Royals (7) | Vanderbilt | Orioles '11 (2) |

**TOTAL UNSIGNED PICKS:** Top 5 Rounds (9), Top 10 Rounds (22)

**Returned to same school.*

Four of the nation's top 10 home run hitters in 2008 were first basemen, including Louisiana State's Matt Clark with 25 and Michigan's Nate Recknagel with 23. Clark was drafted in the 12th round by the Padres. Recknagel was a 19th-round pick of the Cleveland Indians, even though his season ended early because of an elbow injury. All of the college first basemen selected in the first round hit at least 16 homers in their junior season, led by Alonzo and Smoak with 23 each, Wallace with 22, and Cooper with 19.

The 2008 draft pool also included a strong group of college closers, or more appropriately, hard-throwing college pitchers who profiled as relievers in pro ball. Among them were Fields; Texas Christian righthander Andrew Cashner (Cubs, 19th overall); Miami righthander Carlos Gutierrez (Twins, 27th); and the Arizona tandem of righthander Ryan Perry (Tigers, 21st) and lefthander Daniel Schlereth (Diamondbacks, 26th). Cashner and Perry threw fastballs that peaked at 100 mph. Fields was clocked at 99, and Schlereth at 97.

Fields, a second-rounder as a junior in 2007, tied for the NCAA lead in saves with 18 as a senior, and struck out 63 in 37 innings. Cashner went 9-4, 2.32 with nine saves and 80 strikeouts in 54 innings. Gutierrez posted 13 saves. Perry and Schlereth both pitched in set-up roles for Arizona, while sophomore Jason Stoffel was entrusted with the closer's role. Perry went 6-1, 2.89 with 72 strikeouts in 75 innings. Schlereth went 2-0, 1.81 with 76 strikeouts in 55 innings.

Fields, Cashner, Perry and Schlereth all reached the major leagues, but did not distinguish themselves with a combined 13 saves (nine by Fields) through the 2015 season. The Cubs converted Cashner into a starter after he signed, and after six major league seasons, he had a 26-42, 3.59 record.

The best relief pitcher by far from the 2008 draft was righthander Craig Kimbrel, selected in the third round by the Braves out of an Alabama junior college. Kimbrel had 225 saves in his first six major league seasons though 2015.

# 2008 Draft List

**Did not sign. Major leaguers in bold, with first and last years noted. Order of selection indicated in parentheses. For the first five rounds, the peak level of each player is noted.*

## ARIZONA DIAMONDBACKS (26)

**1. Daniel Schlereth, lhp, University of Arizona.—(2009-12)**

DRAFT DROP *Son of Mark Schlereth, guard, National Football League (1989-2000)*

**1. Wade Miley, lhp, Southeastern Louisiana University** (Supplemental choice—43rd—as compensation for Type A free agent Livan Hernandez).**—(2011-15)**

**2. Bryan Shaw, rhp, Long Beach State University.—(2011-15)**

3. Kevin Eichhorn, rhp, Aptos (Calif.) HS.–(High A)

DRAFT DROP *Son of Mark Eichhorn, major leaguer (1982-96)*

4. Ryne White, 1b-of, Purdue University.–(High A)

**5. Collin Cowgill, of, University of Kentucky.—(2011-15)**

6. Justin Parker, ss, Wright State University.

DRAFT DROP *Brother of Jarrod Parker, first-round draft pick, Diamondbacks (2007); major leaguer (2011-13)*

7. Miles Reagan, rhp, El Capitan HS, Lakeside, Calif.

8. Pat McAnaney, lhp, University of Virginia.

9. Brett Moorhouse, rhp, Indian River (Fla.) JC.

10. *Danny Hultzen, lhp, St. Albans HS, Washington, D.C.

DRAFT DROP *First-round draft pick (2nd overall), Mariners (2011)*

11. Kyle Greene, 3b, Lewis-Clark State (Idaho) University.

**12. *Daniel Webb, rhp, Heath HS, Paducah, Ky.—(2013-15)**

13. Ollie Linton, of, UC Irvine.

14. Trevor Harden, rhp, New Mexico JC.

15. Bobby Stone, of, Montgomery (Texas) HS.

16. *Ryan Hughes, lhp, Chabot (Calif.) JC.

17. Ryan Babineau, c, UCLA.

18. *Sam Brown, rhp, North Carolina State University.

19. Joseph Gautier, lhp, Bethune-Cookman College.

20. Jordan Meaker, rhp, Dallas Baptist University.

21. Bryan Woodall, rhp, Auburn University.

22. *Justin La Tempa, rhp, Golden West (Calif.) JC.

23. *Matt Long, of, Santa Clara University.

24. Nelson Gomez, 3b, Keystone (Pa.) College.

**25. *Josh Spence, lhp, Central Arizona JC.—(2011-12)**

26. *Alex Sogard, lhp, North Carolina State University.

DRAFT DROP *Brother of Eric Sogard, major leaguer (2010-15)*

**27. Ryan Cook, rhp, University of Southern California.—(2011-15)**

28. *Adam Smith, ss-rhp, Klein (Texas) HS.

29. *Travis Meiners, ss, Des Moines Area (Iowa) CC.

30. Daniel Rodriguez, of, Miami-Dade CC.

31. *Taylor Cole, rhp, CC of Southern Nevada.

32. *Riccio Torrez, ss, Brophy Prep, Phoenix.

33. *Luke Murton, 1b, Georgia Tech.

DRAFT DROP *Brother of Matt Murton, major leaguer (2005-09)*

**34. Jake Elmore, 2b, Arizona State University.—(2012-15)**

35. Chris Davis, c, University of Central Arkansas.

36. T.J. Hose, rhp, East Carolina University.

37. *Sanders Commings, of, Westside HS, Augusta, Ga.

DRAFT DROP *Defensive back, National Football League (2013)*

38. Jesse Orosco Jr., rhp, Grossmont (Calif.) JC.

DRAFT DROP *Son of Jesse Orosco, major leaguer (1979-2003)*

39. *Josh Godfrey, lhp, Wabash Valley (Ill.) JC.

40. *Taylor Wall, lhp, Westside HS, Houston.

41. Brendan Duffy, of, Oral Roberts University.

42. *Erik Stavert, rhp, Chabot (Calif.) JC.

43. Clayton Suss, rhp, Miami-Dade CC.

44. David Cooper, ss, Mount Olive (N.C.) College.

45. *Jeremy Rathjen, of, Memorial HS, Houston.

46. Dan Kauffman, 1b, Juniata (Pa.) College.

47. *Andrew Maggi, ss, Brophy Prep, Phoenix.

48. *Cecil Richardson, of, Sacramento (Calif.) CC.

49. *Willie Argo, of, Assumption HS, Davenport, Iowa.

50. *Sean Koecheler, rhp, Palm Beach (Fla.) CC.

## ATLANTA BRAVES (18)

1. (Choice to Mets as compensation for Type A free agent Tom Glavine)

1. Brett DeVall, lhp, Niceville (Fla.) HS (Supplemental choice—40th—as compensation for Type B free agent Ron Mahay).—(Low A)

2. Tyler Stovall, lhp, Hokes Bluff (Ala.) HS.–(Low A)

**2. Zeke Spruill, rhp, Kell HS, Marietta, Ga.** (Special compensation—70th—for failure to sign 2007 second-round draft pick Josh Fields).**—(2013-14)**

**3. Craig Kimbrel, rhp, Wallace State-Hanceville (Ala.) CC.—(2010-15)**

4. Braeden Schlehuber, c, CC of Southern Nevada.—(AAA)

5. Jacob Thompson, rhp, University of Virginia.—(AAA)

6. Adam Milligan, of, Walters State (Tenn.) CC.

**7. Paul Clemens, rhp, Louisburg (N.C.) CC.—(2013-14)**

**8. Brett Oberholtzer, lhp, Seminole (Fla.) CC.—(2013-15)**

9. Kyle Farrell, rhp, CC of Western Nevada.

**10. J.J. Hoover, rhp, John C. Calhoun (Ala.) JC.—(2012-15)**

11. Richard Sullivan, lhp, Savannah College of Art & Design.

12. David Francis, rhp, Walters State (Tenn.) CC.

13. Travis Adair, ss, Cleveland State (Tenn.) CC.

14. Jason Hanson, 3b, Sabino HS, Tucson, Ariz.

15. Layton Hiller, of, Blinn (Texas) CC.

**16. *Billy Burns, of, Walton HS, Marietta, Ga.—(2014-15)**

17. *Mark Pope, rhp, Walton HS, Marietta, Ga.

18. *Michael Palazzone, rhp, Lassiter HS, Marietta, Ga.

19. *Zak Fuesser, lhp, York Comprehensive HS, York, S.C.

20. Robert Brooks, ss, Lurleen B. Wallace (Ala.) JC.

21. Tyler Barnett, ss, Eastern Kentucky University.

22. *Dane Carter, 3b, Texas A&M University.

23. Casey Hodges, rhp, Mount Olive (N.C.) College.

24. Shayne Moody, ss, University of North Carolina-Charlotte.

25. *Nick Fuller, rhp, Walters State (Tenn.) CC.

26. Calvin Culver, of, Los Angeles Pierce JC.

**27. *Anthony Rendon, ss, Lamar HS, Houston.—(2013-15)**

DRAFT DROP *First-round draft pick (6th overall), Nationals (2011)*

28. *Quentin Cate, c, Cuesta (Calif.) CC.

29. *Josh Moody, lhp, CC of Western Nevada.

30. Chris Shehan, of, Georgia Southern University.

31. *Jason Stolz, ss, Kell HS, Marietta, Ga.

32. *Pat Lenton, rhp, Minnesota State University-Mankato.

33. *Justin Fowler, rhp, Texarkana (Texas) CC.

34. *Matt Price, rhp, The Walker School, Marietta, Ga.

35. *Zack Osborne, rhp, New Mexico JC.

36. *Cecil Tanner, rhp, Ware County HS, Waycross, Ga.

37. *Lucas Hileman, of, Anna-Jonesboro HS, Anna, Ill.

38. *Jeff Richard, rhp, Coastal Carolina University.

39. *Taylor Wulf, rhp, Alvin (Texas) CC.

40. *Jesse Wierzbicki, c, Walters State (Tenn.) CC.

41. *Ian Gilley, ss, Northside HS, Fort Smith, Ark.

42. *Stephen Foster, lhp, Bellevue (Wash.) CC.

43. Adam Bullard, rhp, Gardner-Webb University.

44. *Taylor Hart, rhp, Madison County HS, Danielsville, Ga.

45. *Nick Croce, c, Mission Bay HS, San Diego.

46. *Matt Harrison, ss, Green Valley HS, Henderson, Nev.

47. *David Walters, rhp, Francis Marion (S.C.) University.

48. *David Holman, rhp, Andale (Kan.) HS.

49. *Josh Adams, rhp, Midland Valley HS, Bath, S.C.

50. *Dylan Lightell, rhp, West Hills (Calif.) JC.

## BALTIMORE ORIOLES (4)

**1. Brian Matusz, lhp, University of San Diego.—(2009-15)**

**2. Xavier Avery, of, Cedar Grove HS, Stockbridge, Ga.—(2012)**

**3. L.J. Hoes, of, St. John's College Prep HS, Washington, D.C.—(2012-15)**

**4. Kyle Hudson, of, University of Illinois.—(2011)**

5. Greg Miclat, ss, University of Virginia.—(AAA)

6. Rick Zagone, lhp, University of Missouri.

**7. Caleb Joseph, c, Lipscomb University.—(2014-15)**

8. Bobby Bundy, rhp, Sperry (Okla.) HS.

DRAFT DROP *Brother of Dylan Bundy, first-round draft pick, Orioles (2011); major leaguer (2012)*

9. Nick Haughian, lhp, University of Washington.

**10. *Chris Herrmann, 3b, Alvin (Texas) CC.—(2012-15)**

11. Nathan Moreau, lhp, University of Georgia.

12. Jason Rook, of-rhp, Appalachian State University.

13. Corey Thomas, 3b, Middleton HS, Tampa.

14. Jesse Beal, rhp, South County HS, Lorton, Va.

**15. Jason Gurka, lhp, Angelina (Texas) JC.—(2015)**

16. Bobby Stevens, ss, Northern Illinois University.

17. Brian Conley, of, Towson University.

18. *Keith Landers, lhp, St. Peter Marian HS, Worcester, Mass.

19. *Jarret Martin, lhp, Centennial HS, Bakersfield, Calif.

20. Ronnie Welty, of, Chandler-Gilbert (Ariz.) CC.

21. Eddie Gamboa, rhp, UC Davis.

22. Pat Kantakevich, rhp, College of William & Mary.

23. Edwin Cintron, of, Antonio Luchetti HS, Arecibo, P.R.

24. T.J. Baxter, of, University of New Orleans.

25. Xavier Lopez, c, Isabel Flores HS, Juncos, P.R.

26. Jose Barajas, rhp, CC of Western Nevada.

27. Ryan O'Shea, rhp, University of New Orleans.

28. Tom Edwards, 3b, Rutgers University.

29. Dennis Perez, c, University of Puerto Rico-Arecibo.

30. *Jeremy Dobbs, lhp, Daviess County HS, Philpot, Ky.

31. Tyler Sexton, lhp, Western Carolina University.

32. *Brandon Loy, ss, Rowlett HS, Houston.

33. *Art Charles, 1b, Ridgeview HS, Bakersfield, Calif.

34. T.R. Keating, rhp, University of Northern Colorado.

35. Buck Britton, 2b, Lubbock Christian (Texas) University.

36. Dan Eastham, rhp, University of Nevada.

37. Chad Durakis, c, University of Maryland.

38. Thomas Phelps, rhp, Whittier (Calif.) College.

39. Lance West, of, Bossier Parish (La.) JC.

40. *Kirk Singer, ss, Los Alamitos (Calif.) HS.

41. *Peter Birdwell, rhp, Riverside (Calif.) CC.

42. Chase Phillips, rhp, Western Oklahoma State JC.

**43. Oliver Drake, rhp, U.S. Naval Academy.—(2015)**

44. *Kevin Brady, rhp, Gaithersburg HS, Montgomery Village, Md.

45. Zach Petersime, rhp, Rend Lake (Ill.) CC.

46. *Michael Mudron, lhp, Martin Luther King HS, Riverside, Calif.

47. *Jared Eskew, lhp, Cal Poly.

48. *Chris Garrison, rhp, Rocklin (Calif.) HS.

49. *Hector Morales, of, University of Puerto Rico-Carolina.

50. *Wes Soto, 2b, Riverview HS, Sarasota, Fla.

## BOSTON RED SOX (30)

**1. Casey Kelly, ss-rhp, Sarasota (Fla.) HS.—(2012-15)**

DRAFT DROP *Son of Pat Kelly, major leaguer (1980)*

**1. Bryan Price, rhp, Rice University** (Supplemental choice—45th—as compensation for Type B free agent Eric Gagne).**—(2014)**

2. Derrik Gibson, ss, Seaford (Del.) HS.—(AAA)

**3. Stephen Fife, rhp, University of Utah** (Special compensation—85th—for failure to sign 2007 second-round draft pick Hunter Morris).**—(2012-14)**

**3. Kyle Weiland, rhp, University of Notre Dame.—(2011-12)**

4. Peter Hissey, of, Unionville HS, West Chester, Pa.—(AAA)

5. Ryan Westmoreland, of, Portsmouth (R.I.) HS.—(Short-season A)

**6. Ryan Lavarnway, c, Yale University.—(2011-15)**

**7. Tim Federowicz, c, University of North Carolina.—(2011-14)**

8. Michael Lee, rhp, Oklahoma City University.

**9. Christian Vazquez, c, Puerto Rico Baseball Academy, Caguas, P.R.—(2014)**

10. Peter Ruiz, rhp, Santa Barbara (Calif.) CC.

11. Bryan Peterson, of, West Valley HS, Spokane, Wash.

12. Lance McClain, lhp, Cumberland (Tenn.) University.

13. Tyler Wilson, rhp, Armuchee HS, Rome, Ga.

14. Tyler Yockey, of, Acadiana HS, Duson, La.

15. *John Lally, lhp, Santa Margarita HS, Rancho Santa Margarita, Calif.

16. Mitch Herold, lhp, University of Central Florida.

17. *Jordan Cooper, rhp, Shawnee Heights HS, Berryton, Kan.

**18. *Brian Flynn, lhp, Owasso (Okla.) HS.—(2013-14)**

19. *Brian Humphries, of, Granite Hills HS, El Cajon, Calif.

**20. *Alex Meyer, rhp, Greensburg (Ind.) HS.—(2015)**

DRAFT DROP *First-round draft pick (23rd overall), Nationals (2011)*

21. Jonathan Hee, 2b, University of Hawaii.

**22. *Anthony DeSclafani, rhp, Colts Neck HS, Freehold, N.J.—(2014-15)**

23. Seth Garrison, rhp, Texas Christian University.

24. *Ricky Oropesa, 1b, Etiwanda HS, Rancho Cucamonga, Calif.

25. *Justin Parker, lhp, Jesuit HS, Rancho Murrieta, Calif.

26. *Navery Moore, rhp, Battle Ground Academy, Franklin, Tenn.

27. Hunter Cervenka, lhp, Ross Sterling HS, Baytown, Texas.

28. *Matt Marquis, of, Immaculata HS, Annandale, N.J.

29. *Jacob Rogers, 3b, Dunedin (Fla.) HS.

30. Alex Hale, rhp, University of Richmond.

31. Andrew Frezza, of, Barry (Fla.) University.

**32. *Travis Shaw, 3b, Washington HS, Washington Courthouse, Ohio.—(2015)**

DRAFT DROP *Son of Jeff Shaw, first overall draft pick, January 1986/regular phase, Indians; major leaguer (1990-2001)*

33. *Brandon Miller, c, Woodward Academy, Tyrone, Ga.

34. *Zak Sinclair, rhp, West Allegheny HS, McDonald, Pa.

**35. Carson Blair, ss, Liberty Christian HS, Dallas.—(2015)**

36. Richie Wasielewski, lhp, Brunswick (Ga.) HS.

37. Thomas Di Benedetto, ss, Trinity (Conn.) College.

38. *Bobby Hernandez, rhp, Barry (Fla.) University.

**39. *Yan Gomes, c, University of Tennessee.—(2012-15)**

40. *Sam Stafford, lhp, Klein Collins HS, Spring, Texas.

41. Dustin Mercadante, rhp, San Diego CC.

42. *Caleb Brown, of, Central Kitsap HS, Silverdale, Wash.

43. *John Killen, lhp, Blue Valley HS, Stilwell, Kan.

44. *Ben Whitmore, lhp, Fresno (Calif.) CC.

45. *Jonathan Griffin, 1b, Manatee (Fla.) CC.

46. *Jeremy Heatley, rhp, North Lake (Texas) CC.

47. Jeremy Kehrt, rhp, University of Southern Indiana.

48. *Kevin Hoef, 3b, University of Iowa.

49. Zach Gentile, 2b, Western Michigan University.

50. Kyle Stroup, rhp, Grant Community HS, Ingleside, Ill.

## CHICAGO CUBS (19)

**1. Andrew Cashner, rhp, Texas Christian University.—(2010-15)**

**1. Ryan Flaherty, ss, Vanderbilt University** (Supplemental choice—41st—as compensation for Type B free agent Jason Kendall).**—(2012-15)**

2. Aaron Shafer, rhp, Wichita State University.–(AA)

**3. Chris Carpenter, rhp, Kent State University.—(2011-12)**

4. Matt Cerda, ss, Oceanside (Calif.) HS.—(AA)

5. Justin Bristow, rhp, East Carolina University.—(Low A)

**6. Josh Harrison, 2b, University of Cincinnati.—(2011-15)**

DRAFT DROP *Nephew of John Shelby, major leaguer (1981-91)*

7. Luis Flores, c, Oklahoma State University.

8. James Leverton, lhp, Texas Tech.
**9. Jay Jackson, rhp, Furman University.—(2015)**
**10.*Alex Wilson, rhp, Texas A&M University.—(2011-15)**
11. Toby Matchulat, rhp, Wabash Valley (Ill.) JC.
12. Jake Opitz, 2b, University of Nebraska.
**13. Tony Campana, of, University of Cincinnati.—(2011-14)**
14. Danny McDaniel, rhp, Chabot (Calif.) JC.
**15. Casey Coleman, rhp, Florida Gulf Coast University.—(2010-14)**
DRAFT DROP *Grandson of Joe Coleman, major leaguer (1942-55) • Son of Joe Coleman, first-round draft pick, Senators (1965); major leaguer (1965-79)*
16. Ryan Keedy, 1b, University of Alabama-Birmingham.
DRAFT DROP *Son of Pat Keedy, major leaguer (1985-89)*
17. Jon Nagel, rhp, Independence (Kan.) CC.
**18. Jeff Beliveau, lhp, Florida Atlantic University.—(2012-15)**
19. David Macias, of, Vanderbilt University.
20. Jericho Jones, of-rhp, Louisiana Tech.
**21. Logan Watkins, ss, Goddard (Kan.) HS.—(2013-14)**
22. Tarlandas Mitchell, rhp, Alto (Texas) HS.
23. Ryan Sontag, of, Arizona State University.
24. David Cales, rhp, St. Xavier (Ill.) University.
25. Rebel Ridling, 1b, Oklahoma State University.
26. Josh Whitlock, rhp, West Virginia University.
**27.*Sonny Gray, rhp, Smyrna (Tenn.) HS.—(2011-15)**
DRAFT DROP *First-round draft pick (18th overall), Athletics (2011)*
28. TeWayne Willis, of, Lincoln Memorial (Tenn.) University.
29.*Sean Buckley, 3b, King HS, Tampa.
30.*Cole White, rhp, Paris (Texas) JC.
31.*Kyle Wilson, 3b, Hill (Texas) JC.
32. Kurt Calvert, of, University of Missouri.
33. Sean Hoorelbeke, 1b, Central Michigan University.
34. Bubba O'Donnell, rhp, High Point University.
35.*Ross Vagedes, rhp, Wright State University.
36. Michael Brenly, c, University of Nevada-Las Vegas.
DRAFT DROP *Son of Bob Brenly, major Leaguer (1981-89); major league manager (2001-04)*
**37. Erik Hamren, rhp, Saddleback (Calif.) CC.—(2011)**
38.*Sean McNaughton, of, Brigham Young University.
39.*Jordan Brown, rhp, Louisiana State University.
40.*Jared McDonald, ss, Pima (Ariz.) CC.
41.*Jordan Petraitis, ss, Miami (Ohio) University.
42.*Derek Riley, rhp, Chandler-Gilbert (Ariz.) JC.
43.*Jesse Ginley, rhp, Dunnellon (Fla.) HS.
44.*David Doss, c, University of South Alabama.
45.*Ashton Florko, lhp, University of British Columbia.
**46.*Tony Zych, rhp, St. Rita HS, Monee, Ill.—(2015)**
47.*Chad Cregar, of, Western Kentucky University.
48.*Dylan Moseley, rhp, Louisiana Tech.
DRAFT DROP *Brother of Dustin Moseley, first-round draft pick, Reds (2000); major leaguer (2006-12)*
49.*Hunter Scantling, rhp, Episcopal HS, Jacksonville, Fla.
50.*Pete Levitt, rhp, Pitt (N.C.) CC.

## CHICAGO WHITE SOX (8)

**1. Gordon Beckham, ss, University of Georgia.—(2009-15)**
2. (Choice to Brewers as compensation for Type A free agent Scott Linebrink)
**3. Brent Morel, 3b, Cal Poly.—(2010-15)**
4. Drew O'Neil, rhp, Penn State University.—(High A)
**5. Daniel Hudson, rhp, Old Dominion University.—(2009-15)**
6. Kenny Williams Jr., of, Wichita State University.
DRAFT DROP *Son of Kenny Williams, major leaguer (1986-91); general manager, White Sox (2000-12)*
**7. Jordan Danks, of, University of Texas.—(2012-15)**
DRAFT DROP *Brother of John Danks, first-round draft pick, Rangers (2003); major leaguer (2007-15)*
8. Kevin Dubler, c, Illinois State University.
9. Ryan Strauss, rhp, Florida State University.
10. Stephen Sauer, rhp, Arizona State University.
**11. Charlie Leesman, lhp, Xavier University.—(2013-14)**
12. Steven Upchurch, rhp, Faith Academy, Mobile, Ala.
13. Dexter Carter, rhp, Old Dominion University.
14.*Jorden Merry, rhp, University of Washington.
15. Tyler Kuhn, ss, West Virginia University.
16.*Brett Basham, c, University of Mississippi.
17.*Jonathan Weaver, rhp, East Leyden HS, Franklin Park, Ill.
18. Josh Billeaud, rhp, University of Southern Mississippi.
19. Justin Kuehn, rhp, Santa Clara University.
20. Justin Greene, of, Francis Marion (S.C.) University.
21. Drew Garcia, 2b, UC Riverside.
DRAFT DROP *Son of Dave Garcia, major league manager (1977-82)*
22. Jose Vargas, 3b, Ventura (Calif.) JC.
23.*Kyle Long, lhp-1b, St. Anne's Belfield School, Ivy, Va.
DRAFT DROP *First-round draft pick, Chicago Bears/ National Football League (2013); guard, NFL (2013-14) • Son of Howie Long, defensive end, NFL (1981-93) • Brother of Chris Long, defensive end, NFL (2008-15)*
24. Brett Graffy, rhp, University of Notre Dame.
**25.*Taylor Thompson, rhp, Auburn University.—(2014)**
26. Jorge Castillo, 1b, Florida International Univ.
27. Doug Thennis, 1b, Texas Tech.
28. Brandon Short, of, St. John's River (Fla.) CC.
29.*Randall Thorpe, of, Heritage HS, Grapevine, Texas.
30. Kevin Asselin, rhp, Sonoma State (Calif.) University.
**31.*James McCann, c, Dos Pueblos HS, Santa Barbara, Calif.—(2014-15)**
32.*Justin Marrero, 2b, Reynoldsburg (Ohio) HS.
33.*Eddie Young, ss, Christian HS, El Cajon, Calif.
**34.*Marcus Semien, ss, St. Mary's HS, El Cerrito, Calif.—(2013-15)**
35.*Harold Riggins, 1b, Normal West HS, Bloomington, Ill.
36.*Jordan Keegan, of, Silverado HS, Las Vegas, Nev.
37. Terry Doyle, rhp, Boston College.
38.*Steve Domecus, c, Moorpark (Calif.) JC.
39.*Rusty Shellhorn, lhp, Central Valley HS, Liberty Lake, Wash.
40.*Mark Hawkenson, rhp, Red Mountain HS, Mesa, Ariz.
41.*Mason Radeke, rhp, Santa Barbara (Calif.) HS.
42.*Steve Sabatino, lhp, Lockport Township HS, Lockport, Ill.
43.*Cory Farris, c, Boone County HS, Florence, Ky.
**44.*C.J. Cron, c, Mountain Pointe HS, Phoenix.—(2014-15)**
DRAFT DROP *First-round draft pick (17th overall), Angels (2011) • Son of Chris Cron, major leaguer (1991-92)*
45.*Julian Kenner, ss, Whitney Young HS, Chicago.
46. Lee Fischer, ss, University of Missouri.
47.*Dan Hayden, c, Xavier University.
DRAFT DROP *Baseball coach, Miami, Ohio (2014-15)*
48.*Ricardo Alvarez, 2b, San Fernando (Calif.) HS.
49.*Travis Otto, 1b, Wheaton North HS, Wheaton, Ill.
DRAFT DROP *Son of Dave Otto, major leaguer (1987-94)*
50.*Steve Florence, ss, Simeon Vocational HS, Chicago.

## CINCINNATI REDS (7)

**1. Yonder Alonso, 1b, University of Miami.—(2010-15)**
2. (Choice to Brewers as compensation for Type A free agent Francisco Cordero)
**3. Zach Stewart, rhp, Texas Tech.—(2011-12)**
4. Tyler Cline, rhp, Cass HS, Cartersville, Ga.—(Rookie)
5. Clayton Shunick, rhp, North Carolina State University.—(AA)
6. Alex Buchholz, 2b-3b, University of Delaware.
**7. Pedro Villarreal, rhp, Howard (Texas) JC.—(2012-15)**
8. Cody Puckett, ss, Cal State Dominguez Hills.
**9. David Sappelt, of, Coastal Carolina University.—(2011-13)**
10. Sean Conner, of, Palm Beach (Fla.) CC.
11. Andrew Means, of, Indiana University.
12. Kyle Day, c, Michigan State University.
13. Blaine Howell, lhp, Pensacola (Fla.) JC.
14. Lance Janke, rhp, San Diego Christian College.
15.*Eric Pfisterer, lhp, Don Bosco Prep, Saddle River, N.J.
16. Carter Morrison, of, Clayton Heights HS, Surrey, B.C.
17. Frank Pfister, 3b, Emory (Ga.) University.
18. Chris McMurray, c, UC Santa Barbara.
19. Mace Thurman, lhp, Baylor University.
20. Tyler Stovall, of, Central Michigan University.
21. Theo Bowe, of, Milford (Del.) HS.
22. Byron Wiley, of, Kansas State University.
23. Will Hudgens, rhp, University of Memphis.
24. Enrique Garcia, rhp, University of Miami.
25. Raul Rodriguez, rhp, Royal HS, Simi Valley, Calif.
26. Michael Bohana, rhp, Kennesaw State University.
27. Matt Stiffler, of, Ohio University.
28.*Bryce Bandilla, lhp, Bella Vista HS, Fair Oaks, Calif.
29.*Ben Hunter, rhp, Wake Forest University.
30. Juan Carlos Sulbaran, rhp, American Heritage HS, Davie, Fla.
31.*Joey Housey, rhp, Nova HS, Hollywood, Fla.
**32. Justin Freeman, rhp, Kennesaw State University.—(2013)**
33.*Taylor Wrenn, 2b, Lakeland (Fla.) HS.
34. Bryan Gardner, lhp, Ithaca (N.Y.) College.
35. Matt Fairel, lhp, Florida State University.
36.*Erik Gregersen, rhp, Stephen F. Austin University.
37. Randall Linebaugh, rhp, Baylor University.
38.*Ricky Bowen, rhp, Mississippi State University.
39. Mike Konstanty, 1b, University of Albany.
DRAFT DROP *Grandson of Jim Konstanty, major leaguer (1944-56)*
40.*David Peterson, rhp, Las Lomas HS, Walnut Creek, Calif.
41. Justin Walker, lhp, Lamar University.
42.*Benson Merritt, rhp, South Lincoln HS, Smithville, Ontario.
43.*Bronson Gagner, rhp, Parkview HS, Lilburn, Ga.
44. Kevin Coddington, c, University of Illinois-Chicago.
45.*Brendan Lobban, lhp, St. Joseph Regional HS, Ramsey, N.J.
46.*Grant Hogue, of, Mississippi State University.
47. David Torcise, lhp, University of South Florida.
48.*Kenny Monteith, rhp, Morristown-Beard HS, Morristown, N.J.
49.*Patrick White, of, West Virginia University.
DRAFT DROP *Quarterback, National Football League (2009-13)*
50.*Kevin Leslie, of, Faulkner (Ala.) University.

## CLEVELAND INDIANS (29)

**1. Lonnie Chisenhall, ss, Pitt (N.C.) CC.—(2011-15)**
2. Trey Haley, rhp, Central Heights HS, Nacogdoches, Texas.—(AAA)
**3. Cord Phelps, 2b, Stanford University.—(2011-14)**
4. Dave Roberts, rhp, Long Beach State University.—(High A)
**5. Zach Putnam, rhp, University of Michigan.—(2011-15)**
6. Jeremie Tice, 3b, College of Charleston.
7. Tim Fedroff, of, University of North Carolina.
8. Eric Berger, lhp, University of Arizona.
9. Clayton Cook, rhp, Amarillo (Texas) HS.
10. Donnie Webb, of, Oklahoma State University.
**11. Matt Langwell, rhp, Rice University.—(2013)**
12. Guido Fonseca, rhp, University of Northern Iowa.
13. Adam Abraham, 3b, University of Michigan.
14. Carlos Moncrief, rhp-of, Chipola (Fla.) JC.
15. Jason Rodriguez, 3b, University of Nevada.
**16. T.J. House, lhp, Picayune Memorial HS, Picayune, Miss.—(2014-15)**
17.*Mitch Mormann, rhp, Des Moines Area (Iowa) CC.
18. Kaimi Mead, lhp, Hawaii Pacific University.
19. Nate Recknagel, 1b, University of Michigan.
20. Marty Popham, rhp, Union (Ky.) College.
21. Ryan Blair, of, Cal State Sacramento.
22. Bryce Stowell, rhp, UC Irvine.
23.*Otto Roberts, rhp, Belleville West HS, Belleville, Ill.
24. Kevin Fontanez, ss, Puerto Rico Baseball Academy, Caguas, P.R.
25. Steve Smith, rhp, Ouachita Baptist (Ark.) University.
26. Moises Montero, c, Chipola (Fla.) JC.
27.*Michael Goodnight, rhp, Westside HS, Houston.
28. Russell Young, lhp, Dartmouth College.
29.*Ryan McCarney, rhp, JC of the Canyons (Calif.).
30. Jeff Walters, rhp, St. Petersburg (Fla.) JC.
31.*Trevor Cousineau, lhp, Davison (Mich.) HS.
**32.*Nick Christiani, rhp, Vanderbilt University.—(2013-14)**
**33. Roberto Perez, c, Lake City (Fla.) CC.—(2014-15)**
34.*Collin Brennan, rhp, Bradley University.
35.*Egan Smith, lhp, CC of Southern Nevada.
**36.*Adam Warren, rhp, University of North Carolina.—(2012-15)**
37.*Chad Bell, lhp, Walters State (Tenn.) CC.
38. Brian Grening, rhp, Cal Poly.
39. Eddie Burns, rhp, Georgia Tech.
40. Tim Palincsar, of, University of Texas-San Antonio.
41.*Adam Matthews, of, White Knoll HS, West Columbus, S.C.
42.*Logan Thompson, ss, Jupiter Community HS, Jupiter, Fla.
DRAFT DROP *Son of Robby Thompson, major leaguer (1986-96) • Brother of Tyler Thompson, 42nd-round draft pick, Giants (2008)*
43. Mike McGuire, rhp, University of Delaware.
44.*Cory White, rhp, Rend Lake (Ill.) JC.
45.*Dean Laganosky, of, Haverford (Pa.) College.
46.*Matt Ramsey, rhp-c, Farragut HS, Knoxville, Tenn.
47.*Randon Henika, ss, Garber (Mich.) HS.
48.*Troy White, 3b, Whitney-Young HS, Chicago.
49.*Devin Jones, rhp, Eupora (Miss.) HS.
50.*Hector Acosta-Carrillo, of, Junction City (Kan.) HS.

## COLORADO ROCKIES (25)

**1. Christian Friedrich, lhp, Eastern Kentucky University.—(2012-15)**
**2. Charlie Blackmon, of, Georgia Tech.—(2011-15)**
3. Aaron Weatherford, rhp, Mississippi State University.—(Low A)
4. Ethan Hollingsworth, rhp, Eastern Michigan University.—(AAA)
**5.*Chris Dominguez, 3b, University of Louisville.—(2014-15)**
DRAFT DROP *Returned to Louisville; re-drafted by Giants, 2008 (3rd round)*
6. Kiel Roling, c, Arizona State University.
7. Daniel Houston, rhp, Boston College.
8. Kurt Yacko, rhp, Chapman (Calif.) College.
9. Craig Bennigson, lhp, University of California.
10. Stephen Dodson, rhp, University of Georgia.
11. Kyle Walker, lhp, University of Texas.
12. Ryan Peisel, 3b, University of Georgia.
13. Erik Wetzel, 2b, Fresno State University.
14. Tyler Massey, 1b, The Baylor School, Chattanooga, Tenn.
15. Juan Rodriguez, rhp, Universidad del Turabo (P.R.)
16. Chad Rose, rhp, Broward (Fla.) CC.
17. Alan DeRatt, rhp, UNC Asheville.
18. Chad Jacobsen, 1b, University of South Carolina-Aiken.
19.*Ben Orloff, 2b, UC Irvine.
20.*Nate Lape, of, Marshall University.
21. Tyler Trice, rhp, University of North Carolina.
22. Nick Schnaitmann, rhp, Cosumnes River (Calif.) CC.
23.*Sam Elam, lhp, University of Notre Dame.
**24. Thomas Field, ss, Texas State University.—(2011-15)**
25.*Andy Burns, ss, Rocky Mountain HS, Fort Collins, Colo.
26. Adam Jorgenson, rhp, Cal State Fullerton.

27. *Tim Matthews, rhp, Baylor University.
28. Mike Zuanich, of, UC Santa Barbara.
29. Matt Baugh, lhp, University of San Francisco.
30. Carlos Luna, rhp, Oral Roberts University.
31. Rod Scurry, rhp, University of Nevada.
DRAFT DROP *Son of Rod Scurry, first-round draft pick, Pirates (1974); major leaguer (1980-88)*
32. *Will Scott, rhp, Kell HS, Marietta, Ga.
33. *Aaron Gates, lhp, Orange Lutheran HS, Villa Park, Calif.
34. *Ryan Radcliff, c, Fairview HS, Fairview Park, Ohio.
35. Maikol Gonzalez, 2b, Tusculum (Tenn.) College.
36. Patrick Rose, of, UC Santa Barbara.
37. Delta Cleary, of, LSU-Eunice JC.
38. *Tyler Pill, rhp, Covina (Calif.) HS.
39. *Kyle Ottoson, lhp, Eaton (Colo.) HS.
40. *Kemer Quirk, of, Rockhurst HS, Kansas City, Kan.
DRAFT DROP *Son of Jamie Quirk, first-round draft pick, Royals (1972); major leaguer (1975-92)*
41. *Dean Espy, ss, Red Mountain HS, Mesa, Ariz.
42. *Taylor Hightower, c, Cartersville (Ga.) HS.
43. Alex Feinberg, 2b, Vanderbilt University.
44. *Jordan Swagerty, c-rhp, Prestonwood Christian Academy, Sachse, Texas.
45. Brad McAtee, rhp, UC Davis.
46. Jimmy Cesario, 2b, University of Houston.
47. *Mark Lincoln, rhp, American River (Calif.) JC.
48. *Austin Nola, ss, Catholic HS, Baton Rouge, La.
DRAFT DROP *Brother of Aaron Nola, first-round draft pick, Phillies (2014); major leaguer (2015)*
49. *Carl Uhl, of, UC Riverside.
50. *Josh Hungerman, lhp, Cleveland State University.

## DETROIT TIGERS (21)

1. **Ryan Perry, rhp, University of Arizona.—(2009-12)**
2. Cody Satterwhite, rhp, University of Mississippi.—(AAA)
3. Scott Green, rhp, University of Kentucky.–(Low A)
4. Brett Jacobson, rhp, Vanderbilt University.—(AAA)
5. **Alex Avila, c, University of Alabama.—(2009-15)**
DRAFT DROP *Brother of Alan Avila, 47th-round draft pick, Tigers (2008) • Son of Al Avila, general manager, Tigers (2015)*
6. Tyler Stohr, rhp, University of North Florida.
7. Jade Todd, lhp, Shades Valley (Ala.) HS.
8. **Andy Dirks, of, Wichita State University.—(2011-13)**
9. Anthony Shawler, rhp, Old Dominion University.
10. **Robbie Weinhardt, rhp, Oklahoma State University.—(2010-11)**
11. Brandon Douglas, ss, University of Northern Iowa.
12. Brett Anderson, ss, Eastern HS, Bristol, Conn.
13. Jared Gayhart, rhp-of, Rice University.
14. Tyler Conn, lhp, University of Southern Mississippi.
15. Alden Carrithers, 2b, UCLA.
16. **Thad Weber, rhp, University of Nebraska.—(2012-13)**
17. Rob Waite, rhp, UC Riverside.
18. *Scott Weismann, rhp, Acton-Boxborough HS, Boxborough, Mass.
19. Ben Guez, of, College of William & Mary.
20. ***Ryan Lollis, of, University of Missouri.—(2015)**
21. Adam Frost, ss, St. Norbert (Wis.) College.
22. *Zach MacPhee, ss, Sandra Day O'Connor HS, Phoenix.
23. Michael Gosse, 2b, University of Oklahoma.
24. Carmelo Jaime, 2b, Miami-Dade CC.
25. Billy Nowlin, c, Golden West (Calif.) JC.
26. Brent Wyatt, ss, Lewis-Clark State (Idaho) College.
27. *James Young, 3b, Southridge HS, Miami.
28. David Stokes, rhp, Liberty University.
29. Keith Stein, of, Sam Houston State University.
30. Tyler Weber, c, Wichita State University.
31. Trevor Feeney, rhp, Northern Illinois University.
32. Mark Sorensen, rhp, Michigan State University.
DRAFT DROP *Son of Lary Sorensen, major leaguer (1977-88)*
33. Jordan Lennerton, 1b, Oregon State University.
34. Bryan Pounds, 3b, University of Houston.
35. Dan DeLucia, lhp, Ohio State University.
36. Steve Gilman, rhp, Yale University.
37. Nick Cassavechia, rhp, Baylor University.
38. Josh Workman, of, Wichita State University.
39. *Chris Gloor, lhp, Quinnipiac University.
40. *Bryan Bingham, rhp, Navarro (Texas) JC.
41. Eric Broberg, rhp, Seminole (Fla.) CC.
42. *Paul Hoenecke, 3b, West Bend West HS, West Bend, Wis.
43. *Tyler Grimes, ss, North HS, Wichita, Kan.
44. *Brian Wheeler, of, Childersburg (Ala.) HS.
45. *Nathan Linseman, lhp, Our Lady of Lourdes Catholic HS, Ariss, Ontario.
46. *Eric Roof, c, Michigan State University.
DRAFT DROP *Son of Phil Roof, major leaguer (1961-77) • Nephew of Gene Roof, major leaguer (1981-83)*
47. *Alan Avila, 2b, Archbishop McCarthy HS, Fort Lauderdale, Fla.
DRAFT DROP *Brother of Alex Avila, sixth-round draft pick, Tigers (2008); major leaguer (2009-15) • Son of Al Avila, general manager, Tigers (2015)*
48. *Casey Moore, c, St. Louis University.
49. *Matt Robertson, rhp, Barton County (Kan.) CC.
DRAFT DROP *Brother of Nate Robertson, major leaguer (2002-10)*
50. *Landon Hernandez, c, University of Hawaii.

## FLORIDA MARLINS (6)

1. **Kyle Skipworth, c, Patriot HS, Riverside, Calif.—(2013)**
2. **Brad Hand, lhp, Chaska (Minn.) HS.—(2011-15)**
3. **Edgar Olmos, lhp, Birmingham HS, Van Nuys, Calif.—(2013-15)**
4. Curtis Petersen, rhp, Billy Ryan HS, Aubrey, Texas.—(Low A)
5. Pete Andrelczyk, rhp, Coastal Carolina University.—(AAA)
6. Graham Johnson, rhp, Westlake HS, Westlake Village, Calif.
7. Paul Gran, 3b, Washington State University.
8. Isaac Galloway, of, Los Osos HS, Rancho Cucamonga, Calif.
9. **Dan Jennings, lhp, University of Nebraska.—(2012-15)**
10. *Trevor Holder, rhp, University of Georgia.
11. Blake Brewer, rhp, Sandy Creek HS, Fairburn, Ga.
12. Brandon Turner, 2b, Mississippi State University.
13. Dan Pertusati, 2b, Damien HS, La Verne, Calif.
14. Bryan Evans, rhp, UC Davis.
15. Johnny Dorn, rhp, University of Nebraska.
16. Andy Loomis, lhp, Purdue University.
17. *Ben Soignier, ss, University of Louisiana-Monroe.
18. **Tom Koehler, rhp, Stony Brook University.—(2012-15)**
19. Justin Bass, of, Stetson University.
20. Wade Korpi, lhp, University of Notre Dame.
21. Lonnie Lechelt, 2b, Oregon State University.
22. Jared Yecker, rhp, St. John's University.
23. Konrad Thieme, c, Sonoma State (Calif.) University.
24. Zach Moore, c, Dundalk (Md.) JC.
25. Robert Taylor, c, University of Arkansas-Little Rock.
26. Jason Peacock, 1b, Florida Gulf Coast University.
27. **Elih Villaneuva, rhp, Florida State University.—(2011)**
28. **Kevin Mattison, of, UNC Asheville.—(2012)**
29. Ricky Orton, 1b, UNC Greensboro.
30. Skyler Crawford, rhp, Hartnell (Calif.) JC.
31. *Marvin Campbell, 1b, Las Vegas (Nev.) HS.
32. Wayman Gooch, rhp, Lewis-Clark State (Idaho) College.
33. *Moses Munoz, lhp, Bossier Parish (La.) JC.
34. Matt Lokken, 3b, St. Helens (Ore.) HS.
35. Brian Schultz, of, Florida Southern College.
36. Brandon Todd, rhp, University of South Carolina.
37. Drew Clothier, lhp, U.S. Military Academy.
38. *Joey DeBernardis, 3b, Lake Zurich (Ill.) HS.
39. ***Mikie Mahtook, of, St. Thomas More HS, Lafayette, La.—(2015)**
DRAFT DROP *First-round draft pick (31st overall), Rays (2011)*
40. *Trent Fuller, ss, Fairfield (Calif.) HS.
41. *Alan Williams, of, Mangham (La.) HS.
42. Jeremy Synan, of, North Carolina State University.
43. *Kes Carter, of, Ravenwood Academy, Nashville, Tenn.
DRAFT DROP *First-round draft pick (56th overall), Rays (2011)*
44. Joel Staples, 3b, St. Mary's (Calif.) College.
45. *Fred Atkins, of, Marin (Calif.) CC.
46. Casey Fry, lhp, Los Angeles Pierce JC.
47. *Jeff Urlaub, lhp, University of Nevada-Las Vegas.
48. *Barrett Serrato, ss, Community HS, West Chicago, Ill.
49. *Taylor Davis, c, Jupiter Community HS, Jupiter, Fla.
50. *Colin Hofmann, of, St. Augustine HS, San Diego.

## HOUSTON ASTROS (10)

1. **Jason Castro, c, Stanford University.—(2010-15)**
1. **Jordan Lyles, rhp, Hartsville (S.C.) HS** (Supplemental choice—38th—as compensation for Type B free agent Trevor Miller).**—(2011-15)**
2. Jay Austin, of, North Atlanta HS, Atlanta.—(High A)
3. *Chase Davidson, of, Milton HS, Alpharetta, Ga.—(Low A)
DRAFT DROP *Attended Georgia; re-drafted by Astros, 2011 (41st round)*
3. Ross Seaton, rhp, Second Baptist HS, Sugar Land, Texas (Special compensation—109th—for failure to sign 2007 third-round draft pick Derek Dietrich).—(AAA)
4. T.J. Steele, of, University of Arizona.—(AA)
5. David Duncan, lhp, Georgia Tech.—(High A)
6. **J.B. Shuck, of-lhp, Ohio State University.—(2011-15)**
7. Jon Gaston, of, University of Arizona.
8. Brad Dydalewicz, lhp, Lake Travis HS, Austin, Texas.
9. Luis Cruz, lhp, Academia Santa Monica, Carolina, P.R.
10. Jarred Holloway, lhp, St. Petersburg (Fla.) JC.
11. Jacob Priday, of, University of Missouri.
12. Jeff Hulett, ss, Okaloosa-Walton (Fla.) JC.
DRAFT DROP *Son of Tim Hulett, major leaguer (1983-95) • Brother of Tug Hulett, major leaguer (2008-09)*
13. Kyle Godfrey, rhp, Hiwassee (Tenn.) JC.
14. Chris Hicks, rhp, Georgia Tech.
15. Phil Disher, 1b, University of South Carolina.
16. *Josh Poytress, lhp, Fowler (Calif.) HS.
17. Andy Simunic, 2b, University of Tennessee.
18. David Flores, 3b, Cal State Sacramento.
19. Ashton Mowdy, rhp, Eastern Oklahoma State JC.
20. *Shea Robin, c, Vanderbilt University.
21. *Rodarrick Jones, of, St. John HS, St. Gabriel, La.
22. *Terrence Jackson, lhp, North Central Texas JC.
23. *Chase Huchingson, lhp, University of Arkansas-Fort Smith JC.
24. Danny Meier, of, University of Portland.
25. Mike Hacker, lhp, Cosumnes River (Calif.) JC.
26. Shane Wolf, lhp, Ithaca (N.Y.) College.
27. Nate Pettus, rhp, Western Oklahoma State JC.
28. Zach Grimmett, rhp, Beggs (Okla.) HS.
29. Chris Jackson, ss, Virginia Commonwealth University.
30. Michael Diaz, 2b, Southern Connecticut State University.
31. Philip Rummel, rhp, Kutztown (Pa.) University.
32. *B.A. Vollmuth, ss, Biloxi (Miss.) HS.
33. ***Shawn Armstrong, rhp, West Craven HS, New Bern, N.C.—(2015)**
34. *Jordan Jankowski, c, Peters Township HS, McMurray, pa.
35. Rene Garcia, c, Sagrada Familia HS, Vega Alta, P.R.
36. Austin Wood, rhp, Niceville (Fla.) HS.
37. Kirkland Rivers, rhp, Texas A&M University.
38. *Kris Castellanos, lhp, Newsome HS, Brandon, Fla.
39. *Tyson Van Winkle, c, Gonzaga University.
40. *Scott Lawson, 2b, Grayson County (Texas) JC.
41. *Tony McClendon, of, Damien HS, La Verne, Calif.
42. *Ryan Danbury, of, North Florida CC.
43. *Austin Green, c, Patrick Henry HS, San Diego.
44. *Edmond Sparks, c, Chipola (Fla.) JC.
45. *Grayson Garvin, lhp, Wesleyan HS, Suwanee, Ga.
DRAFT DROP *First-round draft pick (59th overall), Rays (2011)*
46. *Mike Modica, lhp, George Mason University.
47. Nathan Metroka, of, Compton (Calif.) CC.
48. Danny Meszaros, rhp, College of Charleston.
49. Chase Lehr, rhp, Glendale (Ariz.) CC.
50. *Jamal Austin, of, Harrison HS, Powder Springs, Ga.

## KANSAS CITY ROYALS (3)

1. **Eric Hosmer, 1b, American Heritage HS, Plantation, Fla.—(2011-15)**
1. **Mike Montgomery, lhp, Hart HS, Valencia, Calif.** (Supplemental choice—36th—as compensation for Type B free agent David Riske).**—(2015)**
2. **Johnny Giavotella, 2b, University of New Orleans.—(2011-15)**
3. Tyler Sample, rhp, Mullen HS, Denver.—(AA)
4. Tim Melville, rhp, Wentzville Holt HS, Wentzville, Mo.—(AAA)
5. **John Lamb, lhp, Laguna Hills (Calif.) HS.—(2015)**
6. Alex Llanos, ss, Puerto Rico Baseball Academy, Caguas, P.R.
7. *Jason Esposito, 3b, Amity Regional HS, Amity, Conn.
8. Malcom Culver, rhp, Palmdale (Calif.) HS.
DRAFT DROP *Brother of Tyrone Culver, defensive back, National Football League (2006-12)*
9. J.D. Alfaro, ss, Grayson County (Texas) CC.
DRAFT DROP *Brother of Jason Alfaro, major leaguer (2004)*
10. Mauricio Matos, c, DeWitt Clinton HS, Bronx, N.Y.
11. *Malcolm Bronson, of, Jasper (Texas) HS.
12. Allen Caldwell, of, Spartanburg Methodist (S.C.) JC.
13. John Flanagan, lhp, Southwestern Illinois JC.
14. Chase Hentges, rhp, Shakopee (Minn.) HS.
15. Alberto Espinosa, 1b, Broward (Fla.) CC.
16. Derrick Saito, lhp, Cal Poly.
17. Jake Kuebler, rhp, Lincoln Southeast HS, Lincoln, Neb.
18. Carlo Testa, of, Belmont University.
19. Miguel Moctezuma, c, University of Central Oklahoma.
20. Shawn Griffin, of, University of Tennessee.
21. Jacob Theis, rhp, Mountlake Terrace (Wash.) HS.
22. **Blaine Hardy, lhp, Lewis-Clark State (Idaho) College.—(2014-15)**
23. Dale De Schepper, rhp, Mount San Jacinto (Calif.) JC.
24. Jason Morales, 3b, UNC Pembroke.
25. Carson Bryant, rhp, Azusa Pacific (Calif.) University.
26. Ryan Morgan, rhp, Rockhurst (Mo.) University.
27. Tim Huber, lhp, University of Nebraska-Omaha.
28. Greg Billo, rhp, Carl Sandburg HS, Orland Park, Ill.
29. *Beau Brett, 1b, Ferris HS, Spokane, Wash.
DRAFT DROP *Nephew of George Brett, major leaguer (1973-93)*
30. *Rick Dodridge, lhp, Ogemaw Heights HS, West Branch, Mich.
31. *Ryan Curl, of, St. Francis DeSales HS, Gahanna, Ohio.
32. *Rey Cotilla, rhp, Miami-Dade CC.
33. *Eric Swegman, rhp, Young Harris (Ga.) JC.
34. Brett Richardson, rhp, Wenatchee Valley (Wash.) JC.
35. *Chris Balcom-Miller, rhp, West Valley (Calif.) CC.
36. *Nick Purdy, rhp, St. Marys HS, Hamilton, Ontario.
37. ***Bradin Hagens, rhp, Merced (Calif.) JC.—(2014)**
38. James Thompson, rhp, Columbus State (Ga.) College.
39. *Ryan Modglin, rhp, Scott City (Mo.) HS.
40. Pernell Halliman, rhp, Jackson State University.
41. *Doug Joyce, c, Stanwood (Wash.) HS.
42. *Marc Oslund, rhp, West Torrance HS, Torrance, Calif.
43. *Cory Kiefer, rhp, Valley View HS, Moreno Valley, Calif.
DRAFT DROP *Son of Steve Kiefer, major leaguer (1984-89)*
44. *Patrick Johnson, of, Colony HS, Ontario, Calif.
45. *Ray Anderson, of, Lassiter HS, Marietta, Ga.
46. *William Beckwith, 1b-3b, West Lowndes HS, Crawford, Miss.
47. Stephen Gilgenbach, lhp, University of Arkansas-Little Rock.
48. *Terrence Buchanan, ss, Mount Carmel HS, San Diego.

49. *Alan Salgado, 3b, San Ysidro HS, San Diego.
50. Travis Jones, c, Sabino HS, Tucson, Ariz.

## LOS ANGELES ANGELS (27)

1. (Choice to Twins as compensation for Type A free agent Torii Hunter)
2. **Tyler Chatwood, rhp-of, Redlands East Valley HS, Yucaipa, Calif.—(2011-14)**
DRAFT DROP *First 2008 high school draft pick to reach majors (April 11, 2011)*
3. Ryan Chaffee, rhp, Chipola (Fla.) JC.—(AAA)
3. *Zach Cone, of, Parkview HS, Lilburn, Ga. (Special compensation—112th—for failure to sign 2007 third-round draft pick Matt Harvey).—(AA)
DRAFT DROP *Attended Georgia; re-drafted by Rangers, 2011 (1st round) • Brother of Kevin Cone, wide receiver, National Football League (2011-13)*
4. **Buddy Boshers, lhp, John C. Calhoun (Ala.) CC.—(2013)**
5. *Khiry Cooper, of, Cavalry Academy, Shreveport, La.
DRAFT DROP *Attended Nebraska; re-drafted by Red Sox, 2012 (25th round)*
6. Josh Blanco, lhp, Franklin HS, El Paso, Texas.
7. **Will Smith, lhp, Gulf Coast (Fla.) CC.—(2012-15)**
8. Christian Scholl, rhp, Green River (Wash.) CC.
9. Nick Farnsworth, 1b, Union HS, Tulsa, Okla.
10. Gabe Jacobo, 3b, Cal State Sacramento.
11. Rolando Gomez, ss, Flanagan HS, Pembroke Pines, Fla.
12. Braulio Pardo, c, St. Leo (Fla.) College.
13. **Michael Kohn, rhp, College of Charleston.—(2010-15)**
14. Reyes Dorado, rhp, Arizona State University.
15. Marcel Champagnie, of, Arizona State University.
16. **Johnny Hellweg, rhp, Florida CC.—(2013)**
17. *Jamie Mallard, 1b, Middleton HS, Tampa.
18. Adam Younger, ss, Oral Roberts University.
19. *Marshall Burford, c, Manor (Texas) HS.
20. Beau Brooks, c, Troy University.
21. Dwayne Bailey, 2b, University of Central Florida.
22. Ryan Groth, of, Oral Roberts University.
23. Matt Crawford, of, Mercer University.
24. ***Taylor Jungmann, rhp, Georgetown (Texas) HS.—(2015)**
DRAFT DROP *First-round draft pick (12th overall), Brewers (2011)*
25. Roberto Lopez, of, University of Southern California.
26. Kevin Nabors, rhp, University of South Alabama.
27. Tim Kiely, rhp, Trinity (Conn.) College.
28. Mike Kenney, rhp, Loyola Marymount University.
29. Jeremy Thorne, rhp, Florida Southern College.
30. Jayson Miller, lhp, Washington State University.
31. ***John Hicks, c, Goochland HS, Sandy Hook, Va.—(2015)**
32. *Miguel Starks, rhp, Mundy's Mill HS, Jonesboro, Ga.
33. *Jose Jimenez, 1b, University of Tampa.
34. **Drew Taylor, lhp, North Carolina State University.—(2012)**
35. Demetrius Washington, of, Middle Georgia CC.
36. Kyle Hurst, rhp, South Mountain (Ariz.) CC.
DRAFT DROP *Son of Bruce Hurst, first-round draft pick, Red Sox (1976); major leaguer (1980-94)*
37. *Evan Scott, rhp, Battlefield HS, Haymarket, Va.
38. John Rickard, c, Bishop Gorman HS, Las Vegas, Nev.
39. ***Kyle Hendricks, rhp, Capistrano Valley HS, Mission Viejo, Calif.—(2014-15)**
40. ***Donn Roach, rhp, Bishop Gorman HS, Las Vegas, Nev.—(2014-15)**
41. *Josh Edmondson, rhp, University of Florida.
42. *Chandler Griffin, rhp, Central Arizona JC.
43. *Kevin Ferguson, lhp, University of Tampa.
44. *David Fischer, rhp, Ballston Lake HS, Burnt Hills, N.Y.
45. *Jared Clark, 1b, Cal State Fullerton.
46. *Ryan Hege, c, Maize (Kan.) HS.
47. *Josh Copeland, rhp, University of Alabama.
48. *Chris Vitus, rhp, Mount Hood (Ore.) JC.
49. *Will Roberts, rhp, Maggie Walker Governor's School, Richmond, Va.
50. *Joey Belviso, of, American Heritage HS, Pembroke Pines, Fla.

## LOS ANGELES DODGERS (15)

1. **Ethan Martin, rhp-3b, Stephens County HS, Toccoa, Ga.—(2013-14)**
2. **Josh Lindblom, rhp, Purdue University.—(2011-14)**
3. Kyle Russell, of, University of Texas.—(AAA)
4. **Dee Gordon, ss, Seminole (Fla.) CC.—(2011-15)**
DRAFT DROP *Son of Tom Gordon, major leaguer (1988-2009) • Half-brother of Nick Gordon, first-round draft pick, Twins (2014)*
5. Jon Michael Redding, rhp, Florida CC.—(AA)
6. Tony Delmonico, ss, Florida State University.
7. Cole St. Clair, lhp, Rice University.
8. **Nick Buss, of, University of Southern California.—(2013)**
9. Steve Caseres, 1b, James Madison University.
10. *Chris Joyce, lhp, Dos Pueblos HS, Goleta, Calif.
11. **Nathan Eovaldi, rhp, Alvin (Texas) HS.—(2011-15)**
12. Austin Yount, 3b-rhp, Stanford University.
DRAFT DROP *Son of Larry Yount, major leaguer (1971) • Nephew of Robin Yount, major leaguer (1974-1993)*
13. Lenell McGee, of, Oakton (Ill.) CC.
14. Clay Calfee, of-1b, Angelo State (Texas) University.
15. Albie Goulder, 1b, Louisiana Tech.
16. *Kyle Conley, of, University of Washington.
17. ***Danny Coulombe, lhp, Chaparral HS, Scottsdale, Ariz.—(2014-15)**
18. **Allen Webster, rhp, McMichael HS, Mayodan, N.C.—(2013-15)**
19. ***David Rollins, lhp, First Baptist Academy, Dallas.—(2015)**
20. *Zack Cox, 3b, Pleasure Ridge Park HS, Louisville.
DRAFT DROP *First-round draft pick (25th overall), Cardinals (2010)*
21. *David Sever, rhp, St. Louis University.
22. Matt Smith, rhp, Wichita State University.
23. Brian Ruggiano, 2b, Texas A&M University.
DRAFT DROP *Brother of Justin Ruggiano, major leaguer (2007-15)*
24. Roberto Feliciano, lhp, Puerto Rico Baseball Academy, Caguas, P.R.
25. **Jerry Sands, of, Catawba (N.C.) College.—(2011-15)**
26. *Cody Weiss, rhp, Parkland HS, Allentown, Pa.
27. Clayton Allison, rhp, Fresno State University.
28. Jordan Roberts, lhp, Embry-Riddle (Fla.) University.
29. Jonathan Runnels, lhp, Rice University.
DRAFT DROP *Grandson of Pete Runnels, major leaguer (1951-64); major league manager (1966)*
30. Garett Green, 2b, San Diego State University.
31. **Matt Magill, rhp, Royal HS, Simi Valley, Calif.—(2013)**
32. Shan Sullivan, 3b, Angelo State (Texas) University.
33. Melvin Ray, of, North Florida Christian HS, Tallahassee, Fla.
34. *Andrew Darwin, of, San Jacinto (Calif.) HS.
DRAFT DROP *Son of Bobby Darwin, major leaguer (1962-77)*
35. *Adam Westmoreland, lhp, Brookland-Cayce HS, Cayce, S.C.
36. Jake New, of, Tennessee Tech.
37. *Will Clinard, rhp, East Robertson HS, Cross Plains, Tenn.
38. *Tommy Nurre, 1b, Miami (Ohio) University.
39. *Matt Murray, rhp, Owen J. Roberts HS, Spring City, Pa.
40. *Jimmy Parque, of, Skyline (Calif.) JC.
41. ***Jett Bandy, c, Thousand Oaks (Calif.) HS.—(2015)**
42. *Adam Moskowitz, 2b, Valley HS, West Des Moines, Iowa.
43. *Greg Zebrack, of, Campbell Hall HS, North Hollywood, Fla.
44. *Matt Reed, lhp, West Stanly HS, Albemarle, N.C.
45. Ryan Arp, c, University of Iowa.

## MILWAUKEE BREWERS (16)

1. **Brett Lawrie, c, Brookswood SS, Langley, B.C.—(2011-15)**
1. **Jake Odorizzi, rhp, Highland (Ill.) HS (Supplemental choice—32nd—as compensation for Type A free agent Francisco Cordero).—(2012-15)**
1. Evan Frederickson, lhp, University of San Francisco (Supplemental choice—35th—as compensation for Type A free agent Scott Linebrink).—(High A)
2. Seth Lintz, rhp, Marshall County HS, Lewisburg, Tenn. (Choice from Reds as compensation for Cordero).—(Low A)
2. Cutter Dykstra, of, Westlake HS, Thousand Oaks, Calif. (Choice from White Sox as compensation for Linebrink).—(AAA)
DRAFT DROP *Son of Lenny Dykstra, major leaguer (1985-96)*
2. Cody Adams, rhp, Southern Illinois University.—(Low A)
3. **Logan Schafer, of, Cal Poly.—(2011-15)**
4. Josh Romanski, lhp, University of San Diego.—(AAA)
5. Maverick Lasker, rhp, Sandra Day O'Connor HS, Glendale, Ariz.—(High A)
6. Jose Duran, ss, Texas A&M University.
DRAFT DROP *Brother of German Duran, major leaguer (2008)*
7. Trey Watten, rhp, Abilene Christian (Texas) University.
8. **Erik Komatsu, of, Cal State Fullerton.—(2012)**
9. Michael Bowman, rhp, Virginia Military Institute.
10. Greg Miller, rhp, Seton Hall University.
11. Mikey Marseco, ss, Samford University.
12. Garrett Sherrill, rhp, Appalachian State University.
13. **Rob Wooten, rhp, University of North Carolina.—(2013-15)**
14. Corey Kemp, c, East Carolina University.
15. Mark Willinsky, rhp, Santa Clara University.
16. Stosh Wawrzasek, rhp, Walnut Grove HS, Langley, B.C.
17. Damon Krestalude, rhp, Port St. Lucie HS, Stuart, Fla.
18. Nick Bucci, rhp, St. Patrick HS, Sarnia, Ontario.
19. Blake Billings, rhp, Hillcrest HS, Tuscaloosa, Ala.
20. Liam Ohlmann, rhp, Manchester (Conn.) CC.
21. **Lucas Luetge, lhp, Rice University.—(2012-15)**
22. Ben Jeffers, rhp, Chipola (Fla.) JC.
23. *Marcus Knecht, of, St. Michaels College HS, Toronto, Ontario.
24. Brandon Ritchie, lhp, Grand Rapids (Mich.) CC.
25. John Delaney, ss, Quinnipiac University.
26. Derrick Alfonso, c, University of Louisville.
27. ***Austin Adams, ss, Faulkner (Ala.) University.—(2014-15)**
28. *Brandon Garcia, c, Bishop Gorman HS, Las Vegas, Nev.
29. *Tommy Collier, rhp, Cypress-Fairbanks HS, Cypress, Texas.
30. Wayne Dedrick, of, Hillcrest HS, Tuscaloosa, Ala.
31. Brandon Rapoza, rhp, Flagler (Fla.) College.
32. *Colt Farrar, rhp, First Baptist Academy, Royce City, Texas.
33. *Michael White, rhp, Anderson County HS, Clinton, Tenn.
34. *Calvin Drummond, rhp, Huntington Beach (Calif.) HS.
35. Mike Vass, of, Chapman (Calif.) University.
36. *Evan Bronson, lhp, Trinity (Texas) University.
37. *Kyle Winkler, rhp, Kempner HS, Sugar Land, Texas.
38. Mike Roberts, c, Virginia Military Institute.
39. *Eric Decker, of, University of Minnesota.
DRAFT DROP *Wide receiver, National Football League (2010-15)*
40. *Nick Fogarty, lhp, Thornlea SS, Thornhill, Ontario.
41. *Joe Scott, 2b-ss, Cal State Fullerton.
42. *Ryan Wood, ss, East Carolina University.
43. *Dexter Price, rhp, Air Academy HS, Colorado Springs, Colo.
44. *Kaleb Herren, rhp, North Central Texas CC.
45. *James Kottaras, 2b-3b, Milliken Mills HS, Markham, Ontario.
DRAFT DROP *Brother of George Kottaras, major leaguer (2008-14)*
46. Carlos George, ss, James Monroe HS, Bronx, N.Y.
47. *Kayvon Bahramzadeh, rhp, Catalina Foothills HS, Tucson, Ariz.
48. Rico Salmon, rhp, Miami-Dade CC.
49. Dan Meadows, lhp, Temple (Texas) CC.
50. ***Sean Nolin, lhp, Seaford (N.Y.) HS.—(2013-15)**

## MINNESOTA TWINS (14)

1. **Aaron Hicks, of-rhp, Woodrow Wilson HS, Long Beach, Calif.—(2013-15)**
1. Carlos Gutierrez, rhp, University of Miami (Choice from Twins as compensation for Type A free agent Torii Hunter).—(AAA)
1. Shooter Hunt, rhp, Tulane University (Supplemental choice—31st—as compensation for Hunter).—(High A)
2. **Tyler Ladendorf, ss, Howard (Texas) JC.—(2015)**
3. Bobby Lanigan, of, Adelphi (N.Y.) University.—(AAA)
4. Daniel Ortiz, of, Benjamin Harrison HS, Cayey, P.R.—(AAA)
5. Nick Romero, 3b, San Diego State University.—(AAA)
6. B.J. Hermsen, rhp, West Delaware HS, Masonville, Iowa.
7. Dan Osterbrock, lhp, University of Cincinnati.
8. Jeff Lanning, c, University of New Orleans.
9. Mike Gonzales, 1b, Diablo Valley (Calif.) JC.
10. Evan Bigley, of, Dallas Baptist University.
11. Dominic de la Osa, of-2b, Vanderbilt University.
12. Kyle Carr, lhp, University of Minnesota.
13. Mike Harrington, of, College of Charleston.
14. Blayne Weller, rhp, Key West (Fla.) HS.
15. *David Coulon, lhp, University of Arizona.
16. ***Kolten Wong, 2b, Kamehameha HS, Honolulu, Hawaii.—(2013-15)**
DRAFT DROP *First-round draft pick (22nd overall), Cardinals (2011)*
17. Blake Martin, lhp, Louisiana State University.
18. *Matt Nohelty, of, University of Minnesota.
19. Bruce Pugh, rhp, Hillsborough (Fla.) JC.
20. ***Aaron Barrett, rhp, Wabash Valley (Ill.) JC.—(2014-15)**
21. Steve Blevins, rhp, Marshall University.
22. *Kyle Witten, rhp, Bakersfield (Calif.) JC.
23. *Chris Odegaard, rhp, Minnesota State University-Mankato.
24. *Lionel Morrill, of, Vauxhall (Alberta) HS.
25. Alex Curry, rhp, Cypress (Calif.) JC.
26. Adan Severino, of, University of Miami.
27. *Jerico Weitzel, 2b, Ridgway (Pa.) HS.
28. Nate Hanson, 3b, University of Minnesota.
29. *Joe Loftus, 3b, Academy of Holy Angels, Savage, Minn.
30. **Michael Tonkin, rhp, Palmdale (Calif.) HS.—(2013-15)**
31. *Lee Ridenhour, rhp, Shawnee Mission West HS, Lenexa, Kan.
32. ***Adam Conley, lhp, Olympia (Wash.) HS.—(2015)**
33. *Luke Yoder, of, Cal Poly.
34. *Adam Purdy, rhp, Pell City (Ala.) HS.
35. *Sam Ryan, c, Tartan HS, Oakdale, Minn.
36. *Miers Quigley, lhp, University of Alabama.
37. Javier Brown, ss, Grossmont (Calif.) JC.
38. *Alex Mendez, lhp, Bishop Moore HS, Longwood, Fla.
39. *Steve Proscia, 3b, Don Bosco Prep, Ramsey, N.J.
40. *Wade Kapteyn, rhp, University of Evansville.
41. *Pat Lehman, rhp, George Washington University.
42. *Riley Boening, lhp, University of Texas.
43. *Chase Pickering, lhp, Nitro (W.Va.) HS.
44. *Colby Sokol, of, Emerald Ridge HS, Puyallup, Wash.
45. *Mike Spina, 3b, University of Cincinnati.
46. *Lyndon Eusea, of, Hahnville (La.) HS.
47. *Tom Farmer, rhp, University of Akron.
48. ***George Springer, of, Avon Old Farms HS, Avon, Conn.—(2014-15)**
DRAFT DROP *First-round draft pick (11th overall), Astros (2011)*
49. *Johnny Bromberg, rhp, Los Angeles Pierce JC.
50. *Tyler Anderson, lhp, Spring Valley HS, Las Vegas, Nev.
DRAFT DROP *First-round draft pick (20th overall), Rockies (2011)*

## NEW YORK METS (22)

1. **Ike Davis, 1b-of, Arizona State University** (Choice from Braves as compensation for Type A free agent Tom Glavine).**—(2010-15)**
DRAFT DROP *Son of Ron Davis, major leaguer (1978-88)*
1. Reese Havens, ss, University of South Carolina.—(AAA)
1. Brad Holt, rhp, UNC Wilmington (Supplemental choice—33rd—for loss of Glavine).—(AAA)
2. Javier Rodriguez, of, Puerto Rico Baseball Academy, Caguas, P.R.—(Low A)
3. **Kirk Niewenhuis, of, Azusa Pacific (Calif.) University.—(2012-15)**
4. Sean Ratliff, of, Stanford University.—(AA)
5. Dock Doyle, c, Coastal Carolina University.—(High A)
6. **Josh Satin, 2b, University of California.—(2011-14)**
7. Michael Hebert, rhp, Saugus (Calif.) HS.
8. **Eric Campbell, 3b, Boston College.—(2014-15)**
9. Eric Beaulac, rhp, LeMoyne College.
10. Brian Valenzuela, lhp, Vista Murrieta HS, Murrieta, Calif.
11. Jeff Kaplan, rhp, Cal State Fullerton.
12. Mark Cohoon, lhp, North Central Texas JC.
13. Scott Shaw, rhp, University of Illinois.
14. Brandon Moore, rhp, Indiana Wesleyan University.
15. *Jamie Bruno, 1b, Mandeville HS, Covington, La.
16. Travis Babin, rhp, Sonoma State (Calif.) University.
17. Mitch Houck, lhp, University of Central Florida.
18. **Collin McHugh, rhp, Berry (Ga.) College.—(2012-15)**
19. Zach Rosenbaum, rhp, UNC Charlotte.
20. Michael Moras, c, University of New Haven.
21. Jimmy Fuller, lhp, Southern Connecticut State University.
22. **Chris Schwinden, rhp, Fresno Pacific (Calif.) University.—(2011-12)**
23. Evan LeBlanc, of, Santa Clara University.
24. Kyle Allen, rhp, The Pendleton School, Bradenton, Fla.
25. Erik Turgeon, rhp, University of Connecticut.
26. John Servidio, of, Barry (Fla.) University.
27. Jeff Flagg, 1b, Mississippi State University.
28. Jimmy Johnson, lhp, Biola (Calif.) University.
29. *Mike Giuffre, 2b, Tottenville HS, Staten Island, N.Y.
30. Mike Lynn, rhp, College of Charleston.
31. Michael Powers, rhp, University of Michigan.
32. *Mark Grbavac, rhp, Oregon State University.
33. *Neil Medchill, of, Oklahoma State University.
34. Justin Garber, of, Shippensburg (Pa.) University.
35. Kyle Suire, 2b, University of Louisiana-Monroe.
36. Jake Goldberg, rhp, College of Charleston.
37. Tim Erickson, lhp, Lamar University.
38. Chris Hilliard, lhp, Itawamba (Miss.) JC.
39. Charlie Hinojosa, c, Don Antonio Lugo HS, Chino, Calif.
40. Seth Williams, of, University of North Carolina.
41. Tyler Howe, c, University of Kentucky.
42. Tim Smith, rhp, Catawba (N.C.) College.
43. Mark McGonigle, of, University of New Orleans.
44. *Jean-Francois Ricard, lhp, Ahuntsic (Quebec) College.
45. *David Phillips, 1b, Texarkana (Texas) JC.
46. *Brian Gump, of, UC Santa Barbara.
47. *Matt Bischoff, rhp, Purdue University.
48. *Tyler Baisley, of, Gateway (Ariz.) CC.
49. Doug McNulty, 1b, University of Akron.
50. *Kameron Brunty, of, Gulf Breeze (Fla.) HS.

## NEW YORK YANKEES (28)

1. ***Gerrit Cole, rhp, Orange Lutheran HS, Santa Ana, Calif.—(2013-15)**
DRAFT DROP *Attended UCLA; first overall draft pick, Pirates (2011)*
1. Jeremy Bleich, lhp, Stanford University (Supplemental choice—44th—as compensation for Type B free agent Luis Vizcaino).—(AAA)
2. *Scott Bittle, rhp, University of Mississippi.—(Short-season A)
DRAFT DROP *Returned to Mississippi; re-drafted by Cardinals, 2009 (4th round)*
3. **David Adams, 2b, University of Virginia.—(2013)**
4. **Corban Joseph, ss, Franklin (Tenn.) HS.—(2013)**
5. Chris Smith, of, Centennial HS, Los Angeles.—(Rookie)
6. **Brett Marshall, rhp, Ross S. Sterling HS, Baytown, Texas.—(2013)**
7. Kyle Higashioka, c, Edison HS, Huntington Beach, Calif.
8. Daniel Brewer, of, Bradley University.
9. Mikey O'Brien, rhp, Hidden Valley HS, Roanoke, Va.
10. **D.J. Mitchell, rhp, Clemson University.—(2012)**
11. Ray Kruml, of, University of South Alabama.
12. Luke Greinke, rhp, Auburn University.
DRAFT DROP *Brother of Zack Greinke, first-round draft pick, Royals (2002); major leaguer (2004-15)*
13. Jack Rye, of, Florida State University.
14. **David Phelps, rhp, University of Notre Dame.—(2012-15)**
15. Matt Richardson, rhp, Lake Mary (Fla.) HS.
16. *Luke Anders, 1b, Texas A&M University.
17. Addison Maruszak, ss, University of South Florida.
18. Brandon Braboy, rhp, University of Indianapolis.
19. Mitch Abeita, c, University of Nebraska.
20. **Pat Venditte, rhp-lhp, Creighton University.—(2015)**
21. Mitch Delaney, 1b, Western Texas JC.
22. Cory Arbiso, rhp, Cal State Fullerton.
23. Ryan Wilkes, 2b, University of Kentucky.
24. Mike Lyon, 3b, Northeastern University.
25. Jeff Nutt, c, University of Arkansas.
26. *Blake Monar, lhp, South Spencer HS, Rockport, Ind.
27. Garrison Lassiter, ss, West Forsyth HS, High Point, N.C.
28. Chad Gross, of, Cuesta (Calif.) JC.
DRAFT DROP *Son of Kevin Gross, major leaguer (1983-97)*
29. Mike Jones, of, Arizona State University.
30. *Ben McMahan, c, Bishop Moore HS, Windermere, Fla.
31. Spencer Lucian, 2b, Princeton University.
32. *Andy Suiter, lhp, UC Davis.
33. Tommy Baldridge, of, Coastal Carolina University.
34. Brad Rulon, rhp, Georgia Tech.
35. Andrew Shive, rhp, Azusa Pacific (Calif.) University.
36. ***Chris Dwyer, lhp, Salisbury (Conn.) School.—(2013)**
37. *Justin Harper, rhp, Yavapai (Ariz.) JC.
38. *Clay Caulfield, rhp, College of Charleston.
39. Erik Lovett, 1b, Mount Olive (N.C.) College.
40. *Sam Mende, ss, Clearwater Central Catholic HS, Clearwater, Fla.
41. *Mykal Stokes, of, Tustin (Calif.) HS.
42. Clint Preisendorfer, lhp, San Diego Christian College.
43. *Matt Summers, rhp-of, Chaparral HS, Scottsdale, Ariz.
44. *Evan Ocheltree, of, Wake Forest University.
45. *Creede Simpson, ss, Auburn (Ala.) HS.
46. *Matt Veltmann, rhp, San Diego CC.
47. Ryan Flannery, rhp, Fairleigh Dickinson University.
48. ***Rob Scahill, rhp, Bradley University.—(2012-15)**
49. *John Folino, rhp, University of Connecticut.
50. Nik Turley, lhp, Harvard-Westlake HS, Los Angeles.

## OAKLAND ATHLETICS (12)

1. **Jemile Weeks, 2b, University of Miami.—(2011-15)**
DRAFT DROP *Brother of Rickie Weeks, first-round draft pick, Brewers (2003); major leaguer (2003-14)*
2. **Tyson Ross, rhp, University of California.—(2010-15)**
DRAFT DROP *Brother of Joe Ross, first-round draft pick, Padres (2011)*
3. Preston Paramore, c, Arizona State University.—(AAA)
4. Anthony Capra, lhp, Wichita State Univ.—(AAA)
5. Jason Christian, ss, University of Michigan.–(AA)
6. Tyreace House, of, JC of the Canyons (Calif.).
7. Brett Hunter, rhp, Pepperdine University.
8. Jeremy Barfield, of, San Jacinto (Texas) JC.
DRAFT DROP *Son of Jesse Barfield, major leaguer (1981-92) • Brother of Josh Barfield, major leaguer (2006-09)*
9. Mitch LeVier, c, Fullerton (Calif.) JC.
10. Rashun Dixon, c, Terry HS, Jackson, Miss.
11. Chris Berroa, of, Chipola (Fla.) JC.
12. *Zach Elgie, 1b, Minot (N.D.) HS.
13. Daniel Thomas, rhp, University of South Florida.
14. David Thomas, of, Catawba (N.C.) College.
15. Nino Leyja, ss, Houston Christian HS, Houston.
16. Matt Fitts, rhp, Lewis-Clark State (Idaho) College.
17. ***Brad Glenn, 3b, University of Arizona.—(2014)**
18. *Rayan Gonzalez, rhp, Antonio Luchetti HS, Arecibo, P.R.
19. Mike Hart, rhp, Texas State University.
20. Rodney Rutherford, 3b, Columbus State (Ga.) University.
21. Mathieu LeBlanc-Poirier, rhp, Ahuntsic (Quebec) College.
22. ***Preston Guilmet, rhp, University of Arizona.—(2013-15)**
23. ***Chris Rusin, lhp, University of Kentucky.—(2012-15)**
24. Kenny Smalley, rhp, Delta State University.
25. Trey Barham, lhp, Virginia Military Institute.
26. Ryan Doolittle, rhp, Cumberland County (N.J.) CC.
27. *Brent Warren, of, Xavier HS, Cedar Rapids, Iowa.
28. **Dusty Coleman, ss, Wichita State University.—(2015)**
29. Justin Murray, rhp, Kansas State University.
30. Ryne Jernigan, 2b, University of South Alabama.
31. **Mickey Storey, rhp, Florida Atlantic University.—(2012-13)**
32. Ben Hornbeck, lhp, Kansas State University.
33. Shawn Haviland, rhp, Harvard University.
34. *Riley Welch, rhp, Desert Mountain HS, Scottsdale, Ariz.
DRAFT DROP *Son of Bob Welch, first-round draft pick, Dodgers (1977); major leaguer (1978-94)*
35. *Virgil Hill, of, Los Angeles Mission JC.
36. *Jonathan Berti, ss, Troy (Mich.) HS.
37. *Ryan Doiron, rhp, Barbe HS, Lake Charles, La.
38. *Bobby Crocker, of, Aptos (Calif.) HS.
39. *Denny Clement, rhp, Cascia Hall HS, Tulsa, Okla.
40. *Jeff Dennis, lhp, Binghamton University.
41. *Cody Hawn, 3b, Walters State (Tenn.) JC.
42. *Kent Walton, 2b, Brigham Young University.
43. ***Nick Maronde, lhp, Lexington Catholic HS, Lexington, Ky.—(2012-14)**
44. *Jimmy Messer, rhp, South Caldwell HS, Hudson, N.C.
45. *Derek Benny, rhp, Roseville (Calif.) HS.
46. ***J.R. Graham, rhp, Livermore (Calif.) HS.—(2015)**
47. *Coley Crank, c, Pinole Valley HS, Pinole, Calif.
48. *Brett Holland, rhp, University of Texas-Tyler.
49. *Matt Bowman, 2b, University of Nevada.
50. *Derek Wiley, 1b-3b, Belmont University.

## PHILADELPHIA PHILLIES (24)

1. Anthony Hewitt, 3b, Salisbury (Conn.) School.—(AA)
1. Zach Collier, of, Chino Hills (Calif.) HS (Supplemental choice—34th—as compensation for Type A free agent Aaron Rowand).—(AA)
2. **Anthony Gose, lhp-of, Bellflower (Calif.) HS** (Choice from Giants as compensation for Rowand).**—(2012-15)**
2. Jason Knapp, rhp, North Hunterdon Regional HS, Annandale, N.J.—(High A)
3. **Vance Worley, rhp, Long Beach State University.—(2010-15)**
4. **Jonathan Pettibone, lhp, Esperanza HS, Anaheim, Calif.** (Special compensation—110th—for failure to sign 2007 third-round draft pick Brandon Workman).**—(2013-14)**
4. **Trevor May, rhp, Kelso (Wash.) HS.—(2014-15)**
5. Jeremy Hamilton, 1b, Wright State University.—(Low A)
6. Colby Shreve, rhp, CC of Southern Nevada.
7. *Johnny Coy, 3b, Benton HS, St. Joseph, Mo.
8. Julio Rodriguez, rhp, Puerto Rico Baseball Academy, Caguas P.R.
9. Cody Overbeck, 3b, University of Mississippi.
10. Jean Carlos Rodriguez, c, George Washington HS, Bronx, N.Y.
11. **Mike Stutes, rhp, Oregon State University.—(2011-13)**
12. ***Ryan Weber, rhp, Clearwater Central Catholic HS, Clearwater, Fla.—(2015)**
13. **B.J. Rosenberg, rhp, University of Louisville.—(2012-14)**
14. **Michael Schwimer, rhp, University of Virginia.—(2011-12)**
15. Damarii Saunderson, of, Northville (Mich.) HS.
16. Troy Hanzawa, ss, San Diego State University.
17. Jimmy Murphy, 1b, Washington State University.
18. **Tyler Cloyd, rhp, University of Nebraska-Omaha.—(2012-13)**
19. **Steve Susdorf, of, Fresno State University.—(2013)**
20. Eryk McConnell, rhp, North Carolina State University.
21. Sean Grieve, lhp, College of William & Mary.
22. Daniel Hargrave, 2b, UNC Wilmington.
23. Brandon Haislet, of, University of Hawaii.
24. Korey Noles, lhp, Columbus State (Ga.) University.
25. *Dan Edwards, rhp, Kansas State University.
26. Ryan Bergh, rhp, Old Dominion University.
27. Chad Poe, rhp, Bossier Parish (La.) CC.
28. Jordan Ellis, rhp, Villanova University.
29. ***Keon Broxton, ss, Lakeland (Fla.) HS.—(2015)**
30. *D.J. Henderson, ss, Southeastern HS, Detroit.
31. Spencer Arroyo, lhp, Modesto (Calif.) JC.
DRAFT DROP *Son of Rudy Arroyo, major leaguer (1971)*
32. Shaun Ellis, rhp, Polk (Fla.) CC.
33. *Jamie Simpson, 1b, Dowagiac Union HS, Dowagiac, Mich.
34. *Blaine O'Brien, rhp, Scituate (Mass.) HS.
35. Ruddy Rio-Nunez, rhp, Edouard Montpetit HS, Montreal.
36. Mike Cisco, rhp, University of South Carolina.
DRAFT DROP *Grandson of Galen Cisco, major leaguer (1961-69)*
37. *Matt Johnson, of, John W. North HS, Riverside, Calif.
38. **Jarred Cosart, rhp, Clear Creek HS, League City, Texas.—(2013-15)**
39. *Joe Pond, rhp, Judge Memorial Catholic HS, Centreville, Utah.
40. *Daniel Marrs, rhp, James River HS, Midlothian, Va.
41. *Mike Petello, of, Scottsdale (Ariz.) CC.
42. Mike Bolsenbroek, rhp, Apeldoorn, Netherlands.
43. Bryan Frew, of, University of Nebraska-Omaha.
44. *Charlie Law, rhp, Mainland Regional HS, Linwood, N.J.
45. *Justin Zumwalde, 1b, Sabino HS, Tucson, Ariz.
46. ***Giovanni Soto, lhp, Advanced Central College HS, Carolina, P.R.—(2015)**
47. Nathan Fike, lhp, Potomac State (W.Va.) JC.
48. *Mark Ginther, ss, Jenks HS, Tulsa, Okla.
49. *Michael Russo, rhp, Hun School, Hamilton Square, N.J.
50. *Josh Hake, rhp, Park (Mo.) University.

## PITTSBURGH PIRATES (2)

1. **Pedro Alvarez, 3b, Vanderbilt University.—(2010-15)**
2. ***Tanner Scheppers, rhp, Fresno State University.—(2012-15)**
DRAFT DROP *Signed with St. Paul/American Association (independent); re-drafted by Rangers, 2009 (1st round)*
3. **Jordy Mercer, ss-rhp, Oklahoma State University.—(2012-15)**
4. **Chase d'Arnaud, ss, Pepperdine University.—(2011-15)**
DRAFT DROP *Brother of Travis d'Arnaud, first-round draft pick, Phillies (2007); major leaguer (2013-15)*
5. **Justin Wilson, lhp, Fresno State**

**University.—(2012-15)**

**6. Robbie Grossman, of, Cypress-Fairbanks HS, Cypress, Texas.—(2013-15)**

7. Benji Gonzalez, ss, Puerto Rico Baseball Academy, Caguas, P.R.

8. Jeremy Farrell, 1b-3b, University of Virginia.

DRAFT DROP *Son of John Farrell, major leaguer (1987-96); major league manager (2011-15)*

**9. Matt Hague, 3b-of, University of Washington.—(2012-15)**

10. *Drew Gagnon, rhp, Liberty Union HS, Brentwood, Calif.

11. David Rubinstein, of, Appalachian State University.

12. Calvin Anderson, 1b, Southern University.

13. *Seth Gardner, of, Highland Park HS, Dallas.

14. Mike Colla, rhp, University of Arizona.

15. Chris Aure, lhp, North Pole (Alaska) HS.

16. Wes Freeman, of, All Saints Academy, Lakeland, Fla.

17. *Jaron Shepherd, of, Navarro (Texas) JC.

DRAFT DROP *Son of Ron Shepherd, major leaguer (1984-86)*

18. Jarek Cunningham, ss, Mount Spokane HS, Spokane, Wash.

19. *Jason Haniger, c, Georgia Tech.

20. Quinn Miller, rhp, Shawnee HS, Medford, N.J.

21. Brent Klinger, rhp, Glendale (Ariz.) CC.

22. *Patrick Palmeiro, 3b, Heritage HS, Colleyville, Texas.

DRAFT DROP *Son of Rafael Palmeiro, major leaguer (1986-2005)*

23. *Austin Wright, lhp-1b, James B. Conant HS, Schaumburg, Ill.

24. *Brian Litwin, 3b-of, St. Stephens HS, Hickory, N.C.

25. Brian Leach, rhp, University of Southern Mississippi.

26. *Zach Wilson, 3b, Woodrow Wilson HS, Long Beach, Calif.

27. Edwin Roman, of, Puerto Rico Baseball Academy, Caguas, P.R.

28. Kyle Saukko, rhp, Sierra (Calif.) JC.

29. *Kevin Komstadius, 1b, East Valley HS, Yakima, Wash.

30. *Daniel Martin, rhp, Panola (Texas) JC.

31. *Ryan Hinson, lhp, Clemson University.

32. *T.J. Forrest, rhp, Bossier Parish (La.) JC.

33. Mark Carver, c, UNC Wilmington.

34. Matt Payne, 3b, North Carolina State University.

35. Tyler Cox, lhp, Illinois State University.

36. Kyle Morgan, of, University of San Francisco.

37. *Matt Curry, 1b, Howard (Texas) JC.

38. Alan Knotts, rhp, Louisiana Tech.

39. Albert Fagan, rhp, Rockland (N.Y.) CC.

40. *Beau Didier, 3b, Bellarmine Prep, Federal Way, Wash.

41. Chris Simmons, c, U.S. Military Academy.

42. Cole White, of, U.S. Military Academy.

43. *Johnny Gunter, rhp-c, Chattahoochee Valley (Ala.) CC.

44. Mike Williams, c, Mount Olive (N.C.) College.

45. Allen Ponder, rhp, Auburn University-Montgomery.

**46. *Scott McGough, ss, Plum HS, Pittsburgh.—(2015)**

47. *Jordan Craft, of, Kennesaw Mountain HS, Kennesaw, Ga.

48. Owen Brolsma, rhp, Texas Tech.

49. Zach Foster, rhp-ss, University of Pittsburgh-Bradford.

50. Craig Parry, of, South Dakota State University.

## ST. LOUIS CARDINALS (13)

**1. Brett Wallace, 3b-1b, Arizona State University.—(2010-15)**

**1. Lance Lynn, rhp, University of Mississippi** (Supplemental choice—39th—as compensation for Type B free agent Troy Percival).—**(2011-15)**

**2. Shane Peterson, of-1b, Long Beach State University.—(2013-15)**

3. Niko Vasquez, ss, Durango HS, Las Vegas, Nev.—(AA)

4. Scott Gorgen, rhp, UC Irvine.—(AAA)

DRAFT DROP *Twin brother of Matt Gorgen, 16th-round draft pick, Rays (2008)*

**5. Jermaine Curtis, 3b, UCLA.—(2013)**

**6. Eric Fornataro, rhp, Miami-Dade CC.—(2014)**

7. Anthony Ferrara, lhp, Riverview (Fla.) HS.

8. Ryan Kulik, lhp, Rowan (N.J.) University.

9. Aaron Luna, of, Rice University.

**10. Alex Castellanos, 2b, Belmont-Abbey (N.C.) College.—(2012-13)**

11. Devin Shepherd, of, CC of Southern Nevada.

12. Michael Swinson, of, Coffee HS, Douglas, Ga.

**13. Mitch Harris, rhp, U.S. Naval Academy.—(2015)**

14. Charlie Cutler, of-c, University of California.

15. Scott McGregor, rhp, University of Memphis.

16. Miguel Flores, rhp, Cerritos (Calif.) CC.

17. Josh Hester, rhp, Freed-Hardeman (Tenn.) University.

18. Jared Bradford, rhp, Louisiana State University.

**19. Xavier Scruggs, 1b, University of Nevada-Las Vegas.—(2014-15)**

20. Luis Mateo, ss, Puerto Rico Baseball Academy, Orocovis, P.R.

21. Matt Rigoli, 1b, Pace (N.Y.) University.

22. Colt Sedbrook, 2b, University of Arizona.

23. Jonny Bravo, lhp, Azusa Pacific (Calif.) University.

24. Zach Pitts, rhp, University of Louisville.

25. Jason Buursma, rhp, Bucknell University.

26. Chris Swauger, of, The Citadel.

27. George Brown, lhp, St. John's University.

28. Matt Frevert, rhp, Missouri State University.

29. Brett Lilley, 2b, University of Notre Dame.

30. *Brett Bruening, rhp, Grayson County (Texas) CC.

31. *Justin Leith, lhp, Barron Collier HS, Naples, Fla.

**32. Sam Freeman, lhp, University of Kansas.—(2012-15)**

33. Kevin Thomas, rhp, Stephen F. Austin University.

34. Jack Cawley, c, Pace (N.Y.) University.

35. *Shane Boras, 2b, Junipero Serra Catholic HS, San Juan Capistrano, Calif.

36. Chris Notti, rhp, Moorpark (Calif.) JC.

37. *Danny Jimenez, lhp, St. Charles North HS, St. Charles, Ill.

38. Dan Richardson, lhp, University of Delaware.

39. Curt Smith, 1b, University of Maine.

40. Paul Cruz, of, University of Tampa.

**41. Kevin Siegrist, lhp, Palm Beach (Fla.) CC.—(2013-15)**

42. Blake Murphy, c, Western Carolina University.

43. Joe Babrick, of, King HS, Tampa.

44. Santo Maertz, rhp, St. Peter's College.

45. *Chris Taylor, c, UNC Charlotte.

46. *Brandon Sizemore, 2b, College of Charleston.

47. *Tony Asaro, of, UC Irvine.

48. Adam Prange, rhp, South Mountain (Ariz.) CC.

49. Adam Veres, rhp, St. Petersburg (Fla.) CC.

50. *Danny Miranda, lhp, Killian HS, Miami.

## SAN DIEGO PADRES (23)

**1. Allan Dykstra, 1b, Wake Forest University.—(2015)**

**1. Jaff Decker, of, Sunrise Mountain HS, Phoenix** (Supplemental choice—42nd—as compensation for Type B free agent Doug Brocail).—**(2013-15)**

**1. Logan Forsythe, 3b, University of Arkansas** (Supplemental choice—46th—as compensation for Type B free agent Mike Cameron).—**(2011-15)**

**2. James Darnell, 3b, University of South Carolina.—(2011-12)**

**3. Blake Tekotte, of, University of Miami.—(2011-13)**

3. Sawyer Carroll, of, University of Kentucky (Special compensation—111th—for failure to sign 2007 third-round draft pick Tommy Toledo).—(AAA)

**4. *Jason Kipnis, of, Arizona State University.—(2011-15)**

DRAFT DROP *Returned to Arizona State; re-drafted by Indians, 2009 (2nd round)*

**5. Anthony Bass, rhp, Wayne State (Mich.) University.—(2011-15)**

**6. Cole Figueroa, ss, University of Florida.—(2014-15)**

DRAFT DROP *Son of Bien Figueroa, major leaguer (1992) • Twin brother of Corey Figueroa, 41st-round draft pick, Giants (2008)*

7. Adam Zornes, c, Rice University.

8. Beamer Weems, ss, Baylor University.

9. *Kyle Thebeau, rhp, Texas A&M University.

**10. Andrew Albers, lhp, University of Kentucky.—(2013-15)**

11. Tyson Bagley, rhp, Dallas Baptist University.

**12. Matt Clark, 1b, Louisiana State University.—(2014)**

DRAFT DROP *Son of Terry Clark, major leaguer (1988-97)*

**13. Erik Davis, rhp, Stanford University.—(2013)**

14. Rob Musgrave, lhp, Wichita State University.

15. *Brett Mooneyham, lhp, Buhach Colony HS, Merced, Calif.

DRAFT DROP *Son of Bill Mooneyham, major leaguer (1986)*

16. Tom Davis, rhp, Fordham University.

17. Derek Shunk, ss, Villanova University.

**18. Nick Vincent, rhp, Long Beach State University.—(2012-15)**

19. Robert Lara, c, University of Central Florida.

20. Jason Codiroli, of, West Valley (Calif.) JC.

DRAFT DROP *Nephew of Chris Codiroli, major leaguer (1982-90)*

21. Joey Railey, 2b, University of San Francisco.

22. Chris Wilkes, rhp, Dr. Phillips HS, Orlando, Fla.

23. *Nick Conaway, rhp, Walnut Cove, N.C.

24. Eric Gonzalez, rhp, University of South Alabama.

25. *Logan Power, of, University of Mississippi.

**26. Dean Anna, ss, Ball State University.—(2014-15)**

27. Aaron Murphree, of, University of Arkansas.

28. Nick Schumacher, rhp, Wayne State (Neb.) College.

29. Omar Gutierrez, rhp, Texas A&M-Corpus Christi.

30. Bobby Verbick, of, Sam Houston State University.

**31. *Sean Gilmartin, lhp, Crespi HS, Moorpark, Calif.—(2015)**

DRAFT DROP *First-round draft pick (28th overall), Braves (2011)*

32. Kyle Heyne, rhp, Ball State University.

**33. Dan Robertson, of, Oregon State University.—(2014-15)**

34. Matt Gaski, 2b, UNC Greensboro.

35. Logan Gelbrich, c, University of San Diego.

36. *Jake Shadle, rhp, Graham-Kapowsin HS, Graham, Wash.

37. Matt Means, lhp, Sonoma State (Calif.) University.

38. Zach Herr, lhp, University of Nebraska.

39. Gary Poynter, rhp, Lubbock Christian (Texas) University.

40. Colin Lynch, rhp, St. John's University.

41. *Zack Dascenzo, c, Lake Highlands HS, Uniontown, Pa.

DRAFT DROP *Son of Doug Dascenzo, major leaguer (1988-96)*

**42. Brad Brach, rhp, Monmouth University.—(2011-15)**

43. *James Tunnell, rhp, Oklahoma City, Okla.

DRAFT DROP *Son of Lee Tunnell, major leaguer (1982-89)*

## SAN FRANCISCO GIANTS (5)

**1. Buster Posey, c, Florida State University.—(2009-15)**

**1. Conor Gillaspie, 3b, Wichita State University** (Supplemental choice—37th—as compensation for Type B free agent Aaron Fultz).—**(2008-15)**

DRAFT DROP *First player from 2008 draft to reach majors (Sept. 9, 2008) • Brother of Casey Gillaspie, first-round draft pick, Rays (2014)*

2. (Choice to Phillies as compensation for Type A free agent Aaron Rowand)

**3. Roger Kieschnick, of Texas Tech.—(2013-14)**

**4. Brandon Crawford, ss, UCLA.—(2011-15)**

5. Edwin Quirarte, rhp, Cal State Northridge.—(AAA)

**6. Eric Surkamp, lhp, North Carolina State University.—(2011-15)**

7. Aaron King, lhp, Surry (N.C.) CC.

**8. Scott Barnes, lhp, St. John's University.—(2012-13)**

**9. Ryan Verdugo, lhp, Louisiana State University.—(2012)**

10. *Ryan O'Sullivan, rhp, Valhalla HS, El Cajon, Calif.

DRAFT DROP *Brother of Sean O'Sullivan, major leaguer (2009-15)*

11. Justin Fitzgerald, rhp, UC Davis.

12. Ari Ronick, lhp, University of Portland.

**13. Juan Carlos Perez, of, Western Oklahoma State JC.—(2013-15)**

14. Caleb Curry, of, University of Iowa.

15. Daniel Cook, 3b-2b, Florida Atlantic University.

16. C.J. Ziegler, 1b, University of Arizona.

17. Brian Irving, rhp, Yale University.

18. Brooks Lindsley, ss, Lower Columbia (Wash.) CC.

19. Ryan Mantle, of, Missouri State University.

20. *Trey Sutton, 2b, University of Southern Mississippi.

21. Mike Eifel, rhp, Dominican (Ill.) University.

22. *Carter Bell, ss, Georges P. Vanier SS, Courtenay, B.C.

23. Jason Jarvis, rhp, Lincoln (American Association).

24. *Wes Musick, lhp, University of Houston.

25. Damon Wright, of, Dartmouth College.

26. Ryan Lormand, 2b, University of Houston.

27. Kyle Woodruff, rhp, Chico State (Calif.) University.

28. Shane Kaufman, rhp, San Diego State University.

29. Rob Flanagan, 1b, North Georgia College.

30. Vladimir Frias, ss, Tennessee Wesleyan College.

31. Aaron Davidson, rhp, University of Arkansas-Fort Smith JC.

32. *John Michael Blake, rhp, Lake Sumter (Fla.) CC.

33. Ryne Price, of, University of Kansas.

34. *Francois Lafreniere, rhp, Ahuntsic (Quebec) College.

35. *Dan Black, c, Purdue University.

36. *Matt Way, lhp, Washington State University.

37. *Jeremy Penn, rhp, Western Oklahoma State JC.

38. Chris Wilson, rhp, Trinidad State (Colo.) JC.

39. *Braden Kapteyn, 3b, Illiana Christian HS, Lansing, Ill.

40. *Austin Stadler, 1b, James River HS, Midlothian, Va.

41. *Corey Figueroa, 2b, St. Petersburg (Fla.) JC.

DRAFT DROP *Son of Bien Figueroa, major leaguer (1992) • Twin brother of Cole Figueroa, 6th-round draft pick, Padres (2008); major leaguer (2014-15)*

42. *Tyler Thompson, of, Jupiter Community HS, Jupiter, Fla.

DRAFT DROP *Son of Robby Thompson, major leaguer (1986-96) • Brother of Logan Thompson, 42nd-round draft pick, Indians (2008)*

43. *Zack Thornton, rhp, Ventura (Calif.) JC.

44. Aaron Lowenstein, c, UC Irvine.

45. *Kahlin Villines, Riverside HS, Durham, N.C.

46. *Joey Hainsfurther, ss, Highland Park HS, Dallas.

47. *Abe Ruiz, 3b, Pacific Grove (Calif.) HS.

48. Leonardo Ochoa, 2b, Longeuil, Quebec.

49. *D.J. Hicks, 1b, Lake Brantley HS, Altamonte Springs, Fla.

50. *Chase Ware, rhp, Arkansas State University.

## SEATTLE MARINERS (20)

**1. Josh Fields, rhp, University of Georgia.—(2013-15)**

2. Dennis Raben, of, University of Miami.–(High A)

3. Aaron Pribanic, rhp, University of Nebraska.—(AA)

DRAFT DROP *Grandson of Jim Coates, major leaguer (1956-67)*

4. Steve Hensley, rhp, Elon University.—(AAA)

5. Brett Lorin, rhp, Long Beach State University.—(AAA)

6. Jarrett Burgess, of, Florida Christian HS, Miami.

7. Nate Tenbrink, 3b, Kansas State University.

**8. Bobby LaFromboise, lhp, University of New Mexico.—(2013-15)**

9. *Billy Morrison, rhp, Western Michigan University.

10. *Nate Newman, rhp, Pepperdine University.

11. *Matt Jensen, 2b, Clovis East HS, Clovis, Calif.

12. Kenn Kasparek, rhp, University of Texas.

13. Ryan Royster, of, UC Davis.

DRAFT DROP *Nephew of Jerry Royster, major leaguer (1973-88)*

14. Luke Burnett, rhp, Louisiana Tech.

15. Jake Schaffer, of, Northern Kentucky University.

16. Ben Billingsley, 2b, Lenoir (N.C.) CC.

17. *Mike Dennhardt, rhp, Don Bosco Prep, Oradell, N.J.
18. Travis Howell, c, Long Beach State University.
19. Taylor Lewis, rhp, Yavapai (Ariz.) JC.
20. Fred Bello, ss, Cerro Coso (Calif.) JC.
21. Jordan Alvis, rhp, Middle Tennessee State University.
22. Blake Nation, rhp, Georgia Southern University.
23. **Brandon Maurer, rhp, Orange Lutheran HS, Santa Ana, Calif.—(2013-15)**
24. Henry Contreras, c, Cal State Los Angeles.
25. *Paul Robinson, 2b, Paris (Texas) JC.
26. Taylor Stanton, rhp, Diablo Valley (Calif.) JC.
27. Tommy Johnson, c, Marshall University.
28. Scott Savastano, ss, Franklin Pierce (N.H.) College
29. Stephen Penney, rhp, UC Riverside.
30. Brad Reid, rhp, Bellevue (Wash.) CC.
31. Randy Castillo, rhp, Aiea (Hawaii) HS.
32. Nick Love, rhp, Bellevue (Neb.) University.
33. Kyle Brown, lhp, UC Santa Barbara.
34. *Tyler Tostenson, of, Oak Ridge HS, El Dorado Hills, Calif.
35. Nick Czyz, lhp, University of Kansas.
36. Chris Kirkland, rhp-c, University of Memphis.
37. Brandon Pullen, lhp, San Diego State University.
38. Andres Esquibel, rhp, University of Kansas.
39. Christian Staehely, rhp, Princeton University.
40. *Troy Channing, c, Foothill HS, Pleasanton, Calif.
41. Henry Cotto, of, GateWay (Ariz.) CC.

DRAFT DROP *Son of Henry Cotto, major leaguer (1984-93)*

42. Randy Molina, 1b, Stanford University.
43. *Mike Kindel, of, Springboro (Ohio) HS.
44. Donny Jobe, 2b, Elon University.
45. *Andrew Kittredge, rhp, Ferris HS, Spokane, Wash.
46. *Alvin Rittman, of, Germantown (Tenn.) HS.
47. *Rich O'Donald, rhp, John Dickinson HS, Wilmington, Del.
48. *D.J. Mauldin, rhp, Cal Poly.
49. Josh Rodriguez, c, South Mountain (Ariz.) CC.
50. *Walker Kelly, lhp, Arlington Heights HS, Fort Worth, Texas.

## TAMPA BAY DEVIL RAYS (1)

1. **Tim Beckham, ss, Griffin (Ga.) HS.—(2013-15)**

DRAFT DROP *Brother of Jeremy Beckham, 17th-round draft pick, Rays (2008)*

2. **Kyle Lobstein, lhp, Coconino HS, Flagstaff, Ariz.—(2014-15)**
3. Jake Jefferies, c, UC Davis.—(AAA)
4. Ty Morrison, of, Tigard (Ore.) HS.—(AA)
5. Mike Sheridan, 1b, College of William & Mary.—(AA)
6. Shane Dyer, rhp, South Mountain (Ariz.) CC.
7. Jason Corder, of, Long Beach State University.
8. Anthony Scelfo, 2b, Tulane University.
9. Shawn Smith, lhp, Saugus (Calif.) HS.
10. Matt Hall, ss, Auburn University.
11. Brad Furdal, rhp, Ancaster (Ontario) HS.
12. Brian Bryles, of, North Little Rock (Ark.) HS.
13. Jason McEachern, rhp, St. Stephens HS, Hickory, N.C.
14. Mike McKenna, of, Florida Atlantic University.
15. *Brandon Meredith, of, Montgomery HS, Chula Vista, Calif.
16. Matt Gorgen, rhp, University of California.

DRAFT DROP *Twin brother of Scott Gorgen, fourth-round draft pick, Cardinals (2008)*

17. Jeremy Beckham, 2b, Georgia Southern University.

DRAFT DROP *Brother of Tim Beckham, first overall draft pick, Rays (2008); major leaguer (2013)*

18. David Genao, c, Oral Roberts University.
19. Trevor Shull, rhp, Central Valley HS, Spokane Valley, Wash.
20. Jason Tweedy, 2b, Long Beach State University.
21. *Ryan Carpenter, lhp, Cactus HS, Peoria, Ariz.
22. Jason Appel, of, UNC Wilmington.
23. Neil Schenk, lhp, University of Memphis.
24. Marquis Fleming, rhp, Cal State Stanislaus.
25. Josh Satow, lhp, Arizona State University.
26. Michael Jarman, lhp, Oral Roberts University.
27. Luis Marchena, ss, Otay Ranch HS, San Diego.
28. Tom Rafferty, rhp, Arizona State University.
29. *Brandon Magee, of, Centennial HS, Corona, Calif.

DRAFT DROP *Linebacker, National Football League (2013-14)*

30. *Ryan Turner, rhp, Midland (Texas) JC.
31. *Greg Williams, lhp, Moeller HS, Cincinnati.
32. *Kyle Gaedele, of, Rolling Meadows HS, Arlington Heights, Ill.
33. *Kyle Hunter, lhp, Galesburg (Ill.) HS.
34. Matt Long, rhp, Cal State San Bernardino.
35. Jamie Bagley, rhp, San Jacinto (Texas) JC.
36. *Jordan Leyland, 1b, San Dimas (Calif.) HS.
37. *Kramer Champlin, rhp, Olympia (Wash.) HS.
38. *Anthony Haase, rhp, Rio Rancho (N.M.) HS.
39. *Andrew Gans, of, Coronado HS, Las Vegas, Nev.
40. *Sam Gaviglio, rhp, Ashland (Ore.) HS.
41. *Brett Parsons, 1b-of, Navarro (Texas) JC.
42. *Tim Clubb, rhp, Missouri State University.
43. *Robbie Ross, lhp, Saddleback (Calif.) CC.
44. *Phil Pohl, c, Cooperstown Central HS, Cooperstown, N.Y.
45. *Royce Bollinger, of, Chaparral HS, Scottsdale, Ariz.
46. *Jeff Lease, lhp, American River (Calif.) JC.
47. *Chris Matulis, lhp, Park Vista HS, Boynton Beach, Fla.
48. *Lath Guyer, rhp, Mercer University.
49. *Kash Kalkowski, rhp, Grand Island (Neb.) HS.
50. *Kyle Peterson, c, Hamilton HS, Chandler, Ariz.

## TEXAS RANGERS (11)

1. **Justin Smoak, 1b, University of South Carolina.—(2010-15)**
2. **Robbie Ross, lhp, Lexington Christian Academy, Lexington, Ky.—(2012-15)**
3. Tim Murphy, lhp, UCLA.—(AA)
4. **Joe Wieland, rhp, Bishop Manogue HS, Reno, Nev.—(2012-15)**
5. Clark Murphy, of, Fallbrook Union HS, Fallbrook, Calif.—(Low A)
6. Richard Bleier, lhp, Florida Gulf Coast University.
7. Matt Thompson, rhp, Grace Prep Academy, Burleson, Texas.
8. Mike Bianucci, of, Auburn University.
9. Jared Bolden, of-1b, Virginia Commonwealth University.
10. *Kevin Castner, rhp, Cal Poly.
11. Cliff Springston, lhp, University of Arkansas.
12. Corey Young, lhp, Seton Hall University.
13. Ed Koncel, ss, Joliet (Ill.) JC.
14. Justin Gutsie, rhp, St. John's University.
15. **Joey Butler, of, University of New Orleans.—(2013-15)**
16. **Justin Miller, rhp, Fresno State University.—(2014-15)**
17. Dennis Guinn, 1b, Florida State University.
18. Doug Hogan, c, Clemson University.
19. *Harold Martinez, ss, Braddock HS, Miami.
20. Mike Hollander, ss, Louisiana State University.
21. Dustin Brader, rhp, Arizona State University.
22. Trevor Hurley, rhp, Kansas State University.
23. Eric Evans, lhp, Radford University.
24. Adam Cobb, of, Louisiana Tech.
25. **Tanner Roark, rhp, University of Illinois.—(2013-15)**
26. Chris Dove, of, Elon University.
27. *Charlie Lowell, lhp, Winfield HS, Old Monroe, La.
28. ***Nate Freiman, 1b, Duke University.—(2013-14)**
29. *Charlie Robertson, rhp, Bella Vista HS, Citrus Heights, Calif.
30. Justin King, rhp, Jacksonville State University.
31. Kyle Higgins, ss, Monmouth University.
32. Tyler Tufts, rhp, Indiana University.
33. Ben Petralli, c, Oral Roberts University.

DRAFT DROP *Son of Geno Petralli, major leaguer (1982-93)*

34. Ryan Schlecht, rhp, Mount Olive (N.C.) College.
35. *John Ruettiger, of, Joliet Catholic Academy, Joliet, Ill.
36. *Jack Armstrong, Jupiter Community HS, Jupiter, Fla.

DRAFT DROP *Son of Jack Armstrong, first-round draft pick, Reds (1987); major leaguer (1988-94)*

37. ***Matt Andriese, rhp, Redlands East Valley HS, Redlands, Calif.—(2015)**
38. Jason Ogata, 2b, Oregon State University.
39. ***Brad Miller, ss, Olympia HS, Windermere, Fla.—(2013-15)**
40. Jamie McGraw, of, Corban (Ore.) College.
41. *Brian Feekin, lhp, Iowa Western CC.
42. ***Stephen Pryor, rhp, Cleveland State (Tenn.) CC.—(2012-14)**
43. **Cody Eppley, rhp, Virginia Commonwealth University.—(2011-13)**
44. *Alex Pepe, lhp, Florida Atlantic University.
45. Kevin Torres, c, Puerto Rico Baseball Academy, Caguas, P.R.
46. Erik Morrison, ss, University of Kansas.
47. Rafael Hill, of, Austin Peay State University.
48. *Dan Bowman, of, Turner Ashby HS, Bridgewater, Va.
49. *Matt Sample, rhp, Crowder (Mo.) CC.
50. *Josh Rosecrans, c, Edmond Santa Fe HS, Edmond, Okla.

## TORONTO BLUE JAYS (17)

1. **David Cooper, 1b, University of California.—(2011-12)**
2. Kenny Wilson, of, Sickles HS, Tampa.—(AAA)
3. Andrew Liebel, rhp, Long Beach State University.—(AA)
4. Mark Sobolewski, 3b, University of Miami.—(AAA)
5. **Tyler Pastornicky, ss, The Pendleton School, Bradenton, Fla.—(2012-14)**

DRAFT DROP *Son of Cliff Pastornicky, major leaguer (1983)*

6. Markus Brisker, of, Winter Haven (Fla.) HS.
7. **Eric Thames, of, Pepperdine University.—(2011-12)**
8. **Evan Crawford, lhp, Auburn University.—(2012)**
9. A.J. Jimenez, c, Academy Discipulos de Cristo, Bayamon, P.R.
10. **Danny Farquhar, rhp, University of Louisiana-Lafayette.—(2011-15)**
11. Dustin Antolin, rhp, Mililani HS, Honolulu, Hawaii.
12. Matt Wright, lhp, Shippensburg (Pa.) University.
13. Matt Daly, rhp, University of Hawaii.
14. Chris Holguin, rhp, Lubbock Christian University.
15. Scott Gracey, rhp-ss, University of New Mexico.
16. Michael Crouse, of, Centennial HS, Port Moody, B.C.

DRAFT DROP *Son of Ray Crouse, running back, National Football League (1984)*

17. Jonathan Valdez, c, Puerto Rico Baseball Academy, Caguas, P.R.
18. Bobby Bell, rhp, Rice University.
19. Jason Roenicke, rhp, UC Santa Barbara.

DRAFT DROP *Son of Gary Roenicke, first-round draft pick Expos (1973); major leaguer (1976-88) • Brother of Josh Roenicke, major leaguer (2008-13) • Nephew of Ron Roenicke, major leaguer (1981-88); major league manager (2011-15)*

20. Ryan Page, lhp, Liberty University.
21. Brian Van Kirk, of, Oral Roberts University.
22. Karim Turkamani, c, Miami-Dade CC.
23. Chuck Huggins, lhp, UC Santa Barbara.
24. Chris Hopkins, of, Oregon State University.
25. Brad McElroy, of, UNC Charlotte.
26. *Justin Dalles, c, St. Petersburg (Fla.) CC.
27. Bryan Kervin, ss, Texas Christian University.
28. John Anderson, lhp, Chabot (Calif.) JC.
29. Justin Cryer, rhp, University of Mississippi.
30. Cody Dunbar, rhp, Texas Christian University.
31. *J.R. Betts-Robinson, lhp, New Mexico JC.
32. *Ryan Scott, c, Chaparral HS, Scottsdale, Ariz.

DRAFT DROP *Son of Dick Scott, major leaguer (1989)*

33. Justin McClanahan, 2b, University of Louisville.
34. Austin Armstrong, rhp, Palm Beach (Fla.) CC.
35. Hunter Moody, lhp, University of Louisiana-Lafayette.
36. Ryan Koch, rhp, Florida Southern College.
37. ***Dallas Beeler, rhp, Jenks HS, Tulsa, Okla.—(2014-15)**
38. *Quentin Williams, of, Pittsburgh Central Catholic HS, Pittsburgh.
39. *Jordan Flasher, rhp, George Mason University.
40. Nate Nelson, 1b, Worcester State (Mass.) College.
41. *Kyle Petter, lhp, West Torrance HS, Torrance, Calif.
42. *Andrew Durden, of, Indian River (Fla.) JC.
43. Tyler Ybarra, lhp, Wellington (Kan.) HS.
44. *George Agyapong-Mensah, of, Western Texas JC.

## WASHINGTON NATIONALS (9)

1. ***Aaron Crow, rhp, University of Missouri.—(2011-15)**

DRAFT DROP *Signed with Fort Worth/American Association (independent); re-drafted by Royals, 2009 (1st round)*

2. Destin Hood, of, St. Pauls Episcopal HS, Mobile, Ala.—(AAA)
3. **Danny Espinosa, ss, Long Beach State University.—(2010-15)**
4. Graham Hicks, lhp, George Jenkins HS, Lakeland, Fla.—(Low A)
5. **Adrian Nieto, c, American Heritage HS, Hialeah, Fla.—(2014)**
6. Paul Demny, rhp, Blinn (Texas) JC.
7. Daniel Killian, c, Kellogg (Mich.) CC.
8. Ricardo Pecina, lhp, University of San Diego.
9. J.R. Higley, of-1b, Sacramento (Calif.) CC.
10. **Tommy Milone, lhp, University of Southern California.—(2011-15)**
11. Marcus Jones, of, North Carolina State University.
12. Will Atwood, lhp, University of South Carolina.
13. Blake Stouffer, 2b, Texas A&M University.
14. ***Louis Coleman, rhp, Louisiana State University.—(2011-15)**
15. J.P. Ramirez, of, Canyon HS, New Braunfels, Texas.
16. **Tyler Moore, 1b, Mississippi State University.—(2012-15)**
17. Jose Lozada, ss, Bethune-Cookman College.
18. Bobby Hansen, lhp, Lewis-Palmer HS, Monument, Colo.
19. **Steve Lombardozzi, ss, St. Petersburg (Fla.) JC.—(2011-15)**

DRAFT DROP *Son of Steve Lombardozzi, major leaguer (1985-90)*

20. *Nick Akins, of, Riverside (Calif.) CC.
21. Michael Guerrero, of, University of Mississippi.
22. Chris Curran, 2b, Miami-Dade CC.
23. Derrick Phillips, of, Westminster Christian Academy, St. Louis.
24. Chris Kelley, rhp, Rice University.
25. Austin Garrett, lhp, College of Charleston.
26. ***Cory Mazzoni, rhp, Seneca Valley HS, Evan City, Pa.—(2015)**
27. Chris Solis, c, University of the Incarnate Word (Texas).
28. Nick Arata, ss, Florida Atlantic University.
29. ***Chris Heston, rhp, Seminole (Fla.) CC.—(2014-15)**
30. Casey Whitmer, rhp, University of Texas.
31. *Bryan Harper, lhp, Las Vegas (Nev.) HS.

DRAFT DROP *Brother of Bryce Harper, first overall draft pick, Nationals (2010); major leaguer (2012-15)*

32. *Scott Silverstein, lhp, St. John's College Prep HS, Washington, D.C.
33. *Billy Cather, of, University of Maine.
34. Brian Pruitt, of, Stetson University.
35. Clayton Dill, lhp, Missouri Baptist College.
36. *John Lambert, lhp, Santa Fe (Fla.) CC.
37. *Casey Selsor, lhp, Ronald Reagan HS, San Antonio, Texas.
38. Ronnie LaBrie, 3b, Lynchburg (Va.) College.
39. James Keithley, ss, University of Texas-San Antonio.
40. *Avery Barnes, 2b, University of Florida.
41. *Mike Rayl, lhp, Palm Beach (Fla.) CC.
42. *Naoya Washiya, of, JC of the Desert (Fla.).
43. *Anthony Meo, rhp, Cranston West HS, Cranston, R.I.
44. J.P. Padron, 1b, Rice University.
45. *Colin Rooney, ss, Saddleback (Calif.) JC.
46. ***Rob Brantly, c, Chaparral HS, Temecula, Calif.—(2012-15)**
47. *Anthony Coletti, lhp, South Broward HS, Hollywood, Fla.
48. ***Alex Dickerson, of, Poway (Calif.) HS.—(2015)**
49. *B.J. Zimmerman, of, Osceola HS, Kissimmee, Fla.
50. *Fernando Frias, of, George Washington HS, Bronx, N.Y.

# 2009

## AT A GLANCE

### This Date In History
June 9-11

### Best Draft
**ST. LOUIS CARDINALS.** The Angels had the foresight to draft **MIKE TROUT** with the 25th pick in the first round (along with **GARRETT RICHARDS** and **PATRICK CORBIN**), but the Cardinals reached the playoffs from 2011-15 thanks in large measure to the contributions of **SHELBY MILLER** (1), **JOE KELLY** (3), **MATT CARPENTER** (13), **TREVOR ROSENTHAL** (21) and **MATT ADAMS** (23).

### Worst Draft
**BALTIMORE ORIOLES.** Through the 2015 season, **MYCHAL GIVENS** (2) was the only big leaguer to come from the Orioles 2009 draft. The team's top pick, **MATT HOBGOOD**, selected fifth overall, never came close to fulfilling expectations with a 17-24, 4.98 record through seven minor league seasons.

### First-Round Bust
**DONAVAN TATE, OF, PADRES.** The Padres spent $6.25 million to sign Tate, a record bonus for a high school position player, but had almost nothing to show for their investment. In addition to a substandard performance, Tate's career has been tarnished by injuries and drug suspensions.

### Second Time Around
**JASON KIPNIS, 2B, INDIANS.** Convinced he was better than a fourth-round pick, Kipnis passed up an offer from the Padres in 2008 for a chance to improve his worth as a red-shirt junior at Arizona State. He did that, and then some, performing like a first-rounder in five major league seasons with a pair of all-star performances.

### Late-Round Find
**MATT CARPENTER, 3B, CARDINALS (12TH ROUND).** Signed for just $1,000 as a 23-year-old, fifth-year senior after miss-

# Strasburg comes with big hype, expectations

On April 1, 1985, Sidd Finch was the subject of one of the greatest April Fool's Day hoaxes ever perpetrated.

Sports Illustrated created the legend of Finch, a rookie pitcher in spring training with the New York Mets who had never played baseball before, yet had a fastball that was clocked at an amazing 168 mph. Finch attributed his pitching prowess to "yogic mastery of mind-body," which he learned in Tibet.

Despite the obvious absurdity of the article, written by famed writer George Plimpton, many readers believed that "The Curious Case of Sidd Finch" was real, rather than an April Fool's joke.

Finch still earned a place in baseball lore, though, especially when the latest pitching phenom burst on the scene. In 2009, there may not have been a young pitcher in all the years since SI's spoof on Finch who titillated the baseball world quite like San Diego State pitcher Stephen Strasburg—unofficially, the Second Coming of Sidd Finch.

Strasburg didn't exactly emerge from nowhere, though he wasn't drafted and was barely recruited as an overweight, unmotivated pitcher out of a local high school in 2006. Yet he became such a sensation as a junior righthander for the Aztecs in 2009 that he was heralded as the most dominant arm ever to emerge from the college ranks.

Strasburg became a prohibitive favorite to be the top pick in the 2009 draft far in advance of his actual selection by the Washington Nationals—or pretty much ever since he catapulted himself onto the national stage as a sophomore with his 23-strikeout, one-hit shutout of Utah.

While the 6-foot-5, 225-pound Strasburg was never clocked anywhere close to 168 mph, he threw practically as hard as any pitcher known to man. In most of his outings during his junior season for San Diego State, his fastball was clocked in triple digits and peaked at 103 mph. He wasn't just a one-dimensional pitcher, either.

"He's got the greatest combination of power, command, ability to field his position and hold runners I've ever seen," said Texas Christian coach Jim Schlossnagle, whose team was victimized by 17 strikeouts in eight innings.

Strasburg was compared most often to Southern California righthander Mark Prior, the second overall pick in the 2001 draft, and Vanderbilt lefthander David Price, the No. 1 pick 2007. Both pitchers created a significant buzz within the scouting community in the months leading up to the draft—but nothing quite like Strasburg.

Schlossnagle, who recruited Prior when he was an assistant at Tulane and coached Price on USA Baseball's college national team, said Strasburg was "light years ahead of them in terms of ability."

San Diego Padres general manager Kevin Towers saw Strasburg on a frequent basis, too,

BILL MITCHELL

No pitcher in draft annals attracted the same degree of attention that Stephen Strasburg did, and while he signed a record-breaking deal with the Nationals, he was still fighting to live up to the hype

and marveled at his all-around ability. "He was dominating, as dominating as anyone I've seen. He really has no flaws. You see guys throw in the high 90s, but they usually have no idea where it's going. He can throw in the high 90s comfortably and locate it."

During the 2009 season, Strasburg led NCAA pitchers in ERA (1.32) and strikeouts (193), and his 16.1 strikeouts per nine innings was the best of any starting pitcher in college history. While going 13-1 in 109 innings, he allowed 65 hits and 19 walks. His final home start was a 17-strikeout no-hitter against Air Force.

As a San Diego native, Strasburg would have been a natural fit for the struggling Padres, but as bad as they were a year earlier in winning just 63 games, they won four games too many. The Nationals, with 59 wins in 2008, won the Strasburg sweepstakes.

Even with the No. 1 pick, the Nationals had failed to sign their first-round pick, righthander Aaron Crow, a year earlier, and there were rumblings that Strasburg, who was represented by powerful agent Scott Boras, might be asking for something in the range of $50 million—an amount that only someone in the realm of a real life Sidd Finch might have commanded.

## TROUT UPSTAGES STRASBURG

Strasburg, understandably, was the dominant

## 2009: THE FIRST ROUNDERS

| CLUB: PLAYER, POS., SCHOOL | HOMETOWN | B-T | HT. | WT. | AGE | BONUS | FIRST YEAR | LAST YEAR | PEAK LEVEL (YEARS) |
|---|---|---|---|---|---|---|---|---|---|
| 1. *Nationals: Stephen Strasburg, rhp, San Diego State | San Diego | R-R | 6-5 | 225 | 20 | $7,500,000 | 2010 | Active | Majors (6) |
| Not drafted out of HS, became one of most-hyped pitchers ever three years later; went 13-1, 1.32 (109 IP/195 Ks) as JR, signed record-shattering $15.1M contract. | | | | | | | | | |
| 2. *Mariners: Dustin Ackley, of/2b, North Carolina | Walnut Cove, N.C. | L-R | 6-1 | 190 | 21 | $6,000,000 | 2010 | Active | Majors (5) |
| Hitting machine at UNC stung ball at .412 career clip, slugged 22 HRs as JR; concerns about position, none about bat, but .244 career average in major leagues. | | | | | | | | | |
| 3. Padres: Donavan Tate, of, Cartersville HS | Cartersville, Ga. | R-R | 6-2 | 185 | 18 | $6,250,000 | 2010 | Active | Class A (4) |
| Son of former NFL tailback was high-ceiling athlete, set club bonus record, but injuries, substance abuse short-circuited career; just .229 hitter in A-ball. | | | | | | | | | |
| 4. Pirates: Tony Sanchez, c, Boston College | Miami | R-R | 6-0 | 215 | 21 | $2,500,000 | 2009 | Active | Majors (3) |
| Surprise pick at No. 4, though quality defender, had breakthrough season with bat (.346-14-51); pro career hasn't measured up, has played in just 51 MLB games. | | | | | | | | | |
| 5. Orioles: Matt Hobgood, rhp, Norco HS | Norco, Calif. | R-R | 6-4 | 245 | 18 | $2,422,000 | 2009 | 2015 | Class AA (1) |
| Velocity spike to upper 90s as senior, coupled with 21 HRs, escalated draft stock; ineffectiveness, weight issues, shoulder surgery led to 17-24, 4.98 mark in minors. | | | | | | | | | |
| 6. Giants: Zack Wheeler, rhp, East Paulding HS | Dallas, Ga. | R-R | 6-3 | 180 | 19 | $3,300,000 | 2010 | Active | Majors (3) |
| Dominant prep arm fanned 278 in 142 IP last two HS seasons; premium prospect with high 90s FB, traded to Mets for Carlos Beltran, missed 2015 with TJ surgery. | | | | | | | | | |
| 7. Braves: Mike Minor, lhp, Vanderbilt | Chapel Hill, Tenn. | R-L | 6-3 | 200 | 21 | $2,420,000 | 2009 | Active | Majors (5) |
| Polished southpaw, not overpowering but commanded four-pitch mix; on fast track despite 6-6, 3.90 JR season, won 38 MLB games before 2015 labrum surgery. | | | | | | | | | |
| 8. Reds: Mike Leake, rhp, Arizona State | Fallbrook, Calif. | R-R | 6-0 | 180 | 21 | $2,270,000 | 2010 | Active | Majors (5) |
| Questionable pick as undersized RHP, but athletic, excellent feel for pitching, solid track record at ASU (16-1, 1.71 as JR); went straight to majors, never looked back. | | | | | | | | | |
| 9. *Tigers: Jacob Turner, rhp, Westminster Christian HS | St. Louis | R-R | 6-4 | 205 | 18 | $4,700,000 | 2010 | Active | Majors (4) |
| Big, polished, athletic pitcher with 94-98 mph FB, signed to $5.5M major league deal; career (11-25, 4.97) has never taken off, spent most of 2015 on DL. | | | | | | | | | |
| 10. Nationals: Drew Storen, rhp, Stanford | Brownsburg, Ind. | B-R | 6-1 | 175 | 21 | $1,600,000 | 2009 | Active | Majors (5) |
| Went 7-1 (7 SV, 42 IP/66 SO) as draft-eligible soph at Stanford; was budget pick with Strasburg commanding huge money, but reached MLB after 37 pro IP. | | | | | | | | | |
| 11. Rockies: Tyler Matzek, lhp, Capistrano Valley HS | Mission Viejo, Calif. | L-L | 6-3 | 210 | 18 | $3,900,000 | 2010 | Active | Majors (2) |
| Best prep lefty in draft with 95-98 mph FB, signed record Rockies bonus; wildness haunted him, after respite in 2014, returned with a vengeance in 2015. | | | | | | | | | |
| 12. *Royals: Aaron Crow, rhp, Fort Worth (Independent) | Topeka, Kan. | R-R | 6-2 | 205 | 22 | $1,500,000 | 2010 | Active | Majors (4) |
| Unsigned '08 first-rounder chose independent route instead of returning to Missouri as SR; worked in relief only in MLB with mid-90s FB, was TJ victim in 2015. | | | | | | | | | |
| 13. Athletics: Grant Green, ss, Southern California | Anaheim Hills, Calif. | R-R | 6-3 | 185 | 21 | $2,750,000 | 2009 | Active | Majors (3) |
| High-profile talent in HS/college, three-year regular for USC; had tools but scouts cautious about upside with bat, ability to stick at SS; hit .249 in MLB utility role. | | | | | | | | | |
| 14. Rangers: Matt Purke, lhp, Klein HS | Klein, Texas | L-L | 6-3 | 175 | 18 | Unsigned | 2012 | Active | Class AA (2) |
| Bizarre negotiations with Rangers, ended up at TCU after MLB nixed bonus offer; went 16-0 as freshman, college/pro career never same again after shoulder injury. | | | | | | | | | |
| 15. Indians: Alex White, rhp, North Carolina | Greenville, N.C. | R-R | 6-4 | 190 | 20 | $2,250,000 | 2010 | 2015 | Majors (2) |
| Command issues apparent, even with 27-14 college mark; raw stuff landed him in first round, fast tracked to MLB, career unraveled after trade to Rockies in 2011. | | | | | | | | | |
| 16. Diamondbacks: Bobby Borchering, 3b, Bishop Verot HS | Fort Myers, Fla. | B-R | 6-4 | 195 | 18 | $1,800,000 | 2009 | 2015 | Class AA (1) |
| One-tool talent but switch-hitter with big pop, homered at steady clip in Class A, also strikeout prone; game disappeared in Double-A, after 2012 trade to Astros. | | | | | | | | | |
| 17. Diamondbacks: A.J. Pollock, of, Notre Dame | Hebron, Conn. | R-R | 6-2 | 200 | 21 | $1,400,000 | 2009 | Active | Majors (4) |
| Late bloomer, became first-rounder with big Cape Cod season, evolved into 2015 MLB all-star; bat only plus tool, gets most out of ability with superior makeup. | | | | | | | | | |
| 18. Marlins: Chad James, lhp, Yukon HS | Yukon, Okla. | L-L | 6-3 | 190 | 18 | $1,700,000 | 2010 | 2015 | Class AA (1) |
| Mid-90s FB, plus change justified draft status, but suspect mechanics at root of command issues that plagued career with Marlins (18-41, 4.67), led to 2013 release. | | | | | | | | | |
| 19. Cardinals: Shelby Miller, rhp, Brownwood HS | Brownwood, Texas | R-R | 6-3 | 195 | 18 | $2,875,000 | 2009 | Active | Majors (4) |
| Heralded prep righty with 95-97 mph FB, unflapabble mound presence, shot through minors to pitch in 2012 NLCS at 21, won 15 games following year. | | | | | | | | | |
| 20. Blue Jays: Chad Jenkins, rhp, Kennesaw State | Canton, Ga. | R-R | 6-4 | 235 | 21 | $1,359,000 | 2010 | Active | Majors (3) |
| Sinker/slider pitcher with outstanding control, went 8-1, 2.51 (92 IP, 15 BB/98 SO) as college junior; never profiled as frontline starter, soon relegated to bullpen. | | | | | | | | | |
| 21. Astros: Jiovanni Mier, ss, Bonita HS | La Verne, Calif. | R-R | 6-2 | 175 | 18 | $1,358,000 | 2009 | Active | Class AAA (1) |
| First prep SS drafted, best known for athleticism, defensive tools/arm strength; career slow to progress in minors as bat lagged, just .239 hitter in seven years. | | | | | | | | | |
| 22. Twins: Kyle Gibson, rhp, Missouri | Greenfield, Ind. | R-R | 6-6 | 210 | 21 | $1,850,000 | 2010 | Active | Majors (3) |
| Polished college arm with nasty slider, went 11-3, 3.21 but late-season stress fracture (forearm) hurt chance as top five pick; TJ surgery in 2011 delayed MLB debut. | | | | | | | | | |
| 23. White Sox: Jared Mitchell, of, Louisiana State | New Iberia, La. | L-L | 6-0 | 190 | 20 | $1,200,000 | 2009 | Active | Class AAA (4) |
| Electrifying two-sport athlete; speed was his best tool, but lost some of it due to severe ankle injury in 2010; suspect bat, career .226 hitter (603 G/798 SO). | | | | | | | | | |
| 24. Angels: Randal Grichuk, of, Lamar Consolidated HS | Rosenberg, Texas | R-R | 6-0 | 195 | 17 | $1,242,000 | 2009 | Active | Majors (1) |
| Known best for being picked before Trout; raw power was main selling point, hit .613 with 21 HRs as prep SR; slowed by injuries, took time to grow into power. | | | | | | | | | |
| 25. Angels: Mike Trout, of, Millville HS | Millville, N.J. | R-R | 6-1 | 200 | 17 | $1,215,000 | 2009 | Active | Majors (4) |
| Hard to believe game's best talent wasn't consensus first-rounder; questions about bat, cold/wet New Jersey spring worked against him, but developed quickly. | | | | | | | | | |
| 26. Brewers: Eric Arnett, rhp, Indiana | Pataskala, Ohio | R-R | 6-5 | 230 | 21 | $1,197,000 | 2009 | 2013 | Class A (4) |
| Blossomed as Indiana JR (12-2, 2.50) with 91-94 mph FB after two mediocre seasons; pitched poorly out of gate as a pro, lacked stuff/command, went 8-20, 5.18. | | | | | | | | | |
| 27. Mariners: Nick Franklin, ss, Lake Brantley HS | Altamonte Springs, Fla. | B-R | 6-1 | 170 | 18 | $1,280,000 | 2009 | Active | Majors (3) |
| Switch-hitting middle infielder, huge HS spring (.536, 11 HRs) propelled him up draft lists; made swift climb through minors, hit wall (.203) against MLB pitching. | | | | | | | | | |
| 28. Red Sox: Rey Fuentes, of, Fernando Callejo HS | Manati, P.R. | L-L | 6-0 | 160 | 18 | $1,134,000 | 2009 | Active | Majors (1) |
| Carlos Beltran's cousin drafted for speed/CF defense; traded to Padres in late 2010 as part of Adrian Gonzalez deal, has shown signs with bat but no breakout season. | | | | | | | | | |
| 29. Yankees: Slade Heathcott, of, Texas HS | Texarkana, Texas | L-L | 6-1 | 190 | 18 | $2,200,000 | 2009 | Active | Majors (1) |
| Superior athlete with speed, CF skills; had troubled upbringing, additional off-field problems in pro ball, but litany of injuries also slowed progression to majors. | | | | | | | | | |
| 30. Rays: LeVon Washington, 2b, Buchholz HS | Gainesville, Fla. | L-R | 5-11 | 170 | 17 | Unsigned | 2010 | 2015 | Class A (5) |
| Head-scratcher pick as speed player with no set position, coming off shoulder surgery; negotiations turned sour, ended up at JC, Indians second-rounder in 2010. | | | | | | | | | |
| 31. Cubs: Brett Jackson, of, California | Orinda, Calif. | L-R | 6-2 | 210 | 20 | $972,000 | 2009 | 2015 | Majors (2) |
| CF with power/speed tools to be 30-30 player; struggle to make contact became more acute as moved up minor league ladder, hit .169 (124 AB/60 Ks) in majors. | | | | | | | | | |
| 32. Rockies: Tim Wheeler, of, Sacramento State | Sacramento, Calif. | L-R | 6-4 | 205 | 21 | $900,000 | 2009 | 2015 | Class AAA (4) |
| Big/athletic talent, hit .385-18-72 as college JR, then hit .287-33-86 with 21 SB in Double-A in 2011, but broke hamate bone, power evaporated. | | | | | | | | | |

**Signed to major league contract.*

## AT A GLANCE

ing most of two seasons at TCU while rehabbing from Tommy John surgery, Carpenter proved to be a revelation for the Cardinals. In five seasons, he led the NL in runs and hits once, doubles twice, and was a two-time all-star.

### Never Too Late

**ZACH GODLEY, RHP, METS (50TH ROUND).** An afterthought out of a South Carolina high school, Godley didn't sign and wasn't drafted again for four more years. He signed with the Cubs as a 10th-rounder in 2013 and reached the majors with the Diamondbacks two years later.

### Overlooked

**KENNYS VARGAS, 1B, TWINS.** Dubbed "Bigger Papi" because of his striking resemblance to David Ortiz, along with his propensity to hit tape-measure homers, the 6-foot-3, 275-pound Vargas was signed as a free agent for $90,000 by the Twins—the team Ortiz began his major league career with 12 years earlier. In 111 games with the Twins in 2014-15, Vargas hit .259-14-55.

### International Gem

**XANDER BOGAERTS, SS, RED SOX.** The Red Sox signed two prominent international shortstops in 2009: Bogaerts, a 16-year-old product of Aruba, for $430,000; and **JOSE IGLESIAS**, a 19-year-old Cuban defector, for $8.25 million. Both were big league regulars by 2015—Bogaerts with Boston, Iglesias with Detroit—and Bogaerts emerged as one of the game's top young stars by hitting .320-7-81.

### Minor League Take

**MIKE TROUT, OF, ANGELS.** It was evident from his first full season that Trout was miscast as the 25th pick in the 2009 draft. He hit .342-23-134 with 108 stolen bases in 286 minor league

CONTINUED ON PAGE 658

## AT A GLANCE

CONTINUED FROM PAGE 657

games, and was already a star in the making when he burst into the majors with the Angels in 2011.

### One Who Got Away

**MATT PURKE, LHP, RANGERS (1ST ROUND).** Rangers owner Tom Hicks was in the process of selling his financially strapped club in 2009, so the commissioner's office (which had influence in the team's finances) kept the team from expanding on the $4 million offer they made to Purke, a local high school product, the night before the signing deadline. Rebuffed, he elected to attend college at TCU.

### He Was Drafted?

**COLIN KAEPERNICK, RHP, CUBS (43RD ROUND).** Kaepernick went 11-2, 1.27 with a pair of no-hitters in 13 starts as a high school senior, and intrigued scouts with a 92-94 mph fastball. He went undrafted because of his football commitment to Nevada, but two years later the Cubs took a late-round stab at him. In 2012, he led the San Francisco 49ers to the Super Bowl.

### Did You Know . . .

The Blue Jays failed to sign three players in the top three rounds of the 2009 draft, including two Canadians: supplemental first-rounder **JAMES PAXTON** and second-rounder **JAKE ELIOPOULOS**. The Jays also drafted six more Canadians between the 40th and 50th rounds and didn't sign them, either.

### They Said It

Angels scout **GREG MORHARDT**, on whose recommendation the club drafted **MIKE TROUT** with the 25th pick overall: "He was much faster than everyone in the country. He was much stronger than everyone in the country. He had the timing, the instincts. I'd never seen a 17-year-old who was that fast and that strong."

storyline of the 2009 draft, and made it the most eagerly anticipated event of its kind. It even attracted the attention of the mainstream media, and his last-minute signing at the Aug. 17 deadline was also compelling theatre.

Predictably, he received both the highest signing bonus ($7.5 million) and largest contract (a guaranteed $15,107,104) in major league history, and his debut with the Nationals, a year later, was a must-watch event.

In the meantime, a less-heralded player from the class of 2009 eventually stole Strasburg's thunder and became the dominant talent everyone expected Strasburg to be.

Mike Trout, a New Jersey high school outfielder, went 25th overall and signed with the Los Angeles Angels for a bonus of $1.215 million—less than a tenth of the amount Strasburg received. But it was evident almost from the moment that Trout set foot on the field with the Angels' Rookie-level Arizona League club that he was something special. He quickly blazed a trail through the minors, hitting .342 in 266 games, and received his own share of plaudits when he made his big league debut with the Angels little more than two years later.

Over the next four years, he took the majors by storm like no position player this side of Mickey Mantle more than a half century before him. He became a perennial all-star, won the 2014 American League MVP, led the league in stolen bases in 2012 and RBIs in 2014, and earned plenty of acclaim for his acrobatic catches in center field.

BRIAN BISSELL

Dustin Ackley

With all the hype that Strasburg almost single-handedly generated for the 2009 draft, which was showcased on Major League Baseball's own cable network for the first time, it was Trout who stole the show. He was the only draft pick who was on hand for the made-for-TV event, which was televised in prime time from the MLB Network studios in Secaucus, N.J. Trout unwittingly became the face of the event.

The Nationals not only had first crack at a generational talent like Strasburg, but they were also afforded the greatest opportunity to stockpile talent in the draft's 44-year history because they also had the 10th selection as compensation for failing to sign Crow a year earlier. In keeping with new draft regulations, a team that didn't sign its first-round pick was awarded the corresponding selection in the next draft.

The Nationals used that selection to grab Stanford righthander Drew Storen, who was only too willing to agree to a bonus of $1.6 million, even if it was some $263,000 below the amount allocated for that slot by Major League Baseball. Storen did not project to be drafted in the top half of the first round, but struck a deal with the Nationals prior to the draft. Understandably, the Nationals were looking to save money wherever they could in expectation of breaking the bank to sign Strasburg.

The remainder of the first 10 picks played out according to form, with the Seattle Mariners taking North Carolina outfielder Dustin Ackley, considered the best pure hitter in the draft, with the second pick, while the Padres followed by selecting Georgia high school outfielder Donavan Tate.

The first round featured a record number of 32 picks, with the two extra selections a result of the special compensation for Crow and a second unsigned first-rounder from the 2008 draft, righthander Gerrit Cole, who failed to reach an agreement with the New York Yankees. The Yankees lost their first-round pick, getting the 29th pick overall for losing Cole.

### SLOW ECONOMY CAN'T SLOW SPENDING

Against the backdrop of a global recession that slapped the U.S. economy in 2008 and extended well into 2009, some officials expected to see a resulting drag on signing bonuses, which had increased at a staggering rate in recent years.

"There's no question the economy will have an impact on bonuses this year," an American League

### How They Should Have Done It

Based on the career WAR (Wins Above Replacement, as calculated by Baseball-Reference.com) numbers achieved by all the players eligible for the 2009 draft through the 2015 season, here's how the first round should have unfolded. Numbers in parentheses indicate the round when the player was actually drafted.

| | Player, Pos. | Actual Draft | WAR | Bonus |
|---|---|---|---|---|
| 1. | Mike Trout, of | Angels (1) | 37.9 | $1,215,000 |
| 2. | Paul Goldschmidt, 1b | Diamondbacks (8) | 24.1 | $95,000 |
| 3. | Kyle Seager, 3b | Mariners (3) | 17.5 | $436,500 |
| 4. | Jason Kipnis, of | Indians (2) | 16.1 | $575,000 |
| 5. | A.J. Pollock, of | Diamondbacks (1) | 14.8 | $1,400,000 |
| 6. | Stephen Strasburg, rhp | Nationals (1) | 14.4 | $7,500,000 |
| 7. | Matt Carpenter, 3b | Cardinals (13) | 14.2 | $1,000 |
| 8. | Nolan Arenado, 3b | Rockies (2) | 13.5 | $625,000 |
| 9. | Brandon Belt, 1b | Giants (5) | 12.6 | $200,000 |
| 10. | Mike Leake, rhp | Reds (1) | 12.5 | $2,270,000 |
| 11. | Dallas Keuchel, rhp | Astros (7) | 12.0 | $150,000 |
| 12. | Brian Dozier, ss | Twins (8) | 11.9 | $30,000 |
| 13. | Shelby Miller, rhp | Cardinals (1 ) | 9.3 | $2,875,000 |
| 14. | Yan Gomes, c | Blue Jays (10) | 8.7 | $85,000 |
| 15. | Dustin Ackley, of | Mariners (1) | 8.3 | $6,000,000 |
| 16. | J.D. Martinez, of | Astros (20) | 7.8 | $30,000 |
| 17. | D.J. LeMahieu, 2b | Cubs (2) | 6.2 | $508,000 |
| 18. | Drew Storen, rhp | Nationals (1) | 5.7 | $1,600,000 |
| 19. | Garrett Richards, rhp | Angels (1-S) | 5.6 | $802,800 |
| 20. | Trevor Rosenthal, rhp | Cardinals (21) | 5.3 | $65,000 |
| 21. | Rex Brothers, lhp | Rockies (1-S) | 5.1 | $969,000 |
| | Adam Warren, rhp | Yankees (4) | 5.1 | $195,000 |
| | A.J. Ramos, rhp | Marlins (21) | 5.1 | $1,500 |
| 24. | Patrick Corbin, lhp | Angels (2) | 4.9 | $450,000 |
| | Joe Kelly, rhp | Cardinals (3) | 4.9 | $341,000 |
| | Mike Fiers, rhp | Brewers (22) | 4.9 | $2,500 |
| 27. | Kyle Gibson, rhp | Twins (1) | 4.5 | $1,850,000 |
| 28. | Khris Davis, of | Brewers (7) | 4.3 | $125,000 |
| 29. | Ryan Goins, ss | Blue Jays (4) | 4.2 | $216,000 |
| | Billy Hamilton, ss | Reds (2) | 4.2 | $623,600 |
| 31. | Brock Holt, 2b | Pirates (9) | 4.1 | $125,000 |
| 32. | Scooter Gennett, 2b | Brewers (16) | 4.0 | $260,000 |

| | Top 3 Unsigned Players | | | Year Signed |
|---|---|---|---|---|
| 1. | Corey Dickerson, of | Rockies (29) | 4.6 | 2010 |
| 2. | A.J. Griffin, rhp | Phillies (34) | 4.3 | 2010 |
| 3. | Ken Giles, rhp | Marlins (44) | 4.0 | 2011 |

front office official said. "It had a big impact on free agents in the offseason, and it's pretty clear there's going to be some restraint shown this year."

In 2008, bonus records were set across the board—for total amount spent by all clubs ($188,297,598), by one club (Royals, $11.148 million), to one player (Buster Posey, $6.2 million) and to the average first-rounder ($2,449,785). There was little indication those marks would be eclipsed as most clubs, already mindful of the sour economy, abided by the slot recommendations on bonuses as dictated by the commissioner's office.

Among the encouraging signs were the bonuses signed by Storen, as well as the fourth and fifth overall picks—Boston College catcher Tony Sanchez, who agreed to a predraft deal with the Pittsburgh Pirates for $2.5 million, which was $200,000 below the amount allocated for that slot; and California high school righthander Matt Hobgood, who signed with the Baltimore Orioles for $2.422 million, $98,000 under slot. With a handful of exceptions, no other early-round pick signed for an over-slot amount through the end of July.

But as the Aug. 17 signing deadline approached, it was apparent that more clubs than ever had delayed announcing or hadn't finalized the signing of their premium picks, and Major League Baseball had restricted the flow of bonus information so agents couldn't use the data to strike better deals for their unsigned clients.

With 17 of 32 first-rounders, as well as a number of other high-profile selections, still officially unsigned, a mad scramble was inevitable. Numerous deals, highlighted by Strasburg's, went down in the final hour—even in the final minutes. The final tally demonstrated emphatically that clubs cared more about adding talent, almost at any cost, rather than staying in the good graces of the commissioner's office.

Even before Strasburg agreed to his record-breaking contract, Tate had set—if only temporarily—a new mark for the highest bonus ever as he signed earlier in the day with the Padres for $6.25 million.

Like Strasburg, Ackley and Missouri high school righthander Jacob Turner, selected ninth overall by the Detroit Tigers, agreed to major league contracts. Ackley's deal, worth $7.5 million overall, included a $6 million bonus, while Turner's contract, which guaranteed him $5.5 million, included a $4.7 million bonus. Not coincidentally, Strasburg, Ackley and Tate, the first three selections, and Turner were all represented by Boras.

Seven-figure bonuses were prevalent through-

## Fastest To The Majors

| Player, Pos. | Drafted (Round) | Debut |
|---|---|---|
| 1. # Mike Leake, rhp | Reds (1) | April 11, 2010 |
| 2. Drew Storen, rhp | Nationals (1) | May 17, 2010 |
| 3. Stephen Strasburg, rhp | Nationals (1) | June 8, 2010 |
| 4. Andy Oliver, lhp | Tigers (2) | June 25, 2010 |
| 5. Mike Minor, lhp | Braves (1) | Aug. 9, 2010 |

**FIRST HIGH SCHOOL SELECTION:** Mike Trout, of (Angels/1, July 8, 2011)

*#Debuted in major leagues.*

## DRAFT SPOTLIGHT: MIKE TROUT

**The Angels saw stardom in Mike Trout, but they just had to wait until the 25th pick to draft him**

At age 20, Mike Trout might have been the best player in baseball. He was the American League Rookie of the Year and a close second in balloting for the AL MVP award. He also ranked No. 1 in the majors in Wins Above Replacement.

For all his prowess during the 2012 season, the 6-foot-2, 210-pound Trout was essentially the same physical marvel then that he was three years earlier when he was a senior at Millville (N.J.) High. By slamming a state-record 18 home runs while recording a brisk time of 6.4 seconds over 60 yards, his rare combination of power and speed was already evident.

So why did Trout last until the 25th pick in the 2009 draft before he was snapped up by the Los Angeles Angels? It's a question 21 major league clubs have been asking ever since. In the minds of many, it all had to do with the skepticism associated with him being a New Jersey high school prospect. Almost no one could fathom that a player from that state could be quite this good—not after previous New Jersey hotshot prospects before him like Billy Rowell, Eric Duncan and Corey Smith all went down in flames.

But no one got an accurate reading on Trout's true ability quite like Angels area scout Greg Morhardt, who was infatuated with him from the first time he saw him at a showcase as a 16-year-old.

"When he walked in, he looked like Mickey Mantle," Morhardt said. "He had the same build, the same compact swing."

It didn't hurt that Morhardt had also played with Trout's father Jeff for three years when they were teammates in the Minnesota Twins farm system more than 20 years earlier.

Morhardt saw Trout's obvious physical gifts, but he knew that his desire, intensity and burning drive to excel were traits in the family bloodlines. Even as Jeff Trout never reached the majors, he got every last ounce out of his limited ability. Morhardt was convinced that son Mike, with his superior talent, was a potential superstar in the making.

"He was much faster than everyone in the country. He was much stronger than everyone in the country. He had the timing, the instincts," Morhardt said. "I'd never seen a 17-year-old who was that fast and that strong."

All Morhardt had to do was convince his bosses, especially scouting director Eddie Bane, that Trout was the real deal, the class of the 2009 draft. He did it, even as Trout had one of his worst days as a prep senior with Bane and crosschecker Jeff Malinoff there to see him. But Bane saw in Trout all of the subtle qualities that had drawn Morhardt to him.

"When Eddie and Jeff saw him, he didn't do anything technically, like hitting a home run, getting a stolen base," Morhardt said. "Eddie didn't see the performance, but he saw the ingredients, and to Eddie's credit, he listened to his scouts."

It wasn't lost on Bane, for instance, that on one of the balls Trout popped up that he was almost standing on third base by the time the ball was caught. That, along with Morhardt's unabashed support, sold him on Trout.

"I don't like hearing Mickey Mantle's name when people talk about Mike," Bane said, "but shoot, the kid looks like him. He's got 80 power, and he'd be more than an 80 runner if you could go that high. What's the ceiling for guys like that?"

As the Angels assembled their draft list, Trout ranked second to San Diego State's all-world righthander Stephen Strasburg. Picking deep in the first round, the Angels were dubious about their chances—especially if other clubs saw in Trout what they saw.

Bane ascertained in his detective work that most teams picking ahead of the Angels didn't value Trout quite like his team did. Some clubs had concerns about his bat, others were unsure of his defensive skills. As best as Bane could determine, only the New York Yankees also had Trout ranked as high as second on their board—but their first choice came four picks after the Angels. The 25th pick originally belonged to the Yankees, but they forfeited it to the Angels for signing Mark Teixeira away as a free agent.

The Yankees and other teams had to wonder what might have been as Trout quickly blossomed into the best prospect in the game, and soon into the best all-around young player the game had seen since none other than Mantle—the same player a fortuitous Angels scout compared Trout to from the first day he laid eyes on him.

## WORTH NOTING

■ The 2009 draft ran from June 9-11, which made it the latest in the event's 44-year history. Twice before, in 1976 and 1981, the draft began as late as June 8. The later dates were set, in part, to accommodate both major league teams and college players as they enabled clubs to scout NCAA super-regional tournaments in their entirety for the first time in years, and a Tuesday-Thursday selection process avoided any possibility of players potentially being drafted on the same day they might be playing. The draft was held in the week before the College World Series began.

■ Predictably, San Diego State righthander **STEPHEN STRASBURG** was the No. 1 prospect in the 2009 draft class by the Major League Scouting Bureau. He was graded out with an OFP (overall future potential) grade of 72 on the 20-80 scouting scale. Beyond Strasburg, there was little correlation between the prospects in the bureau's top five with where they were ultimately drafted: No. 2 **KYLE HECKATHORN** (69) was selected 47th overall by the Brewers; No. 3 **MIKE TROUT** (66) was taken 25th overall by the Angels; No. 4 **BEN TOOTLE** (65) was chosen 101st by the Twins; and No. 5 **BLAKE SMITH** (62) went 56th to the Dodgers. Oddly, the two lowest-ranked players actually drafted in the first round—No. 2 **DUSTIN ACKLEY** (49) and No. 27 **NICK FRANKLIN** (48)—were both drafted by the Mariners.

■ Texas' Howard College engineered a near-perfect season at the junior-college level in 2009, opening with a record 57-game winning streak, and capturing the Junior College World Series with a 63-1 record. Only four players were drafted off that team, none higher than the 12th round.

■ The Nationals had the No. 1 pick in the draft for the first time in their brief four-year history, although the old Washington Senators picked

out some of the later rounds, as well, notably the $2 million paid by the Kansas City Royals to third-rounder Wil Myers; $1.625 million by the Tigers to sixth-rounder Daniel Fields and $1.5 million by the A's to fourth-rounder Max Stassi. Some 13 bonuses of $1 million or more were paid beyond the first round, while an additional 77 bonuses of $100,000 or more were paid to players drafted after the 10th round.

Triggered by Strasburg's record-shattering $7.5 million bonus, the Nationals spent a record $11,511,500 to sign all their draft picks, topping the previous mark, set a year earlier by the Royals, by some $500,000. The Mariners ($10.9456 million), Tigers ($9.3951 million), Arizona Diamondbacks ($9.3282 million) and Padres ($9.1365) also spent in excess of $9 million.

Even with all the money flying, three first-rounders were not signed, although Crow, the first-round pick of the Royals, agreed to terms on Sept. 18 for a bonus of $1.5 million as part of a major league contract with a guaranteed value of $3 million. After going unsigned a year earlier, Crow signed on with the Fort Worth Cats of the independent American Association, and by doing so renounced his college eligibility at Missouri and was not subject to the Aug. 17 signing deadline.

A second 2009 draft pick, ex-Fresno State righthander Tanner Scheppers (Pirates, second round), also went unsigned in 2008 and followed a similar path by playing for the American Association's St. Paul Saints. Drafted by the Texas Rangers as a supplemental first-rounder (44th overall), he signed for $1.25 million on Sept. 17.

The average first-round bonus for 2009 was $2,434,800—about $15,000 less than the existing record, set in 2008. But the aggregate amount spent on bonuses in 2009, $189,332,700, was a draft record, topping the 2008 total by little more than $1 million.

### ACKLEY, TATE FALL SHORT

Strasburg, Ackley and Tate were clearly defined as the top three prospects in the 2009 draft, and were drafted and compensated accordingly.

While Strasburg struggled to live up to his considerable press clippings, Ackley proved to be a disappointment in his first five major league seasons. Like Strasburg, he also went undrafted out of high school. He evolved into the most accomplished hitter in the college ranks, batting better than .400 all three seasons at North Carolina, and even showing power as a junior by going deep 22 times.

In 584 games for the Mariners, Ackley hit just .243 with 46 homers before being dispatched to the Yankees in a 2015 trade. The Mariners had expected him to evolve into their center fielder and a consistent .300 hitter, but he was not a force at the plate and never found a home defensively, alternating between second base and left field.

Tate's issues were even more acute.

After starring in baseball and football at Cartersville (Ga.) High, and establishing himself as the best two-sport athlete in the country, Tate bypassed a scholarship to play both sports at North Carolina by signing the largest bonus in Padres history. His career was marred by a string of injuries,

## Top 25 Bonuses

| | Player, Pos. | Drafted (Round) | Order | Bonus |
|---|---|---|---|---|
| 1. | **Stephen Strasburg, rhp** | **Nationals (1)** | **1** | **#$7,500,000** |
| 2. | * Donavan Tate, of | Padres (1) | 3 | $6,250,000 |
| 3. | **Dustin Ackley, of** | **Mariners (1)** | **2** | **#$6,000,000** |
| 4. | *** Jacob Turner, rhp** | **Tigers (1)** | **9** | **#$4,700,000** |
| 5. | *** Tyler Matzek, lhp** | **Rockies (1)** | **11** | **$3,900,000** |
| 6. | *** Zack Wheeler, rhp** | **Giants (1)** | **6** | **$3,300,000** |
| 7. | *** Shelby Miller, rhp** | **Cardinals (1)** | **19** | **$2,875,000** |
| 8. | **Grant Green, ss** | **Athletics (1)** | **13** | **$2,750,000** |
| 9. | **Tony Sanchez, c** | **Pirates (1)** | **4** | **$2,500,000** |
| 10. | * Matt Hobgood, rhp | Orioles (1) | 5 | $2,422,000 |
| 11. | **Mike Minor, lhp** | **Braves (1)** | **7** | **$2,420,000** |
| 12. | **Mike Leake, rhp** | **Reds (1)** | **8** | **$2,270,000** |
| 13. | **Alex White, rhp** | **Indians (1)** | **15** | **$2,250,000** |
| 14. | *** Slade Heathcott, of** | **Yankees (1)** | **29** | **$2,200,000** |
| 15. | *** Wil Myers, c** | **Royals (3)** | **91** | **$2,000,000** |
| 16. | **Kyle Gibson, rhp** | **Twins (1)** | **22** | **$1,850,000** |
| 17. | *** Bobby Borchering, 3b** | **Diamondbacks (1)** | **16** | **$1,800,000** |
| 18. | * Chad James, lhp | Marlins (1) | 18 | $1,700,000 |
| 19. | *** Daniel Fields, ss** | **Tigers (6)** | **180** | **$1,625,000** |
| 20. | **Drew Storen, rhp** | **Nationals (1)** | **10** | **$1,600,000** |
| 21. | **Aaron Crow, rhp** | **Royals (1)** | **12** | **#$1,500,000** |
| | *** Max Stassi, c** | **Athletics (4)** | **123** | **$1,500,000** |
| 23. | **Andy Oliver, lhp** | **Tigers (2)** | **58** | **$1,495,000** |
| 24. | **Chris Dwyer, lhp** | **Royals (4)** | **122** | **$1,450,000** |
| 25. | **A.J. Pollock, of** | **Diamondbacks (1)** | **17** | **$1,400,000** |
| | * David Renfroe, ss | Red Sox (3) | 107 | $1,400,000 |

*Major leaguers in bold. *High school selection. #Major league contract.*

suspensions for substance abuse and a pair of stints in drug rehab centers. Through the 2015 season, he was still mired in the lower minors with just a .229 average and nine homers to show for six mainly wasted seasons in the Padres organization.

Donavan Tate

For all of his failings, Tate was just one of 10 first-rounders who had not played in the majors through the 2015 season, though he was the most noteworthy of the three who had never played above Class A. The others were righthander Eric Arnett (Brewers, 26th overall) and infielder LeVon Washington (Rays, 30th).

Overall, the first round was dominated by pitchers and outfielders. Among the first 22 selections were 15 pitchers (eight from college, seven from high school), while 10 outfielders were spread throughout the round. Outside of Strasburg, the talent level generally drew mixed reviews.

Arizona State righthander Mike Leake, selected eighth overall by the Cincinnati Reds, was not in the same league as Strasburg in the eyes of scouts, mainly because of his 6-foot frame and inferior stuff, but led the nation with 16 wins, and was second to Strasburg in both ERA (1.71) and strikeouts (162). He earned high praise for his ability to throw four pitches for strikes, his feel for pitching and competitive approach.

Like Strasburg, Leake waited to the deadline before signing with the Reds for $2.27 million,

## Largest Bonuses By Round

| | Player, Pos. | Club | Bonus |
|---|---|---|---|
| 1. | **Stephen Strasburg, rhp** | **Nationals** | **$7,500,000** |
| 1-S. | **Tanner Scheppers, rhp** | **Rangers** | **$1,250,000** |
| 2. | **Andy Oliver, lhp** | **Tigers** | **$1,495,000** |
| 3. | ***Wil Myers, c** | **Royals** | **$2,000,000** |
| 4. | *Max Stassi, c | Athletics | $1,500,000 |
| 5. | *Jeff Malm, 1b | Rays | $680,000 |
| 6. | ***Daniel Fields, ss** | **Tigers** | **$1,625,000** |
| 7. | *Madison Younginer, rhp | Red Sox | $975,000 |
| 8. | *Colton Cain, lhp | Pirates | $1,125,000 |
| 9. | *Kevin James, lhp | Rays | $625,000 |
| 10. | *Brandon Jacobs, of | Red Sox | $750,000 |
| 11. | *Mike Ohlman, c | Orioles | $995,000 |
| 12. | Jeff Inman, rhp | Pirates | $425,000 |
| 13. | *Zach Dotson, lhp | Mets | $500,000 |
| 14. | Graham Stoneburner, rhp | Yankees | $675,000 |
| 15. | ***Drew Hutchison, rhp** | **Blue Jays** | **$400,000** |
| 16. | ***Bryan Mitchell, rhp** | **Yankees** | **$800,000** |
| 17. | *Paul Strong, lhp | Rangers | $300,000 |
| 18. | **Daniel Webb, rhp** | **Blue Jays** | **$450,000** |
| 19. | *Sergio Burruel, c | Cubs | $95,500 |
| 20. | Kyle C. Smith, rhp | Indians | $100,000 |
| 21. | *Matt Swilley, rhp | Rays | $120,000 |
| 22. | *Cameron Coffey, lhp | Orioles | $990,000 |
| 23. | Danny Jimenez, lhp | Indians | $125,000 |
| 24. | *Shawn Blackwell, rhp | Rangers | $300,000 |
| 25. | Riley Cooper, of | Rangers | $250,000 |
| Other* | Evan DeLuca, lhp | Yankees (44) | $500,000 |

*Major leaguers in bold. *High school selection.*

and like most of his fellow holdouts didn't pitch at all in 2009. But Leake made such an impression with the Reds the following spring that he debuted in the majors to begin the 2010 season, and became the 22nd (and most recent) player in the draft era to achieve that feat. He won 12 games as a rookie and with 64 victories through six seasons, he had 10 more wins than the Strasburg over a comparable period.

If anyone was expected to jump straight to the majors it was Strasburg, but the Nationals exercised extreme caution in bringing him along and started him in Double-A. He quickly burned through that level, posting a 3-1, 1.64 record in five starts, before making six more starts in Triple-A, where he went 5-1, 1.08. In a combined 55 innings, he walked 13 and fanned 65, and pitched before sell-out throngs everywhere he went.

Storen, who got a jump on Strasburg by signing immediately, also preceded his arrival to Washington, making his debut on May 17, 2010. With the exception of a couple of notable glitches in his performance, he served admirably as the Nationals closer over the better part of six seasons while going 21-13, 3.02 with 95 saves.

Beyond Strasburg, Leake and Storen, most of the remaining first-round arms struggled to achieve meaningful success.

The 6-foot-4, 245-pound Hobgood was a surprise as the first high school pitcher drafted. He went 11-1, 0.92 with 101 strikeouts in 68 innings as a senior at Norco (Calif.) High, while also slamming 40 homers over his high school career, and cemented his stock on the strength of a mid-90s fastball and solid secondary pitches. His pro career, however, was plagued by ineffectiveness, shoulder issues and poor conditioning, and he had a 17-24, 4.98 record to show for seven seasons of work, only one above Class A. He missed the 2012 season entirely after rotator-cuff surgery.

The most polished premium prep pitcher available was the 6-foot-5, 205-pound Turner, who went 7-2, 0.60 with 13 walks and 118 strikeouts in 58 innings at Westminster Christian Academy in St. Louis. Turner's fastball peaked at 98 mph, and he benefited from the tutelage of former big leaguers Andy Benes, Mike Matheny and Todd Worrell, whose sons were his high school teammates. His considerable price tag caused him to slip beyond Hobgood and Zack Wheeler (Giants, sixth overall), a second high school righthander, before the Tigers took him with the ninth pick.

MIKE JANES

Jacob Turner

While Turner's $4.7 million bonus was a record for a high school pitcher and he was the first prep arm from the 2009 class to reach the majors, with Detroit in 2012, he was traded later that season to the Miami Marlins and quickly fell out of favor with that club, as well. Through the 2015 season, his major league record stood at 11-25, 4.97.

Texas high school righthander Shelby Miller (Cardinals, 19th overall) surged ahead of Hobgood, Wheeler and Turner to become the top prep righthander in the class, though he endured a difficult but deceiving 6-17, 3.02 record with the Atlanta Braves in 2015. In time, Wheeler could prove to be Miller's match, but he missed the 2015 season following Tommy John surgery.

Lefthanders Tyler Matzek (Rockies, 11th overall) and Matt Purke (Rangers, 14th) were the top prep lefthanders in the draft with fastballs in the mid-90s, but Matzek struggled to establish himself in the majors because of repeated bouts of wildness, while Purke has been slowed by injuries. After going unsigned by the Rangers, Purke went 16-0 as a freshman at TCU but won 15 games combined over the next five years—five at TCU, 10 in the minors—as he was plagued by shoulder problems and then had Tommy John surgery in 2015.

### DRAFT FOR THE AGES

The St. Louis Cardinals advanced to postseason play every year from 2012-15, in large part because of the contributions of five key players they plucked from the 2009 draft: Miller, third-rounder Joe Kelly, 11th-rounder Matt Carpenter, 21st-rounder Trevor Rosenthal and 23rd-rounder Matt Adams.

All played significant roles, in particular, on the 2013 Cardinals team that won 97 games and advanced to the World Series. Carpenter (.318-11-78, 126 runs, 55 doubles) excelled as the team's second baseman and leadoff hitter, Adams (.284-17-51) provided power in his platoon role at first base, and Miller (15-9, 3.06), Kelly (10-5, 2.69) and Rosenthal (2-4, 2.63, 75 IP/108 SO) were all key components of the pitching staff.

Rarely had one draft so quickly or dramatically

### WORTH NOTING

first overall in 1969, when they selected outfielder **JEFF BURROUGHS**. The Mariners (4) and Padres (5), the teams which selected second and third, had the top pick nine times.

■ All the spending in 2009 wasn't limited to the draft, as the international market became a feeding frenzy of unprecedented proportions. The Red Sox led the way by signing 19-year-old Cuban shortstop **JOSE IGLESIAS** to a four-year major league contract that included a bonus of $6.25 million and a guaranteed value of $8.25 million. Iglesias defected from the 2008 World Junior Championship in Edmonton, Alberta, and signed with the Red Sox a year later after establishing residency in the Dominican Republic. The Red Sox didn't stop there as they signed two other highly rated shortstops: Dominican **JOSE VINCIO**, 16, for $1.95 million, and **XANDER BOGAERTS**, a 16-year-old Aruba product who received $430,000. By 2015, Bogaerts had evolved into one of the top shortstops in the majors. The Rangers also signed a pair of 16-year-old international shortstops, **JURICKSON PROFAR** from Curacao for $1.55 million and **LUIS SARDINAS** from Venezuela for $1.2 million. Righthander **NOEL ARGUELLAS**, who defected from Cuba along with Iglesias, signed a five-year major league contract with the Royals for a guaranteed value of $6.9 million. Among players from the popular Dominican market, the Twins signed third baseman **MIGUEL SANO** for $3.15 million, while the Yankees got catcher **GARY SANCHEZ** for $3 million. Even Nicaragua got into the act as the Royals signed third baseman **CHESLOR CUTHBERT** for $1.35 million, a record for that country.

■ Quarterbacks **COLIN KAEPERNICK** (Nevada), **JAKE LOCKER** (Washington) and **PATRICK WHITE** (West Virginia), and wide receivers

CONTINUED ON PAGE 662

**WORTH NOTING**

CONTINUED FROM PAGE 661

**RILEY COOPER** (Florida) and **ERIC DECKER** (Minnesota) were among the nation's better-known college football players. All had significant ties to baseball and were selected in the 2009 draft, but ultimately pursued careers in the NFL—though Locker and Cooper also signed contracts to play baseball. Locker, a 10th-round pick of the Angels, signed for $200,000, and Cooper, a 25th-round selection of the Rangers, signed for $250,000, though neither played a game of professional baseball. As one of the nation's top quarterback recruits, Locker focused on football in college at Washington, even though he was also a coveted outfield prospect and would have been a near-cinch first-rounder had he decided to make baseball his sport of choice. "The reason I chose not to do both is because I wanted to give myself the best opportunity to be great at one thing," Locker said. Though Locker never played even one baseball game at Washington, the Angels were so infatuated with his raw tools that they went out on a limb and signed him, with no guarantee that Locker would ever play a game for them. After his senior year of football at Washington, Locker was drafted in the first round by the Tennessee Titans and pursued a four-year career in the NFL. Cooper was drafted by the Phillies (2006, 15th round) out of high school, but passed on a chance to sign for an opportunity to play baseball and football in college at Florida, where he was a roommate and favorite target of Tim Tebow. Though he was drafted again in 2009 by the Rangers and signed a deal to play with that club just before returning to Florida to play his senior year of football, he had a change of heart four months later and the contract was voided. Cooper was selected by the Philadelphia Eagles in the fifth round of the 2010 NFL draft, and he played six years for that club as a wide receiver.

affected the fortunes of a team.

Carpenter, in particular, was a coup for the Cardinals and their analytics department, as he was signed for $1,000 as a 23-year-old fifth-year senior.

Early in his junior year at TCU, Carpenter had Tommy John surgery and got a two-year medical redshirt. In the process of rehabilitating his elbow, his future in baseball came into question because his discipline off the field was poor. His grades and conditioning slipped, and he let his weight balloon to 240 pounds. A heart-to-heart conversation with Schlossnagle persuaded him to change his work habits, and in the process of dropping 40 pounds, his baseball career flourished. In 2009, Carpenter had the best season of his college career, hitting .333 with 11 home runs, and the Cardinals took a chance on him. Six years later, he was one of the most productive major leaguers to come out of the 2009 draft.

In contrast to the Cardinals, the Toronto Blue Jays' draft was somewhat of a disaster—initially, at least—as the Blue Jays failed to sign three of their first four picks, including two Canadians: supplemental first-rounder James Paxton and second-rounder Jake Eliopoulos, a pair of lefthanders. The Jays drafted eight Canadians in all, and didn't sign any of them.

MIKE JANES

Tony Sanchez

With unused bonus money at their disposal, the Blue Jays went on a splurge at the deadline and signed four players to bonuses significantly over slot: third-rounder Jake Marisnick ($1 million), sixth-rounder K.C. Hobson ($500,000), 15th-rounder Drew Hutchison ($400,000) and 18th-rounder Daniel Webb ($450,000). All but Hobson later reached the majors, enabling the Jays to recoup some of their losses.

Numerous other clubs went on spending sprees with the deadline at hand. Among the big spenders were big-revenue clubs like the Yankees, Tigers and Boston Red Sox, and notoriously more conservative organizations like the Orioles and Pirates.

The Yankees splurged across the board in 2009, first spending millions to sign Mark Teixeira, C.C. Sabathia and A.J. Burnett as major league free agents prior to the season. As the cost of plunging into free agency, the Yankees forfeited their first three picks in the draft, but that didn't deter them.

With the picks they received for not signing Cole and second-rounder Scott Bittle a year earlier, they took Texas high school outfielder Slade Heathcott and Florida prep catcher J.R. Murphy, and signed them for $2.2 million and $1.4 million, respectively. From there, they signed fifth-rounder Caleb Cotham ($675,000), 14th-rounder Graham Stoneburner ($675,000), 16th-rounder Bryan Mitchell ($800,000) and 44th-rounder Evan DeLuca ($500,000)—a record for that round. Not surprisingly, every one of the signings was announced on Aug. 17.

The Tigers showed little hesitation in taking the high-priced Turner with their top pick and spent the fourth-largest bonus in the draft to sign him. They also showered $1.495 million on second-rounder Andy Oliver, in addition to $1.625 million on Fields, a local high school product. All reached the majors, but none had distinguished himself through the 2015 season.

The Red Sox, meanwhile, played it straight through the first two rounds, but opened their wallet thereafter in signing third rounder David Renfroe for $1.4 million, seventh-rounder Madison Younginer for $975,000, ninth-rounder Kendall Volz for $550,000, 10th-rounder Brandon Jacobs for $750,000, 11th-rounder Jason Thompson for $300,000 and 26th-rounder Miles Head for $335,000. None of the six reached the majors, and only Younginer was still active in 2015.

The Orioles were also conservative in the first round, quickly signing Hobgood for a below-slot deal, but that was the calm before the storm as the O's waited until August to announce the signings of eight players to substantial bonuses, including 11th-rounder Michael Ohlman for $995,000 and 22nd-rounder Cameron Coffey for $990,000. Six years later, only second-rounder Mychal Givens, who signed for $800,000, had reached the majors.

The Pirates were criticized for their selection of Sanchez, who was not regarded as the fourth-best talent. But they planned to save money there and share the wealth with their other picks. Including Sanchez, who signed for $2.5 million, the Pirates signed 14 players for at least $100,000, and eight for more than $200,000, including fourth-rounder Zack Dodson for $600,000, sixth-rounder Zack Von Rosenberg for $1.2 million and eighth-rounder Colton Cain for $1.125 million.

## NCAA CHALLENGES USE OF AGENTS

Louisiana State won its sixth College World Series title in 2009 as outfielder Jared Mitchell,

### One Team's Draft: St. Louis Cardinals

| | Player, Pos. | Bonus | | Player, Pos. | Bonus | | Player, Pos. | Bonus |
|---|---|---|---|---|---|---|---|---|
| **1.** | ***Shelby Miller, rhp** | **$2,875,000** | 10. | *Hector Hernandez, lhp | $85,000 | **19.** | **Travis Tartamella, c** | **$25,000** |
| 2. | Robert Stock, c/rhp | $525,000 | 11. | Alan Ahmady, 1b | $60,000 | 20. | Scott Schneider, rhp | $20,000 |
| **3.** | **Joe Kelly, rhp** | **$341,000** | 12. | Pat Daugherty, lhp | $60,000 | **21.** | **Trevor Rosenthal, rhp** | **$65,000** |
| 4. | Joe Bittle, rhp | $75,000 | **13.** | **Matt Carpenter, 3b** | **$1,000** | 22. | Joey Bergman, 2b | Did not sign |
| **5.** | **Ryan Jackson, ss** | **$157,500** | 14. | Ross Smith, of | $50,000 | **23.** | **Matt Adams, 1b** | **$25,000** |
| 6. | Virgil Hill, of | $150,000 | 15. | *David Washington, 1b | $80,000 | **24.** | **Keith Butler, rhp** | **$25,000** |
| 7. | Kyle Conley, of | $100,000 | 16. | Daniel Bibona, lhp | Did not sign | 25. | Josh Squatrito, rhp | $1,000 |
| 8. | Jason Stidham, ss | $100,000 | 17. | Jonathan Rodriguez, 1b | $45,000 | Other | Travis Lawler (32), rhp | $100,000 |
| 9. | Nick McCully, rhp | $100,000 | 18. | *Anthony Garcia, c | $40,000 | | | |

*Major leaguers in bold. *High school selection.*

## Highest Unsigned Picks

| Player, Pos., Team (Round) | College | Re-Drafted |
|---|---|---|
| Matthew Purke, lhp, Rangers (1) | Texas Christian | Nationals '11 (3) |
| LeVon Washington, 2b, Rays (1) | Chipola (Fla.) JC | Indians '10 (2) |
| James Paxton, lhp, Blue Jays (1) | None | Mariners '10 (4) |
| Jake Eliopoulos, lhp, Blue Jays (2) | Chipola (Fla.) JC | Dodgers '10 (15) |
| Kenny Diekroeger, ss, Rays (2) | Stanford | Royals '12 (4) |
| Jake Barrett, rhp, Blue Jays (3) | Arizona State | D-backs '12 (3) |
| Bryan Morgado, lhp, White Sox (3) | * Tennessee | Phillies '10 (4) |
| Josh Spence, lhp, Angels (3) | * Arizona State | Padres '10 (9) |
| Miguel Pena, lhp, Nationals (5) | San Jacinto (Texas) JC | Padres '10 (13) |
| Damon Magnifico, rhp, Mets (5) | Howard (Texas) JC | Brewers '12 (5) |

**TOTAL UNSIGNED PICKS:** Top 5 Rounds (10), Top 10 Rounds (22)

**Returned to same school.*

a first-round pick of the Chicago White Sox, was named the Most Outstanding Player. Mitchell, an electrifying athlete, also played on LSU's national championship football team in 2007.

He hit .327 with 11 home runs and a team-high 36 stolen bases for the Tigers, and was joined in the early rounds of the draft by teammates like second baseman D.J. LeMahieu (.350-5-43), a second-round pick of the Chicago Cubs; righthander Louis Coleman (14-2, 2.93), a fifth-round selection of the Royals; and outfielder Ryan Schimpf (.336-22-70), a fifth-round choice of the Blue Jays.

Unlike LeMahieu and Coleman, Mitchell never reached the majors as a torn ankle tendon, which caused him to miss the 2010 season, robbed him of his exhilirating speed. He hit just .225 with 46 homers and 83 stolen bases in the minors with the White Sox before being released in 2015.

While Strasburg monopolized most of the attention paid to college talent in what was otherwise regarded as an average crop, the Diamondbacks acquired two future mainstays in Notre Dame outfielder A.J. Pollock, the second of two first-rounders (17th overall), and Texas State third baseman Paul Goldschmidt, an eighth-rounder. The unheralded Goldschmidt, who signed for $95,000, led all NCAA hitters with 87 RBIs in 2009 and the National League in the same category in 2013.

The Mariners made amends for their misstep with Ackley by drafting his less-celebrated UNC teammate, Kyle Seager, in the third round. Seager became an all-star third baseman—the kind of player the Mariners expected Ackley to become.

Three other non-first rounders, Paxton and fellow lefthanders Andy Oliver (Tigers, second round) and Chris Dwyer (Royals, fourth round), also earned notoriety, though for reasons other than their performance on the field.

Oliver was suspended in 2008 by the NCAA, just before he was scheduled to make a regional appearance for Oklahoma State. The NCAA ruled that he had used an agent, Tim Barrata, two years earlier during negotiations with the Minnesota Twins, who had drafted him out of an Ohio high school in 2006. When Oliver later cut ties with Barrata, in favor of Boras, Barrata turned him in.

Oliver then sued the NCAA, and the courts ruled in his favor. On Feb. 12, 2009, an Ohio judge ruled the NCAA could not restrict a player's right to have legal representation when negotiating a professional contract and, in essence, invalidated the NCAA's "no agent" rule. Unfortunately, as part of a $750,000 settlement, the case was dismissed and the "no agent" rule restored.

Not surprisingly, with all the legal issues still hanging over his head, Oliver's junior season was a disappointment as he went just 5-6, 5.30 for the Cowboys after going 7-2, 2.20 a year earlier.

The 6-foot-3, 210-pound lefty had projected as a solid first-round pick on the basis of his sophomore performance and a fastball up to 94 mph, but was still paid like a first-rounder, even as his secondary stuff lacked consistency. His $1.495 million bonus was the largest in the second round.

Before Oliver, the NCAA only investigated the rare accusations of players using agents that were brought to its attention. Since then, the NCAA pursued violations more aggressively.

Paxton ran into the same legal entanglements with the NCAA after he and the Blue Jays failed to reach agreement on a contract, and Paxton attempted to return to Kentucky for his senior year. The Blue Jays acknowledged in public reports that Paxton had used an agent (Boras) in his failed negotiations, which set off a chain of events that ended Paxton's college career.

The NCAA refused to allow him to play until he met with its investigators to answer questions about his eligibility. A judge ruled against Paxton when the matter ended up in the courts, leaving him ineligible to play in 2010. He later hooked on with an independent team before being redrafted by the Mariners.

Dwyer, a 6-foot-2, 200-pound lefthander from Clemson, was eligible for the draft as a freshman because he had already turned 21. That unique circumstance—believed to be a first in draft annals—came about because Dwyer repeated a year in elementary school and then 11th grade. Following his junior year at a Massachusetts high school, he made a decision to transfer to a Connecticut prep school and in the process was re-classified as a junior—in large measure because he was uncertain whether football or baseball offered the best career path in college, and he hoped an extra year would help him make the right decision.

Dwyer's baseball profile skyrocketed while attending Salisbury Prep for two years, as did his price tag, which scared off most clubs in the 2008 draft. The Yankees took him with a token late-round pick, but made little attempt to sign him, paving his way to attend college. He was erratic in his lone college season at Clemson, going 5-6, 4.92, but with a fastball that peaked at 97 mph his potential was evident.

With an opportunity to sign after each of his four years in college, Dwyer was in an enviable situation from a signability standpoint and maximized his leverage by signing with the Royals for $1.45 million—as a fourth-round pick.

Dwyer, Oliver and Paxton all managed to reach the majors, but only Paxton (12-8, 3.16) enjoyed any measurable success. Dwyer and Oliver had still not won a game through the 2015 season.

### IN FOCUS: STEPHEN STRASBURG

Stephen Strasburg was the dominant storyline of the 2009 draft and his debut with the Washington Nationals on June 8, 2010, was one of the most-ballyhooed premieres ever for a major league rookie. He didn't disappoint an electrified home crowd by fanning a club-record 14 and walking none over seven innings in a 5-2 win over the Pirates. His fastball reached 100 mph—and still had plenty of movement when it crossed the plate—and his nasty curve was nearly impossible to hit.

Strasburg showed flashes of brilliance throughout his rookie year with the Nationals, going 5-3, 2.91, along with 17 walks and 92 strikeouts in 68 innings. He gave every indication of becoming one of the dominant major league pitchers of the draft era—before he missed a month with an inflamed shoulder, and was eventually lost for the season with a sore elbow that resulted in Tommy John surgery.

Between his recuperation, which cost him most of the 2011 season, and his comeback a year later that was short-circuited by the Nationals' controversial decision to shut him down after he reached an innings limit, Strasburg's performance had not quite kept pace with all the hype. Through 2015, he assembled a 54-37, 3.09 record, with 901 strikeouts in 777 innings.

# 2009 Draft List

**Did not sign. Major leaguers in bold, with first and last years noted. Order of selection indicated in parentheses. For the first five rounds, the peak level of each player is noted.*

## ARIZONA DIAMONDBACKS (15)

1. Bobby Borchering, 3b, Bishop Verot HS, Fort Myers, Fla.—(AA)
1. **A.J. Pollock, of, University of Notre Dame** (Choice from Dodgers as compensation for Type A free agent Orlando Hudson).**—(2012-15)**
1. **Matt Davidson, 3b, Yucaipa (Calif.) HS** (Supplemental choice—35th—as compensation for Hudson).**—(2013)**
1. **Chris Owings, ss, Gilbert (S.C.) HS** (Supplemental choice—41st—as compensation for Type A free agent Juan Cruz).**—(2013-15)**
1. **Mike Belfiore, lhp, Boston College** (Supplemental choice—45th—as compensation for Type B free agent Brandon Lyon).**—(2013)**
2. Eric Smith, rhp, University of Rhode Island (Choice from Royals as compensation for Cruz).—(AA)
2. **Marc Krauss, of, Ohio University.—(2013-15)**
3. **Keon Broxton, of, Santa Fe (Fla.) CC.—(2015)**
4. David Nick, ss, Cypress (Calif.) HS.—(AA)
5. **Ryan Wheeler, 1b, Loyola Marymount University.—(2012-14)**
6. **Bradin Hagens, rhp, Merced (Calif.) JC.—(2014)**
7. Matt Helm, 3b, Hamilton HS, Chandler, Ariz.
8. **Paul Goldschmidt, 1b, Texas State University.—(2011-15)**
9. **Chase Anderson, rhp, University of Oklahoma.—(2014-15)**
10. Tyson Van Winkle, c, Gonzaga University.
11. Scottie Allen, rhp, Lyman HS, Longwood, Fla.
12. **Charles Brewer, rhp, UCLA.—(2013)**
13. Patrick Schuster, lhp, J.W. Mitchell HS, New Port Richey, Fla.
14. Brent Greer, ss, Western Carolina University.
15. David Narodowski, ss, University of Kansas.
16. Ryan Robowski, lhp, Ohio Dominican University.
17. Andrew Wolcott, rhp, Duke University.
18. Roidany Aguila, c, Colegio Nuestra Senora de la Providencia HS, Rio Piedras, P.R.
19. Randy Hamrick, rhp-ss, Brewton-Parker (Ga.) College.
20. Adam Worthington, rhp, University of Illinois-Chicago.
21. Dan Taylor, lhp, Central Michigan University.
22. Evan Button, ss, University of Mississippi.
23. Chris Odegaard, rhp, Minnesota State University-Mankato.
24. Brad Gemberling, rhp, Princeton University.
25. *Taylor Wrenn, ss, Manatee (Fla.) CC.
26. Dan Kaczrowski, ss, Hamline (Minn.) University.
27. Jake Hale, rhp, Ohio State University.
28. Brian Budrow, rhp, University of Utah.
29. *Jake Williams, 1b, Brophy Prep, Phoenix.
**DRAFT DROP** *Son of Matt Williams, major leaguer (1987-2003); major league manager (2014-15)*
30. *Jack Marder, ss, Newbury Park (Calif.) HS.
31. Keith Cantwell, rhp, Seton Hall University.
32. Will Harvil, rhp, University of Georgia.
33. Brad Wilson, rhp, Cal Poly Pomona.
34. *Patrick Cooper, rhp, Des Moines Area (Iowa) CC.
35. *Zach Morgan, rhp, Shasta (Calif.) JC.
36. *Mike Freeman, ss, Clemson University.
37. *Chris Jacobs, of, Westchester HS, Los Angeles.
38. *Trevon Prince, lhp, Oakland, Calif.
39. *Ryan Jones, of, Wichita State University.
40. Tim Sherlock, of, Duke University.
41. *Cade Kreuter, 3b, William S. Hart HS, Newhall, Calif.
**DRAFT DROP** *Son of Chad Kreuter, major leauer (1988-2003)*
42. *Zach Hendrix, 2b, Emerald Ridge HS, Puyallup, Wash.
43. *Brooklyn Foster, c, Walnut Grove SS, Langley, B.C.
44. Zac Varnell, c, University of Arkansas-Pine Bluff
45. *Beau Amaral, of, Huntington Beach (Calif.) HS.
**DRAFT DROP** *Son of Rich Amaral, major leaguer (1991-2000)*
46. *Matt Ozanne, of, Notre Dame Prep, Scottsdale, Ariz.
47. *Mario Gallardo, lhp, West Los Angeles JC.
48. *Juan Avila, of, Narbonne HS, Harbor City, Calif.
49. *Jordan Luvisi, of, Notre Dame Prep, Scottsdale, Ariz.
50. *Frank Abbl, rhp, Mesa (Ariz.) CC

## ATLANTA BRAVES (7)

1. **Mike Minor, lhp, Vanderbilt University.—(2010-14)**
2. (Choice to Dodgers as compensation for Type A free agent Derek Lowe)
3. **David Hale, rhp, Princeton University.—(2013-15)**
4. Mycal Jones, ss, Miami-Dade JC.—(AAA)
5. Thomas Berryhill, rhp, Newberry (S.C.) College.—(High A)
6. *Ryan Woolley, rhp, University of Alabama-Birmingham
7. Robby Hefflinger, of, Georgia Perimeter JC.
8. Kyle Rose, of, Northwest Shoals (Ala.) CC.
9. Matt Weaver, ss, Burlington County (N.J.) CC.
10. Aaron Northcraft, rhp, Mater Dei HS, Santa Ana, Calif.
11. Chris Masters, lhp, Western Carolina University.
12. Chris Lovett, ss, Columbia State (Tenn.) CC.
13. Jordan Kreke, 3b, Eastern Illinois University.
14. Cory Harrilchak, of, Elon University.
15. *Bennett Pickar, c, Eaton (Colo.) HS.
16. Riaan Spanjer-Furstenburg, 1b, Nova Southeastern (Fla.) University.
17. Jace Whitmer, c, Kennesaw State University.
18. Jakob Dalfonso, 3b, Middle Georgia JC.
19. Ty'Relle Harris, rhp, University of Tennessee
20. Jeff Lorick, lhp, University of Virginia
21. Matt Crim, lhp, The Citadel.
22. **Ryan Weber, rhp, St. Petersburg (Fla.) JC.—(2015)**
23. Lucas LaPoint, rhp, Knight HS, Palmdale, Calif.
24. *Casey Upperman, rhp, Notre Dame Prep, Scottsdale, Ariz.
25. *Ethan Icard, rhp, Wilkes (N.C.) CC.
26. *Will Scott, rhp, Walters State (Tenn.) CC.
27. *Joey Leftridge, of, Howard (Texas) JC.
28. *Eric Swegman, rhp, Young Harris (Ga.) JC.
29. Bobby Rauh, of, Daytona Beach (Fla.) CC.
30. *Vince Howard, of, Sikeston (Mo.) HS.
31. Derek Wiley, 1b, Belmont University.
32. *Jake Montgomery, rhp, Pope HS, Marietta, Ga.
33. *Tyler Stubblefield, ss, Kennesaw State University.
34. *Arby Fields, of, Los Osos HS, Rancho Cucamonga, Calif.
35. *Matt Hartunian, c, Montclair Prep, Van Nuys, Calif.
36. Andrew Wilson, rhp, Liberty University.
37. *Matt Moynihan, of, Cathedral Catholic HS, San Diego.
38. *Tripp Faulk, of, North Myrtle Beach HS, Little River, S.C.
39. *Joey Bourgeois, rhp, LSU-Eunice JC.
40. *Antonio Carrillo, of, San Ysidro HS, San Diego.
41. *Kyle Petter, lhp, El Camino (Calif.) JC.
42. *Josh Conway, of, Smithburg (Md.) HS.
43. *Alan Walden, rhp, Red Bank HS, Chattanooga, Tenn.
44. *Corey Newsome, rhp, Bay HS, Panama City, Fla.
45. *Nathan Dorris, lhp, Marion (Ill.) HS.
46. ***Buck Farmer, rhp, Rockdale County HS, Conyers, Ga.—(2014-15)**
47. *Colby Holmes, rhp, Conway (S.C.) HS.
48. Jamie Hayes, rhp, Rider University.
49. *Gabe Gutierrez, rhp, Apollo HS, Glendale, Ariz.
50. ***Josh Edgin, lhp, Francis Marion (S.C.) University.—(2012-14)**

## BALTIMORE ORIOLES (5)

1. Matt Hobgood, rhp, Norco (Calif.) HS.—(AA)
2. **Mychal Givens, ss-rhp, H.B. Plant HS, Tampa.—(2015)**
3. Tyler Townsend, 1b, Florida International University.—(AA)
4. Randy Henry, rhp, South Mountain (Ariz.) CC.—(AAA)
5. Ashur Tolliver, lhp, Oklahoma City University.—(AA)
6. Justin Dalles, c, University of South Carolina.
7. Aaron Wirsch, lhp, El Toro HS, Lake Forest, Calif.
8. *Devin Harris, of, East Carolina University.
9. Ryan Berry, rhp, Rice University.
10. Jake Cowan, rhp, San Jacinto (Texas) JC.
11. Mike Ohlman, c, Lakewood Ranch HS, Bradenton, Fla.
12. Steve Bumbry, of, Virginia Tech.
**DRAFT DROP** *Son of Al Bumbry, major leaguer (1972-85)*
13. Ty Kelly, 2b, UC Davis.
14. David Baker, rhp, Hemet (Calif.) HS.
15. *Garrett Bush, rhp, Stanton College Prep HS, Jacksonville, Fla.
16. Ryan Palsha, rhp, Diablo Valley (Calif.) JC.
17. *Jeff Walters, rhp, University of Georgia.
18. Jarret Martin, lhp, Bakersfield (Calif.) JC.
19. Kipp Schutz, of, Indiana University.
20. James Brandhorst, rhp, Lamar University.
21. Kevin Landry, rhp, College of William & Mary.
22. Cameron Coffey, lhp, Houston Christian HS, Houston.
23. Mike Mooney, ss, University of Florida.
24. Justin Anderson, lhp, University of Louisiana-Monroe.
25. *Jay Johnson, lhp, Lethbridge (Alberta) CC.
26. Blake Mechaw, lhp, Shelton State (Ala.) CC.
27. Mike Planeta, of, Glendale (Ariz.) CC.
28. Kyle Hoppy, of, Orchard Park (N.Y.) HS.
29. *Brandon Alexander, of, Oakville HS, St. Louis.
30. Brenden Webb, of, Palomar (Calif.) JC.
31. Mike Flacco, 3b, Catonsville (Md.) CC.
**DRAFT DROP** *Brother of Joe Flacco, quarterback, National Football League (2008-14)*
32. *Matt Nadolski, lhp, Casa Grande HS, Petaluma, Calif.
33. *Tyler Naquin, of, Klein Collins HS, Spring, Texas.
**DRAFT DROP** *First-round draft pick (15th overall), Indians (2012)*
34. *Malcolm Clapsaddle, rhp, Oviedo (Fla.) HS.
35. *Jeremy Lucas, c, West Vigo HS, Terre Haute, Ind.
36. *Scott Firth, rhp, Adlai Stevenson HS, Lincolnshire, Ill.
37. *Taylor Rogers, lhp, Chatfield HS, Littleton, Colo.
38. Josh Dowdy, rhp, Appalachian State University.
39. *Kevin Alexander, rhp, Taravella HS, Coral Springs, Fla.
40. *Bobby Shore, rhp, Palomar (Calif.) JC.
41. *Mason Magleby, rhp, Del Oro HS, Loomis, Calif.
42. *Joe Velleggia, c, Old Dominion University.
43. *Brad Decater, of, Cuesta (Calif.) JC.
44. *Kyle Westwood, rhp, University HS, Palm Harbor, Fla.
45. David Rivera, of, Francisco Oller HS, Catano, P.R.
46. *Scott Swinson, rhp, University of Maryland.
47. *Nolan Martz, rhp, McKendree (Ill.) College.
48. *Ryan Burnaman, 3b, San Jacinto (Texas) JC.
49. *Ashley Bulluck, rhp, South Broward HS, Hollywood, Fla.
50. Tim Berry, lhp, San Marcos (Calif.) HS.

## BOSTON RED SOX (27)

1. **Reymond Fuentes, of, Fernando Callejo HS, Manati, P.R.—(2013)**
**DRAFT DROP** *Cousin of Carlos Beltran, major leaguer (1998-2015)*
2. **Alex Wilson, rhp, Texas A&M University.—(2013-15)**
3. David Renfroe, ss, South Panola HS, Batesville, Miss.—(High A)
**DRAFT DROP** *Son of Laddie Renfroe, major leaguer (1991)*
4. Jeremy Hazelbaker, of, Ball State University.—(AAA)
5. Seth Schwindenhammer, of, Limestone Community HS, Bartonville, Ill.—(Short-season A)
6. *Branden Kline, rhp, Thomas Johnson HS, Frederick, Md.
7. Madison Younginer, rhp, Mauldin (S.C.) HS.
8. Shannon Wilkerson, of, Augusta State (Ga.) University.
9. Kendal Volz, rhp, Baylor University.
10. Brandon Jacobs, of, Parkview HS, Lilburn, Ga.
11. Jason Thompson, ss, Germantown (Tenn.) HS.
12. Michael Thomas, c, Southern University.
13. **Chris McGuiness, 1b, The Citadel.—(2013)**
14. Willie Holmes, of, Chaffey (Calif.) JC.
15. Michael Bugary, lhp, University of California
16. *Luke Bard, rhp, Charlotte Christian HS, Charlotte, N.C.
**DRAFT DROP** *First-round draft pick (42nd overall), Twins (2012) • Brother of Daniel Bard, first-round draft pick, Red Sox (2006); major leaguer (2009-13)*
17. *Kraig Sitton, lhp, Oregon State University.
18. Renny Parthemore, rhp, Cedar Cliff HS, Camp Hill, Pa.
19. Tom Ebert, rhp, Florida International University.
20. **Alex Hassan, of-rhp, Duke University.—(2014)**
21. *Randall Fant, lhp, Texas HS, Texarkana, Texas.
22. Jordan Flasher, rhp, George Mason University.
23. Chris Court, rhp, Stephen F. Austin State University.
24. *Dan Kemp, ss, Tantasqua Regional HS, Fiskdale, Mass.
25. *Austin House, rhp, La Cueva HS, Albuquerque, N.M.
26. Miles Head, 3b, Whitewater HS, Fayetteville, Ga.
27. *Reed Gragnani, ss, Godwin HS, Richmond, Va.
28. Eric Curtis, rhp, Miami-Dade JC.
29. *Cody Stubbs, 1b, Tuscola HS, Waynesville, N.C.
30. Jeremiah Bayer, rhp, Trinity (Conn.) University.
31. Tim Webb, lhp, Palm Beach (Fla.) CC.
32. *Michael Clark, lhp, American Heritage HS, Plantation, Fla.
33. *Blaze Tart, rhp, Pendleton School, Bradenton, Fla.
34. *Jimmy Patterson, lhp, Central Arizona JC.
35. *Matt Milroy, rhp, Marmion Academy, Aurora, Ill.
36. *Mike Yastrzemski, of, St. John's Prep, Danvers, Mass.
**DRAFT DROP** *Grandson of Carl Yastrzemski, major leaguer (1961-83)*
37. *Matt Koch, rhp, Washington HS, Cherokee, Iowa.
38. *Zeke DeVoss, of, Astronaut HS, Titusville, Fla.
39. *Gavin McCourt, of, Harvard-Westlake HS, Los Angeles.
**DRAFT DROP** *Son of Frank McCourt, owner, Dodgers (2004-12)*
40. *James Dykstra, rhp, Rancho Bernardo HS, San Diego.
**DRAFT DROP** *Brother of Allan Dykstra, first-round draft pick, Padres (2008); major leaguer (2015)*
41. Kyle Rutter, rhp, North Carolina State University.
42. *Gera Sanchez, rhp, New Mexico JC.
43. ***Luke Maile, c, Covington Catholic HS, Park Hills, Ky.—(2015)**
44. *Derrick Thomas, of, Roswell (Ga.) HS.
45. *Kyle Arnsberg, c, Lamar HS, Arlington, Texas.
**DRAFT DROP** *Son of Brad Arnsberg, major leaguer (1986-92)*
46. *John Pivach, rhp, University of New Orleans.
47. Jordan Sallis, 2b, Arkansas-Fort Smith JC.
48. *Brian Heere, of, University of Kansas
49. *Chris Costantino, 3b, Bishop Hendricken HS, Warwick, R.I.
50. Drew Hedman, 1b, Pomona-Pitzer (Calif.) College.

## CHICAGO CUBS (29)

1. **Brett Jackson, of, University of California.—(2012-14)**
2. **D.J. LeMahieu, 2b, Louisiana State University.—(2011-15)**
3. Austin Kirk, lhp, Owasso (Okla.) HS.—(AA)
4. **Chris Rusin, lhp, University of Kentucky.—(2012-15)**
5. Wes Darvill, ss, Brookswood SS, Langley, B.C.—(AA)
6. **Brooks Raley, lhp, Texas A&M University.—(2012-13)**
7. Blair Springfield, ss, MacArthur HS, Decatur, Ill.
8. Robert Whitenack, rhp, SUNY Old Westbury.
9. Richard Jones, c, The Citadel.
10. Charles Thomas, 3b, Edward Waters (Fla.) College.
11. John Mincone, lhp, Suffolk County (N.Y.) CC.
12. Runey Davis, of, Howard (Texas) JC.
13. *Chad Taylor, ss, Jefferson HS, Tampa.
14. Danny Keefe, rhp, University of Tampa.
15. Cody Shields, of, Auburn University-Montgomery.
16. *Keenyn Walker, of, Judge Memorial HS, Salt Lake

City.

DRAFT DROP *First-round draft pick (47th overall), White Sox (2011)*

17. *B.J. Dail, rhp, Mount Olive (N.C.) College.
18. Matt Williams, c, Duke University.
19. Sergio Burruel, c, Browne HS, Phoenix.
20. *Eric Erickson, lhp, University of Miami.
21. Greg Rohan, 1b, Kent State University.
22. D.J. Fitzgerald, 2b, Dyersburg State (Tenn.) CC.
23. *Jeff Pruitt, of, Cal State Northridge.
24. *Gerardo Esquivel, rhp, De La Salle Institute, Chicago.
25. **Justin Bour, 1b, George Mason University.—(2014-15)**
26. Steve Grife, rhp, Mercyhurst (Pa.) College.
27. Corey Martin, rhp, Western Carolina University.
28. Jordan Petraitis, 3b, Miami (Ohio) University.
29. Tim Clubb, rhp, Missouri State University.
30. *Danny Sheppard, c, Downers Grove (Ill.) North HS.
31. *Andrew Clark, 1b, University of Louisville.
32. Trey McNutt, rhp, Shelton State (Ala.) CC
33. *John Lambert, lhp, North Carolina State University.
34. *Rett Varner, rhp, University of Texas-San Antonio.
35. *Kevin David, c, Oklahoma State University.
36. Brandon May, 2b, University of Alabama
37. *Peter Mooney, ss, Palm Beach (Fla.) CC.
38. Bobby Wagner, 3b, Panola (Texas) JC.
39. Nick Struck, rhp, Mount Hood (Ore.) CC.
40. *Eric Whaley, rhp, Cardinal Gibbons HS, Fort Lauderdale, Fla.
41. Jake Schmidt, rhp, Concordia (Minn.) University.
42. *Trey Ford, ss, Chaparral HS, Scottsdale, Ariz.
43. *Colin Kaepernick, rhp, University of Nevada.

DRAFT DROP *Quarterback, National Football League (2011-15)*

44. *Frank DeJiulio, rhp, Daytona Beach (Fla.) CC.
45. *Addison Dunn, rhp, Warren Area (Pa.) HS.
46. Glenn Cook, of, University of Miami.
47. *Joe Jocketty, 3b, Ladue Horton Watkins HS, St. Louis.

DRAFT DROP *Son of Walt Jocketty, general manager, Cardinals (1994-2007); general manager, Reds (2008-15)*

48. *John Nasshan, rhp, Niles West HS, Skokie, Ill.
49. *Christian Segar, of, McQuaid Jesuit HS, Rochester, N.Y.
50. *Zach Cleveland, rhp, Central Arizona JC.

## CHICAGO WHITE SOX (22)

1. Jared Mitchell, of, Louisiana State University.—(AAA)
1. **Josh Phegley, c, Indiana University** (Supplemental choice—38th—as compensation for Type A free agent Orlando Cabrera).—**(2013-15)**
2. **Trayce Thompson, of, Santa Margarita Catholic HS, Rancho Santa Margarita, Calif.—(2015)**

DRAFT DROP *Son of Mychal Thompson, first overall draft pick, Portland Trail Blazers, National Basketball Association (1978); power forward, NBA (1978-91) • Brother of Mychel Thompson, small forward, NBA (2011-12) • Brother of Klay Thompson, first-round draft pick, Golden State Warriors, NBA (2011); shooting guard, NBA (2011-15)*

2. **David Holmberg, lhp, Port Charlotte (Fla.) HS** (Choice from Athletics as compensation for Cabrera).—**(2013-15)**
3. *Bryan Morgado, lhp, University of Tennessee.—(High A)

DRAFT DROP *Returned to Tennessee; re-drafted by Phillies, 2010 (4th round)*

4. Matt Heidenreich, rhp, Temescal Canyon HS, Lake Elsinore, Calif.—(AA)
5. Kyle Bellamy, rhp, University of Miami.—(AA)
6. Justin Collop, rhp, University of Toledo
7. *Justin Jones, lhp, Oakdale (Calif.) HS.
8. Ryan Buch, rhp, Monmouth University.
9. Matt Hopps, rhp, Cal State Dominguez Hills.
10. Nick Ciolli, of, Indiana State University.
11. J.R. Ballinger, rhp, University of Southern Mississippi
12. Kyle Colligan, of, Texas A&M University.
13. Cameron Bayne, rhp, Concordia (Calif.) University.
14. Dan Black, 1b, Purdue University.
15. *Dane Williams, rhp, Archbishop McCarthy HS, Fort Lauderdale, Fla.
16. Daniel Wagner, 2b, Belmont University.
17. *Brian Goodwin, of, Rocky Mount (N.C.) HS.

DRAFT DROP *First-round draft pick (34th overall), Nationals (2011)*

18. Phil Negus, rhp, Wake Forest University.
19. Brady Shoemaker, of, Indiana State University.
20. *Nate Reed, rhp, University of Pittsburgh.
21. Jared McDonald, ss, Arizona State University.
22. Zach Kayne, ss, Davidson University.
23. Goldy Simmons, rhp, San Diego State University.

DRAFT DROP *Son of Nelson Simmons, major leaguer (1984-87)*

24. Jeff Tezak, 2b, University of Nebraska.
25. *Mike Strong, lhp, Iowa Western CC.
26. Matt Harughty, 2b, University of Oklahoma.
27. Kyle Davis, 2b, University of Delaware.
28. Robby Cummings, 3b, UC Santa Barbara.
29. Trey Delk, rhp, Clemson University.
30. Rob Vaughn, c, Kansas State University.
31. Ryan Hamme, of, Campbell University.
32. Jake Wilson, rhp, New Mexico State University.
33. Chase Cooney, rhp, Volunteer State (Tenn.) CC.
34. Alex Farotto, lhp, University of South Carolina.
35. Danny Wiltz, rhp, University of Tennessee.
36. *Ryan Crowley, lhp, Morton West HS, Berwyn, Ill.
37. Joe Serafin, lhp, University of Vermont.
38. A.J. Casario, of, University of Maryland.
39. Paul Burnside, rhp, Auburn University.
40. Leighton Pangilinan, 1b, Escalon (Calif.) HS.
41. Ryan Lee, of, Cal Poly.
42. Chris Zagyi, rhp, Middlesex (N.J.) CC.
43. *Tyler Williams, 3b, Chaparral HS, Scottsdale, Ariz.

DRAFT DROP *Son of Kenny Williams, major leaguer (1986-91); general manager, White Sox (2000-12)*

44. **Taylor Thompson, rhp, Auburn University.—(2014)**
45. Harold Baines Jr, of, McDaniel (Md.) College.

DRAFT DROP *Son of Harold Baines, first overall draft pick, White Sox (1977); major leaguer (1980-2001)*

46. *Grant Monroe, rhp, Northwest Florida State JC.

DRAFT DROP *Son of Larry Monroe, first-round draft pick, White Sox (1974); major leaguer (1976)*

47. *Jordan Yallen, of, Golden Valley HS, Santa Clarita, Calif.
48. *Matthew Little, lhp, Bryan (Texas) HS.
49. *T.J. Geith, lhp, Scottsdale (Ariz.) CC.
50. ***Kevin Chapman, lhp, University of Florida.—(2013-15)**

## CINCINNATI REDS (8)

1. **Mike Leake, rhp, Arizona State University.—(2010-15)**

DRAFT DROP *First player from 2009 draft to reach majors (April 11, 2010)*

1. **Brad Boxberger, rhp, University of Southern California** (Supplemental choice—43rd—as compensation for Type B free agent Jeremy Affeldt).—**(2012-15)**

DRAFT DROP *Son of Rod Boxberger, first-round draft pick, Astros (1978)*

2. **Billy Hamilton, ss, Taylorsville (Miss.) HS.—(2013-15)**
3. **Donnie Joseph, lhp, University of Houston.—(2013-14)**
4. Mark Fleury, c, University of North Carolina.—(AA)
5. Daniel Tuttle, rhp, Randleman (N.C.) HS.—(Low A)
6. Mark Serrano, rhp, Oral Roberts University.
7. Josh Fellhauer, of, Cal State Fullerton.
8. Juan Silva, of, Puerto Rico Baseball Academy, Gurabo, P.R.
9. Brian Pearl, rhp, University of Washington
10. **Tucker Barnhart, c, Brownsburg (Ind.) HS.—(2014-15)**
11. Jacob Johnson, rhp, Trinity Christian Academy, Lake Worth, Fla.
12. Josh Garton, of, Volunteer State (Tenn.) CC.
13. **Nick Christiani, rhp, Vanderbilt University.—(2013-14)**
14. Tim Crabbe, rhp, Westmont (Calif.) College.
15. Jamie Walczak, rhp, Mercyhurst (Pa.) College.
16. *Chase Fowler, c, South Forsythe HS, Cumming, Ga.
17. ***Deven Marrero, ss, American Heritage HS, Plantation, Fla.—(2015)**

DRAFT DROP *First-round draft pick (24th overall), Red Sox (2012)*

18. *Stephen Perez, ss, Gulliver Prep HS, Miami.
19. Mitch Clarke, lhp, Forest Heights Collegiate Institute, Kitchener, Ontario.
20. *Matt Valaika, 2b, UC Santa Barbara.

DRAFT DROP *Brother of Chris Valaika, major leaguer (2010-14)*

21. *Jon Reed, rhp, Memorial HS, Tulsa, Okla.
22. Dave Stewart, 1b, Grayson County (Texas) CC.
23. Chris Richburg, 1b, Texas Tech.
24. Derrick Lowery, 1b, Young Harris (Ga.) JC.
25. *Mike Monster, rhp, Rutland SS, Kelowna, B.C.
26. Trey Manz, c, University of South Florida.
27. *Stefan Del Pino, lhp, Dorman HS, Roebuck, S.C.
28. *Derek Poppert, ss, University of San Francisco.
29. Jason Braun, rhp, Corban (Ore.) College.
30. Yovan Gonzalez, c, Wabash Valley (Ill.) CC.
31. Adian Kummet, rhp, College of St. Scholastica (Minn.).
32. Shane Carlson, ss, UC Santa Barbara.
33. Will Stramp, 3b, Lubbock Christian (Texas) University.
34. Forest Cannon, rhp, UC Santa Barbara.
35. Oliver Santos, 3b, USC-Salkehatchie JC.
36. Chris Burleson, ss, University of Southern Maine.
37. Dayne Read, of, Chipola (Fla.) JC.
38. Tommy Nurre, 1b, Miami (Ohio) University.
39. *Paul Barton, rhp, Kwalikum SS, Qualicum Beach, B.C.
40. *Michael Robertson, of, Bellevue (Wash.) CC
41. Jake Wiley, rhp, Marist College.
42. Blair Carson, rhp, Anderson (S.C.) University.
43. Ricky Bowen, rhp, Mississippi State University.
44. *Jaron Shepherd, of, Navarro (Texas) JC.
45. *Brian Adams, of, South Forysth HS, Cumming, Ga.
46. *Tim Dunn, rhp, Trevecca Nazarene (Tenn.) University.
47. *Jason Hampton, rhp, Rocklin (Calif.) HS.
48. *Kenny Swab, c, Young Harris (Ga.) JC.
49. *Darion Hamilton, of, Taylorsville (Miss.) HS.
50. *Chris Page, 1b, Genesee (N.Y.) CC.

## CLEVELAND INDIANS (14)

1. **Alex White, rhp, University of North Carolina.—(2011-12)**
2. **Jason Kipnis, 2b-of, Arizona State University.—(2011-15)**
3. Joe Gardner, rhp, UC Santa Barbara.—(AA)
4. Kyle Bellows, 3b, San Jose State University.—(AA)
5. **Austin Adams, rhp-ss, Faulkner (Ala.) University.—(2014-15)**
6. Ben Carlson, 1b, Missouri State University.
7. Jordan Henry, of, University of Mississippi.
8. **Cory Burns, rhp, University of Arizona.—(2012-13)**
9. **Preston Guilmet, rhp, University of Arizona.—(2013-15)**
10. Brett Brach, rhp, Monmouth University.

DRAFT DROP *Brother of Brad Brach, major leaguer (2011-15)*

11. Kirk Wetmore, lhp, Bellevue (Wash.) CC.
12. Joseph Colon, rhp, Caguas, P.R.
13. Jeremy Johnson, rhp, Washington State University.
14. Kyle Smith, ss, Cal Poly.
15. Mike Rayl, lhp, Palm Beach (Fla.) CC.
16. Dale Dickerson, rhp, Nicholls State University.
17. Casey Frawley, of, Stetson University.
18. Dwight Childs, c, University of Arizona.
19. Nick Kirk, lhp, University of Northern Iowa.
20. Kyle C. Smith, rhp, Kent State University.
21. *Jeff Rowland, of, Georgia Tech.
22. *Merrill Kelly, rhp, Yavapai (Ariz.) JC.
23. Danny Jimenez, lhp, John A. Logan (Ill.) JC.
24. *Mike Hamann, rhp, Danbury HS, Lakeside, Ohio.
25. *Blake Hauser, rhp, Manchester HS, Midlothian, Va.
26. Antwonie Hubbard, rhp, University of Oklahoma.
27. Tyler Sturdevant, rhp, New Mexico State University.
28. Nick Sarianides, rhp, Chattahoochee Valley (Ala.) JC.
29. *Xorge Carrillo, c, Central Arizona JC.
30. *Bryson Smith, 3b, Young Harris (Ga.) JC.
31. *Raynor Campbell, 3b, Baylor University.
32. Matt Packer, lhp, University of Virginia.
33. Chris Kersten, 3b, Louisiana Tech.
34. *Westley Moss, of, University of Nevada.
35. ***Chris Beck, rhp, Jefferson (Ga.) HS.—(2015)**
36. *Austin Evans, rhp, University of Alabama.
37. *Steve Ewing, lhp, University HS, Orlando, Fla.
38. *Robert Sabo, rhp, Kent State University.
39. *Brian Hernandez, 3b, UC Irvine.
40. Greg Folgia, ss, University of Missouri.
41. ***Max Muncy, c, Keller (Texas) HS.—(2015)**
42. *Jon Kountis, rhp, Ohio Dominican University.
43. *D.J. Gentile, util, Cal Poly.
44. *Roman Madrid, c, Memorial HS, Victoria, Texas.
45. *James Jones, rhp, John A. Logan (Ill.) CC.
46. *Scott Sommerfeld, of, Parkway South HS, Ballwin, Mo.
47. *Christian Powell, rhp, Greenwood (S.C.) HS.
48. **Vidal Nuno, lhp, Baker (Kan.) University.—(2013-15)**
49. ***Burch Smith, rhp, Howard (Texas) JC.—(2013)**
50. *Tyler Joyner, lhp, Northern Nash HS, Rocky Mount, N.C.

## COLORADO ROCKIES (10)

1. **Tyler Matzek, lhp, Capistrano Valley HS, Mission Viejo, Calif.—(2014-15)**
1. Tim Wheeler, of, Sacramento State University (Choice from Angels as compensation for Type A free agent Brian Fuentes).—(AAA)
1. **Rex Brothers, lhp, Lipscomb University** (Supplemental choice—34th—as compensation for Fuentes).—**(2011-15)**
2. **Nolan Arenado, 3b, El Toro HS, Lake Forest, Calif.—(2013-15)**
3. **Ben Paulsen, 1b, Clemson University.—(2014-15)**
4. Kent Matthes, of, University of Alabama.—(AAA)
5. Joe Sanders, 3b, Auburn University.—(High A)
6. Chris Balcom-Miller, rhp, West Valley (Calif.) JC.
7. Erik Stavert, rhp, University of Oregon.
8. **Rob Scahill, rhp, Bradley University.—(2012-15)**
9. Wes Musick, lhp, University of Houston.
10. Charlie Ruiz, rhp, Long Beach State University.
11. Avery Barnes, of, University of Florida.
12. Jared Clark, 1b, Cal State Fullerton.
13. Paul Bargas, lhp, UC Riverside.
14. Jeff Squier, ss, Mississippi Valley State University.
15. Tyler Gagnon, rhp, Diablo Valley (Calif.) JC.
16. Dom Altobelli, 3b, University of Illinois.
17. Josh Hungerman, lhp, Cleveland State University.
18. Ricky Testa, rhp, Lamar University.
19. **Dustin Garneau, c, Cal State Fullerton.—(2015)**
20. Dallas Tarleton, c, Elon University.
21. Chandler Laurent, of, Delgado (La.) JC.
22. David Born, lhp, Long Beach State University.
23. Jose Rivera, 2b, Universidad Interamericana (P.R.).
24. Joey Wong, ss, Oregon State University.
25. Trevor Gibson, rhp, San Jose State University.
26. Rhett Ballard, rhp, Virginia Tech.
27. Dan Perkins, rhp, Delaware State University.
28. David DiNatale, of, University of Miami.
29. ***Corey Dickerson, of, Meridian (Miss.) CC.—(2013-15)**
30. Bryce Massanari, c, University of Georgia.
31. Clint Tilford, rhp, University of Kentucky.
32. Steve Junker, lhp, Bellevue (Neb.) University.
33. Coty Woods, rhp, Middle Tennessee State University.
34. Brandon Whitby, c, Prairie View A&M University.
35. *Tym Pearson, of, Thurston HS, Springfield, Ore.
36. *Jarrett Higgins, of, Bellaire (Texas) HS.
37. *Brandon Thomas, of, Pace Academy, Atlanta.
38. *Brett Hambright, c, Riverside (Calif.) CC.
39. Eric Federico, rhp, Cal State Stanislaus.

40. *Jason Bagoly, c, Fitch HS, Austintown, Ohio.
41. Matt Sanders, 3b, Clemson University.
42. Joe Scott, 2b, Cal State Fullerton.
43. *Franco Broyles, of, Fayetteville (Ark.) HS.
44. *Micah Green, of, Cherokee Trail HS, Aurora, Colo.
45. *Heath Holliday, c, Bixby (Okla.) HS.
46. *Tyler Wallace, 3b, Eaton (Calif.) HS.
47. *Sterling Monfort, 1b, Eaton (Colo.) HS.
48. Clint McKinney, rhp, Clemson University.
49. *Mark Tracy, c, Duquesne University.
DRAFT DROP *Son of Jim Tracy, major leaguer (1980-18); major league manager (2001-12)*
50. Nathan Hines, of, Middle Tennessee State University.

## DETROIT TIGERS (9)

1. **Jacob Turner, rhp, Westminster Christian Academy, St. Louis.—(2011-14)**
2. **Andy Oliver, lhp, Oklahoma State University.—(2010-11)**
3. Wade Gaynor, 3b, Western Kentucky University.—(AAA)
4. Edwin Gomez, ss, Puerto Rico Baseball Academy, Gurabo, P.R.—(Low A)
5. Austin Wood, lhp, University of Texas.—(AAA)
6. **Daniel Fields, ss, University of Detroit Jesuit HS, Detroit.—(2015)**
DRAFT DROP *Son of Bruce Fields, major leaguer (1986-89)*
7. Jamie Johnson, of, University of Oklahoma.
8. *Craig Fritsch, rhp, Baylor University.
9. John Murrian, c, Winthrop University.
10. Chris Sedon, 2b, University of Pittsburgh.
11. **Adam Wilk, lhp, Long Beach State University.—(2011-12)**
12. *Matt Thomson, rhp, University of San Diego.
13. Michael Rockett, of, University of Texas-San Antonio.
14. Kevan Hess, rhp, Western Michigan University.
15. *Mark Appel, rhp, Monte Vista HS, Danville, Calif.
DRAFT DROP *First overall draft pick, Astros (2012)*
16. Kenny Faulk, lhp, Kennesaw State University.
17. Nate Newman, rhp, Pepperdine University.
18. Eric Roof, c, Michigan State University.
DRAFT DROP *Son of Gene Roof, major leaguer (1981-83)*
19. Rawley Bishop, 3b, Middle Tennessee State University.
20. Jimmy Gulliver, ss, Eastern Michigan University.
DRAFT DROP *Son of Glenn Gulliver, major leaguer (1982-83)*
21. **Giovanni Soto, lhp, Advanced Central College, Carolina, P.R.—(2015)**
22. Matt Mansilla, of, College of Charleston.
23. Cory Hamilton, rhp, UC Irvine.
24. Wade Kapteyn, rhp, University of Evansville.
25. *Victor Roache, of, Lincoln HS, Ypsilanti, Mich.
DRAFT DROP *First-round draft pick (28th overall), Brewers (2012)*
26. Edgar Corcino, 3b, Adolfina Irizarry De Puig HS, Toa Baja, P.R.
27. Pat McKenna, ss, Bryant University.
28. *Tobin Mateychick, rhp, Enid (Okla.) HS.
29. Mike Morrison, rhp, Cal State Fullerton.
30. James Robbins, 1b, Shorecrest HS, Shoreline, Wash.
31. *Andrew Walter, rhp, Cactus HS, Glendale, Ariz.
32. *Parker Markel, rhp, Mountain Ridge HS, Glendale, Ariz.
33. *Cody Keefer, of, Davis (Calif.) HS.
34. *Derek Kline, rhp, Millersville (Pa.) University.
35. *Patrick Biondi, of, Divine Child HS, Dearborn, Mich.
36. *Chuck Crumpton, ss, Lakeside HS, Hot Springs, Ark.
37. *Danny Canela, c, Florida Christian HS, Miami.
38. *Tarran Senay, of, South Park (Pa.) HS.
39. *Chad Duling, ss, Bishop Carroll HS, Wichita, Kan.
40. *Ben Bechtol, c, Neshannock HS, New Castle, Pa.
41. *Larry Balkwill, c, Ursuline College Chatham SS, Chatham-Kent, Ontario.
42. *Nick Avila, rhp, Central Florida CC.
43. *Andrew Allen, 3b, Central Arizona JC.
DRAFT DROP *Son of Rod Allen, major leaguer (1983-88)*
44. *Charlie Markson, of, Whitefish Bay (Wis.) HS.
45. *Jimmy Brennan, of, Suffern (N.Y.) HS.
46. *Nate Goro, 3b, Lafayette HS, Wildwood, Mo.
47. *Kevin Chambers, lhp, Capistrano Valley HS, Mission Viejo, Calif.
48. *Jake Porcello, rhp, Seton Hall Prep, West Orange, N.J.
DRAFT DROP *Brother of Rick Porcello, first-round draft pick, Tigers (2007); major leaguer (2009-15)*
49. *Cameron Giannini, rhp, Hargrave Military Academy, Chatham, Va.
50. *Nico Rosthenhausler, of, South Mountain (Ariz.) CC.

## FLORIDA MARLINS (17)

1. Chad James, lhp, Yukon (Okla.) HS.—(AA)
2. Bryan Berglund, rhp, Royal HS, Simi Valley, Calif.—(Shot-season A)
3. Marquise Cooper, of, Edison HS, Huntington Beach, Calif.—(High A)
4. Dan Mahoney, rhp, University of Connecticut.—(High A)
5. Chase Austin, ss, Elon University.—(High A)
6. Dustin Dickerson, 1b, Baylor University.
7. Josh Hodges, rhp, Ingomar Attendance Center, New Albany, Miss.
8. Stephen Richards, lhp, University of Arkansas.
9. Jobduan Morales, c, Jose S. Alegria HS, Dorado, P.R.
10. Matt Montgomery, rhp, UC Riverside.
11. Chris Wade, ss, University of Kentucky.
12. Kyle Jensen, of, St. Mary's HS, Orchard Lake Village, Mich.
13. *Tyler Curtis, rhp, JC of Southern Idaho.
14. Sequoyah Stonecipher, of, Grossmont (Calif.) JC.
15. Chad Cregar, of, Western Kentucky University.
16. David Peters, c, Lakewood (Calif.) HS.
17. Brent Keys, of, Simi Valley (Calif.) HS.
18. Brett Bukvich, lhp, University of Mississippi.
DRAFT DROP *Brother of Ryan Bukvich, major leaguer (2002-08)*
19. Erick Carrillo, rhp, Cal State San Bernardino.
20. Rand Smith, of, Appalachian State University.
21. **A.J. Ramos, rhp, Texas Tech.—(2012-15)**
22. Terrence Dayleg, ss, Western Kentucky University.
23. Tommy Peale, rhp, Lewis-Clark State (Idaho) College.
24. Mike Brady, ss, University of California.
25. Sean Teague, rhp, Southern Polytechnic State (Ga.) University.
26. Brent Weaver, 3b, Oklahoma City University.
27. Nate Simon, 2b, Pepperdine University.
28. Holden Sprague, rhp, Fresno State University.
29. Jared Eskew, lhp, Cal Poly.
30. Harold Brantley, of, University of Connecticut.
31. Joey O'Gara, rhp, Indiana University.
32. Dallas Hord, c, Missouri State University.
33. *Tom Buske, rhp, University of Minnesota.
34. Isaac Morales, lhp, Cal State Los Angeles.
35. Tyler Topp, rhp, Long Beach State University.
36. *Kaleth Fradera, rhp, Puerto Rico Baseball Academy, Gurabo, P.R.
37. *Alex Glenn, of, Henry County HS, McDonough, Ga.
38. *Kevin Johnson, lhp, University of Cincinnati.
39. Noah Perio, ss, De La Salle HS, Concord, Calif.
40. *Mitch Patito, rhp, Patriot HS, Riverside, Calif.
41. ***Darnell Sweeney, ss, American Heritage HS, Plantation, Fla.—(2015)**
42. *Jordan Poyer, of, Astoria (Ore.) HS.
DRAFT DROP *Defensive back, National Football League (2013-15)*
43. *Donovan Gonzales, rhp, Twentynine Palms (Calif.) HS.
44. ***Ken Giles, rhp, Rio Grande HS, Albuquerque, N.M.—(2014-15)**
45. *Zach Hurley, of, Ohio State University.
46. *Nick Ammirati, c, Seton Hall Prep, West Orange, N.J.
47. *Cody Miller, c, River Valley HS, Yuba City, Calif.
48. *Ryan Gibson, lhp, Yukon (Okla.) HS.
49. *Alan Williams, lhp, Meridian (Miss.) CC.
50. Adam Kam, 1b, Stoneman Douglas HS, Parkland, Fla.

## HOUSTON ASTROS (20)

1. Jiovanni Mier, ss, Bonita HS, La Verne, Calif.—(AAA)
2. Tanner Bushue, rhp, South Central HS, Farina, Ill.—(Low A)
3. Telvin Nash, of, Griffin (Ga.) HS.—(AA)
3. Jonathan Meyer, 3b, Simi Valley (Calif.) HS (Special compensation—111th—for failure to sign 2008 third-round pick Chase Davidson).—(AAA)
4. B.J. Hyatt, rhp, USC Sumter JC.—(Rookie)
5. Brandon Wikoff, ss, University of Illinois.—(AAA)
6. **Enrique Hernandez, ss, American Military Academy, Guaynabo, P.R.—(2014-15)**
7. **Dallas Keuchel, lhp, University of Arkansas.—(2012-15)**
8. Brandt Walker, rhp, Stanford University.
9. Ben Orloff, ss, UC Irvine.
10. Erik Castro, 3b, San Diego State University.
11. Bubby Williams, c, Crowder (Mo.) JC.
12. *Geoff Thomas, rhp, Stephenson HS, Stone Mountain, Ga.
13. **Jake Goebbert, of, Northwestern University.—(2014)**
14. David Berner, lhp, San Jose State University.
15. Ryan Humphrey, of, St. Louis CC-Meramec.
16. Ronald Sanchez, 1b, Manuela Toro Morice HS, Caguas, P.R.
17. Justin Harper, rhp, Oklahoma City University.
18. J.B. MacDonald, rhp, Boston College.
19. Brian Kemp, of, St. John's University.
20. **J.D. Martinez, of, Nova Southeastern (Fla.) University.—(2011-15)**
21. Barry Butera, 2b, Boston College.
22. Mark Jones, rhp, Manheim Township (Pa.) HS.
23. Robby Donovan, rhp, Stetson University.
24. Mike Modica, lhp, George Mason University.
25. Nick Stanley, 1b, Florida Southern College.
26. *Matt Pare, 1b, Pompano Beach (Fla.) HS.
27. Aaron Bray, 3b, UNC Charlotte.
28. *Eric Anderson, rhp, Mountain Vista HS, Highlands Ranch, Colo.
29. Garen Wright, of, Putnam City HS, Oklahoma City, Okla.
30. *Brandon Petite, rhp, Vauxhall (Alberta) Academy.
31. Travis Smink, lhp, Virginia Military Institute.
32. *Greg Peavey, rhp, Oregon State University.
33. Brenden Stines, rhp, Ball State University.
34. Scott Migl, rhp, Texas A&M University.
35. Grant Hogue, of, Mississippi State University.
36. ***Tyler Saladino, ss, Palomar (Calif.) JC.—(2015)**
37. Raul Rivera, rhp, Colegio San Vicente de Paul HS, Santurce, P.R.
DRAFT DROP *Brother of Saul Rivera, major leaguer (2006-10)*
38. Sean Barksdale, of, Temple University.
39. *Rory Young, rhp, R.E. Mountain SS, Langley, B.C.
40. Dan Sarisky, rhp, Oglethorpe (Ga.) College.
41. *Carlos Escobar, c, Chatsworth (Calif.) HS.
42. *Ivory Thomas, of, Downey (Calif.) HS.
43. *Anthony Tzamtzis, rhp, La Salle HS, Miami.
44. Mike Schurz, rhp, University of Iowa.
45. *Adrian Morales, 2b, Miami-Dade JC.
46. *Justin Gonzalez, ss, Christopher Columbus HS, Miami.
47. *Matt Branham, rhp, USC Upstate.
48. ***Paco Rodriguez, lhp, Gulliver Prep, Miami.—(2012-15)**
49. *Matt Smith, 1b, University of Mississippi.
50. Spencer Hylander, lhp, Oklahoma Baptist University.

## KANSAS CITY ROYALS (11)

1. **Aaron Crow, rhp, Fort Worth (American Association).—(2011-14)**
DRAFT DROP *First-round draft pick (9th overall), Nationals (2008)*
2. (Choice to Diamondbacks as compensation for Type A free agent Juan Cruz)
3. **Wil Myers, c/3b, Wesleyan Christian Academy, High Point, N.C.—(2013-15)**
4. **Chris Dwyer, lhp, Clemson University.—(2013)**
5. **Louis Coleman, rhp, Louisiana State University.—(2011-15)**
6. Cole White, rhp, University of New Mexico.
7. Buddy Baumann, lhp, Missouri State University.
8. Dusty Odenbach, rhp, University of Connecticut.
9. Ben Theriot, c, Texas State University.
10. Geoff Baldwin, 1b, Grand Junction (Colo.) HS.
11. Ryan Wood, rhp, East Carolina University.
12. Nick Wooley, rhp, William Woods (Mo.) University.
13. **Lane Adams, of, Red Oak (Okla.) HS.—(2014)**
14. Crawford Simmons, lhp, Statesboro (Ga.) HS.
15. Scott Lyons, ss, University of Arkansas.
16. Eric Diaz, lhp, New Mexico JC.
17. Ben Tschepikow, 2b, University of Arkansas.
18. Brendan Lafferty, lhp, UCLA.
19. Ryan Stovall, 3b, Thomas (Ga.) University.
20. Patrick Keating, rhp, University of Florida.
21. Chanse Cooper, of, Belhaven (Miss.) College.
22. **Ryan Dennick, lhp, Tennessee Tech.—(2014)**
23. Scott Kelley, rhp, Penn State University.
24. *Zack Jones, rhp, Santa Teresa HS, San Jose, Calif.
25. Richard Folmer, rhp, Stephen F. Austin State University.
26. *Matt Frazer, 1b, Nitro (W.Va.) HS.
27. Gabe MacDougall, of, Lynn (Fla.) University.
28. *Eric Peterson, 1b, Liberty HS, Spangle, Wash.
29. *Nick Zaharion, of, South Fork HS, Stuart, Fla.
30. Josh Worrell, rhp, Indiana Wesleyan College.
DRAFT DROP *Son of Todd Worrell, major leaguer (1985-97)*
31. Brian Peacock, lhp, Santa Ana (Calif.) JC.
32. *Luke Voit, c, Lafayette HS, Wildwood, Mo.
33. Claudio Bavera, lhp, Cochise (Ariz.) JC.
34. Justin Trapp, ss, Fairfield Central HS, Winnsboro, S.C.
35. *Levi Cartas, of, Marysville-Pilchuck HS, Marysville, Wash.
36. *Fabian Roman, rhp, Marist HS, Bayonne, N.J.
37. *Tanner Poppe, rhp, Girard (Kan.) HS.
38. *Arthur Owens, ss, Sandy Creek HS, Tyrone, Ga.
39. *Art Charles, 1b, Bakersfield (Calif.) JC.
40. ***Mike Morin, rhp, Shawnee Mission South HS, Overland Park, Kan.—(2014-15)**
41. Joey Lewis, c, University of Georgia.
42. Jon Keck, lhp, Bethel (Tenn.) University.
43. *Jeff Soptic, rhp, Shawnee Mission East HS, Prairie Village, Kan.
44. *Derrick Hudgins, ss, Middleton HS, Tampa.
45. *Derek Spencer, 3b, Bowling Green State University.
46. *Hudson Randall, rhp, Dunwoody (Ga.) HS.
47. Anthony Howard, of, Quince Orchard HS, Gaithersburg, Md.
48. *Kevin Kuntz, ss, Union HS, Tulsa, Okla.
DRAFT DROP *Son of Rusty Kuntz, major leaguer (1979-85)*
49. *Zac Fisher, c, A.B. Miller HS, Fontana, Calif.
50. Anthony Scirrotto, ss, Penn State University.

## LOS ANGELES ANGELS (30)

1. **Randal Grichuk, of, Lamar Consolidated HS, Rosenberg, Texas** (Choice from Mets as compensation for Type A free agent Francisco Rodriguez).**—(2014-15)**
1. **Mike Trout, of, Millville (N.J.) HS** (Choice from Yankees as compensation for Type A free agent Mark Teixeira).**—(2011-15)**
DRAFT DROP *First 2009 high school draft pick to reach majors (July 8, 2011)*
1. (Choice to Rockies as compensation for Type A free agent Brian Fuentes)
1. **Tyler Skaggs, lhp, Santa Monica (Calif.) HS** (Supplemental choice—40th—as compensation for Teixeira).**—(2012-14)**
1. **Garrett Richards, rhp, University of Oklahoma** (Supplemental choice—42nd—as compensation for Rodriguez).**—(2011-15)**
1. Tyler Kehrer, lhp, Eastern Illinois University (Supplemental choice—48th—as compensation for Type B free agent Jon Garland).—(High A)
2. **Pat Corbin, lhp, Chipola (Fla.) JC.—(2012-15)**
3. ***Josh Spence, lhp, Arizona State University.—(2011-12)**
DRAFT DROP *Returned to Arizona State; re-drafted by Padres, 2010 (9th round)*

4. Wes Hatton, 2b, Norco (Calif.) HS.—(Low A)
5. Casey Haerther, 1b, UCLA.—(AA)
6. Danny Reynolds, rhp, Durango HS, Las Vegas, Nev.
7. Jon Karcich, ss, Santa Clara University.
8. Carlos Ramirez, c, Arizona State University.
**9. David Carpenter, rhp, Paris (Texas) JC.—(2012-15)**
10. Jake Locker, of, University of Washington.
DRAFT DROP *First-round draft pick, Tennessee Titans, National Football League (2011); quarterback, NFL (2011-14)*
11. Dillon Baird, 3b, University of Arizona.
12. Travis Witherspoon, of, Spartanburg Methodist (S.C.) JC.
13. Jeremy Cruz, of, Stetson University.
14. *Sam Selman, lhp, St. Andrew's Episcopal HS, Austin, Texas.
15. *Mike Nesseth, rhp, University of Nebraska.
16. *Andrew Del Colle, rhp, Newark Academy, Livingston, N.J.
17. Jeremy Gillan, c, Jacksonville University.
18. Jamie Mallard, 1b, Hillsborough (Fla.) CC.
19. *Adam Hornung, of, Baylor University.
20. Dan Eichelberger, of, East Central (Miss.) CC.
21. Rich Cates, of, Cal State Northridge.
22. Stephen Locke, lhp, University of Florida.
23. Jordan Drake, of, Elsinore HS, Wildomar, Calif.
24. Taylor Kinzer, rhp, Taylor (Ind.) University.
DRAFT DROP *Son of Matt Kinzer, major leaguer (1989-90)*
25. Michael Demperio, 2b, University of Georgia.
26. *Garrett Cannizaro, 2b, Mandeville (La.) HS.
DRAFT DROP *Brother of Andy Cannizaro, major leaguer (2006-08)*
27. *Devon Zenn, of, Benicia (Calif.) HS.
28. Carson Andrew, rhp, Jacksonville University.
29. Heath Nichols, rhp, JC of Southern Idaho.
30. Matt Long, of, Santa Clara University.
31. *Jordan Whatcott, rhp, University of Utah.
32. *Raoul Torrez, 2b, Arizona State University.
33. *Owen Dew, rhp, Seminole (Fla.) CC.
34. Ryan Cisterna, rhp, University of Arkansas.
35. *Robbie Harris, ss, Cardinal Gibbons HS, Baltimore.
36. Eric Oliver, 1b, UC Santa Barbara.
37. *Erik Gregersen, rhp, Stephen F. Austin State University.
38. *Justin Bellez, rhp, Mira Mesa (Calif.) HS.
39. *Ryan Hege, c, Cowley County (Kan.) CC.
40. *Asaad Ali, c, Niles (Mich.) HS.
DRAFT DROP *Son of Muhammad Ali, gold medalist/ boxing, 1960 Olympics (light-heavyweight division); World Boxing Association champion (heavyweight division)*
41. *Joey Rapp, of, Chipola (Fla.) JC.
42. *Sam Wolff, rhp, Stevens HS, Rapid City, S.D.
43. *Seth Harvey, rhp, Washington State University.
44. *R.J. Santigate, 3b, Bishop Gorman HS, Las Vegas, Nev.
45. Phil Bando, 2b, JC of the Canyons (Calif.).
DRAFT DROP *Son of Chris Bando, major leaguer (1981-89) • Nephew of Sal Bando, major leaguer (1966-81)*
46. *Jonathan Paquet, rhp, Cardinal Roy SS, Ancienne-Lorette, Quebec.
47. Jose Jimenez, 1b, University of Tampa.
48. Jake Rife, of, University of Washington.
49. *Chunner Nyberg, rhp, Dixie HS, St. George, Utah.
50. Alibay Barkley, 1b, Washington HS, New York.

## LOS ANGELES DODGERS (16)

1. (Choice to Diamondbacks as compensation for Type A free agent Orlando Hudson)
1. Aaron Miller, lhp, Baylor University (Supplemental choice—36th—as compensation for Type A free agent Derek Lowe).—(AA)
2. Blake Smith, of, University of California (Choice from Braves as compensation for Lowe).—(AA)
2. Garrett Gould, rhp, Maize (Kan.) HS.—(AA)
3. Brett Wallach, rhp, Orange Coast (Calif.) CC.—(High A)
DRAFT DROP *Son of Tim Wallach, major leaguer (1980-96)*
4. Angelo Songco, of, Loyola Marymount University.—(AA)
5. J.T. Wise, c, University of Oklahoma.—(AAA)
6. Jan Vazquez, c, Puerto Rico Baseball Academy, Gurabo, P.R.
7. Brandon Martinez, rhp, Fowler (Calif.) HS.
8. Jon Garcia, of, Luis Munoz Marin HS, Yauco, P.R.
9. Bryant Hernandez, ss, University of Oklahoma.
10. Andy Suiter, lhp, UC Davis.
11. *Connor Powers, 1b, Mississippi State University.
12. Brian Cavazos-Galvez, of, University of New Mexico.
DRAFT DROP *Son of Balvino Galvez, major leaguer (1986)*
13. J.B. Paxson, rhp, Western Kentucky University.
14. Casio Grider, ss, Newberry (S.C.) College.
15. Jeff Hunt, 3b, St. Benedict Catholic SS, Cambridge, Ontario.
16. Mike Pericht, c, St. Joseph's (Ind.) College.
**17. Steve Ames, rhp, Gonzaga University.—(2013)**
18. Greg Wilborn, lhp, University of Louisiana-Lafayette.
19. Nick Akins, of, Vanguard (Calif.) University.
20. *Daniel Palo, rhp, Houston HS, Germantown, Tenn.
21. Chris Henderson, 3b, George Mason University.
22. Stetson Banks, of, Brigham Young University.
23. Jimmy Marshall, rhp, Florida State University.
24. *Chad Kettler, ss, Coppell (Texas) HS.
**25. *Richie Shaffer, 3b, Providence HS, Charlotte, N.C.—(2015)**
DRAFT DROP *First-round draft pick (25th overall), Rays (2012)*
26. *Alex McRee, lhp, University of Georgia.
**27. *Brian Johnson, lhp, Cocoa Beach (Fla.) HS.—(2015)**
DRAFT DROP *First-round draft pick (31st overall), Red Sox (2012)*
28. Bobby Hernandez, rhp, Barry (Fla.) University.
29. *Shawn Payne, 2b, Middle Georgia JC.
30. Nick Gaudi, rhp, Pepperdine University.
31. Austin King, of, Jackson State (Tenn.) CC.
32. Graham Miller, lhp, The Master's (Calif.) College.
33. Steve Cilladi, c, Kansas Wesleyan College.
34. Justin Dignelli, rhp, George Washington University.
35. David Iden, 2b, California Lutheran College.
36. K.J. Childs, rhp, Culver-Stockton (Mo.) College.
37. *Joel Effertz, rhp, Ladysmith (Wis.) HS.
38. *Kirby Pellant, 2b, Corona Del Sol HS, Tempe, Ariz.
39. *Ryan Hander, rhp, Lincoln HS, Sioux Falls, S.D.
40. *Ryan Christenson, lhp, South Mountain (Ariz.) CC.
DRAFT DROP *Son of Gary Christenson, major leaguer (1979-80)*
41. Chris Handke, rhp, Cornell University.
42. *Tony Renda, ss, Serra HS, San Mateo, Calif.
43. *Chad Gough-Fortenberry, c, Northshore HS, Slidell, La.
44. *R.C. Orlan, lhp, Deep Run HS, Glen Allen, Va.
**45. *Stephen Piscotty, ss, Amador Valley HS, Pleasanton, Calif.—(2015)**
DRAFT DROP *First-round draft pick (36th overall), Cardinals (2012)*
46. *James Smith, 2b, Second Baptist HS, Houston.
47. *Cole Pembroke, of, Desert Vista HS, Phoenix.
48. *Travis Burnside, of, Laurens District (S.C.) HS.
**49. *Christian Walker, 3b, Kennedy-Kenrick Catholic HS, Limerick, Pa.—(2014-15)**
50. *David Garcia, ss, John F. Kennedy HS, Granada Hills, Calif.

## MILWAUKEE BREWERS (25)

1. Eric Arnett, rhp, Indiana University.—(High A)
1. Kentrail Davis, of, University of Tennessee (Supplemental choice—39th—as compensation for Type A free agent C.C. Sabathia).—(AAA)
1. Kyle Heckathorn, rhp, Kennesaw State University (Supplemental choice—47th—as compensation for Type B free agent Brian Shouse).—(AAA)
2. Max Walla, of, Albuquerque (N.M.) Academy (Choice from Yankees as compensation for Sabathia).—(Low A)
2. Cameron Garfield, c, Murrieta Valley HS, Murrieta, Calif.—(High A)
**3. Josh Prince, ss, Tulane University.—(2013)**
4. Brooks Hall, rhp, T.L. Hanna HS, Anderson, S.C.—(AA)
5. D'Vontrey Richardson, of, Florida State University.—(AA)
**6. Hiram Burgos, rhp, Bethune-Cookman University.—(2013)**
**7. Khris Davis, of, Cal State Fullerton.—(2013-15)**
8. Chad Stang, of, Midland (Texas) CC.
9. Jon Pokorny, lhp, Kent State University.
10. Tyler Roberts, c, Jones County HS, Gray, Ga.
11. Andre Lamontagne, rhp, Oral Roberts University.
12. Rob Currie, rhp, Tusculum (Tenn.) College.
**13. Sean Halton, 1b, Lewis-Clark State (Idaho) College.—(2013)**
14. Mike Brownstein, 2b, University of New Mexico.
15. Del Howell, lhp, University of Alabama.
**16. Scooter Gennett, ss, Sarasota (Fla.) HS.—(2013-15)**
**17. Tyler Cravy, rhp, Napa Valley (Calif.) CC.—(2015)**
**18. Caleb Thielbar, lhp, South Dakota State University.—(2013-15)**
19. Scott Krieger, of, George Mason University.
20. Franklin Romero, of, Cerro Coso (Calif.) CC.
21. *Brian Vigo-Suarez, ss, Fossil Ridge HS, Keller, Texas.
**22. Mike Fiers, rhp, Nova Southeastern (Fla.) University.—(2011-15)**
23. *Austin Pressley, rhp, Franklin-Monroe HS, Arcanum, Ohio.
24. Peter Fatse, 2b, University of Connecticut.
25. Demetrius McKelvie, of, East Columbus HS, Lake Waccamaw, N.C.
26. *Lex Rutledge, lhp, Tupelo (Miss.) HS.
27. Ryan Platt, rhp, UC Riverside.
28. *Geno Escalante, c, Rodriguez HS, Fairfield, Calif.
29. *Chandler McLaren, of, Guelph Collegiate Vocational Institute, Guelph, Ontario.
30. Brandon Sizemore, 2b, College of Charleston.
31. Jose Oviedo, rhp, Miami-Dade JC.
32. Chris Ellington, of, Texas Christian University.
33. *Jacobbi McDaniel, 3b, Madison County HS, Madison, Fla.
DRAFT DROP *Defensive end, National Football League (2014)*
34. *Mike Ojala, rhp, Rice University.
35. Matt Costello, lhp, Valdosta State (Ga.) University.
36. *Josh Turley, lhp, Texas HS, Texarkana, Texas.
37. *Cullen Sexton, rhp, University of Minnesota.
38. *Casey Stevenson, 2b, UC Irvine.
39. *Brady Rodgers, rhp, Lamar Consolidated HS, Rosenberg, Texas.
40. *Kyle Hansen, rhp, St. Dominic HS, Oyster Bay, N.Y.
DRAFT DROP *Brother of Craig Hansen, first-round draft pick, Red Sox (2005); major leaguer (2005-09)*
41. *Steven Sultzbaugh, of, Rice University.
42. *Brad Schreiber, rhp, Kimberly (Wis.) HS.
43. Kyle Dhanani, 3b, Thompson River (B.C.) University.
44. *Andrew Morris, rhp, Gulf Coast (Fla.) CC.
45. *Richard Stock, c, Agoura HS, Agoura Hills, Calif.
DRAFT DROP *Brother of Robert Stock, second-round draft pick, Cardinals (2009)*
46. *Jordan Wong, rhp, Vauxhall (Alberta) Academy.
47. *Trevor Kirk, of, CC of Southern Nevada.
48. *Rey Cotilla, rhp, Miami-Dade JC.
49. *J.J. Altobelli, ss, Woodbridge HS, Irvine, Calif.
50. *Darren Farmer, c, West Lauderdale HS, Collinsville, Miss.

## MINNESOTA TWINS (21)

**1. Kyle Gibson, rhp, University of Missouri.—(2013-15)**
1. Matt Bashore, lhp, Indiana University (Supplemental choice—46th—as compensation for Type B free agent Dennys Reyes).—(High A)
2. Billy Bullock, rhp, University of Florida.—(AAA)
3. Ben Tootle, rhp, Jacksonville State University.—(Low A)
4. Derek McCallum, 2b, University of Minnesota.—(High A)
5. Tobias Streich, c, West Virginia University.—(AA)
**6. Chris Herrmann, c, University of Miami.—(2012-15)**
7. Brad Stillings, rhp, Kent State University.
**8. Brian Dozier, ss, University of Southern Mississippi.—(2012-15)**
9. Nick Lockwood, ss, Jesuit HS, Tampa.
DRAFT DROP *Brother of Rick Lockwood, 19th-round draft pick, Athletics (2009)*
10. *Blake Dean, of, Louisiana State University.
11. *Ronnie Richardson, of, Lake Region HS, Eagle Lake, Fla.
12. Tony Davis, lhp, University of Florida.
13. *Clarence Davis, ss, Campbell HS, Smyrna, Ga.
14. Matt Tone, lhp, SUNY Cortland.
15. Steven Liddle, of, Vanderbilt University.
16. Dakota Watts, rhp, Cal State Stanislaus.
17. Nick Tindall, c, O'Fallon (Ill.) HS.
18. *Beau Stoker, ss, Bishop Ward HS, Kansas City, Kan.
19. *John Stilson, rhp, Texarkana (Texas) CC.
20. *Tommy Mackoul, lhp, UC Riverside.
21. Kane Holbrooks, rhp, Texas State University.
22. Buddy Munroe, c, University of Florida.
23. *E.J. Encinosa, rhp, Coral Park HS, Miami.
**24. *Mario Hollands, lhp, UC Santa Barbara.—(2014)**
25. *Tony Bryant, rhp, Kennewick (Wash.) HS.
26. *Mike Giovenco, rhp, North Park (Ill.) College.
27. *Eric Decker, of, University of Minnesota.
DRAFT DROP *Wide receiver, National Football League (2010-15)*
28. *Pat Light, rhp, Christian Brothers Academy, Lincroft, N.J.
DRAFT DROP *First-round draft pick (37th overall), Red Sox (2012)*
29. *Beau Wright, lhp, Los Alamitos (Calif.) HS.
30. Trayvone Johnson, c, Los Angeles.
31. *Cody Martin, 3b, Stephens County HS, Toccoa, Ga.
32. *Aaron Senne, of, University of Missouri.
33. Nick Freitas, of, Southern Utah University.
34. *Ricky Claudio, rhp, American HS, Hialeah, Fla.
35. *David Hurlbut, lhp, Diablo Valley (Calif.) JC.
36. *Jason Zylstra, rhp, Jacksonville State University.
37. *David Gutierrez, rhp, University of Miami.
38. Peter Kennelly, rhp, Fordham University.
39. *Ryan Sadler, rhp, Naples (Fla.) HS.
40. *Ryan Abrahamson, of, Tartan HS, Oakdale, Minn.
41. *Pat Butler, rhp, Chatham (N.J.) HS.
42. *Marc Bourgeois, of, Chipola (Fla.) JC.
43. *Jon Hedges, 1b, Olney Central (Ill.) CC.
44. Tyler Herr, rhp, Katy (Texas) HS.
45. Eddie Ahorrio, rhp, Jesus Silverio Delgado HS, Arecibo, P.R.
46. *Jake Kretzer, of, Benton HS, St. Joseph, Mo.
47. Richard Calcano, rhp, Dr. Jose M. Lazaro HS, Carolina, P.R.
48. *Cody Dordan, rhp, Newport (Ore.) HS.
49. Paul-Michael Klingsberg, 1b, Cal State Dominguez Hills.
50. *Alberto Cardenas, rhp, Palmetto Ridge HS, Naples, Fla.

## NEW YORK METS (23)

1. (Choice to Angels as compensation for Type A free agent Francisco Rodriguez)
**2. Steve Matz, lhp, Ward Melville HS, East Setauket, N.Y.—(2015)**
3. Robbie Shields, ss, Florida Southern College.—(High A)
**4. Darrell Ceciliani, of, Columbia Basin (Wash.) CC.—(2015)**
5. *Damien Magnifico, rhp, North Mesquite HS, Mesquite, Texas.—(AA)
DRAFT DROP *Attended Howard (Texas) JC; re-drafted by Brewers, 2012 (5th round)*
**6. *David Buchanan, rhp, Chipola (Fla.) JC.—(2014-15)**
7. Darin Gorski, lhp, Kutztown (Pa.) University.
8. Taylor Freeman, c, McNeese State University.
9. Jeff Glenn, c, Winter Haven (Fla.) HS.
10. Nick Santomauro, of, Dartmouth University.
11. Sam Honeck, 1b, Tulane University.
12. James Ewing, 2b, University of Southern Mississippi.
13. Zach Dotson, lhp, Effingham County HS, Springfield, Ga.
14. R.J. Harris, of, Northwood (Texas) University.

15. *Casey Schmidt, rhp, University of San Diego.
16. Chase Greene, of, West Boca Raton Community HS, Boca Raton, Fla.
17. Alex Gregory, of, Radford University.
18. Cody Holliday, of, Wilmington (Del.) University.
19. Nelfi Zapata, c, English HS, Jamaica Plain, Mass.
20. Joey August, of, Stanford University.
21. Joe Bonfe, 3b, Sierra (Calif.) JC.
22. Zach Von Tersch, rhp, Georgia Tech.
23. John Church, rhp, University of West Florida.
24. Kyle Johnson, rhp, Concordia (Texas) University.
25. Josh Dunn, 3b, Sickles HS, Tampa.
26. John Semel, of, Chapman (Calif.) College.
27. Kurt Steinhauer, of, Point Loma Nazarene (Calif.) University.
28. Brian Needham, rhp, Lamar University.
29. ZeErika McQueen, of, East Central (Miss.) CC.
30. *Jordan Harrison, lhp, New Caney (Texas) HS.
31. *Mitch Haniger, of, Archbishop Mitty HS, San Jose, Calif.

DRAFT DROP *First-round draft pick (38th overall), Brewers (2012)*

32. T.J. Chism, lhp, La Salle University.
33. James Schroeder, 3b, Southern Arkansas University.
34. Cam Maron, c, Hicksville (N.Y.) HS.
35. Wes Wrenn, rhp, The Citadel.
36. Lance Hoge, lhp, Kansas State University.
37. Brandon Sage, lhp, University of South Alabama.
38. Will Cherry, of, Florida Southern College.
39. Taylor Whitenton, rhp, Darton (Ga.) JC.
40. *Jerome Pena, 2b, Western Nevada CC.
41. Travis Ozga, 1b, Florida Atlantic University.
42. *Ryan Gunhouse, c, Clear Creek HS, League City, Texas.
43. *Bobby Rinard, of, Yavapai (Ariz.) JC.
44. *James Wooster, lhp, Alvin (Texas) CC.
45. *Jake Johansen, rhp, Allen (Texas) HS.
46. *Trey Pilkington, rhp, Oxford (Ala.) HS.
47. Ryan Mollica, 2b, Florida International University.
48. *Joe Mantiply, lhp, Tunstall HS, Dry Fork, Va.
49. *Josh Easley, rhp, Weatherford (Texas) HS.
50. ***Zack Godley, rhp, Bamberg-Ehrhardt HS, Bamberg, S.C.—(2015)**

## NEW YORK YANKEES (24)

1. (Choice to Angels as compensation for Type A free agent Mark Teixeira)
1. **Slade Heathcott, of, Texas HS, Texarkana, Texas** (Special compensation—29th—for failure to sign 2008 first-round draft pick Gerrit Cole).**—(2015)**
2. (Choice to Brewers as compensation for Type A free agent C.C. Sabathia)
2. **J.R. Murphy, c, Pendleton School, Bradenton, Fla.** (Special compensation—76th—for failure to sign 2008 second-round Scott Bittle)**—(2013-15)**
3. (Choice to Blue Jays as compensation for Type A free agent A.J. Burnett)
4. **Adam Warren, rhp, University of North Carolina.—(2012-15)**
5. **Caleb Cotham, rhp, Vanderbilt University.—(2015)**
6. Rob Lyerly, 3b, UNC Charlotte.
7. Sean Black, rhp, Seton Hall University.
8. Sam Elam, lhp, University of Notre Dame.
9. Gavin Brooks, lhp, UCLA.
10. ***Tyler Lyons, lhp, Oklahoma State University.—(2013-15)**
11. Neil Medchill, of, Oklahoma State University.
12. Brett Gerritse, rhp, Pacifica HS, Garden Grove, Calif.
13. DeAngelo Mack, of, University of South Carolina.
14. Graham Stoneburner, rhp, Clemson University.
15. **Shane Greene, rhp, Daytona Beach (Fla.) CC.—(2014-15)**
16. **Bryan Mitchell, rhp, Rockingham County HS, Hamlet, N.C.—(2014-15)**
17. *Chad Thompson, rhp, El Toro HS, Lake Forest, Calif.
18. Hector Rabago, c, University of Southern California.
19. Luke Murton, 1b, Georgia Tech.

DRAFT DROP *Brother of Matt Murton, major leaguer (2005-09)*

20. *Thomas Keeling, lhp, Oklahoma State University.
21. Joe Talerico, of, Brookdale (N.J.) CC.
22. *Ben Soignier, ss, University of Louisiana-Monroe.
23. Kevin Mahoney, 3b, Canisius University.
24. Isaac Harrow, 2b, Appalachian State University.
25. Shaeffer Hall, lhp, University of Kansas.
26. *Stephen Bruno, ss, Gloucester Catholic HS, Gloucester City, N.J.
27. Jeff Farnham, c, New Mexico State University.
28. *Aaron Meade, lhp, Missouri State University.
29. *Scott Matyas, rhp, University of Minnesota.
30. *Kyle McKenzie, rhp, Thayer Academy, Braintree, Mass.
31. Judd Golsan, of, Mountain Brook (Ala.) HS.
32. *Nick Ebert, 1b, University of South Carolina.
33. *Andrew Aplin, of, Vanden HS, Fairfield, Calif.
34. ***Jake Petricka, rhp, Indiana State University.—(2013-15)**
35. *Brett Bruening, rhp, Grayson County (Texas) CC.
36. *Kyle Ottoson, lhp, South Mountain (Ariz.) CC.
37. Justin Milo, of, University of Vermont.
38. *Adam Bailey, of, University of Nebraska.
39. *Cody Stiles, rhp, Taravella HS, Coral Springs, Fla.
40. Ben Watkins, rhp, University of Pittsburgh-Johnstown.
41. Mariel Checo, rhp, Norman Thomas HS, New York.
42. *Danny Black, ss, Feather River (Calif.) JC.
43. Isaiah Brown, of, Paradise Valley (Ariz.) CC.
44. Evan DeLuca, lhp, Immaculata HS, Somerville, N.J.
45. *Jeremy Baltz, of, Vestal (N.Y.) HS.
46. *Tony Plagman, 1b, Georgia Tech.
47. *Shane Brown, c, University of Central Florida.
48. *Pat White, of, West Virginia University.

DRAFT DROP *Quarterback, National Football League (2009-13)*

49. *Xavier Esquivel, rhp, Loyola Marymount University.
50. *Stephen Kaupang, 1b, Cypress (Calif.) JC.

## OAKLAND ATHLETICS (12)

1. **Grant Green, ss, University of Southern California.—(2013-15)**
2. (Choice to White Sox as compensation for Type A free agent Orlando Cabrera)
3. **Justin Marks, lhp, University of Louisville.—(2014)**
4. **Max Stassi, c, Yuba City (Calif.) HS.—(2013-15)**
5. Steve Parker, 3b, Brigham Young University.—(AAA)
6. Ryan Ortiz, c, Oregon State University.
7. **Ian Krol, lhp, Neuqua Valley HS, Naperville, Ill.—(2013-15)**
8. Rob Gilliam, rhp, UNC Greensboro.
9. Myrio Richard, of, Prairie View A&M University.
10. ***Sam Dyson, rhp, University of South Carolina.—(2012-15)**
11. Mike Spina, 3b, University of Cincinnati.
12. Connor Hoehn, rhp, St. Petersburg (Fla.) JC.
13. Murphy Smith, rhp, Binghamton University.
14. *Drew Gagnier, rhp, University of Oregon.
15. Anthony Aliotti, 1b, St. Mary's Calif.) College.
16. Josh Leyland, c, San Dimas (Calif.) HS.
17. *Pat Stover, of, Rocklin (Calif.) HS.
18. Max Peterson, lhp, San Jose State University.
19. Daniel Tenholder, rhp, Austin Peay State University.
20. *Tyler Bernard, ss, Valley Center (Calif.) HS.
21. *Mike Faulkner, of, Germantown (Tenn.) HS.
22. Ryan Quigley, lhp, Northeastern University.
23. Kent Walton, of, Brigham Young University.
24. **Dan Straily, rhp, Marshall University.—(2012-15)**
25. Chris Mederos, rhp, Georgia Southern University.
26. Nathan Long, rhp, University of Texas-Arlington.
27. Michael Gilmartin, 2b, Wofford University.
28. Conner Crumbliss, 2b, Emporia State (Kan.) University.
29. ***Mike Zunino, c, Mariner HS, Cape Coral, Fla.—(2013-15)**

DRAFT DROP *First-round draft pick (3rd overall), Mariners (2012)*

30. Royce Consigli, of, Notre Dame HS, Welland, Ontario.
31. *Ian Texidor, 3b, Centro Especializado de Educacion Avanzada, Rio Piedras, P.R.
32. *Garett Claypool, rhp, UCLA.
33. ***Mike Bolsinger, rhp, University of Arkansas.—(2014-15)**
34. *Dylan Brown, of, Oklahoma State University.
35. Paul Smyth, rhp, University of Kansas.
36. Jeremy Wells, 2b, Patten (Calif.) University.
37. *Colin Bates, rhp, University of North Carolina.
38. *Tristan Archer, rhp, Sullivan South HS, Kingsport, Tenn.
39. *Ryan Lockwood, of, University of South Florida.

DRAFT DROP *Brother of Nick Lockwood, ninth-round draft pick, Twins (2009)*

40. *Chris O'Dowd, c, Regis Jesuit HS, Aurora, Colo.

DRAFT DROP *Son of Dan O'Dowd, general manager, Rockies (1999-2014)*

41. *Justin Hilt, of, Elon University.
42. Blake Crosby, 1b, Sacramento State University.

DRAFT DROP *Son of Ed Crosby, major leaguer (1970-76) • Brother of Bobby Crosby, first-round draft pick, Athletics (2001); major leaguer (2003-10)*

43. *Ryan Lipkin, c, University of San Francisco.
44. A.J. Huttenlocker, lhp, Missouri Western State College.
45. Anthione Shaw, of, St. Augustine's (N.C.) University.
46. Joel Eusebio, 3b, Northeastern Oklahoma A&M JC.
47. *Kyle Roller, 1b, East Carolina University.
48. *Addison Johnson, of, Clemson University.
49. *Anthony Giansanti, of, Siena University.
50. *Tanner Biagini, 3b, Virginia Military Institute.

## PHILADELPHIA PHILLIES (26)

1. (Choice to Mariners as compensation for Type A free agent Raul Ibanez)
2. Kelly Dugan, of, Notre Dame HS, Sherman Oaks, Calif.—(AAA)
3. Kyrell Hudson, of, Evergreen HS, Vancouver, Wash.—(High A)
4. Adam Buschini, 2b, Cal Poly.—(AA)
5. Matt Way, lhp, Washington State University.—(High A)
6. Steven Inch, rhp, Vauxhall (Alberta) Academy.
7. Brody Colvin, rhp, St. Thomas More HS, Lafayette, La.
8. **Jon Singleton, 1b, Millikan HS, Long Beach, Calif.—(2014-15)**
9. **Aaron Altherr, of, Agua Fria HS, Avondale, Ariz.—(2014-15)**
10. **Josh Zeid, rhp, Tulane University.—(2013-14)**
11. Jeremy Barnes, ss, University of Notre Dame.
12. Nick Hernandez, lhp, University of Tennessee.
13. Ryan Sasaki, lhp, Connally HS, Austin, Texas.
14. *Jake Stewart, of, Rocky Mountain HS, Fort Collins, Colo.
15. Austin Hyatt, rhp, University of Alabama.
16. ***Andrew Susac, c, Jesuit HS, Carmichael, Calif.—(2014-15)**
17. Mike Dabbs, of, Oklahoma State University.
18. Carl Uhl, of, UC Riverside.
19. Stephen Batts, 1b, East Carolina University.
20. **Darin Ruf, 1b, Creighton University.—(2012-15)**
21. Chase Johnson, rhp, South Mountain (Ariz.) CC.
22. Bronco Lafrenz, c, Indiana State University.
23. Evan Porter, ss, University of Nebraska-Omaha.
24. Justin Long, rhp, Bellevue (Neb.) University.
25. Eric Massingham, rhp, Cal Poly.
26. Brian Gump, of, UC Santa Barbara.
27. Marlon Mitchell, c, Hillsborough HS, Tampa.
28. Justin Beal, rhp, Missouri Southern State College.
29. Mark Doll, rhp, Southern Polytechnic State (Ga.) University.
30. *Stephen Kohlscheen, rhp, Cowley County (Kan.) CC.
31. David Doss, c, University of South Alabama.
32. Kevin Angelle, lhp, San Jacinto (Texas) JC.
33. Colin Kleven, rhp, R.E. Mountain SS, Langley, B.C.
34. ***A.J. Griffin, rhp, University of San Diego.—(2012-13)**
35. Phil Aviola, c, Wilmington (Del.) University.
36. Matt McConnell, 2b, Metro State (Colo.) College.
37. *Brodie Greene, 2b, Texas A&M University.
38. Cory Wine, 1b, Penn State University.

DRAFT DROP *Grandson of Bobby Wine, major leaguer (1960-72) • Son of Robbie Wine, first-round draft pick, Astros (1983); major leaguer (1986-87)*

39. *Sam Kidd, rhp, Ohio County HS, Hartford, Ky.
40. *Rob Amaro, 3b, Penn Charter HS, Philadelphia.
41. *Jeff Gelalich, of, Bonita HS, La Verne, Calif.

DRAFT DROP *First-round draft pick (57th overall), Reds (2012)*

42. *Matt Laney, lhp, Miami-Dade JC.
43. *Frank LaFreniere, rhp, Ahuntsic (Quebec) JC.
44. *Brian Feekin, lhp, Iowa Western CC.
45. *Richard Bain, of, Trinity Christian Academy, Jacksonville, Fla.
46. *Jeff Ames, rhp, Skyview HS, Vancouver, Wash.

DRAFT DROP *First-round draft pick (42nd overall), Rays (2011)*

47. Ryan Bollinger, 1b, Magic City HS, Minot, N.D.
48. *Wander Nunez, of, Frankford HS, Philadelphia.
49. *Chris Gosik, 3b, Malvern Prep, Malvern, Pa.
50. David Hissey, of, Emory (Ga.) University.

## PITTSBURGH PIRATES (4)

1. **Tony Sanchez, c, Boston College.—(2013-14)**
1. **Victor Black, rhp, Dallas Baptist University** (Special compensation—49th—for failure to sign 2008 second-round draft pick Tanner Scheppers).**—(2013-14)**
2. Brooks Pounders, rhp, Temecula Valley HS, Temecula, Calif.—(AA)
3. Evan Chambers, of, Hillsborough (Fla.) CC.—(AA)
4. Zack Dodson, lhp, Medina Valley HS, Castroville, Texas.—(AA)
5. Nate Baker, lhp, University of Mississippi.—(AA)
6. Zack Von Rosenberg, rhp, Zachary (La.) HS.
7. Trent Stevenson, rhp, Brophy Prep, Phoenix.
8. Colton Cain, lhp, Waxahachie (Texas) HS.
9. **Brock Holt, 2b, Rice University.—(2012-15)**
10. Joey Schoenfeld, c, Santiago HS, Garden Grove, Calif.
11. Aaron Baker, 1b, University of Oklahoma.

DRAFT DROP *Grandson of Jerry Mays, lineman, National Football League (1961-70)*

12. Jeff Inman, rhp, Stanford University.
13. Walker Gourley, 3b, Eastern Wayne HS, Goldsboro, N.C.
14. *Marcos Reyna, rhp, Bakersfield (Calif.) JC.
15. *Peter Bako, rhp, Connors State (Okla.) JC.
16. ***Matt den Dekker, of, University of Florida.—(2013-15)**
17. *Jordan Cooper, rhp, Central HS, Shelbyville, Tenn.
18. Ryan Beckman, rhp, Grayson County (Texas) CC.
19. *Josh Urban, rhp, Dripping Springs (Texas) HS.
20. *Sam Spangler, lhp, University of Hawaii.
21. **Phil Irwin, rhp, University of Mississippi.—(2013-14)**
22. *Carmine Giardina, lhp, University of Tampa.
23. Jose Hernandez, of, University of Texas-San Antonio.
24. Jason Erickson, rhp, University of Washington.
25. *Aaron LaFountaine, of, John W. North HS, Riverside, Calif.
26. *Matt Dermody, lhp, Norwalk (Iowa) HS.
27. *Wes Luquette, c, Isadore Newman HS, New Orleans.
28. *Kyle Hooper, rhp, Saugus (Calif.) HS.
29. *Michael Heller, rhp, Cardinal Mooney HS, Bradenton, Fla.
30. Ty Summerlin, ss, University of Southeastern Louisiana.
31. *Zach Taylor, of, Statesboro (Ga.) HS.
32. *Niko Spezial, lhp, Don Bosco Prep, Ramsey, N.J.
33. Pat Irvine, of, Elon University.
34. Zac Fuesser, lhp, Walters State (Tenn.) CC.
35. *Chris McKenzie, rhp, San Jacinto (Texas) JC.
36. *Bobby Doran, rhp, Seward County (Kan.) CC.
37. *Zach Nuding, rhp, Weatherford (Texas) JC.
38. ***Jake Lamb, 3b, Bishop Blanchet HS, Seattle.—(2014-15)**
39. *Keifer Nuncio, rhp, Katy (Texas) HS.
40. *Brett Lee, lhp, West Florida HS, Pensacola, Fla.
41. *Tyler Cannon, ss, University of Virginia.
42. Marc Baca, rhp, University of Nevada-Las Vegas.
43. Teddy Fallon, rhp, USC Upstate.

44. *Dexter Bobo, lhp, Georgia Southern University.
45. *Kevin Gelinas, lhp, Central Arizona JC.
46. *Parker Bangs, rhp, University of South Carolina.
47. *Justin Earls, lhp, University of Georgia.
48. *Blake Brown, of, Normal West HS, Normal, Ill.
49. *Yasser Clor, rhp, University of California.
50. *Matt Taylor, lhp, Columbus (Ga.) HS.

## ST. LOUIS CARDINALS (18)

1. **Shelby Miller, rhp, Brownwood (Texas) HS.—(2012-15)**
2. Robert Stock, c-rhp, University of Southern California.—(AA)

DRAFT DROP *Brother of Richard Stock, 45th-round draft pick, Brewers (2009)*

3. **Joe Kelly, rhp, UC Riverside.—(2012-15)**
4. Scott Bittle, rhp, University of Mississippi.—(Short-season A)
5. **Ryan Jackson, ss, University of Miami.—(2012-15)**
6. Virgil Hill, of, Mission (Calif.) JC.

DRAFT DROP *Son of Virgil Hill, silver medalist/boxing (middleweight division), 1984 Olympics; World Boxing Association champion (light-heavy-weight/cruiserweight divisions)*

7. Kyle Conley, of, University of Washington.
8. Jason Stidham, ss, Florida State University.
9. Nick McCully, rhp, Coastal Carolina University.
10. Hector Hernandez, lhp, Puerto Rico Baseball Academy, Gurabo, P.R.
11. Alan Ahmady, 1b, Fresno State University.
12. Pat Daugherty, lhp, Pearl River (Miss.) CC.
13. **Matt Carpenter, 3b, Texas Christian University.—(2011-15)**
14. Ross Smith, of, Middle Georgia JC.
15. David Washington, 1b, University City HS, San Diego.
16. *Daniel Bibona, lhp, UC Irvine.
17. Jonathan Rodriguez, 1b, Manatee (Fla.) CC
18. Anthony Garcia, c, San Juan Educational HS, San Juan, P.R.
19. **Travis Tartamella, c, Cal State Los Angeles.—(2015)**
20. Scott Schneider, rhp, St. Mary's (Calif.) College.
21. **Trevor Rosenthal, rhp, Cowley County (Kan.) CC.—(2012-15)**
22. *Joey Bergman, 2b, College of Charleston.
23. **Matt Adams, c, Slippery Rock (Pa.) University.—(2012-15)**
24. **Keith Butler, rhp, Wabash Valley (Ill.) CC.—(2013-14)**
25. Josh Squatrito, rhp, Towson University.
26. C.J. Beatty, of, North Carolina A&T University.
27. John Folino, rhp, University of Connecticut.
28. Justin Edwards, lhp, Kennesaw State University.
29. Daniel Calhoun, lhp, Murray State University.
30. Chris Corrigan, rhp, University of Mississippi.
31. Tyler Bighames, ss, Estero (Fla.) HS.
32. Travis Lawler, rhp, Midland (Texas) JC.
33. Devin Goodwin, ss, Delta State (Miss.) University.
34. David Kington, rhp, Southern Illinois University.
35. Andy Moss, rhp, Lincoln (Mo.) University.
36. Justin Smith, rhp, Utah Valley University.
37. Rich Racobaldo, 3b, Mount Olive (N.C.) College.
38. John Durham, lhp, Warner (Fla.) University.
39. *Taylor Terrasas, ss, Santa Fe (Texas) HS.
40. Jesse Simpson, rhp, College of Charleston.
41. Cale Johnson, rhp, McKendree (Ill.) University.
42. Aaron Terry, rhp, Southern Arkansas University.
43. Manuel De La Cruz, lhp, Imperial Valley (Calif.) JC.
44. Kyle Heim, lhp, University of Iowa.
45. *Adam Heisler, of, University of South Alabama.
46. *Jim Klocke, c, Southeast Missouri State University.
47. Michael Thompson, rhp, Bellarmine (Ky.) Colege.
48. Jason Novak, rhp, UCLA.
49. *Andy Hillis, rhp, Brentwood (Tenn.) HS.
50. Tyler Lavigne, rhp, San Diego State University.

## SAN DIEGO PADRES (3)

1. Donavan Tate, of, Cartersville (Ga.) HS.—(High A)

DRAFT DROP *Son of Lars Tate, running back, National Football League (1988-90)*

2. Everett Williams, of, McCallum HS, Austin, Texas.—(AA)

DRAFT DROP *Nephew of Don Baylor, major leaguer (1970-88)*

3. Jerry Sullivan, rhp, Oral Roberts University.—(AAA)
4. **Keyvius Sampson, rhp, Forest HS, Ocala, Fla.—(2015)**
5. Jason Hagerty, c, University of Miami.—(AAA)
6. James Needy, rhp, Santana HS, Santee, Calif.
7. **Miles Mikolas, rhp, Nova Southeastern (Fla.) University.—(2012-14)**
8. **Nate Freiman, 1b, Duke University.—(2013-14)**
9. Chris Fetter, rhp, University of Michigan.
10. Ryan Hinson, lhp, Clemson University.
11. *Drew Madrigal, rhp, Mount San Jacinto (Calif.) JC.
12. Brayden Drake, 3b, Missouri State University.
13. Matt Vern, 1b, Texas Christian University.
14. **Nick Greenwood, lhp, University of Rhode Island.—(2014-15)**
15. Matt Lollis, rhp, Riverside (Calif.) CC.
16. Griffin Benedict, c, Georgia Southern University.

DRAFT DROP *Son of Bruce Benedict, major leaguer (1978-89)*

17. Jorge Reyes, rhp, Oregon State University.
18. *Shuhei Fujiya, rhp, University of Northern Iowa.
19. Chris Tremblay, ss, Kent State University.
20. *John Wooten, 3b, Eastern Wayne HS, Goldsboro, N.C.
21. Kendall Korbal, rhp, Blinn (Texas) JC.
22. **Cody Decker, 1b, UCLA.—(2015)**
23. Jeff Ibarra, lhp, Lee (Tenn.) University.
24. Bo Davis, of, University of Southern Mississippi.
25. Ty Wright, of, Georgia Southern University.
26. Kevin Winn, 2b, Louisiana Tech.
27. Cameron Monger, of, University of New Mexico.
28. **Vince Belnome, 2b, West Virginia University.—(2014)**
29. Robert Poutier, rhp, University of Virginia.
30. Wande Olabisi, of, Stanford University.
31. Matt Jackson, rhp, University of South Alabama.
32. David Erickson, rhp, University of Connecticut.
33. Jon Berger, rhp, San Diego State University.
34. Josh Cephas, rhp, Southern Nazarene (Okla.) University.
35. *Adalberto Santos, of, Oregon State University.
36. Dylan Tonneson, c, University of California.
37. *Gaspar Santiago, lhp, Ranger (Texas) JC.
38. Kyle Loretelli, of, Cal State Stanislaus.
39. Chris Ahearn, ss, Catawba (N.C.) College.
40. Tom Porter, rhp, Elon University.
41. *Dane Hamilton, 2b, University of New Mexico.
42. *Rey Delphey, rhp, Alonso HS, Tampa.
43. Chadd Hartman, of, University of Central Florida.
44. Ryan Skube, 2b, Mountain Ridge HS, Glendale, Ariz.

DRAFT DROP *Son of Bob Skube, major leaguer (1982-83)*

45. *Derek Landis, rhp, Iowa Western CC.
46. *Mykal Stokes, of, Orange Coast (Calif.) CC.
47. *Zach Thomas, lhp, Cypress-Fairbanks HS, Cypress, Texas.
48. *Andrew Ruck, of, Sinclair SS, Whitby, Ontario.
49. Brett Holland, rhp, University of Texas-Tyler.
50. Brett Basham, c, University of Mississippi.

## SAN FRANCISCO GIANTS (6)

1. **Zack Wheeler, rhp, East Paulding HS, Dallas, Ga.—(2013-14)**
2. Tommy Joseph, c, Horizon HS, Scottsdale, Ariz.—(AAA)
3. **Chris Dominguez, 3b, University of Louisville.—(2014-15)**
4. Jason Stoffel, rhp, University of Arizona.—(AAA)
5. **Brandon Belt, 1b, University of Texas.—(2011-15)**
6. Matt Graham, rhp, Oak Ridge HS, Spring, Texas.
7. Nick Liles, 2b, Western Carolina University.
8. Gus Benusa, of, Riverview HS, Oakmont, Pa.
9. Evan Crawford, of, Indiana University.
10. Jeremy Toole, rhp, Brigham Young University.
11. John Eshleman, ss, Mount San Jacinto (Calif.) JC.
12. **Chris Heston, rhp, East Carolina University.—(2014-15)**
13. Shawn Sanford, rhp, University of South Florida.
14. B.J. Salsbury, rhp, Mount San Jacinto (Calif.) JC.
15. Kyle Vazquez, rhp, Franklin Pierce (N.H.) College.
16. Ryan Cavan, ss, UC Santa Barbara.
17. Chris Gloor, lhp, Quinnipiac University.
18. *Jonathan Walsh, c, Coppell (Texas) HS.
19. Jason Walls, rhp, Troy University.
20. *Mitch Mormann, rhp, Des Moines Area (Iowa) CC.
21. *Zak Wasserman, 1b, Lake Shore HS, St. Clair Shores, Mich.
22. Drew Biery, 3b, Kansas State University.
23. *Adam Champion, lhp, University of Arkansas-Little Rock.
24. Alex Burg, c, Washington State University.
25. Taylor Rogers, rhp, Tulane University.
26. Luis Munoz, of, Puerto Rico Baseball Academy, Gurabo, P.R.
27. Kyle Mach, 3b, University of Missouri.
28. *Jamaine Cotton, rhp, Western Oklahoma State JC.
29. Luke Demko, rhp, University of Rhode Island.
30. Craig Westcott, rhp, Bellhaven (Miss.) College.
31. *Diego Seastrunk, c, Rice University.
32. Luke Anders, 1b, Texas A&M University.
33. **Jake Dunning, ss, Indiana University.—(2013-14)**
34. *Brandon Kirby, of, Lake Wales (Fla.) HS.
35. Brandon Graves, lhp, Valdosta State (Ga.) University.
36. Ryan Scoma, of, UC Davis.
37. **Ryan Lollis, of, University of Missouri.—(2015)**
38. A.J. Proszek, rhp, Gonzaga University.
39. Kyle Henson, c, University of Mississippi.
40. Jonathan White, of, Vanderbilt University.
41. Gary Moran, rhp, Sonoma State (Calif.) University.
42. *Nick Schwaner, 3b, University of New Orleans.
43. *Matt Jansen, lhp, Purdue University.
44. *Joe Lewis, 1b, Pittsburg (Calif.) HS.
45. *Kyle Kramp, rhp, Westfield (Ind.) HS.
46. Juan Martinez, ss, Oral Roberts University.
47. *Michael Ness, rhp, Duke University.
48. *Randolph Oduber, of, Western Oklahoma State JC.
49. *Austin Goolsby, c, Embry-Riddle (Fla.) University.
50. Kaohi Downing, rhp, Point Loma Nazarene (Calif.) University.

## SEATTLE MARINERS (2)

1. **Dustin Ackley, of-2b, University of North Carolina.—(2011-15)**
1. **Nick Franklin, ss, Lake Brantley HS, Altamonte Springs, Fla.** (Choice from Phillies as compensation for Type A free agent Raul Ibanez).**—(2013-15)**
1. **Steve Baron, c, John A. Ferguson HS, Miami** (Supplemental choice—33rd—as compensation for Ibanez).**—(2015)**
2. Rich Poythress, 1b, University of Georgia.—(AAA)
3. **Kyle Seager, 2b, University of North Carolina.—(2011-15)**
4. **James Jones, of, Long Island University.—(2014-15)**
5. Tyler Blandford, rhp, Oklahoma State University.—(High A)
6. Shaver Hansen, 3b, Baylor University.
7. Brian Moran, lhp, University of North Carolina.

DRAFT DROP *Brother of Colin Moran, first-round draft pick, Marlins (2013) • Nephew of B.J. Surhoff, first overall draft pick, Brewers (1985); major leaguer (1987-2005)*

8. Jimmy Gillheeney, lhp, North Carolina State University.
9. Trevor Coleman, c, University of Missouri.
10. Vinnie Catricala, 3b, University of Hawaii.
11. Tim Morris, 1b, St. John's University.
12. Andrew Carraway, rhp, University of Virginia.
13. Matt Cerione, of, University of Georgia.
14. *Adam Nelubowich, 3b, Vauxhall (Alberta) Academy.
15. *Blake Keitzman, lhp, Western Oregon University.
16. *Tillman Pugh, of, GateWay (Ariz.) CC.
17. *Joe Terry, 2b, Cerritos (Calif.) CC.
18. **Anthony Vasquez, lhp, University of Southern California.—(2011)**
19. Eric Thomas, rhp, Bethune-Cookman College.
20. Jon Hesketh, lhp, University of New Mexico.
21. Daniel Cooper, rhp, University of Southern California.
22. *Drew Hayes, rhp, Vanderbilt University.
23. ***David Rollins, lhp, San Jacinto (Texas) JC.—(2015)**
24. Carlton Tanabe, c, Pearl City (Hawaii) HS.
25. Brandon Josselyn, rhp, Yale University.
26. Chris Sorce, rhp, Troy University.
27. Austin Hudson, rhp, University of Central Florida.
28. *Regan Flaherty, 1b, Deering HS, Portland, Maine.

DRAFT DROP *Brother of Ryan Flaherty, first-round draft pick, Cubs (2008); major leaguer (2012-15)*

29. Brandon Haveman, of, Purdue University.
30. **Brandon Bantz, c, Dallas Baptist University.—(2013)**
31. *Clint Dempster, lhp, Mississippi Gulf Coast JC.
32. *Ben Whitmore, lhp, University of Oregon.
33. Hawkins Gebbers, 2b, Biola (Calif.) University.
34. *Scott Griggs, rhp, San Ramon Valley HS, Danville, Calif.
35. Eric Valdez, rhp, Indiana State University.
36. John Housey, rhp, University of Miami.
37. Chris Kessinger, rhp, University of Nebraska-Omaha.
38. *Matt Nohelty, of, University of Minnesota.
39. Greg Waddell, of, Florida International University.
40. Jorden Merry, rhp, University of Washington.
41. Kyle Witten, rhp, Cal State Fullerton.
42. *Steve Hagen, 3b, Eastern Oklahoma State JC.
43. *Cam Perkins, of, Southport HS, Indianapolis.
44. Mark Angelo, of, East Stroudsburg (Pa.) University.
45. Kevin Mailloux, 2b, Canisus University.
46. *Clay Cederquist, 1b, Fowler HS, Fresno, Calif.
47. *David Holman, rhp, Hutchinson (Kan.) CC.

DRAFT DROP *Son of Brian Holman, first-round draft pick, Expos (1983); major leaguer (1988-91)*

48. ***Sean Nolin, lhp, San Jacinto (Texas) JC.—(2013-15)**
49. *Dane Phillips, c, Central Heights HS, Nacogdoches, Texas.
50. Evan Sharpley, 3b, University of Notre Dame.

## TAMPA BAY RAYS (28)

1. *LeVon Washington, 2b, F.W. Buchholz HS, Gainesville, Fla.—(High A)

DRAFT DROP *Attended Chipola (Fla) JC; re-drafted by Indians, 2010 (2nd round)*

2. *Kenny Diekroeger, ss, Menlo HS, Atherton, Calif.—(AAA)

DRAFT DROP *Attended Stanford; re-drafted by Royals, 2012 (4th round)*

3. Todd Glaesmann, of, Midway HS, Waco, Texas.—(AAA)
4. Luke Bailey, c, Troup County HS, La Grange, Ga.—(AA)
5. Jeff Malm, 1b, Bishop Gorman HS, Las Vegas, Nev.—(AA)
6. Devin Fuller, rhp, Chandler-Gilbert (Ariz.) CC.
7. Cody Rogers, of, Panola (Texas) JC.
8. Brett Nommensen, of, Eastern Illinois University.
9. Kevin James, lhp, Whitefish Bay HS, Milwaukee.
10. *Derek Dennis, ss, Forest Hills Central HS, Grand Rapids, Mich.
11. Alex Koronis, rhp, University of Tampa.
12. **Andrew Bellatti, rhp, Steele Canyon HS, Spring Valley, Calif.—(2015)**
13. Hunter Hill, rhp, Howard (Texas) JC.
14. Zach Quate, rhp, Appalachian State University.
15. *Pierce Johnson, rhp, Faith Christian Academy, Arvada, Colo.

DRAFT DROP *First-round draft pick (43rd overall), Cubs (2012)*

16. Tyler Bortnick, 2b, Coastal Carolina University.
17. Alex Diaz, of, Puerto Rico Baseball Academy, Gurabo, P.R.
18. Jacob Partridge, lhp, Rogers HS, Spokane, Wash.
19. Scott Shuman, rhp, Auburn University.
20. *Dylan Floro, rhp, Buhach Colony HS, Atwater, Calif.
21. Matt Swilley, rhp, El Camino HS, Oceanside, Calif.
22. Jake Sullivan, lhp, University of Arkansas-Little Rock.

23. *Trevor Petersen, rhp, Hallsville (Texas) HS.
**24. *Andrew Heaney, lhp, Putnam City HS, Oklahoma City.—(2014-15)**
DRAFT DROP *First-round draft pick (9th overall), Marlins (2012)*
25. Ryan Wiegand, 1b, Gonzaga University.
26. Dan Rhault, ss, University of Rhode Island.
27. *Brady Wager, rhp, Globe (Ariz.) HS.
**28. Zac Rosscup, lhp, Chemeketa (Ore.) CC.—(2013-15)**
29. Gabe Cohen, of, UCLA.
30. Marcus Jensen, rhp, Pinnacle HS, Phoenix.
DRAFT DROP *Son of Marcus Jensen, first-round draft pick, Giants (1990); major leaguer (1996-2002)*
31. Aaron Dott, lhp, University of Wisconsin-Whitewater.
32. *Alex Besaw, rhp, Skagit Valley (Wash.) CC.
33. *Ryan McCarney, rhp, Cal State Northridge.
34. Kyle Spraker, ss, Loyola Marymount University.
35. Chris Murrill, of, Nicholls State University.
36. Jeff Cinadr, rhp, University of Toledo.
37. *Austin Maddox, c, Eagle's View HS, Jacksonville, Fla.
38. *Drew Hillman, 3b, Orange Coast (Calif.) CC.
39. Dan April, lhp, Mercer University.
**40. *James Pazos, lhp, Highland HS, Gilbert, Ariz.—(2015)**
41. Matt Stabelfeld, lhp, Lewis-Clark State (Idaho) College.
42. Bennett Davis, 3b, Elon University.
43. Geno Glynn, 3b, University of Minnesota State-Mankato.
44. *Kalani Brackenridge, ss, Kapolei (Hawaii) HS.
DRAFT DROP *Brother of Tyron Brackenridge, defensive back, National Football League (2007-10)*
45. *Cole Nelson, lhp, Des Moines Area (Iowa) CC.
46. *Aaron Oates, 3b, Skyline HS, Oakland, Calif.
47. Jason Patton, of, Kent State University.
48. *Nate Roberts, of, Parkland (Ill.) JC.
49. *Vince Spilker, rhp, Raytown (Mo.) HS.
50. David Wendt, c, Dowling (N.Y.) College.

## TEXAS RANGERS (13)

1. *Matt Purke, lhp, Klein (Texas) HS.—(AA)
DRAFT DROP *Attended Texas Christian; re-drafted by Nationals, third round (2011)*
**1. Tanner Scheppers, rhp, St. Paul/American Association** (Supplemental choice—44th—as compensation for Type B free agent Milton Bradley).**—(2012-15)**
2. Tommy Mendonca, 3b, Fresno State University.—(AAA)
**3. Robbie Erlin, lhp, Scotts Valley (Calif.) HS.—(2013-15)**
4. Andrew Doyle, rhp, University of Oklahoma.—(High A)
5. Nick McBride, rhp, Ragsdale HS, Jamestown, N.C.—(AAA)
6. Ruben Sierra Jr, of, San Juan Educational HS, San Juan, P.R.
DRAFT DROP *Son of Ruben Sierra, major leaguer (1986-2006)*
7. Braxton Lane, of, Sandy Creek HS, Tyrone, Ga.
DRAFT DROP *Nephew of MacArthur Lane, first-round draft pick, St. Louis Cardinals, National Football League (1968); running back, NFL (1968-78)*
8. Braden Tullis, rhp, Skagit Valley (Wash.) CC.
9. *Jabari Blash, of, Miami-Dade JC.
10. *Tom Lemke, rhp, Northwest Christian HS, Phoenix.
11. Johnny Gunter, rhp, Chattahoochee Valley (Ala.) CC.
12. Vinny DiFazio, c, University of Alabama.
13. Justin Jamison, rhp, Strongsville (Ohio) HS.
14. Chad Bell, lhp, Walters State (Tenn.) CC.
15. Keith Campbell, rhp, Everett (Wash.) CC.
16. *Mike Revell, 3b, Florida HS, Tallahassee, Fla.
17. Paul Strong, lhp, Marina HS, Huntington Beach, Calif.
18. *Mike Schaaf, rhp, Arthur Hill HS, Saginaw, Mich.
19. *Jayce Boyd, 3b, Tate HS, Cantonment, Fla.
20. *Jerome Werniuk, rhp, Neil McNeil HS, Toronto.
21. Chris Matlock, rhp, Central Missouri State University.
22. Sam Brown, rhp, North Carolina State University.
23. Danny Lima, ss, Barry (Fla.) University.
24. Shawn Blackwell, rhp, Clear Creek HS, League City, Texas.
25. Riley Cooper, of, University of Florida.
DRAFT DROP *Wide receiver, National Football League (2010-15)*
26. Kevin Castner, rhp, Cal Poly.
**27. *Aaron Barrett, rhp, University of Mississippi.—(2014-15)**
28. *Derek Law, rhp, Seton La Salle Catholic HS, Pittsburgh.
29. *C.C. Watson, lhp, Cleburne County HS, Heflin, Ala.
30. *Bryan Fogle, of, Erskine (S.C.) College.
31. Shon Landry, ss, McNeese State University.
32. *Reggie Williams Jr, of, Brooks-DeBartolo Collegiate HS, Tampa.
DRAFT DROP *Son of Reggie Williams, major leaguer (1985-88)*
33. Kyle Rhoad, of, Eastern Michigan University.
34. Jared Prince, of, Washington State University.
**35. *Eddie Butler, rhp, Greenbrier Christian Academy, Chesapeake, Va.—(2014-15)**
DRAFT DROP *First-round draft pick (46th overall), Rockies (2012)*
36. *Matt Carasiti, rhp, Berlin (Conn.) HS.
37. *Chad Nading, rhp, University of Nevada-Las Vegas.
38. *Anthony Hutting, of, Tesoro HS, Rancho San Margarita, Calif.
39. *Jabari Henry, of, Olympia HS, Orlando, Fla.
40. Taylor Vail, 3b, Cabrillo (Calif.) JC.
41. *Forrest Garrett, lhp, Norcross (Ga.) HS.
42. Shane Zegarac, lhp, St. Joseph's (Ind.) College.
43. Joe Bonadonna, of, University of Illinois.
44. *Tyler Christman, rhp, USC Sumter JC.
45. *Dale Anderson, c, JC of Southern Idaho.
46. *Jerad Grundy, lhp, Johnsburg (Ill.) HS.
47. *Tyler Higgins, rhp, Mount Pleasant (Mich.) HS.
48. *Cole Frenzel, 3b, Dickinson (N.D.) HS.
49. *Cat Kendrick, rhp, Northgate HS, Newnan, Ga.
50. *Ronnie Melendez, of, Cowley County (Kan.) CC.

## TORONTO BLUE JAYS (19)

**1. Chad Jenkins, rhp, Kennesaw State University.—(2012-15)**
**1. *James Paxton, lhp, University of Kentucky** (Supplemental choice—37th—as compensation for Type A free agent A.J. Burnett).—**(2013-15)**
DRAFT DROP *Signed with Grand Prairie/American Association (independent); re-drafted by Mariners, 2010 (4th round)*
2. *Jake Eliopoulos, lhp, Sacred Heart Catholic HS, Newmarket, Ontario.—DNP
DRAFT DROP *Attended Chipola (Fla.) JC; re-drafted by Dodgers, 2010 (15th round)*
3. *Jake Barrett, rhp, Desert Ridge HS, Mesa, Ariz.—(AAA)
DRAFT DROP *Attended Arizona State; re-drafted by Diamondbacks, 2012 (3rd round)*
**3. Jake Marisnick, of, Poly HS, Riverside, Calif.** (Choice from Yankees as compensation for Burnett).**—(2013-15)**
**4. Ryan Goins, ss, Dallas Baptist University.—(2013-15)**
5. Ryan Schimpf, 2b, Louisiana State University.—(AAA)
6. K.C. Hobson, of, Stockdale HS, Bakersfield, Calif.
DRAFT DROP *Son of Butch Hobson, major leaguer (1975-82); major league manager (1992-94)*
7. Egan Smith, lhp, CC of Southern Nevada.
8. Brian Slover, rhp, Cal State Northridge.
**9. Aaron Loup, lhp, Tulane University.—(2012-15)**
**10. Yan Gomes, c, Barry (Fla.) University.—(2012-15)**
11. Sean Ochinko, c, Louisiana State University.
12. Bryson Namba, 3b, Pearl City (Hawaii) HS.
13. Matt Morgal, rhp, Southern Nazarene (Okla.) University.
14. Lance Durham, 1b, University of Cincinnati.
DRAFT DROP *Son of Leon Durham, first-round draft pick, Cardinals (1976); major leaguer (1980-89)*
**15. Drew Hutchison, rhp, Lakeland (Fla.) HS.—(2012-15)**
16. Dave Sever, rhp, Saint Louis University.
17. Steve Turnbull, rhp, University of Iowa.
**18. Daniel Webb, rhp, Northwest Florida State JC.—(2013-15)**
**19. Ryan Tepera, rhp, Sam Houston State University.—(2015)**
20. Kevin Nolan, ss, Winthrop University.
21. *Kurt Giller, rhp, Manhattan (Kan.) HS.
22. Matt Fields, rhp, Gonzaga University.
**23. Brad Glenn, of, University of Arizona.—(2014)**
24. Matt Nuzzo, ss, Brown University.
25. Sam Strickland, lhp, Texas A&M University-Kingsville.
26. Lance Loftin, rhp, Texas State University.
27. Brian Justice, rhp, St. Mary's HS, Orchard Lake, Mich.
28. Zach Outman, rhp, Saint Louis University.
DRAFT DROP *Brother of Josh Outman, major leaguer (2008-14)*
29. Zach Anderson, rhp, University of Buffalo.
30. *T.J. McDonald, of, Edison HS, Fresno, Calif.
DRAFT DROP *Defensive back, National Football League (2013-15)*
31. Jack Murphy, c, Princeton University.
32. Ryan Shopshire, rhp, San Jose State University.
33. *Robert Benincasa, rhp, Armwood HS, Seffner, Fla.
34. Jonathan Fernandez, ss, Guilford Tech (N.C.) CC.
DRAFT DROP *Son of Tony Fernandez, major leaguer (1983-2001)*
35. Evan Teague, lhp, Western Kentucky University.
36. Alex Pepe, lhp, Florida Atlantic University.
37. Shawn Griffith, rhp, George Mason University.
38. Yudelmis Hernandez, 1b, Barry (Fla.) University.
39. *Josh Lucas, rhp, Lakeland (Fla.) HS.
40. *Jonathan Gilbert, of, Ahuntsic (Quebec) JC.
41. *Zach Kirksey, of, LSU-Eunice JC.
42. *Michael Reeves, c, St. Peter's SS, Peterborough, Ontario.
43. *Maxx Tissenbaum, ss, York Mills Collegiate Institute, Toronto.
44. *Nick Wagner, of, Santa Margarita HS, Rancho Santa Margarita, Calif.
45. *Brandon Kaye, rhp, Douglas (B.C.) JC.
46. *Carlos Castro, 3b, Lon Morris (Texas) JC.
47. *John Rigg, of, St. Petersburg (Fla.) JC.
48. *Jeff Gibbs, rhp, Birchmount Park Collegiate Institute, Toronto.
49. *Tommy Collier, rhp, San Jacinto (Texas) JC.
50. *Burke Seifrit, rhp, Semiahmoo SS, Surrey, B.C.

## WASHINGTON NATIONALS (1)

**1. Stephen Strasburg, rhp, San Diego State University.—(2010-15)**
**1. Drew Storen, rhp, Stanford University** (Special compensation—10th—for failure to sign 2008 first-round draft pick Aaron Crow).—**(2010-15)**
**2. Jeff Kobernus, 2b, University of California.—(2013-14)**
3. Trevor Holder, rhp, University of Georgia.—(AA)
4. A.J. Morris, rhp, Kansas State University.—(AAA)
5. *Miguel Pena, lhp, La Joya HS, Mission, Texas.—(AA)
DRAFT DROP *Attended San Jacinto (Texas) JC; re-drafted by Padres, 2010 (13th round)*
**6. Michael A. Taylor, ss, Westminster Academy, Fort Lauderdale, Fla.—(2014-15)**
7. Dean Weaver, rhp, University of Georgia.
8. Roberto Perez, ss, Dorado Academy, Dorado, P.R.
**9. Taylor Jordan, rhp, Brevard (Fla.) CC.—(2013-15)**
10. Paul Applebee, lhp, UC Riverside.
11. Justin Bloxom, of, Kansas State University.
**12. Nate Karns, rhp, Texas Tech.—(2013-15)**
13. Pat Lehman, rhp, George Washington University.
14. Naoya Washiya, of, JC of the Desert (Calif.).
15. *Corey Davis, 1b, Coffee HS, Douglas, Ga.
16. Sean Nicol, ss, University of San Diego.
17. Chad Jenkins, lhp, Cecil (Md.) CC.
**18. *Marcus Stroman, ss, Patchogue-Medford HS, Medford, N.Y.—(2014-15)**
DRAFT DROP *First-round draft pick (22nd overall), Blue Jays (2012)*
19. *Frank Corolla, rhp, University of Houston.
20. Jack Walker, 3b, Concordia (Ill.) University.
21. Mitchell Clegg, lhp, University of Massachusetts.
22. Danny Rosenbaum, lhp, Xavier University.
23. Kyle Breault, ss, Northville (Mich.) HS.
24. Dustin Crane, rhp, Snead State (Ala.) CC.
25. *Matt Ridings, rhp, Western Kentucky University.
26. Gianison Rosa, ss, Carroll HS, Southlake, Texas.
27. Brandon King, rhp, Martinsburg (W.Va.) HS.
28. Matt Swynenberg, rhp, Black Hawk (Ill.) JC.
29. Evan Bronson, lhp, Trinity (Texas) University.
30. Rob Wort, rhp, Jefferson (Mo.) JC.
31. J.J. Sferra, of, University of Nevada-Las Vegas.
32. Kyle Morrison, rhp, Wagner College.
33. *Nick DeSantiago, c, Hays HS, Kyle, Texas.
34. Shane McCatty, rhp, Oakland University.
DRAFT DROP *Son of Steve McCatty, major leaguer (1977-85)*
35. *Jacob Morris, of, Coppell (Texas) HS.
36. *Josh Miller, lhp, O'Connor HS, Helotes, Texas.
37. *Josh Elander, c, Round Rock (Texas) HS.
38. *Chris Manno, lhp, Duke University.
39. *Kyle Martin, rhp, St. Michael's Academy, Austin, Texas.
40. *Joseph Hughes, rhp, McMichael HS, Mayodan, N.C.
41. *Dane Opel, of, Edwardsville (Ill.) HS.
42. *Daniel Cropper, rhp, UNC Wilmington.
43. *Cohl Walla, rhp, Lake Travis HS, Austin, Texas.
44. *Hoby Milner, lhp, Paschal HS, Fort Worth, Texas.
DRAFT DROP *Son of Brian Milner, major leaguer (1978)*
45. *Michael Ratterree, ss, Memorial HS, Houston.
46. *Seth Greene, rhp, Deep Run HS, Glen Allen, Va.
DRAFT DROP *Son of Tommy Greene, first-round draft pick, Braves (1985); major leaguer (1989-97)*
47. *Darius Rudoph, 2b, Snead State (Ala.) CC.
48. *Zach Dygert, c, Ball State University.
49. *Jose Sermo, of, Ileana de Gracia HS, Vega Alta, P.R.
50. *Alvin Hines, of, Pelham (Ala.) HS.

# Nationals hit paydirt, land gem with Harper

Few players in draft history have been as highly regarded and generated more hype than righthander Stephen Strasburg and catcher Bryce Harper, and the Washington Nationals hit the jackpot by drafting each with the No. 1 pick in consecutive years.

The Nationals landed Strasburg, a 21-year-old from San Diego State and arguably the most dominant pitcher in college baseball history, in 2009. A year later they got Harper, just 17 and a power-hitting sensation at the College of Southern Nevada, a two-year school. The Nationals were in position to get both players because they had the worst record in the major leagues in both 2008 and 2009, winning just 59 games each season.

While Strasburg was a virtual unknown at a California high school and blossomed in college, Harper was a teenage prodigy. From his tape-measure home runs, to his daring base-running acumen, to his appearance on a Sports Illustrated cover, Harper stood alone among top prospects, even as he skipped his junior and senior years of high school.

After hitting .626 with 14 home runs, 55 RBIs and 36 stolen bases as a sophomore at Las Vegas High, Harper decided he needed better competition. With the guidance of agent Scott Boras, Harper engineered one of the boldest and most creative maneuvers in draft history, securing his graduate-equivalency diploma and enrolling in junior college, all with the intent of becoming eligible for the draft a year earlier than he would have had he remained in high school.

Any thoughts that Harper, then 16, was biting off more than he could chew quickly evaporated. In one memorable season of junior college, he led the nation in homers (31) and RBIs (98), hit .443 and stole 20 bases. Using wood bats, Harper broke the previous school record of 12 homers in a season, which had been set in 2001 with an aluminum bat. Harper also excelled as a catcher, handing a staff that included some of the best junior college pitchers in the country.

"Certainly, I expected him to have success," Southern Nevada head coach Tim Chambers said, "but I never saw this coming."

The Nationals scouted Harper incessantly in the spring of 2010, and decided long before the draft he would be the first pick. "It was a pretty easy decision," said Nationals general manager Mike Rizzo, who made his mind up after watching Harper play in a weekend series a month before the draft.

The 6-foot-3, 205-pound Harper was drafted as a catcher and profiled as a future all-star at the position with a skill set that included exceptional power, great arm strength and above-average speed. But the Nationals quickly decided to train him as an outfielder, a position move that would enable him to focus on hitting.

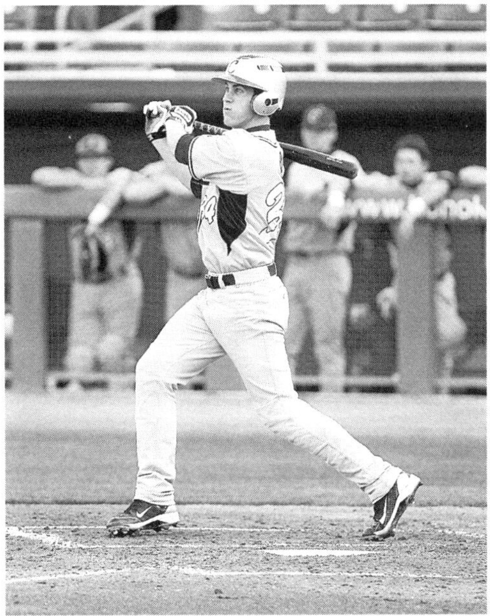

BILL MITCHELL

With consecutive No. 1 overall picks, the Nationals followed their selection of the much hyped Stephen Strasburg by taking the equally hyped Bryce Harper, a Nevada junior-college product

"We're going to take the rigors and the pressure of learning the difficult position of catcher away from him," Rizzo said. "We'll let him concentrate on the offensive part of the game and let his athleticism take over as an outfielder. He's got above-average speed and a plus-plus throwing arm, and we just think it will accelerate his development in the minor leagues and also extend his career."

First, there was the matter of signing Harper, and that didn't promise to be a routine process, not with Boras on Harper's side. A year earlier, the Nationals signed Strasburg, also represented by Boras, just minutes before the deadline. Harper agreed to a major league contract with the Nationals less than a minute before the deadline. The deal included a $6.25 million bonus and was worth $9.9 million overall, both short of the record amounts that Strasburg received, but the most ever for a position player signing with the team that drafted him.

At the end of the news conference introducing Harper, Nationals president Stan Kasten celebrated by giving Rizzo a whipped-cream pie to the face.

### TWO-HORSE RACE INCLUDES TAILLON

In the baseball draft's 45-year history, the first overall pick never had been a high school righthander or a junior college player. That was almost certain to change in 2010, considering the top-rated players most of the spring were Harper and Texas prep righthander Jameson Taillon.

After the Nationals grabbed Harper with the

## AT A GLANCE

### This Date In History
June 7-9

### Best Draft
**NEW YORK METS.** The Mets can point to this draft as a big reason why they returned to postseason play in 2015 for the first time in nine years. It yielded two top starting pitchers, **MATT HARVEY** (1) and **JACOB DEGROM** (9).

### Worst Draft
**CHICAGO CUBS. MATT SZCZUR** (5), **ERIC JOKISCH** (11) and **DALLAS BEELER** (41) became marginal big leaguers. The Cubs botched their first-round selection, **HAYDEN SIMPSON**, an NCAA Division II pitcher who mesmerized Cubs scouts with a sudden increase in velocity late in the spring, and just as quickly fell off the radar by going 5-17, 6.42 in two minor league seasons.

### First-Round Bust
**JOSH SALE, OF, RAYS.** Sale did not advance beyond Class A in four years in the Rays organization, though his career (.238-18-105) was no less productive than **JAKE SKOLE** (Rangers) and Hayden Simpson (Cubs), the two players drafted immediately ahead of him. Sale raised the ante by getting suspended on three occasions, including for the entire 2013 season by the Rays for a Facebook post about his visit to a strip club.

### Second Best
**ANDRELTON SIMMONS, SS, BRAVES.** Simmons, a Curacao native, was a pitcher and shortstop at Western Oklahoma State JC. The Braves developed him as a shortstop, and Simmons quickly became one of the best defensive shortstops in the game.

### Late Round Find
**KEVIN KIERMAIER, OF, RAYS (29TH ROUND).** Kiermaier led Parkland (Ill.) to the junior college

CONTINUED ON PAGE 672

## AT A GLANCE

CONTINUED FROM PAGE 671

Division II national title in 2009 and signed with the Rays a year later. He earned his reputation as a premier defensive outfielder long before playing his first game in the majors in 2013.

### Never Too Late

**A.J. ACHTER, RHP, TWINS (46TH ROUND).** Achter had an 8-13, 4.29 record in three years at Michigan State. The Twins did not offer him a signing bonus until after he pitched well in the Cape Cod League, and he signed for $50,000 just before the deadline. Achter made 18 relief appearances for the Twins during the 2014-15 seasons.

### Overlooked

**RAFAEL MARTIN, RHP, NATIONALS.** Martin's long road to the big leagues began on Feb. 8, 2010, when he signed at age 25 after pitching for Mexico in the Caribbean Series. He had worked four years in construction after graduating from a Southern California high school and pitched for three years in the Mexican League. Martin got to the big leagues in 2015, and went 2-0, 5.11 with 25 strikeouts over 13 relief appearances.

### International Gem

**AROLDIS CHAPMAN, LHP, REDS.** Chapman was 21 when he defected from Cuba in 2009. On Jan. 10, 2010, he signed a six-year, $30.25 million deal with the Reds. He was in the majors to stay later in the 2010 season, reaching 105 mph, the fastest documented pitch in big league history. Entering the 2016 season, he remained one of MLB's elite closers.

### Minor League Take

**CHRIS SALE, LHP, WHITE SOX.** The White Sox drafted Sale in part because they believed he could reach the majors quickly, based on his junior season at Florida Gulf Coast, where he went 11-0, 2.01 with 14 walks and 146 strikeouts in 103 innings. It

## 2010: THE FIRST ROUNDERS

| CLUB: PLAYER, POS., SCHOOL | HOMETOWN | B-T | HT. | WT. | AGE | BONUS | FIRST YEAR | LAST YEAR | PEAK LEVEL (YEARS) |
|---|---|---|---|---|---|---|---|---|---|
| **1. *Nationals: Bryce Harper, c/of, JC of Southern Nevada** | **Las Vegas** | **L-R** | **6-3** | **215** | **17** | **$6,250,000** | **2011** | **Active** | **Majors (4)** |
| Most celebrated teenage prospect of draft era; left HS after soph year, enrolled in JC, hit .443-31-98, became draft-eligible at 17; signed five-year, $9.9M MLB deal. | | | | | | | | | |
| **2. Pirates: Jameson Taillon, rhp, The Woodlands HS** | **The Woodlands, Texas** | **R-R** | **6-6** | **225** | **18** | **$6,500,000** | **2011** | **Active** | **Class AAA (1)** |
| Players picked before/after have four MLB seasons under belt vs. six Triple-A games; missed '14 (TJ), '15 (hernia) with injuries; mid/high-90s FB when healthy. | | | | | | | | | |
| **3. Orioles: Manny Machado, ss, Brito Miami Private HS** | **Miami** | **R-R** | **6-3** | **185** | **17** | **$5,250,000** | **2010** | **Active** | **Majors (4)** |
| Natural comparisons to Alex Rodriguez with similar physique, tools, position evolution, Miami background, MLB debut as teenager; breakout 35-HR season in 2015. | | | | | | | | | |
| **4. Royals: Christian Colon, ss, Cal State Fullerton** | **Santa Clarita, Calif.** | **R-R** | **5-10** | **190** | **21** | **$2,750,000** | **2010** | **Active** | **Majors (2)** |
| Polished college middle infielder considered safe pick/fast mover; hit a deceiving .358-17-68 as Fullerton JR as tools/bat have proven to be marginal for pro ball. | | | | | | | | | |
| **5. Indians: Drew Pomeranz, lhp, Mississippi** | **Collierville, Tenn.** | **L-L** | **6-5** | **240** | **21** | **$2,650,000** | **2010** | **Active** | **Majors (5)** |
| Went 21-9, 3.17, fanned Ole Miss career record 344 with 92-95 mph FB, power curve; has shown flashes in 14-24, 4.17 MLB career, plagued by spotty command. | | | | | | | | | |
| **6. †Diamondbacks: Barret Loux, rhp, Texas A&M** | **Stratford, Texas** | **R-R** | **6-5** | **215** | **21** | **$312,000** | **2011** | **2015** | **Class AAA (2)** |
| Agreed to $2M bonus but failed physical due to labrum/elbow damage, D-backs backed out of predraft deal; signed with Rangers, arm problems persisted. | | | | | | | | | |
| **7. Mets: Matt Harvey, rhp, North Carolina** | **Groton, Conn.** | **R-R** | **6-4** | **225** | **21** | **$2,525,000** | **2011** | **Active** | **Majors (3)** |
| High-profile/unsignable prep arm; after so-so first two years at UNC, showed better command, mid-90s FB as junior; has flourished as big leaguer. | | | | | | | | | |
| **8. Astros: Delino DeShields, of/2b, Woodward Academy** | **College Park, Ga.** | **R-R** | **5-9** | **210** | **17** | **$2,150,000** | **2010** | **Active** | **Majors (1)** |
| Son of '87 first-rounder; fastest player in draft, but surprise pick because he lacked position/power, stole 101 bags in 2012, claimed by Rangers in 2014 Rule 5 draft. | | | | | | | | | |
| **9. Padres: Karsten Whitson, rhp, Chipley HS** | **Chipley, Fla.** | **R-R** | **6-3** | **195** | **18** | **Unsigned** | **2014** | **2014** | **Class A (1)** |
| Dominant fastball/slider in HS, struck out 123 in 55 IP as SR, passed up Padres $2.1 M offer, enrolled at Florida; shoulder problems started in 2012, have persisted. | | | | | | | | | |
| **10. Athletics: Michael Choice, of, Texas-Arlington** | **Arlington, Texas** | **R-R** | **6-0** | **220** | **21** | **$2,000,000** | **2010** | **Active** | **Majors (3)** |
| A's sought elusive combo of power/OBP, found their man in UTA CF (.383-16-59, 76 BBs); more strikeouts/less home runs as a pro, pushed to corner by lack of speed. | | | | | | | | | |
| **11. Blue Jays: Deck McGuire, rhp, Georgia Tech** | **Glen Allen, Va.** | **R-R** | **6-6** | **235** | **20** | **$2,000,000** | **2011** | **Active** | **Class AAA (2)** |
| Went 28-7, 3.28 at Tech, considered safe pick as workhorse with big frame/not overpowering; 40-49, 4.57 in minors, took four years to get over Double-A hurdle. | | | | | | | | | |
| **12. *Reds: Yasmani Grandal, c, Miami** | **Miami Springs, Fla.** | **B-R** | **6-2** | **210** | **21** | **$2,000,000** | **2010** | **Active** | **Majors (4)** |
| Cuban native was nation's top prep catcher in 2007, improved stock with stellar college career, hit .401-15-60 as JR; switch-hitter with raw power, arm strength. | | | | | | | | | |
| **13. White Sox: Chris Sale, lhp, Florida Gulf Coast** | **Lakeland, Fla.** | **L-L** | **6-6** | **180** | **21** | **$1,656,000** | **2010** | **Active** | **Majors (6)** |
| Profiled as reliever with delivery/arm slot, but went 11-0, 2.01 (103 IP, 14 BB/146 SO), commanded three plus pitches as JR, quickly became all-star MLB starter. | | | | | | | | | |
| **14. Brewers: Dylan Covey, rhp, Maranatha HS** | **Pasadena, Calif.** | **R-R** | **6-2** | **195** | **18** | **Unsigned** | **2013** | **Active** | **Class A (3)** |
| Legit mid-first-rounder, but diagnosed as diabetic on eve of signing $1.6M deal; family determined college as better option, became fourth-rounder in 2013. | | | | | | | | | |
| **15. Rangers: Jake Skole, of, Blessed Trinity HS** | **Roswell, Ga.** | **L-R** | **6-1** | **190** | **18** | **$1,557,000** | **2010** | **Active** | **Class AA (2)** |
| Rangers gambled/lost on football-first athlete with limited baseball resume; projected plus power/speed, but neither tool has played consistently in pro career. | | | | | | | | | |
| **16. Cubs: Hayden Simpson, rhp, Southern Arkansas** | **Magnolia, Ark.** | **R-R** | **6-0** | **170** | **21** | **$1,060,000** | **2010** | **2013** | **Class A (2)** |
| Dominant D-II pitcher (career 35-2, 2.39) suddenly hit 94-97 mph before draft; Cubs shocked industry with selection, velocity plummeted, went 5-17, 6.43 in pros. | | | | | | | | | |
| **17. Rays: Josh Sale, of, Bishop Blanchet HS** | **Seattle** | **L-R** | **6-0** | **215** | **18** | **$1,620,000** | **2011** | **2014** | **Class A (2)** |
| Flashed power in three minor league seasons (.238-18-105), but career best known for immaturity, off-field issues that led to three suspensions, release in 2015. | | | | | | | | | |
| **18. Angels: Kaleb Cowart, 3b/rhp, Cook HS** | **Adel, Ga.** | **B-R** | **6-3** | **195** | **18** | **$2,300,000** | **2010** | **Active** | **Majors (1)** |
| Positioned himself as top two-way prospect after starring on showcase circuit; developed by Angels as hitter in pro ball, but spun wheels at plate for six years. | | | | | | | | | |
| **19. Astros: Mike Foltynewicz, rhp, Minooka Comm. HS** | **Minooka, Ill.** | **R-R** | **6-4** | **200** | **18** | **$1,305,000** | **2010** | **Active** | **Majors (2)** |
| Late developer, not considered top rounder until velocity jumped from 87-90 to 93-95 mph, has since reached 100-102 with power curve, but stagnant command. | | | | | | | | | |
| **20. Red Sox: Kolbrin Vitek, 2b/of, Ball State** | **Bryan, Ohio** | **R-R** | **6-2** | **195** | **21** | **$1,359,000** | **2010** | **2013** | **Class AA (2)** |
| Two-way star, one of top college bats in draft; never hit for average/power in four pro seasons (.258-8-103), struggled in field, retired with neck/concussion issues. | | | | | | | | | |
| **21. Twins: Alex Wimmers, rhp, Ohio State** | **Cincinnati** | **L-R** | **6-2** | **195** | **21** | **$1,332,000** | **2010** | **Active** | **Class AA (3)** |
| Two-time Big 10 pitcher of year had dominant pro debut, but struggled afterward with streak of wildness, 2012 TJ surgery, finally saw regular workload in 2015. | | | | | | | | | |
| **22. Rangers: Kellin Deglan, c, R.E. Mountain SS** | **Langley, B.C.** | **L-R** | **6-2** | **195** | **18** | **$1,000,000** | **2010** | **Active** | **Class AA (1)** |
| First prep catcher in draft taken off Canadian junior national team; above-average LH power/arm strength, has struggled to match performance to plus tools. | | | | | | | | | |
| **23. Marlins: Christian Yelich, of, Westlake HS** | **Westlake Village, Calif.** | **L-R** | **6-4** | **190** | **18** | **$1,700,000** | **2010** | **Active** | **Majors (3)** |
| With sweet swing, advanced plate approach, has done nothing but hit in minors (.311), majors (.290); power still evolving, speed is an asset in field/on bases. | | | | | | | | | |
| **24. Giants: Gary Brown, of, Cal State Fullerton** | **Diamond Bar, Calif.** | **R-R** | **6-1** | **190** | **21** | **$1,450,000** | **2010** | **Active** | **Majors (1)** |
| Gifted athlete with excellent speed, skills to excel in CF; hit .438-6-41 as college JR, but scouts questioned style, approach at plate, has struggled at higher levels. | | | | | | | | | |
| **25. *Cardinals: Zack Cox, 3b, Arkansas** | **Louisville, Ky.** | **L-R** | **6-0** | **215** | **21** | **$2,000,000** | **2010** | **2015** | **Class AAA (4)** |
| Regarded as best pure hitter in class, signed major league deal as draft-eligible soph, advanced quickly but fell out of favor with suspect power/plate discipline/defense. | | | | | | | | | |
| **26. Rockies: Kyle Parker, of, Clemson** | **Jacksonville, Fla.** | **R-R** | **6-0** | **200** | **20** | **$1,400,000** | **2011** | **Active** | **Majors (2)** |
| Two-year starting QB at Clemson, only NCAA athlete with 20 TDs/20 HRs in same school year; raw power evident in minors, slow to evolve in majors. | | | | | | | | | |
| **27. Phillies: Jesse Biddle, lhp, Germantown Friends HS** | **Philadelphia** | **L-L** | **6-4** | **225** | **18** | **$1,160,000** | **2010** | **Active** | **Class AAA (1)** |
| Local product went 9-2, 1.06 (59 IP/140 SO) as SR; averaged more than SO/IP first five seasons, but progress slowed by control issues, struggled in Triple-A. | | | | | | | | | |
| **28. Dodgers: Zach Lee, rhp, McKinney HS** | **McKinney, Texas** | **R-R** | **6-4** | **190** | **18** | **$5,250,000** | **2011** | **Active** | **Majors (1)** |
| Puzzling pick with McCourt-owned Dodgers in financial mess, Lee considered unsignable as elite LSU QB recruit; career plagued by inconsistent stuff/command. | | | | | | | | | |
| **29. Angels: Cam Bedrosian, rhp, East Coweta HS** | **Sharpsburg, Ga.** | **R-R** | **6-0** | **205** | **18** | **$1,116,000** | **2010** | **Active** | **Majors (2)** |
| Son of Steve, '87 Cy Young winner; career started slowly with TJ surgery, 4-18, 5.48 mark as starter before switch to bullpen, fastball soon returned to mid-90s. | | | | | | | | | |
| **30. Angels: Chevy Clarke, of, Marietta HS** | **Marietta, Ga.** | **B-R** | **5-11** | **200** | **18** | **$1,089,000** | **2010** | **2014** | **Class A (3)** |
| Third Angels first-round pick from rich Georgia prep ranks; viewed as five-tool talent, but significant holes in swing/poor pitch recognition prompted 2014 release. | | | | | | | | | |
| **31. Rays: Justin O'Conner, c, Cowan HS** | **Muncie, Ind.** | **R-R** | **6-0** | **190** | **18** | **$1,025,000** | **2010** | **Active** | **Class AA (2)** |
| Prep SS/RHP converted to catcher as SR, gunned down runners at 53 percent clip from 2013-15; other catching skills, pitch-recognition ability still evolving. | | | | | | | | | |
| **32. Yankees: Cito Culver, ss, Irondequoit HS** | **Rochester, N.Y.** | **B-R** | **6-0** | **185** | **17** | **$954,000** | **2010** | **Active** | **Class A (1)** |
| Seen by industry as consensus 3rd-4th rounder; average athlete without plus tool, has been solid in field, but bat (.229-23-203) has predictably lagged. | | | | | | | | | |

**Signed to major league contract. †Signed with Rangers after being declared free agent.*

## WAR Heroes

Based on the career WAR (Wins Above Replacement, as calculated by Baseball-Reference.com) numbers achieved by all the players eligible for the 2010 draft, these are the 25 most productive big leaguers through the 2015 season. Numbers in parentheses indicate the round when the player was actually drafted.

| | Player, Pos. | Actual Draft | WAR | Bonus |
|---|---|---|---|---|
| 1. | Chris Sale, lhp | White Sox (1) | 26.2 | $1,656,000 |
| 2. | Bryce Harper, c | Nationals (1) | 19.8 | $6,250,000 |
| 3. | Manny Machado, ss | Orioles (1) | 17.7 | $5,250,000 |
| 4. | Andrelton Simmons, ss | Braves (2) | 17.2 | $522,000 |
| 5. | Matt Harvey, rhp | Mets (1) | 11.0 | $2,525,000 |
| | Kevin Kiermaier, of | Rays (31) | 11.0 | $75,000 |
| 7. | Adam Eaton, of | Diamondbacks (19) | 9.9 | $35,000 |
| 8. | Drew Smyly, lhp | Tigers (2) | 9.6 | $1,100,000 |
| 9. | Jacob deGrom, rhp | Mets (9) | 8.5 | $95,000 |
| | Christian Yelich, 1b | Marlins (1) | 8.5 | $1,700,000 |
| 11. | Kole Calhoun, of | Angels (8) | 7.5 | $36,000 |
| 12. | Yasmani Grandal, c | Reds (1) | 5.9 | $2,000,000 |
| 13. | Corey Dickerson, of | Rockies (8) | 4.6 | $125,000 |
| 14. | A.J. Griffin, rhp | Athletics (13) | 4.3 | $5,000 |
| 15. | Jake Petricka, rhp | White Sox (2) | 3.5 | $540,000 |
| 16. | Evan Gattis, c | Braves (23) | 3.4 | $1,000 |
| 17. | Drew Pomeranz, lhp | Indians (1) | 3.3 | $2,650,000 |
| | Shawn Tolleson, rhp | Dodgers (30) | 3.3 | $20,000 |
| 19. | Aaron Sanchez, rhp | Blue Jays (1-S) | 3.2 | $775,000 |
| | James Paxton, lhp | Mariners (4) | 3.2 | $942,500 |
| 21. | Noah Syndergaard, rhp | Blue Jays (1-S) | 2.5 | $600,000 |
| 22. | Jedd Gyorko, 2b | Padres (2) | 2.4 | $614,700 |
| 23. | J.T. Realmuto, ss | Marlins (3) | 2.3 | $600,000 |
| 24. | Eddie Rosario, of | Twins (4) | 2.2 | $200,000 |
| | Joc Pederson, of | Dodgers (11) | 2.2 | $600,000 |

first pick, the Pittsburgh Pirates drafted the 6-foot-7, 230-pound Taillon, the latest in a line of hard-throwing righthanders from Texas in the draft era that included Nolan Ryan, Roger Clemens, Kerry Wood and Josh Beckett.

Taillon had established himself as the top pitching prospect in the 2010 draft pool the previous summer in national showcase events. His fastball routinely reached 97-98 mph, and he had a dominating performance against Cuba in the gold medal game at the Pan American Baseball Confederation tournament, effectively a qualifying event for the 2010 World Junior Tournament for teams from the Americas. He beat Cuba, 6-1, striking out a tournament-record 16 in 7⅓ innings. As a senior at The Woodlands High in suburban Houston the following spring, Taillon went 8-1, 1.78 with 21 walks and 114 strikeouts in 62 innings.

It was almost a given that the Harper and Taillon negotiations would draw out until the August deadline. They were not alone. Fifteen other first-round picks remained unsigned in the waning hours before the deadline.

Harper's total guarantee topped the previous record of $9.5 million by a position player, set nine years earlier by Mark Teixeira. The $6.5 million bonus the Pirates gave Taillon was the largest ever for a high school player, and second in value only to the record $7.5 million figure the Nationals gave Strasburg a year earlier.

Even with a concerted effort by the commissioner's office to keep spending down by pressuring teams to adhere to a slotting system and delaying approval of the more significant deals, teams spent a record $195,782,830 on bonuses in 2010. That broke the mark set a year earlier by some $7 million.

Harper's $6.25 million bonus pushed the Nationals' bonus total to $11,927,200, eclipsing the record they set in 2009, when Strasburg's record bonus spiked the final amount to $11,511,500. The Pirates ($11,900,400) and Toronto Blue Jays ($11,594,400) also topped the previous mark, and the Boston Red Sox ($10,664,400) were a fourth team to spend more than $10 million.

While overall spending reached record highs, first-round bonuses experienced a notable dip, to an average of $2,220,966, a 9.1 percent decrease from $2,434,800 a year earlier, and the lowest average since 2007.

Unlike 2009, when 14 bonuses of more than $2 million were paid to first-rounders, just nine such deals were executed a year later. That was due in part to three players in the top half of the first round going unsigned. The San Diego Padres did not reach an agreement with Florida high school righthander Karsten Whitson, the ninth pick overall, and the Milwaukee Brewers didn't come to terms with California prep righthander Dylan Covey, selected 14th. Additionally, the Arizona Diamondbacks did not sign Texas A&M righthander Barret Loux after determining he had pre-existing elbow and shoulder injuries. The Texas Rangers signed Loux about a month later for a bonus of $312,000, after he was declared a free agent by Major League Baseball.

Not only was there a flurry of activity involving first-rounders in the final 24 hours before the deadline, but 79 players overall in the first 10 rounds were unsigned. Once midnight struck, 54 had signed for bonuses totaling $83.8 million, a one-day record spree.

Twenty-one players drafted beyond the first round signed contracts in seven figures, and 78 drafted after the 10th round received bonuses of $100,000 or more. Among the record bonuses: $3.45 million to Florida prep third baseman Nick Castellanos, a supplemental first-round pick of the Detroit Tigers; $2 million to Florida high school righthander A.J. Cole, a fourth-round choice of the Nationals; and $1.45 million to North Carolina prep outfielder Ty Linton, a 14th-round pick by the Diamondbacks.

Aroldis Chapman

In addition to Harper, two other first-round picks got major league contracts. University of Miami catcher Yasmani Grandal (Reds, 12th overall) and Arkansas third baseman Zack Cox (Cardinals, 25th) each received bonuses of $2 million, plus an additional $3.45 million in major league guarantees between them.

On the international front, the Reds signed Cuban lefthander Aroldis Chapman to a six-year, $30.25 million contract on Jan. 10, 2010. He quickly became the hardest-throwing pitcher in

### AT A GLANCE

took Sale 47 days to reach Chicago after he dominated in 12 relief appearances in the minors, posting a 1.93 ERA and striking out 30 in 14 innings.

### One Who Got Away

**BARRET LOUX, RHP, DIAMONDBACKS (1ST ROUND).** Arizona's scouting department wanted to pick **MATT HARVEY** or **CHRIS SALE** with the sixth overall pick, but upper management insisted on Loux. He agreed to a $2 million bonus but a physical revealed shoulder and elbow problems, so the Diamondbacks pulled back their offer. Loux signed with the Rangers after being declared a free agent by Major League Baseball.

### He Was Drafted?

**RUSSELL WILSON, 2B, ROCKIES (4TH ROUND).** Wilson won acclaim for his accomplishments as a quarterback, notably for leading the Seattle Seahawks to victory in Super Bowl 48. He also played three years as an infielder for North Carolina State (.282-5-30 in 106 games), was drafted twice in baseball, and played two years as a second baseman in the Rockies system (.226-5-26 in 93 games) after accepting a $200,000 bonus from Colorado in 2010.

### Did You Know . . .

Seventeen first-round picks, along with 79 selections in the top 10 rounds, remained unsigned as of Aug. 16, the 2010 deadline. Before the day was over, 54 players had signed for bonuses totaling $83.8 million, pushing the sum for all drafted players to a record $194.8 million.

### They Said It

**BRYCE HARPER**, 16, when asked his goals in baseball in a 2010 Sports Illustrated cover story: "Be in the Hall of Fame, definitely. Play in the pinstripes. Be considered the best baseball player who ever lived. I can't wait."

## DRAFT SPOTLIGHT: BRYCE HARPER

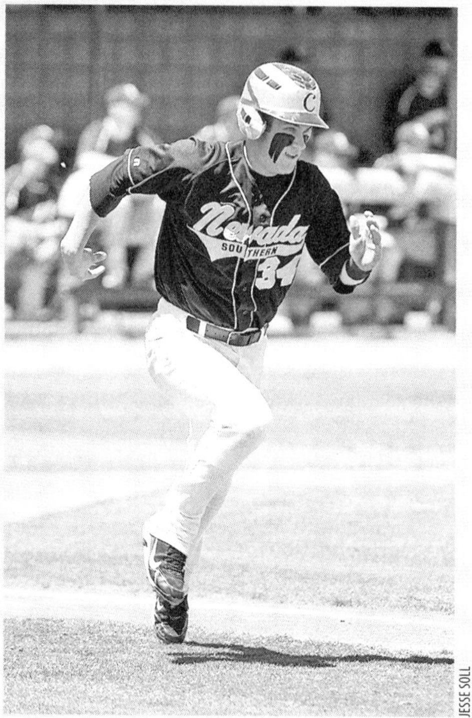

**Bryce Harper dominated his junior college competition in 2010, leading to his selection with the No. 1 overall pick in the draft**

Bryce Harper was so good at such a young age that he played baseball against kids two and three years older in order to have meaningful competition. As a 3-year-old, he played on his 6-year-old brother's tee-ball team. At 10, he played with and against the best 12-year-olds nationally. Almost at every level he played growing up, Harper was the youngest player on the field. And invariably, the best.

Harper dominated the competition as a sophomore at Las Vegas High in 2009, hitting .626 with 14 home runs and 36 stolen bases. As a baseball player, he had little reason to remain in high school. Sports Illustrated had featured him on the cover of the magazine's June 8, 2009, issue, calling him "The Chosen One," and "Baseball's LeBron James."

But at age 16, Harper was at a standstill. He was too young to play in college or turn pro, and playing two more years in high school against inferior competition held no appeal.

Harper had the skills, physique and attitude to perform at a higher level, and he needed the challenge. "High school was a great experience for two years; I loved it," Harper said. "I just want to get out of there where I'm getting walked 40, 50 times a year."

With the guidance of agent Scott Boras, Harper made one of the boldest maneuvers of the draft era, hatching a plan to skip his last two years of high school, earn his GED, and enroll in junior college to become eligible for the 2010 draft a year ahead of schedule.

"He was very bored in school. Maybe it's because he was always around older kids, but he was ready to move on," said Ron Harper, Bryce's father. "College is going to push him academically, and also on the field. He's going to play against a lot of older guys."

The College of Southern Nevada, in Las Vegas, was an ideal fit for Harper. Not only would he be able to live at home, but the Harper family had a long association with head coach Tim Chambers. Brian Harper, Bryce's older brother and a 6-foot-5 lefthander with pro potential himself, planned to transfer to Southern Nevada from Cal State Northridge.

As a 17-year-old, Harper broke a bevy of school and conference records with his explosive lefthanded bat, while transitioning from an aluminum to a wood bat. He homered 31 times in 66 games, 12 more than the entire team had hit the previous season, and 19 more than the previous school record. Harper almost singlehandedly led Southern Nevada to the Junior College World Series, hitting four homers and driving in 10 runs in the regional championship game. He hit .443 and drove in 98 runs for the season.

Harper thrived in all aspects of the game. He displayed superior athletic ability and an ultra-strong throwing arm as a catcher, and his work behind the plate became increasingly more polished. Harper comfortably handled a Southern Nevada staff that featured six pitchers good enough that they might have futures in pro baseball.

"He's really matured," Chambers said. "He's handled a challenging situation very well. His talent is obvious, but the area that has impressed me most is he is no longer showing as much emotion on the field. He has learned to take the game in stride much better.

"Nobody in America knows what it feels like to be him, because it's never been done before. All eyes have been on him all the time, and he's been able to perform. I've known him almost his whole life, and I didn't think he'd do this."

In the face of constant scrutiny from scouts, Harper solidified his standing as a lock to be the No. 1 pick in the 2010 draft, and the Washington Nationals showed no hesitation in taking him with the top selection. By 19, he was the youngest player in the major leagues. He appeared to be a boy among men, but Harper showed no signs of being overmatched or intimidated. After all, he was used to being the youngest player on the field.

major league history with a fastball that reached 105 mph.

Despite the overall downturn in first-round bonuses, the commissioner's office didn't think clubs were doing enough to curb spending, and threatened fines when slot recommendations were not followed. Twenty-eight of the 30 clubs exceeded MLB's bonus guidelines in an least one instance, led by the Blue Jays, who paid 13 players over-slot value. The Atlanta Braves and Minnesota Twins were the only teams that followed the guidelines.

### SALE MAXIMIZES HEAD START

While a majority of the first-round picks were still unsigned on Aug. 6, lefthander Chris Sale, selected 13th overall by the Chicago White Sox, got a significant jump start on his peers by making his big league debut on that date.

Sale had starred the previous summer in the Cape Cod League and was equally dominating as a junior at Florida Gulf Coast University, going 11-0, 2.01 with 146 strikeouts in 103 innings. While most clubs ranked the 6-foot-6 lefty as one of the two best college pitching prospects, he slipped marginally because of questions about his signability. White Sox owner Jerry Reinsdorf, a close ally of commissioner Bud Selig and one of the staunchest proponents for following MLB's bonus recommendations, managed to sign Sale on June 20 for a bonus of $1.656 million.

In exchange for signing quickly and for the slot amount, Sale got a promise that he would get to pitch in the major leagues during the 2010 season. He did, and he did it well, going 2-1, 1.93 with four saves and 32 strikeouts in 23 innings over 21 relief appearances. His ability to throw strikes with three pitches, including a mid-90s fastball, from a deceptive, low three-quarters angle made Sale an instant hit in the majors.

Sale pitched effectively again the next season as a reliever, but the White Sox's plan all along was to use him as a starter. He moved into that role in 2012 and quickly emerged as one of the best starters in the game, as evidenced by four consecutive All-Star Game selections through the 2015 season. At that point, Sale was the most productive major leaguer from the 2010 class, based on career WAR (Wins Above Replacement), followed by Harper.

Louisiana State righthander Anthony Ranaudo entered the 2010 season as a top prospect. He had won the championship game of the 2009 College World Series and was the returning leader in NCAA Division I in wins (12) and strikeouts (159 in 124 innings). But the 6-foot-7 Ranaudo suffered a stress fracture in his pitching elbow in

### Fastest To The Majors

| | Player, Pos. | Drafted (Round) | Debut |
|---|---|---|---|
| 1. | Chris Sale, lhp | White Sox (1) | Aug. 6, 2010 |
| 2. | Josh Spence, lhp | Padres (9) | June 24, 2011 |
| 3. | Bruce Ruffin, rhp | Tigers (1-S) | June 25, 2011 |
| 4. | Addison Reed, rhp | White Sox (3) | Sept. 4, 2011 |
| 5. | Drew Pomeranz, lhp | Indians (1) | Sept. 11, 2011 |

**FIRST HIGH SCHOOL SELECTION:** Manny Machado, ss (Orioles/1, Aug. 9, 2012)

## Top 25 Bonuses

| Player, Pos. | Drafted (Round) | Order | Bonus |
|---|---|---|---|
| 1. * Jameson Taillon, rhp | Pirates (1) | 2 | $6,500,000 |
| **2. Bryce Harper, c** | **Nationals (1)** | **1** | **#$6,250,000** |
| **3. * Manny Machado, ss** | **Orioles (1)** | **3** | **$5,250,000** |
| *** Zach Lee, rhp** | **Dodgers (1)** | **28** | **$5,250,000** |
| **5. * Ryan Castellanos, 3b** | **Tigers (1-S)** | **44** | **$3,450,000** |
| **6. Christian Colon, ss** | **Royals (1)** | **4** | **$2,750,000** |
| **7. Drew Pomeranz, lhp** | **Indians (1)** | **5** | **$2,650,000** |
| **8. Anthony Ranaudo, rhp** | **Red Sox (1-S)** | **39** | **$2,550,000** |
| **9. Matt Harvey, rhp** | **Mets (1)** | **7** | **$2,525,000** |
| **10. * Kaleb Cowart, 3b/rhp** | **Angels (1)** | **18** | **$2,300,000** |
| 11. * Stetson Allie, rhp/3b | Pirates (2) | 52 | $2,250,000 |
| **12. * Delino DeShields, 2b** | **Astros (1)** | **8** | **$2,150,000** |
| **13. Michael Choice, of** | **Athletics (1)** | **10** | **$2,000,000** |
| Deck McGuire, rhp | Blue Jays (1) | 11 | $2,000,000 |
| **Yasmani Grandal, c** | **Reds (1)** | **12** | **#$2,000,000** |
| Zack Cox, 3b | Cardinals (1) | 25 | #$2,000,000 |
| *** A.J. Cole, rhp** | **Nationals (4)** | **116** | **$2,000,000** |
| **18. * Christian Yelich, of** | **Marlins (1)** | **23** | **$1,700,000** |
| **19. Chris Sale, lhp** | **White Sox (1)** | **13** | **$1,656,000** |
| 20. * Josh Sale, of | Rays (1) | 17 | $1,620,000 |
| 21. * Jake Skole, of | Rangers (1) | 15 | $1,557,000 |
| **22. * Luke Jackson, rhp** | **Rangers (1-S)** | **45** | **$1,545,000** |
| 23. * Dickie Joe Thon, ss | Blue Jays (5) | 156 | $1,500,000 |
| **24. Gary Brown, of** | **Giants (1)** | **24** | **$1,450,000** |
| *** Mason Williams, of** | **Yankees (4)** | **145** | **$1,450,000** |

*Major leaguers in bold. *High school selection. #Major league contract.*

his first game of the season and fell out of first-round consideration. The Red Sox, convinced Ranaudo could return to form, drafted him with a supplemental first-round pick and gave him a $2.55 million bonus, the most they spent on a 2010 draft choice.

As Ranaudo faltered, Florida high school shortstop Manny Machado became the third member of a clearly defined big three in the 2010 draft, joining Harper and Taillon. Machado was picked third by the Baltimore Oriole and signed for $5.25 million. Like Alex Rodriguez before him, Machado was a power-hitting shortstop of Dominican descent from a Miami high school. He hit .639 with 12 home runs and 56 RBIs as a senior at Brito Private High, and two years later was in the big leagues as the Orioles third baseman. Machado hit .281 with 68 homers in his first 451 games in the majors, through 2015, and won two Gold Glove awards.

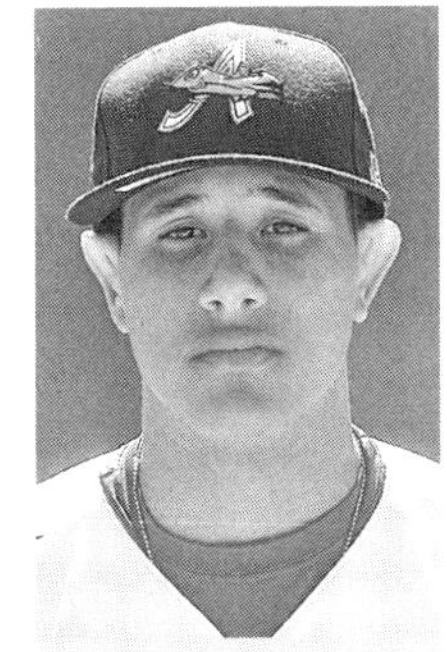

Manny Machado

Harper and Machado justified their selections quickly, reaching the majors in short order and establishing themselves as all-star performers. Taillon's path to the majors was interrupted in 2014, when he suffered an elbow injury during spring training and had Tommy John surgery, and he missed both the 2014 and '15 seasons. Hernia surgery also delayed his comeback in 2015, but he did make his big league debut in 2016—before going on the shelf with a shoulder injury.

Once the first three players came off the 2010 draft board, teams were not certain who would be next.

"Usually you've got a pretty good idea on the morning of the draft the first 10 or 11 picks," said Colorado Rockies scouting director Bill Schmidt. "This year you didn't know who was going where after the first two or three. I think signability really threw the consensus out of whack."

Boras was also a factor in the unpredictable state of the first round. In addition to Harper and Machado, he represented three other first-rounders: University of North Carolina righthander Matt Harvey, and two Cal State Fullerton players, shortstop Christian Colon and outfielder Gary Brown. Boras also represented Ranaudo.

Colon was somewhat of a surprise pick at fourth overall by the Kansas City Royals. A solid but unspectacular player in three years of college, he signed for $2.75 million, little more than half of what Machado received. Colon was attractive to the Royals because of his modest price tag and the expectation he would reach the majors quickly. But his career bogged down in Triple-A, and it was more than four years before he reached the majors, and then only in a utility role. Brown, one of the fastest players in the draft, went 23rd to the San Francisco Giants. He had only seven at-bats to show for his big league career through 2015.

Harvey was selected seventh by the New York Mets. He rebounded from a rough sophomore season at North Carolina and regained his status as an elite pitching prospect, which he had first established in high school. Harvey was developing into one the best starting pitchers in the major leagues in 2013 when he succumbed to Tommy John surgery, and missed the 2014 season. Harvey successfully resumed his career in 2015, helping the Mets advance to the World Series, and was back in the rotation in 2016.

### SURPRISES IN FIRST ROUND

For the second consecutive year, the first round consisted of 32 picks. The Rangers and Tampa Bay Rays were each granted an extra selection as compensation for not signing their 2009 first-round picks, lefthander Matt Purke and outfielder Levon Washington. Washington was selected in the second round in 2010 by the Cleveland Indians.

Through the 2015 season, 16 of the 32 had reached the majors. That number was expected to increase, but for all the success that Harper, Machado, Harvey and Sale, in particular, had enjoyed, the quartet was matched by four first-rounders who were already out of the game.

Six-foot righthander Hayden Simpson was selected by the Chicago Cubs with the 16th pick overall. After agreeing on a predraft, below-slot bonus of $1.06 million, Simpson didn't pitch professionally in 2010. He contracted mononucleosis that cost him 25 pounds on his already lean frame, and had not regained full strength a year later. Simpson's fastball generally resided in the low 80s during the 2011 season, when he went 1-10, 6.27. After failing to regain his velocity, he was released by the Cubs in 2012, with a 5-17, 6.42 record to show for two seasons in the low minors.

One pick after Simpson, Tampa Bay took

### WORTH NOTING

■ The Rays owned the No. 1 pick in the 2007 and 2008 drafts, and the Nationals selected first in both 2009 and 2010. The Astros went them one better, making the first choice in three consecutive drafts from 2012-14. With the No. 1 pick alternating between the American and National Leagues through 2006, the feat never occurred in the first 40 years of the draft's existence.

■ Shortstop **J.T. REALMUTO** set national high school single-season records for hits (88) and RBIs (119), and batted .595 with 28 homers as a senior at Carl Albert High in Midwest City, Okla. Four of his uncles were NCAA wrestling champions at Oklahoma State, including John Smith, who won gold medals in freestyle wrestling in the 1988 and 1992 Olympics. Despite his hitting feats, Realmuto, an Oklahoma State baseball recruit, was relatively unknown nationally, and considered somewhat of a sleeper pick by the Marlins in the third round. Realmuto played shortstop almost exclusively in high school, but the Marlins happened to scout him one day when he was at catcher. They drafted him at that position and signed him for $600,000. Five years later, Realmuto took over the regular catching duties for the Marlins.

■ **BRYCE HARPER** was one of two players who received a predraft grade of 70 (on the 20-80 scouting scale) from the Major League Scouting Bureau. The other was **STETSON ALLIE**, a two-way Ohio high school prospect with one of the top power arms and power bats in the country. He was picked 52nd overall by the Pirates.

■ The Rockies drafted two Atlantic Coast Conference quarterbacks, Clemson's **KYLE PARKER** in the first round and North Carolina State's **RUSSELL WILSON** in the fourth. Both signed contracts—Parker for $1.4 million and Wilson for

CONTINUED ON PAGE 676

## WORTH NOTING

CONTINUED FROM PAGE 675

$200,000—that got them into the Rockies system and also allowed them to continue their college football careers. "Quarterbacks bring some intangibles," said Rockies scouting director Bill Schmidt. "They have leadership skills. They're competitors. They're more about team than self. They see the big picture. You can put them in any environment and they're not going to be fazed after playing in front of some of those college football crowds." The Rockies initially wanted the power-hitting Parker, the first player in NCAA history to hit 20 homers and throw 20 touchdown passes in the same academic year, to agree to a contract that would have compelled him to give up football. For that, he wanted $3 million. The sides compromised at $2.4 million, but didn't reach an agreement before Parker was scheduled to report for fall football practice at Clemson. Two weeks later, at the signing deadline, Parker agreed to the discounted deal that allowed him to play his redshirt sophomore year at Clemson before committing to the Rockies full time. The 6-foot, 205-pound Parker hit 91 homers in the minors before earning an extended trial with the Rockies in 2015. Wilson played parts of two seasons in the Rockies organization, hitting .229 in 93 games. He was a third-round pick of the Seattle Seahawks in the 2012 NFL draft, quit baseball, and developed into a top pro quarterback.

■ Outfielder **RYAN BOLDEN**, a supplemental first-round pick of the Angels (40th overall) and the club's fifth selection overall, retired from baseball in 2013 because of recurring back problems. Less than two years later, a few months after his 23rd birthday, he was shot to death in College Park, Ga., in what began as an argument among children over candy and erupted into violence when adults got involved. Bolden spent four seasons with the Angels without advancing out of Rookie

Washington high school outfielder Josh Sale (pronounced SAH-lay) and signed him for a $1.62 million bonus. He didn't get above Class A in five seasons, hitting a combined .238 with 18 homers, and was suspended on three occasions, twice by Major League Baseball for 50 games for testing positive for drug use in 2012 and '14, and by the Rays for the entire 2013 season for his off-field behavior. Sale's appeal was his bat speed and raw power potential, but he tested the club's resolve from the outset with his immature behavior and arrogant demeanor. The Rays ran out of patience with Sale, releasing him in the spring of 2015.

Kolbrin Vitek, selected 20th by the Red Sox, and Chevy Clarke, the 30th pick and the last of three first-round selections by the Los Angeles Angels, also had brief, unsuccessful careers. Vitek retired after the 2013 season, ending a career that reached Double-A. Clarke was released in 2014 after not advancing past Class A.

The Los Angeles Dodgers and New York Yankees made surprise picks. With the 28th choice, the Dodgers took Texas high school righthander Zach Lee. While he had first-round talent, the 6-foot-4, 195-pound Lee scared off most clubs because he was one of the nation's top quarterback recruits and appeared set on attending Louisiana State. Some thought it might take $6 million to sign Lee, and the Dodgers seemed ill-positioned to pay that much, given the financial troubles of owner Frank McCourt. But Dodgers scouting director Logan White insisted the team planned to sign Lee, even as the player enrolled in summer school classes at LSU.

"We figured he was the best talent on the board, and approached it from that end," said White, whose scouts clocked Lee's fastball at 95-96 mph

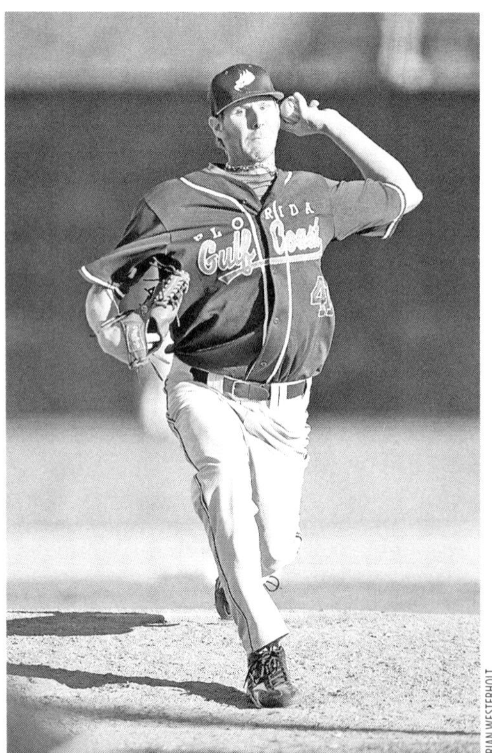

BRIAN WESTERHOLT

**Contrary to many of the top prospects in the 2010 class, Chris Sale signed quickly and was in the big leagues by the end of the season**

### Largest Bonuses By Round

| | Player, Pos. | Club | Bonus |
|---|---|---|---|
| 1. | * Jameson Taillon, rhp | Pirates | $6,500,000 |
| **1-S.** | *** Nick Castellanos, 3b** | **Tigers** | **$3,450,000** |
| 2. | * Stetson Allie, rhp/3b | Pirates | $2,250,000 |
| 3. | * Tony Wolters, ss | Indians | $1,350,000 |
| **4.** | *** A.J. Cole, rhp** | **Nationals** | **$2,000,000** |
| 5. | * Dickie Joe Thon, ss | Blue Jays | $1,500,000 |
| 6. | * Johnny Barbato, rhp | Padres | $1,400,000 |
| 7. | * Ben Wells, rhp | Cubs | $500,000 |
| 8. | * Alex Lavisky, c | Indians | $1,000,000 |
| 9. | * Parker Bridwell, rhp | Orioles | $625,000 |
| **10.** | **Tyler Holt, of** | **Indians** | **$500,000** |
| | * Ben Gamel, of | Yankees | $500,000 |
| **11.** | *** Joc Pederson, of** | **Dodgers** | **$600,000** |
| **12.** | *** Robbie Ray, lhp** | **Nationals** | **$799,000** |
| 13. | Michael Goodnight, rhp | Indians | $315,000 |
| 14. | * Ty Linton, of | Diamondbacks | $1,250,000 |
| 15. | * Will Swanner, c | Rockies | $490,000 |
| 16. | * Jordan Shipers, lhp | Mariners | $800,000 |
| 17. | * Ryan Hafner, rhp | Pirates | $450,000 |
| 18. | Brian Fletcher, of | Royals | $275,000 |
| 19. | * Mark Brown, of | Indians | $125,000 |
| | Tyler Norwood, rhp | Padres | $125,000 |
| 20. | * Kevin Walter, rhp | Phillies | $350,000 |
| 21. | * Jonathan Musser, rhp | Phillies | $350,000 |
| 22. | * Steve Landazuri, rhp | Mariners | $95,000 |
| 23. | * Jared Lakind, 1b | Pirates | $400,000 |
| **24.** | **Erik Goeddel, rhp** | **Mets** | **$350,000** |
| 25. | Rodney Quintero, rhp | Astros | $150,000 |
| Other | * Brian Pointer, of | Phillies (28) | $350,000 |

*Major leaguers in bold. *High school selection.*

late in the spring. "We took him to sign him. Hopefully, he realizes his future is in baseball, and at the end of the day we'll be able to do something."

The day came on the signing deadline, when the Dodgers gave Lee $5.25 million, equaling the third largest bonus in the draft. The amount was more than double the largest bonus in franchise history, although it was payable over five years because of Lee's dual-sport status.

Lee's McKinney (Texas) High teammate, shortstop Matt Lipka, also picked baseball over football. He was a highly regarded wide receiver who caught 22 of Lee's 31 touchdown passes in their senior season and had a football scholarship offer from Alabama. The Braves drafted Lipka in the supplemental first-round after he agreed to a predraft signing bonus of $800,000.

The Yankees, with the 32nd and last pick in the first round, selected high school shortstop Cito Culver, a relatively unknown home-state product. They signed him for $954,000, the only bonus in the first round not in seven figures.

"He wasn't one of the 'names,' " said Yankees scouting director Damon Oppenheimer, "but he's a shortstop with a 65 arm (on the 20-80 scale) and above-average speed, and we liked the way he swung the bat from both sides of the plate." Culver hit .229 with 23 homers in a slow climb through the Yankees system, reaching Triple-A in 2015.

### THREE FIRST-ROUNDERS GO UNSIGNED

With Loux, Whitson and Covey going unsigned, it marked the first time since 1989 that as many as three first-rounders did not reach an agreement. The Diamondbacks spent the sixth overall pick on Loux, a controversial selection from the outset. Most teams considered the 6-foot-5, 220-pound righthander no better than a late first-round or supplemental first-round talent, but Josh Byrnes, Arizona's interim general manager, and Jerry Dipoto, director of player personnel, insisted on drafting Loux because he was willing to accept a below-slot, $2 million bonus. Tom Allison, the club's scouting director, wanted Harvey or Chris Sale. Like others, Allison had concerns about the long-term health of Loux's arm.

Though he appeared healthy during his junior season at Texas A&M, going 11-2, 2.83 with 136 strikeouts in 105 innings, Loux failed his Diamondbacks physical, and the team pulled back its contract offer. The exam showed that Loux had a torn labrum in his shoulder, in addition to a damaged elbow that might need Tommy John surgery.

Recognizing that Loux was in a difficult situation—unable to pitch again in college because he had signed with an agent—MLB took the unprecedented step of declaring him a free agent on Sept. 1. He signed with the Rangers less than three months later for substantially less than what he had agreed to with the Diamondbacks. To avoid a similar situation, the next Collective Bargaining Agreement called for mandatory physical exams for the top 200 prospects prior to the draft. Draft picks who failed a physical and did not receive an offer of at least 40 percent of the assigned value for their slot would be declared free agents.

JOHN WILLIAMSON

Barret Loux

Loux spent two injury-free seasons in the Rangers organization, going 14-1, 3.47 in the Double-A Texas League in 2012. After being traded to the Cubs, he developed elbow problems, had Tommy John surgery, and missed all of the 2014 season and most of 2015. Including Loux, the Rangers signed five of the first 49 selections in the 2010 draft. The team also signed its first 20 selections, the best rate that year.

In perhaps the most shocking development on deadline day, Covey agreed to a $2 million bonus with the Brewers, only for the team to nullify the contract after his physical exam revealed he had Type 1 diabetes. Instead, Covey attended the University of San Diego, close to his home, and went 12-10, 4.78 over three seasons. He was drafted in the fourth round in 2013 by the Oakland A's and signed for $370,000. In three seasons in the A's system, none above Class A, Covey went 16-24, 4.39.

Whitson failed to come to terms with San Diego after the sides disputed the parameters they had agreed to before the draft. The Padres increased their offer to $2.75 million at the deadline, matching what the Royals paid Colon, the No. 4 choice. But Whitson, the consensus second-best high school pitching prospect in the draft pool, after Taillon, opted to attend college at Florida. He went 8-1, 2.40 with 92 strikeouts in 97 innings as a freshman, but Whitson's performance deteriorated in 2012, and he missed the 2013 season while recovering from shoulder surgery. He was drafted by the Nationals in the 37th round in 2013 but returned to college, and was drafted a third time, going to the Red Sox in 2014 in the 11th round and signing for $100,000. Whitson did not win a game in his first two pro seasons.

### BIG BONUSES IN LATER ROUNDS

In addition to record amounts for Harper and fourth-round pick Cole, the Nationals gave University of San Diego lefthander Sammy Solis, their second-round choice, a $1 million signing bonus and signed 12th-rounder Robbie Ray, a lefthander, for $799,000.

Besides Taillon, the Pirates made substantial investments in their second-round pick Stetson Allie ($2.25 million), an Ohio high school player with significant two-way ability, along with 15th-rounder Andrew Maggi ($468,000), 17th-rounder Ryan Hafner ($450,000) and 23rd-rounder Jared Lakind ($400,000).

Taillon and Allie gave the Pirates two of the most electric arms in the draft, if not necessarily the most polished. Allie, a righthander, was projected to be among the first 10 picks when his fastball peaked at 100 mph during his senior season, but his stock dropped, and he was available when the Pirates made the 52nd overall selection. The Pirates also signed the top-rated pitcher on the international market, 16-year-old Luis Heredia, a 6-foot-6 righthander from Mexico, giving him a $2.6 million bonus. The Pirates previously had not spent more than $400,000 on a foreign player.

## One Team's Draft: Toronto Blue Jays

| Player, Pos. | Bonus | Player, Pos. | Bonus | Player, Pos. | Bonus |
|---|---|---|---|---|---|
| 1. Deck McGuire, rhp | $2,000,000 | **6. Sean Nolin, lhp** | **$175,000** | 17. * Myles Jaye, rhp | $250,000 |
| **1. * Aaron Sanchez, rhp** | **$775,000** | 7. * Mitchell Taylor, lhp | $367,500 | **18. * Kris Bryant, 3b** | **Did not sign** |
| **1. * Noah Syndergaard, rhp** | **$600,000** | 8. * Logan Ehlers, lhp | Did not sign | 19. Travis Garrett, rhp | $100,000 |
| **1. Asher Wojciechowski, rhp** | **$815,400** | 9. * Brandon Mims, ss | $230,000 | 20. Art Charles, lhp | $90,000 |
| 2. * Griffin Murphy, lhp | $800,000 | 10. * Tyler Shreve, rhp | Did not sign | 21. Chris Marlowe, rhp | Did not sign |
| 2. * Kellen Sweeney, 3b | $600,000 | 11. * Shane Opitz, ss | $225,000 | 22. Aaron Westlake, of | Did not sign |
| **2. * Justin Nicolino, lhp** | **$615,000** | 12. * Omar Cotto, of | Did not sign | 23. * Angel Gomez, of | $90,000 |
| 3. * Chris Hawkins, 3b | $350,000 | 13. * Tyler Painton, lhp | Did not sign | 24. Ronnie Melendez, of | $40,000 |
| 3. Marcus Knecht, of | $250,000 | 14. Dayton Marze, rhp | $112,500 | 25. * Brando Tessar, rhp | Did not sign |
| **4. Sam Dyson, rhp** | **$600,000** | 15. * Zak Adams, lhp | $250,000 | Other* Adaric Kelly (28), rhp | $250,000 |
| 5. * Dickie Joe Thon, ss | $1,500,000 | **16. * Dalton Pompey, of** | **$150,000** | | |

*Major leaguers in bold. *High school selection.*

## WORTH NOTING

ball, hitting.164 with three homers in 112 games. A Mississippi high school product, he received an $829,800 signing bonus.

■ Outfielder **WAGNER MATEO**, one of the top international prospects in 2009, signed with the Diamondbacks a year later for $512,000. The signing ended a long saga for the 17-year-old Mateo, who had originally agreed to terms with the Cardinals for a $3.1 million bonus, only for the deal to fall apart when he did not pass his physical exam because of a vision issue.

■ South Carolina won the first of two consecutive College World Series titles in 2010, beating UCLA in two games in the best-of-three championship series. The Gamecocks (50-16) got stellar pitching from sophomore lefthander Michael Roth (1-0, 1.10 ERA) and redshirt freshman Matt Price (2-0, 0.93), along with an MVP performance from sophomore outfielder Jackie Bradley Jr. (.368-13-60 for the season). None were eligible for the 2010 draft, and the Gamecocks had only one player selected in the first eight rounds, righthander **SAM DYSON** in the fourth round, and seven picks total. UCLA led all schools with 11 players drafted. The Bruins' best prospects, righthanders Gerrit Cole and Trevor Bauer, also were not eligible for the draft until 2011, when Cole was drafted first overall and Bauer third.

■ The Blue Jays were the biggest spenders in the 2010 draft. They had six extra picks, three for the loss of major league free agents and three for not signing premium picks in the 2009 draft. Toronto showed little regard for the slot recommendations of the commissioner's office. In addition to signing their top pick, Georgia Tech righthander **DECK MCGUIRE**, for $2 million, they spent $1.5 million on fifth-rounder **DICKIE JOE THON**, and at least $100,000 on eight picks beyond the 10th round.

## IN FOCUS: HAYDEN SIMPSON

Hayden Simpson went 35-2, 2.39 in three years at NCAA Division-II Southern Arkansas. He began to generate significant interest from scouts during his junior season, when his fastball reached the high 90s. But perhaps no one was more stunned by his selection by the Cubs in the first round of the 2010 draft than the 6-foot righthander. "I was with a couple of my friends and family," he said. "We were just sitting there, watching the draft. When I heard my name called, everyone was shocked. Then it got real crazy from there."

Simpson's small frame, unorthodox delivery and wide array of pitches reminded the Cubs of 2009 National League Cy Young Award winner Tim Linecum.

"He's got big stuff," Cubs scouting director Tim Wilken said. "He's been a winner, he's stronger than his size, very athletic. He has four average to plus-average pitches, and command, control, and feel to match his stuff."

Simpson didn't pitch in 2010 after contracting mononucleosis and losing 25 pounds. He still hadn't regained full strength a year later, and with his fastball in the low 80s, he went 1-10, 6.27. Simpson's velocity did not return to its college levels in 2012, either, and the Cubs released him after the season. He had a 5-17, 6.42 record to show for two years in the minors.

Neither Taillon, Allie nor Heredia had played in a major league game by the end of the 2015 season. Allie's control problems became so acute in 2012 that he became a position player. In 411 games as a first baseman/outfielder through 2015, he homered 62 times, but also struck out at a high rate. Heredia did not make it out of Class A, plagued by control problems and subpar conditioning.

The Red Sox signed their first two picks, Vitek ($1.359 million) and Bryce Brentz ($889,200), for slot money, but showed little restraint in signing Ranaudo for $2.55 million; third-rounder Sean Coyle for $1.3 million; fourth-rounder Garin Cecchini for $1.31 million; sixth-rounder Kendrick Perkins for $628,000; and 11th-rounder Lucas LeBlanc for $500,000.

Like the Red Sox, the Indians agreed to four million-dollar bonuses. They signed lefthander Drew Pomeranz, their first-round selection and the fifth overall pick, for $2.65 million; Washington, their second-rounder, for $1.2 million; third-rounder Tony Wolters for $1.35 million; and eighth-rounder Alex Lavisky for $1 million.

### GEORGIA ON MY MIND

The state of Georgia developed into fertile ground for talent in the 2000s. Shortstop Tim Beckham of Griffin High was the No. 1 overall pick in 2008, one of seven players from Georgia drafted in the first three rounds. That paled in comparison with 2010, when five Georgia prep players were selected in the first round and 12 in the top three rounds. The Angels took three Georgians in the first round, most notably Cook County High two-way standout Kaleb Cowart, Baseball's America's High School Player of the Year.

Cowart was the 18th pick, after hitting .654 with 11 homers and 36 stolen bases as a switch-hitting third baseman, and posting a 10-1, 1.05 record on the mound. Many scouts favored the 6-foot-3, 190-pound Cowart as a pitcher because of a fastball that touched 95 mph, but he wanted to play every day. The Angels agreed, and signed Cowart for $2.3 million. He struggled to gain a foothold as a power hitter in the Angels organization, hitting 44 home runs in six seasons, but Cowart got to the major leagues in 2015.

JESSEE SOLL

Kaleb Cowart

The Angels' other first-round selections from Georgia were righthander Cam Bedrosian (29th overall) and Clark (30th). The remaining Georgian first-rounders were outfielder Delino DeShields Jr. (Astros, eighth overall) and outfielder Jake Skole (Rangers, 15th).

DeShields and Bedrosian were sons of former major leaguers. DeShields was among the fastest and most athletic players in the draft, and Bedrosian was one of the hardest throwers. The Astros tried to develop DeShields as a second baseman, the same position his father, also named Delino, played for 13 years in the majors, but lost him to the Rangers in the 2014 Rule 5 draft. Shifted to center field by the Rangers, DeShields emerged as a solid big leaguer. Bedrosian made it to the major leagues in 2014 as a relief pitcher.

## Highest Unsigned Picks

| Player, Pos., Team (Round) | College | Re-Drafted |
|---|---|---|
| Barret Loux, rhp, Diamondbacks (1) | None | #Signed |
| Karsten Whitson, rhp, Padres (1) | Florida | Nationals '13 (37) |
| Dylan Covey, rhp, Brewers (1) | San Diego | Athletics '13 (4) |
| Ryne Stanek, rhp, Mariners (3) | Arkansas | Rays '13 (1) |
| Matt Grimes, rhp, White Sox (4) | Georgia Tech | Phillies '13 (31) |
| Austin Wood, rhp, Rays (4) | USC | Angels '11 (6) |
| Cole Green, rhp, Tigers (4) | * Texas | Reds '11 (9) |
| Andrew Toles, of, Marlins (4) | Chipola (Fla.) JC | Rays '12 (3) |
| Scott Frazier, rhp, Phillies (5) | Pepperdine | Cubs '13 (6) |
| Jesus Valdez, rhp, Angels (5) | Oxnard (Calif.) CC | Dodgers '11 (17) |

**TOTAL UNSIGNED PICKS:** Top 5 Rounds (10), Top 10 Rounds (26)

**Returned to same school. #Declared free agent; signed by Rangers.*

### STRENGTH IN JUNIOR COLLEGE RANKS

Starting with Harper as the No. 1 overall pick, eight players from the junior college ranks were selected before the end of the third round, and 29 in the first 10 rounds.

Washington, who didn't strike a deal with the Rays as a 2009 first-round choice and instead went to Chipola (Fla.) JC, was a 2010 second-round choice of the Indians and signed for $1.2 million. Western Oklahoma State shortstop Andrelton Simmons also was picked in the second round, going to the Braves and signing for $522,000. Simmons developed in one of the best defensive shortstops in the major leagues.

Once Simmons got to Western Oklahoma State from Curacao, he quickly impressed scouts with his powerful arm and athletic actions at shortstop. He also showed promise as a pitcher, throwing a fastball at 93-95 mph, but most teams viewed his future at shortstop.

Lefthander James Paxton, a top prospect from Canada, took a circuitous route into professional baseball. A supplemental first-round choice of the Blue Jays in 2009, he sought a $1.35 million signing bonus. When Toronto would go no higher than $1 million, Paxton intended to return to the University of Kentucky for his senior year. However, Blue Jays president Paul Beeston let it slip to a Toronto newspaper that the team had negotiated with Boras, Paxton's agent, a violation of NCAA rules. Kentucky wouldn't allow Paxton back on its baseball team until he submitted to an NCAA interview. He refused, and when he couldn't get a temporary injunction in Kentucky courts, Paxton dropped out of college and signed to pitch in the independent American Association.

Paxton's stuff wasn't as sharp in 2010 as it had been at Kentucky. His fastball was at 88-93 mph rather than the 93-97 mph he had shown in college, and his curveball did not have as much bite. The Mariners drafted him in the fourth round, and with no deadline on negotiations, the sides did not agree to a deal until March 4, 2011. Paxton's $942,000 bonus was the richest for a Mariners draft pick in 2010.

**Did not sign. Major leaguers in bold, with first and last years noted. Order of selection indicated in parentheses. For the first five rounds, the peak level of each player is noted.*

# 2010 Draft List

## ARIZONA DIAMONDBACKS (6)

1. *Barret Loux, rhp, Texas A&M University.—(AAA)

DRAFT DROP *Declared free agent by Major League Baseball; signed by Rangers (Nov. 18, 2010)*

2. J.R. Bradley, rhp, Nitro (W.Va.) HS.—(AA)
3. Robby Rowland, rhp, Cloverdale (Calif.) HS.—(AA)

DRAFT DROP *Son of Rich Rowland, major leaguer (1990-95)*

4. Kevin Munson, rhp, James Madison University.—(AAA)
5. Cody Wheeler, lhp, Coastal Carolina University.—(AAA)
6. Blake Perry, rhp, Pendleton School, Bradenton, Fla.
7. Jeff Shields, rhp, Chattahoochee Valley (Ala.) CC.
8. Tyler Green, rhp, Brazoswood HS, Clute, Texas.
9. **Zach Walters, ss, University of San Diego.—(2013-15)**
10. Kawika Emsley-Pai, c, Lewis-Clark State (Idaho) College.
11. Mike Freeman, ss, Clemson University.
12. Blake Cooper, rhp, University of South Carolina.
13. *Kevin Ziomek, lhp, Amherst Regional HS, Amherst, Mass.
14. Ty Linton, of, Charlotte Christian HS, Charlotte, N.C.
15. **Mike Bolsinger, rhp, University of Arkansas.—(2014-15)**
16. Westley Moss, of, University of Nevada.
17. Derek Eitel, rhp, Rose-Hulman (Ind.) Institute of Technology.
18. Jimmy Comerota, 1b, Rice University.
19. **Adam Eaton, of, Miami (Ohio) University.—(2012-15)**
20. (void) *Michael Hur, of, UC Riverside.
21. Raoul Torrez, 2b, Arizona State University.
22. Jeremy Erben, rhp, University of Oklahoma.
23. *Roberto Padilla, lhp, Ohlone (Calif.) JC.
24. Stephen Cardullo, 3b, Florida State University.
25. *Matt Talley, lhp, The Citadel.
26. Yazy Arbelo, 1b, Keystone (Pa.) College.
27. Niko Gallego, 2b, UCLA.

DRAFT DROP *Son of Mike Gallego, major leaguer (1985-97)*

28. ***Keith Hessler, lhp, Coastal Carolina University.—(2015)**
29. *Jake Floethe, rhp, Cal State Fullerton.
30. *Ryan Zimmerman, rhp, Northwestern State University.
31. *Steven Sultzbaugh, of, Rice University.
32. Greg Robinson, rhp, Wright State University.
33. (void) *Andrew Whittington, c, Southern Arkansas University.
34. Victor Lara, rhp, Keystone (Pa.) College.
35. *Konner Wade, rhp, Chaparral HS, Scottsdale, Ariz.
36. Justin Hilt, of, Elon University.
37. Michael Weber, 2b, Washington State University.
38. *Matt Roberts, c, Graham (N.C.) HS
39. *Garrett Nash, 3b, Oregon State University.
40. *Ryan Casillas, 1b, Hamilton HS, Chandler, Ariz.
41. *Mike McGee, rhp, Florida State University.
42. Chris Jarrett, of, Anderson (Ind.) University.
43. Tom Belza, 2b, Oklahoma State University.
44. Eric Groff, 3b, Keystone (Pa.) College.
45. Javan Williams, of, Contra Costa (Calif.) JC.
46. *Jorge Flores, ss, Hamilton HS, Chandler, Ariz.
47. Casey Upperman, rhp, Yavapai (Ariz.) JC.
48. *Kenny Sigman, rhp, South Mountain (Ariz.) CC.
49. *Tad Barton, rhp, Muhlenberg HS, Laureldale, Pa.

DRAFT DROP *Son of Shawn Barton, major leaguer (1992-96)*

50. *Trey Ford, 3b, South Mountain (Ariz.) CC.

## ATLANTA BRAVES (19)

1. (Choice to Red Sox as compensation for Type A free agent Billy Wagner)
1. Matt Lipka, ss, McKinney (Texas) HS (Supplemental choice--35th—as compensation for Type A free agent Mike Gonzalez).—(AA)
2. **Todd Cunningham, of, Jacksonville State University** (Choice from Orioles as compensation for Gonzalez).**—(2013-15)**
2. **Andrelton Simmons, ss-rhp, Western Oklahoma State JC.—(2012-15)**
3. Joe Leonard, 3b, University of Pittsburgh.—(AAA)
4. Dave Filak, rhp, SUNY Oneonta.—(Low A)
5. **Phil Gosselin, 2b, University of Virginia.—(2013-15)**
6. **Joey Terdoslavich, 3b, Long Beach State University.—(2013-15)**
7. Matt Suschak, rhp, University of Toledo.
8. Kurt Fleming, of, St. Christopher's HS, Richmond, Va.
9. David Rohm, 1b, Fresno (Calif.) CC.
10. Matt Lewis, rhp, UC Davis.
11. **Chasen Shreve, lhp, CC of Southern Nevada.—(2014-15)**
12. Barrett Kleinknecht, ss, Francis Marion (S.C.) University.
13. **Brandon Drury, ss, Grants Pass (Ore.) HS.—(2015)**
14. Richie Tate, rhp, Market Tree (Ark.) HS.
15. Cory Brownsten, c, University of Pittsburgh.
16. Dan Winnie, rhp, Lackawanna (Pa.) JC.
17. *Stefan Sabol, c, Aliso Niguel HS, Aliso Viejo, Calif.
18. *Zach Alvord, 2b, South Forsyth HS, Cumming, Ga.
19. Tyler Hess, rhp, Sonoma State (Calif.) University.
20. Jason Mowry, of, St. Petersburg (Fla.) JC.
21. William Beckwith, 1b, Wallace State (Ala.) CC.
22. *Jordan Buckley, of, New Mexico JC.
23. **Evan Gattis, c, University of Texas-Permian Basin.—(2013-15)**
24. Evan Danieli, rhp, University of Notre Dame.
25. Dan Jurik, rhp, St. John Fisher (N.Y.) College.
26. Jonathan Burns, rhp, St. Edward's (Texas) University.
27. Willie Kempf, rhp, Baylor University.
28. Kyle Mertins, rhp, Cal State Fullerton.
29. *Reid Roper, ss, Harrisburg (Ill.) HS.
30. Kenny Fleming, of, Shelton State (Ala.) CC.
31. *Jack Reinheimer, ss, Ardrey Kell HS, Charlotte, N.C.
32. Ryan Delgado, c, Azusa Pacific (Calif.) University.
33. *Albert Minnis, lhp, Lawrence (Kan.) HS.
34. Matt Fouch, lhp, U.S. Military Academy.
35. *Kenny Swab, c, University of Virginia.
36. Jarred Frierson, 2b, University of Nevada-Las Vegas.
37. *Kollin Dowdy, of, Harrisburg (Ill.) HS.
38. *Jake Wark, 1b, Jesuit HS, Beaverton, Ore.
39. Stephen Foster, lhp, Lewis-Clark State (Idaho) College.
40. Ian Marshall, rhp, University of Richmond.
41. *Spencer Jordan, rhp, Florence-Darlington (S.C.) JC.
42. *Ben Waldrip, 1b, Cypress (Calif.) JC.
43. *LeJon Baker, of, Crenshaw HS, Los Angeles.
44. *Ryan Morrow, c, St. Mary's (Texas) University.
45. Joe Lucas, ss, Dakota County Tech (Minn.) JC.
46. *Kendall Logan, of, Copiah-Lincoln (Miss.) JC.
47. Francois LaFreniere, rhp, St. Petersburg (Fla.) JC.
48. *James Mahler, rhp, Salt Lake (Utah) CC.

DRAFT DROP *Son of Mickey Mahler, major leaguer (1977-86) • Nephew of Rick Mahler, major leaguer (1979-91)*

49. *Ryan Turner, rhp, McLennan (Texas) CC.
50. *Cory Gabella, ss, Notre Dame HS, Burlington, Iowa.

## BALTIMORE ORIOLES (3)

1. **Manny Machado, ss, Brito Miami Private HS, Miami.—(2012-15)**

DRAFT DROP *First 2010 high school draft pick to reach majors (Aug. 9, 2012)*

2. (Choice to Braves as compensation for Type A free agent Mike Gonzalez)
3. Dan Klein, rhp, UCLA.—(AA)
4. Trent Mummey, of, Auburn University.—(High A)
5. Connor Narron, ss, Charles B. Aycock HS, Pikeville, N.C.—(High A)

DRAFT DROP *Son of Jerry Narron, major leaguer (1979-87); major league manager (2005-07)*

6. *Dixon Anderson, rhp, University of California.
7. Matt Bywater, lhp, Pepperdine University.
8. Wynston Sawyer, c, Scripps Ranch HS, San Diego.
9. Parker Bridwell, rhp, Hereford (Texas) HS.
10. Clay Schrader, rhp, San Jacinto (Texas) JC.
11. ***Alex Gonzalez, rhp, Boca Raton Community (Fla.) HS.—(2015)**

DRAFT DROP *First-round draft pick (23rd overall), Rangers (2013)*

12. Riley Hornback, of, San Jacinto (Texas) JC.
13. Jeremy Nowak, of, Mount Olive (N.C.) College.
14. Michael Mosby, 3b, Wabash Valley (Ill.) CC.
15. Joe Oliveira, c, University of the Pacific.
16. *Brandon King, of, Fresno (Calif.) CC.
17. David Richardson, of, Hillsborough (Fla.) CC.
18. Sebastian Vader, rhp, San Marcos (Calif.) HS.
19. Ken Wise, rhp, Santa Fe (Fla.) CC.
20. Matt Drummond, lhp, UCLA.
21. **Scott Copeland, rhp, University of Southern Mississippi.—(2015)**
22. Tanner Murphy, c, Mountain Ridge HS, Glendale, Ariz.
23. Chris Clinton, of, Eckerd (Fla.) College.
24. Tim Adleman, rhp, Georgetown University.
25. Vinny Zazueta, ss, Arizona Western JC.
26. Austin Goolsby, c, Embry-Riddle (Fla.) University.
27. *Austin Urban, rhp, Richland HS, Johnstown, Pa.
28. Jaime Esquivel, rhp, South Houston (Texas) HS.
29. Cameron Roth, lhp, UNC Wilmington.
30. Michael Rooney, ss, UNC Wilmington.
31. Adam Gaylord, 3b, Stanford University.
32. *Joe Robinson, rhp, CC of Southern Nevada.
33. Steven Mazur, rhp, University of Notre Dame.
34. Sammie Starr, ss, University of British Columbia.
35. Auburn Donaldson, ss, Southeastern (Fla.) University.
36. Brad Decater, ss, Cal State Northridge.
37. Austin Knight, 2b, Palm Beach (Fla.) CC.
38. Jeremy Shelby, of, Grambling State University.

DRAFT DROP *Son of Johnny Shelby, major leaguer (1981-91)*

39. Travis Strong, rhp, Wildomar, Calif.
40. Joe Velleggia, c, Old Dominion University.
41. *Coty Blanchard, ss, Cherokee County HS, Centre, Ala.
42. Jake Pettit, lhp, Western Oregon University.
43. Blair Dunlap, of, UCLA.
44. Preston Hale, of, University of North Florida.
45. *Nathan Williams, rhp, Scripps Ranch HS, San Diego.
46. *Dan Torres, c, Countryside HS, Clearwater, Fla.
47. Cody Young, of, Anderson (Ind.) University.
48. Alex Schmarzo, rhp, St. Mary's (Calif.) College.
49. *Hayden Jordan, rhp, Whitewater HS, Fayetteville, Ga.
50. *Philip Walby, rhp, Scripps Ranch HS, San Diego.

## BOSTON RED SOX (28)

1. Kolbrin Vitek, 2b-of, Ball State University (Choice from Braves as compensation for Type A free agent Billy Wagner).—(AA)
1. (Choice to Angels as compensation for Type A free agent John Lackey)
1. **Bryce Brentz, of, Middle Tennessee State University** (Supplemental choice—36th—as compensation for Type A free agent Jason Bay).**—(2014)**
1. **Anthony Ranaudo, rhp, Louisiana State University** (Supplemental choice—39th—as compensation for Wagner).**—(2014-15)**
2. **Brandon Workman, rhp, University of Texas** (Choice from Mets as compensation for Bay).**—(2013-14)**
2. (Choice to Blue Jays as compensation for Type A free agent Marco Scutaro)
3. Sean Coyle, ss, Germantown Academy, Fort Washington, Pa.—(AAA)
4. **Garin Cecchini, ss, Albert M. Barbe HS, Lake Charles, La.—(2014-15)**

DRAFT DROP *Brother of Gavin Cecchini, first-round draft pick, Mets (2012)*

5. Henry Ramos, of, Alfonso Casta Martinez HS, Maunabo, P.R.—(AA)
6. Kendrick Perkins, of, La Porte (Texas) HS.
7. Chris Hernandez, lhp, University of Miami.
8. Matt Price, rhp, Virginia Tech.
9. *Tyler Barnette, rhp, Hickory (N.C.) HS.
10. Jacob Dahlstrand, rhp, Memorial HS, Houston.
11. Lucas LeBlanc, of, Delgado (La.) JC.
12. Garrett Rau, rhp, California Baptist University.
13. Keith Couch, rhp, Adelphi (N.Y.) College.
14. *Mike Hollenbeck, c, Joliet Township (Ill.) HS.
15. *Steve Wilkerson, ss, Pope HS, Marietta, Ga.
16. *Adam Duke, rhp, Spanish Fork (Utah) HS.
17. **Jason Garcia, rhp, Land O'Lakes (Fla.) HS.—(2015)**
18. *Dallas Chadwick, rhp, Shasta HS, Redding, Calif.
19. *Eric Jaffe, rhp, Bishop O'Dowd HS, Oakland.
20. *Rock Shoulders, c, Brandon (Fla.) HS.
21. *Mason Justice, rhp, Holland Hall, Tulsa, Okla.
22. *Trace Tam Sing, 2b, Newport HS, Bellevue, Wash.
23. *Austin Wright, lhp, Chipola (Fla.) JC.
24. *Sean Yost, rhp, University of Nebraska.
25. Tyler Lockwood, rhp, Texas Christian University.
26. *Dillon Overton, lhp, Weatherford (Okla.) HS.
27. *Jay Gonzalez, of, Freedom HS, Orlando, Fla.
28. *Mike Wagner, rhp, Centennial HS, Las Vegas, Nev.
29. *Paul Davis, rhp, Pensacola (Fla.) JC.
30. *DeSean Anderson, of, Ragsdale HS, Jamestown, N.C.
31. *Hunter Renfroe, c, Copiah Academy, Gallman, Miss.

DRAFT DROP *First-round draft pick (13th overall), Padres (2013)*

32. *Jordan Alexander, of, Vista (Calif.) HS.
33. *Mark Donham, rhp, Jupiter (Fla.) Community HS.
34. Mike Gleason, rhp, Cal State Chico.
35. *J.T. Riddle, ss, Western Hills HS, Frankfort, Ky.
36. *Shane Rowland, c, Tampa Catholic HS, Tampa.
37. *Aaron Jones, c, San Clemente (Calif.) HS.
38. *Tom Bourdon, of, Northwest Catholic HS, West Hartford, Conn.
39. Nick Robinson, ss, North Central (Ill.) College.
40. Luke Yoder, of, Cal Poly.
41. Jayson Hernandez, c, Rutgers University.
42. *Dan Slania, rhp, Salpointe Catholic HS, Tucson, Ariz.
43. *Pat Smith, of, Redan HS, Stone Mountain, Ga.
44. Zach Kapstein, c, Tiverton (R.I.) HS.
45. James Kang, ss, Pomona-Pitzer (Calif.) College.
46. *Drake Thomason, rhp, Eastside HS, Taylors, S.C.
47. *David Roseboom, lhp, La Salle Institute, Troy, N.Y.
48. *J.T. Autrey, rhp, Stephenville (Texas) HS.
49. Trygg Larsson-Danforth, 1b, Yale University.
50. *Weston Hoekel, rhp, Bishop Kenny HS, Jacksonville, Fla.

## CHICAGO CUBS (15)

1. Hayden Simpson, rhp, Southern Arkansas University.—(High A)
2. Reggie Golden, of, Wetumpka (Ala.) HS.—(Low A)
3. Micah Gibbs, c, Louisiana State University.—(AAA)
4. Hunter Ackerman, lhp, Louisburg (N.C.) JC.—(Short-season A)
5. **Matt Szczur, of, Villanova University.—(2014-15)**
6. *Ivan DeJesus, of, Cupeyville School, San Juan, P.R.
7. Ben Wells, rhp, Bryant (Ark.) HS.
8. Cam Greathouse, lhp, Gulf Coast (Fla.) CC.
9. Kevin Rhoderick, rhp, Oregon State University.
10. Aaron Kurcz, rhp, CC of Southern Nevada.
11. **Eric Jokisch, lhp, Northwestern University.—(2014)**
12. Austin Reed, rhp, Rancho Cucamonga (Calif.) HS.
13. Pierre LePage, 2b, University of Connecticut.
14. Colin Richardson, rhp, Winter Haven (Fla.) HS.
15. Elliot Soto, ss, Creighton University.
16. Ryan Hartman, rhp, Mount Zion (Ill.) HS.
17. *Steven Brooks, of, Wake Forest University.
18. *Brooks Pinckard, of-rhp, Baylor University.
19. Dustin Fitzgerald, rhp, Hill (Texas) JC.
20. Ryan Cuneo, 1b, University of Delaware.
21. *Cody Cox, rhp, Grassfield HS, Chesapeake, Va.
22. Jeff Vigurs, c, Bryant University.
23. Matt Loosen, rhp, Jacksonville University.
24. Dustin Geiger, of, Merritt Island (Fla.) HS.
25. Eric Rice, rhp, Palm Beach (Fla.) CC.
26. ***Danny Muno, ss, Fresno State University.—(2015)**

27. *Bryan Harper, lhp, CC of Southern Nevada.
DRAFT DROP *Brother of Bryce Harper, first overall draft pick, Nationals (2010)*
28. Joe Zeller, rhp, The Master's (Calif.) College.
29. Casey Harman, lhp, Clemson University.
30. *Karsten Strieby, 1b, Arizona Western JC.
31. *Benito Santiago, 1b, Lon Morris (Texas) JC.
DRAFT DROP *Son of Benito Santiago, major leaguer (1986-2005)*
32. Brent Ebinger, lhp, Lambuth (Tenn.) University.
**33. *Matt Stites, rhp, Jefferson (Mo.) CC.—(2014-15)**
34. Dustin Harrington, 3b, East Carolina University.
35. *Chris Anderson, rhp, Centennial HS, Circle Pines, Minn.
DRAFT DROP *First-round draft pick (18th overall), Dodgers (2013)*
36. *Tyler Bremer, rhp, Yavapai (Ariz.) JC.
37. Chad Noble, c, Northwestern University.
38. *Jeremy Fitzgerald, rhp, Patrick Henry (Va.) CC.
39. *Casey Lucchese, rhp, College of Charleston.
40. Brian Smith, lhp, St. Mary Catholic SS, Pickering, Ontario.
**41. Dallas Beeler, rhp, Oral Roberts University.—(2014-15)**
42. *Trey Nielsen, rhp, Skyline HS, Salt Lake City.
DRAFT DROP *Son of Scott Nielsen, major leaguer (1986-89)*
**43. *Dan Winkler, rhp, Parkland (Ill.) JC.—(2015)**
44. *Jake Rogers, 1b, St. Petersburg (Fla.) JC
45. *Devon Austin, c, Coeur d'Alene (Idaho) HS.
**46. *Jerad Eickhoff, rhp, Olney Central (Ill.) JC.—(2015)**
47. *Clayton Crum, rhp, Klein HS, Spring, Texas.
48. *Eric Paulson, 3b, William Fremd HS, Palatine, Ill.
49. Bryce Shafer, rhp, Valparaiso University.
50. *Eric Jagielo, ss, Downers Grove (Ill.) North HS.
DRAFT DROP *First-round draft pick (26th overall), Yankees (2013)*

## CHICAGO WHITE SOX (13)

**1. Chris Sale, lhp, Florida Gulf Coast University.—(2010-15)**
DRAFT DROP *First player from 2010 draft to reach majors (Aug. 6, 2010)*
**2. Jake Petricka, rhp, Indiana State University.—(2013-15)**
**3. Addison Reed, rhp, San Diego State University.—(2011-15)**
3. Thomas Royse, rhp, University of Louisville (Special compensation—114th—for failure to sign 2009 third-round pick Bryan Morgado).—(Rookie)
4. *Matt Grimes, rhp, Mill Creek HS, Hoschton, Ga.—(Low A)
DRAFT DROP *Attended Georgia Tech; re-drafted by Phillies, 2013 (31st round)*
**5. Andy Wilkins, 1b, University of Arkansas.—(2014)**
6. Rangel Ravelo, 3b, Hialeah (Fla.) HS.
**7. Tyler Saladino, ss, Oral Roberts University.—(2015)**
8. *Joe Terry, 2b, Cerritos (Calif.) JC.
9. Kevin Moran, rhp, Boston College.
10. Ross Wilson, 2b, University of Alabama.
DRAFT DROP *Brother of John Parker Wilson, quarterback, National Football League (2009-12)*
11. *James McDonald, ss, Chaparral HS, Phoenix.
12. Drew Lee, ss, Morehead State University.
13. Ethan Icard, rhp, Wilkes (N.C.) CC.
14. Mike Blanke, c, University of Tampa.
15. Sean O'Connell, c, Chatsworth (Calif.) HS.
16. Stephen McCray, rhp, University of Tennessee.
17. Mike Schwartz, 1b, University of Tampa.
18. Randall Thorpe, of, San Jacinto (Texas) JC.
19. Doug Murray, rhp, University of San Francisco.
20. Jose Ramos, c, Western Oklahoma State JC.
21. *Tyler Jones, rhp, Madison Area Technical (Wis.) JC.
22. *Ozney Guillen, of, Monsignor Pace HS, Opa-Locka, Fla.
DRAFT DROP *Son of Ozzie Guillen, major leaguer (1985-2000); major league manager (2004-12)*
23. Austin Evans, rhp, University of Tampa.
24. Jordan Keegan, of, CC of Southern Nevada.
25. Ethan Wilson, ss, Indiana University.
26. Kevin Rath, lhp, Cal State Fullerton.
27. Pete Gehle, lhp, Azusa Pacific (Calif.) University.
28. *Tom Windle, lhp, Osseo (Minn.) HS.
29. Michael Earley, of, Indiana University.
30. *Kylin Turnbull, lhp, Santa Barbara (Calif.) CC.
31. Robert Young, lhp, Dartmouth University.
32. Jarrett Casey, lhp, University of Northern Kentucky.
33. Jamaal Hollis, rhp, Miami (Ohio) University.
34. Dusty Harvard, of, Oklahoma State University.
35. John Spatola, of, Boston College.
36. *Ben Griset, lhp, Gustine (Calif.) HS.
37. *Chris Lee, lhp, Robinson HS, Tampa.
38. Brad Salgado, ss, Great Oak HS, Temecula, Calif.
39. *Levi Schlick, lhp, Barton County (Kan.) CC.
40. *Conrad Gregor, of, Carmel (Ind.) HS.
41. Sam Phippen, rhp, UC Santa Barbara.
42. Brett Bruening, rhp, Texas Tech.
43. *Luke Irvine, rhp, Northwestern State University.
44. *Matt Chavez, rhp, University of San Francisco.
45. *Ronald Cotton, of, Boone County HS, Florence, Ky.
46. *Ronzelle Fort, lhp, Harlan HS, Chicago.
47. *Matt Reida, 2b, Western HS, Russiaville, Ind.
48. *Audry Santana, 2b, Mariner HS, Cape Coral, Fla.
DRAFT DROP *Son of Rafael Santana, major leaguer (1983-90)*
49. Pat Schatz, rhp, University of Iowa.
50. *David Vazquez, 2b, Archbishop McCarthy HS, Southwest Ranches, Fla.

## CINCINNATI REDS (12)

**1. Yasmani Grandal, c, University of Miami.—(2012-15)**
**2. Ryan LaMarre, of, University of Michigan.—(2015)**
3. Devin Lohman, ss, Long Beach State University.—(AAA)
4. Brodie Greene, 2b, Texas A&M University.—(AA)
5. Wes Mugarian, rhp, Pensacola Catholic HS, Pensacola, Fla.—(High A)
6. Drew Cisco, rhp, Wando HS, Mount Pleasant, S.C.
DRAFT DROP *Grandson of Galen Cisco, major leaguer (1961-69)*
7. Tony Amezcua, rhp, Bellflower (Calif.) HS.
8. David Vidal, 3b, Miami-Dade JC.
9. Tanner Robles, lhp, Oregon State University.
10. Kevin Arico, rhp, University of Virginia.
11. Drew Hayes, rhp, Vanderbilt University.
**12. Kyle Waldrop, of, Riverdale HS, Fort Myers, Fla.—(2015)**
13. Lucas O'Rear, rhp, University of Northern Iowa.
14. Dan Wolford, rhp, University of California.
15. Stephen Hunt, lhp, University of South Florida.
16. *Rob Kral, c, College of Charleston.
17. *Brent Peterson, ss, Liberty HS, Bakersfield, Calif.
18. Robert Maddox, of, Ohio University.
19. *Josh Alexander, of, Mountain Pointe HS, Phoenix.
20. Chris Berset, c, University of Michigan.
**21. Josh Smith, rhp, Lipscomb University.—(2015)**
22. Kurt Muller, of, University of Iowa.
23. *Randy Fontanez, rhp, University of South Florida.
24. Pat Doyle, rhp, Missouri State University.
25. Daniel Renken, rhp, Cal State Fullerton.
26. *Ty Stuckey, lhp, University of Houston.
27. Joel Bender, lhp, Oak Hills HS, Cincinnati.
28. Chad Rogers, rhp, Galveston (Texas) CC.
29. Adam Muenster, 3b, Kansas State University.
30. *Brad Hendrix, rhp, Auburn University.
31. Dominic D'Anna, 1b, Cal State Northridge.
32. Jaren Matthews, 1b, Rutgers University.
33. *David Garner, rhp, Niles (Mich.) HS.
34. Brandon Dailey, ss, Pauline Johnson SS, Brantford, Ontario.
**35. *Tyler Wilson, rhp, University of Virginia.—(2015)**
36. *Chuck Ghysels, rhp, Lincoln Trail (Ill.) CC.
37. *Nick Sawyer, rhp, Hebron HS, Carrollton, Texas.
38. Matt Leonard, lhp, Cal Poly.
39. *Jacob May, ss, Lakota West HS, West Chester, Ohio.
DRAFT DROP *Grandson of Lee May, major leaguer (1965-82) • Son of Lee May Jr., first-round draft pick, Mets (1986)*
40. *Lee Orr, of, McNeese State University.
41. Jonathan Kaskow, 1b, Stanford University.
42. *Mitchell Hopkins, lhp, LSU-Eunice JC.
43. *Matt Campbell, rhp, University of Florida.
44. *Eddie Campbell, lhp, Bridgewater Raynham HS, Bridgewater, Mass.
45. Will Harford, c, University of Notre Dame.
46. Pat Quinn, rhp, St. Petersburg (Fla.) JC.
47. *Tant Shepherd, 1b, University of Texas.
48. *Kaiana Eldredge, c, Punahou HS, Honolulu, Hawaii.
49. El'Hajj Muhammad, rhp, CC of Morris (N.J.).
50. *Dex Kjerstad, of, Randall HS, Amarillo, Texas.

## CLEVELAND INDIANS (5)

**1. Drew Pomeranz, lhp, University of Mississippi.—(2011-15)**
2. LeVon Washington, of, Chipola (Fla.) JC.—(High A)
DRAFT DROP *First-round draft pick (30th overall), Rays (2009)*
3. Tony Wolters, ss, Rancho Buena Vista HS, Vista, Calif.—(AA)
4. Kyle Blair, rhp, University of San Diego.—(AA)
5. Cole Cook, rhp, Pepperdine University.—(AAA)
DRAFT DROP *Son of Peter MacKenzie, actor*
6. Nick Bartolone, ss, Chabot (Calif.) JC.
7. Robbie Aviles, rhp, Suffern (N.Y.) HS.
DRAFT DROP *Brother of Mike Aviles, major leaguer (2008-15)*
8. Alex Lavisky, c, St. Edward HS, Lakewood, Ohio.
9. Jordan Cooper, rhp, Wichita State University.
**10. Tyler Holt, of, Florida State University.—(2014-15)**
11. Hunter Jones, of, Lakewood (Calif.) HS.
DRAFT DROP *Son of Tracy Jones, first overall draft pick, January 1980/secondary phase, Reds; major leaguer (1986-91)*
12. Tyler Cannon, 3b, University of Virginia.
13. Michael Goodnight, rhp, University of Houston.
14. Diego Seastrunk, c, Rice University.
15. *Ben Wetzler, lhp, Clackamas (Ore.) HS.
**16. *Cody Allen, rhp, St. Petersburg (Fla.) JC.—(2012-15)**
17. Aaron Siliga, of, Oceanside (Calif.) HS.
18. Chase Burnette, 1b, Georgia Tech.
19. Mark Brown, of, King HS, Detroit.
**20. *Burch Smith, rhp, Howard (Texas) JC.—(2013)**
21. Owen Dew, rhp, University of Central Florida.
22. Nate Striz, rhp, University of North Carolina.
23. Tony Dischler, rhp, LSU-Eunice JC.
24. *Andrew Triggs, rhp, University of Southern California.
25. *Jay Gause, rhp, West Brunswick HS, Northwest Shallotte, N.C.
26. *Ben Lively, rhp, Gulf Breeze (Fla.) HS.
27. *Jeff Schaus, of, Clemson University.
28. *DeMarcus Tidwell, of, Yavapai (Ariz.) JC.
29. *Kirby Bellow, lhp, Nederland (Texas) HS.
**30. *Taylor Hill, rhp, Vanderbilt University.—(2014-15)**
**31. *David Goforth, rhp, University of Mississippi.—(2015)**
32. *Michael Palazzone, rhp, University of Georgia.
33. Logan Thompson, 2b, Palm Beach (Fla.) CC.
DRAFT DROP *Son of Robby Thompson, major leaguer (1986-96)*
34. Kyle Petter, lhp, El Camino (Calif.) JC.
35. *Ken Ferrer, rhp, Elon University.
36. *Rye Davis, rhp, Western Kentucky University.
37. *Trey Griffin, of, Martin Luther King HS, Lithonia, Ga.
38. *Tyler Pearson, c, Monterey HS, Lubbock, Texas.
39. *Bobby Wahl, rhp, West Springfield HS, Springfield, Va.
40. Jordan Casas, of, Long Beach State University.
41. Brian Heere, of, University of Kansas.
42. Aaron Fields, 2b, Wright State University.
DRAFT DROP *Son of Bruce Fields, major leaguer (1986-89)*
43. *Chris Waylock, ss, Cary-Grove HS, Cary, Ill.
44. *Brock Stassi, lhp, University of Nevada.
45. *Frank DeJiulio, rhp, Daytona Beach (Fla.) CC.
46. *Justin Haley, rhp, Sierra (Calif.) JC.
47. *Luke Malloy, rhp, Alamo Heights HS, San Antonio, Texas.
48. *C.T. Bradford, of, Pace (Fla.) HS.
49. Mark Bradley, of, Central Arizona JC.
50. Henry Dunn, of, Binghamton University.

## COLORADO ROCKIES (25)

**1. Kyle Parker, of, Clemson University.—(2014-15)**
1. Peter Tago, rhp, Dana Hills HS, Dana Point, Calif. (Supplemental choice—47th—for loss of Type B free agent Jason Marquis).—(AA)
**2. Chad Bettis, rhp, Texas Tech.—(2013-15)**
**3. Josh Rutledge, ss, University of Alabama.—(2012-15)**
4. Russell Wilson, of, North Carolina State University.—(Low A)
DRAFT DROP *Quarterback, National Football League (2012-15)*
5. Josh Slaats, rhp, University of Hawaii.—(High A)
6. Jared Simon, of, University of Tampa.
7. Kraig Sitton, lhp, Oregon State University.
**8. Corey Dickerson, of, Meridian (Miss.) CC.—(2013-15)**
9. Geoff Parker, rhp, Florida State University.
10. Brett Tanos, 2b, Santa Ana (Calif.) JC.
11. *Hommy Rosado, 1b, Alfred M. Barbe HS, Lake Charles, La.
12. Matt Crocker, lhp, University of Texas-San Antonio.
13. Josh Mueller, rhp, Eastern Illinois University.
14. Taylor Reid, rhp, St. Mary's (Calif.) College.
15. Will Swanner, c, La Costa Canyon HS, Carlsbad, Calif.
16. Jayson Langfels, 3b, Eastern Kentucky University.
17. Ryan Casteel, c, Cleveland State (Tenn.) JC.
18. Juan Perez, rhp, Bethune-Cookman College.
19. *Ryan Eades, rhp, Northshore HS, Slidell, La.
20. Blake McDade, 1b, Middle Tennessee State University.
21. *Chris Giovinazzo, of, UCLA.
22. Mark Tracy, c, Duquesne University.
DRAFT DROP *Son of Jim Tracy, major leaguer (1980-81); major league manager (2001-12)*
23. Bruce Kern, rhp, St. John's University.
**24. Christian Bergman, rhp, UC Irvine.—(2014-15)**
**25. Kenny Roberts, lhp, Middle Tennessee State University.—(2015)**
26. *Jacob Tanis, 3b, Mercer University.
27. Blake Keitzman, lhp, Western Oregon University.
28. *Tony Rizzotti, rhp, Martin HS, Arlington, Texas.
**29. *Marco Gonzales, lhp, Rocky Mountain HS, Fort Collins, Colo.—(2014-15)**
DRAFT DROP *First-round draft pick (19th overall), Cardinals (2013)*
30. *Jeff Ames, rhp, Lower Columbia (Wash.) JC.
DRAFT DROP *First-round draft pick (42nd overall), Rays (2011)*
31. Russell Brewer, rhp, Vanderbilt University.
32. *Jason Monda, of, Capital HS, Olympia, Wash.
33. Jordan Ballard, 1b, Virginia Military Institute.
34. *Steve Selsky, of, University of Arizona.
35. *Justin Fradejas, of, Auburn University.
36. *Jimmie Koch, of, Sarasota (Fla.) HS.
37. *Dan Kickham, rhp, Crowder (Mo.) CC.
38. *Logan Davis, ss, Cactus Shadows HS, Cave Creek, Ariz.
DRAFT DROP *Son of Mark Davis, major leaguer (1980-97)*
39. Joel McKeithan, ss, T.C. Roberson HS, Asheville, N.C.
40. *Brandon Brennan, rhp, Capistrano Valley HS, Mission Viejo, Calif.
41. *Ben Mordini, rhp, Cherry Creek HS, Greenwood Village, Colo.
42. *Thomas Pereira, rhp, Indian Hills (Iowa) CC.
43. *Kaleb Barlow, 3b, Jackson (Miss.) Prep.
44. *Kyle Richter, lhp, Santa Margarita HS, Rancho Santa Margarita, Calif.
45. *Mike Benjamin Jr., ss, Basha HS, Gilbert, Ariz.
DRAFT DROP *Son of Mike Benjamin, major leaguer (1989-2002)*
46. *Mitch Horacek, lhp, Thunder Ridge HS, Littleton, Colo.
47. *Landon Appling, of, El Campo (Texas) HS.
48. *Hunter Greenwood, rhp, Franklin HS, Elk Grove, Calif.

49. *Brett Thomas, rhp, Poway (Calif.) HS.
50. *James Dykstra, rhp, Yavapai (Ariz.) JC.

## DETROIT TIGERS (18)

1. (Choice to Astros as compensation for Type A free agent Jose Valverde)
**1. Nick Castellanos, 3b, Archbishop McCarthy HS, Southwest Ranches, Fla.** (Supplemental choice—48th—as compensation for Type B free agent Brandon Lyon).**—(2013-15)**
**1. Chance Ruffin, rhp, University of Texas** (Supplemental choice—48th—as compensation for Type B free agent Fernando Rodney).**—(2011-13)**
DRAFT DROP *Son of Bruce Ruffin, major leaguer (1986-97)*
**2. Drew Smyly, lhp, University of Arkansas.—(2012-15)**
**3. Rob Brantly, c, UC Riverside.—(2012-15)**
4. *Cole Green, rhp, University of Texas.—(Low A)
DRAFT DROP *Returned to Texas; re-drafted by Reds, 2011 (9th round)*
5. Alex Burgos, lhp, State College of Florida-Manatee.—(AAA)
**6. Bryan Holaday, c, Texas Christian University.—(2012-15)**
7. Corey Jones, 2b, Cal State Fullerton.
8. Patrick Leyland, c, Bishop Canevin HS, Pittsburgh.
DRAFT DROP *Son of Jim Leyland, major league manager (1986-2013)*
9. Tony Plagman, 1b, Georgia Tech.
10. Cole Nelson, lhp, Auburn University.
11. *Brian Dupra, rhp, University of Notre Dame.
**12. Kyle Ryan, lhp, Auburndale (Fla.) HS.—(2014-15)**
13. P.J. Polk, of, University of Tennessee.
14. Patrick Cooper, rhp, Bradley University.
15. *Collin Kuhn, of, University of Arkansas.
16. Jordan Pratt, rhp, University of Arkansas.
17. Drew Gagnier, rhp, University of Oregon.
18. Josh Ashenbrenner, 2b, Lewis-Clark State (Idaho) College.
19. Jeff Rowland, of, Georgia Tech.
20. Tyler White, rhp, University of Alabama.
21. James Meador, 1b, University of San Diego.
22. *Jake Hernandez, c, Los Osos HS, Rancho Cucamonga, Calif.
23. *Dominic Ficociello, ss, Fullerton Union HS, Fullerton, Calif.
24. Tyler Clark, rhp, University of Missouri.
25. Shawn Teufel, lhp, Liberty University.
DRAFT DROP *Son of Tim Teufel, major leaguer (1983-93)*
**26. Jeff Ferrell, rhp, Pitt (N.C.) CC.—(2015)**
27. Les Smith, of, Meramec (Mo.) CC.
28. Jack Duffey, lhp, Heritage HS, Newnan, Ga.
29. *Chris Joyce, lhp, Central Arizona JC.
30. Logan Hoch, lhp, Wichita State University.
31. Matt Little, rhp, University of Kentucky.
32. Clay Jones, 1b, University of Alabama.
33. Brennan Smith, rhp, Bowling Green State University.
34. *Nolan Sanburn, of, Kokomo (Ind.) HS.
**35. *Cody Hall, rhp, Southern University.—(2015)**
36. Ryan Soares, ss, George Mason University.
37. *Carlos Lopez, 1b, Cal State Fullerton.
38. *Jake Dziubczynski, lhp, Central Arizona JC.
39. Bo McClendon, of, Valparaiso University.
DRAFT DROP *Son of Lloyd McClendon, major leaguer (1987-94); major league manager (2001-15)*
40. Pete Miller, ss, Trinity International (Ill.) University.
41. Matt Perry, 3b, Holy Cross University.
42. *Kevin Grant, of, Millard West HS, Omaha, Neb.
43. *Blake Bell, rhp, Bishop Carroll Catholic HS, Wichita, Kan.
44. *Ricky Knapp, rhp, Port Charlotte (Fla.) HS.
45. *Jake Morton, c, Hudsonville (Mich.) HS.
46. *Ben Verlander, rhp, Goochland (Va.) HS.
DRAFT DROP *Brother of Justin Verlander, first-round draft pick, Tigers (2004); major leaguer (2005-15)*
47. *Chris Triplett, ss, Sandy Creek HS, Fayetteville, Ga.
48. *Tyler Marincov, of, Timber Creek HS, Orlando, Fla.
49. Tyson Kendrick, c, Tabor (Kan.) College.
50. *Jake Ross, lhp, Wor-Wic (Md.) CC.

## FLORIDA MARLINS (22)

**1. Christian Yelich, of, Westlake HS, Westlake Village, Calif.—(2013-15)**
**2. Rob Rasmussen, lhp, UCLA.—(2014-15)**
**3. J.T. Realmuto, ss, Carl Albert HS, Midwest City, Okla.—(2014-15)**
DRAFT DROP *Nephew of John Smith, two-time Olympic gold medalist (1988, 1992), freestyle wrestling; 4-time World freestyle wrestling champion; head wrestling coach, Oklahoma State (1991-2015)*
4. *Andrew Toles, of, Sandy Creek HS, Tyrone, Ga.—(High A)
DRAFT DROP *Attended Chipola (Fla.) JC; re-drafted by Rays, 2012 (3rd round) • Son of Alvin Toles, first-round draft pick, National Football League (1985); linebacker, NFL (1985-88)*
5. Robert Morey, rhp, University of Virginia.—(AAA)
6. Rett Varner, rhp, University of Texas-Arlington.
**7. Mark Canha, of, University of California.—(2015)**
8. Alan Oaks, rhp, University of Michigan.
9. Austin Brice, rhp, Northwood HS, Pittsboro, N.C.
10. Aaron Senne, 1b, University of Missouri.
11. Grant Dayton, lhp, Auburn University.
12. James Wooster, of, Alvin (Texas) CC.
13. Kentrell Dewitt, of, Southeastern (N.C.) CC.
14. Danny Black, 2b, University of Oklahoma.
15. Ryan Fisher, of, UC Irvine.
16. *Randy LeBlanc, rhp, Covington (La.) HS.
17. Zach Neal, rhp, University of Oklahoma.
18. Corey Goudeau, rhp, Frank Phillips (Texas) JC.
19. Dallas Poulk, 2b, North Carolina State University.
20. Alfredo Lopez, ss, Compton (Calif.) CC.
21. Ken Toves, lhp, University of New Mexico.
22. Jeremy Heatley, rhp, University of Arkansas.
**23. *Blake Treinen, rhp, South Dakota State University.—(2014-15)**
24. Gregg Glime, c, Baylor University.
25. Mike Ojala, rhp, Rice University.
26. Todd Muecklisch, ss, Lewis-Clark State (Idaho) College.
**27. Brandon Cunniff, rhp, Cal State San Bernardino.—(2015)**
28. Chad Keefer, c, University of Louisiana-Lafayette.
29. Viosergy Rosa, 1b, Odessa (Texas) JC.
30. Zach Robertson, lhp, University of Iowa.
31. *Taiwan Easterling, of, Florida State University.
32. Eddie Rodriguez, c, University of Oregon.
33. *D'Andre Toney, of, Hardaway HS, Columbus, Ga.
34. *Steve Dennison, lhp, Wheaton (Ill.) College.
35. *Taylor Ard, 1b, Mount Hood (Ore.) CC.
36. Jared Rogers, rhp, Rice University.
37. Chris Squires, rhp, Indiana University.
38. Forrest Moore, lhp, Mississippi State University.
39. *Sam Bates, 1b, Crowder (Mo.) JC.
40. *Dustin Emmons, rhp, UC Riverside.
**41. *Seth Maness, rhp, East Carolina University.—(2013-15)**
42. *Jonathon Crawford, rhp, Okeechobee (Fla.) HS.
DRAFT DROP *First-round draft pick (20th overall), Tigers (2013)*
**43. *Matt Tracy, lhp, University of Mississippi.—(2015)**
44. *Tyler Abbott, lhp, Royal HS, Simi Valley, Calif.
45. Jeremy Weber, rhp, Chaffey (Calif.) JC.
46. *Daniel Johnston, of, Canada (Calif.) JC.
47. *Travis Huber, rhp, JC of Southern Idaho.
48. Beau Wright, lhp, Orange Coast (Calif.) CC.
49. *Cody Lavalli, rhp, Granite Hills HS, Apple Valley, Calif.
50. *Dan Carney, 1b, Notre Dame HS, East Stroudsburg, Pa.

## HOUSTON ASTROS (8)

**1. Delino DeShields, 2b, Woodward Academy, College Park, Ga.—(2015)**
DRAFT DROP *Son of Delino DeShields, first-round draft pick, Expos (1987); major leaguer (1990-2002)*
**1. Mike Foltynewicz, rhp, Minooka Community (Ill.) HS** (Choice from Tigers as compensation for Type A free agent Jose Valverde).**—(2014-15)**
1. Mike Kvasnicka, 3b/c, University of Minnesota (Supplemental choice—33rd—for loss of Valverde).—(AA)
**2. Vince Velasquez, rhp, Garey HS, Pomona, Calif.—(2015)**
3. Austin Wates, 2b, Virginia Tech.—(AAA)
4. Bobby Doran, rhp, Texas Tech.—(AAA)
5. Ben Heath, c, Penn State University.—(AA)
6. *Adam Plutko, rhp, Glendora (Calif.) HS.
7. Roberto Pena, c, Eloisa Pascual HS, Caguas, P.R.
DRAFT DROP *Son of Bert Pena, major leaguer (1981-87)*
**8. Jake Buchanan, rhp, North Carolina State University.—(2014-15)**
9. Tommy Shirley, lhp, Xavier University.
10. Evan Grills, lhp, Sinclair SS, Whitby, Ontario.
11. Kyle Redinger, 3b, Cedar Crest HS, Lebanon, Pa.
12. Andrew Robinson, rhp, Georgia Tech.
13. *Davis Duren, 2b, Oklahoma State University.
14. Jordan Scott, of, Riverside HS, Greer, S.C.
15. Jamaine Cotton, rhp, Western Oklahoma State JC.
16. Chris Wallace, c, University of Houston.
17. Tyler Burnett, 3b, Middle Tennessee State University.
18. Josh Magee, of, Hoover (Ala.) HS.
DRAFT DROP *Son of Wendell Magee, major leaguer (1996-2002)*
19. *JaCoby Jones, ss, Richton (Miss.) HS.
20. Daniel Adamson, of, Jacksonville State University.
21. *Aaron Blair, rhp, Spring Valley HS, Las Vegas, Nev.
DRAFT DROP *First-round draft pick (36th overall), Diamondbacks (2013)*
22. *Zach Dygert, c, Ball State University.
23. Adam Bailey, of, University of Nebraska.
24. Adam Champion, lhp, University of Arkansas-Little Rock.
25. Rodney Quintero, rhp, Chipola (Fla.) JC.
26. Alex Sogard, lhp, North Carolina State University.
DRAFT DROP *Brother of Eric Sogard, major leaguer (2010-15)*
27. Jacke Healey, ss, Youngstown State University.
28. Jason Chowning, rhp, University of Oklahoma.
29. *Broughan Jantz, of, Nevada Union HS, Nevada City, Calif.
30. Kellen Kiilsgaard, of, Stanford University.
31. Travis Blankenship, lhp, University of Kansas.
32. *Austin Chrismon, rhp, Menchville HS, Newport News, Va.
33. Michael Ness, rhp, Duke University.
34. Ryan Cole, rhp, St. John's University.
35. *Esteban Gomez, 1b, Bishop Ford Central Catholic HS, Brooklyn, N.Y.
36. *Ryan Halstead, rhp, Los Osos HS, Rancho Cucamonga, Calif.
37. Brian Streilein, rhp, Villanova University.
38. *Ryan Ford, 1b, Plano West HS, Plano, Texas.
39. Krishawn Holley, rhp, Mid-Carolina HS, Prosperity, S.C.
40. Jeremiah Meiners, lhp, Francis Marion (S.C.) University.
41. Bryce Lane, of, Gulf Coast (Fla.) CC.
42. Paul Gerrish, rhp, Texas Christian University.
43. *DeMarcus Henderson, ss, Wayne County HS, Waynesboro, Miss.
44. *Alexis Garza, rhp, McAllen (Texas) HS.
45. *Ian Vazquez, ss, Perkiomen HS, Pennsburg, Pa.
46. *Lawrence Pardo, lhp, Christopher Columbus HS, Miami.
47. *Joe Carcone, ss, New Hartford (N.Y.) HS.
48. *T.J. Pecoraro, rhp, Half Hollow Hills West HS, Dix Hills, N.Y.
49. Kenny Diaz, c, Colegio Angel David HS, Toa Alta, P.R.
50. *David Donald, of, J.L. Mann HS, Greenville, S.C.

## KANSAS CITY ROYALS (4)

**1. Christian Colon, ss, Cal State Fullerton.—(2014-15)**
2. Brett Eibner, of-rhp, University of Arkansas.—(AAA)
3. Mike Antonio, ss, George Washington HS, New York.—(High A)
**4. Kevin Chapman, lhp, University of Florida.—(2013-15)**
5. Jason Adam, rhp, Blue Valley Northwest HS, Overland Park, Kan.—(AAA)
**6. Scott Alexander, lhp, Sonoma State (Calif.) University.—(2015)**
7. Eric Cantrell, rhp, George Washington University.
**8. Michael Mariot, rhp, University of Nebraska.—(2014-15)**
9. Whit Merrifield, of, University of South Carolina.
10. Tim Ferguson, of, University of Mississippi.
11. Alex McClure, ss, Middle Tennessee State University.
12. Danny Hernandez, rhp, Miami-Dade JC.
**13. *Jonathan Gray, rhp, Chandler (Okla.) HS.—(2015)**
DRAFT DROP *First-round draft pick (3rd overall), Rockies (2013)*
14. Mike Giovenco, rhp, North Park (Ill.) College.
15. Jason Mitchell, rhp, University of Texas-Arlington.
16. Chas Byrne, rhp, East Tennessee State University.
17. Ryan Jenkins, c, Auburn University.
18. Brian Fletcher, of, Auburn University.
DRAFT DROP *Son of Scot Fletcher, major leaguer (1981-95)*
19. Kevin David, c, Oklahoma State University.
20. Cameron Conner, of, Indiana Southeast University.
21. Michael Liberto, ss, University of Missouri.
22. Tyler Graham, rhp, University of Nevada.
23. *Steven Neff, lhp, University of South Carolina.
24. *Brandon Glazer, ss, Clear Spring (Md.) HS.
25. *Buddy Sosnoskie, of, Virginia Tech.
26. Gates Dooley, rhp, Henderson State (Ark.) University.
27. Jose Rodriguez, of, Miami-Dade JC.
28. Murray Watts, 1b, Arkansas State University.
29. Alex Marquez, c, Alfonso Casta Martinez HS, Manaubo, P.R.
30. Chad Blauer, rhp, Point Loma Nazarene (Calif.) University.
31. Parker Bangs, rhp, University of South Carolina.
32. *Justin Hageman, rhp, Hopkinsville (Ky.) HS.
33. Cole Lohden, rhp, Southern Arkansas University.
34. *Mark Blackmar, rhp, Carroll HS, Southlake, Texas.
DRAFT DROP *Son of Phil Blackmar, golfer/PGA tour (1985-2000)*
35. *Kris Carlson, rhp, Wenatchee Valley (Wash.) CC.
36. *Mitchell Beacom, lhp, UCLA.
37. Robbie Penny, rhp, Pitt (N.C.) CC.
38. Nick Graffeo, rhp, University of Alabama-Birmingham.
39. Alex Rivers, rhp, Santa Clara University.
40. Dale Cornstubble, c, Central Michigan University.
41. Matt Ridings, rhp, Western Kentucky University.
42. *Mike Botelho, c, Chabot (Calif.) JC.
43. *Dillon Wilson, lhp, Western Oklahoma State JC.
44. *Shawn Payne, 2b, Georgia Southern University.
45. Tom Zebroski, ss, George Washington University.
46. Drew Robertson, c, Middle Tennessee State University.
47. Darian Sandford, of, Park (Mo.) University.
48. *Jacob Hannemann, of, Lone Peak HS, Highland, Utah.
49. Jordan Propst, rhp, University of South Carolina.
50. *Joe Jackson, c, Mauldin HS, Greenville, S.C.
DRAFT DROP *Great-great nephew of Shoeless Joe Jackson, major leaguer (1908-20)*

## LOS ANGELES ANGELS (29)

**1. Kaleb Cowart, 3b-rhp, Cook HS, Adel, Ga.** (Choice from Mariners as compensation for Type A free agent Chone Figgins).**—(2015)**
**1. Cam Bedrosian, rhp, East Coweta HS, Sharpsburg, Ga.—(2014-15)**
DRAFT DROP *Son of Steve Bedrosian, major leaguer (1981-95)*
1. Chevy Clarke, of, Marietta (Ga.) HS (Choice from Red Sox as compensation for Type A free agent John Lackey).—(High A)
1. Taylor Lindsey, ss, Desert Mountain HS, Scottsdale, Ariz. (Supplemental choice—37th—as compensation for Lackey).—(AAA)
1. Ryan Bolden, of, Madison (Miss.) Central HS (Supplemental choice—40th—as compensation for Figgins).—(Rookie)
2. Daniel Tillman, rhp, Florida Southern College.—(AA)
3. Wendell Soto, ss, Riverview HS, Sarasota, Fla.—

(High A)
**3. Donn Roach, rhp, CC of Southern Nevada** (Special compensation choice—115th—for failure to sign 2009 third-round pick Josh Spence).**—(2014-15)**
4. Max Russell, lhp, Florida Southern College.—(High A)
5. *Jesus Valdez, rhp, Hueneme HS, Oxnard, Calif.—(Low A)
DRAFT DROP *Attended Oxnard (Calif.) JC; re-drafted by Dodgers, 2011 (17th round)*
6. Brian Diemer, rhp, University of California.
**7. *Josh Osich, lhp, Oregon State University.—(2015)**
**8. Kole Calhoun, of, Arizona State University.—(2012-15)**
9. Drew Heid, of, Gonzaga University.
10. Aaron Meade, lhp, Missouri State University.
11. *Jake Rodriguez, ss, Elk Grove (Calif.) HS.
12. Justin La Tempa, rhp, University of Oregon.
13. Bryant George, rhp, Southern Illinois University.
14. James Sneed, of, St. Croix Educational Complex, Christiansted, V.I.
15. Carmine Giardina, lhp, University of Tampa.
16. Thomas Nichols, 3b, Georgia Tech.
17. Kevin Moesquit, ss, Highlands Christian HS, Pompano Beach, Fla.
18. Ryan Broussard, ss, LSU-Eunice JC.
19. *Jonathan Bobea, rhp, Lewis HS, Flushing, N.Y.
20. Kevin Johnson, rhp, University of West Florida.
21. Gary Mitchell, of, Neumann (Pa.) University.
22. Francis Larson, c, UC Irvine.
23. Michael Bolaski, 3b, Hanks HS, El Paso, Texas.
24. Jesus Campos, ss, Cal State Los Angeles.
**25. A.J. Schugel, 3b, Central Arizona JC.—(2015)**
26. Dakota Robinson, lhp, Centenary College.
27. Brandon Decker, of, Valdosta State (Ga.) University.
28. *Tim Helton, c, Upland (Calif.) HS.
29. *Taylor Smith-Brennan, 2b, Meadowdale HS, Lynnwood, Wash.
30. Steven Irvine, 2b, McNeese State University.
31. Mike Sodders, 2b, New Mexico State University.
DRAFT DROP *Son of Mike Sodders, first-round draft pick, Twins (1981)*
32. Drew Beuerlein, c, University of Nevada-Las Vegas.
33. Eric Cendejas, rhp, Cal State Stanislaus.
34. Jerod Yakubik, 1b, Ohio University.
35. Ryan Rivers, of, UNC Charlotte.
36. Hampton Tignor, c, University of Florida.
37. *Tagen Struhs, of, Snohomish, Wash.
38. *Jace Brinkerhoff, 3b, Utah Valley University.
39. *Jimmy Allen, 2b, Rancho Buena Vista HS, Vista, Calif.
40. Drew Oldfield, c, Dixie State (Utah) College.
41. *Justin Poovey, rhp, University of Florida.
42. Chance Mistric, rhp, LSU-Eunice JC.
43. George Barber, of, Broward (Fla.) CC.
44. Mike Turner, of, Chesapeake (Md.) JC.
45. Vinnie St. John, rhp, University of Southern California.
46. *Darren Fischer, lhp, Cumberland Regional HS, Bridgeton, N.J.
47. *Kenny Hatcher, 3b, Chandler-Gilbert (Ariz.) CC.
48. Chad Yinger, rhp, Southern Arkansas University.
49. Alex Burkard, lhp, Georgia College & State University.
50. John Wiedenbauer, lhp, University of Tampa.
DRAFT DROP *Son of Tom Wiedenbauer, major leaguer (1979)*

## LOS ANGELES DODGERS (27)

**1. Zach Lee, rhp, McKinney (Texas) HS.—(2015)**
2. Ralston Cash, rhp, Lakeview Academy, Cornelia, Ga.—(AAA)
3. Leon Landry, of, Louisiana State University.—(AAA)
4. James Baldwin III, of, Pinecrest HS, Southern Pines, N.C.—(High A)
DRAFT DROP *Son of James Baldwin Jr., major leaguer (1995-2005)*
5. Jake Lemmerman, ss, Duke University.—(AAA)
**6. *Kevin Gausman, rhp, Grandview HS, Aurora, Colo.—(2013-15)**
DRAFT DROP *First-round draft pick (4th overall), Orioles (2012)*
7. Ryan Christenson, lhp, South Mountain (Ariz.) CC.
DRAFT DROP *Son of Gary Christenson, major leaguer (1979-80)*
8. Blake Dean, of, Louisiana State University.
9. Steve Domecus, c, Virginia Tech.
10. Bobby Coyle, of, Fresno State University.
**11. Joc Pederson, of, Palo Alto (Calif.) HS.—(2014-15)**
DRAFT DROP *Son of Stu Pederson, major leaguer (1985)*
12. Matt Kirkland, 3b, South Doyle HS, Knoxville, Tenn.
13. Jesse Bosnik, 3b, St. Bonaventure University.
14. Alex McRee, lhp, University of Georgia.
15. *Jake Eliopoulos, lhp, Chipola (Fla.) JC.
16. Andrew Pevsner, lhp, Johns Hopkins (Md.) University.
17. Logan Bawcom, rhp, University of Texas-Arlington.
18. *Chad Arnold, rhp, Washington State University.
19. *Ben Carhart, 3b, Palm Beach (Fla.) CC.
20. *Shane Henderson, rhp, Flower Mound (Texas) HS.
21. Noel Cuevas, of, Universidad Interamericana (P.R.) JC-Arecibo.
22. *Andre Wheeler, of, L.C. Anderson HS, Austin, Texas.
23. B.J. LaRosa, c, Bucknell University.
24. Andrew Edge, c, Jacksonville State University.
25. Chance Gilmore, of, Coastal Carolina University.
**26. Scott Schebler, of, Des Moines Area (Iowa) CC.—(2015)**
27. Yimy Rodriguez, rhp, Peru State (Neb.) College.
28. Mike Drowne, of, Sacred Heart (Conn.) University.
**29. Red Patterson, rhp, Southwestern Oklahoma State University.—(2014)**
**30. Shawn Tolleson, rhp, Baylor University.—(2012-15)**
31. Derek Cone, rhp, Mesa (Ariz.) CC.
32. Devon Ethier, of, GateWay (Ariz.) CC.
DRAFT DROP *Brother of Andre Ethier, major leaguer (2006-15)*
33. *Brett Lee, lhp, Bishop State (Ala.) CC.
34. Joe Lincoln, c, Missouri Southern State University.
35. Beau Brett, 1b, University of Southern California.
DRAFT DROP *Nephew of George Brett, major leaguer (1973-93)*
36. *John Fasola, rhp, Walsh Jesuit HS, Cuyahoga Falls, Ohio.
37. *Cal Vogelsang, 2b, JC of the Canyons (Calif.).
38. *Lucas Witt, of, Lexington Christian HS, Lexington, Ky.
39. Steve Matre, rhp, Mount St. Joseph (Ohio) University.
40. *Kaleb Clark, rhp, Riverton (Kan.) HS.
41. *Kevin Williams, ss, Crespi Carmelite HS, Encino, Calif.
42. *Miles Williams, 3b, Windsor (Calif.) HS.
43. *Chad Wallach, rhp, Calvary Chapel HS, Pacific Grove, Calif.
DRAFT DROP *Son of Tim Wallach, first-round draft pick, Expos (1979); major leaguer (1980-96)*
44. *Nick Baker, rhp, Palm Desert (Calif.) HS.
45. *Logan Gallagher, ss, Louisburg (N.C.) JC.
46. Bret Montgomery, rhp, Cal State Dominguez Hills.
47. *Cody Martin, 1b, Chipola (Fla.) JC.
DRAFT DROP *Brother of Ethan Martin, first-round draft pick, Dodgers (2008); major leaguer (2013-14)*
48. *Anthony Garcia, 2b, Chavez HS, Laveen, Ariz.
DRAFT DROP *Son of Leo Garcia, major leaguer (1987-88)*
49. *Robby Shultz, rhp, Eastside Catholic HS, Sammamish, Wash.
50. *Taylor Kaczmarek, rhp, Desert Ridge HS, Mesa, Ariz.

## MILWAUKEE BREWERS (14)

1. *Dylan Covey, rhp, Maranatha HS, Pasadena, Calif.—(High A)
DRAFT DROP *Attended San Diego; re-drafted by Athletics, 2013 (4th round)*
**2. Jimmy Nelson, rhp, University of Alabama.—(2013-15)**
**3. Tyler Thornburg, rhp, Charleston Southern University.—(2012-15)**
4. Hunter Morris, 1b, Auburn University.—(AAA)
5. Matt Miller, rhp, University of Michigan.—(High A)
6. Cody Hawn, 3b, University of Tennessee.
7. Joel Pierce, rhp, Vincent Massey SS, Windsor, Ontario.
8. Austin Ross, rhp, Louisiana State University.
**9. Yadiel Rivera, ss, Manuela Toro HS, Caguas, P.R.—(2015)**
10. Rafael Neda, c, University of New Mexico.
11. Greg Holle, rhp, Texas Christian University.
DRAFT DROP *Son of Gary Holle, major leaguer (1979)*
12. John Bivens, of, Virginia State University.
13. Michael White, rhp, Walters State (Tenn.) CC.
14. Mike Walker, 3b, University of the Pacific.
15. *Chris Bates, lhp, Regis HS, New York City.
16. *Andrew Morris, rhp, Gulf Coast (Fla.) CC.
17. Brian Garman, lhp, University of Cincinnati.
18. Thomas Keeling, lhp, Oklahoma State University.
19. *Rowan Wick, of, Graham SS, North Vancouver, B.C.
20. Shea Vucinich, ss, Washington State University.
21. Kevin Shackelford, rhp, Marshall University.
22. Kevin Berard, c, Alfred M. Barbe HS, Lake Charles, La.
23. Ryan Bernal, rhp, Florida Atlantic University.
24. Greg Hopkins, 3b, St. John's University.
25. Nick Shaw, ss, Barry (Fla.) University.
26. *Daniel Gibson, lhp, Jesuit HS, Tampa.
27. Alex Jones, rhp, Jacksonville State University.
28. Dane Amedee, lhp, LSU-Eunice JC.
29. Dan Britt, rhp, Elon University.
30. Eric Marzec, rhp, Youngstown State University.
31. Mike Melillo, c, Elon University.
**32. Jason Rogers, 1b, Columbus State (Ga.) University.—(2014-15)**
33. *William Kankel, lhp, University of Houston.
34. *Conor Fisk, rhp, Grafton (Wis.) HS.
35. *T.C. Mark, c, Pinnacle HS, Phoenix.
36. R.J. Johnson, rhp, Starkville (Miss.) HS.
37. Seth Harvey, rhp, Washington State University.
38. Mike Schaub, rhp, Loara HS, Anaheim, Calif.
39. Kenny Allison, of, Angelina (Texas) JC.
40. *Scott Matyas, rhp, University of Minnesota.
41. Derrick Shaw, of, Florida A&M University.
42. Johnny Dishon, of, Louisiana State University.
43. *Steven Okert, lhp, Grayson County (Texas) CC.
44. T.J. Mittelstaedt, of, Long Beach State University.
45. *Lucas Moran, rhp, Lutheran HS North, Houston.
46. *Derek Goodwin, c, Diamond Ranch HS, Pomona, Calif.
47. *Billy Schroeder, c, Grand Canyon University.
48. Marques Kyles, lhp, Limestone (S.C.) College.
49. *Alexander Simone, of, Christian Brothers Academy, Syracuse, N.Y.
50. *Chad Jones, of, Louisiana State University.
DRAFT DROP *Defensive back, National Football League (2010-11)*

## MINNESOTA TWINS (20)

1. Alex Wimmers, rhp, Ohio State University.—(AA)
2. Niko Goodrum, ss, Fayette County HS, Fayetteville, Ga.—(AA)
3. Pat Dean, lhp, Boston College.—(AAA)
**4. Eddie Rosario, of, Rafael Lopez Landron HS, Guayama, P.R.—(2015)**
5. Nate Roberts, of, High Point University.—(High A)
**6. Logan Darnell, lhp, University of Kentucky.—(2014)**
7. Matt Hauser, rhp, University of San Diego.
8. Lance Ray, of, University of Kentucky.
9. Kyle Knudson, c, University of Minnesota.
10. J.D. Williams, ss, Brooks-DeBartolo HS, Tampa.
DRAFT DROP *Son of Reggie Williams, major leaguer (1985-88) • Brother of Reggie Williams, 10th-round draft pick, Cardinals (2010)*
11. *Tyler Kuresa, 1b, Oakmont HS, Roseville, Calif.
12. *Steven Maxwell, rhp, Texas Christian University.
**13. Ryan O'Rourke, lhp, Merrimack (Mass.) College.—(2015)**
14. *DeAndre Smelter, rhp, Tattnall Square Academy, Macon, Ga.
15. *Thomas Girdwood, rhp, Elon University.
16. Clint Dempster, lhp, Nicholls State University.
17. *Devin Grigg, rhp, Cal State East Bay.
18. David Gutierrez, rhp, University of Miami.
19. *Matt Arguello, lhp, Davidson HS, Mobile, Ala.
**20. *Cody Martin, rhp, Gonzaga University.—(2015)**
21. Nathan Fawbush, rhp, Georgia Perimeter JC.
22. *Dillon Moyer, ss, Pendleton School, Bradenton, Fla.
DRAFT DROP *Son of Jamie Moyer, major leaguer (1986-2012)*
23. Dallas Gallant, rhp, Sam Houston State University.
24. Michael Quesada, c, Sierra (Calif.) JC.
25. Andy Leer, ss, University of Mary (N.D.).
26. Kelly Cross, c, Pearland (Texas) HS.
27. Brandon Henderson, of, Fresno (Calif.) CC.
28. Jamaal Hawkins, ss, Jacksonville University.
29. Brian Burke, 3b, Lewis-Clark State (Idaho) College.
30. *Sergio Perez (Dernal), ss, Palmetto Ridge HS, Orangetree, Fla.
31. *Mark Payton, of, St. Rita HS, Chicago.
32. *Tommy Toledo, rhp, University of Florida.
33. Justin Parker, lhp, Cosumnes River (Calif.) JC.
34. Kyle Necke, rhp, UC Irvine.
35. Nick Alloway, rhp, Gloucester (N.J.) CC.
36. Kelvin Mention, of, Brooks-DeBartolo HS, Tampa.
37. *Grant Muncrief, rhp, Wichita State University.
38. *Jared Ray, rhp, University of Houston.
39. Bart Carter, lhp, Western Kentucky University.
40. *Vance Woodruff, rhp, Grayson County (Texas) CC.
41. Sam Spangler, lhp, University of Hawaii.
42. Brett Carroll, lhp, William Paterson (N.J.) College.
43. Derek Christensen, rhp, Salt Lake CC.
44. David Deminsky, lhp, St. Cloud State (Minn.) University.
45. *James Buckelew, lhp, Collins Hills HS, Suwanee, Ga.
**46. A.J. Achter, rhp, Michigan State University.—(2014-15)**
47. *Collin Reynolds, rhp, McLennan (Texas) CC.
48. *Troy Scott, 1b, University of Washington.
49. *LeAndre Davis, ss, Georgia Perimeter JC.
50. *James Harris, 3b, Etowah HS, Woodstock, Ga.

## NEW YORK METS (7)

**1. Matt Harvey, rhp, University of North Carolina.—(2012-15)**
2. (Choice to Red Sox as compensation for Type A free agent Jason Bay)
3. Blake Forsythe, c, University of Tennessee.—(AAA)
DRAFT DROP *Brother of Logan Forsythe, first-round draft pick, Padres (2008); major leaguer (2011-15)*
4. Cory Vaughn, of, San Diego State University.—(AAA)
DRAFT DROP *Son of Greg Vaughn, major leaguer (1989-2003)*
**5. Matt den Dekker, of, University of Florida.—(2013-15)**
6. Greg Peavey, rhp, Oregon State University.
7. Jeff Walters, rhp, University of Georgia.
8. Kenny McDowall, rhp, CC of Southern Nevada.
**9. Jacob deGrom, rhp, Stetson University.—(2014-15)**
**10. Akeel Morris, rhp, Charlotte Amalie HS, St. Thomas, V.I.—(2015)**
11. Adam Kolarek, lhp, University of Maryland.
12. Bret Mitchell, rhp, Minnesota State University-Mankato.
13. Brian Harrison, 3b, Furman University.
14. J.B. Brown, 2b, University of the Pacific.
15. Tillman Pugh, of, Sonoma State (Calif.) University.
16. Ryan Fraser, rhp, University of Memphis.
17. Chad Sheppard, rhp, Northwestern State University.
18. A.J. Pinera, rhp, University of Tampa.
19. Jon Kountis, rhp, Embry-Riddle (Fla.) University.
20. Luke Stewart, 1b, University of Alabama-Birmingham.
21. *Dabias Johnson, 2b, Cook HS, Adel, Ga.
22. Brandon Brown, ss, University of South Alabama.
23. *Drew Martinez, of, University of Memphis.

DRAFT DROP *Son of Chito Martinez, major leaguer (1991-93)*

**24. Erik Goeddel, rhp, UCLA.—(2014-15)**
25. Peter Birdwell, rhp, Vanguard (Calif.) University.
26. Jet Butler, ss, Mississippi State University.
27. Todd Weldon, rhp, Wayland Baptist (Texas) University.
28. Jeremy Gould, lhp, Duke University.
29. Hamilton Bennett, lhp, Tennessee Wesleyan College.
**30. Josh Edgin, lhp, Francis Marion (S.C.) University.—(2012-14)**
31. Steve Winnick, rhp, Point Loma Nazarene (Calif.) University.
32. Patrick Farrell, c, Regis (Colo.) University.
33. Hunter Carnevale, rhp, University of the Pacific.
34. Justin Schafer, 2b, UC Davis.
35. *Josh Easley, rhp, Weatherford (Texas) JC.
36. *Jesen Dygestile-Therrien, rhp, Edouard Montpetit HS, Montreal.
37. Dylan Brown, of, University of Tampa.
38. *Peter Miller, rhp, Cambridge Christian HS, Tampa.
39. *Brian Cruz, ss, Varela HS, Miami.
40. *Brock Stewart, ss, Normal West HS, Normal. Ill.
41. *Taylor Christian, rhp, Weatherford (Texas) JC.
42. *J.J. Franco, ss, Poly Prep Country Day, Brooklyn, N.Y.

DRAFT DROP *Son of John Franco, major leaguer (1984-2005)*

43. Donnie Tabb, ss, East Central (Miss.) CC.
44. *Kevin Gelinas, lhp, UC Santa Barbara.
45. *Terrance Jackson, lhp, Oklahoma City University.
46. *Mike Jefferson, lhp, Louisiana Tech.
47. *Sean O'Connor, rhp, Carroll HS, Southlake, Texas.
48. *Austin Smith, 1b, Pensacola Catholic HS, Pensacola, Fla.
49. *Dillon Newman, rhp, Belton (Texas) HS.
50. *Mark Eveld, c, Jesuit HS, Tampa.

## NEW YORK YANKEES (30)

1. Cito Culver, ss, Irondequoit HS, Rochester, N.Y.—(AAA)
2. Angelo Gumbs, of, Torrance (Calif.) HS.—(High A)
3. Rob Segedin, 3b, Tulane University.—(AAA)
**4. Mason Williams, of, West Orange HS, Winter Garden, Fla.—(2015)**
**5. Tommy Kahnle, rhp, Lynn (Fla.) University.—(2014-15)**
6. Gabe Encinas, rhp, St. Paul HS, Santa Fe Springs, Calif.
7. Jake Anderson, of, Woodlawn HS, Baton Rouge, La.
8. Kyle Roller, 1b, East Carolina University.
9. Taylor Morton, rhp, Bartlett (Tenn.) HS.
10. Ben Gamel, of, Bishop Kenny HS, Jacksonville, Fla.

DRAFT DROP *Brother of Mat Gamel, major leaguer (2008-12)*

11. Zach Varce, rhp, University of Portland.
**12. Danny Burawa, rhp, St. John's University.—(2015)**
13. Tyler Austin, c, Heritage HS, Conyers, Ga.
14. *Travis Dean, rhp, Newton South HS, Newton, Mass.
**15. Chase Whitley, rhp, Troy University.—(2014-15)**
16. Evan Rutckyj, lhp, St. Joseph's HS, St. Thomas, Ontario.
**17. Preston Claiborne, rhp, Tulane University.—(2013-14)**
18. *Kevin Jacob, rhp, Georgia Tech.
19. *Kevin Jordan, of, Northside HS, Columbus, Ga.
20. Mike Ferraro, of, University of San Diego.
21. Dustin Hobbs, rhp, Yavapai (Ariz.) JC.
22. Trevor Johnson, lhp, JC of the Desert (Calif.).
23. Shane Brown, c, University of Central Florida.
24. Conor Mullee, rhp, Saint Peter's (N.J.) University.
25. Casey Stevenson, 2b, UC Irvine.
26. *R.J. Hively, rhp, Santa Ana (Calif.) JC.
27. *Martin Viramontes, rhp, Loyola Marymount University.
28. *Josh Dezse, rhp, Olentangy Liberty HS, Powell, Ohio.
29. *Stewart Ijames, of, University of Louisville.
30. Zach Nuding, rhp, Weatherford (Texas) JC.
31. Mike Gipson, rhp, Florida Atlantic University.
32. Kramer Sneed, lhp, Barton (N.C.) College.
33. *Michael Hachadorian, rhp, San Diego Mesa JC.
34. *Keenan Kish, rhp, Germantown Academy, Fort Washington, Pa.
35. Will Oliver, rhp, Palomar (Calif.) JC.
36. Nick McCoy, c, University of San Diego.
37. *Cameron Hobson, lhp, Dayton University.
38. *James Ramsay, of, Brandon (Fla.) HS.
39. *Jaycob Brugman, of, Desert Vista HS, Phoenix.
40. *Mike Gerber, of, Neuqua Valley HS, Naperville, Ill.
41. *Tym Pearson, of, Columbia Basin (Wash.) JC.
42. *Mike O'Neill, of, Olentangy Liberty HS, Powell, Ohio.

DRAFT DROP *Nephew of Paul O'Neill, major leaguer (1985-2001)*

43. *Kyle Hunter, lhp, Kansas State University.
44. *Dave Middendorf, lhp, Northern Kentucky University.
45. *Tyler Johnson, of, Penn State University.
46. Nathan Forer, rhp, Southern Illinois University.
47. Freddy Lewis, lhp, Tennessee Wesleyan College.
48. *Alex Brown, rhp, Amphitheater HS, Tucson, Ariz.
49. *Will Arthur, of, Abbotsford (B.C.) SS.
50. *Matt Rice, c, Western Kentucky University.

## OAKLAND ATHLETICS (10)

**1. Michael Choice, of, University of Texas-Arlington.—(2013-15)**
2. Yordy Cabrera, 3b, Lakeland (Fla.) HS.—(High A)
3. Aaron Shipman, of, Brooks County HS, Quitman, Ga.—(High A)
4. Chad Lewis, 3b, Marina HS, Huntington Beach, Calif.—(Low A)
5. Tyler Vail, rhp, Notre Dame HS, Easton, Pa.—(Low A)
6. Tony Thompson, 3b, University of Kansas.
7. Jordan Tripp, of, Golden West (Calif.) JC.
8. Blake Hassebrock, rhp, UNC Greensboro.
9. A.J. Kirby-Jones, 1b, Tennessee Tech.
10. Josh Bowman, rhp, University of Tampa.
11. Wade Kirkland, ss, Florida Southern College.
12. Matt Thomson, rhp, University of San Diego.
**13. A.J. Griffin, rhp, University of San Diego.—(2012-13)**
14. J.C. Menna, rhp, Brookdale (N.J.) CC.
15. *Scott Woodward, 3b, Coastal Carolina University.
16. Ryan Hughes, lhp, University of Nebraska.

DRAFT DROP *Son of Ernie Hughes, center, National Football League (1978-83)*

17. Drew Tyson, rhp, Reinhardt (Ga.) College.
18. Jose Macias, rhp, Franklin Pierce (N.H.) College.
19. Logan Chitwood, rhp, University of Texas-Tyler.
20. Rashad Ramsey, of, Chattooga HS, Summerville, Ga.
21. *Michael Anarumo, lhp, LeMoyne University.
22. *Mike Strong, lhp, Oklahoma State University.
23. Zach Thornton, rhp, University of Oregon.
24. Ryan Lipkin, c, University of San Francisco.
25. Josh Whitaker, 3b, Kennesaw State University.
26. Jake Brown, lhp, Georgia Southern University.
27. Seth Frankoff, rhp, UNC Wilmington.
28. Ryan Pineda, 2b, Cal State Northridge.
29. Zach Hurley, of, Ohio State University.
30. Jeff Urlaub, lhp, Grand Canyon University.
31. *Aaron Judge, 1b, Linden (Calif.) HS.

DRAFT DROP *First-round draft pick (32nd overall), Yankees (2013)*

32. *Todd McInnis, rhp, University of Southern Mississippi.
33. Sean Murphy, rhp, Keystone (Pa.) College.
34. Aaron Larsen, rhp, Bethany (Kan.) College.
35. Andrew Bailey, rhp, Concord (W.Va.) University.
36. *Bobby Geren, 3b, San Ramon Valley HS, Danville, Calif.

DRAFT DROP *Son of Bob Geren, first-round draft pick, Padres (1979); major leaguer (1988-93); major league manager (2007-11)*

37. Daniel Petitti, c, North Georgia College and State University.
38. Michael Fabiaschi, 2b, James Madison University.
39. John Nester, c, Clemson University.
40. *Andrew Smith, rhp, Roswell (Ga.) HS.
41. *Andrew Knapp, c, Granite Bay (Calif.) HS.
42. *Louie Lechich, lhp, St. Mary's HS, Stockton, Calif.
43. *Spencer Haynes, ss, Brandon (Fla.) HS.
44. *Lonnie Kauppila, ss, Burbank (Calif.) HS.
45. *Krey Bratsen, of, Bryan (Texas) HS.
46. *Tyler Skulina, rhp, Walsh Jesuit HS, Cuyahoga Falls, Ohio.
47. *Tony McClendon, of, Fullerton (Calif.) JC.
48. *Zach Johnson, 1b, Ohlone (Calif.) JC.
49. *Nick Rosso, of, Lincoln HS, Stockton, Calif.
50. *T.J. Walz, rhp, University of Kansas.

## PHILADELPHIA PHILLIES (26)

1. Jesse Biddle, lhp, Germantown Friends HS, Philadelphia.—(AAA)
2. Perci Garner, rhp, Ball State University.—(AAA)
**3. Cameron Rupp, c, University of Texas.—(2013-15)**
4. Bryan Morgado, lhp, University of Tennessee.—(High A)
5. *Scott Frazier, rhp, Upland (Calif.) HS.—(Low A)

DRAFT DROP *Attended Pepperdine; re-drafted by Cubs, 2013 (6th round)*

6. Gauntlett Eldemire, of, Ohio University.
**7. David Buchanan, rhp, Georgia State University.—(2014-15)**
8. Stephen Malcolm, ss, San Joaquin Delta (Calif.) JC.
9. *Brenton Allen, of, Gahr HS, Cerritos, Calif.
**10. Mario Hollands, lhp, UC Santa Barbara.—(2014)**
11. Garett Claypool, rhp, UCLA.
12. Tyler Knigge, rhp, Lewis-Clark State (Idaho) College.
13. *John Hinson, 3b, Clemson University.
14. Chace Numata, c, Pearl City (Hawaii) HS.
15. Jake Smith, 3b, University of Alabama.
16. Craig Fritsch, rhp, Baylor University.
17. Mike Nesseth, rhp, University of Nebraska.
18. Jeff Cusick, 1b, UC Irvine.
19. *Daniel Palka, 1b, Greer (S.C.) HS.
20. Kevin Walter, rhp, Legacy HS, Westminster, Colo.
21. Jonathan Musser, rhp, Dowling Catholic HS, West Des Moines, Iowa.
22. *Jonathan Paquet, rhp, St. Lawrence (Quebec) JC.
23. Jake Borup, rhp, Arizona State University.
24. *Chad Thompson, rhp, Orange Coast (Calif.) CC.
25. Matt Hutchison, rhp, Nevada-Las Vegas.
26. Chris Duffy, of, University of Central Florida.
27. Matt Payton, 2b, Western Kentucky University.
28. Brian Pointer, of, Galena HS, Reno, Nev.
29. *Patrick Lala, rhp, Kirkwood (Iowa) CC.
30. *Nick Gonzalez, lhp, Leto HS, Tampa.
31. Jim Klocke, c, Southeast Missouri State University.
32. Carlos Alonso, 3b, University of Delaware.
33. Bob Stumpo, c, West Chester (Pa.) University.
34. Pat Murray, 1b, Lewis-Clark State (Idaho) College.
35. Eric Pettis, rhp, UC Irvine.
36. Neal Davis, lhp, University of Virginia.
37. Marshall Schuler, rhp, Colorado School of Mines.
38. *Keenyn Walker, of, Central Arizona JC.

DRAFT DROP *First-round draft pick (47th overall), White Sox (2011)*

39. *Justin Cummings, of, Santa Fe (Fla.) CC.
40. *Jeff Harvill, lhp, Evangel Christian Academy, Shreveport, La.
41. *Taylor Zeutenhorst, of, Sheldon (Iowa) HS.
42. *Tim Chadd, 1b, Bishop Carroll Catholic HS, Wichita, Kan.
43. *Jimmy Hodgskin, lhp, Bishop Moore HS, Orlando, Fla.
44. *Jesse Meaux, rhp, UC Santa Barbara.
45. *Mike Francisco, lhp, Villanova University.
46. *Ty Ross, c, Collier HS, Naples, Fla.
47. Ethan Stewart, lhp, New Mexico JC.
48. *Kyle Ottoson, lhp, South Mountain (Ariz.) CC.
49. *Kyle Hallock, lhp, Kent State University.
50. *Damek Tomscha, 3b, North HS, Sioux Falls, Iowa.

## PITTSBURGH PIRATES (2)

1. Jameson Taillon, rhp, The Woodlands (Texas) HS.—(AAA)
2. Stetson Allie, rhp-3b, St. Edward HS, Lakewood, Ohio.—(AA)
3. Mel Rojas Jr., of, Wabash Valley (Ill.) CC.—(AAA)

DRAFT DROP *Son of Mel Rojas, major leaguer (1990-99)*

4. Nick Kingham, rhp, Sierra Vista HS, Las Vegas, Nev.—(AAA)
5. Tyler Waldron, rhp, Oregon State University.—(AAA)
6. *Jason Hursh, rhp, Trinity Christian HS, Addison, Texas.

DRAFT DROP *First-round draft pick (31st overall), Braves (2013)*

7. *Austin Kubitza, rhp, Heritage HS, Colleyville, Texas.

DRAFT DROP *Brother of Kyle Kubitza, major leaguer (2015)*

8. *Dace Kime, rhp, Defiance (Ohio) HS.
**9. Brandon Cumpton, rhp, Georgia Tech.—(2013-14)**
10. Zack Weiss, rhp, Northwood HS, Irvine, Calif.
11. Dan Grovatt, of, University of Virginia.
12. Vince Payne, rhp, Cypress (Calif.) JC.
13. *Chris Kirsch, lhp, Marple Newtown HS, Newtown Square, Pa.
14. Bryce Weidman, rhp, Southwestern Oregon CC.
15. Drew Maggi, ss, Arizona State University.
16. Matt Curry, 1b, Texas Christian University.
17. Ryan Hafner, rhp, West HS, Lee's Summit, Mo.
18. *Chase Wentz, of, LSU-Shreveport.
19. *Kent Emanuel, lhp, Woodstock (Ga.) HS.
20. Justin Bencsko, of, Villanova University.
21. *Dale Carey, of, Wheeler HS, Marietta, Ga.
22. Adalberto Santos, 2b, Oregon State University.
23. Jared Lakind, 1b, Cypress Woods HS, Cypress, Texas.
24. Justin Howard, 1b, University of New Mexico.
**25. Casey Sadler, rhp, Western Oklahoma State JC.—(2014-15)**
26. *Brandon Pierce, rhp, Gunter (Texas) HS.
27. Kevin Kleis, rhp, Grossmont (Calif.) JC.
28. *Zack Powers, ss, Armwood HS, Seffner, Fla.
29. *Garret Levsen, rhp, Sonora HS, La Habra, Calif.
30. Matt Skirving, c, Eastern Michigan University.
31. Jason Townsend, rhp, University of Alabama.
32. Chase Lyles, 3b, Northwestern State University.
33. Justin Ennis, lhp, LSU-Shreveport.
34. Kelson Brown, ss, Linfield (Ore.) College.
35. *Drew Muren, of, Cal State Northridge.
36. Cliff Archibald, rhp, McLennan (Texas) CC.
37. *Will Allen, c, F.W. Buchholz HS, Gainesville, Fla.
38. *Alex Cox, rhp, Santiago HS, Corona, Calif.
39. Kevin Decker, rhp, College of Charleston.
40. *Harrison Cooney, rhp, Vero Beach (Fla.) HS.
41. Bryton Trepagnier, rhp, East St. John HS, Reserve, La.
42. *Stephen Lumpkins, lhp, American (D.C.) University.
43. *Garrett Hicks, rhp, Yucaipa (Calif.) HS.
44. *Cory McGinnis, rhp, Shelton State (Ala.) CC.
45. *Connor Sadzeck, rhp, Crystal Lake (Ill.) Central HS.
46. *Ryan Wiggins, c, West Seattle HS, Seattle.
47. *Nathan Sorenson, of, Texas HS, Texarkana, Texas.
48. *Dillon Haviland, lhp, South Fayette HS, McDonald, Pa.
49. Logan Pevny, rhp, West Milford (N.J.) HS.
50. *Dusty Isaacs, rhp, Lebanon (Ohio) HS.

## ST. LOUIS CARDINALS (24)

1. Zack Cox, 3b, University of Arkansas.—(AAA)
1. Seth Blair, rhp, Arizona State University (Supplemental choice—46th—for loss of Type B free agent Mark DeRosa).—(AAA)
1. Tyrell Jenkins, rhp, Henderson (Texas) HS (Supplemental choice—50th—for loss of Type B free agent Joel Piniero).—(AAA)
2. Jordan Swagerty, rhp, Arizona State University.—(AA)
**3. Sam Tuivailala, ss, Aragon HS, San Mateo, Calif.—(2014-15)**
**4. Cody Stanley, c, UNC Wilmington.—(2015)**
5. Nick Longmire, of, University of the Pacific.—(AA)
**6. John Gast, lhp, Florida State University.—(2013)**
**7. Greg Garcia, ss, University of Hawaii.—(2014-15)**
8. Daniel Bibona, lhp, UC Irvine.
**9. Tyler Lyons, lhp, Oklahoma State University.—(2013-15)**

10. Reggie Williams Jr., of, Middle Georgia JC.
DRAFT DROP *Son of Reggie Williams, major leaguer (1985-88) • Brother of J.D. Williams, 10th-round draft pick, Twins (2010)*
11. Ben Freeman, lhp, Lake Gibson HS, Lakeland, Fla.
12. *Austin Wilson, of, Harvard-Westlake HS, Studio City, Calif.
13. Colin Walsh, 2b, Stanford University.
14. Cesar Aguilar, rhp, A.B. Miller HS, Fontana, Calif.
15. Geoff Klein, c, Santa Clara University.
16. Anthony Bryant, of, Connally HS, Austin, Texas.
17. Corderious Dodd, of, North Side HS, Jackson, Tenn.
18. Boone Whiting, rhp, Centenary College.
19. *Chad Oberacker, of, Tennessee Tech.
20. Trevor Martin, ss, West Seattle HS.
21. Josh Lucas, rhp, State College of Florida-Manatee.
22. Steve Ramos, of, Ohlone (Calif.) JC.
23. Dyllon Nuernberg, rhp, Western Nevada CC.
24. Pat Biserta, of, Rutgers University.
25. Richard Mendoza, rhp, Isabel Flores HS, Juncos, P.R.
26. Victor Sanchez, 1b, University of San Diego.
27. Aidan Lucas, rhp, Denison (Ohio) University.
28. *Taylor Black, ss, University of Kentucky.
29. Chris Patterson, rhp, Appalachian State University.
30. Iden Nazario, lhp, University of Miami.
31. Mike O'Neill, of, University of Southern California.
32. Ryan Copeland, lhp, Illinois State University.
33. Joey Bergman, 2b, College of Charleston.
34. Matt Valaika, 2b, UC Santa Barbara.
35. Drew Benes, 3b, Arkansas State University.
DRAFT DROP *Son of Andy Benes, first overall draft pick, Padres (1988); major leaguer (1989-2002)*
36. Dean Kiekhefer, lhp, University of Louisville.
37. Packy Elkins, ss, Belmont University.
38. Jeff Nadeau, lhp, LSU-Shreveport.
39. *Ian Parry, rhp, Furman University.
40. Phil Cerreto, 3b, Longwood University.
41. Chase Reid, rhp, Vanderbilt University.
42. Cole Brand, rhp, Bradley Central HS, Cleveland, Tenn.
43. Chris Edmondson, of, Le Moyne University.
44. Adam Melker, of, Cal Poly.
45. *Robert Hansen, rhp, Beech HS, Hendersonville, Tenn.
46. *Peter Mooney, ss, Palm Beach (Fla.) CC.
47. Justin Wright, lhp, Virginia Tech.
48. *Hector Acosta, c, Coffeyville (Kan.) CC.
49. Bob Revesz, lhp, University of Louisville.
50. *Andy Moye, rhp, Georgia Southern University.

## SAN DIEGO PADRES (9)

1. *Karsten Whitson, rhp, Chipley (Fla.) HS.—(Short-season A)
DRAFT DROP *Attended Florida; re-drafted by Nationals, 2013 (37th round)*
2. **Jedd Gyorko, 2b, West Virginia University.—(2013-15)**
3. Zach Cates, rhp, Northeast Texas CC.—(AA)
4. Chris Bisson, 2b, University of Kentucky.—(AA)
5. **Rico Noel, of, Coastal Carolina University.—(2015)**
6. Johnny Barbato, rhp, Felix Varela HS, Miami.
7. *A.J. Vanegas, rhp, Redwood Christian HS, San Lorenzo, Calif.
8. Jose Dore, of, The First Academy, Orlando, Fla.
9. **Josh Spence, lhp, Arizona State University.—(2011-12)**
10. Houston Slemp, of, Eastern Oklahoma State JC.
11. B.J. Guinn, ss, University of California.
12. Chris Franklin, rhp, Southeastern Louisiana University.
13. *Miguel Pena, lhp, San Jacinto (Texas) JC.
14. **Tommy Medica, c, Santa Clara University.—(2013-14)**
15. *Sean Dwyer, 1b, Tavares (Fla.) HS.
16. *Conor Hofmann, of, St. Augustine HS, San Diego.
17. Wes Cunningham, 1b, Murray State University.
18. Dan Meeley, of, Connors State (Okla.) JC.
19. Tyler Norwood, rhp, Southern Union State (Ala.) CC.
20. Paul Bingham, ss, Indiana (Pa.) University.
21. Connor Powers, 1b, Mississippi State University.
DRAFT DROP *Son of John Powers, seventh-round draft pick, New York Giants, National Football League (1981)*
22. Tyler Stubblefield, 2b, Kennesaw State University.
23. *Xorge Carrillo, c, Arizona State University.
24. **Rocky Gale, c, University of Portland.—(2015)**
25. *Josue Montanez, lhp, Ramon Vila Mayo HS, San Juan, P.R.
26. *Cory Hahn, of, Mater Dei HS, Santa Ana, Calif.
27. Matt Branham, rhp, USC Upstate.
28. *Jacoby Almaraz, 3b, Lady Bird Johnson HS, San Antonio, Texas.
29. Mykal Stokes, of, Orange Coast (Calif.) CC.
30. *D.J. Snelten, lhp, Lakes Community HS, Lake Villa, Ill.
31. Oscar Garcia, of, Northwestern State University.
32. Will Scott, rhp, Walters State (Tenn.) CC.
33. Daniel Ottone, rhp, Western Carolina University.
34. Xavier Esquivel, rhp, Loyola Marymount University.
35. *Mike Ellis, rhp, Fleetwood Park SS, Surrey, B.C.
36. Rob Gariano, rhp, Fairfield University.
37. Chase Marona, rhp, Northwest Shoals (Ala.) CC University.
38. Noah Mull, lhp, Wheeling Jesuit (W.Va.) College.
39. Adam Schrader, rhp, Southwest Minnesota State University.
40. Justin Echevarria, c, Stony Brook University.
41. Bryan Altman, 2b, The Citadel.
42. Cole Tyrell, ss, Dayton University.
43. Mark Hardy, lhp, British Columbia.
44. Robert Sabo, rhp, Kent State University.
45. *Michael Fagan, lhp, San Diego Jewish Academy.
46. *Dominick Francia, of, St. Paul's Episcopal HS, Mobile, Ala.
47. *Kraig Kelly, 3b, Collinsville (Okla.) HS.
48. *Dan Child, rhp, Jesuit HS, Sacramento, Calif.
49. *Elliott Glynn, lhp, University of Connecticut.
50. Gunnar Terhune, of, UC Santa Barbara.

## SAN FRANCISCO GIANTS (23)

1. **Gary Brown, of, Cal State Fullerton.—(2014)**
2. **Jarrett Parker, of, University of Virginia.—(2015)**
3. Carter Jurica, ss, Kansas State University.—(AAA)
4. **Seth Rosin, rhp, University of Minnesota.—(2014-15)**
5. **Heath Hembree, rhp, College of Charleston.—(2013-14)**
6. **Mike Kickham, lhp, Missouri State University.—2013-14)**
7. Chuckie Jones, of, Boonville (Mo.) HS.
8. Joe Staley, c, Lubbock Christian (Texas) University.
9. Chris Lofton, of, Jones County (Miss.) JC.
10. Dan Burkhart, c, Ohio State University.
11. **Adam Duvall, 2b, University of Louisville.—(2014-15)**
12. Stephen Harrold, rhp, UNC Wilmington.
13. Tyler Christman, rhp, USC Sumter JC.
14. Raynor Campbell, 2b, Baylor University.
15. *Andrew Barbosa, lhp, University of South Florida.
16. Austin Fleet, rhp, Coastal Carolina University.
17. Ryan Bean, rhp, Edmonds (Wash.) CC.
18. Brandon Allen, rhp, Milton (Fla.) HS.
19. *Austin Southall, of, University HS, Baton Rouge, La.
20. **Brett Bochy, rhp, University of Kansas.—(2014-15)**
DRAFT DROP *Son of Bruce Bochy, major leaguer (1978-87); major league manager (1995-2015)*
21. *Zach Arneson, rhp, Cal State Bakersfield.
22. Bobby Haney, ss, University of South Carolina.
23. ***Alec Asher, rhp, Lakeland (Fla.) HS.—(2015)**
24. *Kyle Wilson, 3b, North Carolina State University.
25. Brett Krill, of, UCLA.
26. Jeff Arnold, c, University of Louisville.
27. Eric Sim, c, University of South Florida.
28. Gaspar Santiago, lhp, Ranger (Texas) JC.
29. Jose Cuevas, ss, Lee (Tenn.) University.
30. Ryan Bradley, lhp, Southern Illinois University.
31. *Kyle Hardy, 3b, Crowder (Mo.) JC.
32. Kevin Couture, rhp, University of Southern California.
33. *Jim Birmingham, lhp, Coastal Carolina University.
34. Johnathan DeBerry, of, Bethel (Tenn.) University.
35. Stephen Shackleford, rhp, Savannah College of Art & Design (Ga.).
36. *John Leonard, rhp, Boston College.
37. *Jake Sisco, rhp, Grace M. Davis HS, Modesto, Calif.
38. *Jake McCasland, rhp, Piedra Vista HS, Farmington, N.M.
39. *Tommy Tremblay, c, Edouard Montpetit (Quebec) JC.
40. Wes Hobson, 2b, Appalachian State University.
41. Ryan Honeycutt, of, University of New Mexico.
42. *James Roberts, rhp, Archbishop Mitty HS, San Jose, Calif.
43. *Raymond Ruggles, rhp, Tusculum (Tenn.) College.
44. Jake Shadle, rhp, Green River (Wash.) CC.
45. *Greg Greve, rhp, Walsh Jesuit HS, Cuyahoga Falls, Ohio.
46. Caleb Hougesen, 3b, Lutheran HS, Indianapolis.
47. *Ray Hanson, rhp, Cypress (Calif.) JC.
48. Devin Harris, of, East Carolina University.
49. *Dan Pellegrino, c, UC Riverside.
50. *Golden Tate, of, University of Notre Dame.
DRAFT DROP *Wide receiver, National Football League (2010-15)*

## SEATTLE MARINERS (17)

1. (Choice to Angels as compensation for Type A free agent Chone Figgins)
1. **Taijuan Walker, rhp, Yucaipa (Calif.) HS** (Supplemental choice—43rd—for loss of Type B free agent Adrian Beltre).**—(2013-15)**
2. Marcus Littlewood, ss, Pine View HS, St. George, Utah.—(AA)
3. *Ryne Stanek, rhp, Blue Valley HS, Stilwell, Kan.—(AA)
DRAFT DROP *Attended Arkansas; re-drafted by Rays, 2013 (1st round)*
4. **James Paxton, lhp, Grand Prairie (American Association).—(2013-15)**
DRAFT DROP *First-round draft pick (37th overall), Blue Jays (2009)*
5. **Stephen Pryor, rhp, Tennessee Tech.—(2012-14)**
6. Christian Carmichael, c, Mililani (Hawaii) HS.
7. Mickey Wiswall, 1b, Boston College.
8. Jabari Blash, of, Miami-Dade JC.
9. Luke Taylor, rhp, Woodinville (Wash.) HS.
10. Tyler Burgoon, rhp, University of Michigan.
11. *Jon Keller, rhp, Xavier HS, Cedar Rapids, Iowa.
12. **Stefen Romero, 3b, Oregon State University.—(2014-15)**
13. Jason Markovitz, lhp, Long Beach State University.
14. *Tyler Linehan, lhp, Sheldon HS, Sacramento, Calif.
15. Charles Kaalekahi, rhp, Campbell HS, Ewa Beach, Hawaii.
16. Jordan Shipers, lhp, South Harrison HS, Bethany, Mo.
17. Danny Lopez, ss, University of Pittsburgh.
18. Willy Kesler, rhp, University of New Mexico.
19. Frankie Christian, of, Upland (Calif.) HS.
20. Matt Bischoff, rhp, Purdue University.
21. *Luke Guarnaccia, c, St. Thomas Aquinas HS, Fort Lauderdale, Fla.
22. Steve Landazuri, rhp, Carter HS, Rialto, Calif.
23. Jandy Sena, rhp, Miami.
24. Ben Whitmore, lhp, Concordia (Calif.) University.
25. Ernesto Zaragoza, rhp, Kaiser HS, Fontana, Calif.
26. Robbie Anston, of, Boston College.
27. *Nick Fleece, rhp, Texas A&M University.
28. Tim Griffin, rhp, Rollins (Fla.) College.
29. *Jon McGibbon, 1b, Lindenhurst (N.Y.) HS.
30. Derek Poppert, ss, University of San Francisco.
31. Jake Schlander, ss, Stanford University.
32. Andrew Giobbi, c, Vanderbilt University.
33. *D.J. Peterson, 3b, Gilbert (Ariz.) HS.
DRAFT DROP *First-round draft pick (12th overall), Mariners (2013)*
34. (void) *Tyler Whitney, lhp, Mississippi State University.
35. Ethan Paquette, 1b, Hofstra University.
36. Forrest Snow, rhp, University of Washington.
37. Ryan Kiel, lhp, Marshall University.
38. Ben Versnik, rhp, University of Wisconsin-Whitewater.
39. Josh Krist, rhp, Cal Poly Pomona.
40. Nate Reed, rhp, Kutztown (Pa.) University.
41. Billy Marcoe, c, Cal State Fullerton.
42. Mike Aviles, rhp, St. Thomas Aquinas (N.Y.) College.
43. Matt Browning, 3b, James Madison University.
44. Tim Boyce, rhp, University of Rhode Island.
45. Stephen Kohlscheen, rhp, Auburn University.
46. ***David Rollins, lhp, San Jacinto (Texas) JC.—(2015)**
47. James Wood, of, Trinity (Conn.) University.
48. Patrick Brady, 2b, Bellarmine (Ky.) College.
49. *Colton Keough, of, Tesoro HS, Las Flores, Calif.
DRAFT DROP *Grandson of Marty Keough, major leaguer (1956-66) • Son of Matt Keough, major leaguer (1977-86)*
50. *David Holman, rhp, Hutchinson (Kan.) CC.
DRAFT DROP *Son of Brian Holman, first-round draft pick, Expos (1983); major leaguer (1988-91)*

## TAMPA BAY RAYS (16)

1. Josh Sale, of, Bishop Blanchet HS, Seattle.—(High A)
1. Justin O'Conner, c, Cowan HS, Muncie, Ind. (Special compensation choice—31st—for failure to sign 2009 first-round pick LeVon Washington).—(AA)
1. Drew Vettleson, of, Central Kitsap HS, Silverdale, Wash. (Supplemental choice—42nd—for loss of Type B Gregg Zaun).—(AA)
2. Jake Thompson, rhp, Long Beach State University.—(AAA)
2. **Derek Dietrich, 3b, Georgia Tech** (Special compensation choice—79th—for failure to sign 2009 second-round pick Kenny Diekroeger).**—(2013-15)**
DRAFT DROP *Grandson of Steve Demeter, major leaguer (1959-60)*
3. **Ryan Brett, 2b, Highline HS, Burien, Wash.—(2015)**
4. *Austin Wood, rhp, St. Petersburg (Fla.) JC.—(AA)
DRAFT DROP *Attended Southern California; re-drafted by Angels, 2011 (6th round)*
5. Ian Kendall, rhp, Ashland (Ore.) HS.—(Low A)
6. **Jesse Hahn, rhp, Virginia Tech.—(2014-15)**
7. ***Michael Lorenzen, of, Fullerton Union HS, Fullerton, Calif.—(2015)**
DRAFT DROP *First-round draft pick (38th overall), Reds (2013)*
8. Merrill Kelly, rhp, Arizona State University.
9. Jake DePew, c, Granite City (Ill.) HS.
10. Deshun Dixon, of, Terry HS, Jackson, Miss.
11. Travis Flores, 1b, Desert Ridge HS, Mesa, Ariz.
12. Phil Wunderlich, 1b, University of Louisville.
13. Robby Price, 2b, University of Kansas.
14. Austin Hubbard, rhp, Auburn University.
15. Brandon Henderson, lhp, Chesnee (S.C.) HS.
16. Nate Garcia, rhp, Santa Clara University.
17. ***Cody Anderson, rhp, Feather River (Calif.) JC.—(2015)**
18. Jimmy Patterson, lhp, Arizona State University.
19. Craige Lyerly, 2b, Catawba (N.C.) College.
20. **C.J. Riefenhauser, lhp, Chipola (Fla.) JC.—(2014-15)**
21. **Adam Liberatore, lhp, Tennessee Tech.—(2015)**
22. *Matt Koch, c, Loyola Marymount University.
23. *Kevin Patterson, 1b, Auburn University.
24. *Daniel Poncedeleon, rhp, La Mirada (Calif.) HS.
25. Matt Spann, lhp, Columbia Central HS, Columbia, Tenn.
26. Justin Woodall, lhp, University of Alabama.
27. Chris Winder, of, Odessa (Texas) JC.
28. *Julio Espinoza, ss, Rialto (Calif.) HS.
29. Scott Lawson, 2b, University of Miami.
30. Nick Schwaner, 3b, University of New Orleans.
31. **Kevin Kiermaier, of, Parkland (Ill.) JC.—(2013-15)**
32. Bryan Fogle, of, Erskine (S.C.) College.

33. *Scott Simon, rhp, Central Valley HS, Spokane, Wash.
34. Steve Tinoco, 1b, Long Beach State University.
35. *Spencer Davis, rhp, The Woodlands (Texas) HS.
36. Robert Dickmann, lhp, Pepperdine University.
37. *Demondre Arnold, rhp, Creekside HS, Fairburn, Ga.
38. *Will Anderson, rhp, Foothill HS, Pleasanton, Calif.
39. Parker Markel, rhp, Yavapai (Ariz.) JC.
40. Wade Broyles, rhp, Belhaven (Miss.) College.
41. **Chris Rearick, lhp, North Georgia College and State University.—(2015)**
42. *Preston Overbey, 3b, University School, Jackson, Tenn.
43. *Ryan Hornback, c, San Jacinto (Texas) JC.
44. Mickey Jannis, rhp, Cal State Bakersfield.
45. *Blake Freeman, lhp, Sunnyslope HS, Phoenix.
46. George Jensen, rhp, Des Moines Area (Iowa) CC.
47. *Hector Montes, 1b, Bonita Vista HS, Chula Vista, Calif.
48. *Blake Barnes, rhp, Howard (Texas) JC.
49. *Paul Hoilman, 1b, East Tennessee State University.
50. *Cory Maltz, rhp, Weatherford (Texas) JC.

## TEXAS RANGERS (21)

1. Jake Skole, of, Blessed Trinity HS, Roswell, Ga. (Special compensation choice—15th—for failure to sign 2009 first-round pick Matt Purke).—(AA)
1. Kellin Deglan, c, R.E. Mountain SS, Langley, B.C.—(AA)
1. **Luke Jackson, rhp, Calvary Christian HS, Fort Lauderdale, Fla.** (Supplemental choice—45th—for loss of Type B free agent Marlon Byrd).**—(2015)**
1. **Mike Olt, 3b, University of Connecticut** (Supplemental choice—49th—for loss of Type B free agent Marlon Byrd).**—(2012-15)**
2. Cody Buckel, rhp, Royal HS, Simi Valley, Calif.—(AA)
3. Jordan Akins, of, Union Grove HS, McDonough, Ga.—(Low A)
4. Drew Robinson, ss, Silverado HS, Las Vegas, Nev.—(AAA)
5. **Justin Grimm, rhp, University of Georgia.—(2012-15)**
6. Brett Nicholas, c, University of Missouri.
7. Jimmy Reyes, lhp, Elon University.
8. Jonathan Roof, ss, Michigan State University.

DRAFT DROP *Son of Gene Roof, major leaguer (1981-83) • Nephew of Phil Roof, major leaguer (1961-77)*

9. Zach Osborne, rhp, University of Louisiana-Lafayette.
10. Jared Hoying, ss, University of Toledo.
11. Chris Hanna, lhp, Stratford HS, Goose Creek, S.C.
12. Josh Richmond, of, University of Louisville.
13. Andrew Clark, 1b, University of Louisville.
14. **Nick Tepesch, rhp, University of Missouri.—(2013-14)**
15. Ryan Rodebaugh, rhp, Kennesaw State University.
16. **Ryan Strausborger, of, Indiana State University.—(2015)**
17. Anthony Haase, rhp, Cochise (Ariz.) JC.
18. *Garrett Buechele, 3b, University of Oklahoma.

DRAFT DROP *Son of Steve Buechele, first-round draft pick, White Sox (1979); major leaguer (1985-95)*

19. Brett Weibley, rhp, Kent State University.
20. *Sam Wilson, lhp, Eldorado HS, Albuquerque, N.M.
21. Joe Van Meter, rhp, Virginia Commonwealth University.
22. **Ben Rowen, rhp, Virginia Tech.—(2014)**
23. Andres Perez-Lobo, rhp, Christopher Columbus HS, Miami.
24. *Jake Cole, rhp, Sahuaro HS, Tucson, Ariz.
25. Kendall Radcliffe, of, Morgan Park HS, Chicago.
26. *Chase Johnson, rhp, Fallbrook (Calif.) HS.
27. **Alex Claudio, lhp, Isabel Flores HS, Juncos, P.R.—(2014-15)**
28. John Kukuruda, rhp, East Nicolaus HS, Nicolaus, Calif.
29. *Trae Davis, rhp, Mexia (Texas) HS.
30. *Brian Ragira, of, James Martin HS, Arlington, Texas.
31. Justin Earls, lhp, University of Georgia.
32. Steve McKinnon, rhp, Cowichan SS, Duncan, B.C.
33. Matt Hill, lhp, Georgia Perimeter JC.
34. Kevin Rodland, ss, University of Nevada.
35. *John Lieske, rhp, Harlem HS, Machesney Park, Ill.
36. Jason Kudlock, of, Cal State Bakersfield.
37. *John Pustay, of, Pine Creek HS, Colorado Springs, Colo.
38. Carson Vitale, c, Creighton University.
39. *Ryan Woolley, rhp, University of Alabama-Birmingham.
40. Travis Meiners, of, Dallas Baptist University.
41. Colby Killian, rhp, Emporia State (Kan.) University.
42. Kevin Johnson, lhp, University of Cincinnati.
43. *Chris Roglen, of, Rocky Mountain HS, Fort Collins, Colo.
44. *Shawn Stuart, rhp, Merced (Calif.) JC.
45. Johnathan Moore, c, Houston Baptist University.
46. *Daryl Norris, rhp, Fairhope (Ala.) HS.
47. *Daniel Ward, rhp, Garfield Heights (Ohio) HS.
48. *Forrest Koumas, rhp, Lugoff-Elgin HS, Lugoff, S.C.
49. *Juan Gomes, c, Southridge HS, Miami.
50. *Trevor Teykl, rhp, Kempner HS, Sugar Land, Texas.

## TORONTO BLUE JAYS (11)

1. Deck McGuire, rhp, Georgia Tech.—(AAA)
1. **Aaron Sanchez, rhp, Barstow (Calif.) HS** (Supplemental choice—34th—for loss of Type A free agent Marco Scutaro).**—(2014-15)**
1. **Noah Syndergaard, rhp, Legacy HS, Mansfield, Texas** (Special compensation choice—38th—for failure to sign 2009 supplemental first-round pick James Paxton).**—(2015)**
1. **Asher Wojciechowski, rhp, The Citadel** (Supplemental choice—41st—for loss of Type B free agent Rod Barajas).**—(2015)**
2. Griffin Murphy, lhp, Redlands East Valley HS. Redlands, Calif.—(High A)
2. Kellen Sweeney, 3b, Jefferson HS, Cedar Rapids, Iowa (Special compensation choice—69th—for failure to sign 2009 second-round pick Jake Eliopoulos).—(High A)

DRAFT DROP *Brother of Ryan Sweeney, major leaguer (2006-14)*

2. **Justin Nicolino, lhp, University HS, Orlando, Fla.** (Choice from Red Sox as compensation or Scutaro).**—(2015)**
3. Chris Hawkins, 3b, North Gwinnett HS, Suwanee, Ga.—(High A)
3. Marcus Knecht, of, Connors State (Okla.) JC (Special compensation choice—113th—for failure to sign 2009 third-round pick Jake Barnett).—(AA)
4. **Sam Dyson, rhp, University of South Carolina.—(2012-15)**
5. Dickie Joe Thon, ss, Academia Perpetio Socorro, San Juan, P.R.—(High A)

DRAFT DROP *Son of Dickie Thon, major leaguer (1979-93)*

6. **Sean Nolin, lhp, San Jacinto (Texas) JC.—(2013-15)**
7. Mitchell Taylor, lhp, Spring (Texas) HS.
8. *Logan Ehlers, lhp, Nebraska City (Neb.) HS.
9. Brandon Mims, ss, Smith HS, Carrollton, Texas.
10. *Tyler Shreve, rhp, Phelps County HS, Redlands, Calif.
11. Shane Opitz, ss, Heritage HS, Centennial, Colo.
12. *Omar Cotto, of, Bonneville School, San Juan, P.R.
13. *Tyler Painton, lhp, Centennial HS, Bakersfield, Calif.
14. Dayton Marze, rhp, University of Louisiana-Lafayette.
15. Zak Adams, lhp, Flower Mound (Texas) HS.
16. **Dalton Pompey, of, John Fraser SS, Mississauga, Ontario.—(2014-15)**
17. Myles Jaye, rhp, Starrs Mill HS, Fayetteville, Ga.
18. ***Kris Bryant, 3b, Bonanza HS, Las Vegas, Nev.—(2015)**

DRAFT DROP *First-round draft pick (2nd overall), Cubs (2013)*

19. Travis Garrett, rhp, Cypress (Calif.) JC.
20. Art Charles, lhp, Bakersfield (Calif.) JC.
21. *Chris Marlowe, rhp, Navarro (Texas) JC.
22. *Aaron Westlake, of, Vanderbilt University.
23. Angel Gomez, of, Maria Cruz Buitrago HS, San Lorenzo, P.R.
24. Ronnie Melendez, of, Cowley County (Kan.) CC.
25. *Brando Tessar, rhp, Chaminade College Prep, West Hills, Calif.
26. *Jay Johnson, lhp, Texas Tech.
27. *Eric Arce, c, Lakeland (Fla.) HS.
28. Adaric Kelly, rhp, Trinity Christian Academy, Lake Worth, Fla.
29. Jonathan Jones, of, Long Beach State University.
30. Steve McQuail, 2b, Canisius University.
31. *Luis Benitez, rhp, Ashworth HS, Carolina, P.R.
32. Andy Fermin, 2b, Chipola (Fla.) JC.

DRAFT DROP *Son of Felix Fermin, major leaguer (1987-96)*

33. Melvin Garcia, of, James Monroe HS, New York City.
34. Tyler Powell, rhp, Belmont-Abbey (N.C.) College.
35. Dan Barnes, rhp, Princeton University.
36. *David Whitehead, rhp, Moeller HS, Cincinnati.
37. *Chad Green, rhp, Effingham (Ill.) HS.
38. Pierce Rankin, c, University of Washington.
39. *Nick Vander Tuig, rhp, Oakdale (Calif.) HS.
40. Brandon Berl, rhp, St. Mary's (Calif.) College.
41. Seth Conner, 3b, Logan-Rogersville HS, Rogersville, Mo.
42. Drew Permison, rhp, Towson University.
43. *Ron Schreurs, lhp, Freedom HS, Orlando, Fla.
44. *Mott Hyde, 2b, Calhoun (Ga.) HS.
45. *Phil Diedrick, of, Pickering HS, Ajax, Ontario.
46. *Connor Smith, rhp, Blessed Trinity SS, Grimsby, Ontario.
47. *Gabriel Romero, rhp, Roosevelt HS, Los Angeles.

DRAFT DROP *Brother of Ricky Romero, first-round draft pick, Blue Jays (2005); major leaguer (2009-13)*

48. *Nick Studer, c, St. Michael's College HS, Toronto.
49. Matt Abraham, 2b, Eckerd (Fla.) College.
50. *Kelly Norris-Jones, c, Lambrick Park SS, Victoria, B.C.

## WASHINGTON NATIONALS (1)

1. **Bryce Harper, c-of, CC of Southern Nevada.—(2012-15)**

DRAFT DROP *Brother of Brian Harper, 27th-round draft pick, Cubs (2010)*

2. **Sammy Solis, lhp, University of San Diego.—(2015)**
3. Rick Hague, ss, Rice University.—(AAA)
4. **A.J. Cole, rhp, Oviedo (Fla.) HS.—(2015)**
5. Jason Martinson, ss, Texas State University.—(AAA)
6. Cole Leonida, c, Georgia Tech.
7. Kevin Keyes, of, University of Texas.
8. **Matt Grace, lhp, UCLA.—(2015)**
9. **Aaron Barrett, rhp, University of Mississippi.—(2014-15)**
10. Blake Kelso, ss, University of Houston.
11. Neil Holland, rhp, University of Louisville.
12. **Robbie Ray, lhp, Brentwood (Tenn.) HS.—(2014-15)**
13. Chris McKenzie, rhp, San Jacinto (Texas) JC.
14. *Tim Smalling, ss, Virginia Tech.
15. David Freitas, c, University of Hawaii.
16. Mark Herrera, rhp, San Jacinto (Texas) JC.
17. Tyler Hanks, rhp, CC of Southern Nevada.
18. Justin Miller, 2b, Middle Tennessee State University.
19. Wade Moore, of, Catawba (N.C.) College.
20. Chad Mozingo, of, Rice University.
21. Connor Rowe, of, University of Texas.
22. Cameron Selik, rhp, University of Kansas.
23. Colin Bates, rhp, University of North Carolina.
24. Russ Moldenhauer, 1b, University of Texas.
25. Christian Meza, lhp, Santa Ana (Calif.) JC.
26. Chris Manno, lhp, Duke University.
27. *Sean Hoelscher, rhp, Texas A&M University-Corpus Christi.
28. *Joey Rapp, 1b, Chipola (Fla.) JC.
29. Rick Hughes, of, CC of Marin (Calif.).
30. *Tim Kiene, 1b, Avon Old Farms HS, Avon, Conn.
31. Jeremy Mayo, c, Texas Tech.
32. Randolph Oduber, of, Western Oklahoma State JC.
33. *Ryan Sherriff, lhp, West Los Angeles JC.
34. *Rolando Botello, rhp, John Jay HS, San Antonio, Texas.
35. Tyler Oliver, 1b, Wabash Valley (Ill.) CC.
36. Wander Nunez, of, Western Oklahoma State JC.
37. Nick Serino, lhp, University of Massachusetts.
38. *Nick Lee, lhp, Weatherford (Texas) JC.
39. *John Simms, rhp, College Park HS, The Woodlands, Texas.
40. *Alejandro Diaz, ss, John A. Ferguson HS, Miami.
41. Kevin Cahill, rhp, Purdue University.
42. *Taylor Stark, 2b, Northwest Rankin HS, Flowood, Miss.
43. *Corey Littrell, lhp, Trinity HS, Louisville, Ky.
44. *Bryce Hines, rhp, Hanahan (S.C.) HS.
45. *Jeff Bouton, of, Hoggard HS, Wilmington, N.C.
46. *Erick Fernandez, c, Georgetown University.
47. *Lance Jarreld, of, Goodpasture HS, Madison, Tenn.
48. *Brandon Miller, c, Northwest Florida State JC.
49. Rashad Hatcher, of, Patrick Henry (Va.) CC.
50. *Harrison Fanaroff, lhp, Winston Churchill HS, Potomac, Md.

## AT A GLANCE

### This Date In History
June 6-8

### Best Draft
**BOSTON RED SOX.** By 2015, the Red Sox had six players from the first five rounds in the major leagues, including **BLAKE SWIHART** (1), **JACKIE BRADLEY JR.** (1-S) and **MOOKIE BETTS** (5).

### Worst Draft
**LOS ANGELES DODGERS.** In contrast to the Padres, who had 10 draft picks reach the major leagues by the end of the 2015 season, the Dodgers had just two, pitchers **CHRIS REED** (1) and **SCOTT MCGOUGH** (5), who both were traded to the Marlins.

### First-Round Bust
**KEVIN MATTHEWS, LHP, RANGERS.** The Rangers lost all-star pitcher Cliff Lee to the Phillies in free agency after the 2010 season. Their compensation pick was Matthews, who went 6-7, 4.56 with 110 walks in 124 innings over four minor league seasons in the Rangers system, none above Class A. He was released by Texas in 2015 after a drunken-driving charge.

### Second Best
**BRAD MILLER, SS, MARINERS.** Among the second-rounders drafted in 2011, Miller was the most productive big leaguer through the 2015 season. He hit .248 with 29 home runs and 118 RBIs in three seasons with the Mariners before being traded to Tampa Bay.

### Late-Round Find
**KEVIN PILLAR, OF, BLUE JAYS (32ND ROUND).** The Blue Jays had seven of the first 78 picks. Four years later, none had performed as well as Pillar, pick No. 979. He played a key role in the Blue Jays getting to the postseason in 2015 for the first time in 22 years, hitting .278 with 12 homers and making highlight-reel plays in center field. Pillar had a 54-game hitting

# Deep class, change on horizon lead to spree

It wasn't a coincidence that the most sweeping changes to the baseball draft in its 46-year history occurred in 2011, just months after almost every bonus record imaginable was broken. Not since the draft was adopted in 1965 as a means of controlling spending on amateur talent had there been such a pronounced cause-and-effect relationship.

Major League Baseball's 30 clubs spent a total of $228,009,050 in 2011 on drafted players, an 8.9 percent increase from 2010. The Pittsburgh Pirates, holding the No. 1 pick, drafted UCLA righthander Gerrit Cole and signed him for a record $8 million bonus, and their $17,005,700 outlay for all their picks easily eclipsed the previous record. Both those standards had been held by the Washington Nationals, who spent $7.5 million on No. 1 pick Stephen Strasburg in 2009 and $11,927,200 overall in 2010.

Not surprisingly, the average first-round bonus of $2,653,375 was a substantial increase from the 2010 figure of $2,220,966, and surpassed the previous record of $2,434,800, set in 2009.

All those marks would take a downturn in 2012, after MLB and the Players Association agreed to significant changes to the draft as part of a new Collective Bargaining Agreement that was ratified in November 2011. The most noteworthy adjustment was the introduction of a threshold on bonuses that penalized clubs in the form of fines and the loss of draft choices if they exceeded budgeted limits to sign their picks.

But the old system still was in effect in 2011, and despite the efforts of the commissioner's office to pressure clubs to keep bonuses in check, there was an onslaught of bonus records and unprecedented spending before the Aug. 15 signing deadline.

The Pirates, coming off a 105-loss season and in the midst of a major league record 19 straight years with a sub-.500 record, were determined to draft the best player available, regardless of cost. They not only signed Cole for a record bonus, but also set a record in the second round by agreeing to a $5 million bonus for Texas high school outfielder Josh Bell. The Pirates also committed $1.2 million to Alabama prep righthander Clay Holmes, a record for an eighth-round selection.

None of those players signed until minutes before the deadline, which had become pretty much standard procedure for a majority of first-rounders, plus an assortment of other players who agreed to deals above the slot values recommended by the commissioner's office. A total of 22 of 33 first-rounders signed on deadline day, and in the process three of the five largest bonuses ever given to players signing with the teams that drafted them were handed out.

A total of 24 players received bonuses of $2 million or more, including 14 of the first 15 selections, and 52 exceeded $1 million. Ten clubs each spent more than $10 million to sign draft picks. Individual bonus records were set in seven different rounds, including the first (Cole), second (Bell), third and fifth.

LARRY GOREN

**Gerrit Cole's losing record during his junior season at UCLA belied his premium ability, and Cole wasted little time reaching the major leagues after the Pirates took him with the No. 1 overall pick**

### TOUGH ACT TO FOLLOW

The 2009 and 2010 drafts were defined by the presence of Strasburg and Bryce Harper, two of the best prospects of the draft era, and the Nationals had the good fortune to pick first each year. The Pirates' options were a little more muddled, though the overall pool of players they had to choose from was considered one of the deepest in years.

Entering the 2011 season, the top three prospects were Cole, an unsigned first-rounder from 2008; Texas Christian lefthander Matt Purke, an unsigned first-rounder from 2009; and Rice University third baseman Anthony Rendon, the 2010 Golden Spikes Award recipient. However, none of the three performed anywhere near the level they had a year earlier, somewhat complicating the Pirates' task.

Cole posted a losing record, going 6-8, 3.31. Rendon hit at a blistering clip as both a freshman (.388-20-72) and sophomore (.394-26-85), and was generally perceived to be the No. 1 prospect

## 2011: THE FIRST ROUNDERS

| CLUB: PLAYER, POS., SCHOOL | HOMETOWN | B-T | HT. | WT. | AGE | BONUS | FIRST YEAR | LAST YEAR | PEAK LEVEL (YEARS) |
|---|---|---|---|---|---|---|---|---|---|
| 1. Pirates: Gerrit Cole, rhp, UCLA | Orange, Calif. | R-R | 6-4 | 220 | 20 | $8,000,000 | 2012 | Active | Majors (3) |
| Pirates locked in on 2008 first-rounder, even as he went 6-8, 3.31 for Bruins; legit power arm with high-90s FB, justified selection with early big league dominance. | | | | | | | | | |
| 2. *Mariners: Danny Hultzen, lhp, Virginia | Bethesda, Md. | L-L | 6-3 | 200 | 21 | $6,350,000 | 2012 | Active | Class AAA (3) |
| Unsignable out of HS, dominated in college (32-5, 2.08, 320 IP/395 Ks); polished arm, legit stuff, dominated early before being beset by major shoulder issues. | | | | | | | | | |
| 3. *Diamondbacks: Trevor Bauer, rhp, UCLA | Santa Clarita, Calif. | R-R | 6-1 | 185 | 20 | $3,400,000 | 2011 | Active | Majors (4) |
| Enrolled at UCLA a year early, went 34-8 in three years, fanned 203 in 136 IP as JR; drew attention for training methods, spotty MLB success because of command. | | | | | | | | | |
| 4. *Orioles: Dylan Bundy, rhp, Owasso HS | Owasso, Okla. | R-R | 6-1 | 195 | 18 | $4,000,000 | 2012 | Active | Majors (1) |
| One of most acclaimed/advanced HS pitchers ever, went 11-0, 0.20 (71 IP, 5 BB/158 SO), dominated minors before 2013 Tommy John surgery, one win since. | | | | | | | | | |
| 5. Royals: Bubba Starling, of, Gardner-Edgerton HS | Gardner, Kan. | R-R | 6-4 | 180 | 18 | $7,500,000 | 2012 | Active | Class AA (1) |
| Small-town three-sport star signed to play QB at Nebraska, but star potential/proximity made him natural fit for Royals; has shown signs of rewarding KC's patience. | | | | | | | | | |
| 6. *Nationals: Anthony Rendon, 3b, Rice | Houston | R-R | 6-0 | 195 | 21 | $6,000,000 | 2012 | Active | Majors (3) |
| Top bat in college ranks hit .391-46-157 in first two years at Rice, .327-6-30 as JR; prone to injuries, but moved quickly to majors, with just 260 ABs in minors. | | | | | | | | | |
| 7. Diamondbacks: Archie Bradley, rhp, Broken Arrow HS | Broken Arrow, Okla. | R-R | 6-4 | 225 | 18 | $5,000,000 | 2011 | Active | Majors (1) |
| Also a top QB recruit, but overshadowed in own state by Bundy, went 12-1, 0.29 (71 IP, 11 BB/137 SO) as SR; made steady climb to MLB, waiting to break through. | | | | | | | | | |
| 8. Indians: Francisco Lindor, ss, Montverde HS | Montverde, Fla. | B-R | 5-11 | 175 | 17 | $2,900,000 | 2011 | Active | Majors (1) |
| Puerto Rico native moved to U.S. as youth to enhance baseball development; switch-hitter with line-drive approach, exceptional instincts, superlative SS skills. | | | | | | | | | |
| 9. Cubs: Javier Baez, ss, Arlington Country Day HS | Jacksonville, Fla. | R-R | 6-1 | 205 | 18 | $2,625,000 | 2011 | Active | Majors (2) |
| Like Lindor, moved to Florida from Puerto Rico in 2005, but different kind of talent; moved to outfield, possesses electric bat speed, though highly prone to strikeout. | | | | | | | | | |
| 10. Padres: Cory Spangenberg, 2b, Indian River (Fla.) JC | Clarks Summit, Pa. | L-R | 6-0 | 185 | 20 | $1,863,000 | 2011 | Active | Majors (2) |
| Transferred from VMI to JC to become draft eligible, attracted scouts with huge spring (.477-5-32, 33 SB); discount price so Padres could go over slot with 25th pick. | | | | | | | | | |
| 11. Astros: George Springer, of, Connecticut | New Britain, Conn. | R-R | 6-3 | 200 | 21 | $2,525,000 | 2011 | Active | Majors (2) |
| Overlooked out of northeast HS, made three-year impact at UConn, hit 46 HRs/stole 76 bases; impressed scouts with CF athleticism, concerns about contact. | | | | | | | | | |
| 12. Brewers: Taylor Jungmann, rhp, Texas | Georgetown, Texas | R-R | 6-6 | 210 | 21 | $2,525,000 | 2012 | Active | Majors (1) |
| Dominant college arm (32-9, 1.85, 356 IP/356 SO) with fastball that peaked at 99; velocity dipped in minors, spun wheels until impressive MLB debut in 2015. | | | | | | | | | |
| 13. Mets: Brandon Nimmo, of, East HS | Cheyenne, Wyo. | L-R | 6-3 | 185 | 18 | $2,100,000 | 2011 | Active | Class AAA (1) |
| First-ever first-rounder from Wyoming; no HS baseball in state, so played American Legion ball; scouts drawn to athleticism (football/track star), hitting instincts. | | | | | | | | | |
| 14. Marlins: Jose Fernandez, rhp, Braulio Alonso HS | Tampa | R-R | 6-3 | 215 | 18 | $2,000,000 | 2011 | Active | Majors (3) |
| Cuban defector battled HS eligibility rules in U.S.; had command/raw stuff (mid-90s fastball, plus slider) to move quickly, dominated in majors before '14 TJ surgery. | | | | | | | | | |
| 15. Brewers: Jed Bradley, lhp, Georgia Tech | Huntsville, Ala. | L-L | 6-4 | 225 | 20 | $2,000,000 | 2012 | Active | Class AAA (1) |
| Stock shot up as college junior (7-3, 3.49) when fastball spiked to mid-90s, tailed off just as quickly in pro ball (22-29, 4.68) with injuries/delivery issues. | | | | | | | | | |
| 16. Dodgers: Chris Reed, lhp, Stanford | Encino, Calif. | L-L | 6-4 | 195 | 21 | $1,589,000 | 2011 | Active | Majors (1) |
| Reliever only at Stanford (6-2, 2.54, 9 SV as JR), but Dodgers made him a starter; showed poor command/inconsistent stuff, went 9-31 before switched back. | | | | | | | | | |
| 17. Angels: C.J. Cron, 1b, Utah | Phoenix | R-R | 6-4 | 235 | 21 | $1,467,000 | 2011 | Active | Majors (2) |
| Son of ex-MLB first baseman and longtime minor league manager Chris; dominant college hitter; value entirely tied to bat, .260-27-88 hitter in 192 MLB games. | | | | | | | | | |
| 18. Athletics: Sonny Gray, rhp, Vanderbilt | Smyrna, Tenn. | R-R | 5-11 | 200 | 21 | $1,540,000 | 2011 | Active | Majors (3) |
| Overcame size bias with superior stuff/athletic ability; went 27-10, 3.19 in Vandy career with mid-90s fastball, knockout curve, quickly settled in as A's ace in 2013. | | | | | | | | | |
| 19. Red Sox: Matt Barnes, rhp, Connecticut | Bethel, Conn. | R-R | 6-4 | 205 | 20 | $1,500,000 | 2012 | Active | Majors (2) |
| Teamed with Springer, went 11-5, 1.93 on best Northeast college team ever; featured mid-90s fastball, but progress as pro stunted by breaking ball/command. | | | | | | | | | |
| 20. Rockies: Tyler Anderson, lhp, Oregon | Las Vegas | L-L | 6-4 | 215 | 21 | $1,400,000 | 2012 | Active | Class AA (1) |
| Went 8-3, 2.34 as Oregon junior, 23-10, 2.39 in first three pro years with deceptive delivery, feel for pitching; injury prone, missed 2015 with elbow stress fracture. | | | | | | | | | |
| 21. Blue Jays: Tyler Beede, rhp, Lawrence Academy | Auburn, Mass. | R-R | 6-4 | 200 | 18 | Unsigned | 2014 | Active | Class AA (1) |
| Committed to Vanderbilt, but Jays gambled anyway, made last-ditch $2.5M offer; had uneven college career but was a first-rounder (Giants) again in 2014. | | | | | | | | | |
| 22. Cardinals: Kolten Wong, 2b, Hawaii | Honolulu, Hawaii | L-R | 5-9 | 190 | 20 | $1,300,000 | 2011 | Active | Majors (3) |
| Excelled in all phases of game at Hawaii (.358-25-145), but it took dominant 2010 summer on Cape Cod to legitimize top-round status; has since justified selection. | | | | | | | | | |
| 23. Nationals: Alex Meyer, rhp, Kentucky | Greensburg, Ind. | R-R | 6-9 | 220 | 21 | $2,000,000 | 2012 | Active | Majors (1) |
| Potential first-round talent out of high school was considered unsignable then, struggled for two years at UK but found command of upper-90s heat/slider. | | | | | | | | | |
| 24. Rays: Taylor Guerrieri, rhp, Spring Valley HS | Columbia, Ga. | R-R | 6-3 | 195 | 18 | $1,600,000 | 2012 | Active | Class AA (1) |
| Emerged as first-rounder with three plus pitches; pro career interrupted in 2013 by TJ surgery, drug suspension, but 12-7, 1.62 in 51 pro outings. | | | | | | | | | |
| 25. Padres: Joe Ross, rhp, Bishop O'Dowd HS | Oakland, Calif. | R-R | 6-3 | 185 | 18 | $2,750,000 | 2011 | Active | Majors (1) |
| Younger brother of Tyson, though little physical/mechanical similarity; Joe has smoother delivery, command of FB/slider, reached MLB with Nationals in 2015. | | | | | | | | | |
| 26. Red Sox: Blake Swihart, c, Cleveland HS | Rio Rancho, N.M. | B-R | 6-1 | 175 | 19 | $2,500,000 | 2011 | Active | Majors (1) |
| Rare top New Mexico prospect; already advanced hitter/athlete, enhanced draft value by becoming switch-hitting catcher; made swift climb through Sox system. | | | | | | | | | |
| 27. Reds: Robert Stephenson, rhp, Alhambra HS | Martinez, Calif. | R-R | 6-2 | 190 | 18 | $2,000,000 | 2012 | Active | Class AAA (1) |
| Routinely compared by scouts to Joe Ross, fellow NorCal prospect; had better stuff of two with fastball up to 97mph/hammer curve, less command. | | | | | | | | | |
| 28. Braves: Sean Gilmartin, lhp, Florida State | Encino, Calif. | L-L | 6-2 | 190 | 21 | $1,134,000 | 2011 | Active | Majors (1) |
| FSU ace for three years as finesse lefty, had breakthrough JR year (12-1, 1.83, 113 IP, 20 BB/122 SO); success tougher to find in minors, but reached majors in 2015. | | | | | | | | | |
| 29. Giants: Joe Panik, ss, St. John's | Hopewell Junction, N.Y. | L-R | 6-1 | 190 | 20 | $1,116,000 | 2011 | Active | Majors (2) |
| Not a consensus first-rounder with no plus tool except bat; hit .398-10-57 as college JR, won batting title as first-year pro, .309 hitter to date as young big leaguer. | | | | | | | | | |
| 30. Twins: Levi Michael, ss, North Carolina | Lexington, N.C. | B-R | 5-10 | 190 | 20 | $1,175,000 | 2012 | Active | Class AA (2) |
| Became first-rounder with polished plate approach/advanced defensive ability, but struggled with injuries, bat in minors (.259-12-121), also shifted to 2B. | | | | | | | | | |
| 31. Rays: Mikie Mahtook, of, Louisiana State | Lafayette, La. | R-R | 6-1 | 200 | 21 | $1,150,000 | 2012 | Active | Majors (1) |
| Son of ex-LSU football star, led Tigers to CWS title as FR, SEC in hitting/steals as JR (.383-14-56, 29 SB); solid in all phases, gets most of ability with drive/makeup. | | | | | | | | | |
| 32. Rays: Jake Hager, ss, Sierra Vista HS | Las Vegas, Nev. | R-R | 6-1 | 170 | 18 | $963,000 | 2011 | Active | Class AA (1) |
| Hit .547-11-57 as prep SR to sneak into first round; solid defender with skills to remain at SS, power still evolving; missed 2015 season with knee injury. | | | | | | | | | |
| 33. Rangers: Kevin Matthews, lhp, Richmond Hill HS | Richmond Hill, Ga. | R-L | 5-11 | 180 | 18 | $936,000 | 2011 | 2015 | Class A (4) |
| Surprise pick won Rangers over with velo spike to mid-90s/power curve; went 6-7, 4.57 in career impacted by shoulder/command issues, released in 2015. | | | | | | | | | |

**Signed to major league contract.*

## AT A GLANCE

streak in 2010 at Cal State Dominguez Hills, and was a .322 hitter on his four-year odyssey through the minor leagues.

### Never Too Late

**C.J. EDWARDS, RHP, RANGERS (48TH ROUND).** The Rangers drafted Edwards after scouting him in an adult league in South Carolina. He signed for a $50,000 bonus, and with a mid-90s fastball quickly established himself as one of the top prospects in the organization. Edwards was one of four prospects sent to the Cubs in a 2013 trade for righthander Matt Garza, and made his big league debut in September 2015.

### Overlooked

**KEITH HESSLER, LHP, DIAMONDBACKS.** Hessler went 5-6, 4.89 in three years at Coastal Carolina, working mostly in relief. The Diamondbacks selected him in the 28th round in 2010 as a draft-eligible sophomore. He didn't sign, but agreed to a contract with Arizona a year later after going undrafted. Hessler reached the majors in 2015, going 0-1, 8.03 in 18 relief appearances.

### International Gem

**LEONYS MARTIN, OF, RANGERS.** The Rangers signed three high-profile Latin American outfielders in 2011. Martin, a 23-year-old Cuban defector, got a five-year, $15.5 million deal, including a $5 million signing bonus. The others were 16-year-old Dominican Republic outfielders **NOMAR MAZARA**, who signed for $4.95 million, and **RONALD GUZMAN**, who got $3.45 million. Through 2015, Martin had spent four years in the majors, hitting .255 with 20 homers, 120 RBIs and 84 stolen bases.

### Minor League Take

**JOSE FERNANDEZ, RHP, MARLINS.** In his only full season in the minors,

CONTINUED ON PAGE 688

## AT A GLANCE

CONTINUED FROM PAGE 687

Fernandez went 14-1, 1.88 with 35 walks and 158 strikeouts in 134 innings between low Class A Greensboro and high-A Jupiter. A year later, he was Baseball America's Rookie of the Year.

### One Who Got Away

**TYLER BEEDE, RHP, BLUE JAYS (1ST ROUND).** The Blue Jays drafted Beede in the first round, but were unable to sign him. They also had failed to sign supplemental first-rounder James Paxton in 2009 and did not sign first-rounder Phil Bickford in 2013. After three years at Vanderbilt, Beede was selected in the first round by the Giants.

### He Was Drafted?

**TREVOR GRETZKY, OF, CUBS (7TH ROUND).** Gretzky, son of all-time hockey great Wayne Gretzky, grew up in Southern California and devoted his attention to baseball. He signed with the Cubs for $375,000. In four minor league seasons through 2015, none above Class A, Gretzy hit .258 with six home runs and 58 RBIs.

### Did You Know ...

The richest bonus contracts for amateur prospects, both domestic and international, were signed in 2011. UCLA righthander **GERRIT COLE** received $8 million from the Pirates as the No. 1 pick in the draft, and 16-year-old Dominican outfielder **NOMAR MAZARA** received $4.95 million.

### They Said It

Marlins first-round pick **JOSE FERNANDEZ**, on what motivated him to defect from Cuba at age 15: "There are a lot of things I won't forget. I can't. When I was in Cuba and decided to get in the boat, you didn't know if you would be alive or not, so that keeps you focused on working hard and achieving your goals. It was all-or-nothing, either you make it or you die, or you're going to be in jail."

entering 2011. But he sustained a shoulder injury early in his junior year that robbed him of bat speed and relegated him to a DH role. Rendon wasn't at his best (.327-6-37), but pitchers still continued to respect him, walking him an NCAA-high 80 times.

Purke led the nation in wins in 2010 as a freshman, going 16-0, 3.02 with 142 strikeouts in 116 innings. As a draft-eligible sophomore, he was hampered early in the season by a blister on his pitching hand and late by a sore shoulder. Purke pitched just 53 innings and won only five games.

With uncertainty surrounding the three players at the top of the list, a handful of other legitimate candidates from both the college and high school ranks emerged over the course of the spring. On the eve of the draft, there was a clearly defined nucleus of six players that had separated from the pack. Joining Cole and Rendon in the top group were University of Virginia lefthander Danny Hultzen and UCLA righthander Trevor Bauer, plus two high school players, righthander Dylan Bundy from Oklahoma and multi-sport star Bubba Starling from Kansas. Meanwhile, Purke's stock had waned because of lingering concerns about his shoulder.

The Pirates' challenge was to get it right after they had misfired on a seemingly endless number of first-round picks over the previous 25 years, plunging the franchise into its current predicament. Over that period, the Pirates had picked first overall on three occasions, in 1986, 1996 and 2002. In the previous five drafts, they had picked no lower than fourth, choosing second in 2008 and 2010, and fourth in 2006, 2007 and 2009.

Danny Hultzen

After careful consideration the Pirates took Cole. Not only did he prove to be the most astute selection from the group of six, but his rise to prominence as a big-leaguer coincided with the Pirates' rise from the ashes to become one of MLB's most consistently competitive teams.

### BIG SIX GO IN RAPID ORDER

The 2011 draft played out pretty much according to script. The six players at the top of most draft boards were the first six picked. Following the Pirates' selection of Cole, the Seattle Mariners took Hultzen, the Arizona Diamondbacks picked Bauer, the Baltimore Orioles selected Bundy, the Kansas City Royals took Starling, and the Nationals picked Rendon.

It marked the first draft ever when pitchers were selected with the first four picks. While Cole struggled as a junior at UCLA, the other three pitchers had breakout seasons. Hultzen went 12-3, 1.37. Bauer was the No. 2 starter at UCLA, but had better success than Cole, going 13-2, 1.25. Bauer and Hultzen finished 1-2 in the NCAA ranks in strikeouts, with Bauer fanning 203 in 137 innings

## WAR Heroes

Based on the career WAR (Wins Above Replacement, as calculated by Baseball-Reference.com) numbers achieved by all the players eligible for the 2011 draft, these are the most productive big leaguers through the 2015 season. Numbers in parentheses indicate the round when the player was actually drafted.

| | Player, Pos. | Actual Draft | WAR | Bonus |
|---|---|---|---|---|
| 1. | Sonny Gray, rhp | Athletics (1) | 10.2 | $1,540,000 |
| 2. | Jose Fernandez, rhp | Marlins (1) | 9.6 | $2,000,000 |
| 3. | Mookie Betts, ss | Red Sox (5) | 8.1 | $750,000 |
| 4. | Gerrit Cole, rhp | Pirates (1) | 7.6 | $8,000,000 |
| 5. | Anthony Rendon, 3b | Nationals (1) | 6.9 | $6,000,000 |
| 6. | Kevin Pillar, of | Blue Jays (32) | 5.9 | $1,000 |
| 7. | George Springer, of | Astros (1) | 5.8 | $2,525,000 |
| 8. | Cody Allen, rhp | Indians (23) | 5.0 | $40,000 |
| 9. | Francisco Lindor, ss | Indians (1) | 4.6 | $2,900,000 |
| 10. | Joe Panik, ss | Giants (1) | 4.5 | $1,116,000 |
| 11. | Kyle Hendricks, rhp | Rangers (8) | 4.3 | $125,000 |
| 12. | Brad Miller, ss | Mariners (2) | 4.1 | $750,000 |
| 13. | Ken Giles, rhp | Phillies (7) | 4.0 | $250,000 |
| 14. | Kolten Wong, 2b | Cardinals (1) | 3.9 | $1,300,000 |
| | Marcus Semien, ss | White Sox (6) | 3.9 | $130,000 |
| 16. | Jackie Bradley, of | Red Sox (1-S) | 2.7 | $1,100,000 |
| | Carson Smith, rhp | Mariners (8) | 2.7 | $215,000 |
| | Billy Burns, of | Nationals (32) | 2.7 | $75,000 |
| 19. | Trevor Bauer, rhp | Diamondbacks (1) | 2.5 | $3,400,000 |
| | Nick Ahmed, ss | Braves (2) | 2.5 | $417,600 |
| 21. | Cory Spangenberg, 2b | Padres (1) | 2.4 | $1,863,000 |
| | Cody Anderson, rhp | Indians (14) | 2.4 | $250,000 |
| 23. | Tony Cingrani, lhp | Reds (3) | 2.1 | $210,000 |
| 24. | Taylor Jungmann, rhp | Brewers (1) | 1.9 | $2,525,000 |
| | Andrew Chafin, lhp | Diamondbacks (1-S) | 1.9 | $875,000 |
| | Seth Maness, rhp | Cardinals (11) | 1.9 | $1,000 |

and Hultzen whiffing 165 in 118 innings. Hultzen enhanced his draft value by adding 4-5 mph to his fastball as a junior. Bauer befuddled hitters with a varied assortment of pitches, including a fastball that peaked at 97 mph.

Bundy dominated the high school ranks like few other pitchers in history. Armed with a high-90s fastball and excellent command of three secondary pitches, he went 11-0, 0.20 with five walks and 158 strikeouts in 71 innings at Owasso (Okla.) High.

The run on pitching ended with the No. 5 pick. The Royals narrowed their selection to Rendon and Starling, the latter a promising power hitter and fleet center fielder from Gardner-Edgerton (Kan.) High, about 35 miles from their home park. Kansas City decided on Starling, even though it meant buying him out of a football commitment to play quarterback at the University of Nebraska.

"We got the player we wanted. We got the most electric athlete and player in the draft," Royals scouting director Lonnie Goldberg said. "He just happened to be in our backyard, as well."

The Nationals were happy to get Rendon with the No. 6 pick overall. It marked the third straight season that Washington landed the preseason No. 1-ranked player according to Baseball America.

Predictably, the first six players drafted received some of the richest contracts in draft history. Four signed major league deals, which enabled their teams to spread out payments over multiple years.

Cole and Starling signed standard minor league deals, but were well compensated. Cole's $8 million bonus broke the record of $7.5 million set a year earlier by Strasburg. Starling's $7.5 million deal tied the previous mark, although it should be noted that Strasburg signed a major league contract that guaranteed him in excess of $15 million. The present value of Starling's deal also was less than the face value, considering the payments were spread out over five years because of his status as a two-sport athlete.

Hultzen's contract provided for a bonus of $6.35 million and guaranteed him $8.5 million overall. Bauer signed for a bonus of $3.4 million and a total guarantee of $4.45 million. Bundy and the Orioles agreed on a bonus of $4 million and $6.25 million in guarantees. Rendon received $7.2 million, including a $6 million bonus. Purke, who tumbled all the way to the third round, where he was drafted by the Nationals, also signed a major league contract. He received a $2.75 million bonus, a record for a third-rounder, and a total guarantee of $4.15 million.

The five major league contracts were the last for drafted players. The Collective Bargaining Agreement that went into effect in 2012 prohibited teams from offering major league deals to draft choices.

Bauer was the only one of the top six picks to sign prior to the Aug. 15 deadline. He signed on July 25, enabling him to begin his professional career during the 2011 season. The other five didn't debut until 2012. Bauer also was the first member of the class of 2011 to reach the majors, joining the Diamondbacks on June 28, 2012.

As the first and third picks overall, Cole and Bauer became the second set of college teammates taken with two of the first three selections. It first happened in 1978, when Arizona State third baseman Bob Horner was selected by the Atlanta Braves with the No. 1 pick and shortstop Hubie Brooks went third to the New York Mets.

## CONTRASTS FOR COLE, BAUER

Cole and Bauer, who both joined the UCLA pitching rotation as freshmen, had radically different pitching styles and backgrounds.

Bauer graduated from high school after one semester of his senior year, and joined the UCLA baseball team in January 2009, making him ineligible for the draft that year. He led the nation in strikeouts in each of his final two seasons at UCLA and firmly established himself as a top prospect.

Cole, a classic power pitcher, was mentioned prominently throughout the spring of 2011 in discussions about the No. 1 pick overall, but he was consistently outpitched by the less imposing Bauer.

### Fastest To The Majors

| | Player, Pos. | Drafted (Round) | Debut |
|---|---|---|---|
| 1. | Trevor Bauer, rhp | Diamondbacks (1) | June 28, 2012 |
| 2. | Chad Allen, rhp | Indians (23) | July 20, 2012 |
| 3. | Carter Capps, rhp | Mariners (3) | Aug. 3, 2012 |
| 4. | Nick Maronde, lhp | Angels (3) | Sept. 2, 2012 |
| 5. | Tony Cingrani, lhp | Reds (3) | Sept. 9, 2012 |

**FIRST HIGH SCHOOL SELECTION:** Dylan Bundy, rhp (Orioles/1, Sept. 23, 2012)

## DRAFT SPOTLIGHT: JOSE FERNANDEZ

MIKE JANES

As a Cuban defector, Jose Fernandez overcame more than his share of challenges to become a first-rounder

Cuba native Jose Fernandez was 8 years old when he first dreamed of playing in the major leagues. His Cuban idols were pitchers Pedro Luis Lazo and Norge Luis Vera, yet Fernandez didn't aspire to pitch in an Olympic gold medal game or in the Cuban National Series championship. His ambitions were loftier, and he was prepared to die for the chance to achieve them.

"The best baseball is in the big leagues," said Fernandez years later, his goal achieved. "I really want to work to be the best, and that's why I wanted to play in the United States. I wanted to prove to myself I could do it. I'm blessed. I've got an amazing opportunity to be here and show what I can do."

Fernandez's path to the majors was considerably more challenging than the average big leaguer, even though he quickly emerged as an elite pitcher after the Florida Marlins selected him in the first round of the 2011 draft.

Fernandez made three unsuccessful attempts on the open seas to defect from Cuba as a teenager, once closing to within 10 miles of Miami before being turned back. With each failed attempt, his stay in a Cuban jail was a little longer. There were days he wondered if he would get out of jail alive, much less pitch again. He was isolated, banned from both school and baseball, and he and his family were ostracized and branded as traitors.

Undeterred, Fernandez, his mother and stepsister made a fourth attempt to escape Cuba, and this time they were successful. After leaving in the dead of night in March 2008, bound for Cancun, Mexico, in an overcrowded speedboat, they encountered violent waves in the Caribbean Sea. Fernandez's mother, Maritza Gomez, who could not swim, was thrown overboard. Fernandez dove into the water and pulled her to safety.

After landing in Mexico more than a week later, Fernandez still faced obstacles. He had to escape detection from Mexican authorities, compelled by law to send defectors back to Cuba. Fernandez and his family kept a low profile for more than a month while making their way through rural Mexico to safety at the Laredo, Texas, border crossing.

Fernandez then reconnected with his stepfather, Ramon Jimenez, who had made 15 unsuccessful attempts to defect from Cuba before finally succeeding and settling in Tampa, waiting for his family to join him. After three arduous years, they made it.

Fernandez quickly turned his attention to baseball, with the help of Orlando Chinea, a renowned pitching coach from Cuba who also defected in 2008. Fernandez was 15, stood 6 feet, weighed 160 pounds and threw 84 mph. But he was a highly motivated pupil, and soon he would grow and throw much faster. Under Chinea, he developed into a star pitcher at Tampa's Alonso High, leading the school to two Florida 6-A titles and compiling a 30-3 record with 59 walks and 314 strikeouts over three years. He was ruled ineligible for his senior year by the Florida High School Athletic Association when it was determined he had exhausted his eligibility because he entered ninth grade in Cuba in 2006. It didn't seem to matter that he missed his sophomore year while in jail or attempting to defect.

Once he was cleared to play, Fernandez, by then a strapping 6-foot-4, 220 pounds, established himself as one of the country's top pitching prospects. His fastball reached 98 mph, he showed command of four pitches, and he was a tenacious competitor. "Mentally, he's pretty advanced for a high school kid," an American League scout said. "I know he wants it a lot. Coming to the U.S. from Cuba isn't easy, and he never seems to forget what he went through to get here."

Fernandez began his pro career in 2012 and blew through Class A, going 14-1, 1.75 with 158 strikeouts in 134 innings. When injuries on the Marlins pitching staff left a void in 2013, the club promoted Fernandez. As a 20-year rookie, he went 12-6, 2.19 with 187 strikeouts in 172 innings, and joined Dwight Gooden and Bob Feller as the only pitchers ever to throw a scoreless inning in the All-Star Game before age 21.

Through all his early success, Fernandez never forgot how far he had come.

"There are a lot of things I won't forget. I can't," Fernandez said. "When I was in Cuba and decided to get in the boat, you didn't know if you would be alive or not, so that keeps you focused on working hard and achieving your goals."

## WORTH NOTING

■ South Carolina won its second straight College World Series title in 2011, beating Southeastern Conference rival Florida in two straight games in the best-of-three final. The Gamecocks (55-14) got stellar pitching from lefthander **MICHAEL ROTH** (14-3, 1.06), who led the nation in wins and was second in ERA, and righthanded closer **MATT PRICE** (7-3, 1.83), who led the country in saves with 20. The soft-tossing Roth lasted until the 31st round of the draft, and the hard-throwing Price, a draft-eligible sophomore, went in the sixth round. Neither player signed.

■ Both Florida and South Carolina had 11 players drafted, but were upstaged by SEC rival Vanderbilt, which not only had a college-high 12 players drafted, but impacted the early rounds like no other team in college history. The Commodores, who finished third in the College World Series, had a first-rounder (**SONNY GRAY**), supplemental first-rounder, second-rounder, three third-rounders and two sixth-rounders. Six of the eight were pitchers with fastballs that were clocked in the mid-90s, led by Gray at 98 mph. The Commodores offset their considerable losses by landing Massachusetts prep righthander **TYLER BEEDE**, the highest unsigned pick from the prep ranks. In addition to Florida and South Carolina, Arizona State and Connecticut each had 11 players drafted.

■ The 2010 draft was a showpiece for the nation's often underappreciated junior-college ranks. Not only did Southern Nevada's **BRYCE HARPER** put the spotlight on junior colleges like no draft before by being taken with the No. 1 overall pick, but five juco players altogether were among the top 100 selections. The highest drafted junior college player in 2011 was Indian River (Fla.) JC infielder **CORY SPANGENBERG**, selected by the Padres with the 10th pick overall. Three junior

BILL MITCHELL

**Righthander Trevor Bauer joined UCLA teammate Gerrit Cole in becoming two of the top three selections in the 2011 draft**

### Top 25 Bonuses

| | Player, Pos. | Drafted (Round) | Order | Bonus |
|---|---|---|---|---|
| **1.** | **Gerrit Cole, rhp** | **Pirates (1)** | **1** | **$8,000,000** |
| 2. | * Bubba Starling, of | Royals (1) | 5 | $7,500,000 |
| 3. | Danny Hultzen, lhp | Mariners (1) | 2 | #$6,350,000 |
| **4.** | **Anthony Rendon, 3b** | **Nationals (1)** | **6** | **#$6,000,000** |
| **5.** | *** Archie Bradley, rhp** | **Diamondbacks (1)** | **7** | **$5,000,000** |
| | * Josh Bell, of | Pirates (2) | 61 | $5,000,000 |
| **7.** | *** Dylan Bundy, rhp** | **Orioles (1)** | **4** | **#$4,000,000** |
| **8.** | **Trevor Bauer, rhp** | **Diamondbacks (1)** | **3** | **#$3,400,000** |
| 9. | Brian Goodwin, of | Nationals (1-S) | 34 | $3,000,000 |
| | *** Austin Hedges, c** | **Padres (2)** | **82** | **$3,000,000** |
| **11.** | *** Francisco Lindor, ss** | **Indians (1)** | **8** | **$2,900,000** |
| **12.** | *** Joe Ross, rhp** | **Padres (1)** | **25** | **$2,750,000** |
| | Matt Purke, lhp | Nationals (3) | 96 | #$2,750,000 |
| **14.** | *** Javier Baez, ss** | **Cubs (1)** | **9** | **$2,625,000** |
| **15.** | **George Springer, of** | **Astros (1)** | **11** | **$2,525,000** |
| | **Taylor Jungmann, rhp** | **Brewers (1)** | **12** | **$2,525,000** |
| **17.** | *** Blake Swihart, c** | **Red Sox (1)** | **26** | **$2,500,000** |
| | Dillon Maples, rhp | Cubs (14) | 429 | $2,500,000 |
| 19. | * Brandon Nimmo, of | Mets (1) | 13 | $2,100,000 |
| **20.** | *** Jose Fernandez, rhp** | **Marlins (1)** | **14** | **$2,000,000** |
| | Jed Bradley, lhp | Brewers (1) | 15 | $2,000,000 |
| | **Alex Meyer, rhp** | **Nationals (1)** | **23** | **$2,000,000** |
| | * Robert Stephenson, rhp | Reds (1) | 27 | $2,000,000 |
| | *** Daniel Norris, lhp** | **Blue Jays (2)** | **74** | **$2,000,000** |
| **25.** | **Cory Spangenberg, 2b** | **Padres (1)** | **10** | **$1,863,000** |

*Major leaguers in bold. *High school selection. #Major league contract.*

While Cole posted a sub-.500 record as UCLA's Friday starter, the 6-foot-1, 175-pound Bauer, the team's Saturday starter, became the most dominant undersized pitcher in college baseball since Washington's Tim Lincecum in 2006. The reference to Lincecum, the two-time National League Cy Young Award winner, was somewhat apt, given that Bauer's style and approach to pitching were similar to Lincecum's.

Despite his unimposing frame, Bauer routinely dialed his fastball up to 97 mph when he reared back for a little extra, but his strikeout pitch was a hard curveball. He also threw a slider, changeup and screwball-like pitch that he referred to as a "reverse slider," and Bauer had near impeccable command of all his pitches.

UCLA coach John Savage thought the competition between Bauer and Cole helped prepare both pitchers for the draft and a future in pro ball.

"They're two of the most competitive guys I've ever been around," Savage said. "Gerrit pitched on Friday, Trevor pitched on Saturday for most of their careers at UCLA. There were a lot of competitions going back and forth—strikeouts, performances, number of hits—and I think they fed off each other. Sometimes it doesn't work, but I think in this case it did for both of them. Coming out of college, being the first and third picks, I don't think a lot of people could argue that both of them performed and fed off it in a positive way."

Bauer beat Cole to the major leagues by almost a full year, but through the 2015 season, Cole had established himself as the superior big league pitcher.

Bauer generally won over scouts with his impressive raw stuff, consistency and competitiveness, but many were skeptical about his unconventional workout and warm-up routines, and somewhat unorthodox max-effort delivery. The pitcher's peculiar work habits and headstrong approach soon caused him problems with the Diamondbacks, who traded Bauer to the Cleveland Indians after he had made just four appearances in the major leagues. After three seasons with the Indians, he had yet to prove himself in the big leagues, showing an overall record of 18-24, 4.50.

The promising careers of Hultzen and Bundy were undermined by major arm problems. After going 32-5, 2.08 with 75 walks and 395 strikeouts in 320 innings in three seasons at Virginia, Hultzen appeared to be on the fast track to the majors when he broke into pro ball at Double-A in 2012 and went 8-3, 1.19 in his first 13 pro starts. But he developed a sore shoulder the following season, had rotator-cuff surgery, and pitched only 44 innings in the minor leagues from 2013-15.

Bundy also debuted in scintillating style, posting a 0.00 ERA in his first eight starts for low Class A Delmarva, while walking two, allowing five hits and striking out 40 in 30 innings. With a fastball that approached 98 mph, he continued to dominate at two more stops in the Orioles organization, going a combined 9-3. Bundy got to the major leagues in the final month of the 2012 season and made two relief appearances, becoming just the fourth teenager to pitch in the majors in a decade.

Bundy, however, soon was beset by arm problems. He missed the 2013 season after Tommy John surgery, and won just one game in the minors over the course of the 2014-15 seasons. Just as his elbow appeared to be healthy, Bundy developed a sore shoulder that curtailed his workload in 2015. He began the 2016 season in the Orioles bullpen.

The 6-foot-4, 195-pound Starling, a five-tool center fielder with an immense ceiling, was the best two-sport athlete in the draft. The Royals paid heavily to pull Starling away from football, and five years later he remained in the minor leagues. Starling wasn't tested against quality pitching in high school, and he struggled at the outset of his pro career, with pitchers exploiting a loop in his swing. He got to Double-A in 2015 as a career .243 hitter with 47 home runs and 58 stolen bases

## Largest Bonuses By Round

| | Player, Pos. | Club | Bonus |
|---|---|---|---|
| **1.** | **Gerrit Cole, rhp** | **Pirates** | **$8,000,000** |
| 1-S. | Brian Goodwin, of | Nationals | $3,000,000 |
| 2. | * Josh Bell, of | Pirates | $5,000,000 |
| 3. | Matt Purke, lhp | Nationals | $2,750,000 |
| 4. | * Kyle Smith, rhp | Royals | $695,000 |
| **5.** | *** Greg Bird, c** | **Yankees** | **$1,100,000** |
| 6. | * Nick Delmonico, 3b | Orioles | $1,525,000 |
| 7. | * Cody Kukuk, lhp | Red Sox | $800,000 |
| | * Christian Lopes, ss | Blue Jays | $800,000 |
| 8. | * Mark Biggs, rhp | Blue Jays | $600,000 |
| 9. | * Clay Holmes, rhp | Pirates | $1,200,000 |
| 10. | * Danny Lockhart, ss | Cubs | $395,000 |
| 11. | * Shawon Dunston Jr., of | Cubs | $1,275,000 |
| 12. | Four tied at | | $125,000 |
| 13. | * Matt Dean, 3b | Blue Jays | $737,500 |
| 14. | Dillon Maples, rhp | Cubs | $2,500,000 |
| 15. | * Phillip Evans, ss | Mets | $650,000 |
| 16. | * Jack Lopez, ss | Royals | $750,000 |
| 17. | * Brady Dragmire, rhp | Blue Jays | $250,000 |
| **18.** | **Shawn Armstrong, rhp** | **Indians** | **$325,000** |
| 19. | * Shawn Morimando, lhp | Indians | $350,000 |
| 20. | * Daniel Camarena, lhp | Yankees | $335,000 |
| 21. | * John Gant, rhp | Mets | $185,000 |
| 22. | * Amir Garrett, lhp | Reds | $1,000,000 |
| 23. | * Sal Romano, rhp | Reds | $450,000 |
| 24. | * Jalen Simmons, of | Orioles | $95,000 |
| 25. | Rock Shoulders, 1b | Cubs | $294,000 |
| Other | * Jake Junis, rhp | Royals (29) | $675,000 |

*Major leaguers in bold. *High school selection.*

in more than 1,700 plate appearances.

Rendon's bat outweighed any concerns the Nationals might have had about his injury history, position or signability. Scouts had long been impressed with his short, quick, fluid swing, along with his discerning eye and plate discipline. Despite a shoulder injury that impacted his 2011 season, Rendon was rated the best college position player in the draft in terms of pure hitting ability and strike-zone judgment. Rendon also sustained major ankle injuries while playing for USA Baseball's college national team following both his freshman and sophomore seasons at Rice. Both injuries required surgery, and effectively cost scouts their one significant opportunity to judge Rendon swinging a wood bat over an extended stretch.

Anthony Rendon

Rendon appeared ready to establish himself as one of the top young stars in the major leagues after hitting .287 with 21 homers, 83 RBIs and an NL-leading 111 runs in 2014. But his progress slowed in 2015, when injuries cost him half the season.

### FIRST ROUND DEEP IN TALENT

Even without a signature player the stature of Strasburg or Harper, the premium talent in the 2011 draft ran deep into the first round and beyond. There was considerable depth in both the college and high school ranks.

"There might be 25 players who would go in the first six to 10 picks in many drafts," said one scouting director. Some in the industry said the overall talent was comparable to the acclaimed draft pools of 2005 and '08.

"I've been doing this for awhile, and I would say no draft in the 2000s, or maybe even before that, do I remember seeing this kind of depth," a National League scouting director said.

For the first time, there were 33 picks in the first round, one more than there had been in both 2009 and 2010. The increase was a result of three teams gaining extra picks for not signing their 2010 first-round picks. The Diamondbacks failed to sign Texas A&M righthander Barret Loux (sixth overall pick), the San Diego Padres didn't agree to terms with Florida prep righthander Karsten Whitson (ninth), and the Milwaukee Brewers failed to sign California prep righty Dylan Covey (14th). The Diamondbacks were compensated with the seventh pick overall in 2011, the Padres got the 10th selection, and the Brewers the 15th pick.

There also were 27 supplemental first-round picks, awarded as compensation to clubs that lost major league free agents during the offseason. With 30 compensation picks in all, second only to 34 in 2007, the second round didn't start until 60 players had been drafted.

As strong as the 2011 class was, the typical hotbed states of California, Texas, Florida and Georgia made fewer contributions than usual.

"There are so many high school guys in small towns this year," said an American League crosschecker. "Typically you can spend 10 days in Atlanta and see a bunch of guys within a little bit of a radius, but not this year. You're all over Oklahoma, Wyoming, out-of-the-way places."

The ultimate example was a player from Wyoming being drafted in the first round, but no high school players from Southern California, two firsts in draft history. Cole and Bauer were products of Southern California high schools before enrolling at UCLA. The first round featured players from 21 different states.

Outfielder Brandon Nimmo, selected 13th by the Mets, became the highest selection ever from Wyoming, which had no formal high school or college programs. Nimmo starred in American Legion competition. The previous high pick from the state was University of Wyoming outfielder Bill Ewing, the NCAA home run leader in 1976. Ewing was selected by the Angels that year in the fourth round. Wyoming later disbanded its baseball program.

### GRAY, FERNANDEZ MAKE IMPRESSIONS

For all the emphasis on the first six players drafted in 2011, the two most productive major leaguers through the 2015 season, according to career WAR (Wins Above Replacement), were righthanders from the second tier of prospects, Jose Fernandez, selected by the Florida Marlins with the 14th pick overall, and Sonny Gray, chosen 18th by the Oakland A's. Both reached the majors in 2013 and quickly became elite starters.

Fernandez, who went 13-1, 1.35 as a senior at

### WORTH NOTING

college players were supplemental first-round picks, including outfielder **BRIAN GOODWIN** (Nationals), from Miami-Dade CC. Goodwin, the 34th pick, received a $3 million signing bonus, while Spangenberg's bonus was just $1.863 million. Goodwin was playing in junior college because he had been suspended from the University of North Carolina baseball team for violating school policy.

■ No. 1 overall pick **GERRIT COLE** received the highest predraft rating from the Major League Scouting Bureau. He had a 67 (on the 20-80 scouting scale), ahead of first-rounders **DYLAN BUNDY** (66, fourth overall pick) and **ALEX MEYER** (65, 23rd overall pick), and supplemental first-rounder **DANIEL NORRIS** (65, 74th overall pick).

■ More players were drafted in 2011 than in any year since the draft was limited to 50 rounds in 1998. With every club drafting its full allotment of picks, plus 30 additional selections awarded as compensation for unsigned 2010 first-rounders or for players lost in major league free agency, there were 1,530 selections. It was a peak that would not soon be approached again. Under terms of a new Collective Bargaining Agreement, the draft would be limited to 40 rounds beginning in 2012.

■ Just six of 33 first-round picks, and one of the first 16 selections signed contracts prior to July 14, marking the slowest signing pace in draft history. All six signed for the slot bonuses recommended by Major League Baseball. The highest draft pick in that group was Spangenberg. This too was a practice not likely to be repeated again with the advent of more formal draft slots and an earlier signing deadline coming in 2012.

■ Two players who were not eligible for the draft

CONTINUED ON PAGE 692

## WORTH NOTING

CONTINUED FROM PAGE 691

as high school players became first-round picks in 2011 as college juniors. UCLA righthander **TREVOR BAUER** (Diamondbacks, third overall) and North Carolina shortstop **LEVI MICHAEL** (Twins, 30th) both enrolled in college in January 2009 after graduating from high school in December, at mid-semester. While they decided to pass up the chance of being drafted out of high school, the tradeoff was they became eligible for the draft a year ahead of schedule coming out of college.

■ University of Utah first baseman **C.J. CRON** (Angels, 17th overall) was the only first-rounder who was the son of a former major leaguer. His father, Chris, played briefly in the majors in 1991-92. Cron's younger brother, **KEVIN**, was a third-round pick of the Mariners, but did not sign. C.J. reached the big leagues in 2014.

■ The Rangers committed only $4.193 million in the draft, less than half what they spent a year earlier. Instead, they used their resources on the international market, signing three highly regarded outfielders. They gave $4.95 million, an international bonus record, to **NOMAR MAZARA**, a 16-year-old from the Dominican Republic, and another $3.45 million to a second 16-year-old from the Dominican, **RONALD GUZMAN**. The Rangers also signed Cuban defector **LEONYS MARTIN**, 23, to a five-year, $15.6 million major league deal.

■ With teams spending bonus money like it was going out of style, the Vanderbilt-bound **TYLER BEEDE** was the only player among the first 50 drafted who did not sign. He turned down a reported bonus offer of $2.4 million from the Blue Jays as the 21st overall pick. His college career was up and down, but the Giants made him a first-round pick again in 2014.

Tampa's Alonso High, debuted in the majors at 20 and had a 22-9, 2.40 record through his first 47 starts, while walking 85 and striking out 330 in 289 innings. He achieved that despite missing the better part of the 2014 and 2015 seasons recovering from Tommy John surgery.

Gray debuted at 23, and was 33-20, 2.88 with 419 strikeouts in 491 innings over his first three seasons. Had he stood taller than 5-foot-11, Gray likely would have factored among the first 10 picks after his dominant college career at Vanderbilt. He defied the conventional bias against short righthanders with his superb athleticism and impressive raw stuff.

One of the quirks in the 2011 draft was with players named Bradley. Only twice previously in draft history had a player with the surname Bradley been a first-round pick (Mark, Dodgers, 1974; and Bobby, Pirates, 1999). But three Bradleys were drafted in the first round and supplemental first round in 2011: Oklahoma prep righthander Archie Bradley (Diamondbacks, 7th overall), Georgia Tech lefthander Jed Bradley (Brewers, 15th) and South Carolina outfielder Jackie Bradley Jr. (Red Sox, 40th).

TONY PARKER

Sonny Gray

Archie Bradley was the most talented of the trio, and except for Starling was the best two-sport athlete in the draft pool. He had a college commitment to Oklahoma to play both football and baseball, and used that leverage to get a $5 million bonus from the Diamondbacks. Bradley, Arizona's compensation pick for not signing Loux a year earlier, and Bauer gave the Diamondbacks two of the top seven selections. No team ever had the opportunity to select two premium picks in such short order. Bradley was selected three picks after Bundy, another Oklahoma prep pitcher, although Bradley was nearly as dominant as Bundy in their senior seasons. In 71 innings at Broken Arrow High, Bradley went 12-1, 0.29 with 11 walks and 137 strikeouts in 71 innings.

### UNPRECEDENTED SPENDING BY CLUBS

The depth of the 2011 draft class, along with the uncertainty regarding future draft parameters with the CBA expiring at the end of the season, created a perfect storm for the record spending that took place at the Aug. 15 signing deadline.

With the possibility of a formal slotting system coming into effect, teams viewed 2011 as the last opportunity to spend whatever it took to sign players who slid in the draft due to strong college commitments, injuries or a desire to play another sport. With teams intent on mining one of the most talented draft pools in recent years, some $132 million in bonuses were committed on deadline day.

The Pirates set the tone by spending upward of $17 million, including $8 million on Cole, which was double the amount recommended by the commissioner's office for the first pick. But the deal that stunned the industry was Pittsburgh's $5 million agreement with Bell, its second-rounder. He hit .575 with 13 homers as a senior at Dallas Jesuit High, and was one of the top power-hitting prospects in the class. But Bell was passed over in the first round after he sent a letter to Major League Baseball, requesting that he not be drafted because he intended to play at the University of Texas.

Ten clubs established records for bonus money expenditures. The Nationals were the biggest spenders in both 2009 ($11,511,500) and 2010 ($11,927,200), and they topped that in 2011 ($15,002,100), but the amount was $2 million less than what the Pirates spent.

In addition to giving $6 million to Rendon and $2 million to righthander Alex Meyer, a second first-round pick (23rd overall), the Nationals committed $3 million to supplemental first-rounder Brian Goodwin, the largest bonus in the sandwich round, and didn't hesitate to draft Purke when he was still available after 95 players had been selected. Those four players alone cost the Nationals nearly $14 million, but only Rendon was an established big leaguer by the 2015 season. Purke had been released, only to re-sign with the Nationals on a minor league contract.

The Royals ($14.066 million), Chicago Cubs ($11.994 million) and Diamondbacks ($11.93 million) also exceeded the previous record for bonus money committed in a single draft.

The rebuilding Cubs, after spending just $4.727 million to sign all their picks in 2010, upped the ante considerably in 2011. They signed 19 players for bonuses of $100,000 or more, including $2.625 million for first-rounder Javier Baez, $1.6 million for second-rounder Daniel Vogelbach and $1.275 million for 11th-rounder Shawon Dunston

## One Team's Draft: Washington Nationals

| Player, Pos. | Bonus | Player, Pos. | Bonus | Player, Pos. | Bonus |
|---|---|---|---|---|---|
| **1. Anthony Rendon, 3b** | **$6,000,000** | 9. Dixon Anderson, rhp | $95,000 | 19. * Hawtin Buchanan, rhp | Did not sign |
| **1. Alex Meyer, rhp** | **$2,000,000** | 10. Manny Rodriguez, rhp | $115,000 | 20. * Josh Laxer, rhp | Did not sign |
| 1. Brian Goodwin, of | $3,000,000 | 11. Caleb Ramsey, of | $2,500 | 21. Todd Simko, lhp | $30,000 |
| 2. No selection | | 12. Blake Monar, lhp | $125,000 | 22. Travis Henke, rhp | $1,000 |
| 3. Matt Purke, lhp | $2,750,000 | 13. Casey Kalenkosky, 1b | Did not sign | 23. Khayyan Norfork, 2b | $1,000 |
| 4. Kylin Turnbull, lhp | $325,000 | 14. Cody Stubbs, of | Did not sign | 24. Kyle Ottoson, lhp | Did not sign |
| 5. Matt Skole, 3b | $161,100 | 15. Zach Houchins, ss | Did not sign | 25. Erick Fernandez, c | $1,000 |
| **6. Taylor Hill, rhp** | **$36,000** | 16. * Deion Williams, ss | $50,000 | **Other Billy Burns (32), of** | **$75,000** |
| 7. Brian Dupra, rhp | $35,000 | 17. Esteban Guzman, rhp | Did not sign | | |
| 8. Greg Holt, rhp | $34,000 | 18. Nick Lee, lhp | $77,000 | | |

*Major leaguers in bold. *High school selection.*

## Highest Unsigned Picks

| Player, Pos., Team (Round) | College | Re-Drafted |
|---|---|---|
| Tyler Beede, rhp, Blue Jays (1) | Vanderbilt | Giants '14 (1) |
| Brett Austin, c, Padres (1) | N.C. State | White Sox '14 (4) |
| Sam Stafford, lhp, Yankees (2) | *Texas | Rangers '12 (13) |
| Kevin Cron, 1b, Mariners (3) | Texas Christian | D-backs '14 (14) |
| Connor Barron, ss, Marlins (3) | Southern Miss. | Never |
| Peter O'Brien, c, Rockies (3) | Miami | Yankees '12 (2) |
| Tyler Palmer, 2b, Marlins (4) | Oakton (Ill.) CC | Never |
| Andrew Chin, lhp, Blue Jays (5) | Boston College | Yankees '14 (15) |
| Brandon Woodruff, rhp, Rangers (5) | Miss. State | Brewers '14 (11) |
| J.D. Davis, 3b, Rays (5) | CS Fullerton | Astros '14 (3) |

**TOTAL UNSIGNED PICKS:** Top 5 Rounds (10), Top 10 Rounds (26)

**Returned to same school.*

Jr., the latter a son of the No. 1 overall pick in the 1982 draft.

The bonus that sent a clear message the Cubs were prepared to spare no expense on talent was the $2.5 million they gave North Carolina high school righthander Dillon Maples, a 14th-round choice. It was the largest bonus in draft history for a player chosen after the third round. Maples went 9-0, 0.53 with 139 strikeouts in 67 innings as a senior at Pinecrest High in Southern Pines. He projected as borderline first-round material, but his seemingly firm college commitment to North Carolina made teams reluctant to draft him. Maples had a 6-11, 5.58 to show for his first four seasons in pro ball, none above Class A.

The Rays spent a club record $11,482,900 to sign all their draft picks, but it was the result of a rare draft windfall, not aggressive spending. Combined with their own first-round pick, the Rays had 10 selections before the start of the second round. It represented the biggest single haul a team had in one draft since 1990, when the Montreal Expos held 10 of the first 53 selections.

"Because of our revenues and the competition we face, the amateur draft is arguably more important to us than to any other club, and this year's draft is easily the most important in our history," Rays executive vice president Andrew Friedman said. "Although we're not picking at the top of the draft, the number of high picks we have is literally unprecedented. It's a tremendous opportunity for us, and we're devoting more energy and resources to the process that we ever have."

The Toronto Blue Jays spent $10,996,500 to sign their picks. That amount fell some $600,000 short of the club record they set in 2010, but was substantial nonetheless, considering they did not sign Massachusetts prep righthander Tyler Beede, their first-round pick (21st overall), and 11 others in the first 20 rounds. The Jays reallocated their unspent bonus money to sign six players at the deadline. Among them were supplemental first-rounder Kevin Comer for $1.5 million, second-rounder Daniel Norris for $2 million, seventh-rounder Christian Lopes for $800,000 and 13th-rounder Matt Dean for $737,500.

### DRAFT CHANGES COMING

A new Collective Bargaining Agreement that was ratified in November 2011 included provisions such as the move of the Houston Astros from the National League to the American League, daily interleague play, the inclusion of extra wild-card teams in postseason play for each 15-team league, expanded rosters for doubleheaders and a plan for mandatory human growth hormone testing.

Another hot topic of discussion during the negotiation process involved a new draft structure, normally a back-burner item in CBA negotiations. Baseball's owners and the Players Association agreed to the most far-reaching changes to the game's primary player procurement process since the draft was implemented in 1965. Almost all measures were aimed at curbing the upward spiral of signing bonuses, an issue that had nettled team owners for a quarter-century and reached new heights in 2011.

Though a proposal that included mandated slotting of individual bonus payments was scrapped, a pseudo-slotting plan was adopted, and it represented the first collectively bargained drag on signing bonuses, involving both drafted players and those signed on the international market. The new language essentially restricted clubs from spending more money than the total value assigned to their allotment for players.

Beginning in 2012, teams would be assigned values for draft bonuses through the first 10 rounds, based on their order in the draft rotation and overall number of picks. If a team exceeded the bonus slot for its pool of players, it would be subject to a penalty, either in the form of a tax or the loss of premium draft picks.

These changes in the draft also would become effective in 2012:

- A shift in the signing deadline from Aug. 15 to July 15
- A reduction in the number of rounds from 50 to 40
- A bonus limit of $100,000 for players picked in the 11th round and beyond, without it counting against a team's pool threshold
- New qualifying standards in the compensation system for teams losing Type A and Type B major league free agents. Now teams had to make a qualifying offer to their free agents that was equal to the average salary of the 125 highest-paid players the previous season in order to be eligible for compensation, which would be a draft pick after the first round. When clubs sign a compensation-eligible player, they would forfeit their own first-round selection, or their second-round selection if their pick is in the top 10
- The elimination of major league contracts for draft picks
- The establishment of a weighted lottery that would assign six extra draft picks after the first round to the 10 lowest-revenue/smallest-market teams.

The implementation of those provisions, along with the new slotting system, was expected to lead to the first sustained drop in bonuses in the draft era, and at the same time protect the interests of teams perceived to be at a competitive disadvantage. Various other changes, including the implementation of a worldwide draft, were tabled for future discussion.

### IN FOCUS: GERRIT COLE

Gerrit Cole's fastball was routinely in the high 90s and peaked at 100 mph at UCLA, and he complemented it with a devastating slider. But he frustrated scouts with his spotty command, inconsistent performance and lack of a reliable changeup, and rarely dominated hitters as one would expect with his electric stuff. Even as he managed to halve his walk total from his sophomore season, when he went 11-4, 3.37 with 153 strikeouts in 123 innings, Cole regressed to a 6-8, 3.31 record with 119 strikeouts in 114 innings as a junior.

Pirates scouting director Greg Smith stuck to his conviction and selected Cole with the No. 1 overall pick, despite Cole's 21-20, 3.38 record in three years at UCLA. Talent is talent, and the Pirates were convinced that Cole had the best stuff of any pitcher in the draft. "Gerrit's been on our radar for a long time," Pirates general manager Neal Huntington said. "You see the size, the strength, the competitor, the arm, the 100 mph fastball, the slider. It's hard to walk away from that."

Through his first three major league seasons, the 6-foot-4, 215-pound Cole had justified the selection, going 40-20, 3.07 with 440 strikeouts in 463 innings. By 2016, he was the Pirates' ace and one of the top starters in the major leagues.

# 2011 Draft List

**Did not sign. Major leaguers in bold, with first and last years noted. Order of selection indicated in parentheses. For the first five rounds, the peak level of each player is noted.*

## ARIZONA DIAMONDBACKS (3)

1. **Trevor Bauer, rhp, UCLA.—(2012-15)**
DRAFT DROP *First player from 2011 draft to reach majors (June 28, 2012)*
1. **Archie Bradley, rhp, Broken Arrow (Okla.) HS** (Special compensation choice—7th—for failure to sign 2010 first-round pick Barret Loux).**—(2015)**
1. **Andrew Chafin, lhp, Kent State University** (Supplemental choice—43rd—for loss of Type B free agent Adam LaRoche).**—(2014-15)**
2. Anthony Meo, rhp, Coastal Carolina University.—(AA)
3. Justin Bianco, of, Peters Township HS, Canonsburg, Pa.—(Short-season A)
4. **Evan Marshall, rhp, Kansas State University.—(2014-15)**
5. Michael Perez, c, Colegio Vocacional Para Adultos, San Juan, P.R.—(High A)
6. *Matt Price, rhp, University of South Carolina.
7. *Ben Roberts, of, Sentinel HS, Missoula, Mont.
8. Jesse Darrah, rhp, Fresno Pacific University.
9. John Leonard, ss, Connellsville Area (Pa.) HS.
10. Kyle Winkler, rhp, Texas Christian University.
11. Will Locante, lhp, Cumberland (Tenn.) University.
12. Josh Parr, ss, University of Illinois.
13. John Pedrotty, lhp, College of the Holy Cross.
14. Cody Geyer, rhp, Walters State (Tenn.) CC.
15. Steven Rodriguez, c, UCLA.
16. Michael Blake, lhp, University of Hawaii.
17. *Adam Choplick, lhp, Ryan HS, Denton, Texas.
18. Taylor Siemens, lhp, California Baptist University.
19. Daniel Pulfer, 2b, University of Oregon.
20. *Tommy Williams, ss, Palm Beach Gardens (Fla.) HS.
21. Jon Griffin, 1b, University of Central Florida.
22. Garrett Weber, ss, Fresno State University.
23. Ryan Court, 3b, Illinois State University.
24. *Matt Ogden, rhp, Smoky Hill HS, Aurora, Colo.
25. *Brett Williams, of, North Carolina State University.
26. Austin Platt, rhp, Bradenton, Fla.
27. *Wyatt Strahan, rhp, Villa Park (Calif.) HS.
28. Mat Sample, rhp, Rogers State (Okla.) University.
29. Carter Bell, 3b, Oregon State University.
30. Dexter Price, rhp, University of South Carolina-Beaufort.
31. Matt Jensen, 2b, Cal Poly.
32. *Alex Vetter, rhp, Feather River (Calif.) JC.
33. *Anthony Banda, lhp, Sinton (Texas) HS.
34. Zach Jones, c, Stanford University.
35. Ross Gerdeman, rhp, Bowling Green State University.
36. Bryan Henry, c, Keystone (Pa.) College.
37. Elroy Urbina, lhp, University of the Incarnate Word (Texas).
38. Kerry Jenkins, of, San Jose State University.
39. Chris Ellison, of, University of Oklahoma.
40. Seth Simmons, rhp, East Carolina University.
41. Michael Cederoth, rhp, Steele Canyon HS, Spring Valley, Calif.
42. Tyler Bream, 3b, Liberty University.
DRAFT DROP *Son of Sid Bream, major leaguer (1983-94)*
43. Alex Capaul, rhp, University of Hawaii.
44. Derek Luciano, 3b, University of Central Florida.
45. *Jake Lane, of, Coral Shores HS, Tavernier, Fla.
46. Joe Loftus, of, Vanderbilt University.
47. *Tucker Ward, rhp, UMS Wright Prep, Mobile, Ala.
48. Ray Hernandez, rhp, Cal State Fullerton.
49. Jake Williams, 1b, South Mountain (Ariz.) CC.
DRAFT DROP *Son of Matt Williams, major Leaguer (1987-2003); major league manager (2014-15)*
50. *David Masters, ss, Timberland HS, Wentzville, Mo.

## ATLANTA BRAVES (25)

1. **Sean Gilmartin, lhp, Florida State University.—(2015)**
2. **Nick Ahmed, ss, University of Connecticut.—(2014-15)**
3. **Kyle Kubitza, 3b, Texas State University.—(2015)**
4. **J.R. Graham, rhp, Santa Clara University.—(2015)**
5. Nick DeSantiago, c, Blinn (Texas) JC.—(Low A)
6. Mark Lamm, rhp, Vanderbilt University.
7. **Cody Martin, rhp, Gonzaga University.—(2015)**
8. **Tommy La Stella, 2b, Coastal Carolina University.—(2014-15)**
9. Chase Larsson, of, Cameron (Okla.) University.
10. Logan Robbins, ss, Western Kentucky University.
11. Seth Moranda, ss, Buchanan HS, Clovis, Calif.
12. Matt Chaffee, lhp, University of Arizona.
13. Tony Mueller, of, Winona State (Minn.) University.
14. Navery Moore, rhp, Vanderbilt University.
15. **John Cornely, rhp, Wofford College.—(2015)**
16. A.J. Holland, rhp, St. Joseph's University.
17. **Gus Schlosser, rhp, Florida Southern College.—(2014)**
18. Greg Ross, rhp, Frostburg State (Md.) University.
19. Troy Snitker, c, North Georgia College and State University.
20. *Carlos Rodriguez, lhp, Iolani HS, Honolulu, Hawaii.
21. Jarrett Miller, rhp, UNC Greensboro.
22. Clint Wright, rhp, Columbia State (Tenn.) CC.
23. Sam Munson, of, Tennessee Weslyan College.
24. Brian Stamps, of, Oregon State University.
25. Will Skinner, of, Middle Tennessee State University.
26. Kirk Walker, ss, Oklahoma City University.
27. Charlie Robertson, rhp, Fresno State University.
28. Matt Talley, lhp, The Citadel.
29. Chad Comer, c, University of Texas-Arlington.
30. *Jon Youngblood, of, Lafayette HS, Lexington, Ky.
31. Jackson Laumann, 1b, Boone County HS, Florence, Ky.
32. *Matt Kimbrel, rhp, Shelton State (Ala.) CC.
DRAFT DROP *Brother of Cole Kimbrel, major leaguer (2010-15)*
33. Nick Popescu, 3b, Texas Tech.
34. Chris Bullard, of, Western Kentucky University.
35. Mike Hashem, lhp, Fisher (Mass.) College.
36. Gardner Adams, rhp, Asbury (Ky.) College.
37. Ryne Harper, rhp, Austin Peay State University.
38. *Nate Williams, rhp, Valley Center (Kan.) HS.
39. *Daniel Arellano, of, Centennial HS, Corona, Calif.
40. *Jacoby Almaraz, 3b, San Jacinto (Texas) JC.
41. *Keelin Rasch, c, Harrisburg (Ill.) HS.
42. Cody Livesay, of, Anna-Jonesboro HS, Jonesboro, Ill.
43. *Jake Lueneberg, 1b, Kishwaukee (Ill.) JC.
44. *Sutton Whiting, 2b, Ballard HS, Louisville, Ky.
45. *Sako Chapjian, 3b, Glendale (Calif.) JC.
46. *John Means, lhp, Gardner-Edgerton HS, Gardner, Kan.
47. *Dane Gronewald, lhp, Jefferson (Mo.) CC.
48. *Alex Real, 3b, Boulder Creek HS, Anthem, Ariz.
49. *Cody Cox, rhp, Thomas Nelson (Va.) CC.
50. *Kevin McKague, rhp, U.S. Military Academy.

## BALTIMORE ORIOLES (4)

1. **Dylan Bundy, rhp, Owasso (Okla.) HS.—(2012)**
DRAFT DROP *First 2011 high school draft pick to reach majors (Sept. 23, 2012)*
2. Jason Esposito, 3b, Vanderbilt University.—(AA)
3. **Mike Wright, rhp, East Carolina University.—(2015)**
4. Kyle Simon, rhp, University of Arizona.—(AAA)
5. Matt Taylor, lhp, Middle Georgia JC.—(High A)
6. Nick Delmonico, 3b, Farragut HS, Knoxville, Tenn.
7. Trent Howard, lhp, Central Michigan University.
8. John Ruettiger, of, Arizona State University.
9. Devin Jones, rhp, Mississippi State University.
10. **Tyler Wilson, rhp, University of Virginia.—(2015)**
11. Adam Davis, c, University of Illinois.
12. *Jason Coats, of, Texas Christian University.
13. *Derek Jones, of, Washington State University.
14. *K.J. Hockaday, 3b, John Carroll School, Bel Air, Md.
15. Eric Wooten, lhp, Central Arizona JC.
16. Mark Blackmar, rhp, Temple (Texas) JC.
DRAFT DROP *Son of Phil Blackmar, golfer, PGA Tour (1985-2000)*
17. *Nick Carmichael, rhp, Palomar (Calif.) JC.
18. *Brad Roney, 3b, Wetumpka (Ala.) HS.
19. Dustin Ward, lhp, University of Central Arkansas.
20. *Marc Wik, of, Chabot (Calif.) JC.
21. Jose Rivera, rhp, Hill (Texas) JC.
22. *Mike Miedzianowski, ss, Martin County HS, Stuart, Fla.
23. *Adam Matthews, of, University of South Carolina.
24. Jalen Simmons, of, Camden County HS, Kingsland, Ga.
25. *Mike Finnigan, lhp, San Bernardino Valley (Calif.) JC.
26. **Zach Davies, rhp, Mesquite HS, Gilbert, Ariz.—(2015)**
27. *Chris Oliver, rhp, Shiloh Christian HS, Springdale, Ark.
28. *Nate Raubinger, 1b, Arroyo Grande (Calif.) HS.
29. Cameron Edman, c, Gonzaga University.
30. *Mikey Reynolds, ss, Paradise Valley (Ariz.) CC.
31. *John Costa, rhp, Summit Christian HS, West Palm Beach, Fla.
32. *Ryan Meyer, rhp, Oviedo (Fla.) HS.
33. *Sander Beck, rhp, University of Maryland.
34. Zach Fowler, lhp, Texas Tech.
35. *Lindsey Caughel, rhp, Stetson University.
36. *Jeffrey Zona, rhp, Hanover HS, Mechanicsville, Va.
37. *Nick Skala, c, Concordia (Ill.) University.
38. Jerome Pena, 2b, Texas Christian University.
39. *Pat Cantwell, c, Stony Brook University.
40. Bennett Parry, lhp, Poway, Calif.
41. *Chris Mariscal, ss, Clovis North HS, Fresno, Calif.
42. Jason McCracken, rhp, Los Angeles Pierce (Calif.) JC.
43. *David Reynolds, rhp, Edmonds (Wash.) CC.
44. *Patrick Merkling, lhp, Chattanooga State (Tenn.) JC.
45. *Andrew Millner, rhp, Feather River (Calif.) JC.
46. *Mark Reyes, lhp, Jessieville HS, Hale, Ark.
47. *Devon Conley, of, New Mexico JC.
48. *Tyler Hunter, of, Lowndes County HS, Valdosta, Ga.
49. *Ronnie Shaban, rhp, Virginia Tech.
50. *Brendan Butler, of, John Carroll School, Bel Air, Md.

## BOSTON RED SOX (21)

1. **Matt Barnes, rhp, University of Connecticut** (Choice from Tigers as compensation for Type A free agent Victor Martinez).**—(2014-15)**
1. (Choice to Rays as compensation for Type A free agent Carl Crawford)
1. **Blake Swihart, c, Cleveland HS, Rio Rancho, N.M.** (Choice from Rangers as compensation for Type A free agent Adrian Beltre).**—(2015)**
1. **Henry Owens, lhp, Edison HS, Huntington Beach, Calif.** (Supplemental choice—36th—for loss of Martinez).**—(2015)**
1. **Jackie Bradley, of, University of South Carolina** (Supplemental choice—40th—for loss of Beltre).**—(2013-15)**
2. Williams Jerez, of, Grand Street Campus HS, Brooklyn, N.Y.—(AA)
3. Jordan Weems, c, Columbus (Ga.) HS.—(High A)
4. **Noe Ramirez, rhp, Cal State Fullerton.—(2015)**
5. **Mookie Betts, ss, Overton HS, Brentwood, Tenn.—(2014-15)**
6. Miguel Pena, lhp, San Jacinto (Texas) JC.
7. Cody Kukuk, lhp, Free State HS, Lawrence, Kan.
8. *Senquez Golson, of, Pascagoula (Miss.) HS.
DRAFT DROP *Second-round draft pick, Pittsburgh Steelers, National Football League (2015)*
9. **Travis Shaw, 3b, Kent State University.—(2015)**
DRAFT DROP *Son of Jeff Shaw, first overall draft pick, January 1986/regular phase, Indians; major leaguer (1990-2001)*
10. Cody Koback, of, University of Wisconsin-Stevens Point.
11. Kevin Brahney, lhp, Cal Chico State.
12. *Deshorn Lake, rhp, Menchville HS, Newport News, Va.
13. Matty Ott, rhp, Louisiana State University.
14. Mike McCarthy, rhp, Cal State Bakersfield.
15. Braden Kapteyn, rhp, University of Kentucky.
16. *Daniel Gossett, rhp, Byrnes HS, Duncan, S.C.
17. *Blake Forslund, rhp, Liberty University.
18. Andrew Jones, rhp, Samford University.
19. *Sikes Orvis, 1b, Freedom HS, Orlando, Fla.
20. Zach Good, lhp, Grayson County (Texas) CC.
21. *Austin Davidson, 2b, Oxnard (Calif.) HS.
22. Joe Holtmeyer, rhp, University of Nebraska-Omaha.
23. *Jarrett Brown, lhp, Salem HS, Conyers, Ga.
24. Drew Turocy, of, Akron University.
25. *Taylor Ard, 1b, Washington State University.
26. *Cody Dill, rhp, Los Osos HS, Rancho Cucamonga, Calif.
27. *Alex Massey, rhp, Catholic HS, Baton Rouge, La.
28. Brenden Shepard, rhp, Stonehill (Mass.) College.
29. Matt Spalding, rhp, St. Xavier HS, Louisville, Ky.
30. Nick Moore, 3b, Brookwood HS, Snellville, Ga.
31. *Tyler Wells, of, Lexington Catholic HS, Lexington, Ky.
32. *Julius Gaines, ss, Luella HS, Locust Grove, Ga.
33. David Chester, 1b, University of Pittsburgh.
34. *Sean Dartnell, lhp, Vauxhall (Alberta) Academy.
35. Carlos Coste, c, Academia Bautista HS, San Juan, P.R.
36. *Jace Herrera, rhp, Wekiva HS, Apopka, Fla.
37. *Robert Youngdahl, of, Hill-Murray HS, Maplewood, Minn.
38. *Tyler Poole, rhp, Hickory (N.C.) HS.
39. Corey Vogt, rhp, Keene State (N.H.) College.
40. *Jordan Gross, lhp, Don Bosco Prep, Ramsey, N.J.
41. Matt Marquis, of, University of Maryland.
42. *Derek O'Dell, 3b, Canyon (Texas) HS.
43. *Brandon Downes, of, South Plainfield (N.J.) HS.
44. *Matt Martin, c, Pendleton School, Bradenton, Fla.
45. Matt Gedman, 2b, University of Massachusetts.
DRAFT DROP *Son of Rich Gedman, major leaguer (1980-92)*
46. ***Mac Williamson, of, Wake Forest University.—(2015)**
47. *Sam Wolff, rhp, CC of Southern Nevada.
48. *David Sosebee, rhp, White County HS, Cleveland, Ga.
49. Jadd Schmeltzer, rhp, Cornell University.
50. *John Gorman, rhp, Catholic Memorial HS, West Roxbury, Mass.

## CHICAGO CUBS (8)

1. **Javier Baez, ss, Arlington Country Day HS, Jacksonville, Fla.—(2014-15)**
2. Dan Vogelbach, 1b, Bishop Verot HS, Fort Myers, Fla.—(AA)
3. Zeke DeVoss, of, University of Miami.—(AAA)
4. **Tony Zych, rhp, University of Louisville.—(2015)**
5. Tayler Scott, rhp, Notre Dame Prep, Scottsdale, Ariz.—(AA)
6. Neftali Rosario, c, Puerto Rico Baseball Academy, Gurabo, P.R.
7. Trevor Gretzky, 1b, Oaks Christian HS, Westlake Village, Calif.
DRAFT DROP *Son of Wayne Gretzky, member, hockey Hall of Fame; center, National Hockey League (1978-99)*
8. *Taylor Dugas, of, University of Alabama.
9. Garrett Schlecht, of, Waterloo (Ill.) HS.
10. Danny Lockhart, ss, Hebron Christian Academy, Dacula, Ga.
DRAFT DROP *Son of Keith Lockhart, major leaguer (1994-2003)*
11. Shawon Dunston Jr., of, Valley Christian HS, San Jose, Calif.
DRAFT DROP *Son of Shawon Dunston, first overall draft pick, Cubs (1982); major leaguer (1985-2002)*
12. ***Jacob Lindgren, lhp, St. Stanislaus HS, Bay St. Louis, Miss.—(2015)**
13. Trey Martin, of, Brookwood HS, Snellville, Ga.
14. Dillon Maples, rhp, Pinecrest HS, Southern Pines, N.C.
15. Justin Marra, c, Michael Power/St. Joseph HS, Toronto.
16. **Rafael Lopez, c, Florida State University.—(2014)**
17. John Andreoli, of, University of Connecticut.

18. James Pugliese, rhp, Mercer County (N.J.) CC.
19. Paul Hoilman, 1b, East Tennessee State University.
20. Ben Klafczynski, of, Kent State University.
**21. Andrew McKirahan, lhp, University of Texas.—(2015)**
22. Ethan Elias, rhp, Grand Trunk HS, Evansburg, Alberta.
23. *Bradley Zimmer, of, La Jolla HS, Country Club, Calif.

DRAFT DROP *First-round draft pick (21st overall), Indians (2014) • Brother of Kyle Zimmer, first-round draft pick, Royals (2012)*

24. *George Asmus, rhp, Ohlone (Calif.) JC.
25. Rock Shoulders, 1b, State College of Florida-Manatee.
26. Michael Jensen, rhp, Hartnell (Calif.) JC.
27. Taiwan Easterling, of, Florida State University.
28. *Chris Garrison, rhp, Western Nevada CC.
29. *Drew Weeks, 3b, Clay HS, Green Cove Springs, Fla.
30. Arturo Maltos-Garcia, rhp, Lamar (Colo.) CC.
31. *Ronnie Richardson, of, University of Central Florida.
32. Pete Levitt, rhp, Mount Olive (N.C.) College.
33. Sheldon McDonald, lhp, University of British Columbia.
34. *Bobby Kelley, of, Calhoun (Ala.) CC.
35. Ian Dickson, rhp, Lafayette College.
36. Travis Garcia, 3b, Martin Methodist (Tenn.) University.
37. Steven Maxwell, rhp, Texas Christian University.
38. *Casey Lucchese, rhp, College of Charleston.
39. *Ricky Jacquez, rhp, Franklin HS, El Paso, Texas.
40. P.J. Francescon, rhp, Trevecca Nazarene (Tenn.) College.
41. Austin Urban, rhp, Des Moines Area (Iowa) CC.
42. Brad Zapenas, ss, Boston College.
43. *Jay Calhoun, rhp, Second Baptist HS, Houston.
44. Kenny Socorro, ss, Marshall University.
45. *Tanner Kichler, rhp, Sherwood (Ore.) HS.
46. Scott Weismann, rhp, Clemson University.
47. *David Ernst, rhp, South HS, Fargo, N.D.
48. *Sam Howard, lhp, Cartersville (Ga.) HS.
49. *Antonio Gonzales, lhp, Damien HS, La Verne, Calif.
50. *Cody Edwards, rhp, Bellevue (Wash.) CC.

## CHICAGO WHITE SOX (20)

1. (Choice to Nationals as compensation for Type A free agent Adam Dunn)
1. Keenyn Walker, of, Central Arizona JC (Supplemental choice—47th—for loss of Type B free agent J.J. Putz).—(AA)
**2. Erik Johnson, rhp, University of California.—(2013-15)**
3. Jeff Soptic, rhp, Johnson County (Kan.) CC.—(High A)
4. Kyle McMillen, rhp, Kent State University.—(Low A)
**5. Scott Snodgress, lhp, Stanford University.—(2014)**
**6. Marcus Semien, ss, University of California.—(2013-15)**
7. Kevan Smith, c, University of Pittsburgh.
8. *Ian Gardeck, rhp, Angelina (Texas) JC.
9. Matt Lane, lhp, Northwest Florida State JC.
10. *Ben O'Shea, lhp, Santa Fe (Fla.) CC.
11. Blair Walters, lhp, University of Hawaii.
12. Andrew Virgili, rhp, Lynn (Fla.) University.
13. *Chadd Krist, c, University of California.
14. *Mark Ginther, 3b, Oklahoma State University.
15. David Herbek, ss, James Madison University.
**16. Chris Bassitt, rhp, University of Akron.—(2014-15)**
17. Collin Kuhn, of, University of Arkansas.
18. Bryan Blough, rhp, Kennesaw State University.
19. Kevin Vance, rhp, University of Connecticut.
20. Martin Medina, c, Cal State Bakersfield.
21. Joe De Pinto, 2b, University of Southern California.
22. Blake Drake, rhp, Indiana State University.
23. Mike Marjama, c, Long Beach State University.
24. Mark Haddow, of, UC Santa Barbara.
25. Chris Devenski, rhp, Cal State Fullerton.
26. Grant Buckner, 3b, West Virginia University.
27. Jake Cose, rhp, San Joaquin Delta (Calif.) JC.
28. Kyle Robinson, 1b, University of Arkansas.
29. Dustin Hayes, of, Langley, B.C.
30. Brandon Parrent, lhp, Texas A&M University.
31. Michael Johnson, ss, Samford University.
32. Brent Tanner, c, University of South Alabama.
33. Bryce Mosier, c, Valhalla HS, El Cajon, Calif.
34. *Dakota Freese, rhp, Washington HS, Cedar Rapids, Iowa.
35. Joe Dvorsky, rhp, Texas State University.
36. Cody Winiarski, rhp, University of Virginia.
37. Todd Kibby, lhp, St. Petersburg (Fla.) JC.
38. Keegan Linza, rhp, Liberty University.
39. *Javier Reynoso, lhp, Brooks-DeBartolo Collegiate HS, Tampa.
40. *Jake Reed, rhp, Helix Charter HS, La Mesa, Calif.
41. *Chandler Shepherd, rhp, Lawrence County HS, Louisa, Ky.
42. *Aaron Pangilinan, rhp, Escalon (Calif.) HS.
43. *Joel Effertz, rhp, Madison Area Tech (Wis.) JC.
44. *Joe Pistorese, lhp, Flathead HS, Kalispell, Mont.
45. Cory Farris, of, Cumberland (Tenn.) University.
46. *Mike Mancuso, rhp, Brecksville-Broadview Heights HS, Broadview Heights, Ohio.
47. *Robert Liera, c, Hialeah (Fla.) HS.
48. *Dontrell Rush, of, Harlan Community HS, Chicago.
49. *Zach Regier, of, Gilbert (Ariz.) HS.
50. *Jack Graham, 2b, Seneca Valley HS, Harmony, Pa.

## CINCINNATI REDS (24)

1. Robert Stephenson, rhp, Alhambra HS, Martinez, Calif.—(AAA)
2. Gabriel Rosa, of, Colegio Hector Urdaneta, Rio Grande, P.R.—(Low A)
**3. Tony Cingrani, lhp, Rice University.—(2012-15)**
4. Kyle McMyne, rhp, Villanova University.—(AA)
5. Ryan Wright, 2b, University of Louisville.—(AA)
6. Sean Buckley, 3b, St. Petersburg (Fla.) JC.
7. James Allen, rhp, Kansas State University.
8. Jon Matthews, of, St. Petersburg (Fla.) JC.
9. Cole Green, rhp, University of Texas.
10. Brooks Pinckard, rhp, Baylor University.
11. Vaughn Covington, rhp, Killarney SS, Vancouver, B.C.
12. *Joe Serrano, ss, Salpointe HS, Tucson, Ariz.
13. Nick Fleece, rhp, Texas A&M University.
14. Ryan Kemp, rhp, St. Joseph's University.
15. *Will Dorton, rhp, Lugoff-Elgin HS, Lugoff, S.C.
16. *Conor Costello, of, Edmond Santa Fe HS, Edmond, Okla.
17. *Morgan Phillips, ss, Frederick Douglas Academy, New York.
18. Jimmy Moran, rhp, University of South Florida.
19. Chris Joyce, lhp, Santa Barbara (Calif.) CC.
20. Dan Jensen, rhp, University of Cincinnati.
21. Carlos Gonzalez, rhp, Cal State Northridge.
22. Amir Garrett, lhp, Henderson (Nev.) International School.
23. Sal Romano, rhp, Southington (Conn.) HS.
24. Nick O'Shea, 1b, University of Minnesota.
25. Justice French, rhp, Mercer University.
26. Juan Perez, 2b, JC of the Canyons (Calif.).
27. Taylor Wrenn, 2b, University of Tampa.
28. Yordanys Perez, of, Calabasas, Calif.
29. *Dariel Delgado, rhp, Miami.
30. Joe Terry, 3b, Cal State Fullerton.
31. Erik Miller, rhp, Texas Christian University.
32. Mike Dennhardt, rhp, Boston College.
33. Steve Selsky, of, University of Arizona.
34. Bryson Smith, of, University of Florida.
35. *Sam Kimmel, 2b, Indian River (Fla.) CC.
36. Randall Yard, rhp, University of Hawaii.
37. *Michael Suiter, of, Punahou HS, Honolulu, Hawaii.
38. *Dan Bowman, of, Coastal Carolina University.
39. *Justin Amlung, rhp, University of Louisville.
40. *Sam Travis, 3b, Providence Catholic HS, New Lenox, Ill.
41. *Carson Baranik, rhp, Parkway HS, Bossier City, La.
42. *Jacob Stallings, c, University of North Carolina.

DRAFT DROP *Son of Kevin Stallings, head basketball coach, Vanderbilt (1999-2015)*

43. Ty Washington, 2b, Plano East HS, Plano, Texas.
44. *Shon Carson, of, Lake City (S.C.) HS.
45. *Travis Radke, lhp, Oaks Christian HS, Westlake Village, Calif.
46. *Jose Brizuela, 3b, Archbishop McCarthy HS, Southwest Ranches, Fla.
47. *Kirby Pellant, 2b, Chandler-Gilbert (Ariz.) CC.
48. *Tyler Webb, lhp, University of South Carolina.
49. Eric Alessio, rhp, Marist College.
50. *Austin Robichaux, rhp, Notre Dame HS, Crowley, La.

## CLEVELAND INDIANS (7)

**1. Francisco Lindor, ss, Montverde (Fla.) Academy.—(2015)**
2. Dillon Howard, rhp, Searcy (Ark.) HS.—(Rookie)
3. Jake Sisco, rhp, Merced (Calif.) JC.—(Low A)
4. Jake Lowery, c, James Madison University.—(AA)
5. Will Roberts, rhp, University of Virginia.—(AAA)
6. Bryson Myles, of, Stephen F. Austin State University.

DRAFT DROP *Brother of Candon Myles, 12th-round draft pick, Pirates (2011)*

7. Eric Haase, c, Divine Child HS, Dearborn, Mich.
8. *Stephen Tarpley, lhp, Gilbert (Ariz.) HS.
9. Jordan Smith, 3b, St. Cloud State (Minn.) University.
10. Jeff Johnson, rhp, Cal Poly.
11. Luis DeJesus, rhp, Angelina (Texas) JC.
12. Grant Sides, rhp, Samford University.
13. Zack MacPhee, 2b, Arizona State University.
**14. Cody Anderson, rhp, Feather River (Calif.) JC.—(2015)**
15. Todd Hankins, 2b, Seminole State (Fla.) JC.
16. Ryan Merritt, lhp, McLennan (Texas) CC.
17. *Kevin Brady, rhp, Clemson University.
**18. Shawn Armstrong, rhp, East Carolina University.—(2015)**
19. Shawn Morimando, lhp, Ocean Lakes HS, Virginia Beach, Va.
20. *Dillon Peters, lhp, Cathedral HS, Indianapolis.
21. Cody Elliott, of, Ball State University.
22. *Matthew Reckling, rhp, Rice University.
**23. Cody Allen, rhp, High Point University.—(2012-15)**
24. *Taylor Sparks, 3b, St. John Bosco HS, Bellflower, Calif.
25. *Kevin Kramer, ss, Turlock (Calif.) HS.
26. *Austin Diemer, of, Rocklin (Calif.) HS.
27. Evan Frazar, ss, Galveston (Texas) JC.
28. *Tyler Nurdin, lhp, Temple (Texas) JC.
29. *Jared Ruxer, rhp, Lawrence Central HS, Indianapolis.
30. *John Polonius, ss, Genesee (N.Y.) CC.
**31. *Michael Roth, lhp, University of South Carolina.—(2013-14)**
32. *Cole Pitts, rhp, Colquitt County HS, Moultrie, Ga.
33. Jack Wagoner, rhp, Florida Gulf Coast University.
34. *Tyler Maloof, rhp, University of Georgia.
35. Mason Radeke, rhp, Cal Poly.
36. Abel Guerrero, lhp, Galveston (Texas) JC.
37. *Taylor Starr, rhp, Oregon State University.
38. Yhoxian Medina, ss, Southeastern (Iowa) CC.
39. John Barr, of, University of Virginia.
40. *Matt Eureste, ss, St. Pius X HS, Houston.
41. Brian Ruiz, of, Lincoln West HS, Cleveland.
42. K.C. Serna, ss, University of Oregon.
43. Geoff Davenport, lhp, University of Arkansas.
44. *Adam Griffin, rhp, Forsyth Country Day HS, Lewisville, N.C.
45. *Will Jamison, of, Evangelical Christian HS, Cordova, Tenn.
46. Rob Nixon, rhp, Adelphi (N.Y.) University.
47. *Cory Embree, of, Moberly (Mo.) HS.
48. *Blaine O'Brien, rhp, Keystone (Pa.) College.
49. *Brian Hansen, of, St. Cloud State (Minn.) University.
50. *Tyler Baker, c, Shawnee Heights HS, Tecumseh, Kan.

## COLORADO ROCKIES (17)

1. Tyler Anderson, lhp, University of Oregon.—(AA)
1. Trevor Story, ss, Irving (Texas) HS (Supplemental choice—45th—for loss of Type B free agent Octavio Dotel).—(AAA)
2. Carl Thomore, of, East Brunswick (N.J.) HS.—(Low A)
**3. *Peter O'Brien, c, Bethune-Cookman College.—(2015)**

DRAFT DROP *Attended Miami (Fla.); re-drafted by Yankees, 2012 (2nd round)*

4. Dillon Thomas, of, Westbury Christian HS, Houston.—(High A)
**5. Taylor Featherston, ss, Texas Christian University.—(2015)**
6. Chris Jensen, rhp, University of San Diego.
7. Harold Riggins, 1b, North Carolina State University.
8. Roberto Padilla, lhp, San Jose State University.
9. *Ross Stripling, rhp, Texas A&M University.
10. Ben Hughes, rhp, St. Olaf (Minn.) College.
11. Alex Gillingham, rhp, Loyola Marymount University.
12. *David Schuknecht, c, Palm Desert (Calif.) HS.
13. Kyle Roliard, lhp, Louisiana Tech.
14. Brian Humphries, of, Pepperdine University.
15. Tim Smalling, ss, Virginia Tech.
**16. *Preston Tucker, 1b, University of Florida.—(2015)**

DRAFT DROP *Brother of Kyle Tucker, first-round draft pick, Astros (2015)*

17. Will Rankin, rhp, Southern Polytechnic State (Ga.) University.
18. Ben Alsup, rhp, Louisiana State University.
19. Jesse Meaux, rhp, UC Santa Barbara.
**20. Danny Winkler, rhp, University of Central Florida.—(2015)**
21. Jordan Ribera, 1b, Fresno State University.
22. Logan Mahon, lhp, Southeast Missouri State University.
23. Brook Hart, lhp, Yale University.
24. *Connor McKay, of, Regis Jesuit HS, Aurora, Colo.
25. Patrick Johnson, rhp, University of North Carolina.
26. Mike Wolford, rhp, UC Riverside.
27. Matt Argyropoulos, 3b, Washington State University.
28. *Joshua Correa, of, Caguas Military Academy, Caguas, P.R.
29. *Matt Dermody, lhp, University of Iowa.
30. *John Curtiss, rhp, Carroll HS, Southlake, Texas.
31. Sam Mende, ss, University of South Florida.
32. Jarod Berggren, of, University of Northern Colorado.
33. Jaron Shepherd, of, Mississippi State University.

DRAFT DROP *Son of Ron Shepherd, major leaguer (1984-86)*

34. Chris Dennis, rhp, University of Portland.
35. Richard Pirkle, c, Georgia College & State University.
36. *Tyler Servais, c, Douglas County HS, Castle Rock, Colo.

DRAFT DROP *Son of Scott Servais, major leaguer (1991-2001)*

37. *Brandon Bonilla, lhp, Pendleton School, Bradenton, Fla.

DRAFT DROP *Son of Bobby Bonilla, major leaguer (1986-2001)*

38. *Boo Vazquez, of, Cardinal Mooney HS, Youngstown, Ohio.
39. *Chase Williams, rhp, Broken Arrow (Okla.) HS.
40. *Drew Stankiewicz, 2b, Gilbert (Ariz.) HS.

DRAFT DROP *Son of Andy Stankiewicz, major leaguer (1992-98); baseball coach, Grand Canyon (2012-15)*

41. *Taylor Martin, rhp, Lexington Catholic HS, Lexington, Ky.
42. *Jordan Johnson, rhp, Franklin HS, Elk Grove, Calif.
43. *Garrett Brown, of, Clyde A. Erwin HS, Asheville, N.C.
44. *Robert Kahana, rhp, Campbell HS, Ewa Beach, Hawaii.
45. *Will Price, of, Greenbrier HS, Evans, Ga.
46. *Nate Causey, c, Gilbert (Ariz.) HS.
47. *Casey Scott, 2b, Notre Dame Prep, Scottsdale, Ariz.
48. *Clay Bauer, rhp, JC of San Mateo (Calif.).
49. *Tyler Bernard, ss, Palomar (Calif.) JC.
50. *Heath Holder, of, Loganville (Ga.) HS.

## DETROIT TIGERS (16)

1. (Choice to Red Sox as compensation for Type A free agent Victor Martinez)

2. **James McCann, c, University of Arkansas.—(2014-15)**
3. Aaron Westlake, 1b, Vanderbilt University.—(AA)
4. Jason King, 3b, Kansas State University.—(High A)
5. Brandon Loy, ss, University of Texas.—(AA)
6. **Tyler Collins, of, Howard (Texas) JC.—(2014-15)**
7. **Brian Flynn, lhp, Wichita State University.—(2013-14)**
8. Jason Krizan, of, Dallas Baptist University.
9. Chad Wright, of, University of Kentucky.
10. **Curt Casali, c, Vanderbilt University.—(2014-15)**
11. Dean Green, 1b, Barry (Fla.) University.
12. Jeff Holm, of, Michigan State University.
13. Ryan Woolley, rhp, University of Alabama-Birmingham.
14. Pat Smith, of, Middle Georgia JC.
15. Tyler Gibson, of, Stratford Academy, Macon, Ga.
16. Ismael Salgado, of, International Baseball Academy, Cieba, P.R.
17. **Chad Smith, rhp, University of Southern California.—(2014-15)**
18. Brett Harrison, 3b, Green Valley HS, Henderson, Nev.
19. Dan Bennett, rhp, Florida State University.
20. Tyler Barrett, lhp, Lewis-Clark State (Idaho) College.
21. *Scott Squier, lhp, Greenway HS, Phoenix.
22. Tommy Collier, rhp, San Jacinto (Texas) JC.
23. *Trent Daniel, lhp, University of Arkansas.
24. Matt Crouse, lhp, University of Mississippi.
25. *Mitch Mormann, rhp, Wichita State University.
26. Colin Kaline, 2b, Florida Southern College.

DRAFT DROP *Grandson of Al Kaline, major leaguer (1953-74)*

27. Scott Matyas, rhp, University of Minnesota.
28. **Guido Knudson, rhp, UC San Diego.—(2015)**
29. Montreal Robertson, rhp, Coahoma (Miss.) CC.
30. *Greg Milhorn, rhp, Arkansas HS, Texarkana, Ark.
31. Brian Stroud, rhp, Western Michigan University.
32. Brandon Eckerle, of, Michigan State University.
33. Dan Kickham, rhp, Missouri State University.

DRAFT DROP *Brother of Mike Kickham, major leaguer (2013-14)*

34. Zach Maggard, c, Florida Southern College.
35. Eric Heckaman, rhp, Western Michigan University.
36. Jake Sabol, rhp, Central Michigan University.
37. Nick Avila, rhp, Nova Southeastern (Fla.) University.
38. *Blaise Salter, c, St. Mary's Prep, Orchard Lake Village, Mich.

DRAFT DROP *Grandson of Bill Freehan, major leaguer (1961-76)*

39. *Cole Brocker, rhp, Sacramento (Calif.) CC.
40. *Ryan Krill, 1b, Portage Central HS, Portage, Mich.
41. *Jimmy Pickens, of, Brother Rice HS, Bloomfield Hills, Mich.
42. *Tucker Chadd, c, Bishop Carroll HS, Wichita, Kan.
43. *Greg Fettes, c, Lamphere HS, Madison Heights, Mich.
44. Chretien Matz, of, University of Arkansas-Pine Bluff.
45. *Andrew Allen, 1b, Cal State Los Angeles.
46. *Alex Fernandez Jr., of, Archbishop McCarthy HS, Southwest Ranches, Fla.

DRAFT DROP *Son of Alex Fernandez, first-round draft pick, Brewers (1988); first-round draft pick, White Sox (1990); major leaguer (1990-2000)*

47. *Ryan MacPhail, c, Dutch Fork HS, Irmo, S.C.
48. *Lavaris McCullough, of, Palatka (Fla.) HS.
49. *Brett Impemba, of, Dakota HS, Macomb, Mich.
50. *Brandon Webber, of, Bishop Carroll HS, Wichita, Kan.

## FLORIDA MARLINS (12)

1. **Jose Fernandez, rhp, Alonso HS, Tampa.—(2013-15)**
2. **Adam Conley, lhp, Washington State University.—(2015)**
3. *Connor Barron, ss, Sumrall (Miss.) HS.

DRAFT DROP *Attended Southern Mississippi; never re-drafted*

4. *Tyler Palmer, 2b, Wayne County HS, Jesup, Ga.—(Rookie)

DRAFT DROP *Attended Oakton (Ill.) JC; never re-drafted*

5. Mason Hope, rhp, Broken Arrow (Okla.) HS.—(Low A)
6. Charlie Lowell, lhp, Wichita State University.
7. Ryan Rieger, 1b, JC of the Sequoias (Calif.).
8. Dejai Oliver, rhp, Seminole State (Fla.) JC.

DRAFT DROP *Son of Joe Oliver, major leaguer (1989-2001)*

9. **Austin Barnes, c, Arizona State University.—(2015)**
10. Scott Lyman, rhp, UC Davis.
11. Jacob Esch, rhp, Georgia Tech.
12. Ryan McIntyre, of, Cal State Bakersfield.
13. Josh Adams, ss, University of Florida.
14. *Nick Grim, rhp, Monterey Peninsula (Calif.) JC.
15. Jhiomar Veras, of, Western Oklahoma State JC.
16. *Adrian Sampson, rhp, Bellevue (Wash.) CC.
17. *Derek Varnadore, rhp, Auburn University.
18. Greg Nappo, lhp, University of Connecticut.
19. Connor Burke, 2b, La Serna HS, Whittier, Calif.
20. *Devon Reed, ss, Milford (Del.) HS.
21. Chase Wier, rhp, Stephen F. Austin State University.
22. Collin Cargill, rhp, University of Southern Mississippi.
23. Tyler Higgins, rhp, Lansing (Mich.) CC.
24. Tony Caldwell, c, Auburn University.
25. Sean Donatello, rhp, University of Connecticut-Avery Point JC.
26. Ryan Goetz, 3b, UC Riverside.
27. Frankie Reed, lhp, Cal Poly.
28. Brad Mincey, rhp, East Carolina University.
29. Matt Neil, rhp, Brigham Young University.
30. Jose Behar, c, Florida International University.
31. Kenny Jackson, 3b, Texas A&M University.
32. Sharif Othman, c, California Baptist University.
33. James Nygren, rhp, Oregon State University.
34. John Schultz, of, University of Pittsburgh.
35. Johnny Omahen, rhp, Cal State San Marcos.
36. *Damek Tomscha, 3b, Iowa Western CC.
37. *Jake Ehret, rhp, San Dimas (Calif.) HS.
38. *Joe Ceja, rhp, Marquette HS, Ottawa, Ill.
39. *Travis Huber, rhp, JC of Southern Idaho.
40. *Trent Gilbert, ss, Torrance (Calif.) HS.
41. *Matt Anderson, rhp, Chaffey (Calif.) JC.
42. *Jerad Grundy, lhp, Heartland (Ill.) CC.
43. *Drew Leenhouts, lhp, Northeastern University.
44. *Zack LaNeve, ss, Pine-Richland HS, Gibsonia, Pa.
45. *Tim Zufall, of, Lamar (Colo.) CC.
46. *Zach Cooper, rhp, Central Michigan University.
47. *Joel Thys, c, Ohlone (Calif.) JC.
48. *Chris Nunez, 2b, Goddard HS, Roswell, N.M.
49. *Connor Little, rhp, University of Hawaii.
50. *Cory Caruso, lhp, Cal State San Bernadino.

## HOUSTON ASTROS (9)

1. **George Springer, of, University of Connecticut.—(2014-15)**
2. **Adrian Houser, rhp, Locust Grove (Okla.) HS.—(2015)**
3. Jack Armstrong Jr., rhp, Vanderbilt University.—DNP

DRAFT DROP *Son of Jack Armstrong, first-round draft pick, Reds (1987); major leaguer (1988-94)*

4. Chris Lee, lhp, Santa Fe (Fla.) CC.—(AA)
5. **Nick Tropeano, rhp, Stony Brook University.—(2014-15)**
6. Brandon Meredith, of, San Diego State University.
7. Javaris Reynolds, of, King HS, Tampa.
8. Brandon Culbreth, rhp, Forsyth Country Day HS, Lewisville, N.C.
9. Jonas Dufek, rhp, Creighton University.
10. Kyle Hallock, lhp, Kent State University.
11. Justin Gominsky, of, University of Minnesota.
12. Miles Hamblin, c, University of Mississippi.
13. John Hinson, 2b, Clemson University.
14. *Gandy Stubblefield, rhp, Lufkin (Texas) HS.
15. Zach Johnson, 1b, Oklahoma State University.
16. Scott Zuloaga, lhp, Scottsdale (Ariz.) CC.
17. Tyson Perez, rhp, Fresno (Calif.) CC.
18. *Kevin Miller, rhp, University of California.
19. Mitchell Lambson, lhp, Arizona State University.
20. **Matt Duffy, 3b, University of Tennessee.—(2015)**
21. Jimmy Howick, ss, Jacksonville University.
22. Drew Muren, of, Cal State Northridge.
23. Ruben Sosa, 2b, Oklahoma City University.
24. Jesse Wierzbicki, 1b, University of North Carolina.
25. *Billy Flamion, of, Central Catholic HS, Modesto, Calif.
26. *Jared Fisher, rhp, Newport HS, Bellevue, Wash.
27. Alex Todd, ss, Sonoma State (Calif.) University.
28. *Jordan John, lhp, University of Oklahoma.
29. Wallace Gonzalez, of, Bishop Amat HS, La Puente, Calif.
30. *Jordan Steranka, 3b, Penn State University.
31. Jarrod McKinney, of, University of Arkansas.
32. Zach Dando, rhp, Central Arizona JC.
33. *Dominique Taylor, of, Salt Lake (Utah) CC.
34. Dustin Kellogg, rhp, Caney Creek HS, Conroe, Texas.
35. *Chris Morales, rhp, Clear Creek HS, League City, Texas.
36. Kevin Gonzalez, c, Texas A&M University.
37. Steve Martin, rhp, Texas A&M University.
38. Brad Propst, rhp, Oklahoma State University.
39. *David Haerle, rhp, JC of the Canyons (Calif.).
40. *Buddy Lamothe, rhp, San Jacinto (Texas) JC.
41. Chase Davidson, 1b, University of Georgia.
42. *Hoke Granger, of, Northside Methodist Academy, Dothan, Ala.
43. *David Grimes, of, Upton Lakes Christian HS, Clinton Corners, N.Y.
44. Blake Ford, rhp, Lamar University.
45. Chris Epps, of, Clemson University.
46. Justin Shults, 1b, UC Riverside.
47. Zack Hardoin, lhp, University of Missouri.
48. *A.J. Murray, c, Westfield (N.J.) HS.
49. *Dave Peterson, rhp, College of Charleston.
50. *Colton Davis, of, Lake Wales (Fla.) HS.

## KANSAS CITY ROYALS (5)

1. Bubba Starling, of, Gardner-Edgerton HS, Gardner, Kan.—(AA)
2. Cameron Gallagher, c, Manheim Township HS, Lancaster, Pa.—(High A)
3. Bryan Brickhouse, rhp, The Woodlands (Texas) HS.—(Low A)
4. Kyle Smith, rhp, Santaluces HS, Lantana, Fla.—(AA)
5. Patrick Leonard, of, St. Thomas HS, Houston.—(AA)
6. Cesar Ogando, lhp, Caribbean (P.R.) University JC.
7. Kellen Moen, rhp, University of Oregon.
8. *Evan Beal, rhp, South County HS, Lorton, Va.
9. **Aaron Brooks, rhp, Cal State San Bernardino.—(2014-15)**
10. Matt Murray, rhp, Georgia Southern University.
11. Jerrell Allen, of, Milford (Del.) HS.
12. *Adam Schemenauer, lhp, Park Hill South HS, Riverside, Mo.
13. Stephen Lumpkins, lhp, American University.
14. D'Andre Toney, of, Gulf Coast (Fla.) CC.
15. Dean Espy, 1b, UCLA.
16. Jack Lopez, ss, Deltona (Fla.) HS.
17. Nic Cuckovich, 3b, Riverside (Calif.) CC.
18. Andy Ferguson, rhp, Arkansas State University.
19. Matt Flemer, rhp, University of California.
20. **Terrance Gore, of, Gulf Coast (Fla.) CC.—(2014-15)**
21. Kenny Swab, c, University of Virginia.
22. Dave Middendorf, lhp, Northern Kentucky University.
23. Lance Harper, c, Scottsdale (Ariz.) CC.
24. **Spencer Patton, rhp, Southern Illinois University-Edwardsville.—(2014-15)**
25. Mark Threlkeld, 3b, Louisiana Tech.
26. *Joseph Moorefield, lhp, Clemson University.
27. *Lee Clubb, of, Iowa Park (Texas) HS.
28. *Jordan Ramsey, rhp, North Davidson HS, Lexington, N.C.
29. Jake Junis, rhp, Rock Falls (Ill.) HS.
30. Christian Binford, rhp, Mercersburg (Pa.) Academy.
31. *Chris Serritella, 1b, Southern Illinois University.
32. *Nick Piscotty, rhp, Amador Valley HS, Pleasanton, Calif.

DRAFT DROP *Brother of Stephen Piscotty, major leaguer (2015)*

33. *Abel Gonzales, lhp, Rice University.
34. Ali Williams, rhp, Charleston Southern University.
35. Gabriel Gray, of, Hazelhurst (Miss.) HS.
36. Christian Witt, rhp, Truman State (Mo.) University.
37. *Matt Wessinger, ss, St. John's University.
38. Andrew Durden, rhp, Nova Southeastern (Fla.) University.
39. *Garrett Mattlage, ss, West HS, Stinnett, Texas.
40. *Ben Waldrip, 1b, Jacksonville State University.
41. Travis Lane, c, Central Arizona JC.
42. *Joey Hawkins, 2b, Sinclair SS, Whitby, Ontario.
43. Tyler Chism, of, Gonzaga University.
44. *Andrew Vasquez, rhp, Los Osos HS, Rancho Cucamonga, Calif.
45. Julio Morales, rhp, Bethune-Cookman College.
46. Adrian Bringas, 3b, Cal State Chico.
47. *Patrick Corbett, rhp, Tabb HS, Yorktown, Va.
48. *Matt Beaty, c, Dresden (Tenn.) HS.
49. Adrian Morales, 3b, University of South Carolina.
50. *Kash Kalkowski, 3b, University of Nebraska.

## LOS ANGELES ANGELS (14)

1. **C.J. Cron Jr., 1b, University of Utah.—(2014-15)**

DRAFT DROP *Son of Chris Cron, major leaguer (1991-92) • Brother of Kevin Cron, third-round draft pick, Mariners (2011)*

2. (Choice to Blue Jays as compensation for Type A free agent Scott Downs)
3. **Nick Maronde, lhp, University of Florida.—(2012-14)**
4. Mike Clevinger, rhp, Seminole State (Fla.) JC.—(AA)
5. Andrew Ray, of, Northeast Texas CC.—(High A)
6. Austin Wood, rhp, University of Southern California.
7. Abel Baker, c, Grayson County (Texas) CC.
8. Logan Odom, rhp, University of Southern California.
9. Nick Mutz, rhp, Cotati, Calif.
10. Drew Martinez, of, Memphis University.

DRAFT DROP *Son of Chito Martinez, major leaguer (1991-93)*

11. Garrett Baker, lhp, Liberty University.
12. Joe Krehbiel, 3b, Seminole (Fla.) HS.
13. Jackson Whitley, 1b, North Augusta (S.C.) HS.
14. *Wayne Taylor, c, Memorial HS, Houston.
15. *Dominic Jose, of, Boca Raton (Fla.) HS.

DRAFT DROP *Son of Felix Jose, major leaguer (1988-2003)*

16. Frazier Hall, 1b, Southern University.
17. *Hunter Lockwood, c, Bell HS, Hurst, Texas.
18. Trevor Hairgrove, ss, UC Riverside.
19. Ryan Crowley, lhp, Northwest Florida State JC.
20. Junior Carlin, lhp, University of South Florida.
21. Shane Riedie, rhp, University of Tampa.
22. Brennan Gowens, of, Fresno State University.
23. Zach Borenstein, of, Eastern Illinois University.
24. Jarrod Parks, 3b, Mississippi State University.
25. Josh Alvarado, rhp, GateWay (Ariz.) CC.
26. *John Gianis, of, North Carolina State University.
27. Brian Hernandez, 3b, UC Irvine.
28. Daniel Vargas-Vila, rhp, University of West Florida.
29. *Greg Larson, rhp, University of Florida.
30. *Mike Papi, of, Tunkhannock (Pa.) Area HS.

DRAFT DROP *First-round draft pick (38th overall), Indians (2014)*

31. **Jett Bandy, c, University of Arizona.—(2015)**
32. John Leonard, rhp, Boston College.
33. *Erik Forgione, ss, West HS, Chehalis, Wash.
34. Andy Workman, of, Arizona State University.
35. Stephen Tromblee, lhp, Lamar University.
36. Brandon Brewer, ss, University of West Florida.
37. Brandon Efferson, rhp, Southeastern Louisiana University.
38. Frank De Julio, rhp, University of Tampa.
39. Chris Giovinazzo, of, UCLA.
40. *Joe Church, rhp, Marshall University.
41. Brandon McNelis, rhp, Northeastern University.
42. Jason Nappi, 3b, Harding (Ark.) University.
43. Kyle Mahoney, c, High Point University.
44. Landis Ware, 2b, Baylor University.
45. Matt Scioscia, c, University of Notre Dame.

DRAFT DROP *Son of Mike Scioscia, first-round draft pick, Dodgers (1976); major leaguer (1980-92); major league manager (2000-15)*
46. Michael Johnson, lhp, Hillsborough (Fla.) CC.
47. Brandon Lodge, rhp, UCLA.
48. Ricky Pacione, c, Marist College.
49. *Matt Vedo, rhp, UC Santa Barbara.
50. *Trent Garrison, c, Fresno State University.

## LOS ANGELES DODGERS (13)

1. **Chris Reed, lhp, Stanford University.—(2015)**
2. Alex Santana, 3b, Mariner HS, Cape Coral, Fla.—(Low A)

DRAFT DROP *Son of Rafael Santana, major leaguer (1983-90)*
3. Pratt Maynard, c, North Carolina State University.—(High A)
4. Ryan O'Sullivan, rhp, Oklahoma City University.—(AA)

DRAFT DROP *Brother of Sean O'Sullivan, major leaguer (2009-15)*
5. **Scott McGough, rhp, University of Oregon.—(2015)**
6. Scott Barlow, rhp, Golden Valley HS, Santa Clarita, Calif.
7. Scott Woodward, of, Coastal Carolina University.
8. Rick Anton, lhp, University of Utah.
9. Tyler Ogle, c, University of Oklahoma.
10. *Jamaal Moore, lhp, Westchester HS, Los Angeles.
11. Scott Wingo, ss, University of South Carolina.
12. O'Koyea Dickson, 1b, Sonoma State (Calif.) University.
13. *David Palladino, rhp, Emerson (N.J.) HS.
14. Justin Boudreaux, ss, Southeastern Louisiana University.
15. Craig Stem, rhp, Trevecca Nazarene (Tenn.) College.
16. Jeff Schaus, of, Clemson University.
17. Jesus Valdez, 3b, Oxnard (Calif.) JC.
18. Chris O'Brien, c, Wichita State University.

DRAFT DROP *Son of Charlie O'Brien, major leaguer (1985-2000)*
19. *Garrett Bush, rhp, Seminole State (Fla.) JC.
20. *Vince Spilker, rhp, Johnson County (Kan.) CC.
21. *Zak Qualls, lhp, Rancho HS, Las Vegas, Nev.
22. *Kyle Conwell, of, Bellevue (Wash.) CC.
23. Garrett Bolt, rhp, Western Illinois University.
24. Matt Shelton, rhp, Sam Houston State University.
25. *Travis Burnside, of, Spartanburg Methodist (S.C.) JC.
26. Freddie Cabrera, rhp, Central Methodist (Mo.) University.
27. *Taylor Garrison, rhp, Fresno State University.
28. Joey Winker, of, Mercer University.
29. *Joe Robinson, rhp, University of Nevada-Las Vegas.
30. *Adam McConnell, ss, University of Richmond.
31. *Mickey McConnell, ss, St. Mary's (Calif.) College.
32. *Hunter Jennings, of, Delgado (La.) CC.
33. Malcolm Holland, 2b, Hamilton HS, Chandler, Ariz.
34. Rob Chamra, rhp, North Carolina State University.
35. Mike Thomas, lhp, Rider University.
36. Kevin Taylor, 2b, Western Nevada CC.
37. *Reid Redman, 3b, Texas Tech.
38. Devin Shines, of, Oklahoma State University.

DRAFT DROP *Son of Razor Shines, major leaguer (1983-87)*
39. *Jordan Kipper, rhp, Mountain Pointe HS, Phoenix.
40. Stefan Jarrin, 2b, San Gabriel, Calif.
41. *Casey Thomas, 2b, Desert Vista HS, Phoenix.
42. *Max Povse, rhp, Green Hope HS, Cary, N.C.
43. *Alex Hermeling, rhp, Glenbrook North HS, Northbrook, Ill.
44. *Austin Slater, ss, Bolles School, Jacksonville, Fla.
45. *James Lynch, of, Salisbury (Conn.) Prep.
46. *Victor Munoz, c, Claremont (Calif.) HS.
47. Gregg Downing, lhp, Franklin Pierce (N.H.) College.
48. Kevin Thompson, ss, Eastern New Mexico University.
49. J.J. Ethel, c, University of Louisville.
50. *Chris Ellis, rhp, Spain Park HS, Birmingham, Ala.

## MILWAUKEE BREWERS (10)

1. **Taylor Jungmann, rhp, University of Texas.—(2015)**
1. Jed Bradley, lhp, Georgia Tech (Special compensation choice—15th—for failure to sign 2010 first-round pick Dylan Covey).—(AAA)
2. **Jorge Lopez, rhp, Academia de Milagrosa, Cayey, P.R.—(2015)**
3. Drew Gagnon, rhp, Long Beach State University.—(AAA)
4. Nick Ramirez, 1b, Cal State Fullerton.—(AA)
5. **Michael Reed, of, Leander (Texas) HS.—(2015)**

DRAFT DROP *Son of Ben Reed, defensive end, National Football League (1987)*
6. Danny Keller, rhp, Newbury Park HS, Thousand Oaks, Calif.
7. **David Goforth, rhp, University of Mississippi.—(2015)**
8. Dustin Houle, c, Brookswood SS, Langley, B.C.
9. Malcolm Dowell, of, La Grange (Ga.) HS.
10. Mike Strong, lhp, Oklahoma State University.
11. Tommy Toledo, rhp, University of Florida.
12. *Andrew Cain, of, UNC Wilmington.
13. *Mailex Smith, of, Rickards HS, Tallahassee, Fla.
14. Jacob Barnes, rhp, Florida Gulf Coast University.
15. Andy Moye, rhp, Georgia Southern University.
16. ***Carlos Rodon, lhp, Holly Springs (N.C.) HS.—(2015)**

DRAFT DROP *First-round draft pick (3rd overall), White Sox (2014)*
17. *Mario Amaral, c, Ronald Reagan HS, Hialeah, Fla.
18. Chris McFarland, ss, Lufkin (Texas) HS.
19. Renaldo Jenkins, ss, Whitewater HS, Fayetteville, Ga.
20. Brandon Williamson, rhp, Dallas Baptist University.
21. Michael Nemeth, 1b, University of Connecticut.
22. *D.J. Jones, of, Jefferson Davis HS, Montgomery, Ala.
23. Ben McMahan, c, University of Florida.
24. *Michael Palazzone, rhp, University of Georgia.
25. Parker Berberet, c, Oregon State University.
26. *Josh Smith, lhp, Wichita State University.
27. Chad Thompson, rhp, Orange Coast (Calif.) CC.
28. *BreShon Kimbell, c, Mesquite (Texas) HS.
29. *David Lucroy, rhp, Umatila (Fla.) HS.

DRAFT DROP *Brother of Jonathan Lucroy, major leaguer (2010-15)*
30. *Trent Boras, 3b, J Serra HS, San Juan Capistrano, Calif.

DRAFT DROP *Brother of Shane Boras, 39th-round draft pick, Athletics (2011)*
31. Sean Albury, rhp, Nova Southeastern (Fla.) University.
32. *Alfredo Rodriguez, ss, University of Maryland.
33. *Steven Okert, lhp, Grayson County (Texas) CC.
34. Adam Weisenburger, c, Miami (Ohio) University.
35. Doug Elliot, c, University of Connecticut.
36. Mitchell Conner, rhp, Elon University.
37. Casey Medlen, rhp, University of North Florida.
38. Chad Pierce, rhp, University of Wisconsin-Milwaukee.
39. Elliott Glynn, lhp, University of Connecticut.
40. *Keaton Aldridge, c, Glenwood School, Smiths Station, Ala.
41. Jalen Harris, 3b, Lambrick Park SS, Victoria, B.C.
42. *Caleb Whalen, ss, Union HS, Camas, Wash.
43. *Clint Wilson, rhp, Navarro (Texas) JC.
44. *Steve Adam, of, Ecole Secondaire L'Essor, Tecumseh, Ontario.
45. Adrian Williams, ss, UCLA.
46. *Ahmad Christian, ss, Trinity Christian Academy, Deltona, Fla.
47. *Jecid Tarazona, of, North Broward Prep, Coconut Creek, Fla.
48. Mike Francisco, lhp, Villanova University.
49. Gant Elmore, 2b, Yale University.
50. Matt Franco, of, St. Thomas Aquinas HS, Fort Lauderdale, Fla.

## MINNESOTA TWINS (27)

1. Levi Michael, ss, University of North Carolina.—(AA)
1. Travis Harrison, 3b, Tustin (Calif.) HS (Supplemental choice—50th—for loss of Type B free agent Orlando Hudson).—(AA)
1. Hudson Boyd, rhp, Bishop Verot HS, Fort Myers, Fla. (Supplemental choice—55th—for loss of Type B free agent Jesse Crain).—(Low A)
2. Madison Boer, rhp, University of Oregon.—(AA)
3. Corey Williams, lhp, Vanderbilt University.—(AA)
4. Matt Summers, rhp, UC Irvine.—(AA)
5. Tyler Grimes, ss, Wichita State University.—(High A)
6. Dereck Rodriguez, of, Monsignor Pace HS, Opa-Locka, Fla.

DRAFT DROP *Son of Ivan Rodriguez, major leaguer (1991-2011)*
7. Steven Gruver, lhp, University of Tennessee.
8. Jason Wheeler, lhp, Loyola Marymount University.
9. Adam Bryant, ss, Troy University.
10. Brett Lee, lhp, St. Petersburg (Fla.) JC.
11. Tyler Jones, rhp, Louisiana State University.
12. Matt Koch, c, Loyola Marymount University.
13. Steven Evans, lhp, Liberty University.
14. *Adam McCreery, lhp, Bonita HS, La Verne, Calif.
15. Josue Montanez, lhp, Miami-Dade JC.
16. Austin Malinowski, lhp, Centennial HS, Circle Pines, Minn.
17. Josh Burris, rhp, LSU-Eunice JC.
18. Corey Kimes, lhp, University of Illinois.
19. Tyler Koelling, of, University of Southern Mississippi.
20. *Brian Anderson, ss, Deer Creek HS, Edmond, Okla.
21. *Michael Howard, lhp, Prescott (Ariz.) HS.
22. *James Ramsey, of, Florida State University.

DRAFT DROP *First-round draft pick (23rd overall), Cardinals (2012)*
23. Tim Shibuya, rhp, UC San Diego.
24. *Nick Burdi, rhp, Downers Grove (Ill.) South HS.
25. Adam Pettersen, ss, University of Minnesota.
26. Trent Higginbotham, rhp, Clay-Chalkville HS, Trussville, Ala.
27. Chris Mazza, rhp, Menlo (Calif.) College.
28. David Hurlbut, lhp, Cal State Fullerton.
29. *Derek Thompson, lhp, Teutopolis (Ill.) HS.
30. *Will Clinard, rhp, Vanderbilt University.
31. Garrett Jewell, rhp, Southern New Hampshire University.
32. *Dylan Chavez, lhp, American River (Calif.) JC.
33. Stephen Wickens, ss, Florida Gulf Coast University.
34. *Ryan Tella, of, Ohlone (Calif.) JC.
35. Phillip Chapman, c, Memphis University.
36. *Austin Barrois, of, Belle Chasse (La.) HS.
37. Drew Leachman, of, Birmingham-Southern College.
38. *Alex Keudell, rhp, University of Oregon.
39. *Rocky McCord, rhp, Spanish Fort (Ala.) HS.
40. ***Kyle Barraclough, rhp, St. Mary's (Calif.) College.—(2015)**
41. *T.J. Oakes, rhp, University of Minnesota.
42. Matt Tomshaw, lhp, Jacksonville University.
43. Bobby O'Neill, rhp, Biola (Calif.) University.
44. Cole Johnson, rhp, University of Notre Dame.
45. Julio Torres, 2b, Puerto Rico Baseball Academy, Gurabo, P.R.
46. *Jared Dettmann, lhp, Somerset (Wis.) HS.
47. *John Hochstatter, lhp, San Ramon Valley HS, Danville, Calif.
48. *Garret Peterson, rhp, DuBois (Pa.) Area HS.
49. *Drake Roberts, 2b, Brenham (Texas) HS.
50. *Bryan Burgher, rhp, Emerald Ridge HS, Puyallup, Wash.

## NEW YORK METS (11)

1. Brandon Nimmo, of, East HS, Cheyenne, Wyo.—(AAA)
1. Michael Fulmer, rhp, Deer Creek HS, Edmond, Okla. (Supplemental choice—44th—for loss of Type B free egent Pedro Feliciano).—(AA)
2. **Cory Mazzoni, rhp, North Carolina State University.—(2015)**
3. **Logan Verrett, rhp, Baylor University.—(2015)**
4. Tyler Pill, rhp, Cal State Fullerton.—(AAA)

DRAFT DROP *Brother of Brett Pill, major leaguer (2011-13)*
5. **Jack Leathersich, lhp, University of Massachusetts-Lowell.—(2015)**
6. Joe Tuschak, of, Northern HS, Dillsburg, Pa.
7. Cole Frenzel, 1b, University of Arizona.
8. **Danny Muno, ss, Fresno State University.—(2015)**
9. Alex Panteliodis, lhp, University of Florida.
10. Matt Budgell, rhp, Woodbridge HS, Irvine, Calif.
11. Christian Montgomery, rhp, Lawrence Central HS, Indianapolis.
12. *Kenny Mathews, lhp, Diamond Bar (Calif.) HS.
13. Robert Gsellman, rhp, Westchester HS, Los Angeles.
14. Xorge Carrillo, c, Arizona State University.
15. Phillip Evans, ss, La Costa Canyon HS, Carlsbad, Calif.
16. Brad Marquez, of, Odessa (Texas) HS.
17. Jonathan Clark, of, Lee (Tenn.) University.
18. Travis Taijeron, of, Cal Poly Pomona.
19. Dustin Lawley, of, University of West Florida.
20. *Mason Robbins, of, George County HS, Lucedale, Miss.
21. John Gant, rhp, Wiregrass Ranch HS, Wesley Chapel, Fla.
22. *Casey Turgeon, ss, Dunedin (Fla.) HS.
23. Jeff Diehl, c, Cranston West HS, Cranston, R.I.
24. Tant Shepherd, 1b, University of Texas.
25. *A.J. Reed, lhp, Terre Haute South HS, Terre Haute, Ind.
26. Casey Hauptman, rhp, University of Nebraska.
27. Randy Fontanez, rhp, University of South Florida.
28. *Jharel Cotton, rhp, Miami-Dade JC.
29. *Josh Ake, ss, Hunterdon Central HS, Flemington, N.J.
30. *Jake Hansen, lhp, Walshe HS, Fort Macleod, Alberta.
31. Chad Zurcher, ss, Memphis University.
32. Carlos Leyva, ss, Cal State Dominguez Hills.
33. Tyson Seng, rhp, University of Oklahoma.
34. Seth Lugo, rhp, Centenary College.
35. Chase Bradford, rhp, University of Central Florida.
36. Ryan Hutson, 1b, University of Texas-San Antonio.
37. Craig Missigman, rhp, Olympic HS, Charlotte, N.C.
38. Dustin Emmons, rhp, UC Riverside.
39. Charley Thurber, of, University of Tennessee.
40. *Alexis Mercado, c, Otay Ranch HS, Chula Vista, Calif.
41. Mark Picca, lhp, University of Texas-Arlington.
42. Greg Pron, of, University of West Florida.
43. *Jacob Decker, ss, Piedmont (Okla.) HS.
44. *Clint Sharp, rhp, Howard (Texas) JC.
45. *Andrew Marra, rhp, St. Thomas of Villanova SS, LaSalle, Ontario.
46. Rich Ruff, rhp, Quincy (Ill.) University.
47. *Cole Limbaugh, rhp, Childersburg (Ala.) HS.
48. *Malcolm Clapsaddle, rhp, Santa Fe (Fla.) CC.
49. *Sean Buckle, lhp, Wilson HS, Long Beach, Calif.
50. Eddie Rohan, c, Winthrop University.

## NEW YORK YANKEES (28)

1. (Choice to Rays as compensation for Type A free agent Rafael Soriano)
1. Dante Bichette Jr., of, Orangewood Christian HS, Orlando, Fla. (Supplemental choice—51st—for loss of Type B free agent Javier Vazquez).—(AA)

DRAFT DROP *Son of Dante Bichette, major leaguer (1988-2001)*
2. *Sam Stafford, lhp, University of Texas.—(High A)

DRAFT DROP *Returned to Texas; re-drafted by Rangers, 2012 (13th round)*
3. Jordan Cote, rhp, Winnisquam HS, Northfield, N.H.—(Low A)
4. Matt Duran, 3b, New Rochelle (N.Y.) HS.—(Short-season A)
5. **Greg Bird, c, Grandview HS, Aurora, Colo.—(2015)**
6. Jake Cave, of, Kecoughtan HS, Hampton, Va.
7. Bubba Jones, 1b, Edmonds-Woodway HS, Edmonds, Wash.
8. Phil Wetherell, rhp, Western Kentucky University.
9. Zach Arneson, rhp, Lewis-Clark State (Idaho) College.

**10. *Jonathan Gray, rhp, Eastern Oklahoma State JC.—(2015)**
DRAFT DROP *First-round draft pick (3rd overall), Rockies (2013)*
11. Mark Montgomery, rhp, Longwood University.
12. Cody Grice, of, Grand Valley State (Mich.) University.
13. Justin James, of, Sacramento (Calif. CC.
DRAFT DROP *Son of Dion James, first-round draft pick, Brewers (1980); major leaguer (1983-96)*
14. Rookie Davis, rhp, Dixon HS, Holly Ridge, N.C.
15. *Tyler Molinaro, of, Pitt (N.C.) CC,
**16. Branden Pinder, rhp, Long Beach State University.—(2015)**
17. *Mathew Troupe, rhp, Chaminade Prep HS, Chatsworth, Calif.
18. Hayden Sharp, rhp, Morris (Okla.) HS.
19. Ben Paullus, rhp, Memphis University.
20. Daniel Camarena, lhp, Cathedral Catholic HS, San Diego.
21. Zach Wilson, 1b, Arizona State University.
**22. *Nick Goody, rhp, State College of Florida-Manatee.—(2015)**
23. Corey Maines, rhp, Illinois State University.
**24. Matt Tracy, lhp, University of Mississippi.—(2015)**
25. Adam Smith, rhp, Texas A&M University.
26. *Jordan Foley, rhp, The Colony (Texas) HS.
27. Chaz Hebert, lhp, Breaux Bridge (La.) HS.
28. *Josean Lazaro, rhp, North Broward Prep, Coconut Creek, Fla.
29. *Scot Hoffman, rhp, Desert Ridge HS, Mesa, Ariz.
30. John Brebbia, rhp, Elon University.
31. *Aaron Bummer, lhp, Sunrise Mountain HS, Peoria, Ariz.
32. *Garrett Nuss, rhp, Mount Dora HS, Sorrento, Fla.
33. *Spencer O'Neil, of, Southridge HS, Kennewick, Wash.
34. *Skylar Janisse, rhp, St. Thomas of Villanova SS, LaSalle, Ontario.
35. *Chris McCue, rhp, Ardrey Kell HS, Charlotte, N.C.
36. *Ryan Thompson, rhp, Franklin Pierce (N.H.) College.
37. *Ryan Harris, rhp, Jupiter (Fla.) HS.
38. Joey Maher, rhp, Bedford (N.H) HS.
39. *Taylor Guilbeau, lhp, Zachary (La.) HS.
40. *Tyler Hanover, ss, Louisiana State University.
41. *Jeremy Rathjen, of, Rice University.
42. *Kevin Cornelius, ss, Weatherford (Texas) HS.
43. *Tyler Farrell, rhp, Galesburg (Ill.) HS.
44. *Adam Ravenelle, rhp, Lincoln-Sudbury HS, Sudbury, Mass.
45. *Cass Ingvardsen, rhp, Weatherford (Texas) JC.
46. *Conner Mach, 3b, University of Missouri.
DRAFT DROP *Grandson of Phil Gagliano, major leaguer (1963-74)*
47. *Ethan Springston, of, Seton Catholic HS, Chandler, Ariz.
48. *Wes Benjamin, lhp, St. Charles (Ill.) East HS.
49. *Tyler Mapes, rhp, Navarro (Texas) JC.
50. *Cody Stewart, of, Great Oak HS, Temecula, Calif.

## OAKLAND ATHLETICS (15)

**1. Sonny Gray, rhp, Vanderbilt University.—(2013-15)**
2. (Choice to Rays as compensation for Type A free agent Grant Balfour)
3. B.A. Vollmuth, 3b, University of Southern Mississippi.—(High A)
4. Bobby Crocker, of, Cal Poly.—(AA)
5. Beau Taylor, c, University of Central Florida.—(AA)
6. Dayton Alexander, of, Feather River (Calif.) JC
**7. Blake Treinen, rhp, South Dakota State University.—(2014-15)**
8. Colin O'Connell, rhp, Cal State Fullerton.
9. *Jace Fry, lhp, Southridge HS, Beaverton, Ore.
10. Dusty Robinson, of, Fresno State University.
11. Chris Lamb, lhp, Davidson University.
12. Xavier Macklin, of, North Carolina A&T University.
13. Jacob Tanis, 3b, Mercer University.
14. Nick Rickles, c, Stetson University.
15. T.J. Walz, rhp, University of Kansas.
16. Tanner Peters, rhp, University of Nevada-Las Vegas.
17. Sean Jamieson, ss, Canisius University.
18. Brent Powers, lhp, Sam Houston State University.
19. Eric Potter, lhp, University of Maryland.
20. Kurt Wunderlich, rhp, Michigan State University.
21. *Brandon Magee, of, Arizona State University.
DRAFT DROP *Linebacker, National Football League (2013-14)*
22. Rhett Stafford, of, Marshall University.
23. Cecil Tanner, rhp, Georgia University.
24. *Max Kuhn, ss, Zionsville Community (Ind.) HS.
25. Chad Oberacker, of, Tennessee Tech.
26. Sam Roberts, rhp, Virginia Military Institute.
27. *Derek Self, rhp, University of Louisville.
28. *Thomas Girdwood, rhp, Elon University.
29. Nate Eppley, rhp, Rider University.
30. Nathan Kilcrease, rhp, University of Alabama.
31. *Sasha Kuebel, lhp, St. Louis University HS, St. Louis.
32. Drew Granier, rhp, University of Louisiana-Monroe.
33. Austin Booker, 2b, University of California.
34. *Alfredo Unzue, lhp, Calabasas, Calif.
35. Max Perlman, rhp, Harvard University.
36. *Brenden Farney, ss, Vacaville (Calif.) HS.
37. *Eric Wood, 3b, Oshawa, Ontario.
38. *Alex Blandino, ss, St. Francis HS, Mountain View, Calif.
DRAFT DROP *First-round draft pick (29th overall), Reds (2014)*
39. Shane Boras, 2b, University of Southern California.
DRAFT DROP *Brother of Trent Boras, 30th-round draft pick, Brewers (2011)*
40. *Nic Coffman, 3b, Wilson HS, Portland, Ore.
41. *Brett Bittiger, ss, Pius X HS, Bangor, Pa.
DRAFT DROP *Son of Jeff Bittiger, major leaguer (1986-89)*
42. *Brett Geren, c, San Ramon Valley HS, Danville, Calif.
DRAFT DROP *Son of Bob Geren, first-round draft pick (1979); major leaguer (1988-93); major league manager (2007-11)*
43. *Adam Frank, lhp, Field HS, Gilbert, Ariz.
44. Chris Bostick, ss, Aquinas Institute, Rochester, N.Y.
45. *C.J. Jacobe, of, Vacaville (Calif.) HS.
46. *Nate Esposito, c, Granite Bay (Calif.) HS.
47. *Jeriel Waller, of, Grossmont (Calif.) JC.
48. *Travis Feeney, of, Pinole Valley HS, Pinole, Calif.
49. *Charles Sheffield, of, Pendleton School, Bradenton, Fla.
50. *Travis Pitcher, rhp, Cypress (Calif.) JC.

## PHILADELPHIA PHILLIES (30)

1. (Choice to Rangers as compensation for Type A free agent Cliff Lee)
1. Larry Greene, of, Berrien County HS, Nashville, Ga. (Supplemental pick—39th—for loss of Type A free agent Jayson Werth).—(Low A)
2. Roman Quinn, ss, Port St. Joe (Fla.) HS (Choice from Nationals as compensation for Werth).—(AA)
2. Harold Martinez, 3b, University of Miami.—(AA)
**3. Adam Morgan, lhp, University of Alabama.—(2015)**
**4. Cody Asche, 3b, University of Nebraska.—(2013-15)**
5. Mitch Walding, ss, St. Mary's HS, Stockton, Calif.—(High A)
6. Zach Wright, c, East Carolina University.
**7. Ken Giles, rhp, Yavapai (Ariz.) JC.—(2014-15)**
8. Austin Wright, lhp, University of Mississippi.
9. Logan Moore, c, Northeastern (Colo.) JC.
10. *Jake Overbey, ss, University School, Jackson, Tenn.
11. Tyler Greene, ss, West Boca Raton (Fla.) HS.
12. Yacksel Rios, rhp, Cuevas HS, Gurabo, P.R.
**13. Colton Murray, rhp, University of Kansas.—(2015)**
14. Trey Ford, 3b, South Mountain (Ariz.) CC.
15. *Ryan Garvey, of, Palm Desert (Calif.) HS.
DRAFT DROP *Son of Steve Garvey, major leaguer (1969-87)*
16. Taylor Black, ss, University of Kentucky.
17. Jesen Dygestile-Therrien, rhp, Ahuntsic (Que.) JC.
18. Drew Hillman, 3b, UC Irvine.
19. John Hill, c, Concordia (Calif.) University.
20. Peter Lavin, of, University of San Francisco.
21. *Riley Moore, c, San Marcos (Calif.) HS.
DRAFT DROP *Son of Brad Moore, major leaguer (1988-90)*
22. Matt Holland, of, Texas A&M University-Corpus Christi.
23. Cody Fick, rhp, University of Evansville.
24. Matt Campbell, rhp, University of Florida.
25. Ryan Duke, rhp, Oklahoma University.
26. *Michael Rocha, rhp, Oklahoma University.
27. Braden Shull, lhp, Mount Pleasant (Iowa) HS.
28. Ian Durham, rhp, California Lutheran University.
29. Paul Cusick, rhp, University of Pennsylvania.
30. Mike Marshall, 1b, Lubbock Christian (Texas) University.
DRAFT DROP *Son of Mike Marshall, major leaguer (1981-91)*
31. *Kyle Olson, c, Henry Jackson HS, Mill Creek, Wash.
32. Greg Herbst, rhp, St. Mary's (Texas) University.
33. Brock Stassi, of, University of Nevada.
34. *Brandon Pletsch, ss, Rancho HS, Las Vegas, Nev.
35. *Kyle Freeland, lhp, Jefferson HS, Denver.
DRAFT DROP *First-round draft pick (8th overall), Rockies (2014)*
36. *Brendon Hayden, rhp, Wilmot Union HS, Wilmot, Wis.
37. *Mike Nastold, rhp, University of Louisville.
38. *Brett Maggard, lhp, Hernando HS, Brooksville, Fla.
39. *Tim Ponto, rhp, Roberts HS, Pottstown, Pa.
40. *Brendan Hendriks, 1b, Vauxhall (Alberta) Academy.
41. *Austin Dicharry, rhp, University of Texas.
42. Andre Kinder, lhp, Peru State (Neb.) University.
43. *Austin Knight, c, Sumrall (Miss.) HS.
44. *Nevin Wilson, lhp, Chaparral HS, Scottsdale, Ariz.
45. *A.J. Ladwig, rhp, Millard West HS, Omaha, Neb.
46. *Scott Tomassetti, c, Sierra Vista HS, Las Vegas, Nev.
47. *Andrew Amaro, 2b, Penn Charter HS, Philadelphia.
DRAFT DROP *Step-brother of Ruben Amaro Jr., major leaguer (1991-98); general manager, Phillies (2008-15)*
48. *Kewby Meyer, 1b, Kamehameha HS, Honolulu, Hawaii.
49. Johnny Knight, of, Sebring (Fla.) HS.
50. *Koyla Stephenson, rhp, Ocean City (N.J.) HS.

## PITTSBURGH PIRATES (1)

**1. Gerrit Cole, rhp, UCLA.—(2013-15)**
DRAFT DROP *First-round draft pick (28th overall), Yankees (2008)*
2. Josh Bell, of, Dallas Jesuit HS, Dallas.—(AAA)
**3. Alex Dickerson, 1b, Indiana University.—(2015)**
4. Colten Brewer, rhp, Canton (Texas) HS.—(Low A)
5. Tyler Glasnow, rhp, William S. Hart HS, Santa Clarita, Calif.—(AAA)
6. Dan Gamache, 3b, Auburn University.
7. Jake Burnette, rhp, Buford (Ga.) HS.
8. Jason Creasy, rhp, Clayton (N.C.) HS.
9. Clay Holmes, rhp, Slocomb (Ala.) HS.
10. Taylor Lewis, of, University of Maine.
11. *Jo-El Bennett, of, Houston Academy, Dothan, Ala.
12. Candon Myles, of, South Grand Prairie (Texas) HS.
DRAFT DROP *Brother of Bryson Myles, sixth-round draft pick, Indians (2009)*
13. *Brandon Platts, rhp, Mason City (Iowa) HS.
14. *Jordan Dunatov, of, Horizon HS, Scottsdale, Ariz.
15. *Kody Watts, rhp, Skyview HS, Vancouver, Wash.
16. *Eric Skoglund, lhp, Sarasota (Fla.) HS.
17. *Aaron Brown, of, Chatsworth (Calif.) HS.
18. Josh Poytress, lhp, Fresno State University.
19. *Taylor Nunez, rhp, Salmen HS, Slidell, La.
**20. *Trea Turner, ss, Park Vista HS, Lake Worth, Fla.—(2015)**
DRAFT DROP *First-round draft pick (13th overall), Padres (2014)*
21. Alex Fuselier, of, University of Louisiana-Lafayette.
22. Mike Jefferson, lhp, Louisiana Tech.
23. Jordan Cooper, rhp, University of Kentucky.
24. Brian Sharp, ss, California Baptist University.
25. *Josh Martin, rhp, Samford University.
26. *Nick Flair, ss, Belle Chasse (La.) HS.
27. Ryan Hornback, c, San Jacinto (Texas) JC.
28. *Brandon Zajac, lhp, Walker Valley HS, Cleveland, Tenn.
29. Kirk Singer, ss, Long Beach State University.
30. Matt Benedict, rhp, Western Carolina University.
31. Derek Trent, c, East Tennessee State University.
32. David Jagoditsh, rhp, Pima (Ariz.) CC.
33. Chris Lashmet, 3b, Northwestern University.
34. *Hommy Rosado, 1b, LSU-Eunice JC.
35. *Reid Matthews, 2b, Dobyns-Bennett HS, Kingsport, Tenn.
36. *Isaac Ballou, of, Marshall University.
37. Rodarrick Jones, of, Southern University.
38. *D.J. Crumlich, ss, UC Irvine.
39. *Rand Ravnaas, of, Georgetown University.
40. *Raph Rhymes, 2b, Louisiana State University.
41. Jonathan Schwind, c, Marist University.
42. *Nick Hibbing, rhp, Lakes Community HS, Antioch, Ill.
43. *Willie Argo, of, University of Illinois.
44. *Bobby LeCount, 3b, Edmonds (Wash.) CC.
45. *Robbie Ingram, lhp, Yavapai (Ariz.) JC.
46. *Jeff Schalk, of, Wheaton North HS, Wheaton, Ill.
47. *Jordan DeLuca, of, Tussey Mountain HS, Saxton, Pa.
48. *Zach Thompson, rhp, Grace Prep Academy, Arlington, Texas.
49. *Austin White, 3b, Arkansas HS, Texarkana, Ark.
50. *Zech Lemond, rhp, Waltrip HS, Houston.

## ST. LOUIS CARDINALS (19)

**1. Kolten Wong, 2b, University of Hawaii.—(2013-15)**
2. Charlie Tilson, of, New Trier HS, Winnetka, Ill.—(AA)
3. C.J. McElroy Jr., of, Clear Creek HS, League City, Texas.—(High A)
DRAFT DROP *Son of Chuck McElroy, major leaguer (1989-2001)*
4. Kenny Peoples-Walls, ss, Westchester HS, Los Angeles.—(Low A)
5. Sam Gaviglio, rhp, Oregon State University.—(AAA)
6. Adam Ehrlich, c, Campbell Hall HS, North Hollywood, Calif.
7. Nick Martini, of, Kansas State University.
8. Danny Miranda, lhp, University of Miami.
9. Tyler Mills, rhp, University of Michigan.
10. Lance Jeffries, of, McCluer HS, St. Louis.
**11. Seth Maness, rhp, East Carolina University.—(2013-15)**
12. Danny Stienstra, 1b, San Jose State University.
13. Kolby Byrd, c, Copiah-Lincoln (Miss.) CC.
14. *Kevin Medrano, 2b, Missouri State University.
15. Matt Williams, ss, Liberty University.
16. Travis Miller, rhp, University of Miami.
17. Dutch Deol, of, Aliso Niguel HS, Aliso Viejo, Calif.
18. Kyle Hald, lhp, Old Dominion University.
19. Nick Gillung, lhp, Mercyhurst (Pa.) University.
20. *Aramis Garcia, c, Pembroke Pines (Fla.) HS.
21. *Chris Kirsch, lhp, Lackawanna (Pa.) JC.
22. *Justin Kamplain, lhp, Walker HS, Jasper, Ala.
23. *Kyle Deese, rhp, Western Carolina University.
24. Jonathan Cornelius, lhp, Florida Tech.
25. Todd McInnis, rhp, University of Southern Mississippi.
26. *Brett Graves, rhp, Howell HS, St. Charles, Mo.
27. Gary Apelian, of, Santa Ana (Calif.) JC.
28. Ryan Sherriff, lhp, Glendale (Calif.) JC.
29. *Chris Matulis, lhp, University of Central Florida.
30. David Bergin, rhp, Tennessee Wesleyan College.
31. Kevin Jacob, rhp, Georgia Tech.
32. Jonathan Keener, c, Cal State Dominguez Hills.
33. Heath Wyatt, rhp, Southeastern Oklahoma State University.
34. Tyler Rahmatulla, 2b, UCLA.
35. *Drew Madrigal, rhp, California Baptist University.
36. Casey Rasmus, c, Liberty University.
DRAFT DROP *Brother of Colby Rasmus, first-round draft pick, Cardinals (2005); major leaguer (2009-15)*

• *Brother of Cory Rasmus, first-round draft pick, Braves (2006); major leaguer (2013-15)*
37. Brad Watson, rhp, Wartburg (Iowa) College.
38. Jeremy Patton, 3b, Florida International University.
39. Tyler Melling, lhp, Miami (Ohio) University.
40. *Kyle Arnsberg, c, McLennan (Texas) CC.

DRAFT DROP *Son of Brad Arnsberg, major leaguer (1986-92)*

41. Mike Knox, 1b, Mount Olive (N.C.) College.
42. *Cody Poarch, rhp, Walters State (Tenn.) CC.
43. Chris Costantino, rhp, Walters State (Tenn.) CC.
44. Brandon Creath, rhp, Embry-Riddle (Fla.) University.
45. *Cooper Moseley, 2b, Central Alabama CC.
46. *Chadwick Kaalekahi, c, Campbell HS, Ewa Beach, Hawaii.
47. *David Schmidt, rhp, Christian Brothers HS, St. Louis.
48. *Brock Asher, of, Aiea (Hawaii) HS.
49. Corey Baker, rhp, University of Pittsburgh.
50. *Tyler Sibley, 2b, Texas State University.

## SAN DIEGO PADRES (22)

1. **Cory Spangenberg, 2b, Indian River (Fla.) JC** (Special compensation choice—10th—for failure to sign 2010 first-round pick Karsten Whitson).**—(2014-15)**
1. **Joe Ross, rhp, Bishop O'Dowd HS, Oakland.—(2015)**

DRAFT DROP *Brother of Tyson Ross, major leaguer (2010-15)*

1. Mike Kelly, rhp, West Boca Raton (Fla.) HS (Supplemental choice—48th—for loss of Type B free agent Jon Garland).—(High A)
1. *Brett Austin, c, Providence HS, Charlotte, N.C. (Supplemental choice—54th—for loss of Type B free agent Yorvit Torrealba).—(High A)

DRAFT DROP *Attended North Carolina State; re-drafted by White Sox, 2014 (4th round)*

1. **Jace Peterson, ss, McNeese State University** (Supplemental choice—58th—for loss of Type B free agent Kevin Correia).**—(2014-15)**
2. **Austin Hedges, c, J Serra HS, San Juan Capistrano, Calif.—(2015)**
3. **Matt Andriese, rhp, UC Riverside.—(2015)**
4. Cody Hebner, rhp, Green River (Wash.) CC.—(AA)
5. Mark Pope, rhp, Georgia Tech.—(AAA)
6. Kyle Gaedele, of, Valparaiso University.

DRAFT DROP *Great nephew of Eddie Gaedel, major leaguer (1951)*

7. **Matt Wisler, rhp, Bryan (Ohio) HS.—(2015)**
8. **Kevin Quackenbush, rhp, University of South Florida.—(2014-15)**
9. Justin Hancock, rhp, Lincoln Trail (Ill.) CC.
10. Robert Kral, c, College of Charleston.
11. Casey McElroy, ss, Auburn University.
12. **Colin Rea, rhp, Indiana State University.—(2015)**
13. Lee Orr, of, McNeese State University.
14. **Burch Smith, rhp, University of Oklahoma.—(2013)**
15. Greg Gonzalez, rhp, Fresno State University.
16. Jeremy Rodriguez, c, Cal State Bakersfield.
17. **Matt Stites, rhp, University of Missouri.—(2014-15)**
18. Mike Gallic, of, Marist University.
19. Jeremy Gigliotti, lhp, East Stroudsburg (Pa.) University.
20. Chris Haney, rhp, Dallas Baptist University.
21. Zach Kometani, 1b, University of San Diego.
22. Matt Colantonio, c, Brown University.
23. R.L. Eisenbach, lhp, Faulkner (Ala.) University.
24. *Erick Fedde, rhp, Las Vegas (Nev.) HS.

DRAFT DROP *First-round draft pick (18th overall), Nationals (2014)*

25. Paul Karmas, 1b, St. John's University.
26. *Roberto Suppa, rhp, St. Thomas Aquinas SS, West London, Ontario.
27. *Arby Fields, of, Cypress (Calif.) JC.
28. Rashaad Ingram, 2b, St. Augustine's (N.C.) College.
29. *Vimeal Machin, c, Puerto Rico Baseball Academy, Gurabo, P.R.
30. Justin Miller, of, Southeastern Oklahoma State University.
31. Clint Moore, ss, U.S. Military Academy.
32. Kyle Brule, rhp, Oklahoma Baptist University.
33. James Jones, rhp, University of Louisiana-Monroe.
34. Dennis O'Grady, rhp, Duke University.
35. Travis Whitmore, 2b, University of Pittsburgh.
36. *Andrew Rash, of, Virginia Tech.
37. *Cody Semler, ss, Allen (Texas) HS.
38. *Pat Connaughton, rhp, St. John's Prep, Danvers, Mass.

DRAFT DROP *Second-round draft pick, Brooklyn Nets/ National Baksetball Association (2015)*

39. *Josh Pond, rhp, Cal State San Bernardino.
40. *Taylor Murphy, 3b, Torrey Pines HS, San Diego.
41. *Dante Flores, 2b, St. John Bosco HS, Bellflower, Calif.
42. *Garrett Boulware, c, T.L. Hanna HS, Anderson, S.C.
43. Cody Gabella, ss, Southeastern (Iowa) CC.
44. *Spenser Linney, lhp, Head-Royce School, Oakland.
45. *Will Gross, of, Tupelo (Miss.) HS.
46. *Eddie Salomon, 2b, Beaumont (Calif.) HS.
47. *Vince Voiro, rhp, University of Pennsylvania.
48. *Kent Rollins, ss, South Gwinnett HS, Snellville, Ga.
49. *Ryan Hutchison, of, Western Kentucky University.

## SAN FRANCISCO GIANTS (26)

1. **Joe Panik, ss, St. John's University.—(2014-15)**
1. Kyle Crick, rhp, Sherman (Texas) HS (Supplemental choice—49th—for loss of Type B free agent Juan Uribe).—(AA)
2. **Andrew Susac, c, Oregon State University.—(2014-15)**
3. Ricky Oropesa, 1b, University of Southern California.—(AA)
4. Bryce Bandilla, lhp, University of Arizona.—(AA)
5. Chris Marlowe, rhp, Oklahoma State University.—(High A)
6. **Josh Osich, lhp, Oregon State University.—(2015)**
7. Ray Black, rhp, University of Pittsburgh.
8. Jean Delgado, ss, Caguas (P.R.) Military Academy.
9. Derek Law, rhp, Miami-Dade JC.
10. Kentrell Hill, of, Arkansas Baptist JC.
11. Christian Diaz, of, Puerto Rico Baseball Academy, Gurabo, P.R.
12. **Kelby Tomlinson, ss, Texas Tech.—(2015)**
13. *Adam Paulencu, rhp, Vancouver Island (B.C.) University.
14. Garrett Buechele, 3b, University of Oklahoma.

DRAFT DROP *Son of Steve Buechele, major leaguer (1985-95)*

15. *Tyler Leslie, rhp, Silverado HS, Victorville, Calif.
16. Clayton Blackburn, rhp, Edmond Santa Fe HS, Edmond, Okla.
17. Paul Davis, rhp, Florida Atlantic University.
18. Cristian Otero, ss, Puerto Rico Baseball Academy, Gurabo, P.R.
19. **Cody Hall, rhp, Southern University.—(2015)**
20. Mitchell Beacom, lhp, UCLA.
21. *Andrew Triggs, rhp, University of Southern California.
22. Cameron McVey, rhp, Biola (Calif.) University.
23. Jonathan Jones, 3b, Vanier (Que.) JC.
24. Keith Bilodeau, rhp, University of Maine.
25. Demondre Arnold, rhp, Middle Georgia JC.
26. Joe Biagini, rhp, UC Davis.
27. Jack Snodgrass, lhp, Austin Peay State University.
28. Tyler Mizenko, rhp, Winthrop University.
29. Eldred Barnett, of, Grambling State University.
30. *David Fischer, rhp, University of Connecticut.
31. Phil McCormick, lhp, University of Missouri.
32. Mike Mergenthaler, of, University of Richmond.
33. *Brock Bennett, c, University of Alabama.
34. Ben Thomas, 1b, Xavier University.
35. Shawn Payne, of, Georgia Southern University.
36. *Austin Lubinsky, rhp, University of Minnesota.
37. *Michael Williams, c, University of Kentucky.
38. Bryan Nicholson, 1b, Concordia (Calif.) University.
39. *Ryan Holland, lhp, Memphis University.
40. *Alan Garcia, rhp, Eastern Arizona JC.
41. Steven Neff, lhp, University of South Carolina.
42. Danny Sandbrink, rhp, Stanford University.
43. Drew Stiner, c, Owasso (Okla.) HS.
44. Travious Relaford, ss, Hinds (Miss.) CC.
45. Brian Maloney, lhp, Franklin Pierce (N.H.) College.
46. Elliott Blair, of, University of Oklahoma.
47. *Marc Frazier, 3b, Newnan (Ga.) HS.
48. Jake Smith, rhp, Campbell University.
49. *Benny Sosnick, 2b, Jewish Community HS of the Bay, San Francisco.
50. *Waldyvan Estrada, of, International Baseball Academy, Cieba, P.R.

## SEATTLE MARINERS (2)

1. Danny Hultzen, lhp, University of Virginia.—(AAA)
2. **Brad Miller, ss, Clemson University.—(2013-15)**
3. *Kevin Cron, 1b, Mountain Pointe HS, Phoenix.—(High A)

DRAFT DROP *Attended Texas Christian; re-drafted by Diamondbacks, 2014 (14th round) • Son of Chris Cron, major leaguer (1991-92) • Brother of C.J. Cron, first-round draft pick, Angels (2011); major leaguer (2014-15)*

3. **Carter Capps, rhp, Mount Olive (N.C.) College** (Special compensation choice—121st—for failure to sign 2010 third-round pick Ryne Stanek).**—(2012-15)**
4. **John Hicks, c, University of Virginia.—(2015)**
5. Tyler Marlette, c, Hagerty HS, Oviedo, Fla.—(AA)
6. James Zamarripa, of, Rancho Cucamonga (Calif.) HS.
7. Steve Proscia, 3b, University of Virginia.
8. **Carson Smith, rhp, Texas State University.—(2014-15)**
9. Cavan Cohoes, ss, Patch HS, Stuttgart, Germany.
10. Dan Paolini, 2b, Siena University.
11. Cameron Hobson, lhp, University of Dayton.
12. Mike Dowd, c, Franklin Pierce (N.H.) College.
13. Jamal Austin, of, University of Alabama-Birmingham.
14. Cody Weiss, rhp, La Salle University.
15. Mike McGee, of, Florida State University.
16. Jack Marder, c, University of Oregon.
17. Nate Melendres, of, University of Miami.
18. Nick Valenza, lhp, Horizon HS, Scottsdale, Ariz.
19. Luke Guarnaccia, c, Palm Beach (Fla.) CC.
20. Dillon Hazlett, 2b, Emporia State (Kan.) University.
21. Joe DiRocco, rhp, Seton Hall University.
22. John Taylor, rhp, University of South Carolina.
23. Richard White, rhp, St. Croix Educational HS, St. Thomas, V.I.
24. *Tanner Chleborad, rhp, Stevens HS, Rapid City, S.D.
25. Gabe Saquilon, rhp, Horizon Christian HS, San Diego.
26. Kenny Straus, 3b, Georgia Perimeter JC.
27. David Colvin, rhp, Pomona Pitzer (Calif.) College.
28. Brett Shankin, rhp, Wayne State (Mich.) University.
29. ***Keone Kela, rhp, Chief Sealth HS, Seattle.—(2015)**
30. Jordan Pries, rhp, Stanford University.

DRAFT DROP *Son of Jeff Pries, first-round draft pick, Yankees (1984)*

31. Kyle Hunter, lhp, Kansas State University.
32. *Ryan Hawthorne, lhp, Loyola Marymount University.
33. Jeremy Dobbs, lhp, Austin Peay State University.
34. *Taylor Smith-Brennan, 2b, Edmonds (Wash.) CC.
35. Cory Scammell, of, St. Francis Xavier HS, Edmonton, Alberta.
36. Bo Reeder, rhp, East Tennessee State University.
37. *Jeremy Null, rhp, Bunker Hill HS, Claremont, N.C.
38. Alex Sunderland, rhp, Claremont McKenna (Calif.) College.
39. Chris Andreas, of, Sam Houston State University.
40. Trevor Miller, rhp, San Joaquin Delta (Calif.) JC.
41. Bobby Shore, rhp, University of Oklahoma.
42. David Villasuso, c, University of Miami.
43. Marcos Reyna, rhp, Bakersfield (Calif.) JC.
44. Josh Corrales, rhp, Cal State Dominguez Hills.
45. Charles Jimenez, of, Milton (Fla.) HS.
46. Maxx Catapano, rhp, Lee (Tenn.) University.
47. Brandon Plotz, rhp, Chabot (Calif.) JC.
48. Max Krakowiak, rhp, Fordham University.
49. *Andrew Grifol, 1b, Santa Fe (Fla.) CC.
50. *Esteban Tresgallo, 1b, Colegio Marista de Guaynabo (P.R.).

## TAMPA BAY RAYS (29)

1. Taylor Guerrieri, rhp, Spring Valley HS, Columbia, S.C. (Choice from Red Sox as compensation for Type A free agent Carl Crawford).—(AA)
1. **Mikie Mahtook, of, Louisiana State University** (Choice from Yankees as compensation for Type A free agent Rafael Soriano).**—(2015)**
1. Jake Hager, ss, Sierra Vista HS, Las Vegas, Nev.—(AA)
1. Brandon Martin, ss, Santiago HS, Corona, Calif. (Supplemental choice—38th—for loss of Soriano).—(Low A)
1. Tyler Goeddel, 3b, St. Francis HS, Mountain View, Calif. (Supplemental choice—41st—for loss of Crawford).—(AA)

DRAFT DROP *Brother of Erik Goeddel, major leaguer (2014-15)*

1. Jeff Ames, rhp, Lower Columbia (Wash.) JC (Supplemental choice—42nd—for loss of Type A free agent Grant Balfour).—(AA)
1. Blake Snell, lhp, Shorewood HS, Shoreline, Wash. (Supplemetal choice—52nd—for loss of Type B free agent Brad Hawpe).—(AAA)
1. Kes Carter, of, Western Kentucky University (Supplemental choice—56th—for loss of Type B free agent Joaquin Benoit).—(AA)
1. Grayson Garvin, lhp, Vanderbilt University (Supplemental choice—59th—for loss of Type B free agent Randy Choate).—(AA)
1. James Harris, of, Oakland Technical HS, Oakland (Supplemental choice—60th—for loss of Type B free agent Chad Qualls).—(AAA)
2. Granden Goetzman, of, Palmetto (Fla.) HS (Choice from Ahletics as compensation for Balfour).—(High A)
2. Lenny Linsky, rhp, University of Hawaii.—(High A)
3. Johnny Eierman, of, Warsaw (Mo.) HS.—(Rookie)
4. Riccio Torrez, 3b, Arizona State University.—(AA)
5. *J.D. Davis, 3b, Elk Grove (Calif.) HS.—(High A)

DRAFT DROP *Attended Cal State Fullerton; re-drafted by Astros, 2014 (3rd round)*

6. Jake Floethe, rhp, Cal State Fullerton.
7. Ryan Carpenter, lhp, Gonzaga University.
8. John Alexander, 1b, Glendora (Calif.) HS.
9. Matt Rice, c, Western Kentucky University.
10. Jacob Faria, rhp, Gahr HS, Cerritos, Calif.
11. Cameron Seitzer, 1b, University of Oklahoma.

DRAFT DROP *Son of Kevin Seitzer, major leaguer (1986-97)*

12. *Trevor Mitsui, 1b, Shorewood HS, Shoreline, Wash.
13. *Tanner English, of, St. James HS, Murrells Inlet, S.C.
14. *Matt Young, of, Compton (Calif.) CC.
15. *Tyler Parmenter, ss, Cibola HS, Yuma, Ariz.
16. *Brett McAfee, ss, Pine Tree HS, Longview, Texas.
17. Taylor Motter, ss, Coastal Carolina University.
18. Andy Bass, rhp, Davidson University.
19. Matt Ramsey, rhp, University of Tennessee.
20. Garret Smith, ss, Boston College.
21. Ryan Terry, 3b, Monmouth University.
22. *Brad Hendrix, rhp, Auburn University.
23. Matt Johnson, of, Arkansas Tech University.
24. Charlie Cononie, rhp, Towson University.
25. Brooks Belter, rhp, Occidental (Calif.) College.
26. Raymond Church, 2b, Florida Atlantic University.
27. Luke Irvine, rhp, Northwestern State University.
28. *Blake Grant-Parks, c, Yuba City (Calif.) HS.

29. Jonathan Koscso, 2b, University of South Florida.
30. *Chris Burgess, rhp, Black Hawk (Ill.) JC.
31. Isaac Gil, rhp, Advanced Software Analysis (N.Y.) JC.
32. Ryan Turner, rhp, Tarleton State (Texas) University.
33. Dan Bream, rhp, Southern Arkansas University.
34. Zach Butler, rhp, McNeese State University.
35. *Johnny Magliozzi, rhp, Dexter HS, Brookline, Mass.
36. Dave Kubiak, rhp, University of Albany
37. *Tanner Poppe, rhp, University of Kansas.
38. Brandon Choate, c, Southern Arkansas University.
39. T.J. Geith, lhp, Scottsdale (Ariz.) CC.
40. *Joe Perricone, rhp, Hersey HS, Arlington Heights, Ill.
41. Shay Crawford, lhp, Lee (Tenn.) University.
42. Mike Bourdon, c, University of Tampa.
43. Stayton Thomas, rhp, University of Texas.
44. *Jordan Leyland, 1b, UC Irvine.
45. *Kevin Lusson, c, University of Texas.
46. *Max Rossiter, c, Central Arizona JC.
47. *Derek Vaughn, rhp, Texas Wesleyan College.
48. *Brandon Liebrandt, lhp, Marist School, Atlanta.
DRAFT DROP *Son of Charlie Liebrandt, major leaguer (1979-93)*
49. *Alan Baldwin, c, Kailua (Hawaii) HS.
50. Ian Tomkins, c, Abilene Christian (Texas) University.

## TEXAS RANGERS (23)

1. (Choice to Red Sox as compensation for Type A free agent Adrian Beltre)
1. Kevin Matthews, lhp, Richmond Hill (Ga.) HS (Choice from Phillies as compensation for Type A free agent Cliff Lee).—(Low A)
1. Zach Cone, of, University of Georgia (Supplemental choice—37th—for loss of Lee).—(AA)
2. Will Lamb, lhp-of, Clemson University.—(AAA)
3. Kyle Castro, rhp, Pleasant Grove HS, Elk Grove, Calif.—(Short-season A)
4. Desmond Henry, of, Centennial HS, Compton, Calif.—(Rookie)
5. *Brandon Woodruff, rhp, Wheeler (Miss.) HS.—(High A)
DRAFT DROP *Attended Mississippi State; re-drafted by Brewers, 11th round (2014)*
6. *Derek Fisher, of, Cedar Crest HS, Lebanon, Pa.
DRAFT DROP *First-round draft pick (37th overall), Astros (2014)*
7. *Max Pentecost, c, Winder-Barrow HS, Winder, Ga.
DRAFT DROP *First-round draft pick (11th overall), Blue Jays (2014)*
**8. Kyle Hendricks, rhp, Dartmouth University.—(2014-15)**
9. Rashad Harlin, of, Helix Charter HS, La Mesa, Calif.
10. Joe Maloney, c, Limestone (S.C.) University.
11. Connor Sadzeck, rhp, Howard (Texas) JC.
12. Greg Williams, lhp, Marshall University.
13. Chris Grayson, of, Lee (Tenn.) University.
**14. Andrew Faulkner, lhp, South Aiken (S.C.) HS.—(2015)**
**15. Jerad Eickhoff, rhp, Olney Central (Ill.) JC.—(2015)**
16. Trever Adams, of, Creighton University.
**17. Ryan Rua, ss, Lake Erie (Ohio) College.—(2014-15)**
**18. Nick Martinez, rhp, Fordham University.—(2014-15)**
19. *Nathan Harsh, lhp, Brunswick (Ga.) HS.
20. Nick Vickerson, ss, Mississippi State University.
21. Chance Sossamon, rhp, Wichita State University.
22. *T.J. Costen, ss, First Colonial HS, Virginia Beach, Va.
23. *Mike Mason, lhp, Marshall University.
24. *Zach Fish, c, Gull Lake HS, Richland, Mich.
25. *Jordan Remer, lhp, University of San Francisco.
26. *Ryan Bores, rhp, Cuyahoga (Ohio) CC.
27. Kyle Devore, rhp, Sacramento (Calif.) CC.
28. Saquan Johnson, of, East Bladen HS, Elizabethtown, N.C.
29. *Nick Sawyer, rhp, Howard (Texas) JC.
**30. Phil Klein, rhp, Youngstown State University.—(2014-15)**
31. Matt Leeds, 3b, College of Charleston.
32. Sam Robinson, lhp, University of Miami.
33. *Jonathan Taylor, of, University of Georgia.
34. Taylor Dennis, rhp, Southern Indiana University.
35. *Cy Sneed, rhp, Twin Falls (Idaho) HS.
36. Jeremy Williams, of, Mobile (Ala.) University.
37. *Bryce Greager, ss, Fountain Hills (Ariz.) HS.
38. *Tucker Donahue, rhp, Stetson University.
39. *Trumon Jefferson, of, Decatur (Ga.) HS.
40. *Josh Peterson, rhp, Unaka HS, Elizabethton, Tenn.
41. *Tyler Scott, of, Marin Catholic HS, Kentfield, Calif.
42. *Joey Pankake, rhp, Easley (S.C.) HS.
43. *Kaleb Merck, rhp, Texas Christian University.
44. *Philip Pfeifer, lhp, Farragut HS, Knoxville, Tenn.
**45. *Brandon Finnegan, lhp, Southwest HS, Fort Worth, Texas.—(2014-15)**
DRAFT DROP *First-round draft pick (17th overall), Royals (2014); first player from 2014 draft to reach majors (Sept. 6, 2014)*
46. *Tyler Powell, rhp, Myers Park HS, Charlotte, N.C.
47. *Kevin Moriarty, rhp, Shorewood HS, Shoreline, Wash.
**48. C.J. Edwards, rhp, Mid-Carolina HS, Prosperity, S.C.—(2015)**
49. *Mick Van Vossen, rhp, Forest Hills Central HS, Grand Rapids, Mich.
50. K.C. Wiser, rhp, Linfield (Ore.) College.

## TORONTO BLUE JAYS (18)

1. *Tyler Beede, rhp, Lawrence Academy, Groton, Mass.—(AA)
DRAFT DROP *Attended Vanderbilt; re-drafted by Giants, 2014 (1st round)*
1. Jake Anderson, of, Chino (Calif.) HS (Supplemental choice—35th—for loss of Type A free agent Scott Downs).—(Rookie)
1. Joe Musgrove, rhp, Grossmont HS, El Cajon, Calif. (Supplemental choice—46th—for loss of Type B free agent John Buck).—(AA)
1. Dwight Smith Jr., of, McIntosh (Ga.) HS (Supplemental choice—53rd—for loss of Type B free agent Kevin Gregg).—(AA)
DRAFT DROP *Son of Dwight Smith, major leaguer (1989-96)*
1. Kevin Comer, rhp, Seneca HS, Tabernacle, N.J. (Supplemental choice—57th—for loss of Type B free agent Miguel Olivo).—(High A)
**2. Daniel Norris, lhp, Science Hill HS, Johnson City, Tenn.** (Choice from Angels as compensation for Downs).**—(2014-15)**
2. Jeremy Gabryszwski, rhp, Crosby (Texas) HS.—(High A)
3. John Stilson, rhp, Texas A&M University.—(AAA)
4. Tom Robson, rhp, Delta SS, Ladner, B.C.—(Low A)
5. *Andrew Chin, lhp, Buckingham Browne & Nichols HS, Cambridge, Mass.—(Short-season A)
DRAFT DROP *Attended Boston College; re-drafted by Yankees, 2014 (15th round)*
**6. Anthony DeSclafani, rhp, University of Florida.—(2014-15)**
7. Christian Lopes, ss, Edison HS, Huntington Beach, Calif.
8. Mark Biggs, rhp, Warren East HS, Bowling Green, Ky.
9. *Andrew Suarez, lhp, Christopher Columbus HS, Miami.
10. *Aaron Garza, rhp, Ball HS, Galveston, Texas.
11. Andy Burns, ss, University of Arizona.
12. *John Norwood, of, Seton Hall Prep, Orange, N.J.
13. Matt Dean, 3b, The Colony (Texas) HS.
14. *Cole Wiper, rhp, Newport HS, Bellevue, Wash.
15. *Cody Glenn, lhp, Westbury Christian HS, Houston.
16. *Richard Prigatano, 1b, St. Francis HS, Mountain View, Calif.
17. Brady Dragmire, rhp, Bradshaw Christian School, Sacramento, Calif.
18. Jon Berti, 2b, Bowling Green State University.
19. *Luke Weaver, rhp, DeLand (Fla.) HS.
DRAFT DROP *First-round draft pick (27th overall), Cardinals (2014)*
20. *Joel Seddon, rhp, St. Clair (Mich.) HS.
21. Peter Mooney, ss, University of South Carolina.
**22. *Aaron Nola, rhp, Catholic HS, Baton Rouge, La.—(2015)**
DRAFT DROP *First-round draft pick (7th overall), Phillies (2014); brother of Austin Nola, 31st-round draft pick, Blue Jays (2011)*
23. *K'Shawn Smith, ss, Indian River (Fla.) JC.
**24. David Rollins, lhp, San Jacinto (Texas) JC.—(2015)**
25. Eric Arce, 1b, Tampa.
26. Justin Atkinson, ss, North Surrey (B.C.) SS.
27. Derrick Loveless, of, Solon (Iowa) HS.
28. Jorge Vega-Rosado, ss, Miami-Dade JC.
29. Taylor Cole, rhp, Brigham Young University.
30. Kevin Patterson, 1b, Auburn University.
31. *Austin Nola, ss, Louisiana State University.
DRAFT DROP *Brother of Aaron Nola, 22nd-round draft pick, Blue Jays (2011); first-round draft pick, Phillies (2014); major leaguer (2015)*
**32. Kevin Pillar, of, Cal State Dominguez Hills.—(2013-15)**
33. Kramer Champlin, rhp, Arizona State University.
34. Aaron Munoz, c, Northwestern State University.
35. *Jerrick Suiter, rhp, Valparaiso (Ind.) HS.
36. Arik Sikula, rhp, Marshall University.
37. Les Williams, rhp, Northeastern University.
38. Nico Taylor, of, Northwood (Texas) University.
39. *Chris Cox, rhp, Canisius University.
40. Nick Baligod, of, Oral Roberts University.
41. Cody Bartlett, ss, Washington State University.
42. Shane Davis, lhp, Canisius University.
43. *Jake Eliopoulos, lhp, Newmarket, Ontario.
44. Colby Broussard, rhp, Faulkner (Ala.) University.
45. *Johnny Coy, 3b, Wichita State University.
46. Shane Farrell, rhp, Marshall University.
DRAFT DROP *Son of John Farrell, major leaguer (1987-96); major league manager (2011-15)*
47. *Austin Davis, 3b, Central Columbia HS, Bloomsburg, Pa.
48. *Jake Wakamatsu, of, Keller (Texas) HS.
DRAFT DROP *Son of Don Wakamatsu, major leaguer (1991); major league manager (2009-10)*
49. *Charlie LaMar, lhp, Clearwater Central Catholic HS, Clearwater, Fla.
50. Eric Brown, rhp, University of British Columbia.

## WASHINGTON NATIONALS (6)

**1. Anthony Rendon, 3b, Rice University.—(2013-15)**
**1. Alex Meyer, rhp, University of Kentucky** (Choice from White Sox as compensation for Type A free agent Adam Dunn).**—(2015)**
1. Brian Goodwin, of, Miami-Dade JC (Supplemental choice—34th—for loss of Dunn).—(AAA)
2. (Choice to Phillies as compensation for Type A free agent Jayson Werth)
3. Matt Purke, lhp, Texas Christian University.—(AA)
DRAFT DROP *First-round draft pick (14th overall), Rangers (2009)*
4. Kylin Turnbull, lhp, Santa Barbara (Calif.) CC.—(High A)
5. Matt Skole, 3b, Georgia Tech.—(AAA)
DRAFT DROP *Brother of Jake Skole, first-round draft pick, Rangers (2010)*
**6. Taylor Hill, rhp, Vanderbilt University.—(2014-15)**
7. Brian Dupra, rhp, University of Notre Dame.
8. Greg Holt, rhp, University of North Carolina.
9. Dixon Anderson, rhp, University of California.
10. Manny Rodriguez, rhp, Barry (Fla.) University.
11. Caleb Ramsey, of, University of Houston.
12. Blake Monar, lhp, Indiana University.
13. *Casey Kalenkosky, 1b, Texas State University.
14. *Cody Stubbs, of, Walters State (Tenn.) CC.
15. Zach Houchins, ss, Louisburg (N.C.) JC.
16. Deion Williams, ss, Redan HS, Stone Mountain, Ga.
DRAFT DROP *Grandson of George Scott, major leaguer (1966-79)*
17. *Esteban Guzman, rhp, San Jose State University.
18. Nick Lee, lhp, Weatherford (Texas) JC.
19. *Hawtin Buchanan, rhp, Biloxi (Miss.) HS.
20. *Josh Laxer, rhp, Madison Central HS, Madison, Miss.
21. Todd Simko, lhp, Texas A&M University-Corpus Christi.
22. Travis Henke, rhp, University of Arkansas-Little Rock.
23. Khayyan Norfork, 2b, University of Tennessee.
24. *Kyle Ottoson, lhp, Arizona State University.
25. Erick Fernandez, c, Georgetown University.
26. Shawn Pleffner, of, University of Tampa.
27. Bobby Lucas, rhp, George Washington University.
28. Ken Ferrer, rhp, Elon University.
29. *Sean Cotten, c, Tusculum (Tenn.) College.
30. Bryan Harper, lhp, University of South Carolina.
DRAFT DROP *Brother of Bryce Harper, first overall draft pick, Nationals (2010); major leaguer (2012-15)*
31. *Josh Tobias, ss, Southeast Guilford HS, Greensboro, N.C.
**32. Billy Burns, of, Mercer University.—(2014-15)**
DRAFT DROP *Son of Bob Burns, running back, National Football League (1974)*
33. Trey Karlen, 2b, University of Tennessee-Martin.
34. *Calvin Drummond, rhp, University of San Diego.
35. Alex Kreis, rhp, Jamestown (N.D.) College.
36. Ben Hawkins, lhp, University of West Florida.
37. *Derrick Bleeker, rhp, Howard (Texas) JC.
38. *Brett Mooneyham, lhp, Stanford University.
DRAFT DROP *Son of Bill Mooneyham, major leaguer (1986)*
39. *Peter Verdin, of, University of Georgia.
40. *Cory Collum, of, Cartersville (Ga.) HS.
41. Bryce Ortega, 3b, University of Arizona.
42. *David Kerian, ss, Bishop Heelan HS, Sioux City, Iowa.
43. *Mitch Morales, ss, Wellington (Fla.) HS.
44. *Matt Snyder, 3b, University of Mississippi.
DRAFT DROP *Son of Brian Snyder, major leaguer (1985-89) • Brother of Brandon Snyder, first-round draft pick (2005); major leaguer (2010-13)*
45. Richie Mirowski, rhp, Oklahoma Baptist University.
46. *Tyler Thompson, of, University of Florida.
47. *Tim Montgomery, lhp, Rockmart (Ga.) HS.
48. *Mike Bisenius, of, Wayne State (Mich.) University.
49. *Hunter Cole, of, Dorman HS, Roebuck, S.C.
50. *Tony Nix, of, UC Riverside.

# New labor agreement brings major changes

Major League Baseball instituted a draft in 1965 to address two issues: provide teams equal access to amateur talent and control how much money teams spent to acquire that talent.

For the better part of 25 years, the draft served its intended purpose. But with the game in a growth spurt and awash in cash in the late 1980s and early 1990s, clubs began spending freely on high school and college players. Bonuses soon skyrocketed and remained on an inflationary spiral for the better part of the next quarter-century. From a first-round average of $176,008 in 1989, the norm grew to $2,653,375 in 2011.

It was evident that history was repeating itself, as spending on amateur players showed no signs of slowing down and it was again leading to an inequitable distribution of talent.

The commissioner's office had accomplished little in its efforts to keep bonuses in check in the first decade of the new century, in part because it had to try piecemeal solutions when bigger issues took center stage in labor negotiations.

Finally in the fall of 2011, after years of labor peace, Major League Baseball's highest priority in negotiations for a new Collective Bargaining Agreement was the draft. It targeted inequities in the process and led to the most sweeping changes since the draft was instituted 47 years earlier. The 2012 draft was the first to feel the effects.

While the Players Association remained opposed to a bonus cap system for the draft, it was amenable to aggregate signing bonus pools, a concept that set a limit on the amount each team could spend collectively on its draft picks. Teams were subject to stiff penalties in the form of a luxury tax and lost draft picks if they exceeded their budgets.

Each slot in the first 10 rounds had a predetermined bonus value, which in 2012 ranged from $7.2 million for the No. 1 choice to $125,000 for pick No. 300 and those that followed. The aggregate value of the pools ranged from $12,368,200 for the Minnesota Twins, who held the No. 2 choice and had three compensation selections for the loss of major league free agents, to $1,645,700 for the Los Angeles Angels, who forfeited their first two picks for signing free agents Albert Pujols and C.J. Wilson. The sum of all the pools was $189,903,500, a slight reduction from the $191,876,250 that clubs spent on bonuses in the first 10 rounds of the 2011 draft.

From the teams' perspective, the 2012 draft was a rousing success. Not only did spending on signing bonuses drop by more than $20 million, but the first-round average dipped 6.7 percent to $2,475,167. The largest bonus was $6 million, given by the Twins to Georgia high school outfielder Byron Buxton, an amount that didn't rank among the top 10 bonuses of all time. The Twins

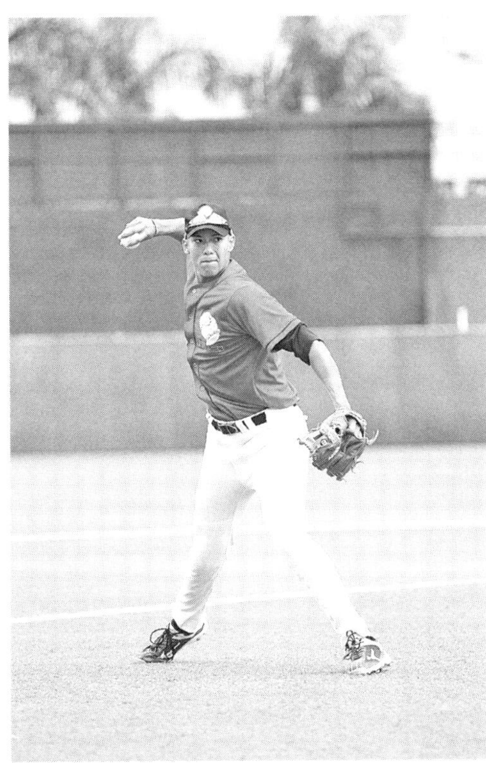

Carlos Correa certainly proved to be a legit No. 1 talent, but the Astros also took him with the first pick because he signed an underslot bonus that allowed them to bring in more premium players

were the biggest spenders overall at $12,602,400, but that figure was almost $5 million less than the Pittsburgh Pirates spent in 2011, when they set a one-year spending record.

The new rules motivated teams to determine a player's signability before selecting him, because if a player didn't sign, the team lost the bonus money for his slot from its budget. And because it now had rules with teeth, MLB no longer had to strong-arm clubs into delaying the announcement of lucrative deals. Combined with a new signing deadline of July 13, players were not only signing more quickly, but also getting their professional careers started earlier than in recent years.

All but six first-rounders signed by the July 13 deadline. A year earlier, 23 of 33 first-rounders remained unsigned on Aug. 16, the deadline day. Players signed at such a prolific clip in 2012 that draft records were set both for the first 10 rounds (330 of 338, 97.6 percent) and overall (913 of 1,231, 73.7 percent).

### ASTROS, TWINS REAP BENEFITS

Teams had operated under a de facto slotting system since 2000, with bonuses recommended by the commissioner's office, but it was ultimately unenforceable because it had not been collectively bargained with the union. Some teams followed

## AT A GLANCE

### This Date In History
June 4-6

### Best Draft
**HOUSTON ASTROS.** The Astros had first pick and the second-largest bonus pool. They selected **CARLOS CORREA** No. 1 and signed him for a $4.8 million bonus, which enabled them to spend significantly over slot on **LANCE MCCULLERS**, the 41st overall pick.

### Second Best
**ALEX WOOD, LHP, BRAVES.** Wood was the most productive big leaguer from the class through the 2015 season, according to career WAR (total of 6.9). Second was lefthander **PACO RODRIGUEZ**, a second-round pick of the Dodgers and the first player to reach the majors, debuting on Sept. 9, 2012.

### Late-Round Find
**MATT DUFFY, 3B, GIANTS (18TH ROUND).** Duffy, a Long Beach State product, was a big hit as the starting third baseman for the Giants in 2015. Righthander **TYLER DUFFEY**, a fifth-round pick of the Twins from Rice, also made an impressive debut in 2015.

### Overlooked
**CHRIS COLABELLO, 1B, TWINS.** Colabello, undrafted out of a Division II school, spent seven years in the independent Can-Am League before the Twins bought his contract in February 2012. Colabello spent 2013-14 with the Twins, hitting .214 with 13 home runs, then landed with the Blue Jays in 2015, and hit .321-15-54.

### International Gem
**YOENIS CESPEDES, OF, ATHLETICS.** Cespedes, a 26-year-old Cuban defector, signed with the A's for $36 million. His biggest competition among international players signed in 2012 came from **YU DARVISH** and **YASIEL PUIG.** Puig also defected from Cuba before

CONTINUED ON PAGE 702

## AT A GLANCE

CONTINUED FROM PAGE 701

signing with the Dodgers for $42 million. Darvish was a Japanese League star before signing with the Rangers, who won his rights with a $51.7 million posting fee and a $60 million contract.

### Minor League Take

**BYRON BUXTON, OF, TWINS.** Buxton had a breakout 2013 season in two Class A stops (.334-12-77, 55 SBs, 18 3Bs) and won Baseball America's Minor League Player of the Year award.

### One Who Got Away

**MARK APPEL, RHP, PIRATES (1ST ROUND).** Appel was on Houston's short list for the No. 1 pick. He slipped to eighth because of signability concerns, and became the only player in the first two rounds who did not sign. A year later, he went No. 1 overall to the Astros and signed quickly.

### He Was Drafted?

**JAMEIS WINSTON, RHP/OF, RANGERS (15TH ROUND).** Had he not been committed to playing quarterback at Florida State, where he won the 2013 Heisman Trophy, Winston might have been picked as early as the first round, as either a pitcher or position player. Three years later, he was the first player selected in the NFL draft, by the Tampa Bay Buccaneers.

### Did You Know . . .

Just eight players from the first 10 rounds went unsigned. The previous low was 14, in 2003 and '04.

### They Said It

Astros scouting director **BOBBY HECK**, on his club's decision to draft **CARLOS CORREA** with the No. 1 pick. "He's a power-hitting shortstop, and that's a pretty good separator. All of the players we considered had strong profiles as well, but it was tough to walk away from the shortstop with power potential."

## 2012: THE FIRST ROUNDERS

| CLUB: PLAYER, POS., SCHOOL | HOMETOWN | B-T | HT. | WT. | AGE | BONUS | FIRST YEAR | LAST YEAR | PEAK LEVEL (YEARS) |
|---|---|---|---|---|---|---|---|---|---|
| **1. Astros: Carlos Correa, ss, Puerto Rico Baseball Acad.** | **Gurabo, P.R.** | **R-R** | **6-4** | **190** | **17** | **$4,800,000** | **2012** | **Active** | **Majors (1)** |
| First Puerto Rican to go No. 1 overall; most clubs favored Buxton, but Astros thought Correa could stay at SS, saved money to spend elsewhere under new draft rules. | | | | | | | | | |
| **2. Twins: Byron Buxton, of, Appling County HS** | **Baxley, Ga.** | **R-R** | **6-1** | **190** | **18** | **$6,000,000** | **2012** | **Active** | **Majors (1)** |
| All-around talent who elicited historical superlatives from scouts, earned perfect 80 grades for speed, arm strength; series of injuries in minors stalled rise to majors. | | | | | | | | | |
| **3. Mariners: Mike Zunino, c, Florida** | **Cape Coral, Fla.** | **R-R** | **6-2** | **220** | **21** | **$4,000,000** | **2012** | **Active** | **Majors (3)** |
| Decorated college catcher combined .327-47-175 career line with high-end defense; bat deemed ready after 96 games in minors, struggled to reach Mendoza line. | | | | | | | | | |
| **4. Orioles: Kevin Gausman, rhp, Louisiana State** | **Centennial, Colo.** | **R-R** | **6-3** | **190** | **21** | **$4,320,000** | **2012** | **Active** | **Majors (3)** |
| On fast track to majors after going 12-2, 2.77 (123 IP/135 SO) with high-90s FB as draft-eligible soph, debuted with O's a year later, has struggled since to stick. | | | | | | | | | |
| **5. Royals: Kyle Zimmer, rhp, San Francisco** | **La Jolla, Calif.** | **R-R** | **6-3** | **215** | **20** | **$3,000,000** | **2012** | **Active** | **Class AA (2)** |
| Had athleticism, raw arm strength to transition from OF to mound at USF, vaulted up draft boards with mid-90s FB, nasty curve, career stalled by injuries. | | | | | | | | | |
| **6. Cubs: Albert Almora, of, Mater Academy** | **Hialeah Gardens, Fla.** | **R-R** | **6-2** | **180** | **18** | **$3,900,000** | **2012** | **Active** | **Class AA (2)** |
| Most-polished/proven, best skill set of six prep outfielders in first round; advanced approach with bat, but has not hit for average, power as expected as a pro. | | | | | | | | | |
| **7. Padres: Max Fried, lhp, Harvard-Westlake HS** | **Studio City, Calif.** | **L-L** | **6-4** | **170** | **18** | **$3,000,000** | **2012** | **Active** | **Class A (2)** |
| Athletic/projectable southpaw joined No. 16 pick Lucas Giolito when his school closed, seventh pair of HS teammates in first round; missed 2015 with TJ surgery. | | | | | | | | | |
| **8. Pirates: Mark Appel, rhp, Stanford** | **Danville, Calif.** | **R-R** | **6-5** | **190** | **20** | **Unsigned** | **2013** | **Active** | **Class AAA (1)** |
| Best raw stuff in class, went 10-2, 2.56 (123 IP/130 SO); one of favorites to go No. 1, Pirates gambled when he slid, but he turned down $3.8M; top pick in '13. | | | | | | | | | |
| **9. Marlins: Andrew Heaney, lhp, Oklahoma State** | **Putnam City, Okla.** | **L-L** | **6-2** | **190** | **20** | **$2,600,000** | **2012** | **Active** | **Majors (2)** |
| Polished lefty with low-90s FB, swing and miss slider, went 8-2, 1.60 (118 IP/140 SO) as JR; dealt to Angels in 2014, already an established MLB starter by 2015. | | | | | | | | | |
| **10. Rockies: David Dahl, of, Oak Mountain HS** | **Birmingham, Ala.** | **L-R** | **6-2** | **185** | **18** | **$2,600,000** | **2012** | **Active** | **Class AA (1)** |
| Impressive tools with middle-of-order power, had big Rookie-league debut (.379-9-57), injury prone since, missed most of 2013 (hamstring), half of 2015 (spleen). | | | | | | | | | |
| **11. Athletics: Addison Russell, ss, Pace HS** | **Pace, Fla.** | **R-R** | **6-0** | **195** | **18** | **$2,625,000** | **2012** | **Active** | **Majors (1)** |
| Longstanding HS prospect lost luster as JR, got in better shape as SR; immediate hit as first-year pro (.369-7-45), surged to majors after being dealt to Cubs. | | | | | | | | | |
| **12. Mets: Gavin Cecchini, ss, Alfred M. Barbe HS** | **Lake Charles, La.** | **R-R** | **6-2** | **180** | **18** | **$2,300,000** | **2012** | **Active** | **Class AA (2)** |
| Brother of Red Sox 2010 fourth-rounder, son of head coach at Barbe High/national prep power; slick fielder, bat light to start pro career but making progress. | | | | | | | | | |
| **13. White Sox: Courtney Hawkins, of, Mary Carroll HS** | **Corpus Christi, Texas** | **R-R** | **6-3** | **220** | **18** | **$2,475,000** | **2012** | **Active** | **Class AA (1)** |
| Primarily pitcher in HS with low-90s FB before getting bigger/stronger, developing raw power; progress at plate in pros (.234-55-220) hindered by irregular contact. | | | | | | | | | |
| **14. Reds: Nick Travieso, rhp, Archbishop McCarthy HS** | **Southwest Ranches, Fla.** | **R-R** | **6-2** | **215** | **18** | **$2,000,000** | **2012** | **Active** | **Class A (3)** |
| Position prospect/part-time reliever until SR year, when fastball hit upper 90s; has made steady progress as starter in four pro seasons (27-17, 3.42). | | | | | | | | | |
| **15. Indians: Tyler Naquin, of, Texas A&M** | **Spring, Texas** | **L-R** | **6-2** | **175** | **21** | **$1,750,000** | **2012** | **Active** | **Class AAA (1)** |
| Earned first-round look with two big tools (arm, bat), won conecutive Big 12 bat titles; lacked power for RF (7 HRs in college, 21 in four pro seasons), speed for CF. | | | | | | | | | |
| **16. Nationals: Lucas Giolito, rhp, Harvard-Westlake HS** | **Studio City, Calif.** | **R-R** | **6-6** | **230** | **17** | **$2,925,000** | **2012** | **Active** | **Class AA (1)** |
| Candidate for No. 1 after touching 100 in early-spring outings, but injured elbow/had TJ surgery; Nationals still took chance on upside, looks like a good bet so far. | | | | | | | | | |
| **17. Blue Jays: D.J. Davis, of, Stone County HS** | **Wiggins, Miss.** | **L-R** | **6-1** | **180** | **17** | **$1,750,000** | **2012** | **Active** | **Class A (3)** |
| High-risk/high-return talent; lightning-fast runner, has flashed raw power as pro, but lacks feel in field/on bases, prone to strikeouts, career slow to evolve. | | | | | | | | | |
| **18. Dodgers: Corey Seager, 3b, Northwest Cabarrus HS** | **Concord, N.C.** | **L-R** | **6-4** | **215** | **18** | **$2,350,000** | **2012** | **Active** | **Majors (1)** |
| More gifted physically than brother Kyle; dominant offensive talent hit .307-62-278 in minors, .337 in majors debut; came up as SS, profiles as Gold Glove 3B. | | | | | | | | | |
| **19. Cardinals: Michael Wacha, rhp, Texas A&M** | **Texarkana, Texas** | **R-R** | **6-6** | **210** | **20** | **$1,900,000** | **2012** | **Active** | **Majors (3)** |
| Went 9-1, 2.06 (113 IP/116 SO) as A&M junior, lost stock in draft with inconsistent breaking stuff; scorched minors, pitched in World Series in 2013, all-star at 23. | | | | | | | | | |
| **20. Giants: Chris Stratton, rhp, Mississippi State** | **Tupelo, Miss.** | **R-R** | **6-3** | **190** | **21** | **$1,850,000** | **2012** | **Active** | **Class AAA (1)** |
| Mediocre first two years in college followed by breakout JR year (11-2, 2.38) with plus FB/SL; enigma again in four pro seasons (22-23, 3.70) as stuff has regressed. | | | | | | | | | |
| **21. Braves: Lucas Sims, rhp, Brockwood HS** | **Snellville, Ga.** | **R-R** | **6-1** | **200** | **18** | **$1,650,000** | **2012** | **Active** | **Class AA (1)** |
| Braves again tapped into local talent; looked like fast tracker after dominant '13 season (12-3, 2.62), has struggled since with command/secondary stuff. | | | | | | | | | |
| **22. Blue Jays: Marcus Stroman, rhp, Duke** | **Medford, N.Y.** | **R-R** | **5-9** | **165** | **21** | **$1,800,000** | **2012** | **Active** | **Majors (2)** |
| SS/RHP for two years at Duke, career took off when he focused on pitching; moved quickly to majors as starter, has bounced back from torn ACL early in 2015. | | | | | | | | | |
| **23. Cardinals: James Ramsey, of, Florida State** | **Norcross, Ga.** | **L-R** | **6-0** | **190** | **22** | **$1,600,000** | **2012** | **Active** | **Class AAA (3)** |
| Only college SR in first round, Cardinals liked his instincts/advanced approach, paid close to slot money; career has stalled in Triple-A with lack of plus tools. | | | | | | | | | |
| **24. Red Sox: Deven Marrero, ss, Arizona State** | **Plantation, Fla.** | **R-R** | **6-1** | **195** | **21** | **$2,050,000** | **2012** | **Active** | **Majors (1)** |
| High-profile HS prospect whose superior defense always has been his calling card; unfortunately, questions about bat have not been answered in pro ball. | | | | | | | | | |
| **25. Rays: Richie Shaffer, 3b, Clemson** | **Charlotte, N.C.** | **R-R** | **6-3** | **220** | **21** | **$1,710,000** | **2012** | **Active** | **Majors (1)** |
| Polished bat with power potential/good eye, hit .336-10-46 with 63 BBs as Clemson JR, solid defender at 3B; slow to develop at plate before breakthrough 2015. | | | | | | | | | |
| **26. Diamondbacks: Stryker Trahan, c/of, Acadiana HS** | **Lafayette, La.** | **L-R** | **6-1** | **215** | **18** | **$1,700,000** | **2012** | **Active** | **Class A (2)** |
| Superior athlete with speed, power, arm strength; longtime concerns over catching ability, but lack of hitting prowess (.224, high strikeout rate) is bigger problem. | | | | | | | | | |
| **27. Brewers: Clint Coulter, c, Union HS** | **Camas, Wash.** | **R-R** | **6-3** | **210** | **18** | **$1,675,000** | **2012** | **Active** | **Class A (3)** |
| State champion wrestler, strong athlete with unconventional but effective hitting style; bat-first prospect with power potential, made conversion to OF in 2015. | | | | | | | | | |
| **28. Brewers: Victor Roache, of, Georgia Southern** | **Ypsilanti, Mich.** | **R-R** | **6-1** | **225** | **20** | **$1,525,000** | **2013** | **Active** | **Class AA (1)** |
| Hit eye-popping 30 HRs as college SO, followed by strong Cape Cod; missed most of JR season with broken wrist, Brewers ignored injury/concerns about long swing. | | | | | | | | | |
| **29. Rangers: Lewis Brinson, of, Coral Springs** | **Coral Springs, Fla.** | **R-R** | **6-3** | **170** | **18** | **$1,625,000** | **2012** | **Active** | **Class AAA (1)** |
| Outstanding athlete with speed/power, but uneven skills/prone to strikeouts; fanned 276 times in first 176 pro games before turned corner, hit .332-20-69 in 2015. | | | | | | | | | |
| **30. Yankees: Ty Hensley, rhp, Edmond Santa Fe** | **Edmond, Ola.** | **B-R** | **6-4** | **220** | **18** | **$400,000** | **2012** | **Active** | **Class A (2)** |
| Mostly catcher until SR year, when fastball hit 96-97 mph; Yankees reduced bonus when physical revealed shoulder problem, career plagued by hip/elbow injuries. | | | | | | | | | |
| **31. Red Sox: Brian Johnson, lhp, Florida** | **Cocoa Beach, Fla.** | **L-L** | **6-3** | **225** | **21** | **$1,575,000** | **2012** | **Active** | **Majors (1)** |
| Mature two-way college performer commands solid-average stuff, made swift rise through minors (24-15, 2.32), reached majors in 2015. | | | | | | | | | |

the recommendations, but many did not, giving them an advantage in stockpiling talent.

Under the revamped CBA, the worst teams generally had the greatest spending power. In 2012, those teams were the Twins and the Houston Astros, who had the first two picks and the largest bonus pools.

The penalties for teams exceeding their spending limit were significant. A team that went over by as much as 5 percent paid a 75 percent tax on the overage. The penalties escalated, with a 75 percent tax and the loss of a first-round pick in the next draft for going over by 5-10 percent; a 100 percent tax and the loss of first- and second-rounders for a 10-15 percent overage; and a 100 percent tax and the loss of two first-rounders for an overage of 15 percent or more. No team exceeded its pool limit by more than 5 percent, and in fact through 2016 no team had ever gone past that threshold.

The signing bonus pools applied to picks in the first 10 rounds, unless a player drafted after the 10th round (and nondrafted free agents) signed for more than $100,000, in which case anything beyond that amount was applied to the team's overall budget as well.

Because the budgeted amounts were for aggregate spending, teams had the latitude to spread their money among picks in the first 10 rounds in any way they chose. At the same time, a team lost the assigned value for any draft pick in the first 10 rounds that it did not sign.

The new system led to an unusual run on college seniors—the easiest and cheapest draft demographic to sign—in the sixth-10th rounds. Teams sought to sign seniors for the lowest amount possible in order to apply the savings to other players with higher price tags. The extra money could also be applied to riskier picks after the 10th round, who carried no budgetary penalty if they didn't sign.

A total of 62 college seniors were drafted in the first 10 rounds, significantly more than in 2011 (23) and 2010 (19). Of the 62 seniors, 34 signed for as little as $10,000.

"The new system turned rounds six to 10 into a joke," a scout said. "It's too bad it's at the expense of having a draft that functions as it should, and potentially at the expense of scouting, because they certainly didn't build a system that accomplishes the proper way that a draft should unfold."

Only the Toronto Blue Jays spent right up to the 5 percent threshold. They paid out bonuses of $9.272 million, $441,200 more than their pool allotment of $8.8308 million. As a result, they were assessed a tax of $330,900.

## Fastest To The Majors

| | Player, Pos. | Drafted (Round) | Debut |
|---|---|---|---|
| 1. | Paco Rodriguez, lhp | Dodgers (2) | Sept. 9, 2012 |
| 2. | Michael Roth, lhp | Angels (9) | April 13, 2013 |
| 3. | Kevin Gausman, rhp | Orioles (1) | May 23, 2013 |
| 4. | Michael Wacha, rhp | Cardinals (1) | May 30, 2013 |
| | Alex Wood, lhp | Braves (2) | May 30, 2013 |

**FIRST HIGH SCHOOL SELECTION:** Addison Russell, ss (Athletics/1, April 21, 2015)

## DRAFT SPOTLIGHT: CARLOS CORREA

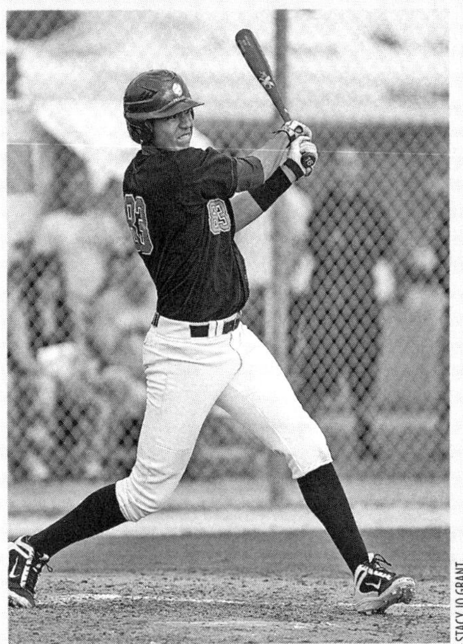
STACY JO GRANT

**Baseball scouts hoped that Carlos Correa's ascent would provide inspiration for more kids from Puerto Rico**

The selection of Carlos Correa with the No. 1 pick in 2012 signaled the beginning of a new era for the Houston Astros and heralded a triumphant new chapter in Puerto Rico's storied baseball tradition.

Not since the island's Dream Team ran roughshod in the 1995 Caribbean Series, or a record 53 native sons populated major league Opening Day rosters in 2001 had there been reason for Puerto Ricans to celebrate a baseball moment quite like the one Correa provided.

The 17-year-old Correa embraced the occasion, happily waving a Puerto Rican mini-flag in a salute to his homeland when baseball commissioner Bud Selig made the announcement of his draft selection on national television.

"I always think about representing Puerto Rico, lifting baseball in Puerto Rico," Correa said. "It's always something I've focused on since I was drafted. I wanted to tell people that, yes, there are good baseball players in Puerto Rico."

His selection recalled the days when Puerto Rico was a major source of major league talent, producing the likes of Roberto Clemente, Orlando Cepeda and Roberto Alomar, all members of the Hall of Fame. And there was the '95 Dream Team roster that included Alomar, Carlos Baerga, Carlos Delgado, Juan Gonzalez, Edgar Martinez and Bernie Williams, all established major league stars in the mid-1990s. The strike of 1994 moved many of Puerto Rico's major leaguers to play winter ball, which culminated with Puerto Rico dominating the Caribbean Series in front of raucous, partisan crowds in San Juan.

All of the Dream Team players had signed as free agents on the open market, because Puerto Ricans were not subject to the draft until 1989. The introduction of the draft coincided with a decline in baseball interest in Puerto Rico, and a resulting dip in talent. That came at a time when other sports such as basketball, boxing and volleyball became popular on the island.

The baseball draft also played a role, considering that major league teams had less incentive to look deep for talent on the island that they might not land. Instead, international scouts redirected their focus to areas such as the Dominican Republic and Venezuela, which were unencumbered by a restrictive draft.

From a record 35 Puerto Ricans drafted in 1995, just seven were selected a decade later, none higher than the 31st round. A record-low 11 Puerto Ricans were on Opening Day rosters in 2012, the year Correa became the first Puerto Rican drafted first overall.

Like his countrymen from another era, Correa pursued baseball with a passion from a young age. With the help of his father, he practiced endlessly to fine-tune his skills, which led to a scholarship at age 15 to the Puerto Rico Baseball Academy, a baseball-centric, accredited high school that opened in 2002 and was funded in part by Major League Baseball, with a mission to rekindle baseball interest among Puerto Rico's youth.

The school provided Correa the finishing touches he needed, both physically and emotionally, and he quickly developed into a top shortstop prospect. His powerful arm, superior speed and thunderous bat reminded some scouts of both Alex Rodriguez, for his size and skill set; and Derek Jeter, for his grace and natural affinity for the game.

Taking a cue from Jeter, Correa understood that his growing fame came with responsibility. From the moment a humble but proud Correa was drafted, he was embraced as a national hero in his homeland, and he enhanced his celebrity status by earning the American League Rookie of the Year award in 2015, edging out another Puerto Rican shortstop, Francisco Lindor.

In the process, Correa not only became the face of a franchise experiencing a turnaround, but a driving force behind the resurgence of top-flight baseball talent from Puerto Rico.

**WORTH NOTING**

■ Stanford righthander **MARK APPEL** received the highest grade from the Major League Scouting Bureau, a 75 on the 20-80 scouting scale. That was 10 points better than the next players on the list, high school righthanders **LUCAS GIOLITO** and **LANCE MCCULLERS**.

■ The bonanza for Puerto Rico that began with **CARLOS CORREA** as the first overall pick continued throughout the first 10 rounds with eight selections overall, the third-most ever. Righthander **JOSE BERRIOS** became the highest Puerto Rican pitcher ever drafted when the Twins took him with the first supplemental round pick (32nd overall). The Dodgers selected infielder **JESMUEL VALENTIN**, son of longtime big league infielder **JOSE VALENTIN**, with the 51st selection.

■ While the 2012 draft wasn't a vintage year for college talent, five of the top six NCAA strikeout leaders were first-round picks. Oklahoma State lefthander **ANDREW HEANEY** (Marlins, ninth overall) led with 140 strikeouts. Duke righthander **MARCUS STROMAN** (Blue Jays, 22nd) was second with 136, and Louisiana State righthander **KEVIN GAUSMAN** (Orioles, fourth) third with 136. Appel (Pirates, eighth) was fifth with 130, and Mississippi State righthander **CHRIS STRATTON** (Giants, 20th) sixth with 127.

■ Three players from Montana were drafted, the most since 1996. Outfielder **JUSTIN BLACK** of Billings West High was picked by the Braves in the fourth round, the first Montana product since 1966 to be selected in the top five rounds. Montana produced two early-round picks in the first two years of the draft: lefthander Les Rohr, second overall in 1965; and lefthander Leo Pinnick in the second round in 1966.

■ The Red Sox' focus on high-ceiling talent was on display in the middle rounds. They picked two future NFL players, outfielders

The Chicago Cubs spent 104.7 percent of their allotment, followed by the Boston Red Sox at 104.1 percent. They were assessed $280,350 and $211,650 in taxes, respectively. A total of 10 teams exceeded their allotments, and two teams (White Sox and Tigers) spent exactly according to the guidelines. The accumulated tax amounted to $1,588,193, which was divided among the 11 teams that received revenue-sharing money from baseball's central fund and did not exceed their bonus pools, per the new draft rules,

The Pirates spent just 49.3 percent of their initial allotment. That was a result of not signing their first-round pick, Stanford righthander Mark Appel (eighth overall), who had an assigned slot value of $2.9 million. The Pirates spent $3,830,700 in bonuses, a monumental drop from the record $17,005,700 they spent a year earlier.

The changes to the draft weren't limited to money issues and moving the signing deadline up a month. The draft also shrank from 50 to 40 rounds, and major league contracts were prohibited. The latter measure meant that teams no longer would be able to spread out payment of a large signing bonus over a number of years.

Changes to the free-agent compensation system resulted in fewer compensation and supplemental picks, though those adjustments didn't come into play until the 2013 draft. The Type A and Type B designations for free agents, which were based on a statistical ranking of the top 30 percent of available free agents, were eliminated. In the final year under the old system, the 2012 draft included 29 compensation and supplemental picks between the first and second rounds.

## MUDDLED CLASS AT THE TOP

With much of the attention focused on draft reform, it was almost lost in the shuffle that the Astros had the first pick, after finishing with a club-record and major league-worst 106 losses in 2011. The team's fall was triggered by a series of unproductive drafts over the previous decade, driven in part by the Astros' adherence to the wishes of the commissioner's office in holding the line on signing bonuses. The team didn't sign some premium picks or did not draft them at all because of what they would cost.

### WAR Heroes

Based on the career WAR (Wins Above Replacement, as calculated by Baseball-Reference.com) numbers achieved by all the players eligible for the 2012 draft, these are the most productive big leaguers through the 2015 season. Numbers in parentheses indicate the round when the player was actually drafted.

| | Player, Pos. | Actual Draft | WAR | Bonus |
|---|---|---|---|---|
| 1. | Alex Wood, lhp | Braves (2) | 6.9 | $700,000 |
| 2. | Michael Wacha, rhp | Cardinals (1) | 5.8 | $1,900,000 |
| 3. | Matt Duffy, 3b | Giants (18) | 4.8 | $50,000 |
| 4. | Carlos Correa, ss | Astros (1) | 4.1 | $4,800,000 |
| 5. | Addison Russell, ss | Athletics (1) | 3.4 | $2,625,000 |
| 6. | Marcus Stroman, rhp | Blue Jays (1) | 3.2 | $1,800,000 |
| 7. | Lance McCullers, rhp | Astros (1-S) | 2.4 | $2,500,000 |
| | Devon Travis, 2b | Tigers (13) | 2.4 | $200,000 |
| 9. | Paco Rodriguez, lhp | Dodgers (2) | 2.1 | $610,800 |
| 10. | Kevin Gausman, rhp | Orioles (1) | 2.0 | $4,320,000 |

NATHAN RODE

Many scouts saw Byron Buxton as the best talent in the 2012 draft, but injuries and his level of competition gave some second thoughts

With a weak major league roster and a barren farm system, the Astros essentially were starting from scratch in 2012 under new owner Jim Crane and new general manager Jeff Luhnow. Crane hired Luhnow away from the St. Louis Cardinals, where he had been the head of a successful scouting and player development operation.

Unfortunately for the Astros, there was plenty of uncertainty about which prospect belonged at the top of the draft order. While that also was the case in 2011, the previous year at least had several legitimate candidates for the No. 1 overall selection. The 2012 crop paled in comparison.

"I think it's fair to say that nobody in this class has separated themselves as an obvious choice," Luhnow said.

If there was a consensus top prospect, it was Buxton, a player with five-tool potential. But he hit just three home runs as a senior against subpar high school competition in rural Georgia, stirring concern that it might be a while before his bat was ready to make an impact at the big league level.

Buxton was on Houston's short list of candidates, along with four college prospects: Appel, Louisiana State righthander Kevin Gausman, San Francisco righthander Kyle Zimmer and Florida catcher Mike Zunino. Puerto Rican high school shortstop Carlos Correa was another option, especially as he made significant strides in the weeks leading up to the draft. But in the minds of the Astros, there wasn't a player deserving of the $7.2 million bonus allocated for the No. 1 slot.

Appel had the best raw stuff among college pitchers and was viewed as the safest, most likely option for the Astros. The 6-foot-4, 195-pound righthander frustrated scouts because he didn't routinely dominate college hitters. Moreover, he was represented by agent Scott Boras, who would be unlikely to accept anything less than the full

## Top 25 Bonuses

| Player, Pos. | Drafted (Round) | Order | Bonus |
|---|---|---|---|
| **1. * Byron Buxton, of** | **Twins (1)** | **2** | **$6,000,000** |
| **2. * Carlos Correa, ss** | **Astros (1)** | **1** | **$4,800,000** |
| **3. Kevin Gausman, rhp** | **Orioles (1)** | **4** | **$4,320,000** |
| **4. Mike Zunino, c** | **Mariners (1)** | **3** | **$4,000,000** |
| 5. * Albert Almora, of | Cubs (1) | 6 | $3,900,000 |
| 6. Kyle Zimmer, rhp | Royals (1) | 5 | $3,000,000 |
| * Max Fried, lhp | Padres (1) | 7 | $3,000,000 |
| 8. * Lucas Giolito, rhp | Nationals (1) | 16 | $2,925,000 |
| **9. Andrew Heaney, lhp** | **Marlins (1)** | **9** | **$2,800,000** |
| **10. * Addison Russell, ss** | **Athletics (1)** | **11** | **$2,625,000** |
| 11. * David Dahl, of | Rockies (1) | 10 | $2,600,000 |
| 12. * Gavin Cecchini, ss | Mets (1) | 12 | $2,550,000 |
| **13. * Lance McCullers, rhp** | **Astros (1-S)** | **41** | **$2,500,000** |
| 14. * Courtney Hawkins, of | White Sox (1) | 13 | $2,475,000 |
| 15. * Nick Travieso, rhp | Reds (1) | 14 | $2,375,000 |
| 16. Tyler Naquin, of | Indians (1) | 15 | $2,250,000 |
| *** Joey Gallo, 3b** | **Rangers (1-S)** | **39** | **$2,250,000** |
| 18. * Matt Smoral, lhp | Blue Jays (1-S) | 50 | $2,000,000 |
| * Walker Weichel, rhp | Padres (1-S) | 55 | $2,000,000 |
| **20. * Corey Seager, ss** | **Dodgers (1)** | **18** | **$1,950,000** |
| **21. Michael Wacha, rhp** | **Cardinals (1)** | **19** | **$1,900,000** |
| 22. Chris Stratton, rhp | Giants (1) | 20 | $1,850,000 |
| 23. * Luke Sims, rhp | Braves (1) | 21 | $1,825,000 |
| 24. James Ramsey, of | Cardinals (1) | 23 | $1,775,000 |
| 25. * D.J. Davis, of | Blue Jays (1) | 17 | $1,750,000 |
| **Deven Marrero, ss** | **Red Sox (1)** | **24** | **$1,750,000** |

*Major leaguers in bold. *High school selection.*

amount the Astros had at their disposal.

The Astros didn't tip their hand throughout the process. When it came time to pick, they pulled a mild surprise, passing on Appel and Buxton in favor of Correa. Astros scouting director Bobby Heck said the team did not settle on Correa, a product of the Puerto Rico Baseball Academy, until the afternoon of the draft.

"He's a power-hitting shortstop, and that's a pretty good separator," Heck said. "All of the players we considered had strong profiles as well, but it was tough to walk away from the shortstop with power potential."

The Astros were also confident Correa would accept a more modest bonus, which would give them more money to sign other players. Their approach became apparent when the Astros selected Florida high school righthander Lance McCullers, a son of former big leaguer Lance McCullers Sr., with their next pick (41st overall).

With a fastball that peaked at 98 mph, along with a 13-0, 0.18 record with 140 strikeouts in 77 innings as a senior at Jesuit High in Tampa, McCullers had been projected to be picked among the top eight to 10 players. But he came with a significant price tag, and once he slipped beyond his projected range, it was apparent that most teams considered him to be out of their price range.

That made the Astros and McCullers a perfect fit. Three days later, the Astros signed Correa for $4.8 million, leaving them with $2.4 million to allocate elsewhere. They signed McCullers for $2.5 million, the 13th-largest bonus in the draft and $1.242 million more than his draft slot.

The Astros also were able to sign California high school third baseman Rio Ruiz, their fourth-round pick, for $1.85 million, more than five times the slot amount of $360,200. Ruiz was a potential first-round selection before he had shoulder surgery in March to alleviate a blood clot, causing him to miss the rest of the 2012 season.

The Astros spent a total of $11,335,200, just $157,500 more than their bonus pool allotment of $11,177,700. While it cost them $118,125 in luxury taxes, no other team secured more high-end talent.

The previous time the Astros had picked first was in 1992, when they chose Cal State Fullerton third baseman Phil Nevin instead of Michigan high school shortstop Derek Jeter. By drafting a shortstop with many of Jeter's qualities, they were determined not to make the same mistake again.

Lance McCullers

It was quickly evident the Astros made the right call on Correa. At 6-foot-3 and 185 pounds, he might have been a little big for a conventional shortstop, but his overall talent reminded scouts of Troy Tulowitzki, and even Alex Rodriguez. Correa was agile, had soft hands and smooth actions, and also had above-average running speed and premium arm strength. Correa showed a smooth righthanded swing, along with excellent balance and bat speed, and projected as a middle-of-the-order run producer.

Correa was the highest-drafted player ever from Puerto Rico, which became part of the draft in 1989. Catcher Ramon Castro previously was the highest-drafted Puerto Rican, selected by the Astros with the 17th overall pick in 1989.

The Astros not only drafted first in 2012, but also had the first selection in the next two drafts after enduring 100-loss seasons. Their plan to rebuild the organization through the draft took hold in 2015, when they reached postseason play for the first time since 2005. Correa was the best player on the team at age 21, and McCullers was a key member of the rotation.

### FIRST ROUND UNFOLDS AS EXPECTED

The Astros set the tone by selecting Correa with the top pick and signing him to a bonus significantly less than the amount allotted for his slot. The Twins followed by selecting Buxton, the Seattle Mariners took Zunino, the Baltimore Orioles picked Gausman, and the Kansas City Royals drafted Zimmer. The Cubs, picking sixth, took Florida high school outfielder Albert Almora.

None of the six players signed for the full bonus assigned to his slot. Buxton's $6 million bonus, while the richest in 2012, was $200,000 below slot for the second pick. Zunino signed for $4 million, $1.2 million under slot. Gausman, a Boras client, received $4.32 million, $120,000 above slot. Zimmer got $3 million, $500,000 under slot. Almora signed for $3.9 million, $650,000 over slot. The first four picks were the only players to sign contracts of $4 million or more. By contrast, four players in 2011 received more than what

### WORTH NOTING

**SHAQ THOMPSON** in the 15th round and **BRANDON MAGEE** in the 23rd. Both players signed—Thompson for $100,000, Magee for $35,000—and played briefly in the Sox system. Thompson's career couldn't have gone much worse, as he was 0-for-39 and struck out 37 times in the Rookie-level Gulf Coast League. A linebacker, he played at the University of Washington and became the NFL's Carolina Panthers' first-round draft pick in 2015. The Red Sox also selected shortstop **ALEX BREGMAN** and righthander **CARSON FULMER**, who both went to college and became the second and eighth overall picks in the 2015 draft.

■ California prep righthander **LUCAS GIOLITO'S** family had deep roots in the entertainment industry. Giolito's mother, Lindsay Frost, was a prominent Hollywood actress, and his father, Rick Giolito, was a producer and video game executive. Giolito's grandfather, Warren Frost, also was an actor, and his uncles, Mart and Scott Frost, were Hollywood writers and producers. Giolito was a first-round pick of the Nationals.

■ While most of the changes to draft rules took effect in 2012, a handful didn't come into play for another year. Going forward, the only major league free agents subject to compensation would be those offered contracts equal to the average salary of the 125 highest-paid players in the game as they entered the free-agent process. Players also had to be with a team for an entire season to be subject to compensation, so pending free agents who were traded at midseason would no longer generate extra picks for the teams that acquired them. Additionally, a team that signed a free agent would be required to surrender its first-round pick. Unlike in the past, when the top 15 picks were protected, only the top 10 would be protected.

CONTINUED ON PAGE 706

## WORTH NOTING

CONTINUED FROM PAGE 705

In such cases, a team would lose its second-highest selection (not necessarily its second-round pick, as in the past). And the forfeited pick would no longer go to the team that lost the free agent; that pick would simply be eliminated. The team that lost the free agent received a supplemental pick after the first round. The new rules also provided for 12 so-called "competitive-balance" selections, six supplemental picks following both the first and second rounds. Major league teams that ranked among the bottom 10 in revenue or market size were placed in a pool, and six were selected by lottery to gain a draft pick after the first round, with the odds of winning based on a team's prior season winning percentage. Teams that didn't get one of those extra picks, along with any other team that received money from revenue-sharing, went into another lottery for six picks after the second round. Lottery picks could be traded, an option that did not apply to other draft choices.

■ Despite failing to reach the NCAA regionals, Arizona State had 10 players drafted, more than any other school. They included shortstop **DEVEN MARRERO**, a first round pick (24th overall) by the Red Sox, three third-rounders and a fifth-rounder. The University of Arizona won the College World Series and had just five players drafted, none higher than the fourth round. Outfielder **ROB REFSNYDER**, a fifth-round pick of the Yankees, was the Series MVP. The Wildcats swept South Carolina in the best-of-three championship series. South Carolina was upstaged in the draft by Southeastern Conference rival Florida, which went winless in the CWS but produced nine draft picks, including first-rounders **MIKE ZUNINO** and lefthander **BRIAN JOHNSON** (Red Sox, 31st). The Gators also had two second-rounders, including lefthander **PACO RODRIGUEZ**.

Buxton got.

Appel's chance for the biggest payday dissipated once he slipped through the first five picks, and it became apparent no team would have enough money left in its pool to meet his expectations. The Pirates drafted Appel with the eighth pick, but never came close to signing him. He was the only 2012 first-rounder to go unsigned.

The first round consisted of 31 picks—the Blue Jays were awarded the 22nd pick as compensation for not signing 2011 first-rounder Tyler Beede—and 19 of the selections signed for the amount assigned to their slot. Eight, including Correa, Buxton, Zunino and Zimmer, received below-slot amounts. Gausman, a draft-eligible sophomore, and Almora were two of just three who earned above-slot deals. The other was California prep righthander Lucas Giolito, who got a $2.925 million bonus, $800,000 over slot, from the Washington Nationals as the 16th pick.

The Nationals, who spent $15,002,100 on bonuses in 2011, had a pool allotment of $4,436,200 in 2012. They managed to get Giolito under contract at the signing deadline, even as it significantly limited what they could spend on other players.

Giolito, from Harvard-Westlake School in Los Angeles, was considered the top pitching prospect in the high school ranks until he injured his elbow in early March and missed two months. He had Tommy John surgery after signing with the Nationals, but by 2016 was regarded as the top pitching prospect in the minor leagues.

BILL MITCHELL
Mark Appel

Giolito's teammate, lefthander Max Fried, was the first prep pitcher picked, going seventh overall to the San Diego Padres. It was just the seventh occasion that high school teammates were first-round picks in the same draft.

The 6-foot-4 Fried spent his senior year at Harvard-Westlake after transferring from nearby Montclair Prep, which cut its entire athletic budget due to financial concerns. Fried developed a sore arm while pitching in the Padres organization and had Tommy John surgery in 2014. He was traded to the Atlanta Braves prior to the 2015 season.

### FIRST-ROUNDERS STILL PROGRESSING

Through the 2015 season, 12 first-rounders from the 2012 draft class had reached the majors. None had enjoyed greater success than Correa, Texas A&M righthander Michael Wacha (Cardinals, 19th overall) and Duke righthander Marcus Stroman (Blue Jays, 22nd).

Correa made his big league debut on June 8, 2015, and became such a force for the upstart Astros that he won the American League Rookie of the Year award. He hit .272 with 22 homers and 68 RBIs. Wacha played an instrumental role for the Cardinals in their charge to the 2013 World Series, first as a late-season starter and more significantly as MVP of the National League Championship Series. With a 17-7, 3.38 record in 2015, he established himself as one of the top young starters in the National League

Stroman went 11-6, 3.65 in his 2014 rookie season with the Blue Jays. After missing most of 2015 while recuperating from knee surgery, he returned in time to contribute to the Jays' trip to the ALCS.

Several other 2012 first-rounders were learning on the job in the big leagues, among them Buxton, who had been a two-way star at Appling County High in Baxley, Ga. Buxton hit .513 with three homers and 35 RBIs in his senior season, and went 10-1, 1.90 with 154 strikeouts in 81 innings, showing a mid-90s fastball.

Buxton made rapid strides in the Twins system, especially in 2013, when he hit .334 with 12 homers, 18 triples and 55 stolen bases in Class A. But a series of injuries in 2014 stalled his progress, and additional injuries were a factor a year later after he was promoted to the Twins. As a major league rookie, Buxton hit just .209 with two homers.

In addition to Correa, two other high school shortstops, Addison Russell (Athletics, 11th) and Corey Seager (Dodgers, 18th), progressed through the minors with relative ease and made their way to the big leagues during the 2015 season.

Russell took quickly to pro ball, hitting .369 with seven home runs at three levels of the A's system in 2012. Traded to the Cubs in 2014, he joined their lineup the following season and hit .242 with 13 homers, in addition to quickly becoming perhaps the league's best defensive shortstop.

Seager, a younger brother of Mariners all-star third baseman Kyle Seager, had a breakout 2014

## Largest Bonuses By Round

| | Player, Pos. | Club | Bonus |
|---|---|---|---|
| **1.** | ***Byron Buxton, of** | **Twins** | **$6,000,000** |
| **1-S.** | ***Lance McCullers, rhp** | **Astros** | **$2,500,000** |
| 2. | *Carson Kelly, 3b/rhp | Cardinals | $1,600,000 |
| 3. | *Tyler Pike, lhp | Mariners | $850,000 |
| 4. | *Rio Ruiz, 3b | Astros | $1,850,000 |
| **5.** | **Chris Taylor, ss** | **Mariners** | **$500,000** |
| 6. | *Timmy Lopes, 2b | Mariners | $550,000 |
| 7. | *Corey Oswalt, rhp | Mets | $475,000 |
| 8. | *Tomas Nido, c | Mets | $250,000 |
| 9. | *Shilo McCall, of | Giants | $200,000 |
| 10. | *Jeremy Kivel, rhp | Reds | $500,000 |
| 11. | Logan Taylor, rhp | Mets | $150,000 |
| 12. | *Max Foody, lhp | Cardinals | $385,000 |
| **13.** | **Devon Travis, 2b** | **Tigers** | **$200,000** |
| 14. | *Chris Flexen, rhp | Mets | $374,400 |
| 15. | *Ryan Borucki, lhp | Blue Jays | $426,000 |
| 16. | *Austin Faircloth, lhp | Royals | $350,000 |
| 17. | *Hayden Hurst, rhp | Pirates | $400,000 |
| 18. | *Brady Lail, rhp | Yankees | $225,000 |
| 19. | Iseha Conklin, ss | Red Sox | $100,000 |
| | *Christian Miller, lhp | Padres | $100,000 |
| 20. | *Zack Larson, of | Twins | $190,000 |
| 21. | Matt Strahm, lhp | Royals | $100,000 |
| 22. | Three tied at | | $100,000 |
| 23. | Kevin Allen, rhp | Royals | $75,000 |
| 24. | Beau Maggi, c | Royals | $100,000 |
| | *Jose Mesa Jr., rhp | Yankees | $100,000 |
| 25. | *Corey Kimber, rhp | Padres | $120,000 |
| Other | Several tied at | | $100,000 |

*Major leaguers in bold. *High school selection.*

## Highest Unsigned Picks

| Player, Pos., Team (Round) | College | Re-Drafted |
|---|---|---|
| Mark Appel, rhp, Pirates (1) | * Stanford | Astros '13 (1) |
| Teddy Stankiewicz, rhp, Mets (2) | Seminole (Okla.) JC | Red Sox '13 (2) |
| Alec Rash, rhp, Phillies (2) | Missouri | Nats '15 (23) |
| Kyle Twomey, lhp, Athletics (3) | USC | Cubs '15 (13) |
| Brandon Thomas, of, Pirates (4) | * Georgia Tech | Yankees '13 (8) |
| Colin Poche, lhp, Orioles (5) | Arkansas | D-backs '16 (14) |
| Nick Halamandaris, 1b, Mariners (8) | California | Never |
| L.J. Mazzilli, 2b, Twins (9) | * Connecticut | Mets '13 (4) |
| Hunter Virant, lhp, Astros (11) | UCLA | Never |
| Matt Gonzalez, ss, Athletics (11) | Georgia Tech | Braves '16 (6) |

**TOTAL UNSIGNED PICKS:** Top 5 Rounds (6), Top 10 Rounds (8)

**Returned to same school.*

season in the minors, hitting .349 with 20 home runs and 97 RBIs. Promoted to the Dodgers late in the 2015 season, he hit .338 with four homers and 17 RBIs in 27 games, and opened the 2016 season as the team's everyday shortstop.

Zunino showed great potential as a power-hitting catcher and capable defender at the University of Florida, but he struggled mightily to hit with any consistency after joining the Mariners in 2013. He had a .193 average through the 2015 season, and had struck out 339 times in 295 games.

Gausman struggled to find consistency as a starter with the Orioles, going 14-19, 4.21 as both a starter and reliever from 2013-15. Zimmer made it to Double-A quickly, but his career stalled because of ongoing arm injuries that limited him to 217 innings in four minor league seasons.

Twenty players (16 first-rounders, four supplemental first-rounders) received bonuses of at least $2 million, down from 23 in 2011. Besides McCullers, the other supplemental first-rounders to get at least $2 million were Nevada high school third baseman Joey Gallo (Rangers, 39th), $2.25 million; Ohio prep lefthander Matt Smoral (Blue Jays, 50th), $2 million; and Florida high school righthander Walker Weichel (Padres, 55th), $2 million. Weichel was one of two supplemental first-rounders from Orlando's Olympia High, joining outfielder Jesse Winker (Reds, 49th).

The Blue Jays navigated the new draft rules as well as any team. Smoral was a potential top 10 draft prospect before missing most of the 2012 season because of a knee injury. And Mississippi high school outfielder Anthony Alford fell to Toronto in the third round because he also was a top-rated quarterback with a college commitment to Southern Mississippi. Alford signed for $750,000.

Smoral's slot value was $1 million and Alford's was $424,400. The Blue Jays would have had little chance to sign either if not for the money they saved by negotiating under-slot bonuses with their first two picks, outfielder D.J. Davis (17th), from the Mississippi prep ranks, and Stroman. Toronto saved $400,000 in the process. And drafting six college seniors and a fourth-year junior from rounds four to 10 helped even more.

In the most noteworthy case of the new rules encouraging a team to walk away from a premium pick rather than losing the player, the Pirates did not come to terms with Appel. Pittsburgh was prepared to offer Appel a $3.8 million bonus, $900,000 over the slot value for the eighth pick, and the highest amount they could go without having to forfeit a 2013 first-round pick. Appel, represented by Boras, wanted more, and after the Pirates refused, he returned to Stanford for his senior year.

A year later, the Astros drafted Appel with the first overall pick and gave him a $6.35 million signing bonus, larger than any bonus in 2012.

The Pirates, by not agreeing to a deal with Appel, received the ninth overall selection in the 2013 draft as compensation. They were able to use money saved on Appel to sign four players at the July 13 deadline, including 16th-rounder Max Moroff for $300,000 and 17th-rounder Hayden Hurst for $400,000.

From 2008-11, the Pirates spent more aggressively in the draft than any other team, paying out $47.6 million in bonuses. But their inability to sign Appel was a setback in their rebuilding efforts.

"The knee-jerk reaction is that you want to sign the player," Pirates assistant general manager Greg Smith said. "When you step back from it, you say he slid, and you knew it was a risk going in."

The Angels did not have a first- or second-round pick, but they signed 36 of their 38 selections, the best rate since the Dodgers signed 33 of 34 picks in the June regular phase in 1985. No team has ever signed all its draft picks in a given year.

With new rules in place that limited bonuses after the 10th round, few players in rounds 11-40 received bonuses that exceeded six figures, and none came close to a seven-figure bonus. The largest bonus for a player after the 10th round went to Illinois prep righthander Ryan Borucki, a 15th-rounder who signed with the Blue Jays for $425,000. Borucki had been targeted as a potential early-round pick before suffering an arm injury during the spring.

### IN FOCUS:: LUCAS GIOLITO

With a fastball that peaked at 100 mph, Lucas Giolito might have been the first high school pitcher drafted in 2012, and perhaps the first prep righthander ever taken first overall, had he not injured his elbow in early March of his senior season that sidelined him for two months.

His health and signability remained uncertain with the draft nearing, but Giolito at least got back on the mound before his senior season at Harvard-Westlake School in Los Angeles was over, posting a 2-1, 0.84 record in 17 innings. The Nationals took a leap of faith, selecting the 6-foot-6, 230-pound Giolito with the 16th overall pick. They knew he would need Tommy John surgery, but still signed him for a $2.925 million bonus.

"We did our homework and due diligence on his makeup and character, and we decided this is the type of player and type of ceiling we want," Nationals general manager Mike Rizzo said.

Giolito did in fact have Tommy John surgery in August 2012, after making just one start in the Nationals system. Once recovered, he was brought along slowly by the Nationals. By 2015 his electric stuff had returned, and Giolito had emerged as one of the top pitching prospects in the game with stuff, size, feel for pitching and makeup. He made his big league debut in 2016.

## One Team's Draft: Houston Astros

| Player, Pos. | Bonus | Player, Pos. | Bonus | Player, Pos. | Bonus |
|---|---|---|---|---|---|
| **1. *Carlos Correa, ss** | **$4,800,000** | 9. Daniel Minor, rhp | $50,000 | 18. Ricky Gingras, c | $30,000 |
| **1. *Lance McCullers, rhp** | **$2,500,000** | 10. Joe Bircher, lhp | $20,000 | 19. Austin Elkins, 2b | $70,000 |
| 2. Nolan Fontana, ss | $875,000 | 11. *Hunter Virant, lhp | Did not sign | 20. Michael Clark, lhp | Did not play |
| 3. Brady Rodgers, rhp | $495,200 | 12. Terrell Joyce, of | $100,000 | 21. Marc Wilk, of | $70,000 |
| 4. *Rio Ruiz, 3b | $1,850,000 | 13. Brian Holmes, lhp | $100,000 | 22. Kenny Long, lhp | $1,000 |
| 5. Andrew Aplin, of | $220,000 | 14. Joe Sclafani, ss | $5,000 | 23. Travis Ballew, rhp | $50,000 |
| 6. *Brett Phillips, of | $300,000 | 15. Erick Gonzalez, rhp | $100,000 | 24. Pat Blair, ss | Did not play |
| **7. Preston Tucker, of** | **$100,000** | 16. Dan Gulbransen, of | $41,000 | 25. Ryan Dineen, ss | $41,000 |
| 8. Tyler Heineman, c | $125,000 | 17. Aaron West, rhp | $50,000 | Other Angel Ibanez (28), 3b | $40,000 |

*Major leaguers in bold. *High school selection.*

# 2012 Draft List

**Did not sign. Major leaguers in bold, with first and last years noted. Order of selection indicated in parentheses. For the first five rounds, the peak level of each player is noted.*

## ARIZONA DIAMONDBACKS (25)

1. Stryker Trahan, c-of, Acadiana HS, Lafayette, La.—(High A)
2. Jose Munoz, 3b, Los Altos HS, Hacienda Heights, Calif.—(Low A)
3. Jake Barrett, rhp, Arizona State University.—(AAA)
4. Chuck Taylor, of, Mansfield Timberview HS, Arlington, Texas.—(High A)
5. Ronnie Freeman, c, Kennesaw State University.—(AA)
6. **Jake Lamb, 3b, University of Washington.—(2014-15)**
7. Andrew Velazquez, ss, Fordham Prep, Bronx, N.Y.
8. Evan Marzilli, of, University of South Carolina.
9. Jeff Gibbs, rhp, University of Maine.
10. Danny Poma, of, Hofstra University.
11. Ben Eckels, rhp, Davis (Calif.) HS.
12. Alex Glenn, of, Arizona Christian University.
13. Phildrick Llewellyn, c, Trinity Christian Academy, Lake Worth, Fla.
14. Derrick Stultz, rhp, University of South Florida.
15. Blake Forslund, rhp, Liberty University.
16. *Landon Lassiter, ss, North Davidson HS, Lexington, N.C.
17. Yogey Perez-Ramos, of, Miami-Dade JC.
18. Kevin Medrano, 2b, Missouri State University.
19. R.J. Hively, rhp, University of Mississippi.
20. Jacob House, 1b, Texas A&M University.
21. Rudy Flores, 1b, Florida International University.
22. *Holden Helmink, rhp, Willis (Texas) HS.
23. *Matt Dermody, lhp, University of Iowa.
24. Mark Ginther, 3b, Oklahoma State University.
25. Vince Spilker, rhp, Lee (Tenn.) University.
26. Chris Capper, rhp, Brigham Young University.
27. Damion Smith, of, Holy Names HS, Windsor, Ontario.
28. *Max Schrock, 2b, Cardinal Gibbons HS, Raleigh, N.C.
29. Adam McConnell, ss, University of Richmond.
30. Chase Stevens, rhp, Oklahoma State University.
31. Andrew Potter, rhp, Eastside HS, Lancaster, Calif.
32. Daniel Watts, lhp, Jacksonville State University.
33. Jonathan Pulley, rhp, Spartanburg Methodist (S.C.) JC.
34. Jared Ray, rhp, University of Houston.
35. Robbie Buller, rhp, Houston Baptist University.
36. Andrew Barbosa, lhp, University of South Florida.
37. Breland Almadova, of, University of Hawaii.
38. *Cam Gibson, of, Grosse Point South HS, Grosse Point, Mich.

DRAFT DROP *Son of Kirk Gibson, first-round draft pick, Tigers (1978); major leaguer (1979-95); major league manager (2010-14)*

39. Bubu Garcia, c, Gilroy (Calif.) HS.
40. *Zane Hemond, rhp, Montrose (Colo.) HS.

## ATLANTA BRAVES (21)

1. Lucas Sims, rhp, Brookwood HS, Snellville, Ga.—(AA)
2. **Alex Wood, lhp, University of Georgia.—(2013-15)**
3. Bryan De La Rosa, c, Bucky Dent Academy, Delray Beach, Fla.—(Low A)
4. Justin Black, of, Billings West HS, Billings, Mont.—(Low A)
5. Blake Brown, of, University of Missouri.—(High A)
6. Josh Elander, c, Texas Christian University.
7. David Starn, lhp, Kent State University.
8. Dave Peterson, rhp, College of Charleston.
9. Steven Schils, rhp, Florida Tech.
10. Mike Dodig, 3b, Columbia-Greene (N.Y.) CC.
11. *Levi Borders, c, Winter Haven (Fla.) HS.

DRAFT DROP *Son of Pat Borders, major leaguer (1988-2005)*

12. Connor Lien, of, Olympia HS, Orlando, Fla.
13. Nate Hyatt, rhp, Appalachian State University.
14. Tyler Tewell, c, Appalachian State University.
15. Alex Wilson, rhp, Wofford College.
16. Fernelys Sanchez, of, George Washington HS, New York City.
17. Chase Anselment, c-of, University of Washington.
18. Ross Heffley, 2b, Western Carolina University.
19. Levi Hyams, 2b, University of Georgia.
20. Eric Garcia, ss, University of Missouri.
21. Jeremy Fitzgerald, rhp, Tennessee Wesleyan College.
22. **Shae Simmons, rhp, Southeast Missouri State University.—(2014)**
23. Kevin McKague, rhp, University.S. Military Academy.
24. Mike Flores, rhp, Grossmont (Calif.) JC.
25. Brandon Rohde, lhp, Central Washington University.
26. Trenton Moses, 3b, Southeast Missouri State University.
27. Chris Barczycowski, rhp, Niagara County (N.Y.) CC.
28. K.C. Clabough, ss, Florida Tech
29. Jaden Dillon, rhp, Texas A&M University-Kingsville.
30. Casey Kalenkosky, 1b, Texas State University.
31. Matt Kimbrel, rhp, Southern Polytechnic State (Ga.) University.

DRAFT DROP *Brother of Craig Kimbrel, major leaguer (2010-15)*

32. *Adam Grantham, rhp, Kennett (Mo.) HS.
33. *Sam Gillikin, of, Hoover (Ala.) HS.
34. *Ben Johnson, of, Westwood HS, Austin, Texas.
35. *Matt Creech, ss, Colquitt County HS, Moultrie, Ga.
36. *Braden Bishop, of, St. Francis HS, Mountain View, Calif.
37. *Gio Brusa, of, St. Mary's HS, Stockton, Calif.
38. *Sean McLaughlin, rhp, Northview HS, Johns Creek, Ga.
39. *Cullen O'Dwyer, of, Eldorado HS, Albuquerque, N.M.
40. *Jimmy Herget, rhp, Jefferson HS, Tampa.

## BALTIMORE ORIOLES (4)

1. **Kevin Gausman, rhp, Louisiana State University.—(2013-15)**
2. Branden Kline, rhp, University of Virginia.—(AA)
3. Adrian Marin, ss, Gulliver Prep, Miami.—(High A)
4. **Christian Walker, 1b, University of South Carolina.—(2014-15)**
5. *Colin Poche, lhp, Marcus HS, Flower Mound, Texas.

DRAFT DROP *Attended Arkansas; never re-drafted*

6. Lex Rutledge, lhp, Samford University.
7. Matt Price, rhp, University of South Carolina.
8. Torsten Boss, 3b, Michigan State University.
9. Brady Wager, rhp, Grand Canyon University.
10. Joel Hutter, ss, Dallas Baptist University.
11. Kevin Grendell, lhp, San Pasqual HS, Escondido, Calif.
12. *Billy Waltrip, lhp, Seminole State (Okla.) JC.
13. *Wade Wass, c, Meridian (Miss.) CC.
14. Sean McAdams, rhp, Cardinal Mooney HS, Sarasota, Fla.
15. *Derick Velasquez, rhp, Merced (Calif.) JC.
16. Luc Rennie, rhp, Torrey Pines HS, San Diego.
17. Nick Grim, rhp, Cal Poly.
18. Sam Kimmel, c, Stetson University.
19. Josh Hader, lhp, Old Mill HS, Millersville, Md.
20. *Ryan Ripken, 1b, Gilman School, Baltimore.

DRAFT DROP *Grandson of Cal Ripken, major league manager, (1987-88) • Son of Cal Ripken Jr., major leaguer (1981-2001) • Nephew of Billy Ripken, major leaguer (1987-98)*

21. *Julian Service, of, Sinclair SS, Whitby, Ontario.
22. Will Howard, of, Kennesaw State University.
23. Gene Escat, rhp, Fresno State University.
24. Tommy Richards, 2b, Washington State University.
25. Creede Simpson, 2b, Auburn University.
26. Lucas Herbst, of, Santa Clara University.
27. Anthony Caronia, ss, University of Tampa.
28. Dennis Torres, rhp, University of Massachusetts.
29. Jake Pintar, rhp, San Juan Hill HS, Cota de Coza, Calif.
30. Anthony Vega, of, Manhattan College.
31. *Anthony Bazzani, rhp, Eastern Kentucky University.
32. Steel Russell, c, Midland (Texas) JC.

DRAFT DROP *Son of John Russell, first-round draft pick, Phillies (1982); major leaguer (1984-93); major league manager (2008-10)*

33. *Colton Plaia, c, Loyola Marymount University.
34. *Johnny Sewald, of, Bishop Gorman HS, Las Vegas, Nev.
35. Duke Porter, lhp, Miami.
36. *Peter Irvin, lhp, Skagit Valley (Wash.) CC.
37. Derrick Bleeker, of-rhp, University of Arkansas.
38. Jack Graham, c, Kenyon (Ohio) College.
39. Scott Kalush, c, UC Davis.
40. Ray Hunnicutt, of, Central HS, Hampshire, Ill.

## BOSTON RED SOX (23)

1. **Deven Marrero, ss, Arizona State University.—(2015)**
1. **Brian Johnson, lhp, University of Florida** (Choice from Phillies for loss of Type A free agent Jonathan Papelbon).**—(2015)**
1. Pat Light, rhp, Monmouth University (Supplemental choice—37th—for loss of Papelbon).—(AAA)
2. Jamie Callahan, rhp, Dillon (S.C.) HS.—(Low A)
3. Austin Maddox, rhp, University of Florida.—(High A)
4. Ty Buttrey, rhp, Providence HS, Charlotte, N.C.—(High A)
5. Mike Augliera, rhp, Binghamton University.—(AA)
6. Justin Haley, rhp, Fresno State University.
7. Kyle Kraus, rhp, University of Portland.
8. Nathan Minnich, 1b, Shepherd (W.Va.) College.
9. Mike Miller, ss, Cal Poly.
10. J.T. Watkins, c, U.S. Military Academy.
11. *Jamal Martin, of, William T. Dwyer HS, West Palm Beach, Fla.
12. Mike Meyers, ss, Silverado HS, Las Vegas, Nev.
13. J.B. Wendelken, rhp, Middle Georgia JC.
14. Dylan Chavez, lhp, University of Mississippi.
15. *Carson Fulmer, rhp, All Saints Academy, Winter Haven, Fla.

DRAFT DROP *First-round draft pick (8th overall), White Sox (2015)*

16. Stephen Williams, rhp, Seminole State (Okla.) JC.
17. Willie Ethington, rhp, Mountain View HS, Mesa, Ariz.
18. Shaq Thompson, of, Grant Union HS, Sacramento, Calif.

DRAFT DROP *First-round draft pick, Carolina Panthers, National Football League (2015); linebacker, NFL (2015)*

19. Iseha Conklin, ss, Iowa Western CC.
20. Greg Larson, rhp, University of Florida.
21. Jake Davies, 1b, Georgia Tech.

DRAFT DROP *Brother of Kyle Davies, major leaguer (2005-15)*

22. *Joe Greenfield, rhp, South Suburban (Ill.) JC.
23. Brandon Magee, of, Arizona State University.

DRAFT DROP *Linebacker, National Football League (2013-14)*

24. Keaton Briscoe, 2b, University of British Columbia.
25. *Khiry Cooper, of, University of Nebraska.
26. *Jake Nelson, rhp, Lake Stevens (Wash.) HS.
27. *Quinn Carpenter, rhp, Goshen Central HS, Goshen, N.Y.
28. *Wes Rogers, of, J.L. Mann HS, Greenville, S.C.
29. *Alex Bregman, 2b, Albuquerque (N.M.) Academy.

DRAFT DROP *First-round draft pick (2nd overall), Astros (2015)*

30. *Justin Taylor, rhp, Farmville Central HS, Farmville, N.C.
31. *Austin Davis, rhp, University of Southern Mississippi.
32. *Hunter Wood, rhp, Rogers Heritage HS, Rogers, Ark.
33. *Chris Carlson, of, Orange Coast (Calif.) CC.
34. *Xavier Turner, 3b, Sandusky (Ohio) HS.
35. *Pat Delano, rhp, Braintree (Mass.) HS.
36. Miguel Rodriguez, c, UNC Charlotte.
37. *Jonathan Dziedzic, lhp, Lamar University.
38. *Donald Smith, c, Claflin (S.C.) University.
39. *Kurt Schluter, rhp, Stetson University.
40. Kevin Heller, of, Amherst (Mass.) College.

## CHICAGO CUBS (6)

1. Albert Almora, of, Mater Academy, Hialeah Gardens, Fla.—(AA)
1. Pierce Johnson, rhp, Missouri State University (Supplemental choice—43rd—for loss of Type B free agent Aramis Ramirez).—(AA)
1. Paul Blackburn, rhp, Heritage HS, Brentwood, Calif. (Supplemental choice—56th—for loss of Type B free agent Carlos Pena).—(High A)
2. Duane Underwood, rhp, Pope HS, Marietta, Ga.—(High A)
3. Ryan McNeil, rhp, Nipomo (Calif.) HS.—(Low A)
4. Josh Conway, rhp, Coastal Carolina University.—(High A)
5. Anthony Prieto, lhp, Americas HS, El Paso, Texas.—(Rookie)
6. Trey Lang, rhp, GateWay (Ariz.) CC.
7. Stephen Bruno, 2b, University of Virginia.
8. Michael Heesch, lhp, University of South Carolina-Beaufort.
9. Chadd Krist, c, University of California.
10. Chad Martin, rhp, Indiana University.
11. Rashad Crawford, of, Mundy's Mill HS, Jonesboro, Ga.
12. Justin Amlung, rhp, University of Louisville.
13. Bijan Rademacher, of, Orange Coast (Calif.) CC.
14. Corbin Hoffner, rhp, St. Petersburg (Fla.) JC.
15. Carlos Escobar, c, University of Nevada.
16. Mike Hamann, rhp, University of Toledo.
17. Nathan Dorris, lhp, Southern Illinois University.
18. David Bote, ss, Neosho County (Kan.) CC.
19. *Damek Tomscha, 3b, Iowa Western CC.
20. *Blake Hickman, c/rhp, Simeon HS, Chicago.
21. Steve Perakslis, rhp, University of Maine.
22. Eddie Orozco, rhp, UC Riverside.
23. *Jake Drossner, lhp, Council Rock North HS, Newton, Pa.
24. *Jameson Fisher, c, Zachary (La.) HS.
25. *Rhett Wiseman, of, Buckingham Browne & Nichols HS, Cambridge, Mass.
26. Jasvir Rakkar, rhp, Stony Brook University.
27. Tyler Bremer, rhp, Baylor University.
28. Lance Rymel, c, Rogers State (Okla.) College.
29. *Austin Pentecost, rhp, Lewis-Clark State (Idaho) College.
30. Izaac Garsez, of, College of Idaho.
31. *Bryan Bonnell, rhp, Centennial HS, Las Vegas, Nev.
32. Tim Saunders, ss, Marietta (Ohio) College.
33. *Tom Pannone, of, Bishop Hendricken HS, Warwick, R.I.
34. *Christian Botnick, rhp, Notre Dame SS, Brampton, Ontario.
35. Ben Carhart, 3b, Stetson University.
36. *Sly Edwards, of, St. Brendan HS, Miami.
37. *Clayton Crum, rhp, Howard (Texas) JC.
38. *Hassan Evans, rhp, Herkimer County (N.Y.) CC.
39. *Rustin Sveum, 3b, Desert Mountain HS, Scottsdale, Ariz.

DRAFT DROP *Son of Dale Sveum, first-round draft pick, Brewers (1982); major leaguer (1986-99); major league manager (2008-13)*

40. Jacob Rogers, 1b, Mount Olive (N.C.) College.

## CHICAGO WHITE SOX (13)

1. Courtney Hawkins, of, Mary Carroll HS, Corpus Christi, Texas.—(AA)
1. Keon Barnum, 1b, King HS, Tampa (Supplemental choice—48th—for loss of Type B free agent Mark Buehrle).—(High A)
2. **Chris Beck, rhp, Georgia Southern University.—(2015)**
3. Joey DeMichele, 2b, Arizona State University.—(AA)
4. Brandon Brennan, rhp, Orange Coast (Calif.) CC.—(High A)
5. Nick Basto, ss, Archbishop McCarthy HS, Southwest Ranches, Fla.—(High A)
6. Kyle Hansen, rhp, St. John's University.

DRAFT DROP *Brother of Craig Hansen, first-round draft pick, Red Sox (2005); major leaguer (2005-09)*

7. Jose Barraza, c, Sunnyside HS, Fresno, Calif.
8. Zach Isler, rhp, University of Cincinnati.
9. **Micah Johnson, 2b, Indiana University.—(2015)**

10. Brandon Hardin, rhp, Delta State (Miss.) University.
11. Eric Jaffe, rhp, UCLA.
12. Zach Stoner, 1b, Boylan Catholic HS, Rockford, Ill.
13. *Derek Thompson, lhp, John A. Logan (Ill.) CC.
14. Tony Bucciferro, rhp, Michigan State University.
15. Jordan Guerrero, lhp, Moorpark (Calif.) HS.
16. Abe Ruiz, 1b, Arizona State University.
17. Sammy Ayala, c, La Jolla (Calif.) Country Day HS.
18. Thomas McCarthy, 3b, University of Kentucky.
19. Alex Williams, 1b, Louisiana Tech.
20. Zach Voight, ss, New Mexico State University.
21. Adam Lopez, rhp, Virginia Military Institute.
22. Cory McGinnis, rhp, Auburn University-Montgomery (Ala.).
23. Kale Kiser, of, University of Nebraska.
24. Eric Grabe, 2b, University of Tampa.
25. Storm Throne, rhp, Morningside (Iowa) College.
26. Zach Toney, lhp, Austin Peay State University.
27. Zac Fisher, c, New Mexico State University.
28. James Hudelson, rhp, Delta State (Miss.) University.
29. Jason Coats, of, Texas Christian University.
30. Jake Brown, ss, Kansas State University.
31. Corey Thompson, 3b, East Carolina University.
32. Steve Nikorak, 3b, Temple University.
33. *Jon Savarise, lhp, Stevenson HS, Lincolnshire, Ill.
34. *Ryan Castellanos, rhp, Archbishop McCarthy HS, Southwest Ranches, Fla.
DRAFT DROP *Brother of Nick Castellanos, first-round draft pick, Tigers (2010); major leaguer (2013-15)*
35. *Kyle Martin, rhp, Texas A&M University.
36. *Mitch Patishall, rhp, Pendleton Heights HS, Pendleton, Ind.
37. Thurman Hall, of, Western Texas CC.
38. *DeJohn Suber, ss, Morgan Park HS, Chicago.
39. Mitch Glasser, 2b, Macalester (Minn.) College.
40. *Sam Mason, rhp, Beverly Hills (Calif.) HS.

## CINCINNATI REDS (14)

1. Nick Travieso, rhp, Archbishop McCarthy HS, Southwest Ranches, Fla.—(High A)
1. Jesse Winker, of, Olympia HS, Orlando, Fla. (Supplemental choice—49th—for loss of Type B free agent Ramon Hernandez).—(AA)
1. Jeff Gelalich, of, UCLA (Supplemental choice—57th—for loss of Type B free agent Francisco Cordero).—(High A)
2. Tanner Rahier, ss, Palm Desert (Calif.) HS.—(Low A)
3. Dan Langfield, rhp, Memphis University.—(Low A)
4. **Jon Moscot, rhp, Pepperdine University.—(2015)**
5. Mason Felt, lhp, Hebron Christian Academy, Dacula, Ga.—(Rookie)
6. Joe Hudson, c, University of Notre Dame.
7. Beau Amaral, of, UCLA.
DRAFT DROP *Son of Rich Amaral, major leaguer (1991-2000)*
8. Seth Mejias-Brean, 3b, University of Arizona.
9. Daniel Pigott, of, University of Florida.
10. Jeremy Kivel, rhp, Spring (Texas) HS.
11. Nolan Becker, lhp, Yale University.
12. Brent Peterson, ss, Bakersfield (Calif.) JC.
13. ***Matt Boyd, lhp, Oregon State University.—(2015)**
14. Luke Moran, rhp, Grayson County (Texas) CC.
15. Ben Klimesh, rhp, Trinity (Texas) University.
16. Nick Routt, lhp, Mississippi State University.
17. Jose Ortiz, c, Colon HS, Comerio, P.R.
18. Jackson Stephens, rhp/3b, Oxford (Ala.) HS.
19. Austin Muehring, rhp, Palomar (Calif.) CC.
20. *Brock Dykxhoorn, rhp, St. Anne's SS, Clinton, Ontario.
21. Jordan Remer, lhp, University of San Francisco.
22. Avain Rachal, rhp, Cy-Fair HS, Cypress, Texas.
23. *Daniel Sweet, of, Northwest Rankin HS, Brandon, Miss.
24. Mike Saunders, rhp, Saginaw Valley State (Mich.) University.
25. Sean Lucas, lhp, University of Albany.
26. *Chase Rezac, rhp, Southern Utah University.
27. Joey Housey, rhp, University of Oregon.
28. Mo Wiley, rhp, University of Houston.
29. Adam Matthews, of, University of South Carolina.
30. *Kyle Wren, of, Georgia Tech.
DRAFT DROP *Son of Frank Wren, general manager, Orioles (1998-99); general manager, Braves (2007-14)*
31. Austin Salter, rhp, Cisco (Texas) JC.
32. *Christian McElroy, rhp, University of Cincinnati.
33. *Justin Topa, rhp, Long Island University.
34. Richard McCaffrey, lhp, UC Santa Barbara.
35. *Mike Sheppard, rhp, Seton Hall Prep, West Orange, N.J.
36. *Jarvis Flowers, 2b, Cy-Ranch HS, Cypress, Texas.
37. Zach Vincej, ss, Pepperdine University.
38. *Daniel Poncedeleon, rhp, Cypress (Calif.) JC.
39. *Jacob Stone, rhp, Weatherford (Texas) JC.
40. *Rafael Pineda, rhp, Texas A&M University.

## CLEVELAND INDIANS (15)

1. Tyler Naquin, of, Texas A&M University.—(AAA)
2. Mitch Brown, rhp, Century HS, Rochester, Minn.—(High A)
3. Kieran Lovegrove, rhp, Mission Viejo (Calif.) HS.—(Short-season A)
4. D'vone McClure, of, Jacksonville (Ark.) HS.—(Short-season A)
5. Dylan Baker, rhp, Western Nevada CC.—(High A)
6. Joey Wendle, 2b, West Chester (Pa.) University.
7. Josh Schubert-McAdams, of, Calhoun (Ga.) HS.
8. Caleb Hamrick, rhp, Cedar Hill (Texas) HS.
9. Jacob Lee, rhp, Arkansas State University.
10. Josh Martin, rhp, Samford University.
11. Logan Vick, of, Baylor University.
12. Jeremy Lucas, c, Indiana State University.
13. Tyler Booth, of, Central Arizona JC.
14. Michael Peoples, rhp, Western Oklahoma State JC.
15. Nellie Rodriguez, 1b, George Washington HS, New York City.
16. Cody Penny, rhp, University of North Carolina.
17. *Andrew Calica, of, Eastlake HS, Chula Vista, Calif.
18. Louis Head, rhp, Texas State University.
19. *Colyn O'Connell, rhp, Dunedin (Fla.) HS.
20. Nick Pasquale, rhp, Diablo Valley (Calif.) JC.
21. Joe Sever, 2b, Pepperdine University.
22. Jim Stokes, rhp, Elon University.
23. Richard Stock, c/1b, University of Nebraska.
24. Walker White, rhp, South Georgia JC.
25. *Cameron Cox, rhp, Weatherford (Texas) JC.
26. *Justin Garza, rhp, Bonita HS, La Verne, Calif.
27. *Ray Castillo, rhp, Russell County HS, Seale, Ala.
28. *Josh Pigg, 3b/rhp, Franklin HS, Elk Grove, Calif.
29. *Randall Fant, lhp, University of Arkansas.
30. *Josh Lester, ss, Columbus (Ga.) HS.
31. *Danny Holst, of, Parkway South HS, Manchester, Mo.
32. *Paul Hendrix, ss, Howard (Texas) JC.
33. *Cory Raley, ss, Uvalde (Texas) HS.
34. *Matt Fultz, c, Lee's Summit (Mo.) West HS.
35. Nick Hamilton, ss, Kent State University.
36. Benny Suarez, rhp, Hill (Texas) JC.
37. *Jacob Morris, of-c, University of Arkansas.
38. Joshua Nervis, rhp, Sonoma State (Calif.) University.
39. D.J. Brown, rhp, James Madison University.
40. *Anthony Hawkins, of, Fresno (Calif.) HS.

## COLORADO ROCKIES (10)

1. David Dahl, of, Oak Mountain HS, Birmingham, Ala.—(AA)
1. **Eddie Butler, rhp, Radford University** (Supplemental choice—46th—for loss of Type B free agent Mark Ellis).**—(2014-15)**
2. Max White, of, Williston (Fla.) HS.—(Low A)
3. **Tom Murphy, c, University of Buffalo.—(2015)**
3. Ryan Warner, rhp, Pine Creek HS, Colorado Springs, Colo. (Special compensation choice—128th—for failure to sign 2011 third-round pick Peter O'Brien).—(Short-season A)
4. Seth Willoughby, rhp, Xavier University.—(Low A)
5. Matt Wessinger, ss, St. John's University.—(High A)
6. Matt Carasiti, rhp, St. John's University.
7. Wilfredo Rodriguez, c, Puerto Rico Baseball Academy, Gurabo, P.R.
8. Derek Jones, of, Washington State University.
9. Zach Jemiola, rhp, Great Oak HS, Temecula, Calif.
10. Ben Waldrip, 1b, Jacksonville State University.
11. T.J. Oakes, rhp, University of Minnesota.
12. Correlle Prime, 1b, Manatee HS, Bradenton, Fla.
13. Kyle Von Tungeln, of, Texas Christian University.
14. Shane Broyles, rhp, Texas Tech.
15. **Scott Oberg, rhp, University of Connecticut.—(2015)**
16. Jeff Popick, of, Colorado Mesa University.
17. Jason Stolz, 2b, Clemson University.
18. *Aaron Jones, c, University of Oregon.
19. Kyle Newton, 3b, Florida Atlantic University.
20. Anthony Seise, lhp, West Orange HS, Winter Garden, Fla.
21. Rayan Gonzalez, rhp, Bethune-Cookman College.
22. Jordan Mejia, rhp, Riverside (Calif.) CC.
23. Andrew Brown, rhp, University of Akron.
24. Mike Mason, lhp, Marshall University.
25. Alec Mehrten, ss, Fresno Pacific University.
26. Adam Paulencu, rhp, Embry-Riddle (Fla.) University.
27. Matt Flemer, rhp, University of California.
28. Ryan Arrowood, rhp, Appalachian State University.
29. Pat Hutcheson, 2b, Fresno State University.
30. Trent Blank, rhp, Baylor University.
31. Shawn Stuart, rhp, Long Beach State University.
32. *A.J. Simcox, ss, Farragut HS, Knoxville, Tenn.
33. Ryan Garvey, of, Riverside (Calif.) CC.
DRAFT DROP *Son of Steve Garvey, major leaguer (1969-87)*
34. Chris Cowell, c, University of Richmond.
35. *Justin Solomon, 2b, Piedra Vista HS, Farmington, N.M.
36. *Kevin Bradley, ss, Hopewell Valley Central HS, Pennington, N.J.
DRAFT DROP *Son of Scott Bradley, major leaguer (1984-92); baseball coach, Princeton (1998-2015)*
37. *Casey Burns, 3b, Grand Junction (Colo.) HS.
38. *Dansby Swanson, ss, Marietta (Ga.) HS.
DRAFT DROP *First overall draft pick, Diamondbacks (2015)*
39. *Justin Dillon, rhp, El Dorado HS, Placentia, Calif.
40. *Brandon Montalvo, c, Langham Creek HS, Houston.

## DETROIT TIGERS (26)

1. (Choice to Brewers as compensation for Type A free agent Prince Fielder)
2. Jake Thompson, rhp, Rockwall-Heath HS, Heath, Texas.—(AA)
3. Austin Schotts, ss, Centennial HS, Frisco, Texas.—(High A)
4. **Drew VerHagen, rhp, Vanderbilt University.—(2014-15)**
5. Joe Rogers, lhp, University of Central Florida.—(AA)
6. Jordan John, lhp, University of Oklahoma.
7. Hudson Randall, rhp, University of Florida.
8. Jeff McVaney, of-lhp, Texas State University.
9. Jake Stewart, of, Stanford University.
10. Charlie Gillies, rhp, The Master's (Calif.) College.
11. Bennett Pickar, c, Oral Roberts University.
12. Julio Felix, rhp, Pima (Ariz.) CC.
13. **Devon Travis, 2b, Florida State University.—(2015)**
14. Hunter Scantling, rhp, Florida State University.
15. Jordan Dean, ss, Central Michigan University.
16. Josh Turley, lhp, Baylor University.
17. Slade Smith, rhp, Auburn University.
18. *Dylan Lavelle, 3b, Lake Stevens (Wash.) HS.
19. Will Clinard, rhp, Vanderbilt University.
20. Logan Ehlers, lhp, Howard (Texas) JC.
21. Alex Phillips, lhp, University of Kentucky.
22. D.J. Driggers, of, Middle Georgia JC.
23. Drew Harrison, rhp, University of Oklahoma.
24. Nick Carmichael, rhp, Palomar (Calif.) JC.
25. Jared Reaves, ss, University of Alabama.
26. Rashad Brown, of, Westlake HS, Atlanta.
27. Miguel Paulino, of, Choctawhatchee HS, Fort Walton Beach, Fla.
28. Josh Carr, rhp, Kennesaw State University.
29. Zach Kirksey, of, University of Mississippi.
30. Preston Jamison, lhp, South Mountain (Ariz.) CC.
31. *Connor Harrell, of, Vanderbilt University.
32. *Blake McFadden, rhp, Savannah (Mo.) HS.
33. Tyler Hanover, 2b, Louisiana State University.
34. Matt Davenport, rhp, College of William & Mary.
35. Jacob Kapstein, c, Tiverton (R.I.) HS.
36. *Clate Schmidt, rhp, Allatoona HS, Acworth, Ga.
37. Charlie Neil, c, Yale University.
38. *Alex Minter, lhp, Brook Hill HS, Bullard, Texas
39. *John Sansone, ss, Neshannock HS, New Castle, Pa.
40. Ryan Longstreth, lhp, Central Michigan University.

## HOUSTON ASTROS (1)

1. **Carlos Correa, ss, Puerto Rico Baseball Academy, Gurabo, P.R.—(2015)**
1. **Lance McCullers Jr., rhp, Jesuit HS, Tampa** (Supplemental choice—41st—for loss of Type B free agent Clint Barmes).**—(2015)**
DRAFT DROP *Son of Lance McCullers, major leaguer (1985-92)*
2. Nolan Fontana, ss, University of Florida.—(AA)
DRAFT DROP *Grandson of Lew Burdette, major leaguer (1950-67)*
3. Brady Rodgers, rhp, Arizona State University.—(AAA)
4. Rio Ruiz, 3b, Bishop Amat HS, La Puente, Calif.—(AA)
5. Andrew Aplin, of, Arizona State University.—(AAA)
6. Brett Phillips, of, Seminole (Fla.) HS.
7. **Preston Tucker, of, University of Florida.—(2015)**
DRAFT DROP *Brother of Kyle Tucker, first-round draft pick, Astros (2015)*
8. Tyler Heineman, c, UCLA.
9. Daniel Minor, rhp, Texas A&M University-Corpus Christi.
10. Joe Bircher, lhp, Bradley University.
11. *Hunter Virant, lhp, Camarillo (Calif.) HS.
12. Terrell Joyce, of, Florida CC-Jacksonville.
13. Brian Holmes, lhp, Wake Forest University.
14. Joe Sclafani, ss, Dartmouth University.
15. Erick Gonzalez, rhp, GateWay (Ariz.) CC.
16. Dan Gulbransen, of, Jacksonville University.
17. Aaron West, rhp, University of Washington.
18. Ricky Gingras, c, Point Loma Nazarene (Calif.) University.
19. Austin Elkins, 2b, Dallas Baptist University.
20. *Michael Clark, lhp, Kent State University.
21. Marc Wik, of, Chabot (Calif.) JC.
22. Kenny Long, lhp, Illinois State University.
23. Travis Ballew, rhp, Texas State University.
24. *Pat Blair, ss, Wake Forest University.
25. Ryan Dineen, ss, Eastern Illinois University.
26. *C.J. Hinojosa, ss, Klein Collins HS, Spring, Texas.
27. *Tanner Mathis, of, University of Mississippi.
28. Angel Ibanez, 3b, University of Texas-Pan American.
29. Christian Garcia, rhp, Florence-Darlington (S.C.) JC.
30. John Neely, rhp, Texas Tech.
31. M.P. Cokinos, c, St. Mary's (Texas) University.
32. *Tyler Manez, lhp, Plainedge HS, North Massapequa, N.Y.
33. Mike Hauschild, rhp, University of Dayton.
34. Jordan Jankowski, rhp, Catawba (N.C.) College.
35. *Jimmy Sinatro, c, Skyline HS, Sammamish, Wash.
DRAFT DROP *Son of Matt Sinatro, major leaguer (1981-92)*
36. Mike Martinez, 3b, Florida International University.
37. Michael Dimock, rhp, Wake Forest University.
38. *Zach Remillard, 3b, LaSalle Institute, Troy, N.Y.
39. *Mitchell Traver, rhp, Houston Christian HS, Houston.
40. *Joe Shaw, rhp, Ennis (Texas) HS.

## KANSAS CITY ROYALS (5)

1. Kyle Zimmer, rhp, University of San Francisco.—(AA)
DRAFT DROP *Brother of Bradley Zimmer, first-round draft pick, Indians (2014)*
2. Sam Selman, lhp, Vanderbilt University.—(AAA)

3. Colin Rodgers, lhp, Parkview Baptist HS, Baton Rouge, La.—(Low A)
4. Kenny Diekroeger, 2b, Stanford University.—(AAA)
5. Chad Johnson, c, Galesburg (Ill.) HS.—(Low A)
6. Zach Lovvorn, rhp, Oxford (Ala.) HS.
7. Fred Ford, of, Jefferson (Mo.) CC.
8. Alfredo Escalera, of, Pendleton School, Bradenton, Fla.
9. Daniel Stumpf, lhp, San Jacinto (Texas) JC.
10. Alexis Rivera, of-1b, Montverde Academy, Kissimmee, Fla.
11. Zeb Sneed, rhp, Northwest Nazarene (Idaho) University.
12. *Jackson Willeford, 2b, Ramona (Calif.) HS.
13. Hunter Haynes, lhp, Mexico (Mo.) HS.
14. Parker Morin, c, University of Utah.
15. Dylan Sons, lhp, Halifax County HS, South Boston, Va.
16. Austin Fairchild, lhp, St. Thomas HS, Houston.
17. Ariel Estades, of, Puerto Rico Baseball Academy, Gurabo, P.R.
18. *Justin Alleman, rhp, Holt (Mich.) HS.
19. Andrew Triggs, rhp, University of Southern California.
20. Shane Halley, of, University of Virginia.
21. Matt Strahm, lhp, Neosho County (Kan.) CC.
22. Alec Mills, rhp, University of Tennessee-Martin.
23. Kevin Allen, rhp, Texas Christian University.
24. Beau Maggi, c, Arizona State University.
25. Matt Tenuta, lhp, Apex (N.C.) HS.
26. Mark Donato, 1b, Indian River (Fla.) JC.
27. Ashton Goudeau, rhp, Maple Woods (Mo.) CC.
28. Sam Bates, 1b, University of Arkansas.
29. John Walter, rhp, Penn State University.
30. Ethan Chapman, of, Cal State San Bernardino.
31. *Hayden Edwards, rhp, Blue Valley HS, Stilwell, Kan.
32. Patrick Conroy, lhp, CC of Marin (Calif.).
33. *Evan Phillips, rhp, Clayton (N.C.) HS.
34. Marsalis Holloway, of, Columbia State (Tenn.) CC.
35. *Tyler Joyner, lhp, East Carolina University.
36. *Raphael Andrades, of, Lincoln HS, Tallahassee, Fla.
37. Jake Newberry, rhp, Mira Mesa HS, San Diego.
38. *Carlos Urena, of, Whitehall (Pa.) HS.
39. *Justin Leeson, of, Georgetown University.
40. *Taylor Kaczmarek, rhp, South Mountain (Ariz.) CC.

## LOS ANGELES ANGELS (19)

1. (Choice to Cardinals as compensation for Type A free agent Albert Pujols)
2. (Choice to Rangers as compensation for Type A free agent C.J. Wilson)
3. **R.J. Alvarez, rhp, Florida Atlantic University.—(2014-15)**
4. Alex Yarbrough, 2b, University of Mississippi.—(AAA)
5. Mark Sappington, rhp, Rockhurst (Mo.) University.—(AA)
6. Eric Stamets, ss, University of Evansville.
7. Chase Patterson, c, Mary Montgomery HS, Semmes, Ala.
8. Austin Adams, rhp, University of South Florida.
9. **Michael Roth, lhp, University of South Carolina.—(2013-14)**
10. Chris O'Grady, lhp, George Mason University.
11. Jonathan Walsh, c, University of Texas.
12. Zach Wright, c, East Carolina University.
13. **Mike Morin, rhp, University of North Carolina.—(2014-15)**
14. Sherman Johnson, 3b, Florida State University.
15. Reid Scoggins, rhp, Howard (Texas) JC.
16. Kody Eaves, 2b, Pasadena Memorial HS, Pasadena, Texas.
17. Yency Almonte, rhp, Christopher Columbus HS, Miami.
18. Ryan Dalton, 3b, University of Texas-San Antonio.
19. Aaron Newcomb, rhp, Delta State (Miss.) University.
20. Quinten Davis, of, McLennan (Texas) CC.
21. Pat Lowery, rhp, Columbia University.
22. Anthony Bemboom, c, Creighton University.
23. Mike Snyder, 3b, Florida Southern College.

DRAFT DROP *Son of Brian Snyder, major leaguer (1985-89) • Brother of Brandon Snyder, first-round draft pick, Orioles (2005); major leaguer (2010-13) • Twin brother of Matt Snyder, 10th-round draft pick, Yankees (2012)*

24. Garrett Bush, rhp, Flagler (Fla.) College.
25. Kyle Johnson, of, Washington State University.
26. Tyler DeLoach, lhp, UNC Wilmington.
27. Wade Hinkle, 1b, Kansas State University.
28. Joel Capote, of, St. Thomas (Fla.) University.
29. Caleb Bushyhead, ss, University of Oklahoma.
30. Nic DellaTorre, lhp, St. John's River (Fla.) JC.
31. *Jeff Kemp, ss, Radford University.
32. Robbie Powell, rhp, Stetson University.
33. Sam Mulroy, c, Princeton University.
34. Zac Livingston, c, Arizona Christian University.
35. Pedro Pizarro, c, Byrd HS, Shreveport, La.
36. Kenny Hatcher, rhp, Dallas Baptist University.

DRAFT DROP *Nephew of Mickey Hatcher, major leaguer (1979-90)*

37. Matt Collins, rhp, University of Central Florida.
38. Jake Boyd, rhp, Stetson University.
39. *Justin Morhardt, c, Gilbert School, Winsted, Conn.

DRAFT DROP *Grandson of Moe Morhardt, major leaguer (1961-62)*

40. Blake Amaral, of, Hawaii Pacific University.

## LOS ANGELES DODGERS (18)

1. **Corey Seager, 3b, Northwest Cabarrus HS, Concord, N.C.—(2015)**

DRAFT DROP *Brother of Kyle Seager, major leaguer (2011-15)*

1. Jesmuel Valentin, 2b, Puerto Rico Baseball Academy, Gurabo, P.R. (Supplemental choice—51st—for loss of Type B free agent Rod Barajas).—(High A)

DRAFT DROP *Son of Jose Valentin, major leaguer (1992-2007)*

2. **Paco Rodriguez, lhp, University of Florida.—(2012-15)**

DRAFT DROP *First player from 2012 draft to reach majors (Sept. 9, 2012)*

3. **Onelki Garcia, lhp, Los Angeles.—(2013)**
4. Justin Chigbogu, 1b, Raytown South HS, Raytown, Mo.—(Low A)
5. Ross Stripling, rhp, Texas A&M University.—(AA)
6. Joey Curletta, 1b-rhp, Mountain Pointe HS, Phoenix.
7. Theo Alexander, of, Lake Washington HS, Kirkland, Wash.
8. Scott Griggs, rhp, UCLA.
9. Zach Bird, rhp, Murrah HS, Jackson, Miss.
10. Zach Babitt, 2b, Academy of Art (Calif.) University.

DRAFT DROP *Son of Shooty Babitt, major leaguer (1981)*

11. Jeremy Rathjen, of, Rice University.
12. James Campbell, rhp, Stony Brook University.
13. **Darnell Sweeney, ss, University of Central Florida.—(2015)**
14. Matthew Reckling, rhp, Rice University.
15. Duke von Schamann, rhp, Texas Tech.

DRAFT DROP *Son of Uwe von Schamann, place kicker, National Football League (1979-84)*

16. Josh Henderson, of, First Baptist Christian HS, Suffolk, Va.
17. *Kevin Maxey, of, Poly HS, Long Beach, Calif.
18. Eric Smith, c, Stanford University.
19. Owen Jones, rhp, University of Portland.
20. Jharel Cotton, rhp, East Carolina University.
21. Jacob Scavuzzo, of, Villa Park (Calif.) HS.
22. Alan Garcia, rhp, Azusa Pacific (Calif.) University.
23. Lindsey Caughel, rhp, Stetson University.
24. Paul Hoenecke, 1b, University of Wisconsin-Milwaukee.
25. **Danny Coulombe, lhp, Texas Tech.—(2014-15)**
26. *Jordan Parr, 1b, University of Illinois.
27. *Justin Gonzalez, ss, Florida State University.
28. Jake Hermsen, lhp, Northern Illinois University.
29. John Cannon, c, University of Houston.
30. *Trent Giambrone, ss, King HS, Metairie, La.
31. *David Graybill, rhp, Brophy Prep, Phoenix.
32. Alfredo Unzue, lhp, Los Angeles.
33. *C.J. Saylor, c, South Hills HS, West Covina, Calif.
34. Jordan Hershiser, rhp, University of Southern California.

DRAFT DROP *Son of Orel Hershiser, major leaguer (1983-2000)*

35. Austin Cowen, c, Western Illinois University.
36. *Jose Vizcaino, 3b, Francis Parker HS, San Diego.

DRAFT DROP *Son of Jose Vizcaino, major leaguer (1989-2006)*

37. John Sgromolo, 1b, Flagler (Fla.) College.
38. Corey Embree, of, Maple Woods (Mo.) CC.
39. *Korey Dunbar, c, Nitro (W.Va.) HS.
40. Pat Stover, of, Santa Clara University.

## MIAMI MARLINS (9)

1. **Andrew Heaney, lhp, Oklahoma State University.—(2014-15)**
2. (Choice to Mets as compensation for Type A free agent Jose Reyes)
3. Avery Romero, 3b, Menendez HS, St. Augustine, Fla.—(High A)
3. Kolby Copeland, of, Parkway HS, Bossier City, La. (Special compensation choice—127th—for failure to sign 2011 third-round pick Connor Barron).—(Short-season A)
4. Austin Dean, 2b, Klein Collins HS, Spring, Texas.—(High A)
5. Austin Nola, ss, Louisiana State University.—(AAA)

DRAFT DROP *Brother of Aaron Nola, first-round draft pick, Phillies (2014); major leaguer (2015)*

6. Anthony Gomez, ss, Vanderbilt University.
7. Ryan Newell, rhp, Shorter (Ga.) University.
8. Drew Steckenrider, rhp, University of Tennessee.
9. Nick Wittgren, rhp, Purdue University.
10. Ron Miller, 1b, Junipero Serra HS, Gardena, Calif.
11. Matt Milroy, rhp, University of Illinois.
12. Christian Rivera, ss, Nueva Superior Vocacional HS, Loiza, P.R.
13. Blake Logan, rhp, Eastern Oklahoma State JC.
14. Michael Vaughn, c, Fresno Pacific University.
15. Cody Keefer, of, UCLA.
16. **Brian Ellington, rhp, University of West Florida.—(2015)**
17. *Bubba Keene, of, Brookhaven (Miss.) Academy.
18. Patrick Merkling, lhp, Lee (Tenn.) University.
19. *Cody Gunter, 3b, Flower Mound (Texas) HS.
20. *Jordan Hillyer, rhp, Hebron Christian Academy, Dacula, Ga.
21. Hayden Fox, lhp, Oakland University.
22. Robert Ravago, rhp, Arizona State University.
23. Cameron Flynn, of, University of Kentucky.
24. Matt Juengel, 3b, Texas A&M University.
25. Dane Stone, rhp, St. Thomas (Fla.) University.
26. *Seth Grant, rhp, Appalachian State University.
27. Justin Jackson, rhp, Sam Houston State University.
28. Casey McCarthy, rhp, Cal State San Bernardino.
29. Blake Barnes, rhp, Oklahoma State University.
30. David Cruz, c, Miami.
31. *Lucas Hunter, ss, Central Catholic HS, Portland, Ore.

DRAFT DROP *Son of Brian L. Hunter, major leaguer (1994-2003)*

32. *Ty Williams, rhp, Sulphur (Okla.) HS.
33. *Steve Weber, rhp, Eastern Michigan University.
34. Patrick Claussen, 3b, Washington State University.
35. *Chad Christensen, of, University of Nebraska.
36. ***Kendall Graveman, rhp, Mississippi State University.—(2014-15)**
37. Eddie Sappelt, of, Southern Alamance HS, Graham, N.C.

DRAFT DROP *Brother of Dave Sappelt, major leaguer (2011-13)*

38. Chipper Smith, lhp, Cumberland (Tenn.) University.
39. *Marcus Greene, c, Vista Del Lago HS, Moreno Valley, Calif.
40. *Alex Polston, ss, Carl Albert HS, Midwest City, Okla.

## MILWAUKEE BREWERS (27)

1. Clint Coulter, c, Union HS, Camas, Wash. (Choice from Tigers for loss of Type A free agent Prince Fielder).—(High A)
1. Victor Roache, of, Georgia Southern University.—(AA)
1. Mitch Haniger, of, Cal Poly (Supplemental choice—38th—for loss of Fielder).—(AA)
2. Tyrone Taylor, of, Torrance (Calif.) HS.—(AA)
3. Zach Quintana, rhp, Arbor View HS, Las Vegas, Nev.—(Low A)
4. **Tyler Wagner, rhp, University of Utah.—(2015)**
5. Damien Magnifico, rhp, University of Oklahoma.—(AA)
6. Angel Ortega, ss, International Baseball Academy, Ceiba, P.R.
7. David Otterman, lhp, University of British Columbia.
8. Edgardo Rivera, of, Inzarry de Puig HS, Toa Baja, P.R.
9. Alex Lavandero, rhp, Belen Jesuit Prep, Miami.
10. Anthony Banda, lhp, San Jacinto (Texas) JC.
11. Preston Gainey, rhp, U.S. Naval Academy.
12. Eric Semmelhack, rhp, University of Wisconsin-Milwaukee.
13. Alan Sharkey, 1b, Coral Springs (Fla.) HS.
14. Ryan Gibbard, rhp, Lynn (Fla.) University.
15. ***Buck Farmer, rhp, Georgia Tech.—(2014-15)**
16. Adam Giacalone, 1b, Neosho County (Kan.) CC.
17. Alfredo Rodriguez, ss, University of Maryland.
18. *Hunter Adkins, rhp, Middle Tennessee State University.
19. *Carlos Garmendia, 3b, Monsignor Pace HS, Miami.
20. Mike Garza, ss, Georgetown University.
21. Austin Blaski, rhp, Marietta (Ohio) College.
22. Taylor Wall, lhp, Rice University.
23. Paul Eshleman, c, Cal State San Bernardino.
24. Michael Turay, c, Cal State Stanislaus.
25. Lance Roenicke, of, UC Santa Barbara.

DRAFT DROP *Son of Ron Roenicke, major leaguer (1981-88); major league manager (2011-15) • Nephew of Gary Roenicke, first-round draft pick, Expos (1973); major leaguer (1976-88)*

26. *Mark McCoy, lhp, Barnegat (N.J.) HS.
27. *Tyler Duffie, rhp, Texas Christian University.
28. Martin Viramontes, rhp, University of Southern California.
29. *Bryan Saucedo, 1b, Vaughan Road Academy, Toronto.
30. Jono Armold, lhp, Flagler (Fla.) College.
31. Brent Suter, lhp, Harvard University.
32. *Nick Anderson, rhp, Mayville State (N.D.) University.
33. Austin Hall, rhp, Brigham Young University.
34. *Tommy Burns, rhp, Don Bosco Prep, Ramsey, N.J.
35. Jose Sermo, ss, Bethany (Kan.) College.
36. *Alex Mangano, c, Southwest Miami HS, Miami.
37. Taylor Smith-Brennan, ss, Edmonds (Wash.) CC.
38. *Chris Shaw, c, Trinity Academy, Okotoks, Alberta.
39. *Derek Jones, of, St. Marguerite d'Youville SS, Brampton, Ontario.
40. *Chucky Vazquez, c, American Senior HS, Miami.

## MINNESOTA TWINS (2)

1. **Byron Buxton, of, Appling County HS, Baxley, Ga.—(2015)**
1. Jose Berrios, rhp, Papa Juan XXIII HS, Bayamon, P.R. (Supplemental chicoie—32nd—for loss of modified Type A free agent Michael Cuddyer).—(AAA)
1. Luke Bard, rhp, Georgia Tech (Supplemental choice—42nd—for loss of Type B free agent Jason Kubel).—(High A)

DRAFT DROP *Brother of Daniel Bard, first-round draft pick, Red Sox (2006); major leaguer (2009-13)*

2. Mason Melotakis, lhp, Northwestern State University.—(AA)
2. J.T. Chargois, rhp, Rice University (Supplemental choice—72nd—for loss of Cuddyer).—(AA)
3. Adam Brett Walker, 1b, Jacksonville University.—(AA)
4. Zack Jones, rhp, San Jose State University.—(AA)
5. **Tyler Duffey, rhp, Rice University.—(2015)**
6. Andre Martinez, lhp, Archbishop McCarthy HS, Southwest Ranches, Fla.
7. Jorge Fernandez, c, International Baseball Academy, Ceiba, P.R.
8. Christian Powell, rhp, College of Charleston.
9. *L.J. Mazzilli Jr., 2b, University of Connecticut.

DRAFT DROP *Son of Lee Mazzilli, first-round draft pick, Mets (1973); major leaguer (1976-89); major league manager (2004-05)*
10. D.J. Baxendale, rhp, University of Arkansas.
11. Taylor Rogers, lhp, University of Kentucky.
12. Alex Muren, rhp, Cal State Northridge.
13. *Erich Knab, rhp, Carolina Forest HS, Myrtle Beach, S.C.
14. Jake Proctor, of, University of Cincinnati.
15. *Jarret Leverett, lhp, Georgia Southern U,
16. Will Hurt, ss, Lexington Catholic HS, Lexington, Ky.
17. D.J. Hicks, 1b, University of Central Florida.
18. *Will LaMarche, rhp, Chabot (Calif.) JC.
19. Jonathan Murphy, of, Jacksonville University.
DRAFT DROP *Brother of Daniel Murphy, major leaguer (2008-15)*
20. Zach Larson, of, Lakewood Ranch HS, Bradenton, Fla.
21. Bo Altobelli, c, Texas Tech.
22. *Josh Graham, c, Roseburg (Ore.) HS.
23. Travis Huber, rhp, University of Nebraska.
24. *Jose Favela, c, Franklin HS, El Paso, Texas.
25. Joel Licon, ss, Orange Coast (Calif.) CC.
26. *Justin Jones, lhp, University of California.
27. *Jerad Grundy, lhp, University of Kentucky.
28. Carson Goldsmith, rhp, Northwestern State University.
29. *Sean Hagan, lhp, St. John's University.
30. Bryan Santy, c, University of Washington.
31. *Timmy Robinson, of, Ocean View HS, Huntington Beach, Calif.
32. Andrew Ferreira, lhp, Harvard University.
33. Kaleb Merck, rhp, Texas Christian University.
34. Bryan Haar, of, University of San Diego.
35. *Jared Wilson, rhp, UC Santa Barbara.
36. *Brandon Bayardi, of, University of Nevada-Las Vegas.
37. *James Marvel, rhp, Campolindo HS, Moraga, Calif.
38. *Austin Rel, c, Campolindo HS, Moraga, Calif.
39. *Alex Liquori, of, Whitewater HS, Fayetteville, Ga.
40. *Brad Schreiber, rhp, Purdue University.

## NEW YORK METS (12)

1. Gavin Cecchini, ss, Alfred M. Barbe HS, Lake Charles, La.—(AA)
DRAFT DROP *Brother of Garin Cecchini, major leaguer (2014-15)*
**1. Kevin Plawecki, c, Purdue University** (Supplemental choice—35th—for loss of Type A free agent Jose Reyes).**—(2015)**
2. Matt Reynolds, 3b, University of Arkansas (Choice from Marlins for loss of Reyes).—(AAA)
2. *Teddy Stankiewicz, rhp, Fort Worth Christian HS, North Richland Hills, Texas.—(High A)
DRAFT DROP *Attended Seminole State (Okla.) JC; re-drafted by Red Sox, 2013 (2nd round)*
3. Matt Koch, rhp, University of Louisville.—(AA)
4. Branden Kaupe, ss, Baldwin HS, Wailuku, Hawaii.—(Short-season A)
5. Brandon Welch, rhp, Palm Beach State (Fla.) JC.—(Short-season A)
6. Jayce Boyd, 1b, Florida State University.
7. Corey Oswalt, rhp, James Madison HS, San Diego.
8. Tomas Nido, c, Orangewood Christian HS, Maitland, Fla.
9. Richie Rodriguez, 2b, Eastern Kentucky University.
10. Paul Sewald, rhp, University of San Diego.
11. Logan Taylor, rhp, Eastern Oklahoma State JC.
12. Rob Whalen, rhp, Haines City (Fla.) HS.
13. Matt Bowman, rhp, Princeton University.
14. Chris Flexen, rhp, Newark Memorial HS, Newark, Calif.
15. *Nick Grant, rhp, Milford (Del.) HS.
16. *Myles Smith, rhp, Miami-Dade JC.
17. Stefan Sabol, c, Orange Coast (Calif.) CC.
18. *Paul Paez, lhp, Rio Hondo (Calif.) CC.
19. Tyler Vanderheiden, rhp, Samford University.
20. Tim Peterson, rhp, University of Kentucky.
21. *Gary Ward, lhp, Bethel (Tenn.) University.
DRAFT DROP *Son of Gary Ward, major leaguer (1979-90)*
22. *Tejay Antone, rhp, Legacy HS, Mansfield, Texas.
23. *Connor Baits, rhp, Point Loma HS, San Diego.
24. Andrew Massie, rhp, Dyer County (Tenn.) HS.
25. *Leon Byrd, ss, Cypress Ranch HS, Cypress, Texas.
26. *Chris Shaw, 1b, Lexington (Mass.) HS.
DRAFT DROP *First-round draft pick (31st overall), Giants (2015)*
27. *Zach Arnold, c, Franklin County HS, Frankfort, Ky.
28. *Jake Marks, rhp, St. Clair SS, Sarnia, Ontario.
29. *Austin Barr, c, Camas (Wash.) HS.
30. *Dustin Cook, rhp, Hargrave HS, Huffman, Texas.
31. *Vance Vizcaino, ss, Wakefield HS, Raleigh, N.C.
32. Jon Leroux, 1b, Northeastern University.
33. *Jared Price, rhp, Twin Valley HS, Elverson, Pa.
34. *Mikey White, of, Spain Park HS, Hoover, Ala.
35. *Brad Markey, rhp, Santa Fe (Fla.) JC.
36. *Donnie Walton, ss, Bishop Kelley HS, Tulsa, Okla.
37. *Benny Distefano, c, Lawrence E. Elkins HS, Missouri City, Texas.
DRAFT DROP *Son of Benny Distefano, major leaguer (1984-92)*
38. Jeff Reynolds, 3b, Harvard University.
39. *Patrick Ervin, 2b, Pace (Fla.) HS.
40. *David Gonzalez, rhp, Gainesville (Ga.) HS.

## NEW YORK YANKEES (29)

1. Ty Hensley, rhp, Edmond Santa Fe HS, Edmond, Okla.—(Short-season A)
2. Austin Aune, of, Argyle (Texas) HS (Special compensation choice—89th—for failure to sign 2011 second-round pick Sam Stafford).—(Low A)
**2. Peter O'Brien, c, University of Miami.—(2015)**
3. Nathan Mikolas, 1b, Bradford HS, Kenosha, Wis.—(Short-season A)
4. Corey Black, rhp, Faulkner (Ala.) University.—(AA)
**5. Rob Refsnyder, 2b, University of Arizona.—(2015)**
**6. Nick Goody, rhp, Louisiana State University.—(2015)**
7. Taylor Garrison, rhp, Fresno State University.
8. Taylor Dugas, of, University of Alabama.
9. Derek Varnadore, rhp, Auburn University.
10. Matt Snyder, 1b, University of Mississippi.
DRAFT DROP *Son of Brian Snyder, major leaguer (1985-89) • Brother of Brandon Snyder, first-round draft pick, Orioles (2005); major leaguer (2010-13) • Twin brother of Mike Snyder, 23rd-round draft pick, Angels (2012)*
11. Caleb Frare, lhp, Custer County HS, Miles City, Mont.
12. Chris Breen, c, Winter Springs (Fla.) HS.
**13. James Pazos, lhp, University of San Diego.—(2015)**
14. Andrew Benak, rhp, Rice University.
15. Dayton Dawe, rhp, A.B. Lucas SS, London, Ontario.
16. Stefan Lopez, rhp, Southeastern Louisiana University.
17. Tim Flight, lhp, Southern New Hampshire University.
18. Brady Lail, rhp, Bingham HS, South Jordan, Utah.
19. Dietrich Enns, lhp, Central Michigan University.
20. *Mikey Reynolds, ss, Texas A&M University.
21. *Jimmy Reed, lhp, University of Maryland.
22. *Bret Marks, rhp, Wallace State (Ala.) CC.
23. *Vincent Jackson, of, Luella HS, McDonough, Ga.
24. Jose Mesa Jr., rhp, Charles W. Flanagan HS, Pembroke Pines, Fla.
DRAFT DROP *Son of Jose Mesa, major leaguer (1987-2007)*
25. *Ty Moore, of, Mater Dei HS, Santa Ana, Calif.
26. Charlie Haslup, rhp, University of Maryland.
27. Danny Oh, of, University of California.
28. *D.J. Stewart, of, Bolles School, Jacksonville, Fla.
DRAFT DROP *First-round draft pick (25th overall), Orioles (2015)*
29. Jose Diaz, lhp, Advantage Learning Institute, Ponce, P.R.
30. *Raph Rhymes, of, Louisiana State University.
31. *Kevin Johnson, rhp, University of Illinois.
32. *Garrett Cannizaro, ss, Tulane University.
DRAFT DROP *Brother of Andy Cannizaro, major leaguer (2006-08)*
33. Saxon Butler, 1b/c, Samford University.
34. Eric Erickson, lhp, University of Miami.
35. *Kyle Farmer, ss, University of Georgia.
36. Dalton Smith, c, University City HS, San Diego.
37. Charles Basford, rhp, Samford University.
38. *David Thompson, of, Westminster Christian HS, Miami.
39. *Bo Decker, of, East Ridge HS, Clermont, Fla.
40. *Sherman Lacrus, of/c, Western Oklahoma State JC.

## OAKLAND ATHLETICS (11)

**1. Addison Russell, ss, Pace (Fla.) HS.—(2015)**
1. Daniel Robertson, 3b, Upland (Calif.) HS (Supplemental choice—34th—for loss of modified Type A free agent Josh Willingham).—(AA)
1. Matt Olson, 1b, Parkview HS, Lilburn, Ga. (Suppemental choice—47th—for loss of Type B free agent David DeJesus).—(AA)
2. Bruce Maxwell, c/1b, Birmingham-Southern College (Supplemental choice—62nd—for loss of Willingham).—(AA)
2. Nolan Sanburn, rhp, University of Arkansas.—(AA)
3. *Kyle Twomey, lhp, El Dorado HS, Placentia, Calif.
DRAFT DROP *Attended Southern California; re-drafted by Cubs, 13th round (2015)*
4. B.J. Boyd, of, Palo Alto (Calif.) HS.—(High A)
**5. Max Muncy, 1b, Baylor University.—(2015)**
6. Seth Streich, rhp, Ohio University.
7. Cody Kurz, rhp, Oxnard (Calif.) JC.
8. Kris Hall, rhp, Lee (Tenn.) University.
9. Dakota Bacus, rhp, Indiana State University.
10. Brett Vertigan, of, UC Santa Barbara.
11. *Matt Gonzalez, ss-c, Harrison HS, Kennesaw, Ga.
12. *John Caputo, 3b, Toronto.
13. Stuart Pudenz, rhp, Dallas Baptist University.
14. Austin House, rhp, University of New Mexico.
15. Vince Voiro, rhp, University of Pennsylvania.
16. Melvin Mercedes, ss, Central Florida CC.
**17. *Tyler Olson, lhp, Gonzaga University.—(2015)**
18. Derek De Young, rhp, Oakton (Ill.) CC.
19. Robert Martinez, of, Quinones Medina HS, Yabucoa, P.R.
20. Boog Powell, of, Orange Coast (Calif.) CC.
21. Tyler Hollstegge, rhp, UNC Greensboro.
22. Matt Hillsinger, of, Radford University.
23. Tucker Healy, rhp, Ithaca (N.Y.) College.
24. Kayvon Bahramzadeh, rhp, Kansas State University.
25. Derek Hansen, rhp/3b, Augustana (S.D.) College.
26. Lee Sosa, rhp, Binghamton University.
27. Ryan Mathews, of, North Carolina State University.
28. Phil Pohl, c, Clemson University.
29. Taylor Massey, lhp, Dallas Baptist University.
30. Chris Wolfe, ss, Grambling State University.
31. Ryan Gorton, c, Oregon State University.
**32. Ryan Dull, rhp, UNC Asheville.—(2015)**
33. Tyler Johnson, rhp, Stony Brook University.
34. *Devon Gradford, ss, Downey (Calif.) HS.
35. *Brett Sunde, c, Bishop Foley HS, Madison Heights, Mich.
36. *Conor Williams, rhp-of, Bingham HS, South Jordan, Utah.
37. John Wooten, 1b-of, East Carolina University.
38. *Calvin Drummond, rhp, University of San Diego.
39. *Dalton Blaser, of, Roseville (Calif.) HS.
40. *David Olmedo-Barrera, ss, St. Francis HS, Mountain View, Calif.

## PHILADELPHIA PHILLIES (30)

1. (Choice to Red Sox as compensation for Type A free agent Jonathan Papelbon)
1. Shane Watson, rhp, Lakewood (Calif.) HS (Supplemental choice—40th—for loss of modified Type A free agent Ryan Madson).—(Low A)
1. Mitch Gueller, rhp, West HS, Chehalis, Wash. (Supplemental choice—54th—for loss of Type B free agent Raul Ibanez).—(Short-season A)
2. Dylan Cozens, of, Chaparral HS, Scottsdale, Ariz. (Supplemental choice—77th—for loss of Madson).—(AA)
2. *Alec Rash, rhp, Adel DeSoto Minburn HS, Adel, Iowa.
DRAFT DROP *Attended Missouri; re-drafted by Nationals, 23rd round (2015)*
3. Zach Green, 3b, Jesuit HS, Sacramento, Calif.—(High A)
4. Chris Serritella, 1b, Southern Illinois University.—(AA)
5. Andrew Pullin, of, Centralia (Wash.) HS.—(High A)
6. Cam Perkins, 3b, Purdue University.
7. Hoby Milner, lhp, University of Texas.
DRAFT DROP *Son of Brian Milner, major leaguer (1978)*
8. Josh Ludy, c, Baylor University.
9. Jordan Guth, rhp, University of Wisconsin-Milwaukee.
10. Kevin Brady, rhp, Clemson University.
11. Willie Carmona, 1b, Stony Brook University.
12. Zach Taylor, of, Armstrong Atlantic State (Ga.) University.
13. Steven Golden, of, San Lorenzo (Calif.) HS.
14. Ricky Bielski, rhp, Servite HS, Anaheim, Calif.
15. Zach Cooper, rhp, Central Michigan University.
16. Nic Hanson, rhp, Golden West (Calif.) JC.
17. *David Hill, rhp, El Modena HS, Orange, Calif.
18. *Tony Blanford, rhp, Boulder Creek HS, Phoenix.
19. Tim Carver, ss, University of Arkansas.
20. Matt Sisto, rhp, University of Hawaii.
21. Drew Anderson, rhp, Galena HS, Reno, Nev.
22. Jeb Stefan, rhp, Louisiana Tech.
23. Geoff Broussard, rhp, Cal Poly Pomona.
24. Chad Carman, c, Oklahoma City University.
25. *Brennan Henry, lhp, Northeastern (Colo.) JC.
26. *Evan Van Hoosier, 2b, Green Valley HS, Henderson, Nev.
27. *Fernando Fernandez, lhp, Edouard Montpetit HS, Montreal.
28. *Joe Mantiply, lhp, Virginia Tech.
29. *Brad Wieck, lhp, Frank Phillips (Texas) JC.
30. *Jordan Kipper, rhp, Central Arizona JC.
31. Chris Nichols, rhp, University of Sioux Falls (S.D.).
DRAFT DROP *Son of Rod Nichols, major leaguer (1988-95)*
32. *Scott Firth, rhp, Clemson University.
33. *Kyle Cody, rhp, Chippewa Falls (Wis.) HS.
34. *Darrell Miller Jr., c, Servite HS, Anaheim, Calif.
DRAFT DROP *Son of Darrell Miller, major leaguer (1984-88); nephew of Cheryl Miller/Reggie Miller, both members of Basketball Hall of Fame*
35. *Steven Wilson, rhp, Dakota Ridge HS, Littleton, Colo.
36. *Charles Galiano, c, Commack (N.Y.) HS.
37. *Daniel Starwalt, rhp, Granite Hills HS, El Cajon, Calif.
38. *Geordy Smith, 1b, Highlands Ranch (Colo.) HS.
39. *Austin Norris, rhp, Trenton (Mo.) HS.
40. *Eric Hanhold, rhp, East Lake HS, Palm Harbor, Fla.

## PITTSBURGH PIRATES (8)

1. *Mark Appel, rhp, Stanford University.—(AAA)
DRAFT DROP *Returned to Stanford; re-drafted by Astros, 2013 (1st overall)*
1. Barrett Barnes, of, Texas Tech (Supplemental choice—45th—for loss of Type B free agent Ryan Doumit).—(AA)
2. Wyatt Mathisen, c, Calallen HS, Corpus Christi, Texas.—(High A)
3. Jon Sandfort, rhp, Winter Springs (Fla.) HS.—(Rookie)
4. *Brandon Thomas, of, Georgia Tech.—(High A)
DRAFT DROP *Returned to Georgia Tech; re-drafted by Yankees, 2013 (8th round)*
5. Adrian Sampson, rhp, Bellevue (Wash.) CC.—(AAA)
6. Eric Wood, 3b, Blinn (Texas) JC.
7. Jacob Stallings, c, University of North Carolina.
DRAFT DROP *Son of Kevin Stallings, basketball coach, Vanderbilt (1999-2015)*
8. Kevin Ross, 3b, Niles West HS, Skokie, Ill.
9. D.J. Crumlich, ss, UC Irvine.
10. Pat Ludwig, rhp, Yale University.
11. Chris Diaz, ss, North Carolina State University.
12. Dalton Friend, lhp, Jefferson (Mo.) CC.
13. Tom Harlan, of/lhp, Fresno State University.
14. *Walker Buehler, rhp, Henry Clay HS, Lexington, Ky.
DRAFT DROP *First-round draft pick (24th overall), Dodgers (2015)*

15. *Jon Youngblood, of, Meridian (Miss.) CC.
16. Max Moroff, ss, Trinity Prep, Winter Park, Fla.
17. Hayden Hurst, rhp, Bolles School, Jacksonville University.
18. John Kuchno, rhp, Ohio State University.
19. *Michael Petersen, rhp, St. Francis HS, Mountain View, Calif.
20. Kyle Haynes, rhp, Virginia Commonwealth University.
21. Jordan Steranka, 3b, Penn State University.
22. *Taylor Hearn, lhp, Royse City (Texas) HS.
23. Lance Breedlove, rhp, Purdue University.
24. Tyler Gaffney, of, Stanford University.
DRAFT DROP *Sixth-round draft pick, Carolina Panthers/ National Footbal League (2014)*
25. Josh Smith, lhp, Wichita State University.
26. Jimmy Rider, ss, Kent State University.
27. *Jake Johansen, rhp, Dallas Baptist University.
28. *Tommy Mirabelli, 2b, St. Edward HS, Lakewood, Ohio.
29. *Jake Post, rhp, Chesterton (Ind.) HS.
30. *Chase McDowell, rhp, Rice University.
31. *Jack Moffit, rhp, Flower Mound (Texas) HS.
32. *Max Rossiter, c, Arizona State University.
33. *Carlos Leal, c, East Central (Miss.) CC.
34. *Ryan Rand, of, Langham Creek HS, Houston.
35. *Jackson McClelland, rhp, East Valley HS, Redlands, Calif.
36. *Brody Russell, 2b, Centennial HS, Bakersfield, Calif.
37. *Jacob Waguespack, rhp, Dutchtown HS, Geismar, La.
38. *Matt Pope, rhp, Science Hill HS, Johnson City, Tenn.
39. *Jared West, lhp, North DeSoto HS, Stonewall, La.
40. *Zarley Zalewski, of, Valley HS, New Kensington, Pa.

## ST. LOUIS CARDINALS (22)

1. **Michael Wacha, rhp, Texas A&M University** (Choice from Angels for loss of Type A free agent Albert Pujols).**—(2013-15)**
1. James Ramsey, of, Florida State University.—(AAA)
1. **Stephen Piscotty, of-3b, Stanford University** (Supplemental choice—36th—for loss of Pujols).**—(2015)**
1. Patrick Wisdom, 3b, St. Mary's (Calif.) College (Supplemental choice—52nd—for loss of Type B free agent Octavio Dotel).—(AA)
1. Steve Bean, c, Rockwall (Texas) HS (Supplemental choice—59th—for loss of Type B free agent Edwin Jackson).—(Low A)
2. Carson Kelly, 3b-rhp, Westview HS, Portland, Ore.—(High A)
3. **Tim Cooney, lhp, Wake Forest University.—(2015)**
4. Alex Mejia, ss, University of Arizona.—(AAA)
5. Cory Jones, rhp, JC of the Canyons (Calif.).—(High A)
6. Kurt Heyer, rhp, University of Arizona.
7. **Kyle Barraclough, rhp, St. Mary's (Calif.) College.—(2015)**
8. Yoenny Gonzalez, of, Central Florida CC.
9. Rowan Wick, c, Cypress (Calif.) JC.
10. Jacob Wilson, 2b, Memphis University.
11. *Trey Williams, 3b, Valencia (Calif.) HS.
DRAFT DROP *Son of Eddie Williams, first-round draft pick, Mets (1983); major leaguer (1986-98)*
12. Max Foody, lhp, Pendleton School, Bradenton, Fla.
13. Brett Wiley, ss, Jefferson (Mo.) CC.
14. Anthony Melchionda, ss, Boston College.
15. Bruce Caldwell, 2b, Spartanburg Methodist (S.C.) JC.
16. Joe Scanio, rhp, Northwestern State University.
17. Chris Perry, rhp, Methodist (N.C.) College.
18. Jeremy Schaffer, 1b, Tulane University.
19. Steven Gallardo, rhp, Long Beach (Calif.) CC.
20. Matt Young, of-rhp, Cal State Dominguez Hills.
21. Jacoby Almaraz, 1b, Angelina (Texas) JC.
22. *Casey Schroeder, c, Ottawa-Glandorf HS, Ottawa, Ohio
23. *Tate Matheny, of, Westminster Christian Academy, St. Louis.
DRAFT DROP *Son of Mike Matheny, major leaguer (1994-2006); major league manager (2012-15)*
24. Lee Stoppelman, lhp, Central Missouri University.
25. Dixon Llorens, rhp, Miami-Dade JC.
26. Steve Sabatino, lhp, University of Notre Dame.
27. Joey Cuda, rhp, Eckerd (Fla.) College.
28. *Dodson McPherson, of, Wingate (N.C.) University.
29. *Andy Hillis, rhp, Lee (Tenn.) University.
30. Kyle Helisek, lhp, Villanova University.
31. Joey Donofrio, rhp, University of California.
32. *Eduardo Oquendo, ss, Olney Central (Ill.) CC.
DRAFT DROP *Son of Jose Oquendo, major leaguer (1983-95)*
33. Ronnie Shaban, rhp, Virginia Tech.
34. *Mark Trentacosta, lhp, UC Irvine.
35. Ben O'Shea, lhp, University of Tampa.
36. *Alex Swim, c, Elon University.
37. *Derrick May, of, Tattnall School, Wilmington, Del.
DRAFT DROP *Grandson of Dave May, major leaguer (1967-78) • Son of Derrick May, first-round draft pick, Cubs (1986); major leaguer (1990-99)*
38. Javier Machuca, lhp, Turabo (P.R.) JC.
39. Mike Aldrete, rhp, San Jose State University.
DRAFT DROP *Son of Mike Aldrete, major leaguer (1986-96)*
40. *Ian Rice, c, Madison Academy, Huntsville, Ala.

## SAN DIEGO PADRES (7)

1. Max Fried, lhp, Harvard-Westlake HS, Studio City, Calif.—(Low A)
1. Zach Eflin, rhp, Hagerty HS, Oviedo, Fla. (Supplemental choice—33rd—for loss of modified Type A free agent Heath Bell).—(AA)
1. **Travis Jankowski, of, Stony Brook University** (Supplemental choice—44th—for loss of Type B free agent Aaron Harang).**—(2015)**
1. Walker Weickel, rhp, Olympia HS, Orlando, Fla. (Special compensation choice—55th—for faiure to sign 2011 supplemental first-round pick Brett Austin).—(High A)
2. Jeremy Baltz, of, St. John's University.—(High A)
2. Dane Phillips, c-1b, Oklahoma City University (Supplemental choice—70th—for loss of Bell).—(High A)
3. Fernando Perez, 3b, Central Arizona JC.—(High A)
4. Walker Lockett, rhp, Providence HS, Jacksonville, Fla.—(Low A)
5. Mallex Smith, of, Santa Fe (Fla.) JC.—(AAA)
6. Jalen Goree, 2b, Bibb County HS, Centreville, Ala.
7. Roman Madrid, rhp, University of Central Florida.
8. Brian Adams, of, University of Kentucky.
9. River Stevens, 2b, Allan Hancock (Calif.) JC.
10. Stephen Carmon, ss, University of South Carolina-Aiken.
11. Maxx Tissenbaum, 2b, Stony Brook University.
12. Drew Harrelson, lhp, Berrien County HS, Nashville, Ga.
13. Malcom Diaz, rhp, International Baseball Academy, Ceiba, P.R.
14. *Andrew Sopko, rhp, Loyola Sacred Heart HS, Missoula, Mont.
15. Cory Bostjancic, rhp, CC of Marin (Calif.).
16. Ronnie Richardson, of, University of Central Florida.
17. Joe Church, rhp, Marshall University.
18. Chris Burke, 3b, Iona University.
19. Christian Miller, lhp, Loganville (Ga.) HS.
20. Cam Stewart, rhp, Valley Christian HS, San Jose, Calif.
21. Matt Chabot, rhp, Riverside (Calif.) CC.
22. *Kevin McCanna, rhp, The Woodlands (Texas) HS.
23. Chris O'Dowd, c, Dartmouth University.
DRAFT DROP *Son of Dan O'Dowd, general manager, Rockies (1999-2014)*
24. Chris Nunn, lhp, Lipscomb University.
25. Corey Kimber, rhp, Dudley HS, Greensboro, N.C.
26. Brandon Alger, lhp, Indiana Tech.
27. Goose Kallunki, 1b, Utah Valley University.
28. Griffin Russell, lhp, Wichita Falls (Texas) HS.
29. Eric Charles, 2b, Purdue University.
30. *Jacob Robson, of, Vincent Massey SS, Windsor, Ontario.
31. Matt Shepherd, rhp, Tennessee Tech.
32. Alexi Colon, of, Tusculum (Tenn.) College.
33. Tony Wieber, rhp, Michigan State University.
34. Kyle Ottoson, lhp, Oklahoma State University.
35. Wynton Bernard, of, Niagara University.
36. *Mac Seibert, 2b, Tate HS, Cantonment, Fla.
37. Cristian Munoz, c, Hector Udraneta HS, Ceiba, P.R.
38. Adam Ford, ss, Trousdale County HS, Hartsville, Tenn.
39. Anthony Renteria, of, Cal State San Marcos.
DRAFT DROP *Son of Rich Renteria, first-round draft pick, Pirates (1980); major leaguer (1986-94); major league manager (2014)*
40. Terrance Owens, lhp, University of Toledo.

## SAN FRANCISCO GIANTS (20)

1. Chris Stratton, rhp, Mississippi State University.—(AAA)
2. Martin Agosta, rhp, St. Mary's (Calif.) College.—(High A)
3. **Mac Williamson, of, Wake Forest University.—(2015)**
4. Steven Okert, lhp, University of Oklahoma.—(AAA)
5. Ty Blach, lhp, Creighton University.—(AAA)
6. Stephen Johnson, rhp, St. Edward's (Texas) University.
7. E.J. Encinosa, rhp, University of Miami.
8. Joe Kurrasch, lhp, Penn State University.
9. Shilo McCall, of, Piedra Vista HS, Farmington, N.M.
10. **Trevor Brown, c, UCLA.—(2015)**
11. *Ryan Tella, of, Auburn University.
12. Jeremy Sy, ss, University of Louisiana-Monroe.
13. Ryan Jones, 2b, Michigan State University.
14. Tyler Hollick, of, Chandler-Gilbert (Ariz.) CC.
15. Leo Rojas, c, Miami-Dade JC.
16. Ian Gardeck, rhp, University of Alabama.
17. Chris Johnson, rhp, University of Portland.
18. **Matt Duffy, ss, Long Beach State University.—(2014-15)**
19. Randy Zeigler, lhp, University of Louisiana-Monroe.
20. Mitch Delfino, inf-rhp, University of California.
21. Ben Turner, c, University of Missouri.
22. Brennan Metzger, of, Long Beach State University.
23. Drew Leenhouts, lhp, Northeastern University.
24. Andrew Cain, of, UNC Wilmington.
25. Sam Eberle, 3b-c, Jacksonville State University.
26. Mason McVay, lhp, Florida International University.
27. Chris Fern, lhp, Union (Ky.) College.
28. Joey Rapp, 1b-of, University of Louisiana-Monroe.
29. Shayne Houck, of, Kutztown (Pa.) University.
30. *Michael Blanchard, of, Austin Peay State University.
31. Jason Forjet, rhp, Florida Gulf Coast University.
32. Chris Pickering, lhp, University of Rhode Island.
33. Brandon Farley, rhp, Arkansas State University.
34. Zak Edgington, lhp, UC Santa Barbara.
35. *Danny Grazzini, rhp, San Mateo (Calif.) JC.
36. *Clint Terry, lhp, San Mateo (Calif.) JC.
37. *Drew Jackson, ss, Miramonte HS, Orinda, Calif.
DRAFT DROP *Brother of Brett Jackson, first-round draft pick, Cubs (2009); major leaguer (2012-14)*
38. *Nolan Long, rhp, Waterford (Conn.) HS.
39. *Kevin Fagan, 2b, North Broward Prep, Coconut Creek, Fla.
40. *Tyler Ferguson, rhp, Clovis West HS, Clovis, Calif.

## SEATTLE MARINERS (3)

1. **Mike Zunino, c, University of Florida.—(2013-15)**
2. Joe DeCarlo, 3b, Garnet Valley HS, Glen Mills, Pa.—(Low A)
3. Edwin Diaz, rhp, Caguas (P.R.) Military Academy.—(AA)
3. Tyler Pike, lhp, Winter Haven (Fla.) HS (Special compensation choice—126th—for failure to sign 2011 third-round pick Kevin Cron).—(AA)
4. Patrick Kivlehan, 3b, Rutgers University.—(AAA)
5. **Chris Taylor, ss, University of Virginia.—(2014-15)**
6. Timmy Lopes, 2b, Edison HS, Huntington Beach, Calif.
7. Taylor Ard, 1b, Washington State University.
8. *Nick Halamandaris, 1b, Stevenson HS, Carmel, Calif.
9. Jamodrick McGruder, 2b, Texas Tech.
10. Grady Wood, rhp, Western Oregon University.
11. Kristian Brito, 1b, Quinones Medina HS, Yabucoa, P.R.
12. Mike Faulkner, of, Arkansas State University.
13. Blake Hauser, rhp, Virginia Commonwealth University.
14. Brock Hebert, ss, Southeastern Louisiana University.
15. Dario Pizzano, of, Columbia University.
16. **Dominic Leone, rhp, Clemson University.—(2014-15)**
17. Isaiah Yates, of, Clovis East HS, Clovis, Calif.
18. Jabari Henry, of, Florida International University.
19. Nate Koneski, lhp, College of the Holy Cross.
20. Steve Ewing, lhp, University of Miami.
21. Scott DeCecco, lhp, USC Upstate.
22. Gabrial Franca, ss, John W. North HS, Riverside, Calif.
23. Levi Dean, rhp, Tennessee Wesleyan College.
24. Matt Vedo, rhp, UC Santa Barbara.
25. Mark Bordonaro, rhp, Fairfield University.
26. Aaron Brooks, rhp, Edmonds (Wash.) CC.
27. Blake Holovach, lhp, University of Missouri.
28. Matt Brazis, rhp, Boston College.
29. Toby DeMello, c, St. Mary's (Calif.) College.
30. *Mike Yastrzemski, of, Vanderbilt University.
DRAFT DROP *Grandson of Carl Yastrzemski, major leaguer (1961-83)*
31. Rusty Shellhorn, lhp, Texas Tech.
32. Richard Palase, 2b, Lynchburg (Va.) College.
33. Logan Seifrit, rhp, Vauxhall (Alberta) Academy.
34. *Alex Ross, c, Bellevue (Wash.) CC.
35. *Tyler Krieger, ss, Northview HS, Johns Creek, Ga.
36. *Trey Wingenter, rhp, Bob Jones HS, Madison, Ala.
37. *Brett Lilek, lhp, Marion Catholic HS, Chicago Heights, Ill.
38. *Richie Martin, ss, Bloomingdale (Fla.) HS.
DRAFT DROP *First-round draft pick (20th overall), Athletics (2015)*
39. *Grayson Long, rhp, Barbers Hill HS, Mont Belvieu, Texas.
40. *James Kaprielian, rhp, Arnold O. Beckman HS, Irvine, Calif.
DRAFT DROP *First-round draft pick (16th overall), Yankees (2015)*

## TAMPA BAY RAYS (24)

1. **Richie Shaffer, 3b, Clemson University.—(2015)**
2. Spencer Edwards, of, Rockwall (Texas) HS.—(Low A)
3. Andrew Toles, of, Chipola (Fla.) JC.—(High A)
DRAFT DROP *Son of Alvin Toles, first-round draft pick, New Orleans Saints/National Football League (1985); linebacker, NFL (1985-88)*
4. Nolan Gannon, rhp, Santa Fe Christian HS, Solana Beach, Calif.—(Short-season A)
5. Bralin Jackson, of, Raytown South HS, Raytown, Mo.—(Low A)
6. Damion Carroll, rhp, King George (Va.) HS.
7. Marty Gantt, of, College of Charleston.
8. **Luke Maile, c-1b, University of Kentucky.—(2015)**
9. Joey Rickard, of, University of Arizona.
10. Sean Bierman, lhp, University of Tampa.
11. Clayton Henning, of, St. Thomas Aquinas HS, Overland Park, Kan.
12. Taylor Hawkins, c, Carl Albert HS, Midwest City, Okla.
13. Dylan Floro, rhp, Cal State Fullerton.
14. Chris Kirsch, lhp, Lackawanna (Pa.) JC.
15. Willie Gabay, rhp, Herkimer County (N.Y.) CC
16. Tommy Coyle, 2b, University of North Carolina.
17. Ryan Dunn, 3b, Oregon State University.
18. Kevin Brandt, lhp, East Carolina University.
19. Miguel Beltran, 1b, Oklahoma City University.
20. R.J. Davis, rhp, Sacramento State University.
21. Jon Weaver, rhp, Central Michigan University.
22. Willie Argo, of, University of Illinois.
23. Reid Redman, 3b, Texas Tech.

24. Daniel Duran, 3b, Cal State Los Angeles.
25. Jordan Harrison, lhp, University of Louisiana-Lafayette.
26. Jason Wilson, rhp, Western Oregon University.
27. Alex Keudell, rhp, University of Oregon.
28. Dayne Quist, lhp, UC Davis.
29. *Keaton Steele, rhp, Iowa Western CC.
30. Michael Williams, c, University of Kentucky.
31. *Taylor Ward, c, Shadow Hills HS, Indio, Calif.
DRAFT DROP *First-round draft pick (26th overall), Angels (2015)*
32. Ben Kline, ss, Embry-Riddle (Fla.) University.
33. Luke Goodgion, rhp, Lewis-Clark State (Idaho) College.
34. Ryan Garton, rhp, Florida Atlantic University.
35. Kris Carlson, rhp, Colorado Mesa College.
36. *Brett McAfee, ss, Panola (Texas) JC.
37. Rob Finneran, rhp, Bentley (Mass.) College.
38. Chad Nacapoy, c, Cal State Los Angeles.
39. Geoff Rowan, c, Northwestern University.
40. Nick Sawyer, rhp, Howard (Texas) JC.

## TEXAS RANGERS (28)

1. Lewis Brinson, of, Coral Springs (Fla.) HS.—(AAA)
1. **Joey Gallo, 3b-rhp, Bishop Gorman HS, Las Vegas** (Supplemental choice—39th—for loss of Type A free agent C.J. Wilson).**—(2015)**
1. Collin Wiles, rhp, Blue Valley West HS, Stilwell, Kan. (Supplemental choice—53rd—for loss of Type B free agent Darren Oliver).—(Low A)
2. Jamie Jarmon, of, Indian River HS, Dagsboro, Del. (Choice from Angels for loss of Wilson).—(High A)
2. Nick Williams, of, Ball HS, Galveston, Texas.—(AA)
3. Pat Cantwell, c, Stony Brook University.—(AAA)
4. **Alec Asher, rhp, Polk State (Fla.) JC.—(2015)**
5. Preston Beck, of, Texas-Arlington.—(AA)
6. Royce Bolinger, of, Gonzaga University.
7. Cam Schiller, 2b, Oral Roberts University.
8. Cody Kendall, rhp, Fresno State University.
9. John Niggli, rhp, Liberty University.
10. Casey Shiver, rhp, Southern Polytechnic State (Ga.) University.
11. Eric Brooks, rhp, McLennan (Texas) CC.
12. **Keone Kela, rhp, Everett (Wash.) CC.—(2015)**
13. Sam Stafford, lhp, University of Texas.
14. *Kwinton Smith, of, Dillon (S.C.) HS.
15. *Jameis Winston, of, Hueytown (Ala.) HS.
DRAFT DROP *Recipient, 2013 Heisman Trophy; first overall draft pick, Tampa Bay Buccaneers/National Football League (2015); quarterback, NFL (2015)*
16. JanLuis Castro, 2b, Colegio Hector Urdaneta, Rio Grande, P.R.
17. Chuck Moorman, c, El Capitan HS, Lakeside, Calif.
18. Ryan Harvey, rhp, Seton Hall University.
19. Tyler Smith, rhp, USC Sumter JC.
20. Josh McElwee, rhp, Newberry (S.C.) College.
21. *Jake Lemoine, rhp, Bridge City (Texas) HS.
22. *Travis Dean, rhp, Kennesaw State University.
23. Coby Cowgill, rhp, Virginia Military Institute.
24. *Chase Mullins, lhp, Bourbon County HS, Paris, Ky.
25. Gabriel Roa, ss, Wabash Valley (Ill.) CC.
26. Austen Thrailkill, lhp, St. Petersburg (Fla.) JC.
27. Ryan Bores, rhp, Kent State University.
28. Joe Burns, lhp, Samford University.
29. Brandon Kuter, rhp, George Mason University.
30. Barrett Serrato, of, Purdue University.
31. Zach Brill, lhp, Mark Morris HS, Longview, Wash.
32. *Alex Young, lhp, Carmel Catholic HS, Mundelein, Ill.
33. *Ryan Burr, rhp, Highlands Ranch (Colo.) HS.
34. David Lyon, c, Kent State University.
35. *Brad Stone, lhp, Ardrey Kell HS, Charlotte, N.C.
36. *Sterling Wynn, lhp, China Spring HS, Waco, Texas.
37. *Matt Withrow, rhp, Midland Christian HS, Midland, Texas.
DRAFT DROP *Brother of Chris Withrow, first-round draft pick, Dodgers (2007); major leaguer (2013-14)*
38. *Zack Fields, 1b, Annapolis (Mich.) HS.
39. *Tevin Johnson, of, Henry County HS, McDonough, Ga.
40. Paul Schwendel, rhp, Emory (Ga.) University.

## TORONTO BLUE JAYS (17)

1. D.J. Davis, of, Stone HS, Wiggins, Miss.–(Low A)
1. **Marcus Stroman, rhp, Duke University** (Special compensation choice—22nd—for failure to sign 2011 first-round pick Tyler Beede).**—(2014-15)**
1. Matt Smoral, lhp, Solon (Ohio) HS (Supplemental choice—50th—for loss of Type B free agent Frank Francisco).—(High A)
1. Mitch Nay, 3b, Hamilton HS, Chandler, Ariz. (Supplemental choice—58th—for loss of Type B free agent Jon Rauch).—(High A)
DRAFT DROP *Grandson of Lou Klimchock, major leaguer (1958-70)*
1. Tyler Gonzales, rhp, James Madison HS, San Antonio, Texas (Supplemental choice—60th—for loss of Type B free agent Jose Molina).—(Rookie)
2. Chase DeJong, rhp, Woodrow Wilson HS, Long Beach, Calif.—(High A)
3. Anthony Alford, of, Petal (Miss.) HS.—(High A)
4. Tucker Donahue, rhp, Stetson University.—(Low A)
5. Brad Delatte, lhp, Nicholls State University.—(Short-season A)
6. Eric Phillips, 2b, Georgia Southern University.
7. Ian Parmley, of, Liberty University.
8. Tucker Frawley, c, Coastal Carolina University.
9. Jordan Leyland, 1b, Azusa Pacific (Calif.) University.
10. Alex Azor, of, U.S. Naval Academy.
11. *Grant Heyman, of, Pittsford Sutherland HS, Pittsford, N.Y.
12. *Ryan Kellogg, lhp, Henry Street HS, Whitby, Ontario.
13. John Silviano, c, Summit Christian School, West Palm Beach, Fla.
14. Zak Wasilewski, lhp, Tazewell (Va.) HS.
15. Ryan Borucki, lhp, Mundelein (Ill.) HS.
16. Will Dupont, 2b, Lafayette HS, Wildwood, Mo.
17. Shane Dawson, lhp, Lethbridge (Alberta) JC.
18. Alonzo Gonzalez, lhp, Glendale (Calif.) CC.
19. Jorge Flores, ss, Central Arizona JC.
20. D.J. Jones, of, Hillsborough (Fla.) CC.
21. Colton Turner, lhp, Texas State University.
22. Josh Almonte, of, Long Island City (N.Y.) HS.
23. Trey Pascazi, ss, East Rochester (N.Y.) HS.
24. *Matt Rose, rhp, Palm Bay (Fla.) HS.
25. Jason Leblebijian, ss, Bradley University.
26. Nathan DeSouza, of, Drury HS, Milton, Ontario.
27. *Daniel Zamora, lhp, Bishop Amat HS, La Puente, Calif.
28. Dan Klein, c, Kansas State University.
29. *Cole Irvin, lhp, Servite HS, Anaheim, Calif.
30. *Devin Pearson, of, Carmel (Calif.) HS.
31. Derrick Chung, ss, Sacramento State University.
32. Jorge Saez, c, Lee (Tenn.) University.
33. *Jonathan Harris, rhp, Hazelwood Central HS, Florissant, Mo.
DRAFT DROP *First-round draft pick (29th overall), Blue Jays (2015)*
34. *Brandon Lopez, ss, American Heritage HS, Plantation, Fla.
35. Devyn Rivera, rhp, California Baptist University.
36. *Brian Cruz, ss, Galveston (Texas) JC.
37. Daniel Devonshire, 1b, Colby (Kan.) CC.
38. *Nick Lovullo, ss, Newbury Park HS, Thousand Oaks, Calif.
DRAFT DROP *Son of Torey Lovullo, major leaguer (1988-99); major league manager (2015)*
39. Shaun Valeriote, 3b, Brock (Ontario) University.
40. *Jose Cuas, ss, Grand Street Campus HS, Brooklyn, N.Y.

## WASHINGTON NATIONALS (16)

1. Lucas Giolito, rhp, Harvard-Westlake HS, Studio City, Calif.—(AA)
2. Tony Renda, 2b, University of California.—(AA)
3. Brett Mooneyham, lhp, Stanford University.—(High A)
DRAFT DROP *Son of Bill Mooneyham, major leaguer (1986)*
4. Brandon Miller, of, Samford University.—(High A)
5. Spencer Kieboom, c, Clemson University.—(High A)
6. Hayden Jennings, of, Evangel Christian Academy, Shreveport, La.
7. Robert Benincasa, rhp, Florida State University.
8. Stephen Perez, ss, University of Miami.
9. Derek Self, rhp, University of Louisville.
10. Craig Manuel, c, Rice University.
11. Brian Rauh, rhp, Chapman (Calif.) College.
12. Carlos Lopez, 1b, Wake Forest University.
13. Elliott Waterman, lhp, University of San Francisco.
14. Jordan Poole, rhp, Chipola (Fla.) JC.
15. *Brandon Smith, of, Woodbridge HS, Irvine, Calif.
16. Ronald Pena, rhp, Palm Beach State (Fla.) CC.
17. Blake Schwartz, rhp, Oklahoma City University.
18. David Fischer, rhp, University of Connecticut.
19. Bryan Lippincott, 3b, Concordia (Minn.) University.
20. James Brooks, ss, University of Utah.
21. Austin Chubb, c, Florida Southern College.
22. Will Hudgins, rhp, University of Notre Dame.
23. Casey Selsor, lhp, University of Texas-San Antonio.
24. Austin Dicharry, rhp, University of Texas.
25. *Freddy Avis, rhp, Menlo School, Atherton, Calif.
26. *Skye Bolt, of, Holy Innocents Episcopal HS, Atlanta.
27. *Cody Poteet, rhp, Christian HS, El Cajon, Calif.
28. Hunter Bailey, ss, Oklahoma State University.
29. L.J. Hollins, rhp, Chipola (Fla.) JC.
30. R.C. Orlan, lhp, University of North Carolina.
31. Mike Boyden, rhp, University of Maryland.
32. Mike Mudron, lhp, Cal State San Bernardino.
33. Mike McQuillan, 2b, University of Iowa.
34. *Jake Jefferies, 2b, Foothill HS, Santa Ana, Calif.
DRAFT DROP *Son of Gregg Jefferies, first-round draft pick, Mets (1985); major leaguer (1987-2000)*
35. *Cory Bafidis, lhp, Texas Wesleyan College.
36. *Max Ungar, c, Smith Jewish Day School, Bethesda, Md.
37. *Tyler Watson, lhp, Georgetown (Texas) HS.
38. *Jared Messer, rhp, Malone (Ohio) College.
39. *Mitchell Williams, c, Coosa HS, Rome, Ga.
40. *Ricky Gutierrez, of, American Senior HS, Miami.
DRAFT DROP *Son of Ricky Gutierrez, first-round draft pick, Orioles (1988); major leaguer (1993-2004)*

# 2013

**AT A GLANCE**

### This Date In History
June 6-8

### International Gem
**JOSE ABREU, 1B, WHITE SOX.** One of the greatest Cuban sluggers ever, Abreu dominated Series Nacional from 2009-12, averaging .412 while hitting 98 home runs in 780 at-bats. He defected in August 2012 at age 26, signed a six-year, $68 million deal with the White Sox and hit .303-66-208 in his first two MLB seasons.

### Minor League Take
**KRIS BRYANT, 3B, CUBS.** Bryant slammed an NCAA-high 31 homers for the University of San Diego in 2013 and 43 more in a 2014 season split between Double-A (.355-22-58) and Triple-A (.295-21-52), and led all major league rookies with 26 homers for the Cubs in 2015.

### One Who Got Away
**PHIL BICKFORD, RHP, BLUE JAYS (1ST ROUND).** Bickford went unsigned as the 10th overall pick out of a California high school; two years later, he signed with the Giants as the 18th selection out of junior college after transferring from Cal State Fullerton.

### Did You Know . . .
A record 74 percent of drafted players signed in 2013. Additionally, the White Sox also set a record by signing their first 32 selections.

### They Said It
Astros scouting director **MIKE ELIAS**, on his club's decision to take Stanford righthander **MARK APPEL** with the No. 1 pick after passing on him with the top selection a year earlier: "This guy was under the microscope for two years. He took every turn. You could set your watch to him, he was so consistent in how he gave Stanford quality start after quality start. The enormity of his consistency really stood out."

# Astros don't miss in second shot at Appel

There was a sense of déjà vu about the 2013 draft.

Not only did the Houston Astros have the No. 1 overall pick again, but Stanford's Mark Appel was also the leading candidate to go first for the second straight year. After passing on the 6-foot-5, 215-pound righthander in 2012 when they couldn't get a handle on his bonus demands, the Astros nabbed Appel the second time around.

For all the angst that surrounded the Astros' decision to bypass Appel in favor of Puerto Rican shortstop Carlos Correa, and Appel's decision to turn down a $3.8 million bonus from the Pittsburgh Pirates after he fell to the eighth pick overall, the saga played out well for all parties.

In the Pirates' case, if they had met Appel's bonus demands, they would have significantly exceeded their bonus pool and would have lost at least one premium draft pick and paid a huge tax bill under the draft rules that went into effect in 2012. Instead, they took advantage of the new rule that gave them a corresponding first-round pick in 2013.

Even though he had no college eligibility remaining, Appel parlayed his talent into a $6.35 million bonus from the Astros—more money than any player had gotten in the two drafts since the new rules changed the landscape, and more than any college senior in draft history.

In between the two drafts, Appel completed his degree in management science and engineering at Stanford. On the mound, his stuff and command got better and he dominated hitters in 2013 like scouts always believed he could. In 106 innings, he went 10-4, 2.12 and his 130 strikeouts enabled him to set a school career mark. He also walked just 24.

Though a year later than expected, Appel wound up in Houston, his hometown until his family moved to northern California when he was 12. He grew up an Astros fan and had every expectation of moving quickly through an organization that was in the midst of a significant overhaul.

The Astros themselves had no regrets waiting an extra year to land Appel. They were just happy to get a second chance to draft him.

"This guy was under the microscope for two years," scouting director Mike Elias said. "He took every turn. You could set your watch to him, he was so consistent in how he gave Stanford quality start after quality start. The enormity of his consistency really stood out.

"Plus he got better. His secondary stuff also took a step forward."

Appel became just the second college senior to go first overall, joining Southern University's Danny Goodwin in 1975. Luke Hochevar, the top pick in 2006, would have been a college senior had he not passed on his final year of college eligibility by joining an independent professional team instead of returning to Tennessee.

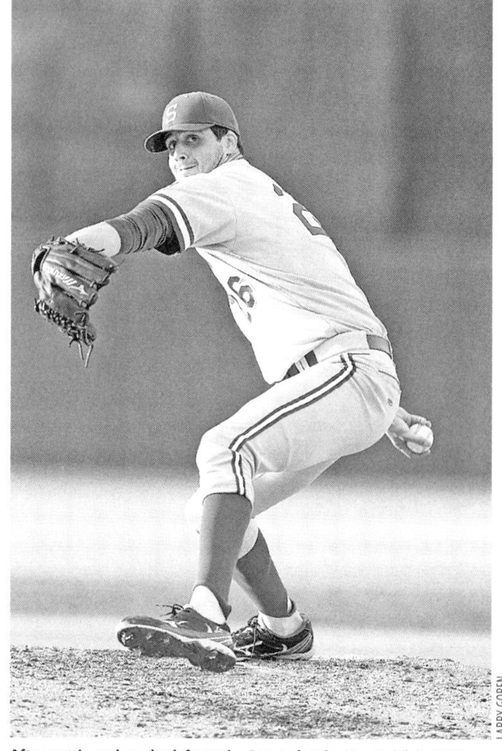

LARRY GOREN

**After getting a long look from the Astros for the No. 1 pick in 2012, Stanford righthander Mark Appel didn't sign and was still available when the Astros had the No. 1 selection again in 2013**

The Astros had been willing to pay Appel as much as $6 million as the No. 1 pick a year earlier, but when they couldn't pin him down on an exact figure, they shifted gears and took Correa. By signing Correa to a discounted bonus of $4.8 million, it left them with $2.4 million to spend elsewhere in the draft from the overall slot value of $7.2 million that was allocated for the first pick, and they landed two other high-profile talents in the 2012 draft.

With an overall bonus pool allotment of $11,698,800 in 2013, including $7,790,400 that was earmarked for the top pick, the Astros hoped to apply the same approach in drafting and signing Appel. He agreed to an amount that was $1,440,400 under slot, meaning the Astros again had money to distribute elsewhere, but they were less judicious in their use of the money. They did benefit by signing high school pitchers Austin Nicely and Devonte German, their 10th- and 11th-round picks, for amounts that were $470,600 and $200,000 over their designated slot values.

With 107 losses in 2012, Houston's ineptitude was rewarded by picking first in the draft for a second straight year.

Only twice in the 48-year history of the draft had a team previously had the No. 1 selection in

## 2013: THE FIRST ROUNDERS

| CLUB: PLAYER, POS., SCHOOL | HOMETOWN | B-T | HT. | WT. | AGE | BONUS | FIRST YEAR | LAST YEAR | PEAK LEVEL (YEARS) |
|---|---|---|---|---|---|---|---|---|---|
| 1. Astros: Mark Appel, rhp, Stanford | San Ramon, Calif. | R-R | 6-4 | 195 | 21 | $6,350,000 | 2013 | Active | Class AAA (1) |
| After Astros passed in 2012, grabbed him a year later after 10-4, 2.12 (104 IP/130) SR year; inconsistent stuff/mechanics dimmed outlook before trade to Phillies. | | | | | | | | | |
| 2. Cubs: Kris Bryant, 3b/of, San Diego | Las Vegas, Nev. | R-R | 6-5 | 215 | 21 | $6,708,400 | 2013 | Active | Majors (1) |
| Premium but unsignable HS prospect had 31 HRs in monster JR season, pounded 43 more in 2014 (only full season in minors), debuted in MLB amid much fanfare. | | | | | | | | | |
| 3. Rockies: Jonathan Gray, rhp, Oklahoma | Chandler, Okla. | R-R | 6-4 | 245 | 21 | $4,800,000 | 2013 | Active | Majors (1) |
| Progressed from 13th-rounder out of HS, 10th-rounder after JC freshman year, blossomed at OU with FB up to 101, went 10-3, 1.64 (126 IP/147 SO) as JR. | | | | | | | | | |
| 4. Twins: Kohl Stewart, rhp, St. Pius X HS | Tomball, Texas | R-R | 6-3 | 210 | 18 | $4,544,400 | 2013 | Active | Class A (2) |
| Two-sport star had chance to succeed Johnny Manziel as Texas A&M QB; brandished lively 93-96 mph FB, pro career (10-13, 2.82) impacted by shoulder issues. | | | | | | | | | |
| 5. Indians: Clint Frazier, of, Loganville HS | Loganville, Ga. | R-R | 5-11 | 185 | 18 | $3,500,000 | 2013 | Active | Class A (2) |
| Best tools in HS class (speed, outstanding power/arm strength); hit .485-17-45 as SR, has posted solid numbers as pro (.279-34-150), though inconsistent contact. | | | | | | | | | |
| 6. Marlins: Colin Moran, 3b, North Carolina | Rye, N.Y. | L-R | 6-4 | 215 | 20 | $3,516,500 | 2013 | Active | Class AA (2) |
| Hit .345-13-91 (68 BBs) as JR to highlight big UNC career; has continued to hit as pro (.300-20-145), but questions remain about power potential, defense at 3B. | | | | | | | | | |
| 7. Red Sox: Trey Ball, lhp, New Castle HS | New Castle, Ind. | L-L | 6-5 | 175 | 18 | $2,750,000 | 2013 | Active | Class A (2) |
| Lean/graceful athlete with two-way pro potential; some scouts liked him as CF with speed/power, Sox preferred 91-94 mph FB, clean delivery, secondary pitches. | | | | | | | | | |
| 8. Royals: Hunter Dozier, ss, Stephen F. Austin | Denton, Texas | R-R | 6-4 | 220 | 21 | $2,200,000 | 2013 | Active | Class AA (2) |
| Money saved here allowed Royals to sign higher-profile/injured Sean Manaea in comp round; hit .396-17-52 as JR, bat has lagged as pro, moved to 3B. | | | | | | | | | |
| 9. Pirates: Austin Meadows, of, Grayson HS | Loganville, Ga. | L-L | 6-2 | 195 | 18 | $3,029,600 | 2013 | Active | Class AA (1) |
| Summer-league teammate/crosstown prep rival of Frazier; advanced hitting skills/plate discipline, .312 hitter through three pro seasons, power/OF skills evolving. | | | | | | | | | |
| 10. Blue Jays: Philip Bickford, rhp, Oaks Christian HS | Westlake Village, Calif | R-R | 6-4 | 200 | 17 | Unsigned | 2015 | Active | Rookie (1) |
| Shot up draft lists after jump in velocity, but honored Cal State Fullerton commitment; stayed one year, transferred to JC, became first-rounder again in 2015. | | | | | | | | | |
| 11. Mets: Dominic Smith, 1b, Serra HS | Los Angeles | L-L | 6-0 | 185 | 17 | $2,600,000 | 2013 | Active | Class A (2) |
| Most polished HS bat in class with sweet LH swing, also exceptional defender, threw in low 90s off mound; has hit in pros (.305-10-149) but power slow to surface. | | | | | | | | | |
| 12. Mariners: D.J. Peterson, 3b, New Mexico | Gilbert, Ariz. | R-R | 6-1 | 205 | 21 | $2,759,100 | 2013 | Active | Class AAA (1) |
| Family draft with brother Dustin to Padres in second round; one of top college bats (.408-18-72), slammed 31 HRs in first full pro season, nosedived to 7 in 2015. | | | | | | | | | |
| 13. Padres: Hunter Renfroe, of, Mississippi State | Crystal Springs, Miss. | R-R | 6-1 | 210 | 21 | $2,678,000 | 2013 | Active | Class AAA (1) |
| Flashed first-round tools as C/RHP with power bat/arm early in college career, settled in as power-hitting RF as JR (.345-16-65), has significant extra-base pop. | | | | | | | | | |
| 14. Pirates: Reese McGuire, c, Kentwood HS | Covington, Wash. | L-R | 6-1 | 195 | 18 | $2,369,000 | 2013 | Active | Class A (3) |
| Second of two Pirates first-rounders; strong defender with excellent arm, receiving skills, leadership; bat has been a little light (.271-3-100 in three pro seasons). | | | | | | | | | |
| 15. Diamondbacks: Braden Shipley, rhp, Nevada | Medford, Ore. | R-R | 6-3 | 190 | 21 | $2,250,000 | 2013 | Active | Class AA (2) |
| Unknown Oregon recruit started college career at SS, converted to pitcher as SO, went 7-3, 2.77 as JR with mid-90s FB, has made modest strides as pro. | | | | | | | | | |
| 16. Phillies: J.P. Crawford, ss, Lakewood HS | Lakewood, Calif. | L-R | 6-2 | 180 | 18 | $2,299,300 | 2013 | Active | Class AA (1) |
| Advanced prospect on both sides of ball; won batting title in first pro season, .290-18-111 hitter through three years; pure SS with arm, actions, instincts to excel. | | | | | | | | | |
| 17. White Sox: Tim Anderson, ss/of, East Central CC | Tuscaloosa, Ala. | R-R | 6-1 | 180 | 19 | $2,164,000 | 2013 | Active | Class AA (2) |
| Prep hoops standout switched focus to baseball in JC; high-risk, high reward talent became immediate hit with speed/raw power, hit .312 in Double-A in 2015. | | | | | | | | | |
| 18. Dodgers: Chris Anderson, rhp, Jacksonville | St. Louis Park, Minn. | R-R | 6-4 | 215 | 20 | $2,109,900 | 2013 | Active | Class AAA (1) |
| Latest upper Midwest prospect who found success at JU; moved into first round when fastball velocity rose to mid-90s; has moved methodically through system. | | | | | | | | | |
| 19. Cardinals: Marco Gonzales, lhp, Gonzaga | Fort Collins, Colo. | L-L | 6-0 | 195 | 21 | $1,850,000 | 2013 | Active | Majors (2) |
| Latest polished/athletic college arm taken by Cards in first round, moved quickly through system, arrived in 2014; dominating change is his signature pitch. | | | | | | | | | |
| 20. Tigers: Jonathan Crawford, rhp, Florida | Okeechobee, Fla. | R-R | 6-2 | 205 | 21 | $2,001,700 | 2013 | Active | Class A (3) |
| Modest college career (3-6. 3.84 as JR), but power arm with FB that peaked at 99 mph; pro career slowed by inconsistent command/secondary stuff, shoulder issue. | | | | | | | | | |
| 21. Rays: Nick Ciuffo, c, Lexington HS | Lexington, S.C. | L-R | 6-1 | 205 | 18 | $1,972,200 | 2013 | Active | Class A (1) |
| Athletic catcher with big arm, leadership skills with mature approach; fringy bat (.249-5-77 in 189 pro games), needs work on plate discipline, developing power. | | | | | | | | | |
| 22. Orioles: Hunter Harvey, rhp, Bandys HS | Catawba, N.C. | R-R | 6-3 | 175 | 18 | $1,947,600 | 2013 | Active | Class A (3) |
| Son of ex-MLB closer Brian; burst on scene as prep senior with 95 mph fastball, plus curve, pro career stymied by elbow soreness, sat out 2015 season. | | | | | | | | | |
| 23. Rangers: Alex Gonzalez, rhp, Oral Roberts | Delray Beach, Fla. | R-R | 6-3 | 200 | 21 | $2,215,000 | 2013 | Active | Majors (1) |
| Florida native better known as "Chi Chi"; polished college arm with plus slider, elevated into top round by adding velocity/cutting action to 92-95 mph fastball. | | | | | | | | | |
| 24. Athletics: Billy McKinney, of, Plano West HS | Plano, Texas | L-L | 6-1 | 195 | 18 | $1,800,000 | 2013 | Active | Class AA (1) |
| A's liked his polished hitting approach, though dealt to Cubs in 2014 trade-deadline deal; .291 hitter in minors, but all about bat as other tools considered fringy. | | | | | | | | | |
| 25. Giants: Christian Arroyo, ss, Hernando HS | Spring Hill, Fla. | R-R | 5-11 | 185 | 18 | $1,866,500 | 2013 | Active | Class A (2) |
| Biggest first-round surprise, viewed as consensus 3rd-5th rounder; Giants liked hitting ability (.303 to date as pro), gamer approach, ability to perform above tools. | | | | | | | | | |
| 26. Yankees: Eric Jagielo, 3b, Notre Dame | Downers Grove, Ill. | L-R | 6-3 | 210 | 21 | $1,839,400 | 2013 | Active | Class AA (1) |
| Sold Yankees as first of three first-round picks with strong Cape Cod performance (.291-13-29), JR season (.388-9-53); has made strides defensively at hot corner. | | | | | | | | | |
| 27. Reds: Philip Ervin, of, Samford | Jackson, Miss. | R-R | 5-10 | 200 | 20 | $1,812,400 | 2013 | Active | Class AA (1) |
| Breakout Cape Cod performance (.323-11-31 in 2012) established credentials; fast-twitch athlete with strength/CF tools, bat has been unexpectedly light as pro. | | | | | | | | | |
| 28. Cardinals: Rob Kaminsky, lhp, St. Joseph HS | Edgewood Cliffs, N.J. | R-L | 5-11 | 190 | 18 | $1,758,300 | 2013 | Active | Class AA (2) |
| Dominated prep competition (10-0, 0.10) with best curve in class to complement low-90s fastball; limited projection, but has enjoyed early pro success. | | | | | | | | | |
| 29. Rays: Ryne Stanek, rhp, Arkansas | Overland Park, Kan. | R-R | 6-4 | 190 | 21 | $1,755,800 | 2013 | Active | Class AA (1) |
| Unsigned 2010 third-rounder, candidate for top 10 with mid-90s FB/power slider, solid performance (10-2, 1.39); early pro career impacted by hip/shoulder issues. | | | | | | | | | |
| 30. Rangers: Travis Demeritte, 3b, Winder Barrow HS | Statham, Ga. | R-R | 6-0 | 180 | 18 | $1,900,000 | 2013 | Active | Class A (2) |
| Led Class A hitters with 25 HRs in 2014 despite .211 BA, 171 Ks; returned to A-ball in 2015, hitting .241-5-19 when suspended 80 games for positive PED test. | | | | | | | | | |
| 31. Braves: Jason Hursh, rhp, Oklahoma State | Carrolton, Texas | R-R | 6-3 | 195 | 21 | $1,704,200 | 2013 | Active | Class AAA (1) |
| Former prep shortstop missed 2012 season with TJ surgery; returned with 95-98 mph sinker; lack of offspeed stuff hurt development as pro, prompted move to pen. | | | | | | | | | |
| 32. Yankees: Aaron Judge, of, Fresno State | Linden, Calif. | R-R | 6-7 | 255 | 21 | $1,800,000 | 2013 | Active | Class AAA (1) |
| Athletic specimen with surprising agility/speed for size; hit .369-12-36 in breakthrough JR year, still tapping into huge raw power after two pro seasons. | | | | | | | | | |
| 33. Yankees: Ian Clarkin, lhp, James Madison HS | San Diego | L-L | 6-2 | 205 | 18 | $1,650,100 | 2013 | Active | Class A (2) |
| Four-pitch lefty starred for Gold-medal-winning U.S. team at 2012 World juniors; has been bothered by injuries as pro, missed 2015 with elbow inflammation. | | | | | | | | | |

## IN FOCUS: CLINT FRAZIER / AUSTIN MEADOWS

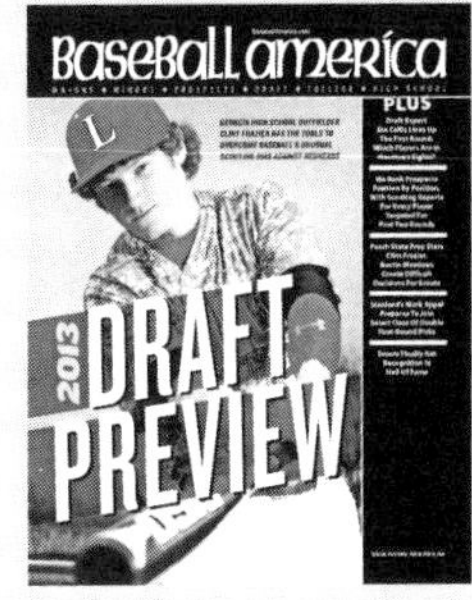


One of the more intriguing developments in the 2013 draft was the selection of high school center fielders **CLINT FRAZIER** by the Indians with the fifth pick overall and **AUSTIN MEADOWS** by the Pirates with the ninth. Frazier and Meadows, the first two prep positions player taken, both hailed from Loganville, Ga., an Atlanta suburb of just 11,000. They had played on the same youth and travel-ball teams since age 9, but competed at rival high schools.

Both players had near-equal ability in the eyes of scouts, but the 6-foot-1, 190-pound Frazier, a righthanded hitter, had the louder tools, with more raw power but a greater propensity to strike out; the 6-foot-3, 190-pound Meadows, a lefthanded bat, was the better, more disciplined hitter overall.

Frazier reached Double-A in the Indians system in 2016, after coming into the season with a .279 career average and 34 homers while also striking out 347 times in 297 games. Meadows had reached Triple-A, after producing a .312 average with 17 homers in 222 games.

Both players, coincidentally, had been bothered by hamstring problems, causing Frazier to miss significant time in 2013, and Meadows the same a year later, but both remained in line to enjoy productive big league careers.

## DRAFT SPOTLIGHT: KRIS BRYANT

ROBERT GURGANUS

Kris Bryant pursued a college career at San Diego before signing with the Cubs out of the 2013 draft

Kris Bryant and Bryce Harper played with and against each other growing up in Las Vegas, on their way to becoming two of the most decorated sluggers in the game. But while the young phenoms shared similar backgrounds and accomplishments, they did not travel the same path or share the same sense of urgency to get to their intended destination.

As products of the same 2010 draft, they went their own ways.

The 6-foot-3, 205-pound Harper, 10 months younger than Bryant, was a player ahead of his time. In his haste to reach the big leagues, he skipped his final two years of high school to make himself eligible for the draft a year ahead of schedule, and fulfilled his goal of being taken with the No. 1 pick overall.

Bryant, at 6-foot-5 and 205 pounds, could have been a first-round pick himself, but he was in no hurry to begin his own professional career coming out of Bonanza High, and elected to fulfill his college commitment to the University of San Diego.

While Harper was a household name as a teenager, Bryant bided his time in relative anonymity in college. But he was no less a dominant force, leading to his selection as the No. 2 pick in the 2013 draft. Like Harper, he accepted the largest signing bonus in his class.

Though Harper, 17 when he signed with the Nationals, got an obvious head start, Bryant was no less an accomplished prospect when he signed with the Cubs at 21. Both were recipients of the Golden Spikes Award, symbolic of the top amateur player in the country—Harper in 2010 in his one season in junior college at the College of Southern Nevada, Bryant for drilling a national-best 31 long balls as a junior at USD in 2013.

Bryant, too, passed quickly through the minors, playing in just 181 games, but he was Baseball America's 2014 Minor League Player of the Year—an award that eluded Harper. A year later, there wasn't a more ballyhooed debut in the big leagues than Bryant's—with the exception of Harper's—and he succeeded in joining Harper by winning the National League rookie of the year award. Yet Harper raised the bar again by winning NL MVP.

"It was only a matter of time before he got up here," Harper said of Bryant. "Great talent, a lot of power. When we were younger, we used to call him 'silk' because he was so smooth with everything he did."

Growing up in Las Vegas, they were an intimidating 1-2 punch while playing on the same teams before they were 10, and later for the Southern Nevada Bulldogs, when Bryant was 12 and Harper 11, and they routinely excelled against older competition.

"We did play together quite a bit when we were 10, 11, 12 years old," Bryant said. "We played on the same club teams. We were pretty good, we won a lot of tournaments, but I don't think I was as highly thought of as him, though. He was on another level. You should have seen some of the baseballs, how far he hit them when he was 12 years old."

Bryant's early recognition that he was never quite as polished or complete a talent as Harper helped him decide that college was the best choice for him.

"Coming to USD was the best decision I've made in my life," he said. "I knew coming here that the coaches would get me a whole lot better, and they have in every area of my game, every year."

"The maturity I've seen in him as a player, it's been leaps and bounds," said Toreros coach Rich Hill, while Bryant was closing out his three-year career by being named BA's College Player of the Year. "His freshman year, he was a wiry, gangly kid with some holes in his swing, and he really had work to do on his defense. To his sophomore year, he kept getting better. To this year, he just blossomed."

Other than their obvious parallel paths, Bryant and Harper were always as different as two stars could be. Harper was always emotional, unfiltered and overly aggressive. Bryant was more mild-mannered and less polarizing.

"We have very different personalities, but I think that's good for the game," Bryant said, just before the two players squared off against one another for the first time in a big league game in 2015. "It's good to have guys who wear their heart on their sleeves and he's one of those guys, and it's awesome to see that. He plays so hard for his team. I think everybody can learn from that, because to play this game, you have to be confident. You have to believe you're the best in the field. I do that in a different way."

consecutive years, as recently as 2006-07, when the Tampa Bay Rays had back-to-back first overall picks, and 2009-10, when the Washington Nationals used the top choices to select San Diego State righthander Stephen Strasburg and junior college catcher-turned-outfielder Bryce Harper.

Tampa Bay was playing in the World Series by 2008, while Strasburg and Harper, two of the most celebrated draft picks ever, played key roles in leading the Nationals to such a significant turnaround that they posted the best regular-season record in the big leagues by 2012.

It was too tall an order to expect the woeful Astros to make the same overnight worst-to-first transformation, and they bottomed out completely in 2013, losing a franchise-worst 111 games, which assured them of making draft history by picking first for the third year in a row in 2014.

Surprisingly, though, the Astros did turn their fortunes in relatively short order, improving from 51 wins in 2013 to 86 in 2015, to reach postseason play in the American League, although Appel had no part in the turnaround. At the end of the season, he was traded to the Philadelphia Phillies

### SYSTEMATIC FIRST ROUND

With Appel going off the board first, the first round as a whole went in a fairly straightforward manner, with few surprises. The top three prospects were Appel, University of San Diego third baseman Kris Bryant, the top power hitter in the draft, and University of Oklahoma righthander Jon Gray, the top power pitcher. Bryant went to the Chicago Cubs with the second selection, while Gray was taken third by the Colorado Rockies.

That the Astros and Cubs ended up with the first two picks was part of an overall rebuilding plan, as those clubs had both made a commitment to rebuild their faltering organizations virtually from scratch, with the draft—especially with new rules that went into effect in 2012—a principal tool to effect the turnaround.

The provisions of a new Collective Bargaining Agreement established parameters in terms of the amounts clubs could spend on all their draft picks, with teams threatened with fines or the loss of premium draft picks if they didn't toe the line.

The new system was designed to benefit weaker teams, and teams at the top of the draft rotation ended up with substantially more money to sign their picks than those at the bottom. The Astros and Cubs, accordingly, had the two largest aggregate bonus pools to sign all their picks in the first 10 rounds.

The Cubs signed Bryant for $6,708,400, the largest bonus paid out in the 2013 draft—and the

### Fastest To The Majors

| | Player, Pos. | Drafted (Round) | Debut |
|---|---|---|---|
| 1. | Kyle Crockett, lhp | Indians (4) | May 16, 2014 |
| 2. | Corey Knebel, rhp | Tigers (1-S) | May 24, 2014 |
| 3. | Marco Gonzalez, lhp | Cardinals (1) | June 25, 2014 |
| 4. | Buck Farmer, rhp | Tigers (5) | Aug. 13, 2014 |
| 5. | Kendall Graveman, rhp | Blue Jays (8) | Sept. 5, 2014 |

**FIRST HIGH SCHOOL SELECTION:** None through 2015

### Top 25 Bonuses

| | Player, Pos. | Drafted (Round) | Order | Bonus |
|---|---|---|---|---|
| **1.** | **Kris Bryant, 3b** | **Cubs (1)** | **2** | **$6,708,400** |
| 2. | Mark Appel, rhp | Astros (1) | 1 | $6,350,000 |
| **3.** | **Jonathan Gray, rhp** | **Rockies (1)** | **3** | **$4,800,000** |
| 4. | * Kohl Stewart, rhp | Twins (1) | 4 | $4,544,000 |
| 5. | Sean Manaea, lhp | Royals (1-S) | 34 | $3,550,000 |
| 6. | Colin Moran, 3b | Marlins (1) | 6 | $3,516,500 |
| 7. | * Clint Frazier, of | Indians (1) | 5 | $3,500,000 |
| 8. | * Austin Meadows, of | Pirates (1) | 9 | $3,029,600 |
| 9. | D.J. Peterson, 3b | Mariners (1) | 12 | $2,759,100 |
| 10. | * Trey Ball, lhp | Red Sox (1) | 7 | $2,750,000 |
| 11. | Hunter Renfroe, of | Padres (1) | 13 | $2,678,000 |
| 12. | * Dominic Smith, 1b | Mets (1) | 11 | $2,600,000 |
| 13. | * Reese McGuire, c | Pirates (1) | 14 | $2,369,800 |
| 14. | * J.P. Crawford, ss | Phillies (1) | 16 | $2,299,300 |
| 15. | Braden Shipley, rhp | Diamondbacks (1) | 15 | $2,250,000 |
| **16.** | **Alex Gonzalez, rhp** | **Rangers (1)** | **23** | **$2,215,000** |
| 17. | Hunter Dozier, ss | Royals (1) | 8 | $2,200,000 |
| 18. | Tim Anderson, ss | White Sox (1) | 17 | $2,164,000 |
| 19. | Chris Anderson, rhp | Dodgers (1) | 18 | $2,109,900 |
| 20. | Jonathon Crawford, rhp | Tigers (1) | 20 | $2,001,700 |
| 21. | * Nick Ciuffo, c | Rays (1) | 21 | $1,972,200 |
| 22. | * Hunter Harvey, rhp | Orioles (1) | 22 | $1,947,600 |
| 23. | * Travis Demeritte, ss | Rangers (1) | 30 | $1,900,000 |
| 24. | * Christian Arroyo, ss | Giants (1) | 25 | $1,866,500 |
| **25.** | **Marco Gonzales, lhp** | **Cardinals (1)** | **19** | **$1,850,000** |

*Major leaguers in bold. *High school selection.*

fourth largest ever—and spent $11,724,900 to sign all their draft picks, more than any club. The $6.35 million bonus the Astros gave Appel was the second-highest on the year, as was their overall commitment of $11,441,000. The Rockies, at $10,368,200, also exceeded the $10 million mark.

Though the Cubs ended up spending more, the Astros had the larger bonus pool of the two clubs, at $11,698,800. The Cubs exceeded their allotment of $10,556,500 by 4.8 percent, requiring them to pay a luxury tax of $383,925, while the Astros didn't spend to their allotment and came in $877,300 under budget.

By contrast, the Nationals, who picked with the 30th and last pick in each round and also forfeited their first-round selection as a result of signing righthander Rafael Soriano as a free agent prior to the 2013 season, had only $2,737,200 to spend for their entire draft.

The new slotting system assigned specific bonus values to every draft pick in the top 10 rounds, and the aggregate of those amounts provided clubs with a limit on what they could spend to sign their selections. The aggregate value of all picks in the first 10 rounds was set at $202 million—an increase of 8.2 percent from 2012, despite 22 fewer picks.

The actual amounts teams spent on all their picks was $219,302,880, second only to the 2011 total of $228,009,050 in the final year before the new draft rules were implemented. The first-round average of $2,641,538 was also the second-highest ever, and at an increase of 6.7 percent effectively negated all the gains that were made in reducing bonuses in the initial year of all the draft changes. Bonuses had fallen by the same 6.7 percent from 2011, when the average was a record $2,653,375.

In all, 53 draft picks signed bonuses of $1 million or more, and 15 players in the 11th round were paid at least $100,000, including $750,000 by the St. Louis Cardinals to California high school righthander Steve Farinaro and $700,000 by the Toronto Blue Jays to Missouri prep lefthander Jake Brentz.

Teams had the latitude to spread their draft pool money among picks in the first 10 rounds in any way they chose, so long as they remained under their total allotment. At the same time, a team forfeited its assigned value for any draft pick in the first 10 rounds if it failed to sign one those selections.

From an actual assigned value of $7,790,400 for the first selection and $6,708,400 for the second pick, the designated amount for each slot dropped to $1,650,100 for the 33rd and last pick in the first round, and all the way to $135,300 for the last 17 picks in the 10th round.

No team overspent its bonus pool by more than 5 percent, which would have triggered the loss of a first-round pick. The Los Angeles Dodgers, at 4.9 percent, pushed the envelope the most, and came within $7,186 of losing a first-rounder. The Atlanta Braves, Cardinals, Cubs, San Francisco Giants and Seattle Mariners also went over by at least 4.6 percent and were among 11 clubs in all that exceeded their pool amounts.

The total tax bill for those 11 clubs came to $1,807,725, which was divided among 10 revenue-sharing recipients who didn't exceed their pools.

## CUBS ZERO IN ON BRYANT

The Cubs never quite sunk to the depths that the Astros did, but the team did see plenty of dark days at Wrigley Field, picking in the top 10 for five straight years from 2011-15, before also suddenly rising from the ashes to reach postseason play in 2015.

By picking second in 2013, the Cubs had a golden opportunity to hasten their rebuilding, especially with three marquee college prospects to choose from. They were believed to be sitting on Appel and Gray because of a need for pitching in the organization, but they decided they couldn't pass up a power hitter of Bryant's stature.

The 6-foot-5, 205-pound slugger led NCAA Division I hitters with 31 homers—10 more than his closest pursuer, and a total greater than 223 of the 296 teams at that level. He also hit more homers in a season than any player had accumulated since college bats were toned down three years earlier, and topped all hitters in slugging (.820), runs (80), total bases (187) and walks (66). He was also Baseball America's College Player of the Year.

"We've always said, especially as it pertains to the draft, the player we feel will have the most impact to the organization for the longest time should be the choice over organizational need," Cubs scouting director Jason McLeod said. "That's what played out."

Bryant was a legitimate first-round candidate coming out of a Nevada high school in 2010. His immense power potential was evident even then, but he slipped to the 18th round when he made his intentions known he would attend college. In

### WORTH NOTING

California colleges proved to be a strength of the 2013 draft with the first two selections in **MARK APPEL** and **KRIS BRYANT**, as well as eight of the first 70 selections, even though none of the players were from UCLA, the College World Series champion. UCLA swept to the NCAA title with a 49-17 record and a 2-0 series sweep over Mississippi State, despite a dearth of premium talent. The Bruins' two primary starters, junior righthanders **NICK VANDER TUIG** (14-4, 2.16) and **ADAM PLUTKO** (10-3, 2.25), were picked in the sixth round by the Giants and 11th round by the Indians, respectively, while shortstop **PAT VALAIKA**, their most productive hitter at .253-5-48, was a ninth-round pick of the Rockies. In going 10-0 in NCAA tournament games, Bruins pitchers gave up just 14 runs. In five College World Series games, the Bruins hit .193 with no homers.

Arkansas, which got bounced in NCAA regional play, had more players drafted than any college team (11), including righthanders **RYNE STANEK** (10-2, 1.39) in the first round (Rays, 29th overall), **COLBY SUGGS** (0-0, 1.74, 13 saves) in the supplemental second and **BARRETT ASTIN** (4-4, 1.79) in the third.

The Cubs spent the most bonus money on the draft in 2013, and dominated the international market by paying out three of the four largest bonuses. They spent $2.8 million to sign 16-year-old Dominican outfielder **ELOY JIMENEZ**, the largest bonus on the year by a full $1 million. Under terms of the new Collective Bargaining Agreement that prescribed how much clubs could spend on international amateurs, the Cubs started the year with the second-largest bonus pool ($4,557,200, second to the Astros), and increased it to $5,520,300 by acquiring two international slot values in a trade with the Orioles, and two more in a trade with the Astros.

CONTINUED ON PAGE 718

## WORTH NOTING

CONTINUED FROM PAGE 717

■ Just like in 2012, Stanford righthander **MARK APPEL** boasted the highest overall future potential grade in the 2013 draft class, as judged by the Major League Scouting Bureau. His score of 73 (on the traditional 20-80 scouting scale) was significantly higher than the grade of 65 turned in by Oklahoma righthander **JONATHAN GRAY**, who was selected third overall. Cal State Fullerton outfielder **MICHAEL LORENZEN** and Arkansas righthander **COLBY SUGGS**, two supplemental picks, also scored 65.

■ One of the most unlikely college success stories in the draft involved 22-year-old Brigham Young freshman outfielder **JACOB HANNEMAN**, who signed with the Cubs for $1 million—the largest bonus signed by a player drafted after the second round. Hanneman had committed to BYU out of high school, but delayed his enrollment for two years by embarking on a Mormon mission. When he completed his service, his intentions were to resume his football career, but injuries caused him to redshirt. That gave him time to pursue a baseball career, and he unexpectedly blossomed. "I wanted to go out and serve (after the 2010 draft), but I missed sports a lot," Hanneman said. "The dream to be a professional baseball player was still there, but it was fuzzy. Now it's clear, like in HD. I never imagined it would come around so quickly."

■ Lefthander **KYLE CROCKETT**, who went 4-1, 1.70 with 12 saves as a closer at Virginia, became the first member of the Class of 2013 to reach the majors. A fourth-round pick of the Indians, he debuted on May 16, 2014.

■ In a nice personal touch, the Diamondbacks picked Arizona State's **CORY HAHN** in the 34th round. Hahn was a highly regarded freshman in 2012 for the Sun Devils when he was paralyzed from the chest down in the third game of the season,

three years at USD, he only enhanced his first-round credentials.

While both Appel and Gray became viable options at the top of the draft board, there was a time early in their college careers that neither pitcher projected as even a first-round candidate.

Appel was never even a regular starter on his high school team; as a freshman at Stanford, his fastball topped out at 92 mph and he had little command of his secondary stuff. Gray committed to Oklahoma out of high school, but diverted to a junior college as a freshman when it was apparent he wasn't ready to pitch at the four-year college level. He threw hard, but struggled with control.

As juniors, both pitchers had breakthrough seasons that catapulted them into prime consideration. In Gray's case, he dominated with a fastball that routinely peaked in triple digits, and even reached 103 mph.

In the short term, at least, the Cubs' decision to go for Bryant proved the most prudent as he tore up the minors over parts of three seasons, hitting .327 with 55 homers in 181 games, before making his highly anticipated debut with the Cubs in 2015, leading to his selection as BA's Rookie of the Year. In 151 games, Bryant hit .275 with 26 homers and played an instrumental role for the Cubs as they improved from 73 wins in 2014 to 99.

Appel, meanwhile, struggled to establish a foothold in pro ball, going just 16-11, 5.12 in three years in the minors. Gray was more effective, leading to a promotion to the Rockies in August of 2015, though he went winless in his first nine major league starts.

Gray signed with the Rockies for $4.8 million ($826,400 under the amount allocated for the No. 3 slot), while the only other 2013 pick who signed for a bonus of at least $4 million was Texas prep righthander Kohl Stewart, who signed with the Minnesota Twins for $4,544,400 (equivalent to slot money) as the fourth pick overall. In addition to being the first high school player drafted, Stewart was one of the nation's top prep quarterbacks, with a commitment to follow in the steps of Heisman Trophy winner Johnny Manziel at Texas A&M.

The 6-foot-3, 205-pound Stewart was clocked up to 96 mph at Houston's St. Pius X High, but struggled to maintain that velocity in the minors while burdened with shoulder problems. In 48 appearances through 2015, none above Class A, he was 10-13, 2.82.

Beyond the top four, the most notable development in the first round was the calculated decision by the Kansas City Royals to draft Stephen F. Austin third baseman Hunter Dozier with the eighth pick, and wait until the 34th pick to select coveted Indiana State lefthander Seth Manaea, who injured his hip while celebrating an early-season win and required surgery.

The Royals signed Dozier to a below-slot deal of $2 million, and applied the money they saved to sign Manaea for $3.55 million—the fifth-largest bonus on the year, and the largest ever given a supplemental first-round pick, breaking the record held by Nick Castellanos, who got $3.45 million from the Detroit Tigers in 2010.

### Largest Bonuses By Round

| | Player, Pos. | Club | Bonus |
|---|---|---|---|
| 1. | **Kris Bryant, 3b** | **Cubs** | **$6,708,400** |
| 1-S. | Sean Manaea, lhp | Royals | $3,550,000 |
| 2. | Austin Wilson, of | Mariners | $1,700,000 |
| 3. | Jacob Hannemann, of | Cubs | $1,000,000 |
| 4. | Tyler Skulina, rhp | Cubs | $800,000 |
| 5. | * Sean Brady, lhp | Indians | $800,000 |
| 6. | * Dom Nunez, 3b | Rockies | $800,000 |
| 7. | Justin Bohn, ss | Marlins | $525,000 |
| 8. | * Adrian De Horta, rhp | Padres | $425,000 |
| | * Neil Kozikowski, rhp | Pirates | $425,000 |
| 9. | * Charcer Burks, of | Cubs | $170,000 |
| 10. | Cole Wiper, rhp | Rangers | $700,000 |
| 11. | * Steve Farinaro, rhp | Cardinals | $750,000 |
| 12. | * Trevor Clifton, rhp | Cubs | $375,000 |
| 13. | Several tied at | | $100,000 |
| 14. | * Nick Buckner, of | Pirates | $135,000 |
| 15. | * Jarrett Freeland, c | Reds | $324,500 |
| 16. | * Billy Roth, rhp | Pirates | $190,000 |
| 17. | * Greg Harris, rhp | Dodgers | $175,000 |
| 18. | * Dustin Fowler, of | Yankees | $278,000 |
| 19. | * Gabe Speier, lhp | Red Sox | $200,000 |
| 20. | * Iolana Akau, c | Athletics | $375,000 |
| 21. | * Luke Lanphere, rhp | Rangers | $400,000 |
| 22. | Several tied at | | $100,000 |
| 23. | Several tied at | | $100,000 |
| 24. | Chase Edwards, rhp | Tigers | $130,000 |
| 25. | * Danny Ayers, lhp | Orioles | $200,000 |
| Other | * Rowdy Tellez, 1b | Blue Jays (30) | $850,000 |

*Major leaguers in bold. *High school selection.*

Manaea's bonus was $1.927 million more than the assigned value for his slot ($1,623,000), but the Royals manipulated their remaining picks in the first 10 rounds to remain within budget. Not only did they sign Dozier for an amount that was $937,800 under his assigned slot, but they signed all but one of their remaining 10 picks in the first 10 rounds for below-slot amounts, and took four inexpensive college seniors. In the end, they spent just $78,700 more than their bonus allotment.

### NEW SIGNING RECORDS SET

With all the money spent in the 2013 draft, it wasn't surprising that players signed contracts at a more prolific rate than any draft in modern history.

Of 1,216 picks overall, 900 signed, a 74.0 percent rate—breaking the previous mark of 73.7 percent, set in 2012. Among players taken in the top 10 rounds, just seven went unsigned, which eclipsed the previous record of eight, also in 2012.

By signing their first 32 picks, the Chicago White Sox established a new standard for most consecutive picks signed, although the Mariners, with 31, also topped the previous mark of 30—set by the Blue Jays in 2000, and tied by the Cardinals in 2008 and Rockies in 2009.

The Los Angeles Angels forfeited their first-round pick but nearly ran the table by signing all of their picks except for Texas prep righthander Blake Goins, a 12th-rounder headed for the University of Texas.

Had the Angels gotten Goins in the fold, they would have become the only team in draft history (June, regular phase) to sign all their draft picks. Previously, the only other team to sign all but one of its selections was the 1985 Dodgers, who signed 33 of 34 picks—the exception being their fourth-rounder, Illinois State outfielder Mike Prior, who opted for a career as a wide receiver in the National Football League.

Even as the Angels came close to signing all their picks, they still committed just $3,168,200 in bonus money to sign them all.

The new draft rules took most of the drama out of the signing process. Before the latest Collective Bargaining Agreement took effect in 2012, bringing with it sweeping new draft regulations, most top draft prospects held out until the mid-August signing deadline. In 2011, 22 of the 33 first-round picks signed on Aug. 15, and teams combined to spend $139.1 million in bonus money on that day alone.

But with a formal slotting process and strict penalties now in place for clubs that surpassed their allocated bonus pools for the first 10 rounds by more than 5 percent, Major League Baseball no longer had to police every individual signing. The new mid-July signing deadline also accelerated the process, enticing players to sign at a much faster clip than in the past. Just six of 33 first-round picks and nine of the top 100 selections didn't sign in June, and only three extended negotiations right to the July 12 deadline—one of whom, California prep righthander Phil Bickford, went unsigned by the Blue Jays. The other two were Bryant and Fresno State outfielder Aaron Judge, the second of three first-round picks of the New York Yankees. Judge signed for $1.8 million ($122,900 above slot), and was one of just three first-rounders who signed for an amount over slot.

BILL MITCHELL
Hunter Dozier

The others were both Texas Rangers picks: Oral Roberts righthander Alex Gonzalez (23rd overall), who signed for $2,215,000 ($294,400 above slot), and Georgia high school shortstop Travis Demeritte (30th overall), who signed for $1.9 million ($122,900 above slot). The Rangers also signed two additional picks that significantly impacted their overall bonus pool amount, 10th-rounder Cole Wiper for $700,000 ($564,700 above slot) and 21st-rounder Lucas Lanphere for $400,000 ($300,000 above slot), but managed to exceed their allotment by just 3.5 percent.

As for Bickford, speculation grew as the signing deadline approached that he was set on attending college at Cal State Fullerton. The day before the deadline, Toronto general manager Alex Anthopoulos announced that he didn't expect his club to land Bickford. He didn't elaborate, beyond saying that the impasse wasn't financial, though no one on either side of the negotiations was willing to discuss exactly what happened.

"We would have liked to have gotten him done, but it didn't work out," Blue Jays scouting director Brian Parker said. "We wish Phil and his family good luck going forward."

A righthander from Oaks Christian High in Westlake Village, Calif., Bickford's stock rose as a senior along with the quality of his fastball. He routinely topped out at 96 mph, and wowed scouts in his final start of the season by striking out 18 in seven innings (including the final 11 hitters he faced) five days before the draft.

Bickford reportedly sought $4.25 million, significantly more than the $2,921,400 assigned value for the No. 10 selection. The Blue Jays weren't in position to pay him more than $3,664,830 without forfeiting a future first-round pick, and they didn't make any further attempts to sign Bickford.

To soften the blow, the Blue Jays made a splash by signing California high school first baseman Rowdy Tellez, their 30th-round pick, for $850,000 (a record for that round) and Brentz for $700,000, less than 15 minutes before the 5 p.m. deadline on July 12. Both players had projected as second- to third-round picks prior to the draft.

The Blue Jays would get the 11th overall pick in the 2014 draft for failing to land Bickford, who attended Cal State Fullerton as a freshman, but then chose to transfer to a junior college to become eligible for the 2015 draft, and was again drafted in the first round.

Because they didn't sign Bickford, the Blue Jays spent a lower percentage (47.7) of their original pool than any club.

The Miami Marlins also secured two compensation picks in 2014 by failing to sign the next two highest unsigned picks: supplemental first-rounder Matt Krook, a California prep lefthander selected 35th overall, and third-rounder Ben Deluzio, a Florida prep shortstop.

Krook failed his physical in late June, stemming from a sore left shoulder, and subsequently rejected a reduced bonus offer from the Marlins before deciding to attend the University of Oregon, while Deluzio ended up at Florida State.

## One Team's Draft: Chicago Cubs

| | Player, Pos. | Bonus | | Player, Pos. | Bonus | | Player, Pos. | Bonus |
|---|---|---|---|---|---|---|---|---|
| 1. | **Kris Bryant, 3b** | **$6,708,400** | 10. | **Zack Godley, rhp** | **$35,000** | 19. | Will Remillard, c | $150,000 |
| 2. | Rob Zastryzny, lhp | $1,361,900 | 11. | Jordan Hankins, c | $90,000 | 20. | Zak Blair, 2b | $1,000 |
| 3. | Jacob Hannemann, of | $1,000,000 | 12. | *Trevor Clifton, rhp | $375,000 | 21. | Josh McCauley, rhp | Did not sign |
| 4. | Tyler Skulina, rhp | $800,000 | 13. | Trevor Graham, rhp | $80,000 | 22. | Kevin Brown, of | $1,000 |
| 5. | Trey Masek, rhp | $357,400 | 14. | Daniel Poncedeleon, rhp | Did not sign | 23. | Tyler Ihrig, lhp | $5,000 |
| 6. | Scott Frazier, rhp | $267,600 | 15. | Michael Wagner, rhp | $100,000 | 24. | *Tyler Alamo, c | $100,000 |
| 7. | David Garner, rhp | $175,000 | 16. | Cael Brockmeyer, c | $40,000 | 25. | *Marcus Doi, of | Did not sign |
| 8. | Sam Wilson, lhp | $130,000 | 17. | Kelvin Freeman, 1b | $7,500 | Other | Brad Renner (28), rhp | $30,000 |
| 9. | *Charcer Burks, of | $170,000 | 18. | Giuseppe Papaccio, ss | $1,000 | | | |

*Major leaguers in bold. *High school selection.*

## WORTH NOTING

after breaking his neck in a collision while trying to steal second base. Hahn, not coincidently, wore No. 34 at ASU. He went on to graduate from Arizona State in 2014 with a business degree and worked for the Diamondbacks as a scout in his native Southern California.

■ The Peterson brothers missed becoming the first brother tandem drafted in the same first round since J.D. and Tim Drew in 1997, but not by much. **D.J. PETERSON**, a power-hitting third baseman from the University of New Mexico, went 12th overall to the Mariners, while younger brother **DUSTIN**, an Arizona high school shortstop, was the 50th overall pick by the Padres.

■ It was a good draft for brothers as identical twins **DAVID** and **RYAN LEDBETTER** were chosen from obscure Division III Cedarville (Ohio) University in the third and 19th rounds, respectively, by the Rangers. Both were righthanders with low- to mid-90s fastballs, although scouts said David had a better delivery and better array of secondary pitches.

■ **CHAD JONES**, a football/baseball star at LSU, signed with the New York Giants after being selected in the third round of the 2010 NFL draft. A near-fatal single-car accident effectively ended his promising football career, though he wasn't released by the Giants until 2012, after two seasons on injured reserve. He turned his attention again to baseball, and though he hadn't pitched since the championship game of the 2009 College World Series, almost four years earlier, and had undergone nearly 20 operations on his badly damaged left leg, his fastball topped out at 92 mph in workouts prior to the 2013 draft. The Reds took a chance on him in the ninth round, but he was never able to overcome his injuries and went just 1-1, 8.76 in 18 relief appearances in Rookie ball in 2013 before calling it quits.

**IN FOCUS: SEAN MANAEA**

Indiana State's Sean Manaea positioned himself to go near the top of the 2013 draft by dominating the Cape Cod League in the summer of 2012 like few pitchers in recent years. But the 6-foot-5 lefthander became damaged goods the following spring when he tore the labrum in his hip.

He still managed to go 5-4, 1.47 with 27 walks and 99 strikeouts in 73 innings, and the Royals, selecting eighth, were determined to take a run at him, knowing he would need surgery and miss the balance of the 2013 season.

Other clubs were hesitant, but the Royals, after reviewing his medical records, determined there would be no long-term damage. They passed on him until their second pick (34th overall), hoping he would still be available. In the meantime, they took shortstop Hunter Dozier at No. 8 and signed him to a money-saving deal of $2 million. They applied the savings to sign Manaea for $3.55 million—the fifth-largest bonus on the year, and the largest ever given a supplemental first-round pick.

After overcoming his hip injury, Manaea made solid strides in the Royals system, reaching Triple-A in 2015, before he was packaged to the A's at the trading deadline in a deal that brought Ben Zobrist to Kansas City. Zobrist, of course, helped the Royals win the World Series, so Manaea had already given the team a return on its investment.

## Highest Unsigned Picks

| Player, Pos., Team (Round) | College | Re-Drafted |
|---|---|---|
| Phil Bickford, rhp, Blue Jays (1) | CS Fullerton | Giants '15 (1) |
| Matt Krook, lhp, Marlins (1) | Oregon | Giants '16 (4) |
| Ben DeLuzio, 3b, Marlins (3) | Florida State | Never |
| Ben Wetzler, lhp, Phillies (5) | * Oregon State | Marlins '14 (9) |
| Jason Monda, of, Phillies (6) | * Washington State | Never |
| Dustin DeMuth, 3b, Twins (8) | * Indiana | Brewers '14 (5) |
| Ross Kivett, 2b, Indians (10) | * Kansas State | Tigers '14 (6) |
| Heath Quinn, of, Indians (12) | Samford | Giants '16 (3) |
| Griffin Jax, rhp, Phillies (12) | Air Force | Twins '16 (3) |
| Blake Goins, rhp, Angels (12) | Texas | Never |

**TOTAL UNSIGNED PICKS:** Top 5 Rounds (4), Top 10 Rounds (7)

**Returned to same school.*

### NEW REALM OF COMPENSATION PICKS

While the new labor agreement that was ratified after the 2011 season put most of the significant changes to the draft into effect in 2012, a number of the changes didn't take effect until 2013, especially as they related to draft pick compensation to teams—both for the loss of major league free agents, as well as the awarding of competitive-balance picks, a new concept.

The familiar Type A and Type B free agents, which were based on a statistical ranking of the top 30 percent of free agents available, were eliminated after 30 years. Going forward, the only free agents subject to compensation would be those agreeing to qualifying offers from their former club equal to the average salary of the 125 highest-paid players in the game as they entered the free-agent process. Players were also required to be with a team for an entire season to be subject to compensation, so pending free agents who were traded at midseason would no longer generate extra picks for the teams that acquired them.

Aaron Judge

Additionally, a team that signed a qualifying free agent would surrender its first-round pick. The forfeited pick would no longer go to the team that lost the free agent; that pick would simply be eliminated. The team that lost the free agent now received a supplemental pick at the end of the first round rotation. But unlike in the past, when the top 15 overall picks were protected, only the top 10 would now be protected.

The net effect of those changes on the 2013 draft was a first round that included 33 picks—seven additional selections as compensation for teams losing free agents, minus four picks that were eliminated for teams signing free agents.

The new rules also provided for 12 competitive-balance selections—six supplemental picks following both the first and second rounds.

The major league teams that were determined to be in the bottom 10 in the game in terms of revenue and/or market size were placed in a pool with six teams drawn by lottery to select after the first round, with the odds of winning based on the prior season's winning percentage. Teams that didn't get one of those picks—along with any other team that received money from revenue-sharing—then went into another lottery for six picks after the second round.

The Royals won the first competitive-balance lottery, meaning they got the pick immediately after the first-round and free-agent compensation choices were made (34th overall), and they chose Manaea with that pick. They were followed in order by the Pirates, Arizona Diamondbacks, Baltimore Orioles, Cincinnati Reds and Marlins.

Another new provision of the competitive-balance picks was that they could be traded—the first baseball draft picks ever allowed to be traded—and that happened three times in 2013.

With the second competitive-balance pick (35th overall), the Pirates traded the selection to the Marlins for Gaby Sanchez, and the Marlins drafted Krook. A trade-deadline deal between the Marlins and Tigers that centered around Anibal Sanchez, Omar Infante and Jacob Turner included two competitive-balance picks—the 39th pick overall that went from the Marlins to the Tigers, and the 73rd choice overall that the Tigers sent to the Marlins. With the 39th pick, the Tigers selected Texas closer Corey Knebel; with the 73rd pick, the Marlins chose Arkansas closer Colby Suggs.

From a college angle, the first round was dominated almost entirely by power arms and power-hitting third basemen. Of 17 collegians who went in the top round, nine were pitchers and five played the hot corner.

Bryant highlighted the crop of third basemen, but his peers included the likes of North Carolina's Colin Moran (.345-13-91), the national RBI leader who was drafted sixth by the Marlins; Dozier (.396-17-52), the top hitter and home run leader in the Southland Conference; New Mexico's D.J. Peterson (.408-18-72), a triple crown winner in the Mountain West Conference who was selected 12th by the Mariners; and Notre Dame's Eric Jagielo (.388-9-53), who fell one point short of winning the Big East Conference batting title and was taken 26th by the Yankees.

Appel was one of three pitchers in the college crop that was an unsigned former first-rounder. The others were Florida righthander Karsten Whitson and USD righthander Dylan Covey, both of whom rejected offers out of high school. Whitson was selected by the San Diego Padres with the ninth pick in the 2010 draft while Covey was chosen by the Milwaukee Brewers with the 14th pick overall in the same draft.

Whitson, who had Tommy John surgery and didn't pitch during the 2013 college season, was a 37th round afterthought of the Nationals, while Covey, who struggled with command issues, went in the fourth round to the A's, and signed for $370,000. Through three years in college, he continued to manage Type 1 diabetes that was diagnosed as part of a routine physical in August of 2010, and was a major contributing factor in his not signing with the Brewers.

# 2013 Draft List

**Did not sign. Major leaguers in bold, with first and last years noted. Order of selection indicated in parentheses. For the first five rounds, the peak level of each player is noted.*

## ARIZONA DIAMONDBACKS (14)

1. Braden Shipley, rhp, University of Nevada.—(AA)

DRAFT DROP *Cousin of Jordan Shipley, wide recever, National Football League (2010-12)*

1. Aaron Blair, rhp, Marshall University (Competitive balance Round 'A' pick—36th).—(AAA)
2. Justin Williams, ss, Terrebonne HS, Houma, La.—(High A)
3. Daniel Palka, 1b, Georgia Tech.—(High A)
4. Matt McPhearson, of, Riverdale Baptist HS, Upper Marlboro, Md.—(Rookie)
5. Jamie Westbrook, ss, Basha HS, Chandler, Ariz.—(High A)
6. Colin Bray, of, Faulkner State (Ala.) CC.
7. Daniel Gibson, lhp, University of Florida.
8. Brad Keller, rhp, Flowery Branch (Ga.) HS.
9. Grant Nelson, c, Saint Louis University.
10. Jimmie Sherfy, rhp, University of Oregon.
11. Jacob Cordero, ss, Puerto Rico Baseball Academy, Gurabo, P.R.
12. Dane McFarland, of, J Serra Catholic HS, San Juan Capistrano, Calif.
13. Taylor Ratliff, of, University of Florida.
14. Steve Hathaway, lhp, Franklin Pierce (N.H.) University.
15. Jordan Parr, 3b, University of Illinois.
16. Elvin Soto, c, University of Pittsburgh.
17. Ryan Gebhardt, ss, Louisiana Tech.
18. Ryan Kinsella, 1b, Elon University.
19. Jake Mayers, 3b, University of Richmond.
20. Adam Miller, rhp, Brigham Young University.
21. *Andy Ravel, rhp, Wilson HS, Reading, Pa.
22. Antonio Alvarez, ss, Elon University.
23. Randy McCurry, ss, Oklahoma State University.
24. Zach Esquerra, of, California Baptist University.
25. Bud Jeter, rhp, Presbyterian University.
26. George Roberts, 1b, Kent State University.
27. Jake Miller, ss, Baylor University.
28. Johnny Shuttlesworth, rhp, Faulkner (Ala.) University.
29. *Matt Foster, rhp, Valley (Ala.) HS.
30. Denver Chavez, 2b, Cal Poly.
31. Joel Thys, c, Arizona Christian University.
32. Dallas Newton, rhp, Pitt (N.C.) CC.
33. Alex Byo, rhp, Tulane University.
34. *Cory Hahn, of, Arizona State University.
35. Tyler Toyfair, rhp, University of Massachusetts-Lowell.
36. *Matt Vogel, rhp, Patchogue-Medford HS, Medford, N.Y.
37. Matt Vinson, of, University of Arkansas.
38. Kurtis Kostuk, rhp, Yale SS, Abbotsford, B.C.
39. *Mark Karaviotis, ss, Maui HS, Kahului, Hawaii.
40. *Frankie Ratcliff, ss, University of Houston.

## ATLANTA BRAVES (27)

1. (Choice forfeited for signing free agent B.J. Upton)
1. Jason Hursh, rhp, Oklahoma State University (Compensation for loss of free agent Michael Bourn—31st).—(AAA)
2. Victor Caratini, c, Miami-Dade JC.—(High A)
3. Carlos Salazar, rhp, Kerman (Calif.) HS.—(High A)
4. Tanner Murphy, c, Malden (Mo.) HS.—(Low A)
5. Mikey Reynolds, ss, Texas A&M University.—(Low A)
6. Stephen Janas, rhp, Kennesaw State University.
7. Ian Stiffler, rhp, Somerset (Pa.) HS.

DRAFT DROP *Grandson of Tom Qualters, major leaguer (1953-58)*

8. Kyle Wren, of, Georgia Tech.

DRAFT DROP *Son of Frank Wren, general manager, Orioles (1998-99); general manager, Braves (2007-14)*

9. Dylan Manwaring, 3b, Horseheads (N.Y.) HS.

DRAFT DROP *Son of Kirt Manwaring, major leaguer (1987-99)*

10. Ian Hagenmiller, 3b, Palm Beach Central HS, Wellington, Fla.
11. Alec Grosser, rhp, T.C. Williams HS, Alexandria, Va.
12. Ryan Gunther, rhp, Charleston Southern University.
13. Joseph Odom, c, Huntingdon (Ala.) College.
14. *Tyler Kuresa, 1b, UC Santa Barbara.
15. **Matt Marksberry, lhp, Campbell University.—(2015)**
16. Michael Swanner, rhp, Pepperdine University.
17. Jared Dettmann, lhp, Century (Minn.) CC.
18. Chuck Buchanan, lhp, Cal State Bakersfield.
19. Jordan Sechler, lhp, Cal State Los Angeles.
20. Tyler Vail, rhp, Temple (Texas) JC.
21. Tyler Brosius, rhp, Walters State (Tenn.) CC.
22. Andrew Waszak, rhp, Michigan State University.
23. Connor Oliver, of, State College of Florida-Manatee.
24. Orrin Sears, c, Arizona Christian University.
25. Reed Harper, ss, Austin Peay State University.
26. Dakota Dill, rhp, Sul Ross State (Texas) University.
27. Jake Schrader, 1b, University of Tampa.
28. *Stephen Wrenn, of, Walton HS, Marietta, Ga.
29. *Tim Hergert, ss, Heritage HS, Vancouver, Wash.
30. *Sterling Sharp, rhp, North Farmington HS, Farmington Hills, Mich.
31. *Johnny Slater, of, Southfield-Lathrup HS, Southfield, Mich.
32. *Jack Klein, of, St. Ignatius HS, San Francisco.
33. *Trevor Sprowl, 2b, Shelton State (Ala.) CC.

DRAFT DROP *Son of Bobby Sprowl, major leaguer (1978-81)*

34. *Mac Seibert, 2b, Meridian (Miss.) CC.
35. *Angel Perez, ss, Collegio San Felipe, Arecibo, P.R.
36. *Tyler Stubblefield, lhp, Lufkin (Texas) HS.
37. *Geoffrey Bramblett, rhp, Hoover (Ala.) HS.
38. *Jacob Heyward, of, Eagle's Landing Christian Academy, McDonough, Ga.

DRAFT DROP *Brother of Jason Heyward, first-round draft pick, Braves (2007); major leaguer (2010-15)*

39. *Francisco Cruz, of, Puerto Rico Baseball Academy, Gurabo, P.R.
40. *Connor Brogdon, rhp, Brentwood HS, Los Angeles.

## BALTIMORE ORIOLES (23)

1. Hunter Harvey, rhp, Bandys HS, Catawba, N.C.—(Low A)

DRAFT DROP *Son of Bryan Harvey, major leaguer (1987-95)*

1. Josh Hart, of, Parkview HS, Lilburn, Ga. (Competitive balance Round 'A' pick—37th).—(High A)
2. Chance Sisco, c, Temescal Canyon HS, Lake Elsinore, Calif.—(AA)
3. Stephen Tarpley, lhp, Scottsdale (Ariz.) CC.—(Low A)
4. Jonah Heim, c, Amherst Central HS, Amherst, N.Y.—(Low A)
5. Travis Seabrooke, lhp, Crestwood SS, North Monaghan, Ontario.—(Short-season A)

DRAFT DROP *Son of Glen Seabrooke, first-round draft pick, Philadelphia Flyers/National Hockey League (1985); center, NHL (1986-89)*

6. Alex Murphy, c, Calvert Hall College HS, Baltimore.
7. Drew Dosch, 3b, Youngstown State University.
8. Trey Mancini, 1b, University of Notre Dame.
9. Mitch Horacek, lhp, Dartmouth University.
10. Austin Wynns, c, Fresno State University.
11. Steven Brault, lhp, Regis (Colo.) University.
12. Jake Bray, rhp, Feather River (Calif.) JC.
13. Jimmy Yacabonis, rhp, St. Joseph's University.
14. Mike Yastrzemski, of, Vanderbilt University.

DRAFT DROP *Grandson of Carl Yastrzemski, major leaguer (1961-83)*

15. *Tyler Walsh, ss, Mater Dei HS, Evansville, Ind.
16. Randolph Gassaway, 1b, Riverwood International HS, Sandy Springs, Ga.
17. Caleb Kellogg, rhp, University of Tampa.
18. *Reed Reilly, rhp, Cal Poly.
19. Dylan Rheault, rhp, Central Michigan University.
20. Nick Cunningham, rhp, University of Arizona.
21. *Levi Scott, 1b, Howard (Texas) JC.
22. Jon Keller, rhp, University of Tampa.
23. Stefan Crichton, rhp, Texas Christian University.
24. Jared Breen, ss, Belmont University.
25. Danny Ayers, lhp, Columbus North HS, Columbus, Ind.
26. *Layne Bruner, lhp, Montesano (Wash.) HS.
27. Donnie Hart, lhp, Texas State University.
28. *Robert Tyler, rhp, Crisp County HS, Cordele, Ga.
29. Conor Bierfeldt, of, Western Connecticut State University.
30. Federico Castagnini, ss, Creighton University.
31. *Dustin Hagy, rhp, Trinity Christian Academy, Deltona, Fla.
32. Max Homick, lhp, University of San Diego.
33. Jeff Kemp, ss, Radford University.
34. *Parker Bugg, rhp, Rancho Bernardo HS, San Diego.
35. *D.J. McKnight, of, Madison County HS, Madison, Fla.
36. Eric Green, lhp, Embry-Riddle (Fla.) University.
37. Justin Viele, ss, Santa Clara University.
38. *Conor Harber, of, Western Nevada CC.
39. Augey Bill, lhp, University of Arizona.
40. Garrett Cortright, rhp, Canisius University.

## BOSTON RED SOX (7)

1. Trey Ball, lhp, New Castle (Ind.) HS.—(High A)
2. Teddy Stankiewicz, rhp, Seminole State (Okla.) JC.—(High A)
3. Jon Denney, c, Yukon (Okla.) HS.—(Rookie)
4. Myles Smith, rhp, Lee (Tenn.) University.—(AAA)
5. Corey Littrell, lhp, University of Kentucky.—(High A)

DRAFT DROP *Grandson of Jack Littrell, major leaguer (1952-57)*

6. Jordon Austin, of, Forest HS, Ocala, Fla.
7. Mike Adams, lhp, University of Tampa.
8. Forrestt Allday, of, University of Central Arkansas.
9. Kyle Martin, rhp, Texas A&M University.
10. Taylor Grover, rhp, University of South Carolina-Aiken.
11. Carlos Asuaje, ss, Nova Southeastern (Fla.) University.
12. Jake Drehoff, lhp, University of Southern Mississippi.
13. *Jordan Sheffield, rhp, Tullahoma (Tenn.) HS.
14. Jake Romanski, c, San Diego State University.
15. Bryan Hudson, of, Mill Creek HS, Hoschton, Ga.
16. Jalen Williams, rhp, Westminster Christian Academy, Opelousas, La.
17. Joseph Monge, of, Carlos Beltran Academy, Florida, P.R.
18. Joe Gunkel, rhp, West Chester (Pa.) University.
19. Gabe Speier, lhp, Dos Pueblos HS, Goleta, Calif.
20. *Derek Burkamper, rhp, Muscatine (Iowa) HS.
21. Reed Gragnani, 2b, University of Virginia.
22. *Ryan Boldt, of, Red Wing (Minn.) HS.
23. *Jimmy Allen, 2b, Cal Poly.
24. Jantzen Witte, 3b, Texas Christian University.
25. *Derik Beauprez, rhp, Cherry Creek HS, Greenwood Village, Colo.
26. Mauricio Dubon, ss, Capital Christian HS, Sacramento, Calif.
27. *Mark Nowaczewski, rhp, Edward C. Reed HS, Sparks, Nev.
28. *Nick Zammarelli, 3b, Lincoln (R.I.) HS.
29. Jeff Driskel, of, University of Florida.
30. Nick Longhi, of, Venice (Fla.) HS.
31. *Ryan Rippee, 1b, Jefferson (Mo.) CC.
32. *Matt Thaiss, c, Jackson Memorial HS, Jackson, N.J.
33. *Andrew Rosa, ss, Owasso (Okla.) HS.
34. Danny Bethea, c, St. John's University.
35. Rafael Oliveras, 3b, Loaiza Cordero Del Rosario HS, Yauco, P.R.
36. Pat Goetze, rhp, Wake County Home Schools, Raleigh, N.C.
37. *Max Watt, rhp, Hillsborough (Fla.) CC.
38. *Trever Morrison, ss, Archbishop Murphy HS, Everett, Wash.
39. K.J. Trader, rhp, Delmar (Del.) HS.
40. *Ryan Lidge, c, Barrington (Ill.) HS.

DRAFT DROP *Son of Brad Lidge, first-round draft pick, Astros (1998); major leaguer (2002-12)*

## CHICAGO CUBS (2)

1. **Kris Bryant, 3b, University of San Diego.—(2015)**
2. Rob Zastryzny, lhp, University of Missouri.—(AA)
3. Jacob Hannemann, of, Brigham Young University.—(AA)
4. Tyler Skulina, rhp, Kent State University.—(High A)
5. Trey Masek, rhp, Texas Tech.—(Short-season A)
6. Scott Frazier, rhp, Pepperdine University.
7. David Garner, rhp, Michigan State University.
8. Sam Wilson, lhp, Lamar (Colo.) CC.
9. Charcer Burks, of, W.B. Travis HS, Richmond, Texas.
10. **Zack Godley, rhp, University of Tennessee.—(2015)**
11. Jordan Hankins, c, Austin Peay State University.
12. Trevor Clifton, rhp, Heritage HS, Maryville, Tenn.
13. Trevor Graham, rhp, Franklin Pierce (N.H.) College.
14. *Daniel Poncedeleon, rhp, University of Houston.
15. Michael Wagner, rhp, University of San Diego.
16. Cael Brockmeyer, c, Cal State Bakersfield.
17. Kelvin Freeman, 1b, North Carolina A&T University.
18. Giuseppe Papaccio, ss, Seton Hall University.
19. Will Remillard, c, Coastal Carolina University.
20. Zak Blair, 2b, Mercyhurst (Pa.) University.
21. *Josh McCauley, rhp, Shepherd (W.Va.) College.
22. Kevin Brown, of, Bryant University.
23. Tyler Ihrig, lhp, CC of Marin (Calif.).
24. Tyler Alamo, c, Cypress (Calif.) HS.
25. *Marcus Doi, of, Mid-Pacific Institute, Honolulu, Hawaii.
26. *Carlos Pena, c, Southwest HS, Miami.
27. *Tyler Sciacca, 2b, Villanova University.
28. Brad Renner, rhp, Florida CC-Jacksonville.
29. *John Garcia, of, Denbigh HS, Newport News, Va.
30. Zak Hermans, rhp, Princeton University.
31. *Sean Johnson, rhp, Iowa Western CC.
32. *Keaton Leach, rhp, Glendale (Calif.) CC.
33. *Chris Madera, of, Northwest Florida State JC.
34. *Jake Thompson, rhp, Central HS, Independence, Ore.
35. *Ramsey Romano, ss, Valhalla HS, El Cajon, Calif.
36. *Derek Campbell, ss, University of California.
37. *Jeremy Martinez, c, Mater Dei HS, Santa Ana, Calif.
38. *Zack Brown, rhp, Seymour (Ind.) HS.
39. *Josh Greene, of, Forest HS, Ocala, Fla.
40. *Bubby Riley, of, Delgado (La.) CC.

## CHICAGO WHITE SOX (17)

1. Tim Anderson, ss, East Central (Miss.) CC.—(AA)
2. Tyler Danish, rhp, Durant HS, Plant City, Fla.—(AA)
3. Jacob May, of, Coastal Carolina University.—(AA)

DRAFT DROP *Grandson of Lee May, major leaguer (1965-82) • Son of Lee May Jr., first-round draft pick, Mets (1986)*

4. Andrew Mitchell, rhp, Texas Christian University.—(Low A)
5. Thaddius Lowry, rhp, Spring (Texas) HS.—(Low A)
6. James Dykstra, rhp, Cal State San Marcos.
7. Trey Michalczewski, 3b, Jenks (Okla.) HS.
8. Chris Freudenberg, lhp, South Mountain (Ariz.) CC.
9. Nick Blount, rhp, Southern Polytechnic State (Ga.) University.
10. Brad Goldberg, rhp, Ohio State University.
11. Matt Ball, rhp, Bonita Vista HS, Chula Vista, Calif.
12. Tyler Shryock, ss, Cal State Fullerton.
13. Danny Hayes, 1b, Oregon State University.
14. Tyler Barnette, rhp, UNC Charlotte.
15. Andre Wheeler, lhp, Texas Tech.
16. Christian Stringer, ss, Rice University.
17. Joey Wagman, rhp, Cal Poly.
18. Michael Carballo, of, Tennessee Wesleyan College.
19. Adam Engel, of, University of Louisville.
20. Dillon Haupt, c, University of San Diego.
21. Toby Thomas, ss, Pensacola State (Fla.) JC.
22. Nolan Earley, of, University of South Alabama.
23. Trey Wimmer, c, Liberty University.
24. Jacob Morris, of, University of Arkansas.
25. Alex Powers, rhp, Southern New Hampshire

University.
26. Charlie Sharrer, rhp, Cal State East Bay.
27. Devin Moore, rhp, Indiana State University.
28. Jeff McKenzie, lhp, Cal State Bakersfield.
29. Matt Abramson, rhp, University of Tampa.
30. Jon Bengard, rhp, California Baptist University.
31. Sean Hagan, lhp, St. John's University.
32. Darian Johnson, of, Lamar University.
33. *Tavo Rodriguez, lhp, Franklin HS, El Paso, Texas.
34. *Tyrell King, lhp, Yavapai (Ariz.) JC.
35. Sam Macias, of, University of San Diego.
36. Nick Parent, 1b, Cal State Monterey Bay.
37. Cody Yount, 1b, Virginia Commonwealth University.
DRAFT DROP *Son of Larry Yount, major leaguer (1971) • Nephew of Robin Yount, first-round draft pick, Brewers (1973); major leaguer (1974-93)*
38. Audry Santana, ss, Eckerd (Fla.) College.
39. *Wolfie Tash, 3b, Venice HS, Los Angeles.
40. *Ro Coleman, 2b, Simeon HS, Chicago.

## CINCINNATI REDS (29)

1. Phil Ervin, of, Samford University.—(AA)
1. **Michael Lorenzen, rhp, Cal State Fullerton** (Competitive balance Round 'A' pick—38th).—**(2015)**
2. Kevin Franklin, 3b, Gahr HS, Cerritos, Calif.—(Rookie)
3. Mark Armstrong, rhp, Clarence (N.Y.) HS.—(Low A)
4. Ben Lively, rhp, University of Central Florida.—(AA)
5. Cory Thompson, ss, Mauldin (S.C.) HS.—(Low A)
6. Zack Weiss, rhp, UCLA.
7. Tyler Mahle, rhp, Westminster (Calif.) HS.
8. Scott Brattvet, rhp, Cal State Bakersfield.
9. Chad Jones, lhp, New Orleans.
DRAFT DROP *Defensive back, National Football League (2010-11)*
10. Daniel Wright, rhp, Arkansas State University.
11. Ty Boyles, lhp, Quartz Hill (Calif.) HS.
12. Shedric Long, c, Jacksonville (Ala.) HS.
13. Evan Mitchell, rhp, Mississippi State University.
14. *Willie Abreu, of, Mater Academy, Hialeah Gardens, Fla.
15. Jarrett Freeland, c, Parkview HS, Lilburn, Ga.
16. Fabian Roman, rhp, Lubbock Christian (Texas) University.
17. Dalton Carter, of, Winder-Barrow HS, Winder, Ga.
18. Joe Mantoni, rhp, Merrimack (Mass.) College.
19. *Alex Krupa, of, Greenwood Community (Ind.) HS.
20. Morgan Lofstrom, c, Mount Boucherie SS, Kelowna, B.C.
21. *Eric Dorsch, rhp, Kent State University.
22. Layne Somsen, rhp, South Dakota State University.
23. Narciso Crook, of, Gloucester County (N.J.) JC.
24. *Brett Morales, rhp, King HS, Tampa.
25. *Eduardo Garcia, rhp, Alexander HS, Laredo, Texas.
26. *Eli White, ss, Wren HS, Anderson, S.C.
27. *Zack Collins, c, American Heritage HS, Plantation, Fla.
28. *Carter Austin, 1b, Maine-Endwell HS, Endwell, N.Y.
29. Alex Greer, of, Iowa Western CC.
30. Taylor Terrasas, 3b, Louisiana Tech.
31. *Andrew Benintendi, of, Madeira HS, Cincinnati.
DRAFT DROP *First-round draft pick (7th overall), Red Sox (2015)*
32. Logan Uxa, 1b, Arkansas State University.
33. *Matt Blandino, rhp, Bristol Central HS, Bristol, Conn.
34. *Luke Bolka, lhp, Atlee HS, Mechanicsville, Va.
35. *Conner Simonetti, of, Fairport (N.Y.) HS.
36. *Taylor Hearn, lhp, San Jacinto (Texas) JC.
37. *Alec Byrd, lhp, St. Thomas Aquinas HS, Fort Lauderdale, Fla.
38. *Dan Grauer, rhp, Liberty University.
39. *Manny Cruz, ss, Wolcott (Conn.) HS.
40. P.J. Cerreto, rhp, Ramapo (N.J.) College.

## CLEVELAND INDIANS (5)

1. Clint Frazier, of, Loganville (Ga.) HS.—(Low A)
2. (Choice forfeited for signing Nick Swisher as free agent)
2. (Competitive balance Round 'B' pick; forfeited for signing Michael Bourn as free agent)
3. Dace Kime, rhp, University of Louisville.—(High A)
4. **Kyle Crockett, lhp, University of Virginia.—(2014-15)**
DRAFT DROP *First player from 2013 draft to reach majors (May 16, 2014)*
5. Sean Brady, lhp, Ida Baker HS, Cape Coral, Fla.—(Low A)
6. Casey Shane, rhp, Centennial HS, Burleson, Texas.
7. Kenny Mathews, lhp, Riverside (Calif.) CC.
8. Trevor Frank, rhp, UC Riverside.
9. Thomas Pannone, lhp, CC of Southern Nevada.
10. *Ross Kivett, 2b, Kansas State University.
11. Adam Plutko, rhp, UCLA.
12. *Heath Quinn, of, Oak Mountain HS, Birmingham, Ala.
13. Sicnarf Loopstok, c, Western Oklahoma State JC.
14. Silento Sayles, of, Port Gibson (Miss.) HS.
15. James Roberts, ss, University of Southern California.
16. *Mark Payton, of, University of Texas.
17. *Ryan Hendrix, rhp, Cypress Woods HS, Cypress, Texas.
18. Paul Hendrix, ss, Texas Christian University.
19. Matt Whitehouse, lhp, UC Irvine.
20. Shane Rowland, c, University of Tampa.
21. *Paul Young, rhp, Central Alabama CC.
22. Ben Heller, rhp, Olivet Nazarene (Ill.) College.
23. Grant Fink, 3b, Missouri Western State University.
24. Kerry Doane, rhp, East Tennessee State University.
25. Cole Sulser, rhp, Dartmouth University.
26. *Danny Cogan, rhp, Rocklin (Ca.) HS.
27. *Juan Gonzalez, c, Puerto Rico Baseball Academy, Gurabo, P.R.
28. *Steven Kane, rhp, Cypress (Calif.) JC.
29. *Ridge Smith, 3b, Germantown (Tenn.) HS.
30. *Aaron Brown, lhp, Pepperdine University.
31. *Wil Crowe, rhp, Pigeon Forge (Tenn.) HS.
32. Cortland Cox, rhp, Riverside (Calif.) CC.
33. *Joey Wise, lhp, Cactus Shadows HS, Cave Creek, Ariz.
34. *Dustin Cook, rhp, San Jacinto (Texas) JC.
35. Jordan Milbrath, rhp, Augustana (S.D.) College.
36. Mike Giuffre, 2b, Brookdale (N.J.) CC.
37. Garrett Smith, 2b, California Lutheran University.
38. Justin Garcia, rhp, Weatherford (Texas) JC.
39. *Frank Duncan, rhp, University of Kansas.
40. *Dan Pellinen, 3b, North Woods HS, Cook, Minn.

## COLORADO ROCKIES (3)

1. **Jonathan Gray, rhp, University of Oklahoma.—(2015)**
2. Ryan McMahon, 3b, Mater Dei HS, Santa Ana, Calif.—(High A)
2. Alex Balog, rhp, University of San Francisco (Competitve balance Round 'B' pick—70th).—(High A)
3. Sam Moll, lhp, Memphis University.—(AA)
4. Jordan Patterson, of, University of South Alabama.—(AA)
5. Blake Shouse, rhp, Middle Georgia JC.—(Low A)
6. Dom Nunez, 3b, Elk Grove (Calif.) HS.
7. Konner Wade, rhp, University of Arizona.
8. Terry McClure, of, Riverwood International HS, Sandy Springs, Ga.
9. Pat Valaika, ss, UCLA.
DRAFT DROP *Brother of Chris Valaika, major leaguer (2010-14)*
10. Mike Tauchman, of, Bradley University.
11. Sean Dwyer, of, Florida Gulf Coast University.
12. Billy Waltrip, lhp, University of Oklahoma.
13. Mike Benjamin Jr., 3b, Arizona State University.
DRAFT DROP *Son of Mike Benjamin, major leaguer (1989-2002)*
14. Dylan Stamey, rhp, University of South Alabama.
15. John Beck, rhp, University of Texas-Arlington.
16. Alex Rodriguez, lhp, Indian River (Fla.) JC.
17. Trent Daniel, lhp, University of Arkansas.
18. Jacob Newberry, rhp, High Point University.
19. Scott Firth, rhp, Clemson University.
20. *M.T. Minacci, rhp, North Florida Christian HS, Tallahassee, Fla.
21. Eric Nedeljkovic, rhp, University of Miami.
22. *Brody Weiss, ss, Regis Jesuit HS, Aurora, Colo.
DRAFT DROP *Son of Walt Weiss, first-round draft pick, Athletics (1985); major leaguer (1987-2000); major league manager (2014-15)*
23. Jerad McCrummen, rhp, Texas Tech.
24. *Hunter Brothers, rhp, Lipscomb University.
DRAFT DROP *Brother of Rex Brothers, major leaguer (2011-15)*
25. *Alec Hansen, rhp, Loveland (Colo.) HS.
26. Matt Pierpont, rhp, Winthrop University.
27. Daniel Palo, rhp, Middle Tennessee State University.
28. *Heath Fillmyer, rhp, Mercer County (N.J.) JC.
29. *Kyle Serrano, rhp, Farragut (Tenn.) HS.
30. *Jacob Stone, rhp, Weatherford (Texas) JC.
31. Wesley Jones, ss, Redan HS, Stone Mountain, Ga.
32. *Thomas Hatch, rhp, Jenks (Okla.) HS.
33. *Alex Haines, lhp, Seton Hill (Pa.) University.
34. *Kyle Thornell, 3b, McLennan (Texas) CC.
35. *Ronnie Gideon, 3b, Hallsville (Texas) HS.
36. *Andy McGuire, ss, Madison HS, Vienna, Va.
37. *Luke Persico, of, Great Oak HS, Temecula, Calif.
38. *Scott Moss, lhp, Deland (Fla.) HS.
39. Cole Norton, of, St. Mary's (Calif.) College.
40. *Tyler Stover, 1b, Vacaville (Calif.) HS.

## DETROIT TIGERS (20)

1. Jonathon Crawford, rhp, University of Florida.—(High A)
1. **Corey Knebel, rhp, University of Texas** (Compective balance Round 'A' pick—39th; obtained from Marlins via trade).**—(2014-15)**
2. Kevin Ziomek, lhp, Vanderbilt University.—(High A)
3. Jeff Thompson, rhp, University of Louisville.—(Low A)
4. Austin Kubitza, rhp, Rice University.—(AA)
DRAFT DROP *Brother of Kyle Kubitza, major leaguer (2015)*
5. **Buck Farmer, rhp, Georgia Tech.—(2014-15)**
6. Calvin Drummond, rhp, Arizona Christian University.
7. Connor Harrell, of, Vanderbilt University.
8. Zac Reininger, rhp, Hill (Texas) JC.
9. Will LaMarche, rhp, Louisiana State University.
10. Kasey Coffman, of, Arizona State University.
11. Chad Green, rhp, University of Louisville.
12. Dominic Ficociello, 3b, University of Arkansas.
13. Austin Green, c, University of San Diego.
14. Ben Verlander, of, Old Dominion University.
DRAFT DROP *Brother of Justin Verlander, first-round draft pick, Tigers (2004); major leaguer (2005-15)*
15. Raph Rhymes, of, Louisiana State University.
16. Duncan McAlpine, c, Dallas Baptist University.
17. Steven Negron, ss, Miami-Dade JC.
18. Jon Maciel, rhp, Long Beach State University.
19. Austin Pritcher, rhp, The Citadel.
20. *Matt Wotherspoon, rhp, University of Pittsburgh.
21. Curt Powell, ss, University of Georgia.
22. Daryl Norris, rhp, Mississippi State University.
23. *Tyler Alexander, lhp, Carroll HS, Southlake, Texas.
24. Chase Edwards, rhp, Hill (Texas) JC.
25. Johnnie Kirkland, rhp, Southeastern (Fla.) University.
26. Adrian Castano, of, Benjamin N. Cardozo HS, Bayside, N.Y.
27. Joe Mantiply, lhp, Virginia Tech.
28. Scott Sitz, rhp, Florida State University.
29. *Charley Sullivan, rhp, University of Alabama.
30. Ryan Beck, lhp, New Mexico State University.
31. Brett Huber, rhp, University of Mississippi.
32. Tanner Bailey, rhp, University of Mississippi.
33. *John Armstrong, 2b, Bishop Carroll Catholic HS, Wichita, Kan.
34. *Brad Holland, 2b, Mesquite HS, Gilbert, Ariz.
35. *A.J. Puk, lhp, Washington HS, Cedar Rapids, Iowa.
36. *Torii Hunter Jr., of, Prosper (Texas) HS.
DRAFT DROP *Son of Torii Hunter, first-round draft pick, Twins (1993); major leaguer (1997-2015)*
37. *Nick Deeg, lhp, Lake Orion (Mich.) HS.
38. *Harrison Wenson, c, University of Detroit Jesuit HS, Detroit.
39. *Anfernee Grier, of, Russell County HS, Seale, Ala.
40. Taylor Johnson, 2b, St. Edward's (Texas) University.

## HOUSTON ASTROS (1)

1. Mark Appel, rhp, Stanford University.—(AAA)
DRAFT DROP *First-round pick (8th overall), Pirates (2012)*
2. Andrew Thurman, rhp, UC Irvine.—(AA)
3. Kent Emanuel, lhp, University of North Carolina.—(AA)
4. Conrad Gregor, 1b, Vanderbilt University.—(AA)
5. Tony Kemp, 2b, Vanderbilt University.—(AAA)
6. Jacob Nottingham, c, Redlands (Calif.) HS.
7. James Ramsay, of, University of South Florida.
8. Jason Martin, of, Orange Lutheran HS, Orange, Calif.
9. Brian Holberton, c, University of North Carolina.
10. Austin Nicely, lhp, Spotswood HS, Penn Laird, Va.
11. Devonte German, rhp, Bishop Manogue HS, Reno, Nev.
12. Chase McDonald, 1b, East Carolina University.
13. Kyle Westwood, rhp, University of North Florida.
14. Chris Cotton, lhp, Louisiana State University.
15. *James Farris, rhp, University of Arizona.
16. *Dillon Newman, rhp, Baylor University.
17. *Alex Schick, rhp, Cathedral Catholic HS, San Diego.
18. Adam Nelubowich, 3b, Washington State University.
19. Jake Rodriguez, c, Oregon State University.
20. *Daniel Pinero, ss, Western Tech HS, Toronto.
21. Jon Kemmer, of, Brewton-Parker (Ga.) College.
22. Sebastian Kessay, lhp, Scottsdale (Ariz.) CC.
23. Thomas Lindauer, ss, University of Illinois.
24. *Nathan Thornhill, rhp, University of Texas.
25. Albert Minnis, lhp, Wichita State University.
26. Austin Chrismon, rhp, Christopher Newport (Va.) College.
27. Pat Christensen, rhp, La Salle University.
28. Jordan Mills, lhp, St. Mary's (Calif.) College.
29. Randall Fant, lhp, University of Arkansas.
30. Jorge Perez, rhp, Seminole State (Okla.) JC.
31. *Scott Burke, rhp, Glendora (Calif.) HS.
32. Zach Morton, rhp, Northwestern University.
33. Tyler White, 3b, Western Carolina University.
34. Brett Booth, c, University of Alabama.
35. *Kacy Clemens, rhp, Memorial HS, Houston.
DRAFT DROP *Son of Roger Clemens, first-round draft pick, Red Sox (1983); major leaguer (1984-2007)*
36. J.D. Osborne, lhp, Wofford College.
37. *Josh Melendez, of, University of New Mexico.
38. Ronnie Mitchell, of, Dallas Baptist University.
39. Juan Santos, rhp, Arlington Country Day School, Jacksonville, Fla.
40. Tyler Brunnemann, rhp, Hardin-Simmons (Texas) University.

## KANSAS CITY ROYALS (8)

1. Hunter Dozier, ss, Stephen F. Austin State University.—(AA)
1. Sean Manaea, lhp, Indiana State University (Competitive balance Round 'A' pick—34th).—(AA)
2. Cody Reed, lhp, Northwest Mississippi CC.—(AA)
3. Carter Hope, rhp, The Woodlands (Texas) HS.—(Rookie)
4. Zane Evans, c, Georgia Tech.—(AA)
5. Amalani Fukofuka, of, Logan HS, Union City, Calif.—(Rookie)
6. Luke Farrell, rhp, Northwestern University.
DRAFT DROP *Son of John Farrell, major leaguer (1987-96); major league manager (2011-15)*
7. Kyle Bartsch, lhp, University of South Alabama.
8. Cody Stubbs, 1b, University of North Carolina.
9. Daniel Rockett, of, University of Texas-San Antonio.
10. Alex Newman, of, Cypress (Calif.) JC.
11. Xavier Fernandez, c, Puerto Rico Baseball Academy, Gurabo, P.R.
12. Brandon Dulin, 1b, Longview (Mo.) CC.
13. Jonathan Dziedzic, lhp, Lamar University.
14. Chase Darhower, rhp, Northwest Florida State

JC.
15. Dominique Taylor, of, UC Irvine.
16. Kevin McCarthy, rhp, Marist College.
17. Kevin Perez, rhp, Miami-Dade JC.
18. Frank Schwindel, c, St. John's University.
19. Andrew Edwards, rhp, Western Kentucky University.
20. Glenn Sparkman, rhp, Wharton (Texas) JC.
21. *Shane Conlon, 1b, Kansas State University.
22. Andrew Brockett, rhp, University of Richmond.
23. Javier Reynoso, lhp, Middle Georgia JC.
DRAFT DROP *Son of Reggie Williams, major leaguer (1985-88)*
24. Riley King, of, Carroll (Mont.) College.
25. *Logan Gray, ss, Rockhurst HS, Kansas City, Mo.
26. *Trace Tam Sing, ss, Washington State University.
27. Christian Flecha, lhp, Caguas (P.R.) Military Academy.
28. Kevin Kuntz, ss, University of Kansas.
DRAFT DROP *Son of Casey Kuntz, major leaguer (1979-85)*
29. Alex Black, rhp, Columbia University.
30. Andrew Ayers, 2b, Sacramento State University.
31. *T.J. Zeuch, rhp, Mason (Ohio) HS.
32. *Michael Shawaryn, rhp, Gloucester Catholic HS, Gloucester City, N.J.
33. *Dalton Moats, lhp, Park Hill HS, Kansas City, Mo.
34. *Isaac Anderson, rhp, JC of Southern Idaho.
35. *Clay Miller, lhp, Bayfield (Colo.) HS.
36. *Ryan McBroom, 1b, West Virginia University.
37. *Will Craig, 3b, Science HIll HS, Johnson City, Tenn.
38. *Jake Matthews, of, Ironwood Ridge HS, Oro Valley, Ariz.
39. *John Sternagel, ss, Rockledge (Fla.) HS.
40. *Keaton Steele, rhp, University of Missouri.

## LOS ANGELES ANGELS (21)

1. (Choice forfeited for signing Josh Hamilton as free agent)
2. Hunter Green, lhp, Warren East HS, Bowling Green, Ky.—(Rookie)
3. Keynan Middleton, rhp, Lane (Ore.) CC.—(Low A)
4. Elliot Morris, rhp, Pierce (Wash.) JC.—(AA)
5. Kyle McGowin, rhp, Savannah State University.—(AA)
6. Harrison Cooney, rhp, Florida Gulf Coast University.
7. Garrett Nuss, rhp, Seminole State (Fla.) CC.
8. Nate Smith, lhp, Furman University.
9. Stephen McGee, c, Florida State University.
10. Grant Gordon, rhp, Missouri State University.
11. Jonah Wesely, lhp, Tracy (Calif.) HS.
12. *Blake Goins, rhp, Pearland (Texas) HS.
13. Angel Rosa, ss, Alcorn State University.
14. Riley Good, of, University of Texas-San Antonio.
15. Chad Hinshaw, of, Illinois State University.
16. Ryan Etsell, rhp, Hillsborough (Fla.) JC.
17. Cal Towey, 3b, Baylor University.
18. Garrett Cannizaro, 3b, Tulane University.
DRAFT DROP *Brother of Andy Cannizaro, major leaguer (2006-08)*
19. Cole Swanson, lhp, Concordia (Calif.) University.
20. Brian Loconsole, rhp, Western Illinois University.
21. Alex Allbritton, ss, University of New Mexico.
22. Trevor Foss, rhp, Texas A&M University-Corpus Christi.
23. Matt Hernandez, lhp, University of Houston.
24. Mark Shannon, of, University of Nevada-Las Vegas.
25. Alan Busenitz, rhp, Kennesaw State University.
26. Kirby Pellant, ss, Ohio State University.
27. Nate Goro, ss, Oral Roberts University.
28. Michael Hermosillo, of, Ottawa (Ill.) HS.
29. Michael Smith, rhp, Dallas Baptist University.
30. Cambric Moye, c, UNC Greensboro.
31. Taylor Johnson, of, Furman University.
32. Mike Fish, of, Siena University.
33. Colin O'Keefe, lhp, Virginia Tech.
34. Eric Aguilera, of, Illinois State University.
35. Eric Weiss, c, Texas A&M University-Corpus Christi.
36. Brandon Bayardi, of, University of Nevada-Las Vegas.
37. Alex Blackford, rhp, Arizona State University.
38. Clint Sharp, rhp, University of Texas-San Antonio.

ANDREW WOOLLEY

**Rockies first-rounder Jonathan Gray made huge strides as a prospect in college at Oklahoma**

39. Dan Tobik, rhp, University of Tennessee-Martin.
DRAFT DROP *Son of Dave Tobik, major leaguer (1978-85)*
40. Ben Carlson, rhp, Furman University.

## LOS ANGELES DODGERS (18)

1. Chris Anderson, rhp, Jacksonville University.—(AAA)
2. Tom Windle, lhp, University of Minnesota.—(AA)
3. Brandon Dixon, 3b, University of Arizona.—(AA)
4. Cody Bellinger, 1b, Hamilton HS, Chandler, Ariz.—(High A)
DRAFT DROP *Son of Clay Bellinger, major leaguer (1999-2002)*
5. J.D. Underwood, rhp, Palm Beach State (Fla.) JC.—(Low A)
DRAFT DROP *Son of Tom Underwood, major leaguer (1974-84) • Nephew of Pat Underwood, first-round draft pick, Tigers (1976); major leaguer (1979-83)*
6. Jacob Rhame, rhp, Grayson County (Texas) CC.
7. Brandon Trinkwon, ss, UC Santa Barbara.
8. Kyle Farmer, c, University of Georgia.
9. Hank Yates, of, Texas Wesleyan College.
10. Nick Keener, rhp, Mansfield (Pa.) University.
11. Spencer Navin, c, Vanderbilt University.
12. Adam Law, 3b, Brigham Young University.
DRAFT DROP *Grandson of Vernon Law, major leaguer (1950-67) • Son of Vance Law, major leaguer (1980-91)*
13. *Ty Damron, lhp, Krum (Texas) HS.
14. Michael Johnson, lhp, Dartmouth University.
15. Billy Flamion, lhp, Grossmont (Calif.) JC.
16. *Peter Miller, rhp, Florida State University.
17. Greg Harris, rhp, Los Alamitos (Calif.) HS.
DRAFT DROP *Son of Greg Harris, majr leaguer (1981-95)*
18. James McDonald, 2b, Arizona State University.
19. Blake Hennessey, ss, Arlington Country Day HS, Jacksonville, Fla.
20. Michael Ahmed, of, College of the Holy Cross.
DRAFT DROP *Brother of Nick Ahmed, major leaguer (2014-15)*
21. Jamie Baune, rhp, Southern Arkansas University.
22. Jake Fisher, lhp, University of Oklahoma.
23. M.J. Villegas, rhp, Seton Catholic HS, Chandler, Ariz.
24. Jose De Leon, rhp, Southern University.
25. Kyle Hooper, rhp, UC Irvine.
26. Thomas Taylor, rhp, University of Kansas.
27. *Tanner Kiest, rhp, Riverside (Calif.) CC.
28. Crayton Bare, lhp, Baylor University.
29. *Sam Finfer, c, Interlake HS, Bellevue, Wash.
30. Ryan Scott, c, Notre Dame HS, Scottsdale, Ariz.
31. *Andrew McWilliam, 3b, Westview HS, San Diego.
32. Rob Rogers, rhp, Keystone (Pa.) College.
33. *Tyger Pederson, 2b, University of the Pacific.
34. *Rob Cerfolio, lhp, Yale University.
35. *Kaleb Holbrook, c, South Georgia JC.
36. *James Lynch, of, Glendale (Ariz.) CC.
37. *Justin Dunn, rhp, The Gunnery School, Washington, Conn.
38. Dillon Moyer, ss, UC San Diego.
DRAFT DROP *Son of Jamie Moyer, major leaguer (1986-2012)*
39. *Jake Sidwell, c, Olympia HS, Orlando, Fla.
40. *Matt Haggerty, of, Seton Catholic HS, Chandler, Ariz.

## MIAMI MARLINS (6)

1. Colin Moran, 3b, University of North Carolina.—(AA)
DRAFT DROP *Nephew of B.J Surhoff, first overall draft pick, Brewers (1985); major leaguer (1987-2005) • Nephew of Rick Surhoff, major leaguer (1985)*
1. *Matt Krook, lhp, St. Ignatius HS, San Francisco (Competitive balance Round 'A' pick—35th; obtained from Pirates via trade).
DRAFT DROP *Attended Oregon*
2. Trevor Williams, rhp, Arizona State University.—(AAA)
2. Colby Suggs, rhp, University of Arkansas (Competitive balance Round 'B' pick—73rd; obtained from Tigers via trade).—(High A)
3. *Ben DeLuzio, ss, The First Academy, Orlando, Fla.
DRAFT DROP *Attended Florida State*
4. K.J. Woods, of, Fort Mill (S.C.) HS.—(Low A)
5. Chad Wallach, c, Cal State Fullerton.—(High A)
DRAFT DROP *Son of Tim Wallach, first-round draft pick, Expos (1979); major leaguer (1980-96)*
6. Ryan Aper, of, Lincoln Land (Ill.) CC.
7. Justin Bohn, ss, Feather River (Calif.) JC.
8. Iramis Olivencia, 2b, Arlington Country Day School, Jacksonville, Fla.
9. Aaron Blanton, ss, Richland (Texas) JC.
10. Carlos Lopez, 1b, Cal State Fullerton.
11. Coco Johnson, of, University of Louisville.
12. C.J. Robinson, rhp, St. John's River (Fla.) JC.
13. J.T. Riddle, 2b, University of Kentucky.
14. Scott Carcaise, 1b, Florida Tech.
15. Miles Williams, of, Cal State Northridge.
16. Tyler Kinley, rhp, Barry (Fla.) University.
17. *Scott Schultz, rhp, Oregon State University.
18. Max Garner, rhp, Baylor University.
19. Will White, lhp, CC of Marin (Calif.).
20. Juan Avila, 3b, Long Beach State University.
21. Sam Alvis, lhp, Louisiana Tech.
22. Nelson Zulueta, rhp, Faith Baptist Christian HS, Brandon, Fla.
23. Josh Easley, rhp, North Carolina State University.
24. Cody Harris, rhp, The Master's (Calif.) College.
25. Sean Townsley, lhp, High Point University.
26. Adam Westmoreland, lhp, University of South Carolina.
27. *Matt Young, rhp, Glendora (Calif.) HS.
28. Joel Effertz, rhp, University of Wisconsin-LaCrosse.
29. *Kevin Williams, ss, UCLA.
30. *Eric Fisher, 1b, University of Arkansas.
31. *Dalton Viner, rhp, Eastern Oklahoma State JC.
32. Cody Crabaugh, rhp, Oklahoma City University.
33. *Blake Douglas, rhp, Weatherford (Texas) JC.
34. Edward Cruz, rhp, Western Oklahoma State JC.
35. *Cole Stapler, rhp, Dutchtown HS, Geismar, La.
36. *Chandler Eden, rhp, Yuba City (Calif.) HS.
37. *Michael Bell, ss, Hughes HS, Fairburn, Ga.
38. Tyler Kane, rhp, University of Washington.
39. *Daulton Jefferies, rhp, Buhach Colony HS, Atwater, Calif.
40. *Timmy Richards, ss, Woodrow Wilson HS, Long Beach, Calif.

## MILWAUKEE BREWERS (16)

1. (Choice forfeited for signing Kyle Lohse as free agent)
2. Devin Williams, rhp, Hazelwood West HS, Hazelwood, Mo.—(Low A)
2. Tucker Neuhaus, ss, Wharton HS, Tampa (Competitive balance Round 'B' pick—72nd).—(Low A)
3. Barrett Astin, rhp, University of Arkansas.—(AA)
4. Taylor Williams, rhp, Kent State University.—(High A)
5. Josh Uhen, rhp, University of Wisconsin-Milwaukee.—(Low A)
6. Garrett Cooper, 1b, Auburn University.
7. Omar Garcia, of, Miami-Dade JC.
8. Brandon Diaz, of, American Heritage HS, Plantation, Fla.
9. Tyler Linehan, lhp, Fresno State University.
10. Michael Ratterree, of, Rice University.
11. Andy Hillis, rhp, Lee (Tenn.) University.
12. Trevor Seidenberger, lhp, Texas Christian University.
13. Tanner Norton, c, Bishop Brossart HS, Alexandria, Ky.
14. Hobbs Johnson, lhp, University of North Carolina.
15. David Denson, 1b, South Hills HS, West Covina, Calif.
16. *Corey Miller, rhp, Pepperdine University.
17. Brandon Moore, rhp, University of Arkansas.
18. Clint Terry, lhp, Lee (Tenn.) University.

19. *Josh Matheson, rhp, Minnesota State University-Mankato.
20. *Ryan Yarbrough, lhp, Old Dominion University.
21. Tristan Archer, rhp, Tennessee Tech.
22. Johnny Davis, of, West Los Angeles JC.
23. Eric Williams, of, Sachse (Texas) HS.
24. Chris Razo, rhp, Illinois State University.
25. Drew Ghelfi, rhp, University of Minnesota.

DRAFT DROP *Son of Tony Ghelfi, major leaguer (1983)*

26. *Kyren Gilmore-Parrott, of, Herndon (Va.) HS.
27. Tyler Alexander, lhp, Florida International University.
28. Alex Moore, rhp, Lee (Tenn.) University.
29. *Nick Eicholtz, rhp, Cambridge Christian HS, Tampa.
30. Luis Aviles, ss, Southwest HS, Miami.
31. Tanner Poppe, rhp, University of Kansas.
32. Ryan Deeter, rhp, UCLA.
33. *Charles LeBlanc, ss, Georges Vanier SS, Toronto.
34. Dylan Brock, rhp, Glendale (Ariz.) CC.
35. *Jesse Travis, rhp, Southwest Mississippi CC.
36. Jesse Weiss, 1b, Kenyon (Ohio) College.
37. *JaVon Shelby, ss, Tates Creek HS, Lexington, Ky.

DRAFT DROP *Son of John Shelby, major leaguer (1981-91)*

38. Charlie Markson, of, University of Notre Dame.
39. Jack Cleary, c, University of Maryland.
40. *Kenny Meimerstorf, of, Bishop Gorman HS, Las Vegas, Nev.

## MINNESOTA TWINS (4)

1. Kohl Stewart, rhp, St. Pius X HS, Houston.—(High A)
2. Ryan Eades, rhp, Louisiana State University.—(High A)
3. Stuart Turner, c, University of Mississippi.—(AA)
4. Stephen Gonsalves, lhp, Cathedral Catholic HS, San Diego.—(High A)
5. Aaron Slegers, rhp, Indiana University.—(AA)
6. Brian Navarreto, c, Arlington Country Day HS, Jacksonville, Fla.
7. Brian Gilbert, rhp, Seton Hall University.
8. *Dustin DeMuth, 3b, Indiana University.
9. Mitch Garver, c, University of New Mexico.
10. C.K. Irby, rhp, Samford University.
11. Nelson Molina, ss, Luchetti HS, Arecibo, P.R.
12. Ethan Mildren, rhp, University of Pittsburgh.
13. Brandon Peterson, rhp, Wichita State University.
14. Zach Granite, of, Seton Hall University.
15. Derrick Penilla, lhp, Mount San Antonio (Calif.) JC
16. Brandon Bixler, lhp, Florida Gulf Coast University.
17. Tanner Mendonca, rhp, Cal State Sacramento.
18. Ryan Walker, ss, University of Texas-Arlington.
19. Jared Wilson, rhp, UC Santa Barbara.
20. Jason Kanzler, of, University of Buffalo.
21. Tyler Stirewalt, rhp, Fresno State University.
22. Alex Swim, c, Elon University.
23. Zach Hayden, rhp, University of South Carolina-Aiken.
24. Brandon Easton, lhp, Lakeland (Ohio) CC.
25. Chad Christensen, of, University of Nebraska.
26. *Ryan Halstead, rhp, Indiana University.
27. *Taylor Blatch, rhp, Jensen Beach (Fla.) HS.
28. *Chris Erwin, lhp, Grayson HS, Loganville, Ga.
29. *Logan Shore, rhp, Coon Rapids (Minn.) HS.
30. Tanner Vavra, 2b, Valparaiso University.
31. *A.J. Bogucki, rhp, Boyertown (Pa.) Area HS.
32. Carlos Avila, ss, Cal State Dominguez Hills.
33. *Steven Sensley, of, University HS, Baton Rouge, La.
34. *Ivory Thomas, of, Cal State Dominguez Hills.
35. *Nick Lemoncelli, lhp, Lower Columbia (Wash.) JC.
36. *Joe Greenfield, rhp, Eastern Illinois University.
37. *Julian Service, of, Northeast Texas CC.
38. *Javi Salas, rhp, University of Miami.
39. Seth Wagner, lhp, Mifflin County HS, Lewistown, Pa.
40. *Kelly Starnes, of, Los Medanos (Calif.) JC.

## NEW YORK METS (10)

1. Dominic Smith, 1b, Serra HS, Gardena, Calif.—(High A)
2. Andrew Church, rhp, Basic HS, Henderson, Nev.—(Short-season A)
3. Ivan Wilson, of, Ruston (La.) HS (Special compensation choice—76th—for failure to sign 2012 second-round pick Teddy Stankiewicz).—(Rookie)
3. Casey Meisner, rhp, Cypress Woods HS, Cypress, Texas.—(High A)
4. L.J. Mazzilli Jr., 2b, University of Connecticut.—(AAA)

DRAFT DROP *Son of Lee Mazzilli, first-round draft pick, Mets (1973); major leaguer (1976-89); major league manager (2004-05)*

5. Jared King, of, Kansas State University.—(AA)
6. Champ Stuart, of, Brevard (N.C.) College.
7. Matt Oberste, 1b, University of Oklahoma.
8. Ricky Knapp, rhp, Florida Gulf Coast University.
9. Patrick Biondi, of, University of Michigan.
10. Luis Guillorme, ss, Coral Springs (Fla.) HS.
11. Ty Bashlor, rhp, South Georgia JC.
12. Jeff McNeil, ss, Long Beach State University.
13. Kevin McGowan, rhp, Franklin Pierce (N.H.) College.
14. *J.D. Leckenby, rhp, Washington State University.
15. Colton Plaia, c, Loyola Marymount University.
16. Zach Mathieu, 1b, Franklin Pierce (N.H.) College.
17. Johnny Magliozzi, rhp, University of Florida.
18. Brent McMinn, rhp, University of Nevada.
19. *Cody Crouse, rhp, Bloomingdale HS, Valrico, Fla.
20. Dan Herrmann, rhp, Christian Brothers HS, St. Louis.
21. *Morgan Earman, rhp, Desert Christian Academy, Bermuda Dunes, Calif.
22. *Daniel Procopio, rhp, Central Technical School, Toronto.
23. Gaither Bumgardner, rhp, USC Upstate.
24. *Matt Brill, rhp, Moline (Ill.) HS.
25. Ricky Jacquez, rhp, Central Arizona JC.
26. *Owen Spiwak, c, Cawthra Park SS, Mississauga, Ontario.
27. *Austin Coley, rhp, Belmont University.
28. Robby Coles, rhp, Florida State University.
29. *Anthony Kay, lhp, Melville HS, East Setauket, N.Y.
30. *David McKay, rhp, Viera (Fla.) HS.
31. *Ben Hecht, rhp, St. Anthony HS, Effingham, Ill.
32. *J.C. Escarra, c, Mater Academy, Hialeah Gardens, Fla.
33. Ryan Chapman, rhp, Santa Ana (Calif.) JC.
34. Cameron Griffin, rhp, Columbus State (Ga.) University.
35. Ty Williams, rhp, Seminole State (Okla.) JC.
36. Brandon Brosher, 1b, Springstead HS, Spring Hill, Fla.
37. *Juan Avena, 1b, Compton (Calif.) JC.
38. Paul Paez, lhp, Rio Hondo (Calif.) JC.
39. *Logan Quimuyog, 1b, Mosley HS, Lynn Haven, Fla.
40. *J.B. Woodman, of, Edgewater HS, Orlando, Fla.

## NEW YORK YANKEES (28)

1. Eric Jagielo, 3b, University of Notre Dame.—(AA)
1. Aaron Judge, of, Fresno State University (Supplemental choice—32nd—for loss of Nick Swisher as free agent).—(AAA)
1. Ian Clarkin, lhp, James Madison HS, San Diego (Supplemental choice—33rd—for loss of Rafael Soriano as free agent).—(High A)
2. Gosuke Katoh, 2b, Rancho Bernardo HS, San Diego.—(Low A)
3. Michael O'Neill, of, University of Michigan.—(High A)

DRAFT DROP *Nephew of Paul O'Neil, major leaguer (1985-2001)*

4. Tyler Wade, ss, Murrieta Valley HS, Murrieta, Calif.—(AA)
5. David Palladino, rhp, Howard (Texas) JC.—(Low A)
6. John Murphy, ss, Sacred Heart University.
7. **Nick Rumbelow, rhp, Louisiana State University.—(2015)**
8. Brandon Thomas, of, Georgia Tech.
9. Conner Kendrick, lhp, Auburn University.
10. Tyler Webb, lhp, University of South Carolina.
11. Kendall Coleman, of, Rockwall (Texas) HS.
12. Philip Walby, rhp, San Diego State University.
13. Cale Coshow, rhp, Oklahoma Christian University.
14. Caleb Smith, lhp, Sam Houston State University.
15. Jordan Barnes, of, Northwest Mississippi CC.
16. *Ryan Butler, rhp, Central Piedmont (N.C.) CC.
17. *Hever Bueno, rhp, Westwood HS, Mesa, Ariz.
18. Dustin Fowler, of, West Laurens HS, Dexter, Ga.
19. Andy Beresford, rhp, University of Nevada-Las Vegas.
20. Drew Bridges, 3b, Carthage (Mo.) HS.
21. Ethan Carnes, lhp, University of Oklahoma.
22. Derek Toadvine, 2b, Kent State University.
23. Alex Polanco, rhp, Western Oklahoma State JC.
24. Sam Agnew-Wieland, rhp, Appalachian State University.
25. *Jordan Floyd, lhp, Shawnee Heights HS, Tecumseh, Kan.
26. *Cal Quantrill, rhp, Trinity College School, Port Hope, Ontario.

DRAFT DROP *Son of Paul Quantrill, major leager (1992-2005)*

27. Dillon McNamara, rhp, Adelphi (N.Y.) University.
28. Trent Garrison, c, Fresno State University.
29. *Charlie White, of, University of Maryland.
30. *Cody Thomas, of, Colleyville Heritage HS, Colleyville, Texas.
31. Kevin Cornelius, ss, Grayson County (Texas) CC.
32. Kale Sumner, 3b, Hawaii Pacific University.
33. *Shane McCarley, rhp, Manvel (Texas) HS.
34. Hector Crespo, 2b, Appalachian State University.
35. *Nick Green, rhp, Fountain-Fort Carson HS, Fountain, Colo.
36. Nestor Cortes, lhp, Hialeah (Fla.) HS.
37. *Josh Pettitte, rhp, Deer Park (Texas) HS.

DRAFT DROP *Son of Andy Pettite, major leaguer (1995-2013)*

38. *Andrew Schmidt, of, Regis Jesuit HS, Aurora, Colo.
39. Ty Afenir, ss, University of Washington.
40. *Kyle Buchanan, of, Florida Gulf Coast University.

## OAKLAND ATHLETICS (25)

1. Billy McKinney, of, Plano West HS, Plano, Texas.—(AA)
2. Dillon Overton, lhp, University of Oklahoma.—(AA)
2. Chad Pinder, ss, Virginia Tech (Competitive balance Round 'B' pick—71st).—(AA)
3. Ryon Healy, 1b, University of Oregon.—(AA)
3. Chris Kohler, lhp, Los Osos HS, Rancho Cucamonga, Calif. (Special compensation choice—106th—for failure to sign 2012 third-round pick Kyle Twomey).—((Short-season A)
4. Dylan Covey, rhp, University of San Diego.—(High A)

DRAFT DROP *First-round draft pick (14th overall), Brewers (2010)*

5. Bobby Wahl, rhp, University of Mississippi.—(AA)
6. Kyle Finnegan, rhp, Texas State University.
7. Dustin Driver, rhp, Wenatchee (Wash.) HS.
8. Tyler Marincov, of, University of North Florida.
9. Matt Stalcup, lhp, Pittsburg State (Kan.) College.
10. Jerad Grundy, lhp, University of Kentucky.
11. Lou Trivino, rhp, Slippery Rock (Pa.) University.
12. Dakota Freese, rhp, Des Moines Area (Iowa) CC.
13. Justin Higley, of, Sacramento State University.
14. *James Lomangino, rhp, St. John's University.
15. Edwin Diaz, ss, Martine HS, Vega Alta, P.R.

DRAFT DROP *Son of Edwin Diaz, major leaguer (1998-99)*

16. Junior Mendez, rhp, Southern New Hampshire University.
17. Jaycob Brugman, of, Brigham Young University.
18. Sam Bragg, rhp, Georgia Perimeter JC.
19. *A.J. Vanegas, rhp, Stanford University.
20. Iolana Akau, c, St. Louis HS, Honolulu, Hawaii.
21. Scott Masik, of, Cal State Los Angeles.
22. Trevor Bayless, rhp, University of San Diego.
23. Josh Miller, c, University of South Carolina-Aiken.
24. *Kevin Johnson, rhp, University of Illinois.
25. Jon Massad, rhp, Southern New Hampshire University.
26. Kyle Wheeler, c, Belhaven (Miss.) College.
27. Ryan Huck, 1b, Western Kentucky University.
28. Joe Bennie, 2b, East Stroudsburg (Pa.) College.
29. Blake McMullen, rhp, Science and Arts of Oklahoma University.
30. Ben McQuown, of, Campbell University.
31. A.J. Burke, rhp, Western Oregon University.
32. Dominique Vattuone, rhp, UNC Greensboro.
33. Joe Michaud, rhp, Bryant University.
34. A.J. Kubala, 1b, Arlington Country Day HS, Jacksonville, Fla.
35. *A.J. Puckett, rhp, De La Salle HS, Concord, Calif.
36. *Cooper Goldby, c, Yuba City (Calif.) HS.
37. *Francis Christy, c, Casa Grande HS, Petaluma, Calif.
38. *Hunter Mercado-Hood, of, De La Salle HS, Concord, Calif.
39. *Hayden Howard, lhp, Seward County (Kan.) CC.
40. *Dominic Miroglio, c, Bishop O'Dowd HS, Oakland.

## PHILADELPHIA PHILLIES (15)

1. J.P. Crawford, ss, Lakewood (Calif.) HS.—(AA)

DRAFT DROP *Son of Larry Crawford, defensive back, Canadian Football League (1981-89) • Cousin of Carl Crawford, major leaguer (2002-15)*

2. Andrew Knapp, c, University of California.—(AA)
3. Cord Sandberg, of, Manatee HS, Bradenton, Fla. (Supplemental choice—89th—for failure to sign 2012 second-round pick Alec Rash).—(Low A)
3. Jan Hernandez, ss, Carlos Beltran Academy, Florida, P.R.—(Low A)
4. Jake Sweaney, c, Garces Memorial HS, Bakersfield, Calif.—(Rookie)
5. *Ben Wetzler, lhp, Oregon State University.—(High A)

DRAFT DROP *Returned to Oregon State; re-drafted by Marlins, 2014 (9th round)*

6. *Jason Monda, of, Washington State University.
7. Trey Williams, 3b, JC of the Canyons (Calif.).

DRAFT DROP *Son of Eddie Williams, first-round draft pick, Mets (1983); major leaguer (1986-98)*

8. Justin Parr, of, University of Illinois.
9. Shane Martin, rhp, Southwestern Oklahoma State University.
10. Jon Prosinski, rhp, Seton Hall University.
11. Denton Keys, lhp, Rye (Colo.) HS.
12. *Griffin Jax, rhp, Cherry Creek HS, Greenwood Village, Colo.
13. *Joey Martarano, 3b, Fruitland (Idaho) HS.
14. Sam Dove, 2b, Georgia Tech.
15. Logan Pierce, 3b, Troy University.
16. Lee Ridenhour, rhp, Austin Peay State University.
17. Rob Marcello, lhp, Appalachian State University.
18. Dan Child, rhp, Oregon State University.
19. Matt Soren, rhp, University of Delaware.
20. Corey Bass, c, University of North Florida.
21. Mark Meadors, rhp, Cowley County (Kan.) CC.
22. Mark Leiter Jr., rhp, New Jersey Tech.

DRAFT DROP *Son of Mark Leiter, major leaguer (1990-2001)*

23. Chris O'Hare, lhp, Fisher (Mass.) College.
24. Will Morris, rhp, CC of Southern Nevada.
25. Cody Forsythe, lhp, Southern Illinois University.
26. Chris Burgess, rhp, Oklahoma Christian University.
27. Tyler Buckley, rhp, University of Arkansas-Little Rock.
28. Matt Southard, rhp, Yavapai (Ariz.) JC.
29. *Cavan Biggio, 2b, St. Thomas HS, Houston.

DRAFT DROP *Son of Craig Biggio, first-round draft pick, Astros (1987); major leaguer (1988-2007)*

30. Venn Biter, of, Rossview HS, Clarksville, Tenn.
31. *Matt Grimes, rhp, Georgia Tech.
32. Tyler Viza, rhp, Desert Vista HS, Phoenix.
33. *Harrison Musgrave, lhp, West Virginia University.
34. David Whitehead, rhp, Elon University.
35. Nick Ferdinand, of, University of Delaware.
36. *Dalton Dulin, 2b, Memphis University HS, Memphis.
37. *Ryley MacEachern, rhp, Salisbury (Conn.) Prep.
38. *Dimitri Casas, rhp, Cherry Creek HS, Greenwood Village, Colo.
39. *Brandon Wagner, 3b, Immaculata HS, Somerville, N.J.
40. *Jose Haros, ss, San Fernando (Calif.) HS.

## PITTSBURGH PIRATES (13)

1. Austin Meadows, of, Grayson HS, Loganville,

Ga. (Special compensation choice—9th—for failure to sign 2012 first-round pick Mark Appel).—(AA)
1. Reese McGuire, c, Kentwood HS, Covington, Wash.—(High A)
2. Blake Taylor, lhp, Dana Hills HS, Dana Point, Calif.—(Short-season A)
3. JaCoby Jones, of, Louisiana State University.—(AA)
4. Cody Dickson, lhp, Sam Houston State University.—(High A)
5. Trae Arbet, ss, Great Oak HS, Temecula, Calif.—(Rookie)
6. Adam Frazier, ss, Mississippi State University.
7. Buddy Borden, rhp, University of Nevada-Las Vegas.
8. Neil Kozikowski, rhp, Avon Old Farms School, Avon, Conn.
9. Chad Kuhl, rhp, University of Delaware.
10. Shane Carle, rhp, Long Beach State University.
11. Erich Weiss, 3b, University of Texas.

DRAFT DROP *Son of Gary Weiss, major leaguer (1980-81)*

12. Beau Wallace, 3b, Hinds (Miss.) CC.
13. Danny Collins, 1b, Troy University.
14. Nick Buckner, of, North Shore HS, Houston.
15. Max Rossiter, c, Arizona State University.
16. Billy Roth, rhp, Vista (Calif.) HS.
17. Justin Topa, rhp, Long Island University-Brooklyn.
18. Jeff Roy, of, University of Rhode Island.
19. Brett McKinney, rhp, Ohio State University.
20. *Ryan Lindemuth, 2b, College of William & Mary.
21. Adam Landecker, 2b, University of Southern California.
22. Henry Hirsch, rhp, University of New Haven (Conn.).
23. Cameron Griffin, lhp, Stetson University.
24. *Carson Cross, rhp, University of Connecticut.

DRAFT DROP *Son of Jeff Cross, forward, National Basketball Association (1986-87)*

25. Justin Maffei, of, University of San Francisco.
26. *Grant Tyndall, of, South Lenoir HS, Deep Run, N.C.
27. Mike Fransoso, ss, University of Maine.
28. Jerry Mulderig, rhp, Rider University.
29. *Jake Stinnett, rhp, University of Maryland.
30. Will Kendall, lhp, Auburn University.
31. *Tevin Johnson, of, Gulf Coast (Fla.) CC.
32. *Christian Ibarra, 3b, Louisiana State University.
33. *Reagan Bazar, rhp, Salado HS, South Bell, Texas.
34. *Connor Goedert, 3b, Neosho County (Kan.) CC.
35. *Cody Beam, rhp, Dallas Baptist University.
36. *Scot Hoffman, rhp, South Mountain (Ariz.) CC.
37. Andrew Dennis, c, Wallace State (Ala.) CC.
38. *Luke Voiron, c, Delgado (La.) CC.
39. *Jacob Smigelski, rhp, UC Riverside.
40. *Bryan Baker, rhp, Choctawhatchee HS, Fort Walton Beach, Fla.

## ST. LOUIS CARDINALS (19)

1. **Marco Gonzales, lhp, Gonzaga University.—(2014-15)**
1. Rob Kaminsky, lhp, Saint Joseph Regional HS, Montvale, N.J. (Supplemental choice—28th—for loss of Kyle Lohse as free agent).—(High A)
2. Oscar Mercado, ss, Gaither HS, Tampa.—(Low A)
3. Mike Mayers, rhp, University of Mississippi.—(AAA)
4. Mason Katz, 2b, Louisiana State University.—(High A)
5. Ian McKinney, lhp, William R. Boone HS, Orlando, Fla.—(High A)
6. Jimmy Reed, lhp, University of Maryland.
7. Chris Rivera, ss, El Dorado HS, Placentia, Calif.
8. Andrew Pierce, rhp, University of Southern Mississippi.
9. Nick Petree, rhp, Missouri State University.
10. Malik Collymore, ss, Port Credit SS, Mississauga, Ontario.
11. Steve Farinaro, rhp, Head Royce HS, Oakland.
12. Ricardo Bautista, of, Martinez HS, Vega Alta, P.R.
13. Jimmy Bosco, of, Menlo (Calif.) College.
14. Elier Rodriguez, c, Immaculata-LaSalle HS, Miami.
15. DeAndre Asbury, of, Brookland-Cayce HS, Cayce, S.C.
16. Blake Higgins, rhp, Jackson (Mich.) CC.
17. Richy Pedroza, ss, Cal State Fullerton.
18. J.J. Altobelli, ss, University of Oregon.
19. Michael Schulze, ss, Missouri Western State College.
20. Chase Brookshire, lhp, Belmont University.
21. Zach Loraine, rhp, Coker (S.C.) College.
22. Luke Voit, c, Missouri State University.
23. Alex DeLeon, c, University of Kansas.
24. Devante Lacy, of, Cedar Valley (Texas) JC.
25. Michael Holback, rhp, Cal Poly.
26. Will Anderson, rhp, Fresno State University.
27. Jake Stone, 1b, Tennessee Wesleyan College.
28. Justin Ringo, 1b, Stanford University.
29. *Bryan Radziewski, lhp, University of Miami.
30. Trey Nielsen, rhp, University of Utah.

DRAFT DROP *Son of Scott Nielsen, major leaguer (1986-89)*

31. *Calvin Munson, rhp, Howell HS, St. Charles, Mo.
32. Kyle Webb, rhp, Elon University.
33. Nick Frey, rhp, Texas Christian University.
34. Nick Lomascolo, lhp, Catawba (N.C.) College.
35. Vaugn Bryan, of, Broward (Fla.) CC.
36. Anthony Ray, of, St. Rita HS, Chicago.
37. *Alan Kruzel, 2b, Sinclair (Ohio) CC.
38. Blake McKnight, rhp, Evangel (Mo.) College.
39. Kevin Herget, rhp, Kean (N.J.) College.
40. Artie Reyes, rhp, Gonzaga University.

## SAN DIEGO PADRES (12)

1. Hunter Renfroe, of, Mississippi State University.—(AAA)
2. Dustin Peterson, ss, Gilbert (Ariz.) HS.—(High A)

DRAFT DROP *Brother of D.J. Peterson, first-round draft pick, Mariners (2013)*

2. Jordan Paroubeck, of, Serra HS, San Mateo, Calif. (Competitive balance Round 'B' pick—69th).—(Rookie)
3. Bryan Verbitsky, rhp, Hofstra University.—(High A)
4. Mason Smith, of, Rocky Mountain HS, Meridian, Idaho.—(Short-season A)
5. Josh Van Meter, ss, Norwell HS, Ossian, Ind.—(Low A)
6. **Trevor Gott, rhp, University of Kentucky.—(2015)**
7. Jake Bauers, 1b, Marina HS, Huntington Beach, Calif.
8. Adrian De Horta, rhp, South Hills HS, West Covina, Calif.
9. Adam Cimber, rhp, University of San Francisco.
10. Justin Livengood, rhp, UNC Wilmington.
11. Erik Schoenrock, lhp, Memphis University.
12. Rod Boykin, of, Edgewood Academy, Elmore, Ala.
13. Travis Remillard, rhp, Northeastern Oklahoma A&M JC.
14. Ryan Miller, c, San Bernardino Valley (Calif.) JC.
15. Tyler Dial, c, Gulf Coast State (Fla.) JC.
16. Payton Baskette, lhp, Grayson County (Texas) CC.
17. Trae Santos, 1b, Troy University.
18. Brandon Fry, lhp, Pearl River (Miss.) CC.
19. *Christian Summers, ss, Angelo State (Texas) University.
20. Michael Miller, c, Dallas Baptist University.
21. *Connor Jones, rhp, Great Bridge HS, Chesapeake, Va.
22. Chase Jensen, ss, Oklahoma City University.
23. Chris Long, rhp, Darton State (Ga.) JC.
24. Marcus Davis, of, Florida State University.
25. Tony Rizzotti, rhp, Tulane University.
26. Josh Richardson, rhp, Liberty University.
27. Michael Bass, 2b, UNC Wilmington.
28. Jace Chancellor, rhp, Lubbock Christian (Texas) University.
29. Kyle Lloyd, rhp, University of Evansville.
30. *Jason Jester, rhp, Texas A&M University.
31. *Chris Okey, c, Eustis (Fla.) HS.
32. Max Beatty, rhp, Pacific Lutheran (Wash.) University.
33. *Garrett Williams, lhp, Calvary Baptist Academy, Shreveport, La.
34. *Sean Carley, rhp, West Virginia University.
35. *Taylor Blair, rhp, Lexington Christian HS, Lexington, Ky.
36. *Cornelius Copeland, ss, Lakewood HS, St. Petersburg, Fla.
37. Jeffrey Enloe, lhp, University of Central Arkansas.
38. Pete Kelich, rhp, Bryant University.
39. *Brock Carpenter, ss, Fife (Wash.) HS.
40. *Chris Thibideau, ss, Vauxhall (Alberta) Academy.

## SAN FRANCISCO GIANTS (26)

1. Christian Arroyo, ss, Hernando HS, Brooksville, Fla.—(High A)
2. Ryder Jones, 3b, Watauga HS, Boone, N.C.—(High A)
3. Chase Johnson, rhp, Cal Poly.—(AA)
4. Brian Ragira, 1b, Stanford University.—(High A)
5. Dan Slania, rhp, University of Notre Dame.—(AA)
6. Nick Vander Tuig, rhp, UCLA.
7. Brandon Bednar, ss, Florida Gulf Coast University.
8. Tyler Horan, of, Virginia Tech.
9. D.J. Snelten, lhp, University of Minnesota.
10. Tyler Rogers, rhp, Austin Peay State University.
11. Johneshwy Fargas, of, Puerto Rico Baseball Academy, Gurabo, P.R.
12. Ty Ross, c, Louisiana State University.
13. Pat Young, rhp, Villanova University.
14. Nick Jones, lhp, Chattahoochee Valley (Ala.) CC.
15. Geno Escalante, c, Mount Olive (N.C.) College.
16. Jonah Arenado, 3b, El Toro HS, Lake Forest, Calif.

DRAFT DROP *Brother of Nolan Arenado, major leaguer (2013-15)*

17. Rene Melendez, c, Caguas (P.R.) Military Academy.
18. Christian Jones, lhp, Oregon.
19. Garrett Hughes, lhp, Stanford University.
20. Brett Kay, ss, Illinois State University.
21. Caleb Simpson, rhp, Seminole State (Okla.) JC.
22. Ethan Miller, rhp, San Diego State University.
23. *Brandon Zajac, lhp, Cleveland State (Tenn.) CC.
24. Nick Gonzalez, lhp, University of South Florida.
25. Blake Miller, ss, Western Oregon University.
26. Jake McCasland, rhp, University of New Mexico.
27. Mike Connolly, rhp, University of Maine.
28. Dusten Knight, rhp, University of Texas-Pan American.
29. Ryan Tuntland, 3b, West Virginia University.
30. Dylan Brooks, rhp, Lord Dorchester SS, North Dorchester, Ontario.
31. John Riley, c, Willow Glen HS, San Jose, Calif.
32. *Nick Cieri, c, Rancocas Valley Regional HS, Mount Holly, N.J.
33. Craig Massoni, 1b, Austin Peay State University.
34. *Rayan Hernandez, rhp, Puerto Rico Baseball Academy, Gurabo, P.R.
35. *Aubrey McCarty, 1b, Colquitt County HS, Moultrie, Ga.
36. *Grant Goodman, rhp, Burlingame (Calif.) HS.
37. Will Callaway, 2b, Appalachian State University.
38. *Osvaldo Garcia, rhp, Miami Southridge HS, Miami.
39. *Chris Viall, rhp, Soquel (Calif.) HS.
40. *Ryan Kirby, of, Granada HS, Livermore, Calif.

## SEATTLE MARINERS (11)

1. D.J. Peterson, 3b, University of New Mexico.—(AAA)

DRAFT DROP *Brother of Dustin Peterson, second-round draft pick, Padres (2013)*

2. Austin Wilson, of, Stanford University.—(High A)
3. Tyler O'Neill, of, Garibaldi SS, Maple Ridge, B.C.—(High A)
4. Ryan Horstman, lhp, St. John's University.—(Low A)
5. Jack Reinheimer, ss, East Carolina University.—(AA)
6. Corey Simpson, of, Sweeny (Texas) HS.
7. **Tyler Olson, lhp, Gonzaga University.—(2015)**
8. Tyler Smith, ss, Oregon State University.
9. Jake Zokan, lhp, College of Charleston.
10. Emilio Pagan, rhp, Belmont Abbey (N.C.) College.
11. Zack Littell, rhp, Eastern Alamance HS, Mebane, N.C.
12. Justin Seager, 1b, UNC Charlotte.

DRAFT DROP *Brother of Kyle Seager, major leaguer (2011-15) • Brother of Corey Seager, first-round draft pick, Dodgers (2012); major leaguer (2015)*

13. Lachlan Fontaine, 3b, Sutherland SS, North Vancouver, B.C.
14. Ian Miller, of, Wagner College.
15. Eddie Campbell, lhp, Virginia Tech.
16. Lonnie Kauppila, ss, Stanford University.
17. Paul Fry, lhp, St. Clair County (Mich.) CC.
18. Troy Scott, rhp, Riverside (Calif.) CC.
19. Jeff Zimmerman, 1b, Northern Illinois University.
20. Dan Torres, c, St. Leo (Fla.) College.
21. Brett Thomas, of, University of Oregon.
22. Tommy Burns, rhp, Howard (Texas) JC.
23. Kyle Petty, 1b, California (Pa.) University.
24. Kevin McCoy, rhp, Kennesaw State University.
25. Will Mathis, lhp, University of New Mexico.
26. Tyler Wright, lhp, University of Arkansas.
27. Ricky Claudio, rhp, St. Thomas (Fla.) University.
28. Zach Shank, ss, Marist College.
29. Chantz Mack, of, University of Miami.
30. Rafael Pineda, rhp, Texas A&M University.
31. Michaelangelo Guzman, lhp, La Selva, Calif.
32. *Nate Maggio, 1b, Blessed Trinity HS, Roswell, Ga.
33. *Corey Ray, of, Simeon HS, Chicago.
34. *Taylor Snyder, 2b, Salem Hills HS, Salem, Utah.

DRAFT DROP *Son of Cory Snyder, first-round draft pick, Indians (1984); major leaguer (1986-94) • Brother of JC Snyder, 36th-round draft pick, Mariners (2013)*

35. *Marshawn Taylor, ss, Simeon HS, Chicago.
36. *JC Snyder, 3b, Salt Lake (Utah) CC.

DRAFT DROP *Son of Cory Snyder, first-round draft pick, Indians (1984); major leaguer (1986-94) • Brother of Taylor Snyder, 34th-round draft pick, Mariners (2013)*

37. Jordan Cowan, ss, Kentlake HS, Kent, Wash.
38. *Michael Sexton, 3b, Rogers HS, Puyallup, Wash.
39. *Sam Hellinger, rhp, West Seattle HS, Seattle.
40. *Mike McCann, c, Columbia River HS, Vancouver, Wash.

## TAMPA BAY RAYS (22)

1. Nick Ciuffo, c, Lexington (S.C.) HS.—(Low A)
1. Ryne Stanek, rhp, University of Arkansas (Supplemental choice—29th—for loss of B.J. Upton as free agent).—(AA)
2. Riley Unroe, ss, Desert Ridge HS, Mesa, Ariz.—(Low A)

DRAFT DROP *Son of Tim Unroe, major leaguer (1995-2000)*

3. Thomas Milone, of, Masuk HS, Monroe, Conn.—(Low A)
4. Kean Wong, 2b, Waiakea HS, Hilo, Hawaii.—(High A)

DRAFT DROP *Brother of Kolten Wong, first-round draft pick, Cardinals (2011); major leaguer (2013-15)*

5. Johnny Field, 2b, University of Arizona.—(AA)
6. *Stephen Woods, rhp, Half Hollow Hills East HS, Dix Hills, N.Y.
7. Ty Young, 3b, University of Louisville.
8. Roel Ramirez, rhp, United South HS, Laredo, Texas.
9. Austin Pruitt, rhp, University of Houston.
10. Aaron Griffin, rhp, Loyola Marymount University.

DRAFT DROP *Brother of A.J. Griffin, major leaguer (2012-13)*

11. Hunter Lockwood, of, Weatherford (Texas) JC.
12. Pat Blair, ss, Wake Forest University.
13. Ben Griset, lhp, St. Mary's (Calif.) College.
14. Jaime Schultz, rhp, High Point University.
15. Coty Blanchard, 2b, Jacksonville State University.
16. Darren Fischer, lhp, Central Florida CC.
17. *Willie Calhoun, 2b, Benicia (Calif.) HS.
18. Julian Ridings, of, Western Carolina University.
19. Josh Kimborowicz, rhp, Everett (Wash.) CC.
20. Harmen Sidhu, rhp, Sonoma State (Calif.) University.
21. John Farrell, rhp, College of William & Mary.
22. Andrew Hanse, rhp, University of Iowa.
23. Rick Teasley, lhp, St. Leo (Fla.) College.
24. Jeremy Hadley, of, Sachse (Texas) HS.
25. Stone Speer, lhp, University of New Orleans.
26. *Christian Talley, rhp, Pearl River (Miss.) CC.
27. Hyrum Formo, rhp, Pima (Ariz.) CC.
28. Derek Loera, lhp, Lubbock Christian (Texas) University.

29. Hunter Wood, rhp, Howard (Texas) JC.
30. Colton Reavis, rhp, Northwood (Texas) University.
31. *Dalton Martinez, of, Dunedin (Fla.) HS.
32. Anthony Tzamtzis, rhp, North Carolina State University.
33. Hector Montes, 3b, Southwestern (Calif.) JC.
34. *Devin Ceciliani, of, Madras (Ore.) HS.
35. Cory Jordan, rhp, Grambling State University.
36. *Ryan Moseley, rhp, Lubbock-Cooper HS, Lubbock, Texas.
37. D.J. Slaton, rhp, San Jose State University.
38. *David Sheaffer, c, North Surry HS, Mount Airy, N.C.

DRAFT DROP *Son of Danny Sheaffer, major leaguer (1987-97)*

39. *Johnny Meszaros, rhp, Service HS, Anchorage, Alaska.
40. Ryan Henley, 2b, Azusa Pacific (Calif.) University.

## TEXAS RANGERS (24)

**1. Alex Gonzalez, rhp, Oral Roberts University.—(2015)**

1. Travis Demeritte, ss, Winder-Barrow HS, Winder, Ga. (Compensation—30th—for loss of free agent Josh Hamilton).—(Low A)
2. Akeem Bostick, rhp, West Florence (S.C.) HS.—(High A)
3. David Ledbetter, rhp, Cedarville (Ohio) University.—(High A)

DRAFT DROP *Twin brother of Ryan Ledbetter, 19th-round draft pick, Rangers (2013)*

4. Isiah Kiner-Falefa, ss, Mid-Pacific Institute, Honolulu, Hawaii.—(High A)
5. Joe Jackson, c, The Citadel.—(High A)

DRAFT DROP *Great-great nephew of Shoeless Joe Jackson, major leaguer (1908-20)*

6. Sam Wolff, rhp, University of New Mexico.
7. Nick Gardewine, rhp, Kaskaskia (Ill.) CC.
8. Evan Van Hoosier, 2b, CC of Southern Nevada.
9. Jose Samayoa, rhp, Lee (Tenn.) University.
10. Cole Wiper, rhp, University of Oregon.
11. Ryan Cordell, of, Liberty University.
12. Derek Thompson, lhp, John A. Logan (Ill.) CC.
13. *Taylor Olmstead, of, Greenwich (Conn.) HS.
14. Jarred Smith, rhp, State College of Florida-Manatee.
15. Cody Ege, lhp, University of Louisville.
16. Marcus Greene, c, New Mexico JC.
17. *Sean Labsan, lhp, Riverview HS, Sarasota, Fla.
18. David Gates, rhp, Howard (Texas) JC.
19. Ryan Ledbetter, rhp, Cedarville (Ohio) College.

DRAFT DROP *Twin brother of David Ledbetter, third-round draft pick, Rangers (2013)*

20. *Jackson Lamb, rhp, Bedford HS, Temperance, Mich.
21. Luke Lanphere, rhp, Citrus Valley HS, Redlands, Calif.
22. *Zach Winn, rhp, Show Low (Ariz.) HS.
23. Luis Pollorena, lhp, Mississippi State University.
24. *Darryn Sheppard, of, Dulles HS, Sugar Land, Texas.
25. Chris Dula, rhp, Catawba (N.C.) College.
26. Travis Dean, rhp, Kennesaw State University.
27. Sherman Lacrus, c, Western Oklahoma State JC.
28. *Ryan Williamson, lhp, Cranford (N.J.) HS.
29. Justin Sprenger, rhp, Tennessee Wesleyan College.
30. Joe Palumbo, lhp, St. John the Baptist HS, West Islip, N.Y.
31. *Michael Petersen, rhp, West Valley (Calif.) JC.
32. John Straka, rhp, North Dakota State University.
33. *Danny de la Calle, c, Miami-Dade JC.
34. Easton Napiontek, rhp, Lower Columbia (Wash.) JC.
35. *Buddy Reed, of, St. George's HS, Middletown, R.I.
36. *Dakota Hudson, rhp, Sequatchie County HS, Dunlap, Tenn.
37. *Cody Lavalli, of, Lewis-Clark State (Idaho) College.
38. *Sheldon Neuse, ss, Fossil Ridge HS, Fort Worth, Texas.
39. *Jay Gonzalez, of, Auburn University.
40. Sal Mendez, lhp, Weehawken (N.J.) HS.

First-round righthander Alex Gonzalez had already reached the big leagues for the Rangers

## TORONTO BLUE JAYS (9)

1. *Phil Bickford, rhp, Oaks Christian HS, Westlake Village, Calif.

DRAFT DROP *Attended Cal State Fullerton; re-drafted by Giants, 2015 (1st round)*

2. Clint Hollon, rhp, Woodford County HS, Versailles, Ky.—(Low A)
3. Patrick Murphy, rhp, Hamilton HS, Chandler, Ariz.—(Rookie)
4. Evan Smith, lhp, Montgomery HS, Semmes, Ala.—(Short-season A)
5. Daniel Lietz, lhp, Heartland (Ill.) CC.—(Short-season A)
6. **Matt Boyd, lhp, Oregon State University.—(2015)**
7. Conner Greene, rhp, Santa Monica (Calif.) HS.
8. **Kendall Graveman, rhp, Mississippi State University.—(2014-15)**
9. Chad Girodo, lhp, Mississippi State University.
10. Garrett Custons, c, Air Force Academy.
11. Jake Brentz, lhp, Parkway South HS, Manchester, Mo.
12. Tim Mayza, lhp, Millersville (Pa.) University.
13. Tim Locastro, ss, Ithaca (N.Y.) College.
14. L.B. Dantzler, 1b, University of South Carolina.
15. Jonathan Davis, of, University of Central Arkansas.
16. Dan Jansen, c, Appleton West HS, Appleton, Wis.
17. *Eric Lauer, lhp, Midview HS, Grafton, Ohio.
18. Sean Ratcliffe, rhp, Pickering HS, Ajax, Ontario.
19. Christian Vazquez, ss, Lubbock Christian (Texas) College.
20. Chaz Frank, of, University of North Carolina.
21. Mike Reeves, c, Florida Gulf Coast University.
22. *Sam Tewes, rhp, Waverly (Neb.) HS.
23. Brenden Kalfus, of, St. Mary's (Calif.) College.
24. Sean Hurley, of, Central Arizona JC.
25. Scott Silverstein, lhp, University of Virginia.
26. *Tanner Cable, rhp, Northwest Mississippi CC.
27. Andrew Florides, ss, Holy Cross HS, Flushing, N.Y.
28. Matt Dermody, lhp, University of Iowa.
29. Garrett Pickens, rhp, Delta State (Miss.) University.
30. Rowdy Tellez, 1b, Elk Grove (Calif.) HS.
31. *Brison Celek, 1b, University of South Carolina.
32. *Josh Sawyer, lhp, Central HS, San Angelo, Texas.
33. *Edgar Cabral, c, Knight HS, Palmdale, Calif.
34. *Dane Dunning, rhp, Clay HS, Green Cove Springs, Fla.
35. *Akoni Arriaga, rhp, Baldwin HS, Wailuku, Hawaii.
36. David Harris, ss, Southern Arkansas University.
37. Brett Barber, rhp, Ohio University.
38. *Jon Nunnally, of, Horizon HS, Scottsdale, Ariz.

DRAFT DROP *Son of Jon Nunnally, major leaguer (1995-2000)*

39. *Zach Levinson, ss, Susan E. Wagner HS, Staten Island, N.Y.
40. *Antonio Ruiz, 1b, San Gabriel (Calif.) HS.

## WASHINGTON NATIONALS (30)

1. (Choice forfeited for signing Rafael Soriano as free agent)
2. Jake Johansen, rhp, Dallas Baptist University.—(High A)
3. Drew Ward, 3b, Leedey (Okla.) HS.—(High A)
4. Nick Pivetta, rhp, New Mexico JC.—(AA)
5. Austin Voth, rhp, University of Washington.—(AA)
6. Cody Gunter, 3b, Grayson County (Texas) CC.
7. Jimmy Yezzo, 1b, University of Delaware.
8. David Napoli, lhp, Tulane University.
9. Jake Joyce, rhp, Virginia Tech.
10. Brennan Middleton, ss, Tulane University.
11. John Simms, rhp, Rice University.
12. Andrew Cooper, rhp, Sierra (Calif.) JC.

DRAFT DROP *Nephew of Joel Quenneville, defenseman, National Hockey League (1978-91); coach, St. Louis Blues, NHL (1996-2004); coach, Colorado Avalanche, NHL (2005-08); coach, Chicago Blackhawks, NHL (2008-15))*

13. John Costa, rhp, Palm Beach State (Fla.) JC.
14. David Masters, ss, Central Arizona JC.
15. Isaac Ballou, of, Marshall University.
16. *Willie Allen, of, Western Oklahoma State JC.
17. Geoff Perrott, c, Rice University.
18. Cory Bafidis, lhp, Texas Wesleyan College.
19. Niko Spezial, lhp, Wake Forest University.
20. Brenton Allen, of, UCLA.

DRAFT DROP *Brother of Tony Fisher, running back, National Football League (2002-06)*

21. Justin Thomas, lhp, Southern Arkansas University.
22. Cody Dent, ss, University of Florida.

DRAFT DROP *Son of Bucky Dent, major leaguer (1973-84); major league manager (1989-90)*

23. Garrett Gordon, of, Wabash Valley (Ill.) CC.
24. Matt Derosier, rhp, Southwestern (Calif.) JC.
25. Travis Ott, lhp, Shippensburg (Pa.) University.
26. *Garrett Hampson, ss, Reno (Nev.) HS.
27. *Bryce Harman, of, Bird HS, Richmond, Va.
28. Joey Webb, lhp, Menlo (Calif.) College.
29. Mike Sylvestri, rhp, Florida Atlantic University.
30. Ryan Ullmann, rhp, Concordia (Texas) University.
31. Willie Medina, ss, High Point University.
32. *Pat Boling, lhp, University of Georgia.
33. *Andrew Dunlap, rhp, University of Houston.
34. Jake Walsh, lhp, University of Missouri.
35. *Lukas Schiraldi, rhp, Navarro (Texas) JC.

DRAFT DROP *Son of Calvin Schiraldi, first-round draft pick, Mets (1983); major leaguer (1984-91)*

36. *Reid Humphreys, ss, Northwest Rankin HS, Flowood, Miss.
37. *Karsten Whitson, rhp, University of Florida.

DRAFT DROP *First-round draft pick (9th overall), Padres (2010)*

38. *Caleb Hamilton, ss, Woodinville (Wash.) HS.
39. *Robbie Tenerowicz, 2b, Campolindo HS, Moraga, Calif.
40. *Shaun Anderson, rhp, American Heritage HS, Plantation, Fla.

# Astros' third straight No. 1 pick goes awry

If nothing else, the Houston Astros were old hands at picking first overall. By finishing with a cumulative 162-324 record from 2011-13—the worst record in the majors over a three-year stretch since the woeful New York Mets of 1962-64—they earned the dubious distinction of choosing first for an unprecedented third draft in a row in 2014.

Rather than lamenting their fate, the Astros saw it as a simple by-product of their long-term blueprint: to strip the team down to its core with ruthless efficiency and build it back up again, stronger and better than ever before with an analytics-based approach.

That became the calculated strategy of new Astros owner Jim Crane after he purchased the team in 2011—just as it hit rock bottom, six years after appearing in the World Series. Crane had made a fortune in the logistics business, which had taught him the value of having superior data at his disposal, and he believed there was a place in baseball for similar application.

One of Crain's first orders of business was to hire a general manager who bought into his way of thinking, and he tapped Jeff Luhnow, who had enjoyed a successful seven-year stint as scouting director of the St. Louis Cardinals. Luhnow was viewed as an industry outsider and alienated himself from traditional thinkers because of some of the concepts he introduced.

Together, Crain and Luhnow embarked on a plan of attack unlike anything baseball had seen before. Their model for rebuilding the Astros as quickly as possible was based more on statistical formulas, and less on human intuition. It didn't make sense, they determined, for the team to pour millions of dollars into fielding a team whose best hope was mediocrity, so they gutted the existing roster in return for stockpiling prospects. They also committed to making the draft the focal point of their rebuilding efforts—even if it practically guaranteed sustained losing in the short term.

With the No. 1 pick in the 2014 draft, Houston had an opportunity to add another critical piece to the rebuilding plan. But it was imperative to get the pick right to sustain the momentum, knowing that the right pick might just be the finishing touch on a future championship team.

After drafting Carlos Correa, a high school shortstop from Puerto Rico with the top selection in 2012, and Mark Appel, a college righthander from Stanford in 2013, the Astros had followed their plan to precision. With eight prep shortstops and 12 college righthanders among the first overall picks since the draft began in 1965, Correa and Appel represented the two most popular demographics.

The 2014 draft shaped up differently, as there were no college righthanders or prep shortstops on the short list of prospects for the Astros to consider

BILL MITCHELL

**The Astros settled on lefthander Brady Aiken with the No. 1 pick and had a deal in place until a physical revealed abnormalities in his elbow that resulted in his decision not to sign**

with the No. 1 pick once they narrowed it to a field of four a day before the draft. North Carolina State lefthander Carlos Rodon was the lone college player on the board, and he was joined by California high school catcher Alex Jackson, and two prep pitchers, California lefthander Brady Aiken and Texas righthander Tyler Kolek.

With his Texas roots and a fastball that was clocked up to 102 mph—the highest recorded velocity ever by a prep pitcher—Kolek was extremely tempting to the Astros, but after careful consideration and weighing all the numbers, they settled on Aiken as their player of choice.

The 6-foot-4, 210-pound lefty appeared to have all the right ingredients. He was exceptionally polished for a high school pitcher; his fastball also sat at a steady 92-93 mph most of the spring and frequently reached 96-97 mph. But Aiken also represented the riskiest demographic in the draft and had nearly 50 years of draft history working against him.

"The tools are in place to get a frontline starter, a big lefthander in our rotation for a long time," Astros scouting director Mike Elias said. "We think he can log innings, with the way he's thrown the ball and the way he's built.

"The mere fact that we were willing to take a high school pitcher 1-1 for the third time in

## 2014

### AT A GLANCE

### This Date In History
June 5-7

### One Who Got Away
**BRADY AIKEN, LHP, ASTROS (1ST ROUND).** Aiken became just the third No. 1 pick not to sign, joining Danny Goodwin in 1971 and Tim Belcher in 1983. After agreeing to terms, pending a physical, the Astros saw something they didn't like in Aiken's elbow, and he balked at a revised offer. Aiken was one of a record low six players in the first 10 rounds to go unsigned; he went 17th overall by the Indians in the 2015 draft.

### He Was Drafted?
**JOHNNY MANZIEL, SS, PADRES (28TH ROUND).** The Padres selected the 2012 Heisman Trophy winner two months after the Cleveland Browns took the former Texas A&M quarterback with the 22nd pick in the 2014 NFL draft. Manziel hadn't played baseball since he was a junior in high school. He became the eighth Heisman winner to be selected in the baseball draft through the years.

### Did You Know . . .
Mets first-round pick **MICHAEL CONFORTO** is the son of 1984 Olympic Games synchronized swimming gold medalist Tracie Ruiz; **JED SPRAGUE**, a 37th-round pick of the White Sox, is the son of 1988 Olympic baseball gold medalist Ed Sprague.

### They Said It
Astros general manager **JEFF LUHNOW**, in announcing his club had failed to sign **BRADY AIKEN**: "We were following the rules all along. We advised MLB of what we were doing every step of the way. We didn't do anything unethical. We didn't try to game the system. We tried to do what was best for the Houston Astros in accordance with the current system. It's frustrating listening to people who are saying we tried to pull a fast one."

## IN FOCUS: BRANDON FINNEGAN

Of all the pitchers in the first round of the 2014 draft, none made a quicker, more dramatic impact than 5-foot-11 lefthander Brandon Finnegan, the 17th pick overall by the Kansas City Royals. After going 0-8 for TCU as a sophomore, he did an about-face as a junior by going 9-3, 2.04 with 134 strikeouts in 106 innings and leading the Horned Frogs to a berth in the College World Series.

After signing with the Royals for a bonus of $2,200,600, Finnegan then made 13 appearances in the minors and was so impressive—with a fastball in the upper 90s and a nasty slider—that he was the first player from the class promoted to the majors, debuting on Sept. 6. Though he made just seven relief appearances over the balance of the 2014 season, the Royals didn't hesitate to add him to their postseason roster, and he was a factor in leading the Royals into the World Series, working as a situational reliever. In the process, he became the first player in baseball history to appear in both the College World Series and World Series in the same year.

The whirlwind rise wasn't lost on Finnegan. "I was sitting in a classroom probably about four months ago," Finnegan said during the World Series. "It's insane to even think of. I lived the college dream and major league dream in one year."

## 2014: THE FIRST ROUNDERS

| CLUB: PLAYER, POS., SCHOOL | HOMETOWN | B-T | HT. | WT. | AGE | BONUS | FIRST YEAR | LAST YEAR | PEAK LEVEL (YEARS) |
|---|---|---|---|---|---|---|---|---|---|
| 1. Astros: Brady Aiken, lhp, Cathedral Catholic HS<br>Polished arm with mid-90s FB, excellent curve/command; signing turned contentious over elbow health, Astros revised offer, vindicated by 2015 TJ surgery. | Jamul, Calif. | L-L | 6-4 | 205 | 17 | Unsigned | 2016 | Active | |
| 2. Marlins: Tyler Kolek, rhp, Shepherd HS<br>Huge, country strong Texan grew up on ranch, posted triple digits with fastball; struggled with mechanics/command, had Tommy John surgery after 2015 season. | Shepherd, Texas | R-R | 6-5 | 260 | 18 | $6,000,000 | 2014 | Active | Class A (1) |
| 3. White Sox: Carlos Rodon, lhp, North Carolina State<br>Consensus No. 1 pick entering season slipped a bit with inconsistent command/uneven performance (6-7, 2.01), but moved quickly and won nine games as a rookie. | Holly Springs, N.C. | L-L | 6-3 | 235 | 21 | $6,582,000 | 2014 | Active | Majors (1) |
| 4. Cubs: Kyle Schwarber, c/of, Indiana<br>Undrafted as prep, made mark with three solid years at Indiana (.341-40-149), summer with Team USA; Cubs so enthralled with bat they ignored position questions. | Middletown, Ohio | L-R | 6-0 | 235 | 21 | $3,125,000 | 2014 | Active | Majors (1) |
| 5. Twins: Nick Gordon, ss, Olympia HS<br>Good bloodlines as son of Tom/half-brother of Dee; consummate yard rat with outstanding defensive tools/arm, projectable LH bat; made easy transition to pro ball. | Windermere, Fla. | L-R | 6-2 | 175 | 18 | $3,851,000 | 2014 | Active | Class A (1) |
| 6. Mariners: Alex Jackson, c/of, Rancho Bernardo HS<br>Top prep bat with outstanding power potential; catcher in HS with big arm, but Mariners immediately moved to OF as pro to maximize offensive potential. | Escondido, Calif. | R-R | 6-2 | 215 | 18 | $4,200,000 | 2014 | Active | Class A (1) |
| 7. Phillies: Aaron Nola, rhp, Louisiana State<br>Most polished arm in draft (23-2, 1.53, 242 IP, 45 BB/256 SO last two years at LSU); excellent command of 93-95 FB, four pitches, already in big leagues by 2015. | Baton Rouge, La. | R-R | 6-2 | 200 | 21 | $3,300,900 | 2014 | Active | Majors (1) |
| 8. Rockies: Kyle Freeland, lhp, Evansville<br>Local product, mediocre in first two college seasons (8-13, 4.44), then blossomed (10-2, 1.90, 99 IP/128 SO) with mid-90s velo, plus slider; slowed by elbow surgery. | Denver | L-L | 6-4 | 185 | 21 | $2,300,000 | 2014 | Active | Class A (2) |
| 9. Blue Jays: Jeff Hoffman, rhp, East Carolina<br>Undrafted out of HS, blossomed in college, was in running for No. 1 overall with mid-90s FB, dominant curve before April TJ surgery; dealt to Rockies for Tulowitzki. | Latham, N.Y. | R-R | 6-4 | 185 | 21 | $3,080,800 | 2015 | Active | Class AA (1) |
| 10. Mets: Michael Conforto, of, Oregon State<br>Intriguing bloodlines (dad played in NFL, mom was Olympic gold medalist); big college bat, shot through minors to make impact in Mets' 2015 pennant drive. | Redmond, Wash. | L-R | 6-1 | 215 | 21 | $2,970,800 | 2014 | Active | Majors (1) |
| 11. Blue Jays: Max Pentecost, c, Kennesaw State<br>Athletic catcher with defensive tools, bat took off JR year (.422-9-61); predraft health concerns proved accurate, missed 2015 after shoulder surgery. | Winder, Ga. | R-R | 6-1 | 190 | 21 | $2,888,300 | 2014 | Active | Class A (1) |
| 12. Brewers: Kodi Medeiros, lhp, Waiakea HS<br>Solid athlete, polarizing prospect; has dominated with extreme movement on mid-90s FB, nasty slider from 3/4 angle, though may be reliever with low arm slot. | Hilo, Hawaii | L-L | 6-2 | 180 | 18 | $2,500,000 | 2014 | Active | Class A (1) |
| 13. Padres: Trea Turner, ss, North Carolina State<br>Blossomed into top prospect in college, answered concerns about offensive ceiling early in pro career; quick trade to Nationals prompted alterations to draft rules. | Lake Worth, Fla. | R-R | 6-1 | 170 | 20 | $2,900,000 | 2014 | Active | Majors (1) |
| 14. Giants: Tyler Beede, rhp, Vanderbilt<br>Unsigned 2011 first-rounder had big soph season (14-1, 2.32) but frustrated scouts as FR (1-5, 4.52), JR (8-8, 4.05) with inconsistent stuff/command. | Auburn, Mass. | R-R | 6-3 | 215 | 21 | $2,613,200 | 2014 | Active | Class AA (1) |
| 15. Angels: Sean Newcomb, lhp, Hartford<br>Overlooked Northeast athlete made rapid improvement in college with FB that touched 97, kept improving while cruising to Double-A in 2015 (now with Braves). | Middleboro, Conn. | L-L | 6-5 | 240 | 20 | $2,518,400 | 2014 | Active | Class AA (1) |
| 16. D'backs: Touki Toussaint, rhp, Coral Springs Academy<br>Haiti native might have had best raw stuff in class with projectable mid-90s FB, hammer curve; mechanics still rough, but developing, dealt to Braves in 2015. | Coral Springs, Fla. | R-R | 6-3 | 185 | 17 | $2,700,000 | 2014 | Active | Class A (1) |
| 17. Royals: Brandon Finnegan, lhp, Texas Christian<br>Only player to pitch in CWS, World Series in same year; went 9-3, 2.04 (105 IP/134 SO) at TCU; Royals put him in bullpen after 27 IP in minors; since traded to Reds. | Fort Worth, Texas | L-L | 5-11 | 185 | 21 | $2,200,600 | 2014 | Active | Majors (2) |
| 18. Nationals: Erick Fedde, rhp, Nevada-Las Vegas<br>Fast-rising prospect destined for top 10 with mid-90s FB/power slider was 8-2, 1.76 before he hurt elbow in May and had TJ surgery; returned as 2015 starter. | Las Vegas | R-R | 6-4 | 180 | 21 | $2,511,100 | 2015 | Active | Class A (1) |
| 19. Reds: Nick Howard, rhp, Virginia<br>Two-way college standout worked as both a starter and reliever; struggled in 2015, but starter potential with athleticism, high-90s fastball, good secondary stuff. | Olney, Va. | R-R | 6-3 | 215 | 21 | $1,990,500 | 2014 | Active | Class A (2) |
| 20. Rays: Casey Gillaspie, 1b, Wichita State<br>Brother of Conor (2008 first-rounder); switch-hitter with raw power/advanced on-base skills, hit .389-15-50 (1.202 OPS) as JR, limited in field to first base. | Omaha, Neb. | B-L | 6-4 | 240 | 21 | $2,033,000 | 2014 | Active | Class A (2) |
| 21. Indians: Bradley Zimmer, of, San Francisco<br>Younger brother of Kyle (2012 first-rounder); different athlete with sweet LH swing, power/speed developed quickly as pro (16 HRs/44 SBs in 2015). | San Diego | L-R | 6-5 | 205 | 21 | $1,900,000 | 2014 | Active | Class AA (1) |
| 22. Dodgers: Grant Holmes, rhp, Conway HS<br>HS arm with mature frame/stuff; impressed in 2015 with mid-90s fastball, low-80s slurvy breaking ball, expected to move quickly through minors. | Conway, S.C. | L-R | 6-1 | 215 | 18 | $2,500,000 | 2014 | Active | Class A (1) |
| 23. Tigers: Derek Hill, of, Elk Grove HS<br>Son of Orsino, scout/ex-minor leaguer; future Gold Glover with exceptional CF skills; bat/power still a question mark, will take time to develop. | Sacramento, Calif. | R-R | 6-2 | 195 | 18 | $2,000,000 | 2014 | Active | Class A (2) |
| 24. Pirates: Cole Tucker, ss, Mountain Pointe HS<br>Surprise pick of first round; lanky athlete with sound SS skills, bat expected to develop with physical maturity; 2015 torn labrum/surgery will slow development. | Phoenix | B-R | 6-3 | 185 | 17 | $1,800,000 | 2014 | Active | Class A (1) |
| 25. Athletics: Matt Chapman, 3b, Cal State Fullerton<br>Outstanding defender with superior arm, hit upper-90s off mound; drafted as 3B after .314-6-48 JR year, power began to play as pro (23 HRs in 80 games in 2015). | Trabuco Canyon, Calif. | R-R | 6-2 | 205 | 21 | $1,750,000 | 2014 | Active | Class AA (1) |
| 26. Red Sox: Michael Chavis, ss, Sprayberry HS<br>Lacks raw tools, projection, but stood out for superior bat speed, performance (.580-13-37, 21 SB as prep SR); settled in at 3B, bat and power will have to carry him. | Marietta, Ga. | R-R | 5-10 | 190 | 18 | $1,870,500 | 2014 | Active | Class A (1) |
| 27. Cardinals: Luke Weaver, rhp, Florida State<br>Possible top 15 pick after dominant 7-2, 2.29 (98 IP, 19 BB/119 SO) soph season, FB that peaked at 97; stuff/command waned as junior, rebounded as pro. | DeLand, Fla. | R-R | 6-2 | 170 | 20 | $1,843,000 | 2014 | Active | Class A (2) |
| 28. Royals: Foster Griffin, lhp, The First Academy<br>Lanky/athletic lefty, strike thrower with advanced feel for pitching, went 7-2, 1.55 (59 IP, 19 BB/99 SO) as prep SR; Royals taking it slow (131 IP/33 career starts). | Orlando, Fla. | R-L | 6-3 | 200 | 18 | $1,925,000 | 2014 | Active | Class A (1) |
| 29. Reds: Alex Blandino, ss, Stanford<br>Hit just .292, flashed power (27 HRs) in regimented hitting style at Stanford, also spent career at 3B; moved to natural SS position in pros, tapped into raw power. | Mountain View, Calif. | R-R | 6-0 | 190 | 21 | $1,788,000 | 2014 | Active | Class AA (1) |
| 30. Rangers: Luis Ortiz, rhp, Sanger HS<br>Overcame weight issue to become dominant closer with mid-90s FB for champion U.S. at 2013 World juniors; stuff inconsistent as SR, still a first-rounder. | Sanger, Calif. | R-R | 6-3 | 230 | 18 | $1,750,000 | 2014 | Active | Class A (2) |
| 31. Indians: Justus Sheffield, lhp, Tullahoma HS<br>Brother Jordan was potential 2013 first-rounder before TJ surgery; different kind of athlete in smaller frame, but four-pitch lefty with low-90s FB, fast start as pro. | Tullahoma, Tenn. | L-L | 5-10 | 195 | 18 | $1,600,000 | 2014 | Active | Class A (1) |
| 32. Braves: Braxton Davidson, of, T.C. Roberson HS<br>Big LH power with advanced feel for strike zone, hit .245-10-45 (84 BBs) in first full pro year; moved from 1B to OF by Braves, still growing into position but big arm. | Arden, N.C. | L-L | 6-2 | 210 | 17 | $1,705,400 | 2014 | Active | Class A (1) |
| 33. Red Sox: Michael Kopech, rhp, Mount Pleasant HS<br>Projectable righty with long/loose frame, whip-like arm action; FB in low 90s in HS, hitting triple digits in pro ball when hit by 50-game drug suspension in 2015. | Mount Pleasant, Texas | R-R | 6-3 | 195 | 18 | $1,500,000 | 2014 | Active | Class A (1) |
| 34. Cardinals: Jack Flaherty, rhp, Harvard-Westlake HS<br>Athletic 3B prospect prior to SR year, but velocity uptick, plus slider, command swayed scouts interest to mound, went 23-0, 0.63 last two years of HS. | Burbank, Calif. | R-R | 6-4 | 205 | 18 | $2,000,000 | 2014 | Active | Class A (1) |

history, even though the first two didn't pan out, showed us how strongly we agreed."

As the third prep arm (all lefthanders) selected with the No. 1 pick—and the first in 23 years—Aiken was following in the infamous footsteps of David Clyde, the top pick in 1973 who went 18-33 in his abbreviated big league career, and Brien Taylor, the first selection in 1991 who never pitched in the majors after injuring his pitching shoulder in an off-field altercation.

Just 63 percent of high school pitchers selected in the first round through the years reached the majors. They had an unenviable track record of flaming out, due to injury or a failure to develop, more than any other category of player.

Despite the inherent risk, the Astros showed little hesitation in taking Aiken.

"We feel in the category of high school pitchers, this is about as safe a player as you can have," Luhnow said. "He's got the polish, he's got the stuff, he's got the command, he has the delivery we like, he's got the makeup, he's got the size. It's really hard to poke any holes in this player at all, except for the fact that he's young, and we really didn't want to hold that against him."

Under draft rules that took effect in 2012 and coincided with Houston landing the first of its three straight first overall selections, a bonus slot of $7,922,100 was allotted to the No. 1 pick.

The Astros had never used the full amount of their No. 1 allotment, and had no intention of doing so now, one of the critical factors they took into account in picking Aiken at the expense of the more proven lefthander, Rodon. Aiken had agreed to sign with the Astros for $6.5 million, and with the savings of roughly $1.4 million, they planned to apply it to other draft picks.

From all indications, everything was in place. Aiken's signing was just a formality.

## PHYSICAL UNCOVERS ELBOW PROBLEM

On July 18, the deadline for teams to sign 2014 draft picks, Aiken dropped a bombshell when he decided not to sign with the Astros.

Though the parties had agreed on the parameters of a $6.5 million deal prior to the draft, Aiken didn't take his physical examination, the final step in making the deal official, until he traveled to Houston in late June. With his family accompanying Aiken, the Astros planned a press conference to announce his signing, but when the Astros read the results of his physical, they didn't like what they saw: a "significant abnormality" in the area of his elbow ligament, making him increasingly susceptible to Tommy John surgery.

The Astros then rescinded their offer, leaving

### Fastest To The Majors

| | Player, Pos. | Drafted (Round) | Debut |
|---|---|---|---|
| 1. | Brandon Finnegan, lhp | Royals (1) | Sept. 6, 2014 |
| 2. | Carlos Rodon, lhp | White Sox (1) | April 21, 2015 |
| 3. | Jacob Lindgren, lhp | Yankees (2) | May 25, 2015 |
| 4. | Kyle Schwarber, c/of | Cubs (1) | June 16, 2015 |
| 5. | Aaron Nola, rhp | Phillies (1) | July 21, 2015 |

**FIRST HIGH SCHOOL SELECTION:** None through 2015.

## DRAFT SPOTLIGHT: BRADY AIKEN

BILL MITCHELL

**Brady Aiken was drafted first overall by the Astros, but the two sides were unable to reach agreement because of an elbow issue**

Brady Aiken was the toast of the baseball world. As the No. 1 pick in the 2014 draft, he was ecstatic about being selected by the Houston Astros, an organization in full rebuild mode but with a seemingly bright future. The $6.5 million signing bonus that he and the Astros agreed to was all but signed.

"It's really a big honor," Aiken said after being drafted. "I think I've worked hard enough and I've done everything I could to put myself in the position that the Astros wanted to make the move, so I'm really excited to get the call. I'm just excited to go out there and start working hard and start helping the team."

Astros officials were equally excited about adding a big, polished lefthander who could become an integral part of their rotation as their makeover was ready to bear fruit.

There was little doubt that the 6-foot-4, 210-pound Aiken was their guy, even though the Astros didn't make their final decision to draft him until the morning of the draft and never divulged their intent to Aiken. "It was a really tough decision," Astros general manager Jeff Luhnow said. "We've been following this kid for a while, we really like him a lot, but what separated it for us was not only the talent, but the makeup of this young man. We really think that's going to separate him and allow him to achieve his potential."

Aiken was just the third high school pitcher selected with the No. 1 pick, and the two first two, David Clyde in 1973 and Brien Taylor in 1991, didn't come close to panning out.

Despite that track record, the Astros showed little hesitation in taking Aiken, who made huge strides in his senior year at San Diego's Cathedral Catholic High, going 7-0, 1.06 with 15 walks and 111 strikeouts in 60 innings.

Aiken began to assemble his credentials as the top pick for 2014 when he starred for USA Baseball's junior national team in the 18-and-under World Cup in Taiwan in September 2013. He won both his starts, including a win over Japan in the gold-medal game in which he allowed one run and struck out 10 in seven innings.

That performance convinced Aiken that he might have a realistic shot at becoming the No. 1 pick, and he set out to get bigger and stronger with that goal in mind.

Aiken had topped out in the low 90s in the past, but his fastball sat at a steady 92-93 mph and frequently reached 96-97 mph during the spring. Combined with a better curve and an advanced feel for his changeup, along with impressive poise, command and approach for a 17-year-old, scouts quickly began looking at Aiken with a different eye that ultimately led to his selection as the No. 1 pick.

As ideal a match as Aiken seemed to be for the Astros, and as happy as both parties were at the time of his selection, the good vibes quickly dissipated when a routine physical exam uncovered previously undetected abnormalities in his pitching elbow.

When the Astros pulled their offer, a war of words soon ensued between the Astros and Aiken's agent, Casey Close, with Aiken caught in the middle. The parties then failed to reach an accord on a compromise deal with a revised bonus offer of $5 million.

Aiken weighed his limited options for several months before deciding to resume his pitching career at the IMG Academy in Bradenton, Fla., in preparation for the 2015 draft. His worst fears were realized when he blew out the tendon in his suspect elbow just 13 pitches into his first start, and shortly thereafter had Tommy John surgery, throwing his once-promising future into more doubt than ever.

Uncertainty over Aikens's elbow obviously remained as the 2015 draft approached, but the Cleveland Indians took him with the 17th pick overall and signed him for $2,513,280 ($119,680 over the slot value of $2,393,600). He had to sit out the balance of the summer while recuperating, making his debut in June 2016 in the Rookie-level Arizona League.

Through all the twists and turns Aiken's career took before he threw even his first pitch as a pro, Aiken remained philosophical about his decision to walk away from the final offer made by the Astros—one that cost him more than $2 million..

"I can honestly say I don't regret not signing," Aiken said. "It was a very difficult decision, but it also was an informed decision based on circumstances only a few people know the truth about. My family and I planned for all the possible outcomes. We weighed the pros and cons, talked with friends and mentors and doctors whose opinions we value and discussed it over a number of family dinners. This wasn't a decision we made lightly."

## WORTH NOTING

Teams signed the highest percentage of drafted players in a single year in 2014: 902 of 1,215, or 74.2 percent. That topped the mark of 74.0 percent set in 2013. Moreover, a record 84 percent of the players signed were from the college and junior-college ranks. Just two of the first 100 picks went unsigned: No. 1 overall pick **BRADY AIKEN**, and Nationals second-rounder **ANDREW SUAREZ** (57th overall), who chose to return to Miami for his senior year. A draft record-low six players went unsigned overall in the first 10 rounds.

Vanderbilt won its first College World Series, even though the team's total of five players that were drafted was the lowest total from that school since 2006. The Commodores, who beat Virginia 2-1 in the best-of-three championship series, weren't exactly lacking in talent, though, as their rotation featured **TYLER BEEDE** (8-8, 4.05), who was selected by the Giants with the 14th overall pick, and a pair of pitchers who would be 2015 first-rounders, **WALKER BUEHLER** (12-2, 2.64) and **CARSON FULMER** (7-1, 1.98). And their leading position player, shortstop **DANSBY SWANSON** (.333-3-34), would go on to be the No. 1 overall pick in 2015. Beede had the distinction of being an unsigned first-round pick from the 2011 draft. He turned down a seven-figure bonus offer from the Blue Jays out of a Massachusetts high school in favor of attending college at Vanderbilt. He tied for the national lead in wins as a sophomore while posting a 14-1 record and projected to be among the top group of talented arms in the 2014 class. Despite his lofty status, Beede was plagued by a string of erratic outings as a junior and slipped marginally into the middle of the first round.

Mississippi, which reached the semifinals of the College World Series, led all colleges with nine selections, while

ALYSON BOYER RODE

**Carlos Rodon had a disappointing junior season at N.C. State, but he moved quickly to the big leagues after the White Sox drafted him**

Aiken in limbo. A few days later, he quietly left town.

Though the Astros subsequently attempted to reach a compromise with Aiken on a contract with a discounted value that took into account the risk involved, it didn't sit well with Aiken's agent, Casey Close of Excel Sports Management, and a highly publicized contract standoff ensued.

Close disputed the assertion that Aiken was damaged goods, and termed the elbow issue "asymptomatic," noting that he had touched 97 mph in his final start before the draft and had never experienced pain in his elbow.

"Brady has been seen by some of the most experienced and respected orthopedic arm specialists in the country," Close said, "and all of those doctors have acknowledged that he's not injured and that he's ready to start his professional career.

"We are extremely disappointed that Major League Baseball is allowing the Astros to conduct business in this manner with a complete disregard for the rules governing the draft and the 29 other clubs who have followed those same rules."

Luhnow's offer provided for a bonus of just $3,168,840, which was equivalent to 40 percent of Aiken's bonus value slot of $7,922,100—the minimum required by the CBA to guarantee a team a compensatory draft pick for an unsigned player in the following year's draft. Close rejected that offer out of hand.

With negotiations still at an impasse on the eve of the signing deadline, Luhnow revised his offer upward to $5 million but relations between the parties had become increasingly testy, and by then it was too little, too late in the minds of Close and Aiken. While it was a significant setback for all parties, Luhnow at least saw it as an opportunity to increase his team's draft haul.

"Not every move is going to be popular, but we did what we thought was in the best interests of the Astros," Luhnow said. "The reality is, we'll get the second pick next year (as compensation) and more money to spend, so there's a very strong possibility that whoever we take gets to the big leagues faster than Brady would have. So it's hard to say it's any sort of setback at all."

Aiken marked just the third time in draft history that the No. 1 pick failed to sign. He joined Illinois high school catcher Danny Goodwin (1971, White Sox) and Mount Vernon Nazarene (Ohio) righthander Tim Belcher (1983, Twins) as a piece of dubious draft history. Goodwin attended Southern and was drafted No. 1 overall again four years later, while Belcher was the first pick again in the January 1984 secondary phase.

### OTHER PICKS TIED TO AIKEN DEAL

With Aiken unexpectedly going unsigned, that only complicated matters for the Astros and a second Excel client, California prep righthander Jacob Nix, the team's fifth-round pick. Nix had also reached a verbal agreement with the Astros on a contract that included a bonus of $1.5 million, but it was contingent on Aiken signing.

The provisions of the existing draft rules, while restrictive, permitted teams to strategically sign their picks in the first 10 rounds for amounts below their assigned value while applying the difference to other selections. That was the intent of the Astros in the cases of Aiken and Nix, as they planned to allocate most of the nearly $1.5 million in savings on Aiken's bonus to the contract they agreed to with Nix. The value of the slot for Nix was just $370,500, meaning the Astros were in no danger of exceeding their overall bonus pool limit.

However, if a team failed to sign any of its draft picks in the first 10 rounds, the slot value of those picks disappeared from the team's overall bonus

### Top 25 Bonuses

| | Player, Pos. | Drafted (Round) | Order | Bonus |
|---|---|---|---|---|
| **1.** | **Carlos Rodon, lhp** | **White Sox (1)** | **3** | **$6,582,000** |
| 2. | * Tyler Kolek, rhp | Marlins (1) | 2 | $6,000,000 |
| 3. | * Alex Jackson, c/of | Mariners (1) | 6 | $4,200,000 |
| 4. | * Nick Gordon, ss | Twins (1) | 5 | $3,851,000 |
| **5.** | **Aaron Nola, rhp** | **Phillies (1)** | **7** | **$3,300,000** |
| **6.** | **Kyle Schwarber, c/of** | **Cubs (1)** | **4** | **$3,125,000** |
| 7. | Jeff Hoffman, rhp | Blue Jays (1) | 9 | $3,080,800 |
| **8.** | **Michael Conforto, of** | **Mets (1)** | **10** | **$2,970,800** |
| **9.** | **Trea Turner, ss** | **Padres (1)** | **13** | **$2,900,000** |
| 10. | Max Pentecost, c | Blue Jays (1) | 11 | $2,888,300 |
| 11. | * Touki Toussaint, rhp | Diamondbacks (1) | 16 | $2,700,000 |
| 12. | Tyler Beede, rhp | Giants (1) | 14 | $2,613,200 |
| 13. | Sean Newcomb, lhp | Angels (1) | 15 | $2,518,400 |
| 14. | Erick Fedde, rhp | Nationals (1) | 18 | $2,511,500 |
| 15. | * Kodi Medeiros, lhp | Brewers (1) | 12 | $2,500,000 |
| | * Grant Holmes, rhp | Dodgers (1) | 22 | $2,500,000 |
| 17. | Kyle Freeland, lhp | Rockies (1) | 8 | $2,300,000 |
| **18.** | **Brandon Finnegan, lhp** | **Royals (1)** | **17** | **$2,200,600** |
| 19. | Casey Gillaspie, 1b | Rays (1) | 20 | $2,035,500 |
| 20. | * Derek Hill, of | Tigers (1) | 23 | $2,000,000 |
| | * Jack Flaherty, rhp | Cardinals (1) | 34 | $2,000,000 |
| | * Forrest Wall, 2b | Rockies (1-S) | 35 | $2,000,000 |
| | * Gareth Morgan, of | Mariners (2-S) | 74 | $2,000,000 |
| 24. | Nick Howard, rhp | Reds (1) | 19 | $1,990,500 |
| 25. | * Foster Griffin, lhp | Royals (1) | 28 | $1,900,000 |

*Major leaguers in bold. *High school selection.*

## Largest Bonuses By Round

| | Player, Pos. | Club | Bonus |
|---|---|---|---|
| 1. | **Carlos Rodon, lhp** | **White Sox** | **$6,582,000** |
| 1-S. | * Forrest Wall, 2b | Rockies | $2,000,000 |
| 2. | * Gareth Morgan, of | Mariners | $2,000,000 |
| 3. | * Austin DeCarr, rhp | Yankees | $1,000,000 |
| 4. | * Carson Sands, lhp | Cubs | $1,100,000 |
| 5. | * Justin Steele, lhp | Cubs | $1,000,000 |
| 6. | * Dylan Cease, rhp | Cubs | $1,500,000 |
| 7. | * Anfernee Seymour, ss | Marlins | $400,000 |
| 8. | * Branden Kelliher, rhp | Athletics | $450,000 |
| 9. | * Kevin Steen, rhp | Red Sox | $255,000 |
| 10. | Dillon Peters, lhp | Marlins | $175,000 |
| 11. | * Gage Hinsz, rhp | Pirates | $580,000 |
| 12. | * Jordan Yamamoto, rhp | Brewers | $330,000 |
| 13. | * Erik Manoah, rhp | Mets | $300,000 |
| 14. | * Zach Sullivan, ss | Marlins | $250,000 |
| 15. | * Gabriel Llanes, rhp | Mets | $300,000 |
| 16. | * Manny Olloque, 3b | Royals | $110,000 |
| 17. | Several tied at | | $100,000 |
| 18. | * Raphael Ramirez, of | Mets | $150,000 |
| | * McKenzie Mills, lhp | Nationals | $150,000 |
| 19. | Aaron Bummer, lhp | White Sox | $100,000 |
| | * Tyler Hill, of | Red Sox | $100,000 |
| 20. | * Jordan Holloway, rhp | Marlins | $400,000 |
| 21. | Several tied at | | $100,000 |
| 22. | Mark Reyes, lhp | Giants | $85,000 |
| 23. | * Zac Law, of | Rays | $127,820 |
| 24. | Lucas Long, rhp | Orioles | $100,000 |
| 25. | * Rudy Martin, of | Royals | $160,000 |
| Other | * Brian Dobzanski, rhp | Cardinals (29) | $700,000 |

*Major leaguers in bold. *High school selection.*

pool. So once Aiken went unsigned, the Astros' bonus pool was reduced accordingly, and they were no longer in position to sign Nix for the amount they agreed to without losing their first-round pick in the 2015 draft.

As a result, the Astros had to renege on their offer to Nix, as well as one to their 20th-round pick, Georgia prep lefthander Mac Marshall, who they had also intended to sign for an over-slot amount by applying even more of the unused portion of Aiken's bonus.

Luhnow came under fire for his handling of both Aiken and Nix, but claimed that his club was just adhering to major league rules. The Players Association still filed a grievance on Nix' behalf.

BILL MITCHELL

Jacob Nix

"Today, two young men should be one step closer to realizing their dreams of becoming major league ballplayers," said Tony Clark, the union's first-year executive director. "Because of the actions of the Houston Astros, they are not."

Nix subsequently received a cash settlement from the Astros to settle his grievance.

Aiken and Nix had both committed to UCLA in the event they didn't sign, but their public involvement with an agent in their failed negotiations with the Astros essentially ruled out that possibility. After weighing their options for several months, both players elected the following spring to enroll at the IMG Academy, a private training institute in Bradenton, Fla., and pitch for the academy's postgraduate team, in preparation for the 2015 draft.

But when Aiken made his first pitching appearance in some 10 months in late March, he tore the very ligament in his elbow that was at heart of his dispute with the Astros after just 13 pitches. He had Tommy John surgery six days later. He was nonetheless drafted in the first round again in June, with the 17th pick by the Cleveland Indians.

Nix, meanwhile, was drafted by the San Diego Padres in the third round (86th overall), and signed for $900,000—$212,700 over the amount slotted for the pick. Marshall, who went on to college at Louisiana State when he didn't sign with the Astros but shortly thereafter transferred to Chipola (Fla.) JC to be eligible for the 2015 draft, was picked in the fourth round by the San Francisco Giants, and signed for $750,000.

The Astros were rewarded in the 2015 draft, as well, for not signing Aiken. With the second and fifth picks overall, they were in the unprecedented position of having a budget of nearly $18 million and were able to influence that draft even more profoundly than they had the previous three years.

### KOLEK, RODON SET EARLY TONE

Houston's selection of Aiken with the No. 1 pick and all the controversy that followed overshadowed most of the other developments in the 2014 draft.

Aiken, along with Kolek and Rodon, were easily considered the cream of the crop in a pitching-rich draft, and Kolek ended up going second overall to the Miami Marlins and Rodon third to the Chicago White Sox.

The 6-foot-4, 240-pound Rodon was the biggest name of the three because he had been projected as a leading candidate to go first overall since he was just a freshman at North Carolina State. He enhanced his status with a dominant sophomore season for the Wolfpack, but after compiling an overall 19-3, 2.33 record with 319 strikeouts in 247 innings in his first two seasons, Rodon struggled to live up to his considerable hype in 2014.

While he still commanded plenty of attention, a mere mortal Rodon rarely dominated his competition like he had in the past, and struggled to even win on a consistent basis in going just 6-7, though his secondary numbers (2.01 ERA, 31 walks/117 strikeouts in 99 innings) were more reflective of his true ability.

Rodon's subpar showing prompted the Astros and Marlins to entertain other options, particularly with the emergence of Aiken and the fireballing Kolek, two hotshot high school arms.

The 6-foot-6, 240-pound Kolek threw harder and was more electrifying than Aiken, but his rise to prominence was considered less surprising than Aiken's as he was generally considered to be the elite prep pitcher in the country entering the 2014 season. He nonetheless elevated his worth with a fastball that routinely reached triple digits, topping at 102 mph, and by opening the 2014 season by hurling 18 straight hitless innings.

### WORTH NOTING

Virginia, the team that knocked out the Rebels to reach the CWS final, had eight, including first-rounder **NICK HOWARD** (Reds, 19th overall), and supplemental first-rounders **STAN PAPI** (Indians, 36th) and **DEREK FISHER** (Astros, 37th).

■ The top college performer during the 2014 season was Kentucky first baseman/lefthander **A.J. REED**, who was drafted in the second round by the Astros (42nd overall) and signed for $1.35 million. He led the nation in homers (23) and slugging (.735), while hitting .336 with 73 RBIs. As a starting pitcher, he went 12-2, 2.09, finishing just one win off the national lead.

■ Oregon State senior lefthander **BEN WETZLER** led the nation in ERA at 0.80, despite being suspended for the first 20 percent of the season by the NCAA for his use of an agent in negotiations a year earlier, when he was picked in the fifth round by the Phillies and turned down a $350,000 offer. The spurned Phillies in turn blew the whistle on him. A year later, as a senior, Wetzler was drafted in the ninth round by the Marlins, and signed for just $30,500.

■ The Orioles signed Notre Dame junior righthander **PAT CONNAUGHTON** as a fourth-round pick, wagering a $428,100 bonus that the two-sport standout would eventually choose baseball as a career. After going winless in six games in the Orioles organization in 2014, despite a fastball that peaked at 96 mph, the 6-foot-5 Connaughton returned to Notre Dame for his senior season of basketball. He made a strong enough impression in leading the Irish to an Atlantic Coast Conference championship that he was taken in the second round of the 2015 NBA draft by the Brooklyn Nets as a shooting guard. He was subsequently traded to the Portland Trail Blazers and

CONTINUED ON PAGE 732

## WORTH NOTING

CONTINUED FROM PAGE 731

chose to pursue a career in the NBA rather than resume his career in the Orioles system. In his first season with Portland, he appeared in 34 games and scored 36 points.

■ Another two-sport star that passed on professional baseball, at least in the short term, was righthander **PAT MAHOMES**, a 37th-round pick of the Tigers. Mahomes, the son of former major league pitcher **PAT MAHOMES**, would have undoubtedly been drafted much earlier if teams considered him signable, but he elected to pursue a college career as a top-rated quarterback recruit. He passed for 4,653 yards and 36 touchdowns, while rushing for 456 yards and 10 more TDs, as a freshman at Texas Tech. Meanwhile, 2012 Heisman Trophy winner **JOHNNY MANZIEL**, who did not play college baseball at Texas A&M, was drafted in the 28th round by the Padres.

■ Of the 20 top-ranked players in the 2014 class as graded by the Major League Scouting Bureau, 17 were pitchers, including the seven highest. Appropriately, the first two players drafted, Texas prep righthander **TYLER KOLEK** (with a grade of 70 on the bureau's standard 20-80 scouting scale) and California prep lefty **BRADY AIKEN** (67) ranked 1-2. A pair of second-round arms—Louisville closer **NICK BURDI** (Twins, 46th overall) and New Jersey prep righthander **JOE GATTO** (Angels, 53rd overall)—were next at 65, followed by first-rounders **TYLER BEEDE**, **JEFF HOFFMAN** and **CARLOS RODON** at 63.

■ Led by the selection of Texas Christian lefthander **BRANDON FINNEGAN** and Florida prep lefty **FOSTER GRIFFIN**, the American League champion Royals drafted more lefthanded pitchers (12) than righthanders (7).

■ Just six players in the

As the Astros gave final consideration to all three pitchers, they ultimately steered away from Rodon when he and agent Scott Boras indicated that they would want the full amount of the slot value for the first pick.

The White Sox didn't hesitate to take Rodon, despite not selecting a Boras client with a premium draft since 1996, when they took lefthander Bobby Seay. Not only were they unable to sign Seay, but that development triggered the controversial loophole free-agency fiasco that led to Seay and three other first-rounders being declared free agents. The four subsequently earned record bonuses totaling almost $30 million.

While Rodon settled for $6.582 million from the White Sox, that was not only the largest bonus paid out in 2014, but $860,500 more than the slot value for the third overall pick, and the discrepancy forced the White Sox to manipulate the remainder of their signings to stay under the 5 percent budget threshold. They were still required to pay $356,175 in the form of a luxury tax.

Teams were taxed at 75 cents on the dollar for everything over their bonus pool allotment, but generally showed a greater willingness to spend up to the 5 percent threshold than in past years. In 2012, the first year under the existing CBA, nine teams spent more than their pool allotment, subjecting them to the tax; that number increased to 10 in 2013 and 15 in 2014. Nine of the 15 exceeded their allotment by at least 4.69 percent, and the Washington Nationals joined the White Sox in tapping out at the full 5 percent. The 15 teams that exceeded their limit were collectively taxed $3,569,219.

MIKE JANES

Tyler Kolek

Had any teams exceeded their bonus pool by more than 5 percent, they would have been subject to losing a first-round pick in the next draft—a price that so far no team has been willing to pay.

Signing bonuses totaled $222,809,919 in 2014, the largest expenditure yet under the new draft rules, and the second-largest outlay in draft history.

Had Aiken and Nix signed with the Astros for the $8 million that they agreed to, the 2014 draft would have been the most expensive in history, surpassing the $228,009,050 spent in 2011, in the last draft under the previous CBA.

The Marlins spent more bonus money than any team at $13,112,900, followed by the White Sox at $10,460,600. The Astros had the largest original signing bonus pool at $13,362,200, but with their failure to sign Aiken they ended up spending $6,154,500—22nd among the 30 big league clubs.

Teams were able to apply bonuses to draft picks in the first 10 rounds as they saw fit, so long as the collective amount did not exceed their bonus pool allotment by more than 5 percent, and it led to a fluctuation in spending throughout the draft, including the first round.

Just 11 first-rounders signed for bonuses equal to the slots assigned by Major League Baseball, while 10 signed for amounts that were greater than the slot and 12 for below-slot amounts.

By signing Kolek for $821,800 under the slot for the second pick, the Marlins freed up enough money to sign seven players in later rounds, including 14th-rounder Zach Sullivan for $250,000 and 20th-rounder Jordan Holloway for $400,000.

After signing Indiana University catcher Kyle Schwarber, the fourth overall pick, for $3.125 million ($1,496,200 under slot), and in turn second-rounder Jake Stinnett for $1 million ($250,400 under slot) and third-rounder Mark Zagunis for $615,000 ($99,900 under slot), the Chicago Cubs were able to aggressively go after their next three picks, signing fourth-rounder Carson Sands for $1.1 million ($619,400 over slot), fifth-rounder Justin Steele for $1 million ($640,100 over slot) and sixth-rounder Dylan Cease for $1.5 million ($1,230,500 over slot).

The Baltimore Orioles spent the least money ($3,410,600) of any team, though they forfeited their first two picks for signing Ubaldo Jimenez and Nelson Cruz as free agents, and didn't make their initial selection until the 90th pick overall.

The New York Yankees lost their first three selections for signing free agents Brian McCann, Carlos Beltran and Jacoby Ellsbury, and spent just $4,050,200 in bonus money—the second-lowest total. But while they were limited in the amount they could spend domestically, they more than made up for it by being the big spenders internationally, paying out three of the five largest bonuses, ranging from $2 million to $3 million, all to 16-year-old Dominicans.

Led by Rodon and Kolek, who signed with the Marlins for $6 million, the average first-round bonus was $2,612,109—a 1.1 percent decrease from 2013. Had Aiken signed for the amount he

## One Team's Draft: Cleveland Indians

| Player, Pos. | Bonus | Player, Pos. | Bonus | Player, Pos. | Bonus |
|---|---|---|---|---|---|
| 1. Brad Zimmer, of | $1,900,000 | 9. * Alexis Pantoja, ss | $144,600 | 19. Argenis Angulo, rhp | $75,000 |
| 1. * Justus Sheffield, lhp | $1,600,000 | 10. Steven Patterson, 2b | $10,000 | 20. * Gianpaul Gonzalez, c | $100,000 |
| 1. Mike Papi, of | $1,250,000 | 11. Jared Robinson, rhp | $100,000 | 21. Bobby Ison, of | $25,000 |
| 2. * Grant Hockin, rhp | $1,100,000 | 12. Jordan Dunatov, rhp | $60,000 | 22. Jordan Carter, rhp | $2,500 |
| 3. * Bobby Bradley, 1b | $912,500 | 13. Austin Fisher, ss | $100,000 | 23. David Armendariz, of | $2,500 |
| 4. * Sam Hentges, lhp | $700,000 | 14. Grayson Jones, rhp | Did not sign | 24. * Jodd Carter, of | $75,000 |
| 5. Julian Merryweather, rhp | $20,000 | 15. Luke Eubank, rhp | $75,000 | 25. K.J. Harrison, c | Did not sign |
| 6. Greg Allen, of | $200,000 | 16. J.P. Feyereisen, rhp | $80,000 | Other Nate Winfrey (28), 3b | $60,000 |
| 7. * Simeon Lucas, c | $168,200 | 17. Cameron Hill, rhp | $75,000 | | |
| 8. * Micah Miniard, rhp | $350,000 | 18. Taylor Murphy, of | $75,000 | | |

*High school selection.

agreed to, that average would been $2,726,459.

A record 67 players signed for bonuses of $1 million or more, the latest of whom were the three players drafted by the Cubs in the fourth, fifth and sixth rounds. Additionally, 23 players earned bonuses of $2 million or more, the latest being Canadian outfielder Gareth Morgan, who accepted a $2 million bonus from the Seattle Mariners as the 74th overall pick.

Meanwhile, 38 players drafted after the 10th round were paid bonuses of more than $100,000—an important threshold because anything in excess of that amount applied to a team's bonus pool. Both the Marlins and New York Mets each exceeded $100,000 on four players beyond the 10th round, though no individual player topped that mark quite so dramatically as New Jersey high school righthander Bryan Dobzanski, the 29th-round pick of the Cardinals. He was paid a bonus of $750,000.

The 6-foot-4, 220-pound Dobzanski boasted a fastball in the mid-90s and planned to pursue baseball in college at Louisville before the Cardinals interceded with the largest bonus ever given to a 29th-rounder. He had devoted limited time to baseball in high school because he was a star wrestler, going 83-0 with 54 pins as a junior and senior.

Rodon's bonus was the fifth-largest in draft history and the second-largest under the current CBA. The White Sox brought him along cautiously, and he pitched in just 25 innings in his first pro season, though made three starts in Triple-A to complete the year. After making two more starts in Triple-A to open the 2015 season, he debuted with the White Sox on April 21 and went 9-6, 3.75 as a rookie.

Kolek struggled with control issues in his first two seasons in the minors while going 4-13, 4.53. He then succumbed to Tommy John surgery in April 2016.

### PITCHING DOMINATES FIRST ROUND

Aiken, Kolek and Rodon were the first three players off the board, as expected, and the rest of the first round went largely according to form.

The Cubs pulled the first surprise by taking Schwarber with the No. 4 pick, at the expense of Jackson, another player with a similar profile. Not only did they rate the 6-foot, 230-pound catcher/outfielder the best all-around hitter in the draft, but he was their No. 2 prospect overall.

Alex Jackson

Jackson, who slugged 47 homers over four years at Rancho Bernardo High in San Diego, had been expected to go in the top four picks and his $4.2 million bonus, the third largest overall, appeared to reflect that. He was taken with the sixth pick by the Mariners, who announced that they intended to move him to the outfield to take full advantage of his offensive potential.

### Highest Unsigned Picks

| Player, Pos., Team (Round) | College | Re-Drafted |
|---|---|---|
| Brady Aiken, lhp, Astros (1) | None | Indians '15 (1) |
| Andrew Suarez, lhp, Nationals (2) | * Miami | Giants '15 (2) |
| Trevor Megill, rhp, Cardinals (3) | * Loyola Marymount | Padres '15 (7) |
| Jacob Nix, rhp, Astros (5) | None | Padres '15 (3) |
| Zach Zehner, of, Blue Jays (7) | * Cal Poly | Yankees '15 (18) |
| Austin Byler, 1b, Nationals (9) | * Nevada | D-backs '15 (11) |
| Jake Latz, lhp, Blue Jays (11) | Louisiana State | Not eligible |
| Justin Bellinger, 1b, Cardinals (11) | Duke | Not eligible |
| Tanner Houck, rhp, Blue Jays (12) | Missouri | Not eligible |
| C.J. Moore, of, Diamondbacks (13) | Lamar | Not eligible |

**TOTAL UNSIGNED PICKS:** Top 5 Rounds (4), Top 10 Rounds (6)

**Returned to same school.*

The Minnesota Twins, picking one spot ahead of the Mariners, took the first high school position player by opting for Florida shortstop Nick Gordon, the son of ex-big leaguer Tom Gordon and half-brother of current big leaguer Dee Gordon.

With the notable exception of Schwarber, Gordon and Jackson, the emphasis in the 2014 draft was on pitching, especially college pitching as nine of the first 19 selections were college arms.

In addition to Rodon, others given a realistic shot of being tabbed in the first 10 picks were righthanders Jeff Hoffman of East Carolina, Tyler Beede of Vanderbilt, Aaron Nola of Louisiana State and Erick Fedde of Nevada-Las Vegas, as well as lefthanders Brandon Finnegan of Texas Christian, Kyle Freeland of Evansville and Sean Newcomb of Hartford.

"You could see as far back as last summer that it would be a pitching-oriented draft this year," said a National League scouting director. "It was apparent just by looking at the Cape Cod League and Team USA that the number of quality bats would be few and far between."

While Rodon's track record and impressive stuff made him the obvious frontrunner to go No. 1 as the 2014 pitching crop began to take shape, Hoffman emerged as a viable candidate to challenge Rodon.

Hoffman didn't enjoy the same success Rodon did through his first two college seasons at ECU, going a combined 9-9, 3.48 with 60 walks and 139 strikeouts in 184 innings. The New York high school product was not drafted coming out of high school either, but was a late bloomer, flashing one of the dominant arms in the Cape Cod League for two summers with a fastball that ranged from 94-99 mph.

Unlike the physically mature Rodon, the 6-foot-4, 190-pound Hoffman was still growing into his lanky frame, and appeared ripe to make a leap forward in the spring of 2014. But after going 3-3, 3.21 in 10 starts for ECU, with the draft less than two months out, Hoffman injured his elbow and had Tommy John surgery. The Toronto Blue Jays, with the ninth and 11th picks, were in position to gamble on Hoffman, and did by taking him with the ninth pick and paying him slot money ($3,080,800).

"We scouted him pretty good early," Jays scouting director Brian Parker said. "This is an athletic,

### WORTH NOTING

10th round signed bonuses in excess of $100,000, while all but two 11th-rounders earned bonuses in six figures, including a high of $580,000 by Montana high school outfielder **GAGE HINSZ**, drafted by the Pirates. While bonuses in the first 10 rounds were tied to a team's overall bonus pool—and teams wanted to be certain they could sign players in the first 10 rounds so they would not lose that money from their signing budgets—bonuses in the 11th round and beyond were not unless they exceeded $100,000, and there were no ramifications to not signing players from those rounds.

■ Even though 15 of the first 21 players drafted were from college, the number of high school selections through the first two rounds (39) outnumbered the number of college and junior-college picks (34). But college talent prevailed by a wide margin from that point on. Once again, teams strategically drafted a wealth of college seniors in the first 10 rounds to give them maximum flexibility with their bonus pool limits and reduce the possibility that they would have unsigned picks in the first 10 rounds. Having exhausted their amateur eligibility, college seniors have significantly less leverage than any draft demographic and in all, 55 seniors were selected in the first 10 rounds, along with 14 fourth-year juniors.

■ The Twins had one of the more unique drafts because of an obvious emphasis on a talent demographic that most teams had ignored in recent years. They picked strong-armed major college relievers with six of their seven picks between the second and eighth rounds, starting off with Burdi and San Diego State righthander **MICHAEL CEDEROTH**, two of the hardest throwers in the college game. Most clubs had begun to develop relievers from pitchers who had backgrounds as starters but were better suited for shorter outings in pro ball.

## IN FOCUS: KYLE SCHWARBER

With his limitations defensively and lack of a defined position, Indiana catcher/outfielder Kyle Schwarber was not a consensus top 10 pick going into the 2014 draft. His bonus of $3.125 million, about $1.5 million under slot for the fourth overall pick, was seen as a compromise and a reflection of his overall ability.

But Schwarber could hit like no player in the 2014 draft and had intangibles to match. The savings also enabled the Chicago Cubs to be aggressive later in the draft, and they signed each of their picks from the fourth-sixth rounds for $1 million or more.

"He does everything that we like from an offensive standpoint in terms of controlling the strike zone, hitting for average, hitting for power," said senior vice president of scouting and player development Jason McLeod. "His makeup is off the charts."

The lefty-swinging Schwarber's advanced hitting ability was prominently on display in a 147-game audition in the minors, where he hit .333 with 34 homers and drew 88 walks. He also homered 16 times in 69 games as a rookie for the Cubs on their unexpected run to a postseason berth in 2015. His bat was so impressive that it didn't seem to matter than he had done little to answer lingering questions where he might eventually fit in defensively.

power, college arm that offers even more upside once he gets into pro ball. We didn't think we'd get a chance to take this player, but when the injury happened, it was something we jumped on."

Hoffman quickly regained his old velocity while making 13 starts in the Blue Jays system in 2015, but was packaged to the Colorado Rockies at the trading deadline in a blockbuster deal that brought all-star shortstop Troy Tulowitzki to Toronto.

Not to be outdone, Fedde was a second elite-level college arm who also hurt his elbow in the midst of the 2014 season. After going 8-2, 1.76 in 11 starts for UNLV, he had Tommy John surgery prior to the draft as well. Like the Blue Jays, the Nationals were undeterred in selecting a pitcher that was considered damaged goods and tagged him with the 18th selection overall. They signed him for $2,511,100—an amount that was actually $365,500 over slot. Like Hoffman, he quickly regained his old form when he began pitching again in 2015.

Jeff Hoffman

Nola, selected seventh overall by the Philadelphia Phillies, was the first college righthander taken. He demonstrated the best command of any pitcher in his class after walking seven in 90 innings as a freshman at LSU. Even as his control wasn't quite as impeccable as a junior, he managed to lead the nation with 134 strikeouts in 116 innings, while walking 27 and posting an 11-1, 1.47 record. His fastball typically only reached the low 90s, but Nola had three above-average pitches and his stuff played up because of his impressive command. Not surprisingly, he breezed through the minors and accorded himself well as a major league rookie in 2015 by going 6-2, 3.59 in 13 starts.

Freeland elevated his stock as much as any college arm as a junior on the strength of his ability to throw quality strikes with a fastball at 91-94 mph that peaked at 96. After going 4-8, 4.34 as a sophomore at Evansville, he went 10-2, 1.90 with 13 walks and 128 strikeouts in 100 innings as a junior, prompting the Rockies to take him with the eighth pick overall. Freeland was appealing to the Rockies because he was a Colorado native and their team doctor had actually performed surgery on his elbow while he was in high school.

Possibly the most dominant college arm of all in the 2014 draft was the 6-foot-4, 220-pound Burdi, who featured a fastball that routinely reached 100-102 mph and a wipeout slider that often topped 90, and went 3-1, 0.49 with 18 saves, while also striking out 65 in 37 innings. Because he profiled as a reliever, he fell to the second round—especially with the less than distinguished record of closers taken in the first round in recent drafts.

While Aiken and Kolek were clearly the class of the high school pitching crop, South Carolina prep righthander Grant Holmes was another prime candidate to crack the top 10 picks. He showcased impressive raw stuff with a fastball that peaked at 100 mph, but the lack of projection in his 6-foot-2, 210-pound frame appeared to work against him as he slipped to the Dodgers with the 22nd pick overall, though he got a $2.5 million bonus.

Virginia righthander Jacob Bukauskas made the most notable rise through the high school draft ranks, mainly on the strength of a fastball that also touched 100 mph. At 17, he was not supposed to be a member of the 2014 draft class initially, but advanced his high school coursework enough to be reclassified as a senior. While he appeared to edge his way into first-round consideration late in the spring, he lasted until the 20th round after advising clubs that he planned to attend college at North Carolina.

### TURNER TRADE LEADS TO RULE CHANGE

With Rodon and Hoffman in contention early in the year to go No. 1 overall, North Carolina already promised to be a popular destination for scouts, but N.C. State had a second candidate capable of going early in the first round in shortstop Trea Turner. The school's banner 2012 freshman class also featured the top unsigned high school selection from the 2011 draft in catcher Brett Austin, a supplemental first-round pick of the Padres.

Austin never progressed in college as expected, but Rodon and Turner obviously did, with Turner going 13th overall in the 2014 draft to the Padres. He played in just 69 games in the organization before a new front office packaged him to the Nationals in a three-way trade also involving the Tampa Bay Rays on Dec. 19, 2014.

Because Turner was dealt before the first anniversary of his signing with the Padres, he was technically classified as a player to be named in the deal, in order to comply with draft rules that prohibited teams from trading picks within 12 months of signing. In an awkward arrangement, Turner was forced to begin the 2015 season at Double-A in the Padres system, while on loan from the Nationals, before finally joining his new organization on June 14. By September, he was in Washington after hitting .322 in the minors between the two organizations.

The existing rule had been implemented in 1985 after the Montreal Expos traded their first-round pick, Pete Incaviglia, to the Texas Rangers as a condition of his signing. The rule had been compromised, though only marginally, on three or four occasions since, but the Turner situation prompted Major League Baseball and the union to agree in May 2015 to amend the terms under which recently drafted players could be traded.

The change wasn't made in time to help Turner because he was dealt under the existing rules, but going forward players from a particular year's draft could be traded the day after the World Series concluded.

Through the 2015 season, Turner was one of just seven players from the 2014 draft, including six first-rounders, who had found their way to the big leagues.

# 2014 Draft List

**Did not sign. Major leaguers in bold, with first and last years noted. Order of selection indicated in parentheses. For the first five rounds, the peak level of each player is noted.*

## ARIZONA DIAMONDBACKS (15)

1. Touki Toussaint, rhp, Coral Springs Christian Academy, Coral Springs, Fla.—(Low A)
2. Cody Reed, lhp, Ardmore (Ala.) HS.—(Short-season A)
2. Marcus Wilson, of, Serra HS, Gardena, Calif. (Competitive balance Round 'B' pick—69th; obtained in trade with Padres).—(Rookie)
2. Isan Diaz, ss, Springfield (Mass.) HS (Competitive balance Round 'B' pick—70th).—(Rookie)
3. Matt Railey, of, North Florida Christian HS, Tallahassee, Fla.—(Rookie)
4. Brent Jones, rhp, Cornell University.—(Low A)
5. Mason McCullough, rhp, Lander (S.C.) University.—(High A)
6. Zac Curtis, lhp, Middle Tennessee State University.
7. Tyler Humphreys, 3b, St. Johns River State (Fla.) JC.
8. Grant Heyman, of, CC of Southern Nevada.
9. Justin Gonzalez, ss, Florida State University.
10. Scott Schultz, rhp, Oregon State University.
11. Jared Miller, lhp, Vanderbilt University.
12. Holden Helmink, rhp, San Jacinto (Texas) JC.
13. *C.J. Moore, of, Suffield (Conn.) Academy.
14. Kevin Cron, 1b, Texas Christian University.

DRAFT DROP *Son of Chris Cron, major leaguer (1991-92) • Brother of C.J. Cron, first-round draft pick, Angels (2011); major leaguer (2014-15)*

15. Tyler Baker, c, Wichita State University.
16. Kevin Simmons, rhp, Wallace CC-Selma (Ala.).
17. Mike Abreu, 2b, Hillsborough (Fla.) CC.
18. *Garrett Mundell, rhp, Fresno State University.
19. Dan Savas, rhp, Illinois State University.
20. *Jacob Bukauskas, rhp, Stone Bridge HS, Ashburn, Va.
21. Gerard Hernandez, of, Pinnacle HS, Phoenix.
22. Michael Branigan, c, Forsyth Central HS, Cumming, Ga.
23. *John Fidanza, c, Georgia Gwinnett College.
24. Mike Cetta, rhp, University of Central Florida.
25. Brando Tessar, rhp, University of Oregon.
26. *Willie Rios, lhp, St. Bernard HS, Montville, Conn.
27. Nate Robertson, ss, Colorado Mesa University.
28. Bennie Robinson, 1b, Florida A&M University.
29. Nick Baker, rhp, Chico State (Calif.) University.
30. Trevor Mitsui, 1b, University of Washington.
31. Roberto Cancio, lhp, Broward (Fla.) CC.
32. *Cameron Bishop, lhp, Brea Olinda HS, Brea, Calif.
33. Tyler Bolton, rhp, East Carolina University.
34. Nate Irving, c, University of Virginia.
35. *Justin Morris, c, DeMatha Catholic HS, Hyattsville, Md.
36. Will Landsheft, rhp, Drury (Mo.) University.
37. *Keith Holcombe, of, Hillcrest HS, Tuscaloosa, Ala.
38. Lawrence Pardo, lhp, University of South Florida.
39. *Drew Rasmussen, rhp, Mount Spokane HS, Mead, Wash.
40. *Zach Gahagan, ss, North Henderson HS, Hendersonville, N.C.

## ATLANTA BRAVES (28)

1. (Choice forfeited for signing Ervin Santana as free agent).
1. Braxton Davidson, of, T.C. Roberson HS, Asheville, N.C. (Compensation for loss of Brian McCann as free agent—32nd).—(Low A)
2. Garrett Fulenchek, rhp, Howe (Texas) HS.—(Rookie)
3. Max Povse, rhp, UNC Greensboro.—(High A)
4. Chad Sobotka, rhp, USC Upstate.—(Low A)
5. Chris Diaz, lhp, University of Miami.—(Low A)
6. Keith Curcio, of, Florida Southern College.
7. Luke Dykstra, 2b, Westlake HS, Westlake Village, Calif.

DRAFT DROP *Son of Lenny Dykstra, major leaguer (1985-96)*

8. Brad Roney, rhp, University of Southern Mississippi.
9. Jordan Edgerton, 3b, UNC Pembroke.
10. Matt Tellor, 1b, Southeast Missouri State University.
11. Luis Gamez, rhp, Cienega HS, Tucson, Ariz.
12. Patrick Dorrian, 2b, Kingston (N.Y.) HS.
13. Caleb Beech, rhp, Shelton State (Ala.) CC.
14. Joseph Daris, of, Azusa Pacific (Calif.) University.
15. Caleb Dirks, rhp, California Baptist University.
16. Brandon Barker, rhp, Mercer University.
17. *Ashton Perritt, rhp-of, Liberty University.
18. Jacob Webb, rhp, Tabor (Kan.) College.
19. Codey McElroy, ss, Cameron (Okla.) University.
20. Wigberto Nevarez, c, Lubbock Christian (Texas) University.
21. *Jake Godfrey, rhp, Providence Catholic HS, New Lenox, Ill.
22. Sean Godfrey, of, Ball State University.
23. Tanner Krietemeier, 1b, Oklahoma State University.
24. Kevin Reiher, c, Prairie State (Ill.) JC.
25. Kyle Kinman, lhp, Bellevue (Neb.) University.
26. Trevor Sprowl, 2b, Auburn University-Montgomery.

DRAFT DROP *Son of Bobby Spowl, major leaguer (1978-81)*

27. *Carl Stajduhar, 1b, Rocky Mountain HS, Fort Collins, Colo.
28. Matt Sims, rhp, University of Texas-San Antonio.
29. *Dazon Cole, rhp, West Bloomfield (Mich.) HS.
30. *Jared James, of, McClatchy HS, Sacramento, Calif.
31. Sal Giardina, c, Lynn (Fla.) University.
32. *Tucker Baca, lhp, North Gwinnett HS, Suwanee, Ga.
33. *Doug Still, lhp, Sikeston (Mo.) HS.
34. *Nick Leonard, rhp, Mountain Vista HS, Highlands Ranch, Colo.
35. *Ryan Kokora, rhp, Fairview HS, Boulder, Colo.
36. *Larry Crisler, of, Bishop Noll Institute, Hammond, Ind.
37. *Gavin Sheets, 1b, Gilman School, Baltimore.

DRAFT DROP *Son of Larry Sheets, major leaguer (1984-93)*

38. J.J. Franco, 2b, Brown University.

DRAFT DROP *Son of John Franco, major leaguer (1984-2005)*

39. *Grayson Byrd, ss, King's Ridge Christian HS, Alpharetta, Ga.

DRAFT DROP *Son of Paul Byrd, major leaguer (1995-2009)*

40. *Randy Santiesteban, 2b, Peru State (Neb.) College.

## BALTIMORE ORIOLES (16)

1. (Choice forfeited for signing Ubaldo Jiminez as free agent).
2. (Choice forfeited for signing Nelson Cruz as free agent)
3. Brian Gonzalez, lhp, Archbishop McCarthy HS, Southwest Ranches, Fla.—(Low A)
4. Pat Connaughton, rhp, University of Notre Dame.—(Short-season A)

DRAFT DROP *Second-round draft pick, Brooklyn Nets/ National Basketball Association (2015); guard, Portland Trail Blazers/NBA (2015-16)*

5. David Hess, rhp, Tennessee Tech.—(AA)
6. Tanner Scott, lhp, Howard (Texas) JC.
7. Max Schuh, lhp, UCLA.
8. Steve Wilkerson, 2b, Clemson University.
9. Austin Anderson, 3b, University of Mississippi.
10. Jay Gonzalez, of, Mount Olive (N.C.) College.
11. John Means, lhp, West Virginia University.
12. Nigel Nootbaar, rhp, University of Southern California.
13. Matt Trowbridge, lhp, Central Michigan University.
14. Gerrion Grim, of, Jefferson (Mo.) JC.
15. Alejandro Juvier, 2b, Doral (Fla.) Academy.
16. Tanner Chleborad, rhp, Washington State University.
17. Jean Cosme, rhp, Colegio Sagrada Familia HS, San Juan, P.R.
18. Matt Grimes, rhp, Georgia Tech.
19. *Connor Seabold, rhp, Newport Harbor HS, Newport Beach, Calif.
20. Zach Albin, rhp, University of Connecticut-Avery Point JC.
21. John McLeod, lhp, Wake Forest University.
22. Josh Walker, rhp, University of New Mexico.
23. Zeke McGranahan, rhp, Georgia Gwinnett College.
24. Lucas Long, rhp, University of San Diego.
25. *Brandon Bonilla, lhp, Grand Canyon University.

DRAFT DROP *Son of Bobby Bonilla, major leaguer (1986-2001)*

26. *Gage Burland, rhp, East Valley HS, Spokane, Wash.
27. Austin Pfeiffer, ss, University of Arkansas-Little Rock.
28. *James Carter, rhp, Chabot (Calif.) JC.
29. Patrick Baker, rhp, Anne Arundel (Md.) CC.
30. Mike Burke, rhp, University of Buffalo.
31. Riley Palmer, 3b, Southern New Hampshire University.
32. Jamill Moquete, of, University of Massachusetts-Boston.
33. Brandon Koch, rhp, Temecula Valley HS, Temecula, Calif.
34. *Garrett Pearson, rhp, St. John's College HS, Washington, D.C.
35. Tad Gold, of, Endicott (Mass.) College.
36. Alexander Lee, 1b, Radford University.
37. *Hunter Hart, rhp, St. Joseph Ogden HS, St. Joseph, Ill.
38. Keegan Ghidotti, rhp, Ouachita Baptist (Ark.) University.
39. *Tucker Simpson, rhp, Chipola (Fla.) JC.
40. T.J. Olesczuk, of, Winthrop University.

## BOSTON RED SOX (29)

1. Michael Chavis, ss, Sprayberry HS, Marietta, Ga.—(Low A)
1. Michael Kopech, rhp, Mount Pleasant (Texas) HS (Compensation for loss of Jacoby Ellsbury as free agent—33rd).—(Low A)
2. Sam Travis, 1b, Indiana University.—(AA)
3. Jake Cosart, rhp, Seminole State (Fla.) JC.—(Short-season A)

DRAFT DROP *Brother of Jarred Cosart, major leaguer (2013-15)*

4. Kevin McAvoy, rhp, Bryant University.—(High A)
5. Josh Ockimey, 1b, Neumann-Goretti HS, Philadelphia.—(Short-season A)
6. Danny Mars, of, Chipola (Fla.) JC.
7. Reed Reilly, rhp, Cal Poly.
8. Ben Moore, c, University of Alabama.
9. Kevin Steen, rhp, Oak Ridge (Tenn.) HS.
10. Cole Sturgeon, of, University of Louisville.
11. Karsten Whitson, rhp, University of Florida.

DRAFT DROP *First-round draft pick (9th overall), Padres (2010)*

12. Jalen Beeks, lhp, University of Arkansas.
13. Chandler Shepherd, rhp, University of Kentucky.
14. Jordan Procyshen, c, Northern Kentucky University.
15. Trenton Kemp, of, Buchanan HS, Clovis, Calif.
16. Michael Gunn, lhp, University of Arkansas.
17. Jeremy Rivera, ss, El Paso (Texas) CC.
18. Jordan Betts, 3b, Duke University.
19. Tyler Hill, of, Delaware Military Academy, Wilmington, Del.
20. Devon Fisher, c, Western Branch HS, Chesapeake, Va.
21. *Ian Rice, c, Chipola (Fla.) JC.
22. *J.J. Matijevic, ss, Norwin HS, North Huntingdon, Pa.
23. Derek Miller, of, University of Texas-Arlington.
24. Cisco Tellez, 1b, UC Riverside.
25. *Gabe Klobosits, rhp, Galveston (Texas) CC.
26. Ryan Harris, rhp, University of Florida.
27. Taylor Nunez, rhp, University of Southern Mississippi.
28. *David Peterson, lhp, Regis Jesuit HS, Aurora, Colo.
29. Josh Pennington, rhp, Lower Cape May Regional HS, Cape May, N.J.
30. *Jeren Kendall, of, Holmen (Wis.) HS.
31. Alex McKeon, c, Texas A&M International University.
32. *Case Rolen, rhp, Sherman (Texas) HS.
33. Luis Alvarado, of, Puerto Rico Baseball Academy, Gurabo, P.R.
34. Kuehl McEachern, rhp, Flagler (Fla.) College.
35. *Ross Puskarich, 3b, Liberty HS, Bakersfield, Calif.
36. *Brad Wilpon, rhp, Brunswick School, Greenwich, Conn.

DRAFT DROP *Son of Jeff Wilpon, chief operating officer, Mets*

37. Hector Lorenzana, ss, University of Oklahoma.
38. Brandon Show, rhp, University of San Diego.
39. *Mike Gretler, ss, Bonney Lake (Wash.) HS.
40. Joe Winterburn, c, La Verne (Calif.) University.

## CHICAGO CUBS (4)

1. **Kyle Schwarber, c, Indiana University.—(2015)**
2. Jake Stinnett, rhp, University of Maryland.—(Low A)
3. Mark Zagunis, c, Virginia Tech.—(High A)
4. Carson Sands, lhp, North Florida Christian HS, Tallahassee, Fla.—(Short-season A)
5. Justin Steele, lhp, George County HS, Lucedale, Miss.—(Short-season A)
6. Dylan Cease, rhp, Milton (Ga.) HS.
7. James Norwood, rhp, Saint Louis University.
8. Tommy Thorpe, lhp, University of Oregon.
9. James Farris, rhp, University of Arizona.
10. Ryan Williams, rhp, East Carolina University.
11. Jordan Brink, rhp, Fresno State University.
12. Tanner Griggs, rhp, Angelina (Texas) JC.
13. Kevonte Mitchell, 3b, Kennett (Mo.) HS.
14. Chesny Young, 2b, Mercer University.
15. Jeremy Null, rhp, Western Carolina University.
16. Jason Vosler, ss, Northeastern University.
17. John Michael Knighton, rhp, Central Alabama CC.
18. Austyn Willis, rhp, Barstow (Calif.) HS.
19. Brad Markey, rhp, Virginia Tech.
20. Alex Tomasovich, ss, Charleston Southern University.
21. Charlie White, of, University of Maryland.
22. Joe Martarano, 3b, Boise State University.
23. *Isiah Gilliam, of, Parkview HS, Lilburn, Ga.
24. *Daniel Spingola, of, Georgia Tech.
25. Tyler Pearson, c, Texas State University.
26. Zach Hedges, rhp, Azusa Pacific (Calif.) University.
27. Calvin Graves, of, Franklin Pierce (N.H.) College.
28. *Jake Niggemeyer, rhp, Olentangy Liberty HS, Powell, Ohio.
29. *Gianni Zayas, rhp, Seminole State (Fla.) JC.
30. *Michael Cantu, c, Moody HS, Corpus Christi, Texas.
31. *Brad Depperman, rhp, East Lake HS, Tarpon Springs, Fla.
32. Andrew Ely, 2b, University of Washington.
33. *Brad Bass, rhp, Lincoln-Way Central HS, New Lenox, Ill.
34. *Stephen Kane, rhp, Cypress (Calif.) JC.
35. Jordan Minch, lhp, Purdue University.
36. *D.J. Peters, of, Glendora (Calif.) HS.
37. *Riley Adams, c, Canyon Crest Academy, San Diego.
38. *Daniel Wasinger, c, Eastlake HS, El Paso, Texas.

DRAFT DROP *Son of Mark Wasinger, major leaguer (1986-88)*

39. *David Petrino, c, Central Arizona JC.
40. *Diamond Johnson, of, Hillsborough HS, Tampa.

## CHICAGO WHITE SOX (3)

1. **Carlos Rodon, lhp, North Carolina State University.—(2015)**
2. Spencer Adams, rhp, White County HS, Cleveland, Ga.—(High A)
3. Jace Fry, lhp, Oregon State University.—(High A)
4. Brett Austin, c, North Carolina State University.—(High A)

DRAFT DROP *First-round draft pick (54th overall), Padres (2011)*

5. Zach Thompson, rhp, University of Texas-Arlington.—(Low A)
6. Louie Lechich, of, University of San Diego.
7. Jake Peter, ss, Creighton University.
8. John Ziznewski, ss, Long Island University.
9. Brian Clark, lhp, Kent State University.
10. Jake Jarvis, 2b, Klein Collins HS, Spring, Texas.
11. Zach Fish, of, Oklahoma State University.
12. Connor Walsh, rhp, University of Cincinnati.
13. Mike Gomez, lhp, Florida International University.
14. *Bryce Montes de Oca, rhp, Lawrence (Kan.) HS.

15. Ben Brewster, lhp, University of Maryland.
16. Matt Cooper, rhp, University of Hawaii.
17. David Trexler, rhp, University of North Florida.
18. Tanner Banks, lhp, University of Utah.
19. Aaron Bummer, lhp, University of Nebraska.
20. Brannon Easterling, rhp, St. Edward's (Texas) University.
21. Ryan Leonards, 3b, University of Louisiana-Lafayette.
22. Kevin Swick, 3b, University of Southern California.
23. Michael Hollenbeck, c, Illinois State University.
24. Michael Suiter, of, University of Kansas.
25. Mason Robbins, of, University of Southern Mississippi.
26. Ethan Gross, ss, Memphis University.
27. Ryan Jones, 1b, Arizona Christian University.
28. Blair Moore, 3b, California Baptist University.
29. Evin Einhardt, rhp, Brewton-Parker (Ga.) College.
30. Marc Flores, 1b, University of Hawaii.
31. Josh Goossen-Brown, rhp-inf, University of San Diego.
32. *Adam Choplick, lhp, University of Oklahoma.
33. Louis Silverio, of, Florida International University.
34. Michael Danner, of, University of Tampa.
35. *Jared Koenig, lhp, Central Arizona JC.
36. *Dayne Wagoner, c, Great Oak HS, Temecula, Calif.
37. *Jed Sprague, 1b, St. Mary's HS, Stockton, Calif.

DRAFT DROP *Son of Ed Sprague, first-round draft pick, Blue Jays (1988); major leaguer (1991-2001) • Grandson of Ed Sprague Sr., major leaguer (1968-76)*

38. *Anthony Justiniano, ss, Clemente HS, Chicago.
39. *James Davison, of, Morgan Park HS, Chicago.
40. *Julian Service, of, Howard (Texas) JC.

## CINCINNATI REDS (20)

1. Nick Howard, rhp, University of Virginia.—(High A)
1. Alex Blandino, ss, Stanford University (Compensation for loss of free agent Shin Soo Choo—29th).—(AA)
2. Taylor Sparks, 3b, UC Irvine.—(High A)
3. Wyatt Strahan, rhp, University of Southern California.—(Low A)
4. Gavin LaValley, 3b, Carl Albert HS, Midwest City, Okla.—(Low A)
5. Tejay Antone, rhp, Weatherford (Texas) JC.—(Low A)
6. Jose Lopez, rhp, Seton Hall University.
7. Shane Mardirosian, 2b, Martin Luther King HS, Riverside, Calif.
8. Brian O'Grady, 1b, Rutgers University.
9. Brian Hunter, rhp, University of Hartford.
10. Seth Varner, lhp, Miami (Ohio) University.
11. Mitch Trees, c, Sacred Heart-Griffin HS, Springfield, Ill.
12. Montrell Marshall, 3b, South Gwinnett HS, Snellville, Ga.
13. Zac Correll, rhp, Joseph Case HS, Swansea, Mass.
14. Jake Ehret, rhp, UCLA.
15. Jimmy Pickens, of, Michigan State University.
16. Garrett Boulware, c, Clemson University.
17. Jacob Moody, lhp, Memphis University.
18. *Roderick Bynum, of, Monroe Catholic HS, Fairbanks, Alaska.
19. *Isaac Anderson, rhp, JC of Southern Idaho.
20. Conor Krauss, rhp, Seton Hall University.
21. Tyler Parmenter, rhp, University of Arizona.
22. *Robert Byckowski, 3b, Blyth Academy, Toronto.
23. Ty Sterner, lhp, University of Rhode Island.
24. Shane Crouse, rhp, Lake Sumter (Fla.) CC.
25. Paul Kronenfeld, 1b, Catawba (N.C.) College.
26. Brennan Bernardino, lhp, Cal State Dominguez Hills.
27. Jake Paulson, rhp, Oakland University.
28. *Dustin Cook, rhp, San Jacinto (Texas) JC.
29. Michael Sullivan, lhp, Gloucester County (N.J.) CC.
30. Josciel Veras, ss, Cumberland (Tenn.) University.
31. *Josh Palacios, of, San Jacinto (Texas) JC.
32. *Dalton Viner, rhp, San Jacinto (Texas) JC.
33. Jose Lopez, c, King HS, Tampa.
34. Keenan Kish, rhp, University of Florida.
35. *Brandon Vicens, of, American Heritage HS, Plantation, Fla.

STEVEN HARRIS

**The Rockies took Evansville's Kyle Freeland, a Colorado native, with the eighth overall pick**

36. *Logan Browning, lhp, Lakeland Christian HS, Lakeland, Fla.

DRAFT DROP *Son of Tom Browning, major leaguer (1984-95)*

37. *Walker Whitworth, 2b, Ada (Okla.) HS.
38. *Bo Tucker, lhp, Rome (Ga.) HS.
39. *Seth Roadcap, c, Capital HS, Charleston, W.Va.
40. *Michael Mediavilla, lhp, Mater Academy, Hialeah Gardens, Fla.

## CLEVELAND INDIANS (23)

1. Bradley Zimmer, of, University of San Francisco.—(AA)

DRAFT DROP *Brother of Kyle Zimmer, first-round draft pick, Royals (2012)*

1. Justus Sheffield, lhp, Tullahoma (Tenn.) HS (Compensation for loss of free agent Ubaldo Jimenez—31st).—(Low A)
1. Mike Papi, of, University of Virginia (Competitive balance Round 'A' pick—38th).—(High A)
2. Grant Hockin, rhp, Damien HS, La Verne, Calif.—(Rookie)

DRAFT DROP *Grandson of Harmon Killebrew, major leaguer (1954-75)*

3. Bobby Bradley, 1b, Harrison Central HS, Gulfport, Miss.—(High A)
4. Sam Hentges, lhp, Mounds View HS, Arden Hills, Minn.—(Short-season A)
5. Julian Merryweather, rhp, Oklahoma Baptist University.—(Low A)
6. Greg Allen, of, San Diego State University.
7. Simeon Lucas, c, Grant Community HS, Fox Lake, Ill.
8. Micah Miniard, rhp, Boyle County HS, Danville, Ky.
9. Alexis Pantoja, ss, Puerto Rico Baseball Academy, Gurabo, P.R.
10. Steven Patterson, 2b, UC Davis.
11. Jared Robinson, rhp, Cerritos (Calif.) JC.
12. Jordan Dunatov, rhp, University of Nevada.
13. Austin Fisher, ss, Kansas State University.
14. *Grayson Jones, rhp, Shelton State (Ala.) CC.
15. Luke Eubank, rhp, Oxnard (Calif.) JC.
16. J.P. Feyereisen, rhp, University of Wisconsin-Stevens Point.
17. Cameron Hill, rhp, Redlands (Calif.) CC.
18. Taylor Murphy, of, University of the Pacific.
19. Argenis Angulo, rhp, Ranger (Texas) JC.
20. Gianpaul Gonzalez, c, Puerto Rico Baseball Academy, Gurabo, P.R.
21. Bobby Ison, of, Charleston Southern University.
22. Jordan Carter, rhp, St. Joseph's University.
23. David Armendariz, of, Cal Poly Pomona.
24. Jodd Carter, of, Hilo (Hawaii) HS.
25. *K.J. Harrison, c, Punahou HS, Honolulu, Hawaii.
26. *Reese Cooley, of, Fleming Island HS, Orange Park, Fla.
27. David Speer, lhp, Columbia University.
28. Nate Winfrey, 3b, Maple Woods (Mo.) CC.
29. Drake Roberts, 2b, St. Mary's (Texas) University.
30. *Nick Hynes, rhp, Riverside (Calif.) CC.
31. Dominic DeMasi, rhp, Valdosta State (Ga.) University.
32. *Jared West, lhp, University of Houston.
33. *Peter Dolan, 3b, Gilmour Academy, Gates Mills, Ohio.
34. *Cody Calloway, 3b, Midview HS, Grafton, Ohio.
35. *Joe Dunand, 3b, Gulliver Prep, Miami.
36. *Max Bartlett, ss, Gulf Coast (Fla.) CC.
37. Juan Gomes, c, Odessa (Texas) JC.

DRAFT DROP *Brother of Yan Gomes, major leaguer (2012-15)*

38. *Cody Jones, of, Texas Christian University.
39. *Jake Morton, rhp, Oakland University.
40. *Ryder Ryan, rhp, North Mecklenburg HS, Huntersville, N.C.

## COLORADO ROCKIES (8)

1. Kyle Freeland, lhp, University of Evansville.—(High A)
1. Forrest Wall, 2b, Orangewood Christian HS, Maitland, Fla. (Competitive balance Round 'A' pick—35th).—(Low A)
2. Ryan Castellani, rhp, Brophy Prep, Phoenix.—(Low A)
3. Sam Howard, lhp, Georgia Southern University.—(Low A)
4. Wes Rogers, of, Spartanburg Methodist (S.C.) JC.—(Low A)
5. Kevin Padlo, 3b, Murrieta Valley HS, Murrieta, Calif.—(Low A)
6. Max George, ss, Regis Jesuit HS, Aurora, Colo.
7. Drew Weeks, of, University of North Florida.
8. Harrison Musgrave, lhp, West Virginia
9. Andrew Rohrbach, rhp, Long Beach State University.
10. Troy Stein, c, Texas A&M University.
11. Richard Prigatano, of, Long Beach State University.
12. Dylan Craig, lhp, Illinois State University.
13. Chris Rabago, ss, UC Irvine.
14. Grahamm Wiest, rhp, Cal State Fullerton.
15. Alec Kenilvort, rhp, Marin (Calif.) CC.
16. Roberto Ramos, 1b, JC of the Canyons (Calif.).
17. Shane Hoelscher, 3b, Rice University.
18. James Lomangino, rhp, St. John's University.
19. Nate Causey, 1b, Arizona State University.
20. Jordan Parris, c, Tennessee Tech.
21. Josh Michalec, rhp, Baylor University.
22. Sam Bumpers, ss, Lamar University.
23. Gavin Glanz, rhp, Oral Roberts University.
24. Jerry Vasto, lhp, Felician (N.J.) College.
25. Alec Crawford, rhp, University of Minnesota.
26. Taylor Black, rhp, Texas State University.
27. Craig Schlitter, rhp, Bryant University.
28. *Landon Lassiter, 3b, University of North Carolina.
29. Logan Sawyer, rhp, Lincoln Memorial (Tenn.) University.
30. Hunter Brothers, rhp, Lipscomb University.

DRAFT DROP *Brother of Rex Brothers, first-round draft pick, Rockies (2009); major leaguer (2011-15)*

31. Dylan Thompson, rhp, UNC Greensboro.
32. *Pavin Smith, 1b, Palm Beach Gardens (Fla.) HS.
33. *Jake Kolterman, rhp, Decatur HS, Federal Way, Wash.
34. *Cory Voss, c, Pueblo South HS, Pueblo, Colo.
35. *Brody Westmoreland, ss, Thunderridge HS, Highlands Ranch, Colo.
36. *Lucas Gilbreath, lhp, Legacy HS, Broomfield, Colo.
37. *Tolly Filotei, of, Daphne (Ala.) HS.
38. *Griffin Canning, rhp, Santa Margarita HS, Rancho Santa Margarita, Calif.
39. *Nathan Rodriguez, c, El Dorado HS, Placentia, Calif.
40. *Taylor Lewis, rhp, Chipola (Fla.) JC.

## DETROIT TIGERS (25)

1. Derek Hill, of, Elk Grove (Calif.) HS.—(Low A)
2. Spencer Turnbull, rhp, University of Alabama.—(Low A)
3. Grayson Greiner, c, University of South Carolina.—(High A)
4. Adam Ravenelle, rhp, Vanderbilt University.—(Low A)
5. Shane Zeile, c, UCLA.—(Low A)

DRAFT DROP *Nephew of Todd Zeile, major leaguer (1989-2004)*

6. Ross Kivett, of, Kansas State University.
7. Joey Pankake, 3b, University of South Carolina.
8. Artie Lewicki, rhp, University of Virginia.
9. Josh Laxer, rhp, University of Mississippi.
10. Paul Voelker, rhp, Dallas Baptist University.
11. A.J. Ladwig, rhp, Wichita State University.
12. Garrett Mattlage, ss, Texas State University.
13. Will Allen, c, University of Mississippi.
14. Josh Heddinger, rhp, Georgia Tech.
15. Mike Gerber, of, Creighton University.
16. *Chase Rader, 3b, Coffeyville (Kan.) CC.
17. Corey Baptist, 1b, St. Petersburg (Fla.) JC.
18. Will Maddox, 3b, University of Tennessee.
19. *Parker French, rhp, University of Texas.
20. Trent Szkutnik, lhp, University of Michigan.

21. Whit Mayberry, rhp, University of Virginia.
22. Michael Thomas, c, University of Kentucky.
23. Brett Pirtle, 2b, Mississippi State University.
24. Gabe Hemmer, rhp, San Diego Christian College.
25. Gage Smith, rhp, Florida State University.
26. Jack Fischer, rhp, Wake Forest University.
27. Tyler Ford, lhp, University of Houston.
28. Will Kengor, ss, Slippery Rock (Pa.) University.
29. Jacob Butler, rhp, College of St. Francis (Ill.).
30. Spenser Watkins, rhp, Western Oregon University.
31. *Grant Reuss, lhp, Cranbrook HS, Bloomfield, Mich.
32. Locke St. John, lhp, University of South Alabama.
33. *Jonathan Perrin, rhp, Oklahoma State University.
34. *Sammy Stevens, c, Brother Rice HS, Bloomfield Hills, Mich.
35. *Dave Hollins, 3b, Orchard Park (N.Y.) HS.

DRAFT DROP *Son of Dave Hollins, major leaguer (1990-2002)*

36. Nate Fury, rhp, Louisiana State University.
37. *Pat Mahomes Jr., rhp, Whitehouse (Texas) HS.

DRAFT DROP *Son of Pat Mahomes, major leaguer (1992-2003)*

38. Magglio Ordonez Jr., 1b, American Heritage HS, Plantation, Fla.

DRAFT DROP *Son of Magglio Ordonez, major leaguer (1997-2011)*

39. *Taylor Sanagorski, c, Bishop Carroll Catholic HS, Wichita, Kan.
40. *Alex Faedo, rhp, Alonso HS, Tampa.

## HOUSTON ASTROS (1)

1. *Brady Aiken, lhp, Cathedral Catholic HS, San Diego.--DNP

DRAFT DROP *Attended IMG Academy, Bradenton, Fla.; re-drafted by Indians, first round (2015)*

1. Derek Fisher, of, University of Virginia (Competitive balance Round 'A' pick—37th; obtained in trade with Orioles).—(High A)
2. A.J. Reed, 1b-lhp, University of Kentucky.—(AA)
3. J.D. Davis, 3b, Cal State Fullerton.—(High A)
4. Daniel Mengden, rhp, Texas A&M University.—(High A)
5. *Jacob Nix, rhp, Los Alamitos (Calif.) HS.—(Rookie)

DRAFT DROP *Attended IMG Academy, Bradenton, Fla.; re-drafted by Padres, third round (2015)*

6. Brock Dykxhoorn, rhp, Central Arizona JC.
7. Derick Velazquez, rhp, Fresno State University.
8. Bobby Boyd, of, West Virginia University.
9. Bryan Radziewski, lhp, University of Miami.
10. Jay Gause, rhp, Faulkner (Ala.) University.
11. Dean Deetz, rhp, Northeastern Oklahoma A&M JC.
12. Ryan Bottger, of, University of Texas-Arlington.
13. Jamie Ritchie, c, Belmont University.
14. Nick Tanielu, 2b, Washington State University.
15. Connor Goedert, 3b, Neosho County (Kan.) CC.
16. Ramon Laureano, of, Northeastern Oklahoma A&M JC.
17. Ben Smith, lhp, Coastal Carolina University.
18. Antonio Nunez, ss, Western Oklahoma State JC.
19. Ruben Castro, c, Puerto Rico Baseball Academy, Gurabo, P.R.
20. Trent Woodward, c, Fresno State University.
21. *Mac Marshall, lhp, Parkview HS, Lilburn, Ga.
22. Bryan Muniz, 1b, Southeastern (Fla.) University.
23. Ryan Thompson, rhp, Campbell University.
24. Vince Wheeland, rhp, Oklahoma State University.
25. Zach Davis, lhp, University of Central Missouri.
26. Mott Hyde, 2b, Georgia Tech.
27. Brandon McNitt, rhp, Stony Brook University.
28. Aaron Greenwood, rhp, University of Mississippi.
29. Richard Gonzalez, c, Alabama State University.
30. Sean McMullen, of, Louisiana State University.
31. Dex McCall, 1b, Hillsborough (Fla.) CC.
32. Robert Kahana, rhp, University of Kansas.
33. Edwin Medina, of, St. Thomas (Fla.) University.
34. Josh James, rhp, Western Oklahoma State JC.
35. Keegan Yuhl, rhp, Concordia (Calif.) University.
36. Justin Ferrell, rhp, Connors State (Okla.) JC.
37. Eric Peterson, rhp, North Carolina State University.
38. *Michael Foster, 2b, Northeastern University.
39. *Brad Antchak, ss, Northeastern Oklahoma A&M JC.
40. Alex Hernandez, 2b, University of Miami.

## KANSAS CITY ROYALS (18)

1. **Brandon Finnegan, lhp, Texas Christian University.—(2014-15)**
1. Foster Griffin, lhp, First Academy, Orlando, Fla. (Compensation for loss of free agent Ervin Santana—28th).—(Low A)
1. Chase Vallot, c, St. Thomas More HS, Lafayette, La. (Competitive balance Round 'A' pick—40th).—(Low A)
2. Scott Blewett, rhp, Charles W. Baker HS, Baldwinsville, N.Y.—(Low A)
3. Eric Skoglund, lhp, University of Central Florida.—(High A)
4. D.J. Burt, ss, Fuquay-Varina (N.C.) HS.–(Rookie)
5. Corey Ray, rhp, Texas A&M University.—(Low A)
6. Logan Moon, of, Missouri Southern State University.
7. Brandon Downes, of, University of Virginia.
8. Ryan O'Hearn, 1b, Sam Houston State University.
9. Brandon Thomasson, of, Tennessee Tech.
10. Nick Green, lhp, University of Utah.
11. Robert Pehl, 1b, University of Washington.
12. Emilio Ogando, lhp, St. Thomas (Fla.) University.
13. Eric Stout, lhp, Butler University.
14. Ian Tompkins, lhp, Western Kentucky University.
15. Corey Toups, ss, Sam Houston State University.
16. Manny Olloque, 3b, Torrance (Calif.) HS.
17. Brennan Henry, lhp, Bellevue (Neb.) University.
18. Alberto Rodriguez, rhp, Northwest Florida State JC.
19. *Scott Heineman, of, University of Oregon.
20. Kyle Pollock, c, University of Evansville.
21. Evan Beal, rhp, University of South Carolina.
22. Mike Hill, ss, Long Beach State University.
23. Eric Sandness, rhp, San Joaquin Delta (Calif.) JC.
24. Brandon Thomas, lhp, San Diego State University.
25. Rudy Martin, of, Lewisburg HS, Olive Branch, Miss.
26. *Michael Arroyo, c, Puerto Rico Baseball Academy, Gurabo, P.R.
27. *Alex Close, c, Liberty University.
28. Josh Banuelos, 1b, Fresno Pacific University.
29. *Vance Vizcaino, 3b, Glendale (Ariz.) CC.
30. *Ryan Lillard, 3b, Urbandale (Iowa) HS.
31. *Rocky McCord, rhp, Auburn University.
32. Tim Hill, lhp, Bacone (Okla.) College.
33. DonAndre Clark, of, St. Mary's (Calif.) College.
34. Todd Eaton, rhp, Southern Illinois University.
35. *Andrew Sykes, lhp, Valparaiso (Ind.) HS.
36. *Brandon Gonzalez, of, Villa Park (Calif.) HS.
37. *David Noworyta, c, Holy Cross HS, Delran, N.J.
38. Cole Way, lhp, Tulsa University.
39. *Jeff Hendrix, of, Oregon State University.
40. *Diego Francisco, 2b, Palm Beach Central HS, Wellington, Fla.

## LOS ANGELES ANGELS (14)

1. Sean Newcomb, lhp, University of Hartford.—(AA)
2. Joe Gatto, rhp, St. Augustine Prep, Richland, N.J.—(Rookie)
3. Chris Ellis, rhp, University of Mississippi.—(AA)
4. Jeremy Rhoades, rhp, Illinois State University.—(High A)
5. Jake Jewell, rhp, Northeastern Oklahoma A&M JC.—(Rookie)
6. Alex Abbott, of, Tift County HS, Tifton, Ga.
7. Bo Way, of, Kennesaw State University.
8. Jake Yacinich, ss, University of Iowa.
9. Jordan Kipper, rhp, Texas Christian University.
10. Caleb Adams, of, University of Louisiana-Lafayette.
11. Andrew Daniel, 3b, University of San Diego.
12. Jared Ruxer, rhp, University of Louisville.
13. Zach Houchins, 3b, East Carolina University.
14. Justin Anderson, rhp, University of Texas-San Antonio.
15. Greg Mahle, lhp, UC Santa Barbara.
16. *Blaine Prescott, 2b, Midland (Texas) JC.
17. Ryan Seiz, 1b, Liberty University.
18. Austin Robichaux, rhp, University of Louisiana-Lafayette.
19. *Justin Bormann, c, University of Texas-San Antonio.
20. *Kyle Martin, 1b, University of South Carolina.
21. Tyler Palmer, of, University of Miami.
22. Adam McCreery, lhp, Azusa Pacific (Calif.) University.
23. Zach Varela, rhp, UC Riverside.
24. Eason Spivey, c, North Georgia College and State University.
25. Tyler Carpenter, rhp, Georgia Gwinnett College.
26. James Connell, rhp, Kennesaw State University.
27. Cody Lavalli, of, Lewis-Clark State (Idaho) College.
28. Jordan Piche, rhp, University of Kansas.
29. Alex Klonowski, rhp, Northern Illinois University.
30. Ronnie Muck, rhp, University of Illinois.
31. Nick Wagner, rhp, Cal State Dominguez Hills.
32. *Kholton Sanchez, c, New Mexico JC.
33. Jake Petersen, lhp, California Lutheran University.
34. Jose Rodriguez, ss, Colegio Hector Urdaneta, Rio Grande, P.R.
35. *Caleb Wallingford, lhp, Memphis University.
36. Brandon Gildea, c, Westmont (Calif.) College.
37. Fran Whitten, 1b, St Leo (Fla.) University.
38. Tyler Watson, lhp, McLennan (Texas) CC.
39. Patrick Armstrong, of, University of Nevada-Las Vegas.
40. Eric Alonzo, rhp, Georgia Southern University.

## LOS ANGELES DODGERS (24)

1. Grant Holmes, rhp, Conway (S.C.) HS.—(Low A)
2. Alex Verdugo, of, Sahuaro HS, Tucson, Ariz.—(High A)
3. John Richy, rhp, University of Nevada-Las Vegas.—(High A)
4. Jeff Brigham, rhp, University of Washington.—(High A)
5. Jared Walker, 3b, McEachern HS, Powder Springs, Ga.—(Rookie)
6. Brock Stewart, rhp, Illinois State University.
7. Trevor Oaks, rhp, California Baptist University.
8. Hunter Redman, c, Texas Tech.
9. Matt Campbell, rhp, Clemson University.
10. Colin Hering, of, Coastal Carolina University.
11. A.J. Vanegas, rhp, Stanford University.
12. Kam Uter, rhp, Pace Academy, Atlanta.
13. Ryan Taylor, rhp, Arkansas Tech University.
14. Kelvin Ramos, ss, San Jacinto (Texas) JC.
15. Joe Broussard, rhp, Louisiana State University.
16. Devan Ahart, of, University of Akron.
17. Tyler Wampler, ss, Indiana State University.
18. Clint Freeman, 1b, East Tennessee State University.
19. *Gary Cornish, rhp, Palomar (Calif.) JC.
20. Brian Wolfe, of, University of Washington.
21. Osvaldo Vela, ss, Oklahoma Baptist University.
22. Bubby Rossman, rhp, Cal State Dominguez Hills.
23. Andrew Godbold, of, Southeastern Louisiana University.
24. Jimmy Allen, 2b, Cal Poly.
25. Matt Jones, of, Hutchinson (Kan.) CC.
26. Deion Ulmer, 2b, Holmes (Miss.) JC.
27. Harlan Richter, rhp, Bossier Parrish (La.) CC.
28. Billy Beresznievicz, of, SUNY Binghamton.
29. *Christian Trent, lhp, University of Mississippi.
30. Brant Whiting, c, Stanford University.
31. Derrick Sylvester, rhp, Southern New Hampshire University.
32. Scott De Jong, 1b, Felician (N.J.) College.
33. Carson Baranik, rhp, University of Louisiana-Lafayette.
34. *Hunter Bross, of, Notre Dame Prep, Scottsdale, Ariz.

DRAFT DROP *Son of Terry Bross, major leaguer (1991-93)*

35. *Tanner Chauncey, ss, Brigham Young University.
36. *Kyle Kocher, rhp, Mountain View HS, Mesa, Ariz.
37. Karch Kowalczyk, rhp, Valparaiso University.
38. Caleb Ferguson, lhp, West Jefferson (Ohio) HS.
39. *Jeff Bain, rhp, San Marino (Calif.) HS.
40. *Sam Moore, rhp, UC Irvine.

## MIAMI MARLINS (2)

1. Tyler Kolek, rhp, Shepherd (Texas) HS.—(Low A)
1. Blake Anderson, c, West Lauderdale HS, Collinsville, Miss. (Special compensation—36th—for failure to sign 2013 supplemental first-round pick Matt Krook).—(Short-season A)
2. Justin Twine, ss, Falls City (Texas) HS.—(Low A)
3. Brian Anderson, 2b, University of Arkansas.—(High A)
3. Michael Mader, lhp, Chipola (Fla.) JC (Special compensation—105th—for failure to sign 2013 third-round pick Ben DeLuzio).—(Low A)
4. Brian Schales, ss, Edison HS, Huntington Beach, Calif.—(Low A)
5. Casey Soltis, of, Granada HS, Livermore, Calif.—(Low A)
6. Chris Sadberry, lhp, Texas Tech.
7. Anfernee Seymour, ss, American Heritage HS, Delray Beach, Fla.
8. Stone Garrett, of, George Ranch HS, Richmond, Texas.
9. Ben Holmes, lhp, Oregon State University.
10. Dillon Peters, lhp, University of Texas.
11. Nick White, rhp, Berryhill HS, Tulsa, Okla.
12. Roy Morales, c, Colegio Angel David HS, San Juan, P.R.
13. Jacob Smigelski, rhp, UC Riverside.
14. Zach Sullivan, ss, Corning-Painted Post East HS, Corning, N.Y.
15. Connor Overton, rhp, Old Dominion University.
16. Scott Squier, lhp, University of Hawaii.
17. Eric Fisher, 1b, University of Arkansas.
18. Brad Haynal, c, San Diego State University.
19. Mason Davis, 2b, The Citadel.
20. Jordan Holloway, rhp, Ralston Valley HS, Arvada, Colo.
21. *D.J. King, ss, Fort Meade (Fla.) HS.
22. *Mitchell Robinson, 3b, Clayton Heights SS, Surrey, B.C.
23. Steven Farnworth, rhp, Cal Poly Pomona.
24. Ryan Cranmer, 2b, Newberry (S.C.) College.
25. Christian MacDonald, lhp, UNC Wilmington.
26. Nick Williams, rhp, University of Tennessee.
27. Chris Hoo, c, Cal Poly.
28. *Christian Williams, 1b, Gulf Coast (Fla.) CC.
29. Greg Greve, rhp, Ohio State University.
30. Kyle Fischer, rhp, St. Cloud State (Minn.) University.
31. Kyle Porter, lhp, University of California.
32. Nestor Bautista, lhp, Ball State University.
33. Austen Smith, 1b, University of Alabama.
34. *Taylor Lehman, lhp, Keystone Oaks HS, Pittsburgh.
35. *Keith Zuniga, rhp, Bethune-Cookman College.
36. Justin Hepner, rhp, San Diego State University.
37. *Chase Williams, rhp, Eastern Oklahoma State JC.
38. *Parker Ray, rhp, Texas A&M University.
39. *Matt Pope, rhp, Walters State (Tenn.) CC.
40. *Hunter Aguirre, of, Westmoore HS, Oklahoma City, Okla.

## MILWAUKEE BREWERS (11)

1. Kodi Medeiros, lhp, Waiakea HS, Hilo, Hawaii.—(Low A)
1. Jake Gatewood, ss, Clovis (Calif.) HS (Competitive balance Round 'A' pick—41st).—(Low A)
2. Monte Harrison, of, Lee's Summit (Mo.) West HS.—(Low A)
3. Cy Sneed, rhp, Dallas Baptist University.—(High A)
4. Troy Stokes, of, Calvert Hall College HS, Baltimore.—(Rookie)
5. Dustin DeMuth, 3b, Indiana University.—(Low A)
6. David Burkhalter, rhp, Ruston (La.) HS.
7. Mitch Meyer, of, Kansas State University.
8. J.B. Kole, rhp, Villanova University.
9. Greg McCall, c, University of Texas-Arlington.
10. Javi Salas, rhp, University of Miami.
11. Brandon Woodruff, rhp, Mississippi State University.
12. Jordan Yamamoto, rhp, St. Louis HS, Honolulu, Hawaii.
13. Kaleb Earls, rhp, Limestone (S.C.) College.
14. Jonathan Oquendo, ss, Maria Teresa Pineiro HS, Toa Baja, P.R.
15. Caleb Smith, rhp, Rice University.
16. *Ben Onyshko, lhp, Vauxhall (Alberta) Academy.
17. *J.J. Schwarz, c, Palm Beach Gardens (Fla.) HS.

18. Luke Curtis, rhp, University of Pittsburgh.
19. Zach Hirsch, lhp, University of Nebraska.
20. *Tate Blackman, ss, Lake Brantley HS, Altamonte Springs, Fla.
21. Donnie Hissa, rhp, University of Notre Dame.
22. *Patrick Weigel, rhp, Oxnard (Calif.) JC.
23. *Kolton Mahoney, rhp, Brigham Young University.
24. Bubba Blau, rhp, Dixie State (Utah) University.
25. *C.D. Pelham, lhp, Spartanburg Methodist (S.C.) JC.
26. *Cre Finfrock, rhp, Martin County HS, Stuart, Fla.
27. Matt Martin, c, Wake Forest University.
28. *Turner Larkins, rhp, James Martin HS, Arlington, Texas.
29. *Aaron Garza, rhp, University of Houston.
30. Taylor Stark, rhp, Delta State (Miss.) University.
31. Brock Hudgens, rhp, UNC Charlotte.
32. *Eric White, rhp, Parkers Chapel HS, El Dorado, Ark.
33. Chad Reeves, lhp, Louisiana State University-Eunice JC.
34. Carlos Leal, rhp, Delta State (Miss.) University.
35. David Carver, lhp, Lamar University.
36. *Hunter Tackett, of, Anderson County HS, Clinton, Tenn.
37. *Eric Ramirez, 1b, Rio Mesa HS, Oxnard, Calif.
38. *Carl Chester, of, Lake Brantley HS, Altamonte Springs, Fla.
39. *John Gavin, lhp, St. Francis HS, Mountain View, Calif.
40. *Taylor Lane, ss, IMG Academy, Bradenton, Fla.

## MINNESOTA TWINS (5)

1. Nick Gordon, ss, Olympia HS, Orlando, Fla.—(Low A)

DRAFT DROP *Son of Tom Gordon, major leaguer (1988-2009) • Brother of Dee Gordon, major leaguer (2011-15)*

2. Nick Burdi, rhp, University of Louisville.—(AA)
3. Michael Cederoth, rhp, San Diego State University.—(Low A)
4. Sam Clay, lhp, Georgia Tech.—(Low A)
5. Jake Reed, rhp, University of Oregon.—(AA)
6. John Curtiss, rhp, University of Texas.
7. Andro Cutura, rhp, Southeastern Louisiana University.
8. Keaton Steele, rhp, University of Missouri.
9. Max Murphy, of, Bradley University.
10. Randy LeBlanc, rhp, Tulane University.
11. Tanner English, of, University of South Carolina.
12. Pat Kelly, 2b, University of Nebraska.
13. Zach Tillery, rhp, Florida Gulf Coast University.
14. Tyler Mautner, 3b, SUNY Buffalo.
15. Roberto Gonzalez, of, University HS, Orlando, Fla.
16. Tyler Kuresa, 1b, UC Santa Barbara.
17. Mat Batts, lhp, UNC Wilmington.
18. T.J. White, 3b, University of Nevada-Las Vegas.
19. Jarrard Poteete, c, Connors State (Okla.) JC.
20. *McCarthy Tatum, 3b, Clovis (Calif.) HS.
21. Onas Farfan, lhp, Ridgewater (Minn.) JC.
22. Trevor Hildenberger, rhp, University of California.
23. Miles Nordgren, rhp, Birmingham-Southern College.
24. Alex Real, c, University of New Mexico.
25. *Taylor Hearn, lhp, San Jacinto (Texas) JC.
26. Blake Schmit, ss, University of Maryland.
27. Gabriel Ojeda, c, Colegio Hector Urdaneta HS, Rio Grande, P.R.
28. Austin Diemer, of, Cal State Fullerton.
29. *Cameron Avila-Leeper, lhp, Grant Union HS, Sacramento, Calif.
30. Mike Theofanopoulos, lhp, University of California.
31. *Sam Hilliard, lhp, Crowder (Mo.) JC.
32. *Orynn Veillon, rhp, St. Thomas More HS, Lafayette, La.
33. Trey Vavra, 1b, Florida Southern College.
34. *Mike Baumann, rhp, Mahtomedi (Minn.) HS.
35. *Brad Mathiowetz, c, Mayo HS, Rochester, Minn.
36. *Kirvin Moesquit, ss, Highlands Christian Academy, Pompano Beach, Fla.
37. Tyree Davis, of, Centennial HS, Compton, Calif.
38. Brett Doe, c, Baylor University.
39. *John Jones, c, Orangewood Christian HS, Maitland, Fla.
40. *Dalton Guthrie, ss, Venice (Fla.) HS.

DRAFT DROP *Son of Mark Guthrie, major leaguer (1989-2003)*

## NEW YORK METS (10)

1. **Michael Conforto, of, Oregon State University.—(2015)**
2. (Choice forfeited for signing Curtis Granderson as free agent).
3. Milton Ramos, ss, American Heritage HS, Plantation, Fla.—(Rookie)
4. Eudor Garcia, 3b, El Paso (Texas) CC.—(Low A)
5. Josh Prevost, rhp, Seton Hall University.—(Low A)
6. Tyler Moore, c, Louisiana State University.
7. Brad Wieck, lhp, Oklahoma City University.
8. Dash Winningham, 1b, Trinity Catholic HS, Ocala, Fla.
9. Michael Katz, of, College of William & Mary.
10. Kelly Secrest, lhp, UNC Wilmington.
11. Connor Buchmann, rhp, University of Oklahoma.
12. Alex Durham, rhp, Southern Alamance HS, Graham, N.C.
13. Erik Manoah, rhp, South Dade HS, Homestead, Fla.
14. Darryl Knight, c, Embry-Riddle (Fla.) University.
15. Gabe Llanes, rhp, Downey (Calif.) HS.
16. Joel Huertas, lhp, Colegio Carmen Sol, Bayamon, P.R.
17. David Roseboom, lhp, University of South Carolina-Upstate.
18. Raphael Ramirez, of, Pace Academy, Atlanta.
19. Bryce Beeler, rhp, Memphis University.
20. Jimmy Duff, rhp, Stonehill (Mass.) College.
21. *Luke Bonfield, of, IMG Academy, Bradenton, Fla.
22. William Fulmer, 2b, University of Montevallo (Ala.).
23. *Richard Moesker, rhp, Trinity Christian Academy, Lake Worth, Fla.
24. Tyler Badamo, rhp, Dowling (N.Y.) College.
25. Nicco Blank, rhp, Central Arizona JC.
26. *Tommy Pincin, c, Upland (Calif.) HS.
27. Alex Palsha, rhp, Sacramento State University.
28. *Keaton McKinney, rhp, Ankeny (Iowa) HS.
29. Matt Blackham, rhp, Middle Tennessee State University.
30. Tucker Tharp, of, University of Kansas.
31. Kurtis Horne, lhp, Milne Community SS, Sooke, B.C.
32. *Chris Glover, rhp, Rockwall (Texas) HS.
33. *Brady Puckett, rhp, Riverdale HS, Murfreesboro, Tenn.
34. *Jordan Hand, c, Shadow Ridge HS, Las Vegas, Nev.
35. *Jonathan Teaney, rhp, Quartz Hill (Calif.) HS.
36. *Garett King, rhp, Orange Lutheran HS, Orange, Calif.
37. *Tristan Gray, ss, Elkins HS, Missouri City, Texas.
38. *Kyle Dunster, rhp, Greenwich (Conn.) HS.
39. Arnaldo Berrios, of, Carlos Beltran Academy, Florida, P.R.
40. Dale Burdick, ss, Summit HS, Spring Hill, Tenn.

## NEW YORK YANKEES (17)

1. (Choice forfeited for signing Brian McCann as free agent).
1. (Compensation for loss of Curtis Granderson as free agent; choice forfeited for signing Jacoby Ellsbury as free agent).
1. (Compensation for loss of Robinson Cano as free agent; forfeited pick for signing Carlos Beltran as free agent).
2. **Jacob Lindgren, lhp, Mississippi State University.—(2015)**
3. Austin DeCarr, rhp, Salisbury (Conn.) School.—(Rookie)
4. Jordan Montgomery, lhp, University of South Carolina.—(High A)
5. Jordan Foley, rhp, Central Michigan University.—(AAA)
6. Jonathan Holder, rhp, Mississippi State University.
7. Mark Payton, of, University of Texas.
8. Connor Spencer, 1b, UC Irvine.
9. Vince Conde, ss, Vanderbilt University.
10. Ty McFarland, 2b, James Madison University.
11. Matt Borens, rhp, Eastern Illinois University.
12. Chris Gittens, 1b, Grayson (Texas) CC.
13. Bo Thompson, 1b, The Citadel.
14. Sean Carley, rhp, West Virginia University.
15. Andrew Chin, lhp, Boston College.
16. Derek Callahan, lhp, Gonzaga University.
17. *Garrett Cave, rhp, South Sumter HS, Bushnell, Fla.
18. Justin Kamplain, lhp, University of Alabama.
19. Joe Harvey, rhp, University of Pittsburgh.
20. Corey Holmes, rhp, Concordia (Texas) University.
21. *Porter Clayton, lhp, University of Oregon.
22. *Jake Kelzer, rhp, Indiana University.
23. *Will Toffey, 3b, Salisbury (Conn.) School.
24. Dominic Jose, of, Stanford University.

DRAFT DROP *Son of Felix Jose, major leaguer (1988-2003)*

25. *Dylan Barrow, rhp, University of Tampa.
26. Collin Slaybaugh, c, Washington State University.
27. Griff Gordon, of, Jacksonville State University.
28. Lee Casas, rhp, University of Southern California.
29. *Mariano Rivera Jr., rhp, Iona University.

DRAFT DROP *Son of Mariano Rivera, major leaguer (1995-2013)*

30. *Jorge Perez, rhp, Grand Canyon University.
31. Devyn Bolasky, of, UC Riverside.
32. *Jordan Ramsey, rhp, UNC Wilmington.
33. *David Graybill, rhp, Arizona State University.
34. Matt Wotherspoon, rhp, University of Pittsburgh.
35. *Chris Hudgins, c, Valhalla HS, El Cajon, Calif.
36. *Will Gaddis, rhp, Brentwood (Tenn.) HS.
37. Ryan Lindemuth, 2b, College of William & Mary.
38. Andre Del Bosque, rhp, University of Houston-Victoria.
39. *Cameron Warren, 1b, Carl Albert HS, Midwest City, Okla.
40. *Madison Stokes, ss, Flora HS, Columbia, S.C.

## OAKLAND ATHLETICS (27)

1. Matt Chapman, 3b, Cal State Fullerton.—(AA)
2. Daniel Gossett, rhp, Clemson University.—(Low A)
3. Brett Graves, rhp, University of Missouri.—(Low A)
4. Jordan Schwartz, rhp, Niagara University.—(Low A)
5. Heath Fillmyer, rhp, Mercer County (N.J.) CC.—(Low A)
6. Trace Loehr, ss, Putnam HS, Milwaukie, Ore.
7. Branden Cogswell, ss, University of Virginia.
8. Branden Kelliher, rhp, Lake Stevens (Wash.) HS.
9. Mike Fagan, lhp, Princeton University.
10. Corey Miller, rhp, Pepperdine University.
11. Joel Seddon, rhp, University of South Carolina.
12. Tyler Willman, rhp, Western Illinois University.
13. Max Kuhn, 2b, University of Kentucky.
14. *Casey Schroeder, c, Polk State (Fla.) JC.
15. Trent Gilbert, 2b, University of Arizona.
16. Jose Brizuela, 3b, Florida State University.
17. *Eric Cheray, c, Missouri State University.
18. Michael Nolan, lhp, Oklahoma City University.
19. *Tom Gavitt, c, Bryant University.
20. Koby Gauna, rhp, Cal State Fullerton.
21. *Tim Proudfoot, ss, Texas Tech.
22. Brendan McCurry, rhp, Oklahoma State University.
23. *Collin Ferguson, 1b, St. Mary's (Calif.) College.
24. Dawson Brown, rhp, University of West Florida.
25. *Joseph Estrada, of, Colegio Hector Urdaneta HS, Ceiba, P.R.
26. Rob Huber, rhp, Duke University.
27. J.P. Sportman, of, Central Connecticut State University.
28. Corey Walter, rhp, West Virginia University.
29. Cody Stull, lhp, Belmont Abbey (N.C.) College.
30. Derek Beasley, lhp, University of South Carolina-Aiken.
31. *Tyler Schimpf, rhp, Capital Christian HS, Sacramento, Calif.
32. *Denz'l Chapman, of, Serra HS, Gardena, Calif.
33. *Michael Rivera, c, Venice (Fla.) HS.
34. John Nogowski, 1b, Florida State University.
35. *Austen Swift, of, Bishop Allen Academy, Toronto.
36. *Tyler Spoon, of, University of Arkansas.
37. *Brock Lundquist, of, Fountain Valley (Calif.) HS.
38. *Colt Atwood, of, Sam Houston State University.
39. *Payton Squier, 2b, Greenway HS, Phoenix.
40. *Bryson Brigman, ss, Valley Christian HS, San Jose, Calif.

## PHILADELPHIA PHILLIES (7)

1. **Aaron Nola, rhp, Louisiana State University.—(2015)**
2. Matt Imhof, lhp, Cal Poly.—(High A)
3. Aaron Brown, of, Pepperdine University.—(High A)
4. Chris Oliver, rhp, University of Arkansas.—(Low A)
5. Rhys Hoskins, 1b, Cal State Sacramento.—(High A)
6. Brandon Leibrandt, lhp, Florida State University.

DRAFT DROP *Son of Charlie Leibrandt, major leaguer (1979-93)*

7. Emmanuel Marrero, ss, Alabama State University.
8. Sam McWilliams, rhp, Beech HS, Hendersonville, Tenn.
9. Matt Hockenberry, rhp, Temple University.
10. Matt Shortall, of, University of Texas-Arlington.
11. Drew Stankiewicz, ss, Arizona State University.

DRAFT DROP *Son of Andy Stankiewicz, major leaguer (1992-98)*

12. Austin Davis, lhp, Cal State Bakersfield.
13. Nathan Thornhill, rhp, University of Texas.
14. Chase Harris, of, University of New Mexico.
15. Jared Fisher, rhp, University of Washington.
16. Calvin Rayburn, rhp, Barry (Fla.) University.
17. Damek Tomscha, 3b, Auburn University.
18. Sean McHugh, c, Purdue University.
19. Joey Denato, lhp, Indiana University.
20. Derek Campbell, 2b, University of California.
21. Tim Zier, 2b, San Diego State University.
22. *Ryan Powers, rhp, Miami (Ohio) University.
23. Joel Fisher, c, Michigan State University.
24. Preston Packrall, rhp, University of Tampa.
25. Bryan Sova, rhp, Creighton University.
26. Jacques de Gruy, rhp, Furman University.
27. Scott Harris, lhp, Buena Vista (Iowa) University.
28. Tanner Kiest, rhp, Chaffey (Calif.) JC.
29. *Al Molina, ss, Red Bank Catholic HS, Red Bank, N.J.
30. *Brandon Murray, rhp, Hobart (Ind.) HS.
31. *Shane Gonzales, rhp, Fullerton (Calif.) JC.
32. *Tom Flacco, of, Eastern HS, Voorhees Township, N.J.

DRAFT DROP *Brother of Joe Flacco, first-round draft pick, Baltimore Ravens/National Football League (2008); quarterback, NFL (2008-15)*

33. *James Harrington, rhp, Mesquite HS, Gilbert, Ariz.
34. Scott Tomassetti, c, CC of Southern Nevada.
35. *Thomas Gamble, of, Moorestown (N.J.) HS.
36. *Blake Wiggins, c, Pulaski Academy, Little Rock, Ark.
37. *Keith Rogalla, rhp, Oak Park & River Forest HS, Oak Park, Ill.
38. *Kollin Schrenk, rhp, Ardrey Kell HS, Charlotte, N.C.
39. *Keenan Eaton, of, Chaparral HS, Parker, Colo.
40. *Jesse Berardi, ss, Commack (N.Y.) HS.

## PITTSBURGH PIRATES (26)

1. Cole Tucker, ss, Mountain Pointe HS, Phoenix.—(Low A)
1. Connor Joe, of, University of San Diego (Competitive balance Round 'A' pick—39th; obtained in trade with Marlins).—(Low A)
2. Mitch Keller, rhp, Xavier HS, Cedar Rapids, Iowa.—(Rookie)
2. Trey Supak, rhp, La Grange (Texas) HS (Competitive balance Round 'B' pick—73rd).—(Rookie)
3. Jordan Luplow, of, Fresno State University.—(Low A)
4. Taylor Gushue, c, University of Florida.—(Low A)
5. Michael Suchy, of, Florida Gulf Coast University.—(Low A)
6. Tyler Eppler, rhp, Sam Houston State University.
7. Nelson Jorge, ss, International Baseball Academy, Ceiba, P.R.
8. Austin Coley, rhp, Belmont University.
9. Kevin Krause, c, Stony Brook University.

10. Alex McRae, rhp, Jacksonville University.
11. Gage Hinsz, rhp, Billings West HS, Billings, Mont.
12. Tyler Filliben, ss, Samford University.
13. Frank Duncan, rhp, University of Kansas.
14. Chase Simpson, 3b, Wichita State University.
15. Eric Dorsch, rhp, Kent State University.
16. Sam Street, rhp, University of Texas-Pan American.
17. Michael Clemens, rhp, McNeese State University.
18. Erik Lunde, 2b, Lander (S.C.) University.
19. Carl Anderson, of, Bryant University.
20. Jon Sever, lhp, Bethune-Cookman College.
21. Eric Thomas, of, Langham Creek HS, Houston.
22. Eric Karch, rhp, Pepperdine University.
23. *Zach Warren, lhp, St. Augustine Prep, Richland, N.J.
24. *Denis Karas, 3b, Campolindo HS, Moraga, Calif.
25. Erik Forgione, ss, University of Washington.
26. Jerrick Suiter, of, Texas Christian University.
27. Jess Amedee, rhp, University of Texas-Arlington.
28. Nick Neumann, rhp, Central Connecticut State University.
29. *Zach Lucas, 2b, University of Louisville.
30. David Andriese, of, UC Riverside.

DRAFT DROP *Brother of Matt Andriese, major leaguer (2015)*

31. Luis Paula, rhp, University of North Carolina.
32. Montana DuRapau, rhp, Bethune-Cookman College.
33. *Zach Lewis, rhp, Wabash Valley (Ill.) CC.
34. *Colin Welmon, rhp, Loyola Marymount University.
35. *Chris Eades, rhp, Delgado (La.) JC.
36. Palmer Betts, rhp, Chipola (Fla.) JC.
37. *Bryant Holtmann, lhp, Florida State University.
38. *Paul DeJong, c, Illinois State University.
39. *Daniel Keating, 3b, Gulfport (Miss.) HS.
40. *Tyler Brown, 2b, CC of Southern Nevada.

## ST. LOUIS CARDINALS (30)

1. Luke Weaver, rhp, Florida State University.—(High A)
1. Jack Flaherty, rhp, Harvard-Westlake HS, Studio City, Calif. (Compensation for loss of free agent Carlos Beltran—34th).—(Low A)
2. Ronnie Williams, rhp, American Senior HS, Hialeah, Fla.—(Rookie)
2. Andrew Morales, rhp, UC Irvine (Competitive balance Round 'B' pick—71st).—(AA)
3. *Trevor Megill, rhp, Loyola Marymount University.—(Short-season A)

DRAFT DROP *Returned to Loyola Marymount; re-drafted by Padres, 2015 (7th round)*

4. Austin Gomber, lhp, Florida Atlantic University.—(Low A)
5. Darren Seferina, 2b, Miami-Dade JC.—(Low A)
6. Andrew Sohn, ss, Western Michigan University.
7. Brian O'Keefe, c, St. Joseph's University.
8. Nick Thompson, of, College of William & Mary.
9. Daniel Poncedeleon, rhp, Embry-Riddle (Fla.) University.
10. Danny Diekroeger, 3b, Stanford University.
11. *Justin Bellinger, 1b, St. Sebastian's HS, Needham, Mass.
12. Jordan DeLorenzo, lhp, University of West Florida.
13. Matt Pearce, rhp, Polk State (Fla.) JC.
14. *Chris Shaw, c, Midland (Texas) JC.
15. *Matt Ditman, rhp, Rice University.
16. *Tristan Hildebrandt, ss, Esperanza HS, Anaheim, Calif.
17. *Dustin Beggs, rhp, Georgia Perimeter JC.
18. Blake Drake, of, Concordia (Ore.) University.
19. *Dom Thompson-Williams, of, Iowa Western CC.
20. Collin Radack, of, Hendrix (Ark.) College.
21. Casey Grayson, 1b, University of Houston.
22. *Derek Casey, rhp, Hanover HS, Mechanicsville, Va.
23. *Joe Gillette, 3b, Scotts Valley (Calif.) HS.
24. Casey Turgeon, 2b, University of Florida.
25. Landon Beck, rhp, Anderson (S.C.) University.
26. Tyler Bray, rhp, University of Louisiana-Monroe.
27. Cole Lankford, c, Texas A&M University.
28. Tyler Dunnington, rhp, Colorado Mesa University.
29. Bryan Dobzanski, rhp, Delsea Regional HS, Franklinville, N.J.

ALYSON BOYER RODE

Trea Turner's stay in the Padres organization was brief, as they traded him to the Nationals

30. Josh Wirsu, rhp, Georgia Southern University.
31. Julian Barzilli, 3b, Whittier (Calif.) College.
32. *Anthony Herron, rhp, Affton HS, St. Louis.
33. *Dominic Moreno, rhp, Texas Tech.
34. *George Iskenderian, ss, Indian River State (Fla.) JC.
35. *Michael Bono, rhp, Buchanan HS, Clovis, Calif.
36. Cody Schumacher, rhp, Missouri State University.
37. Chase Raffield, of, Georgia State University.
38. Sasha Kuebel, lhp, University of Iowa.
39. *Kyle Ruchim, 2b, Northwestern University.
40. Davis Ward, rhp, Ouachita Baptist (Ark.) University.

## SAN DIEGO PADRES (12)

1. **Trea Turner, ss, North Carolina State University.—(2015)**
2. Michael Gettys, of, Gainesville (Ga.) HS.—(Low A)
3. Zech Lemond, rhp, Rice University.—(High A)
4. Nick Torres, of, Cal Poly.—(High A)
5. Auston Bousfield, of, University of Mississippi.—(AA)
6. Zach Risedorf, c, Northwestern Regional HS, Winchester, Conn.
7. Ryan Butler, rhp, UNC Charlotte.
8. Mitch Watrous, rhp, University of Utah.
9. Nick Vilter, ss, UC Riverside.
10. Thomas Dorminy, lhp, Faulkner (Ala.) University.
11. Yale Rosen, of, Washington State University.
12. Seth Lucio, rhp, Tennessee Tech.
13. Joey Epperson, 3b, UC Santa Barbara.
14. Chris Huffman, rhp, James Madison University.
15. Logan Jernigan, rhp, North Carolina State University.
16. Taylor Cox, lhp, University of Tennessee-Martin.
17. T.J. Weir, rhp, Ball State University.
18. Max MacNabb, lhp, University of San Diego.
19. *Justin Lewis, rhp, Greater Atlanta Christian HS, Norcross, Ga.
20. Tyler Wilson, rhp, Tennessee Wesleyan College.
21. *Peter Solomon, rhp, Mount St. Joseph HS, Baltimore.
22. Danny Wissmann, lhp, University of South Carolina-Aiken.
23. Jason Jester, rhp, Texas A&M University.
24. Colby Blueberg, rhp, University of Nevada.
25. Travis Radke, lhp, University of Portland.
26. Aaron Cressley, rhp, University of Pittsburgh-Bradford.
27. Mike Fitzgerald, c, Indiana State University.

DRAFT DROP *Son of Mike Fitzgerald, major leaguer (1983-92)*

28. *Johnny Manziel, ss, Texas A&M University.

DRAFT DROP *First-round draft pick, Cleveland Browns/ National Football League (2014); quarterback, NFL (2014-15)*

29. Mitch Morales, ss, Florida Atlantic University.
30. Ryan Atwood, lhp, Florida Gulf Coast University.
31. *Logan Sowers, of, McCutcheon HS, Lafayette, Ind.
32. Taylor Aikenhead, lhp, Cal State Bakersfield.
33. *Devin Smeltzer, lhp, Bishop Eustace Prep, Pennsauken, N.J.
34. *Brendan McKay, lhp, Blackhawk HS, Beaver Falls, Pa.
35. *Cobi Johnson, rhp, J.W. Mitchell HS, Trinity, Fla.

DRAFT DROP *Son of Dane Johnson, major leaguer (1994-97)*

36. Kyle McGrath, lhp, University of Louisville.
37. Tyler Wood, rhp, Furman University.
38. *Louis-Phillipe Pelletier, 2b, Maisonneuve (Quebec) JC.
39. *Richard Negron, 3b, Tallahassee (Fla.) CC.
40. *Bryce Carter, c, Cascia Hall Prep, Tulsa, Okla.

## SAN FRANCISCO GIANTS (13)

1. Tyler Beede, rhp, Vanderbilt University.—(AA)

DRAFT DROP *First-round draft pick (21st overall), Blue Jays (2011)*

2. Aramis Garcia, c, Florida International University.—(High A)
3. Dylan Davis, of, Oregon State University.—(High A)
4. Logan Webb, rhp, Rocklin (Calif.) HS.—(Short-season A)
5. Sam Coonrod, rhp, Southern Illinois University.—(Low A)
6. Skyler Ewing, 1b, Rice University.
7. Seth Harrison, of, University of Louisiana-Lafayette.
8. Austin Slater, of, Stanford University.
9. Stetson Woods, rhp, Liberty HS, Madera, Calif.
10. Matt Gage, lhp, Siena University.
11. Greg Brody, rhp, Belmont University.
12. Jameson Henning, ss, Western Illinois University.
13. Luis Lacen, of, Carlos Beltran Academy, Florida, P.R.
14. Kevin Rivera, 2b, Carlos Beltran Academy, Florida, P.R.
15. *Benton Moss, rhp, University of North Carolina.
16. *Kevin Ginkel, rhp, Southwestern (Calif.) JC.
17. Caleb Smith, lhp, University of South Carolina-Aiken.
18. *Edrick Agosto, rhp, International Baseball Academy, Cieba, P.R.
19. Richard Amion, of, Alabama State University.
20. *Bret Underwood, of, Northwestern State University.
21. *Matthew Crownover, lhp, Clemson University.
22. Mark Reyes, lhp, Crowder (Mo.) JC.
23. Jordan Johnson, rhp, Cal State Northridge.
24. *Michael Petersen, rhp, Riverside (Calif.) CC.
25. Byron Murray, of, Trinity Christian Academy, Deltona, Fla.
26. Hunter Cole, 3b, University of Georgia.
27. Connor Kaden, rhp, Wake Forest University.
28. Nick Sabo, lhp, Long Beach State University.
29. *Ryan Cruz, rhp, JC of the Canyons (Calif.).
30. *Cliff Covington, 1b, University of West Florida.
31. *Nick Nelson, rhp, Rutherford HS, Panama City, Fla.
32. *Hunter Williams, lhp, Cosby HS, Midlothian, Va.
33. Jared Deacon, c, Cal State Fullerton.
34. *Tim Susnara, c, St. Francis HS, Mountain View, Calif.
35. *Mitch Hart, rhp, Granite Bay HS, Sacramento, Calif.
36. *Zach Taylor, c, Horizon HS, Scottsdale, Ariz.
37. *Garrett Christman, ss, Noblesville (Ind.) HS.
38. *Benito Santiago Jr., c, Coral Springs Christian Academy, Coral Springs, Fla.

DRAFT DROP *Son of Benito Santiago, major leaguer (1986-2005)*

39. *Joe Ryan, rhp, Sir Francis Drake HS, San Anselmo, Calif.
40. *Riles Mahan, ss, Moeller HS, Cincinnati.

## SEATTLE MARINERS (6)

1. Alex Jackson, c-of, Rancho Bernardo HS, San Diego.—(Low A)
2. (Choice forfeited for signing Robinson Cano as free agent).
2. Gareth Morgan, of, North Toronto Collegiate HS, Toronto (Competitive balance Round 'B' pick—74th).—(Rookie)
3. Austin Cousino, of, University of Kentucky.—(Low A)
4. Ryan Yarbrough, lhp, Old Dominion University.—(High A)
5. Dan Altavilla, rhp, Mercyhurst (Pa.) College.—(High A)
6. Lane Ratliff, lhp, Jones County (Miss.) JC.
7. Taylor Byrd, lhp, Nicholls State University.
8. Kody Kerski, rhp, Sacred Heart University.
9. Peter Miller, rhp, Florida State University.
10. Adam Martin, c, Western Carolina University.
11. Jay Muhammad, rhp, Coral Springs Christian Academy, Coral Springs, Fla.
12. Nelson Ward, ss, University of Georgia.
13. Marvin Gorgas, rhp, East Hampton (Conn.) HS.
14. Chris Mariscal, ss, Fresno State University.

15. Lukas Schiraldi, rhp, University of Texas.
DRAFT DROP *Son of Calvin Schiraldi, first-round draft pick, Mets (1983) major leaguer (1984-91)*
16. Wayne Taylor, c, Stanford University.
17. Trey Cochran-Gill, rhp, Auburn University.
18. Nick Kiel, lhp, Bellevue (Wash.) CC.
19. Rohn Pierce, rhp, Canisius University.
20. Hawtin Buchanan, rhp, University of Mississippi.
21. Jay Baum, ss, Clemson University.
22. Jarrett Brown, lhp, University of Georgia.
23. Pat Peterson, lhp, North Carolina State University.
24. Sheehan Planas-Arteaga, 1b, Barry (Fla.) University.
25. Vinny Nittoli, rhp, Xavier University.
26. Taylor Smart, ss, University of Tennessee.
27. Andy Peterson, 2b, Oregon State University.
28. Dominic Blanco, c, Gulf Coast HS, Naples, Fla.
29. Tyler Herb, rhp, Coastal Carolina University.
30. James Alfonso, c, University of Hartford.
31. *DeAires Moses, of, East Nashville Magnet School, Nashville, Tenn.
32. Chase Nyman, 2b, East Mississippi JC.
33. Tom Verdi, ss, University of Connecticut.
34. *Andrew Summerville, lhp, Lakeside HS, Seattle.
35. *Chris McGrath, lhp, Marist School, Atlanta.
36. Spencer Hermann, lhp, Fisher (Mass.) College.
37. Sam Lindquist, rhp, Stanford University.
38. Taylor Zeutenhorst, of, University of Iowa.
39. Kavin Keyes, 3b, Oregon State University.
40. *Scott Manea, c, St. John's HS, Shrewsbury, Mass.

## TAMPA BAY RAYS (22)

1. Casey Gillaspie, 1b, Wichita State University.—(High A)
DRAFT DROP *Brother of Conor Gillaspie, first-round draft pick, Giants (2008); major leaguer (2008-15)*
2. Cameron Varga, rhp, Cincinnati Hills Christian Academy, Cincinnati.—(Short-season A)
2. Brent Honeywell, rhp, Walters State (Tenn.) CC (Competitive balance Round 'B' pick—72nd).—(High A)
3. Brock Burke, lhp, Evergreen (Colo.) HS.–(Rookie)
4. Blake Bivens, rhp, George Washington HS, Danville, Va.—(Rookie)
5. Michael Russell, ss, University of North Carolina.—(Short-season A)
6. Mac James, c, University of Oklahoma.
7. Mike Franco, rhp, Florida International University.
8. Daniel Miles, 3b, Tennessee Tech.
9. Chris Pike, rhp, Oklahoma City University.
10. Bradley Wallace, rhp, Arkansas State University.
11. Spencer Moran, rhp, Mountain View HS, Mesa, Ariz.
12. Braxton Lee, of, University of Mississippi.
13. Jace Conrad, 2b, University of Louisiana-Lafayette.
14. Trevor Lubking, lhp, Pacific Lutheran (Wash.) University.
15. Brian Miller, rhp, Vanderbilt University.
16. Greg Maisto, lhp, McLennan (Texas) CC.
17. Steve Ascher, lhp, SUNY Oneonta.
18. Alec Sole, ss, Saint Louis University.
19. Justin McCalvin, rhp, Kennesaw State University.
20. Kyle McKenzie, rhp, Tulane University.
21. Jaime Ayende, of, Carlos Beltran Academy, Florida, P.R.
22. Ryan Pennell, lhp, Elon University.
23. Zac Law, of, Robinson HS, Waco, Texas.
24. Nic Wilson, 1b, Georgia State University.
25. *Tyler Wells, lhp, University of Nevada.
26. Cade Gotta, of, San Diego Christian College.
27. Grant Kay, 2b, University of Louisville.
28. Carter Burgess, 3b, Sam Houston State University.
29. Tomas Michelson, rhp, University of Illinois-Chicago.
30. Trevor Dunlap, rhp, University of Washington.
31. Andrew Woeck, rhp, North Carolina State University.
32. *Josh Davis, of, Union HS, Tulsa, Okla.
33. Patrick Grady, of, Lander (S.C.) University.
34. Chris Knott, of, East Stroudsburg (Pa.) University.
35. Kyle Bird, lhp, Flagler (Fla.) College.
36. Isias Alcantar, c, University of Arkansas-Pine Bluff.
37. *Matt Plitt, rhp, University of Louisiana-Lafayette.
38. Chris DeMorais, of, University of New Haven.
39. Blake Grant-Parks, 1b, Cal State Monterey Bay.
40. *Conor Harber, rhp, Western Nevada JC.

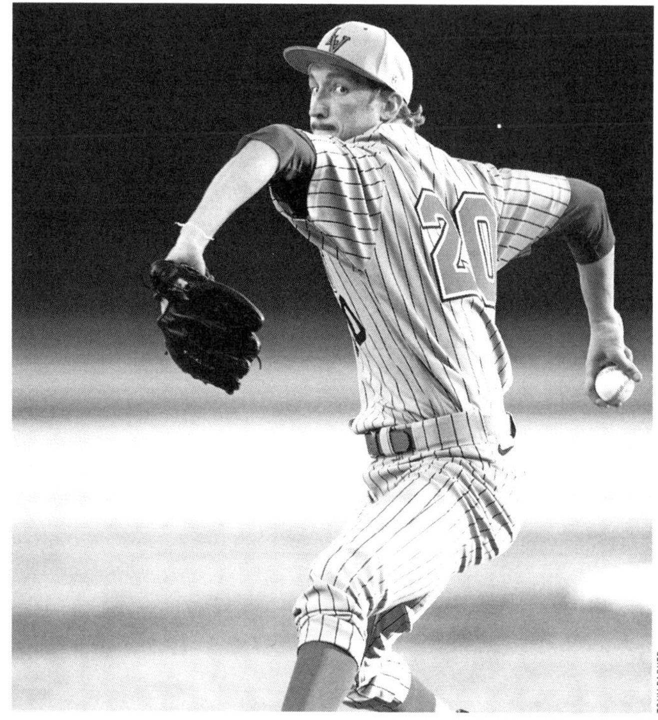
TONY PARKER

**Erick Fedde was drafted first by the Nationals, even as he just had Tommy John surgery**

## TEXAS RANGERS (21)

1. (Choice forfeited for signing Shin Soo Choo as free agent)
1. Luis Ortiz, rhp, Sanger (Calif.) HS (Compensation for loss of Nelson Cruz as free agent—30th).—(Low A)
2. Ti'quan Forbes, ss, Columbia (Miss.) HS.—(Short-season A)
3. Josh Morgan, ss, Orange Lutheran HS, Orange, Calif.—(Low A)
4. Brett Martin, lhp, Walters State (Tenn.) CC.—(Low A)
5. Wes Benjamin, lhp, University of Kansas.—(Rookie)
6. Jose Trevino, 3b, Oral Roberts University.
7. Nick Green, rhp, Indian Hills (Iowa) CC.
8. Erik Swanson, rhp, Iowa Western CC.
9. Doug Votoloto, of, Central Arkansas University.
10. Seth Spivey, c, Abilene Christian (Texas) University.
11. Scott Williams, rhp, State College of Florida-Manatee.
12. Joe Watson, rhp, Catawba (N.C.) College.
13. *Gabe Gonzalez, rhp, Arbor View HS, Las Vegas, Nev.
14. Gio Abreu, rhp, St. Raymond HS, Bronx, N.Y.
15. Joe Filomeno, lhp, University of Louisville.
16. Reed Garrett, rhp, Virginia Military Institute.
17. *David Berg, rhp, UCLA.
18. *J.T. Phillips, rhp, Georgia Perimeter JC.
19. *Tramayne Holmes, 2b, Rickards HS, Tallahassee, Fla.
20. Isaias Quiroz, c, St. Joseph HS, Montvale, N.J.
21. Sterling Wynn, lhp, McLennan (Texas) CC.
22. Tripp Martin, 3b, Samford University.
23. Darius Day, of, Simeon HS, Chicago.
24. Austin Pettibone, rhp, UC Santa Barbara.
DRAFT DROP *Son of Jay Pettibone, major leaguer (1983)*
25. *Daniel Sweet, of, Polk State (Fla.) JC.
26. *Jayce Vancena, rhp, Lake HS, Millbury, Ohio.
27. Jason Hoppe, rhp, Minnesota State University-Mankato.
28. *Chris Mathewson, rhp, Henry J. Kaiser HS, Fontana, Calif.
29. Luke Tendler, of, North Carolina A&T State University.
30. Cody Palmquist, rhp, Palm Beach State (Fla.) JC.
31. John Fasola, rhp, Kent State University.
32. *Andre Jackson, rhp, Cienega HS, Tucson, Ariz.
33. Adam Parks, rhp, Liberty University.
34. Storm Rynard, rhp, Cowley County (Kan.) CC.
35. *Will Carter, rhp, Walters State (Tenn.) CC.
36. Cody Chartrand, rhp, Lewis-Clark State (Idaho) College.
37. *Andrew Bechtold, ss, Garnet Valley HS, Glen Mills, Pa.
38. *Tyree Johnson, lhp, New Hanover HS, Wilmington, N.C.
39. *Travis Jones, of, Atascocita HS, Humble, Texas.
40. Nick Dignacco, lhp, U.S. Milkitary Academy.

## TORONTO BLUE JAYS (9)

1. Jeff Hoffman, rhp, East Carolina University.—(AA)
1. Max Pentecost, c, Kennesaw State University (Special compensation for failure to sign 2013 first-round draft pick Phil Bickford—11th).—(Short-season A)
2. Sean Reid-Foley, rhp, Sandalwood HS, Jacksonville, Fla.—(High A)
3. Nick Wells, lhp, Battlefield HS, Haymarket, Va.—(Short-season A)
4. Matt Morgan, c, Thorsby (Ala.) HS.—(Rookie)
5. Lane Thomas, of, Bearden HS, Knoxville, Tenn.—(Low A)
6. Grayson Huffman, lhp, Grayson (Texas) CC.
7. *Zach Zehner, of, Cal Poly.
8. Justin Shafer, rhp, University of Florida.
9. Ryan Metzler, 2b, University of South Carolina-Aiken.
10. Jordan Romano, rhp, Oral Roberts University.
11. *Jake Latz, lhp, Lemont (Ill.) HS.
12. *Tanner Houck, rhp, Collinsville (Ill.) HS.
13. Gunnar Heidt, 2b, College of Charleston.
14. Chase Mallard, rhp, University of Alabama-Birmingham.
15. Ryan McBroom, 1b, West Virginia University.
16. *Mike Papierski, c, Lemont (Ill.) HS.
17. *Quinn Carpenter, rhp, Iowa Western CC.
18. Dusty Isaacs, rhp, Georgia Tech.
19. Cliff Brantley, of, Adelphi (N.Y.) University.
DRAFT DROP *Son of Cliff Brantley, major leaguer (1991-92)*
20. Aaron Attaway, ss, Western Carolina University.
21. *Drew Lugbauer, c, Arlington HS, Lagrangeville, N.Y.
22. *Todd Isaacs, of, American Heritage HS, Plantation, Fla.
23. *Zach Pop, rhp, Notre Dame SS, Brampton, Ontario.
24. Conor Fisk, rhp, University of Southern Mississippi.
25. *Rob Winemiller, rhp, Case Western Reserve (Ohio) University.
26. Bobby Wheatley, lhp, University of Southern California.
27. *Owen Taylor, 1b, Grand Junction (Colo.) HS.
28. Chris Carlson, of, Cal Poly Pomona.
29. *Chris Murphy, rhp, Billerica Memorial HS, Billerica, Mass.
30. Kevin Garcia, c, Loyola Marymount University.
31. Dave Pepe, 2b, Pace (N.Y.) University.
32. J.T. Autrey, rhp, Lamar University.
33. Chase Wellbrock, rhp, University of Houston.
34. Brandon Hinkle, lhp, University of Delaware.
35. Joey Aquino, rhp, San Diego Christian College.
36. *Yan Rivera, ss, Colegio Catolico Notre Dame HS, Caguas, P.R.
DRAFT DROP *Son of Luis Rivera, major leaguer (1986-98)*
37. Michael Kraft, lhp, University of Texas-San Antonio.
38. *Keith Weisenberg, rhp, Osceola HS, Seminole, Fla.
39. James Lynch, of, Pima (Ariz.) CC.
DRAFT DROP *Son of Ed Lynch, major leaguer (1980-87)*
40. Trent Miller, of, Middle Tennessee State University.

## WASHINGTON NATIONALS (19)

1. Erick Fedde, rhp, University of Nevada-Las Vegas.—(Low A)
2. *Andrew Suarez, lhp, University of Miami.—(High A)
DRAFT DROP *Returned to Miami (Fla.); re-drafted by Giants, second round (2015)*
3. Jakson Reetz, c, Norris HS, Firth, Neb.—(Short-season A)
4. Robbie Dickey, rhp, Blinn (Texas) JC.—(Low A)
5. Drew Van Orden, rhp, Duke University.—(Low A)
6. Austen Williams, rhp, Texas State University.
7. Dale Carey, of, University of Miami.
8. Jeff Gardner, of, University of Louisville.
9. *Austin Byler, 1b, University of Nevada.
10. Matt Page, of, Oklahoma Baptist University.
11. Weston Davis, rhp, Manatee HS, Bradenton, Fla.
12. Domenick Mancini, rhp, Miami-Dade JC.
13. Austin Davidson, 3b, Pepperdine University.
14. James Bourque, rhp, University of Michigan.
15. Ryan Ripken, 1b, Indian River State (Fla.) JC.
DRAFT DROP *Son of Cal Ripken, major leaguer (1981-2001)*
16. Cole Plouck, lhp, Pima (Ariz.) CC.
17. Alec Keller, of, Princeton University.
18. McKenzie Mills, lhp, Sprayberry HS, Marietta, Ga.
19. Clay Williamson, of, Cal State Fullerton.
20. Bryan Langlois, of, Pepperdine University.
21. Connor Bach, lhp, Virginia Military Institute.
22. *Daniel Salters, c, Dallas Baptist University.
23. Chris Riopedre, ss, East Tennessee State University.
24. Kyle Simmons, rhp, Texas Lutheran University.
25. Kyle Bacak, c, Texas Christian University.
26. Chase McDowell, rhp, Rice University.
27. Conor Keniry, ss, Wake Forest University.
28. Kida De la Cruz, rhp, Volunteer State (Tenn.) CC.
29. D.J. Jauss, rhp, University of Massachusetts.
30. Tyler Mapes, rhp, Tulane University.
31. Sam Johns, rhp, University of Evansville.
32. *Elliott Cary, of, Clackamas (Ore.) HS.
DRAFT DROP *Son of Chuck Cary, major leaguer (1985-93)*
33. *Clay Casey, of, DeSoto Central HS, Southaven, Miss.
34. *Evan Skoug, c, Libertyville (Ill.) HS.
35. *Tommy Doyle, rhp, Flint Hill HS, Oakton, Va.
36. *John Henry Styles, lhp, Episcopal HS, Bellaire, Texas.
37. *Quinn Brodey, lhp, Loyola HS, Los Angeles.
38. *Stuart Fairchild, of, Seattle Prep.
39. *Jon Littell, of, Stillwater (Okla.) HS.
40. *Jacob Hill, lhp, Orange Coast (Calif.) JC.

# 2015

# Notable changes mark draft 50th anniversary

On June 8, 1965, the Kansas City Athletics selected Arizona State outfielder Rick Monday with the No. 1 pick in the draft. They signed him for the princely sum of $100,000.

On June 8, 2015, the Arizona Diamondbacks chose Vanderbilt shortstop Dansby Swanson with the initial selection, and signed him to a bonus of $6.5 million.

The simple size of the signing bonuses highlighted the graphic differences between the drafts, set 50 years apart, but they hardly represented the only significant changes in the draft's evolution—not the least of which involved the clubs leading off the proceedings, and their contrasting circumstances.

The Kansas City A's are no more, having long since moved to Oakland and been replaced in Kansas City by the Royals—the 2015 World Series champions, no less. The Diamondbacks were born in a fourth wave of major league expansion in 1998, meaning that College World Series champion Arizona State was the focal point of Arizona's baseball universe in 1965.

Where once there were 20 first-round picks who signed for an average bonus of $42,516, the 2015 draft yielded a record 36 first-round selections who signed, on average, to the tune of $2,774,945—a record, and 6.23 percent greater than a year earlier.

Where once teams drafted in reverse order of finish—according to both the major league team's standing the previous season, as well as their minor league affiliates—in 2015 the Houston Astros had two of the top five picks and paid out three of the six largest bonuses—the greatest advantage one team ever had in a process designed to level the playing field among all major league clubs.

Where once 420 of 826 players drafted actually signed—a success rate of 50.8 percent—the 2015 draft saw 951 of 1,215 selections agree to contracts, a record pace of 78.3 percent. In fact, the three lowest signing rates occurred in the first three years of the draft (including a record-low 49.5 percent in 1967), and the three highest from 2013-15.

Where once the old Milwaukee Braves (now in Atlanta) set the pace by signing their first 11 selections, the Los Angeles Angels (known in 1965 as the California Angels) set a new standard in 2015 by inking their first 37 selections. The Angels might have become the first team ever to sign all its picks had general manager Jerry Dipoto not resigned on July 1, leaving his son, Jonah, a high school righthander taken in the 38th round, in limbo. The Colorado Rockies also broke the old mark of 32 by signing their first 33 picks.

Had Vanderbilt duplicated its 2014 success by repeating as College World Series champions, 2015 might have had at least something in common with 1965 from a draft perspective.

Monday was the only player in draft history to be picked No. 1 while also leading his team to a national title, and Swanson had a realistic chance of duplicating that feat after leading Vanderbilt to a CWS championship and earning Most Outstanding Player honors as a sophomore. The Commodores fell a game short in 2015.

Arizona took aim at Vanderbilt shortstop Dansby Swanson with the No. 1 overall pick after back to back College World Series trips, but traded him to the Braves less than six months after signing him

But Swanson's selection by the Diamondbacks as the top pick remained significant because he was the first college shortstop taken with the first pick since Brown's Bill Almon in 1974. He was followed in quick order by another shortstop from the Southeastern Conference, Louisiana State's Alex Bregman, who was taken by the Astros with the second pick.

Not to be outdone, the Rockies then followed with another shortstop, Brendan Rodgers from Florida's Lake Mary High, making 2015 the most shortstop-oriented draft ever—only a year after the first three players selected were all pitchers. In all, eight shortstops were taken in the first round.

Appropriately, the three shortstops were the highest-paid players in the 2015 draft, with Swanson's $6.5 million bonus followed by Bregman at $5.9 million and Rodgers at $5.5 million.

Though none of the bonuses was historically significant and collectively were some $4.3 million under the bonus values recommended for the first three slots by Major League Baseball, teams spent more bonus money on the 2015 draft than any draft in history, combining to spend $248,833,845, breaking the existing mark of $228,009,050, set in 2011.

Needless to say, it was a lot more money than was ever spent on bonuses in the 1965 draft, when

## AT A GLANCE

### This Date In History
June 8-10

### One Who Got Away
**KYLE FUNKHOUSER, RHP, DODGERS (1ST ROUND SUPPLEMENTAL).** Funkhouser, who went 8-5, 3.20 with 104 strikeouts and 45 walks in 112 innings for Louisville, was projected as a potential top five pick after his fastball reached 100 mph during the 2015 season. But he labored down the stretch as the quality of his stuff regressed, causing his value to erode, and his ties to agent Scott Boras made teams reluctant to take a run at him. The Dodgers finally did, but he returned to Louisville for his senior year. Ultimately, just six players selected in the top 10 rounds didn't sign—a draft record..

### He Was Drafted?
**KODY CLEMENS, SS, ASTROS (35TH ROUND).** Clemens became the third son of Roger Clemens to be drafted by the Astros. Koby Clemens was drafted in the eighth round in 2005, while Kacy Clemens was taken in the 35th round in 2013. Both Kacy and Kody chose to pursue college careers at Texas, Roger's alma mater.

### Did You Know . . .
The Diamondbacks selected righthander Touki Toussaint (16th overall, 2014) and shortstop **DANSBY SWANSON** (first overall, 2015) with first-round picks but didn't hang on to either long. Both were traded to the Braves in separate deals in 2015.

### They Said It
**JOHN HART**, Braves president of baseball operations, on his team's acquisition of Swanson six months after being selected by the Diamondbacks: "It didn't hurt that Dansby was born and raised five minutes from our new ballpark and was an all-world guy at Vanderbilt. He was a No. 1 guy in the draft that our guys loved."

## IN FOCUS: DANSBY SWANSON

After being the No. 1 pick in the 2015 draft and signing with the Diamondbacks for a bonus of $6.5 million at the July 17 deadline, Dansby Swanson's first day as a pro was even more eventful. He was hit in the face with a fastball by Diamondbacks prospect Yoan Lopez, a 22-year old Cuban defector who had signed earlier in the year for $16 million, during a simulated game.

Swanson sustained a mild concussion and needed 14 stitches but missed less than two weeks of action before making his official debut on Aug. 12 at short-season Hillsboro. In 22 games, he hit .289 with a home run and 11 RBIs.

Despite the Diamondbacks' effort to draft and sign Swanson, he was shockingly traded to the Braves during the 2015 Winter Meetings in a five-player blockbuster that featured major leaguer Shelby Miller. Swanson was born and raised in Marietta, Ga., so the trade was considered a coup by the Braves, who were in the midst of a major rebuilding project and had just traded away all-star shortstop Andrelton Simmons as part of that process.

"It didn't hurt that Dansby was born and raised five minutes from our new ballpark and was an all-world guy at Vanderbilt," said John Hart, the Braves president of baseball operations. "He was a No. 1 guy in the draft that our guys loved."

## 2015: THE FIRST ROUNDERS

| CLUB: PLAYER, POS., SCHOOL | HOMETOWN | B-T | HT. | WT. | AGE | BONUS | FIRST YEAR | LAST YEAR | PEAK LEVEL (YEARS) |
|---|---|---|---|---|---|---|---|---|---|
| **1. Diamondbacks: Dansby Swanson, ss, Vanderbilt** | **Kennesaw, Ga.** | **R-R** | **6-1** | **190** | **21** | **$6,500,000** | **2015** | **Active** | **Class A (1)** |
| Track record of success, solid defensive skills established elite prospect status; switch from 2B to SS, jump from 3 HRs to 15 as junior elevated him to No. 1. | | | | | | | | | |
| **2. Astros: Alex Bregman, ss, Louisiana State** | **Albuquerque, N.M.** | **R-R** | **5-11** | **185** | **21** | **$5,900,000** | **2015** | **Active** | **Class A (1)** |
| Comp pick for failure to sign Aiken in 2014; average tools, but consummate performance-based player, expected to max out talent with leadership qualities. | | | | | | | | | |
| **3. Rockies: Brendan Rodgers, ss, Lake Mary HS** | **Longwood, Fla.** | **R-R** | **6-0** | **180** | **18** | **$5,500,000** | **2015** | **Active** | **Rookie (1)** |
| Early favorite to go No. 1, but became third of three shortstops taken after so-so spring; has athleticism to stick at position, also chance to be middle-of-order hitter. | | | | | | | | | |
| **4. Rangers: Dillon Tate, rhp, UC Santa Barbara** | **Claremont, Calif.** | **R-R** | **6-2** | **210** | **21** | **$4,200,000** | **2015** | **Active** | **Class A (1)** |
| Exploded in starting role with 94-98 mph FB/high-80s slider/improved change, though wore down in stretch run after working 3 IP as freshman, closer role as soph. | | | | | | | | | |
| **5. Astros: Kyle Tucker, of, H.B. Plant HS** | **Tampa** | **L-R** | **6-4** | **190** | **18** | **$4,000,000** | **2015** | **Active** | **Rookie (1)** |
| Family reunion as brother Preston promoted by Astros just prior to draft; different kind of athlete with lean/graceful frame, solid speed/arm tools, similar power. | | | | | | | | | |
| **6. Twins: Tyler Jay, lhp, Illinois** | **Lemont, Ill.** | **L-L** | **6-1** | **180** | **21** | **$3,889,500** | **2015** | **Active** | **Class A (1)** |
| Successful reliever in college (5-2, 1.08, 14 SV), despite starter stuff with mid-90s fastball, command of legit curve/change; expected to be developed as starter. | | | | | | | | | |
| **7. Red Sox: Andrew Benintendi, of, Arkansas** | **Cincinnati** | **L-L** | **5-10** | **170** | **20** | **$3,590,400** | **2015** | **Active** | **Class A (1)** |
| Relative unknown as draft-eligible SO after uninspiring FR year (.276-1-27); added strength, exploded in 2015 (.376-20-57, 24 SB), also plus runner/defender. | | | | | | | | | |
| **8. White Sox: Carson Fulmer, rhp, Vanderbilt** | **Lakeland, Fla.** | **R-R** | **6-0** | **195** | **21** | **$3,470,600** | **2015** | **Active** | **Class A (1)** |
| Size, max-effort delivery, command are concerns, but won over scouts with impressive stuff (94-97 FB), dominant college career (24-3, 1.99, 14 SV, 271 IP/313 SO). | | | | | | | | | |
| **9. Cubs: Ian Happ, of, Cincinnati** | **Pittsburgh** | **B-R** | **6-0** | **205** | **20** | **$3,000,000** | **2015** | **Active** | **Class A (1)** |
| Made-to-order pick for offensive-minded Cubs with switch-hit skills, power potential, hit .369-14-44 as JR; profiles in OF, but played all over field in college. | | | | | | | | | |
| **10. Phillies: Cornelius Randolph, ss, Griffin HS** | **Williamson, Ga.** | **L-R** | **5-11** | **205** | **18** | **$3,231,300** | **2015** | **Active** | **Rookie (1)** |
| Best HS bat in class, natural LH hitter, disciplined approach, strength to drive balls consistently for power; prep SS moved immediately to left field in pros. | | | | | | | | | |
| **11. Reds: Tyler Stephenson, c, Kennesaw Mountain HS** | **Kennesaw, Ga.** | **R-R** | **6-4** | **225** | **18** | **$3,141,600** | **2015** | **Active** | **Rookie (1)** |
| Non-factor at beginning of spring, but Georgia Tech recruit had huge, well-timed power displays, also proved agile defensively for size with easy arm strength. | | | | | | | | | |
| **12. Marlins: Josh Naylor, 1b, St. Joan of Arc Catholic SS** | **Mississauga, Ont.** | **L-L** | **6-0** | **225** | **17** | **$2,250,000** | **2015** | **Active** | **Rookie (1)** |
| Biggest surprise of first round; well known to scouts despite Canadian upbringing because of outstanding raw power, though other tools marginal, limited to 1B. | | | | | | | | | |
| **13. Rays: Garrett Whitley, of, Niskayuna HS** | **Niskayuna, N.Y.** | **R-R** | **6-0** | **200** | **18** | **$2,959,600** | **2015** | **Active** | **Class A (1)** |
| Late bloomer as Northeast athlete, came on strong previous summer, maintained stock with impressive bat speed/power, running speed, chance to be elite CF. | | | | | | | | | |
| **14. Braves: Kolby Allard, lhp, San Clemente HS** | **San Clemente, Calif.** | **L-L** | **6-1** | **175** | **17** | **$3,042,400** | **2015** | **Active** | **Rookie (1)** |
| Projected top five pick before missing most of SR year with stress fracture in back, still first HS arm selected with 96 mph FB, outstanding command/offspeed stuff. | | | | | | | | | |
| **15. Brewers: Trent Clark, of, Richland HS** | **Richlands Hills, Texas** | **L-L** | **6-0** | **205** | **18** | **$2,700,000** | **2015** | **Active** | **Rookie (1)** |
| Best pure hitter in HS class with excellent bat speed/plate discipline, track record (.538 for Team USA juniors; .552 as HS senior), despite unusual split grip on bat. | | | | | | | | | |
| **16. Yankees: James Kaprelian, rhp, UCLA** | **Irvine, Calif.** | **R-R** | **6-4** | **200** | **21** | **$2,650,000** | **2015** | **Active** | **Class A (1)** |
| Polished college arm, became safe first-round pick as JR with 10-4, 2.02 record, strong finish, velocity increase to mid-90s to complement curve, his best pitch. | | | | | | | | | |
| **17. Indians: Brady Aiken, lhp, IMG Academy (Fla.)** | **Jamul, Calif.** | **L-L** | **6-4** | **205** | **18** | **$2,513,280** | **2016** | **Active** | **Rookie (1)** |
| Unsigned 2014 No. 1 pick because of elbow concerns, hurt elbow in first inning at IMG Academy, confirmed Astros TJ fears, now high-risk/high-return selection. | | | | | | | | | |
| **18. Giants: Phil Bickford, rhp, CC of Southern Nevada** | **Westlake Village, Calif.** | **R-R** | **6-5** | **205** | **19** | **$2,333,800** | **2015** | **Active** | **Rookie (1)** |
| Two-time first-rounder passed up Blue Jays 2013 offer to attend CS Fullerton, left after one year to attend JC, went 9-1, 1.45 (86 IP/166 SO) with 93-97 mph fastball. | | | | | | | | | |
| **19. Pirates: Kevin Newman, ss, Arizona** | **Poway, Calif.** | **R-R** | **6-1** | **180** | **21** | **$2,175,000** | **2015** | **Active** | **Class A (1)** |
| Polished four-tool shortstop with solid defensive skills; high-contact/high-average offensive player, two-time Cape Cod batting champ, power only drawback. | | | | | | | | | |
| **20. Athletics: Richie Martin, ss, Florida** | **Brandon, Fla.** | **R-R** | **6-0** | **185** | **20** | **$1,950,000** | **2015** | **Active** | **Class A (1)** |
| Natural SS with athleticism, soft hands, easy arm strength, though error-prone; leadoff profile with on-base skills, line-drive/contact approach, occasional power. | | | | | | | | | |
| **21. Royals: Ashe Russell, rhp, Cathedral HS** | **Fairland, Ind.** | **R-R** | **6-4** | **200** | **18** | **$2,190,200** | **2015** | **Active** | **Rookie (1)** |
| Floppy-haired free spirit in mold of Mark "The Bird" Fidrych; loose arm from low 3/4 slot, lively fastball at 92-95 mph, sweeping slider, inconsistent command. | | | | | | | | | |
| **22. Tigers: Beau Burrows, rhp, Weatherford HS** | **Weatherford, Texas** | **R-R** | **6-2** | **200** | **18** | **$2,154,200** | **2015** | **Active** | **Rookie (1)** |
| Physically mature HS prospect, threw mid-90s at 16, has since added tick or two, polished command/secondary pitches; had auspicious pro debut in Rookie ball. | | | | | | | | | |
| **23. Cardinals: Nick Plummer, of, Brother Rice HS** | **Lathrup Village, Mich.** | **L-L** | **5-10** | **200** | **18** | **$2,124,400** | **2015** | **Active** | **Rookie (1)** |
| First Michigan first-rounder in 15 years; late-rising prospect, intrigued scouts with combo of speed/power potential in small frame, advanced, patient hitter. | | | | | | | | | |
| **24. Dodgers: Walker Buehler, rhp, Vanderbilt** | **Lexington, Ky.** | **R-R** | **6-2** | **175** | **20** | **$1,780,000** | **2016** | **Active** | |
| Third Vandy pick in top 24; outstanding raw stuff with mid-90s FB; durability in question with slender frame, concerns over elbow surfaced late, led to TJ surgery. | | | | | | | | | |
| **25. Orioles: D.J. Stewart, of, Florida State** | **Yulee, Fla.** | **L-R** | **6-0** | **230** | **21** | **$2,064,500** | **2015** | **Active** | **Class A (1)** |
| Deceptively good athlete for body type; concern over spread stance at plate, but displayed outstanding power, patience, walked 69 times as JR, hit .311-15-59. | | | | | | | | | |
| **26. Angels: Taylor Ward, c, Fresno State** | **Indio, Calif.** | **R-R** | **6-1** | **190** | **21** | **$1,670,000** | **2015** | **Active** | **Class A (1)** |
| Considered first-round reach, despite sound defensive skills/big arm; made positive first impression by hitting .348-3-31 (39 BBs/23 SOs) in pro debut. | | | | | | | | | |
| **27. Rockies: Mike Nikorak, rhp, Stroudsburg HS** | **Stroudsburg, Pa.** | **R-R** | **6-5** | **205** | **18** | **$2,300,000** | **2015** | **Active** | **Rookie (1)** |
| Excellent athlete in big frame, put himself on draft radar with velo jump to 94-97 mph as JR; uneven performance as SR, control deserted him as first-year pro. | | | | | | | | | |
| **28. Braves: Mike Soroka, rhp, Bishop Carroll HS** | **Calgary** | **R-R** | **6-4** | **195** | **17** | **$1,974,700** | **2015** | **Active** | **Rookie (1)** |
| Rare second Canadian in first round; came on fast with fastball that peaked at 94, but Braves most taken by athletic frame, potential in outstanding breaking ball. | | | | | | | | | |
| **29. Blue Jays: Jon Harris, rhp, Missouri State** | **Florissant, Mo.** | **R-R** | **6-4** | **175** | **21** | **$1,944,800** | **2015** | **Active** | **Class A (1)** |
| Drafted by persistent Blue Jays out of HS, again three years later after velocity jumped from upper-80s to mid-90s, curve/change developed; control still an issue. | | | | | | | | | |
| **30. Yankees: Kyle Holder, ss, San Diego** | **University City, Calif.** | **L-R** | **6-1** | **185** | **21** | **$1,800,000** | **2015** | **Active** | **Class A (1)** |
| Slick fielder with plus arm, considered best defender in deep crop of college shortstops; concerns over bat, contact approach, hit weak .213-0-12 in first pro season. | | | | | | | | | |
| **31. Giants: Chris Shaw, 1b, Boston College** | **Lexington, Mass.** | **L-R** | **6-3** | **235** | **21** | **$1,400,000** | **2015** | **Active** | **Class A (1)** |
| Showcased big power in Cape Cod in 2014 (.275-8-34); hampered by broken hamate bone in spring, still hit .319-11-43, continued to hit (.287-12-30) in pro debut. | | | | | | | | | |
| **32. Pirates: Ke'Bryan Hayes, 3b, Concordia Lutheran HS** | **Tomball, Texas** | **R-R** | **6-1** | **210** | **18** | **$1,855,000** | **2015** | **Active** | **Class A (1)** |
| Son of ex-MLB 3B Charlie, similar kind of player; polished RH hitter with chance for high average, questionable power potential; solid defender at hot corner. | | | | | | | | | |
| **33. Royals: Nolan Watson, rhp, Lawrence HS** | **Lawrence, Ind.** | **R-R** | **6-2** | **195** | **18** | **$1,825,200** | **2015** | **Active** | **Rookie (1)** |
| Second Indianapolis area HS pick snapped up by Royals in first round; more polish, better secondary stuff than Ashe Russell, lower upside with 91-93 mph fastball. | | | | | | | | | |
| **34. Tigers: Christin Stewart, of, Tennessee** | **Lawrenceville, Ga.** | **L-R** | **6-0** | **205** | **21** | **$1,795,100** | **2015** | **Active** | **Class A (1)** |
| Undrafted out of HS, gained momentum by leading 2014 U.S. college team in hitting (.386-2-16); followed up with big spring (.311-15-47), limited to LF defensively. | | | | | | | | | |
| **35. Dodgers: Kyle Funkhouser, rhp, Louisville** | **Oak Forest, Ill.** | **R-R** | **6-2** | **220** | **21** | **Unsigned** | **2016** | **Active** | |
| Contender for top five pick after showcasing mid-90s FB/power slider in summer ball; stock tumbled with inconsistent velocity/command, 8-5, 3.20 record in spring. | | | | | | | | | |
| **36. Orioles: Ryan Mountcastle, ss, Hagerty HS** | **Winter Springs, Fla.** | **R-R** | **6-3** | **185** | **18** | **$1,300,000** | **2015** | **Active** | **Class A (1)** |
| Lowest bonus in first round, reflective of questions about athleticism, future position (likely 3B); bat, power potential legit first-round tools; had sound pro debut. | | | | | | | | | |

the overall tab was on the order of $4,452,906.

## SWANSON'S SHORT SHELF LIFE

For all the bonus money that was spent to mark the 50th anniversary of the baseball draft, the 2015 edition lacked a clearly defined top prospect and the talent overall fell short of expectations.

"There will be the same number of big leaguers, as usual," one veteran scout said in evaluating the entire class, "but there's not the guys perceived to have impact. It will be easier for teams to go safe rather than go for ceiling."

It may not have been the best year for the Diamondbacks to pick first, considering the organization had cleaned house after going a major league-worst 64-98 in 2014, or for the Astros to be the first club in draft history to own two of the top five selections.

Ex-big leaguer Dave Stewart was in his first year as general manager of the Diamondbacks, while new scouting director Deric Ladnier had been on the job for just six months. In many regards, the team played catch-up most of the spring to get a handle on the prospects at their disposal leading up to their selection, but there was never a perception that it was disadvantaged in picking first.

While the team's choice remained a public mystery until the moment was at hand, Ladnier left little doubt that Swanson was the player the Diamondbacks targeted all along. He became convinced Swanson was their man after the team wrapped up its predraft meetings, and his staff was unanimous in its assessment.

"This is the player we wanted," Ladnier said. "We wanted him for awhile."

Swanson learned of his selection while he was in the midst of an on-field celebration after Vanderbilt clinched its NCAA super-regional series at Illinois that paved the way for a return trip to the College World Series.

Getting Swanson signed proved even more dramatic for the Diamondbacks, as negotiations went down to the wire before he finally agreed to terms just before the 5 p.m. deadline on July 17, narrowly avoiding a second straight year in which the first overall pick didn't sign. Lefthander Brady Aiken and the Astros were unable to come to terms in 2014 after a messy negotiation.

Swanson was one of three unsigned first-rounders on the final day. Walker Buehler, Swanson's Vanderbilt teammate, and Louisville's Kyle Funkhouser, both selections of the Los Angeles Dodgers, also went to the wire. Funkhouser went unsigned, the only first-rounder to do so.

DANNY PARKER

Walker Buehler

The circumstances surrounding Swanson's selection were some of the most intriguing in draft history. After winning the first game of its best-of-three super-regional series against Illinois on the Saturday before the draft, Vanderbilt was in position to clinch a return trip to

## DRAFT SPOTLIGHT: ALEX BREGMAN

ANDREW WOOLLEY

**Alex Bregman had to prove himself throughout his amateur career, until the Astros made him a first-rounder**

On the day shortstop Carlos Correa made his major league debut for the Houston Astros, the club drafted another shortstop, Louisiana State's Alex Bregman, with the No. 2 overall pick. Despite the potential conflict, Astros officials were insistent that Bregman would remain a shortstop—but they were no more confident that would happen than Bregman himself.

"There's no question about that. He's got the skills," Astros general manager Jeff Luhnow said. "That's one of the things we watched a lot over the past couple of years is him play shortstop. He can make the spectacular play and he routinely makes the everyday play."

"He will remain a shortstop," scouting director Mike Elias said. "I think you will see him as a shortstop all the way through our system and in the big leagues one day."

The supremely confident Bregman believed he could play shortstop in the big leagues, too, no matter how many scouts may have doubted him along the way.

"Not one person has told me I can't play shortstop," he said. "Until someone does—and until someone tells me why I can't—then I don't understand why I wouldn't be able to."

It's a reflection of the self-assuredness Bregman has about his ability to play baseball. In his mind, he was always destined for greatness—as a shortstop, or at any position.

"Ever since he was 4 or 5, Alex has been consumed and obsessed with the game of baseball," his father, Sam Bregman, said. "No one has worked harder to get where Alex is than Alex. His work ethic is second to none; his passion for the game is unbelievable."

Still, Bregman was a polarizing figure among scouts throughout his high school and college careers. His favorite player growing up was Boston Red Sox sparkplug Dustin Pedroia, who battled many of the same biases that Bregman endured: unremarkable size and average raw tools. The fact that Bregman grew up in the baseball backwater of Albuquerque, N.M., didn't help, either.

But eventually scouts could not ignore his performance. As a slight high school freshman, he hit .514 and led Albuquerque Academy to a state title. In the championship game, he drilled a ball well out of Triple-A Albuquerque's Isotopes Park, a statement from Bregman that he could play with the big boys. Following his sophomore year, he was the shortstop for USA Baseball's 16-and-under national team that won gold at the world championship, and his performance was so electrifying that he was the organization's player of the year, the first time a high school player was so honored.

As a junior in 2011, Bregman hit .678 with a New Mexico record 19 home runs, then followed that up by leading the U.S. to gold again at the world 18-and-under championship.

But the debate over Bregman's pro potential for the 2012 draft got short-circuited when he shattered a knuckle on his right hand five games into his senior year at Albuquerque Academy and missed the rest of the season. His draft stock plummeted. The Red Sox took the overachieving Bregman in the 29th round—a sign of respect after they took his best friend, fellow New Mexico prep product Blake Swihart, in the first round.

Bregman began his freshman year at LSU hitting in the 3-hole and starting at shortstop for a 57-win Tigers team, and never slowed down. He hit .369 with six homers to win Baseball America Freshman of the Year, and continued to excel for two more years, while also starring at shortstop for two summers on USA Baseball's college national team.

While the Astros and a growing legion of teams that were more motivated by performance and less by raw tools took a liking to Bregman by his junior year, some scouts still questioned if he could stay at shortstop over the long haul. They wondered about his power, even as he drilled 34 extra-base hits, including nine homers as a junior; they questioned his speed and athleticism, until he stole 38 bases.

By drafting him, the Astros appeared to create yet another hurdle for Bregman with a potential franchise player at shortstop in Correa, who is actually more than five months younger, and an even more established second baseman in Jose Altuve, 24.

"Everybody can say whatever they want," a resolute Bregman said. "I'm just going to have fun playing the game. If I play second, that's fine. If I play short, that's fine. I just want to help my team win. I definitely think I could play shortstop."

## WORTH NOTING

■ Defending champion Vanderbilt, boasting three first-rounders, was a prohibitive favorite to win the 2015 College World Series, but an injury-riddled Virginia turned the tables on the Commodores (51-21) by winning the best-of-three championship series, two games to one. A year earlier, Vanderbilt beat a favored Cavaliers team that featured three premium picks, also in three games. Virginia squeezed into the NCAA tournament as a No. 3 seed, but caught fire at the right time, winning 10 of 12 games in NCAA play. Still, the team's 44 wins were the fewest by an NCAA champion since 1968. Virginia's top draft pick was injury-plagued lefthander **NATHAN KIRBY**, who was sidelined most of the final eight weeks of the 2015 season by injury and illness but came on to pitch the final two innings of a 4-2 win over Vanderbilt in the third and deciding game, striking out five and earning his only save of the season. Righthander **JOSH SBORZ**, a second-round pick of the Dodgers, was Virginia's go-to arm in the College World Series. He pitched in four games and went 3-0 with a save, while not allowing a run in 13 innings. Though Virginia captured the first CWS title for an ACC team in 60 years, the 2015 season otherwise belonged to the SEC. Not only did it boast four teams that reached Omaha, but the first two picks in the draft and seven selections in the first round came from SEC schools. Oklahoma, which failed to even land a spot in the 64-team NCAA tournament, topped all college teams with 11 selections in the draft, though none higher than fourth rounder **ANTHONY HERMELYN**. UC Santa Barbara, which was bounced in regional play, had 10 players drafted. Vanderbilt had nine players picked, while Virginia had seven.

■ In a banner year for Canadians in the draft, the

Omaha on Sunday. But rain postponed the game until Monday at 3 p.m., four hours before the draft was set to begin.

As Swanson and the rest of the Commodores took the field, more than 1,500 miles away in Phoenix, Ladnier and other Diamondbacks scouts settled in to finish their preparations for the draft and watch the player they would soon make the top overall pick. Swanson didn't disappoint as he went 2-for-4 with a home run, a double and a stolen base to help Vanderbilt defeat Illinois 4-2.

"It was icing on the cake to see him hit a home run, to see him hit a double in the gap and ultimately win the game and advance to the (College) World Series," Ladnier said.

Five minutes after Vanderbilt closed out the victory, baseball commissioner Rob Manfred officially kicked off the draft in Secaucus, N.J., at MLB Network's studios. Swanson was still on the field in Champaign, Ill., surrounded by his teammates and with his family close by, when his name was called a few minutes later.

"It's a surreal moment, especially to be with all my loved ones," Swanson said. "Just to be able to enjoy the moment with the people closest to you, it's pretty phenomenal."

The only previous time the Diamondbacks had the No. 1 pick in the draft was 2005, when they selected Virginia high school shortstop Justin Upton. He was later traded to the Atlanta Braves, though not for more than seven years after his selection. In a case of history repeating itself, Swanson also got shipped to the Braves, in December 2015, by far the quickest a No. 1 overall pick got dispatched by the team that drafted him.

Prior to 2015, drafted players couldn't be traded for at least a year after they signed, but that rule was amended several months before Swanson was dealt. The earliest previous trades of No. 1 picks came when the Astros traded righthander Mark Appel, the 2013 No. 1 pick, to the Philadelphia Phillies on Dec. 12, 2015—just three days after Swansby was dealt—and when outfielder Shawn Abner, the 1984 No. 1 pick, was traded by the New York Mets to the San Diego Padres on Dec. 11, 1986.

Brendan Rodgers

While he was drafted as a shortstop, Swanson spent his sophomore year at Vanderbilt playing second base, while hitting .333 with three homers. That summer, he teamed with Bregman to form the double-play combination on USA Baseball's college national team, but Bregman was solidly entrenched as the shortstop when Swanson reported late because of his participation in the College World Series. Swanson hit .288 in 18 games as Team USA's regular second baseman, while Bregman hit .257 and led the team in RBIs and stolen bases (10).

Naturally, both players were continually compared, and even developed a friendship. And while

### Top 25 Bonuses

| | Player, Pos. | Drafted (Round) | Order | Bonus |
|---|---|---|---|---|
| 1. | Dansby Swanson, ss | Diamondbacks (1) | 1 | $6,500,000 |
| 2. | Alex Bregman, ss | Astros (1) | 2 | $5,900,000 |
| 3. | * Brendan Rodgers, ss | Rockies (1) | 3 | $5,500,000 |
| 4. | Dillon Tate, rhp | Rangers (1) | 4 | $4,200,000 |
| 5. | * Kyle Tucker, of | Astros (1) | 5 | $4,000,000 |
| | * Daz Cameron, of | Astros (1-S) | 37 | $4,000,000 |
| 7. | Tyler Jaye, lhp | Twins (1) | 6 | $3,889,500 |
| 8. | Andrew Benintendi, of | Red Sox (1) | 7 | $3,590,400 |
| 9. | Carson Fulmer, rhp | White Sox (1) | 8 | $3,470,600 |
| 10. | * Cornelius Randolph, ss | Phillies (1) | 10 | $3,231,300 |
| 11. | * Tyler Stephenson, c | Reds (1) | 11 | $3,141,600 |
| 12. | * Kolby Allard, lhp | Braves (1) | 14 | $3,042,400 |
| 13. | Ian Happ, of | Cubs (1) | 9 | $3,000,000 |
| 14. | * Garrett Whitley, of | Rays (1) | 13 | $2,959,600 |
| 15. | * Trent Clark, of | Brewers (1) | 15 | $2,700,000 |
| 16. | James Kaprelian, rhp | Yankees (1) | 16 | $2,650,000 |
| 17. | Brady Aiken, lhp | Indians (1) | 17 | $2,513,280 |
| 18. | Phil Bickford, rhp | Giants (1) | 18 | $2,333,800 |
| 19. | * Triston McKenzie, rhp | Indians (1-S) | 42 | $2,302,500 |
| 20. | * Mike Nikorak, rhp | Rockies (1) | 27 | $2,300,000 |
| 21. | * Josh Naylor, 1b | Marlins (1) | 12 | $2,250,000 |
| 22. | * Ashe Russell, rhp | Royals (1) | 21 | $2,190,200 |
| 23. | Kevin Newman, ss | Pirates (1) | 19 | $2,175,000 |
| 24. | * Beau Burrows, rhp | Tigers (1) | 22 | $2,154,200 |
| 25. | * Nick Plummer, of | Cardinals (1) | 23 | $2,124,400 |

**High school selection.*

they both performed admirably, it would have been hard to predict at the time that they might be drafted 1-2 the next June because they were overshadowed much of the summer by a dominant Team USA pitching staff that posted a cumulative 1.25 ERA and featured Buehler, Funkhouser, Carson Fulmer (Vanderbilt), Tyler Jay (Illinois), James Kaprelian (UCLA) and Dillon Tate (UC Santa Barbara).

But Swanson upstaged the group of elite pitchers by hitting .335 with 15 homers and 64 RBIs in a breakout junior season at Vanderbilt, and enhanced his worth even more by making a smooth transition to shortstop, displaying the kind of athleticism, range, hands and instincts expected in a premier prospect at the position.

By hitting .323 with nine homers and 49 RBIs and an SEC-leading 38 stolen bases, Bregman had a solid junior season himself for LSU. He was steady in all facets of his game, and his long track record of success, as well as his off-the-charts makeup, convinced scouts generally, and the Astros in particular, that he was a player that would get the most out of his ability and was worthy of being picked second overall.

Rodgers was considered the best natural talent of the three shortstops, especially with his superior bat speed and offensive upside, but his standing as a high school player made him a riskier selection.

Led by Swanson and Bregman, a record five college shortstops went in the first round. Arizona's Kevin Newman went 19th overall to the Pittsburgh Pirates, Florida's Richie Martin was taken 20th by the Athletics and San Diego's Kyle Holder was selected 30th by the New York Yankees.

Newman was a two-time Cape Cod League batting champion, Martin's athleticism stood out while Holder was viewed as the best defensive shortstop of the crop. But no shortstop had a better overall package than Swanson.

### ASTROS SPEND EARLY, OFTEN

The Astros selected first overall for a record three straight drafts from 2012-14, but the greatest impetus to their rebuilding efforts may have come in 2015, when they were afforded the largest overall signing budget of $17,289,200 to sign their picks in the first 10 rounds, and ended up spending a draft record $19,103,000 to sign all their picks—more than $2 million more than the Pirates spent in 2011 to set the previous high.

In addition to their own pick, fifth overall, the Astros also had the second selection for failing to sign Aiken a year earlier. No team had ever enjoyed the luxury of having two of the first five picks in a single draft, and after the Astros signed Bregman for $1,520,100 below the assigned slot for the second pick, they also saved $188,700 on the $4 million bonus they paid to the fifth pick, Florida high school outfielder Kyle Tucker.

By applying the savings from those players, and executing numerous other below-slot deals among the other players they took in the first 10 rounds, the Astros positioned themselves to draft and sign a third elite prospect, Georgia high school outfielder Daz Cameron, the son of former big league all-star outfielder Mike Cameron.

MIKE JANES

Daz Cameron

Like Bregman and Tucker, Cameron was also expected to go among the first 10 picks, but with a reported price tag of $5 million, he was available for the Astros with the 37th pick overall. Most other clubs did not have sufficient money in their bonus pools to meet Cameron's demands without risking blowing their budgets if they didn't sign him. The Astros signed him for $4 million, a record for a supplemental first-round pick.

The Astros didn't stop there as they signed their second-rounder, Cal State Fullerton righthander Tom Eshelman, for $1.1 million, and their third-rounder, Texas Christian closer Riley Ferrell, for $1 million. They also spent $900,000 ($800,000 over slot) to sign their 11th-rounder, California prep lefthander Patrick Sandoval.

With all their maneuvering, the Astros paid out three of the six largest bonuses on the year, along with three others in excess of $900,000, and yet were still in compliance with draft rules that penalized teams for spending more than 5 percent over their bonus pool allotment by taking away future draft picks. The Astros did exceed their pool limit by $575,800, though, requiring them to pay a luxury tax of $431,850 (75 percent of the overage).

The Astros took the same calculated approach when drafting shortstop Carlos Correa with the No. 1 pick in 2012 and Appel in 2013. While their plans fell apart in 2014 when they failed to sign Aiken, that led to an even bigger bonanza in 2015 as they turned their compensation pick into Bregman, a more advanced player than Aiken, who had Tommy John surgery in March 2015.

Houston, coincidentally, drafted Bregman the same day it promoted Correa to the majors. More than any player, Correa symbolized the team's massive rebuilding effort that heralded the beginning of a new era in Astros baseball and led to the team's appearance in postseason play in 2015.

The Astros also significantly enhanced their pool of prospects by landing the 6-foot-4, 190-pound Tucker, one of the elite high school bats in the draft, and the 6-foot-2, 185-pound Cameron, one of the best all-around players in the prep class. Tucker hit .484 with 10 homers as a senior at Tampa's H.B. Plant High, and broke the school record for career homers set by his older brother Preston, a seventh-round pick of the Astros in 2012 who made his major league debut a month before the 2015 draft.

In the four-year period from 2012-15, the Astros spent $47,534,700 on signing bonuses—a total that dwarfed the rest of the industry.

### Largest Bonuses By Round

| | Player, Pos. | Club | Bonus |
|---|---|---|---|
| 1. | Dansby Swanson, ss | Diamondbacks | $6,500,000 |
| 1-S. | *Daz Cameron, of | Astros | $4,000,000 |
| 2. | *Eric Jenkins, of | Rangers | $2,000,000 |
| 3. | Michael Matuella, rhp | Rangers | $2,000,000 |
| 4. | *D.J. Wilson, of | Cubs | $1,300,000 |
| 5. | *Brendan Davis, ss | Dodgers | $918,600 |
| 6. | *Justin Cohen, c | Marlins | $540,000 |
| 7. | *Gray Fenter, rhp | Orioles | $1,000,000 |
| 8. | *Logan Allen, lhp | Red Sox | $725,000 |
| 9. | Pierce Romero, rhp | Diamondbacks | $295,000 |
| 10. | Joey Armstrong, of | Diamondbacks | $154,000 |
| 11. | *Imani Abdullah, rhp | Dodgers | $647,500 |
| 12. | *Wesley Rodriguez, rhp | Diamondbacks | $350,000 |
| 13. | Max Schrock, 2b | Nationals | $500,000 |
| 14. | A.J. Simcox, ss | Tigers | $600,000 |
| 15. | Brad Zunica, 1b | Padres | $192,500 |
| 16. | Marcus Brakeman, rhp | Red Sox | $225,000 |
| 17. | *Sam Pastrone, rhp | Angels | $250,000 |
| 18. | *Isaac Anesty, lhp | Reds | $200,000 |
| 19. | *Alan Garcia, of | Padres | $220,000 |
| 20. | Isiah Gilliam, 1b | Yankees | $550,000 |
| 21. | Several tied at | | $100,000 |
| 22. | *Justin Marsden, rhp | Rays | $147,500 |
| 23. | Matt Bower, lhp | Astros | $125,000 |
| 24. | *Reggie Pruitt, of | Blue Jays | $500,000 |
| 25. | Several tied at | | $100,000 |
| Other | *Logan Crouse, rhp | Dodgers (30) | $497,500 |

**High school selection.*

### COLLEGE ARMS TAKE A HIT

The early emphasis in the 2015 draft was an impressive crop of college arms, but few of the bigger names dominated as expected, and the first two pitchers off the board, surprisingly, were Tate and Jay, who had carved their niche in relief roles prior to 2015.

Tate, a 6-foot-2, 165-pound righthander, was the first pitcher taken, going fourth overall to the Texas Rangers. He pitched sparingly as a freshman at UCSB and was the team's closer as a sophomore. It was only as a junior, when he made a successful transition to a starting role, that he moved to the forefront. He went 8-5, 2.26 with 111 strikeouts

### WORTH NOTING

Marlins, the southernmost team in baseball, were the first to go north of the border with their pick. They tabbed 6-foot-1, 225-pound first baseman **JOSH NAYLOR** with the 12th overall selection, the highest draft position ever for a Canadian position player. "There is some **PRINCE FIELDER** in this guy," said Marlins scouting director **STAN MEEK**. "He has that kind of bat speed and power." The Braves took a second Canadian in the first round, 6-foot-4, 195-pound righthander **MIKE SOROKA**. In all, 30 Canadians were drafted, including a record 10 in the first 10 rounds.

■ Pitchers occupied the top six spots on the Major League Scouting Bureau's ranking of the top prospects for the 2015 draft, with Texas prep righthander **ANTONIO SANTILLAN**, a supplemental first-round pick of the Reds, receiving the highest grade: 70 on the standard 20-80 scouting scale. Azusa Pacific (Calif.) righthander **JOSH STAUMONT**, a second-round pick of the Royals, graded as a 68, while Indians first-rounder **BRADY AIKEN** was next at 67. Braves first-rounder **KOLBY ALLARD**, Rockies first-rounder **MIKE NIKORAK** and Indians supplemental first-rounder **TRISTON MCKENZIE** followed at 65.

■ The Cardinals fired scouting director **CHRIS CORREA** in the wake of an investigation into the hacking of the Astros' scouting database. Correa had replaced **JEFF LUHNOW** as Cardinals scouting director after Luhnow left to become general manager of the Astros after the 2011 season. Investigators alleged that he attempted to access the Astros' database to determine whether Luhnow or other former Cardinals employees took proprietary information to their new organization.

■ It was a strong year for Florida, with 13 of the first 63 picks from the Sunshine

CONTINUED ON PAGE 746

## WORTH NOTING

CONTINUED FROM PAGE 745

State, led by prep shortstop **BRENDAN RODGERS** at No. 3 overall. The Padres, in particular, took an interest in Florida as their first three picks and four of their first five came from the state.

■ There are sons of former major leaguers in every draft, but 2015 seemed to be a special year. Ten sons were drafted in the top 10 rounds, led by third baseman **KE'BRYAN HAYES** (son of Charlie), who was taken by the Pirates with the 32nd pick overall. He was followed by outfielder **DAZ CAMERON** (son of Mike) at No. 37 by the Astros, and third baseman **TYLER NEVIN** (son of Phil) one pick later by the Rockies. The Nationals selected righthander **MARIANO RIVERA JR.** in the fourth round, while the Tigers took Michigan State outfielder **CAM GIBSON** (son of Kirk) in the fifth. The Astros picked infielders **CONOR BIGGIO** (son of Craig) and **KODY CLEMENS** (son of Roger) in the 34th and 35th rounds.

■ Royals area scout **MIKE FARRELL**, whose territory included Indiana, had the rare fortune of having two Indianapolis high school pitchers picked in the first round after Kansas City spent the 24th pick overall on righthander **ASHE RUSSELL** and the 33rd pick on righthander **NOLAN WATSON**. Many area scouts, especially in less-fertile regions, can go a whole career without a first-round pick, and Farrell picked up a pair in less than an hour.

■ **LUCIUS FOX**, a shortstop from the Bahamas, signed with the Giants for $6 million as an international free agent—a larger bonus than all but one player in the 2015 draft. Fox was initially believed to be draft eligible because he attended American Heritage High in Plantation, Fla., as a junior and had projected as a second-rounder, but profited handsomely when he returned to the Bahamas and became eligible to sign on the open market.

in 103 innings for the Gauchos. With his high-energy delivery, fast arm and athletic frame, Tate's fastball sat at 94-96 mph, though his hard slider was considered his dominant pitch. He received a $4.2 million bonus, the fourth largest overall, to sign with the Rangers.

Jay, a 6-foot-1, 185-pound lefthander, went sixth overall to the Minnesota Twins and signed for $3,889,500. He emerged as Illinois' closer as a sophomore and dominated in that role as a junior going 5-2, 1.08 with 14 saves; in 67 innings, he walked just seven while striking out 76. His combination of a solid three-pitch mix and ability to hold his fastball velocity made him a candidate to start as a pro, significantly enhancing his worth.

Along with Swanson, the selection of both Fulmer (White Sox, eighth overall) and Buehler (Dodgers, 24th) made Vanderbilt just the fifth team in college history to produce three first-rounders in the same draft. That accomplishment had previously been achieved by Michigan in 1979, Fresno State in 1989, Rice in 2004 and Miami in 2008.

Fulmer was another pitcher who began his college career as a closer before being bumped to the rotation midway through his sophomore year. After going 7-1, 1.98 with 10 saves in 2014, he went 14-2, 1.83 with 167 strikeouts (second in the nation) in 128 innings as Vanderbilt's ace in 2015. Buehler, meanwhile, regressed from a 12-2, 2.64 record as a sophomore to 5-2, 1.95 as a junior, causing his stock to slip marginally.

Despite his 6-foot frame and high-effort delivery, Fulmer won scouts over in the same manner as former Commodores ace Sonny Gray, with a track record of success and a starter's arsenal that included a fastball up to 97 mph. He signed with the Chicago White Sox for $3,470,600. Buehler had a similar repertoire but experienced elbow pain early in the 2015 season, was never quite right all spring and subsequently had Tommy John surgery after signing with the Dodgers for $1,777,500.

Duke's 6-foot-6, 220-pound righthander Michael Matuella profiled as the top pitching prospect in the college class entering the 2015 season on the strength of his combination of stuff and command. As a sophomore, his fastball peaked at 98 mph. But he had never thrown more than 60 innings in a college season, or pitched in the summer or fall, because he had spondylosis, a chronic condition that affects the disks of the neck and spine. Rather than potentially exacerbate the issue, Matuella opted not to pitch in favor of resting and strengthening his back.

It was evident that he was not right physically coming out of the gate for his junior season, though, and he soon succumbed to Tommy John surgery. Scouts said he had altered his delivery to compensate for his back issues, and hurt his elbow in the process. Though he slid to the Rangers in the third round (78th overall), Matuella nonetheless signed for $2 million—a full $1,222,400 above the value for his slot.

Virginia lefthander Nathan Kirby was another pitcher targeted for the top half of the first round, but he was sidelined by a strained lat muscle in April and played a limited role for his team as it overtook Vanderbilt to win the College World Series. He went 40th overall to the Milwaukee Brewers, and after signing for $1.25 million and pitching 12 innings in the minors, he became the latest pitcher to require Tommy John surgery.

The 2015 draft also featured two pitchers who went unsigned as first-rounders in previous drafts and repeated the feat with back-to-back picks. Aiken, the first overall pick in 2014, went 17th overall to the Cleveland Indians, while righthander Phil Bickford went 18th to the San Francisco Giants.

Aiken was the higher-profile arm of the pair and generated considerable intrigue after his 2014 draft debacle. He had agreed to sign with the Astros for $6.5 million, but that deal fell apart after a difference of opinion in the results of an MRI on his elbow from a post-draft physical. He ultimately turned down a reported $5 million from the Astros.

Aiken eventually chose to attend the IMG Academy in Bradenton, Fla., to play for the academy's postgraduate team during the spring in preparation for the 2015 draft, but threw just 13 pitches in his first start before exiting the game with an elbow injury. He had Tommy John surgery six days later.

Brady Aiken

That complex set of circumstances made Aiken one of the biggest wild cards of the 2015 draft and led to him still being on the board through the first 15 picks. The Indians took a leap of faith in selecting him but said they were confident after reviewing his medical files that he would return to his old form by 2016.

### One Team's Draft: Atlanta Braves

| Player, Pos. | Bonus |
|---|---|
| 1. *Kolby Allard, lhp | $3,042,400 |
| 1. *Mike Soroka, rhp | $1,974,700 |
| 1. *Austin Riley, 3b | $1,600,000 |
| 2. *Lucas Herbert, c | $1,125,200 |
| 2. A.J. Minter, rhp | $814,300 |
| 3. *Anthony Guardado, rhp | $550,000 |
| 4. Josh Graham, rhp | $500,000 |
| 5. Ryan Clark, rhp | $352,100 |
| 6. Matt Withrow, rhp | $263,700 |
| 7. Patrick Weigel, rhp | $197,500 |
| 8. Ryan Lawlor, lhp | $171,500 |
| 9. Taylor Lewis, rhp | $200,000 |
| 10. Stephen Moore, rhp | $5,000 |
| 11. Grayson Jones, rhp | $150,000 |
| 12. Justin Ellison, of | $110,000 |
| 13. Chase Johnson-Mullins, lhp | $125,000 |
| 14. Trey Keegan, c | $100,000 |
| 15. *Brad Keller, of | $150,000 |
| 16. Trevor Belicek, lhp | $5,000 |
| 17. Evan Phillips, rhp | $100,000 |
| 18. *Gilbert Suarez, rhp | $100,000 |
| 19. Sean McLaughlin, rhp | $100,000 |
| 20. *Jarret Hellinger, lhp | $300,000 |
| 21. Kurt Hoekstra, 2b | $60,000 |
| 22. Dalton Geekie, rhp | $90,000 |
| 23. Taylor Cockrell, rhp | $120,000 |
| 24. Jacob Lanning, 3b | $3,000 |
| 25. Jonathan Morales, c | $60,000 |
| Other Collin Yelich (29), c | $100,000 |

**High school selection.*

"We've done our due diligence on it and we feel very comfortable," Indians scouting director Brad Grant said. "We're going to work hard with Brody and try to ensure that he gets back to being the pitcher he was before the surgery."

Aiken signed for $2.513 million, and was one of just six first-rounders to receive an amount in excess of his bonus slot value. A bonus of $2,393,600 had been earmarked for the 17th pick.

The Giants selected Bickford out of the College of Southern Nevada, two years after he went unsigned out of a California high school as the 10th overall pick by the Toronto Blue Jays. After a year at Cal State Fullerton, he transferred to a junior college to become eligible for the draft a year ahead of schedule. He signed with the Giants for $2,333.800 after leading all junior-college pitchers with 166 strikeouts.

### BRAVES REBUILD THROUGH DRAFT

As they occupied the first four spots in the draft order, it was appropriate that the Diamondbacks, Astros, Rockies and Rangers were four of the five biggest spenders overall in the draft—just the way the draft was designed to work, by providing the greatest opportunity to acquire talent by those most in need. The Astros easily led the way by spending $19,103,000, and were followed by the Rockies at $14,415,900, the Diamondbacks at $12,270,900 and Rangers at $10,728,300.

The Rangers spent 4.8 percent beyond their bonus pool allotment, while the Astros went over by 3.3 percent, but both the Diamondbacks and Rockies stayed within their limits.

Despite not making their first selection until the 14th pick overall, the Braves were also among the top five spenders, committing $12,659,400 in bonus money. Like the Astros before them, the Braves had started a massive rebuilding job that included unloading almost every veteran player on their big league roster for prospects and utilizing the draft to retool the organization. Their acquisition of Swanson was considered a major building block, but the Braves also had five of the first 75 picks in the draft—two coming via trades with the Padres (for Craig Kimbrel) and Diamondbacks (for Victor Reyes) that netted the competitive balance picks those clubs had obtained.

The rebuilding also included a significant shake-up in the Braves front office that led to the ouster of general manager Frank Wren and brought former scouting director Roy Clark back as assistant to the general manager, overseeing the Braves' draft efforts. Clark immediately returned the Braves to their traditional scouting roots of emphasizing pitching and high school talent in the draft.

With their top pick, the Braves selected California high school lefthander Kolby Allard, the first prep pitcher drafted. The 6-foot-1, 175-pound Allard missed most of the 2015 season with a stress reaction in his back, but the Braves didn't hesitate in signing him for $3,042,400 ($200,000 over slot). Allard didn't show any adverse effects after joining the Braves, though they brought him along slowly. He made just three appearances in August in the Rookie-level Gulf Coast League, totaling 12 strikeouts in six scoreless innings.

Among the Braves' other early picks was catcher Lucas Herbert, one of the best defenders in the draft and Allard's batterymate at San Clemente High. He signed for a slot bonus of $1,125,200.

The Braves signed nine more players to over-slot amounts, including Georgia prep lefthander Jarret Hellinger, a 20th-rounder who signed for $300,000, going 4.4 percent over their bonus allotment and paying $350,475 in luxury tax.

Besides the Braves, the defending World Series champion Giants, as well as the Yankees, with the largest payroll in the game, were among the biggest spenders in the draft—even though neither club had a selection in the first 15 picks.

The Yankees took UCLA righthander James Kaprelian with the 16th pick, their earliest selection since choosing Matt Drews with the 13th pick in 1993. They signed Kaprelian for $2.65 million ($106,700 over slot) and made an even bigger splash by signing third-rounder Drew Finley for $960,000 ($323,400 over slot), 11th-rounder Josh Rogers for $485,000 ($385,000 over slot) and 20th-rounder Isiah Gilliam for $550,000 ($450,000 over slot). The Yankees went 4.7 percent over their allotment and paid a luxury tax of $281,100.

The Giants played it close to the vest with their first three picks, including Bickford, but then signed third-rounder Jalen Miller for $1.1 million ($501,700 over slot) and fourth-rounder Mac Marshall for $750,000 ($306,200 over slot) and five others for over slot amounts. They went to the full 5 percent threshold and paid $281,100 in luxury taxes.

In keeping with all the additional spending in the 2015 draft, there was an 8.7 percent increase in bonus pools in 2015—a reflection of revenue growth in the baseball industry as a whole of some 8.8 percent. A condition of the Collective Bargaining Agreement provided for an annual increase in draft expenditures to correspond with overall revenue growth. The total amount teams had to spend through 10 rounds, as provided by the overall bonus pool, was $223,834,500.

In all, 14 teams exceeded their bonus pool limits, requiring them to pay a luxury tax, though still no one exceeded the 5 percent limit that would result in a lost first-round pick. In all, 13 players received bonuses in excess of $3 million, 28 topped $2 million and 65 exceeded $1 million or more.

## Highest Unsigned Picks

| Player, Pos., Team (Round) | College | Re-Drafted |
|---|---|---|
| Kyle Funkhouser, rhp, Dodgers (1-S) | * Louisville | Tigers '16 (4) |
| Brady Singer, rhp, Blue Jays (2) | Florida | Not eligible |
| Jonathan Hughes, rhp, Orioles (2) | Georgia Tech | Not eligible |
| Kyle Cody, rhp, Twins (2-S) | * Kentucky | Rangers '16 (6) |
| Nick Shumpert, ss, Tigers (7) | San Jacinto (Texas) JC | Braves '16 (28) |
| Kep Brown, of, Cardinals (10) | Spart. Methodist (S.C.) JC | Not eligible |
| Marrick Crouse, rhp, Blue Jays (11) | San Francisco | Not eligible |
| Chandler Newman, rhp, Indians (11) | Georgia Southern | Not eligible |
| Daniel Perry, ss, Blue Jays (13) | Iowa | Not eligible |
| Jake Kelzer, rhp, Cubs (14) | * Indiana | Phillies '16 (18) |

**TOTAL UNSIGNED PICKS:** Top 5 Rounds (4), Top 10 Rounds (6)

**Returned to same school.*

### IN FOCUS: ANDREW BENINTENDI

Outfielder Andrew Benintendi had a record-breaking senior season at Madera (Ohio) High, hitting .564 with 12 homers, 57 RBIs and 38 stolen bases. He set state career records for runs and hits.

After he was selected in the 31st round of the 2013 draft by the Reds, then hit .276 with minimal power in an injury-plagued freshman season at Arkansas and didn't play in the summer, Benintendi didn't register as a premium prospect for the 2015 draft.

"I never felt like I hit my groove at any point," Benintendi said of his freshman year. "Going from high school to the SEC is a big jump, and I had a lot to learn. I really focused the offseason on getting bigger and stronger before my sophomore year."

By hitting .376 with 20 home runs and 24 stolen bases in a breakout 2015 season, the sophomore-eligible Benintendi catapulted to the seventh pick overall by the Red Sox, who handed him a franchise record $3.59 million bonus.

"Andrew made just an incredible jump, just night and day," Arkansas coach Dave Van Horn said. "Last year was probably the first time ever in his life that he failed a little bit. He took it to heart and went home and worked his butt off."

Benintendi proved his worth after signing, hitting .313 with 11 homers in 54 games in his pro debut.

# 2015 Draft List

**Did not sign. Major leaguers in bold, with first and last years noted. Order of selection indicated in parentheses. For the first five rounds, the peak level of each player is noted.*

## ARIZONA DIAMONDBACKS (1)

1. Dansby Swanson, ss, Vanderbilt University.—(Short-season A)
2. Alex Young, lhp, Texas Christian University.—(Short-season A)
3. Taylor Clarke, rhp, College of Charleston.—(Short-season A)
4. Breckin Williams, rhp, University of Missouri.—(Short-season A)
5. Ryan Burr, rhp, Arizona State University.—(Low A)
6. Tyler Mark, rhp, Concordia (Calif.) University.
7. Francis Christy, c, Palomar (Calif.) JC.
8. Kal Simmons, ss, Kennesaw State University.
9. Pierce Romero, rhp, Santa Barbara (Calif.) CC
10. Joey Armstrong, of, University of Nevada-Las Vegas.
11. Austin Byler, 1b, University of Nevada.
12. Wesley Rodriguez, rhp, George Washington HS, New York.
13. Jason Morozowski, of, Mount Olive (N.C.) College.
14. Luke Lowery, c, East Carolina University.
15. Justin Donatella, rhp, UC San Diego.
16. Zach Nehrir, of, Houston Baptist University.
17. Austin Mason, rhp, The Citadel.
18. Daniel Comstock, c, Menlo (Calif.) College.
19. Jacy Cave, of, New Mexico JC.
20. Will Lowman, lhp, Kennesaw State University.
21. Alexis Olmeda, c, Yavapai (Ariz.) JC.
22. Zach Hoffpauir, of, Stanford University.
23. Logan Soole, of, Monarch HS, Louisville, Colo.
24. Bryant Holtmann, lhp, Florida State University.
25. Stephen Dezzi, of, University of Tampa.
26. Kirby Bellow, lhp, University of Texas.
27. Cameron Gann, rhp, Stephen F. Austin State University.
28. *Jesse Wilkening, c, Hanover Central HS, Cedar Lake, Ind.
29. Keegan Long, rhp, St. Joseph's (Ind.) College.
30. Jeff Smith, 2b, Missouri Baptist University.
31. *Vance Vizcaino, 3b, Stetson University.
32. *Bryan Hoeing, rhp, Batesville (Ind.) HS.
33. Luis Silverio, of, Eastern Florida State JC.
34. Jake Peevyhouse, of, Arizona State University.
35. Quinnton Mack, of, New Mexico State University.
36. Cameron Smith, lhp, Texas Tech.
37. Max Brown, of, Kansas State University.
38. Josh Anderson, 3b-of, Florida International University.
39. *Georgie Salem, of, University of Alabama.
40. Tucker Ward, rhp, University of Mobile (Ala.).

DRAFT DROP *Son of Turner Ward, major leaguer (1990-2001)*

## ATLANTA BRAVES (15)

1. Kolby Allard, lhp, San Clemente (Calif.) HS.—(Rookie)
1. Mike Soroka, rhp, Bishop Carroll HS, Calgary, Alberta (Compensation for loss of Ervin Santana as free agent—28th).—(Rookie)
1. Austin Riley, 3b, DeSoto Central HS, Southaven, Miss. (Competitive balance Round 'A' pick—41st; obtained in trade with Padres).—(Rookie)
2. Lucas Herbert, c, San Clemente (Calif.) HS.—(Rookie)
2. A.J. Minter, lhp, Texas A&M University (Competitive balance Round 'B' pick—75th; obtained in trade with Diamondbacks).--DNP
3. Anthony Guardado, rhp, Nogales HS, La Puente, Calif.—(Rookie)
4. Josh Graham, rhp, University of Oregon.—(Rookie)
5. Ryan Clark, rhp, UNC Greensboro.—(Rookie)
6. Matt Withrow, rhp, Texas Tech.

DRAFT DROP *Brother of Chris Withrow, first-round draft pick, Dodgers (2007); major leaguer (2013-14)*

7. Patrick Weigel, rhp, University of Houston.
8. Ryan Lawlor, lhp, University of Georgia.
9. Taylor Lewis, rhp, University of Florida.
10. Stephen Moore, rhp, U.S. Naval Academy.
11. Grayson Jones, rhp, Shelton State (Ala.) CC
12. Justin Ellison, of, Western Oklahoma State JC.
13. Chase Johnson-Mullins, lhp, Shelton State (Ala.) CC.
14. Trey Keegan, c, Bowling Green State University.
15. Brad Keller, of, Crest HS, Shelby, N.C.
16. Trevor Belicek, lhp, Texas A&M University-Corpus Christi.
17. Evan Phillips, rhp, UNC Wilmington.
18. Gilbert Suarez, rhp, San Ysidro HS, San Diego.
19. Sean McLaughlin, rhp, University of Georgia.
20. Jarret Hellinger, lhp, Ola HS, McDonough, Ga.
21. Kurt Hoekstra, 2b, Western Michigan University.
22. Dalton Geekie, rhp, Georgia Highlands JC.
23. Taylor Cockrell, rhp, State College of Florida-Manatee.
24. Jake Lanning, 3b, College of the Holy Cross.
25. Jonathan Morales, c, Miami-Dade JC.
26. Ben Libuda, lhp, Worcester State (Mass.) College.
27. Robby Nesovic, 3b, UC Santa Barbara.
28. *Curtiss Pomeroy, rhp, Georgetown University.
29. Collin Yelich, c, Sam Houston State University.

DRAFT DROP *Brother of Christian Yelich, first-round draft pick, Marlins (2010); major leaguer (2013-15)*

30. *Doug Still, lhp, Jefferson (Mo.) JC.
31. Matt Custred, rhp, Texas Tech.
32. *D.J. Neal, of, Stephenson HS, Stone Mountain, Ga.
33. *Terry Godwin, of, Callaway HS, Hogansville, Ga.
34. *Carter Hall, ss, Wesleyan HS, Norcross, Ga.
35. *Chase Smartt, c, Charles Henderson HS, Troy, Ala.
36. *Luis Lopez, 2b, Colegio Catolico Notre Dame HS, Caguas, P.R.

DRAFT DROP *Son of Luis Lopez, major leaguer (2001-04)*

37. *Jackson Webb, ss, Johnson Ferry Christian Academy, Marietta, Ga.
38. *Liam Scafariello, 1b, Southington (Conn.) HS.
39. *Jeremy Pena, ss, Classical HS, Providence, R.I.

DRAFT DROP *Son of Geronimo Pena, major leaguer (1990-96)*

40. *John Stewart, 3b, Greenwich Central HS, Greenwich, N.Y.

California lefty Kolby Allard led off a high school heavy draft for the rebuilding Braves

ALYSON BOYER RODE

## BALTIMORE ORIOLES (28)

1. D.J. Stewart, of, Florida State University.—(Short-season A)
1. Ryan Mountcastle, ss, Hagerty HS, Oviedo, Fla. (Compensation for loss of Nelson Cruz as free agent—36th).—(Short-season A)
2. *Jonathan Hughes, rhp, Flowery Branch (Ga.) HS.

DRAFT DROP *Attended Georgia Tech*

3. Garrett Cleavinger, lhp, University of Oregon.—(Short-season A)
4. Ryan McKenna, of, St. Thomas Aquinas HS, Dover, N.H.—(Rookie)
5. Jason Heinrich, of, River Ridge HS, New Port Richey, Fla.—(Rookie)
6. Jay Flaa, rhp, North Dakota State University.
7. Gray Fenter, rhp, West Memphis (Ark.) HS.
8. Seamus Curran, 1b, Agawam (Mass.) HS.
9. Jaylen Ferguson, of, Arlington (Texas) HS.
10. Reid Love, lhp, East Carolina University.
11. Ryan Meisinger, rhp, Radford University.
12. Robert Strader, lhp, University of Louisville.
13. Cedric Mullins, of, Campbell University.
14. Drew Turbin, 2b, Dallas Baptist University.
15. Chris Shaw, c, University of Oklahoma.
16. Mike Odenwaelder, of, Amherst (Mass.) College.
17. Branden Becker, ss, Cajon HS, San Bernardino, Calif.
18. Nick Vespi, lhp, Palm Beach State (Fla.) JC.
19. Jerry McClanahan, c, UC Irvine.
20. *Adam Walton, ss, University of Illinois.
21. Juan Echevarria, rhp, Osceola HS, Seminole, Fla.
22. Tristan Graham, of, Northeast Texas CC.
23. Will Dennis, lhp, Seattle University.
24. Kirvin Moesquit, 3b, Seminole State (Fla.) JC.
25. Steve Laurino, 1b, Marist College.
26. Rocky McCord, rhp, Auburn University.
27. Stuart Levy, c, Arkansas State University.
28. Christian Turnipseed, rhp, Georgia Gwinnett College.
29. *Gabriel Garcia, c, Montverde (Fla.) Academy.
30. Andrew Elliot, rhp, Wright State University.
31. Will Shepley, lhp, UNC Wilmington.
32. *Cody Morris, rhp, Reservoir HS, Fulton, Md.
33. Steven Klimek, rhp, St. Bonaventure University.
34. Kory Groves, rhp, Cal State Monterey Bay.
35. *Guillermo Trujillo, rhp, Oral Roberts University.
36. Xavier Borde, lhp, University of Arizona.
37. *Jake Pries, of, J Serra HS, San Juan Capistrano, Calif.

DRAFT DROP *Son of Jeff Pries, first-round draft pick, Yankees (1984)*

38. Jack Graham, 2b, Slippery Rock (Pa.) University.
39. Frank Crinella, 3b, Merrimack (Mass.) College.
40. Mike Costello, rhp, Post (Conn.) University.

## BOSTON RED SOX (6)

1. Andrew Benintendi, of, University of Arkansas.—(Low A)
2. (Choice forfeited for signing Pablo Sandoval as free agent).
2. (Forfeited competitive balance Round 'B' pick for signing Hanley Ramirez as free agent).
3. Austin Rei, c, University of Washington.—(Short-season A)
4. Tate Matheny, of, Missouri State University.—(Short-season A)

DRAFT DROP *Son of Mike Matheny, major leaguer (1994-2006); major league manager (2012-15)*

5. Jagger Rusconi, ss, West Ranch HS, Santa Clarita, Calif.—(Rookie)
6. Travis Lakins, rhp, Ohio State University.
7. Ben Taylor, rhp, University of South Alabama.
8. Logan Allen, lhp, IMG Academy, Bradenton, Fla.
9. Tucker Tubbs, 1b, University of Memphis.
10. Mitchell Gunsolus, 3b, Gonzaga University.
11. Nick Hamilton, of, Lockport (N.Y.) HS.
12. Kevin Kelleher, rhp, University of New Orleans.
13. Matt Kent, lhp, Texas A&M University.
14. Bobby Poyner, lhp, University of Florida.
15. Jerry Downs, of, St. Thomas (Fla.) University.
16. Marc Brakeman, rhp, Stanford University.
17. Chad De la Guerra, 2b, Grand Canyon University.
18. *James Nelson, ss, Redan HS, Stone Mountain, Ga.
19. Logan Boyd, lhp, Sam Houston State University.
20. Yomar Valentin, ss, Puerto Rico Baseball Academy, Florida, P.R.

DRAFT DROP *Son of Jose Valentin, major leaguer (1992-2007)*

21. Danny Zandona, rhp, Cal Poly.
22. Max Watt, rhp, Lynn (Fla.) University.
23. Kyri Washington, of, Longwood University.
24. Brad Stone, lhp, North Carolina State University.
25. Andrew Noviello, c, Bridgewater-Raynham Regional HS, Bridgewater, Mass.
26. *Kevin Ginkel, rhp, Southwestern (Calif.) JC.
27. *Saige Jenco, of, Virginia Tech.
28. *Steve Mangrum, 3b, Western Albemarle HS, Crozet, Va.
29. *Will Stillman, rhp, Wofford University.
30. *Jack Conley, c, Leesville Road HS, Raleigh, N.C.
31. Nick Duron, rhp, Clark (Wash.) JC.
32. *Clate Schmidt, rhp, Clemson University.
33. *Cal Smith, 2b, Fort Worth Christian HS, Richland Hills, Texas.
34. *Nick Lovullo, ss, College of the Holy Cross.

DRAFT DROP *Son of Torey Lovullo, major leaguer (1988-99); major league manager (2015)*

35. Tyler Spoon, of, University of Arkansas.
36. Trevor Kelley, rhp, University of North Carolina.
37. Adam Lau, rhp, University of Alabama-Birmingham.
38. *C.J. Ballard, of, Pike County HS, Zebulon, Ga.
39. *Daniel Reyes, of, Mater Academy Charter HS, Hialeah Gardens, Fla.
40. *D.J. Artis, of, Southeast Guilford HS, Greensboro, N.C.

## CHICAGO CUBS (8)

1. Ian Happ, of, University of Cincinnati.—(Low A)
2. Donnie Dewees, of, University of North

Florida.—(Short-season A)
3. Bryan Hudson, lhp, Alton (Ill.) HS.—(Rookie)
4. D.J. Wilson, of, Canton South HS, Canton, Ohio.—(Rookie)
5. Ryan Kellogg, lhp, Arizona State University.—(Short-season A)
6. David Berg, rhp, UCLA.
7. Craig Brooks, rhp, Catawba (N.C.) College.
8. Preston Morrison, rhp, Texas Christian University.
9. Tyler Peitzmeier, lhp, Cal State Fullerton.
10. Vimael Machin, ss, Virginia Commonwealth University.
11. Matt Rose, 3b, Georgia State University.
12. P.J. Higgins, 2b, Old Dominion University.
13. Kyle Twomey, lhp, University of Southern California.
14. *Jake Kelzer, rhp, Indiana University.
15. Scott Effross, rhp, Indiana University.
16. Michael Foster, of, Northeastern University.
17. Casey Bloomquist, rhp, Cal Poly.
18. *John Cresto, 3b, Cathedral Catholic HS, San Diego.
19. Kyle Miller, rhp, Florida Atlantic University.
20. Blake Headley, 3b, University of Nebraska.
21. Jared Cheek, rhp, University of Georgia.
22. Alex Bautista, of, Lindsey Wilson (Ky.) College.
23. John Williamson, lhp, Rice University.
24. Sutton Whiting, ss, University of Louisville.
25. Marcus Mastrobuoni, c, Cal State Stanislaus.
26. *Jared Padgett, lhp, Graceville (Fla.) HS.
27. Angelo Amendolare, 2b, Jacksonville University.
28. *Delvin Zinn, ss, Pontotoc (Miss.) HS.
29. Ian Rice, c, University of Houston.
30. Tyler Payne, c, West Virginia State University.
31. Daniel Spingola, of, Georgia Tech.
32. *Fitz Stadler, rhp, Glenbrook South HS, Glenview, Ill.
33. M.T. Minacci, rhp, Tallahassee, Fla.
34. *Cody Hawken, of, Union HS, Camas, Wash.
35. *Taylor Jones, 1b, Gonzaga University.
36. *Alonzo Jones, ss, Columbus (Ga.) HS.
37. Donnie Cimino, of, Wesleyan (Conn.) University.
38. *Rayne Supple, rhp, Champlain Valley Union HS, Hinesburg, Vt.
39. *John Kilichowski, lhp, Vanderbilt University.
40. *Domenic DeRenzo, c, Central Catholic HS, Pittsburgh.

## CHICAGO WHITE SOX (7)

1. Carson Fulmer, rhp, Vanderbilt University.—(High A)
2. (Choice forfeited for signing David Robertson as free agent).
3. (Choice forfeited for signing Melky Cabrera as free agent)
4. Zack Erwin, lhp, Clemson University.—(Low A)
5. Jordan Stephens, rhp, Rice University.—(Rookie)
6. Corey Zangari, 1b, Carl Albert HS, Midwest City, Okla.
7. Blake Hickman, rhp, University of Iowa.
8. Casey Schroeder, c, Coastal Carolina University.
9. Ryan Hinchley, lhp, University of Illinois-Chicago.
10. Jackson Glines, of, University of Michigan.
11. Danny Dopico, rhp, Florida International University.
12. Seby Zavala, c, San Diego State University.
13. Ryan Riga, lhp, Ohio State University.
14. Tyler Sullivan, of, University of the Pacific.
15. Chris Comito, rhp, Norwalk (Iowa) HS.
16. Brandon Quintero, rhp, Cal State Los Angeles.
17. Sikes Orvis, 1b, University of Mississippi.
18. Dante Flores, 2b, University of Southern California.
19. Frank Califano, of, Youngstown State University.
20. Jacob Cooper, c, Modesto (Calif.) JC.
21. Landon Lassiter, of, University of North Carolina.
22. Danny Mendick, ss, University of Massachusetts-Lowell.
23. Dylan Barrow, rhp, University of Tampa.
24. Brandon Magallones, rhp, Northwestern University.
25. Richard McWilliams, rhp, Cal Poly Pomona.
26. Grant Massey, ss, Lipscomb University.
27. Alex Katz, lhp, St. John's University.
28. Bradley Strong, 3b, Western Carolina University.
29. Jake Fincher, of, North Carolina State University.
30. Jack Charleston, rhp, Faulkner (Ala.) University.
31. David Walker, 2b, Grand Canyon University.
32. Taylore Cherry, rhp, University of North Carolina.
33. Johnathan Frebis, lhp, Middle Tennessee State University.
34. Drew Hasler, rhp, Valparaiso University.
35. *D.J. King, ss, Hillsborough (Fla.) CC.
36. *Michael Hickman, c, Seven Lakes HS, Katy, Texas.
37. *Garvin Alston, lhp, Mountain Pointe HS, Phoenix.

**DRAFT DROP** *Son of Garvin Alston, major leaguer (1996)*

38. *Cody Staab, of, College Station (Texas) HS.
39. *Jalin McMillan, 3b, Simeon Career Academy, Chicago.
40. *Joseph Reinsdorf, 2b, New Trier HS, Winnetka, Ill.

**DRAFT DROP** *Grandson of Jerry Reinsdorf, owner, White Sox (1981-2015)*

## CINCINNATI REDS (10)

1. Tyler Stephenson, c, Kennesaw Mountain HS, Kennesaw, Ga.—(Rookie)
2. Antonio Santillian, rhp, Seguin HS, Arlington, Texas.—(Rookie)
2. Tanner Rainey, rhp, University of West Alabama (Competitive balance Round 'B' pick—71st).—(Rookie)
3. Blake Trahan, ss, University of Louisiana-Lafayette.—(High A)
4. Miles Gordon, of, St. Ignatius of Loyola Catholic SS, Oakville, Ontario.—(Rookie)
5. Ian Kahaloa, rhp, Campbell HS, Ewa Beach, Hawaii.—(Rookie)
6. Jimmy Herget, rhp, University of South Florida.
7. Jordan Ramsey, rhp, UNC Wilmington.
8. Mitch Piatnik, ss, State College of Florida-Manatee.
9. Sarkis Ohanian, rhp, Duke University.
10. Zach Shields, of, UNC Wilmington.
11. Brantley Bell, ss, State College of Florida-Manatee.

**DRAFT DROP** *Son of Jay Bell, first-round draft pick, Twins (1984); major leaguer (1986-2003)*

12. Alexis Diaz, rhp, Juan Jose Maunez HS, Naguabo, P.R.
13. Andrew Jordan, rhp, Hunter Huss HS, Gastonia, N.C.
14. Austin Orewiler, rhp, Rice University.
15. Blake Butler, 2b, College of Charleston.
16. Jake Johnson, rhp, University of Southeastern Louisiana.
17. J.D. Salmon-Williams, 2b, David Suzuki SS, Brampton, Ontario.
18. Isaac Anesty, lhp, Our Lady of Lourdes Catholic HS, Guelph, Ontario.
19. *Mike Salvatore, rhp-ss, Ewing (N.J.) HS.
20. Rock Rucker, lhp, University of Auburn-Montgomery.
21. Satchel McElroy, of, Clear Creek HS, League City, Texas.
22. Darren Shred, rhp, St. Roch Catholic SS, Brampton, Ontario.
23. Ed Charlton, of, New Jersey Tech.
24. Joe Zanghi, rhp, Cumberland County (N.J.) CC.
25. James Vasquez, 1b, University of Central Florida.
26. *Dwanya Williams-Sutton, of, Greenfield School, Wilson, N.C.
27. Alejo Lopez, ss, Greenway HS, Phoenix.
28. *Ronnie Rossomando, rhp, Bunnell HS, Stratford, Conn.
29. *Elih Marrero, c, Coral Gables (Fla.) HS.

**DRAFT DROP** *Son of Eli Marrero, major leaguer (1997-2006)*

30. *Joe Purritano, 1b, Dartmouth University.
31. *Ethan Skender, 2b, Metamora Township HS, Metamora, Ill.
32. *Will McAffer, rhp, Sentinel SS, West Vancouver, B.C.
33. *Tyler Peyton, rhp, University of Iowa.
34. Connor Bennett, rhp, Buford (Ga.) HS.
35. *Alex Krupa, of, Iowa Western CC.
36. Mitchell Tripp, rhp, University of Central Florida.
37. *Riley Thompson, rhp, Christian Academy of Louisville, Louisville, Ky.
38. *Matt Kroon, 3b, Horizon HS, Scottsdale, Ariz.

**DRAFT DROP** *Son of Marc Kroon, major leaguer (1995-2004)*

39. *Kevin Santiago, ss, Rafaelina E. Lebron Flores HS, Patillas, P.R.
40. *Jonathon Armwood, 1b, St. Edward's (Texas) University.

## CLEVELAND INDIANS (19)

1. Brady Aiken, lhp, IMG Academy, Bradenton, Fla.—DNP

**DRAFT DROP** *First overall draft pick, Astros (2014)*

1. Triston McKenzie, rhp, Royal Palm Beach (Fla.) HS. (Competitive balance Round 'A' pick—42nd).—(Rookie)
2. Juan Hillman, lhp, Olympia HS, Orlando, Fla.—(Rookie)
3. Mark Mathias, 2b, Cal Poly.—(Short-season A)
4. Tyler Krieger, ss, Clemson University.—DNP
5. Ka'ai Tom, of, University of Kentucky.—(Short-season A)
6. Jonas Wyatt, rhp, Quartz Hill (Calif.) HS.
7. Nathan Lukes, of, Cal State Sacramento.
8. Justin Garza, rhp, Cal State Fullerton.
9. Devon Stewart, rhp, Canisius University.
10. Billy Strode, lhp, Florida State University.
11. *Chandler Newman, rhp, Richmond Hill (Ga.) HS.
12. Ryan Perez, lhp, Judson (Ill.) University.
13. Daniel Salters, c, Dallas Baptist University.
14. Matt Esparza, rhp, UC Irvine.
15. *Daniel Sprinkle, rhp, White Hall (Ark.) HS.
16. *Cobie Vance, 2b, Pine Forest HS, Fayetteville, N.C.
17. *Nick Madrigal, ss, Elk Grove (Calif.) HS.
18. Anthony Miller, 1b, Johnson County (Kan.) CC.
19. Todd Isaacs, of, Palm Beach State (Fla.) CC.
20. Luke Wakamatsu, ss, Keller (Texas) HS.

**DRAFT DROP** *Son of Don Wakamatsu, major leaguer (1991); major league manager (2009-10)*

21. Brock Hartson, rhp, University of Texas-San Antonio.
22. *Garrett Benge, 3b, Cowley County (Kan.) CC.
23. *Chad Smith, rhp, Wallace State-Hanceville (Ala.) CC.
24. Sam Haggerty, 2b, University of New Mexico.
25. Connor Marabell, of, Jacksonville University.
26. *A.J. Graffanino, ss, Northwest Christian HS, Phoenix.

**DRAFT DROP** *Son of Tony Graffanino, major leaguer (1996-2009)*

27. *Austin Rubick, rhp, Buena HS, Ventura, Calif.
28. Jack Goihl, c, Augustana (S.D.) College.
29. Christian Meister, rhp, Federal Way, Wash.
30. *Chandler Day, rhp, Watkins Memorial HS, Pataskala, Ohio.
31. *Dillon Persinger, 2b, Golden West (Calif.) JC.
32. *Jacob Hill, lhp, University of San Diego.

**DRAFT DROP** *Brother of David Hill, fourth-round draft pick, Rockies (2015)*

33. *Garrett Wolforth, c, Concordia Lutheran HS, Tomball, Texas.
34. *Andrew Cabezas, rhp, Mater Academy Charter HS, Hialeah Gardens, Fla.
35. *Cade Tremie, c, New Waverly (Texas) HS.

**DRAFT DROP** *Son of Chris Tremie, major leaguer (1995-2004)*

36. Ryan Colegate, rhp, Ohio Dominican University.
37. *Lucas Humphal, rhp, Texas State University.
38. *Braden Webb, rhp, Owasso, Okla.
39. *Tristin English, rhp, Pike County HS, Zebulon, Ga.
40. *Hunter Parsons, rhp, Parkside HS, Salisbury, Md.

## COLORADO ROCKIES (2)

1. Brendan Rodgers, ss, Lake Mary (Fla.) HS.—(Rookie)
1. Mike Nikorak, rhp, Stroudsburg (Pa.) HS (Compensation for loss of Michael Cuddyer as free agent—27th).—(Rookie)
1. Tyler Nevin, 3b, Poway (Calif.) HS (Competitive balance Round 'A' pick—38th).—(Rookie)

**DRAFT DROP** *Son of Phil Nevin, first overall draft pick, Astros (1992); major leaguer (1995-2006)*

2. Peter Lambert, rhp, San Dimas (Calif.) HS.—(Rookie)
3. Javier Medina, rhp, Sahuaro HS, Tucson, Ariz.—(Rookie)
4. David Hill, rhp, University of San Diego.—(Short-season A)

**DRAFT DROP** *Brother of Jacob Hill, 32nd-round draft pick, Indians (2015)*

5. Parker French, rhp, University of Texas.—(Rookie)
6. Jack Wynkoop, lhp, University of South Carolina.
7. Brian Mundell, 1b, Cal Poly.
8. Colin Welmon, rhp, Loyola Marymount University.
9. Trey Killian, rhp, University of Arkansas.
10. Cole Anderson, of, Rocky Mountain HS, Fort Collins, Colo.
11. Michael Zimmerman, lhp, Gulf Coast HS, Naples, Fla.
12. Justin Lawrence, rhp, Daytona State (Fla.) JC.
13. Mylz Jones, ss, Cal State Bakersfield.
14. Sam Thoele, rhp, University of Arkansas-Little Rock.
15. Sam Hilliard, of-lhp, Wichita State University.
16. Ryan McCormick, rhp, St. John's University.
17. Collin Ferguson, 1b, St. Mary's (Calif.) University.
18. Chris Keck, 3b, UCLA.
19. Daniel Koger, lhp, University of Alabama-Huntsville.
20. Bobby Stahel, of, University of Southern California.
21. Logan Cozart, rhp, Ohio University.
22. Eric Toole, of, University of Iowa.
23. Steven Leonard, c, Campbell University.
24. James McMahon, rhp, University of Southern Mississippi.
25. Scotty Burcham, ss, Cal State Sacramento.
26. Drasen Johnson, rhp, University of Illinois.
27. Campbell Wear, c, UC Santa Barbara.
28. Tyler Follis, ss, University of North Dakota.
29. Hayden Jones, rhp, Valdosta State (Ga.) University.
30. Matt Meier, rhp, Lindenwood (Mo.) University.
31. Hector Moreta, rhp, Calusa Prep HS, Miami.
32. Jensen Park, of, University of Northern Colorado.
33. *Wyatt Cross, c, Legacy HS, Broomfield, Colo.
34. *Michael Benson, c, Rancho Buena Vista HS, Vista, Calif.
35. *Ryan Madden, rhp, Fairview HS, Boulder, Colo.
36. *Andy Pagnozzi, rhp, Fayetteville (Ark.) HS.

**DRAFT DROP** *Son of Tom Pagnozzi, major leaguer (1987-98)*

37. *Marc Mumper, ss, Mountain Vista HS, Highlands Ranch, Colo.
38. *Jake Singer, 2b, Torrey Pines HS, San Diego.
39. *Brent Schwarz, rhp, Regis Jesuit HS, Aurora, Colo.
40. *Alexander Carter, 1b, Georgetown University.

## DETROIT TIGERS (25)

1. Beau Burrows, rhp, Weatherford (Texas) HS.—(Rookie)
1. Christin Stewart, of, University of Tennessee (Compensation for loss of Max Scherzer as free agent—34th).—(Low A)
2. Tyler Alexander, lhp, Texas Christian University.—(Short-season A)
3. Drew Smith, rhp, Dallas Baptist University.—(Low A)
4. Kade Scivicque, c, Louisiana State University.—(Low A)
5. Cam Gibson, of, Michigan State University.

**DRAFT DROP** *Son of Kirk Gibson, first-round draft pick, Tigers (1978); major leaguer (1979-95); major league manager (2010-14)*

6. Matt Hall, lhp, Missouri State University.
7. *Nick Shumpert, ss, Highlands Ranch (Colo.) HS.

**DRAFT DROP** *Son of Terry Shumpert, major leaguer (1990-2003)*

8. Dominic Moreno, rhp, Texas Tech.
9. Trey Teakell, rhp, Texas Christian University.
10. Cole Bauml, of, Northern Kentucky University.
11. Jake Shull, rhp, Fresno State University.
12. Kyle Dowdy, rhp, University of Houston.
13. Josh Lester, 3b, University of Missouri.
14. A.J. Simcox, ss, University of Tennessee.
15. Keaton Jones, ss, Texas Christian University.
16. Alec Kisena, rhp, Edmonds (Wash.) CC.
17. *Grant Wolfram, lhp, Hamilton (Mich.) HS.
18. Joey Havrilak, of, University of Akron.
19. *Cam Vieaux, lhp, Michigan State University.
20. Logan Longwith, rhp, Tennessee Wesleyan College.
21. Tanner Donnels, 1b, Loyola Marymount

University.

DRAFT DROP *Son of Chris Donnels, first-round draft pick, Mets (1987); major leaguer (1991-2002)*

22. Toller Boardman, lhp, University of New Mexico.
23. Ryan Milton, rhp, University of Southern Mississippi.
24. Mike Vinson, rhp, University of Florida.
25. Ryan Castellanos, rhp, Nova Southeastern (Fla.) University.

DRAFT DROP *Brother of Nick Castellanos, first-round draft pick, Tigers (2010); major leaguer (2013-15)*

26. Taylor Hicks, rhp, University of Georgia.
27. Tyler Servais, c, Princeton University.

DRAFT DROP *Son of Scott Servais, major leaguer (1991-2001)*

28. Pat MacKenzie, 2b, Central Michigan University.
29. *Dayton Dugas, of, Sam Houston Houston HS, Moss Bluff, La.
30. *Cole McKay, rhp, Smithson Valley HS, Spring Branch, Texas.
31. Blaise Salter, 1b, Michigan State University.

DRAFT DROP *Grandson of Bill Freehan, major leaguer (1961-76)*

32. *Trey Dawson, ss, Hurricane (W.Va.) HS.
33. *Nick Dalesandro, c, Joliet Catholic Academy, Joliet, Ill.

DRAFT DROP *Son of Mark Dalesandro, major leaguer (1994-2001)*

34. *Andrew McWilliam, 3b, San Diego Mesa JC.
35. *Connor Lungwitz, rhp, Maize (Kan.) HS.
36. *Daniel Pinero, ss, University of Virginia.
37. *Andrew Naderer, lhp, Grand Canyon University.
38. *Bryant Harris, of, Luella HS, Locust Grove, Ga.
39. *Travis Howard, rhp, Marana HS, Tucson, Ariz.
40. *Jackson Kowar, rhp, Charlotte Christian HS, Charlotte, N.C.

## HOUSTON ASTROS (4)

1. Alex Bregman, ss, Louisiana State University (Special compensation for failure to sign 2014 first-round pick Brady Aiken).—(High A)
1. Kyle Tucker, of, H.B. Plant HS, Tampa.—(Rookie)

DRAFT DROP *Brother of Preston Tucker, major leaguer (2015)*

1. Daz Cameron, of, Eagle's Landing Christian Academy, McDonough, Ga. (Competitive balance Round 'A' pick—37th; obtained in trade with Marlins).—(Rookie)

DRAFT DROP *Son of Mike Cameron, major leaguer (1995-2011)*

2. Thomas Eshelman, rhp, Cal State Fullerton.—(Low A)
3. Riley Ferrell, rhp, Texas Christian University.—(Low A)
4. Anthony Hermelyn, c, University of Oklahoma.—(Short-season A)
5. Trent Thornton, rhp, University of North Carolina.—(Short-season A)
6. Nestor Muriel, of, Carlos Beltran Academy, Florida, P.R.
7. Michael Freeman, lhp, Oklahoma State University.
8. Garrett Stubbs, c, University of Southern California.
9. Zac Person, lhp, Louisiana State University.
10. Scott Weathersby, rhp, University of Mississippi.
11. Patrick Sandoval, lhp, Mission Viejo (Calif.) HS.
12. Myles Straw, of, St. John's River (Fla.) JC.
13. Kevin McCanna, rhp, Rice University.
14. Johnny Sewald, of, Arizona State University.
15. Pat Porter, of, Ohio State University.
16. Adam Whitt, rhp, University of Nevada.
17. Justin Garcia, of, Nova Southeastern (Fla.) University.
18. Kevin Martir, c, University of Maryland.
19. Drew Ferguson, of, Belmont University.
20. Makay Nelson, rhp, JC of Southern Idaho.
21. Alex Winkelman, lhp, Southeast Missouri State University.
22. *Cole Sands, rhp, North Florida Christian HS, Tallahassee, Fla.
23. Matt Bower, lhp, Washington State University.
24. Chris Murphy, rhp, Millersville (Pa.) University.
25. Jorge Martinez, c, Carlos Beltran Academy, Florida, P.R.
26. Ralph Garza, rhp, University of Oklahoma.
27. *James Carter, rhp, UC Santa Barbara.
28. Zac Grotz, rhp, Embry-Riddle (Fla.) University.
29. Brooks Marlow, 2b, University of Texas.
30. Bobby Wernes, 3b, University of Arkansas.
31. Keach Ballard, ss, Oklahoma Baptist University.
32. Aaron Mizell, of, Georgia Southern University.
33. Kolbey Carpenter, 2b, University of Oklahoma.
34. *Conor Biggio, of, University of Notre Dame.

DRAFT DROP *Son of Craig Biggio, first-round draft pick, Astros (1987); major leaguer (1988-2007)*

35. *Kody Clemens, ss, Memorial HS, Hedwig Village, Texas.

DRAFT DROP *Son of Roger Clemens, first-round draft pick, Red Sox (1983); major leaguer (1984-2007)*

36. Ryan Deemes, rhp, Nicholls State University.
37. *Luken Baker, rhp, Oak Ridge HS, Conroe, Texas.
38. *Nick Rivera, 1b, Florida Gulf Coast University.
39. *Alex Vargas, rhp, Monroe (N.Y.) CC.
40. Steve Naemark, lhp, Angelo State (Texas) University.

## KANSAS CITY ROYALS (24)

1. Ashe Russell, rhp, Cathedral Catholic HS, Indianapolis.—(Rookie)
1. Nolan Watson, rhp, Lawrence North HS, Indianapolis (Compensation for loss of James Shields as free agent—33rd).—(Rookie)
2. Josh Staumont, rhp, Azusa Pacific (Calif.) University.—(Rookie)
3. Anderson Miller, of, Western Kentucky University.—(Low A)
4. Garrett Davila, lhp, South Point HS, Belmont, N.C.--DNP
5. Roman Collins, of, Florida Atlantic University.—(Rookie)
6. Cody Jones, of, Texas Christian University.
7. Gabriel Cancel, ss, Padre Anibal Reyes Belen HS, Florida, P.R.
8. Andre Davis, lhp, University of Arkansas-Pine Bluff.
9. Joey Markus, lhp, Indian River (Fla.) JC.
10. Alex Luna, rhp, University of Alabama-Birmingham.
11. Ben Johnson, of, University of Texas.
12. Daniel Concepcion, rhp, Virginia Commonwealth University.
13. Travis Maezes, ss, University of Michigan.
14. Nick Dini, c, Wagner College.
15. *Marquise Doherty, of, Winnetonka HS, Kansas City, Mo.
16. Matt Ditman, rhp, Rice University.
17. Matt Portland, lhp, Northwestern University.
18. Brian Bayliss, rhp, St. Joseph's (Ind.) College.
19. Emmanuel Rivera, ss, Universidad Interamericana (P.R.) JC.
20. *Junior Harding, rhp, Chipola (Fla.) JC.
21. Austin Bailey, ss, University of San Diego.
22. Drew Milligan, lhp, Delta State (Miss.) University.
23. Colton Frabasilio, of, Saint Louis University.
24. Jonathan McCray, 2b, San Bernardino Valley (Calif.) JC.
25. Tyler Carvalho, rhp, Mesa (Ariz.) CC.
26. Alex Close, c, Liberty University.
27. Jacob Bodner, rhp, Xavier University.
28. *Reed Hayes, rhp, Walters State (Tenn.) CC.
29. Mark McCoy, lhp, Rutgers University.
30. Luke Willis, of, George Mason University.
31. Brian Bien, ss, Bowling Green State University.
32. Jake Kalish, lhp, George Mason University.

DRAFT DROP *Brother of Ryan Kalish, major leaguer (2010-14)*

33. Nate Esposito, c, Concordia (Ore.) University.
34. Taylor Ostrich, 1b, Old Dominion University.
35. Trey Stover, ss, University of Hartford.
36. Tanner Stanley, 2b, University of Richmond.

DRAFT DROP *Son of Mike Stanley, major leaguer (1986-2000)*

37. *Jacob Ruder, rhp, Nixa (Mo.) HS.
38. *Dylan Horne, lhp, Walters State (Tenn.) CC.
39. *Billy Endris, of, Florida Atlantic University.
40. *Ford Proctor, c, Monsignor Kelly Catholic HS, Beaumont, Texas.

## LOS ANGELES ANGELS (30)

1. Taylor Ward, c, Fresno State University.—(Low A)
2. Jahmai Jones, of, Wesleyan HS, Norcross, Ga.—(Rookie)

DRAFT DROP *Son of Andre Jones, linebacker, National Football League (1992)*

3. Grayson Long, rhp, Texas A&M University.—(Rookie)
4. Brendon Sanger, of, Florida Atlantic University.—(Rookie)
5. Jared Foster, of, Louisiana State University.—(Rookie)
6. David Fletcher, ss, Loyola Marymount University.
7. Hutton Moyer, 2b, Pepperdine University.

DRAFT DROP *Son of Jamie Moyer, major leaguer (1986-2012)*

8. Kyle Survance, of, University of Houston.
9. Tanner Lubach, c, University of Nebraska.
10. Adam Hofacket, rhp, California Baptist University.
11. Jimmy Barnes, of, Deep Creek HS, Chesapeake, Va.
12. Dalton Blumenfeld, c, Hamilton HS, Los Angeles.
13. Jeff Boehm, of, University of Illinois-Chicago.
14. Ryan Vega, of, El Paso (Texas) CC.
15. Nathan Bates, rhp, Georgia State University.
16. Nathan Bertness, lhp, McLennan (Texas) CC.
17. Sam Pastrone, rhp, Arbor View HS, Las Vegas, Nev.
18. Travis Herrin, rhp, Wabash Valley (Ill.) JC.
19. Aaron Cox, rhp, Gannon (Pa.) University.
20. Kenny Towns, 3b, University of Virginia.
21. Michael Pierson, 3b, Appalachian State University.
22. Ronnie Glenn, lhp, University of Pennsylvania.
23. Tim Arakawa, 2b, Oklahoma State University.
24. Mitch Esser, of, Concordia (Calif.) University.
25. Trever Allen, of, Arizona State University.

DRAFT DROP *Son of Jamie Allen, first-round pick, Twins (1976); major leaguer (1983)*

26. Taylor Cobb, rhp, University of Houston.
27. Sam Koenig, of, University of Wisconsin-Milwaukee.
28. Aaron Rhodes, rhp, University of Florida.
29. Cody Pope, rhp, Eastern New Mexico University.
30. Nick Lynch, 1b, UC Davis.
31. Izaak Silva, c, UC Davis.
32. Conor Lillis-White, lhp, University of British Columbia.
33. Winston Lavendier, lhp, Cal State Dominguez Hills.
34. Nick Flair, 3b, University of Tampa.
35. Jordan Serena, of, Columbia University.
36. Sam McDonnell, of, Navarro (Texas) JC.
37. Josh Delph, of, Florida State University.
38. *Jonah Dipoto, rhp, Newport Harbor HS, Newport Beach, Calif.

DRAFT DROP *Son of Jerry Dipoto, major leaguer (1993-2000); general manager, Angels (2011-15); general manager, Mariners (2015)*

39. Jared Walsh, 1b, University of Georgia.
40. Jacob McDavid, rhp, Oral Roberts University.

## LOS ANGELES DODGERS (27)

1. Walker Buehler, rhp, Vanderbilt University.--DNP
1. *Kyle Funkhouser, rhp, University of Louisville (Compensation for loss of Hanley Ramirez as free agent—35th).

DRAFT DROP *Returned to Louisville*

2. Mitch Hansen, of, Plano (Texas) HS.—(Rookie)
2. Josh Sborz, rhp, University of Virginia (Competitive balance Round 'B' pick—74th; obtained in trade with Orioles).—(High A)

DRAFT DROP *Brother of Jay Sborz, major leaguer (2010)*

3. Philip Pfeifer, lhp, Vanderbilt University.—(Rookie)
4. Willie Calhoun, 2b, Yavapai (Ariz.) JC.—(High A)
5. Brendon Davis, ss, Lakewood (Calif.) HS.—(Rookie)
6. Edwin Rios, 1b, Florida International University.
7. Andrew Sopko, rhp, Gonzaga University.
8. Tommy Bergjans, rhp, Haverford (Pa.) College.
9. Kevin Brown, rhp, Cal State Dominguez Hills.
10. Logan Landon, of, University of Texas-Pan American.
11. Imani Abdullah, rhp, James Madison HS, San Diego.
12. Matt Beaty, c, Belmont University.
13. Michael Boyle, lhp, Radford University.
14. Garrett Kennedy, c, University of Miami.
15. *Garrett Zech, of, Naples (Fla.) HS.
16. Nolan Long, rhp, Wagner College.
17. *Jason Goldstein, c, University of Illinois.
18. Chris Godinez, 2b, Bradley University.
19. *Joe Genord, c, Park Vista Community HS, Lake Worth, Fla.
20. *John Boushelle, rhp, Fayetteville (Ark.) HS.
21. Jake Henson, c, Saint Louis University.
22. Jordan Tarsovich, 2b, Virginia Military Institute.
23. Andrew Istler, rhp, Duke University.
24. Cameron Palmer, rhp, University of Toledo.
25. Rob McDonnell, lhp, University of Illinois.
26. Marcus Crescentini, rhp, Missouri Baptist University.
27. Ivan Vieitez, rhp, Lenoir-Rhyne (N.C.) University.
28. Kyle Garlick, of, Cal Poly Pomona.
29. *Jason Bilous, rhp, Caravel Academy, Bear, Del.
30. Logan Crouse, rhp, Bloomingdale HS, Valrico, Fla.
31. Corey Copping, rhp, University of Oklahoma.
32. Nick Dean, ss, Maryville (Tenn.) College.
33. Adam Bray, rhp, South Dakota State University.
34. Luis Rodriguez, rhp, Calusa Prep HS, Miami.
35. Gage Green, c, Oklahoma State University.
36. Drayton Riekenberg, rhp, Fresno (Calif.) CC.
37. Casey Mullholland, rhp, University of South Florida.
38. Edwin Drexler, of, Grambling State University.
39. Chris Powell, rhp, Cal Poly Pomona.

DRAFT DROP *Son of Dennis Powell, major leaguer (1985-93)*

40. Isaac Anderson, rhp, Wichita State University.

## MIAMI MARLINS (11)

1. Josh Naylor, 1b, St. Joan of Arc Catholic SS, Mississauga, Ontario.—(Rookie)
2. Brett Lilek, lhp, Arizona State University.—(Short-season A)
3. Isaiah White, of, Greenfield School, Wilson, N.C.—(Rookie)
4. Cody Poteet, rhp, UCLA.—(Short-season A)
5. Justin Jacome, lhp, UC Santa Barbara.—(Short-season A)
6. Justin Cohen, c, Riverview HS, Sarasota. Fla.
7. Travis Neubeck, rhp, Indian Hills (Iowa) CC.
8. Chris Paddack, rhp, Cedar Park (Texas) HS.
9. Reilly Hovis, rhp, University of North Carolina.
10. Kelvin Rivas, rhp, Oklahoma Baptist University.
11. Ryan McKay, rhp, Satellite HS, Satellite Beach, Fla.
12. Terry Bennett, of, Atlantic Coast HS, Jacksonville, Fla.
13. R.J. Peace, rhp, Serrano HS, Phelan, Calif.
14. Jordan Hillyer, rhp, Kennesaw State University.
15. Kyle Barrett, of, University of Kentucky.
16. Justin Langley, lhp, University of Wisconsin-Milwaukee.
17. *Max Whitt, ss, Lewis-Clark State (Idaho) College.
18. Kyle Keller, rhp, Southeastern Louisiana University.
19. Curt Britt, rhp, North Carolina State University.
20. Korey Dunbar, c, University of North Carolina.
21. Giovanny Alfonzo, ss, University of Tampa.
22. L.J. Brewster, rhp, University of Hawaii.
23. Trevor Lacosse, lhp, Bryant University.
24. Octavio Arroyo, rhp, San Ysidro HS, San Diego.
25. Alex Fernandez Jr., of, Nova Southeastern (Fla.) University.

DRAFT DROP *Son of Alex Fernandez, first-round draft pick, Brewers (1988); first-round draft pick, White Sox (1990); major leaguer (1990-2000)*

26. Obed Diaz, rhp, Casiano Cepeda HS, Rio Grande, P.R.
27. Taylor Munden, ss, West Virginia University.
28. Jeff Kinley, lhp, Michigan State University.
29. Ben Meyer, rhp, University of Minnesota.
30. Joe Chavez, ss, UC Riverside.
31. *Griffin Conine, of, Pine Crest HS, Fort Lauderdale, Fla.

DRAFT DROP *Son of Jeff Conine, major leaguer (1990-2007)*

32. Kris Goodman, 3b, University of Iowa.
33. Ryley MacEachern, rhp, Stony Brook University.
34. Brandon Rawe, of, Morehead State University.
35. Cameron Newell, of, UC Santa Barbara.
36. Gunnar Kines, lhp, Mount Olive (N.C.) College.

37. *Ruben Cardenas, of, Bishop Alemany HS, Mission Hills, Calif.
38. *C.J. Newsome, of, Columbia (Miss.) HS.
39. *Bucket Goldby, 3b, Yuba City (HS) Calif.
40. Matt Foley, c, Rhode Island College.

## MILWAUKEE BREWERS (16)

1. Trent Clark, of, Richland HS, North Richland Hills, Texas.—(Rookie)
1. Nathan Kirby, lhp, University of Virginia (Competitive balance Round 'A' pick—40th).—(Low A)
2. Cody Ponce, rhp, Cal Poly Pomona.—(Low A)
3. Nash Walters, rhp, Lindale (Texas) HS.—(Rookie)
4. Demi Orimoloye, of, St. Matthew HS, Orleans, Ontario.—(Rookie)
5. Blake Allemand, ss, Texas A&M University.—(Low A)
6. Eric Hanhold, rhp, University of Florida.
7. George Iskenderian, ss, University of Miami.
8. Nate Griep, rhp, Kansas State University.
9. Karsen Lindell, rhp, West Linn (Ore.) HS.
10. Jake Drossner, lhp, University of Maryland.
11. Jose Cuas, ss, University of Maryland.
12. Drake Owenby, lhp, University of Tennessee.
13. Max McDowell, c, University of Connecticut.
14. Tyrone Perry, 1b, Lakeland (Fla.) HS.
15. Zach Taylor, c, Scottsdale (Ariz.) CC.
16. Conor Harber, rhp, University of Oregon.
17. Michael Petersen, rhp, Riverside (Calif.) CC.
18. Gentry Fortuno, rhp, Charles Flanagan HS, Pembroke Pines, Fla.
19. Steven Karkenny, 1b, The Masters (Calif.) College.
20. David Lucroy, rhp, East Carolina University.

**DRAFT DROP** *Brother of Jonathan Lucroy, major leaguer (2010-15)*

21. Jon Olczak, rhp, North Carolina State University.
22. *Willie Schwanke, rhp, Wichita State University.
23. *Donnie Walton, ss, Oklahoma State University.
24. Christian Trent, lhp, University of Mississippi.
25. *Justin Hooper, lhp, De la Salle HS, Concord, Calif.
26. *Jonathan India, ss, American Heritage HS, Delray Beach, Fla.
27. Jon Perrin, rhp, Oklahoma State University.
28. Mitch Ghelfi, c, University of Wisconsin-Milwaukee.

**DRAFT DROP** *Son of Tony Ghelfi, major leaguer (1983)*

29. *Donny Everett, rhp, Clarksville (Tenn.) HS.
30. *Charlie Donovan, ss, Westmont (Ill.) HS.
31. Colton Cross, rhp, Shorter (Ga.) University.
32. *Sean Chandler, rhp, Papillion-La Vista HS, Papillion, Neb.
33. Connor Baits, rhp, UC Santa Barbara.
34. *Tristan Beck, rhp, Corona (Calif.) HS.
35. Quintin Torres-Costa, lhp, University of Hawaii.
36. Jordan Desguin, rhp, Florida Gulf Coast University.
37. *Brandon Gonzalez, of, Cypress (Calif.) JC.
38. Scott Grist, rhp, Texas State University.
39. *Nolan Kingham, rhp, Desert Oasis HS, Enterprise, Nev.
40. Charles Galiano, c, Fordham University.

## MINNESOTA TWINS (5)

1. Tyler Jay, lhp, University of Illinois.—(High A)
2. (Choice forfeited for signing Ervin Santana as free agent)
2. *Kyle Cody, rhp, University of Kentucky (Competitive balance Round 'B' pick—73rd).

**DRAFT DROP** *Returned to Kentucky*

3. Travis Blankenhorn, 3b, Pottsville (Pa.) HS.—(Rookie)
4. Trey Cabbage, 3b, Grainger HS, Rutledge, Tenn.—(Rookie)
5. Alex Robinson, lhp, University of Maryland.—(Rookie)
6. Chris Paul, 1b, University of California.
7. Jovani Moran, lhp, Carlos Beltran Academy, Florida, P.R.
8. Kolton Kendrick, 1b, Oak Forest Academy, Amite, La.
9. LaMonte Wade, of, University of Maryland.
10. Sean Miller, ss, University of South Carolina-Aiken.
11. Kerby Camacho, c, Carlos Beltran Academy, Florida, P.R.
12. Zander Wiel, 1b, Vanderbilt University.
13. Cody Stashak, rhp, St. John's University.
14. A.J. Murray, c, Georgia Tech.
15. Anthony McIver, lhp, University of San Diego.
16. Lean Marrero, of, Leadership Christian Academy, Guaynabo, P.R.
17. Nate Gercken, rhp, Academy of Art (Calif.) University.
18. Daniel Kihle, of, Wichita State University.
19. *Kyle Wilson, rhp, Raymore-Peculiar HS, Peculiar, Mo.
20. *Colton Eastman, rhp, Central Union HS, Fresno, Calif.
21. Kamran Young, of, Cal State Dominguez Hills.
22. *Blake Cederlind, rhp, Merced (Calif.) JC.
23. Alex Perez, ss, Virginia Tech.
24. Jaylin Davis, of, Appalachian State University.
25. Logan Lombana, rhp, Long Beach State University.
26. *Tyler Williams, of, Raymond S. Kellis HS, Glendale, Ariz.
27. *Dalton Sawyer, lhp, University of Minnesota.
28. *Jonathan Engelmann, of, Burlingame (Calif.) HS.
29. Brad Hartong, c, Indiana University.
30. *Greg Popylisen, of, El Paso (Texas) CC.
31. *Tristan Pompey, of, Jean Vanier Catholic SS, Milton, Ontario.

**DRAFT DROP** *Brother of Dalton Pompey, major leaguer (2014-15)*

32. Andrew Vasquez, lhp, Westmont (Calif.) College.
33. *Colin Theroux, c, San Joaquin Delta (Calif.) JC.
34. Brian Olson, c, Seattle University.
35. Hector Lujan, rhp, Westmont (Calif.) College.
36. Rich Condeelis, rhp, University of Pittsburgh.
37. *Jake Irvin, rhp, Jefferson HS, Bloomington, Minn.
38. *Alex McKenna, of, Bishop Alemany HS, Mission Hills, Calif.
39. *Daniel Tillo, lhp, North HS, Sioux City, Iowa.
40. Max Cordy, rhp, UC Davis.

**The Twins selected Illinois closer Tyler Jay at No. 5, ahead of more heralded college arms**

## NEW YORK METS (14)

1. (Choice forfeited for signing Michael Cuddyer as free agent)
2. Desmond Lindsay, of, Out-of-Door-Academy, Sarasota, Fla.—(Short-season A)
3. Max Wotell, lhp, Marvin Ridge HS, Waxhaw, N.C.—(Rookie)
4. David Thompson, 3b, University of Miami.—(Short-season A)
5. Thomas Szapucki, lhp, William T. Dwyer HS, West Palm Beach, Fla.—(Rookie)
6. Chase Ingram, rhp, Hillsborough (Fla.) CC.
7. Corey Taylor, rhp, Texas Tech.
8. Patrick Mazeika, c, Stetson University.
9. Kevin Kaczmarski, of, University of Evansville.
10. Witt Haggard, rhp, Delta State (Miss.) University.
11. Jake Simon, lhp, Ball HS, Galveston, Texas.
12. Joe Shaw, rhp, Dallas Baptist University.
13. P.J. Conlon, lhp, University of San Diego.
14. Vinny Siena, 2b, University of Connecticut.
15. *Thomas Hackimer, rhp, St. John's University.
16. Dillon Becker, rhp, Angelo State (Texas) University.
17. Sixto Torres, lhp, Faith Baptist Christian HS, Brandon, Fla.
18. Jordan Humphreys, rhp, Crystal River (Fla.) HS.
19. *Nic Enright, rhp, The Steward School, Richmond, Va.
20. Thomas McIlraith, rhp, University of Oklahoma.
21. Taylor Henry, lhp, Centenary (La.) College.
22. *Nick Blackburn, rhp, University of Illinois.
23. Kenneth Bautista, of, Puerto Rico Baseball Academy, Gurabo, P.R.
24. *Jordan Verdon, 3b, Granite Hills (Calif.) HS
25. *Dylan King, rhp, Riverdale HS, Murfreesboro, Tenn.
26. *Shane McClanahan, lhp, Cape Coral (Fla.) HS.
27. *Jake Higginbotham, lhp, Buford (Ga.) HS.
28. Anthony Dimino, c, Belmont Abbey (N.C.) College.
29. Seth Davis, lhp, Augustana (Ill.) College.
30. *Jackson Wark, rhp, Bellerose Composite HS, St. Albert, Alberta.
31. *Tanner Dodson, rhp, Jesuit HS, Carmichael, Calif.
32. *Dustin Beggs, rhp, University of Kentucky.
33. *Brendan Illies, c, Puyallup (Wash.) HS.
34. *L.T. Tolbert, rhp, IMG Academy, Bradenton, Fla.
35. *George Thanopoulos, rhp, Columbia University.
36. *Anthony Gordon, of, Terra Nova HS, Pacifica, Calif.
37. *Geoff Hartlieb, rhp, Lindenwood (Mo.) University.
38. *Jacob Wyrick, lhp, Cleveland State (Tenn.) CC.
39. *Chad Luensmann, rhp, Bellwood-Antis HS, Bellwood, Pa.
40. *Nick Conti, 2b, Dr. Phillips HS, Orlando, Fla.

## NEW YORK YANKEES (18)

1. James Kaprielian, rhp, UCLA.—(Short-season A)
1. Kyle Holder, ss, University of San Diego (Compensation for loss of David Robertson as free agent—30th).—(Short-season A)
2. Jeff Degano, lhp, Indiana State University.—(Short-season A)
3. Drew Finley, rhp, Rancho Bernardo HS, San Diego.—(Rookie)
4. Jeff Hendrix, of, Oregon State University.—(Short-season A)
5. Chance Adams, rhp, Dallas Baptist University.—(High A)
6. Brandon Wagner, 2b-3b, Howard (Texas) JC.
7. Jhalan Jackson, of, Florida Southern College.
8. Donny Sands, 3b, Salpointe Catholic HS, Tucson, Ariz.
9. Ryan Krill, 1b, Michigan State University.
10. James Reeves, lhp, The Citadel.
11. Josh Rogers, lhp, University of Louisville.
12. Terrance Robertson, of, Valley Vista HS, Fountain Valley, Calif.
13. Trey Amburgey, of, St. Petersburg (Fla.) JC.
14. Will Carter, rhp, University of Alabama.
15. Bret Marks, rhp, University of Tennessee.
16. Kolton Mahoney, rhp, Brigham Young University.
17. Brody Koerner, rhp, Clemson University.
18. Zach Zehner, of, Cal Poly.
19. Mark Seyler, rhp, San Diego State University.
20. Isiah Gilliam, 1b, Chipola (Fla.) JC.
21. Josh Roeder, rhp, University of Nebraska.
22. Cody Carroll, rhp, University of Southern Mississippi.
23. Garrett Mundell, rhp, Fresno State University.
24. Paddy O'Brien, rhp, UC Santa Barbara.
25. Audie Afenir, c, Oral Roberts University.
26. Icezack Flemming, rhp, Cal State Los Angeles.
27. *Michael Hicks, 1b, Coeur d'Alene (Idaho) HS.
28. David Sosebee, rhp, University of Georgia.
29. Kane Sweeney, 1b, Morehead State University.
30. Chad Martin, rhp, University of Delaware.
31. Hobie Harris, rhp, University of Pittsburgh.
32. Alex Robinett, rhp, U.S. Military Academy.
33. Christian Morris, rhp, Indiana University.
34. *Andrew Miller, lhp, Sterling HS, Somerdale, N.J.
35. Alex Bisacca, rhp, Sam Houston State University.
36. Dustin Cook, rhp, Oklahoma City University.
37. *Matt Schmidt, 3b, Regis Jesuit HS, Aurora, Colo.
38. *Mike Garzillo, 2b, Lehigh University.
39. *Deacon Liput, ss, Oviedo (Fla.) HS.
40. *Will Albertson, c, Catawba (N.C.) College.

## OAKLAND ATHLETICS (23)

1. Richie Martin, ss, University of Florida.—(Short-season A)
2. Mikey White, ss, University of Alabama.–(Low A)
3. Dakota Chalmers, rhp, North Forsyth HS, Cumming, Ga.—(Rookie)
4. Skye Bolt, of, University of North Carolina.—(Short-season A)
5. Kevin Duchene, lhp, University of Illinois.—(Short-season A)
6. Bubba Derby, rhp, San Diego State University.
7. Kyle Friedrichs, rhp, Long Beach State University.
8. Nick Collins, c, Georgetown University.
9. Jared Lyons, lhp, Liberty University.
10. Steven Pallares, of, San Diego State University.
11. James Terrell, of, St. Patrick-St. Vincent HS, Vallejo, Calif.
12. Chris Iriart, 1b, University of Houston.
13. Brett Siddall, of, Canisius University.

**DRAFT DROP** *Son of Joe Siddall, major leaguer (1993-98)*

14. Boomer Biegalski, rhp, Florida State University.
15. Ryan Howell, 2b, University of Nevada.
16. Dustin Hurlbutt, rhp, Tabor (Kan.) College.
17. *Brent Wheatley, rhp, University of Southern California.
18. Brett Sunde, c, Western Michigan University.
19. Seth Brown, 1b, Lewis Clark State (Idaho) College.
20. James Naile, rhp, University of Alabama-Birmingham.
21. Andrew Tomasovich, lhp, Charleston Southern University.
22. *Brady Bramlett, rhp, University of Mississippi.
23. *Eric Senior, of, York Mills Collegiate Institute, Toronto.
24. Heath Bowers, rhp, Campbell University.
25. Evan Manarino, lhp, UC Irvine.
26. Jordan Devencenzi, c, University of Nevada.
27. Xavier Altamirano, rhp, Oral Roberts University.
28. Marc Berube, rhp, University of Pittsburgh.
29. Armando Ruiz, rhp, Alabama State University.
30. Brendan Butler, rhp, Dowling (N.Y.) College.
31. John Gorman, rhp, Boston College.
32. Michael Murray, rhp, Florida Gulf Coast University.
33. Mike Martin, of, Harvard University.
34. Shane Conlon, 1b, Kansas State University.
35. Tim Proudfoot, ss, Texas Tech.
36. *Troy Rallings, rhp, University of Washington.
37. *Andy Cox, lhp, University of Tennessee.
38. *Chris Cullen, c, West Forsyth HS, Cumming, Ga.
39. *Greg Fettes, c, University of Kentucky.
40. *Nick Maton, ss, Glenwood HS, Chatham, Ill.

## PHILADELPHIA PHILLIES (9)

1. Cornelius Randolph, ss, Griffin (Ga.) HS.—(Rookie)
2. Scott Kingery, 2b, University of Arizona.—(Low A)
3. Lucas Williams, ss, Dana Hills HS, Dana Point, Calif.—(Rookie)
4. Kyle Martin, 1b, University of South Carolina.—(Low A)
5. Bailey Falter, lhp, Chino Hills (Calif.) HS.—(Rookie)
6. Tyler Gilbert, lhp, University of Southern California.
7. Luke Leftwich, rhp, Wofford University.

DRAFT DROP *Son of Phil Leftwich, major leaguer (1993-96) • Grandson of Tom Timmerman, major leaguer (1969-74)*

8. Greg Pickett, of, Legend HS, Parker, Colo.
9. Mark Laird, of, Louisiana State University.
10. Josh Tobias, 3b, University of Florida.
11. Edgar Cabral, c, Mount San Antonio (Calif.) JC.
12. Skylar Hunter, rhp, The Citadel.
13. Zach Coppola, of, South Dakota State University.
14. Austin Bossart, c, University of Pennsylvania.
15. Dylan Bosheers, ss, Tennessee Tech.
16. Brendon Hayden, 1b, Virginia Tech.
17. Kenny Koplove, rhp, Duke University.

DRAFT DROP *Brother of Mike Koplove, major leaguer (2001-07)*

18. Greg Brodzinski, c, Barry (Fla.) University.
19. Rob Tasin, rhp, University of Oklahoma.
20. Will Stewart, lhp, Hazel Green (Ala.) HS.
21. Kevin Walsh, rhp, University of Arkansas-Pine Bluff.
22. Sutter McLoughlin, rhp, Cal State Sacramento.
23. Anthony Sequeira, rhp, Oral Roberts University.
24. Zach Morris, lhp, University of Maryland.
25. *Joey Lauria, rhp, University of Nevada-Las Vegas.
26. Andrew Godail, lhp, Sam Houston State University.
27. Jake Reppert, lhp, Northwest Nazarene (Idaho) College.
28. Gandy Stubblefield, rhp, University of West Alabama.
29. *Von Watson, of, Briarcrest Christian HS, Eads, Tenn.
30. *Kyle Nowlin, of, Eastern Kentucky University.
31. Nick Fanti, lhp, Hauppauge HS, Smithtown, N.Y.
32. Reggie Wilson, of, Oklahoma City University.
33. *Jacob Stevens, rhp, Choate Rosemary Hall HS, Wallingford, Conn.
34. Ben Pelletier, of, Ecole Secondaire des Montagnes, Saint-Michael-des-Saints, Quebec.
35. Andrew Amaro, of, University of Tampa.

DRAFT DROP *Son of Ruben Amaro Jr., major leaguer (1991-98); general manager, Phillies (2008-15) • Grandson of Ruben Amaro Sr., major leaguer (1958-69)*

36. *Gabe Gonzalez, rhp, CC of Southern Nevada.
37. *Malcolm Grady, rhp, Homewood-Flossmoor HS, Flossmoor, Ill.
38. *Beau Brundage, ss, Mill Creek HS, Hoschton, Ga.
39. *Griffin Morandini, of, Garnet Valley HS, Glen Mills, Pa.

DRAFT DROP *Son of Mickey Morandini, major leaguer (1990-2000)*

40. *Thomas McCarthy, 3b, Allentown (N.J.) HS

## PITTSBURGH PIRATES (22)

1. Kevin Newman, ss, University of Arizona.—(Low A)
1. Ke'Bryan Hayes, 3b, Concordia Lutheran HS, Tomball, Texas (Compensation for loss of Russell Martin as free agent—32nd).—(Short-season A)

DRAFT DROP *Son of Charlie Hayes, major leaguer (1988-2001)*

2. Kevin Kramer, ss, UCLA.—(Low A)
3. Casey Hughston, of, University of Alabama.—(Short-season A)
4. Jacob Taylor, rhp, Pearl River (Miss.) CC.—(Rookie)
5. Brandon Waddell, lhp, University of Virginia.—(Short-season A)
6. J.T. Brubaker, rhp, University of Akron.
7. Mitchell Tolman, 3b, University of Oregon.
8. Seth McGarry, rhp, Florida Atlantic University.
9. Bret Helton, rhp, University of Utah.

DRAFT DROP *Son of Barry Helton, punter, National Football League (1988-91)*

10. Logan Sendelbach, rhp, Tiffin (Ohio) University.
11. Christian Kelley, c, Cal Poly Pomona.
12. Ty Moore, of, UCLA.
13. Logan Ratledge, ss, North Carolina State University.
14. Chris Plitt, rhp, South Mountain (Ariz.) CC.
15. Scooter Hightower, rhp, Columbia State (Tenn.) CC.
16. Nick Hibbing, rhp, University of Iowa.
17. *Austin Sodders, lhp, Riverside (Calif.) CC.

DRAFT DROP *Son of Mike Sodders, first-round draft pick, Twins (1981)*

18. Stephan Meyer, rhp, Bellevue (Neb.) University.
19. Ike Schlabach, lhp, Timber Creek HS, Fort Worth, Texas.
20. Tanner Anderson, rhp, Harvard University.
21. Nick Economos, rhp, Mercer County (N.J.) CC.
22. Nathan Trevillian, rhp, Amherst County HS, Amherst, Va.
23. *Jacob McCarthy, of, Scranton (Pa.) HS.
24. John Bormann, c, University of Texas-San Antonio.
25. Logan Hill, of, Troy University.
26. Shane Kemp, rhp, George Washington University.
27. Ryan Nagle, of, University of Illinois.
28. Albert Baur, 1b, Newberry (S.C.) College.
29. *Chris Falwell, lhp, Cisco (Texas) JC.
30. Mike Wallace, rhp, Fairfield University.
31. *Riley Smith, rhp, San Jacinto (Texas) JC.
32. *Cole Irvin, lhp, University of Oregon.
33. Sean Keselica, lhp, Virginia Tech.
34. *Brendan Spillane, 3b, Wheeling (Ill.) HS.
35. Zach George, 1b, Arkansas State University.
36. James Marvel, rhp, Duke University.
37. *Eli White, ss, Clemson University.
38. *Conor Costello, rhp, Oklahoma State University.
39. Tate Scioneaux, rhp, Southeastern Louisiana University.
40. Daniel Zamora, lhp, Stony Brook University.

## ST. LOUIS CARDINALS (26)

1. Nick Plummer, of, Brother Rice HS, Bloomfield Hills, Mich.—(Rookie)
1. Jake Woodford, rhp, H.B. Plant HS, Tampa (Competitive balance Round 'A' pick—39th).—(Rookie)
2. Bryce Denton, 3b, Ravenwood HS, Brentwood, Tenn.—(Rookie)
3. Harrison Bader, of, University of Florida.—(Low A)
3. Jordan Hicks, rhp, Cypress Creek HS, Houston (Special compensation for failure to sign 2014 third-round pick Trevor Megill).—DNP
4. Paul DeJong, 3b, Illinois State University.—(Low A)
5. Ryan Helsley, rhp, Northeastern State (Okla.) University.—(Rookie)
6. Jacob Evans, lhp, University of Oklahoma.
7. Jesse Jenner, c, University of San Diego.
8. Ian Oxnevard, lhp, Shorewood HS, Shoreline, Wash.
9. Andrew Brodbeck, 2b, Flagler (Fla.) College.
10. *Kep Brown, of, Wando HS, Mount Pleasant, S.C.
11. Paul Salazar, rhp, Lutheran South Academy, Houston.
12. Jacob Schlesener, lhp, Logan-Rogersville HS, Rogersville, Mo.
13. Craig Aikin, of, University of Oklahoma.
14. Carson Cross, rhp, University of Connecticut.
15. *Ryan Merrill, ss, Iowa Western CC.
16. Max Almonte, rhp, Villanova University.
17. Chris Chinea, c, Louisiana State University.
18. *Josh Rolette, c, Shawnee (Okla.) HS.
19. Ryan McCarvel, c, Howard (Texas) JC.
20. Luke Doyle, 2b, Yavapai (Ariz.) JC.
21. *Cadyn Grenier, ss, Bishop Gorman HS, Las Vegas.
22. Hunter Newman, 1b, Trevecca Nazarene (Tenn.) University.
23. *Gio Brusa, of, University of the Pacific.
24. Daniel Martin, 2b, Azusa Pacific (Calif.) University.
25. *Kyle Molnar, rhp, Aliso Niguel HS, Aliso Viejo, Calif.
26. Brennan Leitao, rhp, Cal State Sacramento.
27. Greg Tomchick, rhp, Old Dominion University.
28. *Mitchell Traver, rhp, Texas Christian University.
29. Ben Yokley, rhp, Air Force Academy.
30. *Matt Vierling, of, Christian Brothers College HS, St. Louis.
31. *Aaron Coates, lhp, Glasgow HS, Newark, Del.
32. Tom Spitz, of, Wingate (N.C.) College.
33. Chandler Hawkins, lhp, Arkansas State University.
34. *Parker Kelly, rhp, Westview HS, Portland, Ore.
35. Luke Harrison, rhp, Indiana University.
36. Dylan Tice, 2b, West Chester (Pa.) University.
37. Stephen Zavala, c, Whittier (Calif.) College.
38. Orlando Olivera, of, Missouri Baptist University.
39. R.J. Dennard, 1b, Armstrong State (Ga.) University.
40. Joey Hawkins, ss, Missouri State University.

## SAN DIEGO PADRES (12)

1. (Choice forfeited for signing James Shields as free agent)
2. Austin Smith, rhp, Park Vista Community HS, Lake Worth, Fla.—(Rookie)
3. Jacob Nix, rhp, IMG Academy, Bradenton, Fla.—(Rookie)
4. Austin Allen, c, Florida Tech.—(Short-season A)
5. Josh Magee, of, Franklinton (La.) HS.—(Rookie)
6. Jordan Guerrero, rhp, Polk State (Fla.) JC.
7. Trevor Megill, rhp, Loyola Marymount University.
8. Aldemar Burgos, of, Carlos Beltran Academy, Florida, P.R.
9. Jerry Keel, lhp, Cal State Northridge.
10. Justin Pacchioli, of, Lehigh University.
11. Brett Kennedy, rhp, Fordham University.
12. Peter Van Gansen, ss, Cal Poly.
13. Will Headean, lhp, Illinois State University.
14. Kyle Overstreet, c, University of Alabama.
15. Brad Zunica, 1b, State College of Florida-Manatee.
16. Elliott Ashbeck, rhp, Bradley University.
17. Trey Wingenter, rhp, Auburn University.
18. *Justin Harrer, ss, Sisters (Ore.) HS.
19. Alan Garcia, of, Mountain Pointe HS, Phoenix.
20. Phil Maton, rhp, Louisiana Tech.
21. Nick Monroe, rhp, UNC Wilmington.
22. Christian Cecilio, lhp, University of San Francisco.
23. *Chris Chatfield, of, Spoto HS, Riverview, Fla.
24. *Jamar Smith, of, Meridian (Miss.) HS.
25. *Chase Williams, rhp, Wichita State University.
26. Kodie Tidwell, ss, University of Louisiana-Monroe.
27. *Colton Howell, rhp, University of Nebraska.
28. Corey Hale, lhp, University of Mobile (Ala.).
29. Tyler Moore, 2b, University of South Carolina-Aiken.
30. A.J. Kennedy, c, Cal State Fullerton.
31. *Andres Gracia, rhp, Samford University.
32. Lou Distasio, rhp, University of Rhode Island.
33. Braxton Lorenzini, rhp, West Hills (Calif.) JC.
34. Ty France, 3b, San Diego State University.
35. Nathan Foriest, lhp, Middle Tennessee State University.
36. *Alex Webb, rhp, University of British Columbia.
37. Blake Rogers, rhp, University of Oklahoma
38. *Dean Kremer, rhp, San Joaquin Delta (Calif.) JC.
39. *Adam Hill, rhp, T.L. Hanna HS, Anderson, S.C.
40. *Trevor Larnach, of, College Park HS, Pleasant Hill, Calif.

## SAN FRANCISCO GIANTS (21)

1. Phil Bickford, rhp, CC of Southern Nevada.—(Rookie)

DRAFT DROP *First-round draft pick (10th overall), Blue Jays (2013)*

1. Chris Shaw, 1b, Boston College (Compensation for loss of Pablo Sandoval as free agent—31st).—(Short-season A)
2. Andrew Suarez, lhp, University of Miami.—(High A)
3. Jalen Miller, ss, Riverwood International Charter HS, Sandy Springs, Ga.—(Rookie)
4. Mac Marshall, lhp, Chipola (Fla.) JC.—(Short-season A)
5. Ronnie Jebavy, of, Middle Tennessee State University.—(Short-season A)
6. Steven Duggar, of, Clemson University.
7. Jose Vizcaino Jr., ss, Santa Clara University.

DRAFT DROP *Son of Jose Vizcaino, major leaguer (1989-2006)*

8. Cory Taylor, rhp, Dallas Baptist University.
9. David Graybill, rhp, Arizona State University.
10. Tyler Cyr, rhp, Embry-Riddle (Fla.) University.
11. C.J. Hinojosa, ss, University of Texas.
12. Hector Santiago, ss, Colegio Nuestra Senora de Belen, Guaynabo, P.R.
13. Matt Pope, rhp, Walters State (Tenn.) CC.
14. Matt Winn, c, Virginia Military Institute.
15. Cody Brickhouse, c, Sarasota (Fla.) HS.
16. Grant Watson, lhp, UCLA.
17. Cameron Avila-Leeper, lhp, San Joaquin Delta (Calif.) JC.
18. Heath Slatton, rhp, Middle Tennessee State University.
19. Dave Owen, rhp, Arkansas State University.
20. *Travis Eckert, rhp, Oregon State University.
21. Ryan Halstead, rhp, Indiana University.
22. Domenic Mazza, lhp, UC Santa Barbara.
23. Dillon Dobson, 3b, Appalachian State University.
24. Zack Bowers, c, University of Georgia.
25. *Michael Silva, rhp, Loyola Marymount University.
26. Tyler Brown, ss, CC of Southern Nevada.
27. Bryan Case, c, Oklahoma State University.
28. Ashford Fulmer, of, University of Houston.
29. *Matthias Dietz, rhp, John A. Logan (Ill.) JC.
30. *Tucker Forbes, rhp, UCLA.
31. *Ryan Howard, ss, University of Missouri.
32. Jeff Burke, rhp, Boston College.
33. *Rafael Ramirez, rhp, Calusa Prep HS, Miami.
34. *Travis Moniot, ss, Palm Desert (Calif.) HS.
35. Drew Jackson, rhp, Florida Atlantic University.
36. *Brendon Little, lhp, Conestoga HS, Berwyn, Pa.
37. Mark Weist, 3b, Michigan State University.
38. *Nate Pecota, of, Blue Springs (Mo.) South HS.

DRAFT DROP *Son of Bill Pecota, major leaguer (1986-94)*

39. *Hunter Bowling, lhp, American Heritage HS, Delray Beach, Fla.
40. Woody Edwards, of, Gulf Coast State (Fla.) JC

## SEATTLE MARINERS (20)

1. (Choice forfeited for signing Nelson Cruz as free agent).
2. Nick Neidert, rhp, Peachtree Ridge HS, Suwanee, Ga.—(Rookie)
2. Andrew Moore, rhp, Oregon State University (Competitive balance Round 'B' pick—72nd).—(Short-season A)

3. Braden Bishop, of, University of Washington.—(Short-season A)
4. Dylan Thompson, rhp, Socastee HS, Myrtle Beach, S.C.—(Rookie)
5. Drew Jackson, ss, Stanford University.—(Short-season A)

DRAFT DROP *Brother of Brett Jackson, first-round draft pick, Cubs (2009); major leaguer (2012-14).*

6. Kyle Wilcox, rhp, Bryant University.
7. Ryan Uhl, 1b, Indiana (Pa.) University.
8. Cody Mobley, rhp, Mount Vernon (Ind.) HS.
9. Conner Hale, 3b, Louisiana State University.
10. Darin Gillies, rhp, Arizona State University.
11. Dylan Silva, lhp, Florida State University.
12. Logan Taylor, 3b, Texas A&M University.
13. Matt Clancy, lhp, St. John's University.
14. Jio Orozco, rhp, Salpointe Catholic HS, Tucson, Ariz.
15. Ryne Inman, rhp, Parkview HS, Lilburn, Ga.
16. Ricky Eusebio, of, University of Miami.
17. Joe Pistorese, lhp, Washington State University.
18. Anthony Misiewicz, lhp, Michigan State University.
19. P.J. Jones, c, Washington State University.
20. *Parker McFadden, rhp, Yelm (Wash.) HS.
21. Rob Fonseca, 1b, Northeastern University.
22. Joey Strain, rhp, Winthrop University.
23. Art Warren, rhp, Ashland (Ohio) University.
24. Lance Thonvold, rhp, University of Minnesota.
25. Joe Peeler, rhp, East Rowan HS, Salisbury, N.C.
26. Ljay Newsome, rhp, Chopticon HS, Morganza, Md.
27. Michael Rivera, rhp, Colegio Hector Urdaneta HS, Rio Grande, P.R.
28. Taylor Perez, ss, St. Leo (Fla.) University.
29. Jared West, lhp, LSU Shreveport.
30. Gus Craig, of, Columbia University.
31. Logan James, lhp, Stanford University.
32. Colin Tornberg, rhp, University of Texas-Arlington.
33. Julius Gaines, ss, Florida International University.
34. *Kyle Ostrowski, lhp, Lincoln-Way North HS, Frankfort, Ill.
35. Gianni Zayas, rhp, Florida International University.
36. Matt Walker, rhp, Weatherford (Texas) JC.
37. *Colton Sakamoto, of, Westview HS, Portland, Ore.
38. Dalton Kelly, 1b, UC Santa Barbara.
39. *Dante Ricciardi, ss, Worcester (Mass.) Academy.
40. *Mike Rojas, c, Gulf Coast HS, Naples, Fla.

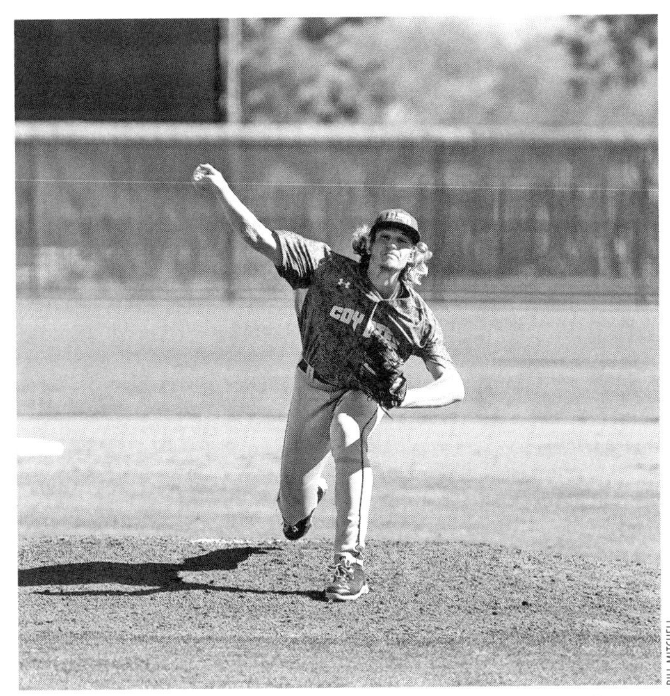
BILL MITCHELL

**The Giants made Phil Bickford a two-time first-round pick by taking him 21st overall**

## TAMPA BAY RAYS (13)

1. Garrett Whitley, of, Niskayuna (N.Y.) HS.—(Short-season A)
2. Chris Betts, c, Woodrow Wilson HS, Long Beach, Calif.--DNP
3. Brandon Lowe, 2b, University of Maryland.--DNP
4. Brandon Koch, rhp, Dallas Baptist University.—(Short-season A)
5. Joe McCarthy, of, University of Virginia.—(Short-season A)
6. Benton Moss, rhp, University of North Carolina.
7. Jake Cronenworth, 2b, University of Michigan.
8. Reece Karalus, rhp, Santa Clara University.
9. Danny De la Calle, c, Florida State University.
10. Sam Triece, rhp, Washington State University.
11. Ian Gibaut, rhp, Tulane University.
12. David Olmedo-Barrera, 1b, Cal State Fullerton.
13. Nicholas Padilla, rhp, Grayson (Texas) CC.
14. Tyler Brashears, rhp, University of Hawaii.
15. Ethan Clark, rhp, Crowder (Mo.) JC.
16. *Joe Davis, c, Bowie (Texas) HS.
17. Brett Sullivan, 2b, University of the Pacific.
18. Landon Cray, of, Seattle University.
19. Porter Clayton, lhp, Dixie State (Utah) University.
20. Edrick Agosto, rhp, International Baseball Academy, Ceiba, P.R.
21. Matt Dacey, 3b, University of Richmond.
22. Justin Marsden, rhp, Mountainview HS, Auburn, Wash.
23. Reign Letkeman, rhp, Big Bend (Wash.) CC.
24. Jesus Ortiz, rhp, Miguel Melendez Munoz HS, Bayamon, P.R.
25. Devin Davis, 1b, Valencia HS, Santa Clarita, Calif.
26. Noel Rodriguez, rhp, Paradise Valley (Ariz.) CC.
27. *Joey Bart, c, Buford (Ga.) HS.
28. *Desmond Chumley, of, Longview (Texas) HS.
29. *Shane Potter, 1b, La Costa Canyon HS, Carlsbad, Calif.
30. *Kyle Teaf, ss, University of South Florida.
31. Tim Ingram, rhp, SUNY Old Westbury.
32. Ty Jackson, rhp, Lewis-Clark State (Idaho) College.
33. Collin Chapman, rhp, Lamar University.
34. Ryan Caldwell, of, Ezell-Harding Christian HS, Antioch, Tenn.
35. Blake Butera, 2b, Boston College.
36. Bryan Bonnell, rhp, University of Nevada-Las Vegas.
37. Kewby Meyer, 1b, University of Nevada.
38. *Steven Sensley, 1b, LSU Eunice JC.
39. *Tyler Rand, of, Langham Creek HS, Houston.
40. *Kahiau Winchester, 2b, Iolani HS, Honolulu, Hawaii.

## TEXAS RANGERS (3)

1. Dillon Tate, rhp, UC Santa Barbara.—(Low A)
2. Eric Jenkins, of, West Columbus HS, Cerro Gordo, N.C.—(Low A)
3. Michael Matuella, rhp, Duke University.--DNP
4. Jake Lemoine, rhp, University of Houston.--DNP
5. Chad Smith, of, South Gwinnett HS, Snellville, Ga.—(Rookie)
6. Tyler Ferguson, rhp, Vanderbilt University.
7. Dylan Moore, ss, University of Central Florida.
8. Blake Bass, rhp, Angelo State (Texas) University.
9. Peter Fairbanks, rhp, University of Missouri.
10. Leon Byrd, ss, Rice University.
11. Scott Heineman, of, University of Oregon.
12. Ladarious Clark, of, University of West Florida.
13. Curtis Terry, 1b, Archer HS, Lawrenceville, Ga.
14. Adam Choplick, lhp, University of Oklahoma.
15. Nick Kaye, of, Glendora (Calif.) HS.
16. Tyler Phillips, rhp, Bishop Eustace Prep HS, Pennsauken Township, N.J.
17. Tyler Sanchez, c, St. John's University.
18. Jason Richman, lhp, Georgia Southern University.
19. Xavier Turner, 3b, Vanderbilt University.
20. *Luke Shilling, rhp, Notre Dame Prep, Pontiac, Mich.
21. Joenny Vazquez, c, Educational Technical (P.R.) JC.
22. Josh Altmann, ss, Olivet Nazarene (Ill.) University.
23. Tyler Davis, rhp, University of Washington.
24. Ashton Perritt, rhp, Liberty University.
25. Demarcus Evans, rhp, Petal (Miss.) HS.
26. Jake Shortslef, rhp, Herkimer County (N.Y.) CC.
27. Clyde Kendrick, lhp, Eastern New Mexico University.
28. Blaine Prescott, 2b, Midland (Texas) JC.
29. Maikor Mora, rhp, Polk State (Fla.) JC.
30. Jeffrey Springs, lhp, Appalachian State University.
31. Jamie Potts, of, Grand Valley State (Mich.) College.
32. John Werner, rhp, St. Catharine (Ky.) College.
33. C.D. Pelham, lhp, Spartanburg Methodist (S.C.) JC.
34. Joeanthony Rivera, lhp, Barry (Fla.) University.
35. *Isaiah Carranza, rhp, Damien HS, La Verne, Calif.
36. *D.J. Peters, of, Western Nevada CC.
37. *Billy Layne, rhp, Old Bridge HS, Matawan, N.J.
38. Dean Long, 3b, Emporia State (Kan.) University.
39. *Shea Murray, rhp, Ohio State University.
40. London Lindley, of, Georgia Perimeter JC.

## TORONTO BLUE JAYS (17)

1. Jon Harris, rhp, Missouri State University (Compensation for loss of Melky Cabrera as free agent).—(Short-season A)
1. (Choice forfeited for signing Russell Martin as free agent)
2. *Brady Singer, rhp, Eustis (Fla.) HS.

DRAFT DROP *Attended Florida*

3. Justin Maese, rhp, Ysleta HS, El Paso, Texas.—(Rookie)
4. Carl Wise, 3b, College of Charleston.—(Short-season A)
5. Jose Espada, rhp, Jose Collazo Colon HS, Juncos, P.R.—(Rookie)
6. J.C. Cardenas, ss, Barry (Fla.) University.
7. Travis Bergen, lhp, Kennesaw State University.
8. Danny Young, lhp, University of Florida.
9. Connor Panas, 3b, Canisius University.
10. Owen Spiwak, c, Odessa (Texas) JC.
11. *Marrick Crouse, rhp, Dana Hills HS, Dana Point, Calif.
12. D.J. McKnight, of, Tallahassee (Fla.) CC.
13. *Daniel Perry, ss, Lassen HS, Susanville, Calif.
14. Ryan Hissey, c, College of William & Mary.
15. Jackson McClelland, rhp, Pepperdine University.
16. Christian Williams, 3b, Gulf Coast State (Fla.) JC.
17. *Chandler Eden, rhp, Yavapai (Ariz.) JC.
18. Geno Encina, rhp, University of Incarnate Word (Texas).
19. John La Prise, 2b, University of Virginia.
20. Tyler Burden, rhp, Chowan (N.C.) College.
21. Tayler Saucedo, lhp, Tennessee Wesleyan College.
22. Nick Sinay, of, SUNY Buffalo.
23. Juandy Mendoza, ss, Otero (Colo.) JC.
24. Reggie Pruitt, of, Kennesaw Mountain HS, Kennesaw, Ga.
25. *Ryan Feltner, rhp, Walsh Jesuit HS, Cuyahoga Falls, Ohio.
26. Gabe Clark, 1b, Oregon State University.
27. Jake Thomas, of, Binghamton University.
28. Levi Scott, 1b, University of Texas-Arlington.
29. *Kyle Davis, rhp, University of Southern California.
30. Earl Burl, of, Alcorn State University.
31. Josh Degraaf, rhp, Taylor (Ind.) University.
32. Andrew Guillotte, 2b, McNeese State University.
33. Kalik May, of, Mississippi Valley State University.
34. Hunter Barnett, lhp, Mount Olive (N.C.) College.
35. Stuart Holmes, lhp, Nicholls State University.
36. Lance Jones, of, Southern University.
37. *Randy Labaut, lhp, Downey (Calif.) HS.
38. Josh Reavis, c, Radford University.
39. Mattingly Romanin, 2b, Chicago State University.
40. Robert Lucido, c, Amherst (Mass.) College.

## WASHINGTON NATIONALS (29)

1. (Choice forfeited for signing Max Scherzer as free agent)
2. Andrew Stevenson, of, Louisiana State University (Special compensation for failure to sign 2014 second-round pick Andrew Suarez as free agent—58th).—(Low A)
2. Blake Perkins, of, Verrado HS, Buckeye, Ariz.—(Rookie)
3. Rhett Wiseman, of, Vanderbilt University.—(Short-season A)
4. Mariano Rivera Jr., rhp, Iona University.—(Short-season A)

DRAFT DROP *Son of Mariano Rivera, major leaguer (1995-2013)*

5. Taylor Hearn, lhp, Oklahoma Baptist University.—(Short-season A)
6. Matt Crownover, lhp, Clemson University.
7. Grant Borne, lhp, Nicholls State University.
8. Koda Glover, rhp, Oklahoma State University.
9. David Kerian, 1b, University of Illinois.
10. Taylor Guilbeau, lhp, University of Alabama.
11. Andrew Lee, rhp, University of Tennessee.
12. Tommy Peterson, rhp, University of South Florida.
13. Max Schrock, 2b, University of South Carolina.
14. *Mack Lemieux, lhp, Jupiter (Fla.) Community HS.
15. Kevin Mooney, rhp, University of Maryland.
16. Ian Sagdal, ss, Washington State University.
17. Dalton Dulin, 2b, Northwest Mississippi CC.
18. Melvin Rodriguez, 2b, Jackson State University.
19. Clayton Brandt, ss, Mid-America Nazarene (Kan.) College.
20. *John Clay Reeves, c, Rice University.
21. Matt Pirro, rhp, Wake Forest University.
22. Adam Boghosian, rhp, North Greenville (S.C.) University.
23. *Alec Rash, rhp, University of Missouri.
24. *Blake Smith, rhp, West Virginia University.
25. Calvin Copping, rhp, Cal State Northridge.
26. Russell Harmening, rhp, Westmont (Calif.) College.
27. Ryan Brinley, rhp, Sam Houston State University.
28. Mick VanVossen, rhp, Michigan State University.
29. Philip Diedrick, of, Western Kentucky University.
30. Jorge Pantoja, rhp, Alabama State University.
31. *Nick Sprengel, lhp, El Dorado HS, Placentia, Calif.
32. Dalton DiNatale, 3b, Arizona State University.
33. Angelo La Bruna, ss, University of Southern California.
34. Tyler Watson, lhp, Perry HS, Gilbert, Ariz.
35. *Coco Montes, ss, Coral Gables (Fla.) HS.
36. *Taylor Bush, ss, The Linfield School, Temecula, Calif.
37. *Stephen DiPuglia, ss, Cooper City (Fla.) HS.
38. *Matt Morales, ss, Wellington (Fla.) Community HS.
39. Jake Jefferies, 2b, Cal State Fullerton.

DRAFT DROP *Son of Gregg Jefferies, first-round draft pick, Mets (1985); major leaguer (1987-2000)*

40. *Parker Quinn, 1b, The Benjamin School, North Palm Beach, Fla.

# 2016

## AT A GLANCE

### This Date In History
June 8-10

### One Who Got Away
**NICK LODOLO, LHP, PIRATES (1ST ROUND SUPPLEMENTAL).** The only unsigned player in the first six rounds, Lodolo (41st overall) chose Texas Christian rather than accept an over-slot $1.75 million offer from the Pirates. Only one other player in the first 10 rounds did not sign, and 75.5 percent of all players drafted signed.

### He Was Drafted?
**TREY GRIFFEY, OF, MARINERS (24TH ROUND).** The Mariners selected the son of Ken Griffey Jr., the No. 1 overall pick in the 1987 draft and a 2016 Hall of Fame inductee, and in a fitting tip of the cap did it in Round 24—Junior's number with the Mariners. Trey had not played baseball since age 14 and was a wide receiver in college at Arizona. The Mariners signed him for the nominal sum of $1,000. "Obviously, he's a good athlete," scouting director Tom McNamara said. "We just want him to know if he's ever interested in playing pro baseball, we have a job for him." In the 23rd round, the Angels took **TORII HUNTER JR.** Like Griffey, Hunter was a wide receiver (at Notre Dame), but he did play for the baseball team, getting 12 at-bats as a little-used outfielder. Hunter signed for $100,000.

### Did You Know?
An unprecedented 209 of the first 210 players drafted in 2016 signed contracts.

### They Said It
**WILL BENSON**, a first-round pick of the Indians: "My primary goal is to make baseball the No. 1 sport in America. It's time to make it the here-and-now sport. It's allowed me to meet different people of different backgrounds with different viewpoints. I think that's a formula for world peace, obviously."

# Moniak leads way in draft devoid of drama

The Philadelphia Phillies had the No. 1 selection in the 2016 draft. They never tipped their hand on the player they would ultimately choose, and it wasn't until commissioner Rob Manfred stepped to the podium and announced that they had selected California high school outfielder Mickey Moniak that the rest of the baseball world knew for certain.

It was the only suspense in a remarkably orderly process that saw the available talent drawn and signed in a systematic manner. The most notable aspect of the 2016 draft was that teams spent more bonus money ($267,351,610) than any draft in history and signed more premium players than ever before. But there was little of the predraft drama or signing deadline suspense that characterized so much of draft history.

While there was uncertainty about whether Moniak would be the Phillies' selection, it was clear the organization would try to strike a balance between talent and value with the No. 1 selection, and spend aggressively later on in the draft.

The No. 1 pick had an assigned bonus value of $9,015,000, but the Phillies were able to sign Moniak for $6,100,000—leaving them with almost $3 million to allocate elsewhere. They used most of it to sign California prep righthander Kevin Gowdy, their second-round pick, for $3.5 million—almost $2 million above his slot value of $1,536,200, and the 11th-highest bonus overall. The Phillies also took advantage of their draft position by signing five other players for above-slot amounts, including their third-, fourth- and fifth-round picks.

Phillies scouting director Johnny Almaraz said the team took Moniak on talent, not because of any potential savings. Above all, they bet on Moniak's bat, a tool that Almaraz said graded out at least a 70 on the standard 20-80 scouting scale.

"We felt as an organization that he was the best high school bat in the country and rated him as one of the top three bats overall," Almaraz said. "This was the type of draft with a lot of talent and depth. There was good high school and college depth, and also lots of hitters and pitchers. We were looking for that one player to separate himself.

"(Moniak is) the type of player who from the get-go, his physical maturity, we could see that he had gotten stronger, and he was getting stronger as the year progressed. We felt like he was one of the few middle-of-the-field players in the draft. He can impact the game on both sides because he can play a really good center field. We liked him and kept going back. We wanted to make sure we were evaluating efficiently."

Moniak, 18, was ecstatic to be the No. 1 pick, and took just 11 days to agree to terms.

"It's indescribable," he said, moments after being selected. "Kids dream to be drafted by an MLB team, but to be the No. 1 pick, it's insane. I'm so grateful for this opportunity to be picked by the Phillies. I'm excited to hopefully prove the Phillies right and be honored as this No. 1 pick."

BILL MITCHELL

**The Phillies took California high school outfielder Mickey Moniak for his bat and his middle-of-the-field potential, but the money they saved by signing him also allowed them to get premium talent later**

Moniak, a UCLA recruit, was the first No. 1 pick by the Phillies since they took infielder Pat Burrell out of Miami in 1998, and the first high school outfielder to go first overall since another Californian, Delmon Young, was taken by the Tampa Bay Devil Rays in 2003. He was the fifth San Diego player to lead off the draft, joining Adrian Gonzalez (Marlins, 2000), Matt Bush (Padres, 2004), Stephen Strasburg (Nationals, 2009) and Brady Aiken (Astros, 2014).

Moniak's $6.1 million bonus was the second-largest in 2016. University of Tennessee third baseman Nick Senzel, selected second by the Cincinnati Reds, signed for $6.2 million.

Because of a supplemental selection (35th overall), the Reds had a larger bonus pool ($13,923,700 through the first 10 rounds) than the Phillies ($13,405,200), though the Phillies spent more money ($14,990,300) than the Reds ($14,679,100) to sign all their draft picks.

The biggest spenders were the Atlanta Braves, who spent $15,516,300—$3.7 million short of the draft record of $19,103,000, set in 2015 by the Houston Astros, who had two of the first five

## 2016: THE FIRST ROUNDERS

| CLUB: PLAYER, POS., SCHOOL | HOMETOWN | B-T | HT. | WT. | AGE | BONUS | FIRST YEAR | LAST YEAR | ENTRY LEVEL |
|---|---|---|---|---|---|---|---|---|---|
| 1. Phillies: Mickey Moniak, of, La Costa Canyon HS | Encinitas, Calif. | L-R | 6-2 | 185 | 18 | $6,100,000 | 2016 | Active | Rookie |
| San Diego area prep product always had impressive bat with speed, CF skills, became legit candidate for top of draft when power evolved as SR, hit .476-7-46. | | | | | | | | | |
| 2. Reds: Nick Senzel, 3b, Tennessee | Knoxville, Tenn. | R-R | 6-1 | 205 | 20 | $6,200,000 | 2016 | Active | Rookie |
| Undrafted out of local HS, broke out as Cape Cod MVP in 2015; surest bat in college ranks (.352-8-59 as JR) with evolving power, made huge strides in field. | | | | | | | | | |
| 3. Braves: Ian Anderson, rhp, Shenendahowa HS | Clifton Park, N.Y. | R-R | 6-4 | 180 | 18 | $4,000,000 | 2016 | Active | Rookie |
| Battled pneumonia, strained oblique to begin senior year, but stock skyrocketed with projectable frame, present combination of mid-90s stuff, polish. | | | | | | | | | |
| 4. Rockies: Riley Pint, rhp, St. Thomas Aquinas HS | Lenexa, Kan. | R-R | 6-5 | 225 | 18 | $4,800,000 | 2016 | Active | Rookie |
| Highest ceiling in draft with 102 mph fastball, secondary stuff, projectable frame, but scouts leery of delivery, command issues; went 7-1, 0.57 (49 IP/87 SO) as SR. | | | | | | | | | |
| 5. Brewers: Corey Ray, of, Louisville | Chicago | L-L | 5-11 | 185 | 21 | $4,125,000 | 2016 | Active | High Class A |
| First of three Louisville first-rounders had best combination of power/speed in draft; hit .310-15-60 with 44 SBs as JR, still proving himself as hitter, defender in CF. | | | | | | | | | |
| 6. Athletics: A.J. Puk, lhp, Florida | Cedar Rapids, Iowa | L-L | 6-7 | 230 | 21 | $4,069,200 | 2016 | Active | Short-season |
| Intimidating size, mid-90s fastball made him obvious candidate to go for top of draft, but inconsistent performance (2-3, 3.05, 74 IP/101 SO) made teams leery. | | | | | | | | | |
| 7. Marlins: Braxton Garrett, lhp, Florence HS | Florence, Ala. | B-L | 6-3 | 190 | 18 | $4,145,900 | 2016 | Active | Rookie |
| Unusually polished lefty dominated Alabama prep ranks in final two years (12-3, 0.65), 129 IP, 26 BB/266 SO); hammer curve best offering in solid three-pitch mix. | | | | | | | | | |
| 8. Padres: Cal Quantrill, rhp, Stanford | Port Hope, Ontario | L-R | 6-3 | 195 | 21 | $3,963,045 | 2016 | Active | Rookie |
| Son of ex-big leaguer Paul would have been likely first college arm taken had he not missed most of 2015, all of 2016 with TJ surgery; has stuff, poise to excel. | | | | | | | | | |
| 9 Tigers: Matt Manning, rhp, Sheldon HS | Elk Grove, Calif. | R-R | 6-6 | 200 | 18 | $3,505,800 | 2016 | Active | Rookie |
| More accomplished at basketball (19.7 ppg as SR) than on diamond (2-1, 1.91, 40 IP/77 SO), but more upside in baseball with high-90s fastball, improving curve. | | | | | | | | | |
| 10. White Sox: Zack Collins, c, Miami | Pembroke Pines, Fla. | L-R | 6-3 | 220 | 21 | $3,380,600 | 2016 | Active | High Class A |
| First of four ACC catchers among top 43 picks; best hitter/power/plate discipline of bunch (.363-16-59), but needs to improve catching skills to stay behind plate. | | | | | | | | | |
| 11. Mariners: Kyle Lewis, of, Mercer | Lithonia, Ga. | R-R | 6-4 | 210 | 20 | $3,286,700 | 2016 | Active | Short-season |
| Lightly recruited talent became offensive force as JR (.395-20-72, 66 BBs) after breakout summer on Cape; impressed scouts with power, arm, imposing frame. | | | | | | | | | |
| 12. Red Sox: Jason Groome, lhp, Barnegat HS | Barnegat, N.J. | L-L | 6-5 | 230 | 17 | $3,650,000 | 2016 | Active | Rookie |
| Prep lefty with impressive size/delivery, advanced raw stuff; was strong candidate to go No. 1 overall before teams became concerned about makeup issues. | | | | | | | | | |
| 13. Rays: Josh Lowe, 3b, Pope HS | Marietta, Ga. | L-R | 6-4 | 190 | 18 | $2,600,000 | 2016 | Active | Rookie |
| With superior power, speed, arm strength, has one of best tools packages in class, though position in question; comes from intriguing baseball family background. | | | | | | | | | |
| 14. Indians: Will Benson, of, Westminster School | Atlanta | L-L | 6-5 | 225 | 17 | $2,500,000 | 2016 | Active | Rookie |
| Intriguing athletic specimen in mold of fellow Georgia prep product Jason Heyward; has similar power/speed package, but boom/bust prospect depending on bat. | | | | | | | | | |
| 15. Twins: Alex Kirilloff, of, Plum HS | New Kensington, Pa. | L-L | 6-3 | 220 | 18 | $2,817,100 | 2016 | Active | Rookie |
| Home-schooled but played for local prep team, hit .540-3-24 (17 BB/1 SO) as SR, also 6-0, 0.74 on mound; LH bat with raw power, needs to refine approach. | | | | | | | | | |
| 16. Angels: Matt Thaiss, c, Virginia | Jackson, N.J. | L-R | 6-1 | 195 | 21 | $2,150,000 | 2016 | Active | Rookie |
| Little doubt among scouts that he has offensive upside to play in majors (hit .323-10-64 as SO, .375-10-59 as JR), but lingering concerns about defensive ability. | | | | | | | | | |
| 17. Astros: Forrest Whitley, rhp, Alamo Heights HS | San Antonio, Texas | R-R | 6-7 | 230 | 18 | $3,148,000 | 2016 | Active | Rookie |
| Made huge strides in HS from sub-6-footer with mid-70s FB to pitcher with 6-7 frame, mid-90s heat; became complete pitcher as SR with improved conditioning. | | | | | | | | | |
| 18. Yankees: Blake Rutherford, of, Chaminade Prep | Simi Valley, Calif. | L-R | 6-3 | 195 | 19 | $3,282,000 | 2016 | Active | Rookie |
| With size, power, athleticism, top-rated prep position prospect at outset of spring; hit .577 with 4 HR, but stock slipped with inconsistency, signability issues. | | | | | | | | | |
| 19. Mets: Justin Dunn, rhp, Boston College | Freeport, N.Y. | R-R | 6-2 | 185 | 20 | $2,378,800 | 2016 | Active | Short-season |
| Stock rose when moved from pen to rotation midway through 2016, went 4-2, 2.06 (66 IP/72 SO); has lightning-quick arm in smaller frame with mid-90s heat. | | | | | | | | | |
| 20. Dodgers: Gavin Lux, ss, Indian Trail HS | Kenosha, Wis. | L-R | 6-2 | 170 | 18 | $2,317,000 | 2016 | Active | Rookie |
| Nephew of Augie Schmidt (No. 2 pick in 1980) became top middle infielder in draft with superior instincts/actions, improvement in swing, strength, speed, arm. | | | | | | | | | |
| 21. Blue Jays: T.J. Zeuch, rhp, Pittsburgh | Mason, Ohio | R-R | 6-7 | 225 | 20 | $2,175,000 | 2016 | Active | Short-season |
| Slowed by groin injury to start 2016 season, but moved up draft boards on strength of size, mid-90s FB; progress of secondary stuff will determine long-term role. | | | | | | | | | |
| 22. Pirates: Will Craig, 3b, Wake Forest | Johnson City, Tenn. | R-R | 6-3 | 235 | 21 | $2,253,700 | 2016 | Active | Low Class A |
| With power (.392-16-65), low-90s FB (2-0, 2.42, 8 SV), was most valuable performer in 2016 college season; has bat/arm for 3B, but lacks athleticism for position. | | | | | | | | | |
| 23. Cardinals: Delvin Perez, ss, Ind. Education HS | Loiza, P.R. | R-R | 6-3 | 180 | 17 | $2,222,500 | 2016 | Active | Rookie |
| Potential top shortstop in draft with superior tools/actions at position, but positive PED test on eve of draft sent stock tumbling; offensive game not as advanced. | | | | | | | | | |
| 24. Padres: Hudson Sanchez, ss, Carroll HS | Grapevine, Texas | R-R | 6-2 | 195 | 17 | $1,000,000 | 2016 | Active | Rookie |
| Biggest surprise of first round, but pick enabled Padres to maximize spending; has impressive bat, age on his side, but unclear where he'll play in field as pro. | | | | | | | | | |
| 25. Padres: Eric Lauer, lhp, Kent State | Elyria, Ohio | R-L | 6-3 | 210 | 21 | $2,000,000 | 2016 | Active | Rookie |
| Polished lefty with exquisite command of four-pitch mix; went 10-2, 0.69 with .141 opponent AVG as JR, lowest ERA by NCAA D-I starter in 37 years; on fast track. | | | | | | | | | |
| 26. White Sox: Zack Burdi, rhp, Louisville | Downers Grove, Ill. | R-R | 6-3 | 210 | 21 | $2,128,500 | 2016 | Active | Double-A |
| Like brother Nick in 2014, dominated as Cardinals closer with magic stuff: 98-101 mph fastball, slider; went 1-3, 3.30 (6-1, 0.92 in 2015) with 11 SV, 47 Ks in 30 IP. | | | | | | | | | |
| 27. Orioles: Cody Sedlock, rhp, Illinois | Rock Island, Ill. | R-R | 6-4 | 205 | 20 | $2,097,200 | 2016 | Active | Short-season |
| Second member of 2015 Illini bullpen to crack first round, joining Tyler Jay (Twins '15); made transition to starter (5-3, 2.49, 101 IP/117 SO) with four-pitch mix. | | | | | | | | | |
| 28. Nationals: Carter Kieboom, ss, Walton HS | Marietta, Ga. | R-R | 6-2 | 190 | 18 | $2,000,000 | 2016 | Active | Rookie |
| Younger brother of Trevor, Nats' fifth-rounder in 2012; has the instincts, athletic actions to remain at shortstop, but also bat, feel for hitting to play hot corner. | | | | | | | | | |
| 29. Nationals: Dane Dunning, rhp, Florida | Fleming Island, Fla. | R-R | 6-4 | 200 | 21 | $2,000,000 | 2016 | Active | Short-season |
| Relegated to set-up role/midweek starter on deep Gators staff (6-3, 2.29, 79 IP/88 SO), but has mid-90s fastball, three-pitch mix to evolve as starter in pro ranks. | | | | | | | | | |
| 30. Rangers: Cole Ragans, lhp, North Florida Christian HS | Tallahassee, Fla. | L-L | 6-3 | 190 | 18 | $2,003,400 | 2016 | Active | Rookie |
| Classic projectable prep arm with command of three pitches, though not overpowering; went 9-2, 0.90 (70 IP/104 SO) as SR, 7-2, 0.89 (63 IP/94 SO) as JR. | | | | | | | | | |
| 31. Mets: Anthony Kay, lhp, Connecticut | Stony Brook, N.Y. | L-L | 5-11 | 185 | 21 | $1,100,000 | 2016 | Active | |
| Mets went local in nabbing Dunn at 19, Kay (previously drafted by Mets in 2013) at 31; polished lefty, has effective FB/change, went 9-2, 2.65 (119 IP/111 SO). | | | | | | | | | |
| 32. Dodgers: Will Smith, c, Louisville | Louisville, Ky. | R-R | 6-0 | 190 | 21 | $1,775,000 | 2016 | Active | Double-A |
| From .242-2-15 in 2015, led Cardinals in hitting (.382-7-43) in breakout JR year; sound defender with plus arm, flashes power, runs adequately for position. | | | | | | | | | |
| 33. Cardinals Dylan Carlson, of, Elk Grove HS | Elk Grove, Calif. | B-L | 6-3 | 195 | 17 | $1,350,000 | 2016 | Active | Rookie |
| Switch-hitter with sweet swing/raw power from both sides; had breakout year at plate (.407-9-40), also went 6-0 on mound; has athleticism, savvy as coach's son. | | | | | | | | | |
| 34. Cardinals Dakota Hudson, rhp, Mississippi State | Dunlap, Tenn. | R-R | 6-5 | 215 | 21 | $2,000,000 | 2016 | Active | Rookie |
| Late-season fade caused stock to slip, though went 9-5, 2.55 (113 IP/115 SO) overall; has deadly fastball/slider combo to profile as either starter/reliever in pros. | | | | | | | | | |

## WORTH NOTING

Upstart Coastal Carolina won the 2016 College World Series, beating Arizona 5-4 in the decisive game of the best-of-three championship series. It was one of the more unlikely finals as neither Coastal, making its first trip to the CWS, nor Arizona, a four-time champion, was a No. 1 seed entering the 64-team NCAA regional field. Neither school factored heavily in the draft, either, as the only noteworthy picks were a pair of fourth-rounders: Arizona third baseman/righthander **BOBBY DALBEC**, selected 118th by the Red Sox, and Coastal Carolina shortstop **MICHAEL PAEZ**, picked 130th by the Mets. By contrast, both Florida and Louisville had seven players drafted apiece by the time that Coastal or Arizona saw their first picks. The bonus tab for Louisville's seven picks, including three first-rounders, was $11,126,000, and for Florida's contingent of seven, including two first-rounders, it was $10,830,800. Arizona had seven players drafted overall for a combined bonus total of $710,500 ($650,000 of which went to Dalbec); Coastal had six players drafted (only five of whom signed), with the total fare a mere $485,000 ($446,500 of which went to Paez). As for their showing in post-season play, Louisville was bounced in two games in the super regionals by UC Santa Barbara, while Florida, the No. 1 national seed, reached Omaha but was eliminated with two straight losses.

Despite the early dominance by Florida and Louisville, Texas A&M led the way among college teams with 13 selections, none higher than outfielder **NICK BANKS** by the Nationals in the fourth round. Southern California had 12 players selected, while Mississippi State and Oklahoma State each produced 11, and Texas Tech 10. Florida and Louisville had eight overall.

Louisville's three first-round picks—outfielder

CONTINUED ON PAGE 756

## DRAFT SPOTLIGHT: MICKEY MONIAK

Mickey Moniak's advanced hitting approach can be traced back to lessons taught by his grandfather

With a name like Mickey and a grandfather who was mentored by Ted Williams, Mickey Moniak was practically born to play professional baseball.

The Philadelphia Phillies obliged him, taking the 18-year-old Carlsbad, Calif., high school outfielder with the first overall selection in the 2016 draft and quickly signing him to a bonus of $6.1 million.

Though Moniak's given name is McKenzie, he has gone by Mickey all his life, and his baseball idol naturally is Hall of Famer Mickey Mantle. "My favorite all-time player is Mickey Mantle and not just because of the name," Moniak said.

One of Mantle's contemporaries was Bill Moniak, Mickey's grandfather, who signed a $25,000 bonus contract with the Boston Red Sox in 1958. Though Bill never advanced beyond Class A in six seasons in the Red Sox system, he was tutored in the finer points of hitting by Williams. He in turn passed some of his basic hitting tips to his grandson and was instrumental in his development as a top prospect. Moniak's first hitting coach, at age 2, was his grandfather.

"My grandpop is my biggest fan," Moniak said. "He definitely influenced my game, my approach, how I hit and play baseball. He's been huge in my development as a baseball player."

Williams stressed having a specific approach at the plate. He told Bill Moniak about what pitches to avoid. A first pitch strike on the outside part of the plate? Let the pitcher have that. Another good pitch on the corner? Lay off it.

"But once you get to 0-2, you have to get up on the plate and look to put the ball in play," Moniak said. "The pitcher is never going to beat you. That's the main mentality. It's just you versus him. That's what he's passed down to me."

The Phillies were drawn to Moniak's advanced offensive skills. In 29 games as a senior at La Costa Canyon High, Moniak hit .476 with seven home runs, 12 triples and 46 RBIs. He finished his four-year career with a .390 average, nine homers and 105 RBIs.

Though his speed, defense and mentality have always been held in high regard, Moniak left little doubt what part of his game excited scouts most. "I love to hit," he said. "I use my speed to help that out, but I'd definitely say hitting. I try to stay within myself, but the main thing I'm working on now is to put on muscle and get more power in my swing."

It was during the summer of 2015, while a member of USA Baseball's junior national team, that Moniak established himself as a top prospect and began believing he had a shot not only at becoming a first-rounder but a top draft pick.

"Obviously, playing with all the tough competition last summer reassured me that I could play with those guys," Moniak said. "Over the summer, there would be 50, 60 scouts at every event you went to. It's good to have an experience like that."

At 6-foot-2 and 180 pounds, the lefthanded-hitting Moniak drew comparisons to fellow Southern California area product Christian Yelich, a rising star with the Miami Marlins. Both are lanky center fielders with speed and Gold Glove potential who are better pure hitters than power hitters. Like Yelich, Moniak has a patient approach and rarely seems to over-stride at the plate—tips that his grandfather gleaned from the Splendid Splinter.

"I take a lot of pride in hitting," Moniak said. "It's something I work on a lot. I definitely think that's what stood out. When I go up to the plate, I have the mentality that the pitcher is not going to beat me. I go up there with a purpose."

Moniak is in tune with the mechanics of his swing and says that his upper half looks pretty similar to how it looked when he was just 10 years old. He sees the ball well and maintains good bat control. He rarely swings and misses.

Phillies scouting director Johnny Almaraz believes Moniak will eventually hit 15-22 homers a season as he matures. "I think you'll have a Gold Glove center fielder who will hit in the middle of the lineup and be a leader on the team," he said.

Mickey's father, Matt, played baseball at San Diego State. "He was a good ballplayer," Bill Moniak confided, "but he liked to surf and things." But it was his grandson who never seemed to want to do or talk about anything else other than baseball.

"That's it in a nutshell," Moniak said. "If there was anyone ever born to play the game, that little kid is it. He played no other sport."

picks. All the Braves' spending came at a cost, as they were taxed $495,900 for exceeding their bonus pool amount of $13,224,100 by 5 percent.

If teams surpass the 5 percent threshold, they lose draft picks, and it is a line that no team has crossed under the current draft rules. The Phillies exceeded their allotment by 3.58 percent, while the Reds were one of nine teams to remain below the threshold amount.

Not only did teams collectively spend a record amount, but they also brought in a record amount of talent as an unprecedented 209 of the first 210 players drafted signed. Pittsburgh Pirates supplemental first-rounder Nick Lodolo (41st overall) was the lone exception. They also did so expeditiously as just two first-rounders, high school lefthanders Braxton Garrett, drafted seventh overall by the Miami Marlins, and Jason Groome, selected 12th by the Boston Red Sox, remained unsigned entering the day of the July 15 signing deadline. Both agreed to terms well in advance of the 5 p.m. deadline, unlike in years past when a last-minute frenzy often characterized the deadline.

With Garrett and Groome in the fold, along with a couple of other stragglers, players signed at the most prolific rate in draft history. Just two players in the first 10 rounds went unsigned. That eclipsed the previous record low of six, set in 2014 and 2015. Overall, players signed at a 75.5 clip—short of the 78.3 percent pace a year earlier.

### MONIAK MOVES TO HEAD OF CLASS

The Phillies opened the 2016 scouting season with Moniak among a group of about 20 players they considered as potential No. 1 overall picks. They eventually narrowed their list to five, with Almaraz later revealing the identity of four of the candidates: Moniak, University of Florida lefthander A.J. Puk, Mercer outfielder Kyle Lewis and California prep outfielder Blake Rutherford.

Though it was not a particularly strong crop overall with no clearly defined top player, a consensus of other clubs also had Senzel, Groome, Louisville outfielder Corey Ray and Kansas prep righthander Riley Pint ranked among the elite candidates. Moniak and Senzel were considered the two best hitters available, and not surprisingly went off the board 1-2.

Few players had more helium as the spring progressed than Moniak, who became a surefire first-rounder after a strong summer with USA Baseball's 18-and-under team in 2015. An above-average runner with center-field skills to go along with an advanced feel for hitting, Moniak soon surfaced as a candidate in the top 10, and eventually for the No. 1 pick overall once he flashed more power during his senior year at La Costa Canyon High. On the season, he hit .476 with seven home runs and 46 RBIs. He also drilled 12 triples while playing in a big home park.

The 6-foot-2, 180-pound Moniak explained his power surge by saying he was committed to putting on weight. As a high school junior, he failed to go deep even once.

"He was No. 1 on my list—he was the best player in the country," Almaraz said. "There was no projection with Mickey Moniak. He possesses the ability that a lot of college players don't possess. He can run. He can throw. He can hit. His abilities are superior, and that's why we took him."

Senzel, undrafted out of a Knoxville, Tenn., high school in 2013, also catapulted into first-round consideration on the strength of a superior summer performance. He was the top prospect in the Cape Cod League in 2015 after leading the league in RBIs while finishing second in batting. He followed that up with a solid junior season at Tennessee, hitting .352 with eight homers and 59 RBIs, along with a 40-21 walk-strikeout ratio.

Considered the best pure hitter in the college class, Senzel featured an advanced approach at the plate, strength and bat speed. His name rarely came up with the Phillies, in part perhaps because his agent Scott Boras was unlikely to cut a deal that would be to the Phillies' liking. Still, he signed for an amount that was more than $1.5 million below the bonus allotted to the second pick.

Lewis also emerged as a top prospect for the 2016 draft with a dominant performance in the Cape Cod League. He had excellent tools across the board, and that helped to address concerns that came with playing at a smaller school in a weaker conference. As a junior at Mercer, Lewis hit .395 with 20 homers and 72 RBIs, along with a .535 on-base percentage. Though he was a serious candidate to go first overall, Lewis lasted until the 11th pick and was scooped up by the Seattle Mariners.

"He looks like a big leaguer," Mariners scouting director Tom McNamara said. "He's talented, he's got power, he's got bat speed. He's short to the ball for a guy with long arms. He's got work to do and he knows it. But he's eager. We called him and he said, 'I'm ready to go.' He's got aptitude for

TOM PRIDDY

Kyle Lewis went from unheralded performer at Mercer to first-round pick, using a big summer in the Cape Cod League as a springboard

baseball, loves the game and has talent. It's a nice combination."

The 6-foot-4, 205-pound Lewis had arguably the highest ceiling and highest floor in the entire draft, in contrast to the 5-foot-11, 185-pound Ray, who projects more as a slash-and-burn leadoff hitter. He also had superior tools with a little less power than Lewis, but a little more speed. Drafted fifth overall by the Milwaukee Brewers, Ray hit .310 with 15 homers and 60 RBIs, along with 44 stolen bases as a junior at Louisville.

As a 6-foot-7 lefthander with a mid-90s fastball and wipeout slider, Puk was in high demand throughout the 2016 college season, but it didn't escape the attention of the Phillies (or the four teams drafting after them) that his stuff and command were inconsistent, and he was the No. 3 starter on a dominant Florida team. He slipped to the Oakland A's with the sixth pick overall after going 2-3, 3.05 with 37 walks and 101 strikeouts in 74 innings.

"As much as anything, it's just consistency of command, and that's one of the things he'll need to work on to move forward, but we've seen him do that," A's scouting director Eric Kubota said. "We think it's just a matter of experience as much as anything else."

Rutherford, from Chaminade Prep in Canoga Park, Calif., was the top-ranked prep position prospect in the draft until Moniak surged past him. He graded out as a potential five-tool talent with the potential to remain in center field as a pro. But a good, not great senior season, along with his age (19) and signability concerns as a Southern California recruit sent his stock tumbling out of the top half of the first round. Rutherford went to the New York Yankees with the 18th pick overall and signed for $3,282,000—more than

## Top 25 Bonuses

| Player, Pos. | Drafted (Round) | Order | Bonus |
|---|---|---|---|
| 1. Nick Senzel, 3b | Reds (1) | 2 | $6,200,000 |
| 2. * Mickey Moniak, of | Phillies (1) | 1 | $6,100,000 |
| 3. * Riley Pint, rhp | Rockies (1) | 4 | $4,800,000 |
| 4. * Braxton Garrett, lhp | Marlins (1) | 7 | $4,145,900 |
| 5. Corey Ray, of | Brewers (1) | 5 | $4,125,000 |
| 6. A.J. Puk, lhp | Athletics (1) | 6 | $4,069,200 |
| 7. * Ian Anderson, rhp | Braves (1) | 3 | $4,000,000 |
| 8. Cal Quantrill, rhp | Padres (1) | 8 | $3,963,045 |
| 9. * Jason Groome, lhp | Red Sox (1) | 12 | $3,650,000 |
| 10. * Matt Manning, rhp | Tigers (1) | 9 | $3,505,800 |
| 11. * Kevin Gowdy, rhp | Phillies (2) | 42 | $3,500,000 |
| 12. Zack Collins, c | White Sox (1) | 10 | $3,380,600 |
| 13. Kyle Lewis, of | Mariners (1) | 11 | $3,286,700 |
| 14. * Blake Rutherford, of | Yankees (1) | 18 | $3,282,000 |
| 15. * Taylor Trammell, of | Reds (1-S) | 35 | $3,200,000 |
| 16. * Forrest Whitley, rhp | Astros (1) | 17 | $3,148,000 |
| 17. * Joey Wentz, lhp | Braves (1-S) | 40 | $3,050,000 |
| 18. * Alex Kirilloff, of | Twins (1) | 15 | $2,817,100 |
| 19. * Josh Lowe, 3b | Rays (1) | 13 | $2,600,000 |
| 20. * Will Benson, of | Indians (1) | 14 | $2,500,000 |
| * Kyle Muller, lhp | Braves (2) | 44 | $2,500,000 |
| 22. Justin Dunn, rhp | Mets (1) | 19 | $2,378,800 |
| 23. * Gavin Lux, ss | Dodgers (1) | 20 | $2,317,000 |
| 24. Will Craig, 3b | Pirates (1) | 22 | $2,253,700 |
| 25. * Nolan Jones, 3b | Indians (2) | 55 | $2,250,000 |

**High school selection*

## WORTH NOTING

**COREY RAY** (Brewers, fifth overall), righthander **ZACK BURDI** (White Sox, 26th) and catcher **WILL SMITH** (Dodgers, 32nd)—marked the sixth time in draft history that one college produced three first-rounders. Vanderbilt turned the trick in 2015. Led by the Cardinals, the Atlantic Coast Conference produced eight first-round selections, and had four catchers taken among the first 42 picks, led by Miami's **ZACK COLLINS** (White Sox, 10th overall).

■ While almost everything related to the drafting and signing of domestic talent in 2016 was orderly, the signing of international talent was marked by controversy and the domination of the process by a few clubs. The Red Sox made headlines just prior to the July 2 international signing period when Major League Baseball handed down unprecedented penalties, granting free agency to several prospects previously signed by the organization and banning the team from signing any international players during the 2016-17 international signing period. MLB ruled that the Red Sox tried to circumvent international bonus restrictions in 2015 by signing several Venezuelan players in "package deals." Meanwhile, the Padres became a major international player by signing Cuban lefthander **ADRIAN MOREJON**, 17, for $11 million, boosting an already formidable international class. The Padres had already exceeded their bonus pool limit and effectively had to pay a 100 percent tax as a result—costing them $22 million in all. In addition to Morejon, the Padres signed three other top international prospects: Dominican shortstop **LUIS ALMANZAR** (for $4 million), Venezuelan shortstop **GABRIEL ARIAS** ($1.9 million) and Dominican outfielder **JEISSEN ROSARIO** ($1.85 million), and 20 players overall. The top-ranked international player signed in 2016, Venezuelan shortstop

CONTINUED ON PAGE 758

## WORTH NOTING

CONTINUED FROM PAGE 757

**KEVIN MAITAN**, signed with the Braves for $4.25 million.

■ The trading of draft picks had not been permitted until the last round of labor negotiations, with the creation of competitive balance draft selections—the first (and so far only) picks that teams are allowed to trade. In both 2015 and '16, the Braves traded for two such selections. In 2016, they acquired the 40th overall selection from the Marlins as part of a 13-player, three-way trade in July 2015 involving the Marlins and Dodgers. They also secured the 76th pick from the Orioles on May 23, 2016, for agreeing to assume the remainder of the contract of major league lefthander Brian Matusz while sending a pair of minor league pitchers to the O's. "We are building for the future and the 76th pick fits within our plan," Braves general manager John Coppolella said. "We recognize value not only in terms of the potential player we select, but also in the flexibility provided with added bonus pool money." Matusz was subsequently designated for assignment by the Braves. In effect, the Braves assumed the remainder of Matusz' $3.9 million salary in order to gain an extra draft pick and sweeten their draft pool by $838,900 (the figure assigned to the 76th selection). With the two extra selections, the Braves added Kansas prep lefthander **JOEY WENTZ** (40th) and University of California catcher **BRETT CUMBERLAND** (76th).

■ The Major League Scouting Bureau, which was formed in 1974 to provide detailed scouting reports to major league clubs and became the jurisdiction of Major League Baseball in 1985, had its mission significantly changed, making its impact on the draft negligible. "In the last decade, the way clubs approach scouting has really changed dramatically," said Bill Bavasi, who became the bureau's director in 2014. "We have to be the bureau that clubs want it to

$800,000 above the slot amount for his pick.

The 2016 draft was more difficult to project than normal because of no clear-cut, top-of-the-draft option, but also because the deepest demographic for first-round talent, high school pitching, was also the one that scared teams the most.

Pint and Groome were the two best prep arms from the outset, though they didn't come without plenty of scrutiny. Pint, a Kansas product whose fastball peaked at 102 mph, was taken fourth overall by the Colorado Rockies, while Groome, a New Jersey lefthander, went to the Boston Red Sox with the 12th selection.

### GROOME, PEREZ SLIP AMID CONCERNS

Groome, a 6-foot-5 lefthander whom many teams considered the best pitching prospect available, fell out of the top 10. He was one of two players, in particular, who saw their stock fall due to off-field questions. Puerto Rican shortstop Delvin Perez also slid, to the St. Louis Cardinals with the 23rd pick overall, after also being considered one of the 10 best players available.

As a big lefty with a low- to mid-90s fastball, hammer curveball and promising changeup, Groome had a chance to be the first pitcher off the board but teams had concerns about his makeup and signability. After 11 clubs passed, the Red Sox gambled on his considerable upside.

Groome was ecstatic to go off the board where he did after it looked like he might drop further. He told reporters following his selection that the Red Sox were his favorite team and that "everything happens for a reason." He waited until the day of the signing deadline before finally agreeing on a $3.65 million bonus.

Perez, meanwhile, tested positive for a performance-enhancing substance during his predraft drug test administered by Major League Baseball.

MIKE JANES

Delvin Perez

Teams scrambled to figure out if they would consider the slick-fielding shortstop if he were available when they picked in the first round. Perez had been discussed as high as No. 2 (Reds), and more frequently at No. 5 (Brewers) or No. 8 (Padres).

"Obviously, when the results of that test came out and we were made aware of it, it was something we had to think about," Cardinals general manager John Mozeliak said. "And it definitely changed our calculus.

"Our takeaway on this is that we understand he made a mistake. We understand that he realizes that this cost him a lot. I certainly hope people understand that he was going to be chosen at some point. If we have to take a black eye for being that team, we'll live with that."

It was a down year for shortstops anyway, and Perez' fall resulted in Wisconsin prep shortstop Gavin Lux becoming the first middle infielder drafted. He went 20th overall to the Los Angeles Dodgers.

### Largest Bonuses By Round

| | Player, Pos. | Club | Bonus |
|---|---|---|---|
| 1. | Nick Senzel, 3b | Reds | $6,200,000 |
| 1-S. | * Taylor Trammell, of | Reds | $3,200,000 |
| 2. | * Kevin Gowdy, rhp | Phillies | $3,500,000 |
| 3. | * Mason Thompson, rhp | Padres | $1,750,000 |
| 4. | * Bryse Wilson, rhp | Braves | $1,200,000 |
| 5. | Cole Irvin, lhp | Phillies | $800,000 |
| 6. | * Luis Curbelo, ss | White Sox | $700,000 |
| 7. | Tyler Ramirez, of | Athletics | $300,000 |
| 8. | Ryan January, c | Diamondbacks | $350,000 |
| 9. | Colin Holderman, rhp | Mets | $400,000 |
| 10. | Dakota Mekkes, rhp | Cubs | $275,000 |
| 11. | * Chad McClanahan, 3b | Brewers | $1,200,000 |
| 12. | * Brady Whalen, ss | Cardinals | $475,000 |
| 13. | Cody Thomas, of | Dodgers | $297,500 |
| 14. | Gabriel Garcia, rhp | Brewers | $150,000 |
| 15. | * Jack Suwinski, of | Padres | $550,000 |
| 16. | * Anthony Churlin, of | Athletics | $175,000 |
| 17. | Several tied at | | $100,000 |
| 18. | * Marcus Mack, of | Rangers | $175,000 |
| 19. | Chris Mathewson, lhp | Dodgers | $202,000 |
| 20. | Jack Kruger, c | Angels | $395,000 |
| 21. | * Dalton Griffin, of | Royals | $105,000 |
| 22. | * Kyle Young, lhp | Phillies | $225,000 |
| 23. | * Dom Abbadessa, of | Blue Jays | $150,000 |
| 24. | Several tied at | | $100,000 |
| 25. | * Blake Lillis, lhp | Brewers | $127,814 |
| Other | Ethan Skender, ss | Padres (28) | $465,000 |

**High school selection.*

The San Diego Padres, with three selections, also had a big effect on the first round. With the eighth pick, they went for Stanford righthander Cal Quantrill, who missed most of the 2015 college season and all of 2016 while recuperating from Tommy John surgery. The Padres didn't hesitate in taking Quantrill, and signed the son of ex-big-leaguer Paul Quantrill to a bonus of $3,963,045. Not only was the amount $333,000 over slot, but Quantrill also was the highest pick to receive an over-slot bonus until Garrett, the seventh pick overall, signed at the deadline for $4,145,900—$389,600 in excess of the allotted amount.

In order to accommodate Quantrill, the Padres saved money with their second pick in the first round, signing Texas prep shortstop Hudson Sanchez, the 24th overall pick, for $1 million, the lowest bonus in the first round and substantially less than the $2,191,200 assigned for the slot. Though he was one of the better hitters in the high school ranks, Sanchez had an uncertain defensive future and projected more as a third-round choice. Instead, the Padres made him the first real shocker in the first round.

The Padres also worked their bonus allotment to sign two high school righthanders to amounts that were significantly over slot: supplemental second-rounder Reggie Lawson for $1.9 million and third-rounder Mason Thompson for $1.75 million. Like Quantrill, Thompson missed the 2016 season because of Tommy John surgery.

The New York Mets targeted University of Connecticut lefthander Anthony Kay with the 31st pick and planned to pay him at least slot money ($1,972,100), but ended up agreeing on a bonus of $1.1 million when a physical revealed concerns with Kay's left elbow. He signed two days before the deadline.

With bonus money suddenly at their disposal, the Mets turned their attention to Kentucky prep righthander Cameron Planck, and signed their 11th-round pick to a bonus of $1,000,001. Players signing after the 10th round do not count against a club's bonus pool unless the bonus exceeds $100,000, but the Mets were able to absorb the excess because of the $872,100 they saved on Kay.

### PREP PITCHERS PROVE POPULAR

The first round comprised 34 picks: 23 regular picks and 11 more awarded to clubs as compensation for the loss of free agents. Seven additional selections were made between the first and second rounds: six competitive balance picks, and the seventh to the Dodgers (36th overall) as compensation for their failure to sign righthander Kyle Funkhouser in the 2015 draft. Funkhouser, then a junior righthander from Louisville, was the highest unsigned selection from 2015.

The first round was an equal 17-17 split between college and high school players, and between pitchers and position players.

Overall, teams drafted 1,216 players, with 766 (or 62.9 percent) coming from the college ranks. The most popular demographic in the first round was college pitchers, with 10 selections, but high school pitchers were the undisputed strength of the 2016 draft. Five went in the first 12 picks, the highest representation from that demographic since 2000, when Mike Stodolka, Matt Harrington, Matt Wheatland, Mark Phillips and Joe Torres were all drafted among the first 10 picks. None ever played in the majors.

Because of the injury epidemic among young arms that has made clubs increasingly leery of taking high school pitchers early in the first round, just seven such pitchers were taken among the first 15 picks in the previous three years. In 2015, no high school pitchers were taken in the first 12 picks and only one in the top 20.

But 2016 was a different story. Besides Pint, Garrett and Groome, righthander Ian Anderson was taken by the Braves with the third pick overall and righthander Matt Manning went to the Detroit Tigers with the ninth selection.

Groome, who spent his junior year at the IMG Academy in Bradenton, Fla., before moving back home to New Jersey for his senior year, was the prep pitcher who appeared to separate himself heading into the 2016 season, though Pint opened eyes with a fastball that reached triple digits.

Groome's senior season at Barnegat High, however, was clouded in controversy. Two weeks in, and a week after a 19-strikeout no-hitter, Groome was suspended for 30 days because he violated a New Jersey State Interscholastic Athletic Association transfer rule, despite returning to his parents' home and former school.

After returning from his suspension, Groome took awhile to regain his groove. Teams also developed concerns about his makeup, and it didn't help his cause that he began to float a $4 million bonus demand to scare off some teams. When the draft arrived, Groome's uncertain status caused his stock to fall, though things worked in his favor when the Red Sox snapped him up with the 12th pick.

"I always said I just wanted to end up somewhere I'm comfortable and feel protected," Groome said. "Like I said, there's no other spot to do that than Boston."

"He's got really good stuff," Red Sox scouting director Mike Rikard said. "He's got a big fastball, a good curveball and he can throw his changeup for strikes as well. He's a big, durable guy, and he's got a nice delivery. He throws the ball easy and he's a strike thrower as well, so we do see him as a starter."

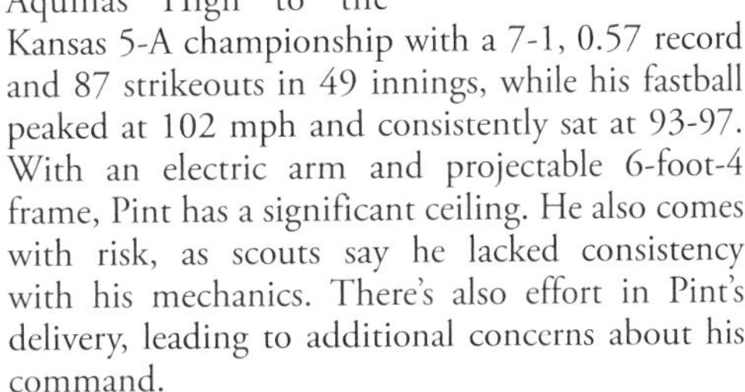
MIKE JANES

Jason Groome

Pint led St. Thomas Aquinas High to the Kansas 5-A championship with a 7-1, 0.57 record and 87 strikeouts in 49 innings, while his fastball peaked at 102 mph and consistently sat at 93-97. With an electric arm and projectable 6-foot-4 frame, Pint has a significant ceiling. He also comes with risk, as scouts say he lacked consistency with his mechanics. There's also effort in Pint's delivery, leading to additional concerns about his command.

The 6-foot-3, 190-pound Garrett's stuff, polished delivery and advanced feel for pitching may allow him to move through the minor league ranks as fast as many college starters. He was regarded as having the best curveball of any prep pitcher on the board. As a junior and senior at Alabama's Florence High, he posted an overall 13-3, 0.65

## One Team's Draft: Cincinnati Reds

| Player, Pos. | Bonus | Player, Pos. | Bonus | Player, Pos. | Bonus |
|---|---|---|---|---|---|
| 1. Nick Senzel, 3b | $6,200,000 | 9. Alex Webb, rhp | $5,000 | 18. *J.C. Flowers, of | Did not sign |
| 1. *Travis Trammell, of | $3,200,000 | 10. Lucas Benenati, rhp | $5,000 | 19. Matt Blandino, rhp | $35,000 |
| 2. Chris Okey, c | $2,000,000 | 11. Joel Kuhnel, rhp | $125,000 | 20. *Todd Lott, of | Did not sign |
| 3. *Nick Hanson, rhp | $925,000 | 12. Cassidy Brown, c | $120,000 | 21. Andrew Wright, lhp | $100,000 |
| 4. Scott Moss, lhp | $577,400 | 13. Ryan Olson, rhp | $250,000 | 22. Aaron Quillen, rhp | $5,000 |
| 5. Ryan Hendrix, rhp | $410,000 | 14. Jesse Adams, lhp | $5,000 | 23. Manny Cruz, ss | $75,000 |
| 6. *Tyler Mondile, rhp | $309,700 | 15. Jesse Stallings, rhp | $150,000 | 24. Bruce Yari, 1b | $30,000 |
| 7. Andy Cox, lhp | $5,000 | 16. *Mauro Conde, of | $100,000 | 25. Colby Wright, 2b | $1,000 |
| 8. John Sansone, 2b | $15,000 | 17. Mitchell Traver, rhp | Did not sign | Other Patrick Riehl (26), rhp | $25,000 |

**High school selection*

## WORTH NOTING

be—that clubs need it to be." That meant shifting away from the current draft class. Instead, the bureau focused on identifying prospects in future classes and took on a more administrative role, gathering medical information and video on young prospects. The change in mission also meant that the bureau laid off many of its scouts.

■ In the third round, the Twins drafted **GRIFFIN JAX**, a righthander from Air Force, making him the highest draft-eligible pick ever out of one of the nation's service academies and the sixth draft ever from the Air Force Academy. Jax accepted a $645,600 bonus from the Twins, slot money for the 93rd pick, even though he is committed to five years of active duty when he graduates in 2017. He could have his commitment deferred while he pursues a professional baseball career. Jax, the son of former NFL linebacker Garth Jax, saw his draft profile skyrocket as a junior by going 9-2, 2.05, while walking 10 and striking out 90 in 105 innings.

■ Yavapai (Ariz.) won the Junior College World Series behind the stellar pitching of lefthander **JOJO ROMERO**, who walked none and struck out 15 in defeating San Jacinto (Texas) 5-2 in the championship game. A night earlier, San Jac lefthander **DEVIN SMELTZER** outdid Romero by striking out 20 in an 8-1 over Chattahoochee Valley (Ala.), propelling his team into the final. Less than a week later, Romero went in the fourth round to the Phillies and Smeltzer a round later to the Dodgers. Romero signed for $800,000; Smeltzer, a childhood cancer survivor, for $500,000. The top-ranked juco talent, Logan (Ill.) JC righthander **MATTHIAS DIETZ**, drafted in the second round (69th overall) by the Orioles, signed for $1.3 million. On the season, the 6-foot-6, 220-pound Dietz went 12-1, 1.22 with 11

CONTINUED ON PAGE 760

## WORTH NOTING

CONTINUED FROM PAGE 759

walks and 117 strikeouts in 103 innings with a fastball that peaked at 98 mph.

■ Since Jeff Luhnow took over as general manager of the Astros prior to the 2012 draft, his club had picked first, first, first and second in consecutive years. In 2016, the Astros picked 17th, dictating a change in strategy. Rather than working their overall bonus pool to get as much talent as possible, the Astros simply took the best player on their board, 6-foot-7 Texas prep righthander **FORREST WHITLEY**, who went 9-1, 0.31 with 126 strikeouts in 68 innings for Alamo Heights High as a senior. Whitley emerged as a top prospect after going on a strict diet after his junior season and dropping nearly 70 pounds.

■ The Rays used their first-round pick on Georgia high school third baseman **JOSH LOWE**, one of the top lefthanded power hitters in the draft, and took his older brother **NATE**, a lefthanded-hitting first baseman from Mississippi State, in the 13th round. Their father David, a righthander, was a fifth-round pick of the Mariners in 1986 out of a Florida high school, but elected to attend the Naval Academy and never played baseball professionally.

■ Righthander **BRANDEN WEBB** was expected to be a top prospect for the 2014 draft after opening his senior season at Owasso (Okla.) High by pitching two straight no-hitters. Two years later, he finally got his first real shot at a professional baseball career, when he was drafted in the third round by the Brewers. Webb was sidetracked two years earlier by Tommy John surgery. After sitting out all of 2015 while rehabbing his elbow, he enrolled at South Carolina and as a 20-year-old freshman dazzled in his only season with the Gamecocks, going 10-6, 3.09 with 128 strikeouts in 102 innings.

### Highest Unsigned Picks

| Player, Pos., Team (Round) | College | Re-Drafted |
|---|---|---|
| Nick Lodolo, rhp, Pirates (1-S) | Texas Christian | N/A |
| Tyler Buffett, rhp, Astros (7) | * Oklahoma State | N/A |
| Nick Quintana, ss, Red Sox (11) | Arizona | N/A |
| Zach Thompson, lhp, Rays (11) | Kentucky | N/A |
| Jason Delay, c, Giants (11) | * Vanderbilt | N/A |
| Jamie Sara, rhp, Padres (12) | William & Mary | N/A |
| Graham Ashcraft, rhp, Dodgers (12) | Mississippi State | N/A |
| Trey Cobb, rhp, Cubs (12) | * Oklahoma State | N/A |
| Nick Eicholtz, rhp, Marlins (13) | * Alabama | N/A |
| Brady Bramlett, rhp, Red Sox (13) | None | N/A |

**TOTAL UNSIGNED PICKS:** Top 5 Rounds (1), Top 10 Rounds (2).

**Returned to same school*

record with 26 walks and 266 strikeouts in 129 innings.

"I think he's one of the more polished high school kids we've probably ever taken," Marlins scouting director Stan Meek said. "He's a lefthander who's already got pitches in place and is a strike-thrower. His delivery is kind of in place. There will be a few tweaks, but nothing major. He has one of the better curveballs I've seen, probably in the top five. He's got plus control of it."

For all the interest in Groome, Pint and Garrett, the first high school pitcher drafted was Anderson, who came on fast to go third overall to the Braves. By signing him for $4 million ($2,510,800 below slot), the Braves were able to load up on three other promising young arms: Kansas lefthander Joey Wentz (40th overall), who signed for $3.05 million; Texas lefthander Kyle Muller (44th), who signed for $2.5 million; and North Carolina righthander Bryse Wilson (third round), who signed for $1.2 million—all significantly above the bonus slots for those picks.

BILL MITCHELL

Ian Anderson

Anderson's senior season at Shenendehowa High in Clifton Park, N.Y., got off to an inauspicious start when he was sidelined first by pneumonia and then by an oblique strain, while warming up in the bullpen for his first scheduled start on April 13. But he regrouped to finish the season on a positive note with a fastball up to 95 mph. In his final outing prior to the draft, with many of Atlanta's top scouts in attendance, Anderson recorded 16 strikeouts over seven shutout innings in a state semifinal playoff game.

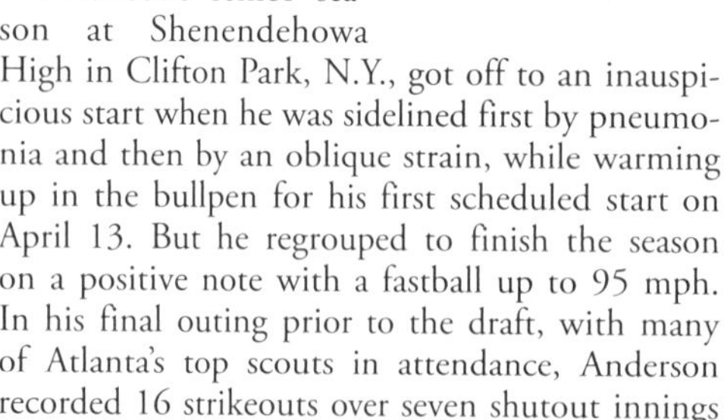

"He's very advanced for a 17-year-old," Braves scouting director Brian Bridges said, citing Anderson's command. "What really sealed the deal was the maturity of this young man at such a young age."

While the Braves admitted they didn't take the highest-ranked pitcher on their board, Bridges said he thought his team got the pitcher that best fit its plan. "I took the best pitcher on the board that we felt as an organization, as a scouting department," Bridges said. "This was a big victory for the Braves today. When you're fortunate to get three of your first 20, you're happy."

Of all the young pitchers drafted in the top half of the first round, none boosted his stock during his senior year of high school as much as Manning, a 6-foot-7 righthander from Sheldon High in Sacramento, Calif., a relative unknown at the outset of the 2016 season and the son of ex-NBA player Rich Manning.

A significant basketball talent with a commitment to play that sport at Loyola Marymount, Manning was late starting his senior baseball season because of his basketball obligation. But he bolted onto the baseball scene with a fastball that was 96-97 mph out of the chute and peaked at 99. The Tigers, always on the lookout for hard throwers, drafted him and quickly him signed for $3,505,800—slot money for the ninth pick.

"I know in my heart that I'm a baseball player," Manning said. "I've been attracted to baseball since I was young. It's going to be a decision that my family is going to make, but I'm ready to make it."

As popular as prep pitchers were, teams also made a run on high school outfielders, led by Moniak. He was accompanied in the first round by Rutherford, Will Benson (Indians, 14th overall), Alex Kirilloff (Twins, 15th) and Dylan Carlson (Cardinals, 33rd).

The 6-foot-6, 220-pound Benson drew instant comparisons to Chicago Cubs outfielder Jason Heyward, who was coincidentally the 14th pick in the 2007 draft. Like Heyward, Benson was a metro Atlanta prep prospect, a lefthanded hitter with a similar build and an outstanding athlete for his size. Scouts say Benson's bat speed and strength give him well above-average raw power; with his aggressive approach, he may even have a better chance than Heyward of tapping into it.

"It's an honor to have that comparison," said Benson, who hit .454 with eight homers and 41 RBIs as a senior at the Westminster Schools. "Defensively, that's a true comparison. I think we both have a lot of range and can throw the ball. I think offensively I can possibly do better. He's always on base and he hits for average. I think that I can hit for a little more power and still hit for average. Defensively, I want to be just like that, but offensively I think I can take it to the next level."

## RECORD SPENDING SETS DRAFT APART

The current Collective Bargaining Agreement, which became effective with the 2012 draft, took much of the drama out of the signing process. Only a handful of picks in the first 10 rounds each year under the new system have gone unsigned, but the 2016 draft took it to a whole new level.

It wasn't a coincidence, though, that more money than ever was spent to sign draft picks.

Overall, bonus payments to first-round picks continued to climb, averaging $2,897,778—an all-time high and a 4.4 percent uptick from 2015, when the first-round average was $2,774,945.

That occurred, even as none of the first five players drafted, led by Moniak, earned bonuses that equaled or topped the assigned value for their slots. In fact, the five were paid, on average,

$1,540,600 below slot, and just six of the 34 players drafted in the first round signed for amounts in excess of their assigned bonus slots.

Yet it was hardly an indicator that teams were on an economy kick, and they paid out numerous significant bonuses through all 40 rounds, including $1.2 million by the Brewers to 11th-rounder Chad McClanahan, $465,000 by the Padres to 28th-rounder Ethan Skender and $248,500 by the Dodgers to 38th-rounder Kevin Malisheski.

Under the current rules, as negotiated by Major League Baseball and the Players Association, each pick in the top 10 rounds comes with an assigned value, and the total for each of a team's choices covers what it can spend without penalty in those rounds. Any bonus money in excess of $100,000 handed out in rounds 11-40 also counts against a club's bonus pool. The aggregate amounts teams can spend changes each year in accordance with MLB's reported revenue, and the amount increased by 4.62 percent compared to 2015. The aggregate pool for all 30 teams in the first 10 rounds in 2016 was $234,331,200.

Not only did seven of the first eight picks in the draft belong to National League clubs, but so did the five largest bonus pools, led by the Reds and Phillies. All had more than $10 million at their disposal, including the Braves ($13,224,100), Padres ($12,869,200) and Rockies ($11,153,400).

At the opposite end were the Cubs, who surrendered their first- and second-round choices for signing Heyward and righthander John Lackey as free agents, and had a mere $2,245,100 to spend. The Cubs' initial selection came with the 104th pick, Oklahoma State righthander Thomas Hatch, who signed for $573,900—slot money.

As was the case in the first four years of the slotting system, no team spent more than 5 percent above its bonus threshold in 2016. A club that exceeds its pool by 0-5 percent pays a 75 percent tax on the overage. At higher thresholds, teams forfeit future draft picks.

From 2012-15, clubs outspent their pools a total of 51 times. In 2016, 21 clubs exceeded their limit, including the Braves. The Dodgers, Brewers, Yankees and Los Angeles Angels were also taxed at the full 5 percent.

Nick Senzel

Senzel's $6.2 million bonus fell short of the $6.5 million bonus the Arizona Diamondbacks gave No. 1 pick Dansby Swanson in 2015, and no records were set in individual rounds, although teams spent liberally in the 11th round, and beyond in some cases.

The Phillies, Reds and Braves all took full advantage of their bonus pool allotments to secure premium first-round picks and at least one other significant player who was worthy of being taken in the first round, and was paid accordingly.

In the case of the Reds, they not only paid out the largest bonus in the first round to Senzel, but also in the supplemental first round ($3.2 million) to Georgia high school outfielder Taylor Trammell, who had initially been targeted as a mid-first round pick. Senzel's bonus, some $1.5 million below the amount allotted for the second pick, enabled the Reds to spend more than $1.4 million above slot to land Trammell with the 35th pick. The Reds then signed Clemson catcher Chris Okey, their second-round pick for $2 million.

The Reds blew well past their previous club record for bonus spending when they spent $9,018,050 in 2015.

In addition to the Braves, the Padres were the other obvious club to benefit from their liberal bonus pool allotment. Besides Quantrill, they gained two extra first-round picks as compensation for the loss of free agents Ian Kennedy and Justin Upton, and a supplemental second-round selection as a competitive balance pick. Their six picks in the top 85 were more than any other club, and five more than they had a year earlier.

"It's a big influx of talent into the system," Padres general manager A.J. Preller said. "Again, the draft, you never really fully know until a few years down the road exactly. But I feel really good. We added a lot of top-end prospects, a lot of depth into the system."

As in recent drafts, teams manipulated their bonus pools by drafting college seniors in the latter part of the first 10 rounds. With little bargaining leverage, seniors usually sign at minimal expense, enabling clubs to allocate money to other, more expensive prospects throughout the draft.

The run on college seniors began in the fourth round, when the Padres took Southeast Missouri State lefthander Joey Lucchesi and the Tigers selected Funkhouser with consecutive picks. Lucchesi received a $100,000 bonus, while Funkhouser got $750,000—significantly above the pick value of $526,200.

Funkhouser was an unconventional senior, but he was considered an elite prospect in the 2015 draft and in line for a bonus upward of $2 million. He labored down the stretch and fell to the 35th pick overall, and decided not to sign, making him the highest unsigned selection from 2015. His ties to Boras also played a role in his slide down the draft board.

After spending his junior season at Louisville in the spotlight, Funkhouser ceded much of the attention in 2016 to a stellar crop of Cardinals juniors as Ray, reliever Zack Burdi and catcher Will Smith all went in the first round. Three other teammates were also taken before Funkhouser was selected after an inconsistent senior year. But the 6-foot-3, 220-pound righthander appeared to recoup some of his lost stature toward the end of the 2016 season, when his fastball rebounded to the mid-90s, and he was paid a bonus more in line with his talent, not his senior standing.

"I don't regret a single thing I did last year, coming back," Funkhouser said. "I wouldn't change a single thing about it. Coming back here, I had a great experience, a great time, got my degree."

In all, some 63 college seniors were taken in the first 10 rounds.

## IN FOCUS: CAL QUANTRILL

BILL MITCHELL

Cal Quantrill was devastated, if not downright angry. When he got the news in March 2015, just as he was embarking on his sophomore year at Stanford, that he needed Tommy John surgery, he was upset about losing all the time he had prepared to be one of the nation's premier pitching prospects.

"It was hours and hours of work, and it was all taken away," Quantrill said. "I sat there for about 15 minutes—sad, angry. But I quickly realized that feeling sorry for myself wasn't going to fix anything."

That is when the son of former big leaguer Paul Quantrill began his comeback quest in earnest. "I wasn't going to just take a break," he said. "It wasn't going to be eight or 10 months of me doing nothing, just sitting around."

Quantrill was the Pacific-12 Conference freshman of the year in 2014, and began his sophomore season at 2-0, 1.93 before injuring his elbow. He never pitched another game for Stanford, but was busy getting ready for the 2016 draft, and the San Diego Padres didn't hesitate in taking him with the eighth pick overall—the first college righthander drafted.

"We feel like we got a value play," general manager A.J. Preller said. "Honestly, if he's healthy all year pitching at Stanford, we probably don't see him there."

"I'm 100 percent ready to go," Quantrill said. "The moment I get the chance, I'll be ready to pitch."

# 2016 Draft List

**Did not sign. Major leaguers in bold, with first and last years noted. Order of selection indicated in parentheses. For the first five rounds, the peak level of each player is noted.*

## ARIZONA DIAMONDBACKS (13)

1. (Choice forfeited for signing Zack Greinke as free agent).
1. Anfernee Grier, of, Auburn University (Competitive balance Round 'A' pick—39th).
2. Andy Yerzy, c, York Mills Collegiate Institute, Toronto.
3. Jon Duplantier, rhp, Rice University.
4. Curtis Taylor, rhp, University of British Columbia.
5. Joey Rose, 3b, Toms River (N.J.) North HS.
6. Mack Lemieux, lhp, Palm Beach State (Fla.) JC.
7. Jordan Watson, lhp, University of Science and Arts of Oklahoma.
8. Ryan January, c, San Jacinto (Texas) JC.
9. Tommy Eveld, rhp, University of South Florida.
10. Stephen Smith, of, Texas Tech.
11. Jake Polancic, rhp, Yale SS, Abbotsford, B.C.
12. Gavin Stupienski, c, UNC Wilmington.
13. Manny Jefferson, 2b, Pepperdine University.
14. Colin Poche, lhp, Dallas Baptist University.
15. Tyler Keele, rhp, Morehead State University.
16. Nick Blackburn, rhp, University of Illinois.
17. Jake Winston, rhp, University of Southern Mississippi.
18. *Bowden Francis, rhp, Chipola (Fla.) JC.
19. Mark Karaviotis, ss, University of Oregon.
20. Connor Grey, rhp, St. Bonaventure University.
21. *Cameron Cannon, ss, Mountain Ridge HS, Glendale, Ariz.
22. Kevin Ginkel, rhp, University of Arizona.
23. Luke Van Rycheghem, c, Ursuline College SS, Chatham, Ont.
24. Riley Smith, rhp, Louisiana State University.
25. Myles Babitt, of, Cal State East Bay.

DRAFT DROP *Son of Shooty Babitt, major leaguer (1981)*

26. Tanner Hill, 1b, Texas State University.
27. Gabe Gonzalez, rhp, JC of Southern Nevada.
28. *Edmond Americaan, of, Trinity Christian Academy, Lake Worth, Fla.
29. *Hunter Kiel, rhp, Pensacola State (Fla.) JC.
30. *Brandon Martorano, c, Christian Brothers Academy, Lincroft, N.J.
31. Williams Durruthy, rhp, Florida International University.
32. Trevor Simms, rhp, Tulane University.
33. Paxton de la Garza, ss, Angelo State (Texas) University.
34. Connor Owings, 2b, Coastal Carolina University.

DRAFT DROP *Brother of Chris Owings, first-round draft pick (2009); major leaguer (2013-15)*

35. Billy Endris, of, Florida Atlantic University.
36. Robert Galligan, lhp, University of Maryland.
37. *Welby Malczewski, lhp, Heartland (Ill.) CC.
38. *Nelson Mompierre, c, Miami-Dade JC.
39. *Jacob Olson, 2b, West Georgia Tech JC.
40. *Jordan Wiley, of, Richland HS, North Richland Hills, Texas.

## ATLANTA BRAVES (3)

1. Ian Anderson, rhp, Shenendehowa HS, Clifton Park, N.Y.

DRAFT DROP *Twin brother of Ben Anderson, 26th-round draft pick, Blue Jays (2016)*

1. Joey Wentz, lhp, Shawnee Mission East HS, Prairie Village, Kan. (Competitive balance Round 'A' pick—40th; obtained in trade with Marlins).
2. Kyle Muller, lhp, Dallas Jesuit Prep, Dallas.
2. Brett Cumberland, c, University of California (Competitive balance Round 'B' pick—76th; obtained in trade with Orioles).
3. Drew Harrington, lhp, University of Louisville.
4. Bryse Wilson, rhp, Orange HS, Hillsborough, N.C.
5. Jeremy Walker, rhp, Gardner-Webb University.
6. Matt Gonzalez, 2b, Georgia Tech.
7. J.B. Moss, of, Texas A&M University.
8. Taylor Hyssong, lhp, UNC Wilmington.
9. Tyler Neslony, of, Texas Tech.
10. Marcus Mooney, ss, University of South Carolina.
11. Matt Rowland, rhp, Pope HS, Marietta, Ga.
12. Brandon White, rhp, Lander (S.C.) University.
13. Brandon White, rhp, Davenport (Mich.) University.
14. Ramon Osuna, 1b, Walters State (Tenn.) CC.
15. Zach Becherer, rhp, Rend Lake (Ill.) JC.
16. *Josh Anthony, 3b, Western Oklahoma State JC.
17. Devan Watts, rhp, Tusculum (Tenn.) College.
18. Zach Rice, lhp, University of North Carolina.
19. Tucker Davidson, lhp, Midland (Texas) JC.
20. Gabe Howell, 2b, Trion (Ga.) HS.
21. Dalton Carroll, rhp, University of Utah.
22. Alex Lee, 1b, Samford University.
23. Griffin Benson, 1b, Aledo (Texas) HS.
24. Matt Hearn, of, Mission (Calif.) JC.
25. Ryan O'Malley, 3b, Sonoma State (Calif.) University.
26. Alan Crowley, c, Reedley (Calif.) JC.
27. Corbin Clouse, lhp, Davenport (Mich.) University.
28. Nick Shumpert, 2b, San Jacinto (Texas) JC.

DRAFT DROP *Son of Terry Shumpert, major leaguer (1990-2003)*

29. Jackson Pokorney, of, Mater Dei HS, Evansville, Ind.
30. Cameron Stanton, rhp, St. Edward's (Texas) University.
31. *Cameron Jabara, rhp, Newport Harbor HS, Newport Beach, Calif.
32. Ryan Schlosser, rhp, Century (Minn.) JC.
33. *Handsome Monica, c, Northwest Florida State JC.
34. Jared James, of, Cal Poly Pomona.

DRAFT DROP *Son of Dion James, first-round draft pick, Brewers (1980); major leaguer (1983-96)*

35. *Michael Gizzi, rhp, State JC of Florida-Manatee.
36. *Andres Perez, c, Pinecrest Academy, Cumming, Ga.

DRAFT DROP *Son of Eddie Perez, major leaguer (1995-2005)*

37. *Zac Kristofak, rhp, Walton HS, Marietta, Ga.
38. *Dayton Tripp, rhp, Rend Lake (Ill.) JC.
39. Parker Danciu, lhp, Marshall University.
40. *Dylan Beasley, rhp, Rome (Ga.) HS.

## BALTIMORE ORIOLES (15)

1. (Choice forfeited for signing Yovani Gallardo as free agent).
1. Cody Sedlock, rhp, University of Illinois (Compensation for loss of Wei-Yin Chen as free agent—27th).
2. Keegan Akin, lhp, Western Michigan University.
2. Matthias Dietz, rhp, John A. Logan (Ill.) JC (Special compensation for failure to sign 2015 second-round pick Jonathan Hughes—69th).
3. Austin Hays, of, Jacksonville University.
4. Brenan Hanifee, rhp, Turner Ashby HS, Bridgewater, Va.
5. Alexis Torres, ss, Angel David HS, San Juan, P.R.
6. Tobias Myers, rhp, Winter Haven (Fla.) HS.
7. Preston Palmeiro, 1b, North Carolina State University.

DRAFT DROP *Son of Rafael Palmeiro, first-round draft pick (1985); major leaguer (1986-2005)*

8. Ryan Moseley, rhp, Texas Tech.
9. Lucas Humpal, rhp, Texas State University.
10. Cody Dube, rhp, Keene State (N.H.) University.
11. Zach Muckenhirn, lhp, University of North Dakota.
12. Max Knutson, lhp, University of Nebraska.
13. *Brandon Bonilla, lhp, Hawaii Pacific University.

DRAFT DROP *Son of Bobby Bonilla, major leaguer (1986-2001)*

14. Ruben Garcia, rhp, Eastern Florida State JC.
15. Nick Jobst, rhp, University of South Carolina-Aiken.
16. Willie Rios, lhp, Florida SouthWestern JC.
17. *Tyler Blohm, lhp, Archbishop Spalding HS, Severn, Md.
18. Layne Bruner, lhp, Washington State University.
19. Cole Billingsley, of, University of South Alabama.
20. Yelin Rodriguez, lhp, Puerto Rico Baseball Academy, Gurabo, P.R.
21. Chris Clare, ss, High Point University.
22. Nick Gruener, rhp, Harvard University.
23. Tyler Erwin, lhp, New Mexico State University.
24. Zach Matson, lhp, Crowder (Mo.) JC.
25. *Will Toffey, 3b, Vanderbilt University.
26. Jaime Estrada, 1b, Central Arizona JC.
27. *Daniel Bakst, 3b, Poly Prep Country Day HS, Brooklyn, N.Y.
28. Matt de la Rosa, rhp, Lenoir-Rhyne (N.C.) University.
29. *Wil Dalton, of, Summit HS, Thompson's Station, Tenn.
30. Garrett Copeland, 2b, Austin Peay State University.
31. Jake Ring, of, University of Missouri.
32. *Ryan Mauch, lhp, South Hills HS, West Covina, Calif.
33. Markel Jones, of, Brunswick (N.C.) CC.
34. Lucas Brown, rhp, Troy University.
35. Tanner Kirk, 2b, Wichita State University.
36. *Ben Brecht, lhp, New Trier HS, Winnetka, Ill.
37. James Teague, rhp, University of Arkansas.
38. Collin Woody, 3b, UNC Greensboro.
39. *Seth Shuman, rhp, Valdosta (Ga.) HS.
40. Joe Johnson, rhp, Erskine (S.C.) College.

## BOSTON RED SOX (12)

1. Jason Groome, lhp, Barnegat (N.J.) HS.
2. C.J. Chatham, ss, Florida Atlantic University.
3. Shaun Anderson, rhp, University of Florida.
4. Bobby Dalbec, 3b-rhp, University of Arizona.
5. Mike Shawaryn, rhp, University of Maryland.
6. Stephen Nogosek, rhp, University of Oregon.
7. Ryan Scott, of, University of Arkansas-Little Rock.
8. Alan Marrero, c, International Baseball Academy, Ceiba, P.R.
9. Matt McLean, of, University of Texas-Arlington.
10. Santiago Espinal, ss, Miami-Dade JC.
11. *Nick Quintana, ss, Arbor View HS, Las Vegas, Nev.
12. Matthew Gorst, rhp, Georgia Tech.
13. *Brady Bramlett, rhp, University of Mississippi.
14. Robby Sexton, lhp, Wright State University.
15. *Michael Wilson, ss, Colonia (N.J.) HS.
16. Alberto Schmidt, c, San Angel David HS, San Juan, P.R.
17. Nick Sciortino, c, Boston College.
18. *Trevor Stephan, rhp, Hill (Texas) JC.
19. Kyle Hart, lhp, Indiana University.
20. Nick Lovullo, ss, Holy Cross University.

DRAFT DROP *Son of Torey Lovullo, major leaguer (1988-99); major league manager (2015)*

21. *Beau Capanna, ss, Bishop Gorman HS, Las Vegas, Nev.
22. Granger Studdard, of, Texas State University.
23. Juan Carlos Abreu, of, Winter Springs (Fla.) HS.
24. Hunter Smith, rhp, UNC Greensboro.
25. Francisco Soto, rhp, Allen (Kan.) CC.
26. Jared Oliver, rhp, Truett-McConnell (Ga.) College.
27. *Vince Arobio, rhp, University of the Pacific.
28. *Jordan Scheftz, rhp, Saddleback (Calif.) JC.
29. *Cam Shepherd, ss, Peachtree Ridge HS, Suwanee, Ga.
30. *Tyler Fitzgerald, ss, Rochester (Ill.) HS.

DRAFT DROP *Son of Mike Fitzgerald, major leaguer (1983-92)*

31. *Christian Jones, of, Federal Way (Wash.) HS.
32. *Jeff Belge, lhp, Henninger HS, Syracuse, N.Y.
33. Chad Hardy, of, Paris (Texas) JC.
34. *Aaron McGarity, rhp, Virginia Tech.
35. *John Rave, of, Central Catholic HS, Bloomington, Ill.
36. *Jordan Wren, of, Georgia Southern University.
37. *Carter Aldrete, ss, Monterey (Calif.) HS.
38. *Austin Bergner, rhp, Windermere Prep, Windermere, Fla.
39. *Jake Wilson, of, Nottawasaga Pines SS, Angus, Ont.
40. *Carter Henry, rhp, Port Neches-Groves HS, Port Neches, Texas

## CHICAGO CUBS (28)

1. (Choice forfeited for signing John Lackey as free agent).
2. (Choice forfeited for signing Jason Heyward as free agent).
3. Thomas Hatch, rhp, Oklahoma State University.
4. Tyson Miller, rhp, California Baptist University.
5. Bailey Clark, rhp, Duke University.
6. Chad Hockin, rhp, Cal State Fullerton.

DRAFT DROP *Grandson of Harmon Killebrew, major leaguer (1954-75)*

7. Michael Cruz, c, Bethune-Cookman University.
8. Stephen Ridings, rhp, Haverford (Pa.) College.
9. Duncan Robinson, rhp, Dartmouth University.
10. Dakota Mekkes, rhp, Michigan State University.
11. Michael Rucker, rhp, Brigham Young University.
12. *Trey Cobb, rhp, Oklahoma State University.
13. Wyatt Short, lhp, University of Mississippi.
14. *Parker Dunshee, rhp, Wake Forest University.
15. Jed Carter, rhp, Auburn University-Montgomery (Ala.).
16. Holden Cammack, rhp, Oral Roberts University.
17. Zack Short, ss, Sacred Heart University.
18. Marc Huberman, lhp, University of Southern California.
19. Matt Swarmer, rhp, Kutztown (Pa.) University.
20. Colton Freeman, lhp, University of Alabama.
21. Sam Tidaback, c, University of North Georgia.
22. *Dante Biasi, lhp, Hazleton Area HS, Hazle Township, Pa.
23. Delvin Zinn, ss, Itawamba (Miss.) CC.
24. *Reynaldo Rivera, 1b, Chipola (Fla.) JC.
25. Trent Giambrone, 2b, Delta State (Miss.) University.
26. *Austin Jones, rhp, University of Wisconsin-Whitewater.
27. Connor Myers, of, Old Dominion University.
28. *Rian Bassett, rhp, Clark (Wash.) JC.
29. Tyler Peyton, rhp, University of Iowa.
30. *Montana Parsons, rhp, San Jacinto (Texas) JC.
31. *Brenden Heiss, rhp, Jacobs HS, Algonquin, Ill.
32. Zach Davis, of, Texas Tech.
33. Nathan Sweeney, rhp, Cherry Creek HS, Greenwood Village, Colo.
34. *Davis Daniel, rhp, St. James School, Montgomery, Ala.
35. *Ryan Kreidler, 3b, Davis (Calif.) HS.
36. *Jake Slaughter, ss, Ouachita Christian HS, Monroe, La.
37. *Davis Moore, rhp, Los Osos HS, Rancho Cucamonga, Calif.
38. Tolly Filotei, of, Faulkner State (Ala.) CC.
39. *Anthony Block, lhp, Newport HS, Bellevue, Wash.
40. *D.J. Roberts, rhp, Atlantic Coast HS, Jacksonville, Fla.

## CHICAGO WHITE SOX (10)

1. Zack Collins, c, University of Miami (Fla.).
1. Zack Burdi, rhp, University of Louisville (Compensation for loss of Jeff Samardzija as free agent—26th).
2. Alec Hansen, rhp, University of Oklahoma.
3. Alex Call, of, Ball State University.
4. Jameson Fisher, c-of, Southeastern Louisiana University.
5. Jimmy Lambert, rhp, Fresno State University.
6. Luis Curbelo, ss, Cocoa (Fla.) HS.
7. Bernardo Flores, lhp, University of Southern California.
8. Nate Nolan, c, St. Mary's (Calif.) College.
9. Max Dutto, ss, Menlo (Calif.) College.
10. Zach Remillard, 3b, Coastal Carolina University.
11. Ian Hamilton, rhp, Washington State University.
12. Mitch Roman, ss, Wright State University.
13. Michael Hickman, c, Chipola (Fla.) JC.
14. Bryan Saucedo, rhp, Davenport (Mich.) University.
15. Jake Elliott, rhp, University of Oklahoma.
16. Ben Wright, rhp, University of Nevada-Las Vegas.
17. Brad Haymes, rhp, Gardner-Webb University.
18. Lane Hobbs, rhp, Concordia (Texas) University.
19. Anthony Villa, 1b, St. Mary's (Calif.) College.
20. Matt Foster, rhp, University of Alabama.
21. Michael Horejsei, lhp, Ohio State University.
22. Joel Booker, of, University of Iowa.
23. Sam Dexter, ss, University of Southern Maine.
24. Brady Conlan, 3b, Cal State Dominguez Hills.
25. *Charlie Madden, c, Mercer University.
26. *Zach Farrar, of, Carroll HS, Southlake, Texas.
27. Mike Morrison, rhp, Coastal Carolina University.
28. Aaron Schnurbusch, of, University of Pittsburgh.
29. *Caleb Henderson, 1b, Central Arizona JC.
30. Pat Cashman, rhp, Southeastern Louisiana University.
31. *Brandon Bossard, ss, Nazareth Academy, La Grange Park, Ill.
32. Sean Renzi, rhp, Central Michigan University.
33. Ryan Boelter, lhp, Gardner-Webb University.
34. *Jaxon Shirley, 2b, Lapel (Ind.) HS.

35. *Garrett Acton, rhp, Lemont (Ill.) HS.
36. *Reese Cooley, of, Chipola (Fla.) JC.
37. *Leo Kaplan, of, Harvard-Westlake HS, Los Angeles.
38. *Tyler Gordon, c, Simeon Career Academy, Chicago.
39. *Justin Lavey, ss, Tremper HS, Kenosha, Wis.
40. *Drew Puglielli, 3b, Gulf Coast HS, Naples, Fla.

## CINCINNATI REDS (2)

1. Nick Senzel, 3b, University of Tennessee.
1. Taylor Trammell, of, Mount Paran Christian School, Kennesaw, Ga. (Competitive balance Round 'A' pick—35th).
2. Chris Okey, c, Clemson University.
3. Nick Hanson, rhp, Prior Lake HS, Savage, Minn.
4. Scott Moss, lhp, University of Florida.
5. Ryan Hendrix, rhp, Texas A&M University.
6. Tyler Mondile, rhp, Gloucester Catholic HS, Gloucester City, N.J.
7. Andy Cox, lhp, University of Tennessee.
8. John Sansone, 2b, Florida State University.
9. Alex Webb, rhp, University of British Columbia.
10. Lucas Benenati, rhp, Kansas State University.
11. Joel Kuhnel, rhp, University of Texas-Arlington.
12. Cassidy Brown, c, Loyola Marymount University.
13. Ryan Olson, rhp, Cal Poly Pomona.
14. Jesse Adams, lhp, Boston College.
15. Jesse Stallings, rhp, Louisiana State University.
16. Mauro Conde, of, Cupeyville School, San Juan, P.R.
17. *Mitchell Traver, rhp, Texas Christian University.
18. *J.C. Flowers, of, Trinity Christian Academy, Jacksonville, Fla.
19. Matt Blandino, rhp, Felician (N.J.) University.
20. *Todd Lott, of, Trinity Christian Academy, Jacksonville, Fla.
21. Andrew Wright, lhp, University of Southern California.
22. Aaron Quillen, rhp, Belmont University.
23. Manny Cruz, ss, Southern New Hampshire University.
24. Bruce Yari, 1b, University of British Columbia.
25. Colby Wright, 2b, University of Kansas.
26. Patrick Riehl, rhp, Mars Hill (N.C.) University.
27. *Dion Henderson, lhp, Dearborn, Mich.
28. *Cooper Johnson, c, Carmel HS, Mundelein, Ill.
29. Daniel Sweet, of, Dallas Baptist University.
30. *Vincent Byrd, 1b, Long Beach (Calif.) CC.
31. *Austin Langworthy, of, Williston (Fla.) HS.
32. *Matt Crohan, lhp, Winthrop University.
33. *Nick Derr, 2b, Sarasota (Fla.) HS.
34. *Ty Weber, rhp, Menomonie (Wis.) HS.
35. *Walker Whitworth, 2b, Northern Oklahoma JC.
36. Ty Blankmeyer, 2b, St. John's University.
37. *Alec Benavides, lhp, Alexander HS, Laredo, Texas.

DRAFT DROP *Son of Freddie Benavides, major leaguer (1991-94)*

38. *John Wilson, lhp, North Hunterdon HS, Annandale, N.J.
39. *Otis Statum, of, Bishop O'Dowd HS, Oakland.
40. *Michael Bienlien, rhp, Great Bridge HS, Chesapeake, Va.

## CLEVELAND INDIANS (16)

1. Will Benson, of, The Westminster Schools, Atlanta.
2. Nolan Jones, ss, Holy Ghost Prep, Bensalem, Pa.
2. Logan Ice, c, Oregon State University (Competitive balance Round 'B' pick—72nd).
3. Aaron Civale, rhp, Northeastern University.
4. Shane Bieber, rhp, UC Santa Barbara.
5. Connor Capel, of, Seven Lakes HS, Katy, Texas.

DRAFT DROP *Son of Mike Capel, major leaguer (1988-91)*

6. Ulysses Cantu, 3b, Boswell HS, Fort Worth, Texas.
7. Michael Tinsley, c, University of Kansas.
8. Andrew Lantrip, lhp, University of Houston.
9. Hosea Nelson, of, Clarendon (Texas) JC.
10. Samad Taylor, ss, Corona (Calif.) HS.
11. Andrew Calica, of, UC Santa Barbara.
12. Zach Plesac, rhp, Ball State University.

DRAFT DROP *Nephew of Dan Plesac, first-round draft pick, Brewers (1983); major leaguer (1986-2003)*

13. Gavin Collins, c, Mississippi State University.
14. Mitch Longo, of, Ohio University.
15. *Zack Smith, c, Eastern Wayne HS, Goldsboro, N.C.
16. Ben Krauth, lhp, University of Kansas.
17. Trenton Brooks, of, University of Nevada.
18. Raymond Burgos, lhp, Pedro Falu Orellano HS, Rio Grande, P.R.
19. Dakody Clemmer, rhp, Central Arizona JC.
20. *Ben Baird, ss, Agoura HS, Agoura Hills, Calif.
21. *Wil Crowe, rhp, University of South Carolina.
22. *Mason Studstill, rhp, Rockledge (Fla.) HS.
23. Michael Letkewicz, rhp, Augustana (S.D.) College.
24. Skylar Arias, lhp, Tallahassee (Fla.) CC.
25. Jonathan Laureno, 3b, Connors State (Okla.) JC.
26. Tanner Tully, lhp, Ohio State University.
27. *Nelson Alvarez, rhp, Braddock HS, Miami.
28. Jamal Rutledge, ss, Contra Costa (Calif.) JC.
29. *Spencer Steer, 3b, Millikan HS, Long Beach, Calif.
30. Ryder Ryan, rhp, University of North Carolina.
31. *Chris Farish, rhp, Wake Forest University.
32. *Kramer Robertson, 2b, Louisiana State University.
33. *Blake Sabol, c, Aliso Niguel HS, Aliso Viejo, Calif.
34. *Austin Shenton, 3b, Bellingham (Wash.) HS
35. *Armani Smith, of, De la Salle HS, Concord, Calif.
36. *Andrew Baker, lhp, Ridge Community HS, Davenport, Fla.
37. *Mike Amditis, c, Boca Raton (Fla.) HS.
38. *Jacob DeVries, lhp, Air Force Academy.
39. *Pedro Alfonseca, of, North Kansas City (Mo.) HS.
40. *Danny Sinatro, of, Skyline HS, Sammamish, Wash.

DRAFT DROP *Son of Matt Sinatro, major leaguer (1981-92)*

## COLORADO ROCKIES (4)

1. Riley Pint, rhp, St. Thomas Aquinas HS, Overland Park, Kan.
1. Robert Tyler, rhp, University of Georgia (Competitive balance Round 'A' pick—38th).
2. Ben Bowden, lhp, Vanderbilt University.
3. Garrett Hampson, ss, Long Beach State University.
4. Colton Welker, 3b, Stoneman Douglas HS, Parkland, Fla.
5. Brian Serven, c, Arizona State University.
6. Willie Abreu, of, University of Miami (Fla.).
7. Reid Humphreys, rhp, Mississippi State University.
8. Ty Culbreth, lhp, University of Texas.
9. Justin Calomeni, rhp, Cal Poly.
10. Vince Fernandez, of, UC Riverside.
11. Bryan Baker, rhp, University of North Florida.
12. Brandon Gold, rhp, Georgia Tech.
13. Taylor Snyder, ss, Colorado State University-Pueblo.

DRAFT DROP *Son of Cory Snyder, first-round draft pick, Indians (1984); major leaguer (1986-94)*

14. Matt Dennis, rhp, Bradley University.
15. Justin Valdespina, rhp, Southern New Hampshire University.
16. Will Haynie, c, University of Alabama.
17. Mike Bunal, rhp, Binghamton University.
18. Hunter Melton, 1b, Texas A&M University.
19. Jacob Bosiokovic, 1b, Ohio State University.
20. Kyle Cedotal, lhp, Southeastern Louisiana University.
21. Tyler Bugner, of, Newman (Kan.) University.
22. Steven Linkous, of, UNC Wilmington.
23. Jared Gesell, rhp, UNC Wilmington.
24. J.D. Hammer, rhp, Marshall University.
25. Heath Holder, rhp, University of Georgia.
26. Austin Moore, rhp, West Texas A&M University.
27. George Thanopoulos, rhp, Columbia University.
28. Ryan Luna, rhp, Sonoma State (Calif.) University.
29. *Josh Shelley, rhp, University of Mobile (Ala.)
30. Rico Garcia, rhp, Hawaii Pacific University.
31. Kenny Oakley, rhp, University of Nevada-Las Vegas.
32. *John Hendry, rhp, Notre Dame College Prep, Niles, Ill.
33. Tyler Orris, ss, Millersville (Pa.) University.
34. *Wyatt Featherston, of, Green Mountain HS, Lakewood, Colo.
35. *Michael Toglia, of, Gig Harbor (Wash.) HS.
36. *Trevor Edior, of, Carson (Calif.) HS.
37. *Troy Bacon, rhp, Santa Fe (Fla.) JC.
38. *Quin Cotton, of, Regis Jesuit HS, Aurora, Colo.
39. *Cuba Bess, c, Fruita Monument HS, Fruita, Colo.
40. *Luca Dalatri, rhp, Christian Brothers Academy, Lincroft, N.J.

## DETROIT TIGERS (9)

1. Matt Manning, rhp, Sheldon HS, Sacramento, Calif.

DRAFT DROP *Son of Rich Manning, power forward, National Basketball Association (1995-97)*

2. (Choice forfeited for signing Jordan Zimmermann as free agent)
3. (Choice forfeited for signing Justin Upton as free agent).
4. Kyle Funkhouser, rhp, University of Louisville.
5. Mark Ecker, rhp, Texas A&M University.
6. Bryan Garcia, rhp, University of Miami (Fla.).
7. Austin Sodders, lhp, UC Riverside.

DRAFT DROP *Son of Mike Sodders, first-round draft pick, Twins (1981)*

8. Jacob Robson, of, Mississippi State University.
9. Daniel Pinero, ss, University of Virginia.
10. Sam Machonis, of, Florida Southern University.
11. Zac Houston, rhp, Mississippi State University.
12. Daniel Woodrow, of, Creighton University.
13. Brady Policelli, c, Towson University.
14. Austin Athmann, c, University of Minnesota.
15. John Schreiber, rhp, University of Northwestern Ohio.
16. Will Savage, 2b, Columbia University.
17. Brandyn Sittinger, rhp, Ashland (Ohio) University.
18. Niko Buentello, 1b, Auburn University.
19. Dustin Frailey, of, Cal State Bakersfield.
20. Clate Schmidt, rhp, Clemson University.
21. Joe Navilhon, rhp, University of Southern California.
22. Burris Warner, rhp, Marshall University.
23. Bryan Torres, c, Carlos Beltran Academy, Florida, P.R.
24. Evan Hill, lhp, University of Michigan.
25. John Hayes, rhp, Wichita State University.
26. Colyn O'Connell, rhp, Florida Atlantic University.
27. Chad Sedio, ss, Miami (Ohio) University.
28. *Alex Cunningham, rhp, Coastal Carolina University.
29. Hunter Swilling, 3b, Samford University.
30. Dalton Lundeen, lhp, Valparaiso University.
31. Dalton Britt, ss, Liberty University.
32. *Connor O'Neil, rhp, Cal State Northridge.
33. *Keegan Thompson, rhp, Auburn University.
34. Geraldo Gonzalez, ss, Puerto Rico Baseball Academy, Gurabo, P.R.
35. *Jacob White, c, Wakeland HS, Frisco, Texas.
36. *Drew Mendoza, 3b, Lake Minneola HS, Minneola, Fla.
37. *David Fleita, 2b, Maine South HS, Park Ridge, Ill.
38. *Josh Smith, ss, Catholic HS, Baton Rouge, La.
39. *Garrett Milchin, rhp, The First Academy, Orlando, Fla.
40. *Dalton Feeney, rhp, Century HS, Bismarck, N.D.

## HOUSTON ASTROS (21)

1. Forrest Whitley, rhp, Alamo Heights HS, San Antonio, Texas.
2. Ronnie Dawson, of, Ohio State University.
3. Jake Rogers, c, Tulane University.
4. Brett Adcock, lhp, University of Michigan.
5. Abraham Toro-Hernandez, 3b, Seminole State (Okla.) JC.
6. Stephen Wrenn, of, University of Georgia.
7. *Tyler Buffett, rhp, Oklahoma State University.
8. Nick Hernandez, rhp, University of Houston.
9. Ryan Hartman, lhp, Tennessee Wesleyan College.
10. Dustin Hunt, rhp, Northeastern University.
11. Chad Donato, rhp, West Virginia University.
12. Carmen Benedetti, lhp, University of Michigan.
13. Ryne Birk, 2b, Texas A&M University.
14. Carson LaRue, rhp, Cowley County (Kan.) CC.
15. Alex DeGoti, ss, Barry (Fla.) University.
16. Spencer Johnson, of, Missouri State University.
17. *Brian Howard, rhp, Texas Christian University.
18. Colin McKee, rhp, Mercyhurst (Pa.) University.
19. Taylor Jones, 1b, Gonzaga University.
20. L.P. Pelletier, 2b, Seminole State (Okla.) JC.
21. Chuckie Robinson, c, University of Southern Mississippi.
22. Ray Henderson-Lozano, c, Grayson (Texas) CC.
23. Tyler Britton, rhp, High Point University.
24. Troy Sieber, c, St. Leo (Fla.) University.
25. Kevin Hill, rhp, University of South Alabama.
26. *Avery Tuck, of, Steele Canyon HS, Spring Valley, Calif.
27. Nathan Thompson, lhp, Oklahoma Baptist University.
28. *Johnny Ruiz, 2b, University of Miami (Fla.).
29. *Elliott Barzilli, 3b, Texas Christian University.
30. Brody Westmoreland, 3b, JC of Southern Nevada.
31. Howie Brey, lhp, Rutgers University.
32. *Darius Vines, rhp, St. Bonaventure HS, Ventura, Calif.
33. *Toby Handley, of, Stony Brook University.
34. Stijin Van Der Meer, ss, Lamar University.
35. *Nick Slaughter, c, Klein (Texas) HS.
36. Ian Hardman, rhp, Seminole State (Okla.) JC.
37. *Anthony DeFrancesco, 3b, Red Mountain HS, Mesa, Ariz.

DRAFT DROP *Son of Tony DeFrancesco, major league manager (2012)*

38. Chaz Pal, of, University of South Carolina-Aiken.
39. Tyler Wolfe, ss, Kansas State University.
40. Lucas Williams, rhp, Central Missouri University.

## KANSAS CITY ROYALS (27)

1. (Choice forfeited for signing Ian Kennedy as free agent).
2. A.J. Puckett, rhp, Pepperdine University.
3. Khalil Lee, of, Flint Hill HS, Oakton, Va.
4. Jace Vines, rhp, Texas A&M University.
5. Nicky Lopez, ss, Creighton University.
6. Cal Jones, of, Dadeville (Ala.) HS.
7. Travis Eckert, rhp, Oregon State University.
8. Chris DeVito, 1b, University of New Mexico.
9. Walker Sheller, rhp, Stetson University.
10. Richard Lovelady, lhp, Kennesaw State University.
11. Vance Vizcaino, of, Stetson University.
12. Jeremy Gwinn, rhp, Colby (Kan.) CC.
13. Logan Gray, 2b, Austin Peay State University.
14. David McKay, rhp, Florida Atlantic University.
15. Mike Messier, lhp, Bellarmine (Ky.) University.
16. Nick Heath, of, Northwestern State University.
17. Dillon Drabble, rhp, Seminole State (Okla.) JC.
18. Vance Tatum, lhp, Mississippi State University.
19. Tyler Fallwell, rhp, Cochise (Ariz.) JC.
20. Anthony Bender, rhp, Santa Rosa (Calif.) JC.
21. Dalton Griffin, of, South Effingham HS, Guyton, Ga.
22. Cody Nesbit, rhp, San Jacinto (Texas) JC.
23. Kort Peterson, of, UCLA.
24. Mike McCann, c, Seattle University.
25. Robby Rinn, 1b, Bryant University.
26. John Brontsema, 3b, UC Irvine.
27. Rex Hill, lhp, Texas Christian University.
28. Yordany Salva, c, Broward (Fla.) CC.
29. Grant Gavin, rhp, Central Missouri University.
30. Geoffrey Bramblett, rhp, University of Alabama.
31. Malcolm Van Buren, rhp, Hanahan (S.C.) HS.
32. *Luke Bandy, of, Providence Classical Christian Academy, Rogers, Ark.
33. *Kameron Misner, of, Poplar Bluff (Mo.) HS.
34. Nathan Webb, rhp, Lee's Summit (Mo.) HS.
35. Mark Sanchez, c, California Baptist University.
36. Alex Massey, rhp, Tulane University.
37. Justin Camp, rhp, Auburn University.
38. *Joey Fregosi, ss, Murrieta Valley HS, Murrieta, Calif.

DRAFT DROP *Grandson of Jim Fregosi, major leaguer (1961-78); major league manager (1978-2000)*

39. Chase Livingston, c, University of Rhode Island.
40. Taylor Kaczmarek, rhp, University of San Diego.

## LOS ANGELES ANGELS (20)

1. Matt Thaiss, c, University of Virginia.
2. Brandon Marsh, of, Buford (Ga.) HS.
3. Nonie Williams, ss, Kansas City, Kan.
4. Chris Rodriguez, rhp, Monsignor Pace HS, Miami Gardens, Fla.
5. Connor Justus, ss, Georgia Tech.
6. Cole Duensing, rhp, Blue Valley Northwest HS, Overland Park, Kan.
7. Jordan Zimmerman, 2b, Michigan State

University.
8. Troy Montgomery, of, Ohio State University.
9. Michael Barash, c, Texas A&M University.
10. Andrew Vinson, rhp, Texas A&M University.
11. Brennon Lund, of, Brigham Young University.
12. Bo Tucker, lhp, University of Georgia.
13. *Anthony Molina, rhp, West Broward HS, Hollywood, Fla.
14. Francisco Del Valle, of, Puerto Rico Baseball Academy, Gurabo, P.R.
15. Mike Kaelin, rhp, University of Buffalo.
16. Keith Grieshaber, ss, Jefferson (Mo.) JC.
17. Zach Gibbons, of, University of Arizona.
18. *David Oppenheim, of, University of Southern California.
19. Cody Ramer, ss, University of Arizona.
20. Jack Kruger, c, Mississippi State University.
21. L.J. Kalawaia, of, UNC Greensboro.
22. *Troy Rallings, rhp, University of Washington.
23. Torii Hunter Jr., of, University of Notre Dame.
DRAFT DROP *Son of Torii Hunter, first-round draft pick (1993); major leaguer (1997-2015)*
24. Brennan Morgan, c, Kennesaw State University.
25. Cameron Williams, of, Howard (Texas) JC.
26. Derek Jenkins, of, Seton Hall University.
27. Greg Belton, rhp, Sam Houston State University.
28. *David Hamilton, ss, San Marcos (Texas) HS.
29. Blake Smith, rhp, West Virginia University.
30. *Robbie Peto, rhp, Monroe Township (N.J.) HS.
31. Johnny Morell, rhp, Basha HS, Chandler, Ariz.
32. Doug Willey, rhp, University of Arkansas.
33. Justin Kelly, lhp, UC Santa Barbara.
34. Justin Nielsen, lhp, University of Illinois.
35. Sean Issac, rhp, Vanguard (Calif.) University.
36. Jose Rojas, ss, Vanguard (Calif.) University.
37. John Schuknecht, of, Cal Poly.
38. Tyler Bates, of, East Texas Baptist University.
39. Richard Fecteau, 2b, Salem State (Mass.) University.
40. Brad Anderson, 1b, Pepperdine University.

## LOS ANGELES DODGERS (25)

1. Gavin Lux, ss, Indian Trail HS, Kenosha, Wis.
1. Will Smith, c, University of Louisville (Compensation for loss of Zack Greinke as free agent—32nd).
1. Jordan Sheffield, rhp, Vanderbilt University (Special compensation for failure to sign 2015 first-rounder Kyle Funkhouser—36th).
DRAFT DROP *Brother of Justus Sheffield, first-round draft pick, Indians (2015)*
2. Mitchell White, rhp, Santa Clara University.
3. Dustin May, rhp, Northwest HS, Justin, Texas.
4. D.J. Peters, of, Western Nevada CC.
5. Devin Smeltzer, lhp, San Jacinto (Texas) JC.
6. Errol Robinson, ss, University of Mississippi.
7. Luke Raley, of, Lake Erie (Ohio) College.
8. Andre Scrubb, rhp, High Point University.
9. Anthony Gonsolin, rhp, St. Mary's (Calif.) College.
10. Kevin LaChance, ss, University of Maryland-Baltimore County.
11. A.J. Alexy, rhp, Twin Valley HS, Elverson, Pa.
12. *Graham Ashcraft, rhp, Huntsville (Ala.) HS.
13. Cody Thomas, of, University of Oklahoma.
14. Dean Kremer, rhp, University of Nevada-Las Vegas.
15. Brayan Morales, of, Hillsborough (Fla.) CC.
16. Darien Tubbs, of, Memphis University.
17. *Dillon Persinger, 2b, Golden West (Calif.) JC.
18. *Cole Freeman, 2b, Louisiana State University.
19. Chris Mathewson, rhp, Long Beach State University.
20. Brock Carpenter, 3b, Seattle University.
21. James Carter, rhp, UC Santa Barbara.
22. Jeff Paschke, rhp, University of Southern California.
23. *Bailey Ober, rhp, College of Charleston.
24. Saige Jenco, of, Virginia Tech.
25. Chandler Eden, rhp, Texas Tech.
26. Brandon Montgomery, 2b, San Jacinto (Texas) JC.
27. Austin French, lhp, Brown University.
28. Jake Perkins, rhp, Ferrum (Va.) College.
29. *Will Kincanon, rhp, Triton (Ill.) JC.
30. Ramon Rodriguez, c, Puerto Rico Baseball Academy, Gurabo, P.R.
31. Stevie Berman, c, Santa Clara University.
32. Connor Costello, rhp, Oklahoma State University.
33. Zack McKinstry, ss, Central Michigan University.
34. Joel Toribio, rhp, Western Oklahoma State JC.
35. Nick Yarnall, of, University of Pittsburgh.
36. *Cal Stevenson, of, Chabot (Calif.) JC.
37. *Enrique Zamora, rhp, Calumet College of St. Joseph (Ind.).
38. Kevin Malisheski, rhp, Wauconda (Ill.) HS.
39. *Ryan Watson, rhp, Auburn (Ala.) HS.
40. *Zach Taglieri, rhp, Port St. Lucie (Fla.) HS.

## MIAMI MARLINS (7)

1. Braxton Garrett, lhp, Florence (Ala.) HS.
2. (Choice forfeited for signing Wei-Yin Chen as free agent).
3. Thomas Jones, of, Laurens (S.C.) HS.
4. Sean Reynolds, of, Redondo Union HS, Redondo Beach, Calif.
5. Sam Perez, rhp, Missouri State University.
6. Remey Reed, rhp, Oklahoma State University.
7. Corey Bird, of, Marshall University.
8. Aaron Knapp, of, University of California.
9. Jarrett Rindfleisch, c, Ball State University.
10. Dylan Lee, lhp, Fresno State University.
11. Chad Smith, rhp, University of Mississippi.
DRAFT DROP *Grandson of Norm Zauchin, major leaguer (1951-59)*
12. Mike King, rhp, Boston College.
13. *Nick Eicholtz, rhp, University of Alabama.
14. Michael Mertz, rhp, Oklahoma State University.
15. James Nelson, ss, Cisco (Texas) JC.
16. Dustin Beggs, rhp, University of Kentucky.
17. Brent Wheatley, rhp, University of Southern California.
18. David Gauntt, c, Washburn (Kan.) University.
19. Shane Sawczak, lhp, Palm Beach State (Fla.) JC.
20. Eric Gutierrez, 1b, Texas Tech.
21. Luis Pintor, ss, New Mexico JC.
22. Alex Mateo, rhp, Nova Southeastern (Fla.) University.
23. Hunter Wells, rhp, Gonzaga University.
24. J.J. Gould, ss, Jacksonville University.
25. Mike Garzillo, 2b, Lehigh University.
26. Gunner Pollman, c, Cal State Sacramento.
27. Parker Bugg, rhp, Louisiana State University.
28. Colby Lusignan, 1b, Lander (S.C.) University.
29. Walker Olis, of, Pacific (Ore.) University.
30. *Garrett Suchey, rhp, Wallace State-Dothan (Ala.) CC.
31. Preston Guillory, rhp, Texas Christian University.
32. Chevis Hoover, rhp, Tennessee Wesleyan College.
33. Branden Berry, 1b, Cal State Northridge.
34. Trenton Hill, lhp, Lee (Tenn.) University.
35. Matt Brooks, 2b, Monroe (N.Y.) CC.
36. *Matt Popowitz, c, Suffern (N.Y.) HS.
37. Zach Daly, of, Lander (S.C.) University.
38. *Dustin Demeter, 3b, Dos Pueblos HS, Goleta, Calif.
39. *Caleb Scires, of, Fairfield (Texas) HS.
40. *Evan Douglas, 2b, Spokane Falls (Wash.) CC.

## MILWAUKEE BREWERS (5)

1. Corey Ray, of, University of Louisville.
2. Lucas Erceg, 3b, Menlo (Calif.) College.
2. Mario Feliciano, c, Carlos Beltran Academy, Florida, P.R. (Competitive balance Round 'B' pick—75th).
3. Braden Webb, rhp, University of South Carolina.
4. Corbin Burnes, rhp, St. Mary's (Calif.) College.
5. Zack Brown, rhp, University of Kentucky.
6. Payton Henry, c, Pleasant Grove (Utah) HS.
7. Daniel Brown, lhp, Mississippi State University.
8. Francisco Thomas, ss, Osceola HS, Kissimmee, Fla.
9. Trey York, 2b, East Tennessee State University.
10. Blake Fox, lhp, Rice University.
11. Chad McClanahan, 3b, Brophy Prep, Phoenix.
12. Trever Morrison, ss, Oregon State University.
13. Thomas Jankins, rhp, Quinnipiac University.
14. Gabriel Garcia, c, Broward (Fla.) JC.
15. Scott Serigstad, rhp, Cal State Fullerton.
16. *Louie Crow, rhp, Buena Park (Calif.) HS.
17. Weston Wilson, 3b, Clemson University.
18. Cooper Hummel, c, University of Portland.
19. Zach Clark, of, Pearl River (Miss.) CC.
20. *Jared Horn, rhp, Vintage HS, Napa, Calif.
21. Nathan Rodriguez, c, Cypress (Calif.) JC.
22. Cam Roegner, lhp, Bradley University.
23. Ronnie Gideon, 1b, Texas A&M University.
24. Michael Gonzalez, rhp, Norwalk (Conn.) HS.
25. Blake Lillis, lhp, St. Thomas Aquinas HS, Overland Park, Kan.
26. Nick Roscetti, ss, University of Iowa.
27. Nick Cain, of, Faulkner (Ala.) University.
28. Andrew Vernon, rhp, North Carolina Central University.
29. *Brennan Price, rhp, Felician (N.J.) University.
30. Dalton Brown, rhp, Texas Tech.
31. Ryan Aguilar, of, University of Arizona.
32. Wilson Adams, rhp, University of Alabama-Huntsville.
33. Emerson Gibbs, rhp, Tulane University.
34. Matt Smith, rhp, Georgetown University.
35. Chase Williams, rhp, Wichita State University.
36. Parker Bean, rhp, Liberty University.
37. Jomar Cortes, ss, Carlos Beltran Academy, Florida, P.R.
38. Caleb Whalen, of, University of Portland.
DRAFT DROP *Brother of Brady Whalen, 12th-round draft pick, Cardinals (2016)*
39. Jose Gomez, of, St. Thomas (Fla.) University.
40. *Kyle Serrano, rhp, University of Tennessee.

## MINNESOTA TWINS (17)

1. Alex Kirilloff, of, Plum HS, Pittsburgh.
2. Ben Rortvedt, c, Verona (Wis.) HS.
2. Jose Miranda, ss, Leadership Christian Academy, Guaynabo, P.R. (Competitive balance Round 'B' pick—73rd).
2. Akil Baddoo, of, Salem HS, Conyers, Ga. (Special compensation for failure to sign 2015 supplemental second-round pick Kyle Cody—74th).
3. Griffin Jax, rhp, Air Force Academy.
DRAFT DROP *Son of Garth Jax, linebacker, National Football League (1986-95)*
4. Tom Hackimer, rhp, St. John's University.
5. Jordan Balazovic, rhp, St. Martin SS, Mississauga, Ont.
6. Alex Schick, rhp, University of California.
7. Matt Albanese, of, Bryant University.
8. Shane Carrier, of, Fullerton (Calif.) JC.
9. Mitchell Kranson, c, University of California.
10. Brandon Lopez, ss, University of Miami (Fla.).
11. Tyler Benninghoff, rhp, Rockhurst HS, Kansas City, Mo.
12. Zach Featherstone, of, Tallahassee (Fla.) CC.
13. Ryan Mason, rhp, University of California.
14. Andre Jernigan, ss, Xavier University.
15. Tyler Wells, rhp, Cal State San Bernardino.
16. Tyler Beardsley, rhp, Cal State Sacramento.
17. Kidany Salva-Rivera, c, Klein Forest HS, Houston.
18. *Timmy Richards, ss, Cal State Fullerton.
19. Sean Poppen, rhp, Harvard University.
20. *Shamoy Christopher, c, Roane State (Tenn.) CC.
21. Domenick Carlini, lhp, Southeastern Louisiana University.
22. Hank Morrison, of, Mercyhurst (Pa.) University.
23. Caleb Hamilton, ss, Oregon State University.
24. *Matt Byars, c, Michigan State University.
25. Colton Davis, rhp, Western Carolina University.
26. *Greg Deichmann, 3b, Louisiana State University.
27. *Scott Ogrin, of, Valencia HS, Santa Clarita, Calif.
28. Matt Jones, lhp, Sinclair SS, Whitby, Ont.
29. Dane Hutcheon, ss, Montevallo (Ala.) University.
30. Quin Grogan, rhp, Lewis-Clark State (Idaho) University.
31. Juan Gamez, c, North Dakota State University.
32. *Matt Wallner, rhp, Forest Lake (Minn.) HS.
33. Clark Beeker, rhp, Davidson College.
34. Joe Cronin, ss, Boston College.
35. Austin Tribby, lhp, University of Missouri.
36. Patrick McGuff, rhp, Morehead State University.
37. *Danny Mayer, of, University of the Pacific.
38. *Brent Rooker, of, Mississippi State University.
39. Casey Scoggins, of, Tampa University.
40. *T.J. Collett, c, North Vigo HS, Terre Haute, Ind.

## NEW YORK METS (24)

1. Justin Dunn, rhp, Boston College.
1. Anthony Kay, lhp, University of Connecticut (Compensation for loss of Daniel Murphy as free agent—31st).
2. Peter Alonso, 1b, University of Florida.
3. Blake Tiberi, 3b, University of Louisville.
4. Michael Paez, ss, Coastal Carolina University.
5. Colby Woodmansee, ss, Arizona State University.
6. Chris Viall, rhp, Stanford University.
7. Austin McGeorge, rhp, Long Beach State University.
8. Placido Torres, lhp, Tusculum (Tenn.) College.
9. Colin Holderman, rhp, Heartland (Ill.) CC.
10. Gene Cone, of, University of South Carolina.
11. Cameron Planck, rhp, Rowan County HS, Morehead, Ky.
12. Matt Cleveland, rhp, Windsor (Conn.) HS.
13. Dan Rizzie, c, Xavier University.
14. Christian James, rhp, East Lake HS, Tarpon Springs, Fla.
15. Jacob Zanon, of, Lewis-Clark State (Idaho) University.
16. Trent Johnson, rhp, Santa Fe (Fla.) CC.
17. Jay Jabs, 3b, Franklin Pierce (N.H.) University.
18. Adam Atkins, rhp, Louisiana Tech.
19. Gary Cornish, rhp, University of San Diego.
20. *Carlos Cortes, 2b, Lake Howell HS, Winter Park, Fla.
21. Max Kuhns, rhp, Santa Clara University.
22. Ian Strom, of, University of Massachusetts-Lowell.
23. Nick Sergakis, 2b, Ohio State University.
24. Dariel Rivera, rhp, Dr. Juan J. Osuna HS, Caguas, P.R.
25. *Cody Beckman, lhp, North Carolina State University.
26. *Rylan Thomas, 3b, Windermere Prep, Windermere, Fla.
27. *Joel Urena, lhp, Gregorio Luperon HS, New York.
28. *William Sierra, rhp, Edouard Montpetit HS, Montreal.
29. *Alex Haynes, rhp, Central HS, Knoxville, Tenn.
30. Eric Villanueva, rhp, Josefina Barcelo HS, Guaynabo, P.R.
31. Jeremy Wolf, of, Trinity (Texas) University.
32. *George Kirby, rhp, Rye (N.Y.) HS.
33. *Duncan Pence, ss, Farragut HS, Knoxville, Tenn.
34. *Anthony Herron, rhp, Jefferson (Mo.) JC.
35. *Andrew Harbin, rhp, Allatoona HS, Acworth, Ga.
36. Garrison Bryant, rhp, Clearwater (Fla.) HS.
37. *Branden Fryman, ss, Tate HS, Cantonment, Fla.
DRAFT DROP *Son of Travis Fryman, first-round draft pick (1987); major leaguer (1990-2002)*
38. *Jaylon McLaughlin, ss, Santa Monica (Calif.) HS.
39. *Jordan Hand, c, JC of Southern Nevada.
40. *Michael Chambers, c, John Paul II HS, Plano, Texas.

## NEW YORK YANKEES (22)

1. Blake Rutherford, of, Chaminade College Prep HS, Canoga Park, Calif.
2. Nick Solak, 2b, University of Louisville.
3. Nolan Martinez, rhp, Culver City (Calif.) HS.
4. Nick Nelson, rhp, Gulf Coast State (Fla.) JC.
5. Dom Thompson-Williams, of, University of South Carolina.
6. Brooks Kriske, rhp, University of Southern California.
7. Keith Skinner, c, University of North Florida.
8. Dalton Blaser, 1b, Cal State Fullerton.
9. Tim Lynch, 1b, University of Southern Mississippi.
10. Trevor Lane, lhp, University of Illinois-Chicago.
11. Connor Jones, lhp, University of Georgia.
12. Taylor Widener, rhp, University of South Carolina.
13. Brian Trieglaff, rhp, Texas Christian University.
14. Jordan Scott, of, IMG Academy, Bradenton, Fla.
15. Tony Hernandez, lhp, Monroe (N.Y.) JC.
16. *Zach Linginfelter, rhp, Sevier County HS, Sevierville, Tenn.
17. Mandy Alvarez, 3b, Eastern Kentucky University.
18. Greg Weissert, rhp, Fordham University.
19. Evan Alexander, of, Hebron HS, Carrollton, Texas.
20. Miles Chambers, rhp, Cal State Fullerton.
21. Timmy Robinson, of, University of Southern California.
22. *Blair Henley, rhp, Arlington Heights HS, Fort Worth, Texas.
23. Braden Bristo, rhp, Louisiana Tech.

24. Joe Burton, of, Harford (Md.) CC.
25. Edel Luaces, of, Globe Institute of Technology (N.Y.).
26. Gage Burland, rhp, Gonzaga University.
27. Phillip Diehl, lhp, Louisiana Tech.
28. Will Jones, rhp, Lander (S.C.) University.
29. *Bo Weiss, rhp, Regis Jesuit HS, Aurora, Colo.

DRAFT DROP *Son of Walt Weiss, first-round draft pick, Athletics (1985); major leaguer (1987-2000); major league manager (2013-15)*

30. Ben Ruta, of, Wagner University.
31. *Miles Sandum, lhp, Granite Hills HS, El Cajon, Calif.
32. *Juan Cabrera, rhp, North Canyon HS, Phoenix.
33. *Bryson Bowman, of, Western Carolina University.
34. *David Clawson, c, Dana Hills HS, Dana Point, Calif.
35. *Zack Hess, rhp, Liberty Christian Academy, Lynchburg, Va.
36. Tyler Honahan, lhp, Stony Brook University.
37. *Corey Dempster, of, University of Southern California.
38. *Sam Ferri, c, Notre Dame College Prep, Niles, Ill.
39. Brian Keller, rhp, University of Wisconsin-Milwaukee.
40. *Nate Brown, rhp, Arrowhead Union HS, Hartland, Wis.

## OAKLAND ATHLETICS (6)

1. A.J. Puk, lhp, University of Florida.
1. Daulton Jefferies, rhp, University of California (Competitive balance Round 'A' pick—37th).
2. Logan Shore, rhp, University of Florida.
3. Sean Murphy, c, Wright State University.
4. Skylar Szynski, rhp, Penn HS, Mishawaka, Ind.
5. JaVon Shelby, 3b, University of Kentucky.

DRAFT DROP *Son of John Shelby, major leaguer (1981-91)*

6. Brandon Bailey, rhp, Gonzaga University.
7. Tyler Ramirez, of, University of North Carolina.
8. Will Gilbert, lhp, North Carolina State University.
9. Dalton Sawyer, lhp, University of Minnesota.
10. Mitchell Jordan, rhp, Stetson University.
11. Eli White, ss, Clemson University.
12. Luke Persico, of, UCLA.
13. Nate Mondou, 2b, Wake Forest University.
14. Nolan Blackwood, rhp, Memphis University.
15. Ty Damron, lhp, Texas Tech.
16. Anthony Churlin, of, Island Coast HS, Cape Coral, Fla.
17. Seth Martinez, rhp, Arizona State University.
18. Skyler Weber, c, University of Georgia.
19. *Sam Gilbert, rhp, University of Kansas.
20. *Brigham Hill, rhp, Texas A&M University.
21. Kyle Nowlin, of, Eastern Kentucky University.
22. Roger Gonzales, c, Winthrop University.
23. *Christian Young, rhp, Niagara County (N.Y.) CC.
24. Robert Bennie, of, East Stroudsburg (Pa.) University.
25. Jeremiah McCray, of, King HS, Riverside, Calif.
26. Charley Gould, 1b, College of William & Mary.
27. Cole Gruber, of, University of Nebraska-Omaha.
28. Josh Vidales, 2b, University of Houston.
29. Matt Milburn, rhp, Wofford University.
30. Nick Highberger, rhp, Creighton University.
31. Sam Sheehan, rhp, Westmont (Calif.) College.
32. Colin Theroux, c, Oklahoma State University.
33. Jarrett Costa, c, Westmont (Calif.) College.
34. Casey Thomas, ss, Texas A&M University-Corpus Christi.
35. *Danny Rafferty, lhp, Bucknell University.
36. *Brady Schanuel, rhp, Parkland (Ill.) JC.
37. *Michael Farley, of, Chico (Calif.) HS.
38. *Matthew Fraizer, of, Clovis North HS, Fresno, Calif.
39. *Shane Martinez, ss, North HS, Riverside, Calif.
40. Brett Bittiger, 2b, Pace (N.Y.) University.

DRAFT DROP *Son of Jeff Bittiger, major leaguer (1986-89)*

## PHILADELPHIA PHILLIES (1)

1. Mickey Moniak, of, La Costa Canyon HS, Carlsbad, Calif.
2. Kevin Gowdy, rhp, Santa Barbara (Calif.) HS.
3. Cole Stobbe, ss, Millard West HS, Omaha, Neb.
4. Jo Jo Romero, lhp, Yavapai (Ariz.) JC.
5. Cole Irvin, lhp, University of Oregon.
6. David Martinelli, of, Dallas Baptist University.
7. Henri Lartigue, c, University of Mississippi.
8. Grant Dyer, rhp, UCLA.
9. Blake Quinn, rhp, Cal State Fullerton.
10. Julian Garcia, rhp, Metro State (Colo.) University.
11. Josh Stephen, of, Mater Dei HS, Santa Ana, Calif.
12. Justin Miller, rhp, Central HS, Fresno, Calif.
13. Andrew Brown, rhp, Granite Hills HS, El Cajon, Calif.
14. Darick Hall, 1b, Dallas Baptist University.
15. *Alex Wojciechowski, 1b, University of Minnesota-Duluth.
16. Brett Barbier, c, Cal Poly.
17. Danny Zardon, 3b, Nova Southeastern (Fla.) University.
18. Jake Kelzer, rhp, Indiana University.
19. Will Hibbs, rhp, Lamar University.
20. Caleb Eldridge, 1b, Cowley County (Kan.) CC.
21. Jonathan Hennigan, lhp, Texas State University.
22. Kyle Young, lhp, St. Dominic HS, Oyster Bay, N.Y.
23. *Camden Duzenack, ss, Dallas Baptist University.
24. Tyler Hallead, rhp, JC of Southern Nevada.
25. Trevor Bettencourt, rhp, UC Santa Barbara.
26. Tyler Kent, of, Otterbein (Ohio) University.
27. *Davis Agle, rhp, Spartanburg Methodist JC (S.C.).
28. Jordan Kurokawa, rhp, University of Hawaii-Hilo.
29. Alexander Kline, lhp, Nova Southeastern (Fla.) University.
30. *Logan Davidson, ss, Providence HS, Charlotte, N.C.
31. Tyler Frohwirth, rhp, Minnesota State University.

DRAFT DROP *Son of Todd Frohwirth, major leaguer (1987-96)*

32. Daniel Garner, c, Northwestern State University.
33. *Jack Klein, rhp, Stanford University.
34. Luke Maglich, of, University of South Florida.
35. *Carter Bins, c, Rodriguez HS, Fairfield, Calif.
36. *Mac Sceroler, rhp, Southeastern Louisiana University.
37. *James Ziemba, lhp, Duke University.
38. *Trevor Hillhouse, lhp, Woodstock (Ga.) HS.
39. *Dante Baldelli, of, Bishop Hendricken HS, Warwick, R.I.

DRAFT DROP *Brother of Rocco Baldelli, first-round draft pick, Rays (2000); major leaguer (2003-10)*

40. *Trey Morris, rhp, Taylor HS, Katy, Texas.

## PITTSBURGH PIRATES (29)

1. Will Craig, 3b, Wake Forest University.
1. *Nick Lodolo, lhp, Damien HS, La Verne, Calif. (Competitive balance Round 'A' pick—41st).
2. Travis MacGregor, rhp, East Lake HS, Tarpon Springs, Fla.
3. Stephen Alemais, ss, Tulane University.
4. Braeden Ogle, lhp, Jensen Beach (Fla.) HS.
5. Blake Cederlind, rhp, Merced (Calif.) JC.
6. Cam Vieaux, lhp, Michigan State University.
7. Brent Gibbs, c, Central Arizona JC.
8. Dylan Prohoroff, rhp, Cal State Fullerton.
9. Clark Eagan, of, University of Arkansas.
10. Matt Anderson, rhp, Morehead State University.
11. Max Kranick, rhp, Valley View HS, Archbald, Pa.
12. Arden Pabst, c, Georgia Tech.
13. John Pomeroy, rhp, Oregon State University.
14. *Hagen Owenby, c, East Tennessee State University.
15. Danny Beddes, rhp, Utah Valley University.
16. Matt Diorio, of, University of Central Florida.
17. Matt Frawley, rhp, Purdue University.
18. Kevin Mahala, rhp, George Washington University.
19. *Pearson McMahan, rhp, St. John's River State (Fla.) JC.
20. Adam Oller, rhp, Northwestern State University.
21. Matt Eckelman, rhp, Saint Louis University.
22. Brandon Bingel, rhp, Bryant University.
23. Garrett Brown, of, Western Carolina University.
24. *Austin Bodrato, 3b, St. Joseph Regional HS, Montvale, N.J.
25. Stephen Owen, of, Indiana State University.
26. Robbie Coursel, rhp, Florida Atlantic University.
27. Tyler Leffler, ss, Bradley University.
28. *Michael Danielak, rhp, Dartmouth University.
29. Geoff Hartlieb, rhp, Lindenwood (Mo.) University.
30. *Chris Cook, ss, East Tennessee State University.
31. Jordan Jess, lhp, University of Minnesota.
32. *Ben Miller, 1b, University of Nebraska.
33. Austin Shields, rhp, St. Mary's Catholic SS, Hamilton, Ont.
34. *Craig Dedelow, of, Indiana University.
35. Pasquale Mazzoccoli, rhp, Texas State University.
36. *Dustin Williams, 1b, Oklahoma State University.
37. *Colin Brockhouse, rhp, Ball State University.
38. *Aaron Maher, of, East Tennessee State University.
39. *Harrison Wenson, c, University of Michigan.
40. *Bret Boswell, ss, University of Texas.

## ST. LOUIS CARDINALS (30)

1. Delvin Perez, ss, International Baseball Academy, Ceiba, P.R.
1. Dylan Carlson, of, Elk Grove (Calif.) HS (Compensation for loss of John Lackey as free agent—33rd).
1. Dakota Hudson, rhp, Mississippi State University (Compensation for loss of Jason Heyward as free agent—34th).
2. Connor Jones, rhp, University of Virginia.
3. Zac Gallen, rhp, University of North Carolina.
4. Jeremy Martinez, c, University of Southern California.
5. Walker Robbins, of, George County HS, Lucedale, Miss.
6. Tommy Edman, ss, Stanford University.
7. Andrew Knizner, c, North Carolina State University.
8. Sam Tewes, rhp, Wichita State University.
9. Matt Fiedler, of, University of Minnesota.
10. Danny Hudzina, 3b, Western Kentucky University.
11. John Kilichowski, lhp, Vanderbilt University.
12. Brady Whalen, ss, Union HS, Camas, Wash.

DRAFT DROP *Brother of Caleb Whalen, 38th-round draft pick, Brewers (2016)*

13. Shane Billings, of, Wingate (N.C.) University.
14. Vincent Jackson, of, University of Tennessee.
15. J.R. Davis, 2b, Oklahoma State University.
16. Tyler Lancaster, c, Spartanburg Methodist (S.C.) JC.
17. *Matt Ellis, rhp, UC Riverside.
18. Austin Sexton, rhp, Mississippi State University.
19. Daniel Castano, lhp, Baylor University.
20. Stefan Trosclair, 1b, University of Louisiana-Lafayette.
21. *Cade Cabbiness, of, Bixby (Okla.) HS.
22. Mick Fennell, of, California (Pa.) University.
23. *John Crowe, of, Francis Marion (S.C.) University.
24. Anthony Ciavarella, lhp, Monmouth University.
25. Spencer Trayner, rhp, University of North Carolina.
26. Eric Carter, rhp, University of Louisiana-Lafayette.
27. Mike O'Reilly, rhp, Flagler (Fla.) College.
28. *Pat Krall, lhp, Clemson University.
29. Noel Gonzalez, rhp, Lewis-Clark State (Idaho) University.
30. *Josh Burgmann, rhp, Vauxhall (Alberta) Academy of Baseball.
31. J.D. Murders, 2b, Bolivar (Mo.) HS.
32. Leland Tilley, rhp, Bellevue (Neb.) University.
33. Caleb Lopes, 2b, University of West Georgia.
34. Jonathan Mulford, rhp, Adelphi (N.Y.) University.
35. *Jackson Lamb, rhp, University of Michigan.
36. Robbie Gordon, rhp, Maryville (Mo.) University.
37. Andy Young, 3b, Indiana State University.
38. Robert Calvano, rhp, University of Nebraska-Omaha.
39. *Aaron Bond, of, San Jacinto (Texas) JC.
40. *Jeremy Ydens, of, St. Francis HS, Mountain View, Calif.

## SAN DIEGO PADRES (8)

1. Cal Quantrill, rhp, Stanford University.

DRAFT DROP *Son of Paul Quantrill, major leaguer (1992-2005)*

1. Hudson Sanchez, ss, Carroll HS, Southlake, Texas (Compensation for loss of Justin Upton as free agent—24th).
1. Eric Lauer, lhp, Kent State University (Compensation for loss of Ian Kennedy as free agent—25th).
2. Buddy Reed, of, University of Florida.
2. Reggie Lawson, rhp, Victor Valley HS, Victorville, Calif. (Competitive balance Round 'B' pick—71st).
3. Mason Thompson, rhp, Round Rock (Texas) HS.
4. Joey Lucchesi, lhp, Southeast Missouri State University.
5. Lake Bachar, rhp, University of Wisconsin-Whitewater.
6. Will Stillman, rhp, Wofford University.
7. Dan Dallas, lhp, Canisius HS, Buffalo, N.Y.
8. Ben Sheckler, lhp, Cornerstone (Mich.) University.
9. Jesse Scholtens, rhp, Wright State University.
10. Boomer White, 2b, Texas A&M University.
11. Trevyne Carter, of, Soddy-Daisy (Tenn.) HS.
12. *Jamie Sara, rhp, West Potomac HS, Alexandria, Va.
13. Joe Galindo, rhp, New Mexico State University.
14. *Jared Poche, lhp, Louisiana State University.
15. Jack Suwinski, of, Taft HS, Chicago.
16. Chris Mattison, c, Southeastern (Fla.) University.
17. Chris Baker, ss, University of Washington.
18. Jaquez Williams, 1b, East Coweta HS, Sharpsburg, Ga.
19. A.J. Brown, of, Starkville (Miss.) HS.
20. Dom DiSabatino, rhp, Harford (Md.) CC.
21. Taylor Kohlwey, of, University of Wisconsin-La Crosse.
22. Evan Miller, rhp, Indiana University-Purdue University Fort Wayne.
23. Nate Easley, 2b, Yavapai (Ariz.) JC.
24. *Hunter Bishop, of, Serra HS, San Mateo, Calif.
25. Luis Anguizola, c, Loyola (Ill.) University.
26. *Grae Kessinger, ss, Oxford (Miss.) HS.

DRAFT DROP *Grandson of Don Kessinger, major leaguer (1964-79); major league manager (1979) • Nephew of Keith Kessinger, major leaguer (1993)*

27. Chasen Ford, rhp, Yale University.
28. Ethan Skender, ss, State JC of Florida-Manatee.
29. *Collin Sullivan, rhp, Fort Pierce Central HS, Fort Pierce, Fla.
30. Dalton Erb, rhp, Chico State (Calif.) University.
31. G.K. Young, 1b, Coastal Carolina University.
32. *Ariel Burgos Garcia, rhp, Northern Oklahoma JC.
33. Mark Zimmerman, rhp, Baldwin-Wallace (Ohio) University.
34. Denzell Gowdy, 3b, Darton State (Ga.) JC.
35. David Bednar, rhp, Lafayette (Pa.) University.
36. *Quinn Hoffman, ss, Cathedral Catholic HS, San Diego.

DRAFT DROP *Son of Trevor Hoffman, major leaguer (1993-2010)*

37. *Ryan Rolison, lhp, University School, Jackson, Tenn.
38. *Will Solomon, lhp, Georgia Gwinnett College.
39. *J.J. Bleday, of, Mosley HS, Lynn Haven, Fla.
40. *Chris Burica, lhp, Orange Lutheran HS, Orange, Calif.

## SAN FRANCISCO GIANTS (19)

1. (Choice forfeited for signing Jeff Samardzija as free agent).
2. Bryan Reynolds, of, Vanderbilt University.
3. Heath Quinn, of, Samford University.
4. Matt Krook, lhp, University of Oregon.
5. Ryan Howard, ss, University of Missouri.
6. Gio Brusa, of, University of the Pacific.
7. Garrett Williams, lhp, Oklahoma State University.
8. Stephen Woods, rhp, University of Albany.
9. Caleb Baragar, lhp, Indiana University.
10. Alex Bostic, lhp, Clemson University.
11. *Jason Delay, c, Vanderbilt University.
12. Ryan Kirby, 1b, University of San Diego.
13. Jose Layer, of, Angel David HS, San Juan, P.R.
14. Conner Menez, lhp, The Masters (Calif.) College.
15. D.J. Myers, rhp, University of Nevada-Las Vegas.
16. Chris Falwell, lhp, Texas A&M University-Corpus Christi.
17. Reagan Bazar, rhp, University of Louisiana-Lafayette.
18. Jacob Heyward, of, University of Miami (Fla.).

DRAFT DROP *Brother of Jason Heyward, first-round draft pick, Braves (2007); major leaguer (2010-15)*

19. Brandon Van Horn, ss, The Master's (Calif.) College.
20. Justin Alleman, rhp, Lee (Tenn.) University.

21. Will Albertson, c, Catawba (N.C.) College.
22. Malique Ziegler, of, North Iowa Area CC.
23. Jacob Greenwalt, rhp, Windsor (Colo.) HS.
24. Jeffrey Parra, c, Ramapo HS, Wyckoff, N.J.
25. *Mike Rescigno, rhp, University of Maryland.
26. Nick Hill, of, Eckerd (Fla.) College.
27. Pat Ruotolo, rhp, University of Connecticut.
28. *Jayden O'Dell, rhp, Angelo State (Texas) University.
29. Mike Bernal, ss, University of Arkansas.
30. Nick Deeg, lhp, Central Michigan University.
31. *Adam Laskey, lhp, Haddon Heights (N.J.) HS.
32. John Timmins, rhp, Bellevue (Neb.) University.
33. *Jarrett Montgomery, rhp, Northwest Florida State JC.
34. C.J. Gettman, rhp, Central Washington University.
35. Sidney Duprey, lhp, Kaskaskia (Ill.) JC.
36. Ryan Matranga, c, University of San Francisco.
37. Christoph Bono, of, UCLA.
DRAFT DROP *Son of Steve Bono, quarterback, National Football League (1985-99)*
38. *David Lee, rhp, Santa Fe (Fla.) JC.
39. *Andrew DiPiazza, rhp, Mercer County (N.J.) CC.
40. *Nick Bennett, lhp, Moeller HS, Cincinnati.

## SEATTLE MARINERS (11)

1. Kyle Lewis, of, Mercer University.
2. Joe Rizzo, 3b, Oakton HS, Vienna, Va.
3. Bryson Brigman, ss, University of San Diego.
4. Thomas Burrows, lhp, University of Alabama.
5. Donnie Walton, ss, Oklahoma State University.
6. Brandon Miller, rhp, Millersville (Pa.) University.
7. Matt Festa, rhp, East Stroudsburg (Pa.) University.
8. Nick Zammarelli, 3b, Elon University.
9. Jason Goldstein, c, University of Illinois.
10. David Greer, 3b, Arizona State University.
11. Michael Koval, rhp, Cal Poly Pomona.
12. Timothy DeWald, lhp, Southern New Hampshire University.
13. Reggie McClain, rhp, University of Missouri.
14. Kyle Davis, rhp, University of Southern California.
15. Danny Garcia, lhp, University of Miami (Fla.).
16. *Lyle Lin, c, J Serra HS, San Juan Capistrano, Calif.
17. Dimas Ojeda, of, McLennan (Texas) CC.
18. Robert Dugger, rhp, Texas Tech.
19. DeAires Moses, of, Volunteer State (Tenn.) CC.
20. Eric Filia, of, UCLA.
21. Austin Grebeck, of, University of Oregon.
DRAFT DROP *Son of Craig Grebeck, major leaguer (1990-2001)*
22. Jansiel Rivera, of, Methuen (Mass.) HS.
23. Jack Anderson, rhp, Penn State University.
24. Trey Griffey, of, University of Arizona.
DRAFT DROP *Grandson of Ken Griffey Sr., major leaguer (1973-91) • Son of Ken Griffey Jr., first-round draft pick, Mariners (1987); major leaguer (1989-2010)*
25. *Ryan Fucci, of, Wright State University.
26. Elliot Surrey, lhp, UC Irvine.
27. Paul Covelle, rhp, Franklin Pierce (N.H.) University.
28. Nathan Bannister, rhp, University of Arizona.
29. Steven Ridings, rhp, Messiah (Pa.) College.
30. *Tyler Duncan, of, Edward Milne SS, Sooke, B.C.
31. *Lincoln Henzman, rhp, University of Louisville.
32. Kenyon Yovan, rhp, Westview HS, Portland, Ore.
33. *Morgan McCullough, ss, West Seattle HS, Seattle.
34. David Ellingson, rhp, Georgetown University.
35. *Will Ethridge, rhp, Parkview HS, Lilburn, Ga.
36. Joe Venturino, 2b, Ramapo (N.J.) College.
37. *Eli Wilson, c, Garfield HS, Seattle.
DRAFT DROP *Son of Dan Wilson, first-round draft pick, Reds (1990); major leaguer (1992-2005)*
38. *James Reilly, rhp, Magnus HS, Bardonia, N.Y.
39. *Camyrn Williams, ss, Gaither HS, Tampa.
DRAFT DROP *Son of Reggie Williams, major leaguer (1985-89)*
40. *Adley Rutschman, c, Sherwood (Ore.) HS.

## TAMPA BAY RAYS (14)

1. Josh Lowe, 3b, Pope HS, Marietta, Ga.
DRAFT DROP *Brother of Nathaniel Lowe, 14th-round draft pick, Rays (2016)*
2. Ryan Boldt, of, University of Nebraska.
2. Jake Fraley, of, Louisiana State University (Competitive balance Round 'B' pick—77th).
3. Austin Franklin, rhp, Paxton (Fla.) HS.
4. Easton McGee, rhp, Hopkinsville (Ky.) HS.
5. Mikey York, rhp, JC of Southern Nevada.
DRAFT DROP *Son of Mike York, major leaguer (1990-91)*
6. Zach Trageton, rhp, Faith Lutheran HS, Las Vegas, Nev.
7. J.D. Busfield, rhp, Loyola Marymount University.
8. Kenny Rosenberg, lhp, Cal State Northridge.
9. Peter Bayer, rhp, Cal Poly Pomona.
10. Spencer Jones, rhp, University of Washington.
11. *Zack Thompson, lhp, Wapahani HS, Selma, Ind.
12. Brandon Lawson, rhp, University of South Florida.
13. Nathaniel Lowe, 1b, Mississippi State University.
DRAFT DROP *Brother of Josh Lowe, first-round draft pick, Rays (2016)*
14. Miles Mastrobuoni, 2b, University of Nevada.
15. Dalton Moats, lhp, Delta State (Miss.) University.
16. *Dominic Miroglio, c, University of San Francisco.
17. *Wyatt Mills, rhp, Gonzaga University.
18. Sam Long, lhp, Cal State Sacramento.
19. Jim Haley, 3b, Penn State University.
20. Kevin Santiago, ss, Miami-Dade JC.
21. *John McMillon, 3b, Jasper (Texas) HS.
22. *Freddy Villarreal, rhp, Veterans Memorial HS, Mission, Texas.
23. Isaac Benard, of, Mount Hood (Ore.) CC.
DRAFT DROP *Son of Marvin Benard, major leaguer (1995-2003)*
24. Joe Serrapica, rhp, Fordham University.
25. Matt Vogel, rhp, University of South Carolina.
26. *Justin Glover, lhp, Buford (Ga.) HS.
27. Robbie Tenerowicz, 2b, University of California.
28. Jean Ramirez, c, Illinois State University.
29. Trek Stemp, 2b, Washington State University.
30. *Kea'von Edwards, ss, Putnam City HS, Oklahoma City, Okla.
31. Joey Roach, c, Georgia State University.
32. Deion Tansel, ss, University of Toledo.
33. *Hayden Wesneski, rhp, Cy Fair HS, Cypress, Texas.
34. Bobby Melley, 1b, University of Connecticut.
35. Alex Estrella, lhp, University of New Mexico.
36. Anthony Parente, rhp, Fullerton (Calif.) JC.
37. *Ryan Zeferjahn, rhp, Seaman HS, Topeka, Kan.
38. Brian McAfee, rhp, Duke University.
39. *Joshua Martinez, of, Caguas Military Academy, Gurabo, P.R.
40. *Andrew Daschbach, 3b, Sacred Heart Prep, Atherton, Calif.

## TEXAS RANGERS (23)

1. (Choice forfeited for signing Ian Desmond as free agent)
1. Cole Ragans, lhp, North Florida Christian HS, Tallahassee, Fla. (Compensation for loss of Yovani Gallardo as free agent—30th).
2. Alex Speas, rhp, McEachern HS, Powder Springs, Ga.
3. Kole Enright, 3b, West Orange HS, Winter Garden, Fla.
4. Charles LeBlanc, ss, University of Pittsburgh.
5. Kyle Roberts, lhp, Henry Ford (Mich.) JC.
6. Kyle Cody, rhp, University of Kentucky.
7. Sam Huff, c, Arcadia HS, Phoenix.
8. Tai Tiedemann, rhp, Long Beach (Calif.) CC.
9. Hever Bueno, rhp, Arizona State University.
10. Josh Merrigan, of, Georgia Gwinnett College.
11. Joe Barlow, rhp, Salt Lake CC.
12. Alex Kowalczyk, c, University of Pittsburgh.
13. Jonah McReynolds, ss, Patrick Henry (Va.) CC.
14. Derek Heffel, rhp, Madison (Wis.) JC.
15. Kobie Taylor, of, Portsmouth (N.H.) HS.
16. Scott Engler, rhp, Cowley County (Kan.) CC.
17. Reid Anderson, rhp, Millersville (Pa.) University.
18. Marcus Mack, of, Bellaire (Texas) HS.
19. Alex Daniele, rhp, University of Oklahoma.
20. Stephen Lohr, 3b, California Baptist University.
21. Kaleb Fontenot, rhp, McNeese State University.
22. Clayton Middleton, c, Bethune-Cookman University.
23. Dylan Bice, rhp, Heritage HS, Ringgold, Ga.
24. Kenneth Mendoza, lhp, Clearview Regional HS, Mullica Hill, N.J.
25. *Tra'mayne Holmes, 2b, Wallace-Dothan (Ala.) CC.
26. Tyree Thompson, rhp, Karr HS, New Orleans, La.
27. Lucas Jacobsen, lhp, Long Beach State University.
28. Marc Isenecker, rhp, St. John Fisher (N.Y.) College.
29. *Robert Harris, of, Marietta (Ga.) HS.
30. Christian Torres, lhp, Faulkner (Ala.) University.
31. *Blair Calvo, rhp, East Florida State JC.
32. Travis Bolin, of, Davenport (Mich.) University.
33. Mark Vasquez, rhp, Faulkner (Ala.) University.
34. Preston Scott, of, Fresno Pacific University.
DRAFT DROP *Son of Tim Scott, major leaguer (1991-97)*
35. Jean Casanova, rhp, Waukegan (Ill.) HS.
36. *Herbie Good, rhp, Puyallup, Wash.
37. Austin O'Banion, of, Fullerton (Calif.) JC.
38. Reilly Peltier, rhp, McHenry County (Ill.) JC.
39. *Tyler Walsh, ss, Belmont University.
40. *Brent Burgess, c, Spartanburg Methodist (S.C.) JC.

## TORONTO BLUE JAYS (26)

1. T.J. Zeuch, rhp, University of Pittsburgh.
2. J.B. Woodman, of, University of Mississippi (Special compensation for failure to sign 2015 second-round pick Brady Singer—57th).
2. Bo Bichette, ss, Lakewood HS, St. Petersburg, Fla.
DRAFT DROP *Son of Dante Bichette, major leaguer (1988-2001)*
3. Zach Jackson, rhp, University of Arkansas.
4. Josh Palacios, of, Auburn University.
5. Cavan Biggio, 2b, University of Notre Dame.
DRAFT DROP *Son of Craig Biggio, first-round draft pick, Astros (1987); major leaguer (1988-2007)*
6. D.J. Daniels, of, Fike HS, Wilson, N.C.
7. Andy Ravel, rhp, Kent State University.
8. Kyle Weatherly, rhp, Grayson (Texas) CC.
9. Nick Hartman, rhp, Old Dominion University.
10. Kirby Snead, lhp, University of Florida.
11. Travis Hosterman, lhp, Hagerty HS, Oviedo, Fla.
12. Ridge Smith, c, Austin Peay State University.
13. *Chris Lincoln, rhp, Rancho Verde HS, Moreno Valley, Calif.
14. Chris Hall, rhp, Elon University.
15. Josh Winckowski, rhp, Estero (Fla.) HS.
16. *Dominic Taccolini, rhp, University of Arkansas.
17. *Clayton Keyes, of, Bishop Carroll HS, Calgary, Alberta.
18. Bradley Jones, 3b, College of Charleston.
19. *Spencer Van Scoyoc, lhp, Jefferson HS, Cedar Rapids, Iowa.
20. Angel Alicea, rhp, Alabama State University.
21. Mitch McKown, rhp, Seminole State (Fla.) JC.
22. Connor Eller, rhp, Ouachita Baptist (Ark.) University.
23. Dom Abbadessa, of, Huntington Beach (Calif.) HS.
24. Mike Ellenbest, rhp, Saginaw Valley State (Mich.) University.
25. *Casey Legumina, rhp, Basha HS, Chandler, Ariz.
26. *Ben Anderson, rhp, Shenendehowa HS, Clifton Park, N.Y.
DRAFT DROP *Twin brother of Ian Anderson, first-round draft pick, Braves (2016)*
27. Ryan Gold, c, Carolina Forest HS, Myrtle Beach, S.C.
28. *Blake Ebo, of, Trenton Catholic Academy, Trenton, N.J.
29. Andrew Deramo, rhp, University of Central Florida.
30. Jake Fishman, lhp, Union (N.Y.) College.
31. *Marcus Still, of, Scottsdale (Ariz.) CC.
32. David Jacob, 1b, Quincy (Ill.) University.
33. Brayden Bouchey, rhp, University of Louisiana-Monroe.
34. *Shea Langeliers, c, Keller (Texas) HS.
35. Jared Carkuff, rhp, Austin Peay State University.
36. *Dustin Skelton, c, Magnolia Heights HS, Senatobia, Miss.
37. Luke Gillingham, lhp, U.S. Naval Academy.
38. *Alex Segal, lhp, Chaparral HS, Scottsdale, Ariz.
39. Chavez Young, of, Faith Baptist Christian Academy, Ludowici, Ga.
40. *Carter Loewen, rhp, Yale SS, Abbotsford, B.C.

## WASHINGTON NATIONALS (18)

1. (Choice forfeited for signing Daniel Murphy as free agent)
1. Carter Kieboom, ss, Walton HS, Marietta, Ga. (Compensation for loss of Jordan Zimmermann as free agent—28th).
1. Dane Dunning, rhp, University of Florida (Compensation for loss of Ian Desmond as free agent—29th).
2. Sheldon Neuse, 3b, University of Oklahoma.
3. Jesus Luzardo, lhp, Stoneman Douglas HS, Parkland, Fla.
4. Nick Banks, of, Texas A&M University.
5. Daniel Johnson, of, New Mexico State University.
6. Tres Barrera, c, University of Texas.
7. Jake Noll, 2b, Florida Gulf Coast University.
8. A.J. Bogucki, rhp, University of North Carolina.
9. Joey Harris, c, Gonzaga University.
10. Paul Panaccione, ss, Grand Canyon University.
11. Armond Upshaw, of, Pensacola State (Fla.) JC.
12. Hayden Howard, lhp, Texas Tech.
13. Conner Simonetti, 1b, Kent State University.
14. Kyle Simonds, rhp, Texas A&M University.
15. Ryan Williamson, lhp, North Carolina State University.
16. Phil Morse, rhp, Shenandoah (Va.) University.
17. Tyler Beckwith, ss, University of Richmond.
18. Ben Braymer, lhp, Auburn University.
19. *Jarrett Gonzales, c, James Madison HS, San Antonio, Texas.
20. Jake Barnett, lhp, Lewis-Clark State (Idaho) University.
21. Jacob Howell, rhp, Delta State (Miss.) University.
22. Sterling Sharpe, rhp, Drury (Mo.) University.
23. Michael Rishwain, rhp, Westmont (Calif.) College.
24. Joseph Baltrip, rhp, Wharton County (Texas) JC.
25. Branden Boggetto, ss, Southeast Missouri State University.
26. Jack Sundberg, of, University of Connecticut.
27. Jeremy McDonald, lhp, California Baptist University.
28. Jonny Reed, lhp, Azusa Pacific (Calif.) University.
29. Sam Held, rhp, University of Nevada.
30. *Tristan Clarke, of, Eastern Oklahoma State JC.
31. C.J. Picerni, c, New York University.
32. *Garrett Gonzales, 3b, James Madison HS, San Antonio, Texas.
33. *Ryan Wetzel, ss, Heritage Christian Academy, Olathe, Kan.
34. *Morgan Cooper, rhp, University of Texas.
35. *Tristan Bayless, lhp, Hutto (Texas) HS.
36. *Jordan McFarland, of, Waterloo (Ill.) HS.
37. *Cory Voss, c, McLennan (Texas) CC.
38. *Noah Murdock, rhp, Colonial Heights (Va.) HS.
39. *Matt Mervis, 1b, Georgetown Prep HS, North Bethesda, Md.
40. *Sean Cook, rhp, Whitman HS, Bethesda, Md.